PRESENTED TO

_____

BY

_____

DATE

_____

OXFORD
UNIVERSITY PRESS

1904 🍁 2004

100 YEARS OF
CANADIAN PUBLISHING

Canadian
Oxford
Dictionary

Canadian Oxford Dictionary

SECOND EDITION

Edited by
Katherine Barber

OXFORD
UNIVERSITY PRESS
1904 ❦ 2004
100 YEARS OF
CANADIAN PUBLISHING

OXFORD
UNIVERSITY PRESS

70 Wynford Drive, Don Mills, Ontario M3C 1J9
www.oup.com/ca

Oxford University Press is a department of the University of Oxford.
It furthers the University's objective of excellence in research, scholarship,
and education by publishing worldwide in

Oxford New York

Auckland   Cape Town   Dar es Salaam   Hong Kong   Karachi
Kuala Lumpur   Madrid   Melbourne   Mexico City   Nairobi
New Delhi   Shanghai   Taipei   Toronto

With offices in

Argentina   Austria   Brazil   Chile   Czech Republic   France   Greece
Guatemala   Hungary   Italy   Japan   Poland   Portugal   Singapore
South Korea   Switzerland   Thailand   Turkey   Ukraine   Vietnam

Oxford is a registered trade mark of Oxford University Press
in the UK and in certain other countries

Published in Canada
by Oxford University Press

Copyright © Oxford University Press Canada 2004

National Library of Canada Cataloguing in Publication

The Canadian Oxford dictionary / edited by Katherine Barber. — 2nd ed.

ISBN-10: 0-19-541816-6
ISBN-13: 978-0-19-541816-3

1. English language—Canada—Dictionaries. 2. English language—Dictionaries.
3. Canadianisms (English)—Dictionaries. I. Barber, Katherine, 1959-

PE3235.C36 2004   423   C2004-902932-0

Cover Design: Brett J. Miller

5 – 08

This book is printed on permanent (acid-free) paper ⊗.
Printed in the United States of America by Quebecor World

Project Team

Project Team for the Second Edition

Editor-in-Chief
Katherine Barber

Senior Lexicographers
W. Alex Bisset
Robert Pontisso

Lexicographers
Heather Fitzgerald
Tom Howell

Citation keyers
Heather Fitzgerald
Elizabeth Marshman

Proofreaders
Michele Melady
Eric Sinkins

IT Support
Owen Eng Technologies Inc.

Project Team for the First Edition

Editor-in-Chief
Katherine Barber

Senior Lexicographer
W. Alex Bisset

Lexicographers
Michele Melady
Robert Pontisso
Eric Sinkins
Ward Stendahl
Rhonda Wauhkonen

Project Assistant
Allison Pelette

Citation keyers
Stephen Albrecht, W. Alex Bisset, Elizabeth Bisset,
Michele Melady, Robert Murray, Kathy Schmidt,
Eric Sinkins, Rick Warden, Rhonda Wauhkonen

Other Contributors

Australian English
Bruce Moore, Australian National Dictionary Centre,
Australian National University

Canadian English - Editorial Adviser
Dr. J. K. Chambers, Dept. of Linguistics, University of Toronto

Canadian Aboriginal Peoples
Maureen Simpkins
Dr. Andrea Laforet, Canadian Ethnology Service,
Canadian Museum of Civilization

Canadian Place Names
Alan Rayburn

Cape Breton Island English
Dr. William Davey, Dr. Richard MacKinnon,
Dept. of Languages, Letters, and Communication
University College of Cape Breton

Etymology
E. S. C. Weiner

Flora
Jenny Bull

History
Dr. Martha Hanna, Dept. of History, University of Colorado

Meteorology
Dave Broadhurst, Environment Canada

Military
Lt. Cdr. M. J. Barber

Newfoundland English
Dr. William Kirwin, English Language Research Centre,
Memorial University of Newfoundland

New Zealand English
Harry Orsman

Pharmacology
Peng Chiang, B.Sc.Phm.

Quebec English
Dr. Pamela Grant-Russell, Département des lettres et
communications, Université de Sherbrooke

South African English
Dr. Penny Silva, Dictionary Unit for South African English,
Rhodes University

Textiles
Dr. Martin King, Dept. of Clothing and Textiles,
University of Manitoba

UK English
Catherine Bailey, Martin Coleman, Judy Pearsall, Della
Thompson, Bill Trumble

Ukrainian-Canadian English
Jars Balan

US English
Frank Abate

Contents

Preface to the First Edition

The *Canadian Oxford Dictionary* is exceptionally reliable in its description of Canadian English because it is based on thorough research into the language: five years of work by five Canadian lexicographers examining almost twenty million words of Canadian text held in databases representing over 8,000 different Canadian publications. Fiction and non-fiction books, newspapers, magazines, even theatre programs, grocery store flyers, and Canadian Tire catalogues were read by the lexicographers to ensure that the vocabulary recorded in this dictionary is the vocabulary of Canadians' everyday life. Indeed, many Canadian magazines and other periodicals provided the dictionary project with free subscriptions for the reading program, and we take this opportunity to acknowledge their generosity.

Furthermore, the sources we read reflect all regions of the country. The publications listed below are just a small sampling: *Inuit Art Quarterly*, *Up Here*, and *The Geography of the Canadian North* provided us with vocabulary from "north of 60". *West Coast Logger*, *Beautiful British Columbia*, and Jack Hodgins brought us the words of the West Coast. *Prairie Fire*, the *Winnipeg Free Press*, and the fiction of Sandra Birdsell and Guy Vanderhaeghe were a breath of prairie air, bringing with them numerous words borrowed from the Ukrainians, Icelanders, and others who settled in the west. Alice Munro spoke the language of Southwestern Ontario while the English of Daniel Richler and the *Montreal Gazette* had a distinct Québécois accent. David Adams Richards, *The Fiddlehead*, and the *Eastern Graphic* from Montague, PEI represented the Maritimes, while Wayne Johnston and other Newfoundland writers supplemented the thorough work of the editors of the *Dictionary of Newfoundland English*, to whom we pay homage.

Special attention has been given to economic activities, sports, and pastimes of particular interest to Canadians. Thus, the vocabulary of logging and wheat farming, of commercial fishing and mining is found alongside the very abundant vocabulary of hockey, figure skating, sport fishing, and hunting. Another area of thorough research was the culture of Aboriginal peoples in Canada.

The result of all this exhaustive research is that this dictionary lists almost two thousand Canadianisms, more than any other general dictionary of English, and, in addition, many words and senses of words which, though not unique to Canadians, are used infrequently by other English speakers and therefore do not appear in other dictionaries of English.

In addition to our Canadian databases, the database of citations which we share with the lexicographers of the *Oxford English Dictionary* gave us over twenty million words of American, British, Australian and other English-language sources to consult. This enabled us to determine with certainty which words and uses are unique to Canada and which we share with some or all other English speakers throughout the world. We were also thankful to be able to call on a group of about thirty Americans, with whom we checked any suspected Canadianisms, as well as the editors of Oxford dictionaries in the UK, Australia, New Zealand, South Africa, and the US. As a result, the geographical labelling in this dictionary is exceptionally accurate.

Our vast and ongoing reading program has also allowed us to detect new words as they become established in the language. Not surprisingly, the explosion of Internet use in the past five years has contributed many new words and meanings to the dictionary: *Web site*, *bookmark*, *browser*, and *firewall* are but a few of these. New foods such as *focaccia* and *jerk chicken* are constantly being borrowed from other cultures, a process that is particularly lively in Canada's highly multicultural society. Ordinary people's everyday shopping practices have been influenced by the introduction of *big box stores* and *power centres*. *Squeegee kids* have rapidly become a fixture at intersections in many urban centres.

Access to large text databases has also allowed us to establish Canadian spelling preferences. When the issue of spelling is raised, most Canadians think of the perennial colour/color debate, and indeed this dictionary does tell users which of the variants (traditionally called "British" and "American") Canadians prefer. But the issue goes far beyond that. One of the thorniest spelling problems is whether to spell a compound as one word, as two words joined by a hyphen or as two separate words. For every compound in the dictionary, we have examined Canadian text to determine what Canadian preference is.

Favoured Canadian pronunciations were determined by surveying a nationwide group of respondents. These very helpful participants eagerly responded to up to ten e-mails a day asking them to indicate their pronunciation for words as varied as *parmesan*, *diocese*, and *schedule*; we thank them for their contribution.

An added feature of this dictionary is its encyclopedic element. It includes short biographies of over 800 Canadians and 5,000 individuals and mythical figures of international significance. Of the almost 6,000 names for countries, provinces and states, cities, bodies of water, and landforms, more than twelve hundred are for Canadian places, and include the origin of the name. Historical events such as wars, treaties, and rebellions also have entries.

Thanks are due to many people in addition to those mentioned as part of the project team. In particular, Gordon and Patricia Barber devoted many hours of volunteer research time to the dictionary, looking into everything from names for Ukrainian garlic sausage to the practices of the Canadian Wheat Board and the death dates of Manitoba premiers. Margery Fee and Janice McAlpine, then of the Strathy Language Unit at Queen's University, were particularly helpful, especially in providing the basis for the corpus used for this project. John Russell, Communications Coordinator of Casey House in Toronto, reviewed our entries for words relating to the gay and lesbian communities. Helpful advice on scientific matters was provided by Jeremy Marshall and Bill Trumble. Michael Proffitt and the other new words editors at the *Oxford English Dictionary* assisted with neologisms. Innumerable but anonymous people answered our telephone calls to sports associations, businesses, cultural organizations, and other institutions with always helpful information to clarify our definitions. Unfailing support was provided by Beryl T. Atkins, John Simpson, Patrick Hanks, Michael Morrow, and Susan Froud.

February 1998   *Katherine Barber*

Preface to the Second Edition

The first edition of the *Canadian Oxford Dictionary* was published in 1998. For this second edition, the text has been completely revised, a major part of that revision being the addition of over 5,000 new words, senses, and phrases to ensure that the dictionary continues to be the most accurate and up-to-date description of English as it is used worldwide and particularly in Canada. The sources for this material continue to be our ongoing Canadian and international reading program and our continually updated Canadian corpus. The explosive growth of the World Wide Web since the appearance of our first edition has also allowed us to check in what parts of the English-speaking world a given word is used, and thus add even more precision to our geographical labelling.

Trends that we identified with the first edition have continued since then. Computer and phone technology have obviously been highly productive, as has medicine (and alternative medicine). Unfortunately we have become all too familiar with military terms like *biowarfare*, *dirty bomb*, and *weapons of mass destruction*. On the lighter side, however, food continues to be a rich source of new vocabulary, with *California rolls*, *bubble tea* and *macchiato*, and of course *carbs* and *supersizing* all becoming part of our everyday parlance. Those who fear that Canadian English may in some way be threatened can be reassured by the addition of 250 Canadianisms to the almost 2000 already in the dictionary.

The encyclopedic element of the dictionary has been revised. Biographical entries for living people have been updated to include significant events in their lives since 1998. Approximately 100 new Canadian biographies and another 100 new international biographies have been added. Geographical entries reflect new political realities such as the division of Czechoslovakia and the creation of Nunavut.

On a related front, currency units have been updated, including all former currencies now superseded by the euro. Municipal restructurings and renamings in Ontario and Quebec have been accounted for, and population figures for Canadian places now reflect the 2001 census. A new useful feature is the inclusion of almost 200 derivatives of Canadian place names (in all cases where we were able to determine that such a derivative exists), so that dictionary users may now quickly find out what to call a person from Moose Jaw.

A new feature of the second edition is the recommended word breaks in headwords. Unlike many other dictionaries, however, which simply allow for breaks at every syllable no matter how misleading that may be to a reader, this one provides "intelligent" word breaks for the greatest ease of comprehension. Thus, misleading breaks like "anal-ogy" (an ever-increasing phenomenon as word-processing programs are allowed to break words without the intervention of human intelligence) are avoided.

Spellings have been updated where necessary to reflect evolving Canadian practice. Our thanks to Warren Clements of *The Globe and Mail* and Patti Tasko of The Canadian Press for an ongoing dialogue on Canadian journalistic spelling preferences.

In short, this edition includes all the features that made the first edition so useful, as well as some new ones for which users have asked. It is our hope that Canadians, who embraced the first edition of this dictionary so enthusiastically, will find the second edition of the *Canadian Oxford Dictionary* equally reliable, up-to-date, and thorough, and even more suited to their needs.

May 2004   *Katherine Barber*

Canadian English: 250 Years in the Making

This dictionary marks the culmination of a century of changing attitudes towards Canadian English. In 1998, we can assert with pride the aspects of Canadian English that distinguish us from other speakers of English worldwide. But in the Victorian era, Canadians were thought to be—nay, expected to be—basically British, and to speak British English. We were, after all, the loyalists who upheld the Anglo-Celtic ethos in North America.

Just how far removed we had already become from Britain even in the nineteenth century was not well understood in the mother country. So it happened that the first person in recorded history who ever spoke of "Canadian English" did so disparagingly. The Rev. A. Constable Geikie, in an address to the Canadian Institute in 1857, ten years before Confederation, stated that "Canadian English" was "a corrupt dialect."

Mr. Geikie was a Canadian, but a fairly new one. He had immigrated to Sarnia, Ontario, with his parents and his older brothers in 1843. His Scottish-born parents had instilled in him the predilections of a breed that came to be known as Anglo-Canadians. Mr. Geikie believed that there was proper English and there was low English, and that proper English was the kind spoken by his family whereas low English was spoken by the people who were already here when his family arrived.

That was quite wrong, of course. The English his family heard spoken and saw written on their arrival at the port of "Muddy York" is the direct ancestor of the English recorded in this dictionary. Mr. Geikie's English is also recorded here, though not as directly. You have to know where to look. It can be found, for instance, in alternate pronunciations for such words as *leisure*, *tomato*, *either*, and *schedule*. For the real linguistic contribution of Mr. Geikie's generation was not to change the speech of the natives, much as they might have wished, but to expose them to a set of alternate forms on the linguistic model of the Old Country.

Their Canadian neighbours heard those alternate forms and, with the kind of tolerance that we occasionally dare to mention as a national virtue, sometimes even adopted them. They did not, in most cases, rid themselves of their old, familiar words and pronunciations. So by the second half of the nineteenth century, Canadians found themselves in possession of a variety of the English language enriched by British forms overlaid on a quite different North American foundation.

That foundation had been laid decades before the arrival of the Geikies and the other 50,000 British immigrants in their cohort. By now it is common knowledge that England's former colonies all speak distinctive varieties of English. They were founded at different times, and naturally the colonizers spoke English appropriate to their own time and place. North America received its first colonists some two centuries before England's other colonies, and as a result, the linguistic starting point was different. Then subsequent independent developments increased those differences.

The varieties spoken are not, however, equally different from one another. Canadian English and American English sound more like one another than they sound like, say, Australian English. Australian English sounds more like New Zealand English than any other variety, and both of them bear many similarities to South African English. Moreover, the Australian-New Zealand-South African accents share more features with the motherland accent than do the Canadian-American accents.

Even before Canada had a significant and widespread population, many distinctive features of the Canadian vocabulary came into being. Explorers and adventurers learned the names of all the places they visited from the native peoples, and in many cases the native names stuck. Our place names resound with words from the native language stocks, from Pugwash and Bouctouche to Wawa, Squamish, Nanaimo, and Tuktoyaktuk. Some places had more than one name because the indigenous name contended with an imperial one: Toronto was called York after the nondescript duke who was George III's second son, but in the end—since 1834—the Mohawk name prevailed.

Indigenous plants and animals usually kept their native names, such as tobacco, tamarack, skunk, raccoon, moose, and caribou. The European adventurers were novices in the wilds, and those who survived were the ones who availed themselves of native know-how: they learned to use foodstuffs such as pemmican, weapons such as tomahawks, watercraft such as kayaks, and apparel such as anoraks, mukluks, and moccasins. Because the first explorers were often francophones, a number of French terms attached themselves permanently to forest and plain: prairie, portage, bateau, snye.

As the population of the country grew, the distinctive vocabulary grew with it. When the land in Upper and Lower Canada was surveyed into lots for the first settlers, the main survey lines, usually one and a quarter miles apart, were called concessions, the French term, and country roads along them are called concession roads to this day.

Some of the earliest political terms used in Canada were either obscure terms in England or obsolete there, so their perpetuation in Canada and the meanings they took on make them unique. Among these are *reeve* as the political head of a municipality, *riding* as an electoral district, and *acclamation* as the election of a candidate without opposition.

The English-speaking population of Canada is largely the result of four significant waves of immigration that took place over slightly less than two centuries. Each wave had linguistic implications—that is, the immigrants influenced the way in which English is spoken in Canada to some extent. But, predictably, the first two were most important linguistically because they took place when the character of Canadian English was not yet formed, and thus they had a formative influence.

The two latest influxes peaked in 1910 and 1960, and brought people from all parts of the globe to Canada.

Ethnically, the new arrivals broke up the old Anglo-Celtic hegemony, but linguistically they have had only a mild influence. The immigrants' grandchildren–the second-generation Canadians–sound much the same as their contemporaries whose Canadian ancestry dates further back.

The first wave of immigrants were refugees from the American Revolution, known as Loyalists. When they arrived in Canada in the last decades of the 18th century, they formed the first permanent population in most regions. There were two main paths of immigration. One was from the coastal New England States, especially Connecticut and Massachusetts, where the first skirmishes of the Revolution took place in 1776, into what would become the provinces of New Brunswick, Prince Edward Island and Nova Scotia.

The other route was taken by Loyalists setting out from the states of Pennsylvania, New Jersey, New York, and Vermont, and they moved inland to entry points at the narrows of the lower Great Lakes, mainly at the upper St. Lawrence, the Niagara River and the Detroit River. There they were met by British governors and sent, with a modest allotment of provisions and tools, to make homesteads in the richly forested parklands of the Great Lakes basin. Where their numbers were concentrated, some of them quit farming to provide goods and services for the others: mills for lumber and mills for flour, blacksmithing, slaughterhouses, tanning, spinning and weaving, rooms and meals for travellers, spelling and arithmetic lessons, Sunday sermons. Towns grew up as central places for distributing goods and services, with markets, stores, churches and schools.

The founding population of any place exerts many subtle and largely unintentional dictates on those who succeed them. They set the pattern for roads in the countryside and streets in the towns, develop routines for land-clearing, crop selection, house construction, religious observance and educational practices, establish norms of communal co-operation (midwifery, health care, sewing bees, barn raising) and set the moral tone of the community.

One of the subtlest dictates–and one seldom considered because it is subconscious–is linguistic. The people who come after the founding population, the second or third generations of settlers, may come from far and wide, but their children will speak, under ordinary circumstances, just like the children whose parents arrived before them. The Loyalists naturally brought with them the sounds and syntax of the middle Atlantic states. Canadian English is directly descended from their speech.

The second wave of immigrants came from Britain and Ireland, and their arrival was a reaction to the growing power of the United States. In June 1812, the United States declared war on Britain and launched a series of raids on the Canadian borders. The war ended in 1814, with the aggressor repelled and the border intact.

British intelligence discovered that the Americans had expected their invading armies to be swelled by anti-English sympathizers as they marched through the colony. Though the Canadians had proven their loyalty, the governors felt uneasy about the broad base of American ancestry in Canada, and they set about diluting it by recruiting British settlers with promises of transport and land.

The British recruits more than doubled the population. Economically, they broadened the consumer base and brought new initiatives. Politically, they brought debating skills and imperialist powerlust; it is an astounding fact that three of our first five Prime Ministers were British-born–Macdonald (in office 1867-73 and 1878-91) and Mackenzie (1873-78) were native Scots, and Bowell (1894-96) was born in England.

Linguistically, their long-term influence was less remarkable. Most of the immigrants settled, naturally, in the towns and villages founded by the Loyalists, and, in the time-honoured pattern, their Canadian-born children grew up speaking not like their parents but like their schoolmates and playmates. The Loyalist base of Canadian English persisted.

Still, the British immigrants did make a lasting impression on Canadian speech. The Rev. Mr. Geikie was not alone in disliking what he heard from the natives, nor in imposing his own linguistic practices. For an entire century, until the 1950s, Anglo-Canadian attitudes enjoyed a special prestige. The most abiding result for Canadian English, as we have seen, is the double standard. Wherever British and North American practices differ from one another in vocabulary, pronunciation or spelling, Canadians usually tolerate both. Not only can Canadians vary their pronunciation of *either* and *leisure* without arousing any comment, but different regions sometimes maintain different norms, as, for instance, Ontarians prefer the spellings *colour* and *neighbour* but Albertans prefer *color* and *neighbor*. These variants–represented in this dictionary more completely than ever before–are the linguistic legacy of the first two immigrations in our history.

Now that Canada has become post-colonial both historically and spiritually, we can expect a great many linguistic changes. Our vocabulary–like the vocabulary of every modern nation–is swelling rapidly with words from technology, medicine, international politics, and other sources. But the changes in Canadian English will come not only from global networking. Our reach may extend around the globe, but in another sense the globe has come to us. Our largest cities and towns make neighbours of people of diverse creeds and colours. The integration of diverse peoples into the social fabric is having subtle effects just as the integration of the Scots and English did in the 1850s.

Just as our oldest vocabulary imported words from Inuit, Indians, and *coureurs de bois*, today the broader base of Canadian ethnicity demands a broadening of vocabulary. Most often, we take the foreign word and adjust it to our own phonology (Italian *bruschetta*, for instance, is often pronounced "brooshetta") and fit it into our own grammar (*teriyaki* is an adjective we use to modify nouns like steak or chicken, *cappuccino* is pluralized as *cappuccinos*). By accommodating foreign words of all kinds, our branch of the language is simply perpetuating an age-old tendency.

That tendency has never served us better than now. Linguistic change is irrepressible even in much more static societies than ours. The Loyalists did not sound like Shakespeare, and we do not sound like the Loyalists. Dr. Johnson's dictionary is a fascinating cornucopia of word lore for scholars but a completely useless guide for modern students and secretaries. It belongs to the Age of Enlightenment. *The Canadian Oxford Dictionary* belongs to the age of the global village, but with a wholesome Canadian bias. This dictionary has dozens of mundane uses–clarifying meanings, settling spellings, suggesting prounciations, providing synonyms, and all the rest– but the sum of all those uses is much greater than the parts. In the living language there is a reflection of where we have been and where we are likely to go next, and what we have considered important on the way. It is the codification of our common understanding.

February 1998

J.K. Chambers
University of Toronto

Guide to the Use of This Dictionary

The *Canadian Oxford Dictionary* is designed to be as straightforward and self-explanatory as possible and the use of special conventions has been kept to a minimum. The following notes will enable the reader to understand more fully the principles involved in assembling the information.

1. HEADWORD

The headword is printed in large bold roman type, or in large bold italic type if the word is originally a foreign word and not naturalized in English.

gran·ary /ˈgreinəri, ˈgran-/ *noun* (*pl.* **-aries**) **1** a storehouse for threshed grain. **2** a region producing, and esp. exporting, much grain. [Latin *granarium* from *granum* grain]

comme il faut /ˌkɒm iːl ˈfoː/ ● *predicative adjective* (esp. of behaviour, etiquette, etc.) proper, correct. ● *adverb* properly, correctly. [French, = as is necessary]

Order of headwords

● Strict alphabetical order is followed even when the headword consists of more than one word or of a hyphenated word (see also *Form of headwords* below).

● Capitalized headwords come before lower case headwords of the same spelling.

Gable, (Wil·liam) Clark (1901–60), US actor. He became famous through his numerous roles as a romantic leading man in Hollywood films of the 1930s; they include *It Happened One Night* (1934), for which he won an Oscar, and *Gone with the Wind* (1939).

gable *noun* **1 a** the triangular upper part of a wall enclosed by the two sloping planes of a ridged roof. **b** (in full **gable end**) a gable-topped wall. **2** a gable-shaped canopy over a window or door. ☐ **gabled** *adjective* (also in *combination*). [Middle English *gable* from Old Norse *gafl*]

● Numerals in headwords take precedence over letters in ordering.

Charles VI (1685–1740), Holy Roman emperor 1711–40. His unsuccessful claim to the Spanish throne instigated the War of the Spanish Succession (1701–14); he attempted to ensure that his daughter Maria Theresa would succeed him to the imperial throne, and the ensuing struggle for power on his death triggered the War of the Austrian Succession (1740–8).

Charles Mar·tel /mɑrˈtel/ (c.688–741), Frankish ruler of the eastern part of the Frankish kingdom from 715 and the whole kingdom from 719. He earned his nickname *Martel* ('the hammer') from his victory at Poitiers in 732, which effectively checked the Muslim advance into Europe; Charlemagne was his grandson.

● Headwords consisting of more than one word where the main headword has been reversed (as in **Versailles, Treaty of** and **Erie, Lake**; see *Form of headwords* below) are listed immediately after headwords with numerals.

Edward VIII (1894–1972), son of George V, king of the United Kingdom 1936, but not crowned. He abdicated 11 months after coming to the throne in order to marry Wallis Simpson, a US divorcee; he was created Duke of Windsor (1936).

Edward, Lake a lake on the border between Uganda and the Democratic Republic of the Congo (formerly Zaire). It is linked to Lake Albert by the Semliki River. [Albert *Edward*, Prince of Wales c.1888–9]

Ed·ward·ian /edˈwɑrdiən, -ˈwɔr-/ ● *adjective* of, characteristic of, or associated with the reign of Edward VII of England (1901–10). ● *noun* a person belonging to this period.

Form of headwords

● All compound nouns, adjectives, and adverbs, whether forming one word (such as **bathroom**, **newspaper**) or consisting of two or more words separated by a space or a hyphen (such as **serial number**, **mega-musical**) are listed as main entries.

● Main headwords consisting of more than one word are entered in the alphabetical place deemed to be most helpful to the user, which may not always correspond to the alphabetical place of the first word. Thus the main entry for **Treaty of Versailles** is entered under 'V' not 'T' and the headword becomes **Versailles, Treaty of**, while **Lake Erie** is entered as **Erie, Lake** (see also *Order of headwords* above).

● In biographical entries the surname of the person forms the main headword, except where the person is better known or only known by a first name, title, sobriquet, etc. (e.g. **Margaret of Anjou**, **Henry IV**).

Variant spellings

Any variant spellings or forms are given at the main headword, in bold type in brackets before the definition. They are also given their own headword entry and cross-reference when these are more than three entries away from the main headword. The main headword represents the most common form in Canadian usage.

phony (also **phon·ey**) *informal* ● *adjective* (**phon·i·er**, **phon·i·est**) **1** sham; counterfeit; fake. **2** insincere. ● *noun* (*pl.* **-ies** or **-eys**) a phony person or thing. ☐ **phon·i·ly** *adverb* **phon·i·ness** *noun* [20th c.: origin unknown]

phoney *var. of* PHONY.

Lazy Su·san *noun* (also **lazy Susan**) **1** a revolving stand on a table to hold condiments etc. **2** *N Amer.* an esp. kitchen cupboard or shelf designed to revolve in order to provide easy access to its contents.

● If the variant spelling or form applies only to one sense or part of an entry it will appear at that sense or part of the entry.

alp·ine ● *adjective* **1 a** of or relating to high mountains. **b** growing or found on high mountains, esp. above the timberline. **2** (**Alpine**) of or relating to the Alps. **3** of or relating to competitive downhill or slalom skiing (*compare* NORDIC 3). ● *noun* a plant native or suited to mountain districts.

Ne·an·der·thal /niˈandər,θɒl, -,tɒl/ ● *adjective* **1** of or belonging to the type of human widely distributed in paleolithic Europe, with a retreating forehead and massive brow ridges. **2** (also **neanderthal**) *jocular* or *derogatory*

a primitive, uncivilized, uncouth. **b** reactionary; extremely conservative. ● *noun* **1** a Neanderthal hominid. **2** (also **neanderthal**) *jocular* or *derogatory* **a** a primitive, uncivilized, or uncouth person. **b** a reactionary or extremely conservative person. [*Neanderthal*, a region in Germany where remains were found]

• Variant spellings chiefly restricted to certain parts of the English-speaking world are introduced by an appropriate restrictive label. Such labels indicate only that the variants are very infrequent in Canadian practice, not that they are unacceptable.

an·emia /əˈniːmiə/ *noun* (also esp. *Brit.* **an·aemia**) a deficiency in the blood, usu. of red cells or their hemoglobin, resulting in pallor and weariness. [modern Latin from Greek *anaimia* (as AN-[1], -EMIA)]

fibre·glass *noun* (also esp. *US* **fiber·glass**) any material consisting of glass filaments woven into a textile or paper, or embedded in plastic etc., for use as a construction or insulation material.

Alternative names

Alternative names or forms are given at the main headword. They are also given their own headword entry and cross-reference when these are more than three entries away from the main headword. The main headword represents the most common form in Canadian usage. The placing of alternative names at the main headword entry depends to a large extent on the context, but the general guidelines are as follows:

• Alternative names in place name entries are given in bold type in brackets before the definition, preceded either by 'also called', or by 'called in German' etc. where the alternative name represents the usual form in the given language. Such alternative forms are included principally for their historical or political importance. Alternative names needing more explanation may also be introduced in the text.

Dan·zig see GDAŃSK.

Gdańsk /gdansk/ (German **Danzig** /ˈdantsɪk/) an industrial port and shipbuilding centre in N Poland, on an inlet of the Baltic Sea; pop. (est. 2000) 456,574. It was a free city under a League of Nations mandate from 1910 until 1939, when it was annexed by Nazi Germany, precipitating hostilities with Poland and the outbreak of the Second World War. It passed to Poland in 1945. In the 1980s the Gdańsk shipyards were the site of the activities of the Solidarity movement, which eventually led to the collapse of the Communist regime in Poland in 1989.

Cit·lal·té·petl /ˌsiːtlalˈteipetəl/ (called in Spanish **Pico de Ori·zaba**) the highest peak in Mexico, in the east of the country, north of the city of Orizaba. It rises to a height of 5 699 m (18,503 ft.) and is an extinct volcano. [Aztec, = star mountain]

Pico de Ori·zaba /ˌpiːkoː dei ˌɒrɪˈzɒbə/ the Spanish name for CITLALTÉPETL.

Galilee, Sea of (also called **Lake Tiberias**) a lake in N Israel. The Jordan River flows through it from north to south.

Ti·ber·ias, Lake /taiˈbiːriəs/ an alternative name for the Sea of Galilee (see GALILEE, SEA OF).

• Alternative names in biographical entries are given in brackets in quotation marks before the definition, introduced by 'known as'.

Fred·erick I (known as 'Frederick Barbarossa' = 'Redbeard') (c.1123–90), king of Germany and Holy Roman emperor 1152–90. He made a sustained attempt to subdue Italy and the papacy, but was eventually defeated at the Battle of Legnano in 1176.

Abbreviations

Most commonly used abbreviations are included at the main headword entry for the full form, in bold, preceded by 'Abbr.',

with a cross-reference from the abbreviation to the main entry. In cases where the abbreviation is significantly more common than the full form, however, the main entry is to be found at the the abbreviation.

Co-operative Commonwealth Federation *noun hist.* (in Canada) a progressive labour party formed in 1932, re-founded as the New Democratic Party in 1961. Abbr.: **CCF**.

CCF *abbreviation Cdn hist.* CO-OPERATIVE COMMONWEALTH FEDERATION. □ **CCFer** *noun*

Registered Retirement Savings Plan *noun Cdn* = RRSP.

RRSP *abbreviation Cdn* Registered Retirement Savings Plan, a tax-sheltered plan for saving for retirement.

Homographs

Words that are different in origin but spelled the same way (called homographs) are treated as separate headwords, distinguished by superscript numbers immediately following the headword. Where necessary, each homograph is given a separate pronunciation.

pug[1] *noun* (in full **pug dog**) a dwarf breed of dog with a broad flat nose and deeply wrinkled face. [16th c.: perhaps from Low German or Dutch]

pug[2] *transitive verb* (**pugged**, **pug·ging**) **1** prepare (clay) for making bricks or pottery, by kneading and working into a soft and plastic condition. **2** pack (the space between floor joists) with earth, sawdust, etc., to provide sound insulation. □ **pug·ging** *noun* [19th c.: origin unknown]

pug[3] *noun slang* a boxer. [abbreviation of PUGILIST]

pug[4] ● *noun* the footprint of an animal. ● *transitive verb* (**pugged**, **pug·ging**) track by pugs. [Hindi *pag* footprint]

• Biographical and geographical entries dealing with people or places of the same name are treated within the same entry. Within biographical entries people are listed in alphabetical order according to their first names; in geographical entries the places are listed by population in descending order.

Greene ▶ **1 (Henry) Gra·ham** (1904–91), English novelist. He converted to Roman Catholicism in 1926, and the moral paradoxes of his faith underlie much of his work, which includes *Brighton Rock* (1938), *The Power and the Glory* (1940), and *Travels with My Aunt* (1969). **2 Lorne (Hyman)** (1915–87), Canadian actor. He was the chief news announcer for CBC Radio (1939–42), and is best known for his portrayal of Ben Cartwright in the popular television program 'Bonanza' (1959–72), and for his television series 'Lorne Greene's New Wilderness'. **3 Nancy** (b.1943), Canadian alpine skier. An outstanding skier, she won the World Cup in 1967, and at the Winter Olympics in 1968 she won a gold and a silver medal.

Cam·bridge /ˈkeimbridʒ/ **1** a city in E England, the county town of Cambridgeshire; pop. (est. 1998) 120,600. Cambridge University is located there. **2** a city in SW central Ontario, about 40 km northwest of Hamilton; pop. (2001) 110,372. **3** a city in E Massachusetts, forming part of the conurbation of Boston; pop. (2000) 101,400. Harvard University and the Massachusetts Institute of Technology are located there. [sense 2 named after an early flour mill in the former town of Preston, now part of Cambridge]

• However, as indicated in *Order of headwords* above, numerals in the names of monarchs etc. are considered an integral part of a headword: only those people sharing both name and numeral are treated in the same entry.

Alexander I ▶ **1** (c.1077–1124), king of Scotland 1107–24, son of Malcolm III. **2** (1777–1825), czar of Russia 1801–25, son of Paul I and grandson of Catherine the Great.

Alexander II ▶ **1** (1198–1249), king of Scotland 1214–49, son of William I. **2** (1818–81), czar of Russia 1855–81, son of Nicholas I. He emancipated the serfs and was assassinated by Nihilists.

2. WORD BREAKS

A small dot (·) indicates a point at which a word can be divided with a hyphen at the end of a line to improve the layout of a page of text. Note that these dots do not necessarily represent the divisions between syllables, which are not always the best places to divide words in print. Breaking **planetary** syllabically as **plane·tary**, for example, would be less helpful than breaking it as **planet·ary**.

When only the final segment of an inflected form is provided, the segment can be taken to indicate an acceptable division point for the inflected word. For example, the plural form **-ties** in the entry for **fifty** indicates that the word can be broken as **fif·ties**.

A word that is shown with recommended division points when it appears on its own, such as **fin·ger**, is not shown with the same breaks when it appears as part of a composite word, e.g. **fore·finger**, **finger·nail**. This is because the user is encouraged to divide the word between its elements rather than break the elements themselves. The elements of hyphenated compound words can be broken if necessary, but it is better not to break them within six letters of the hyphen. Thus only one of the division points in **gov·ern·ment** is given at **self-govern·ment**. Division points for open compound words such as **finger puppet** are not normally provided, since the breaks can be found at the entries for the separate words.

3. PRONUNCIATION

Where necessary, guidance on the pronunciation of a headword will be found in most cases immediately after the headword, enclosed in oblique strokes / /, and is based on thorough surveys of English-speaking Canadians from across the country.

• A pronunciation is not given for headwords consisting of more than one word where the separate words are listed elsewhere in the dictionary with their own pronunciation. For example, the entry **anabolic steroid** is not given its own pronunciation because pronunciations are given at **anabolic** and **steroid**.

• In some cases, more than one pronunciation is given: that given first is generally the most common pronunciation in Canada, though there may in fact be little difference in the frequency of use of the given pronunciations.

• Pronunciations for variant forms are given at the main entry; those for alternative names are given at the alternative name (cross-reference) entry.

• Guidance on the pronunciation of words printed in bold type within an entry (for example, in the derivatives list) is limited to cases in which the pronunciation is substantially different from that of the headword.

Foreign pronunciations

All pronunciations of foreign place names and people's names are transcribed as they are most commonly spoken by English speakers, as are the pronunciations of words recently borrowed from other languages. Whether the pronunciation given is in the 'foreign' or Anglicized form reflects the degree to which the word has been naturalized by English-speaking Canadians.

The International Phonetic Alphabet

Pronunciations are given using a modified version of the International Phonetic Alphabet (IPA). The symbols used, with their values, are to be found on the back endpapers of this volume and along the bottom of each two-page spread in the text.

4. PART OF SPEECH

• A part of speech identifier, such as *noun, verb, adjective*, etc. is given for all main headwords except place name entries, biographical entries, and other proper name entries not including languages and peoples.

• All derivatives are given a part of speech identifier. Compounds and phrases listed under a main headword are given a part of speech when necessary to aid clarity.

• When a headword has more than one part of speech, each successive part of speech is introduced by a bullet marker:

> **lim·ber¹** ● *adjective* **1** lithe, agile, nimble. **2** flexible. ● *verb* (usu. foll. by *up*) **1** *transitive* make (oneself or a part of the body etc.) supple. **2** *intransitive* warm up in preparation for athletic etc. activity. □ **lim·ber·ness** *noun* [16th c.: origin uncertain]

The following additional explanations should also be noted (see also section 8 below):

• *attributive* is used to describe an adjective placed in front of the word it modifies; *attributive adjective* is used as a part of speech identifier for adjectives which can normally only be used attributively, as **breakneck** in *breakneck speed* or **consulting** in *consulting physician*.

• *attributive* is also used to describe a noun which is placed before and used to modify another noun but where its function is not fully adjectival (e.g. **prize** in *a prize poem; the poem is prize* is not acceptable usage).

• *predicative* is used to describe an adjective placed in the predicate of a sentence (usually after a verb); *predicative adjective* is used as a part of speech identifier for adjectives which can normally only be used predicatively, as **asleep** in *she's asleep* (not *the asleep child*), or **bonkers** in *he's bonkers* (not *the bonkers character*).

• 'in *combination*' refers to uses of words (especially adjectives) as an element joined usually by a hyphen with another word, as **bellied**, in *pot-bellied, yellow-bellied*, and so on.

5. INFLECTION

Inflection of words (i.e. plurals, past tenses, etc.) is given after the part of speech concerned:

> **sa·fari** /səˈfɑri/ *noun* (*pl.* **sa·faris**) **1** a hunting or scientific expedition, esp. in East Africa (*go on safari*). **2** a sightseeing trip esp. to see African animals in their natural habitat. [Swahili from Arabic *safara* to travel]

> **char¹** ● *transitive & intransitive verb* (**charred, char·ring**) **1** make or become black by burning; scorch. **2** burn or be burned to charcoal. ● *noun* a charred substance. [apparently back-formation from CHARCOAL]

• The forms given are normally those in use in Canadian English. Variant forms with restricted distribution are identified by the appropriate label.

> **carol** ● *noun* a joyous song or hymn, esp. one celebrating Christmas. ● *verb* (**car·olled, car·ol·ling**; *US* **car·oled, car·ol·ing**) **1** *intransitive* sing carols, esp. outdoors at Christmas. **2** *transitive & intransitive* sing joyfully. □ **carol·ler** *noun* (*US* **carol·er**). [Old French *carole, caroler*, of unknown origin]

• Pronunciation of inflected forms is given when this differs significantly from the pronunciation of the headword. The designation '*pronunc.* same' denotes that the pronunciation, despite a change of form, is the same as that of the headword.

• The inflection of nouns, verbs, adjectives, and adverbs is given when it is irregular (as described below) or when, though regular, it may cause difficulty (as with forms such as **budgeted, coos**, and **taxis**).

Plurals of nouns

Nouns that form their plural regularly by adding -s (or -es when they end in -s, -x, -z, -sh, or soft -ch) receive no comment. Other plural forms are indicated, notably:

- nouns ending in -i or -o.

- nouns ending in -y.

- nouns ending in Latinate forms such as -a and -um.

- nouns with more than one plural form, e.g. **fish** and **aquarium**.

- nouns with plurals involving a change in the stem, e.g. **foot**, **feet**.

- nouns with a plural form identical to the singular form, e.g. **sheep**.

- nouns ending in -ful, e.g. **handful**.

Forms of verbs

The following forms are regarded as regular:

- third person singular present forms adding -s to the stem (or -es to stems ending in -s, -x, -z, -sh, or soft -ch).

- past tenses and past participles adding -ed to the stem, dropping a final silent e (e.g. **changed**, **danced**).

- present participles adding -ing to the stem, dropping a final silent e (e.g. **changing**, **dancing**).

Other forms are given, notably:

- doubling of a final consonant, e.g. **bat**, **batted**, **batting**.

- strong and irregular forms involving a change in the stem, e.g. **come**, **came**, **come**, and **go**, **went**, **gone**.

Comparative and superlative of adjectives and adverbs

- Words of one syllable adding -er or -est, those ending in silent e dropping the e (e.g. **braver**, **bravest**), are regarded as regular. Most one-syllable words have these forms, but participial adjectives (e.g. **pleased**) do not.

- Those that double a final consonant (e.g. **hot**, **hotter**, **hottest**) are given, as are two-syllable words that have comparative and superlative forms in -er and -est (of which very many are forms ending in -y, e.g. **happy**, **happier**, **happiest**), and their negative forms (e.g. **unhappier**, **unhappiest**).

- It should be noted that specification of these forms indicates only that they are used; it is usually also possible to form comparatives with more and superlatives with most (as in more happy, most unhappy), which is the standard way of proceeding with adjectives and adverbs that cannot be inflected.

Adjectives in -able formed from transitive verbs

These are given as derivatives when there is sufficient evidence of their currency; in general they are formed as follows:

- Verbs drop silent final -e except after c and g (e.g. **achievable** but **exchangeable**).

- Verbs of more than one syllable ending in y (preceded by a consonant or qu) change y to i (e.g. **enviable**, **fanciable**).

- A final consonant is often doubled as in normal inflection (e.g. **conferrable**, **regrettable**).

6. DEFINITION

Definitions are listed in a numbered sequence in order of comparative familiarity and importance, with the most current and important senses first. They are subdivided into lettered senses (**a**, **b**, etc.) when these are closely related or call for collective treatment.

> **pan¹** ● *noun* **1 a** a container of metal, earthenware, heat-resistant glass, etc. used for cooking. **b** the contents of this. **2** a panlike vessel in which substances are heated etc. **3** any similar shallow container such as the bowl of a pair of scales or that used for washing gravel etc. to separate gold. **4** *N Amer.* = ICE PAN. **5** part of the lock that held the priming in old guns. **6** a hollow in the ground (*salt pan*). **7** *US slang* the face. **8** a hard substratum of soil. **9 a** a metal drum in a steel band. **b** steel-band music and the associated culture. ● *verb* (**panned**, **pan·ning**) **1** *transitive informal* criticize severely. **2** *transitive slang* hit or punch (a person). **3 a** *transitive* (often foll. by *off*, *out*) wash (gold-bearing gravel) in a pan. **b** *intransitive* search for gold by panning gravel. **c** *intransitive* (foll. by *out*) (of gravel) yield gold. □ **pan out** (of an action etc.) turn out well or in a specified way. □ **pan·ful** *noun* (*pl.* **-fuls**). **pan·like** *adjective* [Old English *panne*, perhaps ultimately from Latin *patina* 'dish']

7. ILLUSTRATIVE EXAMPLES

Many examples of words in use are given to support, and in some cases supplement, the definitions. These appear in italics in brackets. They are meant to amplify meaning and (especially when following a grammatical point) illustrate how the word is used in context:

> **de·sist** *intransitive verb* (often foll. by *from*) stop, cease, or abstain (*please desist from interrupting; when requested, he desisted*). [Old French *desister* from Latin *desistere* (as DE-, *sistere* stop, reduplication from *stare* stand)]

8. GRAMMATICAL INFORMATION

Definitions are often accompanied by explanations in brackets of how the word or phrase in question is used in context. Often, the comment refers to words that usually follow (foll. by) or precede (prec. by) the word being explained. For example, at **sack¹**, shown below, sense 1b usually appears as a *sack of* (something), as the example further illustrates; and senses 2 and 3 always appear as *the sack*:

> **sack¹** ● *noun* **1 a** a large strong bag, esp. one made of heavy fabric, for storing or conveying goods. **b** (usu. foll. by *of*) this with its contents (*a sack of potatoes*). **c** a quantity contained in a sack. **2** (prec. by *the*) *informal* dismissal, esp. from employment. **3** (prec. by *the*) *N Amer. slang* bed. **4** *Baseball* a base. **5** *Football* an act or instance of sacking. **6 a** a woman's short loose dress with a sacklike appearance. **b** *archaic* or *hist.* a woman's loose gown, or a silk train attached to the shoulders of this. **7** a man's or woman's loose-hanging coat not shaped to the back. ● *transitive verb* **1** put into a sack or sacks. **2** *informal* dismiss esp. from employment. **3** *Football* tackle (the quarterback) behind the line of scrimmage before he is able to throw the ball. □ **hit the sack** *informal* go to bed. **sack out** esp. *N Amer. informal* go to bed; go to sleep. □ **sack·ful** *noun* (*pl.* **-fuls**). **sack·like** *adjective* [Old English *sacc* via Latin *saccus* from Greek *sakkos*, of Semitic origin]

- With verbs, the fact that a sense is transitive or intransitive can affect the construction. In the examples given below, both sense 4 of **prevail** and sense 1 of **urge** contain the grammatical note 'foll. by *on*'; because the former is intransitive, the construction is *prevail on a person*), and because the latter is transitive, the construction is *urge a person on*).

> **pre·vail** /prɪ'veɪl/ *intransitive verb* **1** (often foll. by *against*, *over*) be victorious or gain mastery. **2** be the more usual or predominant. **3** exist or occur in general use or experience; be current. **4** (foll. by *on*, *upon*) persuade. [Latin *praevalēre* (as PRAE-, *valēre* have power), influenced by AVAIL]

> **urge** ● *transitive verb* **1** (often foll. by *on*) drive, hasten, or impel with force or encouragement (*he urged the horses forward; she urged her teammates on*). **2** (often foll. by *to* + infin.) encourage or entreat earnestly or persistently; exhort (*we urged them to go*). **3** (often foll. by *on*, *upon*) advocate (an action or argument etc.) pressingly or emphatically (to a person). **4** (often foll. by *that* +

clause) advocate or recommend eagerly or insistently (*we urge caution; we urge that they should be cautious*). **5** present or state earnestly or insistently in argument, justification, or defence (*I must urge the seriousness of this problem*). ● *noun* a strong impulse, desire, or tendency. □ **ur·ging** *noun* [Latin *urgēre* press, drive]

• The formula (foll. by *to* + infin.) means that the word is followed by a normal infinitive with *to*, as in *want to leave* and *eager to learn*.

• The formula (foll. by *that* + clause) indicates the routine addition of a clause with *that*, as in *said that it was late*. (For the omission of *that*, as in *said it was late*, see the usage notes in the entry for **that**.)

• 'pres. part.' and 'verbal noun' denote verbal forms in -*ing* that function as adjectives and nouns respectively, as in *set him laughing* and *tired of asking*.

9. USAGE

If the use of a word is restricted in any way, this is indicated by any of various labels printed in italics, as follows:

Geographical labels

• *Cdn* indicates that the use is found exclusively in Canadian English. To show that a use is restricted to a particular region or regions within Canada, any of the following labels may be included in addition to *Cdn: Alta., BC, Cape Breton, E Ont., Man., Maritimes, NB, Nfld, North, NS, NW Ont., NWT, Nunavut, Ont., PEI, Prairies, Que., Sask., S Ont., West,* and *Yukon*.

• *N. Amer.* indicates that the use is found chiefly in Canada and the US but not in British English.

• *Brit.* indicates that the use is found chiefly in British English (and often also in Australian and New Zealand English and in other parts of the Commonwealth except Canada) but not in North American English.

• *US* indicates that the use is found chiefly in American English but not in Canadian or British English except as a conscious Americanism.

• Other geographical designations (e.g. *Austral.*, NZ, *Scot.*, *S Africa*) restrict uses to the areas named.

• These usage labels should be distinguished from comments of the type '(in the UK)' or '(in Canada)' preceding definitions, which indicate that the thing defined (usually an institution or organization) pertains only to the country named, and that the name given is used by all speakers of whatever nationality to denote the institution or organization.

> **FCC** *abbreviation* **1** (in Canada) Farm Credit Corporation. **2** (in the US) Federal Communications Commission.

Register labels

Levels of usage, or registers, are indicated as follows:

• *formal* indicates uses that are normally restricted to formal (esp. written) English, e.g. **commence**.

• *informal* indicates a use that is normally restricted to informal (esp. spoken) English.

• *slang* indicates a use of the most informal kind, unsuited to formal written English and often restricted to a particular social group.

• *coarse slang* indicates a slang use which is normally taboo.

• *dialect* indicates a word that is restricted to nonstandard or dialect use.

• *archaic* indicates a word that is now obsolete and found only in texts at least a century old, or in special contexts such as legal or religious use, or is used for special effect, e.g. **thereunto**.

• *dated* indicates a word from living memory that is no longer current, which may still be used occasionally by older generations, but would strike most people as old-fashioned, e.g. **galluses**.

• *literary* indicates a word or use that is found chiefly in literature.

• *poet.* (= poetic) indicates uses confined to poetry or other contexts with similar connotations.

• *jocular* indicates uses that are intended to be humorous or playful.

• *derogatory* denotes uses that are intentionally disparaging.

• *offensive* denotes uses that cause offence, whether intentionally or not.

• *disputed* indicates a use that is disputed (and often regarded as erroneous or controversial). Often this is enough to alert the user to a danger or difficulty; when further explanation is needed, a usage note (see note below) is used as well or instead. In using this label the editors are not passing judgment on disputed words and usages; they are merely indicating that these words and usages are in fact current, and warning that their use may provoke criticism.

• *hist.* (= historical) denotes a word or use that is confined to historical reference, normally because the thing referred to no longer exists.

• *proprietary* denotes a term that has the status of a trademark (see Note on proprietary status, found at the end of this guide).

Subject labels

The many subject labels, e.g. *Law, Med., Math., Naut.*, show that a word or sense is current only in a particular field of activity.

Usage notes

These are added to give extra information not central to the definition, and to explain points of grammar and usage. They are introduced by the symbol ¶. The purpose of these notes is not to prescribe usage but to alert the user to a difficulty or controversy attached to a particular use.

10. IDIOMS AND PHRASAL VERBS

These are listed in alphabetical order after the treatment of the main senses, introduced by the symbol □. The words *a, the, one*, and *person* do not count for purposes of alphabetical order:

> **ask** *verb* **1** *transitive* call for an answer to or about (*ask her about it; ask him his name; ask a question of her*). **2** *transitive* seek to obtain from another person (*ask a favour of; ask to be allowed*). **3** *transitive* (usu. foll. by *out* or *over*, or *to* (a function etc.)) invite; request the company of (*must ask them over; asked her to dinner*). **4** *intransitive* (foll. by *for*) seek to obtain, meet, or be directed to (*ask for a donation; ask for the post office; asking for you*). □ **ask after** inquire about (esp. a person). **ask for it** *slang* invite trouble. **ask me another** *informal* I do not know. **for the asking** (obtainable) for nothing. **I ask you!** an exclamation of disgust, surprise, etc. **if you ask me** *informal* in my opinion. □ **ask·er** *noun* [Old English *āscian* etc. from West Germanic]

They are normally defined under the first important word in the phrase, except when a later word is more clearly the key word or is the common word in a phrase with variants (in which case a cross-reference often appears at the entry for the first word):

> **grasp** ● *verb* **1** *transitive* **a** clutch at; seize greedily. **b** hold firmly; grip. **2** *intransitive* (foll. by *at*) try to seize; accept avidly. **3** *transitive* understand or realize (a fact or meaning). ● *noun* **1** a firm hold; a grip. **2** (foll. by *of*) **a** mastery or control (*a grasp of the situation*). **b** a mental hold or understanding (*a grasp of the*

facts). □ **grasp at straws** see STRAW. **within one's grasp** capable of being grasped, achieved, or comprehended by one. □ **grasp·able** *adjective* **grasp·er** *noun* [Middle English *graspe*, *grapse* perhaps from Old English *græpsan* (unrecorded) from Germanic, related to GROPE: compare Low German *grapsen*]

11. DERIVATIVES

Words formed by adding a suffix to another word are in many cases listed at the end of the entry for the main word, introduced in a separate section by the symbol □. In this position they are not given a definition since they can be understood from the sense of the main word and that given at the suffix concerned.

ra·pa·cious /rəˈpeɪʃəs/ *adjective* greedy, grasping, extortionate. □ **ra·pa·cious·ly** *adverb* **ra·pa·cious·ness** *noun* **ra·pa·city** /rəˈpasɪti/ *noun* [Latin *rapax* *-acis* from *rapere* snatch]

Derivatives with the same meaning are listed in alphabetical order. When further definition is called for they are given main entries in their own right (e.g. **changeable**).

12. ETYMOLOGY

A brief account of the etymology, or origin, of words is given in square brackets at the end of entries. Etymologies are not given for compound words of obvious formation (such as **bathroom** and **jellyfish**), for routinely formed derivatives (such as **muddy** and **seller**), or for words consisting of clearly identified elements already explained (such as **Anglo-Irish** and many words in *in-*, *re-*, *un-*, etc.). Etymologies are also not always given for every word of a set sharing the same basic origin (**proprietary** and **proprietor**, for example). Noteworthy features, such as an origin in Old English, are however always given.

Entries for Canadian place names include etymologies; etymologies are not regularly given for foreign place names or for personal names.

The following notes act as a guide to the etymological information in this dictionary.

• The immediate source language is given first. Forms in other languages are not given if they are exactly or nearly the same as the English form given in the headword.

• Words of Germanic origin are described as 'from Germanic' or 'from West Germanic' as appropriate; unrecorded or postulated forms are not normally given.

• 'Old English' is used for words that are known to have been used before AD 1150, and 'Middle English' for words traceable to the period 1150–1500 (no distinction being made between early and late Middle English).

• Words of Romance origin are referred to their immediate source, usually French (or Old French before 1400), and then to earlier sources when known.

• 'Anglo-French' denotes the variety of French current in England in the Middle Ages after the Norman Conquest.

• 'Romanic' denotes the vernacular descendants of Latin that are the source of French, Spanish, Italian, etc. Romanic forms are almost always of the 'unrecorded' or 'postulated' kind, and are not specified except to clarify a significant change of form. Often the formula 'ultimately from Latin' etc. is used to indicate that the route from Latin is via Romanic forms.

• 'Latin' denotes classical Latin up to about AD 200; 'Old Latin', that before about 75 BC; 'Late Latin', that of about 200–600; 'medieval Latin', that of about 600–1500; 'modern Latin', that in use (mainly for technical and scientific purposes) since about 1500.

• Similar divisions for 'late', 'medieval', and 'modern' are made for Greek.

• Many English words have corresponding forms in both French and Latin, and it cannot always be established which was the immediate source. In such cases the formula 'French or Latin' is used (e.g. at **section**: 'French *section* or Latin *sectio*'); in these cases the Latin form is the source of the French word and (either directly or indirectly) of the English word.

• When the origin of a word cannot be reliably established, the forms 'origin unknown' and 'origin uncertain' are used. Often in these cases the century of the first recorded occurrence of the word in English is given.

• An equals sign (=) precedes words in other languages that are parallel formations from a common source (cognates) rather than sources of the English word.

13. PREFIXES, SUFFIXES, AND COMBINING FORMS

A large selection of prefixes (**ex-**, **re-**, etc.), suffixes (**-ion**, **-ness**, etc.), and combining forms (such as **bio-** and **-graphy**) is given in the main body of the text. The entries for prefixes and suffixes should be consulted to explain the many routinely formed derivatives given at the end of entries (see above, section 11).

• The pronunciation given for a prefix, suffix, or combining form is an approximate one for purposes of articulating and (in some cases) identifying the headword; pronunciation and stress may change considerably when they form part of a word.

14. CROSS-REFERENCES

These are introduced by any of a number of reference types, as follows:

• '=' denotes that the meaning of the item at which the cross-reference occurs is the same as that of the item referred to.

• 'see' indicates that information will be found at the point referred to, and is widely used for encyclopedic matter and in the idiom sections of entries to deal with items that can be located at any of a number of words included in the idiom (see also above, section 10).

• 'see also' indicates that further information can be found at the point referred to.

• 'compare' denotes an item related or relevant to the one being consulted, and the reference often completes or clarifies the exact meaning of the item being treated.

• 'opp.' refers to a word or sense that is opposite to the one being treated, and again often completes or clarifies the sense.

• References of the kind '*pl.* of' (= plural of), '*past* of' (= past tense of), etc., are given at entries for inflections and other related forms.

• 'var. of' (= variant of) refers to a word that is the main headword form of one or more variant forms.

Cross-references preceded by any of these reference types appear in small capitals if the reference is to a main headword, and in italics if the reference is to an idiom or phrasal verb to be found within the entry for the first word (or other specified word).

15. ABBREVIATIONS AND SYMBOLS

A complete list of the abbreviations commonly used in this dictionary can be found on the back endpapers of this volume. Abbreviations in general use (such as 'etc.', 'i.e.', and those for books of the Bible) are explained in the dictionary itself.

Symbols used in the dictionary

¶ introduces notes on usage.

□ introduces defined phrases and idioms, or undefined derivatives formed by adding a suffix to the main word.

● introduces a new part of speech.

16. BIOGRAPHICAL ENTRIES

Biographical entries follow place name entries of the same spelling.

Names

● Forenames which are not widely known or used are given in brackets, which are also used to indicate that a person's initials are better known than his or her full forenames.

> **Frost ▸ 1 Les·lie (Mis·camp·bell)** (1895–1963), Canadian politician, Progressive Conservative premier of Ontario 1949–61. **2 Rob·ert (Lee)** (1874–1963), US poet. Considered one of the most accessible of modern poets, he is best known for poems such as 'Mending Wall' (1914), 'The Road Not Taken' (1916), 'Birches' (1916), and 'Stopping by Woods on a Snowy Evening' (1923), which are characterized by simple language and a conversational tone.

> **Cas·son** /'kasən/ **A(l·fred) J(o·seph)** (1898–1992), Canadian painter. A member of the Group of Seven from 1926, he is best known for his sun-drenched paintings of small towns in Ontario, including 'Anglican Church at Magnetawan' (1933) and 'Country Store' (1945).

● Nicknames and shortened forms of forenames are given in brackets after other forenames.

> **Orr, Rob·ert Gor·don** ('Bobby') (b.1948), Canadian hockey player. He joined the NHL Boston Bruins in 1967, and revolutionized the role of the defenceman. He is the only defenceman ever to win the Art Ross Trophy as leading scorer.

● Nicknames, bynames, and alternative names which substitute for a person's full name are given in brackets after forenames, preceded by the words 'known as'. Such names are often given their own headword entry and cross-reference when they are more than three entries away from the main headword.

> **Mary I** (known as Mary Tudor) (1516–58), daughter of Henry VIII, queen of England 1553–8. As queen she attempted to re-establish Catholicism; she married Philip II of Spain, and after putting down several revolts, began a series of religious persecutions which earned her the name 'Bloody Mary'.

> **Mary Tudor** see MARY I.

> **Red Baron** see RICHTHOFEN.

> **Richt·hof·en** /'rɪxtoːfən/ **Baron Man·fred von** (known as 'the Red Baron') (1892–1918), German aviator. He was the top German fighter pilot of the First World War, downing 80 Allied aircraft between 1916 and 1918 before being shot down.

● Full names, names in other languages, etc. are given in brackets following the forenames as appropriate.

● The term 'born' is used when a person has changed his or her name or is normally known by a title or name other than the one he or she was born with. The introductions 'pseudonym of' (for writers) and 'title of' (for political leaders, rulers, etc.), as well as a number of other self-explanatory introductions, are also used.

> **Bono** /'bɒnoː/ (born Paul Hewson) (b.1960), Irish rock singer and songwriter; lead singer for the Irish rock group U2.

> **Se·cord** /'siːkɔrd/ **Laura** (born Laura Ingersoll) (1775–1868), Canadian heroine. In June of 1813 she walked 30 km from Queenston to Beaver Dams to warn the British that she had

overheard American officers discussing a plan to attack; two days later the British ambushed and defeated the American forces as a result of her warning.

Dates

● Dates given for literary works are those of first publication. Dates for dramatic works, musical compositions, etc. are also of first publication, unless the date of first performance is more appropriate: where this is the case it is indicated in the text.

● The abbreviation *fl.* (= *floruit*, flourished) and imprecise periods such as '2nd c. BC' are occasionally used in place of birth and death dates, where the latter are not known.

Nationality

● Where a person has changed his or her nationality both the original and later nationality are indicated.

● Nationalities relating to former names of countries are used where appropriate to the period in question, e.g. Ian Smith is described as 'Rhodesian', Mikhail Gorbachev as 'Soviet'.

● British (rather than English, Scottish, etc.) is used to describe politicians and other public officials of the UK; in most other cases, the appropriate nationality within the UK (English, Welsh, Scottish, or Northern Irish) is used.

Foreign titles of works

Titles of works in a foreign language are normally translated into English, and the original publication date is given. Exceptions to this rule include cases in which the title is better known or only known in the original language (such as *À la recherche du temps perdu*).

17. PLACE NAME ENTRIES

Place names come before biographical names of the same spelling.

Statistics

● Population figures are given for all countries, for all Canadian provinces and territories and US states, for towns and cities, and for some islands and other regions. The most recent census figures available are given; where no census figure is available, the most reliable up-to-date estimate is given.

● Other significant statistics, such as length of rivers, height of mountains, are also given.

Names

● For Chinese names the Pinyin transliteration is given as the main headword; if other transliterations or anglicized forms are well attested they are given as variant forms (e.g. the main headword is **Beijing** but the form **Peking** is also given).

● For other foreign names the form most familiar to speakers of English is given as the main headword, with variant and alternative names if necessary.

● Where a place name has changed, the former name (or names) is given as appropriate.

NOTE ON PROPRIETARY STATUS

Canadian
Oxford
Dictionary

Aa

A¹ *noun* (also **a**) (*pl.* **As** or **A's**) **1** the first letter of the alphabet. **2** *Music* the sixth note of the diatonic scale of C major. **3** the first hypothetical person or example. **4** the highest class or category (of academic marks etc.). **5** (usu. **a**) *Algebra* the first known quantity. **6** a human blood type of the ABO system. □ **from A to B** from one place to another (*takes us from A to B*). **from A to Z** over the entire range, completely.

A² *abbreviation* (also **A.**) **1** ampere(s). **2** answer. **3** Associate of. **4** atomic (energy etc.). **5** alto. **6** analog (recording).

A³ *symbol* adenine.

Å *abbreviation* angstrom(s).

A1 *adjective* **1** *informal* excellent; first-rate. **2** (of a ship) in first-class condition.

a¹ *indefinite article* (also **an** before a vowel) **1** (as an unemphatic substitute) one, some, any. **2** one like (*a Judas*). **3** one single (*not a thing in sight*). **4** the same (*all of a size*). **5** in, to, or for each (*twice a year; $20 a person; five a side*). [weakening of Old English *ān* one; sense 5 originally = A²]

a² *preposition* (usu. as *prefix*) **1** to, towards (*ashore; aside*). **2** (with verb in pres. part. or infin.) in the process of; in a specified state (*a-hunting; a-wandering; abuzz; aflutter*). **3** on (*afire; afoot*). **4** in (*nowadays*). [weakening of Old English prep. *an, on*]

a³ *abbreviation* atto-. **2** are (metric unit).

a-¹ *prefix* not, without (*amoral; agnostic; apetalous*). [Greek *a-*]

a-² *prefix* implying motion onward or away, adding intensity to verbs of motion (*arise; awake*). [Old English *a-*, originally *ar-*]

a-³ *prefix* to, at, or into a state (*adroit; agree; amass; avenge*). [from Latin *ad-* to, at]

a-⁴ *prefix* **1** from, away (*abridge*). **2** of (*akin; anew*). **3** out, utterly (*abash; affray*). **4** in, on, engaged in, etc. (see A²). [sense 1 from Latin *ab*; sense 2 from Old English *of* prep.; sense 3 from Latin *ex*]

a-⁵ *prefix* assimilated form of AD- before *sc, sp, st*.

-a¹ *suffix* forming nouns from Greek, Latin, and Romanic feminine singular, esp.: **1** ancient or Latinized modern names of animals and plants (*amoeba; campanula*). **2** oxides (*alumina*). **3** geographical names (*Africa*). **4** ancient or Latinized modern feminine names (*Lydia; Hilda*).

-a² *suffix* forming plural nouns from Greek and Latin neuter plural, esp. names (often from modern Latin) of zoological groups (*phenomena; Carnivora*).

-a³ *suffix informal* **1** of (*kinda; coupla*). **2** have (*mighta; coulda*). **3** to (*oughta*).

AA *abbreviation* **1** ALCOHOLICS ANONYMOUS. **2** a size of battery, having a voltage of 1.5 V. **3** *Sport* **a** a level of amateur sports competition. **b** *Baseball* a minor league directly below AAA. **4** a level of bond rating below AAA. **5** *Military* anti-aircraft. **6** (in Ontario) ADULT ACCOMPANIMENT. **7** *Brit.* Automobile Association.

aa /ˈɒɒ/ *noun* very rough light-textured lava (*compare* PAHOEHOE). [Hawaiian 'a-'a]

AAA *abbreviation* **1** a size of battery, having a voltage of 1.5 V. **2** Amateur Athletic Association. **3** American Automobile Association. **4** *Sport* **a** a level of amateur sports competition. **b** *Baseball* a minor league directly below the major leagues. **5** the highest level of bond or credit rating assigned to governments etc.

AAC *abbreviation Cdn* (*BC*) *Forestry* ANNUAL ALLOWABLE CUT.

Aachen /ˈɒxən, ˈɒkən/ (called in French **Aix-la-Chapelle**) an industrial city and spa in western Germany, in North Rhine-Westphalia, close to the Belgian and Dutch borders; pop. (est.

2002) 240,300. German emperors were crowned in Aachen from the time of Charlemagne (who was born and buried there) until 1531.

Aalto /ˈɒltoʊ/ **Alvar** (1898–1976), Finnish architect and furniture designer, noted especially for his use of asymmetry, curvilinear shapes, and contrasting natural materials, esp. wood. He invented a style of laminated bent plywood furniture.

AAM *abbreviation* air-to-air missile.

A. & R. *abbreviation* **1** artists and recording. **2** artists and repertoire.

aard·vark /ˈɑrdvɑrk/ *noun* a nocturnal, insectivorous mammal, *Orycteropus afer*, having large ears, a long snout, and a long tongue, native to sub-Saharan Africa. [Afrikaans from *aarde* earth + *vark* pig]

aard·wolf /ˈɑrdwʊlf/ *noun* (*pl.* **aard·wolves** /-wʊlvz/) an African mammal, *Proteles cristatus*, related to the hyena family, with grey fur and black stripes, that feeds on insects. [Afrikaans from *aarde* earth + *wolf* wolf]

Aar·hus /ˈɔrhuːs/ (also **Århus**) a city on the coast of east Jutland, Denmark; pop. (est. 2000) 284,846.

Aaron¹ /ˈɛrən/ (in the Biblical and Quranic traditions) the brother of Moses and traditional founder of the Jewish priesthood (Exod. 4 ff.).

Aaron² /ˈɛrən/ **Henry Louis ('Hank')** (b.1934), US baseball player, holder of the record for home runs (755).

Aaron's rod *noun* any of various tall upright plants, esp. mullein *Verbascum thapsus*. [AARON¹]

AAU *abbreviation* (in the US) Amateur Athletic Union.

AB¹ *noun* a human blood type of the ABO system.

AB² *abbreviation* **1** Alberta (in official postal use). **2** *US* Bachelor of Arts. **3** *Baseball* (times) at bat. **4** able rating or seaman. [sense 2 from Latin *Artium Baccalaureus*; sense 4 from *able-bodied*]

ab *noun* (usu. in *pl.*) *slang* an abdominal muscle. [abbreviation]

ab- *prefix* off, away, from (*abduct; abuse*). [French or Latin]

aba /ˈabə/ *var. of* ABAYA.

Aba /ˈabə/ a city in S Nigeria, on the west bank of the Aba River; pop. (est. 1991) 500,183.

aba·ca /ˈabəkə/ *noun* **1** manila hemp. **2** the plant, *Musa textilis*, yielding this. [Spanish *abacá*]

aback *adverb* **1** *archaic* backwards, behind. **2** *Naut.* (of a sail) pressed against the mast by a headwind. □ **take aback 1** surprise, disconcert (*your request took me aback; I was greatly taken aback by the news*). **2** (as **taken aback**) (of a ship) with the sails pressed against the mast by a headwind. [Old English *on bæc* (as A², BACK)]

aba·cus /ˈabəkəs/ *noun* (*pl.* **aba·cus·es**) **1** an oblong frame with rows of wires or grooves along which beads are slid, used for calculating. **2** *Archit.* the flat slab on top of a capital, supporting the architrave. [Latin from Greek *abax abakos* slab, drawing board, from Hebrew *'ābāk* dust]

Aba·dan /ˌabəˈdan/ a major port and oil-refining centre on an island of the same name on the Shatt al-Arab waterway in W Iran; pop. (1996) 206,073.

Abad·don /əˈbadən/ *noun* **1** hell. **2** the Devil (Rev. 9:11). [Hebrew, = destruction]

abaft /əˈbaft/ *Naut.* ● *adverb* in the stern half of a ship. ● *preposition* nearer the stern than; aft of. [A² + *-baft* from Old English *beæftan* from *be* BY + *æftan* behind]

Aba·kan /ˌabəˈkan/ an industrial city in south central Russia, capital of the republic of Khakassia; pop. (est. 2002) 171,000. It was known as Ustabakanskoe until 1931.

aba·lone /ˌabəˈloːni/ *noun* any mollusc of the genus *Haliotis*, with a shallow ear-shaped shell having respiratory holes, and lined with mother-of-pearl. [Latin American Spanish *abulón*]

aban·don ● *transitive verb* **1** give up completely or before completion (*abandoned hope*; *abandoned the game*). **2 a** forsake or desert (a person or a post of responsibility). **b** leave or desert (a motor vehicle or ship). **3 a** give up to another's control or mercy. **b** *reflexive* yield oneself completely to a passion or impulse. ● *noun* lack of inhibition or restraint; reckless freedom of manner (*wild abandon*). □ **aban·don·er** *noun* **aban·don·ment** *noun* [Old French *abandoner* from *à bandon* under control, ultimately from Late Latin *bannus, -um* BAN¹]

aban·doned *adjective* **1 a** (of a person) deserted, forsaken (*an abandoned child*). **b** (of a building, vehicle, etc.) left empty or unused (*an abandoned cottage*; *an abandoned ship*). **2** (of a person or behaviour) unrestrained, profligate.

abase *transitive verb & reflexive* humiliate or degrade (another person or oneself). □ **abase·ment** *noun* [Old French *abaissier* (as A-³, *baissier* to lower, ultimately from Late Latin *bassus* short of stature): influenced by BASE²]

abash *transitive verb* (usu. as **abashed** *adjective*) embarrass, disconcert. □ **abash·ment** *noun* [Old French *esbaïr* (*es-* = A-⁴ 3, *baïr* astound or *baer* yawn)]

abate *verb* **1** *transitive & intransitive* make or become less strong, severe, intense, etc. **2** *transitive Law* a quash (a writ or action). **b** put an end to (a nuisance). □ **abate·ment** *noun* [Old French *abatre* from Romanic (as A-³, Latin *batt(u)ere* beat)]

aba·tis /ˈabətɪs/ *noun* (also **abat·tis** /əˈbatɪs/) (*pl.* same /-tiːz/; **aba·tis·es**, **abat·tis·es**) *hist.* a defence made of felled trees with the boughs pointing outwards. [French from Old French *abatre* fell: see ABATE]

abat·toir /ˈabəˌtwar/ *noun* a slaughterhouse. [French (as ABATIS, -ORY¹)]

ab·axial /abˈaksiəl/ *adjective Bot.* (esp. of the lower surface of a leaf) facing away from the stem of a plant (*compare* ADAXIAL). [AB- + AXIAL]

abaya /ˈabeɪjə/ *noun* (also **aba**, **abba** /ˈabə/) a sleeveless outer garment worn by Arabs. [Arabic *'abāya*]

ab·bacy /ˈabəsi/ *noun* (*pl.* **-cies**) the office, jurisdiction, or period of office of an abbot or abbess. [ecclesiastical Latin *abbacia* from *abbat-* ABBOT]

Ab·bado /əˈbadoː/ **Clau·dio** (b.1933), Italian conductor, music director of the Vienna State Opera (1986–91), frequently conducted the Vienna Philharmonic Orchestra from 1971, and was principal conductor of the London Symphony Orchestra (1979–88), and the Berlin Philharmonic (1989–2002).

Ab·bas·id /əˈbasɪd/ ● *noun* a member of a dynasty of caliphs ruling in Baghdad 750–1258. ● *adjective* of this dynasty. [*Abbas*, Muhammad's uncle d.652]

ab·ba·tial /əˈbeɪʃəl/ *adjective* of an abbey, abbot, or abbess. [French *abbatial* or medieval Latin *abbatialis* (as ABBOT)]

Abbe /ˈabi/ **Ernst** (1840–1905), German physicist. He worked with Carl Zeiss from 1866, and in 1868 invented the apochromatic lens; he also designed several optical instruments, including a light condenser for use in microscopes and a refractometer.

abbé /aˈbei/ *noun* a francophone priest not belonging to a religious order. [French from ecclesiastical Latin *abbas abbatis* ABBOT]

ab·bess /ˈabes/ *noun* a woman who is the head of certain communities of nuns. [Old French *abbesse* from ecclesiastical Latin *abbatissa* (as ABBOT)]

Abbe·vil·lian /abˈvɪliən/ ● *noun* the culture of the earliest paleolithic period in Europe, characterized by the production of flint hand axes. ● *adjective* of this culture. [French *Abbevillien* from *Abbeville* in N France]

ab·bey *noun* (*pl.* **-beys**) **1** the building(s) occupied by a community of monks or nuns, esp. of a Benedictine order. **2** the community itself. **3** a church or house that was once an abbey. [Old French *abbeie* etc. from medieval Latin *abbatia* ABBACY]

ab·bot *noun* a man who is the head of an abbey of monks. □ **abbot·ship** *noun* [Old English *abbod* from ecclesiastical Latin *abbas -atis* from Greek *abbas* father, from Aramaic *'abbā*]

Abbots·ford a city in southwestern BC, about 70 km southeast of Vancouver, close to the border with Washington State; pop. (2001) 115,463. □ **Abbots·ford·ian** *noun* [H. B. *Abbott*, d.1915, CPR general superintendent and brother of Sir John J. C. Abbott]

Ab·bott, **Sir John Jo·seph Cald·well** (1821–93), 3rd prime minister of Canada (1891–92), succeeding John A. Macdonald as leader of the Conservative Party.

Abbott and Cos·tel·lo a duo comprised of US comics **Bud Abbott** (born William A. Abbott) (1896–1974) and **Lou Costello** (born Louis Francis Cristillo) (1908–59). They appeared on stage, radio, television, and film, and are known for their famous baseball-commentary routine 'Who's on First'; their films include *Buck Privates* (1941) and *The Naughty Nineties* (1945).

ab·brevi·ate *transitive verb* shorten, esp. represent (a word etc.) by a part of it. [Latin *abbreviare* shorten, from *brevis* short: compare ABRIDGE]

ab·brevi·a·tion *noun* **1** an abbreviated form, esp. a shortened form of a word or phrase. **2** the process of abbreviating.

ABC *noun* **1** the alphabet. **2** (**the ABC's**) the rudiments of any subject. **3** an alphabetical guide.

ABC Islands an acronym for the Dutch islands of Aruba, Bonaire, and Curaçao, which lie in the Caribbean Sea near the coast of Venezuela.

ABD *noun* a doctoral candidate whose course work is completed but whose dissertation remains to be written or defended. [acronym from *all* but *d*issertation]

ab·di·cate /ˈabdɪˌkeɪt/ *verb* **1** *intransitive & transitive* give up or renounce (the throne). **2** *transitive* renounce (a responsibility, duty, etc.). □ **ab·di·ca·tion** *noun* **ab·di·ca·tor** *noun* [Latin *abdicare abdicat-* (as AB-, *dicare* declare)]

ab·domen /ˈabdəmən/ *noun* **1** the part of the body containing the stomach, bowels, reproductive organs, etc. **2** *Zool.* the hinder part of an insect, crustacean, spider, etc. [Latin]

ab·dom·in·al /abˈdɒmɪnəl/ ● *adjective* of or pertaining to the abdomen. ● *noun* (usu. in *pl.*) an abdominal muscle. □ **ab·dom·in·al·ly** *adverb* [modern Latin *abdominalis*]

ab·dom·in·o·plasty *noun* (*pl.* **-ties**) cosmetic surgery in which excess abdominal fat and skin is removed. [ABDOMEN + -PLASTY]

ab·duct *transitive verb* **1** carry off or kidnap (a person) illegally by force or deception. **2** (of a muscle etc.) draw (a limb etc.) away from the middle line of the body. □ **ab·duc·tee** *noun* **ab·duc·tion** *noun* **ab·duct·or** *noun* [Latin *abducere abduct-* (as AB-, *ducere* draw)]

Abduh /ˈabdʊ/ **Muhammad** (1849–1905), Egyptian Islamic scholar and jurist, leader of a movement to modernize and revitalize Islam.

Abdul Hamid II /ˌabdʊl ˈhamɪd/ (1842–1918), the last sultan of Turkey, 1876–1909. An autocratic ruler, he suspended parliament and the constitution and ruthlessly suppressed his non-Muslim subjects, notably the Armenians.

Ab·dul·lah /abˈdʊlə/ **Sheik Muhammad** (1905–82), Kashmiri Muslim leader. An activist against the arbitrary rule of the Hindu Maharajah of Kashmir in the 1930s, he eventually won for Kashmir a form of autonomy within India.

Ab·dul·lah ibn Hus·sein /ˌab.dʊlə ˌɪbən hʊˈsein/ (1882–1951), Emir of Transjordan (1921–46) and its first king after the country (later called Jordan) became independent in 1946. He was assassinated in 1951.

Abdul Rah·man /ˌabdʊl ˈrɒman/ **Tunku** (= Prince) (1903–90), Malayan leader. He negotiated Malayan independence from Britain (1957) and the formation of the Federation of Malaysia (1963), becoming Malaya's first prime minister and continuing as the first prime minister of Malaysia (1963–70).

abeam *adverb* **1** on a line at right angles to a ship's or an aircraft's length. **2** (foll. by *of*) opposite the middle of (a ship etc.).

abed *adverb* in bed.

Abed·nego /əˈbednəˌɡoː/ *Bible* see SHADRACH.

Abeg·weit¹ /ˈabəɡˌwɪt/ a name for Prince Edward Island. [Mi'kmaq = cradled in the waves]

Abeg·weit² /ˈabəɡˌwɪt/ *noun* a member of an Algonquian band living on PEI. [ABEGWEIT¹]

Abel¹ /ˈeibəl/ *Bible* the younger son of Adam and Eve, murdered by his brother Cain (Gen. 4).

Abel² /ˈɒbel/ **Niels Henrik** (1802–29), Norwegian mathematician. He proved that equations of the fifth degree cannot be solved by conventional algebraic methods, and made advances in the fields of power series and elliptic functions.

Abel·ard /ˈabəˌlɑrd/ **Peter** (1079–1142), French theologian and philosopher. Twice condemned for heresy, he emphasized the role of reason and logic in the analysis of Christian doctrine. His passionate love affair with his pupil Héloïse led to his being castrated by her family, and he became a monk.

Consonants: b *but* d *dog* f *few* g *get* h *her* j *yes* k *cat* l *leg* m *man* n *no* p *pen* r *red* s *sit*

Abel·ian group /əˈbiːliən/ *noun Math.* a group the members of which are related by a commutative operation (i.e. a×b=b×a). [N.H. ABEL]

Aben·aki /abəˈnaki/ (also **Ab·naki**) ● *noun* **1** (*pl.* same or **-akis**) a member of an Algonquian-speaking Aboriginal people of the eastern woodlands of N America, now living mainly in S Quebec and Maine. **2** the language of the Abenaki. ● *adjective* of or relating to the Abenaki or their culture or language. [French *abénaqui* from Eastern Abenaki *wapánahki* lit. 'person of the dawn land']

Abeo·kuta /abeiˈoːkuːtə/ a city in SW Nigeria, capital of the state of Ogun; pop. (est. 2002) 529,700.

Aber·deen[1] a city and seaport in NE Scotland; pop. (est. 2002) 188,300. It is a centre of the North Sea oil industry.

Aberdeen[2] ▸ **1 George Hamilton Gordon, 4th Earl of** (1784–1860), British Conservative politician, prime minister of a coalition government 1852–55. He was forced to resign over the Crimean War. **2 Ishbel Maria Gordon, Countess of** (1857–1939). Devoted to humanitarian and social causes, she helped to form the National Council of Women of Canada and created the Victorian Order of Nurses during her stay in Canada as wife of the Governor General. **3** her husband, **John Campbell Gordon, 7th Earl of** (1847–1934), Governor General of Canada 1893–98. Later elevated to 1st Marquess of Aberdeen and Temair.

Aberdeen Angus *noun* a breed of hornless black beef cattle, with a compact and low-set body.

Aberdeen Lake a lake in western Nunavut, situated about 140 km west of Baker Lake. [J. C. Gordon, 7th Earl of ABERDEEN]

Aber·deen·shire an administrative region and former county of NE Scotland. Between 1975 and 1996 it was part of Grampian region.

Aber·don·ian /abərˈdoːniən/ ● *adjective* of Aberdeen. ● *noun* a native or citizen of Aberdeen. [medieval Latin *Aberdonia*]

Aber·fan /abərvan/ a village in South Wales where, in 1966, a slag heap collapsed, overwhelming houses and a school and killing 28 adults and 116 children.

Aber·hart /ˈeibərˌhɑrt/ **Wil·liam ('Bible Bill')** (1878–1943), Canadian politician, founder of the Social Credit movement in Canada and premier of Alberta 1935–43. After an early career as a teacher, lay preacher, and radio evangelist, he founded a Social Credit party which he led to a landslide victory in the 1935 Alberta election.

aber·rant /əˈberənt/ *adjective* **1** esp. *Biol.* diverging from the normal type. **2** departing from an accepted standard. □ **aber·rance** *noun* **aber·rancy** *noun* [Latin *aberrare aberrant-* (as AB-, *errare* stray)]

aber·ra·tion /abəˈreiʃən/ *noun* **1** a departure from what is normal or accepted or regarded as right. **2** a moral or mental lapse. **3** *Biol.* deviation from a normal type. **4** *Optics* the failure of rays to converge at one focus because of a defect in a lens or mirror. **5** *Astronomy* the apparent displacement of a celestial body, meteor, etc., caused by the observer's velocity. [Latin *aberratio* (as ABERRANT)]

abet *transitive verb* (**abet·ted, abet·ting**) (often in **aid and abet**) encourage or assist (esp. an offender or offence). □ **abet·ment** *noun* [Old French *abeter* from *à* to + *beter* BAIT]

abet·tor *noun* a person who abets.

abey·ance /əˈbeiəns/ *noun* (usu. prec. by *in, into*) a state of temporary disuse or suspension. □ **abey·ant** *adjective* [Anglo-French *abeiance* from Old French *abeer* from *à* to + *beer* from medieval Latin *batare* gape]

abhor /əbˈhɔr/ *transitive verb* (**ab·horred, ab·hor·ring**) detest; regard with disgust and hatred. □ **ab·hor·rer** *noun* [Latin *abhorrēre* (as AB-, *horrēre* shudder)]

ab·hor·rence /əbˈhɒrəns/ *noun* **1** disgust; detestation. **2** a detested thing.

ab·hor·rent /əbˈhɒrənt/ *adjective* **1** (often foll. by *to*) (of conduct etc.) inspiring disgust, repugnant; hateful, detestable. **2** (foll. by *to*) not in accordance with; strongly conflicting with (*abhorrent to the spirit of the law*).

abide *verb* (*past* **abided** or rarely **abode** /əˈboːd/) **1** *transitive* (usu. in *neg.* or *interrogative*) tolerate, endure (*can't abide him*). **2** *intransitive* (foll. by *by*) **a** act in accordance with (*abide by the rules*). **b** remain faithful to (a promise). **3** *intransitive archaic* **a** remain, continue. **b** dwell. □ **abid·ance** *noun* [Old English *ābidan* (as A-[2], *bidan* BIDE)]

abid·ing *adjective* enduring, permanent (*an abiding love*). □ **abid·ing·ly** *adverb*

Abi·djan /abiˈdʒan/ the chief port of the Ivory Coast and capital (1935–83); pop. (est. 2002) 3,310,400.

Abi·gail /ˈabigeil/ *Bible* the wife of David.

abil·ity *noun* (*pl.* **-ities**) **1** (often foll. by *to* + infin.) capacity or power (*has the ability to write songs*). **2** cleverness, talent; mental power (*natural athletic ability; has many abilities*). [from Latin *habilitas -tatis* from *habilis* able]

-ability *suffix* forming nouns of quality from, or corresponding to, adjectives in *-able* (*capability; vulnerability*). [French *-abilité* or Latin *-abilitas*: compare -ITY]

ab initio /ˌab ɪˈnɪʃioː/ *adverb* from the beginning. [Latin]

abio·gen·esis /ˌeibaioˈdʒenəsɪs/ *noun* **1** the formation of living organisms from non-living substances. **2** the supposed spontaneous generation of living organisms. [A-[1] + Greek *bios* life + GENESIS]

Abi·ola /ˌabiˈoːlə/ **Mos·hood Kashi·mawo Ola·wale** (1937–98), Nigerian Social Democratic politician. He declared himself president-elect in June 1993 after election results showed him to be on the way to a comfortable victory; the election was annulled by the ruling military regime, and in 1994 Abiola was placed under house arrest.

abiot·ic /ˌeibaiˈɒtik/ *adjective* **1** physical rather than biological; not derived from living organisms. **2** devoid of life; sterile. [A-[1] + Greek *bios* life]

Abi·tibi /abɪˈtɪbi/ (in full **Abitibi-Témi·sca·mingue**) an administrative region of W Quebec including the communities of Rouyn-Noranda, Val-d'Or and Amos.

Abi·tibi, Lake a lake in NE Ontario and NW central Quebec, straddling the provincial border and situated roughly midway between James Bay and the Ottawa River. [Cree and Algonquin, = waters of the middle]

Abi·tibi River a river in NE Ontario, 547 km long, draining Lake Abitibi and flowing generally northwestward to join Moose River, just southwest of Moosonee. [see ABITIBI, LAKE]

ab·ject *adjective* **1** miserable, wretched (*abject poverty*). **2** degraded, self-abasing, humble (*abject apology*). **3** despicable. □ **ab·ject·ly** *adverb* **ab·ject·ness** *noun* [Latin *abjectus* past participle of *abicere* (as AB-, *jacere* throw)]

ab·jec·tion *noun* a state of misery or degradation.

ab·jure /əbˈdʒʊr/ *transitive verb* **1** renounce on oath (an opinion, cause, claim, etc.). **2** swear perpetual absence from (one's country etc.). □ **ab·ju·ra·tion** /ˌabdʒʊˈreiʃən/ *noun* [Latin *abjurare* (as AB-, *jurare* swear)]

Ab·khazia /abˈkɒziə/ an autonomous territory in NW Georgia, south of the Caucasus mountains on the Black Sea; pop. (est. 2002) 517,500; capital, Sokhumi. It corresponds to the ancient region of Colchis. □ **Ab·khaz·ian** *noun & adjective*

ab·la·tion /abˈleiʃən/ *noun* **1** the surgical removal of body tissue. **2** *Geol.* the wasting or erosion of a glacier, iceberg, or rock by melting or the action of water. **3** the evaporation or melting of part of the expendable, protective outer surface of a spacecraft through heating by friction with the atmosphere. □ **ab·late** *transitive verb* [Latin *ablat-* (as AB-, *lat-* past participle stem of *ferre* carry)]

abla·tive /ˈablətɪv/ *Grammar* ● *noun* the case (esp. in Latin) of nouns and pronouns (and words in grammatical agreement with them) indicating an agent, instrument, or location. ● *adjective* of or in the ablative. [(as ABLATION)]

ablative absolute *noun* an absolute construction in Latin with a noun and participle or adjective in the ablative case (see ABSOLUTE).

ab·laut /ˈablaʊt/ *noun* a change of vowel in related words or forms, esp. in Indo-European languages, arising from differences of accent and stress in the parent language, e.g. in *sing, sang, sung*. [German]

ablaze *predicative adjective* **1** on fire (*set it ablaze*). **2** (often foll. by *with*) glittering, glowing. **3** (often foll. by *with*) greatly excited.

able *adjective* (**abler, ablest**) **1** having the capacity or power (*was not able to come*). **2** having great ability; clever, skilful. [Latin *habilis* handy, from *habēre* to hold]

-able *suffix* forming adjectives meaning: **1** that may or must be (*eatable; forgivable; payable*). **2** that can be made the subject of (*dutiable; objectionable*). **3** that is relevant to or in accordance with (*fashionable; seasonable*). **4** (with active sense, in earlier word formations) that may (*comfortable; suitable*). [French *-able* or Latin *-abilis*]

able-bodied *adjective* **1** not physically handicapped. **2** fit, healthy.

able-bodied seaman *noun* (also **able-bodied rating**) a non-commissioned member of the Royal Navy.

abled *adjective* able-bodied, not disabled (also in *combination: differently abled*).

able seaman *noun* (also **Able Seaman**) a non-commissioned officer of the second-lowest rank in the Canadian Navy, ranking above Ordinary Seaman and below Leading Seaman. Abbr.: **AB**.

abloom *predicative adjective* blooming; in flower.

ab·lu·tion /əˈbluːʃən/ *noun* (usu. in *pl.*) **1** the ceremonial washing of parts of the body or sacred vessels etc. **2** *informal* the ordinary washing of the body (*to perform one's ablutions*). **3** *Military informal* a building containing washing places etc. □ **ab·lu·tion·ary** *adjective* [Latin *ablutio* (as AB-, *lutio* from *luere lut-* wash)]

ably *adverb* capably, cleverly, competently.

-ably *suffix* forming adverbs corresponding to adjectives in *-able*.

ABM *abbreviation* **1** ANTI-BALLISTIC MISSILE. **2** *Cdn* automated banking machine.

Ab·naki /abˈnaki/ *var. of* ABENAKI.

ab·ne·gate /ˈabnəˌɡeɪt/ *transitive verb* **1** give up or deny oneself (a pleasure etc.). **2** renounce or reject (a right or belief). □ **ab·ne·ga·tion** /ˌabnəˈɡeɪʃən/ *noun* **ab·ne·gator** *noun* [Latin *abnegare abnegat-* (as AB-, *negare* deny)]

ab·nor·mal *adjective* **1** deviating from what is normal or usual; exceptional. **2** relating to or dealing with what is abnormal (*abnormal psychology*). □ **ab·nor·mal·ly** *adverb* [earlier and French *anormal*, *anomal* from Greek *anōmalos* ANOMALOUS, assoc. with Latin *abnormis* (as AB-, *normis* from *norma* rule)]

ab·nor·mal·ity *noun* (*pl.* **-ities**) **1 a** an abnormal quality, occurrence, etc. **b** the state of being abnormal. **2** a physical irregularity.

ABO /ˌeɪbiːˈoʊ/ *adjective* designating or pertaining to the system in which blood is classified into four types (A, AB, B, and O), based on the presence or absence of certain inherited antigens.

Abo /ˈaboʊ/ (also **abo**) *Austral. slang usu. offensive* ● *noun* (*pl.* **Abos**) an Aboriginal. ● *adjective* Aboriginal. [abbreviation]

aboard ● *adverb* **1** on or into a ship, aircraft, train, etc. **2** onto a horse; on horseback. **3** in or into a group, team, etc. **4** *Baseball* on base. **5** *Naut.* alongside. ● *preposition* **1** on or into (a ship, aircraft, train, etc.). **2** on or onto (a horse). □ **all aboard!** a call that warns of the imminent departure of a ship, train, etc. [from A² + BOARD and French *à bord*]

abode¹ *noun* **1** a dwelling place; one's home. **2** *archaic* a stay or sojourn. [verbal noun of ABIDE: compare *ride, rode, road*]

abode² *past of* ABIDE.

aboi·teau /ˌabwɒˈtoʊ/ *noun* (*pl.* **aboi·teaux**) *Cdn* (*Maritimes*) *hist.* **1** a sluice gate in a dike, which allows flood water to flow out but does not allow sea water to enter. **2** the dike system containing such gates. [Acadian French, from Western French dialect *aboteau*, from Old French *bot* dike, influenced by French *bois* wood]

abol·ish *transitive verb* put an end to the existence or practice of (esp. a custom or institution). □ **abol·ish·able** *adjective* **abol·ish·er** *noun* **abol·ish·ment** *noun* [Latin *abolēre* destroy]

abo·li·tion *noun* **1** the act or process of abolishing or being abolished. **2** (**Abolition**) **a** the abolition of slavery in the British Empire or the US. **b** the abolition of capital punishment.

abo·li·tion·ist *noun* a person who favours the abolition of a practice or institution, esp. of capital punishment or of slavery. □ **abo·li·tion·ism** *noun*

abo·ma·sum /ˌabəˈmeɪsəm/ *noun* (*pl.* **abo·masa** /-sə/) the fourth stomach of a ruminant. [modern Latin from AB- + OMASUM]

A-bomb *noun* = ATOMIC BOMB.

abom·in·able /əˈbɒmɪnəbəl/ *adjective* **1** detestable; loathsome; morally reprehensible. **2** very bad or unpleasant (*abominable weather*). □ **abom·in·ably** *adverb* [Latin *abominabilis* from *abominari* deprecate (as AB-, *ominari* from OMEN)]

abominable snowman *noun* an unidentified manlike or bearlike animal said to exist in the Himalayas; a yeti.

abom·in·ate /əˈbɒmɪˌneɪt/ *transitive verb* detest, loathe.

abom·in·a·tion /əˌbɒmɪˈneɪʃən/ *noun* **1** an object of disgust. **2** an odious or degrading habit or act. **3** loathing.

ab·oral /abˈɔrəl/ *adjective* away from or opposite the mouth. [AB- + ORAL]

Ab·orig·in·al /ˌabəˈrɪdʒənəl/ (also **aboriginal**) ● *adjective* **1** (of peoples) inhabiting or existing in a land from the earliest times or from before the arrival of colonists. **2** of or relating to Aboriginal peoples. **3** of the Australian Aboriginals. ● *noun* **1** an Aboriginal inhabitant. **2** an Aboriginal inhabitant of Australia. □ **ab·orig·in·al·ity** /-ˈalɪti/ *noun* **ab·orig·in·al·ly** *adverb* [AS ABORIGINE + -AL]

Aboriginal rights *plural noun* rights enjoyed by a people by virtue of the fact that their ancestors inhabited an area from time immemorial.

Aboriginal title *noun* the communal right of Aboriginal peoples to occupy and use the land inhabited by their ancestors from time immemorial.

ab·orig·ine /ˌabəˈrɪdʒɪni/ *noun* (usu. in *pl.*) **1** an Aboriginal inhabitant. **2** (usu. **Aborigine**) an Aboriginal inhabitant of Australia. **3** an Aboriginal plant or animal. [back-formation from pl. *aborigines* from Latin, prob. from phr. *ab origine* from the beginning]

aborn·ing *esp. N Amer.* ● *predicative adjective* being born or produced. ● *adverb* (esp. in **die aborning**) while being born or produced.

abort ● *verb* **1** *intransitive* **a** (of a woman) undergo abortion; miscarry. **b** (of a fetus) suffer abortion. **2** *transitive* **a** effect the abortion of (a fetus). **b** effect abortion in (a mother). **3 a** *transitive* cause to end fruitlessly or prematurely; stop in the early stages. **b** *intransitive* end unsuccessfully or prematurely. **4 a** *transitive* abandon or terminate (a space flight, computer application, or other technical project) before its completion, usu. because of a fault. **b** *intransitive* terminate or fail to complete such an undertaking. **5** *Biol.* **a** *intransitive* (of an organism) remain undeveloped; shrink away. **b** *transitive* cause to do this. ● *noun* **1** a prematurely terminated space flight or other undertaking. **2** the termination of such an undertaking. [Latin *aboriri* miscarry (as AB-, *oriri ort-* be born)]

abor·ti·fa·cient /əˌbɔrtɪˈfeɪʃənt/ ● *adjective* effecting abortion. ● *noun* a drug or other agent that effects abortion.

abor·tion *noun* **1** the expulsion of a fetus (naturally or esp. by medical induction) from the womb before it is able to survive independently. **2** a stunted or deformed creature or thing. **3** the failure of a project or an action. **4** *Biol.* the arrest of the development of an organ.

abor·tion·ist *noun* **1** a person who carries out abortions, esp. illegally. **2** a person who favours the legalization of abortion.

abortion pill *noun* a pill which induces an early abortion by preventing the implantation of the embryo.

abor·tive *adjective* **1** fruitless, unsuccessful, unfinished. **2** resulting in abortion. **3** *Biol.* (of an organ etc.) rudimentary; arrested in development. □ **abor·tive·ly** *adverb*

abor·tu·ary /əˈbɔrtʃuˌeri/ *noun* (*pl.* **-aries**) *N Amer. derogatory* a place in which abortions are performed; an abortion clinic. [blend of ABORT + MORTUARY]

Abou·kir Bay, Battle of /ˌabuːˈkiːr/ (also called **Battle of the Nile**) a naval battle (1798) in the Mediterranean off Aboukir Bay at the mouth of the Nile, in which the British under Nelson defeated the French fleet.

abou·lia *var. of* ABULIA.

abound *intransitive verb* **1** be plentiful. **2** (foll. by *in, with*) be rich; teem or be infested. [Old French *abunder* etc. from Latin *abundare* overflow (as AB-, *undare* from *unda* wave)]

about ● *preposition* **1 a** on the subject of; in connection with (*a book about birds; what are you talking about?; argued about money*). **b** relating to (*something funny about this*). **c** in relation to (*symmetry about a plane*). **d** so as to affect (*can do nothing about it; what are you going to do about it?*). **2** at a time near to (*come about four*). **3 a** in, around, surrounding (*wandered about the town; a scarf about her neck*). **b** all around from a centre (*look about you*). **4** here and there in; at points throughout (*toys lying about the house*). **5** at a point or points near to (*fighting going on about us*). **6** carried with (*have no money about me*). **7** occupied with (*what are you about?*). ● *adverb* **1 a** approximately (*costs about a dollar; is about right*). **b** *informal* used to indicate understatement (*just about had enough; it's about time they came*). **2** here and there; at points nearby (*a lot of flu about; I've seen him about recently*). **3** all around; in every direction (*look about*). **4** on the move; in action (*out and about*). **5** in partial rotation or alteration from a given position (*the wrong way about*). **6** in rotation or succession (*turn and turn about*). **7** *Naut.* on or to the opposite tack (*go about; put about*). □ **be about to** be on the point of (doing something) (*was about to laugh*). [Old English *onbūtan* (on = A², *būtan* BUT)]

about-face (also **about-turn**) ● *noun* **1** a turn made so as to face the opposite direction. **2** a change of opinion or policy etc. ● *intransitive verb* make an about-face. ● *interjection* (**about turn**) *Military* a command to make an about-face.

above ● *preposition* **1** over; on the top of; higher (vertically, up a slope or stream etc.) than; over the surface of (*head above water; above the din*). **2** more than (*above twenty people; above average*). **3** farther north than (*above the Arctic Circle*). **4** higher in rank, position, importance, etc., than (*above all*). **5 a** too great or good for (*above one's station; is not above cheating at cards*). **b** beyond the reach of; not affected by (*above my understanding; above suspicion*). **6** *archaic* to an earlier time than (*not traced above the third century*). ● *adverb* **1** at or to a higher point; overhead (*the floor above; the clouds above*). **2 a** upstairs (*lives above*). **b** upstream. **3** (of a text reference) further back on a page or in a book (*as noted above*). **4** higher than zero on the temperature scale (*forty above*). **5** on the upper side (*looks similar above and below*). **6** in addition (*over and* *above*). **7** *literary* in heaven (*Lord above!*). ● *adjective* mentioned earlier; preceding (*the above argument*). ● *noun* (prec. by *the*) what is mentioned above (*the above shows*). □ **above one's head** *see* HEAD. **above oneself** conceited, arrogant. [A² + Old English *bufan* from *be* = BY + *ufan* above]

above board *adjective & adverb* without concealment; fair or fairly; open or openly.

above ground *adjective & adverb* not underground.

above-mentioned *adjective* mentioned earlier.

ab ovo /ab 'ɔːvɔ/ *adverb* from the very beginning. [Latin, = from the egg]

Abp. *abbreviation* Archbishop.

abra·ca·dab·ra ● *interjection* a supposedly magic word used by conjurors in performing a trick. ● *noun* a spell or charm. [a mystical word engraved and used as a charm: from Greek]

abrade *transitive verb* scrape or wear away (skin, rock, etc.) by rubbing. □ **abrad·er** *noun* [Latin from *radere ras-* scrape]

Abra·ham /'eɪbrə.ham/ the first of the Hebrew patriarchs, considered by Jews and Christians as the founder of the Hebrew nation (through his son Isaac), and by Muslims as an ancestor of Muhammad and the Arab people (through his son Ishmael).

Abraham, Plains of *see* PLAINS OF ABRAHAM.

abra·sion /ə'breɪʒən/ *noun* **1** the scraping or wearing away (of skin, rock, etc.). **2** a damaged area resulting from this. [Latin *abrasio* (as ABRADE)]

abra·sive /ə'breɪsɪv/ ● *adjective* **1 a** tending to rub or graze. **b** capable of polishing by rubbing or grinding. **2** harsh or hurtful in manner. ● *noun* an abrasive substance. [as ABRADE + -IVE]

ab·reac·tion /.æbri'akʃən/ *noun Psych.* the relief of anxiety by the expression and release of a previously repressed emotion, through reliving the experience that caused it. □ **ab·react** /.æbri'akt/ *transitive verb* **ab·react·ive** *adjective* [AB- + REACTION after German *Abreagierung*]

abreast *adverb* **1** side by side and facing the same way. **2** (usu. foll. by *of*) well-informed, up to date (*abreast of all the changes*). **3** (foll. by *of*) alongside; parallel to (*abreast of the house*). [A² + BREAST]

abridge *transitive verb* **1** shorten (a book, film, etc.) by using fewer words or making deletions. **2** curtail (liberties, rights, etc.). **3** shorten in duration; cut short. □ **abridge·able** *adjective* **abridg·er** *noun* [Old French *abreg(i)er* from Late Latin *abbreviare* ABBREVIATE]

abridge·ment *noun* (also **abridg·ment**) **1 a** a shortened version, esp. of a book; an abstract. **b** the process of producing this. **2** a curtailment (of rights).

abroad *adverb* **1** in or to a foreign country or countries. **2** over a wide area; in different directions; everywhere (*scatter abroad*). **3** at large; freely moving about; in circulation (*there is a rumour abroad*). **4** *archaic* in or into the open; out of doors. **5** *archaic* wide of the mark; erring. □ **from abroad** from another country.

ab·ro·gate /'abrə.geɪt/ *transitive verb* repeal or abolish (a law or custom). □ **ab·ro·ga·tion** /.abrə'geɪʃən/ *noun* [Latin *abrogare* (as AB-, *rogare* propose a law)]

abrupt *adjective* **1** sudden and unexpected; hasty (*her abrupt departure*). **2** (of speech, manner, etc.) uneven; lacking continuity; curt. **3** steep, precipitous. **4** *Bot.* truncated. **5** *Geol.* (of strata) suddenly appearing at the surface. □ **abrupt·ly** *adverb* **abrupt·ness** *noun* [Latin *abruptus* past participle of *abrumpere* (as AB-, *rumpere* break)]

Ab·ruz·zi /ə'brʊtsi/ a mountainous region of east central Italy; capital, Aquila.

ABS *abbreviation* **1** anti-lock braking system (for motor vehicles). **2** acrylonitrile butadiene styrene, a hard, lightweight, durable plastic used in automotive parts, plumbing pipes, luggage, etc.

abs- *prefix* = AB-. [var. of Latin *ab-* used before *c, q, t*]

Absa·lom /'absə.lɒm/ *Bible* the third son of David. Leading a rebellion against his father, he was killed by Joab when he became entangled by the hair in an oak tree (2 Sam. 18–19).

ab·scess /'abses/ *noun* a swollen area accumulating pus within a body tissue. □ **ab·scessed** *adjective* [Latin *abscessus* a going away (as AB-, *cedere cess-* go)]

ab·scis·ic acid /ab'saizɪk/ *noun* a plant hormone which promotes leaf detachment and bud dormancy and inhibits germination. [Latin *abscis-* past participle stem of *abscindere* (as AB-, *scindere* to cut)]

ab·scis·sa /ab'sɪsə/ *noun* (pl. **ab·scis·sae** /-siː/ or **ab·scis·sas**) *Math.* **1** (in a system of coordinates) the shortest distance from a point to the vertical or y-axis, measured parallel to the horizontal or x-axis; the Cartesian x-coordinate of a point (*compare* ORDINATE 2). **2** the part of a line between a fixed point on it and an ordinate drawn to it from any other point. [modern Latin *abscissa* (*linea*) fem. past participle of *abscindere absciss-* (as AB-, *scindere* cut)]

ab·scis·sion /ab'sɪʒən/ *noun* **1** the act or an instance of cutting off. **2** *Bot.* the natural detachment of leaves, branches, flowers, etc. [Latin *abscissio* (as ABSCISSA)]

ab·scond /ab'skɒnd/ *intransitive verb* depart hurriedly and furtively, esp. unlawfully or to avoid arrest. □ **ab·scond·er** *noun* [Latin *abscondere* (as AB-, *condere* stow)]

ab·seil /'abseil, -zail/ esp. *Brit.* = RAPPEL. [German *abseilen* from *ab* down + *Seil* rope]

ab·sence *noun* **1** the state of being away from a place or person. **2** the time or duration of being away. **3** (foll. by *of*) the non-existence or lack of. □ **absence of mind** inattentiveness.

ab·sent ● *adjective* /'absənt/ **1 a** not present. **b** (foll. by *from*) not present at or in. **2** not existing. **3** inattentive to the matter in hand. ● *reflexive verb* /ab'sent/ **1** stay away. **2** withdraw. ● *preposition N Amer. Law* in the absence of. □ **ab·sent·ly** *adverb* (in sense 3 of *adjective*). [Latin *absent-* pres. part. of *abesse* be absent]

ab·sen·tee /.absən'tiː/ *noun* a person not present, esp. one who is absent from work or school.

ab·sen·tee·ism /.absən'tiːɪzəm/ *noun* the practice of absenting oneself from work or school etc., esp. frequently or illicitly.

absentee landlord *noun* a landlord who leases a property while living elsewhere, usu. at a considerable distance.

absent-minded *adjective* habitually forgetful or inattentive; with one's mind on other things. □ **absent-minded·ly** *adverb* **absent-minded·ness** *noun*

ab·sinth /'absɪnθ/ *noun* **1** a shrubby plant, *Artemisia absinthium*, or its essence. *Also called* WORMWOOD. **2** (usu. **ab·sinthe**) a green aniseed-flavoured potent liqueur based on wormwood and turning milky when water is added. [French *absinthe* from Latin *absinthium* from Greek *apsinthion*]

absit omen /.absit 'ɔːmen/ *interjection* may what is threatened not become fact. [Latin, = may this (evil) omen be absent]

ab·so·lute ● *adjective* **1** complete, utter, perfect (*an absolute fool*; *absolute bliss*). **2** unconditional, unlimited (*absolute authority*). **3** despotic; ruling arbitrarily or with unrestricted power (*an absolute monarch*). **4** (of a standard or other concept) universally valid; not admitting exceptions; not relative or comparative. **5** *Grammar* **a** (of a construction) syntactically independent of the rest of the sentence, as in *dinner being over, we left the table*; *let us toss for it, loser to pay*. **b** (of an adjective or transitive verb) used or usable without an expressed noun or object, e.g. *the hungry*; *guns kill*. **6** (of a legal decree etc.) final. ● *noun* **1** a value, standard, etc., which is objective and universally valid, not subjective or relative. **2** (prec. by *the*) **a** *Philos.* that which can exist without being related to anything else. **b** *Theol.* ultimate reality; God. □ **ab·so·lute·ness** *noun* [Latin *absolutus* past participle of *absolvere*: see ABSOLVE]

absolute alcohol *noun Chem.* ethanol containing less than one per cent of water by weight.

ab·so·lute·ly *adverb* **1** completely, utterly, perfectly (*it was absolutely marvellous*; *she absolutely denies it*). **2** independently; in an absolute sense (*God exists absolutely*). **3** (foll. by *neg.*) (no or none) at all (*absolutely no chance of winning*; *absolutely nowhere*). **4** *informal* in actual fact; positively (*it absolutely exploded*). **5** *Grammar* in an absolute way, esp. (of a verb) without a stated object. **6** *informal* (used in reply) quite so; yes.

absolute magnitude *noun* the magnitude, i.e. brightness, of a celestial body as seen at a standard distance of 10 parsecs (opp. APPARENT MAGNITUDE).

absolute majority *noun* **1** a majority over all others combined. **2** more than half.

absolute pitch *noun Music* **1** the ability to recognize the pitch of a note or produce any given note. **2** a fixed standard of pitch defined by the rate of vibration.

absolute temperature *noun* a temperature measured from absolute zero.

absolute zero *noun* a theoretical lowest possible temperature, at which the particles whose motion constitutes heat would be minimal, calculated as −273.15°C (or 0 K).

ab·so·lu·tion /.absə'luːʃən/ *noun* **1** a formal release from guilt, obligation, or punishment. **2** an ecclesiastical declaration of forgiveness of sins or of the remission of penance. **3** forgiveness. [Latin *absolutio -onis* (as ABSOLVE)]

ab·so·lut·ism /'absəluː.tɪzəm/ *noun* **1** the acceptance of or belief in absolute principles in political, philosophical, ethical or theological matters. **2** the principle of absolute government; despotism. □ **ab·so·lut·ist** *noun & adjective*

ab·solve /əb'zɒlv, əb'sɒlv/ *transitive verb* **1** (often foll. by *from, of*) **a** set or pronounce free from blame or obligation etc. **b** acquit; pronounce not guilty. **2** pardon or give absolution for (a sin etc.). □ **ab·solv·er** *noun* [Latin *absolvere* (as AB-, *solvere* solut- loosen)]

ab·sorb *transitive verb* **1** include or incorporate as part of itself or oneself (*the country successfully absorbed its immigrants*). **2** take in; suck up (liquid, heat, knowledge, etc.) (*she quickly absorbed all she was taught*). **3** reduce the effect or intensity of; deal easily with (an impact, sound, difficulty, etc.). **4** consume (income, time, resources, etc.) (*his debts absorbed half his income*). **5** engross the attention of (*television absorbs them completely*). □ **ab·sorb·able** *adjective* **ab·sorb·abil·ity** /-'bɪlɪtɪ/ *noun* **ab·sorb·er** *noun* [Latin *absorbēre absorpt-* (as AB-, *sorbēre* suck in)]

ab·sorbed *predicative adjective* intensely engaged or interested (*she was absorbed in her work*). □ **ab·sorb·ed·ly** /-bədlɪ/ *adverb*

ab·sorb·ent ● *adjective* having a tendency to absorb. ● *noun* a substance that absorbs esp. liquids. □ **ab·sorb·ency** *noun* [Latin *absorbent-* from *absorbēre* ABSORB]

ab·sorb·ing *adjective* engrossing; intensely interesting. □ **ab·sorb·ing·ly** *adverb*

ab·sorp·tion *noun* **1** the process or action of absorbing or being absorbed. **2** disappearance through incorporation into something else. **3** mental engrossment. □ **ab·sorp·tive** *adjective* [Latin *absorptio* (as ABSORB)]

absorption spectrum *noun* Physics a spectrum of electromagnetic radiation transmitted through a substance, with dark lines or bands showing absorption at specific wavelengths.

ab·stain *intransitive verb* **1 a** (usu. foll. by *from*) restrain oneself; refrain from indulging in (*abstained from meat; abstained from mentioning it*). **b** refrain from drinking alcohol. **2** formally decline to use one's vote. □ **ab·stain·er** *noun* [Latin *abstinēre abstent-* (as AB-, *tenēre* hold)]

ab·stemi·ous /ab'stiːmɪəs/ *adjective* (of a person, habit, etc.) moderate, not self-indulgent, esp. in eating and drinking. □ **ab·stemi·ous·ly** *adverb* **ab·stemi·ous·ness** *noun* [Latin *abstemius* (as AB-, *temetum* strong drink)]

ab·sten·tion /əb'stenʃən/ *noun* the act or an instance of abstaining, esp. from voting. [(as ABSTAIN)]

ab·stin·ence /'abstɪnəns/ *noun* the act of abstaining, esp. from food, drugs, or sexual activity.

ab·stin·ent /'abstɪnənt/ *adjective* practising abstinence. □ **ab·stin·ent·ly** *adverb* [(as ABSTAIN)]

ab·stract ● *adjective* **1 a** to do with or existing in thought rather than matter, or in theory rather than practice; not tangible or concrete (*abstract questions rarely concerned him*). **b** (of a word, esp. a noun) denoting a quality or condition or intangible thing rather than a concrete object. **2 a** (of art) achieving its effect by grouping shapes and colours in satisfying patterns rather than by the recognizable representation of physical reality. **b** (of a dance work) not telling a story. ● *verb* **1** *transitive* (often foll. by *from*) take out of; extract; remove. **2** *transitive* summarize (an article, book, etc.). **3** *transitive & reflexive* (often foll. by *from*) disengage (a person's attention etc.); distract. **4** *transitive* (foll. by *from*) consider abstractly or separately from something else. **5** *transitive euphemism* steal. ● *noun* **1** a summary or statement of the contents of a book etc. **2** an abstract work of art. **3** an abstraction or abstract term. □ **in the abstract** in theory rather than in practice. □ **ab·stract·ly** *adverb* **ab·stract·ness** *noun* **ab·stract·or** *noun* (in sense 2 of verb). [Latin *abstractus* past participle of *abstrahere* (as AB-, *trahere* draw)]

ab·stract·ed *adjective* inattentive to the matter in hand; preoccupied. □ **ab·stract·ed·ly** *adverb*

abstract expressionism *noun* a development of abstract art which aims at a subjective emotional expression of an ideal rather than a picture of a physical object.

ab·strac·tion *noun* **1** the act or an instance of abstracting or taking away. **2 a** an abstract or visionary idea. **b** the formation of abstract ideas. **3 a** abstract qualities (esp. in art). **b** an abstract work of art. **4** absent-mindedness.

ab·strac·tion·ism *noun* **1** the principles and practice of abstract art. **2** the pursuit or cult of abstract ideas. □ **ab·strac·tion·ist** *noun*

ab·struse /əb'struːs/ *adjective* hard to understand; obscure. □ **ab·struse·ly** *adverb* **ab·struse·ness** *noun* [Latin *abstrusus* (as AB-, *trusus* past participle of *trudere* push)]

ab·surd /əb'sɜːd, -'zɜːd/ *adjective* **1** (of an idea, suggestion, etc.) wildly unreasonable, illogical, or inappropriate. **2** (of a person) unreasonable or ridiculous in manner. **3** (of a thing) ludicrous, incongruous (*an absurd hat; the situation was becoming absurd*). □ **ab·surd·ly** *adverb* [Latin *absurdus* (as AB-, *surdus* deaf, dull)]

ab·surd·ist ● *adjective* pertaining to or characteristic of the theatre of the absurd. ● *noun* a writer of absurdist drama. □ **ab·surd·ism** *noun*

ab·surd·ity *noun* (*pl.* **-ities**) **1** wild inappropriateness or incongruity. **2** extreme unreasonableness. **3** an absurd thing, esp. a statement or act.

Abu-Bakr /ə,buː'bakɜːr/ (also **Abu-Bekr** /ə,buː'bekɜːr/) (573–634), the first caliph of Islam 632–4, and a close companion of Muhammad.

Abu Dhabi /,abuː 'dabɪ/ **1** the largest of the seven member states of the United Arab Emirates, lying between Oman and the Gulf coast; pop. (est. 2000) 1,186,000. **2** the capital of Abu Dhabi; pop. (est. 2002) 539,800. It is also the federal capital of the United Arab Emirates.

Abuja /ə'buːdʒə/ a newly built city in central Nigeria, designated in 1982 to replace Lagos as the national capital; pop. (est. 2002) 565,100.

abu·lia /ə'buːlɪə/ *noun* (also **abo**u·**lia**) the loss of willpower as a mental disorder. □ **abu·lic** *adjective* [Greek *a-* not + *boulē* will]

Abu Musa /,abuː 'muːsə/ a small island in the Persian Gulf. Formerly held by the emirate of Sharjah, it has been occupied by Iran since 1971.

abun·dance *noun* **1** a very great quantity, usu. considered to be more than enough. **2** plentifulness of the good things in life; prosperity. **3** *Chem., Ecology, etc.* the relative quantity or number (of a species, substance, etc.) present. □ **in abundance** in great quantities.

abun·dant *adjective* **1** existing or available in large quantities; plentiful. **2** (foll. by *in*) having an abundance of (*a sea abundant in fish*). □ **abun·dant·ly** *adverb* [(as ABOUND)]

abuse ● /ə'bjuːz/ *transitive verb* **1 a** use to bad effect or for a bad purpose; misuse (*abused his position of power*). **b** make excessive and habitual use of (alcohol or drugs, esp. illegal ones). **2 a** treat (a person or animal) with cruelty or violence, esp. regularly or repeatedly. **b** assault (esp. a woman or child) sexually. **c** use or treat in such a way as to cause harm or damage (*he had been abusing his body for years*). **3** insult verbally. ● *noun* /ə'bjuːs/ **1 a** incorrect or improper use (*drug abuse*). **b** an instance of this (*an abuse of power*). **2** unjust or corrupt practice (*political abuses*). **3** maltreatment of a person (*compare* CHILD ABUSE, SEXUAL ABUSE). **4** insulting language (*a torrent of abuse*). □ **abus·er** *noun* [Latin *abusus, abuti* (as AB-, *uti us-* USE)]

Abu Sim·bel /,abuː 'sɪmbəl/ a former village in S Egypt, site of two rock-cut temples built by Rameses II (13th c. BC). The facade of the great temple (31 m, 102 ft. high) bears four colossal seated statues of the pharaoh.

abu·sive *adjective* **1** (of a situation) involving maltreatment. **2** (of a person) tending to abuse others; violent. **3** using or containing insulting language. **4** (of language) insulting. □ **abu·sive·ly** *adverb* **abu·sive·ness** *noun*

abut *verb* (**abut·ted, abut·ting**) **1** *transitive & intransitive* (of buildings, sites, etc.) be located next to. **2** *intransitive* (foll. by *on, against*) (of part of a building) touch or lean upon (another) with a projecting end or point (*the shed abutted on the side of the house*). [Old French *abouter* (BUTT¹) and Anglo-Latin *abuttare* from Old French *but* end]

abu·tilon /ə'bjuːtɪlɒn/ *noun* a herbaceous plant or shrub of warm climates, typically bearing showy yellow, red, or mauve flowers and sometimes used for fibre. [modern Latin, from Arabic *ūbūṭīlūn* 'Indian mallow']

abut·ment *noun* **1** the lateral supporting structure of a bridge, arch, etc. **2** the point of junction between such a support and the thing supported.

abuzz *predicative adjective* **1** in a state of excitement or activity. **2** buzzing.

abysm /ə'bɪzm/ *noun archaic or literary* = ABYSS. [Old French *abi(s)me* from medieval Latin *abysmus*]

abys·mal /ə'bɪzməl/ *adjective* **1** extremely bad (*abysmal weather; the food is abysmal*). **2** profound, utter (*abysmal ignorance*). □ **abys·mal·ly** *adverb*

abyss /ə'bɪs/ *noun* **1** a deep or seemingly bottomless chasm. **2 a** an immeasurable depth (*abyss of despair*). **b** a catastrophic situation as contemplated or feared (*his loss brought him a step nearer the abyss*). **3** a vast difference (*unbridgeable cultural abyss*). **4** (prec. by *the*) primal chaos, hell. [Late Latin *abyssus* from Greek *abussos* bottomless (as A-¹, *bussos* depth)]

abys·sal /ə'bɪsəl/ *adjective* **1** at or of the ocean depths or floor. **2** *Geol.* plutonic.

Abys·sinia /,abə'sɪnɪə/ a former name of Ethiopia.

Consonants: b *but*   d *dog*   f *few*   g *get*   h *her*   j *yes*   k *cat*   l *leg*   m *man*   n *no*   p *pen*   r *red*   s *sit*

Abys·sin·ian /ˌabəˈsɪnɪən/ ● *noun* **1** a native or inhabitant of Abyssinia. **2** (in full **Abyssinian cat**) a breed of cat having a long slender body, long ears, and short brown hair. ● *adjective* of or pertaining to Abyssinia or its inhabitants.

AC *abbreviation* **1** (also **ac**) ALTERNATING CURRENT. **2** AIRCRAFTMAN. **3** before Christ. **4** air conditioning. [sense 3 from Latin *ante Christum*]

Ac *symbol Chem.* the element actinium.

a/c *abbreviation* **1** = ACCOUNT *noun* 2, 3. **2** = AIR CONDITIONING. [sense 1 from *account current*]

ac- *prefix* assimilated form of AD- before *c, k, q*.

-ac *suffix* forming adjectives which are often also (or only) used as nouns (*cardiac; maniac*) (*see also* -ACAL). [French *-aque* or Latin *-acus* or Greek *-akos* adj. suffix]

aca·cia /əˈkeɪʃə/ *noun* **1** any frequently thorny leguminous tree or shrub of the genus *Acacia* with usu. yellow flowers, esp. *A. senegal* yielding gum arabic. **2** (also **false acacia**) = LOCUST 4b. [Latin from Greek *akakia*]

Acad. *abbreviation* Academy.

aca·deme /ˈakəˌdiːm/ *noun* **1** the world of learning. **2** universities collectively. [Greek *Akadēmos* (see ACADEMY): used by Shakespeare (*Love's Labour's Lost* I. i. 13) and Milton (*Paradise Regained* iv. 244)]

aca·demia /ˌakəˈdiːmɪə/ *noun* the academic world; scholastic life. [modern Latin: see ACADEMY]

aca·dem·ic /ˌakəˈdɛmɪk/ ● *adjective* **1 a** scholarly; to do with learning. **b** of or relating to a scholarly institution (*academic dress*). **2** abstract; theoretical; not of practical relevance. **3** *Art* conventional, over-formal. **4** (of a person) interested in or excelling at scholarly pursuits and activities. ● *noun* a teacher or scholar in a university or institute of higher education. □ **aca·dem·ic·ally** *adverb*

aca·dem·ic·als /ˌakəˈdɛmɪkəls/ *plural noun Brit.* formal academic attire.

academic freedom *noun* a scholar's freedom to express ideas without risk of official interference.

aca·demi·cian /ˌakədəˈmɪʃən, əˌkadəˈmɪʃən/ *noun* **1** a member of an Academy, esp. of the Royal Academy of Arts, the Académie française, or an Academy of Sciences. **2** an academic.

aca·demi·cism /ˌakəˈdɛmɪˌsɪzəm/ *noun* (also **acad·em·ism** /əˈkadəˌmɪzəm/) academic principles or their application in art, esp. in a conventional or pedantic manner.

aca·dem·ics /ˌakəˈdɛmɪks/ *plural noun* (also treated as *sing.*) studies in the humanities or sciences.

academic year *noun* a period of nearly a year, going from early September to the following summer, during which a school or university is in session.

Aca·dé·mie fran·çaise /a ˌkadeɪˈmiː frɑ̃ˈsɛz/ *noun* a French literary academy founded by Cardinal Richelieu in 1635 to control the development of the French language, esp. by producing a definitive dictionary. Its forty members are significant writers.

acad·emy *noun* (*pl.* **-ies**) **1** a place of study or training in a special field (*military academy; academy of dance*). **2** (usu. **Academy**) a society or institution of distinguished scholars, artists, scientists, etc. (*Royal Academy*). **3 a** a school (esp. in proper names). **b** *US* a private secondary school. **c** *Scot.* a secondary school. **4** *N Amer.* (prec. by *the*) academia. **5** (**Academy**) **a** Plato's followers or philosophical system. **b** the garden near Athens where Plato taught. [Greek *akadēmeia* from *Akadēmos* the hero after whom Plato's garden was named]

Academy Award any of the awards of the Academy of Motion Picture Arts and Sciences (Hollywood) given annually for achievement in the film industry. Also called OSCAR.

Academy of Canadian Cinema and Television a non-profit organization of people involved in the Canadian film and television industry. Founded in 1979, it awards the Genies, Geminis, and Gémeaux.

Acadia /əˈkeɪdɪə/ **1** a former French colony established in 1604 in the territory now forming Nova Scotia, and later occupying the whole of the region between the St. Lawrence River and the Atlantic Ocean, lying in what is now SE Quebec, E Maine, New Brunswick, Nova Scotia, and PEI. Acadia was contested by France and Britain until it was eventually ceded to Britain in 1763. French Acadians were deported to other parts of N America, esp. Louisiana, where the name has survived as Cajun. **2** *Cdn* the francophone regions of the Maritime provinces. [French *Acadie*]

Acad·ian /əˈkeɪdɪən/ ● *noun* **1 a** a native or inhabitant of the French colony of Acadia. **b** esp. *Cdn* a francophone descendant of the early French settlers in Acadia. **2** *US* a descendant of the Acadians deported to Louisiana in the 18th c. (*compare* CAJUN). ● *adjective* of or relating to Acadians.

Acadian forest *noun Cdn* the type of forest, characterized by red spruce, balsam fir, yellow birch, and sugar maple, found in Nova Scotia, PEI, and part of New Brunswick.

Acadian French *noun* the French spoken by Acadians, derived from the dialects spoken in SW France in the 17th c.

-acal *suffix* forming adjectives, often used to distinguish them from nouns in *-ac* (*heliacal; maniacal*).

acan·thus /əˈkanθəs/ *noun* **1** a herbaceous plant or shrub of the genus *Acanthus*, with bold flower spikes and decorative spiny leaves, native to the Mediterranean. **2** a conventionalized representation of an acanthus leaf, used esp. as a decoration for Corinthian column capitals. [Greek *akanthos* from *akantha* thorn, perhaps from *akē* sharp point]

a cap·pella /ˌa kəˈpɛlə/ *adjective & adverb* (also **alla cap·pella** /ˌaləˈ/) (of singing) unaccompanied. [Italian, = in church style]

Aca·pul·co /ˌakəˈpʊlkoː/ (in full **Acapulco de Juárez** /deɪ ˈhwɑːrɛz/) a port and resort in S Mexico, on the Pacific coast; pop. (est. 2000) 620,700.

acari·cide /əˈkɛrəˌsaɪd/ *noun* a preparation for destroying mites. [Greek *akari* mite + -CIDE]

acar·id /ˈakərɪd/ *noun* any small arachnid of the order Acarina, including mites and ticks. [Greek *akari* mite]

Ac·cad·ian *var. of* AKKADIAN.

ACCC *abbreviation* Association of Canadian Community Colleges.

ac·cede /akˈsiːd/ *intransitive verb* (usu. foll. by *to*) **1** assent or agree (*acceded to the request*). **2** take office, esp. become monarch. **3** (foll. by *to*) formally subscribe to a treaty or other agreement. [Latin *accedere* (as AC-, *cedere cess-* go)]

ac·cel·er·ando /akˌsɛləˈrandoː, əˌtʃɛl-/ *adjective & adverb Music* with a gradual increase of speed. [Italian]

ac·cel·er·ant *noun* a substance used to aid the spread of fire.

ac·cel·er·ate /əkˈsɛləˌreɪt/ *verb* **1** *intransitive* **a** (of a moving body, esp. a vehicle) move or begin to move more quickly; increase speed. **b** (of a process) happen or reach completion more quickly. **2** *transitive* **a** cause to increase speed. **b** cause (a process) to happen more quickly. **3** *transitive* (often as **ac·cel·er·at·ed** *adjective*) hasten advancement in (a career, studies, etc.). [Latin *accelerare* (as AC-, *celerare* from *celer* swift)]

ac·cel·er·a·tion *noun* **1** the process or act of accelerating or being accelerated. **2** an instance of this. **3** (of a vehicle etc.) the capacity to gain speed (*the car has good acceleration*). **4** *Physics* the rate of change of velocity measured in terms of a unit of time.

ac·cel·er·ator *noun* **1** a device for increasing speed, esp. the pedal that controls the speed of a vehicle's engine. **2** *Physics* an apparatus for imparting high speeds to charged particles. **3** *Chem.* a substance that speeds up a chemical reaction. **4** (also **accelerator board, accelerator card**) an accessory circuit board which can be plugged into a small computer to increase the speed of its processor or input/output operations.

ac·cel·er·om·eter /akˌsɛləˈrɒmətər/ *noun* an instrument for measuring acceleration (esp. of a rocket) or vibrations.

ac·cent ● *noun* **1** a particular mode of pronunciation, esp. one associated with a particular region or group (*Newfoundland accent; French accent*). **2** prominence given to a syllable by stress or pitch. **3** a mark on a letter or word to indicate pitch, stress, or the quality of a vowel. **4** (usu. foll. by *on*) emphasis (*an accent on comfort*). **5** (often *attributive*) a distinctive or contrasting feature (*blue with accents of red; accent colours*). **6** *Music* emphasis on a particular note or chord. ● *transitive verb* **1** pronounce with an accent; emphasize (a word or syllable). **2** write or print accents on (words etc.). **3** accentuate or enhance (esp. with a contrasting element). **4** *Music* play (a note etc.) with an accent. □ **ac·cen·tual** /akˈsɛntʃʊəl/ *adjective* [Latin *accentus* (as AC-, *cantus* song)]

ac·cen·tor /akˈsɛntər/ *noun* any bird of the genus *Prunella*, native to Europe and Asia, similar to a sparrow, with greyish-brown plumage. [medieval Latin *accentor* from Latin *ad* to + *cantor* singer]

ac·cen·tu·ate /akˈsɛntʃuˌeɪt/ *transitive verb* emphasize; make prominent. □ **ac·cen·tu·a·tion** *noun*

ac·cept *verb* **1** *transitive & intransitive* consent to receive (a thing offered). **2** *transitive & intransitive* give an affirmative answer to (an offer or proposal). **3** *transitive* **a** regard favourably; treat as welcome (*his colleagues never accepted him*). **b** approve for admission (*she was accepted by three universities*). **4** *transitive* **a** believe, receive, recognize (an opinion, explanation, etc.) as adequate or valid. **b** be prepared to subscribe to (a belief, philosophy, etc.). **5** *transitive* receive as suitable (*the hotel accepts traveller's cheques; the machine only accepts tokens*). **6** *transitive* **a** tolerate; submit to (*accepted the umpire's decision*). **b** (often foll. by *that* + clause) be willing to believe (*we accept that you meant well*). **7** *transitive* undertake (an office or responsibility). **8** *transitive* agree to meet (a draft or bill of exchange). [Latin *acceptare* from *accipere* (as AC-, *capere* take)]

ac·cept·able *adjective* **1 a** worthy of being accepted. **b** pleasing, welcome. **2** adequate, satisfactory. **3** tolerable (*an acceptable risk*). □ **ac·cept·abil·ity** *noun* **ac·cept·able·ness** *noun* **ac·cept·ably** *adverb*

ac·cept·ance *noun* **1** the act or fact of accepting or being accepted (*acceptance to university*). **2** willingness to receive (a gift, payment, duty, etc.). **3** an affirmative answer to an invitation or proposal. **4** (often foll. by *of*) a willingness to accept (conditions, a circumstance, etc.). **5 a** approval, belief (*found wide acceptance*). **b** willingness or ability to tolerate. **6 a** agreement to meet a bill of exchange. **b** a bill so accepted.

ac·cep·ta·tion /ˌaksepˈteɪʃən/ *noun* Linguistics a particular sense, or the generally recognized meaning, of a word or phrase.

accepted opinion *noun* an opinion generally held to be correct.

ac·cept·or *noun* **1** Commerce a person who accepts a bill of exchange. **2** *Chem. & Physics* an atom or molecule which receives electrons or which can combine with another atom or molecule, esp. an impurity in a semiconductor. **3** *Electricity* a circuit able to accept a given frequency.

ac·cess ● *noun* **1** a way of approaching or reaching or entering (*a building with rear access*). **2 a** (often foll. by *to*) the right or opportunity to reach or use or visit; admittance (*has access to secret files; was granted access to the prisoner*). **b** Law the right of a parent who does not have legal custody of a child to visit the child and inquire about his or her welfare. **c** the condition of being readily approached; accessibility. **3** *Computing* the action or process of obtaining stored documents, data, etc. (*see also* DIRECT ACCESS, RANDOM ACCESS). **4** (often foll. by *of*) an attack or outburst (*an access of anger*). **5** (*attributive*) Brit. (of broadcasting) undertaken by members of the public by arrangement with broadcasting companies (*access television*) (*see also* COMMUNITY ACCESS, PUBLIC ACCESS). ● *transitive verb* **1** obtain, examine, or retrieve (data, a file, etc.). **2** approach or enter (a place). [Latin *accessus* from *accedere* (as AC-, *cedere* cess- go)]

access code *noun* a series of numbers dialed into a phone or entered into a computerized system to gain access to a certain service, esp. a long-distance phone provider.

ac·cess·ible *adjective* (often foll. by *to*) **1** that can readily be reached, entered, or used. **2** (of a building) posing no obstacles to handicapped people. **3** (of a person) readily available (esp. to subordinates). **4** (in a form) easy to understand or appreciate. □ **ac·cess·ibil·ity** *noun* **ac·cess·ibly** *adverb*

ac·ces·sion /əkˈseʃən/ ● *noun* **1** entering upon an office (esp. the throne) or a condition (as adulthood). **2** (often foll. by *to*) a thing added, e.g. a book to a library; increase, addition. **3** Law the incorporation of one item of property in another. **4** assent; the formal acceptance of a treaty etc. ● *transitive verb* record the addition of (a new item) to a library or museum. [Latin *accessio -onis* (as ACCEDE)]

ac·ces·sor·ize *transitive & intransitive verb* (also esp. Brit. **-ise**) choose or wear accessories to suit (clothing etc.).

ac·ces·sory ● *noun* (*pl.* **-ies**) **1** an additional or extra thing. **2** (usu. in *pl.*) **a** a small attachment or fitting. **b** a small item of (esp. a woman's) dress, e.g. shoes, gloves, purse. **3** (often foll. by *to*) a person who helps in or knows the details of an (esp. illegal) act, esp. one (**accessory before the fact**) who encourages or assists another to commit a crime but is not present when the crime is committed, or one (**accessory after the fact**) who knowingly assists a criminal to escape. ● *adjective* contributing or aiding in a minor way. [medieval Latin *accessorius* (as ACCEDE)]

access road *noun* a road providing access to something, esp. a remote or isolated site, a major construction such as an airport or stadium, or a highway.

access time *noun* Computing the time taken to retrieve data from storage.

access to information *noun* the right of a member of the public to have access to government or official documents, usu. within a specified time from the request and subject to certain exceptions.

acciac·ca·tura /əˌtʃakəˈtʊrə/ *noun* Music a grace note performed as quickly as possible before an essential note of a melody. [Italian]

ac·ci·dence /ˈaksɪdəns/ *noun* the part of grammar that deals with the variable parts or inflections of words. [late Latin *accidentia* (translation

of Greek *parepomena* 'things happening alongside') neuter pl. of *accidere* 'happen']

ac·ci·dent *noun* **1** an event that is without apparent cause, or is unexpected (*their early arrival was just an accident*). **2** an unfortunate event, esp. one causing physical harm or damage, brought about unintentionally. **3** an automobile collision or crash. **4** occurrence of things by chance; the working of fortune (*accident accounts for much in life*). **5** euphemism an occurrence of involuntary urination or defecation. □ **an accident waiting to happen** a potentially disastrous situation, typically caused by negligent or faulty procedures. **by accident** unintentionally. [Late Latin *accidens* from Latin *accidere* (as AC-, *cadere* fall)]

ac·ci·dent·al ● *adjective* **1** happening by chance, unintentionally, or unexpectedly. **2** incidental; subsidiary. ● *noun* Music a sign indicating a momentary departure from the key signature by raising or lowering a note. □ **ac·ci·dent·al·ly** *adverb*

accident-prone *adjective* (of a person) subject to frequent accidents.

ac·cip·iter /əkˈsɪpɪtər/ *noun* a short-winged, long-legged hawk of the genus *Accipiter*, e.g. a goshawk. □ **ac·cipi·trine** *adjective* [Latin, = hawk, bird of prey]

ac·claim ● *transitive verb* **1** (often as **ac·claimed** *adjective*) praise publicly; welcome or applaud enthusiastically. **2** hail as (*acclaimed him king; was acclaimed the winner*). **3** Cdn Politics elect without opposition. ● *noun* **1** public praise; applause; welcome. **2** a shout of acclaim. □ **ac·claim·er** *noun* [Latin *acclamare* (as AC-, *clamare* shout: spelling assimilated to *claim*)]

ac·clam·a·tion /ˌakləˈmeɪʃən/ *noun* **1** Politics (esp. in **by acclamation**) **a** Cdn the act or an instance of election by virtue of being the sole candidate (*she was elected by acclamation*). **b** US a vote by voice (esp. cheering) or applause rather than by formal ballot. **2** loud and eager assent to a proposal. **3** (usu. in *pl.*) shouting in a person's honour. **4** the act or process of acclaiming. **5** Christianity a phrase said or sung by the congregation as part of a liturgy. [Latin *acclamatio* (as ACCLAIM)]

ac·clim·ate /ˈaklɪˌmeɪt, əˈklaɪ-/ *transitive verb* N Amer. acclimatize. □ **ac·clim·a·tion** *noun* [French *acclimater* from *à* to + *climat* CLIMATE]

ac·clima·tize /əˈklaɪməˌtaɪz/ *verb* (also esp. Brit. **-tise**) **1** *transitive* accustom to a new climate or to new conditions. **2** *intransitive* become acclimatized. □ **ac·clima·tiz·a·tion** *noun*

ac·cliv·ity /əˈklɪvɪti/ *noun* (*pl.* **-ities**) an upward slope (*opp.* DECLIVITY). □ **ac·clivi·tous** *adjective* [Latin *acclivitas* from *acclivis* (as AC-, *clivis* from *clivus* slope)]

ac·col·ade /ˈakəˌleɪd/ *noun* **1** the awarding of praise; an acknowledgement of merit. **2** a touch made with a sword at the bestowing of a knighthood. [French from Provençal *acolada* (as AC-, Latin *collum* neck)]

ac·com·mo·date *transitive verb* **1** provide lodging or room for (*the residence can accommodate eighty students*). **2** adapt, harmonize, reconcile (*must accommodate ourselves to new surroundings; cannot accommodate your needs to mine*). [Latin *accommodare* (as AC-, *commodus* fitting)]

ac·com·mo·dat·ing *adjective* obliging, compliant. □ **ac·com·mo·dat·ing·ly** *adverb*

ac·com·mo·da·tion *noun* **1** (in *sing.* or *pl.*) temporary lodging, as at a hotel etc. **2** an adjustment or adaptation to suit a special or different purpose. **3** a convenient arrangement; a settlement or compromise. **4** the automatic adjustment of the focus of the eye by flattening or thickening the lens. **5** (in *pl.*) US a seat, berth, etc. in a train, boat, etc.

accommodation address *noun* Brit. an address used on letters to a person who is unable or unwilling to give a permanent address.

accommodation bill *noun* a bill of exchange co-signed by a guarantor to increase a borrower's credit.

ac·com·mo·da·tion·ist *noun* US a person who seeks (esp. political) compromise.

accommodation ladder *noun* a ladder or flight of steps between a ship's decks, or to and from a small boat alongside.

ac·com·pani·ment *noun* **1** an instrumental or orchestral part supporting or partnering a solo instrument, voice, or group. **2** an accompanying thing. **3** the act or fact of accompanying or escorting someone (*see also* ADULT ACCOMPANIMENT, PARENTAL ACCOMPANIMENT).

ac·com·pan·ist *noun* a person who provides a musical accompaniment.

ac·com·pany *transitive verb* (**-ies, -ied**) **1** go with; escort. **2** (usu. in passive; foll. by *with, by*) **a** be done or found with; supplement (*speech accompanied with gestures*). **b** have as a result (*pills accompanied by side* *effects*). **3** *Music* support or partner with accompaniment. [French *accompagner* from *à* to + Old French *compaing* COMPANION[1]: assimilated to COMPANY]

ac·com·plice /əˈkɒmplɪs/ *noun* a partner in a crime or wrongdoing. [Late Latin *complex complicis* confederate: compare COMPLICATE]

ac·com·plish /əˈkɒmplɪʃ/ *transitive verb* perform; complete; succeed in doing. [Old French *acomplir* from Latin *complēre* COMPLETE]

ac·com·plished *adjective* clever, skilled; well trained or educated.

ac·com·plish·ment *noun* **1** the fulfillment or completion (of a task etc.). **2** an acquired skill, esp. a social one. **3** a thing done; an achievement.

ac·cord ● *verb* **1** *intransitive* (often foll. by *with*) (esp. of a thing) be in harmony; be consistent. **2** *transitive* **a** grant (permission, a request, etc.). **b** give (a welcome etc.). ● *noun* **1** agreement, consent. **2** harmony or harmonious correspondence in pitch, tone, colour, etc. **3** a formal act of agreement; a treaty. □ **of one's own accord** on one's own initiative; voluntarily. **with one accord** unanimously; in a united way. [Old French *acord, acorder* from Latin *cor cordis* heart]

ac·cord·ance *noun* harmony, agreement. □ **in accordance with** in a manner corresponding to (*we acted in accordance with your wishes*). □ **ac·cord·ant** *adjective* **ac·cord·ant·ly** *adverb*

ac·cord·ing *adverb* **1** (foll. by *to*) **a** as stated by or in (*according to my sister; according to their statement*). **b** in a manner corresponding to; in proportion to (*she lives according to her principles*). **2** (foll. by *as* + clause) in a manner or to a degree that varies as (*he pays according as he is able*).

ac·cord·ing·ly *adverb* **1** as suggested or required by the (stated) circumstances (*silence is vital so please act accordingly*). **2** consequently, therefore (*accordingly, he left the room*).

ac·cor·dion /əˈkɔːdɪən/ *noun* **1** a portable musical instrument played by means of keys, buttons, and pleated bellows, which are expanded and contracted to force air through metal reeds. **2** (*attributive*) having folds like the bellows of an accordion (*accordion file; accordion wall*). □ **ac·cor·dion·ist** *noun* [German *Akkordion* from Italian *accordare* to tune]

accordion pleats *plural noun* a series of narrow, symmetrical, zigzag pleats.

ac·cost *transitive verb* approach and address (a person), esp. boldly. [French *accoster* from Italian *accostare*, ultimately from Latin *costa* rib: see COAST]

ac·count ● *noun* **1** a narration or description (*gave a long account of the ordeal*). **2 a** an arrangement at a bank, trust company, etc. for financial transactions, esp. for depositing and withdrawing money (*opened a savings account*). **b** the assets credited by such an arrangement (*has a large account; paid the money into her account*). **c** an arrangement at a store etc. for buying goods or services on credit (*has an account at a department store*). **3** (often in *pl.*) a record or statement of money, goods, or services received or expended, with calculation of the balance (*companies must keep detailed accounts*). **4** a statement of the administration of money in trust (*demand an account*). **5** *Brit.* the period during which transactions take place on a stock exchange; the period from one account day to the next. **6** (in *pl.*) the department of a firm etc. that deals with accounts. **7** a customer or client having an account with a firm. **8** counting, reckoning. ● *transitive verb* consider, regard as (*her trip could not be accounted a success*). □ **account for 1** serve as or provide an explanation or reason for (*that accounts for their misbehaviour*). **2 a** give a reckoning of or answer for (money etc. entrusted). **b** answer for (one's conduct). **3** succeed in killing, destroying, disposing of, or defeating. **4** supply or make up a specified amount or proportion of (*rent accounts for 50 per cent of expenditure*). **by all accounts** in everyone's opinion. **call to account** require an explanation from (a person). **give a good** (or **bad**) **account of oneself** make a favourable (or unfavourable) impression; be successful (or unsuccessful). **keep account of** keep a record of; follow closely. **leave out of account** fail or decline to consider. **of no account** unimportant. **of some account** important. **on account 1** (of goods or services) to be paid for later. **2** (of money) in part payment. **on account of** because of. **on no account** under no circumstances; certainly not. **on one's own account** for one's own purposes; at one's own risk. **settle** (or **square**) **accounts with 1** receive or pay money etc. owed to. **2** have revenge on. **take account of** (or **take into account**) consider along with other factors (*took their age into account*). **turn to account** (or **good account**) turn to one's advantage. [Old French *acont, aconter* (as AC-, *conter* COUNT[1])]

ac·count·able *adjective* **1** responsible; required to account for one's conduct (*accountable for one's actions*). **2** explicable, understandable. □ **ac·count·abil·ity** *noun* **ac·count·ably** *adverb*

ac·count·ancy *noun* the profession or duties of an accountant.

ac·count·ant *noun* a person whose profession is to keep or inspect financial accounts. [legal French from pres. part. of Old French *aconter* ACCOUNT]

account day *noun Brit.* a day of periodic settlement of stock exchange accounts.

account executive *noun* the manager of a client's account, esp. in an advertising agency.

ac·count·ing *noun* **1** the process of or skill in keeping and verifying accounts. **2** *in senses of* ACCOUNT *verb*.

account payable *noun* (*pl.* **accounts payable**) (usu. in *pl.*) an amount owed by a business to a supplier for goods or services.

account receivable *noun* (*pl.* **accounts receivable**) (usu. in *pl.*) an amount owed by a customer to a business for goods or services.

ac·coutre /əˈkuːtər/ *transitive verb* (usu. as **ac·coutred** *adjective*) attire, equip, esp. with a special outfit. [Old French *acoustrer* (as A-[3], *couture* sewing: compare SUTURE)]

ac·coutre·ment /əˈkuːtrəmənt, -tərmənt/ *noun* (usu. in *pl.*) **1** additional items of dress, equipment, etc., or other items carried or worn by a person or used for a particular activity. **2** *Military* a soldier's outfit other than weapons and garments.

Accra /əˈkrɒ/ the capital of Ghana, a port on the Gulf of Guinea; pop. (est. 2000) 1,700,000.

ac·credit *transitive verb* (**ac·credit·ed, ac·credit·ing**) **1** officially recognize as meeting certain standards. **2** (foll. by *to*) attribute (a saying etc.) to (a person). **3** (foll. by *with*) credit (a person) with (a saying etc.). **4** (usu. foll. by *to* or *at*) send (an ambassador etc.) with credentials; recommend by documents as an envoy (*was accredited to the sovereign*). **5** gain belief or influence for or make credible (an adviser, a statement, etc.). □ **ac·credit·ation** *noun* [French *accréditer* (as AC-, *crédit* CREDIT)]

ac·credit·ed /əˈkrɛdɪtəd/ *adjective* **1** (of a person or organization) officially recognized. **2** (of a belief) generally accepted; orthodox.

ac·crete /əˈkriːt/ *verb* **1** *intransitive* grow together or into one. **2** *intransitive* (often foll. by *to*) form around or on, as around a nucleus. **3** *transitive* attract (such additions). [Latin *accrescere* (as AC-, *crescere cret-* grow)]

ac·cre·tion /əˈkriːʃən/ *noun* **1** growth by organic enlargement. **2 a** the growing of separate things into one. **b** the product of such growing. **3 a** extraneous matter added to anything. **b** the adhesion of this. **4** *Law* natural growth of a property, esp. by alluvial deposits. □ **ac·cre·tive** *adjective*

accretion disc *noun Astronomy* a rotating disc of matter formed by accretion around a massive body (such as a black hole) under the influence of gravitation.

ac·crue /əˈkruː/ *verb* (**ac·crues, ac·crued, ac·cru·ing**) (often foll. by *to*) **1** *intransitive* come as a natural increase or advantage, esp. financial. **2** *transitive* esp. *N Amer.* accumulate (esp. interest). □ **ac·crual** *noun* **ac·crued** *adjective* [Anglo-French *acru(e)*, past participle of *acreistre* increase, from Latin *accrescere* ACCRETE]

acct. *abbreviation* account.

ac·cul·tur·ate /əˈkʌltʃəˌreɪt/ *verb* **1** *intransitive* adapt to or adopt a different culture. **2** *transitive* cause to do this. □ **ac·cul·tur·ation** *noun* **ac·cul·tur·ative** *adjective*

ac·cumu·late /əˈkjuːmjʊˌleɪt/ *verb* **1** *transitive* **a** acquire an increasing number or quantity of. **b** produce or acquire (a resulting whole) in this way. **2** *intransitive* grow numerous or considerable; form an increasing mass or quantity. [Latin *accumulare* (as AC-, *cumulus* heap)]

ac·cumu·la·tion /əˌkjuːmjʊˈleɪʃən/ *noun* **1** the act or process of accumulating or being accumulated. **2** an accumulated mass. **3** the growth of capital by the continued addition of interest.

ac·cumu·la·tive /əˈkjuːmjʊlətɪv/ *adjective* **1** arising from accumulation; cumulative (*accumulative evidence*). **2** arranged so as to accumulate. **3** acquisitive; given to hoarding. □ **ac·cumu·la·tive·ly** *adverb*

ac·cumu·la·tor /əˈkjuːmjʊˌleɪtər/ *noun* **1** a person or thing that accumulates. **2** *Brit.* a bet placed on a sequence of events, the winnings and stake from each being placed on the next. **3** a register in a computer used to contain the results of an operation. **4** *Brit.*= STORAGE BATTERY.

ac·cur·acy /ˈakjʊrəsi/ *noun* (*pl.* **-acies**) **1** the quality of being accurate. **2** exactness or precision, esp. arising from careful effort.

ac·cur·ate /ˈakjʊrət/ *adjective* **1** careful, precise; lacking errors. **2** conforming exactly with the truth or with a given standard. **3** able to reach a target or measure a quantity etc. with precision. □ **ac·cur·ate·ly** *adverb* [Latin *accuratus* done carefully, past participle of *accurare* (as AC-, *cura* care)]

---

ac·cursed /ə'kɜrsəd, ə'kɜrst/ *adjective* (*archaic* **ac·curst** /ə'kɜrst/)
1 lying under a curse; ill-fated. **2** (*attributive*) detestable, annoying. [past participle of *accurse*, from A-² + CURSE]

ac·cusal *noun* accusation.

ac·cu·sa·tion *noun* **1** the act or process of accusing or being accused. **2** a statement charging a person with an offence or crime.

ac·cu·sa·tive /ə'kjuːzətɪv/ *Grammar* ● *noun* the case of nouns, pronouns, and adjectives, expressing the object of an action or the goal of motion. ● *adjective* of or in this case. □ **ac·cu·sa·tival** /-'taɪvəl/ *adjective* **ac·cu·sa·tive·ly** *adverb* [Latin (*casus*) *accusativus*, translation of Greek (*ptōsis*) *aitiatikē*]

ac·cu·sa·tor·ial /ə,kjuːzə'tɔriəl/ *adjective* (of judicial proceedings) involving accusation by a prosecutor and a verdict reached by an impartial judge or jury (*opp.* INQUISITORIAL).

ac·cu·sa·tory /ə'kjuːzə,tɔri/ *adjective* (of language, manner, etc.) of or implying accusation.

ac·cuse *transitive verb* **1** (foll. by *of*) charge (a person etc.) with a fault or crime; indict (*accused them of murder*; *was accused of stealing a car*). **2** lay the blame on. □ **ac·cus·er** *noun* **ac·cus·ing** *adjective* **ac·cus·ing·ly** *adverb* [Latin *accusare* (as AC-, CAUSE)]

ac·cused ● *noun* (*pl.* same) a person charged with a crime. ● *adjective* charged with a crime, fault, etc.

ac·cus·tom *transitive verb & reflexive* (foll. by *to*) make (a person or thing or oneself) used to (*the army accustomed him to discipline*; *was accustomed to their strange ways*). [Old French *acostumer* (as AD-, *costume* CUSTOM)]

ac·cus·tomed *adjective* **1** (usu. foll. by *to*) used to (*accustomed to hard work*). **2** customary, usual.

AC/DC ● *abbreviation* alternating current/direct current (of an appliance etc. that can operate on either type of current). ● *adjective* *slang* bisexual.

ACE *abbreviation* angiotensin converting enzyme.

ace ● *noun* **1 a** a playing card, domino, etc., with a single spot and generally having the value 'one' or in card games the highest value in each suit. **b** a single spot on a playing card etc. **2 a** a person who excels in some activity. **b** a fighter pilot who has shot down many enemy aircraft. **c** *Baseball* the best starting or relief pitcher on a team. **3 a** (in racquet sports, volleyball, etc.) a point scored on a service that an opponent fails to touch. **b** a service that achieves this. **4** *Golf* a hole in one. ● *transitive verb* **1** *N Amer. informal* achieve a high grade in (an exam etc.) (*she aced the course*). **2** *Tennis etc.* score an ace against (an opponent). **3** *Golf* complete (a hole) in one stroke. ● *adjective* (also *predicative* **aces**) *slang* excellent. □ **ace up one's sleeve** (or **in the hole**) something effective kept in reserve. **come up aces** *N Amer.* perform exceptionally well. **play one's ace** use one's best resource. **within an ace of** on the verge of. [Latin *as* unity, AS²]

-acea *suffix* forming the plural names of orders and classes of animals (*Crustacea*) (*compare* -ACEAN). [neuter pl. of Latin adj. suffix *-aceus* of the nature of]

-aceae *suffix* forming the plural names of families of plants (*Rosaceae*). [fem. pl. of Latin adj. suffix *-aceus* of the nature of]

-acean *suffix* **1** forming adjectives, = -ACEOUS. **2** forming nouns as the sing. of names in *-acea* (*crustacean*). [Latin *-aceus*: see -ACEA]

acedia /ə'siːdiə/ *noun* laziness, sloth, apathy. [Late Latin *acedia* from Greek *akēdia* listlessness]

ACE inhibitor *noun* any of a class of vasodilatory drugs that act primarily by inhibiting the conversion of angiotensin I to angiotensin II, and are used in the treatment of high blood pressure and heart disease.

acel·lu·lar /eɪ'seljʊlər/ *adjective Biol.* **1** having no cells; not consisting of cells. **2** (esp. of protozoa) consisting of one cell only; unicellular.

-aceous *suffix* forming adjectives, esp. from nouns in *-acea*, *-aceae* (*herbaceous*; *rosaceous*). [Latin *-aceus*: see -ACEA]

aceph·al·ous /ə'sefələs/ *adjective* **1** headless. **2** having no chief. **3** *Zool.* having no part of the body specially organized as a head. **4** *Bot.* with a head aborted or cut off. **5** *Prosody* lacking a syllable or syllables in the first foot. [Greek *akephalos* headless (as A-¹, *kephalē* head)]

acerb /ə'sɜrb/ *adjective US* = ACERBIC.

acer·bic /ə'sɜrbɪk/ *adjective* **1** biting in speech, manner, or temper. **2** astringently sour; harsh-tasting. □ **acer·bic·ally** *adverb* **acer·bity** *noun* (*pl.* **-ties**). [Latin *acerbus* sour-tasting]

acer·ola /,asə'roʊlə/ *noun* a plant of tropical America, *Malpighia glabra*, with edible fruit high in vitamin C used to make syrups, jams and vitamins.

acesul·fame /,asə'sʌlfeɪm/ *noun* a white crystalline compound used as a low-calorie artificial sweetener, typically in the form of a potassium salt (**acesulfame potassium** or **acesulfame K**). [20th c.: origin unknown]

acet·abu·lum /,asə'tabjʊləm/ *noun* (*pl.* **acet·abu·la** -lə/) *Zool.* **1** the socket for the head of the thigh bone, or of the leg in insects. **2** a cup-shaped sucker of various organisms, including tapeworms and cuttlefish. [Latin, = vinegar cup, from *acetum* vinegar + *-abulum* diminutive of *-abrum* holder]

acet·al /'asə,tal/ *noun* any of a class of organic compounds formed by the condensation of two alcohol molecules with an aldehyde molecule. [as ACETIC + -AL]

acet·alde·hyde /,asə'taldə,haɪd/ *noun* a colourless volatile liquid aldehyde, used in the synthesis of acetic acid and other chemical compounds. *Also called* ETHANAL. *Chem.* formula: CH_3CHO. [ACETIC + ALDEHYDE]

aceta·mino·phen /,əsiːtə'mɪnəfən/ *noun N Amer.* a drug used to relieve pain and reduce fever. *Chem.* formula: $C_8H_9NO_2$. [ACETO- + AMINO + PHENO-]

acet·anil·ide /,asət'anɪlaɪd/ *noun* a crystalline solid obtained by acetylation of aniline, used in dye manufacture. [ACETYL + ANILINE + -IDE]

acet·ate /'asə,teɪt/ *noun* **1** a salt or ester of acetic acid, esp. the cellulose ester of acetic acid (CELLULOSE ACETATE) used to make textiles, plastics, etc. **2** a fabric made from cellulose acetate. **3** a disc coated with cellulose acetate, for direct recording by a cutting stylus; any direct-cut disc. **4** a clear plastic film of cellulose acetate, used for overhead transparencies etc.; a sheet of this. [ACETIC + -ATE¹ 2]

acetic /ə'siːtɪk/ *adjective* of or like vinegar. [from Latin *acetum* vinegar]

acetic acid *noun* the clear liquid acid that gives vinegar its characteristic taste. *Chem.* formula: CH_3COOH.

aceto- /'asɪtoː/ *combining form* acetic, acetyl.

acet·one /'asə,toːn/ *noun* a colourless volatile liquid ketone valuable as a solvent for paints, varnishes, nail polish, etc. *Also called* PROPANONE. *Chem.* formula: CH_3COCH_3. [ACETO- + -ONE]

acet·ous /'asətəs/ *adjective* **1** having the qualities of vinegar. **2** producing vinegar. **3** sour. [Late Latin *acetosus* sour (as ACETIC)]

acetyl /'asətəl/ *noun Chem.* the monovalent radical of acetic acid. *Chem.* formula: CH_3CO-. [ACETIC + -YL]

acetyl·a·tion /əsetɪ'leɪʃən/ *noun* a reaction or process in which one or more acetyl groups are introduced into a molecule. □ **acetyl·ated** /ə'setɪleɪtəd/ *adjective*

acetyl·choline /,asətɪl'koːliːn/ *noun* a compound serving to transmit impulses from nerve fibres.

acetyl·ene /ə'setə,liːn/ *noun* a colourless hydrocarbon gas, burning with a bright flame, used esp. in welding and formerly in lighting. *Also called* ETHYNE. *Chem.* formula: C_2H_2. [ACETIC + -YL + -ENE]

acetyl·ide /ə'setə,laɪd/ *noun* any of a class of salts formed from acetylene and a metal.

acetyl·sali·cylic acid /ə'siːtəl,salə,sɪlɪk/ *noun* a drug used to relieve pain and reduce fever, the active ingredient in ASPIRIN. *Chem.* formula: $C_9H_8O_4$. *Abbr.*: **ASA**.

Achaea /ə'kiːə/ a region of ancient Greece on the north coast of the Peloponnese.

Achae·an /ə'kiːən/ ● *adjective* **1** of or relating to Achaea. **2** *literary* (esp. in Homeric contexts) Greek. ● *noun* **1** an inhabitant of Achaea. **2** *literary* (usu. in *pl.*) a Greek.

Achae·menid /ə'kiːmənɪd/ (also **Achae·men·ian** /,akə'miːniən/) ● *adjective* of or relating to the dynasty ruling in Persia from Cyrus I to Darius III (553–330 BC). ● *noun* a member of this dynasty. [Latin *Achaemenius* from Greek *Akhaimenēs*, ancestor of the dynasty]

Acha·tes /ə'koːtiːz/ *Gk & Rom. Myth* a companion of Aeneas. His fidelity to his friend was so exemplary as to become proverbial.

ache ● *noun* **1** a continuous or prolonged dull pain. **2** mental distress. ● *intransitive verb* **1** suffer from or be the source of an ache (*I ached all over*; *my left leg ached*). **2** (foll. by *to* + infin.) desire greatly (*we ached to be at home again*). □ **aching·ly** *adverb* [Old English *æce*, *acan*]

Achebe /ə'tʃeɪbi/ **Chinua** (born Albert Chinualumgu, b.1930), Nigerian novelist, poet, and writer of short stories and essays, awarded the Nobel Prize for literature in 1989. His novels, which include *Things Fall Apart* (1958), show traditional African society in confrontation with European customs and values.

achene /ə'kiːn/ *noun Bot.* a small dry one-seeded fruit that does not open to liberate the seed, e.g. a strawberry pip. [modern Latin *achaenium* (as A-¹, Greek *khainō* gape)]

Acher·nar /'akɜr,nar/ the brightest star in the constellation Eridanus.

Consonants: b *but*   d *dog*   f *few*   g *get*   h *her*   j *yes*   k *cat*   l *leg*   m *man*   n *no*   p *pen*   r *red*   s *sit*

Acher·on /ˈakərɒn/ *Gk & Rom. Myth* one of the rivers of the underworld, sometimes identified as the river over which Charon ferried the souls of the dead.

Ache·son /ˈeitʃəsən/ **Dean Gooder·ham** (1893–1971), US lawyer, politician, and Secretary of State, 1949–53. He urged international control of nuclear power, formulated plans for NATO, and implemented the Marshall Plan and the Truman Doctrine.

Acheu·lian /əˈʃuːliən/ (also **Acheu·lean**) ● *adjective* of the paleolithic period in Europe etc. following the Abbevillian and preceding the Mousterian. ● *noun* the culture of this period. [French *acheuléen* from St-*Acheul* in N France, where remains of it were found]

achieve *verb* **1** *transitive* **a** reach or attain by effort (*achieved victory*). **b** acquire, gain, earn (*achieved notoriety*). **2** *transitive* accomplish or carry out (a feat or task). **3** *intransitive* be successful; attain a desired level of performance. □ **achiev·able** *adjective* **achiev·er** *noun* [Old French *achever* from *a chief* to a head]

achieve·ment *noun* **1** something achieved. **2 a** the act of achieving. **b** an instance of this. **3** *Psych.* performance in a standardized test.

achil·lea /ˌakɪˈliːə/ *noun* any composite herbaceous plant of the genus *Achillea*, with white, purple, or yellow flower heads, esp. the yarrow. [Latin from Greek *Akhilleios* a plant supposed to have been used medicinally by Achilles]

Achil·les¹ /əˈkɪliːz/ *Gk Legend* a hero of the Trojan War, killed by an arrow which struck him in the heel, his only vulnerable spot.

Achilles² /əˈkɪliːz/ = ACHILLES TENDON.

Achilles heel *noun* a person's weak or vulnerable point.

Achilles tendon *noun* the tendon connecting the heel with the calf muscles.

achi·ote /ˌatʃiˈɒti/ *noun* a paste made from ground annatto seeds. [Mexican Spanish, from Nahuatl *achiotl*]

achon·dro·pla·sia /əˌkɒndrəˈpleiʒə/ *noun* a hereditary condition in which the growth of long bones by ossification of cartilage is retarded, resulting in very short limbs and sometimes a face which is small in relation to the (normal sized) skull. □ **achon·dro·plas·tic** *adjective* [A-¹ 'without' + Greek *khondros* 'cartilage' + *plasis* 'moulding' + -IA¹]

achoo *interjection* (also **a-choo**) representing the characteristic sound of a sneeze. [imitative]

achro·mat /ˈakrəˌmat/ *noun* a lens made achromatic by correction.

achro·mat·ic /ˌakrəˈmatɪk/ *adjective Optics* **1** that transmits light without separating it into constituent colours (*achromatic lens*). **2** without colour (*achromatic fringe*). □ **achro·mat·ic·ally** *adverb* **achro·ma·tic·ity** /əˌkrəməˈtɪsɪti/ *noun* **achro·ma·tism** /əˈkrəʊməˌtɪzəm/ *noun* [(as A-¹, CHROMATIC)]

achy /ˈeiki/ *adjective* (**achier, achiest**) full of or suffering from aches.

acid ● *noun* **1** *Chem.* **a** any of a class of substances that liberate hydrogen ions in water, are usu. sour and corrosive, turn litmus red, and have a pH of less than 7. **b** any compound or atom donating protons. **2** (in general use) any sour substance. **3** *slang* the drug LSD. ● *adjective* **1** sharp-tasting, sour. **2** biting, sharp (*an acid wit*). **3** *Chem.* having the essential properties of an acid. **4** (of precipitation) containing acids formed in the atmosphere from industrial waste gases (*compare* ACID RAIN). **5** *Geol.* containing much silica. **6** (of a colour) intense, bright. □ **acid·ic** /əˈsɪdɪk/ *adjective* **acid·ly** *adverb* (in sense 2 of *adjective*) [Latin *acidus* from *acēre* be sour]

acid drop *noun Brit.* a kind of hard candy with a sharp taste.

acid-free *adjective* (of paper) having neutral Ph and thus being resistant to deterioration.

acid·head *noun* (also **acid freak**) *slang* a user of the drug LSD.

acid house *noun* a kind of synthesized music with a simple repetitive beat, often associated with the taking of hallucinogenic drugs.

acid·ify /əˈsɪdɪˌfai/ *transitive & intransitive verb* (**-fies, -fied**) make or become acid. □ **acid·ifi·ca·tion** /-fɪˈkeiʃən/ *noun*

acid·ity *noun* (*pl.* **-ities**) **1** an acid quality or state. **2** an excessively acid condition of the stomach.

acid jazz *noun* a form of jazz combining elements of jazz, funk, and sometimes other musical forms such as hip hop etc.

acido·phil·ic /asidəˈfɪlɪk, əˌsɪd-/ *adjective* **1** *Biol.* (of a cell etc.) readily stained with acid dyes. **2** esp. *Bot.* growing best in acidic conditions.

acid·oph·ilus /ˌasɪˈdɒfɪləs/ *noun* a bacterium, *Lactobacillus acidophilus*, often added to yogurt as being beneficial to the intestinal flora. [modern Latin, = acid-loving]

acid·o·sis /ˌasɪˈdoːsɪs/ *noun* an over-acid condition of body fluids or tissues. □ **acid·otic** /-ˈdɒtɪk/ *adjective*

acid radical *noun* a radical formed by the removal of hydrogen ions from an acid.

acid rain *noun* rain mixed with acid formed in the atmosphere esp. from industrial waste gases.

acid rock *noun* = ACID HOUSE.

acid test *noun* **1** a severe or conclusive test. **2** a test in which acid is used to test for gold etc.

acidu·late /əˈsɪdjʊˌleit/ *transitive verb* make somewhat acid. □ **acidu·la·tion** /-ˈleiʃən/ *noun* [Latin *acidulus* diminutive of *acidus* sour]

acidu·lous /əˈsɪdjʊləs/ *adjective* **1** sharp-tongued, sour-tempered. **2** somewhat acid.

acid-washed *adjective* (of fabric, esp. denim) subjected to a laundering process in which the fabric is washed with porous stones soaked in chlorine bleach, resulting in fading and streaking and softening.

acin·us /ˈasɪnəs/ *noun* (*pl.* **acini** /-ˌnai/) *Anat.* **1** any multicellular gland with sac-like secreting ducts. **2** the terminus of a duct in such a gland. [Latin, = berry, kernel]

-acious *suffix* forming adjectives meaning 'inclined to, full of' (*vivacious; pugnacious; voracious; capacious*). [Latin *-ax -acis*, added chiefly to verbal stems to form adjectives + -OUS]

-acity *suffix* forming nouns of quality or state corresponding to adjectives in *-acious*. [French *-acité* or Latin *-acitas -tatis*]

ack-ack *dated informal* ● *noun* anti-aircraft fire, arms, etc. ● *adjective* anti-aircraft. [formerly signallers' name for the letters AA]

ackee /ˈaki/ *noun* **1** a tropical evergreen tree, *Blighia sapida*. **2** the bland, leathery, red or yellow fruit of this tree, edible only when cooked. [Kru *ākee*]

ac·know·ledge *transitive verb* **1 a** recognize; accept; admit the truth of (*acknowledged the failure of the plan*). **b** recognize as (*acknowledged it to be a great success*). **c** admit that something is so (*acknowledged that he was wrong*). **2** confirm the receipt of (*acknowledged her letter*). **3 a** show that one has noticed (*acknowledged my arrival with a grunt*). **b** express appreciation of (a service etc.). **4** recognize the validity of (*the acknowledged king*). □ **ac·know·ledge·able** *adjective* [obsolete KNOWLEDGE *verb* after obsolete *acknow* (as A-⁴, KNOW), or from obsolete *noun acknowledge*]

ac·know·ledge·ment *noun* (also **ac·know·ledg·ment**) **1** the act or an instance of acknowledging. **2 a** a thing given or done in return for a service etc. **b** a letter confirming receipt of something. **3** (usu. in *pl.*) an author's statement of thanks to others.

aclin·ic line /əˈklɪnɪk/ *noun* = MAGNETIC EQUATOR. [Greek *aklinēs* (as A-¹, *klinō* bend)]

ACLU *abbreviation* (in the US) American Civil Liberties Union.

acme /ˈakmi/ *noun* the highest point or period (of achievement, success, etc.); the peak of perfection (*displayed the acme of good taste*). [Greek, = highest point]

acne *noun* a skin condition, usu. of the face, characterized by red pimples. □ **acned** *adjective* [modern Latin from erroneous Greek *aknas* for *akmas* accusative pl. of *akmē* facial eruption: compare ACME]

aco·lyte /ˈakəˌləit/ *noun* **1** a person assisting a priest in a service or procession. **2** an assistant or follower. [ecclesiastical Latin *acolytus* from Greek *akolouthos* follower]

Acon·cagua /ˌakɒnˈkɒgwə/ an extinct volcano in the Andes, on the border between Chile and Argentina, rising to 6 960 m (22,835 ft.). It is the highest mountain in the western hemisphere.

acon·ite /ˈakəˌnəit/ *noun* **1 a** any poisonous herbaceous plant of the genus *Aconitum*, esp. monkshood or wolfsbane. **b** = ACONITINE. **2** = WINTER ACONITE. [French *aconit* from Greek *akoniton*]

acon·it·ine /əˈkɒnɪˌtiːn/ *noun* a poisonous alkaloid drug obtained from the aconite plant, esp. from the species *A. napellus*, formerly used as a sedative and for reducing fever.

Acorn, Mil·ton (1923–86), Canadian poet whose work focuses on the suffering and virtues of working-class Canadians.

acorn *noun* the fruit of the oak, with a smooth nut in a rough cup-like base. [Old English *æcern*, related to *æcer* ACRE, later assoc. with OAK and CORN¹]

acorn barnacle *noun* a stalkless barnacle, *Balanus balanoides*, living on rocks.

acorn squash *noun N Amer.* = PEPPER SQUASH.

acorn worm *noun* a wormlike hemichordate of the class Enteropneusta, having an acorn-shaped anterior end to its body, a proboscis and gill slits, and inhabiting seashores.

---

t *top*   v *voice*   w *we*   z *zoo*   ʃ *she*   ʒ *vision*   θ *thin*   ð *this*   ŋ *ring*   x *loch*   tʃ *chip*   dʒ *jar*   (*see over for vowels*)

acous·tic /əˈkuːstɪk/ ● *adjective* **1** relating to sound or the sense of hearing. **2** (of music, musicians, or musical instruments) not using electrical amplification (*acoustic guitar*). **3** (of building materials) used for soundproofing or modifying sound. ● *noun* **1** (usu. in *pl.*) the properties or qualities (esp. of a room or hall etc.) in transmitting sound (*good acoustics; a poor acoustic*). **2** (in *pl.*; usu. treated as *sing.*) the science of sound (*acoustics is not widely taught*). **3** an acoustic instrument, esp. a guitar. □ **acous·tic·al** *adjective* **acous·tic·al·ly** *adverb* [Greek *akoustikos* from *akouō* hear]

acoustic coupler *noun Computing* a modem which converts digital signals into audible signals and vice versa, so that the former can be transmitted and received over telephone lines.

acous·ti·cian /ˌakuːˈstɪʃən/ *noun* an expert in acoustics.

ac·quaint *transitive verb & reflexive* (usu. foll. by *with*) make (a person or oneself) aware of or familiar with (*acquaint me with the facts*). □ **acquainted with** having personal knowledge of (a person or thing). [Old French *acointier* from Late Latin *accognitare* (as AC-, *cognoscere cognit-* come to know)]

ac·quaint·ance *noun* **1** a person one knows slightly. **2** the fact or process of being acquainted (*our acquaintance lasted a year*). **3** (usu. foll. by *with*) knowledge (of a person or thing). □ **make someone's acquaintance** first meet or introduce oneself to another person. □ **ac·quaint·ance·ship** *noun*

acquaintance rape *noun N Amer.* = DATE RAPE.

ac·qui·esce /ˌakwiˈes/ *intransitive verb* **1** (often foll. by *to*) agree, esp. tacitly; raise no objection. **2** (foll. by *in*) accept (an arrangement etc.). □ **ac·qui·es·cence** *noun* **ac·qui·es·cent** *adjective* [Latin *acquiescere* (as AC-, *quiescere* rest)]

ac·quire *transitive verb* gain by and for oneself; obtain; come to possess (*acquired fame; acquired much property*). □ **ac·quir·able** *adjective* [Latin *acquirere* (as AC-, *quaerere* seek)]

acquired characteristic *noun Biol.* a characteristic caused by the environment, not inherited.

acquired immune deficiency syndrome *noun see* AIDS.

acquired taste *noun* **1** a liking gained by experience. **2** the object of such a liking.

ac·quire·ment *noun* **1** something acquired, esp. a mental attainment. **2** the act or an instance of acquiring.

ac·qui·si·tion /ˌakwɪˈzɪʃən/ *noun* **1** the act or an instance of acquiring. **2** something acquired, esp. if regarded as useful. [Latin *acquisitio* (as ACQUIRE)]

ac·quisi·tive /əˈkwɪzɪtɪv/ *adjective* keen to acquire things; avaricious; materialistic. □ **ac·quisi·tive·ly** *adverb* **ac·quisi·tive·ness** *noun* **ac·quisi·tor** *noun* [French *acquisitive* or Late Latin *acquisitivus* (as ACQUIRE)]

ac·quit *verb* (**acquit·ted**, **acquit·ting**) **1** *transitive* (often foll. by *of*) declare (a person) not guilty (*were acquitted of the offence*). **2** *reflexive* **a** conduct oneself or perform in a specified way (*we acquitted ourselves well*). **b** (foll. by *of*) discharge (a duty or responsibility). [Old French *aquiter* from medieval Latin *acquitare* pay a debt (as AC-, QUIT)]

ac·quit·tal *noun* **1** the process of freeing or being freed from a charge, esp. by a judgment of not guilty. **2** performance of a duty.

ac·quit·tance *noun* **1** payment of or release from a debt. **2** a written receipt attesting settlement of a debt.

Acre /ˈeɪkɜr/ (also **Akko** /ˈakoː/) an industrial seaport of Israel; pop. (2000) 45,700. Acre was the last Christian stronghold in the Holy Land until taken by the Ottoman Turks in 1517.

acre *noun* **1** a measure of land, 4,840 sq. yds., 0.405 ha. **2** (in *pl.*) a large area. □ **acred** *adjective* (also in *combination*). [Old English *æcer*, designating the amount of land a yoke of oxen could plow in a day]

acre·age *noun* **1** a number of acres. **2** an extent of land, esp. farmland. **3** a plot of land with an area of approximately one acre.

acre-foot *noun* a unit of volume (usually used of water) equivalent to one acre in area and one foot in depth (43,560 cu. ft., 1 233 cubic metres).

acrid /ˈakrɪd/ *adjective* **1** bitterly pungent; irritating; corrosive. **2** bitter in temper or manner. □ **acrid·ity** /əˈkrɪdɪti/ *noun* **acrid·ly** *adverb* [irreg. from Latin *acer acris* keen + -ID¹, prob. after *acid*]

acrid·ine /ˈakrɪˌdiːn/ *noun* a colourless crystalline compound used in the manufacture of dyes and drugs. [ACRID + -INE⁴]

acri·flavine /ˌakrɪˈfleɪvɪn, -viːn/ *noun* a reddish powder used as an antiseptic. [irreg. from ACRIDINE + Latin *flavus* yellow + -INE⁴]

Acri·lan *noun proprietary* a synthetic acrylic fibre used esp. in blankets, carpets, etc.

acri·moni·ous /ˌakrɪˈmoːniəs/ *adjective* extremely bitter in manner or temper. □ **acri·moni·ous·ly** *adverb*

acri·mony /ˈakrɪmoːni/ *noun* extreme bitterness of temper or manner; ill feeling. [Latin *acrimonia* pungency (as ACRID)]

acro *noun* a freestyle skiing event in which competitors perform choreographed acrobatic moves on skis to music. [abbreviation of ACROBATIC (see ACROBAT)]

acro·bat *noun* a person who performs feats of agility, esp. in a circus. □ **acro·bat·ic** /ˌakrəˈbatɪk/ *adjective* **acro·bat·ic·ally** /ˌakrəˈbatɪkli/ *adverb* [French *acrobate* from Greek *akrobatēs* from *akron* summit + *bainō* walk]

acro·bat·ics *plural noun* **1** the feats or skills of an acrobat. **2** (as *sing.*) the art of performing these. **3** a skill requiring dexterity (*mental acrobatics*).

acro·meg·aly /ˌakrəˈmegəli/ *noun Med.* abnormal enlargement of the hands, feet, and face, caused by excessive activity of the pituitary gland. □ **acro·meg·alic** /-məˈgalɪk/ *adjective* [Greek *akron* extremity + *megas megal-* great]

acro·nym /ˈakrənɪm/ *noun* a word, usu. pronounced as such, formed from the initial letters of other words e.g. *laser*, *NATO* (compare INITIALISM). [Greek *akron* end + *-onum-* = *onoma* name]

acrop·etal /əˈkrɒpətəl/ *adjective Bot.* growing or developing from the base upwards, so that the youngest parts are at the tip (compare BASIPETAL). □ **acrop·etal·ly** *adverb* [Greek *akron* tip + Latin *petere* seek]

acro·phobia /ˌakrəˈfoːbiə/ *noun Psych.* an abnormal dread of heights. □ **acro·phob·ic** *adjective* [Greek *akron* peak + -PHOBIA]

acrop·olis /əˈkrɒpəlɪs/ *noun* **1** a citadel or upper fortified part of an ancient Greek city. **2** (**Acropolis**) the ancient citadel at Athens, site of the Parthenon and other notable buildings, mostly dating from the 5th c. BC. [Greek *akropolis* from *akron* summit + *polis* city]

across ● *preposition* **1** to or on the other side of (*walked across the road; lives across the river*). **2** from one side to another side of (*the cover stretched across the opening; a bridge across the river*). **3** at or forming an angle (esp. a right angle) with (*deep cuts across his legs*). **4** from one side of (a country etc.) to the other; throughout. **5** including or applicable to all of a category or range (*works across the network*). ● *adverb* **1** to or on the other side (*ran across; shall soon be across*). **2** from one side to another (*a blanket stretched across*). **3** forming a cross (*with cuts across*). **4** (of a crossword clue or answer) read horizontally (*cannot do mine across*). **5** *Cdn (PEI)* in or to Nova Scotia or New Brunswick (*go across; come from across*). [Old French *a croix, en croix*, later regarded as from A² + CROSS]

acros·tic /əˈkrɒstɪk/ *noun* **1** a poem or other composition in which certain letters in each line form a word or words. **2** a word puzzle constructed in this way. [Greek *akrostikhis* from *akron* end + *stikhos* row, line of verse, assimilated to -IC]

Acrux /ˈakrʊks/ a binary star, the brightest in the constellation Crux.

acryl·a·mide /əˈkrɪləmaɪd/ *noun* a colourless crystalline solid which readily forms water-soluble polymers; the amide of acrylic acid.

acryl·ate /ˈakrɪleɪt/ *noun* a salt or ester of acrylic acid.

acryl·ic /əˈkrɪlɪk/ ● *adjective* **1** of material made with a synthetic polymer derived from acrylic acid. **2** (of paint) having acrylic resin as a vehicle. **3** *Chem.* of or derived from acrylic acid. ● *noun* **1** an acrylic fibre. **2** an acrylic paint. **3** a painting in acrylic paints. [from the liquid aldehyde *acrolein* (from Latin *acer acris* pungent + *olēre* to smell + -IN) + -YL + -IC]

acrylic acid *noun* a pungent liquid organic acid which can be polymerized to make synthetic resins. Chem. formula: $C_3H_4O_2$.

acrylic resin *noun* any of various transparent colourless polymers of acrylic acid.

ACT *abbreviation* Australian Capital Territory.

act ● *noun* **1** something done; a deed; an action. **2** the process of doing something (*caught in the act*). **3 a** a piece of entertainment, usu. one of a series in a program. **b** the performer(s) of this. **4** a pretense; behaviour intended to deceive or impress (*it was all an act*). **5** a main division of a play, opera, or story ballet. **6 a** a written ordinance of a parliament or other legislative body. **b** a document attesting a legal transaction. **7** (often in *pl.*) the recorded decisions or proceedings of a committee, an academic body, etc. **8** (**Acts**) (in full **Acts of the Apostles**) the New Testament book relating the growth of the early Church. ● *verb* **1** *intransitive* behave (*see how they act under stress*). **2** *intransitive* perform actions or functions; operate effectively; take action (*act as referee; the brakes failed to act; we must act quickly*). **3** *intransitive* (also foll. by *on*) exert energy or influence (*the medicine soon began to act; alcohol acts on the brain*). **4** *intransitive* **a** perform a part in a play, film, etc. **b** pretend. **c** embody or portray a character convincingly in a theatrical production (*Martine is a beautiful dancer who is technically strong and can also act*). **5** *transitive* **a** perform the part of (*acted Othello; acts the fool*). **b** perform (a play etc.). **c** portray (an incident) by actions. **d** feign (*we acted indifference*). □ **act for** be the (esp. legal) representative of. **act on** (or **upon**) perform or carry out; put into operation (*acted on my advice*). **act out 1** translate (ideas etc.) into action. **2** *Psych.* represent (one's subconscious desires etc.) in action. **3** (esp. of a child or adolescent) misbehave; behave anti-socially. **act up** *informal* misbehave; give trouble (*my car is acting up again*). **get one's act together** *informal* become properly organized; make preparations for an undertaking etc. **get in on the act** *informal* become a participant (esp. for profit). **a hard act to follow** *informal* a person or thing difficult to be more impressive or successful than. **put on an act** *informal* carry out a pretense. [Middle English, ultimately from Latin *agere act-* do]

ACTA *abbreviation* (in Canada) Alliance of Canadian Travel Agents.

Ac·taeon /ˈæktiːən, -ˈtiːən/ *Gk Legend* a hunter who, because he accidentally saw Artemis bathing, was changed into a stag and killed by his own hounds.

ACTH *abbreviation* ADRENOCORTICOTROPHIC HORMONE.

actin /ˈæktɪn/ *noun* a protein which with myosin forms the contractile filaments of muscle fibres. [Greek *aktin-, aktis* ray + -IN]

act·ing ● *noun* **1** the art or occupation of performing parts in plays, films, etc. **2** *in senses of* ACT *verb*. ● *attributive adjective* serving temporarily or on behalf of another or others (*acting manager; Acting Captain*).

acting sub-lieutenant *noun* (also **Acting Sub-Lieutenant**) a commissioned officer ranking below Sub-Lieutenant in the Canadian Navy. *Abbr.:* **A/SLt**.

ac·tinia /ækˈtɪniə/ *noun* (*pl.* **ac·tiniae** /-nɪˌiː/) any sea anemone, esp. of the genus *Actinia*. [modern Latin, as ACTIN]

ac·tin·ic /ækˈtɪnɪk/ *adjective* (of light etc.) having the ability to cause chemical change. [ACTINISM + -IC]

actin·ide /ˈæktɪˌnaɪd/ *noun* (also **actin·oid** /ˈæktɪˌnɔɪd/) *Chem.* any of the series of 15 radioactive elements having increasing atomic numbers from actinium to lawrencium. [ACTINIUM + -IDE as in *lanthanide*]

actin·ism /ˈæktɪˌnɪzəm/ *noun* the property by which light or other electromagnetic radiation causes chemical changes, as in photography. [as ACTIN + -ISM]

ac·tin·ium /ækˈtɪniəm/ *noun Chem.* a radioactive metallic element of the actinide series, occurring naturally in pitchblende. Symbol: **Ac**; at. no.: 89. [as ACTIN + -IUM]

actin·oid *var. of* ACTINIDE.

ac·tino·lite /ækˈtɪnəlaɪt/ *noun* a green mineral containing calcium, magnesium, and iron silicates, and found esp. in metamorphic rocks.

actin·om·eter /ˌæktɪˈnɒmɪtər/ *noun* an instrument for measuring the intensity of radiation, esp. ultraviolet radiation.

ac·tino·morph·ic /ˌæktɪnəˈmɔrfɪk/ *adjective Biol.* radially symmetrical. [as ACTIN + Greek *morphē* form]

ac·tino·my·cete /ˌæktɪnəˈmaɪsiːt/ *noun* a filamentous anaerobic bacterium of the order Actinomycetales. [as ACTIN + -mycetes from Greek *mukēs -ētos* mushroom]

ac·tion ● *noun* **1** the fact or process of doing or acting (*demanded action; put ideas into action*). **2** forcefulness or energy as a characteristic (*a woman of action*) (also *attributive*: *action photograph*). **3** the exertion of energy or influence (*the action of acid on metal*). **4** something done; a deed or act (*not aware of his own actions*). **5 a** a series of events represented in a story, play, etc. **b** *informal* activity (*arrived late and missed the action; want some action*). **6 a** armed conflict; fighting (*killed in action*). **b** an occurrence of this, esp. a minor military engagement. **7 a** the way in which a machine, instrument, etc. works (*explain the action of an air pump*). **b** the mechanism that makes a machine, instrument, etc. (e.g. a musical instrument, a gun, etc.) work. **c** the mode or style of movement of an animal or human (usu. described in some way) (*a runner with good action*). **8** a legal process; a lawsuit (*bring an action*). **9** (in *imperative*) a word of command to begin, esp. used by a film director etc. ● *transitive verb* bring a legal action against. □ **go into action** start work. **out of action** not working. **take action** act, esp. against something. [Latin *actio -onis* (as ACT)]

action·able *adjective* **1** giving cause for legal action. **2** able to be acted upon; having practical value, useful.

action central *noun N Amer.* a central location where much activity is concentrated.

action committee *noun* (also **action group** etc.) a body formed to take active steps, esp. in politics.

Ac·tion démo·crat·ique du Qué·bec /ˈæksjɔ̃ deimoːkraˈtik duː

keiˈbek/*noun* (in Canada) a Quebec provincial political party, founded in 1994, favouring essentially right-of-centre policies.

Ac·tion Di·recte /ˈæksjɔ̃ drˈrɛkt/ a group of extreme left-wing French terrorists active esp. in the 1980s.

action·er *noun slang* = ACTION FILM.

action figure *noun* a doll representing a person or fictional character capable of or known for vigorous action, e.g. a soldier, athlete, superhero, etc.

action film *noun* (also **action movie** etc.) a feature film containing a great deal of fast-moving (esp. violent) action.

Ac·tion Fran·çaise /ˈæksjɔ̃ frɑ̃ˈsez/ an extreme right-wing anti-republican French nationalist movement of the first half of the 20th c.

action-packed *adjective* full of action or excitement.

action painting *noun* an aspect of abstract expressionism with paint applied by the artist's random or spontaneous gestures.

action plan *noun* a proposed strategy or course of action.

action point *noun* a proposal for action, esp. arising from a discussion etc.

action potential *noun Biol.* the change in electrical potential associated with the passage of an impulse along the membrane of a muscle cell or nerve cell.

action replay *noun Brit.* a playback of part of a television broadcast, esp. a sporting event, often in slow motion.

action stations *plural noun* positions taken up by troops etc. ready for battle.

Ac·tium /ˈæktiəm/ *noun* a promontory off the west coast of Greece, where Octavian defeated Antony and Cleopatra in 31 BC, bringing an end to the Roman republic.

acti·vate *transitive verb* **1** make active; bring into action. **2** *Chem.* cause reaction in; excite (a substance, molecules, etc.). **3** *Physics* make radioactive. □ **acti·va·tion** *noun* **acti·va·tor** *noun*

activated carbon *noun* (also **activated charcoal**) carbon, esp. charcoal, treated to increase its power to adsorb.

activated sludge *noun* aerated sewage containing aerobic bacteria.

act·ive ● *adjective* **1 a** consisting in or marked by action; energetic; diligent (*leads an active life; an active helper*). **b** able to move about or accomplish practical tasks (*infirmity made him less active*). **2** working, operative (*an active volcano*). **3** originating action; not merely passive or inert (*active support; active ingredients*). **4** radioactive. **5** *Grammar* of the form of a verb whose grammatical subject is the person or thing that performs the action, e.g. of the verbs in *guns kill; we saw him*. ● *noun Grammar* the active form or voice of a verb. □ **act·ive·ly** *adverb*

active carbon *noun* = ACTIVATED CARBON.

active culture yogourt *noun* yogourt in which the bacterial culture remains alive, often understood to be specifically yogourt with active acidophilus and bifidum bacteria.

active duty *noun N Amer.* **1** = ACTIVE SERVICE. **2** active involvement in an organization or group.

active layer *noun* the surface layer of soil above permafrost, subject to thawing in summer.

active list *noun Stock Exch.* a list of shares traded in a given period.

active-matrix *noun* (*attributive*) pertaining to or designating a form of liquid crystal display in which each pixel is controlled by its own transistor, thus improving contrast.

active service *noun* full-time service in the armed forces or police.

active·wear *noun* clothing worn primarily during exercise or sports activities.

ac·tiv·ism *noun* the policy or action of using vigorous campaigning to bring about social or political change. □ **ac·tiv·ist** *noun*

ac·tiv·ity *noun* (*pl.* **-ities**) **1 a** the condition of being active or moving about. **b** the exertion of energy; vigorous action. **2** (often in *pl.*) a particular occupation or pursuit (*outdoor activities*). **3** = RADIOACTIVITY.

act of contrition *noun Catholicism* a prayer expressing repentance.

act of God *noun* a usu. disastrous event caused by uncontrollable natural forces.

Act of Supremacy either of two Acts of Parliament of 1534 and 1559, laying down the position of the sovereigns Henry VIII and Elizabeth I as supreme heads of the Church of England and excluding the authority of the Pope. The term is used particularly with reference to the Act of 1534.

Act of Union *Canadian History* an act of the British Parliament (1841) uniting Upper and Lower Canada into the Province of Canada.

---

uː mood aɪ my əɪ pipe au brown ʌu house ei day ɔi boy ɑ̃ franglais ã Canadien ɔ̃ Brayon   (*see over for consonants*)

Acton part of the town of Halton Hills in south central Ontario, west of Brampton; pop. (1996) 7,632. [*Acton* in Northumberland, England]

Acton Vale a town in SE Quebec, in the Eastern Townships, about 30 km south of Drummondville; pop. (2001) 7,299. [ultimately after Acton, part of London, England]

ac·tor *noun* **1** a person who acts a part in a play, film, etc. **2** a person whose profession is performing such parts. **3** a person who is skilled at embodying or portraying characters in theatrical productions. **4** a person who does something; a participant. [Latin, = doer, actor (as ACT, -OR¹)]

ACTRA /ˈaktrə/ *abbreviation* Alliance of Canadian Cinema, Television and Radio Artists, a union for writers, performers, and broadcast journalists and researchers.

ACTRA Award *noun hist.* any of several annual awards presented from 1970–1985 by ACTRA to Canadian broadcast journalists, performers and writers.

ac·tress *noun* **1** a woman or girl who acts a part in a play, film, etc. **2** a woman or girl whose profession is performing such parts. **3** a woman who is skilled at embodying or portraying characters in theatrical productions (*Karen Kain was a marvellous dancer and a wonderful actress*).

ac·tual *adjective* (usu. *attributive*) existing in fact; real (often as distinct from ideal). ¶ Redundant use, as in *tell me the actual facts*, is disputed, but common. □ **ac·tual·ize** *transitive verb* (also esp. *Brit.* **-ise**). **ac·tual·iz·a·tion** *noun* [Late Latin *actualis* from *agere* ACT]

ac·tu·al·ity *noun* (*pl.* **-ities**) **1** reality; what is the case. **2** (in *pl.*) existing conditions. [Old French *actualité* 'entity' or medieval Latin *actualitas* (as ACTUAL)]

ac·tual·ly *adverb* **1** as a fact, really (*I asked for ten, but actually got nine*). **2** as a matter of fact, even (strange as it may seem) (*he actually refused!*).

actual value assessment *noun* assessment of the value of a property for tax purposes based on the current use of the property rather than its speculative value.

ac·tu·ary /ˈaktʃʊeri/ *noun* (*pl.* **-aries**) an expert in statistics, esp. one who calculates insurance risks and premiums. □ **ac·tu·arial** /-ˈeriəl/ *adjective* **ac·tu·arial·ly** /-ˈeriəli/ *adverb* [Latin *actuarius* bookkeeper, from *actus* past participle of *agere* ACT]

ac·tu·ate /ˈaktʃʊeit/ *transitive verb* **1** communicate motion to (a machine etc.). **2** cause the operation of (an electrical device etc.). **3** cause (a person) to act. □ **ac·tu·a·tion** /-ˈeiʃən/ *noun* **ac·tu·ator** *noun* [medieval Latin *actuare* from Latin *actus*: see ACTUAL]

actus reus /ˈaktəs ˈreiəs/ *noun Law* the element of conduct in a crime as distinct from the element of intention (*compare* MENS REA). [Latin, = guilty act]

acu·ity /əˈkjuːiti/ *noun* (of the mind or the senses, esp. vision) sharpness, acuteness. [medieval Latin *acuitas* from *acuere* sharpen: see ACUTE]

acu·leate /əˈkjuːliət/ *adjective* **1** *Zool.* having a sting. **2** pointed, incisive. [Latin *aculeatus* from *aculeus* sting, diminutive of *acus* needle]

acu·men /ˈakjʊmən, əˈkjuːmən/ *noun* the ability to understand and judge things quickly and clearly; shrewdness. [Latin *acumen -minis* anything sharp from *acuere* sharpen: see ACUTE]

acu·min·ate /əˈkjuːminət/ *adjective Biol.* tapering to a point. [Latin *acuminatus* pointed (as ACUMEN)]

acu·pres·sure *noun* = SHIATSU.

acu·punc·ture *noun* a system of complementary medicine in which fine needles are inserted in the skin at specific points along what are considered to be lines of energy (meridians), used in the treatment of various physical and mental conditions. □ **acu·punc·tur·ist** *noun* [Latin *acu* with a needle + PUNCTURE]

acute ● *adjective* **1** (of sensation or senses) keen, penetrating. **2** shrewd, perceptive (*an acute critic*). **3** (of a disease) coming sharply to a crisis; not chronic. **4** (of a difficulty or controversy) critical, serious. **5 a** (of an angle) less than 90°. **b** sharp, pointed. **6** (of a sound) high, shrill. ● *noun* = ACUTE ACCENT. □ **acute·ly** *adverb* **acute·ness** *noun* [Latin *acutus* past participle of *acuere* sharpen from *acus* needle]

acute accent *noun* a mark (´) placed over letters in some languages to show quality, vowel length, pronunciation (e.g. *rosé*), etc.

acute-care *adjective* (of a hospital) providing emergency and general medical treatment for acute conditions rather than long-term care for chronic conditions.

ACW *abbreviation* **1** (in Canada) Anglican Church Women. **2** (in the UK) (preceding a name) AIRCRAFTWOMAN.

-acy *suffix* forming nouns of state or quality (*accuracy*; *piracy*; *supremacy*), or an instance of it (*conspiracy*; *fallacy*) (*see also* -CRACY). [a branch of the suffix -CY from Latin *-acia* or *-atia* or Greek *-ateia*]

acyclo·vir /eiˈsaiklovɪr/ *noun* an antiviral drug used to combat some types of herpes, esp. genital herpes. [A- + CYCLIC + -O- + VIRAL]

acyl /ˈeisail/ *noun Chem.* the monovalent radical of an organic acid. [German (as ACID, -YL)]

AD¹ *abbreviation* (of a date) of the Christian era. ¶ Strictly, AD should precede a date (e.g. AD 410), but uses such as *the tenth century* AD are well established. [*Anno Domini*, 'in the year of the Lord']

AD² *abbreviation* assistant director.

ad *noun informal* an advertisement. [abbreviation]

ad- *prefix* (also **a-** before *sc*, *sp*, *st*, **ac-** before *c*, *k*, *q*, **af-** before *f*, **ag-** before *g*, **al-** before *l*, **an-** before *n*, **ap-** before *p*, **ar-** before *r*, **as-** before *s*, **at-** before *t*) **1** with the sense of motion or direction to, reduction or change into, addition, adherence, increase, or intensification. **2** formed by assimilation of other prefixes (*accursed*; *admiral*; *advance*; *affray*). [(sense 1) (through Old French *a-*) from Latin *ad* to: (sense 2) *a-* representing various prefixes other than *ad-*]

-ad *suffix* forming nouns: **1** in collective numerals (*myriad*; *triad*). **2** in names of poems and similar compositions (*Iliad*; *jeremiad*). [Greek *-as -ada*]

Ada /ˈeidə/ *noun* a programming language used esp. in real-time control situations. [Augusta *Ada*, Lady Lovelace (1815–52), associate of Charles Babbage.]

ad·age /ˈadidʒ/ *noun* a traditional maxim, a proverb. [French from Latin *adagium* (as AD-, root of *aio* say)]

adage /əˈdaʒ, ˈadaʒ/ *noun Dance* **1** slow, flowing movement. **2** a passage of this. [French, from ADAGIO]

ada·gio /əˈdaːʒio, -ʒio/ *Music & Dance* ● *adverb & adjective* in slow time. ● *noun* (*pl.* **-gios**) an adagio movement or passage. [Italian, from *ad agio*, 'at ease']

Adam¹ *noun* the first man, in the Biblical and Quranic traditions. □ **not know a person from Adam** be unable to recognize the person in question. [Hebrew *ādām* man]

Adam² ▶ **1** /aˈdɑ̃/ **Adolphe** (1803–56) French romantic composer. Best known for the ballet *Giselle*, he also composed the Christmas carol *O Holy Night*. **2** /ˈadəm/ **Robert** (1728–92) and **James** (1730–94), Scottish architects. The Adam brothers introduced a lighter, more decorative neoclassical style than the Palladianism of the previous half-century.

Adam³ *noun* the hallucinogenic drug MDMA. [back slang, perhaps influenced by ADAM¹]

ada·mant /ˈadəmənt/ ● *adjective* stubbornly resolute; resistant to persuasion. ● *noun archaic* diamond or other hard substance. □ **ada·mant·ine** /-ˈmantin/ *adjective* **ada·mant·ly** *adverb* [Latin *adamas adamant-* untameable, from Greek (as A-¹, *damaō* to tame)]

Adams ▶ **1 Ansel** (1902–84), US photographer noted for his esp. black and white images of wilderness landscapes. **2 Bryan** (b.1959), Canadian singer, songwriter, guitarist. He has recorded a number of major international hits, including the single 'Straight from the Heart' and the album *Reckless*. **3 Henry (Brooks)** (1838–1918), US historian and writer, who is best known for his autobiography *The Education of Henry Adams* (1918). **4 John** (1735–1826), 1st US vice-president 1789–97; 2nd US president 1797–1801. **5 John Couch** (1819–92), English astronomer. In 1843 he predicted the existence of an eighth planet from perturbations in the orbit of Uranus; similar calculations performed almost simultaneously by Le Verrier resulted in the discovery of Neptune three years later. **6 John Quin·cy** (1767–1848), son of John Adams, 6th US president 1825–9. As Secretary of State under Monroe, he helped to shape the Monroe Doctrine. **7 Sam·uel** (1722–1803), US revolutionary leader and politician, who helped to organize the Boston Tea Party, and signed the Declaration of Independence.

Adams, Mount 1 a mountain in SW Washington, in the Cascade Range (3 751 m, 12,307 ft.). **2** a mountain in N New Hampshire, in the White Mountains (1 767 m, 5,798 ft.).

Adam's ale *noun informal* water.

Adam's apple *noun* a projection of the thyroid cartilage of the larynx, esp. as prominent in men.

Adam's Bridge a line of shoals lying between NW Sri Lanka and the southeast coast of Tamil Nadu in India, separating the Palk Strait from the Gulf of Mannar.

Adam's Peak a mountain in south central Sri Lanka, rising to 2 243 m (7,360 ft.). The mountain is regarded as sacred by Buddhists, Hindus, and Muslims.

Consonants: b *but*   d *dog*   f *few*   g *get*   h *her*   j *yes*   k *cat*   l *leg*   m *man*   n *no*   p *pen*   r *red*   s *sit*

Adana /ˈadənə/ a town in S Turkey, capital of a province of the same name; pop. (est. 2002) 1,162,000.

adapt verb **1** transitive **a** (foll. by to) fit, adjust (one thing to another). **b** (foll. by to, for) make suitable for a purpose. **c** alter or modify (esp. a text). **d** arrange for broadcasting etc. **2** intransitive & reflexive (usu. foll. by to) become adjusted to new conditions. □ **adapt·ive** adjective **adapt·ive·ly** adverb [Latin adaptare (as AD-, aptare from aptus fit)]

adapt·able adjective **1** able to adapt oneself to new conditions. **2** that can be adapted. □ **adapt·abil·ity** noun

adap·ta·tion noun (also **adap·tion**) **1** the act or process of adapting or being adapted. **2** a thing made by adapting something else, esp. a text for production on the stage, radio, etc. **3** Biol. the process by which an organism or species becomes suited to its environment.

adap·ta·tion·ism noun Biology the axiom or assumption that each feature of an organism is the result of evolutionary adaptation for a particular function. □ **adap·ta·tion·ist** noun & adjective

adapt·er noun (also **adapt·or**) **1 a** a device for making equipment compatible. **b** a device for changing voltage or current. **2** a device for connecting several electrical plugs to one socket. **3** a person who adapts.

adapt·o·gen /əˈdaptoːdʒen/ noun (in herbal medicine) a natural substance considered to help the body adapt to stress and to exert a normalizing effect upon bodily processes. The best-known example is ginseng. □ **adapt·o·gen·ic** adjective

Adas·kin /əˈdaskɪn/ **1 Harry** (1901–94), Latvian-born Canadian musician, educator, and broadcaster. **2** his brother **John** (1908–64), Canadian musician and radio producer. Through his CBC radio productions, he encouraged Canadian composers and young Canadian artists; he also promoted the use of Canadian music in schools by commissioning pieces that would be suitable for use in teaching. **3** their brother **Murray** (1906–2002), Canadian composer, teacher, violinist, and conductor. His compositions frequently make use of Canadian folk material.

ad·axial /adˈaksiəl/ adjective Bot. (esp. of the upper surface of a leaf) facing toward the stem of a plant (compare ABAXIAL). [AD- + AXIAL]

ADC abbreviation **1** AIDE-DE-CAMP. **2** analog-digital converter.

ADD abbreviation ATTENTION DEFICIT DISORDER.

add verb **1** transitive join (one thing to another) as an increase or supplement (add your efforts to mine; add insult to injury). **2** transitive & intransitive put together (two or more numbers) to find a number denoting their combined value (children learn to add). **3** transitive say in addition (added a remark; added that I was wrong). □ **add in** include. **add to** increase; be a further item among (this adds to our difficulties). **add up 1** find the total of. **2** (foll. by to) amount to; constitute (adds up to a disaster). **3** informal make sense; be understandable. □ **added** adjective [Latin addere (as AD-, dare put)]

Ad·dams, **Jane** (1860–1935), US social reformer and feminist. She founded Hull House, a social settlement, in Chicago (1889), was prominent in the suffrage movement, and presided over the first Women's Peace Congress at The Hague (1915); she shared the Nobel Peace Prize in 1931.

addax /ˈadaks/ noun a large antelope, Addax nasomaculatus, of Northern Africa, with twisted horns. [Latin from an African word]

ad·den·dum /əˈdendəm/ noun (pl. **ad·den·da** /-də/) **1** a thing (usu. something omitted) to be added, esp. (in pl.) as additional matter at the end of a book. **2** an appendix; an addition. [Latin, gerundive of addere ADD]

ad·der noun **1** any of a variety of non-venomous N American snakes, e.g. the hognose snake. **2** any of various small venomous snakes of Europe and Asia, esp. the common viper, Vipera berus. [Old English nædre: n lost in Middle English by wrong division of a naddre: compare APRON, AUGER, UMPIRE]

adder's tongue noun **1** any of several liliaceous plants of the esp. N American genus Erythronium, with mottled leaves and white, yellow, pink, or purple flowers. **2** any fern of the genus Ophioglossum.

ad·dict ● noun **1** a person addicted to a habit, esp. one dependent on a (specified) drug (drug addict; heroin addict). **2** informal an enthusiastic devotee of a sport or pastime (film addict). ● transitive verb & reflexive (usu. in passive; usu. foll. by to) devote or apply habitually or compulsively; make addicted. [Latin addicere assign (as AD-, dicere dict- say)]

ad·dict·ed adjective (often foll. by to) **1** dependent on as a habit; unable to do without (addicted to heroin). **2** devoted (addicted to football).

ad·dic·tion noun the fact or process of being addicted, esp. the condition of taking a drug habitually and being unable to give it up without incurring adverse effects.

ad·dict·ive adjective (of a drug, habit, etc.) causing addiction or dependence.

add-in noun (usu. attributive) a piece of computer hardware for installation into an existing system.

Ad·ding·ton, **Henry**, **1st Viscount Sidmouth** (1757–1844), British prime minister 1801–4.

Addis Ababa /ˌadɪs ˈabəbə/ (also **Adis Abeba**) the capital of Ethiopia, situated at an altitude of about 2 440 m (8,000 ft.); pop. (est. 2002) 2,638,500.

Ad·di·son ▸ **1 Jo·seph** (1672–1719), English essayist and dramatist who collaborated with Richard Steele on the Spectator and was active in politics. As a dramatist he is best known for his tragedy Cato. **2 Thomas** (1793–1860), English physician, the first to recognize what is now called Addison's disease.

Addison's disease noun a disease characterized by progressive anemia and debility and brown discoloration of the skin. [T. ADDISON]

addi·tion noun **1** the act or process of adding or being added. **2** a person or thing added (a useful addition to the team; built on an addition). □ **in addition** (often foll. by to) furthermore; as something added.

addi·tion·al adjective added, extra, supplementary. □ **addi·tion·al·ly** adverb

addi·tive ● noun a thing added, esp. a substance added to another so as to give it specific qualities (food additive). ● adjective characterized by addition (additive process). [Late Latin additivus (as ADD)]

addle ● verb **1** transitive muddle, confuse. **2** intransitive (of an egg) become addled. ● adjective **1** muddled, unsound (addle-brained; addle-pated). **2** (of an egg) addled. [Old English adela filth, used as adj., then as verb]

ad·dled adjective **1** confused. **2** (of an egg) rotten.

Addled Parliament the parliament of James I of England (James VI of Scotland), summoned in 1614, so known because it refused to accede to the king's financial requests, did not succeed in its attempts to curb his existing powers of taxation, and was dissolved without having passed any legislation.

Addo /aˈdoː/ a national park in South Africa, established in 1931 to protect the last of the Eastern Cape elephants.

add-on noun something added to an existing object or quantity.

ad·dress ● noun **1 a** the place where a person lives or an organization is situated. **b** particulars of this, esp. for postal purposes. **2** Computing **a** the location of an item of stored information. **b** the string of codes representing a person's location on an electronic mail network. **c** a unique name, number, or code that belongs to a device on a network. **3** a discourse delivered to an audience. **4** skill, dexterity, readiness. **5** (in pl.) a courteous approach, courtship (pay one's addresses to). **6** archaic manner in conversation. ● transitive verb **1** write the name and address of the intended recipient on (an envelope etc.). **2** direct in speech or writing (remarks, a protest, etc.). **3** speak or write to, esp. formally (addressed the audience; asked me how to address a duke). **4** direct one's attention to (addressed their concerns). **5** Golf take aim at or prepare to hit (the ball). □ **address oneself to 1** speak or write to. **2** attend to. □ **ad·dress·er** noun [Old French adresse, adresser, ultimately from Latin (as AD-, directus DIRECT)]

ad·dress·able adjective Computing relating to or denoting a memory unit in which all locations can be separately accessed by a particular program. □ **ad·dress·abil·ity** noun

address book noun **1** a book in which are recorded postal addresses, phone numbers, etc. of one's regular correspondents. **2** Computing a function in an email tool which allows the user to save the email addresses of correspondents and also give them shorter aliases.

ad·dres·see noun the person to whom something (esp. a letter) is addressed.

ad·duce transitive verb cite as an instance or as proof of evidence. □ **ad·du·cible** adjective [Latin adducere adduct- (as AD-, ducere lead)]

ad·duct /əˈdʌkt/ transitive verb draw towards a middle line, esp. draw (a limb) towards the middle line of the body. □ **ad·duc·tion** noun [as ADDUCE]

ad·duc·tor /əˈdʌktər/ noun (in full **adductor muscle**) any muscle that moves one part of the body towards another or towards the middle line of the body.

-ade¹ suffix forming nouns **1** an action done (blockade; tirade). **2** the body concerned in an action or process (cavalcade). **3** the product or result of a material or action (arcade; lemonade; masquerade). [from or after French -ade from Latin -ata fem. sing. past participle of verbs in -are]

-ade² suffix forming nouns (decade) (compare -AD¹). [French -ade from Greek -as -ada]

-ade³ *suffix* forming nouns: **1** = -ADE¹ (*brocade*). **2** a person concerned (*renegade*). [Spanish or Portuguese *-ado*, masc. form of *-ada*: see -ADE¹]

Adel·aide /ˈadəˌleid/ a city in Australia, the capital and chief port of the state of South Australia; pop. (2001) 1,110,500. [Queen *Adelaide*, wife of William IV, d.1849]

Adelaide Peninsula /ˈadəˌleid/ a peninsula in Nunavut, south of King William Island. [as ADELAIDE]

adel·gid /əˈdeldʒɪd/ *noun* an insect of the family Adelgidae, which comprises sap-feeding insects resembling aphids and typically covered with white waxy fluff. [perhaps from Greek *adelos* 'unseen' + *-gid* of unknown origin]

Adélie Land /aˈdeili/ (also **Adélie Coast**) a section of the Antarctic continent south of the 60th parallel, between Wilkes Land and King George V Land. [after the wife of J.-S.-C. Dumont d'Urville, French naval explorer, who discovered the area in 1840]

Adélie penguin /əˈdeili/ *noun* a penguin, *Pygoscelis adeliae*, of Antarctica.

Aden /ˈeidən/ a port in Yemen at the mouth of the Red Sea; pop. (est. 2002) 510,400. It was capital of the former South Yemen from 1967 until 1990.

Adena /əˈdiːnə/ ● *noun* (*pl.* same) a prehistoric people living in what is now Kentucky and Ohio from about 500 BC–AD 100. ● *adjective* of or pertaining to the Adena. [*Adena*, Ohio, near where typical Adena burial mounds were found]

Aden, Gulf of a part of the E Arabian Sea lying between the south coast of Yemen and the Horn of Africa.

Aden·auer /ˈadəˌnaur/ **Kon·rad** (1876–1967) German politician, first chancellor of the Federal Republic of Germany (1949–63).

ad·en·ine /ˈadəˌniːn/ *noun* a purine derivative found in all living tissue as a component base of DNA or RNA. Symbol: **A**. [German *Adenin* formed as ADENOIDS: see -INE⁴]

adeno·carcin·oma /ˌadɪnɔˌkɑːsɪˈnoʊmə/ *noun* a malignant tumour formed from glandular structures in epithelial tissue. [Greek *adēn* 'gland' + CARCINOMA]

ad·en·oid·al /ˌadəˈnɔidəl/ *adjective Med.* **1** suffering from enlarged adenoids. **2** (of the voice) having the nasal tones characteristic of a person with enlarged adenoids. □ **ad·en·oid·al·ly** *adverb*

ad·en·oids /ˈadəˌnɔidz/ *plural noun* a mass of lymphatic tissue between the back of the nose and the throat which, when enlarged, hinders speech and breathing. □ **ad·en·oid** *adjective* [Greek *adēn -enos* gland + -OID]

ad·en·oma /ˌadəˈnoʊmə/ *noun* (*pl.* **ad·en·omas** or **ad·en·omata** /-mətə/) a gland-like benign tumour. [modern Latin from Greek *adēn* gland + -OMA]

adeno·sine /əˈdenəˌsiːn/ *noun* a nucleoside of adenine and ribose present in all living tissue in a combined form (*see* ADP, ATP). [ADENINE + RIBOSE]

adenosine triphosphate *noun* a nucleotide important in living cells which, in breaking down adenosine diphosphate, provides energy for physiological processes. Abbr.: **ATP**.

adeno·virus /ˈadɪnoʊˌvairəs/ *noun* any of a group of DNA viruses first discovered in adenoid tissue, most of which cause respiratory diseases.

adept ● *adjective* (often foll. by *at*, *in*) highly gifted or skilled. ● *noun* a skilled performer; an expert. □ **adept·ly** *adverb* **adept·ness** *noun* [Latin *adeptus* past participle of *adipisci* attain]

ad·equate /ˈadəkwət/ *adjective* **1** sufficient, satisfactory. **2** barely sufficient. □ **ad·equa·cy** *noun* **ad·equate·ly** *adverb* [Latin *adaequatus* past participle of *adaequare* make equal (as AD-, *aequus* equal)]

à deux /aˈdɜː/ *adverb & adjective* for or between two people. [French]

ad fin. *abbreviation* at or near the end. [Latin *ad finem*]

Ad·hara /ədˈharə/ the second-brightest star in the constellation Canis Major.

ADHD *abbreviation* ATTENTION DEFICIT HYPERACTIVITY DISORDER.

ad·here *intransitive verb* **1** (usu. foll. by *to*) (of a substance) stick fast to a surface, another substance, etc. **2** (foll. by *to*) behave according to; follow in detail (*adhered to our plan*). **3** (foll. by *to*) give support or allegiance. [French *adhérer* or Latin *adhaerēre* (as AD-, *haerēre haes-* stick)]

ad·her·ent ● *noun* **1** a supporter of a party, person, etc. **2** a devotee of an activity. **3** (in some Protestant denominations) a person who is not officially a member of a congregation but participates in its activities. ● *adjective* **1** (foll. by *to*) faithfully observing a rule etc. **2** (often foll. by *to*) (of a substance) sticking fast. □ **ad·her·ence** *noun*

ad·hesion /ədˈhiːʒən/ *noun* **1** the act or process of adhering. **2** the capacity of a substance to stick fast. **3** *Med.* an unnatural union of surfaces due to inflammation. **4** the maintenance of contact between the wheels of a vehicle and the road. **5** the giving of support or allegiance. ¶ More common in physical senses (e.g. *the glue has good adhesion*), with *adherence* used in abstract senses (e.g. *adherence to principles*). **6** *Cdn* an addition made to a treaty when a new Aboriginal band signs it. [Latin *adhaesio* (as ADHERE)]

ad·hes·ive /ədˈhiːsɪv, ədˈhiːzɪv/ ● *adjective* sticky, enabling surfaces or substances to adhere to one another. ● *noun* an adhesive substance, esp. one used to stick other substances together. □ **ad·hes·ive·ly** *adverb* **ad·hes·ive·ness** *noun* [French *adhésif -ive* (as ADHERE)]

ad hoc /ad ˈhɒk/ *adverb & adjective* for a particular (usu. exclusive) purpose (*an ad hoc committee*). [Latin, = to this]

ad homi·nem /ad ˈhɒmɪˌnem/ *adverb & adjective* **1** relating to or associated with a particular person. **2** (of an argument) characterized by an attack on the person rather than their argument; appealing to the emotions and not to reason. [Latin, = to the person]

adia·bat·ic /ˌeidiəˈbatik, ˌeidaiəˈbatik/ *Physics* ● *adjective* **1** impassable to heat. **2** occurring without heat entering or leaving the system. ● *noun* a curve or formula for adiabatic phenomena. □ **adia·bat·ic·ally** *adverb* [Greek *adiabatos* impassable (as A-¹, *diabainō* pass)]

adieu /əˈdjuː/ ● *interjection* goodbye. ● *noun* (*pl.* **adieus** or **adieux** /əˈdjuːz/) a goodbye (esp. in *bid adieu to*). [Old French from *à* to + *Dieu* God]

Adi Granth /ˌɒdi ˈɡrʌnt/ the canonical work of Sikh sacred scripture. [Hindi (= first book), from Sanskrit]

ad in·fin·itum /ad ˌɪnfɪˈnaitəm/ *adverb* without limit; forever. [Latin]

ad in·ter·im *adverb & adjective* for the meantime. [Latin]

adios /ˌadiˈɔːs/ *interjection* goodbye. [Spanish *adiós* from *a* to + *Dios* God]

adi·po·cere /ˈadipəˌsiːr/ *noun* a greyish fatty or soapy substance generated in dead bodies subjected to moisture. [French *adipocire* from Latin *adeps adipis* fat + French *cire* wax, from Latin *cera*]

adi·pose /ˈadiˌpoʊs, -poːz/ *adjective* (esp. of body tissue) used for the storage of fat. □ **adi·pos·ity** /-ˈpɒsɪti/ *noun* [modern Latin *adiposus* from *adeps adipis* fat]

Adi·ron·dack chair /ˌadəˈrɒndak/ *noun N Amer.* a slatted wooden lawn chair with a fan-shaped back and broad arms; a Muskoka chair.

Adirondack Mountains /ˌadəˈrɒndak/ (also **Adirondacks**) a range of mountains in New York State, source of the Hudson and Mohawk rivers.

Adis Abeba *see* ADDIS ABABA.

adit /ˈadɪt/ *noun* a horizontal entrance or passage in a mine. [Latin *aditus* (as AD-, *itus* from *ire it-* go)]

Adi·vasi /ˌadɪˈvɒsi/ *noun* (*pl.* **Adivasis**) a member of any of the aboriginal peoples of India. [Hindi *adinivāsī* original inhabitant]

Adj. *abbreviation* (preceding a name) Adjutant.

adj. *abbreviation* adjective.

ad·ja·cent /əˈdʒeisənt/ *adjective* (often foll. by *to*) **1** lying near or adjoining. **2** *Math.* (of angles) sharing a vertex and one common line. □ **ad·ja·cency** *noun* [Middle English from Latin *adjacēre* (as AD-, *jacēre* lie)]

ad·jec·tive /ˈadʒəktɪv/ ● *noun* a word or phrase naming an attribute, added to or grammatically related to a noun to modify it or describe it. ● *adjective* additional; not standing by itself; dependent. □ **ad·jec·tival** /ˌadʒəkˈtaivəl/ *adjective* **ad·jec·tival·ly** *adverb* [Old French *adjectif -ive*, ultimately from Latin *adjicere adject-* (as AD-, *jacere* throw)]

ad·join *transitive verb* **1** be close to or joined with. **2** *archaic* = ADD 1. [Old French *ajoindre*, *ajoign-* from Latin *adjungere adjunct-* (as AD-, *jungere* join)]

ad·join·ing *adjective* positioned next to, adjacent; neighbouring.

ad·journ /əˈdʒɜːrn/ *verb* **1** *transitive* **a** put off; postpone. **b** break off (a meeting, discussion, hearing, etc.) with the intention of resuming later. **2** *intransitive* of persons at a meeting: **a** break off proceedings and disperse. **b** (foll. by *to*) transfer the meeting to another place. [Old French *ajorner* (as AD-, *jorn* day, ultimately from Latin *diurnus* DIURNAL): compare JOURNAL, JOURNEY]

ad·journ·ment *noun* adjourning or being adjourned, esp. the postponement of a court case.

ad·judge *transitive verb* **1** adjudicate (a matter). **2** consider. **3** (often foll. by *that* + clause, or *to* + infin.) pronounce judicially (*was adjudged bankrupt*). **4** (foll. by *to*) award judicially. **5** *archaic* condemn. □ **ad·judg·ment** *noun* (also **ad·judge·ment**). [Old French *ajuger* from Latin *adjudicare*: see ADJUDICATE]

ad·judi·cate /əˈdʒuːdɪˌkeit/ *verb* **1** *intransitive* act as judge in a competition, court, tribunal, etc. **2** *transitive* **a** decide judicially regarding (a claim etc.). **b** (foll. by *to be* + *n.* or *adj.*) pronounce. □ **ad·judi·ca·tion** *noun* **ad·judi·ca·tive** *adjective* **ad·judi·ca·tor** *noun* [Latin *adjudicare* (as AD-, *judicare* from *judex -icis* judge)]

ad·junct /ˈadʒʌŋkt/ ● *noun* **1** (usu. foll. by *to*, *of*) something added to something else, and auxiliary to or dependent on it. **2** an assistant; a subordinate person, esp. one with a temporary appointment only. **3** *Grammar* a word or phrase used to explain or amplify the predicate, subject, etc. ● *attributive adjective* connected with in a subordinate or temporary capacity (*adjunct professor*). □ **ad·junct·ive** /əˈdʒʌŋktɪv/ *adjective* [Latin *adjunctus*: see ADJOIN]

ad·jure /əˈdʒʊr, əˈdʒɔr/ *transitive verb* (usu. foll. by *to* + infin.) charge or request (a person) solemnly or earnestly, as if under oath. □ **ad·jur·ation** /ˌadʒʊˈreɪʃən/ *noun* **ad·jura·tory** /-rəˌtɔri/ *adjective* [Latin *adjurare* (as AD-, *jurare* swear) in Late Latin sense 'put a person to an oath']

ad·just *verb* **1** *transitive* **a** arrange; put in the correct order or position. **b** regulate, esp. by a small amount. **2** *transitive* (usu. foll. by *to*) make suitable. **3** *transitive* assess (loss or damages). **4** *intransitive* (usu. foll. by *to*) make oneself suited to; become familiar with; adapt (*adjust to one's surroundings*). **5** *transitive* (foll. by *for*) alter (a statistic etc.) to allow for circumstances (*income adjusted for inflation*). □ **ad·just·able** *adjective* **ad·just·abil·ity** *noun* **ad·just·er** *noun* **ad·just·ment** *noun* [French *adjuster*, ultimately from Latin *juxta* near]

ad·ju·tant /ˈadʒətənt/ *noun* **1 a** *Military* an officer who assists superior officers by communicating orders, conducting correspondence, etc. **b** an assistant. **2** (in full **adjutant bird** or **adjutant stork**) either of two tall Asian storks, *Leptopilus dubius* and *L. javanicus*, with a large bill and a stiff gait. □ **ad·ju·tancy** *noun* [Latin *adjutare* frequentative of *adjuvare*: see ADJUVANT]

adjutant general *noun* a high-ranking army administrative officer.

ad·ju·vant /ˈadʒəvənt/ ● *adjective* helpful, auxiliary. ● *noun* **1** an adjuvant person or thing. **2** a chemical substance or treatment which assists the action of another (*an adjuvant to surgery*). [French from Latin *adjuvare* (as AD-, *juvare jut-* help)]

ad·land *noun informal* the business world of advertising and advertisers.

Adler /ˈadlər/ **Alfred** (1870–1937), Austrian psychologist and psychiatrist. Rejecting Freudian theories, he developed the concept of the 'inferiority complex' and argued that the need for power was a basic human motivation. □ **Adler·ian** /ˌadˈliːriːən/ *adjective*

ad lib ● *intransitive verb* (**ad libbed**, **ad libbing**) speak or perform without formal preparation; improvise. ● *adjective* improvised. ● *adverb* as one pleases, to any desired extent. ● *noun* something spoken or played extempore. [abbreviation of AD LIBITUM]

ad libitum /ad ˈlɪbɪtəm/ *adverb* = AD LIB *adverb*. [Latin, = according to pleasure]

ad litem /ad ˈlaitem/ *adjective* (of a guardian etc.) appointed to act in a lawsuit on behalf of a child or other person who is not considered capable of representing themselves. [Latin, literally 'for the lawsuit']

ADM *abbreviation Cdn* Assistant Deputy Minister.

Adm. *abbreviation* (preceding a name) Admiral.

adman *noun* (*pl.* **admen**) *informal* a person who produces advertisements commercially.

ad·mass *noun* the section of the community that is regarded as readily influenced by advertising and mass communication.

Ad·metus /adˈmiːtəs/ *Gk Myth* a king of Thessaly, the husband of Alcestis.

admin *informal* ● *noun* administration. ● *adjective* administrative.

ad·min·is·ter *verb* **1** *transitive* attend to the running of (business affairs etc.); manage. **2** *transitive* **a** be responsible for the implementation of (the law, justice, punishment, etc.). **b** *Christianity* give out, or perform the rites of (a sacrament). **c** (usu. foll. by *to*) direct the taking of (an oath). **3** *transitive* **a** give, apply (medication etc.). **b** deliver (a rebuke etc.). **4** *transitive* have someone undergo (a test etc.). **5** *intransitive* (foll. by *to*) provide what is necessary to satisfy (a person or their needs). **6** *intransitive* act as administrator. [Latin *administrare* (as AD-, MINISTER)]

ad·min·is·trate *transitive & intransitive verb* administer (esp. business affairs); act as an administrator.

ad·min·is·tra·tion *noun* **1 a** management of a business, institution, etc. **b** management of public affairs. **2** *N Amer.* those responsible for administering a business, institution, etc. (*the administration decided against it*). **3** the government in power. **4** *N Amer.* the term of office of a government or political leader. **5** (in the US) a government agency (*the Food and Drug Administration*). **6** *Law* the management of another

person's estate. **7** (foll. by *of*) **a** the administering of justice, an oath, etc. **b** application of medication etc.

ad·min·is·tra·tive *adjective* concerning or relating to the management of affairs. □ **ad·min·is·tra·tive·ly** *adverb*

administrative assistant *noun* an office worker who assists an executive by handling routine administrative tasks.

ad·min·is·tra·tor *noun* **1** a person who administers a business or public affairs. **2** *Computing* = SYSTEM ADMINISTRATOR. **3** *Law* a person appointed to manage the estate of a person who has died without a will. **4** a person who performs official duties in some sphere, e.g. in religion or justice. □ **ad·min·is·tra·tor·ship** *noun*

ad·min·is·tra·trix /ədˌminiˈstreitriks/ *noun Law* a woman appointed to manage the estate of a person who has died without a will.

ad·mir·able /ˈadmərəbəl/ *adjective* **1** deserving admiration. **2** excellent. □ **ad·mir·ably** *adverb*

ad·miral *noun* **1** (also **Admiral**) a naval officer of high rank: **a** (in Canada) the highest rank in the Maritime Command. Abbr.: **Adm**. **b** (in the US) the second-highest rank in the navy, just below fleet admiral. **c** (in the UK) the second-highest rank in the navy, just below admiral of the fleet. **d** a rear admiral or vice admiral. **2** any of various butterflies (*red admiral*; *white admiral*). □ **ad·miral·ship** *noun* [medieval Latin *a(d)miralis* etc., from Arabic *'amir* commander (compare AMIR), assoc. with ADMIRABLE]

admiral of the fleet *noun* (in the UK) an admiral of the highest rank.

Ad·miral·ty *noun* (*pl.* **-ties**) **1** (*hist.* except in titles) (in the UK) the department administering the Royal Navy. **2** (**admiralty**) *Law* trial and decision of maritime questions and offences.

Admiralty Board *noun hist.* a committee of the British Ministry of Defence which until 1964 superintended the Royal Navy.

Admiralty Islands an island group of Papua New Guinea, in the W Pacific. In 1884 the islands became a German protectorate, but after 1920 they were administered as an Australian mandate.

ad·mir·a·tion *noun* **1** respect, warm approval. **2** an object of this (*was the admiration of the whole town*). **3** pleased contemplation.

ad·mire *transitive verb* **1** regard with approval, respect, or satisfaction. **2** express one's admiration of. [Latin *admirari* (as AD-, *mirari* wonder at)]

ad·mir·er *noun* **1** a person who admires, esp. a devotee of an able or famous person. **2** a person who is sexually attracted to another.

ad·mir·ing *adjective* showing or feeling admiration (*an admiring colleague*; *admiring glances*). □ **ad·mir·ing·ly** *adverb*

ad·mis·sible *adjective* **1** (of an idea or plan) worth accepting or considering. **2** *Law* allowable as evidence. **3** (foll. by *to*) capable of being admitted. □ **ad·mis·si·bil·ity** *noun* [medieval Latin *admissibilis* (as ADMIT)]

ad·mis·sion *noun* **1** an acknowledgement or confession (*admission of guilt*; *admission that he was wrong*). **2 a** the process or right of admitting. **b** a charge for this (*admission is $5*). **3** (in *pl.*) the department (of a university, hospital, etc.) responsible for admitting new students, patients, etc. **4** a person admitted to a hospital. [Latin *admissio* (as ADMIT)]

admit *verb* (**ad·mit·ted**, **ad·mit·ting**) **1** *transitive* **a** (often foll. by *to be*, or *that* + clause) acknowledge; recognize as true. **b** accept as valid or true. **2** *intransitive* (foll. by *to*) acknowledge responsibility for a deed, fault, etc. **3** *transitive* **a** allow (a person) entrance or access. **b** allow (a person) to be a member of (an institution, group, etc.) or to share in (a privilege etc.). **c** (of a hospital etc.) bring in (a person) for treatment. **4** *transitive* (of an enclosed space) have room for; accommodate. **5** *intransitive* (foll. by *of*) allow as possible (*the law admits of many interpretations*). □ **ad·mit·tee** *noun* [Latin *admittere admiss-* (as AD-, *mittere* send)]

ad·mit·tance *noun* **1** the right or process of admitting or being admitted, usu. to a place (*no admittance except on business*). ¶ A more formal and technical word than *admission*. **2** *Electricity* the reciprocal of impedance.

ad·mit·ted·ly *adverb* as an acknowledged fact (*admittedly, there are problems*).

admix *verb* **1** *transitive & intransitive* (foll. by *with*) mingle or mix. **2** *transitive* add as an ingredient.

ad·mix·ture *noun* **1** a combination, esp. of disparate elements. **2** a thing added, esp. a minor ingredient. **3** the act of adding this. [Latin *admixtus* past participle of *admiscēre* (as AD-, *miscēre* mix)]

ad·mon·ish /adˈmɒnɪʃ/ *transitive verb* **1** reprove, esp. gently. **2** (foll. by *to* + infin.) urge. **3** (foll. by *to* + infin.) give advice to. **4** (foll. by *of*) warn.

□ **ad·mon·ish·ment** noun **ad·mon·ition** /ˌadməˈnɪʃən/ noun **ad·mon·itory** /adˈmɒnɪˌtɔrɪ/ adjective [Latin admonēre (as AD-, monēre monit- warn)]

ad nau·seam /ad ˈnɔziˌəm, -ziˌam/ adverb to an excessive or disgusting degree. [Latin, = to sickness]

ad·nom·inal /adˈnɒmɪnəl/ adjective Grammar attached to a noun. [Latin adnomen -minis (added name)]

ado noun fuss, busy activity; trouble, difficulty. □ **without further** (or **more**) **ado** immediately. [originally in much ado = much to do, from northern Middle English at do (= to do) from Old Norse at AT[1] as sign of infin. + DO[1]]

-ado suffix forming nouns (desperado) (compare -ADE[3]). [Spanish or Portuguese -ado from Latin -atus past participle of verbs in -are]

adobe /əˈdoːbɪ/ noun **1** a sun-dried brick made from clay and straw (often attributive: an adobe house). **2** the clay used for making such bricks. [Spanish, from adobar 'to plaster', from Arabic aṭ-ṭūb, from al 'the' + ṭūb 'bricks']

adobo /əˈdoːbo/ noun **1** a Filipino dish of chicken or pork stewed in vinegar, garlic, soy sauce, bay leaves, and peppercorns. **2** the marinade in which this is cooked. **3** (also **adobo sauce**) a paste or marinade made from chilies, vinegar, herbs, and spices, used in Mexican cooking to flavour meat or fish. [Spanish, lit. = 'marinade']

ado·les·cent /ˌadəˈlesənt/ ● adjective **1** between childhood and adulthood. **2** pertaining to or characteristic of this age (adolescent acne; adolescent behaviour). ● noun an adolescent person. □ **ado·les·cence** noun [Old French from Latin adolescere grow up]

Adonai /ˌadoːˈnai/ noun Lord; a name of God used as a substitute for the Hebrew YHVH. [Hebrew ăḏōnāi my lord: see JEHOVAH, YAHWEH]

Adonis[1] /əˈdɒnɪs/ Gk Myth a beautiful youth loved by both Aphrodite and Persephone. After his death, Zeus decreed that he should spend part of the year in the underworld and part on earth. [Greek from Phoenician adōn lord]

Adonis[2] /əˈdɒnɪs/ noun a handsome young man. [ADONIS[1]]

adopt transitive verb **1** take (a person) into a relationship, esp. another's child as one's own. **2** choose to follow (a course of action etc.). **3** assume, take upon oneself (adopt an air of indifference). **4** take over (an idea etc.) from another person. **5** choose as a candidate for office. **6** accept; formally approve (a recommendation, legislation, etc.). **7** choose (a textbook) as standard or required for a course of study. **8** acquire (a pet). **9** (of a community group) assume responsibility for the maintenance and upkeep of (part of a public road, beach, etc.). □ **adopt·able** adjective **adop·tee** noun **adopt·er** noun **adop·tion** noun [Latin adoptare (as AD-, optare choose)]

adopt·ive attributive adjective **1** related by adoption (adoptive parents). **2** (of a city, country, etc.) chosen as residence by one born elsewhere. □ **adopt·ive·ly** adverb

ador·able adjective **1** informal delightful, cute (an adorable baby). **2** deserving adoration. □ **ador·ably** adverb

adore transitive verb **1** regard with honour and deep affection. **2** worship or offer reverence to as divine. **3** informal like very much. □ **ador·ation** noun **ador·er** noun **ador·ing** adjective **ador·ing·ly** adverb [Latin adorare worship (as AD-, orare speak, pray)]

adorn transitive verb **1** add beauty or lustre to; be an ornament to. **2** furnish with ornaments; decorate. □ **adorn·ment** noun [Latin adornare (as AD-, ornare furnish, deck)]

Ador·no /əˈdɔrnoː/ **Theo·dor Wiesen·grund** (1903–69), German philosopher and sociologist. He argued for the systematic rejection of all theory.

ADP abbreviation **1** adenosine diphosphate. **2** automatic data processing.

ADQ abbreviation Cdn ACTION DÉMOCRATIQUE DU QUÉBEC.

ADR abbreviation ALTERNATIVE DISPUTE RESOLUTION.

Adrar des Iforas /aˌdrɑr deiz ɪˈfɔrɔ/ a massif region in the central Sahara, on the border between Mali and Algeria.

ad rem /ad ˈrem/ adverb & adjective to the point; to the purpose. [Latin, = to the matter]

ad·renal /əˈdriːnəl/ adjective **1** of the adrenal glands. **2** at or near the kidneys. [AD- + RENAL]

adrenal gland noun either of two ductless glands above the kidneys, secreting adrenalin.

ad·rena·lin /əˈdrenəlɪn/ noun **1** (also **adrenaline**) a hormone secreted by the adrenal glands, esp. in conditions of stress, increasing rates of blood circulation, breathing, and carbohydrate metabolism and preparing muscles for exertion. **2 Adrenalin** proprietary the same substance obtained from animals or by synthesis, used as a stimulant.

adrenalin junkie noun informal a person who thrives on extreme excitement; a thrill-seeker.

adrenalin rush noun a physical feeling of intense excitement and stimulation caused by the release of adrenalin from the adrenal glands.

ad·rena·lized adjective (also esp. Brit. **-lised**) excited, tense, or highly charged.

ad·reno·cortico·trophic hormone /əˌdriːnəˌkɔrtɪkəˈtrɒfɪk/ noun (also **ad·reno·cortico·tropic** /-ˈtrɒpɪk/) a hormone secreted by the pituitary gland and stimulating the adrenal glands. Abbr.: **ACTH**. [ADRENAL + CORTEX + -TROPHIC, -TROPIC]

ad·reno·cortico·troph·in /əˌdriːnəˌkɔrtɪkəˈtrɒfɪn/ noun = ADRENOCORTICOTROPHIC HORMONE.

Adrian, Edgar Doug·las, 1st Baron (1889–1977), English neurophysiologist, who was awarded the 1932 Nobel Prize for physiology or medicine for his work on the electrical properties of the nervous system.

Adrian IV (born Nicholas Breakspear, c.1100–59), Pope 1154–59, the only English pope.

Adri·atic /ˌeɪdriˈatɪk/ ● adjective of or relating to the Adriatic Sea. ● noun = ADRIATIC SEA.

Adriatic, Marriage of the see MARRIAGE OF THE ADRIATIC.

Adriatic Sea an arm of the Mediterranean Sea between the Balkans and the Italian peninsula.

adrift 1 (of a boat etc.) drifting, esp. without direction. **2** away from the intended course, missing. **3** lacking purpose or guidance, detached (young people adrift in our big cities). **4** informal unfastened.

adroit /əˈdrɔɪt/ adjective **1** dexterous, skilful. **2** clever, astute. □ **adroit·ly** adverb **adroit·ness** noun [French from à droit according to right]

ADSL abbreviation asymmetric digital subscriber line, a technology for transmitting digital information over standard telephone lines, using most of the bandwidth to transmit information to the user and only a small part to receive it from them.

ad·sorb transitive verb (usu. of a solid) hold (molecules of a gas or liquid or solute) to its surface, causing a thin film to form. □ **ad·sorb·able** adjective **ad·sorb·ent** adjective & noun **ad·sorp·tion** noun [AD-, after ABSORB]

ad·sorb·ate /adˈsɔrbeit/ noun a substance adsorbed.

ad·suki var. of ADZUKI.

ADT abbreviation ATLANTIC DAYLIGHT TIME.

adu·late /ˈadjʊˌleɪt/ transitive verb flatter or praise obsequiously. □ **adu·la·tion** /-ˈleɪʃən/ noun **adu·la·tor** noun **adu·la·tory** /ˈadʒʊləˌtɔrɪ/ adjective [Latin adulari adulat- fawn on]

adult ● adjective **1** mature, grown-up. **2** (attributive) **a** of or for adults (adult education). **b** euphemism sexually explicit (adult films). ● noun **1** an adult person. **2** Law a person who has reached the age of majority. □ **adult·hood** noun [Latin adultus past participle of adolescere grow up; compare ADOLESCENT]

Adult Accompaniment noun (in Ontario and the Maritimes) a film classification which requires viewers under 14 years of age to be accompanied by an adult. Abbr.: **AA**.

adul·ter·ant ● adjective used in adulterating. ● noun an adulterant substance.

adul·ter·ate transitive verb corrupt or debase (esp. foods) by adding other or inferior ingredients. □ **adul·ter·a·tion** noun **adul·ter·ator** noun [Latin adulterare adulterat- corrupt]

adul·ter·er noun a person who commits adultery.

adul·ter·ess noun a woman who commits adultery.

adul·ter·ine /əˈdʌltəˌraɪn/ adjective **1** illegal, unlicensed. **2** spurious. **3** born of adultery.

adul·ter·ous adjective of or involved in adultery. □ **adul·ter·ous·ly** adverb

adul·tery noun (pl. **-ies**) **1** voluntary sexual intercourse between a married person and a person (married or not) other than his or her spouse. **2** Law an instance of this; an adulterous relationship. [Latin adulter 'adulterer', from adulterare 'corrupt']

adult·i·cide noun a drug or pesticide that kills the adult forms of a pest or parasite.

adult-onset adjective (esp. of diabetes) developing in adults.

ad·um·brate /ˈadəmˌbreit/ transitive verb **1** outline or indicate faintly. **2** foreshadow, typify. **3** overshadow. □ **ad·um·bra·tion** noun **ad·um·bra·tive** /əˈdʌmbrətɪv/ adjective [Latin adumbrare (as AD-, umbrare from umbra shade)]

Consonants:　b but　d dog　f few　g get　h her　j yes　k cat　l leg　m man　n no　p pen　r red　s sit

adv. *abbreviation* adverb.

ad valorem /ˌad vəˈlɔːrəm/ *adverb & adjective* (of taxes) in proportion to the estimated value of the goods concerned. [Latin, = according to the value]

ad·vance ● *verb* **1** *transitive & intransitive* move or put forward. **2** *intransitive* make progress. **3** *transitive* **a** pay (money) before it is due. **b** lend (money). **4** *transitive* give active support to; promote (a person, cause, or plan). **5** *transitive* put forward (a claim or suggestion). **6** *transitive* cause (an event) to occur at an earlier date (*advanced the meeting three hours*). **7** *transitive* raise (a price). **8** *intransitive* rise (in price). ● *noun* **1** an act of going forward. **2** progress. **3** a payment made before the due time. **4** a loan. **5** (esp. in *pl.*; often foll. by *to*) an amorous or friendly approach. **6** a rise in price. ● *attributive adjective* done or supplied beforehand (*advance warning*; *advance copy*). □ **advance on** approach threateningly. **in advance** ahead in place or time. □ **ad·van·cer** *noun* [Old French *avancer* from Late Latin *abante* in front, from Latin *ab* away + *ante* before]

ad·vanced *adjective* **1** far on in progress (*the work is well advanced*). **2** ahead of the times (*advanced methods*). **3** highly developed, complex (*advanced tool design*).

advanced green *noun Cdn* a flashing green traffic light in advance of the steady green light, indicating that oncoming traffic is halted.

advance guard *noun* a body of soldiers preceding the main body of an army.

advance man *noun N Amer.* a person who arranges security, publicity, etc. before the arrival of a touring politician etc.

ad·vance·ment *noun* the progression or promotion of a person, cause, or plan.

advance poll *noun Cdn* an early poll for voters who expect to be absent from their riding on election day.

advance scout *noun esp. Baseball* a scout who travels ahead of the team in order to gain information about future opponents.

advance team *noun* a team of people who visit a location before the arrival of an important visitor to make the appropriate arrangements.

ad·van·tage ● *noun* **1** a beneficial feature; a favourable circumstance. **2** benefit, profit (*is not to your advantage*). **3** (often foll. by *over*) a better position; superiority in a particular respect. **4** *Tennis* the next point won after deuce. **5** *Hockey* numerical superiority over the opposing team, as on a power play (*scored with a two-man advantage*). ● *transitive verb* **1** be beneficial or favourable to. **2** further, promote. □ **have the advantage of** be in a better position in some respect than. **take advantage of 1** make good use of (a favourable circumstance). **2** exploit or outwit (a person), esp. unfairly. **3** *euphemism* seduce. **to advantage** in a way which exhibits the merits (*was seen to advantage*). **turn to advantage** benefit from. □ **ad·van·ta·geous** /ˌadvənˈteɪdʒəs/ *adjective* **ad·van·ta·geous·ly** *adverb* [Old French *avantage*, *avant* in front, from Late Latin *abante*: see ADVANCE]

ad·van·taged /ədˈvæntɪdʒd/ *adjective* having advantages; privileged.

ad·vec·tion *noun Meteorol.* transfer of heat by the horizontal flow of air. □ **ad·vec·tive** *adjective* [Latin *advectio* from *advehere* (as AD-, *vehere vect-* carry)]

Ad·vent *noun* **1** *Christianity* the season before Christmas, including the four preceding Sundays. **2** *Christianity* the coming or Second Coming of Christ. **3** (**advent**) the arrival of esp. an important person or thing. [Latin *adventus* arrival, from *advenire* (as AD-, *venire vent-* come)]

Advent calendar *noun* a calendar for the month preceding Christmas, esp. one made with flaps or windows opened one each day to reveal a seasonal picture, scene, etc.

Ad·vent·ist /ˈadvɛntɪst/ *noun* a member of a Christian group that believes in the imminent Second Coming of Christ. □ **Ad·vent·ism** /ˈadvɛntɪzəm/ *noun*

ad·ven·ti·tious /ˌadvɛnˈtɪʃəs/ *adjective* **1** accidental, not planned. **2** added from outside, extrinsic. **3** *Biol.* formed accidentally or under unusual conditions. □ **ad·ven·ti·tious·ly** *adverb* [Latin *adventicius* (as ADVENT)]

Advent Sunday *noun Anglicanism* the first Sunday in Advent.

ad·ven·ture ● *noun* **1 a** an unusual and exciting experience. **b** (*attributive*) designating a type of tourism to exotic, esp. wilderness destinations usu. combined with some physical activity, e.g. hiking, canoeing, etc. **2** a daring enterprise; a hazardous activity. **3** enterprise (*the spirit of adventure*). **4** a commercial speculation. ● *intransitive verb* **1** (often foll. by *into*, *upon*) dare to go or come. **2** (foll. by *on*, *upon*) dare to undertake. **3** incur risk; engage in adventure. □ **ad·ven·ture·some** *adjective* [Latin *adventurus* about to happen (as ADVENT)]

adventure playground *noun* a playground where children are provided with functional materials for climbing on, building with, etc.

ad·ven·tur·er *noun* **1** a person who seeks adventure, esp. for personal gain or enjoyment. **2** a financial speculator.

adventure racing *noun* an extreme sport in which teams engage in at least three high-endurance outdoor sports, esp. mountain biking, hiking or trail running, canoeing, kayaking, or rafting, and often rock climbing, over a 24-hour period or longer. □ **adventure race** *noun* **adventure racer** *noun*

ad·ven·tur·ess *noun* **1** *derogatory* a woman who pursues financial gain or social advancement, esp. by sexual means. **2** a woman who engages in adventures.

ad·ven·tur·ism *noun* a tendency to take risks, often imprudently, esp. in foreign policy. □ **ad·ven·tur·ist** *noun*

ad·ven·tur·ous *adjective* **1** rash, venturesome; enterprising. **2** characterized by adventures. □ **ad·ven·tur·ous·ly** *adverb* **ad·ven·tur·ous·ness** *noun*

Advent wreath *noun Christianity* a wreath with four candles lit on successive Sundays in Advent. A fifth central candle completes the group on Christmas.

ad·verb *noun* a word or phrase that modifies or qualifies another word (esp. an adjective, verb, or other adverb) or a word group, expressing a relation of place, time, circumstance, manner, cause, degree, etc., e.g. *gently, quite, then, there*. □ **ad·verb·ial** /ədˈvɜːbɪəl/ *adjective & noun* [French *adverbe* or Latin *adverbium* (as AD-, VERB)]

ad·ver·sar·ial /ˌadvərˈsɛrɪəl/ *adjective* **1** involving conflict or opposition. **2** opposed, hostile.

ad·ver·sary /ˈadvərˌsɛri/ *noun* (*pl.* **-ies**) **1** an enemy. **2** an opponent in a sport or game; an antagonist. [Latin *adversarius* from *adversus*: see ADVERSE]

ad·ver·sa·tive /ədˈvɜːrsətɪv/ *adjective* (of words etc.) expressing opposition or antithesis. □ **ad·ver·sa·tive·ly** *adverb* [Late Latin *adversativus*, from *adversari* oppose, from *adversus*: see ADVERSE]

ad·verse /ədˈvɜːrs, ˈadvɜːrs/ *adjective* **1** contrary, hostile. **2** hurtful, injurious. □ **ad·verse·ly** *adverb* **ad·verse·ness** *noun* ¶ Often confused with *averse*. [Latin *adversus* past participle of *advertere* (as AD-, *vertere vers-* turn)]

ad·ver·sity /ədˈvɜːrsɪti/ *noun* (*pl.* **-ties**) **1** the condition of adverse fortune (*courage in adversity*). **2** a misfortune.

ad·vert¹ /ˈadvɜːrt/ *noun Brit. informal* an advertisement.

ad·vert² /ədˈvɜːrt/ *intransitive verb formal* (foll. by *to*) refer in speaking or writing. [Latin *advertere*: see ADVERSE]

ad·ver·tise *verb* **1** *transitive* draw attention to or describe favourably (goods or services) in a public medium to promote sales. **2** *transitive* make generally or publicly known. **3** *intransitive* (foll. by *for*) seek by public notice, esp. in a newspaper. **4** *transitive* (usu. foll. by *of*, or *that* + clause) notify. □ **ad·ver·tis·er** *noun* [Old French *avertir* (stem *advertiss-*): see ADVERT²]

ad·ver·tise·ment /ədˈvɜːrtɪzmənt, ˈadvɜːrˌtaɪzmənt/ *noun* **1** a public notice or announcement, esp. one advertising goods or services in newspapers etc., on posters, or in broadcasts. **2** a person or thing regarded as a means of recommending something (*unhappy clients are not a good advertisement for the company*).

ad·ver·tor·ial /ˌadvərˈtɔːrɪəl/ *noun* a newspaper or magazine advertisement giving information about a product in the style of an editorial or objective journalistic comment. [blend of ADVERTISEMENT + EDITORIAL]

ad·vice *noun* **1** words offered as an opinion or recommendation about future action; counsel. **2** formal notice of a transaction. □ **take advice 1** obtain advice, esp. from an expert. **2** act according to advice given. [Latin *ad* to + *visum* past participle of *vidēre* see]

ad·vis·able *adjective* (usu. *predicative*) (of a course of action etc.) to be recommended, sensible. □ **ad·vis·abil·ity** /-ˈbɪlɪti/ *noun* **ad·vis·ably** *adverb*

ad·vise *verb* **1** *transitive & intransitive* give advice to. **2** *transitive* recommend; offer as advice (*they advise caution*; *advised me to rest*). **3** *transitive* (usu. foll. by *of*, or *that* + clause) inform, notify. **4** *intransitive* (foll. by *with*) esp. *N Amer.* consult. [Latin *ad* to + *visare* frequentative of *vidēre* see]

ad·vised *adjective* **1** judicious (*ill-advised*). **2** deliberate, considered. **3** recommended (*reservations are advised*). □ **ad·vis·ed·ly** /-zədli/ *adverb*

ad·vise·ment *noun N Amer.* □ **take under advisement** reserve judgment while considering.

ad·vis·er *noun* (also **ad·vis·or**) a person who advises, esp. one appointed to do so and regularly consulted.

ad·vis·ory ● *adjective* having the power to advise; giving advice (*advisory board*; *advisory role*). ● *noun* (*pl.* **-ories**) *N Amer.* an advisory statement, esp. a bulletin about bad weather.

ad·vo·caat /ˌadvəˈkɒt/ *noun* a liqueur of eggs, sugar, and brandy. [Dutch, = ADVOCATE (being originally an advocate's drink)]

ad·vo·cacy /ˈadvəkəsi/ *noun* **1** (usu. foll. by *of*) public support for or recommendation of a cause, policy, etc. (often *attributive*: *an advocacy group*). **2** the function of an advocate.

ad·vo·cate ● *noun* /ˈadvəkət/ **1** (foll. by *of*, *for*) a person who supports or speaks in favour. **2** a person who pleads for another. **3** a lawyer. ● *transitive verb* /ˈadvəˌkeit/ **1** recommend or support by argument (a cause, policy, etc.). **2** plead for, defend. [Latin *advocatus* past participle of *advocare* (as AD-, *vocare* call)]

ad·vow·son /ədˈvauzən/ *noun Brit. Anglicanism* (in ecclesiastical law) the right of recommending a member of the clergy for a vacant benefice, or of making the appointment. [Anglo-French *a(d)voweson* from Latin *advocatio -onis* (as ADVOCATE)]

advt. *abbreviation* advertisement.

ad·ware *noun Computing* software displaying paid advertisements and distributed free of charge (compare SPYWARE).

Ady·gea /ˈɒdəˌgeiə, ˌɒdəˈgjeiə/ (also **Ady·gei Autonomous Republic** /ˈɒdəˌgei, ˌɒdəˈgjei/) an autonomous republic in the NW Caucasus in SW Russia, with a largely Muslim population; pop. (est. 2002) 438,200; capital, Maikop.

ady·tum /ˈaditəm/ *noun* (*pl.* **adyta**) the innermost part of an ancient temple. [Latin from Greek *aduton*, impenetrable (as A-¹, *duō* enter)]

adze /adz/ (*US* also **adz**) ● *noun* a tool for cutting away the surface of wood, like an axe with an arched blade at right angles to the handle. ● *transitive verb* dress or cut with an adze. [Old English *adesa*]

ad·zuki /ədˈzuːki/ *noun* (also **ad·suki**, **azuki**) (*pl.* **-zukis**, **-sukis**) **1** an annual leguminous plant, *Vigna angularis*, native to China and Japan. **2** (usu. **adzuki bean**) the small round red edible bean of this plant. [Japanese *azuki*]

-ae *suffix* forming plural nouns, used in names of animal and plant families, tribes, etc. (*Felidae*; *Rosaceae*) and instead of *-as* in the plural of many non-naturalized or unfamiliar nouns in *-a* derived from Latin or Greek (*larvae*; *actiniae*). [pl. *-ae* of Latin nouns in *-a* or pl. *-ai* of some Greek nouns]

AECB *abbreviation* (in Canada and the US) Atomic Energy Control Board.

ae·dile /ˈiːdail/ *noun hist.* either of a pair of Roman magistrates who administered public works, maintenance of roads, public games, the grain supply, etc. □ **ae·dile·ship** *noun* [Latin *aedilis* concerned with buildings, from *aedes* building]

AEF *abbreviation hist.* American Expeditionary Force.

Ae·gean /əˈdʒiːən/ ● *adjective* of or relating to the Aegean Sea or Islands. ● *noun* = AEGEAN SEA.

Aegean Islands a group of islands in the Aegean Sea, forming a region of Greece. The principal islands of the group are Chios, Samos, Lesbos, the Cyclades, and the Dodecanese.

Aegean Sea a part of the Mediterranean Sea lying between Greece and Turkey, bounded to the south by Crete and Rhodes and linked to the Black Sea by the Dardanelles, the Sea of Marmara, and the Bosporus. It is scattered with numerous islands which are now part of Greece.

Ae·geus /ˈiːdʒiːəs/ *Gk Myth* a king of Athens and father of Theseus.

Aegir /ˈiːdʒiːr/ *Scand. Myth* the god of the sea.

aegis /ˈiːdʒis/ *noun* **1** auspices; control (*under the aegis of the federal government*). **2** a protection; an impregnable defence. [Latin from Greek *aigis* mythical shield of Zeus or Athene]

Aegis·thus /iːˈgisθəs/ *Gk Myth* the son of Thyestes and lover of Agamemnon's wife Clytemnestra.

aegro·tat /ˈagrəˌtat, ˈeigrɒˌtat/ *noun Cdn & Brit.* **1** a certificate stating that a university student is too ill to attend an examination. **2** a passing grade awarded in such circumstances. [Latin, = is sick, from *aeger* sick]

Ael·fric /ˈalfrik/ (*c*.955–*c*.1020) English monk, grammarian, and the best-known prose writer in Old English literature. His most famous work is the *Catholic Homilies*.

-aemia *combining form var.* of -EMIA.

Ae·neas /əˈniːəs/ *Gk & Rom. Myth* a Trojan leader, son of Anchises and Aphrodite. His travels to Carthage and the banks of the Tiber after the fall of Troy are the subject of Virgil's *Aeneid*, in which he is portrayed as the founder of Rome.

ae·olian /eiˈɒːliən/ *adjective* (also **eolian**) borne or produced by the wind (*aeolian erosion*). [Latin *Aeolius* from AEOLUS from Greek *Aiolos*]

aeolian harp *noun* a box-shaped stringed instrument or toy that produces musical sounds when the wind passes through it.

Aeolian Islands the ancient name for the LIPARI ISLANDS.

Aeolian mode *noun Music* the mode represented by the natural diatonic scale A–A. [Latin *Aeolius* from *Aeolis* in Asia Minor from Greek *Aiolis*]

Ae·olus /ˈiːələs/ *Gk Myth* the guardian (later thought of as a god) of the winds. [Greek *Aiolos* from *aiolos* swift, changeable]

aeon *var.* of EON.

aepy·or·nis /ˌiːpiˈɔːrnis/ *noun* a gigantic flightless extinct bird of the genus *Aepyornis*, resembling a moa, known from remains found in Madagascar. [Latin from Greek *aipus* high, *ornis* bird]

aeradio *Cdn var. of* AIR RADIO.

aer·ate *transitive verb* **1** charge (a liquid) with a gas, esp. carbon dioxide, e.g. to produce effervescence. **2** introduce air into (soil etc.). **3** expose to the mechanical or chemical action of the air. □ **aer·ation** *noun* **aer·ator** *noun* [Latin *aer* AIR + -ATE³]

aer·en·chyma /ˌerənˈkaimə/ *noun Bot.* a soft plant tissue containing air spaces found esp. in many aquatic plants. [Greek *aēr* air + *egkhuma* infusion]

aer·ial ● *adjective* **1** by or from or involving aircraft (*aerial navigation*; *aerial photography*). **2 a** existing, moving, or happening in the air. **b** lofty or elevated. **c** of or in the atmosphere, atmospheric. **3 a** thin as air, ethereal. **b** immaterial, imaginary. **c** of air, gaseous. **4** designating events in freestyle skiing in which competitors leap off a ski jump and perform twists and flips in the air before landing. ● *noun* **1** = ANTENNA. **2** *Football* a pass thrown towards the opponent's end zone. **3** (in *pl.*) aerial events in freestyle skiing. [Latin *aerius* from Greek *aerios* from *aēr* air]

aer·ial·ist *noun* **1** a high-wire or trapeze artist. **2** a freestyle skier specializing in aerial events.

aerie /ˈeri, ˈiːri/ *noun* (also **eyrie**) **1** a nest of a bird of prey, esp. an eagle, built high up. **2** a high place or position (*their 15th-floor aerie*). [medieval Latin *aeria*, *aerea*, etc., prob. from Old French *aire* lair, ultimately from Latin *agrum* piece of ground]

aero *attributive adjective informal* aerodynamic. [abbreviation]

aero- *combining form* **1** relating to air or the atmosphere (*aerodynamics*). **2** relating to aircraft (*aerobatics*). [Greek *aero-* from *aēr* air]

aero·bat *noun* a pilot who performs aerobatics. □ **aero·bat·ic** *adjective* **aero·bat·ic·al·ly** *adverb* [AERO- + ACROBAT]

aero·bat·ics *plural noun* feats of expert and usu. spectacular flying and manoeuvring of aircraft.

aer·obe /ˈerɒːb/ *noun* a micro-organism usu. growing in the presence of air, or needing air for growth. [French *aérobie* (as AERO-, Greek *bios* life)]

aer·ob·ic *adjective* **1** increasing or pertaining to oxygen consumption by the body (*aerobic exercise*; *aerobic fitness*). **2** of or relating to aerobics (*aerobic shoes*). **3** *Biol.* of or relating to aerobes. □ **aer·ob·ic·al·ly** *adverb*

aer·ob·i·cized /eˈrɒːbisaizd/ *adjective* (of a person's body) firm, toned, and slender from much aerobic exercise.

aer·ob·ics *plural noun* exercises, esp. those done to music, designed to increase fitness by any maintainable activity that increases oxygen intake and heart rate.

aero·biol·ogy *noun* the study of airborne micro-organisms, pollen, spores, etc., esp. as agents of infection.

aero·brake ● *verb* cause a spacecraft to slow down by flying through a planet's rarefied atmosphere to produce aerodynamic drag. ● *noun* a mechanism for aerobraking.

aero·drome *noun* a small airport or airfield. ¶ Now only *hist.* or in legal contexts to designate any aircraft landing site recognized as such by the Department of Transport. [AERO- + -DROME]

aero·dy·nam·ic *adjective* **1** of or relating to aerodynamics. **2** (of a vehicle etc.) designed to minimize drag. □ **aero·dy·nam·ic·al·ly** *adverb*

aero·dy·nam·ics *plural noun* (usu. treated as *sing.*) **1** the interaction between the air and solid bodies moving through it. **2** the study of this. □ **aero·dy·nami·cist** *noun*

aero·foil *noun Brit.* = AIRFOIL.

aero·gel *noun* an extremely light, porous, foam-like insulating material made from granulated silica.

aero·gram *noun* (also **aero·gramme**) an air letter in the form of a single sheet that is folded and sealed.

Vowels: a cat ɑ arm e bed ɜr her ɜ: *deux* ə ago ɪ sit i cosy iː feed ɒ hot ɔ pore ɔː no ʌ run ʊ put

aero·lite *noun* a stony meteorite.

aer·ol·ogy *noun* the study of the upper levels of the atmosphere. □ **aero·logic·al** *adjective*

aero·naut·ics *plural noun* (usu. treated as *sing.*) the science or practice of motion or travel in the air. □ **aero·naut·ic** *adjective*

aero·naut·ic·al *adjective* [modern Latin *aeronautica* (as AERO-, NAUTICAL)]

aeron·omy /əˈrɒnəmi/ *noun* the science of the upper atmosphere.

aero·plane *noun Brit.* = AIRPLANE. [French *aéroplane* (as AERO-, PLANE[1])]

aero·sol *noun* **1 a** a substance packed under pressure with a device for releasing it as a fine spray (usu. *attributive: aerosol can*). **b** the container holding this. **2** a colloidal suspension of particles dispersed in air or another gas. [AERO- + SOL[2]]

aero·sol·ize *transitive verb* convert into a fine spray or colloidal suspension in air.

aero·space *noun* **1** the earth's atmosphere and outer space. **2 a** the technology of flight in the atmosphere and in space. **b** the industry concerned with this.

aero·stat *noun* any craft which is sustained in the air by buoyancy, esp. a balloon or dirigible. [French *aérostat* from *aéro-* AERO- + Greek *statos* standing]

Aes·chines /ˈiːskɪˌniːz/ (*c.*397–*c.*322 BC) Athenian orator, statesman, and great rival of Demosthenes.

Aes·chylus /ˈiːskələs, ˈe-/ (525/4–456 BC) Athenian dramatist, regarded as the founder of Greek tragedy. His seven extant plays include *Prometheus Bound* and the *Oresteia* trilogy.

Aes·cu·lap·ian /ˌiːskjuˈleipiən, ˈe-/ *adjective* of or relating to medicine or physicians. [AESCULAPIUS]

Aes·cu·lap·ius /ˌiːskjuˈleipiəs/ *Rom. Myth* the god of healing, corresponding to the Greek Asclepius.

Aesir /ˈiːsɜr/ *Scand. Myth* the collective name of the gods.

Aesop /ˈiːsɒp/ the traditional author of Greek animal fables, who possibly lived in Thrace in the 6th c. BC. □ **Aesop·ian** /iːˈsoːpiən/ *adjective* **Aesop·ic** /iːˈsɒpɪk/ *adjective*

aes·thete /ˈesθiːt/ *noun* (also esp. *US* **es·thete**) a person who has or professes to have a special appreciation of beauty. [Greek *aisthētēs* one who perceives, or from AESTHETIC]

aes·thet·ic /esˈθetɪk/ (also **esthetic**) ● *adjective* **1** concerned with beauty or the appreciation of beauty. **2** having such appreciation; sensitive to beauty. **3** in accordance with the principles of good taste. ● *noun* **1** (in *pl.*) the philosophy of the beautiful, esp. in art. **2** (in *pl.*) aesthetically pleasing elements (*designers consider aesthetics and functionality*). **3** a conception of what is beautiful or artistically valid (*a minimalist aesthetic*). □ **aes·thet·ic·ally** *adverb* **aes·thet·ic·ism** /-ˌsɪzəm/ *noun* [Greek *aisthētikos* from *aisthanomai* perceive]

aes·thet·ician /ˌesθəˈtɪʃən/ *noun* **1** a person versed in or devoted to aesthetics. **2** a beautician.

Aesthetic movement *noun* a literary and artistic movement devoted to 'art for art's sake' which blossomed in the 1880s, heavily influenced by the Pre-Raphaelites, Ruskin, and Walter Pater. Its proponents, including Wilde and Beardsley, adopted sentimental archaism as the ideal of beauty.

aes·tival /ˈestivəl/ *adjective* (also **es·tival**) *formal* belonging to or appearing in summer. [Latin *aestivalis* from *aestivus* from *aestus* heat]

aes·tiv·ate /ˈestɪˌveit, ˈiːs-/ *intransitive verb* (also **es·tiv·ate**) **1** *Zool.* spend the summer or dry season in a state of torpor. **2** *formal* pass the summer. [Latin *aestivare aestivat-*]

aes·tiv·a·tion /ˌestɪˈveiʃən, ˌiːs-/ *noun* (also **es·tiv·a·tion**) **1** *Bot.* the arrangement of petals in a flower bud before it opens (*compare* VERNATION). **2** *Zool.* the act of spending the summer or dry season in a state of torpor.

Aethel·red var. of ETHELRED.

aether var. of ETHER 2, 3.

aeti·ol·ogy *Brit.* var. of ETIOLOGY.

AF *abbreviation* **1** *Photog.* AUTOFOCUS. **2** AUDIO FREQUENCY. **3** AIR FORCE.

af- *prefix* assimilated form of AD- before *f*.

afar *adverb* at or to a distance. □ **from afar** from a distance.

AFB *abbreviation* (in the US) Air Force Base.

AFC *abbreviation* **1** (in the US) American Football Conference. **2** (in the UK) Air Force Cross.

af·fable /ˈafəbəl/ *adjective* friendly, good-natured. □ **affa·bil·ity** *noun* **af·fably** *adverb* [Latin *affabilis* from *affari* (as AD-, *fari* speak)]

af·fair *noun* **1** a concern; a business; a matter to be attended to (*that is*

my *affair*). **2 a** a celebrated or notorious happening or sequence of events. **b** a thing or event of a specified sort (*the party was a black-tie affair*). **3** a romantic or sexual relationship between two people, esp. an adulterous one. **4** (in *pl.*) **a** ordinary pursuits of life. **b** business dealings. **c** matters or issues (*current affairs; foreign affairs*). [Old French *afaire* from *à faire* to do: compare ADO]

af·faire *noun* (usu. **l'affaire**) (followed by a proper name) a controversy or notorious event involving the specified person (*l'affaire Ben Johnson*). [French, after *l'affaire* DREYFUS]

af·faire de cœur /aˈfer də ˈkɜr/ *noun* a love affair. [French]

af·fect¹ *transitive verb* **1 a** produce an effect on; influence. **b** (of a disease etc.) attack (*his liver is affected*). **2** move; touch the feelings of (*affected me deeply*). ¶ *Affect* should not be confused with *effect* which means 'to bring about, to accomplish', e.g. *The government effected great changes*. Note also that *effect* is commonly used as a noun as well as a verb. □ **af·fect·ing** *adjective* **af·fect·ing·ly** *adverb* [Latin *afficere affect-* influence (as AD-, *facere* do)]

af·fect² *transitive verb* **1 a** pretend to have or feel (*affected indifference*). **b** (foll. by *to* + infin.) pretend. **2** assume the character or manner of; pose as, usu. pretentiously (*likes to affect the freethinker*). **3** show a preference or liking for, usu. ostentatiously (*she affects fancy hats*). [Latin *affectare* aim at, frequentative of *afficere* (as AFFECT¹)]

af·fect³ /ˈafekt/ *noun Psych.* an emotion or mood associated with certain ideas. [German *Affekt* from Latin *affectus* disposition, from *afficere* (as AFFECT¹)]

af·fect·ation *noun* **1** an assumed or contrived manner of behaviour, esp. in order to impress. **2** (foll. by *of*) a studied display.

af·fect·ed *adjective* **1** in senses of AFFECT¹, AFFECT². **2** artificially assumed or displayed; pretended (*an affected air of innocence*). **3** (of a person) full of affectation; artificial. **4** *archaic* disposed, inclined. □ **af·fect·ed·ly** *adverb*

af·fec·tion *noun* **1** (often foll. by *for, towards*) goodwill; fond or kindly feeling. **2** a mental state; an emotion. **3** a mental disposition. **4** the act or process of affecting or being affected. **5** a disease; a diseased condition. □ **af·fec·tion·al** *adjective* (in sense 2). **af·fec·tion·al·ly** *adverb* [Latin *affectio -onis* (as AFFECT¹)]

af·fec·tion·ate *adjective* loving, fond; showing love or tenderness. □ **af·fec·tion·ate·ly** *adverb*

af·fec·tive *adjective* **1** concerning the affections; emotional. **2** *Psych.* of feeling or mood (*affective disorders*). □ **af·fec·tiv·ity** /ˌafekˈtɪvɪti/ *noun* [Late Latin *affectivus* (as AFFECT¹)]

af·fect·less *adjective* characterized by lack of feeling; emotionless, cold. □ **af·fect·less·ness** *noun*

affen·pin·scher /ˈafənˌpɪnʃər/ *noun* a breed of small dog with a short, wiry coat, resembling the griffon. [German from *Affe* monkey + *Pinscher* terrier]

af·fer·ent /ˈafərənt/ *adjective Physiol.* conducting inwards or towards (*afferent nerves; afferent vessels*) (opp. EFFERENT). [Latin *afferre* (as AD-, *ferre* bring)]

af·fianced /əˈfaiːnst, əˈfaiənst/ *adjective literary* promised in marriage; betrothed, engaged. [Old French *afiancer* from medieval Latin *affidare* (as AD-, *fidus* trusty)]

af·fi·dav·it /ˌafɪˈdeivɪt/ *noun* a written statement confirmed by oath (usu. before an authorized official), for use as evidence in court. [medieval Latin, = has stated on oath, from *affidare*: see AFFIANCED]

af·fili·ate ● *verb* /əˈfɪliːˌeit/ **1** *transitive* (foll. by *to, with*) attach or connect (to a larger organization); adopt as a member, branch, etc. **2** *intransitive* (foll. by *to, with*) associate oneself with a society or organization. ● *noun* /əˈfɪliːˌət/ an affiliated person or organization. □ **af·fili·at·ed** *adjective*

af·fili·a·tion *noun* [medieval Latin *affiliare* adopt (as AD-, *filius* son)]

af·fin·ity /əˈfɪnɪti/ *noun* (*pl.* **-ies**) **1** (often foll. by *for, with, between,* or *to*) a spontaneous or natural liking for or attraction to a person or thing. **2** relationship other than by blood, esp. by marriage or adoption (*compare* CONSANGUINITY 1). **3** resemblance in structure between animals, plants, or languages. **4** a similarity of characters suggesting a relationship. **5** *Chem.* the tendency of certain substances to combine with others. [Latin *affinitas -tatis* from *affinis* related, lit. 'bordering on' (as AD- + *finis* border)]

affinity card *noun* a credit card for which the issuer donates to a specified charity etc. a portion of the money spent using the card.

affinity group *noun* a group of people linked by a common interest or purpose.

af·firm *verb* **1** *transitive* assert strongly; state as a fact. **2** *intransitive* **a** *Law* make an affirmation. **b** make a formal declaration. **3** *transitive Law* confirm, ratify (a judgment). **4** declare one's support for; uphold, defend. [Latin *affirmare* (as AD-, *firmus* strong)]

af·firm·a·tion /ˌafərˈmeɪʃən/ *noun* **1** the act or process of affirming or being affirmed. **2** *Law* a solemn declaration by a person who conscientiously declines to take an oath.

af·firma·tive /əˈfɜrmətɪv/ ● *adjective* **1** affirming; asserting that a thing is so. **2** (of a vote) expressing approval. **3** offering support, help, or encouragement. ● *noun* **1** an affirmative statement, reply, or word. **2** (prec. by *the*) a positive or affirming position. ● *interjection* esp. *N Amer.* yes. □ **in the affirmative** with affirmative effect; so as to accept or agree to a proposal; yes (*the answer was in the affirmative*).
□ **af·firma·tive·ly** *adverb*

affirmative action *noun* esp. *N Amer.* a policy to favour those who often suffer from discrimination, esp. in employment.

affix ● *transitive verb* /əˈfɪks/ **1** (usu. foll. by *to, on*) attach, fasten. **2** impress (a seal, stamp, fingerprint, etc.). **3** add in writing (a signature or postscript). ● *noun* /ˈafɪks/ **1** an appendage; an addition. **2** *Grammar* an addition or element placed at the beginning (*prefix*) or end (*suffix*) of a root, stem, or word, or in the body of a word (*infix*), to modify its meaning. □ **af·fix·a·tion** *noun* [French *affixer, affixe* or medieval Latin *affixare* frequentative of Latin *affigere* (as AD-, *figere* fix-fix)]

af·fla·tus /əˈfleɪtəs/ *noun* a divine creative impulse; inspiration. [Latin from *afflare* (as AD-, *flare flat-* to blow)]

af·flict *transitive verb* distress with bodily or mental suffering.
□ **afflicted with** suffering from. [Latin *afflictare*, or *afflict-* past participle stem of *affligere* (as AD-, *fligere flict-* dash)]

af·flic·tion *noun* **1** physical or mental distress, esp. pain or illness. **2** a cause of this.

af·flu·ence /ˈafluəns/ *noun* an abundant supply of money, commodities, etc.; wealth. [Latin *affluentia* from *affluere*: see AFFLUENT]

af·flu·ent /ˈafluənt/ *adjective* wealthy, rich. [Old French from Latin *affluere* (as AD-, *fluere flux-* flow)]

af·flu·enza /ˌafluˈenzə/ *noun* pursuit of or obsession with wealth, material things, and an affluent lifestyle to a degree that is detrimental to the individual's mental health and to society as a whole. [blend of AFFLUENCE + INFLUENZA]

af·flux /ˈaflʌks/ *noun* a flow towards a point; an influx. [medieval Latin *affluxus* from Latin *affluere*: see AFFLUENT]

af·ford *transitive verb* **1** (prec. by *can* or *be able to*; often foll. by *to* + infin.) **a** have enough money, means, time, etc., for; be able to spare (*can afford $50; can we afford a holiday?; could not afford to worry about it*). **b** be in a position to do something (esp. without risk of adverse consequences) (*can't afford to let him think so*). **2** provide (*affords a view of the lake*). □ **af·ford·able** *adjective* **af·ford·abil·ity** *noun* [Middle English from Old English *geforthian* promote (as FORTH), assimilated to words in AF-]

af·for·est *transitive verb* **1** convert into forest. **2** plant with trees.
□ **af·for·est·a·tion** *noun* [medieval Latin *afforestare* (as AD-, *foresta* FOREST)]

af·fran·chise *transitive verb* release from servitude or an obligation. [Old French *afranchir* (as ENFRANCHISE, with prefix A-³)]

af·fray /əˈfreɪ/ *noun* a public fight; riot. [Anglo-French *afrayer* (v.) from Old French *esfreer* from Romanic]

af·fri·cate /ˈafrɪkət/ *noun* *Phonetics* a composite speech sound in which a plosive or stopped consonant is gradually released with friction, e.g. *ch* in *church*. [Latin *affricare* (as AD-, *fricare* rub)]

af·front ● *noun* an open insult (*feel it an affront; offer an affront to*). ● *transitive verb* **1** insult openly. **2** offend the modesty or self-respect of. [Old French *afronter* slap in the face, insult, ultimately from Latin *frons frontis* face]

Af·ghan /ˈafgan/ ● *noun* **1 a** a native or national of Afghanistan. **b** a person of Afghan descent. **2** the official language of Afghanistan. *Also* called PASHTO. **3** (**afghan**) a knitted or crocheted woollen blanket or shawl. **4** (in full **Afghan coat**) a kind of sheepskin coat with the skin outside and usu. with a shaggy border. **5** = AFGHAN HOUND. ● *adjective* of or relating to Afghanistan or its people or language. [Pashto *afghānī*]

Afghan hound *noun* a tall hunting dog with long silky hair, noted for speed, strength, and endurance.

Af·ghani /afˈgani/ (*pl.* **-is**) ● *noun* **1** a native or national of Afghanistan. **2** (**afghani**) the chief monetary unit of Afghanistan, equal to 100 puls. ● *adjective* of or relating to Afghanistan or its people or language. [Pashto]

Af·ghan·istan /afˈganəˌstan/ a mountainous landlocked republic in central Asia; pop. (est. 2002) 27,756,000; capital, Kabul. In 1996 the fundamentalist Taliban gained control of Kabul and set up an Islamic state; this was overthrown in 2001 by US-led forces in conjunction with Afghan groups following the attacks on the World Trade Centre and the Pentagon by terrorists said to have been harboured by the Taliban.

afi·cion·ado /əfɪʃəˈnadoː, -ˈnɒdoː/ *noun* (*pl.* **-ados**) a devotee, fan or enthusiast. [Spanish, orig. designating a devotee of bullfighting, past participle of *aficionar* 'become fond of', based on Latin *affectio(n-)* 'favourable disposition towards']

afield *adverb* **1** (esp. in **far afield**) away from home; to or at a distance. **2** in the field or the countryside. [Old English (as A², FIELD)]

afire *adverb & predicative adjective* **1** on fire. **2** intensely roused or excited. **3** glittering, glowing; coloured like fire.

aflame *adverb & predicative adjective* **1** in flames. **2** = AFIRE 2. **3** red as if on fire (*his cheeks were aflame*).

af·la·toxin /ˈaflaˌtɒksɪn/ *noun* *Chem.* any of several related toxic compounds produced by the fungus *Aspergillus flavus*, which cause tissue damage and cancer. [*Aspergillus* + *flavus* + TOXIN]

AFL-CIO *abbreviation* American Federation of Labor and Congress of Industrial Organizations, a federation of independent N American trade unions formed by the merger of these two formerly conflicting bodies in 1955.

afloat *adverb & predicative adjective* **1** floating in water or air. **2** at sea; on board ship. **3** out of debt or difficulty. **4** in general circulation; current. **5** full of or covered with a liquid.

aflut·ter *adverb & predicative adjective* fluttering; in a flutter.

AFM *abbreviation* (in the UK) Air Force Medal.

AFN *abbreviation* (in Canada) ASSEMBLY OF FIRST NATIONS.

afoot *adverb & predicative adjective* **1** in operation; progressing. **2** astir; on the move. **3** *N Amer.* **a** on foot (*they arrived afoot*). **b** on one's feet (*slow afoot*).

afore *preposition & adverb* archaic or dialect before; previously; in front (of). [Old English *onforan* (as A², FORE)]

afore- *combining form* before, previously.

afore·mentioned *adjective* (also **afore·said**) denoting a thing or person previously mentioned.

afore·thought *adjective* premeditated (following a noun: *malice aforethought*).

a for·ti·ori /ˌei fɔrtiˈɔri/ *adverb & adjective* with a yet stronger reason (than a conclusion already accepted); more conclusively. [Latin]

afoul *adverb* esp. *N Amer.* (usu. in **run** or **fall afoul of**) into conflict or difficulty with.

AFP *abbreviation* Agence France-Presse, a French independent news agency.

afraid *predicative adjective* **1** (often foll. by *of*, or *that* or *lest* + clause) alarmed, frightened. **2** (foll. by *to* + infin.) unwilling or reluctant for fear of the consequences (*was afraid to go in*). □ **be afraid** (foll. by *that* + clause) admit or declare with (real or politely simulated) regret (*I'm afraid there's none left*). [Middle English, past participle of obsolete *affray* (v.) from Anglo-French *afrayer* from Old French *esfreer*]

A-frame *noun* **1** a frame (of a house etc.) having the shape of a capital letter A. **2** *N Amer.* an A-frame house. **3** *N Amer.* Forestry an A-shaped frame supporting running lines in high-lead logging.

af·reet /ˈafriːt/ *noun* (also **afrit**) a powerful, usu. evil jinni in Arabian stories and Islamic mythology. [Arabic *'ifrīt*]

afresh *adverb* anew; with a fresh beginning.

Af·ri·ca the second largest continent, a southward projection of the Old World land mass, divided roughly in two by the equator and surrounded by sea except where the Isthmus of Suez joins it to Asia. [Latin *Africa (terra)* '(land) of the *Afri*', an ancient people of North Africa]

Af·ri·can ● *noun* **1** a native or inhabitant of Africa. **2** a person of African descent (esp. a dark-skinned person). ● *adjective* of or relating to Africa.

Af·ri·cana *plural noun* things connected with Africa.

African-American *noun* an American citizen of black African origin or descent.

African-Canadian *noun* a Canadian citizen of black African origin or descent.

African elephant *noun* the elephant, *Loxodonta africana*, of Africa, which is larger than the Indian elephant.

Af·ri·can·ize *transitive verb* **1** make African in character. **2** hybridize (honeybees of European stock) with bees of African stock, producing an aggressive strain.

Consonants: b *but* d *dog* f *few* g *get* h *her* j *yes* k *cat* l *leg* m *man* n *no* p *pen* r *red* s *sit*

African National Congress a South African political party and black nationalist organization founded in 1912 with the aim of securing racial equality and black representation in parliament. In South Africa's first democratic elections (April 1994) the party gained 62.6 per cent of the vote and its leader Nelson Mandela became the new President of the country. Abbr.: **ANC**.

African Union an association of African states formed in 2002 from the Organization of African Unity.

African violet *noun* a plant of the genus *Saintpaulia*, with heart-shaped velvety leaves and blue, purple, pink, or white flowers, varieties of which are often grown as a houseplant.

Af·ri·kaans /ˌafrɪˈkɒns/ *noun* the language of the Afrikaner people developed from Dutch, an official language of the Republic of South Africa. [Dutch, = African]

Af·ri·ka Korps /ˈafrɪkə ˌkɔr/ a German army force sent to North Africa in 1941 under the command of General Rommel. After early success the force was defeated at El Alamein in 1942, and was driven out of North Africa in 1943.

Af·ri·kan·er /ˌafrɪˈkɒnər/ *noun* an Afrikaans-speaking white South African, esp. one of Dutch descent. [Afrikaans, alteration of Dutch *Afrikaan*, 'an African']

afrit *var.* of AFREET.

Afro ● *adjective* **1** (also **afro**) (of a hairstyle) shaped into a wide curly or frizzy bush. **2** African. ● *noun* (*pl.* **Afros**) an Afro hairstyle. [AFRO-, or abbreviation of AFRICAN]

Afro- *combining form* African (*Afro-Asian*). [Latin *Afer Afr-* African]

Afro-American /ˌafrəˈmerɪkən/ ● *adjective* of or relating to American blacks or their culture. ● *noun* an American black.

Afro-Asiatic ● *adjective* of or pertaining to a family of languages found in Northern Africa and W Asia, of which Arabic is the most widespread. ● *noun* the Afro-Asiatic language family.

Afro-Canadian *noun & adjective* AFRICAN-CANADIAN.

Afro-Caribbean ● *noun* a person of African descent in or from the Caribbean. ● *adjective* of or relating to the Afro-Caribbeans or their culture.

Afro·cen·tric /ˌafroˈsentrɪk/ *adjective* centred on Africa or on cultures of African origin, esp. N American black culture. □ **Afro·cen·trism** *noun* **Afro·cen·trist** *noun & adjective*

af·ror·mo·sia /ˌafrɔrˈmoziə/ *noun* **1** an African tree, *Pericopsis* (formerly *Afrormosia*) *elata*, yielding a hard wood resembling teak and used for furniture. **2** this wood. [modern Latin, from AFRO- + *Ormosia* genus of trees]

aft[1] *adverb* at or towards the stern of a ship or tail of an aircraft. [prob. from Middle English *baft*: see ABAFT]

aft[2] *noun* *Cdn informal* afternoon (*I'll see you this aft*). [abbreviation]

after ● *preposition* **1 a** following in time; later than (*after six months; after midnight; day after day*). **b** *N Amer.* past the hour of (*a quarter after eight*). **2** (with causal force) in view of (something that happened shortly before) (*after your behaviour tonight what do you expect?*). **3** (with concessive force) in spite of (*after all my efforts I'm no better off*). **4** behind (*shut the door after you*). **5** in pursuit or quest of (*run after them; hanker after it; is after a job*). **6** about, concerning (*asked after her; asked after her health*). **7** in allusion to (*named her Patricia after her mother*). **8** in imitation of (a person, word, etc.) (*a painting after Rubens; 'aesthete' is formed after 'athlete'*). **9** next in importance to (*the best book on the subject after mine*). **10** according to (*after a fashion*). **11** *dialect* (with *to be* + present participle) **a** to have just done (*I was after seeing him just last week*). **b** in the act of, on the point of (*she's after putting the kettle on*). ● *conjunction* in or at a time later than that when (*left after they arrived*). ● *adverb* **1** later in time (*soon after; a week after*). **2** behind in place (*followed on after; look before and after*). ● *adjective* **1** later, following (*in after years*). **2** *Naut.* nearer the stern (*after cabins; after mast*). □ **after all 1** in spite of all that has happened or has been said etc. (*after all, what does it matter?*). **2** in spite of one's exertions, expectations, etc. (*they tried for an hour and failed after all; so you have come after all!*). **3** used in explaining something (*he is the one who suggested it, after all*). **after one's own heart** *see* HEART. **after you** a formula used in offering precedence. [Old English *æfter* from Germanic]

after·birth *noun* *Med.* the placenta and fetal membranes discharged from the uterus after childbirth.

after·burn·er *noun* an auxiliary burner in a jet engine to increase thrust.

after·care *noun* care of a patient after a stay in hospital or of a person on release from prison.

after·deck *noun* *Naut.* the part of a ship's deck nearest the stern.

after-effect *noun* an effect that follows after an interval or after the primary action of something.

after·glow *noun* **1** a light or radiance remaining after its source has disappeared or been removed. **2** a period of happiness, fame, etc. immediately following a successful event.

after-hours *attributive adjective* occurring or operating after the usual or legal operating hours (*after-hours bar*).

after·image *noun* a sensation retained by one of the senses, esp. the eye, after the original stimulus has stopped.

after·life *noun* **1** life after death. **2** life at a later time.

after·market *noun* **1** a market in spare parts and components. **2** *Stock Exch.* a market in shares after their original issue.

after·math *noun* **1** consequences; after-effects (*the aftermath of war*). **2** the period immediately following an event. **3** new grass growing after mowing or after a harvest. [AFTER *adjective* + *math* mowing, from Old English *mæth* from Germanic]

after·most *adjective* furthest aft.

after·noon ● *noun* **1** the time from noon to evening. **2** a time compared with this, esp. the later part of something (*the afternoon of life*). ● *interjection* = GOOD AFTERNOON.

afternoon tea *noun* a light meal served in the afternoon, consisting of tea and usu. sandwiches, small cakes, etc.

after·pains /ˈaftər.peinz/ *plural noun* pains caused by contraction of the uterus after childbirth.

after-party *noun* a party held after another event, esp. a concert or another party.

afters *plural noun* *Brit. informal* dessert (*what's for afters?*).

after·shave *noun* an astringent lotion for use on the face after shaving.

after·shock *noun* **1** a lesser shock following the main shock of an earthquake. **2** an after-effect.

after·taste *noun* **1** a taste remaining or recurring after eating or drinking. **2** a persistent feeling or impression (*defeat left a bitter aftertaste*).

after·thought *noun* **1** an item or thing that is thought of or added later. **2** *informal* the youngest child in a family, esp. one born considerably later than the other children.

after·touch *noun* **1** the resonant effect produced when a pianist sustains the pressure on a key after striking it. **2** a device for reproducing this on an electronic keyboard etc.

after·wards *adverb* (also **after·ward**) later, subsequently. [Old English *æftanwearde* adj. from *æftan* AFT[1] + -WARD]

after·word *noun* concluding remarks in a book, either by the author or by someone else.

after·world *noun* = AFTERLIFE.

AG *abbreviation* **1** ATTORNEY GENERAL. **2** *Cdn* AUDITOR GENERAL.

Ag *symbol* *Chem.* the element silver. [Latin *argentum*]

ag *abbreviation* esp. *N Amer. informal* agriculture, agricultural (*ag college*).

ag- *prefix* assimilated form of AD- before g.

Aga /ˈɑgə/ *noun* *Brit.* proprietary a type of large cooking stove or range burning solid fuel or powered by gas, oil, or electricity. [Swedish from 'Svenska Aktiebolaget Gasackumulator' (Swedish Gas Accumulator Company), the original manufacturer]

aga /ˈɑgə/ *noun* (also **agha**) (in Muslim countries, esp. under the Ottoman Empire) a commander, a chief. [Turkish *ağa* master]

Aga·dir /ˌɑgəˈdiːr/ a seaport and resort on the Atlantic coast of Morocco; pop. (est. 1994) 155,240. It was the centre of a crisis between Britain and Germany in 1911, with war being averted only by the interventions of the French.

again *adverb* **1** another time; once more. **2** as in a previous position or condition (*back again; home again; quite well again*). **3** in addition (*as much again; half as many again*). **4** further, besides (*again, what about the children?*). **5** on the other hand (*I might, and again I might not*). □ **again and again** repeatedly. [originally a northern form of Middle English *ayen* etc., from Old English *ongēan*, *ongægn*, etc., from Germanic]

against *preposition* **1** in opposition to (*fight against the invaders; am against hanging; arson is against the law*). **2** into collision or in contact with (*ran against a rock; lean against the wall; up against a problem*). **3** to the disadvantage of (*her age is against her*). **4** in contrast to (*against a dark background; 3.9 seconds as against 4.2 seconds yesterday*). **5** in anticipation of or preparation for (*against his coming; against a rainy day; protected against the cold; warned against pickpockets*). **6** as a compensating factor to (*income against expenditure*). **7** in return for (*issued against payment of the fee*). □ **against the clock** *see* CLOCK[1]. **against the**

grain *see* GRAIN. **against time** *see* TIME. [Middle English *ayenes* etc. from *ayen* AGAIN + *-t* as in *amongst*: see AMONG]

Aga Khan /ˈɑːɡə ˈkɒn/ *noun* the hereditary spiritual leader of most of the Ismaili Muslims.

Aga·mem·non /ˌæɡəˈmemnɒn/ *Gk Legend* a legendary king of Mycenae who led the Greeks in the Trojan War and was later murdered by his wife, Clytemnestra.

agam·ic /əˈɡæmɪk/ *adjective* characterized by the absence of sexual reproduction. [Greek *agamos* unmarried + -IC]

Agaña /əˈɡɒnjə/ capital of the island of Guam; pop. (est. 1995) 2,000.

aga·pan·thus /ˌæɡəˈpænθəs/ *noun* any plant of the genus *Agapanthus*, native to Africa, having blue or white funnel-shaped flowers. [modern Latin from Greek *agapē* love + *anthos* flower]

agape¹ /əˈɡeɪp/ *adverb & predicative adjective* gaping, open-mouthed, esp. with wonder or expectation.

agape² /ˈæɡəˌpeɪ/ *noun* **1** a Christian feast in token of fellowship, esp. one held by early Christians in commemoration of the Last Supper. **2** *Theol.* Christian fellowship, esp. as distinct from erotic love. [Greek, = brotherly love]

agar /ˈeɪɡɑr/ *noun* (also **agar-agar** /ˌeɪɡɑrˈeɪɡɑr/) a gelatinous substance obtained from any of various kinds of red seaweed, and used as a thickener in food, as a culture medium for bacteria, and as a laxative. [Malay]

aga·ric /ˈæɡərɪk/ *noun* any fungus of the family Agaricaceae, with cap and stalk, including the common edible mushroom. [Latin *agaricum* from Greek *agarikon* 'tree fungus']

Agar·tala /ˈʌɡərtəˌlɑ/ a city in the far northeast of India, capital of the state of Tripura, situated near the border with Bangladesh; pop. (2001) 189,300.

Agas·si /ˈæɡəsi/ **André** (b.1970), US tennis player. Noted for his unconventional on-court appearance and impetuous behaviour, by the age of 18 he was ranked third in the world. He won the Wimbledon men's singles title in 1992.

Agas·siz /ˈæɡəsi/ **Jean Louis Ro·dolphe** (1807–73), Swiss-born zoologist, geologist, and paleontologist, who was the first to propose that vast ice sheets had once covered much of Europe and N America.

Agassiz, Lake /ˈæɡəsi/ a former glacial lake in N America formed by the retreating Laurentide Ice Sheet 11,500 years ago. At its largest, the lake covered most of Manitoba and NW Ontario, and parts of Saskatchewan, N Dakota and Minnesota. [AGASSIZ]

ag·ate /ˈæɡət/ *noun* **1** any of several varieties of hard usu. streaked chalcedony. **2** a coloured toy marble resembling this. [French *agate* from Latin *achates* from Greek *akhatēs*]

agave /əˈɡeɪvi/ *noun* any plant of the genus *Agave*, with rosettes of succulent spiny leaves, and tall inflorescences, e.g. the century plant. [Latin from Greek *Agauē*, proper name in myth, from *agauos* illustrious]

Agawa Bay /ˈæɡəwɒ/ an archaeological site in N Ontario, situated on the northeastern shore of Lake Superior, about 90 km north of Sault Ste. Marie. It is the site of Agawa Rock, a sheer cliff face rising almost 23 m (75 ft.) above the lake, on which have been carved and painted 30 Indian pictographs, now centuries old. [Ojibwa, possibly meaning 'sheltered harbour']

age ● *noun* **1 a** the length of time that a person or thing has existed or is likely to exist (*ten years of age*). **b** (*attributive*) of the age of (*age ten*). **c** a particular point in or part of one's life, often as a qualification (*old age*; *voting age*). **2 a** *informal* (often in *pl.*) a long time (*took an age to answer*; *have been waiting for ages*). **b** a distinct period of the past (*golden age*; *Bronze Age*; *Middle Ages*). **c** a division of geological time, esp. a subdivision of an epoch. **3** a generation. **d** the latter part of life; old age (*the wisdom of age*). ● *verb* (*pres. part.* **aging**, **age·ing**) **1** *intransitive* show signs of advancing age (*has aged a lot recently*). **2** *intransitive* grow old. **3** *intransitive* (esp. of wine or cheese) mature. **4** *transitive* cause or allow to age. □ **of age** adult (esp. in law 18 and over, formerly 21 and over) (*come of age*; *be of age*). ¶ *Age ten* is more common than *aged ten* in Canadian English, but both are acceptable. [Old French, ultimately from Latin *aetas -atis* age]

-age *suffix* forming nouns denoting: **1** an action (*breakage*; *spillage*). **2** a condition or function (*bondage*). **3** an aggregate or number of (*coverage*; *acreage*). **4** fees payable for; the cost of using (*postage*). **5** the product of an action (*dosage*; *wreckage*). **6** a place; an abode (*anchorage*; *orphanage*; *parsonage*). [Old French, ultimately from Latin *-aticum* neuter of adj. suffix *-aticus* -ATIC]

aged *adjective* **1** /eɪdʒd/ **a** of the age of (*aged ten*). **b** that has been subjected to aging. **c** (of a horse) over six years old. **2** /ˈeɪdʒəd/ having lived long; old.

age·ing *var. of* AGING.

age·ism *noun* (also **agism**) prejudice or discrimination on the grounds of age. □ **age·ist** *adjective & noun* (also **agist**).

age·less *adjective* **1** never growing or appearing old or outmoded. **2** eternal, timeless.

age-long *adjective* lasting for a very long time.

agency *noun* (*pl.* **agen·cies**) **1 a** an organization or business providing a (usu. specific) service (*advertising agency*; *car rental agency*). **b** *esp. N Amer.* a government office providing a specific service (*Canadian International Development Agency*). **2** a person or business operating on behalf of another, esp. at a distance (*our Vancouver agency*). **3 a** the duty or function of an agent. **b** the office or place of business of an agent. **4** means; instrumentality; mediation (*fertilized by the agency of bees*). **5** active working or operation; action; activity. [medieval Latin *agentia* from Latin *agere* do]

agen·da *noun* (*pl.* **agen·das**) **1** a list of items of business to be considered at a meeting. **2** a series of things to be done (*on the agenda*). **3** a plan of action (*hidden agenda*; *political agenda*). **4** *N Amer.* a book containing a calendar and usu. an address list etc., used to plan one's activities; an appointment diary. [Latin, neuter pl. of gerundive of *agere* do]

agent *noun* **1** a person who provides a specific service etc. (*travel agent*; *insurance agent*). **2** a person who acts for another in business, politics, etc. (*talk to my agent*). **3** a person or company that represents an organization, company, or government in a particular territory (*the company's Halifax agent*). **4** a person or thing that exerts power or produces an effect. **5** a spy (*enemy agent*). **6 a** the cause of a natural force or effect on matter (*oxidizing agent*). **b** such a force or effect. **7** *Cdn* = INDIAN AGENT. □ **agen·tial** /əˈdʒenʃəl/ *adjective* **agent·ry** *noun N Amer.* [Latin *agent-* part. stem of *agere* do]

agent general *noun* (*pl.* **agents general**) the chief representative of a Canadian province or Australian state in a foreign country or region.

agent·ing *noun* the practice of working as an agent, e.g. for an actor, athlete, etc.

Agent Orange *noun* a highly poisonous herbicide used as a defoliant, esp. by US forces during the Vietnam War. [from the orange stripe on shipping drums]

agent provocateur /aˌʒɑ̃ prəˌvɒkəˈtɜr/ *noun* (*pl.* **agents provocateurs** *pronunc.* same) a person employed to detect suspected offenders by tempting them to overt self-incriminating action. [French, = provocative agent]

age of consent *noun* the age at which marriage or consent to sexual intercourse is valid in law.

age of discretion *noun* the esp. legal age at which a person is able to manage his or her own affairs.

Age of Reason *noun* **1** the late 17th and 18th c. in western Europe and N America, during which cultural life was characterized by faith in human reason. **2** (usu. **age of reason**) the age at which a person is considered capable of making rational judgments.

age-old *adjective* having existed for a very long time.

ager·atum /ˌædʒəˈreɪtəm, -ˈrætəm/ *noun* any of a number of low-growing herbaceous plants of the genus *Ageratum*, bearing clusters of small, long-lasting blue flowers. [modern Latin from Latin *ageraton* from Greek *agēratos* from A-¹ + *gērat-*, *gēras* old age, since the plant originally so-called had everlasting flowers]

Ag·gad·ah /əˈɡɒdə/ *noun* = HAGGADAH.

ag·gie¹ *noun N Amer. informal* a student of agricultural science. [abbreviation]

ag·gie² *noun N Amer. informal* a playing marble, esp. a large one made of or resembling agate. [abbreviation]

ag·glom·er·ate ● *transitive & intransitive verb* /əˈɡlɒməˌreɪt/ **1** collect into a mass. **2** accumulate in a disorderly way. ● *noun* /əˈɡlɒmərət/ **1** a mass or collection of things. **2** *Geol.* a mass of large volcanic fragments bonded under heat (*compare* CONGLOMERATE *noun* 3). ● *adjective* /əˈɡlɒmərət/ collected into a mass. □ **ag·glom·er·a·tion** *noun* **ag·glom·er·a·tive** /əˈɡlɒmərətɪv/ *adjective* [Latin *agglomerare* (as AD-, *glomerare* from *glomus -meris* ball)]

ag·glu·tin·ate /əˈɡluːtɪˌneɪt/ *verb* **1** *transitive* unite as with glue. **2** *transitive & intransitive Biol.* cause or undergo adhesion (of bacteria, red blood cells, etc.). **3** *transitive Linguistics* combine grammatical elements (roots and affixes) into complex words with little or no change of form.

Vowels:　a *cat*　ɑ *arm*　e *bed*　ɜr *her*　ɜ: *deux*　ə *ago*　ɪ *sit*　i *cosy*　iː *feed*　ɒ *hot*　ɔ *pore*　ɔ: *no*　ʌ *run*　ʊ *put*

ag·glu·tin·a·tion noun **ag·glu·tina·tive** /ə'gluːtɪnətɪv/ adjective [Latin agglutinare (as AD-, glutinare from gluten -tinis glue)]

ag·glu·tin·in /ə'gluːtɪnɪn/ noun Biol. a substance or antibody causing agglutination.

ag·grand·ize /ə'grandaɪz/ transitive verb (also esp. Brit. **-ise**) **1** increase the power, rank, or wealth of (a person or nation). **2** cause to appear greater or more important than is the case. □ **ag·grand·ize·ment** /-daizmənt, -dɪzmənt/ noun **ag·grand·iz·er** noun [French agrandir (stem agrandiss-), prob. from Italian aggrandire from Latin grandis large: assimilated to verbs in -IZE]

ag·gra·vate /'agrə,veit/ transitive verb **1** increase the gravity of (an illness, offence, etc.). **2** annoy, exasperate (a person). ¶ The use of aggravate in sense 2 is regarded by some people as incorrect, but it is common in informal use. □ **ag·gra·va·tion** noun [Latin aggravare aggravat- make heavy, from gravis heavy]

ag·gra·vat·ed assault noun Law assault involving wounding, maiming, disfigurement or endangerment of the life of the victim.

ag·gre·gate ● noun /'agrəgət/ **1** a collection of, or the total of, disparate elements. **2** pieces of crushed stone, gravel, etc. used in making concrete. **3 a** Geol. a mass of minerals formed into solid rock. **b** a mass of particles. ● adjective /'agrəgət/ **1** (of disparate elements) collected into one mass. **2** constituted by the collection of many units into one body. **3** Bot. **a** (of fruit) formed from several carpels derived from the same flower (e.g. raspberry). **b** (of a species) closely related. ● transitive & intransitive verb /'agrə,geit/ collect together; combine into one mass. □ **in the aggregate** as a whole. □ **ag·gre·ga·tion** noun [Latin aggregare aggregat- herd together (as AD-, grex gregis flock)]

ag·gre·gat·or noun an Internet company that collects information about other companies' products and services and distributes it through a single website.

ag·gres·sion noun **1** the act or practice of attacking without provocation, esp. beginning a quarrel or war. **2** an unprovoked attack. **3** Psych. hostile or destructive tendency or behaviour. [Latin aggressio attack, from aggredi aggress- (as AD-, gradi walk)]

ag·gres·sive adjective **1** of a person: **a** given to aggression; openly hostile. **b** forceful, assertive; energetic, enterprising (aggressive salespeople). **2** (of an act) offensive, hostile. **3** suggesting assertiveness or hostility (aggressive shoulder pads). **4** growing or multiplying rapidly (an aggressive lesion; a very aggressive ivy). □ **ag·gres·sive·ly** adverb **ag·gres·sive·ness** noun **ag·gres·siv·ity** /,agre'sɪvɪti/ noun

ag·gres·sor noun a person or country that attacks without provocation.

ag·grieved adjective wronged; having a grievance. □ **ag·griev·ed·ly** /-vədli/ adverb [Old French agrever make heavier (as AD-, GRIEVE)]

aggro noun Brit. slang **1** aggressive troublemaking. **2** trouble, difficulty. [abbreviation of AGGRAVATION (see AGGRAVATE)]

agha var. of AGA.

aghast /ə'gast/ predicative adjective (often foll. by at) amazed; filled with dismay or consternation. [Middle English, past participle of obsolete agast, gast frighten: see GHASTLY]

agile /'adʒail, 'adʒəl/ adjective **1** characterized by ease and grace of movement. **2** mentally acute. □ **agile·ly** adverb **agil·ity** /ə'dʒɪlɪti/ noun [Latin agilis from agere do]

agin preposition informal or dialect against. [corruption of AGAINST]

Agin·court, Battle of /'aʒɪn,kɔr/ a battle in northern France in 1415 during the Hundred Years War, in which the longbow helped the English army under Henry V defeat a larger French force, allowing Henry to occupy Normandy and consolidate his claim to the French throne.

aging (also **age·ing**) ● noun **1** the process of growing old. **2** the act or process of causing to age or mature. **3** a change of properties occurring in some metals after heat treatment or cold working. ● adjective becoming or appearing older.

agism var. of AGEISM.

agi·tate verb **1** transitive disturb or excite (a person or feelings). **2** intransitive (often foll. by for, against) stir up or attempt to stir up public interest or concern (agitated for tax reform). **3** transitive shake or move, esp. briskly. □ **agi·tat·ed** adjective **agi·tat·ed·ly** adverb [Latin agitare agitat- frequentative of agere drive]

agi·ta·tion noun **1** the act or process of agitating or being agitated. **2** mental anxiety or concern. □ **agi·ta·tion·al** adjective

agi·tato /,adʒɪ'tɒtoː/ adverb & adjective Music in an agitated manner. [Italian]

agi·ta·tor noun **1** a person who agitates for or against a cause etc. **2** an apparatus for shaking or mixing liquid etc., esp. in a washing machine.

agit·prop /'adʒɪt,prɒp/ noun **1** (**Agitprop**) hist. a Soviet agency for the dissemination of Communist political propaganda, esp. in literature, film, etc. **2** (also attributive) political and usu. pro-communist propaganda, esp. in literature and film. [Russian agitpróp, from agitátsiya agitation + propagánda propaganda]

Ag·laia /ə'glaiə/ Gk Myth one of the three Graces.

ag·let /'aglət/ noun **1** a plastic or metal tag attached to each end of a shoelace etc. **2** = AIGUILLETTE 1. [from French aiguillette small needle, ultimately from Latin acus needle]

agley /ə'glei, -'liː/ adverb Scot. askew, awry. [A² + Scots gley squint]

ag·loo /'agluː/ noun (also **aglu**) Cdn (North) a breathing hole made by a seal through sea ice. [Inuktitut]

aglow predicative adjective glowing.

Aglu·kark /a'gluːkɑrk/ **Susan** (b.1967), Canadian singer and songwriter, the first Inuit recording artist, known for her clear, pure voice and combination of English and Inuktitut lyrics with contemporary pop music.

AGM abbreviation **1** Cdn, Brit., & Austral. ANNUAL GENERAL MEETING. **2** air-to-ground missile.

agma noun **1** the sound represented by the symbol /ŋ/, as in 'ring'. **2** this symbol. [Greek, lit. 'fragment']

ag·nate /'agneit/ noun a person who is descended esp. by male line from the same male ancestor. □ **ag·nat·ic** /-'natɪk/ adjective **ag·na·tion** noun [Latin agnatus from ad to + gnasc be born, from stem gen- beget]

Agnes, St. (died c.304), martyred at the age of 13, patron saint of girls. Her emblem is a lamb.

Agnesi /an'jesi/ **Maria Gae·tana** (1718–99), Italian mathematician and philosopher. She is regarded as the first female mathematician of the Western world.

Agnew /'agnuː, -njuː/ **Spiro Theo·dore** (1918–1996), US Republican politician, vice-president 1969–73.

Agni /'agni/ Hinduism the Vedic god of fire. As mediator between gods and humans, he takes offerings to the gods in the smoke of sacrifice and returns to the earth as lightning. [Sanskrit, = fire, cognitive with Latin ignis]

agnol·otti /,anjə'lɒti/ noun half-moon shaped or triangular pasta filled with meat, cheese, etc. [Italian]

Agnon /'agnɒn/ **Shmuel Yosef** (pseudonym of Samuel Josef Czaczkes) (1888–1970), Polish-born Israeli novelist and short-story writer, whose novels include The Bridal Canopy (1919) and The Day Before Yesterday (1945); he shared the Nobel Prize for literature in 1966.

ag·no·sia /ag'noːsiə/ noun Med. the loss of the ability to interpret sensations. [modern Latin from Greek agnōsia ignorance]

ag·nos·tic /ag'nɒstɪk/ ● noun a person who believes that nothing is known, or can be known, of the existence or nature of God or of anything beyond material phenomena. ● adjective of or relating to agnostics or agnosticism. □ **ag·nos·ti·cism** /-,sɪzəm/ noun [A-¹ + GNOSTIC]

Agnus Dei /,agnus 'deiiː, ,anjus/ noun Christianity **1** a figure of a lamb bearing a cross or flag, as an emblem of Christ. **2 a** a prayer or hymn beginning with the words 'Lamb of God' said or sung before or during Communion in some Christian liturgies. **b** a musical setting of this. [Latin, = lamb of God]

ago adverb earlier, before the present (ten years ago; long ago). ¶ Note the construction it is ten years ago that (not since) I saw them. [Middle English (ago, agone), past participle of obsolete ago (v.) (as A-², GO¹)]

agog predicative adjective eager; excited (en gogue from en in + pl. of gogue fun]

agon /'agɒn/ noun **1** in literature, a struggle, esp. between protagonist and antagonist. **2** hist. in ancient Greece, a contest for prizes. [Greek agōn]

ag·on·ic line /ə'gɒnɪk/ noun a line passing through the two poles, along which a magnetic needle points directly north or south. [Greek agōnios without angle (as A-¹, gōnia angle)]

agon·is·tic /,agə'nɪstɪk/ adjective polemical, combative. □ **agon·is·tic·ally** adverb [Late Latin agonisticus from Greek agōnistikos from agōnistēs contestant, from agōn contest]

ag·on·ize verb (also esp. Brit. **-ise**) **1** intransitive (often foll. by over) undergo (esp. mental) anguish; suffer agony. **2** transitive cause agony to. **3** intransitive struggle, contend. □ **ag·on·iz·ing** adjective **ag·on·iz·ing·ly** adverb [ultimately from Greek agōnizomai contend, from agōn contest]

ag·on·ized *adjective* characterized by or expressing agony (*an agonized look; agonized breathing*).

agony *noun* (*pl.* **ag·on·ies**) **1** extreme mental or physical suffering. **2** a severe struggle. **3** the struggle or suffering preceding death. [Greek *agōnia* from *agōn* contest]

agony aunt *noun Brit. informal* a person (esp. a woman) who answers letters in an agony column.

agony column *noun Brit. informal* **1** a column in a newspaper or magazine offering personal advice to readers who write in. **2** the part of the classified advertisements in a newspaper reserved for messages to lost relatives, etc.

ag·ora[1] /ˈagərə/ *noun Gk Hist.* an assembly or place of assembly, esp. a marketplace. [Greek]

ag·ora[2] /agəˈrɒ/ *noun* (*pl.* **ag·o·rot** /agəˈrɔːt/) a monetary unit of Israel, equal to one-hundredth of a shekel. [Hebrew *agōrāh* 'small coin']

agora·phobia /ˌagərəˈfəʊbɪə/ *noun Psych.* an abnormal fear of open spaces or public places. □ **agora·phobe** *noun* **agora·phob·ic** *adjective & noun* [modern Latin from AGORA + -PHOBIA]

Ag·os·tini /ˌagəˈstiːni/ **Giacomo** (b.1944), Italian racing motorcyclist. Between 1966 and 1975 he won a record fifteen world titles.

agou·ti /əˈguːti/ *noun* (*pl.* **agou·tis**) **1** any burrowing rodent of the genus *Dasyprocta* or *Myoprocta* of Central and S America, related to the guinea pig. **2** any animal whose fur has each hair banded dark and light. [Tupi *aguti*]

AGR *abbreviation* advanced gas-cooled (nuclear) reactor.

Agra /ˈɒgrə/ a city on the Jumna River in Uttar Pradesh state, N India; pop. (2001) 1,260,000. Agra was the capital of the Mogul Empire until 1658. It is the site of the Taj Mahal.

agrar·ian /əˈgrerɪən/ ● *adjective* **1** of or relating to the land or its cultivation. **2** relating to landed property. ● *noun* a person who advocates a redistribution of landed property. [Latin *agrarius* from *ager agri* field]

Agrarian Revolution the transformation of British agriculture during the 18th c., characterized by the acceleration of enclosure of common land, and by the introduction of technological innovations such as the seed drill and the scientific rotation of crops.

agree *verb* (**agrees**, **agreed**, **agree·ing**) **1** *intransitive* hold a similar opinion (*I agree with you about that; they agreed that it would rain*). **2** *intransitive* (often foll. by *to*, or *to* + infin.) consent (*agreed to the arrangement; agreed to go*). **3** *intransitive* (often foll. by *with*) **a** become or be in harmony. **b** suit; be good for (*caviar didn't agree with him*). **c** *Grammar* have the same number, gender, case, or person as. **4** *transitive Brit.* reach agreement about (*agreed a price*). **5** *transitive* consent to or approve of (terms, a proposal, etc.). **6** *transitive* bring (things, esp. accounts) into harmony. **7** *intransitive* (foll. by *on*) decide by mutual consent (*agreed on a compromise*). □ **agree to differ** leave a difference of opinion etc. unresolved. **be agreed** have reached the same opinion. [Old French *agreer*, ultimately from Latin *gratus* pleasing]

agree·able *adjective* **1** pleasant; enjoyable. **2** willing to agree (*was agreeable to going*). **3** (foll. by *to*) acceptable. □ **agree·able·ness** *noun* **agree·ably** *adverb*

agree·ment *noun* **1** the act of agreeing; the holding of the same opinion (*reached agreement*). **2** mutual understanding. **3 a** an arrangement between parties as to a course of action etc. **b** a document outlining such an arrangement. **4** *Grammar* the condition of having the same number, gender, case, or person. **5** a state of being harmonious.

agreement forest *noun Cdn* (in Ontario) a tract of land owned by a municipality, private owner, etc. but managed as forest land by the Ontario Ministry of Natural Resources.

ag rep *noun* (also **ag representative**) *Cdn informal* = AGRICULTURAL REPRESENTATIVE.

agri- *combining form* agriculture, agricultural (*agri-chemical; agribusiness*). [abbreviation]

Agri·bi·tion *noun Cdn* the annual agricultural exhibition in Regina, Saskatchewan. [blend of AGRICULTURE + EXHIBITION]

agri·busi·ness *noun* **1** agriculture conducted on strictly commercial principles, esp. using advanced technology. **2** an organization engaged in this. **3** the group of industries dealing with the produce of, and services to, farming.

Agric·ola /əˈgrɪkələ/ **Gnaeus Jul·ius** (40–93), Roman senator and general, governor of Britain from 78. He extended Roman domination to Scotland and Wales.

agricultural representative *noun Cdn* an employee of an agriculture ministry who advises farmers in a particular region.

agri·cul·ture *noun* the science or practice of cultivating the soil and rearing animals. □ **agri·cul·tur·al** *adjective* **agri·cul·tur·al·ist** *noun* **agri·cul·tur·al·ly** *adverb* **agri·cul·tur·ist** *noun* [Latin *agricultura* from *ager agri* field + *cultura* CULTURE]

agri-food *adjective* esp. *Cdn* (of an industry) concerned with or involved in the production or processing of food.

agri·mony /ˈagrɪˌmɒni/ *noun* (*pl.* **-ies**) any herbaceous plant of the genus *Agrimonia*, with small yellow flowers. [Latin *agrimonia* alteration of *argemonia* from Greek *argemōnē* poppy]

Agrip·pa /əˈgrɪpə/ **1 Mar·cus Vip·san·ius** (64/3–12 BC), Roman general and adviser to Augustus, whose daughter Julia was his third wife. He played an important part in the naval victory over Mark Antony, and paid for the building of baths, aqueducts, and sewers. **2** = HEROD AGRIPPA.

Ag·rip·pina /ˌagrɪˈpiːnə/ **1 the Elder** (*c.*14 BC–AD 33), daughter of Marcus Vipsanius Agrippa, wife of Germanicus, and mother of Caligula. **2** her daughter, **Agrippina the Younger** (AD 15–59), mother of Nero, who had her murdered.

agri-tourism *noun* tourism involving some contact with farmers or farms, including winery tours, farm vacations, pick-your-own operations, farmers' markets, agricultural fairs, etc.

agro *noun Cdn* (*Sask.*) *informal* a student of agricultural science.

agro- *combining form* agricultural (*agro-climatic; agro-ecological*). [Greek *agros* field]

agro·chem·ical *noun* a chemical used in agriculture.

agro·fores·try *noun* agriculture in which there is integrated management of trees or shrubs along with conventional crops or livestock.

agrol·ogy /əˈgrɒlədʒi/ *noun Cdn* the application of science to agriculture. □ **agrol·o·gist** *noun*

agron·omy /əˈgrɒnəmi/ *noun* the science of soil management and crop production. □ **agro·nom·ic** *adjective* **agro·nom·ic·al·ly** *adverb* **agron·o·mist** *noun* [French *agronomie* from Greek *agros* field + *-nomos* from *nemō* arrange]

aground *predicative adjective & adverb* (of a ship) on or onto the bottom of shallow water (*run aground*).

Aguas·ca·lien·tes /ˌagwəskaˈljenteiz/ **1** a state of central Mexico. **2** its capital, a health resort noted for its hot springs; pop. (est. 2000) 594,056.

ague /ˈeigjuː/ *noun* **1** *hist.* a malarial fever, with cold, hot, and sweating stages. **2** a shivering fit. □ **agued** *adjective* [from medieval Latin *acuta* (*febris*) acute (fever)]

Agul·has, Cape /əˈgʌləs/ the most southerly point of the continent of Africa, in the province of Western Cape, South Africa.

Agulhas Current /əˈgʌləs/ an ocean current flowing southward along the east coast of Africa.

AH *abbreviation* of the Muslim era; used to show the year in the Muslim calendar, calculated from the Hegira in AD 622. [Latin *anno Hegirae*]

ah *interjection* expressing surprise, pleasure, sudden realization, resignation, etc.

AHA *abbreviation* ALPHA-HYDROXY ACID.

aha *interjection* expressing discovery, surprise, triumph, mockery, irony, etc.

Ahab /ˈeihab/ *Bible* king of Israel 873–851 BC, and husband of Jezebel.

Ahag·gar Mountains see HOGGAR MOUNTAINS.

ahead *adverb* **1** further forward in space or time. **2** in the lead; further advanced (*ahead 3–1*). **3** in the line of one's forward motion (*construction ahead*). **4** straight forwards. □ **ahead of 1** further forward or advanced than. **2** in the line of the forward motion of. [originally *Naut.*, from A[2] + HEAD]

ahem *interjection* (not usu. clearly articulated) used to attract attention, gain time, or express disapproval.

ahi /ˈaːhi/ *noun* the yellowfin tuna, esp. when caught near Hawaii. [Hawaiian]

ahim·sa /əˈhɪmsɒ/ *noun* (in the Hindu, Buddhist, and Jainist tradition) respect for all living things and avoidance of violence towards others both in thought and deed. [Sanskrit from *a* without + *himsa* injury]

ahis·tor·ic·al *adjective* (also **ahis·tor·ic**) not historic; unrelated to history. □ **ahis·tor·ic·al·ly** *adverb* **ahis·tori·cism** *noun*

AHL *abbreviation* American Hockey League.

Ah·mada·bad /ˈɒmədəˌbad/ (also **Ah·meda·bad**) an industrial city in the state of Gujarat in W India; pop. (2000) 3,515,400.

Consonants: b *but*   d *dog*   f *few*   g *get*   h *her*   j *yes*   k *cat*   l *leg*   m *man*   n *no*   p *pen*   r *red*   s *sit*

-aholic *combining form* (also **-oholic**) denoting addiction (*workaholic*; *chocoholic*). [from ALCOHOLIC]

Ahou·saht /əˈhaʊsət/ *noun* (also **Ahou·sat**) a member of the principal group of Nuu-chah-nulth, living around Clayoquot Sound on the west coast of Vancouver Island. [Nuu-chah-nulth, = 'facing opposite from the ocean']

ahoy *interjection* Naut. a call used to hail a ship or to attract attention. [AH + HOY¹]

Ahri·man /ˈɒrɪmən/ the evil spirit in the dualistic doctrine of Zoroastrianism. [Persian, from Avestan *angramainya* dark or destructive spirit]

Ahura Mazda /əˌhʊrə ˈmazdə/ (later called **Ormazd**) the creator god of ancient Iran (and, in particular, of Zoroastrianism), the force for good and the opponent of Ahriman. [Avestan, = the living wise one]

Ahvaz /ɒˈvɒz/ (also **Ahwaz**) a city in western Iran; pop. (est. 2002) 973,600.

AI *abbreviation* **1** *Computing* artificial intelligence. **2** artificial insemination.

ai /ˈɒɪ/ *noun* (*pl.* **ais**) the three-toed sloth of S America, *Bradypus tridactylus*. [Tupi *ai*, representing its cry]

AID *abbreviation* **1** artificial insemination by donor. **2** Agency for International Development.

aid ● *noun* **1** help. **2** financial or material help, esp. given by one country to another. **3** a material source of help (*teaching aid*). **4** a person or thing that helps. **5** *hist.* a grant of subsidy or tax to a king. ● *transitive verb* **1** (often foll. by *in*) help. **2** promote or encourage (*sleep will aid recovery*). □ **in aid of** in support of. **what's this** (or **all this**) **in aid of?** *informal* what is the purpose of this? [Old French *aide, aidier*, ultimately from Latin *adjuvare* (as AD-, *juvare jut-* help)]

Aidan, St. (d. AD 651), Irish missionary. While a monk in the monastery at Iona he set out to Christianize Northumbria, founding a church and monastery at Lindisfarne in 635 and becoming its first bishop.

aide *noun* **1** an assistant. **2** an aide-de-camp. [short for AIDE-DE-CAMP]

aide-de-camp /ˌeɪd də ˈkɑ̃/ *noun* (*pl.* **aides-de-camp** *pronunc.* same) an officer acting as a confidential assistant to a senior officer. [French = 'camp adjutant']

aide-mémoire /ˌeɪdmeˈmwɑr/ *noun* (*pl.* **aides-mémoire** *pronunc.* same) **1 a** an aid to the memory. **b** a book or document meant to aid the memory. **2** *Diplomacy* a memorandum. [French from *aider* to help + *mémoire* memory]

AIDS *noun* acquired immune deficiency syndrome, a condition caused by a virus transmitted in the blood, marked by severe loss of resistance to infection and so ultimately fatal. [acronym]

AIDS-related complex *noun* a set of symptoms (chronic illness, fever, weight loss, etc.) of a person infected with HIV, which seems to precede the full development of AIDS. Abbr.: **ARC**.

AIDS virus *noun* = HIV.

aig·rette /ˈeɪɡrɛt, eɪˈɡrɛt/ *noun* **1** a tuft of feathers, esp. one worn as a headdress. **2** a spray of gems etc. worn on the head. **3** an egret's white plume. [French]

Aigues-Mortes /eɪɡˈmɔrt/ a town in SE France, in the Rhone delta; pop. (1990) 5,000. The site was chosen by Louis IX as the embarkation port for his two Crusades. The harbour has long been silted up, and the sea is now about 3 miles away. [from Latin *aquae mortuae* dead waters, referring to the saline marshland which surrounds the town]

ai·guille /eɪˈɡwil/ *noun* a sharp peak of rock. [French, lit. 'needle']

ai·guil·lette /ˌeɪɡwiˈlɛt/ *noun* **1** a tagged point hanging from the shoulder on the breast of some uniforms. **2** a thin strip of meat, esp. poultry. [French: see AGLET]

AIH *abbreviation* artificial insemination by husband.

ai·kido /aɪˈkidoʊ, ˈaɪkiˌdoʊ/ *noun* a Japanese form of self-defence and martial art, developed from ju-jitsu and involving holds and throws. [Japanese from *ai* mutual + *ki* mind + *dō* way]

ail *verb* **1** *transitive* trouble or afflict in mind or body (*what ails him?*). **2** *intransitive* be ill or in pain. [Old English *egl(i)an* from *egle* troublesome]

ai·lan·thus /eɪˈlanθəs/ *noun* = TREE OF HEAVEN. [modern Latin *ailantus* from Ambonese *aylanto*]

ail·eron /ˈeɪləˌrɒn/ *noun* a hinged surface in the trailing edge of an airplane wing, used to control lateral balance. [French, diminutive of *aile* wing, from Latin *ala*]

ail·ing *adjective* **1** ill, esp. chronically. **2** in poor condition (*the ailing economy*).

Aille·boust see D'AILLEBOUST.

ail·ment *noun* an illness, esp. a minor one.

AIM *abbreviation* AMERICAN INDIAN MOVEMENT.

aim ● *verb* **1** *intransitive* (foll. by *at* + verbal noun, or *to* + infin.) intend or try (*aim at winning*; *aim to win*). **2** *transitive* (usu. foll. by *at*) direct or point (a weapon, remark, etc.). **3** *intransitive* take aim. **4** *intransitive* (foll. by *at, for*) seek to attain or achieve. ● *noun* **1** a purpose, a design, an object aimed at. **2** the directing of a weapon, missile, etc., at an object. □ **take aim** direct a weapon etc. at an object. [Old French *esmer*, ultimately from Latin *aestimare* reckon]

aim·less *adjective* without aim or purpose. □ **aim·less·ly** *adverb* **aim·less·ness** *noun*

ain't *contraction informal* **1** am not; are not; is not (*you ain't doing it right*; *she ain't nice*). **2** has not; have not (*we ain't seen him*). ¶ Usually regarded as an uneducated use, and unacceptable in spoken and written English, except jocularly or in fixed informal phrases, e.g. *he ain't seen nothing yet!* [contraction of *are not*]

Ain·tree a suburb of Liverpool, site of a racecourse over which the Grand National has been run since 1839.

Ainu /ˈaɪnuː/ ● *noun* **1** (*pl.* same or **Ainus**) a member of the non-Mongoloid aboriginal inhabitants of the Japanese archipelago. **2** their language. ● *adjective* of or pertaining to the Ainu. [Ainu, = man]

aioli /aɪˈjoʊli/ *noun* a garlic mayonnaise, originally a specialty of Provence. [French from Provençal *ai* garlic + *oli* oil]

air ● *noun* **1** an invisible gaseous substance surrounding the earth, a mixture mainly of oxygen and nitrogen. **2 a** the earth's atmosphere. **b** the free or unconfined space in the atmosphere (*birds of the air*; *in the open air*). **c** the atmosphere as a place where aircraft operate. **d** the atmosphere as a medium for transmitting radio waves. **3 a** a distinctive impression or characteristic (*an air of absurdity*). **b** one's manner or bearing, esp. a confident one (*with a triumphant air*). **c** (esp. in *pl.*) an affected manner; pretentiousness (*gave himself airs*; *airs and graces*). **4** *Music* a tune or melody; a melodious composition. **5** a breeze or light wind. **6** *N Amer. informal* air conditioning. **7** (in snowboarding, skateboarding, etc.) a jump which launches one high into the air. ● *verb* **1** *transitive* (usu. foll. by *out*) expose (a room etc.) to the open air; ventilate. **2** *transitive* hang (washed laundry etc.) to remove dampness. **3** *transitive* express publicly (an opinion, grievance, etc.). **4** *transitive & intransitive* broadcast (a program). **5** *transitive* parade; show ostentatiously (esp. qualities). **6** *reflexive* go out in the fresh air. □ **by air** by aircraft; in an aircraft. **in the air** (of opinions or feelings) prevalent; gaining currency. **on** (or **off**) **the air** in (or not in) the process of broadcasting. **take the air** go out of doors. **up in the air 1** aloft. **2** uncertain, undetermined (*his fate is up in the air*). **walk on air** feel elated. [ultimately from Greek *aēr*]

air ambulance *noun* an aircraft specially equipped for transporting the sick or injured to hospital by air, esp. in emergencies.

air·bag *noun* a safety device that fills with air on impact to protect the occupants of a vehicle in a collision.

air ball *noun* *Basketball slang* a shot which results in the ball missing the basket and backboard entirely.

air band *noun* a group of people miming musical performances etc. to the accompaniment of recorded rock or pop music.

air base *noun* a base for the operation of military aircraft.

air bed *noun* an inflatable mattress.

air bladder *noun* **1** a bladder or sac filled with air in fish or some plants (*compare* SWIM BLADDER). **2** any similar bladder or sac made of synthetic material.

air·boat *noun* a flat-bottomed boat with a large propeller mounted above the rear transom generating a rearward thrust of air, capable of travelling very fast and used esp. in shallow and marshy or weedy water but also over ice.

air·borne *adjective* **1** moving through or carried by the air (*airborne pollutants*). **2** (of aircraft) in the air; in flight. **3** (of military activity) involving paratroops.

air brake *noun* **1** a brake worked by air pressure. **2** a movable flap or other device on an aircraft to reduce its speed.

air·brush ● *noun* a device for spraying colour over a surface by means of compressed air, used by artists and to retouch photographs, especially to conceal flaws. ● *transitive verb* **1** paint with an airbrush. **2** gloss over or hide (flaws etc.). □ **air·brushed** *adjective*

air chief marshal *noun* (also **Air Chief Marshal**) **1** *hist.* the highest rank in the RCAF. **2** (in the UK) an RAF officer of high rank, below marshal of the RAF and above air marshal.

air command *noun* **1** a major subdivision of an air force (*Strategic Air*

Command). **2** (**Air Command**) the official name for the Canadian air force.

air commodore *noun* (also **Air Commodore**) (currently in the RAF or *hist.* in the RCAF) an officer above group captain and below air vice marshal.

air-con *noun* esp. *Brit.* air conditioning or an air conditioner.

air-conditioned *adjective* (of a room, building, etc.) equipped with air conditioning.

air conditioner *noun* an air conditioning apparatus.

air conditioning *noun* **1** a system for lowering the temperature and humidity in a building or vehicle. **2** the apparatus for this.

air-cool *transitive verb* cool (an engine etc.) by means of a current of air. □ **air-cooled** *adjective*

air corridor *noun* = CORRIDOR 5.

air·craft *noun* (*pl.* same) a machine capable of flight, esp. an airplane or helicopter.

aircraft carrier *noun* a warship that carries and serves as a base for airplanes.

air·craft·man *noun* (*pl.* **-men**) (also **Aircraftman**) (currently in the RAF or *hist.* in the RCAF) an airman of the lowest rank. Abbr.: **AC**. In the RCAF, the three lowest ranks were **aircraftman second class**, **aircraftman first class**, and **leading aircraftman**.

air·craft·woman *noun* (*pl.* **-women**) (also **Aircraftwoman**) (currently in the WRAF or *hist.* in the RCAF) an airwoman of the lowest rank.

air·crew *noun* **1** the crew of an aircraft. **2** (*pl.* **air·crew**) a member of such a crew.

air cushion *noun* **1** an inflatable cushion. **2** the layer of air supporting a hovercraft or similar vehicle. **3** a layer of air in the sole of a shoe. □ **air-cush·ioned** *adjective*

air·date *noun* the date on which a television or radio program is aired.

Air·drie /'erdri/ a city in SW Alberta, about 25 km north of Calgary; pop. (2001) 20,382. □ **Air·drite** *noun* **Air·dro·nian** *noun* [*Airdrie*, a town in Scotland]

air·drop ● *transitive verb* deliver (food, supplies, etc.) by parachute from an aircraft. ● *noun* a delivery in this way.

air-dry *transitive & intransitive verb* dry (clothing, hair, etc.), or become dry, by exposure to air without added heat.

Aire·dale *noun* a large breed of terrier with a rough coat. [*Airedale* in Yorkshire, England]

air·fare *noun* the price paid by a passenger for transportation by air.

air·field *noun* an area of land where aircraft take off and land, are maintained, etc.

air·flow *noun* a current of air, esp. that encountered by a moving aircraft or vehicle.

air·foil *noun* N *Amer.* a structure with curved surfaces, e.g. a wing, fin, or tailplane, designed to give lift in flight. [AIR + FOIL²]

air force *noun* the branch of a nation's armed forces concerned with fighting or defence in the air.

air force blue *noun* a shade of blue between teal blue and slate blue.

air·frame *noun* the body of an aircraft as distinct from its engine(s).

air freight ● *noun* the transport of goods by air. ● *transitive verb* (usu. **air·freight**) transport goods by air.

air freshener *noun* a fragrant spray or solid used to mask odours in a room, car, etc.

air·glow *noun* radiation from the upper atmosphere, visible at night.

air guitar *noun* an imaginary guitar which one mimes playing while listening to pop music.

air gun *noun* a gun using compressed air to propel pellets etc.

air·head *noun* **1** *Military* a base for aircraft in enemy territory. **2** *slang* usu. *derogatory* a foolish or unintelligent person. □ **air·head·ed** *adjective*

air hockey *noun* N *Amer.* a game in which players use hand-held paddles to direct a plastic disc supported on a cushion of air over an oblong surface, often a large table, into the opponent's goal.

air horn *noun* a horn which produces sound by compressed air.

air hostess *noun* *Brit.* a female flight attendant.

air·ing *noun* **1** exposure to fresh air, esp. for exercise or an excursion. **2** exposure (of laundry etc.) to warm air. **3** public expression of an opinion etc. (*the idea will get an airing at tomorrow's meeting*).

air-kiss *transitive verb* pretend to kiss (someone or something) while actually kissing the air, e.g. near their cheek. □ **air kiss** *noun* **air-kisser** *noun* **air-kiss·ing** *noun*

air lane *noun* a path or course regularly used by aircraft (*compare* LANE 4).

air·less *adjective* **1** stuffy; not ventilated. **2** without wind or breeze; still. □ **air·less·ness** *noun*

air letter *noun* a sheet of light paper forming a letter for sending by airmail.

air·lift ● *noun* the transport of troops and supplies by air, esp. in a blockade or other emergency. ● *transitive verb* transport in this way.

air·line *noun* **1** an organization providing a regular public service of air transport on one or more routes. **2** (usu. **air line**) a pipe or hose supplying air, esp. to a diver.

air·liner *noun* a large passenger aircraft.

air·lock *noun* **1** a stoppage of the flow in a pump or pipe, caused by an air bubble. **2** a compartment with controlled pressure and parallel sets of doors, to permit movement between areas at different pressures.

air·mail ● *noun* **1** a system of transporting mail by air. **2** mail carried by air. ● *transitive verb* send by airmail.

air·man *noun* (*pl.* **-men**) **1** a pilot or member of the crew of an aircraft, esp. in an air force. **2** a member of an air force below commissioned rank.

air marshal *noun* **1** (also **Air Marshal**) (currently in the RAF or *hist.* in the RCAF) an officer of high rank, below air chief marshal and above air vice marshal. **2** = SKY MARSHAL.

air mass *noun* a very large body of air with a roughly uniform temperature and humidity.

air mattress *noun* an inflatable mattress for sleeping on or for floating on water.

air·mobile *adjective* (of troops etc.) that can be moved about by air.

air photo *noun* an aerial photograph.

air·plane *noun* a powered heavier-than-air flying vehicle with fixed wings.

air plant *noun* a plant growing naturally without soil, e.g. an epiphyte.

air·play *noun* broadcasting (of recorded music).

air pocket *noun* **1** an apparent vacuum in the air causing an aircraft to drop suddenly. **2** (in soil, a pipe, etc.) any bubble of air.

air·port *noun* a complex of runways and buildings for the takeoff, landing, and maintenance of civil aircraft, with facilities for passengers.

air power *noun* the ability to defend and attack by means of aircraft, missiles, etc.

air pump *noun* a device for pumping air into or out of a vessel, room, etc.

air purifier *noun* a small electrical appliance which draws air through a filter to remove impurities.

air quality *noun* the degree to which the ambient air is pollution-free, assessed by measuring a number of indicators of pollution, e.g. ozone, nitrogen dioxide, etc.

air quality index *noun* a numerical indicator of the concentration of pollutants in the air.

air radio *noun* (also **aeradio**) *Cdn* a government-operated radio service which broadcasts flight advisory information for pilots and provides air-to-ground communication.

air rage *noun* aggressive or violent behaviour on board an aircraft.

air raid *noun* (also **air strike**) an attack by military aircraft (also *attributive*: *air-raid siren*).

air rifle *noun* a rifle using compressed air to propel pellets etc.

air rights *plural noun* *Law* ownership rights to the air space above a property.

air sac *noun* **1** an extension of the lungs in birds or the tracheae in insects. **2** a lung compartment containing air.

air·screw *noun* *Brit.* an aircraft propeller.

air-sea rescue *noun* rescue from the sea by aircraft.

air·shed *noun* the mass of air over a specific geographical area (*the Fraser Valley airshed*).

air·ship *noun* a powered balloon that can be steered, esp. one having a rigid elongated structure.

air show *noun* a public display of aircraft or aerobatics.

air·sick *adjective* affected with nausea due to travel in an aircraft. □ **air·sick·ness** *noun*

air·some *adjective* *Cdn* (*Nfld*) cold; invigorating.

Vowels: a *cat* ɑ *arm* e *bed* ɜr *her* ɜː *deux* ə *ago* ɪ *sit* i *cosy* iː *feed* ɒ *hot* ɔ *pore* oː *no* ʌ *run* ʊ *put*

air·space *noun* **1** the air available to aircraft to fly in, esp. the part subject to the jurisdiction of a particular country. **2** (usu. **air space**) a space filled with (usu. trapped) air, as between two panes of glass etc. **3** (usu. **air space**) *Law* the space above a piece of land or the buildings constructed on it, extending notionally indefinitely upwards.

air·speed *noun* the speed of an aircraft relative to the air through which it is moving (*compare* GROUNDSPEED).

air·stream *noun* a current of air; an airflow.

air strike *noun* = AIR RAID.

air·strip *noun* a strip of ground suitable for the takeoff and landing of aircraft.

air·tight ● *adjective* **1** not allowing air to pass through. **2** without weakness; unassailable (*an airtight argument*). **●** *noun* (also **airtight stove**) a wood stove in which the air enters through a controlled damper and the door is gasketed to prevent air leaks so that almost all the oxygen is consumed in the combustion of the wood.

air·time *noun* **1** time allotted for a broadcast, commercial, etc. **2** the starting time for a television or radio program. **3** time spent using a cellular phone.

air-to-air *adjective* from one aircraft to another in flight.

air-to-ground *adjective* (also **air-to-surface**) from an aircraft in flight to the earth (*air-to-surface missile*).

air traffic control *noun* an airport department which controls air traffic by giving radio instructions to pilots concerning route, altitude, takeoff, and landing. □ **air traffic controller** *noun*

air·tram *noun Cdn* (*BC*) an aerial cable car.

air·vac ● *noun* evacuation by air ambulance. **●** *transitive verb* (**air·vac·ed**, **air·vac·ing**) evacuate by air ambulance.

air vice marshal *noun* (also **Air Vice Marshal**) (currently in the RAF or *hist.* in the RCAF) an officer of high rank, just below air marshal.

air·waves *plural noun* radio waves used in broadcasting.

air·way *noun* **1 a** a recognized route followed by aircraft. **b** (often in *pl.*) = AIRLINE 1. **2** *Med.* **a** the normal passage for air into the lungs. **b** a tubular device for assisting a patient's breathing. **3** a ventilating passage in a mine.

air·woman *noun* (*pl.* **-women**) **1** a woman pilot or member of the crew of an aircraft, esp. in an air force. **2** (in the UK) a member of the WRAF below commissioned rank.

air·worthy *adjective* (of an aircraft) fit to fly. □ **air·worth·i·ness** *noun*

airy *adjective* (**air·i·er**, **air·i·est**) **1** well-ventilated, breezy. **2** flippant, superficial. **3 a** light as air. **b** graceful, delicate. **4** insubstantial, ethereal, immaterial. □ **air·i·ly** *adverb* **air·i·ness** *noun*

airy-fairy *adjective informal* **1** unrealistic, impractical, foolishly idealistic. **2** light and delicate.

Aisha /ɒˈiːʃə/ (also **Ayesha**) (611–78), the favourite wife of Muhammad, and daughter of Abu-Bakr.

aisle /aɪl/ *noun* **1 a** a passage between rows of pews, seats, etc. **b** a passage between rows of shelves in a supermarket etc. **2** part of a church, esp. one parallel to and divided by pillars from the nave, choir, or transept. □ **roll in the aisles** *see* ROLL. □ **aisled** *adjective* [Middle English *ele*, *ile* from Old French *ele* from Latin *ala* wing: confused with *island* and French *aile* wing]

aitch *noun* the name of the letter H (*drop one's aitches*). [Old French *ache*]

Ait·ken ▶ 1 Rob·ert Mor·ris (b.1939), Canadian composer and flutist. His compositions are highly original and experiment with timbre and technique. **2 Wil·liam Max·well**, *see* BEAVERBROOK.

Aivi·lik /aɪˈvɪlɪk/ *noun* the dialect of Inuktitut of the Aivilingmiut. [Inuktitut, = 'the place that has walrus']

Aivi·ling·miut /aɪvɪˈlɪŋmɪʌt/ *noun* (also **Aivilik Inuit**) a southern branch of the Iglulik Inuit, occupying the northwestern Hudson Bay area. [Inuktitut, = 'people of Aivilik']

Aix-en-Provence /ˌeiksɑ̃prɒˈvɑ̃s/ a city of Provence in S France; pop. (1999) 134,222.

Aix-la-Chapelle /ˌekslaʃaˈpel/ **1** see AACHEN. **2 Treaty of** (1748) a peace treaty which ended the War of the Austrian Succession (also known as King George's War), returning Louisbourg to the French, who had lost it to the English three years previously.

aiyee *interjection* expressing great alarm.

Aizawl /ˈaidʒəl/ a city in the far northeast of India, capital of the state of Mizoram; pop. (2001) 229,700.

Ajac·cio /əˈdʒatsɪˌoː/ a port on the west coast of Corsica; pop. (1999) 52,880. The capital of Corsica until 1975, it is now the capital of the southern department of Corse-du-Sud. Napoleon I was born there in 1769.

Ajanta Caves /əˈdʒʌntə/ a series of caves in the state of Maharashtra, south central India, containing Buddhist frescoes and sculptures dating from the 1st c. BC to the 7th c. AD.

ajar¹ *adverb & predicative adjective* (of a door) slightly open. [A² + obsolete *char* from Old English *cerr* a turn]

ajar² *adverb & predicative adjective* out of harmony. [A² + JAR²]

Ajax¹ a town in S Ontario, situated on Lake Ontario, about 30 km east of Toronto; pop. (2001) 73,753. □ **Aja·cian** /əˈdʒeisiən/ *noun* [HMS *Ajax*, British cruiser]

Ajax² *Gk Legend* **1** a Greek hero of the Trojan War who went mad with jealousy and committed suicide when Agamemnon recognized Odysseus as the greatest Greek warrior by awarding him the dead Achilles' armour. **2** a Greek hero who, for his arrogance, was shipwrecked and killed by Poseidon on his way home from Troy.

Ajman /adʒˈmɒn/ **1** the smallest of the seven emirates of the United Arab Emirates; pop. (est. 2000) 174,000. **2** its capital city.

AK *abbreviation* Alaska (in official postal use).

AK-47 *noun* a Soviet-designed assault rifle, widely used by Communist and guerrilla armies. [Russian (*Avtomat* automatic rifle + KALASHNIKOV name of designer)]

a.k.a. *abbreviation* also known as.

Akan /ˈɒkən/ **●** *noun* **1** (*pl.* same or **Akans**) a member of a people inhabiting Ghana and neighbouring regions of West Africa. **2** their language. **●** *adjective* of or relating to the Akan or their language.

Akbar /ˈakbər/ **Jalal·udin Muham·mad** (1542–1605), Mogul emperor of India. He extended the Mogul Empire over most of India and established administrative efficiency, a coherent commercial system, and religious toleration.

akee *var. of* ACKEE.

Akela /əˈkeilə/ *noun* the adult leader of a group of Cubs. [name of the leader of a wolf pack in Kipling's *Jungle Book*]

Akhe·naten /ˌɑːkəˈnɒtən/ ('Glory of the Sun') the name taken by Amenhotep IV (14th c. BC), the first Egyptian pharaoh to advocate the recognition of Aten (sun disc) as the sole deity, with the king as his only intermediary.

Akhe·taten /ˌɑːkəˈtɒtən/ an ancient Egyptian capital at Tell el-Amarna (see AMARNA, TELL EL-).

Akh·mat·ova /akˈmɒtəvə/ **Anna** (pseudonym of Anna Andreevna Gorenko) (1889–1966), Russian poet, who favoured concrete detail, direct expression, and precision of language as a reaction against the mysticism of contemporary symbolist poetry.

Aki·hito /ˌakiˈhiːtoː/ (b.1933), emperor of Japan from 1989, the son of Hirohito.

akim·bo /əˈkɪmboː/ *adverb* (of the arms) with hands on the hips and elbows turned outwards. [Middle English *in kenebowe*, prob. from Old Norse]

Aki·miski Island /ˌakəˈmɪskɪ/ an island on the west side of James Bay, opposite the mouth of the Attawapiskat River. It is administered by Nunavut. [Cree, = land across]

akin *predicative adjective* **1** related by blood. **2** (usu. foll. by *to*) of similar or kindred character. [A⁴ + KIN]

Akita /əˈkiːtə/ *noun* a breed of Japanese dog, similar to a spitz. [Japanese *Akita* a district in N Japan]

Akkad /ˈakad/ the capital city (as yet undiscovered) which gave its name to an ancient kingdom in N central Mesopotamia (modern Iraq). Traditionally founded by Sargon (2334–2279 BC), it was overwhelmed by invading tribes from the east *c.*2150 BC.

Ak·kad·ian /əˈkeidiən/ (also **Ac·cad·ian**) **●** *noun* **1** the Semitic language of Akkad. **2** an inhabitant of Akkad. **●** *adjective* of Akkad or its people or language.

Akko *see* ACRE.

Akron /ˈakrən/ a city in NE Ohio; pop. (2000) 217,074. It is a centre of the rubber industry.

Aksai Chin /ˌaksai ˈtʃɪn/ a region of the Himalayas occupied by China since 1950, but claimed by India as part of Kashmir.

Aksum /ˈɒksəm/ (also **Axum**) a town in the province of Tigray in N Ethiopia. It was a religious centre and the capital of a powerful kingdom between the 1st and 6th c. AD. □ **Aksum·ite** *noun*

akva·vit *var. of* AQUAVIT.

Ak·we·sasne /ˌakwəˈsasnei/ a Mohawk Indian reserve near Cornwall, Ont., with territory in Ontario, Quebec, and New York State. [Mohawk, lit. 'where the partridge drums']

AL *abbreviation* **1** Alabama (in official postal use). **2** *Baseball* American League.

Al *symbol Chem.* the element aluminum.

al- *prefix assimilated form of* AD- before *-l*.

-al *suffix* **1** forming adjectives meaning 'relating to, of the kind of': **a** from Latin or Greek words (*central*; *regimental*; *colossal*; *tropical*) (*compare* -IAL, -ICAL). **b** from English nouns (*tidal*). **2** forming nouns, esp. of verbal action (*animal*; *rival*; *arrival*; *proposal*; *trial*). [sense 1 from French *-el* or Latin *-alis* adj. suffix related to *-aris* (-AR¹); sense 2 from French *-aille* or from (or after) Latin *-alis* etc. used as noun]

Ala. *abbreviation* Alabama.

à la *preposition* after the manner of (*à la russe*). [French, from À LA MODE]

Al·a·bama a state in the southeastern US, on the Gulf of Mexico; pop. (2000) 4,447,100; capital, Montgomery. □ **Al·a·baman** *adjective & noun* **Al·a·bam·i·an** *adjective & noun*

al·a·bas·ter /ˈaləˌbastər, ˌaləˈb-/ ● *noun* a translucent usu. white form of gypsum, often carved into ornaments. ● *adjective* **1** of alabaster. **2** like alabaster in whiteness or smoothness. □ **al·a·bas·trine** /-ˈbastrɪn/ *adjective* [Latin *alabaster*, *-trum*, from Greek *alabastos*]

à la carte *adverb & adjective* ordered as separately priced item(s) from a menu, not as part of a set meal (*compare* TABLE D'HÔTE). [French]

alack *interjection* (also **alack-a-day** /əˈlakəˌdei/) *archaic* an expression of regret or surprise. [prob. from AH + LACK]

alac·rity /əˈlakrɪti/ *noun* speed or willingness (*he accepted with alacrity*). [Latin *alacritas* from *alacer* brisk]

Alad·din the hero of a story in the *Arabian Nights*, who acquired a lamp which when rubbed produced a genie to do the will of the owner.

Aladdin's cave *noun* a place of great riches.

Aladdin's lamp *noun* a talisman enabling its holder to gratify any wish.

Alain-Fournier /aˈlãˈ furˈnjei/ (pseudonym of Henri-Alban Fournier) (1886–1914), French novelist. His only novel, *Le Grand Meaulnes* (1913), is a lyrical semi-autobiographical narrative set in the countryside of his adolescence.

à la king *adjective* (of poultry etc.) served in a creamy sauce with cooked mushrooms and pimento.

Ala·mein *see* EL ALAMEIN, BATTLE OF.

Alamo /ˈaləmoː/ a mission in San Antonio, Texas, besieged by Mexican forces in 1836 during the Texan struggle for independence from Mexico. It was defended by a handful of volunteers (including Davy Crockett), all of whom were killed.

à la mode /ˌa lə ˈmoːd, ˌɒ lə-/ *adjective* **1** in fashion; fashionable. **2 a** *N Amer.* (of desserts) served with ice cream. **b** (of beef) braised in wine and served with vegetables. [French, = in the fashion]

alan·ine /ˈaləniːn/ *noun* a hydrophobic amino acid present in proteins. [German *Alanin*]

Al-Anon a mutual support organization for the families and friends of alcoholics.

Alar /ˈeilar/ *noun proprietary* a growth-regulating chemical used as a spray on fruit trees to improve the quality of the crop. [20th c.: origin unknown]

alar /ˈeilər/ *adjective* **1** relating to wings. **2** wing-like or wing-shaped. **3** *Bot.* axillary. [Latin *alaris* from *ala* wing]

Alar·cón /ˌalarˈkɒn/ **Pedro An·tonio de** (1833–91), Spanish prose writer whose humorous short story *The Three-cornered Hat* (1874) was used as the basis for a ballet by Massine and de Falla (*Le Tricorne*), and for Hugo Wolf's opera *Der Corregidor*.

Al·aric /ˈalərɪk/ (*c.*370–410), king of the Visigoths who unsuccessfully invaded Greece (395–96) and Italy (400–403) before capturing and sacking Rome in 410.

alarm ● *noun* **1** a warning of danger etc. (*gave the alarm*). **2 a** a sound or device to warn, alert, or signal (*a burglar alarm*). **b** a buzzer etc. on a clock or watch. **c** = ALARM CLOCK. **3 a** frightened expectation of danger or difficulty (*were filled with alarm*). **b** worry, concern, uneasiness. **4** a notification sent to a fire station to dispatch a specified minimum number of fire trucks to a fire, the number of alarms indicating the seriousness of the fire. ● *transitive verb* **1** frighten or disturb. **2** arouse to a sense of danger. [Italian *allarme* from *all'arme!* to arms]

alarm bell *noun* **1** a bell rung as a warning of danger. **2** a thing which alerts people to possible problems or danger and causes anxiety (*the proposal has set alarm bells ringing*).

alarm clock *noun* a clock with a device that can be made to sound at a certain time, usu. to rouse a person from sleep.

alarmed *adjective* **1** frightened or disturbed. **2** fitted or protected with an alarm.

alarm·ing *adjective* disturbing, frightening. □ **alarm·ing·ly** *adverb*

alarm·ist ● *noun* a person given to spreading needless alarm. ● *adjective* creating needless alarm. □ **alarm·ism** *noun*

alar·um /əˈlarəm/ *noun archaic* = ALARM. □ **alarums and excursions** *jocular* confused noise and bustle.

alas /əˈlas/ *interjection* an expression of regret, sorrow, pity, or concern. [Old French *a las(se)* from *a* ah + *las(se)* from Latin *lassus* weary]

Al·as·ka the largest state of the US, in the extreme northwest of N America, with coasts on the Arctic Ocean, Bering Sea, and N Pacific; pop. (2000) 626,932; capital, Juneau. □ **Al·as·kan** *noun & adjective*

Alaska, Gulf of a part of the NE Pacific between the Alaska Peninsula and the Alexander Archipelago.

Alaska Highway a highway constructed by the US Army between 1942–43. Formerly called the Alcan Highway, it extends over 2 400 km (1,490 miles) from Dawson Creek, BC, to Fairbanks, Alaska.

Alaska Peninsula a peninsula on the south coast of Alaska. It extends southwestward into the NE Pacific, between the Bering Sea and the Gulf of Alaska, and is continued in the Aleutian Islands.

Alaska Time *noun* a time zone covering most of Alaska, nine hours behind Greenwich Mean Time.

alate /ˈeileit/ *adjective* having wings or wing-like appendages. [Latin *alatus* from *ala* wing]

alb *noun* a white vestment reaching to the feet, worn by some Christian clergy at church ceremonies. [Latin *albus* white]

Alba /ˈalbə/ *see* ALVA.

alba·core /ˈalbəˌkɔr/ *noun* **1** a long-finned tuna, *Thunnus alalunga*. **2** any of various other related fish. [Portuguese *albacor*, *-cora*, from Arabic *al* the + *bakr* young camel, or *bakūr* premature, precocious]

Alban /ˈɒlbən/ **St.** (3rd c.), the first British martyr. After sheltering the priest who had baptized him, he was beheaded by the Romans on the site of the town outside London which now bears his name.

Al·bani /ɒlˈbɒni/ **Dame Emma** (stage name of Marie-Louise-Cécile-Emma Lajeunesse, 1847–1930), Canadian soprano, the first Canadian-born performer to become known in international opera, oratorio, and concert singing.

Al·ban·ia /alˈbeiniə/ a republic in SE Europe, bordering on the Adriatic Sea; pop. (est. 2002) 3,545,000; capital, Tirana. □ **Al·ban·i·an** *noun & adjective*

Al·bany /ˈɒlbəni/ the state capital of New York, on the Hudson River; pop. (2000) 95,658.

Albany River a river in N Ontario flowing over 980 km (610 miles) from Lake St. Joseph into James Bay, an important transportation route during the fur trade. [James, Duke of York and *Albany*: see JAMES II 2]

alba·tross /ˈalbəˌtrɒs/ *noun* **1** any of several large, long-winged, tube-nosed, stout-bodied birds of the family Diomedeidae, which spend most of their lives at sea, coming ashore only to nest. **2** a source of frustration or guilt; an encumbrance. **3** *Brit. Golf* a score of three strokes under par at any hole. [alteration (after Latin *albus* white) of 17th-c. *alcatras*, applied to various seabirds, from Spanish and Portuguese *alcatraz*, var. of Portuguese *alcatruz* from Arabic *alḳādūs* the pitcher]

al·bedo /alˈbiːdoː/ *noun* (*pl.* **-bedos**) the proportion of light or radiation reflected by a surface, esp. of a planet or moon. [ecclesiastical Latin, = whiteness, from Latin *albus* white]

Albee /ˈalbiː/ **Ed·ward Frank·lin** (b.1928), US playwright whose later works explore sexual fantasy, frustration, and domestic anguish. His best-known play is *Who's Afraid of Virginia Woolf?* (1962).

al·beit /ɒlˈbiːət/ *conjunction* though (*an improvement, albeit a modest one*). [ALL *adverb* + BE + IT *pronoun*, = although it be (that)]

Al·béniz /ˌalˈbeiniθ/ **Isaac** (1860–1909), Spanish composer and pianist. Much of his music, like the piano suite *Iberia*, is inspired by Spanish folk melodies.

Al·bers /ˈalbərz/ **Josef** (1888–1976), German-born US artist, designer, and teacher. He used simple geometric shapes in his furniture designs (which include the first laminated chair for mass production) and in his pictures.

Al·bert, Prince (1819–61), prince of Saxe-Coburg-Gotha, husband to Queen Victoria. He was one of the forces behind the Great Exhibition of 1851 and was instrumental in keeping Britain out of the American Civil War.

Albert I (1875–1934), king of the Belgians 1909–34, who led the Belgian army during the First World War.

Albert II (b.1934), king of the Belgians since 1993.

Albert, Lake a lake in the Rift Valley of east central Africa, on the border between Congo (formerly Zaire) and Uganda. It is linked to Lake Edward by the Semliki River and to the White Nile by the Albert Nile.

Consonants: b *but*   d *dog*   f *few*   g *get*   h *her*   j *yes*   k *cat*   l *leg*   m *man*   n *no*   p *pen*   r *red*   s *sit*

Al·ber·ta a Prairie province in W Canada, bounded on the south by the US and on the west by the Rocky Mountains; pop. (2001) 2,974,807; capital, Edmonton. □ **Al·ber·tan** /alˈbɜrtən/ *adjective & noun* [see ALBERTA, DISTRICT OF]

Alberta, District of *hist.* a provisional district (1882–1905) of the North-West Territories occupying what is now the southern half of the province of Alberta. [Princess Louise Caroline *Alberta*, 4th daughter of Queen Victoria and wife of the Marquess of Lorne, d.1939]

Alberta, Mount a mountain in W Alberta, situated in the Rocky Mountains, in Jasper National Park (3 620 m). [as ALBERTA]

Alberta clipper *noun* *Meteorol.* a low-pressure system forming over Alberta in winter and moving rapidly (usu. 50-60 km/h) southeastward towards New England, often bringing heavy snow.

Alberta Family Day *noun* the official name of FAMILY DAY.

Alberta spruce *noun* a dwarf, cone-shaped variety of the white spruce, *Picea glauca (Conica)*, with dense bright green foliage.

Al·ber·ti /alˈberti/ **Leon Bat·tis·ta** (1404–72), Italian architect, humanist, painter, writer on art, poet, and musician. He designed the facade of Santa Maria Novella in Florence.

al·ber·tite /ˈalbɜrtəit/ *noun* a jet-black, almost infusible form of bitumen found in New Brunswick. [from *Albert* County, New Brunswick + -ITE¹]

al·ber·to·saur·us /alˈbɜrtəˈsɔrəs/ *noun* a large carnivorous dinosaur resembling *Tyrannosaurus*. [from ALBERTA (where its fossilized remains were first discovered) + Greek *sauros* lizard]

Al·ber·tus Mag·nus, St. (*c*.1206–80), Dominican theologian, philosopher, and scientist, a pioneer in the study of Aristotle and teacher of Thomas Aquinas.

Albi /albi/ a town in S France; pop. (1999) 46,300. It was the birthplace, in the 12th c., of the Albigensian movement.

Al·bi·gen·ses /ˌalbɪˈdʒensiːz/ *plural noun* the members of an ascetic Christian sect in S France in the 12th–13th c. Considered heretical, the group was ruthlessly crushed in a crusade (1209–1231).
□ **Al·bi·gen·sian** *adjective & noun* [Latin from ALBI]

al·bino /alˈbaɪnoʊ/ *noun* (pl. **-binos**) **1** a person or animal having a congenital absence of pigment in the skin and hair (which are white), and the eyes (which are usu. pink). **2** a plant lacking normal colouring. □ **al·bin·ism** /ˈalbɪˌnɪzəm/ *noun* **al·bin·otic** /ˌalbɪˈnɒtɪk/ *adjective* [Spanish & Portuguese (originally applied to albinos among black Africans) from *albo* Latin from *albus* white + -ino = -INE¹]

Al·bin·oni /ˌalbɪˈnoʊni/ **Tom·aso** (1671–1751), Italian composer. The popular *Adagio* for organ and strings, attributed to him, was in fact constructed by a 20th-c. musicologist from a manuscript fragment.

Al·binus see ALCUIN.

Al·bion /ˈalbiən/ *noun* (also **perfidious Albion**) Britain or England. [Old English from Latin from Celtic *Albio* (unrecorded): French *la perfide Albion* with reference to alleged treachery to other nations]

al·bite /ˈalbəit/ *noun* a feldspar, usu. white, rich in sodium. [Latin *albus* white + -ITE¹]

Al·boin /ˈalbɔɪn/ (d.572), king of the Lombards *c*.565–72, who led the Lombard invasion of N Italy.

al·bum /ˈalbəm/ *noun* **1** a blank book for the insertion of photographs, stamps, etc. **2 a** a disc or tape comprising several pieces of music. **b** an integral set of discs or tapes. [Latin, = a blank tablet, neuter of *albus* white]

al·bu·men /ˈalˈbjuːmɪn/ *noun* **1** egg white. **2** *Bot.* the substance found between the skin and germ of many seeds, usu. the edible part; = ENDOSPERM. [Latin *albumen -minis* white of egg, from *albus* white]

al·bu·min /ˈalˈbjuːmɪn/ *noun* any of a class of water-soluble proteins found in egg white, milk, blood, etc. □ **al·bu·min·ous** /alˈbjuːmɪnəs/ *adjective* [French *albumine* from Latin *albumin-*: see ALBUMEN]

al·bu·min·oid /alˈbjuːmɪˌnɔɪd/ *noun* = SCLEROPROTEIN.

al·bu·min·uria /ˌalbjuːmɪˈnjʊriə/ *noun* the presence of albumin in the urine, usu. as a symptom of kidney disease.

album-oriented rock *noun* a type of popular music in which a hard rock background is combined with softer, more melodic elements.

Albu·quer·que¹ /ˈalbəˌkɜrki/ the largest city in the state of New Mexico; pop. (2000) 448,607. □ **Albu·quer·quean** *noun*

Albu·quer·que² /ˈalbəˌkɜrki/ **Al·fonso de** (1453–1515), Portuguese colonial statesman. As Viceroy of the Portuguese Indies he conquered and administered Goa, Ceylon, Malacca, Ormuz, and other settlements.

al·bur·num /alˈbɜrnəm/ *noun* = SAPWOOD. [Latin *albus* white]

al·ca·hest *var. of* ALKAHEST.

Al·calá de He·nares /ˌalkaˈla θe eˈnares/ a city in central Spain, on the River Henares, 25 km northeast of Madrid; pop. (est. 2001) 172,418.

al·calde /ɒlˈkɒldei/ *noun* a magistrate or mayor in a Spanish, Portuguese, or Latin American city or town. [Spanish from Arabic *al-ḳāḍī* the judge: see QADI]

Alcan Highway see ALASKA HIGHWAY. [ALASKA + CANADA¹]

Alca·traz /ˈalkəˌtraz/ a rocky island in San Francisco Bay, California. It was, between 1934 and 1963, the site of a top-security Federal prison. [from Spanish *álcatraces* pelicans, which once inhabited the island]

Al·ces·tis /alˈsestɪs/ *Gk Legend* wife of Admetus, king of Pherae in Thessaly, whose life she saved by consenting to die on his behalf. She was brought back from Hades by Hercules.

al·chemy /ˈalkəmi/ *noun* **1** the medieval forerunner of chemistry, esp. seeking to turn base metals into gold or silver. **2** a miraculous transformation or the means of achieving this. □ **al·chem·ic** /alˈkemɪk/ *adjective* **al·chem·ical** /alˈkemɪkəl/ *adjective* **al·chem·ist** *noun* **al·chem·ize** *transitive verb* (also esp. *Brit.* **-ise**). [medieval Latin *alchimia*, from Arabic *alkīmiyā'* from *al* the + *kīmiyā'* from Greek *khēmia*, *-meia* art of transmuting metals]

Al·ci·bi·ades /ˌalsɪˈbaɪədiːz/ (*c*.450–404 BC) Athenian general, statesman, and friend of Socrates. He fought for both Athens and Sparta in the Peloponnesian War, was ultimately forced from Athens, and was assassinated in Phrygia.

alcid /ˈalsɪd/ *noun* a bird of the auk family, Alcidae. [modern Latin *Alcidae* from *Alca* genus name (as AUK)]

Alc·mene /alkˈmiːni/ *Gk Myth* the mother of Hercules by Zeus, who visited her disguised as her husband, Amphitryon.

Al·cock, Sir John Wil·liam (1892–1919), English aviator. In 1919, with Sir Arthur Whitten Brown, he made the first direct non-stop transatlantic flight (16 hours 27 minutes), from Newfoundland to Ireland.

al·co·hol *noun* **1** (in full **ethyl alcohol**) a colourless volatile inflammable liquid forming the intoxicating element in wine, beer, spirits, etc., and also used as a solvent, as fuel, etc. *Also called* ETHANOL. Chem. formula: C_2H_5OH. **2** any liquor containing this. **3** *Chem.* any of a large class of organic compounds that contain one or more hydroxyl groups attached to carbon atoms. [Arabic *al-kuḥl* from *al* the + *kuḥl* KOHL]

al·co·hol·ic ● *adjective* of, relating to, containing, or caused by alcohol. ● *noun* a person suffering from alcoholism.

Alcoholics Anonymous an organization of alcoholics who attempt to overcome their addiction by counselling and mutual support. Abbr.: **AA**.

al·co·hol·ism *noun* **1** an addiction to the consumption of alcoholic liquor. **2** the diseased condition resulting from this.

al·co·hol·om·eter /ˌalkəhɒˈlɒmɪtər/ *noun* an instrument for measuring alcoholic concentration. □ **al·co·hol·om·etry** *noun*

al·cool /ˈalkuːl/ *noun* *Cdn* (esp. *Que.*) a colourless, unflavoured alcoholic spirit distilled from cereal grains. [French, = alcohol]

Al·cott /ˈalkɒt/ **Lou·isa May** (1832–88), US novelist. Her most popular novel is *Little Women* (1868–69), a largely autobiographical work concerning a New England family.

al·cove *noun* **1** a recess, esp. in the wall of a room (*a dining alcove*). **2** an arbour or shady bower. [French from Spanish *alcoba* from Arabic *al-kubba* from *al* the + *kubba* vault]

Al·cuin /ˈalkwɪn/ (*c*.735–804) (also **Al·binus** /alˈbiːnəs/), English scholar and theologian. A guiding force behind the Carolingian renaissance, he established schools and libraries in the Frankish Empire.

Al·cyone /alˈsaɪəni/ *Gk Myth* (also **Hal·cyone**) the daughter of Aeolus, and wife of Ceyx, who drowned herself in grief over the death of her husband, and was transformed into a kingfisher.

Ald. *abbreviation* (preceding a name) Alderman etc.

Al·dabra /alˈdabrə/ a coral island group in the Indian Ocean, northwest of Madagascar. An outlying dependency of the Seychelles, it is administered as a nature reserve.

Al·deb·aran /alˈdebərən/ a conspicuous red giant that is the brightest star in the constellation Taurus. [Arabic, = the following (because it follows the Pleiades)]

Alde·burgh /ˈɒldbrə/ a town on the coast of Suffolk, England; pop. 2,800 (est. 1998). It is the setting for a music festival established by Benjamin Britten.

alde·hyde /ˈaldəˌhaid/ *noun* any of a class of compounds formed by the oxidation of alcohols (and containing the group -CHO). □ **alde·hydic**

/ˌaldəˈhɪdɪk/ *adjective* [abbreviation of modern Latin *alcohol dehydrogenatum* alcohol deprived of hydrogen]

al dente /al ˈdenteɪ/ *adjective* (of pasta etc.) cooked so as to be still firm when bitten. [Italian, lit. 'to the tooth']

alder *noun* any tree or shrub of the genus *Alnus*, related to the birch, with catkins and toothed leaves. [Old English *alor, aler*, related to Latin *alnus*, with euphonic d]

alder·fly *noun* (*pl.* **-flies**) an insect of the genus *Sialis*, found near streams.

alder·man *noun* (*pl.* **-men**) **1** *N Amer. & Austral.* a city councillor, esp. the elected representative of a district or ward. **2** *Brit. esp. hist.* a co-opted member of an English county or borough council, next in dignity to the mayor. □ **alder·man·ic** /-ˈmanɪk/ *adjective* **alder·man·ship** *noun* [Old English *aldor* patriarch from *ald* old + MAN]

Alder·ney[1] /ˈɒldərni/ an island in the English Channel, to the northeast of Guernsey; pop. (2002) 2,160. It is the third-largest of the Channel Islands.

Alder·ney[2] /ˈɒldərni/ *noun* a breed of small dairy cattle that came originally from Alderney.

alder·person *noun* *N Amer.* = ALDERMAN.

alder·woman *noun* (*pl.* **-women**) *N Amer.* a female city councillor.

Al·dine /ˈɒldaɪn/ *adjective* of the Italian printer Aldus Manutius, or the books printed by him or his family, or certain styles of display types. [Latin *Aldinus*, Latinized form of *Aldo*]

Aldis lamp /ˈɒldɪs/ *noun* a hand lamp for signalling in Morse code. [A. C. W. *Aldis*, its inventor]

aldo·ster·one /ˌɒldəʊˈsterəʊn/ *noun* a steroid hormone isolated from the adrenal gland. [ALDEHYDE + STEROL + -ONE]

Al·drin /ˈɒldrɪn/ **Edwin Eu·gene, Jr. ('Buzz')** (b.1930), US astronaut who became the second person to walk on the moon in July 1969.

al·drin /ˈaldrɪn/ *noun* a white crystalline chlorinated hydrocarbon used as an insecticide, now generally banned. [K. *Alder*, German chemist d.1958 + -IN]

Aldus Manu·tius /ˈɒldəs məˈnuːʃiəs/ (Latinized name of Teobaldo Manucci, also known as Aldo Manuzio, 1450–1515), Italian scholar, printer, and publisher. He is known for his fine editions of Greek and Latin classics and for introducing italic type.

ale *noun* **1** *N Amer.* a type of beer fermented rapidly at high temperatures. **2** esp. *Brit.* (usu. as a trade word) any beer other than lager, stout, or porter. [Old English *alu*, = Old Norse *öl*]

alea·tor·ic /ˌeiliəˈtɔrɪk/ *adjective* (also **alea·tory** /ˈeiliəˌtɔri/) **1** *Music & Art* involving random choice by a performer or artist. **2** depending on the throw of a die or on chance. [Latin *aleatorius aleator* dice player, from *alea* die]

Alecto /əˈlektəʊ/ (also **Al·lec·to**) *Gk Myth* one of the Furies. [Greek, = the implacable one]

alee /əˈliː/ *adverb & predicative adjective* **1** on the lee or sheltered side of a ship. **2** to leeward.

ale·house *noun* *hist.* a tavern.

Alei·chem /əlˈeixəm/ **Sho·lem** (pseudonym of Solomon Rabinowitz, 1892–1946), Russian writer of Yiddish plays, novels, and short stories, some of which inspired the musical *Fiddler on the Roof.*

Ale·khine /ˈalɪˌkiːn, ˈaljəkin/ **Alex·an·der** (1892–1946), Russian-born chess player (later a French citizen), world champion 1927–35 and 1937–46.

Alem·bert /ˌaloˈbeɪr/ **Jean le Rond d'** (1717–83), French philosopher and mathematician who collaborated with Diderot in the production of an encyclopedia.

alem·bic /əˈlembɪk/ *noun* *hist.* an apparatus formerly used in distilling. [medieval Latin *alembicus* from Arabic *al-'anbīk* from *al* the + *'anbīk* still, from Greek *ambix, -ikos* cup, cap of a still]

Alen·tejo /ˌalənˈteɪʒʊ/ a region and former province of east central Portugal. [Arabic, = beyond the Tagus]

aleph /ˈɒlef/ *noun* the first letter of the Hebrew alphabet. [Hebrew *'ālep*, lit. 'ox']

Alep·po /əˈlepəʊ/ a city in N Syria; pop. (est. 2002) 1,891,900. This ancient city was formerly an important commercial centre on the trade route between the Mediterranean and the countries of the East.

Alert the site of a Canadian Forces Station, located at the northern tip of Ellesmere Island, Nunavut. [HMS *Alert*, flagship of the British admiralty expedition to the North Pole in 1875–6]

alert ● *adjective* **1** watchful or vigilant; ready to take action. **2** nimble (esp. of mental faculties); attentive. ● *noun* **1** a call or alarm warning of an attack, storm, etc. **2** the duration of this. ● *transitive verb* (often foll.

by *to*) make alert; warn (*were alerted to the danger*). □ **on** (**the**) **alert** on the lookout against danger or attack. □ **alert·ly** *adverb* **alert·ness** *noun* [French *alerte* from Italian *all' erta* to the watchtower]

Alert Bay 1 a small bay on the coast of Cormorant Island, off the northeastern shore of Vancouver Island. **2** a village situated on the bay, famous for its collection of totem poles; pop. (2001) 583. [HMS *Alert* c.1860]

-ales /ˈeiliːz/ *suffix* forming the plural names of orders of plants (*Rosales*). [pl. of Latin adj. suffix *-alis*: see -AL]

Aletsch·horn /ˈɒletʃˌhɔrn/ a mountain in Switzerland, in the Bernese Alps, rising to 4 195 m (13,763 ft.). The Aletsch glaciers are among the largest in Europe.

aleur·one /ˈaljəˌrɔːn, əˈlurˌɔːn/ *noun* (also **aleur·on** /-rən/) *Biochem.* a protein found as granules in the seeds of plants etc. [Greek *aleuron* flour]

Aleut /ˈaljuːt, əˈluːt/ *noun* **1** (*pl.* same or **Aleuts**) a member of an Aboriginal people living in the Aleutian Islands and SW Alaska. **2** the language of the Aleut. □ **Aleu·tian** /əˈluːʃən/ *adjective & noun* [18th c.: origin unknown]

Aleu·tian Islands /əˈluːʃən/ (also **Aleu·tians**) a chain of volcanic islands in US possession, extending southwest from the Alaska Peninsula.

A level *noun* **1** (in the UK) the highest level of examination in secondary education, normally taken at the age of eighteen, and required for university entrance and other types of higher education. **2** a pass in such an examination (*she has three A levels*). [abbreviation of *Advanced* level]

alevin /ˈaləvɪn/ *noun* a very young fish, esp. a salmon or trout. [Old French from Latin *allevare* set up, raise up]

ale·wife /ˈeilwaɪf/ *noun* (*pl.* **ale·wives**) **1** a fish of the herring family, *Alosa pseudoharengus*, found off the Atlantic coast of N America and in the Great Lakes. **2** any of several related fish. [possibly from earlier *alewife* 'woman who keeps an alehouse' with reference to the fish's large belly]

Alex·an·der[1] 'the Great' (356–323 BC), king of Macedon 336–323 BC. Probably the greatest general of antiquity, he successfully invaded the Persian Empire with conquests in Asia Minor, Egypt, Syria, Mesopotamia, and as far east as Bactria and the Punjab.

Alex·an·der[2] *noun* a cocktail made with crème de cacao, sweet cream, and brandy or gin.

Alexander I ▶ 1 (*c.*1077–1124), king of Scotland 1107–24, son of Malcolm III. **2** (1777–1825), czar of Russia 1801–25, son of Paul I and grandson of Catherine the Great.

Alexander II ▶ 1 (1198–1249), king of Scotland 1214–49, son of William I. **2** (1818–81), czar of Russia 1855–81, son of Nicholas I. He emancipated the serfs and was assassinated by Nihilists.

Alexander III ▶ 1 (1241–86), king of Scotland 1249–86, son of Alexander II. **2** (1845–94), czar of Russia 1881–94, son of Alexander II.

Alexander VI (born Rodrigo Borgia) (1431–1503), pope 1492–1503, who was noted for his licentious life and the corruption of his papacy; he was also a noted patron of the arts.

Alexander Archipelago a group of about 1,100 US islands off the coast of SE Alaska, the remnants of a submerged mountain system.

Alexander Nevski (1220–63), Russian saint and national hero, called 'Nevski' from Neva, on the banks of which he defeated the Swedes.

Alexander of Tunis, Har·old Ru·pert Leof·ric George, 1st Earl (1891–1969), the last British Governor General of Canada (1946–52). He was created Viscount Alexander of Tunis (later elevated to earl) for his leadership during the Second World War, supervising the evacuation from Dunkirk, the withdrawal from Burma, and the victorious campaigns in Northern Africa and Italy.

alex·an·ders *noun* any of various umbelliferous plants, esp. of the genus *Zizia*. [from medieval Latin *alexandrum*]

Alexander technique *noun* a technique for controlling posture as an aid to improved well-being. [F. M. *Alexander*, physiotherapist d.1955]

Alex·an·dra (1872–1918), the last tsarina of Russia 1894–1917, wife of Tsar Nicolas II.

Alexandra Falls a waterfall in the southern NWT, 36 m high, situated 42 km from the mouth of the Hay River. [*Alexandra* of Denmark, Princess of Wales, wife of Edward VII (later Queen *Alexandra*) d.1925]

Alex·an·dret·ta the former name for ISKENDERUN.

Alex·an·dria the chief port of Egypt; pop. (est. 2002) 3,806,300.

Founded in 332 BC by Alexander the Great, it became a major centre of Hellenistic culture. It is renowned for the Mouseion library, founded by Ptolemy I, which held a vast store of Greek scholarship in the form of papyrus and vellum scrolls and was burned down by Arab invaders (*c.*641). [ALEXANDER¹]

Alex·an·drian *adjective* **1** of or characteristic of Alexandria. **2** belonging to or akin to the schools of literature and philosophy of Alexandria.

alex·an·drine /ˌaləɡˈzandrɪn/ ● *adjective* (of a line of verse) having six iambic feet. ● *noun* an alexandrine line. [French *alexandrin* from *Alexandre* Alexander (the Great), the subject of an Old French poem in this metre]

alex·an·drite /ˌaləɡˈzandrəit/ *noun* a gem variety of chrysoberyl which appears green in daylight and red in artificial light. [*Alexander I* of Russia + -ITE¹]

alexia /əˈleksiə/ *noun* the inability to understand written words or to read, as a result of brain disorder (*compare* DYSLEXIA). □ **alexic** *adjective* [modern Latin, A-¹ + Greek *lexis* speech from *legein* to speak, confused with Latin *legere* to read]

Alexis Mik·hail·ovich /əˈleksɪs mɪˈkailəˌvitʃ/ (1629–76), tsar of Russia 1645–76, father of Peter I.

Alex·ius I Com·nenus /əˈleksəs kɒmˈniːnəs/ (1048–1118), emperor of Byzantium 1081–1118. With the help of Crusaders, he defended his empire from Turkish and Norman invasions.

al·fal·fa *noun* a leguminous plant, *Medicago sativa*, with clover-like leaves and flowers used for fodder. [Spanish from Arabic *al-faṣfaṣa*, a green fodder]

alfalfa sprouts *plural noun* fine young sprouts of alfalfa, eaten as a salad vegetable or garnish.

Al·fonso XIII (1886–1941), king of Spain 1886–1931. He was forced to abdicate in 1931 after widespread strikes and civil unrest.

Al·fred 'the Great' (849–99), king of Wessex 871–99. In addition to resisting Danish invaders, he was responsible for a considerable revival of learning and literature in W England.

al·fredo *adjective* (often placed after noun) designating a sauce for pasta made of butter, cream, and Parmesan cheese (*fettuccine alfredo*). [*Alfredo* di Lelio, Italian chef (early 20th c.)]

al·fresco *adverb & adjective* (also **al fresco**) in the open air (*we lunched alfresco; an alfresco lunch*). [Italian *al fresco* in the fresh (air)]

Al Fu·jay·rah see FUJAIRAH.

Alf·vén /ˈalven/ **Hannes Olof Gösta** (1908–95), Swedish theoretical physicist. His work was important for controlled nuclear fusion; he shared the Nobel Prize for physics in 1970.

alga /ˈalɡə/ *noun* (pl. **algae** /ˈaldʒiː, ˈalɡiː/) (usu. in pl.) **1** any of a large group of non-vascular, mainly aquatic cryptogams capable of photosynthesis, including seaweeds and many unicellular organisms. **2** (in full **blue-green algae**) = CYANOBACTERIA. □ **algal** *adjective* [Latin]

Al·garve, the /alˈɡɑːv/ the southernmost province of Portugal, on the Atlantic coast; capital, Faro. The Algarve is noted as a holiday resort area. [Arabic *al* the + *gharb* west]

al·ge·bra /ˈaldʒəbrə/ *noun* **1** the branch of mathematics that uses letters and other general symbols to represent numbers and quantities in formulae and equations. **2** a system of this based on given axioms (*linear algebra; the algebra of logic*). □ **al·ge·bra·ic** /ˌaldʒəˈbreiɪk/ *adjective* **al·ge·bra·ic·al·ly** /ˌaldʒəˈbreiɪkli/ *adverb* **al·ge·bra·ist** /ˌaldʒəˈbreiɪst/ *noun* [Italian & Spanish & medieval Latin, from Arabic *al-jabr* from *al* the + *jabr* reunion of broken parts, from *jabara* reunite]

Alge·ciras /ˌaldʒɪˈsiːrəs/ a ferry port and resort in S Spain; pop. (est. 2001) 105,066. It lies on the Strait of Gibraltar.

Alger /ˈaldʒɜr/ **Hor·atio** (1834–1899), US writer of rags-to-riches children's stories with improbable and moralistic plots.

Al·geria /alˈdʒiːriə/ a republic on the Mediterranean coast of North Africa; pop. (est. 2002) 32,278,000; capital, Algiers. The region was colonized by France from the mid-19th c. until 1962, when it achieved independence after a bitter war. □ **Al·ger·ian** *adjective & noun*

-algia /ˈaldʒə/ *combining form Med.* denoting pain in a part specified by the first element (*neuralgia*). □ **-algic** *combining form.* [Greek from *algos* pain]

algi·cide /ˈalɡɪˌsaid/ *noun* a preparation for destroying algae.

Al·giers /alˈdʒiːrz/ the capital of Algeria and one of the leading Mediterranean ports of North Africa; pop. (est. 2002) 3,815,900.

al·gin·ate /ˈaldʒɪˌneit/ *noun* a salt or ester of alginic acid. [ALGA + -IN + -ATE¹]

al·gin·ic acid /alˈdʒɪnɪk/ *noun* an insoluble carbohydrate found (chiefly as salts) in many brown seaweeds. [ALGA + -IN + -IC]

Algol¹ /ˈalɡɒl/ an eclipsing binary star that is the second-brightest in the constellation Perseus. [Arabic, = the destruction]

Algol² /ˈalɡɒl/ *noun* a high-level computer programming language. [ALGORITHMIC (see ALGORITHM) + LANGUAGE]

al·gol·ogy /alˈɡɒlədʒi/ *noun* the study of algae. □ **al·go·logic·al** /-ˈlɒdʒɪkəl/ *adjective* **al·gol·o·gist** *noun*

Al·gon·quian /alˈɡɒŋkwiən, -kiən/ (also **Al·gon·kian** /-kiən/) ● *noun* **1** the largest Aboriginal language group in Canada, including Abenaki, Algonquin, Blackfoot, Cree, Delaware, Maliseet, Mi'kmaq, and Ojibwa. **2** a member of any of the N American Aboriginal peoples speaking languages of this family, living in the Maritimes, Quebec, Ontario, the Prairies, and the east coast of the US. ● *adjective* of or relating to the Algonquian peoples or their languages.

Al·gon·quin /alˈɡɒŋkwɪn, -kɪn/ ● *noun* **1** (also **Al·gon·kin** /-kɪn/ (pl. same or **-s**) a member of an Aboriginal people living along the Ottawa River and its tributaries. **2** (also **Al·gon·kin** /-kɪn/) the dialect of Algonquian spoken by the Algonquin. **3** a type of snowshoe with an upturned front and long tapering tail. ● *adjective* **1** of or relating to the Algonquin or their language. **2** = ALGONQUIAN. ¶ The use of *Algonquin* to refer to the Algonquian peoples or their language is widespread but strictly incorrect. [French from Algonquian, compare Mi'kmaq *algoomeaking* = 'at the place of spearing fish and eels']

al·go·rithm /ˈalɡəˌrɪðəm/ *noun Math.* a process or set of rules used for calculation or problem-solving, esp. with a computer. □ **al·go·rith·mic** /ˌalɡəˈrɪðmɪk/ *adjective* [ultimately from Persian *al-Kuwārizmī* 9th-c. mathematician: *algorithm* influenced by Greek *arithmos* number]

Al·gua·cil /ˌalɡwəˈsɪl, ˈalɡwəsɪl/ *noun* (also **al·gua·zil** /ˌalɡwəˈzɪl, ˈalɡwəzɪl/) **1** a mounted official at a bullfight. **2** a constable or an officer of justice in Spain or Spanish-speaking countries. [Spanish from Arabic *al-wazīr* from *al* the + *wazīr*: see VIZIER]

Al·ham·bra /alˈhambrə/ a fortified palace near Granada in Spain. Built between 1248 and 1354, it was the last stronghold of the Muslim kings of Granada and is an outstanding example of highly ornate Moorish architecture.

Ali /ˈɒliː, ˈaliː/ **1** (*c.*600–61), fourth caliph of Islam 656–61, son-in-law of Muhammad. He is revered by the Shiites as the first caliph. **2** see MUHAMMAD ALI 1. **3** see MUHAMMAD ALI 2.

alias /ˈeiliəs/ ● *adverb* also named or known as. ● *noun* **1** a false or assumed name. **2** *Computing* a command or address which substitutes for another, usu. more complicated one. ● *transitive verb Computing* assign an alias to or employ an alias. [Latin, = at another time, otherwise]

alias·ing *noun* the misidentification of a signal frequency, introducing distortion or error, esp. in a computer image.

Ali Baba the hero of a story supposed to be from the *Arabian Nights*, who discovered the magic formula ('Open Sesame!') which opened the cave in which forty thieves kept the treasure they had accumulated.

alibi /ˈalɪˌbai/ (pl. **alibis**) ● *noun* **1** a claim, or the evidence supporting it, that when an alleged act took place one was elsewhere. **2** *disputed* an excuse of any kind; a pretext or justification. ● *verb* (**alibis**, **alibied**, **alibi·ing**) *informal* **1** *transitive* provide an alibi or offer an excuse for (a person). **2** *intransitive* provide an alibi. [Latin, = elsewhere]

Ali·cante /ˌaləˈkanti/ a seaport on the Mediterranean coast of SE Spain, the capital of a province of the same name; pop. (est. 2001) 283,243.

Alice-in-Wonder·land *adjective* fantastic, absurd. [from the name of the heroine of two books by L. CARROLL]

Alice Springs a railway terminus and supply centre serving the outback of Northern Territory, Australia; pop. (2001) 28,178.

ali·dade /ˈalɪˌdeid/ *noun Surveying* an instrument for determining directions or measuring angles. [Arabic *al-ʿiḍāda* the revolving radius, from *ʿaḍud* upper arm]

alien ● *adjective* **1 a** (often foll. by *to*) unfamiliar; not in accordance or harmony; unfriendly; hostile; unacceptable or repugnant (*army discipline was alien to him; struck an alien note*). **b** (often foll. by *from*) different or separated. **2** foreign; from a foreign country (*help from alien powers*). **3** of or relating to beings supposedly from other worlds. **4** *Bot.* (of a plant) introduced from elsewhere and naturalized in its new home. ● *noun* **1** a foreigner, esp. one who is not a naturalized citizen of the country where he or she is living. **2** a being from another world. **3** *Bot.* an alien plant. □ **alien·ness** *noun* [Latin *alienus* belonging to another (*alius*)]

alien·able /ˈeiliənəbəl/ *adjective Law* able to be transferred to new ownership. □ **alien·abil·ity** *noun*

alien·age /ˈeiliənidʒ/ *noun Law* the state or condition of being an alien.

alien·ate *transitive verb* **1 a** cause (a person) to become unfriendly or hostile. **b** (often foll. by *from*) cause (a person) to feel isolated or estranged from (friends, society, etc.). **2** *Law* transfer ownership of (property) to another person etc. □ **alien·ator** *noun*

alien·at·ed *adjective* **1** withdrawn in feeling or affection, isolated. **2** *Law* transferred to other ownership.

alien·a·tion *noun* **1** the act of estranging or state of estrangement in feeling or affection. **2** (in full **alienation effect**) *Theatre* a dramatic effect whereby an audience remains objective, not identifying with the characters or action of a play. **3** *Psych.* loss of mental faculties; insanity (*mental alienation*).

alien·ist *noun US* a psychiatrist, esp. a legal adviser on psychiatric problems.

Ali·ghieri /ˌaliˈgjeri/ *see* DANTE.

alight¹ *intransitive verb* (*past* and *past participle* **alight·ed**) **1 a** (often foll. by *from*) descend from a vehicle. **b** dismount from a horse. **2** come to rest or settle; descend to earth from the air. **3** (foll. by *on*) find by chance; notice. [Old English *ālīhtan* (as A-², *līhtan* LIGHT² *verb*)]

alight² *predicative adjective* **1** on fire; burning (*they set the old shed alight; is the fire still alight?*). **2** lighted up; excited (*eyes alight with expectation*).

align *transitive verb* **1** put in a straight line or bring into line (*three books were neatly aligned on the shelf; the car's wheels need aligning*). **2** esp. *Politics* (usu. foll. by *with*) bring (oneself etc.) into agreement or alliance with (a cause, policy, political party, etc.). □ **align·ment** *noun* [French *aligner* from phr. *à ligne* into line: see LINE¹]

alike ● *adverb* in a similar way or manner; equally (*all were treated alike*). ● *adjective* (usu. *predicative*) similar, like one another; indistinguishable.

ali·ment /ˈalimənt/ *noun formal* **1** food. **2** support or mental sustenance. [Latin *alimentum* from *alere* nourish]

ali·men·tary /ˌaliˈmentəri/ *adjective* of, relating to, or providing nourishment or sustenance. [Latin *alimentarius* (as ALIMENT)]

alimentary canal *noun Anat.* the passage along which food is passed from the mouth to the anus during digestion.

ali·men·ta·tion /ˌalimenˈteiʃən/ *noun formal* **1** nourishment; feeding. **2** maintenance, support; supplying with the necessities of life. [(as ALIMENT)]

ali·mony /ˈaliˌmoːni/ *noun* a monetary provision for a spouse or former spouse after a separation or divorce. ¶ In legal language, now replaced by *support* or *maintenance*. [Latin *alimonia* nutriment, from *alere* nourish]

A-line *adjective* (of a garment) having a fitted waist or shoulders and somewhat flared skirt.

Alioth /ˈaliːˌɒth/ the brightest star in the Big Dipper.

ali·phat·ic /ˌaliˈfatik/ *adjective* of, denoting, or relating to organic compounds in which carbon atoms form open chains, not aromatic rings. [Greek *aleiphar -atos* fat]

ali·quot /ˈaliˌkwɒt/ ● *adjective* (of a part or portion) contained by the whole an integral or whole number of times (*4 is an aliquot part of 12*). ● *noun* **1** an aliquot part; an integral factor. **2** (in general use) any known fraction of a whole; a sample. [Latin *aliquot* some, so many]

A-list *noun* a list of people or items of the highest importance. □ **A-lister** *noun*

alit·er·ate /eiˈlitərət/ ● *adjective* disinclined to read, despite being able to do so. ● *noun* an aliterate person. □ **alit·eracy** *noun* [A-¹ + LITERATE]

alive *adjective* (usu. *predicative*) **1** (of a person, animal, plant, etc.) living, not dead. **2 a** (of a thing) existing; continuing; in operation or action (*kept his interest alive*). **b** under discussion; provoking interest (*the topic is still very much alive today*). **3** (of a person or animal) lively, active. **4** charged with an electric current; connected to a source of electricity. **5** (foll. by *to*) aware of; alert or responsive to. **6** (foll. by *with*) a swarming or teeming with. **b** full of. □ **alive and kicking** *informal* very active; lively. **alive and well** still alive or active (esp. despite contrary assumptions or rumours). □ **alive·ness** *noun* [Old English *on life* (as A², LIFE)]

aliyah /ˌɒliːˈɒ/ *noun* the migration of Jews to Israel. [Hebrew, lit. 'ascent']

aliz·arin /əˈlizərin/ *noun* **1** the red colouring matter of madder root, used in dyeing. **2** (*attributive*) (of a dye) derived from or similar to this pigment. [French *alizarine* from *alizari* madder, from Arabic *al-ʿiṣara* pressed juice, from ʿaṣara to press fruit]

Al Jizah *see* GIZA.

al·ka·hest /ˈalkəˌhest/ *noun* (also **al·ca·hest**) the universal solvent sought by alchemists. [sham Arabic, prob. invented by Paracelsus]

Al·kaid /alˈkeid/ a star in the constellation Ursa Major (Big Dipper), at the end of the bear's 'tail'. [Arabic, = chief of the mourners]

al·kali /ˈalkəˌlai/ *noun* (*pl.* **al·ka·lis**) **1 a** *Chem.* any of a class of bases that liberate hydroxide ions in water, usu. form caustic or corrosive solutions, turn litmus blue, and have a pH of more than 7, e.g. caustic soda. **b** any other substance with similar but weaker properties, e.g. sodium carbonate. **2** *N Amer.* a soluble salt or mixture of salts existing in excess in soil and having a damaging effect on crops. □ **al·ka·lim·eter** /ˌalkəˈlimitər/ *noun* **al·ka·lim·etry** /ˌalkəˈlimitri/ *noun* [Arabic *al-ḳalī* calcined ashes, from *ḳala* fry]

alkali metals *plural noun* any of the group of metals, lithium, sodium, potassium, rubidium, cesium, and francium, whose hydroxides are alkalis.

al·ka·line /ˈalkəˌlain/ *adjective* **1** of, relating to, or having the nature of an alkali; rich in alkali. **2** *Chem.* having a pH above 7; basic. □ **al·ka·lin·ity** /ˌalkəˈliniti/ *noun*

alkaline battery *noun* a dry cell with an alkaline electrolyte of potassium hydroxide, which provides more power and durability than conventional batteries.

alkaline earth *noun* **1** (in full **alkaline-earth metal**) any of the metals beryllium, magnesium, calcium, strontium, barium, and radium. **2** any of the strongly basic oxides of the alkaline-earth metals.

al·ka·loid /ˈalkəˌlɔid/ *noun* any of a series of nitrogenous organic compounds of plant origin, many of which are used as drugs, e.g. morphine, quinine, nicotine. □ **al·ka·loid·al** *noun* [German (as ALKALI)]

al·ka·losis /ˌalkəˈloːsis/ *noun Med.* an excessive alkaline condition of the body fluids or tissues.

al·kane /ˈalkein/ *noun Chem.* any of a series of saturated aliphatic hydrocarbons having the general formula C_nH_{2n+2}, including methane, ethane, and propane. [ALKYL + -ANE²]

al·kene /ˈalkiːn/ *noun Chem.* any of a series of unsaturated aliphatic hydrocarbons containing a double bond and having the general formula C_nH_{2n}, including ethylene and propylene. [ALKYL + -ENE]

alky *noun* (*pl.* **alkies**) *slang* an alcoholic or drunkard. [abbreviation]

alkyd /ˈalkid/ *noun* any of the group of synthetic resins derived from various alcohols and acids, commonly used in paints etc. [ALKYL + ACID]

alkyl /ˈalkil/ *noun* (in full **alkyl radical**) *Chem.* any radical derived from an alkane by the removal of a hydrogen atom. [German *Alkohol* ALCOHOL + -YL]

alkyl·ate /ˈalkiˌleit/ *transitive verb Chem.* introduce an alkyl radical into (a compound).

al·kyne /ˈalkain/ *noun Chem.* any of a series of unsaturated aliphatic hydrocarbons containing a triple bond and having the general formula C_nH_{2n-2}, including acetylene. [ALKYL + -YNE]

all ● *adjective* **1 a** the whole amount, quantity, or extent of (*waited all day; all his life; we all know why; take it all*). **b** (with *pl.*) the entire number of (*all the others left; all ten men; the children are all boys; film stars all*). **2** any whatever (*beyond all doubt*). **3** greatest possible (*with all speed*). ● *noun* **1 a** all the persons or things concerned (*all were present; all were thrown away*). **b** everything (*all is lost; that is all*). **2** (foll. by *of*) **a** the whole of (*take all of it*). **b** every one of (*all of us*). **c** as much as (*all of three feet tall*). **d** *informal* affected by; in a state of (*all of a dither*). ¶ Use of the preposition *of* after *all* is sometimes criticized, especially before mass nouns (as in *all of the bread*), but is perfectly idiomatic. **3** one's whole strength or resources (*gave her all*). ● *adverb* **1** entirely, quite (*dressed all in black; all round the room; the all-important thing*). **b** as an intensifier (*a book all about ships; stop all this grumbling*). **2** *informal* very (*went all shy*). **3** (foll. by *the* + comparative) by so much; to that extent (*if they go, all the better*). **4** (in games) on both sides (*the score was two all*). □ **all along** all the time (*he knew about it all along*). **all but** very nearly (*it was all but impossible; he was all but drowned*). **all for** strongly in favour of. **as all get-out** *informal* to a high degree (*stubborn as all get-out*). **all in all** everything considered. **all manner of** *see* MANNER. **all of a sudden** *see* SUDDEN. **all one** (or **the same**) (usu. foll. by *to*) a matter of indifference (*it's all the same to me*). **all over 1** completely finished. **2** in or on all parts of (esp. the body) (*went hot and cold all over; mud all over the carpet*). **3** *informal* typically (*that is you all over*). **4** *slang* effusively attentive to (a person). **all the same** nevertheless, in spite of this (*he was innocent but was punished all the same*). **all set** *informal* ready to start. **all that** *informal* particularly; very (*wasn't all that difficult*). **all there** *informal* mentally alert. **all the time** *see* TIME. **all together** all at once; all in one place or in a group (*they came all together*) (*compare*

Consonants: b *but*   d *dog*   f *few*   g *get*   h *her*   j *yes*   k *cat*   l *leg*   m *man*   n *no*   p *pen*   r *red*   s *sit*

ALTOGETHER). **all very well** an expression used to reject or to imply skepticism about a favourable or consoling remark. **all the way** see WAY. **at all** (with *neg.* or *interrogative*) in any way; to any extent (*did not swim at all; did you like it at all?*). **be all up with** see UP. **in all** in total number; altogether (*there were 10 people in all*). **on all fours** see FOUR. **one and all** everyone. [Old English *all, eall*, prob. from Germanic]

alla breve /ˌalə ˈbreɪveɪ/ *noun Music* a time signature indicating 2 or 4 half note beats in a bar; cut time. [Italian, = according to the BREVE]

alla cap·pel·la *var. of* A CAPPELLA.

Allah /ˈalə, ˈɒlə/ *noun* the name of the Supreme Being in Islam. [Arabic *'allāh* contraction of *al-'ilāh* from *al* the + *ilāh* god]

Allah·abad /ˈaləhəˌbad/ a city in the state of Uttar Pradesh, north central India; pop. (2001) 990,300. Situated at the confluence of the sacred Jumna and Ganges rivers, it is a place of Hindu pilgrimage.

all-American ● *adjective* **1** (esp. of an athlete) chosen as one of the best in, or representing the whole of, the US. **2** truly, typically, or exclusively American (*all-American boy; an all-American cast*). ● *noun* an all-American athlete.

Allan, Sir Hugh (1810–82), Scottish-born Canadian shipowner, railway promoter, and financier. The suggestion that his syndicate had paid for being awarded the contract to build the CPR led to the Pacific Scandal and the fall of the Macdonald Conservatives in 1873.

Allan Cup *noun* an annual trophy awarded to the Canadian senior amateur hockey champions. Donated by Sir Hugh Montagu Allan in 1908, it has been awarded by the Canadian Hockey Association since 1928.

al·lan·tois /əˈlantoːɪs/ *noun* (*pl.* **al·lan·to·id·es** /-ɪˌdiːz/) *Zool.* one of several membranes that develop in embryonic reptiles, birds, or mammals. □ **al·lan·toic** /ˌalanˈtoːɪk/ *adjective* [modern Latin from Greek *allantoeidēs* sausage-shaped]

all around (also **all round**) ● *adjective* **1** (of a person) versatile. **2** comprehensive, affecting everything or everyone. ● *adverb* **1** for each person (*he bought drinks all around*). **2** in all respects (*a good performance all around*).

allay /əˈleɪ/ *transitive verb* **1** diminish (fear, suspicion, etc.). **2** relieve or alleviate (pain, hunger, etc.). [Old English *ālecgan* (as A-², LAY¹)]

all-Canadian ● *adjective* **1** (esp. of an athlete) chosen as one of the best in, or representing the whole of, Canada. **2** truly, typically, or exclusively Canadian (*an all-Canadian cast*). ● *noun* an all-Canadian athlete.

all-candidates meeting *noun Cdn* a public meeting held during an election campaign at which all the candidates for an electoral district present their platforms and answer questions from the audience.

all-clear *noun* a signal that danger or difficulty is over.

all-day *attributive adjective* lasting throughout a day (*an all-day meeting*).

all-dressed *adjective Cdn (Que., NB, & E Ont.)* designating an item of food etc. (esp. pizza or a hot dog) served with all the optional garnishes.

Al·lec·to /əˈlɛktoʊ/ *Gk Myth* one of the Furies. [Greek, = the implacable one]

allée /aˈleɪ/ *noun* a walk bordered by trees or clipped hedges in a garden or park. [French]

al·le·ga·tion /ˌaləˈɡeɪʃən/ *noun* **1** an assertion or accusation, esp. an unproven one. **2** the act or an instance of alleging. [Latin *allegatio* from *allegare* allege]

al·lege /əˈlɛdʒ/ *transitive verb* **1** (often foll. by *that* + clause, or *to* + infin.) declare to be the case, esp. without proof. **2** advance as an argument or excuse. □ **al·leged** /əˈlɛdʒd, -dʒəd/ *adjective* [Anglo-French *alegier*, Old French *esligier* clear at law; confused in sense with Latin *allegare*: see ALLEGATION]

al·leg·ed·ly /əˈlɛdʒədli/ *adverb* as is alleged or said to be the case.

Al·leghe·ny Mountains /ˌaləˈɡeɪni/ (also **Al·leghe·nies**) a mountain range of the Appalachian system in the eastern US.

al·le·giance /əˈliːdʒəns/ *noun* **1** loyalty (to a person or cause etc.). **2** the duty of a subject to his or her sovereign or government. [Anglo-French from Old French *ligeance* (as LIEGE): perhaps assoc. with ALLIANCE]

al·legor·ic·al /ˌaləˈɡɒrɪkəl/ *adjective* (also **al·legor·ic**) consisting of or relating to allegory; by means of allegory. □ **al·legor·ic·al·ly** *adverb*

al·legor·ize /ˈaləɡəˌraɪz/ *transitive verb* (also esp. *Brit.* **-ise**) treat as or by means of an allegory. □ **al·legor·iz·a·tion** *noun*

al·legory /ˈaləˌɡɔri/ *noun* (*pl.* **-ies**) **1** a story, play, poem, picture, etc., in which the meaning or message is represented symbolically. **2** the use of such symbols. **3** a symbol. □ **al·legor·ist** /ˈaləɡərˌɪst/ *noun* [ultimately from Greek *allēgoria* from *allos* other + *-agoria* speaking]

al·le·gret·to /ˌaləˈɡrɛtoː/ *Music* ● *adverb & adjective* in a fairly brisk

tempo. ● *noun* (*pl.* **-tos**) an allegretto passage or movement. [Italian, diminutive of ALLEGRO]

Al·le·gri /əˈlɛɡri/ **Gre·gorio** (1582–1652), Italian composer of church music, best known for his *Miserere* for four soloists and five-part choir.

al·le·gro /əˈlɛɡroː/ ● *adverb & adjective Music* in a brisk tempo. ● *noun* (*pl.* **-ros**) a musical passage or dance performed allegro. [Italian, = lively, happy]

al·lele /əˈliːl/ *noun* one of the (usu. two) alternative forms of a gene that occupy the same relative position on a chromosome. □ **al·lel·ic** /əˈliːlɪk/ *adjective* [German *Allel*, abbreviation of ALLELOMORPH]

al·lelo·morph /əˈliːləˌmɔrf/ *noun* = ALLELE. □ **al·lelo·morph·ic** *adjective* [Greek *allēl-* one another + *morphē* form]

al·le·luia /ˌaləˈluːjə, -ˈleɪ-/ (also **hal·le·lu·jah** /hal-/) ● *interjection* God be praised. ● *noun* **1** praise to God. **2** a song of praise to God. **3** *Christianity* an acclamation before the reading of the Gospel containing the word 'Alleluia'. [ultimately from Hebrew *hallĕlūyāh* praise ye the Lord]

alle·mande /ˈalmānd/ *noun* **1 a** the name of several German dances. **b** the music for any of these, esp. as a movement of a suite. **2** a figure in square dancing in which dancers join arms or hands and make a full or partial turn. [French, = German (dance)]

all-embracing *adjective* including everything (*an all-embracing theory*).

Allen ▸ 1 Ethan (1738–89), US soldier during the American Revolution and leader of the Green Mountain Boys, a band of militiamen in Vermont. He captured Fort Ticonderoga, New York, in 1775 and later that year led a failed attack on Montreal. **2 Woody** (born Allen Stewart Konigsberg, b.1935), US film director, writer, and actor, whose films (e.g. *Annie Hall* and *Hannah and Her Sisters*) are noted for their offbeat New York humour and their exploration of modern American neuroses.

Al·len·by, Ed·mund Henry Hyn·man, 1st Viscount (1861–1936), English field marshal. Commander of the Egyptian Expeditionary Force against the Turks, he captured Jerusalem in 1917, and defeated the Turkish forces in Palestine (1918).

Allende /aˈjɛndeɪ/ **Sal·va·dor** (1908–73), President of Chile 1970–73, the first avowed Marxist to win a Latin American presidency in a free election. A military coup, led by General Pinochet with indirect backing from the US, overthrew him in 1973, and he died during the fighting.

Allen key *noun proprietary* (also **Allen wrench**) an L-shaped tool designed to fit into and turn an Allen screw. [*Allen*, name of the US manufacturer]

Allen screw *noun proprietary* a screw with a hexagonal socket in the head.

al·ler·gen /ˈalɜrˌdʒən/ *noun* any substance that causes an allergic reaction. □ **al·ler·gen·ic** /ˌalɜrˈdʒɛnɪk/ *adjective* [ALLERGY + -GEN]

al·ler·gic /əˈlɜrdʒɪk/ *adjective* **1** (foll. by *to*) **a** having an allergy to. **b** *informal* having a strong dislike for (a person or thing). **2** caused by or relating to an allergy.

al·ler·gist /ˈalɜrˌdʒɪst/ *noun* a physician who specializes in the treatment of allergies.

al·lergy /ˈalɜrdʒi/ *noun* (*pl.* **-gies**) **1** a condition of reacting adversely to certain substances, esp. particular foods, pollen, fur, or dust. **2** *informal* an antipathy. [German *Allergie*, after *Energie* ENERGY, from Greek *allos* other]

al·levi·ate /əˈliːviˌeɪt/ *transitive verb* lessen or make less severe (pain, suffering, a problem, etc.). □ **al·levi·a·tion** *noun* **al·levia·tive** /əˈliːviətɪv/ *adjective* **al·levi·ator** *noun* **al·levia·tory** /əˈliːviətɔri/ *adjective* [Late Latin *alleviare* lighten, from Latin *allevare* (as AD-, *levare* raise)]

al·ley¹ *noun* (*pl.* **-leys**) **1** (also **alley·way**) **a** a narrow street. **b** a narrow passageway or lane, esp. between or behind buildings. **2** a path or walk in a park or garden. **3** = BOWLING ALLEY. **4** *Baseball* the area between the outfielders in left-centre or right-centre field. **5** *Tennis* either of the two side strips of a doubles court. **6** (usu. **Alley**) an area known for a specified characteristic, esp. a street or lane with a concentration of similar businesses etc. (*Tornado Alley; Gourmet Alley*). □ **up one's alley** *informal* suited to one's tastes, interests, or abilities. [Old French *alee* 'walking, passage', from *aler* go, from Latin *ambulare* walk]

al·ley² *noun* a large playing marble, often used as a shooter. [perhaps diminutive of ALABASTER]

alley cat *noun* a stray cat in an urban area, often mangy or half wild.

alley-oop ● *interjection* encouraging or drawing attention to the performance of some physical, esp. acrobatic, feat. ● *noun Basketball* **1** (often *attributive*) a high lob or pass caught by a leaping teammate. **2** a basket scored by the receiver of such a pass. [perhaps from French *allez* go on! come on! + representing a supposedly French pronunciation of UP]

alley·way *noun* = ALLEY[1] 1.

All Fools' Day *noun* = APRIL FOOL'S DAY.

All Hal·lows *noun* = ALL SAINTS' DAY.

al·li·aceous /ˌali'eiʃəs/ *adjective* **1** of or relating to the genus *Allium*, including onions, garlic, and leeks. **2** tasting or smelling like onion or garlic. [modern Latin *alliaceus* from Latin *allium* garlic]

al·li·ak /'aliak/ *noun* = KOMATIK. [Inuktitut]

al·li·ance *noun* **1 a** formal union or agreement to co-operate, esp. among nations with a specific goal. **b** a formal grouping of persons having a common aim. **c** the parties involved. **2** union through marriage. **3** a relationship resulting from an affinity in nature or qualities etc. (*the alliance between Church and State*). **4** *Bot.* a group of allied families. **5** (**Alliance**) **a** = CHRISTIAN AND MISSIONARY ALLIANCE. **b** = CANADIAN ALLIANCE.

al·li·cin /'alɪsɪn/ *noun* a pungent oily liquid with antibacterial properties, present in garlic. [from Latin *allium* garlic + -IN[1]]

al·lied /'alaɪd, ə'laɪd/ *adjective* **1 a** united or associated in an alliance. **b** (**Allied**) of or relating to the Allies. **2** connected or related (*studied medicine and allied subjects*).

Al·lies 1 the nations allied against the Central Powers in the First World War, primarily the British Empire (including Canada), France, and the Russian Empire, and later the US. **2** the nations allied against the Axis powers in the Second World War, primarily the United Kingdom and the Commonwealth (including Canada), and France, and later the Soviet Union, the US, and China.

al·li·ga·tor *noun* **1** a large crocodilian reptile of S America, China, and the southeastern US, with upper teeth that lie outside the lower teeth and a head broader and shorter than that of the crocodile. **2** any of several large members of the crocodile family. **3 a** the skin of such an animal or material resembling it. **b** (in *pl.*) shoes of this. [Spanish *el lagarto* the lizard, from Latin *lacerta*]

alligator clip *noun* a metal clip with teeth for gripping wires or other electrical connectors.

alligator pear *noun* an avocado.

alligator snapping turtle *noun* (also **alligator snapper**) a large freshwater snapping turtle, *Macroclemys temmincki*, found in the southern and central US.

all-im·port·ant *adjective* crucial; vitally important.

all in *adjective* **1** (*predicative*) *informal* exhausted. **2** (**all-in**) (*attributive*) *Brit.* all-inclusive.

all-in·clus·ive *adjective* including all or everything.

Al·line /ə'liːn/ **Henry** (1748–84), American-born evangelist and hymn writer. He preached to settlers in the Maritimes and played a major role in the development of the Baptist Church there.

Al·ling·ham /'alɪŋəm/ **Mar·gery** (1904–66), English novelist, best known for her detective stories featuring Albert Campion.

all-in-one ● *attributive adjective* comprising all the necessary features in one indivisible unit. ● *noun* a garment combining parts usually worn separately, e.g a corselette.

all-in wrestling *noun* wrestling with few or no restrictions.

Al·li·son Pass a pass through the Cascade Mountains of southern BC, east of Chilliwack. [J. F. *Allison*, miner and rancher who discovered the pass *c.*1860]

al·lit·er·a·tion /ə,lɪtə'reɪʃən/ *noun* the occurrence of the same letter or sound at the beginning of adjacent or closely connected words (e.g. *cool, calm, and collected*). □ **al·lit·era·tive** /ə'lɪtərətɪv/ *adjective* [modern Latin *alliteratio* (as AD-, *littera* letter)]

al·lium /'aliːəm/ *noun* any plant of the genus *Allium*, usu. bulbous and strong smelling, e.g. onion and garlic. [Latin, = garlic]

all-new *adjective* totally new.

all-night *attributive adjective* lasting or remaining open throughout the night (*all-night party; all-night café*).

all-nighter *noun informal* an event or task that continues throughout the night, esp. a study session before an examination.

allo- *combining form* **1** other, different (*allogamy*). **2** denoting any of several variants (*allomorph; allotrope*). [Greek *allos* other]

al·lo·cate /'aləˌkeɪt/ *transitive verb* assign, designate, or set aside for a specific purpose. □ **al·loc·able** /'aləkəbəl/ *adjective* **al·lo·ca·tion** /ˌalə'keɪʃən/ *noun* **al·lo·ca·tor** *noun* [medieval Latin *allocare* from *locus* place]

al·loch·thon /ə'lɒk,θɒn/ *noun Geol.* a body of rock that has been

transported a considerable distance to its present position (*compare* AUTOCHTHON). □ **al·loch·thon·ous** *adjective* [ALLO- + Greek *khthōn*, *-onos* earth]

al·lo·cu·tion /ˌalə'kjuːʃən/ *noun* a formal speech, esp. one that exhorts. [Latin *allocutio* from *alloqui allocut-* speak to]

al·log·amy /ə'lɒɡəmi/ *noun Bot.* cross-fertilization in plants (*compare* AUTOGAMY). [ALLO- + Greek *-gamia* from *gamos* marriage]

al·lo·morph /'aləˌmɔrf/ *noun Linguistics* any of two or more alternative forms of a morpheme. □ **allo·morph·ic** /ˌalə'mɔrfɪk/ *adjective* [ALLO- + MORPHEME]

al·lo·pathy /ə'lɒpəθi/ *noun* the treatment of disease by conventional means, i.e. with drugs having opposite effects to the symptoms (*compare* HOMEOPATHY). □ **allo·path** /'aləpaθ/ *noun* **allo·path·ic** /ˌalə'paθɪk/ *adjective* [German *Allopathie* (as ALLO-, -PATHY)]

al·lo·pat·ric /alə'patrɪk/ *adjective Biol.* occurring in separate geographical areas. [ALLO- + Greek *patra* 'fatherland']

al·lo·phone[1] *Cdn* ● *noun* (esp. in Quebec) an immigrant whose first language is neither French nor English. ● *adjective* (in Quebec) having a first language other than French, English, or an Aboriginal language. [ALLO-, after FRANCOPHONE]

al·lo·phone[2] *noun Linguistics* any of the variant sounds forming a single phoneme. □ **allo·phon·ic** /ˌalə'fɒnɪk/ *adjective* [ALLO- + PHONEME]

al·lot *transitive verb* (**al·lot·ted, al·lot·ting**) **1** give or apportion to (a person) as a share or task; distribute officially to (*they allotted us each a pair of boots; the men were allotted duties*). **2** assign or allocate. [Old French *aloter* from *a* to + LOT]

al·lot·ment *noun* **1** the action of allotting. **2** a share allotted. **3** a small piece of land, esp. one rented for cultivation.

al·lo·trope /'aləˌtroʊp/ *noun* any of two or more different physical forms in which an element can exist (*graphite, charcoal, and diamond are all allotropes of carbon*). [back-formation from ALLOTROPY]

al·lot·ropy /ə'lɒtrəpi/ *noun* the existence of two or more different physical forms of a chemical element. □ **allo·trop·ic** /ˌalə'trɒpɪk/ *adjective* **allo·trop·ic·al** /ˌalə'trɒpɪkəl/ *adjective* [Greek *allotropos* of another form, from *allos* different + *tropos* manner, from *trepō* to turn]

al·lot·tee *noun* a person to whom something is allotted.

all-out ● *attributive adjective* total; unrestrained (*all-out war*). ● *adverb* (**all out**) with all one's strength; at full speed (*going all out to win*).

all-over *adjective* covering every part (*an all-over pattern*).

al·low *verb* **1** *transitive* permit (a practice, a person to do something, a thing to happen, etc.) (*smoking is not allowed; we allowed them to speak*). **2** *transitive* give or provide; permit (a person) to have (a limited quantity or sum) (*we were allowed $500 a year*). **3** *transitive* provide or set aside for a purpose; add or deduct in consideration of something (*allow 10% for inflation*). **4** *transitive* **a** admit, agree, concede (*he allowed that it was so; 'You know best,' he allowed*). **b** *informal* state the opinion that. **5** *reflexive* permit oneself, indulge oneself in (conduct) (*allowed herself to be persuaded; allowed myself a few angry words*). **6** *intransitive* (foll. by *of*) admit of. **7** *intransitive* (foll. by *for*) take into consideration or account; make addition or deduction corresponding to (*allowing for wastage*). □ **al·low·able** *adjective* **al·low·ably** *adverb* [Middle English, originally = 'praise', from Old French *alouer* from Latin *allaudare* to praise, and medieval Latin *allocare* to place]

al·low·ance ● *noun* **1 a** an amount or sum given to a person, esp. regularly for a stated purpose. **b** *N Amer.* an amount of money given regularly to a child. **2** an amount allowed in reckoning. **3** a deduction or discount (*an allowance for your trade-in*). **4** (foll. by *of*) tolerance of. **5** a portion of something, e.g. land or fabric, allowed for a specified purpose (*road allowance; seam allowance*). ● *transitive verb* **1** make an allowance to (a person). **2** supply in limited quantities. □ **make allowances** (often foll. by *for*) **1** take into consideration (mitigating circumstances) (*made allowances for his demented state*). **2** look with tolerance upon, make excuses for (a person, bad behaviour, etc.).

al·low·ed·ly /ə'lauədli/ *adverb* as is generally allowed or acknowledged.

al·loy ● *noun* /'aloɪ/ **1** a metallic substance made by combining two or more elements at least one of which is a metal, e.g. brass (a mixture of copper and zinc). **2** an inferior metal mixed esp. with gold or silver. ● *transitive verb* /ə'loɪ/ **1** mix (metals). **2** debase (a pure substance) by admixture. [Old French *aloier, aleier* combine, from Latin *alligare* bind]

all-points bulletin *noun US* a generally issued alert among police officers, esp. calling for the apprehension of a wanted person. Abbr.: **APB**. ¶ Not used by police forces in Canada, who use 'general alert' but current in common parlance.

all-purpose *adjective* suitable for many uses.

all right ● *adverb* **1** satisfactorily, as desired (*it worked out all right*). **2** as an intensifier (*that's the one all right*). ● *adjective* satisfactory; safe and sound. ● *interjection* (also *informal* **all righty**) expressing consent or assent to a proposal or order.

all round *var.* of ALL AROUND.

all-rounder *noun* a versatile person.

All Saints' Day *noun* a Christian festival in honour of the souls in heaven, celebrated on 1 Nov. in Western Churches and on the first Sunday after Pentecost in Eastern Churches.

all·sorts *plural noun* an assortment, esp. of licorice candies.

All Souls' Day *noun* 2 Nov., a Roman Catholic holy day with prayers for the souls of the dead in purgatory.

all·spice *noun* **1** the aromatic spice obtained from the ground berry of the pimento tree, *Pimenta dioica*. **2** the berry of this tree. **3** any of various other aromatic shrubs.

all-star ● *noun* **1** *Sport* a player chosen as among the finest in his or her league. **2** a superstar. ● *adjective* relating to or consisting of all-stars (*an all-star cast; an all-star game*).

all-terrain bicycle *noun* = MOUNTAIN BIKE. Abbr.: **ATB**.

all-terrain vehicle *noun* **1** a tank-like military vehicle with treads used to travel over rough terrain. **2** a rugged one-person vehicle with three or four wheels, designed for travel both on and off roads. Abbr.: **ATV**.

all-time *attributive adjective* (of a record etc.) hitherto unsurpassed.

all told *adverb* in all; when everything is considered (*was a good day all told*).

al·lude *intransitive verb* (foll. by *to*) **1** refer, esp. indirectly, covertly, or briefly to. **2** *disputed* mention. [Latin *alludere* (as AD-, *ludere* lus- play)]

all-up weight *noun* the total weight of an aircraft with passengers, cargo, etc., when airborne.

al·lure ● *transitive verb* attract, charm, or fascinate. ● *noun* attractiveness, personal charm, fascination. □ **al·lure·ment** *noun* **al·lur·ing** *adjective* **al·lur·ing·ly** *adverb* [Old French *alurer* attract (as AD-, *luere* LURE noun)]

al·lu·sion *noun* (often foll. by *to*) a reference, esp. a covert, passing, or indirect one. ¶ Often confused with *illusion*. [as ALLUDE]

al·lu·sive *adjective* **1** (often foll. by *to*) containing an allusion. **2** containing many allusions. □ **al·lu·sive·ly** *adverb* **al·lu·sive·ness** *noun*

al·luv·i·al /ə'luːviːəl/ ● *adjective* of or relating to alluvium. ● *noun* alluvium, esp. containing a precious metal.

alluvial fan *noun* a fan-shaped sedimentary deposit formed when a mountain river enters a large valley or plain.

al·luv·ion /ə'luːviːən/ *noun* the formation of new land by the movement of the sea or of a river. [Latin *alluvio -onis* from *luere* wash]

al·luv·ium /ə'luːviːəm/ *noun* (pl. **al·luv·ia** /-viːə/ or **al·luv·iums**) a deposit of usu. fine fertile soil left during a time of flood, esp. in a river valley or delta. [Latin neuter of *alluvius* adj., from *luere* wash]

all-weather *attributive adjective* suitable for use whatever the weather.

all-wheel drive *noun* N Amer. = FOUR-WHEEL DRIVE. Abbr.: **AWD**.

ally ● *noun* (pl. **al·lies**) **1** a state formally co-operating or united with another for a special purpose, esp. by a treaty. **2** a person or organization that co-operates with or helps another. ● *transitive verb* (**al·lies**, **al·lied**) (often foll. by *with*) combine or unite in alliance. [Old French *al(e)ier* from Latin *alligare* bind: compare ALLOY]

-ally *suffix* forming adverbs from adjectives in -al (*compare* -AL, -LY[2], -ICALLY).

allyl /'aləl/ *noun* Chem. the unsaturated monovalent radical $CH_2=CH-CH_2$. [Latin *allium* garlic + -YL; the substance was first obtained from an oil extracted from garlic]

Alma a city in NE central Quebec, situated at the head of the Saguenay River near Lac Saint-Jean; pop. (2001) 30,126. [ultimately after the Crimean War battle of the *Alma*, fought in 1854]

Alma-Ata see ALMATY.

alma·can·tar *var.* of ALMUCANTAR.

Alma·gest /'almə,dʒest/ *noun* **1** the title of an Arabic version of Ptolemy's astronomical treatise. **2** (also **almagest**) any of various other celebrated medieval textbooks on astrology and alchemy. [from Arabic *al* the, Greek *megistē* (*suntaxis*) the great (system)]

alma mat·er /,ɒlmə 'mɒtər, al-, -mat-/ *noun* the university, school, or college which one attended. [Latin, = bounteous mother]

al·ma·nac /'ɔːlmə,nak, 'ɒl-/ *noun* **1** an annual calendar of months and days, usu. with astronomical data and other information. **2** an annual book of general esp. statistical information. [medieval Latin *almanac(h)* from Greek *almenikhiaka*]

al·man·dine /'almən,diːn, -,dain/ *noun* a kind of garnet with a violet tint. [French, alteration of obsolete *alabandine* from medieval Latin *alabandina* from *Alabanda*, ancient city in Asia Minor]

Al·maty /'almɒti/ (also **Alma-Ata** /,almə 'ɑtɒ/) the largest city in the central Asian republic of Kazakhstan; pop. (est. 2002) 1,066,300. It was known as Verny until 1921.

Al·meria /,almə'riːə/ a city in a province of the same name in Andalusia, S Spain; pop. (est. 2001) 171,000.

al·mighty ● *adjective* **1** having complete power; omnipotent. **2** (**the Almighty**) God. **3** *slang* very great (*an almighty crash*). ● *adverb* *slang* extremely; very much. [Old English *ælmihtig* (as ALL, MIGHTY)]

Almighty Voice (also known as Kah-kee-say-mane-too-wayo ('Voice of the Great Spirit') or Jean-Baptiste) (1874–97), Canadian Cree. Arrested in 1895 for illegally butchering a cow, he escaped, killing a NWMP officer. He evaded capture for 19 months, but was eventually cornered, with two young relatives, on a poplar bluff. The three held off 100 police officers and civilians for two days, during which two more NWMP officers and a civilian were killed; the bluff was bombarded by cannon and all three Indians were killed.

Al·mir·ante Brown /,almɪ'ranti/ a city in eastern Argentina, forming part of the conurbation of Buenos Aires; pop. (est. 1999) 550,000.

Almo·dó·var /,almə'doːvar/ **Pedro** (b.1951), Spanish film director. His films, such as *Women on the Verge of a Nervous Breakdown*, are outlandishly inventive and deal outrageously with sexual matters.

Almo·had /'almə,had/ *noun* (also **Almo·hade** /-,heid/) a member of a group of Muslim Berber peoples that conquered the Spanish and North African Empire of the Almoravids in the 12th c., taking the capital Marrakesh in 1147. They were driven out of Spain in 1212 but held on to Marrakesh until 1269.

al·mond /'ɑmənd, 'ɒl-/ *noun* **1** the oval nutlike seed (kernel) of the stone fruit from the tree *Prunus dulcis*, of which there are sweet and bitter varieties. **2** the tree itself, of the rose family and allied to the peach and plum. **3** a very pale beige colour. [medieval Latin *amandula* from Latin *amygdala* from Greek *amugdalē*: assoc. with words in AL-]

almond eyes *plural noun* eyes the shape of almonds, oval and narrowing to a point at both sides.

almond oil *noun* the oil expressed from the seed of the almond (esp. the bitter variety), used for cosmetic preparations, flavouring, and medicinal purposes.

almond paste *noun* = MARZIPAN.

al·mon·er /'ɒmənər/ *noun* **1** *hist.* an official distributor of alms. **2** *Brit.* formerly, a social worker attached to a hospital and seeing to the aftercare of patients. [Old French *aumonier*, ultimately from medieval Latin *eleēmosynarius* (as ALMS)]

Al·monte /'almɒnt/ a former town in east central Ontario, situated on the Mississippi River, southwest of Ottawa, now part of the town of Mississippi Mills; pop. (2001) 4,649. [J. N. *Almonte*, Mexican general and ambassador to the US d.1869]

Al·mora·vid /al'mɔrəvid/ *noun* (also **Al·mora·vide** /-,vaid/) a member of a federation of Muslim Berber peoples that established an empire in Morocco and Algeria in the second half of the 11th c., with Marrakesh as their capital, and went on to take much of Spain from 1086.

al·most *adverb* all but; very nearly. [Old English *ælmæst* for the most part (as ALL, MOST)]

alms /ɒmz/ *plural noun* charitable donations of money or food given to the poor. [Old English *ælmysse, -messe*, from Germanic, ultimately from Greek *eleēmosunē* from *eleēmōn* (adj.) from *eleos* compassion]

alms·giving *noun* the giving of charitable donations. □ **alms·giver** *noun*

alms·house *noun hist.* a house for the poor founded by charity.

almu·can·tar /,almə'kantar/ *noun* (also **almu·can·tar**) *Astronomy* **1** a line of constant altitude above the horizon. **2** an instrument for measuring stellar altitude and azimuth. [ultimately from Arabic *almuḳanṭarāt* sundial, from *ḳanṭara* arch]

Al·ni·lam /'alnɪ,lam/ one of the three bright stars forming Orion's belt. [Arabic, = string of pearls]

Al·ni·tak /'alnɪ,tak/ one of the three bright stars forming Orion's belt. [Arabic, = girdle]

aloe /'aloʊ/ *noun* **1** any plant of the genus *Aloe*, including succulent herbs, shrubs, and trees. **2** (in *pl.*) (in full **bitter aloes**) a strong laxative obtained from the bitter juice of various species of aloe. **3** (in full **American aloe**) = CENTURY PLANT. [Greek *aloē* denoting the fragrant heartwood of certain oriental trees]

aloe vera /ˈaləˈvɛrə/ *noun* a succulent plant, *Aloe vera*, yielding a juice used in cosmetics and as a treatment for burns. [Latin, = true aloe]

aloft *predicative adjective & adverb* **1** in the air, high up; overhead. **2** upwards. [Old Norse *á lopt(i)* from *á* in, on, to + *lopt* air: compare LIFT, LOFT]

alogic·al /eiˈlɒdʒɪkəl/ *adjective* **1** not logical. **2** opposed to logic.

aloha /əˈloːhɒ/ ● *interjection* (in Hawaii and the S Pacific) a greeting or farewell; hello or goodbye. ● *adjective* reflecting characteristics considered typically Hawaiian, such as brightly coloured garments or a relaxed approach to life (*aloha shirt; aloha spirit*). [Hawaiian, lit. 'love, affection, pity']

alone ● *predicative adjective* **1 a** without others present (*they wanted to be alone; the tree stood alone*). **b** without others' help (*succeeded alone*). **c** lonely and isolated (*felt alone*). **2** (often foll. by *in*) standing by oneself in an opinion etc. (*was alone in thinking this*). ● *adverb* only, exclusively (*you alone can help me*). □ **go it alone** act by oneself without assistance. □ **alone·ness** *noun* [Middle English from ALL + ONE]

along ● *preposition* **1** from one end to the other end of (*a handkerchief with lace along the edge*). **2** on or through any part of the length of (*was walking along the road*). **3** beside or through the length of (*shelves stood along the wall*). **4** during the course of (*stop along the way*). ● *adverb* **1** onward; into a more advanced state (*come along; getting along nicely*). **2** at or to a particular place; arriving (*I'll be along soon*). **3** in company with a person, esp. oneself (*bring a book along*). **4** beside or through part or the whole length of a thing. □ **along with** in addition to; together with. [Old English *andlang* from West Germanic, related to LONG¹]

along·shore *adverb* along or by the shore.

along·side ● *adverb* (sometimes foll. by *of*) at or to the side. ● *preposition* **1** close to the side of; next to. **2** in close association with (*the assistants will work alongside the teachers*).

aloof ● *adjective* distant, unsympathetic. ● *adverb* away, apart (*he kept aloof from his colleagues*). □ **aloof·ly** *adverb* **aloof·ness** *noun* [originally Naut., from A² + LUFF]

alo·pecia /ˌaləˈpiːʃə/ *noun Med.* the absence (complete or partial) of hair from areas of the body where it normally grows; baldness. [Greek *alōpekia* fox mange, from *alōpēx* fox]

aloud *adverb* **1** audibly or vocally; not silently or in a whisper. **2** *archaic* loudly. [A² + LOUD]

alow /əˈloː/ *adverb & predicative adjective* in or into the lower part of a ship. [A² + LOW¹]

Aloy·sius /ˌaləˈwɪʃəs/ *St.* (Aloysius Gonzaga, 1568–91), Italian Jesuit. Of noble birth, he abandoned court life to devote himself to God and died nursing plague victims.

alp *noun* **1** a high mountain. (*See also* ALPS, THE.) **2** (in Switzerland) pasture land on a mountainside. [sing. of *Alps*]

al·paca /alˈpakə/ *noun* **1** a S American mammal, *Lama pacos*, related to the llama, with long shaggy hair and usu. brown and white colouring. **2** the wool from this animal. **3** fabric made from the wool, with or without other fibres. [Spanish from Aymara or Quechua]

alpen·glow *noun* the rosy light of the setting or rising sun seen on high mountains. [German *Alpenglühen*, lit. 'Alp-glow']

alpen·horn *var. of* ALPHORN.

alpen·stock *noun* a long iron-tipped staff used in mountain climbing. [German, lit. 'Alp-stick']

al·pha *noun* **1** the first letter of the Greek alphabet (A, α). **2** (*attributive*) designating the first of a series or set. **3** *Astronomy* the chief star in a constellation. **4** *Brit.* a first-class mark given for a piece of work or in an examination. □ **alpha and omega** the beginning and the end; the most important features. [Greek]

alpha·bet *noun* **1** the set of letters used in writing a language (*the Russian alphabet*). **2** a set of symbols or signs representing letters. **3** the rudiments of a branch of knowledge etc.; the ABCs. [Greek *alpha*, *bēta*, the first two letters of the alphabet]

alphabet book *noun* an illustrated book for teaching esp. children the alphabet.

alpha·bet·ic·al *adjective* (also **alpha·bet·ic**) **1** of or relating to an alphabet. **2** in the order of the letters of the alphabet. □ **alpha·bet·ic·al·ly** *adverb*

alpha·bet·ize *transitive verb* (also esp. *Brit.* **-ise**) arrange (words, names, etc.) in alphabetical order. □ **alpha·bet·iz·a·tion** *noun*

alphabet soup *noun* **1** a soup containing letter-shaped pieces of pasta. **2** a jumble of words or letters.

alpha-blocker *noun* a drug preventing stimulation of alpha receptors.

Alpha Cen·tauri /ˌalfə senˈtɔːri/ the brightest star in the constellation Centaurus and the nearest bright star to the Sun.

alpha-hydroxy acid *noun* any of a class of aliphatic carboxylic acids containing a hydroxyl group, some of which are used in skin care preparations for their exfoliating properties. Abbr.: **AHA**.

alpha male *noun* **1** the dominant animal within a single-sex group. **2** a man who embodies characteristics thought of as particularly masculine to a high degree, esp. aggressiveness, dominance, territoriality, and sexuality; a macho man.

alpha·num·er·ic /ˌalfənuːˈmerɪk, -njuː-/ *adjective* (also **alpha·num·er·ic·al**) containing both alphabetical and numerical symbols. [ALPHABETIC (see ALPHABETICAL) + NUMERICAL]

alpha particle *noun* a helium nucleus emitted by a radioactive substance.

alpha ray *noun* (also **alpha radiation**) a stream of alpha particles.

Al·phard /ˈalfard/ the brightest star in the constellation Hydra.

alpha receptor *noun* one of two kinds of receptor in the sympathetic nervous system which increase blood pressure when stimulated.

alpha rhythm *noun* = ALPHA WAVES.

alpha test ● *noun* a preliminary test of computer software etc., usually carried out within the organization developing it (*compare* BETA TEST). ● *transitive verb* submit (a product) to an alpha test.

alpha waves *plural noun* the normal rhythmic activity of the brain recorded in an electroencephalogram, having a frequency of eight to thirteen cycles per second.

alp·horn *noun* (also **alpen·horn**) a very long wooden wind instrument used by cowherds in the Alps and other European mountainous regions to call their cattle. [German *Alpenhorn*]

alp·ine ● *adjective* **1 a** of or relating to high mountains. **b** growing or found on high mountains, esp. above the timberline. **2** (**Alpine**) of or relating to the Alps. **3** of or relating to competitive downhill or slalom skiing (*compare* NORDIC 3). ● *noun* a plant native or suited to mountain districts.

alpine fir *noun* a tall and slender fir tree, *Abies lasiocarpa*, native to northwestern N America and growing at high altitudes.

alpin·ist /ˈalpɪnɪst/ *noun* (also **Alpinist**) a climber of high mountains. □ **alpin·ism** *noun*

Alps, the a mountain system in Europe extending in a curve from the coast of SE France through NW Italy, Switzerland, Liechtenstein, and S Germany, into Austria. Its highest peak, Mont Blanc, rises to a height of 4 807 m (15,771 ft.).

al Qaeda /alˈkaidə/ *noun* a network of Islamic fundamentalist groups founded by Osama bin Laden, advocating and practising terrorism against Western targets and involved in the attacks of September 11th, 2001. [Arabic, lit. + 'the base']

al·ready *adverb* **1** before the time in question (*I knew that already*). **2** as early or as soon as this (*already, at the age of six, he could play the piano*). **3** *N Amer.* used at the end of a phrase as an intensifier to express impatience etc. (*tell the story already!*). [ALL *adv.* + READY]

al·right *disputed var. of* ALL RIGHT.

ALS *abbreviation* AMYOTROPHIC LATERAL SCLEROSIS.

Al·sace /alˈsas, ˈal-/ a region of NE France, on the borders with Germany and Switzerland. Alsace was annexed by Prussia, along with part of Lorraine (forming Alsace-Lorraine), after the Franco-Prussian War of 1870–1, and restored to France after the First World War.

Al·sa·tian /alˈseiʃən/ ● *adjective* of or relating to Alsace. ● *noun* **1** a native or resident of Alsace. **2** a German dialect spoken in Alsace. **3** *Brit.* = GERMAN SHEPHERD. [*Alsatia* (= ALSACE) + -AN]

al·sike /ˈalsəik, ˈalsɪk/ *noun* a species of clover, *Trifolium hybridum*. [*Alsike* in Sweden]

also *adverb* in addition; likewise; besides. [Old English *alswā* (as ALL *adv.*, SO¹)]

also-ran *noun* **1** a contestant not among the winners in a race, election, etc. **2** an undistinguished person.

al·stroe·meria /ˌalstrəˈmiːriə/ *noun* any of various ornamental liliaceous plants of the S American genus *Alstroemeria*, cultivated for their showy flowers. [K. von *Alstroemer*, Swedish naturalist d.1796]

Alt /ɒlt/ *noun Computing* a key on a computer keyboard which alters the function of another key pressed simultaneously. [abbreviation of *alternative*]

Alta. *abbreviation* Alberta.

Altai /ˈaltai/ (also **Altay**) a krai of Russia in SW Siberia, on the border with Kazakhstan; pop. (est. 2001) 2,643,000; capital, Barnaul.

Consonants: b *but* d *dog* f *few* g *get* h *her* j *yes* k *cat* l *leg* m *man* n *no* p *pen* r *red* s *sit*

Al·taic /alˈteiɪk/ ● *noun* a family of languages including Turkic and Mongolian. ● *adjective* denoting or pertaining to this family of languages or its speakers.

Altai Mountains a mountain system of central Asia extending about 1 600 km (1,000 miles) eastward from Kazakhstan into W Mongolia and N China.

Al·tair /ɒlˈteɪr/ the brightest star in the constellation Aquila. [Arabic, = the flying eagle]

Alta·mira /ˌaltəˈmiːrə/ the site of a cave with paleolithic rock paintings, south of Santander in N Spain, discovered in 1879. The paintings were realistic depictions of deer, wild boar, and esp. bison; they are dated to the upper Magdalenian period.

al·tar *noun* **1** a table or flat-topped block, often of stone, for sacrifice or offering to a deity. **2** *Christianity* a table on which bread and wine are consecrated in the Communion service. **3** *Christianity* the raised area in a church on which the communion altar, lecterns, pulpit, etc. are found. □ **lead to the altar** marry. [Latin *altaria* (pl.) burnt offerings, altar, prob. related to *adolēre* burn in sacrifice]

altar boy *noun* a boy who serves as a priest's assistant in a service.

altar call *noun* (esp. in pentecostal Christian worship) an invitation to members of a congregation to gather at the front of the sanctuary, esp. to make a public confession of faith or to request special prayers etc.

altar girl *noun* a girl who serves as a priest's assistant in a service.

altar·piece *noun* a piece of art, esp. a painting, set above or behind an altar.

altar rail *noun* = COMMUNION RAIL.

altar server *noun* a child or adult who serves as a priest's assistant in a service.

Altay see ALTAI.

alt·azi·muth /alˈtazɪməθ/ *noun* an instrument for measuring the altitude and azimuth of celestial bodies. [ALTITUDE + AZIMUTH]

alt-country *noun* a style of country music that is influenced by alternative rock. [abbreviation of ALTERNATIVE, influenced by the *alt.* prefix of some Internet groups]

Alt·dor·fer /ɒltˈdɔrfər/ **Al·brecht** (*c.*1480–1538), German painter. Most of his paintings are religious works, but he is remembered primarily as a leading pioneer of landscape painting.

al·ter *verb* **1** *transitive & intransitive* make or become different; change. **2** *transitive* modify the style or size of (clothing); tailor. **3** *transitive* castrate or spay. □ **alter·able** *adjective* **alter·a·tion** /-ˈreiʃən/ *noun* [Late Latin *alterare* from *alter* other]

alter·ca·tion /ˌɒltərˈkeiʃən/ *noun* a heated argument or dispute; a quarrel. [Latin *altercatio* from *altercari* 'wrangle']

altered state *noun* (also **altered state of consciousness**) any state of mind that differs from the normal state of consciousness of a person, esp. one induced by drugs, hypnosis, or mental disorder.

alter ego *noun* (*pl.* **alter egos**) **1** an intimate and trusted friend. **2** a person's secondary or alternative personality. [Latin, = other self]

al·ter·ity /ɒlˈterɪti/ *noun* the state of being other or different; otherness. [Late Latin *alteritas* from *alter* 'other']

alterna- *combining form* prefixed to a type of popular music to designate an unconventional or idiosyncratic version of that type of music (*alterna-rock*). [shortening of ALTERNATIVE]

alter·nate ● *verb* /ˈɒltərˌneit/ **1** *intransitive* (often foll. by *with*) (of two things) succeed each other by turns (*rain and sunshine alternated; elation alternated with depression*). **2** *intransitive* (foll. by *between*) change repeatedly (between two conditions) (*the patient alternated between hot and cold fevers*). **3** *transitive* (often foll. by *with*) cause (two things) to succeed each other by turns (*the band alternated fast and slow tunes; we alternated criticism with reassurance*). ● *adjective* /ˈɒltərnət/ **1** (with noun in *pl.*) every other (*comes on alternate days*). **2** (of things of two kinds) each following and succeeded by one of the other kind (*alternate joy and misery*). **3** (of a sequence etc.) consisting of alternate things. **4** *Bot.* (of leaves etc.) placed alternately on the two sides of the stem. **5** = ALTERNATIVE. ● *noun* /ˈɒltərnət/ esp. *N Amer.* a person or thing that substitutes for another (*each team carried two alternates*). □ **alter·nate·ly** *adverb* [Latin *alternatus* past participle of *alternare* do things by turns, from *alternus* every other, from *alter* other]

alternate angles *plural noun* two angles, not adjoining one another, that are formed on opposite sides of a line that intersects two other lines.

alternating current *noun* an electric current that reverses its direction at regular intervals (*compare* DIRECT CURRENT). Abbr.: **AC**.

alter·na·tion *noun* the action or result of alternating.

alternation of generations *noun* the occurrence in alternate generations of different forms of an organism having different (usu. sexual and asexual) reproductive processes.

al·terna·tive /ɒlˈtɜrnətɪv/ ● *adjective* **1** (of one or more things) available or usable instead of another (*an alternative route*). ¶ Use with reference to more than two options (e.g. *many alternative methods*) is common, and acceptable. **2** (of two things) mutually exclusive. **3** of or relating to practices that offer a substitute for the conventional ones (*alternative medicine; alternative theatre*). ● *noun* **1** any of two or more possibilities. **2** the freedom or opportunity to choose between two or more things (*I had no alternative but to go*). □ **al·terna·tive·ly** *adverb*

alternative dispute resolution (also **alternate dispute resolution**) *Law* a method of solving a dispute without resorting to litigation, e.g. mediation, arbitration, etc.

alternative rock *noun* rock music (esp. as distributed by an independent record label) characterized by an unorthodox or uncommercial style or approach.

alter·na·tor *noun* a generator that produces an alternating current (*compare* DIRECT CURRENT).

alt·horn /ˈalthɔrn/ *noun Music* a brass instrument of the saxhorn family, esp. the alto or tenor saxhorn in E flat. [German from *alt* high, from Latin *altus* + HORN]

al·though *conjunction* = THOUGH *conjunction* 1–3. [Middle English from ALL *adv.* + THOUGH]

Alt·hus·ser /ˈaltuˌser/ **Louis** (1918–90), French Marxist philosopher. He sought to reassert an anti-humanist approach to Marxism and develop it into a structural analysis of society. His works include *For Marx* (1969) and *Reading Capital* (1970). Found guilty of the murder of his wife, he spent his last years in a mental asylum.

al·tim·eter /alˈtɪmɪtər/ *noun* an instrument for showing height above sea or ground level, esp. one fitted to an aircraft. [Latin *altus* high + -METER]

alti·plano /ˌaltiˈplaːnoː/ *noun* the high tableland of central S America. [Spanish]

alti·tude *noun* **1** the height of an object in relation to a given point, esp. sea level or the horizon. **2** *Astronomy* the angular distance of a celestial body above the horizon. **3** *Geom.* the length of the perpendicular from a vertex to the opposite side of a figure. **4** a high or exalted position. □ **alti·tud·inal** *adjective* [Latin *altitudo* from *altus* high]

altitude sickness *noun* an illness caused by ascent to high altitude, characterized chiefly by nausea and exhaustion.

Alt·man /ˈɒltmən/ **Rob·ert** (b.1925), US film director. He made his name with *MASH* (1970), a black comedy about an army surgical hospital at the front in the Korean War. He has been nominated for an Oscar for best director for four films, including *MASH* and *The Player* (1992).

alto /ˈɒltoː, ˈaltoː/ *noun* (*pl.* **altos**) **1** = CONTRALTO. **2 a** the highest adult male singing voice, above tenor. **b** a singer with this voice. **c** a part written for it. **3 a** (*attributive*) denoting the member of a family of instruments pitched second- or third-highest. **b** an alto instrument, esp. an alto saxophone. [Italian *alto* (*canto*) high (singing)]

alto clef *noun Music* a sign that indicates that the middle line of the staff represents middle C, used chiefly for viola music.

alto·cumu·lus /ˌaltoːˈkjuːmjʊləs/ *noun* cloud formed at medium altitude as a layer of rounded masses with a level base. [Latin *altus* high + CUMULUS]

al·to·geth·er *adverb* **1** totally, completely (*you are altogether wrong*). **2** on the whole (*altogether it had been a good day*). **3** in total (*there are six bedrooms altogether*). ¶ *Altogether* does not mean the same as *all together*. *Altogether* means 'in total', as in *If Paul comes there will be six of us altogether*, whereas *all together* means 'all at once' or 'all in one place' as in *Paul and his friends were all together at the show*. □ **in the altogether** *informal* naked. [Middle English from ALL + TOGETHER]

alto·ist /ˈɒltoːɪst, ˈaltoː-/ *noun* an alto saxophone player.

alto-relievo /ˌaltoːrəˈliːvoː/ *noun* (*pl.* **-relievos**) *Sculpture* **1** a form of relief in which the sculpted shapes stand out from the background to at least half their actual depth. **2** a sculpture characterized by this. [ALTO + RELIEVO]

alto·strat·us /ˌaltoːˈstraːtəs/ *noun* cloud formed at medium altitudes as a continuous flat greyish sheet. [Latin *altus* high + STRATUS]

alt-rock *noun* = ALTERNATIVE ROCK.

al·tru·ism /ˈɒltruːˌɪzəm, ˈal-/ *noun* **1** regard for others as a principle of action. **2** unselfishness; concern for other people. **3** *Zool.* sacrifice so that genetically close younger relatives may survive or otherwise

---

t *top*   v *voice*   w *we*   z *zoo*   ʃ *she*   ʒ *vision*   θ *thin*   ð *this*   ŋ *ring*   x *loch*   tʃ *chip*   dʒ *jar*   (*see over for vowels*)

benefit. □ **al·tru·ist** *noun* **al·tru·is·tic** /ˌɒltruːˈɪstɪk, ˌal-/ *adjective*
al·tru·is·tic·ally /ˌɒltruːˈɪstɪkli, ˌal-/ *adverb* [French *altruisme* from Italian *altrui* somebody else (influenced by Latin *alter* other)]

alum¹ /ˈaləm/ *noun* **1** a double sulphate of aluminum and potassium, having astringent properties. **2** any of a group of compounds of double sulphates of a monovalent metal (or group) and a trivalent metal. [Latin *alumen aluminis*]

alum² /əˈlʌm/ *noun N Amer. informal* alumnus or alumna. [abbreviation]

alum·ina /əˈluːmɪnə/ *noun* the compound aluminum oxide occurring naturally as corundum and emery. Chem. formula: Al_2O_3. [Latin *alumen* alum, after *soda* etc.]

alum·in·ize /əˈluːmɪˌnaɪz/ *transitive verb* (also esp. *Brit.* **-ise**) coat with aluminum. □ **alum·in·iz·a·tion** /-ˈzeɪʃən/ *noun*

alum·ino·sili·cate /əˌluːmɪnoʊˈsɪlɪkeɪt/ *noun* a silicate containing aluminum, esp. a rock-forming mineral of this kind, e.g. a feldspar, a clay mineral.

alum·inum /əˈluːmɪnəm/ *noun* (*Brit.* **alum·in·ium** /ˌaljuːˈmɪniəm/) a silvery, light, and malleable metallic element resistant to tarnishing by air. Symbol: **Al**; at. no.: 13. [alteration (after *sodium* etc.) of *alumium*, from ALUM¹ + -IUM]

aluminum bronze *noun* an alloy of copper and aluminum.

alumna /əˈlʌmnə/ *noun* (*pl.* **alum·nae** /-naɪ, -niː/) **1** a female graduate of a specified university or school. **2** a woman who is a former member of a specified group or organization.

alum·nus /əˈlʌmnəs/ *noun* (*pl.* **alumni** /-naɪ/) **1** a graduate of a specified university or other school. **2** a former member of a specified group or organization. [Latin, = nursling, pupil, from *alere* nourish]

Alva /ˈalvə/ **Duke of** (also **Alba**) (title of Fernando Alvarez de Toledo) (1508–82), Spanish general, noted for his ruthlessness and cruelty as Governor General of the Netherlands (1567–73).

alvar /ˈalvɑr/ *noun* a low-lying area of flat, exposed limestone with shallow soil, covered with shrubs, native grasses, sedges, or wildflowers. Alvars are found only in a few areas surrounding the Great Lakes, Estonia, and Sweden. [Swedish, from *alv* 'stratum, subsoil', compare German dialect *alben* 'loose chalk soil']

al·veo·lar /ˌalviˈoːlɜr, alˈviːələr/ *adjective* **1** of an alveolus. **2** *Phonetics* (of a consonant) pronounced with the tip of the tongue in contact with the alveolar ridge, e.g. *n*, *s*, *t*.

alveolar ridge *noun* the bony ridge behind the upper teeth.

al·veo·lus /ˌalviˈoːləs, alˈviːələs/ *noun* (*pl.* **al·veoli** /-laɪ, -liː/) **1** a cavity, pit, or hollow. **2** any of the many tiny air sacs of the lungs which allow for rapid gaseous exchange. **3** the bony socket for the root of a tooth. **4** the cell of a honeycomb. □ **al·veo·late** *adjective* [Latin diminutive of *alveus* cavity]

Al·ver·stone, Mount /ˈalvɜrstən/ a peak in the St. Elias Mountains, on the Yukon-Alaska border (4 439 m). [R. E. Webster, Viscount *Alverstone*, British judge d.1915]

al·ways *adverb* **1** at all times; on all occasions (*they are always late*). **2** whatever the circumstances (*I can always sleep on the floor*). **3** repeatedly; often (*they are always complaining*).

alys·sum /əˈlɪsəm/ *noun* **1** (in full **sweet alyssum**) a low-growing widely-cultivated plant, *Lobularia maritima*, having very small white or purple flowers. **2** any plant of the genus *Alyssum*, widely cultivated and usu. having yellow or white flowers. [Latin from Greek *alusson*, from *a-* 'without' + *lussa* 'rabies' (referring to early herbalist use)]

Alz·heimer's disease /ˈɒlts.haɪmɜrz, ˈɒls-, ˈalts-, ˈals-/ *noun* (also **Alzheimer's**) a serious disorder of the brain manifesting itself in premature senility. [A. *Alzheimer*, German neurologist d.1915]

AM *abbreviation* **1 a** AMPLITUDE MODULATION. **b** the band of radio stations broadcasting with this system (often *attributive*: *an AM radio*; *the CBC's AM network*). **2** *US* Master of Arts. [(sense 2) Latin *artium Magister*]

Am *symbol Chem.* the element americium.

am *1st person sing. present of* BE.

a.m. *abbreviation* before noon. [Latin *ante meridiem*]

AMA *abbreviation* American Medical Association.

-ama *combining form* = -RAMA.

Amad·juak Lake /əˈmadʒuːak/ a lake situated in the southern part of Baffin Island, northwest of Iqaluit. [Inuktitut, = great water]

Ama·dora /ˌaməˈdɔrə/ a city in W Portugal, part of the conurbation of Lisbon; pop. (est. 2001) 174,788.

amah /ˈɒmə/ *noun* (in the Far East and India) a nursemaid or maid. [Portuguese *ama* nurse]

Amal·fi /əˈmalfi/ a port and resort on the west coast of Italy, on the Gulf of Salerno; pop. (1996) 5,589.

amal·gam /əˈmalgəm/ *noun* **1** a mixture or blend. **2** an alloy of mercury with one or more other metals, used esp. for dental fillings. [medieval Latin *amalgama* from Greek *malagma* an emollient]

amal·gam·ate /əˈmalgəˌmeit/ *verb* **1** *transitive & intransitive* combine or unite to form one structure, organization, etc. **2** *intransitive* (of metals) alloy with mercury. □ **amal·gam·a·tion** /-ˈmeiʃən/ *noun* [medieval Latin *amalgamare amalgamat-* (as AMALGAM)]

Amal·thea /əˈmalθiə/ **1** *Gk Myth* a goat which suckled the infant Zeus. **2** *Astronomy* satellite V of Jupiter, the third closest to the planet, discovered in 1892. It is red in colour and heavily cratered, 262 km long and 146 km across.

aman·dine /ˌamɒnˈdiːn, -mən-/ *adjective* (placed after noun) garnished with (usu. sliced) almonds (*green beans amandine*). [French]

amanu·en·sis /əˌmanjuˈensɪs/ *noun* (*pl.* **amanu·en·ses** /-siːz/) **1** a person who writes from dictation or copies manuscripts. **2** a literary assistant. [Latin from (*servus*) *a manu* secretary + *-ensis* belonging to]

am·ar·anth /ˈaməˌranθ/ *noun* **1** any herbaceous plant of the genus *Amaranthus*, usu. having small green, red, or purple tinted flowers, some species of which are weeds, e.g. pigweed, with other species cultivated as grain crops or ornamentals. **2** an imaginary flower that never fades. **3** a purplish-red dye used esp. to colour foods. □ **amar·anth·ine** /ˌaməˈranθaɪn/ *adjective* [modern Latin from Greek *amarantos* everlasting, from *a-* not + *marainō* wither, alteration of *polyanthus* etc.]

amar·etti /ˌaməˈreti/ *plural noun* (also **amaretti cookies**) small, dry, Italian macaroons. [Italian, diminutive of *amaro* from Latin *amarus* bitter]

amar·etto /ˌaməˈretoː/ *noun* an almond-flavoured liqueur, often used as a flavouring in desserts, coffee, etc. [Italian, as AMARETTI]

Amarna, Tell el- /əˈmɑrnə, ˌtel el/ the site of the ruins of the ancient Egyptian capital Akhetaten, on the east bank of the Nile. The city was built by Akhenaten in *c.*1375 BC, when he established the new worship of the sun disc Aten, and was abandoned four years after his death, when the court returned to the former capital, Thebes.

Amar·one /ˌaməˈroːnei/ *noun* an Italian wine made from dried grapes, with a high alcohol content. [Italian, as AMARETTI]

ama·ryl·lis /ˌaməˈrɪlɪs/ *noun* **1** a plant genus with a single species, *Amaryllis belladonna*, a bulbous lily-like plant native to South Africa with white or rose-pink flowers. *Also called* BELLADONNA LILY. **2** any of various related plants formerly of this genus now transferred to other genera, notably *Hippeastrum*. [Latin from Greek *Amarullis*, name of a country girl]

amass *transitive verb* **1** gather or heap together. **2** accumulate (riches etc.). □ **amass·er** *noun* [French *amasser*, ultimately from Latin *massa* MASS¹]

Ama·ter·asu /əˌmɒtəˈrɒsuː/ the principal deity of the Japanese Shinto religion, the sun goddess and ancestor of Jimmu, founder of the imperial dynasty.

ama·teur /ˈaməˌtʃɜr, -ˌtɜr/ *noun* **1** (often *attributive*) a person who engages in a pursuit, e.g. an art or sport as a pastime rather than a profession (*the actors are amateurs*; *an amateur photographer*). **2** (*attributive*) for or done by amateurs (*amateur athletics*). **3** an unskilful or inexperienced person. **4** (foll. by *of*) a person who is fond of (a thing). □ **ama·teur·ism** *noun* [French from Latin *amator -oris* lover, from *amare* love]

ama·teur·ish /ˈamətʃɜrɪʃ, ˌamətˈʃɜrɪʃ/ *adjective* characteristic of an amateur, esp. unskilful or inexperienced. □ **ama·teur·ish·ly** *adverb* **ama·teur·ish·ness** *noun*

Amati /əˈmɒti/ a family of Italian violin makers. The three generations, all based in Cremona, included **An·drea** (*c.*1520–*c.*1580), his sons **An·tonio** (1550–1638) and **Gi·ro·la·mo** (1551–1635), and, most notable, the latter's son **Nico·lò** (1596–1684). From Nicolò's workshop came the violin makers Antonio Stradivari and Andreas Guarneri (*c.*1626–98), uncle of Giuseppe Guarneri 'del Gesù'. The Amatis developed the basic proportions of the violin, viola, and cello.

ama·tory /ˈaməˌtɔri/ *adjective* of or relating to sexual love or desire. [Latin *amatorius* from *amare* love]

amau·tik /əˈmautɪk/ *noun* (also **amau·ti** /əˈmauti/) *Cdn* (*North*) **1** an Inuit woman's parka with a large hood in which a child may be carried. **2** the large hood of such a parka. [Inuktitut]

amaze *transitive verb* (often foll. by *at*, or *that* + clause, or *to* + infin.) surprise greatly; overwhelm with wonder (*am amazed at your indifference*; *was amazed to find them alive*). □ **amaze·ment** *noun* [Old English *āmasod*, of uncertain origin]

amaz·ing *adjective* **1** causing great surprise. **2** *informal* exceptional (*an amazing book*). □ **amaz·ing·ly** *adverb*

Vowels: a *cat* ɑ *arm* e *bed* ɜr *her* ɜː *deux* ə *ago* ɪ *sit* i *cosy* iː *feed* ɒ *hot* ɔ *pore* ɔː *no* ʌ *run* ʊ *put*

Ama·zon /ˈaməˌzɒn/ noun **1** a member of a mythical race of female warriors which appears in many Greek legends. **2** (**amazon**) a very tall, strong, or athletic woman. □ **Ama·zon·ian** /ˌaməˈzoːniən/ adjective [Greek: explained by the Greeks as 'breastless' (as if A-¹ + mazos breast), but prob. of foreign origin]

Ama·zonia /ˌaməˈzoːniə/ **1** the area around the Amazon River in S America, principally in Brazil, but also extending into Peru, Colombia, and Bolivia. Crossed by the equator in the north, this region comprises approximately one-third of the world's remaining tropical rainforest. **2** a national park protecting 10 000 sq. km (3,850 sq. miles) of tropical rainforest in the state of Pará, N Brazil.

Amazon parrot noun (also **amazon**) any of several short-tailed, chiefly green, Central and S American parrots constituting the genus *Amazona*.

Amazon River /ˈaməzɒn, -zən/ a river in S America, flowing over 6 683 km (4,150 miles) through Peru, Colombia, and Brazil into the Atlantic Ocean. It drains two-fifths of the continent and in terms of water flow it is the largest river in the world. □ **Ama·zon·ian** /ˌaməˈzoːniən/ adjective [AMAZON]

am·bas·sa·dor noun **1** an accredited diplomat sent by a state on a mission to, or as its permanent representative in, a foreign country. **2** a representative or promoter of a specified thing (an ambassador of peace). □ **am·bas·sa·dor·ial** /amˌbasəˈdɔːriəl/ adjective **am·bas·sa·dor·ship** noun [French ambassadeur from Italian ambasciator, ultimately from Latin ambactus servant]

am·bassador-at-large noun N Amer. an ambassador with special duties, not appointed to a particular country.

am·bas·sa·dress noun **1** a female ambassador. **2** an ambassador's wife.

am·ber ● noun **1 a** a yellowish translucent fossilized resin deriving from extinct (esp. coniferous) trees and used in jewellery. **b** the honey-yellow colour of this. **2** a yellow traffic light meaning caution, showing between red for 'stop' and green for 'go'. ● adjective made of or coloured like amber. [Old French ambre from Arabic 'anbar ambergris, amber]

Amber Alert noun N Amer. a public alert issued repeatedly in the event of an abduction. [Amber Hagerman, abducted US child d.1996]

amber·gris /ˈambərgrɪs, -ˌgriːs/ noun a strong-smelling waxlike secretion of the intestine of the sperm whale, found floating in tropical seas and used in perfume manufacture. [Old French ambre gris grey AMBER]

amber·jack noun any large, brightly coloured marine fish of the genus *Seriola* found in tropical and subtropical Atlantic waters.

am·bi·ance var. of AMBIENCE.

ambi·dex·trous /ˌambiˈdekstrəs/ adjective **1 a** (of a person) able to use the right and left hands equally well. **b** (of an object) suited for use with either the right or left hand (ambidextrous scissors). **2** working skilfully in more than one medium. **3** double-dealing; trying to please both parties. □ **ambi·dex·ter·ity** /-ˈsterɪti/ noun **ambi·dex·trous·ly** adverb **ambi·dex·trous·ness** noun [Late Latin ambidexter from ambi- on both sides + dexter right-handed]

am·bi·ence /ˈambiəns, ˈɑ̃mbiˈɑ̃s, ˈambiənz/ noun (also **am·bi·ance**) the surroundings or atmosphere of a place; mood.

am·bi·ent /ˈambiənt/ ● adjective surrounding. ● noun (also **ambient music**) a style of instrumental music with electronic textures and no persistent beat, used to create or enhance a mood or atmosphere. [Latin ambiens -entis pres. part. of ambire go round]

ambi·gu·ity /ˌambɪˈgjuːɪti/ noun (pl. **-ities**) **1 a** a double meaning which is either deliberate or caused by inexactness of expression. **b** an example of this. **2** an expression able to be interpreted in more than one way.

am·bigu·ous /amˈbɪgjuːəs/ adjective **1** having an obscure or double meaning. **2** difficult to classify. □ **am·bigu·ous·ly** adverb **am·bigu·ous·ness** noun [Latin ambiguus doubtful, from ambigere from ambi- both ways + agere drive]

ambi·son·ics /ˌambiˈsɒnɪks/ plural noun a system of sound reproduction designed to reproduce the directional and acoustic properties of the sound source using two or more channels (compare SURROUND SOUND). [Latin ambi- on both sides + SONIC]

ambit noun **1** the scope, extent, or bounds of something. **2** precincts or environs. [Latin ambitus circuit, from ambire: see AMBIENT]

am·bi·tion noun **1** (often foll. by to + infin.) the determination to achieve success or distinction, usu. in a chosen field. **2** the object of this determination. [Latin ambitio -onis from ambire ambit- canvass for votes: see AMBIENT]

am·bi·tious adjective **1 a** full of ambition. **b** showing ambition (an ambitious attempt). **2** (foll. by to + infin.) strongly determined. □ **am·bi·tious·ly** adverb **am·bi·tious·ness** noun

am·biva·lence /amˈbɪvələns/ noun (also **am·biva·lency**) the coexistence in one person of opposing emotions or attitudes towards the same object or situation. □ **am·biva·lent** adjective **am·biva·lent·ly** adverb [German Ambivalenz from Latin ambo both, after equivalence, -ency]

ambi·vert /ˈambɪˌvɜːt/ noun Psych. a person who fluctuates between being an introvert and an extrovert. □ **ambi·ver·sion** /-ˈvɜːʒən/ noun [Latin ambi- on both sides + -vert from Latin vertere to turn, after EXTROVERT, INTROVERT]

amble ● intransitive verb **1** walk at an easy pace. **2** (of a horse etc.) move by lifting the two feet on one side together. **3** ride an ambling horse; ride at an easy pace. ● noun an easy pace; the gait of an ambling horse. [Old French ambler from Latin ambulare walk]

am·bly·opia /ˌambliˈoːpiə/ noun impaired vision without obvious defect or change in the eye. □ **am·bly·opic** /-ˈɒpɪk/ adjective [Greek from ambluōpos (adj.) from amblus dull + ōps, ōpos eye]

ambo /ˈamboː/ noun (pl. **ambos** or **ambo·nes** /-ˈboːniːz/) a pulpit or reading desk in a Christian church. [medieval Latin from Greek ambōn rim (in medieval Greek = pulpit)]

Ambon /ˈambɒn/ (also **Am·boina** /amˈbɔɪnə/) **1** a mountainous island in E Indonesia, one of the Molucca Islands. **2** a port on this island, the capital of the Molucca Islands; pop. (est. 2002) 262,200. □ **Ambon·ese** noun & adjective

am·boyna /amˈbɔɪnə/ noun the decorative wood of the SE Asian tree *Pterocarpus indicus*. Also called PADOUK. [Amboyna Island in Indonesia, now Ambon]

Am·brose, St. (c.339–97), bishop of Milan and a Doctor of the Church; a champion of orthodoxy, he introduced much Eastern theology into the West and encouraged monasticism. The so-called Athanasian Creed has been attributed to him. □ **Am·bro·sian** adjective

am·bro·sia /amˈbroːʒə/ noun **1** (in Greek and Roman mythology) the food of the gods; the elixir of life. **2** anything very pleasing to taste or smell. **3** N Amer. a dessert of sliced oranges and shredded coconut, sometimes also with bananas or pineapple. **4 a** a fungal product used as food by pinhole borers. **b** BEE BREAD. □ **am·bro·sial** adjective **am·bro·sian** adjective [Latin from Greek, = elixir of life, from ambrotos immortal]

ambry /ˈambri/ noun (also **aum·bry** /ˈɒmbri/) (pl. **-bries**) **1** a small recess in the wall of a church. **2** hist. a small cupboard. [Old French almarie, armarie from Latin armarium closet, chest, from arma utensils]

ambu·lac·rum /ˌambjuˈlakrəm, -lei-/ noun (pl. **ambu·lac·ra**) (in an echinoderm) each of the radially arranged bands, together with their underlying structures, through which the double rows of tube feet protrude. □ **ambu·lac·ral** adjective [Latin, 'avenue', from ambulare 'to walk']

ambu·lance /ˈambjʊləns/ ● noun a vehicle specially equipped for conveying the sick or injured to and from a hospital, esp. in emergencies. ● transitive verb convey (someone) somewhere in an ambulance. [French, from hôpital ambulant 'mobile (horse-drawn) field hospital' from Latin ambulant- 'walking']

ambulance chaser noun N Amer. informal derogatory a person who strives to profit from the misfortune of others, esp. a lawyer who specializes in actions for personal injuries. □ **ambulance-chasing** adjective [from the reputation of such lawyers for attending accidents to persuade the victims to sue for damages]

ambulance technician noun = PARAMEDIC.

ambu·lant /ˈambjʊlənt/ adjective Med. = AMBULATORY 1. [Latin ambulare ambulant- walk]

ambu·la·tory /ˈambjʊləˌtɔri/ ● adjective **1** Med. **a** (of a patient) able to walk about; not confining to bed. **b** (of treatment) not confining a patient to bed. **2** of or adapted for walking. **3 a** movable. **b** not permanent. ● noun (pl. **-ies**) Archit. a place for walking, esp. an aisle or cloister in a church or monastery, such as one passing around the apse or chancel. [Latin ambulatorius from ambulare walk]

am·bus·cade /ˌambəˈskeid/ ● noun an ambush. ● verb **1** transitive attack by means of an ambush. **2** intransitive lie in ambush. [French embuscade from Italian imboscata or Spanish emboscada from Latin imboscare: see AMBUSH, -ADE¹]

am·bush /ˈambʊʃ/ ● noun **1** a surprise attack by persons in a concealed position. **2 a** the concealment of persons to make such an attack. **b** the place where they are concealed. **c** the persons concealed. ● transitive verb **1** attack by means of an ambush. **2** lie in wait for. [Old

French *embusche, embuschier*, from a Romanic form = 'put in a wood': related to BUSH[1].

ameba esp. *US var. of* AMOEBA.

ameer *var. of* AMIR.

amel·ior·ate /əˈmiːliəˌreit/ *transitive & intransitive verb formal* make or become better; improve. □ **amel·ior·ation** *noun* **amel·ior·ative** *adjective* [alteration of MELIORATE after French *améliorer*]

amen /ˈɑːmen, ˈei-/ ● *interjection* **1** uttered at the end of a prayer or hymn etc., meaning 'so be it'. **2** (foll. by *to*) expressing agreement or assent (*amen to that*). ● *noun* an utterance of 'amen' (sense 1). [Hebrew *ʾāmēn* certainly]

amen·able /əˈmenəbəl, -miːn-/ *adjective* **1** willing to co-operate; open to suggestion or influence. **2** (often foll. by *to*) (of a person) subject to the authority of (*amenable to the law*). **3** (foll. by *to*) (of a thing) subject or liable. □ **amen·abil·ity** *noun* [Anglo-French (Law) from French *amener* bring to, from *a-* to + *mener* bring, from Late Latin *minare* drive animals, from Latin *minari* threaten]

amend /əˈmend/ *transitive verb* **1** formally revise or alter (a constitution, legislation, etc.). **2** make minor improvements in (a text or a written proposal). **3** correct an error or errors in (a document). **4** make better; improve. ¶ Often confused with *emend*, a more technical word used in the context of textual correction. □ **amend·able** *adjective* **amend·er** *noun* [Old French *amender*, ultimately from Latin *emendare* EMEND]

amending formula *noun* esp. *Cdn* a prescribed method for amending a constitution specifying the proportions of various interested parties that must assent for an amendment to be passed.

amend·ment *noun* **1** a minor improvement in a document (esp. a legal or statutory one). **2** the process or an instance of altering a document. **3** an article officially supplementing a constitution. **4** the act or process of improving, esp. one's conduct. **5** something which is added to soil to improve its texture or fertility, e.g. compost, manure, etc.

amends *noun* □ **make amends** (often foll. by *for*) compensate or make up (for). [Old French *amendes* penalties, fine, pl. of *amende* reparation, from *amender* AMEND]

Amen·hotep /ˌɑːmenˈhoʊtep/ the name of four Egyptian pharaohs of the 18th Dynasty (1550–1307 BC). *Also called* AMENOPHIS.

Amen·hotep IV *see* AKHENATEN.

amen·ity /əˈmenɪti/ *noun* (pl. **-ities**) **1** (usu. in *pl.*) a pleasant or useful feature. **2** pleasantness, agreeableness (of a place, person, etc.). [Latin *amoenitas* from *amoenus* pleasant]

Amen·ophis /ˌɑːmenˈoʊfɪs/ *see* AMENHOTEP.

amen·or·rhea /eiˌmenəˈriə/ *noun* (also **amen·or·rhoea**) *Med.* an abnormal absence of menstruation. [A-[1] + MENO- + Greek *-rrhoia* from *rheō* flow]

ament /ˈeimənt/ *noun* (also **amen·tum** /-təm/) (pl. **aments** or **amenta** /-tə/) a catkin. [Latin, = thong]

Amer. *abbreviation* American.

Amer·asian ● *adjective* of mixed American and Asian parentage. ● *noun* an Amerasian person, esp. a child fathered by a US serviceman stationed in Asia. [blend of AMERICAN + ASIAN]

Amer·ica **1** = THE UNITED STATES OF AMERICA (*see* UNITED STATES). **2** (also **the Americas**) a land mass of the New World or western hemisphere, consisting of the continents of North and South America, joined by the Isthmus of Panama. [prob. from *Americus* Latinized name of *Amerigo* VESPUCCI]

Amer·ican ● *adjective* **1** of, relating to, or characteristic of the US or its inhabitants. **2** (usu. in *combination*) of or relating to the Americas (*Latin-American*). **3** designating plants or animals native to the Americas (*American elk*). ● *noun* **1** a native or citizen of the US. **2** (usu. in *combination*) a native or inhabitant of the Americas (*North Americans*). **3** the English language as it is used in the US. □ **Amer·ican·ness** *noun*

Amer·icana /əˌmerɪˈkɑːnə, -ˈkʌnə/ *plural noun* things pertaining to and typical of American culture, e.g. publications, artifacts, cultural activities, etc.

American aloe *noun see* CENTURY PLANT.

American brook·lime *noun* a kind of speedwell, esp. *Veronica americana*, growing in wet areas.

American Civil War (also **War Between the States**) the war (1861–65) between the northern US states (usually known as the Union) and the Confederate States of the South, fought over the issue of the southern states' right to decide their own policies, esp. in relation to slavery and secession from the Union. The Confederacy was defeated by the more populous northern states.

American cowslip *noun* = SHOOTING STAR 2.

American dream *noun* (also **American Dream**) the traditional American belief that in the US success and material prosperity are available to all.

American eagle *noun* = BALD EAGLE.

American elm *noun* an elm, *Ulmus americana*, native to eastern N America, cultivated as a shade tree, and particularly susceptible to Dutch elm disease. *Also called* WHITE ELM.

American Falls *see* NIAGARA FALLS 1.

American football *noun* a form of football played in the US between two teams of 11 players. It is played on a smaller field than Canadian football, with four downs and slightly different scoring rules (*compare* CANADIAN FOOTBALL).

American Independence, War of *see* AMERICAN REVOLUTION.

American Indian *noun* **1** (also **North American Indian**) a member of a group of Aboriginal peoples of the western hemisphere, excluding the Inuit and Aleuts. **2** *Cdn* a member of these peoples who is a citizen or resident of the US.

American Indian Movement *noun* a militant US Aboriginal organization formed in 1968. Abbr.: **AIM**.

American ipecacuanha *noun see* IPECACUANHA 2.

Amer·ican·ism *noun* **1 a** a word, sense, or phrase peculiar to or originating from the US. **b** a thing or feature characteristic of or peculiar to the US. **2** attachment to or sympathy for the US.

Amer·ican·ize *verb* (also esp. *Brit.* **-ise**) **1** *transitive* **a** make American in character. **b** naturalize as an American. **2** *intransitive* become American in character. □ **Amer·ican·iz·ation** *noun*

American Legion *noun* (in the US) an association of ex-servicemen formed in 1919.

American plan *noun N Amer.* a method of charging for a hotel room which includes meals (*compare* EUROPEAN PLAN, MODIFIED AMERICAN PLAN).

American Revolution (also called the **Revolutionary War** or **War of American Independence**) the war of 1775–83, in which the American colonists won independence from British rule. It was triggered by colonial resentment at the economic policies of Britain, which taxed the colonies while excluding them from participation in political decisions affecting their interests. Fighting broke out at Lexington and Concord in 1775; a year later, in July 1776, the Declaration of Independence was signed. Aided by French sea power, the Americans forced the decisive surrender of a British army at Yorktown, Virginia in 1781. The war was ended by the Peace of Paris in 1783.

American Samoa an unincorporated overseas territory of the US comprising a group of islands in the S Pacific Ocean, to the east of Western Samoa and south of the Kiribati group; pop. (est. 2002) 68,688; capital, Fagatogo.

American Sign Language *noun* a sign language developed for the use of the deaf in the US, also used in English-speaking Canada. Abbr.: **ASL**.

American Standard Version *noun* a version of the Bible, published in the US in 1901, and based on the Revised Version. Abbr.: **ASV**.

American Stock Exchange *noun* the second largest stock exchange in the US, located in New York City.

America's Cup an international yachting trophy, originally won by the schooner *America* in 1851, for which a competition is held every three or four years.

ameri·cium /ˌæməˈrɪʃiəm/ *noun Chem.* an artificially made transuranic radioactive metallic element. Symbol: **Am**; at. no.: 95. [*America* (where first made) + -IUM]

Amer·in·dian /ˌæməˈrɪndiən/ ● *adjective* of or relating to American Indians. ● *noun* an American Indian. ¶ *Amerindian* is much less common in Canadian English than *Indian*. [blend]

Ames test *noun Med.* a test to show the potential carcinogenic properties of chemical substances by observing whether they cause mutations in sample bacteria. [B. *Ames*, US biochemist b.1928]

am·ethyst /ˈæməθɪst/ ● *noun* a precious stone of a violet or purple variety of quartz. ● *adjective* a violet or purple colour. □ **am·ethyst·ine** /-ˈθɪstiːn/ *adjective* [Greek *amethustos* not drunken, the stone being supposed to prevent intoxication]

AMEX /ˈæmeks/ *abbreviation* (also **Amex**) AMERICAN STOCK EXCHANGE.

Am·haric /æmˈherɪk/ ● *noun* the official and commercial language of Ethiopia. ● *adjective* of this language. [*Amhara*, Ethiopian province + -IC]

Consonants: b *but* d *dog* f *few* g *get* h *her* j *yes* k *cat* l *leg* m *man* n *no* p *pen* r *red* s *sit*

Am·herst[1] /'amərst/ a town in N Nova Scotia, situated near the border with New Brunswick; pop. (2001) 9,470. □ **Am·herst·onian** noun [J. AMHERST[2]]

Am·herst[2] /'amərst/ **1 Jef·fery, 1st Baron** (1717–97) British general in command of the successful siege of Louisbourg in 1758. Appointed commander-in-chief in N America in 1759, he captured Montreal in 1760, effectively ending French rule in Canada. **2** his nephew, **Wil·liam Pitt, Earl Amherst of Arakan** (1773–1857), British colonial administrator. After service in Naples (1809–11) and Peking (1816–17), he was Governor General of India 1823–8. In April 1835 he was appointed as Governor General of Canada, but he held the post only 8 days.

Am·herst·burg /'amərst,bərg/ a town in SW Ontario, situated on the Detroit River, about 25 km south of Windsor; pop. (2001) 20,339. [J. AMHERST[2]]

ami·able /'eimiəbəl/ adjective friendly and pleasant in temperament; likeable. □ **ami·abil·ity** noun **ami·able·ness** noun **ami·ably** adverb [Old French from Late Latin amicabilis amicable: confused with French aimable lovable]

ami·an·thus /,ami'anθəs/ noun (also **ami·an·tus** /-təs/) any fine silky-fibred variety of asbestos. [Latin from Greek amiantos undefiled, from a- not + miainō defile, i.e. purified by fire, being incombustible]

am·ic·able /'amɪkəbəl/ adjective showing or done in a friendly spirit (an amicable meeting). □ **am·ic·abil·ity** /,amɪkə'bɪlɪti/ noun **am·ic·able·ness** noun **am·ic·ably** adverb [Late Latin amicabilis from amicus friend]

amice[1] /'amɪs/ noun a white linen cloth worn on the neck and shoulders by a priest celebrating the Eucharist. [medieval Latin amicia, -sia from Latin amictus outer garment]

amice[2] /'amɪs/ noun a cap, hood, or cape worn by members of certain religious orders. [Middle English from Old French aumusse from medieval Latin almucia etc., of unknown origin]

ami·cus curiae /a,mi:kʊs 'kjʊri,ai/ noun (pl. **amici curiae** /-si/) Law an impartial adviser in a court of law. [modern Latin, = friend of the court]

amid preposition (also **amidst**) **1** in the middle of. **2** in the course of. [Middle English amidde(s) from Old English on ON + MID[1]]

amide /'amaid, 'eim-/ noun Chem. a compound formed from ammonia by replacement of one (or sometimes more than one) hydrogen atom by a metal or an acyl radical. [AMMONIA + -IDE]

amid·ships adverb (N Amer. also **amid·ship**) in or into the middle of a ship. [MIDSHIP after AMID]

amidst var. of AMID.

Amiens /'amjã/ the capital of the ancient province and modern region of Picardy, situated on the Somme; pop. (1999) 135,501. Its 13th-c. cathedral is the largest in France. In 1918 Canadian and Australian forces spearheaded a successful four-day Allied attack on the German trenches around Amiens in one of the decisive battles of the last months of World War I.

amigo /a'mi:ɡo:, ə-/ noun (pl. **-gos**) N Amer. informal (often as a form of address) a friend or comrade. [Spanish]

Amin /a'mi:n/ **Idi** (in full **Idi Amin Dada**) (1925–2003) Ugandan soldier, dictator, and head of state 1971–79. His violent rule was characterized by the expulsion of non-Africans.

Amin·divi Islands /,amɪn'di:vi/ the northernmost group of islands in the Indian territory of Lakshadweep in the Indian Ocean.

amine /'ami:n, ə'mi:n/ noun Chem. a compound formed from ammonia by replacement of one or more hydrogen atoms by an organic radical or radicals. [AMMONIA + -INE[4]]

amino /ə'mi:no:/ noun (attributive) Chem. of, relating to, or containing the monovalent group -NH₂. [AMINE]

amino acid /ə'mi:no:, 'aməno:/ noun Biochem. any of a group of organic compounds containing both the carboxyl (COOH) and amino (NH₂) group, occurring naturally in plant and animal tissues and forming the basic constituents of proteins. [AMINE + ACID]

amir /ə'mi:r/ noun (also **ameer**) the title of some Muslim rulers. [Arabic 'amir commander, from amara command: compare EMIR]

Ami·rante Islands /'amɪ,rant/ a group of coral islands in the Indian Ocean, forming part of the Seychelles.

Amis /'eimɪs/ **1 Sir Kings·ley** (1922–95), English novelist and poet; his first novel Lucky Jim (1954) achieved popular success, and in 1986 he won the Booker Prize for The Old Devils. His early works display a deliberate cultivation of a prejudiced and philistine pose which later hardened into an increasingly conservative and hostile view of contemporary life and manners. **2** his son, **Mar·tin** (b.1949), English

novelist, whose works include The Rachel Papers (1974), London Fields (1989), and Time's Arrow (1991).

Amish /'ɒmɪʃ, 'ei-/ ● noun (prec. by the; treated as pl.) the members of a strict Mennonite group whose communal farms are found in S Ontario and parts of the US, esp. Pennsylvania. ● adjective of, pertaining to, or characteristic of this group. □ **Amish·man** noun (pl. **-men**). [prob. from German Amisch from J. Amen or Amman 17th-c. Swiss preacher]

amiss ● predicative adjective wrong; out of order; faulty (knew something was amiss). ● adverb wrong; wrongly; inappropriately (everything went amiss). □ **take amiss** be offended by (took my words amiss). [prob. from Old Norse á mis so as to miss, from á on + mis related to MISS[1]]

ami·tosis /,amɪ'tو:sɪs/ noun a form of cell division that does not involve mitosis. [A-[1] + MITOSIS]

ami·trip·tyl·ine /,amɪ'trɪptɪ,li:n/ noun an antidepressant drug that has a mild tranquilizing action. Chem. formula: $C_{20}H_{23}N$. [AMINE + TRI- + heptyl (see HEPTANE) + -INE[4]]

amity /'amiti/ noun friendship; friendly relations. [Old French amitié, ultimately from Latin amicus friend]

Amman /ə'man/ the capital of Jordan; pop. (est. 2002) 1,252,900.

am·meter /'amɪtər/ noun an instrument for measuring electric current in amperes. [AMPERE + -METER]

ammo /'amo:/ noun informal ammunition. [abbreviation]

am·mol·ite /'amə,ləit/ noun the brilliantly coloured opalescent fossilized shell of an ammonite, found only in southern Alberta, used as a precious gem. [AMMONITE + -LITE]

Ammon var. of AMUN.

am·mo·nia /ə'mo:niə/ noun **1** a colourless strongly alkaline gas with a characteristic pungent smell. Chem. formula: NH_3. **2** a solution of ammonia gas in water. [modern Latin from SAL AMMONIAC]

am·mo·niac·al /,amə'naiəkəl/ adjective of, relating to, or containing ammonia or sal ammoniac. [ultimately from Greek ammōniakos of Ammon (compare SAL AMMONIAC) + -AL]

am·mo·ni·ated /ə'mo:ni,eitəd/ adjective combined or treated with ammonia.

am·mon·ite /'amə,nəit/ noun (also **am·mon·oid** /'amə,nɔid/) any extinct cephalopod mollusc of the order Ammonoidea, with a flat coiled spiral shell found as a fossil. [modern Latin ammonites, after medieval Latin cornu Ammonis, = Latin Ammonis cornu (Pliny), horn of (Jupiter) Ammon]

am·mo·nium /ə'mo:niəm/ noun the monovalent ion NH_4^+, formed from ammonia. [modern Latin (as AMMONIA)]

ammonium chloride noun the salt of ammonia and hydrogen chloride, NH_4Cl, used as an electrolyte in dry cells and as a constituent of soldering fluxes.

am·mu·ni·tion /,amjʊ'nɪʃən/ noun **1** a supply of projectiles (esp. bullets, shells, and grenades). **2** points used or usable to advantage in an argument. [obsolete French amunition, corruption of (la) munition (the) MUNITION]

am·nesia /am'ni:ʒə/ noun a partial or total loss of memory. □ **am·nes·iac** /-zi,ak/ noun **am·nes·ic** /-zɪk/ adjective & noun [Greek, = forgetfulness]

am·nesty /'amnəsti/ ● noun (pl. **-ties**) **1** a general pardon, esp. for political offences. **2** a period during which people may admit an offence without fear of prosecution. ● transitive verb (**am·nes·ties**, **am·nes·tied**, **am·nesty·ing**) grant an amnesty to. [Greek amnēstia oblivion]

Amnesty International noun an independent international organization upholding and campaigning for the human rights of prisoners of conscience.

amnio /'amnio:/ noun informal = AMNIOCENTESIS. [abbreviation]

amnio·cen·tesis /,amnio:sen'ti:sɪs/ noun (pl. **amnio·cen·teses** /-si:z/) Med. the sampling of amniotic fluid by insertion of a hollow needle to determine the condition of an embryo. [AMNION + Greek kentēsis pricking, from kentō to prick]

am·nion /'amniən/ noun (pl. **amnia**) the innermost membrane that encloses the embryo of a reptile, bird, or mammal. [Greek, = caul (diminutive of amnos lamb)]

am·ni·ot·ic /,amni'ɒtɪk/ adjective of or pertaining to the amnion. [irreg. from amnios, obsolete form of AMNION + -OTIC]

amniotic fluid noun the fluid contained within the amnion, in which the fetus effectively floats.

amoeba /ə'mi:bə/ noun (also esp. US **ameba**) (pl. **amoe·bas** or **amoe·bae** /-bi:/) any usu. aquatic protozoan of the genus Amoeba, esp.

A. proteus, capable of changing shape. □ **amoeb·ic** *adjective*
amoeb·oid *adjective* [modern Latin from Greek *amoibē* change]

amoeb·ia·sis /ˌamiˈbaɪəsɪs/ *noun* (also **ameb·ia·sis, amoebic dysentery**) dysentery caused by infection of the intestine with certain amoebae.

amok /əˈmʌk, əˈmɒk/ *adverb* (also **amuck** /əˈmʌk/) □ **go** (or **run**) **amok 1** be out of control. **2** run about wildly in an uncontrollable violent rage. [Malay *amok* rushing in a frenzy]

among *preposition* (also **amongst**) **1** surrounded by; in the company of (*lived among the trees; be among friends*). **2** in the number of (*among us were those who disagreed*). **3** an example of; in the class or category of (*is among the richest men alive*). **4 a** between; within the limits of (collectively or distributively); shared by (*had $5 among us; divide it among you*). **b** by the joint action or from the joint resources of (*among us we can manage it*). **5** with one another; by the reciprocal action of (*was decided among the participants; talked among themselves*). **6** as distinguished from; pre-eminent in the category of (*she is one among many*). [Old English *ongemang* from *on* ON + *gemang* assemblage (related to MINGLE)]

amon·til·lado /əˌmɒntɪˈlɑːdoː, -tiːˈɒdoː/ *noun* (pl. **-dos**) a medium dry sherry. [Spanish from *Montilla* in Spain + *-ado* = -ATE²]

amoral /eiˈmɒrəl, -mɒrəl/ *adjective* **1** not concerned with or outside the scope of morality (compare IMMORAL). **2** having no moral principles. □ **amoral·ism** *noun* **amoral·ist** *noun* **amoral·ity** /-ˈralɪti/ *noun*

amor·etto /ˌaməˈretoː/ *noun* (pl. **amor·etti** /-tiː/) a cupid. [Italian, diminutive of *amore* love, from Latin (as AMOUR)]

Am·or·ite /ˈaməˌraɪt/ ● *noun* **1** a member of a group of Semitic peoples whose semi-nomadic culture flourished in Mesopotamia, Palestine, and Syria from *c.*2000 to *c.*1600 BC. They founded the First Dynasty of Babylon, associated with Hammurabi I (d.1750 BC). **2** their language. ● *adjective* of or pertaining to the Amorites or their language. [Hebrew *'emōrī* from Akkadian *'amurrū* west + -ITE¹]

amor·oso /ˌaməˈroːsoː/ *noun* (pl. **-osos**) a full rich type of sherry. [Spanish, = amorous]

amor·ous /ˈamərəs/ *adjective* **1** showing, feeling, or inclined to sexual love. **2** of or relating to sexual love. □ **amor·ous·ly** *adverb* **amor·ous·ness** *noun* [medieval Latin *amorosus* from Latin *amor* love]

amor·phous /əˈmɔrfəs/ *adjective* **1** shapeless. **2** vague, ill-organized. **3** *Geol. & Chem.* non-crystalline; having neither definite form nor structure. □ **amor·phous·ly** *adverb* **amor·phous·ness** *noun* [medieval Latin *amorphus* from Greek *amorphos* shapeless, from *a-* not + *morphē* form]

amor·tize /ˈamɔrtaɪz, əˈmɔrtaɪz/ *transitive verb* (also esp. *Brit.* **-tise**) *Commerce* **1** gradually pay off (a debt) by money regularly put aside. **2** gradually write off the initial cost of (assets). **3** *hist.* transfer (land) to a corporation in mortmain. □ **amor·tiz·a·tion** *noun* [ultimately from Latin *ad* to + *mors* mort- death]

Amos¹ a town in NW central Quebec, about 50 km northwest of Val-d'Or; pop. (2001) 13,044. [A. *Amos*, wife of Sir J.-L. GOUIN]

Amos² *Bible* **1** a Hebrew minor prophet of the 8th c. BC. **2** a book of the Bible containing his prophecies.

amount ● *noun* a quantity, esp. the total of a thing or things in number, size, value, extent, etc. (*a large amount of money; came to a considerable amount*). ● *intransitive verb* (foll. by *to*) be equivalent to in number, size, significance, etc. (*amounted to $100; amounted to a disaster*). □ **any amount of** a great deal of. **no amount of** not even the greatest possible amount of. [Old French *amunter* from *amont* upward, lit. 'uphill', from Latin *ad montem*]

amour /əˈmʊr/ *noun* a love affair, esp. a secret one. [French, = love]

amour-propre /aˌmʊr ˈprɒpr/ *noun* self-respect. [French]

am·oxi·cil·lin /əˌmɒksiˈsɪlɪn/ *noun* (also **am·oxy·cil·lin**) a broad spectrum semi-synthetic penicillin, closely related to ampicillin but better absorbed when taken orally, used esp. for treating ear and upper respiratory infections. [AMINO + OXY-² + PENICILLIN]

Amoy /əˈmɔɪ/ an alternative name for XIAMEN.

amp¹ *noun Electricity* an ampere. [abbreviation]

amp² *noun informal* an amplifier. [abbreviation]

amp³ *noun informal* an amputee. [abbreviation]

amped *adjective slang* **1** amplified. **2** (also **amped-up**) highly excited and frenetic, from or as if from taking amphetamines.

ampel·op·sis /ˌampɪˈlɒpsɪs/ *noun* any plant of the genus *Ampelopsis* or *Parthenocissus*, usu. a climber supporting itself by twining tendrils, e.g. Virginia creeper. [Greek *ampelos* vine + *opsis* appearance]

amper·age /ˈampərɪdʒ/ *noun* the strength of an electric current in amperes.

Am·père /ˈamper/ **André-Marie** (1775–1836), French physicist, mathematician, and philosopher, best known for his analysis of the relationship between magnetic force and the electric current.

am·pere /ˈamper/ *noun* the SI base unit of electric current. Symbol: **A**. [A.-M. AMPÈRE]

am·per·sand /ˈampər.sand/ *noun* the sign & (= *and*). [corruption of *and per se and* ('&' by itself is '*and*')]

am·phet·a·mine /amˈfetəmiːn/ *noun* a synthetic drug used esp. as a stimulant. Chem. formula: $C_9H_{13}N$. [abbreviation of chemical name *alpha-methyl phenethylamine*]

amphi- /ˈamfi/ *combining form* **1** both. **2** of both kinds. **3** on both sides. **4** around. [Greek]

am·phib·ian /amˈfɪbiən/ ● *adjective* **1** living both on land and in water. **2** *Zool.* of or relating to the class Amphibia. **3** (of a vehicle or airplane) able to operate on land and water. ● *noun* **1** *Zool.* any vertebrate of the class Amphibia, with a life history of an aquatic gill-breathing larval stage followed by a terrestrial lung-breathing adult stage, including frogs, toads, newts, and salamanders. **2** (in general use) a creature living both on land and in water. **3** an amphibian vehicle or airplane. [modern Latin *amphibium* from Greek *amphibion* from AMPHI- + *bios* life]

am·phib·ious /amˈfɪbiəs/ *adjective* **1** living both on land and in water. **2** of or relating to or suited for both land and water. **3** *Military* **a** (of a military operation) involving forces landed from the sea. **b** (of forces) trained for such operations. **4** having a twofold nature; occupying two positions. □ **am·phib·ious·ly** *adverb*

am·phi·bole /ˈamfɪboːl/ *noun* any of a class of rock-forming silicate and aluminosilicate minerals with fibrous or columnar crystals. [French from Latin *amphibolus* ambiguous]

am·phi·mixis /ˌamfɪˈmɪksɪs/ *noun Biol.* true sexual reproduction with the fusion of gametes from two individuals (compare APOMIXIS). □ **am·phi·mic·tic** *adjective* [modern Latin, formed as AMPHI- + Greek *mixis* mingling]

amphi·oxus /ˌamfiˈɒksəs/ *noun* any lancelet of the genus *Branchiostoma* (formerly *Amphioxus*). [modern Latin, formed as AMPHI- + Greek *oxus* sharp]

amphi·path·ic /ˌamfiˈpaθɪk/ *adjective Chem.* **1** of a substance or molecule that has both a hydrophilic and a hydrophobic part. **2** consisting of such parts. [AMPHI- + Greek *pathikos* (as PATHOS)]

amphi·pod /ˈamfiˌpɒd/ *noun* any crustacean of the largely marine order Amphipoda, having a laterally compressed abdomen with two kinds of limb, e.g. sand hoppers. [AMPHI- + Greek *pous podos* foot]

am·phip·ro·style /amˈfɪprəˌstaɪl/ ● *noun* a classical building with a portico at each end. ● *adjective* of or in this style. [Latin *amphiprostylus* from Greek *amphiprostulos* (as AMPHI-, *prostulos* PROSTYLE)]

am·phis·baena /ˌamfɪsˈbiːnə/ *noun* **1** *Zool.* any burrowing wormlike lizard of the family Amphisbaena, having no apparent division of head from body, making both ends look similar. **2** *Myth* a fabulous serpent with a head at each end. [Greek *amphisbaina* from *amphis* both ways + *bainō* go]

am·phi·the·atre /ˈamfiˌθiːətər/ *noun* (also **am·phi·the·ater**) **1** an oval or circular building with seats rising in tiers around a central open space. **2** a piece of level ground surrounded naturally by rising slopes; a large circular hollow. **3** a large lecture theatre with seats rising in tiers. **4** a gallery in a theatre. [as AMPHI-, THEATRE]

Amphi·trite /ˌamfɪˈtraɪti/ *Gk Myth* a sea nymph and goddess, wife of Poseidon.

Am·phit·ryon /amˈfɪtriən/ *Gk Myth* the husband of Alcmene and foster father of Hercules.

am·phora /ˈamfərə/ *noun* (pl. **am·phorae** /-ˌriː/ or **am·phoras**) a Greek or Roman vessel with two handles and a narrow neck. [Latin from Greek *amphoreus*]

ampho·teric /ˌamfəˈterɪk/ *adjective Chem.* able to react as a base and an acid. [Greek *amphoteros* comparative of *amphō* both]

ampi·cil·lin /ˌampɪˈsɪlɪn/ *noun* a semi-synthetic penicillin used esp. in treating infections of the urinary and respiratory tracts. [amino + penicillin]

ample *adjective* (**ampler, amplest**) **1 a** plentiful, abundant, extensive. **b** *euphemism* (esp. of a person) large, stout. **2** enough or more than enough. □ **ample·ness** *noun* **amply** *adverb* [French from Latin *amplus*]

ampli·fier *noun* an electronic device for increasing the strength of electrical signals, esp. for conversion into sound in stereo equipment etc.

ampli·fy *verb* (**-fies**, **-fied**, **-fy·ing**) **1** *transitive* increase the volume or strength of (sound, electrical signals, etc.). **2** *transitive* enlarge upon or add detail to (a story etc.). **3** *intransitive* expand what is said or written. □ **ampli·fi·ca·tion** *noun* [Old French *amplifier* from Latin *amplificare* (as AMPLE, -FY)]

ampli·tude *noun* **1 a** *Physics* the maximum extent of a vibration or oscillation from the position of equilibrium. **b** *Electricity* the maximum departure of the value of an alternating current or wave from the average value. **2 a** spaciousness, breadth; wide range. **b** abundance. [French *amplitude* or Latin *amplitudo* (as AMPLE)]

amplitude modulation *noun* **1** variation of the amplitude of a radio or other wave as a means of carrying information such as an audio signal (*compare* FREQUENCY MODULATION). **2** the system using such modulation. *Abbr.*: **AM**.

am·poule /ˈæmpjuːl/ *noun* (also esp. *US* **ampul** or **am·pule** /ˈæmpuːl/) a small capsule in which measured quantities of liquids or solids, e.g. medications, cosmetics, are sealed ready for use. [French from Latin AMPULLA]

am·pul·la /æmˈpʊlə/ *noun* (*pl.* **am·pul·lae** /-liː/) **1 a** a Roman globular flask with two handles. **b** *Christianity* a vessel for sacred uses, as a cruet for the wine and water used at the Eucharist or to hold the chrism. **2** *Anat.* the dilated end of a vessel or duct. [Latin]

am·pu·tate *transitive verb* cut off by surgical operation (a part of the body, esp. a limb), usu. because of injury or disease. □ **am·pu·ta·tion** *noun* [Latin *amputare* from *amb-* about + *putare* prune]

am·pu·tee *noun* a person who has lost a limb etc. by amputation.

Amqui /æmˈkiː/ a town in E Quebec, in the valley of the Matapédia, about 60 km south of Matane; pop. (2001) 6,473. [from the Rivière *Humqui* on which it is located, from a Mi'kmaq word meaning 'place where it plays', in reference to either the nearby rapids or to festive gatherings by the Mi'kmaq]

Am·rit·sar /æmˈrɪtsər/ a city in the state of Punjab in NW India; pop. (2001) 975,700. Founded in 1577 by Ram Das, fourth guru of the Sikhs, it became the centre of the Sikh faith and the site of its holiest temple, the Golden Temple. It was the scene of a riot in 1919, in the course of which 400 people were killed by British troops.

Am·ster·dam the capital and largest city of the Netherlands; pop. (est. 2002) 719,500. Built on some ninety islands separated by canals, at the southern tip of IJsselmeer, Amsterdam has been an important port since the 14th c. and a financial centre from the early 17th. It is esp. known for its diamond industry, and is a leading cultural centre, housing important art collections. Although Amsterdam is the capital, the country's seat of government and administrative centre is at The Hague. □ **Amster·dam·mer** *noun*

amt. *abbreviation* amount.

amu *abbreviation* ATOMIC MASS UNIT.

amuck *var. of* AMOK.

Amu Darya River /ˌɑːmuː ˈdɑːriə/ a river of central Asia, rising in the Pamirs and flowing 2 400 km (1,500 miles) into the Aral Sea. In classical times it was known as the Oxus.

amu·let /ˈæmjʊlət/ *noun* **1** an ornament or small piece of jewellery worn as a charm against evil. **2** something which is thought to give such protection. [Latin *amuletum*, of unknown origin]

Amun /ˈæmən/ (also **Ammon**) *Myth* a supreme god of the ancient Egyptians. His worship spread to Greece, where he was identified with Zeus, and to Rome, where he was known as Jupiter Ammon. As a national god of Egypt he was associated in a triad with Mut and Khonsu.

Amund Ring·nes Island /ˌɒˌmʌnd ˈrɪŋnəs/ one of the Sverdrup Islands in the Canadian High Arctic, situated west of Axel Heiberg Island. [*Amund Ringnes*, Norwegian promoter of Arctic exploration *c.*1900]

Amund·sen /ˈɒmənsən, ˈɒməndsən/ **Roald** (1872–1928), Norwegian polar explorer who was the first to successfully navigate the Northwest Passage (1903–6), and led the first expedition to reach the South Pole (1911).

Amundsen Gulf an eastern extension of the Beaufort Sea, lying south of Banks Island. [R. AMUNDSEN]

Amur maple *noun* a small maple, *Acer ginnala*, with creamy-white flowers and scarlet autumnal foliage, much cultivated as an ornamental shrub. [named for the region bordering the *Amur*, where it originated]

Amur River /əˈmʊr/ a river of NE Asia, forming for the greater part of its length the boundary between Russia and China. Its length, including its northern headstream, the Shilka, is about 4 350 km (2,737 miles).

amuse *verb* **1** *transitive* cause (a person) to laugh or smile. **2** *transitive* & *reflexive* (often foll. by *with*, *by*) interest or occupy; keep (a person) entertained. □ **amus·ing** *adjective* **amus·ing·ly** *adverb* [Old French *amuser* cause to muse (see MUSE²)]

amuse·ment *noun* **1** something that amuses, esp. a pleasant diversion, game, or pastime. **2 a** the state of being amused. **b** the act of amusing. **3** a mechanical device, e.g. a merry-go-round, for entertainment at a fairground etc.

amusement park *noun* a commercially operated fairground with mechanical rides, e.g. Ferris wheel, roller coaster, etc., and booths for refreshments and games.

amusement tax *noun* N Amer. a tax imposed on the price of admission to entertainments, e.g. plays, sporting events, etc.

amyg·dal·oid /əˈmɪgdəˌlɔɪd/ *adjective* shaped like an almond. [Latin *amygdala* from Greek *amugdalē* almond]

amygdaloid nucleus *noun* a roughly almond-shaped mass of grey matter deep inside each cerebral hemisphere, associated with the sense of smell.

amyl /ˈæmɪl/ *noun* (used *attributive*) *Chem.* **1** the monovalent group C_5H_{11}-, derived from pentane. *Also called* PENTYL. **2** *informal* = AMYL NITRITE. [Latin *amylum* starch, from which oil containing it was distilled]

amyl·ase /ˈæmɪˌleɪz/ *noun* *Biochem.* any of several enzymes that convert starch and glycogen into simple sugars. [AMYL + -ASE]

amyl nitrite *noun* a yellowish volatile synthetic liquid used medicinally as a vasodilator. It is rapidly absorbed by the body on inhalation, and is sometimes used for its stimulatory effects.

amyl·oid /ˈæmɪˌlɔɪd/ *noun* *Biochem.* a glycoprotein deposited in connective tissue in certain diseases. [AMYL + -OID]

amyo·troph·ic lateral sclerosis /ˌæmaɪoˈtroːfɪk/ *noun* a progressive degenerative disease of the central nervous system resulting in weakness and wasting of the muscles and ultimately death. *Abbr.*: **ALS**. *Also called* LOU GEHRIG'S DISEASE. [from A-¹ + Greek *mu*, *mus* muscle + -O- + -TROPHIC.]

Amy·tal /ˈæmɪˌtɒl/ *noun* *proprietary* a name for amobarbital, a barbiturate used as a sedative and a hypnotic. [chemical name *amylethyl barbituric acid*]

an /æn, ən/ *indefinite article* the form of the indefinite article (see A¹) used before words beginning with a vowel sound (*an egg*; *an hour*; *an MP*). ¶ Now less often used before aspirated words beginning with *h* and stressed on a syllable other than the first (so *a hotel*, not *an hotel*).

an-¹ /ən, æn/ *prefix* not, without (*anarchy*) (*compare* A-¹). [Greek *an-*]

an-² /ən, æn/ *assimilated form of* AD- before *n*.

-an /ən/ *suffix* (also **-ean**, **-ian**) forming adjectives and nouns, esp. from names of places, systems, zoological classes or orders, and founders (*Mexican*; *Anglican*; *crustacean*; *European*; *Lutheran*; *Georgian*; *theologian*). [ultimately from Latin adj. endings -(*i*)*anus*, -*aeus*]

ana- /ˈænə/ *prefix* (usu. **an-** before a vowel) **1** up (*anadromous*). **2** back (*anamnesis*). **3** again (*anabaptism*). [Greek *ana* up]

-ana /ˈænə/ *suffix* (also **-iana** /iˈænə/) forming plural nouns meaning 'things associated with' (*Victoriana*; *Canadiana*). [neuter pl. of Latin adj. ending -*anus*]

Ana·bap·tism /ˌænəˈbæptɪzəm/ *noun* the doctrine that baptism should only be administered to believing adults. □ **Ana·bap·tist** *noun* [ecclesiastical Latin *anabaptismus* from Greek *anabaptismos* (as ANA-, BAPTISM)]

ana·batic /ˌænəˈbætɪk/ *adjective* *Meteorol.* (of a wind) caused by air flowing upwards (*compare* KATABATIC). [Greek *anabatikos* ascending]

ana·bol·ic /ˌænəˈbɒlɪk/ *adjective* *Biochem.* of or relating to anabolism.

anabolic steroid *noun* any of a group of synthetic steroid hormones used to increase muscle size.

anab·ol·ism /əˈnæbəˌlɪzəm/ *noun* *Biochem.* the synthesis of complex molecules in living organisms from simpler ones together with the storage of energy; constructive metabolism (*opp.* CATABOLISM). [Greek *anabolē* ascent (as ANA-, *ballō* throw)]

an·achron·ism /əˈnækrəˌnɪzəm/ *noun* **1 a** the attribution of a custom, event, etc., to a period to which it does not belong. **b** a thing attributed in this way. **2 a** anything out of harmony with its period. **b** an old-fashioned or out-of-date person or thing. □ **an·achron·is·tic** *adjective* **an·achron·is·tic·ally** *adverb* [Greek *anakhronismos* (as ANA-, *khronos* time)]

ana·co·lu·thon /ˌænəkəˈluːθɒn/ *noun* (*pl.* **ana·co·lu·tha** /-ˈluːθə/) a sentence or construction which lacks grammatical sequence, e.g. *while in the garden the door banged shut*. [Greek *anakolouthon* (as AN-[1], *akolouthos* following)]

ana·con·da /ˌanəˈkɒndə/ *noun* a S American boa of the genus *Eunectes*, esp. the very large, semi-aquatic *E. murinus*, that kills its prey by constriction. [alteration of *anacondaia* from Sinhalese *henakandayā* whip snake, from *hena* lightning + *kanda* stem: originally of a snake in Sri Lanka]

Anac·re·on /əˈnakriən/ (*c*.570–478 BC) Greek lyric poet; the surviving fragments of his work include love songs and drinking songs.

ana·cru·sis /ˌanəˈkruːsɪs/ *noun* (*pl.* **ana·cru·ses** /-siːz/) **1** (in poetry) an unstressed syllable at the beginning of a verse. **2** *Music* an unstressed note or notes before the strong beat at the beginning of a phrase. [Greek *anakrousis* (as ANA-, *krousis* from *krouō* strike)]

anad·ro·mous /əˈnadrəməs/ *adjective* (of a fish, e.g. the salmon) that swims up a river from the sea to spawn (*opp.* CATADROMOUS). [Greek *anadromos* (as ANA-, *dromos* running)]

an·aemia esp. *Brit. var. of* ANEMIA.

an·aemic esp. *Brit. var. of* ANEMIC.

an·aer·obe /ˈanəˌroːb, əˈneroːb/ *noun* an organism that grows without air, or requires oxygen-free conditions to live. [AN-[1] + AEROBE]

an·aer·obic /ˌanəˈroːbɪk/ *adjective* **1** relating to, involving, or requiring an absence of free oxygen. **2** (of exercise) in which oxygen is used by the muscles faster than it can be supplied by the bloodstream. □ **an·aer·obic·ally** *adverb*

anaes·the·sia /ˌanəsˈθiːziə, -ʒə/ *noun* (also **anes·the·sia**) the absence of sensation, esp. artificially induced insensitivity to pain usu. achieved by the administration of gases or the injection of drugs. [Greek *anaisthēsia* (as AN-[1], *aisthēsis* sensation)]

anaes·the·si·ol·ogy *var. of* ANESTHESIOLOGY.

anaes·thet·ic /ˌanəsˈθetɪk/ (also **anes·thet·ic**) ● *noun* a substance that produces insensibility to pain etc. ● *adjective* producing partial or complete insensibility to pain etc. [Greek *anaisthētos* insensible (as ANAESTHESIA)]

an·aes·the·tist /əˈniːsθətɪst, əˈnes-/ *noun* **1** *Cdn & Brit.* a medical doctor specializing in the administration of anaesthetics. **2** (usu. **an·es·the·tist**) (in the US) a person other than a doctor, e.g. a nurse etc., who administers anaesthetics.

an·aes·the·tize /əˈniːsθəˌtaɪz, əˈnes-/ *transitive verb* (also **an·es·the·tize**, esp. *Brit.* **-tise**) **1** administer an anaesthetic to. **2** deprive of physical or mental sensation. □ **an·aes·the·tiz·a·tion** *noun*

ana·glyph /ˈanəˌglɪf/ *noun* **1** a composite stereoscopic photograph printed in superimposed complementary colours. **2** an embossed object cut in low relief. [Greek *anagluphē* (as ANA-, *gluphē* from *gluphō* carve)]

ana·gram *noun* a word or phrase formed by rearranging the letters of another word or phrase. □ **ana·gram·mat·ic** *adjective* **ana·gram·mat·ic·al** *adjective* **ana·gram·ma·tize** *transitive verb* (also esp. *Brit.* **-tise**). [Greek ANA- + *gramma -atos* letter: compare -GRAM]

Ana·heim /ˈanəˌhaɪm/ a city in California, on the southeast side of the Los Angeles conurbation; pop. (2000) 328,014. It is the site of Disneyland.

anal *adjective* **1 a** relating to or situated near the anus. **b** (of sexual activity) involving the insertion of one partner's penis into the other's anus. **2** *Psych.* designating or pertaining to a stage of infantile psychosexual development that is thought to involve a preoccupation with the anus and defecation. **3** *informal* = ANAL-RETENTIVE. □ **anal·ly** *adverb*

ana·lects /ˈanəˌlekts/ *plural noun* (also **ana·lecta** /ˌanəˈlektə/) a collection of short literary extracts. [Greek *analekta* things gathered, from *analegō* pick up]

an·al·gesia /ˌanəlˈdʒiːziə, -siə/ *noun* the absence or relief of pain. [modern Latin from Greek, = painlessness]

an·al·gesic /ˌanəlˈdʒiːzɪk, -sɪk/ ● *adjective* relieving pain. ● *noun* an analgesic drug.

ana·log *noun* **1** (also **ana·logue**) (*attributive*) (of a watch, clock, etc.) that gives a reading by means of a pointer rather than by displayed digits (*compare* DIGITAL *adjective* 2). **2** (*attributive*) (of a computer or electronic process) operating with signals or information represented by a continuously variable quantity, such as spatial position, voltage, etc. (*compare* DIGITAL *adjective* 3). **3** (*attributive*) (of a recording or recording equipment) in which the signal corresponds to a physical variable, such as the groove on a phonograph record or magnetic particles on

an audio cassette tape (*compare* DIGITAL *adjective* 4). **4** *US var. of* ANALOGUE. [as ANALOGUE]

an·alo·gize /əˈnaləˌdʒaiz/ *verb* (also esp. *Brit.* **-gise**) **1** *transitive* represent or explain by analogy. **2** *intransitive* use analogy.

an·alo·gous /əˈnaləgəs/ *adjective* (usu. foll. by *to*) partially similar or parallel; showing analogy. □ **an·alo·gous·ly** *adverb* [Greek *analogos* proportionate]

ana·logue /ˈanəˌlɒg/ *noun* **1** (*US* **ana·log**) an analogous or parallel thing. **2** *Brit. var. of* ANALOG. [see ANALOGOUS]

an·alogy /əˈnalədʒi/ *noun* (*pl.* **-gies**) **1** (usu. foll. by *to, with, between*) correspondence or partial similarity. **2** *Logic* a process of arguing from similarity in known respects to similarity in other respects. **3** *Linguistics* the imitation of existing words in forming inflections or constructions of others, without the existence of corresponding intermediate stages. **4** *Biol.* the resemblance of function between organs essentially different. **5** an analogue. □ **ana·logic·al** /ˌanəˈlɒdʒɪkəl/ *adjective* **ana·logic·al·ly** /ˌanəˈlɒdʒɪkli/ *adverb* [as ANALOGOUS]

anal-retentive *adjective* (of a person) excessively orderly and fussy (supposedly owing to aspects of toilet training in infancy).

an·aly·sand /əˈnalɪˌsand/ *noun* a person undergoing psychoanalysis. [from ANALYZE + -AND]

ana·lyse *var. of* ANALYZE.

an·aly·sis /əˈnaləsɪs/ *noun* (*pl.* **an·aly·ses** /-ˌsiːz/) **1 a** a detailed examination of the elements or structure of a substance etc. **b** a statement of the result of this. **2** *Chem.* the determination of the constituent parts of a mixture or compound. **3** psychoanalysis. **4** *Math.* the use of algebra and calculus in problem-solving. □ **in the final** (or **last** or **ultimate**) **analysis** after all due consideration; in the end. [Greek *analusis* (as ANA-, *luō* set free)]

ana·lyst /ˈanəlɪst/ *noun* **1** a person engaged or skilled in analysis. **2** a psychoanalyst.

ana·lytic /ˌanəˈlɪtɪk/ *adjective* (also **ana·lytic·al** /-kəl/) **1** of, pertaining to, or using analysis. **2** *Linguistics* using separate words rather than inflected forms to express tense, number, etc. (*compare* SYNTHETIC 5). **3** *Logic* (of a statement etc.) true by virtue of the definition of the terms employed (e.g. *all daughters are female*); self-evident (*compare* SYNTHETIC 3). □ **ana·lytic·al·ly** *adverb* [Greek *analutikos* (as ANALYSIS)]

analytic geometry *noun* (also **analytical geometry**, **coordinate geometry**) geometry involving the use of algebra, with points represented by a pair of numbers, and lines and curves represented by equations.

ana·lyze *transitive verb* (also **ana·lyse**) **1** examine in detail the constitution or structure of. **2** *Chem.* ascertain the constituents of (a sample of a mixture or compound). **3** examine critically (a book, music, etc.) in order to bring out essential elements or structure. **4** *Grammar* resolve (a sentence) into its grammatical elements. **5** psychoanalyze. □ **ana·lyz·able** *adjective* **ana·lyz·er** *noun* [as ANALYSIS]

an·am·nesis /ˌanəmˈniːsɪs/ *noun* (*pl.* **an·am·neses** /-ˌsiːz/) **1** the recalling of things past; reminiscence. **2** a patient's account of his or her medical history. **3** *Christianity* the commemoration of the Passion, Resurrection, and Ascension, recited after the consecration in a Eucharistic liturgy. [Greek, = remembrance]

ana·morph·osis /ˌanəˈmɔːfəsɪs/ *noun* (*pl.* **-oses** /-ˌsiːz/) **1** a distorted projection or drawing which appears normal when viewed from a particular point or by means of a suitable mirror or lens. **2** *Bot. & Zool.* progression to a higher type, esp. development of the adult form through a series of small changes. □ **ana·morph·ic** *adjective* [Greek *anamorphōsis* transformation]

an·an·drous /əˈnandrəs/ *adjective* *Bot.* having no stamens. [Greek *anandros* without males, from *an-* not + *anēr andros* male]

Ana·nias /ˌanəˈnaiəs/ *New Testament* **1** the husband of Sapphira, struck dead because he lied (Acts 5). **2** the Jewish high priest before whom St. Paul was brought (Acts 23).

ana·pest /ˈanəˌpest/ *noun* (also **ana·paest**) *Prosody* a foot consisting of two short or unstressed syllables followed by one long or stressed syllable. □ **ana·pes·tic** (or **-paes·tic**) /-ˈpestɪk/ *adjective* [Latin *anapaestus* from Greek *anapaistos* reversed (because the reverse of a dactyl)]

ana·phase /ˈanəˌfeiz/ *noun* *Biol.* the stage of meiotic or mitotic cell division when the chromosomes move away from one another to opposite poles of the spindle. [ANA- + PHASE]

anaph·ora /əˈnafərə/ *noun* **1** *Rhetoric* the repetition of a word or phrase at the beginning of successive clauses. **2** *Grammar* the use of a word referring to or replacing a word used earlier in a sentence, to avoid

---

Consonants:　b *but*　　d *dog*　　f *few*　　g *get*　　h *her*　　j *yes*　　k *cat*　　l *leg*　　m *man*　　n *no*　　p *pen*　　r *red*　　s *sit*

repetition, e.g. *do* in *I like it and so do they.* **3** *Christianity* the part of the Eucharist which contains the consecration, anamnesis, and communion. □ **ana·phor·ic** /ˌanəˈfɒrɪk/ *adjective* [Latin from Greek, = repetition (as ANA-, *pherō* to bear)]

an·aphro·dis·iac /an͵afrəˈdiːziˌak/ ● *adjective* tending to reduce sexual desire. ● *noun* an anaphrodisiac drug.

an·aphyl·axis /ˌanəfɪˈlaksɪs/ *noun* (*pl.* **an·aphyl·axes** /-ksiːz/) *Med.* an extreme allergic reaction to an antigen, to which the body has become hypersensitive following an earlier exposure. □ **an·aphyl·actic** *adjective* [as ANA- + Greek *phulaxis* guarding]

anap·tyxis /ˌanəpˈtɪksɪs/ *noun* (*pl.* **anap·tyxes** /-siːz/) *Phonetics* the insertion of a vowel between two consonants to aid pronunciation (as in *went thataway*). [Greek *anaptuxis* (as ANA-, *ptussō* fold)]

an·arch·ism /ˈanɑrˌkɪzəm/ *noun* the doctrine that all government should be abolished.

an·arch·ist /ˈanɑrkɪst/ *noun* an advocate of anarchism or of political disorder. □ **an·arch·is·tic** *adjective*

anarcho- /əˈnɑrkoː/ *combining form* anarchic.

an·archy /ˈanɑrki/ *noun* **1** disorder, esp. political or social. **2** lack of government in a society. □ **an·arch·ic** /əˈnɑrkɪk/ *adjective* [Greek *anarkhia* (as AN-¹, *arkhē* rule)]

Ana·sazi /anəˈsɒzi/ ● *noun* a member of a culture of the southwestern US, dating from about AD 100 to the present, of which the Pueblo culture is a continuation. ● *adjective* of or pertaining to the Anasazi culture. [Navajo *anaasází* 'enemy ancestors', applied by the Navajo to the prehistoric inhabitants of ruined Pueblo villages]

ana·stig·mat /əˈnastɪɡˌmat/ *noun* a lens or lens system made free from astigmatism by correction. [German from *anastigmatisch* ANASTIGMATIC]

ana·stig·mat·ic /ˌanəstɪɡˈmatɪk/ *adjective* free from astigmatism.

anas·to·mose /əˈnastəˌmoːz/ *intransitive verb* link by anastomosis.

anas·to·mo·sis /əˌnastəˈmoːsɪs/ *noun* (*pl.* **anas·to·mo·ses** /-siːz/) a cross-connection of arteries, branches, rivers, etc. [Greek from *anastomoō* furnish with a mouth (as ANA-, *stoma* mouth)]

anath·ema /əˈnaθəmə/ *noun* (*pl.* **anath·emas**) **1** a detested thing or person (*is anathema to me*). **2 a** a declaration of the Christian Church, excommunicating a person or denouncing a doctrine. **b** a cursed thing or person. **c** a strong curse. [ecclesiastical Latin, = excommunicated person, excommunication, from Greek *anathema* thing devoted, (later) accursed thing, from *anatithēmi* set up]

anath·ema·tize /əˈnaθəməˌtaiz/ *transitive & intransitive verb* (also esp. *Brit.* **-tise**) curse.

Ana·to·lia /ˌanəˈtoːlia/ the western peninsula of Asia that now forms the greater part of Turkey, bounded by the Black Sea, the Aegean, and the Mediterranean. Most of it consists of a high, largely mountainous, plateau. □ **Ana·to·lian** *adjective & noun* [Greek *anatolē* east]

ana·tom·ic·al /ˌanəˈtɒmɪkəl/ *adjective* (also **ana·tom·ic**) of or relating to anatomy. □ **ana·tom·ic·al·ly** *adverb*

anatomically correct *adjective* (of a doll etc.) having the genitalia, breasts, etc. depicted realistically.

anato·mist /əˈnatəmɪst/ *noun* a person skilled in anatomy.

anato·mize /əˈnatəˌmaiz/ *transitive verb* (also esp. *Brit.* **-mise**) **1** examine in detail. **2** dissect.

anat·omy /əˈnatəmi/ *noun* (*pl.* **-omies**) **1** the science of the bodily structure of animals and plants. **2** this structure. **3** *informal* a human body. **4** analysis. **5** the dissection of the human body, animals, or plants. [Greek, from *ana* 'up' + *tomia* 'cutting']

Anax·agoras /ˈanakˌsagɒrəs/ (*c.*500–*c.*428 BC) Greek philosopher, the last of the Ionian school, who lived in Athens and was a friend of Pericles. He held that all matter was infinitely divisible and initially held together in a motionless uniform mixture until put into a system of circulation directed by Spirit or Intelligence.

Anaxi·man·der /əˈnaksɪˌmandər/ (*c.*610–*c.*545 BC) Greek philosopher and astronomer of the Ionian school, who lived in Miletus. He is reputed to have drawn the earliest map of the inhabited world, to have introduced the gnomon sundial into Greece, and to have taught a primitive form of evolutionary theory, arguing that life began in water and man originated from fish.

Anax·im·enes /ˈanakˌsɪmɪniːz/ (*c.*546 BC) Greek philosopher of the Ionian school, who lived in Miletus. He maintained that the universe consists of 'air' or vapour which when rarefied becomes fire, and when condensed becomes progressively wind, cloud, water, earth, and stone.

ANC *abbreviation* AFRICAN NATIONAL CONGRESS.

An·cas·ter /ˈankastər/ a former town in S Ontario, now the western part of the city of Hamilton; pop. (2001) 27,485. [*Ancaster*, England]

-ance /əns/ *suffix* forming nouns expressing: **1** a quality or state or an instance of one (*arrogance*; *protuberance*; *relevance*; *resemblance*). **2** an action (*assistance*; *furtherance*; *penance*). [from or after French *-ance* from Latin *-antia*, *-entia* (compare -ENCE) from pres. part. stem *-ant-*, *-ent-*]

an·ces·tor *noun* **1** any (esp. remote) person from whom one is descended. **2** an early type of animal or plant from which others have evolved. **3** an early prototype or forerunner (*ancestor of the computer*). □ **an·ces·tress** *noun* [Old French *ancestre* from Latin *antecessor* *-oris* from *antecedere* (as ANTE-, *cedere* *cess-* go)]

an·ces·tral /anˈsestrəl/ *adjective* of, belonging to or inherited from ancestors.

ancestral name *noun* (among some West Coast Aboriginal groups, esp. the Sne Nay Muxw) the personal name of an ancestor, conferred upon a child as a ceremonial name.

an·ces·try *noun* (*pl.* **-tries**) **1** lineage or descent. **2** ancestors collectively.

An·chi·ses /anˈkaisiːz/ *Gk Legend* a prince of Troy, and father of Aeneas.

ancho chili /ˈantʃoː ˌtʃɪli/ *noun esp. N Amer.* **1** a large, fairly hot chili pepper, used (usu. dried) in traditional Mexican dishes. **2** the plant which bears this fruit. [Mexican Spanish *chile ancho*, lit. 'wide pepper']

an·chor ● *noun* **1** a heavy metal weight used to moor a ship to the bottom of a river, lake, sea, etc. or a balloon to the ground. **2** a person or thing that gives stability or security. **3** the main announcer on a news or sports broadcast, who introduces the reports of other broadcasters. **4** a person who plays a crucial part, esp. at the back of a tug-of-war team or as the last runner in a relay race. **5** a bolt or fitting for attaching something to a wall, floor, etc. **6** a store, e.g. a department store, which is the principal tenant of a shopping centre. ● *verb* **1** *transitive* secure (a ship or balloon) by means of an anchor. **2** *transitive* fix firmly. **3** *transitive* cast anchor. **4** *intransitive* be moored by means of an anchor. **5** *transitive* act as an anchor (in senses 3 & 4 of *noun*). □ **at anchor** moored by means of an anchor. **cast** (or **come to**) **anchor** let the anchor down. **weigh anchor** *see* WEIGH. □ (in senses 3 & 4 of *noun*) **anchor·man** *noun* (*pl.* **-men**). **anchor·person** *noun* **anchor·woman** *noun* (*pl.* **-women**). [Old English *ancor* from Latin *anchora* from Greek *agkura*]

An·chor·age the largest city in Alaska, a seaport on an inlet of the Pacific Ocean; pop. (est. 2000) 260,283.

an·chor·age *noun* **1** a place where a ship may be anchored. **2** the act of anchoring or lying at anchor. **3** something that provides security for something else.

anchor ice *noun* ice formed at the bottom of lakes and rivers.

an·chor·ite /ˈaŋkəˌrəit/ *noun* **1** a hermit; a religious recluse. **2** a person of secluded habits. □ **an·chor·ess** /-rəs/ *noun* **an·chor·itic** /-ˈrɪtɪk/ *adjective* [ecclesiastical Latin *anchoreta* from ecclesiastical Greek *anakhōrētēs* from *anakhōreō* retire]

anchor plate *noun* a heavy piece of timber or metal, e.g. as support for suspension bridge cables.

an·cho·veta /ˌantʃəˈveta/ *noun* a small Pacific anchovy, *Cetengraulis mysticetus*, caught for use as bait or to make fish meal. [Spanish, diminutive of *anchova*: compare ANCHOVY]

an·chovy /ˈanˌtʃoːvi, ˈantʃəvi, anˈtʃoːvi/ *noun* (*pl.* **-vies**) a small, mainly Mediterranean fish of the herring family *Engraulis encrasicholus*, which has a rich flavour and is usu. eaten pickled or in pastes, sauces, etc. [Spanish and Portuguese *ancho(v)a*, of uncertain origin]

anchovy pear *noun* the edible fruit of the Jamaican tree *Grias cauliflora*, similar to a mango.

an·cien ré·gime /ˌɑ̃ˌsjɑ̃ reiˈʒiːm/ *noun* **1** the political and social system in France before the Revolution of 1789. **2** any superseded regime. [French, = old rule]

an·cient /ˈeinʃənt/ ● *adjective* **1 a** of long ago. **b** of or pertaining to the world prior to the fall of Rome in 476. **2** having lived or existed long; very old. ● *noun* archaic an old man. □ **the ancients 1** the people of ancient times, esp. the Greeks, Romans, Hebrews, and Egyptians. **2** the writers of classical Greece or Rome. □ **ancient·ness** *noun* [Old French *ancien*, ultimately from Latin *ante* before]

ancient history *noun* **1** the history of the ancient civilizations of the Mediterranean area and the Near East before the fall of the Western Roman Empire in 476. **2** something already long familiar.

ancient lights *noun Law* the right to have access to daylight through a particular window.

---

t *top* ʋ *voice* w *we* z *zoo* ʃ *she* ʒ *vision* θ *thin* ð *this* ŋ *ring* x *loch* tʃ *chip* dʒ *jar*   (*see over for vowels*)

ancient monument *noun Brit.* an old building etc. preserved usu. under Government control.

ancient murrelet *noun* a small black and white seabird, *Synthliboramphus antiquus*, found on the west coast of N America.

an·cil·lary /anˈsɪləri/ ● *adjective* **1** (of a person, activity, or service) providing essential support to a central service or industry. **2** associated, secondary. ● *noun* (*pl.* **-ies**) **1** an ancillary worker. **2** something which is ancillary; an auxiliary or accessory. [Latin *ancillaris* from *ancilla* maidservant]

ancon /ˈaŋkən/ *noun* (*pl.* **an·co·nes** /aŋˈkoːniːz/) *Archit.* **1** a console, usu. of two volutes, supporting or appearing to support a cornice. **2** each of a pair of projections on either side of a block of stone etc. for lifting or repositioning. [Latin from Greek *agkōn* elbow]

An·cona /anˈkoːnə/ a port on the Adriatic coast of central Italy, capital of Marche region; pop. (2001) 100,402. [Greek *agkōn* elbow]

-ancy /ənsi/ *suffix* forming nouns denoting a quality (*constancy; relevancy*) or state (*expectancy; infancy*) (*compare* -ANCE). [from or after Latin *-antia*: compare -ENCY]

and *conjunction* **1 a** connecting words, clauses, or sentences that are to be taken jointly (*meat and potatoes; white and brown bread; buy and sell; two hundred and forty*). **b** implying progression (*better and better*). **c** implying causation (*do that and I'll hit you; she hit him and he cried*). **d** implying great duration (*he cried and cried*). **e** implying a great number (*miles and miles*). **f** implying addition (*two and two are four*). **g** implying variety (*there are books and books*). **h** implying succession (*walking two and two*). **2** *informal* to (*try and open it*). **3** in relation to (*Canada and NATO*). □ **and/or** either or both of two stated possibilities. [Old English *and*]

-and /and/ *suffix* forming nouns meaning 'a person or thing to be treated in a specified way' (*graduand*). [Latin gerundive ending *-andus*]

An·da·lu·sia /ˌandaluˈsiːə/ the southernmost region of Spain, bordering on the Atlantic and the Mediterranean; capital, Seville. □ **An·da·lu·sian** *adjective & noun* [after the *Vandals*, who had settled there in the 5th c.]

An·da·man and Nico·bar Islands /ˈandəmən, ˈnɪkəˌbɑr/ two groups of islands in the Bay of Bengal, constituting a Union Territory of India; pop. (2001) 356,300; capital, Port Blair.

an·dan·te /anˈdɒntei, -ˈdantei/ *Music* ● *adverb & adjective* in a moderately slow tempo. ● *noun* an andante passage or movement. [Italian, part. of *andare* go]

an·dan·tino /ˌandɒnˈtiːnoː, ˌandan-/ *Music* ● *adverb & adjective* somewhat quicker than andante. ● *noun* (*pl.* **-tinos**) an andantino passage or movement. [Italian, diminutive of ANDANTE]

An·der·sen, Hans Chris·tian (1805–75), Danish author of over 150 fairy tales, including *The Little Mermaid*, *The Nightingale*, and *The Ugly Duckling*.

An·der·son ▶ **1 Carl David** (1905–91), US physicist noted for work on cosmic rays; he shared the Nobel prize for physics in 1936. **2 Eliza·beth Gar·rett** (1836–1917), pioneer of medical training for women. Debarred from entry to medical courses in Britain because of her sex, she studied privately, and in 1866 she opened what later became the first hospital to be staffed by medical women. **3 James Thom·as Mil·ton** (1878–1946), Canadian educator, writer, and politician, premier of Saskatchewan 1929–34. **4 Marian** (1902–93), US contralto. In 1955 she became the first black singer to perform at the New York Metropolitan Opera. **5 Phil·ip W(ar·ren)** (b.1923), US physicist. He made contributions to the study of solid-state physics, and research on molecular interactions has been facilitated by his work on the spectroscopy of gases; he shared the Nobel Prize for physics in 1977. **6 Sher·wood** (1876–1941), US novelist and short-story writer, best known for his fictionalized accounts of small-town life in the US Midwest.

Anderson River a river in the NWT, 692 km long, flowing northward into Wood Bay, an inlet of the Beaufort Sea, just east of the Mackenzie Delta. [J. *Anderson*, Hudson's Bay Co. chief factor *c*.1857]

Andes /ˈandiːz/ a major mountain system running the length of the Pacific coast of S America. It extends over some 8 000 km (5,000 miles), with a continuous height of more than 3 000 m (10,000 ft.). □ **An·de·an** /anˈdiːən, ˈandiən/ *adjective*

andes·ite /ˈandɪˌzaɪt/ *noun* a fine-grained brown or greyish intermediate volcanic rock. □ **andes·it·ic** /ˌandɪˈzɪtɪk/ *adjective* [ANDES + -ITE¹]

An·dhra Pra·desh /ˌandrə prəˈdeʃ/ a state in SE India, on the Bay of Bengal; capital, Hyderabad.

and·iron /ˈandˌaɪrn/ *noun* a metal stand (usu. one of a pair) for

supporting burning wood in a fireplace; a firedog. [Old French *andier*, of unknown origin: assimilated to IRON]

An·dorra /anˈdɒrə/ a small autonomous principality in the S Pyrenees, between France and Spain; pop. (2002) 68,403; capital, Andorra la Vella. The sovereignty of Andorra is shared between the President of France and the Spanish bishop of Urgel. □ **An·dor·ran** *adjective & noun*

An·dorra la Vella /anˌdɒrə la ˈveijə/ the capital of Andorra, pop. (est. 1999) 21,513.

an·douille /anˈduːi/ *noun* (in Cajun cuisine) a smoked, spicy, coarse-ground pork sausage. [French, from Latin *inductilia* from *indūcĕre*]

André /ˈɑdrei/ **Brother** (born Alfred Bessette, 1845–1937), Canadian religious. Thousands of healings have been attributed to his intervention with his patron, St. Joseph. His admirers helped him to build a small oratory on Mount Royal in 1904, replaced by an imposing basilica in 1924–25. He was beatified in 1982.

An·drea del Sarto /anˈdreiə del ˈsartoː/ (1486–1531), Italian Renaissance painter influenced by Raphael. His most important works are frescoes and grisailles, as well as dreamy portraits and dark-eyed Madonnas.

An·dret·ti /anˈdreti/ **Mario (Gab·ri·ele)** (b.1940), Italian-born US racing driver. He won sixteen Formula One races and the world championship in 1978. He also won the Indycar championship four times.

An·drew ▶ **1 An·drew Al·bert Chris·tian Ed·ward, Duke of York** (b.1960), second son of Elizabeth II. He married Sarah Ferguson (b.1959) in 1986, and they formally separated in 1993; they have two children, Princess Beatrice Elizabeth Mary (b.1988) and Princess Eugenie Victoria Helena (b.1990). **2 St.** (1st c.), one of the twelve Apostles, brother of St. Peter. Since *c*.750 he has been regarded as the patron saint of Scotland.

An·drews ▶ **1 Julie** (b.1935), English actress and singer, who created the role of Eliza Doolittle in *My Fair Lady* on Broadway, and starred in the films *Mary Poppins* (1964) and *The Sound of Music* (1965). **2 Thom·as** (1813–85), Irish physical chemist. He is best known for his work on the continuity of the gaseous and liquid states; his discovery of the critical temperature of carbon dioxide suggested that any gas could be liquefied if the temperature was sufficiently low.

An·drić /ˈandrɪtʃ/ **Ivo** (1892–1975), Yugoslav novelist, essayist, and short-story writer. His novels *The Bridge* (1945) and *Bosnian Chronicle* (1945) are set in Bosnia and take the history of the province as their theme; he was awarded the Nobel Prize for literature in 1961.

andro *noun informal* = ANDROSTENEDIONE.

andro- *combining form* man, male. [Greek *andro-* male]

andro·cen·tric *adjective* male-centred. □ **andro·cen·trism** *noun*

An·dro·cles /ˈandrəˌkliːz/ a runaway slave in a Roman story who extracted a thorn from the paw of a lion, which later recognized and refrained from attacking him when he faced it in the arena.

an·droe·cium /anˈdriːsiəm, anˈdriːʃiəm/ *noun* (*pl.* **an·droe·cia** /-siə/) *Bot.* the stamens taken collectively. [modern Latin from ANDRO- + *oikion* house]

andro·gen /ˈandrədʒən/ *noun* a male sex hormone or other substance capable of developing and maintaining certain male sexual characteristics. □ **andro·gen·ic** /-ˈdʒenɪk/ *adjective* [ANDRO- + -GEN]

andro·gyne /ˈandrəˌdʒaɪn/ ● *adjective* hermaphrodite. ● *noun* a hermaphrodite person. [Greek *androgunos* (*anēr andros* male, *gunē* woman)]

an·dro·gyn·ous /anˈdrɒdʒɪnəs/ *adjective* **1** partly male and partly female in appearance; of indeterminate sex. **2** having both male and female characteristics; hermaphrodite. **3** *Bot.* with stamens and pistils in the same flower or inflorescence. □ **an·dro·gyny** /-dʒɪni/ *noun* [as ANDROGYNE]

an·droid *noun* a robot with a human appearance. [ANDRO- + -OID]

An·drom·ache /anˈdrɒməki/ *Gk Legend* the wife of Hector. After the fall of Troy she became the slave of Neoptolemus (son of Achilles), and after his death married Helenus, a brother of Hector.

An·drom·eda /anˈdrɒmədə/ **1** *Gk Legend* an Ethiopian princess. Chained to a rock to be eaten by a sea monster after her mother had angered the sea god Poseidon, she was rescued by Perseus, whom she later married. **2** *Astronomy* a constellation lying between Pegasus and Cassiopeia, conspicuous for its great spiral nebula (the **Andromeda Galaxy**), located two million light years away.

An·drop·ov¹ a former name (1984–9) for RYBINSK.

An·drop·ov² /anˈdrɒpɒf/ **Yuri Vlad·imir·ovich** (1914–84), president of the USSR 1983–84.

andro·stene·dione /ˌandrəʊˈstiːndaɪəʊn/ *noun* a naturally occurring androgenic steroid often taken in concentrated form to elevate blood levels of testosterone. [ANDROSTERONE + -ENE + -DIONE]

andro·ster·one /ˌandrəʊˈstɪərəʊn/ *noun* a relatively inactive male sex hormone produced by metabolism of testosterone. [Greek *anēr*, *andr-* 'man' + STEROL + -ONE]

-androus *combining form Bot.* forming adjectives meaning 'having specified male organs or stamens' (*monandrous*). [Greek *-andros* from *anēr andros* male + -OUS]

-ane¹ *suffix var. of* -AN; usu. with distinction of sense (*germane; humane; urbane*) but sometimes with no corresponding form in *-an* (*mundane*).

-ane² /eɪn/ *suffix Chem.* forming names of paraffins and other saturated hydrocarbons (*methane; propane*). [after *-ene, -ine,* etc.]

anec·dot·age /ˈanəkˌdəʊtɪdʒ/ *noun jocular* garrulous old age. [blend of ANECDOTE + DOTAGE]

anec·dot·al /ˌanəkˈdəʊtəl/ *adjective* **1** of, pertaining to, or consisting of anecdotes. **2** based on or consisting of incidental observations or reports rather than systematic research (*anecdotal evidence*). □ **anec·dot·al·ist** *noun*

anec·dote /ˈanəkˌdəʊt/ *noun* a short account of an entertaining or interesting incident. □ **anec·dot·ist** *noun* [Greek *anekdota* things unpublished (as AN-¹, *ekdotos* from *ekdidōmi* publish)]

an·echo·ic /ˌanɪˈkəʊɪk/ *adjective* free from echo.

an·emia /əˈniːmɪə/ *noun* (also esp. *Brit.* **an·aemia**) a deficiency in the blood, usu. of red cells or their hemoglobin, resulting in pallor and weariness. [modern Latin from Greek *anaimia* (as AN-¹, -EMIA)]

an·emic /əˈniːmɪk/ *adjective* (also esp. *Brit.* **an·aemic**) **1** relating to or suffering from anemia. **2** pale; lacking in vitality.

an·emom·eter /ˌanɪˈmɒmɪtər/ *noun* an instrument for measuring the force of the wind. □ **an·emom·etry** *noun* **anemo·met·ric** *adjective* [Greek *anemos* wind + -METER]

anem·one /əˈnɛmənɪ/ *noun* **1** any plant of the genus *Anemone*, related to the buttercup, with flowers of various vivid colours. **2** = PASQUE FLOWER. [Greek *anemōnē* windflower, from *anemos* wind]

an·emoph·il·ous /ˌanəˈmɒfɪləs/ *adjective* wind-pollinated. [Greek *anemos* wind + *-philous* (see -PHILIA)]

an·enceph·aly /anɛnˈsɛfəlɪ/ *noun* a congenital condition where part or all of the cerebral hemispheres and the rear of the skull are absent. □ **an·en·ceph·alic** *adjective* [Greek *anenkephalos* 'without brain']

-aneous *suffix* forming adjectives (*cutaneous; miscellaneous*).

an·er·oid /ˈanəˌrɔɪd/ ● *adjective* (of a barometer) that measures air pressure by its action on the elastic lid of an evacuated box, not by the height of a column of fluid. ● *noun* an aneroid barometer. [French *anéroïde* from Greek *a-* not + *nēros* water]

anes·the·sia etc. *var. of* ANAESTHESIA etc.

anes·the·si·ol·ogy /anəsˌθiːsɪˈɒlədʒɪ/ *noun* the science of administering anaesthetics. □ **anes·the·si·ol·o·gist** *noun*

an·eur·ysm /ˈanjʊˌrɪzəm/ *noun* (also **an·eur·ism**) an excessive localized enlargement of a blood vessel. □ **an·eur·ys·mal** /-ˈrɪzməl/ *adjective* (also **an·eur·is·mal**). [Greek *aneurusma* from *aneurunō* widen out, from *eurus* wide]

anew *adverb* **1** again. **2** in a different way.

an·frac·tu·os·ity /ˌanfraktʃʊˈɒsɪtɪ/ *noun* (*pl.* **-ities**) **1** circuitousness. **2** intricacy. □ **an·frac·tu·ous** /-tʃʊəs/ *adjective* [French *anfractuosité* from Late Latin *anfractuosus* from Latin *anfractus* a bending]

an·ga·kok /ˈaŋɡəkɒk/ *noun* Cdn (North) an Inuit shaman or healer. [Inuktitut]

an·gary /ˈaŋɡərɪ/ *noun Law* the right of a belligerent (subject to compensation for loss) to seize or destroy neutral property under military necessity. [French *angarie*, ultimately from Greek *aggareia* from *aggaros* courier]

an·gel *noun* **1 a** an attendant or messenger of God. **b** a conventional representation of this in human form with wings. **c** an attendant spirit (*evil angel; guardian angel*). **d** *Christianity* a member of the lowest of the nine orders of angelic beings (see ORDER 19). **2 a** a very virtuous person. **b** an obliging person (*be an angel and answer the door*). **3** *N Amer.* = SNOW ANGEL. **4** an old English coin bearing the figure of the archangel Michael piercing the dragon. **5** *slang* a financial backer of an enterprise, esp. in the theatre. **6** *informal* an unexplained radar echo. [ecclesiastical Latin *angelus* from Greek *aggelos* messenger]

angel dust *noun slang* the hallucinogenic drug phencyclidine hydrochloride.

An·gel·eno /ˌandʒəˈliːnəʊ/ *noun* (also **Los Angeleno**) esp. *US* a native or inhabitant of Los Angeles. [US Spanish *angeleño*]

Angel Falls a waterfall in the Guiana Highlands of SE Venezuela. It is the highest waterfall in the world, with an uninterrupted fall of 978 m (3,210 ft.). [J. *Angel*, US aviator and prospector who discovered the falls d.1956]

angel·fish *noun* any of various fish, esp. *Pterophyllum scalare*, with large dorsal and ventral fins.

angel food cake *noun* (also esp. *Brit.* **angel cake**) a light, usu. tall and ring-shaped cake made of beaten egg whites, sugar, and flour.

angel hair *noun* **1** very fine spaghetti. **2** spun glass with very fine filaments forming a fluffy white material used esp. in Christmas decorations.

an·gel·ic *adjective* **1** like or relating to angels. **2** having characteristics attributed to angels, esp. sublime beauty, innocence, or goodness. □ **an·gel·ic·al·ly** *adverb* [Middle English from French *angélique* or Late Latin *angelicus* from Greek *aggelikos* (as ANGEL)]

an·gel·ica /anˈdʒɛlɪkə/ *noun* **1** an aromatic umbelliferous plant, *Angelica archangelica*, used in cooking and medicine. **2** its candied stalks. [medieval Latin (*herba*) *angelica* angelic herb]

An·gel·ico /anˈdʒɛlɪkəʊ/ **Fra** (born Giovanni da Fiesole) (*c.*1400–1455), Italian painter best known for his religious works, e.g. the frescoes in the convent of San Marco, Florence, and the *Scenes from the Lives of St. Stephen and St. Lawrence* in the Vatican.

An·gell /ˈeɪndʒəl/ **Sir Nor·man** (born Ralph Norman Angell-Lane) (1873–1967), English economist and pacifist, who is best known for *The Great Illusion* (1910), which refuted the idea that war was to a nation's economic advantage; he was awarded the Nobel Peace Prize in 1933.

An·ge·lou /ˈandʒəluː/ **Maya** (born Marguerite Johnson, 1928), US novelist, poet, dramatist, and performer. Her most successful work is the series of autobiographical novels beginning with *I Know Why the Caged Bird Sings* (1970).

angel pie *noun N Amer.* a dessert consisting of a meringue base filled with custard and fruit and topped with whipped cream.

angel shark *noun* = MONKFISH 2.

angels-on-horseback *noun* simmered oysters individually wrapped in bacon, served on toast.

an·gelus /ˈandʒələs/ *noun Catholicism* **1** a devotion commemorating the Incarnation and including the recitation of three Hail Marys, traditionally said at morning, noon, and sunset. **2** a bell announcing this. [opening words *Angelus domini* (Latin, = the angel of the Lord)]

an·ger ● *noun* extreme or passionate displeasure. ● *transitive verb* make angry; enrage. [Old Norse *angr* grief, *angra* vex]

An·gers¹ /ãˈʒeɪ/ a city in W France, capital of the former province of Anjou; pop. (1999) 151,279.

An·gers² /ãˈʒeɪ/ **Fé·li·cité** (1845–1924), Canadian writer. Writing under the pen name Laure Conan, she was the first female French-Canadian novelist. Her novels, which deal with the triple concerns of family, nation, and church, include *La Vaine foi* (1921).

An·ge·vin /ˈandʒəvɪn/ ● *noun* **1** a native or inhabitant of Anjou. **2** a Plantagenet, esp. any of the English kings from Henry II to John. ● *adjective* **1** of Anjou. **2** of the Plantagenets. [French]

an·gina /anˈdʒaɪnə/ *noun* **1** (in full **an·gina pec·tor·is** /ˈpɛktərɪs/) pain in the chest brought on by exertion, owing to an inadequate blood supply to the heart. **2** an attack of intense constricting pain often causing suffocation. [Latin, = spasm of the chest, from *angina* quinsy, from Greek *agkhonē* strangling]

angio- *combining form* relating to blood vessels. [modern Latin from Greek *aggeion* vessel]

angio·gen·esis /ˌandʒɪəʊˈdʒɛnəsɪs/ *noun* the development of new blood vessels.

angiogenesis inhibitor /ˌandʒɪəʊˈdʒɛnəsɪs/ *noun* a drug used to prevent tumour growth by preventing the development of new blood vessels to feed the tumour.

angio·gram /ˈandʒɪəˌgram/ *noun* an X-ray made by angiography.

angi·og·raphy /ˌandʒɪˈɒgrəfɪ/ *noun* (*pl.* **-ies**) radiography of blood and lymph vessels, carried out after introduction of a radiopaque substance. □ **angio·graph·ic** *adjective* **angio·graph·ic·ally** *adverb*

angi·oma /ˌandʒɪˈəʊmə/ *noun* (*pl.* **angi·omas**) a tumour produced by the dilatation or new formation of blood vessels or lymph vessels. [as ANGIO-]

angio·plasty /ˈandʒɪəˌplasti/ *noun* (*pl.* **-ties**) surgical repair of a damaged blood vessel.

angio·sperm /ˈandʒɪəˌspɜrm/ *noun* any plant producing flowers and reproducing by seeds enclosed within a carpel, including herbaceous

plants, herbs, shrubs, grasses and most trees (*opp.* GYMNOSPERM).
□ **angio·sperm·ous** /ˌandʒiəˈspɜːrməs/ *adjective* [ANGIO- + *sperma* seed]

angio·tens·in /ˌandʒiəˌˈtensɪn/ *noun* (also **angiotensin II**) a powerful vasoconstricting polypeptide which stimulates the production of aldosterone and vasopressin and results in an increase in blood pressure. [ANGIO- + (HYPER)TENSIN, the former name of the substance, from HYPERTENSION]

angiotensin I *noun* the inactive precursor of angiotensin II, which is formed in the liver by the action of renin on a plasma protein and is converted in the lungs to angiotensin II by a second enzyme.

ang·ishore /ˈaŋəʃɔr/ *Cdn* (*Nfld & Maritimes*) *var. of* HANGASHORE.

Ang·kor /ˈaŋkɔr/ the capital of the ancient kingdom of Khmer in NW Cambodia. It is noted for its temples, esp. the Angkor Wat, decorated with relief sculptures. The site was overgrown with jungle when it was rediscovered in 1860.

Angle *noun* (*usu. in pl.*) a member of a tribe from Schleswig that settled in E Britain in the 5th c., giving their name to England and the English. □ **Angli·an** *adjective* [Latin *Anglus* from Germanic (Old English *Engle*: compare ENGLISH) from *Angul* a district of Schleswig (now in N Germany) (related to ANGLE²)]

angle¹ ● *noun* **1 a** the space between two meeting lines or surfaces. **b** the inclination of two lines or surfaces to each other. **2 a** a corner. **b** a sharp projection. **3 a** the direction from which a photograph etc. is taken. **b** the aspect from which a matter is considered. **4** *Cdn* (*Nfld*) a curved inlet in a lake or pond. ● *verb* **1** *transitive & intransitive* move or place obliquely. **2** *transitive* present (information) from a particular point of view (*was angled in favour of the victim*). □ **angled** *adjective* [Old French *angle* or from Latin *angulus*]

angle² ● *intransitive verb* **1** (often foll. by *for*) fish with hook and line. **2** (foll. by *for*) seek an objective by devious or calculated means (*angled for an invitation*). ● *noun archaic* a fish hook. [Old English *angul*]

angle brackets *plural noun* brackets in the form < > (*see* BRACKET *noun* 3).

angle iron *noun* a piece of iron or steel with an L-shaped cross-section, used to strengthen a framework.

angle of attack *noun* the acute angle between the chord of an airfoil and the direction of the surrounding undisturbed flow of air, water, etc.

angle of incidence *noun* the angle which an incident line, ray, etc., makes with the perpendicular to the surface at the point of incidence.

angle of reflection *noun* the angle made by a reflected ray with a perpendicular to the reflecting surface.

angle of refraction *noun* the angle made by a refracted ray with the perpendicular to the refracting surface.

angle of repose *noun* the angle beyond which an inclined body will not support another on its surface by friction.

angle parking *noun* N Amer. parking of vehicles at an angle to the curb rather than parallel with it. □ **angle-park** *intransitive verb*

an·gler *noun* **1** a person who fishes with a hook and line. **2** = ANGLERFISH.

angler·fish *noun* any of various fishes that prey upon small fish, attracting them by filaments arising from the dorsal fin. *Also called* FROGFISH.

Angle·sey /ˈaŋgəlsi/ an island and (since 1996) county of NW Wales, separated from the mainland by the Menai Strait.

Angli·can ● *adjective* of or relating to the Church of England or any Church in communion with it, e.g. the Anglican Church of Canada. ● *noun* a member of an Anglican Church. □ **Angli·can·ism** *noun* [medieval Latin *Anglicanus* from Latin *Anglus* ANGLE]

Anglican Communion *noun* a group of Christian Churches derived from or related to the Church of England, including the Anglican Church of Canada, the Episcopal Church in the US and other national, provincial, and independent Churches. The body's senior bishop is the Archbishop of Canterbury.

angli·cism *noun* **1** an English word, structure, etc. borrowed into another language. **2** a word or custom peculiar to England. **3** Englishness. **4** preference for what is English. [Latin *Anglicus* (see ANGLICAN) + -ISM]

angli·cize *transitive verb* (also esp. *Brit.* **-cise**) make English in form or character. □ **angli·ciz·a·tion** *noun*

An·glo¹ *noun* (*pl.* **-glos**) *Cdn informal* an anglophone, esp. in Quebec. [abbreviation of ANGLOPHONE]

An·glo² *noun* (*pl.* **-glos**) *US & Austral.* an English-speaking person of British or northern-European origin (in the US esp. as distinct from Hispanic Americans). [abbreviation of ANGLO-SAXON]

Anglo- *combining form* **1** English (*Anglo-Catholic*). **2** of English origin (*an Anglo-Canadian*). **3** English or British and (*an Anglo-French agreement*). [Latin *Anglus* English]

Anglo-American ● *adjective* **1** of American and English (or British) descent. **2** English (or British) and American. ● *noun* an American of English (or British) descent.

Anglo-Canadian ● *adjective* **1** of or pertaining to English-speaking Canadians. **2** English (or British) and Canadian. ● *noun* **1** an English-speaking Canadian. **2** a Canadian of English descent.

Anglo-Catholic ● *adjective* of a High Church Anglican group which emphasizes its Catholic tradition. ● *noun* a member of this group. □ **Anglo-Catholi·cism** *noun*

Anglo·cen·tric *adjective* centred on or considered in terms of England.

Anglo-French ● *adjective* **1** English (or British) and French. **2** of Anglo-French. ● *noun* the French language as retained and separately developed in England after the Norman Conquest.

Anglo-Indian ● *adjective* **1** of or relating to England and India. **2 a** of British descent or birth but living or having lived long in India. **b** of mixed British and Indian parentage. **3** (of a word) adopted into English from an Indian language. ● *noun* an Anglo-Indian person.

Anglo-Irish ● *adjective* **1** of English descent living in Ireland. **2** English (or British) and Irish. **3** of or relating to the English language as spoken in Ireland. ● *noun* **1** the Anglo-Irish language. **2** (*in pl.*) people of English descent but born or resident in Ireland.

Anglo-Irish Treaty an agreement signed in 1921 by representatives of the British government and the provisional Irish Republican government, by which Ireland was partitioned and the Irish Free State created.

Anglo-Latin ● *adjective* of Latin as used in medieval England. ● *noun* this form of Latin.

Anglo·mania *noun* excessive admiration of English customs.

Anglo-Norman ● *adjective* **1** of the Normans in England after the Norman Conquest. **2** of the dialect of French used by them. **3** English and Norman. ● *noun* the Anglo-Norman dialect.

anglo·phile ● *noun* a person who is fond of or greatly admires England, the English, or English-speaking culture. ● *adjective* being or characteristic of an anglophile. □ **anglo·philia** *noun*

anglo·phobe ● *noun* a person who greatly hates or fears anglophones, the English or England. ● *adjective* being or characteristic of an anglophobe. □ **anglo·phobia** *noun* **anglo·phob·ic** *adjective*

anglo·phone esp. *Cdn* ● *adjective* English-speaking. ● *noun* an English-speaking person. [ANGLO-, after FRANCOPHONE]

Anglo-Saxon ● *adjective* **1** of the English Saxons (as distinct from the Old Saxons of the continent, and from the Angles) before the Norman Conquest. **2** of the Germanic peoples (Angles, Saxons, and Jutes) who settled in Britain before the Norman Conquest. **3** of English descent. ● *noun* **1** an Anglo-Saxon person. **2** the Old English language. **3 a** *informal* plain (esp. crude) English. **b** *US* the modern English language.

An·gola /aŋˈgoːlə/ a republic on the west coast of southern Africa; pop. (est. 2002) 10,593,171; capital, Luanda. Independence, achieved in 1975 after a bitter anti-colonial war, was followed by years of civil war. □ **An·go·lan** *adjective & noun*

An·gora /aŋˈgɔrə/ the former name (until 1930) for ANKARA.

an·gora /aŋˈgɔrə/ *noun* **1** a fabric made from the hair of the angora goat or rabbit. **2** a long-haired variety of cat, goat, or rabbit. [ANGORA]

angora wool *noun* a mixture of sheep's wool and angora rabbit hair.

Angos·tura /aŋgəˈstjurə/ the former name for CIUDAD BOLÍVAR.

angos·tura /ˌaŋgəˈsturə/ *noun* (in full **angostura bark**) an aromatic bitter bark used as a flavouring, and formerly used as a tonic and to reduce fever. [ANGOSTURA]

Angos·tura Bit·ters *noun proprietary* a bitter tonic used esp. as a flavouring in cocktails.

angry *adjective* (**angri·er**, **angri·est**) **1** feeling or showing anger; extremely displeased or resentful. **2** (of a wound, sore, etc.) inflamed, painful. **3** suggesting or seeming to show anger (*an angry sky*). □ **angri·ly** *adverb*

angry young man *noun* **1** any of a group of young British writers of the 1950s who criticized the social conventions of the time. **2** any young person who disagrees vehemently with existing attitudes.

Consonants: b *but*   d *dog*   f *few*   g *get*   h *her*   j *yes*   k *cat*   l *leg*   m *man*   n *no*   p *pen*   r *red*   s *sit*

angst /aŋst/ *noun* **1** anxiety. **2** a feeling of guilt or remorse. □ **angsty** *adjective* [German]

Ång·ström /ˈaŋstrəm, ˈɒŋ-/ **An·ders Jonas** (1814–1874), Swedish physicist noted for his work on the measurements of wavelengths in the solar spectrum.

ang·strom /ˈaŋstrəm/ *noun* (also **ång·ström** /ˈɒŋ-/) a unit of length equal to 10^{-10} m, used esp. for electromagnetic wavelengths. Symbol: **Å**. [A.J. ÅNGSTRÖM]

An·guil·la /aŋˈgwɪlə/ the most northerly of the Leeward Islands in the W Indies; pop. (est. 2002) 12,446. □ **An·guil·lan** *adjective & noun*

an·guine /ˈaŋgwɪn/ *adjective* of or resembling a snake. [Latin *anguinus* from *anguis* snake]

an·guish *noun* **1** severe misery or mental suffering. **2** *Cdn* (*Nfld*) inflammation; infection. [Old French *anguisse* choking, from Latin *angustia* tightness, from *angustus* narrow]

an·guished *adjective* suffering or expressing anguish.

angu·lar *adjective* **1 a** having angles or sharp corners. **b** (of a person) having sharp features; lean and bony. **c** awkward in manner. **2** forming an angle. **3** measured by angle (*angular distance*). □ **angu·lar·ity** *noun* **angu·lar·ly** *adverb* [Latin *angularis* from *angulus* ANGLE[1]]

angular momentum *noun* the momentum a body has by virtue of its rotation; the product of its moment of inertia and angular velocity.

angular velocity *noun* the rate of change of angular position of a rotating body.

Angus[1] an administrative region and former county of NE Scotland, known from the 16th c. until 1928 as Forfarshire, and between 1975 and 1996 was part of Tayside region.

Angus[2] *noun* = ABERDEEN ANGUS.

An·halt /ˈɒnhɒlt/ **Ist·ván** (b.1919), Hungarian-born Canadian composer. He combines traditional instruments, electronics and the human voice into a highly complex musical style.

an·hedonia /anhiːˈdoːnɪə/ *noun Psych.* inability to feel pleasure in normally pleasurable activities. [AN-[1] + Greek *hēdonē* pleasure]

an·hed·ral /anˈhiːdrəl/ ● *noun* a downward inclination of an aircraft wing, tailplane, etc. ● *adjective* **1** of or having an anhedral. **2** (of a crystal) not having plane faces. [AN-[1] + -*hedral* (see -HEDRON)]

Anhui /anˈhwiː/ (also **Anhwei**) a province in E China; capital, Hefei.

an·hyd·ride /anˈhaɪdraɪd/ *noun* a substance obtained by removing the elements of water from a compound, esp. from an acid. [as ANHYDROUS + -IDE]

an·hyd·rite /anˈhaɪdrəɪt/ *noun* a naturally occurring, usu. rock-forming, anhydrous mineral form of calcium sulphate. [as ANHYDROUS + -ITE 2]

an·hyd·rous /anˈhaɪdrəs/ *adjective Chem.* without water, esp. water of crystallization. [Greek *anudros* (as AN-[1], *hudōr* water)]

Anik /ˈanɪk/ the name of a series of Canadian geostationary telecommunications satellites.

anil·ine /ˈanɪlaɪn, -lɪn/ *noun* a colourless oily liquid, used in the manufacture of dyes, drugs, and plastics. Chem. formula: $C_6H_5NH_2$. [German *Anilin* from *Anil* indigo (from which it was originally obtained), ultimately from Arabic *an-nīl*]

aniline dye *noun* **1** any of numerous dyes made from aniline. **2** any synthetic dye.

ani·ma *noun Psych.* **1** the inner personality (opp. PERSONA 1). **2** Jung's term for the feminine part of a man's personality (opp. ANIMUS 4). [Latin, = mind, soul]

anim·ad·vert /ˌanɪmadˈvɜrt/ *intransitive verb* (foll. by *on*) criticize, censure (conduct, a fault, etc.). □ **anim·ad·ver·sion** *noun* [Latin *animadvertere* from *animus* mind + *advertere* (as AD-, *vertere vers-* turn)]

ani·mal ● *noun* **1** a living organism which feeds on organic matter, usu. one with specialized sense organs and nervous system, and able to respond rapidly to stimuli. **2** such an organism other than man. **3** a brutish or uncivilized person. **4** *informal* a person or thing of any kind (*there is no such animal*). ● *adjective* **1** characteristic of animals. **2** of animals as distinct from vegetables (*animal fat*). **3** characteristic of the physical needs of animals; carnal, sensual. [Latin *animalis* having breath, from *anima* breath]

animal cracker *noun* (also **animal cookie**) *N Amer.* a small (usu. arrowroot) cookie in the shape of an animal, esp. a circus animal.

ani·mal·cule /ˌanɪˈmalkjuːl/ *noun archaic* a microscopic animal. □ **ani·mal·cu·lar** *adjective* [modern Latin *animalculum* (as ANIMAL, -CULE)]

animal husbandry *noun* the science of breeding and caring for farm animals.

ani·mal·ism *noun* **1** the nature and activity of animals. **2** the belief that humans are not superior to other animals. **3** concern with physical matters; sensuality. □ **ani·mal·is·tic** *adjective*

ani·mal·ity /ˌanɪˈmalɪti/ *noun* **1** the animal world. **2** the nature or behaviour of animals.

ani·mal·ize *transitive verb* (also esp. *Brit.* **-ise**) make into or like an animal. □ **ani·mal·iz·a·tion** *noun*

animal magnetism *noun* **1** power to attract others. **2** *hist.* mesmerism.

animal rights *noun* the right of animals to be free from abuse or exploitation by humans.

animal spirits *noun* natural exuberance.

ani·mate ● *adjective* /ˈanɪmət/ **1** having life. **2** lively. ● *transitive verb* /ˈanɪmeit/ **1** enliven, make lively. **2** give life to. **3** produce (a film etc.) by animation. **4** inspire, actuate. **5** encourage. [Latin *animatus* past participle of *animare* give life to, from *anima* life, soul]

ani·mat·ed *adjective* **1** lively, vigorous. **2** having life. **3** (of a film etc.) using techniques of animation. □ **ani·mat·ed·ly** *adverb*

anima·teur /ˌanɪmaˈtɜr/ *noun* (also **ani·ma·tor** /ˈanɪmeitɜr/) a person who coordinates, or acts as a driving force behind, a cultural or other activity. [French]

ani·ma·tion *noun* **1** vivacity, ardour. **2** the state of being alive. **3** *Film* the technique of filming successive drawings or positions of puppets to create an illusion of movement when the film is shown as a sequence.

ani·ma·tor *noun* **1** a person who makes animated films. **2** *var. of* ANIMATEUR. **3** *Cdn* a person employed at a historic site to act the part of a typical resident of the time or an actual historical figure associated with the site.

anima·tron·ics *noun* the technique of constructing robots resembling animals, people, etc. which are programmed to perform lifelike movements to a pre-recorded soundtrack. □ **anima·tron·ic** *adjective* [blend of ANIMATED + ELECTRONICS]

anime /ˈanimei/ *noun* Japanese film and television animation, typically having a science-fiction theme and sometimes including violent or sexual material. [Japanese *anime* from French *animé* animated]

animé /ˈanɪmei/ *noun* any of various resins, esp. a W Indian resin used in making varnish. [French, of uncertain origin]

ani·mism *noun* **1** the attribution of a living soul to plants, inanimate objects, and natural phenomena. **2** the belief in a supernatural power that organizes and animates the material universe. □ **ani·mist** *noun* **ani·mis·tic** *adjective* [Latin *anima* life, soul + -ISM]

ani·mos·ity /ˌanɪˈmɒsɪti/ *noun* (*pl.* **-ities**) a spirit or feeling of strong hostility. [Late Latin *animositas* from *animosus* spirited]

ani·mus *noun* **1** a display of animosity. **2** ill feeling. **3** a motivating spirit or feeling. **4** *Psych.* Jung's term for the masculine part of a woman's personality (opp. ANIMA 1). [Latin, = spirit, mind]

an·ion /ˈanˌaɪən/ *noun* a negatively charged ion; an ion that is attracted to the anode in electrolysis (opp. CATION). □ **an·ion·ic** /ˌanaɪˈɒnɪk/ *adjective* [ANA- + ION]

anise /ˈanɪs/ *noun* **1** an umbelliferous plant, *Pimpinella anisum*, having aromatic seeds (see ANISEED). **2** any of several trees and shrubs of the genus *Illicium*, which bear fruit with the odour of anise, esp. the star anise, *I. verum*. [Greek *anison* anise, dill]

ani·seed /ˈanɪˌsiːd/ *noun* the seed of the anise, used to give liqueurs, candies, etc. a liquorice-like flavour. [Middle English from ANISE + SEED]

ani·sette /ˌanɪˈset/ *noun* a liqueur flavoured with aniseed. [French, diminutive of *anis* ANISE]

Anishi·nabe /ˌanɪʃɪˈnɒbiː/ (also **Anish·nabe** /ˌanɪʃˈnɒbi/) ● *noun* (*pl.* same) **1** the preferred name for the Ojibwa, an Algonquian people living in northern Quebec, northern and central Ontario, Manitoba, and Saskatchewan. **2** the Algonquian language of this people. ● *adjective* of or relating to this people or their culture or language. [Ojibwa, = the people]

an·iso·trop·ic /ˌanaɪsəˈtrɒpɪk/ *adjective* having physical properties that are different in different directions, e.g. the strength of wood along the grain differing from that across the grain (opp. ISOTROPIC). □ **an·iso·trop·ic·ally** *adverb* **an·isot·ropy** /-ˈsɒtrəpi/ *noun* [AN-[1] + ISOTROPIC]

Anjou /ãˈʒuː/ **1** a former province of W France, on the Loire, noted for its wines. **2** a former city in south central Quebec, on the NE part of the Island of Montreal, now part of the city of Montreal; pop. (2001) 38,015.

Anjou pear *noun* a variety of pear with green skin and white flesh.

Anka /ˈaŋkə/ **Paul Al·bert** (b.1941), Canadian-born singer and songwriter, famous since his teens for songs such as 'Diana', 'Puppy Love', 'Lonely Boy', and Frank Sinatra's 'My Way'.

An·kara /ˈaŋkərə/ the capital of Turkey since 1923; pop. (est. 2002) 3,329,400. It was known until 1930 as Angora.

ankh /aŋk/ noun a device consisting of a looped bar with a shorter crossbar, used in ancient Egypt as a symbol of life. [Egyptian, = life, soul]

an·kle noun 1 the joint connecting the foot with the leg. 2 the part of the leg between this and the calf. [Old Norse *ankul-* (unrecorded) from Germanic: related to ANGLE[1]]

ankle-biter noun slang a child.

ankle bone noun a bone forming the ankle.

ankle sock noun a short sock just covering the ankle.

ank·let noun 1 an ornament or fetter worn around the ankle. 2 esp. US = ANKLE SOCK. [ANKLE + -LET, after BRACELET]

an·kyl·ose /ˈaŋkɪˌloːz/ transitive & intransitive verb (of bones or a joint) stiffen or unite by ankylosis. [back-formation from ANKYLOSIS after *anastomose* etc.]

an·kyl·os·ing spondylitis noun a form of spinal arthritis, chiefly affecting young males, that eventually causes ankylosis of vertebral and sacroiliac joints.

an·kyl·o·sis /ˌaŋkɪˈloːsɪs/ noun 1 the abnormal stiffening and immobility of a joint by fusion of the bones. 2 such fusion. □ **an·kyl·otic** adjective [modern Latin from Greek *agkulōsis* from *agkuloō* crook]

anna /ˈanə/ noun a former monetary unit of India and Pakistan, one sixteenth of a rupee. [Hindustani *ānā*]

An Najaf see NAJAF.

an·nal noun 1 the annals of one year. 2 a record of one item in a chronicle. [back-formation from ANNALS]

an·nal·ist noun a writer of annals. □ **an·nal·is·tic** /-ˈlɪstɪk/ adjective

annals plural noun 1 a narrative of events year by year. 2 historical records. 3 (in proper names) a learned journal. [Latin *annales* (*libri*) yearly (books) from *annus* year]

Annam /ˈanam, aˈnam/ a former French protectorate in central Indochina (1883–1945), now part of Vietnam. □ **An·nam·ese** adjective

Annan /aˈnan/ **Koffi (Atta)** (b.1938), Ghanaian diplomat, Secretary General of the United Nations since 1997. He shared the Nobel Peace Prize with the United Nations in 2001.

An·nand /ˈanənd/ **Wil·liam** (1808–87), Canadian publisher and politician, first premier of Nova Scotia 1867–75.

An·nap·olis /əˈnapəˌlɪs/ the state capital of Maryland, on Chesapeake Bay; pop. (2000) 35,838. It is the home of the US Naval Academy.

Annapolis River a river in W Nova Scotia, flowing southwestward into the Annapolis Basin to empty into the Bay of Fundy. [see ANNAPOLIS ROYAL]

An·nap·olis Royal a town in W Nova Scotia, situated on the south side of the Annapolis River near its mouth, about 90 km northeast of Yarmouth; pop. (2001) 550. □ **Anna·pol·itan** noun [combination of the town's two former names: *Annapolis* (after Queen ANNE + Greek *polis* city) + *Port-Royal*]

An·na·purna /ˌanəˈpərnə/ a ridge of the Himalayas, in north central Nepal. Its highest peak rises to 8 078 m (26,503 ft.).

an·nates /ˈaneɪts/ plural noun Catholicism the first year's revenue of a see or benefice, paid to the Pope. [French *annate* from medieval Latin *annata* year's proceeds, from *annus* year]

an·nat·to /əˈnatoː/ noun 1 a tropical tree, *Bixa orellana*. 2 an orange-red dye obtained from the seed coat of this tree, used esp. as a food colouring. [Carib]

Anne /an/ **1 Anne** (1665–1714), queen of England and Scotland (known as Great Britain from 1707) and Ireland, 1702–14. The last of the Stuart monarchs and daughter of James II, she succeeded her brother-in-law William III; on her death the crown passed to the House of Hanover. **2 Anne Eliza·beth Alice Lou·ise, the Princess Royal** (b.1950), daughter of Elizabeth II. A skilled horsewoman, she rode for Great Britain in the 1976 Olympics; she was married to Captain Mark Philips (b.1948) (1973–92), and in 1992 she married Commander Tim Laurence. She has two children, Peter (b.1977) and Zara (b.1981). **3 St.** (1st c. BC), mother of the Virgin Mary. Patron saint of Brittany and Canada. Her feast day (26 July) is observed with special devotion in Quebec. **4 Anne Boleyn**, see BOLEYN. **5 Anne of Austria** (1601–66), wife of Louis XIII of France and regent (1643–61) during the minority of Louis XIV.

6 Anne of Cleves /kliːvz/ (1517–57), fourth wife of Henry VIII. The marriage was dissolved after six months.

an·neal /əˈniːl/ ● transitive verb 1 heat (metal or glass) and allow it to cool slowly, esp. to toughen it. 2 toughen. ● noun treatment by annealing. □ **an·neal·er** noun [Old English *onælan* from *on* + *ælan* burn, bake, from *āl* fire]

an·nel·id /ˈanəlɪd/ noun an animal of the phylum Annelida, members of which (e.g. marine worms, earthworms, and leeches) have bodies made up of annular segments. □ **an·nel·id·an** /əˈnelɪdən/ adjective & noun [ultimately from Latin *anellus* diminutive of *anulus* ring]

annex ● noun (also esp. *Brit.* **an·nexe**) 1 a separate or added building, esp. for extra accommodation. 2 an addition to a document. 3 *N Amer.* (now esp. in proper names) an area annexed to a city, usu. for housing development. ● transitive verb (also /əˈneks/) 1 add or append as a subordinate part. 2 incorporate (territory of another) into one's own. 3 add as a condition or consequence. 4 informal take without right. □ **an·nex·a·tion** noun [Old French *annexer* from Latin *annectere* (as AN-[2], *nectere nex-* bind)]

an·nex·a·tion·ism noun 1 a policy which favours annexation of territory. 2 *Cdn* any of several historical movements favouring Canadian political union with the US. □ **an·nex·a·tion·ist** noun

An·ni·goni /ˌaniˈɡoːni/ **Pietro** (1910–88), Italian artist, noted for his portraits of Queen Elizabeth II, John F. Kennedy, and others, painted in old-master style.

an·nihi·late /əˈnaɪəˌleɪt/ transitive verb 1 completely destroy. 2 defeat utterly; make insignificant or powerless. 3 *Physics* subject to annihilation. □ **an·nihi·la·tor** noun [Late Latin *annihilare* (as AN-[2], *nihil* nothing)]

an·nihi·la·tion /əˌnaɪəˈleɪʃən/ noun 1 the act or process of annihilating. 2 *Physics* the conversion of a particle and an antiparticle into radiation.

an·ni·ver·sary noun (pl. **-ies**) **1 a** the yearly return of a date on which an event took place in a previous year. **b** the anniversary of a wedding. **2** the celebration of this. [Latin *anniversarius* from *annus* year + *versus* turned]

Anno Dom·ini /ˈanoː ˈdɒmɪˌni, ˈdɒmɪˌnaɪ/ ● adverb in the year of the Christian era. ● noun informal advancing age (*suffering from Anno Domini*). [Latin, = in the year of the Lord]

an·no·tate /ˈanoːˌteɪt, ˈanəˌteɪt/ transitive verb add explanatory notes to (a book, document, etc.). □ **an·no·ta·tion** /-ˈteɪʃən/ noun **an·no·ta·tor** noun [Latin *annotare* (as AD-, *nota* mark)]

an·nounce verb 1 transitive (often foll. by *that*) make publicly known. 2 transitive make known the arrival or imminence of (a guest, dinner, etc.). 3 transitive make known (without words) to the senses or the mind; be a sign of. 4 intransitive US declare one's candidacy for political office. [Old French *annoncer* from Latin *annuntiare* (as AD-, *nuntius* messenger)]

an·nounce·ment noun a statement in written or spoken form that makes something known.

an·noun·cer noun a person who announces speakers, singers, programs, etc., esp. on radio or television.

an·noy transitive verb 1 cause slight anger or mental distress to. 2 (in passive) be somewhat angry (*am annoyed with you; was annoyed at my remarks*). 3 molest; harass repeatedly. □ **an·noy·ance** noun **an·noy·ing** adjective **an·noy·ing·ly** adverb [Old French *anuier*, ultimately from Latin *in odio* hateful]

an·nual ● adjective 1 reckoned by the year. 2 occurring every year. 3 living or lasting for one year. ● noun 1 a book etc. published once a year; a yearbook. 2 a plant that lives only for a year or less. □ **an·nu·al·ly** adverb [Late Latin *annualis* from Latin *annalis* from *annus* year]

annual allowable cut noun *Cdn* (*BC*) *Forestry* the volume of wood which may be cut each year in a specified area.

annual general meeting noun *Cdn, Brit., & Austral.* a yearly meeting of members or shareholders, esp. for holding elections and reporting on the year's events. Abbr.: **AGM**.

an·nu·al·ized adjective (also esp. *Brit.* **-ised**) (of rates of interest, inflation, etc.) calculated on an annual basis, as a projection from figures obtained for a shorter period.

annual report noun a yearly report made by the directors of a company to its shareholders, containing the financial statements and a summary of the year's activities.

annual ring noun a ring in the cross-section of a plant, esp. a tree, produced by one year's growth.

an·nu·it·ant /əˈnjuːɪtənt/ noun a person who holds or receives an annuity.

Vowels: a *cat* ɑ *arm* e *bed* ɜr *her* ɜː *deux* ə *ago* ɪ *sit* i *cosy* iː *feed* ɒ *hot* ɔ *pore* ɔː *no* ʌ *run* ʊ *put*

an·nu·ity /ə'njuːəti, ə'nuː-/ *noun* (*pl.* **-ities**) **1** a yearly grant or allowance. **2** an investment of money entitling the investor to a series of equal annual sums. **3** a sum payable for a particular year. □ **an·nu·it·ize** *transitive verb* [medieval Latin *annuitas -tatis* from Latin *annuus* yearly (as ANNUAL)]

annul /ə'nʌl/ *transitive verb* (**an·nulled**, **an·nul·ling**) **1** declare (a marriage etc.) invalid. **2** cancel, abolish. □ **an·nul·ment** *noun* [Late Latin *annullare* (as AD-, *nullus* none)]

an·nu·lar /'anjʊlər/ *adjective* ring-shaped; forming a ring. [Latin *annularis* from *an(n)ulus* ring]

annular eclipse *noun* an eclipse of the sun in which the moon leaves a ring of sunlight visible round it.

an·nu·late /'anjʊlət/ *adjective* having rings; marked with or formed of rings. □ **an·nu·la·tion** *noun* [Latin *annulatus* (as ANNULUS)]

an·nu·let /'anjʊlət/ *noun* **1** *Archit.* a small fillet or band encircling a column. **2** a small ring. [Latin *annulus* ring + -ET¹]

an·nu·lus /'anjʊləs/ *noun* (*pl.* **an·nuli** /-laɪ/) **1** a ring; a ring-shaped part. **2** the area between two concentric circles. [Latin *an(n)ulus*]

an·nun·ci·a·tion *noun* **1** (**Annunciation**) *Christianity* **a** the announcing of the Incarnation, made by the angel Gabriel to Mary, related in Luke 1:26–38. **b** the festival commemorating this on 25 March. **2 a** the act or process of announcing. **b** an announcement. [Late Latin *annuntiatio -onis* from *annuntiare* announce]

an·nun·ci·ator *noun* **1** a device giving an audible or visible indication of which of several electrical circuits has been activated, of the position of a train, etc. **2** an announcer.

annus hor·ri·bi·lis /'anəs hɒ'rɪbɪlɪs/ *noun* a year of disaster or misfortune. [modern Latin, suggested by ANNUS MIRABILIS]

annus mira·bi·lis /,anəs mɪ'rɑbɪlɪs/ *noun* a remarkable or auspicious year. [modern Latin, = wonderful year]

anoa /ə'noʊə/ *noun* any of several small deer-like water buffalo of the genus *Bubalus*, native to Sulawesi. [name in Sulawesi]

an·ode /'anoʊd/ *noun* *Electricity* **1** the positive electrode in an electrolytic cell or electronic valve or tube. **2** the negative terminal of a primary cell such as a battery (*opp.* CATHODE). □ **anod·al** *adjective* **anod·ic** /ə'nɒdɪk/ *adjective* [Greek *anodos* way up, from *ana* up + *hodos* way]

ano·dize /'anə,daɪz/ *transitive verb* (also esp. *Brit.* **-dise**) coat (a metal, esp. aluminum) with a protective oxide layer by electrolysis. □ **ano·diz·er** *noun*

ano·dyne /'anə,daɪn/ ● *adjective* **1** not likely to cause offence or disagreement and somewhat dull. **2** able to relieve pain. ● *noun* **1** an anodyne drug or medicine. **2** something which alleviates a person's mental distress. [Latin *anodynus* from Greek *anōdunos* painless (as AN-¹, *odunē* pain)]

anoint *transitive verb* **1** apply oil or ointment to, esp. as a religious ceremony, e.g. at baptism, or the consecration of a priest or king, or in ministering to the sick. **2** choose (a leader, successor, etc.) as though by anointing. **3** (usu. foll. by *with*) smear, rub. □ **anoint·er** *noun* [Old French *enoint* past participle of *enoindre* from Latin *inungere* (as IN-², *ungere unct-* smear with oil)]

anoint·ing of the sick *noun* a rite of some Christian denominations in which a gravely ill person is prayed for and anointed with oil as a sign of healing. It is a sacrament in the Roman Catholic Church.

anom·al·is·tic /ə,nɒmə'lɪstɪk/ *adjective* *Astronomy* of the anomaly or angular distance of a planet from its perihelion.

anomalistic month *noun* the period of time (about 27.5 days) between successive perigees of the moon.

anomalistic year *noun* the period of time (about 365 days, 6 hours, 13 minutes and 53 seconds) between successive perihelia of the earth.

anom·al·ous /ə'nɒmələs/ *adjective* having an irregular or deviant feature; abnormal. □ **anom·al·ous·ly** *adverb* **anom·al·ous·ness** *noun* [Late Latin *anomalus* from Greek *anōmalos* (as AN-¹, *homalos* even)]

anom·aly /ə'nɒməli/ *noun* (*pl.* **-alies**) **1** an anomalous circumstance or thing; an irregularity. **2** irregularity of motion, behaviour, etc. **3** *Astronomy* the angular distance of a planet or satellite from its last perihelion or perigee. [Greek *anōmalia* from *anōmalos* ANOMALOUS]

an·omie /'anəmi/ *noun* (also **anomy**) lack of the usual social or ethical standards in an individual or group. □ **anom·ic** /ə'nɒmɪk/ *adjective* [Greek *anomia* from *anomos* lawless]

anon *adverb* archaic or literary soon, shortly (*will say more of this anon*). [Old English *on ān* into one, *on āne* in one]

anon. *abbreviation* anonymous; an anonymous author.

an·onym·ous /ə'nɒnɪməs/ *adjective* **1** of unknown name. **2** of unknown or undeclared source or authorship. **3** without character; featureless, impersonal. **4** (**Anonymous**) (placed after noun) designating a mutual support group in which the members do not have to reveal their names (*Alcoholics Anonymous*). □ **ano·nym·ity** /,anə'nɪmɪti/ *noun* **an·onym·ous·ly** *adverb* [Late Latin *anonymus* from Greek *anōnumos* nameless (as AN-¹, *onoma* name)]

anonymous remailer *noun* = REMAILER.

anoph·eles /ə'nɒfə,liːz/ *noun* any of various mosquitoes of the genus *Anopheles*, many of which are carriers of the malarial parasite. [Greek *anōphelēs* unprofitable]

ano·rak /'anə,rak/ *noun* **1** a waterproof jacket of cloth or plastic, usu. with a hood and with drawstrings at the waist, cuffs, and hood. **2** a light jacket or cardigan with a drawstring waist. **3** *Brit informal* a socially inept and studious or obsessive person with unfashionable and largely solitary interests. [Greenlandic *anoraq*]

an·or·ec·tic /,anə'rektɪk/ ● *adjective* = ANOREXIC. ● *noun* **1** a substance, e.g. a drug, which suppresses the appetite. **2** a person with anorexia. [Greek *anorektos* without appetite (as ANOREXIA)]

an·or·ex·ia /,anə'reksiə/ *noun* **1** a lack or loss of appetite for food. **2** (in full **anorexia ner·vosa** /nɜr'voʊsə/) a psychological illness, esp. in young women, characterized by an obsessive desire to lose weight by refusing to eat. [Late Latin from Greek from *an-* not + *orexis* appetite]

an·or·ex·ic /,anə'reksɪk/ ● *adjective* **1** involving, producing, or characterized by a lack of appetite, esp. in anorexia nervosa. **2** extremely thin. ● *noun* a person with anorexia.

an·ortho·site /ə'nɔrθə,saɪt/ *noun* a granular igneous rock composed largely of plagioclase (usu. labradorite). [French from *anorthose* plagioclase, ultimately from Greek *an-* not + *orthos* straight]

an·osmia /an'ɒːzmiə/ *noun* the loss of the sense of smell. □ **an·osmic** *adjective* [Late Latin from Greek from *an-* not + *osmē* smell]

an·other ● *adjective* **1** an additional; one more (*have another tart; after another six months*). **2** a person like or comparable to (*another Olivier*). **3** a different (*quite another matter*). **4** some or any other (*will not do another man's work*). ● *pronoun* **1** an additional one (*have another*). **2** a different one (*take this book away and bring me another*). **3** some or any other one (*I love another*). □ **such another** another of the same sort. [AN + OTHER]

Anouilh /a'nuːi/ **Jean** (1910–87), French dramatist. Anouilh's characters struggle for personal integrity against the constraints of society and family background. One of his best-known plays, *Antigone* (1944), is a reworking of the Greek myth with undertones of the contemporary situation in Nazi-occupied Paris. Other notable plays include *L'Alouette* (*The Lark*, 1953), and *Becket* (1959).

ANOVA /'anəvɒ/ *abbreviation* analysis of variance.

an·ovu·lant /an'ɒvjʊ,lənt/ ● *noun* a drug preventing ovulation. ● *adjective* preventing ovulation. [AN-¹ + *ovulation* (see OVULATE) + -ANT]

an·ovu·la·tory /an'ɒvjələ,tɔri/ *adjective* (of a menstrual cycle etc.) not accompanied by ovulation.

an·oxia /ən'ɒksiə/ *noun* an absence or deficiency of oxygen. □ **an·oxic** *adjective* [AN-¹ + OXYGEN + -IA¹]

ANSA *abbreviation* Agenzia Nazionale Stampa Associata, an Italian news agency.

Ansan /'ɒnsɒn/ a city on the west coast of S Korea, south of Inchon; pop. (est. 1995) 510,314.

An·schluss /'anʃlʊs/ the annexation of Austria by Germany in 1938 in defiance of the Treaty of Versailles (1919). After Hitler had forced the resignation of the Austrian Chancellor by demanding that he admit Nazis into his cabinet, the new Chancellor, a pro-Nazi, invited German troops to enter the country on the pretext of restoring law and order. [German from *anschliessen* join]

An·selm /'anselm/ **St.** (c.1033–1109), Italian-born philosopher and theologian who became Archbishop of Canterbury in 1093.

An·shan /ɒn'ʃɒn/ a city in Liaoning, China; pop. (est. 1999) 1,285,849. Anshan is situated close to major iron-ore deposits and China's largest iron and steel complex is nearby.

ANSI *abbreviation* American National Standards Institute.

an·swer ● *noun* **1** something said or done to deal with or in reaction to a question, statement, or circumstance. **2** the solution to a problem. **3** (foll. by *to*) an equivalent or rival (*Quebec's answer to the Champs Elysées*). ● *verb* **1** *transitive* make an answer to (*answer me; answer my question*). **2** *intransitive* (often foll. by *to*) make an answer. **3** *transitive* respond to the summons or signal of (*answer the door; answer the telephone*). **4** *transitive* be satisfactory for (a purpose or need). **5** *intransitive* (foll. by *for, to*) be responsible (*you will answer to me for your conduct*). **6** *intransitive* (foll. by *to*) correspond, esp. to a description. **7** *intransitive* be satisfactory or successful. □ **answer back** answer a rebuke etc. impudently.

answer to the name of be called. [Old English *andswaru*, *andswarian* from Germanic, = swear against (charge)]

an·swer·able *adjective* **1** (usu. foll. by *to, for*) responsible (*answerable to them for any accident*). **2** that can be answered. □ **an·swer·abil·ity** *noun*

answering machine *noun* a device which supplies a pre-recorded answer to a telephone call and allows the caller to record a message.

answering service *noun* a business that receives and answers telephone calls for its clients.

an·swer·phone *noun Brit.* a telephone answering machine.

ant *noun* any small insect of a widely distributed hymenopterous family, wingless (except for males in the mating season), and living in complex social colonies. □ **have ants in one's pants** fidget constantly, esp. because of nervousness or impatience. [Old English *æmet(t)e, ēmete* (see EMMET) from West Germanic]

ant- assimilated form of ANTI- before a vowel or *h* (*Antarctic*).

-ant *suffix* **1** forming adjectives denoting attribution of an action (*pendant; repentant*) or state (*arrogant; expectant*). **2** forming nouns denoting an agent (*assistant; celebrant; deodorant*). [French *-ant* or Latin *-ant-, -ent-*, pres. part. stem of verbs: compare -ENT]

Ant·abuse *noun proprietary* = DISULFIRAM. [ANTI- + ABUSE]

ant·acid ● *noun* a substance that prevents or corrects acidity esp. in the stomach. ● *adjective* having these properties.

An·taeus /anˈtiːəs/ *Gk Myth* a giant, son of Poseidon and Earth, who lived in Libya and compelled all comers to wrestle with him. He overcame and killed all opponents until he was defeated by Hercules.

an·tag·on·ism /anˈtagəˌnɪzəm/ *noun* active opposition or hostility.

an·tag·on·ist /anˈtagənɪst/ *noun* **1** an opponent or adversary. **2** a muscle, organism, or substance that partially or completely opposes the action of another. **3** a substance which interferes with or inhibits the physiological action of another. □ **an·tag·on·is·tic** *adjective* **an·tag·on·is·tic·ally** *adverb* [Greek *antagōnistēs* (as ANTAGONIZE)]

an·tag·on·ize /anˈtagəˌnaɪz/ *transitive verb* (also esp. *Brit.* -**ise**) **1** evoke hostility or opposition or enmity in. **2** (of one force etc.) counteract or tend to neutralize (another). □ **an·tag·on·iz·a·tion** *noun* [Greek *antagōnizomai* (as ANTI-, *agōnizomai* from *agōn* contest)]

ant·alkali /antˈalkəlaɪ/ *noun* (*pl.* **ant·alkalis**) any substance that counteracts an alkali.

An·tall /ˈantal/ **Jozsef** (1933 –1993), Hungarian political leader, prime minister 1990–1993. He became leader of the Hungarian Democratic Forum in 1990, and was elected premier in the country's first free elections in over 40 years.

An·talya /anˈtaljə/ a port in southern Turkey; pop. (est. 2002) 606,447.

Anta·nana·rivo /ˌantəˌnanəˈriːvəʊ/ the capital of Madagascar, situated in the central plateau; pop. (est. 2002) 1,359,600. Until 1975 the city was known as Tananarive.

Ant·arc·tic /antˈɑːktɪk, -ˈɑːtɪk/ *adjective & noun* (prec. by *the*) of, relating to, or denoting the south polar region or Antarctica. [Old French *antartique* or Latin *antarcticus* from Greek *antarktikos* (as ANTI-, *arktikos* ARCTIC)]

Ant·arc·tica /antˈɑːktɪkə, -ˈɑːtɪkə/ a continent around the South Pole, situated mainly within the Antarctic Circle. Antarctica is almost entirely covered by ice sheets; it holds 90 per cent of the world's ice, representing 70 per cent of the world's fresh water. In 1911 Roald Amundsen was the first to reach the Pole, and Robert F. Scott reached it a month later. Although there is no permanent human population, Norway, Australia, France, New Zealand, and the UK claim sectors of the continent (Argentina and Chile claim parts of the British sector); its exploitation is governed by an international treaty of 1959, renewed in 1991.

Antarctic Circle the parallel of latitude 66°33′ south of the equator. It marks the southernmost point at which the sun is visible on the southern winter solstice and the northernmost point at which the midnight sun can be seen on the southern summer solstice.

Antarctic Ocean (also called **Southern Ocean**) the sea surrounding Antarctica, consisting of parts of the S Atlantic, the S Pacific, and the S Indian Ocean.

Antarctic Peninsula a mountainous peninsula of Antarctica between the Bellingshausen Sea and the Weddell Sea, extending northwards towards Cape Horn and the Falkland Islands.

An·tares /anˈtɑːriːz/ a red supergiant, the brightest star in the constellation Scorpius.

ant bear *noun Southern Africa* = AARDVARK.

ante /ˈantɪ/ ● *noun* **1** a stake put up by a player in poker etc. before receiving cards. **2** an amount to be paid in advance. ● *transitive verb* (**antes, anted**) **1** put up as an ante. **2 a** bet, stake. **b** (foll. by *up*) pay. □ **up** (or **raise**) **the ante** increase what is at stake, esp. in regard to a challenge. [Latin, = before]

ante- /ˈantɪ/ *prefix* forming nouns and adjectives meaning 'before, preceding' (*antebellum; antedate*). [Latin *ante* (prep. & adv.), = before]

ant·eater *noun* **1** any of several toothless mammals of the family Myrmecophagidae, having a long snout and sticky tongue, and feeding on ants and termites. **2** any animal resembling this, e.g. an aardvark.

ante·bellum /ˌantɪˈbeləm/ *adjective* occurring or existing before a particular war, esp. the American Civil War. [Latin from *ante* before + *bellum* war]

ante·cedent /ˌantɪˈsiːdənt/ ● *noun* **1** a preceding thing or circumstance. **2** *Grammar* a word, phrase, clause, or sentence, to which another word (esp. a pronoun, usu. following) refers. **3** (in *pl.*) history or ancestry, esp. of a person. **4** *Logic* the statement contained in the 'if' clause of a conditional proposition. ● *adjective* **1** (often foll. by *to*) previous. **2** presumptive, a priori. □ **ante·cedence** *noun* **ante·cedent·ly** *adverb* [French *antecedent* from Latin *antecedere* (as ANTE-, *cedere* go)]

ante·chamber *noun* a small room leading to a main one. [as ANTE-, CHAMBER]

ante·date ● *transitive verb* **1** exist or occur at a date earlier than. **2** assign an earlier date to (a document, event, etc.), esp. one earlier than its actual date. ● *noun* a date earlier than the actual one.

ante·dilu·vian /ˌantɪdɪˈluːvɪən/ *adjective* **1** of or belonging to the time before the Biblical Flood. **2** *informal* very old or out of date. [ANTE- + Latin *diluvium* DELUGE + -AN]

ante·lope *noun* (*pl.* same or **ante·lopes**) **1** any of various deer-like ruminants of the family Bovidae, esp. abundant in Africa and typically tall, slender, graceful, and swift-moving with smooth hair and upward-pointing horns, e.g. gazelles, gnus, kudus, and impala. **2** *N Amer.* = PRONGHORN. **3** leather made from the skin of any of these. [medieval Latin *ant(h)alopus* from late Greek *antholops*, of unknown origin]

ante·natal *adjective* esp. *Brit.* = PRENATAL.

an·ten·na *noun* **1** (*pl.* **an·ten·nas**) a metal rod, wire, or other structure by which signals are transmitted or received as part of a radio or television transmitting or receiving system. **2** (*pl.* **an·ten·nae** /-niː/) *Zool.* one of a pair of mobile appendages on the heads of insects, crustaceans, etc., sensitive to touch and taste; a feeler. **3** (**an·ten·nae**) the faculty of instinctively detecting and interpreting subtle signs (*the dulling effect of the suburbs on a person's hipness antennae*). □ **an·ten·nal** *adjective* (in sense 2). [Latin, = sail yard]

ante·nuptial *adjective* esp. *Brit.* = PRE-NUPTIAL.

ante·pendium /ˌantɪˈpendɪəm/ *noun* (*pl.* **ante·pendia** /-dɪə/) a veil or hanging for the front of an altar. [medieval Latin (as ANTE-, *pendēre* hang]

ante·penult /ˌantɪpəˈnʌlt/ *noun* the last syllable but two in a word. [abbreviation of Late Latin *antepaenultimus* (as ANTE-, *paenultimus* PENULT)]

ante·penul·ti·mate /ˌantɪpəˈnʌltəmət/ ● *adjective* last but two. ● *noun* anything that is last but two.

an·ter·ior *adjective* **1** nearer the front, esp. situated in the front of the body, or nearer to the head or forepart (*anterior cruciate ligament*). **2** (often foll. by *to*) earlier, prior. □ **an·ter·ior·ity** *noun* **an·ter·ior·ly** *adverb* [Latin *anterior* from *ante* before]

ante·room *noun* a small room leading to a main one, esp. one used as a waiting room.

anthe·li·on /anˈθiːlɪən/ *noun* (*pl.* **anthe·lia** /-lɪə/) a luminous halo projected on a cloud or fog bank opposite to the sun. [Greek, neuter of *anthēlios* opposite to the sun (as ANTI-, *hēlios* sun)]

anthel·min·tic /ˌanθelˈmɪntɪk/ (also **anthel·min·thic** /-ˈθɪk/) ● *noun* any drug or agent used to destroy parasitic, esp. intestinal, worms, e.g. tapeworms, roundworms, and flukes. ● *adjective* having the power to eliminate or destroy parasitic worms. [ANTI- + Greek *helmins helminthos* worm]

an·them *noun* **1** a solemn song expressing loyalty etc., esp. = NATIONAL ANTHEM. **2** a short choral composition set to a passage of scripture and sung during church services. **3** a song adopted by a group as expressing their feelings, aspirations, etc. (*the anthem of disaffected youth*). [Old English *antefn, antifne* from Late Latin *antiphona* ANTIPHON]

an·them·ic /anˈθemɪk/ *adjective* (of a song) like an anthem in being rousing or uplifting.

an·the·mion /anˈθiːmɪən/ *noun* (*pl.* **an·the·mia** /-mɪə/) *Art* a Greek decorative motif with radiating leaves of honeysuckle, lotus, or palmette. [Greek, = flower]

An·the·mius /an'θiːmiəs/ **of Tralles** (6th c.), Greek mathematician, engineer, and artist who was chosen by Justinian to design the cathedral of St. Sophia in Constantinople.

an·ther noun the apical portion of a stamen containing pollen.
□ **an·ther·al** adjective [Latin anthera 'medicine extracted from flowers' from Greek anthēra flowery, fem. adj. from anthos flower]

an·ther·idium /ˌanθə'rɪdiəm/ noun (pl. **an·ther·idia** /-diə/) Bot. the male sex organ of algae, mosses, ferns, etc. [modern Latin from anthera (as ANTHER) + Greek -idion diminutive suffix]

ant·hill noun 1 a mound-like nest built by ants or termites. 2 a community teeming with people.

antho·cyanin /ˌanθɒ'saɪənɪn/ noun any of several water-soluble nitrogenous pigments which contribute to the red, blue, or violet colours in some plants. [Greek anthocyan from anthos flower + kuanos blue + -IN]

an·thol·o·gize /an'θɒlə,dʒaɪz/ transitive & intransitive verb (also esp. Brit. -gise) compile or include in an anthology.

an·thol·ogy /an'θɒlədʒi/ noun (pl. **-gies**) a published collection of poems, stories, songs, reproductions of paintings, etc.
□ **an·thol·o·gist** noun [Greek anthologia from anthos flower + -logia collection, from legō gather]

An·thony, Susan Brow·nell (1820–1906), US feminist and leader of the women's rights movement. An outspoken advocate of temperance and the abolition of slavery, she concentrated on women's issues after 1863, campaigning for the right to vote, better working conditions, and equitable marriage laws.

An·thony of Egypt, St. (c.251–356), considered the founder of Christian monasticism. He was the first to set out a type of monastic rule by which his disciples lived in a community of hermits.

An·thony of Padua, St. (1195–1231), Portuguese-born Franciscan who converted many by his charismatic preaching. He is invoked as the finder of lost objects.

an·tho·zoan /ˌanθə'zoːən/ ● noun any of the sessile marine coelenterates of the class Anthozoa, including sea anemones and corals. ● adjective of or relating to this class. [modern Latin Anthozoa from Greek anthos flower + zōia animals]

an·thra·cene /'anθrə,siːn/ noun a colourless crystalline aromatic hydrocarbon obtained by the distillation of crude oils and used in the manufacture of chemicals. [Greek anthrax -akos coal + -ENE]

an·thra·cite /'anθrə,saɪt/ noun coal of a hard variety burning with little flame and smoke. □ **an·thra·cit·ic** /-'sɪtɪk/ adjective [Greek anthrakitis a kind of coal (as ANTHRACENE)]

an·thrac·nose /an'θraknoːs/ noun a fungal disease of plants, characterized by dark lesions. [French from Greek anthrak-, anthrax coal + nosos disease]

an·thrax /'anθraks/ noun a lethal disease of sheep and cattle caused by bacterial spores and transmissible to humans. [Greek, = carbuncle]

an·thro noun N Amer. informal anthropology. [abbreviation]

an·throp·ic /an'θrɒpɪk/ adjective of or relating to human beings. [from ANTHROPO- + -IC]

anthropic principle noun the cosmological principle that theories of the origin of the universe are constrained by the necessity to allow individual human existence.

anthropo- /'anθrəpoː/ combining form human, mankind. [Greek anthrōpos human being]

an·thropo·cen·tric /ˌanθrəpoː'sentrɪk, ˌanθrɒpoː-/ adjective regarding human beings as the centre of existence. □ **an·thropo·cen·tric·ally** adverb **an·thropo·cen·trism** noun

an·thropo·gen·ic /ˌanθrəpə'dʒenɪk/ adjective 1 caused by human activity (anthropogenic environmental damage). 2 of or relating to anthropogeny. □ **an·thropo·gen·ic·ally** adjective

an·thro·poid /'anθrə,pɔɪd/ ● adjective 1 esp. Biol. of or relating to the primate suborder Anthropoidea (including humans, apes, and monkeys), esp. designating the larger apes. 2 resembling a human being in form. ● noun esp. Biol. a member of the suborder Anthropoidea, esp. an anthropoid ape. [Greek anthrōpoeidēs (as ANTHROPO-, -OID)]

an·thro·pol·ogy /ˌanθrə'pɒlədʒi/ noun 1 the study of human beings, esp. of their societies and customs. 2 the study of the structure and evolution of human beings as animals. □ **an·thropo·logic·al** adjective **an·thro·pol·o·gist** noun

an·thropo·morph·ic /ˌanθrəpə'mɔrfɪk/ adjective 1 of or characterized

by anthropomorphism. 2 having or representing a human form.
□ **an·thropo·morph·ic·ally** adverb [Greek anthrōpomorphos (as ANTHROPO-, morphē form) + -IC]

an·thropo·morph·ism /ˌanθrəpə'mɔrfɪzəm/ noun the attribution of human characteristics to a god, animal, or thing.
□ **an·thropo·morph·ize** transitive verb

an·thro·poph·agy /ˌanθrə'pɒfədʒi/ noun cannibalism.
□ **an·thro·poph·a·gous** /-fəgəs/ adjective [Greek anthrōpophagia (as ANTHROPO-, phagō eat)]

an·thro·poso·phy /anθrə'pɒsəfi/ noun 1 the knowledge of the nature of humans; human wisdom. 2 a movement inaugurated by Rudolf Steiner to develop the faculty of cognition and the realization of spiritual reality. □ **an·thropo·soph·ical** /-'sɒfɪkəl/ adjective [ANTHROPO- + Greek sophos 'wise']

an·thur·ium /an'θʊriəm/ noun any of various tropical American plants of the arum family, often grown as a houseplant, with colourful, leathery foliage surrounding a spike that bears several flowers. [modern Latin from Greek anthos flower + oura tail]

anti /'anti, 'antaɪ/ ● preposition opposed to (is anti everything). ● noun (pl. **antis**) a person opposed to a particular policy etc. [ANTI-]

anti- /'anti, 'antaɪ/ prefix (also **ant-** before a vowel or h) forming nouns and adjectives meaning: 1 opposed to; against (anticlerical). 2 preventing (antifreeze). 3 designed to destroy or render useless (anti-aircraft, anti-personnel). 4 the opposite of (anticlimax). 5 rival (antipope). 6 unlike the conventional form (anti-hero; antinovel). 7 Physics the antiparticle of a specified particle (antineutrino; antiproton). ¶ Canadians overwhelmingly prefer to pronounce anti- to rhyme with tea; however, a very small minority rhyme it with tie, and some Canadians use tea for some words and tie for others. [Greek anti-against]

anti-abortion adjective opposed to the practice of and legalization of medically induced abortion. □ **anti-abortion·ist** noun

anti-aircraft adjective (of a gun, missile, etc.) used to attack enemy aircraft.

anti-alias·ing /ˌanti'eiliəsɪŋ/ noun the reduction or prevention of aliasing, esp. the smoothing of curved or inclined lines that appear artificially jagged in a computer image.

anti-bac·ter·ial adjective active against bacteria, esp. containing an antibiotic that kills bacteria and prevents them from re-establishing themselves.

anti-ballistic missile noun a missile designed to intercept and destroy a ballistic missile. Abbr.: **ABM**.

An·tibes /ɑ̃'tiːb/ a fishing port and resort in SE France; pop. (1999) 62,412.

anti-bio·sis /ˌantibaɪ'oːsɪs/ noun an antagonistic association between two organisms (esp. micro-organisms), in which one is adversely affected (compare SYMBIOSIS). [as ANTI-, SYMBIOSIS]

anti-biot·ic /ˌantibaɪ'ɒtɪk/ noun any of various substances, e.g. penicillin, produced by micro-organisms or made synthetically, that can inhibit or destroy susceptible micro-organisms, esp. disease-producing bacteria and fungi. ● adjective functioning as an antibiotic. [French antibiotique (as ANTI-, Greek biōtikos fit for life, from bios life)]

anti-body noun (pl. **-bodies**) any of various blood proteins produced in response to and then counteracting antigens. [translation of German Antikörper (as ANTI-, Körper body)]

antic ● noun 1 (usu. in pl.) absurd or foolish behaviour. 2 an absurd or silly action. ● adjective 1 excited, agitated, frenzied. 2 archaic grotesque, bizarre. [Italian antico ANTIQUE, used as meaning 'grotesque']

anti-cathode noun the target (or anode) of an X-ray tube on which the electrons from the cathode impinge and from which X-rays are emitted.

anti-choice adjective opposed to the principle of allowing women to choose to have an abortion. ¶ A derogatory synonym for PRO-LIFE.

anti-cholin·ergic /ˌanti,kɒlɪ'nɜrdʒɪk/ ● adjective (chiefly of a drug) inhibiting the physiological action of acetylcholine, esp. as a neurotransmitter. ● noun an anticholinergic drug.

Anti-christ noun 1 an arch-enemy of Christ. 2 a postulated personal opponent of Christ expected by the early Church to appear before the end of the world.

an·tici·pate transitive verb 1 foresee and deal with ahead of time. 2 disputed expect; regard as probable (did not anticipate any difficulty). 3 forestall (a person or thing). 4 look forward to (anticipate your next letter). □ **an·tici·pator** noun **an·tici·patory** /an'tɪsɪpə,tɔri/ adjective [Latin anticipare from anti- for ANTE- + -cipare from capere take]

an·tici·pa·tion noun **1** the act or process of anticipating. **2** Music the sounding of one note of a chord before the rest of the chord.

anti·clerical ● adjective opposed to the influence of the clergy, esp. in politics. ● noun an anticlerical person. □ **anti·clerical·ism** noun

anti·climax noun a trivial conclusion to something significant or impressive, esp. where a climax was expected. □ **anti·climac·tic** adjective **anti·climac·tic·ally** adverb

anti·cline noun Geol. an arch-shaped fold of stratified rock in which the strata slope down from the crest (opp. SYNCLINE). □ **anti·clinal** adjective [ANTI- + Greek klinō lean, after INCLINE]

anti·clock·wise Brit. = COUNTER-CLOCKWISE.

anti·coagu·lant /ˌantikoːˈaɡjulənt/ ● noun any drug or agent that retards or inhibits coagulation, esp. of the blood. ● adjective retarding or inhibiting coagulation.

anti·codon /ˌantiˈkoːdɒn/ noun Biochem. a sequence of three nucleotides forming a unit of genetic code in a transfer RNA molecule that corresponds to a complementary codon in messenger RNA.

anti·convul·sant /ˌantikənˈvʌlsənt/ ● noun any drug or agent that prevents or reduces the severity of convulsions, esp. epileptic fits. ● adjective preventing or reducing convulsions.

An·ti·costi Island /ˌantiˈkɒsti/ a large island in the Gulf of St. Lawrence, situated at the mouth of the St. Lawrence River and belonging to Quebec. Port-Menier, at its western tip, is the island's only settlement; pop. (2001) 266. [origin uncertain: possibly from Mi'kmaq natigôsteg forward land, or Montagnais natashquan where bears are hunted]

anti·cyclone noun Meteorol. a pressure system characterized by a high central barometric pressure, usu. resulting in dry conditions. □ **anti·cyclon·ic** adjective

anti·depres·sant ● noun any drug or agent that alleviates depression. ● adjective alleviating depression.

anti·diar·rheal /antiˌdaiəˈriːəl/ ● adjective (of a drug) used to alleviate diarrhea. ● noun an antidiarrheal drug.

anti·diuret·ic hormone /ˌantiˌdaijuˈretik/ noun = VASOPRESSIN.

anti·dote noun **1** a medicine etc. taken or given to counteract poison. **2** anything that counteracts something unpleasant or harmful. □ **anti·dotal** adjective [Greek antidotos given against (as ANTI- + stem of didonai give)]

anti·dump·ing adjective aimed at preventing or punishing the practice of dumping goods in a foreign market.

anti·estab·lish·ment adjective against the establishment or established authority.

anti·fog adjective (of lenses or a coating for them) preventing the formation of condensation.

anti·foul·ing noun **1** treatment of a boat's hull with a paint or similar substance designed to prevent fouling. **2** a substance of this kind.

anti·freeze noun **1** a substance (usu. ethylene glycol) added to water to lower its freezing point, esp. in the radiator of a motor vehicle. **2** a biological substance produced by some animals and plants which prevents them from freezing.

anti·fungal ● adjective preventing fungal growth. ● noun a substance, esp. a drug, that is active against fungi.

anti-g adjective (of clothing for an astronaut etc.) designed to counteract the effects of high acceleration (compare G-SUIT). [ANTI- + g symbol for acceleration due to gravity]

anti·gen noun a foreign substance, e.g. a toxin, which causes the body to produce antibodies. □ **anti·genic** adjective [German (as ANTIBODY, -GEN)]

anti·global·iz·ation noun a political movement opposed to the policies of the International Monetary Fund, the World Bank, and the World Trade Organization, esp. increased free trade and open markets, and to the increasing international dominance of multinational corporations and financial institutions to the perceived detriment of the environment and to living standards and human rights in poor countries.

An·tig·one /anˈtɪɡəni/ Gk Legend daughter of Oedipus and Jocasta. Sentenced to death by her uncle Creon for burying the body of her brother Polynices, who was considered an enemy of Thebes, she hanged herself before the sentence was passed.

Antig·onish /ˌantiɡəˈnɪʃ/ a town in NE Nova Scotia, situated at the head of Antigonish Harbour, east of New Glasgow; pop. (2001) 4,754. It is the site of St. Francis Xavier University. □ **Antig·onish·er** noun [alteration of articougnesche, from Mi'kmaq nalegitkoonech, prob. meaning 'flowing through broken marsh']

Antigonish Movement an educational and economic movement of international influence, pioneered in the 1920s at St. Francis Xavier University, which helped rural Maritime communities survive the Depression by establishing credit unions and other co-operatives.

An·tig·onus I /anˈtɪɡənəs/ (known as 'Cyclops') (382–301 BC), Macedonian general, king of Macedon 306–301 BC.

anti·grav·ity noun **1** Physics a hypothetical force opposing gravity. **2** ANTI-G.

An·tigua /anˈtiːɡwə/ (also **Antigua Guatemala** /ˌɡwɒtəˈmɒlə/) a town in the central highlands of Guatemala; pop. (est. 2002) 21,500. Founded in 1543, it was the capital of Spanish Guatemala until devastated by an earthquake in 1773.

An·tigua and Bar·buda /anˈtiːɡə, bɑrˈbuːdə/ a country consisting of two islands in the Leeward Islands in the W Indies; pop. (est. 2002) 67,448; capital, St. John's (on Antigua). □ **An·ti·guan** adjective & noun

anti-hero noun (pl. **-heroes**) a central character in a story or drama who noticeably lacks conventional heroic attributes. □ **anti-heroic** adjective

anti·hista·mine /ˌantiˈhistəmiːn, -min/ noun a substance that counteracts the effects of histamine, used esp. in the treatment of allergies.

anti·hyper·tensive /ˌantihaipərˈtensiv/ ● adjective designating or relating to the treatment of (esp. arterial) hypertension. ● noun a drug used to treat (esp. arterial) hypertension.

anti·inflam·ma·tory ● adjective reducing inflammation of body tissues and associated pain, swelling, etc. ● noun (plural **-ies**) an anti-inflammatory drug or treatment, e.g. cortisone.

anti-knock adjective (of a chemical compound added to motor fuel etc.) preventing premature combustion in an engine.

Anti-Lebanon Mountains a range of mountains running north to south along the border between Lebanon and Syria, east of the Lebanon range.

An·til·les /anˈtɪliːz/ a group of islands, forming the greater part of the West Indies. The **Greater Antilles**, extending roughly east to west, comprise Cuba, Jamaica, Hispaniola (Haiti and the Dominican Republic), and Puerto Rico; the **Lesser Antilles**, to the southeast, include the Virgin Islands, Leeward Islands, Windward Islands, and various small islands to the north of Venezuela. (See also NETHERLANDS ANTILLES.) □ **An·til·lean** noun & adjective

anti-lock brake noun an automobile brake which prevents skidding by alternately locking and momentarily freeing the wheels when applied suddenly.

anti·log noun = ANTILOGARITHM. [abbreviation]

anti·loga·rithm noun the number to which a logarithm belongs (100 is the common antilogarithm of 2).

anti·macas·sar /ˌantiməˈkasɜr/ noun a covering put over furniture, esp. over the back of a chair, as a protection from grease in the hair or as an ornament. [ANTI- + MACASSAR²]

anti·matter noun Physics a hypothetical matter composed solely of antiparticles.

anti·metab·ol·ite /ˌantiməˈtabəˌləit/ noun a drug that interferes with the normal metabolic processes within cells, usu. by combining with enzymes, and used esp. in cancer treatment.

anti·microb·ial ● adjective active against microbes. ● noun an antimicrobial substance.

anti·mony /ˈantiˌmoːni/ noun Chem. a brittle silvery-white metallic element used esp. in alloys. Symbol: **Sb**; at. no.: 51. [medieval Latin antimonium (11th c.), of unknown origin]

anti·node /ˈantiˌnoːd/ noun Physics the position of maximum displacement in a standing wave system.

anti·nomian /ˌantiˈnoːmiən/ ● adjective of or relating to the view that Christians are released by grace from the obligation of observing the moral law. ● noun (**Antinomian**) hist. a person who holds this view. □ **anti·nomian·ism** noun [medieval Latin Antinomi, name of a sect in Germany (1535) alleged to hold this view (as ANTI-, Greek nomos law)]

an·tin·omy /anˈtɪnəmi/ noun (pl. **-omies**) **1** a contradiction between two beliefs or conclusions that are in themselves reasonable; a paradox. **2** a conflict between two laws or authorities. [Greek ANTI- + nomos law)]

anti·novel noun a novel in which the conventions of the form are studiously avoided.

anti·nuclear adjective opposed to the development of nuclear weapons or nuclear power.

An·tioch /ˈantiˌɒk/ **1** a city in S Turkey, near the Syrian border; pop.

(est. 2002) 155,100. Antioch was the ancient capital of Syria under the Seleucid kings, who founded it *c*.300 BC. **2** a city of ancient Phrygia. □ **An·tioch·ian** *adjective*

An·ti·o·chus III /anˈtaɪəkəs/ 'the Great' (*c*.242–187 BC) reigned 223–187 BC, who restored and expanded the Seleucid Empire by regaining the kingdoms of Parthia and Bactria and conquering Armenia, Syria, and Palestine.

An·ti·o·chus IV Epiph·anes /anˈtaɪəkəs, əˈpɪfəniːz/ (*c*.215–163 BC) Seleucid King, reigned 175–163 BC. His attempt to hellenize the Jews resulted in a revival of Jewish nationalism and the Maccabean revolt.

anti·oxidant *noun* **1** a substance (e.g. vitamins C and E) that removes potentially damaging oxidizing agents in a living organism. **2** an agent that inhibits oxidation, esp. used to counteract deterioration of stored food products.

anti·par·ticle *noun Physics* an elementary particle having the same mass as a given particle but opposite electric or magnetic properties.

anti·pasto *noun* (*pl.* **anti·pastos** or **anti·pasti** /-tiː/) **1** a cold appetizer preceding an Italian meal, usu. consisting of meat or fish and vegetables or fruit. **2** a mixture of pickled vegetables served as an appetizer. [Italian, from *anti-* 'before' + *pasto* (from Latin *pastus* 'food')]

anti·path·etic *adjective* (usu. foll. by *to*) having a strong aversion or natural opposition. [as ANTIPATHY after PATHETIC]

an·tip·athy /anˈtɪpəθi/ *noun* (*pl.* **-athies**) (often foll. by *to, for, between*) a strong or deep-seated aversion or dislike. [Greek *antipatheia* from *antipathēs* opposed in feeling (as ANTI-, *pathos -eos* feeling)]

anti·person·nel *adjective* (of a bomb, mine, etc.) designed to kill or injure people rather than to damage buildings or equipment.

anti·perspir·ant /ˌantiˈpərspɪrənt/ ● *noun* a substance applied to the skin to prevent or reduce perspiration. ● *adjective* that acts as an antiperspirant.

anti·phlo·gis·tic /ˌantiflɒˈdʒɪstɪk/ ● *noun* any drug or agent that alleviates or reduces inflammation. ● *adjective* alleviating or reducing inflammation. [ANTI- + Greek *phlogistos* flammable + -IC]

anti·phon /ˈantɪˌfɒn/ *noun* **1** a hymn or psalm, the parts of which are sung or recited alternately by two groups. **2** a versicle or phrase from this. **3** a Biblical verse sung or recited at a specific moment in a Christian liturgy, e.g. at the beginning of the Mass or before Communion, or before or after a psalm or canticle. **4** a response. [ecclesiastical Latin *antiphona* from Greek (as ANTI-, *phōnē* sound)]

an·tiph·on·al /anˈtɪfənəl/ ● *adjective* (of church music) sung or recited alternately by two groups. ● *noun* a collection of antiphons. □ **an·tiph·on·al·ly** *adverb*

an·tiph·on·ary /anˈtɪfəˌneri/ *noun* (*pl.* **-aries**) a book of antiphons.

an·tiph·ony /anˈtɪfəni/ *noun* (*pl.* **-onies**) antiphonal singing or chanting.

anti·pode /ˈantɪˌpoʊd/ *noun* (usu. foll. by *of, to*) the exact opposite. [see ANTIPODES]

an·tip·o·des /anˈtɪpəˌdiːz/ *plural noun* **1** places on opposite sides of the earth to each other. **2** (**Antipodes**) **a** Australia and New Zealand. **b** = ANTIPODES ISLANDS. **3** (usu. foll. by *of*) the exact opposite. □ **an·tip·odal** *adjective* **an·tipo·dean** /-ˈdiːən/ *adjective & noun* [Greek *antipodes* having the feet opposite (as ANTI-, *pous podos* foot)]

Antipodes Islands /anˈtɪpədiːz/ *noun* a small group of uninhabited islands belonging to New Zealand and located southeast of South Island. □ **An·tipo·dean** *noun & adjective*

anti·pope *noun* a person set up as pope in opposition to one (held by others to be) canonically chosen.

anti·proton *noun* the negatively charged antiparticle of a proton.

anti·prur·itic /ˌantipruˈrɪtɪk/ ● *adjective* relieving itching. ● *noun* an antipruritic drug or agent. [ANTI- + PRURITUS + -IC]

anti·psychot·ic ● *adjective* (chiefly of a drug) used to treat psychotic disorders. ● *noun* an antipsychotic drug.

anti·pyr·etic /ˌantipaiˈretɪk/ ● *adjective* preventing or reducing fever. ● *noun* an antipyretic drug or agent.

an·ti·quar·ian /ˌantɪˈkweriən/ ● *adjective* **1** of or dealing in antiques or rare books. **2** of the study of antiquities. ● *noun* an antiquary. □ **an·ti·quar·ian·ism** *noun* [see ANTIQUARY]

anti·quark *noun Physics* the antiparticle of a quark.

an·ti·quary /ˈantɪˌkweri/ *noun* (*pl.* **-ies**) a student or collector of antiques or antiquities. [Latin *antiquarius* from *antiquus* ancient]

an·ti·quat·ed /ˈantɪˌkweɪtəd/ *adjective* old-fashioned; out of date. [ecclesiastical Latin *antiquare antiquat-* make old]

an·tique ● *noun* an object of considerable age, esp. an item of furniture or the decorative arts having a high value. ● *adjective* **1** of or

existing from an early date. **2** old-fashioned, archaic. **3** of ancient times. ● *verb* (**an·tiques, an·tiqued, an·tiqu·ing**) **1** *transitive* give an antique appearance to (furniture etc.) by artificial means. **2** *intransitive* (usu. as **an·tiquing** *noun*) shop for antiques. [Latin *antiquus, anticus* former, ancient, from *ante* before]

an·tiquity /anˈtɪkwɪti/ *noun* (*pl.* **-ties**) **1** ancient times, esp. the period before the Middle Ages. **2** great age (*a city of great antiquity*). **3** (usu. in *pl.*) physical remains or relics from ancient times, esp. buildings and works of art. **4** (in *pl.*) customs, events, etc., of ancient times. **5** the people of ancient times regarded collectively.

anti·racism *noun* the policy or practice of opposing racism and promoting racial tolerance. □ **anti·racist** *noun & adjective*

anti·retro·viral *adjective* (of a drug) active against retroviruses.

anti·roll bar *noun* a rubber-mounted bar fitted in the suspension of a vehicle to increase its stability, esp. when cornering.

an·tir·rhinum /ˌantiˈraɪnəm/ *noun* any flowering plant of the genus *Antirrhinum*, esp. the snapdragon. [Latin from Greek *antirrhinon* from *anti* counterfeiting + *rhis rhinos* nose, from the resemblance of the flower to an animal's snout)]

anti·scor·bu·tic /ˌantiskərˈbjuːtɪk/ ● *adjective* preventing or curing scurvy. ● *noun* an antiscorbutic agent or drug.

anti·Semite /ˌantiˈsemaɪt/ *noun* a person hostile to or prejudiced against Jews. □ **anti·Semitic** /-səˈmɪtɪk/ *adjective* **anti·Semitism** /-ˈsemiˌtɪzəm/ *noun*

anti·sense *adjective Genetics* having a sequence of nucleotides complementary to (and hence capable of binding to) a coding (or sense) sequence, which may be either that of the strand of a DNA double helix which undergoes transcription, or that of a messenger RNA molecule.

anti·sep·sis *noun* the process of using antiseptics to eliminate undesirable micro-organisms such as bacteria, viruses, and fungi that cause disease. [modern Latin (as ANTI-, SEPSIS)]

anti·sep·tic /ˌantɪˈseptɪk/ ● *adjective* **1** counteracting sepsis esp. by preventing the growth of disease-causing micro-organisms. **2** sterile or free from contamination. **3** lacking character or emotion; dispassionate. ● *noun* an antiseptic agent. □ **anti·sep·tic·ally** *adverb*

anti·serum *noun* (*pl.* **anti·sera** /-rə/) a blood serum containing antibodies against specific antigens, injected to treat or protect against specific diseases.

anti·social *adjective* **1** opposed or contrary to normal social instincts or practices. **2** not sociable; unfriendly towards others. □ **anti·social·ly** *adverb*

anti·spasmod·ic ● *adjective* (chiefly of a drug) used to relieve spasm of an involuntary muscle. ● *noun* an antispasmodic drug.

anti·static *adjective* counteracting the effects of static electricity.

an·tis·tro·phe /anˈtɪstrəfi/ *noun* **1** the second section of an ancient Greek choral ode or of one division of it (see STROPHE). **2** lines recited during this. [Late Latin from Greek *antistrophē* from *antistrephō* turn against]

anti·tank *adjective* for use against enemy tanks.

an·tith·esis /anˈtɪθəsɪs/ *noun* (*pl.* **an·tith·eses** /-,siːz/) **1** (foll. by *of, to*) the direct opposite. **2** (usu. foll. by *of, between*) contrast or opposition between two things. **3** a contrast of ideas expressed by parallelism of strongly contrasted words. [Late Latin from Greek *antitithēmi* set against (as ANTI-, *tithēmi* place)]

anti·thet·ic·al /ˌantɪˈθetɪkəl/ *adjective* (also **anti·thet·ic**) **1** contrasted, opposite. **2** connected with, containing, or using antithesis. □ **anti·thet·ic·al·ly** *adverb* [Greek *antithetikos* (as ANTITHESIS)]

anti·toxin *noun* an antibody that counteracts a toxin. □ **anti·toxic** *adjective*

anti·trades /ˌantiˈtreɪdz, ˈanti-/ *plural noun* winds that blow in the opposite direction to (and usu. above) a trade wind.

anti·trust *adjective US* (of a law etc.) opposed to or controlling trusts or other monopolies (see TRUST *noun* 9).

anti·tus·sive /ˈantiˌtʌsɪv/ *Pharm.* ● *adjective* suppressing coughing. ● *noun* an antitussive drug or treatment; a cough medicine.

anti·type *noun* **1** something which a type or symbol represents (see TYPE *noun* 8). **2** a person or thing of the opposite type. □ **anti·typical** *adjective* [Greek *antitupos* corresponding as an impression to the die (as ANTI-, *tupos* stamp)]

anti·venin /ˌantiˈvenɪn/ *noun* (also **anti·venom** /-ˈvenəm/) an antiserum containing antibodies against specific poisons in the venom of esp. snakes, spiders, scorpions, etc. [ANTI- + Latin *venenum* poison + -ENE, -IN]

---

uː m**oo**d   ai m**y**   əi p**i**pe   au br**ow**n   ʌu h**ou**se   ei d**ay**   ɔi b**oy**   ã fr**an**glais   ã Canadi**en**   õ Bray**on**   (*see over for consonants*)

anti·viral *adjective* effective against viruses.

anti·vivi·sec·tion·ism /ˌantiˌvɪvɪˈsekʃəˌnɪzəm/ *noun* opposition to vivisection. □ **anti·vivi·sec·tion·ist** *noun*

ant·ler *noun* **1** each of the branched horns of a stag or other (usu. male) deer. **2** a branch of this. □ **ant·lered** *adjective* [Old French *antoillier*, of unknown origin]

ant·ler·less *adjective* **1** (of a deer, moose, etc.) having no antlers or undeveloped ones. **2** pertaining to the hunting of antlerless animals, e.g. adult females or yearlings of both sexes (*antlerless permit*).

ant-lion *noun* any of various dragonfly-like predatory insects of the family Myrmeleontidae, whose larvae (also called DOODLEBUG) live beneath small pits which they build to trap insects. [translation of Greek *murmēko-leōn*]

An·to·fa·gasta /ˌantoˈfaˈɡastə/ a port in N Chile, capital of a region of the same name; pop. (est. 2002) 277,100.

An·to·nine /ˈantənain/ ● *adjective* of the Roman emperors Antoninus Pius and Marcus Aurelius Antonius or their rule. ● *noun* (in *pl.*) the Antonine emperors.

An·to·ni·nus see CARACALLA.

Antoninus Pius /ˌantəˈnainəs ˈpaiəs/ (86–161), Roman emperor 137–161.

An·toni·oni /ˌantoːniːˈoːni/ **Michel·angelo** (b.1912), Italian film director. His films, which include *L'avventura* (1960) and *Blow-Up* (1967), concentrate on the study of character, often through the use of complex metaphoric plots.

An·to·nius /anˈtoːniəs/ **Mar·cus**, see ANTONY.

an·tono·masia /ˌantənəˈmeizə/ *noun* **1** the substitution of an epithet or title etc. for a proper name, e.g. *the Maid of Orleans* for Joan of Arc, *his Grace* for an archbishop. **2** the use of a proper name to express a general idea, e.g. *a Scrooge* for a miser. [Latin from Greek from *antonomazō* name instead (as ANTI-, + *onoma* name)]

An·tony /ˈantəni/ **Mark** (Marcus Antonius, *c.*83–30 BC), Roman general and supporter of Julius Caesar, after whose murder he was appointed one of the triumvirate of 43 BC, with Octavian and Lepidus. After the battle of Philippi, he took charge of the eastern part of the empire, including Egypt, where he established his association with Cleopatra. Quarrels with Octavian led finally to his defeat at the sea battle of Actium in NW Greece in 31 BC and to his suicide the next year in Alexandria.

an·tonym /ˈantənim/ *noun* a word opposite in meaning to another, e.g. *bad* and *good* (opp. SYNONYM). □ **an·tonym·ous** /anˈtɒniməs/ *adjective* **an·tonymy** /anˈtɒnimi/ *noun* [French *antonyme* (as ANTI-, SYNONYM)]

Antony of Egypt, St. see ANTHONY OF EGYPT, ST.

Antony of Padua, St. see ANTHONY OF PADUA, ST.

An·trim /ˈantrim/ **1** one of the Six Counties of Northern Ireland, formerly an administrative area. **2** a town in this county, on the northeast shore of Lough Neagh; pop. (est. 2002) 20,400.

an·trum /ˈantrəm/ *noun* (pl. **antra** /-trə/) *Anat.* **1** a natural chamber or cavity in the body, esp. one with bony walls. **2** the part of the stomach adjacent to the pylorus. □ **an·tral** *adjective* [Latin from Greek *antron* cave]

antsy *adjective* N Amer. informal agitated, impatient, or fidgety. [from phrase *(have) ants in one's pants*: see ANT]

An·tung /anˈtʊŋ/ the former name for DANDONG.

Ant·werp /ˈantwɜːp/ **1** a province of N Belgium. **2** its capital city, a port on the Scheldt; pop. (est. 2002) 444,100. A former seat of the counts of Flanders, Antwerp had by the 16th c. become a leading European commercial and financial centre.

Anu·bis /əˈnuːbɪs, əˈnjuː-/ *Egyptian Myth* the god of mummification, who was believed to lead the souls of the dead to judgment. He was represented with a dog's or jackal's head, or as a dog lying with head erect, or sometimes (in the Roman period) as a soldier in armour.

Anura·dha·pura /əˌnʊrədəˈpʊrə/ a city in north central Sri Lanka, capital of a district of the same name; pop. (2001) 56,600. It is the ancient capital of Sri Lanka and a centre of Buddhist pilgrimage. A sacred bo tree, brought here as a sapling from the tree in Bodhgaya in India over 2,000 years ago, is alleged to be the oldest living tree in the world.

anur·an /əˈnʊrən, əˈnjʊ-/ ● *noun* any tailless amphibian of the order Anura, including frogs and toads. ● *adjective* of or relating to this order. [modern Latin *Anura* (AN-¹ + Greek *oura* tail)]

anus *noun* (pl. **anus·es**) the excretory opening at the end of the alimentary canal. [Latin]

anvil *noun* **1** a block (usu. of iron) with a flat top, concave sides, and often a pointed end, on which metals are worked in forging. **2** something that resembles an anvil in appearance or use. **3** *Anat.* a bone of the ear; the incus. **4** *Meteorol.* a horizontally extended top of a cumulonimbus cloud. [Old English *anfilte* etc.]

anx·iety *noun* (pl. **-ieties**) **1** the state of being anxious. **2** concern about an imminent danger, difficulty, etc. **3** (usu. foll. by to + infin.) anxious desire. **4** a thing that causes anxiety (*my greatest anxiety is that I will get sick*). **5** *Psych.* a nervous disorder characterized by a state of excessive uneasiness. [French *anxiété* or Latin *anxietas -tatis* (as ANXIOUS)]

anx·ious *adjective* **1** worried or troubled; uneasy in the mind. **2** causing or marked by anxiety (*an anxious moment*). **3** disputed (usu. foll. by to + infin.) earnestly desiring; eager (*anxious to please; anxious for you to succeed*). ¶ Many claim that *anxious* should not be used to mean *eager*, but this use is well established, and standard since the 18th c. □ **anx·ious·ly** *adverb* **anx·ious·ness** *noun* [Latin *anxius* from *angere* choke]

any ● *adjective* **1** (with *interrogative, neg.,* or conditional expressed or implied) **a** one, no matter which, of several (*cannot find any answer*). **b** some, no matter how much or many or of what sort (*if any books arrive; do you have any sugar?*). **2** a minimal amount of (*hardly any difference*). **3** whichever is chosen (*any fool knows that*). **4 a** an appreciable or significant (*did not stay for any length of time*). **b** a very large (*has any amount of money*). ● *pronoun* **1** any one (*did not know any of them*). **2** any number (*are any of them yours?*). **3** any amount (*is there any left?*). **4** *slang* sex (*are you getting any?*). ● *adverb* (usu. with *neg.* or *interrogative*) at all, in some degree (*is that any good?; do not make it any larger; without being any the wiser*). □ **any time** (or **day** or **minute** etc.) **now** *informal* at any time in the near future. [Old English *ænig* from Germanic (as ONE, -Y¹)]

Anyang /ɒnˈjɒŋ/ a city in S Korea, just south of Seoul; pop. (est. 1995) 591,106.

any·body *noun & pronoun* **1 a** a person, no matter who. **b** a person of any kind. **c** whatever person is chosen. **2** a person of importance (*don't worry, he isn't anybody*). □ **anybody's guess** see GUESS.

any·how *adverb* **1** anyway. **2** in a disorderly manner or state (*just does his work anyhow*).

any·more *adverb* **1** any longer; to any further extent (*don't like you anymore*). **2** N Amer. informal nowadays; at the present time (*almost everyone has a computer anymore*). ¶ In Canada, the positive use of *anymore* is strongest in rural Southern Ontario. ¶ Always written as two words when specifying quantity, as in *can't eat any more food*.

any·one /ˈeniˌwʌn/ *pronoun* anybody. ¶ Written as two words when specifying a numerical sense, as in *any one of us can do it*.

any·place /ˈeniˌpleis/ *adverb* N Amer. informal anywhere.

any·thing /ˈeniθɪŋ/ ● *pronoun* **1** a thing, no matter which. **2** a thing of any kind. **3** whatever thing is chosen. ● *adverb* (usu. foll. by *like*) in any way whatsoever; at all (*doesn't sound anything like Mozart*). □ **anything but** not at all (*was anything but honest*). **like anything** *informal* with great vigour, intensity, etc.

any time /ˈeniˌtaim/ *adverb* (also **any·time**) esp. N Amer. at any time.

any·way /ˈeniˌwei/ *adverb* **1** in any way or manner. **2** at any rate. **3** in any case. **4** to resume (*anyway, as I was saying*).

any·ways *adverb* N Amer. informal in any case.

any·where ● *adverb* **1** in or to any place. **2** designating any quantity etc. within a specified range (*anywhere from $10 to $20.*). **3** to any extent (*is it anywhere near full?*). ● *pronoun* any place (*anywhere will do*).

any·wise *adverb* archaic in any manner.

Anzac *noun* **1** hist. a soldier in the Australian and New Zealand Army Corps (1914–18). **2** any member of the armed services of Australia or New Zealand. [acronym]

Anzac Day *noun* (in Australia and New Zealand) 25 April, commemorating the Anzac landing at Gallipoli in 1915.

Anzus /ˈanzəs/ *noun* (also **ANZUS**) an alliance formed in 1951 by Australia, New Zealand, and the US, recognizing the common danger of an armed attack on these countries. After New Zealand's declaration of an anti-nuclear policy (1985) the US suspended its security obligations to that country (1986). [acronym]

AOB *abbreviation* any other business.

A-okay *abbreviation* N Amer. informal excellent; in good order. [all systems okay]

AOR *abbreviation* Music ALBUM-ORIENTED ROCK.

Aor·angi /auˈraŋi/ the Maori name for Mount Cook (see COOK, MOUNT).

Consonants: b *but*   d *dog*   f *few*   g *get*   h *her*   j *yes*   k *cat*   l *leg*   m *man*   n *no*   p *pen*   r *red*   s *sit*

aor·ist /ˈeɪərɪst/ *Grammar* ● *noun* an unqualified past tense of a verb (esp. in ancient Greek), without reference to duration or completion. ● *adjective* of or designating this tense. □ **aor·is·tic** /eɪəˈrɪstɪk/ *adjective* [Greek *aoristos* indefinite, from *a-* not + *horizō* define, limit]

aorta /eɪˈɔrtə/ *noun* (*pl.* **aortas**) the main artery, giving rise to the arterial network through which oxygenated blood is supplied to the body from the heart. □ **aor·tic** *adjective* [Greek *aortē* from *a(e)irō* raise]

Aosta /eɪˈɒstə/ a city in NW Italy, capital of Valle d'Aosta region; pop. (2001) 33,926.

Aou·zou Strip /aʊˈzuː/ a narrow corridor of disputed desert land in N Chad, stretching the full length of the border between Chad and Libya.

AP *abbreviation* **1** Associated Press, an American co-operative news agency. **2** AMERICAN PLAN.

ap-[1] *prefix* assimilated form of AD- before *p*.

ap-[2] *prefix* assimilated form of APO- before a vowel or *h*.

A/P *abbreviation* accounts payable.

apace *adverb* swiftly, quickly. [Old French *à pas* at (a considerable) pace]

Apa·che /əˈpætʃi/ *noun* ● **1** (*pl.* same or **-ches**) a member of an Aboriginal people living in the southwestern US, primarily in Arizona and New Mexico. **2** the Athapaskan language of the Apache. ● *adjective* of or relating to the Apache or their culture or language. [Latin American Spanish, prob. from Zuñi *Apachu*, lit. 'enemy']

apan·age *var.* of APPANAGE.

apart *adverb* **1** separately; not together (*keep your feet apart*). **2** into pieces (*came apart in my hands*). **3** to or on one side; aside (*set apart from the rest*). **4** to or at a distance (*ten kilometres apart*). **5** from one another (*can't tell the twins apart*). □ **apart from 1** except for. **2** in addition to (*apart from roses we grow irises*). □ **apart·ness** *noun* [Old French from *à* to + *part* side]

apart·heid /əˈpɑrtaɪt, -taɪd, -teɪt/ *noun* **1** *hist.* the South African policy of segregation and discrimination against non-whites. **2** segregation or discrimination in other contexts. [Afrikaans (as APART, -HOOD)]

apart·ment *noun* **1** *N Amer.* **a** one or more rooms rented and used as a residence, esp. in a building with other similar dwellings. **b** = APARTMENT BUILDING. **2** (usu. in *pl.*) a room in a house. [French *appartement* from Italian *appartamento* from *appartare* to separate, from *a parte* apart]

apartment building *noun* (also **apartment block**) a building other than a house divided into several apartments.

apartment hotel *noun N Amer.* a hotel with furnished suites of rooms including kitchens, for short-term or long-term rental.

apartment house *noun* esp. *US* = APARTMENT BUILDING.

apa·thet·ic *adjective* having or showing no emotion or interest. □ **apa·thet·ic·ally** *adverb* [APATHY, after PATHETIC]

apathy *noun* lack of interest or feeling; indifference. [Greek *apatheia* from *apathēs* without feeling, from *a-* not + *pathos* suffering]

apa·tite /ˈapəˌtaɪt/ *noun* a naturally occurring crystalline mineral of calcium phosphate and fluoride, used in the manufacture of fertilizers. [German *Apatit* from Greek *apatē* deceit (from its deceptive forms)]

apato·saur·us /əˌpatəˈsɔrəs/ *noun* a huge herbivorous dinosaur of the late Jurassic period, with a long neck and tail. Formerly called BRONTOSAURUS. [modern Latin from Greek *apatē* 'deceit' + *sauros* 'lizard']

APB *abbreviation US* ALL-POINTS BULLETIN.

APC *abbreviation* ARMOURED PERSONNEL CARRIER.

ape ● *noun* **1** any of the various primates of the family Pongidae characterized by the absence of a tail, e.g. the gorilla, chimpanzee, orangutan, or gibbon. **2** (in general use) any monkey. **3** an imitator. **4** a clumsy, coarse, or stupid person. ● *transitive verb* imitate, mimic. □ **go ape** (also **go apeshit**) *slang* become crazy. [Old English *apa* from Germanic]

APEC /ˈeɪpɛk/ *abbreviation* **1** Asia-Pacific Economic Co-operation. **2** Atlantic Provinces Economic Council.

Apel·doorn /ˈapəlˌdɔrn/ a city in the east central Netherlands; pop. (est. 2002) 155,600. Since 1685 it has been the site of the summer residence of the Dutch royal family.

ape·like *adjective* like an ape.

Apel·les /əˈpɛliːz/ (4th c. BC) court portrait painter to Alexander the Great. None of his works survive, but from written sources he is known as the greatest painter of antiquity.

ape man *noun* any of various apelike primates held to be forerunners of present-day humans.

Apen·nines /ˈapəˌnaɪnz/ a mountain range running 1 400 km (880 miles) down the length of Italy, from the northwest to the southern tip of the peninsula.

aper·çu /ˌapɛrˈsuː/ *noun* a comment or brief reference which makes an illuminating or entertaining point. [French, past participle of *apercevoir* perceive]

aper·iod·ic /ˌeɪpɪriˈɒdɪk/ *adjective* **1** not periodic; irregular. **2** *Physics* (of a potentially oscillating or vibrating system, e.g. an instrument with a pointer) that is adequately damped to prevent oscillation or vibration. **3** (of an oscillation or vibration) without a regular period. □ **aperi·od·icity** /-rɪəˈdɪsɪti/ *noun*

aperitif /əˌpɛrɪˈtiːf/ *noun* an alcoholic drink taken before a meal to stimulate the appetite. [French *apéritif* from medieval Latin *aperitivus* from Latin *aperire* to open]

aper·ture /ˈapərˌtʃər/ *noun* **1** an opening; a gap. **2** a space through which light passes in an optical or photographic instrument, esp. a variable space in a camera. [Latin *apertura* (as APERITIF)]

apet·al·ous /eɪˈpɛtələs/ *adjective* (of flowers) having no petals. [Greek *apetalos* leafless, from *a-* not + *petalon* leaf]

Apex *noun* (also **APEX**) (usu. *attributive*) a system of reduced fares for scheduled airline flights when paid for before a certain period in advance of departure. [Advance Purchase Excursion]

apex *noun* (*pl.* **apex·es** or **api·ces** /ˈeɪpɪˌsiːz/) **1** the highest point. **2** a climax; a high point of achievement etc. **3** the vertex of a triangle or cone. **4** a tip or pointed end. [Latin, = peak, tip]

Apgar score *noun* an evaluation of the condition of a newborn by allotting up to two points each for heart rate, breathing effort, muscle tone, response to stimulation, and colour. [V. Apgar, US physician d.1974]

apha·sia /əˈfeɪʒə, -ʒiə/ *noun Med.* the loss of ability to understand or express speech, owing to brain damage. □ **apha·sic** /əˈfeɪzɪk/ *adjective & noun* [modern Latin from Greek from *aphatos* speechless, from *a-* not + *pha-* speak]

apheli·on /apˈhiːliən, əˈfiːliən/ *noun* (*pl.* **aphelia** /-liə/) the point in a body's orbit where it is furthest from the sun (*opp.* PERIHELION). Symbol: **Q**. [Greek *aph' hēliou* from the sun]

apher·esis /əˈfɪrəsɪs, əˈfɛrəsɪs/ *noun* (also **aphaer·esis**) (*pl.* **apher·eses** /-ˌsiːz/) the omission of a letter or syllable at the beginning of a word as a morphological development, e.g. in the derivation of *adder*. [Greek *aphairesis* (as APO-, *haireō* take)]

aphes·is /ˈafɪsɪs/ *noun* (*pl.* **aphes·es** /-ˌsiːz/) the gradual loss of an unstressed vowel at the beginning of a word (e.g. of *e* from *esquire* to form *squire*). □ **aphet·ic** /əˈfɛtɪk/ *adjective* **aphet·ic·ally** /əˈfɛtɪkli/ *adverb* [Greek, = letting go (as APO-, *hiēmi* send)]

aphid /ˈeɪfɪd/ *noun* any small homopterous insect which feeds by sucking sap from leaves, stems, or roots of plants. [back-formation from *aphides*: see APHIS]

aphis /ˈeɪfɪs, ˈafɪs/ *noun* (*pl.* **aphi·des** /-ˌdiːz/) an aphid, esp. of the genus *Aphis*. [modern Latin (Linnaeus) from Greek (1523), perhaps a misreading of *koris* bug]

aphor·ism /ˈafəˌrɪzəm/ *noun* **1** a short pithy maxim. **2** a brief statement of a principle. □ **aphor·ist** *noun* **aphor·is·tic** /-ˈrɪstɪk/ *adjective* **aphor·is·tic·ally** /-ˈrɪstɪkli/ *adverb* **aphor·ize** *intransitive verb* (also esp. *Brit.* **-ise**). [Greek *aphorismos* definition, from *aphorizō* (as APO-, *horos* boundary)]

aphro·dis·iac /afroˈdɪziak/ ● *adjective* that arouses sexual desire. ● *noun* an aphrodisiac substance. [Greek *aphrodisiakos* from *aphrodisios* from APHRODITE]

Aphro·dis·ias /ˌafrəˈdiːsiəs/ an ancient city of W Asia Minor, site of a temple dedicated to Aphrodite. Now in ruins, it is situated 80 km (50 miles) west of Aydin, in western Turkey.

Aphro·dite /ˌafrəˈdaɪti/ *Gk Myth* the goddess of beauty, fertility, and sexual love (*see also* VENUS 1).

aphyl·lous /əˈfɪləs/ *adjective Bot.* (of plants) having no leaves. [modern Latin from Greek *aphullos* from *a-* not + *phullon* leaf]

API *abbreviation Computing* application program interface.

Apia /ˈapiə/ the capital of Western Samoa; pop. (est. 1999) 38,000.

apian /ˈeɪpiən/ *adjective* of or relating to bees. [Latin *apianus* from *apis* bee]

api·ary /ˈeɪpiˌɛri/ *noun* (*pl.* **-aries**) a place where bees are kept. □ **api·ar·ist** *noun* [Latin *apiarium* from *apis* bee]

apical /ˈeɪpɪkəl, ˈap-/ *adjective* of, at, or forming an apex. □ **apical·ly** *adverb* [Latin *apex apicis*: see APEX]

api·ces *pl. of* APEX.

api·cul·ture /ˈeɪpɪˌkʌltʃər/ *noun* beekeeping. □ **api·cul·tur·al** *adjective* **api·cul·tur·ist** *noun* [Latin *apis* bee, after AGRICULTURE]

apiece *adverb* for each one; severally (*ten dollars apiece*).

Apis /ˈeɪpɪs/ *Egyptian Myth* the god of strength in war and fertility, worshipped esp. at Memphis, where a live bull was kept as his incarnation.

apla·sia /əˈpleɪʃə, -zɪə/ *noun Med.* total or partial failure of development of an organ or tissue. □ **aplas·tic** /əˈplastɪk/ *adjective* [modern Latin from a- not + *plasis* formation]

aplen·ty *adverb* in great quantity (placed after noun: *bargains aplenty*).

aplomb /əˈplɒm/ *noun* assurance; self-confidence. [French, = perpendicularity, from *à plomb* according to a plumb line]

ap·nea /apˈniːə/ *noun* (also esp. *Brit.* **ap·noea**) *Med.* a temporary cessation of breathing. [Greek *apnoia* from *apnous* breathless]

apo- *prefix* **1** away from (*apogee*). **2** separate (*apocarpous*). [Greek *apo* from, away, un-, quite]

Apoc. *abbreviation* **1** Apocalypse. **2** Apocrypha.

apoca·lypse /əˈpɒkəlɪps/ *noun* **1** (**the Apocalypse**) Revelation, the last book of the New Testament, recounting a divine revelation of the end of the world to St. John. **2** catastrophic destruction, esp. the end of the world. **3** a revelation, esp. of the end of the world. [Greek *apokalupsis* from *apokaluptō* uncover, reveal]

apoca·lyp·tic /əˌpɒkəˈlɪptɪk/ *adjective* **1** of or resembling the biblical Apocalypse (*apocalyptic imagery*). **2** describing or prophesying the complete destruction of the world. **3** resembling the end of the world; momentous or catastrophic (*the struggle between the two countries is assuming apocalyptic proportions*). □ **apoca·lyp·tic·ally** *adverb*

apo·car·pous /ˌapəˈkɑːpəs/ *adjective Bot.* (of the ovaries of flowering plants) having distinct carpels not joined together (*opp.* SYNCARPOUS). [APO- + Greek *karpos* fruit]

apo·chro·mat /ˈapəkrəˌmat/ *noun* a lens or lens system that reduces spherical and chromatic aberrations. □ **apo·chro·mat·ic** /-krəˈmatɪk/ *adjective* [APO- + CHROMATIC]

apoc·ope /əˈpɒkəpi/ *noun* the omission of a letter or letters at the end of a word as a morphological development, e.g. in the derivation of *curio*. [Greek *apokopē* (as APO-, *koptō* cut)]

Apocr. *abbreviation* Apocrypha.

apo·crine /ˈapəˌkraɪn, -krɪn/ *adjective Biol.* designating or pertaining to glands which lose some of their cytoplasm during secretion, esp. sweat glands opening into hair follicles (as in the armpits and pubic region) (*compare* ECCRINE). [APO- + Greek *krinō* to separate]

Apoc·rypha /əˈpɒkrɪfə/ *plural noun* **1** those books of the Septuagint version of the Hebrew Scriptures which were later rejected from the Jewish canon. Most were accepted as part of the Christian Old Testament and are considered canonical by the Catholic and Orthodox Churches; at the Reformation they were not included in the Protestant Bible. **2** (**apocrypha**) writings or reports not considered genuine. [ecclesiastical Latin *apocrypha* (*scripta*) hidden writings, from Greek *apokruphos* from *apokruptō* hide away]

apoc·ryph·al /əˈpɒkrɪfəl/ *adjective* **1** of doubtful authenticity (originally of some early Christian texts resembling those of the New Testament). **2** invented, mythical (*an apocryphal story*). **3** of or belonging to the Apocrypha.

apo·dic·tic /ˌapəˈdɪktɪk/ *adjective* (also **apo·deic·tic** /-ˈdaɪktɪk/) clearly demonstrated or established. [Latin *apodicticus* from Greek *apodeiktikos* (as APO-, *deiknumi* show)]

apod·o·sis /əˈpɒdəsɪs/ *noun* (*pl.* **apod·o·ses** /-ˌsiːz/) the main (consequent) clause of a conditional sentence, e.g. *I would agree* in *if you asked me I would agree*. [Late Latin from Greek from *apodidōmi* give back (as APO-, *didōmi* give)]

apo·gee /ˈapəˌdʒiː/ *noun* **1** the point in a celestial body's orbit where it is furthest from the earth (*opp.* PERIGEE). **2** the highest or most distant point; maximum. □ **apo·gean** /ˌapəˈdʒiːən/ *adjective* [French *apogée* or modern Latin *apogaeum* from Greek *apogeion* away from earth (as APO-, *gē* earth)]

apolit·ical *adjective* **1** not interested in or concerned with politics. **2** without political bias.

Apol·li·naire /əˌpɒliˈner/ **Guil·laume** (pseudonym of Wilhelm Apollinaris de Kostrowitzki 1880–1918), French poet. Considered a forerunner of surrealism, he used unusual verbal associations and, in *Calligrammes* (1918), exploited typographical arrangement of lines of poetry to create images.

Apol·lo 1 *Gk & Rom. Myth* the sun god, son of Zeus and Leto. He is especially associated with music and the arts, archery, prophecy, and medicine. **2** the name for the US lunar spacecraft program which succeeded in reaching the moon on 20 July 1969.

Apol·lo·nian /ˌapəˈloːnɪən/ *adjective* **1** of or relating to Apollo. **2** orderly, rational, self-disciplined.

Apol·lon·ius /ˌapəˈloːnɪəs/ **1 of Perga** (*c.*260–190 BC), Greek mathematician. In his principal surviving work, *Conics*, he examined and redefined the various conic sections, and was the first to use the terms *ellipse*, *parabola*, and *hyperbola* for the three classes of curve. **2 of Rhodes** (3rd c. BC), Greek poet. His *Argonautica*, a poem in Homeric style on the expedition of the Argonauts, was the first to make the theme of love central to the action of an epic poem.

Apol·lyon /əˈpɒljən/ *New Testament* the Devil, the 'angel of the bottomless pit' (Rev. 9:11). [Latin (Vulgate) from Greek *apolluōn* pres. part. of *apollumi* (as APO-, *ollumi* destroy)]

apolo·get·ic ● *adjective* 1 regretfully acknowledging or excusing an offence or failure. **2** diffident. **3** of reasoned defence or vindication. **● *noun*** (usu. in *pl.*) **1** a reasoned defence, esp. of Christianity. **2** the branch of theology concerned with this. □ **apolo·get·ic·ally** *adverb* [Greek *apologētikos* from *apologeomai* speak in defence]

apo·lo·gia /ˌapəˈloːdʒɪə/ *noun* a formal defence of one's opinions or conduct. [Latin: see APOLOGY]

apolo·gist *noun* a person who defends something by argument. [French *apologiste* from Greek *apologizomai* render account, from *apologos* account]

apolo·gize *intransitive verb* (also esp. *Brit.* **-gise**) make an apology; express regret. [Greek *apologizomai*: see APOLOGIST]

apol·ogy *noun* (*pl.* **-gies**) **1** a regretful acknowledgement of an offence or failure. **2** an assurance that no offence was intended. **3** an explanation or defence. **4** (foll. by *for*) a poor or scanty specimen of (*this apology for a letter*). [French *apologie* or Late Latin *apologia* from Greek (as APOLOGETIC)]

apo·lune /ˈapəˌluːn/ *noun* the point in a body's lunar orbit where it is furthest from the moon's centre (*opp.* PERILUNE). [APO- + Latin *luna* moon, after *apogee*]

apo·mixis /ˌapəˈmɪksɪs/ *noun* (*pl.* **apo·mixes** /-ˌsiːz/) *Biol.* asexual reproduction, esp. in a form outwardly resembling a sexual process (*compare* AMPHIMIXIS). □ **apo·mic·tic** *adjective* [modern Latin, formed as APO- + Greek *mixis* mingling]

apoph·thegm /ˈapəˌθem, ˈapəfˌθem/ *noun* (also **apo·thegm**) a terse saying or maxim, an aphorism. □ **apoph·theg·mat·ic** /-θegˈmatɪk/ *adjective* [Greek *apophthegma -matos* from *apophtheggomai* speak out]

apo·plec·tic /ˌapəˈplektɪk/ *adjective* **1** of, causing, suffering, or liable to apoplexy. **2** *informal* enraged. □ **apo·plec·tic·ally** *adverb* [Greek *apoplēktikos* from *apoplēssō* strike completely (as APO-, *plēssō* strike)]

apo·plexy /ˈapəˌpleksi/ *noun* a sudden loss of consciousness, voluntary movement, and sensation caused by blockage or rupture of a brain artery; a stroke. [Old French *apoplexie* from Late Latin *apoplexia* from Greek *apoplēxia* (as APOPLECTIC)]

apop·to·sis /ˌapəˈtoːsɪs, ˌapɒp-/ *noun Physiology* the death of cells which occurs as a normal and controlled part of an organism's growth or development. [Greek *apoptōsis* 'falling off' from *apo* 'from' + *ptōsis* 'falling, a fall']

apor·ia /əˈpɔːrɪə/ *noun* **1** *Rhetoric* the expression of doubt. **2** a doubtful matter, a perplexing difficulty. [Late Latin from Greek, from *aporos* impassable]

apo·sem·atic /ˌapəsɪˈmatɪk/ *adjective Zool.* (of coloration, markings, etc.) serving to warn or repel. [APO- + Greek *sēma sēmatos* sign]

apos·tasy /əˈpɒstəsi/ *noun* (*pl.* **-ies**) **1** renunciation of a belief or faith, esp. religious. **2** abandonment of principles or of a party. **3** an instance of apostasy. [New Testament Greek *apostasia* from *apostasis* defection (as APO-, *stat-* stand)]

apos·tate /əˈpɒsteɪt/ **● *noun*** a person who renounces a former belief, adherence, etc. **● *adjective*** engaged in apostasy. □ **apos·ta·tize** /əˈpɒstəˌtaɪz/ *intransitive verb* (also esp. *Brit.* **-tise**). [Greek *apostatēs* deserter (as APOSTASY)]

a pos·teri·ori /ˌeɪ pɒˌstiːriˈɔːraɪ/ **● *adjective*** (of reasoning) inductive, empirical; proceeding from effects to causes. **● *adverb*** inductively, empirically; from effects to causes (*opp.* A PRIORI). [Latin, = from what comes after]

apos·tle /əˈpɒsəl/ *noun* **1** (**Apostle**) **a** any of a group of followers of Christ made up of the twelve disciples and Paul and Barnabas, sent out

Vowels: a *cat* ɑ *arm* e *bed* ɜː *her* ɜː *deux* ə *ago* ɪ *sit* i *cosy* iː *feed* ɒ *hot* ɔ *pore* ɔː *no* ʌ *run* ʊ *put*

to preach the gospel after the Resurrection. **b** the first successful Christian missionary in a country or to a people. **2** a leader or outstanding figure, esp. of a reform movement (*apostle of temperance*). **3** a messenger or representative. **4** one of the twelve administrative officials of Mormonism. □ **apostle·ship** *noun* [Greek *apostolos* messenger (as APO-, *stellō* send forth)]

Apostles' Creed *noun* a Christian creed dating from the 4th c., traditionally ascribed to the Apostles, and now used in many Christian liturgies.

apos·tol·ate /əˈpɒstələt/ *noun* **1** the position or authority of an Apostle. **2** an organization dedicated to a religion or doctrine. [ecclesiastical Latin *apostolatus* (as APOSTLE)]

apos·tol·ic /ˌapəˈstɒlɪk/ *adjective* **1** of or relating to the Apostles. **2** of the Pope regarded as the successor of St. Peter. **3** of the character of an Apostle. [Greek *apostolikos* (as APOSTLE)]

Apostolic Fathers *plural noun* the Christian leaders immediately succeeding the Apostles.

apostolic succession *noun* the doctrine of the uninterrupted transmission of spiritual authority from the Apostles through successive popes and bishops.

apos·tro·phe¹ *noun* a punctuation mark used to indicate: **1** the omission of letters or numbers, e.g. *can't*; *he's*; *1 Jan. '97*. **2** the possessive case (e.g. *Harry's book*; *boys' coats*). [Greek *apostrophos* accent of elision, from *apostrephō* turn away (as APO-, *strephō* turn)]

apos·tro·phe² *noun* an exclamatory passage in a speech or poem, addressed to a person (often dead or absent) or thing (often personified). □ **apos·tro·phize** *transitive & intransitive verb* (also esp. *Brit.* **-phise**). [Latin from Greek, lit. 'turning away' (as APOSTROPHE¹)]

apoth·ecaries' measure *noun* (also **apothecaries' weight**) units of weight and liquid volume formerly used in pharmacy. 12 ounces = one pound; 20 fluid ounces = one pint.

apoth·ecary /əˈpɒθəˌkeri/ *noun* (*pl.* **-ies**) *hist.* a person licensed to dispense medicines and drugs. [Late Latin *apothecarius* from Latin *apotheca* from Greek *apothēkē* storehouse]

apo·thegm *var. of* APOPHTHEGM.

apo·them /ˈapəˌθem/ *noun* *Geom.* a line from the centre of a regular polygon at right angles to any of its sides. [Greek *apotithēmi* put aside (as APO-, *tithēmi* place)]

apo·theo·sis /əˌpɒθiˈoːsɪs/ *noun* (*pl.* **apo·theo·ses** /-siːz/) **1** elevation to divine status; deification. **2** a glorification of a thing; a sublime example (*apotheosis of the dance*). **3** a deified ideal. [ecclesiastical Latin from Greek *apotheoō* make a god of (as APO-, *theos* god)]

apo·theo·size /əˈpɒθiəˌsaiz/ *transitive verb* (also esp. *Brit.* **-sise**) **1** make divine; deify. **2** idealize, glorify.

app /ap/ *noun* esp. *N Amer. Computing informal* application. [abbreviation]

app. *abbreviation* **1** appendix. **2** appeal.

Ap·pa·la·chia /ˌapəˈleɪʃiə/ a highland region of the eastern US, in the Appalachian Mountains, including parts of Alabama, Georgia, S Carolina, Tennessee, W Virginia, Kentucky, Virginia, and Pennsylvania.

Ap·pa·la·chian /ˌapəˈleɪʃən/ ● *adjective* **1** of or relating to the Appalachian Mountains. **2** of or relating to the region or people of Appalachia. ● *noun* a native or inhabitant of Appalachia.

Appalachian Mountains (also **Appalachians**) a mountain system of eastern N America, stretching from Quebec and Maine in the north to Georgia and Alabama in the south. Its highest peak is Mount Mitchell in N Carolina, which rises to 2 037 m (6,684 ft.).

Appalachian Region a mountain region of E Canada comprising much of SE Quebec (including Monts Notre-Dame), all of New Brunswick, PEI and Nova Scotia, and most of the island of Newfoundland. It is bounded to the northwest by the St. Lawrence Lowlands.

Appalachian Trail a 3 200 km (2000 mile) hiking trail through the Appalachians from Mount Katahdin in Maine to Springer Mountain in Georgia.

ap·pall /əˈpɒl/ *transitive verb* (also **appal**) (**ap·palled**, **appal·ling**) greatly dismay or horrify. [Old French *apalir* grow pale]

ap·pal·ling /əˈpɒlɪŋ/ *adjective informal* shocking, unpleasant; bad. □ **ap·pal·ling·ly** *adverb*

Ap·pa·loosa /ˌapəˈluːsə/ *noun* a N American breed of horse, having dark spots on a light background. [*Opelousas* in Louisiana, or *Palouse*, a river in Idaho]

ap·pan·age /ˈapənɪdʒ/ *noun* (also **apan·age**) **1** provision for the maintenance of the younger children of kings etc. **2** a natural

accompaniment or attribute. [French, ultimately from medieval Latin *appanare* endow with the means of subsistence (as APO-, *panis* bread)]

ap·pa·rat /ˌapəˈrat/ *noun* the administrative system of a Communist party, esp. in a Communist country. [Russian from German, = apparatus]

ap·pa·rat·chik /ˌapəˈratʃɪk/ *noun* **1 a** a member of a Communist apparat. **b** a Communist agent or spy. **2 a** a member of a political party in any country who executes policy; a zealous functionary. **b** an official of a public or private organization. [Russian: see APPARAT]

ap·par·at·us /ˌapəˈratəs, ˌapəˈreɪtəs/ *noun* **1** the equipment needed for a particular purpose or function, esp. scientific or technical. **2** complex structure of an organization (*apparatus of government*). **3** *Anat.* the organs used to perform a particular process (*digestive apparatus*). **4** (also **critical apparatus** or **apparatus crit·icus**) a collection of variants and annotations accompanying a printed text. [Latin from *apparare apparat-* make ready for]

ap·par·el *noun* clothing, dress. [Old French *apareiller* (v.) from Romanic *appariculare* (unrecorded) make equal or fit, ultimately from Latin *par* equal]

ap·par·ent *adjective* **1** readily visible or perceivable. **2** seeming. [Old French *aparant* from Latin (as APPEAR)]

apparent horizon *noun* see HORIZON 1b.

ap·par·ent·ly *adverb* **1** clearly, plainly. **2** seemingly.

apparent magnitude *noun* the magnitude, i.e. brightness, of a celestial body as seen from the earth (*opp.* ABSOLUTE MAGNITUDE).

apparent time *noun* solar time (see SOLAR *adjective*).

ap·par·ition /ˌapəˈrɪʃən/ *noun* **1** a sudden or dramatic appearance, esp. of a ghost or phantom. **2** a visible ghost. [Latin *apparitio* attendance (as APPEAR)]

ap·peal /əˈpiːl/ ● *verb* **1** *intransitive* make an earnest or formal request; plead (*appealed for calm*; *appealed to us not to leave*). **2** *intransitive* (usu. foll. by *to*) be attractive or of interest; be pleasing. **3** *intransitive* (foll. by *to*) resort to or cite for support. **4** *Law* **a** *intransitive* (often foll. by *to*) apply (to a higher court) for a reconsideration of the decision of a lower court. **b** *transitive* refer to a higher court to review (a case). **c** *intransitive* (foll. by *against*) apply to a higher court to reconsider (a verdict or sentence). **5** *transitive & intransitive* request a review of (a decision) by an authority (*students unhappy with their mark may appeal*). ● *noun* **1** the act or an instance of appealing. **2** a formal or urgent request for public support, esp. financial, for a cause. **3** *Law* the referral of a case to a higher court. **4** attractiveness; appealing quality (*sex appeal*). [Old French *apel*, *apeler* from Latin *appellare* to address]

ap·peal·able *adjective* *Law* (of a case) that can be referred to a higher court for review.

ap·peal·ing *adjective* attractive, likeable. □ **ap·peal·ing·ly** *adverb*

ap·pear *intransitive verb* **1** become or be visible. **2** be evident (*a new problem then appeared*). **3** seem; have the appearance of being (*appeared healthy*; *you appear to be right*). **4** present oneself publicly or formally, esp. on stage or as the accused or counsel in a law court. **5** be published (*it appeared in the papers*; *a new edition will appear*). [Latin *apparēre apparit-* come in sight]

ap·pear·ance *noun* **1** the act or an instance of appearing. **2** an outward form as perceived (whether correctly or not), esp. visually (*very concerned about his appearance*; *has an appearance of prosperity*). **3** a semblance (*gives the appearance of trying hard*). □ **keep up appearances** maintain an impression or pretense of affluence, virtue, etc. **make** (or **put in**) **an appearance** be present, esp. briefly. **to all appearances** as far as can be seen; apparently. [Old French *aparance*, *-ence* from Late Latin *apparentia* (as APPEAR, -ENCE)]

appearance notice *noun* *Cdn Law* a written form given by a police officer to a person accused of a crime at the scene of the crime, stating the date, time, and place that the accused must appear in court.

ap·pease *transitive verb* **1** make calm or quiet, esp. conciliate (a potential aggressor) by making concessions. **2** satisfy (an appetite, scruples). □ **ap·pease·ment** *noun* **ap·peas·er** *noun* [Old French *apaiser* from *à* to + *pais* PEACE]

Appel /ˈɒpəl/ **Karel** (b.1921), Dutch abstract expressionist painter, sculptor, and graphic artist, whose work is characterized by impasto and violent colours.

ap·pel·lant /əˈpelənt/ *noun* *Law* a person who appeals to a higher court. [Middle English from French (as APPEAL, -ANT)]

ap·pel·late /əˈpelət/ *adjective* *Law* (esp. of a court) concerned with or dealing with appeals. [Latin *appellatus* (as APPEAL, -ATE²)]

ap·pel·la·tion /ˌapəˈleɪʃən/ *noun formal* a name or title; nomenclature. [Latin *appellatio -onis* (as APPEAL, -ATION)]

---

uː mo**o**d   ai m**y**   ɔi p**i**pe   au br**ow**n   ʌu h**ou**se   ei d**ay**   ɔi b**oy**   ã fr**an**glais   ã C**ana**dien   ɔ̃ Br**ay**on   (*see over for consonants*)

ap·pel·la·tion con·trô·lée /ˌapela'sjɔ̃ ˌkɔ̃tro:'lei/ *noun* a guarantee of the origin of a French wine (or other item of food) in conformity with statutory regulations. [French = controlled appellation]

ap·pel·la·tive /ə'pelətɪv/ *adjective* **1** naming. **2** *Grammar* (of a noun) that designates a class; common. [Late Latin *appellativus* (as APPEAL, -ATIVE)]

ap·pend *transitive verb* (usu. foll. by *to*) attach, affix, add, esp. to a written document etc. [Latin *appendere* hang]

ap·pend·age *noun* **1** a thing that is added or attached to something larger or more important. **2** *Zool.* a leg or other projecting part of an arthropod.

ap·pen·dec·to·my /ˌapen'dektəmi/ *noun* (*pl.* **-mies**) the surgical removal of the appendix.

ap·pen·di·citis /əˌpendɪ'saɪtɪs/ *noun* inflammation of the appendix.

ap·pen·dix *noun* (*pl.* **ap·pen·di·ces** /-ˌsiːz/; **ap·pen·dix·es**) **1** (in full **vermiform appendix**) *Anat.* a small outgrowth of tissue forming a tube-shaped sac attached to the lower end of the large intestine. **2** subsidiary matter at the end of a book or document. [Latin *appendix -icis* from *appendere* APPEND]

ap·per·ceive *transitive verb* **1** be conscious of perceiving. **2** *Psych.* compare (a perception) to previously held ideas so as to extract meaning from it. □ **ap·per·cep·tion** *noun* **ap·per·cep·tive** *adjective* [Old French *aperceveir*, ultimately from Latin *percipere* PERCEIVE]

ap·per·tain *intransitive verb* (foll. by *to*) **1** pertain. **2** belong as a possession or right. **3** be appropriate. [Old French *apertenir* from Late Latin *appertinēre* from *pertinēre* PERTAIN]

ap·pe·tite *noun* **1** a desire for food. **2** a natural desire to satisfy bodily needs, esp. for sexual activity. **3** (usu. foll. by *for*) an inclination or desire. □ **ap·peti·tive** /ə'petətɪv/ *adjective* [Latin *appetitus* from *appetere* seek after]

ap·pe·tiz·er *noun* (also esp. *Brit.* **-tiser**) a small amount of food or drink which stimulates the appetite before a meal.

ap·pe·tiz·ing *adjective* (also esp. *Brit.* **-ising**) pleasing; stimulating an appetite, esp. for food. □ **ap·pe·tiz·ing·ly** *adverb* [French *appétissant* irreg. from *appétit*, formed as APPETITE]

Ap·pian Way /'apɪən/ (Latin *Via Appia* /ˌviːə 'apɪə/) the principal road southward from Rome to Capua in classical times; it was later extended to Brindisi on the southeast coast of Italy. [after the censor *Appius* Claudius Caecus, who in 312 BC built the section to Capua]

ap·plaud *verb* **1** *intransitive* to clap as an expression of strong approval or praise. **2** *transitive* express approval of (a person or action). [Latin *applaudere applaus-* clap hands]

ap·plause *noun* **1** clapping etc. as an expression of approbation. **2** emphatic approval. [medieval Latin *applausus* (as APPLAUD)]

apple *noun* **1** the fruit of a tree of the genus *Malus*, rounded in form and with a crisp flesh. **2** (in full **apple tree**) the tree bearing this. **3** the most prominent part of the cheek, over the cheekbone and below the eye. **4** *N Amer. slang derogatory* an Aboriginal person who is seen (esp. by other Aboriginals) as part of the white establishment. □ **apples and oranges** irreconcilably different issues etc., esp. when in comparison. **apple of one's eye** a cherished person or thing. **upset the apple cart** spoil careful plans. □ **appley** *adjective* [Old English *æppel* from Germanic]

Apple·baum /'apəlˌbɒm/ **Louis** (1918–2000), Canadian composer and conductor. A prolific composer of ballets, film and theatre scores, and concert pieces, he also chaired (with Jacques Hébert) a 1965 government committee which led to the formation of the National Arts Centre Orchestra in Ottawa.

apple butter *noun N Amer.* a jam-like spread made from stewed spiced apples.

apple-cheeked *adjective* having round, rosy cheeks (esp. as an indication of good health).

apple cider *noun N Amer. see* CIDER 1.

apple doll *noun* a doll with the head made of a dried apple.

apple green ● *noun* a yellow-green colour or pigment like that of a green apple. ● *adjective* having an apple green colour.

apple·jack /'apəlˌdʒak/ *noun N Amer.* a spirit distilled from fermented apple juice. [APPLE + JACK[1]]

apple pan·dowdy /ˌpan'daudi/ *noun esp. US* a baked pudding of sliced apples topped with a tea-biscuit crust. [origin unknown]

apple pear *noun* the common name of the Asian or Oriental pear, which is shaped like an apple.

apple pie *noun* **1** any of various pies with a filling of apples. **2** *US* (*attributive*) embodying qualities thought to be American.

apple-pie bed *noun* a bed made (as a joke) with the sheets folded short, so that a person's legs cannot be accommodated.

apple-pie order *noun* perfect order; extreme neatness.

apple polisher *noun N Amer. informal* a person who curries favour. [from the practice of schoolchildren presenting their teacher with a shiny red apple in order to gain favour]

apple·sauce *noun* **1** a purée of stewed apples, often served with pork or as a dessert. **2** *N Amer. informal* nonsense.

Apple·seed, John·ny (real name John Chapman, 1774–1845), US pioneer known for his zeal in planting apple orchards.

ap·plet *noun Computing* a very small application, esp. a utility program performing one or a few simple functions within a larger program. [blend of APPLICATION + -LET]

Apple·ton, Sir Ed·ward Vic·tor (1892–1965), English physicist. He showed that radio waves are reflected back to earth when they strike the ionized part of the upper atmosphere, and was awarded the Nobel Prize for physics in 1947.

Apple·yard, Peter (b.1928), Canadian jazz musician. Originally a drummer, he is best known for his vibraphone playing.

ap·pli·ance *noun* **1** an electrical or gas-powered device or piece of equipment used for a specific task, esp. for domestic tasks such as washing dishes etc. **2** a prosthetic or orthodontic device. [APPLY + -ANCE]

appliance garage *noun N Amer.* a countertop kitchen cabinet with a roll-up door, used for storing small appliances for immediate use.

ap·plic·able /ə'plɪkəbəl/ *adjective* (often foll. by *to*) **1** that may be applied. **2** having reference; appropriate. □ **ap·plic·abil·ity** /-'bɪlɪti/ *noun* **ap·plic·ably** *adverb* [medieval Latin *applicabilis* (as APPLY, -ABLE)]

ap·pli·cant *noun* a person who applies for something, e.g. a position. [APPLICATION + -ANT]

ap·pli·ca·tion *noun* **1** the act or an instance of applying. **2** a formal request, usu. in writing, for employment, membership, etc. **3 a** relevance. **b** the use to which something can or should be put. **4** sustained or concentrated effort; diligence. **5** a task that a computer can be programmed to do. [Latin *applicatio -onis* (as APPLY, -ATION)]

ap·pli·ca·tor *noun* **1** a device for applying a substance to a surface. **2** a device to aid insertion of something, e.g. a tampon, into a body orifice. **3** a person who applies something, such as pesticide or paint. [APPLICATION + -OR[1]]

ap·plied *adjective* (of a subject of study) put to practical use as opposed to being theoretical (*compare* PURE *adjective* 9).

ap·pli·qué /'aplɪkei/ ● *noun* ornamental work in which fabric is cut out and attached, usu. sewn, to the surface of another fabric to form pictures or patterns. ● *adjective* executed in appliqué. ● *transitive verb* (**ap·pli·qués, ap·pli·quéd, ap·pli·qué·ing**) decorate with appliqué; make using appliqué technique. [French, past participle of *appliquer* apply, from Latin *applicare*: see APPLY]

apply /ə'plaɪ/ *verb* (**ap·plies, ap·plied, ap·ply·ing**) **1** *intransitive* (often foll. by *for, to*, or *to* + infin.) make a formal request for something to be done, given, etc. (*apply for a job; apply for assistance; applied to be sent overseas*). **2** *intransitive* have relevance (*does not apply in this case*). **3** *transitive* **a** make use of as relevant or suitable; employ (*apply the rules*). **b** operate (*apply the brake*). **4** *transitive* (often foll. by *to*) **a** put or spread on (*applied the ointment to the cut*). **b** administer (*applied the remedy; applied common sense to the problem*). **5** *reflexive* (often foll. by *to*) devote oneself (*applied myself to the task*). □ **ap·pli·er** *noun* [Old French *aplier* from Latin *applicare* fold, fasten to]

ap·pog·gia·tura /əˌpɒdʒə'tʊrə/ *noun Music* a grace note performed before, and normally taking half the time value of, an essential note of a melody. [Italian, from *appoggiare* 'lean upon, rest']

ap·point *transitive verb* **1** assign a post or office to (*appoint him treasurer; appoint her to lead the party; appointed to the post*). **2** (often foll. by *for*) fix, decide on (a time, place, etc.) (*8:30 was the appointed time*). **3** prescribe; ordain (*the Bible as appointed to be read in churches*). **4** *Law* declare the destination of (property etc.). **b** declare (a person) as having an interest in property etc. (*Jones was appointed in the will*). □ **ap·poin·tee** *noun* **ap·point·er** *noun* [Old French *apointer* from *à point* to a point]

ap·point·ed *adjective* equipped, furnished (*a well-appointed kitchen*).

ap·point·ive *adjective N Amer.* depending on or filled by appointment (*the Canadian Senate is appointive rather than elective*).

ap·point·ment *noun* **1** an arrangement to meet at a specific time and place. **2 a** a post or office available for applicants, or recently filled (*took up the appointment on Monday*). **b** a person appointed. **3** (usu. in *pl.*) **a** furniture, fittings. **b** equipment.

Ap·po·mat·tox /ˌapə'matəks/ a village in Virginia, site of the surrender on 9 April 1865 of the Confederate army to the Union army, which ended the American Civil War.

ap·por·tion *transitive verb* (often foll. by *to*) share out; assign as a share. □ **ap·por·tion·able** *adjective* [medieval Latin *apportionare* (as AD-, PORTION)]

ap·por·tion·ment *noun* **1** an act or instance of apportioning. **2** *US* the determination of the number of members a state sends to the House of Representatives according to its proportion of the total US population.

ap·pos·ite /ˈapəzɪt/ *adjective* (often foll. by *to*) **1** apt; well chosen. **2** well expressed. □ **ap·pos·ite·ly** *adverb* **ap·pos·ite·ness** *noun* [Latin *appositus* past participle of *apponere* (as AD-, *ponere* put)]

ap·pos·ition /ˌapəˈzɪʃən/ *noun* **1** placing side by side; juxtaposition. **2** *Grammar* the placing of a word next to another, esp. the addition of one noun to another, in order to qualify or explain the first, e.g. *William the Conqueror; my friend Sue*. □ **ap·pos·itive** /əˈpɒzɪtɪv/ *adjective & noun* [Late Latin *appositio* (as APPOSITE, -ITION)]

ap·prais·al *noun* the act or an instance of appraising.

ap·praise *transitive verb* **1** estimate the quality or worth of (*appraised her skills*). **2** evaluate the price of (property, jewellery, etc.). **3** consider (a situation etc.) so as to make a judgment. □ **ap·prais·able** *adjective* **ap·prais·ing·ly** *adverb* [Old French *aprisier* from *à* to + *pris* PRICE by assimilation to PRAISE]

ap·prais·er *noun* a person who assesses the worth or value of something, esp. of property, jewellery, etc.

ap·pre·ci·able *adjective* large enough to be noticed; significant; considerable (*appreciable progress has been made*). □ **ap·pre·ci·ably** *adverb*

ap·pre·ci·ate *verb* **1** *transitive* **a** esteem highly; value. **b** be grateful for (*we appreciate your sympathy*). **c** be sensitive to (*appreciate the nuances*). **2** *transitive* (often foll. by *that* + clause) understand; recognize (*I appreciate that I may be wrong*). **3 a** *intransitive* (of property etc.) rise in value. **b** *transitive* raise in value. □ **ap·pre·cia·tive** *adjective* **ap·pre·cia·tive·ly** *adverb* **ap·pre·ci·ator** *noun* **ap·pre·cia·tory** *adjective* [Late Latin *appretiare* appraise (as AD-, *pretium* price)]

ap·pre·ci·ation *noun* **1** favourable or grateful recognition. **2** an estimation or judgment; sensitive understanding of or reaction to (*a quick appreciation of the problem; music appreciation*). **3** an increase in value. **4** a (usu. favourable) review of a book, film, etc.

ap·pre·hend *transitive verb* **1** understand, perceive (*apprehend your meaning*). **2** seize, arrest (*apprehended the criminal*). **3** anticipate with uneasiness or fear (*apprehending the results*). [French *appréhender* or Latin *apprehendere* (as AD-, *prehendere prehens-* lay hold of)]

ap·pre·hen·sible *adjective* capable of being apprehended by the senses or the intellect. [Late Latin *apprehensibilis* (as APPREHEND, -IBLE)]

ap·pre·hen·sion *noun* **1** uneasiness; dread. **2** grasp, understanding. **3** arrest, capture (*apprehension of the suspect*). **4** an idea; a conception. [Late Latin *apprehensio* (as APPREHEND, -ION)]

ap·pre·hen·sive /ˌapriˈhensɪv/ *adjective* **1** (often foll. by *of, for*) uneasily fearful; dreading. **2** relating to perception by the senses or the intellect. **3** *archaic* perceptive; intelligent. □ **ap·pre·hen·sive·ly** *adverb* **ap·pre·hen·sive·ness** *noun* [medieval Latin *apprehensivus* (as APPREHEND, -IVE)]

ap·pren·tice ● *noun* **1** (often *attributive*) a person who is learning a trade by being employed in it for an agreed period, usu. at lower wages than is normal for that trade. **2** a beginner; a novice. ● *verb* **1** *transitive* (usu. foll. by *to*) engage or bind as an apprentice (*was apprenticed to a builder*). **2** *intransitive N Amer.* serve as an apprentice.

□ **ap·pren·tice·ship** *noun* [Old French *aprentis* from *apprendre* learn (as APPREHEND), after words in *-tis, -tif*, from Latin *-tivus*: see -IVE]

ap·prise *transitive verb* inform. □ **be apprised of** be aware of. [French *appris -ise* past participle of *apprendre* learn, teach (as APPREHEND)]

ap·proach ● *verb* **1** *transitive* come near or nearer to (a place or time). **2** *intransitive* come near or nearer in space or time (*the hour approaches*). **3** *transitive* make a tentative proposal or suggestion to (*approached me about a loan*). **4** *transitive* **a** be similar in character, quality, etc., to (*doesn't approach her for artistic skill*). **b** approximate to; be slightly less than (*a population approaching 5 million*). **5** *transitive* set about (a task etc.). **6** *intransitive* (of an aircraft etc.) prepare to land. **7** *intransitive Golf* play an approach shot. **8** *transitive archaic* bring near. ● *noun* **1** an act or means of approaching (*made an approach; an approach lined with trees*). **2** an approximation (*an approach to an apology*). **3** a way of dealing with a person or thing (*needs a new approach*). **4** (usu. in *pl.*) a sexual advance. **5** the final part of a flight before landing. **6** *Golf* a stroke from the fairway to the green. **7** *Bridge* a bidding method with a gradual advance

to a final contract. [Old French *aproch(i)er* from ecclesiastical Latin *appropiare* draw near (as AD-, *propius* comparative of *prope* near)]

ap·proach·able *adjective* **1** friendly; easy to talk to. **2** able to be approached. □ **ap·proach·abil·ity** *noun*

ap·pro·ba·tion /ˌaprəˈbeɪʃən/ *noun* approval, consent. □ **ap·pro·ba·tory** *adjective* [Latin *approbatio -onis* (as AD-, *probare* test from *probus* good), -ATION)]

ap·pro·pri·ate ● *adjective* /əˈprəʊprɪət/ (often foll. by *to, for*) suitable or proper. ● *transitive verb* /əˈprəʊprɪeɪt/ **1** take possession of, esp. without authority. **2** devote (money etc.) to special purposes. □ **ap·pro·pri·ate·ly** *adverb* **ap·pro·pri·ate·ness** *noun* **ap·pro·pri·a·tion** *noun* **ap·pro·pri·ator** *noun* [Late Latin *appropriatus* past participle of *appropriare* (as AD-, *proprius* own)]

ap·prov·al *noun* **1** the act of approving. **2** an instance of this; consent; a favourable opinion (*with your approval; looked at him with approval*). □ **on approval** (of goods supplied) to be returned if not satisfactory.

approval rating *noun* the percentage of people in an opinion poll who express approval of something or someone, esp. a political figure.

ap·prove *verb* **1** *transitive* confirm; declare acceptable (*approved his application*). **2** *intransitive* give or have a favourable opinion. **3** *transitive* commend (*approved the new hat*). **4** *transitive archaic* (usu. *reflexive*) demonstrate oneself to be (*approved himself a coward*). □ **approve of** **1** pronounce or consider good or satisfactory; commend. **2** agree to. □ **ap·prov·ing·ly** *adverb* [Old French *aprover* from Latin (as APPROBATION)]

approved school *noun Brit. hist.* a residential place of training for young offenders.

approx. *abbreviation* **1** approximate. **2** approximately.

ap·proxi·mate ● *adjective* /əˈprɒksɪmət/ **1** fairly correct or accurate; near to the actual (*the approximate time of arrival; an approximate guess*). **2** near or next (*your approximate neighbour*). ● *transitive & intransitive verb* /əˈprɒksɪˌmeɪt/ **1** (often foll. by *to*) bring or come near, esp. in quality, number, etc. (*approximates to the truth; approximates the amount required*). **2** estimate (*approximate the distance to a kilometre*). □ **ap·proxi·mate·ly** /-mətli/ *adverb* [Late Latin *approximatus* past participle of *approximare* (as AD-, *proximus* very near)]

ap·proxi·ma·tion /əprɒksɪˈmeɪʃən/ *noun* **1** an act or instance of approximating or bringing close. **2** an estimate, guess, or result that is approximately correct, or close enough for a particular purpose.

Apps, Charles Jo·seph Syl·van·us ('Syl') (1915–98), Canadian hockey player. In over ten years with the Toronto Maple Leafs he was renowned for his speed and playmaking ability.

appt. *abbreviation* appointment.

ap·pur·ten·ance /əˈpɜːtɪnəns/ *noun* (usu. in *pl.*) a belonging; an appendage; an accessory. [Old French *apertenance* (as APPERTAIN, -ANCE)]

ap·pur·ten·ant /əˈpɜːtɪnənt/ *adjective* (often foll. by *to*) belonging or appertaining; pertinent. [Old French *apartenant* pres. part. (as APPERTAIN)]

APR *abbreviation* annual or annualized percentage rate (esp. of interest on loans or credit).

Apr. *abbreviation* April.

après- /aˈpreɪ/ *combining form informal* coming after in time, esp. specifying a period following an activity (*après-shopping*). [French, = 'after']

après-ski /ˌapreɪˈskiː/ ● *noun* the evening, esp. its social activities, following a day's skiing. ● *attributive adjective* (of clothes, drinks, etc.) appropriate to social activities following skiing. [French]

apri·cot /ˈeɪprɪˌkɒt/ ● *noun* **1 a** a juicy soft fruit, similar to but smaller than a peach, of an orange-yellow colour. **b** the tree, *Prunus armeniaca*, bearing it. **2** the ripe fruit's orange-yellow colour. ● *adjective* orange-yellow (*apricot dress*). [Portuguese *albricoque* or Spanish *albaricoque* from Arabic *al* the + *barkuk* from late Greek *praikokion* from Latin *praecoquum* var. of *praecox* early-ripe: *apri-* after Latin *apricus* ripe, *-cot* by assimilation to French *abricot*]

April *noun* the fourth month of the year. [Middle English from Latin *Aprilis*]

April Fool *noun* a person successfully tricked on 1 April.

April Fool's Day *noun* 1 April, traditionally a day on which people play practical jokes on one another.

a pri·ori /ˌeɪ praɪˈɔːraɪ/ ● *adjective* **1** (of reasoning) deductive; proceeding from causes to effects (*opp.* A POSTERIORI). **2** (of concepts, knowledge, etc.) logically independent of experience; not derived from experience (*opp.* EMPIRICAL). **3** not submitted to critical investigation (*an a priori* conjecture). ● *adverb* **1** in an a priori manner. **2** as far as one knows; presumptively. □ **apri·or·ism** /ˌeiˈpraiəˌrizəm/ *noun* [Latin, = from what is before]

apron *noun* **1 a** a garment worn to protect the front of a person's clothes from dirt or damage, fastened at the back. **b** a similar garment worn as part of official or ceremonial dress (*Freemason's apron*). **2** *Theatre* the part of a stage in front of the curtain. **3** the hard-surfaced area on an airfield used for manoeuvring or loading aircraft. **4** an endless conveyor belt. □ **tied to a person's apron strings** dominated by or dependent on that person (usu. a woman). □ **aproned** *adjective* [Middle English *naperon* etc. from Old French diminutive of *nape* tablecloth, from Latin *mappa*: for loss of *n* compare ADDER]

apro·pos /ˌæprəˈpoː, ˈæprəˌpoː/ ● *adjective* to the point or purpose; appropriate (*her comment was apropos*). ● *preposition* informal (often foll. by *of*) with respect to; concerning (*apropos the meeting; apropos of the talk*). ● *adverb* **1** appropriately (*spoke apropos*). **2** by the way; incidentally (*apropos, she's not going*). [French *à propos* from *à* to + *propos* PURPOSE]

apse /æps/ *noun* **1** a large semicircular or polygonal recess, arched or with a domed roof, esp. at the eastern end of a church. **2** = APSIS. □ **ap·sid·al** /ˈæpsidəl/ *adjective* [Latin APSIS]

apsis /ˈæpsis/ *noun* (*pl.* **ap·si·des** /-ˌdiːz/) a point in the orbit of a planet or other satellite which is either closest to or farthest from the object around which it moves. □ **ap·sid·al** /ˈæpsidəl/ *adjective* [Latin from Greek (*h*)*apsis, -idos* arch, vault]

apt *adjective* **1** appropriate, suitable. **2** (foll. by *to* + infin.) **a** having a tendency, inclined (*he is too apt to lose his temper*). **b** likely (*there is apt to be local interest*). **3** clever; quick to learn (*an apt pupil; apt at the work*). □ **aptly** *adverb* **apt·ness** *noun* [Latin *aptus* fitted, past participle of *apere* fasten]

apt. *abbreviation* N Amer. apartment.

ap·ter·ous /ˈæptərəs/ *adjective* **1** (of insects) without wings. **2** (of seeds or fruits) having no wing-like expansions. [Greek *apteros* from *a-* not + *pteron* wing]

ap·teryx /ˈæptəriks/ *noun* = KIWI 1. [Greek *a-* not + *pterux* wing]

ap·ti·tude *noun* **1** a natural propensity or talent (*shows an aptitude for drawing*). **2** ability to learn or understand; intelligence. [Late Latin *aptitudo -inis* (as APT, -TUDE)]

aptitude test *noun* a test designed to determine a person's aptitude for a particular task or occupation.

Apu·leius /ˌæpjuˈliːəs/ (2nd c. BC) Latin writer from Africa. Renowned as a declaimer, he wrote a variety of rhetorical and philosophical works. His most famous work is *The Golden Ass*, a picaresque novel.

Apu·lia /əˈpuːliə/ (Italian **Puglia** /ˈpuljа/) a region of SE Italy, extending into the heel of the peninsula; capital, Bari.

Aqaba /ˈækəbə/ Jordan's only port, at the head of the Gulf of Aqaba; pop. (est. 1994) 63,000.

Aqaba, Gulf of a part of the Red Sea extending northward between the Sinai and Arabian peninsulas.

aqua¹ /ˈækwə, ɒ-/ ● *noun* the colour aquamarine. ● *adjective* of this colour. [abbreviation]

aqua² /ˈækwə, ɒ-/ *noun* (esp. in pharmaceutical and commercial use) water.

aqua- /ˈækwə, ɒ-/ *combining form* involving or pertaining to water, esp. with reference to recreational activities (*aquaplane*). [Latin *aqua* water]

aqua·cul·ture /ˈækwəˌkʌltʃər, ˈɒkwə-/ *noun* the cultivation or rearing of fish or aquatic plants for human consumption. □ **aqua·cul·tur·ist** *noun* [Latin *aqua* water + CULTURE, after *agriculture*]

aqua·fit *noun* (also **aqua·fit·ness**) an exercise class conducted in water, often to music.

Aqua·lung /ˈækwəˌlʌŋ/ *noun* proprietary = SCUBA *noun* 1. [Latin *aqua* water + LUNG]

aqua·marine /ˌækwəməˈriːn/ ● *noun* **1** a light bluish-green beryl. **2** its colour. ● *adjective* of this colour. [Latin *aqua marina* sea water]

aqua·naut /ˈækwəˌnɒt/ *noun* an underwater swimmer or explorer, esp. one working for an extended period in a bathysphere. [Latin *aqua* water + Greek *nautēs* sailor]

aqua·plane /ˈækwəˌplein/ ● *noun* a board for riding on the water, pulled by a speedboat. ● *intransitive verb* **1** = HYDROPLANE *verb* 1. **2** ride on an aquaplane. [Latin *aqua* water + PLANE¹]

aqua regia /ˌækwə ˈriːdʒiə/ *noun* Chem. a mixture of concentrated nitric and hydrochloric acids, a highly corrosive liquid attacking many substances unaffected by other reagents. [Latin, = royal water]

aqua·relle /ˌækwəˈrel, ˌɒkwə-/ *noun* a painting in thin, usu. transparent watercolours. [French from Italian *acquarella* watercolour, diminutive of *acqua* from Latin *aqua* water]

aquar·ist /əˈkwerist/ *noun* a person who keeps an aquarium.

aquar·ium *noun* (*pl.* **aquar·iums** or **aquar·ia**) **1** a tank of water with transparent sides containing fish or other live aquatic animals and plants. **2** a building or complex in which live aquatic animals are exhibited and studied. [neuter of Latin *aquarius* of water (*aqua*) after VIVARIUM]

Aquar·ius /əˈkweriəs/ *noun* **1** a constellation between Pisces and Capricorn, traditionally regarded as contained in the figure of a water carrier. **2 a** the eleventh sign of the zodiac. **b** a person born when the sun is in this sign, usu. between 22 January and 18 February. □ **Aquar·ian** *adjective & noun* [Middle English from Latin (as AQUARIUM)]

aqua·tic /əˈkwɒtik/ ● *adjective* **1** of or relating to water. **2** growing or living in or near water. **3** (of a sport) played in or on water. ● *noun* **1** an aquatic plant or animal. **2** (in *pl.*) aquatic sports. [Latin *aquaticus* from *aqua* water]

aqua·tint *noun* **1** a print resembling a watercolour, produced from a copper plate etched with nitric acid. **2** the process of producing this. [Italian *acqua tinta* coloured water]

aqua·vit /ˈækwəvit, -ˌviːt/ *noun* (also **akva·vit** /ˈækvə-/) an alcoholic spirit made from potatoes etc., usu. flavoured with caraway seeds. [Scandinavian *akvavit*]

aqua vitae /ˌækwə ˈviːtai/ *noun* archaic a strong alcoholic spirit, esp. brandy. [Latin, = water of life]

aque·duct /ˈækwəˌdʌkt/ *noun* **1** an artificial channel for conveying water, esp. in the form of a bridge supported by tall columns across a valley. **2** Anat. a small canal, esp. in the head of mammals. [Latin *aquae ductus* conduit, from *aqua* water + *ducere duct-* to lead]

aque·ous /ˈeikwiəs/ *adjective* **1** of, containing, or like water. **2** Chem. dissolved in water (*aqueous formaldehyde*). **3** Geol. created from sediments laid down in water (*aqueous rocks*). [medieval Latin *aqueus* from Latin *aqua* water]

aqueous humour *noun* Physiol. the clear fluid in the eye between the lens and the cornea.

aqui·fer /ˈækwifər/ *noun* Geol. a layer of permeable rock able to store significant quantities of water, through which groundwater moves. [Latin *aqui-* from *aqua* water + *-fer* bearing, from *ferre* bear]

Aquila¹ /əˈkwilə, ˈækwilə/ a small but prominent northern constellation, the Eagle, containing the star Altair.

Aquila² /ˈækwələ/ a city in east central Italy, capital of Abruzzi region; pop. (2001) 63,121.

aqui·legia /ˌækwiˈliːdʒə/ *noun* = COLUMBINE. [modern use of a medieval Latin word: origin unknown]

aqui·line /ˈækwiˌlain/ *adjective* **1** of or like an eagle. **2** (of a nose) curved like an eagle's beak. [Latin *aquilinus* from *aquila* eagle]

Aquin /aˈkã/ **Hu·bert** (1929–1977), Canadian writer, author of the novels *Prochain épisode* (1965) and *Trou de mémoire*, for which he was offered the Governor General's Award in 1969 (which he refused on political grounds). A radical separatist, he was one of the most important cultural figures of his generation in Quebec.

Aqui·nas /əˈkwainəs/ **St. Thom·as** (1225–74), Italian Dominican scholastic philosopher and theologian, a Doctor of the Church, author of the *Summa Contra Gentiles*, the *Summa Theologiae*, which became a standard theological text, as well as several commentaries which made the work of Aristotle acceptable in Christian western Europe.

Aqui·no /aˈkiːnoː/ **Cora·zón** (b.1933), president of the Philippines 1986–92. After the assassination of her husband Benigno Aquino in 1983, she assumed his role as leader of the moral opposition to the regime of President Ferdinand Marcos.

Aqui·taine /ˌækwiˈtein/ a region and former province of SW France, on the Bay of Biscay, centred on Bordeaux. A province of the Roman Empire and a medieval duchy, it became, by the marriage of Eleanor of Aquitaine to Henry II, an English possession and remained so until 1453.

aquiv·er *adverb & predicative adjective* trembling, quivering with excitement.

AR *abbreviation* Arkansas (in official postal use).

Ar *symbol* Chem. the element argon.

ar- *prefix* assimilated form of AD- before *r*.

A/R *abbreviation* ACCOUNT RECEIVABLE.

-ar¹ *suffix* **1** forming adjectives (*angular; linear; nuclear; titular*). **2** forming nouns (*scholar*). [Old French *-aire* or *-ier* or Latin *-aris*]

-ar² *suffix* forming nouns (*pillar*). [French *-er* or Latin *-ar, -are*, neuter of *-aris*]

-ar³ *suffix* forming nouns (*bursar; exemplar; mortar; vicar*). [Old French *-aire* or *-ier* or Latin *-arius, -arium*]

-ar⁴ *suffix* assimilated form of *-ER¹, -OR¹* (*liar*).

Arab ● *noun* **1** a member of a Semitic people originally inhabiting Saudi Arabia and the neighbouring countries, now the Middle East generally. **2** = ARABIAN *noun* 2. ● *adjective* of Arabia or the Arabs. [French *Arabe* from Latin *Arabs Arabis* from Greek *Araps -abos* from Arabic '*arab*]

ara·besque /ˌerəˈbesk, ˌarə-/ *noun* **1** *Dance & Figure Skating* **a** a posture with one leg extended straight backwards and usu. elevated (compare ATTITUDE 2c). **b** a position of the arms in which they are fully extended to the front or side, with the palms facing downwards. **2** a design of intertwined leaves, scrolls, etc. **3** *Music* a florid melodic section or composition. [French from Italian *arabesco* from *arabo* Arab]

Arab·ia /əˈreibiə/ (also **Arabian peninsula**) a peninsula of SW Asia, largely desert, lying between the Red Sea and the Persian Gulf and bounded on the north by Jordan and Iraq. The original homeland of the Arabs and the historic centre of Islam, modern Arabia comprises the states of Saudi Arabia, Yemen, Oman, Bahrain, Kuwait, Qatar, and the United Arab Emirates.

Arab·ian ● *adjective* of or relating to Arabia (*the Arabian desert*). ● *noun* **1** a native of Arabia. ¶ Now less common than *Arab* in this sense. **2** (in full **Arabian horse**) a breed of horse developed in Arabia, renowned for its speed, intelligence and mild disposition.

Arabian camel *noun* a domesticated camel with one hump, *Camelus dromedarius*, native to the deserts of N Africa and Arabia. Also called DROMEDARY.

Arabian Desert (also called the **Eastern Desert**) a desert in E Egypt, between the Nile and the Red Sea.

Arabian Gulf an alternative name for the PERSIAN GULF.

Arabian Nights (in full *Arabian Nights' Entertainment*, also called the 'Thousand and One Nights') a collection of tales of magic and romance written in Arabic dating from the 10th c., including 'Ali Baba and the Forty Thieves' (see SCHEHERAZADE).

Arabian Sea the northwestern part of the Indian Ocean, between Arabia and India.

Arab·ic ● *noun* **1** the Semitic language of the Arabs, now spoken in much of N Africa and the Middle East. **2** = GUM ARABIC. ● *adjective* of or relating to Arabia (esp. with reference to language or literature).

arab·ica /əˈrabikə/ *noun* **1** coffee or coffee beans from the most widely grown species of coffee plant, *Coffea arabica*. **2** the plant itself. [modern Latin from Latin *arabicus*, ARABIC]

Arabic numeral *noun* any of the numerals 0, 1, 2, 3, 4, 5, 6, 7, 8, and 9 (compare ROMAN NUMERAL).

arabi·dop·sis /əˌrabɪˈdɒpsɪs/ *noun* a cruciferous plant much used in genetic research. [from ARABIS + Greek *opsis* 'appearance']

ar·abis /ˈerəbɪs, ˈarə-/ *noun* any plant of the genus *Arabis*, often mat-forming and grown in rock gardens. Also called ROCK CRESS. [medieval Latin from Greek, = Arabian]

Arab·ist *noun* **1** a student of Arabic civilization, language, etc. **2** a supporter of Arab nationalism or political self-assertion.

Arab·ize *transitive verb* (also esp. *Brit.* **-ise**) give (someone or something) an Arab or Arabic character. □ **Arab·iz·ation** *noun* **Arab·ized** *adjective*

ar·able /ˈerəbəl/ ● *adjective* **1** (of land) plowed, or suitable for plowing and crop production. **2** (of crops) that can be grown on arable land. ● *noun* arable land or crops. [Latin *arabilis* from *arare* to plow]

Arab League *noun* = LEAGUE OF ARAB STATES.

Araby /ˈerəbi, ˈarə-/ *noun literary* Arabia.

Ara·cajú /ˌarəkəˈʒuː/ a port in E Brazil, on the Atlantic coast; pop. (2000) 460,898.

ara·chid·onic acid /əˌrakɪˈdɒnɪk/ *noun* a polyunsaturated fatty acid present in animal fats. It is important in metabolism, esp. in the synthesis of prostaglandins and leukotrienes, and is an essential constituent of the diet. [formed irregularly from *arachidic* (a saturated fatty acid) + -ONE + -IC]

Ar·achne /əˈrakni/ *Gk Legend* a skilful weaver who challenged Athene to a contest. After her work was destroyed by Athene, Arachne hanged herself in despair, but was then turned into a spider by Athene.

arach·nid /əˈraknɪd/ *noun* any arthropod of the class Arachnida, having four pairs of walking legs and characterized by simple eyes, e.g. spiders, scorpions, mites, and ticks. □ **arach·nid·an** *adjective & noun* [modern Latin *arachnida* from Greek *arakhnē* spider]

arach·noid /əˈraknɔɪd/ ● *noun Anat.* (in full **arachnoid membrane**) one of the three membranes (see MENINGES) that surround the brain and spinal cord of vertebrates. ● *adjective* **1** *Bot.* covered with long cobweb-like hairs. **2** of or relating to arachnids. [modern Latin *arachnoides* from Greek *arakhnoeidēs* like a cobweb, from *arakhnē*: see ARACHNID]

arach·no·phobia /əˌraknəˈfoːbiə/ *noun Psych.* an abnormal fear of spiders. □ **arach·no·phobe** *noun* [modern Latin from Greek *arakhne* spider + -PHOBIA]

Ara·fat /ˈerəfat, ˈaː-/ **Yas·ser** (b.1929), Palestinian leader, who in 1969 became head of the Palestine Liberation Organization.

Ara·fura Sea /ˌerəˈfurə/ a sea lying between N Australia, the islands of east Indonesia, and New Guinea.

Ara·gon¹ /ˈerəˌgɒn, ˈaː-/ an autonomous region of NE Spain, bounded on the north by the Pyrenees and on the east by Catalonia and Valencia; capital, Saragossa. □ **Aragon·ese** *noun & adjective*

Ara·gon² /araˈɡɔ̃/ **Louis** (1897–1982), French poet, novelist, and essayist, who committed himself to writing for the communist cause.

arag·on·ite /əˈragəˌnaɪt/ *noun* a form of calcium carbonate, harder and denser than calcite, occurring around hot springs and geysers, in pearls, and in the shells of molluscs. [ARAGON¹, where first found, + -ITE¹]

arak /əˈrak/ *noun* (also **ar·rack** /ˈarək/) a Middle Eastern alcoholic spirit, esp. distilled from coco sap or rice. [Arabic '*araḳ* sweat, alcoholic spirit from grapes or dates]

Aral Sea /ˈerəl/ an inland sea in central Asia, on the border between Kazakhstan and Uzbekistan. Its area was reduced to two-thirds of its original size between 1960 and 1990, after water was diverted for irrigation, with serious consequences for the environment of the area.

-arama /ərəmə/ *combining form* = -RAMA.

Ara·maic /ˌerəˈmeiɪk/ ● *noun* a branch of the Semitic family of languages, esp. the language of Syria used as a lingua franca in the Near East from the 6th c. BC, later dividing into varieties one of which included Syriac and Mandaean. ● *adjective* of or in Aramaic. [Latin *Aramaeus* from Greek *Aramaios* of Aram (Biblical name of Syria)]

Aran /ˈerən/ *adjective* designating a type of thick knitwear with cable patterns and large diamond designs. [ARAN ISLANDS, where the design was first devised]

Ar·an·da /əˈrʌntə, ˈarəndə/ ● *noun* (*pl.* same or **Ar·an·das**) **1** a member of an Aboriginal people of central Australia. **2** the language of the Aranda. ● *adjective* of the Aranda or their language.

Aran Islands a group of three islands, Inishmore, Inishmaan, and Inisheer, off the west coast of the Republic of Ireland.

Ara·nyaka /ˌarəˈnjakə/ *noun* each of a set of Hindu sacred treatises based on the Brahmanas, composed in Sanskrit c.700 BC. Intended only for initiates, the Aranyakas contain mystical and philosophical material and explications of esoteric rites. [Sanskrit, = book of the forest]

Arap·aho /əˈrapəhoː/ (also **Arap·ahoe**) ● *noun* **1** (*pl.* same or **-s**) a member of an Aboriginal people of the Great Plains, now living mainly in Wyoming and Oklahoma. **2** the Algonquian language of the Arapaho. ● *adjective* of the Arapaho or their language. [Crow *alappahó*, lit. 'many tattoo marks']

Ara·rat, Mount /ˈerəˌrat/ a pair of volcanic peaks in E Turkey, near the borders with Armenia and Iran. The higher peak, which rises to 5 165 m (16,946 ft.), is the traditional site of the resting place of Noah's ark after the Flood (Gen. 8:4).

Arau·can·ian /ˌerɔːˈkeiniən/ ● *noun* **1** a member of an Aboriginal people of central Chile and adjacent regions of Argentina. **2** the group of languages spoken by the Araucanians. ● *adjective* of the Araucanians or their language. [*Araucanía*, a region of Chile]

arau·caria /ˌerɔːˈkeriə/ *noun* any evergreen conifer of the genus *Araucaria*, e.g. the Norfolk Island pine and the monkey-puzzle tree, originally from S America and Australasia. [*Arauco* a province in Chile]

Ara·wak /ˈerəˌwak/ ● *noun* **1** (*pl.* same or **-waks**) a member of the Aboriginal peoples of the Greater Antilles and northern and western S America, speaking languages of the same linguistic family, forced out of the Antilles by the Carib Indians shortly before the Spanish expansion into the Caribbean. **2** the family of their languages. ● *adjective* of the Arawak or their languages. □ **Ara·wakan** *adjective & noun*

arba·lest /ˈarbəˌlest/ *noun* (also **arba·list** /ˈarbəlɪst/) *hist.* a large, powerful medieval crossbow with a winch and pulley mechanism for drawing the string, capable of firing stones or bolts. [Old French *arbaleste* from Late Latin *arcubalista* from *arcus* bow + BALLISTA]

arbi·ter /ˈarbɪtər/ *noun* **1** = ARBITRATOR. **2** (often foll. by *of*) a judge; an

---

uː m**oo**d   ai m**y**   əi p**i**pe   au br**ow**n   ʌu h**ou**se   ei d**ay**   ɔi b**oy**   ɑ̃ fr**an**glais   ã Canadi**en**   ɔ̃ Brayon   (*see over for consonants*)

authority (*arbiter of taste*). **3** (often foll. by *of*) a person or organization having entire control of something (*supreme arbiter of academic matters*). [Latin]

arbi·ter ele·gan·ti·arum /ˌele̩ˈgantiˈɑrəm/ *noun* (also **arbi·ter ele·gan·tiae** /ˌele̩ˈganʃiːˌiː/) a judge of artistic taste and etiquette. [Latin]

arbi·trage /ˈɑrbɪˌtrɒʒ, -trədʒ/ *noun* the buying and selling of stocks or bills of exchange to take advantage of varying prices in different markets. [French from *arbitrer* (as ARBITRATE)]

arbi·tra·geur /ˌɑrbɪtrɒˈʒɜr/ *noun* (also **arbi·trager** /ˈɑrbɪˌtrɒdʒər/) a person who engages in arbitrage. [French]

arbi·tral /ˈɑrbɪtrəl/ *adjective* concerning arbitration. [French *arbitral* or Late Latin *arbitralis*: SEE ARBITER]

ar·bitra·ment /ɑrˈbɪtrəmənt/ *noun* **1** the deciding of a dispute by an arbitrator. **2** an authoritative decision made by an arbitrator. [medieval Latin *arbitramentum* (as ARBITRATE, -MENT)]

arbi·trary *adjective* **1** based on the unrestricted will of a person, not according to a scheme or plan; capricious. **2** established at random. **3** despotic. □ **arbi·trar·i·ly** *adverb* **arbi·trar·i·ness** *noun* [Latin *arbitrarius* or French *arbitraire* (as ARBITER, -ARY¹)]

arbi·trate *transitive & intransitive verb* decide by arbitration. [Latin *arbitrari* judge]

arbi·tra·tion *noun* *Law* the hearing and resolution of a dispute by a referee, usu. chosen and agreed upon by all disputants, who has the power to impose a settlement. [Latin *arbitratio -onis* (as ARBITER, -ATION)]

arbi·tra·tor /ˈɑrbɪˌtreɪtɜr/ *noun* a person appointed to settle a dispute, usu. with the power to impose a settlement. □ **arbi·tra·tor·ship** *noun*

arbor¹ *noun* an axle or spindle on which something rotates, e.g. one holding a cutter in machine tooling. [French *arbre* tree, axis, from Latin *arbor*: refashioned on Latin]

arbor² *var. of* ARBOUR.

Arbor Day *noun* in Canada, the US, Australia, and other countries, a day dedicated annually to public tree planting. [Latin *arbor* tree]

ar·bor·eal /ɑrˈbɔriəl/ *adjective* of, living in, or pertaining to trees. [Latin *arboreus* from *arbor* tree]

ar·bor·eous /ɑrˈbɔriəs/ *adjective* **1** wooded. **2** arboreal.

arbor·es·cent /ˌɑrbəˈresənt/ *adjective* treelike in growth or general appearance. □ **arbor·es·cence** *noun* [Latin *arborescere* grow into a tree (*arbor*)]

arbor·etum /ˌɑrbəˈriːtəm/ *noun* (pl. **arbor·etums** or **arbor·eta** /-tə/) a botanical garden devoted to trees. [Latin from *arbor* tree]

ar·bori·cul·ture /ɑrˈbɔriˌkʌltʃɜr/ *noun* the cultivation of trees and shrubs. □ **ar·bori·cul·tur·al** /-ˈkʌltʃərəl/ *adjective* **ar·bori·cul·tur·ist** /-ˈkʌltʃərɪst/ *noun* [Latin *arbor -oris* tree, after *agriculture*]

ar·borio rice /ɑrˈbɔrioː/ *noun* a plump, short-grained rice, sticky when cooked, often used in risotto and other Italian dishes. [Italian]

arbor·ist *noun* a person who studies or cultivates trees. [Latin *arbor* tree + -IST]

Arbor·ite *noun* *Cdn proprietary* a plastic laminate used in countertops, tables, etc. [Latin *arbor* tree + -ITE¹]

arbor·iz·a·tion *noun* (also esp. *Brit.* **-isation**) a treelike arrangement, esp. in anatomy or geology.

arbor·vitae /ˌɑrbɔrˈviːtai, -ˈvaiti/ *noun* any of the evergreen conifers of the genus *Thuja*, including the eastern white cedar and the western red cedar, native to N America and N Asia, usu. of columnar habit with flattened shoots bearing scale leaves. [Latin, = tree of life]

arbour *noun* (also **arbor**) **1** a shady garden alcove with the sides and roof formed by trees or climbing plants; a bower. **2** a metal, wooden, or plastic arch for vines etc. to grow on. □ **ar·boured** *adjective* [Anglo-French *erber* from Old French *erbier* from *erbe* herb, from Latin *herba*: phonetic change to *ar-* assisted by assoc. with Latin *arbor* tree]

Arbus /ˈɑrbəs/ **Diane** (1923–71), US photographer. She is best known for her sometimes disturbing images of the poor etc. on the streets of New York and other US cities.

Ar·buth·not /ɑrˈbʌθnət/ **John** (1667–1735), Scottish physician and satirist. His satirical *History of John Bull* (1712), was the origin of 'John Bull', the typical Englishman.

ar·bu·tus /ɑrˈbjuːtəs/ *noun* **1** any evergreen tree or shrub of the genus *Arbutus*, having dark green leaves and clusters of small, fragrant, bell-shaped flowers, esp.: **a** *A. menziesii*, native to the Pacific coast of N America, with peeling red bark, the only broadleaf evergreen tree native to Canada. **b** *A. unedo*, native to S Europe, having strawberry-like berries. *Also called* STRAWBERRY TREE. **2** *N Amer. see* TRAILING ARBUTUS. [Latin]

ARC *abbreviation* AIDS-RELATED COMPLEX.

arc ● *noun* **1** *Geom.* part of the circumference of a circle or any other curve. **2** any curved shape or course. **3** *Electricity* a luminous discharge between two electrodes. **●** *intransitive verb* (**arced**; **arc·ing**) form an arc. [Latin *arcus* bow, curve]

ARCA *abbreviation* Associate of the Royal Canadian Academy (of Arts).

ar·cade *noun* **1** *Archit.* a series of arches supporting or set along a wall. **2** a passageway lined with arches. **3** a public place containing coin-operated game machines. **4** esp. *Brit.* a covered walk with shops along one or both sides. □ **ar·cad·ed** *adjective* [French from Provençal *arcada* or Italian *arcata* from Romanic: related to ARCH¹]

arcade game *noun* a coin-operated game machine, esp. a video game machine or a pinball machine.

Ar·cadia /ɑrˈkeidiə/ a mountainous district in the Peloponnese of S Greece. In poetic fantasy it represents a pastoral paradise, the home of song-loving shepherds. It is, in Greek mythology, the home of Pan.

Ar·cad·ian /ɑrˈkeidiən/ **●** *noun* an idealized peasant or country dweller, esp. in poetry. **●** *adjective* simple and poetically rural. □ **Ar·cad·ian·ism** *noun*

ar·cana /ɑrˈkeinə/ *noun* (sing. **ar·canum**) mysteries or secrets. [Latin neuter plural of *arcanus*: see ARCANE]

Ar·cand /ɑrˈkã/ **(Georges-Henri) Denys** (b.1941) Canadian filmmaker. After establishing himself as a documentary filmmaker with the NFB, he moved on to directing television, then returned to commercial filmmaking, achieving international success with the comedy about sexual mores *The Decline of the American Empire* (1986), which won the Cannes Critics' Prize, and *Jesus of Montreal* (1989), which won the Jury Prize at Cannes. In 2004 he won a Best Foreign-Language Film Oscar for *The Barbarian Invasions* (2003).

ar·cane /ɑrˈkein/ *adjective* mysterious, secret; understood by few. □ **ar·cane·ly** *adverb* [Latin *arcanus* from *arcēre* shut up, from *arca* chest]

arch¹ ● *noun* **1 a** a curved structure spanning an opening, acting as a support for a bridge, roof, floor, etc. **b** an arch used in building as an ornament. **c** a monument whose principal feature is an arch. **2** something shaped like an arch, esp. the curved bony structure on the underside of the foot or the arrangement of teeth in the mouth. **●** *verb* **1** *transitive* form into an arch (*the cat arched its back*). **2** *transitive* span like an arch. **3** *intransitive* form an arch. □ **arched** *adjective* [Old French *arche*, ultimately from Latin *arcus* arc]

arch² *adjective* self-consciously or affectedly playful or teasing. □ **arch·ly** *adverb* **arch·ness** *noun* [ARCH-, originally in *arch rogue* etc.]

arch- *combining form* **1** chief, superior (*archbishop; archdiocese; archduke*). **2** pre-eminent of its kind, extreme (esp. in unfavourable senses) (*arch-villain*). [ultimately from Greek *arkhos* chief]

-arch /ɑrk/ *combining form* denoting a kind of ruler (*matriarch; monarch*). [representing Greek *-arkhos*, *arkhēs* ruling, related to *arkhē* rule, *arkhein* begin, take the lead]

Ar·chaean *var. of* ARCHEAN.

archaeo- /ˈɑrkiɒ/ *combining form* (also **archeo-**) **1** ancient or prehistoric (*archaeopteryx*). **2** involving archaeological research.

ar·chae·ol·ogy /ˌɑrkiˈɒlədʒi/ *noun* (also **ar·che·ol·ogy**) the study of human history and prehistory through the excavation of sites and the analysis of physical remains. □ **ar·chaeo·logic** *adjective* **ar·chaeo·logic·al** *adjective* **ar·chae·olo·gist** *noun* **ar·chae·olo·gize** *intransitive verb* (also esp. *Brit.* **-gise**). [modern Latin *archaeologia* from Greek *arkhaiologia* ancient history, from Greek *arkhaios* ancient, from *arkhē* beginning]

ar·chae·op·teryx /ˌɑrkiˈɒptɜrɪks/ *noun* the oldest known fossil bird, *Archaeopteryx lithographica*, from the Jurassic period, with teeth, feathers, and a reptilian tail. [Greek *arkhaios* ancient + *pterux* wing]

Ar·chae·ozoic *var. of* ARCHEOZOIC.

ar·chaic /ɑrˈkeiɪk/ *adjective* **1 a** antiquated. **b** (of a word etc.) no longer in ordinary use, though retained for special purposes. **2** primitive. **3** (often **Archaic**) of an early period of art or culture, esp. the 7th and 6th c. BC in Greece. **4** (**Archaic**) of the period in N American societies between 6000 BC and 500 AD. □ **ar·chaic·ally** *adverb* [French *archaïque* from Greek *arkhaïkos* (as ARCHEAN)]

ar·cha·ism /ˈɑrkeiˌɪzəm/ *noun* **1** the retention or imitation of the old or obsolete, esp. in language or art. **2** an archaic word or expression. □ **ar·cha·is·tic** *adjective* [as ARCHAIZE, -ISM]

ar·cha·ize /ˈɑrkeiˌaiz/ *verb* (also esp. *Brit.* **-ise**) **1** *intransitive* (usu. as **ar·cha·iz·ing** *adjective*) imitate the archaic. **2** *transitive* make (a work of

Consonants: b *but* d *dog* f *few* g *get* h *her* j *yes* k *cat* l *leg* m *man* n *no* p *pen* r *red* s *sit*

art, literature, etc.) imitate the archaic. [Greek *arkhaizō* be old-fashioned, from *arkhaios* ancient]

Arch·angel /ˈɑːkˌeɪndʒəl/ a port of NW Russia, on the White Sea; pop. (est. 2002) 388,000. From December to April the port is usu. icebound. [after the monastery of the *Archangel* Michael, which is situated there]

arch·angel /ˈɑːkˌeɪndʒəl/ *noun* **1** an angel of the highest rank. **2** *Christianity* a member of the eighth order of the nine ranks of heavenly beings (*see* ORDER *noun* 19). ☐ **arch·angel·ic** /-anˈdʒelɪk/ *adjective* [ecclesiastical Latin *archangelus* from ecclesiastical Greek *arkhaggelos* (as ARCH-, ANGEL)]

arch·bishop *noun* the chief bishop of an ecclesiastical province.

arch·bishop·ric *noun* the office or diocese of an archbishop.

arch·deacon *noun* an Anglican cleric ranking below a bishop, or a member of the clergy of similar rank in other Churches. ☐ **arch·deacon·ry** *noun* (*pl.* **-ries**). **arch·deacon·ship** *noun*

arch·dio·cese /ɑːtʃˈdaɪəsɪs, -sɪːz, -sɪs/ *noun* the diocese of an archbishop. ☐ **arch·dio·cesan** /ˌɑːtʃdaɪˈɒsɪsən -zən/ *adjective*

arch·duch·ess *noun hist.* the wife or daughter of an Austrian archduke.

arch·duke *noun hist.* a chief duke, esp. as the title of a prince of the Austrian Empire. ☐ **arch·ducal** *adjective* **arch·duchy** *noun* (*pl.* **-ies**).

Ar·chean /ɑːˈkiːən/ (also **Ar·chaean**) ● *adjective* of or relating to the earlier part of the Precambrian era, from about 4 billion to 2.5 billion years ago. ● *noun* this time. [Greek *arkhaios* ancient, from *arkhē* beginning]

arche·gon·ium /ˌɑːkɪˈɡoʊniəm/ *noun* (*pl.* **arche·gon·ia** /-iə/) *Bot.* the female sex organ in mosses, ferns, conifers, etc. [Latin, diminutive of Greek *arkhegonos* from *arkhe-* chief + *gonos* race]

arch-enemy *noun* (*pl.* **-enemies**) **1** a chief enemy. **2** Satan.

ar·che·ol·ogy *var. of* ARCHAEOLOGY.

Ar·cheo·zoic /ˌɑːkiːəˈzoʊɪk/ (also **Ar·chaeo·zoic**) = ARCHEAN.

arch·eparch /ɑːtʃˈepɑːk/ *noun* an archbishop in an Eastern-rite Church. ☐ **arch·eparchy** *noun*

arch·er *noun* **1** a person who shoots with a bow and arrows. **2** (**Archer**) the zodiacal sign or constellation Sagittarius. [Old French *archier*, ultimately from Latin *arcus* bow]

arch·ery *noun* shooting with a bow and arrows, esp. as a sport.

arche·type /ˈɑːkɪˌtaɪp/ *noun* **1 a** an original model; a prototype. **b** a typical specimen. **2** (in Jungian psychology) an inherited primitive mental image, supposed to be present in the collective unconscious. **3** a recurrent symbol or motif in literature, art, etc. ☐ **arche·typal** /-ˈtaɪpəl/ *adjective* **arche·typ·ical** /-ˈtɪpɪkəl/ *adjective* [Latin *archetypum* from Greek *arkhetupon* (as ARCH-, *tupos* stamp)]

Archi·bald /ˈɑːtʃəˌbɒld/ **Sir Adams George** (1814–1892), Canadian lawyer and politician, Father of Confederation. After serving as Solicitor General (1856–60) and Attorney General (1860–63) for Nova Scotia, he became the leader of the provincial Liberals (1863). He attended all three Confederation conferences, and entered the federal Cabinet in 1867 as the first secretary of state. From 1870–73 he was Lieutenant-Governor of Manitoba and the North-West Territories, and from 1873–83 Lieutenant-Governor of Nova Scotia.

archi·diac·onal /ˌɑːkɪdaɪˈakənəl/ *adjective* of or relating to an archdeacon.

archi·epis·copal /ˌɑːkiːˈpɪskəpəl/ *adjective* of or relating to an archbishop. ☐ **archi·epis·cop·ate** /-pət, -ˌpeɪt/ *noun* [ecclesiastical Latin *archiepiscopus* from Greek *arkhiepiskopos* archbishop]

archil *var. of* ORCHIL.

archi·man·drite /ˌɑːkɪˈmandraɪt/ *noun* **1** the superior of a large monastery or group of monasteries in the Orthodox Church. **2** an honorary title given to a monastic priest. [ecclesiastical Greek *arkhimandrites* (as ARCH-, *mandra* monastery)]

Archimedean screw *noun* (also **Archimedes' screw**) a device of ancient origin for raising water by means of a rotating spiral tube, or a rotating screw in an inclined cylinder.

Archi·medes /ˌɑːkɪˈmiːdiːz/ (*c.*287–212 BC) Greek mathematician and inventor from Syracuse. He discovered the ratio of the radius of a circle to its circumference, and formulas for the surface area and volume of a sphere and of a cylinder. ☐ **Archi·med·ean** /ˌɑːkɪˈmiːdiən/ *adjective*

Archimedes' principle *noun* the law that a body totally or partially immersed in a fluid is subject to an upward force equal in magnitude to the weight of the fluid it displaces.

archi·pel·ago /ˌɑːkɪˈpeləɡoʊ/ *noun* (*pl.* **-agos** or **-agoes**) **1** a group of islands. **2** a sea with many islands. [Italian *arcipelago* from Greek *arkhi-* chief + *pelagos* sea (originally = the Aegean Sea)]

Archi·pen·ko /ˌɑːkɪˈpeŋkoː/ **Alek·sandr Por·fir·evich** (1887–1964), Russian-born US sculptor, who adapted cubist techniques to sculpture and attempted to unite form and colour in a mixed medium; his works include *Walking Woman* (1912).

archi·tect *noun* **1** a person who designs buildings and supervises their construction. **2** (foll. by *of*) a person who brings about a specified thing (*architect of economic reform*). **3** = LANDSCAPE ARCHITECT (*see* LANDSCAPE ARCHITECTURE). **4** = NAVAL ARCHITECT (*see* NAVAL ARCHITECTURE). [Latin *architectus* from Greek *arkhitektōn* (as ARCH-, *tektōn* builder)]

archi·tec·tonic /ˌɑːkɪtekˈtɒnɪk/ ● *adjective* **1** of or relating to architecture; suggesting architectural design or structure. **2** *Metaphysics* of or relating to the systematization of knowledge. ● *noun* (in *pl.*; usu. treated as *sing.*) **1** the scientific study of architecture. **2** the study of the systematization of knowledge. [Greek *arkhitektonikos* (as ARCHITECT)]

archi·tec·ture *noun* **1** the art or science of designing and constructing buildings. *See also* LANDSCAPE ARCHITECTURE, NAVAL ARCHITECTURE, MARINE ARCHITECTURE. **2** the style of a building as regards design and construction (*Gothic architecture*). **3** buildings or other structures collectively. **4** (usu. foll. by *of*) the structure or design of something (*the architecture of the human body*). **5** *Computing* the conceptual structure of the various processing elements in a computer or computer system, e.g. memory organization, instruction set, user interface, etc., and their interconnection. ☐ **archi·tec·tur·al** *adjective* **archi·tec·tur·al·ly** *adverb* [Latin *architectura* from *architectus* ARCHITECT)]

archi·trave /ˈɑːkɪˌtreɪv/ *noun* **1** (in classical architecture) a main beam resting across the tops of columns. **2** the moulded frame around a doorway or window. **3** a moulding around the exterior of an arch. [French from Italian (as ARCH-, *trave* from Latin *trabs trabis* beam)]

ar·chive /ˈɑːkaɪv/ ● *noun* **1** (usu. in *pl.*) a collection of public, corporate or institutional documents or records. **2** (usu. in *pl.*) the place where these are stored. **3** *Computing* a store of (usu. large amounts of) data kept in machine-readable form but not necessarily on a disk. ● *transitive verb* **1** place or store in an archive. **2** *Computing* transfer (data) to a store of less frequently used files, e.g. from disk to tape. ☐ **ar·chiv·al** /ɑːˈkaɪvəl/ *adjective* [French *archives* (pl.) from Latin *archi(v)a* from Greek *arkheia* public records, from *arkhē* government]

ar·chiv·ist /ˈɑːkɪvɪst/ *noun* a person who maintains and is in charge of archives.

archi·volt /ˈɑːkɪˌvoːlt/ *noun* **1** a band of mouldings around the lower curve of an arch. **2** the lower curve itself from impost to impost. [French *archivolte* or Italian *archivolto* (as ARC, VAULT)]

ar·chon /ˈɑːkɒn, ˈɑːkən/ *noun* each of the nine chief magistrates in ancient Athens. ☐ **ar·chon·ship** *noun* [Greek *arkhōn* ruler, = pres. part. of *arkhō* rule]

arch·rival *noun* a principal rival.

arch·way *noun* **1** a vaulted passage. **2** an arched entrance.

-archy /ɑːki/ *combining form* denoting a type of rule or government (*monarchy*; *oligarchy*). [representing Greek *arkh(e)ia* government, leadership]

arc lamp *noun* (also **arc light**) a light source using an electric arc between carbon electrodes and producing extremely intense white light.

arco *Music* ● *adverb* using a bow to sound the strings of a violin, double bass, etc. (*compare* PIZZICATO). ● *adjective* (of a note, passage, etc.) performed arco. ● *noun* (*pl.* **archi** /ˈɑːki/) a note, passage, etc. played arco. [Italian *arco* bow]

ARCT *abbreviation* (in Canada) Associateship Diploma of the Royal Conservatory of Toronto.

Arc·tic /ˈɑːktɪk, ˈɑːtɪk/ ● *noun* **1 a** the area north of the Arctic Circle. **b** an extremely cold, arid, treeless ecological zone including this and, in Canada, the shores of Hudson Bay, Ungava, and the Labrador coast. *See also* HIGH ARCTIC, LOW ARCTIC. **2** (**arctic**) esp. *US* = ARCTIC BOOT. ● *adjective* **1 a** of the Arctic. **b** designating animals and plants of northern species. **2** (**arctic**) designed for use in arctic conditions (*arctic sleeping bag*). **3** (**arctic**) (esp. of weather) very cold. [Old French *artique* from Latin *ar(c)ticus* from Greek *arktikos* from *arktos* bear, Ursa Major]

Arctic Archipelago the group of islands to the north of mainland Canada, including Baffin, Ellesmere and Victoria Islands.

Arctic Bay 1 a small harbour of Adams Sound, off Admiralty Inlet, situated along the western coast of the Borden Peninsula, Baffin Island. **2** a hamlet situated on the bay; pop. (2001) 646. [*Arctic*, a whaling ship that visited the area *c.*1872]

arctic boot *noun* (in *pl.*) heavy felt-lined rubber-soled boots suitable for extremely cold weather.

Arctic char *noun* a freshwater fish of the north, *Salvelinus alpinus*, with a delicate pink flesh similar to salmon.

Arctic Circle the parallel of latitude 66°33′ north of the equator. It marks the northernmost point at which the sun is visible on the northern winter solstice and the southernmost point at which the midnight sun can be seen on the northern summer solstice.

Arctic Coastal Plain a physiographic region of N Canada comprising that part of the NWT and Nunavut, both mainland and insular, which lies between the Arctic Circle and the 80th parallel and borders on the Arctic Ocean. It includes the Mackenzie Delta region around Tuktoyaktuk and Inuvik.

Arctic cotton *noun* a northern sedge, *Eriophorum callitrix*, bearing fruiting heads with long white cottony hairs.

Arctic fox *noun* a small fox, *Alopex lagopus*, native to the Arctic, whose coat turns white or grey-blue in winter.

Arctic grayling *noun* a highly coloured grayling, *Thymallus arcticus*, abundant in N Canada, much prized by fly fishermen.

Arctic ground squirrel *noun* a large squirrel, *Spermophilus parryii*, with a dappled greyish-brown coat, of N Canada and Asia.

Arctic hare *noun* a large hare, *Lepus arcticus*, whose coat is brown in summer and white in winter, inhabiting the tundra of Canada and Greenland.

Arctic haze *noun* a smog-like form of air pollution found in the Arctic, caused by pollutants originating at northern coal-based industrial centres.

Arctic loon *noun* a loon, *Gavia arctica*, inhabiting the circumpolar regions, esp. the Pacific coast of N America.

Arctic Lowlands (also called **Arctic Platform**) a physiographic region of N Canada including Victoria, Prince of Wales and King William Islands, as well as parts of Somerset, Baffin, Devon and Ellesmere Islands.

Arctic Ocean the ocean surrounding the North Pole, enclosed almost completely by Eurasia, N America and Greenland.

Arctic poppy *noun* any of several golden flowers of the north, including *Papaver radicatum* and *P. macounii*, with four large petals.

Arctic Red River a river flowing north about 500 km (310 mi) from the Yukon–NWT border to the town of Tsiigehtchic, formerly also called Arctic Red River, where it joins the Mackenzie.

Arctic Region a physiographic region of N Canada, north of the Arctic Circle, consisting of the Arctic Coastal Plain and the Arctic Lowlands.

Arctic sea smoke *noun* a steam fog which rises from bodies of water as colder air moves over them.

Arctic tern *noun* a tern, *Sterna paradisaea*, which breeds in the Arctic and migrates to the Antarctic.

Arctic willow *noun* any of several species of small shrubs native to the Arctic and cultivated as ornamentals, esp. *Salix arctica*.

Arc·turus /ɑrkˈtjʊrəs, -ˈtjʊərəs/ the brightest star in the northern sky, in the constellation Boötes. [Greek *arktos* bear + *ouros* guardian, because of its position in a line with the tail of Ursa Major]

arc·u·ate /ˈɔrkjuːət, -eit/ *adjective Med.* shaped like a bow; curved. [Latin *arcuatus* past participle of *arcuare* curve, from *arcus* bow, curve]

arc welding *noun* a method of welding using an electric arc to melt metal.

-ard *suffix* **1** forming nouns in depreciatory senses (*drunkard*; *sluggard*). **2** forming nouns in other senses (*bollard*; *Spaniard*; *wizard*). [Middle English & Old French from German *-hard* hardy (in proper names)]

Arden ▸ 1 Eliza·beth (born Florence Nightingale Graham) (*c.*1880–1966), Canadian-born businesswoman. She built up an international chain of beauty salons and an extensive range of cosmetics. **2 Jann** (born Jann Arden Richards) (b.1962), Canadian pop singer. Her song 'Insensitive' was a smash hit and her albums have consistently achieved huge sales.

Ar·dennes /ɑrˈden/ a forested upland region including parts of Belgium, Luxembourg, and N France, the scene of fierce fighting in both World Wars.

ar·dent *adjective* **1** zealous, eager; (of persons or feelings) fervent, passionate. **2** burning. □ **ar·dent·ly** *adverb* [Old French *ardant* from Latin *ardens -entis* from *ardēre* burn]

Ardna·mur·chan /ˌɑrdnəˈmɜrkən/ a peninsula on the coast of Highland Region in W Scotland. Ardnamurchan Point is the most westerly point on the British mainland.

ar·dour *noun* (also **ardor**) zeal, burning enthusiasm, passion. [Latin *ardor -oris* from *ardēre* burn]

Ardox nail *noun Cdn proprietary* a type of nail with a spiral shaft.

ar·du·ous *adjective* **1** hard to achieve, overcome or endure; laborious, strenuous. **2** steep, difficult (*an arduous path*). □ **ar·du·ous·ly** *adverb* **ar·du·ous·ness** *noun* [Latin *arduus* steep, difficult]

are[1] *2nd sing. present & 1st, 2nd, 3rd pl. present of* BE.

are[2] /er, ɑr/ *noun* a metric unit of measure, one-hundredth of a hectare, equal to 100 square metres. Abbr.: **a**. [French from Latin AREA]

area *noun* **1** the extent or measure of a surface (*over a large area*; *3 hectares in area*; *the area of a triangle*). **2** a region or tract (*the southern area*). **3** a space allocated for a specific purpose (*dining area*; *camping area*). **4** a part of something (*an area of the brain*). **5** the scope or range of an activity or study (*very knowledgeable in the area of botany*). **6** a sunken space in front of a building, usu. leading to the basement. □ **areal** *adjective* [Latin, = vacant piece of level ground]

area code *noun N Amer.* a three-digit prefix to local phone numbers used in making calls from one telephone area to another.

area municipality *noun Cdn* (*Ont.*) a local municipality within a larger regional municipality.

area rug *noun N Amer.* a rug covering part of a floor only, not extending to the walls.

area·way *noun N Amer.* = AREA 6.

areca /ˈarəkə, əˈriːkə/ *noun* any tropical palm of the genus *Areca*, native to Asia. [Portuguese from Malayalam *ádekka*]

areca nut *noun* the astringent seed of a species of areca, *A. catechu*. Also called BETEL NUT.

areg *pl. of* ERG[2].

arena *noun* **1** an enclosed building containing an open, usu. oblong central area (esp. an ice surface) for sports, entertainment or recreation, surrounded by seats for spectators. **2** the central part of an amphitheatre, bullring, stadium, etc., in which the action occurs. **3** a scene of conflict; a sphere of action or discussion (*the political arena*). [Latin (h)*arena* sand, sand-strewn place of combat]

ar·en·aceous /ˌerɪˈneiʃəs, ˌarɪ-/ *adjective* **1** (of rocks) containing sand; having a sandy texture. **2** sand-like. **3** (of plants) growing in sand. [Latin *arenaceus* (as ARENA, -ACEOUS)]

arena rock *noun* rock music as performed in arenas, characterized by extravagant lighting and staging.

arena stage *noun* a stage situated with the audience all around it.

Ar·endt /ˈerənt, ˈɑrənt/ **Han·nah** (1906–75) German-born US political philosopher, known for her work on the nature of totalitarianism, violence, revolution, and other features of modern political life.

aren't *contraction* **1** are not. **2** (in *interrogative*) am not (*aren't I coming too?*).

areola /əˈriələ/ *noun* (*pl.* **areo·lae** /-liː/) **1** *Anat.* a circular pigmented area, esp. that surrounding a nipple. **2** any of the spaces between lines on a surface, e.g. those between the veins of a leaf or an insect's wing. □ **areo·lar** *adjective* [Latin, diminutive of *area* AREA]

Areop·agus /ˌerɪˈɒpəgəs/ *noun* the highest governmental council and (later) a judicial court of ancient Athens. [Greek *Areios pagos* hill of Ares, just west of the Acropolis, where the council met]

Are·quipa /ˌarəˈkiːpə/ a city in the Andes of S Peru; pop. (est. 2002) 733,900.

Ares /ˈeriːz/ *Gk Myth* the war god, son of Zeus and Hera. In Rome he was identified with Mars.

arête /aˈret/ *noun* a sharp narrow mountain ridge formed by the meeting of adjacent glacial valleys. [French from Latin *arista* ear of corn, fishbone, spine]

Are·thusa /ˌarəˈθuːzə/ *Gk Myth* a nymph who was changed into a fountain by Artemis while fleeing from the river god Alpheus.

Are·tino /arəˈtiːnoː/ **Pietro** (1492–1556), Italian poet and dramatist, who is known for his satirical literary attacks on contemporary political figures.

arf *noun* a representation of a dog's bark. [imitative]

ar·gali /ˈɑrgəli/ *noun* (*pl.* same) a large Asiatic wild sheep, *Ovis ammon*, with massive horns. [Mongol]

Argen·son /arʒɑ̃ˈsɔ̃/ **Pierre de Voyer d'** (*c.*1625–1709), governor of New France 1658–61. His suggestion to increase agricultural settlement in the colony was not supported by the French government.

ar·gent /ˈɑrdʒənt/ *noun & adjective Heraldry* silver; silvery white. [French from Latin *argentum*]

argen·tif·er·ous /ˌɑrdʒənˈtɪfərəs/ *adjective* containing natural deposits of silver. [Latin *argentum* + -FEROUS]

Argen·tina /ˌɑːdʒən'tiːnə/ a republic occupying much of the southern part of S America; pop. (2001) 36,223,947; capital, Buenos Aires. Argentina lies between the Andes foothills and the Atlantic coast, and consists mainly of extensive plains, including the treeless and semi-arid pampas. Argentina played a crucial role in the overthrow of European rule in the rest of S America. In 1982 the Argentinian claim to the Falkland Islands led to an unsuccessful war with Britain.
□ **Argen·tine** *adjective & noun* **Argen·tin·ian** /ˌɑːdʒən'tɪnɪən/ *adjective & noun* [Spanish, from Latin *argentum* silver, which the region of the Plate River exported]

Argen·tine /'ɑːdʒən,tain, -,tiːn/ *noun* an older name for Argentina.

argen·tine /'ɑːdʒən,tain, -,tiːn/ *adjective* of silver; silvery. [French *argentin* from *argent* silver]

argh /ɑːg/ *interjection* expressing usu. feigned pain, disgust, or exasperation.

argil /'ɑːdʒɪl/ *noun* clay, esp. that used in pottery. □ **ar·gil·la·ceous** *adjective* [ultimately from Greek *argillos* from *argos* white]

ar·gil·lite /'ɑːdʒɪl,ait/ *noun* a metamorphic rock of a softness between shale and slate, used in Haida sculpture. [Latin *argilla* clay + -ITE[1]]

ar·gin·ine /'ɑːdʒɪ,niːn, -,nain/ *noun* an amino acid present in many animal proteins and an essential nutrient in the vertebrate diet. [German *Arginin*, of uncertain origin]

Ar·give /'ɑːgaiv/ ● *adjective* **1** of Argos in ancient Greece. **2** *literary* (esp. in Homeric contexts) Greek. ● *noun* **1** a citizen of Argos. **2** *literary* (usu. in *pl.*) a Greek. [Latin *Argivus* from Greek *Argeios*]

argol *noun* crude potassium hydrogen tartrate, formed on the sides of wine vats as a by-product of grape fermentation. [Anglo-French *argoile*, of unknown origin]

argon *noun Chem.* an inert gaseous element, of the noble gas group and forming almost 1% of the earth's atmosphere; used in arc welding and semiconductor crystals, and to fill light bulbs and vacuum tubes. Symbol: **Ar**; at. no.: 18. [Greek, neuter of *argos* idle, from *a-* not + *ergon* work]

Argo·nauts /'ɑːgə,nɔːts/ *plural noun Gk Legend* the heroes who accompanied Jason on board the ship *Argo* on the quest for the Golden Fleece. [Greek, 'sailor in the *Argo*']

Argos /'ɑːgɒs/ a city in the NE Peloponnese of Greece; pop. (1991) 22,289. One of the oldest cities of ancient Greece, it was in the 7th c. BC the dominant city of the Peloponnese and the W Aegean.

ar·gosy /'ɑːgəsi/ *noun* (*pl.* **-sies**) *literary* a large merchant ship. [prob. from Italian *Ragusea (nave)* vessel from Ragusa (now Dubrovnik) or Venice]

argot /'ɑːgəʊ, -gət/ *noun* the jargon of a group or class, formerly esp. of criminals. [French: origin unknown]

argu·able *adjective* **1** capable of being argued. **2** supportable by argument. **3** questionable, open to dispute. □ **argu·ably** *adverb*

argue *verb* (**argues**, **argued**, **argu·ing**) **1** *intransitive* (often foll. by *with*, *about*, etc.) exchange views or opinions, especially heatedly or contentiously; quarrel. **2** *transitive & intransitive* (often foll. by *that* + clause) indicate; maintain by reasoning. **3** *intransitive* (usu. foll. by *for*, *against*) provide reasons supporting or challenging something (*argued against the policy*). **4** *transitive* challenge, dispute (*argued the referee's call*). **5** *transitive* treat by reasoning (*argue the point*). **6** *transitive* (foll. by *into*, *out of*) persuade (*argued me into going*). **7** *transitive* suggest, indicate (*a twitch that argued anxiety*). □ **argue the toss** *esp. Brit. informal* dispute a decision or choice already made. □ **argu·er** *noun* [Old French *arguer* from Latin *argutari* prattle, frequentative of *arguere* make clear, prove, accuse]

argu·ment *noun* **1** an exchange of views, esp. a contentious or prolonged one. **2** (often foll. by *for*, *against*) a reason advanced; a reasoning process (*an argument for conscription*). **3** a summary of the subject matter or line of reasoning of a book. **4** *Math.* an independent variable determining the value of a function. **5** *Computing* the part of a command specifying which file etc. the command is to be executed on.

argu·men·ta·tion *noun* **1** methodical reasoning. **2** debate or argument.

argu·men·ta·tive *adjective* **1** fond of arguing; quarrelsome. **2** using methodical reasoning. □ **argu·men·ta·tive·ly** *adverb* **argu·men·ta·tive·ness** *noun*

Argus 1 *Gk myth* a monster with many eyes, used by Hera to watch over Io. He was killed by Hermes, and Hera then used his eyes to deck the peacock's tail. **2** *Gk Legend* Ulysses' dog, who recognized his master on his return from Troy after an absence of 20 years.

argus *noun* **1** (**Argus**) a watchful guardian. **2** an Asiatic pheasant having markings on its tail resembling eyes. **3** a butterfly having markings resembling eyes. [ARGUS]

Argus-eyed *adjective* vigilant.

argy-bargy /ˌɑːdʒi'bɑːdʒi/ *noun esp. Brit. jocular* (*pl.* **-bargies**) a dispute or wrangle. □ **argy-bargy·ing** *noun* [originally Scots]

ar·gyle /'ɑːgail/ (also **ar·gyll**) ● *adjective* designating a knitting pattern with diamonds of various colours on a single background colour. ● *noun* **1** this pattern. **2** (in *pl.*) socks in this pattern. [*Argyll* branch of the Campbell clan, on whose tartan the pattern is based]

Ar·gyll and Bute an administrative region in the west of Scotland, created in 1996.

Argyll·shire /ɑː'gailʃir/ a former county on the west coast of Scotland. It was divided between Strathclyde and Highland regions in 1975 and in 1996 became part of Argyll and Bute.

Århus *see* AARHUS.

aria /'ɑːriə, 'eriə/ *noun Music* a long, accompanied song for solo voice in an opera, oratorio, etc. (*compare* RECITATIVE, ARIOSO). [Italian]

Ari·adne /ˌeri'adni/ *Gk Legend* the daughter of Minos and Pasiphae of Crete. She gave Theseus the thread by which he found his way back out of the Minotaur's labyrinth. Deserted by Theseus on the island of Naxos, she was rescued by Dionysus, who married her and made her immortal.

-arian *suffix* forming adjectives and nouns meaning '(a person) concerned with or believing in' (*agrarian*; *antiquarian*; *humanitarian*; *vegetarian*). [Latin *-arius* (see -ARY[1])]

Arian[1] /'eriən, 'a-/ ● *noun* an adherent of the doctrines of Arius. ● *adjective* of or concerning Arius or his doctrines. □ **Arian·ism** /'eriənɪzəm/ *noun*

Arian[2] /'eriən/ *noun* = ARIES 2b.

Arias Sán·chez /'ɑːriəs 'santʃes/ **Oscar** (b.1941), Costa Rican political leader, president 1986–90, who was awarded the 1987 Nobel Peace Prize for his efforts to achieve peace in Central America.

arid *adjective* **1 a** (of ground, climate, etc.) extremely dry, parched. **b** too dry to support vegetation; barren. **2** emotionless, uninteresting (*arid writing*). □ **arid·ity** *noun* **arid·ly** *adverb* **arid·ness** *noun* [Latin *aridus* from *arēre* be dry]

Ariel /'eriəl/ **1** *Astronomy* satellite I of Uranus, the twelfth closest to the planet, discovered in 1851 (diameter 1,160 km). **2** a series of six American and British satellites devoted to studies of the ionosphere and X-ray astronomy, launched between 1962 and 1979. [the name of a fairy in Shakespeare's *The Tempest*]

Aries /'eriːz/ *noun* (*pl.* same) **1** a constellation between Pisces and Taurus, traditionally regarded as contained in the figure of a ram. **2 a** the first sign of the zodiac. **b** a person born when the sun is in this sign, usu. between 21 March and 19 April. [Latin, = ram]

ari·et·ta /ˌɑːri'etə, ˌa-, ˌe-/ *noun* a shorter and simpler aria. [Italian]

aright *adverb* rightly, correctly.

Arik·ara /ə'rɪkərə/ ● *noun* **1** (*pl.* same or **-aras**) a member of an Aboriginal people of the Great Plains, living mainly in N and S Dakota. **2** the Caddoan language of the Arikara. ● *adjective* of the Arikara or their language. [origin uncertain, possibly = 'horn', referring to a traditional hairstyle]

aril *noun Bot.* an extra seed covering, often coloured and hairy or fleshy, e.g. the outer covering of the nutmeg which yields mace. □ **aril·late** *adjective* [modern Latin *arillus*: compare medieval Latin *arilli* dried grape pits]

ari·oso /ɑːri'ɔːsɔː, ari-, eri-/ *noun Music* **1** a recitative with expressive qualities similar to those of an aria. **2** a short melodious passage at the beginning or end of an aria. [Italian]

Ari·osto /ˌeri'ɒstɔː, ˌari-, ˌari-/ **Ludo·vico** (1474–1533), Italian poet. His *Orlando Furioso* (final version 1532), was the greatest of the Italian romantic epics.

-arious *suffix* forming adjectives (*gregarious*; *vicarious*). [Latin *-arius* (see -ARY[1]) + -OUS]

arise *intransitive verb* (*past* **arose**; *past participle* **arisen**, **aris·ing**) **1** begin to exist; originate. **2** (usu. foll. by *from*, *out of*) result (*accidents can arise from carelessness*). **3** come to one's notice; emerge (*the question of payment arose*). **4** rise, esp. from a seated position or from sleep. [Old English *ārīsan* (as A-[2], RISE)]

Aris·tar·chus /ˌeri'stɑːkəs, ˌari-/ **1 Aristarchus of Samos** (3rd c. BC), Greek astronomer. He advanced the theory of a heliocentric universe, with the earth rotating on its axis and the sun larger than the earth. **2 Aristarchus of Samo·thrace** (*c.*217–145 BC), librarian at Alexandria who produced critical editions of the writings of Homer,

Hesiod, Pindar, and other Greek authors. He is regarded as the originator of scientific scholarship in the West.

Aris·tide /ˌarɪsˈtiːd/ **Jean-Bertrand** (b.1953), Haitian president (1991–96, 2001–). A former Catholic priest, he won the country's first legitimate democratic presidential election in 1990. In September 1991 he was exiled by the military, but with US help was back in power from 1994 to 1996. Amidst general allegations of widespread corruption he was elected again in 2001, but was forced to flee the country again in early 2004.

Aris·tides /ˌerɪˈstaidiːs/ 'the Just' (5th c. BC), Athenian statesman and general, renowned for his honesty. He commanded the Athenian army at the battle of Plataea in 479 BC, and was subsequently prominent in founding the Athenian Empire.

Aris·tip·pus /erɪˈstɪpəs/ (known as Aristippus the Elder) (late 5th c. BC), Greek philosopher, who is generally regarded to be the founder of the Cyrenaic school. His grandson Aristippus the Younger further developed his philosophy.

aristo noun (pl. **aris·tos**) informal an aristocrat. [abbreviation]

aris·toc·ra·cy noun (pl. **-cies**) **1 a** the highest class in society; the nobility. **b** the nobility as a ruling class. **2 a** government by the nobility or a privileged group. **b** a state governed in this way. **3** (often foll. by of) the best representatives or upper echelons (aristocracy of intellect; aristocracy of labour). [Greek aristokratia from aristos best + kratia (as -CRACY)]

aris·to·crat /əˈrɪstəˌkrat/ noun a member of the nobility. [as ARISTOCRACY)]

aris·to·crat·ic /əˌrɪstəˈkratɪk, ˌerɪstəˈkratɪk/ adjective **1** of or relating to the aristocracy. **2** grand; stylish. **b** distinguished in manners or bearing. □ **aris·to·crat·ic·ally** adverb [as ARISTOCRACY]

Aris·topha·nes /ˌerɪˈstɒfəniːz/ (c.450–c.385 BC) Athenian comic playwright. Among his eleven surviving plays are Clouds, Lysistrata, and Frogs, which are characterized by fantasy, exuberance of language, and satirical depictions of prominent people.

Aris·totle /ˈerɪˌstɒtəl, ˈarɪ-/ (384–322 BC), Athenian philosopher. A pupil of Plato and tutor of Alexander the Great, Aristotle founded a school and library (the Lyceum) in Athens in 335 BC. He maintained that knowledge is derived from the experience of the senses and advocated inductive reasoning. His writings on logic, physical science, zoology, psychology, metaphysics, ethics, politics, and rhetoric have been immensely influential in Western thought. □ **Aris·to·tel·ian** /ˌerɪstəˈtiːliən, ˌarɪ-, -ˌrɪstə-/ noun & adjective **Aris·to·tel·ian·ism** noun

Arita /əˈriːtə/ noun (usu. attributive) a type of Japanese porcelain characterized by asymmetric decoration. [Arita in Japan]

arith·met·ic ● noun **1 a** the science of numbers. **b** one's knowledge of this (have improved my arithmetic). **2** the use of numbers; computation (a problem involving arithmetic). **●** adjective (also **arith·met·ic·al**) of or concerning arithmetic. □ **arith·met·ician** /əˌrɪθməˈtɪʃən/ noun [Greek arithmētikē (tekhnē) art of counting, from arithmos number]

arithmetic mean noun Math. **1** the central number in an arithmetic progression. **2** = AVERAGE noun 2.

arithmetic progression noun Math. **1** an increase or decrease by a constant quantity, e.g. 1, 2, 3, 4, etc., 9, 7, 5, 3, etc. **2** (also **arithmetic sequence**) a sequence of numbers showing this.

arithmetic series noun (also **arithmetical series**) Math. **1** the sum of an arithmetic progression. **2** = ARITHMETIC PROGRESSION.

-arium suffix forming nouns usu. denoting a place (aquarium; planetarium). [Latin, neuter of adjectives in -arius: see -ARY¹]

Arius /ˈerɪəs/ (c.250–c.336) a priest of Alexandria who denied the divinity of Christ, maintaining that the Son of God was created by the Father. His views were declared heretical by the Council of Nicaea in 325, but remained widespread until the conversion of the Franks to Catholicism in 496.

Ariz. abbreviation Arizona.

Ari·zona /ˌerəˈzoːnə/ a state of the southwestern US, on the border with Mexico; pop. (2000) 5,130,632; capital, Phoenix. □ **Ari·zon·an** noun & adjective

Ar·juna /ˈardʒunə/ Hinduism a Kshatriya prince in the Mahabharata, one of the two main characters in the Bhagavad-Gita.

Ark. abbreviation Arkansas.

ark noun **1** = NOAH'S ARK 1. **2** = HOLY ARK. **3** (**Ark**) = ARK OF THE COVENANT. **4** archaic a chest or box. □ **out of the ark** informal very antiquated. [Old English ærc from Latin arca chest]

Arkan·sas /ˈarkən.sɒ/ a state of the south central US; pop. (2002) 2,673,400; capital, Little Rock. □ **Arkan·san** /arˈkansən/ noun & adjective

Arkhan·gelsk see ARCHANGEL.

Ark of the Covenant noun (also **Ark of the Testimony**) the wooden chest which in Biblical times contained the tablets of the Law given to Moses by God, the Hebrews' most sacred symbol of God.

Ark of the Law noun = HOLY ARK.

Ark·wright, **Sir Rich·ard** (1732–92), English cotton manufacturer who invented a water-powered machine for spinning cotton thread strong enough to be used in weaving.

Arles /arl/ a city in SE France; pop. (1999) 50,453. It was the capital of the medieval kingdom of Arles, formed in the 10th c. by the union of the kingdoms of Provence and Burgundy.

Ar·ling·ton 1 a county in N Virginia, forming a suburb of Washington on the right bank of the Potomac River. It is the site of the Pentagon and the Arlington National Cemetery. **2** an industrial city in N Texas, between Dallas and Fort Worth; pop. (2002) 332,969.

arm¹ noun **1** each of the two upper limbs of the human body from the shoulder to the hand. **2 a** the forelimb of an animal. **b** the flexible limb of an invertebrate animal, e.g. an octopus. **3** the ability to throw (that pitcher has an impressive arm). **4 a** anything resembling an arm in function or in being attached to a larger mass or main stem (a turntable arm; an arm of the sea). **b** the sleeve of a garment. **c** the side part of a chair etc., used to support a sitter's arm. **d** a large branch of a tree. **e** a branch of a spiral galaxy. **f** Genetics either of the two sections of a chromosome. **g** either of the pieces of an eyeglass frame that extend from the front backwards over the wearer's ears. **5** authority; power (the long arm of the law). □ **an arm and a leg** a large sum of money. **arm in arm** (of two or more persons) with arms linked. **as long as your** (or **my**) **arm** informal very long. **at arm's length 1** as far as an arm can reach. **2** far enough to avoid undue familiarity or influence. **give one's right arm** sacrifice a great deal. **in arms** (of a baby) too young to walk. **in a person's arms** embraced. **on one's arm** supported by one's arm. **under one's arm** between the arm and the body. **within arm's reach** reachable without moving one's position. **with open arms** cordially. □ **arm·ful** noun (pl. **-fuls**). **arm·less** adjective [Old English from Germanic]

arm² ● noun **1** (usu. in pl.) **a** a weapon. **b** = FIREARM. **2** (in pl.) the military profession. **3** a branch of the military, e.g. infantry, cavalry, artillery, etc. **4** a subdivision of an organization, devoted to a specific function or jurisdiction (research arm of a corporation). **5** (in pl.) heraldic devices (coat of arms). **●** transitive verb & reflexive **1** supply with weapons. **2** supply with tools or other requisites or advantages; equip (armed with binoculars and a camera). **3** make (a bomb etc.) able to explode. **4** activate (armed the burglar alarm). □ **in arms** armed. **lay down one's arms** cease fighting. **take up arms** begin fighting. **under arms** ready for war or battle. **up in arms** (usu. foll. by against, about) actively rebelling. □ **arm·less** adjective [Old French armes (pl.), armer, from Latin arma arms, fittings]

ar·mada /arˈmɒdə/ noun **1** a fleet of warships. **2** (**Armada**) = SPANISH ARMADA. [Spanish from Romanic armata army]

arma·dillo /ˌarməˈdɪloː/ noun (pl. **-los**) any nocturnal insect-eating mammal of the family Dasypodidae, native to S America and southern N America, with large claws for digging and a body covered in bony plates, often rolling itself into a ball when threatened. [Spanish diminutive of armado armed man, from Latin armatus past participle of armare ARM²]

Arma·ged·don /ˌarməˈgedən/ noun **1 a** New Testament the last battle between good and evil before the Day of Judgment. **b** the place where this will be fought. **2** a vast and deadly armed conflict, esp. one causing the end of the world through nuclear destruction. [Greek from Hebrew har megiddōn hill of Megiddo: see Rev. 16:16]

Ar·magh /arˈmɒ/ **1** one of the Six Counties of Northern Ireland, formerly an administrative area. **2** the chief town of this county; pop. (est. 2002) 15,200. It was the seat of the kings of Ulster from the 3rd c. BC to AD 333, and became the religious centre of Ireland in AD 445, when St. Patrick was made archbishop of Armagh.

Ar·ma·gnac /ˈarmənjak/ a brandy from the region of Armagnac in SW France.

arma·ment /ˈarməmənt/ noun **1** (often in pl.) military weapons and equipment, esp. guns on a warship or missiles on an airplane. **2** the process of equipping for war. **3** a force equipped for war. [Latin armamentum (as ARM², -MENT)]

arma·men·tar·ium /ˌarməmənˈteriəm/ noun (pl. **arma·men·tar·ia** /-riə/) **1** the instruments, drugs, etc. available for medical use. **2** the resources available for a given task. [Latin, = arsenal]

Ar·mani /arˈmɒni/ **Gior·gio** (b.1936), Italian designer of high-quality fashions, esp. men's suits.

ar·ma·ture /ˈarməˌtʃər/ noun **1 a** the rotating coil or coils of an

---

Consonants: b but   d dog   f few   g get   h her   j yes   k cat   l leg   m man   n no   p pen   r red   s sit

electric motor or generator. **b** any moving part of an electrical machine in which a voltage is induced by a magnetic field. **2** a piece of soft iron placed in contact with the poles of a horseshoe magnet to preserve its power. **3** *Biol.* the protective covering of an animal or plant. **4** a metal framework on which a sculpture is moulded with clay or similar material. **5** *archaic* arms; armour. [French from Latin *armatura* armour (as ARM², -URE)]

arm band *noun* a band worn around the upper arm to hold up a shirt sleeve or as a form of identification etc.

arm candy *noun* an attractive companion of the opposite sex with whom one is seen in public.

arm·chair *noun* **1** a usu. upholstered chair with side supports for the arms. **2** (*attributive*) theoretical rather than active or practical (*an armchair quarterback*).

armed *adjective* **1** equipped with or characterized by the use of weapons. **2** (foll. by *with*) equipped, provided or prepared. **3** (of a weapon, alarm system, etc.) activated.

armed forces *plural noun* **1** (**Armed Forces**) the official name of the united military services in Canada. **2** (also **armed services**) the combined military services of a country or group of countries.

Ar·menia /ɑrˈmiːniə/ **1** a landlocked country in the Caucasus of SE Europe; pop. (est. 2002) 3,330,100; capital, Yerevan. **2** a region south of the Caucasus including the modern Republic of Armenia and parts of the countries bordering it. In 1915 the Turks, fearing their Armenian subjects were sympathizing with Russia and the Allies in the First World War, forcibly deported 1,750,000 Armenians to the deserts of Syria and Mesopotamia; more than 600,000 were killed or died on forced marches.

Ar·men·ian ● *noun* **1 a** a native of the region or the republic of Armenia. **b** a person of Armenian descent. **2** the language of the Armenian people. ● *adjective* of or relating to Armenia, its language, or the Christian Church established there *c.*300.

Armenian Church (in full **Armenian Apostolic Orthodox Church**) an independent Christian Church established in Armenia since *c.*300. Though rejecting the Council of Chalcedon, the Armenian Church has been influenced by Roman and Byzantine as well as Syrian traditions. A small Armenian Catholic Church also exists.

arm·hole *noun* an opening in a garment for the arm.

ar·mil·lary sphere /ɑrˈmɪləri/ *noun hist.* a representation of the celestial globe constructed from metal rings and showing the equator, the tropics, etc. [modern Latin *armillaris* from Latin *armilla* bracelet]

Ar·min·ian /ɑrˈmɪniən/ ● *adjective* relating to the doctrine of Jacobus Arminius. ● *noun* an adherent of this doctrine. □ **Ar·min·ian·ism** *noun*

Ar·min·ius ▸ **1** /ˈɑrmɪniəs/ (*c.*18 BC–AD 19), Germanic chieftain, who led the Germanic resistance to Roman colonization in 9 AD. **2** /ɑrˈmɪniəs/ **Jaco·bus** (Latinized name of Jacob Harmensen, 1560–1609), Dutch Protestant theologian who rejected the Calvinist doctrines of predestination and election.

armis·tice /ˈɑrmɪstɪs/ *noun* a cessation of hostilities by common agreement of the opposing sides; a truce. [French *armistice* or modern Latin *armistitium*, from *arma* arms (ARM²) + *-stitium* stoppage]

Armistice Day *noun* the anniversary of the armistice of 11 Nov. 1918 (*compare* REMEMBRANCE DAY).

arm·let *noun* **1** an ornamental band worn around the arm. **2** a small inlet of the sea or branch of a river.

arm·load *noun* esp. *N Amer.* the quantity that can be carried in the arms; an armful.

ar·moire /ɑrmˈwɑr/ *noun* a large wardrobe or cupboard, esp. one that is ornate or antique. [French]

ar·mor *var.* of ARMOUR.

ar·mor·er *var.* of ARMOURER.

ar·mor·ial /ɑrˈmɔriəl/ *adjective* of or relating to heraldry or heraldic arms. [from *armory* heraldry, from Old French *armoierie* (see ARMOURY) + -AL]

ar·mory *var.* of ARMOURY.

ar·mour (also **armor**) ● *noun* **1** protective clothing, made of fabric, metal plates, or chain mail, designed to deflect or absorb the impact of weapons, bullets, etc. **2 a** (in full **armour-plate**) a protective metal covering for an armed vehicle, ship, etc. **b** armoured fighting vehicles collectively. **3** a protective covering or shell on certain animals and plants. **4** heraldic devices. ● *transitive verb* provide with a protective covering. [Old French *armure* from Latin *armatura*: see ARMATURE]

ar·moured *adjective* (also **ar·mored**) **1** equipped with a protective covering, esp. of metal. **2** (of an infantry division etc.) equipped with tanks and other armoured vehicles.

armoured car *noun* an armour-plated van used for transporting money and valuables.

armoured personnel carrier *noun Military* a tank-like vehicle used for transporting troops.

ar·mour·er *noun* (also **ar·mor·er**) **1** a maker or repairer of arms or armour. **2** an official in charge of a ship's or a regiment's arms. [Anglo-French *armurer*, Old French -*urier* (as ARMOUR, -ER⁵)]

ar·moury *noun* (also **ar·mory**) (*pl.* -**ies**) **1** a place where arms are kept; an arsenal. **2** (in *pl.*) *Cdn* a place where militia units drill and train. **3** an array of weapons, defensive resources, usable material, etc. **4** *US* a place where arms are manufactured. [Old French *armoirie*, *armoierie* from *armoier* to blazon, from *arme* ARM²: assimilated to ARMOUR]

arm·pit *noun* **1** the hollow under the arm at the shoulder. **2** *N Amer. slang* a place considered disgusting or contemptible (*the armpit of the world*).

arm·rest *noun* = ARM¹ 4c.

arms control *noun* international agreement to limit or reduce armaments.

arm's-length *attributive adjective* **1** without friendliness or intimacy; at a distance. **2** (of institutional or commercial relations) with neither party controlled by the other.

arms race *noun* competition between nations in the development and accumulation of weapons.

Arm·strong ▸ **1 Ed·win How·ard** (1890–1954), US electrical engineer, inventor of the superheterodyne radio receiver and the frequency modulation system in radio. **2 Louis** ('Satchmo') (1900–71), US trumpeter, singer, and bandleader who became one of the great masters of Dixieland jazz. **3 Neil Alden** (b.1930), US astronaut, the first person to set foot on the moon (20 July 1969).

arm-twisting *noun* persuasion by the use of moral pressure.

arm wrestling *noun* a trial of strength in which two people, with elbows on a tabletop, grip hands, with each trying to force the other's forearm down onto the table. □ **arm-wrestle** *intransitive verb*

army *noun* (*pl.* -**mies**) **1** an organized force armed for fighting on land. **2** (usu. as **the Army**) the entire body of land forces of a country. **3** (often foll. by *of*) a very large number (*an army of locusts*; *an army of bureaucrats*). **4** a body of people organized for a particular cause (*Salvation Army*). [Old French *armee* from Romanic *armata* fem. past participle of *armare* arm]

army ant *noun* any of various tropical ants of the subfamily Dorylinae, which migrate in large columns and prey mainly on insects and spiders.

army fatigues *plural noun* (also **battle fatigues, combat fatigues**) esp. *N Amer.* loose-fitting clothing, usu. khaki, olive drab, or camouflaged, of a sort worn by soldiers on field duty or when engaged in manual labour, e.g. ditch-digging, sandbagging, etc. ¶ In the Canadian Forces, the word *combat dress* is used.

army-navy store *noun US* a surplus store (*see* SURPLUS *noun* 3b).

army surplus *noun* = SURPLUS *noun* 3.

army worm *noun* any of various moth or fly larvae occurring in destructive swarms.

Arne /ɑrn/ **Thom·as** (1710–78), English composer of esp. theatrical music, best known for the song 'Rule, Britannia'.

Arn·hem /ˈɑrnəm/ a city in the E Netherlands, situated on the Rhine River near its junction with the Ijssel, capital of the province of Gelderland; pop. (est. 2002) 138,500. During the Second World War, in Sept. 1944, British airborne troops made a landing on nearby moorland but were eventually overwhelmed by German forces before the advancing Allied army could cross the Rhine to link up with them.

Arnhem Land a peninsula in Northern Territory, Australia, on the west of the Gulf of Carpentaria. The chief town is Nhulunbuy. In 1976 Arnhem Land was declared an Aboriginal reservation.

ar·ni·ca /ˈɑrnɪkə/ *noun* **1** any composite plant of the genus *Arnica*, having erect stems bearing yellow daisy-like flower heads. **2** a medicine prepared from this, used for bruises etc. [modern Latin: origin unknown]

Ar·nold ▸ **1 Ben·edict** (1741–1801), soldier during the American Revolution. After fighting with conspicuous bravery for the Americans during the invasion of Canada, he defected to the British in 1780, and thereafter his name became synonymous with treason amongst Americans. **2 Sir Mal·colm Henry** (b.1921), English composer and trumpeter. He makes adventurous and colourful use of traditional

---

t *top*   v *voice*   w *we*   z *zoo*   ʃ *she*   ʒ *vision*   θ *thin*   ð *this*   ŋ *ring*   x *loch*   tʃ *chip*   dʒ *jar*   (*see over for vowels*)

forms and is known for his film scores and orchestral music. **3 Mat·thew** (1822–88), English poet, literary critic, and social critic. He is best known for his poem 'Dover Beach' (1867); his prose work *Culture and Anarchy* (1869) challenged Victorian materialism and complacency. **4** his father, **Thom·as** (1795–1842), English educator and historian, who is noted for his introduction of educational reforms while headmaster of Rugby School in England (1828–42). □ **Ar·nold·ian** /ˌɑrˈnoːldiən/ *adjective*

Arno River a river which rises in the Apennines of N Italy and flows westward 240 km (150 miles) through Florence and Pisa to the Ligurian Sea.

Arn·pri·or a town in E Ontario, about 50 km west of Ottawa; pop. (2001) 7,192. □ **Arn·pri·or·ite** *noun* [*Arnpryor*, Scotland, birthplace of brothers G. and A. Buchanan, who named the town]

aroid /ˈerɔid/ *adjective* of or relating to the family Araceae, including arums. [ARUM + -OID]

aro·ma /əˈroːmə/ *noun* **1** a fragrance; a distinctive and pleasing smell, often of food. **2** a subtle pervasive quality. [Latin from Greek *arōma -atos* spice]

aroma·ther·apy *noun* the use of aromatic plant extracts and essential oils, esp. for relief of stress-related symptoms. □ **aroma·thera·peut·ic** /-ˈpjuːtɪk/ *adjective* **aroma·ther·apist** *noun*

aro·mat·ic /ˌærəˈmatɪk/ *adjective* **1** fragrant, spicy; (of a smell) pleasantly pungent. **2** *Chem.* (of organic compounds) having an unsaturated ring, esp. containing a benzene ring. ● *noun* an aromatic substance. □ **aro·mat·ic·ally** *adverb*

aroma·tize /əˈroːməˌtaiz/ *transitive verb Chem.* convert (a compound) into an aromatic structure. □ **aroma·tiz·a·tion** /-ˈzeiʃən/ *noun*

Aroo·stook River /əˈruːstʊk, -tɪk/ a river in W New Brunswick, 225 km long, which rises in N Maine and flows generally northeastward to join the Saint John River south of Grand Falls, New Brunswick. [Maliseet *woolahstook* good river for everything]

arose *past of* ARISE.

around ● *adverb* **1** on every side; so as to surround. **2** in various places; here and there; at random (*shop around*). **3** *informal* **a** in existence; available (*has been around for weeks*). **b** near at hand (*it's good to have you around*). **4** with circular motion (*wheels go around*). **5** with return to the starting point or an earlier state (*summer soon comes around again*). **6 a** with rotation, or change to an opposite position (*she turned around to look*). **b** with change to an opposite opinion etc. (*he came around to her point of view*). **7** to, at, or affecting all or many points of a circumference or an area or the members of a company etc. (*drinks were handed around*; *may I look around?*). **8** in every direction from a centre or within a radius (*spread destruction around*; *everyone for a mile around*). **9** by a circuitous way (*will you jump over or go around?*; *go the long way around*). **10** to a place (*come around to see us*; *brought the car around*). **11** measuring (a specified distance) in girth. ● *preposition* **1** on or along the circuit of. **2** on every side of; enveloping. **3** here and there in or near (*chairs around the room*). **4** approximately at; at a time near to (*come around four o'clock*; *happened around June*). **5** so as to encircle or enclose (*travel around the world*; *has a blanket around him*). **6** at or to points on the circumference of (*sat around the table*). **7** in various directions from or with regard to (*towns around Calgary*; *shells exploding around them*). **8** having as an axis of revolution or as a central point (*turns around its centre of gravity*; *write a book around an event*). **9 a** so as to double or pass in a curved course (*go around the corner*). **b** having passed in this way (*be around the corner*). **c** in the position that would result from this (*find them around the corner*). **10** so as to come close from various sides but not into contact. □ **have been around** *informal* be widely experienced, esp. sexually. **see you around** a noncommittal expression on parting. **what goes around comes around** the consequences of one's actions will have to be dealt with eventually. [A² + ROUND]

arouse *transitive verb* **1** induce; call into existence (esp. a feeling, emotion, etc.). **2** awake from sleep. **3** stir into activity. **4** stimulate sexually. □ **arous·able** *adjective* **arous·al** *noun* **arous·er** *noun* [A-² + ROUSE]

Arp, Jean (or **Hans**) (1887–1966), French painter, sculptor, and poet; one of the founders of the Dada movement.

ar·peg·gio /ɑrˈpedʒɪo/ *noun* (*pl.* **-gios**) *Music* the notes of a chord played or sung in succession, either ascending or descending. □ **ar·peg·giat·ed** *adjective* [Italian from *arpeggiare* play the harp, from *arpa* harp]

ar·pent /ˈɑrpənt, ˈɑrpɑ̃/ *noun Cdn hist.* **1** an old French unit of land area equivalent to 3 420 square metres (about 1 acre), the standard measure of land in those areas settled during the French regime, in use until

the 1970s. **2** a unit of linear measure equivalent to about 58 metres (190 ft.) used in New France. [French]

arr·que·bus *var. of* HARQUEBUS.

arr. *abbreviation* **1** *Music* arranged by. **2** arrives.

arrab·bi·a·ta *adjective* designating a pasta sauce of tomatoes, garlic, bell peppers and hot peppers. [Italian = 'enraged' alluding to the spiciness of the sauce]

ar·rack *var. of* ARAK.

ar·raign /əˈrein/ *transitive verb* **1** call on (a person) to answer a criminal charge before a court; indict; accuse. **2** find fault with; call into question (an action or statement). □ **ar·raign·ment** *noun* [Anglo-French *arainer* from Old French *araisnier* (ultimately as AD-, Latin *ratio -onis* reason, discourse)]

Arran /ˈærən/ an island in the Firth of Clyde, in the west of Scotland.

ar·range *verb* **1** *transitive* put into the required order; classify. **2** *transitive* plan or provide for; cause to occur (*arranged a meeting*). **3** *transitive* settle beforehand the order or manner of. **4** *intransitive* take measures; form plans (*arrange to be there at eight*; *arranged for a taxi to come*). **5** *intransitive* come to an agreement (*arranged with her to meet later*). **6** *transitive* **a** *Music* adapt (a composition) for performance with instruments or voices other than those originally specified. **b** adapt (a play etc.) for broadcasting. **7** *transitive* settle (a dispute etc.). □ **ar·range·able** *adjective* **ar·ran·ger** *noun* (esp. in sense 6). [Old French *arangier* from *à* to + *rangier* RANGE]

ar·ranged marriage *noun* a marriage planned and agreed to by the families or guardians of the couple concerned, rather than by the couple themselves.

ar·range·ment *noun* **1** the act or process of arranging or being arranged. **2** the condition of being arranged; the manner in which a thing is arranged. **3** something arranged (*a flower arrangement*). **4** (in *pl.*) plans, measures (*make your own arrangements*). **5** *Music* a setting of a piece of music for instruments or voices other than those for which it was originally written. **6** settlement of a dispute etc. [French (as ARRANGE, -MENT)]

ar·rant /ˈerənt/ *adjective* downright, utter, notorious (*arrant liar*; *arrant nonsense*). □ **ar·rant·ly** *adverb* [Middle English, var. of ERRANT, originally in phrases like *arrant* (= outlawed, roving) *thief*]

Arras /əˈras/ a city in NE France; pop. (1999) 40,590. It was a centre in medieval times for the manufacture of tapestries. The area surrounding Arras, including Vimy Ridge, was the scene of very heavy fighting in the First World War.

arras /ˈærəs/ *noun hist.* a rich tapestry, often hung on the walls of a room, or to conceal an alcove. [ARRAS]

Arrau /əˈrau/ **Clau·dio** (1903–91), Chilean pianist, a renowned interpreter of the works of Beethoven, Chopin, Liszt, Schumann, and Brahms.

ar·ray ● *noun* **1** an imposing or well-ordered series or display. **2** an ordered arrangement, esp. of troops (*battle array*). **3** attire, dress; an outfit (*in fine array*). **4 a** *Math.* an arrangement of quantities or symbols in rows and columns; a matrix. **b** *Computing* an ordered set of related elements. **5** *Law* a list of jurors empanelled. ● *transitive verb* **1** deck, adorn. **2** set in order; marshal (forces). **3** *Law* empanel (a jury). [Anglo-French *araier*, Old French *areer*, ultimately from a Germanic root, = prepare]

ar·rears *plural noun* an amount still outstanding or uncompleted, esp. work undone or a debt unpaid. □ **in arrears** behind in payments etc. □ **ar·rear·age** *noun* [Old French *arere* from medieval Latin *adretro* (as AD-, *retro* backwards): first used in phr. *in arrear*]

ar·rest ● *transitive verb* **1 a** seize (a person) and take into custody, esp. by legal authority. **b** seize (a ship) by legal authority. **2** stop or check (esp. a process or moving thing). **3 a** attract (a person's attention). **b** attract the attention of (a person). ● *noun* **1** the act of arresting or being arrested, esp. the legal seizure of a person (*they were placed under arrest*). **2** a stoppage or checking of motion (*cardiac arrest*). □ **arrest of judgment** *Law* a stay of proceedings after a verdict, on the ground of error. □ **arrest·ee** *noun* [Old French *arester*, ultimately from Latin *restare* remain, stop]

ar·rest·ing *adjective* attracting attention; striking. □ **ar·rest·ing·ly** *adverb*

ar·rest·or *noun* (also **ar·rest·er**) **1** something which arrests, esp. a device on an aircraft carrier for slowing an aircraft by means of a hook and cable after landing. **2** a device in chimneys, exhausts etc. for preventing smoke or fire, esp. by stopping sparks.

Ar·rhen·ius /əˈreiniəs, əˈriː-/ **Svante Aug·ust** (1859–1927), Swedish chemist, awarded the Nobel Prize for chemistry in 1903 for his work on the physical chemistry of electrolytes.

ar·rhyth·mia /əˈrɪðmɪə/ *noun Med.* deviation from the normal rhythm of the heart. □ **ar·rhyth·mic** *adjective* [Greek *arruthmia* lack of rhythm]

arris /ˈarɪs/ *noun Archit.* a sharp edge formed by the meeting of two flat or curved surfaces. [corruption from French *areste*, modern ARÊTE]

ar·riv·al *noun* **1 a** the act of arriving. **b** an appearance on the scene. **2** a person or thing that has arrived.

ar·rive *intransitive verb* **1** (often foll. by *at, in*) reach a destination; come to the end of a journey or a specified part of a journey (*arrived in Tibet; arrived at the station; arrived late*). **2** (foll. by *at*) reach (a conclusion, decision, etc.). **3** *informal* establish one's reputation or position. **4** (of a child) be born. **5** (of a thing) be brought (*the flowers have arrived*). **6** (of a time) come (*her birthday arrived at last*). **7** come on the scene (*CD-ROMs arrived in the late eighties*). [Old French *ariver*, ultimately as AD- + Latin *ripa* shore]

ar·riv·iste /ˌariːˈviːst/ *noun* an ambitious or ruthlessly self-seeking person. [French from *arriver* from Old French (as ARRIVE, -IST)]

ar·ro·gant /ˈerəgənt, ˈa-/ *adjective* unduly appropriating authority or importance; aggressively conceited or presumptuous; overbearing. □ **ar·ro·gance** *noun* **ar·ro·gant·ly** *adverb* [Old French (as ARROGATE, -ANT)]

ar·ro·gate /ˈerəˌgeɪt/ *transitive verb* **1** (often foll. by *to*) oneself) claim (power, responsibility, etc.) without justification. **2** (often foll. by *to*) attribute unjustly (to a person). □ **ar·ro·ga·tion** *noun*

ar·ron·disse·ment /aˌrɔ̃diːsˈmɑ̃/ *noun* **1** an administrative district of some large cities in France, esp. Paris. **2** a subdivision of a French department, for local government administration purposes. [French]

Arrow, Ken·neth Jo·seph (b.1921), US economist, noted for his work on general economic equilibrium, risk-bearing, and insurance. In 1972 he shared the Nobel Prize for economics with Sir John Hinks.

ar·row *noun* **1** a sharp pointed wooden or metal stick shot from a bow. **2** a drawn or printed etc. representation of an arrow indicating a direction; a pointer. □ **ar·rowy** *adjective* [Old English *ar(e)we* from Old Norse *ǫr* from Germanic]

arrow grass *noun* any of several grasslike marsh plants of the genus *Triglochin*, bearing a slender flowering spike.

arrow·head *noun* **1** the pointed end of an arrow. **2** an aquatic or marsh plant of the genus *Sagittaria*, bearing white flowers and arrowhead-shaped leaves. **3** a decorative device resembling an arrowhead.

arrow·root *noun* **1** a plant of the genus *Maranta*, esp. the Caribbean *M. arundinacea* with fleshy tuberous rhizomes. **2** pure edible starch prepared from the tubers of *M. arundinacea*, or other plants. **3** (in full **arrowroot cookie**) a cookie made with arrowroot flour.

arrow sash *noun Cdn hist.* = CEINTURE FLÉCHÉE.

arrow worm *noun* = CHAETOGNATH.

ar·royo /əˈrɔɪoʊ/ *noun* (pl. **-royos**) esp. *US* a usu. dry channel or gully cut by a stream, esp. in arid regions. [Spanish]

arse *coarse slang* esp. *Brit. & Cdn* (Nfld) var. of ASS². [Old English *ærs*]

arse·hole *coarse slang* esp. *Brit.* var. of ASSHOLE.

arse-licking *coarse slang* esp. *Brit.* see ASS-KISSING.

ar·sen·al /ˈarsənəl/ *noun* **1** a store of weapons. **2** a government establishment for the storage and manufacture of weapons and ammunition. **3** a collection of items, methods, beliefs, etc. available for tackling a problem (*an arsenal of medications*). [obsolete French *arsenal* or Italian *arzanale* from Arabic *dārṣinā'a* from *dār* house + *sinā'a* art, industry, from *ṣana'a* fabricate]

ar·sen·ic ● *noun* /ˈarsənɪk/ **1** a non-scientific name for arsenic trioxide, a highly poisonous white powdery substance used in weed killers, rat poison, etc. **2** *Chem.* a brittle semi-metallic element, used in semiconductors and alloys. Symbol: **As**; at. no.: 33. ● *adjective* /arˈsenɪk/ **1** of or concerning arsenic. **2** *Chem.* containing arsenic with a valence of five. [Old French from Latin *arsenicum* from Greek *arsenikon* yellow orpiment, identified with *arsenikos* male, but in fact from Arabic *al-zarnīk* from *al* the + *zarnīk* orpiment, from Persian from *zar* gold]

ar·sen·ic·al /arˈsenɪkəl/ *adjective* of or containing arsenic.

arsenic hour *noun* the period in the late afternoon when young children become particularly cranky and unmanageable.

arsis /ˈarsɪs/ *noun* (pl. **arses** /-siːz/) a stressed syllable or part of a metrical foot in Greek or Latin verse (*opp.* THESIS 3). [Late Latin from Greek, = lifting, from *airō* raise]

ar·son *noun* the act of maliciously setting fire to property.

ar·son·ist *noun* [legal Anglo-French, Old French, from medieval Latin *arsio -onis* from Latin *ardēre ars-* burn]

art¹ *noun* **1 a** a human creative skill or its application. **b** work exhibiting this. **2 a** (in *pl.*; prec. by *the*) the various branches of creative activity concerned with the production of imaginative designs, sounds, ideas, etc., e.g. painting, music, writing, etc. considered collectively. **b** any one of these branches. **3** creative activity, esp. painting and drawing, resulting in visual representation (*interested in music but not art*). **4** human skill or workmanship as opposed to the work of nature. **5** (often foll. by *of*) a skill, aptitude, or knack (*the art of writing clearly; keeping people happy is quite an art*). **6** (in *pl.*) certain branches of (esp. university) study, esp. the fine arts and humanities, as distinguished from the sciences or technological subjects. [Old French from Latin *ars artis*]

art² *archaic* 2nd *sing.* present of BE.

art. *abbreviation* article.

Ar·taud /arˈtoʊ/ **An·to·nin** (1896–1948), French surrealist actor, director, and dramatist; proponent of the 'Theatre of Cruelty' in which gestures, sounds, and scenic effects are designed to shock the spectator.

Arta·xerxes I /ˌartəˈzɜrksiːz/ a king of ancient Persia, son of Xerxes; reigned 465–425 BC.

Arta·xerxes II /ˌartəˈzɜrksiːz/ a king of ancient Persia, son of Darius II; reigned 404–358 BC.

Arta·xerxes III /ˌartəˈzɜrksiːz/ son of Artaxerxes II, king of ancient Persia 358–338 BC. A ruthless ruler, he secured his throne by killing most of his relatives, and invaded and subjugated both Egypt and Phoenicia during his reign.

art deco *noun* the predominant decorative art style of the period 1910–30, characterized by precise and boldly delineated geometric motifs, shapes, and strong colours. [shortened from French *art décoratif*, from the 1925 *Exposition des Arts décoratifs* in Paris]

art director *noun* **1** the person in charge of the design and production of the costumes and decor for a motion picture. **2** the person in charge of the graphics, layout, etc. of a magazine. □ **art-direct** *transitive verb* **art direction** *noun*

arte·fact var. of ARTIFACT.

Arte·mis /ˈartəmɪs/ *Gk Myth* the goddess of chastity, childbirth, hunting, and wildlife, daughter of Zeus and twin sister of Apollo. She was identified with the Roman goddess Diana, who is often depicted in literature as goddess of the moon.

arte·misia /artəˈmiːʒə, -ˈmiːʃə/ *noun* any of numerous aromatic or bitter-tasting plants of the genus *Artemisia*, of the composite family, which includes silver mound, wormwood, mugwort, sagebrush, etc. [Latin from Greek, = wormwood, from *Artemis*, to whom it was sacred]

ar·ter·ial /arˈtiːrɪəl/ *adjective* **1 a** of or relating to an artery (*arterial disease*). **b** (of blood) oxygenated in the lungs and of a bright red colour (*opp.* VENOUS). **2** (esp. of a road) main, important, esp. providing direct access to the centre of a city. [French *artériel* from *artère* artery]

ar·ter·ial·ize /arˈtiːrɪəˌlaɪz/ *transitive verb* (also esp. *Brit.* **-ise**) **1** convert venous into arterial (blood) by oxygenation esp. in the lungs. **2** provide with an arterial system. □ **ar·ter·ial·iz·a·tion** *noun*

ar·teri·ole /arˈtiːrɪˌoʊl/ *noun* a small branch of an artery leading into capillaries. [French *artériole*, diminutive of *artère* ARTERY]

ar·terio·scler·o·sis /arˌtiːrioʊskləˈroʊsəs/ *noun* abnormal thickening and hardening of the walls of the arteries. □ **ar·terio·scler·otic** /-ˈrɒtək/ *adjective* [ARTERY + SCLEROSIS]

ar·tery *noun* (pl. **-ies**) **1** any of the muscular-walled tubes forming part of the blood circulation system of the body, carrying oxygen-enriched blood from the heart (*compare* VEIN). **2** a major road, railway, river, etc. □ **ar·ter·itis** *noun* [Latin *arteria* from Greek *artēria* prob. from *airō* raise]

ar·tesian well /arˈtiːʒən/ *noun* a well bored perpendicularly, esp. through rock, into water-bearing strata lying at an angle, so that natural pressure produces a constant supply of water with little or no pumping. [French *artésien* from ARTOIS]

art film *noun* a film aiming for aesthetic effect rather than commercial success.

art form *noun* **1** any medium of artistic expression. **2** an established form of composition, e.g. the novel, sonata, sonnet, etc.

art·ful *adjective* **1** skilful, clever. **2** crafty, deceitful. **3** characterized by skill or art. □ **art·ful·ly** *adverb* **art·ful·ness** *noun*

art house *noun* (also **art theatre** etc.) a movie theatre specializing in alternative films, e.g. art films, foreign films, etc.

arth·ral·gia /ɑrˈθraldʒə/ *noun* pain in a joint. [Latin from Greek from *arthron* joint + -ALGIA]

arth·ritis /ɑrˈθraitis/ *noun* inflammation of a joint or joints.
□ **arth·rit·ic** /-ˈθrɪtɪk/ *adjective & noun* [Latin from Greek from *arthron* joint + -ITIS]

arth·ro·pod /ˈɑrθrə,pɒd/ *noun* Zool. any invertebrate animal of the phylum Arthropoda, with a segmented body, jointed limbs, and an external skeleton, e.g. an insect, spider, or crustacean. [Greek *arthron* joint + *pous podos* foot]

arth·ros·copy /ɑrˈθrɒskəpi/ *noun* (pl. **-ies**) Med. examination of, or surgery on, the interior of a joint by the insertion of an instrument called an arthroscope through a small incision. □ **arth·ro·scop·ic** /,ɑrθrəˈskɒpɪk/ *adjective* **arth·ro·scope** /ˈɑrθrə,skoːp/ *noun*

Ar·thur[1] a legendary king of Britain, historically perhaps a 5th- or 6th-c. Celtic chieftain or general. Numerous medieval stories describe the exploits of Arthur, his knights of the Round Table, and the search for the Holy Grail.

Ar·thur[2], **Ches·ter Alan** (1829–86), 21st president of the US, 1881–85. He became president after James Garfield was assassinated while in office.

Ar·thur·ian /ɑrˈθuriən, -ˈθɜriən/ *adjective* relating to or associated with King Arthur or his court.

arti·choke *noun* **1** a plant native to the Mediterranean, *Cynara scolymus*, allied to the thistle. **2** (in full **globe artichoke**) the flower head of the artichoke, the bracts of which have edible bases (*see also* JERUSALEM ARTICHOKE). [Italian *articiocco* from Arabic *al-karšūfa*]

arti·cle ● *noun* **1** a particular or separate thing, esp. one of a set (*articles of clothing*). **2** a piece of writing, complete in itself, in a newspaper, magazine, scholarly journal, etc. **3** a separate clause or portion of any document (*see also* THIRTY-NINE ARTICLES). **4** Grammar the definite or indefinite article. **5** (in pl.) the period of apprenticeship of a law student or (in the UK) an accountant. ● *verb* **1** *transitive* bind by a written contract, esp. for a period of training. **2** *intransitive* Cdn (of a law student) serve one's period of apprenticeship. □ **article of faith 1** a basic point of religious belief. **2** any firmly held belief. **genuine article** something authentic of its kind; not imitative. [Old French from Latin *articulus* diminutive of *artus* joint]

arti·cled clerk *noun* a law student who is articling.

arti·cu·lar /ɑrˈtɪkjʊlər/ *adjective* of or relating to the joints. [Latin *articularis* (as ARTICLE, -AR[1])]

arti·cu·late ● *adjective* /ɑrˈtɪkjʊlət/ **1** able to speak fluently and coherently. **2** (of sound or speech) having clearly distinguishable parts. **3** having joints. ● *verb* /ɑrˈtɪkjʊˌleit/ **1** *transitive* **a** pronounce (words, syllables, etc.) clearly and distinctly. **b** express (an idea etc.) coherently. **2** *intransitive* speak distinctly; enunciate. **3** *transitive* (usu. in *passive*) connect by joints. **4** *transitive* mark with apparent joints. **5** *intransitive* (often foll. by *with*) form a joint. □ **ar·ticu·lacy** *noun* **ar·ticu·late·ly** *adverb* **ar·ticu·late·ness** *noun* **ar·ticu·la·tor** *noun* [Latin *articulatus* (as ARTICLE, -ATE[2])]

ar·ticu·lat·ed /ɑrˈtɪkjʊleitəd/ *adjective* designating a vehicle consisting of two or more sections connected by a flexible joint (*articulated bus*).

ar·ticu·la·tion /ɑr,tɪkjʊˈleiʃən/ *noun* **1 a** the act of speaking. **b** articulate utterance; speech. **2 a** the act or a mode of jointing. **b** a joint, esp. that between two bones, or parts of an invertebrate exoskeleton. [French *articulation* or Latin *articulatio* from *articulare* joint (as ARTICLE, -ATION)]

arti·fact *noun* (also **arte·fact**) **1** a product of human art and workmanship. **2** Archaeology a product of prehistoric or aboriginal workmanship as distinguished from a similar object naturally produced. **3** Biol. etc. a feature not naturally present, introduced during preparation or investigation, e.g. as in the preparation of a slide. □ **arti·fac·tual** *adjective* (in senses 1 and 2). [Latin *arte* (ablative of *ars* art) + *factum* (neuter past participle of *facere* make)]

arti·fice /ˈɑrtəfɪs/ *noun* clever or cunning devices or expedients, esp. as used to trick or deceive others. [French from Latin *artificium* from *ars artis* art, *-ficium* making, from *facere* make]

arti·ficer /ɑrˈtɪfɪsər/ *noun* **1** an inventor. **2** a craftsman. [Anglo-French, prob. alteration of Old French *artificien*]

arti·fi·cial /,ɑrtəˈfɪʃəl/ *adjective* **1** produced by human skill or effort rather than originating naturally (*an artificial lake; artificial flavours*). **2** formed in imitation of something natural (*artificial flowers*). **3** affected, insincere (*an artificial smile*). **4** designating a device etc. that performs the functions of an organ, limb, etc. (*artificial heart; artificial leg*). □ **arti·fi·ci·al·ity** /-ʃiːˈaləti/ *noun* **arti·fi·cial·ly** *adverb*

artificial horizon *noun* a gyroscopic instrument used in an aircraft to indicate its position relative to the horizon.

artificial ice *noun* **1** an ice surface in a skating rink kept frozen by cooling pipes running under the concrete base of the rink. **2** ice frozen by mechanical refrigeration.

artificial insemination *noun* the injection of semen into the vagina or uterus using a syringe. Abbr.: **AI**.

artificial intelligence *noun* the field of study that deals with the capacity of a machine, esp. a computer, to simulate or surpass intelligent human behaviour. Abbr.: **AI**.

artificial language *noun* **1** a composite language, esp. for international use, made from the words and other elements in several languages, e.g. Esperanto. **2** a language invented for use by computers, e.g. a programming language.

artificial life *noun* the production or action of computer programs or computerized systems, e.g. robots, which simulate the behaviour, population dynamics, or other characteristics of living organisms.

artificial reality *noun* = VIRTUAL REALITY.

artificial respiration *noun* the restoration or initiation of breathing by manual or mechanical or mouth-to-mouth methods.

artificial turf *noun* a synthetic surface used as a substitute for grass on sports fields etc.

ar·ti·gi Cdn (North) var. of ATIGI.

ar·til·lery /ɑrˈtɪləri/ *noun* **1** large-calibre guns used in warfare on land. **2** a branch of the armed forces that uses these. [Old French *artillerie* from *artiller* alteration of *atillier, atirier* equip, arm]

ar·til·lery·man *noun* (pl. **-men**) a soldier in the artillery.

arti·san /ˈɑrtɪ,zan, -san/ *noun* **1** a craftsperson specializing in decorative arts, esp. pottery, weaving, etc. **2** a skilled (esp. manual) worker. □ **arti·san·al** *adjective* **artisan·ship** *noun* [French from Italian *artigiano*, ultimately from Latin *artitus* past participle of *artire* instruct in the arts]

art·ist *noun* **1** a person who practises any of the fine arts, esp. painting, sculpting, etc. **2** a person who practises one of the performing arts. **3** a person who shows great skill and inspiration in a particular activity (*a programmer who is a true artist*). **4** a devotee; a habitual practiser of a specified (usu. reprehensible) activity (*con artist; put-down artist*). **5** = RECORDING ARTIST. □ **art·istry** *noun* [French *artiste* from Italian *artista* (as ART[1], -IST)]

ar·tiste /ɑrˈtiːst/ *noun* **1** esp. Brit. a professional performer, esp. a singer or dancer. **2** derogatory a person who cultivates a pretentiously artistic attitude or lifestyle. [French: see ARTIST]

art·is·tic *adjective* **1** having natural skill in art. **2** made or done with art. **3** of art or artists. □ **art·is·tic·al·ly** *adverb*

artistic director *noun* the director of a performing arts organization in charge of programming and casting decisions etc.

art·less *adjective* **1** without guile or deceit. **2** without pretentiousness or effort; natural and simple. **3** clumsy. □ **art·less·ly** *adverb*

art·making *noun* the production of esp. visual art. □ **art·maker** *noun*

art moderne /,ɑrt məˈdern/ *noun* = moderne.

art nou·veau /,ɑrt ˈnuːvoː/ *noun* a European art style of the late 19th c. characterized by flowing lines and natural organic forms.

Ar·tois /ˈɑrtwɒ/ a region and former province of NW France. Known in Roman times as Artesium, the area gave its name to the artesian well, which was first sunk here in the 12th c.

art paper *noun* smooth-coated high-quality paper.

art rock *noun* any type of rock music which is deemed to be produced for artistic rather than commercial reasons, esp. music that is avant-garde, experimental, or pretentious. □ **art rocker** *noun*

arts and crafts *plural noun* decorative design and handicrafts.

Arts and Crafts movement an English aesthetic and social movement of the late 19th c. which sought to revive, in an industrial age, the ideal of the handcrafted object. Led by William Morris, it influenced many artists and designers and was closely associated with the Pre-Raphaelites and the Aesthetic movement.

art·sie *noun* N Amer. slang **1** a student in an arts program at a university or college. **2** an artist or a person who is interested in the arts.

art song *noun* a song produced by an artist and composed with conscious artistry as opposed to a folk song or popular song.

artsy *adjective* (also derogatory **artsy-fartsy**) esp. N Amer. informal pretentiously or affectedly artistic. □ **artsi·ness** *noun*

artsy-craftsy *adjective* informal **1** having a liking for, or engaged in, handicrafts. **2** characterized by the presence of handicrafts.

Consonants: b *but*   d *dog*   f *few*   g *get*   h *her*   j *yes*   k *cat*   l *leg*   m *man*   n *no*   p *pen*   r *red*   s *sit*

art therapy *noun* a form of psychotherapy involving the encouragement of free self-expression through painting, drawing, or modelling, used as a remedial or diagnostic activity. □ **art therapist** *noun*

art·work *noun* **1** a work of art. **2** the illustrations in a printed work or other visual multimedia material, as distinct from the text. **3** prepared or camera-ready copy.

arty *adjective* = ARTSY.

arty-crafty *adjective* esp. *Brit.* = ARTSY-CRAFTSY.

Aruba /əˈruːbə/ an island in the Caribbean Sea, close to the Venezuelan coast; pop. (est. 2002) 70,440; capital, Oranjestad. Formerly part of the Netherlands Antilles, it separated from that group in 1986 as a step towards full independence, becoming a self-governing territory of the Netherlands.

aru·gula /əˈruːgələ/ *noun* a cruciferous plant, *Eruca vesicaria sativa*, having purple-veined pale yellow or white flowers and bitter leaves which are used in salads. *Also called* ROCKET[2] 2. [Italian dial., ultimately diminutive of Latin *eruca*]

arum /ˈerəm/ *noun* **1** any plant of the European genus *Arum*, typically having a white spathe and arrow-shaped leaves, esp. cuckoo pint, *Arum maculatum*. **2** any of various other plants of the family Araceae. [Latin from Greek *aron*]

arum lily *noun* **1** esp. *Brit.* = CALLA 1. **2** = WATER ARUM.

Aru·nachal Pra·desh /ˌɑːrəˌnatʃəl prəˈdeʃ/ a mountainous state in the far northeast of India, lying on the borders of Tibet to the north and Burma (Myanmar) to the east; capital, Itanagar.

Ar·vi·at /ˈɑːrviat/ a hamlet in southern Nunavut, situated on the west coast of Hudson Bay, about 250 km (by air) north of Churchill, Manitoba; pop. (2001) 1,899. □ **Arviaq'miut** /ˈɑːrviˈakmiut/ *noun* [Inuktitut, = place of the bowhead whale]

-ary[1] *suffix* **1** forming adjectives (*budgetary*; *contrary*; *primary*; *unitary*). **2** forming nouns (*dictionary*; *granary*; *January*). [French *-aire* or Latin *-arius* 'connected with']

-ary[2] *suffix* forming adjectives (*military*). [French *-aire* or from Latin *-aris* 'belonging to']

Arya·bhata I /ˌeriəˈbɒtə/ (476–*c*.550), Indian astronomer and mathematician. His surviving work, the *Aryabhatiya* (499), has sections dealing with mathematics, the measurement of time, planetary models, the sphere, and eclipses.

Ary·an /ˈeriən, ˈɑː-/ ● *noun* **1** (in Nazi and neo-Nazi ideology) a Caucasian not of Jewish descent. **2** a member of the peoples speaking any of the languages of the Indo-European (esp. Indo-Iranian) family. **3** the parent language of this family. ● *adjective* of or relating to Aryan or the Aryans. [Sanskrit *āryas* noble]

aryl /ˈarail, ˈarɪl/ *noun Chem.* any radical derived from or related to an aromatic hydrocarbon by removal of a hydrogen atom. [German *Aryl* (as AROMATIC, -YL)]

AS *abbreviation* Anglo-Saxon.

As *symbol Chem.* the element arsenic.

as[1] ● *adverb & conjunction* (*adv.* as antecedent in main sentence; *conj.* in relative clause expressed or implied) ... to the extent to which ... is or does etc. (*I am as tall as he*; *am as tall as he is*; *am not so tall as he*; (*informal*) *am as tall as him*; *as many as six*; *as recently as last week*; *it is not as easy as you think*). ● *conjunction* (with relative clause expressed or implied) **1** (with antecedent *so*) expressing result or purpose (*came early so as to meet us*; *we so arranged matters as to avoid a long wait*; *so good as to exceed all hopes*). **2** (with antecedent adverb omitted) having concessive force (*good as it is* = *although it is good*; *try as he might* = *although he might try*). **3** (without antecedent adverb) **a** in the manner in which (*do as you like*; *was regarded as a mistake*). **b** in the capacity or form of (*I speak as your friend*; *Olivier as Hamlet*; *as a matter of fact*). **c** during or at the time that (*came up as I was speaking*; *fell just as I reached the door*). **d** for the reason that; seeing that (*as you are here, we can talk*). **e** for instance (*port cities, as Vancouver*). ● *relative pronoun* (with verb of relative clause expressed or implied) **1** that, who, which (*I had the same trouble as you*; *she is a writer, as is her husband*; *such money as you have*; *such countries as France*). **2** (with sentence as antecedent) a fact that (*he lost, as you know*). □ **as and when** to the extent and at the time that (*I'll do it as and when I want to*). **as for** with regard to (*as for you, I think you are wrong*). **as from** on and after (a specified date). **as if!** indicating disbelief or disdain. **as if** (or **though**) as would be the case if (*acts as if he were in charge*; *as if you didn't know!*; *looks as though we've won*). **as it is** (or **as is**) in the existing circumstances or state. **as it were** in a way; to a certain extent (*he is, as it were, infatuated*). **as long as** see LONG[1]. **as much** see MUCH. **as of 1** = AS FROM. **2** as at (a specified time). **as per**

see PER. **as regards** see REGARD. **as soon as** see SOON. **as such** see SUCH. **as to** with respect to; concerning (*said nothing as to money*; *as to you, I think you are wrong*). **as was** in the previously existing circumstances or state. **as well** see WELL[1]. **as yet** until now or a particular time in the past (usu. with *neg.* and with implied reserve about the future: *have received no news as yet*). [reduced form of Old English *alswá* ALSO]

as[2] *noun* (*pl.* **asses**) an ancient Roman copper coin. [Latin]

as- *prefix* assimilated form of AD- before *s*.

ASA *abbreviation* **1** *Cdn* ACETYLSALICYLIC ACID. **2** American Standards Association (now replaced by ANSI).

asa·fet·ida /ˌasəˈfiːtɪdə, -ˈfetɪdə/ *noun* (also **asa·foet·ida**) an acrid gum resin with a strong smell like that of garlic, obtained from certain Asian plants of the umbelliferous genus *Ferula*, and used in condiments. [medieval Latin from *asa* from Persian *azā* mastic + *fetida* (as FETID)]

asa·na /ˈɒsənə/ *noun* any of various postures used in yoga. [Sanskrit]

As·ante see ASHANTI[1].

ASAP /ˌeiseiˈpiː, ˈeisap/ *abbreviation* as soon as possible.

As·bes·tos /azˈbestəs, as-/ a town in south central Quebec, about 50 km north of Sherbrooke; pop. (2001) 6,580. [ASBESTOS, discovered there *c*.1879]

as·bes·tos /azˈbestəs, as-/ *noun* **1** a fibrous silicate mineral that is incombustible. **2** this used as a heat-resistant or insulating material. [ultimately from Greek *asbestos* unquenchable, from *a-* not + *sbestos* from *sbennumi* quench]

as·bes·to·sis /ˌazbeˈstoːsɪs, ˌas-/ *noun* a lung disease resulting from the inhalation of asbestos particles.

ASCAP /ˈaskap/ *abbreviation* American Society of Composers, Authors, and Publishers.

as·carid /ˈaskərəd/ *noun* (also **as·caris** /-rəs/) a parasitic nematode worm of the genus *Ascaris*, e.g. the intestinal roundworm of mankind and other vertebrates. [modern Latin *ascaris* from Greek *askaris*]

as·cend /əˈsend/ *verb* **1** *intransitive* move upwards; rise. **2** *intransitive* **a** slope upwards. **b** lie along an ascending slope. **3** *transitive* climb; go up. **4** *intransitive* rise in rank or status. **5** *transitive* mount upon. **6** *intransitive* (of sound) rise in pitch. **7** *transitive* go along (a river) to its source. □ **ascend the throne** become king or queen. [Latin *ascendere* (as AD-, *scandere* climb)]

as·cend·ancy /əˈsendənsi/ *noun* (also **as·cend·ency**) a superior or dominant condition or position.

as·cend·ant /əˈsendənt/ ● *adjective* **1** rising. **2** *Astronomy* rising towards the zenith. **3** *Astrology* just rising above the eastern horizon. **4** predominant. ● *noun Astrology* the point of the ecliptic or sign of the zodiac which at a given moment (esp. at a person's birth) is just rising above the eastern horizon. □ **in the ascendant 1** supreme or dominating. **2** rising; gaining power or authority.

as·cend·er /əˈsendər/ *noun* **1 a** a part of a letter that extends above the main part (as in *b* and *d*). **b** a letter having this. **2** a person or thing that ascends.

as·cen·sion /əˈsenʃən/ *noun* **1** the act or an instance of ascending. **2** *Christianity* (**Ascension**) **a** the ascent of Christ into heaven on the fortieth day after the Resurrection. **b** (in full **Ascension Day**) the day on which Christians annually celebrate the Ascension, either the Thursday forty days after Easter, or the Sunday following this. □ **as·cen·sion·al** *adjective*

Ascension Island a small island in the S Atlantic, incorporated with St. Helena, with which it is a dependency of the UK; pop. (est. 2002) 1,100. It is now a British telecommunications centre and a US air base. [so called because it is said to have been discovered on *Ascension Day* in 1501]

As·cen·sion·tide /əˈsenʃənˌtaid/ *noun Christianity* the period between Ascension Day and the eve of Pentecost.

as·cent /əˈsent/ *noun* **1** the act or an instance of ascending. **2 a** an upward movement or rise. **b** advancement or progress (*the ascent of man*). **3** a way by which one may ascend; an upward slope. [ASCEND, after *descent*]

as·cer·tain /ˌasərˈtein/ *transitive verb* find out as a definite fact. □ **as·cer·tain·able** *adjective* **as·cer·tain·ment** *noun* [Old French *acertener*, stem *acertain-* from *à* to + CERTAIN]

as·cet·ic /əˈsetɪk/ ● *noun* a person who practises severe self-discipline and abstains from all forms of pleasure, esp. for religious or spiritual reasons. ● *adjective* relating to or characteristic of ascetics or asceticism; abstaining from pleasure. □ **as·cet·ic·ally** *adverb* **as·ceti·cism**

---

t top   v voice   w we   z zoo   ʃ she   ʒ vision   θ thin   ð this   ŋ ring   x loch   tʃ chip   dʒ jar   (see over for vowels)

/-tɪ,sɪzəm/ *noun* [medieval Latin *asceticus* or Greek *askētikos* from *askētēs* monk, from *askeō* exercise]

As·cham /'askəm/ **Roger** (1515/16–68), English humanist scholar and writer, tutor to the future Elizabeth I and Latin secretary to Queen Mary and later to Elizabeth.

as·cid·ian /ə'sɪdɪən/ *noun Zool.* any tunicate animal of the class Ascidiacea, often found in colonies, the adults sedentary on rocks or seaweeds, e.g. the sea squirt. [modern Latin *Ascidia* from Greek *askidion* diminutive of *askos* wineskin]

ASCII /'aski/ *noun Computing* a standard code for storing and transmitting information in and between computer systems. [acronym from American Standard Code for Information Interchange]

as·ci·tes /ə'saɪtiːz/ *noun* (pl. same) *Med.* abnormal accumulation of fluid in the abdomen causing swelling. [Late Latin from Greek from *askitēs* from *askos* wineskin]

As·clep·ius /ə'skliːpɪəs/ *Gk Myth* a god of healing, often represented bearing a staff with a serpent coiled around it.

as·cor·bic acid /ə'skɔːbɪk/ *noun* a vitamin found in citrus fruits and green vegetables, essential in maintaining healthy connective tissue, a deficiency of which results in scurvy. *Also called* VITAMIN C. [A¹ + medieval Latin *scorbutus* scurvy + -IC]

Ascot 1 /'askət/ a town in southern England, southwest of Windsor. Its racecourse is the site of an annual series of horse races attended by fashionable English society. **2** /'askɒt/ a former municipality in S Quebec, now part of Sherbrooke; pop. (2001) 6,908.

ascot /'askət, -kɒt/ (in full **ascot tie**) a broad necktie or scarf covering the area of an open neck or waistcoat. [ASCOT 1]

as·cribe *transitive verb* (usu. foll. by *to*) **1** attribute or impute (*ascribes his well-being to a sound constitution*). **2** regard as belonging.
□ **as·crib·able** *adjective* **as·crip·tion** *noun* [Latin *ascribere* (as AD-, *scribere* script- write)]

asdic *noun* an early form of sonar used to detect submarines. [initials of Allied Submarine Detection Investigation Committee]

-ase *suffix Biochem.* forming the name of an enzyme (*amylase*). [DIASTASE]

ASEAN /'asiən/ *abbreviation* Association of South-East Asian Nations.

asep·sis /ei'sepsəs, ə-/ *noun* **1** the absence of harmful bacteria, viruses, or other micro-organisms. **2** a method of achieving asepsis in surgery.

asep·tic /ei'septɪk/ *adjective* **1** free from contamination caused by harmful bacteria, viruses, or other micro-organisms. **2** (of a wound, instrument, or dressing) surgically sterile or sterilized. **3** (of a surgical method etc.) aiming at the elimination of harmful micro-organisms, rather than counteraction (*compare* ANTISEPTIC).

asex·ual /ei'sekʃuəl, a-/ *adjective Biol.* **1** without sex or sexual organs. **2** (of reproduction) not involving the fusion of gametes. **3** without sexuality. □ **asex·u·al·ity** /-'alɪti/ *noun* **asex·ual·ly** *adverb*

As·gard *Scand. Myth* a region in the centre of the universe, inhabited by the gods.

ash¹ *noun* **1 a** (often in *pl.*) the powdery residue left after the burning of any substance. **b** *Chem.* such residue used in chemical analysis, e.g. to assess mineral content (*low ash cat food*). **2** (in *pl.*) the remains of the human body after cremation or disintegration. **3** ash-like material thrown out by a volcano. **4** the colour of esp. wood ashes; pale grey. [Old English *æsce*]

ash² *noun* **1** any forest tree of the genus *Fraxinus*, with silver-grey bark, compound leaves, and tough, flexible, pale wood. **2** the wood of the ash, used to make hockey sticks and implement handles. **3** an Old English runic letter, = æ (named from a word of which it was the first letter). [Old English *æsc* from Germanic]

ashamed *predicative adjective* **1** embarrassed or disconcerted by shame (*ashamed of her aunt; ashamed of having lied; ashamed for you; ashamed to be seen with him*). **2** (foll. by *to* + infin.) hesitant, reluctant (but usu. not actually refusing or declining) (*am ashamed to admit that I was wrong*). □ **asham·ed·ly** *adverb* [Old English *āscamod* past participle of *āscamian* feel shame (as A-², SHAME)]

Ashan·ti¹ /ə'ʃanti/ (also **Asan·te**) a region of central Ghana.

Ashan·ti² /ə'ʃanti/ (also **Asan·te**) ● *noun* **1** a member of the people of the Ashanti region, one of Ghana's principal ethnic groups. **2** the language of this people, a dialect of Twi. ● *adjective* of or relating to the Ashanti or their language. [Twi *Asante*]

ash blond *noun* **1** a very pale blond colour. **2** a person with hair of this colour.

ash·can *noun US* a garbage can.

Ash·croft, Dame Peggy (Edith Margaret Emily) (1907–91), English

stage and film actress, noted for her Shakespearean roles. She won an Oscar for best supporting actress for *A Passage to India* (1984).

Ashe, Ar·thur (Rob·ert) (1943–93), US tennis player. He won the US Open championship in 1968 and Wimbledon in 1975, and was the first black male player to achieve world rankings.

ashen¹ *adjective* **1** ash-coloured; deathly pale. **2** of or resembling ashes.

ashen² *adjective* **1** of or relating to the ash tree. **2** *archaic* made of ash wood.

Asher *Bible* **1** a Hebrew patriarch, son of Jacob and Zilpah (Gen. 30:12, 13). **2** one of the 12 tribes of Israel traditionally descended from him.

Ash·ga·bat /'aʃgə,bat/ (also **Ash·kha·bad** /,aʃkə'bad/) the capital of the central Asian republic of Turkmenistan; pop. (est. 2002) 711,000.

Ash·kelon see ASHQELON.

Ash·ken·azi /,aʃkə'nɒzi/ *noun* (pl. **Ash·ken·azim** /-zɪm/) a Jew of central, northern, or eastern Europe, or of such ancestry (*compare* SEPHARDI). □ **Ash·ken·azic** *adjective* [modern Hebrew, from *Ashkenaz* a descendant of Japheth (Gen. 10:3)]

Ash·ken·azy /,aʃkə'nɒzi/ **Vlad·i·mir David·ovich** (b.1937), Russian-born pianist and conductor, renowned for his interpretations of the music of Mozart, Scriabin, Rachmaninov, and Prokofiev.

Ash·kha·bad see ASHGABAT.

ash·lar /'aʃlər/ *noun* **1** a large square-cut stone used in building. **2** masonry made of ashlars. **3** such masonry used as a facing on a rough rubble or brick wall. [Old French *aisselier* from Latin *axilla* diminutive of *axis* board]

ash-leaved maple *noun* (also **ash-leaf maple**) = MANITOBA MAPLE.

Ash·ley, Laura (1925–85), Welsh designer of textiles, clothing, and home furnishings in traditional floral patterns and romantic neo-Victorian styles.

ashore *adverb* towards or on the shore or land.

ash·pan *noun* a tray under a grate to catch the ash.

Ash·qelon /'aʃkələn/ (also **Ash·kelon**) an ancient Mediterranean city, situated to the south of Tel Aviv, in Israel. A Philistine city state from the 12th to the 8th c. BC, it was known to the Greeks as Ascalon. A modern city of the same name has been built close to the ancient site.

ash·ram /'aʃrəm/ *noun* **1** (in India) a place of religious retreat for Hindus; a hermitage. **2** a place of religious retreat or community life modelled on the Indian ashram. [Sanskrit *āshrama* hermitage]

ash·rama /'aʃrəmə/ *noun Hinduism* any of the four stages of an ideal life, ascending from the status of pupil to the total renunciation of the world. [Sanskrit]

Ash Shari·qah see SHARJAH.

Ash·tanga /aʃ'taŋgə/ *noun* a type of yoga consisting of a series of poses executed in swift succession, combined with deep, controlled breathing. [Sanskrit *ashtanga* having eight parts, from *ashtán* eight, because it is based on eight principles]

Ash·ton, Sir Fred·erick Wil·liam (1904–88), Ecuadorean-born British dancer, choreographer, and ballet director; co-founder of the Royal Ballet. His lyrical classicism is most evident in such works as *La Fille mal gardée* (1960) and *The Dream* (1964).

Ash·tor·eth /'aʃtə,reθ/ (also **Ash·tor·oth**) see ASTARTE.

ash·tray *noun* a small receptacle for cigarette ash, stubs, etc.

Ashur see ASSUR¹, ².

Ashur·bani·pal /,aʃɜr'bɒnəpɒl/ (668–627 BC) the last great king of Assyria, the grandson of Sennacherib, celebrated for his library of over 20,000 clay tablets at Nineveh.

Ash Wednesday *noun Christianity* the first day of Lent, on which the foreheads of penitents are customarily marked with ashes.

ashy *adjective* (**ash·i·er, ash·i·est**) **1** = ASHEN¹. **2** covered with ashes.

Asia /'eiʒə/ the largest of the world's continents, constituting nearly one-third of the land mass, lying entirely north of the equator except for some SE Asian islands. It is connected to Africa by the isthmus of Suez, and borders Europe (part of the same land mass) along the Ural Mountains and across the Caspian Sea. The continent is dominated by China, India, and parts of the former USSR, and contains more than half of the world's population.

Asi·ago /ɒsi'ɒgo/ *noun* a hard light yellow cheese made from cow's milk. [*Asiago* in N Italy]

Asia Minor the western peninsula of Asia, also known as Anatolia, which constitutes the bulk of modern Turkey. The first major civilization established there was that of the Hittites in the 2nd millennium BC. Taken over the centuries by Greeks, Macedonians, and Romans, it eventually fell to the Turks, becoming part of the Ottoman

Empire from the end of the 13th c. until the establishment of modern Turkey after the First World War.

Asian ● *noun* **1** a native of Asia. **2** a person of Asian descent. ● *adjective* of or relating to Asia or its people, customs, or languages.

Asian pear *noun* = APPLE PEAR.

Asiat·ic /ˌeiʃiːˈatək, ˌeiz-/ ● *noun offensive* an Asian. ● *adjective* Asian.

ASIC /ˈasɪk/ *abbreviation Computing* application-specific integrated circuit.

A-side *noun* **1** the first side of a recording, esp. the side of a single featuring the music deemed by the producers to have the greater commercial potential. **2** the music on this side.

aside ● *adverb* **1** to or on one side; away. **2** out of consideration (placed after noun: *joking aside*). ● *noun* **1** words spoken in a play for the audience to hear, but supposed not to be heard by the other characters. **2** an incidental remark. □ **aside from** apart from. **set aside 1** put to one side. **2** keep for a special purpose or future use. **3** reject or disregard. **4** *Law* annul. **5** remove (land) from agricultural production for fallow, forestry, or other use. **take aside** engage (a person) esp. for a private conversation. [originally *on side*: see A²]

Asi·mov /ˈazɪˌmɒf/ **Isaac** (1920–92), Russian-born US author and biochemist; his prolific output included science fiction and books on science for the non-specialist.

asin·ine /ˈasɪˌnain/ *adjective* extremely stupid. □ **asin·in·ity** /-ˈnɪnɪti/ *noun* [Latin *asininus* from *asinus* ass]

Asir Mountains /əˈsiːr/ a range of mountains in SW Saudi Arabia, running parallel to the Red Sea.

-asis *suffix* (usu. as **-iasis**) forming the names of diseases (*psoriasis; satyriasis*). [Latin from Greek *-asis* in nouns of state from verbs in *-aō*]

ask *verb* **1** *transitive* call for an answer to or about (*ask her about it; ask him his name; ask a question of her*). **2** *transitive* seek to obtain from another person (*ask a favour of; ask to be allowed*). **3** *transitive* (usu. foll. by *out* or *over*, or *to* (a function etc.)) invite; request the company of (*must ask them over; asked her to dinner*). **4** *intransitive* (foll. by *for*) seek to obtain, meet, or be directed to (*ask for a donation; ask for the post office; asking for you*). □ **ask after** inquire about (esp. a person). **ask for it** *slang* invite trouble. **ask me another** *informal* I do not know. **for the asking** (obtainable) for nothing. **I ask you!** an exclamation of disgust, surprise, etc. **if you ask me** *informal* in my opinion. □ **ask·er** *noun* [Old English *āscian* etc. from West Germanic]

askance /əˈskans/ *adverb* sideways or squinting. □ **look askance at** regard with suspicion or disapproval. [16th c.: origin unknown]

as·kari /aˈskɑri/ *noun* (pl. same or **as·karis**) a soldier or police officer in E Africa. [Arabic '*askarī* soldier]

askew ● *adverb* obliquely, crookedly; awry. ● *predicative adjective* oblique, crooked; awry.

asking price *noun* the price of an object set by the seller.

ASL *abbreviation* **1** AMERICAN SIGN LANGUAGE. **2** above sea level.

aslant ● *adverb* obliquely or at a slant. ● *preposition* obliquely across (*lay aslant the path*).

asleep *predicative adjective & adverb* **1 a** in or into a state of sleep (*he fell asleep*). **b** inactive, inattentive (*the nation is asleep*). **2** (of a limb etc.) numb. **3** *euphemism* dead. □ **asleep at the switch** *N Amer.* inattentive.

A/SLt *abbreviation Cdn* ACTING SUB-LIEUTENANT.

ASM *abbreviation* air-to-surface missile.

As·mara /asˈmɑrə/ (also **As·mera** /asˈmerə/) the capital of Eritrea; pop. (est. 2002) 392,500.

As·mo·deus /asˈmoːdiəs/ (in Jewish demonology) the king of the demons.

asocial /eiˈsoːʃəl/ *adjective* **1** not social; anti-social. **2** inconsiderate of or hostile to others.

Asoka /əˈsoːkə/ (died *c.*232 BC) emperor of India from *c.*269 BC. After a campaign of conquest he renounced war and embraced Buddhism, adopting a policy of non-violence.

asp *noun* **1** a cobra, *Naja haje*, native to N Africa and Arabia, legendary as the snake which killed Cleopatra. **2** either of two small vipers: **a** (in full **asp viper**) *Vipera aspis*, native to S Europe, resembling a small adder. **b** (in full **horned asp**) *Cerastes cornutus*, with a large head and two small horns above the eyes, found in the deserts of N Africa and SW Asia. *Also called* HORNED VIPER. [Old French *aspe* or Latin *aspis* from Greek]

as·para·gus *noun* any plant of the genus *Asparagus*, esp. *A. officinalis* with edible young shoots used as a vegetable. [Latin from Greek *asparagos*]

asparagus fern *noun* a decorative fern-like plant, *Asparagus setaceus*, having feathery foliage used in flower arrangements.

as·par·tame /ˈaspɑrˌteim/ *noun* a very sweet low-calorie sugar substitute derived from amino acids. Chem. formula: $C_{14}H_{18}N_2O_5$. [ASPARTIC (see ASPARTIC ACID) + -ame, prob. from phenylalanine + methyl + ester]

as·par·tic acid /aˈspɑrtɪk/ *noun* an acidic amino acid present in proteins and important in animal metabolism. [French *aspartique*, formed arbitrarily from ASPARAGUS]

as·pect *noun* **1 a** a particular component or feature of a matter (*only one aspect of the problem*). **b** a particular way in which a matter may be considered. **2** a facial expression; an appearance or look (of a person or thing) (*a cheerful aspect*). **3** the side of a building or location facing a particular direction (*southern aspect*). **4** *Grammar* a verbal category or form expressing inception, duration, or completion. **5** *Astronomy & Astrology* the relative position of planets etc. measured by angular distance. □ **as·pec·tual** *adjective* (in sense 4). [Latin *aspectus* from *adspicere aspect-* look at (as AD-, *specere* look)]

aspect ratio *noun* **1** the ratio of picture width to height on a movie theatre screen, television set, etc. **2** *Aviation* the ratio of the span to the mean chord of an airfoil.

Aspen a resort in south central Colorado; pop. (2000) 5,914. Formerly a silver-mining town, it is now a thriving recreational centre, noted particularly for its skiing facilities.

aspen *noun* any of several poplars characterized by leaves which tremble in the slightest wind, esp. *Populus tremuloides*, widely distributed across N America, and *P. tremula*, found in Europe. [earlier name *asp* from Old English *æspe* + -EN² forming adj. taken as noun]

Asper, Is·rael Har·old ('Izzy') (1932–2003), Canadian politician and media magnate, who turned a local TV station in Winnipeg into CanWest Global Communications, a vast media empire with TV stations in all parts of Canada and broadcast interests in Australia, New Zealand, the UK and elsewhere, as well as extensive newspaper holdings throughout Canada.

as·per·ity /əˈsperɪti/ *noun* (pl. **-ities**) **1** harshness or sharpness of temper or tone. **2** roughness. **3** a rough excrescence. [Latin *asperitas* from *asper* rough]

Asperity Mountain a peak (3 716 m) in the Coast Mountains of southwestern BC, near Mount Waddington. [because of its sharp and daunting appearance]

as·perse /əˈspɜrs/ *transitive verb* attack the reputation of; calumniate. [Middle English, = besprinkle, from Latin *aspergere aspers-* (as AD-, *spargere* sprinkle)]

as·per·sion /əˈspɜrʒən/ *noun* a disparaging remark. □ **cast aspersions on** attack the reputation or integrity of.

as·phalt /ˈasfɒlt, ˈaʃ-/ ● *noun* **1** a dark bituminous pitch occurring naturally or made from petroleum. **2** a mixture of this with sand, gravel, etc., for surfacing roads etc. ● *transitive verb* surface with asphalt. □ **as·phalt·er** *noun* **as·phalt·ic** /-ˈfɒltɪk/ *adjective* [Greek *asphalton*]

aspher·ical /eiˈsferɪkəl/ *adjective* (esp. of an optical lens) not spherical.

as·pho·del /ˈasfəˌdel/ *noun* **1** any liliaceous plant of the genus *Asphodelus*, native to the Mediterranean. **2** *literary* an immortal flower growing in Elysium. [Greek *asphodelos*: compare DAFFODIL]

as·phyxia /asˈfɪksiə/ *noun* a lack of oxygen in the blood, causing unconsciousness or death; suffocation. □ **as·phyx·ial** *adjective* **as·phyxi·ant** *adjective & noun* [modern Latin from Greek *asphuxia* from *a-* not + *sphuxis* pulse]

as·phyxi·ate /asˈfɪksiˌeit/ *transitive verb* cause (a person) to have asphyxia, smother; suffocate. □ **as·phyxi·a·tion** /-ˈeiʃən/ *noun* **as·phyxi·a·tor** *noun*

aspic *noun* **1** a clear savoury jelly prepared from meat or fish stock, used as a garnish or glaze or combined with meat, vegetables, etc. in moulded dishes. **2** a dish of jelled tomato juice with vegetables etc. [French, = ASP, from the colours of the jelly (compared to those of the asp)]

as·pi·dis·tra /ˌaspɪˈdɪstrə/ *noun* any liliaceous foliage plant of the genus *Aspidistra*, with broad tapering leaves, native to E Asia, esp. *A. lurida*, often grown as a houseplant. [modern Latin from Greek *aspis -idos* shield (from the shape of the leaves)]

aspir·ant /ˈaspɪrənt, əˈspairənt/ ● *adjective* aspiring. ● *noun* a person who aspires.

aspir·ate /ˈaspɪrət/ *Phonetics* ● *adjective* **1** pronounced with an exhalation of breath. **2** blended with the sound of *h*. ● *noun* **1** a consonant pronounced in this way. **2** the sound of *h*. ● *verb* /-ˌreit/ **1 a** *transitive* pronounce with a breath. **b** *intransitive* make the sound of *h*.

2 *transitive Med.* draw (fluid) by suction from a vessel or cavity. □ **normally aspirated** (of an internal combustion engine) supplied with air at normal pressure rather than by a supercharger. [Latin *aspiratus* past participle of *aspirare*: see ASPIRE]

aspi·ra·tion /ˌaspɪˈreɪʃən/ *noun* **1** a strong desire to achieve an end; an ambition. **2** the act or process of drawing breath. **3** the action of aspirating. □ **aspir·a·tion·al** *adjective*

aspir·a·tor /ˈaspɪˌreɪtɜr/ *noun* an apparatus for aspirating fluid.

as·pire /əˈspaɪr/ *intransitive verb* (usu. foll. by *to* or *after*, or *to* + infin.) **1** have ambition or strong desire (*aspired to be prime minister*). **2** *archaic* rise high. [Latin *aspirare* from *ad* to + *spirare* breathe]

As·pir·in /ˈasprɪn, ˈaspɪrɪn/ *noun* (*pl.* same or **As·pir·ins**) *proprietary* **1** a white powder, acetylsalicylic acid, used to relieve pain and reduce fever. **2** a tablet of this. [German, formed as ACETYL + *spiraeic* (= SALICYLIC) *acid* + -IN]

as·pir·ing *adjective* **1** desirous of attaining a specified position, career, etc. (*an aspiring actor*). **2** having strong desire for advancement; ambitious.

asquint /əˈskwɪnt/ *predicative adjective & adverb* (usu. *look asquint*) to one side; from the corner of an eye. [perhaps from Dutch *schuinte* slant]

As·quith /ˈaskwɪθ/ **Her·bert Henry** (1852–1928), British prime minister, 1908–16.

ass¹ ● *noun* **1 a** either of two kinds of four-legged long-eared mammal of the horse genus *Equus, E. africanus* of Africa and *E. hemionus* of Asia. **b** (in general use) a donkey. **2** a stupid person. □ **make an ass of** make (a person) look absurd or foolish. [Old English *assa* through Old Celtic from Latin *asinus*]

ass² *noun coarse slang* **1** the buttocks. **2** the rectum. **3 a** sexual gratification. **b** *derogatory* a woman or women regarded as an object providing this. □ **haul ass** *see* HAUL. **kick ass** *see* KICK. **kiss ass** *see* KISS. [variant of ARSE]

Assad /aˈsad/ **Hafez al-** (1928–2000), president of Syria 1971–2000.

as·sa·gai *var. of* ASSEGAI.

assai /aˈsaɪ/ *adverb Music* very (*adagio assai*). [Italian]

as·sail *transitive verb* **1** make a strong or concerted attack on. **2** make a strong or constant verbal attack on (*was assailed with angry questions*). **3** make a resolute start on (a task). □ **as·sail·able** *adjective* [Old French *asaill-* stressed stem of *asalir* from medieval Latin *assalire* from Latin *assilire* (as AD-, *salire salt-* leap)]

as·sail·ant *noun* a person who attacks another, esp. physically.

Assam¹ /aˈsam/ a state in NE India; capital, Dispur.

Assam² /aˈsam/ a strong, dark brown tea from Assam.

As·sam·ese /asəˈmiːz/ ● *noun* (*pl.* same) **1** a native or inhabitant of Assam. **2** the Indic (official) language of Assam. ● *adjective* of or relating to Assam, its people, or its language.

as·sas·sin *noun* **1** a killer, esp. of a political or religious leader. **2** (**Assassin**) *hist.* a member of any of several Muslim sects in the 11th–13th c., notorious for murdering Crusaders and other political and religious opponents. [medieval Latin *assassinus* from Arabic *ḥaššāš* hashish-eater, since the medieval Assassins were reputed to consume hashish to fortify themselves for action]

as·sas·sin·ate *transitive verb* kill (esp. a political or religious leader) for political or religious motives. □ **as·sas·sin·a·tion** *noun*

assassin bug *noun* any insect of the large family Reduviidae, many of which suck blood from their prey.

as·sault ● *noun* **1** a violent physical or verbal attack. **2** *Law* **a** (in civil law) an act that threatens physical harm to a person. **b** (in criminal law) threatened or actual physical contact without consent. **c** = SEXUAL ASSAULT. **3** (*attributive*) relating to or used in a military assault (*assault craft; assault troops*). **4** a vigorous start made to a lengthy or difficult task. **5** a final rush on a fortified place, esp. at the end of a prolonged attack. ● *transitive verb* **1** make an assault on. **2** sexually assault (see SEXUAL ASSAULT). □ **assault and battery** *Law* (in civil law) a threatening act that is followed by physical contact without consent, whether or not harm is caused. □ **as·sault·er** *noun* **as·sault·ive** *adjective* [Old French *asaut* ultimately from Latin (*salire salt-* leap)]

assault course *noun Brit.* an obstacle course used in training soldiers etc.

assault rifle *noun* a lightweight, automatic or semi-automatic military rifle using high-performance ammunition.

assay /əˈseɪ, ˈaseɪ/ ● *noun* a test to determine the composition of a substance, esp. the analysis of an ore or metal to determine its purity. ● *transitive verb* **1** analyze (a substance) to determine its composition or to ascertain the activity of certain substances in it. **2** determine the

presence or activity of (a substance) by testing. **3** analyze or examine. **4** attempt or try. □ **assay·er** *noun* [Old French *assaier, assai,* var. of *essayer, essai:* see ESSAY]

assay office *noun* an establishment which analyzes metals, ores, etc. and is authorized to put hallmarks on precious metals.

ass-backwards *adjective slang* backwards.

as·se·gai /ˈasəˌgaɪ/ *noun* (also **as·sa·gai**) a slender iron-tipped spear made from hardwood, used esp. by southern African peoples. [obsolete French *azagaie* or Portuguese *azagaia* from Arabic *az-zaḡāyah* from *al* the + *zaḡāyah* spear]

as·sem·blage *noun* **1** the act or an instance of bringing or coming together. **2** a collection of things or gathering of people. **3 a** the act or an instance of fitting together. **b** an object made of pieces fitted together. **4** a work of art made by grouping found or unrelated objects.

as·sem·ble *verb* **1** *transitive & intransitive* gather together; collect. **2** *transitive* arrange in order. **3** *transitive* fit together the parts of (*assemble the bicycle*). **4** *transitive Computing* produce (a machine-coded form of a low-level symbolic code). [Old French *asembler,* ultimately from Latin *ad* to + *simul* together]

as·sem·bler *noun* **1** a person who assembles a machine or its parts. **2** *Computing* **a** a program for converting instructions written in low-level symbolic code into machine code. **b** the low-level symbolic code itself; an assembly language.

as·sem·bly *noun* (*pl.* **-blies**) **1** the act or an instance of assembling or gathering together. **2 a** a group of persons gathered together for a specific purpose. **b** a general gathering of the members of a school. **3** (also **Assembly**) a legislative council or deliberative body, esp.: **a** = GENERAL ASSEMBLY. **b** = HOUSE OF ASSEMBLY. **c** = LEGISLATIVE ASSEMBLY. **d** = NATIONAL ASSEMBLY. **4** the assembling of a machine or structure or its parts. **5** a number of component parts fitted together to form a whole. **6** *Military* a call to assemble, given by drum or bugle.

assembly language *noun Computing* a low-level language employing mnemonic symbols which correspond exactly to groups of machine instructions.

assembly line *noun* a sequence of machines and workers along which a product moves as it is assembled in stages.

as·sembly·man *noun* (*pl.* **-men**) **1** a member of an (esp. legislative) assembly. **2** *Cdn hist.* (in PEI) one of the two representatives elected to the Legislative Assembly in each riding (compare COUNCILLOR 3).

Assembly of First Nations a national political organization officially representing status First Nations in Canada. Abbr.: **AFN**.

assembly room *noun* **1** a public room in which meetings or social functions are held. **2** (also **assembly shop**) a place where a machine or its components are assembled.

ass-end *noun slang* the back or rear end of something.

as·sent ● *intransitive verb* (usu. foll. by *to*) **1** consent (*assented to my request*). **2** express agreement (*'That's true,' he assented*). ● *noun* **1** acceptance or agreement (*a nod of assent*). **2** consent or sanction, esp. official (*see also* ROYAL ASSENT). □ **as·sent·er** *noun* (also **as·sent·or**) [ultimately from Latin *assentire* (*ad* to, *sentire* think)]

as·sert *verb* **1** *transitive* declare; state clearly (*assert one's beliefs; assert that it is so*). **2** *reflexive* **a** (of a person) insist on one's rights or opinions; demand recognition. **b** (of a prevailing mood, tendency, etc.) become influential. **3** *transitive* make or enforce a claim to (*assert one's rights*). □ **as·ser·tor** *noun* (also **as·ser·ter**). [Latin *asserere* (as AD-, *serere sert-* join)]

as·ser·tion *noun* **1** a declaration; a forthright statement. **2** the act or an instance of asserting. **3** (also **self-assertion**) insistence on the recognition of one's rights or claims.

as·sert·ive *adjective* **1** tending to assert oneself; forthright, positive. **2** dogmatic. □ **as·sert·ive·ly** *adverb* **as·sert·ive·ness** *noun*

asses *pl.* of AS², ASS¹, ASS².

as·sess *transitive verb* **1** determine or estimate the size, quality, or extent of. **2** judge or evaluate. **3 a** estimate the value of (a property) for taxation. **b** fix the amount of (a tax etc.) and impose it on a person or community. **4** penalize or fine a specific amount (*assessed $100 in damages; assessed a minor penalty*). □ **as·sess·able** *adjective*

as·sess·ment *noun* [French *assesser* from Latin *assidēre* (as AD-, *sedēre* sit)]

as·ses·sor *noun* **1** a person who makes assessments, esp. one who assesses taxes or estimates the value of property for taxation or insurance purposes. **2** a person called upon to advise a judge, committee of inquiry, etc., on technical questions. □ **as·ses·sor·ial** /ˌaseˈsɔriəl/ *adjective* [Latin *assessor -oris* assistant judge (as ASSESS, -OR¹): sense 1 from medieval Latin]

Consonants: b *but*   d *dog*   f *few*   g *get*   h *her*   j *yes*   k *cat*   l *leg*   m *man*   n *no*   p *pen*   r *red*   s *sit*

asset noun **1 a** a useful or valuable quality. **b** a person or thing possessing such a quality or qualities (*is an asset to the company*). **2** (usu. in *pl.*) **a** property and possessions, esp. regarded as having value in meeting debts, commitments, etc. **b** any possession having value. [*assets* (taken as pl.), from Anglo-French *asetz* from Old French *asez* enough, ultimately from Latin *ad* to + *satis* enough]

asset allocation noun investment in a variety of assets, such as stocks, bonds, and property, designed to minimize an investor's risk.

asset-stripping noun *Commerce* the practice of taking over a company in financial difficulty and selling off each of its assets separately at a profit without regard for the company's future. □ **asset-stripper** noun

as·sev·er·ate /əˈsevəˌreɪt/ transitive verb declare solemnly. □ **as·sev·er·a·tion** noun [Latin *asseverare* (as AD-, *severus* serious)]

ass·hole noun *N Amer.* coarse slang **1** the anus. **2** a contemptible person.

as·sibi·late /əˈsɪbɪˌleɪt/ transitive verb *Linguistics* **1** pronounce (a sound) as a sibilant or affricate ending in a sibilant. **2** alter (a syllable) to become this. □ **as·sibi·la·tion** /-ˈleɪʃən/ noun [Latin *assibilare* (as AD-, *sibilare* hiss)]

assi·du·ity /ˌasɪˈdʒuːɪti, -ˈdjuːɪti/ noun (pl. **-ities**) **1** constant or close attention to what one is doing. **2** (usu. in *pl.*) constant attentions to another person. [Latin *assiduitas* (as ASSIDUOUS, -ITY)]

as·sidu·ous /əˈsɪdʒuəs, -djuəs/ adjective **1** persevering, hard-working. **2** attending closely. □ **as·sidu·ous·ly** adverb **as·sidu·ous·ness** noun [Latin *assiduus* (as ASSESS)]

as·sign ● transitive verb **1** (usu. foll. by *to*) **a** allot as a share, responsibility, task, etc. (*assign homework*). **b** appoint to a position, task, etc. **2** fix (a time, place, etc.) for a specific purpose. **3** (foll. by *to*) ascribe or refer to (a reason, date, etc.) (*assigned the manuscript to 1832*). **4** (foll. by *to*) transfer formally (esp. personal property) to (another). ● noun an assignee. □ **as·sign·able** adjective **as·sign·er** noun **as·sign·or** noun (in sense 4 of v.). [Latin *assignare* mark out to (as AD-, *signum* sign)]

as·sig·na·tion /ˌasɪɡˈneɪʃən/ noun **1 a** an appointment to meet. **b** a secret appointment, esp. between illicit lovers. **2** the act or an instance of assigning or being assigned.

as·sign·ee /ˌasaɪˈniː/ noun **1** a person appointed to act for another. **2** a person to whom property or rights are legally transferred.

as·sign·ment noun **1** something assigned, esp. a task allotted to a person. **2** the act or an instance of assigning or being assigned. **3 a** a legal transfer. **b** the document effecting this.

as·simi·late verb **1** transitive **a** absorb and digest (food etc.) into the body. **b** absorb (information etc.) into the mind. **2** transitive absorb (people) into a larger group, esp. by causing a minority culture to acquire the characteristics of the majority culture. **3** intransitive be absorbed into the body, mind, or a larger group. **4** transitive *Linguistics* make (a sound) more like another in the same or next word. **5** transitive (usu. foll. by *to*, *with*) make similar to; cause to resemble. □ **as·simi·la·ble** adjective **as·simi·la·tion** noun **as·simi·la·tion·ism** noun **as·simi·la·tion·ist** noun & adjective **as·simi·la·tive** adjective **as·simi·la·tor** noun **as·simi·la·tory** adjective [Middle English from Latin *assimilare* (as AD-, *similis* like)]

As·sini·boia /əˌsɪnɪˈbɔɪə/ hist. **1** (1811–1870) the area of land granted by the Hudson's Bay Company to Lord Selkirk, encompassing the basins of the Souris, Assiniboine and Red Rivers in present-day S Manitoba, N Dakota, and Minnesota (*compare* RED RIVER SETTLEMENT). **2** (1882–1905) a district of the North-West Territories occupying what is now S Saskatchewan. □ **As·sini·boian** noun & adjective [ASSINIBOINE + -A¹]

As·sini·boine /əˈsɪnɪbɔɪn/ ● noun **1** (pl. same or **-boines**) a member of an Aboriginal people living in S Saskatchewan and NE Montana. **2** the Siouan language of the Assiniboine. ● adjective of or relating to the Assiniboine or their language. [Canadian French from Ojibwa *assini-pwan*, lit. 'stone Sioux', from their practice of cooking by placing heated stones in water]

Assiniboine, Mount a peak (3 618 m) in the Rocky Mountains, situated on the BC–Alberta border, south of Banff.

Assiniboine River a river in SE Saskatchewan and S Manitoba, 1 070 km (665 miles) long, rising north of Yorkton and flowing first southeastward, then eastward through Brandon and Portage la Prairie, before joining the Red River at Winnipeg.

As·sisi /əˈsiːzi/ a town in the province of Umbria in central Italy; pop. (2001) 24,443. It is the birthplace of St. Francis of Assisi, whose tomb is located there.

as·sist ● verb **1** transitive help (a person, process, etc.) (*assisted them in running the classroom*). **2** intransitive act as an assistant (*assisted in the*

ceremony). **3** *Hockey* **a** intransitive (usu. foll. by *on*) score an assist. **b** transitive set up (a goal scorer) with an assist. ● noun **1 a** *Hockey* a point awarded to up to two players who successively touch the puck with their stick immediately before a teammate scores a goal. **b** *Baseball* a fielder's action of helping to put out an opponent. **c** *Basketball* a pass the recipient of which immediately scores a basket. **2** *N Amer.* an act of helping. □ **as·sist·ance** noun **as·sist·er** noun [Latin *assistere* take one's stand by (as AD-, *sistere* take one's stand)]

as·sist·ant noun **1** a helper. **2** (often *attributive*) a person who assists, esp. as a subordinate in a particular job or role. □ **assist·ant·ship** noun

assistant commissioner noun *Cdn* an officer ranking above chief superintendent and below deputy commissioner in the RCMP.

assistant director general noun *Cdn Que.* an officer of the Sûreté du Québec ranking above chief inspector and below director general.

assistant professor noun *N Amer.* a university instructor ranking below an associate professor and above a lecturer.

assist·ed suicide noun suicide effected with the assistance of another person, esp. the taking of lethal drugs, provided by a doctor for the purpose, by a patient considered incurable.

as·size /əˈsaɪz/ noun (usu. in pl.) **1** *Cdn* **a** a session of a court. **b** a trial or lawsuit held before a travelling judge. **2** *Brit. hist.* until 1971, a court sitting at intervals in each county of England and Wales to administer the civil and criminal law. [Old French *as(s)ise*, fem. past participle of *aseeir* sit at, from Latin *assidēre*: compare ASSESS]

ass-kissing noun (also **ass-licking**) *N Amer.* coarse slang obsequiousness for the purpose of gaining favour; toadying. □ **ass-kisser** noun

Assn. abbreviation Association.

Assoc. abbreviation (as part of a title etc.) **1** Association. **2** Associate. **3** Associated.

as·so·ci·ate ● verb /əˈsoːsiˌeɪt, -ˌʃiˌeɪt/ **1** transitive connect in the mind (*associate red with danger*). **2** transitive join or combine. **3** reflexive make oneself a partner; declare oneself in agreement (*did not want to associate myself with the plan*). **4** intransitive combine for a common purpose. **5** intransitive (usu. foll. by *with*) meet frequently or have dealings. ● noun /əˈsoːsiət, -ʃiət/ **1** a business partner or colleague. **2** a friend or companion. **3** a subordinate member of a body, institute, etc. **4** a thing connected with another. ● adjective /əˈsoːʃət, -siət/ **1** joined in companionship, function, or dignity. **2** allied; in the same group or category. **3** of less than full status (*associate member*). □ **as·so·ci·ate·ship** noun **as·so·ci·ator** noun **as·so·ci·atory** adjective [Latin *associatus* past participle of *associare* (as AD-, *socius* sharing, allied)]

associate professor noun *N Amer.* a university instructor ranking below a full professor and above an assistant professor.

as·so·ci·a·tion noun **1** a group of people or organizations united for a joint purpose. **2** the act or an instance of associating. **3** fellowship or companionship. **4** a mental connection between ideas. **5** *Chem.* a loose aggregation of molecules. **6** *Ecology* a group of related plants living in a community. □ **as·so·ci·a·tion·al** adjective

Association Football noun *Brit.* = SOCCER.

as·so·ci·a·tive /əˈsoːsiətɪv, əˈsoːʃi-/ adjective **1** of or involving association. **2** *Math. & Computing* involving the condition that a group of quantities connected by operators (*see* OPERATOR 4) gives the same result whatever their grouping, as long as their order remains the same, e.g. $(a \times b) \times c = a \times (b \times c)$.

As·somp·tion sash /əˌsʌmpʃən/ noun *Cdn hist.* = CEINTURE FLÉCHÉE. [*L'Assomption* in Quebec, where the best sashes were made]

as·son·ance /ˈasənəns/ noun the resemblance of sound between two syllables in nearby words, arising from the rhyming of two or more accented vowels, but not consonants, or the use of identical consonants with different vowels, e.g. *face*, *mail*, and *killed*, *cold*, *culled*. □ **as·son·ant** adjective **as·son·ate** /-ˌneɪt/ intransitive verb [Latin *assonare* respond to (as AD-, *sonus* sound)]

as·sort verb **1** transitive classify or arrange in groups. **2** intransitive suit; fit into; harmonize with (usu. *assort ill* or *well with*). [Old French *assorter* from *à* to + *sorte* SORT]

as·sort·ative mating noun *Biol.* selective mating based on the similarity of the partners' characteristics etc.

as·sort·ed adjective **1** of various sorts put together; miscellaneous. **2** sorted into groups. **3** matched (*ill-assorted*; *poorly assorted*).

as·sort·ment noun a set of various sorts of things or people put together; a mixed collection.

Asst. abbreviation Assistant.

as·suage /əˈsweidʒ/ *transitive verb* **1** calm or soothe (a person, pain, etc.). **2** appease or relieve (an appetite or desire). □ **as·suage·ment** *noun* **as·sua·ger** *noun* [Old French *as(s)ouagier*, ultimately from Latin *suavis* sweet]

As Sulay·ma·ni·yah see SULAYMANIYAH.

as·sume *transitive verb* **1** (often foll. by *that* + clause) take or accept as being true, without proof, for the purpose of argument or action. **2** simulate or pretend (*assumed an air of indifference*). **3** undertake (an office or duty). **4 a** take on (an aspect, attribute, etc.) (*the problem assumed immense proportions*). **b** accept (another's responsibility etc.) as one's own (*assumed the company's debts*). **5** arrogate, usurp, or seize (power etc.) (*assumed the presidency during a coup*). **6** *Cdn* (*Ont.*) (of a municipality) take responsibility for structural repair of (a road etc.). □ **as·sum·able** *adjective* [Latin *assumere* (as AD-, *sumere sumpt-* take)]

as·sump·tion *noun* **1** the act or an instance of assuming. **2 a** the act or an instance of accepting without proof. **b** a thing assumed in this way. **3** arrogance. **4** (**Assumption**) **a** the reception of the Virgin Mary bodily into heaven, according to Roman Catholic doctrine. **b** the feast day in honour of this (15 August). [Latin *assumptio* (as ASSUME, -ION)]

as·sump·tive *adjective* taken for granted. [Latin *assumptivus* (as ASSUME, -IVE)]

Assur¹ /ˈasʊr/ (also **Asur**, **Ashur** /ˈaʃʊr/) an ancient city state of Mesopotamia, situated on the Tigris River to the south of modern Mosul. The Assyrian Empires, the first of which was established early in the 2nd millennium BC, were centred on the city.

Assur² /ˈasʊr, ˈaʃʊr/ (also **Ashur**) the supreme god of the ancient Assyrians.

as·sur·ance *noun* **1** a positive declaration that a thing is true. **2** a solemn promise or guarantee. **3** *esp. Brit.* (or in names of insurance companies) insurance, esp. life insurance. **4** certainty. **5 a** self-confidence. **b** impudence.

Assur·banipal /ˌasʊrˈbɒnɪpəl/ *var. of* ASHURBANIPAL.

as·sure *transitive verb* **1** (often foll. by *of*) **a** make (a person) sure; convince (*assured him of my sincerity*). **b** tell (a person) confidently (*assured him the bus went to Halifax*). **2 a** make certain of; ensure the happening etc. of (*will assure her success*). **b** make safe. **3** *esp. Brit.* insure (esp. a life). □ **as·sur·able** *adjective* **as·sur·er** *noun* [Old French *aseürer*, ultimately from Latin *securus* safe, SECURE]

as·sured *adjective* **1** certain, guaranteed. **2** self-confident. □ **rest assured** remain confident. □ **as·sur·ed·ly** *adverb*

As·syr·ia /əˈsɪriə/ an ancient country in what is now N Iraq. From the early part of the 2nd millennium BC Assyria was the centre of a succession of empires; it was at its peak in the 8th and late 7th c. BC, when its rule stretched from the Persian Gulf to Egypt. It fell in 612 BC to a coalition of Medes and Chaldeans.

As·syr·ian /əˈsɪriən/ ● *noun* **1** an inhabitant of Assyria. **2** the Semitic language of Assyria. ● *adjective* of or relating to Assyria.

As·syr·iol·ogy /əˌsɪriˈɒlədʒi/ *noun* the study of the language, history, and antiquities of Assyria. □ **As·syr·iol·o·gist** *noun*

AST *abbreviation* ATLANTIC STANDARD TIME.

As·taire /əˈster/ **Fred** (born Frederick Austerlitz 1899–1987), US film actor and singer famous for his virtuosic dancing. In a career spanning several decades, he was the epitome of elegance and debonair grace. His best-known films are the 1930s musicals in which he starred with Ginger Rogers, including *Top Hat* (1935), *Follow the Fleet* (1936), and *Shall We Dance?* (1937).

As·tana /əˈstɒnə/ the capital (since 1997) of Kazakhstan; pop. (est. 2002) 293,800.

As·tarte /əˈstɑrti/ (in Phoenician mythology) a goddess of fertility and sexual love, identified with the Egyptian Isis, the Greek Aphrodite, and others. In the Bible she is referred to as Ashtaroth or Ashtoreth, and her worship is linked to that of Baal.

astat·ic /eiˈstatɪk, ə-/ *adjective* **1** not static; unstable or unsteady. **2** *Physics* not tending to keep one position or direction. [Greek *astatos* unstable, from *a-* not + *sta-* stand]

astatic galvanometer *noun* a galvanometer in which the effect of the earth's magnetic field on the meter needle is greatly reduced.

asta·tine /ˈastəˌtiːn/ *noun* a radioactive element, the heaviest of the halogens, which occurs naturally and can be artificially made by nuclear bombardment of bismuth. Symbol: **At**; at. no.: 85. [formed as ASTATIC + -INE⁴]

aster *noun* **1** any composite plant of the genus *Aster*, with bright daisy-like flowers, e.g. the Michaelmas daisy. **2** = CHINA ASTER. [Greek *astēr* star]

-aster *suffix* **1** forming nouns denoting poor quality (*criticaster*; *poetaster*). **2** *Bot.* denoting incomplete resemblance (*oleaster*). [Latin]

aster·isk /ˈastərɪsk/ ● *noun* **1** a symbol (*) used to mark printed or written text, typically as a reference to an annotation or to stand for omitted matter, etc. **2** this symbol used as a wild card in computer searches. ● *transitive verb* mark with an asterisk. [Greek *asteriskos* diminutive (as ASTER)]

aster·ism *noun* **1** a cluster of stars. **2** a group of three asterisks (⁂) calling attention to following text. **3** *Geol.* a figure of light having the form of a six-rayed star, seen in certain crystals. [Greek *asterismos* (as ASTER, -ISM)]

astern *adverb* (often foll. by *of*) *Naut. & Aviation* **1** aft; away to the rear. **2** backwards.

aster·oid *noun* **1** any of the small planetary bodies revolving around the sun, mainly between the orbits of Mars and Jupiter. **2** *Zool.* a starfish. □ **aster·oid·al** *adjective* [Greek *asteroeidēs* (as ASTER, -OID)]

asteroid belt *noun* the region between the orbits of Mars and Jupiter where most asteroids are found.

as·the·nia /asˈθiːniə/ *noun* *Med.* loss of strength; debility. [Greek *astheneia* from *asthenēs* weak]

as·then·ic /asˈθenɪk/ ● *adjective* **1** of lean or long-limbed build. **2** *Med.* of or characterized by asthenia. ● *noun* a lean long-limbed person.

as·theno·sphere /asˈθenəsfɪr/ *noun* *Geol.* the upper layer of the earth's mantle, whose capacity for gradual flow is thought to give rise to continental drift. [Greek *asthenēs* 'weak' + -o- + SPHERE]

asth·ma /ˈazmə/ *noun* a respiratory disorder, often provoked by allergy, causing wheezing and paroxysms of difficult breathing. [Greek *asthma -matos* from *azō* breathe hard]

asth·mat·ic /azˈmatɪk/ ● *adjective* relating to or suffering from asthma. ● *noun* a person suffering from asthma. □ **asth·mat·ic·ally** *adverb*

Asti /ˈasti/ *noun* (*pl.* **Astis**) a sparkling white wine from the province of Asti or neighbouring provinces in NW Italy, south of Turin.

astig·ma·tism /əˈstɪgməˌtɪzəm/ *noun* a defect in the eye or in a lens resulting in distorted images, as light rays are prevented from meeting at a common focus. □ **astig·matic** /ˌastɪgˈmatɪk/ *adjective* [A-¹ + Greek *stigma -matos* point]

as·tilbe /əˈstɪlbi/ *noun* any plant of the genus *Astilbe*, with plumelike heads of tiny white, red, orange, or pink flowers. [modern Latin from Greek *a-* not + *stilbē* fem. of *stilbos* glittering, from the inconspicuous (individual) flowers]

astir *predicative adjective & adverb* **1** in motion. **2** awake and out of bed (*astir early; already astir*). **3** excited. [A² + STIR¹ *noun*]

Asti Spu·mante /ˈasti spuːˈmanti, -ˈmɒntei/ *noun* a light, sweet, sparkling form of Asti. ¶ In 1994, Asti Spumante was officially renamed *Asti*.

ASTM *abbreviation* American Society for Testing and Materials.

Aston, Fran·cis Wil·liam (1877–1945), English physicist. He discovered many of the 287 naturally occurring isotopes of non-radioactive elements, and designed the first mass spectrograph.

as·ton·ish *transitive verb* amaze; surprise greatly. □ **as·ton·ish·ing** *adjective* **as·ton·ish·ing·ly** *adverb* **as·ton·ish·ment** *noun* [obsolete *astone* from Old French *estoner* from Gallo-Roman: see -ISH²]

Astor, Nancy (Witcher), Viscountess (née Langhorne) (1879–1964), US-born English Conservative politician, who became the first woman to sit in the British House of Commons.

astound *transitive verb* overcome with surprise or shock; amaze. □ **astound·ing** *adjective* **astound·ing·ly** *adverb* [obsolete *astound* (adj.) = *astoned* past participle of obsolete *astone*: see ASTONISH]

astrad·dle *adverb & predicative adjective* in a straddling position.

as·tra·gal /ˈastrəgəl/ *noun* *Archit.* a small semicircular moulding round the top or bottom of a column, often decorated with a bead pattern. [ASTRAGALUS]

as·trag·alus /əˈstragələs/ *noun* (*pl.* **-ali** /-ˌlai/) **1** *Anat.* = TALUS¹. **2** a leguminous plant of the large genus *Astragalus*, e.g. the milk vetch. [Latin from Greek *astragalos* ankle bone, moulding, a plant]

As·tra·khan /ˌastrəˈkan/ a city in S Russia, on the delta of the Volga River; pop. (2002) 482,000. Astrakhan fleeces were given their name because traders from the city brought them into Russia from central Asia.

as·tra·khan /ˈastrəˌkan/ *noun* **1** the dark curly fleece of young lambs from the region of Astrakhan. **2** a cloth imitating astrakhan. [ASTRAKHAN]

as·tral *adjective* **1** of or connected with the stars. **2** consisting of stars; starry. **3** relating to or arising from a supposed ethereal existence, esp.

of a counterpart of the body, associated with oneself in life and surviving after death. □ **as·tral·ly** adverb [Late Latin astralis from astrum star]

astray adverb & predicative adjective **1** in or into error or sin (esp. lead astray). **2** out of the right way. □ **go astray 1** be lost or mislaid. **2** wander from the right way. [Old French estraié past participle of estraier, ultimately from Latin extra out of bounds + vagari wander]

astride ● preposition with a leg on each side of; extending across. **●** adverb with a leg on each side, or with legs apart.

astrin·gent /əˈstrɪndʒənt/ **●** adjective **1** causing the contraction of body tissues. **2** checking bleeding. **3 a** severe, austere. **b** sharp, caustic. **●** noun an astringent substance or drug. □ **astrin·gency** noun **astrin·gent·ly** adverb [Latin astringere (as AD-, stringere bind)]

astro- combining form **1** relating to the stars or celestial bodies. **2** relating to outer space. [Greek from astron star]

astro·chem·istry noun the study of molecules and radicals in interstellar space.

astro·labe /ˈastrəˌleib/ noun an instrument, usu. consisting of a graduated disc and a pointer, formerly used to make astronomical measurements, esp. of the altitudes of celestial bodies, and as an aid in navigation. [Greek astrolabon, neuter of astrolabos 'star-taking']

as·trol·ogy noun the study of the movements and relative positions of celestial bodies interpreted as an influence on human affairs. □ **as·trol·oger** noun **astro·logic·al** adjective **as·trol·o·gist** noun [Latin astrologia from Greek (as ASTRO-, -LOGY)]

as·trom·etry /əˈstrɒmətri/ noun the measurement of the positions, motions, and magnitudes of stars.

astro·naut noun **1** a person who is trained to travel in a spacecraft. **2** Cdn (BC) informal a (usu. Asian) immigrant to Canada who commutes back to Hong Kong, Taiwan, etc. frequently to work, while leaving dependants resident in Canada (also attributive: astronaut family). [ASTRO-, after aeronaut]

astro·naut·ics noun the science of space travel.

astro·nomic·al adjective (also **astro·nomic**) **1** of or relating to astronomy. **2** extremely large; too large to contemplate. □ **astro·nomic·al·ly** adverb

astronomical unit noun a unit of measurement in astronomy equal to the mean distance from the centre of the earth to the centre of the sun, 1.495×10^{11} metres or 92.9 million miles.

astronomical year noun see YEAR noun 1.

as·tron·omy noun the study of the universe and its contents beyond the bounds of the Earth's atmosphere. □ **as·tron·omer** noun [Greek astronomia from astronomos (adj.) 'star-arranging', from nemō arrange]

astro·photog·raphy noun the use of photography in astronomy; the photographing of celestial objects and phenomena.

astro·phys·ics noun a branch of astronomy concerned with the physics and chemistry of celestial bodies. □ **astro·physic·al** adjective **astro·physi·cist** noun

Astro·turf noun proprietary a synthetic surface used as a substitute for grass on sports fields etc. [Astrodome, a sports stadium in Houston where it was first used, + TURF]

As·tur·ias¹ /aˈstʊriˌas/ an autonomous region and former principality of NW Spain; capital, Oviedo.

As·tur·ias² /aˈstʊriˌas/ **Mi·guel Ángel** (1899–1974), Guatemalan novelist and poet. His experimental novel The President (1946) deals with the disintegration of human relationships under a repressive dictatorship; he was awarded the Nobel Prize for literature in 1967.

as·tute adjective **1** shrewd; clever. **2** crafty. □ **as·tute·ly** adverb **as·tute·ness** noun [obsolete French astut or Latin astutus from astus craft]

As·tya·nax /aˈstaiəˌnaks/ Gk Myth the son of Hector and Andromache, who was born during the siege of Troy and thrown from its battlements by Neoptolemus after the capture of the city.

Asun·ción /əˌsʊnˈsjɒn/ the capital and chief port of Paraguay; pop. (est. 2002) 546,800.

asun·der adverb literary apart. [Old English on sundran into pieces: compare SUNDER]

Asur see ASSUR¹.

asura /ˈʌsʊrə/ noun a member of a class of divine beings in the Vedic period, which in Indian mythology tend to be evil (opposed to the devas) and in Zoroastrianism are benevolent. (Compare DEVA.) [Sanskrit]

ASV abbreviation AMERICAN STANDARD VERSION.

ASW abbreviation anti-submarine warfare.

Aswan /asˈwɒn/ a city on the Nile in S Egypt, 16 km (10 miles) north of Lake Nasser; pop. (est. 2002) 250,500. It is situated close to two dams across the Nile, one of which produces the greater part of Egypt's electricity.

aswarm adjective crowded or full.

aswirl adjective swirling; covered or surrounded with something swirling.

asy·lum /əˈsailəm/ noun **1 a** a sanctuary; protection, esp. for those pursued by the law (seek asylum). **b** = POLITICAL ASYLUM. **2** hist. any of various kinds of institution offering shelter and support to distressed or destitute individuals, esp. the mentally ill. [Latin from Greek asulon refuge, from a- not + sulon right of seizure]

asym·metry noun (pl. **-ries**) lack of symmetry. □ **asym·met·ric** adjective **asym·met·ric·al** adjective **asym·met·ric·al·ly** adverb

asymp·tom·atic /eɪˌsɪmptəˈmatɪk/ adjective producing or showing no symptoms.

asymp·tote /ˈasɪmpˌtoːt, ˈasɪmˌtoːt/ noun Math. a line that continually approaches a given curve but does not meet it at a finite distance. □ **asymp·tot·ic** /ˌasɪmpˈtɒtɪk/ adjective **asymp·tot·ic·ally** /ˌasɪmpˈtɒtɪkli/ adverb [modern Latin asymptota (linea line) from Greek asumptōtos not falling together, from a- not + sun together + ptōtos falling, from piptō fall]

asyn·chron·ous /eɪˈsɪŋkrənəs/ adjective **1** Computing & Telecommunications (of equipment or methods of working) making use of pulses to control the timing of operations that are sent when the previous operation is completed, rather than at regular intervals. **2** not going at the same rate and exactly together with something else. **3** (of two or more objects or events) not existing or happening at the same time. □ **asyn·chron·ous·ly** adverb

asyn·deton /əˈsɪndətən/ noun (pl. **asyn·deta** /-tə/) Grammar the omission or absence of a conjunction between parts of a sentence, as in I came, I saw, I conquered. □ **asyn·det·ic** /ˌasɪnˈdetɪk/ adjective [modern Latin from Greek asundeton (neuter adj.) from a- not + sundetos bound together]

AT abbreviation ATLANTIC TIME.

At symbol Chem. the element astatine.

at¹ preposition **1** expressing position, exact or approximate (wait at the corner; at the top of the hill; is at school; at a distance). **2** expressing a point in time (see you at three; went at dawn). **3** expressing a point in a scale or range (at boiling point; at her best). **4** expressing engagement or concern in a state or activity (at war; at work; at odds). **5** expressing a value or rate (sell at $10 each). **6 a** with or with reference to; in terms of (at a disadvantage; annoyed at losing; good at math; sick at heart; came at a run; at short notice; work at it). **b** by means of (starts at a touch; drank it at a gulp). **7** expressing: **a** motion towards (arrived at the station; went at them). **b** aim towards or pursuit of (physically or conceptually) (aim at the target; work at a solution; guess at the truth; laughed at us; has been at the booze again). □ **at all** see ALL. **at hand** see HAND. **at home** see HOME. **at it 1** engaged in an activity; working hard (let's get at it). **2** informal repeating a habitual (usu. disapproved of) activity (found them at it again). **at once** see ONCE. **at that** moreover (found one, and a good one at that). **at times** see TIME. **where it's at** slang the fashionable scene or activity. [Old English æt, related to Latin ad to]

at² /at/ noun (pl. same) a monetary unit of Laos, equal to one-hundredth of a kip. [Thai]

at- prefix assimilated form of AD- before t.

Ata·balipa /ˌatəˈbɒlipə/ var. of ATAHUALPA.

Ata·cama Desert /ˌatəˈkɒmə/ an arid region of W Chile, extending from the Peruvian border in the north over a distance of some 965 km (600 miles) to the south.

Ata·hualpa /ˌatəˈwɒlpə/ (also **Ata·balipa**) (c.1502–33), last ruler of the Inca Empire c.1525–33, who was captured and executed by the Spanish conquistador Pizarro.

Ata·lanta /ˈatəˈlantə/ Gk Legend a huntress loved by Meleager. She would marry no one who could not beat her in a foot race, but Melanion (or Hipponemes) won the race by throwing down three golden apples, which were so beautiful that Atalanta stopped to pick them up.

Ata·türk /ˈatəˌtɜrk/ **Kemal** (also **Mus·tafa Kemal**, **Kemal Pasha**) (1881–1938), Turkish general and president of Turkey 1923–1938. He wielded almost dictatorial powers in his struggle to make Turkey a modern secular nation.

atav·is·tic /ˌatəˈvɪstɪk/ adjective related to or characterized by reversion to something ancient or ancestral. □ **atav·ism** noun **atav·is·tic·ally** adverb [from Latin atavus forefather]

ataxia /əˈtaksiə/ noun Med. the loss of full control of bodily movements.

□ **ataxic** *adjective* [modern Latin *ataxia* from Greek from *a-* not + *taxis* order]

ATB *abbreviation* ALL-TERRAIN BICYCLE.

at-bat *noun Baseball* a turn at bat which results in the batter making either a hit or an out.

ATC *abbreviation* AIR TRAFFIC CONTROL.

Ate /ˈeɪti, ˈɒti/ *Gk Myth* the personification of blind folly.

ate *past of* EAT.

-ate[1] *suffix* **1** forming nouns denoting: **a** status or office (*doctorate*; *episcopate*). **b** state or function (*curate*; *magistrate*; *mandate*). **2** *Chem.* forming nouns denoting the salt of an acid with a corresponding name ending in *-ic* (*chlorate*; *nitrate*). **3** forming nouns denoting a group (*electorate*). **4** *Chem.* forming nouns denoting a product (*condensate*; *filtrate*). [from or after Old French *-at* or *é(e)* or from Latin *-atus* noun or past participle: compare -ATE[2]]

-ate[2] *suffix* **1** forming adjectives and nouns (*associate*; *delegate*; *duplicate*; *separate*). **2** forming adjectives from Latin or English nouns and adjectives (*cordate*; *insensate*; *Italianate*). [from or after (French *-é* from) Latin *-atus* past participle of verbs in *-are*]

-ate[3] *suffix* forming verbs (*associate*; *duplicate*; *fascinate*; *hyphenate*; *separate*). [from or after (French *-er* from) Latin *-are* (past participle *-atus*): compare -ATE[2]]

atel·ier /ˌatəlˈjeɪ/ *noun* a workshop or studio, esp. of an artist or designer. [French]

a tempo *adverb Music* in the previous tempo. [Italian, lit. 'in time']

Aten /ˈɒtən/ *Egyptian Myth* the name by which the sun or solar disc was worshipped, particularly during the reign of Akhenaten.

Atha·basca (also **Atha·paska**) the drainage basin of the Athabasca River, important in the early days of the fur trade. [Cree *athapaskaw*, lit. 'there are reeds here and there']

Athabasca, Lake a large lake (7 936 sq. km) straddling the border between NE Alberta and NW Saskatchewan.

Atha·bas·can (also **Atha·bas·kan**) *var. of* ATHAPASKAN.

Athabasca Pass a pass through the Rocky Mountains (1 748 m), situated on the BC–Alberta border, in the southwestern corner of Jasper National Park.

Athabasca River a river in Alberta, flowing over 1 200 km (745 miles) northeastward from the Columbia Icefield to the southwestern tip of Lake Athabasca.

Atha·bas·ka, District of (1882–1905) a district of the North-West Territories occupying what is now northern Alberta, Saskatchewan, and Manitoba.

Atha·na·sian Creed /ˌaθəˈneɪʃən/ *noun* an affirmation of Christian faith formerly much used in the Western Church. Its attribution to St. Athanasius is now generally abandoned (see AMBROSE).

Atha·na·sius /ˌaθəˈneɪʃəs/ **St.** (*c.*296–373), bishop of Alexandria, who vigorously upheld orthodoxy, especially against Arianism. He aided the ascetic movement in Egypt and introduced knowledge of monasticism to the West.

Atha·pas·kan (also **Athaba-, -scan**) ● *noun* **1** an Aboriginal language group, including the Beaver, Carrier, Tsilhqot'in, Chipewyan, Dogrib, Han, Hare, Kaska, Gwich'in, Sarcee, Sekani, Slave, Tagish, Tahltan, and Tutchone, of the subarctic regions of the NWT, Nunavut, Yukon, northern BC, and the northern Prairie provinces. **2** (*pl.* same or **-s**) a member of any of the N American Aboriginal peoples speaking languages of this family. ● *adjective* of or pertaining to the Athapaskan peoples or their languages. [ATHABASCA]

Atharva-Veda /əˌtɑrvəˈveɪdə, -ˈviːdə/ *noun* an ancient collection of sacred Hindu hymns and incantations, traditionally called the fourth Veda but originating outside Vedic society. [Sanskrit *atharvan* priest, *veda* knowledge]

athe·ism /ˈeɪθiˌɪzəm/ *noun* disbelief in the existence of God or gods. □ **athe·ist** *noun* **athe·is·tic** *adjective* **athe·is·tic·al** *adjective* [French *athéisme* from Greek *atheos* without God, from *a-* not + *theos* god]

athel·ing /ˈaθəlɪŋ/ *noun hist.* a prince or lord in Anglo-Saxon England. [Old English *ætheling* from West Germanic, from a base meaning 'race, family']

Athel·stan /ˈaθəlˌstan/ (895–939), king of Wessex and Mercia 924–39. One of the most successful of England's Anglo-Saxon monarchs, he invaded both Scotland and Wales and heavily defeated an invading Danish army.

Athe·na /əˈθiːnə/ (also **Athe·ne** /əˈθiːni/) *Gk Myth* the goddess of wisdom and the arts and patron goddess of Athens, equated with the Roman goddess Minerva. She sprang, fully armed and uttering her war cry, from the head of Zeus.

athen·aeum /ˌaθəˈniːəm, -ˈneɪəm/ *noun* (also **athen·eum**) **1** an institution for literary or scientific study. **2** a library or reading room. [Late Latin *Athenaeum* from Greek *Athēnaion* temple of Athene (used as a place of teaching)]

Athen·ian /əˈθiːniən/ ● *noun* a native or inhabitant of ancient or modern Athens. ● *adjective* of or relating to ancient or modern Athens. [Latin *Atheniensis* from *Athenae* from Greek *Athēnai* ATHENS]

Athenian Empire *see* DELIAN LEAGUE.

Ath·ens /ˈaθənz/ the capital of Greece; pop. (est. 2002) 3,126,600. A flourishing city state of ancient Greece from early times, Athens was an important cultural centre in the 5th c. BC: this was the time of Pericles, who commissioned many of the city's best-known buildings such as the Parthenon. After its capture by the Turks in 1456 Athens declined to the status of a village, until chosen as the capital of a newly independent Greece in 1834.

ath·ero·scler·o·sis /ˌaθəroʊskləˈroʊsɪs/ *noun* a form of arteriosclerosis characterized by the degeneration of the arteries because of the buildup of fatty deposits. □ **ath·ero·scler·ot·ic** /-ˈrɒtɪk/ *adjective* [German *Atherosklerose* from Greek *athērē* groats + SCLEROSIS]

Ather·ton Table·land /ˈaθərtən/ a plateau in the Great Dividing Range in NE Queensland, Australia.

athirst *predicative adjective* **1** (usu. foll. by *for*) eager (*athirst for knowledge*). **2** *archaic* thirsty.

ath·lete *noun* **1** a person who trains to compete in sports and other exercises requiring physical skill, strength, and endurance. **2** a person with a natural talent for sports. [Greek *athlētēs* from *athleō* contend for a prize (*athlon*)]

athlete's foot *noun* a fungal foot condition causing itching, flaking, and cracking of the skin, esp. between the toes.

athletes' village *noun* a concentration of housing usu. built specifically to accommodate athletes attending a large international competition.

ath·let·ic *adjective* **1** of or relating to athletes or athletics (*an athletic competition*). **2** muscular or physically fit. **3** active in, esp. skilled at, sports. □ **ath·let·ic·ally** *adverb* **ath·let·i·cism** /-ˈletɪˌsɪzəm/ *noun*

ath·let·ics *plural noun* (usu. treated as *sing.*) **1** competitive activities requiring physical skill and endurance. **2** esp. *Brit.* track and field events.

athletic shoe *noun* a shoe designed for sports or recreation.

athletic supporter *noun* = JOCKSTRAP.

Ath·lone /aˈθloʊn/ **Alex·an·der Au·gus·tus Fred·erick Cam·bridge, Earl of** (1874–1957), English soldier and Governor General of Canada, 1940–46. He was Governor General of South Africa, 1923–30.

at-home ● *noun* a social reception in a person's home. ● *adjective* occurring in or remaining in the home, as opposed to outside it.

-athon /əˈθɒn/ *combining form* (also **-a-thon**) forming nouns denoting: **1** an extended event involving a single activity, usu. to raise money for a charity (*walkathon*; *dance-a-thon*). **2** an activity of abnormal length (*gab-a-thon*). [after MARATHON]

Athos, Mount /ˈaθɒs, ˈeɪ-/ a narrow, mountainous peninsula in NE Greece, projecting into the Aegean Sea. It is inhabited by monks of the Orthodox Church who live in twenty monasteries founded in the 10th c. They forbid women and even female animals to set foot on the peninsula. □ **Atho·nite** /ˈaθəˌnaɪt/ *adjective & noun*

athwart ● *preposition* from side to side of. ● *adverb* **1** across from side to side (usu. obliquely). **2** *archaic* in opposition. [A[2] + THWART]

-atic *suffix* forming adjectives and nouns (*charismatic*; *fanatic*; *idiomatic*). [French *-atique* or Latin *-aticus*, often ultimately from Greek *-atikos*]

ati·gi /ˈatəgi, əˈtiːgi/ *noun Cdn* (*North*) a type of Inuit parka, made esp. from caribou skin, with the fur on the inside, worn either on its own or as the inner layer of a double-layered parka. [Inuktitut, from *attike* 'covering']

-ation *suffix* **1** forming nouns denoting an action or an instance of it (*alteration*; *flirtation*; *hesitation*). **2** forming nouns denoting a result or product of action (*plantation*; *starvation*; *vexation*) (*see also* -FICATION). [from or after French *-ation* or Latin *-atio -ationis* from verbs in *-are*: see -ION]

-ative *suffix* forming adjectives denoting a characteristic or propensity (*authoritative*; *imitative*; *pejorative*; *qualitative*; *talkative*). [from or after French *-atif -ative* or from Latin *-ativus* from past participle stem *-at-* of verbs in *-are* + *-ivus* (see -IVE): compare -ATIC]

At·lan·ta the state capital of Georgia in the US; pop. (2000) 416,474. □ **At·lan·tan** *noun & adjective*

At·lan·tean /ət'lantiən/ *adjective literary* **1** of or like Atlas, esp. in physical strength. **2** of, like, or relating to Atlantis. [Latin *Atlanteus* (as ATLAS)]

at·lan·tes /ət'lantiːz/ *plural noun Archit.* male figures carved in stone and used as columns to support the entablature of a Greek or Greek-style building (*compare* CARYATID). [Greek, pl. of *Atlas*: see ATLAS]

At·lan·tic ● *adjective* of or adjoining the Atlantic Ocean. ● *noun* = ATLANTIC OCEAN. [Greek *Atlantikos* (as ATLAS, -IC): originally of the Atlas Mountains, then of the sea near the W African coast]

Atlantic, Battle of the a succession of sea operations during the Second World War, in which Canadian, British, and US naval forces defended Allied shipping in the Atlantic from German U-boat attacks. About 2,800 Allied merchant ships, mainly British, were lost before the U-boat threat was eliminated.

Atlantic Canada = ATLANTIC PROVINCES. □ **Atlantic Canadian** *noun & adjective*

Atlantic Charter a declaration of eight common principles in international relations intended to guide a postwar peace settlement, drawn up by Winston Churchill and Franklin D. Roosevelt at their meeting off the coast of Newfoundland in August 1941.

Atlantic City a seaside resort city with many casinos in SE New Jersey; pop. 40,199.

Atlantic Daylight Time *noun* daylight time in the Atlantic Time zone. Abbr.: **ADT**.

At·lan·ti·cist /at'lantɪsɪst/ ● *adjective* advocating or favouring a close relationship between N America and Europe. ● *noun* a person who advocates or favours such a relationship.

Atlantic Ocean the ocean lying between Europe and Africa to the east and North and S America to the west. It is divided by the equator into the North Atlantic and the South Atlantic oceans. A submarine ridge known as the Mid-Atlantic Ridge runs down the centre from north to south, deep basins lying on either side.

Atlantic provinces *plural noun* (also **Atlantic Canada**) New Brunswick, Nova Scotia, PEI, and Newfoundland and Labrador (*compare* MARITIMES).

Atlantic puffin *noun see* PUFFIN.

Atlantic salmon *noun* a salmon, *Salmo salar*, inhabiting the coastal N Atlantic and its freshwater tributaries.

Atlantic Standard Time *noun* standard time in the Atlantic Time zone. Abbr.: **AST**.

Atlantic Time *noun* the time in a zone including the Maritime provinces, parts of Labrador and E Quebec, and eastern Central and S America. Atlantic Standard Time is four hours behind Greenwich Mean Time; Atlantic Daylight Time is three hours behind Greenwich Mean Time. Abbr.: **AT**.

At·lan·tis *Gk Legend* a fabled island reputedly overwhelmed by the sea.

Atlas *Gk Myth* one of the Titans, who was punished for his part in the revolt against Zeus by being made to support the heavens.

atlas *noun* **1** a book of maps or charts. **2** the cervical vertebra of the backbone articulating with the skull at the neck. [ATLAS]

Atlas Mountains a range of mountains in North Africa extending from Morocco to Tunisia in a series of chains. These include the Anti-Atlas, High Atlas, Middle Atlas, Rif Mountains, Tell Atlas, and Sahara Atlas.

at·latl /'atlatəl/ *noun* a device consisting of a wooden rod, used historically by N American Aboriginal peoples as a spear thrower. [Nahuatl *ahtlatl*]

Atlin Lake /'atlɪn/ a lake in northwestern BC, 95 km in length, situated southeast of Whitehorse. It is the source of the Yukon River and is a noted mining and hunting centre. [Inland Tlingit *ahklen* or *aht'lah* big lake]

ATM *abbreviation* AUTOMATED TELLER MACHINE.

atm *abbreviation Physics* atmosphere(s).

atman /'ɒtmən/ *noun Hinduism & Buddhism* **1** the real self. **2** the supreme spiritual principle. [Sanskrit *ātmán* essence, breath]

atmos·phere *noun* **1 a** the envelope of gases surrounding the earth, any other planet, or any substance. **b** the air in any particular place, esp. if unpleasant. **2 a** the pervading tone or mood of a place or situation, esp. with reference to the feelings or emotions evoked. **b** the feelings or emotions evoked by a work of art, a piece of music, etc. **3** *Physics* a unit of pressure equal to mean atmospheric pressure at sea level, 101.325 kilopascals. Abbr.: **atm**. [modern Latin *atmosphaera* from Greek *atmos* vapour: see SPHERE]

atmos·pher·ic /,atməs'fiːrɪk, -'ferɪk/ *adjective* **1** of, relating to, or occurring in the atmosphere. **2** possessing or evoking a particular or characteristic tone, mood, or set of associations. □ **atmos·pher·ic·al·ly** /-'fiːrɪkli, -'ferɪkli/ *adverb*

atmospheric pressure *noun* the pressure exerted on the earth's surface by the weight of the air above it.

atmos·pher·ics /,atməs'fiːrɪks, -'ferɪks/ *plural noun* **1** electrical disturbance in the atmosphere, esp. caused by lightning. **2** interference with telecommunications caused by this. **3** = ATMOSPHERE 2.

at. no. *abbreviation* atomic number.

at·oll /'atɒl/ *noun* a ring-shaped coral reef enclosing a lagoon. [Maldivian *atolu*]

atom *noun* **1 a** the smallest particle of a chemical element that can take part in a chemical reaction. **b** this particle as a source of nuclear energy. **2** *Cdn* **a** a level of children's sports, usu. involving children aged 9–11. **b** a player in this age group. **3** (often with *neg.*) a very small portion of a thing or quality (*not an atom of pity*). [Greek *atomos* indivisible]

atom bomb *noun* = ATOMIC BOMB.

atom·ic *adjective* **1** concerned with or using atomic energy or atomic bombs. **2** of or relating to an atom or atoms. □ **atom·ic·ally** *adverb*

atomic age *noun* the current historical period, beginning with the development of the atomic bomb near the end of the Second World War, characterized by the use of atomic energy.

atomic bomb *noun* a bomb involving the release of energy by nuclear fission.

atomic clock *noun* an extremely accurate type of clock which is regulated by the vibrations of an atomic or molecular system, such as caesium or ammonia.

atomic energy *noun* (also **atomic power**) energy obtained by nuclear fission or fusion.

atom·icity /,atə'mɪsɪti/ *noun* **1** the number of atoms in the molecules of an element. **2** the state or fact of being composed of atoms.

atomic mass *noun* the mass of an atom measured in atomic mass units.

atomic mass unit *noun* a unit of mass used to express atomic and molecular weights that is equal to one twelfth of the mass of an atom of carbon-12. Abbr.: **amu**.

atomic number *noun* the number of protons in the nucleus of an atom, which is characteristic of a chemical element and determines its place in the periodic table. Symbol: Z.

atomic particle *noun* any one of the particles of which an atom is constituted.

atomic physics *noun* the branch of physics concerned with the structure of the atom and the characteristics of the elementary particles of which it is composed.

atomic pile *noun* a nuclear reactor.

atomic power *noun* = ATOMIC ENERGY.

atomic spectrum *noun* the emission or absorption spectrum arising from electron transitions inside an atom and characteristic of the element.

atomic structure *noun* the structure of an atom as being a central positively charged nucleus surrounded by negatively charged orbiting electrons.

atomic theory *noun* **1** *Physics* the concept of an atom as being composed of elementary particles. **2** *Physics* the theory that all matter is made up of small indivisible particles called atoms, and that the atoms of any one element are identical in all respects but differ from those of other elements and only unite to form compounds in fixed proportions. **3** *Philos.* atomism.

atomic weight *noun* = RELATIVE ATOMIC MASS.

atom·ism /'atə,mɪzəm/ *noun Philos.* the theory that all matter consists of tiny individual particles. □ **atom·ist** *noun* **atom·is·tic** /-'mɪstɪk/ *adjective*

atom·ize *transitive verb* (also esp. *Brit.* **-ise**) **1** reduce to atoms or fine particles. **2** break up (a society etc.) into small constituent parts; fragment. □ **atom·iz·a·tion** *noun*

atom·iz·er *noun* (also esp. *Brit.* **-iser**) a device for emitting water, perfume, or other liquids as a fine spray.

atom-smasher *noun informal* = ACCELERATOR 2.

Aton *var.* of ATEN.

atonal /eɪˈtoːnəl/ *adjective Music* not written in any key or mode. □ **atonal·ity** /-ˈnalɪti/ *noun*

atone *intransitive verb* (usu. foll. by *for*) make amends; expiate (for a wrong). [back-formation from ATONEMENT]

atone·ment *noun* **1** expiation; reparation for a wrong or injury. **2** (**Atonement**) *Christianity* the reconciliation of God and humanity, esp. the expiation by Christ of mankind's sin. [*at one* + -MENT, after medieval Latin *adunamentum* and earlier *onement* from obsolete *one* (v.) unite]

aton·ic /əˈtɒnɪk/ *adjective* **1** *Phonetics* without accent or stress. **2** *Med.* lacking bodily tone. □ **atony** /ˈatəni/ *noun*

atop ● *preposition* on the top of. ● *adverb* on the top.

atopy /ˈatəpi/ *noun* (*pl.* **-pies**) an allergic reaction which is associated with a hereditary predisposition to allergy in some form. □ **atop·ic** /əˈtɒpɪk/ *adjective* [Greek *atopia* unusualness, from *atopos* unusual, from A-¹ + *topos* place]

-ator *suffix* forming agent nouns, usu. from Latin words (sometimes via French) (*agitator*; *creator*; *equator*; *escalator*). *See also* -OR¹. [Latin *-ator*]

-atory *suffix* forming adjectives meaning 'relating to or involving (a verbal action)' (*amatory*; *explanatory*; *predatory*). *See also* -ORY². [Latin *-atorius*]

ATP *abbreviation* ADENOSINE TRIPHOSPHATE.

atra·bil·ious /ˌatrəˈbɪljəs/ *adjective literary* melancholy; ill-tempered. [Latin *atra bilis* black bile, translation of Greek *melagkholia* MELANCHOLY]

atra·zine /ˈatrəziːn/ *noun* a selective, highly persistent herbicide, used alone and with other herbicides to control esp. annual weeds in a wide range of crops. [AMINO + TRIAZINE]

Atre·us /ˈeɪtriəs/ *Gk Legend* a Mycenaean king, father of Agamemnon and Menelaus. He invited his brother Thyestes to a banquet and served him the flesh of Thyestes' own children, at which the sun turned back on its course in horror.

atri·um /ˈeɪtriəm/ *noun* (*pl.* **atri·ums** or **atria** /-triə/) **1 a** the central court of an ancient Roman house. **b** a usu. skylit central hall or court, often rising through several storeys, with galleries and rooms opening off it. **2** *Anat.* a cavity in the body, esp. one of the two upper cavities of the heart, receiving blood from the veins. □ **atri·al** *adjective* [Latin]

atro·cious /əˈtroʊʃəs/ *adjective* **1** very bad or unpleasant (*atrocious weather*; *their manners were atrocious*). **2** extremely savage or wicked (*atrocious cruelty*). □ **atro·cious·ly** *adverb* **atro·cious·ness** *noun* [Latin *atrox -ocis* cruel]

atroc·ity /əˈtrɒsɪti/ *noun* (*pl.* **-ties**) **1** an extremely wicked or cruel act, esp. one involving physical violence or injury. **2** extreme wickedness. **3** something that evokes outrage or disgust. [French *atrocité* or Latin *atrocitas* (as ATROCIOUS, -ITY)]

atro·phy /ˈatrəfi/ ● *verb* (**-phies**, **-phied**, **-phy·ing**) **1** *intransitive* waste away through undernourishment, aging, or lack of use; become emaciated. **2** *transitive* cause to atrophy. ● *noun* the process of atrophying; emaciation. □ **atroph·ic** /əˈtrɒfɪk/ *adjective* [Late Latin *atrophia* from Greek from *a-* not + *trophē* food]

atro·pine /ˈatrəˌpiːn, -pɪn/ *noun* a poisonous alkaloid found in deadly nightshade and other plants, used medicinally esp. to relax muscles and inhibit secretion. [modern Latin *Atropa belladonna* deadly nightshade, from Greek ATROPOS]

Atro·pos /ˈatrəˌpɒs/ *Gk Myth* one of the three Fates, thought to cut the thread of human life with her shears.

at sign *noun* the symbol @

At·sina /atˈsiːnə/ *noun* = GROS VENTRE. [Blackfoot *ăt-sé-na* 'gut people']

atta·boy *interjection* esp. *N Amer.* expressing encouragement or admiration. [prob. reproducing a pronunciation of *that's the boy!*]

at·tach *verb* **1** *transitive* **a** fasten, affix, join. **b** link (an electronic file) to an email message to be sent with it. **2** *transitive* (in *passive*; foll. by *to*) be very fond of or devoted to (*am deeply attached to her*). **3** *transitive* attribute, assign (some function, quality, or characteristic) (*can you attach a name to it?*; *attaches great importance to it*). **4 a** *transitive* accompany; form part of (*no conditions are attached*). **b** *intransitive* (foll. by *to*) be an attribute or characteristic (*great prestige attaches to the job*). **5** *reflexive* (usu. foll. by *to*) take part in; join (*attached themselves to the expedition*). **6** *transitive* appoint for special or temporary duties. **7** *transitive* *Law* seize (a person or property) by legal authority. □ **at·tach·able** *adjective* **at·tach·er** *noun* [Old French *estachier* fasten, from Germanic]

at·ta·ché /aˈtaˌʃeɪ/ *noun* **1** a person appointed to an ambassador's staff, usu. with a special sphere of activity (*military attaché*; *cultural attaché*). **2** *N Amer.* an attaché case. [French, past participle of *attacher*: see ATTACH]

attaché case *noun* a small flat rectangular case for carrying documents etc.; a briefcase.

at·tached *adjective* **1** joined or fastened to something. **2** (of a building or room) adjacent to and typically connected with another building or room (*an attached garage*). **3** full of affection or fondness. **4** (of a person) appointed to (an organization or group) for special or temporary duties (*he was attached to military intelligence*). **5** (of an organization or body) affiliated to (another organization or body).

at·tach·ment *noun* **1** a thing attached or to be attached, esp. to a machine, device, etc., for a special function. **2** affection, devotion. **3** a means of attaching. **4** the act of attaching or the state of being attached. **5** legal seizure. **6** a temporary position in an organization. **7** a computer file sent with an email message (*our mailer has trouble with some attachments*; *the virus is sent as an email attachment*).

at·tack ● *verb* **1** *transitive* act violently against. **2** *transitive* *Military* begin an offensive against. **3** *transitive* criticize adversely. **4** *transitive* act harmfully upon (*a virus attacking the nervous system*). **5** *transitive* vigorously apply oneself to; begin work on (*attacked his meal with gusto*). **6** *intransitive* make an attack. **7** *intransitive* be in a mode of attack. ● *noun* **1** the act or process of attacking. **2** an offensive military operation. **3** *Music* the action or manner of beginning a piece, passage, etc. **4** gusto, vigour. **5** a sudden occurrence of esp. an illness. **6** *Sport* **a** offensive action. **b** the players seeking to score goals etc. □ **at·tack·er** *noun* [French *attaque*, *attaquer* from Italian *attacco* attack, *attaccare* ATTACH]

at·tain *verb* **1** *transitive* arrive at; reach (a goal etc.). **2** *transitive* gain, accomplish (an aim, distinction, etc.). **3** *intransitive* (foll. by *to*) arrive at by conscious development or effort. □ **at·tain·able** *adjective* **at·tain·abil·ity** /-ˈbɪlɪti/ *noun* [Old French *ataindre* from Latin *attingere* (as AD-, *tangere* touch)]

at·tain·der *noun* *hist.* the forfeiture of land and civil rights suffered as a consequence of a sentence of death for treason or felony. □ **act** or **bill of attainder** *hist.* an item of legislation inflicting attainder without judicial process. [Old French *ateindre* ATTAIN used as noun: see -ER⁶]

at·tain·ment *noun* **1** (often in *pl.*) something attained or achieved; an accomplishment. **2** the act or an instance of attaining.

at·taint *transitive verb* **1** *hist.* subject to attainder; condemn (for treason). **2** *archaic* **a** (of disease etc.) strike, affect. **b** taint. [Old French *ataint*, *ateint* past participle formed as ATTAIN: confused in meaning with TAINT]

At·ta·lid /ˈatəlɪd/ ● *adjective* of the Hellenistic dynasty which ruled from Pergamum in Asia Minor, founded by Philetaerus (son of Attalus) in 282 BC and bequeathed to Rome by Attalus III in 133 BC. ● *noun* a member of this dynasty.

at·tar /ˈatər/ *noun* (also **otto** /ˈɒtoː/) a fragrant essential oil, esp. from rose petals. [Persian *'atar* from Arabic from *iṭr* perfume]

At·ta·wapis·kat River /ˌatəˈwɒpɪskat/ a river in N Ontario, flowing 748 km from Attawapiskat Lake to James Bay. [perhaps from Cree *atawao* he trades + *pisket* divided, suggesting a trading post with rooms]

at·tempt ● *transitive verb* **1** (often foll. by *to* + infin.) seek to achieve or complete (a task or action) (*attempted the exercise*; *attempted to explain*). **2** seek to climb or master (a mountain etc.). ● *noun* (often foll. by *at*, *on*, or *to* + infin.) an act of attempting; an endeavour (*made an attempt at winning*; *an attempt to succeed*; *an attempt on his life*). [Latin *attemptare* (as AD-, *temptare* TEMPT)]

At·ten·bor·ough /ˌatənˈbarə/ **Rich·ard (Sam·uel)**, **Baron Attenborough of Richmond-upon-Thames** (b.1923), English film actor, producer, and director. The films he directed include *Oh! What a Lovely War* (1969), *Gandhi* (1982, for which he won an Oscar), and *Shadowlands* (1993).

at·tend *verb* **1** *transitive* **a** be present at (*attended the meeting*). **b** go regularly to (*attend school*). **2** *intransitive* **a** be present (*many members failed to attend*). **b** be present in a serving capacity; wait. **3 a** *transitive* escort, accompany (*she was attended by three bridesmaids*). **b** *intransitive* (foll. by *on*) wait on; serve. **4** *intransitive* **a** (usu. foll. by *to*) turn or apply one's mind; focus one's attention (*attend to what I am saying*; *was not attending*). **b** (foll. by *to*) deal with (*shall attend to the matter myself*). **5** *transitive* (usu. in *passive*) follow as a result from (*the error was attended by serious consequences*). □ **at·tend·er** *noun* [Latin *attendere* (as AD-, *tendere* tent-stretch)]

at·tend·ance *noun* **1** the act of attending or being present. **2** the number of people present (*a high attendance*).

at·tend·ant ● *noun* a person employed to wait on others or provide a service (*flight attendant*; *parking lot attendant*). ● *adjective* **1** accompanying (*attendant circumstances*). **2** waiting on; serving (*ladies attendant on the queen*).

at·ten·dee noun a person who attends (a meeting etc.).

at·ten·tion ● noun 1 the act or faculty of applying one's mind (*give me your attention; attract his attention*). 2 a consideration (*give attention to the problem*). b care (*give special attention to your handwriting*). 3 (in *pl.*) a ceremonious politeness (*he paid his attentions to her*). b wooing, courting (*she was the subject of his attentions*). 4 a soldier's drill position, standing upright with feet together and arms stretched downwards (*stand at attention*). ● interjection 1 calling people to listen to an announcement etc. (*Attention, please! The bus will leave in ten minutes.*). 2 ordering soldiers to come to attention. □ **atten·tion·al** adjective [Latin *attentio* (as ATTEND, -ION)]

attention deficit disorder noun *Psych.* any behavioural disorder (usu. of a child or adolescent) characterized by a marked degree of inattention that is not considered to be a sign of another disorder (esp. attention deficit hyperactivity disorder). Abbr.: **ADD**.

attention deficit hyperactivity disorder noun a behavioural disorder in which the predominant features are inattention, impulsivity, and hyperactivity, typically beginning in early childhood and often persisting into adulthood, and usu. affecting school performance most severely though also manifesting itself in work and social situations. Abbr.: **ADHD**.

attention-getter noun something or someone who attracts a great deal of public attention. □ **attention-getting** noun

attention span noun the length of time for which a person is able to concentrate mentally on a particular activity.

at·ten·tive adjective 1 concentrating; paying attention. 2 assiduously polite. □ **at·ten·tive·ly** adverb **at·ten·tive·ness** noun [French *attentif* from *attente* fem. past participle of *atendre* ATTEND]

at·ten·u·ate ● transitive verb /əˈtɛnjʊˌeɪt/ 1 reduce in force, value, or virulence. 2 *Electricity* reduce the amplitude of (a signal or current). 3 make thin. ● adjective /əˈtɛnjʊət/ 1 slender. 2 tapering gradually. 3 archaic rarefied. □ **at·ten·u·at·ed** adjective **at·ten·u·a·tion** /-ˈeɪʃən/ noun **at·ten·u·a·tor** noun [Latin *attenuare* (as AD-, *tenuis* thin)]

at·test verb 1 transitive confirm the validity or truth of. 2 transitive be evidence or proof of. 3 intransitive (foll. by *to*) bear witness to. □ **at·test·able** adjective **at·test·or** noun [French *attester* from Latin *attestari* (as AD-, *testis* witness)]

at·test·a·tion /ˌatɛˈsteɪʃən/ noun 1 the act of attesting. 2 a testimony.

Attic ● adjective of ancient Athens or Attica, or the form of Greek spoken there. ● noun the form of Greek used by the ancient Athenians. [Latin *Atticus* from Greek *Attikos*]

attic noun 1 the highest storey of a house, usu. immediately under the beams of the roof. 2 a room in the attic area. [French *attique*, as ATTIC: originally a small architectural order above a taller one]

At·ti·ca /ˈatɪkə/ a triangular promontory of E Greece. With the islands in the Saronic Gulf it forms a department of Greece, of which Athens is the capital.

At·ti·ka·mek /aˈtɪkəˌmɛk/ ● noun 1 (pl. same or **-meks**) a member of an Aboriginal people living in the upper St. Maurice River valley in Quebec. 2 the Algonquian language of this people. ● adjective of or relating to the Attikamek or their culture or language. [French *Attikameg* from Cree (Montagnais dialect) *atihkame:kw* = whitefish]

At·ti·la /əˈtɪlə/ (406–53), king of the Huns 434–53, known for his savage attacks. He devastated much of the eastern Roman Empire (445–50) and then invaded the Western Empire, but was defeated in 451 by the Romans and the Visigoths.

at·tire ● transitive verb (usu. as **at·tired** adjective) dress, esp. in fine clothes or formal wear. ● noun clothes, esp. fine or formal. [Old French *atir(i)er* equip, from *à tire* in order, of unknown origin]

Attis /ˈatɪs/ *Gk & Rom. Myth* the youthful consort of Cybele. His death and resurrection were celebrated in a spring festival, with a sacrifice for the crops; his symbol was the pine tree.

at·ti·tude noun 1 a a settled opinion or way of thinking. b behaviour reflecting this (*I don't like his attitude*). 2 a a bodily posture. b a pose adopted in a painting or a play, esp. for dramatic effect (*strike an attitude*). c *Dance* a pose in which the dancer stands on one leg, with the other raised and bent in front or behind (compare ARABESQUE 1a). 3 informal an uncooperative or hostile disposition (*a teenager with attitude*). 4 the position of an aircraft, spacecraft, etc., in relation to specified directions. □ **at·ti·tud·inal** adjective [French from Italian *attitudine* fitness, posture, from Late Latin *aptitudo -dinis* from *aptus* fit]

at·ti·tud·in·ize intransitive verb (also esp. *Brit.* **-ise**) 1 practise or adopt attitudes, esp. for effect. 2 speak, write, or behave affectedly.

Att·lee /ˈatli/ **Clem·ent Rich·ard, 1st Earl** (1883–1967), British politician and prime minister (1945–51). His Labour government

nationalized many industries and introduced social security, thus laying the foundations of the British welfare state.

attn. abbreviation 1 attention. 2 for the attention of.

atto- /ˈatɔː/ combining form *Math.* denoting a factor of 10^{-18} (*attometre*). [Danish or Norwegian *atten* eighteen + -o-]

at·tor·ney /əˈtɜːrni/ noun (pl. **-neys**) 1 a person, esp. a lawyer, appointed to act for another in business or legal matters. See also CROWN ATTORNEY, POWER OF ATTORNEY. 2 *US* a lawyer, esp. one representing a client in a law court. □ **attorney·ship** noun [Old French *atorné* past participle of *atorner* assign, from *à* to + *torner* turn]

Attorney General noun (pl. **Attorneys General**) 1 (in Canada) the minister of the Crown (federally and provincially) responsible for the administration of justice and also acting as legal adviser to the government. 2 a similar chief legal officer in other countries, e.g. the head of the Department of Justice in the US or the member of the UK government who is its chief legal adviser.

at·tract verb 1 transitive draw or bring to oneself or itself (*attracts many admirers; attracts attention*). 2 transitive & intransitive be attractive to; fascinate (*he attracts me; opposites attract*). 3 transitive (of a magnet, gravity, etc.) exert a pull on (an object). □ **at·tract·or** noun [Latin *attrahere* (as AD-, *trahere tract-* draw)]

at·tract·ant ● noun a substance which attracts something. ● adjective attracting.

at·trac·tion noun 1 a the act or power of attracting (*the attraction of foreign travel*). b a person or thing that attracts by arousing interest (*the fair is a big attraction*). 2 *Physics* the force by which bodies attract or approach each other (opp. REPULSION). 3 *Grammar* the influence exerted by one word on another which causes it to change to an incorrect form, e.g. *the wages of sin is death*.

at·trac·tive adjective 1 attracting or capable of attracting; interesting (*an attractive proposition*). 2 aesthetically pleasing or appealing. □ **at·trac·tive·ly** adverb **at·trac·tive·ness** noun

at·trib·ute ● transitive verb /əˈtrɪbjuːt/ (usu. foll. by *to*) 1 regard as belonging or appropriate to (*a poem attributed to Shakespeare*). 2 ascribe to; regard as the effect of a stated cause (*the delays were attributed to the heavy traffic*). ● noun /ˈatrɪˌbjuːt/ 1 a a quality ascribed to a person or thing. b a characteristic quality. 2 a material object recognized as appropriate to a person, office, or status (*a sceptre is an attribute of majesty*). 3 *Grammar* an attributive adjective or noun. □ **at·trib·ut·able** /əˈtrɪbjʊtəbəl/ adjective **at·tri·bu·tion** /ˌatrɪˈbjuːʃən/ noun [Latin *attribuere attribut-* (as AD-, *tribuere* assign)]

at·tribu·tive /əˈtrɪbjʊtɪv/ adjective *Grammar* (of an adjective or noun) preceding the word described and expressing an attribute, as *old* in *the old dog* (but not in *the dog is old*) and *expiry* in *expiry date* (opp. PREDICATIVE). □ **at·tribu·tive·ly** adverb

at·tri·tion /əˈtrɪʃən/ noun 1 *N Amer. & Austral.* reduction of a workforce by processes other than firing, as by non-replacement of employees who retire, die, etc. 2 a the act or process of gradually wearing out, esp. by friction. b abrasion. 3 see also WAR OF ATTRITION. □ **at·tri·tion·al** adjective [Late Latin *attritio* from *atterere attrit-* rub]

at·tune transitive verb (usu. foll. by *to*) 1 make receptive or aware. 2 accustom or acclimatize. [AT- + TUNE]

Atty. abbreviation Attorney.

ATV abbreviation ALL-TERRAIN VEHICLE.

At·wood /ˈatwʊd/ **Mar·garet Elea·nor** (b.1939), Canadian poet, novelist, and writer of short stories, children's books, and literary criticism. She is best known for her novels, often with themes of feminism and human rights: they include *The Edible Woman* (1969), *Surfacing* (1972), *The Handmaid's Tale* (1986), *Cat's Eye* (1988), and *Alias Grace* (1996). She was awarded the Booker Prize in 2000 for *The Blind Assassin*.

atyp·ical /eɪˈtɪpɪkəl/ adjective not typical; not conforming to a type. □ **atyp·ical·ly** adverb

AU abbreviation 1 (also **au.**) astronomical unit. 2 ångström unit.

Au symbol *Chem.* the element gold. [Latin *aurum*]

au·bade /oːˈbɒd/ noun a poem or piece of music appropriate to the dawn or early morning. [French from Spanish *albada* from *alba* dawn]

au·berge /oːˈbɛrʒ/ noun an inn. [French]

auber·gine /ˈoʊbərˌʒiːn/ noun 1 a dark purple colour. 2 *Brit.* = EGGPLANT. [French from Catalan *alberginia* from Arabic *al-bādinjān* from Persian *bādingān* from Sanskrit *vātiṃgaṇa*]

au·brie·tia /ɒˈbriːʃə/ noun (also **au·bre·tia**, **au·brie·ta**) any dwarf perennial rock plant of the genus *Aubrieta*, having purple or pink flowers in spring. [Claude Aubriet, French botanist d.1743]

au·burn adjective reddish brown (usu. of a person's hair). [Middle

u: mood ai my əi pipe au brown ʌu house ei day ɔi boy ã franglais ã Canadien ɔ̃ Brayon (*see over for consonants*)

English, originally yellowish white, from Old French *auborne*, *alborne*, from Latin *alburnus* whitish from *albus* white]

Au·bus·son /ˈoːbuːˌsɔ̃/ *noun* (usu. *attributive*) **1** a kind of tapestry depicting esp. pastoral or chinoiserie designs. **2** a floral-pattern carpet woven by the tapestry process. [*Aubusson* in central France]

AUC *abbreviation* (of a date) from the foundation of the city (esp. of Rome, 753 BC). [Latin *ab urbe condita*]

Auck·land the largest city and chief seaport of New Zealand, on North Island; pop. (2001) 380,154. It was the site of the first parliament of New Zealand in 1854, remaining the capital until 1865.

au con·traire /oː kɒnˈtrɛr/ *interjection* on the contrary; not true. [French]

au cou·rant /ˌoː kuːˈrɑ̃/ *predicative adjective* **1** aware of what is going on; well-informed. **2** trendy; fashionable. [French, = in the (regular) course]

auc·tion ● *noun* **1** a sale of goods, usu. in public, in which articles are sold to the highest bidder. *See also* DUTCH AUCTION, SILENT AUCTION. **2** the sequence of bids made at auction bridge. ● *transitive verb* sell by auction. □ **at auction** in an auction sale. [Latin *auctio* increase, auction, from *augēre auct-* increase]

auction block *noun* N Amer. a place or facility for the auction of goods. □ **on the auction block** available for auction or sale.

auction bridge *noun* a form of bridge in which players bid for the right to name trumps.

auc·tion·eer *noun* a person who conducts auctions professionally, by calling for bids and declaring goods sold. □ **auc·tion·eer·ing** *noun*

auction house *noun* a company which specializes in sales by auction.

au·da·cious /ɔˈdeɪʃəs/ *adjective* **1** daring, bold. **2** impudent. □ **au·da·cious·ly** *adverb* **au·da·cious·ness** *noun* **au·da·city** /ɔˈdasɪti/ *noun* [Latin *audax -acis* bold, from *audēre* dare]

Auden, Wys·tan Hugh (1907–73), English poet, a master of verse form, accommodating traditional patterns to fresh contemporary language.

aud·ible ● *adjective* capable of being heard. ● *noun* Football a play called by the quarterback at the line of scrimmage to replace one previously agreed on. □ **audi·bil·ity** /-ˈbɪlɪti/ *noun* **aud·ible·ness** *noun* **aud·ibly** *adverb* [Late Latin *audibilis* from *audire* hear]

audi·ence *noun* **1 a** the assembled listeners or spectators at an event, esp. a stage performance, concert, etc. **b** the people addressed by a film, book, play, etc. **2** a formal interview with a person in authority. **3** *archaic* a hearing (*give audience to my plea*). [Latin *audientia* from *audire* hear]

aud·ile /ˈɒdaɪl/ *adjective* of or referring to the sense of hearing. [irreg. from Latin *audire* hear, after *tactile*]

audio *noun* (usu. *attributive*) **1** sound or its (esp. electrical) reproduction. **2** equipment for electrical reproduction of sound, e.g. amplifiers, speakers, etc. (*what's new in home audio*). [AUDIO-]

audio- *combining form* hearing or sound. [Latin *audire* hear + -o-]

audio·book *noun* a recording on audio cassette or CD of a reading of a book, usu. a work of fiction.

audio·confer·ence *noun* a meeting that is conducted by telephone or other audio telecommunications device. □ **audio·confer·enc·ing** *noun*

audio frequency *noun* a frequency capable of being perceived by the human ear.

audio·gram *noun* a graphic record of a measurement of the range and sensitivity of a person's hearing.

audi·ol·ogy *noun* the scientific study of hearing, including the treatment of hearing disorders. □ **audi·ol·o·gist** *noun*

audi·om·eter /ˌɒdiˈɒmɪtər/ *noun* an instrument for testing hearing. □ **audi·om·etry** *noun*

audio·phile /ˈɒdioˌfaɪl/ *noun* a person who has a particularly strong interest in high-fidelity sound reproduction.

audio·tape ● *noun* **1** a magnetic tape on which sound can be recorded. **2** a sound recording on tape. ● *transitive verb* record (sound, speech, etc.) on tape.

audio·vis·ual *adjective* (esp. of teaching methods) using electrical equipment, e.g. projectors, tape recorders, etc. that are directed at the senses of sight and hearing.

aud·it ● *noun* **1** an official examination and verification of accounts. **2** a detailed examination or analysis, esp. to assess strengths and weaknesses (*environmental audit; safety audit*). ● *transitive & intransitive verb* (**audit·ed**, **audit·ing**) **1** conduct an audit (of). **2** N Amer. attend (a

class) informally, without working for credits. [Latin *auditus* hearing, from *audire audit-* hear]

au·di·tion ● *noun* **1** a practical demonstration of one's abilities as a singer, actor, dancer, etc., with the aim of winning a role or a position. **2** the power of hearing or listening. ● *verb* **1** *transitive* interview (a candidate at an audition). **2** *intransitive* be interviewed at an audition. [Latin *auditio* from *audire audit-* hear]

aud·it·or *noun* **1** a person who audits accounts. **2** N Amer. a person who audits a class. **3** a listener. □ **audi·tor·ial** /-ˈtɔriəl/ *adjective* [Latin *auditor -oris* (as AUDITION, -OR¹)]

Auditor General *noun* (*pl.* **Auditors General**) Cdn the official responsible for auditing the accounts of a (federal or provincial) government's agencies, departments, and some Crown corporations, and presenting an annual report on government spending to the House of Commons or legislature.

audi·tor·ium /ˌɒdɪˈtɔriəm/ *noun* (*pl.* **audi·tor·iums** or **audi·tor·ia** /-riə/) **1** the part of a theatre etc. in which the audience sits. **2** N Amer. a building incorporating a large hall for public gatherings, performances, sports events, etc. **3** N Amer. a large room, esp. in a school, used for assemblies, theatrical performances, etc. and also usu. as a gymnasium. [Latin neuter of *auditorius* (adj.): see AUDITORY, -ORIUM]

audi·tory /ˈɒdɪˌtɔri/ *adjective* **1** concerned with hearing. **2** received by the ear. [Latin *auditorius* (as AUDITOR, -ORY²)]

Audu·bon /ˈɒdəbɒn/ **John James** (1785–1851), US naturalist and artist, famous for his lifelike paintings of birds in his book *The Birds of America* (1827–38).

Auer /ˈaʊər/ **Carl, Baron von Wels·bach** (1858–1929), Austrian chemist, who patented the incandescent gas mantle, and discovered that the so-called element of didymium was actually a mixture of the two rare-earth elements neodymium and praseodymium (1885).

au fait /oː ˈfeɪ/ *predicative adjective* (usu. foll. by *with*) having current knowledge; conversant (*fully au fait with the arrangements*). [French]

au fond /oː ˈfɔ̃/ *adverb* basically. [French]

Aug. *abbreviation* August.

Au·geas /ɒˈdʒiːəs/ Gk Myth a legendary king whose vast stables had never been cleaned. Hercules cleaned them in a day by diverting the Alpheus river to run through them. □ **Au·gean** *adjective*

aug·er /ˈɒgər/ *noun* **1** a tool resembling a large corkscrew, for boring holes in wood, the ground, ice, etc. **2** a similar device enclosed in a cylinder for moving grain etc. [Old English *nafogār* from *nafu* NAVE², + *gār* pierce: for loss of *n* compare ADDER]

augh *interjection* expressing despair, frustration, etc.

aught¹ *pronoun* (also **ought**) *archaic* (usu. implying *neg.*) anything whatever (esp. in **for aught I know**). [Old English *āwiht* from Germanic]

aught² var. of OUGHT².

aug·ite /ˈɒgaɪt, ˈɒdʒ-/ *noun* a complex silicate mineral, chiefly of calcium, magnesium, and aluminum, occurring in many igneous rocks. [Greek *augitēs* from *augē* lustre]

aug·ment ● *transitive & intransitive verb* /ɒgˈment/ make or become greater; increase or enhance. ● *noun* /ˈɒgment/ Grammar a vowel prefixed to the past tenses in some Indo-European languages. □ **aug·ment·er** *noun* [Late Latin *augmentum*, *augmentare* from Latin *augēre* increase]

aug·men·ta·tion /ˌɒgmenˈteɪʃən/ *noun* **1** enlargement; growth; increase. **2** Music the lengthening of the time values of notes in melodic parts.

aug·menta·tive /ɒgˈmentətɪv/ *adjective* **1** having the property of increasing. **2** Grammar (of an affix or derived word) reinforcing the idea of the original word.

aug·ment·ed interval *noun* Music a perfect or major interval that is increased by a semitone.

aug·ment·ed reality *noun* a technology that superimposes a computer-generated image on a user's view of the real world, thus providing a composite view.

Au·gra·bies Falls /əˈgrɒbiːz/ a series of waterfalls on the Orange River in the province of Northern Cape, South Africa.

au gra·tin /oː graˈtɑ̃/ *adjective* Cooking cooked with a crisp brown crust usu. of bread crumbs or melted cheese. [French from *gratter*, = by grating, from GRATE¹]

Augs·burg /ˈaʊgzbɜrg/ a city in S Germany, in Bavaria; pop. (est. 2002) 252,300.

Augsburg Confession a statement of essential Lutheran doctrines and of abuses for which remedies were sought, mainly drawn up by

Consonants: b *but* d *dog* f *few* g *get* h *her* j *yes* k *cat* l *leg* m *man* n *no* p *pen* r *red* s *sit*

Philipp Melanchthon but approved by Martin Luther before being presented to the Emperor Charles V at Augsburg on 25 June 1530.

aug·ur /ˈɒgər/ ● *verb* **1** *intransitive* **a** (of an event, circumstance, etc.) suggest a specified outcome (usu. *augur well* or *ill*). **b** portend, bode (*all augured well for our success*). **2** *transitive* **a** foresee, predict. **b** portend. ● *noun* Rom. Hist. a religious official who observed natural signs, esp. the behaviour of birds, interpreting these as an indication of divine approval or disapproval of a proposed action. □ **aug·ur·al** *adjective* [Latin]

aug·ury /ˈɒgjəri/ *noun* (pl. **-ies**) **1** an omen; a portent. **2** the work of an augur; the interpretation of omens.

Aug·ust *noun* the eighth month of the year. [Old English from Latin AUGUSTUS]

au·gust /ɒˈgʌst/ *adjective* inspiring reverence and admiration; venerable, impressive. □ **au·gust·ly** *adverb* **au·gust·ness** *noun* [Latin *augustus* consecrated, venerable]

Au·gus·ta 1 a city in E Georgia in the US; pop. (2000) 199,800. **2** the state capital of Maine; pop. (1990) 18,560.

Augusta, Mount a peak in the St. Elias Mountains, situated on the Yukon–Alaska border (4 289 m). [J. *Augusta* Russell, wife of US geologist I. C. Russell *c.*1891]

Au·gus·tan /ɒˈgʌstən/ ● *adjective* **1** connected with, occurring during, or influenced by the reign of the Roman emperor Augustus, esp. as an outstanding period of Latin literature. **2** (of a literary period, esp. the 18th c. in England) characterized by a refined and classical style. ● *noun* a writer of the Augustan age of any literature.

Au·gus·tine /əˈgʌstɪn, ˈɒgʌˌstiːn/ **1 St.** (354–430), a Doctor of the Church, and Bishop of Hippo (in N Africa) from 395. His theology has had a dominant influence on later Western Christian theology, with its conception of humanity's dependence on grace, expressed in his doctrine of predestination. **2 St.** (died *c.*604), the first archbishop of Canterbury, sent to England by Pope Gregory the Great in 597.

Au·gus·tin·ian /ˌɒgəˈstɪniən/ ● *adjective* **1** of or relating to St. Augustine of Hippo or his doctrines. **2** belonging to a religious order observing a rule derived from St. Augustine's writings. ● *noun* **1** an adherent of the doctrines of St. Augustine. **2** (also **Au·gus·tine**) a member of an Augustinian religious order.

Au·gus·tus (63 BC–AD 14), the first Roman emperor. Born Gaius Octavius (subsequently known as Octavian). He was adopted by the will of his great-uncle Julius Caesar. By defeating Antony at Actium in 31 BC, he became supreme ruler. His rule was marked by a series of expansionist military campaigns and by moral and religious reforms intended to restore old Roman values. He energetically patronized the arts; the literature of his age represents the high point of Roman classicism.

au jus /oː ˈʒuː/ *adjective* (of meat, esp. roast beef) served with its natural juices. [French]

auk /ɒk/ *noun* any of various marine diving birds of the family Alcidae, with a heavy body, short wings, and black and white plumage, e.g. the guillemot, puffin, and razorbill. [Old Norse *álka*]

auk·let /ˈɒklət/ *noun* any of various small auks, chiefly of the N Pacific. [AUK + -LET]

Au·la·vik National Park /ˈaʊləvɪk/ a park in NWT, situated in the northern part of Banks Island. The Thomsen River, Canada's northernmost navigable waterway, flows through its varied landscape. [Inuvialuktun, = 'place where people travel']

auld /ɒld/ *adjective* Scot. old. [Old English *ald*, Anglian form of OLD]

auld lang syne /ˌɒːld laŋ ˈsain, ˌɒld-/ *noun* times long past. [Scots, = old long since: also as the title and refrain of a song]

aum·bry /ˈɒmbri/ *var. of* AMBRY.

au naturel /oː natʃəˈrel/ *predicative adjective & adverb* **1** naked. **2** in a natural, untouched, or unimproved state. **3** uncooked; (cooked) in the most natural or simplest way. [French, = in the natural state]

Aung San /aʊŋ ˈsan/ (1914–47), Burmese national leader, who was instrumental in securing Burma's independence from British rule. He was assassinated by political rivals after negotiating a promise of full self-government from the British.

Aung San Suu Kyi /aʊŋ ˌsan suː ˈtʃiː/ (b.1945) Burmese political leader, daughter of Aung San. She became leader of the National League for Democracy (NLD) in 1988. Although she was under house arrest (1989–95) and not allowed to stand as a candidate, the NLD won 80 per cent of the seats in the 1990 elections; however the military government refused to recognize the result. Nobel Peace Prize (1991).

aunt /ant, Maritimes ɒnt/ *noun* **1** the sister of one's father or mother. **2** an uncle's wife. **3** *informal* an unrelated woman friend of a child or

children. □ **my** (or **my sainted** etc.) **aunt** *slang* an exclamation of surprise, disbelief, etc. [Old French *ante*, from Latin *amita*]

aunt·ie /ˈanti, Maritimes ˈɒnti/ *noun* (also **aunty**) (pl. **-ies**) *informal* **1** = AUNT. **2** (**Auntie**) Brit. an institution considered to be conservative or cautious, esp. the BBC.

Aunt Sally *noun* Brit. & Austral. **1** a game in which players throw sticks or balls at a wooden dummy. **2** the object of an unreasonable attack.

au pair /oː ˈpeə/ *noun* a young person from another country, esp. a woman, helping with housework etc. in exchange for room and board, esp. as a means of learning a language. [French]

aura *noun* (pl. **auras**) **1** the distinctive atmosphere diffused by or attending a person, place, etc. **2** (in mystic or spiritualistic use) a supposed subtle emanation, visible as a sphere of white or coloured light, surrounding the body of a living creature. **3** a subtle emanation or aroma from flowers etc. **4** Med. a sensation, as of flashing lights, immediately preceding an attack of migraine or epilepsy. □ **aural** *adjective* **auric** *adjective* [Greek, = breeze, breath]

aural /ˈɔːrəl/ *adjective* of or relating to or received by the ear. □ **aur·al·ly** *adverb* [Latin *auris* ear]

Aur·ang·zeb /ˈɔːrəŋˌzeb, ˈau-/ (1618–1707), Mughal emperor of Hindustan 1658–1707, a period of great wealth and splendour for the empire.

aurar *pl. of* EYRIR.

aur·eate /ˈɔːriət/ *adjective* **1** golden, gold-coloured. **2** (of a language) highly ornamented. [Late Latin *aureatus* from Latin *aureus* golden, from *aurum* gold]

Aurel·ian /ɔːˈriːliən/ (Lucius Domitius Aurelianus, *c.*215–75), Roman emperor. Originally a common soldier, he rose through the ranks and was acclaimed emperor by the army in 270 and murdered in a military plot in 275.

Aurel·ius /ɔːˈriːliəs/ **Mar·cus** (121–80), Roman emperor (161–80), the adopted successor of Antoninus Pius. Although he was by nature a philosophic contemplative, much of his reign was occupied with wars against Germanic tribes invading the empire from the north.

aur·eole /ˈɔːriˌoːl/ *noun* (also **aur·eo·la** /ɔːˈriːələ/) **1** a halo or circle of light, esp. around the head or body of a portrayed religious figure. **2** a corona around the sun or moon. [Latin *aureola* (*corona*), = golden (crown) from *aurum* gold]

Aur·eo·mycin /ˌɔːriəˈmaisɪn/ *noun* proprietary an antibiotic of the tetracycline family used esp. to treat lung diseases. [Latin *aureus* golden + Greek *mukēs* fungus + -IN]

au re·voir /oː rəˈvwɑːr/ *interjection & noun* goodbye (until we meet again). [French]

aur·icle /ˈɔːrɪkəl/ *noun* Anat. **1 a** a small muscular pouch on the surface of each atrium of the heart. **b** the atrium itself. **2** the external ear of animals. *Also called* PINNA. **3** an appendage shaped like the ear. [AURICULA]

aur·icu·la /ɔːˈrɪkjʊlə/ *noun* a primula, *Primula auricula*, with a dark purple outer ring and pale yellow centre. [Latin, diminutive of *auris* ear, from its ear-shaped leaves]

aur·icu·lar /ɔːˈrɪkjʊlər/ *adjective* **1** of or relating to the ear or hearing. **2** of or relating to the auricle of the heart. **3** shaped like an auricle. [(as AURICULA)]

aur·icu·late /ɔːˈrɪkjʊlət/ *adjective* having one or more auricles or ear-shaped appendages. [(as AURICULA)]

aur·if·er·ous /ɔːˈrɪfərəs/ *adjective* containing or yielding gold. [Latin *aurifer* from *aurum* gold]

Auriga /ɔːˈraigə/ a constellation in the northern hemisphere near Orion, including the brilliant yellow star Capella. [Latin = charioteer]

Aurig·na·cian /ˌɔːrɪgˈneiʃən/ ● *noun* a culture of the early stages of the upper paleolithic period in Europe and the near East, dating from about 34,000–29,000 years ago. It is associated with Cro-Magnon man and witnessed the first appearance of cave paintings. ● *adjective* of this culture. [French *Aurignacien* from *Aurignac* in SW France, where remains of it were found]

aur·ochs /ˈɔːrɒks/ *noun* (pl. same) an extinct wild ox, *Bos primigenius*, ancestor of domestic cattle and formerly native to many parts of the world. *Also called* URUS. [German from Old High German *ūrohso* from *ūr-urus* + *ohso* ox]

Au·rora[1] **1** a city in Colorado; pop. (est. 2000) 276,393. **2** a town in south central Ontario, about 35 km north of downtown Toronto; pop. (2001) 40,167. □ **Au·ro·ran** *noun* [sense 2 after AURORA[2], to symbolize a new dawn of prosperity in the area]

Au·rora[2] Rom. Myth the goddess of the dawn, corresponding to the Greek Eos.

au·ro·ra *noun* (*pl.* **au·ro·ras** or **au·ro·rae** /-riː/) **1** a luminous phenomenon, usu. of shimmering colours, seen in the upper atmosphere in high northern or southern latitudes, and caused by the interaction of charged solar particles with atmospheric gases, under the influence of the earth's magnetic field. **2** *literary* the dawn. □ **au·ror·al** *adjective* [Latin, = dawn]

aurora aus·tral·is /ɒ'strɑlɪs/ *noun* a southern occurrence of the aurora. *Also called* SOUTHERN LIGHTS.

aurora bor·eal·is /ˌbɔri'ɑlɪs/ *noun* a northern occurrence of the aurora. *Also called* NORTHERN LIGHTS.

aurora trout *noun* a rare type of brook trout, *Salvelinus fontinalis timagamiensis*, found in N Ontario. [AURORA (because of its coloration)]

Ausch·witz /'auʃvɪts/ a Nazi concentration camp in the Second World War, near the town of Oświęcim (Auschwitz) in Poland.

aus·cul·ta·tion /ˌɒskəl'teiʃən/ *noun* the act of listening, esp. to sounds from the heart, lungs, etc., as a part of medical diagnosis. □ **aus·cul·ta·tory** /-'kʌltə,tɔri/ *adjective* [Latin *auscultatio* from *auscultare* listen to]

Aus·lese /'ausleizə/ *noun* a white wine made esp. in Germany from selected bunches of grapes picked later than the general harvest. [German from *aus* out + *lese* picking, vintage]

aus·pice /'ɒspɪs/ *noun* **1** (in *pl.*) patronage, support (*under the auspices of*). **2** a forecast. [originally 'observation of bird flight in divination': Latin *auspicium* from *auspex* observer of birds, from *avis* bird]

aus·pi·cious /ɒ'spɪʃəs/ *adjective* of good omen; favourable. □ **aus·pi·cious·ly** *adverb* **aus·pi·cious·ness** *noun* [AUSPICE + -OUS]

Aus·sie /'ɒzi, 'ɒsi/ (also **Os·sie**, **Oz·zie**) *informal* ● *noun* **1** an Australian. **2** Australia. ● *adjective* Australian. [abbreviation]

Aus·ten, **Jane** (1775–1817), English novelist. Her major works, which portray the social life of the upper classes and praise the virtues of reason and intelligence rather than those of passion and impulse, all end with a happy marriage achieved after the surmounting of obstacles, and include *Sense and Sensibility* (1811), *Pride and Prejudice* (1813), *Emma* (1816), and *Persuasion* (1818).

aus·tere /ɒ'stiːr/ *adjective* **1** severely simple. **2** morally strict. **3** harsh, stern. □ **aus·tere·ly** *adverb* [Greek *austēros* severe]

aus·ter·ity /ɒ'sterɪti/ *noun* (*pl.* **-ities**) **1** sternness; moral severity. **2** frugality or money-saving practices. **3** (esp. in *pl.*) an austere practice (*the austerities of a monk's life*).

Aus·ter·litz, Battle of /'ɒstərlɪts, 'auster-/ a battle in 1805 near the town of Austerlitz (now **Slavkov u Brna** in the Czech Republic), in which Napoleon defeated the Austrians and Russians.

Aus·tin¹ the state capital of Texas; pop. (2000) 656,562.

Aus·tin² ▶ **1** John (1790–1859), English jurist. His work is significant for its strict delimitation of the sphere of law and its distinction from that of morality. **2** John Lang·shaw (1911–60), English philosopher who, as an exponent of the linguistic school of philosophy, sought to elucidate philosophical problems by analysis of the words in which they are expressed.

Aus·tin³ *noun* (also **Austin Friar**) = AUGUSTINIAN *noun*. [contraction of AUGUSTINE]

aus·tral /'ɒstrəl/ *adjective* **1** southern. **2** (**Austral**) of Australia or Australasia (*Austral English*). [Latin *australis* from *Auster* south wind]

Austral·asia the region consisting of Australia, New Zealand, New Guinea, and the neighbouring islands of the Pacific. □ **Austral·asian** *adjective & noun*

Aus·tralia an island country and continent of the southern hemisphere, in the SW Pacific, a member state of the Commonwealth; pop. (2001) 19,485,278; capital, Canberra. Much of the continent has a hot dry climate and a large part of the central area is desert or semi-desert; the most fertile areas are the eastern coastal plains and the southwestern corner of Western Australia. □ **Aus·tral·ian** *noun & adjective* **Aus·tral·ian·ism** *noun*

Australian Antarctic Territory an area of Antarctica administered by Australia, lying between longitudes 142° east and 136° east.

Australian Capital Territory a federal territory in New South Wales, Australia, formerly consisting of two enclaves ceded by New South Wales, one in 1911 to contain Canberra, the other in 1915 containing Jervis Bay; the latter separated from the Capital Territory in 1988 to become the Jervis Bay Territory.

Australian cattle dog *noun* a breed of dog with short hair and a dark speckled body, used for herding cattle.

Australian crawl *noun* *Swimming* = CRAWL *noun* 3.

Australian Rules *noun* a form of football played with an oval ball on an oval field by teams of 18, having very few rules.

Australian terrier *noun* a wire-haired breed of terrier, ranging in colour from blue-black to reddish brown.

Austral Islands /'ɒstrəl/ an alternative name for the TUBUAI ISLANDS.

Aus·tral·oid ● *adjective* of or relating to the broad division of humankind represented by Australian Aboriginal peoples. ● *noun* a person belonging to this division of humankind.

Aus·tralo·pith·ecus /ˌɒstrələ'pɪθɪkəs/ *noun* any extinct bipedal primate of the genus *Australopithecus* having apelike and human characteristics, or its fossilized remains. □ **aus·tralo·pith·ecine** /-ˌɪˌsiːn/ *noun & adjective* [modern Latin from Latin *australis* southern + Greek *pithēkos* ape]

Aus·tria a republic in central Europe; pop. (2001) 8,065,465; capital, Vienna. Austria is largely mountainous, with the Danube River flowing through the northeast. It was dominated from the early Middle Ages by the Hapsburg family, and became the centre of a massive central European empire. □ **Aus·trian** *adjective & noun*

Austria-Hungary (also called **Austro-Hungarian Empire**) the 'Dual Monarchy', established in 1866, in which Austria and Hungary were autonomous states under a common sovereign. The failure of the empire to resolve the nationalist aspirations of other subject nations, including Croatians, Serbs, Slovaks, Romanians, and Czechs, was one of the causes of the First World War; the Versailles peace settlement dissolved the empire in 1919.

Austrian pine *noun* a pine, *Pinus nigra*, native to Europe and W Asia, with a dense branch system, widely cultivated as an ornamental.

Austrian Succession, War of the (1740–48), a collection of related wars in which the key issue was the right of Maria Theresa of Austria to succeed to the Austrian throne after the death of her father, the emperor Charles VI. Austria was challenged by Bavaria, Saxony, and Spain, all of whom had rival claimants to the throne, and by Prussia, who had designs on Austrian territory; Britain, Hungary, and the Netherlands supported Austria, while France backed Bavaria and Prussia. The settlement in 1748 preserved most of the Austrian inheritance for Maria Theresa. The N American phase of this war was called KING GEORGE'S WAR.

Austro- *combining form* **1** Austrian; Austrian and (*Austro-Hungarian*). **2** Australian; Australian and (*Austronesian*).

Austro·nesian /ɒstrɒ'niːʒən/ ● *noun* a family of languages spoken widely in Malaysia, Indonesia, and other parts of SE Asia, and in the islands of the central and S Pacific. ● *adjective* of or relating to this language family. [German *austronesisch*, from Latin *australis* 'southern' + -o- + Greek *nēsos* 'island']

aut·archy /'ɒtɑrki/ *noun* (*pl.* **-ies**) **1** absolute sovereignty. **2** despotism. **3** an autarchic country or society. □ **aut·arch·ic** /ɒ'tɑrkɪk/ *adjective* **aut·arch·ic·al** /ɒ'tɑrkɪkəl/ *adjective* [modern Latin *autarchia* (as AUTO-, Greek -*arkhia* from *arkhō* rule)]

aut·arky /'ɒtɑrki/ *noun* (*pl.* **-ies**) **1** self-sufficiency, esp. as an economic system. **2** a state etc. run according to such a system. □ **aut·ark·ic** /ɒ'tɑrkɪk/ *adjective* **aut·ark·ic·al** /ɒ'tɑrkɪkəl/ *adjective* **aut·ark·ist** *noun* [Greek *autarkeia* (as AUTO-, *arkeō* suffice)]

au·teur /oː'tɜr/ *noun* a director who so greatly influences the films directed as to be able to rank as their author. [French, = author]

au·then·tic *adjective* **1 a** of undisputed origin; genuine. **b** reliable or trustworthy. **2** *Music* performed on instruments dating from and with techniques typical of the same period as the piece performed. **3** *Music* (of a church mode) containing notes between a final note and an octave higher (*compare* PLAGAL). □ **au·then·tic·ally** *adverb* **au·then·ti·city** /ˌɒθen'tɪsɪti/ *noun* [Greek *authentikos* principal, genuine]

au·then·ti·cate *transitive verb* **1** establish the truth or genuineness of. **2** validate. □ **au·then·ti·ca·tion** *noun* **au·then·ti·ca·tor** *noun*

auth·or ● *noun* **1** a writer, esp. of books. **2** the originator of an event, a condition, etc. (*the author of all my woes*). ● *transitive verb* be the author of. □ **author·ial** /ɒ'θɔriəl/ *adjective* [Old French *autor* from Latin *auctor* from *augēre auct-* increase, originate, promote]

author·ess *noun* a female writer, esp. of books. ¶ *Author* is now usu. preferred.

au·thori·tar·ian ● *adjective* **1** favouring, encouraging, or enforcing strict obedience to authority, as opposed to individual freedom. **2** tyrannical or domineering. ● *noun* a person favouring absolute obedience to a constituted authority. □ **au·thori·tar·ian·ism** *noun*

au·thori·ta·tive *adjective* **1** recognized as true or dependable. **2** (of a person, behaviour, etc.) commanding or self-confident. **3** official; supported by authority (*an authoritative document*). □ **au·thori·ta·tive·ly** *adverb* **au·thori·ta·tive·ness** *noun*

au·thor·ity *noun* (*pl.* **-ities**) **1 a** the power or right to enforce obedience. **b** (often foll. by *for*, or *to* + infin.) delegated power. **2** a person or organization having power or control in a particular, esp. political or administrative, sphere. **3 a** an expert in a particular subject (*an authority on vintage cars*). **b** a book etc. that can supply reliable information or evidence. **4** considerable force or strength (*delivered her speech with authority*). **5** testimony, evidence (*took it on their authority*). [Old French *autorité* from Latin *auctoritas* from *auctor*: see AUTHOR]

au·thor·ize *transitive verb* (also esp. *Brit.* **-ise**) give official permission for or approval to (an undertaking or agent). □ **au·thor·iz·a·tion** *noun* [Old French *autoriser* from medieval Latin *auctorizare* from *auctor*: see AUTHOR]

Authorized Version *noun* = KING JAMES VERSION. Abbr.: **AV**.

au·thor·ship *noun* **1** the origin of a book or other written work (*of unknown authorship*). **2** the occupation of writing.

aut·ism /ˈɔːtɪzəm/ *noun Psych.* a mental condition, usu. present from childhood, characterized by complete self-absorption and a reduced ability to respond to or communicate with the outside world. □ **au·tis·tic** /ɔːˈtɪstɪk/ *adjective* [modern Latin *autismus* (as AUTO-, -ISM)]

auto (*pl.* **autos**) *N Amer.* ● *noun* an automobile (usu. *attributive: auto insurance; auto mechanic*). ● *adjective* automatic. [abbreviation]

auto- *combining form* (usu. **aut-** before a vowel) **1** originating with, induced by, or pertaining to the self (*autobiography; autosuggestion; autism*). **2** self-operating, automatic (*autofocus*). **3** relating to automobiles or the automobile industry (*automaker*). [from or after Greek *auto-* from *autos* self]

auto·anti·body *noun* (*pl.* **-bodies**) an antibody produced by an organism in response to a constituent of its own tissues.

auto·bahn /ˈɔːtəˌbɑːn/ *noun* an expressway in Germany, Austria, or other German-speaking region. [German from *Auto* automobile + *Bahn* path, road]

auto·biog·raphy *noun* (*pl.* **-ies**) **1** a personal account of one's own life, esp. for publication. **2** this as a process or literary form. □ **auto·biog·raph·er** *noun* **auto·bio·graph·ic** *adjective* **auto·bio·graph·ic·al** *adjective*

auto·body *noun* the shell of a motor vehicle, distinguished from its chassis, esp. in contexts of maintenance or repair.

auto·ceph·al·ous /ˌɔːtəˈsefələs/ *adjective* **1** (esp. of an Eastern church) appointing its own head. **2** (of a bishop, church, etc.) independent. [Greek *autokephalos* (as AUTO-, *kephalē* head)]

au·toch·thon /ɔːˈtɒkθən/ *noun* (*pl.* **au·toch·thons** or **au·toch·thon·es** /-θəˌniːz/) **1** (in *pl.*) the original or earliest known inhabitants of a country; aboriginals. **2** *Geol.* an autochthonous rock formation (*compare* ALLOCHTHON). [Greek, = sprung from the earth (as AUTO-, *khthōn*, *-onos* earth)]

au·toch·thon·ous /ɔːˈtɒkθənəs/ *adjective* **1** *Geol.* (of a rock formation) originating in the place in which it is found. **2** indigenous. [as AUTOCHTHON + -OUS]

auto·clave /ˈɔːtəˌkleɪv/ ● *noun* **1** a sterilizer using high-pressure steam. **2** a strong vessel used for chemical reactions at high pressures and temperatures. ● *transitive verb* heat or sterilize in an autoclave. [AUTO- + Latin *clavus* nail or *clavis* key]

au·toc·racy /ɔːˈtɒkrəsi/ *noun* (*pl.* **-cies**) **1** absolute government by one person. **2** the power exercised by such a person. **3** an autocratic country or society. [Greek *autokrateia* (as AUTOCRAT)]

auto·crat *noun* **1** an absolute ruler. **2** a dictatorial person. □ **auto·crat·ic** *adjective* **auto·crat·ic·ally** *adverb* [French *autocrate* from Greek *autokratēs* (as AUTO-, *kratos* power)]

auto·cross *noun* a competition in which drivers manoeuvre cars around a winding course. [blend of AUTOMOBILE + CROSS-COUNTRY]

auto-da-fé /ˌɔːtəʊdɑːˈfeɪ/ *noun* (*pl.* **autos-da-fé** /ˌɔːtəʊz-/) **1** a sentence of punishment by the Spanish Inquisition. **2** the execution of such a sentence, esp. the burning of a heretic. [Portuguese, = act of the faith]

auto·dial *noun* a facility that enables an electronic device (as a telephone, fax machine, modem, etc.) to initiate a telephone call to a particular number stored in its memory, either automatically or when activated by a simple command. □ **auto·dial·ler** *noun* **auto·dial·ling** *noun*

auto·didact /ˌɔːtəʊˈdaɪdakt/ *noun* a self-taught person. □ **auto·didac·tic** /-ˈdaktɪk/ *adjective* [AUTO- + *didact* as DIDACTIC]

auto-eroticism /ˌɔːtəʊɪˈrɒtɪˌsɪzəm/ *noun* (also **auto-erotism** /-ˈerəˌtɪzəm/) *Psych.* sexual excitement generated by stimulating or fantasizing about one's own body. □ **auto-erotic** /-ɪˈrɒtɪk/ *adjective*

auto·focus *noun* a device for focusing a camera etc. automatically. □ **auto·focus·ing** *noun*

au·tog·amy /ɔːˈtɒɡəmi/ *noun* **1** *Bot.* self-fertilization in plants (*compare* ALLOGAMY). **2** *Biol.* a type of cell conjugation in which a nucleus divides itself and then reunites to form a zygote. □ **au·tog·am·ous** *adjective* [AUTO- + Greek *-gamia* from *gamos* marriage]

auto·genic /ˌɔːtəʊˈdʒɛnɪk/ *adjective* self-produced; originating within one's own body.

autogenic training *noun* a relaxation technique in which the patient learns a form of self-hypnosis and biofeedback as a way of managing stress.

au·togen·ous /ɔːˈtɒdʒənəs/ *adjective* **1** self-produced; originating within one's own body. **2** (of a weld or welding) formed by or involving the melting of the joined ends, without added filler. **3** (of a vaccine) derived from the patient's own infecting micro-organisms.

auto·giro *var. of* AUTOGYRO.

auto·graft *noun* a graft of tissue from one point to another of the same person's body.

auto·graph ● *noun* **1 a** a signature, esp. that of a celebrity. **b** handwriting. **2** a manuscript in an author's own handwriting. **3** a document signed by its author. ● *transitive verb* **1** sign (a photograph, autograph album, etc.). **2** write (a letter etc.) by hand. [(as AUTO-, -GRAPH)]

au·tog·raphy /ɔːˈtɒɡrəfi/ *noun* **1** writing done with one's own hand. **2** the facsimile reproduction of writing or illustration. □ **auto·graph·ic** /-ˈɡrafɪk/ *adjective*

auto·gyro /ˌɔːtəʊˈdʒaɪrəʊ/ *noun* (also **auto·giro**) (*pl.* **-gyros**) an early form of helicopter with a frontal propeller and freely rotating horizontal vanes which provide lift. [Spanish (as AUTO-, *giro* gyration)]

auto·harp *noun* a kind of zither played by strumming the strings while selecting chords with keys that dampen certain strings and leave others to vibrate freely.

auto·immune *adjective* (of a disease) caused by antibodies produced against substances naturally present in the body. □ **auto·immun·ity** *noun*

auto·intoxi·ca·tion *noun* poisoning by a toxin formed within the body itself.

au·tol·o·gous /ɔːˈtɒləɡəs/ *adjective Med.* (of a graft, transfusion, etc.) obtained from the same individual who receives it.

au·toly·sis /ɔːˈtɒlɪsɪs/ *noun* the destruction of cells by their own enzymes. □ **auto·lytic** /ˌɔːtəˈlɪtɪk/ *adjective* [German *Autolyse* (as AUTO-, -LYSIS)]

auto·maker *noun* a company which manufactures automobiles.

Auto·mat *noun US* a now obsolete type of cafeteria, common esp. in New York and Philadelphia in the first half of the 20th c., in which food was obtained from compartments by the insertion of coins.

au·tom·ata *pl. of* AUTOMATON.

auto·mate *transitive verb* convert to or operate by automation (*the ticket office has been automated*). [back-formation from AUTOMATION]

auto·mat·ed teller machine *noun* (also **automated banking machine**) an electronic machine which allows users to perform banking transactions by inserting an encoded plastic card. Abbr.: **ATM**. Also called BANK MACHINE.

auto·matic ● *adjective* **1** (of a machine, device, etc., or its function) working by itself, without direct human intervention. **2 a** done spontaneously, without conscious thought or intention (*an automatic reaction*). **b** necessary and inevitable (*an automatic penalty*). **3** *Psych.* performed unconsciously or subconsciously. **4 a** (of a firearm) that continues firing until the pressure on the trigger is released or the ammunition is exhausted. **b** (of a pistol) that fires each time the trigger is pulled, without requiring manual reloading. **5** (of a motor vehicle or its transmission) using gears that change automatically according to speed and acceleration. ● *noun* **1** an automatic device, esp. a gun or transmission. **2** a vehicle with automatic transmission. □ **auto·matic·ally** *adverb* **auto·mati·city** /ˌɔːtəməˈtɪsɪti/ *noun* [formed as AUTOMATON + -IC]

automatic pilot *noun* **1** a device for keeping an aircraft on a set course. **2** the state of a person doing something by routine or habit, without concentration.

auto·mation *noun* **1** the use of automatic equipment to save mental and manual labour. **2** the state of being automated.

au·toma·tism /ɔːˈtɒməˌtɪzəm/ *noun* **1** *Psych.* **a** the performance of actions unconsciously or subconsciously (*epileptic automatism*). **b** such action. **2** *Law* an involuntary action for which one is not held legally responsible. **3** unthinking routine. [French *automatisme* from *automate* AUTOMATON]

au·to·ma·tize /ɒˈtɒməˌtaɪz/ *transitive verb* (also esp. *Brit.* **-tise**) **1** make (a process etc.) automatic. **2** = AUTOMATE. □ **au·to·ma·tiz·a·tion** /-ˈzeɪʃən/ *noun* [AUTOMATIC + -IZE]

au·tom·a·ton /ɒˈtɒmətɒn/ *noun* (*pl.* **au·tom·a·ta** /-tə/ or **au·tom·a·tons**) **1** a mechanism which operates with concealed motive power, esp. one simulating a living being. **2** a person who behaves without active intelligence or mechanically in a set pattern or routine. [Latin from Greek, neuter of *automatos* acting of itself: see AUTO-]

au·to·mobile *noun* N Amer. a car (often *attributive*: *automobile industry*). [French (as AUTO-, MOBILE)]

au·to·motive *adjective* concerned with motor vehicles.

au·to·nomic /ˌɒtəˈnɒmɪk/ *adjective* esp. *Physiol.* functioning involuntarily.

autonomic nervous system *noun* the part of the nervous system responsible for control of the bodily functions not consciously directed, e.g. heartbeat.

au·to·no·mous /ɒˈtɒnəməs/ *adjective* **1** having self-government. **2** acting or existing independently or having the freedom to do so. □ **au·to·no·mous·ly** *adverb*

au·ton·omy /ɒˈtɒnəmi/ *noun* **1** the right of self-government. **2** personal freedom or independence. **3** freedom of the will. **4** a self-governing community. □ **au·tono·mist** *noun* [Greek *autonomia* from *autos* self + *nomos* law]

Auto·pac /ˈɒtoˌpak/ *noun* Cdn (Man.) proprietary the vehicle insurance provided by the Manitoba government through the Manitoba Public Insurance Corporation.

Auto Pact *noun* Cdn the familiar name for the Canada-US Automotive Products Agreement (signed 1965), which removed tariffs from the sale of vehicles and automotive parts between the two countries, with the provision that to import cars duty-free into Canada, US manufacturers had to use a minimum proportion of Canadian components and build in Canada a number of vehicles proportionate to their Canadian sales.

auto·pilot *noun* = AUTOMATIC PILOT.

aut·opsy /ˈɒˌtɒpsi/ *noun* (*pl.* **-opsies**) **1** a post-mortem examination conducted to determine the cause of death. **2** a critical analysis of an event etc. after its completion. [modern Latin *autopsia* from Greek from *autoptēs* eyewitness]

auto·radio·graph *noun* a photograph of an object produced by radiation from radioactive material in the object. □ **auto·radio·graphic** *adjective* **auto·radi·og·raphy** *noun*

auto·route *noun* an expressway in Quebec, France, or other French-speaking region. [French (as AUTOMOBILE, ROUTE)]

auto·strada /ˈɒtoˌstradə/ *noun* (*pl.* **auto·stradas**) an expressway in Italy. [Italian (as AUTOMOBILE, *strada* road)]

auto·sugges·tion *noun* a hypnotic or subconscious suggestion made to oneself which affects behaviour.

auto·telic /ˌɒtəˈtelɪk/ *adjective* having or being a purpose in itself. [AUTO- + Greek *telos* end]

au·tot·omy /ɒˈtɒtəmi/ *noun* Zool. the voluntary severance of a body part, e.g. the tail of a lizard, to escape a predator.

auto·toxin *noun* a product of an organism's metabolism which is poisonous to the organism itself. □ **auto·toxic** *adjective*

auto·troph·ic /ˌɒtəˈtrɒfɪk/ *adjective* Biol. able to form complex nutritional organic substances from simple inorganic substances such as carbon dioxide (*compare* HETEROTROPHIC). [AUTO- + Greek *trophos* feeder]

auto worker *noun* a labourer employed by an automobile manufacturer.

aut·oxi·dation /ɒˌtɒksɪˈdeɪʃən/ *noun* Chem. oxidation by exposure to air at room temperature.

au·tumn *noun* **1** the third season of the year, associated with harvests and falling leaves, in the northern hemisphere from September to November and in the southern hemisphere from March to May. *Also called* FALL (sense 2). **2** *Astronomy* the period from the autumnal equinox to the winter solstice. **3** a time of maturity or incipient decay. [Latin *autumnus*]

autum·nal *adjective* **1** of, characteristic of, or appropriate to autumn (*autumnal colours*). **2** occurring in autumn (*autumnal equinox*). **3** maturing or blooming in autumn. **4** past the prime of life.

autumnal equinox *noun* (also **autumn equinox**) the equinox occurring on or about 22 Sept. in the northern hemisphere and on or about 21 March in the southern hemisphere.

autumn crocus *noun* any plant of the genus *Colchicum*, esp. meadow saffron, of the lily family and unrelated to the true crocus.

Au·vergne /oˈvɛrn/ a region of south central France. The region is mountainous and contains the extinct volcanic cones known as the Puys. [the *Arverni*, a Celtic tribe who lived there in Roman times]

aux·iliary /ɒɡˈzɪljəri, -ˈzɪləri/ ● *adjective* **1** (of a person or thing) helpful, giving support. **2** (of services or equipment) subsidiary, additional. **3** (of a sailing vessel) equipped with an engine. ● *noun* (*pl.* **-ies**) **1** an auxiliary person or thing. **2** *N Amer.* a group of volunteers who assist a church, hospital, etc. with fundraising and other charitable activities. **3** (in *pl.*) Military foreign or allied troops in a belligerent nation's service. **4** *Grammar* an auxiliary verb. [Latin *auxiliarius* from *auxilium* help]

auxiliary bishop *noun* Catholicism a bishop who assists a diocesan bishop.

auxiliary verb *noun* Grammar a verb used in forming tenses, moods, and voices of other verbs, e.g. *will* in *she will go*.

auxin /ˈɒksɪn/ *noun* a plant hormone that regulates growth. [German from Greek *auxō* increase + -IN]

Au·yu·it·tuq National Park /ˌaujuˈiːtʊk/ a park located at the southeastern end of Baffin Island. It was established in 1972 as Baffin Island National Park. [Inuktitut, lit. 'place that does not melt']

AV *abbreviation* **1** AUDIOVISUAL (teaching aids etc.). **2** AUTHORIZED VERSION.

AVA *abbreviation* ACTUAL VALUE ASSESSMENT.

avail ● *verb* **1** *transitive* help, benefit. **2** *reflexive* (foll. by *of*) profit by; take advantage of. ● *noun* **1** (usu. in *neg.* phrases) use, profit (*to no avail*; *without avail*). **2** (in *pl.*) esp. *Cdn* proceeds or profits, esp. those produced by another person's labour (*living off the avails of prostitution*). [Middle English from obsolete *vail* (v.) from Old French *valoir* be worth, from Latin *valēre*]

avail·able *adjective* **1** capable of being used; at one's disposal; obtainable. **2** (of a person) **a** free for consultation or service. **b** presently uninvolved in a romantic relationship. **3** (of a feature on a vehicle etc.) that can be acquired as an option but is not part of the base price. □ **avail·abil·ity** /-ˈbɪlɪti/ *noun* **avail·able·ness** *noun* **avail·ably** *adverb* [Middle English from AVAIL + -ABLE]

ava·lanche ● *noun* **1** a mass of snow, ice, rock, etc. tumbling rapidly down a mountainside. **2** a sudden appearance or arrival of anything in large quantities (*faced with an avalanche of work*). ● *verb* **1** *intransitive* descend like an avalanche. **2** *transitive* carry down like an avalanche. [French, alteration of dial. *lavanche* after *avaler* descend]

avalanche lily *noun* a liliaceous plant of the genus *Erythronium*, commonly found near the snow line on mountains, esp. *E. grandiflorum*, with a large, brilliant yellow flower. *Also called* GLACIER LILY.

Avalanche Peak a mountain (4 212 m) in the St. Elias Mountains of SW Yukon Territory. [because an avalanche was observed at the time of its discovery]

Ava·lon /ˈavəlɒn/ **1** (in Arthurian legend) the place to which Arthur was conveyed after death. **2** (in Welsh mythology) the kingdom of the dead.

Avalon Peninsula /ˈavələn/ a peninsula joined to SE Newfoundland by a narrow isthmus and surrounded by several large bays. St. John's is located on its northeastern shore. [AVALON 1]

avant-garde /ˌavɒntˈɡɑrd/ ● *noun* pioneers or innovators esp. in art and literature. ● *adjective* (of ideas, works of art, etc.) experimental, progressive. □ **avant-gardism** *noun* **avant-gardist** *noun* [French, = vanguard]

avant la let·tre /aˌvɑ̃ la ˈletr/ *adverb phrase* before the name was coined; before the concept (or person) referred to was formally recognized or in existence. [French, lit. 'before the letter']

Avar /ˈɒvɑr/ a member of a Turkic people prominent in SE Europe in the 6th–8th c. before being subdued by Charlemagne (791–99). In the 7th c. their kingdom extended from the Black Sea to the Adriatic.

avar·ice /ˈavərɪs/ *noun* extreme greed for money or gain; cupidity. □ **avar·icious** /ˌavəˈrɪʃəs/ *adjective* **avar·icious·ly** /-ˈrɪʃəsli/ *adverb* **avar·icious·ness** /-ˈrɪʃəsnəs/ *noun* [Latin *avaritia* from *avarus* greedy]

avast /əˈvast/ *interjection* Naut. stop, cease. [Dutch *houd vast* hold fast]

ava·tar /ˈavəˌtar/ *noun* **1** Hinduism a manifestation of a deity or released soul in bodily form on earth; an incarnate divine teacher. **2** an incarnation, embodiment, or manifestation of a person or idea (*he set himself up as a new avatar of Arab nationalism*). **3** a movable icon representing a person in cyberspace or virtual reality graphics. [Sanskrit *avatāra* descent, from *áva* down + *tṛ*- pass over]

avaunt /əˈvɒnt/ *interjection archaic* begone. [Old French *avant*, ultimately from Latin *ab* from + *ante* before]

Ave. *abbreviation* Avenue.

ave /ˈɒveɪ/ ● *noun* **1** (in full **Ave Maria** /ˈɒveɪ məˈriːə/) = HAIL MARY 1. **2** *archaic* or *literary* a shout of welcome or farewell. ● *interjection archaic* or *literary* welcome or farewell. [Latin, 2nd sing. imperative of *avēre* fare well]

Ave·bury /ˈeɪvbəri/ a village in Wiltshire, site of one of Britain's major henge monuments of the late neolithic period. The monument, about 425 m (1,400 ft.) across, consists of a massive bank and ditch surrounding the largest known stone circle, with two smaller circles and other stone settings within it. It is the centre of a complex ritual landscape that also contains a stone avenue, chambered tombs, and various other monuments.

avenge *transitive verb* **1** inflict retribution on behalf of (a person, a violated right, etc.). **2** take vengeance for (an injury). ● **be avenged** avenge oneself. □ **aven·ger** *noun* [Old French *avengier* from *à* to + *vengier* from Latin *vindicare* vindicate]

avens /ˈavənz/ *noun* **1** any of various rosaceous plants of the genus *Geum*. **2** = MOUNTAIN AVENS. [Old French *avence* (medieval Latin *avencia*), of unknown origin]

aven·tur·ine /əˈventʃəˌriːn/ *noun* **1** brownish ornamental glass containing sparkling gold-coloured particles usu. of copper or gold. **2** a variety of spangled quartz or feldspar resembling this. [French from Italian *avventurino* from *avventura* chance (because of its accidental discovery)]

av·enue *noun* **1 a** an urban road or street. **b** (in many N American grid-layout cities) a road running perpendicular to a street, esp. east-west (*compare* STREET 1d). **2** a road, driveway, or path with trees at regular intervals along its sides. **3** a way of approaching or dealing with something (*explored every avenue to find an answer*). [French, fem. past participle of *avenir* from Latin *advenire* come to]

aver /əˈvɜːr/ *transitive verb* (**averred**, **aver·ring**) *formal* assert or affirm. [Old French *averer* (as AD-, Latin *verus* true)]

aver·age ● *noun* **1 a** the usual amount, extent, or rate. **b** the ordinary standard. **2** the result of adding several amounts together and dividing the total by the number of amounts (*the average of 4, 5, and 9 is 6*). **3** *Baseball* = BATTING AVERAGE. **4** *N Amer.* the overall mean of a student's marks, expressed as a percentage, number, or letter grade (*had an 82% average in Grade 12*) (*compare* GRADE POINT AVERAGE). **5** *Law* damage to or loss of a ship or its cargo. ● *adjective* **1** usual, ordinary. **2** estimated or calculated by average. ● *transitive verb* **1** amount on average to (*the sale of the product averaged one hundred a day*). **2** do on average (*averages six hours' work a day*). **3 a** estimate the average of. **b** estimate the general standard of. □ **average out** result in an average. **law of averages** the principle that if one of two extremes occurs the other will also tend to so as to maintain the normal average. **on average** as an average rate or estimate. □ **aver·age·ly** *adverb* [French *avarie* damage to ship or cargo (see sense 5), from Italian *avaria* from Arabic *'awārīya* damaged goods, from *'awār* damage at sea, loss: *-age* after *damage*]

aver·ment /əˈvɜːrmənt/ *noun* **1** a positive statement or affirmation. **2** *Law* an allegation.

Aver·nus /əˈvɜːrnəs/ a lake near Naples in Italy, which fills the crater of an extinct volcano. It was described by Virgil and other Latin writers as the entrance to the underworld.

Aver·roës /əˈveroʊˌiːz/ (c.1126–98) Spanish Islamic philosopher whose Neoplatonic commentaries on Aristotle exercised a strong and controversial influence upon the succeeding centuries of Western philosophy and science.

averse /əˈvɜːrs/ *predicative adjective* (foll. by *to*) opposed, disinclined (*was not averse to helping me*). ¶ Often confused with *adverse*. [Latin *aversus* (as AVERT)]

aver·sion /əˈvɜːrʒən/ *noun* **1** (usu. foll. by *to*) a dislike or unwillingness (*has an aversion to hard work*). **2** an object of dislike (*my pet aversion*). [Latin *aversio* (as AVERT, -ION)]

aversion therapy *noun* behaviour therapy designed to cause the patient to give up an undesirable habit by associating it with an unpleasant effect.

avert *transitive verb* **1** (often foll. by *from*) turn away (one's eyes or thoughts). **2** prevent or ward off (an undesirable occurrence). [Latin *avertere* (as AB-, *vertere* vers- turn)]

Aves·ta /əˈvestə/ *noun* (usu. prec. by *the*) the sacred writings of Zoroastrianism (*compare* ZEND). [Persian]

Aves·tan /əˈvestən/ ● *adjective* of or relating to the Avesta. ● *noun* the ancient E Iranian language of the Avesta, closely related to Vedic Sanskrit.

avgas *noun* gasoline for aircraft. [aviation + gasoline]

avgo·lemono /ˌavɡoʊˈlemənoʊ/ *noun* (in Greek cuisine) a sauce or soup made with eggs and lemon juice. [Greek, from *avgo* egg + *lemon* lemon]

avian /ˈeɪviən/ *adjective* of or relating to birds. [Latin *avis* bird]

avian influenza *noun* **1** an acute, infectious, often fatal disease affecting birds (esp. poultry) and caused by any of several strains of influenza virus. **2** influenza in humans and other mammals caused by the same type of virus or one that is closely related.

avi·ary /ˈeɪviˌeri/ *noun* (*pl.* **-ies**) a large enclosure or building for keeping birds. [Latin *aviarium* (as AVIAN, -ARY¹)]

avi·ation *noun* **1** the skill or practice of operating aircraft. **2** aircraft manufacture. [French from Latin *avis* bird]

aviation snips *noun* metal snips having a compound lever action to make cutting easier.

avi·ator *noun* an aircraft pilot. [French *aviateur* from Latin *avis* bird]

aviator glasses *plural noun* a style of lightweight wire-rimmed glasses with rather large usu. tinted lenses resembling a pilot's goggles.

avia·trix /ˌeɪviˈeɪtrɪks/ *noun* a female aircraft pilot, esp. in the early days of flying.

Avi·cen·na /ˌavɪˈsenə/ (980–1037) Persian Islamic philosopher whose writings on Neoplatonic philosophy exercised a dominant influence on medieval Islam and scholasticism and whose *Canon of Medicine* was a popular text in the Middle Ages.

avi·cul·ture /ˈeɪviˌkʌltʃər/ *noun* the rearing and keeping of birds. □ **avi·cul·tur·ist** /-ˈkʌltʃərɪst/ *noun* [Latin *avis* bird, after AGRICULTURE]

avid *adjective* **1** eager or enthusiastic (*an avid cyclist*). **2** greedy. □ **avid·ity** /əˈvɪditi/ *noun* **avid·ly** *adverb* [Latin *avidus* from *avēre* crave]

avi·fauna /ˈeɪviˌfɒnə/ *noun* birds of a region or country collectively. [Latin *avis* bird + FAUNA]

Avi·gnon /avi·ˈnjɔ̃/ a city on the Rhone in SE France; pop. (est. 2002) 85,854. From 1309 until 1377 it was the residence of the popes during their exile from Rome, becoming papal property in 1348. After the papal court had returned to Rome, two successive antipopes re-established a rival papal court in Avignon, which lasted until 1408. The city remained in papal hands until the French Revolution.

avi·on·ics /ˌeɪviˈɒnɪks/ *plural noun* **1** (treated as *sing.*) electronics as applied to aviation. **2** electronic equipment fitted in an aircraft, e.g. altimeter, artificial horizon, etc. □ **avi·onic** *adjective* [blend of AVIATION + ELECTRONICS]

Avi·son /ˈeɪvɪsən/ **Mar·garet** (b.1918), Canadian poet. She won the Governor General's Award for her first collection, *Winter Sun* (1960), and another for *No Time* (1990).

avita·min·osis /ˌeɪˌvaɪtəmɪˈnoʊsɪs/ *noun Med.* a condition resulting from a deficiency of one or more vitamins.

avo /ˈavoʊ/ *noun* a monetary unit of Macao, equal to one-hundredth of a pataca. [Portuguese]

avo·cado *noun* (*pl.* **-dos**) **1 a** (in full **avocado pear**) a pear-shaped fruit with rough leathery skin, a smooth oily edible flesh, and a large pit. **b** the tropical evergreen tree, *Persea americana*, native to Central America, bearing this fruit. *Also called* ALLIGATOR PEAR. **2** (also **avocado green**) the light green colour of the flesh of this fruit. [Spanish, = advocate (substituted for Aztec *ahuacatl*)]

avo·ca·tion /ˌavəˈkeɪʃən/ *noun* **1** a secondary activity undertaken in addition to one's main work. **2** *informal* a vocation or calling. [Latin *avocatio* from *avocare* call away]

avo·cet /ˈavəˌset/ *noun* any wading bird of the genus *Recurvirostra* with long legs and a long slender upward-curved bill and usu. black and white plumage. [French *avocette* from Italian *avosetta*]

Avo·gadro /ˌavəˈɡadroʊ/ **Ama·deo** (1776–1856), Italian physicist, best known for his discovery in 1811 of the law that bears his name.

Avogadro's constant *noun* (also **Avogadro's number**) the number of atoms or molecules in one mole of a substance, equal to 6.02×10^{23}.

Avogadro's law *noun* the law that equal volumes of all gases at the same temperature and pressure contain the same number of molecules.

avoid *transitive verb* **1** keep away or refrain from (a thing, person, or action). **2** escape; evade. **3** *Law* nullify, quash (a contract or ruling). □ **avoid·able** *adjective* **avoid·ably** *adverb* **avoid·ance** *noun* **avoid·er**

noun [Anglo-French *avoider*, Old French *evuider* clear out, get quit of, from *vuide* empty, VOID]

avoidance behaviour *noun* (also **avoidance tactics**) behaviour which tends to remove an individual or organism from a stimulus or situation that is or may be unpleasant.

avoir·du·pois /ˌavərdəˈpɔɪz/ *noun* **1** (in full **avoirdupois weight**) a system of weights based on a pound of 16 ounces or 7,000 grains. **2** (usu. /ˌavwardu:ˈpwɒ/) *informal* excess body weight. [Middle English from Old French *aveir de peis* goods of weight, from *aveir* from Latin *habēre* have + *peis* (see POISE¹)]

Avon *noun* a former county of SW England, formed in 1974 from parts of north Somerset and Gloucestershire, and replaced in 1996 by four smaller districts.

Avon River **1 a** a river of central England which rises near the Leicestershire–Northamptonshire border and flows 154 km (96 miles) southwest through Stratford to the Severn River. **b** a river of SW England which rises near the Gloucestershire–Wiltshire border and flows 121 km (75 miles) through Bath and Bristol to the Severn River. **2** a river in SW Ontario, a tributary of the North Thames River.

avouch *transitive & intransitive verb archaic* guarantee, affirm, confess. □ **avouch·ment** *noun* [Old French *avochier* from Latin *advocare* (as AD-, *vocare* call)]

avow /əˈvaʊ/ *transitive verb* admit, confess. □ **avow·al** *noun* [Old French *avouer* acknowledge, from Latin *advocare* (as AD-, *vocare* call)]

avowed *adjective* admitted (*the avowed author*). □ **avow·ed·ly** *adverb*

avul·sion *noun* **1** esp. *Med.* a forcible separation or detachment. **2** *Law* a sudden removal of land by a flood etc. to another person's property. □ **avulse** *transitive verb* [Latin *avulsio* from *avellere avuls-* pluck away]

avun·cular /əˈvʌŋkjʊlər/ *adjective* **1** (of an older man, esp. in relation to younger people) benevolent and friendly. **2** of or pertaining to an uncle. [Latin *avunculus* maternal uncle, diminutive of *avus* grandfather]

aw *interjection N Amer. & Scot.* expressing mild protest, entreaty, commiseration, sympathy, or disapproval. [imitative]

AWACS /ˈeɪwaks/ *noun* a long-range radar system for detecting enemy aircraft. [acronym from airborne warning and control system]

await *verb* **1** *transitive* wait for. **2** *transitive* (of an event or thing) be in store for (*a surprise awaits you*). **3** *intransitive* wait. [Anglo-French *awaitier*, Old French *aguaitier* (as AD-, *waitier* WAIT)]

awake ● *verb* (*past* **awoke**; *past participle* **awoken**) **1** *intransitive* **a** cease to sleep. **b** become active. **2** *intransitive* (foll. by *to*) become aware of. **3** *transitive* rouse from sleep. **4** *transitive* arouse; provoke (*awoke our interest*). ● *predicative adjective* **1** not asleep. **2** vigilant. **3** (foll. by *to*) aware of. [Old English *āwæcnan, āwacian* (as A-², WAKE¹)]

awak·en *verb* **1** *transitive & intransitive* = AWAKE *verb*. **2** *transitive* (often foll. by *to*) make aware. [Old English *onwæcnan* etc. (as A-², WAKEN)]

awak·en·ing ● *noun* an arousal from sleep, inaction, indifference, ignorance, etc. (*a rude awakening*). ● *attributive adjective* incipient.

award ● *transitive verb* **1** give or order to be given as a prize, payment, or penalty (*awarded them a trophy*; *was awarded damages*). **2** grant, assign. ● *noun* **1** a prize or payment awarded. **2 a** a judicial decision. **b** the penalty awarded by a judicial decision. □ **award·er** *noun* [Anglo-French *awarder*, ultimately from Germanic: see WARD]

award-winning *adjective* that has won an award or several awards.

aware *predicative adjective* **1** (often foll. by *of*, or *that* + clause) conscious; not ignorant; having knowledge. **2** concerned and well-informed about a particular subject. □ **aware·ness** *noun* [Old English *gewær*]

awash *predicative adjective* **1** (usu. foll. by *in, with*) overrun as if by a flood (*the country is awash in natural resources*). **2** level with the surface of water, so that it just washes over. **3** carried or washed by the waves; flooded.

away ● *adverb* **1** to or at a distance from the place, person, or thing in question (*go away*; *give away*; *look away*; *they are away*; *5 kilometres away*). **2** towards or into non-existence (*sounds die away*; *explain it away*; *idled their time away*). **3** constantly, persistently, continuously (*work away*; *laugh away*). **4** without delay (*fire away!*). **5** *Baseball* out (*one away in the inning*). **6** *Cdn* (*Nfld & Maritimes*) in a place other than the speaker's home province or Atlantic Canada in general (*they're from away*). ● *adjective Sport* played in an opponent's venue (*away game*). □ **away with** (as imperative) take away; let us be rid of. [Old English *onweg, aweg* on one's way from A² + WAY]

AWD *abbreviation* ALL-WHEEL DRIVE.

Awdry, Reverend Wil·bert Vere (1911–1997), English author of children's stories about railway engines in the immensely popular *Thomas the Tank Engine* series.

awe ● *noun* a feeling of respect combined with fear or wonder (*stand in awe of*). ● *transitive verb* inspire with awe. [Middle English *age* from Old Norse *agi* from Germanic]

aweigh *predicative adjective Naut.* (of an anchor) clear of the bed of a body of water; hanging. [A² + WEIGH]

awe-inspiring *adjective* causing awe or wonder; amazing, magnificent.

awe·some *adjective* **1** inspiring awe; dreaded. **2** *slang* excellent, marvellous. □ **awe·some·ly** *adverb* **awe·some·ness** *noun*

awe·struck *adjective* (also **awe·stricken**) affected or overcome with awe.

awful ● *adjective* **1 a** unpleasant or horrible (*awful weather*). **b** poor in quality; very bad (*has awful handwriting*). **c** *informal* (*attributive*) excessive; large (*an awful lot of money*). **2** *literary* inspiring awe. ● *adverb informal* very. □ **something awful** *informal* to a great extent (*it started to rain something awful*). □ **aw·ful·ness** *noun* [AWE + -FUL]

aw·ful·ly *adverb* **1** in an unpleasant, bad, or horrible way (*he played awfully*). **2** *informal* very (*she's awfully young*).

awhile *adverb* for an unspecified length of time.

awk·ward *adjective* **1** ill-adapted for use; unwieldy. **2** clumsy or bungling. **3 a** embarrassed or ill at ease (*felt awkward in such company*). **b** embarrassing (*an awkward silence*). **4** difficult to deal with (*an awkward situation*; *an awkward customer*). □ **awk·ward·ly** *adverb*

awk·ward·ness *noun* [obsolete *awk* backhanded, untoward, from Old Norse *afugr* turned the wrong way + -WARD]

awl *noun* a small pointed tool used for piercing holes, esp. in leather or wood. [Old English *æl*]

awn *noun* a bristle-like projection growing from the grain sheath of barley, oats, and other grasses, or terminating a leaf etc. □ **awned** *adjective* [Old Norse *ögn*]

awn·ing *noun* a sheet of canvas, plastic, etc. sloping outward from the top of a window, storefront, or doorway or suspended above a ship's deck or other area to provide protection from the sun or rain. □ **awn·inged** *adjective* [17th c. (Naut.): origin uncertain]

awoke *past of* AWAKE.

awoken *past participle of* AWAKE.

AWOL /ˈeɪwɒl/ *abbreviation informal* absent without leave.

awry /əˈraɪ/ ● *adverb* **1** crookedly or askew. **2** improperly or amiss. ● *predicative adjective* **1** crooked. **2** amiss or wrong. □ **go awry** go or do wrong. [Middle English from A² + WRY]

aw-shucks *adjective N Amer. informal* marked by a self-deprecating, self-conscious, or shy manner.

axe (*US* usu. **ax**) ● *noun* **1** a chopping tool, usu. of iron with a steel edge and wooden handle. **2** the drastic cutting or elimination of expenditure, staff, etc. **3** dismissal, cancellation, etc. (*he and his program have both been given the axe*). **4** *slang* **a** an electric guitar used in jazz or rock music. **b** a saxophone used in jazz. ● *transitive verb* (**axing**) **1** cut (esp. costs or services) drastically. **2** remove or dismiss. □ **an axe to grind** private ends to serve. [Old English *æx* from Germanic]

Axel /ˈaksəl/ *noun* (also **axel**) *Figure Skating* a one-and-a half turn jump from the front outside edge of one skate to the back outside edge of the other. [*Axel R. Paulsen*, Norwegian figure skater d.1938]

Axel Hei·berg Island /ˈaksəl ˈhaɪbɜrg/ one of the Sverdrup Islands in the Canadian High Arctic, situated off the northwest coast of Ellesmere Island. [*Axel Heiberg*, Norwegian consul and promoter of Arctic exploration *c*.1900]

Axel·rod /ˈaksəlrɒd/ **Jul·ius** (b.1912), US biochemist and pharmacologist, who shared the 1970 Nobel Prize for physiology or medicine for his research on neurotransmitters.

axe·man *noun* (*US* usu. **ax·man**) (*pl.* **-men**) **1** a person who works with an axe, esp. one who fells trees. **2** *slang* a jazz or rock guitarist.

axe murderer *noun* a person who commits murder with an axe, often taken as the epitome of a violent psychopathic criminal.

axes *pl.* of AXIS¹.

axial /ˈaksɪəl/ *adjective* **1** forming or belonging to an axis. **2** around an axis (*axial rotation*; *axial symmetry*). □ **axi·al·ity** /ˌaksɪˈalɪti/ *noun* **axi·al·ly** *adverb*

axil /ˈaksɪl/ *noun Bot.* the upper angle between a leaf and the stem it springs from, or between a branch and the trunk. [Latin *axilla*: see AXILLA]

ax·il·la /akˈsɪlə/ *noun* (*pl.* **ax·il·lae** /-liː/) **1** *Anat.* the armpit. **2** the corresponding part of a bird or other creature. [Latin, = armpit, diminutive of *ala* wing]

Vowels: a *cat* ɑ *arm* e *bed* ɜr *her* ɜː *deux* ə *ago* ɪ *sit* i *cosy* iː *feed* ɒ *hot* ɔ *pore* ɔː *no* ʌ *run* ʊ *put*

ax·il·lary /akˈsɪləri/ *adjective* **1** *Anat.* of or relating to the armpit. **2** *Bot.* in or growing from the axil.

axi·ology /ˌaksiˈɒlədʒi/ *noun* the theory of values, esp. as they apply to ethics and aesthetics. [Greek *axia* value + -OLOGY]

axiom /ˈaksiəm/ *noun* **1** an established or widely accepted principle. **2** esp. *Geom.* a self-evident truth. [Greek *axiôma axiōmat-* from *axios* worthy]

axio·mat·ic /ˌaksiəˈmatɪk/ *adjective* **1** self-evident. **2** relating to or containing axioms. □ **axio·mat·ic·ally** *adverb*

axis¹ *noun* (*pl.* **axes** /-siːz/) **1 a** an imaginary line about which a body rotates or about which a plane figure is conceived as generating a solid. **b** a line which divides a regular figure symmetrically. **2** *Math.* a fixed reference line for the measurement of coordinates etc. **3** *Bot.* the central column of an inflorescence or other growth. **4** *Anat.* the second cervical vertebra. **5** *Physiol.* the central part of an organ or organism. **6 a** an agreement or alliance between two or more countries forming a centre for an eventual larger grouping of nations sharing an ideal or objective. **b** (**the Axis**) *see* AXIS POWERS. [Latin, = axle, pivot]

axis² *noun* (*pl.* same) a S Asian deer with a white-spotted coat, *Axis axis.* Also called CHITAL. [Latin]

Axis Powers (also **Axis**) the group of nations opposed to the Allies in the Second World War. Initially comprising Germany and Italy, which formed a political association in 1936 and a military alliance in 1939, and later extended to include Japan and other countries, the Axis collapsed with the fall of Mussolini and the surrender of Italy in 1943.

axle *noun* a rod or spindle (either fixed or rotating) on which a wheel or group of wheels is fixed. [originally *axle-tree* from Middle English *axel-tre* from Old Norse *öxull-tré*]

ax·man *US var. of* AXEMAN.

Ax·min·ster *noun* (in full **Axminster carpet**) a kind of machine-woven patterned carpet with a cut pile. [*Axminster* in S England]

axo·lotl /ˈaksəˌlɒtəl/ *noun* any of a number of Central American salamanders of the genus *Ambystoma* (esp. *A. Mexicanum*), which live in lakes and retain many larval characteristics, including external gills, throughout life, although capable in certain conditions of developing full adult form. [Nahuatl from *atl* water + *xolotl* servant]

axon /ˈaksɒn/ *noun Anat. & Zool.* a long threadlike part of a nerve cell, conducting impulses from the cell body. [Greek *axōn* axis]

Axum *see* AKSUM.

ay *var. of* AYE¹.

Aya·cucho /ˌaiəˈkuːtʃoː/ a city in the Andes of south central Peru; pop. (est. 2002) 111,100. The modern city was founded by Francisco Pizarro in 1539. At the battle of Ayacucho in Dec. 1824, the Spanish forces were defeated and the independence of Peru secured.

ayah *noun* a nursemaid or female servant esp. in India and other former British territories in Asia. [Anglo-Indian from Portuguese *aia* nurse]

aya·huas·ca /ˌaiəˈwaskə/ *noun* (also **yage**) **1** a tropical vine of the Amazon region, noted for its hallucinogenic properties. **2** a hallucinogenic drink prepared from the bark of this. [Quechua *ayawáska*, from *aya* 'corpse' + *waskha* 'rope']

aya·tol·lah /ˌaijəˈtoːlə/ *noun* a Shiite religious leader in Iran. [Persian from Arabic, = token of God]

ayaya /aijɒˈjɒ/ *noun* singing, typically among the Inuit, in which the sounds *ay-ay-a* are used rather than words. [imitative]

Ayck·bourn, Alan (b.1939), popular English playwright and director whose plays are comic and sometimes disturbing explorations of suburban and middle-class life.

aye¹ /ai/ (also **ay**) ● *adverb* **1** archaic or *Scot.*, N Ireland, & Northern England yes. **2** (in voting) I assent. **3** (as **aye aye**) *Naut.* a response accepting an order. ● *noun* an affirmative answer or assent, esp. in voting. □ **the ayes have it** the affirmative votes are in the majority. [16th c.: prob. from the pronoun *I* expressing assent]

aye² /ei/ *adverb* archaic ever, always. □ **for aye** forever. [Old Norse *ei, ey* from Germanic]

aye-aye /ˈaiai/ *noun* an insectivorous tree-dwelling primate of Madagascar, *Daubentonia madagascariensis*, which is closely related to the lemurs and has a narrow elongated finger on each hand for prying insects from bark. [Malagasy *aiay*]

Ayer /er/ **Sir Al·fred Jules** (1910–89), English utilitarian philosopher. His theories of 'logical positivism' were set out in his book *Language, Truth and Logic* (1936) and qualified in later works.

Ayers Rock /erz/ a red rock mass in Northern Territory, Australia, southwest of Alice Springs. The largest monolith in the world, it is 348 m (1,143 ft.) high and about 9 km (6 miles) in circumference. (Official name **Uluru**.) [Sir Henry *Ayers*, Premier of South Australia in 1872–3.]

Ayesha var. of AISHA.

Ayk·royd, Dan·iel Ed·ward ('Dan') (b.1952), Canadian comedian and actor, known especially for the movies *The Blues Brothers* (1980) and *Ghostbusters* (1984). He was nominated for an Academy Award for Best Supporting Actor for *Driving Miss Daisy* (1989).

Ayles·bury¹ a town in south central England, the county town of Buckinghamshire; pop. (est. 2002) 61,000.

Ayles·bury² *noun* (*pl.* **Ayles·burys**) a breed of large white duck, domesticated for its meat. [AYLESBURY¹]

Ayl·mer 1 a former city in SW Quebec, situated on the Ottawa River, just southwest of Hull, now part of Gatineau; pop. (2001) 36,085. **2** a town in SW Ontario, east of St. Thomas; pop. (2001) 7,126. [5th Baron *Aylmer*, Governor General of British North America d.1850]

Ayl·ward, Gladys May (1902–70), English missionary. In 1932 she helped found an inn in Yangsheng (later portrayed in the 1959 film *The Inn of the Sixth Happiness*). During the Sino-Japanese war she made a perilous journey to lead a hundred children to safety.

Ay·mara /ˌaimɒˈrɒ/ *noun* (*pl.* same or **Ay·maras**) **1** a member of an Aboriginal people of modern Bolivia and Peru, mainly inhabiting the plateaus near Lake Titicaca. **2** a group of languages spoken by the Aymara. [Bolivian Spanish]

Ayr·shire¹ /ˈerʃir/ a former county of SW Scotland, on the Firth of Clyde. From 1975 to 1996 it was part of Strathclyde region, and is now divided into North Ayrshire, East Ayrshire, and South Ayrshire.

Ayr·shire² /ˈerʃir/ *noun* a hardy breed of dairy cattle, mainly white with spots of red or brown, originating in Ayrshire.

Ayur·veda /aijurˈveidə/ *noun* a form of traditional Hindu medicine based on the idea of balance in bodily systems and using diet, herbal treatment, and yogic breathing. □ **Ayur·vedic** *adjective* [Sanskrit *āyur-veda* = science of life, medicine]

AZ *abbreviation* Arizona (in official postal use).

Azad Kashmir /ˌʌzɑd kaʃˈmiːr/ an autonomous state in NE Pakistan, formerly part of Kashmir; administrative centre, Muzzafarabad. It was established in 1949 after Kashmir was split as a result of the partition of India. The name means 'Free Kashmir'.

aza·lea /əˈzeiliə/ *noun* any of various flowering deciduous shrubs of the genus *Rhododendron*, with pink, purple, white, or yellow flowers. [Greek, fem. of *azaleos* dry (from the dry soil in which it was believed to flourish)]

Azazel /əˈzeizɛl, ˈazəˌzɛl/ **1** *Bible* a demon in the wilderness to whom the scapegoat was sent on the Day of Atonement, after Aaron had placed his hands on it and confessed the people's sins (Lev. 16:1–28). **2** *Islam* a demon.

azeo·trope /əˈziːəˌtroːp/ *noun Chem.* a mixture of liquids in which the boiling point remains constant during distillation, at a given pressure, without change in composition. □ **azeo·trop·ic** /əˌziːəˈtrɒpɪk/ *adjective* [A-¹ + Greek *zeō* boil + *tropos* turning]

Azer·bai·jan /ˌazərbaiˈdʒɒn/ a country in the Caucasus of SE Europe, on the western shore of the Caspian Sea; pop. (est. 2002) 7,798,497; capital, Baku. Historically, the name Azerbaijan referred to a larger Transcaucasian region which formed part of Persia. The northern part was ceded to Russia in the early 19th c., the southern part remaining a region of NW Iran.

Azer·bai·jani /ˌazərbaiˈdʒɒni/ ● *noun* **1** (also **Azeri** /əˈzeri/) a native or inhabitant of Azerbaijan. **2** the Turkic language of Azerbaijan. ● *adjective* of or pertaining to Azerbaijan or its people.

Azil·ian /əˈzɪliən/ *Archaeology* ● *adjective* of an early mesolithic industry in S France and N Spain, dating to 10,000–8,000 BC. Items from this period include flat bone harpoons, painted pebbles, and microliths. ● *noun* the Azilian industry. [Mas d'*Azil* in the French Pyrenees, where remains of the industry were found]

azi·muth /ˈazɪməθ/ *noun* **1** the angle between the most northerly point of the horizon and the point directly below a given celestial body, usu. measured clockwise using due north as the zero point. **2** the horizontal angle or direction of a compass bearing. **3** the angle of a recording head on a VCR in relation to the tape. □ **azi·muth·al** /-ˈmuːθəl/ *adjective* [Old French *azimut* from Arabic *as-sumūt* from *al* the + *sumūt* pl. of *samt* way, direction]

azine /ˈeiziːn/ *noun Chem.* an organic compound with at least one nitrogen atom in a six-membered ring. [AZO- + -INE⁴]

azo- /ˈazoː, ˈei-/ *prefix Chem.* containing two adjacent nitrogen atoms between carbon atoms. [French *azote* nitrogen, from Greek *azōos* without life]

azoic /əˈzoːɪk/ *adjective* **1** having no trace of life. **2** *Geol.* (of an age etc.) having left no organic remains. [Greek *azōos* without life]

Azores /əˈzɔrz/ a group of volcanic islands in the Atlantic Ocean, west of Portugal, in Portuguese possession but partially autonomous; pop. (est. 1999) 246,030; capital, Ponta Delgada.

Azov, Sea of /ˈazɒf/ an inland sea of S Russia and Ukraine, separated from the Black Sea by the Crimea and linked to it by a narrow strait.

Az·rael /ˈazreɪəl/ *Judaism & Islam* the angel who severs the soul from the body at death. [Hebrew, = help of God]

AZT *noun* an antiviral drug used to treat HIV infection and AIDS. Chem. formula: $C_{10}H_{13}N_5O_4$. [chemical name *azidothymidine*]

Aztec /ˈaztek/ ● *noun* **1** a member of the Aboriginal people dominant in central and southern Mexico before the Spanish conquest of 1519. **2** the language of the Aztecs. ● *adjective* of the Aztecs or their language (*see also* NAHUATL). [Nahuatl *aztecatl* men of the north]

Aztec lily *noun* a Mexican lily, *Sprecklia formosissima*, with red flowers, cultivated as an ornamental.

azuki *var. of* ADZUKI.

azure /ˈaʒɜr, -zjɜr/ ● *noun* **1 a** a deep sky-blue colour. **b** *Heraldry* blue. **2** *literary* the clear sky. ● *adjective* **1** of the colour azure. **2** *Heraldry* blue. [Old French *azur*, from medieval Latin *azzurum* from Arabic *al* the + *lāzaward* from Persian *lāžward* lapis lazuli]

azy·gous /ˈeizaigəs/ *Anat.* ● *adjective* (of any organic structure) single, not existing in pairs. ● *noun* an organic structure occurring singly. [Greek *azugos* unyoked, from *a-* not + *zugon* yoke]

Bb

B¹ /biː/ *noun* (also **b**) (*pl.* **Bs** or **B's**) **1** the second letter of the alphabet. **2** *Music* the seventh note of the diatonic scale of C major. **3** the second hypothetical person or example. **4** the second highest class or category (of academic marks etc.). **5** *Math.* (usu. **b**) the second known quantity. **6** a human blood type of the ABO system. **7** designating the degree of softness of a pencil lead (*a 4B pencil is darker than a 2B pencil*).

B² *symbol* **1** *Chem.* the element boron. **2** *Physics* magnetic flux density.

B³ *abbreviation* (also **B.**) **1** Bachelor. **2** bel(s). **3** billion. **4** bishop. **5** Blessed. **6** bass.

b *symbol Physics* barn.

b. *abbreviation* **1** born. **2** billion.

BA *abbreviation Baseball* BATTING AVERAGE.

B.A. *abbreviation* Bachelor of Arts.

Ba *symbol Chem.* the element barium.

B.A.A. *abbreviation N Amer.* Bachelor of Applied Arts.

baa ● *intransitive verb* (**baas**, **baaed**, **baa·ing**) (of a sheep) bleat. ● *noun* (*pl.* **baas**) the bleat of a sheep or lamb. [imitative]

Baade /ˈbɒdə/ **Wil·helm Hein·rich Wal·ter** (1893–1960), German-born US astronomer. He proved that the Andromeda galaxy was much further away than had been thought, which implied that the universe was much older and more extensive than had been thought.

Baal /bɒl/ (also **Bel** /bel/) a male fertility god whose cult was widespread in ancient Phoenician and Canaanite lands. [Hebrew *ba'al* lord]

Baal·bek /ˈbɒlbek/ a town in E Lebanon, site of the ancient city of Heliopolis. Its principal monuments date from the Roman period; they include the Corinthian temples of Jupiter and Bacchus and private houses with important mosaics.

Baal Shem Tov /bɒl ˈʃem tɒv/ (also **Baal Shem Tob**; born Israel ben Eliezer) (*c.*1700–60), Polish Jewish religious leader and educator, the founder of Hasidism.

baas /bɒs/ *noun South Africa* boss, master (often as a form of address). [Dutch: compare BOSS¹]

baas·skap /ˈbɒskɒp/ *noun South Africa* domination, esp. of non-whites by whites. [Afrikaans from *baas* master + *-skap* condition]

Baath /bɒθ/ *noun* (also **Ba'ath**) a pan-Arab socialist movement founded in Syria in the early 1940s. □ **Baath·ism** *noun* **Baath·ist** *noun* [Arabic *ba't*, lit. 'resurrection']

Bab /bɒb/ *the* (title of Sayyid Ali Muhammad Shirazi) (1819–50), Persian religious leader, who founded Babism (see BABI).

baba¹ /ˈbɒbə/ *noun* (in full **rum baba**) a small rich cake leavened with yeast, usu. soaked in rum-flavoured syrup. [French from Polish, lit. 'peasant woman']

baba² /ˈbɒbə/ *noun* **1** (among people of E European descent) grandmother. **2** *informal* an old woman of E European descent. [Ukrainian]

baba³ /ˈbɒbə/ *noun* **1** (among people of Indian descent) father. **2** (also **Baba**) a spiritual leader or holy man in India. [Hindi *bābā*]

baba gha·nouj /ˈbɒbə gə,nuːʃ/ *noun* a dip, originally Middle Eastern, made from mashed baked eggplant, tahini, garlic and other seasonings. [Arabic]

Bab·bage, Charles (1791–1871), English mathematician and inventor who designed and built several machines which could perform mathematical computations. He is generally considered the pioneer of modern computing.

Bab·bitt¹, Mil·ton Byron (b.1916), US composer and mathematician. His compositions developed from the 12-note system of Schoenberg and Webern, and later employed electronic devices such as synthesizers and tape.

Bab·bitt² *noun* **1** (in full **Babbitt metal**) any of a group of soft alloys of tin, antimony, copper, and usu. lead, used for lining bearings etc., to diminish friction. **2** (**babbitt**) a bearing lining made of this. [I. *Babbitt*, US inventor d.1862]

Bab·bitt³ *noun* a materialistic, complacent business person. □ **Bab·bit·try** *noun* [George *Babbitt*, a character in the novel *Babbitt* (1922) by S. Lewis]

bab·ble ● *verb* **1** *intransitive* **a** talk in an inarticulate or incoherent manner. **b** chatter excessively or irrelevantly. **c** (of a stream, bird, etc.) produce a succession of indistinct sounds. **2** *transitive* repeat foolishly; divulge through chatter. ● *noun* **1 a** incoherent speech. **b** foolish, idle, or childish talk. **2** the murmur of voices, water, etc. [Middle Low German *babbelen*, or imitative]

-babble *combining form* forming nouns denoting the jargon characteristic of a specified subject or group (*psychobabble*).

bab·bler *noun* **1** a chatterer. **2** a person who reveals secrets. **3** any of a large group of passerine birds with loud chattering voices.

babe *noun* **1** a baby. **2** an innocent or helpless person. **3** esp. *N Amer. slang* a young and attractive person, esp. a woman. ¶ Sometimes *offensive* when used of women. □ **babe in arms 1** a small baby, esp. one too young to walk. **2** an innocent or naive person. [Middle English: imitative of child's *ba, ba*]

babel /ˈbeibəl, ˈbabəl/ *noun* **1** a confused noise, esp. of voices. **2** a noisy assembly. **3** a scene of confusion. [from *Babel* (see TOWER OF BABEL), where, according to the biblical story, God confused the language of the builders]

babe magnet *noun* (also **chick magnet**) *slang* a person or thing that attracts much attention from women.

Babi /ˈbabi/ *noun* a member of a Persian eclectic sect founded in 1844 by Mirza Ali Muhammad of Shiraz (called *the Bab*), emphasizing the coming of a new prophet or messenger of God. The Baha'i faith is derived from Babism. □ **Bab·ism** *noun* [Persian *Bab-ed-Din*, gate (= intermediary) of the Faith]

ba·biche /baˈbiːʃ/ *noun N Amer.* strips of rawhide or sinew used as laces, thread, webbing, etc., e.g. in snowshoes. [Canadian French from Mi'kmaq *aːpapiːč*]

Ba·bine Lake /baˈbiːn/ a long, narrow lake in west central BC, situated near the centre of the province. [French, = large lip, with reference to the distended lip of labret-wearing Carrier women]

babka /ˈbɒbkə/ *noun* a sweet E European yeast cake flavoured with rum. [as BABA¹]

ba·boon *noun* **1** any of various African and Arabian monkeys of the genus *Papio*, having a long doglike snout and large teeth. **2** an ugly or uncouth person. [Old French *babuin* or medieval Latin *babewynus*, of unknown origin]

Babur /ˈbabər/ (born Zahir al-Din Muhammad) (1483–1530), the first Mogul emperor of India 1526–30.

ba·bush·ka /bəˈbuːʃkə/ *noun* **1** a kerchief tied under the chin. **2** an old Russian woman. [Russian, = grandmother]

baby ● *noun* (*pl.* **babies**) **1** a very young child or infant, esp. one not yet able to walk. **2** an unduly childish person (*don't be such a baby!*). **3** the youngest member of a family, team, etc. **4** (often *attributive*) **a** a young or newly born animal. **b** a thing that is small of its kind (*baby corn; baby rose*). **c** *informal* a junior member in a hierarchy, e.g. a farm team or junior team in a major-league team's organization (*the baby Habs lost to Laval*). **5** *slang* a young woman; a sweetheart (often as a form of address). ¶ Often *offensive* if used to a stranger. **6** *slang* a person or thing regarded with affection or familiarity. **7** one's own responsibility, invention, concern, achievement, etc., regarded in a personal way. ● *transitive verb* (**babies**, **babied**) **1** treat like a baby. **2** pamper. □ **carry** (or **hold**) **the baby** bear unwelcome responsibility. **throw out the baby with the bathwater** reject the essential with the inessential. □ **baby·hood** *noun* [Middle English, formed as BABE, -Y²]

baby beef *noun* meat from young cattle older than those producing veal.

Baby Bell *noun* any of the regional US telephone companies into which the Bell company split in 1984 (*compare* MA BELL).

baby blue soft, pale blue.

baby blue eyes *noun* a N American ornamental annual plant, *Nemophila menziesii*, having bowl-shaped blue flowers with white centres.

baby blues *plural noun* **1** *informal* attractive blue eyes. **2** *informal* postpartum depression.

baby bonus *noun Cdn* family allowance or child tax benefit.

baby boom *noun* a temporary marked increase in the birth rate.

baby boomer *noun* a person born during a baby boom, esp. after the war of 1939–45.

baby boomlet *noun* a small baby boom, esp. that at the end of the 1980s caused by baby boomers having children.

baby bottle *noun N Amer.* a bottle with a rubber nipple for feeding babies and small toddlers.

baby buggy *noun N Amer.* = BABY CARRIAGE.

baby bust *noun* a temporary marked decrease in the birth rate.

baby buster *noun* a person born during a baby bust, esp. in the late 1960s and early 1970s.

baby carriage *noun N Amer.* a four-wheeled carriage for a baby, pushed by a person on foot.

baby carrier *noun* a pouch for carrying a baby, typically designed to be worn slung on the back or across the chest, and usu. having openings for the baby's legs.

baby doll *noun* **1** a doll resembling a baby. **2 a** (in *pl.*) (in full **baby-doll pyjamas**) women's or girls' pyjamas consisting of a hip-length top of a delicate fabric and matching panties. **b** (in full **baby-doll dress**) a short, loose-fitting, usu. sleeveless dress, extending to just below the buttocks.

baby face *noun* a youthful or innocent face. □ **baby-faced** *adjective*

baby farm *noun* a place where babies are lodged and cared for in exchange for payment. □ **baby-farming** *noun*

baby fat *noun* the fatty tissue which gives babies and young children their characteristic plumpness, peaking at nine months of age and diminishing until about the age of seven.

baby finger *noun* the little finger.

baby food *noun* a light, usu. puréed diet suitable for babies.

baby grand piano *noun* (also **baby grand**) the smallest size of grand piano.

baby·ish *adjective* **1** childish, simple. **2** immature. □ **baby·ish·ly** *adverb* **baby·ish·ness** *noun*

Baby·lon¹ /ˈbabəˌlɒn/ an ancient city in Mesopotamia, which first came to prominence in the second millennium BC under Hammurabi, who made it the capital of Babylonia. The city lay on the Euphrates and was noted for its luxury, its fortifications, and particularly for the Hanging Gardens (see HANGING GARDENS OF BABYLON). [Greek *Babulōn* from Hebrew *bābel* BABEL]

Baby·lon² /ˈbabɪˌlon/ *noun* **1** any magnificent and decadent city. **2** *derogatory* (among some blacks, esp. Rastafarians): **a** white society. **b** any representation of this, esp. the police. [BABYLON¹]

Baby·lonia /ˌbabəˈləʊnɪə/ an ancient region of Mesopotamia, formed when the kingdoms of Akkad and Sumer combined in the first half of the 2nd millennium BC. It was eventually conquered by Cyrus the Great of Persia in 539 BC.

Baby·lon·ian /ˌbabɪˈləʊnɪən/ ● *noun* **1** an inhabitant of Babylon or Babylonia. **2** the Akkadian dialect of the Babylonians. ● *adjective* of or relating to Babylon or Babylonia.

Babylonian Captivity 1 (also **Babylonian exile**) the captivity of the Israelites in Babylon, lasting from their deportation by Nebuchadnezzar in 586 BC until their release by Cyrus the Great in 538 BC. **2** the exile of seven Popes at Avignon from 1309 to 1377.

baby monitor *noun* an intercom which allows parents to listen to a baby while in another room.

baby oil *noun* a mineral oil used to soften skin, in massaging, and to remove makeup.

baby powder *noun* a usu. scented talcum powder used on babies' skin.

baby's breath *noun N Amer.* a plant of the pink family, *Gypsophila paniculata*, with tiny usu. white flowers, often used to ornament bouquets of larger flowers.

baby shower *noun N Amer.* a party given for a pregnant woman at which her female friends and relatives give her presents for the baby.

baby·sit *transitive & intransitive verb* (**-sit·ting**; *past and past participle* **-sat**) look after a child or children while the parents are out. □ **baby·sit·ter** *noun* **baby·sit·ting** *noun*

baby snatcher *noun informal* **1** a person who kidnaps babies. **2** = CRADLE-ROBBER.

baby's tears *noun* (also **baby tears**) a houseplant, *Helxine soleirolii*, with small, round leaves.

baby step *noun* a very small metaphorical step.

baby talk *noun* childish talk used by or to young children.

baby tooth *noun* a tooth belonging to a person's first set of teeth, shed between the ages of five and thirteen. *Also called* PRIMARY TOOTH.

bac·ca·la /bakəˈlɒ, bɒkəˈlɒ/ *noun* (also **baca·lao** /bakəˈlaʊ/, **baca·lhau** /bɒkəˈljuː/) cod, esp. dried and salted. [Italian *baccalà*, Spanish *bacal(l)ao*, Portuguese *bacalhau*]

bac·ca·laure·ate /ˌbakəˈlɔrɪət/ *noun* **1** the university degree of bachelor. **2** an examination intended to qualify successful candidates for higher education. *See also* INTERNATIONAL BACCALAUREATE. [French *baccalauréat* or medieval Latin *baccalaureatus* from *baccalaureus* bachelor]

bac·ca·lieu bird /bakəˈluː/ *noun Cdn* (*Nfld*) any of various seabirds, esp. the Atlantic common murre (*Uria aalge aalge*) or the Atlantic common puffin (*Fratercula arctica arctica*). [as BACCALA]

bac·carat /ˈbakəˌrɒ, ˌbakəˈrɒ, bɒ-/ *noun* a card game similar to blackjack, in which players take turns betting against the dealer. [French]

bac·cate /ˈbakeɪt/ *adjective Bot.* **1** bearing berries. **2** of or like a berry. [Latin *baccatus* berried, from *bacca* berry]

Bac·chae /ˈbakiː/ *plural noun* the priestesses or female devotees of the Greek god Bacchus. [Latin from Greek *Bakkhai*]

bac·cha·nal /ˌbakəˈnɒl, ˌbɒk-/ ● *noun* **1** a wild and drunken revelry. **2** a drunken reveller. **3** a priest, worshipper, or follower of Bacchus. ● *adjective* of or like Bacchus, the Greek or Roman god of wine, or his rites. [Latin *bacchanalis* from *Bacchus* god of wine]

Bac·cha·nalia /ˌbakəˈneɪlɪə, ˌbɒk-/ *plural noun* **1** the Roman festival of Bacchus. **2** (**bacchanalia**) a drunken revelry. □ **bac·cha·nal·ian** *adjective & noun* [Latin, neuter pl. of *bacchanalis*: see BACCHANAL]

bac·chant /ˈbakənt/ *noun* (*pl.* **bac·chants** or **bac·chant·es** /bəˈkantiːz/) **1** a priest, worshipper, or follower of Bacchus. **2** a drunken reveller. □ **bac·chan·tic** /bəˈkantɪk/ *adjective* [French *bacchante* from Latin *bacchari* celebrate Bacchanal rites]

bac·chan·te /bəˈkanti/ *noun* a female bacchant.

Bac·chic /ˈbakɪk, ˈbɒkɪk/ *adjective* pertaining to or characteristic of Bacchus or his cult. [Latin *bacchicus* of Bacchus]

Bac·chus /ˈbakəs, ˈbɒkəs/ *Gk & Rom. Myth* the Roman name for DIONYSUS, used occasionally in Greece as well.

baccy *noun slang* tobacco. [abbreviation]

Bach /bɒx/ **1 Carl Phil·ipp Eman·uel** (1714–88), German composer, son of J.S. Bach, known for developing the sonata form through more than 200 keyboard sonatas, and for a celebrated treatise on keyboard playing. **2 Jo·hann Chris·tian** (1735–1782), German composer, son of J.S. Bach, and as music master to the British royal family, known as 'the English Bach'. He is noted for his 13 operas, which influenced Mozart. **3 Jo·hann Sebas·tian** (1685–1750), German baroque composer, whose music has been considered by many as supreme. Among his most celebrated works are the six Brandenburg Concertos, the *St. Matthew* and *St. John Passions*, the *Christmas Oratorio*, the *Goldberg Variations*, the *Mass in B minor*, and his collection of preludes and fugues known as the *Well-Tempered Clavier*. **4 Wil·helm Friede·mann** (1710–84), German composer, son of J.S. Bach, also regarded as one of the greatest organists of his day. □ **Bach·ian** *adjective*

Bacha·rach /ˈbakəˌrak/ **Burt** (b.1929), US writer of popular songs and film scores. His songs include 'Alfie' (1966), and 'Raindrops Keep Falling on my Head' (1969).

bach·elor *noun* **1** an unmarried man. **2 a** (in full **bachelor's degree**) a degree awarded to someone who has completed undergraduate studies. **b** a person who has been awarded a bachelor's degree. **3** *Cdn* = BACHELOR APARTMENT. **4** a male animal, esp. a male fur seal, which is prevented from breeding by more dominant males in a social group. **5** *hist.* a young knight serving under another's banner. □ **bachelor·hood** *noun* [Old French *bacheler* aspirant to knighthood, of uncertain origin]

bachelor apartment *noun* **1** *Cdn & S Africa* an apartment consisting of a single large room serving as bedroom and living room, with a separate bathroom. **2** any apartment occupied by a bachelor.

bachelor button *noun* (also **bachelor's button**) any of various flowers with tightly-petalled heads, esp. the cornflower.

bachelor·ette *noun* **1** *N Amer.* a young unmarried woman. **2** *Cdn* a very small bachelor apartment.

bachelorette party *noun* *N Amer.* a party, usu. attended by women only, given for a woman soon to be married.

bachelor girl *noun* an independent unmarried young woman. ¶ Used disparagingly at the beginning of the 20th century.

bachelor party *noun* a party, usu. attended by men only, given for a man soon to be married.

Bach flower remedies /batʃ/ *plural noun* preparations of the flowers of various plants used in a system of complementary medicine intended to relieve ill health by influencing underlying emotional states. [named after E. Bach, British physician d.1936]

ba·cil·lary /bəˈsɪləri, ˈbasəˌleri/ *adjective* relating to or caused by bacilli.

ba·cil·li·form /bəˈsɪlɪˌfɔrm/ *adjective* rod-shaped.

ba·cil·lus /bəˈsɪləs/ *noun* (*pl.* **ba·cil·li** /-laɪ/) **1** any rod-shaped bacterium. **2** (usu. in *pl.*) any pathogenic bacterium. [Late Latin, diminutive of Latin *baculus* stick]

ba·cil·lus thur·in·gien·sis /ˌθɜrɪndʒiˈensɪs, θəˌrɪndʒiˈensɪs/ *noun* **1** a bacterium containing a glycoprotein that is toxic to insects but not to vertebrates. **2** a bacterial pesticide used against spruce budworm, gypsy moth, mosquitoes, etc. Abbr.: **Bt, BT**. [from *Thuringia* in Germany, where the bacterium was first discovered in moth larvae]

Back, 1 Fré·dé·ric (b.1924) Canadian animator, winner of Oscars for *Crac* and *The Man Who Planted Trees*. **2 Sir George** (1796–1878), English explorer who accompanied John Franklin on two Arctic voyages, and who led his own Arctic expedition in search of John Ross in 1833.

back ● *noun* **1 a** the rear surface of the human body from the shoulders to the hips. **b** the corresponding upper surface of an animal's body. **c** the spine (*fell and broke his back*). **d** the keel of a ship. **2 a** any surface regarded as corresponding to the human back, e.g. of the head or hand, or of a chair. **b** the part of a garment that covers the back. **3 a** the less active or visible or important part of something functional, e.g. of a knife or a piece of paper (*write it on the back*). **b** the side or part normally away from the spectator or the direction of motion or attention, e.g. of a car, house, or room (*stood at the back*). **4 a** (in football etc.) a player positioned behind the front line of play (*see* RUNNING BACK, DEFENSIVE BACK). **b** this position. ● *adverb* **1** to the rear; away from what is considered to be the front (*go back a bit; ran off without looking back*). **2 a** in or into an earlier or normal position or condition (*came back late; went back home; ran back to the car; put it back on the shelf*). **b** in return (*pay back*). **3** in or into the past (*back in June; three years back*). **4** at a distance (*stand back from the road*). **5** in check (*hold him back*). **6** *N Amer.* behind (*the team was five points back*). ● *verb* **1** *transitive* **a** help with moral or financial support. **b** bet on the success of (a horse etc.). **2** *transitive & intransitive* (usu. foll. by *up*) move, or cause (a vehicle etc.) to move, backwards. **3** *transitive* a put or serve as a back, background, or support to. **b** *Music* accompany. **4** *transitive* lie at the back of (*a beach backed by steep cliffs*). **5** *intransitive* (of the wind) move round in a counter-clockwise direction. ● *adjective* **1** situated behind, esp. as remote or subsidiary (*back street; back teeth*). **2** of or relating to the past; not current (*back pay; back issue*). **3** reversed, backward (*back flow, back somersault*). **4** *Phonetics* formed at the back of the mouth. □ **at a person's back** in pursuit or support. **at the back of one's mind** remembered but not consciously thought of. **back and fill** go backward and forward. **back and forth** to and fro. **back down** withdraw one's claim or point of view etc.; concede defeat in an argument etc. (**in**) **back of** *N Amer.* behind. **the back of beyond** a

very remote or inaccessible place. **back off 1** draw back, retreat. **2** abandon one's intention, stand, etc. **back on to** have its back adjacent to (*the house backs on to a field*). **back out** (often foll. by *of*) withdraw from a commitment. **back up 1** give (esp. moral) support to. **2** *Computing* make a spare copy of (data, a disk, etc.). **3** (of running water) accumulate behind an obstruction. **4** reverse (a vehicle) into a desired position. **5** *N Amer.* form a line of vehicles in congested traffic. **back water** reverse a boat's forward motion using oars. **get** (or **put**) **a person's back up** annoy or anger a person. **get off a person's back** stop troubling a person. **go back on** fail to honour (a promise or commitment). **in back** *N Amer. informal* in or at the back. **know like the back of one's hand** be entirely familiar with. (**flat**) **on one's back** injured or ill in bed. **on the backs of** by exploiting or causing to suffer (*it wants to reduce the deficit on the backs of the unemployed*). **pat** (or **slap** or **clap**) **on the back** a gesture of approval or congratulation. **pat** (or **slap** or **clap**) **a person on the back** congratulate a person. **put one's back into** approach (a task etc.) with vigour. **see the back of** *see* SEE¹. **turn one's back on 1** abandon. **2** ignore. **with one's back to** (or **up against**) **the wall** in a desperate situation; hard-pressed. □ **back·er** *noun* (in sense 1 of *verb*). **back·less** *adjective* [Old English *bæc* from Germanic]

back·ache *noun* a (usu. prolonged) pain in one's back.

back alley *noun* *N Amer.* **1** a passageway behind buildings. **2** the hidden aspects of something (*the back alleys of international business*).

back bacon *noun* *Cdn & Brit.* round, lean bacon cut from the eye of a pork loin.

back·bar *noun* esp. *US* a structure behind a bar, with shelves for holding bottles etc.

back bay *noun* *Cdn* a shallow bay off a lake.

back·beat *noun* **1** an accented secondary beat, esp. as played by a drummer in various forms of popular music. **2** the rhythm created by a series of these.

back·bench *noun* *Cdn, Brit., Austral., & NZ* **1** (often in *pl.*) a backbencher's seat. **2** the backbenchers' seats collectively. **3** (often *attributive*) the backbenchers collectively (*a backbench Tory MP*).

back·bench·er *noun* *Cdn, Brit., Austral., & NZ* a member of a legislative assembly who is not a member of the cabinet, an opposition critic, or a party leader.

back bend *noun* **1** a bend backwards from the waist. **2** a gymnastic manoeuvre in which a person bends backwards until the hands reach the floor.

back·biting *noun* speaking maliciously of an absent person. □ **back·biter** *noun*

back·blocks *plural noun* *Austral. & NZ* land in the remote and sparsely inhabited interior.

back·board *noun* **1** *Basketball* the vertical board to which the basket is attached. **2** (in *pl.*) *Hockey* the boards behind the net at each end of the rink. **3** a board placed at or forming the back of anything. **4** a board used to support or straighten a person's back, esp. after an accident.

back boiler *noun* *Brit.* a tank or pipes attached to the back of a fireplace, used for heating water.

back·bone *noun* **1** the spine. **2** the main support or most important element in a structure, organization, etc. (*trout are the backbone of the recreational fishery*). **3** firmness of character. **4** *US* the spine of a book. **5** a high-speed, high-capacity digital connection which forms the basis of a local or wide-area computer network, and to which subsidiary parts of the network may be connected.

back-breaker *noun* **1** an extremely arduous task. **2** *N Amer. esp. Sport* a decisive event or action, esp. one that ensures an opponent's defeat (*their third-period goal was the back-breaker*).

back-breaking *adjective* (esp. of manual work) extremely hard.

back burner *noun* **1** a position receiving little attention or low priority (*the project has been put on the back burner*). **2** a heating element at the rear of a stove. □ **back-burner** *transitive verb*

back·cast *noun* *N Amer. Angling* the action of casting a fishing line backwards before casting it into the water.

back·catch·er *noun* *Cdn* = CATCHER 2.

back channel *noun* **1** *Cdn* a backwater or side channel of a river. **2** a person who acts as a secret intermediary in diplomatic negotiations. **3** (often *attributive*) a secretive, covert action.

back·chat *noun* esp. *Brit.* = BACKTALK.

back·check *intransitive verb* *Hockey* (of a forward) return to the defensive zone and check attacking opponents. □ **back·check·er** *noun* **back·check·ing** *noun*

back·cloth *noun* *Brit.* = BACKDROP 1.

back·comb *transitive verb* comb (the hair) from the ends towards the scalp to make it look thicker.

back concession *noun Cdn (Ont. & Que.)* **1** a concession at some distance from a more heavily settled road or area. **2** (in *pl.*) rural areas, esp. viewed as conservative or unsophisticated.

back·country *noun N Amer., Austral., & NZ* an area away from settled districts.

back·court *noun* **1** *Tennis* the area between the baseline and the service line. **2** *Basketball* **a** the half of the court which a team defends. **b** a team's guards.

back crawl *noun* = BACKSTROKE 2.

back·cross ● *transitive verb* cross (a hybrid) with one of its parents. ● *noun* (usu. *attributive*) an instance or the product of this.

back·date *transitive verb* **1** put an earlier date to (an agreement etc.) than the actual one. **2** make retrospectively valid.

back door ● *noun* **1** a door at the back of a house, vehicle, etc. **2** an alternative, usu. ingenious, indirect, or less conspicuous means of gaining an objective. ● *adjective* (**back·door**) **1 a** secondary, alternative (*backdoor route*). **b** clandestine, underhanded (*backdoor deal*; *backdoor attempt*). **2** *Basketball* involving a pass from the top of the key to a player who has just run to the side of the basket.

back·draft *noun* (also esp. *Brit.* **back·draught**) **1** a reverse draft of air or other gas. **2** the violent explosion occurring when air reaches an oxygen-starved fire.

back·drop *noun* **1** a painted cloth hung across the back of a stage as the principal part of the scenery. **2** the setting for an event or situation (*against the backdrop of modernism*).

back eddy *noun Cdn* (esp. *BC*) **1** an area of water behind an obstruction in a watercourse in which the current is the reverse of the general direction of flow. **2** = BACKWATER 2.

back end *noun* **1** the rearmost part of something. **2** the final stage of a process, esp. the profits generated by a film etc., or the termination of an agreement (often *attributive*: *back-end deal*; *back-end charges*). **3** *Computing* (often *attributive*) the elements of a computer's architecture pertaining to data stored in a database (compare FRONT END 3).

back·fat *noun* a layer of fat between the skin and muscle of animals, esp. along the back, a measurement of which is used in grading the meat.

back·field *noun Football* **1** the area of play behind the line of scrimmage. **2** the players who line up in the backfield collectively, esp. the running backs and quarterback. □ **back·field·er** *noun*

back·fill ● *transitive verb* refill an excavated hole with the material dug out of it. ● *noun* excavated material used to refill an excavation.

back·fire ● *intransitive verb* **1** undergo a mistimed explosion, as in the cylinder or exhaust of an internal combustion engine. **2** (of a plan etc.) rebound adversely on the originator; have the opposite effect to what was intended. ● *noun* **1** an instance of backfiring. **2** *N Amer.* a fire set deliberately to stop the advance of a forest fire or prairie fire.

back·flip *noun* a backwards aerial somersault.

back-forma·tion *noun* **1** the formation of a word from its seeming derivative, e.g. *laze* from *lazy*. **2** a word formed in this way.

back forty *noun N Amer.* the area at the back of (esp. a rural) property.

back·gam·mon *noun* **1** a game for two played on a board with pieces moved according to throws of the dice. **2** the most complete form of win in this. [BACK + GAMMON²]

back garden *noun* esp. *Brit.* = BACKYARD 1.

back·ground *noun* **1** part of a scene, picture, or description, that serves as a setting to the chief figures or objects and foreground. **2** an inconspicuous or obscure position (*kept in the background*). **3** a person's education, knowledge, or social circumstances. **4** explanatory or contributory information or circumstances. **5** *Electronics* unwanted signals, such as noise in the reception or recording of sound. **6** = BACKGROUND RADIATION.

back·ground·er *noun N Amer.* an official briefing or handout giving background information.

background music *noun* music intended as an unobtrusive accompaniment to some activity, or to provide atmosphere in a film etc.

background radiation *noun* **1** the normal, low-intensity electromagnetic radiation present in the natural environment. **2** (in full **cosmic microwave background radiation**) electromagnetic radiation which appears to pervade the whole universe, believed to be the remnant of the radiation generated by the big bang.

back·hand ● *noun* **1** (often *attributive*) any arm motion performed with the arm initially across and in front of the torso, esp.: **a** *Tennis etc.* a stroke made with the back of the hand turned towards the opponent. **b** a blow made with the back of the hand. **2** *Hockey* (often *attributive*) a shot or pass made by striking the puck with the back of the stick's blade. ● *transitive verb* strike with a backhand.

back·hand·ed *adjective* **1** (of an arm motion) performed with the arm initially across the torso, or with the back of the hand (*backhanded catch*; *backhanded blow*). **2** indirect; ambiguous (*a backhanded compliment*).

back·hand·er *noun* **1** a backhand shot, blow, stroke, etc. **2** *informal* an indirect attack. **3** *Brit. slang* a bribe.

back·hoe *noun* a mechanical excavator which operates by drawing towards itself a bucket attached to a hinged boom.

back·house *noun N Amer.* = OUTHOUSE 1.

back·ing *noun* **1** support. **2** material used to form a back or support. **3** (often *attributive*) musical accompaniment, esp. to a singer.

back kitchen *noun* (in older houses) a room, often one built as an extension, used originally as a summer kitchen or pantry or for storage etc.

back·lands *plural noun* sparsely settled areas.

back lane *noun Cdn & Brit.* = BACK ALLEY 1.

back·lash *noun* **1** an excessive or marked adverse reaction. **2 a** a sudden recoil or reaction between parts of a mechanism. **b** excessive play between such parts.

back·light ● *noun* (also **back·light·ing**) light illuminating something (esp. a photographic subject or a computer screen) from behind. ● *transitive verb* (*past* and *past participle* **back·lit** or **back·light·ed**) illuminate (esp. a photographic subject, a computer screen, etc.) from behind. □ **back·light·ing** *noun* **back·lit** *adjective*

back line *noun* **1** *Hockey* the blue line. **2** *Sport* a team's defencemen collectively.

back·liner *noun Sport* a defenceman, esp. in hockey.

back·list *noun* a publisher's list of books published before the current season and still in print.

back·log ● *noun* an accumulation of uncompleted work etc. ● *verb* (**-logged**, **-log·ging**) **1** *transitive* overload (a system, process, etc.). **2** *intransitive* accumulate unfinished tasks or unprocessed material. [originally a large log placed at the back of a fire to sustain it]

back·lot *noun* an outdoor area attached to a film studio, where street scenes are recreated and filmed.

back matter *noun* the parts of a book which follow the main text, e.g. the index, bibliography and appendices.

back·most *adjective* farthest back.

back nine *noun Golf* the final nine holes on an 18-hole course.

back office *noun* an office or centre in which the administrative work of a business is carried out, as opposed to its dealings with customers, orig. situated behind the main office or shop, now often in larger companies located at a separate site.

back order *noun* a retailer's order (for merchandise) yet to be filled by a supplier. □ **on back order** (of merchandise) ordered by a retailer but not yet received from the supplier.

back·pack ● *noun* a knapsack. ● *intransitive verb* travel or hike with a backpack. □ **back·pack·er** *noun* **back·pack·ing** *noun*

back·paddle *intransitive verb* paddle a canoe etc. by moving the paddle towards the bow.

back passage *noun informal* the rectum.

back-patting *noun* the act or an instance of administering a pat on the back or congratulating.

back·pedal *intransitive verb* (**-pedalled** or **-pedaled**, **-pedal·ling** or **-pedal·ing**) **1** pedal backwards on a bicycle etc. **2** reverse one's previous action or opinion. **3** walk or sprint backwards.

back·plane *noun* a board to which the main circuit boards of a computer may be connected, and which provides connections between them.

back·plate *noun* **1** a plate placed at or forming the back of something. **2** a plate of armour for the back.

back-projec·tion *noun* the projection of a picture from behind a translucent screen for viewing or filming.

back·rest *noun* a support for the back.

back ribs *plural noun* a cut of pork consisting of the ribs and adhering meat from the back of the pig.

Back River a river in Nunavut, 974 km (605 miles) long, flowing northeastward into Franklin Lake, to empty into the Arctic Ocean south of King William Island. [Sir George BACK]

back road noun a little-used road or highway, esp. through the countryside.

back·room noun 1 a room at the back of a store, office, etc., usu. off limits to the public. 2 (usu. *attributive*) a place where secret (esp. political or corporate) plans are made (*backroom deal*; *backroom boys*).
□ **back·room·er** noun

back rub noun a massage of the back.

back·saw noun a saw with a short rectangular blade reinforced by a metal strip along the upper edge.

back·scat·ter noun (also **back·scat·ter·ing**) the reflection of radiation with more or less complete reversal of direction.

back-scratch·er noun 1 a rod terminating in a clawed hand for scratching one's own back. 2 a person who performs services for another for mutual gain. □ **back-scratch·ing** noun

back seat noun a seat at the back of a vehicle, airplane, etc. □ **take a back seat** occupy a subordinate place.

back-seat driver noun 1 a person who rides in the back seat of a car and gives unwanted advice to its driver. 2 a person who criticizes or attempts to control without responsibility.

back·sheesh var. of BAKSHEESH.

back·side noun informal the buttocks.

back sight noun 1 the sight of a rifle etc. that is nearer the stock. 2 Surveying a sight or reading taken backwards or towards the point of starting.

back slang noun slang using words spelled backwards, e.g. *yob*.

back·slap ● transitive & intransitive verb slap jovially on the back as an (often excessive) expression of camaraderie. ● noun such a slap.
□ **back·slap·per** noun

back·slap·ping adjective 1 characterized by (often excessive) displays of camaraderie. 2 vigorously hearty.

back·slash noun a backward-sloping diagonal line; a reverse solidus (\).

back·slide intransitive verb (past and past participle **-slid**) relapse into bad ways or error, esp. in ideology. □ **back·slid·er** noun

back·space ● intransitive verb move a cursor, typewriter carriage, etc. back one or more spaces. ● noun the key on a keyboard which performs this function.

back·spin noun a backward spin imparted to a ball causing it to slow down or roll or bounce back on hitting a surface.

back·splash noun N Amer. a covering, usu. ceramic, behind a sink, counter, etc., to protect the wall from splashes.

back·split noun Cdn a house with floors raised half a storey at the rear, having an upper and lower main floor, and an upper and lower basement.

back·stab·ber noun a person who betrays a friend or associate.
□ **back·stab·bing** noun & adjective

back·stage ● adverb 1 Theatre out of view of the audience, esp. in the wings or dressing rooms. 2 not known to the public. ● adjective that is backstage; concealed.

back stairs plural noun 1 stairs at the back or side of a building. 2 (**back·stairs**) (*attributive*) denoting underhand or clandestine activity.

back·stay noun a rope etc. leading downwards and aft from the top of a mast.

back·stitch ● noun a stitch or stitching in which the thread overlaps the preceding stitch. ● verb 1 transitive & intransitive sew using backstitch. 2 intransitive stitch backwards over existing stitching.

back·stop ● noun 1 Baseball a catcher. 2 a goaltender. 3 Sport a wall, fence, etc. used to keep the ball in the playing area, esp. behind home plate in baseball. 4 a source of esp. financial support. ● transitive verb 1 Sport serve (a team) as goaltender, catcher, etc. 2 provide money as security for (a project, loan, company, etc.); underwrite.

back·story noun (pl. **-ies**) a history or background, esp. one created for a fictional character or thing, e.g. in a movie.

back·strap noun N Amer. any of various cuts of meat from the back of an animal, esp. a tenderloin.

back street noun 1 a street in a quiet part of a city, away from the main streets. 2 (**back-street**) (*attributive*) denoting illicit or illegal activity (*a backstreet abortion*).

back·stretch noun 1 the straight section of a racetrack opposite the home stretch. 2 the area adjacent to a race course where the horses are stabled and stable employees have temporary living accommodations.

back·stroke noun Swimming 1 a stroke performed on the back. See also ELEMENTARY BACKSTROKE. 2 such a stroke in which the arms are lifted alternately out of the water in a backward circular motion and the legs extended in a kicking action. Also called BACK CRAWL.

back·swing noun Sport the upward or backward motion bringing a golf club, racquet, bat, etc. into position for the stroke.

back·talk noun N Amer. informal a rude or impudent reply.

back-to-back ● adjective 1 N Amer. (of two events) consecutive (*back-to-back victories*). 2 esp. Brit. (of houses) separated by a common back wall. ● adverb (**back to back**) 1 with backs adjacent and opposite each other (*we stood back to back*). 2 N Amer. consecutively (*challenge two opponents back to back*).

back to front ● adverb 1 with the back at the front and the front at the back. 2 in disorder. ● adjective backwards.

back-to-nature adjective (usu. *attributive*) applied to a movement or enthusiast for the reversion to a simpler, more natural way of life.

back-to-school adjective (usu. *attributive*) pertaining to the start of a new school year (*back-to-school sale*).

back-to-work attributive adjective Law denoting legislation etc. requiring striking workers to return to work.

back·track intransitive verb 1 retrace one's steps. 2 reverse one's previous action or opinion.

back·up noun 1 moral or technical support (*called for extra backup*). 2 a something kept in reserve, esp. for emergency replacement. b Sport (often *attributive*) an alternate player (*a backup goalie*; *she played backup*). 3 Computing (often *attributive*) a the procedure for making security copies of data (*backup facilities*). b the copy itself (*made a backup*). 4 N Amer. a line of vehicles in congested traffic. 5 (*attributive*) N Amer. designating a light, beeper, etc. activated when a vehicle is in reverse gear. 6 (often *attributive*) musical accompaniment (*backup singers*; *she sang backup*).

back·ward ● adverb = BACKWARDS. ¶ *Backwards* is somewhat more common, esp. in literal senses. ● adjective 1 directed to the rear or starting point (*a backward look*). 2 reversed. 3 mentally retarded or slow. 4 reluctant, shy, unassertive. 5 unsophisticated, underdeveloped.
□ **back·ward·ly** adverb **back·ward·ness** noun [earlier *abackward*, assoc. with BACK]

back·ward·a·tion noun esp. Brit. Stock Exch. the percentage paid by a person selling stock for the right of delaying the delivery of it (*compare* CONTANGO).

backward compatibility noun (of new technology) the capacity to interact with products designed to be used with an earlier version of that technology. □ **backward-compatible** adjective

backward masking noun the practice of recording a message in a piece of music so that it can only be understood if the music is played backwards, though the message may allegedly be perceived subliminally during normal playing.

back·wards adverb 1 away from one's front (*lean backwards*; *look backwards*). 2 a with the back foremost (*walk backwards*). b in reverse of the usual way (*count backwards*; *spell backwards*). 3 a into a worse state (*new policies are taking us backwards*). b into the past (*looked backwards over the years*). c (of a thing's motion) back towards the starting point (*rolled backwards*). □ **backwards and forwards** in both directions alternately; to and fro. **bend over backwards** informal (often foll. by *to* + infin.) make every effort, esp. to be fair or helpful. **know backwards** be entirely familiar with.

back·wash ● noun 1 a receding waves created by the motion of a ship etc. b a backward current of air created by a moving aircraft. 2 repercussions. 3 water pumped backwards through a swimming pool filter to clean it. 4 slang liquid which flows from the mouth back into the bottle etc. while one is drinking. 5 the motion of a receding wave. ● transitive verb clean (a swimming pool filter) by pumping water through it backwards.

back·water noun 1 stagnant water fed from a stream. 2 a place or condition remote from the centre of activity or thought.

back·woods plural noun (often *attributive*) 1 remote uncleared forest land. 2 any remote or sparsely inhabited region.

back·woods·man noun (pl. **-men**) 1 an inhabitant of backwoods. 2 an uncouth person.

back·yard noun 1 N Amer. a piece of ground, usu. landscaped, behind a house and belonging to it. 2 Brit. a paved or gravelled enclosure behind a house. 3 a place near at hand (*not in my backyard*).

Ba·co·lod /bɒˈkoːlɒd/ a city on the northwest coast of the island of

Negros in the central Philippines; pop. (est. 2002) 440,700. It is the chief city of the island and a major port.

Bacon /'beikən/ **1 Sir Fran·cis** (1561–1626), English philosopher, politician and essayist, he became Lord Chancellor under James I. His *Novum Organum* (1620) is celebrated for its espousal of inductive reasoning and rejection of a priori hypotheses. **2 Fran·cis** (1909–92), Irish-born British painter, known for his horrific depictions of human figures in repulsively distorted postures. His most famous works include *Three Studies for Figures at the Base of a Crucifixion* and the collection known as 'The Screaming Popes'. **3 Roger** (c.1214–94), English scholar and Franciscan monk, one of the earliest advocates of experimental science. He is known for his experiments in optics, his description of gunpowder, his prophecies about mechanical devices, and his *Opus Majus*, an attempted compendium of all branches of knowledge.

bacon *noun* cured meat from the back or sides of a pig. □ **bring home the bacon** *informal* **1** succeed in one's undertaking. **2** supply material provision or support. [Old French from Frankish *bako* = Old High German *bahho* ham, flitch]

Bacon·ian /bei'koːniən/ ● *adjective* of or relating to Sir Francis Bacon, or to his inductive method of reasoning and philosophy. ● *noun* **1** a follower of Bacon. **2** a supporter of the view that Bacon was the author of the plays attributed to Shakespeare.

bac·ter·emia /ˌbaktə'riːmiə/ *noun* (also **bac·ter·aemia**) the presence of bacteria in the blood. [from BACTERIUM + -EMIA]

bac·teria *plural noun* (*sing.* **bac·ter·ium**) any of various groups of unicellular micro-organisms lacking organelles and an organized nucleus, some of which can cause disease. □ **bac·ter·ial** *adjective* [Greek *baktērion* diminutive of *baktron* stick]

bac·teri·cide /bak'tiːrɪˌsaid/ *noun* a substance capable of destroying bacteria. □ **bac·teri·cid·al** *adjective*

bac·teri·ol·ogy *noun* the study of bacteria. □ **bac·terio·logic·al** *adjective* **bac·terio·logic·al·ly** *adverb* **bac·teri·ol·o·gist** *noun*

bac·teri·oly·sis /bakˌtiːri'ɒləsɪs/ *noun* the rupture of bacterial cells. □ **bac·terio·lytic** /bakˌtiːriə'lɪtɪk/ *adjective* [BACTERIUM + -LYSIS]

bac·terio·phage /bak'tiːriəˌfeidʒ/ *noun* a virus parasitic on a bacterium, by infecting it and reproducing inside it. [BACTERIUM + Greek *phagein* eat]

bac·terio·stat *noun* a substance which inhibits the multiplying of bacteria without destroying them. □ **bac·terio·stat·ic** *adjective* [BACTERIUM + Greek *statos* standing]

bac·ter·ium *sing. of* BACTERIA.

bac·teri·uria /bakˌtiːri'jʊəriə/ *noun* the presence of bacteria in the urine.

Bac·tria an ancient country in central Asia, corresponding to the northern part of modern Afghanistan. Traditionally the home of Zoroaster, it was the seat of a powerful Indo-Greek kingdom in the 3rd and 2nd c. BC.

Bac·trian camel *noun* a camel, *Camelus bactrianus*, native to central Asia, with two humps.

bad ● *adjective* (**worse; worst**) **1** inferior, inadequate, defective (*bad work; a bad driver; bad light*). **2 a** unpleasant, unwelcome (*bad weather; bad news*). **b** unsatisfactory, unfortunate (*a bad business*). **3** harmful (*is bad for you*). **4** (of food) decayed, putrid. **5** *informal* ill, injured (*am feeling bad today; a bad leg*). **6** *informal* regretful, guilty, ashamed (*feels bad about it*). **7** (of an unwelcome thing) serious, severe (*a bad headache; a bad mistake*). **8 a** morally wicked or offensive (*a bad man; bad language*). **b** naughty; badly behaved (*a bad child*). **9** worthless; not valid (*a bad cheque*). **10** (of a loan, debt, etc.) unlikely to be paid. **11** (**bad·der, bad·dest**) *esp. N Amer. slang* admirable, excellent. ● *noun* **1 a** ill fortune (*take the bad with the good*). **b** ruin; a degenerate condition (*go to the bad*). **2** the debit side of an account (*$500 to the bad*). **3** (as *pl.*; prec. by *the*) bad or wicked people. ● *adverb N Amer. disputed* badly (*he's hurt bad*). □ **from bad to worse** into an even worse state. **in a bad way** ill; in trouble (*looked in a bad way*). **my bad** *slang* (said as an apology) it is my fault; my mistake (*sorry I lost your CD—it's my bad*). **not** (or **not so**) **bad** *informal* fairly good. **too bad** *informal* (of circumstances etc.) regrettable but now beyond helping. □ **bad·ness** *noun* [perhaps from Old English *bæddel* hermaphrodite, womanish man: for loss of *l* compare MUCH, WENCH]

bada bing *interjection* (also **bada bing bada boom, bada boom bada bing**) *N Amer. informal* used to denote a decisive, rapid, and forceful achievement, effect, or resolution of a problem. [prob. imitative of a drum roll]

Bada·lona /ˌbɒðə'loːnə/ a city on the northeast coast of Spain, near Barcelona; pop. (est. 1998) 209,606.

bad apple *noun* **1** an apple that has gone bad. **2** (also **rotten apple**) *N Amer.* a member of an otherwise admirable group whose actions disgrace it.

bad·ass *esp. N Amer. slang* ● *adjective* belligerent or intimidating; tough. ● *noun* an aggressive, uncooperative person; a troublemaker.

bad blood *noun* ill feeling, animosity.

bad boy *noun* a man who cultivates an uncooperative or rebellious attitude.

bad breath *noun* unpleasant-smelling breath.

bad cholesterol *noun* = LOW-DENSITY LIPOPROTEIN.

Bad·deck /bə'dek/ a village in central Cape Breton Island, situated on the shore of Bras d'Or Lake, about 70 km west of Sydney; pop. (1996) 937. It was the site of the summer residence of Alexander Graham Bell. □ **Bad·deck·er** *noun* [from Mi'kmaq *petecook* lying on the backward turn, with reference to the entrance to the Baddeck River]

baddy *noun* (also **bad·die**) (*pl.* **-dies**) *informal* a villain or criminal, esp. in a story, film, etc.

bade *see* BID.

Baden /'bɒdən/ a spa town in Austria, south of Vienna; pop. (2001) 24,500. It was a royal summer retreat and fashionable resort in the 19th c.

Baden-Baden /ˌbɒdən'bɒdən/ a spa town in the Black Forest of SW Germany, a fashionable resort, esp. in the 19th c.; pop. (est. 2002) 52,400.

Baden-Powell /ˌbeidən'pauəl/ **Sir Rob·ert Ste·phen·son Smyth, 1st Baron Baden-Powell of Gil·well** (1857–1941), English soldier, founder of the Boy Scouts (1908), Girl Guides (1910), and related organizations.

Baden-Württem·berg /ˌbɒdən'vʊtəmˌbɜrg/ a state of SW Germany; capital, Stuttgart.

bad faith *noun* intent to deceive.

bad form *noun* an offence against social conventions.

badge *noun* **1** a distinctive emblem worn as a mark of office, membership, achievement, licensed employment, etc. **2** any feature or sign which reveals a characteristic condition or quality. [Middle English: origin unknown]

badg·er ● *noun* **1** an omnivorous grey-coated nocturnal mammal of the family Mustelidae, with a white stripe flanked by black stripes on its head. **2** a fishing fly, brush, etc., made of its hair. ● *transitive verb* pester, harass, tease. [16th c.: perhaps from BADGE, with reference to its white forehead mark]

bad guy *noun informal* a villain.

bad hair day *noun* **1** a day when one's hair is unmanageable. **2** a day when everything seems to be going wrong.

Badham, Mount /'badəm/ a peak in the St. Elias Mountains of SW Yukon Territory (3 848 m). [F. M. *Badham*, boundary surveyor d. c.1915]

Badian /'beidiən/ *noun* = BARBADIAN (*see* BARBADOS). [abbreviation]

bad·in·age /'badɪˌnɒʒ/ *noun* humorous or playful ridicule. [French from *badiner* to joke]

bad·lands *plural noun* extensive, barren, strikingly-eroded tracts in arid areas, as along the Red Deer River in S Alberta. [translation of French *mauvaises terres*]

bad lot *noun* a person of bad character.

badly *adverb* (**worse; worst**) **1** in a bad manner (*works badly*). **2** *informal* very much (*wants it badly*). **3** severely (*was badly defeated*).

B.Admin. *abbreviation* Bachelor of Administration.

bad·min·ton *noun* a game in which players use racquets to hit a shuttlecock back and forth across a high net. [*Badminton* in S England]

bad·mouth *transitive verb N Amer.* subject to malicious gossip or criticism.

bad news *noun* **1** alarming or disheartening information. **2** *informal* an unpleasant or troublesome person or thing.

Badon Hill, Battle of /'beidən/ an ancient British battle (AD 516) in which the forces of King Arthur successfully defended themselves against the Saxons. The location of the battlefield is uncertain, and some sources do not connect the battle with King Arthur.

bad-tempered *adjective* having a bad temper; irritable; easily annoyed. □ **bad-tempered·ly** *adverb*

Baeck /bek/ **Leo** (1873–1956), German rabbi and theologian, one of the leading exponents of liberal Jewish theology in the 20th c. He was

Vowels: a *cat* ɑ *arm* e *bed* ɜr *her* ɜː *deux* ə *ago* ɪ *sit* i *cosy* iː *feed* ɒ *hot* ɔ *pore* ɔː *no* ʌ *run* ʊ *put*

the spiritual leader of Germany's Jews during their struggle against Nazi persecution before and during the Second World War.

Baeda /ˈbiːdə/ see BEDE.

Baed·eker /ˈbeidəkər/ *noun* any of various travel guidebooks published by the firm founded by the German Karl *Baedeker* (d.1859).

Baer /ber/ **Karl Er·nest von** (1792–1876), German biologist. He discovered that ova were particles within the ovarian follicles, and formulated the principle that in the developing embryo general characters appear before special ones; his studies were used by Darwin in the theory of evolution.

Baeyer /ˈbaiər/ **(Jo·hann Frie·drich Wil·helm) Adolf von** (1835–1917), German organic chemist. He prepared the first barbiturates and investigated dyes, synthesizing indigo and determining its structural formula; he was awarded the Nobel Prize for chemistry in 1905.

Baez /ˈbaiez, baiˈez/ **Joan** (b.1941), US folksinger. A prominent figure in the US folk revival, she is best known for her performances at civil-rights demonstrations in the early 1960s.

Baf·fin, Wil·liam (c.1584–1622), English navigator who in 1616 explored the northern coast of the Canadian Arctic's largest island, which was named after him.

Baffin, the an administrative region comprising Baffin Island and adjoining islands and mainland and the eastern High Arctic islands.

Baffin Bay an extension of the N Atlantic between Baffin Island and Greenland, linked to the Arctic Ocean by three passages. Lying to the north of the Arctic Circle and traversed by the Labrador Current, it is largely icebound in winter. [W. BAFFIN]

Baffin Island the largest island in Canada, 507 451 sq. km, situated in the Arctic at the mouth of Hudson Bay. It is separated from Greenland by Baffin Bay and Davis Strait. [W. BAFFIN]

Baffin·land *noun* the area of the Canadian Arctic including Baffin Island and adjoining islands and mainland and the eastern High Arctic islands.

Baffinland Inuit *noun* the Inuit living on Baffin Island and the eastern High Arctic islands, esp. coastal southern and south central Baffin Island.

baf·fle ● *transitive verb* **1** confuse or perplex (a person, one's faculties, etc.). **2 a** frustrate or hinder (plans etc.). **b** restrain or regulate the progress of (fluids, sounds, etc.). ● *noun* **1** (also **baffle plate**) a device used to restrain the flow of fluid, air, etc., or to prevent the spreading of sound or light in a particular direction. **2** a device used to impede or block access etc. (*a bird feeder with squirrel baffles*). □ **baffle·ment** *noun* **baf·fler** *noun* **baf·fling** *adjective* **baf·fling·ly** *adverb* [perhaps related to French *bafouer* ridicule, Old French *beffer* mock]

baffle board *noun* a device to prevent sound from spreading in different directions, esp. round a loudspeaker cone.

baffle·gab *noun N Amer.* official or professional jargon which confuses more than it clarifies.

bag ● *noun* **1** a receptacle of flexible material with an opening at the top. **2 a** (usu. in *pl.*) a piece of luggage (*put the bags in the trunk*). **b** a woman's handbag. **3** (in *pl.*; usu. foll. by *of*) *informal* a large amount; plenty. **4** (in *pl.*) *Brit. informal* pants. **5** *slang derogatory* a woman, esp. regarded as unattractive or unpleasant. **6** an animal's sac containing poison, honey, etc. **7** an amount of game or fish taken by a sportsman. **8** (usu. in *pl.*) baggy folds of skin under the eyes. **9** *slang* the scrotum. **10** *slang* a person's particular interest or preoccupation, esp. in a distinctive style or category of music (*country music is not my bag*). **11** *Baseball* first, second, or third base. **12** an udder. ● *verb* (**bagged**, **bag·ging**) **1** *transitive* put in a bag. **2** *transitive informal* **a** attain, secure (*bagged three awards*). **b** apprehend (a criminal etc.). **c** shoot (game). **d** *informal* steal. **e** (often in phr. **bags I**) *Brit. informal* claim on grounds of being the first to do so (*bagged first go; bags I go first*). **3 a** *intransitive* hang loosely; bulge; swell. **b** *transitive* cause to do this. □ **bag and baggage** with all one's belongings. **bag of bones** *informal* an extremely emaciated person. **bag of tricks** *informal* one's (usu. ingenious) resources or techniques (*flattery is in his bag of tricks*). **in the bag** *informal* as good as secured; achieved. **left holding the bag** *N Amer. informal* left with unwelcome responsibility. □ **bag·ful** *noun* (*pl.* **-fuls**). [perhaps from Old Norse *baggi*]

ba·gasse /bəˈgas/ *noun* the dry pulpy residue left after the extraction of juice from sugar cane, usable as fuel or to make paper etc. [French from Spanish *bagazo*]

baga·telle /ˌbagəˈtel/ *noun* **1** a mere trifle; a negligible amount. **2** *Music* a short piece of music, esp. for the piano. **3** a game in which small balls are struck into numbered holes on a board, with pins as

obstructions. [French from Italian *bagatella*, perhaps from *baga* BAGGAGE]

bag boy *noun* a boy employed by a grocery store to bag purchases at the checkout.

Bage·hot /ˈbadʒət/ **Wal·ter** (1826–77), English economist and journalist, editor of *The Economist* from 1860 until his death. His remarkable insight into economic and political questions is shown in his *The English Constitution* (1867), *Lombard Street* (1873), and *Economic Studies* (1880).

bagel *noun* a chewy, ring-shaped bread roll that is simmered before baking. [Yiddish *beygel*]

bag·gage *noun* **1** suitcases, bags, etc. packed for travelling; luggage. **2** an encumbrance (esp. psychological). **3** the portable equipment of an army. **4** *jocular* or *derogatory* a girl or woman. [Old French *bagage* from *baguer* tie up, or *bagues* bundles: perhaps related to BAG]

baggage car *noun N Amer.* a railway car for travellers' luggage.

baggage claim *noun N Amer.* (in full **baggage claim area**) an area in an airport, railway station, etc. where passengers retrieve their checked baggage.

baggage handler *noun* a person whose job it is to load and unload luggage.

bag·gata·way /bəˈgatəwei/ *noun* a forerunner of lacrosse played by the Aboriginal peoples of eastern N America, in which opposing teams attempt to propel a ball into the other's goal using a mesh attached to a curved stick. [Ojibwa *paka'atowe* he plays lacrosse]

bagged *adjective* **1** packaged in a bag. **2** *N Amer. informal* fatigued, exhausted.

bag·ger ● *noun* a person or thing that packages something in bags. ● *combining form Baseball* a run which reaches a specified number of bases (*an extra-inning four-bagger*).

Bag·gie *noun* *proprietary* a small bag made of clear plastic, used for storing sandwiches etc.

baggy ● *adjective* (**bag·gi·er, bag·gi·est**) **1** (of clothes) loosely fitting. **2** puffed out. ● *noun* (*pl.* **-gies**) *informal* loose, wide-legged trousers or shorts. □ **bag·gi·ly** *adverb* **bag·gi·ness** *noun*

Bagh·dad /ˈbagdad, bagˈdad/ the capital of Iraq, on the Tigris River; pop. (est. 2002) 5,605,000. The city flourished under the Abbasid caliphs in the 8th and 9th centuries. Although the discovery of oil brought renewed prosperity to the city, it suffered damage in the Iran-Iraq war (1980–88), the Gulf War (1991), and during the overthrow of Saddam Hussein (2003).

bag lady *noun* esp. *N Amer.* a homeless woman who carries her possessions around in shopping bags.

bag·man *noun* (*pl.* **-men**) **1** *Cdn* a political fundraiser. **2** *US informal* an agent who collects or distributes money for illicit purposes. **3** *Brit. informal* a travelling salesman.

bagnio /ˈbanjoʊ/ *noun* (*pl.* **bagnios**) **1** a brothel. **2** an oriental prison. [Italian *bagno* from Latin *balneum* bath]

Bagot /ˈbagət/ **Sir Charles** (1781–1843), British colonial administrator. In 1817 he negotiated a treaty for disarmament on the Great Lakes. Appointed Governor General of Canada in 1841, he attempted a number of minor reforms in colonial government, but many of his policies were reversed by his successor.

bag·pipe *noun* (usu. in *pl.*) a musical instrument consisting of a windbag connected to two kinds of reeded pipes: drone pipes which produce single sustained notes and a fingered melody pipe or 'chanter'. □ **bag·piper** *noun*

ba·guette /baˈget/ *noun* **1** a long narrow loaf of bread. **2** a gem cut in a long rectangular shape. **3** *Archit.* a small moulding, semicircular in section. [French from Italian *bacchetto* diminutive of *bacchio* from Latin *baculum* staff]

bah *interjection* an expression of contempt or disbelief. [prob. French]

Baha'i /bəˈhai/ *noun* (*pl.* **Baha'is**) a member of a monotheistic religion founded in Persia in 1863 as a branch of Babism (see BABI), emphasizing the unity of all religions, and world peace. □ **Baha'ism** *noun* [Persian *bahá* splendour]

Ba·ha·mas /bəˈhɒməz/ a country consisting of an archipelago off the southeast coast of Florida, part of the W Indies; pop. (est. 2002) 300,529; capital, Nassau. It was here that Columbus made his first landfall in the New World (12 Oct. 1492).

Ba·ha·mian /bəˈheimiən/ ● *noun* **1** a native or national of the Bahamas in the W Indies. **2** a person of Bahamian descent. ● *adjective* of or relating to the Bahamas.

Ba·hasa /bəˈhɒsə/ *noun* **1** (in full **Bahasa Indonesia**) the form of

Malay spoken as the official language of Indonesia. **2** (in full **Bahasa Malaysia**) the form of Malay spoken as the official language of Malaysia. [from Malay *bahasa* language]

Baha'ullah /bɒ'hʊʊˌlɒ/ (title of Mirza Hosein Ali) (1817–92), Persian religious leader. He was a follower of the Bab, and founded the Baha'i faith.

Ba·hawal·pur /bɑ'hɒwəlˌpʊr/ a city of central Pakistan, in Punjab province; pop. (1998) 403,400. It was formerly the capital of a princely state established by the nawabs of Bahawalpur.

Bahia /bɒ'iːə/ the former name for SALVADOR.

Bahía Blanca /bɒ'iːə 'blaŋkə/ a port in Argentina serving the southern part of the country; pop. (est. 1999) 281,161.

Bah·rain /bɒ'reɪn/ a sheikdom consisting of a group of islands in the Persian Gulf; pop. (est. 2002) 656,397; capital, Manama. □ **Bah·raini** *adjective & noun*

baht /bɒt/ *noun* (*pl.* same) the basic monetary unit of Thailand, equal to 100 stangs. [Thai *bāt*]

bai·dar·ka /baɪ'dɑrkə/ *noun* (also **bai·dar** /'baɪdɑr/) a long, kayak-like boat for two or more people, used around the Aleutian Islands. [Russian, diminutive of *baidara*, from Aleut]

Baie-Comeau /ˌbeɪ'koːmoː/ a city in E Quebec, situated on the north shore of the St. Lawrence, about 450 km northeast of Quebec City; pop. (2001) 23,079. [N.A. *Comeau*, celebrated North Shore writer and naturalist d.1923]

Baie des Cha·leurs /beɪdeɪʃə'lɜr/ see CHALEUR BAY.

Baie-Saint-Paul /beɪsɑ̃'pɒl/ a town in E Quebec, on the north shore of the St. Lawrence about 80 km downstream from Quebec City; pop. (2001) 7,290. [in honour of St. PAUL]

Bai·kal, Lake /baɪ'kɒl/ (also **Lake Bay·kal**) a large lake in S Siberia, the largest freshwater lake in Europe and Asia and, with a depth of 1 743 m (5,714 ft.), the deepest lake in the world.

Baiko·nur /ˌbaɪkə'nʊr/ (also **Bayko·nyr**) a mining town in central Kazakhstan. The world's first satellite (1957) and the first manned space flight (1961) were launched from the former Soviet space centre nearby.

bail[1] ● *noun* **1** money etc. required as security against the temporary release of a prisoner pending trial. **2** a person or persons giving such security. **3** (also **pretrial release** or **judicial interim release**) the temporary release of a prisoner who provides such security (*grant bail*). ● *transitive verb* **1** (usu. foll. by *out*) **a** release or secure the release of (a prisoner) on payment of bail. **b** release from a difficulty; come to the rescue of (esp. financially). **2** *Law* deliver (goods) in trust for a specified purpose. □ **jump** (or **skip** or *formal* **forfeit**) **bail** fail to appear for trial after being released on bail. **stand** (or **post**) **bail** (often foll. by *for*) act as surety (for an accused person). □ **bail·able** *adjective* [Old French *bail* custody, *bailler* take charge of, from Latin *bajulare* bear a burden]

bail[2] *noun* ● **1** the bar on a typewriter holding the paper against the platen. **2** *Cricket* either of the two crosspieces bridging the stumps in a wicket. **3** = BAILEY. [Old French *bail(e)*, perhaps from *bailler* enclose]

bail[3] *transitive verb* (*Brit.* **bale**) **1** (usu. foll. by *out*) scoop water out of (a boat etc.). **2** scoop (water etc.) out. □ **bail·er** *noun* [obsolete *bail* (n.) bucket, from French *baille*, ultimately from Latin *bajulus* carrier]

bail[4] *verb* (*Brit.* **bale**) □ **bail out 1** make an emergency parachute jump from an aircraft. **2** desert a difficult situation. **bail on** *N Amer. informal* let (someone) down. [originally *bale out*, as though dropping a bale through a trap door (see BALE[1])]

bail bond *noun* the document executed to secure the release of a person awaiting trial.

bail bondsman *noun* (*pl.* **-men**) a person who posts bail for another, esp. as a business.

bailee *noun Law* a person or party to whom goods are committed for a purpose, e.g. custody or repair, without transfer of ownership.

Bailey ▶ **1 Don·ovan** (b.1967), Jamaican-born Canadian sprinter, winner of Olympic gold medals for the 100m (for which he set a new world record) and 4 x 100m relay in 1996. **2 Ir·vine Wal·lace** ('Ace') (1903–92) Canadian hockey player, a star forward with the Toronto Maple Leafs until a near-fatal injury during a game in 1934 ended his career prematurely. **3 Nathan** (or **Na·than·iel**) (d.1742), English lexicographer, compiler of the *Universal Etymological English Dictionary* (1721).

bail·ey *noun* (*pl.* **-eys**) **1** the outer wall of a castle. **2** a court enclosed by it. [Middle English, var. of BAIL[2]]

Bailey bridge *noun* a temporary bridge of lattice steel designed for

rapid assembly from prefabricated standard parts, used esp. in military operations. [Sir D. *Bailey*, British engineer d.1985]

bailie /'beɪli/ *noun* esp. *hist.* a municipal officer and magistrate in Scotland. [Old French *bailli(s)* BAILIFF]

bail·iff *noun* **1** (in full **court bailiff**) an officer of the court who serves processes and enforces orders, esp. warrants authorizing the seizure of a debtor's goods. **2** (in full **private bailiff**) *Cdn* a person who repossesses property for private clients. **3** *N Amer.* an official in a court of law who keeps order, looks after prisoners, etc. **4** *Brit.* (*hist.* except in formal titles) the sovereign's representative in a district, esp. the chief officer of a hundred. **5** the first civil officer in the Channel Islands. **6** *Brit.* the agent or steward of a landlord. [Old French *baillif*, ultimately from Latin *bajulus* carrier, manager]

baili·wick *noun* **1** *Law* the district or jurisdiction of a sheriff or bailiff. **2** a person's sphere of operations or particular area of interest. [BAILIE + WICK[2]]

bail·ment *noun Law* the transfer of the possession of goods from a bailor to a bailee for a specified purpose, with the bailor retaining ownership.

bail·or *noun Law* a person or party that entrusts goods to a bailee while maintaining ownership.

bail·out *noun* a financial rescue.

bails·man *noun* (*pl.* **-men**) a person who stands bail for another.

Baily's beads *noun Astronomy* the appearance of the sun's crescent as a string of bright points just before or after the sun's disc is totally eclipsed by the moon. [F. *Baily*, English astronomer d.1844]

bain-marie /ˌbãma'riː/ *noun* (*pl.* **bains-marie** *pronunc.* same) a cooking vessel containing hot water into which a second vessel containing a sauce etc. is placed so as to cook gently. [French, translation of medieval Latin *balneum Mariae* bath of Maria (an alleged Jewish alchemist)]

Bai·ram /baɪ'ram, 'baɪram/ *noun* either of two annual Muslim festivals, the Lesser Bairam, lasting one day, which follows the fast of Ramadan, and the Greater Bairam, lasting three days, seventy days later. [Turkish & Persian]

Baird, John Logie (1888–1946), Scottish pioneer of television, who made the first transatlantic transmission and demonstration of colour television in 1928.

Baird Peninsula a small peninsula of the west central coast of Baffin Island.

Baird's sandpiper *noun* a small sandpiper, *Calidris bairdii* that breeds in the High Arctic. [S. F. *Baird*, US zoologist d.1887]

Bai·riki /baɪ'riːki/ the capital of Kiribati, situated on the island of Tarawa; pop. (est. 1999) 32,000.

bairn *noun Scot. & Northern England* a child. [Old English *bearn*]

bait ● *noun* **1** food used to entice prey. **2** an allurement; something intended to tempt or entice. **3** *archaic* a halt on a journey for refreshment or a rest. ● *verb* **1** *transitive* **a** harass or annoy (a person, community, etc.) (*red-baiting*). **b** torment (a chained animal). **2** *transitive* put bait on (a hook, trap, etc.) to entice a prey. **3** *archaic* **a** *transitive* give food to (horses on a journey). **b** *intransitive* stop on a journey to take food or a rest. □ **bait·ed** *adjective* [Old Norse *beita* hunt or chase]

bait and switch *noun* (often *attributive*) the practice of luring customers with a limited supply of bargains in order to sell them more expensive items.

bait·cast·er *noun* (also **baitcasting reel**) esp. *N Amer.* a fishing reel mounted on top of the rod, with an open rotating spool (*compare* SPINCASTER, SPINNING REEL).

bait·cast·ing rod *noun* a fishing rod with eyes along the top and a finger grip, used with baitcasters and spincasters.

bait·fish *noun* (*pl.* same or **-fish·es**) any small fish eaten by larger fish, often used to lure game fish.

baiza /'baɪzə/ *noun* a monetary unit of Oman, equal to one thousandth of a rial. [Arabic]

baize /beɪz/ *noun* a coarse usu. green woollen material resembling felt used as a covering or lining, esp. on the tops of billiard tables and card tables. [French *baies* (pl.) fem. of *bai* chestnut-coloured (BAY[4]), treated as sing.: compare BODICE]

Baja California /'bɒhɒ/ (also called **Lower California**) a mountainous peninsula in NW Mexico, which extends southward from the border with California and separates the Gulf of California from the Pacific Ocean. It consists of two states of Mexico: **Baja California (Norte)** (capital, Mexicali) and **Baja California Sur** (capital, La Paz).

Consonants: b *but*   d *dog*   f *few*   g *get*   h *her*   j *yes*   k *cat*   l *leg*   m *man*   n *no*   p *pen*   r *red*   s *sit*

Bajan /ˈbeɪdʒən/ = BARBADIAN (see BARBADOS). [representative of a certain pronunciation of BADIAN]

bake ● *verb* **1 a** *transitive* cook (food) by dry heat in an oven or on a hot surface, without direct exposure to a flame. **b** *intransitive* undergo the process of being baked. **2** *intransitive informal* **a** (usu. as **be baking**) (of weather etc.) be very hot. **b** (of a person) become hot. **3 a** *transitive* harden (clay etc.) by heat. **b** *intransitive* (of clay etc.) be hardened by heat. **4 a** *transitive* (of the sun) affect by its heat, e.g. ripen (fruit). **b** *intransitive* (e.g. of fruit) be affected by the sun's heat. ● *noun* **1** the act or an instance of baking. **2** (esp. in *combination*) baked goods (*bake table*). **3** (in *combination*) N Amer. a social gathering, esp. a picnic, at which baked food is eaten (*clambake*). **4** a baked dish, esp. a casserole (*sausage and rigatoni bake*). [Old English *bacan*]

bake·apple *noun* (also **baked-apple berry**) N Amer. (esp. Nfld & Maritimes) = CLOUDBERRY. [corruption of Inuit *appik* + APPLE]

baked Alaska *noun* a dessert consisting of ice cream on a slab of cake, covered with meringue and browned quickly.

baked beans *plural noun* dried white beans baked in a tomato sauce.

baked custard *noun* = CUSTARD 1.

bake·house *noun* a house or room with an oven for baking bread.

Bake·lite /ˈbeɪkəˌlaɪt/ *noun* proprietary any of various thermosetting resins or plastics made from formaldehyde and phenol and used for cables, buttons, plates, etc. [German *Bakelit* from L.H. *Baekeland* its Belgian-born inventor d.1944]

Bake-Off *noun* proprietary a competition at which (esp. amateur) cooks prepare baked goods for judging.

Baker ▶ 1 Car·roll (b.1949), Canadian country singer, winner of several Juno Awards. Her recordings include 'I've Never Been This Far Before' (1976). **2 Chet** (1929–88), US trumpet player and singer, very popular in the 1950s for his light, clear playing of modern jazz. **3 Dame Janet** (b.1933), English mezzo-soprano singer of opera, lieder, English and French songs, and oratorio, noted for her rich voice and intensity of feeling. **4 Jo·seph·ine** (1906–75), US-born French singer and dancer whose appearance in *La Revue Nègre* in Paris (1925) made her one of the most popular entertainers in France. She was awarded the Legion of Honour for her role in the resistance. **5 Peggy Laur·ayne** (b.1952), Canadian dancer and choreographer, acknowledged as one of the finest modern dancers Canada has produced. From 1981 to 1988 she danced with the Lar Lubovitch Dance Company in New York, and shortly thereafter launched a successful solo career. **6 Sir Sam·uel White** (1821–93), English explorer, who led an exploration of the Nile tributaries, during which he discovered and named Lake Albert Nyanza (Lake Albert) (1864).

baker *noun* **1** a person who bakes and sells bread, cakes, etc., esp. professionally. **2** an appliance or dish in which something is baked (*clay baker; waffle baker*).

Baker Lake 1 a lake in central Nunavut, situated just south of the geographic centre of Canada, about 200 km west of Hudson Bay. **2** a hamlet situated on its northern shore, a centre for Inuit art; pop. (2001) 1,507. [Sir W. and R. *Baker*, brothers associated with the Hudson's Bay Co.]

baker's dozen *noun* thirteen. [so called from bakers' former custom of adding an extra loaf to a dozen sold; the exact reason for this is unclear]

baker's rack *noun* a set of superimposed shelves consisting of rods of metal with wide spaces between them, suitable for cooling baked goods but used also as bookshelves etc.

bakery *noun* (pl. **-ies**) a place where bread and cakes are made or sold.

bake sale *noun* N Amer. a sale of home-baked goods, usu. to raise money for a charity etc.

bake·shop *noun* N Amer. = BAKERY.

bake·ware *noun* pans, pie plates, etc., used in baking.

Bake·well, Rob·ert (1725–95), English agriculturist, who pioneered scientific methods of livestock breeding and husbandry.

Bakewell tart /ˈbeɪkwel/ *noun* a baked open pie consisting of a pastry case lined with jam and filled with a rich almond paste. [*Bakewell* in Derbyshire]

baking parchment *noun* see PARCHMENT 2b.

baking powder *noun* a mixture of sodium bicarbonate and an acid such as cream of tartar, etc., used as leavening in baking.

baking powder biscuit *noun* N Amer. = TEA BISCUIT.

baking sheet *noun* a large shallow pan, used for baking cookies, rolls, etc.

baking soda *noun* sodium bicarbonate used as an antacid, as leavening in baked goods, or as a household cleaner and deodorizer.

bak·la·va /ˈbaklɒvə, ˌbaklɑˈvɒ/ *noun* a rich sweet dessert of flaky pastry, honey, and nuts. [Turkish]

bak·sheesh /ˈbakʃiːʃ/ *noun* (also **back·sheesh**) (in some oriental countries) a small sum of money given as a gratuity or as alms. [ultimately from Persian *bakšīš* from *bakšīdan* give]

Bakst /bakst/ **Léon** (born Lev Semuilovich Rosenberg, 1866–1924), Russian painter and stage designer, one of the most influential members of Diaghilev's Ballets Russes, whose work revolutionized European stage design.

Baku /baˈkuː/ the capital of Azerbaijan, on the Caspian Sea; pop. (est. 2002) 2,071,600. It is an industrial port and a centre of the oil industry.

Baku·nin /baˈkuːnɪn/ **Mik·hail Alek·san·dro·vich** (1814–76), Russian revolutionary, a leading exponent of anarchism. He participated in the First International, founded in 1864, but conflicted with Marx in calling for violent means to destroy the existing political and social order, splitting the two factions for years to come.

Balaam /ˈbeɪlam/ *Bible* a non-Israelite prophet who, on being summoned by the Moabites to put a curse on Israel, is first rebuked by the ass he is riding when he is unable to recognize an angel, and then prophesies great blessings for Israel (Num. 22–24).

bala·clava /ˌbaləˈklavə/ *noun* a tight knitted garment covering the whole head and neck with holes for the eyes and mouth. [*Balaklava* in the Crimea, where soldiers first wore them]

bala·fon /ˈbaləˌfɒn/ a wooden musical instrument from Africa, precursor of the xylophone.

Bala·ki·rev /ˌbaˈlaːkɪrev/ **Mily (Alex·sey·evich)** (1837–1910), Russian composer. A leader of Russian composers of his time, Balakirev reflected his passionate interest in Russian folk music.

bala·lai·ka /ˌbaləˈlaɪkə/ *noun* a guitar-like musical instrument having a triangular body and 2 to 4 strings, popular in Russia and other Slavic countries. [Russian]

bal·ance ● *noun* **1** an apparatus for weighing, esp. one with a central pivot, beam, and two scales. **2 a** a counteracting weight or force. **b** (in full **balance wheel**) the regulating device in a clock etc. **3 a** an even distribution of weight or amount. **b** stability of body or mind (*regained his balance*). **4** a preponderating weight or amount (*the balance of opinion*). **5 a** an agreement between or the difference between credits and debits in an account. **b** the amount of money held in a bank account at a given moment. **c** the difference between an amount due and an amount paid (*will pay the balance next week*). **d** an amount left over; the rest. **6** *Art* harmony of design and proportion. **7 a** the relative volume of various musical parts (*bad balance between violins and trumpets*). **b** the relative volume of two or more stereo speakers. **c** a dial on a stereo for adjusting this. **8** (**the Balance**) the zodiacal sign or constellation Libra. ● *verb* **1** *transitive* (foll. by *with, against*) offset or compare (one thing) with another (*must balance the advantages with the disadvantages*). **2** *transitive* counteract, equal, or neutralize the weight or importance of. **3 a** *transitive* bring into or keep in equilibrium (*balanced a book on her head*). **b** *intransitive* be in equilibrium (*balanced on one leg*). **4** *transitive* (usu. as **balanced** *adjective*) establish equal or appropriate proportions of elements in (*a balanced diet; balanced opinion*). **5** *transitive* weigh (arguments etc.) against each other. **6 a** *transitive* compare and esp. equalize debits and credits of (an account) (*balance the budget*). **b** *intransitive* (of an account) have credits and debits equal. □ **in the balance** uncertain; at a critical stage. **off balance 1** in danger of falling. **2** unprepared, confused. **on balance** all things considered. **strike a balance** choose a moderate course or compromise. □ **bal·an·cer** *noun* [Old French, ultimately from Late Latin (*libra*) *bilanx bilancis* two-scaled (balance)]

balance beam *noun* **1** a long narrow wooden beam on which female gymnasts perform feats of balance and agility. **2** the gymnastics event in which this is used.

balanced fund *noun* an investment fund comprising a mixture of stocks, bonds, and other investments such as money market funds.

balance of payments *noun* the difference in value between payments into and out of a country.

balance of power *noun* **1** a situation in which the chief nations of the world have roughly equal power. **2** the power held by a small group when larger groups are of equal strength.

balance of trade *noun* (also **trade balance**) the difference in value between imports and exports.

balance sheet *noun* **1** a written statement of the assets and

---

t *top*   v *voice*   w *we*   z *zoo*   ʃ *she*   ʒ *vision*   θ *thin*   ð *this*   ŋ *ring*   x *loch*   tʃ *chip*   dʒ *jar*   (*see over for vowels*)

liabilities of an organization on a given date. **2** an organization's financial state.

Bal·an·chine /ˈbalən.ʃiːn/ **George** (1904–83), Russian-born US choreographer and ballet director, founder of the New York City Ballet. A dominant force in neoclassicism, he favoured an athletic, abstract style and tall, long-legged ballerinas. His works include *Serenade* (1934) and *The Four Temperaments* (1946).

balancing act *noun* the dexterous handling of several different tasks simultaneously.

bal·ata /ˈbalətə/ *noun* **1** any of several latex-yielding trees of Central America, esp. *Manilkara bidentata*. **2** the dried sap of this used as a substitute for gutta percha, esp. in golf balls. [ultimately from Carib]

Bala·ton, Lake /ˈbɒlə.tɒn/ a large shallow lake in west central Hungary, situated in a resort and wine-producing region.

Bal·boa /balˈboːə/ **Vasco Núñez de** (1475–1517), Spanish explorer, the first European to see the Pacific Ocean (1513, from Darien in Panama).

bal·boa /balˈboːə/ *noun* the basic monetary unit of Panama, equal to 100 cents. [V. N. de BALBOA]

Bal·brig·gan /balˈbrɪgən/ *noun* a knitted cotton fabric used for underwear etc. [*Balbriggan* in Ireland, where it was originally made]

bal·cony *noun* (*pl.* **-ies**) **1** a usu. balustraded platform on the outside of a building, with access from an upper-floor window or door. **2** a projecting tier of seats above the main floor in a theatre. □ **bal·con·ied** *adjective* [Italian *balcone*]

bald *adjective* **1** (of a person) with the scalp wholly or partly lacking hair. **2** (of an animal, plant, etc.) not covered by the usual hair, feathers, leaves, etc. **3** (of a landscape) treeless (*bald prairie*). **4** with the surface worn away (*a bald tire*). **5 a** blunt, without elaboration (*a bald statement*). **b** undisguised (*the bald effrontery*). **6** meagre or dull (*a bald style*). **7** marked with white, esp. on the face (*a bald horse*). □ **bald·ing** *adjective* (in senses 1 & 2). **bald·ish** *adjective* **bald·ly** *adverb* (in sense 5). **bald·ness** *noun* [Middle English *ballede*, originally 'having a white blaze', prob. from an Old English root *ball-* 'white patch']

bal·da·chin /ˈbɒldəkɪn/ *noun* (also **bal·da·quin**) **1** an ornamental canopy of cloth or stone over an altar, throne, etc. **2** a rich brocade. [Italian *baldacchino* from *Baldacco* Baghdad, its place of origin]

bald cypress *noun* either of two coniferous trees of the genus *Taxodium* growing in swamps of southern N America, having knee-like pointed roots which project above the water.

bald eagle *noun* an eagle of N America (*Haliaeetus leucocephalus*), with large brown wings and body, a white head and a yellow bill, used as the emblem of the United States. *Also called* AMERICAN EAGLE.

Bal·der /ˈbɒldər/ *Scand. Myth* a son of Odin and Frigga. He was killed when Loki tricked the blind god Hödur into striking him with a sprig of mistletoe, the only substance to which he was not invulnerable.

bal·der·dash *noun* senseless talk or writing; nonsense. [17th c., earlier = 'mixture of drinks': origin unknown]

bald-faced *adjective* = BAREFACED.

bald·head·ed *adjective* having little or no hair on the head; bald.

bald·ie *noun* *informal* a bald person.

bald·pate *noun* **1** a baldheaded person. **2** a N American widgeon, *Anas americana*, the male of which has a white crown.

bal·dric /ˈbɒldrɪk/ *noun* *hist.* a belt for a sword, bugle, etc., hung from the shoulder across the body to the opposite hip. [Old French *baudrei*: compare Middle High German *balderich*, of unknown origin]

Bald·win ▶ 1 James Ar·thur (1924–87), US writer and civil rights activist, born in Harlem. His first novel, *Go Tell it on the Mountain* (1953), was followed by several novels and essays dealing with homosexuality and race relations. **2 Stan·ley** (1867–1947), British prime minister 1923–24, 1924–29, and 1935–37. **3 Wil·liam War·ren** (1775–1844) and his son **Rob·ert** (1804–58), Upper Canadian politicians and lawyers. The elder Baldwin was the first to propose the principle of responsible government (1828), and his son's developments of the idea influenced Lord Durham's report of 1839.

Bald·win I (1058–1118), first king of the Latin kingdom of Jerusalem. A French nobleman who embarked on the First Crusade in 1096, he established the kingdom of Jerusalem in 1100.

bale¹ ● *noun* **1** a bundle of material tightly wrapped or bound (*a bale of hay*). **2** the quantity in a bale as a unit of measure, esp. *US* 500 lb. of cotton. ● *transitive verb* make up into bales. [Middle English prob. from Middle Dutch, ultimately identical with BALL¹]

bale² *noun* *archaic* or *literary* evil, destruction, woe, pain, misery. [Old English *b(e)alu*]

bale³ *Brit. var. of* BAIL³, BAIL⁴.

Bale·ar·ic Islands /ˌbaliˈerɪk/ (also **Bale·ar·ics**) a group of Mediterranean islands off the east coast of Spain, forming an autonomous region of that country, with four large islands (Majorca, Minorca, Ibiza, Formentera) and seven smaller ones; capital, Palma (on Majorca).

ba·leen /bəˈliːn/ *noun* whalebone. [Old French *baleine* from Latin *balaena* whale]

baleen whale *noun* any of various whales of the suborder Mysticeti, having plates of baleen fringed with bristles for straining plankton from the water.

bale·ful *adjective* **1** (esp. of a manner, look, etc.) gloomy, menacing. **2** harmful, malignant, destructive. □ **bale·ful·ly** *adverb* **bale·ful·ness** *noun* [BALE² + -FUL]

baler *noun* a machine for making bales of hay, straw, or other material.

baler twine *noun* *N Amer.* = BINDER TWINE.

Bal·four /ˈbalfɔr/ **Ar·thur James** (1848–1930), British politician, philosopher, and prime minister 1902–5. As foreign secretary in 1917, he issued the Balfour Declaration, advocating a Jewish national home in Palestine.

Bali /ˈbɒli/ a mountainous island of Indonesia, to the east of Java; chief city, Denpasar; pop. (est. 1995) 2,902,200. It is noted for its beauty and the richness of its culture. □ **Bali·nese** /ˌbɒləˈniːz/ *adjective & noun*

baling wire *noun* wire used for fastening bales of hay etc., often invoked as a type of something used for improvised repairs.

balk /bɔk/ (also esp. *Brit.* **baulk**) ● *verb* **1** *intransitive* **a** refuse to go on. **b** (often foll. by *at*) hesitate. **2** *transitive* **a** thwart, hinder. **b** disappoint. **3** *transitive* **a** miss, let slip (a chance etc.). **b** ignore, shirk. **4** *intransitive Baseball* commit a balk. ● *noun* **1** a hindrance; a stumbling block. **2** a rafter or beam used for building. **3** *Billiards* the area immediately behind the balk line on a billiard table. **4** *Baseball* an illegal motion made by a pitcher which allows the baserunners to advance one base. **5** a ridge left unplowed between furrows. **6** a roughly hewed beam of timber. □ **balk·er** *noun* [Old English *balc* from Old Norse *bálkr* from Germanic]

Bal·kan /ˈbɒlkən/ *adjective* of or relating to the people or nations of the Balkan Peninsula. [Turkish *balkan* chain of wooded mountains]

bal·kan·ize /ˈbɒlkənaɪz/ *transitive verb* (also esp. *Brit.* **-ise**) divide (a country etc.) into smaller mutually hostile units. □ **bal·kan·iz·a·tion** *noun* **bal·kan·ized** *adjective* [BALKAN PENINSULA, which was divided into quarrelsome units in the late 19th and early 20th c.]

Balkan Mountains a range of mountains stretching across central Bulgaria from the Serbian border to the Black Sea.

Balkan Peninsula a large peninsula in SE Europe, south of the Danube and bordered by the Adriatic, Ionian, Mediterranean, Aegean, and Black Seas.

Balkans, the /ˈbɒlkənz/ the countries occupying the Balkan Peninsula. After the First World War the peninsula was divided between Greece, Albania, Bulgaria, and Yugoslavia (see YUGOSLAVIA), with Turkey retaining only a small area including Constantinople (Istanbul). In 1991–93 the former federal republic of Yugoslavia broke up, the constituent republics of Serbia and Montenegro retaining the name 'Yugoslavia' (now the UNION OF SERBIA AND MONTENEGRO) while Slovenia, Croatia, Macedonia, and Bosnia and Herzegovina became independent against a background of civil conflict.

Balkan Wars two wars of 1912–13 that added to the tension in the Balkans before the First World War. In the first (1912), Bulgaria, Serbia, Greece, and Montenegro attacked Ottoman Turkey and forced it to give up Albania and Macedonia; in the second (1913), Bulgaria disputed with Serbia, Greece, and Romania for possession of Macedonia, which was partitioned between Greece and Serbia.

Bal·kis /ˈbɒlkɪs/ the name of the Queen of Sheba in Arabic literature.

balk line *noun* *Billiards* a line on a billiard table on or behind which the cue ball is placed at the beginning of a game or following a scratch.

balky /bɔki/ *adjective* (also esp. *Brit.* **baulky**) (**balk·i·er**, **balk·i·est**) reluctant, perverse. □ **balk·i·ness** *noun*

Ball ▶ 1 John (d.1381), English rebel. A Wycliffite priest who preached an egalitarian social message, he was excommunicated and imprisoned for heresy, and following the Peasants' Revolt was hanged as a traitor. **2 Lu·cille** (1911–89), US comic actress, star of the enormously popular television series *I Love Lucy* (1951–5).

ball¹ ● *noun* **1** a solid or hollow sphere, esp. for use in a game. **2 a** any roughly spherical object resembling a ball (*ball of snow*; *ball of wool*; *rolled himself into a ball*). **b** a rounded part of the body (*ball of the foot*).

Vowels: a *cat* ɑ *arm* e *bed* ɜr *her* ɜ: *deux* ə *ago* ɪ *sit* i *cosy* iː *feed* ɒ *hot* ɔ *pore* oː *no* ʌ *run* ʊ *put*

3 a game played with a ball, esp. baseball. **4** *Baseball* **a** a pitch that is out of the designated strike zone and is not swung at. **b** a pitched ball, or one which has been struck by the batter (*breaking ball; fair ball*). **5** esp. *Brit.* a passing of the ball in soccer. **6** (in *pl.*) *coarse slang* **a** the testicles. **b** (usu. as an exclamation of contempt) nonsense. **c** courage. ¶ Sense 6 is often considered a taboo use. ● *verb* **1** *transitive* squeeze or wind into a ball. **2** *intransitive* (often foll. by *up*) form or gather into a ball or balls. **3** *transitive & intransitive* esp. *N Amer. coarse slang* have sexual intercourse (with). □ **the ball is in your** etc. **court** you etc. must be next to act. **ball** (or **balls**) **up** *coarse slang* bungle; make a mess of. **on the ball** *informal* alert. **play ball** *informal* co-operate. **start** (or **keep**) **the ball rolling** begin (or maintain the momentum of) an activity. [Old Norse *böllr* from Germanic]

ball² *noun* **1** a formal social gathering for dancing. **2** *informal* an enjoyable time (esp. *have a ball*). [French *bal* from Late Latin *ballare* to dance]

bal·lad *noun* **1** a poem or song narrating a popular story. **2** a slow sentimental or romantic song. [Old French *balade* from Provençal *balada* dancing song from *balar* to dance]

bal·lade /baˈlɒd/ *noun* **1** a poem of one or more triplets of stanzas with a repeated refrain and an envoy. **2** *Music* a short lyrical piece, esp. for piano. [earlier spelling and pronunciation of BALLAD]

bal·lad·eer *noun* a singer or composer of ballads.

ballad metre *noun* (also **ballad stanza**) the usual metre of ballads, consisting of a four-line stanza in which the first and third lines are unrhymed and have four stressed syllables, while the second and fourth lines rhyme and have three stressed syllables.

bal·lad·ry *noun* ballads collectively.

ball and chain *noun* **1** a heavy metal ball secured by a chain to the leg of a prisoner etc. to prevent escape. **2** *informal* **a** a severe hindrance. **b** *derogatory* a wife.

ball-and-socket joint *noun* a joint in which a rounded end lies in a concave cup or socket, allowing considerable freedom of movement.

Bal·lan·tyne ▸ Rob·ert Mich·ael (1825–94), Scottish author. His early stories, including *The Young Fur Traders* (1856) and *The Coral Island* (1857), drew on his experiences in N Canada.

Bal·la·rat /ˈbaləˌrat/ a mining and sheep-farming centre in Victoria, Australia; pop. (2001) 80,045. It is the site of the discovery in 1851 of the largest gold reserves in Australia.

Bal·lard /ˈbalɑrd/ **James Gra·ham** (b.1930), British novelist and short-story writer. He is known for dystopian science fiction such as his first novel, *The Drowned World* (1962).

Ballard fuel cell *noun* *proprietary* a type of fuel cell that combines hydrogen and oxygen, without combustion, to generate electricity. [*Ballard Power Systems*, the Canadian company that invented the technology]

bal·last /ˈbaləst/ ● *noun* **1** any heavy material carried by a ship or balloon etc. to secure stability. **2** coarse stone etc. used to form the bed of a railway track or road. **3** *Electricity* any device used to stabilize the current in a circuit. **4** anything that affords stability or permanence. ● *transitive verb* **1** provide with ballast. **2** afford stability or weight to. [16th c.: from Low German or Scandinavian, of uncertain origin]

ball bearing *noun* **1** a bearing in which the two halves are separated by a ring of small metal balls which reduce friction. **2** one of these balls.

ball·boy *noun* (in tennis, baseball, etc.) a boy who retrieves balls that go out of play during a game.

ball-breaker *noun* (also **ball-buster**) *coarse slang* an extremely difficult or demanding person, esp. a sexually manipulative woman.

ball club *noun* a team of players of a ball game, esp. a baseball team.

ball·cock *noun* a valve which controls the water level in a tank by means of a floating ball on a hinged arm.

bal·ler·ina *noun* a female ballet dancer. [Italian, from *ballare* dance, from Late Latin: see BALL²]

Bal·le·steros /ˌbaləˈsterɒs/ **Sev·eri·ano** 'Sevvy' (b.1957), Spanish golfer. In 1979 he became the youngest player in the 20th c. to win the British Open (also taking the title in 1984 and 1988). The following year he was the youngest-ever winner of the US Masters.

bal·let /ˈbalei, baˈlei/ *noun* **1 a** a theatrical style of dancing using set steps and techniques and characterized by movement with the legs turned out in the hip sockets and by the women dancing on pointe. **b** a theatrical work using ballet abstractly or to tell a story. **c** a piece of music composed for a ballet. **d** a performance of ballet (*went to the ballet seven times this week*). **2** a company performing ballet. **3** = ACRO.

□ **bal·let·ic** /baˈletɪk/ *adjective* [French from Italian *balletto* diminutive of *ballo* BALL²]

ballet master *noun* (also **ballet mistress**) an employee of a ballet company who teaches and rehearses dancers.

bal·leto·mane /baˈletɔːˌmein/ *noun* a devotee of ballet. □ **bal·leto·mania** /-ˈmeiniə/ *noun* [BALLET + French *-mane*, = -MANIAC]

ball field *noun* *N Amer.* a field on which baseball is played.

ball game *noun* **1** any game played with a ball, esp. a game of baseball. **2** esp. *N Amer. informal* a particular affair or concern (*a whole new ball game*).

ball·girl *noun* (in tennis, baseball, etc.) a girl who retrieves balls that go out of play during a game.

ball hockey *noun* *Cdn* **1** a version of hockey played in a gymnasium or in an arena without ice, using a hard plastic ball in place of a puck. **2** a version of hockey, usu. without formal rules, played on a paved surface, using a tennis ball instead of a puck.

balli·cat·ter /ˈbalɪˌkatər/ *noun* *Cdn* (*Nfld*) ice formed along a shoreline from waves and freezing spray. [alteration of BARRICADE]

bal·lista /bəˈlɪstə/ *noun* (*pl.* **bal·lis·tae** /-ˌstiː/) an ancient weapon resembling a catapult or large crossbow used for hurling stones or other missiles. [Latin from Greek *ballō* throw]

bal·lis·tic /bəˈlɪstɪk/ *adjective* **1** of or relating to projectiles. **2** moving under the force of gravity only. □ **go ballistic** esp. *N Amer. slang* become incensed or act in a hysterical manner. □ **bal·lis·tic·ally** *adverb* [BALLISTA + -IC]

ballistic missile *noun* a missile which is initially powered and guided but falls under gravity on its target.

ballistic nylon *noun* a durable, tightly woven nylon used in bulletproof vests, luggage, etc.

bal·lis·tics /bəˈlɪstɪks/ *plural noun* (usu. treated as *sing.*) the science of projectiles and firearms.

ball lightning *noun* a rare and little known kind of lightning having the form of a moving globe of light several centimetres across which persists for periods of up to a minute.

bal·locks *var. of* BOLLOCKS.

bal·lon /baˌlõ/ *noun* **1** a ballet dancer's ability to prolong a jump by appearing to pause in mid-air. **2** a ballet dancer's general skill in jumping. [French, = balloon]

bal·loon ● *noun* **1** a small inflatable rubber pouch with a neck, used as a toy or as decoration. **2** a large usu. round bag inflated with hot air or gas to make it rise in the air, often carrying a basket for passengers. **3** an outline enclosing the words or thoughts of characters in a comic strip or cartoon. **4** a window covering falling in wide, puffy bands (usu. *attributive*: *balloon blind*). **5** *Med.* a tiny inflatable pouch attached to a catheter and used to dilate an artery etc. during angioplasty or other procedures. **6** a large globular drinking glass for brandy or wine. ● *verb* **1** *intransitive & transitive* **a** swell out or cause to swell out like a balloon. **b** grow or increase dramatically (*the deficit has ballooned*). **2** *intransitive* travel by balloon. □ **when the balloon goes up** *informal* when the action or trouble starts. □ **bal·loon·ist** *noun* **bal·loon·ing** *noun & adjective* [French *ballon* or Italian *ballone* large ball]

balloon flower *noun* a plant of the genus *Platycodon*, having usu. blue or purple balloon-shaped buds which open to form five-petalled flowers.

balloon tire *noun* a wide pneumatic tire inflated at low pressure to absorb shock.

bal·lot ● *noun* **1** a system of secret voting, usu. by marking a paper with one's choice of candidate etc. **2 a** a single round of voting (*won on the second ballot*). **b** the total number of votes recorded in a ballot. **3** a paper or ticket etc. used in voting. **4** the drawing of lots. ● *verb* (**bal·lot·ed, bal·lot·ing**) **1** *intransitive* (usu. as **bal·lot·ing** *noun*) **a** vote by ballot. **b** draw lots for precedence etc. **2** *transitive* solicit votes from (*the union balloted its members*). [Italian *ballotta* diminutive of *balla* BALL¹]

ballot box *noun* **1** a sealed box into which voters put completed ballots. **2** an election (*defeated at the ballot box*).

ball·park *noun* *N Amer.* **1** a field or stadium designed for baseball. **2** (*attributive*) *informal* approximate, rough (*a ballpark figure*). □ **in the ballpark** *informal* approximately correct.

ball-peen hammer *noun* a hammer with a ball-shaped head, used for metalworking etc.

ball·player *noun* a player in a ball game, esp. a baseball player.

ball·point *noun* (in full **ballpoint pen**) a pen in which the writing point is a tiny rotating ball which rolls ink from an internal cartridge onto the writing surface.

---

uː mood ai my əi pipe au brown ʌu house ei day ɔi boy ɑ̃ franglais ã Canadien ɔ̃ Brayon (*see over for consonants*)

ball·room *noun* a large room or hall for dancing.

ballroom dancing *noun* formal or recreational social dancing for couples, including the foxtrot, waltz, tango, and rumba.

balls-up *noun Brit. coarse slang* a mess; a confused or bungled situation.

ballsy *adjective* (**balls·i·er**, **balls·i·est**) *slang* courageous, tough, gutsy.

bally /ˈbali/ *adjective & adverb Brit. slang* a mild form of *bloody* (see BLOODY *adjective* 3) (*took the bally lot*). [alteration of BLOODY]

bally·hoo /ˈbaliˌhuː, ˌbaliˈhuː/ ● *noun* **1** extravagant or brash publicity; hype. **2** a confused state or commotion. ● *transitive verb* (**bally·hooed**, **bally·hooing**) **1** promote using sensational publicity or hype. **2** praise extravagantly. □ **bally·hooed** *adjective* [19th or 20th c., origin unknown]

Bally·mena /ˌbaliˈmiːnə/ a town in Northern Ireland, to the north of Lough Neagh, capital of a district of the same name; pop. (est. 2002) 29,900.

balm /bɑːm/ *noun* **1** an aromatic ointment for anointing, soothing, or healing. **2** a fragrant and medicinal exudation from certain trees and plants. **3** a healing or soothing influence or consolation. **4** = BALM OF GILEAD 1a. **5** any aromatic herb, esp. one of the genus *Melissa*. **6** a pleasant perfume or fragrance. [Old French *ba(s)me* from Latin *balsamum* BALSAM]

Bal·main /balˈmã/ **Pierre Alex·andre Claud·ius** (1914–1982), French fashion designer. His designs, especially for evening dresses, were renowned for their elegance, especially in the years following the Second World War.

balm of Gil·ead *noun* **1 a** any of various evergreen trees of the genus *Commiphora*, native to W Asia and N Africa. **b** a fragrant resin exuded by such a tree. **2** a frequently planted hybrid poplar. **3** a balsam fir, *Abies balsamea*. [with reference to Jer. 8:22 or Gen. 37:25]

bal·moral /balˈmɒrəl/ *noun* **1** a brimless hat with a cockade or ribbons attached. **2** a leather walking boot with laces up the front. [*Balmoral* Castle in Scotland]

balmy /ˈbɑːmi/ *adjective* (**balm·i·er**, **balm·i·est**) **1** (of weather) warm. **2** mild and fragrant; soothing. **3** yielding balm. **4** *Brit. slang* = BARMY. □ **balm·i·ly** *adverb* **balm·i·ness** *noun*

bal·ne·ol·ogy /ˌbalniˈɒlədʒi/ *noun* the scientific study of bathing and medicinal springs. □ **bal·ne·ol·o·gist** *noun* [Latin *balneum* bath + -LOGY]

ba·loney *noun* **1** *N Amer.* = BOLOGNA. **2** *informal* nonsensical or absurd ideas. [corruption of BOLOGNA]

Bal·qash, Lake /balˈkaʃ/ (also **Bal·khash**) a shallow salt lake in Kazakhstan.

balsa /ˈbɒlsə/ *noun* **1** (in full **balsa wood**) a tough lightweight wood used for making boats, model airplanes, etc. **2** the tropical American tree, *Ochroma lagopus*, from which it comes. [Spanish, = raft]

bal·sam /ˈbɒlsəm/ *noun* **1** any of several aromatic resins, such as balm, obtained from various trees and shrubs and used as a base for certain fragrances and medical preparations (*see also* CANADA BALSAM). **2** an ointment, esp. one composed of a substance dissolved in oil or turpentine. **3** any of various trees or shrubs which yield balsam. **4** any of several flowering plants of the genus *Impatiens*. **5** a healing or soothing agent. □ **bal·sam·ic** /-ˈsamɪk/ *adjective* [Old English from Latin *balsamum*]

balsam fir *noun* a N American fir, *Abies balsamea*, which yields Canada balsam. **2** any of several other firs of northwestern N America, esp. the alpine fir.

bal·sam·ic vinegar *noun* an aged sweet red-wine vinegar made from white grapes. [Italian *aceto balsamico*, lit. 'medicinal vinegar', because originally sipped after a meal as a restorative]

balsam poplar *noun* any of various N American poplars, esp. *Populus balsamifera*, yielding a resin formerly used in cough medicines, ointments, and as waterproofing in birchbark canoes. *Also called* TACAMAHAC.

balsam root *noun* any of several herbaceous plants of the genus *Balsamorhiza* of western N America, esp. *B. sagittata*, with yellow sunflower-like flowers and arrow-shaped leaves. *Also called* SPRING SUNFLOWER.

Balt /bɒlt/ *noun* a native or inhabitant of one of the Baltic States. [late Latin *Balthae*]

Bal·tha·sar /ˈbalθəˌzar/ one of the three Magi.

balti /ˈbalti/ *noun* **1** a type of Pakistani cuisine in which the food is cooked in a small two-handled pan. **2** a meal prepared in this way. [Urdu *bāltī*, literally 'pail']

Bal·tic /ˈbɒltɪk/ ● *adjective* of or relating to the Baltic Sea, the Baltic States, their people, or their language group. ● *noun* **1** an Indo-European branch of languages including Old Prussian, Lithuanian, and Latvian. **2** = BALTIC SEA. **3** (in *pl.*) = BALTIC STATES. [medieval Latin *Balticus* from Late Latin *Balthae* dwellers near the Baltic Sea]

Baltic Sea a sea in N Europe. Almost landlocked, it is linked with the North Sea by the Kattegat strait and the Øresund channel.

Baltic States 1 the independent republics of Estonia, Latvia, and Lithuania. **2** the ten states bordering the Baltic Sea: Denmark, Estonia, Finland, Germany, Latvia, Lithuania, Norway, Poland, Russia, and Sweden.

Bal·ti·more a seaport in north Maryland; pop. (2000) 651,154. □ **Bal·ti·mor·ean** /ˌbɒltəˈmɔːriən/ *noun & adjective* [G. Calvert, 1st Baron *Baltimore*, who obtained a grant of land for the colony later to become Maryland *c.*1632]

Baltimore oriole *noun* a bright orange and black N American oriole, a subspecies of the northern oriole, *Icterus galbula galbula*.

Bal·ti·stan /ˌbɒltɪˈstan/ (also called **Little Tibet**) a region of the Karakoram range of the Himalayas, to the south of K2.

Ba·luch·istan /bəˌluːtʃəˈstan/ **1** a mountainous region of W Asia, which includes part of SE Iran, SW Afghanistan, and W Pakistan. **2** a province of west Pakistan; capital, Quetta.

bal·us·ter /ˈbaləstər/ *noun* each of a series of often ornamental short posts supporting a railing etc. [French *balustre* from Italian *balaustro* from Latin from Greek *balaustion* wild pomegranate flower]

bal·us·trade /ˌbaləˈstreɪd/ *noun* a railing supported by balusters, esp. forming an ornamental parapet to a balcony, bridge, or terrace. □ **bal·us·trad·ed** *adjective* [French (as BALUSTER)]

Bal·zac /ˈbɒlzak, ˈbalzak/ **Hon·oré de** (1799–1850), French novelist. His more than 90 works of fiction, including the 17 volumes of *The Human Comedy* (1842–48), provide a sweeping picture of 19th-c. France. □ **Bal·zac·ian** /bɒlˈzakiən/ *adjective*

bam *interjection* **1** expressing the sound of a hard blow. **2** indicating suddenness. [imitative]

Bam·ako /ˈbaməˌkoː/ the capital of Mali, in the south of the country, on the Niger River; pop. (est. 2002) 906,700.

bam·bino /bamˈbiːnoː/ *noun* (*pl.* **bam·binos** or **bam·bini** /-ni/) **1** *informal* a young (esp. Italian) child. **2** an image of the infant Jesus in a painting etc. [Italian, diminutive of *bambo* silly]

bam·boo *noun* **1** a mainly tropical giant woody grass of the genus *Bambusa* and related genera. **2** its hollow jointed stem, used as building material or to make furniture etc. [Dutch *bamboes* from Portuguese *mambu* from Malay]

bamboo curtain *noun* a political and economic barrier between China and non-Communist countries. [after IRON CURTAIN]

bamboo shoot *noun* a young shoot of bamboo, eaten as a vegetable.

bam·boozle *transitive verb informal* **1** cheat, deceive, swindle. **2** mystify, perplex. □ **bam·boozle·ment** *noun* **bam·booz·ler** *noun* [*c.*1700: prob. of cant origin]

Bamian /ˈbamiˌɒn/ a city in central Afghanistan; pop. (est. 2002) 29,800. Two colossal statues of Buddha nearby, dating from the fifth and third centuries AD, were destroyed by the Taliban in 2001. The ruins of the city of Ghulghuleh, which was destroyed by Genghis Khan *c.*1221, are also nearby.

ban¹ ● *transitive verb* (**banned**, **ban·ning**) forbid, prohibit, esp. formally. ● *noun* **1** a formal or authoritative prohibition (*a ban on smoking*). **2** a tacit prohibition by public opinion. **3** *archaic* a denunciation or curse. [Old English *bannan* summon, from Germanic]

ban² *noun* (*pl.* **bani**) a monetary unit of Romania and Moldova, equal to one-hundredth of a leu. [Romanian]

banal /bəˈnal/ *adjective* trite, trivial, commonplace. □ **ban·al·ity** *noun* (*pl.* **-ities**). **ban·al·ly** *adverb* [originally in sense 'compulsory', hence 'common to all', from French from *ban* (as BAN¹)]

ba·nana *noun* **1** a long curved fruit with soft pulpy flesh and yellow skin when ripe, growing in clusters. **2** (in full **banana tree**) any of several tropical and subtropical treelike plants of the genus *Musa* bearing this fruit. **3** *N Amer. slang derogatory* an Oriental person regarded, esp. by other Orientals, as part of the white establishment. **4** *See also* TOP BANANA, SECOND BANANA. [Portuguese or Spanish, from a name in Guinea]

banana belt *noun informal* a region having a relatively warm climate, esp. (for Canadians) the Niagara Peninsula or southern BC.

banana peel *noun* (also **banana skin**) **1** the skin of a banana. **2** a cause of upset or humiliation; a blunder.

banana pepper *noun* a small, yellow, banana-shaped hot pepper.

banana republic *noun* often *derogatory* a small tropical nation, esp. in Central or S America, economically dependent on fruit exports or similar trade.

ba·nanas *predicative adjective informal* **1** crazy or angry. **2** extremely enthusiastic. [perhaps from *banana oil* nonsense]

banana seat *noun* a long and narrow bicycle seat.

banana split *noun* a dessert consisting of a split banana, ice cream, sauce, whipped cream, and garnishes.

ban·ausic /bəˈnɔːsɪk/ *adjective* **1** uncultivated, unsophisticated. **2** utilitarian, practical. [Greek *banausikos* 'for artisans']

Ban·bury tart /ˈbanbəri/ *noun* a flat pastry with a spicy currant filling. [*Banbury* in S England, where it was originally made]

banc /bæŋk/ *noun* (also **banco**) *see* EN BANC. [Anglo-French (= bench) from medieval Latin (as BANK²)]

band¹ ● *noun* **1 a** a flat, thin strip or loop of material, e.g. paper, metal, or cloth, put around something esp. to hold it together or decorate it (*headband*). **b** a strip of material forming part of a garment (*hatband*; *waistband*). **2** a stripe of a different colour or material on an object. **3** any long and narrow strip or grouping (*band of forest*; *band of thunderstorms*). **4** *Biochem.* a transverse region in a chromosome which reacts characteristically to staining. **5 a** a range of frequencies or wavelengths in a spectrum (esp. of radio frequencies). **b** a range of values within a series. **6** a ring without a prominent precious stone. **7** a section of a phonograph record, usu. comprising a single song etc. **8** a loop of metal or plastic attached to the leg of a bird etc. for identification. **9** *Mech.* a belt connecting wheels or pulleys. **10** (in *pl.*) a collar having two hanging strips, worn by some lawyers, ministers, and academics in formal dress. ● *transitive verb* **1** put a band on, esp. attach an identification band to a bird etc. **2** mark with stripes. □ **band·ed** *adjective* [Old French *bande*, *bende* from Germanic]

band² ● *noun* **1** an organized group of people having a common objective (*a band of protesters*). **2** (in Canada) an Indian community officially recognized as an administrative unit by the federal government. **3** *Anthropology* a basic organizational unit in nomadic societies, consisting of several families; a subgroup of a tribe. **4 a** a group of musicians, esp. playing wind and percussion instruments (*brass band*; *military band*). **b** a group of musicians playing jazz, rock, or pop music. **c** *informal* an orchestra. **5** *N Amer.* a herd or flock. ● *transitive & intransitive verb* form into a group for a purpose (*band together for mutual protection*). □ **to beat the band** *see* BEAT. [Old French *bande*, *bander*, medieval Latin *banda*, prob. of Germanic origin]

ban·dage ● *noun* **1** a strip of material for binding up a wound etc. **2** any piece of material used for binding or covering up. ● *transitive verb* bind (a wound etc.) with a bandage. [French from *bande* (as BAND¹)]

Band-Aid *noun* *proprietary* **1** an adhesive bandage with a gauze pad for dressing small cuts etc. **2** (also **band-aid**) (often *attributive*) a makeshift or temporary solution.

ban·dana *noun* (also **ban·danna**) a coloured handkerchief or head scarf, usu. of cotton, and often having a figured design. [prob. Portuguese from Hindi]

Ban·da·ra·naike /ˌbandərəˈnaikə/ **Siri·mavo Rat·watte Dias** (1916–2000), prime minister of Sri Lanka 1960–65 and 1970–77, the world's first woman prime minister.

Ban·dar Lam·pung /ˌbandər ˈlampʊŋ/ a city at the southern tip of Sumatra, in Indonesia; pop. (est. 2002) 727,400. It was created in the 1980s as a result of the amalgamation of the city of Tanjungkarang and the nearby port of Telukbetung.

Band·ar Seri Be·ga·wan /ˌbandər ˌseri bəˈɡʊwən/ the capital of Brunei; pop. (est. 2002) 74,700.

Banda Sea /ˈbandə/ a sea in E Indonesia, between the central and southern Molucca Islands.

B & B *abbreviation* **1** bed and breakfast. **2** *Cdn* bilingualism and biculturalism.

band·box *noun* a usu. circular box for carrying hats. [such boxes being orig. used to carry neckbands]

band council *noun* *Cdn* a local form of Aboriginal government, consisting of a chief and councillors who are elected for two or three year terms to carry on band business. □ **band councillor** *noun*

B and E *abbreviation slang* BREAKING AND ENTERING.

ban·deau /ˈbandoː, -ˈdoː/ *noun* (*pl.* **ban·deaus** or **ban·deaux** /-doːz/) **1** a strapless band of material worn around the breasts, esp. as part of a swimsuit. **2** a narrow headband. [French]

ban·der·illa /ˌbandəˈrijə, -riljə/ *noun* a decorated dart thrust into a bull's neck or shoulders during a bullfight. [Spanish]

ban·der·ole /ˈbandəˌroːl/ *noun* (also **ban·der·ol**) **1** a long narrow flag with a cleft end, flown from the masthead of a ship. **2** *hist.* an ornamental streamer on a knight's lance. **3** a ribbon-like scroll bearing an inscription. [French *banderole* from Italian *banderuola* diminutive of *bandiera* BANNER]

bandi·coot /ˈbandɪˌkuːt/ *noun* **1** any of the small insect- and plant-eating marsupials of the family Peramelidae, found in Australasia. **2** (in full **bandicoot rat**) any of several S Asian rats of the genera *Bandicota* and *Nesokia*, destructive to crops. [Telugu *pandikokku* pig-rat]

band·ing *noun* **1** *in senses of* BAND¹ *verb*, BAND² *verb*. **2** *Biochem.* an analytical technique involving making the bands of a chromosome visible by staining.

ban·dit *noun* **1** a robber, esp. a member of a gang; a gangster. **2** an outlaw. □ **ban·dit·ry** *noun* [Italian *bandito*, past participle of *bandire* ban, = medieval Latin *bannire* proclaim: see BANISH]

ban·dit·ti /banˈdiːti/ *rare pl. of* BANDIT.

Band·jar·masin *see* BANJARMASIN.

band·leader *noun* the leader of a band of musicians.

band list *noun* *Cdn* a list of members of an Aboriginal band, as recognized by the federal government.

band·master *noun* the conductor of a (esp. military or brass) band.

band·mate *noun* a fellow member of a band of musicians.

band office *noun* the administrative office of a band council.

ban·do·lier /ˌbandəˈliːr/ *noun* (also **ban·do·leer**) a belt or strap worn diagonally across the chest with loops or pockets for ammunition. [Dutch *bandelier* or French *bandoulière*, prob. formed as BANDEROLE]

band·pass *noun* *Electronics* the range of frequencies (of sound, electrical signals, etc.) which are transmitted through a filter.

band saw *noun* an electric saw with a seamless toothed band which rotates clockwise around two wheels.

band·shell *noun* a bandstand in the form of a large concave shell with special acoustic properties.

bands·man *noun* (*pl.* **-men**) a player in esp. a military or brass band.

band·stand *noun* **1** a covered outdoor platform for a band to play on, usu. in a park. **2** any stage or platform for a band.

Ban·dung /ˈbandʊŋ/ a city in Indonesia; pop. (est. 2002) 2,884,300. Founded by the Dutch in 1810, it was the capital of the former Dutch East Indies.

ban·dura /banˈdʊrə/ *noun* a Ukrainian stringed instrument resembling a large lopsided lute and held almost vertically on the lap when played. □ **ban·dur·ist** *noun* [Ukrainian]

B & W *abbreviation* (of film etc.) black and white.

band·wagon *noun* **1** a wagon used for carrying a band in a parade etc. **2** (esp. in **jump** (or **climb**) **on the bandwagon**) a party, cause, or group that is fashionable or seems likely to succeed.

band·width *noun* the range of frequencies within a given band, esp. the transmission capacity of a computer network or other telecommunication system.

bandy¹ *adjective* (**ban·di·er**, **ban·di·est**) **1** (of the legs) curved so as to be wide apart at the knees. **2** (also **bandy-legged**) (of a person) bowlegged. [perhaps from BANDY³]

bandy² *transitive verb* (**-dies**, **-died**) **1** (often foll. by *about*) **a** pass (a story, rumour, etc.) to and fro. **b** throw or pass (a ball etc.) to and fro. **2** (often foll. by *about*) discuss disparagingly (*bandied her name about*). **3** (often foll. by *with*) exchange (blows, insults, etc.) (*don't bandy words with me*). [perhaps from French *se bander* take sides, from *bande* BAND²]

bandy³ *noun* **1** an early form of hockey played on a field or on ice with a ball and large curved sticks. **2** (*pl.* **ban·dies**) the curved stick used in this sport. [perhaps from BANDY²]

bane *noun* **1** the cause of ruin or trouble (*the bane of my existence*). **2** *literary* ruin; woe. **3** *archaic* (except in *combination*) poison (*ratsbane*). □ **bane·ful** *adjective* **bane·ful·ly** *adverb* [Old English *bana* from Germanic]

bane·berry *noun* (*pl.* **-berries**) **1** a plant of the genus *Actaea*, related to the buttercup. **2** the bitter poisonous berry of this plant, usu. white with a black dot. Also called DOLL'S EYES.

Banff a town in SW Alberta, situated in the Rocky Mountains, about 110 km west of Calgary; pop. (2001) 7,135. □ **Banff·ite** *noun* [*Banff*, Scotland]

Banff National Park a park in SW Alberta, situated in the Rocky Mountains, west of Calgary. Established in 1885, it is Canada's oldest national park and, together with the other Rocky Mountain parks, has been designated a World Heritage Site.

t top   v voice   w we   z zoo   ʃ she   ʒ vision   θ thin   ð this   ŋ ring   x loch   tʃ chip   dʒ jar   (see over for vowels)

Banff·shire /ˈbamfʃɪr/ a former county of NE Scotland which became a part of Grampian region in 1975, and in 1996 was divided between Aberdeenshire and Moray.

bang ● *noun* **1 a** a loud sudden sound. **b** an explosion. **c** the firing of a gun. **2 a** a sharp blow. **b** the sound of this. **3** *N Amer. informal* a thrill (*got a bang out of it*). **4** (in *pl.*) esp. *N Amer.* a fringe of hair cut across the forehead. **5** *coarse slang* an act of sexual intercourse. **6** *slang* an exclamation mark. ● *verb* **1** *transitive & intransitive* strike or shut noisily (*banged the door shut; banged on the table*). **2** *transitive & intransitive* make or cause to make the sound of a blow or an explosion. **3** *transitive* esp. *N Amer.* cut (hair) into bangs. **4** *coarse slang* **a** *intransitive* have sexual intercourse. **b** *transitive* have sexual intercourse with. ● *adverb* **1** with a bang or sudden impact. **2** *informal* exactly (*bang in the middle*). ● *interjection* indicating suddenness or swiftness. □ **bang on** *Cdn & Brit. informal* exactly right. **bang on about** *Brit. informal* talk tediously and at length about. **bang out** *informal* produce (a piece of work etc.) quickly and without attention to detail. **bang to rights** *Brit. slang* (of a criminal) caught red-handed. **bang up 1** damage or injure. **2** *Brit. slang* imprison. **bang for one's buck** *N Amer.* value for one's money. **with a bang 1** quickly and noisily. **2** with great commotion, publicity, success, etc. [16th c.: perhaps from Scandinavian, compare Old Norse *banga* to hammer]

Banga·lore /ˌbaŋɡəˈlɔr/ a city in south central India, capital of the state of Karnataka; pop. (2001) 4,292,200.

bang-bang *adjective N Amer.* (esp. of a play in sports) consisting of two actions happening in quick succession.

bang·belly *noun Cdn (Nfld)* a dense cake made of cooked rice, flour, molasses, raisins, salt pork, and spices.

bang·er *noun* **1** a thing that makes a banging noise, e.g. a firecracker or device for scaring away birds etc. **2** *Brit. slang* a sausage. **3** *Brit. slang* a jalopy. **4** (in *combination*) *slang* an engine having a specified number of cylinders (*four-banger*).

Bang·kok /baŋˈkok/ the capital and chief port of Thailand on the Chao Phraya waterway, 40 km (25 miles) upstream from its outlet into the Gulf of Thailand; pop. (est. 2000) 6,320,200.

Ban·gla·desh /ˌbaŋɡləˈdɛʃ/ a Muslim country of the Indian subcontinent, in the Ganges delta; pop. (est. 2002) 133,376,684; capital, Dhaka. Formerly part of British India, the region became (as East Pakistan) one of the two geographical units of Pakistan. In response to civil war an independent republic was proclaimed in East Pakistan in 1971, taking the name of Bangladesh. □ **Ban·gla·deshi** *adjective & noun* [Bengali, = land of Bengal]

ban·gle *noun* a rigid bracelet, usu. without a clasp, worn around the arm or ankle. [Hindi *bangri* glass bracelet]

bang·tail *noun* a horse, esp. one with its tail cut straight across.

Ban·gui /ˈbaŋɡi/ the capital of the Central African Republic; pop. (est. 2002) 652,900.

bang-up *adjective N Amer. informal* first-class, excellent (esp. *bang-up job*).

ban·ish *transitive verb* **1** formally expel (a person), esp. from a country. **2** dismiss from one's presence or mind. □ **ban·ish·ment** *noun* [Old English *banir*, ultimately from Germanic]

ban·is·ter *noun* (also **ban·nis·ter**) **1** the handrail at the side a staircase. **2** (in *pl.*) a handrail and its supporting uprights. **3** (usu. in *pl.*) an upright supporting a handrail. [earlier *barrister*, corruption of BALUSTER]

Ban·jar·masin /ˌbandʒɑrˈmɒsɪn/ (also **Ban·djar·masin**) a deepwater port and capital of the province of Kalimantan in Indonesia, on the island of Borneo; pop. (est. 2002) 548,900.

ban·jax *transitive verb Brit. informal* ruin, incapacitate. [20th c.: orig. Anglo-Irish, of unknown origin]

banjo *noun* (*pl.* **ban·jos** or **ban·joes**) a four- or five-stringed musical instrument with a neck and head like a guitar and an open-backed body consisting of parchment stretched over a metal hoop. □ **banjo·ist** *noun* [US southern corruption of earlier *bandore*, ultimately from Greek *pandoura* three-stringed lute]

Ban·jul /banˈdʒuːl/ the capital of Gambia; pop. (est. 2000) 57,800. Until 1973 it was known as Bathurst.

bank[1] ● *noun* **1** the sloping ground bordering a body of water. **2** the area of ground alongside a river (*the left bank of the Seine*). **3** a slope or raised shelf of ground. **4** an underwater ridge of land (*Grand Banks*). **5** the slope built into a road etc., enabling vehicles to maintain speed around a curve. **6** the tilt of an aircraft etc. to one side during a turn. **7** a mass of cloud, fog, snow, etc. **8** the cushioned rim around the playing surface of a billiard table. ● *verb* **1 a** *transitive & intransitive* (often foll. by *up*) heap or rise into banks. **b** *transitive N Amer.* (*PEI & New England*) insulate (a house) by piling seaweed, hay, earth, etc. up against the outside walls. **2 a** *intransitive* (of a vehicle or aircraft) tilt to one side while rounding a curve. **b** *transitive* cause (a vehicle or aircraft) to do this. **3** *transitive* contain or confine within a bank or banks. **4** *transitive* build (a road etc.) higher at the outer edge of a bend to enable fast cornering. **5** *transitive* heap up (a fire) tightly so that it burns slowly. **6** *transitive* cause (a ball) to strike the cushion of a billiard table. **7** *transitive* cause (a puck) to rebound off the boards of a hockey rink. [Old Norse *banki* (unrecorded: compare Old Icelandic *bakki*): related to BENCH]

bank[2] ● *noun* **1 a** a financial establishment which uses money deposited by customers for investment, pays it out when required, lends money at interest, exchanges currency, etc. **b** a building in which this business takes place. **2 a** an institution which collects a product and stores it for future use (*blood bank; food bank*). **b** a place where information is stored in a computer (*data bank*). **3 a** the money or tokens held by the banker in some games. **b** the banker or dealer in such games. **4** = PIGGY BANK. ● *verb* **1** *transitive* deposit (money or valuables) in a bank. **2** *intransitive* engage in business as a banker. **3** *intransitive* (often foll. by *at*, *with*) keep money (at a bank). **4** *intransitive* act as banker in a game. □ **bank on** rely on (*I'm banking on your help*). [medieval Latin *banca*, *bancus*, from Germanic: related to BANK[1]]

bank[3] *noun* **1** a row of similar objects, esp. of keys, lights, or switches. **2** a tier of oars. [Old French *banc* from Germanic: related to BANK[1], BENCH]

bank·able *adjective* **1** acceptable at a bank. **2** reliable (*a bankable reputation*). **3** certain to bring in a profit. □ **bank·abil·ity** *noun*

bank barn *noun N Amer.* (esp. *Ont. & US Midlands*) a barn built into the side of a hill with an entrance to the top storey on one side and to the lower storey on the other.

bank bill *noun* **1** esp. *US* = BANKNOTE. **2** *Brit.* a bank draft.

bank book *noun* = PASSBOOK.

bank card *noun* a plastic card with an encoded magnetic strip, used for accessing one's account at automated teller machines.

bank draft *noun* an order for payment drawn by one bank on another.

bank·er[1] *noun* **1** a person who manages or owns a bank or group of banks. **2 a** a keeper of the bank or dealer in some gambling games. **b** a card game involving gambling.

bank·er[2] *noun* **1** a fishing boat operating in the waters off Newfoundland, esp. the Grand Banks. **2** a Newfoundland fisherman.

banker's hours *plural noun* very restricted working hours, traditionally from 10 a.m. to 3 p.m. on weekdays.

banker's lamp *noun* a table lamp, usu. of brass, with a long cylindrical light bulb and a green glass shade.

Bank·head, Tal·lu·lah (1903–68), US actress. Making her stage debut in New York in 1918, she became noted for her uninhibited public persona, rich laugh and harsh drawl. Her most successful film appearance was in Alfred Hitchcock's *Lifeboat* (1944).

bank holiday *noun* **1** a weekday on which banks are closed. **2** *Brit.* a legal public holiday on which most business are closed.

bank·ing[1] *noun* **1** *Cdn (Nfld)* fishing for cod off the southeast coast of Newfoundland. **2** *N Amer.* (*PEI & New England*) seaweed, hay, etc. piled up against a building to insulate it.

bank·ing[2] *noun* **1** the business conducted by a bank. **2** the custom given to a bank by a customer.

bank machine *noun* = AUTOMATED TELLER MACHINE.

bank·note *noun* a piece of paper money issued by a central bank, circulating as a nation's currency.

Bank of Canada *noun* the federally owned central bank which controls Canada's bank rate and other fiscal policies.

Bank of England *noun* the central bank of England and Wales, issuing banknotes and having the Government as its main customer.

bank rate *noun* esp. *Cdn* the central bank's minimum interest rate on short-term loans to banks etc.

bank·roll ● *noun N Amer.* **1** a roll of banknotes. **2** a sum of money; available funds. ● *transitive verb* esp. *N Amer. informal* support financially.

bank·rupt ● *adjective* **1 a** legally declared unable to pay debts; insolvent. **b** undergoing the legal process resulting from this. **2** (often foll. by *of*) exhausted or drained (of some quality etc.); deficient, lacking. ● *noun* **1** an insolvent debtor whose estate is administered and disposed of for the benefit of the creditors. **2** a person exhausted of or deficient in a certain attribute (*a moral bankrupt*). ● *transitive verb* make bankrupt. □ **bank·rupt·cy** /-ˌrʌpsi/ *noun* (*pl.* **-cies**). [16th c.: from Italian *banca rotta* broken bench (as BANK[2], Latin *rumpere rupt-* break), assimilated to Latin]

Vowels: a *cat* ɑ *arm* e *bed* ɜr *her* ɜː *deux* ə *ago* ɪ *sit* i *cosy* iː *feed* ɒ *hot* ɔ *pore* ɔː *no* ʌ *run* ʊ *put*

Banks, Sir Jo·seph (1743–1820), English naturalist and scientist who accompanied Captain James Cook on his first voyage around the world (1768–71) and collected many species of New World plants.

bank·sia *noun* any evergreen flowering shrub of the genus *Banksia*, native to Australia. [Sir J. BANKS]

bank·side *noun* the sloping side of a river bank.

Banks Island a large island in the W Arctic Archipelago, bordered by the Beaufort Sea to the west and Amundsen Gulf to the south. [Sir J. BANKS]

bank swallow *noun* a greyish-brown and white swallow, *Riparia riparia*, which nests in tunnels burrowed in banks of sand, soil, etc.

ban·ner ● *noun* **1** a large sign or strip of cloth etc. bearing a slogan or design, usu. carried in a procession or hung in a public place. **2** a belief or principle serving as a rallying point. **3** (in full **banner headline**) a large newspaper headline, esp. one across the top of the front page. **4 a** a national flag. **b** *hist.* a flag on a pole used as the standard of a king, knight, etc., esp. in battle. ● *attributive adjective N Amer.* excellent, outstanding (*a banner year in sales*). □ **ban·nered** *adjective* [Anglo-French *banere* from Romanic, ultimately from Germanic]

banner ad *noun* an advertisement appearing as a banner across the top or bottom of a web page.

ban·ner·et /'banərət, -'ret/ *noun hist.* **1 a** a knight who commanded his own troops in battle under his own banner. **b** a knighthood given on the battlefield for courage. **2** (also **ban·ner·ette**) a small banner.

Ban·nis·ter, Sir Roger Gil·bert (b.1929), English middle-distance runner who became the first athlete to run a mile in less than four minutes (6 May 1954), which in its day was the most coveted feat in track and field.

ban·nis·ter *var. of* BANISTER.

ban·nock *noun* **1** *Cdn* a bread similar to tea biscuits, made of flour, water, and fat, sometimes leavened with baking powder, and cooked on a griddle or over a fire. **2** esp. *Scot.* a round flat unsweetened cake made from oatmeal, barley, flour, etc., usu. unleavened. [Old English *bannuc*, perhaps from Celtic]

Ban·nock·burn a former town in central Scotland, the scene of a decisive battle in 1314 in which the Scottish, led by Robert the Bruce, defeated the English army to regain their independence.

banns *plural noun* an oral or published notice announcing an intended marriage and giving the opportunity for objections, esp. one repeated on three successive Sundays in a church. [pl. of BAN[1]]

ban·offi pie *noun* (also **ban·offee pie**) esp. *Brit.* a pie or tart made with toffee, bananas, and cream. [blend of BANANA and TOFFEE]

ban·quet ● *noun* **1** an elaborate and extensive feast. **2** a dinner for many people followed by speeches in favour of a cause or in celebration of an event. ● *verb* (**ban·quet·ed, ban·quet·ing**) **1** *intransitive* hold a banquet; feast. **2** *transitive* entertain with a banquet. □ **ban·quet·er** *noun* [French, diminutive of *banc* bench, BANK[2]]

banquet burger *noun Cdn* a hamburger with bacon and cheese.

banquet hall *noun* **1** a large room in which banquets are held. **2** a building containing one or more of these.

ban·quette /baŋ'ket/ *noun* **1** an upholstered bench along a wall, esp. in a restaurant or bar. **2** a raised step behind a rampart. [French from Italian *banchetta* diminutive of *banca* bench, BANK[2]]

ban·shee /'banʃiː/ *noun* (in Gaelic mythology) a female spirit whose wailing warns of imminent death in a family. [Irish *bean sídhe* from Old Irish *ben síde* woman of the fairies]

ban·tam *noun* **1** any of several small breeds of domestic fowl, of which the rooster is very aggressive. **2** a small but aggressive person. **3** *Cdn* **a** a level of amateur sport, usu. involving children aged 13–15. **b** a player in this age group. [apparently from *Bāntān* in Java, although the fowl is not native there]

bantam·weight *noun* **1** a weight class in certain sports between flyweight and featherweight, in the professional boxing scale not more than 118 lbs. (53 kg) but differing for amateur boxers and wrestlers. **2** an athlete of this weight.

ban·ter ● *noun* good-humoured teasing. ● *verb* **1** *transitive* ridicule in a good-humoured way. **2** *intransitive* talk humorously or teasingly. □ **ban·ter·er** *noun* [17th c.: origin unknown]

Ban·ting, Sir Fred·erick Grant (1891–1941), Canadian surgeon who, with Charles Best, was the first to isolate insulin as the internal secretion of the pancreas. The discovery immediately revolutionized the treatment of diabetes, and Banting shared the Nobel Prize for medicine in 1923.

Bantu /'bantuː/ ● *noun* **1** a group of Niger-Congo languages spoken in equatorial and southern Africa, including Swahili, Xhosa, and Zulu.

2 (*pl.* same or **Bantus**) a member of the peoples speaking these languages. ● *adjective* of or relating to these languages or peoples. [in certain Bantu languages, pl. of *-ntu* person]

Bantu·stan /ˌbantuː'stan/ *noun hist.* often *offensive* any of several partially self-governing areas in South Africa set aside for blacks during the apartheid era (*see also* HOMELAND 2). [BANTU + *-stan* as in *Hindustan*]

banty *noun* (*pl.* **-ties**) *informal* a bantam rooster or hen.

ban·yan /'banjən/ *noun* an Indian fig tree, *Ficus benghalensis*, the branches of which produce aerial roots to form new trunks. [Portuguese *banian* from Gujarati *vāṇiyo* man of trading caste, from Sanskrit: applied originally by Europeans to one such tree under which merchants had built a pagoda]

ban·zai /bɒn'zai, ban'zai/ *interjection* **1** a Japanese battle cry. **2** a form of greeting used to the Japanese emperor. [Japanese, = ten thousand years (of life to you)]

bao·bab /'beɪoː,bab/ *noun* an African tree, *Adansonia digitata*, with an enormously thick trunk and large fruit containing edible pulp. [Latin, prob. from a central African language]

Bao·tou /bau'toː/ an industrial city in Inner Mongolia, northern China, on the Yellow River; pop. (est. 2002) 1,437,000.

bap /bap/ *noun Brit.* a soft flattish bread roll. [16th c.: origin unknown]

bap·tism *noun* **1 a** a religious rite symbolizing admission to the Christian Church, involving sprinkling the forehead with water or total immersion and generally accompanied by naming. **b** the act of baptizing or being baptized. **2** any similar rite of initiation, purification, or naming. □ **bap·tis·mal** *adjective* [ecclesiastical Greek *baptismos* from *baptizō* BAPTIZE]

baptism of fire *noun* **1** initiation into battle. **2** a painful new undertaking or experience.

bap·tist *noun* **1** a person who baptizes (esp. *John the Baptist*). **2** (**Baptist**) a member of a Protestant denomination advocating baptism by total immersion, esp. of adults, as a symbol of membership of and initiation into the Church.

bap·tis·tery *noun* (also **bap·tis·try**) (*pl.* **-ies**) **1 a** the part of a church used for baptism. **b** *hist.* a building next to a church, used for baptism. **2** (in a Baptist church) a tank used for total immersion.

bap·tize *transitive verb* (also esp. *Brit.* **-tise**) **1** administer baptism to. **2** give a name or nickname to; christen. [ecclesiastical Latin *baptizare* from Greek *baptizō* immerse, baptize]

bar¹ ● *noun* **1** a long rod or piece of rigid wood, metal, etc., esp. used as an obstruction, confinement, fastening, weapon, etc. **2 a** something resembling a bar in being (thought of as) straight, narrow, and rigid (*bar of soap*; *chocolate bar*). **b** a band of colour or light, esp. on a flat surface. **c** = CROSSBAR. **d** a metal strip below the clasp of a medal, awarded as an extra distinction. **e** a bank of sand etc. across the mouth of a river or harbour (*compare* SANDBAR). **f** the element of an electric heater. **g** a rail (*towel bar*). **3 a** a barrier of any shape. **b** a restriction (*a bar to promotion*). **c** *Law* a legal obstacle preventing an action or claim. **4 a** a counter in a pub, restaurant, or home across which alcohol or refreshments are served. **b** a room in a restaurant, hotel, etc. in which customers may sit and drink. **c** *N Amer.* an establishment serving alcoholic drinks; a pub. **5** a small shop, stall, department, etc. which specializes in a particular product (*gas bar*; *snack bar*). **6** *Music* **a** any of the sections of usu. equal time value into which a musical composition is divided by vertical lines across the staff. **b** = BAR LINE. **7 a** a rail in a law court separating the space occupied by the judge, lawyers, and parties to a case from the general public. **b** an enclosure in which an accused person stands before a court of law. **c** a rail marking the end of the chamber in the House of Commons. **8** a public standard of acceptability, before which a person is said to be tried (*bar of conscience*). **9** *Law* (prec. by the) **a** *N Amer.* lawyers collectively. **b** *N Amer.* the profession of lawyer. **c** (**Bar**) *Brit.* barristers collectively. ● *transitive verb* (**barred, bar·ring**) **1 a** fasten (a door, window, etc.) with a bar or bars. **b** (usu. foll. by *in, out*) shut or keep in or out (*barred him in*). **2** obstruct, prevent (*bar her progress*). **3 a** (usu. foll. by *from*) prohibit, exclude (*bar them from attending*). **b** exclude from consideration (*compare* BARRING). **4** mark with stripes. **5** *Law* prevent or delay (an action) by legal obstacle. ● *preposition* except (*this is the best ever, bar none*). □ **at (the) bar** (of a lawsuit, defendant, etc.) currently before the courts. **be called** (or **admitted**) **to the bar** be formally admitted into the legal profession. **behind bars** in prison. **raise** (or **lower**) **the bar** increase (or decrease) standards, a level of difficulty or expectations, etc. [Old French *barre, barrer*, from Romanic]

bar² *noun* esp. *Meteorol.* a unit of pressure equal to 100 kilopascals. [Greek *baros* weight]

uː m**oo**d   ai m**y**   ɔi p**i**pe   au br**ow**n   ʌu h**ou**se   ei d**ay**   ɔi b**oy**   ã fr**anglais**   ã Cana**dien**   ɔ Br**ayon**   (*see over for consonants*)

Bar·ab·bas /bəˈrabəs/ *New Testament* the condemned thief whom Pontius Pilate released from prison at Passover instead of Jesus (Matt. 27:16).

bara·chois /ˈbarəˌʃwɒ/ *noun* (also **barachois pond**) *Cdn* (*Nfld & Maritimes*) a shallow coastal lagoon or pond created by the formation of a sandbar a short distance offshore from a beach. [Canadian French]

Baraka /bəˈrɒkə/ **Imamu Amiri**, Muslim name of E.L. JONES.

bara·thea /ˌbarəˈθiə/ *noun* a fine woollen cloth, sometimes mixed with silk or cotton, used esp. for coats, suits, etc. [19th c.: origin unknown]

barb ● *noun* **1** a secondary backward-projecting point of an arrow, fish hook, etc., angled to make extraction difficult. **2** a deliberately hurtful remark. **3** a beard-like filament at the mouth of some fish, e.g. barbel and catfish. **4** any one of the fine hairlike filaments growing from the shaft of a feather, forming the vane. ● *transitive verb* furnish (an arrow, fish hook, etc.) with a barb or barbs. [Latin *barba* beard]

Bar·bados /bɑːˈbeidoːs, -oːz/ the most easterly of the Caribbean islands, one of the Windward Islands group; pop. (est. 2002) 276,607; capital, Bridgetown. □ **Bar·bad·ian** *adjective & noun*

bar band *noun* a band which performs in bars.

bar·bar·ian /bɑːˈbeəriən/ ● *noun* **1** an uncultured or brutish person. **2** a member of a people regarded as primitive or uncivilized. **3** *hist.* (in the ancient world) a foreigner or pagan, esp. a non-Greek or non-Roman. ● *adjective* **1** rough and uncultured. **2** uncivilized. [originally of any foreigner with a different language or customs: French *barbarien* from *barbare* (as BARBAROUS)]

bar·bar·ic /bɑːˈberik/ *adjective* **1** brutal; cruel (*flogging is a barbaric punishment*). **2** rough and uncultured; unrestrained. **3** of or like barbarians; primitive. □ **bar·bar·ic·ally** *adverb* [Greek *barbarikos* from *barbaros* foreign]

bar·bar·ism /ˈbɑːbəˌrɪzəm/ *noun* **1 a** the absence of culture and civilized standards; ignorance and rudeness. **2 a** word or expression not considered correct; a solecism. **3** anything considered to be in bad taste. [Greek *barbarismos* from *barbarizō* speak like a foreigner, from *barbaros* foreign]

bar·bar·ity /bɑːˈberiti/ *noun* (pl. **-ities**) **1** savage cruelty. **2** an example of this.

bar·bar·ize *transitive & intransitive verb* (also esp. *Brit.* **-ise**) make or become barbarous. □ **bar·bar·iz·a·tion** *noun*

Bar·ba·rossa /bɑːbəˈroːsə/ **1** (real name Khair ed-Din, d.1546), Barbary pirate and admiral. He conquered much of the eastern Mediterranean after being made commander of the Ottoman fleet in 1533. **2** see FREDERICK I.

bar·bar·ous /ˈbɑːbərəs/ *adjective* **1** uncivilized. **2** cruel. **3** coarse and unrefined. □ **bar·bar·ous·ly** *adverb* **bar·bar·ous·ness** *noun* [originally of any foreign language or people: from Latin from Greek *barbaros* foreign]

Bar·bary /ˈbɑːbəri/ (also **Barbary States**) *hist.* the Saracen countries of North and NW Africa, together with Moorish Spain. The area was noted between the 16th and 18th c. as a haunt of pirates. See also MAGHRIB. [ultimately from Arabic *Barbar* BERBER, applied by ancient Arab geographers to the natives of North Africa west and south of Egypt]

Barbary ape *noun* a tailless light brown macaque, *Macaca sylvana*, of N Africa and Gibraltar.

Bar·beau /bɑːˈboː/ **1** (**Charles**) **Mar·ius** (1883–1969), Canadian folklorist and ethnologist. He was a leading figure in the study of Québécois and Aboriginal legends and folk songs. **2 Jean** (b.1945), Canadian dramatist. His plays, often concerning contemporary Quebec values, are characterized by acerbic humour and a strong political sensibility.

Barbeau Peak a mountain on Ellesmere Island. Rising over 2 600 m, it is the highest mountain in the Arctic and the highest in eastern N America. [C. M. BARBEAU]

bar·be·cue (also **bar·be·que**) ● *noun* **1 a** a meal, esp. of meat, cooked on an open fire or grill out of doors. **b** a party at which such a meal is cooked and eaten. **2 a** a metal appliance equipped with a grill on which meat etc. is cooked over charcoal or gas flame. **b** a fireplace, usu. of brick, containing a grill for cooking. ● *transitive verb* (**bar·be·cues, bar·be·cued, bar·be·cu·ing**) cook (esp. meat) on a barbecue. [Spanish *barbacoa* from Arawak *barbacoa* wooden frame on posts]

barbecue sauce *noun* a highly seasoned sauce, usu. tomato-based, used to baste barbecued meat.

barbed *adjective* **1** equipped with barbs. **2** (of a remark etc.) deliberately hurtful.

barbed wire *noun* (*N Amer.* also **barb·wire**) wire bearing sharp pointed spikes close together and used in fencing, or in warfare as an obstruction.

bar·bel *noun* **1** any large European freshwater fish of the genus *Barbus*, with fleshy filaments hanging from its mouth. **2** such a filament growing from the mouth of any fish. [Old French from Late Latin *barbellus* diminutive of *barbus* barbel, from *barba* beard]

bar·bell *noun* a metal bar with a series of weighted discs at each end, used for weightlifting exercises. [BAR¹ + BELL¹]

bar·be·que *var. of* BARBECUE.

Barber, Sam·uel (1910–81), US composer whose works, including the *Adagio for Strings* (1936) and the opera *Vanessa* (1958), are largely lyrical and of the conservative European tradition.

barber ● *noun* a person who cuts men's hair and shaves or trims beards as an occupation; a men's hairdresser. ● *transitive verb* **1** cut the hair, shave or trim the beard of. **2** cut or trim (grass etc.) closely. [Old French *barbeor* from medieval Latin *barbator -oris* from *barba* beard]

barber chair *noun* **1** a chair used by hairdressers, esp. one which can be raised or lowered with a foot pedal. **2** *Cdn* a tree stump with a large splintered point of wood left above the undercut as a result of improper sawing.

barber pole *noun* a pole with spiral red and white stripes, hung outside a barbershop as a business sign.

bar·berry *noun* (pl. **-berries**) **1** any shrub of the genus *Berberis*, with spiny shoots, yellow flowers, and ovoid red berries. **2** its berry. [Old French *berberis*, of unknown origin: assimilated to BERRY]

barber·shop *noun* esp. *N Amer.* **1** a shop where a barber works. **2** (also **barbershop quartet**) a style of close harmony singing for four male voices.

barber·shop·per *noun* a person who sings barbershop music.

bar·bet /ˈbɑːbət/ *noun* any small brightly coloured tropical bird of the family Capitonidae, with bristles at the base of its beak. [French from *barbe* beard]

bar·bette /bɑːˈbet/ *noun* **1** a platform in a fort from which guns can be fired over a parapet etc. and not through an embrasure. **2** a cylindrical armoured gun mounting in a warship on which a turret revolves. [French, diminutive of *barbe* beard]

bar·bi·can /ˈbɑːbikən/ *noun* the outer defence of a city, castle, etc., esp. a double tower above a gate or drawbridge. [Old French *barbacane*, of unknown origin]

Bar·bie *noun* (also **Barbie doll**) **1** *proprietary* a doll representing a slim, fashionably dressed, conventionally attractive young woman. **2** a woman with similar physical characteristics, esp. (*derogatory*) an unintelligent one.

bar·bie *noun* esp. *Austral. informal* a barbecue. [abbreviation]

bar·bi·tal *noun* (*Brit.* **bar·bi·tone**) a long-acting hypnotic and sedative drug. [as BARBITURIC ACID + -*al* as in *veronal*]

bar·bit·ur·ate /bɑːˈbitʃurət, -ˌreit/ *noun* any derivative of barbituric acid used in the preparation of sedative and sleep-inducing drugs. [BARBITURIC + -ATE¹]

bar·bi·tur·ic acid /ˌbɑːbiˈtʃurik, -ˈtjurik/ *noun* an organic acid from which various sedatives and sleep-inducing drugs are derived. [French *barbiturique* from German *Barbitursäure* (*Säure* acid) from the name *Barbara*]

Bar·bi·zon school /ˈbɑːbizɒn/ a group of French landscape painters of the 1840s, who reacted against classical conventions and based their art on direct study of nature. Led by Théodore Rousseau and including Charles Daubigny, Narcisse Virgile Diaz (1807–76), Jean François Millet, and Jules Dupré (1811–89), they took their name from a small village in the forest of Fontainebleau where Rousseau and others worked.

barb·less *adjective* (of a fish hook) not having a barb.

bar·botte¹ /ˈbɑːbət/ *noun* (also **bar·bot**) *Cdn* (*Que. & Ont.*) a large catfish, esp. *Ictalurus punctatus*. [Canadian French]

bar·botte² /bɑːˈbɒt/ *noun* *Cdn* (esp. *Que.*) a gambling game similar to craps but played with three dice. [Canadian French from Turkish *barbut*]

Bar·bour /ˈbɑːbər/ **1 Doug·las** (b.1940), Canadian poet, publisher, and critic. His poetry is marked by the use of sound patterns and vibrant imagery. **2 John** (c.1320–95), Scottish poet. The only poem ascribed to him with certainty is *The Bruce*, a chronicle relating the deeds of Robert I of Scotland.

Bar·buda see ANTIGUA AND BARBUDA.

barb·ule /ˈbɑːbjuːl/ *noun* a minute filament projecting from the barb of a feather. [Latin *barbula*, diminutive of *barba* beard]

Consonants: b *but*   d *dog*   f *few*   g *get*   h *her*   j *yes*   k *cat*   l *leg*   m *man*   n *no*   p *pen*   r *red*   s *sit*

barb·wire *N Amer. var. of* BARBED WIRE.

bar·ca·role /ˈbɑːkəˌroːl/ *noun* (also **bar·ca·rolle** /-ˌrɒl/) **1** a song sung by Venetian gondoliers. **2** music in imitation of this. [French *barcarolle* from Venetian Italian *barcarola* boatman's song, from *barca* boat]

Bar·ce·lona /ˌbɑːsəˈloːnə/ a city and port on the Mediterranean in NE Spain; pop. (est. 2001) 1,505,325.

B.Arch. *abbreviation* Bachelor of Architecture.

bar chart *var. of* BAR GRAPH.

bar clam *noun Cdn* (*PEI*) a large clam with a corrugated shell, found on underwater sandbars.

Bar-Cochba /bɑːˈkɒkbə/ the name found in Christian sources (Jewish sources call him Simeon) for the leader of a Jewish revolt in AD 132 against Hadrian's project to rebuild Jerusalem as a non-Jewish city. He claimed to be, and was accepted by some as, the Messiah.

bar code *noun* a code in the form of a pattern of stripes, used for identification by an optical scanner. □ **bar-coded** *adjective* **bar-coding** *noun*

bard[1] *noun* **1 a** *hist.* a Celtic minstrel. **b** the winner of a prize for Welsh verse at an eisteddfod. **2** *literary* a poet, esp. one treating heroic themes. □ **the Bard** (or **the Bard of Avon**) Shakespeare. □ **bard·ic** *adjective* [Gaelic & Irish *bárd*, Welsh *bardd*, from Old Celtic]

bard[2] *noun* a slice of fat, e.g. salt pork or bacon, placed on meat or game before roasting. ● *transitive verb* cover (meat etc.) with bards. [French *barde*, originally = horse's breastplate, ultimately from Arabic]

Bar·deen /bɑːˈdiːn/ **John** (1908–91), US physicist, who shared the 1956 and 1972 Nobel Prizes for physics for his work on solid state devices and superconductivity.

Bar·dot /bɑːˈdoː/ **Bri·gitte** (b.1934), French film actress and animal rights activist, considered a sex symbol because of her coquettish appeal.

bare ● *adjective* **1** (esp. of part of the body) unclothed or uncovered (*bare feet*). **2** without appropriate covering or contents: **a** (of a tree) leafless. **b** unfurnished; empty (*bare rooms; the cupboard was bare*). **c** (of a floor) uncarpeted. **d** (of ground) without vegetation (*bare rock*). **3** *N Amer.* (of a road, sidewalk, etc.) clear of snow and ice. **4 a** undisguised (*the bare truth*). **b** unadorned (*bare facts*). **5** (*attributive*) **a** scanty (*a bare majority*). **b** mere (*bare necessities*). ● *transitive verb* **1** uncover, unsheathe (*bared his teeth*). **2** reveal (*bared his soul*). □ **bare of** without. **lay bare** expose, reveal. **with one's bare hands** without using tools or weapons. □ **bare·ness** *noun* [Old English *bær*, *barian* from Germanic]

bare·back *adjective & adverb* **1** on an unsaddled horse etc. **2** *slang* (of sex) without a condom.

bare·boat *noun* (usu. *attributive*) a boat, esp. a sailboat, that is rented without a crew (*bareboat charter*).

bare bones *plural noun* essential parts or components (*pare the story down to its bare bones*). □ **bare-bones** *adjective*

Bare·bones Par·lia·ment the nickname of Oliver Cromwell's Parliament of 1653. [from one of its members, Praise-God Barbon]

bare·faced *adjective* undisguised; impudent (*barefaced lie*). □ **bare·faced·ly** *adverb* **bare·faced·ness** *noun*

bare·foot *adjective & adverb* (also **bare·foot·ed**) with nothing on the feet.

barefoot doctor *noun* a paramedical worker with basic medical training, esp. in China.

ba·rège /bəˈreːʒ/ *noun* a silky gauze made from wool or other material. [French from *Barèges* in SW France, where it was originally made]

bare-handed *adjective & adverb* with bare hands; without gloves.

bare-headed *adjective & adverb* without a covering for the head.

bare-knuckle *adjective* (also **bare-knuckled**) **1** *Boxing* without gloves; with bare fists. **2** without niceties (*bare-knuckle political campaign*).

bare-legged *adjective* not wearing hosiery or trousers.

bare·ly *adverb* **1** only just; scarcely (*barely escaped*). **2** scantily (*barely furnished*). **3** *archaic* openly, explicitly.

barely-there *attributive adjective informal* **1** inconspicuous. **2** (of clothing) skimpy.

Bar·en·boim /ˈberənˌboim/ **Dan·iel** (b.1942), Israeli pianist and conductor. He became musical director of the Orchestre de Paris (1975–88) and subsequently of the Chicago Symphony Orchestra in 1991.

Bar·ents /ˈberənts/ **Wil·lem** (d.1597), Dutch explorer. Searching for the Northeast Passage, Barents reached Spitsbergen and Novaya Zemlya, off the coast of which he died.

Barents Sea a shallow part of the Arctic Ocean, bounded by Norway,

Russia, and the islands of Novaya Zemlya, Spitsbergen, and Franz Josef Land.

barf *informal* ● *intransitive verb* vomit or retch. ● *noun* **1** vomited food, etc. **2** an attack of vomiting. ● *interjection* expressing disgust (*I have to clean the fridge. Barf!*). [prob. imitative]

barfi *noun var. of* BURFI.

bar·fly *noun* (*pl.* **-flies**) *informal* a person who frequents bars.

bar·gain ● *noun* **1 a** an agreement on the terms of a transaction or sale. **b** this seen from the buyer's viewpoint (*a bad bargain*). **2** something acquired or offered cheaply. ● *intransitive verb* (often foll. by *with, for*) discuss the terms of a transaction (*expected him to bargain, but he paid up; bargained with her; bargained for the table*). □ **bargain away** part with for something worthless (*had bargained away the farm*). **bargain for** (or **on**) (usu. with *neg.* actual or implied) be prepared for; expect (*didn't bargain on having bad weather; more than I bargained for*). **bargain on** rely on. **drive a hard bargain** pursue one's own profit in a transaction keenly. **into** (or **in**) **the bargain** moreover; in addition to what was expected. **make** (or **strike**) **a bargain** agree to a transaction. □ **bar·gain·er** *noun* [Old French *bargaine*, *bargaignier*, prob. from Germanic]

bargain basement ● *noun* a store, or basement of a store, where bargains are available. ● *adjective* **1** inexpensive, cheap. **2** inferior, poor-quality.

bargain bin *noun* a receptacle in a store where cheap or discounted items are placed.

bar·gain·ing agent *noun* an organization, e.g. a trade union, that negotiates on behalf of employees in collective bargaining.

bargaining chip *noun* something, as a potential concession etc., which can be used to advantage in negotiations.

bargaining table *noun* a table around which negotiations are conducted.

bargaining unit *noun* a group of workers united for the purpose of collective bargaining.

bargain price *noun* a price that is much less than usual or than one would expect. □ **bargain-priced** *adjective*

barge ● *noun* **1** a long flat-bottomed boat for carrying freight etc. **2** *Cdn* (*Nfld*) a large boat used to collect, hold, and process cod. **3** a long ornamental boat used for pleasure or ceremony. **4** a boat used by the chief officers of a man-of-war. ● *verb* **1 a** *transitive* transport (goods) on a barge. **b** *intransitive* travel by barge. **2** *intransitive* (often foll. by *around*) lurch or rush clumsily about. **3** *intransitive* (foll. by *in, into*) **a** intrude or interrupt rudely or awkwardly (*barged in while we were kissing*). **b** collide with (*barged into her*). [Old French perhaps from medieval Latin *barica* from Greek *baris* Egyptian boat]

barge·board *noun* a board (often ornamental) fixed to the gable end of a roof to hide the ends of the roof timbers. [perhaps from medieval Latin *bargus* gallows]

bar·gee *noun Brit.* a person in charge of or working on a barge.

barge pole *noun* a long pole used for punting barges etc. and for fending off obstacles. □ **would not touch with a barge pole** see TOUCH.

bar·goon *noun Cdn slang* a bargain. [alteration of BARGAIN]

bar graph *noun* (also **bar chart**) a graph using bars to represent quantity.

bar harbour *noun N Amer.* a harbour with an entrance that is partially obstructed by a sandbar.

bar-hop *intransitive verb N Amer.* (**-hopped**, **-hopping**) *informal* go from one bar to another, drinking but not staying long in each.

Bari an industrial seaport on the Adriatic coast of SE Italy, capital of Apulia region; pop. (2001) 312,452.

bari·at·ric /ˌberiˈatrik/ *adjective* (of medical care etc.) aimed at treating obesity. [Greek *barus* 'heavy' + *iatreia* 'healing']

Bari·loche see SAN CARLOS DE BARILOCHE.

Bari·sal /ˈbɑːrɪˌsal/ a river port in southern Bangladesh, on the Ganges delta; pop. (2002) 260,400.

bar·ista /bɑːˈriːstə/ *noun* (*pl.* **-tas**) a person who makes and serves coffee in a specialty coffee shop. [Italian, = bartender]

bar·ite /ˈberaɪt/ *noun* (also **bar·yte**) a mineral form of barium sulphate. *Also called* BARYTES. [Greek *barus* heavy, partly assimilated to mineral names in *-ites*]

bari·tone /ˈberɪˌtoːn/ ● *noun* **1 a** the second-lowest adult male singing voice. **b** a singer with this voice. **c** a part written for it. **2 a** an instrument that is second-lowest in pitch in its family. **b** its player.

● *adjective* of the second-lowest range. [Italian *baritono* from Greek *barutonos* from *barus* heavy + *tonos* TONE]

bar·ium /'beriəm, 'ba-/ *noun Chem.* **1** a white reactive soft metallic element of the alkaline-earth group. Symbol: **Ba**; at. no.: 56. **2** (usu. *attributive*) a mixture of barium sulphate and water, which is opaque to X-rays, and is given to patients requiring radiological examination of the stomach and intestines (*barium enema*; *barium X-ray*). [BARYTA + -IUM]

bark¹ ● *noun* **1** the sharp explosive cry of a dog, fox, etc. **2** a sound resembling this cry. ● *verb* **1** *intransitive* (of a dog, fox, etc.) give a bark. **2** *transitive & intransitive* speak or utter sharply or brusquely. **3** *intransitive* cough fiercely. **4** *transitive US* sell or advertise publicly by calling out. □ **one's bark is worse than one's bite** one is not as ferocious as one appears. **bark up the wrong tree** be on the wrong track; make an effort in the wrong direction. [Old English *beorcan*]

bark² ● *noun* **1** the tough protective outer sheath of the trunks, branches, and twigs of trees or woody shrubs. **2** this material used for tanning leather or dyeing material. **3** *N Amer.* a type of flat usu. chocolate candy containing nuts. ● *transitive verb* **1** graze or scrape (one's shin etc.). **2** strip bark from (a tree etc.). **3** tan or dye (leather etc.) using the tannins found in bark. **4** *Cdn (Nfld)* boil (nets, sails, etc.) in an infusion of conifer buds and bark as a preservative. [Old Icelandic *börkr* *bark-*: perhaps related to BIRCH]

bark³ *noun literary* a ship or boat. [= BARQUE]

bar·keep *noun* (also **bar·keep·er**) *N Amer. informal* a bartender.

bar·ken·tine *esp. US var. of* BARQUENTINE.

Bark·er, Wil·liam George 'Billy' (1894–1930), Canadian fighter pilot. Credited with 53 aerial victories during World War I, he was awarded the Victoria Cross for single-handed combat against some 60 enemy aircraft in October 1918. He was also the first director of the RCAF.

bark·er *noun* **1** a person who calls out loudly to attract customers to an auction, a stall at a fair, etc. **2** a dog etc. that barks persistently.

Bark·er·ville a restored urban site and historic park in east central BC, about 70 km east of Quesnel. It was the site of a large gold strike in 1862, a find which spawned the Cariboo gold rush. [W. *Barker*, who first discovered gold there d.1894]

bark·ing *adjective* (also **barking mad**) *Brit.* completely mad or demented.

Bark·ley Sound a wide bay of the Pacific Ocean, situated on the southwestern coast of Vancouver Island. It has several inlets, the longest of which is Alberni Inlet, and many small islands. [C. W. *Barkley*, captain of a sailing vessel d.1832]

Bark·ly Tableland a plateau region lying to the northeast of Tennant Creek in Northern Territory, Australia.

bar·ley *noun* any of various hardy awned cereals of the genus *Hordeum*, widely used as food and in malt liquors and spirits such as whisky. [Old English *bærlic* (adj.) from *bære, bere* barley]

barley·corn *noun* **1** the grain of barley. **2** a former unit of measure (about a third of an inch) based on the length of a grain of barley.

barley sandwich *noun esp. Cdn slang* a beer.

barley sugar *noun* an amber-coloured candy made of boiled sugar, traditionally shaped as a twisted stick.

barley water *noun* a drink made from water and a boiled barley mixture.

bar line *noun Music* a vertical line used to mark divisions between bars.

barm *noun* **1** the froth on fermenting malt liquor. **2** *archaic* or *dialect* yeast or leaven. [Old English *beorma*]

bar·maid *noun* a female bartender.

bar·man *noun* (pl. **-men**) a male bartender.

barm·brack *noun* (also **barn·brack**) *Irish* soft spicy bread with currants etc. [Irish *bairigen breac* speckled cake]

Bar·me·cide /'bɑrmə,said/ ● *adjective* illusory, imaginary; such as to disappoint. ● *noun* a giver of benefits that are illusory or disappointing. [the name of a wealthy man in the *Arabian Nights' Entertainments* who gave a beggar a feast consisting of ornate but empty dishes]

bar mitz·vah /bɑr 'mɪtzvə/ ● *noun* **1** the religious initiation ceremony of a Jewish boy who has reached the age of 13. **2** the boy undergoing this ceremony. ● *transitive verb* (in *passive*) cause to undergo this ceremony. [Hebrew, = 'son of the commandment']

barmy *adjective* (**barm·i·er, barm·i·est**) *esp. Brit. informal* crazy, stupid. □ **barm·i·ly** *adverb* **barm·i·ness** *noun* [earlier = frothy, from BARM]

barn¹ *noun* **1** a large farm building for housing animals, storing grain, etc. **2** *derogatory* a large plain or unattractive building. **3** *N Amer.* a large

shed for storing road or railway vehicles. [Old English *bern, beren* from *bere* barley + *ern, ærn* house]

barn² *noun Physics* a unit of area, 10^{-28} square metres, used esp. in particle physics. Symbol: **b**. [perhaps from phrase 'as big as a barn']

Bar·na·bas /'bɑrnəbəs/ **St.** (1st c.), a Levite, born in Cyprus, who became one of the earliest disciples of Christ at Jerusalem. He introduced St. Paul to the Apostles and accompanied him in the first missionary journey to Cyprus and Asia Minor.

bar·nacle /'bɑrnəkəl/ *noun* **1** any of various species of small marine crustaceans of the class Cirripedia which in adult form cling to rocks, ships' bottoms, etc. **2** a tenacious attendant or follower who cannot easily be shaken off. □ **bar·nacled** *adjective* [Middle English *bernak* (= medieval Latin *bernaca*), of unknown origin]

barnacle goose *noun* an Arctic goose, *Branta leucopsis*, which winters in N Europe.

Bar·nard ▸ **1 Chris·ti·aan Neeth·ling** (1922–2001), South African surgeon, who performed the first human heart transplant in Dec. 1967. **2 Ed·ward Emer·son** (1857–1923), US astronomer. He pioneered celestial photography, and discovered Jupiter's fifth satellite (1892) and the second-nearest star to the sun (1916), which is named after him.

Bar·nar·do /bɑr'nɑrdo,/ **Thom·as John** (1845–1905), British philanthropist and founder of a chain of homes for destitute children. Approximately 30,000 of these children, known as **Barnardo children**, were sent as immigrants to Canada after 1870.

Bar·naul /,bɑrnə'uːl/ a city in SW Siberia; pop. (est. 2002) 580,100.

barn·board *noun N Amer.* (also **barn·wood**) wide softwood boards that have not been planed, used esp. for building barns.

barn·brack *var. of* BARMBRACK.

barn·burn·er *noun N Amer. informal* **1** something exciting or successful. **2** a lively or exciting esp. political speech (*delivered a two-hour barnburner*). **3** a game or competition that has a close result (*the game was a 2–1 barnburner*). [originally the nickname of a radical wing of the US Democratic Party in 19th c.]

barn dance *noun* **1** an informal social gathering for dancing, originally in a barn. **2** a dance for a number of couples forming a line or circle, with couples moving along it in turn.

bar·ney *noun* (pl. **-neys**) *Brit. informal* a noisy quarrel. [origin unknown]

barn owl *noun* an owl of the genus *Tyto*, esp. *T. alba*, which usu. has a white face and underside and frequently nests in farm buildings.

barn rais·ing *noun N Amer.* a gathering of people to put up the framework of a neighbour's barn, usu. followed by a dance.

Barns·ley a town in South Yorkshire, England; pop. (est. 1999) 221,000.

barn·storm *verb* **1** *N Amer.* **a** *intransitive* make a rapid tour holding political meetings. **b** *transitive* visit (an area) to hold such meetings. **2** *intransitive N Amer.* give informal flying exhibitions, esp. at country fairs etc.; do stunt flying. **3** *intransitive* tour rural districts giving theatrical performances (formerly often in barns). **4** *intransitive* (of a sports team) tour through an area playing exhibition games. □ **barn·storm·er** *noun*

barn swallow *noun N Amer.* the common swallow, *Hirundo rustica*, which builds mud nests on buildings such as barns.

Bar·num, Phin·eas Tay·lor (1810–91), US circus impresario famous for his extravagant advertising. He created the Greatest Show on Earth (1871) and, with J.A. Bailey, founded the Barnum and Bailey Circus (1881).

barn·wood *noun N Amer.* = BARNBOARD.

barn·yard *noun* **1** the usu. fenced area around a barn. **2** (*attributive*) earthy, coarse (*barnyard humour*).

barnyard grass *noun* a millet, *Echinochloa crus-galli*, which is a common weed in many parts of the world.

Bar·oda /bə'roːdə/ see VADODARA.

baro·graph /'bærə,graf/ *noun* a barometer equipped to record its readings. [Greek *baros* weight + -GRAPH]

Ba·ro·ja /bə'roːxə/ **Pio** (full name Pio Baroja y Nessi) (1872–1956), Spanish Basque novelist. His series of 22 novels known as *Memorias de un hombre de acción* (1913–34) provides a panoramic portrait of Spain.

Ba·ro·lo /bə'roːloː/ *noun* (pl. **Ba·ro·los**) a full-bodied red Italian wine from the Barolo region of Piedmont in N Italy.

bar·om·eter /bə'rɒmɪtər/ *noun* **1** an instrument measuring atmospheric pressure, esp. in forecasting the weather and determining altitude. **2** anything which reflects changes in circumstances, opinions, etc. □ **baro·met·ric** /,berə'metrɪk/ *adjective*

bar·on *noun* **1** a member of the lowest order of nobility in the United

Kingdom or other countries. **2** an important businessman or other powerful or influential person (*timber baron*; *newspaper baron*). **3** *hist.* a person who held lands or property from the sovereign or a powerful overlord. [Old French *baron* from medieval Latin *baro, -onis* man, of unknown origin]

baron·age *noun* barons or nobles collectively.

baron·ess *noun* **1** a woman holding the rank of baron either as a life peerage or as a hereditary rank. **2** the wife or widow of a baron.

baron·et *noun* a member of the lowest hereditary titled British order, below a baron but above a knight. [Anglo-Latin *baronettus* (as BARON)]

baron·et·age *noun* baronets collectively.

baron·etcy *noun* (*pl.* **-cies**) the domain, rank, or tenure of a baronet.

baron·ial /bəˈroːniəl/ *adjective* **1** of or relating to a baron or barons. **2** in the turreted style characteristic of Scottish country houses.

baron of beef *noun* a roast of beef consisting of two sirloins left joined at the backbone.

bar·ony /ˈberəni/ *noun* (*pl.* **-ies**) **1** the domain, rank, or tenure of a baron. **2** (in Ireland) a division of a county. **3** (in Scotland) a large manor or estate.

bar·oque /bəˈroːk/ ● *noun* **1** a style of architecture and decorative art of the late 16th to early 18th c., characterized by extensive ornamentation. **2** a style of music from the period 1600–1750, characterized by increasing harmonic complexity and emphasis on contrast. ● *adjective* **1** of or relating to this period or style. **2** highly ornate and complex. [French (originally = 'irregular pearl') from Portuguese *barroco*, of unknown origin]

bar·ouche /bəˈruːʃ/ *noun* a horse-drawn carriage with four wheels and a collapsible hood over the rear half, used esp. in the 19th c. [German (dial.) *Barutsche* from Italian *baroccio*, ultimately from Latin *birotus* two-wheeled]

barque /bark/ *noun* **1** a sailing ship with the rear mast fore-and-aft-rigged and the remaining (usu. two) masts square-rigged. **2** *literary* any boat. [French prob. from Provençal *barca* from Latin *barca* ship's boat]

bar·quen·tine /ˈbarkənˌtiːn/ *noun* (also esp. *US* **bar·ken·tine**) a sailing ship with the foremast square-rigged and the remaining (usu. two) masts fore-and-aft-rigged. [BARQUE after *brigantine*]

Bar·quisi·meto /ˌbarkəsəˈmeitoː/ a city in NW Venezuela; pop. (est. 2002) 919,500.

bar·rack¹ ● *noun* (usu. in *pl.*, often treated as *sing.*) **1** a building or building complex used to house soldiers. **2** *Cdn* a building housing a local detachment of the RCMP. **3** any building used to accommodate large numbers of people. **4** a large building with a bleak or plain appearance. **5** *Cdn* (*Maritimes*) a structure, consisting of four posts and an adjustable roof, which protects hay etc. from rain or snow. ● *transitive verb* place (soldiers etc.) in barracks. [French *baraque* from Italian *baracca* or Spanish *barraca* soldier's tent, of unknown origin]

bar·rack² *verb Brit., Austral., & NZ* **1** *transitive* shout or jeer at (players in a game, a performer, speaker, etc.). **2** *intransitive* (of spectators at games etc.) shout or jeer. [prob. from Irish *barrack* 'brag']

bar·ra·cuda /ˌberəˈkuːdə/ *noun* (*pl.* same or **bar·ra·cudas**) a large and voracious tropical marine fish of the family Sphyraenidae. [Latin American Spanish *barracuda*]

bar·rage /bəˈrɒʒ/ ● *noun* **1** a concentrated artillery bombardment over a wide area. **2** a rapid succession of questions or criticisms. **3** an artificial barrier, esp. in a river. **4** a heat or deciding event in fencing, show jumping, etc. ● *transitive verb* subject to a barrage of artillery fire, questions, etc. [French from *barrer* (as BAR¹)]

barrage balloon *noun* a large anchored balloon, often with netting suspended from it, used (usu. as one of a series) as a defence against low-flying aircraft.

bar·ra·mundi /ˌberəˈmʌndi/ *noun* (*pl.* same or **bar·ra·mundis**) any of various edible Australian freshwater fishes, esp. *Lates calcarifer*. [prob. Aboriginal (Queensland)]

Bar·ran·quilla /ˌbarənˈkiːjə/ the chief port of Colombia, at the mouth of the Magdalena River, near the Caribbean; pop. (est. 2002) 1,298,400.

bar·ra·sway /ˈbarəˌswai/ *noun Cdn* (*Nfld*) = BARACHOIS.

bar·ra·try /ˈbarətri/ *noun* **1** fraud or gross negligence of a ship's master or crew at the expense of its owners or users. **2** *hist.* vexatious litigation or incitement to it. **3** *hist.* trade in the sale of Church or state appointments. □ **bar·ra·tor** *noun* **bar·ra·trous** *adjective* [Old French *baraterie* deceit, from *barat* deceit, fraud, trouble, etc.]

Bar·rault /baˈroː/ **Jean-Louis** (1910–94), French actor and director. He directed a number of acclaimed films, including *Les Enfants du paradis* (1945) and *The Longest Day* (1962).

Barr Colonists a group of about 2000 English colonists, led originally by the Rev. Isaac Barr, who settled the area west of Saskatoon from 1903 onward.

barre *noun* **1** a waist-level horizontal bar to help dancers keep their balance during some exercises. **2** dance exercises done at a barre. [French]

barré /ˈbarei/ *noun Music* a method of playing a chord on the guitar etc. with a finger laid across the strings at a particular fret, raising their pitch. [French, past participle of *barrer* bar]

barred owl *noun* a large owl, *Strix varia*, with large brown vertical streaks on its breast, which inhabits the southern boreal forest of N America.

bar·rel ● *noun* **1** a cylindrical container usu. bulging out in the middle, made of wooden staves with metal hoops around them, or of plastic or metal. **2** the contents of this. **3** a measure of capacity, usu. varying from 30 to 40 imperial gallons (136 to 182 litres). **4** a unit of capacity for oil and petroleum products equal to 35 imperial gallons (about 159 litres). **5** the cylindrical body or trunk of an object, e.g. a pump, pen, etc. **6** the metal tube of a gun, through which the shot is discharged. **7** the fuel outlet from the carburetor on a gasoline engine. **8** the trunk of a horse etc. ● *verb* (**bar·relled**, **bar·rel·ling**; also esp. *US* **bar·reled**, **bar·rel·ing**) **1** *transitive* put into a barrel or barrels. **2** *intransitive N Amer. informal* move quickly (*barrel along the road*). □ **barrel of fun** (or **laughs**) *informal* a great deal of fun. **over a barrel** *informal* in a helpless position; at a person's mercy. **scrape** (**the bottom of**) **the barrel** see SCRAPE. [Old French *baril* perhaps from Romanic: related to BAR¹]

barrel cactus *noun* a cactus of the genus *Echinocactus* with spiny ribs, grown as a houseplant.

barrel-chested *adjective* having a large rounded chest.

barrel·head *noun* the flat top of a barrel. □ **on the barrelhead** *N Amer.* immediately and up front (*paid cash on the barrelhead*).

barrel·house *noun* **1** a disreputable or cheap bar. **2** (often *attributive*) an unrestrained and uninhibited style of jazz music.

barrel-jumping *noun Cdn* a sport in which a skater jumps over a row of barrels lying on their sides.

barrel organ *noun* a mechanical musical instrument in which a rotating pin-studded cylinder acts on a series of pipe valves, strings, or metal tongues.

barrel race *noun N Amer.* a women's rodeo event in which a mounted rider must navigate a triangular arrangement of three barrels and return to the starting line. □ **barrel racer** *noun* **barrel racing** *noun*

barrel roll *noun* an aerobatic manoeuvre in which an aircraft rolls once about its longitudinal axis.

barrel vault *noun Archit.* a vault formed by an extended round arch or series of arches. □ **barrel-vaulted** *adjective*

bar·ren ● *adjective* (**barren·er**, **barren·est**) **1 a** unable to bear young. **b** unable to produce fruit or vegetation. **2** meagre, unprofitable. **3** dull, unstimulating. **4** (foll. by *of*) lacking in (*barren of wit*). ● *noun* **1** (in eastern N America) a tract of elevated flat land that supports shrubs and bushes but no trees. **2** *Cdn* (*NB & NS*) an expanse of marsh or muskeg. **3** (in *pl.*) *Cdn* see BARRENS, THE. □ **bar·ren·ly** *adverb* **barren·ness** *noun* [Anglo-French *barai(g)ne*, Old French *barhaine* etc., of unknown origin]

barren ground caribou *noun* a caribou, *Rangifer tarandus groenlandicus*, native to the tundra of N Canada.

Barrens, the *plural noun* (also **bar·rens**, **Barren Grounds**, **Barren Lands**) *Cdn* the treeless, sparsely populated region of N Canada, lying between Hudson Bay and Great Slave and Great Bear lakes.

Bar·rett see BROWNING, Elizabeth Barrett.

bar·rette /bəˈret/ *noun* a bar-shaped clip or ornament for a woman's or girl's hair. [French]

bar·ri·cade ● *noun* a barrier, esp. one improvised across a street etc. ● *transitive verb* block or defend with a barricade. [French from *barrique* cask, from Spanish *barrica*, related to BARREL]

Bar·rie¹ a city in south central Ontario, situated on Lake Simcoe, about 75 km north of Toronto; pop. (2001) 103,710. [Sir R. *Barrie*, naval officer d.1841]

Bar·rie², **Sir James Mat·thew** (1860–1937), Scottish dramatist and novelist, author of *Peter Pan* (1904).

bar·rier *noun* **1** a fence or other obstacle that bars advance or access. **2** an obstacle or circumstance that keeps people or things apart, or prevents communication (*class barriers*; *a language barrier*). **3** anything that prevents progress or success. **4** a gate at a parking garage etc., that controls access. **5** an exposed sandbar that parallels a coast, as on the

uː **m**ood aɪ **m**y əɪ **p**ipe aʊ **br**own ʌu **h**ouse eɪ **d**ay ɔɪ **b**oy ã **fr**anglais ã **Cana**dien ɔ̃ **Bra**yon   (*see over for consonants*)

north shore of PEI (*barrier island; barrier beach*). **6** *informal* = SOUND BARRIER. **7** something that prevents transmission of a substance. *See also* VAPOUR BARRIER. [Old French *barriere*]

barrier cream *noun Brit.* a cream used to protect the skin from damage or infection.

barrier-free *adjective* designating buildings etc that offer no barriers to freedom of movement by people in wheelchairs.

barrier method *noun* a method of contraception using a device or preparation that prevents live sperm from reaching an ovum.

barrier reef *noun* a coral reef separated from the shore by a broad deep channel.

bar·ring *preposition* in the absence of (*barring complications, all should go well*).

bar·rio /ˈbɑːrɪoː, ˈbaˌ-/ *noun* (*pl.* **-rios**) **1** a ward or quarter of town in Spain and Spanish-speaking countries. **2** (in the US) the Spanish-speaking quarter of a town or city. [Spanish, = district of a town]

bar·rique /baˈriːk/ *noun* **1** a wine barrel, varying in size according to place of origin, esp. that of Bordeaux. **2** a small cask of new oak in which wine is aged. [French]

bar·ris·ter *noun* (in full **barrister-at-law**) **1** *Cdn* a lawyer who pleads cases before the courts. ¶ In Canada the term is used mainly by members of the legal profession. All lawyers in Canadian common law provinces are both barristers and solicitors. **2** *Brit.* a person called to the bar and entitled to practise as an advocate in the higher courts. *Compare* SOLICITOR 2. [16th c.: from BAR[1], perhaps after *minister*]

barrister and solicitor *noun Cdn* a lawyer.

bar·room *noun* = BAR[1] 4b.

bar·row[1] *noun* **1** = WHEELBARROW. **2** *Cdn* (*Nfld*) a flat, rectangular wooden frame with handles at both ends, used by two people to carry fish etc. **3** *Brit.* a two-wheeled handcart used esp. by street vendors. **4** *Brit.* a metal frame with two wheels used for transporting luggage etc. [Old English *bearwe* from Germanic]

bar·row[2] *noun Archaeology* a mound of earth constructed in ancient times to cover one or more burials. [Old English *beorg* from Germanic]

bar·row[3] *noun N Amer.* a castrated boar. [Old English *b(e)arg*]

barrow boy *noun Brit.* a man who sells goods from a barrow.

barrow pit *noun* = BORROW PIT. [possibly with reference to BARROW[2], possibly altered to reflect regional pronunciation of BORROW]

Barry, Sir Charles (1795–1860), English architect, who designed the Houses of Parliament in London (1840–60).

Barry·more ▸ 1 Ethel (1879–1959), US actress. She appeared on stage, radio, television and film, and the Ethel Barrymore Theater in New York was named in her honour in 1928. **2** her brother **John** (1882–1942), US theatre and film actor and light comedian, considered one of the greatest and handsomest actors of his time. **3** their brother **Lionel** (1878–1954), US film and theatre actor. In later life he often played testy, irascible characters from his wheelchair.

Bar·sac *noun* a sweet white wine from the district of Barsac, department of Gironde, in SW France.

bar sinister *noun* = BEND SINISTER.

bar stool *noun* a high, usu. cushioned stool for sitting at bars or counters.

Bart, Lionel (1930–99), English composer and lyricist, whose *Oliver!* achieved 2,618 performances, setting a new record for a musical.

Bart. *abbreviation* Baronet.

bar·tend·er *noun* a person serving drinks at a bar. □ **bar·tend** *intransitive verb* **bar·tend·ing** *noun*

bar·ter ● *verb* **1** *transitive* exchange (goods or services) without using money. **2** *intransitive* make such an exchange. ● *noun* trade by exchange of goods. □ **bar·ter·er** *noun* [prob. Old French *barater*: see BARRATRY]

Barth ▸ 1 John Sim·mons (b.1930), US novelist, whose complex, experimental novels include *The Sot-Weed Factor* (1960) and *Letters* (1979). **2 Karl** (1886–1968), Swiss Protestant theologian who sought a return to the Reformation and the teachings of the Bible. He stressed humanity's utter dependence on divine grace, and argued that human reason was worthless in comparison to the supremacy and transcendence of God. □ **Barth·ian** *noun & adjective*

Barthes /bɑrt/ **Ro·land** (1915–80), French literary critic. A prominent structuralist and post-structuralist, Barthes was severely criticized for his attack on traditional methods of literary analysis. □ **Barthes·ian** *adjective*

Bar·tholdi /bɑrˈtoːldi/ **Fré·dé·ric Au·guste** (1834–1904), French

sculptor and architect, best known for designing the Statue of Liberty (1886).

Bar·tholo·mew /bɑrˈθɒləˌmjuː/ **St.** (1st c.), one of the twelve Apostles. He is said to have been flayed alive, and is hence regarded as the patron saint of tanners.

bar·ti·zan /ˈbɑrtɪzən, ˌbɑrtɪˈzan/ *noun Archit.* a battlemented parapet or an overhanging corner turret at the top of a castle or church tower. □ **bar·ti·zaned** *adjective* [var. of *bertisene*, erroneous spelling of *bratticing*: see BRATTICE]

Bart·lett pear *noun* esp. *N Amer.* a large, yellow, juicy variety of pear. [E. *Bartlett*, US merchant d.1860]

Bar·tók /ˈbɑrtɒk/ **Béla** (1881–1945), Hungarian composer. His work owes much to Hungarian folk music, and includes six string quartets, three piano concertos, and the *Concerto for Orchestra* (1943).

Bar·tolom·meo /ˌbɑrtɒlɒˈmeɪɔ/ **Fra Baccio della Porta** (c.1472–1517), Florentine painter of the period of transition between the early and the High Renaissance. His large-scale works are restrained and austere, and his ideals were balance and simplicity.

Bar·ton ▸ 1 Sir Derek H(ar·old) R(ich·ard) (1918–98), English organic chemist, who shared the 1969 Nobel Prize for chemistry for his research on conformational analysis. **2 Sir Ed·mund** (1849–1920), Australian political leader and jurist. He was co-leader of the Australian Federation movement from 1896, and he became the first prime minister of Australia (1901–3).

Bar·uch /ˈbɑrʊk/ a book of the Apocrypha, attributed in the text to Baruch, the scribe of Jeremiah.

bary·on /ˈberiˌɒn/ *noun Physics* any of the heavier elementary particles (protons, neutrons, hyperons). □ **bary·on·ic** /-ˈɒnɪk/ *adjective* [Greek *barus* heavy + -ON]

Barysh·nikov /bəˈrɪʃnɪkɒf/ **Mik·hail Niko·lai·evich** (b.1948), Soviet-born US dancer, generally considered the greatest of his generation. He defected while on tour in Canada in 1974, and was the director of American Ballet Theatre from 1980–1990. Since 1990 he has danced with and been the director of the White Oak Dance Project, a modern dance group.

bary·sphere /ˈberiˌsfɪːr/ *noun* the dense interior of the earth, including the mantle and core, enclosed by the lithosphere. [Greek *barus* heavy + *sphaira* sphere]

baryta /bəˈraɪtə/ *noun* barium oxide or hydroxide. □ **ba·ryt·ic** /-ˈrɪtɪk/ *adjective* [BARYTES, after *soda* etc.]

ba·rytes /bəˈraɪtiːz/ *noun* = BARITE.

BAS *abbreviation Anglicanism* Book of Alternative Services.

basal *adjective* **1** of, at, or forming a base. **2** fundamental.

basal metabolism *noun* the chemical processes occurring in an organism at complete rest.

bas·alt /ˈbasɒlt/ *noun* a dark basic volcanic rock whose strata sometimes form columns. □ **bas·alt·ic** /bəˈsɒltɪk/ *adjective* [Latin *basaltes* var. of *basanites* from Greek from *basanos* touchstone]

B.A.Sc. *abbreviation* Bachelor of Applied Science.

bas·cule bridge /ˈbaskjuːl/ *noun* a type of drawbridge which is raised and lowered using counterweights. [French, earlier *bacule* see-saw, from *battre* bump + *cul* buttocks]

base[1] ● *noun* **1 a** a part that supports from beneath or serves as a foundation for an object or structure. **b** a notional structure or entity on which something draws or depends (*power base*). **2** a principle or starting point; a basis. **3 a** a place from which an operation or activity is directed. **b** *Military* a military installation from which operations are conducted and where equipment and supporting facilities are concentrated. **4 a** a main or important ingredient of a mixture. **b** a substance, e.g. water, in combination with which pigment forms paint etc. **5** a substance used as a foundation for makeup. **6** *Chem.* a substance capable of combining with an acid to form a salt and water and usu. producing hydroxide ions when dissolved in water. **7** *Math.* a number in terms of which other numbers or logarithms are expressed (see RADIX). **8** *Archit.* the part of a column between the shaft and pedestal or pavement. **9** *Geom.* a line or surface on which a figure is regarded as standing. **10** *Surveying* a known line used as a geometrical base for trigonometry. **11** *Electronics* the middle part of a transistor separating the emitter from the collector. **12** *Linguistics* a root or stem as the origin of a word or a derivative. **13** *Baseball* one of the four stations that must be reached in turn when scoring a run. **14** *Bot. & Zool.* the end at which a part or organ is attached to the main part. **15** *Heraldry* the lowest part of a shield. ● *transitive verb* **1** (usu. foll. by *on*, *upon*) found or establish (*a theory based on speculation; her opinion was soundly based*). **2** (foll. by *at*, *in*, etc.) station (*troops were based in Cyprus*).

Consonants: b *but*   d *dog*   f *few*   g *get*   h *her*   j *yes*   k *cat*   l *leg*   m *man*   n *no*   p *pen*   r *red*   s *sit*

☐ **cover** (or **touch**) **all the bases** *N Amer. informal* deal with all the related details. **make it to** (or **reach** etc.) **first base** *esp. N Amer. informal* achieve the first step of an objective, plan, etc. **off base 1** *Baseball* not touching a base. **2** *esp. N Amer. informal* **a** mistaken. **b** unprepared, unawares. **touch base** *esp. N Amer. informal* contact or communicate (with someone). [French *base* or Latin *basis* stepping, from Greek]

base² *adjective* **1** lacking moral worth; cowardly, despicable. **2** menial. **3** not pure; alloyed (*base coin*). **4** (of a metal) low in value (compare PRECIOUS METAL, NOBLE METAL). ☐ **base·ly** *adverb* **base·ness** *noun* [Middle English in sense 'of small height', from French *bas* from medieval Latin *bassus* short (in Latin as a cognomen)]

base·ball *noun* **1** a game played with teams of nine in which a batter must hit a ball (thrown by the opposing team's pitcher) with a bat, and then complete a diamond-shaped circuit of four bases to score a run. **2** the ball used in this game.

baseball cap *noun* (also **baseball hat**) a cap with a rounded visor and soft, rounded crown, often with a crest on the front.

base·board *noun N Amer.* a strip of wood along the bottom of a wall in a house.

baseboard heater *noun N Amer.* a heater attached to a wall near the floor, esp. one which provides heat by means of a radiant electric coil.

base camp *noun* a camp from which mountaineering expeditions set out or from which a particular activity can be carried out.

base·head *noun slang* a person who habitually takes freebased cocaine or crack.

base hit *noun Baseball* a hit that enables the batter to reach base without a fielder's error and without forcing out a runner already on base.

BASE jump *noun* a parachute jump from a fixed point, typically a high building or promontory, rather than an aircraft. ☐ **BASE jumper** *noun* **BASE jumping** *noun* [acronym of building, *a*ntenna, *s*pan, *e*arth, denoting the types of structures used]

Basel /ˈbɒzəl/ a commercial, industrial and administrative city on the Rhine in NE Switzerland; pop. (est. 2002) 163,800.

base·less *adjective* unfounded, groundless. ☐ **base·less·ness** *noun*

base·line *noun* **1** a line used as a base or starting point. **2** the area on a baseball diamond within which a runner must remain when running between bases. **3** (in tennis, basketball, etc.) the line marking each end of the court. **4** (usu. *attributive*) a basic level or standard; something which serves as a basis (*baseline health study; a baseline for further observation*). **5** a line which serves as the basis for subsequent surveying lines in a town or township.

base·load *noun* the permanent load on power supplies etc.

base lodge *noun* a building at the foot of the slopes in a ski resort, offering various services such as restaurants, equipment sales, lodging, etc.

base·man *noun* (pl. **-men**) (usu. in *combination*) *Baseball* a player whose position is first, second, or third base (*first baseman*).

base·ment *noun* **1** the lowest floor of a building, at least partly below ground level. **2** *N Amer. Sport informal* the lowest position in the standings. [prob. Dutch, perhaps from Italian *basamento* column base]

ba·sen·ji /bəˈsendʒɪ/ *noun* a smallish hunting dog of a central African breed, which growls and yelps but does not bark. [Bantu]

base pair *noun Biochem.* a pair of complementary bases, one in each strand of double-stranded nucleic acid, held together by a hydrogen bond.

base·path *noun Baseball* **1** the prescribed path for a baserunner extending between consecutive bases or between first or third base and home plate. **2** (in *pl.*) *informal* the aspect of the game concerned with running or stealing bases (*this team is a disaster on the basepaths*).

base rate *noun Brit.* the interest rate set by the Bank of England, used as the basis for other banks' rates.

base·run·ner *noun Baseball* a member of the batting team who is on base or running between bases. ☐ **base·run·ning** *noun*

bases pl. of BASE¹, BASIS.

base station *noun* **1** a stationary installation serving to facilitate the transmission or reception of mobile wireless communications of various kinds. **2** a Citizens' Band radio transceiver intended for use at a fixed location. **3** a relay station located at the centre of any of the cells of a cellular telephone network. **4** a short-range transceiver which connects a portable cordless telephone to the normal telephone network.

base unit *noun* a unit (of measurement etc.) that is defined arbitrarily and not by combinations of other units.

bash ● *verb* **1** *transitive* **a** strike bluntly or heavily. **b** *informal* attack violently. **c** (often foll. by *in, down,* etc.) damage or break by striking forcibly. **2** *intransitive* (foll. by *into*) collide with. **3** *transitive* (often as **bash·ing** *noun*) *informal* deride, criticize (*bashing the government; Toronto-bashing*). ● *noun* **1** a heavy blow. **2** *informal* a party or social event. ☐ **have a bash at** *Brit. informal* make an attempt at (*had a bash at painting*). ☐ **bash·er** *noun* [imitative, perhaps from *bang, smash, dash,* etc.]

bash·ful *adjective* **1** shy, diffident, self-conscious. **2** sheepish. ☐ **bash·ful·ly** *adverb* **bash·ful·ness** *noun* [obsolete *bash* (v.), = ABASH]

bash·ing *noun* = GAY BASHING.

Bash·kiria /baʃˈkiːrɪə/ (also called **Bash·kir Autonomous Republic**, **Bash·kor·to·stan**) an autonomous republic in central Russia, west of the Urals; pop. (est. 1990) 3,964,000; capital, Ufa. ☐ **Bash·kir** *noun*

Basho /bɒˈʃoː/ (full name Matsuo Basho; born Matsuo Munefusa) (1644–94), Japanese poet, known for his haiku.

BASIC /ˈbeɪsɪk/ *noun* a computer programming language using familiar English words, designed for beginners and widely used on microcomputers. [*B*eginner's *A*ll-purpose *S*ymbolic *I*nstruction *C*ode]

basic ● *adjective* **1** forming or serving as a base. **2** fundamental. **3 a** simplest or lowest in level (*basic requirements*). **b** vulgar (*basic humour*). **4** *Chem.* having the properties of or containing a base. **5** *Geol.* (of volcanic rocks etc.) having less than 50 per cent silica. **6** *Metallurgy* of or produced in a furnace etc. which is made of a basic material. ● *noun* (usu. in *pl.*) the fundamental facts or principles. ☐ **back to (the) basics** a catch phrase applied to a movement or enthusiasm for a return to the fundamental principles in education etc. or to policies reflecting this.

basic·ally *adverb* **1** in the most essential respects; fundamentally. **2** used to indicate that a statement summarizes the most important aspects, or gives a roughly accurate account, of a more complex situation.

basic cable *noun* the package of cable television channels offered to all subscribers, usu. not including specialty channels.

basic dye *noun* a dye consisting of salts of organic bases.

Basic English *noun* a simplified form of English, limited to 850 selected words, intended for international communication.

basic industry *noun* an industry of fundamental economic importance.

bas·icity /beɪˈsɪsɪtɪ/ *noun Chem.* the number of hydrogen atoms replaceable by a base in a particular acid.

basic slag *noun* phosphate-rich slag from basic steelmaking, frequently used as a fertilizer.

basic training *noun* a period of initial training in the police, armed forces, etc.

ba·sid·ium /bəˈsɪdɪəm/ *noun* (pl. **ba·sidia** /-dɪə/) a microscopic spore-bearing structure produced by certain fungi. [modern Latin from Greek *basidion* diminutive of BASIS]

Basie /ˈbeɪsi/ **Wil·liam** ('Count') (1904–84), US jazz bandleader. The big band he formed in 1935 became one of the most successful bands of the swing era.

Basil /ˈbazəl/ **St.** (*c.*330–79), a Doctor of the Church who defended orthodoxy against the Arian heresy, and developed a monastic rule.

bas·il /ˈbazəl, ˈbeɪzəl/ *noun* an aromatic herb of the genus *Ocimum*, esp. *O. basilicum* (in full **sweet basil**), whose leaves are used as a flavouring in savoury dishes. [Old French *basile* from medieval Latin *basilicus* from Greek *basilikos* royal]

basi·lar /ˈbazɪlər/ *adjective* of or at the base (esp. of the skull). [modern Latin *basilaris* (as BASIS)]

Ba·sil·ian /bəˈzɪlɪən/ ● *noun* **1** a member of the Congregation of St. Basil (Basilian Fathers), an esp. teaching order of Roman Catholic priests. **2** a member of any of several Eastern-rite religious orders following the rule of St. Basil. ● *adjective* of or relating to St. Basil, or to these religious orders. [Latin *Basilius* Basil]

ba·sil·ica /bəˈsɪlɪkə, bəˈzɪl-/ *noun* **1** an ancient Roman public hall with an apse and colonnades, used as a law court and place of assembly. **2** a similar building used as a Christian church. **3** a title of honour awarded to certain Catholic churches by the Pope. ☐ **ba·sil·ican** *adjective* [Latin from Greek *basilikē* (*oikia, stoa*) royal (house, portico) from *basileus* king]

Ba·sili·cata /bə·sɪlɪˈkɒtə/ a region of southern Italy, lying between Apulia and Calabria; capital, Potenza.

basi·lisk /ˈbazɪlɪsk/ noun **1** a mythical reptile with a lethal breath and look. **2** any small tropical American lizard of the genus *Basiliscus*, with a crest from its back to its tail. **3** *Heraldry* a cockatrice. [Latin *basiliscus* from Greek *basiliskos* kinglet, serpent]

basin noun **1 a** a wide shallow open container, esp. one for holding water. **b** a bathroom sink. **2** a hollow rounded depression. **3** any sheltered area of water where boats can moor safely. **4** a round valley. **5** an area drained by rivers and tributaries. **6** *Geol.* **a** a rock formation where the strata dip towards the centre. **b** an accumulation of rock strata formed in this dip as a result of subsidence and sedimentation. □ **basin·ful** noun (pl. **-fuls**). [Old French *bacin* from medieval Latin *ba(s)cinus*, perhaps from Gaulish]

basip·etal /beɪˈsɪpɪtəl/ adjective *Bot.* (of each new part produced) growing or developing nearer the base than the previous one did (compare ACROPETAL). □ **basip·etal·ly** adverb [BASIS + Latin *petere* seek]

basis noun (pl. **bases** /-siːz/) **1** the foundation or support of something, esp. an idea or argument. **2** the main or determining principle or ingredient (*on a purely friendly basis*). **3** the starting point for a discussion etc. [Latin from Greek, = BASE¹]

basis point noun one-hundredth of one per cent (of interest rates etc.).

bask intransitive verb **1** sit or lie back lazily in warmth and light (*basking in the sun*). **2** (foll. by *in*) derive great pleasure (from) (*basking in glory*). [Middle English, apparently from Old Norse: related to BATHE]

Bas·ka·tong, Réservoir /baskɒˈtɒŋ/ a reservoir in SW central Quebec, situated along the Gatineau River, about 150 km north of Gatineau. [Algonquin, = place where sand holds back the water]

Bas·ker·ville, John (1706–75), English printer, who designed the typeface that bears his name.

bas·ket noun **1** a container made of interwoven cane etc. **2** a container resembling this. **3** the amount held by a basket. **4** *Basketball* **a** a net fixed on a ring attached to a backboard and raised usu. about 10 feet above the surface of the court. **b** a goal scored through this. **5** a group, category; a range (*the consumer price index measures a broad basket of goods and services*). **6** a list of items which one has selected for purchase while shopping online. **7** *Brit. euphemism informal* bastard. □ **basket·ful** noun (pl. **-fuls**). [Anglo-French *basket*, Anglo-Latin *baskettum*, of unknown origin]

basket·ball noun **1** a game between two teams of five, in which goals are scored by throwing a ball through a basket suspended at either end of a court. **2** the ball used in this game.

basket case noun *informal* a person or thing that is incapacitated, esp. by emotional or mental disturbance or bankruptcy. [originally applied to a person with both legs and both arms amputated]

Basket Maker noun a member of a culture of the southwestern US, forming the early stages of the Anasazi culture from the 1st c. BC until *c.*700 AD, so called from the basketry and other woven fragments found in early cave sites.

basket-of-gold noun = ALYSSUM 2.

bas·ketry noun **1** the art of making baskets. **2** baskets collectively.

basket sled noun (also **basket sleigh**) a sled used in dogsledding, with a row of stanchions lashed in a criss-cross pattern supporting side rails.

basket weave noun a weave resembling that of a basket.

basket·work noun **1** material woven in the style of a basket. **2** the art of making this.

bask·ing shark noun a very large shark, *Cetorhinus maximus*, which often lies near the surface.

Basle /bɒl/ the French spelling of BASEL.

bas·mati /baz'mati/ noun (in full **basmati rice**) a kind of rice with very long thin grains and a delicate fragrance. [Hindi, = fragrant]

Basov /ˈbasɒf/ **Niko·lai Gen·nediy·evich** (1922–2001), Russian physicist, who shared the 1964 Nobel Prize for physics for his research leading to the development of the maser.

Basque /bask, bɒsk/ ● noun **1** a member of a people inhabiting the western Pyrenees in central northern Spain and the extreme southwest of France. **2** the language of this people. ● adjective of or relating to the Basques or their language. [French from Latin *Vasco -onis*]

basque /bask/ noun a close-fitting bodice extending from the shoulders to the waist and often with a short continuation below waist level. [BASQUE]

Basque Country a region of the western Pyrenees in both France and Spain, the homeland of the Basque people. The region comprises the autonomous Basque Provinces of northern Spain, together with the SW part of Aquitaine in France.

Basque Provinces an autonomous region of northern Spain, on the Bay of Biscay, consisting of the provinces of Àlava, Guipùzcoa, and Vizcaya; capital, Vitoria. Its chief industrial cities are Bilbao and San Sebastiàn.

Basra /ˈbazrə/ an oil port of Iraq, on the Shatt al-Arab waterway; pop. (est. 2002) 1,337,600.

bas-relief /ˌbɒrɪˈliːf, ˌbas-/ noun sculpture or carving in which the figures project slightly from the background. [earlier *basse relieve* from Italian *basso rilievo* low relief: later altered to French form]

bass¹ /beis/ ● noun **1 a** the lowest adult male singing voice. **b** a singer with this voice. **c** a part written for it. **2** (also **bass line**) the lowest part in harmonized music. **3 a** an instrument that is the lowest in pitch in its family. **b** its player. **4 a** a bass guitar or double bass. **b** its player. **5** the low-frequency output of a radio, record player, etc., corresponding to the bass in music. ● adjective **1** lowest in musical pitch. **2** deep-sounding. [alteration of BASE² after BASSO]

bass² /bas/ noun (pl. same or **bass·es**) any of various edible freshwater and marine fishes of the families Serranidae and Centrarchidae, having spiny fins. See also LARGEMOUTH, ROCK BASS, SEA BASS, SMALLMOUTH. [earlier *barse* from Old English *bærs*]

bass³ /bas/ noun **1** = BAST. **2** *var. of* BASSWOOD. [alteration of BAST]

bass-ackwards adverb *slang* backwards. [alteration of *ass-backwards*]

bass clef noun *Music* a sign that indicates that the second highest line of the staff represents the F below middle C.

Basse-Norman·die /ˌbasnɔrmɑ̃ˈdiː/ a region of NW France, on the coast of the English Channel, including the Cherbourg peninsula and the city of Caen.

Basse·terre /basˈtɛr/ the capital (on the island of St. Kitts) of St. Kitts and Nevis; pop. (est. 2002) 11,600.

Basse-Terre /basˈtɛr/ **1** the main island of Guadeloupe in the West Indies. **2** its capital city, situated on the SW corner of the island; pop. (est. 1990) 14,000.

bas·set horn noun a clarinet in F, with a range between that of a common clarinet and a bass clarinet. [German, translation of French *cor de bassette* from Italian *corno di bassetto* from *corno* horn + *bassetto* diminutive of *basso* BASE²]

bas·set hound noun (also **basset**) a breed of hunting dog with a long body, short legs, and long, droopy ears. [French, diminutive of *bas basse* low: see BASE²]

bas·si·net noun a portable basket-like bed for a young baby, often with a hood. [French, diminutive of *bassin* BASIN]

bass·ist noun a person who plays a bass guitar or a double bass.

basso /ˈbasɒ/ noun (pl. **bas·sos** or **bassi** /-si/) a singer with a bass voice. [Italian, = BASS¹]

bas·soon noun **1** a bass instrument of the oboe family, with a double reed. **2** its player. □ **bas·soon·ist** noun [French *basson* from *bas* BASS¹]

basso pro·fun·do /prɒˈfundɒ/ noun a bass singer with an exceptionally low range. [Italian *basso profondo* deep bass]

Bass Strait /bas/ a channel separating Tasmania from the mainland of Australia. [G. *Bass*, English explorer d.1812?]

bass viol noun **1 a** a viola da gamba. **b** its player. **2** *N Amer.* a double bass.

bass·wood /ˈbaswʊd/ noun (also **bass**) **1** any of several trees of the linden family, esp. *Tilia americana*, native to the deciduous forests of eastern N America. **2** the wood of this tree, which is very soft and light. [BASS³ + WOOD]

bast noun the inner bark of lindens, or other flexible fibrous bark, used as fibre in matting etc. [Old English *bæst* from Germanic]

bas·tard ● noun **1** a person born of parents not married to each other. ¶ Offensive in other than legal or historical contexts. **2** *coarse slang* **a** an unpleasant or despicable person. **b** a person of a specified kind (*poor bastard; rotten bastard; lucky bastard*). **3** *coarse slang* a difficult or awkward thing, undertaking, etc. ● adjective **1** born of parents not married to each other; illegitimate. **2** (of things): **a** unauthorized, counterfeit. **b** hybrid. □ **bas·tardy** noun (in sense 1 of *noun*). [Old French from medieval Latin *bastardus*, perhaps from *bastum* packsaddle]

bastard canoe noun *Cdn hist.* a birchbark canoe used in the fur trade, about 9 m (30 ft.) long and capable of carrying about 2000 kg (two tons) of freight. [Canadian French *canot bâtard*]

bas·tard·ize transitive verb (also esp. *Brit.* **-ise**) **1** corrupt, debase. **2** declare (a person) illegitimate. □ **bas·tard·iz·a·tion** /-'zeɪʃən/ noun

bastard maple noun *Cdn* = MANITOBA MAPLE.

baste¹ transitive verb moisten (meat) with gravy, melted fat, etc. during cooking. □ **bast·er** noun [16th c.: origin unknown]

baste[2] *transitive verb* stitch loosely together in preparation for sewing; tack. [Old French *bastir* sew lightly, ultimately from Germanic]

baste[3] *transitive verb* beat soundly; thrash. [perhaps figurative use of BASTE[1]]

Bas·tet /'bastet/ *Egyptian Myth* a goddess usually shown as a woman with the head of a cat, wearing one gold earring.

Bas·tia /'bastjə/ the chief port of Corsica; pop. (1999) 37,884.

Bas·tille /ba'stiːl/ a fortress in Paris built in the 14th c. and used in the 17th–18th c. as a state prison. It became a symbol of despotism and its storming by the mob on 14 July 1789 marked the start of the French Revolution. [Old French *bastille* fortress, from Provençal *bastide* built]

Bastille Day *noun* July 14, a French national holiday marking the storming of the Bastille.

bas·tin·ado /ˌbastɪ'neɪdoʊ/ ● *noun* punishment by beating with a stick on the soles of the feet. ● *transitive verb* (**-adoes**, **-adoed**) punish (a person) in this way. [Spanish *bastonada* from *baston* BATON]

bas·tion /'bastʃən/ *noun* **1** a projecting part of a fortification built at an angle of, or against the line of, a wall. **2** a thing regarded as protecting (*bastion of freedom*). **3** a natural rock formation resembling a bastion. [French from Italian *bastione* from *bastire* build]

Ba·suto·land /bə'suːtoʊˌland/ the former name (until 1966) for LESOTHO.

bat[1] ● *noun* **1** an implement with a rounded usu. wooden handle and a solid head with a flat or rounded surface, used for hitting a ball in various games, such as baseball or cricket. **2** a turn at using this; an at-bat. **3** a batter in baseball etc., usu. described in some way (*the team needs a right-handed bat*). **4** *Cdn* (*Nfld*) a pole 1.5–2.5 m (5–8 ft.) long, having an iron hook and spike on one end, used to kill seals and assist a sealer on the ice. ● *verb* (**bat·ted**, **bat·ting**) **1** *transitive* hit with or as with a bat. **2** *intransitive* take a turn at batting. □ **bat around 1** discuss (an idea or proposal). **2** *Baseball* have an inning in which all nine players have an at-bat. **3** *Brit. slang* potter aimlessly. **go to bat for** *N Amer. informal* defend the interests of. **off one's own bat** *Brit.* unprompted, unaided. **right off the bat** *N Amer.* immediately. [Old English *batt* club, perhaps partly from Old French *batte* club, from *battre* strike]

bat[2] *noun* any mouselike nocturnal mammal of the order Chiroptera, capable of flight by means of membranous wings extending from its forelimbs. □ **have bats in the belfry** be eccentric or crazy. **like a bat out of hell** very fast. **old bat** see OLD BAT. [16th c., alteration of Middle English *bakke* from Scandinavian]

bat[3] *transitive verb* (**bat·ted**, **bat·ting**) blink (one's eyelid); flutter (one's eyelashes). □ **bat an eye** (or **eyelash** or **eyelid**) *informal* show reaction or emotion. [var. of obsolete *bate* flutter]

Bata /'batə/ **Thom·as John** (b.1914), Czech-born Canadian shoe manufacturer. He joined his father's shoe company in Zlin, Czechoslovakia in 1929, moving to Canada to open a new factory in 1939. The family-run company now operates in over 65 countries worldwide.

Batan Islands /bə'tɑn/ a group of islands in the northern Philippines, lying between the Babuyan Islands and Taiwan.

ba·tard /bə'tɑr/ *noun Cdn hist.* = BASTARD CANOE.

Ba·tavia /bə'teɪviə/ the former name (until 1949) of JAKARTA.

bat boy *noun Baseball* a person who takes care of the bats etc. of a baseball team.

batch[1] ● *noun* **1** a number of things or persons forming a group or dealt with together. **2** an instalment (*have sent off the latest batch of proofs*). **3** a quantity produced by one operation, or the amount of material necessary for this (*a batch of doughnuts; a batch of concrete*). **4** (*attributive*) using or dealt with in batches, not as a continuous flow (*batch production*). **5** *Computing* a group of records processed as a single unit. ● *transitive verb* arrange or deal with in batches. □ **batch of snow** *Cdn* (*Nfld*) a flurry or snowfall. [Old English *bæcce* from *bacan* BAKE]

batch[2] *transitive & intransitive verb N Amer., Austral., & NZ* (esp. in **batch it**) live alone and keep house for oneself, esp. temporarily.

ba·teau /ba'toː, 'batoː/ *noun Cdn hist.* (also **bat·teau**) (*pl.* **-teaux** /-'toː, -'toːz/) a light, shallow-draft, flat-bottomed boat with pointed bow and stern, esp. of the kind used by fur traders, propelled by oars, poles, or sails, or drawn by horses. [French, = boat]

bated *adjective* □ **with bated breath** very anxiously. [past participle of obsolete *bate* (v.) restrain, from ABATE]

Bate·man, Rob·ert Mc·Lel·lan (b.1930), Canadian painter and naturalist. His paintings depict wildlife in a realistic natural environment.

Bates ▶ **1 Henry Wal·ter** (1825–92), English naturalist. Noting the similarity of some animals to their natural backgrounds and of some species of edible butterflies to poisonous ones, Bates suggested that, by natural selection, those who 'mimic' in this way are more likely to survive. **2 H(er·bert) E(r·nest)** (1905–74), English novelist and writer of short stories. His novels include *Love for Lydia* (1952) and *The Darling Buds of May* (1958).

BATF *abbreviation* (in the US) Bureau of Alcohol, Tobacco and Firearms.

Bath a town in SW England, formerly in Somerset and Avon; pop. (est. 2002) 86,300. A fashionable spa in the 18th c., Bath is still famous for its hot springs, its Roman remains, notably the baths, and its Regency architecture.

bath ● *noun* (*pl.* **baths**) **1** the act or process of immersing the body for washing or therapy (*have a bath; take a bath*). **2 a** = BATHTUB. **b** this with its contents (*your bath is ready*). **3 a** a vessel containing liquid in which something is immersed, e.g. a film for developing, a dish to be cooked at a controlled temperature, etc. **b** this with its contents. **4** esp. *N Amer.* = BATHROOM. **5** (usu. in *pl.*) a building with baths or a swimming pool, usu. open to the public. ● *verb Cdn & Brit.* **1** *transitive* wash (esp. a person) in a bath. **2** *intransitive* wash oneself in a bath. □ **take a bath** *informal* suffer a heavy financial loss. [Old English *bæth* from Germanic]

Bath chair *noun hist.* a usu. hooded wheelchair for invalids. [BATH]

bathe ● *verb* **1** *intransitive* swim. **2** *intransitive N Amer.* wash oneself. **3** *transitive* immerse in or wash or treat with liquid esp. for cleansing or medicinal purposes. **4** *transitive* (of sunlight etc.) envelop. ● *noun Brit.* a swim. □ **bath·ing** *noun* [Old English *bathian* from Germanic]

bath·er *noun* **1** a swimmer. **2** a person taking a bath.

ba·the·tic /bə'θɛtɪk/ *adjective* characterized by bathos; anticlimactic.

bath·house *noun* **1 a** a building with baths for public use. **b** such a place used esp. by homosexual men for sexual encounters. **2** a building for changing one's clothes on a beach or at a swimming pool.

bathing cap *noun* a cap made of rubber or elasticized polyurethane fabric, worn when swimming.

bathing costume *noun* **1** esp. *Brit.* a bathing suit. **2** *N Amer.* an old-fashioned bathing suit.

bathing suit *noun* a garment worn for swimming.

bath mat *noun* **1** a small mat for standing on before and after a bath. **2** a rubber mat for standing or sitting on inside a bathtub, esp. to prevent slipping.

batho·lith /'baθəlɪθ/ *noun* a dome of igneous rock extending inwards to an unknown depth. [German from Greek *bathos* depth + -LITH]

ba·thos /'beɪθɒs/ *noun* an unintentional lapse in mood from the sublime to the absurd or trivial; a commonplace or ridiculous feature offsetting an otherwise sublime situation; an anticlimax. [Greek, = depth]

bath·robe *noun* a loose usu. belted robe worn over nightwear or while resting, esp. one made of thick terry cloth.

bath·room *noun* **1** a room containing a bath and usu. other washing facilities. **2** esp. *N Amer.* a room containing a toilet or toilets. **3** (*attributive*) designating humour based on urinating or defecating. □ **go to the bathroom** *N Amer. euphemism* urinate or defecate.

bathroom tissue *noun* = TOILET PAPER.

bath salts *noun* soluble salts used for softening or scenting bathwater.

Bath·sheba /baθ'ʃiːbə, 'baθʃɪbə/ the wife of Uriah the Hittite (2 Sam. 11). She became one of the wives of David, who had caused her husband to be killed in battle, and was the mother of Solomon.

bath sheet *noun* a very large bath towel, usu. about 85×155 cm.

bath towel *noun* a towel large enough to be suitable for drying oneself after bathing or showering, usu. about 70×135 cm.

bath·tub *noun* a tub for bathing in, especially one that is permanently fixed in a bathroom.

bathtub gin *noun* illicitly produced liquor, esp. during times of prohibition.

bathtub race *noun Cdn* an event in which bathtubs are motorized and piloted across bodies of water.

Bath·urst /'baθrst/ **1** a city in NE New Brunswick, situated at the mouth of the Nepisiguit River at Chaleur Bay; pop. (2001) 12,924. **2** the former name (until 1973) of BANJUL. □ **Bath·urst·onian** *noun* in sense 1 [H. *Bathurst*, colonial secretary and 3rd Earl *Bathurst* d.1834]

Bathurst Inlet a deep inlet of the northwestern coast of mainland Nunavut, east of Coronation Gulf. [as BATHURST]

Bathurst Island one of the Parry Islands in the Canadian High

Arctic, between Melville and Devon islands. The north magnetic pole is located in the vicinity of its northern shore. [as BATHURST]

bath·water *noun* the water in a bath. □ **throw out the baby with the bathwater** *see* BABY.

ba·thym·etry /bəˈθɪmɪtri/ *noun* the measurement of depth of water in seas, lakes, etc. □ **ba·thym·eter** *noun* **bathy·met·ric** /ˌbaθɪˈmɛtrɪk/ *adjective* [Greek *bathus* deep + -METRY]

bathy·scaphe /ˈbaθɪˌskaf/ *noun* a self-propelled vessel for deep-sea diving. [Greek *bathus* deep + *skaphos* ship]

bathy·sphere /ˈbaθɪˌsfɪr/ *noun* a spherical vessel for deep-sea observation, lowered on cables from the surface. [Greek *bathus* deep + SPHERE]

batik /bəˈtiːk/ ● *noun* **1** a method (originally used in Java) of producing coloured designs on textiles by waxing the parts not to be dyed. **2** a piece of cloth treated in this way. ● *transitive verb* (usu. as **ba·tiked** *adjective*) produce coloured designs in this way. [Javanese, = painted]

Bat·ista /bəˈtiːstə/ **Ful·gen·cio** (full name Batista y Zalvídar, 1901–73), Cuban soldier and dictator, president of Cuba 1940–44 and 1954–9. His second government was notoriously corrupt and ruthless, and was overthrown by an uprising under the leadership of Fidel Castro.

bat·iste /baˈtiːst/ ● *noun* a fine linen or cotton cloth. ● *adjective* made of batiste. [French (earlier *batiche*), perhaps related to *battre* BATTER[1]]

bat·man *noun* (*pl.* **-men**) *Military* (in the UK) an officer's personal servant. [Old French *bat, bast* from medieval Latin *bastum* packsaddle + MAN]

bat mitz·vah /bat ˈmɪtsvə/ *noun* **1** a religious initiation ceremony for a Jewish girl aged twelve years and one day, regarded as the age of religious maturity. **2** the girl undergoing this ceremony. [Hebrew *baṯ miṣwāh* daughter of commandment, after BAR MITZVAH]

Ba·toche /bəˈtɒʃ/ part of the rural municipality of St. Louis in central Saskatchewan, situated on the South Saskatchewan River, northeast of Saskatoon. A historic locality, it was the site of a major confrontation during the Riel Rebellion of 1885. The Metis, Cree and Dakota defenders were greatly outnumbered by Canadian soldiers, and more than 25 people were killed; Riel surrendered a few days later. [X. Letendre *dit Batoche*, ferry operator and founder of the village *c.*1871]

baton /baˈtɒn/ *noun* **1** a thin stick used by a conductor to direct an orchestra, choir, etc. **2** *Athletics* a short stick or tube carried and passed on by the runners in a relay race. **3** a stick carried and twirled by a drum major or majorette. **4** a staff of office or authority. **5** a police officer's truncheon. □ **pass the baton** transfer a duty or responsibility to another; allow someone else to continue with the next part of a task etc. [French *bâton, baston*, ultimately from Late Latin *bastum* stick]

bâton·nier /batɔnˈjei/ *noun* (in Quebec) a president of a Bar Association. [French, lit. 'staff bearer', from *bâton* staff]

Baton Rouge /ˌbatən ˈruːʒ/ the capital of Louisiana, situated on the east bank of the Mississippi; pop. (2000) 227,818.

bat·ra·chian /bəˈtreikiən/ ● *noun* a frog or toad. ● *adjective* of or relating to frogs or toads. [from modern Latin *Batrachia* former name (now Anura) from Greek *batrakhos* frog]

bats *predicative adjective* *slang* crazy. [from phr. *have bats in the belfry*: see BAT[2]]

bat·shit *adjective* *N Amer.* *slang* crazy. □ **go batshit** become mentally unstable; lose one's composure.

bats·man *noun* (*pl.* **-men**) a person who bats or is batting, esp. in cricket. □ **bats·man·ship** *noun*

batt *noun* **1** a sheet of usu. fibreglass insulation sized to fit between studs, joists, or rafters. **2** = BATTING 2. [var. of BAT[1]]

bat·tal·ion /bəˈtalian/ *noun* **1** a large body of soldiers ready for battle, esp. an infantry unit forming part of a brigade. **2** a large group of people pursuing a common aim or sharing a major undertaking. [French *bataillon* from Italian *battaglione* from *battaglia* BATTLE]

bat·teau *var. of* BATEAU.

bat·ten[1] ● *noun* **1** a long flat strip of wood or metal used to hold something in place (*board-and-batten siding*). **2** *Naut.* **a** a thin, narrow strip of wood or plastic inserted in pockets in a sail to maintain its proper shape. **b** a strip of wood or metal for securing a tarpaulin over a ship's hatchway. ● *transitive verb* strengthen, fasten, or secure with or as if with battens. □ **batten down the hatches** *Naut.* secure a ship's tarpaulins. **2** prepare for a difficulty or crisis. [Old French *batant* part. of *batre* beat, from Latin *battuere*]

bat·ten[2] *noun* *Cdn var. of* BATTING 2 (*cotton batten*).

Batten·berg lace *noun* *N Amer.* a type of lace made of thin strips of

fabric with large openings crossed by heavy thread. [*Battenberg* in Germany]

bat·ter[1] *verb* **1 a** *transitive* strike repeatedly with hard blows. **b** *intransitive* (often foll. by *against, at*, etc.) strike repeated blows; pound heavily and insistently (*batter at the door*). **2** *transitive* (often in *passive*) **a** handle roughly, esp. over a long period. **b** censure or criticize severely. **3** *intransitive* *Cdn* (*Nfld*) (of a bird) flap the wings and take off from a body of water. □ **bat·ter·er** *noun* [Old French *batre* beat, from Latin *battuere*]

bat·ter[2] *noun* **1** a fluid mixture of flour, egg, and a liquid, used for coating food before frying. **2** a mixture of flour and other raw ingredients for a cake etc., more liquid than a dough. [Old French *bateüre* from *batre*: see BATTER[1]]

bat·ter[3] *noun* a player batting, esp. in baseball.

bat·ter[4] ● *noun* **1** a wall etc. with a sloping face. **2** a receding slope. ● *intransitive verb* have a receding slope. [Middle English: origin unknown]

bat·tered[1] *adjective* **1** (of a person, esp. a woman or child) subjected to repeated violence from a spouse, parent, etc. (*battered wife*). **2** damaged by age, adversity, or heavy use (*a battered old truck*).

bat·tered[2] *adjective* (esp. of fish) coated in batter and deep-fried.

battered woman syndrome *noun* (also **battered wife syndrome**) the psychologically helpless condition in which abused women find themselves, esp. as used in court to extenuate guilt for violent action against the abuser.

bat·ter·ing ram *noun* *hist.* a heavy beam, originally with an end in the form of a carved ram's head, used in breaching fortifications.

bat·tery *noun* (*pl.* **-ies**) **1** a device, consisting of one or more cells, in which chemical energy is converted into electricity. **2** a set of similar units of equipment, esp. connected (*a battery of clocks*). **3** a usu. exhaustive series of tests. **4 a** a fortified emplacement for heavy guns. **b** an artillery unit of guns, personnel, and vehicles. **5** *Law* an act, including touching, inflicting unlawful personal violence on another person, even if no physical harm is done (*see* ASSAULT 2). **6** *Baseball* the pitcher and the catcher. **7** (often *attributive*) esp. *Brit.* a series of cages for the intensive breeding and rearing of poultry or cattle. □ **recharge one's batteries** restore one's strength, enthusiasm, etc. [French *batterie* from *batre, battre* strike, from Latin *battuere*]

bat·ting *noun* **1** the action of hitting with a bat. **2** wadding of cotton, polyester, etc. prepared in sheets for use in quilts etc.

batting average *noun* *Baseball* a statistic indicating a batter's proficiency, calculated by dividing the number of hits by the number of at-bats.

batting cage *noun* *Baseball* a mesh enclosure in which baseball players can practise batting.

batting order *noun* *Baseball* the order in which baseball players take their turn at bat.

bat·tle ● *noun* **1 a** a prolonged fight between large organized armed forces. **b** a fight or violent altercation between opposed groups (*street battles between rival gangs*). **2** a contest; a prolonged or difficult struggle (*life is a constant battle; a battle of wits*). ● *verb* **1** *intransitive* struggle, strive; fight persistently (*battled against the elements; battled for women's rights*). **2** *transitive* struggle against. **3** *transitive* *N Amer.* engage in battle with. □ **battle it out** fight to a conclusion. **half the battle** the key to the success of an undertaking. □ **bat·tler** *noun* [Old French *bataille*, ultimately from Late Latin *battualia* gladiatorial exercises, from Latin *battuere* beat]

battle-axe *noun* **1** a large axe used in ancient warfare. **2** (**battle·axe**) *informal* a formidable or domineering older woman.

battle cruiser *noun* *hist.* a heavy-gunned ship faster and more lightly armoured than a battleship.

battle cry *noun* **1** a rallying cry used in battle. **2** a rallying cry or slogan of a group of people fighting for the same cause.

battle·dore *noun* *hist.* **1 a** (in full **battledore and shuttlecock**) a game played with a shuttlecock and racquets. **b** the racquet used in this. **2** a kind of wooden utensil like a paddle, formerly used in washing, baking, etc. [15th c., perhaps from Provençal *batedor* beater, from *batre* beat]

battle·dress *noun* **1** attire worn for battle. **2** *hist.* a soldier's or airman's everyday khaki uniform of tunic and trousers.

battle fatigue *noun* (also **combat fatigue**) **1** (in *pl.*) = ARMY FATIGUES. **2** a mental disorder caused by stress in wartime combat.

battle·field *noun* **1** the piece of ground on which a battle is or was fought. **2** = BATTLEGROUND.

battle·ground *noun* **1** an area of disputation, contention, or hostility. **2** = BATTLEFIELD.

battle group *noun* a military force created to fight together, typically consisting of several different types of troops.

battle lines *plural noun* **1** the lines along which opposing armies are drawn up for battle. **2** the entrenched ideas, ideological positions, etc. held by opposing groups (*with two weeks left before the vote, the battle lines in the Legislature have been drawn*).

battle·ment *noun* (usu. in *pl.*) **1** an alternately high and low parapet along the top of a wall, as part of a fortification. **2** a section of roof enclosed by this (*walking on the battlements*). □ **battle·ment·ed** *adjective* [Old French *bataillier* furnish with ramparts + -MENT]

Battle of the Atlantic a succession of sea operations during the Second World War in which Axis naval and air forces attempted to destroy ships carrying supplies from North America to the UK.

battle royal *noun* **1** a battle in which several combatants or all available forces engage; a free fight. **2** a heated argument.

battle-scarred *adjective* (also **battle-weary**) *N Amer.* **1** (of a soldier) scarred or weary from battle. **2** (of a person, group of people, etc.) exhausted from activity, esp. of a particular kind (*battle-scarred government*). **3** (of a building, city, etc.) **a** damaged by war or violence. **b** *informal* dilapidated or worn out through use.

battle·ship *noun* a warship of the most heavily armed and armoured class, of sufficient size to take part in a main attack.

battleship grey ● *adjective* of a drab, slightly bluish-grey colour (often used for warships as reducing their visibility). ● *noun* this colour.

bat·tue /baˈtjuː, baˈtuː/ *noun* **1** the driving of game towards hunters by beaters. **2** a hunting party arranged in this way. [French, fem. past participle of *battre* beat, from Latin *battuere*]

batty *adjective* (**bat·ti·er, bat·ti·est**) *informal* crazy. □ **bat·ti·ly** *adverb* **bat·ti·ness** *noun*

bat·wing *adjective* (of a sleeve etc.) shaped like the wing of a bat.

bau·ble *noun* **1** a showy trinket or toy of little value. **2** a baton formerly used as an emblem by jesters. [Old French *ba(u)bel* child's toy, of unknown origin]

Bau·cis /ˈbɔːkɪs/ *Gk Myth* the wife of Philemon (see PHILEMON).

baud /bɔːd/ *noun* (*pl.* same or **bauds**) *Computing etc.* **1** a unit used to express the speed of electronic code signals, corresponding to one information unit per second. **2** (loosely) a unit of data transmission speed of one bit per second. [J. M. E. Baudot, French engineer d.1903]

Baude·laire /ˈbɔːdəˌler/ **Charles** (1821–67), French poet and critic, perhaps the most influential of the 19th c. *Les Fleurs du mal* (1857), his most famous work, expresses his almost mystic view of beauty and evil in the real world, but was condemned as offensive when it appeared. □ **Baude·lair·ean** /-ˈleriən/ *adjective*

Bau·douin I /bɔːˈdwæ̃/ (1930–93), king of the Belgians 1951–93. He restored confidence in the Belgian monarchy after the abdication of his father, Leopold III, and oversaw the granting of independence to the Belgian Congo (now Congo).

Bau·dril·lard /ˈbɔːdrɪˌjar/ **Jean** (b.1929), French sociologist and cultural critic, associated with postmodernism.

Bauer /ˈbaʊər/ **David Wil·liam** (1925–1988), Canadian priest, educator, and hockey coach. He founded a Canadian national amateur hockey team in 1962, and coached the team to a bronze medal at the 1968 Olympics.

Bau·haus /ˈbaʊhaʊs/ *noun* **1** a German school of architectural design (1919–33). **2** its principles, based on functionalism and development of existing skills. [German from *Bau* building + *Haus* house]

Bauld, Cape /bɔːld/ the northernmost point of the island of Newfoundland, situated on Quirpon Island at the entrance to the Strait of Belle Isle.

baulk esp. *Brit. var. of* BALK.

baulky esp. *Brit. var. of* BALKY.

Baum /baʊm/ **L(yman) Frank** (1856–1919), US novelist and dramatist, author of *The Wonderful Wizard of Oz* (1900).

baux·ite *noun* a claylike mineral containing varying proportions of alumina, the chief source of aluminum. □ **baux·it·ic** /-ˈsɪtɪk/ *adjective* [French from *Les Baux* near Arles in S France + -ITE¹]

Bav·aria /bəˈveriə/ a state of S Germany; capital, Munich. □ **Bav·arian** *adjective & noun*

Bavarian cream *noun* a usu. moulded dessert of flavoured whipped cream stiffened with gelatin.

bawd *noun* a woman who runs a brothel. [Middle English *bawdstrot* from Old French *baudetrot, baudestroyt* procuress]

bawdy ● *adjective* (**bawd·i·er, bawd·i·est**) humorously indecent. ● *noun* bawdy talk or writing. □ **bawd·i·ly** *adverb* **bawd·i·ness** *noun*

bawdy house *noun* a brothel.

bawk *noun* *Cdn (Nfld)* = GREATER SHEARWATER. [origin unknown]

bawl *verb* **1** *transitive* speak or call out noisily. **2** *intransitive* weep loudly. **3** *intransitive* (of a cow, seal, etc.) cry out, wail. □ **bawl out** *informal* reprimand angrily. □ **bawl·er** *noun* [imitative: compare medieval Latin *baulare* bark, Icelandic *baula* (Swedish *böla*) to low]

bawn *noun* *Cdn (Nfld)* **1** a meadow near a house etc. **2** a stretch of rocks on which salted cod are spread for drying. [Irish *badún*, perhaps from *ba* cows + *dún* fortress]

Bax·ter, John Bab·ing·ton Mac·aulay (1868–1946), Canadian lawyer and politician, premier of New Brunswick 1925–31. He played a leading role in the growth of the New Brunswick Conservative party.

Bay *noun* *Cdn proprietary* the Hudson's Bay Company, or one of its posts or retail stores.

bay¹ *noun* **1** a body of water where the coastline curves inwards. **2** an indentation or recess in a range of hills etc. **3** *Cdn (Nfld)* (often *attributive*) a large indentation on the coast, including several harbours, islands, outports, fishing grounds, etc. [Old French *baie* from Old Spanish *bahia*]

bay² *noun* **1** (in full **bay laurel** or **bay tree**) a Mediterranean laurel, *Laurus nobilis*, having deep green leaves and purple berries. Also called SWEET BAY. **2** = BAY LEAF. **3** (in *pl.*) a wreath made of bay leaves, for a victor or poet. [Old French *baie* from Latin *baca* berry]

bay³ *noun* **1** a space created by a window-line projecting outwards from a wall. **2** a recess; a section of wall between buttresses or columns, esp. in the nave of a church etc. **3** a compartment (*bomb bay; drive bay*). **4** an area specially allocated or marked off (*sick bay; loading bay*). [Old French *baie* from *ba(y)er* gape, from medieval Latin *batare*]

bay⁴ ● *adjective* (esp. of a horse) dark reddish-brown. ● *noun* a bay horse with a black mane and tail. [Old French *bai* from Latin *badius*]

bay⁵ ● *verb* **1** *intransitive* (esp. of a large dog) bark or howl loudly and plaintively. **2** *transitive* bay at. ● *noun* the sound of baying, esp. in chorus from hounds in close pursuit. □ **at bay 1** cornered, apparently unable to escape. **2** in a desperate situation. **bring to bay** gain on in pursuit; trap. **hold** (or **keep**) **at bay** hold off (a pursuer). **stand at bay** turn to face one's pursuers. [Old French *bai, baïer* bark, from Italian *baiare*, of imitative origin]

Bay·ard /ˈbeɪɑrd/ **Pierre du Ter·rail, Sei·gneur de** (1473–1524), French soldier of great valour and chivalry, known as 'fearless and above reproach'.

Bay Area *noun* the area surrounding San Francisco Bay.

bay·berry *noun* (*pl.* **-berries**) **1** any of various N American shrubs or small trees of the genus *Myrica*, having aromatic leaves and bearing berries covered in a wax coating. **2** the fruit of the bay tree, *Laurus nobilis*. **3** a fragrant, oil-bearing Caribbean tree, *Pimenta acris*. [BAY² + BERRY]

bay boat *noun* *Cdn (Nfld)* a boat that carries passengers, mail, and supplies to coastal areas of Newfoundland.

Bay Cha·leur /beɪ ʃəˈlɜr/ see CHALEUR BAY.

Bay d'Espoir /beɪ dəˈsper/ see ESPOIR, BAY D'.

Ba·yeux Tapestry /ˈbaɪjɜ/ *noun* an embroidered cloth, about 70 m (230 ft) long, illustrating events leading up to the Norman Conquest, made between 1066 and 1077 for the bishop of Bayeux in Normandy, where it is still kept.

Bay·field, Henry Wol·sey (1795–1885), British naval officer and surveyor. He surveyed the Canadian Great Lakes, the St. Lawrence River, and the shores of E Canada.

bay·front *noun* *N Amer.* the shoreline of a bay.

bay ice *noun* *Cdn (Nfld)* ice formed in a single winter on the surface of a bay or harbour.

Bay·kal, Lake see BAIKAL, LAKE.

Bayko·nyr see BAIKONUR.

Bayle /beil, bel/ **Pierre** (1647–1706), French philosopher, a forerunner of 18th-c. rationalism, and author of the influential *Dictionnaire historique et critique* (1697).

bay leaf *noun* the aromatic (usu. dried) leaf of the bay tree, used in cooking (see BAY² 1).

Bay·lis /ˈbeilɪs/ **Lil·lian Mary** (1874–1937), English theatre manager. She founded the Old Vic (1912) and reopened the Sadler's Wells Theatre (1931), which led to the formation of the Royal Ballet and the English National Opera.

bay·man *noun* (*pl.* **-men**) **1 a** *Cdn (Nfld)* an inhabitant of an outport, esp.

as opposed to someone living in a town. **b** esp. *US* a person living on or near a bay. **2** (**Bay man**) *Cdn hist.* an employee of the Hudson's Bay Company.

bay·nod·dy *noun Cdn* (*Nfld*) (*pl.* **-dies**) = BAYMAN 1a. [BAY¹ + NODDY]

Bay of Pigs a bay on the SW coast of Cuba, scene of an unsuccessful attempt on 17 Apr. 1961 by US-backed Cuban exiles to invade the country and overthrow the regime of Fidel Castro. The newly inaugurated President Kennedy refused the expected US air support, and the operation was a fiasco, resulting in a rise in Castro's prestige and power.

bay·on·et /ˌbeɪəˈnɛt/ ● *noun* **1** a stabbing blade attachable to the muzzle of a rifle. **2** an electrical or other fitting engaged by being pushed into a socket and twisted. ● *transitive verb* (**bay·on·et·ted**, **bay·on·et·ting** or **bay·on·et·ed**, **bay·on·et·ing**) stab with a bayonet. [French *baïonnette*, perhaps from *Bayonne* in SW France, where they were first made]

bayou /ˈbaɪuː/ *noun* a marshy offshoot of a river etc. in the southern US. [Louisiana French from Choctaw]

Bay·reuth /ˈbaɪrɔɪt, -ˈrɔɪt/ a town in Bavaria, Germany, where Wagner lived from 1874 and where he is buried. Festivals of his operas are held regularly in a theatre specially built (1872–6) to house performances of *Der Ring des Nibelungen*.

Bay Roberts a town in SE Newfoundland, situated on the Avalon Peninsula, on the west shore of Conception Bay; pop. (2001) 5,237. [possibly from an English surname]

bay rum *noun* a perfume, esp. for the hair, distilled originally from leaves of the bayberry (*Pimenta acris*) in rum.

bay scallop *noun* **1** a scallop, *Aequipecten irradians*, of the Atlantic coast of Canada and New England. **2** the edible adductor muscle of this scallop.

bay·side ● *adjective* situated at or near a (usu. specified) bay. ● *noun* (**Bayside**) *Cdn* the area around Hudson Bay (also *attributive*: *Bayside post*).

Bay State, the Massachusetts.

Bay Street *noun Cdn* **1** a street in Toronto where the headquarters of many financial institutions are located. **2** the moneyed interests of Toronto, esp. as opposed to other regions of Canada (*Bay Street is nervous about the election*).

bay window *noun* a window, usu. with glass on three sides, projecting from an outside wall.

bay·wop *noun Cdn* (*Nfld*) *derogatory* = BAYMAN 1a. [back-formation from BAY¹ + wops, imitation of outport pronunciation of WASP]

ba·zaar *noun* **1** (esp. in the Middle East) a marketplace or shopping quarter. **2** a fundraising sale of various articles, esp. for charity. **3** a large store selling miscellaneous items. **4** a place where items of a specified sort are sold (*when did playgrounds become drug bazaars?*). [Persian *bāzār*, prob. through Turkish and Italian]

ba·zil·lion *noun* esp. *N Amer. informal* an exaggeratedly large number (*they mailed out a bazillion flyers*). [alteration of BILLION after GAZILLION]

ba·zooka *noun* **1** a tubular short-range rocket launcher used against tanks. **2** a crude trombone-like musical instrument. [apparently from *bazoo* mouth, of unknown origin]

ba·zoom *noun slang* (usu. in *pl.*) a woman's breast. [deformation of BOSOM]

bazz *transitive verb Cdn* (*Nfld*) throw (a stone, marble, etc.). [origin unknown]

BB¹ *abbreviation* double-black (pencil lead).

BB² /ˈbiːbiː/ *noun* a small pellet for shooting out of an air rifle or shotgun. [designation of size]

B.B.A. *abbreviation* Bachelor of Business Administration.

b-ball *noun N Amer. slang* basketball.

BBC *abbreviation* British Broadcasting Corporation.

BBC English *noun* a form of standard British English regarded as characteristic of BBC announcers, often identified with Received Pronunciation.

bbl. *abbreviation* barrels (esp. of oil).

b-boy *noun* a young man involved in hip hop culture. [*b* perhaps from BREAKDANCING]

BBQ *abbreviation informal* barbecue.

BBS *abbreviation* (*pl.* **BBSs**) bulletin board service, a computerized system for the exchange of software and electronic messages.

BC *abbreviation* **1** British Columbia. **1** (of a date) before Christ.

BC Bud *noun informal* high-potency marijuana grown in BC, with a THC content of 15% to 25%. [from British Columbia + BUD¹, the buds of the cannabis plant being the richest source of THC]

BCD *noun Computing* a code representing decimal numbers as a string of binary digits. [acronym from binary coded decimal]

BC Day *noun Cdn* the name of the August civic holiday in British Columbia.

BCE *abbreviation* before the Common Era. ¶ Used to denote years before the traditional date of the birth of Christ.

B.C.E. *abbreviation* Bachelor of Civil Engineering.

B cell *noun* (also **B lymphocyte**) an antibody-producing lymphocyte which, in adult mammals, develops within bone marrow and lymph nodes, and has immunoglobulins on its surface. [B from *Bursa of Fabricius*, a glandular sac that opens into a bird's cloaca, where their development was first observed]

BCG *abbreviation* Bacillus Calmette-Guérin, an anti-tuberculosis vaccine.

B.Com. *abbreviation* (also **B.Comm.**) Bachelor of Commerce.

B complex *noun* = VITAMIN B COMPLEX.

B.C.S. *abbreviation* Bachelor of Computer Science.

B.D. *abbreviation* Bachelor of Divinity.

b'day *noun informal* birthday.

BDC *abbreviation* (in Canada) Business Development Bank of Canada.

Bde *abbreviation* Brigade.

bdel·lium /ˈdɛliəm/ *noun* **1** any of various trees, esp. of the genus *Commiphora*, yielding resin. **2** this fragrant resin used in perfumes. [Latin from Greek *bdellion* from Hebrew bᵉ*dhōlah*]

Bdr *abbreviation* (before a name) Bombardier.

bdrm *abbreviation* bedroom.

B.E. *abbreviation* **1** Bachelor of Education. **2** Bachelor of Engineering. **3** bill of exchange.

Be *symbol Chem.* the element beryllium.

be (*sing. present* **am**; **are**; **is**; *pl. present* **are**; *1st and 3rd sing. past* **was**; *2nd sing. past and pl. past* **were**; *present subjunctive* **be**; *past subjunctive* **were**; *pres. part.* **being**; *past participle* **been** /biːn, bɪn/) ● *intransitive verb* **1** (often *prec. by there*) exist, live (*I think, therefore I am*; *there is a house on the corner*). **2 a** occur; take place (*dinner is at eight*). **b** occupy a position in space (*he is in the garden*; *she is from abroad*; *have you been to Paris?*). **3** remain, continue (*let it be*). **4** linking subject and predicate, expressing: **a** identity (*she is the person*; *today is Thursday*). **b** condition (*he is ill today*). **c** state or quality (*she is very kind*; *they are my friends*). **d** opinion (*I am against hanging*). **e** total (*two and two are four*). **f** cost or significance (*it is $5 to enter*; *it is nothing to me*). ● *auxiliary verb* **1** with a past participle to form the passive voice (*it was done*; *it is said*; *we shall be helped*). **2** with a present participle to form progressive tenses (*we are coming*; *it is being cleaned*). **3** with an infinitive to express duty or commitment, intention, possibility, destiny, or hypothesis (*I am to tell you*; *we are to wait here*; *she is to come at four*; *it was not to be found*; *they were never to meet again*; *if I were to die*). **4** *archaic* with the past participle of intransitive verbs to form perfect tenses (*the sun is set*; *Babylon is fallen*). □ **be about** occupy oneself with (*is about her business*). **be at** occupy oneself with (*what is he at?*; *mice have been at the food*). **been** (or **been and gone**) **and** *slang* an expression of protest or surprise (*he's been and taken my car!*). **been there, done that** indicating that the speaker has already experienced something or is familiar with it, esp. to the point of boredom or complacency. **be off** *informal* go away; leave. **be that as it may** *see* MAY. **-to-be** of the future (*in combination*: *bride-to-be*). [Old English *beo(m)*, *(e)am*, *is*, *(e)aron*; past from Old English *wæs* from *wesan* to be; there are numerous Germanic cognates]

be- *prefix* forming verbs: **1** (from transitive verbs) **a** all over; all round (*beset*; *besmear*). **b** thoroughly, excessively (*begrudge*; *belabour*). **2** (from intransitive verbs) expressing transitive action (*bemoan*; *bestride*). **3** (from adjectives and nouns) expressing transitive action (*befool*; *befoul*). **4** (from nouns) **a** affect with (*befog*). **b** treat as (*befriend*). **c** (forming adjectives in *-ed*) having; covered with (*bejewelled*; *bespectacled*). [Old English *be-*, weak form of *bī* BY as in *bygone*, *byword*, etc.]

beach ● *noun* **1** a pebbly or sandy shore of a body of water, esp. a lake or ocean. **2** *Cdn* (*Nfld*) a stretch of shingle or smooth rocks used for drying salt cod. ● *transitive verb* run or haul up (a boat etc.) on to a beach. [16th c.: origin unknown]

beach ball *noun* a large lightweight inflated ball, esp. for games on the beach.

beach bird *noun Cdn* (*Nfld*) any of a variety of shorebirds, such as the spotted sandpiper.

beach buggy *noun* = DUNE BUGGY.

Vowels: a cat ɑ arm e bed ɜr her ɜ: deux ə ago ɪ sit i cosy iː feed ɒ hot ɔ pore oː no ʌ run ʊ put

beach·comb·er *noun* **1** *Cdn* (*BC*) a person who earns a living by collecting logs that have broken loose from log booms and returning them to logging companies. **2** a person who searches beaches for articles of value. **3** a long wave rolling in from the sea.
□ **beach·comb** *transitive & intransitive verb*

beached *adjective* (of a sea mammal etc.) stranded on the shore, esp. by the action of tides etc. (*beached whale*).

beach·front *esp. N Amer.* ● *noun* land that fronts onto a beach.
● *adjective* located on or overlooking a beach.

beach grass *noun* any of various grasses which grow on sand dunes, esp. marram.

beach·head *noun* **1** *Military* a fortified position established on a beach by landing forces. **2** a foothold; an initial position from which one may advance. [after *bridgehead*]

Beach-la-mar /ˌbiːtʃləˈmɑr/ *noun* an English-based pidgin formerly used as a trade language and contact vernacular in the SW Pacific. [corruption from Portuguese *bicho do mar* BÊCHE-DE-MER 'sea cucumber' (traded as a commodity: the word then applied to the language of trade)]

beach pea *noun* a wild pea of the genus *Lathyrus* found on the shores of lakes and oceans throughout the northern hemisphere.

beach plum *noun* **1** a maritime N American shrub, *Prunus maritima*. **2** its edible fruit.

beach·side *attributive adjective* on or along a beach.

beach towel *noun* a very large terry towel, suitable for lying on on a beach.

beach volleyball *noun* a form of volleyball played by teams of two on a beach or other surface covered deeply with sand.

bea·con *noun* **1 a** a fire or light set up in a high or prominent position as a warning etc. **b** *Brit.* (now often in place names) a hill suitable for this. **2** a visible warning or guiding point or device, e.g. a lighthouse, navigation buoy, etc. **3** a radio transmitter whose signal helps fix the position of a ship, aircraft, etc. [Old English *bēacn* from West Germanic]

Bea·cons·field a former city in south central Quebec, on the SW shore of the Island of Montreal, now part of the city of Montreal; pop. (2001) 19,310. [ultimately after B. Disraeli, Earl of *Beaconsfield*, prime minister of Great Britain d.1881]

bead ● *noun* **1 a** a small usu. rounded and perforated piece of glass, stone, etc., for threading with others to make jewellery, or sewing on to fabric, etc. **b** (in *pl.*) a string of beads. **c** (in *pl.*) a rosary. **2** a drop of liquid; a bubble. **3** a small knob in the foresight of a gun. **4** the inner edge of a pneumatic tire that grips the rim of the wheel. **5** *Archit.* **a** a moulding like a series of beads. **b** a narrow moulding with a semicircular cross-section. ● *verb* **1** *transitive* furnish or decorate with beads. **2** *transitive* string together. **3** *intransitive* form or grow into beads.
□ **draw a bead on** take aim at. **say the** (or **tell one's**) **beads** *dated* use the beads of a rosary etc. in counting prayers. □ **bead·ed** *adjective* [originally = 'prayer' (for which the earliest use of beads arose): Old English *gebed* from Germanic, related to BID]

bead·ing *noun* **1** decoration in the form of or resembling a row of beads, esp. lace-like looped edging. **2** *Archit.* a bead moulding. **3** the bead of a tire.

Bea·dle, George Wells (1903–89), US geneticist, who shared the 1958 Nobel Prize for physiology or medicine for his research in biochemical genetics which resulted in the hypothesis that a single gene codes for a single kind of enzyme.

bea·dle *noun* **1** a ceremonial usher, mace bearer, etc. in certain universities etc. **2** a Presbyterian church officer attending on the minister. **3** a layperson employed by a church, synagogue, etc., to perform various minor functions. □ **beadle·ship** *noun* [Old French *bedel*, ultimately from Germanic]

beads·man *noun* (*pl.* -**men**) *hist.* **1** a pensioner provided for by a benefactor in return for prayers. **2** an inmate of an almshouse.

bead·work *noun* ornamental work with beads. □ **bead·work·er** *noun*

beady *adjective* (**bead·i·er, bead·i·est**) **1** (of the eyes) small, round, and bright. **2** covered with beads or drops. □ **bead·i·ly** *adverb* **bead·i·ness** *noun*

beady-eyed *adjective* **1** with beady eyes. **2** observant.

bea·gle ● *noun* a short-legged breed of dog with a short black and white or brown and white coat. ● *intransitive verb* (often as **beag·ling** *noun*) hunt with beagles. □ **beag·ler** *noun* [Old French *beegueule* noisy person, prob. from *beer* open wide + *gueule* throat]

Beagle Channel a channel in the islands of Tierra del Fuego at the southern tip of S America. It is named after HMS *Beagle*, the ship of Charles Darwin's voyage of 1831–6.

beak¹ *noun* **1 a** a bird's horny projecting jaws; a bill. **b** the similar projecting jaw of other animals, e.g. a turtle. **2** *slang* a hooked nose. **3** *Naut. hist.* the projection at the prow of a warship. **4** a spout.
□ **beaked** *adjective* **beak·like** *adjective* **beaky** *adjective* [Old French *bec* from Latin *beccus*, of Celtic origin]

beak² *noun* *Brit. slang* **1** a magistrate. **2** a schoolmaster. [19th c.; prob. from thieves' cant]

beaked willow *noun* = DIAMOND WILLOW.

beak·er *noun* **1** a lipped cylindrical glass vessel for scientific experiments. **2** *Brit.* **a** a tall drinking vessel, usu. of plastic and tumbler-shaped. **b** a metal or plastic mug. **3** *archaic* or *literary* a large drinking vessel with a wide mouth. [Old Norse *bikarr*, perhaps from Greek *bikos* drinking bowl]

Beaker Folk *noun* *Archaeology* a people thought to have come to Britain from central Europe in the early Bronze Age, named after beaker-shaped pottery found in their graves.

Beale, Doro·thea (1831–1906), pioneer in higher education for women in Britain, and an enthusiastic advocate of women's suffrage.

beal·ing *dialect* ● *adjective* (of a part of the body) infected. ● *noun* (also **beal**) an infected or festering sore. [alteration of BOIL²]

be-all and end-all *noun* *informal* (often foll. by *of*) the whole being or essence.

Beals, Car·lyle Smith (1899–1979), Canadian astronomer. He contributed to the development of instrumentation for astronomy, and initiated a program to identify and study meteorite craters in Canada.

beam ● *noun* **1** a long sturdy piece of metal or squared timber etc. spanning an opening or room, usu. to support the structure above. **2 a** a ray or shaft of light. **b** a directional flow of particles or radiation. **3** a bright look or smile. **4 a** a series of radio or radar signals as a guide to a ship or aircraft. **b** the course indicated by this (*off beam*). **5** the crossbar of a balance, from which the pans or weights are suspended. **6 a** a ship's breadth at its widest point. **b** *informal* (esp. in **broad in the beam**) the width of a person's hips. **7** (in *pl.*) the horizontal cross timbers of a ship supporting the deck and joining the sides. **8** the side of a ship (*land on the port beam*). **9** = BALANCE BEAM. **10** the central shaft of a plow. **11** the cylinder in a loom on which the warp or cloth is wound. **12** the main stem of a stag's antlers. **13** the lever in an engine connecting the piston rod and crank. **14** the shank of an anchor. ● *verb* **1** *transitive* emit or direct (light, radio waves, etc.). **2** *intransitive* **a** shine. **b** look or smile radiantly. □ **beam down** (in science fiction) transport or be transported instantaneously to another place, esp. to or from a spaceship or another planet. **the beam in one's eye** a fault that is greater in oneself than in the person one is finding fault with (see Matt. 7:3). **off beam** *informal* mistaken. **on the beam** right. **on her** (or **its**) **beam ends** (of a ship) on its side; almost capsizing. **on one's beam ends** near the end of one's resources. [Old English *bēam* tree, from West Germanic]

beam compass *noun* a compass with the legs connected by a beam with sliding sockets, used for large circles.

beamed *adjective* having a beam or beams (*beamed ceiling*).

Bea·mon, Rob·ert ('Bob'), (b.1946), US athlete. He set a world record of 8.90 metres (29 ft. 2 ½ in.) in the long jump at the 1968 Olympic Games in Mexico City; this was not beaten until 1991.

beamy *adjective* (of a ship) broad-beamed.

bean ● *noun* **1 a** any kind of leguminous plant with edible usu. kidney-shaped seeds in long pods. **b** one of these seeds. **2** a similar seed of coffee and other plants. **3** *N Amer. informal* the head. **4** (in *pl.*; with *neg.*) *N Amer. informal* anything at all (*doesn't know beans about it*). ● *transitive verb* *N Amer. informal* hit on the head. □ **be full of beans** *informal* **1** be lively or mischievous. **2** *N Amer.* talk nonsense. **not a bean** *Brit. slang* no money. **not a hill of beans** *N Amer. slang* an insignificant amount. **old bean** *Brit. slang* a friendly form of address, usu. to a man. [Old English *bēan* from Germanic]

bean·bag *noun* **1** a small bag filled with dried beans and used esp. in children's games. **2** a large cushion filled usu. with polystyrene beads and used as a seat.

bean·ball *noun* *Baseball* a pitch thrown at the batter's head.

bean-counter *noun* *informal derogatory* a person, esp. an accountant or bureaucrat, perceived as placing excessive emphasis on numbers, budgets, etc., esp. to the detriment of vision or creativity.
□ **bean-counting** *noun*

bean curd *noun* = TOFU.

bean·ery noun (pl. **-eries**) N Amer. informal a cheap restaurant.

bean·feast noun Brit. informal a celebration; a merry time. [BEAN + FEAST, beans and bacon being regarded as an indispensable dish]

beanie noun a skullcap, esp. of a sort worn formerly by small boys. [perhaps from BEAN 'head' + -IE]

beano noun (pl. **beanos**) Brit. slang a celebration; a party. [abbreviation of BEANFEAST]

bean·pole noun 1 a stick for supporting bean plants. 2 informal a tall thin person.

bean sprout noun (usu. in pl.) a sprout of a bean seed, esp. of the mung bean, eaten raw or cooked.

bean·stalk noun the stem of a bean plant.

Bean·town informal Boston.

bear¹ verb (past **bore**; past participle **borne**, **born**) ¶ In the passive born is used with reference to birth (e.g. was born in July), except for borne by foll. by the name of the mother (e.g. was borne by Sarah). 1 transitive carry, bring, or take (esp. visibly) (bear gifts). 2 transitive show; be marked by; have as an attribute or characteristic (bear marks of violence; bears no relation to the case; bore no name). 3 transitive a produce, yield (fruit etc.). b give birth to (has borne a son; was born last week). 4 transitive a sustain (a weight, responsibility, cost, etc.). b stand, endure (an ordeal, difficulty, etc.). 5 transitive (usu. with neg. or interrogative) a tolerate; put up with (can't bear her; how can you bear it?). b admit of; be fit for (does not bear thinking about; does not bear repeating). 6 transitive carry in thought or memory (bear a grudge). 7 intransitive veer in a given direction (bear left). 8 transitive bring or provide (something needed) (bear him company). 9 reflexive behave (in a certain way). □ **bear arms 1** carry weapons; serve as a soldier. 2 wear or display heraldic devices. **bear away** (or **off**) win (a prize etc.). **bear down** exert downward pressure. **bear down on** approach rapidly or purposefully. **bear fruit** have results. **bear a hand** help. **bear in mind** take into account having remembered. **bear on** (or **upon**) be relevant to. **bear out** support or confirm (an account or the person giving it). **bear up** raise one's spirits; not despair. **bear with** tolerate patiently. **bear witness** testify. [Old English beran from Germanic]

bear² noun 1 any large heavy mammal of the family Ursidae, having thick fur and walking on its soles. 2 a rough, unmannerly, or uncouth person. 3 Stock Exch. a person who sells shares hoping to buy them back later at a lower price. 4 (**the Bear**) informal Russia. □ **like a bear with a sore head** Brit. informal very irritable. □ **bear·like** adjective [Old English bera from West Germanic]

bear·able adjective that may be endured or tolerated. □ **bear·ably** adverb

bear-baiting noun hist. an entertainment involving setting dogs to attack a captive bear.

bear·berry noun (pl. **-berries**) 1 a small trailing evergreen shrub of the chiefly N American genus Arctostaphylos, esp. A. uva-ursi, with bright red astringent berries. 2 the berries of this plant.

beard ● noun 1 hair growing on the chin and lower cheeks of the face, esp. a man's face. 2 a similar tuft or part on an animal (esp. a goat). 3 the awn of a grass, sheath of barley, etc. ● transitive verb oppose openly; defy. □ **beard·ed** adjective **beard·less** adjective [Old English from West Germanic]

bearded collie noun a medium-sized breed of shaggy sheepdog.

bearded iris noun a variety of iris with numerous hairs on the lower petals, the most common type of cultivated iris.

bearded seal noun an Arctic seal, Erignathus barbatus, characterized by a large mouth surrounded by beard-like bristles.

Beard·more Glacier a glacier in Antarctica, flowing from the Queen Maud Mountains to the Ross Ice Shelf, at the southern edge of the Ross Sea. One of the world's largest glaciers, it is 418 km (260 miles) long.

Beards·ley, **Aub·rey Vin·cent** (1872–98), English artist and illustrator. He is known for his illustrations of Malory's Morte d'Arthur, Wilde's Salome, and Pope's The Rape of the Lock.

beard·tongue noun any of various plants of the chiefly western N American genus Penstemon, with tubular flowers.

bear·er noun 1 a person or thing that bears, carries, or brings. 2 a carrier of equipment on an expedition etc. 3 a person who presents a cheque or other order to pay money. 4 (attributive) payable to the possessor (bearer stock). 5 hist. (esp. in India) a personal servant.

bear·grass noun 1 a plant of western N America, Xerophyllum tenax, whose leaves were used by Aboriginal peoples to make watertight baskets. 2 any of various plants of the agave family, e.g. the yucca or the Spanish bayonet.

bear hug noun a tight embrace.

bear·ing noun 1 a person's bodily attitude or outward behaviour. 2 (foll. by on, upon) relation or relevance to (her comments had no bearing on the subject). 3 endurability (beyond bearing). 4 a part of a machine that supports a rotating or other moving part. 5 direction or position relative to a fixed point, measured esp. in degrees. 6 (in pl.) a one's position relative to one's surroundings. b awareness of this; a sense of one's orientation (get one's bearings; lose one's bearings). 7 Heraldry a device or charge. 8 = BALL BEARING.

bear·ing rein noun a fixed rein from bit to saddle that forces a horse to arch its neck.

bear·ish adjective 1 a Stock Exch. causing, predicting, or associated with a fall in prices. b pessimistic. 2 like a bear, esp. in temper; rough, surly. □ **bear·ish·ly** adverb **bear·ish·ness** noun

Bear Lake noun = SAHTU DENE. [GREAT BEAR LAKE]

bear market noun Stock Exch. a market with falling prices.

Béar·naise sauce /ˌbeiərˈneiz/ noun a rich sauce containing egg yolks, butter, vinegar and tarragon. [French, fem. of béarnais of Béarn in SW France]

bear·paw noun 1 the paw of a bear. 2 (in full **bearpaw snowshoe**) Cdn an almost circular, tailless type of snowshoe.

bear-pit session noun Cdn an esp. political meeting in which audience members question one or more representatives, leaders, candidates, etc.

bear root noun = LICORICE ROOT 2.

bear's breech noun a kind of acanthus, Acanthus mollis.

bear's ear noun = AURICULA.

bear's foot noun a hellebore, Helleborus foetidus.

bear·skin noun 1 a the skin of a bear. b a rug etc. made of this. 2 a tall furry hat worn ceremonially by some regiments.

beast noun 1 an animal other than a human being, esp. a wild quadruped. 2 a a brutal person. b informal an objectionable or unpleasant person or thing (he's a beast for not inviting her; a beast of a problem). 3 (prec. by the) a human being's brutish or uncivilized characteristics (saw the beast in her). □ **the nature of the beast** the undesirable but unchangeable inherent or essential quality or character of the thing. [Old French beste from Romanic besta from Latin bestia]

beast·ie noun jocular 1 a small animal. 2 a small malevolent creature.

beast·ly ● adjective (**beast·li·er**, **beast·li·est**) 1 informal objectionable, unpleasant. 2 like a beast; brutal. ● adverb informal very, extremely. □ **beast·li·ness** noun

beast of burden noun an animal, e.g. an ox, used for carrying loads.

beast of prey noun an animal which hunts animals for food.

beat ● verb (past **beat**; past participle **beaten**) 1 transitive a strike (a person or animal) persistently or repeatedly, esp. to harm or punish. b strike (a thing) repeatedly, e.g. to remove dust from (a carpet etc.), to sound (a drum etc.). 2 intransitive (foll. by against, at, on, etc.) a pound or knock repeatedly (waves beat against the shore; beat at the door). b = BEAT DOWN 3. 3 transitive a overcome; surpass; win a victory over. b complete an activity before (another person etc.). c be too hard for; perplex. 4 transitive mix or stir (ingredients) vigorously so as to incorporate air. 5 transitive (often foll. by out) fashion or shape (metal etc.) by blows. 6 intransitive (of the heart, a drum, etc.) pulsate rhythmically. 7 transitive (often foll. by out) indicate (a tempo or rhythm) by gestures, tapping, etc. b sound (a signal etc.) by striking a drum or other means (beat a tattoo). 8 a intransitive (of a bird's wings) move up and down. b transitive cause (wings) to move in this way. 9 transitive make (a path etc.) by trampling. 10 transitive strike (bushes etc.) to rouse game. 11 intransitive Cdn (Nfld) (of herd animals, esp. seals) migrate. 12 intransitive Naut. sail in the direction from which the wind is blowing. ● noun 1 a a main accent or rhythmic unit in music or verse (three beats to the bar; missed a beat and came in early). b the indication of rhythm by a conductor's movements (watch the beat). c (in popular music) a strong rhythm. d (attributive) characterized by a strong rhythm (beat music). 2 a a stroke or blow, e.g. on a drum. b a measured sequence of strokes (the beat of the waves on the rocks). c a throbbing movement or sound (the beat of his heart). 3 a a route or area allocated to a police officer, reporter, etc. b a person's area of interest or specialization (a reporter on the entertainment beat). 4 Physics a pulsation due to the combination of two sounds or electric currents of similar but not equivalent frequencies. 5 informal = BEATNIK. ● adjective 1 (predicative) informal exhausted, tired out. 2 (attributive) of the beat generation or its philosophy. □ **beat about** (often foll. by for) search (for an excuse etc.). **beat around the bush** discuss a matter without coming to the point. **to beat the band** in such a way as to defeat all competition. **beat one's breast** strike one's chest in anguish or sorrow. **beat the bushes** N Amer. search thoroughly (beating the bushes for work). **beat the clock** complete a task within a stated time. **beat down 1 a** bargain with (a seller) to lower the price. **b** cause a seller to lower (the price). **2** strike (a resisting object) until it falls (beat the door down). **3** (of the sun, rain, etc.) radiate heat or fall continuously and vigorously. **beat the drum for** publicize, promote. **beaten at the post** defeated at the last moment. **beat in** crush. **beat it** informal go away. **beat off** drive back (an attack etc.). **beat oneself up (over)** criticize oneself excessively for a mistake etc. **beat a retreat** withdraw; abandon an undertaking. **beat time** indicate or follow a musical tempo with a baton or other means. **beat a person to it** arrive or achieve something before another person. **beat up** give a beating to, esp. with punches and kicks. **beat up on** abuse, attack, or defeat. (**it**) **beats me** I do not understand (it). **miss a beat** see MISS¹. **two hearts that beat as one** two people who are perfectly united in thought. □ **beat·able** adjective [Old English bēatan from Germanic]

beat box noun **1** = DRUM MACHINE. **2** = BOOM BOX.

beat·en adjective **1** outwitted; defeated. **2** exhausted; dejected. **3** (of gold or any other metal) shaped by a hammer. **4** (of a path etc.) well-trodden, much used. □ **off the beaten track** (or **path**) **1** in or into an isolated place. **2** unusual.

beat·er noun **1** an implement used for beating (e.g. eggs, a drum, etc.). **2** N Amer. informal an old or dilapidated vehicle. **3** a person who beats metal. **4** Cdn (Nfld) a young harp seal, about three to four weeks old. **5** a person employed to rouse game for shooting.

beat generation noun the members of a movement of young people esp. in the 1950s who rejected conventional society in their dress, habits, and beliefs.

bea·tif·ic /ˌbiːəˈtɪfɪk/ adjective **1** informal blissful (a beatific smile). **2** making blessed; imparting supreme happiness. □ **bea·tif·ic·ally** adverb [Latin beatificus from beatus blessed]

be·ati·fi·ca·tion /biːˌatɪfɪˈkeɪʃən/ noun **1** Catholicism the act of formally declaring a dead person 'blessed', often a step towards canonization. **2** the act or fact of making or being blessed. [ecclesiastical Latin beatificatio (as BEATIFY)]

be·ati·fy /biːˈatɪˌfaɪ/ transitive verb (**-fies**, **-fied**) **1** Catholicism announce the beatification of. **2** make happy. [ecclesiastical Latin beatificare from Latin beatus blessed]

beat·ing noun **1** a physical punishment or assault. **2** a defeat. □ **take some** (or **a lot of**) **beating** be difficult to surpass.

be·ati·tude /biːˈatɪˌtuːd, -tjuːd/ noun **1** blessedness. **2** (in pl.) the declarations of blessedness in Matt. 5:3–11. **3** a title given to patriarchs in the Orthodox Church. [Latin beatitudo from beatus blessed]

beat·nik noun a member of the beat generation. [BEAT + -nik after Sputnik, perhaps influenced by use of Yiddish -nik agent-suffix]

Bea·ton, Sir Cecil Wal·ter Hardy (1904–80), English photographer, noted for his fashion features and portraits of celebrities.

Bea·trix /ˈbiːətrɪks/ (full name Beatrix Wilhelmina Armgard) (b.1938), queen of the Netherlands from 1980.

Beat·ty /ˈbiːti/ (**Henry**) **War·ren** (b.1937), US actor, film director, and screenwriter. He starred in and produced Bonnie and Clyde (1967), co-directed Heaven Can Wait (1978), and was producer, director, co-writer, and star of Reds (1981), which won an Oscar for best director.

beat-up adjective informal dilapidated; in a state of disrepair.

beau /bəʊ/ noun (pl. **beaux** or **beaus** /bəʊz, bəʊ/) **1** esp. N Amer. dated or jocular an admirer; a boyfriend. **2** hist. a fop; a dandy. [French, = handsome, from Latin bellus]

Beauce·ron /bəʊsəˈrɔ̃/ noun (in Canada) a native or inhabitant of Quebec's Beauce region along the Chaudière river.

Beauce·ville /bəʊsvɪl/ a town in SE Quebec, on the Chaudière river southeast of Quebec City; pop. (2001) 6,261. [from the region of Beauce in which it is located]

Beau·fort /ˈbəʊfərt/ **Henry** (c.1374–1447), English cardinal and bishop of Westminster, a dominant political figure in the reigns of Henry IV, Henry V, and Henry VI, during whose minority and reign Beaufort effectively controlled the government.

Beaufort scale /ˈbəʊfərt/ noun a scale of wind speed ranging from 0 (calm) to 12 (hurricane). [Sir F. Beaufort, English admiral d.1857]

Beaufort Sea /ˈbəʊfərt/ a part of the Arctic Ocean lying to the north of the Yukon and Alaska. [Sir F. Beaufort, English admiral d.1857]

beau geste /bəʊ ˈʒest/ noun (pl. **beaux gestes** pronunc. same) a generous or gracious act. [French, = splendid gesture]

Beau·har·nais /bəʊarˈneɪ/ see JOSEPHINE.

Beau·har·nois¹ /ˌbəʊarˈnwɒ/ a town in S Quebec, situated on the south shore of the St. Lawrence, southwest of Montreal; pop. (2001) 11,464. [after seigneurs C. de Beauharnois de Beaumont de Villechauve d.1738, and C. de BEAUHARNOIS]

Beau·har·nois² /ˌbəʊarˈnwɒ/ **1 Charles de Beauharnois de La Boische, Marquis de** (1671–1749), French colonial administrator. As governor of New France 1726–47, he checked the expansion of the British Empire in N America. With the help of his Aboriginal allies he was able to defend key positions in Acadia and on Lake Ontario. **2** his brother, **Fran·çois de Beauharnois de La Chaus·saye, Baron de Beau·ville** (1665–1746), French colonial administrator. As intendant of New France (1702–05), he attempted to develop agriculture and bolster the fur trade, but his term of office was too short for his initiatives to have much effect.

beau ideal /ˌbəʊ iːdeɪˈal/ noun (pl. **beaux ideals** /ˌbəʊz iːdeɪˈal/) the highest type of excellence or beauty. [French beau idéal = ideal beauty: see BEAU, IDEAL]

Beau·jo·lais /ˈbəʊʒəˌleɪ/ noun a red or white burgundy wine from the Beaujolais district of France.

Beau·mar·chais /ˌbəʊmarˈʃeɪ/ **Pierre Au·gus·tin Caron de** (1732–99), French dramatist, best known for his comedies Le Barbier de Séville (1775) and Le Mariage de Figaro (1784), which inspired operas by Rossini and Mozart.

beau monde /bəʊ ˈmɒnd/ noun fashionable society. [French]

Beau·mont¹ /ˈbəʊmɒnt/ a town in central Alberta, immediately south of Edmonton; pop. (2001) 7,006. [French beau mont beautiful mountain]

Beau·mont² /ˈbəʊmɒnt/ **Fran·cis** (1584–1616), English dramatist. He collaborated with John Fletcher on Philaster (1609) and many other plays; The Knight of the Burning Pestle (?1607) is attributed to Beaumont alone.

Beaune /bəʊn/ noun a red burgundy wine from the region around the town of Beaune in east central France.

Beau·port /bəʊˈpɔr/ a former city in SE central Quebec, now part of the city of Québec; pop. (2001) 72,813. [French beau port beautiful port]

beaut informal ● noun esp. N Amer., Austral., & NZ an excellent or beautiful person or thing. ● adjective Austral., & NZ excellent; beautiful. [abbreviation of BEAUTY]

beaut·eous /ˈbjuːtiəs/ adjective literary beautiful.

beaut·ician noun **1** a person who gives beauty treatment. **2** a person who runs or owns a beauty salon.

beauti·ful adjective **1** delighting the aesthetic senses (a beautiful voice). **2** pleasant, enjoyable (had a beautiful time). **3** excellent (a beautiful specimen). □ **beauti·ful·ly** adverb

beauti·fy transitive verb (**-fies**, **-fied**) make beautiful; adorn. □ **beauti·fi·ca·tion** noun **beauti·fi·er** noun

beauty ● noun (pl. **-ies**) **1 a** a combination of qualities such as shape, colour, etc., that pleases the aesthetic senses, esp. the sight. **b** a combination of qualities that pleases the intellect or moral sense (the beauty of the argument). **c** something beautiful. **2 a** an excellent specimen (what a beauty!). **b** an attractive feature; an advantage (that's the beauty of the plan!). **3** a beautiful woman. ● interjection N Amer. expressing satisfaction etc. □ **beauty is only skin deep** a pleasing appearance is not a guide to character. [Old French beauté, ultimately from Latin (as BEAU)]

beauty·bush noun a shrub, Kolkwitzia amabilis, with pink and white flowers, planted as an ornamental.

beauty contest noun (also **beauty pageant**) a competition in which participants, usu. women, are judged on their physical attractiveness.

beauty queen noun the woman judged most beautiful in a beauty contest.

beauty salon noun (also **beauty parlour**) an establishment in which beauty treatment, esp. hairdressing, is practised professionally.

beauty sleep noun sleep as contributing to one's beauty.

beauty spot noun **1** a place known for its beauty. **2** (also **beauty mark**) a small natural or artificial mark such as a mole on the face, considered to enhance another feature.

beauty treatment noun the use of cosmetics, manicuring, hairdressing, etc. to enhance personal appearance.

Beau·voir /ˈbəʊvwar/ **Si·mone de** (1908–86), French existentialist novelist and feminist whose best-known work is the treatise Le Deuxième Sexe (The Second Sex, 1949). She formed a lifelong association with Sartre, whom she met in 1929.

beaux *pl. of* BEAU.

beaux arts /boː'zɑr/ *plural noun* **1** fine arts. **2** (*attributive*) relating to the classical decorative style maintained by the École des Beaux-Arts in Paris, esp. in the 19th c. [French *beaux-arts*]

Bea·ver *noun & adjective* ● *noun* (*pl.* same or **-vers**) = DUNNE-ZA. [translation of Chipewyan *tsa-tinné*, 'dwellers among the beaver']

bea·ver¹ ● *noun* (*pl.* same or **bea·vers**) **1 a** any large semi-aquatic broad-tailed rodent of the genus *Castor*, native to N America, Europe, and Asia, and able to gnaw down trees and build dams. **b** this as an emblem of Canada. **2 a** the soft, light brown fur of this animal. **b** = BEAVER HAT. **3** (**Beaver**) a member of the youngest level (ages 5, 6, and 7) in Scouting. **4** *Cdn hist.* **a** = MADE BEAVER. **b** a coin used during the fur trade, having a value equal to one made beaver. **5** *coarse slang* the female genitals. **6** (in full **beaver cloth**) a heavy woollen cloth like beaver fur. ● *intransitive verb informal* (usu. foll. by *away*) work hard. [Old English *be(o)for* from Germanic]

bea·ver² *noun hist.* the lower face guard of a knight's helmet. [Old French *baviere* bib, from *baver* slaver, from *beve* saliva, from Romanic]

beaver·board *noun* a kind of wood-fibre board used for building partitions etc. [BEAVER¹ + BOARD]

Beaver·brook, Wil·liam Max·well Ait·ken, 1st Baron (1879–1964), Canadian-born entrepreneur and politician. He became a millionaire before moving to England in 1910; there he held several cabinet posts and built a newspaper empire.

beaver bundle *noun* (esp. among the Blackfoot) a medicine bundle containing the skin of a beaver and other objects.

Beaver Club *noun Cdn hist.* a Montreal social club founded in the 18th c. by members of the North West Company.

beaver dam *noun N Amer.* a dam of mud and sticks built by beavers across a stream or river.

Beaver Dams a former British outpost in the Niagara Peninsula near the present-day Thorold, Ontario. In June 1813, attacking US troops were ambushed and routed by Mohawk and Caughnawaga warriors led by Lt James FitzGibbon, who had been warned of the attack by Laura Secord.

beaver fever *noun N Amer. informal* = GIARDIASIS.

beaver hat *noun hist.* a hat made from beaver wool.

beaver house *noun* (also **beaver lodge**) *N Amer.* a den constructed by beavers from sticks and mud, usu. in a beaver pond.

beaver lamb *noun* lambskin cut and dyed to resemble beaver fur.

beaver meadow *noun N Amer.* a flat, fertile, usu. treeless area created by the silting up of a beaver pond.

beaver pond *noun N Amer.* a pool of water formed behind a beaver dam, often containing several lodges.

beaver root *noun Cdn* (*Nfld*) any of several varieties of water lily, esp. *Nymphaea odorata*.

beaver tail *noun* **1** the broad, flat tail of a beaver. **2** *N Amer.* (*attributive*) (usu. **beaver·tail**) having the round, broad shape of a beaver tail (*beavertail snowshoe; beavertail paddle*). **3** (**Beaver Tail**) *Cdn proprietary* a flat oval of deep-fried dough served with various garnishes, esp. sugar and cinnamon.

beaver wool *noun N Amer.* the short smooth hair under the thick fur of a beaver pelt.

Bebb willow *noun* (also **Bebb's willow**) = DIAMOND WILLOW. [M. S. *Bebb*, US botanist d.1895]

Bebel /'beibəl/ (**Fer·di·nand**) **Aug·ust** (1840–1913), German socialist leader, who helped to found the German Social Democratic Party (1869).

bebop /'biːbɒp/ *noun* a type of jazz originating in the 1940s and characterized by complex harmony and rhythms. □ **bebop·per** *noun* [imitative of the typical rhythm]

be·calmed /bɪ'kɑmd/ *adjective* (of a sailing ship) deprived of wind and unable to move.

be·came *past of* BECOME.

Bé·can·cour /beikɑ'kur/ a town in south central Quebec, situated near the mouth of the Rivière Bécancour, across the St. Lawrence from Trois-Rivières; pop. (2001) 11,051. [ultimately from the name of the seigneury]

be·cause *conjunction* for the reason that; since. □ **because of** on account of; by reason of. [Middle English from BY *preposition* + CAUSE, after Old French *par cause de* by reason of]

bé·cha·mel /'beiʃə,mel/ *noun* = WHITE SAUCE. [Louis (Marquis de) Béchamel, French courtier who invented it, d.1703]

bêche-de-mer /,beʃ də 'mer/ *noun* (*pl.* same or **bêches-de-mer**, *pronunc.* same) **1** any of several sea cucumbers used to make Chinese soups, usu. cut into long strips and dried. *Also called* TREPANG. **2** = BEACH-LA-MAR. [French, alteration of *biche de mer* from Portuguese *bicho do mar* sea worm]

Bech·uana·land /,betʃu'ɒnə,land/ the former name (until 1966) of BOTSWANA.

beck¹ *noun* a gesture requesting attention, e.g. a nod, wave, etc. □ **at a person's beck and call** always having to be ready to obey a person's orders immediately. [*beck* (v.) from BECKON]

beck² *noun Northern England* a brook or mountain stream. [Old Norse *bekkr* from Germanic]

Beck·er, Boris (b.1967), German tennis player who became the youngest-ever men's singles champion at Wimbledon in 1985. He took the Wimbledon title again in 1986 and 1989.

Beck·et, St. Thom·as (à) (*c*.1118–70), English clergyman and statesman. He was chancellor of England under Henry II (1155–62), who named him archbishop of Canterbury in 1162, hoping to control the English Church. Becket came increasingly into conflict with Henry. Acting (as they thought) on the king's orders, four knights murdered Becket in Canterbury cathedral, which became a centre of pilgrimage.

beck·et *noun Naut.* a contrivance such as a hook, bracket, or looped rope, for securing loose lines, tackle, or spars. [18th c.: origin unknown]

Beck·ett, Sam·uel Barc·lay (1906–89), Irish-born dramatist, novelist, and poet in both French and English best known for his absurdist plays, including *Waiting for Godot* (1953) and *Endgame* (1957). He was awarded the Nobel Prize in 1969. □ **Beck·ett·ian** *adjective & noun*

Beck·ham /'bekəm/ **David (Rob·ert Jo·seph)** (b.1975), British soccer player. A midfielder, he became captain of the English national team in 2001, and was transferred from Manchester United to Real Madrid in 2003.

Beck·mann ▸ 1 Ernst Otto (1853–1923), German chemist, who devised a method of determining a compound's molecular weight by measuring the rise in boiling point of a solvent containing the compound. **2 Max** (1884–1950), German expressionist painter and graphic artist. His paintings typically reflect his first-hand experience of human evil during the First World War.

beck·on *verb* **1** *transitive* attract the attention of; summon by gesture. **2** *intransitive* (usu. foll. by *to*) make a signal to attract a person's attention; summon a person by doing this. □ **beck·on·ing** *adjective* [Old English *bīecnan*, *bēcnan*, ultimately from West Germanic *baukna* BEACON]

Beck·with /'bekwɪθ/ **John** (b.1927), versatile Canadian composer, educator, and music critic. His works, often written in collaboration with James Reaney and other poets, are in the N American tradition of Ives and Copland.

be·cloud *transitive verb* **1** obscure, confuse (*becloud the argument*). **2** cover with clouds. □ **be·cloud·ed** *adjective*

be·come *verb* (*past* **be·came**; *past participle* **be·come**) **1** *intransitive* begin to be (*became president; will become famous*). **2** *transitive* **a** look well on; suit (*blue becomes him*). **b** befit (*behaviour that becomes a professional*). □ **become of** happen to (*what will become of me?*). [Old English *becuman* from Germanic: compare BE-, COME]

be·com·ing *adjective* **1** flattering the appearance. **2** suitable; decorous. □ **be·com·ing·ly** *adverb*

Bec·querel /'bekə,rel/ **Antoine-Henri** (1852–1908), French physicist who shared the 1903 Nobel Prize with the Curies for his discovery of natural radioactivity in uranium salts.

bec·querel /'bekə,rel/ *noun Physics* the SI unit of radioactivity, corresponding to one disintegration per second. [A.-H. BECQUEREL]

B.Ed. *abbreviation* Bachelor of Education.

bed ● *noun* **1 a** a piece of furniture used for sleeping or resting on, usu. a box spring and a mattress. **b** a mattress and covers. **2** any place used by a person or animal for sleep or rest. **3** a bed and associated facilities: **a** for a patient in a hospital. **b** for a guest in a hotel etc. **4** the act of or usual time for being in bed. **5** the use of a bed: **a** *informal* for sexual intercourse. **b** for rest. **6** a place where something is embedded. **7** a level surface or other base upon which something rests as in: **a** the foundations of a road or railway. **b** a layer of rice, vegetables, etc. upon which another food is served. **c** the surface on a printing press etc. upon which a form is placed. **8** the body or floor of a truck. **9** a plot of land in which plants are grown, esp. a garden plot for planting flowers. **10** the bottom of a lake, sea, or river. **11** a layer of oysters etc. congregated in a particular spot. **12** *Geol.* a layer of stratified rock.

Vowels: a *cat* ɑ *arm* e *bed* ɜr *her* ɜ: *deux* ə *ago* ɪ *sit* i *cosy* iː *feed* ɒ *hot* ɔ *pore* oː *no* ʌ *run* ʊ *put*

● *verb* (**bed·ded**, **bed·ding**) **1** *transitive & intransitive* (usu. foll. by *down*) **a** put or go to bed. **b** settle, make oneself comfortable. **2** *transitive informal* have sexual intercourse with. **3** *transitive* (often foll. by *down*) furnish (a stable etc.) with bedding for livestock. **4** *transitive* (often foll. by *out*) plant in a garden bed. **5** *transitive* embed; fix firmly in something. **6 a** *transitive* arrange as a layer. **b** *intransitive* be or form a layer. □ **bed of roses** a position of ease and luxury. **brought to bed** *archaic* delivered of a child. **get up on the wrong side of the bed** be bad-tempered during the day. **go to bed 1** retire for the night. **2** (foll. by *with*) have sexual intercourse. **3** (of a publication) go to press. **be** (or **get**) **in bed with 1** have sexual intercourse with. **2** fraternize or consort with. **make the bed** tidy and arrange the covers of a bed after use. **make one's bed and lie in it** accept the consequences of one's actions. **put to bed 1** cause to go to bed. **2** make (a publication) ready for press. **take to one's bed** retire to bed because of illness. [Old English *bed(d)*, *beddian* from Germanic]

bedad /bəˈdad/ *interjection Irish archaic* by God! [corruption: compare GAD[2]]

bed and board *noun* = ROOM AND BOARD.

bed and breakfast *noun* **1** one night's accommodation and breakfast the next morning in a hotel etc. **2** an establishment providing this for one inclusive price.

Bé·dard /beiˈdɑr/ **Myriam** (b.1969), Canadian biathlete, winner of gold medals at the 1993 world championships and the 1994 Olympics, the first non-European to win gold in Olympic biathlon.

be·daub /bɪˈdɔb/ *transitive verb* **1** smear or daub with paint etc. **2** decorate gaudily.

be·dazzle *transitive verb* **1** dazzle thoroughly. **2** confuse by excess of brilliance. □ **be·dazzle·ment** *noun*

bed·bug *noun* any of several flat, wingless, bloodsucking insects of the genus *Cimex*, esp. *C. lectularius*, which infest beds and houses.

bed·chamber *noun* **1** *archaic* a bedroom. **2** *Brit.* (**Bedchamber**) part of the title of some of the monarch's attendants (*Lady of the Bedchamber*).

bed·clothes *plural noun* covers for a bed, such as sheets, blankets, etc.

bed·cover *noun* a cover for a bed, such as a quilt, etc.

bed·dable *adjective informal* sexually attractive.

bed·der *noun* = BEDDING PLANT.

bed·ding *noun* **1** the articles which compose a bed, esp. a mattress and bedclothes. **2** a layer of straw etc. on which livestock sleep. **3** a bottom layer. **4** *Geol.* the stratification of rocks, esp. when clearly visible.

bedding plant *noun* a plant, esp. an annual, suitable for a garden bed.

beddy-bye *noun* (also **beddy-byes**) *informal* bed, sleep. [BED + -Y[2] + BYE-BYE[2]]

Bede /biːd/ **St.** (also **Venerable Bede**) (*c.*673–735), English monk and historian. His *Ecclesiastical History of the English People*, completed in 731, is the first serious work of English history. Feast day, 27 May.

be·deck *transitive verb* adorn.

bedel *noun* (in some universities) an official with largely ceremonial duties. [archaic spelling of BEADLE]

be·devil *transitive verb* (**be·dev·illed**, **be·dev·il·ling**; esp. *US* **be·dev·iled**, **be·dev·il·ing**) **1** plague; afflict. **2** confound; confuse. **3** possess as if with a devil; bewitch. □ **be·devil·ment** *noun*

be·dew *transitive verb* cover or sprinkle with dew or drops of moisture.

bed·fellow *noun* **1** a person who shares a bed with another. **2** an associate or companion. □ **strange bedfellows** an oddly assorted group of persons, things, etc.

Bed·ford[1] a former town in central Nova Scotia, situated at the head of Bedford Basin, just north of Halifax, now part of the regional municipality of Halifax; pop. (2001) 16,102. □ **Bedford·ite** *noun* [see BEDFORD BASIN]

Bed·ford[2], **Duke of** (title of John of Lancaster) (1389–1435), English general, son of Henry IV of England, who was appointed protector of England on several occasions between 1415 and 1421, and regent of France (1422–35).

Bedford Basin an inlet of the Atlantic Ocean, situated at the head of Halifax Harbour, Nova Scotia. [J. Russell, 4th Duke of *Bedford*, British statesman d.1771]

Bedford cord *noun* a tough woven fabric having prominent ridges, similar to corduroy. [*Bedford* in S England]

Bed·ford·shire /ˈbɛdfərdˌʃɪr/ a county of south central England; county town, Bedford.

bed-head *noun* **1** esp. *N Amer. slang* a dishevelled head of hair such as results from a night's sleep. **2** *Brit.* the headboard of a bed.

bed-hopping *informal* ● *adjective* sexually promiscuous. ● *noun* sexual promiscuity.

be·dight /bɪˈdaɪt/ *adjective archaic* arrayed; adorned. [as BE-, DIGHT]

bedim *transitive verb* (**be·dimmed**, **be·dimming**) *archaic* make (the eyes, mind, etc.) dim.

be·dizen /bɪˈdaɪzən, -ˈdɪzən/ *transitive verb literary* deck out gaudily. [BE- + obsolete *dizen* deck out]

bed jacket *noun* a woman's short, light jacket worn in bed over a nightgown, esp. by invalids.

bed·lam /ˈbedləm/ *noun* **1** a scene of uproar and confusion (*there was bedlam in the finish area after the race*). **2** *archaic* a lunatic asylum. [alteration of Hospital of St. Mary of *Bethlehem*, an asylum in medieval London]

bed·lam·er /ˈbedləmər/ *noun Cdn* (*Nfld*) a young harp seal. [possibly from BEDLAM, reflecting the apparently manic behaviour of the seals]

bed·lam·ite /ˈbedləmaɪt/ *noun* a mentally ill person.

bed linen *noun* sheets and pillowcases.

bed·liner *noun N Amer.* a protective sheet of heavy plastic etc. placed in the bed of a pickup truck.

Bed·ling·ton terrier *noun* a breed of terrier with a narrow head, long legs, and curly grey hair. [*Bedlington* in Northumberland, England]

bed·mate *noun* **1** a person who shares a bed with another. **2** a sexual partner.

Bed·ouin /ˈbeduːɪn/ (also **Bed·uin**) (*pl.* same) ● *noun* **1** a member of an Arabic-speaking nomadic people inhabiting the desert regions of the Middle East, traditionally herders of camels, goats, and sheep. **2** a wanderer; a nomad. ● *adjective* **1** of or relating to the Bedouin. **2** wandering; nomadic. [ultimately from Arabic *badwiyyin* dwellers in the desert, from *badw* desert]

bed·pan *noun* a receptacle used by a bedridden patient for urine and feces.

bed·plate *noun* a metal plate forming the base of a machine.

bed·post *noun* any of the four upright supports of a bedstead.

bed race *noun* a race in which teams push people in wheeled beds along a course.

be·drag·gled /bɪˈdragəld/ *adjective* **1** untidy; dishevelled. **2** tattered; dilapidated. [BE- + DRAGGLE]

bed·rest *noun* confinement of an invalid to bed.

bed·rid·den *adjective* confined to bed by infirmity, esp. permanently. [Old English *bedreda* from *ridan* ride]

bed·rock *noun* **1** solid rock underlying loose superficial material, alluvial deposits, etc. **2** the underlying principles or facts of a theory, character, etc.

bed·roll *noun* esp. *N Amer.* portable bedding rolled into a bundle.

bed·room *noun* **1** a room for sleeping in. **2** (*attributive*) of or referring to sexual suggestiveness (*bedroom comedy*; *bedroom eyes*).

bedroom community *noun* (also **bedroom suburb**) *N Amer.* a residential suburb outside a larger city, inhabited largely by commuters.

Beds. *abbreviation* Bedfordshire.

bed·sheet *noun* = SHEET[1] 1.

bed·side *noun* **1** the space beside a bed. **2** (*attributive*) of or relating to the side of a bed (*bedside table*).

bedside manner *noun* the manner of a doctor when attending a patient.

bed-sitting room *noun* (also *informal* **bed-sitter**, *Brit.* **bed-sit**) *Cdn & Brit.* = BACHELOR APARTMENT 1.

bed·skirt *noun N Amer.* a usu. gathered fabric covering concealing the box spring and legs or frame of a bed.

bed·sock *noun* esp. *Brit.* each of a pair of thick warm socks worn in bed.

bed·sore *noun* an ulceration of the buttocks, heels, etc. developed by the constant pressure of the mattress on an invalid's skin.

bed·spread *noun* a top cover placed over a bed.

bed·spring *noun N Amer.* **1** a set of springs contained in a mattress or box spring. **2** any of the individual springs.

bed·stead *noun* a framework of wood or metal supporting the springs and mattress of a bed.

bed·straw *noun* **1** any herbaceous plant of the genus *Galium* having tiny flowers and whorls of leaves, once used as straw for bedding. *See also* CLEAVERS. **2** = OUR LADY'S BEDSTRAW.

bed·time *noun* **1** the usual time for going to bed. **2** (*attributive*) of or relating to bedtime (*bedtime story*).

Bed·uin *var. of* BEDOUIN.

bed·wet·ting *noun* urination in bed while asleep. □ **bed·wet·ter** *noun*

bee *noun* **1 a** a stinging hymenopterous insect of the genus *Apoidea*, which collects nectar and pollen, produces wax and honey, and lives in large communities. **b** a related insect of the family Apoidea, either social or solitary. **2** esp. *N Amer.* a social gathering at which communal work is performed (*quilting bee*). **3** a competition, e.g. in spelling etc., in which competitors take turns answering questions and are eliminated if their answers are incorrect. □ **a bee in one's bonnet** an obsession. **the bee's knees** *slang* something outstandingly good (*thinks he's the bee's knees*). **busy bee** a busy person. [Old English *béo* from Germanic]

Beeb *noun* (prec. by *the*) *Brit. informal* the BBC. [abbreviation]

bee balm *noun* = BERGAMOT[1] 3b.

bee bread *noun* a mixture of honey and pollen that comprises the food of bee larvae.

beech *noun* **1** any large deciduous tree of the genus *Fagus*, growing in temperate regions and having smooth grey bark and glossy leaves. **2** (also **beech·wood**) its wood. **3** any of various similar trees of the genus *Nothofagus* growing in Australasia and S America. [Old English *béce* from Germanic]

Bee·cham /'biːtʃəm/ **Thom·as** (1879–1961), British conductor and founder of the London Philharmonic (1932) and the Royal Philharmonic (1947). He excelled in Mozart and Haydn and was an important interpreter of his contemporaries Delius, Sibelius and Richard Strauss.

Bee·cher, Henry Ward (1813–87), US Congregational minister, who was a noted orator and outspoken advocate of the abolition of slavery.

Bee·cher Stowe *see* STOWE, HARRIET ELIZABETH BEECHER.

Bee·chey, Fred·erick Wil·liam (1796–1856), English naval officer, explorer, and artist. He participated in voyages of Arctic exploration under John Franklin (1818) and W.E. Parry (1819–20). In 1825–7 he commanded a voyage exploring the western Arctic.

Bee·chey Island /'biːtʃi/ a small island in the Canadian Arctic, situated off the southwestern coast of Devon Island. [F.W. BEECHEY]

beech fern *noun* a fern of the genus *Thelypteris* esp. *T. phegopteris*, found in damp woods.

beech·mast *noun* (*pl.* same) the beechnut, esp. used as food for animals.

beech·nut *noun* the small rough-skinned fruit of the beech tree.

bee dance *noun* the ritualized dance-like behaviour performed by worker honeybees to inform the colony of the location and quality of a food source.

bee-eater *noun* any bright-plumaged insect-eating bird of the family Meropidae, with a slender curved bill.

beef ● *noun* **1** the flesh of a cow, steer, or bull used as food. **2** (*pl.* **beeves**) **a** a cow, steer, or bull raised for its meat. **b** its carcass. **3** *informal* muscle or flesh; strength, size, or power. **4** (*pl.* **beefs**) *slang* a complaint; a protest. **5** *N Amer. slang* a criminal charge. ● *intransitive verb slang* complain. □ **beef up** *slang* strengthen, reinforce, augment. [Old French *boef* from Latin *bos bovis* ox]

beef·alo *noun* (*pl.* same or **-aloes**) a hybrid breed of bovine, usu. five-eighths buffalo and three-eighths domestic cow, raised for its meat. [blend of BEEF + BUFFALO]

beef·burger *noun* = HAMBURGER 1, 2.

beef·cake *noun informal* muscular male physique, esp. when prominently displayed in photographs etc. [after CHEESECAKE 2]

beef·eat·er *noun* a warder at the Tower of London; a Yeoman of the Guard. [from obsolete sense 'well-fed menial']

beef ring *noun N Amer. hist.* a co-operative butchering arrangement for the provision of fresh beef throughout the summer months.

beef·steak *noun* a slice of beef, usu. for grilling or frying.

beefsteak fungus *noun* an edible fungus, *Fistulina hepatica*, resembling raw meat in appearance.

beefsteak tomato *noun* any of several large and firm varieties of tomato.

beef stroganoff *noun see* STROGANOFF.

beef tea *noun* a hot beverage made from stewed extract of beef.

beef Wellington *noun* tenderloin of beef spread with pâté de foie gras, enclosed in puff pastry, and baked. [20th c.: origin uncertain]

beefy *adjective* (**beef·i·er, beef·i·est**) **1** like beef. **2** solid; muscular. □ **beef·i·ly** *adverb* **beef·i·ness** *noun*

bee·hive *noun* **1** an artificial habitation for keeping bees, traditionally in the shape of a dome but now usu. a box containing the combs on wooden slides. **2** a busy place. **3** a woman's high cone-shaped hairstyle. **4** (*attributive*) anything having a domed shape. □ **bee·hived** *adjective* (in sense 3).

beehive burner *noun Cdn* (*BC*) a dome-shaped incinerator used to burn waste at a sawmill.

bee·keep·er *noun* a person who raises honeybees for their honey and beeswax. □ **bee·keep·ing** *noun*

bee·line *noun* a straight line between two places. □ **make a beeline for** hurry directly to.

Beel·ze·bub /biː'elzə,bʌb/ *New Testament* the Devil. [Greek *beelzeboub* & Hebrew *ba'al z'bûb* lord of the flies, name of a Philistine god]

been *past participle of* BE.

bee orchid *noun* a kind of European orchid, *Ophrys apifera*, pollinated by insects who attempt to copulate with the flower, which resembles a female bee.

beep ● *noun* **1** a high-pitched noise, esp. one produced electronically. **2** the sound of a car horn. ● *verb* **1** *intransitive* emit a beep. **2** *transitive* cause to beep. **3** *transitive* summon or alert by means of a beeping device. [imitative]

beep·er *noun* **1** *N Amer.* a small electronic device which emits a high-pitched signal when the user is contacted, usu. by telephone. **2** anything that emits a beep.

bee plant *noun* any of various plants of the genus *Cleome* with protruding stamens which give the flower a bristly look.

bee pollen *noun* pollen gathered by bees, extracted and ingested as an antioxidant and to strengthen the immune system.

beer *noun* **1 a** an alcoholic drink made from yeast-fermented malt etc., flavoured with hops. **b** a bottle, can, or glass of this. **2** any of several other carbonated drinks flavoured with various plant extracts (*root beer; ginger beer*). □ **beer and skittles** *Brit.* amusement (*life is not all beer and skittles*). [Old English *béor* from Late Latin *biber* drink, from Latin *bibere*]

beer belly *noun* a protruding stomach caused by drinking large quantities of beer etc. □ **beer-bellied** *adjective*

Beer·bohm /'biːrboːm/ **Sir (Henry) Max·imil·ian** (1872–1956), English caricaturist, essayist, and critic. A central figure of the Aesthetic movement, he completed one novel, *Zuleika Dobson* (1911), a satire of *fin-de-siècle* Oxford.

beer cellar *noun* **1** an underground room for storing beer. **2** a pub located in a basement or cellar.

beer garden *noun* an outdoor garden with tables and chairs where beer is sold and consumed.

beer gut *noun Brit.* a beer belly.

beer hall *noun* a large room where beer is sold and consumed.

beer league *noun* **1** a sports minor league of the lowest rank. **2** a league of recreational hockey, baseball, etc. players.

beer mat *noun Brit.* a small cardboard coaster for beverages served in a bar.

beer·nut *noun N Amer.* a shelled roasted peanut with a crisp sweet coating.

beer parlour *noun Cdn* a room in a hotel or tavern where beer is served.

Beers, Wil·liam George (1843–1900), Canadian dentist and lacrosse player. His efforts to have lacrosse declared Canada's national game were ultimately unsuccessful, but did result in a tremendous increase in the game's popularity in the years immediately following Confederation.

Beer·sheba /biːr'ʃiːbə/ a city in S Israel on the northern edge of the Negev desert; pop. (est. 2000) 172,900. In biblical times it marked the southern limit of the Hebrew kingdom of ancient Israel (Judges 20; *see also* DAN 3).

beer slinger *noun Cdn informal* a bartender. □ **beer sling·ing** *noun*

beery *adjective* (**beer·i·er, beer·i·est**) **1** showing the influence of drink in one's appearance or behaviour. **2** smelling or tasting of beer. □ **beer·i·ly** *adverb* **beer·i·ness** *noun*

bee-stung *adjective* (of lips) full and pouty.

bees·wax ● *noun* **1** the wax secreted by bees to make honeycombs. **2** this wax refined and used to make candles, ointments, polishes, etc.

Consonants: b *but*   d *dog*   f *few*   g *get*   h *her*   j *yes*   k *cat*   l *leg*   m *man*   n *no*   p *pen*   r *red*   s *sit*

3 *N Amer. informal* business (*mind your own beeswax; none of your beeswax*). ● *transitive verb* polish (furniture etc.) with beeswax.

beet *noun* any plant of the genus *Beta*, esp. *B. vulgaris*, having an edible spherical dark red root used as a vegetable (*see also* SUGAR BEET). [Old English *bête* from Latin *beta*, perhaps of Celtic origin]

Beethov·en /'bei,to:vən/ **Lud·wig van** (1770–1827), German composer who settled in Vienna in 1792. Despite increasing deafness which became total around 1819, he revolutionized the genres of symphony, sonata, and concerto by incorporating both late classical and early romantic elements. □ **Beethov·en·ian** /ˌbeitoː'viːniən/ *adjective & noun*

bee·tle¹ ● *noun* **1** any insect of the order Coleoptera, with modified front wings forming hard protective cases closing over the back wings. **2** any similar. usu. black, insect. ● *intransitive verb informal* hurry, scurry. [Old English *bitula* biter from *bītan* BITE]

bee·tle² ● *noun* **1** a usu. wooden tool with a heavy head and a handle, used for ramming, crushing, driving wedges, etc. **2** a machine used for heightening the lustre of cloth by pressure from rollers. ● *transitive verb* **1** ram, crush, drive, etc., with a beetle. **2** finish (cloth) with a beetle. [Old English *bētel* from Germanic]

bee·tle³ ● *adjective* (esp. of the eyebrows) projecting, shaggy, scowling. ● *intransitive verb* project, overhang. [Middle English: origin unknown]

beetle-browed *adjective* with shaggy, projecting, or scowling eyebrows.

bee·tling *adjective* (of brows, cliffs, etc.) projecting; overhanging threateningly.

beet red ● *noun* an extremely dark shade of red, esp. describing a deep blush of embarrassment. ● *adjective* of this colour.

beet·root *noun Brit.* the edible red beet.

beeves *pl.* of BEEF 2.

BEF *abbreviation hist.* British Expeditionary Force.

be·fall *verb* (*past* **be·fell**; *past participle* **be·fall·en**) **1** *transitive* happen to (a person etc.) (*a similar fate befell the Romans*). **2** *intransitive* happen (*so it befell*). [Old English *befeallan* (as BE-, *feallan* FALL)]

befit *transitive verb* (**be·fit·ted**, **be·fit·ting**) **1** be fitted or appropriate for; suit. **2** be incumbent on. □ **be·fit·ting** *adjective* **be·fit·ting·ly** *adverb*

befog *transitive verb* (**be·fogged**, **be·fog·ging**) **1** confuse; obscure. **2** envelop in fog.

be·fool *transitive verb* make a fool of; delude.

be·fore ● *conjunction* **1** earlier than the time when (*crawled before he walked*). **2** rather than that (*would starve before she stole*). ● *preposition* **1 a** in front of (*before her in the line*). **b** ahead of (*crossed the finish line before him*). **c** under the impulse of (*recoiled before the attack*). **d** awaiting (*the future before them*). **2** earlier than; preceding (*spring comes before summer*). **3** rather than (*death before dishonour*). **4 a** in the presence of (*appear before the judge*). **b** for the attention of (*a plan put before the committee*). ● *adverb* **1 a** earlier than the time in question; already (*heard it before*). **b** in the past (*happened long before*). **2** ahead (*go before*). **3** on the front (*hit before and behind*). □ **before God** a solemn oath meaning 'as God sees me'. **not before time** *see* TIME. [Old English *beforan* from Germanic]

Before Christ *adverb* (of a date) reckoned backwards from the birth of Christ. Abbr.: BC.

be·fore·hand *adverb* in anticipation; in advance; in readiness (*had prepared the meal beforehand*).

be·foul *transitive verb* **1** make foul or dirty. **2** degrade; defile (*befouled her name*). □ **be·foul·ment** *noun*

be·friend *transitive verb* be or become friendly with.

be·fuddle *transitive verb* **1** confuse. **2** make drunk. □ **be·fuddle·ment** *noun*

beg *verb* (**begged**, **beg·ging**) **1 a** *intransitive* (usu. foll. by *for*) ask for (esp. food, money, etc.) (*begged for alms*). **b** *transitive* ask for (food, money, etc.) as a gift. **c** *intransitive* live by begging. **2** *transitive & intransitive* (usu. foll. by *for*, or *to* + infin.) ask earnestly or humbly (*begged for forgiveness; begged to be allowed out; please, I beg of you; beg your indulgence for a time*). **3** *transitive* ask formally for (*beg leave*). **4** *intransitive* (of a dog etc.) sit up with the front paws raised expectantly. **5** *transitive* take or ask leave (to do something) (*I beg to differ*). **6** *intransitive* demand, need urgently (*stories begging to be written*). □ **beg one's bread** live by begging. **beg off** decline to take part or attend. **beg a person's pardon** apologize. **beg pardon** *see* PARDON. **beg the question 1** assume the truth of an argument or proposition to be proved, without arguing it. **2** *disputed* pose the question. **3** *informal* evade a difficulty. ¶ Many people use the phrase *beg the question* in the disputed sense (sense 2 above). It

originally meant, and still means, 'to assume the truth of the thing that is to be proved', e.g. *By devoting such a large part of the budget for the fight against drug addiction to education, we are begging the question of its significance in the battle against drugs*, i.e. we are assuming that through education we can radically reduce drug taking. Over the years *beg the question* has been misunderstood and another meaning has arisen, 'to raise the question', or 'invite the obvious question', and this is now the more common use of the phrase, e.g. *Most people continue to live in cities, which begs the question as to whether city life or country life is more desirable.* This use has been extended even further in phrases such as *The question that still needs to be begged is . . . .* **go begging** (of a chance or a thing) not be taken; be unwanted. [Middle English, prob. from Old English *bedecian* from Germanic: related to BID]

begad /bi'gad/ *interjection archaic informal* by God! [corruption: compare GAD²]

began *past of* BEGIN.

begat *past of* BEGET.

Beg·bie /'begbi/ **Sir Mat·thew Bail·lie** (1819–94), English-born lawyer and judge. Appointed the first judge of the new colony of British Columbia in 1858, he helped to ensure that the colony remained British and eventually entered Confederation. In 1871 he was appointed the first chief justice of the province of British Columbia.

beget *transitive verb* (**be·get·ting**; *past* **begat**; **begot**; *past participle* **be·got·ten**) **1** be the parent, esp. the father of. **2** give rise to; cause (*violence begets violence*). □ **be·get·ter** *noun* [Old English *begietan*, formed as BE- + GET = procreate]

beg·gar ● *noun* **1** a person who begs, esp. one who lives by begging. **2** a poor person. **3** *informal* a person; a fellow (*poor beggar*). ● *transitive verb* **1** reduce to poverty. **2** exhaust the resources of (*beggar description*). □ **beggars can't be choosers** those without other resources must take what is offered.

beg·gar·ly *adjective* **1** poverty-stricken; needy. **2** mean; sordid. **3** ungenerous. □ **beg·gar·li·ness** *noun*

beggar-thy-neighbour *noun* (also **beggar-my-neighbour**) **1** a card game in which a player seeks to capture an opponent's cards. **2** (*attributive*) (of a policy) self-aggrandizing at the expense of competitors.

beg·gary *noun* extreme poverty.

begging bowl *noun* a bowl etc. held out for food or alms.

Begin /'beigin/ **Men·achem Wolf·ovitch** (1913–92), Israeli prime minister 1977–83. A militant Zionist leader in the 1930s and 1940s, he later opened peaceful negotiations with Anwar Sadat, President of Egypt, with whom he shared the 1978 Nobel Peace Prize.

begin *verb* (**be·gin·ning**; *past* **began**; *past participle* **begun**) **1** *transitive* start; perform the first part of (*begin work; begin crying; begin to understand*). **2** *intransitive* come into being; arise: **a** in time (*the strike began last week*). **b** in space (*our property begins beyond the river*). **3** *transitive* (usu. foll. by *to* + infin.) start at a certain time (*then began to feel ill*). **4** *intransitive* be begun (*the meeting will begin at 7*). **5** *intransitive* **a** start speaking ('*No,*' *she began*). **b** take the first step; be the first to do something (*who wants to begin?*). **6** *intransitive informal* (usu. with *neg.*) show any attempt or likelihood (*can't begin to compete*). □ **begin at** start from. **begin on** (or **upon**) set to work at. **begin with** take (a subject, task, etc.) first or as a starting point. **to begin with** in the first place. [Old English *beginnan* from Germanic]

be·gin·ner *noun* a person just beginning to learn a skill etc.

beginner's luck *noun* good luck supposed to attend a beginner at games etc.

be·gin·ning *noun* **1** the time or place at which anything begins. **2** a source or origin. **3** the first part. □ **the beginning of the end** the first clear sign of the end of something.

Bégon /bei'ɡɔ̃/ **Michel Bégon de La Picar·dière** (1667–1747), French colonial administrator. As intendant of New France 1712–26, he was faced with a depressed economy; his attempts to liberalize the fur trade and establish new industries failed, and he was recalled under suspicion of embezzlement.

be·gone *interjection literary* go away at once!

be·gonia /bə'ɡoːnjə, -niə/ *noun* any plant of the genus *Begonia* with brightly coloured sepals and no petals, and often having brilliant glossy foliage. [M. *Bégon*, French patron of science d.1710]

be·gorra /bə'ɡɒrə/ *interjection Irish* by God! [corruption]

begot *past of* BEGET.

be·got·ten *past participle of* BEGET.

be·grimed *adjective* grimy, soiled.

---

t top　v voice　w we　z zoo　ʃ she　ʒ vision　θ thin　ð this　ŋ ring　x loch　tʃ chip　dʒ jar　　　(*see over for vowels*)

be·grudge *transitive verb* **1** resent; be dissatisfied at. **2** envy (a person) the possession of. □ **be·grudg·ing·ly** *adverb*

be·guile /bɪˈgaɪl/ *transitive verb* **1** charm; amuse. **2** divert attention pleasantly from (toil etc.). **3** (usu. foll. by *of*, *out of*, or *into*) delude; cheat (*beguiled him into paying*). □ **be·guile·ment** *noun* **be·guil·er** *noun* **be·guil·ing** *adjective* **be·guil·ing·ly** *adverb* [BE- + obsolete *guile* to deceive]

be·guine /bɪˈɡiːn/ *noun* (also **bi·guine**) **1** a popular dance of W Indian origin. **2** its rhythm. [West Indian French from French *béguin* infatuation]

begum /ˈbeɪɡəm/ *noun* **1** (in the Indian subcontinent) a Muslim woman of high rank. **2** (**Begum**) (in the Indian subcontinent) the title of a married Muslim woman, equivalent to Mrs. [Urdu *begam* from Eastern Turkish *bīgam* princess, fem. of *big* prince: compare BEY]

begun *past participle of* BEGIN.

be·half *noun* □ **on behalf of** (also esp. *US* **in behalf of**) **1** in the interests of (a person, principle, etc.). **2** as representative of (*acting on behalf of my client*). [mixture of earlier phrases *on his halve* and *bihalve him*, both = on his side: see BY, HALF]

Behan /ˈbiːən/ **Bren·dan Fran·cis** (1923–94), Irish writer and nationalist. His autobiography *Borstal Boy* (1958) describes his detention for IRA activity; his plays include the tragicomedies *The Quare Fellow* (1956) and *The Hostage* (1958).

be·have *verb* **1** *intransitive* **a** act or react (in a specified way) (*behaved well*). **b** (esp. to or of a child) conduct oneself properly. **c** (of a machine etc.) work well (or in a specified way) (*the computer is not behaving today*). **2** *reflexive* (esp. of or to a child) show good manners (*behaved herself*). □ **behave towards** treat (in a specified way). [BE- + HAVE]

be·hav·iour *noun* (also **be·hav·ior**) **1 a** the way one conducts oneself; manners. **b** the treatment of others; moral conduct. **2** the way in which a vehicle, machine, chemical substance, etc., acts or works. **3** *Psych.* an observable pattern of actions (of a person, animal, etc.), esp. in response to a stimulus. **4** an instance of behaving in a specific way (*the sequence of behaviours typical of nesting loons*). □ **be on one's best behaviour** behave well when being observed. [BEHAVE on the pattern of *demeanour* and influenced by obsolete *haviour* from *have*]

be·hav·iour·al *adjective* (also **be·hav·ior·al**) of or relating to behaviour. □ **be·hav·iour·al·ist** *noun* (also **be·hav·ior·al·ist**) **be·hav·iour·al·ly** *adverb* (also **be·hav·ior·al·ly**).

behavioural science *noun* the scientific study of human behaviour (*see* BEHAVIOURISM).

be·hav·iour·ism *noun* (also **be·hav·ior·ism**) *Psych.* **1** the theory that objective investigation of stimuli and responses is the only valid psychological method, and that psychological disorders are best treated by altering behaviour patterns. **2** such study and treatment in practice. □ **be·hav·iour·ist** *noun* (also **be·hav·ior·ist**). **be·hav·iour·is·tic** *adjective* (also **be·hav·ior·is·tic**).

behaviour therapy *noun* the treatment of neurotic symptoms by training the patient's reactions (*see* BEHAVIOURISM; *compare* PSYCHOANALYSIS).

be·head *transitive verb* cut off the head of (a person), esp. as a form of execution; decapitate. □ **be·head·ing** *noun* [Old English *behēafdian* (as BE-, *hēafod* HEAD)]

be·held *past and past participle of* BEHOLD.

be·he·moth /bəˈhiːməθ, ˈbiːəˌməθ/ *noun* an enormous creature or thing. [Hebrew *bᵉhēmōt* intensive pl. of *bᵉhēmāh* beast (see Job 40:15), perhaps from Egyptian *p-ehe-mau* water ox]

be·hest /bɪˈhest/ *noun* (in phr. **at the behest of**) a command; a request. [Old English *behǣs* from Germanic]

be·hind ● *preposition* **1 a** in, towards, or to the rear of. **b** on the farther side of (*behind the bush*). **c** hidden by (*something behind that remark*). **2 a** in the past in relation to (*trouble is behind me now*). **b** late in relation to (*behind schedule*). **3** inferior to; weaker than (*behind the others in math*). **4 a** in support of (*she's behind the idea*). **b** responsible for; giving rise to (*the woman behind the project*; *the reasons behind his resignation*). **5** in the tracks of; following. ● *adverb* **1 a** in or to or towards the rear; further back (*the street behind*; *glance behind*). **b** on the further side (*a high wall with a field behind*). **2** remaining after departure (*leave behind*; *stay behind*). **3 a** in arrears (*behind with the rent*). **b** late in accomplishing a task etc. (*working too slowly and getting behind*). **4** in an inferior position (*the team was two points behind*). **5** following (*her dog running behind*). ● *noun informal* the buttocks. □ **behind a person's back** without a person's knowledge. **behind the scenes** *see* SCENE. **behind the times** antiquated. **come from behind** win after trailing. **fall** (or **lag**) **behind** not keep up; begin to trail. **put behind one 1** refuse to

consider. **2** get over (an unhappy experience etc.). [Old English *behindan*, *bihindan* from *bi* BY + *hindan* from behind, *hinder* below]

behind·hand *adverb & predicative adjective* **1** (usu. foll. by *with*, *in*) late (in discharging a duty, paying a debt, etc.). **2** out of date; less advanced.

Behn /ben/ **Aphra** (1640–89), English author. Her novel *Oroonoko* (1688) influenced the development of the genre, and her plays, including *The Rover* (final version 1681), enjoyed considerable success during her lifetime.

be·hold *transitive verb* (*past* and *past participle* **be·held**) *literary* **1** see, observe. **2** (in *imperative*) pay attention. [Old English *bihaldan* (as BE-, *haldan* hold)]

be·hold·en /bɪˈhoʊldən/ *predicative adjective* (usu. foll. by *to*) under obligation. [past participle (obsolete except in this use) of BEHOLD, = bound]

be·hold·er *noun literary* a person who beholds. □ **in the eye of the beholder** (of a quality, trait, etc.) to be judged subjectively. [Old English *bihaldan* (as BE-, *haldan* hold)]

be·hoof /bɪˈhuːf/ *noun archaic* (prec. by *to*, *for*, *on*; foll. by *of*) benefit; advantage. [Old English *behōf*]

be·hoove *transitive verb* (also esp. *Brit.* **be·hove**) *formal* (prec. by *it* as subject; foll. by *to* + infin.) **1** be incumbent on. **2** (usu. with *neg.*) befit (*it ill behooves him to protest*). [Old English *behōfian* from *behōf*: see BEHOOF]

Behr·ens /ˈbeɪrənz/ **Peter** (1868–1940), German architect, a leading influence in the growth of modern architecture and industrial design in Germany 1900–14.

Behr·ing /ˈbeɪrɪŋ/ **Emil Adolf von** (1854–1917), German bacteriologist and one of the founders of immunology. He discovered that diphtheria and tetanus could be cured by injecting patients with blood serum from animals previously exposed to the disease. He received the Nobel Prize in 1901.

Beider·becke /ˈbaɪdərˌbek/ **Leon Bis·marck** ('Bix') (1903–31), US jazz musician and composer, who was noted for his bell-like tone and lyrical improvisations on the cornet.

beige /beɪʒ/ ● *noun* a very pale yellowish brown. ● *adjective* of this colour. [French: origin unknown]

bei·gnet /ˈbeɪnjeɪ/ *noun* **1** a fritter. **2** a light doughnut, esp. in Creole cuisine. [French]

Beijing /beɪˈdʒɪŋ/ (also **Pe·king** /piːˈkɪŋ/) the capital of China, in the northeast of the country; pop. (est. 2002) 9,267,300. Kublai Khan developed his capital on the site in the late 13th c. At the centre of modern Beijing lies the Forbidden City, containing the former imperial palaces, to which entry was forbidden to all except the members of the imperial family and their servants. □ **Bei·jing·er** *noun* [Chinese, = northern capital]

be-in *noun* a mass public gathering, esp. of hippies in the sixties.

be·ing *noun* **1** existence. **2** the nature or essence (of a person etc.) (*his whole being revolted*). **3** a human being. **4** anything that exists or is imagined.

Beira /ˈbaɪərə/ a port on the coast of Mozambique, capital of the province of Sofala; pop. (est. 2002) 447,600.

Bei·rut /beɪˈruːt/ the capital and chief port of Lebanon; pop. (est. 2002) 1,878,200.

Bé·jart /beɪˈʒɑr/ **Mau·rice** (real name Maurice Jean Berger) (b.1927), French-born choreographer. He founded The Ballet of the 20th Century in Brussels in 1959, and his choreography is a fusion of classic and modern dance, in particular developing virile acrobatics. He currently leads a dance company in Lausanne.

be·jesus *noun* (also **be·jasus**, **be·jab·bers**, **be·jab·ers**) *N Amer.*, *Scot. & Irish* used as an intensifier (*beat the bejesus out of him*). [corruption of *by Jesus!*]

be·jew·elled *adjective* (also esp. *US* **be·jew·eled**) adorned with jewels.

Bekaa /bɪˈkɒ/ (also **El Beqa'a**) a fertile valley in central Lebanon between the Lebanon and Anti-Lebanon mountain ranges.

Be·kasi /bəˈkɒsi/ a city in NW Java, Indonesia, east of Jakarta; pop. (est. 1995) 644,284.

bel /bel/ *noun* a unit used in the comparison of power levels in electrical communication or intensities of sound, corresponding to an intensity ratio of 10 to 1 (compare DECIBEL). [A. G. BELL]

be·labour *transitive verb* (also **be·labor**) **1** argue or elaborate (a subject) in excessive detail. **2** attack verbally. **3** thrash; beat. [BE- + LABOUR = exert one's strength]

Bela·fonte /ˌbeləˈfɒnteɪ/ **Har·old George ('Harry')** (b.1927), US singer who specialized in calypso and had great success in the 1950s and 1960s with songs such as 'Mary's Boy Child' and 'Day O'.

Bel and the Dragon a book of the Apocrypha containing stories of Daniel, including his exposure of the fraudulent priests of Bel and his destruction of a serpent; in Catholic and Orthodox Bibles the stories are included in the Book of Daniel.

Bel·aney /bə'leini/ see GREY OWL.

Bela·rus /ˌbelə'ruːs/ (also **Belo·rus·sia** /ˌbelə'rʌʃə/; also called **White Russia**) a country in E Europe; pop. (est. 2002) 10,335,352; capital, Minsk. Successively part of Imperial Russia then a republic of the USSR, Belarus gained independence as a member of the Commonwealth of Independent States in 1991.

Bela·ru·sian /ˌbelə'ruːsiən/ (also **Belo·rus·sian** /ˌbelə'rʌʃən/) ● noun **1** a native or national of Belarus. **2** the Slavic language of Belarus. ● adjective of or relating to Belarus, its people, or language.

be·lated adjective **1** coming late or too late. **2** archaic overtaken by darkness. □ **be·lated·ly** adverb **be·lated·ness** noun [past participle of obsolete belate delay (as BE-, LATE)]

Belau see PALAU.

be·lay /bi'lei/ (past and past participle **be·layed**) ● verb **1** transitive secure (a rope) around a cleat, pin, rock, etc. **2** transitive & intransitive (usu. in imperative) Naut. stop, halt (belay there!). ● noun **1** a spike of rock etc. used for belaying a rope in climbing. **2** an act of belaying. □ **belay·er** noun [Dutch beleggen]

belay·ing pin noun a fixed wooden or iron pin used for fastening a rope around.

bel canto /bel 'kantoː/ noun **1** a lyrical style of operatic singing using a full rich broad tone and smooth phrasing. **2** (attributive) (of a type of aria or voice) characterized by this type of singing. [Italian, = fine song]

belch ● verb **1** intransitive emit gas noisily from the stomach through the mouth; burp. **2** transitive **a** (of a chimney, volcano, gun, etc.) send (smoke etc.) out or up. **b** gush forth. **c** utter forcibly. ● noun an act of belching. [Old English belcettan]

Bel·cher, Jona·than (1710–76), US-born Canadian lawyer and judge. He was appointed the first chief justice of the colony of Nova Scotia in 1754 and was its lieutenant-governor 1760–63.

Belcher Islands /'beltʃər/ (also **Belchers**) a group of islands in SE Hudson Bay. Administered by Nunavut, the islands are inhabited by a small number of Inuit. [J. Belcher, Hudson's Bay Co. supplier c.1720]

bel·dam /'beldəm/ noun (also **bel·dame**) archaic **1** an old woman; a hag. **2** a virago. [Old French bel beautiful + DAM², DAME]

be·lea·guer /bə'liːgər/ transitive verb **1** vex, harass. **2** lay siege to. [Dutch belegeren camp around (as BE-, leger a camp)]

be·lea·guered /bə'liːgərd/ adjective beset with difficulties.

Belém /be'lem/ a city and port of N Brazil, at the mouth of the Amazon; pop. (2000) 1,271,615. It is the country's chief commercial centre.

belem·nite /'beləm,nəit/ noun any extinct cephalopod of the order Belemnoidea, having a bullet-shaped internal shell often found in fossilized form. [modern Latin belemnites from Greek belemnon dart + -ITE¹]

Bel·fast the capital of Northern Ireland; pop. (est. 2001) 277,391. The city suffered a dramatic population decline from the early 1970s as a result of sectarian violence by the IRA and Loyalist paramilitary groups.

bel·fry /'belfri/ noun (pl. **-fries**) **1** a bell tower or steeple housing bells, esp. forming part of a church. **2** a space for hanging bells in a church tower. □ **have bats in the belfry** see BAT². [Old French berfrei from Frankish: altered by assoc. with bell]

Bel·gae /'beldʒiː/ plural noun an ancient Celtic people inhabiting Gaul north of the Seine and Marne rivers, eventually defeated by Julius Caesar in the Gallic Wars of 58–51 BC.

Bel·gian /'beldʒən/ ● noun **1** a native or national of Belgium. **2** a person of Belgian descent. **3** = BELGIAN HORSE. ● adjective of or relating to Belgium.

Belgian Congo the former name (1908–60) of CONGO 1.

Belgian endive noun N Amer. the crown of the chicory plant which has been whitened by blanching, used in salads.

Belgian hare noun a domestic breed of rabbit having long ears and dark red fur.

Belgian horse noun a draft horse of a large, heavy, and short-legged breed of Flemish origin.

Belgian waffle noun a type of waffle with very deep indentations.

Bel·gic /'beldʒik/ adjective **1** of or relating to the Belgae. **2** of the Low Countries. [Latin Belgicus from BELGAE]

Bel·gium /'beldʒəm/ a low-lying country in W Europe on the south shore of the North Sea and English Channel; pop. (est. 2002) 10,274,595; capital, Brussels. Flemish is mainly spoken in the north of the country, and French and Walloon in the south. [BELGAE]

Bel·gorod /'bjelgərət/ an industrial city in southern Russia, on the Donets river close to the border with Ukraine; pop. (est. 2002) 300,000.

Bel·grade /'belgreid, -'greid/ the capital of Serbia and the federal capital of the Union of Serbia and Montenegro, situated at the junction of the Sava and Danube rivers; pop. (est. 2002) 1,127,500. □ **Bel·grad·er** noun

Belial /'biːliəl/ noun Bible the Devil. [Hebrew bᵉliyyaʻal worthless]

belie /bə'lai/ transitive verb (**be·lying**) **1** give a false notion of; fail to corroborate (its appearance belies its age). **2 a** fail to fulfill (a promise etc.). **b** fail to justify (a hope etc.). [Old English belēogan (as BE-, lēogan LIE²)]

be·lief noun **1 a** a firm opinion or conviction (my belief is that he did it). **b** an acceptance (of a thing, fact, statement, etc.) (belief in the afterlife). **c** a person's religion; religious conviction. **2** (usu. foll. by in) trust or confidence. □ **beyond belief** incredible. **to the best of my belief** in my genuine opinion. [(as BELIEVE)]

belief system noun a set of tenets held by a person or group, which constitute a religion, philosophy, ethos, etc.

be·lieve verb **1** transitive accept as true or as conveying the truth (I believe it; don't believe him; believes what she is told). **2** transitive think, suppose (I believe it's raining; Mr. Smith, I believe?). **3** intransitive (foll. by in) **a** have faith in the existence of (believes in God). **b** have confidence in (a remedy, a person, etc.) (believes in alternative medicine). **c** have trust in the advisability of (believes in telling the truth). **4** intransitive have (esp. religious) faith. □ **believe me** (or **believe you me**) used to emphasize the truth of a statement or assertion. **believe one's eyes** (or **ears**) (usu. in neg.) accept that what one apparently sees or hears etc. is true. **believe it or not** informal it is true though surprising. **make believe** (often foll. by that + clause) pretend (children like to make believe that they're adults). □ **be·liev·abil·ity** noun **be·liev·able** adjective **be·liev·ably** adverb [Old English belȳfan, belēfan, with change of prefix from gelēfan from Germanic: related to LIEF]

be·liev·er noun **1** an adherent of a specified religion. **2** a person who believes, esp. in the efficacy of something (a great believer in exercise).

be·like adverb archaic likely, probably.

Beli·sar·ius /ˌbelə'seriəs/ (c.505–65), a general under Justinian. His victories against the Persians, Vandals, Ostrogoths, and others made him perhaps the most successful of Byzantine generals.

Be·li·sha beacon /bə'liːʃə/ noun Brit. a striped post with a flashing orange light marking a crosswalk. [L. Hore-Belisha, British transport minister d.1957]

be·little transitive verb **1** make (a person, action, etc.) seem unimportant or worthless. **2** make small; dwarf. □ **be·little·ment** noun **be·lit·tler** noun **be·lit·tling·ly** adverb

Béli·veau /'belivoː/ **Jean** (b.1931), Canadian hockey player. During his career as a centreman with the Montreal Canadiens (1951–71) he scored over 500 goals and won 10 Stanley Cups.

Bel·ize /be'liːz/ a country on the Caribbean coast of Central America; pop. (est. 2002) 263,000; capital, Belmopan. Known as British Honduras from the 17th c. until 1973, the territory has always been claimed by Guatemala on the basis of old Spanish treaties. □ **Beliz·ean** /bə'liːziən/ noun & adjective

Belize City the principal seaport and former capital (until 1970) of Belize; pop. (2000) 49,100.

Bell ▸ 1 Alex·an·der Gra·ham (1847–1922), Scottish-born scientist and inventor who spent most of his career in the northeastern US and Canada, inventor of the telephone (between 1874 and 1876) and the gramophone. He also founded the Bell Telephone Company and was a pioneer in aviation. **2 Cur·rer, Ellis,** and **Acton,** see BRONTË. **3 Mari·lyn** (b.1937), Canadian swimmer. In September 1954 she became the first person to swim across Lake Ontario, swimming from Youngstown, New York, to Toronto in just under 21 hours; she later became the youngest person to swim the English Channel and Strait of Juan de Fuca.

bell¹ ● noun **1** a hollow usu. metal object in the shape of a deep upturned cup usu. widening at the lip, made to sound a clear musical note when struck (either externally or by means of a clapper inside). **2 a** a sound or stroke of a bell, esp. as a signal. **b** Naut. (prec. by a numeral) the time as indicated every half-hour of a watch by the

uː m**oo**d ai m**y** əi p**i**pe au br**ow**n ʌu h**ou**se ei d**ay** ɔi b**oy** ã franglais ã Canadien ɔ̃ Brayon (see over for consonants)

striking of the ship's bell one to eight times. **3** anything that sounds like or functions as a bell, esp. an electronic device that rings etc. as a signal. **4 a** any bell-shaped object or part, e.g. of a musical instrument. **b** the corolla of a flower when bell-shaped. **5** *Music* (in *pl.*) a set of cylindrical metal tubes of different lengths, suspended in a frame and played by being struck with a hammer. **6** *Cdn* the dangling appendage under a moose's neck. ● *transitive verb* **1** provide with a bell or bells; attach a bell to. **2** (foll. by *out*) form into the shape of the lip of a bell. □ **bells and whistles** *informal* attractive but non-essential components; gimmicks. **bell the cat** attempt something daring or dangerous. **clear** (or **sound**) **as a bell** perfectly clear or sound. **ring a bell** *informal* revive a distant recollection; sound familiar. **saved by the bell** spared (from an unpleasant occurrence) at the last moment. **with bells on** enthusiastically. [Old English *belle*: perhaps related to BELL²]

bell² ● *noun* the cry of a stag or buck at rutting time. ● *intransitive verb* make this cry. [Old English *bellan* bark, bellow]

Bella Bella = HEILTSUK. [altered form of Heiltsuk *pélbálá*, the name of a fort and village on Milbanke Sound]

Bella Coola = NUXALK. [perhaps from Kwagiulth *Bílxula*]

bella·don·na *noun* **1** a poisonous plant, *Atropa belladonna*, with purple flowers and purple-black berries. *Also called* DEADLY NIGHTSHADE. **2** a drug prepared from its root and leaves (*see also* ATROPINE). [modern Latin from Italian, = fair lady, perhaps from its use as a cosmetic]

belladonna lily *noun* a southern African amaryllis with white or pink flowers, *Amaryllis belladonna*.

Bella·trix /ˈbelətrɪks/ a giant star, the third brightest in the constellation Orion. [Latin, = female warrior]

Bel·lay /beˈleɪ/ **Joa·chim du** (*c.*1522–60), French poet, who was a leader with Ronsard of the group known as the Pléiade; his treatise *The Defence and Illustration of the French Language* (1549) asserted the value of French as a literary language at a time when Latin was still considered the language of prestige.

bell·bird *noun* any of various birds with a bell-like song, esp. any Central or S American bird of the genus *Procnias*, or a New Zealand honeyeater, *Anthornis melanura*.

bell-bottom *noun* **1** a wide flare below the knee of a trouser leg. **2** (in *pl.*) trousers with bell bottoms. □ **bell-bottomed** *adjective*

bell·boy *noun* esp. *N Amer.* = BELLHOP.

bell buoy *noun* a buoy equipped with a warning bell rung by the motion of the waves.

bell captain *noun N Amer.* a supervisor of a group of bellhops.

bell·cast *adjective* designating a style of roof typical of traditional architecture in Quebec, with gables having the shape of a squared-off bell.

bell curve *noun* a bell-shaped line on a graph showing normal distribution.

belle /bel/ *noun* **1** a beautiful woman. **2** a woman recognized as the most beautiful (*the belle of the ball*). [French from Latin *bella* fem. of *bellus* beautiful]

belle époque /ˌbel eiˈpɒk/ *noun* the period of settled comfort and prosperity before the First World War. [French, = fine period]

Belle·feuille /belˈfɜːj/ a former town in south central Quebec, now part of Saint-Jérôme; pop. (2001) 14,066. [French, = 'beautiful leaf']

Belle Isle, Strait of /ˌbel ˈaɪl/ a strait between Labrador and the island of Newfoundland, connecting the N Atlantic Ocean and the Gulf of St. Lawrence. [French, lit. 'beautiful island', with reference to the island at its entrance]

Belle Province *see* LA BELLE PROVINCE.

Bel·lero·phon /bəˈlerəfɒn/ *Gk Myth* a hero who slew the monster Chimera with the help of the winged horse Pegasus.

belles let·tres /bel ˈletr/ *plural noun* (also treated as *sing.*) writings or studies of a purely literary nature, esp. essays and criticisms. □ **bel·let·rism** /beˈletrɪzəm/ *noun* **bel·let·rist** /beˈletrɪst/ *noun* **bel·let·ris·tic** /ˌbeləˈtrɪstɪk/ *adjective* [French, = fine letters]

Belle·ville a city in SE Ontario, situated on the Bay of Quinte, west of Kingston; pop. (2001) 45,986. □ **Belle·vil·lian** *noun* [Lady Arabella (*Bella*) Gore, wife of Lt.-Gov. Sir Francis Gore]

bell·flower *noun* = CAMPANULA.

bell glass *noun* a bell-shaped glass cover for plants.

bell·hop *noun N Amer.* a hotel employee who helps guests with luggage, shows them to rooms, etc.

bel·li·cose /ˈbelɪˌkoʊs/ *adjective* inclined to war or fighting; warlike. □ **bel·li·cos·ity** /-ˈkɒsɪti/ *noun* [Latin *bellicosus* from *bellum* war]

bel·lied *adjective* (in *combination*) having a belly of a specified kind (*pot-bellied*).

bel·liger·ence /bəˈlɪdʒərəns/ *noun* (also **bel·liger·ency**) **1** aggressive or warlike behaviour. **2** the status of a belligerent.

bel·liger·ent /bəˈlɪdʒərənt/ ● *adjective* **1** engaged in war or conflict. **2** given to repeated fighting; pugnacious. ● *noun* a nation or person engaged in war or conflict. □ **bel·liger·ent·ly** *adverb* [Latin *belligerare* wage war, from *bellum* war + *gerere* wage]

Bel·lings·hau·sen Sea /ˈbelɪŋzˌhaʊzən/ a part of the SE Pacific off the coast of Antarctica, bounded to the east and south by the Antarctic Peninsula and Ellsworth Land. [Fabian Gottlieb von Bellingshausen, Russian explorer d.1852, who in 1819–21 became the first to circumnavigate Antarctica]

Bel·lini /beˈliːni/ **1 Gen·tile** (*c.*1429–1507), Venetian artist, a prominent portraitist and narrative painter. **2** his brother **Gio·van·ni** (*c.*1430–1516), who transformed Venice into a major centre of Renaissance painting. Both his sacred and secular subjects are characterized by serene contemplative qualities and subtle transitions in light and colour. **3** their father **Jac·opo** (*c.*1400–70). Few of his paintings survive but over 230 drawings are preserved in two extant sketchbooks. **4 Vin·cen·zo** (1801–35), Italian composer of 11 operas, including *La Sonnambula* (1831), *Norma* (1831), and *I Puritani* (1835). The soprano aria 'Casta diva' from *Norma* is the supreme example of his gift for long legato melody.

Bell Island an island in Conception Bay, SE Newfoundland. [origin uncertain: possibly after *Belle-Île*, an island in the Bay of Biscay, NW France]

bell jar *noun* a bell-shaped glass esp. for covering instruments or containing gas in a laboratory.

bell lap *noun* the final lap of a race, signalled by a bell.

bell·man *noun* (*pl.* **-men**) **1** *N Amer.* = BELLHOP. **2** *hist.* a town crier.

bell metal *noun* an alloy of copper and tin for making bells (the tin content being greater than in bronze).

Bel·loc /ˈbelɒk/ **Hi·laire** (1870–1953), French-born British writer of essays, biographies, travelogues, novels, best known for his books of light verse.

Bel·lona /bəˈloʊnə/ *Rom. Myth* the goddess of war.

Bel·lot Strait /ˈbelət/ a small, narrow strait in the Canadian Arctic, separating Somerset Island from the Boothia Peninsula of mainland Nunavut. [J. R. *Bellot*, French naval officer and Arctic explorer d. *c.*1853]

Bel·low, Saul (b.1915), US novelist born in Canada of Russian-Jewish parents. His work is rooted in the postwar Jewish community of the northeastern US. He was awarded the Nobel Prize in 1976. □ **Bel·lo·vian** *adjective & noun*

bel·low ● *verb* **1** *intransitive* **a** emit a deep loud roar. **b** cry or shout with pain. **2** *transitive* utter loudly and usu. angrily. ● *noun* a bellowing sound. [Middle English: perhaps related to BELL²]

bel·lows *plural noun* (also treated as *sing.*) **1** a device with an air bag that emits a stream of air when squeezed, esp.: **a** (in full **pair of bellows**) a kind with two handles used for blowing air onto a fire. **b** a kind used in a harmonium or small organ. **2** an expandable component, e.g. joining the lens to the body of a camera. [Middle English prob. from Old English *belga* pl. of *belig* belly]

Bell Peninsula an extension of the eastern coast of Southampton Island, Nunavut.

bell pepper *noun see* PEPPER *noun* 2.

bell pull *noun* a cord or handle which rings a bell when pulled.

bell push *noun* a button that operates an electric bell when pushed.

bell-ringer *noun* a person who rings church bells or handbells.

bell-ringing *noun* **1** the ringing of church bells or handbells, esp. change ringing. **2** *Cdn* the ringing of bells in a legislative assembly to summon members for a vote, esp. when provoked or prolonged by Opposition members as a tactic for stalling debate.

Bell's palsy *noun Med.* paralysis of the facial nerve causing muscular weakness in one side of the face with drooping of the corner of the mouth and inability to close the eye. [Sir C. *Bell*, Scottish anatomist d.1842]

bell tent *noun* a cone-shaped tent supported by a central pole.

bell·wether *noun* **1** (often *attributive*) an indicator or predictor of something. **2** the leading sheep of a flock, on whose neck a bell is hung. [BELL¹ + WETHER]

bell·wort /ˈbelwɜːt, -wɔːt/ *noun* any of various liliaceous plants of the genus *Uvularia* of eastern N America, with yellow bell-shaped flowers.

belly ● *noun* (*pl.* **-lies**) **1** the part of the human body below the chest, containing the stomach and bowels. **2** the stomach, esp. representing the body's need for food. **3** the front surface of the body from the waist to the groin. **4** the corresponding part or surface of the body of an animal. **5 a** a cavity or bulging part of anything. **b** the surface of a violin etc. across which the strings pass. ● *transitive & intransitive verb* (**-lies, -lied, belly·ing**) (often foll. by *out*) swell or cause to swell; bulge. □ **belly up** approach closely (*bellied up to the bar*). **go belly up** esp. *N Amer.* fail; become bankrupt; die (*the company went belly up*). [Old English *belig* (originally = bag) from Germanic]

belly·ache *informal* ● *noun* a stomach pain. ● *intransitive verb* complain noisily or persistently. □ **belly·acher** *noun*

belly·band *noun* **1** a band placed around the belly, e.g. of a horse or baby. **2** a band encircling a number of pieces of paper, banknotes, books, etc.

belly·boat *noun* a water safety device, chiefly used in angling, consisting of a large, circular inflated rubber tube attached around a person's waist. □ **belly·boat·ing** *noun*

belly button *noun informal* the navel.

belly dance *noun* a solo dance of Middle Eastern origin performed by a woman and involving the rippling of the abdominal muscles. □ **belly dancer** *noun* **belly dancing** *noun*

belly·flop *informal* ● *noun* a dive into water in which the body lands with the belly flat on the water. ● *intransitive verb* (**-flopped, -flop·ping**) perform this dive.

belly·ful *noun* (*pl.* **-fuls**) **1** enough to eat. **2** *informal* enough or more than enough of anything (esp. unwelcome).

belly landing *noun* a crash landing of an aircraft on the underside of the fuselage, with the landing gear up.

belly laugh *noun* a deep unrestrained laugh.

Bel·mo·pan /ˌbelmoːˈpan/ the capital of Belize. Founded in 1970, it is one of the smallest capital cities in the world; pop. (est. 2000) 8,100.

Belœil /belˈɔj/ a city in south central Quebec, situated on the Richelieu, east of Montreal; pop. (2001) 19,053. [French, lit. 'beautiful eye', prob. with reference to the beautiful view from the peak of Mont Saint-Hilaire]

Belo /ˈbeloː/ **Car·los Filipe Xim·enes** (b.1948), East Timorese activist. A Roman Catholic bishop, he shared the Nobel Peace Prize in 1996 for his work toward a peaceful resolution of the crisis in East Timor.

Belo Hori·zonte /ˌbeloː ˌɒrɪˈzɒnti/ a city in E Brazil; pop. (2000) 2,229,697.

be·long *intransitive verb* **1** (foll. by *to*) **a** be the property of. **b** be rightly assigned to as a duty, right, part, member, characteristic, etc. **c** be a member of (a club, family, group, etc.). **2** have the right personal or social qualities to be a member of a particular group (*he's nice but just doesn't belong*). **3** (foll. by *in, under*): **a** be rightly placed or classified. **b** fit a particular environment. **4** *Cdn* (*Nfld*) be related to; be within a family group. □ **be·long·ing** *noun* **be·long·ing·ness** *noun* [Middle English from intensive BE- + *longen* belong, from Old English *langian* (*gelang* at hand)]

be·long·ings *plural noun* personal possessions or effects.

Belo·rus·sia see BELARUS.

Belo·rus·sian see BELARUSIAN.

Belo·stok see BIAŁYSTOK.

be·lov·ed ● *adjective* dearly loved. ● *noun* a dearly loved person. [obsolete *belove* (v.)]

below ● *preposition* **1** lower in position (vertically, down a slope or stream, etc.) than. **2** beneath the surface of; at or to a greater depth than (*head below water; below 50 metres*). **3** lower in rank, position, or importance than. **4** unworthy of; beneath. ● *adverb* **1** at or to a lower point or level. **2 a** on or to a lower floor or deck; downstairs (*went below*). **b** downstream. **3** (of a text reference) further down on a page or later in an article, book, etc. (*as noted below*). **4** on the lower side (*looks similar above and below*). **5** lower than zero on a temperature scale (*temperature is 20 below*). **6** *literary* **a** on earth. **b** in hell. □ **below stairs** in the basement of a house esp. as the part occupied by servants. [BE- + LOW[1]]

Bel Paese /ˌbel paˈezeɪ/ *noun proprietary* a rich, white, mild-flavoured creamy cheese originally made in Italy. [Italian, = beautiful country]

Bel·sen /ˈbelsən/ a village in NW Germany, site of a Nazi concentration camp (Bergen-Belsen) during the Second World War.

Bel·shazzar /belˈʃazər/ (in the Bible) son of Nebuchadnezzar and last king of Babylon, who was killed in the sack of the city by Cyrus (538 BC) and whose doom was foretold by writing which appeared on the walls of his palace at a great banquet.

bel·snickle /ˈbelˌsnɪkl/ *noun N Amer.* (in Nova Scotia, Virginia, and areas of German settlement) a person in disguise who seeks admission to the homes of neighbours and relatives, esp. during Christmas (*compare* MUMMER). [corruption of German *Pelz* fur + *Nickel* diminutive of (Saint) *Nicholas*, from the German custom of a person disguised in furs visiting children on the eve of St. Nicholas's day (6th December) to dispense warnings and gifts]

belt ● *noun* **1** a flat encircling strip of leather, cloth, etc., worn around the waist or from the shoulder to the opposite hip to support clothes, tools, weapons, etc., or as a decorative accessory. **2 a** a belt worn as a sign of rank or achievement. **b** a belt of a specified colour indicating the wearer's level of proficiency in judo, karate, etc. (*compare* BLACK BELT). **3 a** a circular band of material used as a driving medium in machinery etc. **b** a conveyor belt. **c** a flexible strip for feeding a machine gun with ammunition. **4** a seat belt. **5** a strip of colour or texture etc. differing from that on either side. **6** a zone or region of distinct character or occupancy (*wheat belt; Bible belt*). **7** *informal* a heavy blow or stroke. **8** a strip of reinforcing material (esp. steel) placed beneath the tread of a tire for durability. **9** *informal* a drink. ● *verb* **1** *transitive* put a belt around. **2** *transitive* (often foll. by *on*) fasten with a belt. **3** *transitive* **a** beat with a belt. **b** *informal* hit hard. **4** *intransitive informal* rush, hurry (*belted along; belted home*). **5** *transitive* drink quickly. **6** sing very loudly and forcefully, esp. as a technique in musical theatre. □ **below the belt** unfair or unfairly. **belt and braces** *Brit.* (of a policy etc.) of twofold security. **belt out** *informal* sing or utter loudly and forcibly. **belt up** *informal* **1** be quiet. **2** put on a seat belt. **tighten one's belt** curtail expenditure. **under one's belt 1** (of food or drink) consumed. **2** securely acquired (*has a degree under her belt*). □ **belt·er** *noun* (esp. in sense of *belt out*). [Old English from Germanic from Latin *balteus*]

Bel·tane /ˈbeltein/ *noun* an ancient Celtic festival celebrated on May Day. [Gaelic *bealltainn*]

belt·ed *adjective* **1** fastened or ornamented with a belt. **2** (of a tire) having a strip of reinforcing material beneath the tread.

belted kingfisher *noun* a N American kingfisher, *Ceryle alcyon*, having a greyish-blue upper body and white breast with a blue band in the male, and a second light brown band in the female.

belt·line *noun* **1** the waistline. **2** the area where the hood and doors of an automobile meet the windshield and windows.

belt-tightening *noun* curtailing of expenditure.

belt·way *noun esp. US* **1** a highway that encircles a city or metropolitan area. **2** (usu. **Beltway**) (often *attributive*) Washington, DC, esp. as representing the perceived intellectual and social insularity of the US government.

be·luga /bəˈluːɡə/ *noun* **1** a whale, *Delphinapterus leucas*, of the Arctic Ocean which is found as far south as the St. Lawrence estuary, and is white when adult. *Also called* WHITE WHALE. **2 a** a large kind of sturgeon, *Huso huso*, of the Caspian and Black Seas. **b** caviar obtained from it. [Russian *beluga* from *belyi* white]

bel·ve·dere /ˈbelvəˌdiːr/ *noun* a raised turret or summer house commanding a fine view. [Italian from *bel* beautiful + *vedere* see]

bely·ing *pres. part. of* BELIE.

BEM *abbreviation* British Empire Medal.

Bembo *noun* a typeface modelled on that used in the Aldine edition of the tract *De Aetna* by Pietro Bembo. [P. *Bembo*, Italian scholar d.1547]

be·med·alled *adjective* adorned with medals.

be·moan *transitive verb* **1** express regret or sorrow over; lament. **2** complain about.

be·muse *transitive verb* (usu. as **be·mused** *adjective*) cause (often somewhat amused) puzzlement. □ **be·mus·ed·ly** *adverb* **be·muse·ment** *noun* [BE- + MUSE[2]]

ben *noun Scot. & Irish* a high mountain or mountain peak, esp. in names (*Ben Nevis*). [Gaelic *beann*]

Ben·a·dryl *noun proprietary* an antihistamine preparation containing diphenhydramine hydrochloride. [*ben*(zene) + *-a-* + *-dr* (in HYDROCHLORIDE + -YL]

Ben·ares see VARANASI.

Bena·vente y Mar·tínez /benəˈvente iː marˈtiːnəs/ **Ja·cin·to** (1866–1954), Spanish dramatist and critic, writer of satirical comedies, including *Saturday Night* (1903) and *Vested Interests* (1907); he was awarded the Nobel Prize for literature in 1922.

Ben Bella, Ahmad (b.1916), Algerian leader, who worked for the independence of his country and became its first prime minister (1962–65) and president (1963–65).

bench ● *noun* **1** a long seat, with or without a back, for several people.

---

t *top*   v *voice*   w *we*   z *zoo*   ʃ *she*   ʒ *vision*   θ *thin*   ð *this*   ŋ *ring*   x *loch*   tʃ *chip*   dʒ *jar*   (see over for vowels)

2 a work table used by a carpenter etc., or in a laboratory. **3** (prec. by *the*) **a** the office or status of a judge. **b** the seat on which the judge or judges sit in court. **c** a court of law (see also QUEEN'S BENCH). **d** judges and magistrates collectively. **4** *Sport* **a** a seat used by players when not participating in a game. **b** the substitute players collectively. **5** *Parl.* a seat (*front bench*; *back bench*). **6 a** a bank or shelf of ground. **b** a level ledge in earthwork, masonry, etc. **c** esp. *Geomorph.* = BENCHLAND. **7** a platform on which dogs etc. are exhibited at a show. ● *transitive verb* **1** *N Amer. & Austral. Sport* remove or retire (a player) to the bench esp. for poor performance. **2** exhibit (a dog etc.) at a show. □ **behind the bench** *Hockey* serving as a coach. **on the bench** serving as a judge or magistrate. [Old English *benc* from Germanic]

bench-clearing *noun* (esp. *attributive*) *N Amer.* an incident in which an entire sports team leaves the players' bench and enters the playing area, usu. to engage in a brawl.

bench·er *noun* **1** (in combination) *Parl.* an occupant of a specified bench (*backbencher*). **2** *Cdn Law* a member of the regulating body of the law society in all provinces except New Brunswick. **3** *Brit. Law* a senior member of any of the Inns of Court.

bench·land *noun N Amer.* a relatively narrow, naturally occurring terrace often backed by a steep slope.

bench·mark ● *noun* **1** a surveyor's mark cut in a wall, post, etc., used as a reference point in measuring comparative elevations. **2** a standard or point of reference. **3** (in full **benchmark test**) a means of testing a computer, usu. by a set of programs run on a series of different machines. ● *transitive verb* test or check by comparison with a benchmark.

bench penalty *noun* (also **bench minor**) *Hockey* a minor penalty assessed to a team as a whole and served by a single player.

bench press ● *noun* an exercise in which a person lying face upwards on a bench with feet on the floor raises a barbell by extending both arms upward from the chest. ● *transitive & intransitive verb* (usu. **bench-press**) raise (a weight) in a bench press.

bench strength *noun N Amer.* notable skill, competence, etc. among the secondary members of a team or group.

bench test ● *noun* a test performed on an automobile engine, computer, etc. before installation. ● *transitive verb* subject to a bench test.

bench·warm·er *noun N Amer. informal* an athlete who routinely is not selected to play. □ **bench-warming** *noun & adjective*

bench warrant *noun* a warrant issued by a judge or court for the arrest of a person who fails to appear.

bend[1] ● *verb* (*past* **bent**; *past participle* **bent**) **1 a** *transitive* force or adapt (esp. something straight) into a curve or angle. **b** *intransitive* (of an object) be altered in this way. **2** *intransitive* move or stretch in a curved course (*the road bends to the left*). **3** *intransitive & transitive* (often foll. by *down, over*, etc.) incline or cause to incline from the vertical (*bent down to pick it up*). **4** *transitive & reflexive* (foll. by *to, on*) direct or devote (oneself or one's attention, energies, etc.). **5** *transitive* turn (one's steps or eyes) in a new direction. **6** *transitive* (in *passive*; foll. by *on*) have firmly decided; be determined (*was bent on selling*). **7 a** *intransitive* stoop or submit. **b** *transitive* force to submit. **8** *transitive Naut.* attach (a sail or cable) with a knot. ● *noun* **1** a curve in a road or other course. **2** a departure from a straight course. **3** a bent part of anything. **4** (in *pl.*; prec. by *the*) *informal* = DECOMPRESSION SICKNESS. □ **bend over backwards** see BACKWARDS. **bend someone's ear** importune someone with persistent talk; have a word with someone. **bend the rules** interpret or modify rules etc. to suit oneself. **on bended knee** kneeling, esp. in reverence, supplication, or submission. **round the bend** *informal* crazy, insane. □ **bend·able** *adjective* [Old English *bendan* from Germanic]

bend[2] *noun* **1** *Naut.* any of various knots for tying ropes (*fisherman's bend*). **2** *Heraldry* a diagonal stripe from top right to bottom left of a shield (i.e. from top left to bottom right for the observer). [Old English *bend* band, bond, from Germanic]

bend·er *noun* **1** *slang* a wild drinking spree. **2** an instrument for bending (pipes etc.).

bend sinister *noun Heraldry* a diagonal stripe from top left to bottom right on a shield (i.e. from top right to bottom left for the observer), as a sign of bastardy.

bendy *adjective* (**bend·i·er**, **bend·i·est**) *informal* capable of bending; soft and flexible. □ **bend·i·ness** *noun*

be·neath ● *preposition* **1** below, under. **2** not worthy of; too demeaning for (*it was beneath him to reply*). ● *adverb* below, under, underneath. □ **beneath contempt** see CONTEMPT. [Old English *binithan*, *bineothan* from *bi* BY + *nithan* etc. below, from Germanic]

bene·di·cite /ˌbenəˈdiːtʃɪteɪ/ *noun* a blessing, esp. a grace said at table in religious communities. [Latin, = bless ye: see BENEDICTION]

Bene·dict, St. (*c.*480–*c.*547), a hermit, the 'Patriarch of Western monasticism', compiler of a monastic rule (chiefly at Monte Cassino in Italy) though he does not seem to have contemplated founding an order.

Benedict XV /ˈbenədɪkt/ (born Giacomo della Chiesa) (1854–1922), Pope 1914–22. Throughout the First World War he made attempts at peacemaking and alleviating the suffering of its victims.

Bene·dict·ine /ˌbenəˈdɪktiːn/ ● *noun* **1** a monk or nun of an order following the rule of St. Benedict. **2** *proprietary* a liqueur of brandy and herbs, originally made by Benedictines in France. ● *adjective* of St. Benedict or the Benedictines. [French *bénédictine* or modern Latin *benedictinus* from *Benedictus* Benedict]

bene·dic·tion /ˌbenəˈdɪkʃən/ *noun* **1** the utterance of a blessing, esp. at the end of a religious service. **2** (**Benediction**) a chiefly Roman Catholic service in which the congregation is blessed with the Host, usu. displayed in a monstrance. **3** the state of being blessed. [Latin *benedictio -onis* from *benedicere -dict-* bless]

Bene·dic·tus /ˌbenəˈdɪktʊs/ *noun* **1** the section of the Mass beginning *Benedictus qui venit in nomine Domini* (Blessed is he who comes in the name of the Lord). **2** a canticle beginning *Benedictus Dominus Deus* (Blessed be the Lord God) from Luke 1:68–79. **3** a musical setting of either of these. [Latin, = blessed: see BENEDICTION]

bene·fac·tion /ˌbenəˈfakʃən/ *noun* **1** a donation or gift. **2** an act of giving or doing good. [Late Latin *benefactio* (as BENEFIT)]

bene·fac·tor /ˈbenəˌfaktər/ *noun* a person who gives support (esp. financial) to a person or cause. □ **bene·fac·tress** /-trəs/ *noun* [as BENEFIT]

bene·fice /ˈbenəfɪs/ *noun* **1** a position held by a member of the clergy that ensures an income or a specified property. **2** the income from such a position. □ **bene·ficed** *adjective* [Latin *beneficium* favour, from *bene* well + *facere* do]

be·nefi·cent /bɪˈnefɪsənt/ *adjective* doing good; generous, actively kind. □ **be·nefi·cence** *noun* **be·nefi·cent·ly** *adverb* [Latin *beneficent-* (as BENEFICE)]

bene·fi·cial /ˌbenəˈfɪʃəl/ *adjective* **1** advantageous; having benefits. **2** *Law* of, pertaining to, or having the use or benefit of property etc. □ **bene·fi·cial·ly** *adverb* [Late Latin *beneficialis* (as BENEFICE)]

bene·fici·ary /ˌbenəˈfɪʃəri, -ˈfɪʃəri/ *noun* (pl. **-aries**) **1** a person who receives or is entitled to receive benefits, esp. under a will or life insurance policy. **2** a person who benefits from a particular event, action, etc. (*the beneficiaries of law reform*). **3** a holder of a benefice. [Latin *beneficiarius* (as BENEFICE)]

bene·fit /ˈbenəfɪt/ ● *noun* **1** a favourable or helpful factor or circumstance; advantage, profit. **2** (often in *pl.*) allowance of money etc. to which a person is entitled from a pension plan, government support programs, etc. (*unemployment insurance benefits*). **3** (often in *pl.*) an advantage other than salary associated with a job, e.g. dental coverage, life insurance, etc. **4** a public performance, sporting event, etc. held in order to raise money for a particular player, charity, etc. ● *verb* (**bene·fit·ed**, **bene·fit·ing**; also **bene·fit·ted**, **bene·fit·ting**) **1** *transitive* do good to; be of advantage to; improve. **2** *intransitive* (often foll. by *from, by*) receive an advantage or gain. □ **the benefit of the doubt** assumption of a person's innocence, rightness, etc., rather than the contrary in the absence of proof. [Anglo-French *benfet*, Old French *bienfet*, from Latin *benefactum* from *bene facere* do well]

benefit of clergy *noun* **1** *hist.* exemption from the jurisdiction of secular courts of law because of membership in the clergy. **2** ecclesiastical sanction or approval (*marriage without benefit of clergy*).

Bene·lux /ˈbenəˌlʌks/ *noun* a collective name for Belgium, the Netherlands, and Luxembourg, esp. with reference to their economic co-operation established in the Benelux Customs Union of 1948. [*Belgium + Netherlands + Luxembourg*]

Beneš /ˈbeneʃ/ **Ed·vard** (1884–1948), Czechoslovak politician; co-founder (with Tomáš Masaryk) of modern Czechoslovakia. President of his country 1935–38 and 1946–48 and of its government-in-exile during the Second World War, he resigned in 1948 after the Communist coup.

Benesh Notation /ˈbeneʃ/ *noun* (in full **Benesh Movement Notation**) a system of dance notation in which symbols representing the positions and movements of the body are written into a five-line staff according to the musical development. [Rudolf (d.1975) and Joan (b.1920) *Benesh*, British dance notators]

Benét /bəˈneɪ/ **Ste·phen Vin·cent** (1898–1943), US poet, novelist, and short-story writer. He won a Pulitzer Prize (1929) for his long narrative poem on the American Civil War, *John Brown's Body*; he also wrote the short story 'The Devil and Daniel Webster'.

be·nev·o·lent /bə'nevələnt/ *adjective* **1** wishing to do good; actively friendly and helpful. **2** charitable (*benevolent fund; benevolent society*). □ **be·nevo·lence** *noun* **be·nevo·lent·ly** *adverb* [Latin *bene volens -entis* well wishing, from *velle* wish]

B.Eng. *abbreviation* Bachelor of Engineering.

Ben·gal /ben'gɒl/ a region in the northeast of the Indian subcontinent, containing the Ganges and Brahmaputra river deltas. In 1947, with the end of British rule, the area was divided into West Bengal, which has remained a state of India, and East Bengal, now Bangladesh.

Bengal, Bay of a part of the Indian Ocean lying between India to the west and Burma (Myanmar) and Thailand to the east.

Ben·gali /ben'gɒli, -gɑli/ ● *noun* **1** a native of Bengal. **2** the language of this people, descended from Sanskrit. ● *adjective* of or relating to Bengal or its people or language.

ben·ga·line /ˌbeŋgə'liːn/ *noun* a lustrous fabric with the weft of a thicker, coarser thread than the warp. [French, from BENGAL, whence striped fabrics were imported to Europe]

Bengal tiger *noun* a tiger of a variety found in the Indian subcontinent, distinguished by unbroken stripes.

Ben·ghazi /ben'gɒzi/ a Mediterranean port in NE Libya; pop. (est. 2002) 708,000. It was the joint capital (with Tripoli) of Libya from 1951 to 1972.

Ben·guela /ben'gwelə/ a port and railway terminal in Angola, on the Atlantic coast; pop. (est. 2002) 131,400. The Benguela railway line provides a link with the copper-mining regions of Zambia and Congo (formerly Zaire).

Ben-Gurion /ˌben'gʊriən/ **David** (1886–1973), Israeli leader, born in Russian Poland. As Israel's first prime minister (1948–53, 1955–63) and minister of defence, he played the largest part in shaping the State of Israel during its formative years.

be·night·ed /bə'naɪtəd/ *adjective* **1** intellectually or morally ignorant. **2** unfortunate. **3** overtaken by night or darkness. □ **be·night·ed·ness** *noun* [obsolete *benight* (v.)]

be·nign /bə'naɪn/ *adjective* **1** gentle, mild, kindly. **2** fortunate, salutary. **3** (of climate etc.) mild, favourable. **4** *Med.* (of a disease, tumour, etc.) not malignant. □ **be·nign·ly** *adverb* [Old French *benigne* from Latin *benignus* from *bene* well + *-genus* born]

be·nig·nant /bə'nɪgnənt/ *adjective* **1** kindly, gracious. **2** salutary, beneficial. □ **be·nig·nancy** *noun* **be·nig·nant·ly** *adverb* [BENIGN or Latin *benignus*, after *malignant*]

be·nig·nity /bə'nɪgnɪti/ *noun* (pl. **-ties**) **1** kindliness. **2** an act of kindness. [Old French *benignité* or Latin *benignitas* (as BENIGN)]

benign neglect *noun* lack of attention reflecting confidence in or a favourable disposition towards a person or thing; well-intentioned or beneficial neglect.

Benin /be'niːn/ a country of West Africa, immediately west of Nigeria; pop. (est. 2002) 6,787,625; capital, Porto Novo. Formerly known as Dahomey and a centre of the slave trade, the country was conquered by the French in 1893 and became part of French West Africa. In 1960 it became fully independent and in 1975 adopted the name of Benin, a former African kingdom centred on southern Nigeria that was powerful in the 14th–17th c. and was famous for its bronze and ivory sculptures. □ **Benin·ese** /ˌbenə'niːz/ *adjective & noun*

Benin, Bight of a wide bay on the coast of Africa north of the Gulf of Guinea, bordered by Togo, Benin, and SW Nigeria. Lagos is its chief port.

Benin City a city in south central Nigeria, pop. (est. 1991) 762,719.

beni·son /'benɪzən/ *noun literary* a blessing. [Old French *beneiçun* from Latin *benedictio -onis*]

Ben·ja·min ▸ **1** /'bendʒəmɪn/ **a** a Hebrew patriarch, the youngest and favourite son of Jacob (Gen. 43 etc.). **b** the smallest tribe of Israel, traditionally descended from him. **2** /'benjəmɪn/ **Wal·ter** (1892–1940), German literary critic and cultural theorist who wrote extensively on literature, art, and drama from a Marxist perspective.

ben·ja·mina ficus /bendʒə'miːnə/ *noun* (also **Benjamin's fig**) = FICUS BENJAMINA.

Ben·nett ▸ **1** (**Enoch**) **Ar·nold** (1867–1931), English novelist, best known for his portrayal of English provincial life, esp. in the pottery-producing towns of Staffordshire, in documentary detail. **2 Rich·ard Bed·ford, Viscount** (1870–1947), Canadian businessman and lawyer, prime minister 1930–35. A prosperous lawyer

in Calgary before becoming Conservative prime minister during the Depression, Bennett introduced reform measures but was widely regarded as an ineffective leader; he retired to Surrey, England in 1939, and in 1941 was made a viscount. **3 Rich·ard Rod·ney** (b.1936), English composer. He studied in Paris with Pierre Boulez (1956–8), then settled in London. He is known for his film scores, notably those for *Far from the Madding Crowd* (1967) and *Murder on the Orient Express* (1974). **4 Wil·liam An·drew Cecil** ('Wacky') (1900–79), Canadian politician, premier of BC 1952–72. During his term as Social Credit premier, BC saw unprecedented growth and prosperity. **5** his son **Wil·liam Rich·ards** (b.1932), Canadian politician, premier of BC 1975–86, who oversaw a rigorous program of fiscal restraint.

Bennett buggy *noun Cdn hist.* an automobile hitched to horses or oxen, used during the Depression by owners who could no longer afford gasoline and operating expenses. [R. B. BENNETT]

Ben Nevis /ben 'nevɪs/ a mountain in W Scotland. Rising to 1 343 m (4,406 ft.), it is the highest mountain in the British Isles.

Benny, Jack (born Benjamin Kubelsky) (1894–1974), US comedian and actor. Benny made his radio debut in 1932 on Ed Sullivan's radio show and launched his own series in 1932. *The Jack Benny Show* was successfully transplanted to television in 1950 and ran until 1965. He was renowned for his timing, delivery and self-effacing mordant humour.

benny *noun* (pl. **-nies**) *slang* an amphetamine tablet, esp. as a stimulant. [abbreviation of BENZEDRINE]

ben·omyl /'benəmɪl/ *noun* a systemic fungicide used on fruit and vegetable crops. [*benzo* + *-o-* + *methyl*]

bent¹ ● *verb* past and past participle of BEND¹ *verb.* ● *adjective* **1** curved or having an angle. **2** (foll. by *on*) determined to do or have. **3** *slang* homosexual. **4** esp. *Brit. slang* dishonest, illicit. ● *noun* **1** an inclination or bias. **2** (foll. by *for*) a talent for something specified (*a bent for mimicry*). □ **bent out of shape** *N Amer. informal* upset or annoyed, esp. unreasonably so.

bent² *noun* **1 a** (also **bent grass**) any stiff grass of the genus *Agrostis*, a hardy grass used esp. in golf courses. **b** any of various grasslike reeds, rushes, or sedges. **2** a stiff stalk of a grass usu. with a flexible base. **3** *Brit. archaic* or *dialect* a heath or unenclosed pasture. [Middle English representing Old English *beonet-* (in place names), from Germanic]

Ben·tham /'benθəm, -təm/ **Jer·emy** (1748–1832), English philosopher, the first major proponent of utilitarianism. Bentham exercised a decisive influence over 19th-c. British thought, particularly with reference to political reform. □ **Ben·tham·ism** /'benθə,mɪzəm/ *noun* **Ben·tham·ite** *noun & adjective*

ben·thos /'benθɒs/ *noun* the flora and fauna at the bottom of a sea or lake. □ **ben·thic** *adjective* [Greek, = depth of the sea]

Ben·tinck, Wil·liam Henry Cav·en·dish, 3rd Duke of Portland, (1738–1809), English political leader, prime minister 1783 and 1807–9, and home secretary 1794–1801.

Bent·ley, Ed·mund Cleri·hew (1875–1956), English journalist and novelist. Examples of his comic verse form, the clerihew, were first published along with some sketches by his friend G. K. Chesterton in *Biography for Beginners* (1905).

bento box *noun* esp. *N Amer.* a portable lunch of Japanese food, typically rice, vegetables, sashimi, etc. served in a decorated lacquered wood box divided into compartments. [Japanese *bento* 'lunch']

ben·ton·ite /'bentə,naɪt/ *noun* a kind of highly absorbent clay having numerous uses, esp. as a filler. [Fort *Benton* in Montana]

bent·wood *noun* wood that is artificially curved for use in making furniture.

bentwood box *noun* a square or rectangular chest made from steamed and bent cedar, used traditionally by Aboriginal peoples of the Pacific Northwest for storage, cooking, etc.

be·numb *transitive verb* **1** make numb; deaden. **2** paralyze (the mind or feelings). [originally = deprived, as past participle of Middle English *benimen* from Old English *beniman* (as BE-, *niman* take)]

Benxi /ben'ʃiː/ a city in NE China, in the province of Liaoning; pop. (est. 2002) 1,170,100.

Benz, Karl Frie·drich (1844–1929), German engineer, who built the first car (a three-wheeled vehicle) to be driven by an internal combustion engine, at Mannheim in 1885.

Ben·ze·drine /'benzə,driːn/ *noun proprietary* a type of amphetamine. [BENZOIC + EPHEDRINE]

ben·zene /'benziːn/ *noun* a colourless carcinogenic volatile liquid found in coal tar, petroleum, etc., and used as a solvent and in the manufacture of plastics etc. Chem. formula: C_6H_6. □ **ben·zen·oid** *adjective* [BENZENE + -ENE]

benzene ring *noun* the hexagonal unsaturated ring of six carbon atoms in the benzene molecule.

ben·zine /ˈbenziːn/ *noun* a mixture of liquid hydrocarbons obtained from petroleum, used as a solvent and fuel. [BENZOIN + -INE⁴]

ben·zo·di·azep·ine /ˈbenzəˌdaiˈazepiːn/ *noun* any of a class of heterocyclic compounds used as tranquilizers, including Librium and Valium. [BENZOIC + DIAZO- + -EPINE]

ben·zo·ic /benˈzoːɪk/ *adjective* containing or derived from benzoin or benzoic acid. [BENZOIN + -IC]

benzoic acid *noun* a white crystalline substance used esp. as a food preservative. Chem. formula: $C_7H_6O_2$.

ben·zo·in /ˈbenzoːɪn/ *noun* **1** a fragrant gum resin obtained from various E Asian trees of the genus *Styrax*, and used in the manufacture of perfumes and incense. **2** the white crystalline constituent of this. *Also called* GUM BENJAMIN. [earlier *benjoin*, ultimately from Arabic *lubān jāwī* incense of Java]

ben·zol /ˈbenzɒl/ *noun* (also **ben·zole** /-zoːl/) benzene, esp. unrefined and used as a fuel.

benzo·quin·one /ˌbenzoːˈkwɪnoːn/ *noun* a yellow crystalline compound related to benzene but having two hydrogen atoms replaced by oxygen.

ben·zoyl /ˈbenzoːɪl/ *noun* (usu. *attributive*) Chem. the radical C_6H_5CO.

benzoyl peroxide *noun* a white crystalline solid, used as a bleaching agent, as a catalyst and initiator in polymerization, and applied topically in the treatment of acne.

ben·zyl /ˈbenzail, -zɪl/ *noun* (usu. *attributive*) Chem. the radical $C_6H_5CH_2$.

Beo·grad the Serbian name for BELGRADE.

Beo·thuk /biːˈʊθʊk/ (also **Beo·thuck**) ● *noun* **1** (*pl.* same or **-s**) a member of an Aboriginal people formerly inhabiting Newfoundland but extinct since the early 19th c. **2** the Algonquian language of this people. ● *adjective* of or relating to the Beothuk or their language. [Beothuk, = people]

Beo·wulf /ˈbeiəwulf/ a hero in Scandinavian folklore, whose exploits in defeating the monster Grendel and fighting to his death with a dragon are recounted in the Old English epic poem *Beowulf*, the first major poem in a European vernacular language.

be·queath /biˈkwiːθ, biˈkwiːð/ *transitive verb* **1** leave (an estate or piece of property) to a person by will. **2** hand down to posterity. □ **be·queath·able** *adjective* **be·queath·al** *noun* **be·queath·er** *noun* [Old English *becwethan* (as BE-, *cwethan* say: compare QUOTH)]

be·quest *noun* **1** the act or an instance of bequeathing. **2** a thing bequeathed. [Middle English from BE- + obsolete *quiste* from Old English -*cwiss*, *cwide* saying]

be·rate *transitive verb* scold, rebuke. [BE- + RATE²]

Ber·ber ● *noun* **1** a member of the indigenous mainly Muslim Caucasian peoples of N Africa (now mainly in Morocco and Algeria) speaking related languages. **2** the Afro-Asiatic language or group of languages of these peoples. **3** (**berber**) a type of sturdy carpet having large tightly woven loops, and often having the appearance of tweed. ● *adjective* of the Berbers or their language. [Arabic *barbar*]

ber·beris /ˈbɜːrbərɪs/ *noun* any shrub of the genus *Berberis*, esp. one grown for ornament (*see* BARBERRY). [medieval Latin from Arabic *berberys*, the name of the fruit]

ber·ceuse /ˌberˈsɜːz/ *noun* (*pl.* **berceuses** pronunc. same) **1** a lullaby. **2** an instrumental piece in the style of a lullaby. [French]

Berch·tes·gaden /ˈberktəsˌgadən/ a town in S Germany, in the Bavarian Alps close to the border with Austria; pop. (1997) 7,966. Hitler had an alpine retreat there.

Berczy /ˈbɜːrkzi/ **Wil·liam** (born Johann Albrecht Ulrich Moll, 1744–1813), German portrait painter and architect who settled in Upper Canada in 1794. He is best known for his portraits of Joseph Brant (c.1805) and *The Woolsey Family* (1808).

ber·dache /ˈbɜːrdaʃ/ *noun* (also **ber·dash**) a N American Aboriginal male, either celibate or homosexual, who assumes an intermediate social role between that of men and women in Aboriginal society. □ **ber·dach·ism** *noun* [French *bardache* 'boy prostitute' from Italian *bardascia* perhaps from Arabic *bardaj* slave]

be·reave *transitive verb* (*past* and *past participle* **be·reaved** or **be·reft**) (usu. foll. by *of*) deprive of a relation, friend, etc., esp. by death. □ **be·reave·ment** *noun* [Old English *berēafian* (as BE-, REAVE)]

be·reaved *adjective* saddened by the death of a loved one.

be·reft *adjective* (foll. by *of*) deprived (esp. of a non-material asset) (*bereft of hope*). □ **bereft·ness** *noun* [past participle of BEREAVE]

Beren·son /ˈberənsən/ **Ber·nard** (1865–1959), Lithuanian-born US art historian, whose work on Italian Renaissance art set new standards of criticism.

Beres·ford /ˈberəzfərd/ a town in NE New Brunswick, situated on Chaleur Bay, immediately northwest of Bathurst; pop. (2001) 4,414. [W. C. Beresford, Viscount *Beresford*, military commanding officer d.1854]

Beresford-Howe /ˈberəzfərdˌhau/ **Con·stance** (b.1922), Canadian novelist. A member of the English departments at McGill University (1946–71) and Ryerson Polytechnic, she has written seven novels, all dealing with the day-to-day and emotional lives of contemporary women, including *Night Studies* (1985).

beret /bəˈrei, beˈrei/ *noun* a round brimless cap of felt or cloth that is close-fitting and lies flat on the head. [French *béret* Basque cap, from Provençal *berret*]

Berg /berg/ **Alban** (1885–1935), Austrian composer. A student of Schoenberg's, he was one of the leading exponents of twelve-tone composition, and is known for his Violin Concerto (1935), and two operas, *Wozzeck* (1914–21) and *Lulu* (1928–35).

berg /bɜːrg/ *noun* = ICEBERG. [abbreviation]

ber·ga·mot¹ /ˈbɜːrgəˌmɒt/ *noun* **1** a citrus tree, *Citrus bergamia*, bearing fruit similar to an orange, from the rind of which a fragrant essential oil is extracted. **2** the oil or essence itself, used esp. in perfumes, Earl Grey tea, etc. **3** any of several herbaceous plants of the mint family smelling like bergamot, esp.: **a** N Amer. (in full **wild bergamot**) a N American plant, *Monarda fistulosa*, having purple or pink flowers. **b** a related plant, *Monarda didyma*, grown for its showy heads of scarlet flowers. *Also called* BEE BALM, OSWEGO TEA. **c** a Mediterranean mint, *Mentha citrata*, grown for its fragrance. [*Bergamo* in N Italy]

ber·ga·mot² /ˈbɜːrgəˌmɒt/ *noun* a large, round, yellow and russet variety of pear cultivated in Britain. [French *bergamotte* from Italian *bergamotta* from Turkish *begarmüdi* prince's pear, from *beg* prince + *armudi* pear]

Ber·gen a seaport in SW Norway; pop. (est. 2002) 200,600. It is a centre of the fishing and North Sea oil industries.

Bergen-Belsen a Nazi concentration camp during the Second World War, near the German villages of Bergen and Belsen.

ber·genia /bɜːrˈɡiːniə/ *noun* any of various perennial plants of the genus *Bergenia*, of the saxifrage family, having large, thick leaves and usu. pink, red or purple flowers. [K.A. von *Bergen*, German botanist d.1760]

Ber·ger, Hans (1873–1941), German psychiatrist. He attempted to correlate mental activity with brain physiology, detecting electric currents in the exposed cortex in 1924; finding that these could also be detected through the intact skull, he developed electroencephalography.

Ber·gerac¹ /ˈberʒəˌrak/ **1** a wine-producing region in the Dordogne valley in SW France. **2** a town on the Dordogne River; pop. (1999) 26,053.

Ber·gerac² /ˈberʒəˌrak/ *see* CYRANO DE BERGERAC.

Ber·gius /ˈbɜːrgiəs/ **Fried·rich (Karl Ru·dolf)** (1884–1949), German industrial chemist. He developed a process for producing petroleum and other hydrocarbons from coal dust, using hydrogen and a catalyst under high pressure; he shared the Nobel Prize for chemistry in 1931.

Berg·man ▸ **1 Ing·mar** (b.1918), Swedish film and theatre director. His films often explore complex psychological and metaphysical issues, and include *The Seventh Seal* (1956), *Wild Strawberries* (1956), *Autumn Sonata* (1978), and *Fanny and Alexander* (1983). **2 Ing·rid** (1915–82), Swedish film and stage actress, whose films include *Casablanca* (1943), *For Whom the Bell Tolls* (1943), and *Anastasia* (1956).

berg·schrund /ˈberkʃrʊnt/ *noun* a crevasse or gap at the head of a glacier or névé. [German, from *Berg* 'mountain' + *Schrund* 'crevice']

Berg·son /ˈbɜːrgsən, ˈberk-/ **Henri** (1859–1941), French philosopher, awarded the Nobel Prize for literature in 1927. His best-known work, *Creative Evolution* (1907), proposed that life possessed an inherent creative drive that led to the production of new forms. □ **Berg·son·ian** /ˌbɜːrgˈsoːniən, ˌberg-/ *adjective*

bergy bit /ˈbɜːrgi/ *noun* an iceberg about the size of a small house. [abbreviation of ICEBERG]

Beria /ˈberiə/ **Lav·renti Pav·lo·vich** (1899–1953), Soviet politician and head of the secret police (MVD). Following Stalin's death (1953) he became a victim of the ensuing struggle for power, and he was executed after a secret trial.

be·ribboned *adjective* decorated with ribbons.

Consonants: b *but* d *dog* f *few* g *get* h *her* j *yes* k *cat* l *leg* m *man* n *no* p *pen* r *red* s *sit*

beri·beri /ˌberiˈberi/ *noun* a disease causing inflammation of the nerves due to a deficiency of vitamin B₁ (thiamine), and mainly associated with rice-based diets. [Sinhalese, from *beri* weakness]

Ber·ing /ˈberiŋ/ **Vitus Jonas·sen** (1681–1741), Danish navigator and explorer of Arctic Asia, who led several Russian expeditions to discover whether Asia and N America were connected by land. He reached Alaska in 1741, but on the return voyage his ship was wrecked.

be·ringed /biˈriŋd/ *adjective* adorned with rings.

Ber·in·gia /bəˈrɪŋiə/ a land mass formerly linking Alaska with Siberia (most recently from *c.* 23,000 BC to 8,000 BC), now beneath the Bering Strait. □ **Ber·in·gian** *adjective & noun*

Bering Sea an arm of the N Pacific lying between NE Siberia and Alaska, bounded to the south by the Aleutian Islands. It is linked to the Arctic Ocean by the Bering Strait. [V.J. BERING]

Bering Strait a narrow sea passage, which separates the eastern tip of Siberia from Alaska, and links the Arctic Ocean with the Bering Sea. At its narrowest point it is about 85 km (53 miles) wide. During the ice age, as a result of a drop in sea levels, the area formed a bridge of land between the two continents, allowing migration of plants and animals. [V.J. BERING]

Berio /ˈberiɔː/ **Lu·ciano** (1925–2003), Italian composer whose works are influenced by serialism, electronic devices, and indeterminacy.

berk *noun* (also **burk**) *Brit. slang* a fool; a stupid person. [abbreviation of *Berkeley* or *Berkshire Hunt*, rhyming slang for *cunt*]

Berke·ley[1] /ˈbɑrkli/ a city in W California, on San Francisco Bay, site of a campus of the University of California; pop. (2000) 102,700.

Berke·ley[2] ▶ **1** /ˈbɜrkli/ **Busby** (born William Berkeley Enos, 1895–1976), US choreographer and film director, noted for his elaborate choreography and innovative camerawork in film musicals. **2** /ˈbɑrkli/ **George** (1685–1753), Irish-born philosopher and Anglican bishop. In his philosophical system Berkeley denied the existence of matter, and maintained that material objects exist only by being perceived. **3** /ˈbɑrkli/ **Sir Len·nox (Ran·dall Fran·cis)** (1903–89), English composer. His works, which are noted for their intensity of feeling and technical elegance, include four operas, among them *Nelson* (1953) and *Ruth* (1956), four symphonies, music for ballet and film, and sacred choral music.

ber·kel·ium /bɜrˈkiːliəm, ˈbɑrkliəm/ *noun* *Chem.* a transuranic radioactive metallic element produced by bombardment of americium. Symbol: **Bk**; at. no.: 97. [*Berkeley*, California (where first made) + -IUM]

Berks. /bɑrks/ *abbreviation* Berkshire.

Berk·shire /ˈbɑrkʃɪr/ a county of S England, west of London, subdivided in 1998 into six jurisdictions.

Berle, Mil·ton (born Milton Berlinger) (1908–2002), US comedian and entertainer whose steady appearances on television from the 1940s to the 1960s earned him the nickname 'Mr. Television'.

Ber·lin[1] **1** the capital of Germany; pop. (est. 2002) 3,289,500. Following the Second World War the city was divided into two parts: **West Berlin**, a state of the Federal Republic of Germany, forming an enclave within the German Democratic Republic; and **East Berlin**, capital of the German Democratic Republic. Between 1961 and 1989 the Berlin Wall separated the two sectors, which were reunited in 1990. **2** the former name (1833–1916) for Kitchener, Ontario. □ **Ber·lin·er** *noun*

Ber·lin[2] ▶ **1** **Irv·ing** (born Israel Baline, 1888–1989), Russian-born US songwriter. He wrote more than fifteen hundred songs, many of which acquired worldwide familiarity, e.g. 'White Christmas'. **2 Sir Isaiah** (1909–97), Latvian-born British philosopher. He devoted his career to the history of ideas. Notable works include *Karl Marx* (1939), *Four Essays on Liberty* (1959), and *Vico and Herder* (1976).

Berlin airlift an operation by British and American aircraft to airlift food and supplies to Berlin during the Russian blockade of the city in 1948–9. The airlift thwarted Russian plans to isolate the city from the West, and after the blockade was lifted, the city was formally divided into East and West Berlin.

Berlin Wall a fortified and heavily guarded wall built in 1961 by the Communist authorities on the boundary between East and West Berlin, chiefly to curb the flow of East Germans to the West. Regarded as a symbol of the division of Europe into the Communist countries of the East and the democracies of the West, the wall was opened in November 1989 after the collapse of the Communist regime in East Germany and subsequently dismantled.

Ber·lioz /ˈberliɔːz/ **Hec·tor** (1803–69), French composer, one of the most innovative orchestrators of his time. His works include the *Symphonie fantastique* (1830), the dramatic cantata *La Damnation de Faust*

(1846), and the operas *Les Troyens* (1855–58) and *Béatrice et Bénédict* (1860–62).

Ber·lus·coni /berluːˈskoːniː/ **Sil·vio** (b.1936), Italian media entrepreneur and politician, prime minister of Italy in 1994 and since 2001.

berm *noun* **1 a** a flat strip of land, raised bank, or terrace bordering a river etc. **b** a narrow path or grass strip beside a road. **2** a narrow ledge, esp. in a fortification between a ditch and the base of a parapet. □ **bermed** *adjective* [French *berme* from Dutch *berm*, prob. related to Old Norse *barmr* brim]

Ber·muda (also **the Bermudas**) a country (a British dependency with full internal self-government) consisting of about 150 small islands off the coast of N Carolina; pop. (est. 2002) 63,690; capital, Hamilton. □ **Ber·mud·an** *adjective & noun* **Ber·mud·ian** *adjective & noun* [J. *Bermúdez*, Spaniard who sighted the islands in the early 16th c.]

Bermuda grass *noun* N Amer. a creeping grass, *Cynodon dactylon*, common in warmer parts of the world, and used for lawns and pastures.

Bermuda onion *noun* a large, relatively mild, yellow or white onion having flattened ends.

Bermuda shorts *plural noun* (also **Bermudas**) knee-length shorts.

Bermuda Triangle *noun* **1** an area of the W Atlantic between Bermuda and Florida where ships and aircraft are reported to have disappeared without trace. **2** an area, activity, etc. where things are lost and never seen again (*he was swallowed up in the Bermuda Triangle of environmental politics*).

Bern *see* BERNE.

Ber·na·dette, St. (1844–79), Marie Bernarde Soubirous (*see* LOURDES).

Ber·na·dotte /ˌbɜrnəˈdɒt/ **1 Folke, Count** (1895–1948), Swedish statesman. He served as vice-president of the Swedish Red Cross during the Second World War; appointed UN mediator in Palestine in 1948, he was assassinated by Jewish extremists. **2 Jean Bapt·iste Jules** *see* CHARLES XIV.

Ber·nanos /ˈbernanɒs/ **Georges** (1888–1948), French writer. His works, such as *Sous le soleil de Satan* (1926), *Journal d'un curé de campagne* (1937), and *Dialogue des Carmélites* (1948) depict the struggle between extremes of good and evil from a strongly Roman Catholic perspective.

Ber·nard /bɜrˈnɑrd/ **1 Claude** (1813–78), French physiologist, pioneer of modern knowledge of the functioning of the body. Bernard determined the role of the pancreas in digestion, the method of regulation of body temperature, and the function of the nerves supplying the body's internal organs. **2 St.** (of Clairvaux) (1090–1153), Cistercian monk who founded a monastery at Clairvaux, France. Enjoying papal favour, he was an important religious force in Europe, and the Cistercian order grew rapidly under his influence; he preached the Second Crusade, and had Abelard condemned for heresy. **3 St.** (*c*.996–*c*.1081), a priest who founded two hospices to aid travellers in the Alps. The St. Bernard passes, where the hospices were situated, and St. Bernard dog, once kept by the monks and trained to aid travellers, are named after him.

Ber·nardi /ˌbɜrˈnɑrdi/ **Mario** (b.1930), Canadian conductor. He was the first conductor of the National Arts Centre Orchestra in Ottawa (1968–82), conductor of the CBC Vancouver Orchestra (now the CBC Radio Orchestra) from 1983, and music director of the Calgary Philharmonic Orchestra (1984–92).

Berne /bɜrn/ (also **Bern**) **1** a canton of Switzerland. **2** its capital, the capital of Switzerland; pop. (est. 2002) 121,900. □ **Bern·ese** *adjective & noun*

Berners-Lee, Tim (b.1955), British computer engineer who proposed the World Wide Web in 1989 and designed its first software.

Bernese mountain dog *noun* a dog of a large Swiss breed with long coats.

Bern·hardt /ˈbɜrn.hɑrt/ **Sarah** (born Rosine Bernard, 1844–1923), French romantic and tragic actress. Known as the 'divine Sarah', she was considered one of the foremost actresses of her day.

Ber·nières /bernˈjer/ an urban community in SE central Quebec, part of the city of Bernières-Saint-Nicolas. [*Bernières*-sur-Mer in Normandy, NW France]

Bernières-Saint-Nicolas /bernˌjersãnikɔˈlɒ/ a city in SE central Quebec, situated on the south shore of the St. Lawrence, southwest of Quebec City; pop. (1996) 15,594. [BERNIÈRES + SAINT-NICOLAS]

Ber·nini /berˈniːni/ **Gian·lor·enzo** (1598–1680), Italian sculptor, painter, and architect, the outstanding figure of the Italian baroque.

Bernini used a variety of materials (bronze, stucco, stone, and marble) to fuse sculpture, architecture, and painting into a decorative whole.

Ber·noul·li /bɜrˈnuːli/ **1 Dan·iel** (1700–82), Swiss mathematician, professor of mathematics at St. Petersburg before holding successively the chairs of botany, physiology, and physics at Basel. He is best remembered for explaining that the pressure in a fluid decreases as the flow speed increases. **2** his uncle **Jakob** (Jacques or James) (1654–1705), Swiss mathematician, professor of mathematics at Basel. He made substantial discoveries in calculus, which he used to solve minimization problems, and he contributed to geometry and the theory of probabilities. **3** Daniel's father **Jo·hann** (Jean or John) (1667–1748), Swiss mathematician, professor of mathematics at Basel, who also contributed to differential and integral calculus.

Bern·stein /ˈbɜrnstaɪn/ **Leon·ard** (1918–90), US composer, conductor, and pianist; conductor of the New York Philharmonic (1958–69). His works include the symphony *The Age of Anxiety* (1947–49), musicals such as *West Side Story* (1957), and film music such as that for *On the Waterfront* (1954).

Ber·ra /ˈbɛrə/ **Law·rence Peter** ('Yogi') (b.1925), US baseball player. As a catcher with the New York Yankees from 1946 to 1963 he played in fourteen World Series.

ber·ried *adjective* **1** (of a plant) bearing berries (also in *combination*: *yellow-berried*). **2** (of a lobster) egg-bearing.

Berry[1] a former province of central France; chief town, Bourges.

Berry[2], **Charles Ed·ward** ('Chuck') (b.1931), US guitarist, singer, and prolific songwriter, whose music and distinctive style were an early influence on rock 'n' roll.

berry *noun* (*pl.* **-ries**) **1** any small roundish juicy fruit without a stone. **2** *Bot.* a fruit with its seeds enclosed in pulp, e.g. the grape, gooseberry, tomato, etc. **3** any of various kernels or seeds, esp. of wheat etc. **4** an egg of a fish or lobster. [Old English *berie* from Germanic]

berry ground *noun Cdn* (*Nfld*) an elevated, treeless area where wild berries are found.

berry·ing *noun* gathering berries.

Berry·man, John (1914–72), US poet, writer, and critic, who was extremely influential in the US during the 1950s and 1960s.

berry spoon *noun* a serving spoon with a large, usu. perforated bowl, used for serving berries.

berry sugar *noun Cdn* very fine granulated white sugar.

ber·serk /bəˈzɜrk, bɜr-/ ● *adjective* (esp. in **go berserk**) wild, frenzied; in a violent rage. ● *noun* (also **ber·serk·er**) an ancient Norse warrior who fought with frenzied fury. [Icelandic *berserkr* (n.) prob. from *bern-* BEAR[2] + *serkr* coat]

berth ● *noun* **1** a fixed bunk on a ship, train, etc., for sleeping in. **2** a ship's place at a wharf. **3** room for a ship to swing at anchor. **4** sufficient room for a ship to manoeuvre. **5** *Sport* an opportunity for a team or athlete to compete (*a berth on the Olympic team; a playoff berth*). **6** *informal* a situation or appointment. **7** the proper place for anything. **8** *Cdn Forestry* a specified area of timberland in which a company or individual is entitled to fell trees. **9** *Cdn* (*Nfld*) a particular area claimed by a boat on fishing grounds. ● *verb* **1** *transitive* moor (a ship) in its berth. **2** *transitive* provide a sleeping place for. **3** *intransitive* (of a ship) come to its mooring place. □ **give a wide berth to** stay away from; avoid. [prob. from naut. use of BEAR[1] + -TH[2]]

bertha *noun* a deep falling collar (often of lace) or small cape on a dress. [French *berthe* from *Berthe* Bertha]

Ber·to·lucci /ˌbɛrtəˈluːtʃi/ **Ber·nar·do** (b.1940), Italian film director, whose films include *The Spider's Stratagem* (1970), *Last Tango in Paris* (1972), and *The Last Emperor* (1987).

Ber·ton, Pierre (b.1920), Canadian popular historian and journalist, one of Canada's best-known writers. His books include *Klondike* (1958), *The National Dream* (1970), *The Last Spike* (1971), and *Vimy* (1986).

Ber·wick·shire /ˈbɛrɪkˌʃɪr/ a former county of SE Scotland, on the border with England. It became a part of Borders region (now Scottish Borders) in 1975.

Berwick-upon-Tweed /ˈbɛrɪk/ a town at the mouth of the Tweed River in NE England, close to the Scottish border; pop. (est. 2002) 14,000.

beryl *noun* **1** a kind of transparent precious stone, esp. pale green, blue, or yellow, and consisting of beryllium aluminum silicate in a hexagonal form. **2** a mineral species which includes this, emerald, and aquamarine. [Latin *beryllus* from Greek *bērullos*]

beryl·lium /bəˈrɪliəm/ *noun Chem.* a hard white metallic element used in the manufacture of light corrosion-resistant alloys. Symbol: **Be**; at. no.: 4. [BERYL + -IUM]

Ber·zel·ius /bɜrˈziːliəs/ **Jöns Jakob** (1779–1848), Swedish chemist. He discovered several elements, suggested the basic principles of the modern notation of chemical formulae, and introduced the terms isomerism, polymer, protein, and catalysis.

Bes /bɛs/ *Egyptian Myth* a grotesque god depicted as having short legs, an obese body, and an almost bestial face, whose comic but frightening aspect was believed to dispel evil spirits.

B.E.S. *abbreviation* Bachelor of Environmental Studies.

Besan·çon /bəzɑ̃ˈsɔ̃/ the capital of Franche-Comté in NE France; pop. (1999) 117,733.

Bes·ant /ˈbɛzənt/ **Annie** (1847–1933), British social reformer and theosophist, who was active in the Indian independence movement.

be·seech *transitive verb* (*past* and *past participle* **be·sought** /-ˈsɒt/ or **be·seeched**) **1** (foll. by *for*, or *to* + infin.) entreat, implore. **2** ask earnestly for. □ **be·seech·ing** *adjective* **be·seech·ing·ly** *adverb* [Middle English from BE- + *secan* SEEK]

beset *transitive verb* (**beset·ting**; *past* and *past participle* **beset**) **1** attack or harass persistently (*beset by worries*). **2** surround or hem in (a person etc.). **3** *archaic* cover or surround with (*beset with pearls*). [Old English *besettan* from Germanic]

beset·ting *adjective* characteristic or predominant (*his besetting sin is greed*).

be·side *preposition* **1** at the side of; near. **2** compared with. **3** irrelevant to (*beside the point*). □ **beside oneself** overcome with worry, anger, etc. [Old English *be sīdan* (as BY, SIDE)]

be·sides ● *preposition* **1** in addition to; as well as. **2** other than; apart from; except; excluding. ● *adverb* in addition; as well; moreover.

be·siege /bɪˈsiːdʒ/ *transitive verb* **1** lay siege to. **2** crowd around oppressively. **3** harass with requests. **4** assail, beset. □ **be·sieger** *noun* [Middle English from *assiege* by substitution of BE-, from Old French *asegier* from Romanic]

be·smear *transitive verb* **1** smear with a greasy or sticky substance. **2** sully (a reputation etc.).

be·smirch *transitive verb* **1** soil, discolour. **2** dishonour; sully the reputation or name of.

besom /ˈbiːzəm/ *noun* **1** a broom made of twigs tied around a stick. **2** esp. *Scot.* & *Northern England derogatory* or *jocular* a woman or girl. [Old English *besema*]

be·sot·ted *adjective* **1** infatuated. **2** intoxicated, stupefied. **3** foolish, confused. [*besot* (v.) (as BE-, SOT)]

be·sought *past* and *past participle* of BESEECH.

be·spatter *transitive verb* spatter (liquid etc.) about.

be·speak *transitive verb* (*past* **be·spoke**; *past participle* **be·spoken** or as *adjective* **bespoke**) **1** suggest; be evidence of (*his gift bespeaks a kind heart*). **2** arrange for; engage in advance. **3** *archaic* speak to; address. [Old English *bisprecan* (as BE-, SPEAK)]

be·spec·tacled *adjective* wearing eyeglasses.

be·spoke ● *verb past* and *past participle* of BESPEAK. ● *adjective* **1** (of goods, esp. clothing) made to order. **2** (of a tailor etc.) making goods to order.

be·spoken *past participle* of BESPEAK.

be·sprinkle *transitive verb* **1** sprinkle or dot all over with liquid etc. **2** sprinkle (liquid etc.) over.

Bes·sar·abia /ˌbɛsəˈreɪbiə/ a region in E Europe between the Dniester and Prut rivers, from 1918 to 1940 part of Romania. The major part of it now falls in Moldova, the remainder in Ukraine. □ **Bes·sar·abian** *adjective* & *noun*

Bess·bor·ough /ˈbɛsbərə/ **Vere Brab·azon Pon·son·by, 9th Earl of** (1880–1956), Governor General of Canada 1931–35, founder of the Dominion Drama Festival.

Bes·sel /ˈbɛsəl/ **Frie·drich Wil·helm** (1784–1846), German astronomer and mathematician. He determined the positions of some 75,000 stars, was the first to obtain accurate measurements of stellar distances using the parallax resulting from the earth's changing position, and worked intensively on the orbits of planets and binary stars, developing mathematical functions that are named after him.

Bes·semer /ˈbɛsəmər/ **Sir Henry** (1813–98), English engineer and inventor, noted for the steelmaking process which bears his name.

Bessemer converter *noun* a special furnace used to purify pig iron using the Bessemer process. [BESSEMER]

Bessemer process *noun* a steelmaking process once widely used, in which air is blown through molten pig iron to remove carbon, silicon, and other impurities.

Bes·sette /beˈsɛt/ **Gé·rard** (b.1920), Canadian novelist and literary critic, who is best known for his satirical novels about Quebec society *La Bagarre* (1958), *Le Libraire* (1960), and *Les Pédagogues* (1961).

Best, Charles Her·bert (1899–1978), Canadian physiologist who assisted Frederick Banting in the discovery of insulin (*see also* BANTING).

best ● *adjective* (*superlative of* GOOD) of the most excellent or outstanding or desirable kind (*my best work*; *the best solution*; *the best thing to do would be to confess*). ● *adverb* (*superlative of* WELL¹). **1** in the best manner (*does it best*). **2** to the greatest degree (*like it best*). **3** most usefully (*is best ignored*). ● *noun* **1** that which is best (*the best is yet to come*). **2** the chief merit or advantage (*brings out the best in him*). **3** (foll. by *of*) a winning majority of (a certain number of games etc. played) (*the best of five*). **4** a best performance recorded to date (*her personal best*). ● *transitive verb informal* defeat, outwit, outbid, etc. □ **all the best** an expression of goodwill. **as best one can** (or **may**) as effectively as possible under the circumstances. **at best** on the most optimistic view. **at one's best** in peak condition etc. **at the best of times** even in the most favourable circumstances. **be for** (or **all for**) **the best** be desirable in the end. **the best of both worlds** the benefits of two different desirable outcomes, possibilities, etc., without having to choose between them. **the best part of** most of. **do** (or **give it**) **one's best** do all one can. **get the best of** defeat, outwit. **give a person one's best** express one's best wishes to a person. **had best** would find it wisest to. **make the best of** derive what limited advantage one can from (something unsatisfactory or unwelcome); put up with. **to the best of one's ability, knowledge,** etc. as far as one can do, know, etc. **with the best of them** as well as anyone. [Old English *betest* (adj.), *bet(o)st* (adv.), from Germanic]

best-before date *noun* the date marked on food showing the period after which it can be expected to deteriorate.

best bet *noun* the most favourable option under the circumstances.

best boy *noun* the assistant to the chief electrician of a film crew.

best buy *noun* the purchase giving the best value in proportion to its price; a bargain.

best friend *noun* a person's closest friend.

best girl *noun* N Amer. dated a girlfriend.

bes·tial /ˈbiːstɪəl, ˈbes-/ *adjective* **1** brutish, cruel, savage. **2** sexually depraved; lustful. **3** of or like a beast. □ **bes·tial·ly** *adverb* [Late Latin *bestialis* from *bestia* beast]

bes·ti·al·ity /ˌbiːstiˈalɪti, ˌbest-/ *noun* (*pl.* **-ities**) **1** sexual intercourse between a person and an animal. **2** bestial behaviour or an instance of this.

bes·ti·ary /ˈbiːstɪˌeri, ˈbestɪəri/ *noun* (*pl.* **-aries**) a moralizing medieval treatise on real and imaginary animals. [medieval Latin *bestiarium* from Latin *bestia* beast]

be·stir /bɪˈstɜr/ *reflexive verb* (**be·stirred, be·stir·ring**) exert or rouse (oneself).

best man *noun* the bridegroom's chief attendant at a wedding.

best of breed *noun* **1** the animal in a competitive show which is judged to be the best representative of its breed. **2** any item or product considered to be the best in its category.

be·stow *transitive verb* (foll. by *on, upon*) confer (a gift, right, etc.). □ **be·stow·al** *noun* **be·stow·er** *noun* [Middle English from BE- + Old English *stow* a place]

best practice *noun* that practice which is most appropriate, esp. that practice in the conduct of commercial or professional activities which is accepted by consensus or prescribed by regulation as being correct.

be·strew *transitive verb* (*past participle* **be·strewed** or **be·strewn**) **1** (foll. by *with*) cover or partly cover (a surface). **2** scatter (things) about. **3** lie scattered over.

be·stride *transitive verb* (*past* **be·strode** /-ˈstroːd/; *past participle* **be·strid·den** /-ˈstrɪdən/) **1** sit astride on. **2** stand astride over. **3** dominate.

best·sell·er *noun* **1** a book or other item that has sold in large numbers. **2** the author of such a book etc. □ **best·sell·ing** *adjective* **best·sell·er·dom** *noun*

be·suit·ed *adjective* wearing a suit.

bet ● *verb* (**bet·ting**; *past and past participle* **bet** or **bet·ted**) **1** *intransitive* (foll. by *on* or *against* with reference to the outcome) risk a sum of money etc. against another's on the basis of the outcome of an unpredictable event (esp. the result of a race, game, etc., or the outcome in a game of chance). **2** *transitive* risk (an amount) on such an outcome or result (*bet $20 on a horse*). **3** *transitive* risk a sum of money against (a person). **4** *transitive informal* feel sure (*bet they've forgotten it*). ● *noun* **1** the act of betting (*make a bet*). **2** the money etc. staked (*put a*

bet on). **3** *informal* an opinion, esp. a quickly formed or spontaneous one (*my bet is that he won't come*). **4** *informal* a choice or course of action (*she's a good bet*). □ **all bets are off** *informal* the outcome of a situation is unpredictable. **don't bet on it** *informal* used to express doubt about an assertion or situation. **want to bet?** *informal* used to express vigorous disagreement with a confident assertion. **you bet** you can be certain. [16th c.: perhaps a shortened form of ABET]

Beta *noun* = BETAMAX.

beta /ˈbeɪtə/ *noun* **1** the second letter of the Greek alphabet (Β, β). **2** (attributive) designating the second of a series or set. **3** Astronomy the second brightest star in a constellation. **4** Brit. a second-class mark given for a piece of school work or in an examination. [Greek]

beta blocker *noun* a drug preventing stimulation of beta receptors.

beta carotene *noun* an isomer of carotene found in carrots, tomatoes, etc., and converted in the body to vitamin A.

be·take *reflexive verb* (*past* **be·took**; *past participle* **be·taken**) (foll. by *to*) go to (a place or person).

Beta·max /ˈbeɪtəmaks/ *noun* proprietary (also **Beta** /ˈbeɪtə/) a standard format for video and videotapes using the whole area of the tape to record. [Japanese *beta-beta* all over (influenced by BETA) + *max*, abbreviation of maximum, after the condensed format in which the signal is recorded]

beta particle *noun* a high-speed electron or positron emitted by a radioactive substance.

beta ray *noun* (also **beta radiation**) a stream of beta particles.

beta receptor *noun* one of two kinds of receptor in the sympathetic nervous system, which increase cardiac activity when stimulated.

beta test ● *noun* a test of computer hardware or software in the final stages of development, carried out by the users for whom it is intended (*compare* ALPHA TEST). ● *transitive verb* (also **beta-test**) submit (a product) to a beta test.

beta·tron /ˈbeɪtəˌtrɒn/ *noun* Physics an apparatus for accelerating electrons in a circular path by magnetic induction. [BETA + -TRON]

beta version *noun* a version of a computer program or component used in beta testing.

bet·cha *verb* a non-standard contraction of 'bet you', used in representing informal speech.

betel /ˈbiːtəl/ *noun* the leaf of the Asian evergreen climbing plant *Piper betle*, commonly chewed with parings of the areca nut in SE Asia. [Portuguese from Malayalam *veṭṭila*]

Betel·geuse /ˈbiːtəlˌdʒuːs/ a first-magnitude variable red giant star in the constellation Orion. [French, alteration of Arabic *yad al-jauzā'* = hand of the giant (Orion)]

betel nut *noun* = ARECA NUT.

bête noire /bet ˈnwɑr/ *noun* (*pl.* **bêtes noires** *pronunc.* same) a person or thing one particularly dislikes or fears. [French, = black beast]

Bethe /ˈbeɪtə/ **Hans Al·brecht** (b.1906), German-born US physicist, who was awarded the 1967 Nobel Prize for physics for discovering the source of energy in the sun and stars.

be·think *reflexive verb* (*past and past participle* **be·thought**) (foll. by *of, how*, or *that* + clause) archaic **1** reflect; stop to think. **2** be reminded by reflection. [Old English *bithencan* from Germanic (as BE-, THINK)]

Beth·le·hem a small town 8 km (5 miles) south of Jerusalem, in the West Bank; pop. (est. 2002) 21,950. The native city of King David and reputed birthplace of Jesus, it contains a church built by Constantine in 330 over the supposed site of Christ's birth.

Beth·mann Holl·weg /ˈbetman ˈhɒlveig/ **Theo·bald von** (1856–1921), chancellor of Germany 1909–17. He opposed the introduction of unrestricted submarine warfare during the First World War, and in 1916 attempted to obtain US mediation.

Be·thune /beˈθjuːn, beˈθuːn/ **(Henry) Nor·man** (1890–1939), Canadian surgeon and political activist. A noted thoracic surgeon, Bethune served with the Communist forces in the Spanish Civil War (during which he organized the first mobile blood-transfusion service) and in China, where he is viewed as a hero thanks to a memorial essay by Mao Zedong.

be·tide *verb* (only in infin. and 3rd sing. subjunctive) **1** *transitive* happen to (*woe betide you if you do!*). **2** *intransitive* archaic happen (*whate'er may betide*). [Middle English from obsolete *tide* befall, from Old English *tīdan*]

be·times *adverb* **1** literary early; in good time. **2** N Amer. occasionally. [Middle English from obsolete *betime* (as BY, TIME)]

bêt·ise /beiˈtiːz/ *noun* **1** a foolish or ill-timed remark or action. **2** a piece of folly. [French]

Betje·man /'betʃəmən/ **Sir John** (1906–84), English poet, appointed Poet Laureate in 1972. His popular poems are witty and gently satiric, a comedy of manners, place names, and contemporary allusions.

be·token transitive verb **1** be a sign of; indicate. **2** augur. [Old English (as BE-, tācnian signify: see TOKEN)]

bet·ony /'betəni/ noun (pl. **-onies**) **1** a purple-flowered herbaceous plant of the mint family, Stachys officinalis. **2** any of various similar plants. [Old French betoine from Latin betonica]

be·took past of BETAKE.

be·tray transitive verb **1** place (a person, one's country, etc.) in the hands or power of an enemy. **2** be disloyal to (another person, a person's trust, etc.). **3** reveal involuntarily or treacherously; be evidence of (his shaking hands betrayed his fear). **4** lead astray or into error. □ **be·tray·al** noun **be·tray·er** noun [Middle English from obsolete tray, ultimately from Latin tradere hand over]

be·troth /bi'troʊð/ transitive verb formal bind with a promise to marry. □ **be·troth·al** noun [Middle English from BE- + trouthe, treuthe TRUTH, later assimilated to TROTH]

be·trothed /bi'troʊðd, -ðəd/ formal ● noun the person to whom one is betrothed; one's fiancé or fiancée. ● adjective engaged to be married.

Bet·tel·heim /'betəl,haɪm/ **Bruno** (1903–90), Austrian-born US psychologist, noted for his work with emotionally disturbed children. His book The Uses of Enchantment (1976) deals with the psychological significance of fairy tales.

bet·ter ● adjective (comparative of GOOD). **1** of a more excellent or outstanding or desirable kind (a better product; it would be better to go home). **2** partly or fully recovered from illness (feeling better). ● adverb (comparative of WELL[1]). **1** in a better manner (she sings better). **2** to a greater degree (like it better). **3** more usefully or advantageously (is better forgotten). ● noun **1** that which is better (the better of the two). **2** (usu. in pl.; prec. by my etc.) one's superior in ability or rank (take notice of your betters). ● verb **1** transitive improve on; surpass (I can better his offer). **2** transitive make better; improve. **3** reflexive improve one's position etc. **4** intransitive become better; improve. □ **better off** in a better (esp. financial) position. **better than** more than (lived there for better than twenty years). **the better part of** most of. **the better to …** so as to … better (the better to see). **for better or for worse** whatever changes may take place; whatever happens. **get the better of** defeat, outwit; win an advantage over. **go one better 1** outbid etc. by one. **2** outdo another person. **had better** would find it wiser to. **no better than** merely. **no better than one should** (or **ought to**) **be** of doubtful moral character, esp. sexually promiscuous. [Old English betera from Germanic]

better half noun informal jocular one's spouse.

better·ment noun **1** making better; improvement. **2** Law an improvement made to real property that enhances the property's value.

Bet·ter·ton, Thom·as (1635–1710), the leading English actor of the Restoration period.

Betti /'beti/ **Ugo** (1892–1953), Italian dramatist, who also wrote poetry, short stories, and a novel. His plays include Crime on Goat Island (1950, 1960) and Corruption in the Palace of Justice (1949, 1962).

bet·ting noun **1** gambling by risking money on an unpredictable outcome. **2** the odds offered in this.

betting shop noun Brit. (US **betting parlor**) an establishment licensed to handle bets on horse races etc.

bet·tor noun a person who bets.

be·tween ● preposition **1 a** at or to a point in the area or interval bounded by two or more other points in space, time, etc. (broke down between Edmonton and Red Deer; we must meet between now and Friday). **b** along the extent of such an area or interval (there are five houses between here and the main road; works best between five and six; the numbers between 10 and 20). **2** separating, physically or conceptually (the distance between here and Regina; the difference between right and wrong). **3 a** by combining the resources of (great potential between them; between us we could afford it). **b** shared by; as the joint resources of ($5 between them). **c** by joint or reciprocal action (an agreement between us; sorted it out between themselves). ¶ Use in sense 3 with reference to more than two people or things is established and acceptable (e.g. relations between Canada, the United States, and Mexico). **4** to and from (runs between Ottawa and Montreal). **5** taking one and rejecting the other of (decide between eating here and going out). ● adverb (also **in between**) at a point or in the area bounded by two or more other points in space, time, sequence, etc. (not fat or thin but in between). □ **between ourselves** (or **you and me**) in confidence. **between times** (or **whiles**) in the

intervals between other actions; occasionally. [Old English betwēonum from Germanic (as BY, TWO)]

be·twixt preposition & adverb archaic between. □ **betwixt and between** informal neither one thing nor the other. [Old English betwēox from Germanic: compare AGAINST]

Beur·ling /'bɜrlɪŋ/ **George Fred·erick** ('Buzz') (1921–1948), Canadian fighter pilot of both the RAF and the RCAF during the Second World War. Although considered undisciplined, he shot down more than 30 enemy aircraft and received a number of military awards.

beurre blanc /bɜr blɑ̃/ noun a sauce made of heated butter, shallots, and white wine, vinegar, or lemon juice, often served with fish. [French, = white butter]

Beuys /bɔɪs/ **Jo·seph** (1921–86), German sculptor and performance artist. A leading avant-garde artist of the 1970s and 1980s, he is known for his sculptures employing animal fat and felt, and for performances such as How to Explain Pictures to a Dead Hare (1965).

BeV abbreviation a billion electron volts. Also called GEV.

Bevan /'bevən/ **An·eurin** ('Nye') (1897–1960), English Labour politician, responsible for the creation of the National Health Service (1948) during his time as Minister of Health (1945–51).

bevel /'bevəl/ ● noun **1** a sloping surface or edge; a slope from the horizontal or vertical in carpentry, stonework, etc. **2** (in full **bevel square**) an adjustable tool for marking angles in carpentry, stonework, etc. ● verb (**bev·elled, bevel·ling**; also **bev·eled, bevel·ing**) **1** transitive reduce (a square edge) to a sloping edge. **2** intransitive slope at an angle; slant. [Old French bevel (unrecorded) from baif from baer gape]

bevel gear noun a gear working another gear at an angle to it by means of bevel wheels.

bevel wheel noun a toothed wheel whose working face is oblique to the axis.

bev·er·age /'bevərɪdʒ/ noun a drink (hot beverage; alcoholic beverage). [Old French be(u)vrage, ultimately from Latin bibere drink]

beverage room noun Cdn a lounge, bar, etc. where alcoholic drinks are sold.

Bev·er·idge /'bevərɪdʒ/ **Wil·liam Henry, 1st Baron** (1879–1963), British economist, author of the Beveridge Report (1942), which led to the creation of the national social insurance program in Britain.

Bev·er·ly Hills a largely residential city in California, on the northwest side of the Los Angeles conurbation; pop. (2000) 33,784. It is famous as the home of many film stars.

Bevin /'bevɪn/ **Er·nest** (1881–1951), English Labour politician and union leader. As foreign secretary (1945–51), he helped form the Organization for European Economic Cooperation (1948) and NATO (1949).

bevy /'bevi/ noun (pl. **-ies**) **1** a group or company of any kind. **2** a flock of quails or larks. [15th c.: origin unknown]

be·wail transitive verb **1** greatly regret or lament. **2** wail over; mourn for. □ **be·wail·er** noun

be·ware verb (only in imperative or infinitive) **1** intransitive (often foll. by of, or that, lest, etc. + clause) be cautious, take heed (beware of the dog; told us to beware; beware that you don't fall). **2** transitive be cautious of (beware the Ides of March). [BE + WARE[3]]

be·whis·kered adjective having whiskers.

be·wil·der transitive verb utterly perplex or confuse. □ **be·wil·dered** adjective **be·wil·dered·ly** adverb **be·wil·der·ing** adjective **be·wil·der·ing·ly** adverb **be·wil·der·ment** noun [BE- + obsolete wilder lose one's way]

be·witch transitive verb **1** enchant; greatly delight. **2** subject to the influence of magic or witchcraft; cast a spell on. □ **be·witch·ing** adjective **be·witch·ing·ly** adverb **be·witch·ment** noun

bey /beɪ/ noun hist. the governor of a district or province in the Ottoman Empire. [Turkish]

Bey·non /'beɪnən/ **Wil·liam** (1888–1958), Canadian ethnographer. A hereditary chief of the Nisga'a, he worked as an interpreter and field researcher among the Tsimshian, Nisga'a and Gitksan. His notes on the social structure and mythology of these peoples form a major source of data for the study of their cultures.

be·yond ● preposition **1** at or to the further side of (beyond the river). **2** outside the scope, range, or understanding of (beyond repair; beyond a joke; it is beyond me). **3** more than. ● adverb **1** at or to the further side. **2** further on. ● noun (prec. by the) the unknown after death. □ **the back of beyond** see BACK. [Old English beg(e)ondan (as BY, YON, YONDER)]

Consonants: **b** but **d** dog **f** few **g** get **h** her **j** yes **k** cat **l** leg **m** man **n** no **p** pen **r** red **s** sit

bez·ant /'bezənt, bɪ'zant/ *noun* **1** *hist.* a gold or silver coin originally minted at Byzantium, widely used in the currency of medieval Europe. **2** *Heraldry* a gold roundel. [Old French *besanz -ant* from Latin *Byzantius* Byzantine]

bez·el /'bezəl/ *noun* **1** the sloped edge of a chisel. **2** the oblique faces of a cut gem. **3 a** a groove holding a watch glass or gem. **b** a rim holding a glass etc. cover, e.g. on a clock, navigational instrument, etc. [Old French *besel* (unrecorded: compare French *béseau, bizeau*) of unknown origin]

Bé·zier /'beiziei/ *noun* (*attributive*) designating a polynomial curve expressed in such a way that its shape and curvature is specified by the position of two or more control points, which do not themselves lie on the curve. [P. *Bézier*, French mathematician]

bez·ique /bə'ziːk/ *noun* **1** a card game for two with a double pack of 64 cards, including the seven to ace only in each suit. **2** a combination of the queen of spades and the jack of diamonds in this game. [French *bésigue*, perhaps from Persian *bāzīgar* juggler]

be·zoar /'biːzɔr, 'bezoːˌɑr/ *noun* a small stone which may form in the stomachs of certain animals, esp. ruminants, and which was once used as an antidote for various ills. [ultimately from Persian *pādzahr* antidote, Arabic *bāzahr*]

BF *abbreviation* = BUTTERFAT.

b.f. *abbreviation* **1** *Printing* bold face. **2** *Brit. informal* bloody fool.

BFA *abbreviation* Bachelor of Fine Arts.

B-52 *noun* a cocktail consisting of Kahlúa, Irish Cream, and Grand Marnier layered in a small shot glass. [after the massive *B-52* bomber plane]

BGen *abbreviation Cdn* = BRIGADIER GENERAL.

BGH *abbreviation* BOVINE GROWTH HORMONE.

B.G.S. *abbreviation* Bachelor of General Studies.

Bhagavad-Gita /ˌbɒɡəvɒd'ɡiːtə/ the most famous religious text of Hinduism, an independent devotional work incorporated into the Mahabharata. [Sanskrit, = Song of the Lord]

bhajan /'bɒdʒən/ *noun Hinduism* a devotional song. [Sanskrit *bhajana*]

bhaji /'bɒdʒi/ *noun* (*pl.* **bhajis**) **1** an Indian dish of fried vegetables. **2** a small flat cake or ball of this, fried in batter (*onion bhaji*). [Hindi *bhājī* 'fried vegetables']

bhakti /'bʌkti/ *noun Hinduism* religious devotion or piety as a means of salvation, the most common form of Hinduism. [Sanskrit]

Bhakti·vedan·ta /ˌbʌktɪvə'dɒntə/ **Abhay Chara·na·ra·vinda** (1891–1977), Indian religious leader, founder of the International Society for Krishna Consciousness, known as the Hare Krishna movement, in 1965.

bhang /baŋ/ *noun* the leaves and flower tops of Indian hemp used as a narcotic. [Portuguese *bangue*, Persian & Urdu *bang* later assimilated to Hindi *bhāṅ*, from Sanskrit *bhaṅgā*]

bhan·gra /'baŋɡrə/ *noun* a style of popular (esp. dance) music combining Punjabi folk music with rock or disco elements. [Punjabi *bhāngrā* a traditional harvest dance]

bhar·al /'bʌrəl/ *noun* a Himalayan wild sheep, *Pseudois nayaur*, with a blue-black coat and horns curved rearward. [Hindi]

Bha·ra·tiya Jan·ata Party /bɒˌrɒtijə 'dʒʌnətɒ/ an Indian political party promoting Hindu nationalism.

Bhar·at·pur /ˌbʌrət'pʊr/ a sanctuary for migratory birds, near an 18th-c. fort in Rajasthan in NW India.

Bhav·nagar /bʌv'nʌɡər/ an industrial port in NW India, in Gujarat, on the Gulf of Cambay; pop. (2001) 511,000. It was the capital of a former Rajput princely state of the same name.

B.H.E. *abbreviation* Bachelor of Human Ecology.

bhel·puri /'beilˌpuːri/ *noun* an Indian dish of puffed rice, onions, spices, and hot chutney. [Hindi *bhel* 'mixture']

Bho·pal /boː'pɒl/ a city in central India, the capital of the state of Madhya Pradesh; pop. (2001) 1,433,900. In Dec. 1984 leakage of poisonous gas from an American-owned pesticide factory caused the death of about 2,500 people and thousands of injuries.

b.h.p. *abbreviation* BRAKE HORSEPOWER.

BHT *abbreviation* butylated hydroxytoluene, an antioxidant used to retard rancidity in foods containing fats and oils.

Bhuba·nes·war /ˌbuba'neiʃwɜr/ a city in E India, capital of the state of Orissa; pop. (2001) 647,300.

Bhu·tan /buː'tan/ a small independent kingdom on the southeastern slopes of the Himalayas, a protectorate of the Republic of India; pop. (est. 2002) 721,000; capital, Thimphu. □ **Bhu·tan·ese** /ˌbuːtə'niːz/ *adjective & noun*

Bhut·to /'buːtoː/ **1 Bena·zir** (b.1953), Pakistani politician, president of Pakistan 1988–90 and again 1993–96. In 1988 she was elected head of the Pakistan People's Party, which her father Zulfikar Ali Bhutto had founded, and became the first woman prime minister of a Muslim country, a position she held until 1996. She now lives in self-imposed exile in the UK. **2 Zul·fikar Ali** (1928–79) Pakistani politician, the first civilian president (1971–73) and later prime minister (1973–77) of his country. He was ousted by a military coup and executed for conspiring to murder a political rival.

Bi *symbol Chem.* the element bismuth.

bi /bai/ *adjective & noun informal* bisexual. [abbreviation]

bi- *combining form* (often **bin-** before a vowel) forming nouns and adjectives meaning: **1** having two; a thing having two (*bilateral; binaural; biplane*). **2 a** occurring twice in every one or once in every two (*biweekly*). **b** lasting for two (*biennial*). **3** doubly; in two ways (*biconcave*). **4** *Chem.* a substance having a double proportion of the acid etc. indicated by the simple word (*bicarbonate*). **5** *Bot. & Zool.* (of division and subdivision) twice over (*bipinnate*). [Latin]

BIA *abbreviation* **1** *Cdn* Business Improvement Association, a grouping of businesses which promotes commerce in a designated area and lobbies for the area's interests. **2** *Cdn* Business Improvement Area, the area served by a Business Improvement Association. **3** (in the US) Bureau of Indian Affairs.

Bi·afra /bi'afrə/ a state proclaimed in 1967, when part of E Nigeria, inhabited chiefly by the Ibo people, sought independence from the rest of the country. In the ensuing civil war the new state's troops were overwhelmed by numerically superior forces, and by 1970 it had ceased to exist. □ **Bi·af·ran** *adjective & noun*

Biały·stok /bja'wɪstɒk/ (Russian **Belo·stok** /ˌbjila'stɒk/) an industrial city in NE Poland, close to the border with Belarus; pop. (est. 2000) 285,507.

bi and bi *noun Cdn jocular* bilingualism and biculturalism. [abbreviation]

bi·annu·al *adjective* occurring, appearing, etc., twice a year (*compare* BIENNIAL). □ **bi·annu·al·ly** *adverb*

Biar·ritz /biə'rɪts/ a seaside resort in SW France, on the Bay of Biscay; pop. (1999) 30,055.

bias ● *noun* **1** (often foll. by *towards, against*) a predisposition or prejudice. **2** *Statistics* a systematic distortion of a statistical result due to a factor not allowed for in its derivation. **3** a diagonal line or cut across the weave of a fabric. **4 a** the irregular shape given to a ball in lawn bowling. **b** the oblique course this causes it to run. **5** *Electronics* **a** a steady voltage, magnetic field, etc., applied to an electronic system or device. **b** (in tape recording) a high-frequency waveform on which the signal is superimposed in order to avoid distortion. ● *transitive verb* (**biased**, **bias·ing**) **1** influence (usu. unfairly); prejudice. **2** give a bias to. □ **on the bias** obliquely, diagonally. [French *biais*, of unknown origin]

bias binding *noun* a strip of fabric cut obliquely and used to bind edges.

bias-cut *adjective* (of a garment or fabric) cut obliquely or diagonally across the grain.

biased *adjective* having a bias; prejudiced.

bias-ply *adjective N Amer.* (of a tire) having fabric layers with cords lying crosswise (*compare* RADIAL *adjective* 4).

bi·ath·lon /bai'aθlɒn/ *noun Sport* an athletic contest in cross-country skiing and shooting or in cycling and running. □ **bi·ath·lete** *noun* [BI-, after PENTATHLON]

bi·axial /bai'aksiəl/ *adjective* **1** having two axes. **2** (of crystals) having two optical axes along which polarized light travels with equal velocity.

bib[1] *noun* **1** a piece of cloth or plastic fastened around the neck, esp. of a baby, to keep the clothes clean during a meal. **2** the top front part of an apron, overalls, etc. **3** *N Amer.* a simple loose sleeveless jersey worn over sports attire to identify participants as members of a team, esp. during practice. **4** a coloured patch on the chest of certain dogs, cats, etc. **5** the edible marine fish, *Trisopterus luscus*, of the cod family, having a distensible membrane able to cover its head. Also called POUT[2]. □ **best bib and tucker** best clothes. [perhaps from BIB[2]]

bib[2] *intransitive verb* (**bibbed**, **bib·bing**) *archaic* drink much or often. [Middle English, perhaps from Latin *bibere* drink]

bibb *noun* a mild and tender head lettuce with loose, dark green leaves. [John *Bibb*, US horticulturalist d.1884, who developed it]

bib·ber *noun* a drinker, esp. of alcohol (*wine bibbers*). □ **bib·bing** *noun*

bib·cock *noun* a tap with a bent nozzle fixed at the end of a pipe. [perhaps from BIB[1] + COCK[1]]

bibe /baib/ *noun Cdn* (*Nfld*) a creature said to cry at night as an omen of someone's death.

bibe·lot /ˈbiːblo/ *noun* a small curio or artistic trinket. [French]

Bible *noun* **1 a** the Christian scriptures consisting of the Old and New Testaments. **b** the Jewish scriptures. **c** (*also* **bible**) any copy of these (*three bibles on the table*). **d** a particular edition of the Bible (*New English Bible*). **2** (usu. **bible**) any authoritative book (*the gardener's bible*). **3** the scriptures of any non-Christian religion. [ecclesiastical Latin *biblia* from Greek *biblia* books (pl. of *biblion*), originally diminutive of *biblos*, *bublos* papyrus]

Bible belt *noun esp. N Amer.* any area known for its fundamentalist Christian beliefs.

Bible oath *noun* a solemn oath taken on the Bible.

Bible school *noun* **1** (*also* **Bible college**) a post-secondary educational institution offering courses in Bible study and theology, esp. for evangelical Protestants. **2** *N Amer.* an organized course of study devoted to the Bible (*vacation Bible school*).

Bible-thumping *noun* (*Brit.* **Bible-bashing**) *informal* aggressive fundamentalist preaching. □ **Bible-thumper** *noun* (*Brit.* **Bible-basher**).

Bib·lical /ˈbɪblɪkəl/ *adjective* (*also* **biblical**) **1** of, concerning, or contained in the Bible. **2** resembling the language of the King James Bible. **3** very great; on a large scale (*a catastrophe of biblical proportions*). □ **bib·lical·ly** /ˈbɪblɪkli/ *adverb*

biblio- /ˈbɪblio/ *combining form* denoting a book or books. [Greek from *biblion* book]

bibli·og·raphy /ˌbɪbliˈɒɡrəfi/ *noun* (*pl.* **-ies**) **1 a** a list of the books referred to in a scholarly work, usu. printed as an appendix. **b** a list of the books of a specific author or publisher, or on a specific subject, etc. **2 a** the history or description of books, including authors, editions, etc. **b** any book containing such information. □ **bibli·og·raph·er** *noun* **bib·lio·graph·ic** /ˌbɪblioˈɡrafɪk/ *adjective* **bib·lio·graph·ic·al** /ˌbɪblioˈɡrafɪkəl/ *adjective* **bib·lio·graph·ic·al·ly** /ˌbɪblioˈɡrafɪkli/ *adverb* [modern Latin *bibliographia* from Greek (as BIBLE, -GRAPHY)]

bib·lio·mancy /ˈbɪblioˌmansi/ *noun* foretelling the future by the analysis of a randomly chosen passage from a book, esp. the Bible.

bib·lio·mania /ˌbɪblioˈmeiniə/ *noun* an extreme enthusiasm for collecting and possessing books. □ **bib·lio·maniac** /-niak/ *noun & adjective*

bib·lio·phile /ˈbɪblioˌfail/ *noun* a person who collects or is fond of books. □ **bib·lio·phil·ic** /-ˈfɪlɪk/ *adjective*

bib·lio·pole /ˈbɪblioˌpoʊl/ *noun* a seller of (esp. rare) books. [Greek *bibliopōlēs* from *biblion* book + *pōlēs* seller]

bib overalls *noun N Amer.* loose-fitting pants with fabric extending up to cover the front torso, fastened around the neck or over the shoulders.

bibu·lous /ˈbɪbjuləs/ *adjective* **1** fond of drinking alcoholic liquor. **2** relating to drink. □ **bibu·lous·ly** *adverb* **bibu·lous·ness** *noun* [Latin *bibulus* freely drinking, from *bibere* drink]

Bic *noun proprietary* a small disposable lighter.

bi·cam·eral /baiˈkamərəl/ *adjective* (esp. of a parliament or legislative body) having two chambers. □ **bi·cam·eral·ism** *noun* [BI- + Latin *camera* chamber]

bi·carb /ˈbaikɑrb/ *noun informal* = BICARBONATE 2. [abbreviation]

bi·car·bon·ate /baiˈkɑrbəneit, -nət/ *noun* **1** *Chem.* any acid salt of carbonic acid. **2** (in full **bicarbonate of soda**) = BAKING SODA.

bi·cen·ten·ary /ˌbaisənˈtenɑri, -ˈtiːnəri/ ● *noun* (*pl.* **-aries**) **1** a bicentennial. **2** a celebration of this. ● *adjective* of or concerning a bicentenary.

bi·cen·ten·nial /ˌbaisənˈteniəl/ *esp. N Amer.* ● *noun* a two-hundredth anniversary. ● *adjective* **1** lasting two hundred years or occurring every two hundred years. **2** of or concerning a bicentennial.

bi·cep /ˈbaisep/ *noun informal* a biceps muscle. ¶ Although *bicep* is becoming more common in informal use, *biceps* remains standard as the singular noun. [back-formation from BICEPS]

bi·ceph·al·ous /baiˈsefələs/ *adjective* having two heads.

bi·ceps /ˈbaiseps/ *noun* (*pl.* same) the flexor muscle at the front of the upper arm or at the back of the thigh. [Latin, = two-headed, (because the muscle has two attachments at one end) formed as BI- + *-ceps* from *caput* head]

bi·chon frise /biːˌʃɒn ˈfriːz/ *noun* a small dog of a breed with a fine, curly white coat. [French *barbichon* 'little water spaniel' + *frisé* 'curly-haired']

bick·er *intransitive verb* **1** quarrel pettily; wrangle. **2** *archaic* **a** (of a stream, rain, etc.) patter (over stones etc.). **b** (of a flame, light, etc.) flash, flicker. □ **bick·er·er** *noun* [Middle English *biker, beker*, of unknown origin]

Bick·ert, Ed·ward Isaac (b.1932), Canadian jazz guitarist, noted for his work with Moe Koffman and Rob McConnell's Boss Brass.

bi·coast·al *adjective* living on or pertaining to two coasts, esp. of the US.

bi·col·our ● *adjective* (*also* **bi·col·oured**) having two colours. ● *noun* a bicolour blossom or animal.

bi·con·cave *adjective* (esp. of a lens) concave on both sides.

bi·con·vex *adjective* (esp. of a lens) convex on both sides.

bi·cultur·al *adjective* having or involving two cultures, esp. (in Canada) English-Canadian and French-Canadian. □ **bi·cultur·al·ism** *noun*

bi-curious *adjective* (of a heterosexual person) interested in experiencing a first encounter or relationship with a person of the same sex.

bi·cus·pid ● *adjective* having two cusps or points. ● *noun* **1** the premolar tooth in humans. **2** a tooth with two cusps. □ **bi·cus·pid·ate** *adjective* [BI- + Latin *cuspis -idis* sharp point]

bi·cycle ● *noun* a vehicle with two wheels held in a frame one behind the other, propelled by pedals and steered with handlebars attached to the front wheel. ● *intransitive verb* ride a bicycle. □ **bi·cyc·list** *noun* [French from BI- + Greek *kuklos* wheel]

bicycle chain *noun* a chain connecting a bicycle's pedals to the rear wheel.

bicycle clip *noun* either of two metal clips used to confine a cyclist's pants at the ankles.

bicycle path *noun* a paved route for bicycling, often also open to pedestrians.

bicycle pump *noun* a portable pump for inflating bicycle tires.

bicycle shorts *plural noun* **1** tight-fitting, thigh-length elastic shorts with a padded crotch, worn esp. by cyclists. **2** a tight-fitting undergarment extending from the waist to mid-thigh.

bi·cyclic /baiˈsaiklɪk, -ˈsɪk-/ *adjective Chem.* having two (usu. fused) rings of atoms in the molecular structure.

bid ● *verb* **1** *transitive & intransitive* (**bid·ding**; *past* and *past participle* **bid**) (often foll. by *for, against*) **a** (esp. at an auction) offer (a certain price) (*did not bid for the vase; bid against the dealer; bid $100*). **b** offer to do work etc. for a stated price. **2** *transitive* (**bidding**; *past* **bid, bade** /beid, bad/; *past participle* **bid, bid·den**) **a** command; order (*bid the soldiers shoot*). **b** invite (*bade her start*). **3** *transitive* (**bidding**; *past* **bade** /beid, bad/, **bid**; *past participle* **bidden** /ˈbɪdən/, **bid**) utter (greeting or farewell) to (*I bade him welcome*). **4** (**bidding**; *past* and *past participle* **bid**) *Cards* **a** *intransitive* state before play how many tricks one intends to make. **b** *transitive* state (one's intended number of tricks). ● *noun* **1 a** (esp. at an auction) an offer (of a price) (*a bid of $5*). **b** an offer to do work, supply goods, etc.) at a stated price; a tender. **2** *Cards* a statement of the number of tricks a player proposes to make. **3** an attempt; an effort (*a bid for power*). □ **bid fair to** seem likely to. (**make a) bid for** try to gain (*made a bid for freedom; a rookie goalie bidding for his first shutout*). □ **bid·der** *noun* [Old English *biddan* ask, from Germanic, & Old English *bēodan* offer, command]

bid·dable *adjective* **1** obedient. **2** *Cards* (of a hand or suit) suitable for being bid. □ **bid·dabil·ity** *noun*

bid·den *past participle* of BID.

bid·ding *noun* **1** the offers made for something being sold. **2** *Cards* the act of making a bid or bids. **3** a command, request, or invitation.

bidding prayer *noun Anglicanism* a prayer inviting the congregation to join in.

bidding war *noun* a situation in which competitors outbid one another repeatedly to gain an advantage.

Bid·dle, John (1615–1662), English theologian. His strongly anti-Trinitarian views resulted in repeated prison terms, but by 1652 he was able to establish the first English Unitarian congregation.

biddy *noun* (*pl.* **-dies**) *slang derogatory* a woman (esp. *old biddy*). [pet form of the name *Bridget*]

bide *intransitive verb archaic* or *dialect* remain; stay. □ **bide one's time** await one's best opportunity. [Old English *bidan* from Germanic]

bidet /biːˈdei/ *noun* a low oval bathroom fixture used for washing the genital and anal regions. [French, originally = pony]

bi·direc·tion·al *adjective* functioning in two directions.

Bid·well, Mar·shall Spring (1799–1872), US-born Canadian lawyer and politician. A leader of the Reform interests in Upper Canada, he sat in the Assembly 1824–36, serving as Speaker in 1828 and 1834. He rejected the radicalism of William Lyon Mackenzie and did not take part in the Upper Canada Rebellion, but left the province in 1837 after being criticized by Sir Francis Bond Head for his disloyalty.

Bieder·meier /ˈbiːdərˌmaɪər/ *attributive adjective* denoting or relating to a style of furniture and interior design current in Germany in the period 1815–48, characterized by restraint, conventionality, and utilitarianism. [*Biedermaier* a fictitious German poet (1854)]

Biele·feld /ˈbiːləˌfelt/ an industrial city in North Rhine-Westphalia in western Germany; pop. (est. 2002) 322,000.

bi·en·nale /biːeˈnɒli/ *noun* a large (esp. biennial) art exhibition or music festival, esp. the one (**Biennale**) held biennially in Venice, Italy. [Italian (as BIENNIAL)]

bi·enni·al /baɪˈeniəl/ ● *adjective* **1** recurring every two years (compare BIANNUAL). **2** lasting two years. ● *noun* **1** *Bot.* a plant that takes two years to grow from seed to fruition and die (compare ANNUAL, PERENNIAL). **2** an event celebrated or taking place every two years. □ **bi·enni·al·ly** *adverb* [Latin *biennis* (as BI-, *annus* year)]

bi·enni·um /baɪˈeniəm/ *noun* (pl. **bi·enni·ums** or **bi·ennia** /-niə/) a period of two years. [Latin (as BIENNIAL)]

bien pen·sant /ˌbjã pãˈsã/ usu. *derogatory* ● *noun* a right-thinking or orthodox person. ● *adjective* right-thinking, orthodox. [French, lit. 'well-thinking', from *penser* think]

bier /biːr/ *noun* a movable frame on which a coffin or a corpse is placed, or taken to a grave. [Old English *bēr* from Germanic]

Bierce /biːrs/ **Am·brose Gwin·nett** (1842–?1914), US journalist and author, whose realistic and sardonic short stories were influenced by Poe. In 1913 he went to Mexico and disappeared mysteriously.

bier·wurst /ˈbiːrwɜrst/ *noun* a cooked, smoked salami of ground beef and pork seasoned with mustard, garlic, onion, and pepper. [German, = beer sausage, because traditionally served with beer.]

bi·face *noun* a type of prehistoric stone implement flaked on both sides. □ **bi·facial** *adjective* **bi·facial·ly** *adverb*

biff *Brit. slang* ● *noun* a sharp blow. ● *transitive verb* strike (a person). [imitative]

bif·fin *noun Brit.* a deep red cooking apple. [= *beefing* from BEEF + -ING¹, with reference to the colour]

biffy *noun* (pl. **-fies**) *N Amer.* (esp. *West*) *informal* **1** an outhouse. **2** a toilet. [origin unknown: possibly a childish deformation of *privy*]

bifid /ˈbaɪfɪd/ *adjective* divided by a deep cleft into two parts. [Latin *bifidus* (as BI-, *fidus* from stem of *findere* cleave)]

bif·id·um /ˈbɪfɪdəm/ *noun* a bacterium, *Lactobacillus bifidum*, often added to yogourt as being beneficial to the intestinal flora. [as BIFID]

bi·focal ● *adjective* having two focuses, esp. of a lens with a part for distant vision and a part for near vision. ● *noun* (in pl.) bifocal glasses.

bi·fold /ˈbaɪfoʊld/ ● *adjective* designating a two-piece door which moves on tracks and folds along a hinge down the centre. ● *noun* a bifold door.

bi·fur·cate /ˈbaɪfərˌkeɪt, baɪˈfɜrkeɪt, -kət/ ● *transitive & intransitive verb* divide into two branches; fork. ● *adjective* forked; branched. [medieval Latin *bifurcare* from Latin *bifurcus* two-forked (as BI-, *furca* fork)]

bi·fur·ca·tion /ˌbaɪfərˈkeɪʃən/ *noun* **1 a** a division into two branches. **b** either or both of such branches. **2** the point of such a division.

big ● *adjective* (**bigger**, **biggest**) **1 a** of considerable size, amount, intensity, etc. (*a big mistake*; *a big helping*). **b** of a large or the largest size (*big toe*; *big drum*). **2 a** important; significant; outstanding (*my big chance*). **b** famous, popular (*a big celebrity*; *big in Japan*). **3 a** grown up (*a big boy now*). **b** elder (*big sister*). **4** *informal* **a** boastful (*big words*). **b** often *ironic* generous (*big of him*). **c** ambitious (*big ideas*). **d** (of a game etc.) well-played (*a big inning*; *he had a big game*). **5** (usu. foll. by *with*) **a** advanced in pregnancy (*big with child*). **b** fecund (*big with consequences*). ● *adverb informal* in a big manner, esp.: **1** effectively (*went over big*). **2** boastfully (*talk big*). **3** ambitiously (*think big*). **4** to a considerable extent (*win big*). ● *noun N Amer.* (in pl.) the major baseball leagues (*made it to the bigs*). □ **be big on** be enthusiastic about. **come** (or **go**) **over big** make a great effect. **come up big** perform successfully when relied upon to do so. **in a big way 1** on a large scale. **2** *informal* with great enthusiasm, display, etc. **look** (or **talk**) **big** boast. **make it big** achieve great success. **too big for one's britches** (or **boots**) *slang* conceited. □ **big·gish** *adjective* **big·ness** *noun* [Middle English: origin unknown]

big air *noun* a very high jump in snowboarding, freestyle skiing, etc.

big·amy /ˈbɪɡəmi/ *noun* (pl. **-ies**) the crime of marrying when one is lawfully married to another person. □ **biga·mist** *noun* **biga·mous** *adjective* [Old French *bigamie* from *bigame* bigamous, from Late Latin *bigamus* (as BI-, Greek *gamos* marriage)]

Big Apple, the *N Amer. slang* New York City.

big band *noun* (often *attributive*) a large jazz or swing orchestra.

big bang *noun* **1** *Astronomy* the violent explosion of all matter from a state of high density and temperature, postulated as the origin of the universe. **2** any sudden or dramatic beginning of drastic change. **3** (in the UK) the introduction in 1986 of important changes in the regulations and procedures for trading on the Stock Exchange, esp. the widening of membership, the relaxation of rules for brokers, and the introduction of computerized communications.

Big Bear (*Mistahimaskwa c.*1825–88), Canadian Plains Cree leader, their chief during the Northwest Rebellion. Despite his calls for moderation among his followers, he was convicted of treason-felony in 1885 and sentenced to three years imprisonment.

Big Ben *noun* the great clock tower of the Houses of Parliament in London, and its bell.

Big Bend National Park a US national park in a bend of the Rio Grande, in the desert lands of S Texas on the border with Mexico, in which were discovered, in 1975, fossil remains of the pterosaur.

Big Blue Machine *noun Cdn* the Ontario Progressive Conservative Party during the premiership of William Davis (1971–85).

Big Board *noun US informal* the New York Stock Exchange.

big-boned *adjective* **1** having large bones. **2** *euphemism* (of a person) large; heavy-set.

big box *noun N Amer.* a very large, warehouse-style store, often specializing in one kind of merchandise (e.g. hardware, books, etc.), usu. at lower prices than in other stores.

Big Brother *noun* **1** an all-powerful dictator or government which keeps the populace under close observation and strict control (as in Orwell's *1984*). **2** an adult who befriends a fatherless child, esp. through an agency. □ **Big Brother·ism** *noun* (in sense 1).

big bucks *noun N Amer. slang* a great deal of money.

big business *noun* large commercial, industrial, or financial companies, esp. when having a significant social, economic, or political influence.

big C *noun informal* cancer.

big cat *noun* any of the larger members of the feline family, e.g. lions, leopards, tigers, etc.

big cheese *noun informal* a very important person. [CHEESE³]

big crunch *noun Astronomy* the hypothetical total inward collapse of the universe following a sufficient slowing-down of its expansion. [after BIG BANG]

big deal *noun informal* something important.

Big Dipper *noun N Amer.* the constellation Ursa Major or its seven bright stars.

Big Easy *noun informal* New Orleans.

big end *noun* (in a motor vehicle) the end of the connecting rod attached to the crankpin.

Big·foot /ˈbɪɡfʊt/ *noun* = SASQUATCH.

big game *noun* large animals hunted for sport.

big·gie *noun informal* a very important person, company, event, etc. □ **no biggie** *informal* no big deal.

big government *noun* government characterized by large-scale or expensive participation in domestic affairs.

big gun *noun informal* **1** an important person, company, etc. **2** *Sport* a high-scoring player.

big hair *noun informal* a bouffant hairstyle with the hair standing upwards or outwards from the head.

big head *noun informal* a conceited person. □ **have a big head** be conceited. □ **big-headed** *adjective* **big-headed·ness** *noun*

big heart *noun* a generous nature. □ **big-hearted** *adjective*

big·horn *noun* a N American sheep, *Ovis canadensis*, with large curving horns, esp. native to the Rocky Mountains.

big house *noun* (also **Big House**) **1** *slang* a prison. **2** *N Amer.* a communal dwelling, sometimes up to 18 m (60 ft.) in length, used by West Coast Aboriginal peoples, with a section for each family as well as a central common area. **3** *Brit. or hist.* the principal house in a village etc. **4** *Cdn hist.* the residence of the chief trader at a fur-trading post.

bight /baɪt/ *noun* **1** a curve or recess in a coastline, river, etc. **2** a loop of rope. [Old English *byht*, Middle Low German *bucht* from Germanic: see BOW²]

---

uː m**oo**d   aɪ m**y**   əi p**i**pe   au br**ow**n   ʌv h**ou**se   ei d**ay**   ɔi b**oy**   ā fr**an**glais   ã Cana**di**en   ɔ̃ Br**ay**on   (see over for consonants)

big idea *noun* often *ironic* the important intention or scheme.

big iron *noun informal* large powerful mainframe computers or supercomputers.

Big Island *informal* the island of Hawaii, the largest of the Hawaiian islands.

big kahuna *noun N Amer. slang* **1** an important person; a big shot. **2** anything very large, esp. a large wave. [Hawaiian *kahuna* priest, wise man]

big·leaf maple *noun* a maple tree, *Acer macrophyllum*, native to the Pacific coast of N America, with very large lobed leaves.

big league *noun* **●** *noun* **1** the highest professional league in a sport, esp. baseball. **2** the highest class in any field (*made it to the big leagues*). **●** *adjective* (**big-league**) first-class; worthy of being in the big leagues. □ **big-leaguer** *noun*

big lie *noun esp. N Amer.* an intentional distortion of facts, esp. by a politician, official body, etc.

big money *noun* **1** a great deal of money, esp. as pay or profit. **2** large corporations, the very wealthy, etc.

big·mouth *noun* a talkative, indiscreet, or boastful person.

big name *noun* a famous person (often *attributive*: *big-name stars*).

big noise *noun esp. Brit. informal* = BIGWIG.

Big O *noun* **1** *slang* orgasm. **2** *Cdn slang* the Olympic Stadium in Montreal.

big one *noun informal* **1** a major event. **2** (also **Big One**) (usu. prec. by *the*) an anticipated massive earthquake along the San Andreas Fault in California. **3** a sum of money or a banknote representing it (*it'll cost you fifty big ones*).

Bigot /biˈɡoː/ **Fran·çois** (1703–78), French-born intendant of New France (1748–60), whose corrupt administration has been blamed for leaving Canada vulnerable to the British.

big·ot /ˈbɪɡət/ *noun* a person intolerant of another's beliefs, race, politics, etc. □ **big·otry** *noun* [16th c. from French: origin unknown]

big·ot·ed /ˈbɪɡətɪd/ *adjective* unreasonably prejudiced and intolerant.

big picture *noun* (prec. by *the*) an issue etc. viewed or understood as a whole (*concentrating so much on the details, we overlooked the big picture*).

big science *noun* enormously expensive, usu. large-scale scientific research.

big screen *noun* **1** the screen in a movie theatre. **2** (usu. prec. by *the*) motion pictures collectively, esp. as seen in theatres (*their first appearance on the big screen*).

big shot *noun informal* **1** an important person, esp. in a corporation etc. **2** a pretentious person.

Big Sister *noun* an adult who befriends a motherless child, esp. through an agency.

Big Six *noun Cdn* (prec. by *the*) the six leading Canadian banks.

big smoke *noun informal* (prec. by *the*) any large city, esp. (in Canada) Toronto, (in the US) New York, (in the UK) London.

big spender *noun* an extravagant person.

big stick *noun* a display of force.

big tent *noun* a political party's policy of permitting and encouraging a broad spectrum of views among its members.

Big Three *noun* (usu. prec. by *the*) (in N America) the three largest automakers.

big-ticket *attributive adjective* expensive (*sales of big-ticket items have increased*).

big time *informal* **●** *noun* (usu. prec. by *the*) the highest level of success in a profession, esp. entertainment (*dreams of the big time*). **●** *adverb* esp. *N Amer.* as an intensifier (*they lost big time*). □ **big-time** *adjective* **big-timer** *noun*

big toe *noun* either of the innermost and largest toes.

big·tooth aspen *noun* = LARGETOOTH ASPEN.

big top *noun* **1** the main tent of a circus. **2** a circus. **3** a tent capable of holding a large gathering.

big tree *noun* a giant evergreen conifer, *Sequoiadendron giganteum*, of the Sierra Nevada in California, the most massive of all trees.

bi·guine *var. of* BEGUINE.

big wheel *noun* **1** *N Amer. informal* = BIGWIG. **2** a Ferris wheel.

big·wig *noun informal* an important person.

Bihar /bɪˈhɑr/ a state in NE India; capital, Patna.

Bi·hari /biˈhɑri/ *noun* **1** a native of Bihar. **2** a group of three closely related languages, descended from Sanskrit, spoken principally in Bihar.

bijou /ˈbiːʒuː, biˈʒuː/ **●** *noun* (*pl.* **bijoux** *pronunc.* same) a jewel; a trinket. **●** *attributive adjective* small and elegant. [French]

bi·jural·ism /baiˈdʒʊrəlɪzəm/ *noun esp. Cdn Law* the existence of two legal systems within a single jurisdiction. □ **bi·jural** *adjective* [BI- + Latin *jus juris* law]

bike *informal* **●** *noun* a bicycle or motorcycle. **●** *intransitive verb* ride a bicycle or motorcycle. [abbreviation]

biker *noun* **1** a cyclist, esp. a motorcyclist. **2** a member of a motorcycle gang.

bike·way *noun N Amer.* a transportation route reserved for or specially adapted for bicycles.

Biki·ni an atoll in the Marshall Islands, in the W Pacific, used by the US between 1946 and 1958 as a site for testing nuclear weapons.

biki·ni *noun* **1** a two-piece bathing suit for women, the bottom half of which consists of skimpy briefs which do not extend above the top of the pelvis. **2** a skimpy bathing suit for men, similar to the bottom half of a bikini. **3** = BIKINI BRIEFS. **4** (*attributive*) designating the pubic hairline, esp. of a woman (*bikini line; bikini cut; bikini wax*). □ **bi·ki·nied** *adjective* [BIKINI, from the supposed 'explosive' effect]

bikini briefs *plural noun* (also **bikini underwear**) skimpy briefs which do not extend above the top of the pelvis.

Biko /ˈbiːkoː/ **Ste·phen** (1946–77), South African student leader, an active opponent of apartheid and founder of the 'black consciousness' movement. His brutal death while in police custody made him a symbol of heroism in Black townships and beyond.

bi·labi·al /baiˈleibiəl/ *adjective Phonetics* (of a sound etc.) made with closed or nearly closed lips.

bi·lat·eral /baiˈlatərəl/ *adjective* **1** of, on, or with two sides. **2** affecting or between two parties, countries, etc. (*bilateral negotiations*). □ **bi·lat·eral·ly** *adverb*

bilateral symmetry *noun* a type of body arrangement in which there is only one plane along which an organism can be divided into two symmetrical halves.

bi·layer /ˈbaileiэr/ *noun* a film two molecules thick, in which each molecule is arranged with its hydrophilic end directed outwards.

Bil·bao /bɪlˈbau/ a seaport and industrial city in N Spain; pop. (est. 2001) 353,943.

bil·berry *noun* (*pl.* **-berries**) **1** any of several shrubs of the genus *Vaccinium*, with single, edible, blue or black berries. **2** a berry from such a shrub. [origin uncertain: compare Danish *bøllebær*]

bilbo *noun* (*pl.* **-bos** or **-boes**) *hist.* a sword noted for the temper and elasticity of its blade. [*Bilboa* = BILBAO]

bil·boes /ˈbɪlboːz/ *plural noun hist.* an iron bar with sliding shackles for a prisoner's ankles. [16th c.: origin unknown]

Bild·ungs·roman /ˈbɪldʊŋzroːˌmɒn/ *noun* a novel dealing with one person's early life and development. [German, from *Bildung* education + *Roman* novel]

bile *noun* **1** a bitter greenish-brown alkaline fluid which aids digestion and is secreted by the liver and stored in the gallbladder. **2** bad temper; peevish anger. [French from Latin *bilis*]

bile duct *noun* the duct which conveys bile from the liver and the gallbladder to the duodenum.

bi-level **●** *adjective* **1** having or functioning on two levels; arranged on two planes. **2** *N Amer.* designating a style of two-storey house in which the lower storey is partially sunk below ground level, and the main entrance is between the two storeys. **●** *noun N Amer.* a bi-level house.

bilge **●** *noun* **1 a** the lowest area inside a ship, where water collects. **b** the area on the outer surface of a ship's hull where the flat bottom meets the vertical side. **2** (in full **bilge water**) **a** a filthy water that collects inside the bilge. **b** *informal* nonsense. **●** *verb* **1** *transitive* stave in the bilge of (a ship). **2** *intransitive* spring a leak in the bilge. **3** *intransitive* swell out; bulge. [prob. var. of BULGE]

bilge keel *noun* either of two keel-like projections pointing downwards from the bilges of a ship and running parallel to the centre keel.

bil·har·zia /bɪlˈhɑrtsiə/ *noun* **1** a tropical flatworm of the genus *Schistosoma* (formerly *Bilharzia*) which is parasitic in blood vessels in the human pelvic region. *Also called* SCHISTOSOME. **2** (also **bil·har·zia·sis** /ˌbɪlhɑrˈtsaiəsɪs/) the chronic tropical disease produced by its presence. *Also called* SCHISTOSOMIASIS. [modern Latin from T. *Bilharz*, German physician d.1862]

bili·ary /ˈbɪliˌeri, ˈbɪljəri/ *adjective* of the bile. [French *biliaire*: see BILE, -ARY²]

bi·lin·gual /baiˈlɪŋɡwəl, baiˈlɪŋgjuːəl/ **●** *adjective* **1** able to speak two

Consonants: b *but*   d *dog*   f *few*   g *get*   h *her*   j *yes*   k *cat*   l *leg*   m *man*   n *no*   p *pen*   r *red*   s *sit*

languages, esp. fluently. **2** spoken or written in or involving two languages. ● *noun* a bilingual person. □ **bi·lin·gual·ly** *adverb* [Latin *bilinguis* (as BI-, *lingua* tongue)]

bi·lin·gual·ism /baiˈlɪŋgwəˌlɪzəm, baiˈlɪŋgjuːəˌlɪzəm/ *noun* **1** the ability to speak two languages, esp. (in Canada) English and French. **2** a policy promoting this among a population.

bi·lin·gual·ize /baiˈlɪŋgwəˌlaiz, -ˈlɪŋgjuːəl-/ *transitive verb* (also **-ise**) *Cdn* make bilingual (*bilingualizing the public service*).

bil·ious /ˈbɪljəs, ˈbɪliəs/ *adjective* **1** affected by a disorder of the bile. **2** bad-tempered. **3** of or like bile; nauseating (*bilious haze*). □ **bil·ious·ly** *adverb* **bil·ious·ness** *noun* [Latin *biliosus* from *bilis* bile]

bili·rubin /ˌbɪliˈruːbɪn/ *noun* the orange-yellow pigment occurring in bile. [German from Latin *bilis* BILE + *ruber* red]

bilk *transitive verb informal* **1** cheat. **2** avoid paying (a creditor or debt). □ **bilk·er** *noun* [origin uncertain, perhaps = BALK: earliest use (17th c.) in cribbage, = spoil one's opponent's score]

bill¹ ● *noun* **1 a** a printed or written statement of charges for goods supplied or services rendered. **b** the amount owed; the cost of something (*ran up a bill of $300; the taxpayers will pay the bill for this new program*). **2** = BILL OF EXCHANGE. **3** a draft of a proposed law. **4 a** a printed list, esp. a concert or theatre program. **b** the entertainment itself (*double bill*). **5** *N Amer.* a banknote (*ten-dollar bill*). **6** *Cdn* (*Nfld*) the share of a fishing or sealing season's profit paid as wages to each fisherman or sealer. **7 a** a poster; a placard. **b** = HANDBILL. ● *transitive verb* **1** (usu. in *passive*) (*the trip was billed as a fact-finding tour*). **2** invoice (*please bill me for the books*). □ **bill·able** *adjective* [Anglo-French *bille*, Anglo-Latin *billa*, prob. alteration of medieval Latin *bulla* seal, sealed documents, BULL²]

bill² ● *noun* **1** the beak of a bird, esp. when it is slender, flattened, or weak, or belongs to a web-footed bird or a bird of the pigeon family. **2** the muzzle of a platypus. **3** the long, pointed upper jaw of marlins, sailfish, etc. **4** *N Amer.* the visor on a baseball cap. **5** a narrow promontory. **6** the point of an anchor fluke. ● *intransitive verb* (of doves etc.) stroke a bill with a bill. □ **bill and coo** behave or talk in a very loving or sentimental way. □ **billed** *adjective* (usu. in *combination*). [Old English *bile*, of unknown origin]

bill³ *noun* **1** *hist.* a weapon like a halberd with a hook instead of a blade. **2** = BILLHOOK. [Old English *bil*, ultimately from Germanic]

bil·la·bong /ˈbɪləˌbɒŋ/ *noun Austral.* a branch of a river forming a backwater or a stagnant pool. [Wiradjuri *bilabang* (originally as the name of the Bell River, New South Wales)]

bill·board *noun* a large outdoor board for advertisements etc.

bil·let¹ ● *noun* **1 a** a place, esp. a private home, where a student, travelling athlete, soldier, etc. is provided with accommodation, usu. without charge. **b** a written order requiring a householder to lodge the bearer. **2** *informal* a situation; a job. ● *verb* (**bil·let·ed, bil·let·ing**) **1** *transitive* (usu. foll. by *on, in, at*) arrange temporary free lodging for. **2** *transitive* (of a householder) provide with board and lodging. **3** *intransitive* take lodging with a billet. □ **bil·let·ee** /-ˈtiː/ *noun* **bil·let·er** *noun* [Anglo-French *billette*, Anglo-Latin *billetta*, diminutive of *billa* BILL¹]

bil·let² *noun* **1** a thick piece of wood, esp. one cut for firewood. **2** a metal bar. [French *billette* small log, ultimately prob. of Celtic origin]

billet-doux /ˌbɪleiˈduː, ˌbɪli-/ *noun* (pl. **billets-doux** /-ˈduːz/) often *jocular* a love letter. [French, = 'sweet note']

bill·fish *noun* (pl. same or **-fish·es**) any of various large marine game fishes of the family Istiophoridae, with long spear-like upper jaws, comprising marlins and sailfishes.

bill·fold *noun N Amer.* a wallet for keeping paper money.

bill·hook *noun* a sickle-shaped tool with a sharp inner edge, used for pruning, lopping, etc.

bil·liards /ˈbɪljərdz/ *noun* **1 a** any of various games played on an oblong cloth-covered table, with a cue used to strike a number of balls. **b** a version of this using three balls, either with pockets around the edge of the table (**English billiards**) or without (**carom**, or **French billiards**). **2** (**bil·liard**) (in *combination*) used in billiards (*billiard ball; billiard table*). [originally pl., from French *billard* billiards, cue, diminutive of *bille* log: see BILLET²]

bill·ing *noun* **1** in senses of BILL¹ *verb*. **2** placement in a list of performers (*received top billing*).

Bil·lings·gate a London fish market dating from the 16th c., known for the invective traditionally ascribed to the porters who worked there.

bil·lion ● *noun* (pl. same or (in sense 3) **bil·lions**) (in *sing.* prec. by *a* or *one*) **1** a thousand million (1,000,000,000 or 10⁹). **2** *Brit.* a million million (1,000,000,000,000 or 10¹²). **3** (in *pl.*) *informal* a very large number (*billions of years*). ● *adjective* that amount to a billion. □ **bil·lionth** *adjective & noun* [French (as BI-, MILLION)]

bil·lion·aire *noun* a person possessing over a billion dollars, pounds, etc.

bill of exchange *noun* a written order to pay a sum of money on a given date to the drawer or to a named payee.

bill of fare *noun* **1** a menu. **2** an offering of entertainment.

bill of goods *noun N Amer.* a quantity of merchandise. □ **sell a person a bill of goods** persuade a person to accept something undesirable; swindle.

bill of health *noun* **1** *Naut.* a certificate relating to the incidence of infectious disease on a ship or in a port at the time of sailing. **2** (**clean bill of health**) **a** such a certificate stating that there is no disease. **b** a declaration that a person or thing examined has been found to be free of illness or in good condition.

bill of indictment *noun Law* a written accusation against a defendant, presented during arraignment.

bill of lading *noun* a list of goods delivered to a carrier by a shipper, including a shipping agreement.

Bill of Rights *noun Law* **1** = CANADIAN BILL OF RIGHTS. **2** a bill passed by the English Parliament in Oct. 1689 confirming the deposition of James II and the accession of William and Mary, guaranteeing the Protestant succession, and laying down principles of parliamentary supremacy. **3** the first ten amendments to the Constitution of the US, ratified in 1791, spelling out individual rights that are regarded as inalienable. The amendments guarantee the freedom of religion, assembly, speech, and the press, as well as the right to bear arms, and specify the rights of persons accused of crimes. **4** (also **bill of rights**) a statement of the rights of a group of people.

bill of sale *noun* **1** a printed record of a purchase; a receipt. **2** a certificate of transfer of personal property, esp. as a security against debt.

bil·lon /ˈbɪlən/ *noun* an alloy of gold or silver with a predominating admixture of a base metal. [French from *bille* BILLET²]

bil·low ● *noun* **1** a wave. **2** a soft rising flow, as of smoke or clouds. **3** any large soft mass. ● *intransitive verb* **1** (of the sea, smoke, etc.) rise in billows; surge. **2** (of sails, clothing, etc.) swell or undulate, as in the wind. □ **bil·lowy** *adjective* [Old Norse *bylgja* from Germanic]

bill·post·er *noun* a person who pastes up advertisements on billboards. □ **bill·post·ing** *noun*

billy¹ *noun* (pl. **-lies**) (in full **billy·can**) a tin or enamel cooking pot with a lid and wire handle, for use out of doors. [Scots dialect *billy-pot* cooking utensil]

billy² *noun* (pl. **-lies**) = BILLY GOAT.

billy club *noun N Amer.* a police officer's truncheon. [*Billy*, pet form of the name *William*]

billy goat *noun* a male goat. [*Billy*, pet form of the name *William*]

billy-oh *noun* □ **like billy-oh** *slang* very much, hard, strongly, etc. (*raining like billy-oh*). [19th c.: origin unknown]

Billy the Kid see BONNEY.

bi·lob·ate /baiˈloːbeit/ *adjective* (also **bi·lobed** /ˈbailoːbd, -ˈloːbd/) having or consisting of two lobes.

bil·tong *noun esp. S African* lean meat which is salted and dried in strips. [Afrikaans, from Dutch *bil* 'buttock' + *tong* 'tongue']

bimah /ˈbiːmə/ *noun* (also **bima**) a raised platform for readers in a synagogue.

bi·manu·al /baiˈmanjuəl/ *adjective* performed with two hands.

bim·bette *noun derogatory slang* = BIMBO 1. [after BIMBO]

bim·bo *noun* (pl. **-bos**) *slang usu. derogatory* **1** a woman, esp. a young, sexually attractive, unintelligent one. **2** a person. [Italian, = little child]

bi·metal·lic /ˌbaiməˈtalɪk/ *adjective* **1** (also **bi·metal**) made of two metals. **2** of or relating to bimetallism.

bimetallic strip *noun* a sensitive element in some thermostats made of two bands of different metals that expand at different rates when heated, causing the strip to bend.

bi·metal·lism /baiˈmetəlɪzəm/ *noun Currency* a system using gold and silver as legal tender to any amount at a fixed ratio to each other.

bi·mil·len·ary /ˌbaimiˈlenəri/ ● *adjective* of or relating to a two-thousandth anniversary. ● *noun* (pl. **-aries**) a bimillenary year or festival.

bim·ini /ˈbɪməni/ *noun* (on a yacht or other vessel of similar size) an awning attached to the bridge. [the *Bimini* Islands in the western Bahamas]

bi·modal /baɪˈmoːdəl/ *adjective* esp. *Statistics* having two modes. □ **bi·modal·ity** /ˌbaɪmoːˈdalətɪ/ *noun*

bi·molecu·lar /baɪməˈlekjʊlər/ *adjective* involving two molecules.

bi·month·ly ● *adjective* occurring every two months or twice a month. ● *adverb* every two months or twice a month. ● *noun* (*pl.* **-lies**) a periodical produced bimonthly. ¶ Often avoided, because of the ambiguity of meaning, in favour of *biweekly* or *twice-monthly*.

bin ● *noun* **1** a large receptacle for storage or display or for depositing rubbish, recyclables, etc. **2** a partitioned stand for storing bottles of wine. **3** *slang* = LOONY BIN. ● *transitive verb* (**binned**, **bin·ning**) *informal* **1** store or put in a bin. **2** *Brit.* throw away. [Old English *bin(n)*, *binne*]

bin- *prefix var. of* BI- before a vowel.

bi·nary /ˈbaɪnərɪ, -ˌnerɪ/ ● *adjective* **1 a** dual. **b** of or involving a pair or pairs. **2** of the arithmetical system using 2 as a base. ● *noun* (*pl.* **-ies**) **1** something having two parts. **2** a binary star. **3** a binary number. [Late Latin *binarius* from *bini* two together]

binary code *noun Computing* a coding system using the binary digits 0 and 1 to represent a letter, digit, or other character in a computer (*see* BCD).

binary compound *noun Chem.* a compound having two elements or radicals.

binary fission *noun* the division of a cell or organism into two parts.

binary number *noun* (also **binary digit**) one of two digits (usu. 0 or 1) in a binary system of notation.

binary system *noun* **1** (also **binary star**) a system of two stars orbiting each other. **2** a system in which information can be expressed by combinations of the digits 0 and 1 (corresponding to 'off' and 'on' in computing).

binary tree *noun* a data structure in which a record is branched to the left when greater and to the right when less than the previous record.

bi·nate /ˈbaɪneɪt/ *adjective Bot.* **1** growing in pairs. **2** composed of two equal parts. [modern Latin *binatus* from Latin *bini* two together]

bi·nation·al *adjective* involving two nations.

bin·aural /baɪˈnɔrəl/ *adjective* **1** of or used with both ears. **2** (of sound) recorded using two microphones and usu. transmitted separately to the two ears.

bind ● *verb* (*past* and *past participle* **bound**) (*see also* BOUNDEN). **1** *transitive* (often foll. by *to*, *on*, *together*) tie or fasten tightly, attach. **2** *transitive* restrain; put in bonds. **3** *transitive* **a** esp. *Cooking* cause (ingredients) to cohere using another ingredient. **b** hold by chemical bonding; combine with. **4** *transitive* fasten or hold together as a single mass. **5** *transitive* compel; impose an obligation or duty on. **6** *transitive* **a** edge (fabric etc.) with braid etc. **b** fix together and fasten (the pages of a book) in a cover. **7** *transitive* constipate. **8** *transitive* ratify (a bargain, agreement, etc.). **9** *transitive* (in *passive*) be required by an obligation or duty (*am bound to answer*). **10** *transitive* (often foll. by *up*) **a** put a bandage or other covering around. **b** fix together with something put around (*bound her hair*). **11** *transitive* indenture as an apprentice. **12** *intransitive* (of snow etc.) cohere, stick. **13** *intransitive* be prevented from moving freely. ● *noun* **1** a difficult situation; a position that prevents free action. **2** *informal* a nuisance; a restriction. **3** = BINE. □ **bind over** *Law* order (a person) to do something, esp. keep the peace. **bind up** bandage. [Old English *bindan*]

bind·er *noun* **1** a detachable cover for sheets of paper, magazines, etc. **2** a substance that acts cohesively. **3** esp. *hist.* a machine for binding grain into sheaves. **4** a bookbinder.

binder twine *noun* a coarse twine used esp. to tie bales of hay, straw, etc.

bind·ery *noun* (*pl.* **-ies**) a workshop or factory for binding books.

bindi /ˈbɪndiː/ *noun* a decorative mark worn in the middle of the forehead by South Asian women, esp. Hindus. [Hindi]

bind·ing ● *noun* **1** the strong covering of a book holding the sheets together. **2** the fastening attaching a boot to a ski. **3** a trim for binding raw edges of fabric. ● *adjective* **1** legally enforceable (*binding arbitration*). **2** that binds physically; causing or tending to cohere.

bind·weed *noun* **1** any of various twining plants of the morning glory family (Convolvulaceae), with funnel-shaped flowers, esp. of the genera *Convolvulus* and *Calystegia*. **2** any of various species of climbing plants such as honeysuckle.

bine *noun* **1** the twisting stem of a climbing plant, esp. the hop. **2** a flexible shoot. [originally a dial. form of BIND]

Binet /biːˈneɪ/ **Al·fred** (1857–1911), French psychologist. With the psychiatrist Théodore Simon (1873–1961) he produced tests (now known as **Binet** or **Binet-Simon tests**) intended to examine a child's general reasoning capacities rather than perceptual-motor skills; he also devised a mental age scale which described performance in relation to the average performance of students of the same physical age.

Bing, Sir Ru·dolph (1902–97), Austrian-born British impresario. He helped to found the Edinburgh Festival and from 1950 to 1972 was general manager of the Metropolitan Opera in New York.

bing *interjection* indicating a sudden action or event. [imitative]

Bing cherry *noun N Amer.* a variety of large, dark red cherry. [named for the Chinese nursery foreman who cultivated test rows of the variety in Oregon in the 1880s]

binge ● *noun* a period of uncontrolled indulgence in some activity, esp. eating or drinking. ● *intransitive verb* (**binge·ing** *past* and *past participle* **binged**) indulge in uncontrolled eating, drinking, shopping, etc. □ **bin·ger** *noun* [prob. originally dial., = soak]

binge-and-purge *noun* (*attributive*) designating an eating disorder characterized by alternate overeating and vomiting or the use of laxatives to purge the body of the food. □ **bingeing and purging** *noun*

bingo ● *noun* a game for any number of players, each having a card of squares with numbers, which are marked off as numbers are randomly drawn by a caller. ● *interjection* indicating a sudden action or event, or satisfaction, etc., as in winning at bingo. [prob. imitative: compare BING]

bin liner *noun Brit.* a garbage bag.

bin Laden /bɪnˈlɑdən/ **Osama** (b.1957), Saudi-born leader of the al-Qaeda terrorist network. He has been linked to bombings of US embassies in Kenya and Tanzania (1998), and is widely believed to be the mastermind behind the September 11 attacks in the US (2001).

bin·nacle /ˈbɪnəkəl/ *noun* a built-in housing for a ship's compass. [earlier *bittacle*, ultimately from Latin *habitaculum* habitation, from *habitare* inhabit]

bin·ocu·lar /bɪˈnɒkjʊlər, baɪ-/ ● *adjective* adapted for or using both eyes. ● *noun* /bɪˈnɒkjʊlər/ = BINOCULARS. [BIN- + Latin *oculus* eye]

bin·ocu·lars /bɪˈnɒkjʊlərz/ *plural noun* an optical instrument with lenses for each eye, for viewing distant objects.

binocular vision *noun* vision using two eyes with overlapping fields of view, allowing good perception of depth.

bi·nom·ial /baɪˈnoːmɪəl/ ● *noun* **1** an algebraic expression of the sum or the difference of two terms. **2** a two-part name, esp. in taxonomy. ● *adjective* consisting of two terms. □ **bi·nom·ial·ly** *adverb* [French *binôme* or modern Latin *binomium* (as BI-, Greek *nomos* part, portion)]

binomial distribution *noun* a frequency distribution of the possible number of successful outcomes in a given number of trials in each of which there is the same probability of success.

binomial nomenclature *noun* a system of naming plants and animals using two terms, the first one indicating the genus and the second the species.

binomial theorem *noun* a formula for finding any power of a binomial without multiplying at length.

bint *noun Brit. slang* usu. *offensive* a girl or woman. [Arabic, = daughter, girl]

bi·nucle·ate /baɪˈnjuːklɪət/ *adjective* having two nuclei.

bio *noun informal* **1** *N Amer.* a biography. **2** biology. [abbreviation]

bio- *combining form* **1** life (*biography*). **2** of living beings (*biochemistry*). **3** biology (*biomathematics*). [Greek *bios* (course of) human life]

bio·accumu·late *intransitive verb* (of poisons, chemicals, etc.) collect in animal tissue in progressively higher concentrations towards the top of the food chain.

bio·assay *noun* a measurement of the concentration or strength of a substance by means of its effect on a living organism.

bio·avail·abil·ity *noun* the rate at which a drug etc. is absorbed by the body or exerts an effect after absorption. □ **bio·avail·able** *adjective*

bio·cen·trism *noun* the belief or view that all life is important, and that no single species should occupy a privileged position. □ **bio·cen·tric** *adjective* **bio·cen·trist** *noun*

biochem. *abbreviation* biochemistry.

bio·chem·istry *noun* the study of the chemical and physicochemical processes of living organisms. □ **bio·chem·ical** *adjective* **bio·chem·ical·ly** *adverb* **bio·chem·ist** *noun*

Vowels: a *cat* ɑ *arm* e *bed* ɜr *her* ɜː *deux* ə *ago* ɪ *sit* i *cosy* iː *feed* ɒ *hot* ɔ *pore* oː *no* ʌ *run* ʊ *put*

bio·cide /ˈbaɪəˌsaɪd/ *noun* **1** a poisonous substance, esp. a pesticide, herbicide, etc. **2** the destruction of life. [BIO- + -CIDE]

bio·com·pat·ible *adjective* not harmful or toxic to living tissue. □ **bio·com·pat·ibil·ity** *noun*

bio·degrad·able *adjective* capable of being decomposed by bacteria or other living organisms. □ **bio·degrad·abil·ity** *noun*

bio·degrade *intransitive verb* decompose through the action of bacteria or other living organisms. □ **bio·deg·rad·a·tion** *noun*

bio·diesel *noun* a biofuel intended as a substitute for diesel.

bio·divers·ity *noun* variety of species.

bio·dynam·ic *adjective* **1** (of farming) using only organic fertilizers etc. **2** of or pertaining to dynamic effects brought about or experienced by living organisms. □ **bio·dynam·ics** *noun*

bio·ener·get·ics *noun* the study of the transformation of energy in living organisms.

bio·engineer·ing *noun* **1** the application of engineering techniques to biological processes. **2** the use of artificial tissues, organs, or organ components to replace damaged or absent parts of the body, e.g. artificial limbs, heart pacemakers, etc. **3** the industrial use of biological processes. □ **bio·engin·eer** *noun & verb*

bio·ethics *plural noun* (treated as *sing.*) the ethics of medical and biological research and practice. □ **bio·ethic·al** *adjective* **bio·ethi·cist** *noun*

bio·feed·back *noun* the use of electronic monitoring of a normally automatic bodily function, e.g. temperature, in order to train a person to acquire voluntary control of it.

bio·flavon·oid /ˌbaɪoˈfleɪvəˌnɔɪd/ *noun* any of a group of substances occurring mainly in citrus fruits and blackcurrants, and formerly thought to be a vitamin.

bio·fuel *noun* fuel derived immediately from living matter.

bio·gas *noun* gaseous fuel (usu. methane) produced by fermentation of organic matter.

bio·gen·esis /ˌbaɪoˈdʒenəsɪs/ *noun* **1** the synthesis of substances by living organisms. **2** the hypothesis that a living organism arises only from another similar living organism. □ **bio·gen·etic** /-dʒəˈnetɪk/ *adjective*

bio·genic /ˌbaɪoˈdʒenɪk/ *adjective* produced by living organisms.

bio·geog·raphy *noun* the scientific study of the geographical distribution of plants and animals. □ **bio·geo·graph·ic** *adjective* **bio·geo·graph·ic·al** *adjective*

biog·raphee *noun* a person who is the subject of a biography.

biog·raphy /baɪˈɒɡrəfi/ *noun* (*pl.* **-ies**) **1 a** a written account of a person's life, usu. by another. **b** such writing as a branch of literature. **2** the course of a living (usu. human) being's life. □ **biog·raph·er** *noun* **bio·graph·ic** *adjective* **bio·graph·ic·al** *adjective* [modern Latin *biographia* from medieval Greek]

bio·hazard *noun* a risk to human health or the environment arising from biological work, esp. with micro-organisms.

bio·inform·atics *noun* the science of collecting and analysing complex biological data such as genetic codes.

Bioko /biˈoːkoː/ an island of Equatorial Guinea, in the eastern part of the Gulf of Guinea. Its chief town is Malabo, the capital of Equatorial Guinea. It was known as Fernando Póo until 1973, and from 1973 to 1979 as Macias Nguema.

bio·logic·al ● *adjective* **1** (also **bio·logic**) of or relating to biology or living organisms. **2** (of a parent) involved in the procreation of the child in question, as opposed to its rearing (*biological father*). ● *noun* a biological product, esp. one used therapeutically or in biological control. □ **bio·logic·al·ly** *adverb*

biological clock *noun* **1** an innate mechanism controlling the rhythmic physiological activities of an organism, e.g. sleep. **2** an innate mechanism regulating the aging process, esp. in relation to the ability to bear children.

biological control *noun* the control of a pest by the introduction of a natural enemy.

biological warfare *noun* warfare involving the use of toxins or micro-organisms.

biological weapon *noun* a weapon which unleashes toxins or harmful micro-organisms.

biol·ogy *noun* **1** the study of living organisms. **2** the plants and animals of a particular area. □ **biol·o·gist** *noun* [as BIO-, -LOGY]

bio·lumin·es·cence /ˌbaɪoˌluːmɪˈnesəns/ *noun* the emission of light by living organisms such as the firefly and glow-worm. □ **bio·lumin·es·cent** *adjective*

bio·marker *noun* a naturally occurring molecule, gene, or characteristic by which a particular pathological or physiological process, disease, etc. can be identified.

bio·mass *noun* **1** the total quantity or weight of organisms in a given area or of a given species. **2** non-fossilized organic matter (esp. regarded as fuel).

bi·ome /ˈbaɪoːm/ *noun* **1** a large, naturally occurring community of flora and fauna adapted to the particular conditions in which they occur, e.g. tundra. **2** the geographical region containing such a community. [BIO- + -OME]

bio·mech·an·ics *noun* the study of the mechanical laws relating to the movement or structure of living organisms. □ **bio·mech·an·ical** *adjective* **bio·mech·an·ical·ly** *adverb*

bio·medi·cine *noun* the application of biology to clinical medicine. □ **bio·med·ical** *adjective*

bio·met·rics /ˌbaɪoˈmetrɪks/ *noun* (also **biom·etry** /baɪˈɒmətri/) **1** the application of statistical analysis to biological investigation. **2** technologies for personal identification that use measurements of a part of the human body or characteristics, e.g. fingerprints, irises, keystroke rhythms, voice patterns, etc. □ **bio·met·ric** *adjective* **bio·met·ric·al** *adjective* **bio·met·ri·cian** /ˌbaɪoməˈtrɪʃən/ *noun*

bio·mimet·ic *adjective* **1** designating synthetic techniques that mimic naturally occurring biological processes. **2** designating artificial structures, materials, or systems modelled on those found in nature.

bio·morph /ˈbaɪoːˌmɔrf/ *noun* a decorative form based on a living organism. □ **bio·morph·ic** /-ˈmɔrfɪk/ *adjective* [BIO- + Greek *morphē* form]

bi·on·ic /baɪˈɒnɪk/ *adjective* **1** having artificial body parts or the superhuman powers resulting from these. **2** relating to bionics. □ **bi·on·ic·ally** *adverb* [BIO- after ELECTRONIC]

bi·on·ics /baɪˈɒnɪks/ *plural noun* (treated as *sing.*) the study of mechanical systems that function like living organisms or parts of living organisms.

bio·phys·ics *plural noun* (treated as *sing.*) the science of the application of the laws of physics to biological phenomena. □ **bio·physic·al** *adjective* **bio·physi·cist** *noun*

bio·pic *noun informal* a biographical film. [*biographical* + PIC]

bio·prospect·ing *n.* the action or process of searching for plant and animal species that may yield commercially valuable biochemicals or genetic material.

bi·op·sy ● *noun* (*pl.* **-sies**) the removal and examination of tissue taken from a living body to discover the presence, cause, or extent of a disease. ● *transitive verb* (**-sies**, **-sied**) examine (tissue) for diagnostic purposes. [Greek *bios* life + *opsis* sight, after NECROPSY]

bio·react·or *noun* an apparatus or structure in which a biological reaction or process is carried out, esp. on a commercial scale.

bio·region *noun* an area or region that constitutes a natural ecological community. □ **bio·region·al** *adjective*

bio·remedi·a·tion *noun* encouragement of the natural microbial degradation of environmental pollutants, e.g. by the introduction of materials such as appropriate micro-organisms (in addition to those present naturally) and substances which promote the microbial metabolism of specific pollutants.

bio·rhythm *noun* any of the recurring cycles of biological processes thought to affect a person's emotional, intellectual, and physical activity. □ **bio·rhyth·mic** *adjective*

BIOS /ˈbaɪoːs/ *abbreviation Computing* firmware which controls many basic operations, such as keyboard control and booting. [basic input output system]

bio·sensor *noun* a device which uses a living organism or active biological molecules, esp. enzymes or antibodies, combined with an electrochemical transducer, to detect the presence of chemicals.

bio·solid *noun* (usu. in *pl.*) solidified sludge retrieved after sewage has been treated, used as fertilizer.

bio·sphere *noun* the regions of the earth's crust and atmosphere occupied by living organisms.

biosphere reserve *noun* an area of land designated by UNESCO, the biological and cultural diversity of which is protected through conservation and ecologically sustainable activity.

bio·statis·tics *plural noun* **1** the branch of statistics that deals with data relating to life. **2** vital statistics. □ **bio·statis·tical** *adjective* **bio·statis·ti·cian** *noun*

bio·synth·esis /ˌbaɪoˈsɪnθəsɪs/ *noun* the production of organic molecules by living organisms. □ **bio·syn·thet·ic** /-ˈθetɪk/ *adjective*

biota /baɪ'ɔːtə/ noun the animal and plant life of a region. [modern Latin: compare Greek biotē life]

bio·tech informal ● noun biotechnology. ● adjective biotechnological. [abbreviation]

bio·tech·nol·ogy noun (pl. **-gies**) the exploitation of biological processes for industrial and other purposes, esp. genetic manipulation of micro-organisms (for the production of antibiotics, hormones, etc.). □ **bio·tech·no·logic·al** adjective

bio·terror·ism noun the use of harmful biological or biochemical substances as weapons of terrorism. □ **bio·terror** noun **bio·terror·ist** noun

biot·ic /baɪ'ɒtɪk/ adjective **1** relating to life or to living things. **2** of biological origin. [Greek biōtikos from bios life]

bio·tin /'baɪətɪn/ noun a vitamin of the B complex, found esp. in egg yolk, liver, and yeast, and involved in the metabolism of carbohydrates, fats, and proteins. Also called VITAMIN H. [German from Greek bios life + -IN]

biot·ite /'baɪə,taɪt/ noun Geol. a black, dark brown, or green micaceous mineral occurring as a constituent of metamorphic and igneous rocks. [J. B. Biot, French physicist d.1862]

bio·type noun a group of organisms having an identical genetic constitution.

bio·warfare noun = BIOLOGICAL WARFARE.

bio·weapon noun = BIOLOGICAL WEAPON.

bi·par·tisan /baɪ'pɑːtɪzən/ adjective of or involving two (esp. political) parties. □ **bi·par·tisan·ship** noun

bi·part·ite /baɪ'pɑːtaɪt/ adjective **1** consisting of two parts. **2** shared by or involving two parties. **3** (of a contract, treaty, etc.) drawn up in two corresponding parts or between two parties. [Latin bipartitus from bipartire (as BI-, partire PART)]

bi·ped /'baɪped/ ● noun a two-footed animal. ● adjective two-footed. □ **bi·pedal** adjective **bi·pedal·ism** noun **bi·pedal·ity** /baɪpɪ'dalɪti/ noun [Latin bipes -edis (as BI-, pes pedis foot)]

bi·phenyl /baɪ'fenəl, -fiːnəl/ noun Chem. a crystalline hydrocarbon containing two benzene rings.

bi·pin·nate /baɪ'pɪneɪt/ adjective (of a pinnate leaf) having leaflets that are further subdivided in a pinnate arrangement.

bi·plane noun an early type of airplane having two sets of wings, one above the other (compare MONOPLANE).

bi·polar adjective **1** having two poles or extremities. **2** characterized by two extremes. **3** (of psychiatric illness) characterized by both manic and depressive episodes, or manic ones only (bipolar disorder). □ **bi·polar·ity** /-'lerɪti/ noun

bi·racial adjective concerning or containing members of two racial groups.

birch ● noun **1** any tree of the genus Betula, having thin peeling bark and slender branches, found predominantly in northern temperate regions. **2** (in full **birch·wood**) the hard fine-grained pale wood of these trees. **3** (in full **birch rod**) a bundle of birch twigs used for flogging. ● transitive verb beat with a birch (in sense 3). ● adjective made of or derived from birch. □ **birch·en** adjective [Old English bi(e)rce from Germanic]

birch·bark noun **1** the bark of Betula papyrifera, traditionally used by some Algonquian peoples to make canoes etc. **2** N Amer. such a canoe.

birchbark biting noun a modern Aboriginal handicraft, made by biting designs into birch bark.

birch broom noun Cdn (Nfld) a broom made from bundles of birch twigs or whittled from a single stick of birch.

Birch·er noun (in full **John Bircher**) (in the US) a member of the John Birch Society, an extreme right-wing and anti-Communist organization founded in 1958. [J. Birch, a USAF officer killed by Chinese Communists in 1945]

bird noun **1** a feathered, warm-blooded vertebrate of the class Aves, having a beak and wings, laying eggs, and usu. able to fly. **2** a game bird. **3** informal a person of a specified type (a tough old bird). **4** a shuttlecock. **5** Brit. slang a young woman. **6** slang a hissing or booing etc. as an expression of disapproval. **b** N Amer. a gesture of contempt made by raising the middle finger. **7** Brit. slang **a** a prison. **b** a prison sentence. □ **a bird in the hand** something secured or certain. **the bird is** (or **has**) **flown** the prisoner etc. has escaped. **the birds and the bees** euphemism sexual activity and reproduction. **birds of a feather** people of like character. **for the birds** informal useless, not worth consideration. **have a bird** N Amer. slang become agitated (Mom had a bird when I told her). **eat like a bird** eat very small amounts. **a little bird** informal an unnamed informant. □ **bird·like** adjective [Old

English brid, of unknown origin; sense 7 rhyming slang from birdlime = time]

bird bath noun a basin in a garden etc. with water for birds to bathe in.

bird·brain noun informal a silly or stupid person. □ **bird·brained** adjective

bird·cage noun **1** a cage for birds usu. made of wire or cane. **2** an object of a similar design.

bird call noun **1** a bird's natural call. **2** an imitation of this. **3** an instrument imitating this.

bird cherry noun = PIN CHERRY.

bird course noun Cdn derogatory slang a university or high school course requiring little work or intellectual ability.

bird dog ● noun **1** a hunting dog trained to retrieve birds. **2** N Amer. informal a scout for a talent agency or sports team. **3** Cdn a small aircraft that acts as a spotter and guide for water bombers. ● transitive verb (**bird-dog**) search and pursue with dogged determination.

bird·er noun a birdwatcher.

bird feeder noun a raised platform or other receptacle for holding birdseed, erected outdoors to attract wild birds.

bird flu noun avian influenza, esp. disease caused in humans by an avian influenza virus or a closely related virus.

bird·house noun a box, usu. of wood, designed to attract nesting birds.

bird·ie ● noun **1** informal a small bird. **2** Golf a score of one stroke under par at any hole. **3** a shuttlecock. ● transitive verb (**bird·ies**, **bird·ied**, **birdie·ing**) Golf play (a hole) in one stroke under par.

bird·ing noun observing birds in their natural surroundings; birdwatching.

bird·life noun the birds of a region or country collectively.

bird·lime noun sticky material painted on to twigs to trap small birds.

bird of paradise noun **1** any bird of the family Paradiseidae found chiefly in New Guinea, the males having brilliantly coloured plumage. **2** a southern African plant with orange and blue flowers, Strelitzia reginae, cultivated for flower arrangements.

bird of passage noun **1** a migratory bird. **2** any transient visitor.

bird of prey noun a bird which hunts animals for food.

bird·seed noun a blend of seed used in bird feeders or for feeding caged birds.

Bird·sell /'bɜːdzəl/ **San·dra** (b.1942), Canadian author. Her story collections and novels, including The Missing Child (1989) and The Chrome Suite (1992), are often set in her home province of Manitoba.

bird's-eye noun **1** any of several plants having small bright round flowers, esp.: **a** (in full **bird's-eye primrose**) a Eurasian primrose, Primula farinosa. **b** = GERMANDER SPEEDWELL. **2** (often attributive) a pattern with many small spots.

bird's-eye maple noun the wood of the sugar maple used in panelling, cabinetmaking, etc., having a wavy grain with a characteristic pattern of round dark eye-like markings.

bird's-eye view noun **1** a view (of a landscape etc.) from overhead. **2** a general overview (of a subject etc.).

bird's-foot noun (pl. **bird's-foots**) any plant resembling the foot of a bird, esp. of the genera Lotus, Trifolium, and Ornithopus.

bird's-foot trefoil noun a leguminous plant of the genus Lotus, esp. L. corniculatus, having yellow flowers and claw-shaped pods.

bird's-foot violet noun a N American violet, Viola pedata, having purple flowers and cleft leaves.

bird·shot noun a small variety of shotgun pellets used for hunting birds.

bird's nest fern noun a fern, Asplenium nidus, with undivided fronds, often cultivated as a houseplant.

bird's nest soup noun a Chinese soup made from the dried gelatinous coating of the nests of swifts and other birds.

bird·song noun the musical call or sound of a bird or birds.

bird strike noun a collision between a bird and an aircraft.

bird table noun Brit. = BIRD FEEDER.

bird·watch·er noun a person who observes birds in their natural surroundings. □ **bird·watch·ing** noun

bi·refrin·gent /,baɪrə'frɪndʒənt/ adjective Physics having two different refractive indices. □ **bi·refrin·gence** noun

bi·reme /'baɪriːm/ noun hist. an ancient warship with two tiers of oars on each side. [Latin biremis (as BI-, remus oar)]

bir·etta /bɪ'retə/ noun a square usu. black cap with three flat projections on top, worn (esp. formerly) by (esp. Roman Catholic) clergymen. [Italian *berretta* or Spanish *birreta* from Late Latin *birrus* cape]

bir·i·ani *var. of* BIRYANI.

Bir·ken·stock /'bɜrkənstɒk/ *noun proprietary* a kind of flat-soled sandal with a contoured cork insole and broad leather straps, frequently perceived as typically worn by hippies, students, and people concerned with the environment.

Birks, Henry (1840–1928), Canadian silversmith. In 1879 he opened his own jewellery and silver store, which remained in the Birks family until the 1990s.

birl *transitive verb N Amer.* cause (a floating log) to rotate by using one's feet; spin. □ **birl·ing** *noun* [perhaps related to Scots *birr* a whirring sound + WHIRL]

Bir·ming·ham 1 /'bɜrmɪŋəm/ an industrial city in west central England; pop. (est. 2001) 977,100. **2** /'bɜrmɪŋham/ an industrial city in north central Alabama; pop. (2000) 242,820.

Bir·ney, Earle (1904–95), Canadian poet. He won the Governor General's Award for his first collection, *David* (1942) and a second in 1945. His later volumes are marked by technical virtuosity, playfulness, and experimentation.

Biro /'baɪroː/ *noun Brit. proprietary* (*pl.* **Biros**) a ballpoint pen. [L. Biró, Hungarian inventor d.1985]

birr /bɜr/ *noun* (*pl.* same or **birrs**) the chief monetary unit of Ethiopia, divided into 100 cents. [Amharic]

birth ● *noun* **1** the emergence of a (usu. fully developed) infant or other young from the body of its mother. **2** the beginning or coming into existence of something (*the birth of civilization; the birth of socialism*). **3 a** origin, descent, ancestry (*of noble birth*). **b** high or noble birth; inherited position. **4** (*attributive*) designating the parent who gave birth to or fathered a child (*birth mother*). ● *verb N Amer.* **1** *transitive* give birth to. **2** *intransitive* give birth. □ **give birth** bear a child etc. **give birth to 1** produce (young) from the womb. **2** cause to begin, found. [Old Norse *byrth* from Germanic: see BEAR¹, -TH²]

birth canal *noun* the canal comprising the cervix, vagina, and vulva, through which the fetus passes during delivery.

birth certificate *noun* an official document identifying a person by name and place and date of birth.

birth control *noun* the practice or methods of preventing pregnancy, esp. by contraception.

birth control pill *noun* an oral contraceptive containing progesterone and often estrogen, used to prevent ovulation.

birth·date *noun* one's date of birth.

birth·day *noun* **1** the anniversary of a person's birth. **2** the day on which a person etc. was born. **3** the anniversary of the day on which something came into being (*July 1 is Canada's birthday*).

birthday honours *plural noun Brit.* titles etc. given on a sovereign's official birthday.

birthday suit *noun jocular* the bare skin; nakedness.

birth·ing *noun* the act or process of giving birth (also *attributive*: *birthing centre*).

birth·mark *noun* an unusual brown or red mark on one's body at or from birth.

birth·place *noun* **1** the place where a person was born. **2** a place of origin or commencement (*the birthplace of Confederation*).

birth rate *noun* the number of live births per thousand of population per year.

birth·right *noun* a right of possession or privilege belonging to one from birth.

birth·stone *noun* a gemstone popularly associated with the month of one's birth.

birth weight *noun* the weight of a baby at birth.

birth·wort *noun* any of several climbing vines of the genus *Aristolochia*, reputed to have medicinal properties.

Birt·wistle /'bɜrt,wɪsəl/ **Sir Har·ri·son (Paul)** (b.1934), English composer and clarinetist. His early work was influenced by Stravinsky, while later compositions are more experimental; they include the opera *Punch and Judy* (1966–7).

biry·ani /,bɪri'ani/ *noun* (also **biri·ani**) an originally Indian dish made with highly seasoned rice, and meat or fish etc. [Urdu]

Bis·cay, Bay of /'bɪskei/ a part of the N Atlantic between the north coast of Spain and the west coast of France, noted for its strong currents and storms.

bis·cotti /bɪ'skɒti/ *plural noun N Amer.* hard, dry, Italian cookies, usu. containing ground nuts. [Italian, = biscuits]

bis·cuit ● *noun* **1** a dry, hard, flat, baked foodstuff (*ship's biscuit; dog biscuit*). **2** *N Amer.* = TEA BISCUIT. **3** *Brit.* a cookie. **4** fired unglazed pottery. **5** a light brown colour. ● *adjective* biscuit-coloured. □ **have had the biscuit** *Cdn slang* be no longer good for anything; be done for. □ **bis·cuity** *adjective* [Old French *bescoit* etc., ultimately from Latin *bis* twice + *coctus* past participle of *coquere* cook]

bi·sect *transitive verb* **1** divide into two (strictly, equal) parts. **2** cut across. □ **bi·sec·tion** *noun* **bi·sect·or** *noun* [BI- + Latin *secare sect-* cut]

bi·sex·ual ● *adjective* **1** sexually attracted to persons of both sexes. **2** *Biol.* having characteristics of both sexes. **3** of or concerning both sexes. ● *noun* a bisexual person. □ **bi·sex·u·al·ity** /-'aliti/ *noun*

bish *noun slang* a bishop. [abbreviation]

Bish·kek /bɪʃ'kek/ the capital of Kyrgyzstan; pop. (est. 2002) 808,900. From 1926 to 1991 the city was named Frunze. Before 1926 it was known as Pishpek.

Bish·op ▶ 1 Eliza·beth (1911–79), US poet. Bishop's first two collections, *North and South* (1946) and *A Cold Spring* (1955), received the Pulitzer Prize when published as a combined edition in 1955. Her poetry contrasts her experiences in South America (1952–67) with her New England origins. Other notable works include *Geography III* (1976). **2 Wil·liam Avery ('Billy')** (1894–1956), Canadian fighter pilot. A legendary ace during the First World War, Bishop was credited with destroying 72 German aircraft and became the first Canadian pilot to win the Victoria Cross.

bish·op *noun* **1** a member of the highest rank of clerical hierarchy in some Christian denominations, usu. in charge of a diocese, and empowered to confer holy orders. **2** a chess piece which is moved diagonally and has the upper part shaped like a mitre. **3** mulled and spiced wine, esp. port. [Old English *biscop*, ultimately from Greek *episkopos* overseer (as EPI-, *-skopos* -looking)]

bish·op·ric *noun* **1** the office of a bishop. **2** a diocese. [Old English *bisceoprīce* (as BISHOP, *rīce* realm)]

Bis·la·ma /,bɪʃlə'mɒ/ *noun* an English-based pidgin used as a lingua franca in Fiji and as an official language in Vanuatu. [alteration of BEACH-LA-MAR]

Bis·marck¹ the state capital of N Dakota; pop. (2000) 55,532. [BISMARCK², so named to attract German capital for railroad building]

Bis·marck² ▶ Otto Ed·uard Leo·pold, Prince von (1815–98), German political leader. The driving force behind German unification, he orchestrated wars with Denmark (1864), Austria (1866), and France (1870–71), forged important alliances within Europe, and became the first chancellor of the German Empire (1870–91).

bis·marck *noun N Amer.* **1** *Alta., Sask., & US Midwest* a sugar-coated jam-filled doughnut. **2** *Man.* a cream-filled doughnut, often with a chocolate glaze. [origin unknown, possibly after BISMARCK²]

Bismarck Sea an arm of the Pacific Ocean northeast of New Guinea and north of New Britain. In March 1943 the US destroyed a large Japanese naval force in these waters.

bis·muth /'bɪzməθ/ *noun Chem.* **1** a brittle reddish-white metallic element, occurring naturally and used in alloys. Symbol: **Bi**; at. no.: 83. **2** any compound of this element used medicinally. [modern Latin *bisemutum*, Latinization of German *Wismut*, of unknown origin]

bison /'baizən, 'bəisən/ *noun* (*pl.* same) either of two heavily built bovines of the genus *Bison*, *B. bison*, native to the N American plains (*also called* BUFFALO), or *B. bonasus*, native to Europe (*also called* WISENT), both having a high shoulder hump, shaggy hair, and a large head with short horns. *See also* PLAINS BISON, WOOD BISON. [Middle English from Latin from Germanic]

bisque¹ /bɪsk/ *noun* **1** a rich soup usu. made from shellfish but also from game or vegetables. **2** a dark beige colour. [French]

bisque² /bɪsk/ *noun Tennis, Croquet, & Golf* an advantage of scoring one free point, or taking an extra turn or stroke. [French]

bisque³ /bɪsk/ *noun* **1** a variety of unglazed white porcelain used for statuettes etc. **2** = BISCUIT 4. [from BISCUIT]

Bis·sagos Islands /bɪ'sɒgəs/ a group of islands off the coast of Guinea-Bissau, West Africa.

Bis·sau /bɪ'sau/ the capital of Guinea-Bissau; pop. (est. 2002) 288,300.

Bis·soon·dath /bɪ'sundaθ/ **Neil** (b.1955), Canadian author born in Trinidad of E Indian descent. His short-story collections and novels include *Digging up the Mountains* (1985), *A Casual Brutality* (1988), and *On the Eve of Uncertain Tomorrows* (1990).

bi·stable /bai'steibəl/ *adjective* (of an electrical circuit etc.) having two stable states.

bis·ter var. of BISTRE.

bis·tort /ˈbɪstɔrt/ noun any of various polygonums with twisted roots, esp. *Polygonum bistorta* of Europe, with a cylindrical spike of pink flowers, or *P. bistortoides* of N America. [medieval Latin *bistorta* from *bis* twice + *torta* fem. past participle of *torquēre* twist]

bistre /ˈbɪstər/ (also **bis·ter**) ● noun 1 a brownish pigment made from the soot of burnt wood. 2 the brownish colour of this. ● adjective of this colour. [French, of unknown origin]

bis·tro /ˈbiːstrəʊ, ˈbɪstrəʊ/ noun (pl. **-tros**) a small restaurant or bar. [French, perhaps related to *bistouille*, a northern colloquial term meaning 'bad alcohol', perhaps from Russian *bystro* 'rapidly']

bi·sul·phate /baɪˈsʌlfeɪt/ noun (also **bi·sul·fate**) Chem. a salt or ester of sulphuric acid.

bit¹ noun 1 a small piece or quantity (*a bit of cheese; give me another bit; that bit is too small*). 2 (prec. by a) **a** a fair amount (*sold quite a bit; needed a bit of persuading*). **b** informal somewhat (*am a bit tired*). **c** (foll. by *of*) informal rather (*a bit of an idiot*). 3 a short time or distance (*wait a bit; move up a bit*). 4 a part, esp. of a film or play (*I liked the bit where they fell in love*). 5 N Amer. informal a unit of 12 $1/2$ cents (used only in even multiples). 6 (*attributive*) relating to a minor speaking role in a play or film (*bit part; bit player*). 7 informal a characteristic way of behaving (*the dog did its protective bit*). □ **bit by bit** gradually. **bit of all right** Brit. slang a pleasing person or thing, esp. a woman. **bit of fluff** (or **skirt** or **stuff**) a woman regarded as an object of sexual desire. **bit on the side** slang 1 a sexual relationship involving infidelity to one's partner. 2 the person with whom one is unfaithful. **bits and pieces** (or **bobs**) an assortment of small items. **do one's bit** informal make a useful contribution to an effort or cause. **every bit as** see EVERY. **not a bit** (or **not a bit of it**) not at all. **to bits** into pieces. [Old English *bita* from Germanic, related to BITE]

bit² past of BITE.

bit³ ● noun 1 a metal mouthpiece on a bridle, used to control a horse. 2 a (usu. metal) tool or piece for boring or drilling. 3 **a** the cutting or gripping part of a plane, pincers, etc. **b** the cutting blade or edge of an edged tool, axe, etc. 4 the part of a key that engages with the lock lever. 5 the copper head of a soldering iron. ● transitive verb (**bit·ted**, **bit·ting**) 1 put a bit into the mouth of (a horse). 2 restrain. □ **chomp** (or **champ** or **chafe**) **at the bit** be restlessly impatient. **take the bit between** (or **in**) **one's teeth 1** take decisive personal action. 2 escape from control. [Old English *bite* from Germanic, related to BITE]

bit⁴ noun Computing a unit of information expressed as a choice between two possibilities; a 0 or 1 in binary notation. [blend of BINARY + DIGIT]

bitch ● noun 1 a female dog or other canine animal. 2 offensive slang a malicious, spiteful, or unpleasant woman. 3 coarse slang a very unpleasant or difficult thing or situation. ● intransitive verb 1 (often foll. by *about*) speak scathingly. 2 complain. □ **bitch·ery** noun [Old English *bicce*]

bitch·in' adjective N Amer. slang excellent.

bitch-slap transitive verb N Amer. slang deliver a stinging blow to (someone), typically in order to humiliate them. [orig. Black English, with reference to a woman hitting or haranguing her male partner]

bitchy adjective (**bitch·i·er**, **bitch·i·est**) slang spiteful; bad-tempered. □ **bitch·i·ly** adverb **bitch·i·ness** noun

bite ● verb (past **bit**; past participle **bit·ten**) 1 transitive cut or puncture using the teeth. 2 transitive (foll. by *off*, *away*, etc.) detach with the teeth. 3 transitive (of an insect, snake, etc.) wound with a sting, fangs, etc. 4 intransitive **a** (of a wheel, screw, etc.) grip, penetrate. **b** Curling (of a rock) come to a stop. 5 intransitive **a** (of fish) accept bait. **b** (of a person) accept inducement or be taken in by a deception. 6 intransitive have a (desired) adverse effect. 7 transitive (in passive) a take in; swindle. **b** (foll. by *by*, *with*, etc.) be infected by (enthusiasm etc.). 8 intransitive (foll. by *at*) snap at. 9 intransitive N Amer. slang be extremely bad or unpleasant (*this movie bites*). ● noun 1 an act of biting. 2 a wound or sore made by biting. 3 **a** a mouthful of food. **b** a snack or light meal. 4 the taking of bait by a fish. 5 pungency (esp. of flavour). 6 incisiveness, sharpness. 7 a pithy quotation or excerpt (*sound bite*). 8 a portion exacted (*the tax bite rose to 20 per cent.*). 9 = OCCLUSION 3. □ **bite back** restrain (one's speech etc.) by or as if by biting the lips. **bite the big one** N Amer. slang 1 die. 2 be very bad or unpleasant. **bite the bullet** informal behave bravely or stoically. **bite the dust** slang 1 die. 2 fail; break down. **bite the hand that feeds one** hurt or offend a benefactor. **bite a person's head off** informal respond fiercely or angrily. **bite one's lip** see LIP. **bite one's tongue** refrain from speaking, esp. reluctantly. **bite off more than one can chew** take on a commitment one cannot fulfill. **once bitten twice shy** an unpleasant experience induces caution. **put the bite on** N Amer. & Austral. slang borrow or extort money from. **take a bite out of** informal reduce by a significant amount. **what's biting you?** slang what is annoying you? □ **biter** noun [Old English *bītan* from Germanic]

bite-sized adjective (also **bite-size**) 1 small enough to be eaten in one mouthful. 2 very small or short.

Bi·thynia /bɪˈθɪniə/ the ancient name for the region of NW Asia Minor west of Paphlagonia, bordering the Black Sea and the Sea of Marmara.

bit·ing adjective 1 that bites (*biting insects*). 2 stinging; intensely cold (*a biting wind*). 3 sharp; effective (*biting wit; biting sarcasm*). □ **bit·ing·ly** adverb

bit·map noun Computing 1 a representation, e.g. of a computer memory, in which each item is represented by one bit. 2 a graphic display in which characters are formed by assigning a bit value to each individual pixel. □ **bit·mapped** adjective

bit·stream noun a stream of data in binary form.

bit·ten past participle of BITE.

bit·ter ● adjective 1 having a sharp pungent taste; not sweet. 2 **a** caused by or showing mental pain or resentment (*bitter memories; bitter response*). **b** painful or difficult to accept (*bitter disappointment*). 3 **a** harsh; virulent (*bitter animosity*). **b** piercingly cold. ● noun 1 (in pl.) liquor with a bitter flavour (esp. of wormwood) used as an additive in cocktails. 2 Brit. beer strongly flavoured with hops and having a bitter taste. □ **to the bitter end** to the very end in spite of difficulties. □ **bit·ter·ly** adverb **bit·ter·ness** noun [Old English *biter* prob. from Germanic]

bitter apple noun = COLOCYNTH.

bitter·brush noun a shrub of western N America of the genus *Purshia*, esp. *P. tridentata*, grown as an ornamental.

bitter cassava noun see CASSAVA.

bitter cherry noun 1 a cherry tree, *Prunus emarginata*, of the Pacific coast of N America. 2 the extremely bitter fruit of this tree.

bitter cress noun any herbaceous plant of the genus *Cardamine* of the mustard family, bearing slender seed pods.

bit·tern /ˈbɪtərn/ noun 1 any of several marsh birds of the heron family, esp. of the genus *Botaurus*, with a distinctive booming call. 2 Chem. the liquid remaining after the crystallization of common salt from sea water. [Old French *butor*, ultimately from Latin *butio* bittern + *taurus* bull; *-n* perhaps from assoc. with HERON]

bitter·nut noun a hickory, *Carya cordiformis*, of eastern N America, bearing a bitter nut covered with a thin, ridged husk.

bitter orange noun = SEVILLE ORANGE.

bitter pill noun something unpleasant that must be accepted or endured.

bitter·root noun any of various plants with bitter roots, esp. of the western N American genus *Lewisia*, of the purslane family, with edible roots and pink or white flowers.

bitter·sweet ● adjective 1 sweet with a bitter aftertaste. 2 arousing pleasure tinged with pain or sorrow. ● noun 1 **a** a sweetness with a bitter aftertaste. **b** pleasure tinged with pain or sorrow. 2 any of several N American climbing vines of the genus *Celastrus*, esp. *C. scandens*. 3 = WOODY NIGHTSHADE (see NIGHTSHADE 1).

bitts plural noun Naut. a pair of posts on the deck of a ship, for fastening cables etc. [prob. from Low German: compare Low German & Dutch *beting*]

bitty adjective (**bit·ti·er**, **bit·ti·est**) 1 N Amer. informal (usu. in **little bitty** or **itty-bitty**) very small. 2 esp. Brit. made up of unrelated bits.

bitu·men /ˈbɪtjuːmən, -ˈtuːmən/ noun 1 any of various tar-like mixtures of hydrocarbons derived from petroleum naturally or by distillation and used for road surfacing and roofing. 2 Austral. informal a tarred road. [Latin *bitumen -minis*]

bi·tu·min·ous /bɪˈtjuːmɪnəs, -ˈtuːmɪnəs/ adjective of, relating to, or containing bitumen.

bituminous coal noun a volatile form of coal burning with a smoky flame.

bi·valent /baɪˈveɪlənt/ ● adjective 1 Chem. having a valence of two. 2 Biol. (of homologous chromosomes) associated in pairs. ● noun Biol. any pair of homologous chromosomes. □ **bi·valence** noun [BI- + *valent-* pres. part. stem formed as VALENCE]

bi·valve /ˈbaɪvalv/ noun any of a group of aquatic molluscs of the class Bivalvia, with laterally compressed bodies enclosed within two hinged shells, e.g. oysters, mussels, etc. ● adjective 1 with a hinged double shell. 2 Biol. (of a seed capsule) having two valves.

biv·ou·ac /ˈbɪvʊˌwak/ ● noun a temporary open encampment e.g. of soldiers or mountaineers. ● *intransitive verb* (**biv·ou·acked**, **biv·ou·acking**) camp in a bivouac, esp. overnight. [French, prob. from Swiss German *Beiwacht* additional guard at night]

bi·week·ly ● *adverb* **1** every two weeks. **2** twice a week. ● *adjective* produced or occurring biweekly. ● *noun* (*pl.* **-lies**) a biweekly periodical. ¶ See the note at *bimonthly*.

bi·year·ly ● *adverb* **1** every two years. **2** twice a year. ● *adjective* produced or occurring biyearly. ¶ See the note at *bimonthly*.

biz *noun informal* business. [abbreviation]

Bi·zard, Île /ˈbɪˈzɑr/ an island in Lac des Deux Montagnes in south central Quebec, just off the western corner of Île de Montréal. [J. Bizard, French governor d.1692]

bi·zarre *adjective* strange in appearance or effect; eccentric; grotesque. □ **bi·zarre·ly** *adverb* **bi·zarre·ness** *noun* [French, originally = handsome, brave, from Spanish & Portuguese *bizarro* from Basque *bizarra* beard]

bi·zar·rerie /bɪˈzɑrəri/ *noun* a bizarre quality; bizarreness. [French]

bi·zar·ro *adjective N Amer. slang* bizarre. [alteration of BIZARRE]

Bizet /ˈbiːzei/ **Alex·andre Cé·sar Léo·pold** (known as **Georges**) (1838–75), French composer. His first major work was his Symphony in C major (1855); his opera *Carmen* (1875) is one of the most popular works in the repertory.

B.J. *abbreviation* Bachelor of Journalism.

Bjerk·nes /ˈbjɜrknəs/ **Vil·helm F(ri·mann) K(oren)** (1862–1951), Norwegian geophysicist and meteorologist. He developed mathematical models for weather prediction, formulated a theory which accounted for the generation of cyclones, and introduced the term *front* to meteorology.

Bjørn·son /ˈbjɜrnsən/ **Bjørn·stjerne Mar·tin·ius** (1832–1910), Norwegian poet, dramatist, and novelist, who is known for works such as the epic poem *Arnljot Gelline* (1870) and the drama *The Bankrupt* (1875); he was awarded the Nobel Prize for literature in 1903.

BJP *abbreviation* BHARATIYA JANATA PARTY.

Bk *symbol Chem.* the element berkelium.

bk. *abbreviation* book.

BL *abbreviation* **1** Bachelor of Law. **2** British Library. **3** BILL OF LADING.

bl. *abbreviation* **1** barrel. **2** black.

B.L.A. *abbreviation* Bachelor of Landscape Architecture.

blab ● *verb* (**blabbed**, **blab·bing**) **1** *intransitive* **a** talk foolishly or indiscreetly. **b** reveal secrets. **2** *transitive* reveal (a secret etc.) by indiscreet talk. ● *noun archaic* a person who blabs. □ **blab·by** *adjective* [Middle English prob. from Germanic]

blab·ber ● *noun* (also **blabber·mouth**) a person who blabs. ● *intransitive verb* (often foll. by *on*) talk foolishly or inconsequentially, esp. at length.

Black ▸ **1 Con·rad Mof·fat, Lord Black of Cross Harbour** (b.1944), Canadian financier and newspaper magnate, who, at various times, has owned or controlled many major newspapers in Canada and abroad. **2 David·son** (1884–1934), Canadian anthropologist who conducted pioneering studies in the origins of early humans in China, and in 1926 identified a distinct species which he called *Sinanthropus pekinensis* (see PEKING MAN). **3 Jo·seph** (1728–99), Scottish chemist. He formulated the concepts of latent heat and heat capacity, and isolated a distinct gas which he termed 'fixed air,' now known to be carbon dioxide. **4 Shir·ley Tem·ple** see S. TEMPLE.

black ● *adjective* **1** very dark, having no colour from the absorption of all or nearly all incident light. **2** completely dark from the absence of a source of light (*black night*). **3** (also **Black**) **a** belonging or relating to any of various peoples having dark-coloured skin, esp. of African or Australian origin. **b** of or relating to black peoples or their culture (*black studies*). **4** (of the sky, a cloud, etc.) dusky; heavily overcast. **5** angry, threatening (*a black look*). **6** implying disgrace or condemnation (*in his black books*). **7** wicked, sinister, deadly (*black-hearted*). **8** gloomy, depressed, sullen (*a black mood*). **9** portending trouble or difficulty (*things looked black*). **10** (of hands, clothes, etc.) dirty, soiled. **11** (of humour or its representation) with sinister or macabre, as well as comic, import (*a black comedy*). **12** (of coffee or tea) without milk. **13** dark in colour as distinguished from a lighter variety (*black bear; black pine*). **14** *Cards* belonging to spades or clubs. **15** *Brit.* **a** (of industrial labour or its products) boycotted, esp. by a trade union, in an industrial dispute. **b** (of a person) doing work or handling goods that have been boycotted. ● *noun* **1** a black colour or pigment. **2** black clothes or material (*dressed in black*). **3 a** (in a game or sport) a black piece, ball, etc. **b** the player using such pieces. **4** the absence of light on a stage or film set (*fade to black*). **5** the credit side of an account (*in*

the black). **6** (also **Black**) a black person. ● *transitive verb* **1** make black (*blacked his face*). **2** polish with blacking. **3** *Brit.* declare (goods etc.) 'black'. □ **black out 1 a** effect a blackout on. **b** undergo a blackout. **2** obscure windows etc. or extinguish all lights for protection esp. against an air attack. □ **black·ish** *adjective* **black·ly** *adverb* **black·ness** *noun* [Old English *blæc*]

black Africa *noun* Africa south of the Sahara, inhabited predominantly by blacks (as opposed to Arabs) or governed by blacks (as opposed to whites).

black·amoor /ˈblakəˌmʊr, -ˌmɔr/ *noun archaic* a black person. [BLACK + MOOR]

black and blue *adjective* discoloured by bruises.

Black and Tans an armed auxiliary force recruited by the British government to fight Sinn Fein in Ireland 1920–1, whose harsh methods caused an international outcry. [from the colours of the mixed military (khaki) and constabulary (black) uniforms they wore]

black and white ● *noun* writing or printing (*in black and white*). ● *adjective* **1** (of film etc.) not in colour. **2** consisting of extremes only, oversimplified (*interpreted the problem in black and white terms*).

black Angus *noun* = ABERDEEN ANGUS.

black art *noun* = BLACK MAGIC.

black ash *noun* an ash of eastern N America, *Fraxinus nigra*, growing in swampy woodland. *Also called* SWAMP ASH.

black·ball *transitive verb* **1** reject (a candidate) in a vote (originally by voting with a black ball). **2** ostracize or exclude.

black bass *noun* any freshwater fish of the genus *Micropterus*, native to N America and introduced elsewhere (*compare* LARGEMOUTH, SMALLMOUTH).

black bean *noun* **1** any of several leguminous plants of the genus *Phaseolus*. **2** the edible black seed of this plant. **3** a fermented soybean, used as flavouring in oriental cooking.

black bear *noun* either of two bears with black or blue-black fur, the American black bear *Ursus americanus* of N American forests, or the Asian black bear *Selenarctos thibetanus*, a small, mainly herbivorous bear of SE Asia.

Black·beard see E. TEACH.

black belt *noun* **1** a black belt worn by an expert in one of the martial arts. **2** a person qualified to wear this.

black·berry ● *noun* (*pl.* **-berries**) **1** any thorny shrub of the genus *Rubus*, esp. *R. fruticosus* and *R. allegheniensis*, bearing white or pink flowers. *Also called* BRAMBLE. **2** a black fleshy edible fruit of this plant. **3** *Cdn* (*Nfld*) = CROWBERRY. ● *intransitive verb* (**-ries**, **-ried**) gather blackberries.

black birch *noun* any of several species of birch, e.g. water birch.

black·bird *noun* **1** *N Amer.* any of various birds of the subfamily Icterinae with mainly black plumage, esp. the red-winged blackbird and the grackle. **2** a common European thrush, *Turdus merula*, of which the male is black with an orange beak, and the female brown. **3** *hist.* a kidnapped black or Polynesian slave.

black blizzard *noun N Amer.* a dust storm of soil blown by high winds on the prairies.

black·board *noun* a board with a smooth dark surface used in schools etc. for writing on with chalk.

black·body *noun* (*pl.* **-bodies**) *Physics* a hypothetical perfect absorber and radiator of energy, with no reflecting power.

black book *noun* a record of valuable, esp. confidential information.

black box *noun* **1** a flight data or cockpit voice recorder in an aircraft, designed to survive a crash. **2** any complex piece of equipment, usu. a unit in an electronic system, with contents which are mysterious to the user. **3** a theatre consisting of a large bare space usu. painted black, which can be configured in any way.

black bread *noun* a coarse dark-coloured type of rye bread.

black bryony *noun* a rooted Eurasian climbing plant, *Tamus communis*, with clusters of red poisonous berries.

black·buck *noun* a small Indian gazelle, *Antilope cervicapra*, with a black back and white underbelly.

black·cap *noun N Amer.* = BLACK RASPBERRY.

black-capped chickadee *noun see* CHICKADEE.

black cherry *noun* **1** a cherry, *Prunus serotina*, of eastern N America, bearing dark, edible fruit. **2** the fruit of this.

black cod *noun* a large edible fish, *Anoplopoma fimbria*, found throughout the N Pacific, having a dark-coloured back. *Also called* SABLEFISH.

Black·comb, Mount a peak (1 609 m) in SW central BC, situated in the Coast Mountains, adjacent to Mount Whistler.

Black Country the western part of the West Midlands in England. [so named after the smoke and dust produced by the coal and iron industries of the 19th c.]

black·currant noun **1** a widely cultivated shrub, *Ribes nigrum*, bearing flowers in racemes. **2** the small dark edible berry of this plant.

black damp noun = CHOKEDAMP.

Black Death noun a pandemic of bubonic and pneumonic plague that killed perhaps one-third of the population of Europe in the mid-14th c. and resurfaced at irregular intervals throughout the next few centuries.

black diamond noun **1** (in pl.) coal. **2** = CARBONADO. **3** (attributive) designating a particularly difficult ski run.

black duck noun a wild duck, *Anas rubripes*, predominantly dark brown with a purple patch on the wings, found throughout Canada east of Manitoba and much prized as a game bird.

black earth noun = CHERNOZEM.

black economy noun Brit. = UNDERGROUND ECONOMY.

black·en verb **1** transitive & intransitive make or become black or dark. **2** transitive speak evil of, defame (*blacken someone's character*).

black·ened adjective (of food, esp. in Cajun dishes) covered with spices and cooked quickly over high heat.

black English noun the form of English used by some N American blacks, esp. as an urban dialect.

Black·ett, Pat·rick May·nard Stu·art, Baron (1897–1974), English physicist who studied cosmic rays by observing the effect of bombarding atomic nuclei with alpha particles. He was awarded the 1948 Nobel Prize for physics.

black eye noun **1** bruised or discoloured skin around the eye, esp. resulting from a blow. **2** a severe blow or rebuff.

black-eyed pea noun **1** a leguminous plant, *Vigna unguiculata* or *V. sinensis*, commonly grown for forage in the southern US. Also called COWPEA. **2** the edible seed of this plant (so called from its black hilum).

black-eyed Susan noun (also **brown-eyed Susan**) any of several plants having yellow flowers with dark centres, esp. *Thunbergia alata* and species of *Rudbeckia*.

black·face noun **1** facial makeup used by a non-black performer playing a black role. **2** a variety of sheep with a black face.

black·fish noun **1** any of several species of dark-coloured fish, esp.: **a** = TAUTOG. **b** a freshwater fish of Alaska and Siberia, *Callia pectoralis*. **2** a salmon at spawning.

black flag noun **1** a pirate's ensign. **2** hist. a flag hoisted outside a prison to announce an execution.

black·fly noun (pl. **-flies**) **1** N Amer. any of various gnat-like flies, esp. of the genus *Simulium*, of which the females bite and may carry disease. **2** Brit. any of various thrips or aphids, esp. *Aphis fabae*, infesting plants.

Black·foot ● noun **1** (pl. same or **-feet**) a member of a group of N American Aboriginal peoples comprising the Siksika, Blood, and Peigan now largely found in S Alberta and Montana. **2** = SIKSIKA. **3** the Algonquian language of this people. ● adjective of or relating to the Blackfoot or their language.

black-footed albatross noun a dark-bodied albatross, *Diomedea nigripes*, with black feet and a dark bill, which ranges over the N Pacific.

Black Forest a hilly wooded region of SW Germany lying to the east of the Rhine valley.

Black Forest cake noun (also **Black Forest torte**) a layered chocolate cake with a filling of cherries and whipped cream, originally from S Germany.

Black Forest ham noun N Amer. a variety of sweetened and smoked ham.

Black Friar noun a Dominican friar. [from the black mantle worn over their white habit]

black frost noun a frost without white dew, occurring at very low temperatures and causing plants to wither.

black gold noun informal crude oil.

black grouse noun a Eurasian grouse, *Lyrurus tetrix*.

black·guard /'blagɑrd, -gɔrd, 'blak,gɑrd/ noun a scoundrel; an unscrupulous, unprincipled person. □ **black·guard·ly** adjective [BLACK + GUARD: originally applied collectively to menial workers etc.]

black guillemot noun a circumpolar guillemot, *Cepphus grylle*, which is predominantly black except for a white patch on the wings.

black gum noun a deciduous tree of eastern N America, *Nyssa sylvatica*, with a sour, plum-like fruit.

black-hat noun **1** a malicious hacker; a computer criminal. **2** any potential threat to a network or network security.

black haw noun **1** a black-fruited hawthorn of N America, *Crataegus douglasii*. **2** a viburnum, *Viburnum prunifolium*, of eastern N America, bearing edible black fruit.

black·head noun a black-tipped plug of fatty matter in a skin follicle, esp. on the face.

Black Hills a range of mountains in E Wyoming and western South Dakota. The highest point is Harney Peak (2 207 m, 7,242 ft.); the range also includes the sculptured granite face of Mount Rushmore. [so called because the densely forested slopes appear dark from a distance]

black hole noun **1** a region of space having a gravitational field so intense that no matter and radiation can escape. **2** any inescapable void or place of confinement.

Black Hole of Calcutta see CALCUTTA, BLACK HOLE OF.

black ice noun thin hard transparent ice, esp. on a road surface or body of water.

black·ing noun any black paste or polish, esp. for shoes.

black·jack¹ ● noun **1 a** a card game in which players try to acquire cards with a face value exceeding the dealer's but no more than 21. Also called TWENTY-ONE. **b** two cards totalling 21 in this game. **2** N Amer. a flexible bludgeon of leather-covered lead. **3** a shrubby oak of eastern N America, *Quercus marilandica*. **4** a pirates' black flag. ● transitive verb strike or beat with a blackjack. [BLACK + JACK¹]

black·jack² noun hist. a large tar-coated leather jug or tankard for beer. [BLACK + JACK²]

Black Jew noun see FALASHA.

black·lead /'blakled/ ● noun graphite. ● transitive verb polish with graphite.

black·leg ● noun **1** an acute infectious bacterial disease of cattle and sheep, causing necrosis in the legs. **2** any of various bacterial or fungal diseases of plants, usu. causing the blackening of the stem. **3** (often attributive) Brit. = SCAB noun 2. ● intransitive verb (**-legged**, **-leg·ging**) Brit. = SCAB verb 1.

black letter noun a medieval European typeface, characterized by heavy vertical and angular strokes without curves.

black light noun Physics the invisible ultraviolet or infrared radiations of the electromagnetic spectrum.

black·list ● noun a list of persons under suspicion, in disfavour, etc. ● transitive verb put the name of (a person) on a blacklist.

black locust noun a leguminous tree native to eastern N America, *Robinia pseudoacacia*, with pinnate leaves and black pods.

black lung noun a form of pneumoconiosis caused by the inhalation of coal dust.

black magic noun magic involving supposed invocation of evil spirits.

black·mail ● noun **1 a** an extortion of payment in return for not disclosing discreditable information, a secret, etc. **b** any payment extorted in this way. **2** the use of threats or moral pressure. ● transitive verb **1** extort or try to extort money etc. from (a person) by blackmail. **2** threaten, coerce. □ **black·mail·er** noun [BLACK + obsolete mail rent, Old English māl from Old Norse mál agreement]

black maple noun a maple of eastern N America, *Acer nigrum*, with usu. three-lobed leaves.

Black Maria /'blak mə'raiə/ noun slang a police vehicle for transporting prisoners. [mid 19th c.: said to be named after a black woman *Maria Lee*, who kept a boarding house in Boston and helped police to escort drunk and disorderly customers to jail]

black mark noun a mark of discredit.

black market noun an illicit traffic in officially controlled or scarce commodities. □ **black marketeer** noun

Black Mass noun **1** a travesty of the Roman Catholic Mass said to be used in the cult of Satanism. **2** a requiem Mass in which the celebrant wears black vestments.

black medick noun a low-growing leguminous plant, *Medicago lupulina*, with small yellow flower heads.

Black Monday Monday 19 Oct. 1987, when massive falls in the value of stocks on Wall Street triggered similar falls in markets around the world.

Black·more, R(ich·ard) D(od·dridge) (1825–1900), English author of the romantic novel *Lorna Doone* (1869), set in 17th-c. Exmoor, SW England.

Black Mountain poets an influential group of writers based in N Carolina in the 1950s. Led by Charles Olson and Robert Creeley, the group encouraged free verse and published several important writers including Denise Levertov and Allan Ginsberg.

Black Muslim *noun* a follower of the Nation of Islam.

black nationalism *noun* a political and social movement originating in the US in the 1960s, advocating solidarity, pride, and self-government among blacks.

black nightshade *noun* a poisonous plant, *Solanum nigrum*, with black berries.

black oak *noun* any of several oaks, esp. *Quercus velutina* of eastern N America, having dark-coloured bark.

black olive *noun* the fully ripe fruit of the olive tree.

black·out *noun* **1** a temporary or complete loss of vision, consciousness, or memory. **2** a loss of power, radio reception, etc. **3** a compulsory period of darkness as a precaution against air raids. **4** a temporary suppression of the release of information, esp. from police or government sources. **5** a sudden darkening of a theatre stage. **6** *N Amer.* (often *attributive*) a period in which discounts, esp. on airfare, do not apply. **7** *N Amer.* a ban on the local broadcast of a sports event for which tickets are still available.

Black Panther a member of a militant political organization set up in the US in 1966 to fight for black rights. Internal conflict and the arrest of some of its leaders led to its decline in the 1970s.

black pepper *noun* a condiment made from the unripe ground or whole berries of *Piper nigrum*.

black·poll /ˈblakpoːl/ *noun* (in full **blackpoll warbler**) a N American warbler, *Dendroica striata*, the male of which has a black crown in spring.

Black·pool a seaside resort in NW England, formerly in Lancashire; pop. (2001) 142,284.

black poplar *noun* a European poplar, *Populus nigra*.

black powder *noun* = GUNPOWDER.

black power *noun* a movement in support of civil rights and political power for blacks.

Black Prince the 16th-c. name given to Edward Plantagenet (1330–76), eldest son of Edward III and father of Richard II.

black pudding *noun Brit.* = BLOOD SAUSAGE.

black raspberry *noun* a N American raspberry, *Rubus occidentalis*, having black berries.

black robe *noun Cdn hist.* a Christian priest working as a missionary among Aboriginal peoples.

Black Rod *noun* **1** (in full **Usher of the Black Rod**) (in Canada) the principal usher of the Senate, who summons the Commons to the Senate at the opening of Parliament. ¶ Until 1997 the term in full was **Gentleman Usher of the Black Rod. 2** (in full **Gentleman Usher of the Black Rod**) (in the UK) the principal usher of the Lord Chamberlain's department and the House of Lords. [so called from the ebony wand carried as a symbol of the office]

black rot *noun* any of various bacterial or fungal plant diseases producing decay and dark discoloration.

black salsify *noun* = SCORZONERA.

Black Sea a tideless almost landlocked sea bounded by Ukraine, Russia, Georgia, Turkey, Bulgaria, and Romania, and connected to the Mediterranean through the strait of Bosporus and the Sea of Marmara.

black sheep *noun informal* an unsatisfactory member of a family, group, etc.; an outcast.

black·shirt *noun* a member of a militant Fascist organization, esp. (in Italy) a member of a paramilitary group founded by Mussolini, (in Nazi Germany) a member of the SS, or (in the UK) a supporter of Oswald Moseley's British Union of Fascists. [from the colour of the Italian Fascist uniform]

black·smith *noun* **1** a smith who works in iron. **2** *N Amer.* = FARRIER 1. □ **black·smith·ing** *noun*

black smoker *noun* a geothermal vent on the seabed which ejects superheated water containing much suspended matter, typically black sulphide minerals.

black spot *noun* **1** any of various diseases of plants causing the appearance of black spots. **2** *Brit.* a place of danger or difficulty, esp. a section of road noted for accidents.

black spruce *noun* a widely distributed spruce of Canada and the northeastern US, *Picea mariana*, growing in both wet and dry places.

black squirrel *noun* a black phase of the grey squirrel.

Black·stone, Sir Wil·liam (1723–80), English jurist whose 4-volume *Commentaries on the Laws of England* was the most influential legal treatise in England and the US in the 19th c.

black·strap *noun* (in full **blackstrap molasses**) *N Amer.* a low grade of molasses from which the maximum amount of sugar has been extracted.

black swan *noun* a swan of Australia and New Zealand, *Cygnus atratus*, with black plumage and a red beak.

black·tail *noun* (in full **blacktail deer**, **black-tailed deer**) = MULE DEER.

black tea *noun* tea that is fully fermented before drying.

black tern *noun* a small dark tern, *Chlidonias niger*, breeding in the northern hemisphere and feeding on insects which it catches on the wing.

black·thorn *noun* **1** a N American hawthorn, esp. *Crataegus calpodendron*. **2** a thorny rosaceous European shrub, *Prunus spinosa*, bearing white-petalled flowers before small blue-black fruits. *Also called* SLOE. **3** a cudgel or walking stick made from the blackthorn.

black tie *noun* **1** a black bow tie worn with a tuxedo etc. **2** an occasion requiring that men wear a tuxedo (also *attributive*: *black-tie dinner*) (*compare* WHITE TIE).

black tiger shrimp *noun* a large shrimp with dark stripes, of the genus *Penaeus*.

black·top ● ** *noun* **1 a type of bituminous road-surfacing material; asphalt. **2** a road surfaced with this. **●** *transitive verb* (**black·topped**, **black·top·ping**) surface (a road etc.) with blacktop.

black tracker *noun Austral.* an Aboriginal employed to help find persons lost or hiding in the bush.

Black Tuesday Tuesday 29 Oct. 1929, on which 16 million shares were sold on the American stock market, causing it to collapse and ushering in the Great Depression.

black velvet *noun* a drink of stout and champagne.

black walnut *noun* **1** a walnut tree, *Juglans nigra*, of the northeastern US and southern Canada, planted for its edible nut and as an ornamental. **2** the rich, dark brown wood of this tree, much prized in cabinetmaking. **3** the edible nut of this tree.

Black Watch *noun* **1** the Royal Highland Regiment of the Canadian Forces (historically a regiment of the regular army and currently a reserve regiment). **2** the Royal Highland Regiment of the British army. **3** a very dark green and navy blue tartan. [from the darkness of the tartan, worn as the regimental uniform]

black·water fever *noun* a complication of malaria, in which blood cells are rapidly destroyed, resulting in dark urine.

black widow *noun* a venomous black spider of the genus *Latrodectus*, esp. *L. mactans*, the female of which usu. devours the male after mating.

black willow *noun* a large willow tree, *Salix nigra*, of moist places of eastern N America.

Black·wood, David Lloyd (b.1941), Canadian printmaker and painter. His work, which he sees as telling stories in the ballad tradition, using visual images, portrays his boyhood in Newfoundland.

blad·der *noun* **1** any of various membranous sacs in some animals, containing urine (**urinary bladder**), bile (**gallbladder**), or air (**swim bladder**). **2** an inflated pericarp or vesicle in various plants. **3** anything inflated and hollow. [Old English *blǣdre* from Germanic]

bladder·nut *noun* any of various shrubs or small trees of the genus *Staphylea*, esp. *S. trifolia*, with seeds borne in an inflated capsule.

bladder·wort /ˈbladər,wɜrt, -wɔrt/ *noun* any insect-consuming aquatic plant of the genus *Utricularia*, with underwater leaves having small bladders for trapping insects.

bladder·wrack /ˈbladər,rak/ *noun* a common brown seaweed, *Fucus vesiculosus*, with fronds containing air bladders which give buoyancy to the plant.

blade ● ** *noun* **1 a the flat part of a knife, chisel, etc. that forms the cutting edge. **b** = RAZOR BLADE. **2** the flattened functional part of an oar, propeller, skate, hockey stick, etc. **3 a** the flat, narrow, usu. pointed leaf of grass and cereals. **b** *Bot.* the broad thin part of a leaf apart from the petiole. **4 a** a broad flat bone, esp. in the shoulder. **b** a cut of beef from behind the neck and above the shoulder. **5** the flat part of the tongue behind the tip. **6** *Archaeology* a long narrow flake (*see* FLAKE[1] 3). **7** *literary* a sword. **8** a dashing, pleasure-seeking young man. **●** *intransitive verb N Amer.* = ROLLERBLADE *verb*. □ **blad·ed** *adjective* (also in combination). **blad·er** *noun* **blad·ing** *noun* [Old English *blæd* from Germanic]

blag /blag/ *Brit. slang* **●** *noun* robbery, esp. with violence. **●** *transitive & intransitive verb* (**blagged**, **blag·ging**) **1** rob (esp. with violence).

2 obtain (something) by clever talk or lying. □ **blag·ger** *noun* [19th c.: origin unknown]

blah *informal* ● *noun* **1** (also **blah-blah**) pretentious nonsense. **2** (in *pl.*) a general feeling of depression. ● *adjective* **1** dull, unexciting, bland. **2** lethargic, lacking in enthusiasm. ● *interjection* (usu. **blah blah blah**) indicating long-winded and tedious speech or writing. [imitative]

blain *noun* an inflamed swelling or sore on the skin. [Old English *blegen* from West Germanic]

Blain·ville /ˈblăvil/ a city in south central Quebec, northwest of Laval; pop. (2001) 36,029. [L.-J.-B. Céleron de *Blainville*, local seigneur d.1756]

Blair ▸ 1 An·drew George (1844–1907), Canadian lawyer and politician, Liberal premier of New Brunswick 1883–1896 and minister of railways and canals in the Laurier Cabinet 1896–1903. **2 An·thony Charles Lyn·ton** 'Tony' (b.1953), British politician. Elected leader of the Labour Party in 1994, he achieved a landslide victory in the election of 1997, which gave his party its biggest-ever majority and made him the youngest Prime Minister since Lord Liverpool in 1812. □ **Blair·ite** *adjective & noun*

Blais /blei/ **Marie-Claire** (b.1939), Canadian author. Many of her characters are young Quebecers who struggle against the constraints of family and Church, as in the tragic novel *Une Saison dans la vie d'Emmanuel* (1965), and her trilogy of semi-autobiographical novels (1968–70) about Pauline Archange.

Blake ▸ 1 Ed·ward (1833–1912), Canadian politician and lawyer. Serving as both a provincial and federal Liberal, he was the second premier of Ontario (1872) and a member of Alexander Mackenzie's cabinet (1873–78). **2 Hec·tor** ('Toe') (1912–95), Canadian hockey player and coach. After a 12-season career as a left-winger with the Montreal Canadiens he coached the team to 8 Stanley Cups between 1956 and 1968. **3 James Huber** ('Eubie') (1883–1983), US jazz pianist and composer, whose musical *Shuffle Along* (1927), featured the song 'I'm Just Wild about Harry'. **4 Rob·ert** (1599–1657), English admiral, a Parliamentarian commander during the English Civil War; he had notable successes against the Royalists (1649–51), the Dutch (1652–4), and Spain (1656–7). **5 Wil·liam** (1757–1827), English poet and artist. His poetry expresses a mystic spirituality and a protest against hypocrisy and constraint in conventional religion. His major works, many engraved and illuminated with his own watercolours, include *Songs of Innocence* (1789), *Songs of Experience* (1794), and *The Marriage of Heaven and Hell* (c.1790–93).

Blak·ean /ˈbleikiən/ *adjective* (also **Blake·ian**) relating to or characteristic of William Blake or his work, esp. in its visionary aspects.

Blake·ney /ˈbleikni/ **Allan Emrys** (b.1925), Canadian politician, NDP premier of Saskatchewan 1971–82.

Blakey, Ar·thur 'Art' (1919–90), US jazz drummer. In 1955 Blakey formed the influential jazz group known as the Jazz Messengers. A pioneer in the early days of the bebop movement, he continued to hold a leading position in the jazz world.

blam ● *noun* a loud sharp sound, as of a gunshot or an explosion. ● *intransitive verb* (**blammed, blam·ming**) make such a loud sound. [imitative]

blame ● *transitive verb* **1** assign fault or responsibility to. **2** (foll. by *on*) assign the responsibility for (an error or wrong) to a person etc. (*blamed his death on a poor diet*). ● *noun* **1** responsibility for a bad result; culpability (*shared the blame equally; put the blame on the bad weather*). **2** the act of blaming or attributing responsibility; censure (*she got all the blame*). ● *adjective* (also **blamed**) *N Amer. informal* damned, confounded. □ **be to blame** (often foll. by *for*) be responsible; deserve censure (*she is not to blame for the accident*). **have only oneself to blame** be solely responsible (for something one suffers). **I don't blame you** etc. I think your etc. action was justifiable. □ **blame·able** *adjective* (also **blam·able**). [Old French *bla(s)mer* (v.), *blame* (n.) from popular Latin *blastemare* from ecclesiastical Latin *blasphemare* reproach, from Greek *blasphēmeō* blaspheme]

blame·ful *adjective* deserving blame; guilty. □ **blame·ful·ly** *adverb*

blame game *noun informal* a situation in which one party blames others, esp. rather than attempting to seek a solution.

blame·less *adjective* innocent; free from blame. □ **blame·less·ly** *adverb* **blame·less·ness** *noun*

blame·worthy *adjective* deserving blame. □ **blame·worthi·ness** *noun*

blanc de blancs /ˈblādəblā/ *noun* a (usu. sparkling) white wine made from white grapes only. [French, lit. = 'white of whites']

blanch /blantʃ/ *verb* **1** *transitive* make white or pale by extracting colour.

2 *intransitive & transitive* grow or make pale from shock, fear, etc. **3** *transitive Cooking* **a** peel (almonds etc.) by scalding. **b** immerse (vegetables or meat) briefly in boiling water. **4** *transitive* clean or whiten (a metal) by immersion in acid or by coating with tin. **5** *transitive* whiten (a plant) by depriving it of light. [Old French *blanchir* from *blanc* white, BLANK]

Blan·chard /blāˈʃar/ **Jean Pierre Fran·çois** (1753–1809), French aviation pioneer. With Dr. John Jefferies he made the first crossing of the English Channel by air, flying by balloon from Dover to Calais on 7 Jan. 1785.

blanc·mange /bləˈmɒndʒ/ *noun* a sweet opaque gelatinous dessert made with flavoured milk and thickened with cornstarch. [Old French *blancmanger* from *blanc* white + *manger* eat, from Latin *manducare* MANDUCATE]

bland *adjective* **1 a** mild, not irritating. **b** tasteless. **2** not stimulating, insipid. **3** expressionless, mild-tempered. □ **bland·ly** *adverb* **bland·ness** *noun* [Latin *blandus* soft, smooth]

blan·dish *transitive verb* flatter; coax, cajole. [Old French *blandir* (-ISH²) from Latin *blandiri* from *blandus* soft, smooth]

blan·dish·ment *noun* (usu. in *pl.*) flattery; cajolery.

blank ● *adjective* **1 a** (of paper) not written or printed on. **b** (of a document) with spaces left for a signature or details. **c** (of a tape, disk, etc.) containing no recorded sound, information, etc. **d** (of a computer monitor, television screen, etc.) not displaying any images, characters, etc. **2 a** not filled; empty (*a blank space*). **b** lacking contrast; sheer (*a blank wall*). **3 a** having or showing no interest or expression (*a blank face*). **b** void of incident or result. **c** puzzled, nonplussed. **d** having (temporarily) no knowledge or understanding (*my mind went blank*). **4** (with neg. import) complete, downright (*a blank refusal; blank despair*). **5** *Curling* (of an end) played without either rink scoring a point. **6** *euphemism* used in place of an adjective regarded as coarse or abusive. ● *noun* **1 a** a space left to be filled in a document. **b** a document having blank spaces to be filled. **2** (in full **blank cartridge**) a cartridge containing gunpowder but no bullet, used for training etc. **3** an empty space or period of time. **4 a** a coin disc before stamping. **b** a metal or wooden block before final shaping. **5 a** a dash written instead of a word or letter, esp. instead of an obscenity. **b** *euphemism* used in place of a noun regarded as coarse. **6** a blank domino or tile in some games. **7** a lottery ticket that gains no prize. **8** the white centre of the target in archery etc. ● *transitive verb* **1** (usu. foll. by *off, out*) screen, obscure (*clouds blanked out the sun*). **2** (usu. foll. by *out*) cut (a metal blank). **3** *N Amer. Sport* defeat without allowing to score; shut out. **4** *Curling* play (an end) without either rink scoring a point. **5** (often foll. by *out*) cause the mind to become empty of memories, or incapable of conscious thought or feeling. □ **draw a blank** elicit no response; fail. **shoot** (or **fire**) **blanks** *informal* **1** (of a man) be infertile. **2** (of a sports team) be unable to score or win. **3** be unsuccessful. □ **blank·ly** *adverb* **blank·ness** *noun* [Old French *blanc* white, ultimately from Germanic]

blank cheque *noun* **1** a cheque with the amount left for the payee to fill in. **2** *informal* unlimited freedom of action (*compare* CARTE BLANCHE).

blan·ket ● *noun* **1** a large piece of woollen or other material used esp. as a bedcover or to wrap up a person or an animal for warmth. **2** (usu. *attributive*) a type of woollen cloth similar to a woollen blanket (*blanket coat*). **3** (usu. foll. by *of*) a thick mass or layer that covers something (*blanket of fog; blanket of silence*). **4** *Printing* a rubber surface transferring an impression from a plate to paper etc. in offset printing. **5** *N Amer.* (often *attributive*) traditional Indian life or culture. ● *adjective* covering all cases or classes; inclusive (*blanket condemnation; blanket agreement*). ● *transitive verb* (**blan·ket·ed, blan·ket·ing**) **1** cover with or as if with a blanket (*snow blanketed the land*). **2** stifle; keep quiet (*blanketed all discussion*). **3** *Naut.* take wind from the sails of (another craft) by passing to windward. □ **born on the wrong side of the blanket** illegitimate. [Old French *blancquet* from *blanc* white, BLANK]

blanket box *noun* (also **blanket chest**) a wooden chest with a hinged top, used for storing bedding or clothing.

blanket coat *noun* esp. *N Amer.* a coat made from a blanket or blanket cloth, esp. (in Canada) = HUDSON'S BAY BLANKET COAT.

blanket flower *noun* = GAILLARDIA.

blanket stitch *noun* a buttonhole stitch worked on the edge of blankets or other material too thick to be hemmed.

blanket toss *noun* an Inuit game in which a large circle of animal skin or canvas held around the edges by several people is used to toss a person in the air.

blan·kety *adjective* (also **blankety-blank**) *informal* = BLANK *adjective* 6.

blan·kie *noun N Amer. informal* a child's blanket, esp. a security blanket. [abbreviation]

Vowels: a cat ɑ arm e bed ɜr her ɜː deux ə ago ɪ sit i cosy iː feed ɒ hot ɔ pore oː no ʌ run ʊ put

blank slate *noun* a person, situation, etc. seen as having no innate characteristics and capable of becoming whatever outside influences determine.

blank verse *noun* unrhymed verse, esp. iambic pentameters.

blan·quette /blɔ̃'ket/ *noun* a stew of light-coloured meat, esp. veal, in a white sauce. [French (as BLANKET)]

Blan·tyre /blan'taɪr/ the chief commercial and industrial city of Malawi; pop. (est. 2002) 533,000 (with Limbe, a town 8 km southeast of Blantyre). [*Blantyre*, Scotland, birthplace of D. LIVINGSTONE²]

blare ● *verb* **1** *intransitive* make a loud harsh sound (*car horns blared*). **2** *transitive & intransitive* produce or utter (such sounds) loudly (*the radio was blaring*). ● *noun* a loud harsh sound. [Middle Dutch *blaren, bleren*, imitative]

blar·ney ● *noun* **1** cajoling talk; flattery. **2** nonsense. ● *verb* (**-neys, -neyed**) **1** *transitive* flatter (a person) with blarney. **2** *intransitive* talk flatteringly. [*Blarney*, a castle near Cork, Ireland, with a stone said to confer a cajoling tongue on whoever kisses it]

Blas·co Ibá·ñez /'blasko: iː'banjes/ **Vi·cente** (1867–1928), Spanish novelist, whose works include *Blood and Sand* (1909) and *The Four Horsemen of the Apocalypse* (1916).

blasé /blɑ'zeɪ/ *adjective* **1** unimpressed or indifferent because of overfamiliarity. **2** tired of pleasure; surfeited. [French, past participle of *blaser* 'cloy', prob. from Germanic]

blas·pheme /blas'fiːm, 'blasfiːm/ *verb* **1** *intransitive* swear or curse, making use of religious names etc. **2** *intransitive* speak irreverently about God or sacred things. □ **blas·phem·er** *noun* [Greek *blasphēmeō*: compare BLAME]

blas·phemy /'blasfəmi/ *noun* (*pl.* **-ies**) **1** the action or offence of speaking sacrilegiously about God or sacred things. **2** something shocking that deeply offends people's idea of what is correct. □ **blas·phem·ous** *adjective* **blas·phem·ous·ly** *adverb* [Greek *blasphēmia* slander, blasphemy]

blast ● *noun* **1** a strong gust of wind. **2 a** an explosion. **b** a destructive wave of highly compressed air spreading outwards from an explosion. **c** the quantity of explosive used in a blasting operation. **3** a single loud note emitted by a car horn, whistle, brass instrument, etc. **4** a gunshot. **5** *informal* a severe reprimand. **6** a strong current of air used in smelting etc. **7** *informal* a good time; an enjoyable experience (*was having a blast*). **8** *Sport* a vigorous hit, throw, etc. **9** *Computing* (*attributive*) designating an esp. advertising email message sent to a number of recipients. ● *verb* **1** *transitive* blow up (rocks etc.) with explosives. **2** *transitive* create out of or from rocks etc. by blasting (*blasted a tunnel through the Rockies*). **3** *intransitive & transitive* make or cause to make a loud or explosive noise (*blasted away on his trumpet*). **4 a** *transitive informal* reprimand severely. **b** *intransitive* exclaim vehemently or loudly. **5** *informal* **a** *transitive* shoot; shoot at. **b** *intransitive* shoot. **6** *transitive Sport* hit or throw forcefully. **7** *transitive* destroy, ruin (*blasted her hopes*). **8** *transitive* wither, shrivel, or blight (a plant etc.) (*blasted oak*). **9** *transitive* strike with divine anger; curse. ● *interjection* expressing annoyance. □ **full blast** *informal* working at maximum speed etc. **blast from the past** *informal* a forcefully nostalgic event or thing. **blast off** (of a rocket etc.) take off from a launching site. [Old English *blǣst* from Germanic]

-blast *combining form Biol.* **1** an embryonic cell (*erythroblast*) (*compare* -CYTE). **2** a germ layer of an embryo (*epiblast*). [Greek *blastos* sprout]

blast·ed *adjective* **1** (*attributive*) damned; annoying (*that blasted dog!*). **2** (*predicative*) *informal* drunk.

blast·er *noun* **1** in senses of BLAST *verb*. **2** *N Amer.* = GHETTO BLASTER.

blast furnace *noun* a smelting furnace into which compressed hot air is driven.

blast·hole *noun* a hole containing an explosive charge for blasting.

blast-off *noun* the launching of a rocket etc.

blas·tula /'blastjʊlə/ *noun* (*pl.* **blas·tu·las** or **blas·tu·lae** /-,liː/) *Biol.* an animal embryo at an early stage of development when it is a hollow ball of cells. [modern Latin from Greek *blastos* sprout]

blasty *adjective Cdn* (*Nfld*) (of a branch of a spruce or fir tree) dead and dry, with the needles (now brown or red) still attached.

blat ● *noun* a loud discordant noise, e.g. the sounding of a horn. ● *intransitive verb* (**blat·ted, blat·ting**) make a loud discordant sound. [imitative]

bla·tant /'bleɪtənt/ *adjective* **1** flagrant, unashamed (*blatant attempt to steal*). **2** offensively noisy or obtrusive. □ **bla·tancy** *noun* **bla·tant·ly** *adverb* [perhaps after Scots *blatand* = bleating]

blath·er (also **bleth·er**) ● *noun* foolish chatter. ● *transitive & intransitive verb* (also **blith·er**) chatter foolishly. □ **blath·er·ing** *noun* [Old Norse *blathra* talk nonsense, from *blathr* nonsense]

blather·skite *noun* **1** a person who blathers. **2** = BLATHER *noun*, [BLATHER + *skite*, corruption of SKATE³]

Bla·vat·sky /blə'vatski/ **Helen Pet·rovna** (1831–91), Russian spiritualist, founder of the Theosophical Society.

blax·ploi·ta·tion *noun US informal* (usu. *attributive*) the exploitation of blacks, esp. as actors in films. [blend of BLACK *noun* 6 + EXPLOITATION]

blaze¹ ● *noun* **1** a bright flame or fire. **2 a** a bright glaring light (*the sun set in a blaze of orange*). **b** a blaze (of publicity). **3** a violent outburst (of passion etc.) (*a blaze of patriotic fervour*). **4 a** a glow of colour (*roses were a blaze of scarlet*). **b** a bright display (*a blaze of glory*). ● *intransitive verb* **1** burn with a bright flame. **2** be brilliantly lighted. **3** be consumed with anger, excitement, etc. **4 a** show bright colours (*blazing with jewels*). **b** emit light (*stars blazing*). **5** esp. *Sport* move quickly. □ **blaze away** (often foll. by *at*) **1** fire continuously with rifles etc. **2** work enthusiastically. **blaze up 1** burst into flame. **2** burst out in anger. **go to blazes** *informal* go to hell. **like blazes** *informal* **1** with great energy. **2** very fast. **what in blazes** *informal* what on earth. [Old English *blǣse* torch, from Germanic, ultimately related to BLAZE²]

blaze² ● *noun* **1** a white mark on an animal's face. **2** a mark made on or affixed to a tree etc. to mark a route. ● *transitive verb* mark (a tree or a path) by chipping bark. □ **blaze a trail** (or **path**) **1** mark out a path or route. **2** be the first to do, invent, or study something; pioneer. [17th c., ultimately related to BLAZE¹]

blaze³ *transitive verb* proclaim as with a trumpet. [Low German or Dutch *blāzen* blow, from Germanic *blǣsan*]

blaze orange *N Amer.* ● *adjective* of a vivid orange colour (often used for hunting attire to increase its visibility). ● *noun* this colour.

blaz·er *noun* **1** a jacket of a solid colour, often with a crest and patch pockets, worn as part of a uniform. **2** a plain jacket of a dark solid colour, often blue, that is not part of a suit. [BLAZE¹ + -ER¹]

blaz·ing *adjective* **1** in senses of BLAZE¹ *verb*. **2** very hot (*a blazing hot day*). □ **blaz·ing·ly** *adverb*

blazing star *noun* any of various plants, esp. of the genera *Mentzelia* and *Liatris*, bearing clusters of star-shaped flowers.

blaz·on /'bleɪzən/ ● *transitive verb* **1** display prominently or vividly (*their company name was blazoned all over the media*). **2** *Heraldry* **a** describe or paint (arms). **b** inscribe or paint (an object) with arms, names, etc. ● *noun* **1** *Heraldry* a shield, coat of arms, bearings, or a banner. **2** a correct description of these. [Old French *blason* shield, of unknown origin; verb also from BLAZE³]

blaz·onry /'bleɪzənri/ *noun Heraldry* **1** the art of describing or painting heraldic devices or armorial bearings. **2** such devices or bearings.

bldg. *abbreviation* building.

bleach ● *transitive & intransitive verb* **1** whiten by a chemical process or by exposure to sunlight. **2** (of coral) lose colour and die as a result of ejecting their symbiotic algae in response to undetermined stresses of which one may be a rise in temperature of sea water. ● *noun* **1** a bleaching substance, esp. a solution of sodium hypochlorite used domestically for whitening laundry and as a disinfectant. **2** the process of bleaching. [Old English *blǣcan* from Germanic]

bleach·er *noun* **1** (usu. in *pl.*) esp. *N Amer.* **a** uncovered, tiered, inexpensive bench seating at a sports ground, stadium, etc. **b** a similar type of seating in a gymnasium etc. **2 a** a person who bleaches (esp. textiles). **b** a vessel or chemical used in bleaching.

bleak¹ *adjective* **1** bare, exposed; windswept. **2** unpromising; dreary (*bleak prospects*). **3** cold or harsh (*a bleak wind*). □ **bleak·ly** *adverb* **bleak·ness** *noun* [16th c.: related to obsolete adjectives *bleach, blake* (from Old Norse *bleikr*) pale, ultimately from Germanic: compare BLEACH]

bleak² *noun* any of various species of small silvery European river fish of the carp family, esp. *Alburnus alburnus*. [prob. from Old Norse *bleikja*, Old High German *bleicha* from Germanic]

blear *archaic* ● *adjective* **1** (of the eyes or the mind) dim, dull, filmy. **2** indistinct. ● *transitive verb* make dim or obscure; blur. [Middle English, of uncertain origin]

bleary *adjective* (**blear·i·er, blear·i·est**) **1** (of the eyes or mind) dim; blurred. **2** indistinct. □ **blear·i·ly** *adverb* **blear·i·ness** *noun*

bleary-eyed *adjective* having irritated, tired, and unfocused eyes, esp. from lack of sleep or inebriation.

bleat ● *verb* **1** *intransitive* (of a sheep, goat, calf, etc.) give its natural tremulous cry. **2** *intransitive & transitive* (often foll. by *out*) speak or say feebly, foolishly, or plaintively. ● *noun* **1** the sound made by a sheep, goat, etc. **2** a weak, plaintive, or foolish exclamation, statement, etc. □ **bleat·er** *noun* **bleat·ing·ly** *adverb* [Old English *blǣtan* (imitative)]

bleb noun **1** esp. Med. a small blister or swelling. **2** a small bubble in glass or on water. [var. of BLOB]

blech /blex/ interjection N Amer. expressing disgust.

bleed ● verb (past and past participle **bled**) **1** intransitive emit blood. **2** transitive draw blood from surgically. **3** transitive extort money from. **4** intransitive spend or lose money in large quantities. **5** intransitive (of a plant) emit sap. **6** intransitive **a** (of dye) come out in water. **b** (of colour) transfer or spread from one thing to another; run. **7** transitive **a** allow (fluid or gas) to escape from a closed system through a valve etc. **b** treat (such a system) in this way. **8** intransitive (often foll. by for) suffer wounds or violent death (bled for the Revolution). **9** Printing **a** intransitive (of a printed area) be cut into when pages are trimmed. **b** transitive cut into the printed area of when trimming. **c** transitive extend (an illustration) to the cut edge of a page. ● noun **1** a draining of fluid or gas from a closed system. **2** (usu. in combination) an act of bleeding (nosebleed). □ **bleed dry** (or **white**) drain (a person, country, etc.) of wealth etc. **one's heart bleeds** usu. ironic one is very sorrowful. [Old English blēdan from Germanic]

bleed·er noun **1** a person or thing that bleeds. **2** Brit. slang a person (esp. as a term of contempt or disrespect) (you bleeder; lucky bleeder). **3** informal a hemophiliac.

bleed·ing adjective & adverb Brit. slang expressing annoyance or antipathy (a bleeding nuisance).

bleeding edge noun the very forefront of technological development, esp. when experimental or risky. [after LEADING EDGE, CUTTING EDGE.]

bleeding heart noun **1** informal a person perceived as overly sentimental, esp. in regard to social problems. **2** any of various plants, esp. Dicentra spectabilis, having heart-shaped pinkish-red flowers hanging from an arched stem.

bleep ● noun **1** an intermittent high-pitched sound made electronically. **2** this sound or the word itself used as a substitute for an expletive. ● verb **1** intransitive & transitive make or cause to make such a sound, esp. as a signal. **2** transitive (often foll. by out) substitute a bleep for. [imitative]

bleep·er noun Brit. = BEEPER.

blem·ish ● noun **1** a flaw or defect (not a blemish on her character). **2** a mark on the skin, esp. a pimple, blackhead, scar, etc. ● transitive verb spoil the perfection or beauty of (plagiarism will blemish a student's record). [Old French ble(s)mir make pale, prob. of Germanic origin; see -ISH²]

blench¹ intransitive verb flinch; quail. [Old English blencan, ultimately from Germanic]

blench² intransitive verb turn pale; blanch. [var. of BLANCH]

blend ● verb **1** transitive **a** mix (esp. sorts of coffee, spirits, tobacco, etc.) together to produce a desired flavour etc. **b** produce by this method (blended whisky). **2** intransitive form a harmonious compound; become one. **3** transitive & intransitive (often foll. by with, in) mingle or be mingled (her voice blends in with the others). **4 a** transitive (often foll. by in) mix thoroughly. **b** transitive & intransitive combine (ingredients) using an electric blender. **5** intransitive (esp. of colours) **a** pass imperceptibly into each other. **b** go well together; harmonize. ● noun **1 a** a mixture, esp. of various sorts of coffee, spirits, tobacco, fibre, etc. **b** a combination (of different abstract or personal qualities). **2** a word blending the sounds and combining the meanings of two others, e.g. motel, Agribition. [prob. from Old Norse blanda mix]

blende /blɛnd/ noun any naturally occurring metal sulphide, esp. zinc blende. [German from blenden deceive, so called because while often resembling galena it yielded no lead]

blended family noun a family consisting of children from more than one marriage.

blend·er noun **1** an electric kitchen appliance with rotating blades, used for puréeing, liquefying, or finely chopping. **2** a person or thing that blends.

Blen·heim /ˈblɛnəm/ **1** a village in Bavaria, scene of a battle (1704) during the War of the Spanish Succession, in which the English, under the Duke of Marlborough, defeated the French and the Bavarians. **2** a former town in SW Ontario, now part of the city of Chatham-Kent; pop. (2001) 4,780.

blen·ny noun (pl. **-nies**) any of various small spiny-finned marine fishes belonging to the Blenniidae or a related family, most of which are bottom-dwelling fishes of intertidal and shallow inshore waters. [Latin blennius from Greek blennos mucus, with reference to its mucous coating]

blent archaic past and past participle of BLEND.

bleph·ar·itis /ˌblɛfəˈraɪtɪs/ noun inflammation of the eyelids. [as BLEPHARO- + -ITIS]

blepharo- /ˈblɛfərɔː/ combining form of or relating to the eyelids. [Greek blepharon eyelid]

bleph·aro·plasty /ˈblɛfərɔːˌplasti/ noun the surgical repair or reconstruction of an eyelid. [BLEPHARO- + -PLASTY]

Blé·riot /ˈblɛriˌɔː/ (1872–1936), French pioneer in aviation. On 25 July 1909 he became the first to fly across the English Channel, from Calais to Dover, in a monoplane.

bles·bok /ˈblɛsbɒk/ noun (also **bles·buck** /-bʌk/) a white-faced southern African antelope, Damaliscus dorcas, having small lyre-shaped horns. [Afrikaans from bles BLAZE² (from the white mark on its forehead) + bok goat]

bless transitive verb (past and past participle **blessed**, archaic **blest**) **1 a** (of a priest etc.) pronounce words, esp. in a religious rite, to confer or invoke divine favour on. **b** bestow divine favour on (bless this house). **2 a** consecrate (esp. bread and wine). **b** sanctify. **3** call (God) holy; adore. **4** reflexive make the sign of the cross. **5** attribute one's good fortune to (an auspicious time, one's fate, etc.); thank (bless the day I met her; bless my stars). **6** (usu. in passive; often foll. by with) make happy or successful (blessed with children; they were truly blessed). ● (**God**) **bless me** (or **my soul**) an exclamation of surprise, pleasure, indignation, etc. (**God**) **bless you!** **1** an exclamation of endearment, gratitude, etc. **2** an exclamation made to a person who has just sneezed. **I'm blessed** (or **blest**) an exclamation of surprise etc. **not have a penny to bless oneself with** be impoverished. [Old English blǣdsian, blēdsian, blētsian, from blōd blood (hence mark with blood, consecrate): meaning influenced by its use at the conversion of the English to translate Latin benedicare praise]

blessed /ˈblɛsəd, blɛst/ adjective (also archaic **blest**) **1** sanctified, revered. **2** /blɛst/ (usu. foll. by with) often ironic fortunate (in the possession of) (blessed with good health; blessed with children). **3** euphemism cursed; damned (blessed nuisance!). **4** in paradise. **5** (**Bless·ed**) Catholicism a title given to a beatified person. **6** bringing happiness; blissful (blessed ignorance). □ **bless·ed·ly** adverb

blessed event noun the birth of a child.

bless·ed·ness /ˈblɛsədnəs/ noun **1** happiness. **2** the enjoyment of divine favour. □ **single blessedness** jocular the state of being unmarried (perversion of Shakespeare Midsummer Night's Dream I. i. 78).

Bless·ed Sacrament noun esp. Catholicism the Eucharist, esp. the consecrated bread and wine.

Bless·ed Virgin Mary the mother of Jesus (see MARY).

bless·ing noun **1** the act of declaring, seeking, or bestowing (esp. divine) favour (sought God's blessing; mother gave them her blessing). **2** grace said before or after a meal. **3** a gift of a deity, nature, etc.; a thing one is glad of (what a blessing he brought it!). □ **blessing in disguise** an apparent misfortune that eventually has good results.

blest archaic var. of BLESSED.

bleth·er var. of BLATHER.

bleu /blu/ noun Cdn esp. hist. a Quebec supporter of a Conservative party.

blew past of BLOW¹, BLOW³.

blew·its /ˈbluːəts/ noun an edible European mushroom of the genus Lepista with a pale buff or mauve cap and a mauve or bluish stem. [prob. from BLUE¹]

Bligh /blaɪ/ **Wil·liam** (1754–1817), British naval officer. He was captain of HMS Bounty on a voyage to the West Indies. In 1789 part of his crew, led by the first mate Fletcher Christian, mutinied and Bligh was set adrift in an open boat, arriving safely at Timor, nearly 6 400 km (4,000 miles) distant, a few weeks later.

blight /blaɪt/ ● noun **1** any plant disease caused by mildews, rusts, smuts, fungi, or insects. **2** any insect or parasite causing such a disease. **3** any obscure force which is harmful or destructive. **4** the act or state of deteriorating or being destroyed (urban blight). ● transitive verb **1** affect with blight. **2** harm, destroy. **3** spoil. [17th c.: origin unknown]

blight·er /ˈblaɪtər/ noun esp. Brit. informal a person (esp. as a term of contempt or disparagement). [BLIGHT + -ER¹]

Bligh·ty /ˈblaɪti/ noun (also **old Blighty**) slang Britain, esp. England. [Urdu b'lāytī, informal form of wilāyatī foreign, (esp.) European, from Arabic wilāya(t) dominion, district: used by soldiers, esp. during the war of 1914–18]

blimey /ˈblaɪmi/ interjection (also **cor blimey** /kɔrˈblaɪmi/) Brit. slang an expression of surprise, contempt, etc. [corruption of (God) blind me!]

blimp noun **1** a small non-rigid airship. **2** (also **Blimp, Colonel Blimp**) a proponent of reactionary establishment opinions. **3** an obese person. **4** a soundproof cover for a movie camera. [20th. c., of uncertain origin: in sense 2, a pompous, obese, elderly character invented by cartoonist David Low (d.1963), and used in anti-German or anti-government drawings before and during the war of 1939–45]

blimp·ery *noun* pomposity or reactionary attitudes.

blimp·ish *adjective* stupidly complacent and pompous.

blind ● *adjective* **1** lacking the power of sight. **2 a** without foresight, discernment, intellectual perception, or adequate information (*blind effort*). **b** (often foll. by *to*) unwilling or unable to appreciate (a factor, circumstance, etc.) (*blind to argument*). **3** not governed by purpose or reason (*blind forces*). **4** reckless (*blind hitting*). **5** concealed, obscured (*blind corner*). **6 a** (of a door, window, etc.) walled up. **b** (of a street, alley, etc.) closed at one end. **c** (of a geographical feature) terminating abruptly (*blind gully*). **7** (of flying) without direct observation, using instruments only. **8** (of a pie shell, etc.) baked without a filling. **9** (of a wall) having no windows. **10** (of a test or experiment) conducted in a way that does not allow the subject or examiner to prejudice the results. **11** *informal* drunk. **12** (of a joint, rivet, etc.) invisible. ● *transitive verb* **1** deprive of sight, permanently or temporarily (*blinded by tears*). **2** (often foll. by *to*) rob of judgment; deceive (*blinded them to the danger*). ● *noun* **1 a** a screen for a window, esp. on a roller, or with slats (*roller blind*; *Venetian blind*). **b** an awning over a store window. **2 a** something designed or used to hide the truth; a pretext. **b** a legitimate business concealing a criminal enterprise (*she's a spy, and her job is just a blind*). **3** *N Amer.* a camouflaged shelter used for observing or hunting wildlife. **4** any obstruction to sight or light. **5** *Cards* a stake put up by a poker player before the cards dealt are seen. **6** *Brit. slang* a heavy drinking bout. ● *adverb* **1** *Aviation* without direct observation, using instruments only (*fly blind*). **2** without guidance (*buy it blind*). **3** to a great extent (*robbed them blind*). **4** *Cooking* without a filling (*bake it blind*). □ **blind as a bat** completely blind. **the blind leading the blind** people without knowledge or experience attempting to guide or advise those in a similar position. **blind with science** overawe with a display of (often spurious) knowledge. **not a blind bit of** *informal* not the slightest amount of (*didn't do a blind bit of good*). **turn a blind eye to** pretend not to notice. □ **blind·ness** *noun* [Old English from Germanic]

blind alley *noun* **1** a street, alley, etc. with one end closed off. **2** a course of action leading nowhere.

blind copy *noun* a copy of a letter etc. of which the original shows no indication that a copy was sent to another recipient.

blind date *noun* **1** a social engagement between two people who have not previously met. **2** either of the two people on a blind date.

blind drunk *adjective informal* extremely drunk.

blind·er *noun informal* **1** (usu. in *pl.*) *N Amer.* = BLINKER *noun* 1. **2** *Brit.* an excellent piece of play in a game.

blind·fold ● *transitive verb* **1** deprive (a person) of sight by covering the eyes, esp. with a tied cloth. **2** deprive of understanding; hoodwink. ● *noun* **1** a bandage or cloth used to blindfold. **2** any obstruction to understanding. ● *adjective & adverb* **1** with eyes bandaged. **2** without care or circumspection (*went into it blindfold*). **3** *Chess* without sight of board and men. [replacing (by assoc. with FOLD[1]) Middle English *blindfellen*, past participle *blindfelled* (FELL[2]) strike blind]

blind gut *noun* the cecum.

blind·ing ● *noun* **1** the act of causing blindness. **2** the process of covering a newly made road etc. with grit to fill cracks. **3** such grit. ● *adjective* **1** causing temporary or permanent inability to see (*a blinding snowstorm*). **2** dazzlingly bright (*blinding white beaches*). **3** extreme; severe (*blinding speed*; *blinding headaches*). □ **blind·ing·ly** *adverb*

blind·ly *adverb* **1** without being able to see (*groped blindly down the hall*). **2** without understanding or thought; ignorantly (*plunged in blindly*).

blind man's bluff *noun* (also esp. *Brit.* **blind man's buff**) a game in which a blindfolded player tries to catch others while being pushed about by them.

blind pig *noun N Amer. informal* an illegal bar.

blind side ● *noun* a direction in which one cannot see the approach of danger etc. ● *transitive verb* (usu. **blind·side**) *N Amer.* **1** attack or strike on the blind side. **2** surprise, take unawares; take advantage of.

blind spot *noun* **1** *Anat.* the point of entry of the optic nerve on the retina, insensitive to light. **2** an area where vision is obscured or hindered, esp. that part of the road which a driver of a motor vehicle cannot see using mirrors. **3** an area in which a person lacks understanding or impartiality. **4** a point of unusually weak radio reception.

blind stamping *noun* (also **blind tooling**) embossing a book cover without the use of colour or foil.

blind·stitch ● *noun* sewing visible on one side only. ● *transitive & intransitive verb* sew with this stitch.

blind trust *noun* **1** a trust independently administering the private business affairs of a person in public office to prevent conflict of interest. **2** complete, unthinking faith.

blind·worm *noun* = SLOW-WORM.

bling *noun* (also **bling-bling**) *slang* flashy and expensive clothing or jewellery. [perhaps imitative of light reflecting off jewellery, or of jewellery clashing together]

blini /ˈblɪni/ *noun* (*pl.* same or **blinis**) an originally Russian pancake made from buckwheat flour and yeast. [pl. of Russian *blin*]

blink ● *verb* **1** *intransitive & transitive* shut and open the eyes quickly and usu. involuntarily. **2** *intransitive* (often foll. by *at*) look with eyes opening and shutting, esp. in surprise or bewilderment. **3** *transitive* **a** (often foll. by *back*) prevent (tears) by blinking. **b** (often foll. by *away, from*) clear (dust etc.) from the eyes by blinking. **4** *transitive & intransitive* shirk consideration of; ignore; condone. **5** *intransitive* shine with an unsteady or intermittent light; flash. **b** *transitive* cause (a light) to flash briefly. **6** *intransitive* back down in a confrontation; yield. ● *noun* **1** an act of blinking. **2** a momentary gleam or glimpse. **3** = ICEBLINK. □ **on the blink** *informal* out of order, esp. intermittently. **the blink of an eye** a very short time. [partly var. of *blenk* = BLENCH[1], partly from Middle Dutch *blinken* shine]

blink·er ● *noun* **1** (usu. in *pl.*) either of a pair of screens attached to a horse's bridle to prevent it from seeing sideways. **2** a device that blinks, esp. a vehicle's turn signal. ● *transitive verb* obscure with blinkers.

blink·ered *adjective* having narrow and prejudiced views.

blink·ing *adjective & adverb Brit. slang* an intensive, esp. expressing disapproval (*a blinking idiot; a blinking awful time*). [BLINK + -ING[2] (euphemism for BLOODY)]

blintz *noun* (also **blintze**) (*pl.* **-es**) a thin pancake wrapped around a filling, usu. of cottage or cream cheese. [Yiddish *blintse* from Russian *blinets* diminutive of *blin*]

blip ● *noun* **1** a quick popping sound; a short bleep. **2** a small image of an object on a radar screen. **3** a temporary movement in statistics, usu. in an unexpected or unwelcome direction. ● *intransitive verb* (**blipped**, **blip·ping**) **1** make a blip. **2** (of figures etc.) rise suddenly and temporarily. [imitative]

Bliss, Sir Ar·thur (1891–1975), English composer. He was director of music at the BBC from 1942–44 and Master of the Queen's Music from 1953 to 1975.

bliss ● *noun* **1 a** perfect joy or happiness. **b** enjoyment; gladness. **2 a** the state of being in heaven. **b** a state of blessedness. ● *intransitive verb* (foll. by *out*) esp. *N Amer. slang* reach a state of ecstasy. [Old English *blīths*, *bliss* from Germanic *blīthsjō* from *blithiz* BLITHE: sense influenced by BLESS]

blissed-out *adjective* esp. *N Amer. slang* in a state of bliss; ecstatic.

bliss·ful *adjective* perfectly happy; joyful. □ **blissful ignorance** fortunate unawareness of something unpleasant. □ **bliss·ful·ly** *adverb* **bliss·ful·ness** *noun*

B-list *noun* a group of people or things not of the first rank, quality, or importance.

blis·ter ● *noun* **1** a small bubble on the skin filled with serum and caused by friction, burning, etc. **2** a similar swelling on any other surface. ● *verb* **1** *transitive* raise a blister on. **2** *intransitive* come up in a blister or blisters. **3** *transitive* attack sharply (*blistered them with his criticisms*). □ **blis·tery** *adjective* [Middle English perhaps from Old French *blestre*, *blo(u)stre* swelling, pimple]

blister copper *noun* impure copper with a blistered appearance, obtained during smelting.

blister gas *noun* a poison gas causing blisters on the skin.

blis·ter·ing *adjective* **1** very harsh (*a blistering attack on her character*). **2** very intense (*blistering sun*; *blistering cold*). **3** very fast (*a blistering shot*). □ **blis·ter·ing·ly** *adverb*

blister pack *noun* (also **bubble pack**) a small package enclosing goods in a rigid transparent case on a flat backing.

blister rust *noun* a disease of pine trees caused by a fungus of the genus *Cronartium* and characterized by blistering of the stem.

blithe /blaɪð, blaɪθ/ *adjective* (usu. *attributive*) **1** happy, joyous. **2** careless, casual (*with blithe indifference*). □ **blithe·ly** *adverb* **blithe·ness** *noun* [Old English *blīthe* from Germanic]

blith·er /ˈblɪðər/ *var. of* BLATHER.

blith·er·ing /ˈblɪðərɪŋ/ *adjective informal* **1** senselessly talkative.
2 a (*attributive*) utter; hopeless (*blithering idiot*). **b** contemptible.

B.Litt. *abbreviation* Bachelor of Letters. [Latin *Baccalaureus Litterarum*]

blitz *informal* ● *noun* **1 a** an intensive or sudden (esp. aerial) attack.
b *informal* any sudden or concentrated effort, esp. on a large scale (*a nationwide publicity blitz*). **2** (**the Blitz**) the intensive German air raids on Britain in 1940. **3** *Football* a play in which one or more defensive backs charge the quarterback of the opposing team. ● *verb* **1** *transitive* attack, damage, or destroy by a blitz. **2** *intransitive Football* charge into the offensive backfield. □ **blitz·er** *noun* [abbreviation of BLITZKRIEG]

blitzed *adjective slang* drunk.

blitz·krieg /ˈblɪtskriːg/ *noun* an intense military campaign intended to bring about a swift victory. [German, = lightning war]

Blix·en /ˈblɪksən/ **Baroness Karen**, see DINESEN.

bliz·zard ● *noun* **1** a severe snowstorm with high winds. **2** *informal* a large amount of something (*a blizzard of paperwork*). ● *intransitive verb* (of a snowstorm) attain blizzard conditions (*they would stay in only when it was really blizzarding*). □ **bliz·zard·y** *adjective* [19th c.: origin unknown]

bloat ● *verb* **1** *transitive & intransitive* inflate, swell (*wind bloated the sheets*; *bloated with gas*). **2** *transitive* cure (a herring) by salting and smoking lightly. ● *noun* **1** an accumulation of gas in the stomach or abdomen.
2 the quality of something which has grown beyond manageable size (*administrative bloat*). [obsolete *bloat* swollen, soft and wet, perhaps from Old Norse *blautr* soaked, flabby]

bloat·ed *adjective* **1** swollen, puffed. **2** suffering from an excess of gas or water. **3** larger than necessary (*bloated bureaucracy*). **4** puffed up with pride or excessive wealth (*bloated plutocrat*).

bloat·er *noun* a herring cured by bloating.

blob *noun* **1** a small roundish mass; a drop of matter. **2** a drop of liquid.
3 a spot of colour. **4** *informal* a large shapeless person. □ **blobby** *adjective* (**blob·bi·er**, **blob·bi·est**). [imitative: compare BLEB]

bloc *noun* **1** a combination of nations, parties, groups, or people, formed to promote a particular purpose. **2** (**Bloc**) (in Canada) = BLOC QUÉBÉCOIS. [French, = block]

Bloch /blɒx/ **1 Er·nest** (1880–1959), US composer. Many of his works are inspired by Jewish folk music and liturgy. **2 Felix** (1905–83), Swiss-born US physicist, who was awarded the 1952 Nobel Prize for physics for his work on the magnetic properties of atomic nuclei.
3 Kon·rad Emil (1912–2000), German-born US biochemist, who shared the 1964 Nobel Prize for physiology or medicine for his study of cholesterol and fatty acid metabolism.

block ● *noun* **1** a solid hewn or unhewn piece of hard material, esp. of stone, wood, or ice. **2** a hollow usu. rectangular masonry building unit (*concrete block*). **3** a flat-topped block used as a base for chopping, beheading, standing something on, hammering on, or for mounting a horse from. **4** = AUCTION BLOCK. **5 a** a large building, esp. when subdivided (*apartment block*; *East Block of the Parliament Buildings*). **b** = CELLBLOCK. **6 a** an area bounded by (usu. four) streets. **b** *N Amer.* the length of one side of this, esp. as a measure of distance (*lives three blocks away*). **7 a** an obstruction (*a block in the drain*). **b** anything preventing normal progress or operation (*mental block*; *writer's block*). **8** the metal casting containing the cylinders of an internal combustion engine. **9 a** pulley or system of pulleys mounted in a case. **10** (*in pl.*) = BUILDING BLOCK. **11** *Printing* a piece of wood or metal engraved for printing on paper or fabric. **12** a head-shaped mould used for shaping hats or wigs.
13 *informal* the head (*knock his block off*). **14** a large quantity or allocation of things treated as a unit, esp. shares, seats in a theatre, etc.
15 *Computing* a collection of data that can be stored and processed as a single unit. **16** part of a body of text, etc. (*move this block to the conclusion*). **17** *Geol.* a body of rock bounded by faults. **18** a pad of paper, esp. for drawing. **19** *Athletics* = STARTING BLOCK. **20** *Sport* an obstruction of an opponent or an opponent's play. **21** a sheet of four or more unseparated postage stamps not in a strip. **22 a** a tract of land offered to an individual settler by a government. **b** a large area of land. **23** one of the small usu. square pieces of which a quilt, afghan, etc. is made. **24** a chock for stopping the motion of a wheel etc. ● *transitive verb* **1 a** (often foll. by *up*) obstruct (a passage etc.) (*the road was blocked*; *you are blocking my view*). **b** put obstacles in the way of (progress etc.).
2 a restrict the use or conversion of (currency or any other asset). **b** prevent or impede (a physiological or mental function or effect, esp. the passage of nerve impulses); interrupt the action of (a nerve, organ, etc.). **3 a** use a block for making or shaping (a hat, wig, etc.). **b** stretch (a sweater etc.) into its proper shape. **4** emboss or impress a design on (a book cover). **5** *Sport* intercept (an opponent or the ball, puck, etc.) with one's body. **6** *Theatre* plan or direct (the movements or positions of actors on stage). ● *attributive adjective* treating (many similar things) as

one unit (*block booking*). □ **block in 1** sketch roughly; plan. **2** confine.
block out 1 a shut out (light, noise, etc.). **b** exclude from memory, as being too painful. **2** sketch roughly; plan. **block up 1** confine; shut (a person etc.) in. **2** infill (a window, doorway, etc.) with bricks etc. **have been around the block** have experience. **on the block** *N Amer.* = ON THE AUCTION BLOCK (see AUCTION BLOCK). [Old French *bloc, bloquer* from Middle Dutch *blok*, of unknown origin]

block·ade ● *noun* **1** the surrounding or blocking of access to a place to prevent entry and exit of supplies etc., as a military tactic or act of protest etc. **2** anything that prevents access or progress. **3** obstruction or prevention of a physiological or mental function. ● *transitive verb* **1** subject to a blockade. **2** obstruct (a passage etc.). □ **run a blockade** enter or leave a blockaded port by evading the blockading force. □ **block·ad·er** *noun* [BLOCK + -ADE¹, prob. after *ambuscade*]

blockade-runner *noun* a vessel or person that attempts to pass through a blockade. □ **blockade-running** *noun*

block·age *noun* **1** an obstruction. **2** a blocked state.

block and tackle *noun* a system of pulleys and ropes, esp. for lifting.

block·board *noun Brit.* a plywood board with a core of wooden strips.

block·bust·er *noun* **1** an extremely popular or financially successful film, book, etc. **2** a huge bomb capable of destroying a whole block of buildings. **3** *N Amer.* (also **blockbuster trade**) *Sport* a trade involving several usu. high-profile players.

block capitals *plural noun* capital block letters.

block diagram *noun* a diagram in which squares and other conventional symbols show the general arrangement of parts of an apparatus.

blocked *adjective* **1** in senses of BLOCK *verb*. **2** *Cdn* (*Nfld*) **a** crowded, overflowing. **b** *informal* replete, full.

block·er *noun* **1** a person or thing that blocks. **2** *Hockey* a glove with a rectangular pad worn by a goaltender to protect the hand which holds the stick. **3** *Football* a player whose role is to block the opponent's play. **4** a substance which prevents or inhibits a given physiological function.

block·head *noun* a stupid person. □ **block·head·ed** *adjective*

block heater *noun N Amer.* an electric heater used to warm the coolant and hence the engine block of a motor vehicle in winter, allowing for easier starting.

block·house *noun* **1** a reinforced concrete shelter used as an observation point etc. **2** *hist.* a one- or two-storey timber building with loopholes, used as a fort.

block·ish *adjective* stupid; obtuse.

block letters *plural noun* (esp. capital) letters written without serifs and separate from each other.

block mountain *noun Geol.* a mountain formed by natural faults.

Block Parent *noun esp. Cdn proprietary* one of a number of police-screened volunteers who offer their home, identified by an easily recognizable sign, as an emergency refuge to children or others who are lost or in danger.

block party *noun N Amer.* a usu. outdoor party to which all the residents of a block or neighbourhood are invited.

block system *noun* (also **block signalling**) a system by which no railway train may enter a section of track that is not clear.

block vote *noun* a vote proportional in power to the number of people a delegate represents.

blocky *adjective* like a block; solid, chunky.

Bloc popu·laire cana·dien /blɒk ˈpɒpjuːˌler ˈkanəˌdjã/ a Canadian federal and Quebec provincial political movement formed in 1942, which favoured Canadian neutrality, provincial autonomy, a co-operative economy, and social reforms such as health insurance. It was disbanded provincially in 1948 and federally in 1949.

Bloc Québécois /blɒk keibekˈwɒ/ a federal political party advocating Quebec separatism, founded in 1990.

Bloem·fon·tein /ˈbluːmfɒnˌtein/ the capital of Free State province and judicial capital of South Africa; pop. (est. 2002) 371,200.

blog ● *noun* = WEBLOG. ● *intransitive verb* maintain a weblog. □ **blog·ger** *noun* **blog·ging** *noun* [shortening]

bloke *noun esp. Brit. informal* a man, a fellow. [Shelta]

bloke·ish *adjective* (also **blokey**) *Brit. informal* indulging in or relating to stereotypically male behaviour and interests.

Blom·idon, Cape /ˈblɒmɪdən/ the easternmost point on Cape Blomidon Peninsula, a hooked peninsula on the northwest central coast of Nova Scotia. The cape extends into Minas Basin. [contraction

---

Vowels:　a *cat*　ɑ *arm*　e *bed*　ɜr *her*　ɜː *deux*　ə *ago*　ɪ *sit*　i *cosy*　iː *feed*　ɒ *hot*　ɔ *pore*　ɔː *no*　ʌ *run*　ʊ *put*

of the nautical phrase 'blow me down', with reference to the area's susceptibility to high winds]

blond (also **blonde**) ● *adjective* **1** (of hair or the complexion) light-coloured; fair. **2** (of wood) of a light yellowish colour. ● *noun* a person with fair hair and skin. ¶ The form *blonde* is more likely to be used of females than of males, while *blond* can be used of both males and females. □ **blond·ish** *adjective* **blond·ness** *noun* [medieval Latin *blondus*, *blundus* yellow, perhaps of Germanic origin]

Blon·din /ˈblɒndɪn, blɔ̃ˈdɑ̃/ **Charles** (born Jean-François Gravelet, 1824–97), French acrobat, best known for walking across a tightrope suspended over the Niagara River gorge in 1859 and on subsequent occasions.

Blood *noun* **1** a member of an Aboriginal people of S Alberta. **2** the Algonquian language of the Blood.

blood ● *noun* **1** a usu. red liquid circulating in the arteries and veins of vertebrates that carries oxygen to and carbon dioxide from the tissues of the body. **2** a corresponding fluid in invertebrates. **3** bloodshed, esp. killing. **4** passion, temperament. **5** the blood as the vehicle of hereditary characteristics or relationship; family descent (*related by blood; musical ability runs in their blood*). **6** a relationship; relations (*own flesh and blood; blood is thicker than water*). **7** *archaic* a dandy; a man of fashion. ● *transitive verb* **1** give (a hound) a first taste of blood. **2** initiate (a person) by experience. □ **bad blood** ill feeling. **blood and guts** violence and bloodshed, esp. in fiction. **blood-and-thunder** (*attributive*) *informal* sensational, melodramatic. **one's blood is up** one is in a fighting mood. **first blood 1** the first shedding of blood, esp. in boxing. **2** the first point gained in a contest etc. **in one's blood** inherent in one's character. **make one's blood boil** infuriate one. **make one's blood run cold** horrify one. **new** (or **fresh**) **blood** new members admitted to a group, esp. as an invigorating force. **of the blood** royal. **out for a person's blood** set on getting revenge. **taste blood** be stimulated by an early success. **young blood 1** a younger member or members of a group. **2** a rake or fashionable young man. [Old English *blōd* from Germanic]

blood-alcohol level *noun* (also **blood-alcohol concentration**, **blood alcohol**) the concentration of alcohol in the blood expressed usu. as a decimal fraction representing the number of grams of alcohol per 100 ml of blood.

blood bank *noun* **1** a place where supplies of blood or plasma for transfusion are stored. **2** any supply of blood for transfusions.

blood·bath *noun* a massacre.

blood blister *noun* a blister containing blood.

blood-borne *adjective* (typically of a disease or pathogen) carried by the blood.

blood-brain barrier *noun* a semi-permeable membrane separating circulating blood from the tissue fluids surrounding brain cells.

blood brother *noun* a brother by birth or by the ceremonial mingling of blood.

blood count *noun* **1** the counting of the number of corpuscles in a specific amount of blood. **2** the number itself.

blood-curdling *adjective* horrifying.

blood donor *noun* a person who gives blood for transfusion.

blood donor clinic *noun Cdn* a usu. temporary location where people can give blood.

blood doping *noun* the practice of removing some of an athlete's blood, storing it, and replacing it just before an event to increase oxygenation.

blood·ed *adjective* **1** (in *combination*) having blood or a disposition of a specified kind (*cold-blooded; red-blooded*). **2** (of horses etc.) of good pedigree.

blood feud *noun* a feud between families involving killing or injury.

blood group *noun* = BLOOD TYPE.

blood heat *noun* the normal body temperature of a healthy human being, about 37°C or 98.4°F.

blood·hound *noun* a large hound of a breed used in tracking, having a very keen sense of smell.

blood·less *adjective* **1** without blood. **2** unemotional; cold. **3** pale. **4** without bloodshed (*a bloodless coup*). **5** feeble; lifeless. □ **blood·less·ly** *adverb* **blood·less·ness** *noun*

blood·let·ting *noun* **1** the removal of some of a person's blood for some purpose, esp. surgically or ritually. **2** bloodshed. **3** *informal* (in a workplace etc.) bitter quarrelling, esp. accompanied by reductions in staff etc.

blood·line *noun* (usu. in *pl.*) **1** (of animals) pedigree. **2** family; ancestry.

blood lust *noun* the desire for shedding blood.

blood meal *noun* dried blood used for feeding animals and as a fertilizer.

blood money *noun* **1** money paid to the next of kin of a person who has been killed. **2** money paid to a hired murderer. **3** money paid for information about a murder or murderer.

blood orange *noun* an orange with red or red-streaked pulp.

blood poisoning *noun* a diseased state caused by the presence of micro-organisms or toxins in the blood.

blood pressure *noun* the pressure of the blood in the circulatory system, often measured for diagnosis since it is closely related to the force and rate of the heartbeat and the diameter and elasticity of the arterial walls. Abbr.: **BP**.

blood-red *adjective* red as blood.

blood relative *noun* (also **blood relation**) a relative by birth, not by marriage.

blood·root *noun* an eastern N American woodland plant, *Sanguinaria canadensis*, of the poppy family, with white flowers, red sap, and a red root.

blood royal *noun* the royal family.

blood sausage *noun* (also **blood pudding**) esp. *N Amer.* a black sausage containing pork, dried pig's blood, suet, etc.

blood serum *noun see* SERUM 1, 2.

blood·shed *noun* **1** the spilling of blood. **2** slaughter.

blood·shot *adjective* (of an eyeball) inflamed, tinged with blood.

blood sport *noun* sport, esp. hunting, involving the wounding or killing of animals.

blood·stain *noun* a discoloration caused by blood.

blood·stained *adjective* **1** stained with blood. **2** guilty of bloodshed.

blood·stock *noun* thoroughbred horses.

blood·stone *noun* a type of green chalcedony spotted or streaked with red, often used as a gemstone.

blood·stream *noun* blood in circulation.

blood·suck·er *noun* **1** an animal or insect that sucks blood, esp. a leech. **2** an extortionist. □ **blood·suck·ing** *adjective*

blood sugar *noun* **1** the amount of glucose in the blood. **2** the glucose itself.

blood test *noun* a scientific examination of a blood sample, esp. for diagnosis, measurement of sugar or alcohol level, etc.

blood·thirsty *adjective* (**blood·thirst·i·er**, **blood·thirst·i·est**) **1** having a longing for blood (*bloodthirsty mosquitoes*). **2 a** eager to kill; murderous (*bloodthirsty killer*). **b** taking pleasure or showing interest in killing or violence (*bloodthirsty spectators*). **3** (of a book, film, etc.) describing or depicting killing or violence. □ **blood·thirst·i·ly** *adverb* **blood·thirst·i·ness** *noun*

blood transfusion *noun* the injection of a volume of blood, previously taken from a healthy person, into a patient.

blood type *noun* (also **blood group**) any one of the various types of human blood determining compatibility in transfusion.

blood vessel *noun* a vein, artery, or capillary carrying blood.

blood work *noun* = BLOOD TEST.

blood·worm *noun* **1** any of a variety of bright red worms of the genus *Arenicola* or *Tubifex*. **2** the aquatic larva of a midge of the genus *Chironomus*.

blood-wort *noun* any of various plants having red roots or leaves.

bloody ● *adjective* (**blood·i·er**, **blood·i·est**) **1 a** of or like blood. **b** running or smeared with blood (*bloody bandage*). **2 a** involving, loving, or resulting from bloodshed (*bloody battle*). **b** cruel (*bloody murderer*). **3** esp. *Cdn*, *Brit.*, *Austral.*, & *NZ informal* expressing annoyance or antipathy, or as an intensive (*a bloody shame; a bloody sight better; not a bloody chocolate left*). **4** red. ● *adverb informal* as an intensive (*you can bloody well think what you like*). ● *transitive verb* (**-ies**, **-ied**) make bloody; stain with blood. □ **bloodied but unbowed** proud of what one has achieved despite having suffered great difficulties or losses. **bloody murder** *N Amer.* vociferously (*screaming bloody murder*). □ **blood·i·ly** *adverb* **blood·i·ness** *noun* [Old English *blōdig* (as BLOOD, -Y¹)]

Bloody Assizes the trials of the supporters of the Duke of Monmouth after their defeat at Sedgemoor, held in SW England in 1685. Several hundred rebels were sentenced to death and about 1,000 others to slavery in America.

Bloody Caesar *noun Cdn* a drink composed of vodka and tomato clam cocktail, usu. garnished with celery.

Bloody Falls a rapids situated 16 km from the mouth of the

Coppermine River, NU. [so called with reference to an 18th-c. massacre of local Inuit]

Bloody Mary[1] see MARY I.

Bloody Mary[2] *noun* (*pl.* **Marys**) a drink composed of vodka and tomato juice.

bloody-minded *adjective informal* **1** esp. *Cdn*, *Brit.*, & *Austral.* deliberately uncooperative. **2** bloodthirsty. □ **bloody-minded·ly** *adverb* **bloody-minded·ness** *noun*

Bloody Sunday 1 in Northern Ireland, 30 January 1972, when British troops shot dead thirteen marchers in Londonderry who were protesting against the government's policy of internment. **2** in Russia, 9 January 1905 (22 January in the New Style calendar), when troops attacked and killed hundreds of unarmed workers who had gathered in St. Petersburg to present a petition to the czar. **3** in Britain, Sunday 13 Nov. in Trafalgar Square, London, 1887, when police violently broke up a socialist demonstration against the British government's Irish policy.

bloom[1] ● *noun* **1 a** a flower, esp. one cultivated for its beauty. **b** the state of flowering (*in bloom*). **2** a state of perfection or loveliness; the prime (*in full bloom*). **3 a** (of the complexion) a flush; a glow. **b** a delicate powdery surface deposit on plums, grapes, leaves, etc., indicating freshness. **c** a cloudiness on a shiny surface. **4** a scum formed by the rapid proliferation of microscopic algae on water. ● *verb* **1** *intransitive* bear flowers; be in flower. **2** *intransitive* **a** come into, or remain in, full beauty. **b** flourish; be in a healthy, vigorous state. **3** *transitive Photog.* coat (a lens) so as to reduce reflection from its surface. □ **take the bloom off** make stale. [Old Norse *blóm*, *blómi* etc. from Germanic: compare BLOSSOM]

bloom[2] ● *noun* a mass of puddled iron hammered or squeezed into a thick bar. ● *transitive verb* make into bloom. [Old English *blōma*]

bloom·er[1] *noun* **1** a plant that blooms (in a specified way) (*early autumn bloomer*). **2** *N Amer.* a person who develops or matures later (**late bloomer**) or earlier (**early bloomer**) than normal.

bloom·er[2] *noun Brit.* an oblong loaf with a rounded diagonally slashed top. [20th c.: origin uncertain]

bloom·er[3] *noun Brit. slang* = BLOOPER. [from BLOOMING *error*]

bloom·ers *plural noun* **1** women's loose-fitting almost knee-length underpants. **2** *informal* any women's underpants. **3** *hist.* women's loose-fitting trousers, gathered at the knee or (originally) the ankle. [Amelia *Bloomer*, US social reformer d.1894, who advocated a similar costume]

bloom·ery *noun* (*pl.* **-eries**) a factory that makes puddled iron into blooms.

Bloom·field, Leon·ard (1887–1949) US linguist. One of the founders of American linguistic structuralism, he is best known for his textbook *Language* (1933), which was largely dedicated to an account of the aims and techniques of the new descriptive linguistics. □ **Bloom·field·ian** *adjective & noun*

bloom·ing ● *adjective* **1** flourishing; healthy. **2** *Brit. slang* an intensive (*a blooming miracle*). ● *adverb Brit. slang* an intensive (*was blooming difficult*). [BLOOM[1] + -ING[2]: euphemism for BLOODY]

Blooms·bury (in full **Bloomsbury Group**) a group of writers, artists, and philosophers living in or associated with Bloomsbury in London, England, in the early 20th c.

bloop esp. *N Amer. Baseball* ● *transitive verb* hit (a ball) as a blooper. ● *noun* a blooper (also *attributive*: *bloop single*). [imitative; originally v., = 'howl']

bloop·er *noun informal* **1** an embarrassing blunder. **2** *Baseball* **a** a fly ball hit just beyond the infield. **b** a ball thrown high by the pitcher. [BLOOP + -ER[1]]

Bloore /blʊr/ **Ron·ald** (b.1925), Canadian painter, organizer of a group of artists (including himself) known as the Regina Five. His work is characterized by limited subject matter and a restricted palette.

Blo·quiste /blɒˈkiːst/ *noun Cdn* a member of the Bloc Québécois. [Canadian French]

blos·som ● *noun* **1** a flower or a mass of flowers, esp. of a fruit tree. **2** the stage or time of flowering (*the cherry tree in blossom*). **3** a promising stage (*the blossom of youth*). ● *intransitive verb* **1** open into flower. **2** reach a promising stage; mature, thrive. □ **blos·somy** *adjective* [Old English *blōstm(a)* prob. formed as BLOOM[1]]

blot ● *noun* **1** a spot or stain of ink etc. **2** a moral defect in an otherwise good character; a disgraceful act or quality. **3** any disfigurement or blemish. ● *verb* (**blot·ted, blot·ting**) **1 a** *transitive* spot or stain with ink; smudge. **b** *intransitive* (of a pen, ink, etc.) make blots. **2** *transitive* **a** use blotting paper or other absorbent material to absorb (liquid), esp. by dabbing or pressing rather than rubbing. **b** (of

blotting paper etc.) soak up (liquid). **3** *transitive* disgrace (*blotted her reputation*). □ **blot one's copybook** damage one's reputation. **blot on the escutcheon** a disgrace to the family name. **blot out 1 a** obliterate (writing). **b** obscure (a view, sound, etc.). **2** obliterate (from the memory) as too painful. **3** destroy. [prob. from Scandinavian: compare Icelandic *blettr* spot, stain]

blotch ● *noun* **1** a discoloured or inflamed patch on the skin. **2** an irregular patch of colour. ● *transitive verb* cover with blotches. □ **blotchy** *adjective* (**blotch·i·er, blotch·i·est**). [17th c.: from obsolete *plotch* and BLOT]

blot·ter *noun* **1** a sheet or sheets of blotting paper, usu. inserted into a frame. **2** *N Amer.* a record of arrests and charges in a police station. **3** a small piece of paper impregnated with LSD.

blotting paper *noun* unsized absorbent paper used for soaking up excess ink.

blot·to *adjective slang* very drunk. [20th c.: perhaps from BLOT]

blouse /blaʊz, blaʊs/ ● *noun* **1** a woman's or girl's lightweight upper garment, usu. with buttons and a collar. **2** a waist-length, somewhat full, belted jacket worn as part of an airman's or soldier's uniform in some military forces. **3** a loose linen or cotton garment, usu. hanging above the knees and belted at the waist. ● *transitive verb* make (a bodice etc.) loose like a blouse. [French, of unknown origin]

blous·on /ˈbluːzɒn/ *noun* a jacket cinched at the waist so that the fabric covering the torso is full. [French]

blow[1] ● *verb* (*past* **blew** /bluː/; *past participle* **blown** /bloʊn/) **1 a** *intransitive* (of the wind or air, or impersonally) move along; act as an air current (*it was blowing hard*). **b** *intransitive* be driven by an air current (*papers blew along the sidewalk*). **c** *transitive* drive with an air current (*blew the door open; blew the sign down*). **2 a** *transitive* send out (esp. air) by breathing (*blew cigarette smoke*). **b** *intransitive* send a directed air current from the mouth. **3** *transitive & intransitive* sound or be sounded by blowing (*the whistle blew; they blew the trumpets*). **4** *transitive* direct an air current at (*blew the embers*). **b** (foll. by *off, away*, etc.) clear of by means of an air current (*blew the dust off*). **5** *transitive* (*past participle* **blowed**) *slang* (esp. in *imperative*) curse, confound (*blow it!; I'll be blowed!*). **6** *transitive* **a** clear (the nose) of mucus by blowing. **b** remove contents from (an egg) by blowing through it. **7 a** *intransitive* puff, pant. **b** *transitive* (esp. in *passive*) exhaust of breath. **8** *slang* **a** *transitive* depart suddenly from (*blew the town yesterday*). **b** *intransitive* depart suddenly. **9** *transitive & intransitive* explode or cause to explode (*blew a tire; the bomb blew the building apart*). **10** *transitive & intransitive* melt or cause to melt from overloading (*the fuse has blown*). **11** *transitive* make or shape (glass or a bubble) by blowing air in. **12** *intransitive* (of a whale) eject air and water through a blowhole. **13** *transitive* break into (a safe etc.) with explosives. **14** *transitive informal* **a** squander, spend recklessly (*blew $50 on a meal*). **b** spoil, bungle (an opportunity etc.) (*he's blown his chance*). **c** waste, esp. by incompetence (*blew a two-goal lead*). **d** reveal (a secret etc.) (*blew her cover*). **15** *transitive* work the bellows of (an organ). **16** *transitive* (of flies) deposit eggs in. **17** *transitive coarse slang* fellate. **18** *transitive slang* inhale (cocaine, heroin, etc.). ● *noun* **1** an act of blowing (e.g. one's nose, a wind instrument). **b** *informal* a session of jazz playing (on any instrument). **2 a** a gust of wind or air. **b** *N Amer.* a storm. **3** *N Amer. slang* cocaine. □ **blow away** *slang* **1** kill or destroy, esp. with a gun. **2** defeat soundly. **3** impress greatly. **blow a person's cover** reveal a person's secret identity. **blow the doors off something** *N Amer.* be outstandingly more successful than something. **blow in** *informal* arrive unexpectedly. **blow a kiss** pretend to place a kiss on one's hand and blow it to a distant person. **blow a person's mind** *slang* **1** impress a person greatly; overwhelm. **2** cause a person to have drug-induced hallucination. **blow off 1** remove or be removed by the force of an air current, esp. the wind. **2** remove by an explosive force, esp. a bomb or bullet. **3** *N Amer. slang* disregard; consider insignificant. **4** *N Amer. slang* waste (time). **5** *N Amer. slang* fail to do (work) or attend (classes etc.). **blow off steam** see STEAM. **blow out 1** extinguish (esp. a flame) by blowing. **2** send outwards by an explosion. **3** (of a tire) burst. **4** (of a fuse etc.) melt. **5** *N Amer. slang* **a** defeat convincingly. **b** render useless, break (*he blew out his knee*). **6** cause to lose strength by blowing (*the storm blew itself out*). **blow out of the water** *N Amer.* defeat overwhelmingly or completely. **blow over** (of trouble etc.) fade away without serious consequences. **blow one's own horn** etc. praise oneself. **blow one's top** (or *N Amer.* **stack**) *informal* explode in rage. **blow up 1 a** shatter or destroy by an explosion. **b** explode, erupt. **2** inflate (a tire etc.). **3** *informal* **a** enlarge (a photograph). **b** exaggerate. **4** *informal* come to notice; arise. **5** *informal* lose one's temper. **blow the whistle on** see WHISTLE. [Old English *blāwan* from Germanic]

blow[2] *noun* **1** a hard stroke with a hand or weapon. **2** a sudden shock or misfortune. □ **come to blows** end up fighting. **in** (or **at**) one

blow by a single stroke; in one operation. **strike a blow for** (or **against**) help (or oppose). [15th c.: origin unknown]

blow³ /bləʊ/ *archaic* ● *intransitive verb* (*past* **blew**; *past participle* **blown**) burst into or be in flower. ● *noun* blossoming, bloom (*in full blow*). [Old English *blōwan* from Germanic]

blow·back *noun* **1** a process in which gases expand or travel in a direction opposite the usual one, esp. through escape of pressure or delayed combustion. **2** *slang* the unintended consequences of an action, esp. of covert political action.

blow-by-blow *attributive adjective* (of a description etc.) giving all the details in sequence.

blow·down *noun N Amer.* **1** the uprooting of trees by the wind. **2** a tree so felled.

blow-dried *adjective* **1** (of hair) dried with a blow-dryer. **2** (of a person) well-groomed and usu. superficially or pretentiously suave; slick.

blow-dry ● *transitive verb* arrange (the hair) while drying it with a hand-held dryer. ● *noun* an act of doing this. □ **blow-dryer** *noun*

blow·er *noun* **1** *in senses of* BLOW¹ *verb*. **2** a device for creating a current of air. **3** *informal* a telephone.

blow·fish *noun* = PUFFERFISH.

blow·fly *noun* (*pl.* **-flies**) any of various flies of the family Calliphoridae, which deposit their eggs on meat and carcasses, e.g. the bluebottle.

blow·gun *noun* a hunting weapon consisting of a tube from which arrows or darts are propelled by blowing.

blow·hard *informal* ● *noun* a boastful or pompous person. ● *adjective* boastful; blustering.

blow·hole *noun* **1** the nostril of a whale, on the top of its head. **2** a hole in ice through which seals or other animals breathe. **3** a vent for air, smoke, etc., in a tunnel etc. **4** a hole in a coastal rock or cliff through which jets of spray and water are intermittently forced upward. **5** a hole or bubble in metal formed by escaping gas during solidification.

blowing snow *noun* snow whipped up by the wind to a height of two metres or more from accumulations on the ground.

blow job *noun coarse slang* an act of fellatio.

blow·lamp *noun Brit.* = BLOWTORCH.

blown *past participle of* BLOW¹, BLOW³.

blow·out *noun* **1** *informal* a burst tire. **2** *N Amer. informal* a game, election, etc. with a lopsided result. **3** *informal* an elaborate party or feast; an extravaganza. **4** *N Amer. informal* a sale in a retail store featuring drastic price reductions. **5** a rapid uncontrolled uprush from an oil or gas well. **6** a rockburst. **7** *N Amer.* a hollow in the ground caused by wind erosion.

blow·pipe *noun* **1** = BLOWGUN. **2** a tube used to intensify the heat of a flame by blowing air or other gas through it at high pressure. **3** a tube used in glass-blowing.

blowsy /ˈblaʊzi/ *adjective* (also **blowzy**) (**blows·i·er**, **blows·i·est**) **1** coarse and red-faced. **2** dishevelled, slovenly. □ **blows·i·ly** *adverb* **blows·i·ness** *noun* [obsolete *blowze* beggar's wench, of unknown origin]

blow·torch *noun* a portable device which creates a very hot flame, used for welding etc.

blow-up ● *noun* **1** an enlargement (of a photograph etc.). **2** an explosion. **3** *N Amer. informal* a quarrel. ● *attributive adjective* **1** inflatable (a *blow-up toy*). **2** enlarged (a *blow-up photograph*).

blowy *adjective* (**blow·i·er**, **blow·i·est**) windy, windswept.

blowzy *var. of* BLOWSY.

B.L.S. *abbreviation* Bachelor of Library Science.

BLT *noun* a bacon, lettuce, and tomato sandwich. [abbreviation]

blub *intransitive verb* (**blubbed**, **blub·bing**) *Brit. slang* sob. [abbreviation of BLUBBER¹]

blub·ber¹ ● *noun* **1** an insulating layer of fat in whales, seals, polar bears and other swimming mammals. **2** body fat. **3** a period of weeping. ● *verb* **1** *intransitive* weep loudly. **2** *transitive* sob out (words). □ **blub·ber·er** *noun* **blub·bery** *adjective* [Middle English perhaps imitative (obsolete meanings 'foaming, bubble')]

blub·ber² *adjective* (of the lips) swollen, protruding. [earlier *blabber*, *blobber*, imitative]

Blü·cher /ˈbluːkər/ **Geb·hard Lebe·recht von** (1742–1819), Prussian field marshal, commander of the Prussian forces which helped to defeat Napoleon at Waterloo (1815).

blu·chers /ˈbluːkərz, -tʃərz/ *plural noun* laced half-boots or high shoes in which the vamp and tongue are formed from a single piece of strong leather. [G. L. von *Blücher*, Prussian general d.1819]

bludg·eon /ˈblʌdʒən/ ● *noun* a club with a heavy end. ● *transitive verb* **1** beat with a bludgeon. **2** coerce. [18th c.: origin unknown]

blue¹ ● *adjective* **1** having a colour between green and violet in the spectrum, like that of a clear sky. **2** sad, depressed; (of a state of affairs) gloomy, dismal (*feel blue*). **3** with bluish skin through cold, fear, anger, etc. **4** having blue or a bluish shade as a distinguishing colour (*blue jay*; *blue whale*). **5** indecent, pornographic (a *blue film*). **6** *Cdn & Brit.* politically conservative. **7** (of cooked beef, esp. steak) very rare, almost raw. ● *noun* **1** a blue colour or pigment. **2** blue clothes or material (*dressed in blue*). **3** (also **Blue**) *Cdn & Brit.* a supporter of a Conservative party. **4** any of various small blue butterflies of the family Lycaenidae. **5** *Brit.* **a** a person who has represented a university in a sport, esp. Oxford or Cambridge. **b** this distinction. **6** *Brit.* = BLUING. **7** a blue ball, piece, etc. in a game or sport. **8** *Cdn* (usu. in *pl.*) a blue seat in a hockey arena etc., usu. a less expensive one at some distance from the playing surface. **9** *N Amer. Printing* (usu. in *pl.*) a print made on photosensitive paper, usu. blue on white, used to produce proofs before printing plates are made from the film. **10** (prec. by *the*) the clear sky. ● *transitive verb* (**blues**, **blued**, **blu·ing** or **blue·ing**) **1** make blue. **2** treat (laundry) with bluing. □ **do something until one is blue in the face** do something repeatedly and at great length until one becomes frustrated, exasperated, angry, etc. **blue murder** = BLOODY MURDER (see BLOODY). **once in a blue moon** very rarely. **out of the blue** unexpectedly. **talk etc. a blue streak** esp. *N Amer.* speak etc. in a swift and continuous stream of words. □ **blue·ness** *noun* [Old French *bleu* from Germanic]

blue² *transitive verb* (**blues**, **blued**, **blu·ing** or **blue·ing**) *Brit. slang* squander (money). [perhaps var. of BLOW¹]

blue baby *noun* a baby with bluish-tinged skin from lack of oxygen in the blood due to a congenital defect of the heart or major blood vessels.

blue·back *noun* **1** any of several fishes, esp. two species of Pacific coast salmon: **a** *Cdn* a small or immature coho. **b** = SOCKEYE. **2** *Cdn* a very young hooded seal. **3** (also **blueback herring**) a herring, *Alosa aestivalis*, very similar to the alewife, with a dark blue or greyish back.

blue-bead lily *noun* = CLINTONIA.

Blue·beard *noun* a man who murders his wives. [a character in a fairy tale told originally in French (*Barbe-Bleue*) by Perrault]

blue beech *noun* a tree of eastern N America, *Carpinus caroliniana*, with strong wood and smoothly ridged bark. Also called HORNBEAM, MUSCLEWOOD, IRONWOOD.

blue·bell *noun* **1** = HAREBELL. **2** any of several liliaceous Eurasian plants of the genus *Endymion*, esp. *E. nonscriptus*, with clusters of bell-shaped blue flowers on a stem arising from a rhizome. **3** any of several other plants with blue bell-shaped flowers, esp. of the genus *Mertensia*.

blue beret *noun* = BLUE HELMET.

blue·berry *noun* (*pl.* **-berries**) **1** any of several plants of the genus *Vaccinium*, cultivated for their edible fruit. **2** the small blue-black fruit of these plants.

blueberry buckle *noun Cdn* (*Maritimes*) a cake topped with blueberries and a crumbly topping.

blueberry grunt *noun see* GRUNT 6.

blueberry tea *noun* a mixed drink of Amaretto, Grand Marnier, and tea.

blue·bird *noun* any of various N American songbirds of the thrush family, esp. of the genus *Sialia*, the males having distinctive blue plumage usu. on the back or head.

blue-black ● *noun* a black colour with a tinge of blue. ● *adjective* of this colour.

blue·blood *noun* **1** *N Amer.* a wealthy or socially prominent person. **2** an aristocrat. **3** (**blue blood**) noble birth. □ **blue-blooded** *adjective* [translation of Spanish *sangre azul*, claimed by certain families of Castile, as having no admixture of other races]

blue book *noun* **1** (**Blue Book**) *Cdn* a report of estimated government expenditures tabled annually in the House of Commons. **2** *N Amer.* a reference book listing the market value of certain consumer items, esp. used cars. **3** *Brit.* a parliamentary or Privy Council report. **4** a directory listing people considered socially important. **5** *US* a university examination booklet.

blue·bottle *noun* **1** any of several large blowflies with a metallic-blue body, esp. *Calliphora vomitoria*. **2** a dark blue cornflower. **3** *Brit. informal* a police officer. **4** esp. *Austral.* a Portuguese man-of-war.

---

t top   v voice   w we   z zoo   ʃ she   ʒ vision   θ thin   ð this   ŋ ring   x loch   tʃ chip   dʒ jar   (*see over for vowels*)

blue box *noun* **1** *Cdn* a blue plastic box for the collection of recyclable household materials. **2** *esp. US* an electronic device used to access long-distance telephone lines illegally.

blue cheese *noun* any of several strong cheeses produced with veins of blue mould, e.g. Gorgonzola or roquefort.

blue chip ● *noun* a stock exchange investment considered to be fairly reliable though not entirely without risk. ● *attributive adjective* (usu. **blue-chip**) **1** (of an investment, company, etc.) reliable; consistently giving a good yield. **2** of the highest quality. [from *blue chip*, a high-value counter in gambling games]

blue chipper *noun N Amer. informal* **1** a blue-chip company. **2** an excellent athlete.

blue-collar *adjective* of or relating to manual or industrial labourers, usu. paid wages rather than salary (*compare* WHITE-COLLAR).

blue crab *noun* a large edible crab of the N American Atlantic coast, *Callinectes sapidus*, having a pale green shell and bluish legs.

Blue Ensign *noun* (in the UK) the ensign of government departments and formerly of the naval reserve etc.

blue-eyed *adjective* **1** having blue eyes. **2** *esp. Brit.* = FAIR-HAIRED 2.

blue-eyed grass *noun* any of several plants of the genus *Sisyrinchium*, related to the iris, having grassy leaves and blue or violet flowers.

blue-eyed Mary *noun* **1** any of several western N American plants of the genus *Collinsia*, having mauve or purplish-blue flowers. **2** a blue-flowered European ornamental plant, *Omphalodes verna*.

Bluefields a port on the Mosquito Coast of Nicaragua, situated on an inlet of the Caribbean Sea; pop. (est. 2002) 43,200.

bluefin *noun* (in full **bluefin tuna**) the common tuna, *Thunnus thynnus*.

bluefish *noun* **1** a voracious blue marine fish, *Pomatomus saltatrix*, inhabiting warmer waters of the Atlantic and Indian oceans and popular as a food and game fish. *Also called* SNAPPER. **2** (in full **Boston bluefish**) = POLLOCK 1.

blue funk *noun informal* **1** *N Amer.* a state of dejection or depression. **2** *Brit.* a state of great nervousness or panic.

bluegill *noun* a small colourful N American freshwater sunfish, *Lepomis macrochirus*.

blue goose *noun* a colour phase of the snow goose having bluish-grey plumage.

blue grama *noun* a grass of the shortgrass prairie, *Bouteloua gracilis*, also grown as an ornamental. *Also called* SPEAR GRASS, JUNE GRASS.

bluegrass *noun* **1** any of several bluish-green grasses of the genus *Poa*, esp. Kentucky bluegrass. **2** a kind of country music characterized by close harmony and virtuosic playing of banjos, guitars, fiddles, etc.

blue-green algae *plural noun* = CYANOBACTERIA.

blue ground *noun* = KIMBERLITE.

blue grouse *noun* a large grouse of the mountains of western N America, *Dendragapus obscurus*, with feathered legs and a slaty blue colouring.

blue gum *noun* any Australasian tree of the genus *Eucalyptus*, esp. *E. regnans* or *E. globulus* with blue-green aromatic leaves.

blue-haired *adjective informal* elderly.

blue helmet *noun* (also **blue beret**) *informal* a United Nations peacekeeping soldier. [with reference to their pale blue headgear]

blue heron *noun* = GREAT BLUE HERON.

blue ice *noun Cdn* a vivid blue ice formed when a large amount of water freezes quickly.

bluejacket *noun informal* a sailor in the navy.

blue jay *noun* a crested jay of central and eastern N America, *Cyanocitta cristata*, having a large tail and blue, black, and white plumage.

blue jeans *plural noun* pants made of blue denim. □ **blue-jeaned** *adjective*

blue-joint *noun* a N American grass, *Calamagrostis canadensis*, growing in wet places.

blue law *noun N Amer.* (usu. in *pl.*) a law considered severely puritanical or restrictive, e.g. those forbidding all secular activities on Sunday.

blue line *noun Hockey* **1** one of the two lines on the ice surface between the centre and the goal. **2** a team's defencemen collectively.

blue-liner *noun N Amer. informal* a hockey defenceman.

blue mould *noun* a bluish fungus of the genus *Penicillium* growing on food (esp. cheeses) and other organic matter.

Blue Mountains 1 a section of the Great Dividing Range in New South Wales, Australia. Part of it is a national park and nature reserve.

2 a range of mountains in E Jamaica. **3** a range of mountains running from central Oregon to SE Washington state in the US.

Blue Mountains, The a town in south central Ontario, on the south shore of Nottawasaga Bay about 22 km west of Collingwood, including the former town of Thornbury; pop. (2001) 6,116.

Blue Nile one of the two principal headwaters of the Nile. Rising from Lake Tana in NW Ethiopia, it flows some 1 600 km (1,000 miles) southward then northwestward into Sudan, where it meets the White Nile at Khartoum.

Bluenose *noun* **1** (also **Bluenoser**) *Cdn informal* a Nova Scotian. **2** *US* (**bluenose**) a puritanical or prudish person. [origin unknown: variously explained as referring to fishermen's noses blue from cold, to the name of a potato with a blue protuberance, or to Scots Presbyterians referred to as 'true blue' in the 17th c.]

blue note *noun Music* a flatted third, fifth, or seventh in a chord, often used in the blues.

blue pages *plural noun N Amer.* the pages of a telephone directory containing listings of government departments and services.

blue-pencil *transitive verb* (**-pencilled**, **-pencil·ling**; also **-penciled**, **-pencil·ing**) edit or alter (a manuscript etc.).

blue peter *noun* a blue flag with a white square, representing *P* and raised on board a ship leaving port.

blue plate *adjective N Amer.* (of a restaurant meal) consisting of a full main course ordered as a single menu item (*blue plate special*).

blueprint ● *noun* **1** a photographic print of the final stage of engineering or other plans in white on a blue background. **2** a detailed plan, esp. in the early stages of a project or idea. ● *transitive verb N Amer.* plan, project; make a blueprint of (a building, etc.).

Blue Puttees *plural noun* the first 500 volunteers to join the Royal Newfoundland Regiment at the outbreak of war in 1914. [so-called because there was not enough of the standard khaki material available for the soldiers' puttees and blue cloth was used instead]

blue ribbon ● *noun* **1** the highest honour in a competition etc. **2** (in Canada) a ribbon awarded to the second-place finisher in a competition. ● *attributive adjective* (usu. **blue-ribbon**) **1** of the highest quality. **2** (of a committee, jury, etc.) carefully or specially selected.

Blue Ridge Mountains a range of the Appalachian Mountains in the eastern US, stretching from S Pennsylvania to N Georgia.

blue rinse ● *noun* a preparation for tinting grey hair. ● *adjective* (also **blue-rinse**, **blue-rinsed**) composed of or relating to esp. conservative elderly women.

blue roan ● *adjective* black mixed with white. ● *noun* a blue roan animal.

blues /bluːz/ *plural noun* **1** (prec. by *the*) a bout of depression (*had a fit of the blues*). **2 a** (prec. by *the*; often treated as *sing.*) a melancholic musical style characterized by frequent blues notes and often in a twelve-bar sequence. **b** (*attributive*) of or relating to such music (*the band played a blues number*). □ **bluesy** *adjective* (in sense 2).

blue screen *noun* a special-effects technique used in films and TV in which scenes shot against a blue background are superimposed on other scenes.

blue shark *noun* a large common shark, *Prionace glauca*, having a deep blue body and a white underbelly.

blue shift *noun* the shift of spectral lines toward shorter wavelengths, arising when a galaxy or celestial body and its observer are moving toward each other (*compare* RED SHIFT). □ **blue·shift·ed** *adjective*

blue-sky *adjective* **1** *N Amer.* **a** (of a security) having no value. **b** (of a law) intended to prevent the sale of worthless securities. **2** not practical; unrealistic.

bluesman /'bluːzmən/ *noun* (*pl.* **-men**) a musician, esp. a professional, who plays the blues.

blue spruce *noun* a N American spruce with bluish-green needles, *Picea pungens*, widely grown as an ornamental. *Also called* COLORADO SPRUCE.

bluestem *noun* any of several tall N American grasses of the genus *Andropogon*, growing in prairie regions and often used for forage.

blue·stock·ing *noun* usu. *derogatory* a woman having or affecting scholarly or literary interests. [originally a frequenter of the 'blue-stocking' literary assemblies held in London *c*.1750 (from the less formal blue stockings worn by some men): later applied only to women]

bluestone *noun* any of various bluish or grey building stones.

bluet /'bluːət/ *noun* (usu. in *pl.*) a N American blue-flowered plant of the madder family, *Hedyotis caerulia*.

blue tit *noun* a common European bird, *Parus caeruleus*, with a distinct blue crest on a black and white head.

blue·tongue *noun* a non-contagious viral disease of sheep and other animals, characterized by fever, lameness, and swelling of the mouth and tongue.

Blue·water a town in south central Ontario, on the east shore of Lake Huron, south of Goderich; pop. (2001) 6,916.

blue water *noun* open sea.

blue·weed *noun N Amer.* = VIPER'S BUGLOSS.

blue whale *noun* a baleen whale, *Balaenoptera musculus*, the largest of all living animals, reaching a length of up to 30 m (100 ft.).

blue willow *noun* = WILLOW PATTERN.

blue-winged teal *noun see* TEAL *noun* 1.

bluey *adjective* = BLUISH.

bluff¹ ● *verb* 1 *intransitive* make a pretense of strength or confidence to gain an advantage. 2 *transitive* mislead by bluffing. ● *noun* an act of bluffing; a show of confidence or assertiveness intended to deceive. □ **call a person's bluff** challenge a person thought to be bluffing. □ **bluff·er** *noun* [19th c. (originally in poker) from Dutch *bluffen* brag]

bluff² ● *noun* 1 a steep cliff or bank. 2 *Cdn* (*Prairies*) a grove or clump of trees, usu. poplars or willows. ● *adjective* 1 (of a person or manner) good-naturedly blunt, frank, hearty. 2 (of a cliff, or a ship's bows) having a vertical or steep broad front. □ **bluff·ly** *adverb* (in sense 1 of *adjective*). **bluff·ness** *noun* (in sense 1 of *adjective*). [17th-c. Naut. word: origin unknown]

blu·ing /ˈbluːɪŋ/ *noun* a blue powder or liquid used to prevent white laundry from yellowing.

blu·ish *adjective* somewhat blue.

Blum /bluːm/ **Léon** (1872–1950), French Socialist politician, prime minister 1936–7, 1938, 1946–7. He introduced significant labour reforms, and was arrested (1940), tried (1942), and imprisoned (1943–5) by the Vichy government during the Second World War.

Blumen·bach /ˈbluːmənˌbɒx/ **Jo·hann Frie·drich** (1752–1840), German physiologist and comparative anatomist, who classified humans into five broad categories (Caucasian, Mongoloid, Malayan, Ethiopian, and American), based mainly on cranial measurements.

Blun·den /ˈblʌndən/ **Ed·mund Charles** (1869–1974), English poet whose work, rooted in rural life, includes *Undertones of War* (1928), an account of his experiences in the First World War.

blun·der ● *noun* a careless or foolish mistake, esp. an important one. ● *verb* 1 *intransitive* make a blunder; act clumsily or ineptly. 2 *transitive* deal incompetently with; mismanage. 3 *intransitive* move about blindly or clumsily; stumble. □ **blun·der·er** *noun* **blun·der·ing·ly** *adverb* [prob. from Scandinavian: compare Middle Swedish *blundra* shut the eyes]

blunder·buss ● *noun hist.* a short large-bored gun which sprays several balls or slugs simultaneously at close range. ● *adjective* (of a method, approach, etc.) ostensibly wide-ranging but poorly focused and ineffective. [alteration of Dutch *donderbus* thunder gun, assoc. with BLUNDER]

Blunt, An·thony Fred·erick (1907–83), English art historian, Foreign Office official, and spy. A leading art historian and Surveyor of the King's (later the Queen's) Pictures (1945–72), he confessed in 1965 that he had been a Soviet agent since the 1930s and had facilitated the escape of the spies Guy Burgess and Donald Maclean in 1951.

blunt ● *adjective* 1 (of a knife, pencil, etc.) lacking in sharpness; having a worn-down point or edge. 2 (of a person or manner) direct, uncompromising, outspoken. 3 short and with a squared-off end (*blunt fingers*). ● *transitive verb* 1 make blunt or less sharp. 2 weaken or reduce the sensitivity of (the senses, one's feelings, etc.). ● *noun* a short cigar, esp. one containing drugs. □ **blunt·ly** *adverb* (in sense 2 of *adjective*). **blunt·ness** *noun* [perhaps from Scandinavian: compare Old Norse *blunda* shut the eyes]

blur ● *verb* (**blurred, blur·ring**) 1 *transitive & intransitive* make or become unclear or less distinct. 2 *transitive* smear; partially efface. 3 *transitive* make (one's memory, perception, etc.) dim or less clear. ● *noun* something that appears or sounds indistinct or unclear. □ **blur·ry** *adjective* (**blur·ri·er, blur·ri·est**). **blur·ri·ness** *noun* [16th c.: perhaps related to BLEAR]

blurb ● *noun* a promotional (usu. complimentary) description, esp. printed on a book's jacket by its publisher. ● *transitive & intransitive verb* print or utter a blurb. [coined by G. Burgess, US humorist d.1951]

blurt *transitive verb* (usu. foll. by *out*) utter abruptly, thoughtlessly, or tactlessly. [prob. imitative]

blush ● *intransitive verb* 1 **a** develop a pink tinge in the face from embarrassment or shame. **b** (of the face) redden in this way. 2 feel embarrassed or ashamed. 3 be or become red or pink. ● *noun* 1 the act of blushing. 2 a pink tinge. 3 *N Amer.* (also **blush·er**) a cosmetic used to give a pinkish colour to the cheeks. 4 a fairly sweet, pale pink wine made from black-skinned grapes. □ **at first blush** on the first glimpse or impression. **save a person's blushes** refrain from causing embarrassment. [Old English *blyscan*]

blus·ter ● *intransitive verb* 1 behave pompously and boisterously; utter empty threats. 2 (of the wind etc.) blow fiercely. ● *noun* 1 noisily self-assertive talk. 2 empty threats. □ **blus·te·rer** *noun* **blus·tery** *adjective* [16th c.: ultimately imitative]

Blvd *abbreviation* Boulevard.

B lymphocyte *noun* = B CELL.

Bly·ton /ˈblaɪtən/ **Enid** (1897–1968), English writer of over 400 children's books and creator of the popular character Noddy.

BM *abbreviation* 1 British Museum. 2 Bachelor of Medicine. 3 *informal* bowel movement.

BMI *abbreviation* BODY MASS INDEX.

B movie *noun* a film regarded as second-rate, esp. one which relies on stereotypes and formulas.

B.Mus. *abbreviation* Bachelor of Music.

B.Mus.A. *abbreviation* Bachelor of Musical Arts.

B.Mus.Ed. *abbreviation* Bachelor of Music Education.

BMX *noun* 1 organized bicycle racing on a dirt track, esp. for youngsters. 2 the sturdy, manoeuvrable kind of bicycle used for this. 3 (*attributive*) of or related to such racing or the equipment used (*BMX gloves*). [abbreviation of bicycle *moto-cross*]

B.N. *abbreviation* Bachelor of Nursing.

Bn. *abbreviation* Battalion.

bn. *abbreviation* billion.

BNA *abbreviation hist.* British North America.

BNA Act *abbreviation* = BRITISH NORTH AMERICA ACT.

B'nai Brith /bəˌneɪ bəˈriːθ, brɪθ/ a Jewish organization founded in New York in 1843, which pursues educational, humanitarian, and cultural activities and attempts to safeguard the rights and interests of Jews around the world. [Hebrew, = sons of the covenant]

B.N.R.N. *abbreviation* Bachelor of Nursing (Registered Nurse).

B.O. *abbreviation* 1 *informal* BODY ODOUR. 2 BOX OFFICE.

boa /ˈboːə/ *noun* 1 any of several large snakes of the subfamily Boinae, found mainly in warm regions, which crush and suffocate their prey. 2 any related snake which is similar in appearance, such as the python or anaconda. 3 a long thin scarf made of feathers or fur. [Latin]

Boab·dil /boːəbˈdel/ (born Abu Abdallah) (d.1527), the last Moorish sultan of Granada 1482–3 and 1486–92.

boa constrictor *noun* a large snake, *Constrictor constrictor*, native to tropical America and the West Indies, which crushes its prey.

Boa·di·cea *see* BOUDICCA.

boar *noun* 1 (in full **wild boar**) a tusked wild pig of Eurasia and Africa, *Sus scrofa*, from which domestic pigs are descended. 2 an uncastrated male pig. 3 its flesh. 4 a male guinea pig etc. [Old English *bār* from West Germanic]

board ● *noun* 1 **a** a flat thin piece of sawn timber, usu. long and narrow. **b** a material resembling this, made from compressed or synthetic fibres (*cardboard; particleboard*). **c** a thin slab of wood or a similar substance, often with a covering, used for any of various purposes (*chessboard; ironing board; notice board*). **d** thick stiff card used in bookbinding. 2 = CIRCUIT BOARD. 3 the provision of regular meals, usu. with accommodation, for payment. 4 **a** the directors of a company or other organization. **b** a specially constituted administrative body. 5 *N Amer.* (in *pl.*) the wooden fence-like structure enclosing the ice surface of a skating rink. 6 (in *pl.*) the stage of a theatre (*compare* TREAD THE BOARDS, *see* TREAD). 7 (in *pl.*) *slang* skis. 8 *Naut.* the side of a ship. 9 *archaic* a table spread for a meal. 10 *Basketball slang* a rebound. ● *verb* 1 **a** *transitive & intransitive* go on board (a ship, aircraft, train, etc.). **b** *transitive* force one's way on board (a ship etc.) in attack. **c** *intransitive* receive passengers (*the plane is now boarding*). **d** *transitive* allow (passengers) on board; load (an airplane) (*passengers with children are boarded first; we will board the plane by seat and row number*). 2 **a** *intransitive* receive regular meals, or meals and lodging, for payment. **b** *transitive* (often foll. by *out*) arrange accommodation away from home for (*boarded the dog while we were on vacation*). **c** *transitive* provide (a lodger etc.) with regular meals. 3 *transitive* (usu. foll. by *up*) cover with boards; seal or close. 4 *transitive Hockey* bodycheck (an opponent) into the boards with excessive force. □ **across the board** general; generally; applying to all. **go by the board** be neglected, omitted, or discarded. **on board 1** on or in a ship, aircraft, train, etc. **2** present and functioning as a member of a team, corporation, etc. **3** *Baseball* on base. **take on board** consider (a new idea etc.). [Old English *bord* from Germanic]

board and batten *noun* a siding of vertical plywood sheets with battens at the joints between one sheet and the next.

board book *noun* a book for very small children, with the pages pasted to heavy cardboard.

board·er *noun* **1** a person who boards (*see* BOARD *verb* 2a), esp. a lodger or a pupil at a boarding school. **2** a person who boards a ship, esp. an enemy. **3** a person who takes part in a sport using a board, such as snowboarding, skateboarding, or surfing.

board foot *noun* N Amer. a unit of volume for lumber equal to 144 cubic inches, or one square foot of one-inch-thick board.

board game *noun* a game played on a board, usu. with special pieces, dice, etc.

board·ing *noun* **1** *Hockey* the infraction of bodychecking an opponent into the boards with excessive force. **2** snowboarding (*Tristan loves to go boarding*).

boarding house *noun* an establishment providing board and lodging for paying guests.

boarding-house reach *noun* N Amer. informal jocular the practice of reaching for food at a dining table with total disregard for one's dinner companions.

boarding kennel *noun* (often in *pl.*) a boarding establishment for dogs.

boarding pass *noun* a pass which permits a passenger to board an airplane, usu. indicating the departure gate and seat number etc.

boarding school *noun* a school at which most or all pupils are resident during the school term.

board of control *noun* Cdn (in Ontario) an elected body in municipal government having executive powers, comprising the mayor of a municipality and controllers elected on a city-wide basis rather than to represent wards.

board of education *noun* N Amer. (*Ont.* & *US*) **1** a body responsible for administering public schools within a stated jurisdiction. **2** the jurisdiction covered by such a board.

board of trade *noun* N Amer. a chamber of commerce.

board·room *noun* a meeting room in which the directors of a company etc. convene.

board·sail·ing *noun* = WINDSURFING. □ **board·sail·or** *noun* (also **board·sail·er**).

board shorts *plural noun* long shorts of a kind orig. worn by surfers.

board·walk *noun* N Amer. a walkway of crosswise wooden boards, constructed esp. on sand etc.

boart *var. of* BORT.

Boas /ˈboːaz/ **Franz** (1858–1942), German-born US anthropologist. Studying Inuit and other N American Aboriginal societies, he revolutionized his field by insisting on relativism rather than assuming a single, hierarchical, racially correlated culture.

boast¹ ● *verb* **1** *intransitive* declare one's achievements, possessions, or abilities with indulgent pride and satisfaction. **2** *transitive* own or have as something praiseworthy etc. (*the hotel boasts magnificent views*). ● *noun* **1** an act of boasting. **2** something one is proud of. □ **boast·er** *noun* **boast·ing·ly** *adverb* [Anglo-French *bost*, of unknown origin]

boast² ● *noun* (in squash etc.) a shot in which the ball strikes either of the side walls before hitting the end wall. ● *transitive & intransitive verb* play a shot of this type. [perhaps from French *bosse* a projection of the wall in a French tennis court]

boast·ful *adjective* **1** given to boasting. **2** characterized by boasting (*boastful talk*). □ **boast·ful·ly** *adverb* **boast·ful·ness** *noun*

boat ● *noun* **1** a small vessel propelled on water by an engine, oars, or sails. **2** (in general use) a ship of any size. **3** an elongated boat-shaped container for holding gravy, sauce, etc. ● *verb* **1** *intransitive* travel or go in a boat, esp. for pleasure. **2** *transitive* catch (a fish) and bring it into a boat. □ **off the boat** often *offensive* recently arrived from a foreign country. **in the same boat** sharing the same (usu. adverse) circumstances. □ **boat·ful** *noun* (*pl.* **-fuls**). [Old English *bāt* from Germanic]

boat·er *noun* **1** a person who boats, esp. as a recreation. **2** a flat-topped hardened straw hat with a brim.

boat·hook *noun* a long pole with a hook and a spike at one end, for pulling or pushing a boat.

boat·house *noun* a shed at the edge of a river, lake, etc., for housing boats.

boat·ing *noun* the use of boats as a form of recreation or sport.

boat launch *noun* a place or contrivance for launching a boat.

boat·load *noun* **1** enough to fill a boat. **2** *informal* a large number of people or things.

boat·man *noun* (*pl.* **-men**) a man who hires out boats or provides transport by boat.

boat neck *noun* a wide neckline passing just below the collarbone.

boat people *plural noun* refugees who have fled a country by sea.

boat·port *noun* a floating roofed enclosure for boats, usu. with open sides.

boat shoe *noun* = DECK SHOE.

boat·swain /ˈboːsən/ *noun* (also **bo'sun, bosun, bo's'n**) a ship's officer in charge of equipment and the duties of the crew. [Old English *bātswegen* (as BOAT, SWAIN)]

boatswain's chair *noun* a seat suspended from ropes for work on the side of a ship or building.

boat train *noun* a train scheduled to connect with the arrival or departure of a boat.

boat·yard *noun* a place where boats are built, repaired, stored, etc.

Boa Vista /ˌboːə ˈvɪstə/ a city in N Brazil; pop. (est. 2002) 221,100.

Boaz /ˈboːaz/ *Bible* the husband of Ruth (Ruth 2–4).

Bob *noun* □ **Bob's your uncle** Cdn & Brit. slang an expression of completion or satisfaction. [pet form of the name *Robert*]

bob¹ ● *verb* (**bobbed, bob·bing**) **1** *intransitive* move quickly up and down, esp. on water. **2** *transitive* move (the body or part of it) up and down with a slight jerk. **3** *intransitive* curtsy. ● *noun* **1** a jerking or bouncing movement, esp. upward. **2** a curtsy. **3** = BOBBER. □ **bob for** try to catch (floating apples etc.) with the mouth alone, as a game. **bob up** come to the surface or reappear suddenly. [14th c.: prob. imitative]

bob² ● *noun* **1** a woman's or child's hairstyle cut short and even all around. **2** a weight on a pendulum, plumb line, or kite tail. **3 a** a short runner on a sled etc. **b** = BOBSLED. **4** a horse's docked tail. **5** a short line at or towards the end of a stanza. ● *transitive verb* (**bobbed, bob·bing**) cut (hair) short and even all around. [Middle English: origin unknown]

bob³ *noun* (*pl.* same) Brit. slang hist. a shilling. □ **a few bob** an unspecified amount of money. [19th c.: origin unknown]

bob·ber *noun* N Amer. a float used in fishing to suspend a line or net at a fixed depth.

bob·bin *noun* **1** a cylinder or cone holding thread, yarn, wire, etc., used esp. in weaving and machine sewing. **2** a spool or reel. [French *bobine*]

bobbin lace *noun* lace made by hand with thread wound on bobbins and worked on a pillow. Also called PILLOW LACE.

bob·ble¹ ● *verb* **1** *intransitive* move with continual bobbing. **2** *transitive* N Amer. mishandle or fumble (a ball). ● *noun* N Amer. a mistake or error, esp. a fumble of a ball. [diminutive of BOB¹]

bob·ble² *noun* a small woolly or tufted ball as a decoration or trimming. □ **bob·bled** *adjective* [diminutive of BOB²]

bobble-head doll *adjective* a small figurine with a disproportionately large bobbing head, esp. representing a popular sports figure or celebrity.

bobby *noun* (*pl.* **-bies**) Brit. informal a police officer. [Sir *Robert* Peel, d.1850, founder of the British metropolitan police force]

bobby pin *noun* N Amer., Austral., & NZ a flat hairpin of metal bent double. [BOB² + -Y²]

bobby socks *plural noun* esp. N Amer. socks reaching just above the ankle, esp. worn by teenage girls in the 1940s and 1950s.

bobby soxer *noun* esp. N Amer. an adolescent girl, esp. one of the 1940s, wearing bobby socks.

Bob·Cat *noun* proprietary a type of small, highly manoeuvrable front-end loader.

bob·cat *noun* a small N American lynx, *Felis rufus*, with a spotted reddish-brown coat and a short tail. [BOB² + CAT]

bobo·link /ˈbɒbəlɪŋk/ *noun* a N American songbird, *Dolichonyx oryzivorus*, the male of which is black with yellow and white markings, and the female yellowish buff. [originally *Bob (o') Lincoln*: imitative of its call]

Consonants: b *but*   d *dog*   f *few*   g *get*   h *her*   j *yes*   k *cat*   l *leg*   m *man*   n *no*   p *pen*   r *red*   s *sit*

bob·skate *noun* esp. *Cdn* a child's skate consisting of two parallel blades which are attached with straps to a shoe or boot.

bob·sled (also **bob·sleigh** /ˈbɒbsleɪ/) ● *noun* a mechanically steered and braked sled for two or four people, used for racing down a steep ice-covered run with many turns. ● *verb* (**-sled·ded, -sled·ding**) *intransitive* race in a bobsled. □ **bob·sled·der** *noun* [BOB² + SLED]

bob·stay *noun* the chain or rope holding down a ship's bowsprit. [prob. BOB¹ + STAY²]

bob·tail *noun* **1** a docked or short tail. **2** an animal with a bobtail, esp. a horse or dog. [BOB² + TAIL¹]

bob·white *noun* any N American quail of the genus *Colinus*, esp. *C. virginianus*. [imitative of its call]

Boc·caccio /bɔːˈkatʃɪəʊ/ **Gio·van·ni** (1313–75), Italian poet, humanist, and influential figure in the history of narrative fiction. His most enduring work, the *Decameron* (1348–58), is a collection of prose tales told by ten young people fleeing from the Black Death in Florence.

bocce /ˈbɒtʃɪ/ *noun* (also **boccie, bocci**) an Italian form of lawn bowling, usu. played on a narrow dirt-covered court. [Italian, pl. of *boccia* ball]

Boc·cher·ini /bɒkeˈriːni/ **Luigi** (1743–1805), Italian composer. A virtuoso cellist, he is important chiefly for his several hundred string quartets, quintets, and trios.

Boccio·ni /bɒtˈʃoːni/ **Um·ber·to** (1882–1916), Italian painter and sculptor. A leading exponent of the futurist movement, he is known for works such as *Riot in the Gallery* (1909) and *The City Rises* (1910–11), which attempt to express movement through dots and whirling strokes of vibrant colour.

boc·con·cini /bɒkɒnˈtʃiːni/ *noun* a mild Italian cheese similar to mozzarella, in the form of a small ball. [Italian, pl. of *bocconcino* little mouthful, from *boccone* mouthful]

Boche /bɒʃ/ *dated slang derogatory* ● *noun* **1** a German, esp. a soldier. **2** (prec. by *the*) Germans, esp. German soldiers, collectively. ● *adjective* German. [French slang, originally = rascal: applied to Germans in the First World War]

Bochum /ˈbɔːkəm/ an industrial city in the Ruhr valley, North Rhine-Westphalia, Germany; pop. (est. 2002) 387,000.

bock *noun* (in full **bock beer**) a strong dark German beer. [French from German abbreviation of *Eimbockbier* from *Einbeck* in Hanover]

BOD *abbreviation* biochemical oxygen demand.

bod *noun informal* **1** *N Amer.* a body (*has a gorgeous bod*). **2** *Brit.* a person. [abbreviation of BODY]

bo·da·cious /bɔːˈdeɪʃəs/ *adjective N Amer. slang* **1** outstanding, excellent. **2** esp. *US* (*South*) daring, audacious. [blend of BOLD + AUDACIOUS]

bode *transitive verb* **1** portend, foreshow. **2** *archaic* foresee, foretell (evil). □ **bode well** (or **ill**) show good (or bad) signs for the future. □ **bod·ing** *noun* [Old English *bodian* from *boda* messenger]

bo·dega /bɔːˈdeɪgə/ *noun* a cellar or store selling wine and food, esp. in Spanish-speaking areas. [Spanish from Latin *apotheca* from Greek *apothēkē* storehouse]

Bode's law /bɔːdz, ˈbɒdəz/ *noun Astronomy* a formula by which the distances of the first seven planets from the sun are roughly derived in terms of powers of two. [J.E. *Bode*, German astronomer d.1826]

Bodh·gaya /ˌbɒdgəˈjɑː, bɔːd-/ (also **Buddh Gaya** /ˌbud gəˈjɑː/) a village in the state of Bihar, NE India, where Siddhartha Gautama (see BUDDHA) attained enlightenment. A bo tree here is said to be a descendant of the tree under which he meditated.

Bodhi·sat·tva /ˌbɔːdiˈsatvə/ *noun* in Mahayana Buddhism, a person who is able to reach nirvana but delays doing so through compassion for suffering beings. [Sanskrit, = one whose essence is perfect knowledge]

bodh·ran /bɒˈran, bɔː-/ *noun* an Irish folk instrument resembling a large, deep tambourine without jingles, played with a wooden beater knobbed at both ends. [Gaelic]

bod·ice /ˈbɒdɪs/ *noun* **1** the part of a woman's dress or blouse (excluding sleeves) which is above the waist. **2** a woman's sleeveless garment, usu. laced in the front, worn over a blouse or dress. [originally *pair of bodices* = stays, corsets]

bodice-ripper *noun informal* a romantic (esp. historical) novel or film with scenes of seduction and sometimes violence.

bod·ied *combining form* having a body of the specified shape, colour, character, etc. (*full-bodied*).

bod·i·less *adjective* **1** lacking a body. **2** incorporeal, insubstantial.

bod·i·ly ● *adjective* of or concerning the body. ● *adverb* **1** with the whole bulk; as a whole (*threw them bodily*). **2** in the body; as a person.

bod·kin *noun* **1** a blunt thick needle with a large eye used esp. for drawing tape etc. through a hem. **2** a long pin for fastening hair. **3** a small pointed instrument for piercing cloth, removing a piece of type for correction, etc. [Middle English perhaps from Celtic]

Bod·ley, Sir Thom·as (1545–1613), English scholar and diplomat. He greatly enlarged the Oxford University library, which was opened in 1602 and in 1604 was renamed the Bodleian by King James I.

Bo·doni /bəˈdoːni/ **Giam·bat·tista** (1740–1813), Italian printer. The typeface he designed, and others based on it, are named after him.

Bod·rum /ˈbɒdrəm/ a resort town on the Aegean coast of W Turkey, site of the ancient city of Halicarnassus.

body ● *noun* (*pl.* **-ies**) **1 a** the physical structure, including the bones, flesh, and organs, of a person or an animal, whether dead or alive. **b** the torso apart from the head and the limbs. **c** a corpse. **2 a** the main or central part of a thing (*body of the car; body of the attack; body of the essay*). **b** the bulk or majority; the aggregate (*body of opinion*). **3 a** a group of persons regarded collectively, esp. as having a corporate function (*governing body*). **b** (usu. foll. by *of*) a collection (*body of facts*). **4** a quantity (*body of water*). **5** a piece of matter; a mass (*celestial body*). **6** *informal* a person. **7 a** a full or substantial quality of flavour, tone, etc., e.g. in wine, musical sounds, etc. **b** an appearance of fullness and usu. waviness of the hair. ● *transitive verb* (**-ies, -ied**) (usu. foll. by *forth*) give body or substance to. □ **in a body** all together. **keep body and soul together** keep alive, esp. barely. **over my dead body** *informal* entirely without my assent. **take the body** *Hockey* bodycheck. [Old English *bodig*, of unknown origin]

body armour *noun* armour, esp. made of bulletproof etc. fabric.

body art *noun* **1** the practice of decorating the body by means of tattooing, painting, piercing, plastic surgery, etc. **2** art carried about the body, as jewellery, clothing, etc. **3** an artistic movement in which the physical presence of the artist (or of a model) is regarded as an integral part of the work.

body awareness *noun* a heightened consciousness of one's body, its functioning, posture, etc.

body bag *noun* a bag for carrying a corpse from the scene of an accident, crime, battle, etc.

body blow *noun* a severe setback.

body·board *noun* a short, light type of surfboard ridden in a prone position. □ **body·board·er** *noun* **body·board·ing** *noun*

body·building *noun* the practice of strengthening, shaping, and enlarging the muscles by lifting weights and systematic exercise. □ **body·build·er** *noun*

body·check *Hockey* ● *noun* an instance of using one's body to hit or obstruct an opposing player. ● *transitive verb* hit or obstruct in this way.

body clock *noun* the human body's biological clock.

body conditioning *noun* exercises done to improve the strength and muscle tone of the body.

body count *noun* a list or total of people killed, esp. in a military operation.

body double *noun* a stand-in for a film actor during stunt or nude scenes.

body dys·morphic disorder *noun* a psychological disorder in which a person becomes obsessed with imaginary defects in their appearance.

body English *noun N Amer.* **1** = BODY LANGUAGE. **2** the use of gesticulation, inclination of the body, etc. as if to influence the motion of an object.

body·guard *noun* a person or group of persons escorting and protecting another person (esp. a celebrity or dignitary).

body image *noun* one's perception of how one's body looks.

body language *noun* the process of communicating through conscious or unconscious gestures and expressions.

body·man *noun* (*pl.* **-men**) *N Amer.* a person whose job it is to do autobody repair work.

body mass index *noun* an indicator of weight relative to height, calculated by dividing one's weight in kilograms by the square of one's height in metres. Abbr.: **BMI**.

body odour *noun* the smell of the human body, esp. when unpleasant.

Body of Christ *noun* **1** the Christian Church. **2** the consecrated Host.

body paint *noun* a coloured liquid used as theatrical makeup on all parts of the body.

body piercing *noun* the piercing of holes in parts of the body other than the earlobes.

body politic *noun* organized society; a people or nation regarded as a political entity.

body rub *noun* a massage, esp. one given for sexual stimulation.

body-rub parlour *noun Cdn* an establishment at which body rubs and often other sexual services are provided.

body search *noun* a search of a person's entire body and clothing for a hidden weapon, concealed drugs, etc.

body shop *noun* a shop or garage where repairs to the bodywork of vehicles are carried out.

body-slam *transitive verb informal* throw (a person) violently against a wall or against the floor (e.g. in wrestling).

body·snatch·er *noun* a person who illicitly exhumes corpses, esp. for dissection. □ **body·snatch·ing** *noun*

body stocking *noun* a one-piece undergarment, usu. made of nylon, which covers the feet, legs, and torso.

body·suit *noun* a close-fitting one-piece stretch garment worn esp. for sporting activities.

body·surf *intransitive verb* ride the crest of a wave without a surfboard. □ **body·surf·er** *noun* **body·surf·ing** *noun*

body wash *noun* a moisturizing liquid soap for use all over the body.

body wave *noun* (also **body perm**) a soft light permanent wave designed to give the hair fullness.

body weight *noun* the weight of a person's body.

body·work *noun* **1** the structure of a vehicle body. **2** the manufacture or repair of vehicle bodies. **3** therapies and techniques in complementary medicine which involve touching or manipulating the body. □ **body·work·er** *noun* in sense 3

body wrap *noun* a type of beauty treatment involving the application of skin-cleansing ingredients to the body followed by wrapping it in hot bandages, intended to result in a reduction in body measurements.

Boe·otia /bɪˈoːʃə/ a department of central Greece, to the north of the Gulf of Corinth, and a region of ancient Greece of which the chief city was Thebes. Hesiod, Pindar, and Plutarch all came from Boeotia. □ **Boe·otian** *adjective & noun*

Boer /bɔr, bɔːr, bʊr/ ● *noun* a South African of Dutch descent. ● *adjective* of or relating to the Boers. [Dutch: see BOOR]

Boer War either of two wars between Great Britain and the Boers in South Africa, esp. the second (1899–1902), caused by the Boer refusal to grant political rights to recent British immigrants, a situation exacerbated by the discovery of coveted gold deposits in the Transvaal. *Also called* SOUTH AFRICAN WAR.

Bo·eth·ius /bəʊˈiːθɪəs/ (Anicius Manlius Severinus, *c.*480–524) Roman political leader and philosopher. While in prison on a charge of treason (for which he was ultimately executed) he wrote *The Consolation of Philosophy*, which argued that happiness can be attained by realizing the value of goodness and meditating on the reality of God.

boff *transitive & intransitive verb N Amer. slang* have sexual intercourse (with). [dial. var. of *buff* hit, prob. imitative; compare Old French *buffer* to slap in the face]

bof·fin *noun* esp. *Brit. informal* a scientist or expert in a technical field, e.g. computers. [20th c.: origin unknown]

boffo *adjective N Amer. slang* **1** (esp. of a film, theatrical performance, etc.) resoundingly successful; highly lucrative. **2** (of a person) very popular. [*box office* + -*o*]

Bo·fors gun /ˈbəʊfɔrz/ *noun* a type of light anti-aircraft gun with single or twin 40-mm barrels. [*Bofors* in Sweden, where it was originally made]

bog ● *noun* **1 a** a wet spongy ground too soft to support any heavy body, composed largely of mosses, sedges, rushes, and decomposing plant matter. **b** a stretch of such ground. **2** *Brit. slang* a toilet. ● *transitive & intransitive verb* (**bogged**, **bog·ging**) (foll. by *down*; usu. in *passive*) **1** make or become unable to proceed (*was bogged down in paperwork*). **2** sink into mud or wet ground. □ **bog off** (usu. in *imperative*) *Brit. slang* go away. □ **boggy** *adjective* (**bog·gi·er, bog·gi·est**). **bog·gi·ness** *noun* [Irish or Gaelic *bogach* from *bog* soft]

bogan /ˈbɒɡən/ *noun N Amer.* (*Maritimes & Maine*) a stagnant backwater adjacent to a river, lake, etc. [prob. of Algonquian origin]

Bo·gart /ˈbəʊɡɑrt/ **Hum·phrey** (**'Bogey'**) (1899–1957) US film actor whose roles were often those of tough reckless characters with romantic appeal. His films include *The Maltese Falcon* (1941), *Casablanca* (1942), and *The African Queen* (1951), for which he won an Oscar.

bog asphodel *noun* any liliaceous yellow-flowered marsh plant of the genus *Narthecium*, esp. *N. americanum* of N America or *N. ossifragum* of Europe.

bog·bean *noun* = BUCKBEAN.

bog cranberry *noun* a creeping cranberry of sphagnum bogs, *Vaccinium oxycoccus* or *V. vitis-idaea*, with small edible pink to purple berries.

bogey¹ *Golf* ● *noun* (*pl.* **bogeys**) **1** a score of one stroke over par at any hole. **2** (formerly) = PAR 3. ● *transitive verb* (**bogeys, bogeyed**) play (a hole) in one stroke over par. [perhaps from BOGEY² as an imaginary player]

bogey² *noun* (also **bogy**) (*pl.* **bogeys** or **bogies**) **1** an evil or mischievous spirit. **2** an awkward or threatening thing or circumstance. **3** *slang* = BOOGER. [19th c., originally as a proper name: compare BOGLE]

bogey·man *noun* (also **bogy·man, boogey·man**) (*pl.* -**men**) **1** an imaginary evil spirit, esp. invoked to frighten children. **2** a person or thing that is widely regarded as an object of fear.

bog·gle *verb informal* **1** *intransitive & transitive* be or cause to be startled or baffled (esp. *the mind boggles; boggles the mind*). **2** *intransitive* (usu. foll. by *at*) hesitate, demur. [prob. from dial. *boggle* BOGEY²]

bog·hole *noun* a natural hole in the ground with a swampy bottom.

bogie /ˈbəʊɡi/ *noun* **1** esp. *Brit.* the swivelling assembly containing the wheels on a railway car. **2** a similar non-swivelling assembly in the rear of a truck. **3** a small trolley or cart. [19th-c. English dial. word: origin unknown]

bog iron *noun* soft, spongy limonite deposited in bogs.

bog·land *noun* an expanse of boggy land.

bog laurel *noun* a shrub of swamps and bogs of N America, *Kalmia polifolia*, with pink flowers.

bogle /ˈbəʊɡəl/ *noun* **1** = BOGEY². **2** a scarecrow. [originally Scots (16th c.), prob. related to BOGEY²]

bog myrtle *noun* a deciduous shrub, *Myrica gale*, which grows in damp open places and has short upright catkins and aromatic grey-green leaves. *Also called* SWEET GALE.

bog oak *noun* ancient oak wood which has been preserved in a blackened state in peat.

Bo·gotá /ˌbəʊɡəˈtɒ/ the capital of Colombia, situated in the E Andes at about 2 610 m (8,560 ft.); pop. (est. 2002) 6,680,500.

bog rosemary *noun* a shrub of swamps and bogs of northern and eastern N America, of the genus *Andromeda*, with white or pink flowers.

bog-standard *adjective Brit. slang* basic, standard, unexceptional.

bog·trot·ter *noun derogatory* an Irish person.

bogus *adjective* sham, fictitious, spurious. □ **bogus·ly** *adverb* **bogus·ness** *noun* [19th-c. US word, originally an apparatus for counterfeiting coins]

bog violet *noun* = BUTTERWORT.

bogy *var. of* BOGEY².

bogy·man *var. of* BOGEYMAN.

Bo Hai /bɔːˈhaɪ/ (also **Po Hai** /pɔː/; also called the **Gulf of Chihli**) a large inlet of the Yellow Sea, on the coast of E China.

Bo·hem·ia /bəʊˈhiːmɪə/ a region forming the western part of the Czech Republic.

Bo·hem·ian /bəʊˈhiːmɪən/ ● *noun* **1** a native of Bohemia. **2** (also **bohemian**) a socially unconventional person, esp. an artist or writer. ● *adjective* **1** of, relating to, or characteristic of Bohemia or its people. **2** (also **bohemian**) socially unconventional. □ **bo·hem·ian·ism** *noun* (in sense 2). [BOHEMIA + -AN: sense 2 from French *bohémien* gypsy]

Bohemian waxwing *noun* a waxwing, *Bombycilla garrulus*, which breeds in woodlands of northwestern N America and northern Eurasia and wanders widely in winter.

boho *informal* ● *noun* (*pl.* **bohos**) = BOHEMIAN *noun* 2. ● *adjective* = BOHEMIAN *adjective* 2. [abbreviation of BOHEMIAN + -O]

Bohol /bɔːˈhɒl/ an island lying to the north of Mindanao in the central Philippines; pop. (2000) 1,139,130; chief town, Tagbilaran.

Bohr /bɔr/ **Niels Hen·drik David** (1885–1962), Danish physicist who postulated that electrons orbit the nucleus at fixed distances, each having a quantum (fixed amount) of energy, and proposed the theory of 'complementarity' which accounted for the paradox of wave-particle duality. He was awarded the 1922 Nobel Prize.

bohr·ium *noun* a very unstable chemical element made by high-energy atomic collisions. Symbol: **Bh**; at. no. 107. [modern Latin, from BOHR]

bo·hunk /ˈbəʊhʌŋk/ *noun N Amer.* **1** *derogatory* an immigrant from central or SE Europe. **2** a rough or muscular person. [prob. from BOHEMIAN + HUNGARIAN; compare HUNK 2]

boil[1] ● *verb* **1** *intransitive* **a** (of a liquid) start to bubble up and turn to vapour; reach a temperature at which this happens. **b** (of a vessel) contain boiling liquid (*the kettle is boiling*). **2 a** *transitive* bring (a liquid or vessel) to a temperature at which it boils. **b** *transitive* cook (food) by boiling. **c** *intransitive* (of food) be cooked by boiling. **d** *transitive* subject to the heat of boiling water, e.g. to clean. **3** *intransitive* **a** (of the sea etc.) undulate or seethe like boiling water. **b** (of a person or feelings) be greatly agitated, esp. by anger. ● *noun* **1** the act or process of boiling; boiling point (*bring to a boil; on the boil*). **2** *N Amer.* a party at which (a usu. specified) food is boiled and eaten (*corn boil*). □ **boil down 1** reduce volume by boiling. **2** reduce to essentials. **3** (foll. by *to*) amount to; signify basically. **boil over 1** spill over in boiling. **2** lose one's temper; become overexcited. **make one's blood boil** see BLOOD. [Old French *boillir* from Latin *bullire* to bubble, from *bulla* bubble]

boil[2] *noun* an inflamed pus-filled swelling caused by infection of a hair follicle etc. □ **lance the boil** see LANCE. [Old English *bȳl(e)* from West Germanic]

Boi·leau(-Despréaux) /ˈbwʌloː ˌdespreiˈoː/ **Nico·las** (1636–1711), French poet and a founder of French literary criticism. His influential didactic poem *Art Poétique* (1674) defines neoclassical principles of composition and criticism.

boiled dinner *noun N Amer. (Maritimes, Nfld, US North & US North Midlands)* a dish of meat and vegetables, esp. beef brisket, potatoes, cabbage and root vegetables, stewed together in water.

boiled sweet *noun Brit.* a hard candy.

boil·er *noun* **1** a strong vessel for generating steam under pressure, used to power a locomotive, ship, etc. **2** a tank for heating a hot-water supply. **3** a metal tub or other vessel used for boiling.

boiler·maker *noun* **1** a worker who makes and repairs boilers. **2** *N Amer.* a drink of whisky with a beer chaser.

boiler·plate *noun* **1** a piece of rolled steel for making boilers. **2** a standard form, computer subroutine, etc. which can easily be replicated. **3** *N Amer.* (often *attributive*) hackneyed or predictable ideas, language, or writing.

boiler room *noun* **1** a room with a boiler and other heating equipment, esp. in the basement of a large building. **2** *N Amer.* a room, business, etc., in which many operators engage in high-pressure, often illicit, telephone marketing.

boiler suit *noun Brit.* = COVERALL.

boil·ing *adjective* (also **boiling hot**) *informal* very hot.

boiling point *noun* **1** the temperature at which a liquid starts to boil. **2** a state of high excitement or extreme agitation (*his temper reached the boiling point*).

boing (also **boing-boing**) ● *noun* a twanging sound, such as that of a compressed spring suddenly released. ● *interjection* indicating this sound. [imitative]

boink *N Amer.* var. of BONK.

Bois·briand /bwɒbriˈã/ a city in south central Quebec, northwest of Montreal; pop. (2001) 26,729. [M.-S. Dugué de *Boisbriand*, local seigneur d.1688]

bois-brûlé /bwɒ bruːˈlei/ *noun N Amer. archaic* a Metis. [French, = burnt wood, with reference to their dark complexion]

Bois-des-Filion /ˌbwɒdeifilˈjõ/ a town in south central Quebec, east of Blainville; pop. (2001) 7,712. [French, lit. 'Filions' wood', with reference to a maple bush belonging to a man by the name of *Filion*]

Boise /ˈbɔisi/ the state capital of Idaho; pop. (2000) 185,787.

bois·ter·ous /ˈbɔistərəs/ *adjective* **1** (of a person or thing) rough; noisily exuberant. **2** (of the sea, weather, etc.) stormy, rough. □ **bois·ter·ous·ly** *adverb* **bois·ter·ous·ness** *noun* [var. of Middle English *boist(u)ous*, of unknown origin]

boîte /bwɒt/ *noun* a bar or nightclub. [French, lit. = 'box']

Bo·kas·sa /boˈkasə/ **Jean Bédel** (1921–1996), African military leader who became president (1966–77) and later self-styled emperor of the Central African Republic. In 1987 he was convicted of massacring some 100 children and accused of cannibalism.

bok choy *noun N Amer.* a cabbage-like plant of the mustard family, *Brassica chinensis*, having dark green outer leaves, white stalks, and a yellow centre. [Cantonese *paak-ts'oi* 'white vegetable']

Bo·khara see BUKHORO.

bolas /ˈboːləz/ *noun* (as *sing.* or *pl.*) (esp. in S America) a hunting weapon consisting of a number of balls connected by strong cord, which when thrown entangles the limbs of an animal. [Spanish & Portuguese, pl. of *bola* ball]

bold ● *adjective* **1** confidently assertive; adventurous, courageous. **2** forthright, impudent. **3** vivid, distinct, well-marked (*bold colours*). **4** (in full **bold·face**, **bold·faced**) printed in a thick black typeface. ● *noun* (also **bold·face**) bold type. ● *transitive verb* (also **bold·face**) set or present in bold type. □ **as bold as brass** excessively bold or self-assured. **be** (or **make**) **so bold as to** presume to; venture to. □ **bold·ly** *adverb* **bold·ness** *noun* [Old English *bald* dangerous, from Germanic]

Bol·den /ˈboːldən/ **Buddy** (born Charles Bolden) (1868–1931), US jazz cornetist and bandleader, a pioneer of New Orleans jazz.

bole[1] *noun* the stem or trunk of a tree. [Old Norse *bolr*, perhaps related to BALK]

bole[2] *noun* fine compact earthy clay. [Late Latin BOLUS]

bol·ero /bəˈlɛroː/ *noun* (*pl.* **-eros**) **1 a** a Spanish dance in simple triple time. **b** music for or in the time of a bolero. **2** a sleeved or sleeveless open jacket just reaching the waist. [Spanish]

bol·etus /bəˈliːtəs/ *noun* (also **bol·ete** /boːˈliːt/) a mushroom or toadstool of the genus *Boletus*, having many pores on the underside of the cap. [Latin from Greek *bōlitēs*, perhaps from *bōlos* lump]

Bol·eyn /bəˈlɪn/ **Anne** (1507–36), second wife of Henry VIII and mother of Elizabeth I. Henry divorced Catherine of Aragon to marry her, but had her beheaded on dubious adultery charges after she failed to bear him a son.

Bolí·var /ˌboːˈliːvar/ **Simón** (1783–1830), Venezuelan leader who was more than any other man responsible for liberating S America from Spanish rule. Though his plan for a united continent was never realized, he led successful revolutions in what are now Colombia, Venezuela, Ecuador, Peru, and Bolivia.

boli·var /ˈbɒləvar/ *noun* the basic monetary unit of Venezuela, equal to 100 centimos. [S. BOLÍVAR]

Bo·livia /bəˈlɪviə/ a landlocked country in S America; pop. (est. 2002) 8,445,134; capital, La Paz; legal capital and seat of the judiciary, Sucre. □ **Bo·liv·ian** *adjective & noun* [S. BOLÍVAR]

bo·liv·iano /bəlɪviˈɒnoː/ *noun* (*pl.* **-nos**) the basic monetary unit of Bolivia (1863–1962 and since 1987), equal to 100 centavos or cents. [BOLÍVAR]

Böll /bɜːl/ **Hein·rich** (1917–85), German novelist and short-story writer whose work is often set in wartime or postwar Germany. A Catholic humanist and pacifist, he was awarded the Nobel Prize for literature in 1972.

boll /boːl/ *noun* a rounded capsule containing seeds, esp. cotton or flax. [Middle Dutch *bolle*: see BOWL[1]]

bol·lard /ˈbɒlard/ *noun* **1** a short post on a pier or ship for securing a rope. **2** *Brit.* any of a series of short posts in the road, esp. as part of a traffic island. [Old Norse *bolr* BOLE[1] + -ARD]

bol·lix /ˈbɒlɪks/ *coarse slang* ● *transitive verb* (usu. foll. by *up*) bungle or confuse. ● *plural noun* = BOLLOCKS. [alteration of BOLLOCKS]

bol·lock·ing /ˈbɒləkɪŋ/ *noun* esp. *Brit. coarse slang* a severe reprimand.

bol·locks /ˈbɒləks/ *plural noun* esp. *Brit. coarse slang* **1** the testicles. **2** (usu. as an exclamation of contempt) nonsense, rubbish. [Old English *bealluc*, related to BALL[1]]

boll weevil *noun* a small weevil of Mexico and the southern US, *Anthonomus grandis*, whose larvae destroy cotton bolls.

Bolly·wood *noun* the Indian popular film industry, based in Bombay, esp. designating very formulaic romantic musicals. [blend of BOMBAY + HOLLYWOOD]

bolo[1] /ˈboːloː/ *noun* (*pl.* **bolos**) a large and heavy knife, used esp. in the Philippines. [prob. Spanish dial.]

bolo[2] /ˈboːloː/ *noun* (*pl.* **bolos**) (in full **bolo tie**) *N Amer.* a necktie made of cord or thick string, fastened at the collar with a decorative clasp. [prob. from Spanish & Portuguese *bola*, related to BOLAS]

Bol·ogna /bəˈloːnjə/ a city in N Italy, capital of Emilia-Romagna region; pop. (2001) 369,955. Its university, which dates from the 11th c., is the oldest in Europe.

bol·ogna /bəˈloːni, -nə/ *noun* (also **ba·loney**) *N Amer.* a smoked luncheon meat made from finely minced pork and beef. [BOLOGNA]

bol·ognese /ˌbɒləˈneiz/ ● *adjective* **1** (often placed after noun) designating a sauce for pasta made of ground beef, tomatoes, onions, etc. **2** (**Bolognese**) of or pertaining to Bologna. ● *noun* (**Bolognese**) a resident of Bologna. [Italian, = of Bologna]

bo·lom·eter /bəˈlɒmətər/ *noun* an instrument for measuring electromagnetic radiation (esp. infrared and microwaves) electrically.

☐ **bo·lom·etry** *noun* **bolo·met·ric** /ˌbəʊlə'metrɪk/ *adjective* [Greek *bolē* ray + -METER]

Bol·she·vik /'bɒlʃəvɪk/ ● *noun* **1** *hist.* a member of the radical faction of the Russian socialist party, which became the communist party in 1918 (*compare* MENSHEVIK). **2** a Russian communist. **3** (in general use) any revolutionary socialist. ● *adjective* **1** of, relating to, or characteristic of the Bolsheviks. **2** communist. ☐ **Bol·she·vism** *noun* **Bol·she·vist** *noun* [Russian, = a member of the majority, one who (in 1903) favoured extreme measures, from *bol'she* greater]

Bol·shie /'bɒlʃi/ (also **Bol·shy**) esp. *Brit. slang* ● *adjective* (usu. **bolshie**) **1** left-wing, socialist. **2** uncooperative, rebellious, awkward; bad-tempered. ● *noun* (*pl.* **-shies**) a Bolshevik. [abbreviation]

bol·ster[1] /'bəʊlstər/ ● *noun* **1** a long, often cylindrical pillow or cushion. **2** a pad or support, esp. in a machine. **3** *Archit.* a short timber cap over a post to increase the bearing of the beams it supports. ● *transitive verb* **1** support, reinforce (*bolstered our morale*). **2** support with a bolster or pillow; prop up. ☐ **bol·ster·er** *noun* [Old English from Germanic]

bol·ster[2] /'bəʊlstər/ *noun* a chisel for cutting bricks. [20th c.: origin uncertain]

Bolt, Rob·ert (Ox·ton) (1924–95), English dramatist. His acclaimed play *A Man for All Seasons* (1960) was filmed in 1967. His screenplay for this won an Oscar, as did that for *Dr Zhivago* (1965). He also wrote screenplays for *Lawrence of Arabia* (1962) and *The Mission* (1986).

bolt[1] ● *noun* **1** a sliding bar and socket used to fasten or lock a door, gate, etc. **2** a large usu. metal pin with a head, usu. riveted or used with a nut, to hold things together. **3** a discharge of lightning. **4** the sliding piece of the breech mechanism of a rifle. **5** an act of bolting (*compare* sense 4 of *verb*); a sudden escape or dash for freedom. **6** *hist.* an arrow for shooting from a crossbow. **7** a roll of fabric, paper, etc. ● *verb* **1** *transitive* fasten or lock with a bolt. **2** *transitive* (foll. by *in*, *out*) keep (a person etc.) from leaving or entering by bolting a door. **3** *transitive* fasten together with bolts. **4** *intransitive* **a** dash suddenly away, esp. to escape. **b** (of a horse) suddenly gallop out of control. **5** *transitive* gulp down (food or drink) hurriedly. **6** *intransitive* (of a plant) run to seed. ☐ **a bolt from** (or **out of**) **the blue** a complete surprise. **bolt upright** rigidly, stiffly. **shoot one's bolt** do all that is in one's power. ☐ **bolt·er** *noun* (in sense 4 of *verb*). [Old English *bolt* arrow]

bolt[2] *transitive verb* (also **boult**) sift (flour etc.). [Old French *bulter*, *buleter*, of unknown origin]

bolt cutters *plural noun* a type of shears with very short blades and long handles, which provide a great deal of leverage to cut through bolts.

bolt·hole *noun* **1** a means of escape. **2** a secret refuge. **3** (**bolt hole**) a hole for inserting a bolt to fasten something.

Bol·ton a city in NW England, near Manchester; pop. (est. 1999) 258,600.

bolt-on ● *adjective* **1** able to be fastened or attached by bolts. **2** able to be added when required. ● *noun* a thing that can be bolted on.

Boltz·mann /'bɒltsmən/ **Lud·wig** (1844–1906), Austrian physicist who made fundamental contributions to the kinetic theory of gases, classical statistical mechanics, and thermodynamics.

bolus /'bəʊləs/ *noun* (*pl.* **bo·lus·es**) **1** a soft ball, esp. of chewed food. **2** *Vet.* a large pill. **3** *Med.* a single dose of a pharmaceutical preparation given intravenously. [Late Latin from Greek *bōlos* clod]

Bol·zano /bɒl'tsɒnɔ/ a city in NE Italy, capital of the Trentino-Alto Adige region; pop. (2001) 93,079.

bomb ● *noun* **1 a** a container with explosive, incendiary material, smoke, or gas etc., designed to explode on impact or by means of a time mechanism or remote-control device. **b** an ordinary object fitted with an explosive device (*letter bomb*). **2** (prec. by *the*) the atomic or hydrogen bomb considered as a weapon with supreme destructive power. **3** a mass of solidified lava thrown from a volcano. **4** *N Amer. informal* a bad failure (*her latest play is a real bomb*). **5** an aerosol can or its contents (*touch up the car with a paint bomb*). **6** *N Amer. Sport* a long pass, kick, shot, or hit. ● *verb* **1** *transitive* attack with bombs; drop bombs on. **2** *transitive* (foll. by *out*) drive (a person etc.) out of a building or refuge by using bombs. **3** *intransitive* throw or drop bombs. **4** *intransitive* esp. *N Amer. informal* (often foll. by *out*) fail badly. **5** *intransitive informal* move or go very quickly. ☐ **go down a bomb** *Brit. informal* be very well received. **go like a bomb** *Brit. informal* **1** be very successful. **2** go very fast. [French *bombe* from Italian *bomba* from Latin *bombus* from Greek *bombos* hum]

bom·bard *transitive verb* **1** attack with a number of bombs, shells, etc. **2** (often foll. by *with*) subject to persistent questioning, abuse, etc. **3** *Physics* direct a stream of high-speed particles at (a substance).

bom·bard·ment *noun* [French *bombarder* from *bombarde*, from medieval Latin *bombarda* a stone-throwing engine: see BOMB]

bom·barde /'bɒmbɑːd/ *noun* a medieval alto-pitched shawm. [Old French *bombarde*, medieval Latin *bombarda* prob. from Latin *bombus* (see BOMB)]

Bom·bar·dier[1] /ˌbɒbɑː'djeɪ/ **(Jo·seph) Ar·mand** (1907–64), Canadian inventor. In 1959 his company began to produce the Ski-Doo. Bombardier has become a major international company involved in aviation, rail transport, recreational equipment, and engineering.

Bom·bar·dier[2] /bɒm'bɑːdiːr/ *noun Cdn proprietary* an enclosed vehicle for travelling over snow or ice, driven by rear caterpillar treads and steered by front skis, and capable of carrying several passengers. [BOMBARDIER[1]]

bom·bar·dier /ˌbɒmbɑː'diːr/ *noun* **1** *N Amer.* a member of a bomber crew responsible for sighting and releasing bombs. **2** *Cdn & Brit.* a non-commissioned officer in the artillery, of a rank equivalent to corporal. Abbr.: **Bdr**. [French (as BOMBARD)]

bom·bar·don /bɒm'bɑːdən, 'bɒmbədən/ *noun* **1** a type of valved bass tuba. **2** an organ stop imitating this. [Italian *bombardone* from *bombardo* bassoon]

bom·bast /'bɒmbast/ *noun* pompous or extravagant language. ☐ **bom·bas·tic** /-'bastɪk/ *adjective* **bom·bas·tic·ally** /-'bastɪkəli/ *adverb* [earlier *bombace* cotton wool, from French from medieval Latin *bombax -acis* alteration of *bombyx*; see BOMBAZINE]

Bom·bay /bɒm'beɪ/ a city and port on the west coast of India, capital of the state of Maharashtra; pop. (2000) 12,147,100. In 1995 the city's official name was changed to the Hindi form Mumbai. ☐ **Bombay·ite** *noun*

Bombay duck *noun* a dried fish, esp. bummalo, usu. eaten with curried dishes. [corruption of *bombil*: see BUMMALO]

Bombay mix *noun* an Indian snack consisting of lentils, peanuts, and spiced, deep-fried strands of gram flour.

bom·ba·zine /'bɒmbəˌziːn, -'ziːn/ *noun* a twilled dress material of worsted, sometimes blended with silk or cotton, esp., when black, formerly used for mourning. [French *bombasin* from medieval Latin *bombacinum* from Late Latin *bombycinus* silken, from *bombyx -ycis* silk or silkworm, from Greek *bombux*]

bomb bay *noun* a compartment in an aircraft used to hold bombs.

bombe /bɒm/ *noun* a dome-shaped frozen dessert, usu. consisting of an outer layer of ice cream filled with custard, cake crumbs, or another type of ice cream. [French, = BOMB]

bom·bé /'bɒmbeɪ/ *adjective* (esp. of furniture) rounded; convex. [French, past participle of *bomber* swell out]

bombed *adjective informal* **1** intoxicated. **2** subjected to bombing.

bombed-out *adjective* **1** (of a person) driven out by bombing. **2** (of a building etc.) rendered uninhabitable by bombing. **3** *slang* = BOMBED 1.

bomb·er *noun* **1** an aircraft equipped to carry and drop bombs. **2** a person using bombs, esp. illegally. **3** *Cdn* = WATER BOMBER.

bomber jacket *noun* a short leather or cloth jacket tightly gathered at the waist and cuffs.

bomb·let *noun* a very small bomb.

bom·bon·iere /bɒmbɒn'jereɪ/ *noun* (*pl.* same or **-ieres**) a small favour or keepsake, usu. accompanied by sugared almonds, given to guests at an Italian wedding, christening, etc. [Italian, from French *bonbonnière* 'candy dish' (as BONBON)]

bom·bora /bɒm'bɔːrə/ *noun Austral.* a dangerous sea area where waves break over a submerged reef. [Aboriginal, perhaps Dharuk *bumbora*]

bomb·proof *adjective* strong enough to resist the effects of blast from a bomb.

bomb·shell *noun* **1** an overwhelming surprise or disappointment. **2** an artillery bomb. **3** *informal* a very attractive woman (*blond bombshell*).

bomb shelter *noun* a room or building built to withstand bombs, used as a shelter during an air raid.

bomb·sight *noun* a device in an aircraft for aiming bombs.

bomb site *noun* an area where buildings have been destroyed by bombs.

bomb squad *noun* a division of a police force etc., responsible for defusing or safely detonating unexploded bombs.

Bon, Cape /bɒn/ a peninsula of NE Tunisia, extending into the Mediterranean Sea, noted for its resorts and its wine.

bona fide /ˌbəʊnə 'faɪd, ˌbɒnə 'faɪd/ ● *adjective* genuine; sincere. ● *adverb Law* in good faith. [Latin, ablative sing. of BONA FIDES]

bona fides /ˌbəʊnə 'faɪdiːz/ *noun* **1** esp. *Law*. an honest intention;

sincerity. **2** (as *pl.*) *informal* documentary evidence of acceptability (*his bona fides are in order*). [Latin, = good faith]

Bon·aire /bɒˈneɪr/ one of the two principal islands of the Netherlands Antilles (the other is Curaçao); chief town, Kralendijk.

bon·an·za /bəˈnænzə/ ● *noun* **1** a source of wealth or good fortune. **2** a large output (esp. of a mine). **3 a** prosperity; good luck. **b** a run of good luck. ● *adjective* greatly prospering or productive. [Spanish, = fair weather, from Latin *bonus* good]

Bona·parte /ˈbəʊnəˌpɑːt/ (also **Buona·parte**) **1 Jé·rôme** (1784–1860), brother of Napoleon I, king of Westphalia 1807. **2 Jo·seph** (1768–1844), brother of Napoleon I, king of Naples 1806–8; king of Spain 1808–13. **3 Louis** (1778–1846), brother of Napoleon I, king of Holland 1806–10. **4 Louis Napo·leon** see NAPOLEON III. **5 Lu·cien** (1775–1840), brother of Napoleon I, prince of Canino. **6 Napo·leon** see NAPOLEON I. **7 Napo·leon** see NAPOLEON II.

Bona·parte's gull *noun* a small gull, *Larus philadelphia*, having a grey mantle and white wing tips with black borders, which breeds in western and central Canada. [C. L. *Bonaparte*, nephew of Napoleon I and ornithologist d.1857]

Bona·part·ism *noun* (in 19th-c. France) attachment to or advocacy of the autocratic style of government of Napoleon I and his dynasty.
□ **Bona·part·ist** *noun & adjective*

bon ap·pé·tit /ˌbɒnapeɪˈtiː/ *interjection* expressing a wish that someone will enjoy what they are about to eat. [French]

Bona·ven·ture /ˈbɒnəˌvɛntʃər/ **St.** (*c.*1218–74), Franciscan friar, bishop, cardinal, and Doctor of the Church. He was head of the Franciscan order from 1257, and is seen as its second founder. He played a prominent role at the Council of Lyons in 1274.

Bonaventure, Île de /bɒnəˈvɛntʃər/ a small island in the Gulf of St. Lawrence, E Quebec, situated just offshore the Gaspé Peninsula, opposite the town of Percé. A noted site for migratory birds, the island is today a provincial park. [French *bon aventure* good venture, perhaps because of its thriving fishery in the 17th c.]

Bona·vista /ˌbɒnəˈvɪstə/ a town in E Newfoundland, situated on the tip of Bonavista Peninsula, southeast of Gander; pop. (1996) 4,021. [see BONAVISTA, CAPE]

Bonavista, Cape the northernmost point of the Bonavista Peninsula, overlooking the southeastern entrance to Bonavista Bay, Newfoundland. [possibly after *Boa Vista*, one of the Cape Verde Islands]

Bonavista Bay a large inlet of the N Atlantic Ocean, situated on the eastern coast of Newfoundland, east of Gander. Its coastline is heavily indented and contains a large number of islands. [see BONAVISTA, CAPE]

Bonavista Peninsula a peninsula in E Newfoundland, between Bonavista Bay and Trinity Bay. [see BONAVISTA, CAPE]

bon·bon *noun* a candy, esp. a fancy one. [French from *bon* good, from Latin *bonus*]

bonce /bɒns/ *noun Brit. slang* the head. [19th c.: origin unknown]

bond ● *noun* **1 a** a thing that ties another down or together. **b** (usu. in *pl.*) a thing restraining bodily freedom (*broke his bonds*). **2** (often in *pl.*) **a** a uniting force (*sisterly bond*). **b** a restraint; a responsibility (*bonds of duty*). **3** a binding engagement; an agreement (*my word is my bond*). **4 a** certificate issued by a government or a public company promising to repay borrowed money at a fixed rate of interest at a specified time; a debenture. **5** adhesiveness. **6** *Law* a sum of money put up as recognizance, esp. as a guarantee of good conduct (*released on $50,000 bond; offered to put up a bond*). **7** *Chem.* a strong force of attraction holding atoms together in a molecule or crystal. **8** = BOND PAPER. **9** the laying of bricks in one of various patterns in a wall in order to ensure strength (*English bond; Flemish bond*). ● *verb* **1** *transitive* bind together with an adhesive. **2** *intransitive* adhere; hold together. **3** *transitive* connect with a bond. **4** *transitive* place (goods) in bond. **5 a** *intransitive* become emotionally attached. **b** *transitive* link by an emotional or psychological bond. **6** *transitive* lay (bricks) overlapping. □ **in bond** (of goods) stored in a bonded warehouse until the importer pays the duty owing.
□ **bond·able** *adjective* [Middle English var. of BAND¹]

bond·age *noun* **1** serfdom; slavery. **2** subjection to constraint, influence, obligation, etc. **3** sado-masochistic practices, including the use of physical restraints or mental enslavement. [Anglo-Latin *bondagium*: influenced by BOND]

bond·ed *adjective* **1** (of goods) placed in bond. **2** (of material) reinforced by or cemented to another. **3** (of a person's or company's behaviour or performance) secured by a deposit of money. **4** (of a debt) secured by bonds. **5** (of a worker or workforce) obliged to work for a particular employer, typically in a condition close to slavery.

bonded warehouse *noun* a warehouse for the retention of imported goods until the customs duty owed is paid.

bond·hold·er *noun* a person holding a bond granted by a private person, company, or government.

Bondi /ˈbɒndaɪ/ a coastal resort in New South Wales, Australia, a suburb of Sydney. It is noted for its popular beach.

Bond·ian *adjective* (also **Bond·ish**) characteristic or evocative of the fictional character James Bond or the spy novels and films in which he appeared, esp. (of a person) suavely charismatic and resourceful, or (of a situation) action-packed or (of a technology) highly ingenious.

bond·ing *noun* **1** the binding or connecting together of any substances esp. by adhesion. **2** the formation of a chemical bond. **3** the formation of an emotional bond between two individuals, or between an individual and a group, esp. the establishment of strong ties between a parent and a child.

bond paper *noun* high-quality writing paper, usu. containing cotton fibre.

bonds·man *noun* (*pl.* **-men**) **1** a person who posts a bond for another. **2** a slave. **3** a person in thrall to another. [var. of *bondman* (from archaic *bond* in serfdom or slavery) as though from *bond's*, genitive of BOND]

bond store *noun Cdn* (*Nfld*) a liquor store.

bone ● *noun* **1** any of the pieces of hard tissue making up the skeleton in vertebrates. **2** (in *pl.*) **a** the skeleton, esp. as remains after death. **b** the body, esp. as a seat of intuitive feeling (*felt it in my bones*). **3 a** the material of which bones consist. **b** a similar substance such as ivory, dentine, or whalebone. **4** (also *attributive*) a thing made of bone. **5** (in *pl.*) the essential part of a thing (*the bare bones*). **6** (in *pl.*) **a** dice. **b** castanets. **7** a strip of stiffening in a corset etc. **8** a pale ivory colour like that of bone. ● *verb* **1** *transitive* take out the bones from (meat or fish). **2** *transitive* stiffen (a garment) with bone etc. **3** *transitive Brit. slang* steal. □ **bone of contention** a source or ground of dispute. **bone up** (often foll. by *on*) *informal* study (a subject) intensively. **close to** (or **near**) **the bone 1** tactless to the point of offensiveness. **2** destitute; hard up. **have a bone to pick** (usu. foll. by *with*) have a cause for dispute (with another person). **jump a person's bones** *slang* have sexual intercourse with a person. **make no bones about 1** make no attempt to conceal; admit openly (*made no bones about the parking ticket*). **2** not hesitate (*made no bones about revealing her income*). **throw someone a bone** give someone something to appease them partially and temporarily. **to the bone 1** to the bare minimum (*cut expenses to the bone*). **2** completely (*chilled her to the bone*). **work one's fingers to the bone** work very hard, esp. thanklessly. □ **bone·less** *adjective* [Old English *bān* from Germanic]

bone·bed *noun N Amer.* an area of land containing esp. dinosaur fossils.

bone-chilling *adjective* **1** extremely cold. **2** frightening.

bone china *noun* fine china made of clay mixed with the ash from bones.

boned *adjective* **1** (in *combination*) having bones of a specified sort (*fine-boned*). **2** (of meat or fish) having the bones removed. **3** (of a corset etc.) having bones as stays.

bone-dry *adjective* extremely dry.

bone·fish *noun* any of several species of large game fish, esp. *Albula vulpes*, having many small bones.

bone·head *informal* ● *noun* a stupid person. ● *adjective* stupid.
□ **bone·head·ed** *adjective*

bone idle *adjective* (also **bone lazy**) utterly idle or lazy.

bone marrow *noun* a soft fatty substance in the cavities of bones, of major importance in blood cell formation.

bone meal *noun* crushed or ground bones used esp. as a fertilizer.

boner *noun informal* **1** a stupid mistake. **2** *N Amer. coarse slang* an erection.

bone·set *noun* a herbaceous plant of the composite family, *Eupatorium perfoliatum*, bearing white flowers. [prob. from BONE + SET¹, from its medicinal uses]

bone-setter *noun* a person who sets broken or dislocated bones, esp. without being a qualified surgeon.

bone·shak·er *noun* **1** *informal* a decrepit or uncomfortable old vehicle. **2** *hist.* a type of bicycle with solid tires.

bone-weary *adjective* (also **bone-tired**) exhausted.

bone·yard *noun informal* a cemetery.

bon·fire *noun* a large open-air fire for burning rubbish, as part of a celebration, or as a signal. [earlier *bonefire* from BONE (bones being the chief material formerly used) + FIRE]

Bonfire Night *noun* **1** *Cdn* (*Nfld*) 5 Nov., on which people light very large bonfires of combustible items, e.g. oil barrels and tires, often on prominent heights. **2** *Brit.* = GUY FAWKES' NIGHT.

bong¹ *noun* a low pitched sound as of a bell. [20th c.: origin uncertain]

bong² *noun* a type of water pipe for smoking marijuana etc. [Thai *baung*, lit. 'cylindrical wooden tube']

bongo¹ *noun* (*pl.* **bon·gos**) either of a pair of small long-bodied drums usu. held between the knees and played with the fingers. [Latin American Spanish *bongó*]

bongo² *noun* (*pl.* same or **bon·gos**) a rare antelope, *Tragelaphus euryceros*, native to the forests of central Africa, having spiralled horns and a chestnut-red coat with narrow white vertical stripes. [Congolese]

bon·homie /ˌbɒnɒˈmiː/ *noun* geniality; good-natured friendliness. [French from *bonhomme* good fellow]

bon·hom·ous /ˈbɒnəməs/ *adjective* full of bonhomie.

Boni·face VIII /ˈbɒnɪˌfəs/ (born Benedict Caetani) (*c.*1228–1303), pope 1294–1303. He challenged Philip IV of France over the king's right to tax the clergy, and in response Philip had him seized (1303).

Boni·face, St. /ˈbɒnɪˌfəs/ (real name Wynfrith; 'apostle of Germany') (680–754), Anglo-Saxon missionary. He was appointed primate of Germany (732), was given authority to reform the whole Frankish Church (741), and greatly assisted the spread of papal influence. Feast day, 5 June.

bon·ito /bəˈniːtoʊ/ *noun* (*pl.* **-itos**) any of various striped tuna, esp. *Sarda sarda* of the Atlantic and Mediterranean. [Spanish]

bonk ● *verb* **1** *transitive* hit resoundingly. **2** *intransitive* bang; bump. **3** *coarse slang* **a** *intransitive* have sexual intercourse. **b** *transitive* have sexual intercourse with. **4** *intransitive slang* suffer total exhaustion or aerobic collapse. ● *noun* an instance of bonking (*a bonk on the head*). [imitative: compare BANG, BUMP 1, CONK²]

bonk·ers /ˈbɒŋkərz/ *predicative adjective slang* crazy. [20th c.: origin unknown]

bon mot /bɔ̃ ˈmoʊ, bɒn-/ *noun* (*pl.* **bons mots** *pronunc.* same or /-moʊz/) a witty saying.

Bonn /bɒn/ a city in the state of North Rhine-Westphalia in Germany; pop. (est. 2002) 311,800. From 1949 until the reunification of Germany in 1990 Bonn was the capital of the Federal Republic of Germany.

Bon·nard /bɒˈnɑr/ **Pierre** (1867–1947), French painter and graphic artist, whose works continue and develop the Impressionist tradition; they are notable for their rich, glowing colour harmonies, and typically depict intimate domestic interior scenes, nudes, and landscapes.

bon·net *noun* **1 a** a woman's or child's hat tied under the chin and usu. with a brim framing the face. **b** a soft round brimless hat like a beret worn by men and boys in Scotland. **c** *informal* any hat. **2** = WAR BONNET. **3** the cowl of a chimney etc. **4** a protective cap in various machines. **5** *Brit.* = HOOD¹ 3. □ **bon·net·ed** *adjective* [Old French *bonet* short for *chapel de bonet* cap of some kind of material (medieval Latin *bonetus*)]

bonnet monkey *noun* an Indian macaque, *Macaca radiata*, with a bonnet-like tuft of hair.

Bon·ney /ˈbɒni/ **Wil·liam H.** (born Henry McCarty; known as Billy the Kid) (1859–81), US outlaw. He killed a man in New Mexico when only 12 years old and subsequently became a notorious robber and murderer. Sheriff Pat Garrett captured him in 1880, but he escaped, only to be shot by Garrett at Fort Sumner, New Mexico.

Bon·nie Prince Char·lie see Charles Edward STUART.

bonny *adjective* (**bon·ni·er**, **bon·ni·est**) esp. *Scot. & Northern England* **1 a** physically attractive. **b** healthy-looking. **2** good, fine, pleasant. [16th c.: perhaps from French *bon* good]

Bonny·ville /ˈbɒnivɪl/ a town in east central Alberta, northeast of Edmonton; pop. (2001) 5,709. [Fr. F. S. Bonny, who built the community's first Catholic church]

Bono /ˈbɒnoʊ/ (born Paul Hewson) (b.1960), Irish rock singer and songwriter; lead singer for the Irish rock group U2.

bon·obo /ˈbɒnəboʊ/ *noun* (*pl.* **-obos**) a chimpanzee, *Pan paniscus*, with a black face and black hair found in the Congo rainforests. It is believed to be the closest living relative of humans. [local name]

bon·sai /ˈbɒnzaɪ, -saɪ/ *noun* (*pl.* same) **1** the art of cultivating ornamental artificially dwarfed varieties of trees and shrubs. **2** a tree or shrub grown by this method. [Japanese]

bon·spiel /ˈbɒnspiːl/ *noun* a curling tournament. [16th c.: perhaps from Low German; compare West Flemish *bonespel* a children's game]

bon·te·bok /ˈbɒntɪˌbʌk/ *noun* (also **bont·bok** /ˈbɒntbʌk/) (*pl.* same or **-boks**) a large chestnut antelope, *Damaliscus dorcas*, native to southern Africa, having a white tail and a white patch on its head and rump. [Afrikaans from *bont* spotted + *bok* BUCK¹]

bonus *noun* (*pl.* **bo·nus·es**) **1** an unsought or unexpected extra benefit. ¶ The phrase *added bonus*, although common, is regarded as tautologous by some people and is to be avoided in formal usage. **2 a** an amount of money given in addition to normal pay, in recognition of exceptional performance or as a supplement at Christmas etc. **b** *Brit.* an extra dividend or issue paid to the shareholders of a company. **c** *Brit.* a distribution of profits to holders of an insurance policy. [Latin *bonus*, *bonum* good (thing)]

bo·nus·ing *noun Cdn* an act of subsidizing something, esp. as an inducement for development etc.

bon vi·vant /ˌbɔ̃ viːˈvɑ̃/ *noun* (*pl.* **bon vi·vants** or **bons vi·vants** *pronunc.* same) a person indulging in good living; a gourmand. [French, lit. 'good liver' from *vivre* to live]

bon vi·veur /ˌbɔ̃ viːˈvɜr/ *noun* (*pl.* **bon vi·veurs** or **bons vi·veurs** *pronunc.* same) = BON VIVANT. [pseudo-French, after *bon vivant*: *viveur* 'a living person']

bon voyage /ˌbɒn vɔɪˈjɒʒ, bɔ̃-, bɔ̃ vwɑˈjɒʒ/ *interjection & noun* an expression of good wishes to a departing traveller. [French]

bony *adjective* (**bon·i·er**, **bon·i·est**) **1** (of a person) thin with prominent bones. **2** having many bones. **3** of or like bone. **4** (of a fish) having bones rather than cartilage. □ **bon·i·ness** *noun*

bonze *noun* a Japanese or Chinese Buddhist priest. [French *bonze* or Portuguese *bonzo* perhaps from Japanese *bonzō* from Chinese *fanseng* religious person, or from Japanese *bō-zi* from Chinese *fasi* teacher of the law]

bon·zer *adjective Austral. slang* excellent, first-rate. [perhaps from BONANZA]

boo ● *interjection* **1** an expression of disapproval or contempt. **2** a sound, made esp. to a child, intended to surprise. ● *noun* an utterance of *boo*, esp. as an expression of disapproval or contempt made to a performer etc. ● *verb* (**boos**, **booed**) **1** *intransitive* utter a boo or boos. **2** *transitive* jeer at (a performer etc.) by booing. □ **not say boo to a goose** remain silent, esp. from shyness or timidity. [imitative]

boob¹ *slang* ● *noun* **1** a foolish or stupid person. **2** *Brit.* an embarrassing mistake. ● *intransitive verb Brit.* make an embarrassing mistake. [abbreviation of BOOBY]

boob² *noun informal* a woman's breast. [earlier *bubby*, *booby*, of uncertain origin]

boo-bird *noun N Amer.* a member of an audience, esp. at a sports event, who boos loudly or frequently.

boo-boo *noun informal* **1** a mistake. **2** *N Amer.* a minor scrape, cut, bump, or other injury. [BOOB¹]

boob tube *noun informal* **1** (usu. prec. by *the*) *N Amer.* television; a television set. **2** *Brit.* a woman's low-cut close-fitting usu. strapless top.

booby *noun* (*pl.* **-ies**) **1** a stupid or childish person. **2** *slang* = BOOB². **3** any of various seabirds of the genus *Sula*, related to the gannet. [prob. from Spanish *bobo* (in senses 1 & 3) from Latin *balbus* stammering]

booby prize *noun* a prize given to the least successful competitor in a contest.

booby trap ● *noun* **1** a trap intended to surprise someone as a practical joke. **2** *Military* an apparently harmless explosive device intended to kill or injure anyone touching it. ● *transitive verb* (usu. **booby-trap**) place a booby trap or traps in or on.

boo·dle *noun slang* money, esp. when gained or used dishonestly, e.g. as a bribe. [Dutch *boedel* possessions]

boo·ga·loo *noun* a dance to rock and roll music performed with swivelling and shuffling movements of the body, orig. popular in the 1960s. [perhaps an alteration of BOOGIE-WOOGIE]

boog·er /ˈbʊgər/ *noun N Amer. informal* a piece of dried nasal mucus. [alteration of BOGEY²]

boogey·man *var.* of BOGEYMAN.

boog·ie /ˈbʊgi, ˈbuːgi/ ● *intransitive verb* (**boog·ies**, **boog·ied**, **boogy·ing**) *informal* **1** dance enthusiastically to rock music. **2** move or go quickly (*let's boogie on out of here*). ● *noun* **1** = BOOGIE-WOOGIE. **2** *informal* a dance to rock music. [BOOGIE-WOOGIE]

Boogie Board *noun N Amer. proprietary* a small, flexible plastic surfboard. □ **boogie boarding** *noun*

boogie-woogie /ˌbuːgiˈwʊgi/ *noun* a style of playing blues or jazz on the piano, marked by a persistent bass rhythm. [20th c.: origin unknown]

boo hoo ● *interjection* (also **boo hoo hoo**) expressing weeping. ● *noun*

(**boo-hoo**) (*pl.* **boo-hoos**) loud sobbing; bewailing. ● *intransitive verb*
(**boo-hoo**) (**boo-hoos**, **boo-hooed**) (esp. of a child) weep loudly.
[imitative]

book ● *noun* **1 a** a written or printed work consisting of pages glued or sewn together along one side and bound in covers. **b** a literary composition intended for publication (*is working on her book*). **2** a bound set of blank sheets for writing or keeping records in. **3** a set of tickets, stamps, matches, cheques, etc., bound up together. **4** (in *pl.*) a set of records or accounts. **5** a main division of a literary work, or of the Bible (*the Book of Deuteronomy*). **6** a libretto, script of a play, etc. **7** a telephone directory (*my number's in the book*). **8** a record of bets made and money paid out by a bookmaker. **9** (in bridge etc.) a set of six tricks collected together. **10** an imaginary record or list (*the book of life*; *broke every rule in the book*). ● *verb* **1** *transitive* **a** engage (a seat etc.) in advance; make a reservation of. **b** engage (a guest, supporter, etc.) for some occasion. **2** *transitive* **a** take the personal details of (an offender or rule breaker). **b** enter in a book or list. **3** *transitive* issue a railway etc. ticket to. **4** *intransitive* make a reservation (*no need to book*). □ **book in** esp. *Brit.* register one's arrival at a hotel etc. **book off** *Cdn* stay home from work, esp. when sick (*phoned my boss to book off sick*). **booked up** with all places reserved. **bring to book** call to account. **by the book** according to the rules. **close the books** ensure that all pertinent information is entered at the end of an accounting period. **in a person's bad** (or **good**) **books** in disfavour (or favour) with a person. **in my book** in my opinion. **make book 1** give odds, take bets, and pay out winnings. **2** bet (*no one's making book on who will win the election*). **off the books** unofficially, not appearing in payroll reports etc. **on the books 1** (of a rule, law, etc.) publicly recorded. **2** contained in a list of members etc. **throw the book at** *informal* charge or punish to the utmost. □ **book·er** *noun* [Old English *bōc*, *bōcian*, from Germanic, usu. taken to be related to BEECH (the bark of which was used for writing on)]

book·able *adjective* **1** that may be reserved or engaged in advance. **2** *Soccer* (of an offence) serious enough to be entered in the referee's book.

book·bag *noun* N Amer. a bag or knapsack used esp. by students to carry books, papers, etc.

book·bind·er *noun* a person who binds books professionally. □ **book·bind·ing** *noun*

book·case *noun* a set of shelves for books in the form of a cabinet.

book club *noun* **1** a society which sells its members selected books on special terms. **2** a group of people who meet on a regular basis to discuss a book or books that they have read.

book·end ● *noun* **1** one of a pair of props used to keep a row of books upright. **2** one of a pair of e.g. television commercials etc. situated at either end of something. **3** *Football* a player positioned at either end of a team's defensive line. ● *transitive verb* **1** serve as or provide with something which frames a larger item on either side. **2** (of two people) flank a (third) person.

book·ie *noun* informal = BOOKMAKER.

book·ing *noun* an act of reserving accommodations etc. or of buying a ticket in advance.

book·ish *adjective* **1** studious; fond of reading. **2** acquiring knowledge from books rather than practical experience. **3** (of a word, language, etc.) literary; not colloquial. □ **book·ish·ly** *adverb* **book·ish·ness** *noun*

book·keep·er *noun* a person who keeps accounts for a trader, a public office, etc. □ **book·keep·ing** *noun*

book learning *noun* knowledge gained from books; mere theory.

book·let *noun* a small book consisting of a few sheets usu. with paper covers.

book·louse *noun* a minute insect of the order *Psocoptera*, often damaging to books.

book·maker *noun* a person who takes bets, calculates odds, and pays out winnings. □ **book·making** *noun*

book·mark ● *noun* **1** a strip of leather, card, etc., used to mark one's place in a book. **2** a tag or character which can be inserted by a user at a particular point in an electronic text, and can be located quickly by a search through the document, making it easier to return to that point. **3** an electronic reference to a particular Internet site, which a reader has chosen to store permanently in the browser software, so as to reconnect rapidly with it. ● *transitive verb* mark (an Internet site) with a bookmark.

book·mobile /ˈbʊkməˌbiːl/ *noun* N Amer. a truck, van, etc., fitted to hold shelves of books and serve as a mobile library. [after AUTOMOBILE]

Book of Changes see I CHING.

Book of Common Prayer the official service book of the Church of England. It was compiled through the efforts of Thomas Cranmer and others as a simplified and condensed English version of the Latin service books used by the medieval Church and was first issued in 1549.

book of hours *noun* Christianity a book containing the prayers or offices appointed to be said at certain times of day.

book·plate *noun* a decorative label stuck in the front of a book bearing the owner's name.

book·rest *noun* an adjustable support for an open book on a table.

book·sell·er *noun* a person who sells books, esp. the proprietor of a bookstore.

book·shelf *noun* (*pl.* **-shelves**) **1** a single shelf for books, either attached to a wall or as part of a bookcase. **2** = BOOKCASE. **3** (*attributive*) designating stereo equipment etc. that is small enough to place on a bookshelf (*bookshelf speakers*).

book-signing *noun* a publicity event at which an author appears in person to autograph books being sold.

book·stall *noun* a stand for selling books, newspapers, etc., esp. out of doors or at an airport etc.

book·stand *noun* **1** a bookstall. **2** a stand or rack, usu. sloped, for supporting a book.

book·store *noun* (also **book·shop**) a store where books are sold.

book value *noun* the value of an asset as entered in business or other records (*opp.* MARKET VALUE).

book·worm *noun* **1** informal a person devoted to reading. **2** the larva of a moth or beetle which feeds on the paper and glue used in books.

Boole /buːl/ **George** (1815–64), English mathematician, chiefly remembered for his development of an algebraic description of reasoning.

Bool·ean /ˈbuːliən/ *adjective* pertaining to a system in which logical propositions are manipulated using the operators 'and', 'or', and 'not'. [from G. BOOLE]

boom¹ ● *noun* **1** a deep resonant sound, as of a distant explosion or a bass drum. **2** the resonant cry made by some birds and animals, esp. the prairie chicken and bittern. **3** a period of prosperity or sudden activity in commerce. ● *verb* **1** *intransitive* make a deep hollow resonant sound. **2** *transitive* (usu. foll. by *out*) speak or utter with a booming sound. **3** *intransitive* (esp. of commercial ventures) be suddenly prosperous or successful. □ **boom·ing** *adjective* **boomy** *adjective* [ultimately imitative: perhaps from Dutch *bommen* hum, buzz]

boom² ● *noun* **1 a** a movable arm used for lifting, manoeuvring, etc. **b** a movable arm supporting a camera, microphone, etc. **2 a** a barrier stretched across a river, harbour, etc. to obstruct navigation. **b** N Amer. Forestry a barrier of floating timber used to contain, restrain or guide floating logs. **c** a similar barrier used to contain oil spills etc. on water. **3** N Amer. Forestry a raft of timber or logs fastened together for transportation on water. **4** Naut. a pivoted spar to which the foot of a sail is attached, allowing the angle of the sail to be changed. ● *transitive verb* N Amer. Forestry **1** gather or confine (logs) in a boom. **2** move or transport (logs) by forming them into a boom. [Dutch, = BEAM *noun*]

boom and bust *noun* a period of economic expansion and prosperity followed by a recession or depression, often seen as a naturally occurring economic cycle.

boom box *noun* a usu. large and powerful portable stereo.

boom chain *noun* Cdn Forestry a chain linking two boomsticks, used to hold booms of logs together.

boom·er *noun* = BABY BOOMER.

boom·er·ang ● *noun* **1** a curved flat hardwood projectile used by Australian Aboriginals to kill prey, and often of a kind able to return in flight to the thrower. **2** a plan or scheme that recoils on its originator. ● *intransitive verb* **1** act as a boomerang. **2** (of a plan or action) backfire. [Dharuk *bumarin*ʸ]

booming ground¹ *noun* Cdn a section of a lake, river, etc. where logs are collected into booms. [BOOM²]

booming ground² *noun* N Amer. the mating ground of the prairie chicken. [from the booming sound made by the males]

boom·let *noun* a small boom, as in business or population.

boom man *noun* N Amer. Forestry a person who collects logs into booms.

boom·stick *noun* N Amer. Forestry one of the logs that surrounds a boom and holds it together.

boom town *noun* a town owing its origin, growth, or prosperity to a boom in some commodity or activity.

uː mo**od**　ai my　əi p**i**pe　au br**ow**n　ʌu h**ou**se　ei d**ay**　ɔi b**oy**　ā fr**a**nglais　ã Canadi**e**n　ɔ̃ Brayon　(*see over for consonants*)

boomy adjective (**boom·i·er**, **boom·i·est**) **1** having a loud, deep, resonant sound. **2** of or relating to a boom in business etc.

boon[1] noun **1** an advantage; a blessing. **2** archaic **a** a thing asked for; a request. **b** a gift; a favour. [Middle English, originally = prayer, from Old Norse *bón* from Germanic]

boon[2] adjective close, intimate, favourite (*boon companion*). [Middle English, originally = jolly, congenial, from Old French *bon* from Latin *bonus* good]

boon·docks noun N Amer. informal rough or isolated country; backwoods. [Tagalog *bundok* mountain]

boon·dog·gle N Amer. informal ● noun **1** work of little or no value done merely to appear busy. **2** a government-funded project with no purpose other than political patronage. ● verb **1** transitive deceive (a person etc.). **2** intransitive do work for the purpose of appearing to be busy. [origin unknown]

Boone, **Dan·iel** (1734–1820), US frontiersman, central figure in the settlement of Kentucky, and folk hero.

boon·ies plural noun N Amer. slang = BOONDOCKS.

boor noun **1** a rude, ill-mannered person. **2** a clumsy person. □ **boor·ish** adjective **boor·ish·ly** adverb **boor·ish·ness** noun [Low German *būr* or Dutch *boer* farmer: compare BOWER[3]]

boost ● transitive verb **1** promote or increase the reputation of (a person, scheme, commodity, etc.) by praise or advertising. **2** increase or raise (*boost her spirits*; *boost prices*). **3** push from below; assist (*boosted me up the tree*). **4** raise the voltage in (an electric circuit etc.). **5** N Amer. recharge (a car battery). **6** N Amer. slang steal. **7** amplify (a radio signal). ● noun **1** a lift or push from below (*asked for a boost up the tree*). **2** an improvement in spirits, confidence, etc. (*praising your children will give them a boost*). **3** an increase (*he is enjoying a boost in popularity*). **4** N Amer. the action of recharging a car battery. [19th c.: origin unknown]

boost·er noun **1** a device for increasing electrical power or voltage. **2** an auxiliary engine or rocket used to give initial acceleration. **3** Med. a dose of an immunizing agent increasing or renewing the effect of an earlier one (also attributive: *booster shot*). **4** a person who boosts by helping or encouraging. **5** = BOOSTER SEAT.

booster cable noun N Amer. (usu. in pl.) = JUMPER CABLE.

boost·er·ism noun N Amer. the tendency to praise, advertise, or promote oneself or one's own (town, country, product, etc.). □ **boost·er·ish** adjective

booster seat noun a small seat placed on another seat, e.g. in a car or at a table, to elevate a toddler or child.

boot[1] ● noun **1** an outer covering for the foot usu. reaching above the ankle, often to the knee. **2** informal a kick. **3** (prec. by the) informal dismissal, esp. from employment (*gave them the boot*). **4** Brit. = TRUNK 5. **5** a covering to protect the lower part of a horse's leg. **6** hist. an instrument of torture encasing and crushing the foot. ● transitive verb **1** kick. **2** (often foll. by *out*) dismiss (a person) forcefully. □ **die with one's boots on** die in action. **put the boots to** (also Brit. **put the boot in**) kick brutally. **you bet your boots** informal it is quite certain. □ **boot·ed** adjective [Old Norse *bóti* or from Old French *bote*, of unknown origin]

boot[2] Computing ● noun the operation or procedure of booting a computer or an operating system. ● verb **1** transitive prepare (a computer) for operation by causing an operating system to be loaded into its memory. **2** transitive cause (an operating system) to be loaded in this way. **3** transitive (often foll. by *up*) load (a routine) into a computer's memory. **4** intransitive (of a computer, operating system, or program) undergo booting. □ **boot·able** adjective [abbreviation of BOOTSTRAP 2]

boot[3] noun □ **to boot** as well; to the good; in addition. [originally = 'advantage': Old English *bót* from Germanic]

boot·black noun US dated a person who polishes boots and shoes.

boot camp noun N Amer. informal **1** a centre for basic military training. **2** a penal institution in which young, esp. first-time, offenders undergo rigorous exercise and work and military-style discipline.

boot-cut adjective (of jeans or pants) cut with a leg that is flared very slightly from the knee to the ankle, so as to be worn comfortably over boots.

boot·ee var. of BOOTIE.

Bo·ötes /bəʊˈəʊtiːz/ a constellation of the northern sky, dominated by the bright orange star Arcturus, and said to represent a herdsman driving a bear (the constellation Ursa Major). [Latin from Greek *boōtes* ploughman, from *bous* ox + *ōthein* push]

Booth ▸ **1 Ed·win Thom·as** (1833–93), US actor, who was a noted tragedian, esp. in Shakespearean roles. **2 John Wilkes** (1838–65), US actor who assassinated Abraham Lincoln in 1865. **3 Jun·ius Brut·us**

(1796–1852), English-born US actor and father of Edwin Booth, who was also a noted tragedian. **4 Wil·liam** (1829–1912), English revivalist preacher. Concerned with the physical needs of those to whom he preached, he founded the Salvation Army in 1865.

booth /buːθ/ noun (pl. **booths** /buːðs, buːðz/) **1** a small temporary structure or stall for the display or sale of goods, e.g. at an exhibition or market. **2** an enclosure or compartment for various purposes, e.g. telephoning, broadcasting, or voting. **3** a set of a table and benches in a restaurant or bar. [Middle English from Scandinavian]

Booth·ia, Gulf of /ˈbuːθɪə/ a large inlet of the Arctic Ocean, situated between the Boothia Peninsula and Baffin Island. [Sir F. *Booth*, promoter of Arctic exploration d.1850]

Booth·ia Peninsula a large peninsula of central Nunavut, situated between Victoria and Baffin islands. Its northern tip represents the most northerly point of the N American mainland. [Sir F. *Booth*, promoter of Arctic exploration d.1850]

boot·ie noun (also **boot·ee**) **1** a soft woollen or cloth shoe. **2** a woman's short boot.

boot·jack noun a device for holding a boot by the heel to ease withdrawal of the leg.

boot·lace noun a cord or leather thong for lacing boots.

boot·leg ● adjective **1** (of alcoholic beverages, drugs, etc.) illicitly produced, transported, or sold. **2** (of a recording) made without authorization, e.g. by illicitly recording a live concert. **3** Football of or relating to a play in which a player feigns a pass to another player, then continues with the ball concealed near his hip. ● noun **1** something produced or sold illegally. **2** Football a bootleg play. ● transitive verb (**-legged**, **-leg·ging**) make, distribute, or smuggle illicit goods (esp. alcohol). □ **boot·leg·ger** noun [from smugglers' practice of concealing bottles in their boots]

boot·less adjective archaic unavailing, useless. [Old English *bótlēas* (as BOOT[3], LESS)]

boot·lick·er noun informal a person who behaves obsequiously or servilely. □ **boot·lick·ing** adjective

boot·strap ● noun **1** a loop at the back of a boot used to pull it on. **2** Computing the action of bootstrapping; a bootstrapping routine. ● verb **1** make one's way or get oneself into a new state using existing resources; modify or improve by making use of what is already present. **2** Computing = BOOT[2] verb. □ **pull oneself up by one's bootstraps** better oneself by one's own efforts.

booty noun **1** plunder gained by force or violence. **2** informal something gained or won. [Middle Low German *būte*, *buite* exchange, of uncertain origin]

booze informal ● noun **1** alcoholic drink. **2** a drinking bout. ● intransitive verb drink alcoholic liquor, esp. excessively or habitually. [earlier *bouse*, *bowse*, from Middle Dutch *būsen* drink to excess]

booze can noun Cdn an illegal bar, esp. one operating in a private home.

booze·hound noun N Amer. informal = BOOZER 1.

booz·er noun informal **1** a person who drinks alcohol, esp. to excess. **2** Brit. a bar or pub.

booze-up noun slang a drinking bout.

boozy adjective (**booz·i·er**, **booz·i·est**) informal **1** intoxicated; addicted to drink. **2** involving a great deal of alcoholic drink (*a boozy party*; *a boozy dessert*). □ **booz·i·ly** adverb **booz·i·ness** noun

bop[1] informal ● noun **1** = BEBOP. **2** esp. Brit. a dance to pop music. ● intransitive verb (**bopped**, **bop·ping**) **1** dance, esp. to pop music. **2** move, go. □ **bop·per** noun **bop·pish** adjective **bop·py** adjective [abbreviation of BEBOP]

bop[2] informal ● transitive verb (**bopped**, **bop·ping**) hit, punch lightly. ● noun a light blow or hit. [imitative]

Bophu·tha·tswa·na /ˌbɒpuːtətˈswɒnə/ a former homeland established in South Africa for the Tswana people, now part of North-West Province and Mpumalanga. (See also HOMELAND 2).

bora /ˈbɔːrə/ noun a strong cold dry NE wind blowing in the upper Adriatic. [Italian dial. from Latin *boreas* north wind: see BOREAL]

Bora-Bora /ˌbɔːrəˈbɔːrə/ an island of the Society Islands group in French Polynesia.

bor·acic /bəˈrasɪk/ adjective of, containing, or derived from borax. [medieval Latin *borax -acis*]

boracic acid noun = BORIC ACID.

bor·age /ˈbɒrɪdʒ, ˈbʌ-/ noun any plant of the genus *Borago*, esp. *Borago officinalis*, which has hairy leaves and bright blue flowers, and is sometimes used in salads etc. [Old French *bourrache* from medieval

Latin *borrago* from Arabic *'abu 'ārak* father of sweat (from its use as a diaphoretic)]

bor·ane /ˈbɔːreɪn/ *noun Chem.* any hydride of boron.

bor·ate /ˈbɔːreɪt/ *noun* a salt or ester of boric acid.

borax /ˈbɔːraks/ *noun* **1** the mineral salt sodium borate, occurring in alkaline deposits as an efflorescence or as crystals. **2** the purified form of this salt, used in making glass and china, as an antiseptic, and as a household cleanser. [medieval Latin from Arabic *būrak* from Persian *būrah*]

bora·zon /ˈbɔːrəˌzɒn/ *noun* a hard form of boron nitride, resistant to oxidation. [BORON + AZO- nitrogen +-*on*]

bor·boryg·mus /ˌbɔːbəˈrɪgməs/ *noun* (*pl.* **bor·boryg·mi** /-maɪ/) a rumbling of gas in the intestines. [modern Latin from Greek]

Bor·deaux¹ /bɔːˈdəʊ/ *a* a port of SW France on the Garonne River, capital of Aquitaine; pop. (1999) 215,363. It is a centre of the wine trade.

Bor·deaux² /bɔːˈdəʊ/ *noun* (*pl.* same /-ˈdəʊz/) any of various red, white, or rosé wines from the district of Bordeaux in SW France.

Bordeaux mixture *noun* a fungicide for vines, fruit trees, etc., composed of equal quantities of copper sulphate and calcium oxide in water.

bor·del·lo /bɔːˈdeləʊ/ *noun* (*pl.* **-los**) a brothel. [Italian from Old French *bordel* small farm, diminutive of *borde*, ultimately from Frankish: see BOARD]

Bor·den ▶ 1 Liz·zie (An·drew) (1860–1927) suspected murderess of her father and stepmother. In 1892, her parents were found hacked to death with a sharp instrument in their home in Fall River, Massachusetts. Lizzie's murder trial in 1893 caused a sensation throughout the US, but she was acquitted. **2 Rob·ert Laird** (1854–1937), Canadian Conservative prime minister (1911–20), remembered for wartime leadership which included conscription (1917), the introduction of income tax (1917), and international recognition of the autonomy of the Dominions.

Borden Island the most northerly of the Parry Islands in the Canadian High Arctic, situated west of Ellef Ringnes Island. [R. L. BORDEN]

Borden Peninsula a large peninsula of the northern coast of Baffin Island. It is flanked to the west by Brodeur Peninsula and to the east by Bylot Island. [R. L. BORDEN]

bor·der • *noun* **1** the edge or boundary of anything, or the part near it. **2 a** the line separating two political or geographical areas, esp. countries. **b** the district on each side of this. **3** a distinct edging around anything, esp. for strength or decoration. **4** a long narrow bed of flowers or shrubs in a garden (*herbaceous border*). • *verb* **1** *transitive* be a border to. **2** *transitive* provide with a border. **3** *intransitive* (usu. foll. by *on*, *upon*) **a** adjoin; be situated alongside. **b** come close to being (*this borders on madness*). □ **border·less** *adjective* [Old French *bordure*: compare BOARD]

border collie *noun* a long-haired usu. black and white breed of dog, often used for herding sheep. [with reference to the Borders, the region along the border between England and Scotland]

border crossing *noun* **1** a place at which one may officially cross an international border. **2** the act of passing through customs and immigration formalities when crossing a border.

bor·der·er *noun Brit.* a person who lives near the border between Scotland and England.

border·land *noun* **1** the district near a border. **2** an intermediate condition between two extremes.

border·line • *noun* **1** a marginal position between two categories or qualities. **2** a line marking a boundary. • *adjective* **1** on the borderline. **2** verging on each of two categories or conditions without clearly being identifiable as one or the other.

Bor·ders the former name for SCOTTISH BORDERS.

border terrier *noun* a small rough-haired breed of terrier. [with reference to the border between England and Scotland]

Bor·det /bɔːˈdeɪ/ **Jules** (1870–1961), Belgian bacteriologist and immunologist. He discovered the heat-sensitive complements found in blood serum, demonstrated their role in antibody–antigen reactions and bacterial lysis, and developed a vaccine for whooping cough; he was awarded a Nobel Prize in 1919.

Bor·duas /ˈbɔːduːɒ/ **Paul-Émile** (1905-60), Canadian painter. His early work is figurative, but his later work, like the masterpiece *L'Étoile noire* (1957), explores the abstract contrasts of black and white.

bor·dure /ˈbɔːdjʊə/ *noun Heraldry* a border around the edge of a shield. [Middle English form of BORDER]

bore¹ • *verb* **1** *transitive* make a hole in, esp. with a revolving tool. **2** *transitive* hollow out (a tube etc.). **3** *transitive* **a** make (a hole) by boring or excavation. **b** make (one's) way through a crowd etc. **4** *intransitive* drill a well (for oil etc.). **5** *transitive* (of an animal) move by burrowing. • *noun* **1** the hollow of a firearm barrel or of a cylinder in an internal combustion engine. **2** the diameter of this; the calibre. **3** = BOREHOLE. [Old English *borian* from Germanic]

bore² • *noun* a tiresome or dull person or thing. • *transitive verb* cause to lose all interest by tedious talk or dullness. □ **bore a person to tears** cause (a person) intense boredom. □ **bored** *adjective* [18th c.: origin unknown]

bore³ *noun* (in full **tidal bore**) a high wave caused by rapidly rising tide entering a long shallow narrow inlet. [perhaps from Old Norse *bára* wave]

bore⁴ *past of* BEAR¹.

bor·eal /ˈbɔːrɪəl/ *adjective* **1** of the North or northern regions. **2** of the north wind. [Late Latin *borealis* from Latin *Boreas* from Greek *Boreas* god of the north wind]

boreal chickadee *noun* a chickadee of coniferous forests in North America, with a brown crown and back.

boreal forest *noun* the northernmost and coldest forest zone of the northern hemisphere, which forms a 1 000 km-wide belt across N America, Europe, and Asia; in Canada, it is dominated by evergreens and small-leaf deciduous trees.

boreal owl *noun* a small brown and white owl, *Aegolius funereus*, of boreal woodlands of N America and Eurasia.

Bor·eas /ˈbɔːrɪəs/ *Gk Myth* the personification of the north wind.

bore·dom *noun* the state of being bored.

bore·hole *noun* a deep narrow hole, esp. one made in the earth to find water, oil, etc.

bor·er *noun* **1** any of several worms, molluscs, insects, or insect larvae which bore into wood, other plant material, and rock. **2** a tool for boring.

Borg, Bjorn (b.1956), Swedish tennis player. In 1980 he won the men's singles championship at Wimbledon for the fifth year in succession, beating the previous record of three consecutive wins set in 1936.

Borges /ˈbɔːxes/ **Jorge Luis** (1899–1986), Argentinian writer. His stories tend to be labyrinthine in form and metaphysical in speculation. □ **Borges·ian** *adjective*

Borgia /ˈbɔːʒə/ **1 Cesare** (*c.*1476–1507), Italian statesman. The illegitimate son of Cardinal Rodrigo Borgia (later Pope Alexander VI) and brother of Lucrezia Borgia, he became a cardinal in 1493. As captain-general of the papal army from 1499, he became master of a large portion of central Italy until he was defeated at Naples in 1504. **2 Lu·cre·zia** (1480–1519), Italian noblewoman. The illegitimate daughter of Cardinal Rodrigo Borgia (later Pope Alexander VI), she married three times, according to the political alliances useful to her father and to her brother, Cesare Borgia. Always associated with the scandals of her birth and marriages, after her third marriage in 1501 she established herself as a patron of the arts and became increasingly religious.

Bor·glum /ˈbɔːɡləm/ **(John) Gut·zon** (1867–1941), US sculptor, whose colossal portrait busts of US presidents Washington, Jefferson, Lincoln, and Theodore Roosevelt are carved into Mount Rushmore in South Dakota (1930–41).

boric /ˈbɔːrɪk/ *adjective* of or containing boron.

boric acid *noun* an acid derived from borax, used as a mild antiseptic and in the manufacture of heat-resistant glass and enamels.

bor·ing *adjective* that makes one bored; uninteresting, tedious, dull. □ **bor·ing·ly** *adverb* **bor·ing·ness** *noun*

Bor·laug /ˈbɔːlɒɡ/ **Nor·man (Er·nest)** (b.1914), US agronomist, awarded the 1970 Nobel Peace Prize for his development of high-yielding cereal varieties for the Third World.

Bor·mann /ˈbɔːmən/ **Mar·tin** (1900–*c.*1945), German Nazi politician. He succeeded Hess as Party chancellor in 1941. Considered to be Hitler's closest collaborator, he disappeared at the end of the Second World War. He was sentenced to death *in absentia* at the Nuremberg trials in 1945; his skeleton, exhumed in Berlin, was identified in 1973.

Born, Max (1882–1970), German theoretical physicist, one of the founders of quantum mechanics. He was awarded the Nobel Prize for physics in 1954 for his work on wave mechanics and quantum theory.

born *adjective* **1** existing as a result of birth. **2 a** being such or likely to become such by natural ability or quality (*a born leader*). **b** (usu. foll. by *to* + infin.) having a specified destiny or prospect (*born lucky*; *born to be king*; *born to shop*). **3** (in *combination*) of a certain status by birth

(*Canadian-born*; *well-born*). **4** created or caused; brought into existence (*anger born of frustration*; *a new religion was born out of this experience*). □ **born and bred** by birth and upbringing. **in all one's born days** *informal* in one's life so far. **not born yesterday** *informal* not stupid; shrewd. [past participle of BEAR[1]]

born-again *attributive adjective* **1** of or relating to a Christian who has made a new or renewed commitment to esp. evangelical faith. **2** full of enthusiastic and esp. new-found zeal for a cause.

borne 1 *past participle of* BEAR[1]. **2** (in *combination*) carried or transported by (*airborne*).

Bor·ne·o /ˈbɔːnɪˌəʊ/ a large island of the Malay Archipelago, comprising Kalimantan (a region of Indonesia), Sabah and Sarawak (states of Malaysia), and Brunei. □ **Born·ean** *adjective*

Born·holm /ˈbɔːnhəʊm/ a Danish island in the Baltic Sea, southeast of Sweden.

boro- /ˈbɔːrəʊ/ *combining form* boron.

Bo·ro·bu·dur /ˌbɔːrəʊbʊˈdʊr/ a Buddhist monument in central Java, built *c.*800, abandoned *c.*1000, restored in 1907–11 and again in the 1980s. It consists of five square successively smaller terraces, one above the other, surmounted by three concentric galleries and a stupa. Illustrations on the terrace walls show the life of the Buddha and successive stages towards perfection.

Bo·ro·din /ˈbɔːrədɪn/ **Alex·an·der** (1833–87), Russian composer. One of the group known as 'The Five' or 'The Mighty Handful' (the others were Balakirev, Mussorgsky, Rimsky-Korsakov, and Cui), he composed symphonies, string quartets, songs, and piano music, and is best known for his epic opera *Prince Igor.*

Bo·ro·di·no, Battle of /ˌbɔːrəˈdiːnəʊ/ a battle in 1812 at Borodino, a village about 110 km west of Moscow, between Napoleon's forces and the Russian army. Though the French were victorious in the battle, the heavy losses they suffered contributed to their eventual defeat in the campaign against Russia.

boron /ˈbɔːrɒn/ *noun Chem.* a non-metallic brown amorphous or black crystalline element extracted from borax and boric acid and mainly used for hardening steel. Symbol: **B**; at. no.: 5. [BORAX + -*on* from *carbon* (which it resembles in some respects)]

bor·o·nia /bəˈrəʊnɪə/ *noun* any sweet-scented Australian shrub of the genus *Boronia.* [F. *Borone*, Italian botanist d.1794]

bor·o·sili·cate /ˌbɔːrəʊˈsɪlɪˌkeɪt, -kət/ *noun* any of many substances containing boron, silicon, and oxygen generally used in glazes and enamels and in the production of glass.

bor·ough /ˈbʌrə/ *noun* **1** *Brit.* **a** a town (as distinct from a city) with a corporation and privileges granted by a royal charter. **b** *hist.* a town sending representatives to Parliament. **2 a** *hist.* (in Ontario) a municipality with the status of a township. **b** (in Quebec) one of the municipal electoral divisions of the amalgamated city of Montreal. **3** an administrative division of London, England. **4** a municipal corporation in certain US states. **5** each of five divisions of New York City. **6** (in Alaska) a county. [Old English *burg*, *burh* from Germanic: compare BURGH]

Bor·ro·mini /ˌbɒrəˈmiːni, bɒ-/ **Fran·cesco** (1599–1667), Italian architect, one of the leading figures of Roman baroque. His style, both passionate and mathematical, using subtle architectural forms but austere methods of decoration, was of tremendous importance in the development of the baroque in Italy, Germany, and Austria.

bor·row *verb* **1 a** *transitive* acquire temporarily with the promise or intention of returning. **b** *intransitive* obtain money in this way. **2** *transitive* use (an idea, invention, etc.) originated by another; plagiarize. **3** *transitive & intransitive* (in subtraction) take (one) from a digit of the minuend in order to add it as 10 to the digit holding the next lower place. **4** *transitive Linguistics* (of a language) adopt (a word form) from another language. □ **borrowed time** an unexpected extension, esp. before an imminent disaster. **borrow trouble** *N Amer.* go out of one's way to find trouble. □ **bor·row·er** *noun* **bor·row·ing** *noun* [Old English *borgian* give a pledge]

borrow pit *noun* a pit or ditch created by removing earth for use in building up an adjacent road, embankment, etc.

borscht /bɔːʃt/ *noun* an originally Eastern European soup with various ingredients including beets and cabbage, and served with sour cream. □ **cheap like borscht** *Cdn informal* extremely cheap. [Russian *borshch*]

Borscht Belt *noun N Amer.* the resort area of the Catskill mountains in New York State, much frequented by Jewish vacationers, and known for its cabarets and stand-up comics. [borscht being a staple of Eastern European Jewish cooking]

Bor·stal /ˈbɔːstəl/ *noun Brit. hist.* an institution for reforming and training young offenders. [*Borstal* in S England, where the first of these was established]

bort *noun* (also **boart**) **1** an inferior or malformed diamond, used for cutting. **2** fragments of diamonds produced in cutting. [Dutch *boort*]

bor·zoi /ˈbɔːzɔɪ/ *noun* a breed of large Russian wolfhound with a narrow head and silky, usu. white, coat. [Russian from *borzyi* swift]

bosc·age /ˈbɒskɪdʒ/ *noun* (also **bosk·age**) **1** masses of trees or shrubs. **2** wooded scenery. [Old French *boscage* from Germanic: compare BUSH[1]]

Bosch /bɒʃ/ **Hier·ony·mus** (*c.*1450–1516), Dutch painter. His works, most having a moral theme, are characterized by half-human, half-animal creatures of fantasy and demons, interspersed with human figures in a setting of imaginary architecture and landscape.

Bosc pear /bɒsk/ *noun N Amer.* a firm, sweet, fairly elongated russet winter pear. [L. A. G. *Bosc*, French naturalist d.1828]

Bose /ˈbəʊs/ **Sat·yen·dra Nath** (1894–1974), Indian physicist. With Einstein, he described fundamental particles which later came to be known as bosons.

bosh *noun & interjection slang* nonsense; foolish talk. [Turkish *boş* empty]

bosky *adjective* (**bosk·i·er**, **bosk·i·est**) *literary* wooded, bushy. [Middle English *bosk* thicket]

bo's'n *var. of* BOATSWAIN.

Bos·nia and Herze·go·vina /ˌbɒznɪə, hɜːtsəˈɡɒvɪnə, -ɡəˈviːnə/ (also **Bosnia-Herzegovina**) a country in the Balkans, formerly a constituent republic of Yugoslavia; pop. (est. 2002) 3,964,388; capital, Sarajevo. In 1992 Bosnia and Herzegovina followed Slovenia and Croatia in declaring independence from Yugoslavia, but ethnic conflict amongst Muslims, Serbs and Croats created a state of civil war. In 1994 Bosnian Muslims and Croats reached an accord establishing a federation; a year later a peace agreement was reached between Bosnia, Croatia and Serbia, effectively dividing Bosnia into separate self-governing parts, the Muslim-Croat Federation and the Bosnian Serb Republic. (See also HERZEGOVINA.) □ **Bos·nian** *noun & adjective*

bosom /ˈbʊzəm/ *noun* **1 a** a person's breast or chest, esp. a woman's. **b** *informal* each of a woman's breasts. **c** the enclosure formed by a person's breast and arms. **2** an emotional centre, esp. as the source of an enfolding relationship (*in the bosom of one's family*). **3** the part of a woman's dress covering the breast. [Old English *bōsm* from Germanic]

bosomed /ˈbʊzəmd/ *adjective* (in *combination*) having breasts of a specified type (*big-bosomed*).

bosom friend *noun* (also **bosom buddy**) a very close or intimate friend.

bosomy /ˈbʊzəmi/ *adjective* (of a woman) having large breasts.

boson /ˈbəʊzɒn/ *noun Physics* any of several elementary particles obeying the relations stated by Bose and Einstein, with a zero or integral spin, e.g. photons (compare FERMION). [S. N. *Bose*]

Bos·porus /ˈbɒspərəs/ (also **Bos·phorus** /ˈbɒsfərəs/) a strait connecting the Black Sea with the Sea of Marmara, separating Europe from the Anatolian peninsula of W Asia. Istanbul is located at its south end. [Greek *bos* ox, cow + *poros* passage, crossing; the name is linked with the story of Io]

boss[1] ● *noun* **1** a person in charge of employees; an employer, manager, or supervisor. **2** a person who controls or manages an organization, e.g. a political party, union, organized crime syndicate, etc. **3** a person who asserts authority (*let them know who's boss*). ● *transitive verb* **1** (usu. foll. by *around*) treat domineeringly; give constant peremptory orders to. **2** be the master or manager of. ● *adjective slang* first-rate, excellent. [Dutch *baas* master]

boss[2] *noun* **1** a round knob, stud, or other protuberance, esp. on the centre of a shield or in ornamental work. **2** *Archit.* a piece of ornamental carving etc. covering the point where the ribs in a vault or ceiling cross. **3** *Geol.* a protuberant mass of igneous rock. **4** *Mech.* an enlarged part of a shaft. [Old French *boce* from Romanic]

bossa nova /ˌbɒsə ˈnəʊvə/ *noun* **1** a dance like the samba, originating in Brazil. **2** a piece of music for this or in its rhythm. [Portuguese, lit. 'new flair']

boss man *noun* a man in charge.

Bos·suet /ˈbɒsueɪ/ **Jacques Bé·nigne** (1627–1704), French bishop, whose funeral orations are considered eminent examples of French classical style and the art of oratory.

Bossy /ˈbɒsi/ **Mi·chael ('Mike')** (b.1957), Canadian hockey player. A right winger with the New York Islanders from 1977–87, he became the only player to score more than 50 goals in nine consecutive seasons.

Vowels: a *cat* ɑ *arm* e *bed* ɜr *her* ɜː *deux* ə *ago* ɪ *sit* i *cosy* iː *feed* ɒ *hot* ɔ *pore* ɔː *no* ʌ *run* ʊ *put*

bossy[1] *adjective* (**boss·i·er**, **boss·i·est**) *informal* domineering; tending to boss. □ **boss·i·ly** *adverb* **boss·i·ness** *noun*

bossy[2] *noun* (*pl.* **-ies**) *N Amer.* a cow (also as a nickname).

bossy-boots *noun informal* a domineering person.

Bos·ton the state capital of Massachusetts; pop. (2000) 589,141. An early centre of New England Puritanism, Boston was the scene of disturbances leading to the American Revolution at the end of the 18th c. (*see* BOSTON TEA PARTY). □ **Bos·ton·ian** /bɒsˈtoːniən/ *noun & adjective*

Boston baked beans *noun N Amer.* baked beans with salt pork and molasses.

Boston bluefish *noun Cdn* = POLLOCK 1.

Boston brown bread *noun N Amer.* a steamed bread made with wheat flour, rye flour, cornmeal, and molasses.

Boston cream *noun* a doughnut with a custard or cream filling and chocolate icing.

Boston cream pie *noun N Amer.* a round, vanilla cake with a custard filling and chocolate icing.

Boston fern *noun esp. N Amer.* an ornamental fern, *Nephrolepis exaltata bostoniensis*, having long narrow fronds.

Boston ivy *noun N Amer.* an ornamental climbing vine, *Parthenocissus tricuspidata*, the leaves of which turn a vivid red in autumn.

Boston lettuce *noun N Amer.* a cultivated salad lettuce having a round head and soft pale leaves.

Boston rocker *noun N Amer.* a wooden rocking chair with a high back with spindles, a curved solid seat and arms, and a usu. decorated panel across the top.

Boston States *plural noun Cdn* (*Maritimes & Nfld*) New England.

Boston Tea Party a demonstration by American colonists on 16 Dec. 1773. Angered by the imposition of a tax on tea by the British Parliament (in which the colonists had no representation), citizens of Boston, Massachusetts, boarded vessels moored in the harbour and threw the cargoes of tea into the water.

Boston terrier *noun* a small breed of dog with a smooth coat, originating from a crossing of the bulldog and terrier.

bosun (also **bo'sun**) *var.* of BOATSWAIN.

Bos·well /ˈbɒzwel/ **James** (1740–95), Scottish author whose *Life of Samuel Johnson* (1791) is one the most celebrated biographies in English.

Bos·worth Field /ˈbɒzwɜːθ/ (also **Battle of Bosworth**) a battle of the Wars of the Roses fought in 1485 near Market Bosworth in Leicestershire. Henry Tudor defeated and killed the Yorkist king Richard III, enabling him to take the throne as Henry VII.

bot[1] *noun* (also **bott**) the parasitic larva of the botfly, infesting horses, sheep, etc. [prob. of Low German origin]

bot[2] *noun* a program on a network, esp. the Internet, which operates independently, often having reasoning and decision-making capabilities, esp. a program which locates information or responds and behaves like a human in games. [shortening of ROBOT]

bot. *abbreviation* **1** botanic; botanical; botany. **2** bottle.

bo·tan·ic·al /bəˈtanɪkəl/ ● *adjective* (also **bo·tan·ic** /bəˈtanɪk/) **1** of or relating to botany. **2** of, relating to, or derived from plants. ● *noun* a drug, insecticide, or cosmetic etc. derived from parts of a plant. □ **bo·tan·ic·al·ly** *adverb* [Greek *botanikos* from *botanē* plant]

botanical garden *noun* (also **botanic garden**) a large garden in which plants are studied and displayed.

bot·an·ize /ˈbɒtəˌnaɪz/ *intransitive verb* (also esp. *Brit.* **-ise**) study plants, esp. in their habitat.

bot·any /ˈbɒtəni/ *noun* **1** the study of the physiology, structure, genetics, ecology, distribution, and classification of plants. **2** the plant life of a particular area or time. □ **bot·an·ist** *noun* [BOTANICAL + -Y]

Botany Bay an inlet of the Tasman Sea in New South Wales, Australia, just south of Sydney. It was the site of Captain Cook's landing in 1770 and of an early penal settlement. [so called after the large variety of plants collected there by Cook's companion, Sir J. Banks]

botch ● *transitive verb* **1** bungle; do badly. **2** patch or repair clumsily. ● *noun* (also **botch-up**) bungled or spoiled work. □ **botch·er** *noun* [Middle English: origin unknown]

bot·fly *noun* (*pl.* **-flies**) any dipterous fly of the family Oestridae, having a stout hairy body.

both ● *adjective & pronoun* the two, not only one (*both girls; both the girls; both of the girls; the girls are both here*). ● *adverb* with equal truth in two cases (*both the boy and his sister are here; are both here and hungry*).

□ **have it both ways** alternate between two incompatible points of view to suit the needs of the moment. [Old Norse *báthir*]

Botha /ˈbɔːtə/ **1 Louis** (1862–1919), South African general and political leader. He was commander of the Transvaal forces during the Boer War and in 1910 became the first president of the Union of South Africa. **2 Pieter Wil·lem** (b.1916), South African prime minister (1978–84) and president (1984–89).

both·er ● *verb* **1** *transitive* **a** give trouble to; worry, disturb. **b** *reflexive* (often foll. by *about*) be anxious or concerned. **2** *intransitive* **a** (often foll. by *about*, or *to* + infin.) worry or trouble oneself; go to an effort (*don't bother about that; didn't bother to tell me*). **b** (foll. by *with*) be concerned. ● *noun* **1 a** a person or thing that bothers or causes worry. **b** a minor nuisance. **2** trouble, worry, fuss. ● *interjection* esp. *Brit.* expressing annoyance or impatience. □ **cannot be bothered** will not make the effort needed. [Irish *bodhraim* deafen]

both·er·a·tion *noun & interjection informal* = BOTHER *noun, interjection*.

both·er·some *adjective* causing bother; troublesome.

Both·nia, Gulf of /ˈbɒθniə/ a northern arm of the Baltic Sea, between Sweden and Finland.

Both·well /ˈbɒθwel/ **4th Earl of** (title of James Hepburn) (*c*.1536–78), Scottish nobleman and third husband of Mary, Queen of Scots. Mary's chief adviser, he was implicated in the murder of Lord Darnley (1567); tried for the crime but acquitted, he married Mary later the same year.

bothy /ˈbɒθi/ *noun* (*pl.* **-ies**) *Scot.* a small hut or cottage, esp. one for housing labourers. [18th c.: origin unknown: perhaps related to BOOTH]

Botox /ˈbɔːtɒks/ *noun proprietary* a drug prepared from botulinum toxin, used medically to treat certain muscular conditions and cosmetically to remove wrinkles by temporarily paralyzing facial muscles. [from BOTULINUM TOXIN]

bo tree *noun* an Indian fig tree, *Ficus religiosa*, regarded as sacred by Buddhists. *Also called* PEEPUL *or* PIPAL. [representing Sinhalese *bogaha* tree of knowledge (Buddha's enlightenment having occurred beneath such a tree)]

botry·oid·al /ˈbɒtriˌɔɪdəl/ *adjective* (esp. of a mineral) shaped like a cluster of grapes. [Greek *botruoeidēs* from *botrus* bunch of grapes]

botry·tis /bəˈtraɪtɪs/ *noun* a fungus of the genus *Botrytis*, esp. the grey mould *B. cinerea*, deliberately cultivated on the grapes used for certain wines (also called NOBLE ROT). □ **botry·tised** /bəˈtraɪtaɪzd/ *adjective* [modern Latin, from Greek *botrus* 'cluster of grapes']

Bot·swana /bɒtˈswɒnə/ a landlocked country in southern Africa; pop. (est. 2002) 1,591,232; capital, Gaborone. Much of Botswana is an arid tableland, with the Kalahari Desert occupying the western half of the country. It is inhabited by Sotho people and, in the Kalahari, San (Bushmen). □ **Bot·swan·an** *adjective & noun*

bott *var.* of BOT[1].

Bot·ti·celli /ˌbɒtiˈtʃeli/ **San·dro** (born Alessandro di Mariano Filipepi, 1445–1510), Florentine painter. A student of Filippo Lippi, he worked under the patronage of the Medici from 1475. His work, most famously *Primavera* (*c*.1478) and *The Birth of Venus* (*c*.1480), displays an interest in mythological subjects and is characterized by a delicate and ornamental linear style.

bot·tle ● *noun* **1** a container, usu. of glass or plastic and with a narrow neck, for storing liquid, pills, etc. **2** the amount that will fill a bottle. **3** = BABY BOTTLE. **4 a** (prec. by *the*) *informal* liquor or other alcoholic drink (*problems drove him to the bottle*). **b** a bottle of an alcoholic drink. **5** a metal cylinder for liquefied gas. **6** *Brit. slang* courage, confidence. ● *transitive verb* **1 a** put into bottles or jars. **b** *Brit., Cdn* (*Nfld*), *Austral.*, & *NZ* preserve in glass jars; can (*bottled moose*). **2** (usu. foll. by *up*) **a** conceal or restrain for a time (esp. a feeling). **b** keep (people) contained or entrapped. □ **hit the bottle** *informal* drink heavily. **on the bottle** *informal* drinking (alcoholic drink) heavily. □ **bottle·ful** *noun* (*pl.* **-fuls**). [Old French *botele, botaille* from medieval Latin *butticula* diminutive of Late Latin *buttis* BUTT[4]]

bottle blond ● *adjective* **1** (of hair) dyed blond. **2** (of a person) having dyed blond hair. ● *noun* a person with dyed blond hair.

bottle·brush *noun* **1** a cylindrical brush for cleaning the insides of bottles. **2** any of various plants with colourful flowers of this shape, esp. several Australian shrubs of the myrtle family.

bottlebrush grass *noun* a grass, *Hystrix patula*, with long stiff bristles resembling a bottlebrush, cultivated for bouquets.

bot·tled *adjective* **1** (of a liquid) contained in a bottle. **2** (of a gas) compressed to a liquid and contained in a tank. **3** *Brit. slang* drunk.

bottle-feed *transitive verb* (*past* and *past participle* **-fed**) feed (a baby) with milk by means of a bottle.

uː mood   ai my   əi pipe   au brown   ʌu house   ei day   ɔi boy   ɑ̃ franglais   ã Canadien   ɔ̃ Brayon   (*see over for consonants*)

bottle green ● *noun* dark green. ● *adjective* (**bottle-green**) of this colour.

bottle·neck *noun* **1** a point at which the flow of traffic, production, etc., is constricted. **2** a narrow place causing constriction. **3 a** a smooth cylinder worn on a guitarist's finger used to produce sliding effects on the strings. **b** the guitar style characterized by this technique.

bottle·nose dolphin *noun* (also **bottle·nosed dolphin**) any of several dolphins of the genus *Tursiops*, with an elongated beak.

bot·tler *noun* **1** a person or company which bottles drinks etc. **2** *Austral. & NZ slang* an excellent person or thing.

bottle tree *noun* an Australian tree of the genus *Brachychiton* with a swollen bottle-shaped trunk.

bottle-washer *noun* (esp. in phr. **chief cook and bottle-washer**) *informal* a person who performs menial tasks.

bot·tom ● *noun* **1 a** the lowest point or part (*bottom of the stairs*). **b** the part on which a thing rests (*bottom of a saucepan*). **c** the underside (*scraped the bottom of the car*). **d** the furthest or inmost part (*bottom of the garden*). **e** (in pl.) *N Amer.* = BOTTOMLAND. **2** *informal* the buttocks. **3** the seat of a chair. **4** the less honourable, important, or successful portion (*at the bottom of his class*). **5** the ground under the water of a lake, a river, etc. (*swam until she touched the bottom*). **6** the basis; the origin (*get to the bottom of the problem*). **7** *Baseball* **a** the second half of an inning, in which the home team bats. **b** the lower third of a batting order where the team's poorer batters tend to be included. **c** the batters making up this part of the batting order. **8** (in pl.) the part of a two-piece garment, esp. pyjamas or a bathing suit, worn below the waist. **9** *Naut.* **a** the keel or hull of a ship. **b** a ship, esp. a cargo carrier. **10** staying power; endurance. ● *adjective* **1** lowest (*bottom button*). **2** last (*got the bottom score*). ● *verb* **1** *transitive* provide with a bottom. **2** *intransitive* (of a ship) reach or touch the bottom. **3** *transitive* find the extent or real nature of; work out. **4** *transitive* (usu. foll. by *on*) base (an argument etc.) (*reasoning bottomed on logic*). **5** *transitive* touch the bottom or lowest point of. □ **at bottom** basically, essentially. **be at the bottom of** be the cause of. **bet one's bottom dollar** *slang* be assured. **bottom falls out** collapse occurs. **bottom out** reach the lowest level. **the bottom of the hour** the midpoint of the hour. **bottoms up!** a toast made when drinking. **bottom up** upside down. **get to the bottom of** fully investigate and explain. □ **bottom·most** *adjective* [Old English *botm* from Germanic]

bottom drawer *noun Brit.* = HOPE CHEST.

bottom-feeder *noun N Amer.* **1** a fish or other organism living and feeding near the bottom of a body of water. **2** *derogatory* a person who exploits or lives parasitically off others. □ **bottom-feeding** *adjective*

bottom fishing *noun* **1** fishing for bottom-feeders. **2** *informal* purchasing stocks, companies, etc. when they are at their lowest value. □ **bottom fish** *noun* **bottom fisher** *noun*

bottom·land *noun N Amer.* low-lying, fertile land along a watercourse; a flood plain.

bottom·less *adjective* **1** without a bottom. **2** very deep (*a bottomless pit*). **3 a** (of a supply etc.) inexhaustible. **b** (of drinks provided in a restaurant etc.) refilled at no extra charge. **4** naked below the waist (*bottomless dancers*). **5** featuring bottomless dancers etc. (*a bottomless bar*).

bottom line *noun* **1** the last line of a set of accounts, showing the final profit or loss. **2** net profit or loss. **3** *informal* the deciding or crucial factor; the essential point (in an argument etc.).

bottom round *noun N Amer.* a steak or other cut of meat from the outer portion of a round of beef.

bottom-up *attributive adjective* **1** proceeding from detail to general theory, or from the bottom upwards. **2** non-hierarchical.

botu·lin·um toxin /bɒtjuˈlainəm/ *noun* the bacterial toxin involved in botulism.

botu·lism /ˈbɒtʃuˌlizəm/ *noun* poisoning caused by a toxin produced by the bacillus *Clostridium botulinum* growing in poorly preserved food. [German *Botulismus* from Latin *botulus* sausage]

Bou·chard /buːˈʃar/ **Lu·cien** (b.1938), Canadian lawyer and politician. He served as chair of the 'Oui' side during the 1980 Quebec referendum. In 1990 he formed the Bloc Québécois, serving as Leader of the Opposition 1993–96. He resigned to become leader of the Parti Québécois and premier of Quebec 1996–2001.

Bou·cher /buːˈʃei/ **1 Fran·çois** (1703–70), French painter and decorative artist whose elegant and often frivolous work typifies the French rococo style. **2 Gaë·tan** (b.1958), Canadian speed skater and winner of four Olympic medals, including two gold medals from the 1984 Winter Games.

Boucher·ville /buːˈʃeiˈvil/ a former city in south central Quebec, situated on the St. Lawrence, opposite Montreal, now part of Longueuil; pop. (2001) 36,253. [P. Boucher de Grosbois, Canadian soldier, interpreter and governor d.1717]

bou·clé /ˈbuːklei/ *noun* **1** yarn (esp. wool) with a looped or curled ply. **2** a fabric knitted or woven from this yarn, having a knotted and curled appearance. [French, = buckled, curled]

Bou·dicca /ˈbuːdikə/ (also **Boa·di·cea** /boːdəˈsiːə/) (d. AD 62), a queen of the ancient Iceni tribe in present-day Norfolk, E England, who led a revolt against the Romans during which her forces sacked Colchester, St. Albans, and London before being defeated.

bou·doir /ˈbuːdwar, buːˈdwar/ *noun* a woman's small private room or bedroom. [French, lit. 'sulking place' from *bouder* sulk]

bouf·fant /buːˈfɒnt/ ● *adjective* (of a dress, hair, etc.) puffed out. ● *noun* a bouffant hairstyle. [French, present part. of *bouffer* swell]

Bou·gain·ville[1] /ˈbuːgən,vil/ a volcanic island in the S Pacific, the largest of the Solomon Islands chain, but belonging to Papua New Guinea. [BOUGAINVILLE[2]]

Bou·gain·ville[2] /ˌbuːgãˈviːl/ **Louis-Antoine de** (1729–1811), French explorer. After a military career during which he served as aide-de-camp to Montcalm in French Canada (1759), he led the first successful French circumnavigation of the globe, visiting and studying many islands of the S Pacific.

bou·gain·vil·lea /ˌbuːgənˈviliə/ *noun* any widely cultivated tropical plant of the genus *Bougainvillaea*, with large coloured bracts (usu. purple, red, or white) almost concealing the inconspicuous flowers. [BOUGAINVILLE[1]]

bough /bau/ *noun* a branch of a tree, esp. a main one. [Old English *bōg, bōh* from Germanic]

bought *past and past participle of* BUY.

bought·en /ˈbɒtən/ *adjective N Amer.* bought, as opposed to homemade. ¶ This usage is more current in non-urban than in urban areas. Although this leads some people to think it dialectal, old-fashioned, or ungrammatical, it has been used by such respected Canadian writers as Margaret Laurence. [var. of past participle of BUY]

bou·gie /ˈbuːʒi, buːˈʒi/ *noun Med.* a thin flexible surgical instrument for exploring, dilating, etc. the passages of the body. [French, lit. 'wax candle', from Arabic *Bujiya* Algerian port with a wax trade]

bouil·la·baisse /ˈbuːjəˌbeis/ *noun* a rich, spicy fish stew, originally from Provence. [French]

bouil·lon /ˈbuljən, ˈbuːljɒn/ *noun* a clear broth made by cooking meat or fish in water. [French from *bouillir* to boil]

bouillon cube *noun* a cube of concentrated soup stock which dissolves in boiling water to make broth.

Bou·lan·ger /buːlãˈʒei/ **1 Georges (Er·nest Jean Marie)** (1837–91), French general and minister of war 1886–7, who was accused of treason, and fled into exile in Belgium, where he committed suicide. **2 Nadia (Juli·ette)** (1887–1979), French music teacher, conductor, and composer, who played an important role in the Monteverdi revival and in the performance of French renaissance and baroque music.

boul·der *noun* a large stone, esp. one worn smooth by erosion. □ **boul·dery** *adjective* [short for *boulderstone*, Middle English from Scandinavian]

boulder clay *noun Geol.* = TILL[4].

boul·der·ing *noun* the sport of climbing large boulders.

boule[1] /buːl/ *noun* (also **boules** *pronunc.* same) a French form of lawn bowling, played on rough ground with usu. metal balls. [French, = BOWL[2] *noun*]

boule[2] /ˈbuːli/ *noun* a legislative body of ancient or modern Greece. [Greek *boulē* senate]

boule[3] *var. of* BUHL.

boule·vard /ˈbuːlə,vard/ *noun* **1** *N Amer.* a broad urban road. **2** a broad street, esp. with rows of trees planted along it. **3** *N Amer.* (*Cdn & Upper Midwest & North Central US*) a strip of grass or other vegetation between a sidewalk and a roadway. **4** *N Amer.* (*Cdn & Upper Midwest & North Central US*) a median in the centre of a road, separating opposite directions of traffic. □ **boule·vard·ed** *adjective* [French from German *Bollwerk* BULWARK, originally of a promenade on a demolished fortification]

boule·var·dier /buːləvarˈdjei/ *noun* a man who lives luxuriously and frequents fashionable places. [French, originally referring to those who frequented the theatrical district along the *Grands Boulevards* of Paris]

Bou·lez /buːˈlez/ **Pierre** (b.1925), French composer and conductor. His avant-garde compositions include aleatory and serial (twelve-tone) music, and feature both traditional and electronic instruments.

boulle var. of BUHL.

Bou·logne /buːˈlɔɪn/ a ferry port and fishing town in N France; pop. (1999) 44,859.

Boult /boːlt/ **Sir Ad·rian Ced·ric** (1889–1983), English conductor of the BBC Symphony Orchestra (1930–49) and the London Philharmonic (1950–57).

boult var. of BOLT[2].

bounce ● verb **1 a** intransitive (of a ball etc.) rebound. **b** transitive cause to rebound. **c** transitive & intransitive bounce repeatedly. **2 a** intransitive (of light, radio waves, etc.) reflect. **b** transitive cause (light, radio waves, etc.) to reflect. **3** informal **a** intransitive (of a cheque) be returned by a bank when there are insufficient funds to meet it. **b** transitive write or present a cheque for which there are insufficient funds. **c** transitive refuse to pay (the bank bounced my rent cheque). **4** intransitive **a** (foll. by about, up) (of a person, dog, etc.) jump or spring energetically. **b** (foll. by in, out, etc.) rush noisily, angrily, enthusiastically, etc. (bounced into the room; bounced out in a temper). **5** transitive informal **a** eject forcibly (from a bar, club, etc.). **b** dismiss (from a job). **6** intransitive Baseball hit a ground ball (bounced to the shortstop). **7** intransitive (of an electronic mail message) be returned to the sender. ● noun **1 a** a rebound. **b** the power of rebounding (this ball has good bounce). **c** a springy quality (blow-drying gives your hair bounce). **2** a boost or rise (a bounce in popularity). **3** informal **a** swagger, self-confidence (has a lot of bounce). **b** liveliness. **4** slang an instance of luck (the bounces went our way tonight). **5** slang an act of ejection or dismissal. □ **bounce back** regain one's good health, spirits, prosperity, etc. **bounce off the walls** N Amer. informal be extremely excited, agitated, etc. [Middle English bunsen beat, thump, (perhaps imitative), or from Low German bunsen, Dutch bons thump]

boun·cer noun **1** a person employed to eject troublemakers from a bar, club, etc. **2** Baseball a high-bouncing ground ball. **3** a person or thing that bounces.

boun·cing adjective **1** (esp. of a baby) big and healthy. **2** boisterous.

bouncing Bet noun = SOAPWORT.

bouncy adjective (**boun·ci·er**, **boun·ci·est**) **1** (of a ball etc.) tending to bounce well. **2** cheerful and lively. **3** resilient, springy (a bouncy sofa). □ **boun·ci·ness** noun

bound[1] ● intransitive verb **1 a** spring, leap (bounded out of bed). **b** walk or run with leaping strides. **2** (of a ball etc.) recoil from a wall or the ground; bounce. ● noun **1** a springy movement upwards or outwards; a leap. **2** a bounce. □ **by leaps and bounds** see LEAP. [French bond, bondir (originally of sound) from Late Latin bombitare from Latin bombus hum]

bound[2] ● noun (usu. in pl.) **1** a limitation; a restriction (beyond the bounds of possibility). **2** a border of a territory; a boundary. ● transitive verb **1** (esp. in passive; foll. by by) set bounds to; limit (views bounded by prejudice). **2** be the boundary of. □ **in bounds** inside the part of a playing field, court, etc. in which play is conducted. **out of bounds 1** outside the part of a playing field, court, etc. in which play is conducted. **2** outside of the area in which one is allowed to go according to regulations, e.g. of a school. **3** beyond what is acceptable; forbidden. [Anglo-French bounde, Old French bonde etc., from medieval Latin bodina, earlier butina, of unknown origin]

bound[3] adjective (usu. foll. by for or in combination) moving in a specified direction or toward a specified goal (boxcars bound for Edmonton; bound for stardom; northbound; outward bound). [Old Norse búinn past participle of búa get ready: -d euphonic, or partly after BIND]

bound[4] ● verb past and past participle of BIND. ● adjective **1** tied or secured with rope, cord, etc. (bound bundles; a bound hostage). **2** certain (the dictionary's bound to be a hit; there's bound to be a catch). **3** required; obligated (bound by the law). **4** (in combination) constricted, prevented from advancing (snowbound; theory-bound academics). **5** (of the pages in a book etc.) held together by a binding. **6** Linguistics (of a linguistic element) occurring only in combination with another form. □ **bound up with** (or **in**) closely associated with.

bound·ary noun (pl. **-aries**) a line marking the limits of an area, territory, etc. (shipments across provincial boundaries; boundary between liberty and licence). [dial. bounder from BOUND[2] + -ER[1] perhaps after limitary]

boundary layer noun the fluid immediately surrounding an object that is immersed and moving.

bound·en adjective archaic obligatory. [archaic past participle of BIND]

bounden duty noun a solemn responsibility.

bound·er noun **1** esp. Brit. dated informal a man whose behaviour is

morally unacceptable. **2** Baseball a high-bouncing ground ball. [BOUND[1] + -ER]

bound·less adjective unlimited; immense (boundless enthusiasm). □ **bound·less·ly** adverb **bound·less·ness** noun

boun·teous /ˈbaʊntɪəs/ adjective literary **1** = BOUNTIFUL. **2** freely given (bounteous affection). □ **boun·teous·ly** adverb **boun·teous·ness** noun [Middle English from Old French bontif from bonté BOUNTY after plenteous]

boun·ti·ful adjective **1** generous, liberal, plentiful. **2** ample. □ **boun·ti·ful·ly** adverb

Bounty a ship of the British navy, part of whose crew mutinied against their commander, Captain Bligh, on 28 Apr. 1789, and fled to found a settlement on Pitcairn Island which was not discovered until 1808. Bligh and eighteen companions, left in an open boat, drifted nearly 6,400 km (4,000 miles) before reaching land safely.

bounty noun (pl. **-ties**) **1** liberality; generosity. **2** a gift or reward, made usu. by a government, esp.: **a** a sum paid for the killing of dangerous or undesirable animals. **b** a sum paid for bringing criminals to justice. **c** a sum paid to encourage a trading enterprise etc. **3** an abundance. [Old French bonté from Latin bonitas -tatis from bonus good]

bounty hunter noun a person who pursues criminals or kills wild animals for a reward. □ **bounty hunting** noun

bou·quet /boːˈkeɪ, buː-/ noun **1** an arrangement of cut flowers, esp. bound together for carrying. **2** the scent of wine etc. **3** a favourable comment; a compliment. [French from dial. var. of Old French bos, bois wood]

bouquet garni /buːˈkeɪ ɡɑrˈniː/ noun (pl. **bou·quets gar·nis** pronunc. same) a small bundle of herbs, usu. including parsley, thyme, and bay leaf, used for flavouring stews etc. [French, lit. 'garnished bouquet']

Bou·ras·sa /bʊrəˈsɑ/ **1 Henri** (1868–1952), Canadian politician and journalist. A Liberal member of both the federal and provincial legislatures, he was founder and editor (1910–32) of the Montreal newspaper Le Devoir. **2 Rob·ert** (1933–96), Canadian politician. As Liberal premier of Quebec from 1970–76 and 1986–93, he was a strong federalist and a supporter of the Meech Lake and Charlottetown Accords.

Bour·baki /bʊrˈbaki/ **Nico·las**, the pseudonym under which a group of mathematicians, mainly French, began publishing an encyclopedic survey of pure mathematics. Despite its idiosyncrasies, it has remained an influential work since first appearing in 1939.

Bour·bon /ˈbʊrbən, ˈbʊrbɔ̃/ the surname of a branch of the royal family of France which succeeded to the throne with Henry IV in 1589, reached the peak of its power under Louis XIV in the late 17th c., and provided the last king of France, Louis Philippe, whose overthrow in 1848 marked the end of the French monarchy. Members of this family have also been kings of Spain (1700–1931, with a few interruptions, and from 1975) and of Naples.

bour·bon /ˈbɜrbən/ noun an American whisky distilled from corn mash and rye. [Bourbon County, Kentucky, where it was first made]

Bour·bon·nais /ˈbʊrbɔneɪ/ a former duchy and province of central France; chief town, Moulins. It forms part of the Auvergne and Centre regions.

bour·don /ˈbʊrdən/ noun Music **1** a low-pitched stop in an organ or harmonium. **2** the lowest bell in a peal of bells. **3** the drone pipe of a bagpipe. [French, = bagpipe drone, from Romanic, prob. imitative]

Bour·geois /bʊrˈʒwɒ/ **Léon (Vic·tor Au·guste)** (1851–1925), French politician. He was the French representative to the League of Nations (1919), and was awarded the Nobel Peace Prize in 1920.

bour·geois /bʊrˈʒwɒ, ˈbʊr-/ often derogatory ● adjective **1 a** conventionally middle class. **b** humdrum, unimaginative. **c** selfishly materialistic. **2** upholding the interests of the capitalist class; non-communist. ● noun (pl. same) **1** a bourgeois person. **2** Cdn hist. = WINTERING PARTNER. [French: see BURGESS]

bour·geoi·sie /ˌbʊrʒwɒˈziː/ noun **1** the capitalist class. **2** the middle class. [French]

bour·geoi·si·fy /bʊrˈʒwɒzɪfaɪ/ transitive verb (**-fies**, **-fied**) convert to a bourgeois outlook or way of life. □ **bour·geoi·si·fi·ca·tion** /bʊrˌʒwɒzɪfɪˈkeɪʃən/ noun

Bour·geoys /bʊrˈʒwɒ/ **St. Mar·guer·ite** (1620–1700), French-born teacher who opened several schools in New France and founded a religious order, the Congrégation de Notre-Dame de Montréal. She was beatified in 1950 and canonized in 1982.

Bour·get /bʊrˈʒeɪ/ **Ignace** (1799–1885), Canadian Catholic bishop. Overseeing the diocese of Montreal from 1840–76, he was a staunch ultramontane who is best remembered for his opposition to Joseph Guibord and the Institut Canadien.

bour·gui·gnon /ˈbʊrɡɪnjɔ̃/ *adjective* designating a sauce, esp. for beef, of red wine, beef stock, mushrooms, and onions. [French, 'Burgundian']

Bouri·not /ˈbʊriˌnoː/ **Sir John George** (1837–1902), Canadian writer and historian. His book *Bourinot's Rules of Order* outlined the procedures of the House of Commons in Ottawa and has been through four editions.

Bourke-White /bɜrkˈwʌit/ **Mar·garet** (1906–71), US photojournalist, known for her photographs of the rural poor in the southern US during the Depression, and for her coverage of the Second World War.

bourn[1] /bɔrn, bʊrn/ *noun* a small stream. [Middle English: S English var. of BURN[2]]

bourn[2] /bɔrn, bʊrn/ *noun* (also **bourne**) *archaic* **1** a goal; a destination. **2** a limit. [French *borne* from Old French *bodne* BOUND[2]]

Bourne and Kraatz Canadian figure skating duo consisting of Shae-Lynn Bourne (b.1976) and Victor Kraatz (b.1971), noted for their innovative energetic dance style and particularly for their trademark 'hydroblading' (skating while crouched low to the ice), ten times Canadian ice dance champions and 2003 world dance champions. The duo split up in December 2004 with the retirement from skating of Kraatz.

Bourne·mouth /ˈbɔrnməθ/ a resort on the south coast of England, formerly in Dorset; pop. (2001) 163,441.

Bour·non·ville /ˌbʊrnɔ̃ˈvil/ **Au·gust** (1805–1879), Danish choreographer and director of the Royal Danish Ballet from 1830–77. His choreography, including *La Sylphide* (1836) and *Napoli* (1842), is characterized by agile footwork, light bouncy and running steps, and musicality.

bour·rée /ˈbʊrei/ *noun* **1** a lively French dance like a gavotte. **2** the music for this dance. **3** a ballet step consisting of a series of very fast little steps, with the feet close together, usu. performed on pointe and giving the impression that the dancer is gliding over the floor. [French]

bourse /bʊrs/ *noun* (also **Bourse**) a stock exchange, esp. in Europe. [French, = purse, from medieval Latin *bursa*: compare PURSE]

bous·tro·phedon /ˌbʌustrəˈfiːdən, ˌbuː-/ *adjective & adverb* (of written words) from right to left and from left to right in alternate lines. [Greek (adv.) = as an ox turns in plowing, from *bous* ox + *-strophos* turning]

bout *noun* (often foll. by *of*) **1 a** a limited period (of intensive work or exercise). **b** a drinking session. **c** a period (of illness) (*a bout of the flu*). **2 a** a wrestling or boxing match. **b** a fight. **c** a trial of strength. [16th c.: apparently the same as obsolete *bought* bending]

bou·tique /buːˈtiːk/ *noun* a small shop or department of a store selling specialized goods or services, esp. fashionable clothes or accessories. *attributive adjective* designating products, services, etc. produced on a small scale and marketed to a specialized clientele. □ **bou·tiquey** *adjective* [French, = small shop, from Latin (as BODEGA)]

boutique hotel *noun* a hotel with no more than 150–200 rooms, often in a renovated older or architecturally distinctive building, with luxurious appointments and much attention paid to unusual interior design, distinctive touches, etc. but not usu. having convention facilities etc.

bouton·niere /ˌbuːtənˈiːr/ *noun* a flower or spray of flowers worn in a buttonhole or on a lapel. [French]

Boutros-Ghali /buːtrɔːsˈɡaliː/ **Bou·tros** (b.1922), Egyptian politician, diplomat, and Secretary-General of the United Nations (1992–96).

Bou·troue /buːˈtruː/ **Claude de Boutroue d'Aubigny** (1620–80), intendant of New France 1668–70.

Bou·vet Island /ˈbuːvei/ an uninhabited Norwegian island in the S Atlantic. [F. Lozier-*Bouvet*, French navigator who visited the island d.1786]

Bou·vier des Flan·dres /ˈbuːvjei dei flɒndrə/ *noun* (also **Bouvier**) a large Belgian breed of dog having a shaggy coat, used as a livestock herder or guard dog. [French, lit. 'cowherd of Flanders']

bou·zouki /buːˈzuːki/ *noun* a Greek form of mandolin. [modern Greek]

Bovet /bɔːˈvei/ **Dan·iel** (1907–1992), Swiss physiologist. He researched antihistamine drugs and for his work on muscle relaxants used in anaesthesia he was awarded the Nobel prize for medicine in 1957.

bo·vine /ˈboːvain/ *adjective* **1** of or resembling oxen or cattle. **2** stupid, dull. *noun* a bovine animal. [Late Latin *bovinus* from Latin *bos bovis* ox]

bovine growth hormone *noun* a growth hormone of cattle, administered in genetically engineered form to dairy cows to increase milk production. Abbr.: **BGH**.

bovine spongiform encephalopathy *noun see* BSE.

Bov·ril /ˈbɒvril/ *noun proprietary* a concentrated essence of beef diluted with hot water to make a drink. [Latin *bos bovis* ox, cow]

bov·ver *noun Brit. slang* deliberate troublemaking. [cockney pronunciation of BOTHER]

bov·ver boot *noun Brit. slang* = COMBAT BOOT.

Bow /boː/ **Clara** (1905–65), US actress. One of the most popular stars and sex symbols of the 1920s, she was known as the 'It Girl'; her best-known roles were in the silent films *It* (1927) and *The Wild Party* (1929).

bow[1] /boː/ *noun* **1 a** a slip knot with a double loop. **b** a ribbon, shoelace, etc., tied with this. **c** a decoration (on a gift, in the hair, etc.) in the form of a bow. **2** a device for shooting arrows with a taut string joining the ends of a curved piece of wood etc. **3 a** a rod with horsehair stretched along its length, used for playing the violin, cello, etc. **b** a single stroke of a bow over strings. **4 a** a shallow curve or bend. **b** a rainbow. **5** a metal ring forming the handle of scissors, a key, etc. **6** *N Amer.* the frame or temple of a pair of eyeglasses. **7** = ARCHER. **8** = SADDLE-BOW. *verb* **1** *transitive & intransitive* use a bow on (a violin etc.) (*he bowed vigorously*). **2** *intransitive* curve outward like a bow. [Old English *boga* from Germanic: compare BOW[2]]

bow[2] /bau/ *verb* **1** *intransitive* **a** incline the head or upper body, esp. in greeting, reverence, assent, or acknowledgement of applause. **b** incline or bend downward (*the grass bowed before the wind*). **2** *intransitive* submit (*bowed to the inevitable*). **3** *transitive* cause to incline (*bowed his head; bowed his will to hers*). **4** *transitive* express (thanks, assent, etc.) by bowing. **5** *transitive* (foll. by *in, out*) usher or escort obsequiously (*bowed us out of the restaurant*). *noun* an inclining of the head or body in greeting, assent, or in the acknowledgement of applause, etc. □ **bow and scrape** be obsequious or fawning. **bow down 1** bend or kneel in submission or reverence (*bowed down before the king*). **2** (usu. in *passive*) crush under the weight of (*was bowed down by the burden*). **bow out 1** make one's exit (esp. formally). **2** retreat, withdraw; retire gracefully. **make one's bow** make a formal exit or entrance. **take a bow** acknowledge applause. [Old English *būgan*, from Germanic: compare BOW[1]]

bow[3] /bau/ *noun Naut.* **1** (often in *pl.*) the front end of a boat or ship. **2** = BOWMAN[2]. □ **shot across the bow(s)** a warning. [Low German *boog*, Dutch *boeg*, ship's bow, originally shoulder: see BOUGH]

bow compass /boː/ *noun* a drawing compass with the legs connected by a bow-shaped flexible metal joint.

bowd·ler·ize /ˈbaudləˌraiz/ *transitive verb* (also esp. *Brit.* **-ise**) expurgate (a book etc.) by removing or altering material considered improper or offensive. □ **bowd·ler·ism** *noun* **bowd·ler·iz·ation** /-ˈzeiʃən/ *noun* [T. *Bowdler*, expurgator of Shakespeare d.1825]

bow drill /boː/ *noun* a drill turned by means of a bow, the string of which is twisted around the drill.

bowel /ˈbauəl/ *noun* **1 a** the part of the alimentary canal below the stomach. **b** (usu. in *pl.*) the intestines. **2** (in *pl.*) the depths; the innermost parts (*the bowels of the earth*). [Old French *buel* from Latin *botellus* little sausage]

Bow·ell /ˈboːəl/ **Sir Mac·ken·zie** (1823–1917), Canadian politician. As a Conservative MP he held several cabinet posts before becoming the country's fifth prime minister (1894–96).

bowel movement *noun* **1** discharge from the bowels; defecation. **2** the feces discharged from the body.

Bowen Island /ˈboːən/ an island off the southwestern coast of BC, situated at the entrance to Howe Sound, just northwest of Vancouver. [J. *Bowen*, English naval commander d.1835]

bower[1] /ˈbauər/ *noun* **1 a** a secluded place, esp. in a garden, enclosed by foliage; an arbour. **b** a small hut providing shade in a park or garden. **2** *literary* an inner room; a boudoir. *transitive verb literary* embower. □ **bow·ery** *adjective* [Old English *būr* from Germanic]

bower[2] /ˈbauər/ *noun* (in full **bower anchor**) either of two anchors carried at a ship's bow. [BOW[3] + -ER[1]]

bower[3] /ˈbauər/ *noun* either of the two highest cards in euchre, the jack of trumps (**right bower**) and the other jack of the same colour (**left bower**). [German *Bauer* peasant, jack (in cards), related to Dutch *boer*: see BOOR]

bower·bird /ˈbauərˌbɜrd/ *noun* any of various birds of the Ptilonorhynchidae family, native to Australia and New Guinea, the males of which construct elaborate bowers of feathers, grasses, shells, etc. during courtship.

bower cable *noun* the cable attached to a bower anchor.

Bow·er·ing /ˈbauərɪŋ/ **George** (b.1935), Canadian poet, fiction writer, and critic whose work is textually innovative with postmodern elements. One of the dominant figures of the Vancouver literary scene since the 1960s, he has won Governor General's Awards for poetry (1969) and fiction (1980). In 2002, he became Canada's first official Poet Laureate.

Bow·ery /ˈbauəri/ *noun* a district in New York City notorious for its prostitutes, drunks, disreputable establishments, etc. [Dutch *bouwerij* farm, the district being originally a Dutch governor's farm]

bow·fin /ˈboːfɪn/ *noun* a voracious freshwater fish, *Amia calva*, inhabiting eastern N America. [BOW¹ + FIN¹]

bow front /boː/ *adjective* (esp. of a piece of furniture) with the front curving outward. □ **bow-fronted** *adjective*

bow·head /ˈboːhed/ *noun* a large baleen whale, *Balaena mysticetus*, inhabiting Arctic waters and having a massive bow-shaped lower jaw.

bow·hunt /ˈboːˌhʌnt/ *transitive & intransitive verb* hunt (game) with a bow and arrows. □ **bow·hunt·er** *noun* **bow·hunt·ing** *noun*

Bowie /ˈboːi/ **1 David** (born David Robert Jones) (b.1947), English rock singer and songwriter whose recordings include 'Space Oddity' (1969), *Ziggy Stardust* (1973), and *Let's Dance* (1983). He has also appeared in several films. **2 James** ('Jim') (1799–1836), US frontiersman. He became a leader among the American settlers who opposed Mexican rule. He shared command of the garrison that resisted the attack on the Alamo, where he died.

bowie knife /ˈboːi/ *noun* a long hunting knife with a short hilt and a guard for the hand. [J. BOWIE]

bow·ing /ˈboːɪŋ/ *noun* the manner of playing a violin etc. with a bow.

bowl¹ *noun* **1 a** a usu. round deep basin used for food or liquid. **b** the quantity (of soup etc.) a bowl holds. **c** the contents of a bowl. **2 a** any deep-sided container shaped like a bowl (*toilet bowl*). **b** the bowl-shaped part of a tobacco pipe, spoon, balance, etc. **3 a** esp. *N Amer.* a bowl-shaped natural basin. **b** a bowl-shaped structure, esp. an amphitheatre or stadium (*Hollywood Bowl*). **4** (also **bowl game**) *Football* a post-season game or tournament between leading football teams (*Atlantic Bowl*; *Super Bowl*). □ **bowl·ful** *noun* (*pl.* **-fuls**). [Old English *bolle*, *bolla*, from Germanic]

bowl² ● *verb* **1 a** *transitive* roll (a ball etc.) along the ground. **b** *intransitive* play a game of bowling. **2** *intransitive* go along rapidly by revolving, esp. on wheels (*the cart bowled along the road*). **3** *transitive & intransitive Cricket* **a** deliver (a ball) in a straight-arm overhand motion so that it bounces before reaching the batsman. **b** (often foll. by *out*) dismiss (a batsman) by knocking down the wicket with a ball. ● *noun* **1** a wooden or hard rubber ball, slightly asymmetrical so that it runs on a curved course, used in lawn bowling. **2** (in *pl.*; usu. treated as *sing.*) = LAWN BOWLING. **3** *Cricket* an instance or turn of bowling. □ **bowl over 1** knock down. **2** *informal* **a** impress greatly. **b** overwhelm (*bowled over by the performance*). [French *boule* from Latin *bulla* bubble]

bow legs /boː/ *plural noun* legs which are curved outward so as to be wide apart below the knee. □ **bow·legged** *adjective*

bowl·er¹ *noun* **1** a person who participates in bowling. **2** a member of a cricket team who bowls or is bowling.

bowl·er² *noun* (in full **bowler hat**) a derby hat. [W. *Bowler*, English hatter who designed it in 1850]

bow·line /ˈboːlən/ *noun Naut.* **1** a rope attaching the weather side of a square sail to the bow. **2** a simple knot for forming a non-slipping loop at the end of a rope.

bowl·ing *noun* a game in which players roll a ball down an alley toward an arrangement of usu. five or ten pins with the intent of knocking down as many as possible.

bowling alley *noun* **1** a long and narrow hardwood lane along which the ball is rolled in the game of bowling. **2** a building containing several of these.

bowling green *noun* an area of grass used for lawn bowling.

Bow·man /ˈboːmən/ **Wil·liam Scott** (**'Scotty'**) (b.1933), Canadian hockey coach who won five Stanley Cups with the Montreal Canadiens in the 1970s, a sixth with the Pittsburgh Penguins in 1992, and three more with the Detroit Red Wings in 1997, 1998, and 2002.

bow·man¹ /ˈboːmən/ *noun* (*pl.* **-men**) an archer.

bow·man² /ˈbaumən/ *noun* (also **bows·man** /ˈbauzmən/) (*pl.* **-men**) the paddler or rower nearest the bow of a boat, esp. a canoe or racing boat.

Bow·man·ville /ˈboːmənvɪl/ part of the municipality of Clarington in S Ontario, situated about 15 km east of Oshawa. [C. *Bowman*, merchant and landowner *c.*1824]

Bow River /boː/ a river in S Alberta, rising in the Rocky Mountains

and flowing 644 km southeastward through Banff and Calgary to join the Oldman River west of Medicine Hat. [translation from Cree, with reference to the bows made from fir saplings growing along its banks]

bow·saw *noun* a saw with a narrow blade stretched tightly on a bow-shaped light frame.

bow·ser *noun* **1** *Brit.* a truck with a large tank for fuelling aircraft etc., or for supplying water. **2** *Cdn, Austral. & NZ* a gasoline pump. [origin unknown]

bow·shot /ˈboːʃɒt/ *noun* the distance an arrow can be shot from a bow.

bow·sprit /ˈboːsprɪt/ *noun Naut.* a spar running out from a ship's bow to which the forestays are fastened.

Bow Street runner /ˈboː/ *noun* (also **Bow Street officer**) *Brit. hist.* a London police officer. [*Bow Street* in London, containing the chief metropolitan police court]

bow·string /ˈboːstrɪŋ/ *noun* the string of an archer's bow.

bow tie /boː/ *noun* **1** a necktie in the form of a bow (BOW¹ *noun* 1). **2** something in the shape of a bow tie, esp. a form of pasta. □ **bow-tied** *adjective*

bow wave /bau/ *noun* a wave set up at the bow of a moving ship or in front of a body moving in air.

bow window /boː/ *noun* a curved bay window.

bow-wow ● *interjection* an imitation of a dog's bark. ● *noun* **1** *informal* a dog. **2** a dog's bark. [imitative]

bow·yer /ˈboːjər/ *noun* a maker or seller of archers' bows.

box¹ ● *noun* **1** a container, usu. with flat sides and of firm material such as wood or cardboard, esp. for holding solid objects. **2** the amount that will fill a box. **3** *Brit.* a boxed gift. **4** a separate compartment for any of various purposes, esp.: **a** a private seating area for a small group in a theatre or sports stadium (also *attributive*: *box seat*). **b** a stand for a witness or prisoner in a courtroom. **c** a stall for a horse in a stable. **d** the rectangular body of a truck, wagon, sleigh, etc., in which goods are transported. **5 a** a rectangular arrangement of people or things, e.g. of four hockey players killing a penalty. **b** an enclosed area or space. **6** an enclosure or receptacle for holding a specified item or items (*shoe box*; *jewellery box*). **7 a** a box, either at a post office or at the side of a road, where mail is delivered. **b** a compartment at a newspaper office for receiving replies to a private advertisement. **8** (prec. by *the*) *informal* television. **9 a** *N Amer.* = BOOM BOX. **b** any of various electric or electronic devices housed in a box. **c** *slang* a computer. **10** a space or area enclosed by a border on a printed sheet or computer screen. **11** a protective casing for a piece of a machine etc. **12** (prec. by *the*) any of several specially demarcated areas in various sports, esp.: **a** *Hockey* the penalty box. **b** *Baseball* any of the areas designating the positions to be taken by the batter, pitcher, catcher, or coaches. **c** *Soccer* the penalty area. **d** the enclosed area in which box lacrosse is played. **13** *N Amer., Austral., & NZ coarse slang* the female genitals. **14** a coach driver's seat. ● *transitive verb* **1** put in or provide with a box. **2** (foll. by *in, up, out*) surround or confine (a person, vehicle, etc.); restrain from movement. **3** mix up, esp. shuffle (cards) improperly so that some face the wrong way. □ **box the compass** *Naut.* recite the points of the compass in the correct order. **think outside the box** think creatively or in an unorthodox manner; not be bound by convention. □ **box·ful** *noun* (*pl.* **-fuls**). **box·like** *adjective* [Old English *box* from Late Latin *buxis* from Latin PYXIS]

box² ● *verb* **1 a** *transitive* fight (an opponent) in a boxing match. **b** *intransitive* participate in boxing. **2** *transitive* slap or punch (esp. a person's ear). ● *noun* a slap or punch, esp. on the ear. □ **box clever** *Brit. informal* act in a clever or effective way. [Middle English: origin unknown]

box³ *noun* **1** = BOXWOOD. **2** any of various shrub-like trees in Australasia, esp. those of several species of *Eucalyptus*. [Old English from Latin *buxus*, Greek *puxos*]

box ball *noun N Amer.* = WALL BALL.

box·board *noun* a lightweight cardboard used in packaging etc.

box camera *noun* a simple usu. non-adjustable box-shaped camera.

box canyon *noun* a narrow canyon with a flat bottom and vertical walls.

box·car *noun N Amer.* **1** an enclosed railway freight car, usu. having sliding doors on the sides. **2** (in *pl.*) a roll of double sixes on a pair of dice, esp. in craps.

box cutter *noun* esp. *US* = UTILITY KNIFE.

box elder *noun* = MANITOBA MAPLE.

Boxer *noun hist.* a member of a fiercely nationalistic Chinese secret society responsible for an unsuccessful rebellion in 1900 against

---

uː mood   aɪ my   əɪ pipe   au brown   ʌu house   eɪ day   ɔɪ boy   ū franglais   ã Canadien   ɔ̃ Brayon   (*see over for consonants*)

Western domination. [translation of Chinese *yi hé quán*, lit. 'righteous harmonious fists']

box·er noun **1** a person who participates in boxing, esp. for sport. **2** a breed of medium-sized dog with a smooth brown coat and pug-like face. **3** (in *pl.*) = BOXER SHORTS.

Boxer·cise noun *proprietary* a form of exercise based on boxing training and using boxing equipment. [blend of BOXER + EXERCISE]

boxer shorts noun **1** men's loose-fitting underwear with an elasticized waistband. **2** men's or women's shorts of a similar design.

box girder noun a hollow girder with a rectangular cross-section.

box·ing noun the sport of fighting with the fists, esp. in padded gloves.

Boxing Day noun (in parts of the Commonwealth) a holiday celebrated on Dec. 26 or the first weekday after Christmas. [from the British custom of giving tradespeople gifts: see BOX[1] noun 3]

boxing glove noun each of a pair of heavily padded gloves used in boxing.

Boxing Week noun *Cdn* the week between Christmas and New Year's Day. [after BOXING DAY]

box kite noun a tailless kite with a light rectangular frame at each end.

boxla /ˈbɒkslə/ noun *Cdn informal* = BOX LACROSSE. [abbreviation]

box lacrosse noun *Cdn* a form of lacrosse played in an enclosed area (usu. a hockey rink without ice) by teams of six players.

box lunch noun *N Amer.* a cold meal packed in a box, bag, etc.

box number noun a number of a postal or newspaper box.

box office noun **1** an office for booking seats and buying tickets at a theatre, cinema, stadium, etc. **2** the financial aspect of the arts and entertainment industry (often *attributive*: *a box-office failure*).

box pew noun a type of pew, found in older churches, enclosed by low wooden walls.

box pleat noun a pleat consisting of two parallel creases forming a raised band.

box score noun *N Amer.* a table summarizing a baseball game etc., showing the score, names of players, their statistics, and other information.

box set noun **1** a collection of several compact discs, cassettes, books, etc. sold together in a box. **2** a theatre set representing the three walls and ceiling of a room.

box social noun *N Amer.* a fundraising event at which box lunches are auctioned to raise funds, often such that the purchaser shares the meal with the person who prepared it.

box spanner noun *Brit.* = BOX WRENCH.

box spring noun *N Amer.* a rectangular wooden frame containing vertical springs and used as a support for a mattress.

box stall noun *N Amer.* an enclosed, usu. square stall in a barn, esp. for a horse.

box trap noun *N Amer.* a device for trapping small animals with a box which falls or closes when the bait is disturbed.

box turtle noun (also **box tortoise**) a N American land turtle of the genus *Terrapene*, able to enclose itself completely within its shell by means of a hinged lower carapace.

box·wood noun (also **box**) **1** any small slow-growing evergreen tree or shrub of the genus *Buxus*, esp. *B. sempervirens*, having glossy dark green leaves and popular as hedging. **2** the hard wood of this, used for carving, engraving, etc.

box wrench noun *N Amer.* (also *Brit.* **box spanner**) a wrench with a closed end fitting over the head of a nut.

boxy adjective (**box·i·er**, **box·i·est**) (esp. of a building) resembling a box in shape.

boy ● noun **1** a male child or youth. **2** a young man, esp. regarded as not yet mature. **3** a son. **4** *offensive* a male servant, esp. one belonging to a race perceived to be inferior. **5** a male belonging to a specified group (*a country boy*; *backroom boys*). **6** (**the boys**) *informal* a group of men mixing socially. **7** (usu. as a form of address) a male animal (*Down, boy!*). ● interjection expressing pleasure, surprise, etc. □ **boys will be boys** such behaviour from young males is to be expected.
□ **boy·hood** noun **boy·ish** adjective **boy·ish·ly** adverb **boy·ish·ness** noun [Middle English = servant, perhaps ultimately from Latin *boia* fetter]

boyar /bɔːˈjɑr/ noun *hist.* a member of an order of the Russian aristocracy (abolished by Peter the Great), next in rank to a prince. [Russian *boyarin* grandee]

boy band noun a pop group composed of young attractive men, appealing esp. to a young audience.

Boyce, Wil·liam (1711–79), English composer and organist who compiled *Cathedral Music* (1760–73), an important anthology covering 200 years of English sacred music.

boy·cott ● transitive verb **1** combine to coerce or punish (a person, company, nation, etc.) by a systematic refusal of normal commercial or social relations. **2 a** refuse to handle or purchase (goods) to this end. **b** refuse to attend (a meeting etc.) with this aim. ● noun such a refusal. [Capt. C. C. *Boycott*, Irish land agent d.1897, so treated from 1880]

Boyd, Liona (b.1950), Canadian classical guitarist.

Boyd Orr, John, 1st Baron Boyd Orr of Brechin Mearns (1880–1971), Scottish biologist and nutritionist, who served as director general of the United Nations Food and Agriculture Organization (1945–8); he was awarded the Nobel Peace Prize in 1949.

Boyer /bwɒˈjei/ **Charles** (1897–1978), French-born US actor, who is known for his romantic leading roles in films such as *Mayerling* (1936), *Gaslight* (1944), and *Barefoot in the Park* (1968).

boy·friend noun **1** a regular male companion or lover. **2** any male friend.

Boyle, Rob·ert (1627–91), Irish-born natural philosopher and scientist. He advanced a corpuscular theory of matter, a precursor of the modern theory of chemical elements, and is best known for his experiments with gases which led to the discovery of the law which bears his name.

Boyle's law noun the law that the pressure of a given mass of gas is inversely proportional to its volume at a constant temperature. [R. BOYLE]

Boyne, Battle of the a battle fought near the River Boyne in Ireland in 1690, in which the Protestant army of William of Orange (the newly crowned William III), defeated the Catholic army (including troops from both France and Ireland) led by the recently deposed James II, preventing him from regaining the throne.

boyo noun (pl. **boyos**) esp. *Irish informal* boy, lad (esp. as a form of address).

Boy Scout noun = SCOUT[1] 4.

boysen·berry /ˈbɔizənˌberi/ noun (pl. **-berries**) **1** a hybrid of several species of bramble. **2** the large red edible fruit of this plant. [R. *Boysen*, 20th-c. US horticulturalist]

boys in blue plural noun *informal* (often prec. by *the*) police officers; the police.

boy toy noun *N Amer. slang derogatory* **1** an attractive young man who is the lover of an older person. **2** a woman considered to have an overtly sexual image.

boy wonder noun an exceptionally talented young man or boy.

bozo noun (pl. **bozos**) esp. *N Amer. slang* a stupid or annoying person. [origin unknown]

BP abbreviation **1** boiling point. **2** blood pressure. **3** before the present (era).

Bp. abbreviation Bishop.

B.P.E. abbreviation Bachelor of Physical Education.

BPH abbreviation benign prostatic hyperplasia, an enlargement of the prostate gland common in elderly men.

B.Phil. abbreviation Bachelor of Philosophy.

bpm abbreviation beats per minute.

bps abbreviation *Computing* bits per second.

BQ abbreviation (in Canada) BLOC QUÉBÉCOIS.

Bq abbreviation BECQUEREL.

BR abbreviation bedroom.

Br symbol *Chem.* the element bromine.

Br. abbreviation **1** Brother. **2** Britain; British.

bra noun (pl. **bras**) **1** an undergarment worn by women and adolescent girls to support the breasts. **2** *N Amer. & Austral.* a piece of vinyl or other material designed to fit over the front end of a car to protect the finish. □ **bra·less** adjective [abbreviation of BRASSIERE]

Bra·bant /brəˈbant/ a former duchy in W Europe, lying between the Meuse and Scheldt rivers. Its capital was Brussels. It is now divided into two provinces in two countries: North Brabant in the Netherlands, of which the capital is 's-Hertogenbosch; and Brabant in Belgium, of which the capital remains Brussels.

brace ● noun **1 a** a device that clamps or fastens tightly. **b** a strengthening piece of iron or timber used in building. **2** (in *pl.*) *Cdn, Brit., Austral. & NZ* suspenders. **3** (in *pl.*) an orthodontic appliance

Consonants: b *but*   d *dog*   f *few*   g *get*   h *her*   j *yes*   k *cat*   l *leg*   m *man*   n *no*   p *pen*   r *red*   s *sit*

consisting of metal wires and brackets worn on the teeth to straighten them. **4** a device to support an injured joint or other body part (*neck brace*). **5** (*pl.* same) a pair. **6** a large hand drill consisting of a simple crank handle and a chuck to hold a bit. **7** a rope attached to the yard of a ship for trimming the sail. **8 a** a connecting mark { or } used in printing. **b** *Music* a similar mark connecting staffs to be performed at the same time. ● *transitive verb* **1** fasten tightly, give firmness to. **2** make steady by supporting. **3** invigorate, refresh. **4** (often *reflexive*) prepare for a difficulty, shock, etc. [Old French *brace* two arms, *bracier* embrace, from Latin *bra(c)chia* arms]

Brace·bridge a town in south central Ontario, north of Lake Simcoe; pop. (2001) 13,751. [after the literary figure of Squire *Bracebridge*, from W. Irving's novel *Bracebridge Hall*]

brace·let *noun* **1** an ornamental band, hoop, or chain worn on the wrist or arm, or sometimes on the ankle. **2** a band or chain worn around the wrist for identification, esp. for medical purposes. **3** *slang* a handcuff. [Old French, diminutive of *bracel* from Latin *bracchiale* from *bra(c)chium* arm]

bracer¹ *noun informal* **1** an invigorating, usu. alcoholic, drink. **2** a toner for the skin. [BRACE + -ER¹]

bracer² *noun* (also **brace**) a protective wristband worn by an archer. [Old French *braciere*, from *bras* arm]

bra·chial /'braɪəl, 'breɪ-/ *adjective* **1** of or relating to the arm (*brachial artery*). **2** like an arm. [Latin *brachialis* from *bra(c)chium* arm]

brachi·ate /'braɪkiət, 'breɪ-, -,eɪt/ ● *intransitive verb* (of certain apes and monkeys) move by using the arms to swing from branch to branch. ● *adjective Biol.* **1** having arms. **2** having paired branches on alternate sides. □ **brachi·a·tion** *noun* **brachi·at·or** *noun* [Latin *bra(c)chium* arm]

brachio·pod /'braɪkiə,pɒd, 'breɪk-/ *noun* any marine invertebrate of the phylum Brachiopoda (esp. a fossil one) having a two-valved chalky shell and a ciliated feeding arm. [modern Latin from Greek *brakhiōn* arm + *pous podos* foot]

brachio·saur·us /,braɪkiə'sɔːrəs, ,breɪk-/ *noun* (*pl.* **-es**) (also **brachio·saur** /'braɪkiə,sɔr, 'breɪk-/) a sauropod of the genus *Brachiosaurus*, the heaviest of all dinosaurs, with forelegs longer than its hind legs. [modern Latin from Greek *brakhiōn* arm + *sauros* lizard]

bra·chis·to·chrone /bra'kɪstə,krɒn/ *noun Math.* a curve joining two points such that a body travelling along it (e.g. under gravity) takes a shorter time than is possible for any other curve between the points. [Greek *brakhistos* shortest + *khronos* time]

brachy- /'braɪki/ *combining form* short. [Greek *brakhus* short]

brachy·ceph·alic /,braɪksə'falɪk/ *adjective* having a broad short head. □ **brachy·ceph·al·ous** /,braɪkɪ'sefələs/ *adjective* [BRACHY- + Greek *kephalē* head]

brachy·ther·apy *noun* the treatment of cancer, esp. prostate cancer, by the insertion of small radioactive implants directly into the cancerous tissue.

bracing ● *adjective* invigorating, refreshing (*the cool wind was bracing*). ● *noun* a system or series of braces. □ **bracing·ly** *adverb*

Brack·en, John (1883–1969), Canadian politician, premier of Manitoba 1922–42. He was asked to become premier of Manitoba with a United Farmers government (1922). From 1942 to 1948 he was leader of the federal Progressive Conservative party.

brack·en *noun* **1** (also **bracken fern**) a large branching fern, *Pteridium aquilinum*, having long coarse fronds. **2** a mass of such ferns. [Middle English from Old Norse]

brack·et ● *noun* **1** a right-angled or other support attached to and projecting from a vertical surface. **2** a shelf fixed with such a support to a wall. **3** each of a pair of marks ( ) [ ] { } < > used to enclose words or figures. **4** a group classified as containing similar elements or falling between given limits (*income bracket*). **5** the distance between two artillery shots fired either side of the target to establish range. ● *transitive verb* (**brack·et·ed, brack·et·ing**) **1 a** link or couple (names, lines, etc.) with a brace. **b** imply a connection or equality between. **2 a** enclose in brackets as parenthetic or spurious. **b** *Math.* enclose in brackets as having specific relations to what precedes or follows. **3** enclose on either side. **4** establish the range of (a target) by firing two preliminary shots one short of and the other beyond it. **5** *Photography* shoot (film) at exposures lower and higher than the estimated correct exposure. [French *braguette* or Spanish *bragueta* codpiece, diminutive of French *brague* from Provençal *braga* from Latin *braca*, pl. *bracae* breeches]

bracket fungus *noun* a fungus forming shelf-like projections on tree trunks etc.

brack·ish *adjective* (of water etc.) slightly salty. □ **brack·ish·ness** *noun* [obsolete *brack* (adj.) from Middle Low German, Middle Dutch *brac*]

bract *noun* a modified and often brightly coloured leaf, with a flower or an inflorescence in its axil. □ **brac·teal** *adjective* [Latin *bractea* thin plate, gold leaf]

brad *noun* a thin flat nail with a head in the form of a slight enlargement at the top. [var. of Middle English *brod* goad, pointed instrument, from Old Norse *broddr* spike]

brad·awl *noun* a small tool with a pointed end for making holes in wood for the insertion of brads etc. [BRAD + AWL]

Brad·bury ▸ **1 Mal·colm Stan·ley** (1932–2000), English novelist and critic whose works include *The History Man* (1975) and *Rates of Exchange* (1983). **2 Ray Doug·las** (b.1920), US author of science fiction novels, including *The Martian Chronicles* (1950) and *Fahrenheit 451* (1953).

Brad·ford an industrial city in West Yorkshire, England; pop. (est. 1999) 457,344. It was noted for the production of woollen cloth until the decline of the textile industry in the 1970s.

Bradford West Gwil·lim·bury /'gwɪləm,beri/ a town in south central Ontario, situated about 10 km north of Newmarket; pop. (2001) 22,228. [BRADFORD + perhaps after Lt.-Col. T. Gwillim (father-in-law of John Graves Simcoe) d.1762]

Brad·ley ▸ **1 Fran·cis Her·bert** (1846–1924), English idealist philosopher, whose works include *Principles of Logic* (1883) and *Appearance and Reality* (1893). **2 James** (1693–1762), English astronomer who in 1728 discovered that the apparent change in the position of stars is due to the combined effect of the velocity of light and the earth's annual orbital motion. He also observed the oscillation of the earth's axis, which he termed 'nutation.'

Brad·street, Anne (Dud·ley) (c.1612–72), English-born US poet. She is considered one of the first colonial US poets, and her works include *The Tenth Muse Lately Sprung Up in America* (1650).

brady·car·dia /,bradɪ'kɑrdiə/ *noun Med.* abnormally slow heart rate (usually taken as 60 beats per minute or less). [Greek *bradus* slow + *kardia* heart]

brae /breɪ/ *noun Scot.* a steep bank or hillside. [Old Norse *brá* eyelash]

Brae·burn /'breɪbɜrn/ *noun* a crisp, flavourful, tart-sweet apple with a greenish-gold to red skin. [*Braeburn* Valley in Nelson, NZ, the orchard in which it was discovered in 1950]

brag ● *verb* (**bragged, brag·ging**) **1** *intransitive* talk boastfully. **2** *transitive* boast about. ● *noun* **1** a boastful statement; boastful talk. **2** a card game like poker. □ **brag·ger** *noun* **brag·ging·ly** *adverb* **brag·gy** *adjective* (**brag·gi·er, brag·gi·est**). [Middle English, originally adj., = spirited, boastful; origin unknown]

Braga /'brɒgə/ a city in N Portugal, capital of a mountainous district of the same name; pop. (est. 2001) 105,000.

Bra·ganza¹ /brə'ganzə/ a city in NE Portugal, capital of a mountainous district of the same name; pop. (est. 2001) 19,885. It was the original seat of the Braganza dynasty.

Bra·ganza² /brə'ganzə/ the dynasty that ruled Portugal from 1640 until the end of the monarchy in 1910, and Brazil (on its independence from Portugal) from 1822 until the formation of a republic in 1889.

Bragg, Sir Wil·liam Henry (1862–1942), English physicist and founder of solid state physics. He shared the 1915 Nobel Prize for physics with his son, William (later Sir Lawrence) Bragg (1890–1971), for determining the atomic structure of crystals using X-ray diffraction.

brag·ga·do·cio /,bragə'doʊtʃioʊ, -'doʊʃioʊ/ *noun* empty boasting; a boastful manner of speech and behaviour. [*Braggadochio*, a braggart in Spenser's *Faerie Queene*, from BRAG or BRAGGART + Italian augmentative suffix -*occio*]

brag·gart /'bragərt/ ● *noun* a person given to bragging. ● *adjective* boastful. [French *bragard* from *braguer* BRAG]

bragging rights *plural noun* entitlement to boast of one's obvious superiority.

Brahe /'brɒhi, -hə/ **Tycho** (1546–1601), Danish astronomer. His observations, the most accurate ever made with the naked eye, were used by Kepler in formulating his laws of planetary motion.

Brah·ma¹ /'brɒmə/ *Hinduism* the creator god, who forms a triad with Vishnu and Shiva. Brahma was an important god of late Vedic religion, but has been little worshipped since the 5th c. AD and has only one major temple dedicated to him in India today. [masculine form of neuter BRAHMAN]

Brah·ma² /'brɒmə/ *noun* (also **Brah·man**) a breed of cattle from India, with a humped shoulder and neck, much used in crossbreeding for its tolerance of heat and drought.

---

t *top*   v *voice*   w *we*   z *zoo*   ʃ *she*   ʒ *vision*   θ *thin*   ð *this*   ŋ *ring*   x *loch*   tʃ *chip*   dʒ *jar*   (*see over for vowels*)

brah·ma /ˈbrɒmə/ *noun* a large Asian breed of domestic fowl. [shortening of brahmaputra, after the BRAHMAPUTRA RIVER, from where it was brought]

Brah·man /ˈbrɒmən/ *noun* (also **brahman**) (*pl.* **-mans**) **1** a member of the highest Hindu caste, whose members are traditionally eligible for the priesthood. **2** = BRAHMA². □ **Brah·man·ic** /-ˈmanɪk/ *adjective* **Brah·man·ic·al** /-ˈmanɪkəl/ *adjective* [Sanskrit *brāhmaṇas* from *brahmaṇ* priest]

Brah·mana /ˈbrɒmənə/ *noun* any of the lengthy commentaries on the Vedas, composed in Sanskrit *c.*900–700 BC, containing exegetical material relating to Vedic sacrificial ritual. [as BRAHMAN]

Brah·man·ism /ˈbrɒmənɪzm/ *noun* the complex sacrificial pantheistic religion that emerged in post-Vedic India (*c.*900 BC), characterized by the caste system.

Brah·ma·putra River /ˌbrɒməˈpuːtrə/ a river of S Asia, rising in the Himalayas and flowing 2 900 km (1,800 miles) through Tibet, NE India, and Bangladesh, to join the Ganges at its delta on the Bay of Bengal.

Brah·min /ˈbrɒmɪn/ *noun* **1** = BRAHMAN. **2** *US* a socially or intellectually superior person, esp. from New England. □ **Brah·min·ic** /-ˈmɪnɪk/ *adjective* **Brah·min·ic·al** /-ˈmɪnɪkəl/ *adjective* [var. of BRAHMAN]

Brahms /brɒmz/ **Jo·han·nes** (1833–97), German composer and pianist. Eschewing program music and opera, he concentrated his energies on 'pure' and traditional forms. Among his most famous works are his four symphonies, his Violin Concerto, and his great choral work, *A German Requiem.* □ **Brahms·ian** *adjective*

braid ● *noun* **1** a length of hair, straw, etc. in three or more interlaced strands. **2** a woven band of fabric or thread used for edging or trimming. ● *transitive verb* **1** plait or intertwine (hair, rope, etc.). **2** trim or decorate with braid. □ **braid·er** *noun* [Old English *bregdan* from Germanic]

braid·ed *adjective* **1** intertwined in a braid. **2** (of a river) split by deposits into interconnected streams.

braided rug *noun N Amer.* a rug made of a braid of long strips of cloth wound around itself and sewed together to form a mat.

braid·ing *noun* **1** various types of braid collectively. **2** braided work.

Braille¹ /breɪl/ **Louis** (1809–52), French educator. Blind from the age of three, he devised the system of printing and writing for the blind that is named after him.

Braille² /breɪl/ ● *noun* a system of writing and printing for the blind, in which characters are represented by patterns of raised dots. ● *transitive verb* print or transcribe in Braille. [BRAILLE¹]

brain ● *noun* **1** an organ of soft nervous tissue contained in the skull of vertebrates, functioning as the coordinating centre of sensation, and of intellectual and nervous activity. **2** (in *pl.*) the substance of the brain, esp. as food. **3 a** a person's intellectual capacity (*has a poor brain*). **b** (often in *pl.*) intelligence; high intellectual capacity (*has a brain*; *has brains*). **4** *informal* an intelligent person. **5** (often in *pl.*; prec. by *the*) *informal* **a** the cleverest person in a group. **b** a person who originates a complex plan or idea (*the brains behind the robbery*). **6** an electronic device with functions comparable to those of a brain. ● *transitive verb* **1** dash out the brains of. **2** strike hard on the head. □ **on the brain** *informal* obsessively in one's thoughts. [Old English *brægen* from West Germanic]

brain candy *noun N Amer. slang* = MIND CANDY.

brain·case *noun* the cranium.

brain·child *noun* (*pl.* **brain·chil·dren**) *informal* an idea, plan, or invention regarded as the result of a person's mental effort.

brain coral *noun* coral forming a compact mass with a surface resembling the convolutions of the brain.

brain damage *noun* injury to the brain permanently impairing its functions. □ **brain-damaged** *adjective*

brain-dead *adjective* **1** having suffered brain death. **2** *informal derogatory* lacking signs of mental activity; stupid.

brain death *noun* permanent cessation of the functions of the brain stem that control breathing etc., regarded as indicative of death.

brain drain *noun informal* the loss of skilled personnel by emigration.

brain fever *noun* inflammation of the brain.

brain food *noun N Amer.* food, esp. fish, considered to be beneficial to the intellect.

brain·iac *noun N Amer. slang* a very intelligent or clever person; an expert. [the name of *Brainiac*, a super-intelligent alien character in Superman comics, from BRAIN + MANIAC]

brain·less *adjective* stupid, foolish.

brain·pan *noun informal* the skull.

brain·power *noun* mental ability or intelligence.

brain scan *noun* a diagnostic radiographic scan of the brain.

brain stem *noun* the central trunk of the brain, upon which the cerebrum and cerebellum are set, and which continues downwards to form the spinal cord.

brain·storm ● *noun* **1** a concerted intellectual treatment of a problem by discussing spontaneous ideas about it. **2** *N Amer.* = BRAINWAVE 2. **3** a violent or excited outburst often as a result of a sudden mental disturbance. **4** *informal* mental confusion. ● *transitive & intransitive verb* seek solutions to a problem by discussing spontaneous ideas about it in a group. □ **brain·storm·ing** *noun*

brain·teas·er *noun informal* a puzzle or problem.

brain trust *noun* esp. *N Amer.* (also esp. *Brit.* **brains trust**) a group of expert advisers.

brain·wash *transitive verb* subject (a person) to a prolonged process by which ideas other than and at variance with those already held are implanted in the mind. □ **brain·wash·ing** *noun*

brain·wave *noun* **1** (usu. in *pl.*) an electrical impulse in the brain. **2** *informal* a sudden bright idea.

brainy *adjective* (**brain·i·er**, **brain·i·est**) intellectually clever or active. □ **brain·i·ly** *adverb* **brain·i·ness** *noun*

braise /breɪz/ *transitive verb* fry lightly and then stew slowly with a little liquid in a closed container. [French *braiser* from *braise* live coals]

brake¹ ● *noun* **1** (often in *pl.*) a device for stopping the motion of a mechanism, esp. a wheel or vehicle, or for keeping it at rest. **2** anything that has the effect of hindering or impeding (*shortage of money was a brake on their enthusiasm*). ● *verb* **1** *intransitive* **a** apply a brake. **b** slow or come to a stop upon application of a brake. **2** *transitive* retard or stop with a brake. □ **put on the brakes** slow down. [prob. obsolete *brake* in sense 'machine handle, bridle']

brake² *noun* = BRACKEN. [Middle English, perhaps shortened from BRACKEN, *-en* being taken as a pl. ending]

brake³ *archaic past of* BREAK¹.

brake block *noun* a block used to hold a brake shoe or brake pad.

brake drum *noun* a cylinder attached to a wheel, whose inner surface is gripped by brake shoes when drum brakes are applied.

brake fluid *noun* fluid used in a hydraulic brake system.

brake horsepower *noun* the power of an engine reckoned in terms of the force needed to brake it.

brake light *noun* (usu. in *pl.*) a red light at the rear of a motor vehicle, lit when the brakes are applied.

brake lining *noun* a strip of fabric which increases the friction of the brake shoe or brake pad.

brake·man *noun* (*pl.* **-men**) **1** *N Amer.* an employee on a train, responsible for maintenance on a journey. **2** a person in charge of brakes.

brake pad *noun* **1** either of two metal pads which squeeze the disc when disc brakes are applied. **2** either of two pieces of hard rubber applied to the rim of a bicycle wheel as a brake.

brake shoe *noun* a long curved metal block which presses on the inside of a brake drum when drum brakes are applied.

brake van *noun Brit.* a railway coach or vehicle from which the train's brakes can be controlled.

Bram·ah /ˈbrɑmə/ **Jo·seph** (1749–1814), English inventor. One of the most influential engineers of the Industrial Revolution, he is best known for his hydraulic press, used for heavy forging.

Bra·mante /brəˈmɒntei, -ˈmantei/ **Do·nato** (1444–1514), the outstanding architect of the High Renaissance. His work, including his plans for the new St. Peter's (begun in 1506), expressed the Renaissance striving for the ideal of classical perfection.

bram·ble *noun* **1** any of various thorny shrubs bearing fleshy red or black berries, esp. the blackberry bush. **2** the edible berry of these shrubs. **3** any of various other rosaceous shrubs with similar foliage, esp. a wild rose. □ **bram·bly** *adjective* [Old English *bræmbel* (earlier *bræmel*): see BROOM]

Bram·ley *noun* (*pl.* **-leys**) (in full **Bramley's seedling**) a large green variety of cooking apple, popular in Britain. [M. *Bramley*, English butcher in whose garden it may have first grown *c.*1850]

Bramp·ton a city in south central Ontario, to the north of Mississauga; pop. (2001) 325,428. [the name of a town in Cumberland, England]

bran *noun* edible husks of grain separated from flour after grinding. [Middle English from Old French of unknown origin]

Bran·agh /ˈbranə/ **Ken·neth Charles** (b.1960), Northern Irish actor, producer, and director, whose acclaimed performances include several major Shakespearean roles.

branch ● *noun* **1** a limb extending from a tree or bough. **2** a lateral extension or subdivision, esp. of a river, road, or railway. **3** a conceptual extension or subdivision, as of a family, knowledge, etc. **4** a local division or office etc. of a large business, bank, library, etc. ● *intransitive verb* (often foll. by *off*) **1** diverge from the main part. **2** divide into branches. **3** (of a tree) bear or send out branches. □ **branch out** extend one's field of interest. □ **branched** *adjective* **branch·let** *noun* **branch·like** *adjective* **branchy** *adjective* [Old French *branche* from Late Latin *branca* paw]

bran·chia /ˈbraŋkɪə/ *plural noun* (also **bran·chiae** /-kiˌiː/) gills. □ **bran·chi·al** *adjective* **bran·chi·ate** /-kiˌeɪt/ *adjective* [Latin *branchia*, pl. *-ae*, from Greek *bragkhia* pl.]

branch line *noun* a rail line connecting outlying centres to a main line.

branch plant *noun Cdn* a factory etc. owned by a company based in another country (often *attributive*: *branch-plant economy*).

Bran·cusi /branˈkuːzi/ **Con·stan·tin** (1876–1957), Romanian sculptor, active mainly in Paris, one of the most influential of 20th-c. artists. He is noted for his originality in reducing forms to their ultimate—almost abstract—simplicity.

brand ● *noun* **1 a** a particular make of goods. **b** an identifying trademark, label, etc. **2** (usu. foll. by *of*) a special or characteristic kind (*brand of humour*). **3** an identifying mark burned on livestock or (formerly) prisoners etc. with a hot iron. **4** an iron used for this. **5** a piece of burning, smouldering, or charred wood. **6** a stigma; a mark of disgrace. **7** *literary* **a** a torch. **b** a sword. **8** a kind of blight, giving leaves a burnt appearance. ● *transitive verb* **1** mark with a hot iron. **2** stigmatize; mark with disgrace (*they branded him a liar; was branded for life*). **3** impress unforgettably on one's mind. **4** assign a trademark or label to. **5** make (a product or line of products) instantly recognizable as being produced by a particular manufacturer etc. □ **brand·er** *noun* **brand·ing** *noun* [Old English from Germanic]

bran·dade /brɑ̃ˈdad/ *noun* a dish made from puréed fish, esp. salted cod. [French from modern Provençal *brandado*, lit. 'thing which has been moved or shaken']

Bran·den·burg /ˈbrandənˌbərg/ a state of NE Germany; capital, Potsdam. The city of Berlin lies in the centre of the state, but is administratively independent of it. The modern state corresponds to the western part of the former Prussian electorate, of which the eastern part was ceded to Poland after the Second World War.

Brandenburg Gate one of the city gates of Berlin, the only one that survives. It was built in 1788–91 in neoclassical style. After the construction of the Berlin Wall in 1961, it stood in East Berlin, a conspicuous symbol of a divided city. It was reopened in Dec. 1989.

bran·died *adjective* preserved or flavoured with brandy.

branding iron *noun* an iron used to brand livestock etc.

bran·dish *transitive verb* wave or flourish as a threat or in display. □ **bran·dish·er** *noun* [Old French *brandir*, ultimately from Germanic, related to BRAND]

brand loyalty *noun* consumers' willingness to continue purchasing products from the same manufacturer.

brand name *noun* (often *attributive*) **1** a trade or proprietary name. **2** a product with a brand name.

brand new *adjective* completely or obviously new.

Bran·do, Mar·lon (b.1924), US film actor, an exponent of Stanislavsky's 'method' style. His films include *A Streetcar Named Desire* (1951), *On the Waterfront* (1954), *The Godfather* (1972), and *Last Tango in Paris* (1972).

Bran·don a city in SW Manitoba, situated on the Assiniboine River, about 200 km west of Winnipeg; pop. (2001) 39,716. □ **Brandon·ite** *noun* [from *Brandon House*, a nearby Hudson's Bay Co. trading post, after the 8th Duke of Hamilton, also known as the Duke of *Brandon*, after a place in Suffolk, England]

Brandt, Willy (born Herbert Ernst Karl Frahm, 1913–92), German politician, Chancellor of West Germany 1969–74, winner of the Nobel Peace Prize in 1971 for promoting more cordial relations between West and East Germany. He also chaired the Brandt Commission on the state of the world economy, whose report was published in 1980.

brandy *noun* (pl. **-dies**) a strong alcoholic spirit distilled from wine or fermented fruit juice. [earlier *brand(e)wine* from Dutch *brandewijn* burnt (distilled) wine]

brandy butter *noun* a rich sweet hard sauce made with brandy, butter, and sugar.

brandy glass *noun* = SNIFTER 1.

brandy snap *noun* a crisp rolled gingerbread wafer usu. served filled with whipped cream.

Brandy·wine Falls a waterfall in southwestern BC, situated on Brandywine Creek at Daisy Lake, between Squamish and Whistler. It has a vertical drop of 61 m.

brank-ursine /braŋkˈɜrsaɪn/ *noun* the plant *Acanthus mollis* or *A. spinosus*, with three-lobed flowers and spiny leaves, used as a motif for the Corinthian capital. *Also called* BEAR'S BREECH. [French *branche ursine*, medieval Latin *branca ursina* bear's claw: see BRANCH, URSINE]

Brant[1] a city in SW Ontario, including the former town of Paris; pop. (2001) 31,669. [after Joseph BRANT[2]]

Brant[2] ▸ **1 Jo·seph** (Thayendanegea 1742–1807), Mohawk chief, captain in the British military, and Christian missionary. He led the Iroquois on the British side during the American Revolution. **2** his sister, **Mary** ('Molly') (c.1736–96), Mohawk leader. As head of a society of Six Nations matrons, and later as the wife of Sir William Johnson, first superintendent of the northern Indians of British N America, she exercised enormous influence over her people. She encouraged the Six Nations to maintain the alliance with England during the American Revolution.

brant *noun* (also *Brit.* **brent**) *N Amer.* an Arctic goose, *Branta bernicla*, similar to the Canada goose but smaller and darker. [Middle English: origin unknown]

Brant·ford a city in SW Ontario, situated on the Grand River, about 35 km west of Hamilton; pop. (2001) 86,417. [J. BRANT]

Bran·ting /ˈbrantɪŋ/ **Karl Hjal·mar** (1860–1925), Swedish politician, prime minister 1920, 1921–3, and 1924–5; he shared the Nobel Peace Prize in 1921.

Braque /brak/ **Georges** (1882–1963), French painter, inaugurator, with Picasso, of cubism; he was the first to make the collages which developed into synthetic cubism.

Bras D'Or Lake /bridˈɔr/ a small inland sea forming the core of Cape Breton Island and virtually splitting the island in two. [corruption of LABRADOR[1]]

brash[1] *adjective* **1** vulgarly or ostentatiously self-assertive. **2** hasty, rash. **3** impudent. □ **brash·ly** *adverb* **brash·ness** *noun* [originally dial., perhaps from RASH[1]]

brash[2] *noun* **1** loose broken rock or ice. **2** clippings from hedges, shrubs, etc. [18th c.: origin unknown]

brash[3] *adjective US* (esp. of timber) brittle, fragile. □ **brash·ness** *noun* [16th c., perhaps imitative]

brash[4] *noun* an eruption of fluid from the stomach. [16th c., perhaps imitative]

Bra·silia /brəˈzɪliə/ the capital, since 1960, of Brazil; pop. (2000) 2,043,169. Designed in 1956, the city was located in the centre of the country with the intention of drawing people away from the crowded coastal areas.

Bra·şov /braˈʃɒv/ a city in Romania; pop. (est. 2002) 309,600. It belonged to Hungary until after the First World War, and was ceded to Romania in 1920.

brass ● *noun* **1** a yellow alloy of copper and zinc. **2 a** an ornament or other decorated piece of brass. **b** brass objects collectively. **3** *Music* brass wind instruments (including trumpet, horn, trombone) forming a band or a section of an orchestra. **4** *Brit. slang* money. **5** (in full **horse brass**) a round flat brass ornament for the harness of a draft horse. **6** (in full **top brass**) *informal* persons in authority or of high (esp. military) rank. **7** an inscribed or engraved memorial tablet of brass. **8** *informal* effrontery (*then had the brass to demand money*). ● *adjective* made of brass. □ **brassed off** *Brit. slang* fed up. **not a brass farthing** *informal* the least possible amount. [Old English *bræs*, of unknown origin]

Bras·sard /braˈsɑr/ **Jean-Luc** (b.1972) Canadian freestyle skier, winner of an Olympic gold medal in 1994 and the World Cup in 1996 and 1997.

brass band *noun* a group of musicians playing brass instruments, sometimes also with percussion.

brass bed *noun* a bedstead with the head and usu. the foot of brass spindles.

bras·serie /ˈbrasɜri/ *noun* **1** a restaurant, originally one serving beer with food. **2** *Cdn (Que.)* a pub. [French, = brewery]

Bras·sey /ˈbrasi/ **Thom·as** (1805–70), English engineer. The greatest railway contractor of the 19th c., he built more than 10,000 km (6,500 miles) of railways worldwide; his one failure was Canada's Grand Trunk Railway, where costs greatly exceeded estimates.

brass hat *noun informal* a person, esp. a military officer, of high rank or position.

bras·sica /ˈbrasɪkə/ *noun* any cruciferous plant of the genus *Brassica*, having taproots and erect branched stems, including cabbage, mustard, cauliflower, kohlrabi, broccoli, kale, and turnip. [Latin, = cabbage]

brass·ie *noun* (also **brassy**) (*pl.* **-ies**) *Golf* the second-largest wooden-headed club; a 2 wood. [BRASS + -IE, from its metal base.]

bras·siere /brəˈzɪːr/ *noun* = BRA 1. [French, = woman's bodice]

brass knuckles *plural noun* connected metal rings worn on the fingers to make punches more severe.

brass monkey *noun coarse slang* used in various phrases to indicate extreme cold (*brass-monkey weather*).

brass ring *noun N Amer.* noteworthy success, esp. as viewed as a reward for ambition, hard work, etc. (*reach for the brass ring*).

brass rubbing *noun* **1** the rubbing of chalk etc. over paper laid on an engraved brass to take an impression of its design. **2** the impression obtained by this.

brass tacks *plural noun informal* actual details; real business (*get down to brass tacks*).

brassy[1] *adjective* (**brass·i·er**, **brass·i·est**) **1** impudent. **2** showy, flamboyant. **3** loud and blaring. **4** of or like brass. □ **brass·i·ly** *adverb* **brass·i·ness** *noun*

brassy[2] *var.* of BRASSIE.

brat *noun* **1** usu. *derogatory* a child, esp. an ill-behaved one. **2** a child brought up in a specified milieu (*Forces brat*). □ **brat·tish** *adjective* **brat·tish·ness** *noun* **brat·ti·ness** *noun* **brat·ty** *adjective* [perhaps abbreviation of Scots *bratchet* 'infant', or from *brat* 'rough garment']

Brati·slava /ˌbratɪˈslɒvə/ the capital of Slovakia, a port on the Danube; pop. (2001) 428,672. From 1526 to 1784 it was the capital of Hungary.

brat pack *noun slang* a rowdy and ostentatious group of young celebrities, esp. film stars. □ **brat packer** *noun*

brat·tice /ˈbratɪs/ *noun* a wooden partition or shaft lining in a mine. [Middle English, ultimately from Old English *brittisc* BRITISH]

brat·wurst /ˈbratwɜrst/ *noun* a type of small German pork sausage. [German from *braten* fry, roast + *Wurst* sausage]

Braun /braun/ **1 Eva** (1912–45), mistress of Adolf Hitler, whom she married the day before they both committed suicide. **2 Karl Fer·di·nand** (1850–1918), German physicist who made notable contributions to wireless telegraphy and to the development of the cathode ray tube. He shared the 1909 Nobel Prize for physics with Marconi. **3 Wern·her Mag·nus Max·imil·ian von** (1912–77), German designer of rocket engines in the 1930s and during the Second World War. After the war he worked in the US space program.

Braun·schweig /ˈbraunʃvaɪk/ **1** (also **Bruns·wick**) a former duchy and state of Germany, mostly incorporated into Lower Saxony. **2** the capital of this former duchy, an industrial city in Lower Saxony, Germany; pop. (est. 2002) 242,400.

brava /ˈbrɒvɑ/ *interjection* expressing approval of a female performer. [feminine of BRAVO[1]]

bra·vado /brəˈvɑːdoː, -ɑdoː/ *noun* a bold manner or a show of boldness intended to impress. [Spanish *bravata* from *bravo*: compare BRAVE, -ADO]

brave ● *adjective* **1** able or ready to face and endure danger, pain, adversity, etc. **2** *literary* splendid, spectacular (*make a brave show*). ● *noun hist.* a N American Aboriginal warrior. ● *transitive verb* defy; encounter bravely. □ **brave it out** behave defiantly under suspicion or blame. □ **brave·ly** *adverb* **brave·ness** *noun* [Middle English from French, ultimately from Latin *barbarus* BARBAROUS]

brave new world *noun* usu. *ironic* an era of supposed happiness brought on by technological or social developments. [with reference to A. Huxley's dystopian novel *Brave New World*, the title being an ironic use of a line in Shakespeare's *Tempest*]

brav·ery *noun* **1** brave conduct. **2** a brave nature. [French *braverie* or Italian *braveria* (as BRAVE)]

bravo[1] /ˈbrɒvoː, brɒˈvoː/ ● *interjection* expressing approval of a performer etc. ● *noun* (*pl.* **-vos**) a cry of bravo. [French from Italian]

bravo[2] /ˈbrɒvoː/ *noun* (*pl.* **-voes** or **-vos**) a hired ruffian or killer. [Italian: see BRAVE]

bra·vura /brəˈvʊrə/ ● *adjective* requiring or displaying brilliant or

virtuosic skill (*a bravura performance*). ● *noun* brilliant or virtuosic skill, esp. in artistic performance. [Italian]

braw *adjective Scot.* fine, good. [var. of *brawf* BRAVE]

brawl ● *noun* **1** a rowdy fight, usu. involving several people. **2** a noisy quarrel. ● *intransitive verb* **1** fight or quarrel noisily or roughly. **2** (of a stream) run noisily. □ **brawl·er** *noun* [Middle English from Old Provençal, related to BRAY]

brawn *noun* **1** muscular strength. **2** muscle; lean flesh. **3** Brit. = HEADCHEESE. [Anglo-French *braun*, Old French *braon* from Germanic]

brawny *adjective* (**brawn·i·er**, **brawn·i·est**) muscular, strong. □ **brawn·i·ness** *noun*

Brax·ton Hicks contractions *plural noun* intermittent weak contractions of the uterus occurring during pregnancy. [J. *Braxton Hicks*, English gynecologist d.1897]

bray ● *noun* **1** the cry of a donkey. **2** a sound like this cry, e.g. that of a harshly-played brass instrument, a laugh, etc. ● *verb* **1** *intransitive* make a braying sound. **2** *transitive* utter harshly. [Old French *braire*, perhaps ultimately from Celtic]

Bra·yon /breiˈjɔ̃/ *Cdn* ● *noun* an inhabitant of the Madawaska region of NW New Brunswick. ● *adjective* denoting the Brayons, their mixed francophone and anglophone culture, etc. [from French *brayer* break flax before spinning]

braze[1] ● *transitive verb* solder with an alloy of copper and zinc at a high temperature. ● *noun* **1** a brazed joint. **2** the alloy used for brazing. [French *braser* solder from *braise* live coals]

braze[2] *transitive verb* **1 a** make of brass. **b** cover or ornament with brass. **2** make hard like brass. [Old English *bræsen* from *bræs* BRASS]

braz·en ● *adjective* **1** (also **brazen-faced**) flagrant and shameless; insolent. **2** made of brass. **3** of or like brass, esp. in colour or sound. ● *transitive verb* (usu. in phr. **brazen it out**) face (censure) in a defiantly unrepentant manner. □ **braz·en·ly** *adverb* **braz·en·ness** *noun* [Old English *bræsen* from *bræs* brass]

bra·zier /ˈbreizjər, -ʒər/ *noun* **1** *N Amer.* a charcoal grill for cooking. **2** a portable heater consisting of a pan or stand for holding lighted coals. [French *brasier* from *braise* hot coals]

Bra·zil the largest country in S America; pop. (est. 2002) 176,029,560; capital, Brasília. Brazil is the fifth largest country in the world, occupying almost half of the continent and containing most of the Amazon basin with its tropical rainforests. □ **Bra·zil·ian** *adjective & noun* [so called after *brazilwood*, of which the country was a major source]

Brazil nut *noun* the large three-sided nut of the S American tree *Bertholletia excelsa*. [BRAZIL]

brazil·wood *noun* a hard red wood of various tropical trees, esp. of the genus *Caesalpinia*, which yields dyes. [Spanish and Portuguese *brasil*, ultimately from medieval Latin *brasilium*, of uncertain origin]

Braz·za·ville /ˈbrazəˌvɪl/ the capital and a major port of the Republic of the Congo; pop. (est. 2002) 1,133,800. It was capital of French Equatorial Africa from 1910 to 1958. [S. de *Brazza*, French explorer who founded it d.1905]

breach ● *noun* **1** (often foll. by *of*) the breaking of or failure to observe a law, contract, regulations, procedures, etc. **2 a** a breaking of relations; an estrangement. **b** a quarrel. **3 a** a broken state. **b** a gap, esp. one made by artillery in fortifications. ● *verb* **1** *transitive* break through; make a gap in. **2** *transitive* break (a law, contract, etc.). **3** *intransitive* (of a whale) leap clear out of the water. □ **step into** (or **fill**) **the breach** give help in a crisis, esp. by replacing someone who has dropped out. [Old French *breche*, ultimately from Germanic]

breach of promise *noun* the breaking of a promise, esp. a promise to marry.

breach of the peace *noun* an infringement or violation of the public peace by any disturbance or riot etc.

bread ● *noun* **1** baked food made of flour and a liquid and often leavened with yeast, eaten as a staple food. **2 a** necessary food. **b** (also **daily bread**) one's livelihood. **3** *slang* money. ● *transitive verb* coat with bread crumbs for cooking. □ **bread and wine** the Eucharist. **break bread** share a meal. **know which side one's bread is buttered (on)** know where one's advantage lies. **take the bread out of a person's mouth** take away a person's living, esp. by competition etc. [Old English *bréad* from Germanic]

bread and butter (also **bread-and-butter**) ● *noun* **1** bread spread with butter. **2** an essential element, esp. that which provides one's livelihood. ● *adjective* (usu. **bread-and-butter**) **1** designating something basic and fundamental to one's livelihood (*bread-and-butter* concerns). **2** commonplace, humdrum. **3** expressing gratitude, esp. for hospitality (*bread-and-butter letter*).

bread-and-butter pickles *plural noun N Amer.* thinly sliced cucumbers, onions, and peppers pickled in brine.

bread-and-butter plate *noun N Amer.* a small plate, usu. about 15 cm in diameter, used esp. as a side plate for bread and butter, salad, etc.

bread and circuses *plural noun* public provision of food and entertainment, esp. to assuage the populace. [Latin *panem et circenses*, Juvenal's description of what would satisfy the Roman populace]

bread·basket *noun* **1** a basket for bread or rolls. **2** a region producing much grain. **3** *slang* the abdomen or stomach.

bread bin *noun Brit.* a bread box.

bread·board *noun* **1** a board for cutting bread on. **2** a board for making an experimental model of an electric circuit.

bread·box *noun N Amer.* a container in which bread is kept.

bread crumb *noun* **1** a very small fragment of bread. **2** (in *pl.*) bread crumbled for use in cooking.

bread flour *noun* flour, usu. milled from hard wheat, with a high proportion of gluten, suitable for making bread.

bread·fruit *noun* **1** a tropical evergreen tree, *Artocarpus altilis*, bearing edible usu. seedless fruit. **2** the fruit of this tree which when roasted becomes soft like new bread.

bread·knife *noun* (*pl.* **-knives**) a knife with a long serrated blade, for slicing bread.

bread·line *noun* **1** *N Amer.* a line of people waiting to receive free food. **2** *Brit.* subsistence level (esp. *on the breadline*).

bread pudding *noun* a baked, usu. sweet, custard containing pieces of bread.

bread·root *noun* a leguminous plant, *Psoralea esculenta*. Also called PRAIRIE TURNIP.

bread sauce *noun Brit.* a white sauce thickened with bread crumbs.

bread stick *noun* a long, thin, stick-like piece of crisp bread.

breadth *noun* **1** the distance or measurement from side to side of a thing; broadness. **2** a piece (of cloth etc.) of standard or full breadth. **3** extent, range. **4** freedom from limitations, esp. in opinion or interests. **5** *Art* unity of the whole, achieved by the disregard of unnecessary details. □ **breadth·ways** *adverb* **breadth·wise** *adverb* [obsolete *brede*, Old English *brǣdu*, from Germanic, related to BROAD]

bread·win·ner *noun* a person who earns the money to support a family. □ **bread·win·ning** *noun & adjective*

break[1] ● *verb* (*past* **broke** /broːk/ or *archaic* **brake** /breɪk/; *past participle* **broken** /ˈbroːkən/ or *archaic* **broke**) **1** *transitive & intransitive* **a** separate into pieces under a blow or strain; shatter; fracture. **b** make or become inoperative, esp. from damage (*the toaster broke*). **c** break a bone in or dislocate (part of the body). **d** break the skin of (the head or crown). **2 a** *transitive* cause or effect an interruption in (*broke our journey; the spell was broken; broke the silence*). **b** *intransitive* have an interval between spells of work (*let's break now; let's break for coffee*). **3** *transitive* fail to observe or keep (a law, promise, etc.). **4 a** *transitive & intransitive* make or become subdued or weakened; yield or cause to yield (*broke his spirit; they broke under the strain*). **b** *transitive* weaken the effect of (a fall, blow, etc.). **c** *transitive* = BREAK IN 3c. **d** *transitive* defeat, destroy (*broke the enemy's power*). **e** *transitive* defeat the object of (a strike, e.g. by employing other personnel). **5** *transitive* surpass (a record). **6** *intransitive* (foll. by *with*) quarrel or cease association with (another person etc.). **7** *transitive* **a** be no longer subject to (a habit). **b** (foll. by *of*) cause (a person) to be free of a habit (*broke them of their addiction*). **8** *transitive & intransitive* reveal or be revealed; (cause to) become known (*how can I break it to you gently?; the story broke on Friday*). **9** *intransitive* **a** (of the weather) change suddenly, esp. after a hot spell. **b** (of waves) curl over and dissolve into foam. **c** (of the day) dawn. **d** (of clouds) move apart; show a gap. **e** (of a storm) begin violently. **10** *transitive Electricity* disconnect (a circuit). **11** *intransitive* **a** (of the voice) change with emotion. **b** (of a boy's voice) change in register etc. at puberty. **12** *transitive* **a** (often foll. by *up*) divide (a set etc.) into parts, esp. by selling to different buyers. **b** change (a bill, banknote, etc.) for coins. **13** *transitive* ruin (an individual or institution) financially (*see also* BROKE *adjective*). **14** *transitive* penetrate, e.g. a safe, by force. **15** *transitive* decipher (a code). **16** *transitive* make (a way, path, etc.) by separating obstacles. **17** *intransitive* burst forth (*the sun broke through the clouds*). **18** *Military* **a** *intransitive* (of troops) disperse in confusion. **b** *transitive* make a rupture in (ranks). **19 a** *intransitive* (usu. foll. by *free, loose, out,* etc.) escape from constraint suddenly. **b** *transitive* escape or emerge from (prison, bounds, cover, etc.). **20** *transitive Tennis etc.* win a game against (an opponent's service). **21** *intransitive Boxing etc.* (of two fighters, usu. at

the referee's command) come out of a clinch. **22** *transitive Military* demote (an officer). **23** *intransitive* esp. *Stock Exch.* (of prices) fall sharply. **24** *intransitive Baseball* (of a pitch) curve or drop. **25** *intransitive Billiards etc.* disperse the balls at the beginning of a game. **26** *transitive* unfurl (a flag etc.). **27** *transitive Phonetics* subject (a vowel) to fracture. **28** *transitive* fail to rejoin (one's ship) after absence on leave. **29** *transitive* disprove (an alibi). **30** *transitive* bring an end to (an undecided condition, state of affairs, etc.) (*the goal broke a scoreless tie; an effort to break the impasse*). **31** *transitive* (in golf, bowling, etc.) achieve or surpass (a noteworthy score) (*broke 70, hopes to break 200*). **32** *transitive N Amer., Austral., & NZ* (often foll. by *in*) bring (virgin land) under cultivation. ● *noun* **1 a** an act or instance of breaking. **b** a point where something is broken; a gap. **2 a** an interval, an interruption; a pause in work. **b** a holiday (*spring break*). **3** a sudden dash (esp. to escape). **4** *informal* an instance of luck, esp. of a specified kind (*lucky break; bad break*). **5** *Sport* = BREAKAWAY 1. **6** *Billiards etc.* **a** a series of points scored during one turn. **b** the opening shot that disperses the balls. **7** *Music* (in jazz) a short unaccompanied passage for a soloist, usu. improvised. **8** *Electricity* a discontinuity in a circuit. □ **break away** make or become free or separate (*see also* BREAKAWAY). **break the back of 1** overburden (a person). **2** exert (oneself) greatly. **3** do the hardest or greatest part of (a task). **4** *N Amer.* defeat, destroy, crush. **break the bank 1** exhaust all one's financial resources. **2** (in gaming) exhaust the bank's resources; win spectacularly. **break bread** *see* BREAD. **break down 1 a** fail in mechanical action; cease to function. **b** (of human relationships etc.) fail, collapse. **c** fail in (esp. mental) health. **d** be overcome by emotion; collapse in tears. **2 a** demolish, destroy. **b** suppress (resistance). **c** force (a person) to yield under pressure. **3** analyze into components (*see also* BREAKDOWN). **4** decompose. **break even** emerge from a transaction etc. with neither profit nor loss. **break a game (wide) open** decisively turn a close game in one's favour with dramatic scoring. **break a person's heart** *see* HEART. **break the ice 1** begin to overcome formality or shyness, esp. between strangers. **2** make a start. **break in 1** enter premises by force, esp. with criminal intent. **2** interrupt. **3 a** accustom to a habit etc. **b** wear etc. until comfortable. **c** tame or discipline (an animal); accustom (a horse) to saddle and bridle etc. **break in on** disturb; interrupt. **break into 1** enter forcibly or violently. **2 a** suddenly begin, burst forth with (a song, laughter, etc.). **b** suddenly change one's pace for (a faster one) (*broke into a gallop*). **3** interrupt. **break a leg** (as *interjection*) *Theatre slang* good luck. **break loose 1** escape from constraint or a fixed position suddenly (*the icicle broke loose and fell to the ground*). **2** (of a condition, state, etc.) develop suddenly (*all hell broke loose*). **break new ground** innovate. **break of day** dawn. **break off 1** detach by breaking. **2** bring to an end. **3** cease talking etc. **break open** open forcibly. **break out 1** escape by force, esp. from prison. **2** begin suddenly; burst forth (*then violence broke out*). **3** (usu. foll. by *in*) become covered in (a rash, pimples, etc.). **4** exclaim. **5** release (a raised flag). **6 a** open up (a receptacle) and remove its contents. **b** remove (articles) from a place of storage. **break step** get out of step. **break (into) a sweat** begin sweating, esp. because of nervousness or physical exertion. **break trail** *N Amer.* **1** beat a path, e.g. through deep snow or undergrowth. **2** innovate. **break up 1** break into small pieces. **2** disperse; disband. **3 a** terminate a relationship. **b** cause to do this. **4** (of the weather) change suddenly (esp. after a fine spell). **5** (of a frozen body of water) break into blocks of ice at the spring thaw. **6** esp. *N Amer.* **a** upset or be upset. **b** excite or be excited. **c** convulse or be convulsed (*see also* BREAKUP). **7** *Brit.* end the school term. **break wind** release gas from the anus. **break one's word** *see* WORD. **give me a break** *informal* expressing skepticism, exasperation, scorn, etc. [Old English *brecan* from Germanic]

break[2] *noun* a carriage frame without a body, for breaking in young horses. [perhaps = *brake* framework: 17th c., of unknown origin]

break·able ● *adjective* that may or is apt to be broken easily. ● *noun* (esp. in *pl.*) a breakable thing.

break·age *noun* **1 a** a broken thing. **b** damage caused by breaking. **2** an act or instance of breaking.

break and enter *noun* = BREAKING AND ENTERING.

break·away ● *noun* **1** (also **break**) (in hockey, soccer, basketball, etc.) a long rush towards the goal or net after having passed all defenders (*scored on a breakaway*). **2** the act or an instance of breaking away or seceding. **3** a false start in a race. ● *attributive adjective* **1** broken away or separated from a larger body (*breakaway republic*). **2** designed to break or disengage easily to prevent more serious damage (*the actors were using breakaway bottles; tore off the car's breakaway mirror*).

break·beat *noun* a style of hip hop music incorporating altered sampled beats, usu. to create a syncopated rhythm.

break·dan·cing *noun* an energetic style of (usu. solo) street dancing, frequently involving spinning on the back or head. □ **break·dance** *noun & verb* **break·dan·cer** *noun*

break·down *noun* **1** a mechanical failure. **2** a loss of (esp. mental) health and strength. **3** a collapse or disintegration (*communication breakdown*). **4** chemical or physical decomposition. **5** a detailed analysis (of statistics etc.).

break·er *noun* **1** a person or thing that breaks something (*circuit breaker; record-breaker*). **2** a heavy wave that breaks. **3** *Cdn (Nfld)* a submerged rock with waves breaking above it. **4** a person who breaks in a horse. **5** *N Amer.* a breakdancer. **6** *N Amer.* a person who interrupts the conversation of others on a CB radio.

break-even ● *adjective* designating the point at which earnings equal expenditures. ● *noun* a break-even point.

break·fast ● *noun* the first meal of the day. ● *intransitive verb* have breakfast. □ **eat for breakfast** *slang* destroy (something) or defeat (a person) easily. □ **break·fast·er** *noun* [BREAK¹ 2 + FAST²]

breakfast nook *noun* a small area in or off a kitchen, with a table or counter and seating, designed for eating breakfast.

breakfast television *noun* early-morning television.

break·front *noun* a cabinet etc. whose front edge projects outwards at the centre (often *attributive: breakfront bookcase*).

break-in *noun* **1** an illegal forced entry into premises, esp. with criminal intent. **2** an illegal accessing of information from a computer.

break·ing *adjective* (often in *combination*) (of news, events, etc.) happening, occurring, esp. at the moment (*late-breaking story*).

breaking and entering *noun* the illegal entering of a building with the intent to commit an indictable offence.

breaking ball *noun* (also **breaking pitch**) *Baseball* a pitch that drops or curves just before reaching the batter.

breaking point *noun* the point of greatest strain, at which a thing breaks or a person gives way.

break·neck *attributive adjective* (of speed) dangerously fast.

break-open *noun* (usu. *attributive*) a lottery ticket on which perforated paper covering strips are torn away to reveal a series of images which, if matching, constitute a win. *Also called* NEVADA².

break·out *noun* **1** (in hockey etc.) a sudden offensive rush. **2** a forcible escape. **3** *N Amer.* an outbreak, esp. of pimples etc. **4** the breaking of a gathering into smaller groups for discussion (usu. *attributive: breakout groups; breakout rooms*). **5** (*attributive*) designating a book, song, etc. which achieves widespread popularity for its author, performer etc. (*a breakout book that appeals to more than just industry insiders*).

break point *noun* **1** a place or time at which an interruption or change is made. **2** (usu. **break·point**) *Computing* a place in a computer program where the sequence of instructions is interrupted, esp. by another program. **3** *Tennis* **a** a point which would win the game for the player(s) receiving service. **b** the situation at which the receiver(s) may break service by winning such a point. **4** = BREAKING POINT.

Break·spear /'breɪkspɪr/ **Nicho·las**, see ADRIAN IV.

break·through *noun* **1** a major advance or discovery. **2** an act of breaking through an obstacle etc. **3** = BREAKOUT 5.

breakthrough bleeding *noun* vaginal bleeding between menstrual periods.

break·up *noun* **1** disintegration, collapse. **2** the termination of a relationship. **3** dispersal. **4** *Cdn* (also **spring breakup**) **a** the breaking of a frozen river etc. into blocks of ice at the spring thaw. **b** the time during which this happens.

break·wall *noun* *N Amer.* (*Eastern Great Lakes*) a breakwater.

break·water *noun* a structure which breaks the force of waves, esp. at the entrance to a harbour.

Bream /briːm/ **Jul·ian (Alex·an·der)** (b.1933), English guitarist and lutenist, who formed the Julian Bream Consort for the performance of early consort music and has revived and edited much early music.

bream /briːm/ *noun* (*pl.* same) **1** a carp-like freshwater fish of Europe, *Abramis brama*, with an arched back. **2** (in full **sea bream**) a similarly shaped marine fish of the family Sparidae. **3** *N Amer.* = BLUEGILL. [Old French *bre(s)me* from West Germanic]

breast ● *noun* **1 a** either of two milk-secreting organs on the upper front of a woman's body. **b** a corresponding organ on females of other mammals, esp. primates. **c** the corresponding usu. rudimentary part of a man's body. **2 a** the upper front part of a human body; the chest. **b** the corresponding part of an animal. **3** a portion of poultry cut from the breast. **4** the part of a garment that covers the breast. **5** the breast as a source of nourishment or emotion. ● *transitive verb* **1** face, meet in

full opposition (*breast the waves*). **2** contend with. **3** reach the top of (a hill). □ **make a clean breast of** confess fully. □ **breast·ed** *adjective* (also in *combination*). **breast·less** *adjective* [Old English *brēost* from Germanic]

breast-beating *noun* an ostentatious display of remorse, sorrow, etc.

breast·bone *noun* a thin flat vertical bone and cartilage in the chest connecting the ribs.

breast·feed *verb* (*past* and *past participle* **-fed**) **1** *transitive & intransitive* feed (a baby) from the breast. **2** *intransitive* (of a baby) feed from the breast.

breast implant *noun* a small silicone pouch filled with silicone gel or saline solution, surgically inserted in a breast to enlarge it.

breast·plate *noun* a vestment or piece of armour covering the breast.

breast pump *noun* an instrument for drawing milk from the breasts by suction.

breast·stroke *noun* *Swimming* a stroke performed by a swimmer floating face down, extending the joined hands outward from the chest to above the head and then sweeping them down on either side of the body, while the legs execute a frog kick.

breast·work *noun* a temporary defence or parapet, usu. chest-high.

breath *noun* **1 a** the air taken into or expelled from the lungs. **b** one respiration of air. **c** an exhalation of air that can be seen, smelled, or heard (*cloudy breath in the cold air; bad breath*). **2 a** a slight movement of air; a breeze. **b** a whiff of perfume etc. **3** a whisper, a murmur (esp. of a scandalous nature). **4** the power of breathing; life (*while I still have breath*). □ **below** (or **under**) **one's breath** in a whisper. **breath of fresh air 1** a small amount of or a brief time in the fresh air. **2** a refreshing change. **breath of life** a necessity. **catch one's breath 1** cease breathing momentarily in surprise, suspense, etc. **2** rest after exercise to restore normal breathing. **draw breath** breathe; live. **hold one's breath** cease breathing temporarily. **don't hold your breath** *informal* do not expect something to happen imminently. **in the same breath** (esp. of saying two contradictory things) within a short time. **out of breath** gasping for air, esp. after exercise. **take breath** pause for rest. **take one's breath away** astound; surprise; awe; delight. **waste one's breath** talk or give advice without effect. [Old English *brǣth* from Germanic]

breath·able *adjective* **1** (of air) fit to be breathed. **2** (of textiles, clothing, etc.) allowing the passage of air and inhibiting condensation. □ **breath·abil·ity** /briːðəˈbɪlɪti/ *noun*

Breath·alyz·er *noun* *proprietary* an instrument for measuring the amount of alcohol in the breath (and hence in the blood) of a driver. □ **breath·alyze** *transitive verb* (also **-lyse**). [BREATH + ANALYZE + -ER¹]

breathe *verb* **1** *intransitive* take air into and expel it from the lungs. **2** *intransitive* be or seem alive (*is she breathing?*). **3** *transitive* **a** utter; say (esp. quietly) (*breathed her forgiveness*). **b** express; display (*breathed defiance*). **4** *intransitive* take breath, pause. **5** *transitive* **a** send out (as if) with exhaled air (*breathed a sigh of relief*). **b** take in (as if) with breathed air (*breathed the fumes*). **6** *intransitive* (of wine, fabric, etc.) be exposed to fresh air. **7** *intransitive* **a** (of textiles, clothing, etc.) allow the passage of air and inhibit condensation. **b** (of the skin) absorb oxygen and get rid of moisture. **8** *intransitive* (of wind) blow softly. **9** *transitive* allow (a horse etc.) to breathe; give rest after exertion. □ **breathe easy** (or **freely**) be relieved from tension, suspense, etc. **breathe down a person's neck** be close behind a person, esp. in mistrust or pursuit. **breathe (new) life into** invigorate; make lively. **breathe one's last** die. **not breathe a word of** keep quite secret. [Middle English from BREATH]

breath·er *noun* **1** *informal* a brief pause for rest. **2** a person or animal that breathes, esp. a specified substance or in a specified way (*seals are air-breathers; heavy breathers*). **3** a safety vent in the crankcase of a car etc.

breath·ing *noun* **1** the process of taking air into and expelling it from the lungs. **2** *Phonetics* a sign in ancient Greek indicating the presence of an aspirate (**rough breathing**) or the absence of an aspirate (**smooth breathing**).

breathing hole *noun* a hole made by seals through the ice covering a body of water, used for breathing.

breathing space *noun* (also **breathing room**) **1** a pause or respite; a time to rest, recover, reconsider, etc. **2** a space or area which allows for easy movement, rest, etc. (*our breathing space in the city*).

breath·less *adjective* **1** panting, out of breath. **2** holding the breath because of excitement, suspense, etc. (*a state of breathless expectancy*). **3** (of air) calm and still. **4** causing shortness of breath, esp. through exertion, excitement, etc. □ **breath·less·ly** *adverb* **breath·less·ness** *noun*

breath mint *noun* a usu. mint-flavoured lozenge for sweetening the breath.

breath·taking *adjective* astounding; awe-inspiring. □ **breath·taking·ly** *adverb*

breath test *noun* a test of a person's alcohol consumption, using a Breathalyzer.

breathy /'breθi/ *adjective* (**breath·i·er**, **breath·i·est**) (of a singing voice etc.) containing the sound of breathing. □ **breath·i·ly** *adverb* **breath·i·ness** *noun*

Bré·beuf /breɪ'bəf/ **St. Jean de** (1593–1649), French-born Jesuit missionary to New France, who lived among the Hurons and produced a Huron grammar and dictionary. Captured by invading Iroquois, he was tortured and killed. He was canonized in 1930.

B.Rec. *abbreviation* Bachelor of Recreation.

brec·cia /'bretʃiə/ ● *noun* a rock of angular stones etc. cemented by finer material. ● *transitive verb* form into breccia. □ **brecci·ate** *transitive verb* **brecci·a·tion** /-'eiʃən/ *noun* **brecci·at·ed** *adjective* [Italian, = gravel, from Germanic, related to BREAK[1]]

Brecht /brext/ **Ber·tolt** (1898–1956), German dramatist, producer and poet, known for his attempt to develop a Marxist 'epic theatre' employing the 'alienation effect', which rejected Aristotelian dramatic principles. His works include *The Threepenny Opera* (1928) and *Mother Courage* (1941). □ **Brecht·ian** *adjective*

Brecon·shire /'brekən.ʃiːr/ (also **Breck·nock·shire** /'breknɒk.ʃiːr/) a former county of south central Wales. It was divided between Powys and Gwent in 1974.

bred *past and past participle of* BREED.

Breda /'briːdə/ a manufacturing city in the SW Netherlands; pop. (est. 2002) 160,000. It is noted for the Compromise of Breda of 1566, a protest against Spanish rule over the Netherlands; the 1660 manifesto of Charles II (who lived there in exile), stating his terms for accepting the throne of Britain; and the Treaty of Breda, which ended the Anglo-Dutch war of 1665–7.

breech ● *noun* **1 a** the part of a cannon behind the bore. **b** the back part of a rifle or gun barrel. **2** (*attributive*) designating a birth in which the baby presents in the birth canal with the buttocks or feet foremost. **3** *archaic* the buttocks. ● *transitive verb archaic* put (a boy) into breeches after being in petticoats since birth. [Old English *brōc*, pl. *brēc* (treated as sing. in Middle English), from Germanic]

breech·block *noun* a metal block which closes the breech aperture in a gun.

breech·cloth *noun* (also **breech·clout** /-klaut/) = LOINCLOTH.

breech·es /'britʃəz/ *plural noun* (also **pair of breeches** *singular*) **1** short trousers, esp. fastened below the knee, now used esp. for riding or in court costume. **2** = BRITCHES. [pl. of BREECH]

breeches buoy *noun* a lifebuoy suspended from a rope which has canvas breeches for the user's legs.

breech-loader *noun* a gun loaded at the breech, not through the muzzle. □ **breech-loading** *adjective*

breed ● *verb* (*past and past participle* **bred** /bred/) **1** *transitive & intransitive* bear, generate (offspring). **2** *transitive & intransitive* propagate or cause to propagate; raise (livestock). **3** *transitive* **a** yield, produce; result in (*war breeds famine*). **b** spread (*discontent bred by rumour*). **4** *intransitive* arise; spread (*disease breeds in the tropics*). **5** *transitive* bring up; train (*bred to the law*; *Hollywood breeds stars*). **6** *transitive Physics* create (fissile material) by nuclear reaction. ● *noun* **1** a stock of animals or plants within a species, having a similar appearance, and usu. developed by deliberate selection. **2** a race; a lineage. **3** a sort, a kind. **4** *offensive* a person of mixed racial descent; a half-breed. □ **bred and born** = BORN AND BRED (see BORN). **bred in the bone** hereditary. **breed in** mate with or marry near relations. □ **breed·er** *noun* [Old English *brēdan*: related to BROOD]

breeder reactor *noun* a nuclear reactor that can create more fissile material than it consumes. *Also called* FAST-BREEDER.

breed·ing *noun* **1** the process of developing or propagating (animals, plants, etc.). **2** generation; child-bearing. **3 a** upbringing or education. **b** behaviour, esp. good manners. **4** wealthy or aristocratic family background.

breeding ground *noun* **1** an area of land where an animal, esp. a bird, habitually breeds. **2** a thing that favours the development or occurrence of something, esp. something unpleasant (*breeding ground for organized crime*).

breeks *Scot. var. of* BREECHES.

breeze[1] ● *noun* **1** a gentle wind. **2** *Meteorol.* a wind of 1.6–13.8 m/s (4–31 mph) and between force 2 and force 6 on the Beaufort scale. **3** a wind blowing from land at night or a large body of water during the day. **4** esp. *N Amer. informal* an easy task. ● *intransitive verb* **1** (foll. by *in, out, along*, etc.) *informal* come or go in a casual or lighthearted manner. **2** (usu. foll. by *through*) emerge successfully and easily from (a test, competition, etc.). □ **breeze up** *N Amer.* (*Maritimes, Nfld & New England*) (of a wind) increase to gale force. **shoot the breeze** *N Amer. informal see* SHOOT. [prob. from Old Spanish & Portuguese *briza* NE wind]

breeze[2] *noun* small cinders. [French *braise* live coals]

breeze block *noun Brit.* = CINDER BLOCK.

breeze·way *noun N Amer.* a covered passageway, as between a house and a garage.

breezy *adjective* (**breez·i·er**, **breez·i·est**) **1 a** windswept. **b** pleasantly windy. **2** *informal* lively; jovial; spirited. **3** *informal* careless (*with breezy indifference*). □ **breez·i·ly** *adverb* **breez·i·ness** *noun*

Bre·genz /breɪ'gentz/ a city in W Austria, on the eastern shores of Lake Constance; pop. (est. 2002) 26,853. It is the capital of the state of Vorarlberg.

brek·kie *noun Cdn, Brit.,* & *Austral. slang* breakfast.

Brel, Jacques (1929–78), Belgian singer and composer. He gained a reputation in Paris as an original songwriter whose satirical wit was balanced by his idealism and hope. His cabaret-revue, which opened in New York in 1968, ran for 1,847 performances. His last album, *Brel* (1977), sold over two million copies.

Bre·men /'breɪmən/ **1** a state of NW Germany. Divided into two parts, which centre on the city of Bremen and the port of Bremerhaven, it is surrounded by the state of Lower Saxony. **2** its capital, an industrial city linked by the Weser River to the port of Bremerhaven and the North Sea; pop. (est. 2002) 528,200.

brems·strah·lung /'bremz.ʃtrʊləŋ/ *noun Physics* the electromagnetic radiation produced by the acceleration or esp. the deceleration of a charged particle after passing through the electric and magnetic fields of a nucleus. [German, = braking radiation]

Bren *noun* (in full **Bren gun**) a lightweight quick-firing machine gun. [*Brno* in the Czech Republic (where originally made) + *Enfield* in England (where later made)]

Bren·dan, St. (*c*.486–*c*.575), Irish abbot, whose mythical voyage with a band of monks to a promised land was described in the 9th-c. epic, 'The Navigation of St. Brendan'.

Bren·del /'brendəl/ **Al·fred** (b.1931), Austrian pianist best known for his interpretations of Beethoven and Schubert.

Bren·ner Pass an Alpine pass at the border between Austria and Italy, on the route between Innsbruck and Bolzano, at an altitude of 1 371 m (4,498 ft.).

brent *noun* (in full **brent goose**) *Brit.* = BRANT.

bre·sao·la /bre'saʊlə/ *noun* an Italian dish of raw beef cured by salting and air-drying, typically served in slices with an olive oil, lemon juice, and pepper dressing. [Italian, from Italian regional *bresada*, past participle of *brasare* 'braise']

Bre·scia /'breʃə/ an industrial city in Lombardy, in N Italy; pop. (2001) 187,865.

Bres·lau /'breslaʊ/ *noun* the German name for WROCŁAW.

Bres·son /bre'sɔ̃/ **Rob·ert** (1907–99), French film director whose austere intellectual style has had a profound influence on the cinema. His films include *Diary of a Country Priest* (1951), *The Trial of Joan of Arc* (1962), *The Devil, Probably* (1977), and *L'Argent* (1983).

Brest /brest/ **1** a port and naval base on the Atlantic coast of Brittany, in NW France; pop. (1999) 149,634. **2** a river port and industrial city in Belarus, situated close to the border with Poland; pop. (est. 2002) 305,800. The peace treaty between Germany and Russia was signed there in March 1918. It was known until 1921 as Brest-Litovsk.

breth·ren *plural noun see* BROTHER.

Bre·ton[1] /brə'tɔ̃/ **André** (1896–1966), French poet, essayist, and critic, founder and chief theorist of surrealism.

Bre·ton[2] /'bretən/ ● *noun* **1** a native of Brittany. **2** the Brythonic Celtic language of Brittany. ● *adjective* of or relating to Brittany or its people or language. [Old French, = BRITON]

Breton, Cape /'bretən/ the most southeasterly point of Cape Breton Island, near the community of Louisbourg. [origin uncertain: either in honour of English fishermen (see BRITON) or after *Cap Breton* near Bayonne, France (see BRETON[2])]

Bret·ton Woods Conference /'bretən/ *noun* an international financial conference held in the resort town of Bretton Woods, New Hampshire, which led to the foundation of the World Bank and the International Monetary Fund.

Breuer /ˈbrɔɪɜr/ **Mar·cel (Lajos)** (1902–81), Hungarian-born US architect and designer, who produced the first tubular-steel chair while at the Bauhaus; his most influential concrete buildings were the UNESCO secretariat in Paris (1953–8) and the Whitney Museum in New York (1966).

Breu·ghel var. of BRUEGEL.

Breuil /brɜj/ **Henri Édouard Pros·per** (1877–1961), French archaeologist. He authenticated the paleolithic cave paintings at Altamira in Spain and made detailed studies of those in the Dordogne region of France and southern Africa.

breve /briːv/ noun **1** Music a note, now rarely used, having the time value of two semibreves or whole notes. **2** a written or printed mark (˘) indicating a short or unstressed vowel. [Middle English var. of BRIEF]

brevet ● noun **1** /ˈbrevət/ (often attributive) a document conferring a privilege from a sovereign or government, esp. a rank in the army, without the appropriate pay (was promoted by brevet; brevet major). **2** /ˈbreveɪ/ an identifying badge with one wing worn by members of the aircrew other than pilots in the RAF and hist. in the RCAF. ● transitive verb /ˈbrevət/ (**brev·et·ed, brev·et·ing** or **brev·et·ted, brev·et·ting**) confer brevet rank on. [Old French diminutive of bref BRIEF]

brevi·ary /ˈbriːviəri, ˈbriːviˌeri, ˈbrev-/ noun (pl. **-aries**) Catholicism a book containing the divine office for each day, to be recited by those in orders. [Latin breviarium summary from breviare abridge: see ABBREVIATE]

brev·ity /ˈbreviti/ noun **1** economy of expression; conciseness. **2** shortness (of time etc.). [Anglo-French breveté, Old French brieveté from bref BRIEF]

brew ● verb **1** transitive **a** make (beer etc.) by infusion, boiling, and fermentation. **b** make (tea, coffee, etc.) by infusion. **2** intransitive undergo either of these processes (the tea is brewing). **3** intransitive (of trouble, a storm, etc.) gather force; threaten (mischief was brewing). **4** transitive bring about; set in train; concoct (brewed their fiendish scheme). ● noun **1** an amount (of beer etc.) brewed at one time (this year's brew). **2** what is brewed (esp. with regard to its quality) (a good strong brew). **3 a** beer. **b** a serving of beer. **4** the action or process of brewing. **5** a mixture, esp. of disparate elements. □ **brew up** Brit. make tea. [Old English brēowan from Germanic]

brew·er noun a person or company that makes beer.

brewer's yeast noun a non-leavening dry yeast of the genus Saccharomyces, used in the fermentation of beer and wine, and added to some foods as a nutritive agent.

brew·ery noun (pl. **-eries**) a place where beer etc. is brewed commercially.

brew·house noun a place where beer is brewed.

brewis /bruːz/ noun Cdn (Nfld) **1** a stew made of hardtack soaked in water and boiled. **2** = FISH AND BREWIS. [English dial. 'bread soaked in fat or broth' from Old French bro(u)ez broth, ultimately from Germanic]

brew·master noun N Amer. a master brewer.

brew pub noun a bar with on-site brewing facilities.

brew·ski noun (pl. **-skis** or **-skies**) N Amer. slang a beer. [BREW noun 3, ending possibly fancifully after common Eastern European surname suffix -ski]

Brew·ster, Sir David (1781–1868), Scottish physicist, who is best known for his work on the laws controlling the polarization of light, and for his invention of the kaleidoscope.

brew-up noun Brit. informal an instance of making tea.

Brezh·nev /ˈbreʒnjef/ **Leo·nid Ilich** (1906–82), Soviet political leader, General Secretary of the Communist Party of the USSR 1966–82 and President 1977–82. His period in power was marked by intensified persecution of dissidents at home and by attempted détente followed by renewed cold war in 1968. He was largely responsible for the decision to invade Czechoslovakia in 1968.

Brian Boru /ˈbraɪən bəˈruː/ (c.941–1014), the last king of Ireland 1002–14.

Briand /briˈɑ̃/ **Ari·stide** (1862–1932), French radical socialist politician, prime minister of France eleven times between 1909 and 1929. An outspoken advocate of the League of Nations, he negotiated the Locarno Pact (1925), which attempted to restore relations between Germany and its former enemies, and the Kellogg-Briand Pact (1928), in which 60 countries renounced war; he was awarded the Nobel Peace Prize in 1926.

Bri·ansk see BRYANSK.

briar[1] var. of BRIER[1].

briar[2] var. of BRIER[2].

bribe ● noun a sum of money or another reward offered or demanded in order to procure an (often illegal or dishonest) action or decision in favour of the giver. ● transitive verb persuade (a person etc.) by means of a bribe (bribed the guard to release the suspect). □ **brib·able** adjective

brib·er noun **brib·ery** noun [Old French briber, brimber beg, of unknown origin]

bric-a-brac noun miscellaneous, often old, ornaments, trinkets, furniture, etc., of no great value. [French from obsolete à bric et à brac at random]

Brice, Fanny (born Fannie Borach) (1891–1951), US actress, comedienne, and singer, who appeared in numerous Ziegfeld Follies revues between 1911 and 1923.

brick ● noun **1 a** a small, usu. rectangular, block of fired or sun-dried clay, used in building. **b** the material to make these. **c** a similar block of concrete etc. **2** a brick-shaped solid object (a brick of ice cream). **3** a white, smooth, firm cow's-milk cheese with a brick-like shape. **4** Brit. = BUILDING BLOCK 3. **5** dated slang a generous or loyal person. ● adjective **1** built of brick (brick wall). **2** of a dull red colour. □ **like a ton of bricks** informal with crushing weight, force, or authority. **run into a brick wall** come up against an insurmountable obstacle. **two** (or **a few**) **bricks short** (or **shy**) **of a load** lacking in intelligence. [Middle Low German, Middle Dutch bri(c)ke, of unknown origin]

brick·bat noun **1** a piece of brick, esp. when used to throw at someone. **2** an uncomplimentary remark.

brick·lay·er noun a worker who builds with bricks. □ **brick·lay·ing** noun

brick red ● noun the dull red colour typical of bricks. ● adjective (hyphenated when attributive) of this colour.

bricks and clicks noun (attributive) designating a commercial operation that operates both online and through traditional retail outlets.

bricks and mortar noun buildings, esp. housing or traditional retail businesses in stores, as opposed to electronic retailing.

brick·work noun **1** construction using brick. **2** a wall, building, etc. made of brick.

brick·yard noun a place where bricks are made.

brico·lage /ˌbrɪkəˈlɒʒ/ noun **1** construction or creation from whatever is immediately available for use. **2** something constructed or created in this way. □ **brico·leur** noun [French, from bricoler 'do odd jobs', from Provençal bricola or Italian briccola, of unknown origin]

bridal adjective of or concerning a bride or a wedding. [originally as noun, = wedding feast, from Old English brȳd-ealu from brȳd BRIDE + ealu ale-drinking]

Bridal Veil Falls a waterfall in southwestern BC, situated on Bridal Creek, just northeast of Chilliwack. It has a vertical drop of 122 m.

bridal wreath noun any of various ornamental plants with white flowers, esp. shrubs of the genus Spiraea of the rose family.

bride noun a woman on her wedding day and for some time before and after it. [Old English brȳd from Germanic]

bride·groom noun a man on his wedding day and for some time before and after it. [Old English brȳdguma (as BRIDE, guma man, assimilated to GROOM)]

bride price noun a payment of money or goods made to a bride or her parents by the bridegroom or his parents.

brides·maid noun **1** a girl or woman attending a bride on her wedding day. **2** N Amer. a person or group that never quite attains a desired goal (the team is the league's perennial bridesmaid). [earlier bridemaid, from BRIDE + MAID]

bride·well noun archaic a prison; a reformatory. [St. Bride's Well in London, England, near which such a building stood]

Bridge, Frank (1879–1941), English composer, conductor, and violist. His later works, such as the string trio Rhapsody (1928) and Oration (for cello and orchestra, 1930), show stylistic elements akin to those of Schoenberg. Benjamin Britten was one of his pupils.

bridge[1] ● noun **1 a** a structure carrying a road, path, railway, etc., across a stream, ravine, road, railway, etc. **b** anything providing a connection between different things (a bridge between cultures). **2** the superstructure on a ship from which the captain and officers direct operations. **3 a** the upper bony part of the nose. **b** the central part of a pair of eyeglasses, which rests on this and connects the two lenses. **4** Music a piece of wood, plastic, etc. on a violin, guitar, etc. over which the strings are stretched. **5** Music a transitional piece between main themes. **6** a dental structure used to cover a gap, joined to and

---

Consonants: b but d dog f few g get h her j yes k cat l leg m man n no p pen r red s sit

supported by the teeth on either side. **7** *Billiards* **a** a long stick with a structure at the end which is used to support a cue for a difficult shot. **b** a support for a cue formed by a raised hand. **8** = LAND BRIDGE. **9** an electric circuit with two branches across which a detector or load is connected. These circuits are used to measure resistance or other property by equalizing the potential across the two ends of a detector, or to rectify an alternating voltage or current. ● *transitive verb* **1 a** be a bridge over (*a fallen tree bridges the stream*). **b** make a bridge over; span. **2** span as if with a bridge (*bridged the gap between east and west*). □ **cross that bridge when one comes to it** deal with a problem when and if it arises. □ **bridge·able** *adjective* [Old English *brycg* from Germanic]

bridge² *noun* a card game for four players derived from whist, in which one player's cards are exposed at a certain point and are thereafter played by his or her partner (*compare* AUCTION BRIDGE, CONTRACT BRIDGE). [19th c.: origin unknown]

bridge-building *noun* **1** the activity of building bridges. **2** the promotion of friendly relations, esp. between countries. □ **bridge-builder** *noun*

bridge financing *noun N Amer.* = BRIDGE LOAN.

bridge·head *noun* **1** a fortified position held on the enemy's side of a river or other obstacle. **2** an initial position established as a basis for advancing further.

bridge loan *noun* (*also esp. Brit.* **bridg·ing loan**) a short-term loan covering the interval between two transactions, e.g. the purchase of a second house before the closing of the sale of the first.

Bridge Mixture *noun* (*also* **Bridge Mix**) *N Amer.* proprietary an assortment of small chocolates with a variety of fillings, e.g. peanuts, raisins, jellies, etc.

bridge roll *noun Brit.* a small soft oval bread roll.

Bridg·es, Rob·ert (Sey·mour) (1844–1930), English poet and literary critic, Poet Laureate 1913–30. Among his best-known works are the long philosophical poem *The Testament of Beauty* (1929) and two important critical essays, *Milton's Prosody* (1893) and *John Keats* (1895).

Bridget, St. ▸ **1 of Ireland** (*also* **Bride** /ˈbriːdə, braid/, **Brigid** /ˈbrɪdʒɪd/) (6th c.), Irish abbess. She was venerated in Ireland as a virgin saint and noted in miracle stories for her compassion; her cult soon spread over most of western Europe. It has been suggested that she may represent the Irish goddess Brig. **2 of Sweden** (*also* **Bir·gitta** /bɪərˈɡɪtə/) (c.1303–73), Swedish nun and visionary. She experienced her first vision of the Virgin Mary at the age of 7. After her husband's death she was inspired by further visions to devote herself to religion and she founded the Order of Bridgettines (c.1346) at Vadstena in Sweden.

Bridge·town the capital of Barbados, a port on the south coast; pop. (est. 1999) 133,000.

Bridge·water a town in central Nova Scotia, situated on the LaHave River, southwest of Halifax; pop. (2001) 7,621. [named after a nearby bridge spanning the river]

bridge·work *noun* **1** = BRIDGE¹ *noun* 6. **2** the art or process of building bridges.

Bridg·man, P(ercy) W(il·liams) (1882–1961), US physicist. He worked mainly on the properties of liquids and solids under very high pressures, and his techniques were later used in making artificial diamonds and other minerals; he was awarded the Nobel Prize for physics in 1946.

bridie *noun* an originally Scottish turnover filled with meat and onions. [apparently from 'bridie's pie', a large pie traditionally baked by a bride's family or friends for her wedding guests]

bridle ● *noun* **1 a** the headgear used to control a horse, consisting of buckled leather straps, a metal bit, and reins. **b** a restraining thing or influence (*put a bridle on your tongue*). **2** *Naut.* a mooring cable. ● *verb* **1** *transitive* put a bridle on (a horse etc.). **2** *transitive* bring under control; curb. **3** *intransitive* (*often foll. by up*) express offence, resentment, etc. [Old English *bridel*]

bridle path *noun* (*also* **bridle·way**) a rough path or road fit only for riders or walkers, not vehicles.

bri·doon /brɪˈduːn/ *noun Riding* a small snaffle used in a double bridle. [French *bridon* from *bride* bridle]

brie /briː/ *noun* a kind of ripened soft cheese with a white mould skin. [*Brie*, a former province in N France]

brief ● *adjective* **1** of short duration. **2** concise in expression. **3** abrupt, brusque. **4** short; scanty (*a brief halter top*). ● *noun* **1** (in *pl.*) close-fitting legless underpants. **2** *N Amer. Law* a written statement of the arguments for a case. **3** *Brit. Law* **a** a summary of the facts and legal points of a case

drawn up by a solicitor for a barrister. **b** a piece of work for a barrister. **4** instructions given for a task, operation, etc. **5** esp. *Brit.* a set of instructions, as a job description etc. (*your brief will include managing the payroll*). **6** *Journalism* a brief news article or summary. **7** *Catholicism* a letter from the Pope to a person or community on a matter of discipline. ● *transitive verb* **1** instruct (an employee, a participant, etc.) in preparation for a task; inform or instruct thoroughly in advance (*briefed him for the interview*) (*compare* DEBRIEF). **2** *Brit. Law* **a** instruct (a barrister) by brief. **b** retain as counsel in a suit. □ **hold no brief for** not support or argue in favour of. **in brief** in short. □ **brief·er** *noun* **brief·ly** *adverb* **brief·ness** *noun* [Anglo-French *bref*, Old French *brief*, from Latin *brevis* short]

brief·case *noun* a flat rectangular case for carrying documents etc.

brief·ing *noun* **1** a meeting for giving information or instructions. **2** the information or instructions given. **3** the action of informing or instructing.

Brier /ˈbraɪr/ *noun* the bonspiel for the Canadian men's national curling championship. [the name of the trophy, originally sponsored by the Macdonald tobacco company]

brier¹ /ˈbraɪr/ *noun* (*also* **briar**) any prickly bush esp. of a wild rose. □ **briery** *adjective* [Old English *brǣr*, *brēr*, of unknown origin]

brier² /ˈbraɪr/ *noun* (*also* **briar**) **1** a white plant of the heath family, *Erica arborea*, native to S Europe. **2** a tobacco pipe made from its root. [19th-c. *bruyer* from French *bruyère* heath]

brier rose *noun* a dog rose.

Brig. *abbreviation* BRIGADIER.

brig¹ *noun* **1** a two-masted square-rigged ship. **2** a prison, esp. on a warship. [abbreviation of BRIGANTINE]

brig² *noun Scot. & Northern England var. of* BRIDGE¹.

brig·ade /brɪˈɡeɪd/ ● *noun* **1 a** a subdivision of an army. **b** a British infantry unit consisting usu. of 3 battalions and forming part of a division. **c** a corresponding armoured unit. **2** an organized or uniformed band of workers (*fire brigade*). **3** *informal* any group of people with a characteristic in common (*the couldn't-care-less brigade*). **4** *Cdn hist.* a group or fleet of canoes, bateaux, Red River carts, pack horses, etc., travelling together to the same trading post etc. ● *transitive verb* form into a brigade. [French from Italian *brigata* company, from *brigare* be busy with, from *briga* strife]

brigade trail *noun Cdn* a trail built for or used by brigades of pack horses.

briga·dier /ˌbrɪɡəˈdɪr/ *noun Military* (*also* **Brigadier**) (in the UK and *hist.* in the Canadian Army) **1** an officer commanding a brigade. **2** a staff officer of similar standing, above a colonel and below a major general. Abbr.: **Brig.** [French (as BRIGADE, -IER)]

brigadier general *noun* (*also* **Brigadier General**) (in the Canadian Army and Air Force and US Army, Air Force, and Marines) an officer ranking next above colonel. Abbr.: **BGen** (*Cdn*) or **Brig. Gen.**

bri·gand /ˈbrɪɡənd/ *noun* a member of a robber band living by pillage and ransom, usu. in wild terrain. □ **bri·gand·age** *noun* **bri·gand·ry** *noun* [Old French from Italian *brigante* from *brigare*: see BRIGADE]

bri·gan·tine /ˈbrɪɡən,tiːn/ *noun* a two-masted sailing ship with a square-rigged foremast and a fore-and-aft-rigged mainmast. [Old French *brigandine* or Italian *brigantino* from *brigante* BRIGAND]

Brig. Gen. *abbreviation* Brigadier General. ¶ The Canadian Forces use the abbreviation BGen.

Briggs, Henry (1561–1630), English mathematician. He was renowned for his work on logarithms, in which he introduced the decimal base, made the thousands of calculations necessary for the tables, and popularized their use.

bright ● *adjective* **1 a** emitting or reflecting much light; shining. **b** full of light (*a bright apartment*). **2** (of colour) intense, vivid. **3** clever, talented, quick-witted (*a bright idea; a bright child*). **4** cheerful, vivacious. **5** full of hope; auspicious, promising (*has a bright future*). ● *adverb* esp. *literary* brightly (*the moon shone bright*). ● *noun* (in *pl.*) **1** bright colours. **2** *N Amer.* headlights switched to high beam. □ **bright and early** very early in the morning. **bright-eyed and bushy-tailed** *informal* alert and sprightly. **look on the bright side** be optimistic. □ **bright·ish** *adjective* **bright·ly** *adverb* **bright·ness** *noun* [Old English *beorht*, (adv.) *beorhte*, from Germanic]

bright·en *transitive & intransitive verb* **1** make or become brighter. **2** make or become more cheerful. □ **bright·en·er** *noun*

bright lights *plural noun* (prec. by *the*) the glamour and excitement of the city.

Bright·on 1 a resort city on the south coast of England, formerly part of Sussex; pop. (est. 2002) 122,500. It was patronized by the Prince of

Wales (later George IV) from *c.*1780 to 1827, and is noted for its Regency architecture. **2** a town in SE Ontario, between Belleville and Cobourg; pop. (2001) 9,449. [sense 2 after sense 1]

bright·work *noun* polished metal or metal-like parts on a car, boat, etc.

Brigid, St. /ˈbrɪdʒɪd/ see BRIDGET, ST. 1.

brill[1] *noun* a European flatfish, *Scophthalmus rhombus*, resembling a turbot. [15th c.: origin unknown]

brill[2] *adjective Brit. informal* = BRILLIANT *adjective* 4. [abbreviation]

Brillat-Savarin /briːˈjo savaˈrɑ̃/ **(Jean) An·thelme** (1755–1826), French jurist and gourmet, whose *Physiologie du goût ou Méditations sur la gastronomie transcendente* (1825) is a collection of anecdotes and aphorisms on food.

bril·liance *noun* **1** great brightness; sparkling or radiant quality. **2** outstanding talent or intelligence. □ **bril·lian·cy** *noun*

bril·liant ● *adjective* **1** very bright; sparkling. **2** outstandingly talented or intelligent. **3** showy; outwardly impressive. **4** *informal* excellent, superb. ● *noun* a diamond of the finest cut with many facets. □ **bril·liant·ly** *adverb* [French *brillant* part. of *briller* shine, from Italian *brillare*, of unknown origin]

bril·liant·ine /ˈbrɪljən.tiːn/ *noun* **1** an oily liquid dressing for making the hair glossy. **2** *US* a lustrous dress fabric. [French *brillantine* (as BRILLIANT)]

Brillo *noun* (also **Brillo pad**) *proprietary* a scouring pad of steel wool impregnated with soap.

brim ● *noun* **1** the edge or lip of a cup or other vessel, or of a hollow. **2** the projecting edge of a hat. ● *transitive & intransitive verb* (**brimmed**, **brim·ming**) **1** fill or be full to the edge. **2** (usu. foll. by *with*) be full of a particular quality, feeling, etc. □ **brim over** overflow. □ **brim·less** *adjective* **brimmed** *adjective* (usu. in *combination*). [Middle English *brimme*, of unknown origin]

brim·ful *adjective* (usu. *predicative*; often foll. by *of*) filled to the brim.

brim·stone *noun archaic* the element sulphur. [prob. from Old English *bryne* burning + STONE]

brin *noun Cdn* (*Nfld*) burlap (*brin bag*). [obsolete Devonshire dialect, = 'strong linen', possibly from archaic *brinded*, of a tawny brown colour]

brin·dled /ˈbrɪndəld/ *adjective* (also **brin·dle**) (esp. of domestic animals) brownish or tawny with streaks of other colour. [earlier *brinded*, *brended* from *brend*, perhaps of Scandinavian origin]

brine ● *noun* **1** water saturated or strongly impregnated with salt. **2** sea water. ● *transitive verb* soak in or saturate with brine. [Old English *brine*, of unknown origin]

brine shrimp *noun* a small crustacean of the genus *Artemia*, inhabiting salt lakes etc. and used as food for aquarium fish.

bring *transitive verb* (*past and past participle* **brought**) **1** come carrying or leading (something) or accompanying (someone). **2** cause to come or be present (*what brings you here?*). **3** cause or result in (*war brings misery; the pills brought some relief*). **4** be sold for; produce as income. **5 a** make (a legal charge). **b** initiate (legal action). **6** cause to become or to reach a particular state (*brought them to their senses; cannot bring myself to agree*). **7** adduce (evidence, an argument, etc.). **8** make (something) move in the direction or way specified (*the roof was brought down by the weight of the snow*). □ **bring about 1** cause to happen. **2** turn (a ship) around. **bring back** call to mind. **bring down 1** cause to fall. **2** lower (a price). **3** *informal* make unhappy or less happy. **4** *informal* damage the reputation of; demean. **5** *Cdn, Austral.,* & *NZ esp. Parl.* present (a budget, law, report, etc.). **bring down the house** get loud applause. **bring forth 1** *give birth to. **2** produce, emit, cause. **bring forward 1** move to an earlier date or time. **2** transfer from the previous page or account. **3** draw attention to; adduce. **bring home to** cause to realize fully (*brought home to me that I was wrong*). **bring in 1** introduce (legislation, a custom, fashion, topic, etc.). **2** yield as income or profit. **bring into play** cause to operate; activate. **bring low** overcome. **bring off** achieve successfully. **bring on 1** cause to happen or appear. **2** accelerate the progress of. **bring out 1** emphasize; make evident. **2** publish. **bring over** convert to one's own side. **bring round** (or **around**) **1** restore to consciousness. **2** persuade. **bring tears to the eyes** cause to weep. **bring through** aid (a person) through adversity, esp. illness. **bring to 1** restore to consciousness (*brought her to*). **2** check the motion of (a ship. usu. foll. by *on*) direct and concentrate (forces). **bring to mind** recall; cause one to remember. **bring to pass** cause to happen. **bring under** subdue. **bring up 1** rear (a child). **2** vomit, regurgitate. **3** call attention to. **4** stop suddenly. **bring on** (or **upon**) **oneself** be responsible for

(something one suffers). □ **bring·er** *noun* [Old English *bringan* from Germanic]

Brink, André (b.1935), South African novelist, short-story writer, and playwright. He gained international recognition with his seventh novel *Looking on Darkness* (1973), which became the first novel in Afrikaans to be banned by the South African government. Subsequent novels include *A Dry White Season* (1979) and *A Chain of Voices* (1982).

brink *noun* **1** the extreme edge of land before a precipice, river, etc., esp. when a sudden drop follows. **2** the point or state very close to something unknown, dangerous or exciting. □ **on the brink of** about to experience or suffer; in imminent danger of. [Middle English from Old Norse: origin unknown]

brink·man·ship *noun* (also **brinks·man·ship**) the art or policy of pursuing a dangerous course to the brink of catastrophe before desisting.

briny /ˈbraɪni/ ● *adjective* (**brin·i·er, brin·i·est**) of brine or the sea; salty. ● *noun* (prec. by *the*) *slang* the sea.

brio /ˈbriːoʊ/ *noun* style, vigour, vivacity. [Italian]

bri·oche /briːˈɒʃ, ˈbriːɒʃ, -ˈɒːʃ/ *noun* a sweet roll or small loaf made with a yeast dough rich in eggs. [French]

bri·quette /brɪˈkɛt/ *noun* (also **bri·quet**) a block of compressed charcoal or coal dust etc. used as fuel. [French *briquette*, diminutive of *brique* brick]

bris /brɪs/ *noun Judaism* the rite of circumcision, usu. performed eight days after birth.

Bris·bane[1] /ˈbrɪzbən/ the capital of Queensland, Australia; pop. (est. 2002) 1,536,000. [Sir T. BRISBANE]

Bris·bane[2] /ˈbrɪzbən/ **Sir Thom·as Mak·doug·all** (1773–1860), Scottish soldier, governor of New South Wales (1821–5) and an acclaimed astronomer.

brisk *adjective* **1** quick, lively, keen (*a brisk pace; brisk trade*). **2** cold but pleasantly fresh (*a brisk wind*). □ **brisk·ly** *adverb* **brisk·ness** *noun* [prob. French *brusque* BRUSQUE]

bris·ket /ˈbrɪskət/ *noun* **1** the breast of an animal. **2** a cut of beef used esp. to make corned beef. [Anglo-French from Old French *bruschet*, perhaps from Old Norse]

bris·ling /ˈbrɪzlɪŋ, ˈbrɪs-/ *noun* a small herring or sprat. [Norwegian & Danish, = sprat]

bris·tle /ˈbrɪsəl/ ● *noun* **1** a short stiff hair, esp. one of those on an animal's back. **2** this, or a synthetic substitute, used in clumps to make a brush. ● *verb* **1 a** *intransitive* (of the hair) stand upright, esp. in anger or pride. **b** *transitive* make (the hair) do this. **2** *intransitive* show irritation or defensiveness. **3** *intransitive* (usu. foll. by *with*) be covered or abundant (in). [Middle English *bristel, brestel* from Old English *byrst*]

bristle·cone pine *noun* a very slow-growing, shrubby pine, *Pinus aristata*, native to the southwest US; some specimens are over 4,000 years old.

bristle·tail *noun* = SILVERFISH 1.

brist·ly /ˈbrɪsli/ *adjective* (**brist·li·er, brist·li·est**) full of bristles; rough, prickly.

bristly sarsaparilla *noun* see SARSAPARILLA 4.

Bris·tol /ˈbrɪstəl/ a city in SW England; pop. (est. 2002) 409,300. Situated on the Avon River about 10 km (6 miles) from the Bristol Channel, it has been a leading port since the 12th c.

bris·tol board /ˈbrɪstəl/ *noun* a kind of fine smooth pasteboard. [BRISTOL]

Bristol Channel a wide inlet of the Atlantic between South Wales and the southwestern peninsula of England, narrowing into the estuary of the Severn River.

Bristol fashion *adverb & adjective* (in full **shipshape and Bristol fashion**) *Brit.* with all in good order.

bris·tols /ˈbrɪstəlz/ *plural noun Brit. slang* a woman's breasts. [rhyming slang from *Bristol cities* = *titties*]

Brit *informal* ● *noun* a British person. ● *adjective* British. [abbreviation]

Brit. *abbreviation* **1** British. **2** Britain.

Brit·ain the island containing England, Wales, and Scotland, and including the small adjacent islands (see also GREAT BRITAIN). The name is broadly synonymous with Great Britain. [13th c. *Bretayne* from Old French *Bretaigne* from Latin *Britannia* (Old English *Breoton* and variants]

Britain, Battle of the series of air battles fought over Britain (Aug.-Oct. 1940), in which the RAF successfully resisted raids by the numerically superior German air force. The failure to establish control in the air led Hitler to abandon plans to invade Britain.

Vowels: a *cat* ɑ *arm* e *bed* ɜr *her* ɜː *deux* ə *ago* ɪ *sit* i *cosy* iː *feed* ɒ *hot* ɔ *pore* oː *no* ʌ *run* ʊ *put*

Britan·nia /brɪˈtanjə/ *noun* the personification of Britain, esp. as a helmeted woman with shield and trident. [Latin from Greek *Brettania* from *Brettanoi* Britons]

Britan·nic /brɪˈtanɪk/ *adjective* of Britain (*Her Britannic Majesty*). [Latin *Britannicus* (as BRITANNIA)]

britch·es *plural noun informal* any pants, shorts, or underwear. □ **too big for one's britches** more arrogant than one's situation or knowledge allows. [alteration of BREECHES]

Brit·com *noun* a British situation comedy.

Briti·cism /ˈbrɪtɪˌsɪzəm/ *noun* (also **Brit·ish·ism** /-ˌʃɪzəm/) a word or idiom used in Britain but not in other English-speaking countries.

Brit·ish ● *adjective* **1** of or relating to Great Britain or the United Kingdom, or to its people or language. **2** of the British Commonwealth or (formerly) the British Empire (*British subject*). **●** *noun* (prec. by *the*; treated as *pl.*) the British people. □ **Brit·ish·ness** *noun* [Old English *Brettisc* etc. from *Bret* from Latin *Britto* or Old Celtic]

British Antarctic Territory that part of Antarctica claimed by Britain. Designated in 1962 from territory that was formerly part of the Falkland Islands Dependencies, it includes some 388 500 sq. km (150,058 sq. miles) of the continent of Antarctica as well as the South Orkney Islands and South Shetland Islands in the S Atlantic.

British bulldog *noun* a children's game in which one person tries to catch the other players as they run across a field; those caught join the player in the middle, the winner being the last one caught.

British Columbia a province on the west coast of Canada; pop. (2001) 3,907,738; capital, Victoria. Formed in 1866 by the union of Vancouver Island (a former British colony) and the mainland area, then called New Caledonia, the province includes the Queen Charlotte Islands. □ **Brit·ish Col·um·bian** *adjective & noun* [see COLUMBIA RIVER]

British connection *noun Cdn hist.* the relationship that existed between Canada and Great Britain.

British Empire British overseas possessions, from the 17th to the mid-20th c., acquired for commercial, strategic, and territorial reasons. The colonization of North America and the domination of India started in the early 17th c., and by the end of the 19th c. the empire also included Australia, New Zealand, some of the West Indies, various possessions in the Far East (notably Hong Kong), and large areas of Africa. The movement of the British colonies towards independence began with the American Revolution late in the 18th c., and starting in the mid-19th c. self-government was granted to Canada, Australia, New Zealand, and South Africa. Most of the remaining colonies gained independence in the decade and a half following the end of the Second World War.

British Empire Range a mountain range situated at the northern end of Ellesmere Island.

Brit·ish·er *noun* a British subject, esp. of British descent. ¶ Not used in Britain.

British Honduras the former name (until 1973) for BELIZE.

British India that part of the Indian subcontinent administered by the British from 1765, when the East India Company acquired control over Bengal, until 1947, when India became independent and Pakistan was created. By 1850 British India was coterminous with India's boundaries in the west and north and by 1885 it included Burma (Myanmar) in the east.

British Indian Ocean Territory a British dependency in the Indian Ocean, comprising the islands of the Chagos Archipelago and (until 1976) some other groups now belonging to the Seychelles. There are no permanent inhabitants, but British and US naval personnel occupy the island of Diego Garcia.

British Isles a group of islands lying off the coast of NW Europe, from which they are separated by the North Sea and the English Channel. They include Britain, Ireland, the Isle of Man, the Hebrides, the Orkney Islands, the Shetland Islands, the Scilly Isles, and the Channel Islands.

Brit·ish·ism *var. of* BRITICISM.

British North America Act *noun* an act passed by the British Parliament on 29 March 1867, creating the Dominion of Canada with the provinces of Nova Scotia, New Brunswick, Quebec and Ontario. Abbr.: **BNA Act.**

British soldiers *plural noun* a lichen with red-tipped fruiting bodies.

Brit·ish So·mali·land /səˈmɒlɪˌland/ a former British protectorate established on the Somali coast of East Africa in 1884. In 1960 it united with former Italian territory to form the independent republic of Somalia.

British Summer Time *noun* daylight time in the United Kingdom, one hour ahead of Greenwich Mean Time. Abbr.: **BST**.

British thermal unit *noun* the amount of heat needed to raise 1 lb. of water at maximum density through one degree Fahrenheit, equivalent to 1.055×10^3 joules. Abbr.: **BTU**.

British Virgin Islands see VIRGIN ISLANDS.

Briton *noun* **1** a native or inhabitant of Great Britain or (formerly) of the British Empire. **2** one of the people of southern Britain before the Roman conquest. [Latin *Britto -onis* from Old Celtic]

Brit·pop *noun* British pop music of the nineties, showing influences from a variety of British musical traditions and perceived as a reaction against American grunge music.

Brit·tany a region and former duchy of NW France, forming a peninsula between the Bay of Biscay and the English Channel. It was occupied in the 5th and 6th c. by Britons fleeing the Saxon invasions of Britain.

Brit·ten, (Ed·ward) Ben·jam·in, Lord Britten of Aldeburgh (1913–76), English composer, pianist, and conductor. Chiefly known for his operas, he made settings of a wide and varied range of writers, including George Crabbe (*Peter Grimes*, 1945), Shakespeare (*A Midsummer Night's Dream*, 1960), and Thomas Mann (*Death in Venice*, 1973). His many choral works include the *War Requiem* (1962), based on Wilfred Owen's war poems.

brit·tle ● *adjective* **1 a** hard but easily broken; fragile. **b** insecure; easily damaged (*brittle nerves*). **2** (of a sound) unpleasantly hard and sharp (a *brittle laugh*). **3** (of a person) lacking in warmth. **●** *noun* a brittle candy made from nuts and set melted sugar. □ **brittle·ly** *adverb*

brittle·ness *noun* [ultimately from a Germanic root related to Old English *brēotan* break up]

brittle bone disease *noun* = OSTEOPOROSIS.

brittle·star *noun* an echinoderm of the class Ophiuroidea, with long brittle arms radiating from a small central body.

Brit·ton·ic *var. of* BRYTHONIC.

Brno /ˈbɜːrnoː/ an industrial city in the Czech Republic; pop. (2001) 379,185. It is the capital of Moravia.

bro *noun* (*pl.* **bros**) *N Amer. slang* brother; buddy.

Bro. *abbreviation* Brother.

broach *verb* **1** *transitive* raise (a subject) for discussion. **2** *transitive* pierce (a cask) to draw liquor. **3** *transitive* open and start using the contents of (a box, bale, bottle, etc.). **4** *transitive* begin drawing (liquor). **5** *intransitive* (of a fish, submarine, etc.) break the surface of the water. **6 a** *intransitive* (of a ship) veer to windward. **b** *transitive* cause (a ship) to veer to windward. [Old French *brocher* ultimately from Latin *brocc(h)us* projecting]

broad ● *adjective* **1** large in extent from one side to the other; wide. **2** (following a measurement) in breadth (*2 metres broad*). **3** spacious or extensive (*broad acres; a broad plain*). **4** full and clear (*broad daylight*). **5** explicit, unmistakable (*broad hint*). **6** general; not taking account of detail (*a broad inquiry; in the broadest sense of the word*). **7** of or including a great variety of people, things, or experiences; extensive (*a broad range of options; broad experience*). **8** chief or principal (*the broad facts*). **9** tolerant, liberal (*take a broad view*). **10** somewhat coarse (*broad humour*). **11** (of speech) markedly regional (*a broad Newfoundland accent*). **●** *noun* **1** the broad part of something (*broad of the back*). **2** *N Amer. slang* offensive a woman. □ **broad·ness** *noun* [Old English *brād* from Germanic]

broad·axe *noun* a large axe with a broad blade, used esp. for shaping or trimming rather than felling.

broad·band *noun* a transmission technique utilizing a wide range of frequencies, which enables messages to be communicated simultaneously.

broad bean *noun* = FAVA BEAN.

Broad·bent, (John) Ed·ward (b.1936), Canadian politician and political scientist. He was leader of the federal NDP 1975–89.

broad-brush *attributive adjective* as if painted with a broad brush; general; lacking in detail (*adopted a broad-brush approach*).

broad·cast ● *verb* (*past* **broad·cast** or **broad·cast·ed**; *past participle* **broad·cast**) **1** *transitive* **a** transmit (programs or information) by radio or television. **b** disseminate (information) widely. **2** *intransitive* undertake or take part in a radio or television transmission. **3** *transitive* scatter (seed etc.) over a large area, esp. by hand. **●** *noun* a radio or television program or transmission. **●** *adjective* **1** transmitted by radio or television. **2 a** scattered widely. **b** (of information etc.) widely disseminated. **●** *adverb* over a large area. □ **broad·cast·er** *noun* **broad·cast·ing** *noun*

Broad Church *noun* a group within the Anglican Church favouring a liberal interpretation of doctrine.

broad·cloth *noun* **1** a closely woven fabric of wool, cotton, silk, or a mixture of the three. **2** a densely woven woollen cloth in a plain or twill weave and having a lustrous finish. [originally with reference to width and quality]

broad·en *transitive & intransitive verb* make or become broader.

broad gauge *noun* a railway track with a gauge wider than the standard one.

broad jump *noun N Amer.* = LONG JUMP.

broad·leaf ● *adjective* (also **broad-leaved**, **broad-leafed**) **1** designating any of a number of weeds, e.g. dandelion, burdock, plantain, etc., having broad leaves. **2** (of a tree) deciduous and hard-timbered. ● *noun* (*pl.* **-leaves**) **1** a broadleaf weed. **2** a broadleaf tree.

broad·loom *noun* carpet woven in broad widths. □ **broad·loomed** *adjective*

broad·ly *adverb* in a broad manner; widely (*grinned broadly*). □ **broadly speaking** disregarding minor exceptions.

broad-minded *adjective* tolerant or liberal in one's views. □ **broad-minded·ly** *adverb* **broad-minded·ness** *noun*

Broads a low-lying, flat region of E England, characterized by many lakes and wide rivers.

broad·sheet *noun* **1** a sheet of paper printed for posting or distribution, esp. for spreading information. **2** a newspaper with a large format.

broad·side ● *noun* **1** the firing of all guns from one side of a ship. **2** a vigorous verbal onslaught. **3** the side of a ship above the water between the bow and quarter. **4** = BROADSHEET. ● *adverb* with the side turned towards a given object (*the car hit the wall broadside*). ● *adjective* sideways. ● *transitive verb N Amer.* run into or collide with on the side (*the truck broadsided the car*).

broad spectrum *adjective* **1** (of a drug) effective against a wide range of pathogens. **2** (of a sunscreen) effective against most wavelengths of sunlight. **3** having a wide range of applications.

broad·sword *noun* a sword with a broad blade, for cutting rather than thrusting.

broad·tail *noun* the lustrous pelt of a young karakul lamb.

Broad·way a street traversing the length of Manhattan, New York. It is famous for its theatres, and its name has become synonymous with show business. It is also known as the Great White Way, in reference to its brilliant street illuminations.

Brob·ding·nag·ian /ˌbrɒbdɪŋˈnagiən/ ● *adjective* gigantic, colossal (*a Brobdingnagian mistake*). ● *noun* a giant; a huge person. [*Brobdingnag* (a land in Swift's *Gulliver's Travels* where everything is on a gigantic scale) + -IAN]

bro·cade ● *noun* a rich fabric with a silky finish woven with a raised pattern, and often with gold or silver thread. ● *transitive verb* (usu. as **bro·cad·ed** *adjective*) weave with this design. [Spanish & Portuguese *brocado* from Italian *broccato* from *brocco* twisted thread]

Broca's area /ˈbrəʊkəz/ *noun* part of the premotor cortex in the inferior frontal convolution of the brain, concerned with the movements required for speech. [P. *Broca*, French surgeon and anthropologist d.1880]

brocco·flower *noun* a hybrid vegetable, the result of a genetic cross between broccoli and cauliflower, resembling a green cauliflower that tastes like broccoli. [blend of BROCCOLI + CAULIFLOWER]

broc·coli /ˈbrɒkəli/ *noun* **1** a brassica, related to the cauliflower, with a loose cluster of usu. greenish flower buds. **2** the flower stalk and head used as a vegetable. [Italian, pl. of *broccolo* diminutive of *brocco* sprout]

brocco·lini /brɒkəˈliːni/ *noun proprietary* a hybrid of broccoli and a variety of kale, eaten as a vegetable.

broch /brɒk, brɒx/ *noun* (in Scotland) a prehistoric circular stone tower. [Old Norse *borg* castle]

broch·ette /brɒˈʃet, brəˈʃet/ *noun* a dish consisting of chunks of food, esp. meat, threaded on a skewer and grilled. [French, = skewer, as BROACH]

bro·chure /brəʊˈʃʊr, -ˈʃɜr/ *noun* a pamphlet or leaflet, esp. one giving descriptive information. [French, lit. 'stitching', from *brocher* stitch]

Brock, **Sir Isaac** (1769–1812), English military commander. Made provisional administrator of Upper Canada in 1811, his early victories at the outset of the War of 1812 inspired the vastly outnumbered Canadian colonists. He was killed while leading an attack against a battery on Queenston Heights.

brock *noun Brit.* a badger. [Old English *broc(c)* from Celtic]

brock·et *noun* any small deer of the genus *Mazama*, native to Central and S America, having short straight antlers. [Anglo-French *broque* (= *broche* BROACH)]

Brock·house, **Ber·tram** (1918–2003), Canadian physicist. His development of neutron-scattering techniques led to his sharing the Nobel Prize for physics in 1994.

Brock·ville a city in SE Ontario, situated on the St. Lawrence, about 75 km northeast of Kingston; pop. (2001) 21,375. □ **Brock·vill·ian** *noun* [I. BROCK]

bro·de·rie an·glaise /ˌbrɒdəri ɑ̃ˈgleiz/ *noun* open embroidery on white linen or cambric, esp. in floral patterns. [French, = 'English embroidery']

Bro·deur Peninsula /brəˈdɜr/ a large peninsula of the northwestern coast of Baffin Island. [L.-P. *Brodeur*, Canadian politician and judge d.1924]

Brod·sky /ˈbrɒtski/ **Jo·seph** (real name Iosif Aleksandrovich Brodsky) (1940–1996), Russian-born US poet. Written in both Russian and English, his poetry is preoccupied with themes of loss and exile. He was awarded the Nobel Prize for literature in 1987.

bro·gan /ˈbrəʊɡən/ *noun* a coarse leather work shoe reaching to the ankle. [Irish *brógán*, Gaelic *brógan* diminutive of *bróg* BROGUE²]

brogue¹ /brəʊɡ/ *noun* a marked accent, esp. Irish. [18th c.: origin unknown: perhaps allusively from BROGUE²]

brogue² /brəʊɡ/ *noun* **1** a strong outdoor shoe with ornamental perforated bands. **2** a rough shoe of untanned leather. [Gaelic & Irish *bróg* from Old Norse *brók*]

broil¹ *verb esp. N Amer.* **1** *transitive* cook (meat etc.) by direct exposure to heat (*compare* CHARBROIL, PAN-BROIL). **2** *transitive & intransitive* make or become very hot. [Old French *bruler* burn, from Romanic]

broil² *noun* a row; a tumult. [obsolete *broil* to muddle: compare EMBROIL]

broil·er *noun* **1** *N Amer.* an appliance or the element in an oven used for broiling. **2** a young chicken raised for broiling or roasting. **3** *informal* a very hot day.

broiler house *noun* a building for rearing broiler chickens in close confinement.

broil·ing *adjective N Amer.* very hot (*a broiling summer day*).

broke ● *verb past of* BREAK¹. ● *predicative adjective informal* having no money; financially ruined. □ **go for broke** *slang* risk everything in a strenuous effort. [(adj.) archaic past participle of BREAK¹]

bro·ken ● *verb past participle of* BREAK¹. ● *adjective* **1 a** that has been broken. **b** out of order. **2** (of a person) reduced to despair; beaten. **3** (of a language or of speech) spoken falteringly and with many mistakes (*broken English*). **4** disturbed, interrupted (*broken time*). **5** uneven (*broken ground*). **6** (of a horse, etc.) trained, tamed (*broken to the saddle*). **7** (of a marriage, family, etc.) divided by separation or divorce. □ **bro·ken·ly** *adverb* **bro·ken·ness** *noun*

broken chord *noun Music* a chord in which the notes are played successively.

broken-down *adjective* **1** worn out by age, use, or ill-treatment. **2** out of order.

broken-hearted *adjective* overwhelmed with sorrow or grief. □ **broken-hearted·ness** *noun*

Broken Hill 1 a town in New South Wales, Australia; pop. (est. 2002) 22,200. It is a centre of lead, silver, and zinc mining. **2** the former name (1904–65) for KABWE.

broken wind *noun* heaves (*see* HEAVE *noun* 3). □ **broken-winded** *adjective*

brok·er ● *noun* **1** an agent who buys and sells or acts for others; an intermediary. **2** a member of a stock exchange who deals in stocks and shares. **3** *Brit.* an official appointed to sell or appraise distrained goods. ● *transitive verb* act as a broker; negotiate, esp. as an intermediary. [Anglo-French *brocour*, of unknown origin]

broker·age *noun* **1** the action or service of a broker. **2** a company providing such a service. **3** a broker's fee or commission.

brok·ing *noun* the action or service of a broker.

brol·ga /ˈbrɒlɡə/ *noun* a large Australian crane, *Grus rubicunda*, with a booming call. [Kamilaroi (and other Aboriginal languages) *burralga*]

brol·ly *noun* (*pl.* **-lies**) *esp. Brit. informal* an umbrella. [alteration of UMBRELLA]

bro·mate /ˈbrəʊmeit/ *noun Chem.* a salt or ester of bromic acid.

brome *noun* (also **brome grass**) any oatlike grass of the genus *Bromus* of the temperate zone, having slender stems with flowering spikes. [modern Latin *Bromus* from Greek *bromos* oat]

bro·meli·ad /broˈmiːliəd/ *noun* (also **bro·melia** /-liə/) any tropical plant of the family Bromeliaceae (esp. of the genus *Bromelia*), having short stems with rosettes of stiff usu. spiny leaves, e.g. pineapple. [O. *Bromel*, Swedish botanist d.1705]

bro·mic /ˈbroːmɪk/ *adjective Chem.* of or containing bromine.

bromic acid *noun* a strong acid used as an oxidizing agent. Chem. formula: HBrO₃.

bro·mide /ˈbroːmaɪd/ *noun* **1** *Chem.* a compound of bromine with a less electronegative element or radical; a salt or ester of bromic acid. **2** *Pharm.* a preparation of usu. potassium bromide, used as a sedative. **3** a trite remark.

bro·mine /ˈbroːmiːn/ *noun Chem.* a dark fuming liquid element with a choking irritating smell, used in the manufacture of chemicals for photography and medicine. Symbol: **Br**; at. no.: 35. [French *brome* from Greek *brōmos* stink]

bromo- /ˈbroːmoː/ *combining form Chem.* bromine.

Bromp·ton·ville a former city in S Quebec, now part of Sherbrooke; pop. (2001) 5,571. [prob. ultimately after Brompton, Yorkshire]

bronc *noun N Amer. informal* = BRONCO. [abbreviation]

bron·chi *pl. of* BRONCHUS.

bron·chi·al /ˈbrɒŋkiəl/ *adjective* of or relating to the bronchi or bronchioles.

bron·chi·ole /ˈbrɒŋkiˌoːl/ *noun* any of the minute divisions of a bronchus. □ **bron·chi·ol·ar** /-ˈoːlɜr/ *adjective*

bron·chitis /brɒŋˈkaɪtɪs/ *noun* inflammation of the mucous membrane in the bronchial tubes. □ **bron·chit·ic** /-ˈkɪtɪk/ *adjective & noun*

broncho- /ˈbrɒŋkoː/ *combining form* bronchi.

bron·cho·cele /ˈbrɒŋkəˌsiːl/ *noun* a goitre.

bron·cho·dila·tor /ˌbrɒŋkoːdaɪˈleɪtər/ *noun* a substance which causes widening of the bronchi, used esp. to alleviate asthma.

bron·cho·pneu·monia /ˌbrɒŋkoːnəˈmoːniə, -nuːˈmoː-, -njuːˈmoː-/ *noun* inflammation of the lungs, arising in the bronchi or bronchioles.

bron·cho·scope /ˈbrɒŋkəˌskoːp/ *noun* a usu. fibre optic instrument for inspecting the bronchi. □ **bron·chos·copy** /-ˈkɒskəpi/ *noun*

bron·cho·spasm /ˈbrɒŋkəˌspazəm/ *noun* spasm of the bronchial smooth muscle, producing narrowing of the bronchi.

bron·chus /ˈbrɒŋkəs/ *noun* (pl. **bron·chi** /-kaɪ/) any of the major air passages of the lungs, esp. either of the two main divisions of the windpipe. [Late Latin from Greek *brogkhos* windpipe]

bron·co *noun* (pl. **-cos**) *N Amer.* a wild or half-tamed horse. [Spanish, = rough]

bronco·bust·er *noun N Amer. informal* a person who breaks in horses. □ **bronco·bust·ing** *noun*

Bron·të /ˈbrɒntei/ **Char·lotte** (1816–55), **Emily** (1818–48), and **Anne** (1820–49), English novelists. Raised in the village of Haworth in a remote part of Yorkshire and all dying young, they had an unusually limited experience of the outside world, apart from work as governesses and, for Emily and Charlotte, a visit to Brussels. Emily's poems are now valued for their originality and vision and her novel *Wuthering Heights* (1847) is recognized as a masterpiece. Anne's novels are *Agnes Grey* (1845) and *The Tenant of Wildfell Hall* (1847). Charlotte achieved fame for her romantic tour de force *Jane Eyre* (1847) and for *Shirley* (1849) and *Villette* (1853). Their works were published under the pseudonyms Currer, Ellis, and Acton Bell.

bron·to·saur·us /ˌbrɒntəˈsɔrəs/ *noun* (pl. **bron·to·saur·us·es**) (also **bron·to·saur** /ˈbrɒntəˌsɔr/) the former name for the APATOSAURUS. [Greek *brontē* thunder + *sauros* lizard]

Bronx, the a borough in the northeast of New York City. [J. *Bronck*, Dutch settler who purchased land there in 1641]

Bronx cheer *noun N Amer.* = RASPBERRY 3.

bronze ● *noun* **1** any of a group of alloys of copper and tin. **2** its brownish colour. **3** a thing made of bronze, esp. as a work of art. **4** = BRONZE MEDAL. ● *adjective* made of or coloured like bronze. ● *verb* **1** *transitive* give a bronze-like surface to. **2** *transitive & intransitive* make or become brown; tan. □ **bronzy** *adjective* [French from Italian *bronzo*, prob. from Persian *birinj* copper]

Bronze Age *noun* the period preceding the Iron Age, when weapons and tools were usu. made of bronze.

bronze medal *noun* a medal usu. awarded to a competitor who comes third (esp. in sport).

bronz·er *noun* a cosmetic applied to the skin to make it look tanned.

brooch /broːtʃ/ *noun* an ornament fastened to clothing with a hinged pin. [Middle English *broche* (as BROACH)]

brood ● *noun* **1** the young of an animal (esp. a bird) produced at one hatching or birth. **2** *informal* the children in a family. **3** a group of related things. **4** bee or wasp larvae. **5** (*attributive*) kept for breeding (*brood sow*). ● *verb* **1** *intransitive* (often foll. by *on*, *over*, etc.) worry or ponder (esp. resentfully). **2 a** *intransitive* (of a bird) sit on eggs to hatch them. **b** *transitive* sit on (eggs) to hatch them. **3** *intransitive* (usu. foll. by *over*) (of silence, a storm, etc.) hang or hover closely. [Old English *brōd* from Germanic]

brood·er *noun* **1** a heated device or structure for raising chicks etc. **2** a person who broods.

brood·ing *adjective* **1** (of a person) melancholy, glum. **2** (of a landscape etc.) sombre and giving the impression of hovering over the surroundings. □ **brood·ing·ly** *adverb*

brood·mare *noun* a mare kept for breeding.

broody *adjective* (**brood·i·er**, **brood·i·est**) **1** (of a hen) wanting to brood. **2** sullenly thoughtful or depressed. □ **brood·i·ly** *adverb* **brood·i·ness** *noun*

Brook, Peter Ste·phen Paul (b.1925), English theatre director. Appointed co-director of the Royal Shakespeare Company in 1962, he earned critical acclaim with *King Lear* (1963) and *A Midsummer Night's Dream* (1970). In 1971 he founded the International Centre for Theatre Research in Paris, developing new acting techniques drawn from mime and other cultures.

brook¹ *noun* a small stream. □ **brook·let** *noun* [Old English *brōc*, of unknown origin]

brook² *transitive verb* (usu. with *neg.*) tolerate, allow. [Old English *brūcan* from Germanic]

Brooke, Ru·pert (Chaw·ner) (1887–1915), English poet best known for his war poems and for his lighter verse, such as 'The Old Vicarage, Granchester'.

brook·ie *noun N Amer. informal* = BROOK TROUT.

Brook·lyn a borough of New York City, at the southwestern corner of Long Island. The Brooklyn Bridge (1869–83) links Long Island with lower Manhattan. □ **Brooklyn·ese** *noun* **Brooklyn·ite** *noun*

Brooks¹ a town in south central Alberta, southeast of Calgary; pop. (2001) 11,604. [N. E. *Brooks*, CPR divisional engineer at Calgary d.1926]

Brooks² ▶ **1 Cle·anth** (1906–94), US teacher and critic, a leading proponent of the New Criticism movement; his critical works include *Modern Poetry and Tradition* (1939) and *The Well-Wrought Urn* (1947). **2 Gwen·do·lyn Eliza·beth** (1917–2000), American writer. She became the first black woman to win the Pulitzer Prize (1949) for her second collection of poetry, *Annie Allen*. **3 Mel** (born Melvin Kaminsky) (b.1927), US film director and actor. His film debut *The Producers* (1967) was followed by the spoofs *Blazing Saddles* (1974) and *Silent Movie* (1976), which established Brooks's characteristic style. Later films include *Spaceballs* (1987), a parody of *Star Wars*.

Brooks Range a section of the Rocky Mountains in N Alaska, with peaks rising to 2 816 m (9,239 ft.).

brook trout *noun* a trout, *Salvelinus fontinalis*, found widely throughout eastern N America.

broom *noun* **1** a brush of bristles, straw, etc. on a long handle, used for sweeping. **2** *Curling* the long-handled implement used for sweeping the ice surface, orig. a normal straw broom, now more typically with a rectangular flat head covered with foam rubber and nylon or carpet, sheepskin, etc. **3** any of various shrubs, esp. *Cytisus scoparius*, bearing bright yellow flowers. [Old English *brōm*, first applied to the plant, the brushes originally being made of twigs of this plant]

broom·ball *noun N Amer.* a game similar to hockey in which players run rather than skate and use rubber brooms or broom handles to propel a ball, esp. a volleyball, into the goal. □ **broom·ball·er** *noun*

broom closet *noun* (also **broom cupboard**) **1** a closet in which brooms and cleaning supplies are kept. **2** an extremely small room.

broom·rape *noun* any of various parasitic plants, esp. of the genus *Orobanche*, with tubular flowers on a leafless brown stem, and living on the roots of other plants, e.g. dandelions. [BROOM + Latin *rapum* tuber]

broom·stick *noun* the handle of a broom.

Bros. *abbreviation* Brothers (esp. in the name of a company).

Bros·sard¹ /brɒˈsɑr, -ˈsɒrd/ a former city in south central Quebec, situated on the south shore of the St. Lawrence, southeast of Montreal, now part of Longueuil; pop. (2001) 65,026. [G.-H. *Brossard*, mayor 1944–67]

Bros·sard² /brɒˈsɑr/ **Ni·cole** (b.1943), Canadian writer and publisher. A leading exponent of formalist poetry in Quebec, she is also a feminist theorist. Her work, including the poetry collection *Double impression* (1985) and the novel *Le Désert mauve* (1987), is abstract and non-lyrical. She won the Governor General's Award for poetry in 1974 and 1980.

broth *noun* **1** *Cooking* **a** a thin soup of meat or fish stock. **b** meat or fish stock that has not been clarified. **2** *Biol.* meat stock as a nutrient medium for bacteria. □ **a broth of a boy** a fine boy. [Old English from Germanic: related to BREW]

broth·el /ˈbrɒθəl/ *noun* a house etc. where prostitution takes place. [originally *brothel-house* from Middle English *brothel* worthless man, prostitute, from Old English *brēothan* go to ruin]

brothel creepers *plural noun informal* suede shoes with rubber crepe soles.

broth·er ● *noun* **1** a man or boy in relation to other sons and daughters of his parents. **2 a** (often as a form of address) a close male friend or associate. **b** a male fellow member of a union, fraternity, etc. **3** (*pl.* also **breth·ren** /ˈbreðrɪn/) **a** a member of a male religious order, esp. a monk. **b** a fellow member of a religion, esp. the Christian Church. **c** an associate in a common cause, association, etc. **d** *hist.* a member of a guild etc. **4** a fellow human being. ● *interjection* esp. *N Amer.* expressing mild deprecation or annoyance. □ **one's brother's keeper** one who is responsible for the well-being of one's fellow humans. □ **brother·less** *adjective* **brother·ly** *adjective & adverb* **brother·li·ness** *noun* [Old English *brōthor* from Germanic]

brother german *noun* see GERMAN.

brother·hood *noun* **1 a** the relationship between brothers. **b** brotherly friendliness; companionship. **2 a** an association, society, or community of people linked by a common interest, religion, trade, etc. **b** its members collectively. **3** *N Amer.* (in proper names) a labour union. **4** community of feeling between all human beings. [Middle English alteration of *brotherrede* from Old English *brōthor-rǣden* (compare KINDRED) after words in -HOOD, -HEAD]

brother-in-law *noun* (*pl.* **brothers-in-law**) **1** the brother of one's spouse. **2** the husband of one's sister. **3** the husband of one's sister-in-law.

brother uterine *noun* see UTERINE 2.

Brott, **Boris** (b.1944), Canadian violinist, conductor, and composer. He made his violin debut at age 5, and was assistant conductor of the Toronto Symphony 1963–5. From 1969 to 1992 he was conductor of the Hamilton Philharmonic; he also conducted Symphony Nova Scotia 1983–6.

brougham /ˈbruːəm, bruːm, ˈbrɒəm/ *noun hist.* **1** a horse-drawn closed carriage with a driver perched outside in front. **2** (formerly) an automobile with an open driver's seat. [Lord *Brougham* (d.1868), who designed the carriage]

brought *past and past participle of* BRING.

brou·haha /ˈbruːhɑːhɑː/ *noun* **1** commotion, sensation; hubbub, uproar. **2** an instance of this. [French]

Brou·wer /ˈbraʊər/ **Adri·aen** (*c.*1605–38), Flemish painter. An important bridge between Dutch and Flemish genre painting, he typically painted peasant scenes in taverns, his delicate use of colour contrasting with the coarseness of the subject matter.

brow *noun* **1** the forehead. **2** (usu. in *pl.*) an eyebrow. **3** the summit of a hill or pass. **4** the edge of a cliff, riverbank, etc. □ **browed** *adjective* [Old English *brū* from Germanic]

brow·beat *transitive verb* (*past* **-beat**; *past participle* **-beat·en**) intimidate; bully. □ **brow·beat·er** *noun*

brow·bone *noun* the ridge of bone above the eye socket.

brow log *noun N Amer. Forestry* a large log laid horizontally beside a log car or truck, used to protect the vehicle from damage during loading.

Brown ▸ 1 Sir Ar·thur Whit·ten (1886–1948), Scottish aviator. He made the first transatlantic flight in 1919 with Sir John William Alcock. **2 Ford Madox** (1821–93), English painter. A number of his early paintings, including *The Last of England* (1855), were inspired by the Pre-Raphaelites. In 1861 he became a founding member of William Morris's company, for which he designed stained glass and furniture. He also designed a cycle of twelve frescoes in Manchester Town Hall (1878–93). **3 George** (1818–80), Scottish-born Canadian journalist and politician. The founder and editor of the Toronto *Globe* (1844), he was a noted Reform politician and supporter of Confederation. **4 James** (b.1928), US soul and funk singer and songwriter. Influenced by gospel and early rhythm and blues, he became known as 'Soul Brother Number One' in the 1960s, playing a leading role in the development of funk and going on to exert a significant influence on many other areas of popular music. His many hits include 'Papa's Got a Brand New

Bag' (1965) and 'Sex Machine' (1970). **5 John** (1800–59), US abolitionist. He was captured and executed after raiding Harper's Ferry in 1859, intending to arm the black slaves and start a revolt, becoming a hero of the American abolitionists. He is commemorated in the popular marching song 'John Brown's Body'. **6 Lan·ce·lot** ('Capability') (1716–83), English landscape gardener. He evolved an English style of landscape parks, contrived to look natural by serpentine waters, clumps of trees, and other artifices. **7 Rob·ert** (1773–1858), Scottish botanist, who discovered the phenomenon known as Brownian motion.

brown ● *adjective* **1** having the colour produced by mixing red, yellow, and black, as of dark wood or rich soil. **2** dark-skinned or suntanned. **3** (of bread) made from a dark flour, e.g. whole wheat. **4** (of species or varieties) distinguished by brown coloration. ● *noun* **1** a brown colour or pigment. **2** brown clothes or material (*dressed in brown*). **3** *N Amer.* = BROWN TROUT. **4** (in a game or sport) a brown ball, piece, etc. **5** brown bread. ● *transitive & intransitive verb* make or become brown by cooking, sunburn, etc. □ **in a brown study** see STUDY. □ **brown·ish** *adjective* **brown·ness** *noun* **browny** *adjective* [Old English *brūn* from Germanic]

brown ale *noun* a dark, mild, bottled beer.

brown alga *noun* (*pl.* **brown algae**) an alga containing xanthophyll in addition to chlorophyll, including many seaweeds.

brown bag *N Amer.* ● *noun* a plain brown paper bag in which a lunch is packed and carried to work etc. ● *transitive verb* take (a packed lunch) to work, school, etc. □ **brown bagger** *noun*

brown bear *noun* a bear of the species *Ursus arctos*, of northern N America, Europe, and Asia, including the grizzly bear (*U. arctos horribilis*), kodiak bear (*U. arctos middendorffi*), and Siberian brown bear (*U. arctos beringianus*).

brown belt *noun* **1** a belt of a brown colour marking a high level of proficiency in judo, karate, or other martial arts, below that of a black belt. **2** a person qualified to wear such a belt.

brown Betty *noun* **1** esp. *N Amer.* a baked pudding consisting of sliced apples layered with bread crumbs, butter, and sugar. **2** a round teapot made of red clay earthenware, usu. with a brown glaze.

brown coal *noun* = LIGNITE.

brown cow *noun Cdn* a cocktail of coffee liqueur and milk or cream.

brown creeper *noun* a small brown and white bird of the creeper family, *Certhia americana*, which creeps up tree trunks in search of insects.

brown dwarf *noun Astronomy* a hypothetical cool star with a mass too low for nuclear reactions to be ignited in the core.

Browne, **Sir Thom·as** (1605–82), English author and physician. His *Religio Medici* (1642), a confession of Christian faith, drew together a collection of imaginative and erudite opinions on a vast number of subjects more or less connected with religion.

browned off *adjective Brit. & Cdn slang* fed up, disheartened.

brown·er *noun Cdn* (*Ont.*) *informal* = BROWN-NOSER.

brown-eyed Susan *noun* = BLACK-EYED SUSAN.

brown fat *noun* a dark-coloured adipose tissue with a rich supply of blood vessels.

brown·field *noun* an urban site for potential building development that has had previous development on it, esp. one that has industrial contamination.

Brown·ian motion *noun* (also **Brownian movement**) *Physics* the erratic random movement of microscopic particles in a liquid, gas, etc., as a result of continuous bombardment from molecules of the surrounding medium. [R. BROWN]

brown·ie *noun* **1** (usu. **Brownie**; in full **Brownie Guide**) a member of the junior branch of the Guides. **2** a small square of rich, usu. chocolate, cake with nuts. **3** a benevolent elf said to haunt houses and do household work secretly.

brownie point *noun informal* a notional credit for something done to please or win favour.

Brown·ing ▸ 1 Eliza·beth Bar·rett (1806–61), English poet. Her *Poems* (1844) were so well received that she was seriously considered as a possible successor to Wordsworth as Poet Laureate. In 1846, after a year of passionate correspondence with Robert Browning, she eloped with him to Italy to escape the wrath of her domineering father. Modern readers know her best for her love poems *Sonnets from the Portuguese* (1850), her experimental verse novel *Aurora Leigh* (1857), and her posthumous *Last Poems* (1862). **2 Kurt** (b.1966), Canadian figure skater. He took the Canadian and world men's championships in 1989, 1990, and 1991, winning the worlds again in 1993. He has since led a successful professional career. **3 Rob·ert** (1812–89), English poet. The publication of *Dramatic Lyrics* (1842), containing such well-loved poems as 'The Pied Piper of Hamelin' and 'My Last Duchess', established his name. *Dramatic Romances and Lyrics* (1845), which included 'Home Thoughts from Abroad', built on this success. *The Ring and the Book*, a series of dramatic monologues published in 1868–9, is considered his greatest work.

brown·ing *noun* (in full **gravy browning**) *Cdn & Brit.* browned flour or any other additive used to colour gravy.

Brown·lee, John Ed·ward (1883–1961), Canadian lawyer and politician, premier of Alberta 1925–34. He helped form the United Grain Growers (1917) and the Alberta Wheat Pool. As premier he negotiated the deal in 1929 by which Alberta gained control over its natural resources.

brown-noser *noun* esp. *N Amer.* a person who behaves obsequiously in the hope of advancement. □ **brown-nose** *intransitive verb* **brown-nosing** *noun*

brown·out *noun* esp. *N Amer.* a temporary reduction in electrical power, esp. for conservation. [BROWN + OUT, after BLACKOUT]

brown owl *noun* **1** any of various owls, esp. the tawny owl. **2** (**Brown Owl**) *Cdn* an adult leader of a Brownie pack. ¶ Also used colloquially but not officially in Britain.

brown paper *noun* a coarse unbleached paper used esp. for wrapping.

brown rat *noun* = NORWAY RAT.

brown rice *noun* unpolished rice with only the husk of the grain removed.

brown·shirt *noun* **1** (**Brownshirt**) a member of an early Nazi militia, the Storm Troopers (German *Sturmabteilung*, abbr. **SA**), whose violent intimidation of political opponents played a key role in Hitler's rise to power. In order to appease the army, which was hostile to the growing power of the Brownshirts, Hitler had more than seventy members of the SA summarily executed on 29–30 June 1934, the 'night of the long knives'. **2** a fascist; a member of a fascist organization. □ **brown-shirted** *adjective* [colour of uniforms worn by members of the SA]

brown·stone *noun N Amer.* **1** a kind of reddish-brown sandstone used for building. **2** a building faced with this.

brown sugar *noun* **1** refined sugar to which molasses has been added. **2** unrefined or partially refined sugar.

brown thrasher *noun* see THRASHER[2].

brown trout *noun* a trout, *Salmo trutta*, native to Europe and W Asia and introduced into large parts of N America.

browse ● *verb* **1** *intransitive & transitive* **a** survey objects superficially and in a leisurely fashion, esp. goods for sale. **b** scan through a book or magazine superficially to gain an impression of the contents. **2** *intransitive & transitive Computing* read or survey (data files etc.), esp. via a network. **3** *intransitive* (often foll. by *on*) feed (on leaves, twigs, or scanty vegetation). **4** *transitive* crop and eat. ● *noun* **1** twigs, young shoots, etc., as fodder for cattle etc. **2** an act of browsing. □ **brows·abil·ity** *noun* **brows·able** *adjective* [(n.) from earlier *brouse* from Old French *brost* young shoot, prob. from Germanic; (v.) from French *broster*]

browse line *noun* the height to which deer etc. browse the foliage of trees.

brows·er *noun* **1** a person who looks casually through books or magazines or at things for sale. **2** an animal which feeds mainly on high-growing vegetation. **3** a computer program with a graphical user interface for displaying HTML files, used to navigate the World Wide Web.

Broz /'brɔːz, 'brɒz/ **Josip**, see TITO.

brr *interjection* expressing cold or shivering.

Bru·beck /'bruːbek/ **David War·ren** (b.1920), US jazz pianist, composer, and bandleader. After forming the Dave Brubeck Quartet in 1951, he gained a reputation as an experimental musician and won international recognition with the album *Time Out*, which included 'Take Five'.

Bruce ▶ **1 James** ('the Abyssinian') (1730–94), Scottish explorer. Bruce set off from Cairo in 1768 on an expedition to Abyssinia, becoming the first European to discover the source of the Blue Nile in 1770. His *Travels to Discover the Sources of the Nile* (1790), containing an account of his expedition, was dismissed by his contemporaries as fabrication. **2 Rob·ert the**, see ROBERT I.

bru·cel·lo·sis /ˌbruːsəˈloʊsɪs/ *noun* a disease caused by bacteria of the genus *Brucella*, causing spontaneous abortion in cattle and other farm animals, and undulant fever in humans. [*Brucella* from Sir D. *Bruce*, Scottish physician d.1931 + -OSIS]

Bruce Peninsula a peninsula in south central Ontario, stretching

from Owen Sound to Tobermory Bay. It separates Georgian Bay from Lake Huron and forms part of the Niagara Escarpment. [J. *Bruce*, 8th Earl of Elgin and Governor General of Canada d.1863]

Bruce Peninsula National Park a park in south central Ontario, located at the northern tip of the Bruce Peninsula. It was established in 1987.

Bruch /brʊx/ **Max** (1838–1920), German composer. He is best known for his virtuoso violin and cello pieces, especially his first violin concerto.

bru·cite /'bruːsaɪt/ *noun* a mineral form of magnesium hydroxide. [A. *Bruce*, US mineralogist d.1818]

Bruck·ner /'brʊknər/ **(Josef) Anton** (1824–96), Austrian composer and organist, who is known for his nine symphonies, four masses, and *Te Deum* (1884). □ **Bruck·ner·ian** *adjective*

Brue·gel /'brɔɪɡəl/ (also **Breu·ghel, Brue·ghel**) **1 Jon** ('Velvet') (1568–1623), a celebrated Flemish painter of flower, landscape, and mythological pictures, son of Pieter Bruegel the Elder. **2 Pieter** ('the Elder') (*c.*1525–69), Flemish artist. His landscapes and peasant scenes are remarkable for their detail and witty observation. His major works include *The Procession to Calvary* (1564), *The Blind Leading the Blind* (1568), and *The Peasant Dance* (1568). **3 Pieter ('Hell')** ('the Younger') (1564–1638), his son, known primarily as a very able copyist of his father's work; he is also noted for his paintings of devils (hence his diabolic nickname).

Bruges /bruːʒ/ (Flemish **Brugge** /'bryxə/) a city in NW Belgium, capital of the province of West Flanders; pop. (est. 2002) 115,400. A centre of the Flemish textile trade until the 15th c., it is a well-preserved medieval city surrounded by canals.

bruin /'bruːɪn/ *noun informal* a bear. [Middle English from Dutch, = BROWN: used as a name in *Reynard the Fox*]

bruise ● *noun* **1** an injury appearing as an area of discoloured skin on a human or animal body, caused by a blow or impact. **2** a similar area of damage on fruit etc. ● *verb* **1** *transitive* **a** inflict a bruise on. **b** hurt mentally. **2** *intransitive* be susceptible to bruising. **3** *transitive* crush or pound. [Old English *brȳsan* crush, reinforced by Anglo-French *bruser*, Old French *bruisier* break]

bruis·er *noun informal* **1** a large tough-looking person. **2** a professional boxer.

bruit /bruːt/ ● *transitive verb* (often foll. by *abroad, about*) spread (a report or rumour). ● *noun archaic* a report or rumour. [French, = noise from *bruire* roar]

Brû·lé /bruːˈleɪ/ **Étienne** (*c.*1592–*c.*1633), French explorer. In 1610 he went to live among the Huron, the first Frenchman to live with the Aboriginal peoples of N America. He was probably the first European to see Lakes Ontario, Huron, and Superior.

Brum *noun informal* Birmingham (in England). [abbreviation of BRUMMAGEM]

brume *noun literary* mist, fog. [French from Latin *bruma* winter]

Brum·ma·gem /'brʌmədʒəm/ *adjective* **1** cheap and showy (*Brummagem goods*). **2** counterfeit. [dial. form of *Birmingham*, England, with reference to counterfeit coins and plated goods once made there]

Brum·mell /'brʌməl/ **George Bryan ('Beau')** (1778–1840), English dandy. He was the arbiter of British fashion for the first decade and a half of the 19th c.

Brum·mie (also **Brummy**) *Brit. informal* ● *noun* (*pl.* **-mies**) a native of Birmingham. ● *adjective* of or characteristic of a Brummie (*a Brummie accent*).

brunch ● *noun* a late-morning meal intended to combine breakfast and lunch. ● *intransitive verb* eat brunch. □ **brunch·er** *noun* [blend of BREAKFAST + LUNCH]

Brundt·land /'brʌntlænd/ **Gro Har·lem** (b.1939), Norwegian Labour stateswoman, prime minister 1981, 1986–89, 1990–96. Norway's first woman prime minister, she chaired the World Commission on Environment and Development (known as the Brundtland Commission), which produced the report *Our Common Future* in 1987.

Bru·nei /'bruːnaɪ/ (official name **Brunei Darus·salam**) a small oil-rich sultanate on the northwest coast of Borneo, pop. (est. 2002) 350,898; capital, Bandar Seri Begawan. □ **Bru·nei·an** /bruːˈnaɪən/ *adjective*

Bru·nel /bruːˈnel/ **1 Isam·bard King·dom** (1806–59), English engineer. He designed the famous Clifton suspension bridge in Bristol (1829–30), then in 1833 became chief engineer of the Great Western Railway, before turning to steamship construction with the *Great Western* (1838), the first successful transatlantic steamship. His *Great Eastern* (1858) remained the world's largest ship until 1899. **2** his father, **Sir Marc Isam·bard** (1769–1849), French-born English engineer. His machines for woodworking, knitting, and printing represented a first step in automation. A versatile civil engineer, he built bridges, landing stages, and the first tunnelling shield, which he used to construct the first tunnel under the Thames (1825–43).

Bru·nel·les·chi /ˌbruːnəˈleski/ **Filip·po** (born Filippo di Ser Brunellesco) (1377–1446), Italian architect. He revived Roman architectural forms, and is esp. noted for the dome of Florence cathedral (1420–61).

brun·ette /bruːˈnet/ ● *noun* a woman with dark brown hair. ● *adjective* (of a woman) having dark brown hair. [French, fem. of *brunet*, diminutive of *brun* BROWN]

Brun·hild /ˈbruːnhɪlt/ (also **Brunn·hilde** /ˈbruːnhɪldə/) (in the *Nibelungenlied*) the wife of Gunther, who instigated the murder of Siegfried. In the Norse versions she is a Valkyrie whom Sigurd (the counterpart of Siegfried) wins by penetrating the wall of fire behind which she lies in an enchanted sleep.

Bruno ▶ **1 Gior·dano** (1548–1600), Italian philosopher. He was a supporter of the heliocentric Copernican view of the solar system, envisaging an infinite universe of numerous worlds moving in space; tried by the Inquisition for heresy, he was later burned at the stake. **2 St.** (*c.*1032–1101), German-born French churchman. After withdrawing to the mountains of Chartreuse in 1084, he founded the Carthusian order at La Grande Chartreuse in SE France in the same year. Feast day, 6 October.

Bruns·wick *var. of* BRAUNSCHWEIG.

brunt *noun* the chief or initial impact of an attack, task, etc. (*bore the brunt of the damage*). [Middle English: origin unknown]

brus·chet·ta /ˌbruːˈʃetə, -ˈsketə/ *noun* slices of toasted bread drizzled with olive oil and usu. topped with diced tomatoes, garlic, etc. [Italian from *bruscare* roast over coals]

brush ● *noun* **1 a** an implement with bristles, hair, wire, etc. varying in firmness set into a block or projecting from the end of a handle, for any of various purposes, esp. cleaning or scrubbing, painting, grooming the hair, etc. **b** *Curling* = BROOM 2. **2** the application of a brush; brushing. **3 a** (usu. foll. by *with*) a short esp. unpleasant encounter (*a brush with the law*). **b** a skirmish. **4 a** the bushy tail of a fox. **b** a brushlike tuft. **5** either of a pair of thin sticks with long wire bristles for softly playing a drum, cymbal, etc. **6** *Electricity* **a** a piece of carbon or metal, ending in wires or strips, serving as an electrical contact esp. with a moving part. **b** (in full **brush discharge**) a brushlike discharge of sparks. **7** esp. *N Amer. & Austral.* **a** undergrowth; small trees and shrubs. **b** *N Amer.* such wood cut and bundled as kindling. **c** land covered with brush. **d** *Austral.* dense forest. **8** *Austral. & NZ informal* a girl or young woman. ● *verb* **1** *transitive* **a** sweep or scrub or put in order with a brush. **b** treat (a surface) with a brush so as to change its nature or appearance. **2** *transitive* **a** remove (dust etc.) with a brush. **b** apply (a liquid preparation) to a surface with a brush. **3** *transitive & intransitive* graze or touch in passing. **4** *intransitive* perform a brushing action or motion. □ **brush aside** dismiss or dispose of (a person, idea, etc.) curtly or lightly. **brush off** rebuff; dismiss abruptly. **brush over** paint lightly. **brush up** (usu. foll. by *on*) revive one's former knowledge of (a subject). □ **brush·like** *adjective* **brushy** *adjective* [Old French *brosse*]

brush·back *noun* *Baseball* a fastball deliberately pitched close to the batter's head or body.

brush cut *noun* *N Amer.* a very short haircut with the hair resembling the short, straight bristles of a brush.

brush·cut·ter *noun* a device with blades for cutting heavy undergrowth.

brushed *adjective* **1** swept or smoothed with a brush. **2** (of metallic surfaces) treated so as to be lustreless (*brushed aluminum*). **3** (of fabric) brushed so as to raise the nap (*brushed cotton*).

brush fire *noun* *N Amer. & Austral.* **1** a fire in brush or scrub. **2** (often *attributive*) a localized, small-scale flare-up or skirmish.

brush·land *noun* *N Amer.* = BRUSH 7c.

brush·less *adjective* **1** without a brush. **2** not requiring the use of a brush (*brushless shaving cream*).

brush-off *noun* a rebuff; an abrupt dismissal.

brush stroke *noun* **1** the trace of paint left on a painting by one application of a loaded brush. **2** a painter's style in this.

brush wolf *noun* *N Amer.* a coyote.

brush·wood *noun* **1** cut or broken twigs etc. **2** undergrowth; a thicket.

brush·work *noun* **1** manipulation of the brush in painting. **2** a painter's style in this.

brusque /brʌsk/ *adjective* abrupt or offhand in manner or speech. □ **brusque·ly** *adverb* **brusque·ness** *noun* [French from Italian *brusco* sour]

Brus·sels the capital of Belgium and of the Belgian province of Brabant; pop. (est. 2002) 958,800. The headquarters of the European Commission is located there.

Brussels sprouts *plural noun* **1** a variety of cabbage, *Brassica oleracea gemmifera*, with small compact cabbage-like buds borne close together along a tall single stem. **2** these eaten as a vegetable.

brut /bruːt/ *adjective* (of wine) unsweetened; very dry. [French]

brutal *adjective* **1** savagely or coarsely cruel. **2** harsh, merciless (*brutal cold*). **3** *N Amer. slang* very bad (*a brutal haircut*). □ **bru·tal·ity** *noun* (pl. **-ities**). **brutal·ly** *adverb* [French *brutal* or medieval Latin *brutalis* from *brutus* BRUTE]

brutal·ism *noun* **1** brutality. **2** a heavy plain style of architecture etc. □ **brutal·ist** *noun & adjective*

brutal·ize *transitive verb* (also esp. *Brit.* **-ise**) **1** make brutal. **2** treat brutally. □ **brutal·iz·a·tion** *noun*

brute ● *noun* **1 a** a brutal or violent person or animal. **b** *informal* an unpleasant person. **2** an animal as opposed to a human being. **3** a large and very strong person, animal, etc. ● *adjective* **1** unthinking; entirely physical (*brute force; brute strength*). **2** not possessing the capacity to reason. **3** animal-like, cruel. □ **brut·ish** *adjective* **brut·ish·ly** *adverb* **brut·ish·ness** *noun* [French from Latin *brutus* stupid]

brute fact *noun* a simple inescapable or unexplained fact; the plain truth.

Bru·tus /ˈbruːtəs/ **1** legendary Trojan hero, great-grandson of Aeneas and supposed ancestor of the British people. He is said to have brought a group of Trojans to England, becoming the progenitor of a line of kings. **2 Lu·cius Jun·ius**, legendary founder of the Roman Republic. Traditionally he led a popular uprising, after the rape of Lucretia, against the king (his uncle) and drove him from Rome. He and the father of Lucretia were elected as the first consuls of the Republic (509 BC). **3 Mar·cus Jun·ius** (85–42 BC), Roman senator. With Cassius he was a leader of the conspirators who assassinated Julius Caesar in the name of the Republic in 44. He and Cassius were defeated by Caesar's supporters, Antony and Octavian, at the battle of Philippi in 42, after which he committed suicide.

brux·ism /ˈbrʌksɪzəm/ *noun* the involuntary or habitual grinding or clenching of the teeth. [Greek *brukhein* gnash the teeth]

Bryan /ˈbraiən/ **William Jen·nings** (1860–1925), US lawyer and politician. He campaigned unsuccessfully for the presidency three times. He acted for the prosecution during the Scopes Trial in 1925, upholding the fundamentalist and creationist view.

Bry·ansk /briˈansk/ (also **Bri·ansk**) an industrial city in European Russia, southwest of Moscow, on the Desna River; pop. (est. 2002) 452,000.

Bryl·creem /ˈbrɪlkriːm/ *noun proprietary* a cream for working into the hair to give it a smooth shiny appearance. □ **Bryl·creemed** *adjective* [corruption of BRILLIANT + CREAM]

Bryn·hild /ˈbrɪnhɪld/ *Scand. Myth* a valkyrie who is awoken from an enchanted sleep by Sigurd.

bry·ol·ogy /braiˈɒlədʒi/ *noun* the study of bryophytes. □ **bryo·logic·al** *adjective* **bry·ol·o·gist** *noun* [Greek *bruon* moss]

bry·ony /ˈbraiəni/ *noun* (pl. **-ies**) any climbing plant of the genus *Bryonia*, esp. *B. dioica*, bearing greenish-white flowers and red berries. [Latin *bryonia* from Greek *bruõnia*]

bryo·phyte /ˈbraiəˌfait/ *noun* any plant of the phylum Bryophyta, including mosses and liverworts. □ **bryo·phyt·ic** /-ˈfitik/ *adjective* [modern Latin *Bryophyta* from Greek *bruon* moss + *phuton* plant]

bryo·zoan /ˌbraiəˈzoʊən/ ● *noun* any aquatic invertebrate animal of the group Bryozoa (now regarded as comprising the phyla Ectoprocta and Entoprocta), which form colonies often suggesting mossy growths on rocks, seaweeds, etc. Also called POLYZOAN. ● *adjective* of or relating to the phylum Bryozoa. [Greek *bruon* moss + *zõia* animals]

Bry·thon·ic /brɪˈθɒnɪk/ (also **Brit·ton·ic** /brɪˈtɒnɪk/) ● *noun* the language group comprising Welsh, Cornish, and Breton. ● *adjective* of or pertaining to the ancient Britons or their languages. [Welsh *Brython* Britons, from Old Celtic]

BS[1] *abbreviation* **1** *US* Bachelor of Science. **2** Blessed Sacrament. **3** British Standard(s).

Consonants: b *but*   d *dog*   f *few*   g *get*   h *her*   j *yes*   k *cat*   l *leg*   m *man*   n *no*   p *pen*   r *red*   s *sit*

BS² *abbreviation* esp. N Amer. slang (**BS's**, **BS'd**, **BS'ing**) BULLSHIT.
□ **BSer** *noun*

B.S.A. *abbreviation* Bachelor of Science in Agriculture.

B.Sc. *abbreviation* Bachelor of Science.

B.Sc. (Agr.) *abbreviation* Bachelor of Science in Agriculture.

B.Sc.F. *abbreviation* Bachelor of Science in Forestry.

B.Sc.N. *abbreviation* Bachelor of Science in Nursing.

B.Sc.O.T. *abbreviation* Bachelor of Science in Occupational Therapy.

B.Sc. (Pharm.) *abbreviation* Bachelor of Science in Pharmacy.

B.Sc.P.T. *abbreviation* Bachelor of Science in Physiotherapy.

BSE *abbreviation* **1** bovine spongiform encephalopathy, a usu. fatal disease of cattle involving the central nervous system and causing extreme agitation. **2** breast self-examination.

BSI *abbreviation* British Standards Institution.

B-side *noun* **1** the second side of a recording, esp. the usu. less commercial side of a single. **2** the music on this side.

bsmt. *abbreviation* basement.

B.S.N. *abbreviation* Bachelor of Science in Nursing.

BST *abbreviation* **1** bovine somatotropin, a growth hormone occurring naturally in cows that has been added to cattle feed in some countries to boost milk production. **2** BRITISH SUMMER TIME.

B.S.W. *abbreviation* Bachelor of Social Work.

BT *abbreviation* (also **Bt**) BACILLUS THURINGIENSIS.

B.T. *abbreviation* Bachelor of Technology.

Bt. *abbreviation* Baronet.

B.Th. *abbreviation* Bachelor of Theology.

bth *abbreviation* bath(room).

BTU *abbreviation* (also **Btu**) BRITISH THERMAL UNIT.

BTW *abbreviation* by the way.

B2B *abbreviation* business-to-business (*B2B transactions*).

B2C *abbreviation* business-to-consumer, denoting trade conducted via the Internet between businesses and consumers.

bu. *abbreviation* bushel(s).

bub *noun* N Amer. informal a boy or a man, often used as a form of address. [earlier *bubby*, perhaps a childish form of BROTHER or from German *Bube* boy]

bub·ba /ˈbʌbə/ *noun* esp. N Amer. slang a conservative, blue-collar white male, esp. of the southern US; redneck.

bub·be /ˈbʊbə/ *noun* (also **bub·bie** /ˈbʊbi/) a Jewish grandmother. [Yiddish]

bub·ble ● *noun* **1 a** a thin sphere of liquid enclosing air etc. **b** an air-filled cavity in a liquid or a solidified liquid such as glass or amber. **2** the sound or appearance of boiling. **3** a transparent domed cavity. **4** a situation in which investments, sales, etc. increase rapidly and then collapse (*the South Sea Bubble*). ● *intransitive verb* **1 a** rise in or send up bubbles. **b** become manifest; arise as if from a depth. **2** make the sound of boiling. **3** be exuberant with laughter, excitement, anger, etc. □ **on the bubble** N Amer. Sport (of a player, team, etc.) occupying the last qualifying position (on a team, for a tournament, etc.) and liable to be replaced by another. [Middle English: prob. imitative]

bubble and squeak *noun* Brit. cooked cabbage fried with cooked potatoes or meat.

bubble bath *noun* **1** a preparation for adding to bathwater to make it foam. **2** a bath with this added.

bubble chamber *noun* Physics a container of superheated liquid used to detect charged particles by the trails of bubbles which they produce.

bubble economy *noun* an economy characterized by unsustainable surges in the price or availability of a commodity etc.

bubble gum *noun* **1** chewing gum that can be blown into bubbles. **2** N Amer. slang derogatory (often *attributive*) bland, repetitive pop music intended to appeal esp. to children and young teenagers. **3** (often *attributive*) a pink or purple colour like that of bubble gum.

bubble·head *noun* esp. N Amer. slang usu. derogatory a foolish, unintelligent, or empty-headed person, esp. a woman.
□ **bubble·head·ed** *adjective*

Bubble Jet printer *noun* proprietary a type of ink-jet printer in which the ink is heated to boiling to produce a bubble.

bubble memory *noun* Computing a type of memory which stores data as a pattern of magnetic regions (or bubbles) in a thin layer of magnetic material.

bubble pack *noun* = BLISTER PACK.

bubble tea *noun* an orig. Taiwanese beverage consisting of cold tea, milk, and cooked tapioca balls, sometimes with fruit flavouring.

bubble wrap *noun* a flexible, clear plastic packaging material consisting of small bubbles, used to protect fragile objects during transport etc.

bub·bly ● *adjective* (**bub·bli·er**, **bub·bli·est**) **1** having or resembling bubbles. **2** exuberant. ● *noun* (pl. **-blies**) informal sparkling wine, esp. champagne.

Buber /ˈbuːbər/ **Mar·tin** (1878–1965), Israeli religious philosopher, born in Austria. In his existentialist work *I and Thou* (1923), he argues that religious experience involves reciprocal relationships with a personal subject, rather than knowledge of some 'thing'.

bub·kes *noun* (also **bup·kes**, **bup·kis**, **bup·kus**) informal nothing; something worthless. [Yiddish *bobke* 'goat or sheep dung']

bubo /ˈbjuːbəʊ, ˈbuː-/ *noun* (pl. **bu·boes**) a swollen inflamed lymph node esp. in the armpit or groin. [medieval Latin *bubo -onis* swelling, from Greek *boubōn* groin]

bu·bon·ic /bjuːˈbɒnɪk, buː-/ *adjective* relating to or characterized by buboes.

bubonic plague *noun* a highly contagious bacterial disease characterized by fever, delirium, and the formation of buboes.

Buca·ra·manga /ˌbuːkərəˈmaŋɡə/ a city in N Colombia; pop. (est. 1999) 515,555.

buc·cal /ˈbʌkəl/ *adjective* **1** of or relating to the cheek. **2** of or in the mouth. [Latin *bucca* cheek]

buc·can·eer /ˌbʌkəˈniːr/ ● *noun* **1** a pirate, esp. one who plundered the Spanish colonies of the Caribbean and South American coasts in the late 17th c. **2** an unscrupulous adventurer. ● *intransitive verb* be a buccaneer. □ **buc·can·eer·ing** *noun & adjective* [French *boucanier* from *boucaner* cure meat on a barbecue, from *boucan* from Tupi *mukem*]

buc·cin·ator /ˈbʌksɪˌneɪtər/ *noun* a flat thin cheek muscle. [Latin from *buccinare* blow a trumpet (*buccina*)]

Bu·ceph·alus /bjuːˈsefələs/ the favourite horse of Alexander the Great, who tamed it as a boy and took it with him on his campaigns until its death, after a battle, in 326 BC.

Buch·an /ˈbʌkən/ **John, 1st Baron Tweeds·muir** (1875–1940), Scottish novelist, Governor General of Canada 1935–40. His action-packed adventure stories, many of which feature recurring heroes such as Richard Hannay, include *The Thirty-Nine Steps* (1915), *Greenmantle* (1916), and *The Three Hostages* (1924). As Governor General, he toured Canada extensively, including the Arctic, supported peace initiatives in the buildup to the Second World War, and instituted the Governor General's Literary Awards.

Bu·chan·an /bjuːˈkanən/ **James** (1791–1868), US Democratic politician, 15th President of the US 1857–61. He consistently leaned towards the pro-slavery side in the developing dispute over slavery. Towards the end of his term the issue grew more fraught and he retired from politics in 1861.

Bucha·rest /ˌbuːkəˈrest/ the capital of Romania; pop. (est. 2002) 1,977,200.

Buchen·wald /ˈbʊkənˌvɒlt, ˈbuːxən-/ a Nazi concentration camp in the Second World War, near the village of Buchenwald in eastern Germany.

Buch·ner /ˈbʌknər, ˈbuːxnər/ **Ed·uard** (1860–1917), German organic chemist, who discovered that certain enzymes in yeast were responsible for alcoholic fermentation; he was awarded the Nobel Prize for chemistry in 1907.

Buck, Pearl S(yden·strick·er) (1892–1973), US writer. Her earliest novels, including *The Good Earth* (Pulitzer Prize, 1931) and *Dragon Seed* (1942), were inspired by China, where she was brought up and where she worked as a missionary and teacher until 1935, when she returned to the US. She was awarded the Nobel Prize for literature in 1938.

buck¹ ● *noun* **1** (also *attributive*) the male of various animals, esp. the deer, hare, or rabbit (*buck antelope*). **2** a self-assured young man. **3** (*attributive*) US Military of the lowest grade of a specific military rank (*buck sergeant*). **4** (in pl.) buckskin clothes or shoes etc. ● *verb* **1** *intransitive* **a** (of a horse) jump upwards with back arched and feet drawn together. **b** (of a vehicle, aircraft, etc.) move jerkily and with a strong up-and-down motion. **2** *transitive* (usu. foll. by *off*) throw (a rider or burden) in this way. **3** *transitive* esp. N Amer. **a** oppose, resist (*bucking the trend*). **b** make one's way with difficulty against (*bucking southeasterly winds*). **4** *transitive* Football charge into (an opponent's line) while carrying the ball. □ **buck for** N Amer. informal strive for (a promotion, advantage, etc.). **buck up** informal make or become more cheerful. [Old English *buc* male deer, *bucca* male goat, from Old Norse]

buck² *noun* N Amer., Austral. & NZ informal a dollar. □ **a fast** (or **quick**) **buck** easy money. [19th c.: origin unknown]

buck³ *noun* slang an object placed as a reminder before a player whose turn it is to deal at poker. □ **pass the buck** informal shift responsibility (to another). [19th c.: origin unknown]

buck⁴ ● *transitive verb* N Amer. cut (a tree) into logs. ● *noun* **1** N Amer. a frame supporting wood for sawing. **2** a vaulting horse. [shortened from SAWBUCK]

buck⁵ *adverb* □ **buck-naked** (also **butt-naked**) N Amer. slang completely naked. [origin unknown]

buck⁶ *transitive verb* (**bucked, buck·ing**) Cdn (Nfld) collect surreptitiously; steal. [origin unknown]

buck and doe *noun* Cdn (Ont.) = STAG AND DOE.

buck·a·roo *noun* N Amer. a cowboy. [alteration of Spanish *vaquero* cowboy]

buck·bean *noun* a bog plant, *Menyanthes trifoliata*, with white or pinkish hairy flowers. Also called BOGBEAN.

buck·board *noun* N Amer. a horse-drawn four-wheeled vehicle with the body formed by a flexible plank fixed to the axles. [obsolete *buck* body + BOARD]

buck·brush *noun* N Amer. any of various shrubs on which deer browse, esp. the shrubby cinquefoil, *Potentilla fruticosa*, or *Symphoricarpos occidentalis* of the honeysuckle family.

buck·er *noun* N Amer. **1** a horse or bull that bucks. **2** Forestry a person who cuts felled trees into logs for transporting.

buck·et ● *noun* **1 a** a roughly cylindrical open container of metal, plastic, etc. with a handle, used for carrying, drawing, or holding water etc. **b** the amount contained in this (*need three buckets to fill the tub*). **2** (in *pl.*) large quantities of liquid, esp. rain or tears (*wept buckets*). **3** the scoop of a backhoe etc. **4** one of a series of containers on the outer edge of a water wheel, on a mechanical conveyor, etc. ● *verb* (**buck·et·ed, buck·et·ing**) **1** *intransitive & transitive* (often foll. by *along*) move or drive jerkily or bumpily. **2** *intransitive* (often foll. by *down*) (of liquid, esp. rain) pour heavily. □ **bucket·ful** *noun* (pl. **-fuls**). [Anglo-French *buket, buquet*, perhaps from Old English *būc* pitcher]

bucket brigade *noun* N Amer. a line of people formed to put out a fire by passing buckets of water.

bucket·load *noun* **1** a quantity conveyed in a bucket. **2** a large amount.

bucket·mouth *noun* N Amer. slang a largemouth bass.

bucket seat *noun* a seat with a rounded back to fit one person, esp. in a car.

bucket shop *noun* US & Brit. **1** an office for gambling in stocks, speculating on markets, etc. **2** informal a travel agency specializing in cheap air tickets.

buck·eye *noun* **1** any tree or shrub of the genus *Aesculus*, with large sticky buds and showy red or white flowers. **2** the shiny brown fruit of this plant.

Buck·ing·ham¹ /ˈbʌkɪŋˌham/ a former town in SW Quebec, situated on the Ottawa River, now part of eastern Gatineau; pop. (2001) 11,668. [possibly after the 1st Marquess of *Buckingham* d.1813]

Buck·ing·ham² /ˈbʌkɪŋəm/ **1 George Vil·liers, 1st Duke of** (1592–1628), English courtier and statesman. The favourite of James I and Charles I, he was noted for his personal extravagance and political incompetence. **2** his son, **George Vil·liers, 2nd Duke of** (1628–87), English courtier and writer, an influential figure in the reign of Charles II, and famed for his debauchery; his works include the comedy *The Rehearsal* (1672).

Buck·ing·ham·shire /ˈbʌkɪŋəmˌʃɪr/ a county of south central England; county town, Aylesbury.

buck knife *noun* N Amer. a sturdy, all-purpose hunting knife.

Buck·land, Wil·liam (1784–1856), English geologist, who supported the idea of a past catastrophic event, first interpreting this as being the biblical flood and later moving to the idea of an ice age.

buckle ● *noun* **1** a flat often rectangular frame with a hinged pin, used for joining the ends of a belt, strap, etc. **2** a similarly shaped ornament on a shoe etc. ● *verb* **1** *transitive* (often foll. by *up, on*, etc.) fasten with a buckle. **2** *transitive & intransitive* (often foll. by *up*) give way or cause to give way under longitudinal pressure; crumple up. **3** *intransitive* (often foll. by *under*) submit under pressure. □ **buckle down** make a determined effort. **buckle up** fasten one's seat belt. [Old French *boucle* from Latin *buccula* cheek strap of a helmet, from *bucca* cheek: sense 2 of *verb* from French *boucler* bulge]

buck·ler *noun* **1** hist. a small round shield usu. held by a handle. **2** Bot.

any of several ferns of the genus *Dryopteris*, having buckler-shaped indusia. [Old French *bocler*, lit. 'having a boss' from *boucle* BOSS²]

buck·min·ster·ful·ler·ene /ˌbʌkmɪnstərˈfʊləriːn/ *noun* an extremely unstable form of carbon whose molecule consists of 60 carbon atoms forming a structure suggestive of a geodesic dome. Also called BUCKYBALL. [B. FULLER + -ENE]

bucko *noun* slang (pl. **buck·oes**) a swaggering or domineering fellow. [BUCK¹ + -O]

buck-off *noun* N Amer. an instance of being bucked off a horse or a bull, esp. in a rodeo.

buck-passing *noun* the act of passing the buck or shifting responsibility to another person. □ **buck-passer** *noun*

buck·ram /ˈbʌkrəm/ *noun* a coarse linen or other cloth stiffened with gum or paste, and used as interfacing or in bookbinding. [Anglo-French *bukeram*, Old French *boquerant*, perhaps from *Bokhara* in central Asia]

Bucks. *abbreviation* Buckinghamshire.

buck·saw *noun* N Amer. a woodcutting saw having the blade set within an H-shaped upright frame.

buck·shot *noun* a coarse lead shot used in shotgun shells.

buck·skin *noun* **1 a** the skin of a male deer. **b** a yellowish-tan usu. suede leather made from this or sheepskin. **c** (in *pl.*) N Amer. clothing made from buckskin. **2** a thick smooth cotton or woollen cloth resembling buckskin. **3** a yellowish-tan horse.

buck·tail *noun* N Amer. a fishing lure made of hairs from the tail of a deer etc.

buck·thorn *noun* any thorny shrub or small tree of the genus *Rhamnus*, esp. R. *cathartica* with berries formerly used as a cathartic, and R. *purshiana*, source of cascara sagrada.

buck·tooth *noun* (pl. **-teeth**) an upper front tooth that projects. □ **buck·toothed** *adjective* [BUCK¹ (deer) + TOOTH]

buck·wheat *noun* any cereal plant of the genus *Fagopyrum*, esp. F. *esculentum* with seeds used for fodder and for flour to make bread and pancakes. [Middle Dutch *boecweite* beech wheat, its grains being shaped like beechmast]

bucky·ball *noun* Chem. a molecule of buckminsterfullerene, or more generally of any fullerene. [BUCKMINSTERFULLERENE + -Y² + BALL¹]

bu·col·ic /bjuˈkɒlɪk/ ● *adjective* **1** of or pertaining to an idyllic life in the countryside. **2** of shepherds, pastoral. ● *noun* (usu. in *pl.*) a pastoral poem or poetry. □ **bu·col·ic·ally** *adverb* [Latin *bucolicus* from Greek *boukolikos* from *boukolos* herdsman, from *bous* OX]

bud¹ ● *noun* **1 a** an immature knob-like shoot from which a stem, leaf, or flower develops. **b** a flower or leaf that is not fully open. **2** Biol. an asexual outgrowth from a parent organism that separates to form a new individual. **3** anything still undeveloped. **4** informal marijuana. ● *verb* (**bud·ded, bud·ding**) **1** *intransitive* Bot. & Zool. form a bud or buds. **2** *intransitive* begin to grow or develop (*a budding actor*). **3** *transitive* Hort. graft a bud (of a plant) on to another plant. □ **in bud** having newly formed buds. [Middle English: origin unknown]

bud² *noun* N Amer. informal = BUDDY. [abbreviation]

Buda·pest /ˈbuːdəˌpɛst/ the capital of Hungary; pop. (est. 2002) 1,858,100. [blend of *Buda* + *Pest*, cities located on opposite banks of the Danube River, amalgamated in 1873]

Bud·dha /ˈbuːdə, ˈbʊdə/ *noun* **1** a title given to successive teachers (past and future) of Buddhism, although it usually denotes the founder of Buddhism, Siddhartha Gautama (*c*.563–*c*.480 BC). Although born an Indian prince (in what is now Nepal), he renounced his kingdom, wife, and child to become an ascetic, taking religious instruction until he attained enlightenment (nirvana) through meditation. **2** a statue or picture of the Buddha. □ **Buddha·hood** *noun* [Sanskrit, = enlightened, past participle of *budh* know]

Buddh Gaya see BODHGAYA.

Bud·dhism /ˈbuːdɪzəm, ˈbʊd-/ *noun* a widespread Asian religion or philosophy, founded by Gautama Buddha in India in the 5th c. BC, which teaches that elimination of the self and earthly desires is the highest goal (compare NIRVANA). □ **Bud·dhist** *noun & adjective* **Bud·dhis·tic** *adjective*

bud·dleia /ˈbʌdliə/ *noun* any shrub of the genus *Buddleia*, with fragrant lilac, yellow, or white flowers attractive to butterflies. [A. *Buddle*, English botanist d.1715]

buddy esp. N Amer. ● *noun* (pl. **-dies**) **1** informal a close friend or companion. **2** informal (esp. as a form of address) any male. **3** a person's assigned or chosen companion for some (esp. dangerous) activity. ● *intransitive verb* (**-dies, -died**) (often foll. by *up*) become friendly. [perhaps corruption of *brother*, or var. of BUTTY¹]

Vowels: a cat ɑ arm e bed ɜr her ɜː deux ə ago ɪ sit i cosy iː feed ɒ hot ɔ pore oː no ʌ run ʊ put

buddy-buddy *adjective* esp. *N Amer. informal* exceptionally close or friendly; intimate.

buddy movie *noun* (also **buddy film**) a film in which camaraderie between two characters of the same sex (usu. men) is a central theme.

buddy system *noun* a co-operative arrangement whereby individuals are paired or teamed up and assume responsibility for one another's welfare or safety.

Budge, John Don·ald (**'Don'**) (1915–2000), US tennis player, who was the first to win the four major singles championships (Australia, Britain, France, and the US) in one year (1938).

budge *verb* (usu. with *neg.*) **1** *intransitive* **a** make the slightest movement. **b** change one's opinion (*he's stubborn, he won't budge*). **2** *transitive* cause or compel to budge (*nothing will budge him*). [French *bouger* stir, ultimately from Latin *bullire* boil]

budg·eri·gar /ˈbʌdʒəriˌgɑr/ *noun* a small Australian parakeet, *Melopsittacus undulatus*, green in the wild state, although captive birds are often bred in a variety of colours. [Aboriginal, perhaps alteration of Kamilaroi (and related languages) *gijirrigaa*]

budget ● *noun* **1** a periodic (esp. annual) estimate of the revenue and expenditure of a country, organization, etc. **2** a similar estimate for a private individual or family, often over a short period. **3** (*attributive*) inexpensive. **4** the amount of money needed or available (for a specific item etc.) (*a budget of $200; can't exceed the budget*). ● *verb* (**budget·ed**, **budget·ing**) **1** *transitive & intransitive* (often foll. by *for*) allow or arrange for in a budget (*have budgeted for a new car; can budget $60*). **2** *transitive* plan the expenditure or allotment of (money, time, etc.). □ **on a budget** with a restricted amount of money. □ **budget·ary** *adjective* [Middle English = pouch, from Old French *bougette* diminutive of *bouge* leather bag, from Latin *bulga* (from Gaulish) knapsack: compare BULGE]

budgie *noun informal* = BUDGERIGAR. [abbreviation]

bud vase *noun* a small, narrow vase suitable for a single flower.

bud·worm *noun* **1** SPRUCE BUDWORM. **2** a larva destructive to the buds of plants.

Buena·ven·tura /ˌbweinəvenˈtʊrə/ the chief Pacific port of Colombia; pop. (est. 2002) 230,700.

Buenos Aires /ˌbweinəs ˈeriːz/ the capital city and chief port of Argentina, on the Plate River; pop. (est. 1999) 2,904,200.

buff ● *adjective* **1** of a yellowish beige colour (*buff envelope*). **2** (also **buffed**) *informal* (of a person) having a well-toned body with highly sculpted muscles. ● *noun* **1** a yellowish beige colour. **2** *informal* an enthusiast or expert in a specified subject or activity (*film buff*). **3 a** a thick ox or buffalo leather of a dull yellow colour and velvety surface. **b** (*attributive*) (of a garment etc.) made of this (*buff gloves*). ● *transitive verb* **1** polish (metal, fingernails, etc.). **2** make (leather) velvety like buff, by removing the surface. □ **in the buff** *informal* naked. [original sense 'buffalo', prob. from French *buffle*; sense 2 of *n.* originally from buff uniforms formerly worn by New York volunteer firemen, applied to enthusiastic fire-watchers]

Buf·falo an industrial city in New York State, at the eastern end of Lake Erie; pop. (2000) 292,648. □ **Buf·falo·nian** *noun & adjective*

buf·falo *noun* (*pl.* same or **buf·fa·loes**) **1** esp. *N Amer.* the N American bison, *Bison bison*. **2** either of two species of ox, the Cape buffalo *Syncerus caffer*, native to Africa, or the water buffalo *Bubalus arnee*, native to Asia with heavy back-swept horns. **3** = BUFFALO FISH. [prob. from Portuguese *bufalo* from Late Latin *bufalus* from Latin *bubalus* from Greek *boubalos* antelope, wild ox]

buffalo bean *noun* a leguminous plant of western N America, *Astragalus crassicarpus*, with yellow flowers and edible pods. Also called GOLDEN BEAN.

buffalo berry *noun* **1** a shrub of the N American genus *Shepherdia* of the oleaster family, esp.: **a** *S. argentea* (in full **silver buffalo berry**) found from BC to Manitoba. **b** *S. canadensis* (in full **Canada buffalo berry**) found in wooded areas across Canada. Also called SOAPBERRY, SOOPOLLALIE. **2** the edible red or yellow fruit of these plants.

Buffalo Bill (born William Frederick Cody) (1846–1917), US showman. Working as a frontier scout in the American West, he got his nickname as a hunter of buffalo. He became famous with his Wild West Show, which claimed to show what life was like on the American frontier and travelled throughout N America and Europe.

buffalo chip *noun N Amer.* **1** a piece of dried buffalo dung, esp. when used as fuel by early settlers on the Prairies. **2** (usu. in *pl.*) thickly cut french fries.

buf·fa·loed *adjective N Amer. slang* overawed, outwitted. [BUFFALO]

buffalo fish *noun N Amer.* a large freshwater fish of the genus *Ictiobus*, of the sucker family.

buffalo grass *noun* **1** a grass, *Buchloe dactyloides*, of the N American plains. **2** a grass, *Stenotaphrum secundatum*, of Australia and New Zealand.

buffalo jump *noun N Amer. hist.* a cliff or precipice over which Plains Indians drove herds of buffalo to slaughter them.

buffalo pound *noun Cdn hist.* a sturdy corral or enclosure into which Plains Indians drove buffalo in order to slaughter them.

buffalo robe *noun N Amer.* **1** a lap robe, blanket, or rug made of the hairy hide of the N American bison. **2** clothing made from bison skins.

buffalo rubbing stone *noun* a rock against which buffalo rub up to scrape off their winter coat.

buffalo run *noun N Amer. hist.* **1** a buffalo hunt conducted on horseback. **2** a trail made by buffalo.

buffalo runner *noun N Amer. hist.* a horse trained for the buffalo hunt.

buffalo stone *noun* a small fossil found on the prairies, believed by Plains Aboriginal peoples to give their finders great power with the buffalo.

Buffalo wings *plural noun* (also **Buffalo style chicken wings**) *N Amer.* deep-fried chicken wings coated in a spicy sauce and served with blue cheese dressing. [BUFFALO, where the style originated]

buf·fer[1] ● *noun* **1 a** a device that protects against or reduces the effect of an impact. **b** such a device (usu. one of a pair) on the front and rear of a railway vehicle or at the end of a track. **2** *Chem.* a substance that maintains the hydrogen ion concentration of a solution when an acid or alkali is added. **3** (often *attributive*) **a** a country or area between two potential belligerents, regarded as reducing the likelihood of open hostilities (*buffer zone; buffer state*). **b** an area, person, thing, etc., that protects from the potentially damaging impact of one person, activity, etc. on another. **4** *Computing* an intermediate memory for the temporary storage of information during data transfers, e.g. before printing. ● *transitive verb* **1** act as a buffer to. **2** *Chem.* treat with a buffer. [prob. from obsolete *buff* (v.), imitative of the sound of a soft body struck]

buf·fer[2] *noun* a device for buffing or polishing.

buf·fet[1] /bʌˈfei, bəˈfei, ˈbʌfei/ *noun* **1 a** a meal consisting of several dishes set out from which guests serve themselves (*buffet lunch*). **b** a table or counter from which such meals are served. **c** a restaurant having such a table or counter. **2** a sideboard or cabinet for china, silverware, etc. [French from Old French *bufet* stool, of unknown origin]

buf·fet[2] /ˈbʌfət/ ● *verb* (**buf·fet·ed**, **buf·fet·ing**) **1** *transitive* **a** strike or knock repeatedly (*wind buffeted the trees*). **b** strike, esp. repeatedly, with the hand or fist. **2** *transitive* (usu. in *passive*) attack; plague (*businesses buffeted by the recession*). **3 a** *intransitive* struggle; fight one's way (through difficulties etc.). **b** *transitive* contend with (waves etc.). ● *noun* **1** a blow, esp. of the hand or fist. **2** a shock. □ **buf·fet·ing** *noun* [Old French diminutive of *bufe* blow]

buffle·head *noun* a black and white N American diving duck, *Bucephala albeola*, with a relatively large head. [obsolete *buffle* buffalo + HEAD]

buf·fo /ˈbʊfoː/ ● *noun* (*pl.* **-fos**) a comic actor, esp. in Italian opera. ● *adjective* comic, burlesque. [Italian]

Buf·fon /buːˈfɔ̃/ **Georges-Louis Le·clerc, Comte de** (1707–88), French naturalist. He was one of the founders of paleontology, and is noted for his 36-volume compilation of the animal kingdom, the *Histoire Naturelle* (1749–88).

buf·foon *noun* **1** a stupid person. **2** a jester; a mocker. □ **buf·foon·ery** *noun* **buf·foon·ish** *adjective* [French *bouffon* from Italian *buffone* from medieval Latin *buffo* clown, from Romanic]

buffy *adjective* yellowish beige.

bug[1] ● *noun* **1 a** *N Amer.* any small insect. **b** *Zool.* any of various hemipterous insects with oval flattened bodies and mouthparts modified for piercing and sucking. **2** *informal* a micro-organism, esp. a bacterium, or a disease caused by it. **3** *informal* a concealed microphone or other device used in electronic surveillance. **4** *informal* a mistake or malfunction in a computer program or system etc. **5** *informal* an obsession, enthusiasm, etc. ● *verb* (**bugged, bug·ging**) **1** *transitive informal* annoy, bother. **2** *transitive informal* conceal a microphone in (a room etc.). **3** *intransitive* (often foll. by *out*) *N Amer.* (of the eyes) bulge. □ **put a bug in a person's ear** *N Amer.* suggest something to a person, esp. confidentially. [17th c.: origin unknown]

bug[2] *intransitive verb N Amer.* **1** (foll. by *off*) *informal* go away. **2** (foll. by *out*) esp. *Military slang* leave quickly. [sense 1 abbreviation of BUGGER OFF (see BUGGER); sense 2 origin uncertain]

buga·boo *noun* **1** a bugbear. **2** an object of fear or anxiety. [prob. of dial. origin: compare Welsh *bwcibo* the Devil, *bwci* hobgoblin]

Buga·boos, the (also **the Bugaboo Mountains**) a series of peaks in southeastern BC, situated in the Purcell Mountains, east of Revelstoke. They are accessible only by helicopter. [with reference to the desolation of the surrounding area]

Bu·gan·da /buːˈɡandə, bjuː-/ a former kingdom of East Africa on the north shore of Lake Victoria, now part of Uganda.

bug·bear noun **1** a cause of annoyance or anger. **2** an object of baseless fear. **3** archaic a goblin or other imaginary being invoked to intimidate children. [obsolete bug + BEAR²]

bug-eyed adjective having bulging eyes.

bug·ger ¶ Often considered a coarse or taboo word. ● noun **1** slang **a** a person, esp. of a specified kind (the old bugger). **b** an unpleasant or awkward person or thing (the bugger won't fit). **2** a person who commits buggery. ● transitive verb **1** slang as an exclamation of annoyance (bugger it). **2** slang (often foll. by up) a ruin; spoil (really buggered it up). **b** Brit. exhaust, tire out. **3** commit buggery with. ● interjection expressing annoyance. □ **bugger about** (or **around**) (often foll. by with) **1** mess about. **2** mislead; persecute. **bugger off** (often in imperative) esp. Brit. go away. [Old French bougre, originally 'heretic', from medieval Latin Bulgarus Bulgarian (member of the Greek Church)]

bugger all noun esp. Brit. coarse slang nothing.

bug·gery noun **1** anal intercourse. **2** = BESTIALITY 1.

buggy¹ noun (pl. **-gies**) **1** a light horse-drawn vehicle for one or two people, with two or four wheels. **2** a small, sturdy, esp. open, automobile (beach buggy; dune buggy). **3** N Amer. = BABY BUGGY. **4** N Amer. = SHOPPING CART. [18th c.: origin unknown]

buggy² adjective (**bug·gi·er**, **bug·gi·est**) **1** infested with bugs. **2** (of software) having programming errors. **3** N Amer. slang mad or crazy.

bug·house noun N Amer. slang a mental hospital.

bugle¹ ● noun **1** a brass instrument like a small trumpet, used esp. for military signals. **2** the call of a bull elk at rutting time. ● verb **1** intransitive sound a bugle. **2** transitive sound (a note, a call, etc.) on a bugle. **3** intransitive (of a bull elk etc.) make a loud bellowing call. □ **bugler** noun [Middle English, originally = 'buffalo', from Old French from Latin buculus diminutive of bos ox]

bugle² noun a tube-shaped bead sewn on a dress etc. for ornament. [16th c.: origin unknown]

bugle·weed noun a creeping plant of the genus Ajuga, of the mint family, esp. A. reptans, which bears blue flowers and is cultivated as a ground cover. [Middle English from Late Latin bugula]

bu·gloss /ˈbjuːɡlɒs/ noun **1** any of various bristly plants related to borage, esp. of the genus Anchusa with bright blue tubular flowers. **2** = VIPER'S BUGLOSS. [Latin buglossus from Greek bouglōssos ox-tongued]

buhl /buːl/ noun (also **boule**, **boulle**) **1** pieces of brass, tortoiseshell, etc., cut to make a pattern and used as decorative inlays esp. on furniture. **2** work inlaid with buhl. **3** (attributive) inlaid with buhl. [(buhl Germanized) from A. C. Boule, French woodcarver d.1732]

build ● verb (past and past. part. **built**) **1** transitive **a** construct (a house, vehicle, fire, road, model, etc.) by putting parts or material together. **b** commission, finance, and oversee the building of (the city built two new hospitals). **2** transitive **a** (often foll. by up) establish, develop, make, or accumulate gradually (built the business up from nothing). **b** (often foll. by on) base (hopes, theories, etc.) (ideas built on a false foundation). **3** intransitive (of sounds, sensations, pressure, etc.) become more intense. ● noun **1** the proportions of esp. the human body (a slim build). **2** a style of construction; a make. □ **build in** (or **into**) **1** incorporate as part of a structure. **2** integrate as part of a plan, policy, activity, etc. **build on 1** add (an extension etc.). **2** make further advances after achieving (a success etc.). **build up 1** increase in size or strength. **2** praise; boost. **3** gradually become established. □ **build·able** adjective [Old English byldan from bold dwelling, from Germanic: compare BOWER¹, BOOTH]

build·er noun a person who builds, esp. a contractor for building houses etc. **2** a substance added to a soap or detergent to increase its efficiency.

build·ing noun **1** a permanent fixed structure forming an enclosure and providing protection from the elements etc. (e.g. an office building, school, house, etc.) **2** the constructing of such structures.

building block noun **1** a basic component or element (the building blocks of DNA). **2** a block of stone or other material used in building. **3** one of a set of wooden or plastic cubes etc. that fit together, as a child's toy.

building code noun the body of regulations governing standards of construction.

building society noun Brit. a public finance company which accepts investments at interest and lends capital for mortgages on houses etc.

build-out noun **1** the exhaustion of land available for continued development. **2** planned expansion, esp. of infrastructure.

build·up noun **1** a favourable description in advance; publicity. **2** a gradual approach to a climax or maximum (the buildup was slow but sure). **3** an accumulation (flossing will prevent tartar buildup).

built ● verb past and past participle of BUILD. ● adjective **1** having a specified build (sturdily built). **2** produced by building (the built environment). **3** slang (of a woman) having large breasts.

built-in ● adjective **1** forming an integral part of a structure (a built-in flash). **2** inherent, integral, innate (a built-in bias). ● noun a built-in cabinet, appliance, etc.

built-up adjective **1** (of a locality) densely covered by houses etc. **2** increased in height etc. by the addition of parts. **3** composed of separately prepared parts.

Bu·jum·bura /ˌbuːdʒəmˈbʊrə/ the capital of Burundi, at the northeastern end of Lake Tanganyika; pop. (est. 2002) 323,200. It was known as Usumbura until 1962.

Bu·kha·rin /buˈkɑːrɪn/ **Niko·lai Ivan·ovich** (1888–1938), Russian revolutionary activist and theorist. Editor of Pravda (1917–29) and Izvestia (1934–7), he was a prominent opponent of Stalin's policies and was arrested and executed during the purges.

Bu·khoro /buˈkɔːrə/ (also **Bu·khara** /bəˈkɑːrə/, **Bo·khara**) a city in the central Asian republic of Uzbekistan; pop. (est. 2002) 268,000.

Buko·vina /ˌbuːkəˈviːnə/ a region of SE Europe in the Carpathians, divided between Romania and Ukraine. □ **Buko·vin·ian** noun & adjective

Bula·wayo /ˌbuːləˈweɪəʊ/ an industrial city in western Zimbabwe; pop. (est. 2002) 927,600.

bulb noun **1 a** the globular underground organ of an onion, lily, or similar plant, which contains the following year's bud and scale leaves that serve as food reserves. **b** a plant grown from this, e.g. a daffodil. **2** = LIGHT BULB. **3** any object or part shaped like a bulb. [Latin bulbus from Greek bolbos onion]

bul·bil /ˈbʌlbɪl/ noun Bot. **1** a small bulb which grows among the leaves or flowers of a plant. **2** a small bulb at the side of an ordinary bulb. [modern Latin bulbillus, diminutive of bulbus 'bulb']

bul·bous /ˈbʌlbəs/ adjective **1** shaped like a bulb; fat or bulging. **2** having a bulb or bulbs. **3** (of a plant) growing from a bulb.

bul·bul /ˈbʊlbʊl/ noun any songbird of the family Pycnonotidae, of dull plumage with contrasting bright patches. [Persian from Arabic, of imitative origin]

Bul·ga·nin /bʊlˈɡɒnɪn/ **Niko·lai Alek·san·dro·vich** (1895–1975), Soviet military and political leader, chairman of the council of ministers (premier) 1955–8.

Bul·gar /ˈbʌlɡɑr/ noun **1** a member of an ancient Turkic people who settled in what is now Bulgaria in the 7th c. **2** a Bulgarian. [medieval Latin Bulgarus from Old Bulgarian Blŭgarinŭ]

bul·gar var. of BULGUR.

Bul·garia /bʌlˈɡeriə/ a country in SE Europe on the western shores of the Black Sea; pop. (est. 2002) 7,621,337; capital, Sofia. [BULGAR]

Bul·gar·ian /bʌlˈɡeriən/ ● noun **1 a** a native or national of Bulgaria. **b** a person of Bulgarian descent. **2** the language of Bulgaria. ● adjective of or relating to Bulgaria or its people or language. [medieval Latin Bulgaria from Bulgarus: see BULGAR]

bulge ● noun **1 a** a convex part of an otherwise flat or flatter surface. **b** an irregular swelling; a lump. **2** informal a temporary increase in quantity or number. ● verb **1** intransitive swell outwards. **2** intransitive be full or replete. **3** transitive swell (a bag, cheeks, etc.) by stuffing. □ **bul·ging·ly** adverb **bulgy** adjective [Old French boulge, bouge from Latin bulga: see BUDGET]

Bulge, Battle of the in the Second World War, a German counteroffensive in the Ardennes (1944–early 1945) aimed at preventing an invasion of Germany by the western Allies. The Germans drove a salient or 'bulge' about 110 km (60 miles) deep in the front line, but were later forced to retreat.

bul·gur /ˈbʌlɡər/ noun (also **bul·gar**, **bul·ghur**) a cereal food of whole wheat partially boiled then dried. [Turkish]

bu·limia /buˈliːmiə/ noun Med. **1** (in full **bu·limia ner·vosa**) an emotional disorder in which bouts of extreme overeating are followed by self-induced vomiting, purging, or fasting. **2** insatiable overeating. □ **bu·lim·ic** adjective & noun [modern Latin from Greek boulimia from bous ox + limos hunger]

bulk ● noun **1 a** size; magnitude (esp. large). **b** a large mass, body, or person. **c** a large quantity. **2** a large shape, body, or person (jacket barely covered his bulk). **3** (usu. prec. by the; treated as pl.) the greater part or

---

Consonants: b *but* d *dog* f *few* g *get* h *her* j *yes* k *cat* l *leg* m *man* n *no* p *pen* r *red* s *sit*

number (*the bulk of the applicants are women*). **4** roughage. **5** cargo, esp. when not packaged. ● *verb* **1** *intransitive* seem, as regards size or importance (*bulks large in his reckoning*). **2** *transitive* make (a substance) seem bulkier. **3** *transitive* combine (consignments of a commodity) together. ● *attributive adjective* pertaining to material bought, sold, handled, etc. in bulk. □ **in bulk 1** loose, not packaged. **2** in large quantities. **bulk up** increase in bulk or mass. [sense 'cargo' from Old Icelandic *búlki*; sense 'mass' etc. perhaps alteration of obsolete *bouk*]

bulk buying *noun* **1** buying in large amounts at a discount. **2** the purchase by one buyer of all or most of a producer's output.

bulk carrier *noun* (also **bulk·er**) a ship that carries cargo in bulk.

bulk·head *noun* an upright partition separating the compartments in a ship, aircraft, vehicle, etc. [*bulk* stall, from Old Norse *bálkr* + HEAD]

bulk mail *noun* a category of mail for mailing out large numbers of identical items at a reduced rate.

bulky *adjective* (**bulk·i·er**, **bulk·i·est**) **1** taking up much space, large. **2** awkwardly large, unwieldy. □ **bulk·i·ness** *noun*

bull[1] ● *noun* **1 a** an uncastrated male bovine animal. **b** the male of various other large animals, e.g. whale, elephant, moose, and seal. **2** (**the Bull**) the constellation and zodiacal sign Taurus. **3** *Stock Exch.* a person who buys shares hoping to sell them at a higher price later (*compare* BEAR[2]). **4** *slang* = BULLSHIT. **5** *N Amer. slang* a policeman. ● *adjective* **1** like that of a bull (*bull neck*). **2** (in combination) *N Amer. Forestry* chief or head. ● *verb* **1** *transitive & intransitive* act or treat violently. **2** *Stock Exch.* **a** *intransitive* speculate for a rise. **b** *transitive* produce a rise in the price of (stocks, etc.). □ **bull ahead** progress regardless of opposition. **bull in a china shop** a reckless or clumsy person. **take the bull by the horns** meet a difficulty boldly. **bull through** *N Amer.* force through with great effort. □ **bull·ish** *adjective* [Old Norse *boli* = Middle Low German, Middle Dutch *bulle*]

bull[2] *noun* a papal edict. [Old French *bulle* from Latin *bulla* rounded object, in medieval Latin 'seal']

bull[3] *noun* (also **Irish bull**) an expression containing a contradiction in terms or implying ludicrous inconsistency. [17th c.: origin unknown]

bul·lace /ˈbʊləs/ *noun* a thorny shrub, *Prunus institia*, bearing globular yellow or purple-black fruits, of which the damson plum is the cultivated form. [Old French *buloce*, *beloce*]

bull bird *noun Cdn* (*Nfld*) = DOVEKIE.

bull block *noun N Amer. Forestry* a large pulley through which the mainline passes in yarding.

bull bucker *noun N Amer. Forestry* a person in charge of a team of fallers and buckers.

bull·cook *noun N Amer.* a person who performs various chores in a logging camp etc. (e.g. chopping wood, cleaning bunkhouses, etc.). [so-called with reference to the job of caring for oxen once used in logging camps]

bull·dog *noun* **1** a sturdy, powerful breed of dog with a large head, protruding lower jaw, and smooth hair. **2** a tenacious and courageous person.

bulldog clip *noun* a strong sprung metal device with two flat plates that close so as to hold large quantities of paper together.

bull·dog·ging *noun N Amer. slang* = STEER WRESTLING. □ **bull·dog·ger** *noun*

bull·doze *transitive verb* **1** clear with a bulldozer. **2** *informal* **a** intimidate. **b** make (one's way) forcibly. [perhaps from BULL[1] + alteration of DOSE]

bull·doz·er *noun* **1** a powerful tractor with a broad curved vertical blade at the front for clearing ground. **2** a forceful and domineering person.

bull-dyke *noun* (also **bull-dike**) *slang* usu. *derogatory* a lesbian with masculine tendencies.

bul·let *noun* **1** a projectile of lead etc. for a rifle, revolver, machine gun etc. **2** *Printing* a small usu. solid circle used to introduce and emphasize a line, an item in a list, etc. □ **dodge a bullet** narrowly avoid death, defeat, etc. [French *boulette* diminutive of *boule* ball, from Latin *bulla* bubble]

bul·letin *noun* **1** a short official account, statement, or broadcast report of news. **2** a regular list of information etc. issued by an organization or society. [French from Italian *bullettino* diminutive of *bulletta* passport, diminutive of *bulla* seal, BULL[2]]

bulletin board *noun* **1** *N Amer.* a board for displaying notices. **2** a system for storing information in a computer so that any authorized user can access and add to it from a remote terminal or personal computer.

bullet point *noun* each of several items in a list e.g. a summary of the

arguments in a presentation or the features of a product in point form, printed with a typographical bullet before each for emphasis.

bullet·proof ● *adjective* **1** impenetrable by bullets (*bulletproof vest*). **2** unassailable, safe from criticism etc. (*financially bulletproof*). ● *transitive verb* make bulletproof.

bullet train *noun* a high-speed passenger train, esp. in Japan.

bull·fight *noun* a sport of baiting and (usu.) killing bulls as a public spectacle, esp. in Spain. □ **bull·fight·er** *noun* **bull·fight·ing** *noun*

bull·finch *noun* any of a number of Eurasian finches of the genus *Pyrrhula*, esp. *Pyrrhula pyrrhula*, with a short stout beak and bright plumage.

bull·frog *noun* any of several large frogs with bellowing calls, esp. the largest N American kind, *Rana catesbeiana*.

bull·head *noun* **1** any N American freshwater catfish of the genus *Ictalurus* having a large head with several barbels. **2** any of various northern fishes of the family Cottidae with large heads bearing spines.

bull·head·ed *adjective* obstinate; impetuous; blundering. □ **bull·head·ly** *adverb* **bull·head·ness** *noun*

bullhead lily *noun* a yellow pond lily, *Nuphar variegatum*, of northern N America.

bull·horn *noun* an electronically amplified megaphone.

bul·lion /ˈbʊliən/ *noun* a metal (esp. gold or silver) in bulk before coining, or valued by weight. [Anglo-French = mint, var. of Old French *bouillon*, ultimately from Latin *bullire* boil]

bull·ish *adjective* **1 a** *Stock Exch.* causing or associated with a rise in prices. **b** aggressively optimistic. **2** like a bull. □ **bull·ish·ly** *adverb* **bull·ish·ness** *noun*

bull market *noun* a market with shares rising in price.

bull-necked *adjective* having a short, thick neck.

bull-nose *adjective* (also **bull-nosed**) with a rounded end.

bul·lock /ˈbʊlək/ *noun* = STEER[2]. [Old English *bulluc*, diminutive of BULL[1]]

bull of the woods *noun N Amer. Forestry* a logger renowned for his ability.

bull·pen *noun* **1** *Baseball* **a** an area where pitchers, esp. relief pitchers, warm up. **b** the relief pitchers on a baseball team. **2** a large cell in which prisoners are held temporarily, in a courthouse, police station, or jail.

bull riding *noun N Amer.* a rodeo event in which a rider attempts to remain on a bucking bull for eight seconds while holding onto a rope tied around the animal's middle with one hand. □ **bull rider** *noun*

bull·ring *noun* an arena for bullfights.

bull session *noun N Amer.* an informal group discussion.

bull's eye *noun* **1 a** the centre of a target. **b** a shot, dart, etc. hitting this. **2** a hemisphere or thick disc of glass in a ship's deck or side to admit light. **3** a small circular window. **4 a** a hemispherical lens. **b** a lantern fitted with this. **5** a boss of glass at the centre of a blown glass sheet. **6** an accurate remark or guess.

bull·shit *coarse slang* ● *noun* (often as *interjection*) nonsensical, foolish, or deceptive talk or writing. ● *intransitive verb* (**-shit·ted**, **-shit·ting**) talk nonsense; bluff. □ **bull·shit·ter** *noun*

bull snake *noun* a large yellowish-brown N American constricting snake of the genus *Pituophis*, which feeds on small rodents.

bull team *noun N Amer. hist.* a team of several pairs of oxen.

bull terrier *noun* a stocky, short-haired breed of dog that is a cross between a bulldog and a terrier.

bull thistle *noun* any of several large thistles of the genus *Cirsium*, esp. *C. vulgare*, a widespread weed.

bull trout *noun* **1** *N Amer.* = DOLLY VARDEN 1. **2** *Brit.* a salmon trout.

bull·whack·er *noun N Amer.* esp. *hist.* a person driving a team of oxen.

bull·whip esp. *N Amer.* ● *noun* a whip with a long heavy lash. ● *transitive verb* thrash with such a whip.

bull work *noun N Amer.* heavy or strenuous physical labour.

bully[1] ● *noun* (pl. **-lies**) a person who uses strength or power to coerce others by fear. ● *transitive verb* (**-lies**, **-lied**) **1** persecute or oppress by force or threats. **2** (foll. by *into* + verbal noun) pressure or coerce (a person) to do something (*bullied him into agreeing*). [originally as a term of endearment, prob. from Middle Dutch *boele* lover]

bully[2] *slang* ● *adjective* dated very good; first-rate. ● *interjection* (foll. by *for*) expressing admiration or approval, or *ironic* (*bully for you!*). [perhaps from BULLY[1]]

bully[3] *noun* (pl. **-lies**) (also **bul·ley**, **bully boat**) *Cdn* (*Nfld*) a two-masted decked boat used for fishing on the coasts of NE Newfoundland and Labrador. [origin unknown]

bully beef *noun* corned beef. [French *bouilli* boiled beef, from *bouillir* BOIL[1]]

bully boy *noun* a young bully, esp. a hired ruffian.

bully pulpit *noun* N Amer. a prominent or advantageous position used to promote one's cause.

bully·rag *transitive verb* (**-ragged, -rag·ging**) *slang* bully, harass. [18th c.: origin unknown]

Bülow /ˈbjuːloː/ **Prince Bern·hard von** (1849–1929), German statesman, chancellor of Germany 1900–9. His support of the Austrian annexation of Bosnia-Herzegovina helped to precipitate the First World War.

bul·rush *noun* **1** any rushlike water plant of the genus *Scirpus*, esp. *S. lacustris*, used for weaving. **2** a tall water plant, *Typha latifolia*, having a brown cigar-shaped flower head. *Also called* CATTAIL, REED MACE. **3** *Bible* a papyrus plant. [perhaps from BULL[1] = large, coarse, as in *bullfrog*, *bull trout*, etc.]

bul·wark /ˈbʊlwɜrk, -wɔrk/ *noun* **1** a defensive wall, esp. of earth; a rampart; a mole or breakwater. **2** a person, principle, etc., that acts as a defence. **3** (usu. in *pl.*) a ship's side above deck. [Middle Low German, Middle Dutch *bolwerk*: see BOLE[1], WORK]

Bulwer-Lytton /ˌbʊlwərˈlɪtən/ *see* LYTTON.

bum[1] *noun* Cdn, Brit., Austral., & NZ informal the buttocks. ◻ **bums in seats** paying customers in a theatre etc. [Middle English *bom*, of unknown origin]

bum[2] ● *noun* **1** a street person or vagrant. **2** a lazy or irresponsible person. **3** N Amer. an obnoxious person. **4** N Amer. a person who devotes a great deal of time to a specified activity (*beach bum*). ● *verb* (**bummed, bum·ming**) *informal* **1** *intransitive* (often foll. by *around*) loaf or wander around. **2** *transitive* acquire by begging; scrounge. **3** *transitive* N Amer. (foll. by *out*) disappoint. ● *attributive adjective* **1** malfunctioning (*Josh has a bum knee*). **2** worthless (*a bum cheque*). **3** unfair, disappointing (*a bum deal*). ◻ **give a person the bum's rush** N Amer. **1** forcibly eject. **2** abruptly dismiss. [prob. abbreviation or back-formation from BUMMER]

bum·bag *noun* Brit. informal = FANNY PACK.

bum-bailiff *noun* hist. a bailiff empowered to collect debts or arrest debtors for nonpayment. [BUM[1], so called as approaching from behind]

bum·ble *intransitive verb* **1** (often as **bum·bling** *adjective*) move or act ineptly; blunder. **2** (foll. by *on*) speak in a rambling incoherent way. **3** make a buzz or hum. ◻ **bum·bler** *noun* [BOOM[1] + -LE[4]: partly from *bumble* = blunderer]

bumble·bee *noun* any large hairy bee of the genus *Bombus* with a loud buzz, common in temperate regions.

bumble·berry *noun* Cdn a mixture of berries, e.g. blackberries, raspberries, blueberries, strawberries, etc., sometimes also containing apples and rhubarb, used esp. as a pie filling but also in jams, yogourt, etc. [English dialect *bumble*, = rosehip, blackberry, possibly deformation of BRAMBLE]

bum·boat *noun* a small boat carrying or selling provisions etc. to ships. [BUM[1] (originally a scavenger's boat removing refuse etc. from ships)]

bum·boy *noun* slang a young male homosexual, esp. a prostitute.

bumf var. of BUMPH.

bum·malo /ˈbʌməˌloː/ *noun* (pl. same) a small fish, *Harpodon nehereus*, of S Asian coasts, dried and used as food (see BOMBAY DUCK). [perhaps from Marathi *bombil(a)*]

bummed *adjective* N Amer. informal (also **bummed out**) disappointed.

bum·mer *noun* N Amer. informal **1** an unpleasant occurrence. **2** an idler; a loafer. [19th c.: perhaps from German *Bummler* person who strolls around]

bump ● *noun* **1** a dull-sounding blow or collision. **2** a swelling or dent caused by this. **3** an uneven patch on a road, field, etc. **4** any of various prominences on the skull thought by phrenologists to indicate different mental faculties. **5** Cdn & Brit. (in *pl.*) a custom in which a person celebrating a birthday is either lifted by the legs and arms and lowered to the ground or hit in the buttocks with a knee once for each year of age. **6** a rising air current causing an irregularity in the aircraft's motion. ● *verb* **1 a** *transitive* hit or come against with a bump. **b** *intransitive* (of two objects) collide. **2** *intransitive* (foll. by *against*, *into*) hit with a bump; collide with. **3** *transitive* (often foll. by *against*, *on*) hurt or damage by striking (*bumped my head on the ceiling*; *bumped the car while parking*). **4** *intransitive* (usu. foll. by *along*) move or travel with much jolting (*we bumped along the road*). **5** *transitive* N Amer. displace, e.g. from a job (by seniority) or airline reservation. ◻ **bump and grind** move

(one's hips etc.) to music, esp. as part of an erotic dance. **bump into** *informal* meet by chance. **like a bump on a log** N Amer. inertly. **bump off** *slang* murder. **bump up** *informal* increase (prices etc.). **things that go bump in the night 1** supernatural beings regarded as the cause of unidentifiable nighttime noises. **2** unspecified objects of fear. [16th c., imitative: perhaps from Scandinavian]

bump·er *noun* **1** a horizontal bar or strip fixed across the front or back of a motor vehicle to reduce damage in a collision or as a trim. **2** (usu. *attributive*) an unusually large or fine example (*a bumper crop*). **3** a brimful glass of wine etc. ◻ **bumper to bumper 1** (of traffic) backed up. **2** N Amer. (of automobile insurance etc.) covering the entire vehicle from one bumper to the other.

bumper boat *noun* each of a number of padded round boats steered around a pond at an amusement park etc. and bumped into each other.

bumper car *noun* each of a number of small electrically driven cars in an enclosure at an amusement park etc., driven around and bumped into each other.

bumper pad *noun* N Amer. (usu. in *pl.*) a long pad attached around the inside of a crib to stop drafts and provide cushioning.

bumper shining *noun* Cdn (Man. & Sask.) the practice, engaged in by children, of holding on to a car's rear bumper on a snowy or icy road so as to be dragged along for a ride.

bumper sticker *noun* N Amer. a sticker with a slogan, advertisement, etc., to be displayed on a vehicle's bumper.

bumph *noun* (also **bumf**) *derogatory slang* **1** Cdn & Brit. **a** publicity materials, e.g. press releases, campaign flyers, etc. **b** papers, documents. **2** Brit. toilet paper. [abbreviation of *bum-fodder*]

bump·kin *noun* (also **country bumpkin**) an unsophisticated and socially inept rural person. [perhaps Dutch *boomken* little tree or Middle Dutch *bommekijn* little barrel]

bump·tious /ˈbʌmpʃəs/ *adjective* offensively self-assertive or conceited. ◻ **bump·tious·ly** *adverb* **bump·tious·ness** *noun* [BUMP, after FRACTIOUS]

bumpy *adjective* (**bump·i·er, bump·i·est**) **1** having many bumps (*a bumpy road*). **2** affected by bumps (*a bumpy ride*). ◻ **bump·i·ly** *adverb* **bump·i·ness** *noun*

bum rap *noun* informal **1** imprisonment on a false charge. **2** a false accusation.

bum-rush *transitive verb* esp. US slang force or barge one's way into (esp. a rock concert or sports stadium); gatecrash.

bum steer *noun* informal a piece of false information. [BUM[2] + STEER[1]]

bum·wad *noun* Cdn slang toilet paper.

bun *noun* **1** N Amer. a small unsweetened bread roll. **2 a** a small sweetened bread roll or cake, often with dried fruit. **b** Cdn (Nfld) a tea biscuit; a scone (*stop by for a cup of tea and a bun*). **3** (in *pl.*) N Amer. informal the buttocks. **4** hair worn in a tight coil at the back of the head. ◻ **have a bun in the oven** *slang* be pregnant. [Middle English: origin unknown]

bunch ● *noun* **1** a cluster of things growing or fastened together (*bunch of grapes*; *bunch of keys*). **2** a collection; a set or lot (*best of the bunch*). **3** *informal* a group; a gang. **4** *informal* a large amount; lots (*a bunch of ideas*; *thanks a bunch*). ● *verb* **1** *transitive* make into a bunch or bunches; gather into close folds. **2** *intransitive* form into a group or crowd. ◻ **bunch·er** *noun* **bunchy** *adjective* [Middle English: origin unknown]

bunch·berry *noun* (pl. **-berries**) a dwarf dogwood, *Cornus canadensis*, or its red fruit. *Also called* CRACKERBERRY, DWARF DOGWOOD.

Bunche /ˈbʌntʃ/ **Ralph (John·son)** (1904–71), US political scientist and diplomat, who played a leading role in drafting the United Nations charter, and was awarded the 1950 Nobel Peace Prize for his efforts to bring about a settlement in the Arab-Israeli conflict.

bunch·grass *noun* any of various N American grasses that grow in clumps.

bun·co /ˈbʊŋkoː/ N Amer. slang ● *noun* (pl. **-cos**) a swindle, esp. by card-sharping or a confidence game. ● *transitive verb* (**-coes, -coed**) swindle, cheat. [perhaps from Spanish *banca* a card game]

bun·combe var. of BUNKUM.

Bundes·bank /ˈbʊndəsˌbaŋk/ *noun* the central bank of Germany. [German from *Bund* federation + *Bank* bank]

Bundes·rat /ˈbʊndəsˌrɑt/ *noun* the Upper House of Parliament in Germany or in Austria. [German from *Bund* federation + *Rat* council]

Bundes·tag /ˈbʊndəsˌtɑg/ *noun* the Lower House of Parliament in Germany. [German from *Bund* federation + *tagen* confer]

bun·dle ● *noun* **1** a collection of things tied or fastened together. **2** a set of nerve fibres etc. banded together. **3** *informal* a large amount of money. ● *verb* **1** *transitive* (usu. foll. by *up*) tie in or make into a bundle (*bundled up my books and papers*). **2** *transitive* (usu. foll. by *into*) throw or push, esp. quickly or confusedly (*bundled the papers into the drawer*). **3** *transitive* (usu. foll. by *out*, *off*, *away*, etc.) send (esp. a person) away hurriedly or unceremoniously (*bundled them off the premises*). **4** *transitive* dress (*bundled them into their snowsuits*). **5** *transitive* (in *passive*) sell as a unit (*software bundled with the computer*). **6** *intransitive* sleep clothed with another person, esp. a fiancé(e), as a local custom. □ **bundle of joy** *jocular* a baby. **be a bundle of nerves** be extremely nervous. **bundle up** dress warmly or cumbersomely. **go a bundle on** *Brit. slang* be very fond of. [Middle English, perhaps from Old English *byndelle* a binding, but also from Low German, Dutch *bundel*]

bundle buggy *noun* (*pl.* **-gies**) *N Amer.* a two-wheeled collapsible cart used for shopping etc.

Bundt cake /bʌnt/ *noun N Amer.* proprietary a cake, e.g. a pound cake, baked in a Bundt pan.

Bundt pan /bʌnt/ *noun N Amer.* proprietary a tube pan with fluted sides used for baking cakes.

bun·fight *noun Cdn, Brit., & Austral. slang* **1** a large, crowded, usu. boisterous party or dinner. **2** an occasion characterized by vigorous disputes or general chaos.

bung ● *noun* a stopper for closing a hole in a container, esp. a cask. ● *transitive verb* **1** stop with a bung. **2** *Brit. slang* throw, toss. □ **bunged up** *informal* **1** *N Amer.* damaged; malfunctioning. **2** closed, blocked. **3** constipated. [Middle Dutch *bonghe*]

bun·ga·low /ˈbʌŋɡəˌlo/ *noun* **1** a one-storey house. **2** *Cdn* (*Cape Breton*) a summer cottage, esp. a modest one. [Gujarati *bangalo* from Hindustani *banglā* belonging to Bengal]

Bun·gee *noun var. of* BUNGI.

bun·gee cord /ˈbʌndʒi/ *noun* **1** strong elasticized cord or cable. **2** a piece of this, usu. with a hook on each end and used esp. for securing baggage etc. [origin unknown]

bun·gee jump *intransitive verb* jump from a height, as from a bridge or crane, while attached to it by a bungee cord. □ **bun·gee jump·er** *noun* **bun·gee jump·ing** *noun*

bung·hole *noun* a hole for filling or emptying a cask etc.

Bungi /bʌnˈɡi/ *noun* **1** (*pl.* same) the Ojibwa living on the plains of Manitoba, North Dakota, and Montana. **2** a dialect of English formerly spoken by some Aboriginal peoples around the Red River settlement, incorporating elements of Cree, Scots, Gaelic, and French. [corruption of Cree *pahki*, Ojibwa *panki* 'part, thing, a little']

bun·gle ● *verb* **1** *transitive* blunder over, mismanage, or fail at (a task). **2** *intransitive* work badly or clumsily. ● *noun* a bungled attempt; bungled work. □ **bun·gler** *noun* **bun·gling** *noun & adjective* [imitative: compare BUMBLE]

bun·head *noun slang* a female ballet student or ballet dancer, esp. one obsessively interested with ballet.

Bunin /ˈbuːnɪn/ **Ivan Alek·se·evich** (1870–1953), Russian poet and prose writer. Love and peasant life are the most prominent themes in his prose works, which include the novel *The Village* (1910); he was awarded the Nobel Prize for literature in 1933.

bun·ion /ˈbʌnjən/ *noun* a swelling on the foot, esp. at the first joint of the big toe. [Old French *buignon* from *buigne* bump on the head]

bunk¹ ● *noun* **1** a simple bed, esp. one of two or more arranged on top of one another. **2** *N Amer.* a large trough for feeding cattle in a feedlot etc. **3** a crossbeam on a logging truck on which the logs rest. ● *intransitive verb* **1** sleep in or lie on a bunk or improvised bed. **2** share a room with. □ **bunk down** go to bed. [18th c.: origin unknown]

bunk² *noun* □ **do a bunk** *Brit. slang* leave or abscond hurriedly. [19th c.: origin unknown]

bunk³ *noun slang* nonsense; humbug. [abbreviation of BUNKUM]

bunk bed *noun* each of two or more beds one above the other, forming a unit.

bun·ker ● *noun* **1** a large container or compartment for storing fuel. **2** *Military* a reinforced underground shelter. **3** a hollow filled with sand, used as an obstacle in a golf course. ● *transitive verb* **1** fill the fuel bunkers of (a ship etc.). **2** (usu. in *passive*) **a** trap in a bunker (in sense 3). **b** bring into difficulties. [19th c.: origin unknown]

bunker-buster *noun informal* a bomb capable of penetrating a military bunker. □ **bunker-busting** *noun & adjective*

bunker C *noun* a thick, sticky, black fuel oil, produced by blending the residual oil from the refining process with lighter oil, used in large marine diesel engines, in power stations, industrial furnaces, etc. [the

heaviest of three previously available fuel oils, the lighter ones being designated 'bunker A' and 'bunker B']

Bunker Hill the first pitched battle (1775) of the American Revolution (actually fought on Breed's Hill near Boston, Massachusetts). Although the British were able to drive the Americans from their positions, the good performance of the untrained American irregulars gave considerable impetus to the Revolution.

bunker mentality *noun* a feeling of excessive defensiveness amongst a group perceiving itself as besieged.

bunk·house *noun* **1** a house where workers etc. are lodged. **2** *Cdn* = BUNKIE.

bunk·ie *noun Cdn* (*S Ont.*) a small outbuilding on the property of a summer cottage providing extra sleeping accommodation for guests. [abbreviation of BUNKHOUSE]

bun·kum *noun* (also **bun·combe**) nonsense; humbug. [originally *buncombe* from *Buncombe* County in N Carolina, mentioned in a nonsense speech by its Congressman, *c.*1820]

bunny *noun* (*pl.* **-nies**) **1** *informal* a rabbit. **2** *derogatory* (usu. in *combination*) a young, attractive woman, esp. one who is sexually available, involved in a particular activity (*beach bunny*; *ski bunny*). **3** *N Amer.* (*attributive*) designating an easy hill for beginner skiers (*bunny run*; *bunny hill*). [dialect *bun* rabbit]

bunny-hop ● *noun* **1** a jump in a crouched position. **2** a dance of hopping steps in which the participants face the same direction and form a line by placing their hands on the waist or shoulders of the person in front of them. ● *verb* (**-hopped**, **-hop·ping**) *intransitive* jump forward with a jerky motion.

bunny hug *noun Cdn* (*Sask.*) a hooded sweatshirt.

Bun·sen /ˈbʌnsən/ **Rob·ert Wil·helm Eber·hard** (1811–99), German chemist. With G. Kirchhoff he developed spectroscopy, using it to detect new elements (cesium and rubidium) and to determine the composition of substances and of the sun and stars; he designed numerous items of chemical apparatus, besides the burner (developed in 1855) for which he is best known.

Bunsen burner *noun* a small adjustable gas burner used in scientific work as a source of great heat. [BUNSEN]

bunt¹ ● *verb* **1** *transitive & intransitive* push with the head or horns; butt. **2** *Baseball* **a** *transitive* strike or tap (the ball) with the bat without swinging. **b** *intransitive* bunt the ball. ● *noun* **1** an act of bunting. **2** a bunted ball. □ **bunt·er** *noun* [19th c.: compare BUTT¹]

bunt² *noun* the baggy centre of a fishing net, sail, etc. [16th c.: origin unknown]

bunt³ *noun* a disease of wheat caused by the fungus *Tilletia caries*. [18th c.: origin unknown]

bunt·ing¹ *noun* any of numerous seed-eating birds related to the finches and sparrows. [Middle English: origin unknown]

bunt·ing² *noun* **1** flags and other decorations. **2** a loosely woven fabric used for these. [18th c.: origin unknown]

bunt·ing³ *noun* (also **bunting bag**) *N Amer.* a snug, hooded sleeping bag for infants. [special use of BUNTING² 2]

bunt·line *noun* a line for confining the bunt (see BUNT²) when furling a sail.

Bu·ñuel /buːˈnwɛl/ **Luis** (1900–83), Spanish film director. Remarkable for their shocking and terrifying images, his films often attacked the Establishment (in particular the Church); they include *Un Chien andalou* (1928), *Belle de jour* (1967), and *The Discreet Charm of the Bourgeoisie* (1972).

Bun·yan ▶ **1 John** (1628–88), English writer, who is best known for *The Pilgrim's Progress* (1678–84), an allegory recounting the spiritual journey of its hero Pilgrim. **2 Paul** (in N. American folklore) a giant lumberjack famed for his strength and exploits. □ **Bun·yan·esque** *adjective*

bun·yip /ˈbʌnjɪp/ *noun Austral.* **1** a fabulous monster inhabiting swamps and lagoons. **2** an imposter. [Wemba-wemba *banib*]

Buona·parte /ˌbwɒnəˈpɑːteɪ/ *see* BONAPARTE.

Buon·ar·roti *see* MICHELANGELO.

buoy /bɔɪ, ˈbuːi/ ● *noun* **1** an anchored float serving as a navigation mark or to show reefs etc. **2** a lifebuoy. ● *transitive verb* **1** (usu. foll. by *up*) **a** keep afloat. **b** sustain the courage or spirits of (a person etc.); uplift, encourage. **2** mark with a buoy or buoys. □ **buoy·age** *noun* [prob. from Middle Dutch *bo(e)ye*, from a Germanic base meaning 'signal']

buoy·ancy /ˈbɔɪənsi/ *noun* **1** the capacity to be or remain buoyant. **2** resilience; recuperative power. **3** cheerfulness.

buoy·ant /ˈbɔɪənt/ *adjective* **1 a** able or apt to keep afloat or rise to the top of a liquid or gas. **b** (of a liquid or gas) able to keep something afloat. **2** lighthearted. □ **buoy·ant·ly** adverb [French *buoyant* or Spanish *boyante* part. of *boyar* float, from *boya* BUOY]

bup·kes noun (also **bup·kis, bup·kus**) = BUBKES.

bup·pie noun informal a black yuppie. [blend of BLACK adjective 3 + YUPPIE]

bur var. of BURR[1].

burb noun N Amer. informal (usu. in pl.) = SUBURB. [abbreviation]

Bur·bage /ˈbɜːbɪdʒ/ **Rich·ard** (c.1567–1619), English actor. He was the first performer of most of Shakespeare's great tragic roles (Hamlet, Othello, Lear, and Richard III), and was also associated with the building of the Globe Theatre.

Bur·bank a city in S California, to the north of Los Angeles; pop. (2000) 100,316. It is a centre of the film and television industries.

bur·ble ● intransitive verb **1** make a murmuring noise. **2** speak ramblingly. ● noun **1** a murmuring noise. **2** rambling speech. [19th c.: imitative]

bur·bot /ˈbɜːbət/ noun a freshwater fish, *Lota lota*, of the cod family, with a broad head and barbels. [Old French *borbete*, prob. from *borbe* 'mud, slime']

bur·den ● noun **1** a load, esp. a heavy one. **2** an oppressive duty, obligation, expense, emotion, etc. **3** a ship's carrying capacity, tonnage. **4 a** the refrain or chorus of a song. **b** the chief theme or gist of a speech, book, poem, etc. ● transitive verb load with a burden; encumber, oppress. □ **burden of proof** the obligation to prove one's case. □ **bur·den·some** adjective [Old English *byrthen*: related to BEAR[1]]

bur·dock noun a large herbaceous plant of the genus *Arctium*, with prickly flowers and large leaves. [BUR + DOCK[3]]

bur·eau /ˈbjʊərəʊ/ noun (pl. N Amer. **bur·eaus**, Brit. **bur·eaux** /-rəʊz/) **1 a** Cdn & Brit. a writing desk with drawers and usu. an angled top opening downwards to form a writing surface. **b** N Amer. a chest of drawers. **2 a** an office or business with a specified function (*tourist bureau*). **b** a government department. [French, = desk, originally its baize covering, from Old French *burel* from *bure*, *buire* dark brown, ultimately from Greek *purros* red]

bureau·cracy /bjʊˈrɒkrəsi/ noun (pl. **-cies**) **1 a** government by central administration. **b** a nation or organization so governed. **2** the officials of such a government, esp. regarded as oppressive and inflexible. **3** conduct typical of such officials. [French *bureaucratie*: see BUREAU]

bureau·crat /ˈbjʊərəˌkrat, -rɒˌkrat/ noun **1** an official in a bureaucracy. **2** an inflexible or insensitive administrator. □ **bureau·crat·ic** adjective **bureau·crat·ic·ally** adverb [French *bureaucrate* (as BUREAUCRACY)]

bureau·crat·ese /ˌbjʊərəˌkraˈtiːz/ noun a style of language believed to be characteristic of bureaucrats, marked by jargon, abstractions, circumlocution, etc. [BUREAUCRAT + -ESE]

bureau·crat·ize /bjʊˈrɒkrəˌtaɪz/ transitive verb (also esp. Brit. **-ise**) govern by or transform into a bureaucratic system. □ **bureau·crat·iz·a·tion** noun

bur·ette /bjʊˈrɛt/ noun (also **buret**) a graduated glass tube with an end tap for measuring small volumes of liquid in chemical analysis. [French]

burfi noun an Indian dessert made from milk solids and sugar, cut into squares or diamonds, and typically flavoured with cardamom or nuts. [Hindi, from Persian *barfi*, literally 'icy, snowy']

burg noun N Amer. informal a town or city. [see BOROUGH]

bur·gee /bɜːˈdʒiː/ noun a triangular or swallow-tailed flag flown by yachts etc., usu. bearing distinguishing colours or the emblem of a yacht club or sailing club. [18th c.: perhaps = (ship)owner, ultimately French *bourgeois*: see BURGESS]

Bur·gen·land /ˈbʊərɡənˌlant/ a state of E Austria; capital, Eisenstadt.

bur·geon /ˈbɜːdʒən/ intransitive verb **1** begin to grow rapidly; flourish. **2** literary put forth young shoots; bud. [Old French *burjon* 'bud' ultimately from Late Latin *burra* wool]

bur·geon·ing /ˈbɜːdʒənɪŋ/ adjective growing; flourishing (*a burgeoning population*).

bur·ger noun **1** informal a hamburger. **2** (in combination) a certain kind of hamburger or savoury patty shaped like one (*cheeseburger*; *fishburger*; *veggie burger*). [abbreviation]

Bur·gess /ˈbɜːdʒɪs/ **1 An·thony** (pseudonym of John Anthony Burgess Wilson) (1917–93), English novelist and critic. His novels include *A Clockwork Orange* (1962), a disturbing, futuristic vision of juvenile delinquency, violence, and high technology, and *Earthly Powers* (1980), in which the hero lives through some of the most dramatic real events of the 20th c. **2 Guy (Fran·cis de Moncy)** (1911–63), British

Foreign Office official and spy. Acting as a Soviet agent from the 1930s, he was charged with espionage in 1951 and fled to the USSR with Donald Maclean.

bur·gess /ˈbɜːdʒəs/ noun Brit. **1** an inhabitant of a town or borough, esp. of one with full municipal rights. **2** hist. a Member of Parliament for a borough, corporate town, or university. [Old French *burgeis* ultimately from Late Latin *burgus* BOROUGH]

Burgess Shale noun a block of shale in Yoho National Park, BC, unique in having fossil remains of over 140 invertebrate species.

burgh /ˈbʌrə/ noun hist. a Scottish borough or chartered town. [Scots form of BOROUGH]

bur·gher /ˈbɜːrɡər/ noun **1** N Amer. a middle-class inhabitant of a (usu. specified) city or town. **2** hist. a citizen, esp. of a European town. **3** South Africa hist. a citizen of a Boer republic. [German *Burger* or Dutch *burger* from *Burg*, *burg* BOROUGH]

Burgh·ley /ˈbɜːrli/ **Wil·liam Cecil, 1st Baron** (also **Bur·leigh**) (1520–98), English statesman. As Secretary of State to Queen Elizabeth I (1558–72) and Lord High Treasurer (1572–98), he was the queen's most trusted councillor and minister and the driving force behind the successful policies of the Elizabethan age.

bur·glar noun a person who commits burglary. [legal Anglo-French *burgler*, related to Old French *burgier* pillage]

bur·glar·ize transitive & intransitive verb N Amer. (also **-ise**) = BURGLE.

bur·glary noun (pl. **-ies**) **1** entry into a building illegally with intent to commit theft, do bodily harm, or do damage. **2** an instance of this. ¶ In Canadian law, now replaced by BREAKING AND ENTERING.

bur·gle verb **1** transitive commit burglary on (a building or person). **2** intransitive commit burglary. [back-formation from BURGLAR]

burgo·master noun the mayor of a Dutch or Flemish town. [Dutch *burgemeester* from *burg* BOROUGH: assimilated to MASTER]

bur·goo noun **1** esp. US (South) a stew or thick soup, typically one made for an outdoor meal. **2** hist. a thick porridge served aboard ship.

Bur·gos /ˈbʊərɡɒs/ a city in N Spain; pop. (2000) 166,251. The capital of the former kingdom of Castile during the 11th c., it became politically significant again during the Spanish Civil War, when Franco made it the official seat of his Nationalist government (1936–9).

Bur·goyne /bɜːˈɡɔɪn/ **John ('Gentleman Johnny')** (1722–92), English general and playwright. He is largely remembered for capitulating to the Americans at Saratoga (1777) in the American Revolution. His plays include the comedies *The Maid of the Oaks* (1774) and *The Heiress* (1786).

Bur·gundy a region and former duchy of east central France, centred on Dijon. The region is noted for its wine. □ **Bur·gun·di·an** noun & adjective

bur·gundy ● noun (pl. **-dies**) **1** (also **Burgundy**) **a** the wine (usu. red) of Burgundy. **b** a similar wine from another place. **2** the reddish purple colour of burgundy wine. ● adjective of this colour.

bur·ial /ˈbɛriəl, ˈbɜːriəl/ noun **1 a** the burying of a dead body. **b** a funeral. **2** Archaeology a grave or its remains.

burial ground noun a cemetery.

burin /ˈbjʊərɪn/ noun **1** a steel tool for engraving on copper or wood. **2** Archaeology a flint tool with a chisel point. [French, perhaps related to Old High German *bora* 'boring tool']

Burin Peninsula /ˈbjʊərɪn/ a long peninsula of the southern coast of the island of Newfoundland. It extends southwestward and is separated from the Avalon Peninsula to the east by Placentia Bay. [origin uncertain: possibly from French *burin* engraving tool or Basque *burua* head]

burk var. of BERK.

burka /ˈbɜːrkə/ noun a long enveloping garment traditionally worn in public by Muslim women. [Urdu from Arabic *burka'*]

Burke /bɜːrk/ **1 Ed·mund** (1729–97), British man of letters and Whig politician. Burke wrote prolifically on political emancipation and moderation, supporting proposals for relaxing anti-Catholic laws in Britain and protesting against the harsh handling of the American colonies. Vehemently opposing the radical excesses of the French Revolution, he called on European leaders to resist the new regime in his influential *Reflections on the Revolution in France* (1790). **2 John** (1787–1848), Irish genealogical and heraldic writer. He compiled *Burke's Peerage* (1826), the first reference guide of peers and baronets in alphabetical order. **3 Wil·liam** (1792–1829), Irish murderer. A notorious bodysnatcher operating in Edinburgh, he was hanged for a series of fifteen or more murders carried out for profit. □ **Burk·ean** /ˈbɜːrkiən/ adjective

Bur·kina Faso /bɜːrˈkiːnə ˈfasoː/ a landlocked country of western

---

Consonants: **b** *but* **d** *dog* **f** *few* **g** *get* **h** *her* **j** *yes* **k** *cat* **l** *leg* **m** *man* **n** *no* **p** *pen* **r** *red* **s** *sit*

Africa, in the Sahel, known until 1984 as Upper Volta; pop. (est. 2002) 12,603,185; capital, Ouagadougou. □ **Bur·kinan** adjective & noun

Bur·kitt's lymphoma /ˈbɜːkɪts/ noun a malignant tumour of the lymphatic system, caused by the Epstein-Barr virus, esp. affecting children in central Africa. [D. P. Burkitt, British surgeon d.1993]

burl /bɜːl/ noun **1** N Amer. a flattened knotty growth on a tree. **2** = BURR³. **3** a knot or lump in wool or cloth. □ **burled** adjective [Old French bourle tuft of wool, diminutive of bourre coarse wool, from Late Latin burra wool]

bur·lap /ˈbɜːlap/ noun **1** coarse canvas esp. of jute used for sacking etc. **2** a similar lighter material for use in dressmaking or furnishing. [17th c.: origin unknown]

Bur·leigh /ˈbɜːli/ var. of BURGHLEY.

bur·lesque /bɜːˈlesk/ ● noun **1 a** a comic imitation, esp. in parody of a dramatic or literary work. **b** a performance or work of this kind. **c** bombast, mock-seriousness. **2** N Amer. a variety show, often including striptease. ● adjective of or in the nature of burlesque. ● transitive verb (**bur·lesques, bur·lesqued, bur·les·quing**) make or give a burlesque of. [French from Italian burlesco from burla mockery]

Bur·ling·ton /ˈbɜːlɪŋtən/ a city in S Ontario, situated on Lake Ontario, about 50 km southwest of Toronto; pop. (2001) 150,836.
□ **Bur·ling·ton·ian** noun [the name of the bay (now officially called Hamilton Harbour), an alteration of Bridlington, a town in the East Riding of Yorkshire, England]

Burlington bun noun Cdn (NS) = JELLY DOUGHNUT. [origin unknown]

burly adjective (**bur·li·er, bur·li·est**) of stout sturdy build; big and strong. □ **bur·li·ness** noun [Middle English borli prob. from an Old English form = 'fit for the bower' (BOWER¹)]

Burma (official name **My·an·mar**) a country in SE Asia, on the Bay of Bengal; pop. (est. 2002) 42,238,224; capital, Rangoon. The official name of the country was changed to the Union of Myanmar in 1989.

Bur·man adjective & noun (pl. **Bur·mans**) = BURMESE.

Burm·ese /bɜːˈmiːz/ ● noun (pl. same) **1 a** a native or national of Burma (now Myanmar) in SE Asia. **b** a person of Burmese descent. **2 a** member of the largest ethnic group of Burma. **3** the language of this group. **4** (in full **Burmese cat**) a short-haired breed of domestic cat with a usu. brown coat. ● adjective of or relating to Burma or its people or language.

burn¹ ● verb (past and past participle **burned** or **burnt**) **1** transitive & intransitive be or cause to be consumed or destroyed by fire. **2** intransitive **a** blaze or glow with fire. **b** be in the state characteristic of fire. **3** transitive & intransitive be or cause to be injured or damaged by fire or great heat or by radiation. **4** transitive & intransitive use or be used as a source of heat, light, or other energy (the lights burned all night). **5** transitive & intransitive char or scorch in cooking (burned the vegetables; the vegetables are burning). **6** transitive produce (a hole, a mark, etc.) by fire or heat. **7** transitive **a** subject (clay, chalk, etc.) to heat for a purpose. **b** harden (bricks) by fire. **c** make (lime or charcoal) by heat. **8** transitive colour, tan, or parch with heat or light (we were burnt brown by the sun). **9** transitive & intransitive put or be put to death by fire. **10** transitive **a** cauterize, brand. **b** (foll. by in) imprint by burning. **11** transitive & intransitive make or be hot, give or feel a sensation or pain of or like heat. **12** transitive & intransitive (often foll. by with) make or be passionate; feel or cause to feel great emotion (burn with shame). **13** intransitive slang drive fast. **14** transitive N Amer. informal anger, infuriate. **15** intransitive (of acid etc.) gradually penetrate (into) causing disintegration. **16** transitive metabolize in the body (burn calories). **17** transitive produce (a CD) by copying from an original or master copy. **18** transitive & intransitive cause or feel a sharp sensation (the alcohol burned in her throat). **19** transitive informal swindle or cheat. **20** transitive Curling touch (a rock in play) with one's foot, broom, etc. ● noun **1 a** a mark or injury caused by burning. **b** a mark or injury caused by friction or abrasion (razor burn). **2** the ignition of a rocket engine in flight, giving extra thrust. **3** N Amer., Austral., & NZ **a** an area of forest destroyed by a forest fire. **b** a forest area cleared by intentional burning. □ **burn one's bridges** (or **boats**) commit oneself irrevocably. **burn the candle at both ends** exhaust one's strength or resources by undertaking too much. **burn down 1 a** destroy (a building) by burning. **b** (of a building) be destroyed by fire. **2** burn less vigorously as fuel fails. **burn one's fingers** or **get one's fingers burned** suffer for meddling or rashness. **burn a hole in one's pocket** (of money) be quickly spent. **burn low** (of fire) be nearly out. **burn the midnight oil** read or work late into the night. **burn off 1** remove by fire. **2** expend (kids need to burn off energy). **3** lose (weight) through physical activity. **burn out 1** be reduced to nothing by burning. **2** fail or cause to fail by burning. **3** esp. N Amer. suffer physical or emotional exhaustion.

4 consume the contents of by burning. **5** make (a person) homeless by burning his or her house. **burn up 1** get rid of by fire. **2** begin to blaze. **3** N Amer. slang be or make furious. **have money to burn** have more money than one needs. [Old English birnan, bærnan from Germanic]

burn² noun Scot. a small stream. [Old English burna etc. from Germanic]

Bur·naby /ˈbɜːnəbi/ a city in southwestern BC, immediately east of Vancouver; pop. (2001) 193,954. [R. Burnaby, private secretary to the commanding officer of the Royal Engineers during a survey of New Westminster in 1859 d.1878]

burned-out adjective var. of BURNT-OUT.

Burne-Jones, **Sir Ed·ward Coley** (1833–98), English painter and designer. A leading member of the Pre-Raphaelite brotherhood, he was preoccupied by medieval and literary themes; major works include the tapestry The Adoration of the Magi in Exeter College Chapel, Oxford, and the paintings The Golden Stairs (1880) and The Mirror of Venus (1867–77).

burn·er noun **1** a person or thing that burns. **2 a** the part of a gas stove, lamp, etc. that emits and shapes the flame. **b** N Amer. the heating element of an electric stove. **3** a furnace, esp. of a specified kind (oil burner). **4** = CD BURNER.

bur·net /ˈbɜːnət/ noun **1** any plant of the genus Sanguisorba of the rose family, with pink or red flowers. **2** a day-flying moth of the genus Zygaena, typically dark green with crimson-spotted wings. [obsolete burnet (adj.) dark brown, from Old French burnete]

Bur·nett, **Fran·ces (Eliza) Hodg·son** (1849–1924), English-born US novelist. She is remembered chiefly for her novels for children, including Little Lord Fauntleroy (1886), The Little Princess (1905), and The Secret Garden (1911).

Bur·ney, **Fran·ces** ('Fanny') (1752–1840), English novelist. Her satire Evelina (1778) and the novel Cecilia (1782) brought her fame and the patronage of Samuel Johnson, but she is best remembered for her diaries and letters, which record her experiences at the English court and abroad.

burn-in noun **1** damage to a computer or television screen, caused by being left on for an excessive period. **2** a reliability test in which a device is switched on for a long time.

burn·ing adjective **1** ardent, intense (burning desire). **2** hotly discussed, exciting (burning question). **3** flagrant (burning shame). □ **burn·ing·ly** adverb

burning bush noun **1** any of various shrubs with red fruits or red autumn leaves, esp. of the genus Euonymus. **2** fraxinella. [with biblical allusion to Exodus 3:2 in which God appears to Moses in a burning bush]

bur·nish ● transitive verb polish by rubbing. ● noun a polished lustre. □ **bur·nish·er** noun [Old French burnir = brunir from brun BROWN]

bur·noose /bɜːˈnuːs/ noun (also **bur·nous**) a hooded Arab cloak. [French from Arabic burnus from Greek birros cloak]

burn·out noun **1** physical or emotional exhaustion, esp. caused by stress. **2** depression, disillusionment. **3** informal a dropout or drug abuser, esp. a teenage one.

burn rate noun the rate at which a new company uses up its venture capital to fund fixed overheads before cash begins to come in from its trading activities.

Burns ▸ **1 George** (born Nathan Birnbaum) (1896–1996), US comedian and actor, who with his wife Gracie Allen, was popular for over thirty years in vaudeville, radio, television, and film. He won an Academy Award for best supporting actor in The Sunshine Boys (1975). **2 Pat·rick** (1856–1937), Canadian rancher and businessman. He built up one of the largest meat-packing businesses in Canada between 1885 and 1928. **3 Rob·ert** (1759–96), Scottish poet. He is considered the national poet of Scotland, and his works, written in the Scottish dialect, include the lyric 'Auld Lang Syne', and the narrative poem 'Tam o' Shanter' (1791).

Burns Night noun 25 January, the birthday of Robert Burns, celebrated by Scots and other admirers of the poet. Traditionally haggis and other Scottish dishes are eaten while bagpipe music is played and some of Burns's most popular poems are read aloud.

burnt ● verb past and past participle of BURN¹. ● adjective **1** marked or affected by burning or as if burning. **2** (of a pigment) made darker by burning (burnt umber).

burnt offering noun an offering burned on an altar as a sacrifice.

burnt-out adjective **1** physically or emotionally exhausted. **2** destroyed by burning so that only a shell remains.

burnt sienna noun a dark reddish-orange colour.

bur oak var. of BURR OAK.

burp ● *verb* **1** *intransitive* belch. **2** *transitive* make (a baby) belch, usu. by patting its back. ● *noun* a belch. [imitative]

bur·pee *noun* a physical exercise consisting of a squat thrust made from and ending in a standing position. [Royal H. *Burpee*, US psychologist b.1897]

burp gun *noun* US *slang* a small submachine gun.

Burr, Aaron (1756–1836), US Democratic Republican politician, vice-president 1800–4. He killed his political rival Alexander Hamilton in a duel (1804), and subsequently plotted to annex Mexico to the western US and establish a separate empire; he was tried for treason and acquitted in 1807.

burr[1] *noun* (also **bur**) **1 a** a prickly clinging seed case or flower head. **b** any plant producing these. **2** a rough edge left on cut or punched metal, paper, etc. **3** a surgeon's or dentist's small drill. **4 a** a siliceous rock used for millstones. **b** a whetstone. □ **burr under** (or **in**) **one's saddle** N Amer. a source of irritation, esp. a persistent one. [Middle English: compare Danish *burre* burr, burdock, Swedish *kard-borre* burdock]

burr[2] ● *noun* **1** a whirring sound. **2** a rough sounding of the letter *r*. ● *verb* **1** *transitive* pronounce with a burr. **2** *intransitive* speak indistinctly. **3** *intransitive* make a whirring sound. [prob. imitative, but perhaps also from BURR[1]]

burr[3] *noun* **1** a swirled pattern in the grain of wood (also *attributive*: *burr walnut*). **2** the rounded knob forming the base of deer's horn. [perhaps from French; compare BURL]

Bur·rard Inlet /ˈbʌrˈɑrd/ an arm of the Strait of Georgia in southwestern BC. It extends eastward, separating Vancouver from North Vancouver. [Sir H. *Burrard*, English general d.1813]

bur reed *noun* a plant of wet ground or shallow water of the genus *Sparganium* with burr-like seed heads.

bur·rito /bəˈriːtoː/ *noun* (*pl.* **-tos**) N Amer. a tortilla rolled around a spicy filling of meat, beans, etc. [Latin American Spanish, diminutive of *burro* BURRO]

burro /ˈbʌroː/ *noun* (*pl.* **-ros**) esp. US a small donkey used as a pack animal. [Spanish]

burr oak *noun* (also **bur oak**) a N American oak, *Quercus macrocarpa*, with large fringed acorn cups.

Bur·roughs /ˈbʌroːz/ **1 Edgar Rice** (1875–1950), US novelist and science-fiction writer, the creator of the jungle hero Tarzan, who first featured in *Tarzan of the Apes* (1914). **2 Wil·liam Sew·ard** (1914–97), US novelist. He became associated with leading figures of the beat generation in the 1940s, and his best-known writing deals, in a surreal style, with life as a drug addict (*Junkie*, 1953; *The Naked Lunch*, 1959).

bur·row ● *noun* a hole or tunnel dug by a small animal as a dwelling. ● *verb* **1** *intransitive* make or live in a burrow. **2** *transitive* make (a hole etc.) by digging. **3** *intransitive* hide oneself. **4** *intransitive* (foll. by *into*) investigate, search. □ **bur·row·er** *noun* [Middle English, apparently var. of BOROUGH]

burrow·ing owl *noun* a small, sandy-coloured, round-headed, long-legged owl, *Athene cunicularia*, which nests in burrows and is found in central N America, and Central and South America.

Bursa /ˈbɜrsə/ a city in NW Turkey, capital of a province of the same name; pop. (est. 2002) 1,190,000. Captured by the Turks in 1326, it was the capital of the Ottoman Empire from then until 1402.

bursa /ˈbɜrsə/ *noun* (*pl.* **bur·sae** /-siː/ or **bur·sas**) Anat. a fluid-filled sac of fibrous tissue, esp. one serving to lessen friction between moving parts (e.g. at a joint). □ **bur·sal** *adjective* [medieval Latin = bag: compare PURSE]

bur·sar /ˈbɜrsər/ *noun* **1** a treasurer or other financial officer, esp. of a university or college. **2** Brit. the holder of a bursary. □ **bursar·ship** *noun* [French *boursier* or (in sense 1) medieval Latin *bursarius* from *bursa* bag]

bur·sary /ˈbɜrsəri/ *noun* (*pl.* **-ies**) **1** Cdn a financial award to an esp. university student made primarily on the basis of financial need or some other criterion in addition to academic merit. **2** Scot. a scholarship. □ **bur·sar·ial** /-ˈseriəl/ *adjective* [medieval Latin *bursaria* (as BURSAR)]

bur·sitis /bɜrˈsaɪtɪs/ *noun* inflammation of a bursa.

burst ● *verb* (*past* and *past participle* **burst**) **1 a** *intransitive* break suddenly and violently apart by expansion of contents or internal pressure. **b** *transitive* cause to do this. **2 a** *transitive* open forcibly. **b** *intransitive* come open or be opened forcibly. **3 a** *intransitive* (usu. foll. by *in*, *out*) make one's way suddenly, dramatically, or by force. **b** *transitive* break away from or through (*the river burst its banks*). **4** *intransitive* (usu. foll. by *with*) be full to overflowing; have in abundance (*bursting with flavour*). **5** *intransitive* appear or come suddenly (*burst into flame*; *burst upon the view*; *sun burst out*). **6** *intransitive* (foll. by *into*) give sudden expression to (*burst into tears*). **7** *intransitive* be as if about to burst because of effort, excitement, etc. **8** *transitive* suffer bursting of (*burst a blood vessel*). ● *noun* **1** the act of or an instance of bursting; a split. **2** a sudden issuing forth (*burst of flame*). **3** a sudden outbreak (*burst of applause*). **4 a** a short sudden effort; a spurt. **b** a gallop. **5** an explosion. □ **bursting at the seams** full to overflowing. **burst out 1** suddenly begin (*burst out laughing*). **2** exclaim. [Old English *berstan* from Germanic]

bur·then *archaic var.* of BURDEN.

Bur·ton ▶ 1 Rich·ard (born Richard Jenkins) (1925–84), Welsh actor. He played a number of Shakespearian roles before becoming well known in films. He had a famous screen partnership with Elizabeth Taylor, to whom he was twice married, in films such as *Who's Afraid of Virginia Woolf* (1966) and *Cleopatra* (1963). **2 Sir Rich·ard (Fran·cis)** (1821–90), English explorer, anthropologist, and translator. He discovered Lake Tanganyika with John Speke (1858); as a translator, he is best remembered for his unexpurgated versions of the *Arabian Nights* (1885–8), the *Kama Sutra* (1883), and other works of Arabian erotica. **3 Rob·ert** (1577–1640), English scholar, cleric, and writer, who is best known for his *Anatomy of Melancholy* (1621), a treatise on melancholy which is, in effect, a satire on the inefficacy of human learning and endeavour.

bur·ton *noun* a light two-block tackle for hoisting. [Middle English *Breton tackles*: see BRETON[2]]

Bur·undi /buˈrʌndi/ a central African country on the east side of Lake Tanganyika; pop. (est. 2002) 6,373,000; capital, Bujumbura. Ethnic violence in the mid-1990s between the majority Hutu and minority Tutsi peoples resulted in the deaths of at least 150,000. □ **Bur·und·ian** *adjective & noun*

bury /ˈberi, ˈbɜːri/ *transitive verb* (**-ies**, **-ied**) **1** place (a dead body) in the earth, in a tomb, or in the sea, a large lake, etc. **2** lose by death (*has buried three children*). **3 a** put under ground (*bury alive*). **b** hide (treasure, a bone, etc.) in the earth. **c** cover up; submerge. **4 a** put out of sight (*buried his face in his hands*). **b** consign to obscurity (*the idea was buried after brief discussion*). **c** put away; forget. **5** involve deeply (*buried herself in her work*; *was buried in a book*). □ **bury the hatchet** cease to quarrel. [Old English *byrgan* from West Germanic]

Bury (in full **Bury St. Ed·munds**) a town in E England, in the county of Suffolk; pop. (est. 1999) 176,760.

Bur·yat·ia /burˈjɒtiə/ (also called **Bur·yat Autonomous Republic**) an autonomous republic in SE Russia, between Lake Baikal and the Mongolian border; pop. (est. 2002) 1,013,800; capital, Ulan-Ude.

bury·ing ground *noun* (also **burying place**) a cemetery.

bus ● *noun* (*pl.* **buses**) **1** a large motor vehicle designed to carry several passengers, esp. one serving the public on a fixed route or as a chartered service. **2** *informal* a car, airplane, etc., functioning like a bus. **3** Computing a defined set of conductors carrying data and control signals within a computer. **4** Electricity a system of conductors in a generating or receiving station on which power is concentrated for distribution. ● *verb* (**buses, bused, bus·ing**) **1** *intransitive* go by bus. **2** *transitive* N Amer. transport by bus. **3** *transitive* N Amer. carry or remove (dishes etc.) in a cafeteria; clear (a table in a cafeteria etc.) of dishes. [abbreviation of OMNIBUS]

bus·boy *noun* N Amer. a waiter's assistant who clears tables etc.

busby /ˈbʌzbi/ *noun* (*pl.* **-bies**) a tall fur hat worn by hussars etc. [18th c.: origin unknown]

bus depot *noun* N Amer. a bus station.

Bush ▶ 1 George Her·bert Walk·er (b.1924), US Republican politician, 41st president of the US 1989–93. He was director of the CIA (1976–7), and vice-president (1981–8); while in office he negotiated further arms reductions with the Soviet Union and organized international action to liberate Kuwait following the Iraqi invasion in 1990. **2** his son **George Walk·er** (b.1946), 43rd president of the US 2001– . A Texas Republican, he became president in one of the closest and most controversial presidential elections in US history. After the terrorist attacks against the US on September 11, 2001, he sent US forces to bring down the Taliban government of Afghanistan, and in 2003 invaded Iraq to topple the regime of Saddam Hussein.

bush[1] ● *noun* **1** a shrub or clump of shrubs with stems of moderate length. **2** a thing resembling this, esp. a clump of hair or fur. **3** Cdn a wooded piece of land on a farm etc.; a woodlot. **4** (esp. in N and S America, Australia and Africa) a wild uncultivated district; woodland or forest. **5** (*attributive*) (of a plant) shaped like a bush (*bush beans*). **6** *hist.* a bunch of ivy as a vintner's sign. ● *verb* **1** *intransitive* (usu. foll. by *out*) branch or spread like a bush. **2** *transitive* N Amer. mark a road across (ice) with bushes or trees set at intervals. □ **go bush** *Austral.* leave one's usual surroundings; run wild. [ultimately from Germanic]

bush² ● *noun* **1** a metal lining for a round hole enclosing a revolving shaft etc. **2** a sleeve providing electrical insulation. ● *transitive verb* provide with a bush. [Middle Dutch *busse* BOX¹]

bush baby *noun* = GALAGO.

bush basil *noun* a culinary herb, *Ocimum minimum*.

bush·buck *noun* a small antelope, *Tragelaphus scriptus*, of southern Africa, having a chestnut coat with white stripes. [BUSH¹ + BUCK¹, after Dutch *boschbok* from *bosch* bush]

bush camp *noun Cdn* **1** the living quarters, offices, etc., of a mining or lumbering operation in the bush. **2** a camp set up for living in the bush.

bush country *noun* a wooded wilderness area; an extensive tract of bush.

bush·craft *noun N Amer.* the knowledge or experience needed to survive in the bush.

bushed *adjective* **1** (*predicative*) *informal* tired out. **2** forested; wooded. **3** *Cdn informal* (of a person) **a** living in the bush. **b** crazy; insane (due to isolation). **4** *Austral. & NZ informal* lost or confused.

bushel /ˈbʊʃəl/ *noun* **1** (in Canada and other Commonwealth countries) a measure of capacity for grain, fruit, etc., equal to 8 imperial gallons or 36.4 litres. **2** (in the US) a similar unit of measure equal to 64 US pints or 35.24 litres. □ **bushel·ful** *noun* (*pl.* **-fuls**). [Old French *buissiel* etc., perhaps of Gaulish origin]

bush farm *noun Cdn hist.* a farm in the bush, esp. one that has not been completely or properly cleared of trees.

bush fever *noun Cdn* any of various physical or emotional disorders caused by protracted isolation in the bush.

bush·fire *noun* a fire in a forest or in scrub, often spreading widely.

bu·shido /buːˈʃiːdoʊ/ *noun* the code of honour and morals evolved by the Japanese samurai. [Japanese, = military knight's way]

bush·ing *noun* = BUSH² *noun.*

bush jacket *noun Cdn* = LUMBERJACK JACKET.

bush·land *noun* = BUSH¹ 4.

bush league *N Amer.* ● *noun* = MINOR LEAGUE. ● *adjective* (also **bush-league**) inferior, unsophisticated. □ **bush leaguer** *noun*

bush·lot *noun Cdn* = WOODLOT.

bush·man /ˈbʊʃmən/ *noun* (*pl.* **-men**) **1** a person who lives or gains his livelihood in the bush, e.g. a logger. **2** (**Bushman**) **a** a member of an aboriginal people in southern Africa. **b** the language of this people. [BUSH¹ + MAN: sense 2 after Dutch *boschjesman* from *bosch* bush]

bush·master *noun* a venomous viper, *Lachesis muta*, of Central and S America. [perhaps from Dutch *boschmeester*]

bush party *noun Cdn* a usu. large social gathering, esp. of young people, held in a woodlot or bush etc., and usu. with the object of consuming beer.

bush pilot *noun N Amer.* a pilot who flies small aircraft into isolated areas.

bush plane *noun N Amer.* a small plane used for flying into isolated areas, usu. equipped with floats or skis.

bush·ranger *noun hist.* an Australian outlaw living in the bush.

bush road *noun* a usu. dirt road through a forested area.

bush telegraph *noun* rapid spreading of information, a rumour, etc.

bush·whack *verb* **1** *intransitive N Amer., Austral., & NZ* **a** clear a way through underbrush, dense vegetation, etc. **b** clear land in bush country and establish a settlement. **2** *transitive N Amer.* ambush.

bush·whack·er *noun* **1** *N Amer., Austral., & NZ* **a** a person who clears land in bush country and settles there. **b** a person who hikes in bush country. **2** *US* a guerrilla fighter (originally in the American Civil war).

bush·work·er *noun Cdn* a logger; a person who works in the bush. □ **bush work** *noun*

bushy¹ *adjective* (**bush·i·er**, **bush·i·est**) **1** growing thickly like a bush. **2** having many bushes. **3** covered with bush. □ **bush·i·ness** *noun*

bushy² *noun* (*pl.* **-ies**) *Austral. & NZ informal* a person who lives in the bush (as distinct from in a town).

bushy-tailed woodrat *noun* = PACK RAT 1.

busi·ly *adverb see* BUSY.

busi·ness /ˈbɪznəs/ *noun* **1** one's regular occupation, profession, or trade. **2** a thing that is one's concern (*none of your business*). **3 a** a task or duty. **b** a reason for coming (*what is your business?*). **4** serious work or activity (*get down to business*). **5** *derogatory* an affair, a matter (*sick of the whole business*). **6** a thing or series of things needing to be dealt with

(*the business of the day*). **7** volume of trade (*did a lot of business*). **8 a** a company or corporation. **b** commercial enterprises collectively (*the government needs the support of business*). **9** patronage; custom (*take my business elsewhere*). **10** *N Amer.* euphemism (esp. of pets) an occurrence of defecation or urination. **11** *Theatre* action on stage, as opposed to dialogue. □ **business as usual** an ongoing, unchanging state of affairs, esp. in adversity. **has no business** has no right. **in business 1** engaged in commercial activity. **2** able to begin operations. **the business end** *informal* the functional part of a tool or device. **in the business of** engaged in. **like nobody's business** *informal* extraordinarily. **make it one's business to** undertake to. **mean business** be in earnest. **mind one's own business** not meddle. **on business** with purpose relating to one's regular occupation. **send a person about his or her business** dismiss a person; send a person away. [Old English *bisignis* (as BUSY, -NESS)]

business administration *noun* a program of study at a university or college which trains students for managerial positions in businesses etc.

business card *noun* a card printed with one's name and professional details.

business casual *adjective* designating clothing that is more casual than formal business attire but still suitable for office wear.

business class *noun* a more expensive class of seating than economy class in an aircraft, typically offering roomier seating, better food, and other advantages.

business cycle *noun* recurring periods of increased and decreased economic activity.

business day *noun* a day on which a business is open to the public.

business end *noun* **1** the functional part of a tool or device (*he found himself facing the business end of six lethal-looking weapons*). **2** the essential or basic part of a process or operation.

business hours *plural noun* the hours during which stores or offices are open to the public.

business jet *noun* a small, usu. twin-engined jet airplane, with seating for four to eight passengers.

busi·ness·like *adjective* efficient, systematic, practical.

busi·ness·man *noun* (*pl.* **-men**) a male business person.

business park *noun* an area designed to accommodate businesses and light industry.

business person *noun* (*pl.* **business people**) a person engaged in trade or commerce, esp. at a senior level.

business plan *noun* a detailed plan setting out the objectives of a business over a stated period, providing figures for projected cash flow, production, and profit and loss, and outlining its strategy for achieving its objectives.

business school *noun* an institution of higher education, usu. part of a university, at which students learn business-related skills.

business studies *plural noun* training in economics, management, etc.

busi·ness·woman *noun* (*pl.* **-women**) a female business person.

busk *intransitive verb* perform (esp. music) for donations, usu. in the street or in subways. □ **busk·er** *noun* **busk·ing** *noun* [*busk* peddle etc. (perhaps from obsolete French *busquer* seek)]

bus·kin *noun* **1** either of a pair of thick-soled laced boots worn by an ancient Athenian tragic actor to gain height. **2** (usu. prec. by *the*) tragic drama; its style or spirit. **3** *hist.* either of a pair of calf- or knee-high boots of cloth or leather worn in the Middle Ages. [prob. from Old French *bouzequin*, var. of *bro(u)sequin*, of unknown origin]

bus lane *noun* a lane on a road reserved for use by buses.

bus·load *noun* the number of people travelling in a bus.

bus·man *noun* (*pl.* **-men**) *dated* the driver of a bus.

busman's holiday *noun* leisure time spent in an activity similar to one's regular work.

buss *N Amer. informal* ● *noun* a kiss. ● *transitive verb* kiss. [earlier *bass* (n. & v.): compare French *baiser* 'kiss' from Latin *basiare*]

bus shelter *noun* a shelter from rain etc. beside a bus stop.

bus station *noun* a place in a city or town where intercity buses depart and arrive.

bus stop *noun* **1** a regular stopping place of a bus. **2** a sign marking this.

bust¹ *noun* **1 a** the human chest, esp. that of a woman; the bosom. **b** the circumference of the body at bust level (*a 36-inch bust*). **c** the part of a woman's garment fitting over the bust (*too small in the bust*). **2** a sculpture of a person's head, shoulders, and chest. [French *buste* from Italian *busto*, of unknown origin]

bust² *informal* ● *verb* (*past and past participle* **bust·ed** or **bust**) **1** *transitive & intransitive* burst, break. **2** *transitive* esp. *US* reduce (a soldier etc.) to a lower rank; dismiss. **3** *transitive* esp. *N Amer.* **a** raid, search. **b** arrest. **4** *transitive N Amer.* tame (esp. broncos). ● *noun* **1** a failure. **2** a depression; a sudden economic downturn. **3** a police raid. **4** esp. *N Amer.* a punch; a hit. ● *adjective* **1** (also **bust·ed**) broken, burst, collapsed. **2** bankrupt. □ **bust one's ass** (or **butt**) *slang* give oneself a great deal of trouble. **bust someone's ass** (or **butt**) *slang* beat or chastise someone. **bust a gut 1** become excited, upset, etc. **2** exert oneself exceedingly. **3** laugh hysterically. **bust a move** perform a dance move. **bust up 1** bring or come to collapse; explode. **2** (of esp. a married couple) separate. **go bust** become bankrupt; fail. [originally a (dial.) pronunciation of BURST]

bus·tard /ˈbʌstərd/ *noun* any large terrestrial bird of the family Otididae, with long neck, long legs, and stout tapering body. [Old French *bistarde* from Latin *avis tarda* slow bird (? = slow on the ground; but possibly a perversion of a foreign word)]

bus·tee /ˈbʌstiː/ *noun* (in India) a shantytown; a slum. [Hindustani *bastī* dwelling]

bust·er *noun* **1** a person or thing that busts. **2** *informal* fellow (used esp. as a disrespectful form of address). **3** (in *combination*) something that eradicates an undesirable or unpleasant phenomenon (*vitamin C has a reputation as a cold buster*).

bus·tier /ˈbʌstiˌei/ *noun* **1** a woman's form-fitting, sleeveless, and often strapless bodice or top, sometimes laced at the front. **2** a short camisole reaching just below the bustline. [French]

-busting *combining form* eradicating or defeating a phenomenon or thing perceived as undesirable or unpleasant (*union-busting*).

bus·tle¹ /ˈbʌsəl/ ● *verb* **1** *intransitive* (often foll. by *about*) **a** work etc. showily, energetically, and officiously. **b** hasten (*bustled about the kitchen banging saucepans*). **2** *transitive* make (a person) hurry or work hard (*bustled him into his overcoat*). **3** *intransitive* (often foll. by *with*) (of a place) be full of activity. ● *noun* excited activity; a fuss. [perhaps from *buskle* frequentative of *busk* prepare]

bus·tle² /ˈbʌsəl/ *noun* **1** *hist.* a pad or frame worn under a skirt and puffing it out behind. **2** a traditional dance outfit for Aboriginal men, featuring a circular ruffle of eagle feathers. [18th c.: origin unknown]

bust·line *noun* **1** the shape or outline of a woman's breasts. **2** the part of a garment covering this.

bust-up *noun informal* **1** a quarrel. **2** a marital separation or other breakup. **3** a collapse.

busty *adjective* (**busti·er**, **busti·est**) (of a woman) having a prominent bust. □ **busti·ness** *noun*

busy ● *adjective* (**busi·er**, **busi·est**) **1** (often foll. by *in*, *with*, *at*, or *pres. part.*) occupied or engaged in work etc. with the attention concentrated (*she was busy packing*; *busy at work*). **2** full of activity (*a busy evening*). **3** (of a street etc.) having heavy traffic. **4** (of patterns etc.) overwhelmed by an excess of detail, variety, etc. (*the fabric was a very busy print*). **5** employed continuously; unresting (*busy as a bee*). **6** esp. *N Amer.* (of a telephone line) already in use. **7** *archaic* meddlesome; prying. ● *transitive verb* (**busies**, **busied**) (*reflexive*) keep busy; occupy (*busied herself with the accounts*). □ **busi·ly** /ˈbɪzɪli/ *adverb* **busy·ness** /ˈbɪzinəs/ *noun* (compare BUSINESS). [Old English *bisig*]

busy·body *noun* (*pl.* **-ies**) **1** an overly inquisitive or meddlesome person. **2** a mischief-maker.

busy Liz·zie *noun* a houseplant, *Impatiens walleriana*, which blooms almost constantly under the right conditions.

busy signal *noun N Amer.* a sound indicating that a telephone line is in use.

busy·work *noun* work that keeps a person busy but has little value in itself.

but ● *conjunction* **1 a** nevertheless, however (*tried hard but did not succeed*; *I am old, but I am not weak*). **b** on the other hand; on the contrary (*I am old but you are young*). **2** (*prec. by can etc.*; in *neg.* or *interrogative*) except, other than, otherwise than (*cannot choose but do it*; *what could we do but run?*). **3** without the result that (*it never rains but it pours*). **4** prefixing an interruption to the speaker's train of thought (*the weather is ideal – but is that a cloud on the horizon?*). ● *preposition* except; apart from; other than (*everyone went but me*; *nothing but trouble*). ● *adverb* **1** only; no more than; only just (*we can but try*; *is but a child*; *had but arrived*; *did it but once*). **2** introducing emphatic repetition; definitely (*wanted to see nobody, but nobody*). ● *relative pronoun* who not; that not (*there is not a man but feels pity*). ● *noun* an objection (*ifs and buts*). ● *transitive verb* (in phr. **but me no buts**) do not raise objections. □ **but for** without the help or

hindrance etc. of (*but for you I'd be rich by now*). **but one** (or **two** etc.) excluding one (or two etc.) from the number (*next door but one*; *last but one*). **but that** (*prec. by neg.*) that (*I don't deny but that it's true*). **but that** (or *informal* **what**) other than that; except that (*who knows but that it is true?*). **but then** (or **yet**) however, on the one hand (*I won, but then the others were beginners*). [Old English *be-ūtan*, *būtan*, *būta* outside, without]

bu·ta·di·ene /ˌbjuːtəˈdaiiːn/ *noun* a colourless gaseous hydrocarbon used in the manufacture of synthetic rubbers. Chem. formula: C_4H_6. [BUTANE + DI-² + -ENE]

bu·tane /ˈbjuːtein, bjuːˈtein/ *noun* a gaseous hydrocarbon of the alkane series used in liquefied form as fuel. Chem. formula: C_4H_8. [BUTYL + -ANE²]

butch *slang* ● *adjective* masculine; tough-looking. ● *noun* **1** (often *attributive*) **a** a mannish woman. **b** a mannish lesbian. **2** a tough, usu. muscular, youth or man. [perhaps abbreviation of BUTCHER]

butch·er ● *noun* **1 a** a person whose trade is dealing in meat. **b** a person who slaughters animals for food. **2** a person who kills or has people killed indiscriminately or brutally. **3** (**butcher's**) *Brit. slang* a look. ● *transitive verb* **1** slaughter or cut up (an animal) for food. **2** kill (people) wantonly or cruelly. **3** ruin (a job, musical composition, etc.) through incompetence. [Old French *bo(u)chier* from *boc* BUCK¹; sense 3 of *noun* rhyming slang from *butcher's hook*]

butcher bird *noun* **1** a shrike. **2** a predatory songbird of the genus *Cracticus*, native to Australia and New Guinea.

butcher block *noun N Amer.* laminated strips of hardwood, usu. in alternating dark and light colours, used to make countertops and similar surfaces.

butcher knife *noun* a large, broad-bladed knife used for cutting meat.

butcher paper *noun N Amer.* a heavy paper, usu. pinkish-brown, coated to make it moisture proof, used for wrapping meat.

butcher's broom *noun* an evergreen shrub of the chiefly Mediterranean genus *Ruscus*, esp. *R. aculeatus* having flat spiny leaflike shoots.

butch·ery *noun* (*pl.* **-eries**) **1** needless or cruel slaughter (of people). **2** a butcher's trade. **3** *Brit.* a slaughterhouse.

Bute Inlet /bjuːt/ an arm of the Strait of Georgia, extending northward into the Coast Mountains of mainland BC, northwest of Powell River. [John Stuart, 3rd Earl of Bute and prime minister of the United Kingdom d.1792]

Buten·andt /ˈbuːtənɒnt/ **Adolf (Fred·erick Jo·hann)** (1903–95), German biochemist, who shared the 1939 Nobel Prize for chemistry for his work on sex hormones.

buteo /ˈbjuːtiːoː/ *noun* any of several birds of prey of the genus *Buteo*, having a broad wingspan and a wide rounded tail. [Latin *buteo* falcon; compare BUZZARD]

Buthe·lezi /ˌbuːtəˈleizi/ **Chief Man·go·suthu Gat·sha** (b.1928), South African Inkatha politician, Chief Minister of KwaZulu since 1976. He was elected leader of Zululand in 1970 and was responsible for the revival of the Inkatha movement in 1975.

But·ler ▸ **1 Sam·uel** (1612–80), English poet whose satirical work *Hudibras* (1663–80, 3 parts) is a mock romance which includes attacks on academic pedantry, Puritan theology, and the politics of the English Civil War. **2 Sam·uel** (1835–1902), English novelist whose important works include *Erewhon* (1872), *Erewhon Revisited* (1901), and the autobiographical *The Way of All Flesh* (1903).

but·ler *noun* the principal male servant of a household, usu. in charge of wines and liquor, the serving of meals, receiving visitors, and supervising other servants. [Anglo-French *buteler*, Old French *bouteillier*: see BOTTLE]

bu·toh /ˈbuːtoː/ *noun* a style of Japanese modern dance featuring nude or nearly nude dancers in white body paint, often performing feats such as lowering themselves on ropes from roofs of buildings. [Japanese 'dance']

butt¹ ● *verb* **1** *intransitive & transitive* push or strike with the head or horns. **2** *intransitive* (usu. foll. by *out*) project, jut. **3** *intransitive & transitive* (usu. foll. by *against*, *on*) lie or place with one end flat against, meet end to end with, abut. ● *noun* **1** a push or blow made with the head or horns. **2** (also **butt joint**) a simple joint in which two pieces of wood etc. are bonded without overlapping. □ **butt heads** be in tenacious conflict. **butt in 1** interrupt, meddle. **2** push into (a line of people) out of turn. **butt out** esp. *N Amer.* cease to interrupt or meddle. [Anglo-French *buter*, Old French *boter* from Germanic: influenced by BUTT² and ABUT]

butt² *noun* **1** (often foll. by *of*) an object of ridicule etc. (*the butt of his jokes*). **2 a** a mound behind a target to stop stray bullets etc. **b** (in *pl.*) a shooting range. **c** a target. **3** a low wall or mound of earth concealing a bird hunter; a blind. [Old French *but* goal, of unknown origin]

butt³ ● *noun* **1** (also **butt end**) the thicker end, esp. of a tool or a weapon (*gun butt*). **2** *N Amer.* a cut of pork from the shoulder. **3 a** the stub of a cigar or a cigarette. **b** *slang* a cigarette. **4** esp. *N Amer. slang* the buttocks. **5** the trunk of a tree, esp. the part just above the ground. ● *transitive verb N Amer.* extinguish (a cigarette) by pressing it into an ashtray etc. □ **butt out** *N Amer.* **1** extinguish (a cigarette) by pressing it into an ashtray etc. **2** stop smoking, esp. permanently. [Dutch *bot* stumpy]

butt⁴ *noun* **1** a large cask for wine or ale. **2** a former unit of measure equal to two hogsheads. [Anglo-French *but*, from Old French *bo(u)t* from Late Latin *buttis*]

butte /bjuːt/ *noun* a high isolated hill with steep sides and a flat top, esp. in western N America. [French, = mound]

butt-ending *noun Hockey* the infraction of jabbing an opponent with the butt end of the stick. □ **butt-end** *transitive verb*

but·ter ● *noun* **1 a** a pale yellow edible fatty substance made by churning cream and used as a spread or in cooking. **b** a substance of a similar consistency or appearance (*peanut butter; cocoa butter*). **2** excessive flattery. ● *transitive verb* spread, cook, or serve with butter (*butter the bread; buttered carrots*). □ **butter up** *informal* flatter excessively. **look as if butter wouldn't melt in one's mouth** seem demure or innocent, probably deceptively. [Old English *butere* from Latin *butyrum* from Greek *bouturon*]

butter-and-eggs *noun* a common plant of the figwort family, *Linaria vulgaris*, having a long stalk of flowers in two shades of yellow. Also called TOADFLAX.

butter·ball *noun* **1** a piece of butter shaped into a ball. **2** *N Amer.* = BUFFLEHEAD. **3** *N Amer. slang* a plump person, animal, etc.

butter bean *noun* **1** a flat, dried, white lima bean. **2** = WAX BEAN.

butter·bur *noun* any of several plants of the genus *Petasites* with large soft leaves and spikes of purple flowers. Also called SWEET COLTSFOOT.

butter·cream *noun* a mixture of butter, sugar, etc. used as a filling or icing for a cake.

butter·cup *noun* any of various common plants of the genus *Ranunculus*, bearing usu. yellow cup-shaped flowers.

buttercup squash *noun N Amer.* a winter squash, a variety of *Cucurbita maxima*, with dark green skin and orange flesh.

butter·fat *noun* the natural fats derived from milk, consisting mainly of glycerides, which make up the main constituent of butter. Abbr.: **BF**.

butter·fingers *noun informal* a clumsy person prone to drop things. □ **butter·fingered** *adjective*

butter·fish *noun* a food fish of N American Atlantic waters, *Peprilus triacanthus*.

butter·flied *adjective* (of shrimp, a steak, etc.) sliced down the centre and spread apart.

butter·fly ● *noun* (*pl.* **-flies**) **1** any diurnal insect of the order Lepidoptera, with knobbed antennae, a long thin body, and four usu. brightly coloured wings erect when at rest. **2** a showy or frivolous person. **3** (in *pl.*) *informal* a nervous sensation felt in the stomach. **4** a swimming stroke in which both arms are lifted out of the water and the legs are kept together while kicking. **5** *Hockey* a kneeling position assumed by a goaltender in which the lower legs are spread apart to cover the bottom part of the goal. **6** *Cdn* a social dance in which trios of people alternate between promenading slowly around the dance floor and whirling each other around in circles. ● *transitive verb* (**-flies**; **-fly·ing**; *past* **-flied**) slice (meat, shrimp, etc.) down the centre and spread apart before cooking. [Old English *buttor-flēoge* (as BUTTER, FLY²)]

butterfly bush *noun* a buddleia, esp. *Buddleia davidii*.

butterfly chair *noun* a lawn chair consisting of a canvas sling hung loosely over a tubular metal frame.

butterfly effect *noun* (in chaos theory) the phenomenon whereby a minute localized change in a complex system can have large effects elsewhere. [from the notion that a butterfly fluttering in Rio de Janeiro could change the weather in Chicago]

butterfly fish *noun* any of various small tropical fishes characterized by quick movements and bright colours, esp. of the genus *Chaetodon*.

butterfly flower *noun* a S American annual plant of the genus *Schizanthus*, grown for its showy flowers.

butterfly knife *noun* a long broad knife used in pairs in some forms of kung fu.

butterfly net *noun* a fine net on a ring attached to a pole, used for catching butterflies.

butterfly nut *noun* = WING NUT 1.

butterfly valve *noun* **1** a valve consisting of hinged semicircular plates, permitting flow in only one direction. **2** a valve, e.g. the damper in a stovepipe or the throttle valve in a carburetor, that pivots on a central axis.

butterfly weed *noun* a N American milkweed, esp. the orange-flowered *Asclepias tuberosa*.

butter·head *noun* (also **butter lettuce**) any of several varieties of lettuce having soft and tender leaves and crisp hearts, e.g. bibb or Boston lettuce.

butter·horn *noun N Amer.* a flaky bread roll, sometimes crescent-shaped, made with a high proportion of butter.

butter knife *noun* a blunt knife used for cutting or spreading butter.

butter·milk *noun* **1** a slightly acid liquid left after churning butter. **2** a dairy product prepared commercially by adding bacterial culture to milk.

butter·nut *noun* **1** a deciduous, eastern N American tree of the walnut family, *Juglans cinerea*, having light grey bark and soft wood. **2** the oily nut of this tree. **3** the soft, light brown wood of this tree, used esp. in cabinetmaking etc. **4** *N Amer.* a light brownish-grey colour.

butternut squash *noun N Amer.* a pear-shaped variety of winter squash with light yellowish-brown skin and orange flesh.

butter·scotch *noun* **1** a brittle candy made from butter, brown sugar, etc. **2** the flavour of this. [SCOTCH]

butter tart *noun Cdn* a tart with a filling of butter, eggs, brown sugar, and usu. raisins.

butter·wort /'bʌtər,wɜrt, -wɔrt/ *noun* any bog plant of the genus *Pinguicula*, esp. *P. vulgaris* with violet-like flowers and fleshy leaves that secrete a fluid to trap small insects.

but·tery¹ *adjective* like, containing, or spread with butter. □ **butter·i·ness** *noun*

but·tery² *noun* (*pl.* **-ies**) *Brit.* a room in a college where provisions are kept and sold to students etc. [Anglo-French *boterie* cellar for storing casks (as BUTT⁴)]

butt·in·sky /bʌt'ɪnski/ *noun* (also **butt·in·ski**) esp. *N Amer. informal* (*pl.* **-skies**) a person who meddles or intrudes, esp. habitually. [*butt in* (see BUTT¹) + *-sky* final element in many Slavic names]

but·tle *intransitive verb jocular* work as a butler. [back-formation from BUTLER]

butt-naked *adjective informal* see BUCK⁵.

but·tock /'bʌtək/ *noun* (usu. in *pl.*) **1** each of two fleshy protuberances on the lower rear part of the human trunk. **2** the corresponding part of an animal. [*butt* ridge + -OCK]

but·ton ● *noun* **1** a small disc or knob sewn on to a garment, either to fasten it by being pushed through a buttonhole, or as an ornament. **2 a** a knob on a piece of mechanical or electronic equipment which performs a particular function when pressed. **b** a small box depicted on a computer screen, representing a function which can be selected by clicking with a mouse. **3** *N Amer.* a usu. round badge bearing a slogan etc. fastened to the clothing with a pin. **4** a small round object resembling a button (often *attributive*: *button nose*). **5 a** a bud. **b** a button mushroom. **6** *Curling* the four-foot circle in the centre of the house. **7** *Fencing* a knob covering the point of a foil to make it harmless. **8** (in *pl.*) *Brit. informal* a pageboy. ● *verb* **1** *transitive & intransitive* = BUTTON UP 1. **2** *transitive* supply with buttons. □ **button it** *informal* cease talking. **button one's lip** *informal* remain silent. **button up 1** fasten with buttons. **2** *informal* become silent. **3** *informal* complete (a task etc.) satisfactorily. **on the button** esp. *N Amer. informal* exactly on target; precise. **push a person's buttons** esp. *N Amer. informal* touch or exploit a person's fears, emotions, prejudices, etc. **push** (or **press** or **hit**) **the right buttons** play expertly on a person's emotions so as to elicit a desired response. □ **but·toned** *adjective* **button·less** *adjective* [Old French *bouton*, ultimately from Germanic]

button-back *noun* (often *attributive*) a chair or sofa with a quilted back, the stitching hidden by buttons.

button·ball *noun* = SYCAMORE 1.

button blanket *noun* a colourful blanket elaborately ornamented with mother-of-pearl, traditionally worn by leaders of Aboriginal peoples of the Pacific Coast of North America.

button·bush *noun* a N American shrub of the madder family, *Cephalanthus occidentalis*, having white globular flower heads.

button chrysanthemum *noun* a variety of chrysanthemum with small spherical flowers.

button-down *adjective* **1** (of a collar) having the points buttoned to the shirt. **2** (of a shirt) having a button-down collar.

buttoned-down *adjective* (also **buttoned-up**) *informal* **1** formal and inhibited in manner. **2** conservative, traditional.

button·hole ● *noun* **1** a loop or slit made in a garment through which a button may be passed for fastening. **2** *Brit.* a boutonniere. ● *transitive verb* **1** *informal* accost and detain (a reluctant listener). **2** make buttonholes in.

button·hol·er *noun* a device for making buttonholes.

buttonhole stitch *noun* a tightly looped stitch used for reinforcing the edges of buttonholes.

button·hook *noun* **1** a small hook for drawing small buttons into place, formerly used on some styles of boots. **2** *Football* a play in which a receiver runs straight downfield and then doubles back a few steps before receiving the pass.

button mushroom *noun* a young unopened mushroom.

button·wood *noun* = SYCAMORE 1.

but·tress /ˈbʌtrəs/ ● *noun* **1** a projecting support of stone or brick etc. built against a wall. **2** a source of help or support. **3** a projecting portion of a hill or mountain. ● *transitive verb* (often foll. by *up*) **1** support with a buttress. **2** provide with support (a *claim buttressed by facts*). [Old French (*ars*) *bouterez* thrusting (arch) from *bouteret* from *bouter* BUTT[1]]

butt·stock *noun* = STOCK 16.

butt-ugly *adjective* *slang* very ugly.

butt weld *noun* a welded butt joint (*see* BUTT[1] 2).

butty[1] *noun* (*pl.* **-ties**) *Brit.* **1** *informal* or *dialect* a fellow worker; a companion. **2** *hist.* a middleman negotiating between a mine owner and the miners. **3** a barge or other craft towed by another. [19th c.: perhaps from BOOTY in phr. *play booty* join in sharing plunder]

butty[2] *noun* (*pl.* **-ties**) *Northern England* **1** a sandwich. **2** a slice of bread and butter. [BUTTER + -Y[2]]

butut /ˈbuːtuːt/ *noun* (*pl.* same or **bu·tuts**) a monetary unit of Gambia, equal to one-hundredth of a dalasi. [a local word]

butyl /ˈbjuːtəl/ *noun Chem.* the monovalent alkyl radical C_4H_9. [BUTYRIC (ACID) + -YL]

butyl·ated hy·droxy·tolu·ene /ˈbjuːtəˌleitəd ˌhaidrɒksəˈtɒljuːiːn/ *noun* = BHT.

butyl rubber *noun* a synthetic rubber used in the manufacture of tire inner tubes.

buty·rate /ˈbjuːtəˌreit/ *noun Chem.* a salt or ester of butyric acid. [BUTYRIC (ACID) + -ATE[1]]

bu·tyr·ic acid /bjuːˈtɪrɪk/ *noun Chem.* a colourless syrupy liquid organic acid found in two isomeric forms in rancid butter or arnica oil. Chem. formula: $C_4H_8O_2$. [Latin *butyrum* BUTTER + -IC]

buxom /ˈbʌksəm/ *adjective* **1** (of a woman) having large breasts. **2** (of a woman) plump and healthy-looking. □ **buxom·ness** *noun* [earlier sense *pliant*: Middle English from stem of Old English *būgan* BOW[2] + -SOME[1]]

Bux·te·hude /ˈbʊkstəˌhuːdə/ **Diet·rich** (*c.*1637–1707), Danish organist and composer. His skill as an organist inspired Bach to walk more than 200 miles from Anstadt to hear him play. His toccatas, preludes, fugues, and choral variations give some idea of his mastery of the instrument as well as of his gifts as a composer.

buy ● *verb* (**buys**, **buy·ing**; *past* and *past participle* **bought**) **1** *transitive* **a** purchase; obtain in exchange for money etc. **b** serve to obtain (*money can't buy happiness*). **2** *transitive* **a** procure (the loyalty etc.) of a person by bribery, promises, etc. **b** win over (a person) in this way. **3** *transitive* get by sacrifice, great effort, etc. (*dearly bought*; *bought with our sweat*). **4** *transitive informal* accept, believe in, approve of (*the police bought our story*). **5** *intransitive* be a buyer for a store etc. (*buys for the furniture chain*). ● *noun informal* a purchase (*that car is a good buy*). □ **buy in 1** buy a stock of. **2** withdraw (an item) at auction because of failure to reach the reserve price. **buy into 1** obtain a share in (an enterprise) by payment. **2** *informal* accept (a line of reasoning etc.). **buy it** (*N Amer.* also **buy the farm**) (usu. in *past*) *slang* be killed. **buy off 1** get rid of (a claim, a claimant, a blackmailer) by payment. **2** bribe. **buy oneself out** (or **off**) obtain one's release (esp. from the armed services) by payment. **buy out** pay (a person, company, etc.) to give up an ownership, interest, etc. **buy time** delay an event, conclusion, etc., temporarily. **buy up 1** buy as much as possible of. **2** absorb (another firm etc.) by purchase. [Old English *bycgan* from Germanic]

buy·back *noun* the purchase of a thing (esp. stock in a company) after having sold it.

buy-down *noun* a sum of money provided by a third party to a lender on behalf of a borrower, resulting in reduced interest rates on a loan.

buy·er *noun* **1** a purchaser, a customer. **2** a person employed to select and purchase stock for a large store etc.

buyer's market (also **buyers' market**) an economic position in which goods are plentiful and cheap and buyers have the advantage over sellers.

buy-in *noun* **1** a purchase of shares by a broker after a seller has failed to deliver similar shares, the original seller being charged any difference in cost. **2** *informal* agreement to support a decision (*there should be a moral buy-in from everyone in the organization*).

buy·out *noun* the purchase of a controlling share in a company etc.

buzz ● *noun* **1** the humming sound of an insect or a machine etc. **2** the sound of a buzzer. **3 a** a confused low sound as of people talking; a murmur. **b** a stir; hurried activity (*a buzz of excitement*). **c** *informal* a rumour. **d** *informal* publicity, esp. created by word of mouth. **4** *slang* a telephone call (*give me a buzz*). **5** *slang* a thrill; a feeling of mild intoxication, esp. from drink or drugs. **6** (also **buzz cut**) *N Amer. slang* a very short haircut. ● *verb* **1** *intransitive* make a humming sound. **2 a** *transitive* & *intransitive* signal or call with a buzzer. **b** *transitive informal* telephone. **3** *intransitive* **a** (often foll. by *about*) move or hover busily. **b** (of a place) have an air of excitement or purposeful activity. **4** *transitive informal* throw hard. **5** *Aviation transitive informal* fly fast and very close to (another aircraft, the ground, etc.). **6** (of a person's mind or head) be filled with excited or confused thoughts. □ **buzz in** allow (someone) into a building by activating a switch that unlocks a door with an accompanying buzzing sound. **buzz off** *slang* go or hurry away. □ **buzzy** *adjective* (**buzz·i·er**, **buzz·i·est**). [imitative]

buz·zard /ˈbʌzərd/ *noun* **1** any of a group of predatory birds of the hawk family, esp. of the genus *Buteo*, with broad wings well adapted for soaring flight. **2** *N Amer.* = TURKEY VULTURE. **3** *slang* an old person. [Old French *busard*, *buson* from Latin *buteo -onis* falcon]

buzz·bait *noun* a fishing lure with a spinning spoon-shaped blade which emits vibrations.

buzz bomb *noun* a flying bomb, esp. one used in the Second World War.

buzzed *adjective* *slang* intoxicated.

buzz·er *noun* an electromagnetic device, similar to an electric bell, that makes a buzzing noise. □ **at the buzzer** *N Amer.* at the end of a game etc. (*scored at the buzzer*).

buzz saw *noun* *N Amer.* a circular saw, esp. a very noisy one.

buzz·word *noun* (also **buzz phrase**) **1** a fashionable piece of jargon, esp. one that sounds technical. **2** a catchword or slogan, esp. one of little exact meaning.

BVM *abbreviation* Blessed Virgin Mary.

b/w *adjective* black and white (used esp. to describe printing, movies, photographs, or television pictures).

bwana /ˈbwɒnə/ *noun* (in Africa) master, sir. [Swahili]

BWR *abbreviation* boiling water (nuclear) reactor.

BWV *abbreviation* *Music* Bach Werke-Verzeichnis (indicating the cataloguing system of the works of J. S. Bach, compiled by Wolfgang Schmieder in 1950). [German, = Index to Bach's Works]

By, **John** (1779–1836), British military officer and engineer. He supervised the building of the Rideau Canal (1826–32) from Bytown (now Ottawa) to Kingston.

by ● *preposition* **1** near, beside, in the region of (*stand by the door*; *sit by me*; *path by the river*). **2** through the agency, means, instrumentality, or causation of (*by proxy*; *a play by Shakespeare*; *went by bus*; *had two children by his first wife*; *divide four by two*). **3** not later than; as soon as (*by next week*; *by now*; *by the time he arrives*). **4 a** past, beyond (*drove by the church*; *came by us*). **b** passing through; via (*went by Montreal*). **5** in the circumstances of (*by day*; *by daylight*). **6** to the extent of (*missed by a foot*; *better by far*). **7** according to; using as a standard or unit (*judge by appearances*; *paid by the hour*). **8** with the succession of (*worse by the minute*; *day by day*; *one by one*). **9** concerning (*Smith by name*; *all right by me*). **10** used in mild oaths (originally = as surely as one believes in) (*by God*; *by George*; *swear by all that is sacred*). **11** placed between specified lengths in two directions (*three feet by two*). **12** avoiding, ignoring (*pass by her*; *passed us by*). **13** (esp. in names of compass points) inclining to (*northeast by north*). ● *adverb* **1** near (*sat by*, *watching*; *lives close by*). **2** aside; in reserve (*put $5 by*). **3** past (*they marched by*). ● *noun* (*pl.* **bys**) = BYE[1]. □ **by and by** before long; eventually. **by and large** on the whole, everything considered. **by the by** (or **bye**) incidentally, parenthetically. **by oneself 1 a** unaided. **b** without prompting. **2** alone; without company. [Old English *bī, bi, be* from Germanic]

by- *prefix* (also **bye-**) subordinate, incidental, secondary (*by-product*; *byroad*).

Byatt /ˈbaiət/ **An·tonia Susan** (b.1936), English novelist and literary critic. Her fiction is noted for its wealth of literary and historical allusion and pastiche. Major novels include *The Virgin in the Garden* (1978) and *Possession* (1990), which won the Booker Prize. She is the elder sister of novelist Margaret Drabble.

Byb·los /ˈbiblɒs/ an ancient Mediterranean seaport, situated on the site of modern Jubayl, or Jebeil, to the north of Beirut in Lebanon. An important trading centre with strong links with Egypt, it became a thriving Phoenician city in the 2nd millennium BC. It was particularly noted for the export of papyrus and cedar wood.

by-blow *noun* **1** an incidental blow not at the main target. **2** an illegitimate child.

by-boat *noun* (also **bye-boat**) *Cdn hist.* a small fishing boat used by Europeans who travelled to the Maritimes to fish in the summer.

by·catch *noun* fish of species other than the species being fished for, caught in fishing nets and usually discarded.

Byd·goszcz /bɪdˈɡɒʃtʃ/ an industrial river port in north central Poland; pop. (est. 2000) 384,537. A monument commemorates the massacre of 20,000 of its citizens by Nazis in Sept. 1939.

bye¹ *noun* **1** the status of an unpaired competitor in a tournament, who proceeds to the next round as if having won. **2** *Golf* one or more holes remaining unplayed after the match has been decided. **3** *Cricket* a run scored from a ball that passes the batsman without being hit. [BY as *noun*]

bye² *interjection* = GOODBYE. [abbreviation]

bye- *prefix var.* of BY-.

bye-bye¹ *interjection informal* = GOODBYE. [childish corruption]

bye-bye² *noun* (also **bye-byes**) (a child's word for) sleep. [Middle English, from the sound used in lullabies]

by-election *noun Cdn, Brit., Austral.,* & *NZ* an election held in a single constituency to fill a vacancy arising during a government's term of office.

Byelo·rus·sia /ˌbjelɒˈrʌʃə/ a former name of Belarus.
  □ **Byelo·rus·sian** *noun* & *adjective*

by-form *noun* a secondary form of a word etc.; a variant.

by·gone ● *attributive adjective* past, antiquated (*bygone years*). ● *noun* (in *pl.*) past events, esp. offences. □ **let bygones be bygones** forgive and forget.

by·law *noun* (also *Brit.* **bye-law**) **1** a rule made by a company or society for its members. **2** *Cdn, Brit.,* & *Austral.* a law made by a body subordinate to a legislature, esp. a municipal government. [Middle English prob. from obsolete *byrlaw* local custom (Old Norse *bȳjar* genitive sing. of *bȳr* town, but assoc. with BY)]

by·line *noun* **1** a line in a newspaper or magazine naming the writer of an article. **2** *Soccer* the goal line or touchline.

Bylot Island /ˈbailət/ an island situated off the northern coast of Baffin Island. Currently uninhabited, it is the site of a bird sanctuary. [R. *Bylot*, explorer of the Northwest Passage *fl.* 1610–16]

by·name *noun* a secondary name; a nickname.

Byng, Jul·ian Hed·worth George, Vis·count Byng of Vimy (1862–1935), English cavalry officer. Appointed to lead the Canadian Corps in May 1916, he directed the attack on Vimy Ridge. Serving as Governor General of Canada 1921–6, he refused Prime Minister King's request to dissolve parliament in 1926, naming Meighen as prime minister instead.

BYO *abbreviation informal* (also **BYOB**) bring your own (bottle of liquor), e.g. to a social gathering (*the party was BYO*).

by·pass ● *noun* **1** a road passing around a town or its centre to provide an alternative route for through traffic. **2** a secondary channel

or pipe etc. to allow a flow when the main one is closed or blocked. **3** *Med.* **a** an alternative passage for diverting blood or other fluids around an obstruction or away from a particular area during surgery. **b** = CORONARY BYPASS. ● *transitive verb* **1** avoid; go around. **2** provide with a bypass.

by·play *noun* a secondary action or sequence of events, esp. in a play.

by-product *noun* **1** an incidental or secondary product made in the manufacture of something else. **2** a secondary result.

Byrd /bɜrd/ **1 Rich·ard Eve·lyn** (1888–1957), US naval officer, aviator, and explorer. He made the first flight over the South Pole in 1929 and led four Antarctic survey expeditions from 1928 to 1941. **2 Wil·liam** (1543–1623), English composer. Joint organist of the Chapel Royal with Tallis, he was one of the finest Tudor composers. As a Roman Catholic under the Anglican Elizabeth I, he wrote for both Churches and is most famous for his Latin masses for three, four, and five voices and his Anglican Great Service. He composed a great quantity of music for virginals in addition to more than forty consort songs.

byre /ˈbair/ *noun Brit.* a cowshed. [Old English *bȳre*: perhaps related to BOWER¹]

by·road *noun* a minor road.

Byron /ˈbairən/ **George Gor·don, 6th Baron** (1788–1824), English Romantic poet whose most famous works include *Childe Harold's Pilgrimage* (1812–18) and *Don Juan* (1819–24). Debts, licentiousness, and accusations of incest forced him to spend much of his life in exile, and he became a symbol of the melancholy and rebellious romantic hero. He died of fever while aiding the Greek struggle against the Turks.

By·ron·ic /baiˈrɒnɪk/ *adjective* **1** characteristic of Byron or his romantic poetry. **2** (of a man) handsomely dark, mysterious, or moody.

bys·sus /ˈbisəs/ *noun* (pl. **bys·sus·es** or **byssi** /-sai/) **1** *hist.* a fine textile fibre and fabric of flax. **2** a tuft of tough silky filaments by which some molluscs adhere to rocks etc. □ **bys·sal** *adjective* [Latin from Greek *bussos* fine linen fabric]

by·stand·er *noun* a person who is present but does not take part; a spectator or passive witness.

byte /bait/ *noun Computing* a group of usu. eight binary digits, often used to represent one character. [20th c.: perhaps based on BIT¹ and BITE]

by-the-book *adjective* designating a person who acts strictly by the rules.

by-the-numbers *adjective* showing no originality or creativity.

By·town the former name (until 1855) for Ottawa. [J. BY]

by·way *noun* **1** a minor road. **2** a minor activity.

by·word *noun* **1** a person or thing cited as a notable example (*is a byword for luxury*). **2** a familiar saying; a proverb.

by-your-leave *noun* a request for permission or an expression of apology for taking a liberty (*barged in here without so much as a by-your-leave*).

Byzan·tine /ˈbizən,tiːn, -tain/ ● *adjective* **1** of or relating to Byzantium. **2** (of a political situation etc.) **a** extremely complicated. **b** inflexible. **c** carried on by underhand methods. **3** (of art or architecture) of a highly decorated style developed in the Byzantine Empire. ● *noun* a citizen of Byzantium. [French *byzantin* or Latin *Byzantinus* from BYZANTIUM]

Byzantine Empire the eastern branch of the Roman Empire as it existed from the 4th–15th c. The birthplace of Orthodox Christianity, the empire was centred on the Balkans and Asia Minor and included parts of the Middle East until the 7th c. It rose to the height of its power *c.*850–1000 before its capital at Constantinople fell to the Ottomans in 1453.

Byzan·tium /bɪˈzantiəm, bai-/ an ancient Greek city, founded in the 7th c. BC, at the southern end of the Bosporus, site of the modern city of Istanbul. It was rebuilt by Constantine the Great in AD 324–30 as Constantinople.

Cc

C¹ *noun* (also **c**) (*pl.* **Cs** or **C's**) **1** the third letter of the alphabet. **2** *Music* the first note of the diatonic scale of C major (the major scale having no sharps or flats). **3** the third hypothetical person or example. **4** the third highest class or category (of academic marks etc.). **5** *Math.* (usu. **c**) the third known quantity. **6** (as a Roman numeral) 100. **7** (**c**) the speed of light in a vacuum. **8** (also ©) copyright. **9** a size of battery, having a voltage of 1.5 V.

C² *symbol Chem.* the element carbon. **2** cytosine.

C³ *abbreviation* (also **C.**) **1** Cape. **2** Conservative. **3** Celsius, Centigrade. **4** coulomb(s), capacitance. **5** *Cdn* Commons (designating bills introduced in the House of Commons).

C⁴ *noun Computing* a programming language, originally developed for the Unix operating system, combining the features of high-level and assembly languages.

c. *abbreviation* **1** century; centuries. **2** chapter. **3** cent(s). **4** cold. **5** cubic. **6** centi-. **7** cup(s).

c. *abbreviation circa*, about.

CA *abbreviation* **1** (in Canada and Scotland) = CHARTERED ACCOUNTANT. **2** California (in official postal use). **3** Canadian Alliance.

Ca *symbol Chem.* the element calcium.

Ca. *abbreviation* California.

ca. *abbreviation circa*, about.

CAA *abbreviation* **1** Canadian Automobile Association. **2** (in the UK) Civil Aviation Authority.

Caaba *var. of* KAABA.

CAAT *abbreviation* (in Canada) College of Applied Arts and Technology.

CAB *abbreviation* **1** (in the US) Civil Aeronautics Board. **2** (in the UK) Citizens' Advice Bureau.

cab¹ ● *noun* **1** a taxi. **2** the driver's compartment in a truck, train, tractor, crane, etc. **3** *hist.* a carriage kept for hire. ● *intransitive verb* travel by taxi. [abbreviation of CABRIOLET]

cab² *noun* Cabernet. [abbreviation]

ca·bal /kəˈbal/ *noun* **1** a secret intrigue or conspiracy. **2** a political clique or faction. [French *cabale* from medieval Latin *cabala*, CABBALA]

ca·bala 1 *var. of* CABBALA 1. **2** (**Cabala**) *var. of* KABBALAH.

ca·bal·lero /ˌkabəˈljeroː/ *noun* (*pl.* **-leros**) a Spanish gentleman. [Spanish: see CAVALIER]

ca·bana /kəˈbanə/ *noun N Amer.* a cabin or other shelter, esp. at a beach or swimming pool. [Spanish *cabaña* from Late Latin (as CABIN)]

ca·bane à sucre /kəˈban a ˌsuːkrə/ *noun* (*pl.* **ca·banes à sucre** *pronunc.* same) *Cdn* (*Que.*) = SUGAR SHACK. [Canadian French]

caba·ret /ˈkabəˌrei/ *noun* **1** a nightclub or restaurant, esp. one in which entertainment is provided while guests eat or drink at tables. **2** the entertainment provided. [French, = wooden structure, tavern]

cab·bage *noun* any of several cultivated varieties of *Brassica oleracea*, with a head of thick green or purple leaves eaten as a vegetable. □ **cab·bagy** *adjective* [earlier *cabache*, *-oche* from Old French (Picard) *caboche* head, Old French *caboce*, of unknown origin]

cabbage butterfly *noun* (also **cabbage white**) any white butterfly of the genus *Pieris*, whose caterpillars feed on cabbage leaves.

cabbage palm *noun* any of several palm trees with edible cabbage-like terminal buds.

cabbage roll *noun* (usu. in *pl.*) *N Amer.* a boiled cabbage leaf wrapped

around a filling of rice and usu. ground meat to form a roll and baked, usu. with tomato sauce.

cabbage rose *noun* a double garden rose, *Rosa centifolia*, with a large round compact flower.

cab·bala /kəˈbɒlə, ˈkabələ/ *noun* **1** (also **ca·bala**, **kab·bala**, **kab·balah**) mystic interpretation; any esoteric doctrine or occult lore. **2** (**Cabbala**) *var. of* KABBALAH. □ **cab·bal·ism** *noun* **cab·bal·ist** *noun* **cab·bal·is·tic** *adjective* [medieval Latin from Rabbinical Hebrew *kabbālā* 'tradition']

cab·bie *noun* (also **cabby**) (*pl.* **-bies**) *informal* a taxi driver.

caber /ˈkeibər/ *noun* a roughly trimmed tree trunk thrown in a Scottish Highland sport as a test of physical strength. [Gaelic *cabar* pole]

Cab·er·net /ˈkabərˌnei/ *noun* **1** a variety of black grape (esp. **Cabernet Franc** /frɑ̃/ or **Cabernet Sauvignon** /ˌsoːvɪˈnjɔ̃/) used in winemaking. **2** a vine on which these grow. **3** a wine made from these grapes. [French]

cab·in ● *noun* **1 a** a small shelter or house, esp. of wood. **b** *N Amer.* a summer cottage. **2** a room or compartment in an aircraft or ship for passengers or crew. **3** a driver's cab. ● *transitive verb* (**cab·ined**, **cab·in·ing**) confine in a small place, cramp. [Old French *cabane* from Provençal *cabana* from Late Latin *capanna*, *cavanna*]

cabin boy *noun* a boy employed as an attendant to a ship's officers or passengers.

cabin class *noun* the class of accommodation in a ship between first class and tourist class.

cabin crew *noun* the crew members on an airplane attending to passengers and cargo.

cabin cruiser *noun* a large yacht equipped with a cabin and living accommodation.

Cab·inda /kəˈbɪndə/ **1** an enclave of Angola at the mouth of the Congo River, separated from the rest of Angola by a wedge of Congo (formerly Zaire). **2** its capital; pop. (est. 2002) 208,900.

cab·inet /ˈkabɪnət/ *noun* **1 a** a cupboard or case with drawers, shelves, etc., for storing or displaying articles. **b** a piece of furniture housing a stereo, television set, etc. **2** (also **Cabinet**) **a** (in Canada, the UK, and other Commonwealth countries) a committee of senior ministers responsible for controlling government policy. **b** (in the US) a body of advisers to the President, composed of the heads of the executive departments of the government. **3** *archaic* a small private room. [CABIN + -ET¹, influenced by French *cabinet*]

cabinet·maker *noun* a person skilled in making furniture and light woodwork. □ **cabinet·making** *noun*

cabinet minister *noun* a member of a parliamentary cabinet.

cabinet order *noun* *Cdn* = ORDER-IN-COUNCIL.

cabinet pudding *noun* *Brit.* a steamed pudding with dried fruit.

cab·in·etry *noun* cabinets or fine woodwork collectively.

cabin fever *noun* *N Amer.* a condition characterized by lassitude, irritability, anxiety, etc. resulting from long confinement or isolation indoors, esp. during the winter.

cable ● *noun* **1** a thick rope of wire or hemp. **2** an encased group of insulated wires for transmitting electricity or electrical signals. **3** = CABLE TELEVISION. **4** = CABLEGRAM. **5 a** *Naut.* the chain of an anchor. **b** (in full **cable length**) a unit of measure, equal to one-tenth of a nautical mile (185 m) or 100 fathoms in Canadian and British use, and 120 fathoms in the US. **6** (in full **cable stitch**) a knitted stitch resembling twisted rope. **7** *Archit.* a rope-shaped ornamental moulding. ● *verb* **1 a** *transitive* transmit (a message) by cablegram. **b** *transitive* inform (a person) by cablegram. **c** *intransitive* send a cablegram. **2** *transitive* furnish or fasten with a cable or cables. **3** *transitive Archit.* furnish with cables. □ **cab·ling** *noun* [Old French *chable*, ultimately from Late Latin *capulum* halter, from Arabic *ḥabl*]

cable car *noun* **1** a small passenger car (often one of a series) suspended on an endless cable and drawn up and down a mountainside etc. by an engine at one end. **2** a vehicle drawn along a cable railway.

cable·cast *N Amer.* ● *transitive verb* broadcast (a program) on cable television. ● *noun* a program broadcast in this way. □ **cable·cast·er** *noun* [blend of CABLE + BROADCAST]

cable·gram *noun* a telegraph message sent by undersea cable etc.

cable-knit ● *adjective* (of a knitted garment) having a design of cables. ● *noun* a cable-knit garment.

cable-laid *adjective* (of rope) having three triple strands twisted together.

cable modem *noun Computing* a modem that allows users to access the Internet through their television cable.

cable railway *noun* a railway along which vehicles are drawn by an endless cable moving underneath the road.

cable television *noun* (also **cable TV**) a broadcasting system with signals transmitted and received by cable (as opposed to antenna), allowing subscribers access to a large number of channels.

cable·vision *noun* = CABLE TELEVISION. [blend]

cable·way *noun* a system for transporting goods etc. by means of a usu. elevated cable.

cabo·chon /ˈkabəˌʃɒn/ *noun* a convex gem polished but not faceted. [French, diminutive of *caboche*: see CABBAGE]

Ca·bonga, Réservoir /kaˈbōgə/ a reservoir in NW central Quebec, situated southeast of Val-d'Or. It was created in 1928–29 with the intention of regulating the headwaters of the Ottawa and Gatineau rivers. [Algonquin *kakibonga* blocked entirely by sand]

ca·boo·dle /kəˈbuːdəl/ *noun* □ **the whole (kit and) caboodle** *informal* the whole lot (of persons or things). [19th-c.: perhaps from KIT[1] + BOODLE]

ca·boose /kəˈbuːs/ *noun* **1** *N Amer.* a railway car, usu. at the end of the train, for housing the crew etc. **2** a ship's kitchen. **3** *Cdn* a portable wooden cabin, esp. one on runners which can be pulled over snow. **4** *informal* the buttocks. [Dutch *cabuse* or *combuse*, of unknown origin]

Ca·bora Bassa /kəˌbɔrə ˈbasə/ a lake on the Zambezi River in W Mozambique. Its waters are impounded by a dam and massive hydroelectric complex supplying power mainly to Maputo and South Africa.

Cabot /ˈkabət/ **1 John** (Giovanni Caboto, d. *c.*1498), Venetian explorer and navigator whose English-backed voyages were the basis of Britain's claim to Canada. On his voyage of 1497 he became the first known European to land in N America, arriving possibly in Cape Breton Island, Labrador, or Newfoundland. His second voyage in 1498 never returned, and he is believed to have perished somewhere in the NW Atlantic. **2** his son, **Sebas·tian** (*c.*1476-1557), a cartographer who may have accompanied the elder Cabot in 1497 and later charted parts of the S American mainland under Spanish patronage.

cabo·tage /ˈkabəˌtɒʒ, -tədʒ/ *noun* **1** *Naut.* coastal navigation and trade. **2** esp. *Aviation* the restrictions imposed by a country on (esp. air) traffic operation within its territory. **3** esp. *Aviation* the transportation of passengers by a foreign carrier between two points within domestic airspace. [French from *caboter* to coast, perhaps from Spanish *cabo* CAPE[2]]

Cabot Strait a strait between N Cape Breton Island and SW Newfoundland, connecting the Atlantic Ocean and the Gulf of St. Lawrence. [J. CABOT]

Cabot Trail a 300-km highway through N Cape Breton Island, famous for its mountainous and coastal scenery. [J. CABOT]

cab·ri·ole /ˈkabriˌoːl/ *noun* **1** a kind of ornamental and curved leg characteristic of 18th-c. furniture. **2** a springing dance step in which one leg is extended and the other brought up to it. [French from *cabrioler*, *caprioler* from Italian *capriolare* to leap in the air; from the resemblance to a leaping animal's foreleg: see CAPRIOLE]

cab·ri·o·let /ˌkabriɔːˈlei/ *noun* **1** a light two-wheeled carriage with a hood, drawn by one horse. **2** an automobile with a folding top. [French from *cabriole* goat's leap (compare CAPRIOLE), applied to its motion]

caca *noun slang* **1** excrement. **2** nonsense. [Spanish]

ca·canny /kaˈkani/ *noun Brit.* **1** a trade union policy of limiting workers' output; a slowdown. **2** extreme caution. [Scots, = proceed warily: see CALL *verb* 18, CANNY]

ca·cao /kəˈkaoː, -ˈkeioː/ *noun* (*pl.* **-caos**) **1** a seed pod from which cocoa and chocolate are made. **2** a small widely cultivated evergreen tree, *Theobroma cacao*, bearing these. [Spanish from Nahuatl *cacauatl* (*uatl* tree)]

caccia·tore /ˌkatʃəˈtɔri/ *adjective* (placed after noun) cooked with tomatoes, mushrooms, and herbs (*chicken cacciatore*). [Italian, lit. 'hunter']

ca·chaca /kəˈʃaːkə/ *noun* a Brazilian white rum made from sugar cane. [Brazilian Portuguese, from Portuguese *cacaça* (white) rum]

cacha·lot /ˈkaʃəˌlɒt, -ˌloːt/ *noun* a sperm whale. [French from Spanish & Portuguese *cachalote*, of unknown origin]

cache /kaʃ/ ● *noun* **1** a hiding place. **2** *Cdn (North)* a place, structure, or device used for storing fuel, food, supplies, equipment, etc. **3** the contents of a cache. **4** an auxiliary computer memory from which high-speed retrieval is possible. ● *transitive verb* (**cached**, **cach·ing**) put in a cache. [French from *cacher* to hide]

ca·chec·tic /kəˈkektɪk/ *adjective* relating to or having the symptoms of cachexia.

cache·pot /ˈkaʃpɔː, -pɒt/ *noun* an ornamental holder for a flower pot. [French *cacher* hide + *pot* pot]

ca·chet /kaˈʃei, ˈkaʃei/ *noun* **1** a distinguishing mark or seal. **2** prestige. **3** *Med.* a flat capsule enclosing a dose of unpleasant-tasting medicine. [French from *cacher* press, ultimately from Latin *coactare* constrain]

ca·chex·ia /kəˈkeksiə/ *noun* (also **ca·chexy** /-ksi/) a condition of weakness of body or mind associated with chronic disease. [French *cachexie* or Late Latin *cachexia* from Greek *kakhexia* from *kakos* bad + *hexis* habit]

ca·chu·cha /kəˈtʃuːtʃə/ *noun* a lively Spanish solo dance with castanets. [Spanish]

ca·cique /kəˈsiːk/ *noun* **1** an Aboriginal chief in the W Indies or S America. **2** a political boss in Spain or Latin America. [Spanish, of Carib origin]

cack-handed *adjective Brit. informal* **1** awkward, clumsy. **2** left-handed. □ **cack-handed·ly** *adverb* **cack-handed·ness** *noun* [dial. *cack* excrement]

cackle ● *noun* **1** a clucking sound as of a hen or a goose. **2** a loud silly laugh. **3** noisy inconsequential talk. ● *verb* **1** *intransitive* emit a cackle. **2** *intransitive* talk noisily and inconsequentially. **3** *transitive* utter or express with a cackle. □ **cut the cackle** esp. *Brit. informal* stop talking aimlessly and come to the point. [prob. from Middle Low German, Middle Dutch *kākelen* (imitative)]

caco·mistle /ˈkakəˌmɪsəl/ *noun* any raccoon-like animal of several species of the genus *Bassariscus*, native to Central America, having a black and white ringed tail. [Latin American Spanish *cacomixtle* from Nahuatl *tlacomiztli*]

cac·oph·ony /kəˈkɒfəni/ *noun* (*pl.* **-onies**) **1** a harsh discordant mixture of sound. **2** dissonance; discord. □ **cac·o·phon·ic** /ˌkakəˈfɒnɪk/ *adjective* **cac·oph·on·ous** *adjective* [French *cacophonie* from Greek *kakophōnia* from *kakophōnos* from *kakos* bad + *phōnē* sound]

cac·ta·ceous /kakˈteiʃəs/ *adjective* of or pertaining to the family Cactaceae.

cac·tus *noun* (*pl.* **cacti** or **cac·tus·es**) **1** any succulent plant of the family Cactaceae, found in arid regions, having a thick fleshy stem, usu. spines but no leaves, and brilliantly coloured flowers. **2** any of various other succulent or spiny plants. [Latin from Greek *kaktos* cardoon]

ca·cu·min·al /kaˈkjuːmɪnəl/ *adjective Phonetics* = RETROFLEX 1. [Latin *cacuminare* make pointed, from *cacumen -minis* summit, top]

CAD *abbreviation* **1** computer-aided design. **2** Canadian dollars.

cad *noun* a person (esp. a man) who behaves dishonourably. □ **cad·dish** *adjective* **cad·dish·ly** *adverb* **cad·dish·ness** *noun* [abbreviation of CADDY[2] in sense 'odd-job man']

cad·as·tral /kəˈdastrəl/ *adjective* of or showing the extent, value, and ownership of land, esp. for taxation. [French from *cadastre* 'register of property' via Provençal *cadastro* from Italian *catast(r)o* (earlier *catastico*), from late Greek *katastikhon* 'list, register', from *kata stikhon* 'line by line']

cad·av·er /kəˈdavər/ *noun* a corpse, esp. used for dissection. □ **cad·av·er·ic** *adjective* [Latin from *cadere* fall]

cad·av·er·ous /kəˈdavrəs/ *adjective* **1** corpse-like. **2** deathly pale or gaunt. [Latin *cadaverosus* (as CADAVER)]

Cad·boro·saur·us /ˌkadbərəˈsɔrəs/ *Cdn* a large serpentine sea creature supposedly inhabiting the waters off Victoria, BC. [*Cadboro Bay* + Greek *sauros* lizard]

Cad·bury /ˈkadbəri/ **George** (1839–1922), English manufacturer, Quaker, and social reformer who, with his brother Richard (1835–99), built the Cadbury Brothers chocolate factory and became known for greatly improving the working conditions and housing of his employees.

CAD/CAM *abbreviation* computer-aided design and computer-aided manufacturing.

cad·die *var. of* CADDY².

cad·dis fly *noun* any small hairy-winged nocturnal insect of the order Trichoptera, living near water. [17th c.: origin unknown]

caddis·worm *noun* (also **cad·dis**) a larva of the caddis fly, living in water and making protective cylindrical cases from bits of sand, wood, leaves, etc.

Caddo /ˈkado/ ● *noun* (*pl.* same or **-dos**) **1** a member of an Aboriginal people once inhabiting present-day Louisiana and Arkansas but now living mostly in Oklahoma. **2** the Caddoan language of this people. ● *adjective* of or relating to this people or their language or culture. [Caddo *Kãdohãdãcho* 'Caddo proper, real Caddo']

Cad·do·an /ˈkadoən/ ● *noun* a family of N American Aboriginal languages related to Siouan and spoken by indigenous peoples of the central US. ● *adjective* of or relating to the Caddo or their language.

Caddy *Cdn informal* = CADBOROSAURUS.

caddy¹ *noun* (*pl.* **-dies**) **1** a small container, sometimes with subdivisions, for holding small items. **2** (in full **tea caddy**) a small decorative container for tea leaves. [earlier *catty* weight of 1¹/₃ lb., from Malay *kãti*]

caddy² (also **cad·die**) ● *noun* (*pl.* **-dies**) a person who assists a golfer by carrying clubs etc. ● *intransitive verb* (**cad·dies, cad·died, caddy·ing**) act as a caddy. [originally Scots from French CADET]

ca·dence /ˈkeidəns/ *noun* **1** a fall in pitch of the voice, esp. at the end of a phrase or sentence. **2** intonation, tonal inflection. **3** *Music* the resolution at the end of a musical phrase. **4** rhythm; the measure or beat of sound or movement. □ **ca·denced** *adjective* [Old French from Italian *cadenza*, ultimately from Latin *cadere* fall]

ca·den·tial /kəˈdenʃəl/ *adjective* of a cadence or cadenza.

ca·den·za /kəˈdenzə/ *noun Music* a virtuosic passage for a solo voice or instrument, usu. near the close of an aria or a concerto movement, sometimes improvised. [Italian: see CADENCE]

ca·det /kəˈdet/ *noun* **1 a** a member of a corps receiving elementary military or police training, esp. for the rank of an officer. **b** (in Canada) a member of a paramilitary organization for young people aged 12 to 18, run by the reserve forces of the army, navy, or air force. **c** (in the UK) a member of a similar organization. **2** an apprentice. **3** a younger son. □ **cadet·ship** *noun* [French from Gascon dial. *capdet*, ultimately from Latin *caput* head]

cadge *verb* **1** *transitive* get or seek by begging or scrounging. **2** *intransitive* beg or scrounge. □ **cadg·er** *noun* [19th c.: origin unknown]

cadi *var. of* QADI.

Cad·il·lac *noun* something or someone of high quality, desirable, expensive, or otherwise comparable to a Cadillac luxury car (*the Cadillac of health care services*). [proprietary name of a luxury car]

Cadiz /kəˈdɪz/ a city and port on the coast of SW Spain; pop. (est. 2001) 137,971.

cad·mium *noun* a soft bluish-white metallic element occurring naturally with zinc ores, and used in the manufacture of solders and in electroplating. Symbol: **Cd**; at. no.: 48. [obsolete *cadmia* calamine, from Latin *cadmia* from Greek *kadm(e)ia* (*gē*) Cadmean (earth), from CADMUS + -IUM]

cadmium yellow *noun* an intense yellow pigment containing cadmium sulphide and used in paints etc.

Cad·mus *Gk Legend* the brother of Europa who killed a dragon and sowed its teeth, from which grew a harvest of armed soldiers. With five of these men he founded Thebes; he is also reputed to have introduced the alphabet into Greece.

cadre /ˈkadrə, ˈkadrei, ˈkɒd-/ *noun* **1** a small, usu. exclusive group with a common objective, occupation, etc. **2 a** a group of activists in a communist or revolutionary party. **b** a member of such a group. **3** a permanent establishment of trained soldiers, workers, etc. that can be enlarged when necessary. [French from Italian *quadro* from Latin *quadrus* square]

ca·du·ceus /kəˈduːsiəs, kəˈdjuː-, -ʃiəs, -ʃəs/ *noun* (*pl.* **ca·ducei** /-si,ai/) **1** *Gk & Rom. Myth* a staff with a winged top and two serpents coiled around it, esp. as carried by Hermes or Mercury. **2** this staff as a

symbol of the medical profession. [Latin from Doric Greek *karuk(e)ion* from *kērux* herald]

ca·du·cous /kəˈduːkəs, kəˈdjuː-/ *adjective Bot. & Zool.* (of organs and parts) easily detached or shed at an early stage, after serving their purpose. [Latin *caducus* falling, from *cadere* fall]

cae·cil·ian /siːˈsɪliən/ *noun* (also **coe·cil·ian**) any burrowing wormlike amphibian of the order Gymnophiona, having poorly developed eyes and no limbs. [Latin *caecilia* kind of lizard]

cae·cum *var. of* CECUM.

Cæd·mon /ˈkadmən/ (7th c.), English poet and monk. The only authentic fragment of his work is his song in praise of creation, quoted by Bede.

Caen /kɑ̃/ an industrial city and river port in Normandy in N France, on the Orne River, capital of the region of Basse-Normandie; pop. (1999) 113,987. It is the burial place of William the Conqueror. The city was the scene of fierce fighting between the Germans and the Allies (esp. British and Canadian) in June and July 1944.

Caeno·zoic *var. of* CENOZOIC.

Caer·nar·fon /kərˈnɑrvən/ (also **Caer·nar·von**) a town in NW Wales on the shore of the Menai Strait, the administrative centre of Gwynedd; pop. (est. 2002) 9,600. Its 13th-c. castle was the birthplace of Edward II.

Caerns. *abbreviation* Caernarvonshire (a former county in Wales).

Caer·philly /kərˈfɪli, kɑr-/ *noun* a kind of mild white cheese. [*Caerphilly* in S Wales where it was originally made]

Caesar¹ /ˈsiːzər/ **(Gaius) Jul·ius** (100–44 BC), Roman general and leader. He established the first triumvirate with Pompey and Crassus (60), conquered Gaul (58–51), invaded Britain (55–54), and during a civil war defeated Pompey at Pharsalus (48). After making himself dictator of the Roman Empire (46), he initiated a series of reforms, including the introduction of the Julian calendar; he was assassinated in a conspiracy led by Brutus and Cassius.

Caesar² /ˈsiːzər/ *noun* **1** the title of the Roman emperors, esp. from Augustus to Hadrian. **2** an autocrat. **3** *N Amer.* = CAESAR SALAD. **4** *Cdn* = BLOODY CAESAR. [Latin, family name of J. CAESAR¹]

Caesa·rea /ˌsiːzəˈriːə/ an ancient port on the Mediterranean coast of Israel. Founded in 22 BC by Herod the Great on the site of a Phoenician harbour, it became one of the principal cities of Roman Palestine. It later declined as its harbour silted up. [Augustus *Caesar*: see AUGUSTUS]

Caes·ar·ean /səˈzeriən/ (also **Caes·ar·ian, Ces-**) ● *adjective* **1** of Julius Caesar or the Caesars. **2** (of a birth) effected by Caesarean section. ● *noun* a Caesarean section. [Latin *Caesarianus*]

Caesarean section *noun* an operation for delivering a child by cutting through the wall of the abdomen and uterus. [J. CAESAR¹ supposedly having been born this way]

Caesa·rea Phil·ip·pi /ˈfɪlɪ,pai, fɪˈlɪpai/ a city in ancient Palestine, on the site of the present-day village of Baniyas in the Golan Heights. It was the scene of a Hellenistic shrine to the god Pan, and then of a temple built towards the end of the 1st c. BC by Herod the Great. [Augustus *Caesar*: see AUGUSTUS]

Caesar salad *noun* a salad of romaine lettuce tossed usu. with Parmesan cheese, garlic croutons, bacon bits, and a dressing of oil, lemon juice, raw egg, and anchovies. [*Caesar* Cardini, Mexican restaurateur who created it in 1924]

caes·ious /ˈsiːziəs/ *adjective Bot.* bluish or greyish green. [Latin *caesius*]

caes·ium *var. of* CESIUM.

caes·ura /sɪˈzjʊrə/ *noun* (*pl.* **caes·uras**) *Prosody* **1** (in Greek and Latin verse) a break between words within a metrical foot. **2** (in modern verse) a pause near the middle of a line. □ **caes·ur·al** *adjective* [Latin from *caedere caes-* cut]

CAF *abbreviation* **1** CANADIAN ARMED FORCES. **2** cost and freight.

caf *noun* (also **caff**) *informal* **1** *Cdn* a cafeteria. **2** *Brit.* a café. [abbreviation]

ca·fard /kaˈfɑr/ *noun* melancholia. [French, lit. 'cockroach', 'hypocrite']

café /kaˈfei/ *noun* **1** a restaurant serving coffee and other beverages and light meals. **2** *N Amer.* a bar or nightclub. [French, = coffee, coffee house]

café au lait /kaˈfei oː ˈlei/ *noun* **1** strong coffee with a roughly equal portion of hot milk, usu. served in a large mug or bowl. **2** the colour of this. [French]

café curtain *noun* a short curtain, usu. of lightweight fabric, covering the bottom half of a window, usu. with a matching ruffle across the top of the window.

café noir /ˈnwar/ *noun* strong black coffee. [French]

Vowels: a *cat* ɑ *arm* e *bed* ɜr *her* ɜː *deux* ə *ago* ɪ *sit* i *cosy* iː *feed* ɒ *hot* ɔ *pore* oː *no* ʌ *run* ʊ *put*

café society *noun* the regular patrons of fashionable restaurants and nightclubs. [French]

cafe·teria /ˌkafəˈtiːriə/ *noun* **1** a restaurant in which customers collect their meals on trays at a counter and usu. pay before sitting down to eat. **2** a lunch room in a school, office, etc. [Latin American Spanish *cafetería* coffee shop]

cafe·tor·ium /ˌkafəˈtɔriəm/ *noun N Amer.* a large room serving as both a cafeteria and an auditorium, esp. in a school. [blend of CAFETERIA + AUDITORIUM]

caff *var. of* CAF.

caf·fein·at·ed /ˈkafɪneitəd/ *adjective* **1** (of a beverage) containing caffeine. **2** *informal* (of a person) energetic or frenetic from or as from having ingested much caffeine.

caf·feine /kaˈfiːn/ *noun* an alkaloid drug with stimulant action found in coffee, tea, chocolate, cola beverages, etc. [French *caféine* from *café* coffee]

caffe latte /ˈkafei ˌlatei/ *noun* espresso coffee with hot milk. [Italian]

caf·tan /ˈkaftan/ *noun* (also **kaf·tan**) **1** an ankle-length tunic, usu. belted at the waist, worn by men in E Europe and the Middle East. **2 a** a woman's long loose dress. **b** a loose shirt or top. [Turkish *kaftān*, partly through French *cafetan*]

Caga·yan Islands /ˌkɒɡəˈjɒn/ a group of seven small islands in the Sulu Sea in the W Philippines.

Cage, John (1912–1992), US composer. A student of Schoenberg, he is best known for his innovative and aleatory compositions such as *Music for Changes* (for piano, 1951), which was composed according to decisions made by tossing a coin, and the notorious *4′ 33″* (1952), in which the performer remains silent for four minutes and thirty-three seconds.

cage ● *noun* **1** a structure of bars, wires, wood, etc. used as a place of confinement for birds or animals. **2** any similar framework, esp.: **a** an enclosed platform used as an elevator, esp. in a mine. **b** a protective structure of strong metal bars built into the body of an automobile. **c** a barred enclosure for a teller, formerly found in banks. **3** a system of netting or mesh strung around a metal framework, esp.: **a** a hockey net. **b** = BATTING CAGE. **4** a wire face mask attached to a helmet, e.g. of a baseball catcher or hockey goaltender. **5** *informal* a jail or prison camp. ● *transitive verb* place or keep in a cage. [Old French from Latin *cavea*]

cage bird *noun* any bird of a type popularly kept in a cage as a pet, e.g. a budgie.

cager *noun N Amer. slang* a basketball player.

cagey *adjective* (also **cagy**) (**cagier, cagiest**) *informal* cautious and uncommunicative; wary. □ **cagily** *adverb* **cagi·ness** *noun* (also **cagey·ness**) [20th-c.: origin unknown]

Ca·glia·ri /ˈkaljəri/ the capital of Sardinia, a port on the south coast; pop. (2001) 158,351.

Cag·ney, James (1899–1986), US film actor whose roles often included those of aggressive and arrogant criminals in films such as *G-Men* (1935) and *Angels With Dirty Faces* (1938).

ca·goule /kəˈɡuːl/ *noun* a light hooded waterproof garment pulled over the head and worn in mountaineering etc. [French, literally 'cowl']

ca·hoots /kəˈhuːts/ *plural noun* □ **in cahoots** (often foll. by *with*) *slang* in collusion. [19th c.: origin uncertain]

CAI *abbreviation* computer-assisted (or -aided) instruction.

cai·man /ˈkeimən/ *noun* (also **cay·man**) any of various Central and S American alligator-like reptiles, esp. of the genus *Caiman*. [Spanish & Portuguese *caiman*, from Carib *acayuman*]

Cain in the Bible, the eldest son of Adam. He murdered his brother Abel (Gen. 4:1–16). □ **raise Cain** *informal* make a disturbance; create trouble.

Caine, Mi·chael (born Maurice Micklewhite) (b.1933), English actor. He first gained fame as an anti-heroic spy in the film *The Ipcress File* (1965), and *Alfie* (1966) established his reputation in laconic cockney parts; his other films include *Educating Rita* (1983) and *Hannah and Her Sisters* (1986), for which he won an Oscar.

-caine *suffix* forming nouns denoting drugs, esp. ones with anaesthetic properties (*Novocaine*). [from COCAINE]

Caino·zoic *var. of* CENOZOIC.

cai·pi·rinha /ˌkɒipiˈrɪnjə/ *noun* a Brazilian cocktail made with cachaca, lime or lemon juice, sugar, and crushed ice. [Brazilian Portuguese, from *caipira* yokel]

ca·ique /kaiˈiːk/ *noun* **1** a light rowboat or skiff used on the Bosporus. **2** an eastern Mediterranean sailing ship. [French from Italian *caicco* from Turkish *kayɪk*]

cairn *noun* **1** a mound of rough stones as a monument or landmark. **2** (in full **cairn terrier**) a small breed of terrier with short legs, a longish body, and a shaggy coat (perhaps so called from its being used to hunt among cairns). [Gaelic *carn*]

cairn·gorm /ˈkɛrnɡɔrm/ *noun* a yellow or smoky semi-precious form of quartz. [CAIRNGORM MOUNTAINS, where it was first found]

Cairn·gorm Mountains (also **Cairn·gorms**) a mountain range in N Scotland. Its highest peak, Ben Macdhui (1 309 m; 4,296 ft.) is the second highest mountain in the British Isles. [Gaelic *carn gorm* blue cairn]

Cairo /ˈkairoː/ the capital of Egypt, a port on the Nile near the head of its delta; pop. (est. 2002) 15,546,100.

caisse popu·laire /ˌkes pɒpjuˈler/ *noun Cdn* (in Quebec and other francophone communities) a co-operative financial institution similar to a credit union. [French]

cais·son /ˈkeisɒn, ˈkeisən/ *noun* **1** a watertight chamber in which underwater construction work can be done. **2** a floating vessel used as a floodgate in docks. **3** a wagon or chest for carrying ammunition. [French (from Italian *cassone*) assimilated to *caisse* CASE²]

caisson disease *noun* = DECOMPRESSION SICKNESS.

Caith·ness /keiθˈnes/ a former county in the extreme northeast of Scotland. It became part of Highland region in 1975.

cai·tiff /ˈkeitɪf/ *archaic* ● *noun* a base or despicable person; a coward. ● *adjective* base, despicable, cowardly. [Old French *caitif, chaitif* ultimately from Latin *captivus* CAPTIVE]

Caius *var. of* GAIUS.

ca·jole /kəˈdʒoːl/ *verb* (often foll. by *into*) **1** *transitive* persuade by flattery, deceit, etc. **2** *intransitive* use cajolery. □ **ca·jol·ery** *noun* [French *cajoler*]

Cajun /ˈkeidʒən/ ● *noun* **1** a descendant of the French-speaking settlers who were expelled from Acadia in the mid-18th c., living primarily in S Louisiana. **2** the French patois of the Cajuns. ● *adjective* **1** of or relating to the Cajuns or their language. **2** designating a type of cooking originating amongst Cajuns, characterized esp. by the use of strong seasonings and often blackened fish or meat (*Cajun chicken*). [alteration of ACADIAN]

cake ● *noun* **1** a baked sweet food usu. containing flour, eggs, and sugar, and often containing fat and leavening. **2** any of several other foods in a flat round shape (*fish cake*). **3** a flattish compact mass (*a cake of soap*). **4** *Scot. & Northern England* a thin bread made from oats. ● *verb* **1** *transitive & intransitive* form into a compact mass. **2** *transitive* (usu. foll. by *with*) cover (with a hard or sticky mass) (*boots caked with mud*). □ **cakes and ale** earthly pleasures, merrymaking. **have one's cake and eat it** (**too**) *informal* enjoy both of two mutually exclusive alternatives. **a piece of cake** *informal* something easily achieved. **take the cake** *see* TAKE. □ **cakey** *adjective* [Old Norse *kaka*]

cake doughnut *noun N Amer.* a doughnut made from a cake-like batter rather than from a yeast-leavened dough.

cake flour *noun* (also **cake and pastry flour**) *N Amer.* a flour made from soft wheat, containing more starch and less gluten than all-purpose flour or bread flour.

cake·walk ● *noun* **1 a** *hist.* a competition in promenade dancing, originally organized by American blacks, having a cake as a prize. **b** a high-stepping dance developed from this. **2** *informal* an easy task. ● *intransitive verb* perform a cakewalk.

CAL *abbreviation* computer-assisted learning.

Cal. *abbreviation* California.

cal (often in *combination* or *attributive*) large calorie(s) (*see* CALORIE 1) (*low-cal*).

Cala·bar /ˈkaləˌbar/ a seaport in Nigeria; pop. (est. 2002) 431,200.

Calabar bean *noun* a poisonous seed of the tropical African climbing plant *Physostigma venenosum*, containing alkaloids used in medicine. [CALABAR]

cala·bash /ˈkaləˌbaʃ/ *noun* **1 a** an evergreen tree, *Crescentia cujete*, native to tropical America, bearing fruit in the form of large gourds. **b** a gourd from this tree. **2** the shell of this or a similar gourd used as a vessel for water, to make a tobacco pipe, etc. [French *calebasse* from Spanish *calabaza* perhaps from Persian *karbuz* melon]

cala·bogus *Cdn var. of* CALLIBOGUS.

cala·boose /ˈkaləˌbuːs/ *noun US slang* a jail or prison. [Louisiana French *calabouse* from Spanish *calabozo* dungeon]

cala·brese /ˌkaləˈbreizei/ *noun* **1** esp. *Cdn* a round white crusty Italian bread. **2** *Brit.* a large variety of broccoli. [Italian, = Calabrian]

Ca·lab·ria /kəˈlabriə/ a region of SW Italy, forming the 'toe' of the Italian peninsula; capital, Reggio di Calabria. The name was formerly applied by the Byzantines to the eastern promontory forming the 'heel', but was transferred to the 'toe' in the west when the area was seized by the Lombards AD *c.*700. □ **Ca·la·brian** *adjective & noun*

ca·la·di·um /kə'leidiəm/ *noun* any of several plants of the tropical American genus *Caladium*, of the arum family, having starchy tubers and colourful leaves. [modern Latin from Malay *keladi* + -IUM]

Calais /ka'lei/ a ferry port in N France; pop. (1999) 77,333. It was an English possession from 1347 to 1558.

cala·man·der /'kalə,mandər/ *noun* a fine-grained red-brown ebony streaked with black, from the Asian tree *Diospyros quaesita*, used in furniture. [19th c.: origin unknown: perhaps related to Sinhalese word for the tree *kalu-madiriya*]

cala·mari /kalə'mɑri/ *noun* the flesh of the squid when used as food. [Italian (as CALAMARY)]

cala·mary /'kaləmɛri/ *noun* (*pl.* **-ies**) a squid with a long, tapering, horny, internal shell, esp. one of the common genus *Loligo*. [medieval Latin *calamarium* pen case, from Latin *calamus* pen (with reference to its inky secretion)]

cala·mata *var. of* KALAMATA.

cala·mine /'kalə,main/ *noun* **1** a pink powder consisting of zinc carbonate and a small quantity of ferric oxide used as a lotion or ointment, e.g. for sunburn, insect bites, or rashes. **2** an ore of zinc, esp. zinc carbonate. [French from medieval Latin *calamina* alteration of Latin *cadmia*: see CADMIUM]

cala·mint /'kaləmint/ *noun* any aromatic herb or shrub of the genus *Calamintha* (now usu. included in *Clinopodium* or *Satureja*) of the mint family, with purple, lilac, or white flowers. [Old French *calament* from medieval Latin *calamentum* from Late Latin *calaminthe* from Greek *kalaminthē*]

ca·lam·ity /kə'lamiti/ *noun* (*pl.* **-ities**) **1** a disaster, a great misfortune. **2 a** adversity. **b** deep distress. □ **ca·lami·tous** *adjective* **ca·lami·tous·ly** *adverb* [French *calamité* from Latin *calamitas -tatis*]

Calamity Jane /kə'lamiti 'dʒein/ (born Martha Jane Cannary) (*c.*1852–1903), US frontierswoman. A colourful character noted for her skill at shooting and riding, she also became known for her wild behaviour and heavy drinking.

cala·mon·din /kalə'mɒndin/ *noun* **1** a small hybrid citrus tree frequently grown as a houseplant. **2** the acidic fruit of this tree, resembling a small tangerine. [Tagalog *kalamunding*]

cala·mus *noun* (in full **sweet calamus**) = SWEET FLAG. [Greek *kalamos* reed]

ca·lan·do /ka'lando:/ *adverb Music* gradually decreasing in speed and volume. [Italian, = slackening]

ca·lash /kə'laʃ/ *noun hist.* **1 a** a light low-wheeled carriage with a removable folding hood. **b** the folding hood itself. **2** a large and folding hooped hood worn by women in the 18th c. [see CALÈCHE]

cala·thea /kalə'θi:ə/ *noun* a plant of the genus *Calathea*, with colourful, patterned leaves, often grown as a houseplant. [from Latin *calathus* 'flower-shaped basket']

calc- /kalk/ *combining form* lime or calcium. [German *Kalk* from Latin CALX]

cal·ca·neus /kal'keiniəs/ *noun* (also **cal·ca·neum** /-niəm/) (*pl.* **cal·ca·nei** /-niai/ or **cal·ca·nea** /-niə/) the bone forming the heel. [Latin]

cal·car·eous /kal'kɛriəs/ *adjective* of or containing calcium carbonate; chalky. [Latin *calcarius* (as CALX)]

cal·ceo·laria /kalsiə'lɛriə/ *noun* any plant of the genus *Calceolaria*, native to Central and S America, with slipper-shaped flowers. *Also called* SLIPPERWORT. [modern Latin from Latin *calceolus* diminutive of *calceus* shoe + -*aria* fem. = -ARY[1]]

cal·ceo·late /'kalsiə,leit/ *adjective Bot.* slipper-shaped.

cal·ces *pl. of* CALX.

cal·cif·erol /kal'sifə,rɒl/ *noun* one of the D vitamins, routinely added to dairy products, essential for the deposition of calcium in bones. *Also called* VITAMIN D$_2$. [CALCIFEROUS + -OL[1]]

cal·cif·er·ous /kal'sifərəs/ *adjective* yielding calcium salts, esp. calcium carbonate. [Latin CALX lime + -FEROUS]

cal·ci·fy /'kalsə,fai/ *transitive & intransitive verb* (**-fies**, **-fied**) **1** harden or become hardened by deposition of calcium salts; petrify. **2** convert or be converted to calcium carbonate. **3** make or become inflexible or rigid. □ **cal·ci·fi·ca·tion** *noun*

cal·cine /'kalsain, -sin/ *verb* **1** *transitive* **a** reduce, oxidize, or desiccate by strong heat. **b** burn to ashes; consume by fire; roast. **c** reduce to calcium oxide by roasting or burning. **2** *intransitive* undergo any of these.

cal·cin·a·tion *noun* [Old French *calciner* or medieval Latin *calcinare* from Late Latin *calcina* lime, from Latin CALX]

cal·cite /'kalsait/ *noun* natural crystalline calcium carbonate. [German *Calcit* from Latin CALX lime]

cal·ci·tonin /,kalsi'tonin/ *noun* a polypeptide hormone secreted by the thyroid, having the effect of lowering blood calcium. [CALC- + TONIC + -IN]

cal·cium /'kalsiəm/ *noun* a soft greyish-white metallic element of the alkaline-earth group occurring naturally in limestone, chalk, etc., and in animal bones and teeth, and whose ions and salts are essential to life. Symbol: **Ca**; at. no.: 20. [Latin CALX lime + -IUM]

calcium carbide *noun* a greyish-black solid used in the production of acetylene. Chem. formula: CaC_2.

calcium carbonate *noun* a white insoluble solid occurring naturally as chalk, limestone, marble, and calcite, and used in the manufacture of lime and cement. Chem. formula: $CaCO_3$.

calcium channel blocker *noun* any of a class of drugs that inhibit the uptake of calcium by smooth muscle and myocardial cells, thus reducing the strength of muscular contractions, and are used in the management of angina and high blood pressure.

calcium hydroxide *noun* a white crystalline powder used in the manufacture of plaster and cement; slaked lime. Chem. formula: $Ca(OH)_2$.

calcium oxide *noun* = LIME[1] *noun* 1.

calcium phosphate *noun* a white insoluble powder, the main constituent of animal bones and used as a fertilizer and food additive.

calcium sulphate *noun* a white crystalline solid occurring as anhydrite and gypsum. Chem. formula: $CaSO_4$.

cal·crete /'kalkri:t/ *noun Geol.* a conglomerate formed by the cementation of sand and gravel with calcium carbonate. [Latin *calc* lime + concrete]

calc·spar *noun* = CALCITE. [CALC- + SPAR[3]]

cal·cul·able /'kalkjʊləbəl/ *adjective* able to be calculated or estimated. □ **cal·cul·abil·ity** *noun* **cal·cul·ably** *adverb*

cal·cu·late /'kalkjʊ,leit/ *verb* **1** *transitive* ascertain or determine by using mathematics or one's judgment; estimate. **2** *transitive* intend or design for a particular purpose (*his speech was calculated to stir up the crowd*). **3** *intransitive* (foll. by *on*) rely or depend on; make an essential part of one's reckoning (*calculated on a quick response*). □ **cal·cu·la·tive** /-lətiv/ *adjective* [Late Latin *calculare* (as CALCULUS)]

cal·cu·lat·ed /'kalkjʊ,leitəd/ *adjective* **1** (of an action) done with awareness of the likely consequences (*a calculated risk*). **2** (foll. by *to* + infin.) designed or suitable; intended. □ **cal·cu·lat·ed·ly** *adverb*

cal·cu·lat·ing /'kalkjʊ,leitiŋ/ *adjective* (of a person) shrewd, scheming. □ **cal·cu·lat·ing·ly** *adverb*

cal·cu·la·tion /,kalkjʊ'leiʃən/ *noun* **1** the act or process of calculating. **2** a result obtained by calculating. **3** a reckoning or forecast.

cal·cu·la·tor /'kalkjʊ,leitər/ *noun* **1** a device (esp. a small electronic one) used for making mathematical calculations. **2** a person or thing that calculates. **3** a set of tables used in calculation.

cal·cu·lus /'kalkjʊləs/ *noun* (*pl.* **cal·cu·li** /-,lai/ or **cal·cu·lus·es**) **1** *Math.* **a** a particular method of calculation or reasoning (*calculus of probabilities*). **b** the infinitesimal calculi of integration or differentiation (see INTEGRAL CALCULUS, DIFFERENTIAL CALCULUS). **2 a** *Med.* a stone or concretion of minerals formed within the body, esp. in the kidney or gallbladder. **b** = TARTAR 1. □ **cal·cu·lous** *adjective* (in sense 2). [Latin, = small stone used in reckoning on an abacus]

Cal·cutta /kal'kʌtə/ a port and industrial centre in E India, capital of the state of West Bengal and one of the largest cities in India; pop. (est. 2002) 13,821,600. It is situated on the Hooghly River near the Bay of Bengal. Founded *c.*1690 by the East India Company, Calcutta was the capital of India from 1772 to 1912.

Calcutta, Black Hole of a dungeon in Fort William, Calcutta, where, following the capture of Calcutta by the Nawab of Bengal in 1756, perhaps as many as 146 English prisoners were confined in a narrow cell 6 m (20 ft) square for the night of 20 June, only 23 of them still being alive the next morning.

Cal·der /'kɒldər/ **Alex·an·der** (1898–1976), US sculptor and painter. The inventor of the mobile in the early 1930s, he was one of the first artists to introduce movement into sculpture.

cal·dera /kal'dɛrə, kɒl-/ *noun* a large volcanic crater, esp. one whose breadth greatly exceeds that of the vent or vents within it, created by a volcanic explosion. [Spanish from Late Latin *caldaria* pot for boiling]

Cal·de·rón de la Barca /,kɒldə,rɒːn də lə 'barkə/ **Pedro** (1600–81),

Spanish dramatist and poet. He wrote some 120 plays, more than 70 of them religious dramas.

cal·dron *var. of* CAULDRON.

Cald·well /ˈkɒldwel/ **Ers·kine** (1903–87), US novelist, best known for his graphic portrayal of the rural poor in the southern US, as in *Tobacco Road* (1932) and *God's Little Acre* (1933).

ca·lèche /kəˈleʃ/ *noun Cdn* a two-wheeled one-horse vehicle with a seat for the driver on the splashboard, commonly used in tourist areas of Quebec. [French from German *Kalesche* from Polish *kolaska* or Czech *kolesa*]

Cal·edon /ˈkalədən/ a town in south central Ontario, northwest of Toronto; pop. (2001) 50,595. [shortening of Latin *Caledonia*, a poetic name for Scotland]

Cal·edon·ian /ˌkaləˈdoːniən/ ● *adjective* **1** of or relating to Scotland. **2** *Geol.* of a mountain-forming period in NW Europe in the Paleozoic era. ● *noun literary* a Scottish person. [Latin *Caledonia* N Britain]

cal·en·dar /ˈkaləndər/ ● *noun* **1** a system by which the beginning, length, and subdivisions of the year are fixed. **2** a chart or series of pages showing the days, weeks, and months of a particular year, or giving special seasonal information. **3** a timetable or program of appointments, special events, etc. **4** *Cdn* a book containing a list of courses offered at a university or college, along with general information on registration etc. **5** a list or register, esp. of canonized saints, cases for trial, etc. ● *transitive verb* register or enter in a calendar or timetable etc. □ **ca·len·dric** /-ˈlendrɪk/ *adjective* **ca·len·dric·al** /-ˈlendrɪkəl/ *adjective* [Anglo-French *calender*, Old French *calendier* from Latin *calendarium* account book (as CALENDS)]

calendar month *noun* = MONTH 1a.

calendar year *noun* = YEAR 2.

cal·en·der /ˈkaləndər/ ● *noun* a machine in which cloth, paper, etc., is pressed by rollers to glaze or smooth it. ● *transitive verb* press in a calender. [French *calendre(r)*, of unknown origin]

cal·ends /ˈkalendz/ *plural noun* (also **kal·ends**) the first of the month in the ancient Roman calendar. [Old French *calendes* from Latin *kalendae*]

ca·len·dula /kəˈlendjʊlə/ *noun* any plant of the genus *Calendula*, with large yellow or orange flowers, e.g. marigold. [modern Latin, diminutive of *calendae* (as CALENDS), perhaps = little clock]

cal·en·ture /ˈkalentʃər/ *noun* a form of delirium formerly supposed to afflict sailors in the tropics, in which the sea is mistaken for green fields. [French from Spanish *calentura* fever, from *calentar* be hot, ultimately from Latin *calēre* be warm]

calf[1] *noun* (*pl.* **calves**) **1** a young bovine animal. **2** the young of other animals, e.g. elephant, whale, and seal. **3** = CALFSKIN. **4** *Naut.* a floating piece of ice detached from an iceberg. □ **in calf** (of a cow) pregnant. □ **calf·hood** *noun* **calf·like** *adjective* [Old English *cælf* from West Germanic]

calf[2] *noun* (*pl.* **calves**) the fleshy hind part of the human leg below the knee. [Old Norse *kálfi*, of unknown origin]

calf love *noun* = PUPPY LOVE.

calf roping *noun N Amer.* a rodeo event in which contestants on horseback chase and attempt to lasso a calf before dismounting and tying its legs. □ **calf roper** *noun*

calf·skin *noun* the hide of a calf, esp. as leather used in bookbinding and shoemaking.

Cal·gary /ˈkalgəri/ a city in SW Alberta, situated on the Bow River, about 275 km south of Edmonton; pop. (2001) 878,866. The Calgary Stampede, an annual rodeo inaugurated in 1912, is held there. □ **Cal·gar·ian** /kalˈgeriən/ *noun & adjective* [after an estate on the Isle of Mull, from Gaelic *calgary* clear running water]

Cali /ˈkɒli/ an industrial city in W Colombia; pop. (est. 2002) 2,203,800.

cali·brate /ˈkalə,breit/ *transitive verb* **1** mark (a gauge) with a standard scale of readings. **2** correlate the readings of (an instrument) with a standard. **3** determine the calibre of (a gun). **4** determine the correct capacity or value of. □ **cali·bra·tor** *noun*

cali·bra·tion /kalɪˈbreiʃən/ *noun* **1** the act or process of calibrating something. **2** each of a set of graduations on an instrument etc.

cali·bre /ˈkaləbər/ *noun* (esp. *US* **cali·ber**) **1 a** the internal diameter of a gun or tube. **b** the diameter of a bullet or shell. **2** strength or quality of character; ability, importance (*we need someone of your calibre*). [French *calibre*, Italian *calibro*, from Arabic *ḳālib* mould]

cali·che /kəˈliːtʃi/ *noun* **1** a mineral deposit of gravel, sand, and nitrates found in dry areas of N or S America, esp. Chile saltpetre. **2** = CALCRETE. [Latin American Spanish]

cal·ico /ˈkalə,koː/ ● *noun* (*pl.* **-icoes** or **-icos**) **1** *N Amer.* a cotton fabric with a printed pattern. **2** *Brit.* a cotton cloth, esp. plain white or

unbleached. ● *adjective* **1** made of calico. **2** *N Amer.* **a** (of an animal etc.) having irregular patches of colours, mottled. **b** (of a domestic cat) having a coat with patches of orange tabby, black, and white. [earlier *calicut* from CALICUT]

Cali·cut /ˈkalɪ,kʌt/ a seaport in the state of Kerala in SW India, on the Malabar Coast; pop. (2001) 436,500. In the 17th and 18th c. Calicut became a centre of the textile trade with Europe. The cotton fabric known as calico originated there.

Calif. *abbreviation* California.

Cali·for·nia /ˌkaləˈfɔːrnjə/ a state of the US, on the Pacific coast; pop. (2000) 33,871,684; capital, Sacramento. □ **Cali·for·nian** *adjective & noun*

California, Gulf of an arm of the Pacific Ocean separating the Baja California peninsula from mainland Mexico.

California poppy *noun* a plant of the poppy family, *Eschscholzia californica*, with brilliant yellow or orange flowers.

California roll *noun* a type of sushi consisting of rice, avocado, crabmeat, and cucumber rolled in seaweed.

California sea lion *noun* a dark brown seal of the eastern Pacific, *Zalophus californianus*, often trained in captivity.

California shutter *noun* a shutter with louvres that can be opened and closed, for the interior of a window.

Cali·for·ni·cation /ˌkalɪfɔːrnɪˈkeiʃən/ *noun informal* a region's assumption of undesirable features seen to be characteristic of California, e.g. suburban sprawl. [blend of CALIFORNIA + FORNICATION]

cali·for·nium /ˌkaləˈfɔːrniəm/ *noun Chem.* a transuranic radioactive metallic element produced artificially from curium. Symbol: **Cf**; at. no.: 98. [University of *California*, where it was first made + -IUM]

Ca·lig·ula /kəˈlɪɡjʊlə/ (full name Gaius Julius Caesar Germanicus) (12–41), Roman emperor 37–41. Brought up in a military camp, he was nicknamed 'Caligula' (= baby boot) as an infant on account of the military boots he wore; his brief reign as emperor was notorious for its tyrannical excesses, and he was assassinated.

cali·per /ˈkaləpər/ (also **cal·liper**) ● *noun* (usu. in *pl.*) **1** an instrument with two pivoting bowed legs for measuring the diameter of convex bodies (**outside calipers**), or with out-turned points for measuring internal dimensions (**inside calipers**). **2** the part of an automobile or bicycle brake assembly which houses the brake pads and grips the disc or wheel. **3** *Brit.* a metal splint to support the leg. ● *transitive verb* measure with calipers. [apparently var. of CALIBRE]

ca·liph /ˈkeilɪf, ˈkal-/ *noun hist.* the chief Muslim civil and religious ruler, regarded as the successor of Muhammad. The first caliph was Abu-Bakr (573–634), chosen following the death of Muhammad in AD 632. Subsequently the caliphate became a hereditary position with the establishment of the Umayyad and Abbasid dynasties (respectively 661–750 and from 750). The latter ruled in Baghdad until 1258 and then in Egypt until the Ottoman conquest (1517). The title was then held by the Ottoman sultans until the nationalist revolution of 1922, and the caliphate was abolished by Atatürk in 1924. □ **ca·liph·ate** *noun* [Old French *caliphe* from Arabic *Kalīfa* successor]

cal·is·then·ics /ˌkalɪsˈθenɪks/ *plural noun* (also **cal·lis·then·ics**) gymnastic exercises to achieve bodily fitness and grace of movement. □ **cal·is·then·ic** *adjective* [Greek *kallos* beauty + *sthenos* strength]

Cal-Ital /kalˈɪtal/ *adjective* (of cuisine) combining Californian and Italian elements. [abbreviation]

calk esp. *US var. of* CAULK[1], [2].

call ● *verb* **1 a** *intransitive* (often foll. by *out*) cry, shout; speak loudly. **b** *intransitive* (of a bird or animal) emit its characteristic note or cry. **c** *transitive N Amer.* attract (an animal, bird, etc.) by mimicking its sound. **2** *transitive* communicate or converse with by telephone or radio. **3** *transitive* **a** bring to one's presence by calling; summon (*will you call the children?*). **b** arrange for (a person or thing) to come or be present (*called a taxi*). **4** *intransitive* (often foll. by *at, in, on*) pay a brief visit (*called at the house; called in to see you; come and call on me*). **5** *transitive* **a** order to take place; fix a time for (*called a meeting*). **b** direct to happen; announce (*called a stop to it*). **6 a** *intransitive* require one's attention or consideration (*duty calls*). **b** *transitive* urge, invite, nominate (*call to the bar*). **7** *transitive* name; describe as (*call her Liz*). **8** *transitive* consider; regard or estimate as (*I call that silly*). **9** *transitive* rouse from sleep (*call me at 8*). **10** *intransitive* guess the outcome of tossing a coin etc. **11** *intransitive* (foll. by *for*) order, require, demand (*called for silence*). **12** *transitive* read out (a list of names to determine those present). **13** *intransitive* (foll. by *on, upon*) invoke; appeal to; request or require (*called on us to be quiet*). **14** *transitive Sport* (of an umpire or referee) **a** rule; assess (*called a penalty*). **b** officiate (a game). **15** *Cards* **a** *transitive* specify (a suit or contract) in bidding. **b** *intransitive* (in poker) make a demand for a show of hands. **16** *transitive*

N Amer. = CALL OFF 3. **17** *transitive* N Amer. (foll. by *on*) **a** require (of someone) proof or support for a statement (*they called him on the numbers he presented*). **b** criticize, condemn (*the boss called them on their behaviour*). **18** *transitive Scot.* drive (an animal, vehicle, etc.). ● *noun* **1** a shout or cry; an act of calling. **2 a** the characteristic cry of a bird or animal. **b** an imitation of this. **c** an instrument for imitating it. **3** a brief visit (*paid them a call*). **4 a** an act of telephoning. **b** a telephone conversation. **5 a** an invitation or summons to appear or be present. **b** an appeal or invitation (from a specific source or discerned by a person's conscience etc.) to follow a certain profession, set of principles, etc. **6** (foll. by *for*, or *to* + infin.) a duty, need, or occasion (*no call to be rude; no call for violence*). **7** (foll. by *for*, *on*) a demand (*not much call for it these days; a call on one's time*). **8 a** *Sport* a ruling made by an official (*you're the boss; you make the call*). **9** a signal on a bugle etc.; a signalling whistle. **10** *Stock Exch.* an option of buying stock at a fixed price at a given date. **11** *Cards* **a** a player's right or turn to make a bid. **b** a bid made. □ **call away** divert, distract, summon elsewhere. **call down 1** invoke. **2** reprimand. **call forth** elicit. **call in 1** withdraw from circulation. **2** seek the advice or services of. **call in** (or **into**) **question** dispute; doubt the validity of. **call into play** make use of. **call a person names** abuse a person verbally. **call off 1** cancel (an arrangement etc.). **2** order (an attacker or pursuer) to desist. **3** N Amer. chant (the directions) for a square dance etc. **call of nature** a need to urinate or defecate. **call out 1** CALL *verb* 1a. **2** summon (troops etc.) to action. **3** order (workers) to strike. **call the shots** (or **tune**) be in control; take the initiative. **call to account** *see* ACCOUNT. **call to mind** recollect; cause one to remember. **call to order 1** request to be orderly. **2** declare (a meeting) open. **call up 1** reach by telephone. **2** imagine, recollect. **3** summon, esp. to serve in the army. **4** *Sport* promote (a player) to the major leagues. **on** (or **at**) **call 1** (of a doctor etc.) available if required but not formally on duty. **2** (of money lent) repayable on demand. **within call** near enough to be summoned by calling. [Old English *ceallian* from Old Norse *kalla*]

cal·la /ˈkalə/ *noun* **1** (in full **calla lily**) the arum lily, *Zantedeschia aethiopica*, with an esp. white funnel-shaped spathe and a yellow spadix. **2** (in full **wild calla**) = WATER ARUM. [modern Latin]

Cal·laghan /ˈkaləhan/ **1 (Leon·ard) James, Baron Cal·laghan of Car·diff** (b.1912), English Labour politician, prime minister 1976–9. He became prime minister during a period of increasing union unrest, and following widespread strikes in the so-called 'winter of discontent' (1978–9), Callaghan received a vote of no confidence and his party was defeated by the Conservatives in the subsequent election. **2 Mor·ley Ed·ward** (1903–90), Canadian novelist and short-story writer. His novels are noted for their subtle exploration of character and use of moral symbolism, and include *More Joy in Heaven* (1937), about a paroled convict, and *The Loved and the Lost* (1951).

cal·la·loo /kaləˈluː/ *noun* a West Indian soup or stew containing salt pork, crabmeat, okra, coconut milk, and greens, esp. the leaves of the taro plant. [Latin American Spanish *calalú*]

Cal·lan·der /ˈkaləndər/ a place in NE central Ontario, situated on Lake Nipissing, just southeast of North Bay. It is famous as the nearest railway centre to Corbeil, birthplace of the Dionne quintuplets. [*Callander* in Stirling, Scotland, birthplace of G. Morrison, first settler and postmaster *c*.1881]

call-and-response *noun* (often *attributive*) a style of singing in which a line is sung by one person and then repeated by a group.

Cal·lao /kaˈljoʊ/ the principal seaport of Peru; pop. (est. 1998) 424,300.

Cal·las /ˈkaləs/ **Maria** (born Maria Cecilia Anna Kalageropoulos) (1923–77), US-born operatic soprano, of Greek parentage.

call·back *noun* an instance of calling back, e.g by a salesperson or service person, or for a job interview or theatrical audition.

call board *noun* a bulletin board in a theatre, rehearsal space, etc., on which announcements for the cast and crew are posted.

call box *noun* **1** esp. *Brit.* = TELEPHONE BOOTH. **2** N Amer. a direct telephone line, e.g. for reporting emergencies to the police.

call boy *noun* **1** a theatre attendant who summons actors when needed on stage. **2** a male prostitute who accepts appointments by telephone.

call centre *noun* a business employing staff to answer toll-free customer service telephone calls.

call display *noun* Cdn = CALLER ID.

called strike *noun Baseball* a pitch that is not swung at by the batter but is ruled a strike by the umpire.

call·er *noun* **1** a person who calls, esp. one who pays a visit or makes a telephone call. **2** a person who announces something, esp. the directions in a square dance or the numbers in a bingo game.

caller ID *noun* (also **caller identification**) a telephone service which displays the telephone number of an incoming call on a screen on the subscriber's telephone.

call forwarding *noun* N Amer. a service which allows users to have telephone calls automatically forwarded to another line.

call girl *noun* a female prostitute who accepts appointments by telephone.

calli·bogus /kaləˈboːgəs/ *noun* (also **cala·bogus**) Cdn (esp. *Nfld*) a beverage made from spruce beer and rum mixed with molasses. [18th c.: origin unknown]

Cal·lic·ra·tes /kəˈlɪkrəˌtiːz/ (5th c. BC), Greek architect. He was the leading architect in Periclean Athens, and with Ictinus designed the Parthenon (447–438 BC). Other structures attributed to him include the Ionic temple of Athena Nike on the Acropolis in Athens (448–after 421 BC).

Cal·lière /kalˈjer/ **Louis-Hector de** (also **Cal·lières**) (1648–1703), French soldier, governor of Montreal 1684–98 and New France 1699–1703. A noted military commander and administrator, he oversaw the signing of a peace treaty (1701) between the Iroquois and the Huron, Odawa, and Abenaki.

cal·lig·ra·phy /kəˈlɪɡrəfi/ *noun* **1** handwriting, esp. when fine or pleasing. **2** the art of stylized or beautiful handwriting. □ **cal·lig·raph·er** *noun* **cal·li·graph·ic** /ˌkalɪˈɡrafɪk/ *adjective* **cal·lig·raph·ist** *noun* [Greek *kalligraphia* from *kallos* beauty]

Cal·lima·chus /kəˈlɪməkəs/ (*c*.305–*c*.240 BC), Greek poet and scholar. He wrote hymns and epigrams and was head of the library at Alexandria.

call-in *noun* = PHONE-IN.

call·ing *noun* **1** a profession or occupation. **2** an inwardly felt call or summons; a vocation.

calling card *noun* **1** a small card with one's name and often address and telephone number, presented when visiting. **2** (**Calling Card**) a credit card issued by a telephone company allowing a customer to charge long-distance calls to an account. **3** a distinctive mark or feature by which someone can be recognized.

Cal·li·ope /kəˈlaɪəpi/ Gk & Rom. Myth the Muse of epic poetry. [Greek, = beautiful-voiced]

cal·li·ope /kəˈlaɪəpi/ *noun* N Amer. **1** a keyboard instrument resembling an organ, with a set of steam whistles producing musical notes. **2** (in full **calliope hummingbird**) a tiny hummingbird, *Stellula calliope*, the male of which has purple streaks on the throat, of mountainous areas of western N America. [CALLIOPE]

cal·li·per var. of CALIPER.

cal·lis·then·ics var. of CALISTHENICS.

Cal·listo /kəˈlɪstoʊ/ **1** Gk Myth a nymph who was changed into a bear by Zeus. **2** Astronomy satellite IV of Jupiter, the eighth closest to the planet, and one of the Galilean moons (diameter 4 800 km).

call letters *plural noun* N Amer. the letters identifying a radio or television station.

call loan *noun* = DEMAND LOAN.

call number *noun* the cataloguing numbers and letters assigned to a book or other item in a library.

cal·los·ity /kəˈlɒsɪti/ *noun* (*pl.* **-ities**) a hard thick area of skin usu. occurring in parts of the body subject to pressure or friction. [French *callosité* or Latin *callositas* (as CALLOUS)]

cal·lous /ˈkaləs/ ● *adjective* **1** unfeeling, insensitive. **2** (of skin) hardened or hard. ● *noun* = CALLUS 1. □ **cal·loused** *adjective* **cal·lous·ly** *adverb* (in sense 1 of *adjective*). **cal·lous·ness** *noun* [Latin *callosus* (as CALLUS) or French *calleux*]

call-out *noun* a paid duty or service performed by a worker or police officer, esp. outside of normal business hours.

cal·low /ˈkaloʊ/ *adjective* inexperienced, immature. □ **cal·low·ly** *adverb* **cal·low·ness** *noun* [Old English *calu*]

Cal·lo·way /ˈkaləweɪ/ **Cabell** ('Cab'), (1907–94), US jazz singer, composer, and bandleader. As a New York bandleader in the 1930s he gained enduring fame as the 'Hi-De-Ho man', in recognition of his exuberance and trademark scat singing.

call sign *noun* **1** a conventional signal identifying a particular radio transmitter. **2** *Aviation* a name by which a person communicating by radio, esp. an aircraft pilot, is identified.

call to arms *noun* **1** an instance of calling up for active military service. **2** an instance of inciting or encouraging people to vigorous, usu. defensive action.

cal·luna /kəˈluːnə/ *noun* any common heather of the genus *Calluna*, native to Europe and N Africa. [modern Latin from Greek *kallunō* beautify, from *kallos* beauty]

call-up *noun* **1** the act or process of calling up, esp. being summoned to the army or promoted to the major leagues. **2** a person who is called up.

cal·lus /ˈkaləs/ *noun* (*pl.* **cal·lus·es**) **1** a hard thick area of skin or tissue. **2** a hard tissue formed around bone ends after a fracture. **3** *Bot.* a new protective tissue formed over a wound. □ **cal·lused** *adjective* [Latin]

call waiting *noun* a telephone service which alerts subscribers that a second call is coming through (by causing a tone to sound) and allows the user to switch back and forth between the two calls.

Call·wood /ˈkɒlwʊd/ **June** (b.1924), Canadian journalist and activist, who is known for her work on behalf of homeless youth and battered women; her writings include *The Law is not for Women* (1976) and *Twelve Weeks in Spring* (1986).

calm /kɒm, kɒlm/ ● *adjective* **1** tranquil, quiet, windless (*a calm sea; a calm night*). **2** (of a person or disposition) settled; not agitated (*remained calm throughout the ordeal*). **3** self-assured, confident (*his calm assumption that we would wait*). ● *noun* **1** a state of being calm; stillness, serenity. **2 a** a period without wind or storm. **b** *Meteorol.* absence of wind, force 0 on the Beaufort scale. **3** (in *pl.*) an area, esp. of the sea, with predominantly calm weather. ● *transitive & intransitive verb* (often foll. by *down*) make or become calm. □ **calm·ly** *adverb* **calm·ness** *noun* [Middle English ultimately from Late Latin *cauma* from Greek *kauma* heat]

calma·tive /ˈkɒmətɪv, ˈkalm-/ *Med.* ● *adjective* tending to calm or sedate. ● *noun* a calmative drug etc.

calo·mel /ˈkaləˌmɛl/ *noun* a compound of mercury and chlorine, formerly used medicinally as a purgative. [modern Latin perhaps from Greek *kalos* beautiful + *melas* black]

Calor gas /ˈkalər/ *noun* *Brit.* liquefied butane gas stored under pressure in containers for domestic use. [Latin *calor* heat]

ca·lor·ic /kəˈlɒrɪk/ ● *adjective* of heat or calories. ● *noun* *hist.* (in the late 18th and early 19th centuries) a hypothetical fluid substance that was thought to be responsible for the phenomena of heat. [French *calorique* from Latin *calor* heat]

cal·orie /ˈkaləri/ *noun* a unit of quantity of heat: **1** (in full **large calorie**) the amount needed to raise the temperature of 1 kilogram of water through 1°C, often used to measure the energy value of foods. Also called KILOCALORIE. **2** (in full **small calorie**) the amount needed to raise the temperature of 1 gram of water by 1°C. [French, arbitrary alteration of Latin *calor* heat + *-ie*]

cal·or·if·ic /ˌkaləˈrɪfɪk/ *adjective* **1** producing heat. **2** pertaining to or high in calories. □ **cal·or·if·ic·al·ly** *adverb* [Latin *calorificus* from *calor* heat]

calorific value *noun* the amount of heat produced by a specified quantity of fuel, food, etc.

cal·or·im·eter /ˌkaləˈrɪmətər/ *noun* any of various instruments for measuring quantity of heat, esp. to find calorific values. □ **cal·or·i·met·ric** /-ˈmɛtrɪk/ *adjective* **cal·or·im·etry** *noun* [Latin *calor* heat + -METER]

calque /kalk/ *Linguistics* ● *noun* an expression adopted by one language from another in a more or less literally translated form. Also called LOAN TRANSLATION. ● *transitive verb* (**calqued**, **cal·quing**) form (a word or phrase) as a calque. [French, = copy, tracing, from *calquer* 'trace', ultimately from Latin *calcare* tread]

cal·trop /ˈkaltrəp/ *noun* (also **cal·trap**) **1** *hist.* an iron ball with four spikes placed so that one point always faces upwards, thrown on the ground to impede cavalry horses. **2** *Heraldry* a representation of this. **3** any creeping plant of the genus *Tribulus*, with woody carpels usu. having hard spines. [(sense 3) Old English *calcatrippe* from medieval Latin *calcatrippa*: (senses 1–2) Old French *chauchetrape* from *chauchier* tread, *trappe* trap: ultimately the same word]

calu·met /ˈkaljuˌmɛt/ *noun* a N American Aboriginal tobacco pipe with a clay bowl and long reed stem, smoked esp. as a sign of peace. [French, ultimately from Latin *calamus* reed]

calum·ni·ate /kəˈlʌmniˌeɪt/ *transitive verb* slander. □ **calum·ni·ator** *noun* [Latin *calumniari*]

calum·ny /ˈkaləmni/ ● *noun* (*pl.* **-nies**) **1** slander; malicious representation. **2** an instance of this. ● *transitive verb* (**-nies, -nied**) slander. □ **calum·ni·ous** /kəˈlʌmniəs/ *adjective* [Latin *calumnia*]

Cal·va·dos /ˈkalvəˌdɒs/ *noun* (also **calvados**) a French apple brandy. [*Calvados*, a region in Normandy, France, where it was first distilled]

Cal·vary /ˈkalvəri/ *noun* the place where Christ was crucified. [Late

Latin *calvaria* skull, translation of Greek *golgotha*, Aramaic *gûlgûltâ* (Matt. 27:33)]

calve *verb* **1 a** *intransitive* give birth to a calf. **b** *transitive* (esp. in *passive*) give birth to (a calf). **2** *transitive & intransitive* (of an iceberg) break off or shed (a mass of ice). [Old English *calfian*]

Cal·vert /ˈkalvɜrt/ **1 Sir George, 1st Baron Bal·ti·more** (*c.*1579–1632), English statesman. He established a colony in Newfoundland (1621), obtained a charter for the Avalon Peninsula (1623), and later left Newfoundland with his family and settlers to establish the colony of Maryland (1632). **2** his son, **Leon·ard** (1606–1647), English statesman, first governor of the colony of Maryland (1634–1647).

calves *pl. of* CALF[1], CALF[2].

Cal·vin /ˈkalvɪn/ **1 John** (1509–64), French Protestant theologian and reformer. He spent most of his life in Geneva, and was one of the most important figures of the Reformation; he taught that doctrine should come directly from the Bible, that Christians are saved by believing and not by doing good works, and that God chooses those who will be saved. **2 Mel·vin** (1911–97), US biochemist. He investigated the metabolic pathways involved in photosynthesis, discovering the cycle of reactions which is named after him, and was awarded the Nobel Prize for chemistry in 1961.

Cal·vin·ism /ˈkalvəˌnɪzəm/ *noun* the theology of John Calvin or his followers. □ **Cal·vin·ist** *noun* **Cal·vin·is·tic** *adjective* [French *calvinisme* or modern Latin *calvinismus*]

Cal·vino /kalˈviːnoʊ/ **Italo** (1923–85), Italian novelist and short-story writer. His novels frequently blend fantasy with elements of folklore and innovative narrative structures; they include *Invisible Cities* (1972) and *If on a Winter's Night a Traveller* (1979).

calx /kalks/ *noun* (*pl.* **cal·ces** /ˈkalsiːz/) **1** a powdery metallic oxide formed when an ore or mineral has been heated. **2** calcium oxide. [Latin *calx calcis* lime, prob. from Greek *khalix* pebble, limestone]

Ca·lyp·so /kəˈlɪpsoʊ/ *Gk Myth* a nymph who kept Odysseus on her island, Ogygia, for seven years. [Greek, = she who conceals]

ca·lyp·so /kəˈlɪpsoʊ/ *noun* (*pl.* **-sos**) **1** a kind of West Indian music in syncopated African rhythm, usu. improvised on a topical theme. **2** a song in this style. **3** an orchid found across Canada and parts of the US, *Calypso bulbosa*, with pink, slipper-shaped flowers. Also called FAIRY SLIPPER. □ **calyp·son·ian** *noun* [20th c.: origin unknown]

calyx /ˈkeɪlɪks, ˈkal-/ *noun* (also **calix**) (*pl.* **caly·ces** /-lɪˌsiːz/ or **calyx·es**) **1** *Bot.* the sepals collectively, forming the protective layer of a flower in bud. **2** *Biol.* any cup-like cavity or structure. [Latin from Greek *kalux* case of bud, husk: compare *kaluptō* hide]

cal·zone /kalˈzoʊneɪ/ *noun* a type of baked turnover of bread dough filled with tomato sauce, cheese, and vegetables or meat. [Italian dialect, prob. related to *calzone*, 'trouser leg']

CAM *abbreviation* computer-aided manufacturing.

cam *noun* a projection on a rotating part in machinery, shaped to impart reciprocal or variable motion to the part in contact with it. [Dutch *kam* comb: compare Dutch *kamrad* cogwheel]

cama·rad·erie /ˌkɒməˈrɒdəri, ˌkamɑˈradəri, ˌkaməˈrɒdəri/ *noun* mutual trust and sociability among friends. [French]

Cam·argue, the /kaˈmɑrɡ/ a region of the Rhone delta in SE France, characterized by numerous shallow salt lagoons. The region is known for its white horses and as a nature reserve.

cama·rilla /ˌkaməˈrɪlə/ *noun* a cabal or clique. [Spanish, diminutive of *camara* chamber]

camas /ˈkaməs/ *noun* **1** any of several N American plants of the lily family, esp. *Camassia quamash*, the edible bulbs of which were a staple of Aboriginal peoples. **2** = DEATH CAMAS. [Chinook Jargon *kamass*, perhaps from Nuu-chah-nulth]

Camb. *abbreviation* Cambridge.

Cam·bay, Gulf of /kamˈbeɪ/ (also **Gulf of Kham·bat** /kamˈbat/) an inlet of the Arabian Sea on the Gujarat coast of W India, north of Bombay (Mumbai).

cam·ber ● *noun* **1** the slightly convex or arched shape of the surface of a road, ship's deck, aircraft wing, etc. **2** a slight sideways inclination of the wheels of a motor vehicle. ● *verb* **1** *intransitive* (of a surface) have a camber. **2** *transitive* give a camber to; build with a camber. [French *cambre* arched, from Latin *camurus* curved inwards]

Camber·well beauty *noun* *Brit.* = MOURNING CLOAK. [*Camberwell* in London]

cam·bium /ˈkambiəm/ *noun* (*pl.* **cam·bia** /-biə/ or **cam·biums**) *Bot.* a cellular plant tissue responsible for the increase in girth of stems and roots. □ **cam·bial** *adjective* [medieval Latin, = change, exchange]

Cam·bo·dia /kamˈboʊdiə/ a country in SE Asia between Thailand and southern Vietnam; pop. (est. 2002) 12,775,324; capital, Phnom Penh. It was bombed and then invaded by US forces during the Vietnam War, and then embroiled in a civil war in 1970–5, which was won by the Khmer Rouge; more than 2 million Cambodians died before the regime was toppled by a Vietnamese invasion in 1979. The country was known officially as the Khmer Republic from 1970 to 1975 and as Kampuchea from 1976 to 1989.

Cam·bo·dian /kamˈbəʊdiən/ ● *noun* **1 a** a native or national of Cambodia in SE Asia. **b** a person of Cambodian descent. **2** the Khmer language. ● *adjective* of or relating to Cambodia or its people or the Khmer language.

cam·boose /kamˈbuːs/ *noun Cdn hist.* **1** (in full **camboose shanty**) a large wooden cabin with a central fireplace, serving as a winter shelter in a logging camp. **2** an open fireplace or cooking stove. [French *cambuse* from Dutch *combuse*, as CABOOSE]

Cam·bo·zola /kambəˈzəʊlə/ *noun proprietary* a type of German blue soft cheese with a Camembert-like rind, and produced using Gorgonzola blue mould. [invented name, from CAMEMBERT + -bo- + GORGONZOLA]

Cam·brian /ˈkeɪmbriən, ˈkam-/ ● *adjective* **1** Welsh. **2** *Geol.* of or relating to the first period of the Paleozoic era, lasting from about 590 to 505 million years BP, between the end of the Precambrian era and the beginning of the Ordovician period. It was a time of widespread seas, and is the first period in which fossils can be used in geological dating. ● *noun* this period or system. [Latin *Cambria* var. of *Cumbria* from Welsh *Cymry* Welshman or *Cymru* Wales]

Cambrian explosion *noun* the appearance about 570 million years ago, over a relatively short time, of almost all major groups of modern animals.

cam·bric /ˈkambrɪk/ *noun* a fine white linen or cotton fabric. [*Kamerijk*, Flemish form of *Cambrai* in N France, where it was originally made]

Cam·bridge /ˈkeɪmbrɪdʒ/ **1** a city in E England, the county town of Cambridgeshire; pop. (est. 1998) 120,600. Cambridge University is located there. **2** a city in SW central Ontario, about 40 km northwest of Hamilton; pop. (2001) 110,372. **3** a city in E Massachusetts, forming part of the conurbation of Boston; pop. (2000) 101,400. Harvard University and the Massachusetts Institute of Technology are located there. [sense 2 named after an early flour mill in the former town of Preston, now part of Cambridge]

Cambridge Bay 1 a small bay on the eastern half of the southern coast of Victoria Island. **2** a hamlet situated on the bay; pop. (2001) 1,309. [prob. after Adolphus Frederick, Duke of *Cambridge* and seventh son of George III d.1850]

Cambridge blue *noun & adjective* a pale blue. [CAMBRIDGE]

Cam·bridge·shire /ˈkeɪmbrɪdʒˌʃɪr/ a county of E England; county town, Cambridge.

Cambs. *abbreviation* Cambridgeshire.

Cam·by·ses /kamˈbaɪsiːz/ (d.522 BC), king of Persia 529–522 BC, son of Cyrus the Great. He conquered Egypt in 525 BC.

cam·cord *transitive verb* videotape using a camcorder. [back-formation from CAMCORDER]

cam·corder /ˈkamˌkɔːrdər/ *noun* a portable video camera which records picture and sound on a videocassette etc. [blend of *camera* + re*corder*]

came *past of* COME.

camel *noun* **1** either of two kinds of large cud-chewing mammals having slender cushion-footed legs and one hump (**Arabian camel**, *Camelus dromedarius*) or two humps (**Bactrian camel**, *Camelus bactrianus*). **2** a fawn colour. **3** an apparatus for providing additional buoyancy to ships etc. [Old English from Latin *camelus* from Greek *kamēlos*, of Semitic origin]

camel·back *noun* **1** the humped back of a camel. **2** (often *attributive*) a curved shape, esp. of a sofa back, which is higher in the centre than at the sides.

camel·eer *noun* a camel driver.

camel hair *noun* (also **camel's hair**) **1 a** the hair of a camel. **b** a fabric made of this. **2** a fine soft hair used in artists' brushes.

camel·lia /kəˈmiːliə/ *noun* any evergreen shrub of the genus *Camellia*, native to E Asia, with shiny leaves and red, pink, or white roselike flowers. [J. *Camellus* or *Kamel*, 17th-c. Moravian botanist]

cam·elo·pard /ˈkamələˌpɑrd, kəˈmel-/ *noun archaic* a giraffe. [Latin *camelopardus* from Greek *kamēlopardalis* (as CAMEL, PARD)]

Cam·elo·par·dalis /kəˌmeləˈpɑrdələs/ a large but inconspicuous constellation found near the north celestial pole. [Latin *camēlopardalis* giraffe (as CAMELOPARD)]

Cam·elot /ˈkaməˌlɒt/ *noun* **1** (in Arthurian legend) the English town where King Arthur's court was located. **2** a period of perceived

prosperity and cultural renaissance, esp. (in the US) during the years of John F. Kennedy's presidency (1961—63).

camel spin *noun Figure Skating* an arabesque spin.

Camem·bert /ˈkaməmˌber/ *noun* a kind of soft creamy cheese with a whitish rind, usu. with a strong flavour. [*Camembert* in N France, where it was originally made]

cameo /ˈkamiˌoʊ/ *noun* (*pl.* **cameos**) **1** a piece of jewellery, typically oval in shape, consisting of a portrait in profile carved in relief on a background of a different colour. **2 a** a small character part in a play or film, usu. brief and played by a distinguished actor or actress. **b** a short descriptive literary sketch or acted scene. [Old French *camahieu* and medieval Latin *cammaeus*]

cam·era *noun* **1** an apparatus for taking photographs, consisting of a lightproof box to hold light-sensitive film, a lens, and a shutter mechanism, either for still photographs or for motion picture film. **2** a piece of equipment which forms an optical image and converts it into electrical impulses for video transmission or storage. □ **in camera 1** privately; not in public. **2** *Law* in a judge's private room. **on** (or **off**) **camera** (esp. of an actor or actress) being (or not being) filmed or televised at a particular moment. [originally = chamber, from Latin *camera* from Greek *kamara* vault etc.]

cam·era lu·cida /ˈluːsɪdə/ *noun* (*pl.* **cam·era lu·cidas**) an apparatus, now often attached to a microscope, by which an image is reflected on to a screen by a prism as an aid to drawing. [Latin, = bright chamber]

camera·man *noun* (*pl.* **-men**) a camera operator, esp. a male one.

cam·era ob·scura /ɒbˈskjʊrə/ *noun* a darkened box or room with a tiny aperture through which light is admitted, thereby projecting the inverted image of an external object on a screen inside it. [Latin, = dark chamber]

camera operator *noun* (also **camera·person**) a person who operates a film or television camera, esp. professionally.

camera phone *noun* a mobile phone that incorporates a small digital camera.

camera-ready *adjective Printing* (of copy or artwork) in a form suitable for immediate photographic reproduction.

camera·woman *noun* (*pl.* **-women**) a female camera operator.

camera·work *noun* the technique of using cameras in films or television.

Cam·eron ▸ 1 James (b.1954) Canadian-born American film director, producer, and screenwriter, who made his breakthrough as a director with *The Terminator* (1984), and gained huge success for the immensely popular epic *Titanic* (1997), which won 11 Academy Awards including Best Picture and Best Director. **2 Julia Mar·garet** (1815–79), English photographer. She quickly gained acclaim for her portraits of prominent figures such as Tennyson, Darwin, and Carlyle.

Cameron Highlands a hill resort region in Pahang, Malaysia. [W. *Cameron*, surveyor who mapped the area in 1885]

Cam·er·oon /ˌkaməˈruːn/ a country on the west coast of Africa between Nigeria and Gabon; pop. (est. 2002) 16,184,748; capital, Yaoundé. □ **Cam·er·oon·ian** *adjective & noun*

cami *noun informal* = CAMISOLE. [abbreviation]

cami·knick·ers /ˈkaməˌnɪkərz/ *plural noun Brit.* a one-piece close-fitting undergarment worn by women. [CAMISOLE + KNICKERS]

cami·sole /ˈkaməˌsoʊl/ *noun* **1** a woman's waist-length sleeveless undergarment with shoulder straps. **2** a similar outer garment. [French from Italian *camiciola* or Spanish *camisola*: see CHEMISE]

camo *noun slang* **1** = CAMOUFLAGE. **2** (*pl.* **camos**) camouflage clothing. [abbreviation]

Camo·ëns /ˈkaməˌens/ **Luis Vaz de** (also **Camões**) (c.1524–80), Portuguese poet, whose epic poem *The Lusiads* (1572), about Vasco da Gama's discovery of the sea route to India, is considered the national poem of Portugal.

camo·mile /ˈkaməˌmaɪl/ *noun* (also **chamo·mile**) any of various aromatic plants of the composite family, esp. *Chamaemelum nobilis* and plants of the genera *Anthemis* and *Matricaria*, with daisy-like flowers. [Old French *camomille* from Late Latin *camomilla* or *chamomilla* from Greek *khamaimēlon* earth apple (from the apple smell of its flowers)]

Cam·orra /kəˈmɒrə/ a secret criminal society that evolved and grew powerful in Naples and Neapolitan emigrant communities in the 19th century; in the US it has formed links with the Mafia. [Italian, perhaps from Spanish *camorra* 'dispute, quarrel']

cam·ou·flage /ˈkaməˌflɒʒ/ ● *noun* **1 a** the disguising of military vehicles, aircraft, ships, personnel, artillery, and installations by painting or covering them to make them blend with their

Consonants: b *but*   d *dog*   f *few*   g *get*   h *her*   j *yes*   k *cat*   l *leg*   m *man*   n *no*   p *pen*   r *red*   s *sit*

surroundings. **b** such a disguise or uniform etc. **2** the natural colouring of an animal which enables it to blend in with its surroundings. **3** a misleading or evasive precaution or expedient. ● *transitive verb* **1** hide or disguise by means of camouflage. **2** conceal or disguise (a flaw, emotion, etc.). [French from *camoufler* disguise, from Italian *camuffare* disguise, deceive]

Camp ▶ Dal·ton Kings·ley (1920-2002), Canadian political adviser and writer. As president of the federal Progressive Conservative Party (1964-9), he helped to bring about the removal of Diefenbaker as party leader (1967); he was subsequently a prominent adviser to many of the party's leaders.

camp¹ ● *noun* **1** temporary overnight lodging in tents etc. in the open. **2** temporary accommodation of various kinds, usu. consisting of huts or tents, for detainees, homeless persons, and other emergency use. **3 a** a complex of buildings for holiday accommodation, usu. with extensive recreational facilities. **b** a summer holiday program for children, offering various recreational or educational activities, often in a lakeside setting. **c** a place where such a program is offered. **d** *N Amer. (N Ont., Maritimes, US Northeast & Gulf States)* a summer cottage. **4** *N Amer.* a place of accommodation for workers at a particular place of employment, esp. in the bush etc. (*logging camp; mining camp*). **5 a** a place where troops are lodged or trained. **b** the military life. **6** an ancient fortified site or its remains. **7** the adherents of a particular party or doctrine regarded collectively (*the Conservative camp was crushed*). **8** = TRAINING CAMP. **9** *South Africa* a portion of veld fenced off for pasture on farms. **10** *Austral. & NZ* an assembly place of sheep or cattle. ● *intransitive verb* **1** set up or spend time in a camp (in senses 1 and 5 of *noun*). **2** (often foll. by *out*) lodge in temporary quarters or in the open. □ **camp·ing** *noun* [French from Italian *campo* from Latin *campus* level ground]

camp² *informal* ● *adjective* **1** affected, effeminate. **2** homosexual. **3** done in an exaggerated way for effect. ● *noun* a camp manner or style. ● *transitive & intransitive verb* behave or do in a camp way. □ **camp it up** overact; behave affectedly. □ **campy** *adjective* (**camp·i·er, camp·i·est**). **camp·i·ly** *adverb* **camp·i·ness** *noun* [20th c.: origin uncertain]

cam·paign /kam'pein/ ● *noun* **1** an organized course of action for a particular purpose, esp. to arouse public interest (e.g. before a political election). **2 a** a series of military operations in a definite area or to achieve a particular objective. **b** military service in the field (*on campaign*). ● *intransitive verb* conduct or take part in a campaign. □ **cam·paign·er** *noun* [French *campagne* open country, from Italian *campagna* from Late Latin *campania*]

campaign trail *noun* the series of public appearances, speeches, etc. made by a candidate in the course of a political campaign.

Cam·pa·nia /kam'paniə/ a region of west central Italy; capital, Naples.

cam·pa·nile /ˌkampə'niːlei/ *noun* a usu. free-standing bell tower, esp. in Italy. [Italian from Late Latin *campana* bell]

cam·pan·ol·ogy /ˌkampə'nɒlədʒi/ *noun* **1** the study of bells. **2** the art or practice of bell-ringing. □ **cam·pano·logic·al** /-nə'lɒdʒɪkəl/ *adjective* **cam·pan·ol·o·gist** *noun* [modern Latin *campanologia* from Late Latin *campana* bell]

cam·pan·ula /kam'panjulə/ *noun* any plant of the genus *Campanula*, with usu. blue, purple, or white bell-shaped flowers. *Also called* BELLFLOWER. [modern Latin diminutive of Latin *campana* bell]

cam·panu·late /kam'panjulət/ *adjective* *Bot. & Zool.* bell-shaped.

camp bed *noun* a folding portable bed or cot.

Camp·bell /'kambəl/ **1 Sir Alex·an·der** (1822-92), English-born Canadian politician, Father of Confederation. He was appointed to the legislative council in 1858, attended the Quebec Conference in 1864, and at Confederation was appointed to the Senate; he later held a number of ministerial posts and was Lieutenant-Governor of Ontario (1887-92). **2 Alex·an·der Brad·shaw** (b.1933), Canadian politician, Liberal premier of PEI 1966-78. His government negotiated the Comprehensive Development Plan with Ottawa (1969) to encourage the growth of tourism, agriculture, and industry in PEI. **3 (Avril) Kim** (b.1947), Canadian politician, Progressive Conservative prime minister 1993. After serving for two years as an MLA in BC, she was elected to the House of Commons in 1988. She was minister of Justice and Attorney General 1990-1992, then moved to National Defence, and was elected leader of the federal PC party in June 1993. The party suffered the worst defeat in Canadian history in the ensuing election, with Campbell losing her own seat; she resigned as party leader soon after. **4 Clar·ence** (1905-84), Canadian sports administrator, who served as president of the National Hockey League (1946-77). **5 Doug·las Lloyd** (1895-1995), Canadian politician, Liberal premier of Manitoba

1948-58. A farmer's candidate and Liberal minister of agriculture before becoming premier, he was noted for his conservative policies while in office. **6 Jo·seph** (1904-1987), US mythologist. A prolific writer, his works examine comparative mythology and the archetype of the hero, and include *The Hero with a Thousand Faces* (1949) and the 4 volume *The Masks of God* (1959-67). **7 Mrs. Pat·rick** (née Beatrice Stella Tanner) (1865-1940), English actress. She gave notable performances in roles ranging from Shakespeare to Ibsen, and when George Bernard Shaw wrote the part of Eliza Doolittle in *Pygmalion* (1914) for her they began a long correspondence. **8 Thane Alex·an·der** (1895-1978), Canadian politician, Liberal premier of PEI 1936-43. He served as Attorney General (1930-1 and 1935-6) and as chief justice of PEI (1943-70).

Campbell-Bannerman /ˌkambəl'banɜrmən/ **Sir Henry** (1836-1908), British Liberal politician, prime minister 1905-8. During his term of office self-government was granted to the defeated Boer republics of the Transvaal (1906) and the Orange River Colony (1907).

Campbell River /'kambəl ˌrɪvɜr/ a district municipality in BC, located on the east coast of Vancouver Island, 46 km northwest of Courtenay; pop. (2001) 28,456. □ **Campbell River·ite** *noun* [perhaps after Dr. S. *Campbell*, assistant surgeon on the survey ship *Plumper* c.1907]

Camp·bell·ton /'kambəltən/ a city in N New Brunswick, located near the mouth of the Restigouche River, on the border with Quebec; pop. (2001) 7,798. □ **Camp·bell·ton·ian** /kambəl'toːniən/ *noun* [Sir A. *Campbell*, British general d.1843]

camp·craft *noun* the skills and knowledge required for outdoor camping.

Cam·peche /kam'peitʃi/ **1** a state of SE Mexico, on the Yucatán Peninsula. **2** its capital, a seaport on the Gulf of Mexico; pop. (2000) 190,800.

camp·er *noun* **1** a person who camps out as a recreation, or lives temporarily at a camp. **2** a vehicle or trailer equipped for camping.

campe·sino /kampə'siːnoː/ *noun* (pl. **-sinos**) (in Central or S America) a farmer or peasant. [Spanish]

camp·fire *noun* an outdoor fire in a camp etc.

camp follower *noun* **1** a civilian, esp. a prostitute, who provides services to personnel in a military camp. **2** a disciple or adherent, esp. a hanger-on.

camp·ground *noun* an outdoor area with facilities for camping.

cam·phor /'kamfɜr/ *noun* a white translucent crystalline volatile substance with an aromatic smell and bitter taste, used to make celluloid and in medicine. Chem. formula: $C_{10}H_{16}O$. □ **cam·phor·ic** /-'fɒrɪk/ *adjective* [Old French *camphore* or medieval Latin *camphora* from Arabic *kāfūr* from Sanskrit *karpūram*]

cam·phor·ate /'kamfəˌreit/ *transitive verb* impregnate or treat with camphor.

camphor tree *noun* a tree of the laurel family, *Cinnamomum camphora*, which is native to E Asia and the major source of natural camphor.

Cam·pin·as /kam'piːnəs/ a city in SE Brazil, northwest of São Paulo; pop. (2000) 951,824. It is a major centre of the coffee trade.

Cam·pion /'kampiən/ **1 St. Ed·mund** (1540-81), English Jesuit priest and martyr. Originally a deacon in the Church of England, he went abroad because of his Roman Catholic sympathies and became a Jesuit priest (1573); as a member of the first Jesuit mission to England (1580) he was arrested, charged with conspiracy against the Crown, tortured, and executed. Feast day, 1 December. **2 Jane** (b.1954), New Zealand film director and screenwriter. Campion's films reflect her interest in awkward, shy, or marginal young women who possess great strength of private vision and tranquility. Among these are *An Angel at My Table* (1990) and *The Piano* (1993), for which she received an Oscar for Best Screenplay. **3 Thom·as** (1567-1620), English poet and composer, known for his four *Bookes of Ayres* for lute and voice.

cam·pion /'kampiən/ *noun* **1** any plant of the genus *Silene*, with usu. pink or white flowers with notched petals. **2** any of several similar cultivated plants of the genus *Lychnis*. [perhaps from obsolete *campion* from Old French, = CHAMPION: translation of Greek *lukhnis stephanōmatikē* a plant used for (champions') garlands]

camp meeting *noun* *N Amer.* an evangelical Christian worship service held outdoors or in a tent, often lasting several days.

Campo·basso /ˌkampoː'basoː/ a city in central Italy, capital of Molise region; pop. (2001) 46,860.

Campo·bello Island /ˌkampə'beloː/ an island at the southwestern entrance to Passamaquoddy Bay, New Brunswick. It is connected to the state of Maine by bridge. [ultimately from Spanish or Italian *campo bello* fair field, so named also to honour Lord W. *Campbell*, Nova Scotia governor c.1770]

Campo Gran·de /ˌkampoː ˈɡrandi/ a city in SW Brazil; pop. (2000) 654,832.

camp-out *noun N Amer.* an instance of camping out.

camp robber *noun N Amer.* a grey jay.

camp·site *noun* any place used for camping.

camp stove *noun* a portable cooking stove used by campers etc., usu. using naphtha as fuel.

cam·pus *noun* (*pl.* **cam·pus·es**) **1 a** the grounds of a university or college. **b** *N Amer. & Austral.* one of several local branches of a large university. **2** (often *attributive*) a university or college (*campus newspaper*). [Latin, = field]

cam·pylo·bac·ter /ˌkampələːˈbaktɜr/ *noun* a bacterium of the genus *Campylobacter*, occurring in unpasteurized dairy products, poultry, and other foods, capable of causing food poisoning in humans. [Greek *kampulos* bent, twisted + BACTERIUM]

Cam·rose a city in east central Alberta, southeast of Edmonton; pop. (2001) 14,854. □ **Cam·ros·ian** *noun* [*Camrose*, in Wales]

cam·shaft *noun* a shaft with one or more cams attached to it.

Camus /ˈkamuː/ **Al·bert** (1913–60), Algerian-born French novelist, dramatist, and essayist. His most famous works, the essay *The Myth of Sisyphus* (1942), and the novels *The Outsider* (1942) and *The Plague* (1947) all convey his existentialist conception of the absurdity of human existence; he was awarded the Nobel Prize for literature in 1957.

cam·wood *noun* a hardwood tree, *Pterocarpus soyauxii*, native to W Africa and yielding a red wood. *Also called* PADOUK. [perhaps from Temne]

Can. *abbreviation* Canada; Canadian.

can¹ *auxiliary verb* (*3rd sing. present* **can**; *past* **could**) (foll. by infin. without *to*, or *absol.*; present and past only in use) **1 a** be able to; know how to (*I can run fast, can he?; can you speak French?*). **b** be potentially capable of (*you can do it if you try*). **2** be permitted to (*can we go to the party?*). [Old English *cunnan* know]

can² ● *noun* **1** a metal vessel for liquid. **2** a metal container in which food or drink is hermetically sealed to enable storage over long periods. **3** a bin or other similar receptacle (*garbage can*). **4** (prec. by *the*) *slang* **a** a prison. **b** *N Amer.* a washroom or toilet. **5** *N Amer.* the buttocks. ● *transitive verb* (**canned**, **can·ning**) **1** put or preserve in a can or jar. **2** *N Amer. informal* **a** cease, end. **b** remove. **c** fire, dismiss. **3** record on film or tape for future use. □ **can it** *N Amer. informal* be quiet. **in the can** *informal* completed, ready (originally of filmed or recorded material). [Old English *canne*]

Cana /ˈkeinə/ an ancient small town in Galilee, where Christ is said to have performed his first miracle by changing water into wine during a marriage feast (John 2:1–11).

Canaan /ˈkeinən/ *noun* **1** the land, later known as Palestine, which the Israelites gradually conquered and occupied during the latter part of the 2nd millennium BC. In the Bible it is the land promised by God to Abraham and his descendants (Gen. 12:7). **2** a promised land. **3** heaven. □ **Canaan·ite** *noun & adjective* [ecclesiastical Latin from ecclesiastical Greek *Khanaan* from Hebrew *kʰnaʻan*]

Can·ada¹ 1 the second largest country in the world, covering the entire northern half of N America with the exception of Alaska; pop. (2001) 30,007,094; capital, Ottawa. Canada became a federation of provinces with dominion status in 1867, and the last step in attaining legal independence from the UK was taken with the signing of the Constitution Act of 1982. Canada is a member of the Commonwealth. **2** *hist.* (often in *pl.*, prec. by *the*) **a** Lower Canada and Upper Canada. **b** Canada East and Canada West. [Iroquoian *kanata* cluster of dwellings, village]

Can·ada² *noun N Amer.* (usu. in *pl.*) a Canada goose.

Canada balsam *noun* a yellow resin obtained from the balsam fir (*Abies balsamea*) and used for mounting preparations on microscope slides (its refractive index being similar to that of glass).

Canada buffalo berry *noun see* BUFFALO BERRY.

Canada Day *noun* the annual holiday commemorating the creation of the Dominion of Canada (then New Brunswick, Nova Scotia, Quebec, and Ontario) on 1 July 1867 (formerly called DOMINION DAY).

Canada dogwood *noun* = BUNCHBERRY.

Canada East *hist.* that part of the Province of Canada (1841–67) previously known as Lower Canada.

Canada Games *plural noun* a national sports competition, with

events divided into summer and winter sports, held in Canada every four years since 1967.

Canada goose *noun* a wild goose native to N America, *Branta canadensis*, with a brownish-grey back, black head and neck, and white cheeks and breast.

Canada jay *noun* = GREY JAY.

Canada lily *noun* a lily of eastern N America, *Lilium canadense*, with large yellow, orange or red spotted flowers.

Canada lynx *noun* a larger subspecies of lynx, often classified separately as *Felis canadensis*, found in northern N America.

Canada mayflower *noun* a woodland plant of eastern N America, *Maianthemum canadense*, of the lily family, with white flowers and pale red berries. *Also called* WILD LILY OF THE VALLEY.

Canada Pension Plan *noun* a pension plan funded by contributions from employees and employers and administered by the Canadian government.

Canada plum *noun* **1** a plum tree, *Prunus nigra*, found chiefly in SE Canada and the northeastern US. **2** the red or yellow juicy sour fruit of this.

Canada poplar *noun* = CAROLINA POPLAR.

Canad·arm *noun* a type of mechanical arm on a space shuttle's cargo bay, used for releasing, retrieving, and repairing satellites and other equipment. [blend of CANADA¹ + ARM¹]

Canada Savings Bond *noun* a savings bond issued by the Canadian federal government.

Canada thistle *noun N Amer.* a perennial thistle with pink or purple flowers, *Cirsium arvense*, native to Europe, now a flourishing weed in N America.

Canada violet *noun* a violet, *Viola canadensis*, of eastern N America, bearing flowers with white petals tinged with purple on the back.

Canada West *hist.* that part of the Province of Canada (1841–67) previously known as Upper Canada.

Canada yew *noun* = GROUND HEMLOCK.

Can·ad·ian ● *noun* **1** a native or inhabitant of Canada. **2** (in *pl.*) *informal* the Canadian national championships in a given sport. ● *adjective* of or relating to Canada or its people. □ **Can·ad·ian·ness** *noun*

Can·adi·ana *noun* things pertaining to and typical of Canadian culture, e.g. publications, artifacts, cultural activities.

Canadian Alliance *noun* a right-wing Canadian political party (2000-03) created through the joining of the Reform Party and some members of the Progressive Conservative Party. In 2003 the party officially merged with the federal Progressive Conservative Party to form the Conservative Party of Canada.

Canadian Armed Forces *noun* an unofficial name for the Canadian Forces.

Canadian bacon *noun US* = BACK BACON.

Canadian Bill of Rights *noun* a charter of human rights which guarantees all Canadians the rights of life, liberty, security of person and enjoyment of property, the right to protection of and equality before the law, and the freedoms of religion, speech, assembly and association, and the press, introduced by John Diefenbaker in 1960.

Canadian canoe *noun* a small, lightweight two-person canoe, usu. about 6 m (20 ft.) long.

Canadian Charter of Rights and Freedoms *noun* a charter of rights entrenched in Canada's Constitution Act, 1982, covering fundamental political freedoms and democratic, legal, equality, mobility, and language rights, and affirming the Aboriginal rights that existed in 1982.

Canadian English *noun* the English language as it is spoken and written by anglophone Canadians.

Canadian football *noun* a form of football played on a field 110 by 65 yards in which teams of 12 players attempt to throw, carry, or kick an oval ball across their opponents' goal line (*compare* AMERICAN FOOTBALL).

Canadian Forces *noun* the official name of the Canadian military, comprised of the former army, navy, and air force.

Canadian French *noun* the French language as it is spoken and written by francophone Canadians.

Canadian horse *noun* a sturdy black draft horse of a breed developed in Canada by early French settlers.

Can·ad·ian·ism *noun* **1 a** a word or expression originating in Canada. **b** an English or French word or expression used only in Canada. **2** loyalty or devotion to Canada. **3 a** the state of being Canadian. **b** Canadian character or spirit.

Vowels: a *cat* ɑ *arm* e *bed* ɜr *her* ɜː *deux* ə *ago* ɪ *sit* i *cosy* iː *feed* ɒ *hot* ɔ *pore* oː *no* ʌ *run* ʊ *put*

Can·ad·ian·ist *noun* a specialist in Canadian studies.

Can·ad·ian·ize *transitive verb* (also esp. *Brit.* **-ise**) make or become Canadian in content, character, style, ownership, etc. □ **Can·ad·ian·iz·a·tion** *noun*

Canadian Shield (also called **Laurentian Shield, Precambrian Shield**) a very large area of extremely old rock which occupies over two-fifths of the land area of Canada encircling Hudson Bay. It extends from the Arctic to the Great Lakes, with its surface made up of hills, plains, and low mountains with over 25 % covered by swamps and lakes and much exposed bedrock.

Canadian Tire money *noun Cdn* coupons having the appearance of play money issued in varying small denominations to customers by associate stores of the Canadian Tire Corp. Ltd. for redemption on purchases.

Canadian whisky = RYE 2a.

Cana·dien /ˌkanaˈdjã/ *noun* a French Canadian. [Canadian French]

Cana·dienne /ˌkanaˈdjen/ *noun* a French-Canadian woman or girl. [Canadian French]

ca·naille /kəˈnai/ *noun* the rabble. [French from Italian *canaglia* pack of dogs, from *cane* dog]

Can·ajun /ˌkəˈneidʒən/ (also **Cana·jan**) *Cdn jocular* ● *adjective* typically or purely Canadian. ● *noun* **1** a Canadian. **2** Canadian English, esp. as allegedly spoken by unsophisticated Canadians. [an alleged Canadian pronunciation of *Canadian*]

can·al *noun* **1** an artificial waterway for inland navigation or irrigation. **2** any of various tubular ducts or passages in a plant or animal body. **3** *Astronomy* any of a network of apparent linear markings on the planet Mars, which are observed from earth but not at close range. [Old French (earlier *chanel*) from Latin *canalis* or Italian *canale*]

canal boat *noun* a long narrow boat designed for carrying freight on canals.

Cana·letto /ˌkanəˈletoː/ (born Giovanni Antonio Canale) (1697–1768), Italian painter. He is primarily known for his topographically precise and detailed urban scenes, esp. those of his native city of Venice.

can·al·ize *transitive verb* (also esp. *Brit.* **-ise**) **1** make a canal through. **2** convert (a river) into a canal. **3** provide with canals. **4** give the desired direction or purpose to. □ **can·al·iz·a·tion** *noun* [French *canaliser*: see CANAL]

canal rays *plural noun Physics* streams of positive ions moving through holes bored in the cathode of a high-vacuum discharge tube.

Canal Zone see PANAMA CANAL.

Can-Am *Cdn* ● *adjective* designating an event, esp. a sporting event, for Canadian and American participants. ● *noun* a Can-Am event. [abbreviation]

can·apé /ˈkanəpei/ *noun* **1** a cracker or small piece of bread with a savoury food on top, often served as an hors d'oeuvre. **2** a sofa. [French, as CANOPY]

can·ard /kəˈnɑrd/ *noun* **1** an unfounded rumour or story. **2** an extra surface attached to a boat etc. for added stability or control. [French, = duck]

Can·ar·ese *var.* of KANARESE.

can·ary /kəˈneri/ ● *noun* (*pl.* **-aries**) **1** any of various small finches of the genus *Serinus*, esp. *S. canaria*, a songbird native to the Canary Islands, of which wild varieties are green and the numerous cage varieties usu. bright yellow. **2** (in full **canary yellow**) a bright yellow colour. **3** *hist.* a sweet wine from the Canary Islands. ● *adjective* having a bright yellow colour. □ **canary in a coal mine** something that serves as a warning of imminent disaster. [CANARY ISLANDS]

canary creeper *noun* a climbing plant, *Tropaeolum peregrinum*, with bright yellow flowers with deeply toothed petals.

canary grass *noun* a grass of the genus *Phalaris*, esp. *P. canariensis*, grown as a crop plant for birdseed. *See also* REED CANARY GRASS.

Canary Islands (also **Canaries**) a group of islands in the Atlantic Ocean, off the northwest coast of Africa, forming an autonomous region of Spain; capital, Las Palmas; pop. (2000) 1,716,276. It includes the islands of Tenerife, Gomera, La Palma, Hierro, Gran Canaria, Fuerteventura, and Lanzarote. [ultimately from Latin *canis* dog, because one of the islands was noted in Roman times for its large dogs]

can·asta /kəˈnastə/ *noun* **1** a card game using two decks and resembling rummy, the aim being to collect sets (or melds) of cards. **2** a set of seven cards in this game. [Spanish, = basket]

Can·av·eral, Cape /kəˈnavərəl/ a cape on the east coast of Florida, known as Cape Kennedy from 1963 until 1973. It is the location of the John F. Kennedy Space Center, from which space missions are launched.

Can·berra /ˈkanbərə/ the capital of Australia and seat of the federal government, in Australian Capital Territory, an enclave of New South Wales; pop. (2001) 321,700.

can·can *noun* a lively stage dance with high kicking, usu. performed by women holding up the front of their long ruffled skirts. [French, child's word for *canard* 'duck', designating a dance popular in Louis Philippe's time, with reference to a duck's waddle, ultimately from Old French *caner* 'to quack']

cancel ● *verb* (**can·celled, can·cel·ling**; also esp. *US* **can·celed, can·cel·ing**) **1** *transitive* **a** announce that (something already arranged and decided upon) will not be done or take place; call off. **b** discontinue (an arrangement in progress) (*cancelled my subscription*; *they've cancelled our favourite program*). **2** *transitive* obliterate or delete (writing etc.). **3** *transitive* mark or pierce (a cheque, stamp, etc.) so that it may not be used again. **4** *transitive* annul; make void; abolish. **5** (often foll. by *out*) **a** *transitive* (of one factor or circumstance) neutralize or counterbalance (another). **b** *intransitive* (of two factors or circumstances) neutralize each other. **6** *transitive Math.* strike out (an equal factor) on each side of an equation or from the numerator and denominator of a fraction. ● *noun* **1** an order revoking a previous one. **2** the cancellation of a postage stamp. □ **can·cel·ler** *noun* [French *canceller* from Latin *cancellare* from *cancelli* crossbars, lattice]

can·cel·late /ˈkansələt, -leit/ *adjective* (also **can·cel·lat·ed** /-ˌleitəd/) *Biol.* **1** marked with crossing lines. **2** = CANCELLOUS. [Latin *cancelli* lattice]

can·cel·la·tion /ˌkansəˈleiʃən/ *noun* **1** the act or an instance of cancelling or being cancelled. **2** something that has been cancelled, esp. a booking or reservation. **3** the marks made by cancelling, esp. a stamp.

can·cel·lous /ˈkansələs/ *adjective* (of a bone) with pores; spongy. [Latin *cancelli* lattice]

can·cer *noun* **1 a** any malignant growth or tumour from an abnormal and uncontrolled division of body cells. **b** a disease characterized by this. **2** an evil influence or corruption spreading uncontrollably. **3** (**Cancer**) a constellation between Gemini and Leo, traditionally regarded as contained in the figure of a crab. **4** (**Cancer**) **a** the fourth sign of the zodiac. **b** a person born when the sun is in this sign, usu. between 21 June and 22 July. □ **Can·cer·ian** /-ˈseriən, -ˈsiːriən/ *noun & adjective* (in sense 4). **can·cer·ous** *adjective* [Latin, = crab, cancer, after Greek *karkinos*]

cancer stick *noun slang* a cigarette.

Can·Con *noun* (also **Cancon**) *Cdn informal* Canadian content, esp. with reference to regulated quotas in broadcasting. [abbreviation]

Can·Cult *noun* (also **Cancult**) *Cdn informal* Canadian culture. [abbreviation]

Can·cún /kanˈkuːn/ a resort in SE Mexico, on the northeast coast of the Yucatán Peninsula; pop. (2000) 397,200.

can·dela /kanˈdiːlə, -ˈdelə/ *noun* the SI unit of luminous intensity. Abbr.: **cd**. [Latin, = candle]

can·del·abra /ˌkandəˈlabrə, -lɒb-/ *noun* a large branched candlestick holder for several candles or lamps. [Latin from *candela* CANDLE]

can·del·abrum /ˌkandəˈlabrəm, -lɒb-/ *noun* (*pl.* **can·del·abra**) = CANDELABRA.

Can·diac /kãˈdjak/ a town in south central Quebec, situated on the south shore of the St. Lawrence, just southwest of Montreal; pop. (2001) 12,675. [after an estate in the former province of Languedoc, S France]

can·did ● *adjective* **1** frank; not hiding one's thoughts. **2** (of a photograph) taken informally, usu. without the subject's knowledge. ● *noun* a candid photograph. □ **can·did·ly** *adverb* **can·did·ness** *noun* [French *candide* or Latin *candidus* white]

can·dida /kanˈdiːdə, ˈkandɪdə/ *noun* **1** any yeastlike parasitic fungus of the genus *Candida*, esp. *C. albicans*, causing thrush. **2** = CANDIDIASIS. [modern Latin fem. of Latin *candidus*: see CANDID]

can·di·date /ˈkandɪdeit, -ˌdət/ *noun* **1** a person who seeks or is nominated for an office, award, etc. **2** a person or thing likely to gain some distinction or position. **3** a person entered for an examination. □ **can·di·dacy** *noun* **can·di·da·ture** *noun Brit.* [French *candidat* or Latin *candidatus* white-robed (Roman candidates wearing white)]

candid camera *noun* a small camera for taking candid photographs.

can·di·dia·sis /ˌkandɪˈdaiəsɪs/ *noun* an infection with candida, esp. causing oral or vaginal thrush.

can·died *adjective Cooking* **1** (esp. of fruit) preserved by being coated or impregnated with sugar. **2** cooked with a large quantity of sugar (*candied parsnips*).

can·dle ● *noun* **1 a** a cylinder or block of wax or tallow with a central wick that is burned for light. **b** = VOTIVE CANDLE 1. **2** = CANDLEPOWER. ● *verb* **1** *transitive* test (an egg) for freshness by holding it to the light. **2** *intransitive* esp. *Cdn* (of ice) deteriorate into candle ice. □ **cannot hold a candle to** cannot be compared with; is much inferior to. **not worth the candle** not justifying the cost or trouble. [Old English *candel* from Latin *candela* from *candēre* shine]

candle·fish *noun* N Amer. = EULACHON. [CANDLE + FISH¹, from the practice of inserting a cloth wick into the fish, which has a very high oil content, and using it as a candle.]

candle holder *noun* = CANDLESTICK.

candle ice *noun* (also **candled ice**) esp. *Cdn* ice which has deteriorated into candle-like icicles before breaking up.

candle·light *noun* light provided by candles (also *attributive*: *candlelight dinner*). □ **candle·lit** *adjective*

Candle·mas /ˈkandləs/ *noun* Christianity (in some churches) a feast with blessing of candles (2 Feb.), commemorating the Purification of the Virgin Mary and the presentation of Christ in the Temple. [Old English *Candelmæsse* (as CANDLE, MASS²)]

candle·power *noun* a unit of luminous intensity.

candle·stick *noun* a holder for one or more candles.

candle·wick *noun* **1** a thick soft cotton yarn. **2** material made from this, usu. with a tufted pattern.

can-do *attributive adjective* informal displaying enthusiasm, confidence, and efficiency (*can-do attitude*).

Can·dolle /kãˈdɒl/ **Au·gus·tin Pyr·ame de** (1778–1841), Swiss botanist. His prolific writings on taxonomy and botany were highly influential, and his scheme of classification prevailed for many years.

Can·dom·blé /kandəmˈbleɪ/ *noun* an Afro-Brazilian folk religion or cult based on traditional African religious practices modified by elements of Roman Catholicism and spiritualism. [Brazilian Portuguese, ultimate origin obscure]

can·dour *noun* (also **can·dor**) candid behaviour or action; frankness. [French *candeur* or Latin *candor* whiteness]

CANDU *noun* (*pl.* **CANDUs**) proprietary a nuclear reactor using easily replaceable fuel bundles and a heavy water cooling and moderating system. [CANADA¹ + DEUTERIUM + URANIUM]

C. & W. *abbreviation* country and western.

Candy, John (1950–94), Canadian comedian and movie actor. A key member of the SCTV comedy TV show, he subsequently had roles in films such as *Planes, Trains, and Automobiles* (1987) and *Uncle Buck* (1989).

candy ● *noun* (*pl.* **-dies**) **1** esp. *N Amer.* **a** a confection with a high proportion of sugar, often also including chocolate, nuts, etc. **b** such confections collectively. **2** sugar crystallized by repeated boiling and slow evaporation. ● *transitive verb* (**-dies, -died**) (usu. as **can·died** *adjective*) preserve by coating and impregnating with a sugar syrup (*candied fruit*). [French *sucre candi* candied sugar, from Arabic *kand* sugar]

candy apple *noun* N Amer. an apple covered with a hard, usu. bright red, sugar glaze and impaled on a stick.

candy-apple red *N Amer.* ● *noun* a bright, glossy red. ● *adjective* of this colour.

candy-ass *noun* N Amer. slang a timid or cowardly person. □ **candy-assed** *adjective*

candy bar *noun* esp. *US* = CHOCOLATE BAR.

candy cane *noun* a hard, thin, striped candy with a curved end resembling a walking stick, often eaten at Christmastime.

candy colours *plural noun* N Amer. bright colours, esp. pink, orange, yellow, and green. □ **candy-coloured** *adjective*

candy corn *noun* N Amer. candy resembling kernels of corn.

candy floss *noun* Cdn & Brit. a fluffy mass of spun sugar wrapped around a stick.

candy stripe *noun* a pattern consisting of stripes (usu. red or pink) on a white background. □ **candy-striped** *adjective*

candy·striper *noun* N Amer. a usu. young volunteer at a hospital. [from the candy-striped uniform often worn]

candy thermometer *noun* N Amer. a thermometer used in cooking jam and confectionery with graduations marking significant stages of concentration of the sugar syrup.

candy·tuft *noun* any of various plants of the genus *Iberis*, native to W Europe, with white, pink, or purple flowers in tufts. [obsolete *Candy* (*Candia* Crete) + TUFT]

cane ● *noun* **1 a** the hollow jointed stem of giant reeds or grasses (*bamboo cane*). **b** the solid stem of slender palms (*malacca cane*). **2** = SUGAR CANE. **3** a raspberry cane. **4** material of cane used for wickerwork etc. **5 a** a cane used as a walking stick or a support for a plant or an instrument of punishment. **b** any slender walking stick. ● *transitive verb* **1** beat with a cane. **2** weave cane into (a chair etc.). □ **caner** *noun* (in sense 2 of verb). **caning** *noun* [Old French from Latin *canna* from Greek *kanna*]

cane·brake *noun* esp. *US* a tract of land overgrown with canes.

cane chair *noun* a chair with a seat made of woven cane strips.

cane sugar *noun* sugar obtained from sugar cane.

cane toad *noun* a large brown toad, *Bufo marinus*, native to tropical America and introduced elsewhere originally for pest control.

Can·etti /kaˈneti/ **Elias** (1905–97), Bulgarian-born English novelist and playwright, whose works, written in German, often explore issues of alienation and crowd psychology, and include *Auto da Fé* (1935) and *Crowds and Power* (1960). He was awarded the Nobel Prize for literature in 1981.

CANEX *noun* Cdn a store for military personnel on a Canadian military base. [acronym from *Canadian Forces Exchange*]

can·id /ˈkanɪd/ *noun* an animal of the family Canidae, which includes dogs, wolves, foxes, etc. [modern Latin *canidae* from Latin *canis* dog]

ca·nine /ˈkeɪnaɪn/ ● *adjective* **1** of a dog or dogs. **2** of or belonging to the family Canidae, including dogs, wolves, foxes, etc. ● *noun* **1** a dog. **2** (in full **canine tooth**) a pointed tooth between the incisors and premolars. [Latin *caninus* from *canis* dog]

canine distemper *noun* see DISTEMPER² 1a.

Canis Major /ˈkeɪnɪs/ a small constellation, just south of the celestial equator and next to Orion, containing the brightest star in the sky, Sirius. [Latin, = greater dog]

Canis Minor /ˈkeɪnɪs/ a small constellation bordering the celestial equator, close to Orion. [Latin, lit. 'lesser dog']

can·is·ter /ˈkanɪstər/ *noun* **1** a container, often one of a set, for holding flour, sugar, coffee, tea, etc. **2 a** a cylinder of shot, tear gas, etc., that explodes on impact. **b** such cylinders collectively. **3** a metallic cylindrical container for storing toxic waste etc. [Latin *canistrum* from Greek *kanastron* wicker basket, from *kanna* CANE]

can·ker ● *noun* **1 a** a destructive fungus disease of trees and plants. **b** an open wound in the stem of a tree or plant. **2** Zool. an ulcerous ear disease of animals esp. cats and dogs. **3** Med. (also **canker sore**) esp. N Amer. an ulceration esp. on the lips or the inside of the mouth. **4** a corrupting influence. ● *transitive verb* **1** consume with canker. **2** infect with a pervasive and corrupting bitterness. □ **can·ker·ous** *adjective* [Old English *cancer* & Old Northern French *cancre*, Old French *chancre* from Latin *cancer* crab]

canker·worm *noun* any caterpillar of various wingless moths which consume the buds and leaves of shade and fruit trees in N America.

Can·Lit *abbreviation* Cdn informal Canadian literature. [abbreviation]

Can·more a town in SW Alberta, situated in the Rocky Mountains, about 100 km west of Calgary; pop. (2001) 10,792. □ **Can·mor·ite** *noun* [Malcolm *Canmore*: see MALCOLM III]

can·na *noun* any tropical plant of the genus *Canna* with bright flowers and ornamental leaves. [Latin: see CANE]

can·na·bin·oid /ˈkanəbɪnɔɪd/ *noun* any of a group of closely related compounds which include cannabinol and the active constituents of cannabis.

can·na·bin·ol /ˈkanəbɪnɒl/ *noun* a crystalline compound whose derivatives, esp. THC, are the active constituents of cannabis.

can·na·bis /ˈkanəbɪs/ *noun* **1** any hemp plant of the genus *Cannabis*, esp. Indian hemp. **2** a preparation of parts of this used as an intoxicant or hallucinogen (marijuana, hashish, bhang, etc.). [Latin from Greek]

cannabis resin *noun* a sticky product containing the active principles of cannabis, esp. from the flowering tops of the female cannabis plant.

Can·nary /ˈkanəri/ **Mar·tha Jane**, see CALAMITY JANE.

canned *adjective* **1** supplied in a can (*canned peas*). **2** pre-recorded (*canned laughter; canned music*). **3** informal drunk. **4** informal (of a speech etc.) prepared in advance to suit many different occasions.

can·nel·lini *noun* (also **cannellini bean**) a kidney-shaped bean of a medium-sized creamy-white variety. [Italian, lit. = 'small tubes']

can·nel·loni /ˌkanəˈloːni/ *plural noun* tubes or rolls of pasta stuffed with meat or a vegetable mixture. [Italian from *cannello* stalk]

can·nel·ure /ˈkanəlʊr/ *noun* the groove around a bullet etc. [French from *canneler* from *canne* reed, CANE]

Consonants: b *but*   d *dog*   f *few*   g *get*   h *her*   j *yes*   k *cat*   l *leg*   m *man*   n *no*   p *pen*   r *red*   s *sit*

can·ner *noun* **1** a large cooking vessel in which jars of preserves are immersed to be sterilized. **2** *Cdn* (*Maritimes*) a lobster designated for canning because it is too small for the market. **3** a person who preserves food by canning (*home canners*).

can·nery *noun* (pl. **-ies**) a factory where food is canned.

Cannes /kan/ a resort on the Mediterranean coast of France; pop. (1999) 67,304. An international film festival is held there annually.

can·ni·bal /ˈkanəbəl/ ● *noun* **1** a person who eats human flesh. **2** an animal that feeds on flesh of its own species. ● *adjective* of or like a cannibal. □ **can·ni·bal·ism** *noun* **can·ni·bal·is·tic** /-bəˈlɪstɪk/ *adjective* [originally pl. *Canibales* from Spanish: var. of *Caribes* name of a West Indian nation]

can·ni·bal·ize /ˈkanəbəˌlaɪz/ *transitive verb* (also esp. *Brit.* **-ise**) use (a machine etc.) as a source of spare parts for others. □ **can·ni·bal·iza·tion** /-ˈzeɪʃən/ *noun*

can·ni·kin /ˈkanɪkɪn/ *noun* a small drinking cup or can. [Dutch *kanneken* (as CAN², -KIN)]

Can·ning, Charles John, 1st Earl (1812–62), English statesman, Governor General of India 1856–8, and first viceroy 1858–62. His term as Governor General saw the suppression of the Indian Mutiny (1857).

can·ning *noun* the process of preserving food in cans or hermetically sealed glass jars.

Can·niz·zaro /ˌkanɪˈzɑːro/ **Stan·is·lao** (1826–1910), Italian chemist. He revived Avogadro's hypothesis, using it to distinguish clearly between atoms and molecules, and introducing the unified system of atomic and molecular weights; he also discovered a reaction (named after him) in which an aldehyde is converted into an acid and an alcohol in the presence of a strong alkali.

can·noli /kəˈnoːli/ *plural noun* a dessert consisting of small deep-fried pastry tubes filled with sweetened ricotta cheese and pieces of chocolate etc. [Italian, from *canna* reed]

can·non ● *noun* (pl. same or **can·nons**) **1** a large heavy gun installed on a carriage or mounting. **2** a similar device for discharging a specific substance (*water cannon*; *snow cannon*). **3** an automatic aircraft gun firing shells. **4** *Brit. Billiards* = CAROM. **5** *Mech.* a hollow cylinder moving independently on a shaft. ● *intransitive verb* **1** (usu. foll. by *against*, *into*) collide heavily or obliquely. **2** *Brit. Billiards* = CAROM. [French *canon* from Italian *cannone* large tube, from *canna* CANE: see CAROM]

can·non·ade /ˌkanəˈneɪd/ ● *noun* a period of continuous heavy gunfire. ● *transitive verb* bombard with a cannonade. [French from Italian *cannonata*]

cannon·ball ● *noun* **1** a large usu. metal ball fired by a cannon. **2** *Cdn* (*BC*) a cannonball-like weight tied to commercial fishing lines to control depth and angle. **3** *N Amer.* a jump (into a swimming pool etc.) with the knees clasped close to the chest. ● *intransitive verb* move with the speed and force of a cannonball.

cannon bone *noun* the tube-shaped bone between the hock and fetlock of a horse and other hoofed mammals.

cannon fodder *noun* people, esp. soldiers, regarded merely as material to be expended in war.

can·not *auxiliary verb* can not.

can·nula /ˈkanjʊlə/ *noun* (pl. **can·nu·lae** /-liː/ or **can·nu·las**) *Med.* a small tube inserted into the body to allow fluid to enter or escape. [Latin, diminutive of *canna* cane]

can·nu·late /ˈkanjʊˌleɪt/ *transitive verb Med.* introduce a cannula into. □ **can·nu·la·tion** *noun*

canny *adjective* (**can·ni·er, can·ni·est**) **1 a** shrewd, worldly-wise. **b** thrifty. **c** circumspect, cautious. **2** sly, drily humorous. **3** *Scot. & Northern England* pleasant, agreeable. □ **can·ni·ly** *adverb* **can·ni·ness** *noun* [CAN¹ (in sense 'know') + -Y¹]

canoe /kəˈnuː/ ● *noun* a small narrow boat with pointed upcurved ends usu. propelled by paddling (also *attributive*: *canoe route*; *canoe trip*). ● *verb* (**ca·noes, ca·noed, canoe·ing**) **1** *intransitive* travel in a canoe. **2** *transitive* paddle a canoe on or along (a lake, river, etc.). □ **canoe·ist** *noun* **canoe·ing** *noun* **canoe·able** *adjective* [Spanish and Haitian *canoa*]

canoe-camping *noun N Amer.* camping in which campgrounds are reached by canoe. □ **canoe-camper** *noun*

canoe·man *noun* (pl. **-men**) esp. *Cdn* **1** *hist.* a voyageur. **2** a canoeist.

can of worms *noun informal* a complicated problem.

can·ola /kəˈnoːlə/ *noun* any of several varieties of rapeseed low in erucic acid, producing an oil used in cooking (also *attributive*: *canola oil*). [CANADA¹ + -ola (with reference to Latin *oleum* oil)]

can·on *noun* **1 a** a general law, rule, principle, or criterion. **b** a church decree or law. **2 a** a member of a cathedral chapter. **b** a title in the Anglican Church, bestowed as an honorary title for distinguished service. **c** a member of certain Roman Catholic orders. **3 a** a collection or list of sacred books etc. accepted as genuine. **b** the recognized genuine works of a particular author, composer, etc.; a list of these. **c** a collection or list of books generally regarded as most important in a given field (*the literary canon*). **4** the part of the Roman Catholic Mass containing the words of consecration. **5** *Music* a piece with different parts taking up the same theme successively, either at the same or at a different pitch. [Old English from Latin from Greek *kanōn* rule]

canon·ess *noun* a member of a community of women living according to an ecclesiastical rule but not under a perpetual vow. [CANON + -ESS¹]

ca·non·ic·al /kəˈnɒnəkəl/ (also **ca·non·ic**) ● *adjective* **1 a** according to or ordered by canon law. **b** included in the canon of Scripture. **2** authoritative, standard, accepted. **3** of a cathedral chapter or a member of it. **4** *Music* in canon form. ● *noun* (in *pl.*) the canonical dress of the clergy. □ **ca·non·ic·al·ly** *adverb*

canonical hours *plural noun Christianity* **1** the times fixed for a formal set of prayers. **2** the offices appointed for these times, e.g. matins, vespers, compline, etc.

can·on·icity /ˌkanəˈnɪsɪti/ *noun* the status of being canonical.

can·on·ist *noun* an expert in canon law.

can·on·ize *transitive verb* (also esp. *Brit.* **-ise**) **1 a** declare officially to be a saint, usu. with a ceremony. **b** regard as a saint. **2 a** admit to the canon of Scripture. **b** accept as canonical. **3** sanction by Church authority. □ **can·on·iza·tion** *noun* [medieval Latin *canonizare*: see CANON]

canon law *noun* ecclesiastical law.

canon regular *noun* (also **regular canon**) see REGULAR *adjective* 14b.

can·onry *noun* (pl. **-ries**) the office or benefice of a canon.

ca·noo·dle /kəˈnuːdəl/ *intransitive verb informal* kiss and cuddle amorously. [19th-c.: origin unknown]

can opener *noun* a device for opening cans of food etc.

Ca·no·pic jar /kəˈnoːpɪk/ *noun* (also **Canopic vase**) an urn used for holding the entrails of an embalmed body in an ancient Egyptian burial. [Latin *Canopicus* from *Canopus* in ancient Egypt]

Ca·no·pus /kəˈnoːpəs/ a supergiant star, the brightest in the constellation Carina and the second brightest in the sky. [*Canopus*, the pilot of the fleet of Menelaus]

can·opy /ˈkanəpi/ ● *noun* (pl. **-opies**) **1 a** a covering hung or held up over a throne, bed, person, etc. **b** the sky. **c** an overhanging shelter. **2** *Archit.* a roof-like projection over a niche etc. **3** the uppermost layers of foliage etc. in a forest. **4 a** the expanding part of a parachute. **b** the cover of an aircraft's cockpit. ● *transitive verb* (**-opies, -opied**) (usu. in *passive*) cover with a canopy. [medieval Latin *canopeum* from Latin *conopeum* from Greek *kōnōpeion* couch with mosquito netting, from *kōnōps* gnat]

canopy bed *noun N Amer.* a four-poster bed with a canopy.

canot du maître /kaˌnoːduːˈmetrə/ *noun Cdn hist.* the largest birchbark canoe of the fur trade, up to 12 m (40 ft.) long, used between the St. Lawrence River and Lake Superior. Also called MONTREAL CANOE. [French, = canoe of the master]

canot du nord /kaˌnoːduːˈnɔr/ *noun Cdn hist.* a birchbark canoe of the fur trade, about 9 m (30 ft.) long, used on the rivers and lakes northwest of Lake Superior. Also called NORTH CANOE. [French, = canoe of the north]

Ca·nova /kəˈnoːvə/ **An·to·nio** (1757–1822), Italian sculptor. A leading exponent of neoclassicism, his most famous works range from classical subjects such as *Cupid and Psyche* (1792) and *The Three Graces* (1813–16) to funeral monuments and life-size busts of contemporaries such as Napoleon.

Canso a town situated on Chedabucto Bay, at the easternmost point of peninsular Nova Scotia; pop. (2001) 992. [ultimately from Mi'kmaq *kamsook* opposite the lofty cliff]

Canso, Strait of a narrow, deep passage of the N Atlantic, separating Cape Breton Island from peninsular Nova Scotia. [see CANSO]

canst *archaic* 2nd person sing. of CAN¹.

Cant. *abbreviation Bible* Canticles.

cant¹ ● *noun* **1** insincere pious or moral talk. **2** ephemeral or fashionable catchwords. **3** language peculiar to a class, profession, sect, etc.; jargon. ● *intransitive verb* talk hypocritically or sanctimoniously. [earlier of musical sound, of intonation, and of beggars' whining; perhaps from the singing of religious mendicants: prob. from Latin *canere* sing]

cant² ● *noun* **1 a** a slanting surface, e.g. of a bank. **b** a bevel of a crystal etc. **2** an oblique push or movement that upsets or partly upsets something. **3** a tilted or sloping position. **4** a partly trimmed log. ● *verb* **1** *transitive* push or pitch out of level; tilt. **2** *intransitive* take or lie in a slanting position. **3** *transitive* impart a bevel to. **4** *intransitive Naut.* swing around. [Middle Low German *kant, kante*, Middle Dutch *cant*, point, side, edge, ultimately from Latin *cant(h)us* corner of the eye]

can't *contraction* can not.

Cantab. *abbreviation* of Cambridge University. [Latin *Cantabrigiensis*]

can·ta·bile /kan'tabilei/ *Music* ● *adverb & adjective* in a smooth singing style. ● *noun* a cantabile passage or movement. [Italian, = singable]

Can·tab·ria /kan'tabriə/ an autonomous region of N Spain; capital, Santander. □ **Can·tab·rian** *adjective & noun*

Can·ta·brig·ian /ˌkantə'bridʒiən/ ● *adjective* **1** of Cambridge, England or Cambridge University. **2** of Cambridge, Massachusetts or Harvard University. ● *noun* **1** a member or graduate of Cambridge University or Harvard University. **2** a native of Cambridge, England or Cambridge, Massachusetts. [Latin *Cantabrigia* Cambridge]

can·ta·loupe /'kantə,lo:p/ *noun* (also **can·ta·loup**) a small round variety of melon with netted skin and orange flesh. [French *cantaloup* from *Cantaluppi* near Rome, where it was first grown in Europe]

can·tan·ker·ous /kan'taŋkərəs/ *adjective* bad-tempered, quarrelsome. □ **can·tan·ker·ous·ly** *adverb* **can·tan·ker·ous·ness** *noun* [perhaps from Irish *cant* outbidding + *rancorous*]

can·ta·ta /kan'tatə, -tɒtə/ *noun Music* a short narrative or descriptive composition with vocal solos and usu. chorus and orchestral accompaniment. [Italian *cantata (aria)* sung (air), from *cantare* sing]

can·teen *noun* **1** a soldier's or camper's water flask. **2 a** a restaurant for employees in an office or factory etc. **b** a shop selling provisions or liquor in a barracks or camp. **3** a case or box of cutlery. **4** a set of eating or drinking utensils. [French *cantine* from Italian *cantina* cellar]

can·ter ● *noun* a gentle gallop. ● *verb* **1** *intransitive* (of a horse or its rider) go at a canter. **2** *transitive* make (a horse) canter. [short for *Canterbury pace*, from the supposed easy pace of medieval pilgrims to Canterbury]

Can·ter·bury /'kantərberi/ a city in Kent, SE England; pop. (est. 2002) 40,400. St. Augustine established a church and monastery there in 597 and its cathedral became a place of medieval pilgrimage after the murder there of St. Thomas Becket. It is the seat of the Archbishop of Canterbury, Primate of the Anglican Church.

Canterbury, Archbishop of the archbishop of the southern province of England, first peer of the realm, and Primate of All England of the Anglican Church.

Canterbury bell *noun* a cultivated campanula with large flowers. [after the bells of Canterbury pilgrims' horses]

Canterbury Plains a region on the central east coast of South Island, New Zealand.

can·thar·i·des /kan'θeri,di:z/ *plural noun* a preparation made from dried bodies of a beetle, *Lytta vesicatoria*, causing blistering of the skin and formerly used in medicine and sometimes taken as an aphrodisiac. *Also called* SPANISH FLY. [Latin from Greek *kantharis* Spanish fly]

cant hook *noun* an iron hook at the end of a long handle, used for rolling logs. [CANT² *verb* 1]

can·thus /'kanθəs/ *noun* (pl. **can·thi** /-θi/) the outer or inner corner of the eye, where the upper and lower lids meet. [Latin from Greek *kanthos*]

can·ticle /'kantikəl/ *noun* **1** a song or chant with a Biblical text. **2 Canticles** (also **Canticle of Canticles**) the Song of Solomon. [Old French *canticle* (var. of *cantique*) or Latin *canticulum* diminutive of *canticum* from *canere* sing]

can·ti·lena /ˌkantı'li:nə, -'leinə/ *noun Music* a simple or sustained melody. [Italian]

can·ti·lever /'kantə,li:vər/ ● *noun* **1** a long bracket or beam etc. projecting from a vertical support. **2** a beam or girder fixed at only one end. ● *intransitive verb* **1** project as a cantilever. **2** be supported by cantilevers. □ **can·ti·levered** *adjective* [17th c.: origin unknown]

cantilever brake *noun* a bicycle brake in which the brake pads are attached to outward-pointing metal arms that pivot on the frame.

cantilever bridge *noun* a bridge made of cantilevers projecting from the piers and connected by girders.

can·tina /kan'ti:nə/ *noun* a bar or wine shop, esp. in a Spanish-speaking area. [Spanish & Italian]

can·tle *noun* the protuberant part at the back of a saddle. [see CANT²]

can·to /'kantoʊ/ *noun* (pl. **-tos**) a division of a long poem. [Italian, = song, from Latin *cantus*]

Can·ton see GUANGZHOU.

can·ton ● *noun* **1** /'kantɒn/ **a** a subdivision of a country. **b** a state of the Swiss confederation. **2** /'kantɒn/ *Heraldry* a square division, less than a quarter, in the upper (usu. dexter) corner of a shield. ● *transitive verb* **1** put (troops) into quarters. **2** /kan'tɒn/ divide into cantons. □ **can·ton·al** /'kantənəl, kan'tɒnəl/ *adjective* [Old French, = corner (see CANT²): (v.) also partly from French *cantonner*]

Can·ton·ese /ˌkantə'ni:z/ ● *adjective* of Canton or the Cantonese dialect of Chinese. ● *noun* (pl. same) **1** a native of Canton. **2** the dialect of Chinese spoken in SE China and Hong Kong.

can·ton·ment /kan'tɒnmənt/ *noun* a lodging assigned to troops.

Can·tor, **Georg** (1845–1918), Russian-born German mathematician. Cantor's work on numbers laid the foundations of the theory of sets. He introduced the concept of transfinite numbers, and his work stimulated 20th-c. exploration of number theory and the logical foundation of mathematics.

can·tor /'kantər, -tɔr/ *noun* **1** the leader of the singing in church. **2** a person employed to sing the solo prayers in a synagogue. [Latin, = singer, from *canere* sing]

can·tor·ial /kan'tɔriəl/ *adjective* **1** of or relating to the cantor. **2** (in a church with choir stalls facing inward) of the left side of the choir (when facing the front of the church) (*compare* DECANAL).

can·toris /kan'tɔris/ *adjective Music* to be sung by the cantorial side of the choir in antiphonal singing (*compare* DECANI). [Latin, genitive of CANTOR precentor]

can·trip *noun Scot.* **1** a witch's trick. **2** a piece of mischief; a playful act. [18th c.: origin unknown]

Can·uck *informal* ● *noun* a Canadian. ● *adjective* Canadian. [apparently from *Canada*]

Ca·nute /kə'nu:t/ (also **Cnut, Knut**) (d.1035), Danish king of England 1016–35, Denmark 1018–35, and Norway 1028–35. His reign ended a prolonged struggle for power, and was a period of relative peace; it is recounted that he proved to his fawning courtiers that he was not all-powerful by showing that he could not stop the rising tide.

can·vas ● *noun* **1 a** a strong coarse kind of cloth usu. made from cotton or other coarse yarn and used for sails, tents, sturdy bags, etc. and as a surface for oil painting. **b** a piece of this. **2** a painting on canvas, esp. in oils. **3** an open kind of canvas used as a basis for tapestry and embroidery. **4** the floor of a boxing or wrestling ring. ● *transitive verb* (**can·vassed, can·vas·sing**; US **can·vased, can·vas·ing**) cover with canvas. □ **under canvas 1** in a tent or tents. **2** with sails spread. [Old Northern French *canevas*, ultimately from Latin *cannabis* hemp]

canvas·back *noun* a wild duck, *Aythya valisineria*, of N America, the male of which has back feathers the colour of unbleached canvas, and a chestnut head and neck.

can·vass /'kanvəs/ ● *verb* **1 a** *intransitive* solicit votes, charitable donations, support, custom, etc., esp. by going door to door. **b** *transitive* solicit votes etc. from (people). **c** *transitive* visit (a building, area, etc.) in order to do this. **2** *transitive* **a** ascertain opinions of. **b** discuss thoroughly. **3** *transitive* propose (an idea or plan etc.). ● *noun* the process of or an instance of canvassing. □ **can·vass·er** *noun* [originally = toss in a sheet, agitate, from CANVAS]

can·yon *noun* **1** a deep gorge, often with a stream or river. **2** a street hemmed in by tall buildings (*the canyons of downtown Toronto*). □ **canyon·land** *noun* [Spanish *cañón* tube, ultimately from Latin *canna* CANE]

canyon·ing *noun* the sport or activity of jumping into a fast-flowing mountain stream and allowing oneself to be carried downstream at high speed.

CAO *abbreviation* Chief Administrative Officer.

Caou·ette /kau'et/ (**Joseph-David**) **Réal** (1917–76), Canadian politician, who was a leading figure of the Social Credit movement in Quebec as head of the Ralliement des Créditistes party (1962–76).

caou·tchouc /'kautʃʊk/ *noun* raw rubber. [French from Carib *cahuchu*]

cap ● *noun* **1 a** a close-fitting brimless head covering, often of a soft material and usu. with a visor (*baseball cap*). **b** a head covering worn in a particular profession (*nurse's cap*). **c** esp. *Brit.* a cap awarded as a sign of membership of an (esp. national) sports team. **d** an academic mortarboard or soft hat. **e** a special hat as part of Highland costume. **2 a** a cover like a cap in shape or position (*kneecap*). **b** a device to seal a bottle or protect the point of a pen, lens of a camera, etc. **c** the top of a bird's head, esp. when distinctively coloured. **3** = CROWN noun 9b. **4** the pileus of a mushroom or toadstool. **5** (also **percussion cap**) a small amount of explosive powder contained in metal or paper and exploded by striking, used esp. in toy guns and formerly in some firearms. **6** an upward limit put on something (salary cap). ● transitive verb (**capped**, **cap·ping**) **1 a** put a cap on. **b** cover the top or end of. **c** set a limit to (rate-capping). **d** seal (a well) to prevent or control the loss of gas or oil. **2** esp. Brit. award a sports cap to. **3 a** lie on top of; form the cap of. **b** surpass, excel. **c** improve on (a story, quotation, etc.) esp. by producing a better or more apposite one. **d** serve as a final climax or culmination to; complete (capped the season with a shutout). □ **cap in hand** humbly. **if the cap fits** = IF THE SHOE FITS (see SHOE). **set one's cap at** try to attract as a suitor. □ **cap·ful** noun (pl. **-fuls**). **capped** adjective (also in combination). **cap·ping** noun [Old English cæppe from Late Latin cappa, perhaps from Latin caput head]

cap. abbreviation **1** capital. **2** capital letter. **3** chapter. **4** capitalization. [Latin capitulum or caput]

Capa /ˈkapə/ **Rob·ert** (born André Friedmann) (1913–54), Hungarian-born US photographer. An internationally acclaimed war photojournalist, he covered the Spanish Civil War and served as a correspondent for Life magazine during the Second World War.

ca·pabil·ity /ˌkeipəˈbiləti/ noun (pl. **-ities**) **1** (often foll. by of, for, to) ability, power; the condition of being capable. **2** an undeveloped or unused faculty.

ca·pable /ˈkeipəbəl/ adjective **1** competent, able, gifted. **2** (foll. by of) **a** having the ability or fitness or necessary quality for. **b** susceptible or admitting of (explanation or improvement etc.). □ **ca·pably** adverb [French from Late Latin capabilis from Latin capere hold]

cap·acious /kəˈpeiʃəs/ adjective roomy; able to hold much. □ **cap·acious·ly** adverb **cap·acious·ness** noun [Latin capax -acis from capere hold]

cap·aci·tance /kəˈpasitəns/ noun Electricity **1** the ability of a system to store an electric charge. **2** the ratio of the change in an electric charge in a system to the corresponding change in its electric potential. Symbol: **C**. [CAPACITY + -ANCE]

cap·aci·tor /kəˈpasitər/ noun Electricity a device of one or more pairs of conductors separated by insulators used to store an electric charge.

cap·acity /kəˈpasəti/ ● noun (pl. **-ies**) **1 a** the power of containing, receiving, experiencing, or producing. **b** the maximum amount that can be contained or produced etc. **c** the volume, e.g. of the cylinders in an internal combustion engine. **2 a** mental power. **b** a faculty or talent. **3** a position or function (in a civil capacity; in my capacity as a critic). **4** legal competence. **5** Electricity capacitance. ● attributive adjective filling all available space (capacity crowd). □ **to capacity** fully; using all resources (working to capacity). □ **cap·aci·tive** adjective (in sense 5). [French from Latin capacitas -tatis (as CAPACIOUS)]

ca·pari·son /kəˈperisən/ ● noun **1** (usu. in pl.) a horse's trappings. **2** equipment, finery. ● transitive verb put caparisons on; adorn richly. [obsolete French caparasson from Spanish caparazón saddle cloth, from capa CAPE[1]]

Cap-de-la-Madeleine /ˌkapdəlamadˈlen/ a former city in south central Quebec, situated on the east side of the Rivière Saint-Maurice near its mouth, now part of Trois-Rivières; pop. (2001) 32,534. [ultimately after J. de La Ferté de La Madeleine, abbot of Sainte-Marie-Madeleine de Châteaudun, France]

cape[1] ● noun **1** a sleeveless cloak. **2** a short sleeveless cloak as a fixed or detachable part of a longer cloak or coat. ● transitive verb N Amer. skin the head and neck of (an animal) to prepare a hunting trophy. □ **caped** adjective [French from Provençal capa from Late Latin cappa CAP]

cape[2] noun **1** a headland or promontory. **2** (**the Cape**) **a** the Cape of Good Hope. **b** the former Cape Province of South Africa. [Old French cap from Provençal cap, ultimately from Latin caput head]

Cape Ann noun Cdn (Nfld) a broad-brimmed rain hat with an extended back flap. [Cape Ann in Massachusetts]

Cape Breton 1 a regional municipality of E Cape Breton Island, comprising the urban communities of Dominion, Glace Bay, Louisbourg, New Waterford, North Sydney and Sydney Mines, as well as the metropolitan area of Sydney; pop. (2001) 105,968. **2** = CAPE BRETON ISLAND. □ **Cape Bret·on·er** noun [see BRETON, CAPE]

Cape Breton Highlands National Park a park at the northern end of Cape Breton Island, Nova Scotia. Established in 1936, it encompasses a large part of the Cabot Trail.

Cape Breton Island an island forming the northeastern part of the province of Nova Scotia. It is separated from peninsular Nova Scotia by the Strait of Canso.

Cape Breton pork pie noun Cdn a date-filled tart with short pastry.

Cape Cod 1 a sandy peninsula in SE Massachusetts, forming a wide curve enclosing Cape Cod Bay, and having many resort towns. **2** a style of rectangular house, usu. one-and-a-half storeys, with a steeply gabled roof (also attributive: Cape Cod house). □ **Cape Cod·der** noun

Cape Colony an early name (1814–1910) for the former CAPE PROVINCE.

Cape Coloured South Africa ● adjective of the Coloured (see COLOURED 2) population of Cape Province. ● noun a member of this population.

Cape Dorset a hamlet in Nunavut, situated on Dorset Island, just off the southwest coast of Baffin Island; pop. (2001) 1,148. It is a noted Inuit art and crafts centre. [E. Sackville, 7th Earl of Dorset d.1652]

ca·peesh interjection var. of CAPISCE.

Cape gooseberry noun **1** an edible soft roundish yellow berry enclosed in a lantern-like husk. **2** the S American plant, Physalis peruviana, bearing these.

Cape Island boat noun (also **Cape Islander**) Cdn a boat used by inshore fishermen esp. in Nova Scotia, with a high prow and a low stern. [after Cape Sable Island, NS, where first built in 1905]

Cape Johnson Depth the deepest point of the Philippine Trench, off the east coast of the Philippines, dropping to 10 497 m (34,440 ft.) below sea level. [USS Cape Johnson, which took soundings there in 1945]

Čapek /ˈtʃɒpek/ **Karel** (1890–1938), Czech novelist and playwright. He wrote several plays with his brother Josef (1887–1945), including the satirical The Insect Play (1921); his best-known independent work, R.U.R. (1920), a cautionary drama about the dangers of mechanization, introduced the word 'robot'.

cape·let /ˈkeiplet/ noun a small cape covering the shoulders.

cape·lin /ˈkaplin, ˈkeiplin/ noun (also **cap·lin**) a small smelt-like fish, Mallotus villosus, of the N Atlantic, used as food and as bait for catching cod etc. [French from Provençal capelan: see CHAPLAIN]

capelin scull noun Cdn (Nfld) **1** the seasonal migration of capelin from the sea to inshore waters to spawn. **2** the season when this occurs, usu. June and July.

Ca·pella /kəˈpelə/ a yellow star, the brightest in the constellation Auriga, and the sixth-brightest in the night sky. [Latin = she-goat]

cap·el·lini /ˌkapəˈliːni/ noun very fine spaghetti. Also called ANGEL HAIR. [Italian, diminutive of capelli hair]

Cape of Good Hope a mountainous promontory south of Cape Town, South Africa, near the southern extremity of Africa.

Cape Province the former province of South Africa containing the Cape of Good Hope. In 1994 it was divided into the provinces of Northern Cape, Western Cape, and Eastern Cape.

Caper noun a native or resident of Cape Breton.

caper[1] ● intransitive verb jump or run about playfully. ● noun **1** a playful jump or leap. **2 a** a fantastic proceeding; a prank. **b** informal any (esp. disreputable) activity or occupation. □ **cut a caper** (or **capers**) act friskily. □ **caper·er** noun [abbreviation of CAPRIOLE]

caper[2] noun **1** a bramble-like S. European shrub, Capparis spinosa. **2** (in pl.) its flower buds cooked and pickled for use as flavouring esp. for a savoury sauce. [French câpres from Latin capparis from Greek kapparis, treated as pl.: compare CHERRY, PEA]

caper·cail·lie /ˌkapərˈkeili/ noun (also **caper·cail·zie** /-lzi/) a large European grouse, Tetrao urogallus. [Gaelic capull coille horse of the wood]

Cape Sable Island a small island off the southwestern tip of Nova Scotia, to which it is connected by a causeway. [see SABLE, CAPE]

Capet /kaˈpei, ˈkapət/ **Hugh** (or **Hugues**) (938–96), king of France 987–96. His election as king marked the foundation of the Capetian dynasty.

Cap·etian /kəˈpiːʃən/ noun a member of a dynasty of kings of France, founded by Hugh Capet in 987 in succession to the Carolingian dynasty. It survived until 1328, when its extinction gave rise to Edward III's claim to the French throne and the start of the Hundred Years War.

Cape Town the legislative capital of South Africa and administrative capital of the province of Western Cape; pop. (est. 2002) 2,686,000. It is situated at the foot of Table Mountain. □ **Cape·ton·ian** /keipˈtoːniən/ noun & adjective

Cape Verde /vɜrd/ a country consisting of a group of islands in the Atlantic off the coast of Senegal; pop. (est. 2002) 408,760; capital, Praia. □ **Cape Verd·ean** /ˈvɜrdiən/ adjective & noun [named after the most westerly cape of Africa]

capi·as /ˈkapi,əs, ˈkeip-/ noun Law a writ ordering the arrest of the person named. [Latin, = you are to seize, from capere take]

capi·col·lo /ˌkapɪˈkoːloː/ noun (also **capi·col·la** /-lə/) spicy Italian cured pork shoulder butt, usu. served in thin slices. [Italian]

Capi·lano River /ˌkapɪˈlanoː/ a river flowing south from Capilano Lake through a spectacular canyon into Burrard Inlet.

cap·il·lar·ity /ˌkapɪˈlerɪti/ noun (also **capillary action**) a phenomenon at liquid boundaries resulting in the rise or depression of liquids in narrow tubes. [French *capillarité* (as CAPILLARY)]

cap·il·lary /kəˈpɪləri/ ● adjective 1 of or like a hair. 2 (of a tube) of hairlike internal diameter. 3 of one of the delicate ramified blood vessels intervening between arteries and veins. ● noun (pl. **-ies**) 1 a capillary tube. 2 a capillary blood vessel. [Latin *capillaris* from *capillus* hair]

ca·pisce /kəˈpiːʃ/ interjection N Amer. slang do you understand? [Italian *capisce* formal for 'do you understand?']

cap·ital¹ ● noun 1 the city or town in a country, province, etc. at which the principal government institutions (the legislature, judiciary, the government administrative headquarters) are located. 2 the most noteworthy place for a specified quality (*sunshine capital; crime capital*). 3 a the money or other assets with which a company starts in business. b accumulated wealth, esp. as used in further production. c money invested or lent at interest. 4 the holders of wealth as a class; capitalists, employers of labour. 5 a capital letter. ● adjective 1 a principal; most important; leading. b informal excellent, first-rate. 2 a involving or punishable by death (*capital punishment; a capital offence*). b (of an error etc.) vitally harmful; fatal. 3 (of letters of the alphabet) large in size and of the form used to begin sentences and names etc. ● interjection expressing approval or satisfaction. □ **make capital out of** use to one's advantage. **with a capital —** emphatically such (*art with a capital A*). □ **cap·ital·ly** adverb [Old French from Latin *capitalis* from *caput -itis* head]

cap·ital² noun Archit. the head or cornice of a pillar or column. [Old French *capitel* from Late Latin *capitellum* diminutive of Latin *caput* head]

capital campaign noun a campaign to raise money to be invested in permanent assets such as land, buildings, machinery, etc. rather than spent on operating costs.

capital flight noun the movement of capital out of a region of economic instability.

capital gain noun a profit from the sale of investments or property.

capital gains tax noun a tax levied on the profit from the sale of investments or property.

capital goods plural noun goods, esp. machinery etc., used or to be used in producing commodities (opp. CONSUMER GOODS).

Capital Hill the capital of the Northern Marianas, situated on the island of Saipan; pop. (est. 1995) 2,698.

capital-intensive adjective Business requiring much use of capital.

cap·ital·ism noun 1 a an economic system in which the production and distribution of goods depend on invested private capital and profit-making. b the possession of capital or wealth. 2 the dominance of private owners of capital and of production for profit.

cap·ital·ist ● noun 1 a person using or possessing capital; a rich person. 2 an advocate of capitalism. ● adjective of or favouring capitalism. □ **cap·ital·is·tic** adjective **cap·ital·is·tic·ally** adverb

cap·ital·ize /ˈkapɪtəˌlaɪz/ verb (also esp. Brit. **-ise**) 1 transitive a convert into or provide with capital. b calculate or realize the present value of an income. c reckon (the value of an asset) by setting future benefits against the cost of maintenance. 2 transitive a write (a letter of the alphabet) as a capital. b begin (a word) with a capital letter. 3 intransitive (foll. by *on*) use to one's advantage; profit from. □ **cap·ital·iz·a·tion** noun

capital sum noun a lump sum of money, esp. payable to an insured person.

capi·ta·tion /ˌkapɪˈteɪʃən/ noun a tax or fee at a set rate per person (also attributive: *capitation grant*). [French *capitation* or Late Latin *capitatio* poll tax, from *caput* head]

Cap·itol /ˈkapɪtəl/ noun a building housing a legislature in the US, esp. the federal legislative building in Washington. [Latin *capitolium* from *caput* head]

Capitol Hill noun 1 the hill in Washington, DC, on which the Capitol sits. 2 the US Congress.

Cap·ito·line /kəˈpɪtəlaɪn/ noun (prec. by the) (also **Capitoline Hill**) the hill in Rome on which the temple of Jupiter stood in ancient times.

ca·pitu·lar /kəˈpɪtʃʊlər/ adjective 1 of or relating to a cathedral chapter. 2 Anat. of or relating to a terminal protuberance of a bone. [Late Latin *capitularis* from Latin *capitulum* CHAPTER]

ca·pitu·late /kəˈpɪtʃʊˌleɪt/ intransitive verb surrender, esp. on stated conditions. □ **ca·pitu·la·tor** noun **ca·pitu·la·tory** /-ləˌtɔri/ adjective [medieval Latin *capitulare* draw up under headings, from Latin *caput* head]

ca·pitu·la·tion /kəˌpɪtjʊˈleɪʃən/ noun 1 the act of capitulating; surrender. 2 a statement of the main divisions of a subject. 3 hist. an agreement or set of conditions.

ca·pitu·lum /kəˈpɪtʃʊləm/ noun (pl. **ca·pitu·la** /-lə/) Bot. an inflorescence with flowers clustered together like a head, as in the daisy family. [Latin, diminutive of *caput* head]

cap·let noun an oblong medicinal tablet, usu. coated. [blend of CAPSULE + TABLET]

cap·lin var. of CAPELIN.

cap'n noun slang captain. [contraction]

capo¹ /ˈkeɪpoː/ noun (in full **capo tasto** /ˈtastoː/) (pl. **capos** or **capo tas·tos**) Music a device secured across the neck of a fretted instrument to raise equally the tuning of all strings by the required amount. [Italian *capo tasto* head stop]

capo² /ˈkapoː/ noun (pl. **capos**) esp. N Amer. the head of a crime syndicate, esp. the Mafia, or one of its branches. [Italian, = 'boss' from Latin *caput* head]

capo di tutti capi /ˈkapoː diː ˈtuːti ˈkapiː/ noun esp. N Amer. the overall head of a crime syndicate. [Italian, = 'boss of all bosses' (as CAPO²)]

capo·eira /kapoˈeːrə/ noun a system of physical discipline and movement emphasizing leg and foot movements and performed inside a circle formed by onlookers, originating among Brazilian slaves, treated as a martial art and dance form. □ **capo·eir·is·ta** noun [Brazilian Portuguese]

ca·pon /ˈkeɪpɒn/ noun a cockerel castrated and fattened for eating. □ **capon·ize** transitive verb (also Brit. **-ise**). [Old English from Anglo-French *capun*, Old French *capon*, ultimately from Latin *capo -onis*]

capo·nata /ˌkapoˈnatə/ noun a dish of eggplant, olives, and onions in a tomato sauce, seasoned with herbs, served typically as an appetizer. [Italian *capponata*]

Ca·pone /kəˈpoːn/ **Al·phonse** (also called **Scar·face**) (1899–1947), Italian-born US gangster. He was notorious for his domination of organized crime in Chicago in the 1920s, and although indirectly responsible for many murders, it was for federal income tax evasion that he was eventually imprisoned in 1931.

Ca·po·te /kəˈpoːti/ **Tru·man** (1924–84), US writer. His works range from the lighthearted novella *Breakfast at Tiffany's* (1958) to the grim and meticulous recreation of a brutal multiple murder in *In Cold Blood* (1966).

ca·pote /kəˈpɒt/ noun (also **capot**) hist. a long coat with a hood, esp. (in Canada) tied with a colourful sash. [French, diminutive of *cape* CAPE¹]

Cap·pa·do·cia /ˌkapəˈdoːʃə/ an ancient region of central Asia Minor, between Lake Tuz and the Euphrates, north of Cilicia. It was an important centre of early Christianity. □ **Cap·pa·do·cian** adjective & noun

cap·per noun 1 informal an event etc. that surpasses or completes others. 2 a device or person that applies caps.

cap·puc·cino /ˌkapəˈtʃiːnoː/ noun (pl. **-cinos**) espresso coffee with milk made frothy with pressurized steam. [Italian, = CAPUCHIN]

Capra /ˈkaprə/ **Frank** (1897–1991), Italian-born US film director. His reputation rests on the comedies which he directed in the 1930s and early 1940s, such as *It Happened One Night* (1934), *Arsenic and Old Lace* (1944), and *It's a Wonderful Life* (1946); he won six Oscars for his films. □ **Capra·esque** adjective

Capri /kəˈpriː/ an island off the west coast of Italy, south of Naples.

ca·pri /kəˈpriː/ noun (pl. **ca·pris**) (usu. attributive) women's close-fitting, tapered pants or leggings extending to just above the ankles (*capri pants; capri tights*). [CAPRI]

ca·pric·cio /kəˈpriːtʃio/ noun (pl. **-cios**) 1 a lively and usu. short musical composition. 2 a painting etc. representing a fantasy or a mixture of real and imaginary features. [Italian, from *capo* 'head' + *riccio* 'hedgehog', literally 'head with the hair standing on end', hence 'horror', later 'a sudden start' (influence by *capra* 'goat', associated with frisky movement]

ca·pric·cio·so /kəˌpriːtʃiˈoːsoː/ adverb & adjective Music in a free and impulsive style. [Italian, = capricious]

ca·price /kəˈpriːs/ noun 1 a an unaccountable or whimsical change of mind or conduct. b a tendency to this. 2 a work of lively fancy in painting, drawing, or music; a capriccio. [French from Italian CAPRICCIO]

Consonants: b but d dog f few g get h her j yes k cat l leg m man n no p pen r red s sit

ca·pri·cious /kəˈprɪʃəs, -prɪʃ-/ *adjective* **1** guided by or given to caprice. **2** irregular, unpredictable. □ **ca·pri·cious·ly** *adverb* **ca·pri·cious·ness** *noun*

Cap·ri·corn /ˈkaprɪˌkɔrn/ *noun* **1** (also **Cap·ri·corn·us** /-ˈkɔrnəs/) a constellation between Sagittarius and Aquarius, traditionally regarded as contained in the figure of a goat's horns. **2 a** the tenth sign of the zodiac. **b** a person born when the sun is in this sign, usu. between 22 December and 19 January. □ **Cap·ri·corn·ian** *noun & adjective* [Old French *capricorne* from Latin *capricornus* from *caper -pri* goat + *cornu* horn]

cap·rine /ˈkaprain/ *adjective* of or like a goat. [Latin *caprinus* from *caper -pri* goat]

cap·ri·ole /ˈkaprɪˌoʊl/ ● *noun* **1** a leap or caper. **2** a trained horse's high leap and kick without advancing. ● *verb* **1** *intransitive* (of a horse or its rider) perform a capriole. **2** *transitive* make (a horse) capriole. [French from Italian *capriola* leap, ultimately from *caper -pri* goat]

Ca·pri·vi Strip /kəˈpriːvi/ a narrow strip of Namibia, which extends towards Zambia from the northeast corner of Namibia and reaches the Zambezi River. [Leo Graf von *Caprivi*, German imperial Chancellor d.1899]

cap·rock *noun* **1** a hard rock or stratum overlying a salt dome or a deposit of oil, gas, coal, etc. **2** a hard rock or stratum at the top of a hoodoo, butte, etc.

Cap-Rouge /kapˈruːʒ/ a former town in SE central Quebec, now part of the city of Québec; pop. (2001) 13,700. [French, lit. 'red cape', with reference to the cape's red-coloured schistose rock]

caps. *abbreviation* capital letters.

cap·sai·cin /kapˈseɪəsɪn/ *noun* a compound responsible for the pungency of capsicums. [earlier *capsicine* CAPSICUM + -IN]

Cap·si·an /ˈkapsiən/ ● *adjective* of or relating to a mesolithic culture surrounding the salt lakes of Tunisia (8000–2700 BC). ● *noun* this culture. [Latin *Capsa* = Gafsa in Tunisia]

cap·si·cum /ˈkapsɪkəm/ *noun* **1** any plant of the genus *Capsicum*, having edible capsular fruits containing many seeds, esp. *C. annuum*, varieties of which yield paprikas, green or red peppers, chilies, and cayenne pepper. **2** the fruit of any of these plants. [modern Latin, perhaps from Latin *capsa* box]

cap·sid[1] *noun* = MIRID. [modern Latin *Capsus* a genus of them]

cap·sid[2] *noun* the protein coat or shell of a virus. [French *capside* from Latin *capsa* box]

cap·size /ˈkapsaiz, kapˈsaiz/ *verb* **1** *transitive* upset or overturn (a boat). **2** *intransitive* be capsized. [*cap-* as in Provençal *capvirar*, French *chavirer*: -*size* unexplained]

cap sleeve *noun* a short sleeve which extends over the shoulder but not under the arm.

cap·stan /ˈkapstən/ *noun* **1** a thick revolving cylinder with a vertical axis, for winding an anchor cable or a halyard etc. **2** a revolving spindle on a tape recorder, that guides the tape past the head. [Provençal *cabestan*, ultimately from Latin *capistrum* halter, from *capere* seize]

cap·stone *noun* **1 a** a stone which caps a structure. **b** = CAPROCK. **2** a culmination or highest point.

cap·sule /ˈkapsəl, -sjəl/ *noun* **1** a small soluble case of gelatin enclosing a dose of medicine and swallowed with it. **2** (in full **space capsule**) a detachable compartment of a spacecraft or nose cone of a rocket. **3** a membranous or fibrous envelope around an organ, joint, etc. **4** a top or cover for a bottle, esp. the foil or plastic covering the cork of a wine bottle. **5 a** a dry fruit that releases its seeds when ripe. **b** the spore-producing part of mosses and liverworts. **6** *Biol.* an enveloping layer surrounding certain bacteria. **7** a concise or highly condensed report (also *attributive*: *a capsule review*). □ **cap·su·lar** *adjective* **cap·su·late** *adjective* **cap·su·lat·ed** *adjective* [French from Latin *capsula* from *capsa* CASE[2]]

cap·su·lize /ˈkapsəˌlaiz/ *transitive verb* (also esp. *Brit.* -**ise**) put (information etc.) in compact form.

Capt *abbreviation* Captain.

cap·tain /ˈkaptən/ ● *noun* **1 a** a chief or leader. **b** the leader of a team, esp. in sports. **c** a powerful or influential person (*captain of industry*). **2 a** the person in command of a ship. **b** the pilot of a civil aircraft. **3** (also **Captain**) *Military* **a** (in Canada, the US, and the UK) an officer in land-based forces ranking below major and above lieutenant. **b** (in Canada and the US) an officer in the air force ranking below major and above lieutenant. **c** (in Canada, the US, and the UK) a naval officer ranking above commander. **d** (in the US) an officer in the Marine Corps ranking below major and above first lieutenant. **e** (in the Sûreté du

Québec) an officer ranking above lieutenant and below inspector. **f** (in some Canadian police forces) a municipal police officer ranking above lieutenant and below inspector. **4 a** a foreman. **b** *N Amer.* a supervisor of waiters or bellboys. **5 a** a great soldier or strategist. **b** an experienced commander. ● *transitive verb* be captain of; lead.
□ **cap·tain·cy** *noun* (*pl.* -**cies**). **captain·ship** *noun* [Old French *capitain* from Late Latin *capitaneus* chief, from Latin *caput capit-* head]

captain's bed *noun N Amer.* a bed consisting of a wooden frame for the mattress with drawers beneath it.

captain's chair *noun N Amer.* a wooden chair whose spindled back curves around to form armrests.

cap·tion ● *noun* **1** a title or brief explanation appended to an illustration, cartoon, etc. **2** wording appearing on a cinema or television screen as part of a film or broadcast. **3** the heading of a chapter or article etc. **4** *Law* the heading on a document, containing information concerning the parties involved etc. ● *transitive verb* provide with a caption. [Latin *captio* from *capere capt-* take]

cap·tious /ˈkapʃəs/ *adjective* given to finding fault or raising petty objections. □ **cap·tious·ly** *adverb* **cap·tious·ness** *noun* [Old French *captieux* or Latin *captiosus* (as CAPTION)]

cap·tiv·ate /ˈkaptəˌveit/ *transitive verb* attract and hold the interest of; charm. □ **cap·tiv·at·ing·ly** *adverb* **cap·tiv·a·tion** *noun* [Late Latin *captivare* take captive (as CAPTIVE)]

cap·tive /ˈkaptɪv/ ● *noun* a person or animal that has been taken prisoner or confined. ● *adjective* **1** imprisoned or confined (*held them captive in a farmhouse*). **2 a** unable to escape. **b** in a position of having to comply (*captive audience*; *captive market*). **3** of or like a prisoner (*captive state*). **4** pertaining to animals kept in captivity (*captive breeding*). [Latin *captivus* from *capere capt-* take]

captive breeding *noun* a program of breeding animals held in captivity. □ **captive-bred** *adjective*

cap·tiv·ity /kapˈtɪvɪti/ *noun* (*pl.* -**ities**) **1** the condition or circumstances of being held or confined against one's will. **2** a period of captivity.

Capt(N) *abbreviation Cdn* captain (in the Navy).

cap·tor /ˈkaptər, -tər/ *noun* a person who takes or holds (a person etc.) captive. [Latin (as CAPTIVE)]

cap·ture /ˈkaptʃər/ ● *transitive verb* **1 a** take prisoner. **b** seize as a prize. **c** obtain by force or trickery. **2** win control of (something) (*captured our imagination*; *captures public support*). **3** portray or preserve faithfully, esp. in permanent form (*captured their adventure on film*; *captures the spirit of the twenties*). **4** *Physics* absorb (a subatomic particle). **5** (in board games) make a move that secures the removal of (an opposing piece) from the board. **6** cause (data) to be stored in a computer. **7** *Astronomy* (of a star, planet, etc.) bring (a less massive body) permanently within its gravitational influence. ● *noun* **1** the act of capturing. **2** a thing or person captured. □ **cap·tur·er** *noun* [French from Latin *captura* from *capere capt-* take]

Capu·chin /ˈkapjuːtʃɪn, -puːʃɪn, -juː-/ *noun* **1** a Franciscan friar of a branch established in 1529 to re-emphasize the ideals of poverty and austerity. **2** (**capuchin**) any monkey of the genus *Cebus* of S America, with cowl-like fur on its head. [French from Italian *cappuccino* from *cappuccio* cowl, from *cappa* CAPE[1]]

capy·bara /ˌkapəˈbarə/ *noun* a very large semi-aquatic rodent of the genus *Hydrochoerus*, resembling a guinea pig, native to S America. [Tupi]

car *noun* **1** a road vehicle with an enclosed passenger compartment, powered by an internal combustion engine; an automobile. **2 a** wheeled vehicle, esp. of a specified kind (*cable car*). **3** *N Amer.* a railway vehicle for carrying passengers or freight. **4** the passenger compartment of an elevator, cableway, balloon, etc. **5** *N Amer.* = STREETCAR. **6** *archaic* a wheeled vehicle; a chariot. □ **car·ful** *noun* (*pl.* -**fuls**). [Anglo-French & Old Northern French *carre*, ultimately from Latin *carrum, carrus*, of Old Celtic origin]

cara·bi·neer /ˌkarəbəˈniːr/ *noun* (also **cara·bi·nier**) *hist.* a soldier whose principal weapon is a carbine. [French *carabinier* from *carabine* CARBINE]

cara·biner /ˌkarəˈbinər/ *noun* (also **kara·biner**) a clip with a spring latch used for securing a rope in climbing or mountaineering. [German *Karabiner* from *Karabinerhaken* carbine hook: see CARBINE]

cara·bi·niere /ˌkarəbɪnˈjeri, ˈkarə-/ *noun* (*pl.* **cara·bi·nieri** /-eri/) a member of an Italian army corps which serves as one of Italy's three national police forces. [Italian]

cara·cal /ˈkarəˌkal/ *noun* a lynx-like feline, *Felis caracal*, native to

N Africa and SW Asia, having tufted black ears. [French or Spanish from Turkish *karakulak* from *kara* black + *kulak* ear]

Cara·calla /ˌkerəˈkalə/ (full name Marcus Aurelius Antoninus) (188–217), Roman emperor 211–17. Sole ruler after the murder of his brother in 212, he campaigned first in Germany and then in the east, where he hoped to repeat the conquests of Alexander the Great, but was assassinated in Mesopotamia. By an edict of 212 he granted Roman citizenship to all free inhabitants of the Roman Empire.

cara·cara /ˌkarəˈkarə/ *noun* any of several mainly tropical American birds of prey related to falcons but resembling vultures. [Spanish or Portuguese *caracará*, from Tupi-Guarani (imitative)]

Ca·ra·cas /kəˈrakəs/ the capital of Venezuela; pop. (est. 2002) 1,763,100.

cara·cole /ˈkerəˌkoːl/ ● *noun* a horse's half turn to the right or left. ● *intransitive verb* (of a horse or its rider) perform a caracole. [French]

cara·cul *var. of* KARAKUL.

ca·rafe /kəˈraf/ *noun* 1 a wide-mouthed glass container for beverages, esp. water or wine. 2 the contents of a carafe. 3 an insulated, decorative jug for serving hot or cold beverages, esp. coffee. [French from Italian *caraffa*, ultimately from Arabic *ġarrāfa* drinking vessel]

cara·gana /kerəˈganə/ *noun* any Asian leguminous shrub of the genus *Caragana*, esp. the Siberian pea (*C. arborescens*), widely planted as hedging. [of Turkic origin; compare Kyrgyz *karaghan* Siberian pea]

ca·ramba /kəˈrɒmbə/ *interjection* (also **ay caramba**) expressing exasperation, surprise, etc. [Spanish]

caram·bola /ˌkerəmˈboːlə/ *noun* 1 a small tree, *Averrhoa carambola*, native to SE Asia, bearing golden-yellow ribbed fruit. 2 this fruit. *Also called* STARFRUIT. [Portuguese, prob. from Marathi *karambal*]

cara·mel /ˈkerəˌmel, ˈkarməl/ ● *noun* 1 sugar or syrup heated until it turns brown, then used as a flavouring, garnish, or colour in food or drink. 2 a kind of soft candy made with sugar, butter, milk, etc., melted and further heated. 3 the light brown colour of caramel. ● *adjective* 1 flavoured with caramel. 2 of the light brown colour of caramel. ¶ *Caramel* and *caramelize* are often misspelled *carmel* or *carmelize*. [French from Spanish *caramelo*]

cara·mel·ize /ˈkarməˌlaiz, ˈkerə-/ *verb* (also esp. *Brit.* **-ise**) 1 a *transitive* convert (sugar or syrup) into caramel. b *intransitive* (of sugar or syrup) be converted into caramel. 2 *transitive* coat or cook (food) with caramelized sugar or syrup. □ **cara·mel·iz·a·tion** *noun*

cara·pace /ˈkerəˌpeis/ *noun* 1 the hard upper shell of a turtle or a crustacean. 2 something serving as a shell or protection (*the writer's carapace of selfishness and separateness*). [French from Spanish *carapacho*]

Cara·quet¹ /ˈkarəˌket/ a town in NE New Brunswick, situated on an inlet of the southern shore of Chaleur Bay, 66 km (41 miles) northeast of Bathurst; pop. (2001) 4,442. It is a centre of Acadian culture and religion. [possibly from Mi'kmaq *pkalge* junction of two rivers, with reference to the point where the Rivière du Nord joins the Caraquet River]

Cara·quet² /ˈkarəˌket/ *noun Cdn* a small variety of edible oyster found in the waters off New Brunswick. [CARAQUET¹]

carat /ˈkerət, ˈka-/ *noun* 1 a unit of weight for precious stones, now equivalent to 200 milligrams. 2 *var. of* KARAT. [French from Italian *carato* from Arabic *kīrāt* weight of four grains, from Greek *keration* fruit of the carob (diminutive of *keras* horn)]

Cara·vag·gio /ˌkerəˈvadʒioː, ˌka-/ **Michel·angelo Merisi da** (1573–1610), Italian painter. He was an important figure in the transition from late mannerism to baroque, and his work is characterized by naturalistic realism (achieved partly by the use of ordinary people as models for Biblical characters) and dramatic use of light and shade. □ **Cara·vag·gesque** *adjective*

cara·van ● *noun* 1 a company of people with vehicles or pack animals travelling together, esp. across a desert. 2 a *N Amer.* a covered motor vehicle with living accommodations. b *Brit.* a trailer equipped with living accommodations. 3 a covered cart or carriage. ● *intransitive verb* (**cara·vanned, cara·van·ning; cara·vaned, cara·van·ing**) travel or live in a caravan. □ **cara·van·ner** *noun* [French *caravane* from Persian *kārwān*]

cara·van·serai /ˌkerəˈvansərai, -səri/ *noun* (also **cara·van·sary** /-səri/) (in the Middle East) an inn with a central court where caravans (*see* CARAVAN 1) may rest. [Persian *kārwānsarāy* from *sarāy* palace]

cara·vel /ˈkerəˌvel/ *noun* (also **car·vel** /ˈkarvəl/) *hist.* a small light fast ship, used from the 15th–17th c. chiefly by the Spanish and Portuguese. [French *caravelle* from Portuguese *caravela* from Greek *karabos* horned beetle, light ship]

cara·way /ˈkerəˌwei/ *noun* 1 an umbelliferous plant, *Carum carvi*,

bearing clusters of tiny white flowers. 2 (also **caraway seed**) the fruit of the caraway plant used as flavouring and as a source of oil. [prob. Old Spanish *alcarahueya* from Arabic *alkarāwiyā*, perhaps from Greek *karon, kareon* cumin]

carb¹ *noun informal* a carburetor. [abbreviation]

carb² *noun informal* carbohydrate. [abbreviation]

car·ba·mate /ˈkarbəˌmeit/ *noun Chem.* a salt or ester containing the anion NH_2CO_2- or the group NH_2CO_2-m derived from the hypothetical carbamic acid NH_2COOH. [CARBON + AMIDE + -IC + -ATE¹]

carba·mazep·ine /ˌkarbəˈmeizəpiːn/ *noun* a synthetic compound of the benzodiazepine class, used as an anticonvulsant and analgesic drug. [from CARBO- and AMIDE, on the pattern of *benzodiazepine*]

car barn *noun N Amer.* a large garage for streetcars, buses, etc.

car·bide *noun Chem.* 1 a binary compound of carbon with a lower or comparable electronegativity. 2 = CALCIUM CARBIDE. 3 a very hard material manufactured by sintering a pulverized mixture of cobalt or nickel and carbides of metals such as tungsten and tantalum, used in the cutting parts of tools.

car·bine /ˈkarbain/ *noun* a short firearm, usu. a rifle, originally for cavalry use. [French *carabine* (this form also earlier in English), weapon of the *carabin* mounted musketeer]

car·bo *noun N Amer. slang* carbohydrate. [abbreviation]

carbo- *combining form* carbon (*carbohydrate; carbolic; carboxyl*).

carbo·hy·drate /ˌkarboˈhaidreit/ *noun* 1 any of a large group of energy-producing organic compounds containing carbon, hydrogen, and oxygen, e.g. starch, glucose, and other sugars. 2 (usu. in *pl.*) a foodstuff that is high in carbohydrates, e.g. bread, sweets, pasta, etc.

car·bol·ic /karˈbɒlik/ *noun* (in full **carbolic acid**) phenol, esp. when used as a disinfectant. [CARBO- + -OL¹ + -IC]

carbo-loading *noun N Amer.* the practice of eating large amounts of carbohydrate, esp. before a sporting event to improve stamina. □ **carbo-load** *intransitive verb*

car bomb *noun* a terrorist bomb concealed in or under a parked car.

car·bon *noun* 1 a non-metallic element occurring naturally as diamond, graphite, and charcoal, and in all organic compounds. Symbol: **C**; at. no.: 6. 2 a = CARBON COPY 1. b = CARBON PAPER. 3 a rod of carbon in an arc lamp. [French *carbone* from Latin *carbo -onis* charcoal]

carbon-12 *noun* a carbon isotope of mass 12, used in calculations of atomic mass units.

carbon-14 *noun* a long-lived radioactive carbon isotope of mass 14, used in radiocarbon dating and as a tracer in biochemistry.

car·bon·aceous /ˌkarbəˈneiʃəs/ *adjective* 1 consisting of or containing carbon. 2 of or like coal or charcoal.

car·bon·ado /ˌkarbəˈneidoː/ *noun* (*pl.* **-ados**) a dark opaque or impure kind of diamond used as an abrasive, for drilling etc. [Portuguese]

car·bon·ara /ˌkarbəˈnarə/ *adjective* (often placed after noun) designating a sauce for pasta made of eggs, cream, Parmesan cheese, and pieces of bacon (*linguine carbonara*). [Italian, perhaps from *carbonata* 'salt pork grilled over a charcoal fire' after *carbonara*, dialect 'charcoal burner's wife']

car·bon·ate ● *noun Chem.* a salt of carbonic acid. ● *transitive verb* 1 impregnate (a liquid) with carbon dioxide to produce effervescence. 2 convert into a carbonate. □ **car·bon·a·tion** *noun* [French *carbonat* from modern Latin *carbonatum* (as CARBON)]

car·bon·at·ed *adjective* (of a beverage) having an effervescent quality due to the presence of carbon dioxide.

carbon black *noun* an amorphous form of carbon suitable for use as a pigment.

carbon copy *noun* 1 a copy made with carbon paper. 2 an exact duplicate (*is a carbon copy of his father*).

carbon cycle *noun* 1 *Biol.* the continuous transfer of carbon in various forms from the atmosphere to living organisms by plant photosynthesis, and back to the atmosphere by respiration and decay. 2 *Astronomy* a thermonuclear chain reaction postulated to occur within stars, in which carbon nuclei act as catalysts in the fusion of hydrogen to form helium.

carbon dating *noun* (also **carbon-14 dating**) = RADIOCARBON DATING.

carbon dioxide *noun* a colourless odourless gas occurring naturally in the atmosphere and formed by respiration. Chem. formula: CO_2.

carbon disulphide *noun* a colourless liquid used as a solvent for rubber. Chem. formula: CS_2.

Car·bon·ear /ˈkarbənˈeːr/ a town situated on the Avalon Peninsula of

SE Newfoundland, on a bay along the west shore of Conception Bay; pop. (2001) 4,759. [the name of the bay, originally *Carbonera Bay*, from Spanish or French, prob. with reference to the area's production of carbon]

carbon fibre *noun* a thin strong crystalline filament of carbon used as strengthening material in plastic etc.

car·bon·ic /kɑrˈbɒnɪk/ *adjective* containing carbon.

carbonic acid *noun* a very weak acid formed from carbon dioxide dissolved in water. Chem. formula: H_2CO_3.

car·bon·if·er·ous /ˌkɑrbəˈnɪfərəs/ ● *adjective* **1** producing carbon or coal. **2** (**Carboniferous**) *Geol.* of or relating to a period of the Paleozoic era, lasting from about 360 to 286 million years BP, between the Devonian and the Permian. During this period seed-bearing plants appeared and luxuriant vegetation developed on coastal swamps; this vegetation was later drowned and buried under mud and sand, and subsequently became coal. ● *noun* (**Carboniferous**) *Geol.* this geological period or system.

car·bon·ize *transitive verb* (also esp. *Brit.* **-ise**) **1** convert into carbon by heating. **2** reduce to charcoal or coke. **3** coat with carbon. □ **car·bon·iz·a·tion** *noun*

carbon monoxide *noun* a colourless odourless toxic gas formed by the incomplete burning of carbon. Chem. formula: CO.

car·bon·nade /ˌkɑrbəˈnɑd/ *noun* a Belgian dish of beef and onions braised in beer. [French, denoting a piece of meat or fish cooked on hot coals]

carbon paper *noun* a thin carbon-coated paper placed between two ordinary sheets of paper so that what is written or typed on the top sheet will be reproduced on the bottom sheet.

carbon sink *noun* a forest, ocean, or other natural environment viewed in terms of its ability to absorb carbon dioxide from the atmosphere.

carbon steel *noun* a steel with properties dependent on the percentage of carbon present.

carbon tax *noun* a tax levied on fuels whose utilization results in the production of carbon emissions.

carbon tetrachloride *noun* a colourless volatile liquid used as a refrigerant and a solvent in dry cleaning. Chem. formula: CCl_4.

car·bonyl /ˈkɑrbəˌnɪl/ *noun* (used *attributive*) *Chem.* the divalent radical CO.

car boot sale *noun Brit.* an outdoor sale at which participants sell unwanted possessions from the trunks of their cars or from tables set up nearby.

car·bor·un·dum /ˌkɑrbəˈrʌndəm/ *noun* proprietary a compound of carbon and silicon used esp. as an abrasive. [CARBON + CORUNDUM]

carb·oxyl /kɑrˈbɒksɪl/ *noun Chem.* the monovalent acid radical (-COOH), present in most organic acids. □ **carb·oxyl·ic** *adjective* [CARBON + OXYGEN + -YL]

car·boy *noun* a large bottle, usu. of coloured glass and protected by a frame, used chiefly for holding acids and other corrosive liquids. [Persian *karāba* large glass flagon]

car·bun·cle /ˈkɑrbʌŋkəl/ *noun* **1** a collection of boils forming a large abscess. **2** a bright red gem, esp. a garnet cut with a convex back. □ **car·bun·cu·lar** /-ˈbʌŋkjulər/ *adjective* [Old French *charbucle* etc. from Latin *carbunculus* small coal, from *carbo* coal]

car·bur·et /ˌkɑrbəˈreit/ *transitive verb* (**car·bur·eted**, **car·bur·et·ing**; also **car·bur·et·ted**, **car·bur·et·ting**) charge (air etc.) with a spray of liquid hydrocarbon fuel, esp. in an internal combustion engine. □ **car·bur·a·tion** *noun* [earlier *carbure* from French from Latin *carbo* (as CARBON)]

car·bur·etor /ˈkɑrbəˌreitər/ *noun* (also **car·bur·et·tor**) an apparatus for controlling the mixture of gasoline and air in an internal combustion engine. [as CARBURET + -OR[1]]

car·ca·jou /ˈkɑrkəˌdʒuː, -kəˌʒuː/ *noun N Amer.* = WOLVERINE. [Canadian French, prob. of Algonquian origin]

car·cass /ˈkɑrkəs/ *noun* (*Brit.* also **car·case**) **1** the dead body of an animal, esp. one slaughtered for its meat. **2** the bones of a cooked bird. **3** *informal* a human body, living or dead. **4** the skeleton or framework of a building, ship, etc. **5** worthless remains. [Anglo-French *carcois* (Old French *charcois*) & from French *carcasse*: ultimate origin unknown]

Car·cas·sonne /kɑrkaˈsɒn/ a walled city in SW France; pop. (1999) 44,000. It is noted for its medieval fortifications.

car·cino·gen /kɑrˈsɪnədʒən/ *noun* any substance that produces cancer. □ **car·cino·gen·ic** /-ˈdʒɛnɪk/ *adjective* **car·cino·gen·icity** /-ˈnɪsɪti/ *noun* [as CARCINOMA + -GEN]

car·cino·gen·esis /ˌkɑrsɪnəˈdʒɛnəsɪs/ *noun* the production of cancer.

car·cin·oma /ˌkɑrsɪˈnoʊmə/ *noun* (*pl.* **car·cin·omas** or **car·cin·omata** /-tə/) a cancer, esp. one arising in epithelial tissue. □ **car·cin·oma·tous** *adjective* [Latin from Greek *karkinōma* from *karkinos* crab]

car coat *noun* an overcoat extending to just below the hips, originally designed for wear while driving.

Card. *abbreviation* Cardinal.

card[1] ● *noun* **1** thick stiff paper or thin pasteboard. **2 a** a flat piece of this, esp. for writing or printing on. **b** = POSTCARD. **c** a card used to send greetings, issue an invitation, etc. (*birthday card*). **d** = CALLING CARD 1. **e** = BUSINESS CARD. **f** a card with a photograph of a sports figure etc., collected as part of a set. **g** a card indicating membership or entitling admission. **3 a** = PLAYING CARD. **b** a similar card in a set designed for a particular game. **c** (in *pl.*) card playing; a card game. **d** a specified advantageous usu. political factor (*politicians will play the crime card yet again*). **4 a** a program of events at a race, boxing match, etc. **b** a scorecard. **c** a list of holes on a golf course, on which a player's scores are entered. **5** *informal* an amusing person (*he's a real card!*). **6** a printed or written notice or advertisement. **7** a small rectangular piece of plastic issued by a bank or other institution with personal (often machine-readable) data on it (*bank card; credit card; health card*). **8** *Computing* **a** = PUNCH CARD. **b** a circuit board. **9** (in *pl.*) *Brit. & Austral. informal* an employee's documents, esp. for tax and national insurance, held by the employer. ● *transitive verb* **1** affix to a card. **2** write on a card, esp. for indexing. **3** demand identification from (a person), esp. as evidence of legal drinking age. **4** *Cdn* (in *passive*) (of an amateur athlete) receive government funding to pursue one's training. □ **ask for** (or **get**) **one's cards** *Brit. & Austral.* ask (or be told) to leave one's employment. **card up one's sleeve** a plan in reserve. **hold all the cards** be in a very strong or advantageous position. **in** (or *Brit.* **on**) **the cards** possible or likely. **play one's cards right** (or **well**) act carefully; carry out a scheme successfully. **put** (or **lay**) **one's cards on the table** reveal one's resources, intentions, etc. [Old French *carte* from Latin *charta* from Greek *khartēs* papyrus leaf]

card[2] ● *noun* **1** a machine through which fibre is fed past a series of wire teeth to align and disentangle the fibre before spinning. **2** a toothed instrument or wire brush for raising the nap on cloth. ● *transitive verb* prepare (fibre) with a card. □ **card·er** *noun* [Old French *carde* from Provençal *carda* from *cardar* tease, comb, ultimately from Latin *carere* card]

car·da·mom /ˈkɑrdəməm/ *noun* (also **car·da·mon** /-mən/) **1** an aromatic SE Asian plant, *Elettaria cardamomum*. **2** the seed capsules of this used as a spice. [Latin *cardamomum* or French *cardamome* from Greek *kardamōmon* from *kardamon* cress + *amōmon* a spice plant]

Cardamom Mountains a range of mountains in W Cambodia, rising to a height of 1 813 m (5,886 ft.) at its highest point.

card·board ● *noun* pasteboard or stiff paper, esp. for making cards or boxes. ● *adjective* **1** made of cardboard. **2** flimsy, insubstantial, artificial. □ **card·boardy** *adjective*

cardboard cut-out *noun* a person, character, or thing lacking depth or individuality.

card-carrying *attributive adjective* **1** registered as a member (esp. of a political party or trade union). **2** devoted to a specified party or cause.

card catalogue *noun* a file of cards which serves as an index to the holdings of a library.

card·ed *adjective Cdn* (of an amateur athlete) receiving government funding to pursue training.

Cár·denas /ˈkɑrdenəs/ **Láz·aro** (1895–1970), Mexican revolutionary leader and president 1934–40. As president he redistributed land to the peasants, expropriated foreign-owned oil companies, and nationalized the railways.

card game *noun* a game in which playing cards are used.

card·holder *noun* a person who has a specific card, esp. a credit card.

car·diac /ˈkɑrdiˌak/ ● *adjective* **1** of or relating to the heart. **2** of or relating to the part of the stomach nearest the esophagus. ● *noun* a person with heart disease. [French *cardiaque* or Latin *cardiacus* from Greek *kardiakos* from *kardia* heart]

cardiac arrest *noun* a sudden cessation of the heartbeat.

Car·diff /ˈkɑrdɪf/ the capital of Wales, a seaport on the Bristol Channel; pop. (est. 2002) 279,500.

car·di·gan /ˈkɑrdɪgən/ *noun* a knitted jacket or sweater fastening down the front, usu. with long sleeves. [7th Earl of *Cardigan* d.1868]

Car·din /kɑrdæ/ **Pierre** (b.1922), French fashion designer. He was the first designer to show a collection of clothes for men as well as women (1960).

Car·din·al /'kɑrdɪnəl/ **1 Doug·las (Jo·seph)** (b.1934), Canadian architect, of Metis descent. His highly individual architectural style, as in St. Mary's Church in Red Deer (1965–8) and the Canadian Museum of Civilization in Hull (1983–9), is characterized by undulating, curvilinear forms suggestive of prairie landscapes. **2 Har·old** (b.1945), Canadian Indian leader. A member of the Sucker Creek Reserve, he is noted for promoting Native culture and instituting reforms as president of the Indian Association of Alberta (1968–77); his works include *The Unjust Society* (1969) and *The Rebirth of Canada's Indians* (1977).

car·din·al /'kɑrdɪnəl/ ● *noun* **1** (as a title **Cardinal**) a leading dignitary of the Roman Catholic Church, one of the college electing the Pope. **2** a N American songbird, *Cardinalis cardinalis* (formerly *Richmondena cardinalis*), the males of which have scarlet plumage. **3** *hist.* a woman's cloak, originally of scarlet cloth with a hood. ● *adjective* **1** chief, fundamental; on which something hinges (*a cardinal rule*). **2** deep scarlet in colour. □ **car·din·al·ate** /-ˌleɪt/ *noun* (in sense 1 of *noun*). **car·din·al·ly** *adverb* **car·din·al·ship** *noun* (in sense 1 of *noun*). [Old French from Latin *cardinalis* from *cardo -inis* hinge: in English first applied to the four virtues on which conduct 'hinges']

cardinal flower *noun* a Central and N American herbaceous plant, *Lobelia cardinalis*, bearing scarlet flowers.

cardinal humour *see* HUMOUR *noun* 5.

cardinal number *noun* a number denoting quantity (one, two, three, etc.), as opposed to an ordinal number (first, second, third, etc.).

cardinal point *noun* one of the four main points of the compass: north, south, east, west.

cardinal sin *noun* **1** a deadly sin. **2** an action perceived as unforgivable.

cardinal virtue *noun* **1** one the chief moral virtues (originally of scholastic philosophy); justice, prudence, temperance, and fortitude. **2** each of seven chief virtues comprising these with the three theological virtues of faith, hope, and charity. **3** an outstanding quality.

card index *noun* an index in the form of a file with each item entered on a separate card. □ **card-index** *transitive verb*

car·dio *noun slang* **1** cardiovascular exercise. **2** cardiovascular fitness. [abbreviation]

cardio- *combining form* heart (*cardiogram*; *cardiology*). [Greek *kardia* heart]

cardio·gram *noun* = ELECTROCARDIOGRAM.

cardio·graph *noun* = ELECTROCARDIOGRAPH. □ **cardi·og·raph·er** /ˌkɑrdɪˈɒɡrəfɜr/ *noun* **cardi·og·raphy** /ˌkɑrdɪˈɒɡrəfɪ/ *noun*

cardi·ol·ogy /ˌkɑrdɪˈɒlədʒɪ/ *noun* the branch of medicine concerned with diseases and abnormalities of the heart. □ **cardi·ol·o·gist** *noun*

cardio·myop·athy /ˌkɑrdɪoˌmaɪˈɒpəθɪ/ *noun* (*pl.* **-athies**) chronic disease of the heart muscle.

cardio·pulmon·ary /ˌkɑrdɪoˈpʌlmə,nerɪ, -ˈpʊl-/ *adjective* of or relating to the heart and the lungs.

cardiopulmonary resuscitation *noun* a series of emergency techniques used to revive a patient whose heart has stopped, including artificial respiration and heart massage. Abbr.: **CPR**.

cardio·vascu·lar /ˌkɑrdɪoˈvaskjʊlɜr/ *adjective* of or relating to the heart and blood vessels.

car·doon /kɑrˈduːn/ *noun* a thistle-like plant, *Cynara cardunculus*, related to the artichoke, with leaves used as a vegetable. [French *cardon*, ultimately from Latin *cardu(u)s* thistle]

card sharp *noun* (also **card sharper**, *N Amer.* **card shark**) a person who professionally or habitually cheats at card games. □ **card-sharp** *intransitive verb*

card table *noun* a square table designed for playing card games, esp. one with folding legs.

Car·ducci /kɑrˈduːtʃɪ/ **Gio·suè** (1835–1907), Italian poet. His poetry celebrates Italy's classical heritage at the expense of romanticism and the Church. He was awarded the Nobel Prize for literature in 1906.

care ● *noun* **1 a** the process of looking after or providing for someone or something; the provision of what is needed for health or protection (*child care*; *health care*; *skin care*). **b** *Cdn & Brit.* protective custody or guardianship provided by a child welfare agency for a child whose parents are deemed unable to provide proper care (*was taken into care*). **2** serious attention or thought in doing something properly or avoiding damage to something (*assembled with care*; *handle with care*). **3** a troubled state of mind arising from worry or anxiety. **4** maintenance

(*car care*). **5** a matter of concern; something to be done or seen to. ● *intransitive verb* **1 a** (usu. foll. by *about, for, whether*) feel concern or interest. **b** have an objection; mind (*she won't care if we leave early*). **2** (usu. foll. by *for, about*, and with neg. expressed or implied) feel liking, affection, regard, or deference (*don't care for jazz*). **3** (foll. by *to* + infin.) wish or be willing (*do not care to be seen with him*; *would you care to try them?*). **4** in conventional polite offers, esp. of food or drink (*would you care for a cup of tea?*). □ **care for 1** look after, esp. an old or sick person. **2** love or be fond of. **care of** at the address of (*sent it care of his sister*). **for all one cares** *informal* denoting a lack of interest or concern (*for all I care they can leave tomorrow; I could be dying for all you care*). **have a care** take care; be careful. **I** (etc.) **couldn't** (or *N Amer. disputed* **could**) **care less** *informal* an expression of complete indifference. **take care 1** be careful. **2** (foll. by *to* + infin.) not fail or neglect. **3** a conventional expression of good wishes on parting, at the end of a communication, etc. **take care of 1** look after; keep safe. **2** deal with. **3** dispose of. **who cares?** no one cares; I don't care. [Old English *caru, carian*, from Germanic]

ca·reen *verb* **1** *intransitive N Amer.* rush headlong; hurtle unsteadily. **2 a** *intransitive* tilt; lean over. **b** *transitive* cause to do this. **3** *transitive Naut.* turn (a ship) on one side for cleaning, caulking, or repair. [earlier as noun, = careened position of ship, from French *carène* from Italian *carena* from Latin *carina* keel]

ca·reer ● *noun* **1 a** one's advancement through life, esp. in a profession. **b** the progress through history of a group or institution. **2** a profession or occupation, esp. as offering advancement. **3** swift course; impetus (*in full career*). ● *adjective* **1** (*attributive*) **a** pursuing or wishing to pursue a career (*career woman*). **b** working permanently in a specified profession (*career diplomat*). **2** (*attributive*) *Sport* **a** (of a sports statistic, etc.) accumulated over one's career (*scored 500 career goals*). **b** constituting a high point in one's career (*the pitcher had a career night*). ● *intransitive verb* **1** move or swerve about wildly. **2** go swiftly. [French *carrière* from Italian *carriera*, ultimately from Latin *carrus* CAR]

career·ist *noun* a person predominantly concerned with personal advancement. □ **career·ism** *noun*

career path *noun* a recognized pattern of advancement within a job or profession.

care·free *adjective* free from anxiety or responsibility. □ **care·free·ness** *noun*

care·ful *adjective* **1** painstaking, thorough. **2** cautious. **3** done with care and attention. **4** showing care or concern for; not neglecting. □ **care·ful·ly** *adverb* **care·ful·ness** *noun*

care·giver *noun* **1** a parent or guardian who cares for a child. **2** (also *Brit.* **carer**) a person who cares for a sick or elderly person. **3** a person employed to look after a child. □ **care·giving** *noun*

care label *noun* a label attached to clothing, with instructions for washing etc.

Care·less, James Mau·rice Stock·ford (b.1919), Canadian historian, whose works include *Canada: A Story of Challenge* (1953) and *Brown of the Globe* (1963), a biography of George Brown.

care·less *adjective* **1** not taking care or paying attention. **2** unthinking, insensitive. **3** done without care; inaccurate. **4** lighthearted. **5** (foll. by *of*) not concerned about; taking no heed of. **6** effortless. □ **care·less·ly** *adverb* **care·less·ness** *noun*

care package *noun* **1** a parcel of food, clothing, or other staple items sent to the needy in a foreign country. **2** a parcel of luxuries (esp. homemade foods) sent to a person who is living away from home.

ca·ress ● *transitive verb* **1** touch or stroke gently or lovingly. **2** treat fondly or kindly. ● *noun* a loving or gentle touch or kiss. □ **ca·ress·ing·ly** *adverb* [French *caresse* (n.), *caresser* (v.), from Italian *carezza*, ultimately from Latin *carus* dear]

caret /'kɑrət/ *noun* a mark (^) indicating a proposed insertion in printing or writing. [Latin, = is lacking]

care·taker *noun* **1** a person employed to look after a building; a custodian or janitor. **2** = CAREGIVER. **3** (*attributive*) exercising temporary authority (*caretaker government*). □ **care·taking** *noun*

care·worn *adjective* showing the effects of prolonged worry.

Carey, George (Leon·ard) (b.1935), English Anglican churchman, Archbishop of Canterbury 1991–2002.

car·fare *noun N Amer. dated* a passenger's fare to travel by public transit, esp. by streetcar.

cargo *noun* (*pl.* **-goes** or **-gos**) goods carried on a ship, aircraft, or other vehicle. [Spanish (as CHARGE)]

cargo cult *noun* a chiefly Melanesian religious belief in the imminent arrival of ships bringing cargoes of food, arising after the Aboriginal peoples observed colonial deliveries and traffic in goods.

cargo pants *plural noun* esp. *N Amer.* a pair of esp. loose-fitting, cotton pants with large, external pockets halfway up the side of each leg.

car·hop *noun N Amer.* a waiter or waitress at a drive-in restaurant.

Caria /ˈkeriə/ an ancient region of SW Asia Minor, south of the Maeander River and northwest of Lycia. □ **Carian** *adjective & noun*

Carib /ˈkerɪb/ ● *noun* **1** an aboriginal inhabitant of the southern W Indies or the adjacent coasts. **2** the language of this people. ● *adjective* of or relating to this people. [Spanish *Caribe* from Haitian]

Carib·bean /ˌkerəˈbiːən, kəˈrɪbiən/ ● *noun* **1** (also **Caribbean Sea**) the part of the Atlantic between the southern W Indies and Central America. **2** the islands of this region. ● *adjective* **1** of or relating to this region or its people or culture. **2** of the Caribs or their language.

cari·boo *rare var. of* CARIBOU.

Cariboo gold rush a gold rush that occurred in the Cariboo Mountains between 1860 and 1863.

Cariboo Mountains a mountain range in east central BC, lying just west of the Fraser River.

cari·bou /ˈkerɪˌbuː/ *noun* (*pl.* same) **1** any of several subspecies of reindeer (*Rangifer tarandus*) inhabiting N Canada and Alaska, esp. the woodland or barren ground caribou. **2** the meat or hide of this animal. **3** *Cdn* (esp. *Que.*) a beverage made from red wine and whisky blanc. [Canadian French from Mi'kmaq *ɣalipu*, lit. 'snow-shoveller']

Cari·bou Inuit *plural noun* an inland Inuit people formerly inhabiting the Barrens and relying almost entirely on caribou for food and clothing.

caribou moss *noun* = REINDEER MOSS.

cari·ca·ture /ˈkerɪkətʃər/ ● *noun* **1** a grotesque usu. comic representation of a person by exaggeration of characteristic traits, in a picture, writing, or mime. **2** a ridiculously poor or absurd imitation or version. ● *transitive verb* make or give a caricature of. □ **cari·ca·tu·ral** *adjective* **cari·ca·tur·ist** *noun* [French from Italian *caricatura* from *caricare* load, exaggerate: see CHARGE]

CARICOM *abbreviation* Caribbean Community and Common Market.

caries /ˈkeriːz/ *noun* (*pl.* same) decay and crumbling of a tooth or bone. [Latin]

Car·ignan[1] /kariˈnjɑ̃/ a town in south central Quebec, near Chambly; pop. (2001) 5,915. [in honour of the men from the *Carignan*-Salières Regiment, many of whom were settlers in the Chambly area, after *Carignano*, a town in Italy]

Car·ignan[2] /kariˈnjɑ̃/ **Jean** (known as 'Ti-Jean') (1916–88), Canadian fiddler, known for his performances of traditional French-Canadian and Celtic music.

car·il·lon /ˈkerələn, -ɒn/ *noun* **1** a set of bells sounded either from a keyboard or mechanically. **2** a tune played on bells. **3** an organ stop imitating a peal of bells. [French from Old French *quarregnon* peal of four bells, alteration of Romanic *quaternio* from Latin *quattuor* four]

Car·il·lon Canal /kariˈjɔ̃/ a historic canal in south central Quebec, situated on the Ottawa River, 65 km northwest of Montreal. Built in 1825, it was used for military, then commercial, navigation. [the name of a village nearby]

car·il·lon·neur /ˌkerɪlɒnˈɜr/ *noun* a person who plays a carillon. [French]

Carina /kəˈriːnə/ a large constellation in the southern Milky Way, containing Canopus, the second-brightest star in the sky. [Latin *carina* keel]

carina /kəˈriːnə/ *noun Biol.* a keel-shaped structure, esp. the ridge of a bird's breastbone. □ **carin·al** *adjective* [Latin, = keel]

carin·ate /ˈkerɪˌneɪt/ *adjective* (of a bird) having a deep keel-like ridge on the breastbone for the attachment of flight muscles (*opp.* RATITE). [Latin *carinatus* having a keel, from *carina* keel]

car·ing *adjective* compassionate or considerate, esp. towards other people. □ **car·ing·ly** *adverb*

cari·oca /ˌkeriˈoːkə/ *noun* **1 a** a Brazilian dance like the samba. **b** the music for this. **2** (**Carioca**) a native of Rio de Janeiro. [Portuguese]

cario·gen·ic /ˌkerioˈdʒɛnɪk/ *adjective* causing caries.

cari·ole *var. of* CARRIOLE.

cari·ous /ˈkeriəs/ *adjective* (of bones or teeth) decayed. [Latin *cariosus*]

car·jack·ing *noun* the hijacking of a car or its passengers. □ **car·jack** *transitive verb* **car·jack·er** *noun* [CAR + HIJACKING]

car jock·ey *noun N Amer.* a person employed to park customers' cars, esp. at a restaurant, hotel, etc.

cark·ing *adjective archaic* burdensome, nagging (*carking doubts*). [part. of obsolete *cark* (v.) from Old Northern French *carkier* from Romanic, related to CHARGE]

carl *noun Scot.* a man; a fellow. [Old English from Old Norse *karl*, related to CHURL]

Carl XVI Gus·taf /kɑrl ˈɡʊstɒv/ (b.1946), king of Sweden since 1973. He became king during a period of constitutional change which saw the monarch assume an essentially symbolic role.

Carle /ˈkɑrl/ **Gilles** (b.1929), Canadian film director and screenwriter, whose films include *La Vraie Nature de Bernadette* (1972), *Maria Chapdelaine* (1983), and the documentary *Cinéma, cinéma* (1985).

Carle·ton /ˈkɑrltən/ **1 Guy, 1st Baron Dorchester** (1724–1808), Irish-born British army officer, who served as governor of Quebec (1768–78 and 1785–95) and commander-in-chief of British forces in N America (1782–3); as governor-in-chief of British North America (1786–1798) he opposed the Constitutional Act (1791) dividing Quebec into Upper and Lower Canada. **2** his brother, **Thom·as** (*c.*1735–1817), Irish-born British army officer, who served as the first Lieutenant-Governor of New Brunswick (1784–1817).

Carleton Place a town in east central Ontario, about 35 km southwest of Ottawa; pop. (2001) 9,083. [originally *Carlton Place*, after a street in central Glasgow]

car·line /ˈkɑrlɪn/ *noun* a Eurasian plant of the genus *Carlina*, esp. the thistle-like *C. vulgaris*. [French from medieval Latin *carlina* perhaps for *cardina* (Latin *carduus* thistle), assoc. with *Carolus Magnus* Charlemagne]

Car·ling, Sir John (1828–1911), Canadian Conservative politician and brewer. He inherited the Carling Brewing and Malting Company from his father (1849), and later served as postmaster general (1882–5) and minister of agriculture (1885–92).

Car·lisle /kɑrˈlail/ a town in NW England, the county town of Cumbria; pop. (est. 2002) 73,100. Founded as a Roman settlement close to Hadrian's Wall, Carlisle served for centuries as a fortress town in defence of the northwestern borders of England against the Scots.

car·load *noun* **1** the quantity of freight that can be shipped in a railway car. **2** *N Amer.* the number of people that can travel in an automobile.

Car·los /ˈkɑrlɒs/ **Don** (born Carlos María Isidro de Borbón) (1788–1855), Spanish prince, pretender to the throne. The second son of Charles IV, he asserted his right to the Spanish throne and was leader of the unsuccessful Carlists in the civil war which ensued (1834–40).

Car·lo·vin·gian *var. of* CAROLINGIAN.

Car·low /ˈkɑrloː/ **1** a county of the Republic of Ireland, in the southeast, in the province of Leinster. **2** its county town; pop. (1991) 11,275.

Car·lyle /kɑrˈlail, ˈkɑrlail/ **Thom·as** (1795–1881), Scottish historian and political philosopher. He attacked social injustice and materialistic attitudes that resulted from the Industrial Revolution. His major works include *Sartor Resartus* (1833–4), the three-volume *The French Revolution* (1837), and *On Heroes, Hero Worship, and the Heroic in History* (1841).

car·maker *noun* = AUTOMAKER.

Car·man /ˈkɑrmən/ **(Wil·liam) Bliss** (1861–1929), Canadian poet, journalist, and editor. His poetry is noted for its mystical and visionary quality. He is best known for his nature lyrics; his verse collections include *Low Tide on Grand Pré* (1893), the five-volume *The Pipes of Pan* (1903–5), and *Sappho* (1905).

Car·mel, Mount /ˈkɑrməl/ a group of mountains near the Mediterranean coast in NW Israel, sheltering the port of Haifa. Caves on the southwestern slopes provided evidence of human occupation dating from the palaeolithic to the mesolithic periods. The Carmelite order was founded on Mount Carmel during the Crusades.

Car·mel·ite /ˈkɑrməˌlait/ ● *noun* **1** a member of an order of mendicant friars (also known as the White Friars), founded in the 12th c. **2** a nun of a contemplative order modelled on this order of friars. ● *adjective* of or relating to the Carmelites. [French *Carmelite* or medieval Latin *carmelita* from Mt. CARMEL, where the order was founded]

Car·michael /ˈkɑrˌmaikəl/ **1 Frank·lin** (1890–1945), Canadian painter. A founding member of the Group of Seven, he is known for works such as *Autumn Hillside* (1920) and *Jackfish Village* (1926). **2 Hoag·land How·ard** ('Hoagy') (1899–1981), US jazz pianist, composer, and singer. His best-known songs include 'Stardust' (1929), 'Two Sleepy People' (1938), and 'In the Cool, Cool, Cool of the Evening' (1951).

car·mina·tive /kɑrˈmɪnətɪv, ˈkɑr-/ ● *adjective* relieving flatulence. ● *noun* a carminative drug. [French *carminatif -ive* or medieval Latin *carminare* heal (by incantation): see CHARM]

car·mine /ˈkɑːmaɪn/ ● *adjective* of a vivid crimson colour. ● *noun* **1** this colour. **2** a vivid crimson pigment made from cochineal. [French *carmin* or medieval Latin *carminium* perhaps from *carmesinum* crimson + *minium* cinnabar]

Car·nac /ˈkɑːnak/ the site, in NW France, in Brittany near the Atlantic coast, of a group of stone monuments dating from the neolithic period. There are nearly 3,000 stones, which include single standing stones (menhirs), dolmens, and long avenues of grey monoliths arranged in order of height; some of these avenues end in semicircular or rectangular enclosures of standing stones.

car·nage /ˈkɑːnɪdʒ/ *noun* the killing of many people, animals, etc., usu. with much bloodshed. [French from Italian *carnaggio* from medieval Latin *carnaticum* from Latin *caro carnis* flesh]

car·nal /ˈkɑːnəl/ *adjective* **1** of the body or flesh; worldly. **2** sensual, sexual. □ **car·nal·ity** /-ˈnalɪti/ *noun* **car·nal·ly** *adverb* [Late Latin *carnalis* from *caro carnis* flesh]

carnal knowledge *noun* sexual intercourse.

Car·nap /ˈkɑːnap/ **Ru·dolf** (1891–1970), German-born US philosopher. One of the originators of logical positivism, he emphasized the scientific method in philosophy and the need to verify statements through observation.

car·nas·sial /kɑːˈnasɪəl/ ● *adjective* (of a carnivore's upper premolar and lower molar teeth) adapted for shearing flesh. ● *noun* such a tooth. [French *carnassier* carnivorous]

car·na·tion¹ *noun* **1** any of several cultivated varieties of the clove pink (*see* CLOVE¹ 2), with variously coloured showy flowers. **2** this flower. [origin uncertain: in early use varying with *coronation*]

car·na·tion² ● *noun* a rosy pink colour. ● *adjective* of this colour. [French from Italian *carnagione*, ultimately from Latin *caro carnis* flesh]

car·nauba /kɑːˈnaʊbə, -ˈnɒbə, -ˈnɔːbə/ *noun* **1** a fan palm, *Copernicia cerifera*, native to NE Brazil. **2** (in full **carnauba wax**) the yellowish wax obtained from the leaves of this tree, used as a polish etc. [Portuguese]

Car·negie /ˈkɑːnəgi, kɑːˈneɪgi/ **An·drew** (1835–1919), Scottish-born US industrialist and philanthropist. After amassing a considerable fortune in the US steel industry, he retired in 1901 and devoted his wealth to charitable purposes on both sides of the Atlantic, supporting many educational institutions, libraries, and the arts.

car·nel·ian /kɑːˈniːlɪən/ *noun* (also **cor·nel·ian** /kɔː-/) a dull red or reddish-white variety of chalcedony. [Old French *corneline*; *car-* after Latin *caro carnis* flesh]

car·ni·val /ˈkɑːnəvəl/ *noun* **1 a** the festivities usual during the period before Lent in some countries. **b** any festivities, esp. those occurring during a regular season (*winter carnival*). **2** *N Amer.* a travelling fair with exhibits, games, rides, and other amusements. **3** merrymaking, revelry. **4** *Cdn Figure Skating* a non-competitive performance given by the members of a figure skating club. □ **car·ni·val·esque** *adjective* [Italian *carne-*, *carnovale* from medieval Latin *carnelevarium* etc. Shrovetide, from Latin *caro carnis* flesh + *levare* put away]

car·ni·vore /ˈkɑːnəˌvɔː/ *noun* **1 a** any mammal of the order Carnivora (cats, dogs, bears, seals, etc.) with powerful jaws and teeth adapted for stabbing, tearing, and eating flesh. **b** any other flesh-eating mammal. **2** any insect-eating plant. **3** a person who eats (esp. large amounts of) meat; a non-vegetarian. □ **car·ni·vory** *noun*

car·niv·or·ous /kɑːˈnɪvərəs/ *adjective* **1** (of an animal) feeding on flesh. **2** (of a plant) digesting trapped insects or other animal substances. **3** of or relating to the order Carnivora. **4** (of a person) not vegetarian. □ **car·niv·or·ous·ly** *adverb* **car·niv·or·ous·ness** *noun* [Latin *carnivorus* from *caro carnis* flesh + -VOROUS]

Car·not /ˈkɑːnoʊ/ **1 La·zare (Nico·las Mar·guer·ite)** (1753–1823), French military engineer and administrator who mobilized the French Revolutionary armies and became known as the *Organizer of Victory*. **2** his son, **(Nico·las Léo·nard) Sadi** (1796–1832), French scientist. An army officer for most of his life, he developed a private interest in the principles and efficiency of steam engines, and his work was recognized after his death as being of crucial importance to the theory of thermodynamics.

carny *noun* (also **car·nie**, **car·ney**) (*pl.* **-nies** or **-neys**) *N Amer. informal* **1** a person who works at a travelling fun fair. **2** a travelling fun fair. [abbreviation of CARNIVAL]

carob /ˈkerəb/ *noun* **1** (in full **carob tree**) an evergreen tree, *Ceratonia siliqua*, native to the Mediterranean, bearing edible pods. **2** its bean-shaped edible seed pod. **3** the powdered pulp of these pods, used esp. as a substitute for chocolate. [obsolete French *carobe* from medieval Latin *carrubia*, *-um* from Arabic *ḵarrūba*]

Carol II (1893–1953), king of Romania 1930–40, who ruled a corporatist dictatorship until he was forced to abdicate by the pro-Nazi Iron Guard.

carol ● *noun* a joyous song or hymn, esp. one celebrating Christmas. ● *verb* (**car·olled**, **car·ol·ling**; *US* **car·oled**, **car·ol·ing**) **1** *intransitive* sing carols, esp. outdoors at Christmas. **2** *transitive & intransitive* sing joyfully. □ **carol·ler** *noun* (*US* **carol·er**). [Old French *carole*, *caroler*, of unknown origin]

Caro·lina *noun* (in *pl.*) the states of North and South Carolina collectively.

Carolina poplar *noun* a hybrid poplar tree between a European poplar species and the N American eastern cottonwood. *Also called* CANADA POPLAR.

Caro·line *adjective* (also **Caro·lean** /ˌkarəˈliːən/) of the time of Charles I or II of England. [Latin *Carolus* Charles]

Caroline Islands (also **Carolines**) a group of islands in the W Pacific Ocean, north of the equator, forming the Federated States of Micronesia.

Caro·lin·gian /ˌkerəˈlɪndʒɪən/ (also **Car·lo·vin·gian** /ˌkɑːləˈvɪndʒɪən/) ● *adjective* **1** of or relating to the second Frankish dynasty, founded by Charlemagne (d.814). **2** of a style of script developed in France at the time of Charlemagne. ● *noun* **1** a member of the Carolingian dynasty. **2** the Carolingian style of script. [French *carlovingien* from *Karl* Charles, after *mérovingien* (see MEROVINGIAN): re-formed after Latin *Carolus*]

Carolingian Renaissance a period marked by achievements in art, architecture, learning, and music during the reign of the Frankish emperor Charlemagne (800–14) and his successors.

Caro·lin·ian /kerəˈlɪnɪən/ ● *adjective* **1** of or relating to a forest region extending from S Ontario to North and South Carolina, characterized by broadleaf deciduous trees such as the tulip tree, magnolia, and eastern flowering dogwood. **2** of or relating to the states of South or North Carolina. ● *noun* a native or inhabitant of South or North Carolina.

carom /ˈkerəm/ *N Amer.* ● *noun* **1** *Billiards* a shot in which the cue ball strikes two other balls in succession. **2** an instance of striking and rebounding. ● *intransitive verb* **1** *Billiards* make a carom. **2** (usu. foll. by *off*) strike and rebound. [abbreviation of *carambole* from Spanish *carambola*, apparently from *bola* 'ball']

Caron /kaˈrɔ̃/ **Louis** (b.1942), Canadian journalist and novelist. His novels include *L'emmitouflé* (1977), *Bonhomme sept-heures* (1978), and *Le canard de bois* (1981), the first volume of a trilogy entitled 'Les Fils de la liberté', about the Lower Canada Rebellion.

car·ot·ene /ˈkerəˌtiːn/ *noun* any of several orange-coloured plant pigments found in carrots, tomatoes, etc., acting as a source of vitamin A. [German *Carotin* from Latin *carota* CARROT]

car·ot·en·oid /kəˈrɒtəˌnɔɪd/ *noun* any of a class of mainly yellow, orange, or red fat-soluble pigments, including carotene, giving colour to plant parts, e.g. ripe tomatoes, autumn leaves.

Ca·roth·ers /kəˈrʌðərz/ **Wal·lace Hume** (1896–1937), US industrial chemist. He studied long-chain molecules, now called polymers, and developed the first synthetic rubber, neoprene, and the first synthetic fibre, Nylon 6.6.

ca·rotid /kəˈrɒtɪd/ ● *noun* each of the two main arteries carrying blood to the head and neck. ● *adjective* of or relating to either of these arteries. [French *carotide* or modern Latin *carotides* from Greek *karōtides* (pl.) from *karoō* stupefy (compression of these arteries being thought to cause stupor)]

ca·rouse /kəˈraʊz/ ● *intransitive verb* **1** participate in a noisy or lively drinking party. **2** drink heavily. ● *noun* a noisy or lively drinking party. □ **ca·rous·al** *noun* **ca·rous·er** *noun* [originally as adv. = right out, in *phr. drink carouse* from German *gar aus trinken*]

car·ou·sel /ˌkerəˈsel, ˈkerə-/ *noun* **1** *N Amer.* **a** a large revolving device in a playground, for children to ride on. **b** a merry-go-round. **2** a rotating delivery or conveyor system, esp. for passengers' luggage at an airport. **3** a rotating tray for holding specific objects, esp. on a slide projector or compact disc player. **4** *hist.* a kind of equestrian tournament. [French *carrousel* from Italian *carosello*]

carp¹ *noun* (*pl.* same) any freshwater food fish of the family Cyprinidae, esp. *Cyprinus carpio*, having large scales and barbels on either side of its mouth. [Old French *carpe* from Provençal or from Late Latin *carpa*]

carp² *intransitive verb* find fault; complain pettily. □ **carp·er** *noun* [obsolete Middle English senses 'talk, say, sing' from Old Norse *karpa* to brag: modern sense (16th c.) from or influenced by Latin *carpere* pluck at, slander]

Car·pac·cio /kɑːˈpɒtʃɪoʊ/ **Vit·tore** (c.1455–c.1525), Italian painter. He is noted esp. for his paintings of Venice and for his lively narrative cycle of paintings *Scenes from the Life of St. Ursula* (1490–5).

car·pac·cio /kɑrˈpatʃioː/ *noun* a thin strip of marinated raw meat, esp. beef, as an appetizer. [CARPACCIO]

car·pal /ˈkɑrpəl/ ● *adjective* of or relating to the bones in the wrist. ● *noun* any of the bones forming the wrist. [CARPUS + -AL]

carpal tunnel syndrome *noun* a painful disorder of the hand caused by compression of a major nerve in the wrist, often brought about by overexertion.

car park *noun Cdn., Brit., Austral.,* & *NZ* = PARKING LOT.

Car·path·ian Mountains /kɑrˈpeɪθiən/ (also **Car·path·ians**) a mountain system extending southeastward from S Poland and Slovakia into Ukraine and Romania.

carpe diem /ˌkɑrpeɪ ˈdiːem/ *interjection* seize the day; enjoy the present and give little thought to the future. [Latin]

car·pel /ˈkɑrpəl/ *noun Bot.* the female reproductive organ of a flower, consisting of a stigma, style, and ovary. □ **car·pel·lary** *adjective* [French *carpelle* or modern Latin *carpellum* from Greek *karpos* fruit]

Car·pen·taria, Gulf of /ˌkɑrpənˈteriə/ a large bay on the north coast of Australia, between Arnhem Land and the Cape York Peninsula.

car·pen·ter ● *noun* a person skilled in woodwork, esp. of a structural kind. ● *verb* **1** *intransitive* do carpentry. **2** *transitive* make by means of carpentry. **3** *transitive* construct; fit together. [Old French *carpentier* from Late Latin *carpentarius* from *carpentum* wagon, from Gaulish]

carpenter ant *noun* any large ant of the genus *Camponotus* which bores into wood to nest.

carpenter bee *noun* any of various solitary bees which bore into wood.

car·pen·try *noun* **1** the work or occupation of a carpenter. **2** woodwork constructed by a carpenter.

car·pet ● *noun* **1 a** a thick fabric for covering a floor or stairs. **b** a piece of this fabric. **2** an expanse or layer resembling a carpet in being smooth, soft, bright, or thick (*carpet of violets*). ● *transitive verb* (**car·pet·ed, car·pet·ing**) ● cover with or as with a carpet. □ **call** (or **have up**) **on the carpet** reprimand; reprove. **sweep under the carpet** conceal (a problem or difficulty) in the hope that it will be forgotten. [Old French *carpite* or medieval Latin *carpita*, from obsolete Italian *carpita* woollen counterpane, ultimately from Latin *carpere* pluck, pull to pieces]

carpet bag *noun* a travelling bag of a kind originally made of carpet-like material.

carpet·bag·ger *noun* **1** esp. *N Amer.* a political candidate in an area where the candidate has no local connections. **2** an unscrupulous opportunist. □ **carpet·bag·ging** *adjective* & *noun* [originally applied to a northerner in the southern US after the Civil War]

carpet beetle *noun* any of various beetles of the genus *Antherenus* or *Attagenus*, whose larvae are destructive to carpets and other fabrics.

carpet bombing *noun* the dropping of a large number of bombs uniformly over an area.

carpet bowling *noun* an indoor game similar to lawn bowling, played with either round balls or asymmetrical bowls.

carpet·ing *noun* **1** material for carpets. **2** carpets collectively.

carpet slipper *noun* a kind of slipper with the upper made originally of carpet-like material.

carpet sweeper *noun* a household implement with a revolving brush or brushes for sweeping carpets.

carpet tile *noun* one of a number of small squares of carpet laid like tiles for flooring.

car phone *noun* a cellphone for use in a motor vehicle.

car·pol·ogy /kɑrˈpɒlədʒi/ *noun* the study of the structure of fruit and seeds. [Greek *karpos* fruit]

car·pool *noun N Amer.* an arrangement between people to travel together in a single vehicle, usu. with each member taking a turn at driving the others. □ **car·pool** *intransitive verb* **car·pool·er** *noun* **car·pool·ing** *noun*

car·port *noun* a shelter with a roof and open sides for a car, usu. beside a house.

car·pus /ˈkɑrpəs/ *noun* (*pl.* **carpi** /-paɪ/) the small bones between the forelimb and metacarpus in terrestrial vertebrates, forming the wrist in humans. [modern Latin from Greek *karpos* wrist]

Carr, Emily (1871–1945), Canadian landscape painter and writer. Her paintings, inspired by the wilderness of British Columbia, often drew on the motifs of West Coast Indian art; from 1927 she came into

contact with the Group of Seven and produced such expressionist works as *Forest Landscape II* and *Sky* (both 1934–5).

Car·racci /kəˈrɒtʃi/ **1 Agos·tino** (1557–1602), Italian painter. He worked with his brother in the Farnese Gallery, but was chiefly known as an engraver. **2** his brother, **Anni·bale** (1560–1609), Italian painter, who is known esp. for his work in Rome, such as the ceiling of the Farnese Gallery (1597–1600); he developed a style which proved to be a foundation of the Italian baroque, and is also remembered for his invention of the caricature. **3** their cousin **Ludo·vico** (1555–1619), Italian painter, who is remembered chiefly as a distinguished teacher and with his cousins established an Academy at Bologna, which trained many important painters.

car·rack /ˈkerək, ˈka-/ *noun hist.* a large armed merchant ship. [French *caraque* from Spanish *caraca* from Arabic *karākir*]

car·ra·geen /ˈkerəˌgiːn/ *noun* (also **car·ra·gheen**) an edible purplish-red seaweed, *Chondrus crispus*, of the northern hemisphere. *Also called* IRISH MOSS. [origin uncertain: perhaps from Irish *cosáinín carraige* carrageen, lit. 'little stem of the rock']

car·ra·geen·an /ˌkerəˈgiːnən/ *noun* (also **car·ra·geen·in**) a mixture of polysaccharides extracted from carrageen or similar seaweed and used as a gelling, thickening, and emulsifying agent in food products.

Car·rara /kəˈrɑrə/ a town in Tuscany in NW Italy, famous for the white marble quarried there since Roman times; pop. (2001) 65,650.

Car·rel /kəˈrel/ **Alexis** (1873–1944), French surgeon and biologist. He developed improved techniques for suturing arteries and veins, performed some of the first organ transplants, and succeeded in keeping organs alive outside the body by perfusion. He spent much of his career in the US, and received a Nobel Prize in 1912.

car·rel /ˈkerəl/ *noun* **1** a small cubicle or desk with high sides in a library, designed for individual study. **2** *hist.* a small enclosure or study in a cloister. [Old French *carole*, medieval Latin *carola*, of unknown origin]

Car·reras /kəˈrerəs/ **José** (b.1946), Spanish operatic tenor. Noted for his soft voice in the upper register, he has had significant success in the operas of Verdi, Puccini, and Donizetti.

Car·rey, James ('Jim') (b.1962), Canadian comedian and actor. Known for his highly physical comedy, rubber face, and taste for excess, he has starred in *The Mask* (1994) and the two *Ace Ventura* movies (1994 and 1995).

car·riage /ˈkerɪdʒ, ˈka-/ *noun* **1** a wheeled passenger vehicle, esp. one with four wheels and pulled by horses. **2** = BABY CARRIAGE. **3** *Brit.* a railway passenger car. **4 a** the conveying of goods. **b** the cost of this. **5** the part of a machine (e.g. a typewriter) that carries other parts into the required position. **6** = GUN CARRIAGE. **7** a manner of carrying oneself; one's bearing or deportment. [Old Northern French *cariage* from *carier* CARRY]

carriage bolt *noun* a bolt with a smooth oval head and with the part of the shank nearest the head unthreaded.

carriage clock *noun* a portable clock in a rectangular case with a handle on top.

carriage house *noun* = COACH HOUSE.

carriage lamp *noun* an exterior lamp having a light bulb enclosed by four square glass panels.

carriage return *noun* = RETURN *noun* 7.

carriage trade *noun* the wealthy clients or customers of a business.

carriage·way *noun Brit.* the part of a road intended for vehicles.

car·rick bend *noun Naut.* a round knot to join ropes required to go round a capstan. [BEND² : *carrick* perhaps from CARRACK]

Carrick-on-Shannon the county town of Leitrim, in the Republic of Ireland, on the Shannon River; pop. (est. 2002) 2,600.

Car·ri·er¹ /ˈkeriei/ **Roch** (b.1937), Canadian novelist, poet, and playwright. His work presents a humorous, ironic, and occasionally sentimental view of rural life in Quebec, and includes the novel *La guerre, yes sir!* (1968), about a village at the start of the Second World War; he is also known for the collection *Les enfants du bonhomme dans la lune* (1979, translated as *The Hockey Sweater and Other Stories*).

Car·ri·er² /ˈkeriər/ ● *noun* a member of an Athapaskan people inhabiting the BC interior. ● *adjective* of or relating to this people or their language. [so called from their custom of a widow's carrying (for a period) the cremated remains of her husband in a bag]

car·ri·er *noun* **1** a person or thing that carries or in which something is carried. **2** a person or company undertaking to convey goods or passengers for payment. **3** a part of a bicycle etc. for carrying luggage or a passenger. **4** a person who delivers newspapers, flyers, etc. **5** a person or animal that may transmit a disease or a hereditary characteristic without suffering from or displaying it. **6** = AIRCRAFT CARRIER. **7** a substance used to support or convey a pigment, a catalyst, radioactive material, etc. **8** *Physics* a mobile electron or hole that carries a charge in a semiconductor. **9** (in full **carrier wave**) a high-frequency electromagnetic wave modulated in amplitude or frequency to convey a signal. **10** (in full **carrier bag**) *Brit.* a plastic or paper shopping bag with handles.

carrier pigeon *noun* a homing pigeon trained to carry messages tied to its neck or leg.

Car·ring·ton, Dora (de Hough·ton) (1893–1932), English painter. She became involved with the Bloomsbury Group, in particular Lytton Strachey, with whom she continued a relationship despite her marriage in 1921. When he died in 1932 she committed suicide.

car·ri·ole /ˈkeri,oːl, ˈka-/ *noun* (also **cari·ole**) **1** a small open carriage for one person. **2** a covered light cart. **3** *Cdn hist.* **a** a horse-drawn sleigh with seats for a driver and often one or more passengers. **b** (*North*) a type of dogsled designed to carry a passenger or load in the front, with a rear platform for the driver to stand on. [French from Italian *carriuola*, diminutive of *carro* CAR]

car·rion /ˈkeriən/ *noun* **1** dead putrefying flesh. **2** something vile or filthy. [Anglo-French & Old Northern French *caroine, -oigne*, Old French *charoigne*, ultimately from Latin *caro* flesh]

carrion crow *noun* a black crow, *Corvus corone*, native to Europe, feeding mainly on carrion.

carrion flower *noun* **1** a N American climbing plant of the lily family, *Smilax herbacea*, having fetid flowers. **2** = STAPELIA.

Car·roll, Lewis (pseudonym of Charles Lutwidge Dodgson) (1832–98), English mathematician and writer. He is best known for his fantasies *Alice's Adventures in Wonderland* (1865) and *Through the Looking Glass* (1871), and his nonsense verse, notably *The Hunting of the Snark* (1876).

car·rot *noun* **1 a** an umbelliferous plant, *Daucus carota*, with a tapering orange-coloured root. **b** this root as a vegetable. **2** a means of enticement or persuasion. **3** (in *pl.*) *informal* = CARROT TOP. [French *carotte* from Latin *carota* from Greek *karōton*]

carrot-and-stick *noun* (*attributive*) designating an approach, procedures, etc., combining rewards for desirable behaviour and punishment for undesirable behaviour.

carrot cake *noun* a cake made of eggs, oil, sugar, flour, grated carrots and spices, typically served with cream cheese icing.

carrot pudding *noun* a sweet steamed suet pudding including grated carrots, grated potato, spices, and raisins, often served as Christmas pudding.

carrot top *noun informal* (often as a form of address) a person with red hair. □ **carrot-topped** *adjective*

car·roty *adjective* (of hair) orangey-red.

carry ● *verb* (**-ries, -ried**) **1** *transitive* support or hold up, esp. while moving. **2** *transitive* convey with one from one place to another. **3** *transitive* have on one's person (*should the police carry guns?; I never carry much money with me*). **4** *transitive* conduct or transmit (*pipe carries water; wire carries electric current*). **5** *transitive* take (a process etc.) to a specified point (*carry into effect; carry a joke too far*). **6** *transitive* (foll. by *to*) continue or prolong (*carry modesty to excess*). **7** *transitive* involve, imply; have as a feature or consequence (*carries a two-year guarantee; privilege carries responsibility*). **8** *transitive* (in calculations) transfer (a figure) to a column of higher value. **9 a** *reflexive* conduct oneself in a specified way, esp. in reference to one's bearing (*carries herself with pride*). **b** *transitive* hold (a part of the body) in a specified way (*the horse carries his head low*). **10** *transitive* **a** (of a newspaper or magazine) publish; include in its contents, esp. regularly. **b** (of a radio or television station) broadcast, esp. regularly. **11** *transitive* (of a retailing outlet) keep a regular stock of (particular goods for sale) (*have stopped carrying that brand*). **12** *transitive* make regular payments towards (a mortgage, loan, etc.). **13** *intransitive* **a** (of sound, esp. a voice) be audible at a distance. **b** (of a missile) travel, penetrate. **14** *transitive* (of a gun etc.) propel a specified distance. **15** *transitive* **a** win victory or acceptance for (a proposal etc.). **b** win acceptance from (*carried the audience with them*). **c** win, capture (a prize, a fortress, etc.). **d** *N Amer.* win (a constituency) in an election. **e** *Golf* cause the ball to pass beyond (a bunker etc.). **16** *intransitive Football* attempt to gain yardage by rushing with the ball. **17** *transitive* **a** endure the weight of; support (*columns carry the dome*). **b** be the chief cause of the effectiveness of; be the driving force in (*you carry the sales department*). **18** *transitive* be pregnant with (*is carrying twins*). **19** *transitive* **a** (of a motive, money, etc.) cause or enable (a person) to go to a specified place. **b** (of a journey) bring (a person) to a specified point. **20** *transitive* sing (a tune) on pitch. ● *noun* (*pl.* **-ries**) **1** an act of carrying. **2** *Golf* the distance a ball travels before reaching the ground. **3** a

portage between rivers etc. **4** the range of a gun etc. **5** *Football* an instance of rushing with the ball. □ **carry all before one** succeed; overcome all opposition. **carry away 1** remove. **2** inspire; affect emotionally or spiritually. **3** deprive of self-control (*got carried away*). **4** *Naut.* **a** lose (a mast etc.) by breakage. **b** break off or away. **carry back** take (a person) back in thought to a past time. **carry the can** *Cdn & Brit. informal* bear the responsibility or blame. **carry conviction** be convincing. **carry the day** be victorious or successful. **carry forward** transfer to a new page or account. **carry it off** (or **carry it off well**) do well under difficulties. **carry off 1** take away, esp. by force. **2** win (a prize). **3** (esp. of a disease) kill. **4** render acceptable or passable. **carry on 1** continue (*carry on eating; carry on, don't mind me*). **2** engage in (a conversation or a business). **3** *informal* behave strangely or excitedly. **4** (often foll. by *with*) *informal* flirt or have a love affair. **5** advance (a process) by a stage. **carry out 1** put (ideas, instructions, etc.) into practice. **2** perform or conduct (an investigation, test, etc.). **carry over** be temporarily suspended and resumed later; postpone. **carry through 1** complete successfully. **2** bring safely out of difficulties. **carry weight** be influential or important. **carry with one** remember; bear in mind. [Anglo-French & Old Northern French *carier* (as CAR)]

carry·all *noun* **1** *N Amer.* a large bag or case for carrying things. **2** *US* a large car or truck with seats facing each other along the sides. **3** *hist.* a light carriage (compare CARRIOLE).

carry·cot *noun Brit.* a portable cot for a baby.

carry·ing capacity *noun* **1** the capacity of something, e.g. a vehicle, to hold passengers or cargo. **2** the maximum population of a certain species that can be supported by a given environment.

carry·ing charge *noun* **1** the interest on a loan etc. **2** an unproductive expense, e.g. for goods stored in a warehouse.

carrying-on *noun* (also **carryings-on** *plural noun*) **1** a state of excitement or fuss. **2** a questionable piece of behaviour. **3** a flirtation or love affair.

carry·ing place *noun N Amer. hist.* = PORTAGE *noun* 2.

carry-on ● *adjective* (of a suitcase etc.) suitable for carrying onto an airplane, bus, etc., rather than loading as checked baggage. ● *noun* a carry-on suitcase.

carry-out *attributive adjective & noun* esp. *US & Scot.* = TAKEOUT 1.

carry-over *noun* **1** something retained or carried over. **2** the act of retaining something or carrying something over.

car seat *noun* **1** a portable chair that fastens to the seat of a car and is used for securing young children. **2** the seat of a car.

car sharing *noun* a system whereby several people buy shares in a car so that each may reserve the use of it for short periods when required.

car·sick *adjective* affected with nausea caused by the motion of a car. □ **car·sick·ness** *noun*

Car·son ▸ 1 Chris·to·pher ('Kit') (1809–68), US frontiersman, guide, and soldier. A US folk hero, he was a renowned guide during the 1840s and fought for the Union during the American Civil War. **2 John Wil·liam** ('Johnny') (b.1925), US television personality. Carson's monologues on the daytime *The Johnny Carson Show* convinced NBC executives to engage him as permanent host of *The Tonight Show* in 1962, a position which he held with enormous popularity until he retired from the show in 1992. **3 Rachel Lou·ise** (1907–64), US zoologist. A pioneer ecologist and popularizer of science, she wrote *The Sea Around Us* (1951) and *Silent Spring* (1962), an attack on the indiscriminate use of pesticides and weed killers.

Carson City the state capital of Nevada; pop. (2000) 52,457.

car·spiel /ˈkɑːrspiːl/ *noun Cdn* a bonspiel in which curlers compete for a car or cars. [CAR + BONSPIEL]

cart ● *noun* **1** a strong vehicle with two or four wheels for carrying loads, drawn by a horse, ox, etc. **2** a light vehicle for pushing or pulling by hand (*shopping cart*). **3** a light vehicle with two wheels for driving in, drawn by a single horse. **4** = GOLF CART. **5** = SHOPPING CART 3. ● *transitive verb* **1** convey in or as in a cart. **2** *informal* carry (esp. a cumbersome thing) with difficulty or over a long distance (*carted it all the way home*). □ **cart off** remove, esp. by force. **put the cart before the horse 1** reverse the proper order or procedure. **2** take an effect for a cause. □ **cart·er** *noun* **cart·ful** *noun* (*pl.* **-fuls**). [Old Norse *kartr* cart & Old English *cræt*, prob. influenced by Anglo-French & Old Northern French *carete* diminutive of *carre* CAR]

cart·age /ˈkɑːrtɪdʒ/ *noun* **1** the act of carting or conveying goods. **2** the price paid for carting.

CART *abbreviation proprietary* Championship Auto Racing Teams.

Car·ta·gena /ˌkɑːrtəˈheinə, -ˈdʒiːnə/ **1** a port in SE Spain; pop. (est.

Consonants: **b** *but* **d** *dog* **f** *few* **g** *get* **h** *her* **j** *yes* **k** *cat* **l** *leg* **m** *man* **n** *no* **p** *pen* **r** *red* **s** *sit*

2001) 183,799. **2** a port, resort, and oil-refining centre in NW Colombia, on the Caribbean Sea; pop. (est. 2002) 853,900.

carte blanche /kɑːt ˈblɑ̃ʃ/ noun complete freedom to act as one thinks best. [French, = blank paper]

car·tel /kɑːˈtel/ noun **1** a group of manufacturers or suppliers who collude to maintain prices at a high level, and control production, marketing arrangements, etc. **2** a political combination between parties. □ **car·tel·ize** /ˈkɑːtəˌlaɪz/ transitive & intransitive verb (also esp. Brit. **-ise**). [German Kartell from French cartel from Italian cartello diminutive of carta CARD[1]]

Car·ter ▶ **1 Sir Fred·er·ick Bow·ker Ter·ring·ton** (1819–1900), Canadian politician, prime minister of Newfoundland 1865–9 and 1875–8. He was the Newfoundland representative at the Quebec Conference, but failed to gain sufficient support for union with the other British North American provinces. **2 How·ard** (1873–1939), English archaeologist and Egyptologist who discovered (1922) and excavated the tomb of Tutankhamen. **3 James Earl** ('Jimmy') (b.1924), US Democratic politician, 39th president of the US 1977–81. A progressive and reformist governor of Georgia (1970–4), he was elected president on a platform of civil rights and economic reform. Although his administration was notable for achieving the Panama Canal Treaty (1977) and the Camp David agreements (1979), it was dogged in the last few years by his inability to resolve the crisis caused by the seizure of US hostages in Iran. He was awarded the Nobel Peace Prize in 2002 for his work in international conflict resolution and social development. **4 Wil·fred Ar·thur Charles** ('Wilf') (1904–1996), Canadian country singer and songwriter, whose most popular songs include 'My Swiss Moonlight Lullaby' and 'The Capture of Albert Johnson' (both 1932).

Car·te·sian /kɑːˈtiːʒən, -iːzjən/ ● adjective of or relating to Descartes, his philosophy, or his mathematical methods. ● noun a follower of Descartes. □ **Car·te·sian·ism** noun [modern Latin Cartesianus from Cartesius, name of DESCARTES]

Cartesian coordinates plural noun a system for locating a point by reference to its distance from two or three axes intersecting at right angles.

Car·thage /ˈkɑːθɪdʒ/ an ancient city on the coast of North Africa near present-day Tunis, founded by the Phoenicians traditionally in 814 BC. It became a major force in the Mediterranean, with interests throughout North Africa, Spain, and Sicily that brought it into conflict with Greece until the 3rd c. BC and then with Rome in the Punic Wars; the Romans finally destroyed it in 146 BC. □ **Car·tha·gin·ian** /ˌkɑːθəˈdʒɪnɪən/ adjective & noun

cart horse noun a thickset horse suitable for heavy work.

Car·thu·sian /kɑːˈθjuːzɪən, -ˈθuːʒən/ ● noun a Christian monk or nun of a strictly contemplative order founded at Chartreuse in SE France by St. Bruno in 1084, leading a hermitic way of life remarkable for its austerity and self-denial. ● adjective of or relating to the Carthusians. [medieval Latin Carthusianus from Latin Cart(h)usia Chartreuse]

Car·tier /kɑːˈtjei/ **1 Sir George-Étienne** (1814–73), Canadian politician, prime minister of the Province of Canada 1857–8 and 1858–62, Father of Confederation. He attended all three conferences leading to Confederation, and was largely responsible for gaining French-Canadian support for union. **2 Jacques** (1491–1557), French explorer. The first to establish France's claim to N America, he made three voyages to Canada between 1534 and 1541, sailing up the St. Lawrence River as far as present-day Montreal and building a fort at Cap Rouge (a few miles upstream of what is now Quebec City).

Cartier-Bresson /kɑːtˌjeibreˈsɔ̃/ **Henri** (b.1908), French photographer. Intent on capturing the 'decisive moment' of a scene or event, he travelled widely, recording in black and white the lives of ordinary people, and establishing a reputation as a humane and perceptive observer.

car·ti·lage /ˈkɑːtəlɪdʒ/ noun a firm, elastic, semi-opaque connective tissue of the vertebrate body; gristle. □ **car·ti·la·gin·ous** /-ˈladʒɪnəs/ adjective [French from Latin cartilago -ginis]

cart·load noun **1** an amount filling a cart. **2** a large quantity of anything.

carto·gram noun a map with diagrammatic statistical information. [French cartogramme from carte map, card]

car·tog·raphy /kɑːˈtɒɡrəfi/ noun the science or practice of map drawing. □ **car·tog·raph·er** noun **carto·graph·ic** /-təˈɡrafɪk/ adjective **carto·graph·ic·al** /-təˈɡrafɪkəl/ adjective [French cartographie from carte map, card]

carto·mancy /ˈkɑːtəˌmansi/ noun fortune-telling by interpreting a random selection of playing cards. [French cartomancie from carte CARD[1]]

car·ton noun **1** a light cardboard or plastic box or container. **2** the contents of a carton. [French (as CARTOON)]

car·toon ● noun **1** a humorous drawing in a newspaper, magazine, etc., esp. as a topical comment. **2** = COMIC STRIP. **3** a filmed sequence of drawings using the technique of animation. **4** an artist's full-size preliminary design for a painting, tapestry, mosaic, etc. ● verb **1** transitive draw a cartoon of. **2** intransitive draw cartoons. □ **car·toon·ist** noun **cartoon-like** adjective [Italian cartone from carta CARD[1]]

car·toon·ish adjective resembling a comic cartoon or its style, esp. by showing simplification or exaggeration of some features. □ **car·toon·ish·ly** adverb

car·toony adjective visually resembling a comic cartoon.

car·touche /kɑːˈtuːʃ/ noun **1 a** Archit. a scroll-like ornament, e.g. the volute of an Ionic capital. **b** a tablet imitating, or a drawing of, a scroll with rolled-up ends, used ornamentally or bearing an inscription. **c** an ornate frame. **2** Archaeology an oval ring enclosing Egyptian hieroglyphs, usu. representing the name and title of a king. [French, = cartridge, from Italian cartoccio from carta CARD[1]]

car·tridge noun **1** a case containing a charge of propelling explosive for firearms or blasting, with a bullet or shot if for small arms. **2** a spool of film, magnetic tape, etc., in a sealed container ready for insertion into a particular mechanism. **3** a component carrying the stylus on the pickup head of a record player. **4** a container of ink, toner, etc., for insertion in a pen, printer, photocopier, etc. [corruption of CARTOUCHE (but recorded earlier)]

cartridge belt noun a belt with pockets or loops for cartridges (see CARTRIDGE 1).

cart track noun (also **cart trail**) a track or road for cart traffic.

cart·wheel ● **1** the (usu. spoked) wheel of a cart. **2** a circular sideways handspring with the arms and legs extended. ● intransitive verb **1** perform cartwheels. **2** turn end over end.

Cart·wright /ˈkɑːtraɪt/ **Ed·mund** (1743–1823), English engineer, inventor of the power loom. Initially a clergyman, he became interested in textile machinery, developing machines for wool combing and rope making, and an engine which used alcohol rather than steam.

cart·wright noun a maker of carts.

carun·cle /ˈkerəŋkəl, kəˈrʌŋkəl/ noun **1** a fleshy excrescence, e.g. a turkey's wattles or the red prominence at the inner angle of the eye. **2** Bot. an outgrowth from a seed near the micropyle. □ **car·uncu·lar** /-kjʊlər/ adjective [obsolete French from Latin caruncula from caro carnis flesh]

Ca·ruso /kəˈruːsəʊ/ **En·rico** (1873–1921), Italian operatic tenor. One of the most highly acclaimed singers of the 20th c., he had his greatest successes in operas by Verdi, Puccini, and Massenet; he was also the first major tenor to be recorded on gramophone records.

carve verb **1** transitive produce or shape (a statue, representation in relief, etc.) by cutting into a hard material (carved a figure out of rock; carved it in wood). **2** transitive **a** cut patterns, designs, letters, etc. in (hard material). **b** (foll. by into) form a pattern, design, etc., from (carved it into a bust). **c** (foll. by with) cover or decorate (material) with figures or designs cut in it. **3** transitive & intransitive cut (meat etc.) into slices for eating. **4** transitive cut (a way, passage, etc.). **5** intransitive (in skiing, snowboarding, etc.) make a sharp turn in snow with minimal sideslipping. □ **carved in stone** (of a decision etc.) unchangeable. **carve out 1** take from a larger whole. **2** establish (a career etc.) purposefully (carved out a name for themselves). **carve (out) a niche** establish oneself in a particular area of a market etc. in order to excel. **carve up 1** divide into several pieces; subdivide (territory etc.). **2** cut (a person) with a knife. □ **carv·er** noun [Old English ceorfan cut, from West Germanic]

car·vel var. of CARAVEL.

carvel-built adjective (of a boat) made with planks flush, not overlapping (compare CLINKER-BUILT).

carv·en archaic past participle of CARVE.

Carv·er, George Wash·ing·ton (1860–1943), US botanist, agricultural chemist, and educator. He dedicated his life to improving the condition of blacks in the southern US, and developed hundreds of food and industrial products from peanuts, soybeans, and sweet potatoes.

carv·ery noun (pl. **-ies**) esp. Brit. a buffet restaurant, esp. one serving roast beef.

carve-up *noun informal* a sharing-out, esp. of spoils.

carv·ing *noun* a carved object, esp. as a work of art.

carving knife *noun* a knife with a long blade, for carving meat.

car wash *noun* a business or building with equipment for washing cars.

cary·atid /ˌkeriˈatɪd/ *noun* (*pl.* **cary·atids** or **cary·atid·es** /-ˌdiːz/) *Archit.* a pillar in the form of a draped female figure, supporting an entablature (compare ATLANTES). [French *caryatide* from Italian *cariatide* or Latin from Greek *karuatis -idos* priestess at Caryae (*Karuai*) in Laconia]

cary·op·sis /ˌkeriˈɒpsɪs/ *noun* (*pl.* **cary·op·ses** /-siːz/) *Bot.* a dry one-seeded indehiscent fruit, as in wheat and corn. [modern Latin from Greek *karuon* nut + *opsis* appearance]

CAS *abbreviation* (in Canada) CHILDREN'S AID SOCIETY.

ca·saba /kəˈsɒbə/ *noun* a type of melon, *Cucumis melo inodorus*, having a yellow wrinkled skin and whitish flesh. [prob. from *Kasaba*, former name of Turgutlu, a town in W Turkey]

Casa·blanca /ˌkasəˈblaŋkə/ the largest city of Morocco, a seaport on the Atlantic coast; pop. (est. 2002) 3,344,300.

Ca·sals /kəˈsalz, -ˈsɒlz/ **Pablo** (or **Pau**) (1876–1973), Spanish cellist, conductor, and composer. The foremost cellist of his time, he was noted esp. for his performances of Bach suites and the Dvořák *Cello Concerto*.

Casa·nova[1] /ˌkasəˈnoːvə/ **Gio·van·ni Jac·opo** (full surname Casanova de Seingalt) (1725–98), Italian adventurer. He is famous for his memoirs (first published in French 1828–38), describing his adventures in Europe and esp. his sexual encounters.

Casa·nova[2] /ˌkasəˈnoːvə/ *noun* a man notorious for seducing women. [with reference to CASANOVA[1]]

cas·bah /ˈkazbɒ/ *noun* (also **kas·bah**) **1** the citadel of a N African city. **2** an Arab quarter near this. [French from Arabic *kas(a)ba* citadel]

CASBY /ˈkazbi/ *noun* (*pl.* **CASBIES**) (in Canada) any of several awards presented annually to Canadian popular music performers; voting is conducted by ballot among the general public. [acronym from *Canadian Artists Selected By You*]

cas·cade ● *noun* **1** a small waterfall, esp. forming one in a series or part of a large broken waterfall. **2 a** a succession of electrical devices or stages in a process. **b** a rapid sequence of events. **3** a quantity of material etc. draped in descending folds. **4** a process of disseminating information from senior to junior levels in an organization. **5** a thing that falls or hangs in a way suggestive of a waterfall (*cascades of blond hair*). ● *intransitive verb* fall in or like a cascade. [French from Italian *cascata* from *cascare* to fall, ultimately from Latin *casus*: see CASE[1]]

Cascade Mountains a mountain range in western N America, extending southward over 1 100 km from southwestern BC to N California. [after the impressive cascades near the Columbia River gorge, situated at the Washington–Oregon border]

cas·cara /kasˈkɑrə/ *noun* (in full **cascara sag·rada** /səgˈrɒdə/) the dried bark of the western N American cascara buckthorn, *Rhamnus purshiana*, used as a purgative. [Spanish, = (sacred) bark]

case[1] *noun* **1** an instance of something occurring. **2** a state of affairs, hypothetical or actual. **3** the position or circumstances in which one is (*in your case, we are prepared to be lenient*). **4 a** an instance of a person receiving professional advice, e.g. from a doctor or social worker. **b** this person or the circumstances involved. **5** a matter under official investigation, esp. by the police. **6** *Law* **a** a cause or suit for trial. **b** a statement of the facts or evidence for a trial etc. **7 a** the sum of the arguments on one side, esp. in a lawsuit (*that is our case*). **b** a set of arguments, esp. in relation to persuasiveness (*have a good case; have a weak case*). **c** a valid set of arguments (*have no case*). **8** *Grammar* **a** the relation of a word to other words in a sentence. **b** a form of a noun, adjective, or pronoun expressing this. □ **as the case may be** according to the situation. **get off** (or **on**) **one's case** *N Amer.* stop (or start) harassing one. **in any case** whatever the truth is; whatever may happen. **in case 1** in the event that; if. **2** lest; in provision against a stated or implied possibility (*take an umbrella in case it rains; took it in case*). **in the case of** in the event of. **in the case of** as regards. **in no case** under no circumstances. **in that case** if that is true; should that happen. **is** (or **is not**) **the case** is (or is not) so. [Old French *cas* from Latin *casus* fall, from *cadere cas-* to fall]

case[2] ● *noun* **1** a container or covering serving to enclose, hold, or contain. **2** a container with its contents. **3** an outer protective covering. **4** an item of luggage, esp. a suitcase. **5** *Printing* a partitioned receptacle for type. ● *transitive verb* **1** enclose in a case. **2** (foll. by *with*) surround. **3** *slang* reconnoitre (a house etc.) esp. with a view to robbery.

□ **have got it cased** have got everything under control. [Old French *casse, chasse*, from Latin *capsa* from *capere* hold]

case·book *noun* a book containing a record of legal or medical cases.

case·bound *adjective* (of a book) hardcover.

case-harden *transitive verb* **1** harden the surface of, esp. give a steel surface to (iron) by carbonizing. **2** make callous. □ **case-hardened** *adjective*

case history *noun* information about a person for use in professional treatment, e.g. by a doctor.

ca·sein /ˈkeisiːn, ˈkeisiiːn/ *noun* **1** the main protein in milk, esp. in coagulated form as in cheese. **2** this protein used in making plastics, etc. **3 a** a paint containing casein as a vehicle. **b** a painting in casein paints. [Latin *caseus* cheese]

case law *noun* the law as established by the outcome of former cases (compare COMMON LAW, STATUTE LAW).

case·load *noun* the cases with which a doctor etc. is concerned at one time.

case lot *noun* a large amount of something (*buys wine in case lots*).

case·mate /ˈkeismeit/ *noun* **1** a chamber in the thickness of the wall of a fortress, with embrasures. **2** an armoured enclosure for guns on a warship. [French from Italian *casamatta*, perhaps from Greek *khasma -atos* gap]

Case·ment, **Sir Roger (David)** (1864–1916), Irish nationalist and British public official. Shortly after the outbreak of the First World War he visited Germany to seek support for an Irish uprising. He was captured on his return to Ireland before the Easter rebellion of 1916, and subsequently hanged by the British for treason.

case·ment *noun* **1** a window or part of a window hinged vertically to open like a door. **2** *literary* a window. [Anglo-Latin *cassimentum* from *cassa* CASE[2]]

case-sensitive *adjective Computing* **1** (of a program or function) differentiating between capital and lower case letters. **2** (of input) treated differently depending on whether it is in capitals or lower case letters.

case study *noun* **1** an attempt to understand a person, institution, etc., from collected information. **2** a record of such an attempt. **3** the use of a particular instance as an exemplar of general principles.

case·work *noun* social work concerned with individuals, esp. involving understanding of the client's family and background. □ **case·work·er** *noun*

Cas·grain /kazˈgrɑ̃/ **Thé·rèse** (1896–1981), Canadian feminist and politician. A leading figure in the Quebec campaign for women's suffrage in the 1920s and 1930s, she served as Quebec leader of the Co-operative Commonwealth Federation (1951–7), and helped to found the League for Human Rights (1960).

Cash, **John·ny** (1932–2003), US country singer and songwriter. He was known for his trademark black clothing, deep voice, and songs about characters who are unlucky in life or love; his most famous hits include 'I Walk the Line' (1956), 'Ring of Fire' (1963), and 'A Boy Named Sue' (1969).

cash[1] ● *noun* **1** money in coins or banknotes, as distinct from cheques, money orders, or payment on credit. **2** (also **cash down**) money given as full payment at the time of purchase, as distinct from credit. **3** *informal* money. **4** *Cdn informal* = CASH REGISTER. ● *transitive verb* give or obtain cash for (a note, cheque, etc.). □ **cash in 1** obtain cash for. **2** *informal* (usu. foll. by *on*) profit (from); take advantage (of). **3** (in full **cash in one's chips**) *informal* die. **cash out** (*Brit.* **up**) **1** count and check cash takings at the end of a day's business. **2** convert one's winnings or earnings from an investment into cash. □ **cash·able** *adjective* [obsolete French *casse* box or Italian *cassa* from Latin *capsa* CASE[2]]

cash[2] *noun* (*pl.* same) *hist.* any of various southern Indian, SE Asian, and Chinese coins of small value. [ultimately from Portuguese *ca(i)xa* from Tamil *kāsu* from Sanskrit *karsha*]

cash and carry ● *adjective* (of a store, sale, etc.) operated on a system of cash payments and with no delivery available. ● *noun* a store where this system operates.

cash·back *noun* **1** a form of incentive offered to buyers of certain products, mortgage applicants, etc. whereby they receive a cash sum after making their purchase or negotiating their loan etc. **2** a facility offered by certain retailers whereby the customer may withdraw cash when making a debit card purchase, the amount of which is added to their bill.

cash bar *noun* a bar at a special function at which guests buy drinks rather than having them provided free (compare OPEN BAR).

Vowels: a *cat* ɑ *arm* e *bed* ɜr *her* ɜː *deux* ə *ago* ɪ *sit* i *cosy* iː *feed* ɒ *hot* ɔ *pore* oː *no* ʌ *run* ʊ *put*

cash·book *noun* a book in which receipts and payments of cash are recorded.

cash box *noun* a box for storing money used in sales, usu. having a tray divided into compartments for bills and coins.

cash card *noun* = BANK CARD.

cash cow *noun* *informal* a business, product, or operation that provides a steady and abundant cash flow.

cash crop *noun* a crop produced for sale. □ **cash crop·per** *noun* **cash crop·ping** *noun*

cash desk *noun* *Cdn & Brit.* a counter in a store where goods are paid for.

cash dispenser *noun* = AUTOMATED TELLER MACHINE.

cash·ew /ˈkaʃuː, kaˈʃuː/ *noun* **1** a bushy evergreen tree, *Anacardium occidentale*, native to Central and S America, bearing kidney-shaped nuts attached to fleshy fruits. **2** the edible nut of this tree. [Portuguese from Tupi *(a)caju*]

cash flow *noun* the movement of money as affecting liquidity or as a measure of profitability.

cash grab *noun* an instance of an organization, e.g. a government, creating a policy or regulation the real but unacknowledged purpose of which is to generate more money for itself (*the city's building permit requirements are just a cash grab*).

cash·ier[1] /kaˈʃiːr/ *noun* **1** a person handling customer payments in a store. **2** a person in charge of a bank's or company's cash. [Dutch *cassier* or French *caissier* (as CASH[1])]

cash·ier[2] /kaˈʃiːr/ *transitive verb* dismiss from service, esp. from the armed forces with disgrace. [Flemish *kasseren* disband, revoke, from French *casser* from Latin *quassare* QUASH]

cash·less *adjective* (of a society, economic system, etc.) functioning without cash, all financial transactions being executed electronically or by credit card.

cash machine *noun* = AUTOMATED TELLER MACHINE.

cash·mere /ˈkaʒmiːr/ *noun* **1** a fine soft wool, esp. that of a Kashmir goat. **2** a material made from this. [*Kashmir* in Asia]

cash on delivery *noun* a system of paying the carrier for goods when they are delivered.

cash·point *noun* *Brit.* = AUTOMATED TELLER MACHINE.

cash-poor *adjective* (of a person or business) lacking cash for immediate purchases, although usu. having non-liquid wealth such as real estate.

cash register *noun* a machine in a store etc. with a drawer for money, recording the amount of each sale, totalling receipts, etc.

cash·spiel /ˈkaʃspiːl/ *noun* *Cdn* a bonspiel in which curlers compete for cash prizes.

cash-strapped *adjective* extremely short of money.

cas·ing *noun* **1** a protective or enclosing cover or shell. **2** the material for this.

ca·sino /kaˈsiːnoː/ *noun* (*pl.* **-sinos**) a public room or building for gambling. [Italian, diminutive of *casa* house, from Latin *casa* cottage]

cask *noun* **1** a large barrel-like container made of wood, metal, or plastic, esp. one for alcoholic liquor. **2** its contents. **3** its capacity. **4** *Cdn* (*Nfld*) a wooden container for shipping dried and salted cod, containing four hundredweight (about 200 kg). [French *casque* or Spanish *casco* helmet]

cask·et *noun* **1** esp. *N Amer.* a coffin. **2** a small often ornamental box or chest for jewels, letters, etc. [perhaps from Anglo-French form of Old French *cassette* from Italian *cassetta* diminutive of *cassa* from Latin *capsa* CASE[2]]

Cas·par /ˈkaspɑr, -spɜr/ one of the three Magi.

Caspar Milque·toast *noun* = MILQUETOAST.

Cas·pian Sea /ˈkaspiən/ a large landlocked salt lake, bounded by Russia, Kazakhstan, Turkmenistan, Azerbaijan, and Iran. It is the world's largest body of inland water. Its surface lies 28 m (92 ft.) below sea level.

casque /kask/ *noun* **1** *hist.* or *literary* a helmet. **2** *Anat.* a helmet-like structure, e.g. the process on the bill of the cassowary. [French from Spanish *casco*]

Cas·san·dra[1] /kaˈsandrə/ *Gk Myth* a daughter of the Trojan king Priam. Apollo loved her and gave her the gift of prophecy, but when she rejected him he caused her prophecies, though true, to be disbelieved.

Cas·san·dra[2] /kaˈsandrə/ *noun* a prophet of disaster, esp. one who is disregarded. [with reference to CASSANDRA[1]]

cas·sata /kaˈsɒtə/ *noun* **1** a type of ice cream containing candied or dried fruit and nuts. **2** a rich layered dessert consisting of ricotta cheese and sponge cake, covered with marzipan or chocolate icing. [Italian]

Cas·satt /kaˈsat/ **Mary** (*c.*1844–1926), US painter and printmaker. She exhibited with the Impressionists in Paris, and is known chiefly for her paintings of mothers and children (e.g. *The Bath, c.*1892), and her pastels, which show the influence of Japanese art.

cas·sava /kaˈsɒvə/ *noun* **1 a** any plant of the genus *Manihot*, esp. the cultivated varieties *M. esculenta* (**bitter cassava**) and *M. dulcis* (**sweet cassava**), having starchy tuberous roots. **b** the roots themselves. **2** a starch or flour obtained from these roots. *Also called* TAPIOCA, MANIOC. [earlier *cas(s)avi* etc., from Taino *casavi*, influenced by French *cassave*]

casse-croûte /kasˈkruːt/ *noun* *Cdn (Que.)* a snack bar. [Canadian French from French *casse-croûte* snack, lit. 'break crust (of bread)']

cas·ser·ole /ˈkasəˌroːl/ *noun* **1** a covered dish, usu. of earthenware or glass, in which food is cooked, esp. in an oven. **2** food cooked in a casserole, esp. a savoury dish combining meat or fish, vegetables, pasta, sauce, etc. [French from *cassole* diminutive of *casse* from Provençal *casa* from Late Latin *cattia* ladle, pan, from Greek *kuathion* diminutive of *kuathos* cup]

cas·sette /kaˈset/ *noun* a sealed case containing a length of tape, ribbon, etc., ready for insertion in a machine, esp.: **1** a length of magnetic tape wound on to spools, ready for insertion in a tape recorder. **2** a length of photographic film, ready for insertion in a camera. [French, diminutive of *casse* CASE[2]]

cas·sia /ˈkasiə, ˈkaʃə/ *noun* **1** any plant of the genus *Cassia*, esp. one yielding senna. **2 a** (in full **cassia bark**) the cinnamon-like bark of *Cinnamomum cassia* used as a spice. **b** (in full **cassia tree**) the tree yielding this. [Latin from Greek *kasia* from Hebrew *k'ṣī'āh* bark like cinnamon]

Cas·siar Mountains /ˈkasiˌɑr/ a mountain range extending southeastward from S Yukon Territory into north central BC. [after the KASKA]

Cas·sini /kaˈsiːni/ **Gio·van·ni Domen·ico** (1625–1712), Italian-born French astronomer. He helped to establish the Paris Observatory, and is noted for determining the rotational periods of Jupiter and Saturn, calculating the movements of the Galilean moons of Jupiter, discovering four of the moons of Saturn, and describing a gap in the rings of Saturn (now known as Cassini's division).

Cassin's auklet /ˈkasɪnz/ *noun* a small black and white auklet, *Ptychoramphus aleuticus*, of the N Pacific. [J. *Cassin*, US ornithologist d.1869]

Cas·sio·dor·us /ˌkasioˈdɔrəs/ **Fla·vius Mag·nus Aurel·ius** (*c.*490–*c.*585), Roman statesman, historian, and monk, who wrote *Chronicon*, a history extending from Adam to 519, and *Institutiones*, a compendium of knowledge compiled for his monastery.

cas·sio·pe /kaˈsaiəpi/ *noun* any of several circumboreal heathers of the genus *Cassiope* with small white bell-shaped flowers. [from CASSIOPEIA]

Cas·sio·peia /ˌkasiəˈpiːə/ **1** *Gk Myth* the wife of Cepheus, king of Ethiopia, and mother of Andromeda. She boasted that she herself (or, in some versions, her daughter) was more beautiful than the nereids, thus incurring the wrath of Poseidon. **2** *Astronomy* a constellation near the north celestial pole, recognizable by the conspicuous 'W' pattern of its brightest stars. It contains a supernova remnant which is the strongest radio source in the sky.

cas·sis /kaˈsiːs/ *noun* a syrupy blackcurrant liqueur. [French, = blackcurrant]

cas·sit·er·ite /kaˈsɪtəˌrait/ *noun* a naturally occurring ore of tin dioxide, from which tin is extracted. *Also called* TINSTONE. [Greek *kassiteros* tin]

Cas·sius /ˈkasiəs/ **Gaius** (full name Gaius Cassius Longinus) (d.42 BC), Roman general. With Brutus he was one of the leaders of the conspiracy in 44 BC to assassinate Julius Caesar. He and Brutus were defeated by Caesar's supporters, Antony and Octavian, at the battle of Philippi in 42 BC.

cas·sock /ˈkasək/ *noun* a close-fitting garment with sleeves, fastened at the neck and reaching to the heels, worn under a surplice, alb, or gown by some clerics, members of choirs, etc. □ **cas·socked** *adjective* [French *casaque* long coat, from Italian *casacca* horseman's coat, prob. from Turkic: compare COSSACK]

Cas·son /ˈkasən/ **A(l·fred) J(o·seph)** (1898–1992), Canadian painter. A member of the Group of Seven from 1926, he is best known for his sun-drenched paintings of small towns in Ontario, including 'Anglican Church at Magnetawan' (1933) and 'Country Store' (1945).

uː mood   ai my   əi pipe   au brown   ʌu house   ei day   ɔi boy   ɑ̃ franglais   ā Canadien   ɔ̃ Brayon   (*see over for consonants*)

cas·sou·let /ˈkasʊˌleɪ/ noun a stew of beans with pork, mutton, and either duck or goose. [French, diminutive of dial. *cassolo* stew pan, from Old Provençal *cassa*, related to CASSEROLE]

cas·so·wary /ˈkasəˌweri/ noun (pl. **-ies**) any large flightless Australasian bird of the genus *Casuarius*, with heavy body, stout legs, a wattled neck, and a bony crest on its forehead. [Malay *kasuāri, kasavāri*]

cast ● verb (past and past participle **cast**) **1** transitive throw, esp. deliberately or forcefully. **2** transitive (often foll. by on, over) **a** direct or cause to fall (one's eyes, a glance, light, a shadow, a spell, etc.). **b** express (doubts, aspersions, etc.). **3** transitive throw out (a fishing line) into the water. **4** transitive let down (an anchor etc.). **5** transitive **a** throw off, get rid of. **b** shed (skin etc.) esp. in the process of growth. **c** (of a horse) lose (a shoe). **d** (of an animal) bring forth (young), esp. abortively. **6** transitive record, register, or give (a vote). **7** transitive **a** shape (molten metal or plastic material) in a mould. **b** make (a product) in this way. **8** intransitive (of dogs etc.) search for a scent. **9** transitive Printing make (type). **10 a** transitive (usu. foll. by as) assign (a theatrical performer) to the role of a particular character. **b** transitive allocate roles in (a play, film, etc.). **c** intransitive select performers for the roles in (a play, film, etc.). **11** transitive Cdn (Nfld) catch (capelin) using a cast net. **12** transitive (foll. by in, into) arrange or formulate (facts etc.) in a specified form. **13** transitive & intransitive reckon, add up, calculate (accounts or figures). **14** transitive calculate and record details of (a horoscope, tides, etc.). ● noun **1 a** the throwing of a missile etc. **b** the distance reached by this. **2** a throw or a number thrown at dice. **3** a throw of a net, fishing line, etc. **4** Fishing **a** that which is cast, esp. the line with hook, fly, etc. **b** a place for casting (a good cast). **5 a** an object of metal, clay, etc., made in a mould. **b** a moulded mass of solidified material, esp. plaster protecting a broken limb. **6** the performers taking part in a play, film, etc. **7** form, type, or quality (cast of features; cast of mind). **8** a tinge or shade of colour. **9 a** (in full **cast in the eye**) a slight squint. **b** a twist or inclination. **10 a** a mass of earth excreted by a worm. **b** a mass of indigestible food thrown up by a hawk, owl, etc. **11** the form into which any work is thrown or arranged. **12 a** a wide area covered by a dog or pack to find a trail. **b** Austral. & NZ a wide sweep made by a sheepdog in mustering sheep. □ **cast about** (or **around** or **round**) make an extensive search (actually or mentally) (cast about for a solution). **cast adrift** leave to drift. **cast ashore** (of waves etc.) throw to the shore. **cast aside** give up using; abandon. **cast away 1** reject. **2** (in passive) be shipwrecked (compare CASTAWAY). **cast down** depress, deject (compare DOWNCAST). **cast in stone** (of a decision etc.) irrevocably set. **cast loose** detach; detach oneself. **cast lots** see LOT. **cast one's mind back** think back; recall an earlier time. **cast a wide net** (or **one's net wide**) cover a wide field of supply, activity, inquiry, etc. **cast off 1** abandon. **2** Knitting take the stitches off the needle by looping each over the next to finish the edge. **3** Naut. **a** set a ship free from a quay etc. **b** loosen and throw off (rope etc.). **4** Printing estimate the space that will be taken in print by manuscript copy. **cast on** Knitting make the first row of loops on the needle. **cast out** expel. **cast up 1** (of water) deposit (something) on the shore. **2** add up (figures etc.). [Old Norse *kasta*]

cas·ta·nets /ˌkastəˈnets/ plural noun a pair of shell-shaped pieces of wood, plastic, or ivory clicked together with the fingers, esp. as a rhythmic accompaniment to Spanish dance. [Spanish *castañeta* diminutive of *castaña* from Latin *castanea* chestnut]

cast·away ● noun **1** a shipwrecked person. **2** an outcast; a drifter. **3** a castoff. ● adjective **1** shipwrecked. **2** cast aside; rejected.

caste /kast/ noun **1** any of the Hindu hereditary classes whose members have no social contact with other classes, but are socially equal with one another and often follow the same occupations. **2** a more or less exclusive social class. **3** a system of such classes. **4** the position it confers. **5** Zool. a form of social insect having a particular function. □ **lose caste** descend in the social order. □ **caste·ism** /ˈkastɪzəm/ noun [Spanish and Portuguese *casta* lineage, race, breed, fem. of *casto* pure, CHASTE]

Cas·tel Gan·dol·fo /ˌkastel ganˈdɒlfɔː/ the summer residence of the Pope, situated on the western edge of Lake Albano, 16 km (10 miles) southeast of Rome.

cas·tel·lan /ˈkastələn/ noun hist. the governor of a castle. [Old Northern French *castelain* from medieval Latin *castellanus*: see CASTLE]

cas·tel·lat·ed /ˈkastəˌleɪtəd/ adjective **1** having battlements. **2** castle-like. □ **cas·tel·la·tion** noun [medieval Latin *castellatus*: see CASTLE]

caste mark noun a symbol on the forehead denoting a person's caste.

cast·er noun **1** a person who casts. **2** (also **cast·or**) a small swivelled wheel (often one of a set) fixed to a leg (or the underside) of a piece of

furniture. **3** (also **cast·or**) a small container with holes in the top for sprinkling the contents (sugar caster). □ **cast·ered** adjective (in sense 2).

caster sugar noun (also **castor sugar**) Brit. finely granulated white sugar.

cas·ti·gate /ˈkastɪˌgeɪt/ transitive verb rebuke or punish severely. □ **cas·ti·ga·tion** noun **cas·ti·ga·tor** noun [Latin *castigare* reprove from *castus* pure]

Cas·ti·glione /ˌkastɪlˈjɔːni/ **Count Bal·das·sare** (1478–1529), Italian diplomat, courtier, and writer, whose influential *Il Libro del Cortegiano* (*The Book of the Courtier*) (1528) discusses in dialogue form the ideal of the aristocratic gentleman in Renaissance Italy.

Cas·tile /kaˈstiːl/ a region of central Spain, on the central plateau of the Iberian peninsula. It was formerly an independent Spanish kingdom. The marriage of Isabella of Castile to Ferdinand of Aragon in 1469 linked these two powerful kingdoms and led eventually to the unification of Spain.

Castile soap noun a fine hard white or mottled soap made with olive oil and soda.

Cas·til·ian /kəˈstɪlɪən/ ● noun **1** a native of Castile in Spain. **2** the language of Castile, standard spoken and literary Spanish. ● adjective of or relating to Castile.

Castilla-La Man·cha /kaˌstiːljəlɔ ˈmantʃə/ an autonomous region in central Spain; capital, Toledo.

Castilla-León /kaˌstiːljəleiˈɒn/ an autonomous region of N Spain; capital, Valladolid.

cast·ing noun **1** an object made by casting, esp. of molten metal. **2** the action of allocating roles to performers. **3** the list of roles with the performers assigned to them (when will the casting be announced?). **4** the action of throwing out a fishing line into the water.

casting call noun an open audition for parts in a play, film, etc.

casting couch noun a couch in the office of a casting director, esp. as representative of the exchange of sexual favours for parts in films etc.

casting director noun a director responsible for assigning roles in a film, play, etc.

cast iron ● noun a hard alloy of iron, carbon, and silicon cast in a mould. ● adjective **1** made of cast iron. **2** hard, unchallengeable, unchangeable.

castle ● noun **1 a** a large fortified building or group of buildings; a stronghold. **b** a formerly fortified mansion. **2** Chess = ROOK². ● verb Chess **1** intransitive make a special move (once only in a game on each side) in which the king is moved two squares along the back rank and the nearer rook is moved to the square passed over by the king. **2** transitive move (the king) by castling. □ **castles in the air** (or **in Spain**) a visionary unattainable scheme; a daydream. [Anglo-French & Old Northern French *castel, chastel* from Latin *castellum* diminutive of *castrum* fort]

Castle·bar the county town of Mayo, in the Republic of Ireland; pop. (est. 2002) 8,900.

Castle·gar a city in southern BC, located at the confluence of the Columbia and Kootenay rivers, about 35 km north of the US border; pop. (2001) 7,002. [the name of a CPR station, a shortening of *Castle Garden*, the name of an immigration centre in New York]

Castle Hill a historic site in SE Newfoundland, located on the Avalon Peninsula, on Placentia Bay. Originally an important French settlement and fishing centre, it became the focal point of an Anglo-French rivalry, eventually passing to the British with the Treaty of Utrecht in 1713.

Castle·reagh /ˈkasəlˌreɪ/ **Rob·ert Stew·art, Viscount** (1769–1822), Irish-born British Tory statesman. He was chief secretary for Ireland (1798–1801), when he secured the passing of the Act of Union, and as foreign secretary (1812–22) he represented Britain at the Congress of Vienna (1815), playing a central part in reviving the Quadruple Alliance.

cast net noun Fishing a net thrown out and immediately drawn in.

cast-off ● adjective abandoned, discarded. ● noun (**cast·off**) a cast-off person or thing.

Cas·tor /ˈkastər/ **1** Gk Myth the twin brother of Pollux. See DIOSCURI. **2** Astronomy the second brightest star in the constellation of Gemini, close to Pollux. It is a multiple star system, the three components visible in a moderate telescope being close binaries.

cas·tor¹ var. of CASTER 2, 3.

cas·tor² /ˈkastər/ noun a pungent, bitter-tasting, reddish-brown substance obtained from two perineal sacs of the beaver, formerly used in medicine and perfumes. [French or Latin from Greek *kastōr* beaver]

cas·tor·eum /kas'tɔːriəm/ *noun* = CASTOR².

castor gras /grɒ/ *noun hist.* a beaver pelt worn as clothing for several months to soften it and increase its value before being traded. [French, lit. 'greasy beaver']

castor oil /ˈkastər/ *noun* **1** an oil from the seeds of a plant, *Ricinus communis*, used as a purgative and lubricant. **2** (in full **castor oil plant**) this plant. [18th c.: origin uncertain: perhaps so called as having succeeded CASTOR² in the medical sense]

castor oil bean *noun* (also **castor bean**) a seed of the castor oil plant.

castor sugar *Brit. var. of* CASTER SUGAR.

cas·trate *transitive verb* **1** remove the testicles of; geld. **2** deprive of vigour or power. □ **cas·tra·tion** *noun* **cas·tra·tor** *noun* [Latin *castrare*]

cas·tra·to /kaˈstrɒtɒ/ *noun* (*pl.* **cas·trati** -tiː/) *hist.* a male singer castrated in boyhood so as to retain a soprano or alto voice. [Italian, past participle of *castrare*: see CASTRATE]

Cas·tries /ˈkastriːs/ the capital of the Caribbean island of St. Lucia, a seaport on the northwest coast; pop. (est. 2000) 60,200.

Cas·tro, Fidel (full name Fidel Castro Ruz) (b.1927), Cuban political leader, prime minister 1959–76 and president since 1976. He led the successful Communist revolution against Batista in 1959, and has maintained a hardline political attitude in the face of prolonged international isolation.

cas·ual /ˈkaʒʊəl, -ʒjʊəl/ ● *adjective* **1** accidental; due to chance. **2** not regular or permanent; temporary, occasional (*casual work*). **3 a** unconcerned, uninterested (*was very casual about it*). **b** made or done without great care or thought (*a casual remark*). **c** acting carelessly or unmethodically. **4** (of clothes) informal. **5** (of sexual activity) happening between individuals who are not regular or established sexual partners. ● *noun* **1** a casual worker. **2** (usu. in *pl.*) casual clothes or shoes. □ **cas·ual·ly** *adverb* **cas·ual·ness** *noun* [Old French *casuel* & Latin *casualis* from *casus* CASE¹]

casual day *noun* a day when office workers are allowed to dress more casually than usual.

casual Friday *noun* Friday as a day when office workers are allowed to dress more casually than usual.

cas·ual·iz·a·tion *noun* (also esp. *Brit.* **-isation**) **1** the practice or process of transforming a workforce from one employed chiefly on permanent contracts to one engaged on a short-term temporary basis. **2** the process of making or becoming more casual. □ **cas·ual·ized** *adjective*

cas·ual·ty /ˈkaʒʊəlti/ *noun* (*pl.* **-ties**) **1** a person killed or injured in a war or accident. **2** a thing lost or destroyed. **3** an accident, mishap, or disaster. **4** *Brit.* (in full **casualty department**, **casualty ward**) = EMERGENCY 4.

casual·wear *noun* casual clothing.

cas·uar·in·a /ˌkasjʊəˈriːnə/ *noun* any tree of the genus *Casuarina*, native to Australia and the E Indies, with jointed branches resembling gigantic horsetail plants. [modern Latin *casuarius* cassowary (from the resemblance of the branches to the bird's feathers)]

casu·ist /ˈkaʒjuːɪst, ˈkaʒʊɪst/ *noun* **1** a person, esp. a theologian, who resolves problems of conscience, duty, etc., often with clever but false reasoning. **2** a sophist or quibbler. □ **casu·is·tic** *adjective* **casu·is·tic·al** *adjective* **casu·is·tic·al·ly** *adverb* **casu·istry** *noun* [French *casuiste* from Spanish *casuista* from Latin *casus* CASE¹]

casus belli /ˌkasəs ˈbeli, ˌkeisəs/ *noun* an act or situation provoking or justifying war. [Latin]

CAT *abbreviation Med.* COMPUTERIZED AXIAL TOMOGRAPHY.

Cat *noun proprietary* = CATERPILLAR 2b.

cat ● *noun* **1** a small soft-furred four-legged domesticated animal, *Felis catus*. **2** any wild animal of the genus *Felis*, e.g. a lion, tiger, or leopard. **3** a catlike animal of any other species (*civet cat*). **4** *informal* a malicious or spiteful woman. **5** *slang* **a** a person; a fellow (*cool cat*). **b** a jazz enthusiast. **6** *Naut.* = CATHEAD. **7** = CATFISH. **8 a** = CATBOAT. **b** = CATAMARAN. **9** = CAT-O'-NINE-TAILS. **10** *Cdn* (*Nfld*) a young or newborn seal; a pup. ● *transitive & intransitive verb* (**cat·ted**, **cat·ting**) *Naut.* raise (an anchor) from the surface of the water to the cathead. □ **cat got your tongue?** *informal* don't you have anything to say? **cat's pyjamas** (or **meow** or **whiskers** or **ass**) *informal* an excellent person or thing. **first** (or **last**) **kick at the cat** one's first (or last) opportunity to do something. **let the cat out of the bag** reveal a secret, esp. involuntarily. **like a cat on a hot tin roof** (or **on hot bricks**) very agitated or agitatedly. **put** (or **set**) **the cat among the**

pigeons cause trouble. **rain cats and dogs** rain very hard. [Old English *catt(e)* from Late Latin *cattus*]

cata- *prefix* (usu. **cat-** before a vowel or *h*) **1** down, downwards (*catadromous*). **2** wrongly, badly (*catachresis*). [Greek *kata* down]

ca·tab·ol·ism /kəˈtabəˌlɪzəm/ *noun Biochem.* the breakdown of complex molecules in living organisms to form simpler ones with the release of energy; destructive metabolism (*opp.* ANABOLISM). □ **cata·bol·ic** /ˌkatəˈbɒlɪk/ *adjective* [Greek *katabolē* descent, from *kata* down + *bolē* from *ballō* throw]

cata·chres·is /ˌkatəˈkriːsɪs/ *noun* (*pl.* **cata·chres·es** /-siːz/) an incorrect use of words. □ **cata·chres·tic** /-ˈkriːstɪk, -ˈkrestɪk/ *adjective* [Latin from Greek *katakhrēsis* from *khraomai* use]

cata·clysm /ˈkatəˌklɪzəm/ *noun* **1 a** a violent, esp. social or political, upheaval or disaster. **b** a great change. **2** a great flood or deluge. □ **cata·clys·mic** /-ˈklɪzmɪk/ *adjective* **cata·clys·mic·ally** /-ˈklɪzmɪkli/ *adverb* [French *cataclysme* from Latin *cataclysmus* from Greek *kataklusmos* from *klusmos* flood, from *kluzō* wash]

cata·comb /ˈkatəˌkoːm/ *noun* (often in *pl.*) **1** an underground cemetery, esp. a Roman subterranean gallery with recesses for tombs. **2** a similar underground construction; a cellar. [French *catacombes* from Late Latin *catacumbas* (name given in the 5th c. to the cemetery of St. Sebastian near Rome), of unknown origin]

ca·tad·ro·mous /kəˈtadrəməs/ *adjective* (of a fish, e.g. the eel) that swims down rivers to the sea to spawn (*compare* ANADROMOUS). [Greek *katadromos* from *kata* down + *dromos* running]

cata·falque /ˈkatəˌfɒlk/ *noun* a decorated wooden framework for supporting the coffin of a distinguished person during a funeral or while lying in state. [French from Italian *catafalco*, of unknown origin]

Cata·lan /ˈkatəlan/ ● *noun* **1** a native of Catalonia in Spain. **2** the language of Catalonia. ● *adjective* of or relating to Catalonia or its people or language. [French from Spanish]

cata·lase /ˈkatəˌleɪz/ *noun Biochem.* an enzyme that catalyzes the reduction of hydrogen peroxide. [CATALYSIS]

cata·lepsy /ˈkatəˌlepsi/ *noun* a state of trance or seizure with loss of sensation and consciousness accompanied by rigidity of the body. □ **cata·lep·tic** /-ˈleptɪk/ *adjective & noun* [Greek *katalēpsis* (as CATA-, *lēpsis* seizure)]

cata·logne /ˌkatəˈlɒnjə/ *noun Cdn* (*Que.*) a kind of weaving using rags as the weft and widely spaced threads as the warp. [Canadian French]

cata·logue /ˈkatəˌlɒg/ (also esp. *US* **cata·log**) ● *noun* **1** a complete list of items (e.g. articles for sale, books held by a library), usu. in alphabetical or other systematic order and often with a description of each. **2** an extensive list (*a catalogue of crimes*). **3** *US* a college or university course calendar. ● *transitive verb* (**cata·logues**, **cata·logued**, **cata·logu·ing**; *US* **cata·logs**, **cata·loged**, **cata·log·ing**) **1** make a catalogue of. **2** enter in a catalogue. □ **cata·loguer** *noun* (*US* **cata·log·er**). [French from Late Latin *catalogus* from Greek *katalogos* from *katalegō* enrol (as CATA-, *legō* choose)]

cata·logue rai·son·né /ˈkatəˌlɒg ˌreizɔˈnei/ *noun* (*pl.* **cata·logues rai·son·nés**) a descriptive catalogue of an art exhibit etc., with explanations or comments. [French, = explained catalogue]

Cata·lonia /ˌkatəˈloːniə/ an autonomous region of NE Spain; capital, Barcelona. The region has a strong separatist tradition; the normal language for everyday purposes is Catalan, which has also won acceptance in recent years for various official purposes. □ **Cata·lon·ian** *noun & adjective*

ca·tal·pa /kəˈtalpə/ *noun* any tree of the genus *Catalpa*, with heart-shaped leaves, trumpet-shaped flowers, and long pods, planted as ornamentals. *Also called* CATAWBA, INDIAN BEAN TREE. [Creek]

cata·lyse *var. of* CATALYZE.

cat·aly·sis /kəˈtalɪsɪs/ *noun* (*pl.* **cat·aly·ses** /-ˌsiːz/) the acceleration of a chemical or biochemical reaction by a catalyst. [Greek *katalusis* dissolution (as CATA-, *luō* set free)]

cata·lyst /ˈkatəlɪst/ *noun* **1** *Chem.* a substance that, without itself undergoing any permanent chemical change, increases the rate of a reaction. **2** a person or thing that precipitates a change. [as CATALYSIS after *analyst*]

cata·lytic /ˌkatəˈlɪtɪk/ *adjective Chem.* relating to or involving catalysis. □ **cata·lytic·ally** *adverb*

catalytic converter *noun* a device fitted in the exhaust system of some motor vehicles which converts pollutant gases into less harmful ones by catalytic action.

catalytic cracker *noun* a device for cracking (*see* CRACK *verb* 9) petroleum oils by catalysis.

---

t *top*   v *voice*   w *we*   z *zoo*   ʃ *she*   ʒ *vision*   θ *thin*   ð *this*   ŋ *ring*   x *loch*   tʃ *chip*   dʒ *jar*   (*see over for vowels*)

cat·a·lyze /'katə,laiz/ *transitive verb* (also **cata·lyse**) *Chem.* **1** produce (a reaction) by catalysis. **2** cause (an action or process) to begin. [as CATALYSIS after *analyze*]

cata·ma·ran /,katəmə'ran/ *noun* **1** a boat with twin hulls in parallel. **2** a raft of yoked logs or boats. **3** *Cdn* (*Nfld*) a heavy sled used for hauling wood. [Tamil *kattumaram* tied wood]

cata·mite /'katə,moit/ *noun* a boy who is having a sexual relationship with a man. [Latin *catamitus* through Etruscan from Greek *Ganumēdēs* Ganymede, cupbearer of Zeus]

cata·mount /'katə,maunt/ *noun* **1** a lynx, leopard, cougar, or similar cat. **2** a wild quarrelsome person. [Middle English from *cat of the mountain*]

cat and mouse *noun* a situation in which two opposing parties engage in prolonged wary manoeuvres (also *attributive*: *the police and the criminals were playing a cat-and-mouse game*).

Ca·tania /kə'taniə/ a seaport situated at the foot of Mount Etna, on the east coast of Sicily; pop. (2001) 306,464.

cata·plexy /'katə,pleksi/ *noun* sudden temporary paralysis due to fright etc. □ **cata·plec·tic** /-'plektɪk/ *adjective* [Greek *kataplēxis* stupefaction]

cata·pult /'katə,pult, -pʌlt/ ● *noun* **1** *hist.* a military machine worked by a lever and ropes for hurling large stones etc. **2** a mechanical device for launching a glider, an aircraft from the deck of a ship, etc. **3** *Brit.* = SLINGSHOT. ● *verb* **1** move suddenly and unexpectedly from one state or situation to another (*catapulted from obscurity to prominence*). **2** *transitive* **a** hurl from or launch with a catapult. **b** fling forcibly. **3** *intransitive* leap or be hurled forcibly. [French *catapulte* or Latin *catapulta* from Greek *katapeltēs* (as CATA-, *pallō* hurl)]

cata·ract /'katə,rakt/ *noun* **1 a** a large waterfall or cascade. **b** a downpour; a rush of water. **2** *Med.* **a** a disease in which the lens of the eye becomes cloudy, causing partial or total blindness. **b** an eye clouded in this way (*an operation to remove cataracts*). [Latin *cataracta* from Greek *katarrhaktēs* down-rushing; in medical sense prob. from obsolete sense 'portcullis']

Cata·raqui /,katə'rɒkwiː/ the former name (*c.*1673) for Kingston, Ont. [Iroquois, = rocks rising out of the water]

ca·tarrh /kə'tɑr/ *noun* **1** inflammation of the mucous membrane of the nose, air passages, etc. **2** a watery discharge in the nose or throat due to this. □ **ca·tar·rhal** *adjective* [French *catarrhe* from Late Latin *catarrhus* from Greek *katarrhous* from *katarrheō* flow down]

cat·ar·rhine /'katə,rain/ *Zool.* ● *noun* any of various primates having nostrils close together and directed downwards, e.g. baboons, chimpanzees, and humans (*compare* PLATYRRHINE). ● *adjective* of or relating to such animals. [CATA- + *rhis rhinos* nose]

catas·tro·phe /kə'tastrəfi/ *noun* **1** a great and usu. sudden disaster. **2** the denouement of a tragedy. **3** a disastrous end; ruin. □ **cat·as·troph·ic** /-'strɒfɪk/ *adjective* **cat·as·troph·ic·ally** /-'strɒfɪkli/ *adverb* [Greek *katastrophē* (as CATA-, *strophē* turning from *strephō* turn)]

catas·troph·ism /kə'tastrə,fɪzəm/ *noun* *Geol.* the theory that changes in the earth's crust have occurred in sudden violent and unusual events. □ **catas·troph·ist** *noun*

cata·tonia /,katə'toːniə/ *noun* **1** schizophrenia with intervals of catalepsy and sometimes violence. **2** catalepsy. [German *Katatonie* (as CATA-, TONE)]

cata·ton·ic /,katə'tɒnɪk/ *adjective* **1** affected by catatonia. **2** inert or unemotional, as if affected by catatonia.

cata·wam·pus /,katə'wɒmpəs/ *adjective* esp. *N Amer.* dialect askew, awry.

Ca·taw·ba /kə'tɔbə/ *noun* **1** a member of an American Aboriginal people living in S Carolina. **2** the Siouan language of this people. [origin obscure: prob. from Choctaw *Katápa*, lit. 'divided, separated']

ca·taw·ba /kə'tɒbə/ *noun* **1** a reddish variety of grape grown in the eastern US. **2** a white wine made from these grapes. **3** = CATALPA. [*Catawba* River in the Carolinas, from CATAWBA]

cat·bird *noun* any of various birds with a characteristic mewing cry, esp. the N American songbird *Dumetella carolinensis*, having slate-grey plumage. □ **catbird seat** a position of power or prominence.

cat·boat *noun* a sailing boat with a single mast placed well forward and carrying only one sail. [perhaps from *cat* a former type of coal boat in NE England, + BOAT]

cat·brier /'katbraiər/ *noun* = GREENBRIER.

cat burglar *noun* a burglar who enters by climbing to an upper storey.

cat·call ● *noun* a shrill whistle of disapproval made at sports events, concerts, etc. ● *verb* **1** *intransitive* make a catcall. **2** *transitive* make a catcall at.

catch ● *verb* (*past* and *past participle* **caught** /kɒt/) **1** *transitive* **a** lay hold of so as to restrain or prevent from escaping; capture in a trap, in one's hands, etc. **b** (also **catch hold of**) get into one's hands so as to retain, operate, etc. (*caught hold of the handle*). **2** *transitive* detect or surprise (a person, esp. in a wrongful or embarrassing act) (*caught me in the act*). **3** *transitive* intercept and hold (a moving thing) in the hands etc. (*failed to catch the ball; a bowl to catch the drips*). **4** *transitive* **a** contract (a disease) by infection or contagion. **b** acquire (a quality or feeling) from another's example (*caught her enthusiasm*). **5** *transitive* **a** reach in time and board (an airplane, bus, etc.). **b** be in time to see etc. (a person or thing about to leave or finish) (*if you hurry you'll catch them; caught the end of the performance*). **6** *transitive* **a** attend (*catch a movie tonight*). **b** meet with (*catch you later*). **7** *transitive* apprehend (*didn't catch what he said; do you catch my meaning?; caught it out of the corner of my eye*). **8** *transitive* (of an artist etc.) reproduce faithfully. **9 a** *intransitive* become fixed or entangled; be checked (*the bolt began to catch*). **b** *transitive* cause to do this (*caught the kite in a tree*). **c** *transitive* (often foll. by *on*) hit, deal a blow to (*caught him on the nose; caught her elbow on the table*). **10** *transitive* draw the attention of; captivate (*caught my eye*). **11** *intransitive* **a** begin to burn. **b** (of an engine) start. **12** *transitive* capture and absorb or reflect (light) (*catch some sun*). **13** *transitive* be the recipient of (*catch hell*). **14** *transitive* (often foll. by *up*) reach or overtake (a person etc. ahead). **15** *transitive* check suddenly (*caught her breath*). **16** *transitive* (foll. by *at*) grasp or try to grasp. **17** *reflexive* stop (oneself) just in time (*caught myself before I said it*). **18** *intransitive* *Baseball* play as catcher. **19** *transitive* take (sleep) (*catch forty winks*). ● *noun* **1 a** an act of catching. **b** *Baseball* a chance or act of catching the ball. **2 a** an amount of a thing caught, esp. of fish. **b** a thing or person caught or worth catching, esp. in marriage. **3** a game in which a ball is thrown back and forth between two or more players. **4 a** a question, trick, etc., intended to deceive, incriminate, etc. **b** an unexpected or hidden difficulty or disadvantage. **5** a device for fastening a door, window, bag, etc. **6** a check or impediment in the voice, breath, throat, etc. **7** a snag in a sweater etc. **8** a fragment of a song. **9** *Music* a round, esp. with words arranged to produce a humorous effect. □ **catch-as-catch-can 1** a style of wrestling with few holds barred. **2** a situation where there are no rules; a free-for-all. **catch one's death** *see* DEATH. **catch fire** *see* FIRE. **catch it** *slang* be punished or in trouble. **catch on** *informal* **1** (of a practice, fashion, etc.) become popular. **2** (of a person) understand what is meant. **catch out 1** detect in a mistake etc. **2** take unawares; cause to be bewildered or confused. **catch up 1 a** (often foll. by *with*) reach a person etc. ahead (*he caught up in the end; he caught us up; he caught up with us*). **b** (often foll. by *with, on*) make up arrears (of work etc.) (*must catch up on my housework*). **2** snatch or pick up hurriedly. **3** (often in *passive*) **a** involve; entangle (*caught up in suspicious dealings*). **b** fasten up (*hair caught up in a ribbon*). □ **catch·able** *adjective* [Anglo-French & Old Northern French *cachier*, Old French *chacier*, ultimately from Latin *captare* try to catch]

Catch-22 *noun* (often *attributive*) a dilemma or circumstance from which there is no escape because of mutually conflicting or dependent conditions. [title of a novel by J. HELLER featuring a dilemma of this kind]

catch-all *noun* (often *attributive*) a thing designed to be all-inclusive.

catch-and-release *noun* (often *attributive*) *N Amer.* a method of sport fishing in which anglers release fish immediately after catching them in order to preserve stocks.

catch basin *noun* **1 a** a storm sewer or artificial pond for catching excess rainwater. **b** a receptacle to trap debris before it enters a storm sewer. **2** an area or organization which attracts people of a specific kind.

catch·er *noun* **1** a person or thing that catches. **2** *Baseball* the fielder positioned behind home plate.

catch·fly *noun* (*pl.* **-flies**) any of various campions with sticky stems, chiefly of the genera *Silene* and *Lychnis*.

catch·ing *adjective* **1 a** (of a disease) infectious. **b** (of a practice, habit, etc.) likely to be imitated. **2** attractive; captivating.

catch·ment *noun* **1** the act or process of collecting water. **2** a place where water is collected; a reservoir. **3** = CATCHMENT AREA.

catchment area *noun* **1** the area from which rainfall flows into a river etc. **2** the area served by a school, hospital, etc.

catch·penny *adjective* intended merely to sell quickly; superficially attractive.

catch·phrase *noun* a phrase or slogan in frequent use.

catch-up *noun* (often *attributive*) the act of attempting to reach someone or something which is ahead. □ **play catch-up** *N Amer.* & *Austral.* attempt to overtake an opponent or competitor.

catch·word noun **1** a word or phrase in common (often temporary) use; a topical slogan. **2** a word placed so as to draw attention. **3** *Theatre* an actor's cue. **4** *Printing* the first word of a page given at the foot of the previous one.

catchy adjective (**catch·i·er**, **catch·i·est**) **1** (of a tune, phrase, etc.) easy to remember; attractive. **2** capable of snaring or entrapping; deceptive. □ **catch·i·ly** adverb **catch·i·ness** noun

cat door noun = CAT FLAP.

cat·eche·sis /ˌkatəˈkiːsɪs/ noun religious instruction. [as CATECHIZE]

cat·echet·ic·al /ˌkatəˈketɪkəl/ adjective (also **cat·echet·ic**) **1** of or by oral teaching. **2** according to the catechism of a Christian religion. **3** consisting of or proceeding by question and answer. **4** of or relating to religious instruction. □ **cat·echet·ic·al·ly** adverb **cat·echet·ics** noun [ecclesiastical Greek *katēkhētikos* from *katēkhētēs* oral teacher: see CATECHIZE]

cat·echin /ˈkatəˌtʃɪn/ noun a crystalline compound which is the major constituent of catechu. [CATECHU + -IN]

cat·ech·ism /ˈkatəˌkɪzəm/ noun **1 a** a summary of the principles of a Christian religion. **b** such a summary in the form of questions and answers. **c** a book containing this. **2** esp. *Catholicism* **a** a religious instruction. **b** a class in this. **3** a series of questions put to anyone. [ecclesiastical Latin *catechismus* (as CATECHIZE)]

cat·ech·ist /ˈkatəkɪst/ noun a teacher giving instruction in Christianity by means of a catechism.

cat·ech·ize /ˈkatəˌkaiz/ transitive verb (also esp. *Brit.* **-ise**) **1** instruct by means of question and answer, esp. from a catechism. **2** put questions to; examine. □ **cat·ech·iz·er** noun [Late Latin *catechizare* from ecclesiastical Greek *katēkhizō* from *katēkheō* make hear (as CATA-, *ēkheō* sound)]

cat·echol·amine /ˈkatəˌtʃɒːləmiːn, -tʃɒl-, -main/ noun any of various amines that function as neurotransmitters or hormones, e.g. dopamine, adrenalin. [CATECHU + -OL[1] + AMINE]

cat·echu /ˈkatəˌtʃuː/ noun (also **ca·chou** /ˈkaʃuː/) gambier or a similar vegetable extract containing tannin. [modern Latin from Malay *kachu*]

cat·ech·umen /ˌkatəˈkjuːmən/ noun a Christian convert under instruction before baptism. [Old French *catechumene* or ecclesiastical Latin *catechumenus* from Greek *katēkheō*: see CATECHIZE]

cat·egor·ic·al /ˌkatəˈɡɒrɪkəl, -ɡɒr-/ adjective (also **cat·egor·ic**) unconditional, absolute; explicit, direct (*a categorical refusal*). □ **cat·egor·ic·al·ly** adverb [French *catégorique* or Late Latin *categoricus* from Greek *katēgorikos*: see CATEGORY]

categorical imperative noun (in Kantian ethics) an unconditional moral obligation derived from pure reason; the bidding of conscience as ultimate moral law.

cat·egor·ize /ˈkatəɡəˌraiz/ transitive verb (also esp. *Brit.* **-ise**) place in a category or categories. □ **cat·egor·iz·a·tion** noun

cat·egory /ˈkatəˌɡɒri/ noun (pl. **-ies**) **1** a class or division. **2** *Philos.* **a** one of a possibly exhaustive set of classes among which all things might be distributed. **b** (in Kantian philosophy) one of the a priori conceptions applied by the mind to sense impressions. **c** any relatively fundamental philosophical concept. □ **cat·egor·ial** /-ˈɡɔriəl/ adjective [French *catégorie* or Late Latin *categoria* from Greek *katēgoria* statement, from *katēgoros* accuser]

category killer noun a wholesaler or retail store which dominates the market in a particular product.

cat·en·ary /ˈkatəneri/ ● noun (pl. **-aries**) **1** a curve formed by a uniform chain hanging freely from two points not in the same vertical line. **2** a cable suspended in this fashion on a cableway, bridge, etc. ● adjective of or resembling such a curve. [Latin *catenarius* from *catena* chain]

cat·en·ate /ˈkatəˌneit/ transitive verb connect like links of a chain. □ **cat·en·a·tion** noun [Latin *catenare catenat-* (as CATENARY)]

cater verb **1 a** intransitive (often foll. by *for*) provide food, drink, etc. for a reception etc. **b** transitive *N Amer.* provide food for (a party etc.). **2** intransitive **a** (foll. by *to*, *for*) provide for; meet the needs of. **b** (foll. by *to*) pander to (one's whims etc.). [obsolete noun *cater* (now *caterer*), from *acater* from Anglo-French *acatour* buyer, from *acater* buy, from Romanic]

cat·eran /ˈkatərən/ noun *Scot. hist.* an irregular fighting man of the Highlands; a marauder. [medieval Latin *cateranus* & Gaelic *ceathairne* peasantry]

cater-cornered /ˈkatərˌkɔrnərd/ (also **cater-corner**) *N Amer.* var. of KITTY-CORNER.

cater·er noun a person who supplies food for social events, esp. professionally.

cater·ing noun the profession or work of a caterer.

cater·pil·lar noun **1 a** the larva of a butterfly or moth. **b** (in general use) any similar larva of various insects. **2** (often *attributive*) **a** an endless articulated steel tread passing around the wheels of a tractor etc. for travel on rough ground. **b** (**Caterpillar**) proprietary a vehicle equipped with these treads. [perhaps Anglo-French var. of Old French *chatepelose*, lit. 'hairy cat', influenced by obsolete *piller* ravager]

cater·waul /ˈkatərˌwɒl/ ● intransitive verb make the shrill howl of a cat. ● noun a caterwauling noise.

cat·face noun *N Amer.* a knot, burn mark, or other imperfection on a log which reduces its value as timber.

cat fight noun **1** a dispute in which the participants are spiteful, malicious, and unrestrained. **2** a malicious fight or dispute between women. **3** a fight between cats.

cat·fish noun (pl. same) any of numerous fishes of the order Siluriformes, usu. inhabiting fresh water and characterized by whisker-like barbels around the mouth.

cat flap noun (also **cat door**) a small swinging flap in an outer door or wall allowing a cat to pass in and out.

cat·gut noun a material made from the twisted intestines of a cow, sheep, horse, or other animal, and used esp. formerly to make the strings of musical instruments, racquets, and surgical sutures.

Cath. abbreviation **1** Cathedral. **2** Catholic.

Cath·ar /ˈkaθɑr/ noun (pl. **Cath·ars** or **Cathari** /-ri/) a member of a medieval sect which sought to achieve great spiritual purity. □ **Cath·ar·ism** noun **Cath·ar·ist** noun [medieval Latin *Cathari* (pl.) from Greek *katharoi* pure]

cath·ar·sis /kəˈθɑrsɪs/ noun (pl. **cath·ar·ses** /-siːz/) **1** a release or relieving of emotions, esp. through drama or art. **2** *Psych.* the process of freeing repressed emotion by association with the cause, and elimination by abreaction. **3** *Med.* purgation. [modern Latin from Greek *katharsis* from *kathairō* cleanse: sense 1 from Aristotle's *Poetics*]

cath·ar·tic /kəˈθɑrtɪk/ ● adjective **1** effecting catharsis. **2** purgative. ● noun a cathartic drug. □ **cath·ar·tic·ally** adverb [Late Latin *catharticus* from Greek *kathartikos* (as CATHARSIS)]

Ca·thay /kaˈθei/ the name by which China was known to medieval Europe. [medieval Latin *Cataya* from Turkic *Khitāy*]

Cath·cart, Charles Mur·ray, 2nd Earl (1783–1859), English general, who served as commander-in-chief of British forces in N America (1845–7) and as Governor General of British North America (1846–7).

cat·head noun *Naut.* a horizontal beam from each side of a ship's bow for raising and carrying the anchor.

cath·ec·tic adjective see CATHEXIS.

cath·edral /kəˈθiːdrəl/ noun the principal church of a diocese, containing the bishop's throne. [Old French *cathedral* or from Late Latin *cathedralis* from Latin from Greek *kathedra* seat]

cathedral ceiling noun *N Amer.* a high usu. sloping or vaulted ceiling, esp. one with exposed rafters, e.g. in the entryway or living room of a house.

Cather /ˈkaθər/ **Willa (Sibert)** (1873–1947), US novelist and short-story writer. Her home state of Nebraska provides the setting for some of her best writing; major novels include *O Pioneers!* (1913) and *My Antonia* (1918), while among her later works is the bestselling *Death Comes for the Archbishop* (1927).

Cath·er·ine I (1684–1727), second wife of Peter I the Great, empress of Russia 1725–27. Born a Lithuanian peasant, she became Peter the Great's mistress and wife, and was proclaimed empress when he died without naming an heir.

Catherine II ('the Great') (1729–96), empress of Russia 1762–96. A German princess, she was made empress following a plot which deposed her husband Peter III (1728–62). During her reign Russia expanded southward and eastward and played an important part in European affairs, participating in the three partitions of Poland and forming close links with Prussia and Austria; she was a noted patron of literature and the arts.

Catherine de' Med·ici /ˌkaθrɪn də ˈmediːtʃi, ˌkaθərɪn/ (1519–89), queen of France. The wife of Henry II of France, Catherine ruled as regent during the minority reigns of their three sons, Francis II (1544–60), Charles IX (1550–74), and Henry III (1551–89); it was on her instigation that several thousand Huguenots were massacred on St. Bartholomew's Day (August 24th, 1572).

Catherine of Alexandria, St. (died *c.*307), early Christian martyr, possibly legendary. According to tradition, she opposed the persecution of Christians, debated with fifty scholars sent to undermine her position, refused to recant, and is said to have been tortured on a spiked wheel and beheaded when it broke; the Catherine wheel subsequently became her emblem.

Catherine of Aragon (1485–1536), first wife of Henry VIII, youngest daughter of Ferdinand and Isabella of Spain, mother of Mary I. Henry VIII divorced her on the debatable grounds that her prior marriage to his elder brother Arthur made the marriage illegal; Catherine was sent into retirement, but never accepted the annulment of her marriage (a view supported by the Pope) or the Act of Succession, which declared Mary to be illegitimate.

Catherine of Braganza (1638–1705), wife of Charles II of England, daughter of John IV of Portugal.

Catherine wheel /ˈkaθərɪn/ *noun* **1** = PINWHEEL 2. **2** a circular window with radial divisions. [after CATHERINE OF ALEXANDRIA]

cath·eter /ˈkaθətər/ *noun Med.* a tube for insertion into a body cavity or blood vessel for introducing or removing fluid etc. [Late Latin from Greek *kathetēr* from *kathiēmi* send down]

cath·eter·ize /ˈkaθətəˌraiz/ *transitive verb* (also esp. *Brit.* **-ise**) *Med.* insert a catheter into. □ **cath·eter·iz·a·tion** *noun* **cath·eter·ized** *adjective*

cath·exis /kəˈθeksɪs/ *noun* (*pl.* **cath·exes** /-siːz/) *Psych.* concentration of mental energy on a particular object. □ **cath·ec·tic** *adjective* [Greek *kathexis* retention]

cath·ode /ˈkaθəʊd/ *noun Electricity* **1** the negative electrode in an electrolytic cell or electronic valve or tube. **2** the positive terminal of a primary cell such as a battery (*opp.* ANODE). □ **cath·od·ic** /kəˈθɒdɪk/ *adjective* [Greek *kathodos* descent from *kata* down + *hodos* way]

cathode ray *noun* a beam of electrons emitted from the cathode of a high-vacuum tube.

cathode ray tube *noun* a high-vacuum tube in which cathode rays produce a luminous image on a fluorescent screen, used in televisions, computer screens, etc. Abbr.: **CRT**.

cath·olic /ˈkaθlɪk/ ● *adjective* **1** (**Catholic**) of the Roman Catholic religion. **2** pertaining to or designating the ancient Church before the great schism between East and West, or the Western or Latin Church after the schism and before the Reformation, or to any Church standing in historical continuity with it. **3** all-embracing; of wide sympathies or interests (*has catholic tastes*). **4** of interest or use to all; universal. ● *noun* (**Catholic**) a Roman Catholic. □ **Cath·oli·cism** /kəˈθɒlɪˌsizəm/ *noun* **cath·olic·ly** *adverb* [Old French *catholique* or Late Latin *catholicus* from Greek *katholikos* universal, from *kata* in respect of + *holos* whole]

Catholic Emancipation the granting of full political and civil liberties to Roman Catholics in Britain and Ireland, who were barred from holding public office and restricted in many other ways (*see* PENAL LAWS, TEST ACTS). After the Act of Union (1801), heavy pressure was applied from Ireland for the admission of Catholics to Parliament, but emancipation was strongly opposed by George III. The election to Parliament of Daniel O'Connell in 1828 led to the passing of the Catholic Emancipation Act of 1829, which repealed most of the discriminatory laws.

cath·ol·icity /ˌkaθəˈlɪsɪti/ *noun* **1** the quality of having sympathies with all or being all-embracing. **2** (**Catholicity**) the character of belonging to or being in accordance with a catholic church, esp. the Roman Catholic Church.

cath·oli·cize /kəˈθɒləˌsaiz/ *transitive & intransitive verb* (also esp. *Brit.* **-cise**) **1** make or become catholic. **2** (**Catholicize**) make or become a Roman Catholic.

Catholic League *see* HOLY LEAGUE.

Catholic Reformation *noun* = COUNTER-REFORMATION.

cat·house *noun* a brothel.

cat ice *noun* a thin layer of ice unsupported by water.

Cati·line /ˈkatiˌlain/ (Latin name Lucius Sergius Catilina) (d.62 BC), Roman nobleman. Thwarted in his ambition to be elected consul, in 63 BC he planned an uprising against Cicero; he died in a battle in Etruria.

cat·ion /ˈkatˌaiən, -aiɒn/ *noun* a positively charged ion; an ion that is attracted to the cathode in electrolysis (*opp.* ANION). [CATA- + ION]

cat·ion·ic /ˌkataiˈɒnɪk/ *adjective* **1** of a cation or cations. **2** having an active cation.

cat·kin *noun* a spike of usu. downy or silky unisexual flowers hanging from a willow, hazel, or other tree. [obsolete Dutch *katteken* kitten]

cat·like *adjective* **1** like a cat. **2** stealthy.

cat·lin·ite /ˈkatlənait/ *noun* = PIPESTONE. [G. Catlin, US artist d.1872 + -ITE¹]

cat litter *noun* granular absorbent material, usu. clay, for lining a box for a cat to urinate and defecate in indoors.

cat·mint *noun* esp. *Brit.* = CATNIP.

cat·nap ● *noun* a short sleep. ● *intransitive verb* (**-napped**, **-nap·ping**) have a catnap.

cat·nip *noun* a herb of the mint family, *Nepeta cataria*, having a pungent smell attractive to cats. [CAT + dial. *nip* catnip, var. of dial. *nep*]

Cato /ˈkeitəʊ/ **1 Mar·cus Por·cius** (**'the Elder'** or **'the Censor'**) (234–149 BC), Roman statesman, orator, and writer. An implacable enemy of Carthage, and rigorous moral and social reformer, he attempted to stem the growing influence of Greek culture on Roman life. **2** his grandson, **Cato the Younger** (95–46 BC), Roman statesman, who was an opponent of the dictatorial ambitions of Julius Caesar.

cat-o'-nine-tails *noun hist.* a rope whip with usu. nine knotted lashes used for flogging.

cat·op·tric /kəˈtɒptrɪk/ *adjective* of or relating to a mirror, a reflector, or reflection. □ **cat·op·trics** *noun* [Greek *katoptrikos* from *katoptron* mirror]

CAT scan *noun* a medical examination using an X-ray apparatus which produces a series of detailed cross-sectional pictures of internal organs, esp. the brain. □ **CAT scanner** *noun* [abbreviation of computerized axial tomography]

cat's cradle *noun* a child's game in which a loop of string is held between the fingers and patterns are formed.

cat's eye *noun* **1** one of a series of small reflector studs set into the centre of a road as lane markers. **2** any of several convex gemstones with a characteristic lustre, esp. a variety of chalcedony or chrysoberyl.

cat's-foot *noun* (also **cat's ears**) a small European plant of the daisy family, *Antennaria dioica*, cultivated for its woolly leaves.

Cats·kill Mountains (also **Cats·kills**) a range of mountains in the state of New York, part of the Appalachian system.

cat·skin·ner *noun N Amer.* the operator of a vehicle equipped with caterpillar treads.

cat's paw *noun* **1** a person used as a mere instrument by another. **2** a slight breeze rippling the surface of an area of water.

cat spruce *noun* = WHITE SPRUCE.

cat·suit *noun* a close-fitting garment with trouser legs, covering the body from neck to feet.

cat·sup esp. *US var. of* KETCHUP.

cat·tail *noun N Amer.* (*Brit.* **cat's tail**) = BULRUSH 2.

cat·tery *noun* (*pl.* **-ies**) a place where cats are boarded or bred.

cat·tish *adjective* = CATTY. □ **cat·tish·ly** *adverb* **cat·tish·ness** *noun*

cat·tle *plural noun* **1** large ruminant animals with horns and cloven hoofs, e.g. cows, bison, and buffalo, esp. of the genus *Bos*. **2** *archaic* livestock. [Old French *chatel* CHATTEL]

cattle beast *noun* a cow, bull, steer, heifer, or calf.

cattle cake *noun Brit.* a concentrated food for cattle, in cake form.

cattle call *noun N Amer. slang* an open audition for parts in a play, film, etc., usu. attended by many performers.

cattle egret *noun* a small white heron, *Bubulais ibis*, often associated with grazing cattle.

cattle guard *noun N Amer.* (also *Cdn* **Texas gate**, *Brit.* **cattle grid**) a ditch covered by metal bars spaced so as to allow vehicles and pedestrians to pass over but not cattle or other animals.

cattle·man *noun* (*pl.* **-men**) *N Amer.* a person who tends or rears cattle.

catt·leya /ˈkatliə/ *noun* any epiphytic orchid of the genus *Cattleya*, cultivated for its showy flowers. [modern Latin from W. *Cattley*, English patron of botany d.1832]

cat train *noun Cdn* (*North*) a series of linked freight-carrying sleds hauled over snow by a tractor equipped with caterpillar treads.

catty *adjective* (**cat·ti·er**, **cat·ti·est**) **1** sly, spiteful; deliberately hurtful in speech. **2** catlike. □ **cat·ti·ly** *adverb* **cat·ti·ness** *noun*

catty-corner (also **catty-cornered**) *var. of* KITTY-CORNER.

Catul·lus /kəˈtʌləs/ **Gaius Valer·ius** (*c.*84–*c.*54 BC), Roman poet. His one book of verse contains poems on a variety of subjects, but he is best known for his love poems to a married woman nicknamed 'Lesbia'.

cat·walk *noun* **1** a narrow footway along a bridge, above a theatre stage, etc. **2** a narrow platform along which models walk during a fashion show.

Cau·ca·sian /kɒˈkeizən/ ● *adjective* **1** of or relating to the white or light-skinned race of human beings originally inhabiting Europe,

N Africa, and the Middle East. **2** of or relating to the Caucasus or its people. **3** of or relating to the non-Indo-European languages of this region, e.g. Georgian. ● *noun* a Caucasian person. [the CAUCASUS, believed by BLUMENBACH to be the place of origin of this race]

Cau·cas·oid /'kɒkəˌsɔɪd/ *adjective* of or relating to the Caucasian division of humankind.

Cau·ca·sia, the /'kɒkəsəs/ (also **Cau·ca·sia** /kɒˈkeɪʒə, -ˈkeɪziə/) a mountainous region of SE Europe, lying between the Black Sea and the Caspian Sea, in Georgia, Armenia, Azerbaijan, and SE Russia.

Cauchy /'kauʃi, koːʃi/ **Au·gus·tin Louis, Baron** (1789–1857), French mathematician. His numerous writings introduced new standards of criticism and rigorous argument in calculus, from which grew the field of mathematics known as analysis; he also founded the modern theory of elasticity, and contributed substantially to the founding of group theory.

cau·cus /'kɒkəs/ ● *noun* (*pl.* **cau·cus·es**) **1** *N Amer. & NZ* **a** the members of a legislative assembly belonging to a particular party. **b** a subgroup of these comprising the members from a particular region. **c** a closed-door meeting of either of these groups to discuss policy etc. **2** a group sharing common political goals, esp. a faction within a larger group. **3** a usu. secret meeting of a small group of people to discuss matters concerning a larger group. **4** *US* a local meeting of members of a political party to select candidates, delegates, etc., esp. as an early step in preparing for an election. ● *intransitive verb* (**cau·cused, cau·cus·ing**) hold or form a caucus. [18th-c., perhaps from Algonquian *cau'-cau'-as'u* adviser]

cau·dal /'kɒdəl/ *adjective* **1** of or like a tail. **2** of the posterior part of the body. □ **cau·dal·ly** *adverb* [modern Latin *caudalis* from Latin *cauda* tail]

cau·date /'kɒdeɪt/ *adjective* having a tail or an appendage resembling a tail. [see CAUDAL]

cau·dillo /kauˈdiːjoː, -ˈdiːljoː/ *noun* (*pl.* **-dillos**) (in Spanish-speaking countries) a military or political leader. [Spanish from Late Latin *capitellum* diminutive of *caput* head]

Caugh·na·waga the former spelling for KAHNAWAKE.

caught *past and past participle of* CATCH.

caul *noun* **1 a** the inner membrane enclosing a fetus. **b** part of this occasionally found on a child's head at birth, thought to bring good luck. **2 a** the omentum. **b** the omentum of cattle, pigs, and other animals used as food. **3** *hist.* **a** a woman's close-fitting indoor headdress. **b** the plain back part of a woman's indoor headdress. [perhaps from Old French *cale* small cap]

caul·dron *noun* (*US* also **cal·dron**) **1 a** a large deep bowl-shaped vessel for boiling over an open fire. **b** an ornamental vessel resembling this. **2** a volatile or chaotic situation. [Anglo-French *caudron*, ultimately from Latin *caldarium* hot bath, from *calidus* hot]

cauli·flower *noun* **1** a variety of cabbage with a large white flower head of immature buds in its centre. **2** the flower head eaten as a vegetable. [earlier *cole-florie* etc. from obsolete French *chou fleuri* flowered cabbage, assimilated to COLE and FLOWER]

cauliflower ear *noun* an ear thickened and disfigured by repeated blows, esp. as suffered by a boxer.

caulk[1] /kɒk/ (also esp. *US* **calk**) ● *transitive verb* **1** fill (a seam, crack, etc.) with a watertight or airtight material. **2** make (esp. a boat or window) watertight or airtight by this method. ● *noun* (also **caulk·ing**) a substance used to caulk. □ **caulk·er** *noun* [Old French dial. *cauquer* tread, press with force, from Latin *calcare* tread, from *calx* heel]

caulk[2] /kɒk, kɔːk/ (also esp. *US* **calk**) *N Amer.* ● *noun* **1** a small spike fitted to the sole of a boot to resist slipping. **2** (in full **caulk boot**) a boot equipped with such spikes, used esp. by loggers. ● *transitive verb* furnish (a boot) with caulks. [apparently ultimately from Latin *calc-*, *calcaneum* heel, or *calcar* spur; may be related to *calkin*, a similar projection on a horseshoe, from Middle Dutch *kalkoen* or Old French *calcain*]

cauri *noun* a monetary unit of Guinea, equal to one-hundredth of a franc.

caus·al *adjective* **1** of, forming, or expressing a cause or causes. **2** relating to, or of the nature of, cause and effect. □ **caus·al·ly** *adverb*

caus·al·ity /kɒˈzalɪti/ *noun* **1** the relation of cause and effect. **2** the principle that everything has a cause.

caus·a·tion /kɒˈzeɪʃən/ *noun* **1** the act of causing or producing an effect. **2** = CAUSALITY.

caus·a·tive /'kɒzətɪv/ *adjective* **1** acting as cause. **2** (foll. by *of*) producing; having as effect. **3** *Grammar* expressing cause.
 □ **caus·a·tive·ly** *adverb*

cause ● *noun* **1 a** that which produces an effect, or gives rise to an action, phenomenon, or condition. **b** a person or thing that occasions something. **c** a reason or motive; a ground that may be held to justify something (*no cause for complaint*). **2** a reason adjudged adequate (*he was asked to show cause why he shouldn't be held in contempt of court*). **3** a principle, belief, or purpose which is advocated or supported (*faithful to the cause*). **4 a** a matter to be settled at law. **b** an individual's case offered at law (*plead a cause*). **5** the side taken by any party in a dispute. ● *transitive verb* **1** be the cause of, produce, make happen (*caused a commotion*). **2** (foll. by *to* + infin.) induce (*caused me to smile; caused it to be done*). □ **cause and effect 1** a cause and the effect it produces; the doctrine of causation. **2** the operation or relation of a cause and its effect. **in the cause of** to maintain, defend, or support (*in the cause of justice*). **make common cause with** join the side of. □ **caus·able** *adjective* **cause·less** *adjective* **caus·er** *noun* [Old French from Latin *causa*]

'cause *conjunction & adverb informal* = BECAUSE. [abbreviation]

cause cé·lèbre /ˌkɒz seˈleb, koːz, sei-, -ˌlebrə/ *noun* (*pl.* **causes célèbres** *pronunc.* same) a lawsuit or other affair that attracts much attention. [French]

caus·erie /'koːzəri/ *noun* (*pl.* **causeries** *pronunc.* same) an informal article or talk, esp. on a literary subject. [French from *causer* talk]

cause·way *noun* **1** a raised road or track across low or wet ground or a stretch of water. **2** a raised path by a road. [earlier *cauce, causeway* from Old Northern French *caucié*, ultimately from Latin CALX lime, limestone]

caus·tic ● *adjective* **1** capable of burning or corroding organic tissue. **2** sarcastic, biting. **3** *Chem.* strongly alkaline. **4** *Physics* formed by the intersection of reflected or refracted rays of light from a curved surface. ● *noun* **1** a caustic substance. **2** *Physics* a caustic surface or curve. □ **caus·tic·ally** *adverb* **caus·tic·ity** *noun* [Latin *causticus* from Greek *kaustikos* from *kaustos* burned, from *kaiō* burn]

caustic potash *noun* potassium hydroxide.

caustic soda *noun* sodium hydroxide.

caut·er·ize /'kɒtəˌraɪz/ *transitive verb* (also esp. *Brit.* **-ise**) *Med.* burn or coagulate (tissue) with a heated instrument or caustic substance, esp. to stop bleeding. □ **caut·er·iz·a·tion** *noun* [French *cautériser* from Late Latin *cauterizare* from Greek *kautēriazō* from *kautērion* branding iron]

caut·ery /'kɒtəri/ *noun* (*pl.* **-eries**) *Med.* **1** an instrument or caustic for cauterizing. **2** the action of cauterizing. [Latin *cauterium* from Greek *kautērion*: see CAUTERIZE]

cau·tion ● *noun* **1** attention to safety; prudence, carefulness. **2** a warning. **3** *Cdn, Brit., & Austral. Law* a warning to an arrested person that his or her statements may be used as evidence in court. **4** *informal* an amusing or surprising person or thing. ● *verb* **1** *transitive & intransitive* (often foll. by *against*, or *to* + infin.) warn or admonish. **2** *transitive Cdn, Brit., & Austral. Law* issue a caution to. □ **throw caution to the wind** act imprudently or rashly, esp. intentionally. [Old French from Latin *cautio -onis* from *cavēre caut-* take heed]

cau·tion·ary *adjective* giving or serving as a warning (*a cautionary tale*).

cau·tious *adjective* careful, prudent. □ **cau·tious·ly** *adverb* **cau·tious·ness** *noun*

Cau·very River /'kɒvəri/ (also **Kav·eri River**) a river in S India which rises in N Kerala and flows 765 km (475 miles) eastward to the Bay of Bengal, south of Pondicherry. It is held sacred by Hindus.

cava /'kɑːvə/ *noun* a Spanish sparkling wine made in the same way as champagne. [Spanish, = 'cellar']

caval·cade /ˌkavəlˈkeɪd/ *noun* a procession or formal company of riders, motor vehicles, etc. [French from Italian *cavalcata* from *cavalcare* ride, ultimately from Latin *caballus* pack horse]

cava·lier /ˌkavəˈliːr/ ● *noun* **1** a gallant or fashionable man, esp. escorting a woman. **2** *hist.* (**Cavalier**) a supporter of Charles I in the English Civil War. **3** *archaic* a horseman. ● *adjective* offhand, haughtily careless in manner, supercilious. □ **cava·lier·ly** *adverb* [French from Italian *cavaliere*: see CHEVALIER]

cav·al·ry /'kavəlri/ *noun* (*pl.* **-ries**) (usu. treated as *pl.*) **1** soldiers on horseback. **2** soldiers in armoured vehicles. [French *cavallerie* from Italian *cavalleria* from *cavallo* horse, from Latin *caballus*]

cav·al·ry·man /'kavəlrimən, -man/ *noun* (*pl.* **-men**) a soldier of a cavalry regiment.

cavalry twill *noun* a strong fabric woven in a double twill.

Cavan /'kavən/ **1** a county of the Republic of Ireland, part of the old province of Ulster. **2** its county town; pop. (est. 2002) 3,600.

cava·tina /ˌkavəˈtiːnə/ *noun* **1** a short simple song. **2** a similar piece of instrumental music, usu. slow and emotional. [Italian]

cave ● *noun* **1** a large natural underground hollow, esp. with a roughly horizontal opening. **2** a cellar for storing wine etc. ● *intransitive verb* **1** explore caves, esp. interconnecting or underground. **2** *US slang* = CAVE IN. □ **cave in 1 a** (of a wall, earth over a hollow, etc.) subside, collapse. **b** cause (a wall, earth, etc.) to do this. **2** yield or submit under pressure; give up. □ **cave·like** *adjective* [Old French from Latin *cava* from *cavus* hollow]

ca·veat /ˈkaviˌat/ *noun* **1** a warning or proviso. **2** *Law* a notice entered in a legal registry advising a court official to halt a specific proceeding until the party entering the notice has been contacted. [Latin, = let a person beware]

caveat emp·tor /ˈkaviˌat ˈemptɔr/ *noun* the principle that the buyer alone is responsible if dissatisfied. [Latin, = let the buyer beware]

cave bear *noun* an extinct species of large bear, *Ursus spelaeus*, the remains of which have been discovered in European caves.

cave dweller *noun* a prehistoric human using a cave as shelter.

cave-in *noun* a collapse, submission, etc.

Cav·ell /ˈkavəl, kaˈvel/ **Edith (Lou·isa)** (1865–1915), English nurse executed by the Germans in the First World War for helping Allied troops to escape from occupied Belgium.

cave·man *noun* (*pl.* **-men**) **1** a prehistoric human, esp. one using a cave as shelter. **2** a primitive or crude person.

Cav·en·dish[1] /ˈkavəndɪʃ/ an unincorporated place in PEI, situated about 35 km northwest of Charlottetown. Cavendish was the hometown of the novelist Lucy Maud Montgomery. [prob. after Lord F. *Cavendish*, British field marshal and patron of a local landowner d.1803]

Cav·en·dish[2] /ˈkavəndɪʃ/ **Henry** (1731–1810), English chemist and physicist. Cavendish identified hydrogen as a separate gas, studied carbon dioxide, and determined their densities relative to atmospheric air. He also established that water was a compound, determined the density of the earth, and made a number of discoveries in the field of electrostatics.

caver *noun* a person who explores caves as a sport or recreation; a spelunker.

cav·ern /ˈkavɜrn/ *noun* an underground hollow; a vast cave. [Old French *caverne* or from Latin *caverna* from *cavus* hollow]

cav·ern·ous /ˈkavɜrnəs/ *adjective* of or resembling a cavern in size or appearance (a *cavernous hall*). □ **cav·ern·ous·ly** *adverb*

cavi·ar /ˈkaviˌɑr/ *noun* the pickled roe of sturgeon or other large fish, eaten as a delicacy. [early forms representing Italian *caviale*, French *caviar*, prob. from medieval Greek *khaviári*, related to Turkish *havyar*]

cavil /ˈkavəl/ ● *intransitive verb* (**cav·illed, cavil·ling; cav·iled, cavil·ing**) (usu. foll. by *at, about*) make petty objections; carp. ● *noun* a trivial objection. □ **cavil·ler** *noun* [French *caviller* from Latin *cavillari* from *cavilla* mockery]

cav·ing *noun* the exploration of caves as a sport or recreation; speleology.

cavi·ta·tion /ˌkavəˈteɪʃən/ *noun* **1** the formation and subsequent collapse of air bubbles or cavities in a liquid, caused by the rapid movement of a propeller etc. through it. **2** *Med.* the formation of cavities in diseased tissue.

cav·ity /ˈkavɪti/ *noun* (*pl.* **-ities**) **1** a hollow within a solid body. **2** a decayed part of a tooth. [French *cavité* or Late Latin *cavitas* from Latin *cavus* hollow]

cavity wall *noun* a wall formed from two separate walls with a space between for insulation etc.

ca·vort /kəˈvɔrt/ *intransitive verb* prance; jump, dance, or behave excitedly or happily. [perhaps from *curvet* a horse's leap, from Italian *corvetta* diminutive of *corva* CURVE]

Ca·vour /kəˈvʊr/ **Cam·illo Benso, Count di** (1810–61), Italian political leader, prime minister 1861. He was the driving force behind the unification of Italy under Victor Emmanuel II, obtaining international support for Italian unity as prime minister of Piedmont (1852–59; 1860–1), and becoming the first prime minister of united Italy in 1861.

cavy /ˈkeɪvi/ *noun* (*pl.* **cavies**) any small rodent of the family Caviidae, native to S America and having a sturdy body and vestigial tail, including guinea pigs. [modern Latin *cavia* from Galibi *cabiai*]

CAW *abbreviation* Canadian Auto Workers.

caw ● *noun* the harsh cry of a crow, raven, etc. ● *intransitive verb* utter this cry. [imitative]

Cawn·pore see KANPUR.

Cax·ton, Wil·liam (*c.*1422–91), the first English printer. He printed his first English text in 1474 and produced about 80 other texts, including editions of Malory's *Le Morte d'Arthur*, Chaucer's *Canterbury Tales*, and his own translations of French romances.

cay /keɪ/ *noun* a low insular bank or reef of coral, sand, etc. (compare KEY[2]). [Spanish *cayo* shoal, reef, from French *quai*: see QUAY]

Cay·enne /keɪˈen/ *noun* the capital and chief port of French Guiana; pop. (1999) 50,600.

cay·enne /kaiˈen, ˈkaien, keiˈen, ˈkeien/ *noun* (in full **cayenne pepper**) a pungent red powder obtained from the ground fruit and seeds of various capsicums, used as a seasoning. [Tupi *kyynha* assimilated to CAYENNE]

Cay·ley /ˈkeili/ **1 Ar·thur** (1821–95), English mathematician and barrister. He wrote almost a thousand mathematical papers in algebra and geometry, including articles on determinants, the newly developing group theory, and the algebra of matrices. The Cayley numbers, a generalization of complex numbers, are named after him. **2 Sir George** (1773–1857), English engineer and aeronautical pioneer. Among his numerous inventions were the first piloted glider (1853) and what was later called the caterpillar tractor.

cay·man *var. of* CAIMAN.

Cay·man Islands /ˈkeimən/ (also **Cay·mans**) a British dependency consisting of a group of three islands in the Caribbean Sea, south of Cuba; pop. (est. 2002) 36,272; capital, George Town.

Cay·uga /keiˈuːgə/ *noun* **1** a member of an Iroquoian people originally inhabiting central New York State, now living mainly on the Six Nations reserve near Brantford, Ont. **2** the Iroquoian language of this people. □ **Cay·u·gan** *adjective* [*Cayuga* Lake in New York]

cay·use /ˈkaiuːs, ˈkei-/ *noun N Amer.* **1** a feral or domesticated mustang or pony in the N American west, esp. one tamed by Aboriginal peoples. **2** *informal* a horse. [*Cayuse*, an Aboriginal people of Washington and Oregon who domesticated horses]

cazh *adjective & adverb slang* casual(ly).

CB *abbreviation* citizens' band (radio).

Cb *symbol Chem.* the element columbium.

CBA *abbreviation* **1** Canadian Bar Association. **2** Canadian Booksellers Association. **3** Canadian Basketball Association.

CBC *abbreviation* Canadian Broadcasting Corporation.

CBD *abbreviation* CENTRAL BUSINESS DISTRICT.

CBE *abbreviation* Commander of the Order of the British Empire.

CC *abbreviation* **1** Companion of the Order of Canada. **2** (in the UK) **a** City Council. **b** County Council; County Councillor.

cc ● *abbreviation* (also **c.c.**) **1** cubic centimetre(s). **2** used on letters, emails, etc. as an indication that a duplicate has been or should be sent to another person. ● *noun* (*pl.* **cc's**) a cubic centimetre.

CCD *abbreviation* CHARGE-COUPLED DEVICE.

CCF *abbreviation Cdn hist.* CO-OPERATIVE COMMONWEALTH FEDERATION. □ **CCFer** *noun*

C-clamp *noun* a clamp shaped like a letter C.

C clef *noun Music* a clef which can be moved on the staff to indicate the position of middle C (*see also* ALTO CLEF, TENOR CLEF).

CCRA *abbreviation* (in Canada) Canada Customs and Revenue Agency.

CCTV *abbreviation esp. Brit.* closed-circuit television.

CD[1] *abbreviation* **1** Civil Defence. **2** *Corps Diplomatique*.

CD[2] /siːˈdiː/ *noun* **1** a compact disc. **2** a CD-ROM. [abbreviation]

Cd *symbol Chem.* the element cadmium.

cd *abbreviation* candela.

CD burner *noun* a device used for copying data onto a compact disc.

CD-I *abbreviation* compact disc-interactive.

CDIC *abbreviation* Canada Deposit Insurance Corporation.

Cdn. *abbreviation* Canadian.

CD-R *noun* compact disc (recordable).

Cdr *abbreviation* COMMANDER.

Cdre. *abbreviation* Commodore.

CD-ROM /ˌsiːdiːˈrɒm/ *abbreviation* compact disc read-only memory (for storage and retrieval of text or data on a computer).

CD-RW *noun* compact disc (rewritable).

CDT *abbreviation* CENTRAL DAYLIGHT TIME.

CE *abbreviation* **1** Church of England. **2** civil engineer. **3** Common Era.

Ce *symbol Chem.* the element cerium.

cea·noth·us /ˌsiːəˈnoʊθəs/ *noun* (*pl.* **cea·noth·us·es**) any shrub of the

Vowels:　a *cat*　ɑ *arm*　e *bed*　ɜr *her*　ɜː *deux*　ə *ago*　ɪ *sit*　i *cosy*　iː *feed*　ɒ *hot*　ɔ *pore*　oː *no*　ʌ *run*　ʊ *put*

N American genus *Ceanothus*, with small starry blue or white flowers. *Also called* REDROOT. [modern Latin from Greek *keanōthos* kind of thistle]

cease *transitive & intransitive verb* stop; bring or come to an end (*cease fire*; *ceased to exist*). □ **without cease** continually, unrelentingly. [Old French *cesser*, Latin *cessare* frequentative of *cedere cess-* yield]

cease·fire *noun Military* **1** an order to stop firing. **2** a period of truce; a suspension of hostilities.

cease·less *adjective* without end; not ceasing. □ **cease·less·ly** *adverb*

Ceau·şescu /tʃauˈʃɛskuː/ **Nico·lae** (1918–89), Romanian Communist political leader, first president of the Socialist Republic of Romania 1974–89. A popular uprising in Dec. 1989 led to the downfall of his totalitarian and corrupt regime; he and his wife Elena were arrested, summarily tried, and executed.

Cebu /səˈbuː/ **1** an island of the south central Philippines. **2** its chief city and port; pop. (2000) 718,821. Ferdinand Magellan landed there in 1521.

Cec·chet·ti[1] /tʃəˈketi/ **En·rico** (1850–1928), Italian dancer, ballet master, and teacher. Among his students were Pavlova, Nijinsky, and Fokine. He developed a style of dance teaching that is one of the principal methods used today.

Cec·chet·ti[2] /tʃəˈketi/ *noun* the method of teaching or performing ballet devised by Enrico Cecchetti.

Cecil /ˈsɛsəl/ **1 Rob·ert**, see SALISBURY[2]. **2 Wil·liam**, see BURGHLEY.

Ce·ci·lia, St. /səˈsiːljə/ (2nd or 3rd c.), Roman martyr. According to legend, she took a vow of celibacy, but was forced to marry a young Roman; she converted her husband to Christianity and both were martyred. She is frequently pictured playing the organ and is the patron saint of church music. Feast day, 22 Nov.

cecum /ˈsiːkəm/ *noun* (also **cae·cum**) (*pl.* **ceca** /-kə/) a pouch-like cavity at the junction of the small and large intestines. □ **cecal** *adjective* [Latin for *intestinum caecum* from *caecus* blind, translation of Greek *tuphlon enteron*]

cedar /ˈsiːdər/ *noun* **1** any evergreen conifer of the genus *Cedrus*, native to the region from the E Mediterranean to central Asia, having tufts of short needles and cones of papery scales. **2** any of various similar conifers yielding timber, including species of arborvitae, cypress, and juniper. **3** (in full **cedar·wood**) the fragrant durable wood of any cedar tree, often used to line closets, chests, etc. because of its insect-repellent qualities. □ **cedary** *adjective* [Old French *cedre* from Latin *cedrus* from Greek *kedros*]

Cedar Lake a lake in west central Manitoba, immediately north of Lake Winnipegosis. [because it is situated at the northern limit of the cedar tree]

cedar shake *noun N Amer.* a type of shingle made from cedarwood, with at least one face split rather than sawn.

cedar·strip *noun Cdn* (usu. *attributive*) a technique for making boats, esp. canoes, consisting of long strips of cedar.

cedar swamp *noun N Amer.* an area of swamp or bog in which cedars are the predominant trees.

cedar waxwing *noun* (also **cedar bird**) a N American waxwing, *Bombycilla cedrorum*, having brownish plumage with red-tipped wings and a yellow belly and tail tip.

cede /siːd/ *transitive verb* **1** give up one's rights to or possession of. **2** transfer possession of. [French *céder* or Latin *cedere* yield]

cedi /ˈsiːdi/ *noun* (*pl.* same or **cedis**) the chief monetary unit of Ghana, equal to 100 pesewas. [Ghanaian, perhaps from alteration of SHILLING]

ced·illa /sɪˈdɪlə/ *noun* **1** a mark written under the letter *c* in French and Portuguese to show that it is sibilant (as in *façade*). **2** a similar mark under *c* or *s* to distinguish voiceless from voiced consonants in modern Turkish. [Spanish *cedilla* diminutive of *zeda* from Greek *zēta* letter Z]

CEF *abbreviation hist.* Canadian Expeditionary Force.

CEGEP /ˈsiːdʒɛp, ˈseɪʒɛp/ *abbreviation* (also **Cegep**) (in Quebec) Collège d'enseignement général et professionnel, a post-secondary educational institution offering two-year programs for preparation for university and three-year training programs in professions and trades.

cei·lidh /ˈkeɪli/ *noun* **1** a party featuring traditional Scottish or Irish music, dancing, songs, and stories. **2** a concert at which traditional Scottish music and dancing are performed. [Gaelic, from Old Irish *céilidhe* 'visit, visiting' from *céile* 'companion']

ceil·ing /ˈsiːlɪŋ/ *noun* **1 a** the upper interior of a room or other similar compartment. **b** the material forming this. **2** an upper limit on prices, wages, performance, etc. **3** *Aviation* the maximum altitude a given aircraft can reach. **4** the altitude of the base of a cloud layer.

5 *Naut.* the inside planking of a ship's bottom and sides. □ **ceil·inged** *adjective* (in *combination*). [Middle English *celynge*, *siling*, perhaps ultimately from Latin *caelum* heaven or *celare* hide]

ceiling fan *noun* a fan suspended from a ceiling, having long blades to circulate cooling air when operated counter-clockwise and force warm air down from the ceiling when operated clockwise.

cein·ture flé·chée /sãtuːr fleiˈʃei/ *noun* (*pl.* **cein·tures flé·chées** pronunc. same) *Cdn hist.* a long, brightly coloured sash woven with an arrow-shaped pattern and worn around the waist, esp. by voyageurs. *Also called* ARROW SASH, ASSOMPTION SASH, VOYAGEUR SASH. [Canadian French, lit. 'arrowed sash' (see CINCTURE)]

cel /sɛl/ *noun* a transparent sheet of celluloid or cellulose acetate, which can be drawn on and used in combination with others in the production of animated films. [abbreviation of CELLULOID]

cela·don /ˈselə,dɒn/ ● *noun* **1** a pale greyish shade of green. **2** a grey-green glaze used on some pottery or porcelain. **3** Chinese pottery or porcelain glazed in this way. ● *adjective* of a grey-green colour. [French, from the name of a character in d'Urfé's *L'Astrée* (1607–27)]

Ce·laeno /səˈliːnoː/ *Gk Myth* one of the Pleiades.

celan·dine /ˈselən,daɪn, -diːn/ *noun* **1** either of two yellow-flowered plants, the greater celandine, *Chelidonium majus*, and the lesser celandine, *Ranunculus ficaria*. **2** (in full **celandine poppy**) = WOOD POPPY. [Old French *celidoine*, ultimately from Greek *khelidōn* swallow: the flowering of the plant was associated with the arrival of swallows]

-cele /siːl/ *combining form* (also **-coele**) *Med.* swelling, hernia (*gastrocele*). [Greek *kēlē* tumour]

celeb /səˈlɛb/ *noun informal* a celebrity. [abbreviation]

Cel·ebes /ˈseli,biːz/ the former name for SULAWESI.

Celebes Sea a part of the W Pacific between the Philippines and Sulawesi, bounded to the west by Borneo. It is linked to the Java Sea by the Makassar strait.

cele·brant /ˈseləbrənt/ *noun* **1** a person who performs a rite, esp. a priest who officiates at the Eucharist. **2** a person participating in a celebration. **3** a person who celebrates or praises someone or something. [French *célébrant* or Latin *celebrare celebrant-*: see CELEBRATE]

cele·brate /ˈselə,breit/ *verb* **1** *transitive* mark (a festival or special event) with festivities etc. **2** *intransitive* engage in festivities, usu. after a special event etc. **3** *transitive* perform publicly and duly (a religious ceremony etc.). **4 a** *transitive* officiate at (the Eucharist). **b** *intransitive* officiate, esp. at the Eucharist. **5** *transitive* make publicly known; extol, praise widely. □ **cele·bra·tion** *noun* **cele·bra·tor** *noun* **cele·bra·tory** /ˈseləbrə,tɔri, səˈlebrə,tɔri/ *adjective* [Latin *celebrare* from *celeber -bris* frequented, honoured]

cele·brat·ed /ˈseləbreitəd/ *adjective* publicly honoured, widely known.

ce·leb·rity /səˈlebriti/ *noun* (*pl.* **-ties**) **1** a well-known person. **2** fame. □ **ce·leb·rity·hood** *noun* [French *célébrité* or Latin *celebritas* from *celeber*: see CELEBRATE]

celebrity culture *noun* a culture which values celebrity for its own sake and is obsessed with the minutiae of celebrities' lives.

ce·leri·ac /səˈleri,ak/ *noun* a variety of celery with a swollen turnip-like root used as a vegetable. [CELERY: *-ac* is unexplained]

ce·ler·ity /səˈleriti/ *noun archaic* or *literary* swiftness (esp. of a living creature). [French *célérité* from Latin *celeritas -tatis* from *celer* swift]

cel·ery /ˈseləri/ *noun* an umbelliferous plant, *Apium graveolens*, with closely packed succulent leaf stalks used as a vegetable. [French *céleri* from Italian dial. *selleri* from Latin *selinum* from Greek *selinon* parsley]

celery salt *noun* a seasoning made from salt and finely ground celery seed.

ce·lesta /səˈlestə/ *noun* (also **ce·leste**) a small keyboard instrument resembling a glockenspiel, with hammers striking steel plates suspended over wooden resonators, giving an ethereal bell-like sound. [French *céleste* heavenly, from Latin *caelestis* from *caelum* heaven]

ce·les·tial /səˈlestiəl/ *adjective* **1** heavenly; divinely good or beautiful; sublime. **2 a** of the sky; of the part of the sky commonly observed in astronomy etc. **b** of heavenly bodies. □ **ce·les·tial·ly** *adverb* [Old French from medieval Latin *caelestialis* from Latin *caelestis*: see CELESTA]

celestial equator *noun* the great circle of the sky in the plane perpendicular to the earth's axis.

celestial horizon *noun* see HORIZON 1c.

celestial navigation *noun* navigation using the observed positions of the stars and other celestial bodies.

celestial sphere *noun* an imaginary sphere of which the observer is the centre and in which celestial objects are represented as lying.

ce·li·ac /ˈsiːli,ak/ *adjective* (also **coe·li·ac**) **1** of or pertaining to the abdominal cavity. **2** (of a person) afflicted with celiac disease. [Latin *coeliacus* from Greek *koiliakos* from *koilia* belly]

celiac disease *noun* a digestive disorder of the small intestine, causing chronic failure to digest food properly unless gluten is excluded from the diet.

celi·bate /ˈsɛlɪbət/ ● *adjective* **1** committed to abstention from sexual relations and from marriage, esp. for religious reasons. **2** abstaining from sexual relations. ● *noun* a celibate person. □ **celi·bacy** *noun* [French *célibat* or Latin *caelibatus* unmarried state, from *caelebs -ibis* unmarried]

cell *noun* **1** a small room, esp. in a prison or monastery. **2** a compartment, e.g. in a honeycomb. **3** a small group operating as a local branch of a political movement, esp. of a subversive kind. **4** *Computing* a location or address where a piece of information is stored, esp. in a spreadsheet or database. **5** the local area covered by one of the short-range radio transmitters in a cellphone system. **6** *Biol.* **a** the basic structural and functional unit of an organism, usu. microscopic, consisting of cytoplasm and a nucleus enclosed in a membrane. **b** an enclosed cavity in an organism etc. **7** *Electricity* **a** a battery or other device for generating electricity or producing electrolysis from chemical energy. **b** = SOLAR CELL. **8** an atmospheric mass with roughly uniform properties (*high-pressure cell*). **9** *hist.* a small monastery or convent dependent on a larger one. **10** a cellphone. [Old French *celle* or from Latin *cella* storeroom etc.]

cel·lar ● *noun* **1** a room below ground level in a house, often used for storage of food and wine. **2** a stock of wine in a cellar (*has a good cellar*). **3** *N Amer. Sport informal* = BASEMENT 2. ● *transitive verb* store or put in a cellar. [Anglo-French *celer*, Old French *celier* from Late Latin *cellarium* storehouse]

cellar·age *noun* **1** space in a cellar. **2** the charge for the use of a cellar or storehouse.

cellar-dweller *noun* *N Amer.* a sports team habitually in last place in the standings. □ **cellar-dwelling** *adjective*

cellar·er *noun* an officer in a monastery etc. in charge of food and drink.

cel·lar·et /ˌsɛləˈrɛt/ *noun* a buffet or case for holding wine bottles in a dining room etc.

cell·block *noun* one of several sections of cells into which a large prison is divided.

-celled *combining form* possessing the specified number of cells (*single-celled animal*).

Cel·lini /tʃɛˈliːni/ **Ben·ven·uto** (1500–71), Italian goldsmith and sculptor. His bronze *Perseus* (1545–54), considered his masterpiece, is typical of his elaborate and virtuosic style; his autobiography is famous for its vivid picture of Italian Renaissance life.

cell·mate *noun* a prisoner occupying the same cell as another.

cello /ˈtʃɛloʊ/ *noun* (pl. **cellos**) the second-largest instrument of the violin family, held upright on the floor between the knees of the seated player. □ **cel·list** *noun* [abbreviation of VIOLONCELLO]

Cello·phane /ˈsɛləˌfeɪn/ *noun* proprietary a thin transparent wrapping and packaging material made from viscose. [CELLULOSE + -*phane* (compare DIAPHANOUS)]

cellophane noodle *noun* (in Oriental cuisine) a fine noodle made from mung bean starch, which becomes almost transparent when heated.

cell·phone *noun* a portable telephone which operates by means of a cellular network (see CELLULAR *adjective* 5). [blend of CELLULAR + TELEPHONE]

cel·lu·lar /ˈsɛljʊlər/ ● *adjective* **1 a** of or having small compartments or cavities. **b** porous. **2** of or consisting of biological cells. **3** (of a fabric etc.) having an open texture. **4** (of a plant) having no distinct stem, leaves, etc. **5** (of a telephone system) using a number of short-range radio transmitters to cover a large area, the signal being automatically switched from one transmitter to the next as the user travels about. ● *noun* a cellphone system. [French *cellulaire* from modern Latin *cellularis*: see CELLULE]

cellular automaton *noun* *Computing* one of a set of units in a mathematical model which have simple rules governing their replication and destruction. They are used to model complex systems composed of simple units such as living things or parallel processors.

cel·lule /ˈsɛljuːl/ *noun* *Biol.* a small cell or cavity. [French *cellule* or Latin *cellula* diminutive of *cella* CELL]

cel·lu·lite /ˈsɛljʊˌlaɪt/ *noun* fatty tissue regarded as causing a dimpled or lumpy texture on the hips and thighs (esp. of women). [French (as CELLULE)]

cel·lu·litis /ˌsɛljʊˈlaɪtɪs/ *noun* inflammation of cellular tissue.

cel·lu·loid /ˈsɛljʊˌlɔɪd/ ● *noun* **1** a transparent flammable plastic made from camphor and nitrocellulose. **2** motion picture film. ● *adjective* **1** made of celluloid. **2** relating to film or motion pictures. [irreg. from CELLULOSE]

cel·lu·lose /ˈsɛljʊˌloʊs, -ˌloʊz/ *noun* **1** *Biochem.* a carbohydrate forming the main constituent of the cell walls of plants, used in the production of textile fibres. **2** a compound of this (esp. cellulose acetate or nitrocellulose) in solution, used as a base for paints, lacquers, etc. □ **cel·lu·losic** /-ˈloʊsɪk/ *adjective* [French (as CELLULE)]

cellulose acetate *noun* an insoluble compound made by treating cellulose (usu. from wood pulp) with a mixture of acetic anhydride, acetic acid, and concentrated sulphuric acid, used to make lacquers, textiles, etc.

cellulose nitrate *noun* = NITROCELLULOSE.

celom *var. of* COELOM.

celo·sia /səˈloʊsiə/ *noun* a plant of a genus that includes cockscomb. [modern Latin, from Greek *kēlos* 'burnt or dry' (from the burnt appearance of the flowers in some species)]

Cel·sius[1] /ˈsɛlsiəs/ **An·ders** (1701–44), Swedish astronomer, best known for the temperature scale (**Celsius scale**) which bears his name; although the thermometer first advocated by him in 1743 had 100° as the freezing point of water and 0° as the boiling point, the modern Celsius scale is the reverse.

Cel·sius[2] /ˈsɛlsiəs/ *adjective* of or denoting a temperature on the Celsius scale.

Celt /kɛlt, sɛlt/ *noun* (also **Kelt**) a member of a group of W European peoples, including the pre-Roman inhabitants of Britain and Gaul and their descendants, esp. in Ireland, Wales, Scotland, Cornwall, Brittany, and the Isle of Man. [Latin *Celtae* (pl.) from Greek *Keltoi*]

celt /sɛlt/ *noun* *Archaeology* a stone or metal prehistoric implement with a chisel edge. [medieval Latin *celtes* chisel]

Celt·ic /ˈkɛltɪk, ˈsɛltɪk/ ● *adjective* of or relating to the Celts. ● *noun* a group of languages spoken by Celtic peoples, including Gaelic, Welsh, Cornish, Manx, and Breton. □ **Celt·i·cism** /-ˌsɪzəm/ *noun*

Celtic Church the Christian Church in the British Isles from its foundation in the 2nd or 3rd c. until its assimilation into the Roman Catholic Church. It was largely driven out of England by the Saxons in the 5th c., surviving in Scotland, Wales, and Ireland and attempting to convert the invaders by means of missionaries.

Celtic cross *noun* a Latin cross with a circle around the intersection.

Celtic Sea the part of the Atlantic Ocean between S Ireland and SW England.

ce·ment /səˈmɛnt/ ● *noun* **1 a** a powdery substance made by calcining lime and clay, mixed with water to form mortar or used in concrete. **b** concrete. ¶ The use of *cement* to mean *concrete* rather than the binding substance in concrete has been much criticized. *Cement* is, however, the older word, and in non-technical use such uses as *cement floor* or *cement sidewalk* are unambiguous. **2** any substance that hardens and fastens on setting. **3** a uniting factor or principle. **4** a substance for filling cavities in teeth. **5** (also **ce·men·tum**) *Anat.* a thin layer of bony material forming the outer layer of the root of a tooth. ● *transitive verb* **1 a** unite with or as with cement. **b** establish or strengthen (a friendship etc.). **2** line or cover with cement. [Old French *ciment* from Latin *caementum* quarry stone, from *caedere* hew]

ce·men·ta·tion /ˌsiːmɛnˈteɪʃən, ˌsɛmən-/ *noun* **1** the act or process of cementing or being cemented. **2** the heating of iron with charcoal powder to form steel.

ce·men·ti·tious /ˌsɛmɛnˈtɪʃəs/ *adjective* of the nature of cement.

cement mixer *noun* a machine (usu. with a revolving drum) for mixing cement with water.

cem·etery /ˈsɛməˌtɛri, -tri/ *noun* (pl. **-ies**) a graveyard. [Late Latin *coemeterium* from Greek *koimētērion* dormitory, from *koimaō* put to sleep]

ceno·bite /ˈsɛnəˌbaɪt/ *noun* (also **coeno·bite** /ˈsiː-/) a member of a monastic community. □ **ceno·bit·ic** /-ˈbɪtɪk/ *adjective* **ceno·bit·ic·al** /-ˈbɪtɪkəl/ *adjective* [Old French *cenobite* from Late Latin *coenobium* from Greek *koinobion* convent, from *koinos* common + *bios* life]

ceno·taph /ˈsɛnəˌtaf/ *noun* a tomb-like monument, esp. a war memorial, to a person or persons whose bodies are interred elsewhere. [French *cénotaphe* from Late Latin *cenotaphium* from Greek *kenos* empty + *taphos* tomb]

Ceno·zoic /ˌsiːnəˈzoʊɪk, ˌsɛn-/ *Geol.* (also **Caino·zoic** /ˌkaɪnə-/, **Caeno·zoic** /ˌsiːn-/) ● *adjective* of, relating to, or denoting the most recent geological era, following the Mesozoic and lasting from about

65 million years ago to the present day. The Cenozoic includes the Tertiary and Quaternary periods, and has seen the rapid evolution of mammals. ● *noun* this geological era (*compare* MESOZOIC, PALEOZOIC). [Greek *kainos* new + *zōion* animal]

cens /sãs/ *noun* (*pl.* same) *Cdn hist.* a token payment made to a seigneur by a habitant, reaffirming the feudal nature of the land tenure. [French, as CENSUS]

cense /sens/ *transitive verb* direct smoke from burning incense at, esp. as a religious rite. [aphetic from Old French *encenser*]

cens·er /'sensər/ *noun* a vessel in which incense is burned, esp. during a religious procession or ceremony. [Anglo-French *censer*, Old French *censier* aphetic form of *encensier* from *encens* INCENSE¹]

cen·si·taire /sãsi'ter/ *noun* *Cdn hist.* a tenant on a seigneury. [French, from CENS]

cen·sor /'sensər/ ● *noun* **1** an official authorized to examine printed matter, films, news, etc., before public release, and to suppress any parts on the grounds of obscenity, threats to security, etc. **2** *Rom. Hist.* either of two annual magistrates responsible for holding censuses and empowered to supervise public morals. **3** *Psych.* an impulse which is said to prevent certain ideas and memories from emerging into consciousness. ● *transitive verb* **1** act as a censor of. **2** make deletions or changes in. ☐ **cen·sor·ial** /-'sɔriəl/ *adjective* **cen·sor·ship** *noun* [Latin from *censēre* assess]

cen·sor·ious /sen'sɔriəs/ *adjective* severely critical; fault-finding; quick or eager to criticize. ☐ **cen·sor·ious·ly** *adverb* **cen·sor·ious·ness** *noun*

censor·ware *noun* filtering software intended to prevent access to websites identified by the software as offensive, unsuitable, or pornographic by the use of criteria (e.g. key words) written into the program.

cen·sure /'senʃər/ ● *transitive verb* criticize harshly; reprove. ¶ Often confused with *censor*. ● *noun* harsh criticism; expression of disapproval. ☐ **cen·sur·able** *adjective* [Old French from Latin *censura* from *censēre* assess]

cen·sus /'sensəs/ ● *noun* (*pl.* **cen·sus·es**) an official count of a population or of a class of things, often with various statistics noted. ● *transitive verb* (**cen·sused**, **cen·sus·ing**) conduct a census of; count, enumerate. [Latin from *censēre* assess]

cent *noun* **1 a** a monetary unit in various countries, equal to one-hundredth of a dollar or other decimal currency unit. **b** a coin of this value. **2** *informal* a very small sum of money. **3** *see* PER CENT. [French *cent* or Italian *cento* or Latin *centum* hundred]

cent. *abbreviation* century.

cen·taur /'sentɔr/ *noun* a creature in Greek mythology with the head, arms, and torso of a man and the body and legs of a horse. [Latin *centaurus* from Greek *kentauros*, of unknown origin]

Cen·taur·us /sen'tɔrəs/ *noun* a large southern constellation lying in the Milky Way. [Latin *Centaurus* (as CENTAUR)]

cen·taury /'sentɔri/ *noun* (*pl.* **-ies**) any plant of the genus *Centaurium*, esp. *C. erythraea*, formerly used in medicine. [Late Latin *centaurea*, ultimately from Greek *kentauros* CENTAUR: from the legend that it was discovered by the centaur Chiron]

cen·tavo /sen'tavɔ/ *noun* a small coin and monetary unit of some Latin American countries, worth one-hundredth of the standard unit. [Spanish from Latin *centum* hundred]

cen·ten·ar·ian /ˌsentə'neriən/ ● *noun* a person a hundred or more years old. ● *adjective* a hundred or more years old.

cen·ten·ary /sen'tenəri, -ti'nɛri/ ● *noun* (*pl.* **-aries**) **1** a centennial. **2** a celebration of this. ● *adjective* of or relating to a centenary. [Latin *centenarius* from *centeni* a hundred each, from *centum* a hundred]

cen·ten·nial /sen'teniəl/ esp. *N Amer.* ● *noun* a hundredth anniversary. ● *adjective* **1** lasting for a hundred years or occurring every hundred years. **2** of or concerning a centennial; in Canada, esp. that of Confederation, in 1967. [Latin *centum* a hundred, after BIENNIAL]

cen·ter etc. *var. of* CENTRE etc.

cen·tes·i·mal /sen'tesiməl/ *adjective* reckoning or reckoned by hundredths. ☐ **cen·tes·i·mal·ly** *adverb* [Latin *centesimus* hundredth, from *centum* hundred]

cen·tési·mo /sen'tesi,mɔ/ *noun* (*pl.* **-mos**) a monetary unit of Uruguay, equal to one-hundredth of a peso. [Spanish]

centi- *combining form* **1** one-hundredth, esp. of a unit in the metric system (*centimetre*; *centigram*). **2** hundred. Abbr.: **c**. [Latin *centum* hundred]

centi·grade *adjective* **1** = CELSIUS². **2** having a scale of a hundred degrees. [French from Latin *centum* hundred + *gradus* step]

centi·gram *noun* a metric unit of mass, equal to one-hundredth of a gram.

centi·litre *noun* (also esp. *US* **centi·liter**) a metric unit of capacity, equal to one-hundredth of a litre.

cen·time /sã'tiːm/ *noun* **1 a** a monetary unit in various countries, equal to one-hundredth of a franc or other decimal currency unit. **b** a coin of this value. **2** a monetary unit equal to one-hundredth of a gourde in Haiti or of a dirham in Morocco. [French from Latin *centum* a hundred]

centi·metre *noun* (also esp. *US* **centi·meter**) a metric unit of length, equal to one-hundredth of a metre (0.394 in.).

centimetre-gram-second system *noun* the system using the centimetre, the gram, and the second as basic units of length, mass, and time respectively. Abbr.: **cgs system**.

cen·timo /'senti,mɔ/ *noun* (*pl.* **-timos**) a monetary unit of a number of Latin American countries, equal to one-hundredth of the basic unit. [Spanish]

centi·pede /'senti,piːd/ *noun* any arthropod of the class Chilopoda, with a wormlike body of many segments each with a pair of legs. [French *centipède* or Latin *centipeda* from *centum* hundred + *pes pedis* foot]

cen·to /'sentɔ/ *noun* (*pl.* **-tos**) a composition made up of quotations from other authors. [Latin, = patchwork garment]

cen·tral ● *adjective* **1** of, at, or forming the centre. **2** from the centre. **3** chief, essential, most important. **4** *attributive adjective* denoting a house's heating, air conditioning, or vacuum system in which the rooms are connected via pipes, ducts, or tubes to a single source of heat, cool air, or suction. ● *noun* *N Amer.* *informal* a place with a high concentration of a specified thing etc. (*looks like cowboy central*). ☐ **cen·tral·ity** /-'traliti/ *noun* **cen·tral·ly** *adverb* [French *central* or Latin *centralis* from *centrum* CENTRE]

Central African Republic a country of central Africa; pop. (est. 2002) 3,642,739; capital, Bangui. It was formerly known as the French colony of Ubanghi Shari.

Central America the southernmost part of N America linking the continent to S America and consisting of the countries of Guatemala, Belize, Honduras, El Salvador, Nicaragua, Costa Rica, and Panama. ☐ **Central American** *noun & adjective*

central bank *noun* a national bank that provides financial and banking services for its country's government and commercial banking system, as well as implementing the government's monetary policy, setting interest rates, issuing currency etc.

central business district *noun* the area of a town or city where business, shopping, administrative, and entertainment facilities are most densely located. Abbr.: **CBD**.

Central Canada see CENTRAL PROVINCES.

central casting *noun* *N Amer.* a department of a motion picture production company that hires actors, esp. for bit parts as stock characters.

Central Daylight Time *noun* daylight time in the Central Time zone. Abbr.: **CDT**.

Central European Time *noun* the standard time in a zone including Western Europe, one hour ahead of Greenwich Mean Time. Abbr.: **CET**.

Central Intelligence Agency *noun* a US federal agency, established in 1947, responsible for coordinating government intelligence activities. Abbr.: **CIA**.

cen·tral·ism *noun* a system that centralizes (esp. an administration) (see also DEMOCRATIC CENTRALISM). ☐ **cen·tral·ist** *noun*

cen·tral·ize *verb* (also esp. *Brit.* **-ise**) **1** *transitive & intransitive* bring or come to a centre. **2** *transitive* **a** concentrate (administration) at a single centre. **b** subject (a state) to this system. ☐ **cen·tral·iz·a·tion** *noun* **cen·tral·iz·er** *noun*

central locking *noun* a locking system in motor vehicles whereby the locks of several doors can be operated from a single lock.

central nervous system *noun* *Anat.* the complex of nerve tissues that controls the activities of the body, in vertebrates the brain and spinal cord.

Central Park a large public park in the city of New York, in the centre of Manhattan.

central planning *noun* the complete planning of an economy by a central authority which controls all prices, wages, and production.

Central Powers a Triple Alliance of Germany, Austria-Hungary, and Italy, between 1882 and 1914.

---

t top   v voice   w we   z zoo   ʃ she   ʒ vision   θ thin   ð this   ŋ ring   x loch   tʃ chip   dʒ jar   (*see over for vowels*)

central processing unit *noun* (also **central processor**) the part of a computer which controls the system and performs arithmetical and logical operations on data. Abbr.: **CPU**.

Central provinces *plural noun* (also **Central Canada**) Ontario and Quebec (*compare* ATLANTIC PROVINCES, WESTERN PROVINCES).

Central Region a former local government region in central Scotland, dissolved in 1996 and mainly replaced by Stirling.

central reservation *noun see* RESERVATION 6.

Central Saanich /'sanɪtʃ/ a district municipality on the Saanich Peninsula of Vancouver Island, situated between the district municipalities of Saanich and North Saanich; pop. (2001) 15,348. [SAANICH¹]

Central Standard Time *noun* standard time in the Central Time zone. Abbr.: **CST**.

Central Time *noun* the time in a zone including Saskatchewan and Manitoba as well as the central states of the US. Central Standard Time is six hours behind Greenwich Mean Time; Central Daylight Time is 5 hours behind Greenwich Mean Time. Abbr.: **CT**.

Centre /'sãtrə/ a region of central France, including the cities of Orleans, Tours, Chartres and Bourges.

centre (also **cen·ter**) ● *noun* **1** the middle point, esp. of a line, circle, or sphere, equidistant from the ends or from any point on the circumference or surface. **2** a pivot or axis of rotation. **3 a** a place or group of buildings forming a central point in a district, city, etc., or a main area for an activity (*the city's shopping centre; town centre*). **b** a place or group of buildings with a specified function (*detention centre; drop-in centre*). **c** (with preceding word) a piece or set of equipment for a number of connected functions (*entertainment centre*). **4** a point of concentration or dispersion; a nucleus or source. **5** a political party or group holding moderate opinions. **6** the filling in a chocolate etc. **7** *Sport* the middle player in a line or group in some games, esp.: **a** (in hockey) the forward who takes faceoffs at centre ice. **b** (in football) the offensive lineman who snaps the ball to the quarterback, punter, etc. **c** (in basketball) the forward who plays near the net, usu. the tallest player on the team. **8** *Sport* a pass from the side to the centre of the playing area, esp. in the offensive zone. **9** (in a lathe etc.) a conical adjustable support for the workpiece. **10** (*attributive*) of or at the centre. ● *verb* **1** *intransitive* (foll. by *in, on, around*) have as its main centre or focus. **2** *transitive* place in the centre. **3** *transitive* mark with a centre. **4** *transitive* (foll. by *in* etc.) concentrate. **5** *transitive Sport* pass (the ball, puck, etc.) from the side to the centre of the playing area, esp. in the offensive zone. **6** *transitive Hockey* be a centreman for (two wingers) or on (a line) (*centres the checking line*).□ **centre·most** *adjective* **cen·tric** *adjective* **cen·tri·city** /-'trɪsɪti/ *noun* [Old French *centre* or Latin *centrum* from Greek *kentron* sharp point]

centre bit *noun* a boring tool with a centre point and side cutters.

centre·board *noun* a retractable keel on a sailboat.

cen·tred *adjective* (also **cen·tered**) **1** (in *combination*) taking a specified subject as the most important or focal element (*child-centred learning*). **2** (in *combination*) (of a chocolate) having a centre or filling of a specified type (*soft-centred truffles*). **3** *N Amer.* (of a person) well-balanced and confident or serene.□ **centred·ness** *noun* (usu. in *combination*).

centre field *noun Baseball* **1** the part of the outfield between left field and right field. **2** the position of the player who covers this area.□ **centre fielder** *noun*

centre·fire *adjective* **1** (of a cartridge) having the charge in the centre of the base. **2** (of a firearm) designed for use with such cartridges.

centre·fold *noun* **1** a centre spread of a magazine laid out as a unit, often with a portion that folds out. **2** a usu. naked or scantily clad model pictured on such a spread.

centre forward *noun* (in soccer etc.) the middle player or position in a forward line.

centre half *noun Sport* the middle player or position in a halfback line.

centre ice *noun* the central area of a rink, esp. the spot precisely in the centre of a hockey rink where faceoffs take place at the start of each period and after every goal.

centre·man *noun* = CENTRE *noun* 7a.

centre of attention *noun* **1** a person or thing that draws general attention. **2** *Physics* the point to which bodies tend by gravity.

centre of gravity *noun* **1** a point from which the weight of a body or system may be considered to act. **2** the point or object of greatest importance or interest.

centre of mass *noun* a point representing the mean position of matter in a body or system.

centre·piece *noun* **1** an ornament for the middle of a table. **2** a principal item.

centre spread *noun* the two facing middle pages of a newspaper etc.

centre stage ● *noun* **1** the central, most prominent area on a theatrical stage. **2** the most prominent position (*funding took centre stage in their discussions*). ● *adverb* in or into this position.

-centric *combining form* forming adjectives with the sense 'having a (specified) centre or focus' (*anthropocentric; eccentric; egocentric*).□ **-centrism** *combining form* **-centrist** *combining form* [after *concentric* etc. from Greek *kentrikos*: see CENTRE]

cen·tri·fu·gal /ˌsenˈtrɪfəgəl, -ˈtrɪfjə-, sentrɪ'fjuːgəl/ *adjective* moving or tending to move from a centre (*compare* CENTRIPETAL).□ **cen·tri·fu·gal·ly** *adverb* [modern Latin *centrifugus* from Latin *centrum* centre + *fugere* flee]

centrifugal force *noun* an apparent force that acts outwards on a body moving about a centre.

cen·tri·fuge /'sentrɪˌfjuːdʒ/ ● *noun* a machine with a rapidly rotating device designed to separate liquids from solids or other liquids (e.g. cream from milk). ● *transitive verb* **1** subject to the action of a centrifuge. **2** separate by centrifuge.□ **cen·tri·fu·ga·tion** /-fjuˈgeɪʃən/ *noun*

centring *noun* (also **center·ing**) **1** the action or process of placing something in the middle of something else. **2** *Building* framing used to support an arch or dome while it is under construction.

cen·tri·ole /'sentriˌoːl/ *noun Biol.* a minute organelle usu. within a centrosome, involved esp. in the development of spindles in cell division. [medieval Latin *centriolum* diminutive of *centrum* centre]

cen·trip·etal /sen'trɪpətəl/ *adjective* moving or tending to move towards a centre (*compare* CENTRIFUGAL).□ **cen·trip·etal·ly** *adverb* [modern Latin *centripetus* from Latin *centrum* centre + *petere* seek]

centripetal force *noun* the force acting on a body in circular motion directing it towards the centre of rotation.

cen·trist *noun Politics* a person who holds moderate views.□ **cen·trism** *noun*

cen·troid /'sentroɪd/ *noun Math.* **1** the point within an area or volume at which the centre of mass would be if the surface or body had a uniform density. **2** the point whose coordinates are the mean values of the corresponding coordinates of points in a given set.

cen·tro·mere /'sentrəˌmiːr/ *noun Biol.* the point on a chromosome to which the spindle is attached during cell division.□ **cen·tro·mer·ic** /-'merɪk, -'miːrɪk/ *adjective* [Latin *centrum* centre + Greek *meros* part]

cen·tro·some /'sentrəˌsoːm/ *noun Biol.* a distinct part of the cytoplasm in a cell, usu. near the nucleus, that contains the centriole. [German *Centrosoma* from Latin *centrum* centre + Greek *sōma* body]

cen·trum /'sentrəm/ *noun Anat.* the solid central part of a vertebra. [Latin = centre]

cen·tuple /sen'tʌpəl/ *transitive verb* multiply by a hundred; increase a hundredfold. [French *centuple* or ecclesiastical Latin *centuplus, centuplex* from Latin *centum* hundred]

cen·tur·ion /sen'tʃʊriən, -'tʃʊriən/ *noun* the commander of a century in the ancient Roman army. [Latin *centurio -onis* (as CENTURY)]

cen·tury /'sentʃəri/ *noun* (*pl.* **-ies**) **1 a** a period of one hundred years. **b** any of the centuries reckoned from the supposed date of the birth of Christ. ¶ In older use, the twentieth century was reckoned from 1901–2000. In modern use it is often reckoned as 1900–1999. **2** *Sport* **a** a score etc. of a hundred, esp. a hundred runs by one batsman in cricket. **b** a group or total of a hundred (*first to reach the century mark this season*). **3 a** a company in the ancient Roman army, originally of 100 men. **b** an ancient Roman political division for voting. [Latin *centuria* from *centum* hundred]

century home *noun Cdn* (also **century house**) **1** a house which is approximately one hundred years old. **2** any house designed or decorated in century-old styles.

century plant *noun* a plant, *Agave americana*, flowering once in many years and yielding sap from which tequila is distilled. *Also called* AMERICAN ALOE.

CEO *abbreviation* = CHIEF EXECUTIVE OFFICER.

cep /sep/ *noun* an edible mushroom, *Boletus edulis*, with a stout stalk and brown smooth cap. [French *cèpe* from Gascon *cep* from Latin *cippus* stake]

ceph·alic /sə'falɪk/ *adjective* of or in the head. [French *céphalique* from Latin *cephalicus* from Greek *kephalikos* from *kephalē* head]

-cephalic /sə'falɪk/ *combining form* = -CEPHALOUS.

cephalic index *noun Anthropology* the ratio of the maximum breadth of a skull (multiplied by 100) to its maximum length.

Vowels: a *cat* ɑ *arm* e *bed* ɜr *her* ɜː *deux* ə *ago* ɪ *sit* i *cosy* iː *feed* ɒ *hot* ɔ *pore* ɔː *no* ʌ *run* ʊ *put*

cephalo- /ˈsefələʊ/ *combining form* (also **cephal-** before a vowel) forming nouns and adjectives concerning the head or skull. [from Greek *kephalē* head]

ceph·al·om·etry /sefəˈlɒmətri/ *noun Med.* measurement of the head. ☐ **ceph·alo·met·ric** /-ˈmetrɪk/ *adjective*

ceph·alo·pod /ˈsefələˌpɒd/ *noun* any mollusc of the class Cephalopoda, having a well-developed head surrounded by tentacles, e.g. octopus, squid, and cuttlefish. [Greek *kephalē* head + *pous podos* foot]

ceph·alo·spor·in /ˌsefələˈspɔːrɪn/ *noun* any of a class of semi-synthetic antibiotics derived from a mould of the genus *Cephalosporium*. [from modern Latin *Cephalosporium* + -IN]

ceph·alo·thor·ax /ˌsefələˈθɔːraks/ *noun* (*pl.* **-thor·aces** /-θɔrəˌsiːz/ or **-thor·ax·es**) *Anat.* the fused head and thorax of a spider, crab, or other arthropod.

-cephalous /ˈsefələs/ *combining form* -headed (*brachycephalous*; *dolichocephalic*). [Greek *kephalē* head]

Ceph·eid /ˈsiːfiɪd, ˈsefiɪd/ *noun* (in full **Cepheid variable**) *Astronomy* any of a class of variable stars with regular cycles of brightness, which can be used to measure distances. [named after *Delta Cephei*, which typifies the class]

Ceph·eus /ˈsiːfiəs, -fjuːs/ a constellation near the north celestial pole. [Latin, from Greek *Kēpheus*, a legendary king of Ethiopia, husband of Cassiopeia and father of Andromeda]

cer·am·ic /səˈramɪk/ ● *adjective* **1** designating or pertaining to hard brittle substances produced by the process of strong heating of a non-metallic mineral, esp. clay (*a ceramic bowl*). **2** of or relating to pottery (*the ceramic arts*). ● *noun* **1** a ceramic article or product. **2** a substance, esp. clay, used to make ceramic articles. [Greek *keramikos* from *keramos* pottery]

cer·ami·cist /səˈramɪsɪst/ *noun* (also **cer·am·ist** /ˈserəmɪst, səˈramɪst/) a person who makes ceramics.

cer·am·ics /səˈramɪks/ *plural noun* **1** ceramic products collectively (*exhibition of ceramics*). **2** (usu. treated as *sing.*) the art of making ceramic articles.

Ceram Sea /ˈseirəm/ (also **Seram Sea**) the part of the W Pacific Ocean at the centre of the Molucca Islands.

cer·as·tes /səˈrastiːz/ *noun* (*pl.* same) any viper of the genus *Cerastes*, of N Africa, esp. the horned viper *C. cerastes* having a sharp upright spike over each eye and moving forward in a diagonal motion. [Latin from Greek *kerastēs* from *keras* horn]

cera·tops·ian /ˌserəˈtɒpsiən/ ● *noun* a gregarious quadrupedal herbivorous dinosaur of a group found in the Cretaceous period, including triceratops. It had a large beaded and horned head and a bony frill protecting the neck. ● *adjective* of or relating to the ceratopsians. [modern Latin *Ceratopsia* (plural) from Greek *keras, kerat-* 'horn' + *ops* 'face' + -AN]

Cer·ber·us /ˈsɜːbərəs/ **1** *Gk Myth* a monstrous watchdog with three (or fifty) heads, which guarded the entrance to Hades; one of the twelve labours of Hercules was to bring him up from the underworld. **2** a person who vigorously protects something from all who would attempt to take it.

cer·caria /sɜːˈkeriə/ *noun* (*pl.* **-iae** /-iiː/) *Zool. & Med.* a free-swimming larval stage in which a parasitic fluke passes from an intermediate host (often a snail) to another intermediate host or to the final vertebrate host. [modern Latin, formed irregularly from Greek *kerkos* 'tail']

cer·cus /ˈsɜːkəs/ *noun* (*pl.* **cerci** /-kai/) *Zool.* either of a pair of small appendages at the end of the abdomen of some insects and other arthropods. [modern Latin, from Greek *kerkos* 'tail']

cere /siːr/ *noun* a waxy fleshy covering at the base of the upper beak in some birds, e.g. parrots, birds of prey. [Latin *cera* wax]

cer·eal /ˈsiːriəl/ ● *noun* **1** (usu. in *pl.*) **a** any kind of grain used for food. **b** any grass producing this, e.g. wheat, corn, rye, etc. **2** a breakfast food made from a cereal. ● *adjective* of edible grain or products of it. [Latin *cerealis* from *Ceres* goddess of agriculture]

cereal bar *noun* a granola bar or a small oatmeal-cookie-like bar, usu. with a fruit filling.

cereal cream *noun Cdn* cream containing 10% milk fat.

cere·bel·lum /ˌserəˈbeləm/ *noun* (*pl.* **cere·bel·lums** or **cere·bel·la** /-lə/) the part of the brain at the back of the skull in vertebrates, which coordinates and regulates muscular activity. ☐ **cere·bel·lar** *adjective* [Latin diminutive of CEREBRUM]

ce·re·bral /səˈriːbrəl, ˈserəbrəl/ *adjective* **1** of the brain. **2** intellectual rather than emotional. **3** = RETROFLEX 1. ☐ **ce·re·bral·ly** *adverb* [Latin *cerebrum* brain]

cerebral cortex *noun* the intricately folded outer layer of the cerebrum.

cerebral hemisphere *noun* each of the two halves of the vertebrate cerebrum.

cerebral palsy *noun* a condition marked by weakness and impaired coordination of the limbs, esp. caused by damage to the brain before or at birth.

cere·bra·tion /ˌserəˈbreɪʃən/ *noun* working of the brain. ☐ **cere·brate** /ˈserəˌbreɪt/ *intransitive verb*

cerebro- /səˈriːbrəʊ/ *combining form* brain (*cerebrospinal*).

cere·bro·spin·al /səˈriːbrəʊˈspainəl/ *adjective* of the brain and spine.

cerebrospinal fluid *noun* a clear fluid surrounding the brain and spinal cord. Abbr.: **CSF**.

cere·bro·vascu·lar /ˌserəbrəʊˈvaskjʊlər/ *adjective* of the brain and its blood vessels.

ce·re·brum /səˈriːbrəm, ˈserə-/ *noun* (*pl.* **ce·re·bra** /-brə/) the principal part of the brain in vertebrates, located in the front area of the skull, which integrates complex sensory and neural functions. [Latin, = brain]

cere·cloth /ˈsiːrklɒθ/ *noun hist.* waxed cloth used as a waterproof covering or (esp.) as a shroud. [earlier *cered cloth* from *cere* to wax, from Latin *cerare* from *cera* wax]

Cere·dig·ion /ˌkerəˈdɪgiən/ a county of west central Wales; administrative centre, Aberaeron.

cere·ment /ˈsiːrmənt/ *noun* (usu. in *pl.*) *archaic* grave clothes; cerecloth. [first used by Shakespeare in *Hamlet* (1602): apparently from CERECLOTH]

cere·mon·ial /ˌserəˈmoːniəl/ ● *adjective* **1** concerning or used in ritual or ceremony. **2** formal (*a ceremonial bow*). ● *noun* **1** a system of rites etc. to be used esp. at a formal or religious occasion. **2** one of these rites. ☐ **cere·mon·ial·ism** *noun* **cere·mon·ial·ist** *noun* **cere·mon·ial·ly** *adverb*

cere·moni·ous /ˌserɪˈmoːniəs/ *adjective* behaving or performed in a formal, ritualistic, or elaborate way. ☐ **cere·moni·ous·ly** *adverb* **cere·moni·ous·ness** *noun*

cere·mony /ˈserəˌmoːni/ *noun* (*pl.* **-ies**) **1** a formal religious or public rite, observance, or occasion, esp. celebrating a particular event or anniversary. **2** formalities, esp. of an empty or ritualistic kind (*ceremony of exchanging compliments*). **3** excessively polite behaviour (*bowed low with great ceremony*). ☐ **stand on ceremony** insist on the observance of formalities. **without ceremony** informally. [Latin *caerimonia* religious worship]

Cerenkov radiation /tʃeˈrenkɒf/ *noun* (also **Cherenkov radiation**) the electromagnetic radiation emitted by particles moving in a medium at speeds faster than that of light in the same medium. [CHERENKOV]

Ceres /ˈsiːriːz/ **1** *Rom. Myth* an ancient Italian goddess of agriculture, commonly identified in antiquity with Demeter. **2** *Astronomy* the first asteroid to be discovered, found by the Italian astronomer Giuseppe Piazzi (1746–1826) on 1 Jan. 1801.

ce·rise /səˈriːz, -ˈriːs/ ● *adjective* of a dark clear red. ● *noun* this colour. [French, = CHERRY]

cer·ium /ˈsiːriəm/ *noun Chem.* a silvery metallic element of the lanthanide series occurring naturally in various minerals and used in the manufacture of lighter flints. Symbol: **Ce**; at. no.: 58. [named after the asteroid *Ceres*, discovered (1801) about the same time as this]

Cer·lox *noun proprietary Cdn* a type of reusable plastic spiral binding with teeth that lock into rectangular holes punched in the paper.

cer·met /ˈsɜːrmet/ *noun* a heat-resistant material made of ceramic and sintered metal. [*ceramic* + *metal*]

CERN /sɜːrn/ *abbreviation* European Laboratory for Particle Physics. [French *Conseil Européen pour la Recherche Nucléaire*, its former title]

cert *noun slang* (esp. **dead cert**) **1** an event or result regarded as certain to happen. **2** a racehorse etc. regarded as certain to win. [abbreviation of CERTAIN, CERTAINTY]

cert. *abbreviation* **1** certificate. **2** certified.

cer·tain /ˈsɜːrtən/ ● *adjective* **1 a** (often foll. by *of*, or *that* + clause) confident, convinced (*certain that I put it here*). **b** (often foll. by *that* + clause) indisputable; known for sure (*it is certain that he is guilty*). **2** (often foll. by *to* + infin.) **a** that may be relied on to happen (*it is certain to rain*). **b** destined (*certain to become a star*). **3** definite, unfailing, reliable (*a certain indication of the coming storm*). **4** (of a person, place, etc.) that might be specified, but is not (*a certain lady*; *of a certain age*). **5** some though not much (*a certain reluctance*). **6** (of a person, place, etc.) existing, though probably unknown to the reader or hearer (*a certain John Smith*). ● **pronoun** (as *pl.*) some but not all (*certain of them were wounded*). □ **for certain** without doubt. **make certain** = MAKE SURE (see SURE). [Old French, ultimately from Latin *certus* settled]

cer·tain·ly *adverb* **1** undoubtedly, definitely. **2** confidently. **3** (in affirmative answer to a question or command) yes; by all means.

cer·tain·ty *noun* (*pl.* **-ties**) **1 a** an undoubted fact. **b** a certain prospect (*his return is a certainty*). **2** (often foll. by *of*, or *that* + clause) an absolute conviction (*has a certainty of his own worth*). **3** (often foll. by *to* + infin.) a thing or person that may be relied on (*a certainty to win the game*). □ **for a certainty** beyond the possibility of doubt.

cer·ti·fi·able /ˌsɜrtɪˈfaɪəbəl/ *adjective* **1** able or needing to be certified. **2** *informal* insane.

cer·tifi·cate /sɜrˈtɪfɪkɪt/ ● *noun* a formal document attesting a fact, esp. birth, marriage, or death, a medical condition, a level of achievement, a fulfillment of requirements, ownership of shares, etc. ● *transitive verb* /-ˌkeɪt/ (esp. as **cer·tifi·cat·ed** *adjective*) provide with or license or attest by a certificate. □ **cer·tifi·ca·tion** /ˌsɜrtɪfɪˈkeɪʃən/ *noun* [French *certificat* or medieval Latin *certificatum* from *certificare*: see CERTIFY]

certified cheque *noun* a cheque the validity of which is guaranteed by a bank.

certified general accountant *noun Cdn* a person trained and licensed to practise accounting. Abbr.: **CGA**.

certified mail *noun N Amer.* a postal service which requires the receiver to sign on delivery, and which provides the sender with confirmation of delivery.

certified management accountant *noun* (in Canada) an accountant qualified to manage the finances of an organization for internal purposes. Abbr.: **CMA**.

cer·tify /ˈsɜrtɪfaɪ/ *transitive verb* (**-fies**, **-fied**) **1** make a formal statement of; attest; attest to (*certified that he had witnessed the crime*). **2 a** declare by certificate that a person is qualified or competent (*certified as a bookkeeper*). **b** declare by certificate that something has met esp. safety standards (*the car has been certified*). **3** officially declare insane (*he should be certified*). □ **cer·ti·fied** *adjective* [Old French *certifier* from medieval Latin *certificare* from Latin *certus* certain]

cer·tior·ari /ˌsɜrʃiˈoːrɑri/ *noun Law* a writ from a higher court requesting the records of a case tried in a lower court for purposes of judicial review. [Late Latin passive of *certiorare* inform, from *certior* comparative of *certus* certain]

cer·ti·tude /ˈsɜrtɪˌtuːd, -ˌtjuːd/ *noun* **1** a feeling of absolute certainty or conviction. **2** a belief held with absolute certainty. [Late Latin *certitudo* from *certus* certain]

ceru·lean /səˈruːliən/ *literary* ● *adjective* deep blue like a clear sky. ● *noun* this colour. [Latin *caeruleus* sky blue, from *caelum* sky]

ceru·men /səˈruːmən/ *noun* the yellow waxy substance in the outer ear; earwax. □ **ceru·min·ous** *adjective* [modern Latin from Latin *cera* wax]

Cer·van·tes /sɜrˈvæntiːz, -teiz, ser-, -vɒn-/ **Mi·guel de** (1547–1616) (full surname Cervantes Saavedra), Spanish novelist and dramatist. His *Don Quixote* (1605, 1615), a satire on chivalric romances, tells the story of an amiable knight who imagines himself called upon to roam the world in search of adventure, accompanied by his shrewd squire Sancho Panza.

cer·vic·al /ˈsɜrvɪkəl/ *adjective Anat.* **1** of or relating to the neck (*cervical vertebrae*). **2** of or relating to the cervix (*cervical cancer*). [French *cervical* or modern Latin *cervicalis* from Latin *cervix -icis* neck]

cervical cap *noun* a contraceptive device consisting of a small cap of a rubber-like plastic placed over the cervix to prevent the passage of sperm.

cervical collar *noun* a band worn round the neck to support it after whiplash injuries etc.

cervical screening *noun* examination of a large number of apparently healthy women for cervical cancer.

cervical smear *noun* esp. *Brit.* = PAP SMEAR.

cer·vine /ˈsɜrvaɪn/ *adjective* of or like a deer. [Latin *cervinus* from *cervus* deer]

cer·vix /ˈsɜrvɪks/ *noun* (*pl.* **cer·vi·ces** /-ˌsiːz/) *Anat.* **1** the narrow lower part of the uterus, extending into the vagina. **2** the neck. [Latin]

Cesar·ean (also **Cesar·ian**) *var. of* CAESAREAN.

ces·ium /ˈsiziəm/ *noun* (also **caes·ium**) a soft silver-white element of the alkali metal group, occurring naturally in a number of minerals, and used in photoelectric cells. Symbol: **Cs**; at. no.: 55. [as CAESIOUS (from its spectrum lines)]

cesium clock *noun* an atomic clock that uses cesium.

České Budě·jo·vice /ˌtʃeskei ˈbʊdjeˌjoːvɪtsə/ a city in the south of the Czech Republic, on the Vltava River; pop. (2001) 180,314.

cess[1] /ses/ *noun Scot., Irish,* & *Ind.* etc. a tax, a levy. [properly *sess* for obsolete *assess* n.: see ASSESS]

cess[2] /ses/ *noun Irish* □ **bad cess to** may evil befall (*bad cess to their clan*). [perhaps from CESS[1]]

ces·sa·tion /seˈseɪʃən/ *noun* a ceasing (*cessation of hostilities*). [Latin *cessatio* from *cessare* CEASE]

ces·sion /ˈseʃən/ *noun* **1** (often foll. by *of*) the ceding or giving up (of rights, property, and esp. of territory). **2** the territory etc. so ceded. [Old French *cession* or Latin *cessio* from *cedere cess-* go away]

cess·pit *noun* **1** a pit for the disposal of refuse. **2** = CESSPOOL. [*cess* in CESSPOOL + PIT[1]]

cess·pool *noun* **1** an underground container for the temporary storage of liquid waste or sewage. **2** a centre of corruption, depravity, etc. [perhaps alteration, after POOL[1], of earlier *cesperalle*, from *suspiral* vent, water pipe, from Old French *souspirail* air hole, from Latin *suspirare* breathe up, sigh (as SUB-, *spirare* breathe)]

ces·tode /ˈsestoːd/ *noun* any flatworm of the class Cestoda, including tapeworms. [Latin *cestus* from Greek *kestos* girdle]

CET *abbreviation* CENTRAL EUROPEAN TIME.

cet·acean /səˈteiʃən/ ● *noun* any marine mammal of the order Cetacea with a streamlined hairless body and dorsal blowhole for breathing, including whales, dolphins, and porpoises. ● *adjective* of cetaceans. □ **cet·aceous** *adjective* [modern Latin *Cetacea* from Latin *cetus* from Greek *kētos* whale]

cetane /ˈsiːtein/ *noun Chem.* a colourless liquid hydrocarbon of the alkane series used in standardizing ratings of diesel fuel. [Latin *cetus* whale + -ANE[2]; related compounds were isolated from spermaceti]

cetane number *noun* a measure of the ignition properties of diesel fuel.

cet·eris pari·bus /ˌsetərɪs ˈpɑriˌbʊs/ *adverb* other things being equal. [Latin]

cetol·ogy /siːˈtɒlədʒi/ *noun* the branch of zoology that deals with whales, dolphins, and porpoises. □ **cetol·o·gist** *noun* [Latin *cetus* 'whale' + -OLOGY]

Cetus /ˈsiːtəs/ *noun* a large constellation between Taurus and Aquarius. [Latin, = whale]

Ceuta /ˈseiuːtə/ a Spanish enclave on the coast of North Africa, in Morocco; pop. (2001) 71,500 (with Melilla). It consists of a free port and a military post and overlooks the Mediterranean approach to the Strait of Gibraltar.

Cé·vennes /seiˈven/ a mountain range on the southeastern edge of the Massif Central in France.

ce·viche /seˈviːtʃei/ *noun* (also **se·viche**) a Latin American dish of raw fish or seafood marinated in lime or lemon juice, usu. garnished and served as an appetizer. [Latin American Spanish *seviche*, *cebiche*]

Cey·lon /səˈlɒn/ the former name (until 1972) for SRI LANKA. □ **Cey·lon·ese** *noun & adjective*

Ceylon moss *noun* a red seaweed, *Gracilaria lichenoides*, from E India, the major source of agar.

Ceylon satinwood *noun see* SATINWOOD 1.

Ceylon tea *noun* a Pekoe tea produced in Sri Lanka.

Ceyx /ˈsiːɪks/ *Gk Myth* the husband of Alcyone.

Cé·zanne /seiˈzan/ **Paul** (1839–1906), French painter. From the 1880s his work was dominated by the use of simplified geometrical forms (the cylinder, the sphere, and the cone), which he regarded as being the structural basis of nature; he is esp. known for his landscapes, many of which depict Mont Sainte-Victoire near Aix-en-Provence, and still lifes such as *Still Life with Cupid* (1895).

CF *abbreviation* **1** cystic fibrosis. **2** Canadian Forces.

Cf *symbol Chem.* the element californium.

cf. *abbreviation* compare. [Latin *confer* imperative of *conferre* compare]

CFA *abbreviation Cdn* (*Maritimes* & *Nfld*) = COME FROM AWAY.

CFA franc *noun* the Communauté Financière Africaine franc, the chief monetary unit of several African countries, including Cameroon, Mali, Niger, and Senegal, equal to 100 centimes.

CFB *abbreviation* Canadian Forces Base.

CFC *abbreviation Chem.* chlorofluorocarbon, any of various usu. gaseous compounds of carbon, hydrogen, chlorine, and fluorine, used in refrigerants, aerosol propellants, etc., and thought to be harmful to the ozone layer in the earth's atmosphere.

Consonants: b *but*   d *dog*   f *few*   g *get*   h *her*   j *yes*   k *cat*   l *leg*   m *man*   n *no*   p *pen*   r *red*   s *sit*

CFIA *abbreviation* Canadian Food Inspection Agency.

CFL *abbreviation* Canadian Football League.

CFM *abbreviation* cubic feet per minute.

CFO *abbreviation* CHIEF FINANCIAL OFFICER.

CFR *abbreviation* Canadian Finals Rodeo.

CFS *abbreviation* **1** Canadian Forces Station. **2** CHRONIC FATIGUE SYNDROME.

cfs *abbreviation* cubic feet per second.

cg *abbreviation* centigram(s).

CGA *abbreviation* (in Canada) CERTIFIED GENERAL ACCOUNTANT.

CGI *abbreviation* computer-generated imagery.

CGIT *abbreviation* *Cdn* (in the United Church) Canadian Girls in Training.

CGS *abbreviation* Chief of General Staff.

cgs *abbreviation* centimetre-gram-second.

CGT *abbreviation* capital gains tax.

CH *abbreviation* (in the UK) Companion of Honour.

ch. *abbreviation* **1** church. **2** chapter. **3** channel.

Cha·blis /ʃaˈbliː, ʃə-, ˈʃabli/ *noun* (*pl.* same /-liːz/) **1** a dry white wine from N Burgundy. **2** *N Amer. & Austral.* any dry white wine. [*Chablis* in E France]

cha-cha (also **cha-cha-cha**) ● *noun* **1** a ballroom dance with a Latin-American rhythm. **2** music for or in the rhythm of a cha-cha. ● *intransitive verb* (**cha-chas, cha-chaed** or **cha-cha'd, cha-chaing**) dance the cha-cha. [Latin American Spanish]

Chaco see GRAN CHACO.

cha·conne /ʃaˈkɒn/ *noun Music* **1a** a musical form consisting of variations on a ground bass. **b** a musical composition in this style. **2** *hist.* a dance performed to this music. [French from Spanish *chacona*]

Chaco War a war in 1932–5 between Bolivia and Paraguay, a boundary dispute triggered by the discovery of oil in the northern part of the Gran Chaco.

Chad a landlocked country in northern central Africa; pop. (est. 2002) 8,997,237; capital, N'Djamena. Much of the country lies in the Sahel and, in the north, the Sahara Desert. The population includes several ethnic groups with a variety of languages and religions. □ **Chad·ian** *adjective & noun*

Chad, Lake a shallow lake on the borders of Chad, Niger, and Nigeria in north central Africa. Its size varies seasonally from c.10 000 sq. km (4,000 sq. miles) to c.26 000 sq. km (10,000 sq. miles).

chad·or /ˈtʃʌdʒr/ *noun* a large piece of cloth worn in some countries by Muslim women, wrapped around the body to leave only the face exposed. [Persian *chador*, Hindi *chādor*]

Chad·wick, Sir James (1891–1974), English physicist. He studied the artificial disintegration of elements such as beryllium when bombarded by alpha particles; this led to the discovery of the neutron, for which he received the 1935 Nobel Prize for physics.

chae·bol /ˈtʃeibɒl/ *noun* (*pl.* same or **chae·bols**) (in South Korea) a large esp. family-owned business conglomerate. [Korean, lit. 'money clan']

chaet·og·nath /ˈkiːtəɡˌnaθ/ *noun* any dart-shaped worm of the phylum Chaetognatha, usu. living among marine plankton, and having a head with external thorny teeth. *Also called* ARROW WORM. [modern Latin *Chaetognatha* from Greek *khaitē* long hair + *gnathos* jaw]

chafe /tʃeif/ ● *verb* **1** *transitive & intransitive* make or become sore or damaged by rubbing. **2** *transitive* rub (esp. the skin to restore warmth or sensation). **3** *transitive & intransitive* make or become annoyed; fret (*they chafed at the delay*). ● *noun* **1a** an act of chafing. **b** a sore resulting from this. **2** a state of annoyance. [Old French *chaufer*, ultimately from Latin *calefacere* from *calēre* be hot + *facere* make]

chaf·er /ˈtʃeifər/ *noun* any of various large slow-moving beetles of the family Scarabaeidae, esp. the cockchafer. [Old English *ceafor*, *cefer* from Germanic]

chaff ● *noun* **1** the husks of grain etc. separated from the seed by winnowing or threshing. **2** chopped hay and straw used as fodder. **3** lighthearted joking; banter. **4** worthless things; rubbish. **5** strips of metal foil released in the air to obstruct radar detection. ● *transitive & intransitive verb* tease; banter. □ **separate the wheat from the chaff** distinguish good from bad. □ **chaffy** *adjective* [Old English *ceaf*, *cæf* prob. from Germanic: sense 3 of *n.* & 1 of *v.* perhaps from CHAFE]

chaf·finch *noun* a common European finch, *Fringilla coelebs*, the male of which has a blue-grey head with pinkish cheeks. [Old English *ceaffinc*: see CHAFF, FINCH]

chaf·ing dish /ˈtʃeifiŋ/ *noun* a dish supported on a stand and heated from below by an alcohol burner for cooking at table. [obsolete sense of CHAFE = warm]

Cha·gall /ʃəˈɡɒl/ **Marc** (1887–1985), Russian-born French painter and graphic artist. His style of painting was influenced by Russian folk art and avant-garde art forms, and often uses rich emotive colour and dream imagery, as in *Maternity* (1913); he is also known for his book illustrations, theatre design, stained glass windows, and murals.

Chagas' disease /ˈtʃaɡəs/ (also **Chagas's disease**) *noun* a kind of sleeping sickness caused by a protozoan transmitted by bloodsucking insects. [C. *Chagas*, Brazilian physician d.1934]

Chagos Archipelago /ˈtʃaɡəs/ an island group in the Indian Ocean, formerly a dependency of Mauritius and now forming the British Indian Ocean Territory.

cha·grin /ˈʃəˈɡrɪn/ ● *noun* acute vexation or mortification. ● *transitive verb* affect with chagrin. □ **cha·grined** *adjective* [French *chagrin(er)*, of uncertain origin]

chai¹ /tʃai/ *noun* tea, esp. when made by boiling the tea leaves with milk, sugar, and cardamom. [ultimately from Chinese *ch'a* tea, possibly through Russian *tchaï*]

chai² /ʃe/ *noun* a shed for aging wine. [French, from Poitou dialect for *quai* quay]

Chain, Sir Ernst Boris (1906–79), German-born English biochemist (*see* FLOREY).

chain ● *noun* **1 a** a connected flexible series of esp. metal links. **b** something resembling this (*formed a human chain*). **c** such a device used to impart motion from the pedals of a bicycle to the rear wheel. **2** (in *pl.*) **a** fetters used to confine prisoners. **b** any restraining force. **3** a sequence, series, or set (*chain of events*; *mountain chain*; *food chain*). **4** a group of associated hotels, stores, restaurants, newspapers, etc., esp. with the same owners or management. **5** a badge of office in the form of a chain worn around the neck (*mayoral chain*). **6** *Surveying* **a** a jointed measuring line consisting of one hundred linked metal rods. **b** its length (66 ft., approx. 20 m). **7** *Chem.* a group of (esp. carbon) atoms bonded in sequence in a molecule. **8** a figure in a quadrille or similar dance. **9** (in *pl.*) a set of linked chains fastened around a vehicle's tires to prevent skidding in snow. **10** a chain for fastening a door to its jamb as a security device. ● *verb* **1** *transitive* (often foll. by *up*) secure or confine with a chain. **2** *transitive* confine or restrict (a person) (*chained to her desk till the dictionary's finished*). **3** *transitive & intransitive Computing* link (a file etc.) or be linked with another by the inclusion in each item of an address by which a successor may be located. □ **pull** (or **jerk** or **yank**) **someone's chain** *N Amer. informal* tease someone, typically by leading them to believe something untrue. [Old French *cha(e)ine* from Latin *catena*]

chain drive *noun* a system of transmission by endless chains.

chain fern *noun* a fern of wet places of the genus *Woodwardia* with spores clustered in chain-like rows.

chain gang *noun* a team of convicts chained together and forced to work in the open air.

chain letter *noun* one of a sequence of letters the recipient of which is requested to send copies to a specific number of other people.

chain-link *adjective* made of wire in a diamond-shaped mesh (*chain-link fence*).

chain mail *noun* armour made of interlaced rings.

chain·man *noun* (*pl.* **-men**) (also **chain·er**) *N Amer.* a member of a survey party who holds the measuring chain.

chain of command *noun* a hierarchical arrangement in an organization through which orders are carried out.

chain pickerel *noun* a N American pike, *Esox niger*, of the eastern seaboard, with markings resembling chain links on the flanks.

chain reaction *noun* **1** *Physics* a self-sustaining nuclear reaction, esp. one in which a neutron from a fission reaction initiates a series of these reactions. **2** *Chem.* a self-sustaining molecular reaction in which intermediate products initiate further reactions. **3** a series of events, each caused by the previous one.

chain·saw ● *noun* a motor-driven saw with teeth on an endless chain. ● *transitive verb* (**chain·sawed, chain·saw·ing**) cut with a chainsaw.

chain-smoke *transitive & intransitive verb* smoke (cigarettes etc.) continually, esp. lighting each from the stub of the last one smoked. □ **chain-smoker** *noun* **chain-smoking** *noun*

chain stitch *noun* an ornamental embroidery or crochet stitch resembling chains.

chain store *noun* one of a series of stores owned by one company and selling the same sort of goods.

chair ● *noun* **1** a separate seat for one person, of various forms, usu. having a back. **2 a** a professorship (*offered the chair in physics*). **b** a seat of authority, esp. on a board of directors. **c** a position as a musician in an orchestra. **3 a** a chairperson. **b** the seat or office of a chairperson (*will you take the chair?; I'm in the chair*). **4** *US* = ELECTRIC CHAIR. **5** *hist.* = SEDAN CHAIR (see SEDAN). ● *transitive verb* **1** act as chairperson of or preside over (a meeting). **2** *Brit.* carry (a person) aloft in a chair or in a sitting position, in triumph. **3** install in a chair, esp. as a position of authority. □ **take a chair** sit down. [Old French *chaiere* from Latin *cathedra* from Greek *kathedra*: see CATHEDRAL]

chair·lift *noun* a series of chairs on an endless cable for carrying passengers up and down a mountain etc.

chair·man *noun* (*pl.* **-men**) **1** a person chosen to preside over a meeting. **2** the permanent president of a committee, a board of directors, a company, etc. **3** (**Chairman**) (since 1949) the leading figure in the Chinese Communist Party. **4** the master of ceremonies at an entertainment etc. □ **chair·man·ship** *noun*

chair·person *noun* (*pl* **-persons** or **-people**) a chairman or chairwoman (used as a neutral alternative).

chair rail *noun N Amer.* a moulding around an inside wall, at about the height of the top of a chair back, to prevent marks on the wall when chairs are pushed against it.

chair·woman *noun* (*pl.* **-women**) a female chairperson.

chaise /ʃeiz/ *noun* **1** *esp. hist.* a horse-drawn carriage for one or two persons, esp. one with a folding top and two wheels. **2** = POST-CHAISE. **3** = CHAISE LONGUE. [French var. of *chaire*, formed as CHAIR]

chaise longue /ʃeiz 'lɑundʒ, -lɒŋ/ *noun* (*pl.* **chaise longues** or **chaises longues**) (also **chaise lounge**) a chair with an extended seat on which to rest the legs. [French, lit. 'long chair']

chak·ra /'tʃʌkrə/ *noun* (in yoga) each of the seven centres of spiritual power in the human body. [Sanskrit *cakra* wheel]

cha·laza /kə'leizə/ *noun* (*pl.* **cha·lazae** /-ziː/ or **-lazas**) each of two twisted membranous strips joining the yolk to the ends of an egg. [modern Latin from Greek, = hailstone]

Chal·ce·don /kal'sɪdən/ a former city on the Bosporus in Asia Minor, now a district of Istanbul. □ **Chal·ce·don·ian** /ˌkalsɪ'dɔːniən/ *adjective*

chal·ce·dony /kal'sedəni/ *noun* a type of quartz occurring in several different forms, e.g. onyx, agate, tiger's eye, etc. □ **chal·ce·don·ic** /ˌkalsə'dɒnɪk/ *adjective* [Latin *c(h)alcedonius* from Greek *khalkēdōn*]

chal·cid /'kalsɪd/ *noun* (in full **chalcid fly**, **chalcid wasp**) any insect of the superfamily Chalcidoidea, esp. the parasitic hymenopterous ones of the family Chalcididae. [modern Latin *Chalcis* from Greek *khalkos* copper, brass, from their metallic sheen]

chal·co·lith·ic /ˌkalkə'lɪθɪk/ *adjective Archaeology* of a prehistoric period in which both stone and bronze implements were used. [Greek *khalkos* copper + *lithos* stone]

chal·co·pyr·ite /ˌkalkə'pairɑit/ *noun* a yellow mineral consisting of a sulphide of copper and iron, which is the principal ore of copper. [Greek *khalkos* copper + PYRITE]

Chal·dea /kal'diːə/ an ancient country in what is now S Iraq inhabited by the Chaldeans, forming the southern part of Babylonia from *c.*800 to 539 BC.

Chal·dean /kal'diːən/ ● *noun* **1 a** a native of ancient Chaldea or Babylonia. **b** the language of the Chaldeans. **2** an astrologer. **3** a member of an Eastern Catholic (formerly Nestorian) Church sect in Iran etc. ● *adjective* **1** of or relating to ancient Chaldea or its people or language. **2** of or relating to astrology. **3** of or relating to the Chaldean Church in Iran etc. [Latin *Chaldaeus* from Greek *Khaldaios* from Assyrian *Kaldu*]

Chal·dee /kal'diː/ *noun* a native of ancient Chaldea. [as CHALDEAN]

cha·let /ʃa'lei/ *noun* **1** a style of wooden house, typical of the European Alps, having a steeply pitched roof with very deep overhanging eaves. **2** the main building at a ski resort, usu. with rental facilities and a restaurant. **3** *Cdn* (*Que.*) a holiday cottage. [Swiss French, diminutive of Old French *chasel* from Latin *casa* hut, cottage]

Cha·leur Bay /ʃa'lɜr/ (also **Baie des Cha·leurs**, **Bay Chaleur**) a bay of the Gulf of St. Lawrence, situated between the Gaspé Peninsula and New Brunswick. [French *chaleur* heat, with reference to the hot weather in July 1534, when it was named]

Cha·lia·pin /ʃa'liɒpɪn/ **Feo·dor Ivan·ovich** (1873–1938), Russian operatic bass, widely renowned as the greatest singing actor of his age.

chal·ice /'tʃalɪs/ *noun Christianity* a wine cup used in the Eucharist. [Old French from Latin *calix -icis* cup]

chalk /tʃɒk/ ● *noun* **1** a white soft earthy limestone (calcium carbonate) formed from the skeletal remains of sea creatures. **2 a** a similar substance (calcium sulphate), sometimes coloured, used for writing or drawing. **b** a piece of this (*take a new chalk from the box*). **3** a series of strata consisting mainly of chalk. **4** *Billiards* a small blue chalklike cube, rubbed against the tip of a pool cue to reduce slippage. **5** a kind of steatite used for marking cloth and removing grease and, in powder form, as a dry lubricant. ● *transitive verb* rub, mark, draw, or write with chalk. □ **as different as chalk and** (or **from**) **cheese** fundamentally different. **by a long chalk** *Brit.* by far. **chalk and talk** traditional teaching methods (employing blackboard, chalk, and interlocution). **chalk out** sketch or plan a thing to be accomplished. **chalk up 1** (foll. by *to*) attribute, charge (*chalk it up to my upbringing*). **2** register (a point scored, a success, etc.). □ **chalk·like** *adjective* [Old English *cealc*, ultimately from West Germanic from Latin CALX; *by a long chalk* from the use of chalk to mark the score in games]

chalk·board *noun N Amer.* = BLACKBOARD.

chalk line *noun* **1 a** an instrument for marking straight lines, consisting of a chalk-covered cord stretched between two points. **b** a line marked with this. **2** any line marked with chalk, e.g. those on a baseball diamond, or those made on textiles by garment makers.

chalk pit *noun* a quarry in which chalk is dug.

chalk-stripe *noun* a pattern of thin white stripes on a dark background. □ **chalk-striped** *adjective*

chalk talk *noun N Amer. informal* an instructional talk, lecture, etc. in which the speaker uses a blackboard and chalk.

chalky *adjective* (**chalk·i·er**, **chalk·i·est**) **1 a** abounding in chalk. **b** white as chalk. **2** having the consistency of chalk. □ **chalk·i·ness** *noun*

chal·lah /'hɒlə/ *noun* (*pl.* **-lahs**, **-loth**) a loaf of white leavened egg bread, often braided, traditionally baked to celebrate the Jewish Sabbath. [Hebrew *ḥalah*]

chal·lenge ● *noun* **1 a** a summons to take part in a contest or a trial of strength etc. **b** a summons to prove or justify something. **2 a** a demanding or difficult task (*getting out of bed on time is a challenge*). **b** a difficult but stimulating task (*welcomed the challenge of his new job*). **3** *Law* an objection made to a jury member. **4** a call to respond, esp. a sentry's call for a password etc. **5** an invitation to a sporting contest, esp. one issued to a reigning champion. **6** *Med.* a test of immunity after immunization treatment. ● *transitive verb* **1** (often foll. by *to* + infin.) **a** invite to take part in a contest, game, debate, duel, etc. **b** invite to prove or justify something. **2** dispute, deny (*I challenge that remark*). **3** stretch, stimulate (*challenges him to produce his best*). **4** (of a sentry) call to respond. **5** claim (attention, etc.). **6** *Law* object to (a jury member, evidence, etc.). **7** *Med.* test by a challenge. □ **chal·lenge·able** *adjective* **chal·len·ger** *noun* [Old French *c(h)alenge*, *c(h)alenger* from Latin *calumnia calumniari* calumny]

chal·lenged *adjective* **1** (often in *combination*) (of a person) disabled (*physically challenged*). **2** (in *combination*) *jocular* not having a specified quality, e.g. *vertically challenged* for short.

Challenger Deep /'tʃalɒndʒɜr/ the deepest part (11 022 m, 36,161 ft.) of the Mariana Trench in the N Pacific, discovered by HMS *Challenger II* in 1948.

chal·len·ging *adjective* demanding; stimulatingly difficult.

chal·lis /ʃa'liː, 'ʃali/ *noun* a lightweight soft clothing fabric. [perhaps from a surname]

Chal·mers /'tʃɒmɜrz/ **Floyd (Sher·man)** (1898–1993), Canadian publishing executive and arts patron, who established the Floyd S. Chalmers Foundation (1964) to promote and develop the performing arts in Canada.

cha·lyb·eate /kə'lɪbiət, -'lɪbieɪt/ *adjective* (of mineral water etc.) impregnated with iron salts. [modern Latin *chalybeatus* from Latin *chalybs* from Greek *khalups -ubos* steel]

chamae·phyte /'kaməˌfaɪt/ *noun* a plant whose buds are on or near the ground. [Greek *khamai* on the ground + -PHYTE]

cham·ber *noun* **1 a** a hall used by a legislative or judicial body. **b** the body that meets in it. **c** any of the houses of a parliament (*Chamber of Deputies; Red Chamber*). **2** (in *pl.*) *esp. Brit.* lawyers' offices, esp. (in the UK) those used by barristers in the Inns of Court. **3** (in *pl.*) a judge's room used for hearing cases not needing to be taken in court. **4** *poet.* or *archaic* a room, esp. a bedroom. **5** *Music* (*attributive*) of or for a small group of instruments (*chamber orchestra; chamber music*). **6** an enclosed space in machinery etc. (esp. the part of a gun that contains the cartridge or shell). **7 a** a cavity in a plant or in the body of an animal. **b** a compartment in a structure. **8** a space, cavity, or room constructed for a specific purpose (*decompression chamber*). **9** = CHAMBER POT. □ **cham·bered** *adjective* [Old French *chambre* from Latin CAMERA]

Cham·ber·lain /ˈtʃeɪmbərlɪn/ **1 Sir (Jo·seph) Aus·ten** (1863–1937), English Conservative statesman, foreign secretary 1924–9. He helped to negotiate the Locarno Pact and was awarded the Nobel Peace Prize in 1925. **2** his father, **Jo·seph** (1836–1914), English Liberal statesman and colonial secretary 1895–1903, who was a spokesman for imperialist interests, and played a leading role in the handling of the Second Boer War. **3** his son, **(Ar·thur) Nev·ille** (1869–1940), English Conservative politician, prime minister 1937–40. As prime minister he pursued a policy of appeasement towards Germany, Italy, and Japan, intending to postpone war until Britain had rearmed; he was forced to prepare for war when Hitler invaded Czechoslovakia in 1939, and when his war leadership proved inadequate he was replaced by Winston Churchill. **4 Owen** (b.1920), US physicist. He worked on the Manhattan project during the war, after which he investigated subatomic particles, discovering the antiproton with E. G. Segrè in 1955; they shared the Nobel Prize for physics in 1959.

cham·ber·lain /ˈtʃeɪmbərlɪn/ *noun* **1** an officer managing the household of a sovereign or a great noble. **2** the treasurer of a corporation etc. □ **cham·ber·lain·ship** *noun* [Old French *chamberlain* etc. from Frankish from Latin *camera* CAMERA]

chamber·maid *noun* **1** a housemaid at a hotel etc. **2** *N Amer.* a housemaid.

chamber of commerce *noun* an association to promote local commercial interests.

Chamber of Deputies *noun* the lower legislative assembly in some parliaments.

chamber of horrors *noun* a place full of horrors (originally a room of criminals etc. in Madame Tussaud's waxworks).

chamber pot *noun* a receptacle for urine etc., used in a bedroom.

Cham·bly /ʃɑ̃ˈbliː/ a city in south central Quebec, situated on the Richelieu, southeast of Montreal; pop. (2001) 20,342. [see FORT CHAMBLY]

Chambly Canal a historic canal in south central Quebec, situated on the Richelieu, linking Chambly and Saint-Jean-sur-Richelieu. Opened in 1843, the canal was formerly of great commercial importance, particularly with respect to the forest industry in Quebec.

cham·bray /ʃɒmˈbreɪ/ *noun* a linen-finished gingham cloth with a white weft and a coloured warp. [irreg. from *Cambrai*: see CAMBRIC]

cham·bré /ˈʃɑ̃breɪ/ *adjective* (of red wine) brought to room temperature. [French, past participle of *chambrer* from *chambre* room: see CHAMBER]

cha·meleon /kəˈmiːliən/ *noun* **1** any of a family of small lizards having grasping tails, long tongues, protruding eyes, and the power of changing colour. **2** a variable or inconstant person or thing. □ **cha·mele·on·ic** /-ˈɒnɪk/ *adjective* [Latin from Greek *khamaileōn* from *khamai* on the ground + *leōn* lion]

cham·fer /ˈtʃamfər/ ● *transitive verb* bevel symmetrically (a right-angled edge or corner). ● *noun* a bevelled surface at an edge or corner. [back-formation from *chamfering* from French *chamfrain* from *chant* edge (CANT²) + *fraint* broken, from Old French *fraindre* break, from Latin *frangere*]

cham·ois *noun* **1** /ˈʃamwɒ/ (*pl.* same /-wɒz/) an agile goat-antelope, *Rupicapra rupicapra*, native to the mountains of Europe and Asia. **2** /ˈʃami/ (*pl.* same /-iːz/) **a** a soft pliable leather from sheep, goats, deer, etc. **b** a piece of this for polishing etc. [French]

chamo·mile *var. of* CAMOMILE.

Cha·mo·nix /ʃamɔˈniː/ (in full **Chamonix-Mont-Blanc** /mɔ̃blɑ̃/) a ski resort at the foot of Mont Blanc, in the Alps of E France; pop. (1999) 9,830.

champ¹ *noun informal* a champion. [abbreviation]

champ² = CHOMP. [prob. imitative]

Cham·pagne¹ /ʃamˈpeɪn/ a region and former province of NE France, which now corresponds to the Champagne-Ardenne administrative region. The region is noted for the white sparkling wine first produced there in about 1700.

Cham·pagne² /ʃɑ̃ˈpɒnjə/ **Claude** (1891–1965), Canadian composer and educator. His work is characterized by its romanticism, and includes the *Symphonie gaspésienne* (1945), *Suite canadienne* (1927), and *Altitude* (1959).

cham·pagne /ʃamˈpeɪn/ *noun* **1 a** a white sparkling wine from Champagne. **b** a similar wine from elsewhere. ¶ Strictly speaking, use in sense b is incorrect. **2** a pale cream or straw colour. [CHAMPAGNE¹]

Champagne-Ardenne /ʃam.peɪnɑrˈden/ a region of NE France, comprising part of the Ardennes forest and the vine-growing area of Champagne.

champagne socialist *noun* a person who espouses socialist ideals while enjoying a wealthy and luxurious lifestyle.

cham·paign /ʃamˈpeɪn/ *noun literary* an expanse of open country. [Old French *champagne* from Late Latin *campania*: compare CAMPAIGN]

cham·pers /ˈʃampərz/ *noun* esp. *Brit. slang* champagne.

cham·perty /ˈtʃampərti/ *noun* (*pl.* **-ties**) *Law* an illegal agreement in which a person not naturally interested in a lawsuit finances it with a view to sharing the disputed property. □ **cham·per·tous** *adjective* [Anglo-French *champartie* from Old French *champart* feudal lord's share of produce, from Latin *campus* field + *pars* part]

Cham·pigny /ʃɑ̃piˈnjiː/ **Jean Bo·chart de** (d.1720), French chevalier, intendant of New France 1686–1702, who was noted as an administrator and for his work strengthening the defence of New France.

cham·pion ● *noun* **1** (often *attributive*) a person (esp. in a sport or game), animal, plant, etc., that has defeated or surpassed all rivals in a competition etc. **2 a** a person who fights or argues for a cause or on behalf of another person. **b** *hist.* a knight etc. who fought in single combat on behalf of a king etc. ● *transitive verb* support the cause of, defend, argue in favour of. ● *adjective informal* first-class, splendid. [Old French from medieval Latin *campio -onis* fighter, from Latin *campus* field]

cham·pion·ship *noun* **1** (often in *pl.*) a contest for the position of champion in a sport etc. **2** the position of champion over all rivals. **3** the advocacy or defence (of a cause etc.).

Cham·plain /ʃamˈpleɪn/ **Sam·uel de** (1567–1635), French explorer and governor of New France 1633–5. He made his first voyage to Canada in 1603, and between 1604 and 1607 explored the eastern coast of N America; in 1608 he was sent to establish a settlement at Quebec, where he developed alliances with the Aboriginal peoples for trade and defence, and extensively explored the Canadian interior.

Champlain, Lake /ˈʃampleɪn/ a lake straddling the Canada-US border between Quebec, New York State, and Vermont. [CHAMPLAIN]

champ·levé /ˌʃɑ̃ləˈveɪ/ ● *noun* a type of enamelwork in which hollows made in a metal surface are filled with coloured enamels. ● *adjective* of or relating to champlevé (compare CLOISONNÉ). [French, = raised field]

Cham·pol·lion /ʃɑ̃pɒljɔ̃/ **Jean-François** (1790–1832), French Egyptologist. A pioneer in the study of ancient Egypt, he is best known for his success in deciphering some of the hieroglyphic inscriptions on the Rosetta Stone in 1822.

Champs Ély·sées /ˌʃɑ̃zeiliˈzei/ an avenue in Paris, leading from the Place de la Concorde to the Arc de Triomphe. It is noted for its fashionable shops and restaurants.

chana /tʃʌnə/ *noun* (in Indian cuisine) chick peas, esp. when roasted and prepared as a snack. [Hindi *canā*]

chance ● *noun* **1 a** a possibility (*just a chance we will catch the train*). **b** (often in *pl.*) probability (*chances are that you will be promoted*). **2** a risk (*have to take a chance*). **3 a** an unplanned occurrence (*just a chance that they met*). **b** the absence of design or discoverable cause (*leave nothing to chance*). **4** an opportunity (*didn't have a chance to speak to him*). **5** the way things happen; fortune; luck (*we'll just leave it to chance*). **6** (often **Chance**) the course of events regarded as a power; fate (*blind Chance rules the universe*). ● *adjective* fortuitous, accidental (*a chance meeting*). ● *verb* **1** *transitive informal* risk (*we'll chance it and go*). **2** *intransitive* (often foll. by *to* + infin.) happen without intention (*I chanced to find it*). □ **by any chance** as it happens; perhaps. **by chance** without design; unintentionally. **chance one's arm** *Brit. informal* make an attempt though unlikely to succeed. **chance on** (or **upon**) happen to find, meet, etc. **no chance** there is no possibility of that. **on the chance** (often foll. by *of*, or *that* + clause) in view of the possibility. **stand a chance** have a prospect of success etc. **take a chance** (or **chances**) behave riskily; risk failure. **take a** (or **one's**) **chance on** (or **with**) consent to take the consequences of; trust to luck. [Anglo-French *ch(e)aunce*, Old French *chëance chëoir* fall, ultimately from Latin *cadere*]

chan·cel /ˈtʃansəl/ *noun* a part of some (esp. Anglican) churches, located near the altar, which is usu. separated from the nave by steps or enclosed by a screen. [Old French from Latin *cancelli* lattice]

chan·cel·lery /ˈtʃansələri, -sləri/ *noun* (*pl.* **-ies**) **1 a** the position, office, staff, department, etc., of a chancellor. **b** the official residence of a chancellor. **2** *US* an office attached to an embassy or consulate. [Old French *chancellerie* (as CHANCELLOR)]

chan·cel·lor /ˈtʃansələr/ *noun* **1** a State or legal official of various kinds. **2** the head of the government in Germany and Austria. **3** *Cdn & Brit.* the non-resident honorary head of a university. **4** *Catholicism* a priest in charge of a chancery. **5** *US* the president of a chancery court.

□ **chan·cellor·ship** *noun* [Old English from Anglo-French *c(h)anceler*, Old French *-ier* from Late Latin *cancellarius* porter, secretary, from *cancelli* lattice]

Chancellor of the Exchequer *noun* the finance minister of the United Kingdom.

chan·cery /ˈtʃɑːnsərɪ/ *noun* (*pl.* **-ies**) **1** an office attached to an embassy or consulate. **2** the administrative office of a Catholic diocese. **3** *Law* (**Chancery**) the Lord Chancellor's court, a division of the High Court of Justice. **4** *US* a court of equity. **5** a public record office. **6** *hist.* the records office of an order of knighthood. [Middle English, contracted from CHANCELLERY]

Chan Chan /tʃan ˈtʃan/ the capital of a pre-Inca civilization, the extensive adobe ruins of which are situated on the coast of N Peru.

chan·cre /ˈʃaŋkər/ *noun* a hard, painless ulcer developing as the primary lesion of syphilis and certain other infectious diseases. [French from Latin CANCER]

chan·croid /ˈʃaŋkrɔɪd/ *noun* a venereal infection with the bacterium *Haemophilus ducreyi*, causing enlarged, ulcerated lymph nodes of the groin.

chancy *adjective* (**chan·ci·er**, **chan·ci·est**) subject to chance; uncertain; risky. □ **chan·ci·ly** *adverb* **chan·ci·ness** *noun*

chan·de·lier /ˌʃandəˈlɪər/ *noun* an ornamental branched hanging support for several light bulbs or candles. □ **chan·de·liered** *adjective* [French from *chandelle* as CANDLE]

Chan·di·garh /ˌtʃʌndɪˈɡɑr/ **1** a Union Territory in NW India, created in 1966. **2** a city in this territory; pop. (2001) 808,000. The present city was designed in 1950 by Le Corbusier as a new capital for the Punjab, the old capital, Lahore, having been lost to Pakistan in 1947. Chandigarh is the capital of both the modern Indian state of Punjab, which lies to the west of it, and Haryana, which lies to the south of it.

Chand·ler[1] /ˈʃɑːdlər/ a town in E Quebec, on the south coast of the Gaspé peninsula; pop. (2001) 5,662. [P. *Chandler*, president of a pulp and paper company which established a mill there in 1912]

Chand·ler[2] /ˈtʃandlər/ **1 Ed·ward Baron** (1800–1880), Canadian politician, Lieutenant-Governor of New Brunswick 1878–80, Father of Confederation. At the Quebec Conference (1864) he spoke in favour of granting strong powers to the provincial governments, but was outvoted. **2 Ray·mond Thorn·ton** (1888–1959), US novelist and screenwriter. A writer of detective fiction and thrillers, he is particularly remembered as the creator of the private investigator Philip Marlowe in works such as *The Big Sleep* (1939), *Farewell, My Lovely* (1940), and *The Long Goodbye* (1953). □ **Chand·ler·esque** *adjective*

chand·ler /ˈtʃandlər/ *noun* **1** a dealer of supplies or goods for a specific purpose, esp. of boating supplies (*ship chandler*). **2** a person who makes or sells items of tallow or wax, e.g. candles, soap, etc. [Anglo-French *chaundeler* (as CANDLE)]

chand·lery /ˈtʃandlərɪ/ *noun* (*pl.* **-ies**) **1** goods sold by a chandler. **2** a chandler's store.

Chan·dra·gupta Mau·rya /ˌtʃʌndrəˈɡuptə ˈmauriə/ (*c.*325–297 BC), Indian emperor. He founded the Mauryan Empire. From his capital at Paliputra he expanded westwards, annexing provinces deep into Afghanistan from Alexander's Greek successors. The empire continued to expand after his death, but ended in 185 BC.

Chan·dra·sekhar /ˌtʃʌndrəˈsiːkər/ **Sub·rah·man·yan** (1910–95), Indian-born US astronomer. He suggested the process whereby some stars eventually collapse to form a dense white dwarf while others collapse further to form neutron stars; he shared the Nobel Prize for physics in 1983.

Cha·nel /ʃəˈnɛl/ **Gab·ri·elle Bon·heur ('Coco')** (1883–1971), French fashion designer. She is known for her simple but sophisticated designs and her range of perfumes (notably Chanel No. 5, launched in 1922), costume jewellery, and textiles.

Chanel jacket *noun* a round-necked women's jacket without lapels. [CHANEL]

Chaney /ˈtʃeɪnɪ/ **1 Lon** (born Alonso Chaney) (1883–1930), US actor. He was known as 'the Man of a Thousand Faces' for his macabre roles in horror films such as *The Hunchback of Notre Dame* (1923) and *The Phantom of the Opera* (1925). **2** his son, **Lon, Jr.** (born Creighton Chaney) (1907–73), US actor who also starred in a number of horror films, including *The Wolf Man* (1941).

Chang·an /tʃaŋ ˈan/ the former name (202 BC until AD 618) for XIAN.

Chang·chun /tʃaŋˈtʃun/ an industrial city in NE China, capital of Jilin province; pop. (2002) 2,690,300.

change ● *noun* **1 a** the act or an instance of making or becoming different. **b** an alteration or modification (*the change in her expression*).

2 a money given in exchange for money in larger units or a different currency. **b** money returned as the balance of that given in payment. **c** coins (*a pocketful of change*). **d** *N Amer.* a relatively small amount of something, esp. money (*spent $10 million and change*). **3** a new experience; variety (*time for a change*). **4 a** the substitution of one thing for another; an exchange (*change of scene*). **b** a set of clothes etc. put on in place of another. **5** (in full **change of life**) *informal* menopause. **6** (usu. in *pl.*) the different orders in which a peal of bells can be rung. **7** (**Change**) (also **'Change**) *hist.* a place where merchants etc. met to do business. **8** (of the moon) arrival at a fresh phase, esp. at the new moon. ● *verb* **1** *transitive & intransitive* undergo, show, or subject to change; make or become different (*the wig changed his appearance*; *changed from an introvert into an extrovert*). **2** *transitive* **a** take or use another instead of; go from one to another (*changed the tire*; *changed his doctor*; *changed trains*). **b** (usu. foll. by *for*) give up or get rid of in exchange (*changed the car for a van*). **3** *transitive* **a** give or get change in smaller denominations for (*can you change a twenty-dollar bill?*). **b** (foll. by *for*) exchange (a sum of money) for (*changed our dollars for pounds*). **4** *transitive & intransitive* put fresh clothes or coverings on (*change the baby*; *changed into something more comfortable*). **5** *transitive* (often foll. by *with*) give and receive, exchange (*changed places with her*; *we changed places*). **6** *intransitive* change trains etc. (*changed at Montreal*). **7** *intransitive* (of the voice) become deeper in tone. **8** *intransitive* (of the moon) arrive at a fresh phase, esp. become new. □ **change of air** a different climate; variety. **change colour** blanch or flush. **change down** *Brit.* = GEAR DOWN 3 (*see* GEAR). **change gear** engage a different gear in a vehicle. **change hands 1** pass to a different owner. **2** substitute one hand for another. **change of heart** a conversion to a different view. **change over** change from one system or situation to another. **change step** begin to keep step with the opposite leg when marching etc. **change the subject** begin talking of something different, esp. to avoid embarrassment. **change one's tune 1** voice a different opinion from that expressed previously. **2** change one's style of language or manner, esp. from an insolent to a respectful tone. **change up** *Brit.* = GEAR UP (*see* GEAR). **get no change out of** *Brit. slang* **1** fail to get information from. **2** fail to get the better of (in business etc.). **ring the changes** (**on**) vary the ways of expressing, arranging, or doing something. □ **change·ful** *adjective* **chan·ger** *noun* [Old French *change*, *changer* from Late Latin *cambiare*, Latin *cambire* barter, prob. of Celtic origin]

change·able *adjective* **1** irregular, inconstant. **2** that can change or be changed. □ **change·abil·ity** *noun* **change·able·ness** *noun* **change·ably** *adverb*

change agent *noun* a person who initiates a movement toward social or corporate change in a group.

change·less *adjective* unchanging. □ **change·less·ly** *adverb* **change·less·ness** *noun*

change·ling *noun* a child or thing believed to have been secretly substituted for another.

change of life *noun see* CHANGE *noun* 5.

change·over *noun* an act or the process of changing over.

change purse *noun* *N Amer.* a small, usu. leather, container for carrying coins.

change ringing *noun* the ringing of a set of esp. church bells in a constantly varying order. □ **change ringer** *noun*

change room *noun* (also **chan·ging room**) a room where people may change their clothes, esp. before and after physical activity.

change table *noun* (also **chan·ging table**) a table designed for use in changing a baby's diaper.

change·up *noun* *Baseball* a slow pitch, thrown with the motions of a fastball, to deceive the batter.

Chan·ging of the Guard *noun* **1** a ceremonial replacement of one body of guards by another, esp. at parliament buildings etc. **2** a profound change in management, approach, etc.

Chang·sha /tʃaŋˈʃɑ/ the capital of Hunan province in east central China; pop. (est. 2002) 1,544,700.

chan·nel[1] ● *noun* **1 a** a length of water wider than a strait, joining two larger areas. **b** the bed of a river, stream, or other watercourse. **c** the navigable part of a waterway. **d** (**the Channel**) = ENGLISH CHANNEL. **2** a medium of communication; an agency for conveying information (*through the usual channels*). **3** *Broadcasting* **a** a band of frequencies used in radio and television transmission, esp. as used by a particular station. **b** a service or station using this. **4** the course in which anything moves; a direction. **5** a tubular passage for liquid. **6** *Electronics* a lengthwise strip on recording tape etc. **7** a groove or a flute, esp. in a column. ● *transitive verb* (**chan·nelled, chan·nel·ling**;

also esp. *US* **chan·neled**, **chan·nel·ing**) **1** guide or convey through or as if through a channel (*channelled them through customs*). **2** direct (funds, energy, emotions, etc.) toward a goal. **3** act as a medium for (a spirit). **4** form channels in; groove. [Old French *chanel* from Latin *canalis* CANAL]

chan·nel² *noun Naut.* any of the broad thick planks projecting horizontally from a sailing ship's side abreast of the masts, used to widen the basis for the shrouds. [for *chain-wale*: compare *gunnel* for *gunwale*]

channel cat *noun* (in full **channel catfish**) a large edible freshwater catfish, *Ictalurus punctatus*, of central N America.

channel changer *noun* a remote control for changing the channels and adjusting the volume etc. of a television set.

Channel Country an area of SW Queensland and NE South Australia, watered intermittently by natural channels, where rich grasslands produced by the summer rains provide grazing for cattle.

Channel Islands a group of islands in the English Channel off the northwest coast of France, of which the largest are Jersey, Guernsey, and Alderney; pop. (2001) 149,800. They are the only portions of the former dukedom of Normandy that still owe allegiance to England, to which they have been attached since the Norman Conquest in 1066.

chan·nel·ize *transitive verb* (also esp. *Brit.* **-ise**) convey in, or as if in, a channel; guide. □ **chan·nel·iz·a·tion** *noun*

chan·nel·ler *noun* (also **chan·nel·er**) a person who claims to be in psychic contact with spirits or otherworldly entities; a medium.

Channel-Port aux Basques /ˈtʃanəl,pɔːr oː ˌbask/ a town situated at the southwestern tip of the island of Newfoundland, on Cabot Strait; pop. (2001) 4,637. [*Channel*, after a narrow channel at the same location, + *Port aux Basques*, prob. after Basque whalers who passed by the coast on their way to Labrador in the 16th c.]

channel surfing *noun N Amer. informal* the act of flipping from one television channel to another in rapid succession using a remote control. □ **channel surfer** *noun*

Channel Tunnel *noun* a 49-km long railway tunnel under the English Channel, linking the coasts of England and France.

chan·son /ʃɑ̃ˈsɔ̃/ *noun* a French song, usu. sung by a solo singer with minimal accompaniment and characterized by political or social commentary. [Old French from Latin *cantio(n-)* singing, from *cant-*, past participle of *canere* sing]

chanson de geste /ʃɑ̃,sɔ̃ də ˈʒest/ *noun* (pl. **chansons** pronunc. same) any of a group of medieval French epic poems. [French, = song of heroic deeds]

chan·son·nier /ˌʃɑ̃sɔnˈjei/ *noun* a singer of chansons. [French (see CHANSON)]

chan·son·ni·ère /ˌʃɑ̃sɔnˈjɛr/ *noun* a female singer of chansons. [French (see CHANSON)]

chant ● *noun* **1 a** a spoken singsong phrase, esp. one performed in unison by a crowd etc. **b** a repetitious singsong way of speaking. **2** *Music* **a** a religious song or prayer in which many of the words are sung on the same note. **b** the style of music so sung. **c** a song, esp. monotonous or repetitive. **3** a musical recitation, esp. of poetry. **4** = GREGORIAN CHANT. ● *transitive & intransitive verb* **1** intone monotonously or repetitiously, esp. in a singsong voice (*a crowd chanting slogans*). **2** sing or intone (a psalm etc.). [Old French *chanter* sing, from Latin *cantare* frequentative of *canere cant-* sing]

chant·er *noun* **1** a person who chants. **2** the pipe of a bagpipe, with finger holes, on which the melody is played.

chan·ter·elle /ˌtʃantəˈrel/ *noun* an edible fungus, *Cantharellus cibarius*, with a yellow funnel-shaped cap. [French from modern Latin *cantharellus* diminutive of *cantharus* from Greek *kantharos* a kind of drinking vessel]

chant·euse /ʃɒnˈtɜːz/ *noun* a female singer of popular songs. [French]

chan·ti·cleer /ˌtʃantɪˈkliːr, ˌtʃɒn-, ˌʃan-, ˌʃɒn-/ *noun literary* a name given to a rooster, esp. in fairy tales etc. [Old French *chantecler* (as CHANT, CLEAR), a name in *Reynard the Fox*]

Chan·tilly /ʃanˈtɪli, ˌʃɑ̃tiːˈjiː/ *noun* **1** a delicate kind of bobbin lace. **2** sweetened or flavoured whipped cream. [*Chantilly* near Paris]

chan·try /ˈtʃɑːntri/ *noun* (pl. **-tries**) **1** an endowment for a priest or priests to celebrate masses for the founder's soul. **2** the priests, chapel, altar, etc., endowed. [Old French *chanterie* from *chanter* CHANT]

chanty *var.* of SHANTY².

Cha·nu·kah *var.* of HANUKKAH.

Chao Phra·ya /ˈtʃau prəˈjɒ/ a major waterway of central Thailand, formed by the junction of the Ping and Nan rivers.

Chaos /ˈkeɪɒs/ *Gk Myth* the first created being, scarcely personified, from which came the primeval deities Gaia (Earth), Tartarus, Erebus (Darkness), and Nyx (Night). [Greek, = gaping void]

chaos /ˈkeɪɒs/ *noun* **1** utter confusion. **2** the formless matter supposed to have existed before the creation of the universe. □ **cha·ot·ic** /keiˈɒtɪk/ *adjective* **cha·ot·ic·ally** /-ˈɒtɪkli/ *adverb* [French or Latin from Greek *khaos*: -*otic* after *erotic* etc.]

chaos theory *noun* the theory that provides mathematical methods to explain the chaotic behaviour of systems, such as weather, that seem unpredictable but have an underlying order. Chaos theory shows that tiny changes in the starting conditions of a system can have enormous consequences on the state of the system later on.

chap¹ *noun informal* a man; a boy; a fellow. [abbreviation of CHAPMAN]

chap² ● *verb* (**chapped**, **chap·ping**) **1** *intransitive* (esp. of the skin; also of dry ground etc.) crack in fissures, esp. because of exposure and dryness. **2** *transitive* (of the wind, cold, etc.) cause to chap. ● *noun* (usu. in pl.) a crack in the skin. [Middle English, perhaps related to Middle Low German, Middle Dutch *kappen* chop off]

chap³ *noun* the lower jaw or half of the cheek, esp. of a pig as food. [16th c.: var. of CHOP², of unknown origin]

chap. *abbreviation* chapter.

Cha·pais /ʃaˈpei/ **Jean-Charles** (1811–85), Canadian Conservative politician, Father of Confederation. He was commissioner of works in the Great Coalition ministry of 1864–7, and attended the Quebec Conference; he later served as minister of agriculture (1867–9) and as receiver general (1869–73).

chapa·rajos /ˌʃapəˈreiɒːs, ˌtʃap-/ *plural noun N Amer.* = CHAPS. [Mexican Spanish, from *chaparrerras* from *chaparra* (with reference to protection from thorny vegetation: see CHAPARRAL); probably influenced by Spanish *aparejo* 'equipment']

chap·ar·ral /ˌʃapəˈral, ˌtʃap-/ *noun N Amer.* vegetation consisting chiefly of tangled shrubs and thorny bushes in southwestern North America. [Spanish from *chaparra* dwarf evergreen oak]

cha·pati /tʃəˈpɒti, -ˈpati/ *noun* (also **cha·pat·ti**) (pl. **-patis**) a flat thin Indian cake of unleavened whole wheat bread. [Hindi *capātī*]

chap·book *noun* **1** a small and often self-published booklet of poetry, stories, etc., usu. saddle-stitched or stapled. **2** *hist.* a small pamphlet containing tales, ballads, tracts, etc., sold by chapmen. [19th c.: see CHAPMAN]

chape /tʃeip/ *noun* **1** the metal cap of a scabbard point. **2** the back piece of a buckle attaching it to a strap etc. [Old French, = cope, hood, formed as CAP]

chap·eau /ʃapɔ/ *noun* (pl. **chap·eaux** pronunc. same) a hat, esp. an extravagant one. [French]

chap·el *noun* **1** *Christianity* **a** a small sanctuary within a larger church or cathedral, often having its own altar and dedication (*Lady chapel*). **b** a place of worship attached to a hospital, school, private house, etc. **c** any other place of worship that is neither a parish church nor a cathedral. **2** a chapel service. **3** a funeral home, or the room in a funeral home in which funerals are held. **4** *Brit.* **a** a place of worship for nonconformist denominations. **b** (*predicative*) an attender at or believer in nonconformist worship (*they are strictly chapel*). **5** the members or branch of a printers' trade union at a specific place of work. [Old French *chapele* from medieval Latin *cappella* diminutive of *cappa* cloak: the first chapel was a sanctuary in which St. Martin's sacred cloak (*cappella*) was preserved]

chapel royal *noun* a chapel in a royal palace.

chap·er·one /ˈʃapə,rəʊn/ (also **chap·er·on**) ● *noun* **1** a person who supervises young people on trips etc. **2** a person who ensures that no improper behaviour occurs on a date, at a dance, etc. **3** esp. *hist.* a person, esp. an older woman, who ensures propriety by accompanying a young unmarried woman on social occasions. ● *transitive verb* act as a chaperone to. □ **chap·er·on·age** /ˈʃapərənɪdʒ/ *noun* [French, = hood, chaperone, diminutive of *chape* cope, formed as CAP]

chap·er·on·in /ˌʃapˈrəʊnɪn/ *noun* a protein that aids the assembly and folding of other protein molecules in living cells. [CHAPERONE + -IN¹]

chap·fallen *adjective* dispirited, dejected. [CHAP³]

chap·lain /ˈtʃaplɪn/ *noun* a member of the clergy attached to a private chapel, institution, ship, regiment, etc. □ **chap·lain·cy** *noun* (pl. **-cies**) [Old French *c(h)apelain* from medieval Latin *cappellanus*, originally custodian of the cloak of St. Martin: see CHAPEL]

Chap·leau /ʃaˈplɔː/ **Sir Joseph-Adolphe** (1840–98), Canadian lawyer and politician, Conservative premier of Quebec 1879–82, who also served as secretary of state (1882–92) and Lieutenant-Governor of Quebec (1892–8).

chap·let /'tʃaplət/ *noun* **1** a garland or circlet for the head. **2** a string of 55 beads (one-third of the rosary number) for counting prayers. **3** a necklace. **4** a moulding made to resemble a string of beads. [Old French *chapelet*, ultimately from Late Latin *cappa* CAP]

Chap·lin, **Sir Charles Spen·cer ('Char·lie')** (1889–1977), English film actor and director. He is generally regarded as one of the greatest comic actors of silent film, famous for his portrayal of a kind-hearted bowler-hatted tramp. A master of mime who combined pathos with slapstick clowning, his most successful films include *The Kid* (1920), *The Gold Rush* (1925), *Modern Times* (1936), and *The Great Dictator* (1940). □ **Chapl·in·esque** *adjective*

Chap·man, **George** (*c.*1560–1634), English poet and dramatist. Although acclaimed as a dramatist in his day, he is now chiefly known for his translations of Homer's *Iliad* (1611–16) and *Odyssey* (1616).

chap·man *noun* (*pl.* **-men**) *hist.* a peddler. [Old English *cēapman* from *cēap* barter]

chap·pal /'tʃapəl/ *noun* an Indian sandal, usu. of leather. [Hindi]

chapped *adjective* (esp. of the lips or skin) dry and cracking.

chap·pie *noun informal* = CHAP¹.

chaps /tʃaps, ʃaps/ *plural noun N Amer.* **1** thick leather leggings worn by western riders over trousers as protection against thorns etc. **2** similar protective leather leggings worn by loggers. [abbreviation of CHAPARAJOS]

Chap Stick *noun N Amer. proprietary* a soothing, waxlike balm applied to chapped lips, usu. packaged in a tube.

chap·tal·iz·a·tion /tʃaptəlai'zeiʃən/ *noun* (in winemaking) the correction or improvement of must by the addition of calcium carbonate to neutralize acid or of sugar to increase alcoholic strength. □ **chap·tal·ize** *transitive verb* [J.A. *Chaptal* d.1832, French naturalist who invented the process + -IZATION]

chap·ter *noun* **1** a main division of a book, treatise, etc. **2** *N Amer.* a local branch of a society. **3** a period of time (in a person's life, a nation's history, etc.). **4 a** the canons of a cathedral or other religious community or knightly order. **b** a meeting of these. **5** an Act of Parliament numbered as part of a session's proceedings. □ **chapter and verse** an exact reference or authority. [Old French *chapitre* from Latin *capitulum*, diminutive of *caput -itis* head]

chapter book *noun* a children's book consisting of a single story divided into chapters, as opposed to a picture book or collection of stories.

Chapter 11 *noun* (in the US) a section of the Bankruptcy Code which grants corporations temporary protection from creditors while they reorganize, provided that they can pay all current expenses.

chapter house *noun* **1** a building or room in a cathedral or monastery where the chapter holds its meetings. **2** *US* the place where a college fraternity or sorority meets.

char¹ ● *transitive & intransitive verb* (**charred**, **char·ring**) **1** make or become black by burning; scorch. **2** burn or be burned to charcoal. ● *noun* a charred substance. [apparently back-formation from CHARCOAL]

char² *noun* (also **charr**) (*pl.* same) **1** a small trout of the genus *Salvelinus*, esp. the Arctic char. **2** a Dolly Varden trout or brook trout. [17th c.: origin unknown]

char³ *Brit. informal* ● *noun* = CHARWOMAN. ● *intransitive verb* (**charred**, **char·ring**) work as a charwoman. [earlier *chare* from Old English *cerr* a turn, *cierran* to turn]

chara·banc /'ʃarəˌbaŋ/ *noun Brit. hist.* an early type of bus, used esp. for pleasure trips. [French *char à bancs* seated carriage]

chara·cin /'karəsɪn/ *noun* a freshwater fish of the family Characidae, mainly of South and Central America, including piranhas and tetras. [modern Latin *Characinus* genus name, from Greek *kharax*, a kind of fish]

char·ac·ter /'karəktər/ ● *noun* **1** the collective qualities or characteristics, esp. mental and moral, that distinguish a person or thing. **2** moral strength (*has a weak character*). **3** reputation (*a blot on her character*). **4** distinctive or unusual features (*a house with character*). **5 a** a person in a novel, play, etc. **b** a part played by a performer; a role. **6** (*attributive*) **a** designating an acting role requiring strong delineation of individual and esp. eccentric character, or an actor who plays such roles. **b** designating roles in dramatic ballets, or the artists performing them, which require more acting than dancing. **7** *informal* a person, esp. an eccentric or outstanding individual (*he's a real character*). **8 a** a printed or written letter, symbol, or distinctive mark (*Chinese characters*). **b** *Computing* any of a group of symbols representing a letter etc. **9** a written description of a person's qualities; a reference. **10** a

characteristic (esp. of a biological species). **11** = CHARACTER DANCE. ● *transitive verb archaic* inscribe; describe. □ **in** (or **out of**) **character** consistent (or inconsistent) with a person's character. □ **char·ac·ter·ful** *adjective* **char·ac·ter·less** *adjective* [Latin from Greek *kharaktēr* stamp, impress]

character assassination *noun* a malicious attempt to harm or destroy a person's good reputation.

character dance *noun* a style of dance in classical ballet based on national or folk dances. □ **character dancer** *noun*

char·ac·ter·is·tic /ˌkarəktə'rɪstɪk/ ● *adjective* typical, distinctive (*with characteristic expertise*). ● *noun* **1** a characteristic feature or quality. **2** *Math.* the whole number or integral part of a logarithm. □ **char·ac·ter·is·tic·ally** *adverb*

char·ac·ter·ize /'karɪktəˌraiz/ *transitive verb* (also esp. *Brit.* **-ise**) **1 a** describe or portray the character of. **b** (foll. by *as*) describe as. **2** be characteristic of. □ **char·ac·ter·iz·a·tion** /-'zeiʃən/ *noun*

char·ac·ter·o·logic·al /ˌkarəktərə'lɒdʒɪkəl/ *adjective* of or relating to character or the study of character.

character set *noun Computing* a set of letters, digits, and other characters that can be drawn on to represent data, usu. varying according to the hardware involved.

character witness *noun* a person who attests to another's good reputation in a court of law.

cha·rade /ʃə'reid/ *noun* **1 a** (usu. in *pl.*, treated as *sing.*) a game of guessing a word from a written or acted clue given for each syllable and for the whole. **b** one such clue. **2** an absurd pretense. [French from modern Provençal *charrado* conversation, from *charra* chatter]

charas /'tʃarəs/ *noun* = HASHISH. [Hindi]

char·broil *transitive verb* cook (meat etc.) on a grill over a charcoal fire. □ **char·broiled** *adjective* [CHARCOAL + BROIL¹]

char·coal ● *noun* **1** an amorphous form of carbon consisting of a porous black residue from partially burnt wood, bones, etc. **2** a piece of this, or a pencil made from it, used for drawing. **3** a drawing in charcoal. **4** (in full **charcoal grey**) a dark grey colour. ● *adjective* (in full **charcoal grey**) dark grey. [Middle English COAL = charcoal: first element perhaps *chare* turn (compare CHAR¹, CHAR²)]

charcoal burner *noun* esp. *hist.* a person who makes charcoal by burning wood.

Char·cot /ʃarko/ **Jean-Martin** (1825–93), French neurologist. He established links between various neurological conditions and particular lesions in the central nervous system, and is regarded as one of the founders of modern neurology; his work on hysteria was taken up by his pupil Sigmund Freud.

char·cu·terie /ʃar'kuːtəriː/ *noun* **1** assorted meats such as cold cuts, sausages, pâté, etc. **2** a store that specializes in selling such meats. [French, from obsolete *char* (modern *chair*) *cuite* cooked flesh; see -ERY]

chard *noun* (in full **Swiss chard**) a kind of beet, *Beta vulgaris*, with edible broad white leaf stalks and green blades. [French *carde*, and *chardon* thistle: compare CARDOON]

Char·don·nay /'ʃardəˌnei/ *noun* **1** a variety of white grape used in winemaking. **2** a dry white wine made from Chardonnay grapes. [French]

Cha·rente River /ʃa'rɑ̃t/ a river of W France, which rises in the Massif Central and flows 360 km (225 miles) westward to enter the Bay of Biscay at Rochefort.

cha·rette /ʃə'ret/ *noun* **1** a workshop-like public meeting to brainstorm community design issues. **2** an intensive last-minute group effort to finish an architectural or design project. [French *charrette*, lit. = 'cart', possibly from the idiom *être en charrette* 'be faced with a deadline', with reference to the use of *charrette* to designate the tumbrils transporting people to the guillotine during the French Revolution]

charge ● *verb* **1** *transitive* **a** ask (an amount) as a price (*charges $5 a ticket*). **b** ask (a person) for an amount as a price (*you forgot to charge me*). **2** *transitive* **a** (foll. by *to*, *up to*) debit the cost of to (a person or account) (*charge it to my account*; *charge it up to me*). **b** debit (a person or an account) (*bought a new car and charged the company*). **3** *transitive* **a** (often foll. by *with*) accuse (of an offence) (*charged him with theft*). **b** (foll. by *that* + clause) make an accusation that. **4** *transitive* **a** (foll. by *to* + infin.) instruct or command. **b** (of a judge) instruct (a jury). **5** *transitive* (foll. by *with*) entrust with. **6 a** *intransitive* make a rushing attack; rush headlong. **b** *transitive* make a rushing attack on; throw oneself against. **7** (often foll. by *up*) **a** *transitive* give an electric charge to (a body). **b** *transitive* store energy in (a battery). **c** *intransitive* (of a battery etc.) receive and store energy. **8** *transitive* (often foll. by *with*) load or fill (a vessel, gun, etc.) to the full or proper extent. **9** *transitive* (usu. as **charged** *adjective*) **a** (foll.

by *with*) saturated with (*air charged with vapour*). **b** (usu. foll. by *with*) pervaded (with strong feelings etc.) (*atmosphere charged with emotion*; *a charged atmosphere*). ● *noun* **1 a** a price asked for goods or services. **b** a financial liability or commitment. **2** an accusation, esp. against a prisoner brought to trial. **3 a** a task, duty, or commission. **b** care, custody, responsible possession. **c** a person or thing entrusted. **d** the congregation or congregations for which a minister is responsible. **4 a** an impetuous rush or attack, esp. in a battle. **b** the signal for this. **5** the appropriate amount of material to be put into a receptacle, mechanism, etc. at one time, esp. of explosive for a gun. **6 a** a property of matter that is a consequence of the interaction between its constituent particles and exists in a positive or negative form, causing electrical phenomena. **b** the quantity of this carried by a body. **c** energy stored chemically for conversion into electricity. **d** the process of charging a battery. **7** an exhortation; directions, orders, esp. instructions given by a judge to a jury, or by a bishop to his clergy. **8** esp. *N Amer. informal* a thrill. **9** a burden or load. **10** *Heraldry* a device; a bearing. □ **charge up 1** recharge (a battery etc.). **2** (usu. as **charged up** *adjective*) excite. **free of charge** at no cost. **in charge** having command. **lay to a person's charge** *Brit.* accuse a person of. **put a person on a charge** charge a person with a specified offence. **return to the charge** begin again, esp. in argument. **take charge** (often foll. by *of*) assume control or direction. □ **charge·able** *adjective* [Old French *charger* from Late Latin *car(ri)care* load, from Latin *carrus* CAR]

charge account *noun N Amer.* an account with a store etc. for obtaining goods or services before payment.

charge·back *noun* the action of recovering expenses from those who have caused them to be incurred.

charge card *noun* a credit card, esp. one for which the account must be paid in full when a statement is issued.

charge-coupled device *noun* a light-sensitive grid on a silicon chip which creates digital signals from images, used in video recorders, photocopiers, etc. Abbr.: **CCD**.

char·gé d'af·faires /ˌʃɑrʒeɪ daˈfer/ *noun* (also **chargé**) (*pl.* **char·gés** *pronunc.* same) **1** an ambassador's deputy. **2** an envoy to a country to which an ambassador has not been sent. [French, = in charge (of affairs)]

charge nurse *noun Brit.* a nurse in charge of a ward etc.

Charge of the Light Brigade a British cavalry charge during the Battle of Balaclava in the Crimean War. A misunderstanding led to British cavalry being committed to an attack up a valley strongly held on three sides by the Russians. Immortalized in verse by Tennyson, the charge in fact destroyed some of the finest light cavalry in the world to very little military purpose.

char·ger[1] *noun* **1** an apparatus for charging a battery. **2** a cavalry horse. **3** a person or thing that charges.

char·ger[2] *noun* a large flat dish. [Anglo-French *chargeour*, from *chargier* 'to load' from Late Latin *carricare*]

charge sheet *noun Cdn & Brit.* a record of cases and charges made at a police station.

char·ging *noun Hockey* an illegal play involving a forward attack of more than two steps against a member of the opposing team in order to take him or her out of play.

char·grill *transitive verb* grill (food, typically meat or fish) quickly at a very high heat.

char·iot /ˈtʃɛrɪət/ ● *noun* **1** *hist.* **a** a two-wheeled vehicle drawn by horses, used in ancient warfare and racing. **b** a light four-wheeled carriage used in the 18th c. **2** *literary* a stately or triumphal vehicle. ● *transitive verb literary* convey in or as in a chariot. [Old French, augmentative of *char* CAR]

char·iot·eer /ˌtʃɛrɪəˈtɪr/ *noun* a chariot driver.

char·is·ma /kəˈrɪzmə/ *noun* **1 a** the ability to inspire followers with devotion and enthusiasm. **b** an attractive aura; great charm. **2** (*pl.* **cha·ris·mata** /kəˈrɪzmətə/) a divinely conferred power or talent. [ecclesiastical Latin from Greek *kharisma* from *kharis* favour, grace]

char·is·matic /ˌkɛrɪzˈmatɪk/ ● *adjective* **1** having charisma; inspiring enthusiasm. **2** (of Christian worship) characterized by spontaneity, ecstatic utterances, etc. ● *noun* a Christian who emphasizes charismatic worship and experiences. □ **char·is·matic·ally** *adverb*

char·it·able /ˈtʃɛrɪtəbəl/ *adjective* **1** generous in giving to those in need. **2** of, relating to, or connected with a charity or charities. **3** apt to judge favourably of persons, acts, and motives. □ **char·it·able·ness** *noun* **char·it·ably** *adverb*

char·ity /ˈtʃɛrɪti/ *noun* (*pl.* **-ities**) **1 a** voluntary giving to those in need.

b the help, esp. money, so given. **2 a** an institution or organization for helping those in need. **b** a non-profit organization (*see* NON-PROFIT). **3 a** kindness, benevolence. **b** tolerance in judging others. **c** love of one's fellow humans. □ **charity begins at home** a person's first responsibility is for the needs of their own family and friends. [Old English from Old French *charité* from Latin *caritas -tatis* from *carus* dear]

chari·vari /ˌʃɑriˈvɑri/ *noun* **1** = SHIVAREE 2. **2** a medley of sounds; a hubbub. [French, = a serenade with pans, trays, etc., to an unpopular person]

char·lady *noun* (*pl.* **-ladies**) *Brit.* = CHARWOMAN.

char·la·tan /ˈʃɑrlətən/ *noun* a person falsely claiming a special knowledge or skill. □ **char·la·tan·ism** *noun* **char·la·tan·ry** *noun* [French from Italian *ciarlatano* from *ciarlare* babble]

Charle·bois /ˈʃɑrləbwɒ/ **Rob·ert** (b.1945), Canadian pop singer and songwriter, noted for singing in *joual*.

Charle·magne[1] /ˈʃɑrləmɑɲ/ a town in south central Quebec, northeast of Montreal; pop. (2001) 5,662. [R.-*Charlemagne* Laurier, Canadian politician and half-brother of Sir W. Laurier, d.1906]

Charle·magne[2] /ˈʃɑrləˌmeɪn/ (Latin *Carolus magnus* Charles the Great) (742–814), King of the Franks 768–814 and Holy Roman emperor (as Charles I) 800–14. He subdued the Lombards (774), Saxons (772–7; 782–5), and Avars (791–9), and his coronation by Pope Leo III in Rome on Christmas Day, 800, is taken to have inaugurated the Holy Roman Empire. He promoted commerce, agriculture, the arts, and education, and under Alcuin his principal court at Aachen became a major centre of learning.

Charle·roi /ˈʃɑrləˈrwɒ/ an industrial city in SW Belgium; pop. (est. 2002) 201,000.

Charles ► **1** Charles Philip Arthur George, Prince of Wales (b.1948), heir apparent to Elizabeth II. He has two children, Prince William Arthur Philip Louis (b.1982) and Prince Henry Charles Albert David (b.1984). **2 Ray** (born Ray Charles Robinson) (b.1930), US singer, pianist, and songwriter. Blind from the age of seven, he is known as a versatile performer of blues, gospel, jazz, soul, and country music; his most popular songs include 'Georgia on My Mind' (1960), and 'I Can't Stop Loving You' (1962).

Charles I (1600–49), son of James I, king of England, Scotland, and Ireland 1625–49. His reign was dominated by the deepening religious and constitutional crisis that eventually resulted in the English Civil War; when the Royalist forces were defeated in 1648 he was tried by a special Parliamentary court and beheaded.

Charles II 1 (1630–85), son of Charles I, king of England, Scotland, and Ireland 1660–85. After his father's execution in 1649 Charles was declared king in Scotland and then crowned there in 1651, but was forced into exile on the Continent where he remained for nine years until the collapse of the Commonwealth. **2** (1661–1700), king of Spain 1665–1700. The last Hapsburg to be king of Spain, he inherited a kingdom already in decline. Childless, he chose Philip of Anjou, grandson of Louis XIV of France, as his successor; this ultimately gave rise to the War of the Spanish Succession (1701–14).

Charles IV (1748–1819), king of Spain 1788–1808. His reign was dominated by the influence of his mother Maria Louisa and her lover, Manuel de Godoy (prime minister from 1792). Following the French invasion of Spain in 1807, Charles was forced to abdicate; he died in exile in Rome.

Charles V (1500–58), son of Philip I, Holy Roman emperor 1519–56, king of Spain (as Charles I) 1516–56. He united the Spanish and imperial thrones but his reign was marked by the spread of Protestantism, revolt in Spain, and war with France (1512–44).

Charles VI (1685–1740), Holy Roman emperor 1711–40. His unsuccessful claim to the Spanish throne instigated the War of the Spanish Succession (1701–14); he attempted to ensure that his daughter Maria Theresa would succeed him to the imperial throne, and the ensuing struggle for power on his death triggered the War of the Austrian Succession (1740–8).

Charles VII (1403–61), king of France 1422–61. At the time of his accession to the throne, much of N France was under English occupation, including Reims (thus denying Charles his coronation). After the intervention of Joan of Arc, however, the French experienced a dramatic military revival; Charles was crowned, and his reign eventually saw the defeat of the English and the end of the Hundred Years War.

Charles XII (also **Karl XII**) (1682–1718), king of Sweden 1697–1718. In 1700 he embarked on the Great Northern War against the encircling powers of Denmark, Poland–Saxony, and Russia, and in 1709 his army was destroyed by the Russians at Poltava. Charles was interned in

Turkey until 1715; he resumed his military career after his return but was killed while besieging a fortress in Norway.

Charles XIV (born Jean Baptiste Jules Bernadotte) (1763–1844), French soldier, king of Sweden and Norway 1818–44. A revolutionary general and marshal under Napoleon, he was elected crown prince of Sweden in 1810, and became king in 1818, thus founding the present royal house.

Charles·bourg /ʃɑrləˈbʊr/ a former city in SE central Quebec, now part of the city of Québec; pop. (2001) 70,310. [named after the chapel at *Bourg-Royal*, dedicated to St. *Charles* Borromeo d.1584]

Charles' Law /ˈtʃɑrlz/ (also **Charles's Law**) *noun Chem.* the law stating that the volume of an ideal gas at constant pressure is directly proportional to the absolute temperature. [J. A. C. *Charles*, French scientist d.1823]

Charles Mar·tel /mɑrˈtel/ (*c.*688–741), Frankish ruler of the eastern part of the Frankish kingdom from 715 and the whole kingdom from 719. He earned his nickname *Martel* ('the hammer') from his victory at Poitiers in 732, which effectively checked the Muslim advance into Europe; Charlemagne was his grandson.

Charles's Wain *noun Brit.* = BIG DIPPER. [Old English *Carles wægn* the wain of Carl (Charles the Great, Charlemagne), perhaps by assoc. of the star Arcturus with legends of King Arthur and Charlemagne]

Charles·ton¹ 1 the state capital of West Virginia; pop. (2000) 53,421. **2** a city and port in S Carolina; pop. (2000) 96,650. The bombardment in 1861 of Fort Sumter, in the harbour, by Confederate troops marked the beginning of the American Civil War.

Charles·ton² ● *noun* a fast dance, popular in the 1920s, in which the knees are turned inwards and the legs kicked sideways. ● *intransitive verb* dance the Charleston. [CHARLESTON]

char·ley horse *noun N Amer.* cramp or soreness in a muscle, esp. in the leg. [19th c.: origin uncertain]

char·lock *noun* a wild mustard, *Sinapis arvensis*, with yellow flowers. Also called FIELD MUSTARD. [Old English *cerlic*, of unknown origin]

Char·lotte /ˈʃɑrlət/ a commercial city and transportation centre in southern N Carolina; pop. (2000) 540,828.

char·lotte /ˈʃɑrlət/ *noun* any of various desserts consisting of a filling of fruit, custard, cream, etc. encased in strips of bread, sponge cake, etc. [French]

Char·lotte Ama·lie /əˈmɑliə/ the capital of the US Virgin Islands, on the island of St. Thomas; pop. (est. 2002) 13,800. [after the wife of King Christian V of Denmark]

charlotte russe /ˈruːs/ *noun* a dessert consisting of flavoured cream or custard stiffened with gelatin and encased in strips of sponge cake. [CHARLOTTE + French *russe* Russian]

Char·lottes /ˈʃɑrləts/ an informal name for the Queen Charlotte Islands.

Char·lotte·town /ˈʃɑrləˌtaʊn/ the capital city of PEI, situated on the south central shore of the island, on Charlottetown Harbour, an inlet of the Northumberland Strait; pop. (2001) 32,245.

☐ **Char·lotte·tonian** *noun* [*Charlotte* Sophia, queen of George III d.1818]

Charlottetown Conference a conference held in Charlottetown in September 1864, which was initially proposed to discuss a union of the three Maritime colonies; the Province of Canada asked to attend to discuss a more general union, and the delegates agreed in general terms to a plan for Confederation.

charm ● *noun* **1 a** the power or quality of giving delight or arousing admiration. **b** fascination, attractiveness. **c** (usu. in *pl.*) an attractive or enticing quality. **2** a trinket on a bracelet etc. **3 a** an object, act, or word(s) supposedly having occult or magic power; a spell. **b** a thing worn to avert evil etc.; an amulet. **4** *Physics* a property of matter manifested by some quarks and other subatomic particles. **5** *Cdn* (*Nfld*) a confused noise or sound (of voices etc.). ● *transitive verb* **1** delight, captivate (*charmed by the performance*). **2** influence or protect as if by magic (*leads a charmed life*). **3 a** gain by charm (*charmed agreement out of him*). **b** influence by charm (*charmed her into consenting*). **4** cast a spell on; bewitch. **5** *Cdn* (*Nfld*) cure (an illness, bleeding, etc.) by supernatural means. ☐ **like a charm** perfectly, wonderfully. ☐ **charm·er** *noun* [Old French *charme*, *charmer* from Latin *carmen* song]

charm bracelet *noun* a bracelet hung with small trinkets.

charm·euse /ʃɑrˈmɜːz/ *noun* a soft smooth silk fabric with a satin-like surface. [French, fem. of *charmeur* (as CHARM)]

charm·ing *adjective* **1** delightful, attractive, pleasing. **2** (often as *interjection*) ironic expressing displeasure or disapproval.
☐ **charm·ing·ly** *adverb*

charm·less *adjective* lacking charm; unattractive. ☐ **charm·less·ly** *adverb* **charm·less·ness** *noun*

charm offensive *noun* a campaign of flattery, friendliness, and cajolement designed to achieve the support or agreement of others.

charm school *noun* a school at which social graces, grooming, etc. are taught.

char·nel house /ˈtʃɑrnəl/ *noun* a house or vault in which dead bodies or bones are piled. [Old French *charnel* burying place, from medieval Latin *carnale* from Late Latin *carnalis* CARNAL]

Char·ny /ʃɑrˈniː/ a former town in SE central Quebec, south of Quebec City, now part of Lévis; pop. (2001) 10,507. [J. de Lauson de *Charny*, grand seneschal of New France d.1661]

Charo·lais /ˈʃɑrəˌleɪ/ *noun* (*pl.* same) a breed of large white beef cattle. [Monts du *Charolais* in E France]

Charon /ˈkɛrən/ **1** *Gk Myth* an aged ferryman who, for a fee of one obol, ferried the souls of the dead across the rivers Styx and Acheron to Hades. **2** *Astronomy* the only satellite of Pluto, discovered in 1978. Its diameter of 1 200 km is more than half that of Pluto.

char·poy /ˈtʃɑrpɔɪ/ *noun* (in India) a light bedstead. [Hindustani *chārpāī*]

charr var. of CHAR².

chart ● *noun* **1** information in the form of a table, graph, or diagram. **2** a geographical map or plan, esp. for marine or aerial navigation. **3** (usu. in *pl.*) a listing of the most popular songs, albums, etc., for a given period. **4** a record of medical information concerning a patient. ● *verb* **1** *transitive* make a chart of; map. **2** *transitive* outline, plan (*chart a new course*). **3** *transitive* trace systematically (*charted its progress from its beginnings*). **4** *intransitive* (of a recording or an artist) appear on the charts. [French *charte* from Latin *charta* CARD¹]

chart·bust·er *noun informal* a bestselling popular song, album, artist, etc.

char·ter ● *noun* **1 a** a written grant of rights, by the sovereign or legislature, esp. the creation of a company, university, etc. **b** a written constitution or description of an organization's functions etc. **2** (**the Charter**) (in Canada) the Canadian Charter of Rights and Freedoms. **3 a** the hiring of an aircraft, ship, etc., for a special purpose (also *attributive*: *charter flight*; *charter company*). **b** a contract for this. **c** the aircraft, ship, etc. chartered. ● *transitive verb* **1** grant a charter to. **2** hire (an aircraft, ship, bus, etc.). ☐ **char·ter·er** *noun* [Old French *chartre* from Latin *chartula* diminutive of *charta* CARD¹]

charter community *noun Cdn* (*NWT & Nunavut*) a small municipality having some bylaw authority and at least 25 residents who are eligible to vote.

char·tered *adjective Brit.* (of an accountant, engineer, librarian, etc.) qualified as a member of a professional body that has a royal charter.

chartered accountant *noun* an accountant authorized to sign audit statements. Abbr.: **CA**.

chartered bank *noun* (in Canada) a large, privately-owned bank chartered by Parliament and operating under the provisions of the Bank Act.

charter member *noun* an original member of a society, corporation, etc.

charter school *noun N Amer.* a publicly funded school run by parents, teachers, and members of the business community, operating by contract or charter to the local school board or government.

Chart·ism *noun hist.* the principles of a popular reformist movement in Britain (1837–48) calling for universal suffrage for men, equal electoral districts, voting by secret ballot, abolition of the property qualification for Parliament, payment of MPs, and annual parliaments. Despite mass support and petitions to Parliament, the movement collapsed before most of its demands became law. ☐ **Chart·ist** *noun* [from *The People's Charter*, the movement's manifesto]

Char·tres /ˈʃɑrtrə/ a city in N France; pop. (1999) 40,361. It is noted for its Gothic cathedral.

char·treuse /ʃɑrˈtrɜːz/ ● *noun* **1** (**Chartreuse**) *proprietary* a pale green or yellow liqueur of brandy and aromatic herbs etc. **2** a pale yellowish green. ● *adjective* pale yellowish-green. [La Grande *Chartreuse* (Carthusian monastery near Grenoble)]

chart-topping *adjective* (of a popular singer, group, or recording) having reached the top of the music charts. ☐ **chart-topper** *noun*

char·woman *noun* (*pl.* **-women**) esp. *Brit.* a woman employed as a cleaner in houses or offices.

chary /ˈtʃɛri/ *adjective* (**char·i·er**, **char·i·est**) (often foll. by *of*) **1** cautious, wary (*chary of major economic reform*). **2** sparing; ungenerous

Consonants: b *but*   d *dog*   f *few*   g *get*   h *her*   j *yes*   k *cat*   l *leg*   m *man*   n *no*   p *pen*   r *red*   s *sit*

(*chary of giving praise*). **3** shy. □ **char·i·ly** *adverb* **char·i·ness** *noun* [Old English *cearig*]

Cha·ryb·dis /kə'rıbdıs/ *Gk Myth* a dangerous whirlpool in a narrow channel of the sea, opposite the cave of the sea monster Scylla; it was later identified with the Strait of Messina.

Chas. *abbreviation* Charles.

chase¹ ● *verb* **1** *transitive* pursue in order to catch. **2** *transitive* **a** (foll. by *from, out of, to*, etc.) force to leave. **b** (foll. by *away*) dispel (*chase away all fears*). **3** *intransitive* **a** (foll. by *after*) hurry in pursuit of (a person). **b** (foll. by *around* etc.) *informal* act or move about hurriedly. **4** *transitive* (usu. foll. by *up, down*) *informal* make efforts to find or obtain quickly. **5** *transitive informal* **a** try to attain. **b** court persistently and openly. ● *noun* **1** the act or an instance of pursuing. **2** *Brit.* unenclosed but private hunting land. **3** (prec. by *the*) hunting esp. as a sport. **4** an animal etc. that is pursued. **5** = STEEPLECHASE. □ **give chase** pursue a person, animal, etc.; hunt. **go and chase oneself** (usu. in *imperative*) *informal* depart. [Old French *chace chacier*, ultimately from Latin *capere* take]

chase² *transitive verb* emboss or engrave (metal). [apparently from earlier *enchase* from French *enchâsser* (as EN-¹, CASE²)]

chase³ *noun Printing* a metal frame holding composed type. [French *châsse* from Latin *capsa* CASE²]

chase⁴ *noun* **1** the part of a gun enclosing the bore. **2** a trench or groove cut to receive a pipe etc. [French *chas* enclosed space, from Provençal *ca(u)s* from medieval Latin *capsum* thorax]

chas·er *noun* **1** a person or thing that chases. **2** *informal* a drink taken after another of a different kind, e.g. beer after hard liquor. **3** *N Amer.* a logger who unhooks logs at a landing. **4** a horse for steeplechasing.

Chasid *var. of* HASID.

chasm /'kazəm/ *noun* **1** a deep fissure or opening in the earth, rock, etc. **2** a wide difference of feeling, interests, etc.; a gulf. □ **chas·mic** *adjective* [Latin *chasma* from Greek *khasma* gaping hollow]

chas·sé /'ʃaseɪ/ ● *noun* a sliding step in dance, in which one foot displaces the other as if by chasing it. ● *intransitive verb* (**chas·séd**; **chas·sé·ing**) make this step. [French, = chased]

Chas·sid *var. of* HASID.

chas·sis /'ʃasi, 'ʃasi/ *noun* (*pl.* same /-si:z/) **1** the basic frame of a motor vehicle, trailer, etc., including the engine, wheels, and other mechanical parts, but not the body. **2** the frame of a stereo, television set, etc. [French *châssis*, ultimately from Latin *capsa* CASE²]

chaste /tʃeɪst/ *adjective* **1** abstaining from extramarital, or from all, sexual intercourse. **2** (of behaviour, speech, etc.) pure, virtuous, decent. **3** (of artistic etc. style) simple, unadorned. □ **chaste·ly** *adverb* **chaste·ness** *noun* [Old French from Latin *castus*]

chas·ten /'tʃeɪsən/ *transitive verb* **1** (esp. as **chas·ten·ing** *adjective*, **chas·tened** *adjective*) subdue, humble (*a chastening experience*; *chastened by his failure*). **2** discipline, punish. □ **chas·ten·er** *noun* [obsolete *chaste* (v.) from Old French *chastier* from Latin *castigare* CASTIGATE]

chas·tise /'tʃastaɪz, tʃas'taɪz/ *transitive verb* **1** rebuke or reprimand severely. **2** punish, esp. by beating. □ **chas·tise·ment** *noun* **chas·tis·er** *noun* [Middle English, apparently irreg. formed from obsolete verbs *chaste, chasty*: see CHASTEN]

chas·tity /'tʃastɪti/ *noun* **1** being chaste. **2** sexual abstinence; virginity. **3** simplicity of style or taste. [Old French *chasteté* from Latin *castitas -tatis* from *castus* CHASTE]

chastity belt *noun hist.* a locking belt-like device fitting over a woman's genitals to prevent her from having sexual intercourse.

chas·uble /'tʃazʊbəl, 'tʃazjʊbəl, 'tʃasʊbəl/ *noun Christianity* a loose sleeveless usu. ornate outer vestment worn by some clergy when celebrating the Eucharist. [Old French *chesible*, later *-uble*, ultimately from Latin *casula* hooded cloak, little cottage, diminutive of *casa* cottage]

chat¹ ● *intransitive verb* (**chat·ted, chat·ting**) talk in a light familiar way. ● *noun* **1** informal conversation or talk. **2** an instance of this. □ **chat up** *informal* chat to, esp. flirtatiously or with an ulterior motive. [Middle English: shortening of CHATTER]

chat² *noun* **1** any of various small birds with harsh calls, esp. a N American warbler of the genus *Granatellus* or *Icteria*. **2** a Eurasian thrush of the genus *Saxicola*. [prob. imitative]

châ·teau /'ʃatoː, 'ʃatoː/ *noun* (*pl.* **châ·teaux** /-toːz/) **1** a large French country house or castle, often giving its name to wine made in its neighbourhood. **2** *hist.* (in French Canada) the residence of a seigneur or a governor. [French from Old French *chastel* CASTLE]

Cha·teau·briand /ʃatoːbriˈɑ̃/ **François-René, Vi·comte de** (1768–1848), French writer and diplomat. An important figure in early French Romanticism, he established his literary reputation with *Atala*

(1801) and *Le Génie du Christianisme* (1802); his autobiography *Mémoires d'outre-tombe* (1849–50) gives an eloquent account of his life against a background of political upheaval.

cha·teau·briand /ʃaˌtoːbriˈɑ̃/ *noun* a thick beef steak from the tenderloin, grilled and served with a sauce or herbs etc. [CHATEAUBRIAND]

Château Clique *noun Cdn hist.* a name given to the small group of powerful citizens appointed to important political positions by the governor in Lower Canada prior to 1830. Mostly English-speaking merchants, they tended to promote their own interests instead of addressing the problems of the French-speaking majority (compare FAMILY COMPACT).

Châ·teau·guay /ʃatoˈgeɪ/ a city in south central Quebec, situated at the mouth of the Rivière Châteauguay, southwest of Montreal; pop. (2001) 41,003. It was the site in 1813 of a battle between British North American troops, consisting mostly of French Canadians, and an American invasion force. Though greatly outnumbered, the Canadians prevailed, compelling the US force to retreat and abandon any plans for an attack on Montreal. [C. LE MOYNE]

Château style *noun Cdn* a style of architecture derived from the French château, characterized by steep, often copper-covered, roofs and round towers, used esp. in building railway hotels in Canada in the early 20th c.

chat·el·aine /'ʃatəˌleɪn/ *noun* **1** the mistress of a large house. **2** *hist.* a set of short chains attached to a woman's belt, for carrying keys etc. [French *châtelaine*, fem. of *chatelain* lord of a castle, from medieval Latin *castellanus* CASTELLAN]

chat group *noun* a group of people who communicate regularly via the Internet, usu. in real time but also via email.

Chat·ham¹ /'tʃatəm/ a former city in SW Ontario, situated on the Thames River, about 100 km southwest of London, now part of the city of Chatham-Kent; pop. (2001) 43,690. □ **Chatham·ite** *noun* [*Chatham, England*]

Chat·ham² /'tʃatəm/ **1st Earl of**, see PITT 1.

Chatham Islands a group of two islands, Pitt Island and Chatham Island, in the SW Pacific to the east of New Zealand.

Chatham-Kent a city in SW Ontario encompassing the former city of Chatham and Kent County, between the eastern shore of Lake St. Clair and Lake Erie; pop. (2001) 107,431. [*Chatham, England*, and KENT ¹]

chat line *noun* a telephone or email service which enables users to exchange casual conversation, either individually or by means of a conference line, with other subscribers or with employees of the service.

chat room *noun* an area on the Internet or another computer network where users can communicate, esp. one dedicated to a particular topic.

chat show *noun* = TALK SHOW.

chat·tel /'tʃatəl/ *noun* (usu. in *pl.*) **1** a movable possession; any possession or piece of property other than real estate or a freehold. **2** a slave. □ **goods and chattels** personal possessions. [Old French *chatel*: compare CATTLE]

chattel mortgage *noun N Amer.* a loan in which movable possessions (e.g. equipment or appliances) are used as security.

chat·ter ● *intransitive verb* **1** talk quickly, incessantly, trivially, or indiscreetly. **2** (of an animal) emit short quick sounds. **3** (of the teeth) click repeatedly together (usu. from cold). **4** (of a tool) rattle from vibration. ● *noun* **1** chattering talk or sounds. **2** the vibration of a tool. **3** the exchange of electronic communications by means of email, text messaging, interactive chat sessions, etc., esp. as intercepted by intelligence agencies. □ **chat·ter·er** *noun* **chat·tery** *adjective* [Middle English: imitative]

chatter·box *noun* a talkative person.

chat·ter·ing classes *plural noun* usu. *derogatory* the educated members of the middle and upper classes who consider themselves politically liberal and socially aware.

Chat·ter·ton, Thom·as (1752–70), English poet. He is chiefly remembered for his fabricated poems professing to be the work of Thomas Rowley, an imaginary 15th-c. monk. Poverty and lack of recognition drove him to suicide at the age of 17, and his tragic life was much romanticized by Keats and Wordsworth.

chatty *adjective* (**chat·ti·er, chat·ti·est**) **1** fond of chatting; talkative. **2** *informal* and lively (*a chatty letter*). □ **chat·ti·ly** *adverb* **chat·ti·ness** *noun*

Chatty Cathy *noun N Amer.* a talkative person; a chatterbox. [proprietary name of a talking doll]

Chau·cer, Geof·frey (c.1342–1400), English poet. He is best known for his *Canterbury Tales* (*c.*1387–*c.*1400), a cycle of linked tales told by a group of pilgrims who meet in a London tavern before their pilgrimage to Canterbury; many regard his work as the starting point of English literature.

Chau·cer·ian /ʃɔːˈsɪriən/ ● *adjective* of or relating to Chaucer or his style. ● *noun* a person who specializes in studying Chaucer.

chaud-froid /ʃəʊˈfrwɑ/ *noun* a dish of cold cooked meat or fish in jelly or sauce. [French from *chaud* hot + *froid* cold]

Chau·dière, Ri·vière /ʃəʊˈdjer/ a river in SE Quebec, about 200 km long, which rises in Lac Mégantic and flows generally northward, then northwestward, to empty into the St. Lawrence just south of Quebec City. [French, = boiler, so called with reference to a deep circular hole in the soft rock of its falls, from which the water appears to boil]

chauf·feur /ʃəʊˈfɜːr, ˈʃəʊ-/ ● *noun* a person employed to drive a limousine or other automobile. ● *transitive verb* **1** drive (a car) as a chauffeur. **2** transport by car (*chauffeuring the kids to hockey practice*). [French, lit. 'stoker' (by association with steam engines) from *chauffer* 'to heat']

chaul·moo·gra /tʃɔːlˈmuːɡrə/ *noun* any of various tropical Asian trees, esp. *Hydnocarpus kurzii*, with seeds yielding an oil formerly used in the treatment of leprosy. [Bengali *cāulmugrā*]

chau·tau·qua /ʃəˈtɒkwə, tʃə-/ *noun hist.* (in Canada and the US) a cultural program for adults combining lectures with music and theatre, popular in the late 19th and early 20th c. [*Chautauqua* in New York State, where the movement originated]

Chau·veau /ʃəʊˈvoː/ **Pierre-Joseph-Olivier** (1820–90), Canadian politician and writer, first premier of Quebec 1867–73, who is also known for his novel *Charles Guérin: roman de moeurs canadiennes* (1846).

chau·vin·ism /ˈʃəʊvə.nɪzəm/ *noun* **1** exaggerated or aggressive patriotism. **2** prejudice against or lack of consideration for those of a different sex, class, nationality, culture, etc. (*male chauvinism*). [*Chauvin*, a Napoleonic veteran noted for his extreme patriotism in the Cogniards' *Cocarde Tricolore* (1831)]

chau·vin·ist /ˈʃəʊvənɪst/ *noun* a person who exhibits chauvinism. □ **chau·vin·is·tic** *adjective* **chau·vin·is·tic·ally** *adverb*

Cha·vez /ˈtʃɑveɪz, ˈʃɑvez/ **Cesar (Es·tra·da)** (1927–1993), US labour organizer, who helped to unionize migrant Mexican-American grape workers in California, and organized a boycott (1965–70) of California grapes; he founded the National Farm Workers Association (1962), which eventually became the United Farm Workers of America (1971).

Cha·vín /tʃɑˈviːn/ a civilization that flourished in Peru 1000–200 BC, uniting a large part of the country's coastal region in a common religious culture, remains of which include characteristic fanged figures, presumably gods.

chaw *noun* esp. *US* **1** chewing tobacco. **2** a wad of this. [var. of CHEW]

chay·ote /tʃaɪˈoːti/ *noun* **1** a vine, *Sechium edule*, native to tropical America and cultivated elsewhere for its fruit. **2** the pear-shaped fruit of this plant, resembling a squash with a green exterior and succulent white flesh. *Also called* MIRLITON. [Spanish from Nahuatl *chayotli*]

CHD *abbreviation* coronary heart disease.

cheap ● *adjective* **1** low in price, inexpensive; worth more than its cost (*a cheap holiday*; *cheap labour*). **2** charging low prices; offering good value (*a cheap restaurant*). **3** of poor quality; inferior (*cheap housing*). **4** *N Amer. informal* (of a person) careful with money; parsimonious. **5 a** requiring little effort or acquired by discreditable means (*talk is cheap*; *scored a cheap goal*). **b** contemptible, despicable (*a cheap criminal*; *a cheap joke*). **c** ashamed; of low esteem (*made us feel cheap*). **d** unwarranted, uncalled for (*a cheap penalty*). ● *adverb* inexpensively (*got it cheap*). □ **cheap and nasty** *Brit.* of low cost and bad quality. **dirt cheap** very inexpensive. **on the cheap** inexpensively. □ **cheap·ish** *adjective* **cheap·ly** *adverb* **cheap·ness** *noun* [obsolete phr. *good cheap* from *cheap* 'a bargain' from Old English *cēap* barter, ultimately from Latin *caupo* innkeeper]

cheap·en *transitive & intransitive verb* make or become cheap or cheaper; depreciate, degrade.

cheap·jack ● *noun* a seller of inferior goods at low prices. ● *adjective* inferior, shoddy. [CHEAP + JACK¹]

cheapo (also **cheap·ie**) *informal* ● *adjective* inexpensive or of low quality. ● *noun* (pl. **cheapos**) **1** something inexpensive or of low quality. **2** a stingy person.

cheap shot *noun N Amer.* **1** a malicious or cruel comment directed at a defenceless person. **2** *Sport* the act of striking an unsuspecting player in an illegal manner.

cheap·skate *noun informal* a stingy or parsimonious person; a miser. [CHEAP + SKATE³]

cheat ● *verb* **1** *transitive* **a** gain an advantage over or deprive of something by using unfair or deceitful methods; defraud (*cheated him out of his savings*). **b** deprive someone of something to which they are entitled (*this plot treatment cheats moviegoers*). **2** *intransitive* act dishonestly or unfairly in order to gain an advantage, esp. in a game or examination. **3** *transitive* avoid (something undesirable) by luck or skill (*cheated fate*). **4** *intransitive* (usu. foll. by *on*) **a** be sexually unfaithful to. **b** lapse from strict adherence to (a diet). **5** *intransitive* use different and inferior materials or methods unobtrusively, esp. in order to save time or money. ● *noun* **1** a person who cheats. **2** a trick, fraud, or deception. **3** an act of cheating. **4** (also **cheat code**) (with reference to computer games) a means that is not strictly within the rules of a game by which gamers can gain an advantage. [Middle English *chete* from *achete*, var. of ESCHEAT]

cheat·er *noun* **1** a person who cheats. **2** (in *pl.*) *N Amer. slang* eyeglasses.

cheat sheet *noun N Amer.* a usu. small piece of paper with written notes carried surreptitiously into an exam etc.

Cheb·ok·sary /ˌtʃebəkˈsɑri/ a city in west central Russia, on the Volga River, west of Kazan, capital of the autonomous republic of Chuvashia; pop. (est. 2002) 430,000.

Chech·en /ˈtʃetʃən/ ● *noun* **1** a member of a Muslim people of the Chechen Republic, an autonomous republic in SE Russia. **2** the Caucasian language of this people. ● *adjective* of or relating to this people.

Chechen Republic /ˈtʃetʃen/ (also **Chech·nya** /ˌtʃetʃnjə/) an autonomous republic in the Caucasus in SW Russia, on the border with Georgia; pop. (1990) 1,290,000; capital, Grozny. The republic declared itself independent in 1991, resulting in a protracted armed conflict with Russia.

check ● *verb* **1** *transitive & intransitive* **a** examine the accuracy, quality, or condition of; inspect. **b** (often foll. by *that* + clause) make sure; verify; establish to one's satisfaction (*checked that the doors were locked*; *checked the train times*). **c** search; look through (*checked the house for the lost item*). **2** *transitive* **a** stop or slow the motion of; curb, restrain (*checked his anger*). **b** find fault with; rebuke. **3** *transitive Hockey* **a** physically obstruct the progress of (an opponent). **b** cause (an opponent) to lose possession of the puck. **4** *transitive Chess* move a piece into a position that directly threatens (the opposing king). **5** *intransitive Cards* (in poker) choose not to make a bet when called upon, allowing another player to do so instead. **6** *transitive* (often foll. by *off*) make a mark next to an item to indicate that it has been dealt with, chosen, or verified. **7** *transitive N Amer.* deposit (a coat, luggage, etc.) for temporary storage or dispatch. **8** *intransitive* (of a hunting dog) pause to ensure or regain a scent. ● *noun* **1** a means or act of testing or ensuring accuracy, quality, satisfactory condition, etc. **2** a measure or policy to ensure against fraud or abuse (*checks and balances*). **3 a** a stopping or slowing of motion; a restraint on action. **b** a rebuff or rebuke. **c** a person or thing that restrains. **4** *Hockey* an instance of checking an opponent; a bodycheck. **5** *Chess* **a** the exposure of a king to direct attack from an opposing piece. **b** (also as *interjection*) an announcement of this by the attacking player. **6** *N Amer.* = CHECK MARK. **7 a** a pattern of small squares or intersecting lines. **b** fabric having this pattern. **8** esp. *US var.* of CHEQUE etc. **9** *N Amer.* a bill in a restaurant. **10** a ticket used to claim an item which has been temporarily stored. **11** *N Amer.* a counter used in various card games. **12** a temporary loss of the scent (by a hunting dog). **13** a crack or flaw in timber. ● *interjection N Amer.* expressing assent or agreement. □ **check in 1** arrive or register at a hotel, airport, etc. **2** record the arrival of. **check into 1** register one's arrival at (a hotel etc.). **2** investigate. **check (up) on 1** examine carefully or in detail; ascertain the truth about. **2** keep a watch on (a person, work done, etc.). **check out 1** leave a hotel etc. after paying the appropriate fees. **2 a** investigate; examine for authenticity or suitability. **b** *informal* look at; give consideration to (*check out that outfit*). **3** (of two or more items, accounts, etc.) agree or correspond when compared. **4** *N Amer. informal* die. **5** borrow (an item) from a library, video store, etc. **check over** examine for errors; verify. **check something at the door** suppress or ignore something (*judges are expected to check any personal or national bias they have at the door*). **in check** under control, restrained. □ **check·able** *adjective* [Old French *eschequier* play chess, give check to, and Old French *eschec*, ultimately from Persian *šāh* king]

checked *adjective* = CHECKERED 1.

check·er¹ *noun* **1** a person or thing that verifies or examines (*fact checker*; *spell-checker*). **2** esp. *US* a cashier in a supermarket or store. **3** *Hockey* **a** a forward whose role is primarily defensive. **b** any player who checks an opponent.

check·er² (also esp. *Brit.* **chequer**) ● *noun* **1** (often in *pl.*) a pattern of squares, often alternately coloured. **2 a** (in *pl.*; usu. treated as *sing.*)

N Amer. a game for two, played on a checkerboard, in which players attempt to capture all of their opponent's 12 pieces. **b** one of the small round pieces used in this game. ● *transitive verb* **1** mark with a checkered pattern. **2** diversify with a different colour or shade; break the uniformity of. [Middle English from EXCHEQUER]

checker·berry *noun* (*pl.* **-berries**) **1** a N American wintergreen, *Gaultheria procumbens*. **2** the edible red fruit of this plant. [English dial. *chequers* berries of the service tree]

checker·board *noun* (also *Brit.* **chequer·board**) **1** a board with a pattern of squares of alternating colours, arranged in 8 vertical and 8 horizontal rows, used in the game of checkers. **2** something with a pattern resembling this.

check·ered *adjective* (also esp. *Brit.* **chequered**) **1** marked with a pattern of small squares, often of alternating colours. **2** having undergone varied fortunes; having discreditable episodes (*a checkered career*).

checkered flag *noun* (also **chequered flag**) *Motorsport* a flag with a black and white checkered pattern, displayed to drivers or riders at the moment of finishing a race.

checker lily *noun* = CHOCOLATE LILY.

check-in *noun* **1** the act of registering one's arrival at a hotel, airport, etc. (often *attributive*: *check-in counter*). **2** the place where one registers arrival at a hotel, airport, etc.

check·list *noun* an inventory or other (usu. complete) list of items for comparison or verification.

check mark *noun N Amer.* a mark placed beside an item to indicate that it has been dealt with, chosen, or verified.

check·mate ● *noun* **1** *Chess* **a** a check from which a king cannot escape, indicating that the game is over. **b** (also as *interjection*) an announcement of this. **2** a final defeat or deadlock. ● *transitive verb* **1** *Chess* put into checkmate. **2** defeat; frustrate. [Old French *eschec mat* from Persian *šāh māt* the king is dead]

check·out *noun* **1** an act of registering one's departure from a hotel etc. **2** a counter at which goods are paid for in a supermarket or store. **3** the point during an online shopping transaction where one confirms purchase of the goods one has selected.

check·point *noun* a place, esp. a roadblock or manned entrance, where documents, vehicles, etc. are officially inspected.

check·rein *noun* a rein attaching one horse's rein to another's bit, or preventing a horse from lowering its head.

check·room *noun N Amer.* a room where coats, luggage, etc. may be temporarily deposited for a fee.

checks and balances *plural noun* **1** (esp. in the US) constitutional means of limiting or counteracting the wrongful use of governmental or administrative power, esp. in the form of guarantees and counterbalancing influences. **2** counterbalancing influences by which any system is regulated.

check·stop *noun Cdn* (*Alta.*) a roadside checkpoint where drivers are randomly tested with a Breathalyzer.

check·sum *noun Computing* a code transmitted with a data item to provide a check of any errors which may arise in it.

check·up *noun* a thorough examination, esp. of a person's general medical condition.

check valve *noun* a valve allowing flow in one direction only.

Ched·a·buc·to Bay /tʃedəˈbʌktoː/ an inlet of the Atlantic Ocean on the east coast of Nova Scotia between Cape Breton Island and the mainland. [Mi'kmaq *Sedabooktook* 'a bay running far back']

ched·dar *noun* (also **Cheddar**) any of several firm varieties of cheese ranging in colour from white to orange and becoming increasingly strong with age. [*Cheddar* in S England, where it was originally made]

che·der /ˈxeidər, ˈhei-/ *noun* (also **heder**) a school for Jewish children in which Hebrew and religious knowledge are taught. [Hebrew *ḥēder*, lit. 'room']

chee·chako /tʃiˈtʃakoː/ *noun N Amer.* a newcomer or tenderfoot, esp. in the Yukon and Alaska (*compare* SOURDOUGH 3). [Chinook Jargon]

Chee Chee, Ben·ja·min (born Kenneth Thomas Benjamin) (1944–77), Canadian Ojibwa artist. He is known for his linear drawings and modernist acrylics, both of which often depict birds and animals.

cheek ● *noun* **1 a** the side of the face below the eye. **b** the side wall of the mouth. **c** *Cdn* the edible tender flesh around the mouth of a fish, esp. cod. **2 a** impertinent speech. **b** impertinence; cool confidence (*had the cheek to ask for more*). **3** *slang* either of the buttocks. **4 a** either of the side posts of a door etc. **b** either of the jaws of a vise. **c** either of the side pieces of various parts of machines arranged in lateral pairs.

● *transitive verb* speak impertinently to. □ **cheek by jowl** close together; side by side; intimate. **turn the other cheek** accept attack etc. meekly; refuse to retaliate. [Old English *cē(a)ce, cēoce*]

cheek·bone *noun* the bone below the eye that forms the prominent part of the cheek. *Also called* ZYGOMATIC BONE.

-cheeked *combining form* having cheeks of a specified kind (*ruddy-cheeked*).

cheeky *adjective* (**cheek·i·er, cheek·i·est**) impertinent, impudent. □ **cheek·i·ly** *adverb* **cheek·i·ness** *noun*

cheep ● *noun* the weak shrill cry of a young bird. ● *intransitive verb* make such a cry. [imitative: compare PEEP[2]]

cheer ● *noun* **1 a** a shout of encouragement or applause. **b** an organized chant or other series of actions performed by cheerleaders or by a crowd at a sporting event etc. **2** mood, disposition (*full of good cheer*). **3** cheerfulness, gladness (*little cause for cheer*). **4** food and drink (*Christmas cheer*). ● *verb* **1** *transitive* **a** applaud with shouts. **b** (usu. foll. by *on*) urge or encourage. **2** *intransitive* shout for joy. **3** *transitive* (usu. foll. by *up*) make or become less depressed. □ **three cheers** three successive hurrahs for a person or thing honoured. [Anglo-French *chere* face etc., Old French *chiere* from Late Latin *cara* face, from Greek *kara* head]

cheer·ful *adjective* **1** in good spirits, noticeably happy (*a cheerful disposition*). **2** bright, pleasant (*a cheerful room*). **3** willing, not reluctant. □ **cheer·ful·ly** *adverb* **cheer·ful·ness** *noun*

cheer·io *interjection* esp. *Brit. informal* expressing good wishes on parting.

cheer·lead·er *noun* **1** a person who leads a crowd in formal cheers at a sporting event. **2** a person who rouses his or her colleagues into action; a fervent supporter. □ **cheer·lead·ing** *noun*

cheer·less *adjective* gloomy, dreary, miserable. □ **cheer·less·ly** *adverb* **cheer·less·ness** *noun*

cheer·ly *adverb* heartily, with vigour (used as a cry of encouragement amongst sailors).

cheers *interjection* **1** an informal drinking toast. **2** esp. *Brit.* expressing good wishes or gratitude. **3** as a closing salutation in an email.

cheery *adjective* (**cheer·i·er, cheer·i·est**) lively; in good spirits; genial, cheering. □ **cheer·i·ly** *adverb* **cheer·i·ness** *noun*

cheese[1] *noun* **1 a** a food made from the curds of milk separated from the whey, often coagulated by rennet and pressed into a solid mass. **b** a complete cake of this with rind. **2** *Brit.* a food having the consistency of soft cheese. **3** an object with a round flattened shape. □ **hard cheese** *Brit. slang* tough luck; too bad. **say cheese** smile for a photograph. [Old English *cēse* etc., ultimately from Latin *caseus*]

cheese[2] *transitive verb slang* **1** (foll. by *off*) frustrate or exasperate someone. **2** *dated* (foll. by *it*) stop, desist; flee. [19th c.: origin unknown]

cheese[3] *noun* (also **big cheese**) *slang* an important person. [perhaps from Hindustani *chīz* thing]

cheese·board *noun* **1** a board or tray from which cheese is served. **2** a selection of cheeses.

cheese·burger *noun* a hamburger topped with melted cheese.

cheese·cake *noun* **1** a rich sweet cake made with cream cheese or cottage cheese. **2** *informal* the portrayal of women in a sexually provocative manner in photographs.

cheese·cloth *noun* thin loosely woven cloth resembling gauze. [originally used for wrapping cheese]

cheese cutter *noun* **1** any of various utensils used for slicing cheese with a blade or by pulling a wire through it. **2** *Cdn* (*Que. & E Ont.*) *slang* = BOBSKATE.

cheese·monger /ˈtʃiːz,mʌŋɡɜr, -mʌŋɡɜr/ *noun* a dealer in cheese, butter, etc.

cheese-paring ● *adjective* stingy. ● *noun* stinginess.

cheese plant *noun* = SWISS CHEESE PLANT.

cheese straw *noun* a thin cheese-flavoured strip of pastry.

cheese strings *plural noun Cdn & Brit.* cheese, usu. mozzarella or cheddar, that has been pulled into strands which are braided together into a cylinder but may be pulled off to be eaten individually.

cheesy *adjective* (**chees·i·er, chees·i·est**) **1** like cheese in taste, smell, appearance, etc. **2** *slang* inferior in quality, cheap. **3** *slang* unsophisticated, corny. □ **chees·i·ness** *noun*

chee·tah /ˈtʃiːtə/ *noun* a spotted feline native to the plains of Africa and SW Asia, *Acinonyx jubatus*, the world's fastest-running land animal. [Hindi *cītā*, perhaps from Sanskrit *citraka* speckled]

Chee·ver, John (1912–82), US short-story writer and novelist. His work often satirizes middle-class suburban New England life, and his novels include *The Wapshot Chronicle* (1957), *Bullet Park* (1969), and *Falconer* (1977).

uː mood ai my əi pipe au brown ʌu house ei day ɔi boy ã franglais ã Canadien ɔ̃ Brayon (*see over for consonants*)

Cheez·ies *plural noun Cdn proprietary* a snack food consisting of finger-sized pieces of extruded corn meal coated with powdered cheese.

chef /ʃef/ *noun* a cook, esp. the chief cook in a restaurant. [French, = head]

chef de cuisine /ʃef ˌdə kwiˈziːn/ *noun* (*pl.* **chefs de cuisine**) = CHEF. [French, lit. 'head of cooking']

chef de mis·sion /ʃef ˌde mɪˈsjɔ̃/ *noun* (*pl.* **chefs de mission**) the person in charge of a sports delegation, esp. a national team attending international games. [French, lit. 'head of mission']

chef-d'oeuvre /ʃeiˈdɜːvrə/ *noun* (*pl.* **chefs-d'oeuvre** *pronunc.* same) a masterpiece. [French]

chef's knife *noun* a large kitchen knife having a long, gently curved, triangular pointed blade.

chef's salad *noun* a salad, usu. eaten as a main course, consisting of mixed greens, various raw vegetables, strips of ham, chicken, beef, etc., and usu. hard-boiled eggs.

Chekh·ov /ˈtʃekɒf/ **Anton (Pav·lov·ich)** (1860–1904), Russian dramatist and short-story writer. He is best known for his plays *The Seagull* (1896), *Uncle Vanya* (c.1900), *The Three Sisters* (1901), and *The Cherry Orchard* (1904). His work, portraying upper-class life in pre-revolutionary Russia, has had a considerable influence on 20th-c. drama. □ **Che·khov·ian** /tʃeˈkoːviən/ *adjective*

Che·kiang see ZHEJIANG.

chela[1] /ˈkiːlə/ *noun* (*pl.* **che·lae** /-liː/) a prehensile claw of crabs, lobsters, scorpions, etc. [modern Latin from Latin *chele*, or Greek *khēlē* claw]

chela[2] /ˈtʃeilə/ *noun* (in Hinduism) a religious disciple or pupil. [Hindi, = servant]

che·late /ˈkiːleit/ ● *noun Chem.* a chemical compound containing a bonded ring of atoms including a metal atom. ● *adjective* **1** *Chem.* of a chelate. **2** *Zool. & Anat.* of or having chelae. ● *intransitive verb Chem.* form a chelate. □ **che·la·tion** *noun* **che·la·tor** *noun*

Chel·lean /ˈʃeliən/ *adjective Archaeology* = ABBEVILLIAN. [French *chelléen* from *Chelles* near Paris]

Chelms·ford /ˈtʃelmzfərd/ a cathedral city in SE England, the county town of Essex; pop. (est. 2002) 100,700.

chelo·nian /kəˈloːniən/ ● *noun* any reptile of the order Testudines (formerly Chelonia), including turtles, terrapins, and tortoises. ● *adjective* of or relating to this order. [modern Latin *Chelonia* from Greek *khelōnē* tortoise]

Chel·sea /ˈtʃelsi/ **1** a residential district of London, on the north bank of the Thames. **2** a municipality in SW central Quebec, northwest of Gatineau; pop. (2001) 6,036. [sense 2 from *Chelsea*, Vermont]

Chelsea bun *noun* a spiral-shaped yeast bun containing currants and coated with sugar. [CHELSEA 1]

Chelsea pensioner *noun Brit.* an inmate of the Chelsea Royal Hospital for old or disabled soldiers.

Chel·ten·ham /ˈtʃeltənəm/ a town in W England, in Gloucestershire. Noted for its saline springs, it became a fashionable spa town in the 19th c.

Chel·ya·binsk /ˌtʃeljaˈbɪnsk/ an industrial city in S Russia on the eastern slopes of the Ural Mountains; pop. (est. 2002) 1,107,000.

chem /ˈkem/ *noun N Amer. informal* a chemistry class or course. [abbreviation]

chem. *abbreviation* **1** chemical. **2** chemistry. **3** chemist.

chemi- *combining form* var. of CHEMO-.

chem·ical /ˈkemikəl/ ● *adjective* of, made by, or employing chemistry or chemicals. ● *noun* a compound or substance that has been purified or prepared, esp. artificially. □ **chem·ical·ly** *adverb* [*chemic* alchemic, from French *chimique* or modern Latin *chimicus*, *chymicus*, from medieval Latin *alchymicus*: see ALCHEMY]

chemical bond *noun* = BOND *noun* 7.

chemical castration *noun* the use of testosterone-suppressing drugs to eliminate sexual desire as a punishment for sex offenders and to prevent them from reoffending.

chemical dependency *noun* drug or alcohol addiction.

chemical engineering *noun* the science of the utilization of chemical processes in manufacturing and industry. □ **chemical engineer** *noun*

chemical reaction *noun* a process whereby compounds or elements undergo a change in structure and form new compounds.

chemical warfare *noun* the military deployment of chemical weapons.

chemical weapon *noun* a weapon that depends for its effect on the release of a toxic or noxious substance, e.g. poison gas.

chemico- /ˈkemɪkə/ *combining form* chemical; chemical and (*chemico-physical*).

chemi·lumin·es·cence /ˌkeməˌluːməˈnesəns, -ˌljuː-/ *noun* the emission of light during a chemical reaction. □ **chemi·lumin·es·cent** *adjective*

che·min de fer /ʃəˌmã də ˈfer/ *noun* a form of baccarat in which the deal passes from player to player. [French, = railway, lit. 'road of iron']

che·mise /ʃəˈmiːz/ *noun* a woman's loose-fitting undergarment or dress hanging straight from the shoulders. [Old French from Late Latin *camisia* shirt]

chemi·sorp·tion /ˌkeməˈsɔrpʃən/ *noun* adsorption by chemical bonding. [CHEMI- + ADSORPTION (see ADSORB)]

chem·ist /ˈkemɪst/ *noun* **1** a scientist practising or trained in chemistry. **2** *Brit.* = PHARMACIST. [French *chimiste* from modern Latin *chimista* from *alchimista* ALCHEMIST (see ALCHEMY)]

chem·istry /ˈkeməstri/ *noun* (*pl.* **-tries**) **1** the study of the elements, the compounds they form, and the reactions they undergo. **2 a** the chemical constituents or properties of a substance or organism (*the chemistry of sea water*). **b** the elements that make up an emotional process etc. (*the chemistry of fear*). **3** *informal* the interaction, attraction, or rapport existing among two or more people.

Chem·nitz /ˈkemnɪts/ an industrial city in eastern Germany, on the Chemnitz River; pop. (est. 2002) 256,100. Between 1953 and 1990 it was called Karl-Marx-Stadt.

chemo /ˈkiːmoː/ *noun N Amer. informal* = CHEMOTHERAPY. [abbreviation]

chemo- /ˈkiːmoː/ *combining form* (also **chemi-** /ˈkemi/) chemical.

chemo·preven·tion *noun* the use of pharmaceuticals to prevent disease.

chemo·recep·tor *noun* a sensory cell or organ responsive to chemical stimuli. □ **chemo·recep·tion** *noun*

chemo·synth·esis /ˌkiːmoːˈsɪnθəsɪs/ *noun* the synthesis of organic compounds by energy derived from chemical reactions.

chemo·taxis /ˌkiːmoːˈtaksɪs/ *noun Biol.* motion of a motile cell, organism, or part towards or away from a chemical stimulus. □ **chemo·tac·tic** /-ˈtaktɪk/ *adjective*

chemo·ther·apy /ˌkiːmoːˈθerəpi/ *noun* the treatment of disease, esp. cancer, by use of highly toxic chemical substances which target rapidly-dividing cells to slow cell division. □ **chemo·thera·peut·ic** /-ˈpjuːtɪk/ *adjective* **chemo·ther·apist** *noun*

Chenab River /tʃɪˈnab/ a river of N India and Pakistan, which rises in the Himalayas and flows through Himachal Pradesh and Jammu and Kashmir, to join the Sutlej River in Punjab. It is one of the five rivers that gave Punjab its name.

Cheng·chow see ZHENGZHOU.

Cheng·du /tʃeŋˈduː/ the capital of Sichuan province in west central China; pop. (est. 2002) 3,312,200.

Ché·nier /ʃeiˈnjei/ **Jean-Olivier** (1806–37), Canadian physician and reformer, who became a leader of the Patriotes of the Deux-Montagnes region, and was killed at Saint-Eustache during the Rebellion of 1837.

che·nille /ʃəˈniːl/ *noun* **1** a velvety cord or yarn surrounded with pile, used in trimming furniture, bedspreads, or clothing. **2** fabric made from this. [French, lit. 'hairy caterpillar' from Latin *canicula* diminutive of *canis* dog]

Che·nin Blanc /ˌʃenɪn ˈblɒŋk/ *noun* **1** a variety of white grape, native to the Loire valley but now also cultivated in North America, and used to make wine with a distinctive flowery taste. **2** a white wine made from this grape. [French, perhaps from the name of the manor of Mont-*Chenin* near Tours]

Chen·nai /ˈtʃɪnai/ a seaport (formerly Madras) on the east coast of India, capital of Tamil Nadu; pop. (2001) 4,298,600.

cheong·sam /tʃɒŋˈsam/ *noun* a woman's garment with a high neck and slit skirt, worn in China and E Asia. [Cantonese var. of Mandarin *chángshān*, lit. 'long dress']

Che·ops /ˈkiːɒps/ (Egyptian name Khufu) (early 26th c. BC), Egyptian pharaoh of the 4th dynasty, who commissioned the building of the great pyramid at Giza.

cheque /tʃek/ *noun* (also esp. *US* **check**) **1** a written order to a bank to pay the stated sum from the drawer's account to a specified person or company. **2** the printed form on which such an order is written. [special use of CHECK to mean 'device for checking the amount of an item']

cheque·book *noun* **1** a book of forms for writing cheques and

---

Consonants: b *but* d *dog* f *few* g *get* h *her* j *yes* k *cat* l *leg* m *man* n *no* p *pen* r *red* s *sit*

recording the transactions of a chequing account. **2** one's financial means, esp. when seen as a source of donations.

chequebook journalism *noun* the payment of large sums by a news medium for exclusive rights to material for (esp. personal or scandalous) stories.

cheque card *noun Brit.* a card issued by a bank to guarantee the honouring of cheques up to a stated amount.

chequer *esp. Brit. var. of* CHECKER².

chequer·board *esp. Brit. var. of* CHECKERBOARD.

chequered *esp. Brit. var. of* CHECKERED.

chequing account *noun N Amer.* a bank account against which cheques may be written (*compare* SAVINGS ACCOUNT).

Cher·bourg /ˈʃɛrˈbuːr/ a seaport and naval base in Normandy, N France; pop. (1999) 25,370.

Cher·en·kov /tʃɪˈrɛŋkɒf/ **Pavel (Alek·sey·evich)** (also **Cer·en·kov**) (1904–90), Soviet physicist. He investigated the effects of high-energy particles, in particular, the blue light emitted from water containing a radioactive substance, and suggested the cause of this radiation (an example of what is now called *Cerenkov radiation*); he shared the 1958 Nobel Prize for physics.

Cherenkov radiation *var. of* CERENKOV RADIATION.

Cher·epo·vets /ˌtʃɛrəpəˈvjets/ a city in NW Russia, on the Rybinsk reservoir; pop. (est. 2002) 324,800.

cheri·moya /ˌtʃɛrɪˈmɔɪə/ *noun* **1** a kind of custard apple with a pineapple-like flavour and scaly green skin. **2** the small tree, *Annona cherimola*, which bears this fruit, native to the Andes of Peru and Ecuador. [Spanish, from Quechua, from *chiri* 'cold or refreshing' + *muya* 'circle']

cher·ish /ˈtʃɛrɪʃ/ *transitive verb* **1** protect or tend to lovingly. **2** hold dear, cling to (emotions, memories, etc.). [Old French *cherir* from *cher* from Latin *carus* dear]

Cher·kasy /tʃɜrˈkasi/ a port in central Ukraine, on the Dnieper River; pop. (est. 2001) 295,000.

Cher·kessk /tʃɜrˈkesk/ a city in the Caucasus in S Russia, capital of the republic of Karachai-Cherkessia; pop. (est. 2002) 121,700.

Cher·nenko /tʃɜrˈnjeŋkɔː/ **Kon·stan·tin (Ustin·ovich)** (1911–85), Soviet political leader, General Secretary of the Communist Party of the USSR and president 1984–5. He became a full member of the Politburo in 1978, and succeeded Andropov in the presidency, but died after only thirteen months in office.

Cher·ni·hiv /tʃɜrˈniːhɪv/ (Russian **Cher·ni·gov** /tʃɜrˈnigɒf/) a city in N Ukraine, on the Desna River; pop. (est. 2001) 301,000.

Cher·niv·tsi /tʃɜrˈnɪvtsi/ a city in W Ukraine, in the foothills of the Carpathians, close to the border with Romania; pop. (est. 2001) 240,000. It was part of Romania between 1918 and 1940.

Cher·nobyl /tʃɜrˈnoːbəl/ a town near Kiev in Ukraine where, in April 1986, an accident at a nuclear power station resulted in a serious escape of radioactive material and the subsequent contamination of Ukraine, Belarus and other parts of Europe.

Cher·no·reche /ˌtʃɜrnəˈretʃə/ a former name (until 1919) for DZERZHINSK.

cher·no·zem /tʃɜrnɒˌzem/ *noun* a fertile black soil rich in humus, found in temperate or cool grasslands. *Also called* BLACK EARTH. □ **cher·no·zem·ic** /ˌtʃɜrnɒːˈzemɪk/ *adjective* [Russian from *chernyi* black + *zemlya* earth]

Chero·kee /ˈtʃɛrəki/ ● *noun* **1** a member of an Iroquoian people formerly inhabiting much of the southeastern US, now largely confined to Oklahoma and N Carolina. **2** the language of this people. ● *adjective* of or relating to the Cherokees or their language. [Cherokee *Tsálági*]

che·root /ʃəˈruːt/ *noun* a cigar with both ends open. [French *cheroute* from Tamil *shuruttu* roll]

Cher River /ʃer/ a river of central France, which rises in the Massif Central, flowing 350 km (220 miles) northward to meet the Loire near Tours.

cherry ● *noun* (*pl.* **-ries**) **1 a** a small soft round fruit, usu. red when ripe, with a single stone in its centre. **b** any of several trees of the genus *Prunus* bearing this fruit or grown for its ornamental flowers. **2** (also **cherry·wood**) the reddish wood of a cherry tree. **3** *N Amer. slang* **a** virginity. **b** a virgin. **4** *N Amer. slang* the red light on the roof of a police car. ● *adjective* of a light red colour. □ **bowl of cherries** a consistently pleasurable, carefree experience (*life is not a bowl of*

cherries). [Old Northern French *cherise* (taken as pl.: compare PEA) from medieval Latin *ceresia* perhaps from Latin from Greek *kerasos*]

cherry bomb *noun N Amer.* a small firecracker which explodes loudly when ignited.

cherry brandy *noun* a dark red liqueur of brandy in which cherries have been steeped.

cherry laurel *noun* a small evergreen tree, *Prunus laurocerasus*, with white flowers and cherry-like fruits.

cherry-pick *transitive & intransitive verb N Amer.* **1** select only those items which are desirable or require little effort. **2** select items individually from various places, esp. to obtain the best value.

cherry picker *noun* **1** a crane with an articulated arm and a bucket for raising and lowering workers, firefighters, etc. **2** *Cdn* (*BC*) a tractor-like machine with a crane for retrieving logs lost along a road or railway. **3** = GOAL SUCK.

cherry plum *noun* **1** a tree, *Prunus cerasifera*, native to SW Asia, with solitary white flowers and red fruits. **2** the fruit of this tree. *Also called* MYROBALAN.

cherry·stone *noun* (also **cherrystone clam**) a small edible northern quahog clam.

cherry tomato *noun* a small red or yellow variety of tomato.

Cher·so·nese /ˈkɜrsəˌniːs/ an ancient name for the Gallipoli peninsula.

chert /tʃɜrt/ *noun* a flint-like form of quartz composed of chalcedony. □ **cherty** *adjective* [17th c.: origin unknown]

cher·ub /ˈtʃɛrəb/ *noun* **1** (*pl.* **cher·ub·im** /-bɪm/) **a** *Bible* a supernatural being resembling a winged lion with a human face. **b** *Christianity* a member of the second order of the nine ranks of heavenly beings (*see* ORDER *noun* 19). **2** (*pl.* **cher·ubs**) *Art* a representation of a winged child or the head of a winged child. **3** (*pl.* **cher·ubs**) a beautiful or innocent child. [Old English *cherubin* and from Hebrew *kᵉrūb*, pl. *kᵉrūbīm*]

che·rub·ic /tʃɪˈruːbɪk, -rʌb-, ˈtʃɛrəbɪk/ *adjective* of, pertaining to, or resembling a cherub or cherubs, esp. in having a round face, cheerful disposition, etc. □ **che·rub·ic·ally** *adverb*

Cheru·bini /ˌkeruˈbiːni/ **(Maria) Luigi (Carlo Zeno·bio Sal·va·tore)** (1760–1842), Italian composer. He spent most of his composing career in Paris and is principally known for his church music and operas, which include *Les Deux Journées* (1800).

cher·vil /ˈtʃɜrvɪl/ *noun* an umbelliferous plant, *Anthriscus cerefolium*, with small white flowers, used as a herb for flavouring soup, salads, etc. [Old English *cerfille* from Latin *chaerephylla* from Greek *khairephullon*]

Cher·well /ˈtʃɑːrwel/ **Fred·erick Alex·an·der Linde·mann, 1st Viscount** (1886–1957), German-born English physicist. A number of theories and items are named after him, including a theory of specific heat, a formula concerning the melting point of crystals, and an electrometer; he was scientific adviser to Churchill during the Second World War.

Ches. *abbreviation* Cheshire.

Chesa·peake Bay /ˈtʃesəˌpiːk/ a large inlet of the N Atlantic on the US coast, extending 320 km (200 miles) northward through the states of Virginia and Maryland.

Chesh·ire¹ /ˈtʃeʃər, ˈtʃeʃiːr/ a county of west central England; county town, Chester.

Chesh·ire² *noun* a kind of firm crumbly cheese resembling cheddar. [CHESHIRE¹, where it was originally made]

Cheshire cat *noun* an imaginary cat with a broad fixed inexplicable grin. □ **grin like a Cheshire cat** smile with a broad, contented grin as if highly amused or knowing a secret. [a character in Lewis Carroll's *Alice in Wonderland*]

Chesil Beach /ˈtʃezəl/ (also **Chesil Bank**) a shingle beach in S England, on the Dorset coast. Separated from the mainland by a tidal lagoon, it is over 25 km (17 miles) long.

chess *noun* a game for two, played on a chessboard with 16 pieces each, in which players attempt to place their opponent's king in checkmate. [Old French *esches* pl. of *eschec* CHECK]

chess·board *noun* a board with a pattern of squares of alternating colours, arranged in 8 vertical and 8 horizontal rows, used in the game of chess.

chess·man *noun* (*pl.* **-men**) any of the 32 pieces used in the game of chess.

chest *noun* **1 a** the part of a human or animal body enclosed by the ribs. **b** the upper front surface of the body; the breast. **2** a large strong box, esp. for storage or transport of items. **3** a small cabinet for toiletries, medicines, etc. **4** *Brit.* **a** the treasury or financial resources of an institution. **b** the money available from it. □ **get a thing off one's chest** *informal* disclose a fact, secret, etc., to relieve one's anxiety about it. **play (one's cards, a thing,** etc.) **close to one's chest** *informal* be cautious or secretive about. [Old English *cest, cyst* from Germanic from Latin from Greek *kistē*]

-chested *combining form* having a chest of a specified kind (*bare-chested*).

Ches·ter 1 a town in W England, the county town of Cheshire; pop. (est. 2002) 80,800. **2** a village on the southeastern coast of Nova Scotia, situated on Mahone Bay, about 70 km west of Halifax; pop. (2001) 10,781. [sense 2 possibly after *Chester*, Pennsylvania]

Ches·ter·field, Phil·ip Dor·mer Stan·hope, 4th Earl of (1694–1773), English statesman, diplomat, and writer. He was ambassador to Holland 1728–32, and Lord Lieutenant of Ireland 1745–6, but is chiefly remembered for his *Letters to His Son* (1732–68), which consist of instruction in etiquette and social advancement.

ches·ter·field *noun* **1 a** *Cdn* any couch or sofa. **b** a padded sofa with arms the same height as the back. **2** a man's plain overcoat usu. with a velvet collar. [19th-c. Earl of *Chesterfield*]

Chesterfield Inlet a long, narrow inlet on the northwestern shore of Hudson Bay, extending over 150 km westward to Baker Lake. [CHESTERFIELD]

Ches·ter·ton, Gil·bert Keith (1874–1936), English essayist, novelist, and critic. He is best known for his series of stories about the crime-solving priest Father Brown (1911–35); he became a Roman Catholic in 1922.

chest·nut ● *noun* **1** any of several trees of the genus *Castanea* of the beech family, bearing flowers in catkins and nuts enclosed in a spiny fruit, esp.: **a** *C. dentata* of N America. **b** *C. sativa* of Eurasia. *Also called* SWEET CHESTNUT. **2** the large edible nut of any of these trees. **3** the heavy wood of any of these trees. **4** = HORSE CHESTNUT. **5** a horse of a reddish-brown or yellowish-brown colour. **6** a small hard callus on a horse's leg. **7** *informal* a stale joke or anecdote. **8** a reddish-brown colour. ● *adjective* reddish brown in colour. [obsolete *chesten* from Old French *chastaine* from Latin *castanea* from Greek *kastanea*]

chest of drawers *noun* a piece of furniture consisting of a set of drawers in a frame.

chest-thumping *noun* vociferous self-congratulation that draws attention to oneself.

chest voice *noun* the lowest register of the voice in singing or speaking.

chesty *adjective* (**chest·i·er, chest·i·est**) **1** *informal* having a large chest or prominent breasts. **2** *N Amer. slang* arrogant. **3** *Brit.* (of a cough etc.) symptomatic of a chest ailment.

Chet·nik /ˈtʃetnɪk/ *noun* a member of a Serbian nationalist and anti-Communist guerrilla force which operated during both World Wars and re-emerged in the late 1980s. [Serbo-Croat *četnik* from *četa* band, troop]

chet·rum /ˈtʃetruːm/ *noun* (*pl.* same or **chet·rums**) a monetary unit of Bhutan, equal to one-hundredth of a ngultrum. [Dzongkha]

Chetu·mal /ˌtʃetuˈmɒl/ a port in SE Mexico, on the Yucatán Peninsula at the border with Belize, capital of the state of Quintana Roo; pop. (2000) 121,600.

che·val glass /ʃəˈval/ *noun* a tall mirror designed to pivot on an upright frame. [French *cheval* horse, frame]

Che·va·lier /ʃəˈvaljei/ **Mau·rice** (1888–1972), French singer and actor. He first gained international fame as a singer and dancer in Paris during the 1920s, and went on to star in Hollywood musicals such as *Innocents of Paris* (1929), *Love Me Tonight* (1932), and *Gigi* (1958).

cheva·lier /ʃevaˈliːr, ʃəˈvaljei/ *noun* **1 a** a member of certain orders of knighthood or distinction, as the Legion of Honour in France. **b** *hist.* a minor member of the former French nobility. **c** *archaic* or *hist.* a knight. **2 (Chevalier)** *Brit. hist.* the title of the Old and Young Pretenders. **3** a chivalrous man; a cavalier. [Old French from medieval Latin *caballarius* from Latin *caballus* horse]

che·vet /ʃəˈvei/ *noun* the apsidal end of a church, sometimes with an attached group of apses. [French, = pillow, from Latin *capitium* from *caput* head]

Chev·iot /ˈtʃeviət, ˈtʃ-/ *noun* **1** a sheep of a hardy and hornless breed with wool of moderate length and thickness. **2 (cheviot)** the wool or cloth obtained from this breed. [CHEVIOT HILLS]

Cheviot Hills (also **Cheviots**) a range of hills on the border between England and Scotland.

chèvre /ˈʃevr/ *noun* a soft goat's-milk cheese of a kind orig. from France, usu. made in a log shape. [French, = goat]

chev·ron /ˈʃevrən, -rɒn/ *noun* **1** a badge in a V shape on the sleeve of a uniform indicating rank or length of service. **2** an ornamental representation of this. **3** any V-shaped line or stripe. [Old French, ultimately from Latin *caper* goat: compare Latin *capreoli* pair of rafters]

chev·ro·tain /ˈʃevrəˌtein/ (also **chev·ro·tin** /-tɪn/) *noun* any small hoofed mammal of the family Tragulidae, native to Africa and SE Asia, resembling a rodent with slender legs, reddish-brown fur spotted with white, and tusks in the male. [French, diminutive of Old French *chevrot* diminutive of *chèvre* goat]

chevy *var.* of CHIVVY.

chew ● *verb* **1** *transitive & intransitive* work (food etc.) between the teeth; crush or indent with the teeth. **2** *transitive* (often foll. by *up*) shred, mangle, mutilate, or otherwise damage (*the car chewed up the road*). **3** *transitive* (foll. by *on* or *over*) think about, meditate on, discuss. **4** *intransitive* use chewing tobacco, esp. habitually. ● *noun* **1** an act of chewing. **2** something intended for chewing, esp. tobacco or candy. □ **chew the cud 1** (of an animal) ruminate. **2** reflect, ponder. **chew the fat** (or **rag**) *slang* chat; converse informally. **chew out** *N Amer. informal* reprimand harshly. □ **chew·able** *adjective* **chew·er** *noun* [Old English *cēowan*]

chew·ing gum *noun* flavoured and sweetened gum, esp. chicle, for chewing.

chew·ing tobacco *noun* flavoured tobacco designed for chewing rather than smoking.

chew toy *noun* an item designed for a dog to chew on, e.g. a rawhide or nylon bone.

chewy *adjective* (**chew·i·er, chew·i·est**) **1** needing much chewing. **2** suitable for chewing. □ **chew·i·ness** *noun*

Chey·enne[1] /ʃaiˈan, -ˈen/ the state capital of Wyoming; pop. (2000) 53,011.

Chey·enne[2] /ʃaiˈan, -ˈen/ ● *noun* **1** (*pl.* same or **-ennes**) a member of an Algonquian people formerly living between the Missouri and Arkansas rivers, now inhabiting Oklahoma and Montana. **2** the language of this people. ● *adjective* of or relating to the Cheyenne or their language. [Canadian French from Dakota *Sahiyena*]

Cheyne-Stokes /ˌtʃein ˈstoːks/ *adjective* *Med.* (of a breathing pattern) involving a cycle of gradual decrease, cessation, and gradual increase. [J. *Cheyne*, Scottish physician d.1836, and W. *Stokes*, Irish physician d.1878]

chez /ʃei/ *preposition* at the house or home of. [French from Old French *chiese* from Latin *casa* cottage]

Chhat·tis·garh /ˌtʃatɪzˈɡar/ a state in central India, formed in 2000 from the southeast part of Madhya Pradesh; capital, Raipur.

chi /kai/ *noun* the twenty-second letter of the Greek alphabet (Χ, χ). [Greek *khi*]

ch'i /ˈtʃiː/ *noun* (also **qi, chi**) (in Chinese philosophy) the immaterial substance which composes all things, esp. the vital life force residing within the breath and body. [Chinese, = breath]

chia /ˈtʃiːə/ *noun* **1** a plant of the mint family, *Salvia columbaria*, with clusters of small two-lipped purple flowers, common throughout California. **2** a related plant, *S. hispanica* whose seeds can be sprouted on clay planters, e.g. in the shape of animals. [Mexican Spanish from Nahuatl]

Chiang Kai-shek /ˌtʃjaŋ kaiˈʃek/ (also **Jiang Jie Shi** /ˌdʒjaŋ dʒiːˈʃiː/) (1887–1975), Chinese general and Kuomintang leader, president of China 1928–31 and 1943–9 and of Taiwan 1950–75. A general in the army of Sun Yat-sen, in the 1930s he concentrated more on defeating the Chinese Communists than on resisting the invading Japanese. He was defeated by the Communists after the Second World War, retreated to Taiwan, and set up a separate Nationalist Chinese State in 1949.

Chiang·mai /tʃjaŋˈmai/ a city in NW Thailand; pop. (2000) 167,800.

Chi·anti /kiˈanti/ *noun* (*pl.* **Chi·antis**) a dry usu. red Italian wine. [*Chianti*, an area in Tuscany, Italy]

Chi·apas /tʃiˈɒpɒs/ a state of S Mexico, on the border with Guatemala; capital, Tuxtla Gutiérrez.

chiaro·scuro /kiˌɑrəˈskuːroː, -skjɑroː/ *noun* **1** the treatment of light and shade in drawing and painting. **2** a monochrome print or woodcut. **3** any contrast of light and dark. [Italian from *chiaro* CLEAR + *oscuro* dark, OBSCURE]

chi·asma /kaiˈazmə/ *noun* (*pl.* **chi·as·mata** /-tə/) **1** *Anat.* an intersection or crossing, esp. (in full **optic chiasma**) the point where the two optic nerves are joined. **2** *Biol.* the point at which paired chromosomes remain in contact after crossing over during meiosis. [modern Latin from Greek *chiasma* a cross-shaped mark]

chi·as·mus /kai'azməs/ noun (pl. **chi·as·mi** /-mai/) inversion in the second of two parallel phrases of the order followed in the first (e.g. *to stop too fearful and too faint to go*). □ **chi·as·tic** adjective [modern Latin from Greek *khiasmos* crosswise arrangement, from *khiazō* mark with letter CHI]

Chiba /'tʃiːbə/ a city in Japan, on the island of Honshu, east of Tokyo; pop. (est. 2002) 902,600.

Chi·bou·ga·mau /ʃiːbuːgaˈmoː, ʃhəˈbuːgəˌmuː/ a mining and forestry town in north central Quebec, northwest of Lac Saint-Jean; pop. (2001) 7,992. [Cree, = 'lake traversed by a river' or 'meeting place']

chi·bouk /tʃɪˈbuːk/ noun (also **chi·bouque**) a long Turkish tobacco pipe. [Turkish *çubuk* tube]

chic /ʃiːk/ ● adjective (**chic·er**, **chic·est**) stylish, elegant (in dress or appearance). ● noun stylishness, elegance. □ **chic·ness** noun **chic·ly** adverb [French, prob. from German *Schick* 'skill']

Chi·ca·go /ʃɪˈkɒɡoʊ/ a city in Illinois, on Lake Michigan; pop. (2000) 2,896,016. □ **Chi·ca·go·an** noun & adjective

Chi·cana /tʃɪˈkɒnə, -ˈkɑnə/ noun esp. US a female American of Mexican origin. [Spanish *mejicana* Mexican female (see CHICANO)]

chi·cane /ʃɪˈkeɪn/ ● noun 1 a an artificial barrier or obstacle on an automobile racetrack. b a similar barrier on a road intended to reduce the speed of traffic. 2 *Cards* (in bridge) a hand without trumps, or without cards of one suit. ● verb archaic 1 intransitive use chicanery. 2 transitive (usu. foll. by into, out of, etc.) cheat (a person). [French *chicane(r)* quibble]

chi·can·ery /ʃɪˈkeɪnəri/ noun (pl. **-eries**) 1 clever but misleading talk; a false argument. 2 trickery, deception. [French *chicanerie* (as CHICANE)]

Chi·cano /tʃɪˈkɒnoʊ, -ˈkɑnoʊ/ noun (pl. **-canos**) esp. US an American, esp. a male, of Mexican origin. [Spanish *mejicano* Mexican]

Chic-Chocs, Monts /ʃikˈʃɒk/ a chain of mountains in E Quebec, situated along the northern shore of the Gaspé Peninsula. They are an extension of the Monts Notre-Dame. [from Mi'kmaq *sigsôg* steep rocks]

Chi·ches·ter /'tʃɪtʃɪstər/ a city in S England, the county town of West Sussex; pop. (est. 2002) 27,200.

chi-chi /'ʃiːʃiː/ adjective 1 (of a thing) ostentatiously stylish or fashionable. 2 (of a person or behaviour) fussy, affected. [French]

chick noun 1 a young or newly hatched bird, esp. a chicken. 2 slang often offensive a young woman. 3 a child. □ **neither chick nor child** no children at all. [Middle English: shortening of CHICKEN; idiom from sense 3]

chick·a·dee noun any of various small N American birds of the titmouse family, esp. the black-capped chickadee, *Parus atricapillus*, with a distinctive dark-crowned head. [imitative]

Chick·a·saw noun 1 a member of a Muskogean people formerly resident in Mississippi and Alabama, and subsequently in Oklahoma. 2 the language spoken by this people and the Choctaw. [Chickasaw *čikašša*]

chick drink noun slang derogatory a cocktail perceived as being favoured by or suitable to women, esp. by being sweet, coloured, etc.

chick·en ● noun 1 any of several varieties of domestic fowl raised for their flesh or eggs, esp. a young one. 2 the flesh of the chicken prepared as food. 3 Cdn (BC & Prairies) = PRAIRIE CHICKEN. 4 informal a cowardly person. 5 informal a contest for testing courage in which participants attempt dangerous or reckless feats, usu. to see which one will yield first. ● adjective informal cowardly. ● intransitive verb (foll. by out) informal withdraw from some activity through fear or lack of nerve. □ **count one's chickens** (**before they are hatched**) be over-optimistic. [Old English *cicen*, *cȳcen* from Germanic]

chicken-and-egg adjective of or pertaining to the unresolved question as to which of two things caused the other.

chicken cholera noun an infectious disease of fowls, produced by a bacterium of the genus *Pasteurella*, originally thought to coincide with cholera epidemics.

chicken coop noun a coop for keeping poultry in.

chicken feed noun 1 food for domestic fowl. 2 informal a small amount of money.

Chicken Finger noun proprietary a breaded, deep-fried strip of chicken.

chicken-fried steak noun US a cut of beef which is pounded thin, lightly battered, and fried until crisp.

chicken hawk noun any of several raptors preying on other birds, esp. domestic fowls.

chicken-hearted adjective (also **chicken-livered**) easily frightened; lacking nerve or courage.

chicken Kiev noun boneless chicken breasts filled with seasoned garlic butter, breaded, and deep-fried. [KIEV]

Chicken Little noun a person who is hysterically convinced of imminent doom with no evidence to sustain the claim. [with reference to the character in the nursery tale who claims that the sky is falling]

chicken nugget noun a small, roughly oval piece of chicken that is breaded and deep-fried.

chicken pox noun an infectious disease, esp. of children, with a rash of small blisters. Also called VARICELLA.

chicken scratch noun informal 1 illegible handwriting. 2 a a style of music resembling polka, originating in Aboriginal communities in the US southwest. b a dance performed to this music.

chicken·shit N Amer. coarse slang ● adjective 1 petty, trivial. 2 cowardly. ● noun 1 trivialities, petty concerns; nonsense. 2 a coward.

chicken wire noun a light wire netting with a hexagonal mesh.

chick flick noun informal a movie that is perceived or marketed to appeal esp. to women, usu. featuring strong female characters and themes of romance, relationships, and female solidarity.

chick magnet noun = BABE MAGNET.

chick·pea noun 1 a leguminous plant, *Cicer arietinum*, with short swollen pods containing yellowish-brown pea-shaped seeds. 2 this seed used as a vegetable. Also called GARBANZO. [originally *ciche pease* from Latin *cicer*: see PEASE]

chick·weed noun any of several plants of the genera *Cerastium* and *Stellaria*, esp. *S. media*, a common weed with slender stems and tiny white flowers.

chicle /'tʃɪkəl, -liː/ noun the milky juice of the sapodilla tree, used in the manufacture of chewing gum. [Latin American Spanish from Nahuatl *tzietli*]

chic·ory /'tʃɪkəri/ noun (pl. **-ories**) 1 a blue-flowered plant, *Cichorium intybus*, cultivated for its salad leaves and its root (compare BELGIAN ENDIVE). 2 its root, roasted and ground as a substitute for or an additive to coffee. [obsolete French *cicorée* endive, from Latin *cichorium* from Greek *kikhorion*]

chi·cot /ʃiːˈkoː/ noun Forestry a dead tree or dead part of a tree. [French, = 'stump']

Chi·cou·timi /ʃɪˈkuːtəmiː, ʃiːkuːtiːˈmiː/ a former city in NE central Quebec, located at the confluence of the Chicoutimi and Saguenay rivers, now merged with Jonquière, La Baie, Laterrière, and other communities into the city of Saguenay; pop. (2001) 60,008. [Montagnais, = end of the deep waters]

chide transitive & intransitive verb (past **chid·ed** or **chid**; past participle **chid·ed** or **chid·den**) 1 scold, rebuke. 2 compel by chiding; goad. □ **chid·er** noun **chid·ing·ly** adverb [Old English *cīdan*, of unknown origin]

Chid·ley, Cape /'tʃɪdli/ a cape at the northern tip of the Labrador coast, part of Nunavut politically. [prob. after J. *Chidley*, friend of explorer John Davis *c*.1587]

chief ● noun 1 a a leader or ruler. b the head of a tribe, clan, or Aboriginal band. c the leader of a Canadian Aboriginal community under the band council system. 2 the head of a police or fire department etc.; the highest official. 3 *Heraldry* the upper third of a shield. ● adjective 1 first in position, importance, influence, etc. (*chief engineer*). 2 prominent, leading. □ **-in-chief** (in combination) principal, head (*editor-in-chief*). □ **chief·dom** noun [Old French *ch(i)ef*, ultimately from Latin *caput* head]

Chief Constable noun (esp. in the UK) the head of the police force of a county etc.

chief electoral officer noun Cdn an official appointed to oversee the conduct of federal, provincial, and territorial elections.

chief executive noun 1 = CHIEF EXECUTIVE OFFICER. 2 US the governor of a state or (**Chief Executive**) the president of the US.

chief executive officer noun the highest-ranking executive of a corporation or other institution. Abbr.: **CEO**.

chief factor noun Cdn hist. (in the fur trade) the senior officer overseeing a major trading post and its surrounding district.

chief financial officer noun the senior executive in charge of financial affairs for a corporation or other institution. Abbr.: **CFO**.

chief inspector noun (in the Sûreté du Québec) an officer ranking above inspector.

chief justice noun (also **chief judge**) (in Canada, the US, and several Commonwealth countries) the presiding judge of the Supreme Court or of a court which has several judges, e.g. a provincial court of appeal etc.

uː mood ai my əi pipe au brown ʌu house ei day ɔi boy ũ franglais ã Canadien ɔ̃ Brayon (*see over for consonants*)

chief·ly *adverb* above all; mainly but not exclusively.

Chief of Defence Staff *noun* **1** (in Canada) the senior military official responsible for the control and administration of the Canadian Forces. **2** the senior military official of some other countries.

Chief of Naval Operations *noun* (in the US) the highest-ranking officer in the navy (see JOINT CHIEFS OF STAFF).

chief of police *noun* (in some municipal police forces and in the Royal Newfoundland Constabulary) the highest ranking police officer.

chief of staff *noun* **1** *Military* **a** the senior staff officer of a branch of the armed forces. **b** (Chief of Staff) (in the US) the highest-ranking officer in the army or air force (see JOINT CHIEFS OF STAFF). **2** the head of any government staff, esp. the adviser to a prime minister, president, etc.

chief operating officer *noun* the senior executive in charge of directing the operations of a corporation or other institution. Abbr.: **COO**.

chief petty officer *noun* (also **Chief Petty Officer**) **1** *Cdn* (in the Canadian navy) an officer of either of two ranks: chief petty officer first class (Abbr.: **CPO1**), the highest non-commissioned rank, or chief petty officer second class (Abbr.: **CPO2**), ranking next below it. **2** an officer of the highest non-commissioned rank in other navies. Abbr.: **CPO**.

chief superintendent *noun* **1** (in the Ontario Provincial Police) an officer ranking above superintendent and below deputy commissioner. **2** (in the RCMP) an officer ranking above superintendent and below assistant commissioner.

chief·tain /ˈtʃiːftən/ *noun* the leader of a tribe or clan; chief. □ **chief·tain·cy** *noun* (pl. **-cies**). **chief·tain·ship** *noun* [Old French *chevetaine* from Late Latin *capitaneus* CAPTAIN: assimilated to CHIEF]

chief·tain·ess /ˌtʃiːftəˈnes/ *noun* a female leader of a tribe or clan.

chief warrant officer *noun* (also **Chief Warrant Officer**) **1** (in the Canadian Army and Air Force) the highest-ranking non-commissioned officer. Abbr.: **CWO**. **2** (in the US armed services) the highest of four ranks of warrant officer. Abbr.: **CWO**.

Ch'ien-lung /tʃiˈanˈlʊŋ/ see QIAN LONG.

chiff·chaff *noun* a small European bird of the warbler family, *Phylloscopus collybita*. [imitative]

chif·fon /ʃəˈfɒn/ ● *noun* a light diaphanous fabric of silk, nylon, etc. ● *adjective* **1** made of chiffon. **2** (of a pie filling, dessert, etc.) light in texture. [French from *chiffe* rag]

chiffon cake *noun* a light-textured cake made from a batter of flour, sugar, oil, and egg yolks folded into beaten egg whites, usu. baked in a tube pan.

chif·fon·ier /ˌʃɪfəˈniːr/ *noun* a tall and narrow cabinet with drawers or shelves, often having a small mirror on top. [French *chiffonnier*, -*ière* ragpicker, chest of drawers for odds and ends]

chiffon pie *noun* a pie with a light-textured jelled filling into which beaten egg whites have been folded.

chig·ger *noun* **1** the larva of any of various mites, several of which are parasitic. *Also called* HARVEST MITE. **2** = CHIGOE. [var. of CHIGOE]

Chig·nec·to, Cape /ˈʃɪgnekˌtoː/ a point on the northwestern coast of Nova Scotia. It extends into the Bay of Fundy, separating Chignecto Bay from Minas Channel. [possibly from Mi'kmaq *sigunikt* carpet]

Chig·nec·to Bay the northeastern arm of the Bay of Fundy, separating New Brunswick from Nova Scotia. [see CHIGNECTO, CAPE]

chi·gnon /ˈʃiːnjɔ̃/ *noun* a coil or knot of hair at the back of a woman's head. [French, originally = nape of the neck, based on Latin *catena* 'chain']

chig·oe /ˈtʃɪgoː/ *noun* a tropical flea, *Tunga penetrans*, the pregnant females of which burrow beneath the skin of humans and animals and cause painful sores. *Also called* CHIGGER. [Carib]

Chihli, Gulf of /ˈtʃiːliː/ an alternative name for BO HAI.

Chi·hua·hua /tʃɪˈwɒwə/ **1** a state of N Mexico. **2** its capital, a principal city of north central Mexico; pop. (2000) 657,900.

chi·hua·hua /tʃəˈwɒwə/ *noun* a very small breed of dog with smooth hair, large eyes, and prominent ears. [CHIHUAHUA, where this breed originated]

chi kung *noun* = QIGONG.

chil·blain /ˈtʃɪlblein/ *noun* (usu. in pl.) an itching swelling of the skin, usu. on the hands or feet, caused by exposure to cold and by poor circulation. □ **chil·blained** *adjective* [CHILL + BLAIN]

Chil·cotin /tʃɪlˈkoːtən/ *var. of* TSILHQOT'IN.

Chilcotin, the a region of west central BC, between the Fraser River and the Coast Mountains.

Chilcotin River a river in southwestern BC, 235 km long, which rises west of Quesnel and flows southeastward to join the Fraser south of Williams Lake. [CHILCOTIN]

Child, Julia (b.1912), US cooking expert, known for her books and television series on esp. French cooking.

child *noun* (pl. **chil·dren**) **1 a** a young human being below the age of puberty. **b** an unborn or newborn human being. **2** one's son or daughter (at any age). **3** (foll. by *of*) a descendant, follower, adherent, or product of (*children of Israel*; *child of the TV generation*). **4** a childish person. □ **child·less** *adjective* **child·less·ness** *noun* [Old English *cild*]

child abuse *noun* maltreatment of a child, esp. by beating, neglect, or sexual molestation.

child-bearing ● *noun* the act of giving birth to a child. ● *adjective* of, relating to, or suitable for the bearing of a child or children (*women of child-bearing age*).

child·bed *noun* = CHILDBIRTH.

child benefit *noun* **1** *Cdn* = CHILD TAX BENEFIT. **2** *Brit.* a State monetary allowance for each child in a family.

child·birth *noun* the act of giving birth to a child.

child care *noun* **1** the care and rearing of a child or children. **2** = DAYCARE. **3** (usu. **child·care**) *Brit.* the care of homeless, orphaned, or neglected children by a local authority.

childe /tʃaild/ *noun archaic* (as a title **Childe**) a youth of noble birth (*Childe Harold*). [var. of CHILD]

child·hood *noun* the state or period of being a child.

child·ish *adjective* **1** of, like, or proper to a child. **2** immature, silly. □ **child·ish·ly** *adverb* **child·ish·ness** *noun*

child·like *adjective* **1** of or resembling a child (*a childlike appearance*). **2** having the qualities of a child, esp. positive ones such as innocence or frankness.

child·mind·er *noun* *Brit.* a person who looks after children for payment.

child·proof ● *adjective* **1** unable to be damaged, operated, or opened by a child (*childproof locks*). **2** designed so as to be safe for young children (*childproof kitchen*). ● *transitive verb* render childproof.

chil·dren pl. *of* CHILD.

Children's Aid Society *noun* (also **Children's Aid**) (in Canada) an organization sanctioned to provide assistance or guardianship for homeless or abused children. Abbr.: **CAS**.

Children's Crusade a movement in 1212 in which tens of thousands of children (mostly from France and Germany) were organized for a crusade to the Holy Land. Most of the children never reached their destination, many being sold into slavery before embarking from French and Italian ports.

child's play *noun* an easy task.

child support *noun* money paid to a divorced spouse or guardian for the support of one's children.

child tax benefit *noun* (in Canada) a federal government program providing tax-free monthly payments to low- and moderate-income families with children under 18 years of age.

Chile /ˈtʃɪli/ a country occupying a long coastal strip down the southern half of the west of S America, between the Andes and the Pacific Ocean; pop. (est. 2000) 15,498,930; capital, Santiago. □ **Chil·ean** /ˈtʃɪliən, tʃɪˈleiən/ *adjective & noun*

chile var. *of* CHILI.

Chile pine *noun* = MONKEY PUZZLE.

chile rel·leno *noun* a battered, deep-fried, stuffed green pepper. [Latin American Spanish = 'stuffed pepper']

Chile saltpetre *noun* (also **Chile nitre**) naturally occurring sodium nitrate.

chili /ˈtʃɪli/ *noun* (pl. **-ies**) (also **chile**, *Brit.* **chil·li**) **1** (in full **chili pepper**) the small hot-tasting red pod of a capsicum, often dried and ground and used as a seasoning and in several spices. **2 a** = CHILI CON CARNE. **b** a spicy meatless dish made usu. with chilies or chili powder, cooked tomatoes, beans, and onions. [Spanish *chile*, *chili*, from Aztec *chilli*]

chili·ad /ˈkɪliˌad/ *noun* **1** a thousand. **2** a thousand years. [Late Latin *chilias chiliad-* from Greek *khilias -ados*]

chili·asm /ˈkɪliˌazəm/ *noun* the doctrine of or belief in Christ's prophesied reign of one thousand years on earth (see MILLENNIUM). □ **chili·ast** *noun* **chili·as·tic** *adjective* [Greek *khiliasmos*: see CHILIAD]

chili con carne /kɒn ˈkɑrni/ *noun* a spicy dish of chopped or ground meat, chilies or chili powder, and usu. cooked tomatoes, beans, and onions. [Spanish, = chili with meat]

Consonants: b *but*   d *dog*   f *few*   g *get*   h *her*   j *yes*   k *cat*   l *leg*   m *man*   n *no*   p *pen*   r *red*   s *sit*

chili dog *noun N Amer.* a hot dog garnished with chili con carne.

chili powder *noun* a hot condiment made usu. with cayenne or dried chilies, garlic, cumin, and other spices.

chili sauce *noun* a spicy sauce made with tomatoes, chilies, and spices.

Chil·kat /ˈtʃɪlkat/ *noun* a member of a subdivision of the Tlingit people inhabiting the Alaskan coast. [Tlingit *jílkáat*]

Chilkat blanket *noun* a pentagonal ceremonial blanket worn by West Coast Aboriginal peoples, woven from mountain goat hair and shredded cedar bark and covered with symbolic designs in yellow, blue, black, and white.

Chil·koot Pass /ˈtʃɪlkuːt/ a famous pass through the Coast Mountains, situated on the BC–Alaska border, just to the west of White Pass. From 1897 to 1898 it was crossed by as many as 30,000 Klondike gold seekers. [after the CHILKAT]

chill ● *noun* **1 a** an unpleasant cold sensation; lowered body temperature. **b** a feverish cold (*catch a chill*). **2** unpleasant coldness (of air, water, etc.). **3 a** a depressing influence (*cast a chill over*). **b** a feeling of fear or dread accompanied by coldness. **4** coldness of manner. **● verb 1** *transitive & intransitive* make or become cold. **2** *transitive* depress, dispirit. **3** *transitive* cool (food or drink); preserve by cooling. **4** *intransitive* esp. *N Amer. slang* **a** (often foll. by *out*) relax, settle down. **b** loiter, hang out. **5** *transitive* harden (molten metal) by contact with cold material. **● adjective** chilly. □ **take the chill off** warm slightly. □ **chill·er** *noun* **chill·ing·ly** *adverb* **chill·ness** *noun* [Old English *cele, ciele* 'cold, coldness']

chil·li *Brit. var. of* CHILI.

Chil·li·wack¹ /ˈtʃɪləˌwak/ a district municipality in southwestern BC, situated on the south shore of the Fraser River, about 100 km east of Vancouver; pop. (2001) 62,927. [CHILLIWACK²]

Chil·li·wack² /ˈtʃɪləˌwak/ *noun* **1** a member of a Salishan people, a division of the Halq'emeylem, living in part of the Fraser River valley in BC. **2** the Halkomelem language of these people. [lit., 'quieter water on the head' or 'travel by way of a backwater']

chilly *adjective* (**chill·i·er, chill·i·est**) **1** (of the weather or an object) somewhat cold. **2** (of a person or animal) feeling somewhat cold; sensitive to the cold. **3** unfriendly; unemotional. □ **chill·i·ness** *noun*

Chil·pan·cingo /ˌtʃɪlpanˈsiŋgoʊ/ a city in SW Mexico, capital of the state of Guerrero; pop. (2000) 142,746.

Chil·tern Hills /ˈtʃɪltərn/ (also **Chil·terns**) a range of chalk hills in S England, north of the Thames and west of London.

Chiltern Hundreds /ˈtʃɪltərn/ *plural noun* (in the UK) a crown property whose administration is given as a nominal office to an MP as a way of resigning from the House of Commons (a member cannot by law resign his or her seat). [*Chiltern* Hills in S England]

chi·maera *var. of* CHIMAERA.

Chim·bo·razo /ˌtʃɪmbəˈrɑːzoʊ/ the highest peak of the Andes in Ecuador, rising to 6 310 m (20,487 ft.).

chime¹ ● *noun* **1** a set of attuned bells. **2** the series of sounds given by this. **3** (in *pl.*) a musical instrument comprising a set of attuned bells or bars. **4** (often in *pl.*) a doorbell. **● verb 1 a** *intransitive* (of bells) ring. **b** *transitive* sound (a bell or chime) by striking. **2** *transitive* (of a clock or bell) indicate (the hour) by chiming. □ **chime in 1** interject a remark. **2** join in harmoniously. **3** (foll. by *with*) agree with. □ **chim·er** *noun* [Middle English, prob. from *chym(b)e* bell, from Old English *cimbal* from Latin *cymbalum* from Greek *kumbalon* CYMBAL]

chime² *noun* the projecting rim at the end of a cask. [Middle English: compare Middle Dutch, Middle Low German *kimme*]

chi·mera /kaɪˈmɪːrə, kɪ-/ (also **chi·maera**) *noun* **1 a** *Gk Myth* (**Chimera**) a fire-breathing female monster with a lion's head, a goat's body, and a serpent's tail. **b** any mythical beast with parts taken from various animals. **2** a thing that is hoped or wished for but in fact is illusory or impossible to achieve. **3** *Biol.* an organism containing genetically different tissues, formed by grafting, mutation, etc. **4** any cartilaginous fish of the family Chimaeridae, typically having erect pointed fins and a long tail. □ **chi·mer·ic** /-ˈmerɪk/ *adjective* **chi·mer·ic·al** /-ˈmerɪkəl/ *adjective* [Latin from Greek *khimaira* she-goat, chimera]

chimi·chan·ga /ˌtʃɪmiˈtʃæŋgə/ *noun* a tortilla wrapped around a filling of meat etc. and deep-fried. [Mexican Spanish, = 'trinket']

chi·mi·nea /ˌtʃɪmiˈneɪə/ *noun* (also **chi·me·nea**) an earthenware outdoor fireplace shaped like a light bulb, with the bulbous end housing the fire and typically supported by a wrought-iron stand. [Mexican Spanish]

chim·ney *noun* (*pl.* **-neys**) **1** a vertical shaft conducting smoke or combustion gases etc. up and away from a fire, furnace, etc. **2** the part of this which projects above a roof. **3** a glass tube protecting the flame of a lamp. **4** a narrow vertical crack in a rock face, often used by mountaineers to ascend. [Old French *cheminée* from Late Latin *caminata* having a fireplace, from Latin *caminus* from Greek *kaminos* oven]

chimney breast *noun* a projecting wall surrounding a chimney on the inside of a building.

chimney piece *noun* esp. *Brit.* an ornamental structure around an open fireplace; a mantelpiece.

chimney pot *noun* an earthenware or metal pipe at the top of a chimney, narrowing the aperture and increasing the updraft.

chimney stack *noun* **1** a number of chimneys grouped in one structure. **2** = CHIMNEY 2.

chimney sweep *noun* a person whose job is removing soot from inside chimneys.

chimp *noun informal* = CHIMPANZEE. [abbreviation]

chim·pan·zee /ˌtʃɪmpanˈziː/ *noun* a Central and W African anthropoid ape of the genus *Pan*, of which there are two species, *P. troglodytes*, which resembles man more closely than does any other ape, and the pygmy chimpanzee, *P. paniscus*. [French *chimpanzé* from Kongo]

Chin *var. of* JIN.

chin *noun* the front of the lower jaw. □ **chin up** *informal* cheer up. **keep one's chin up** *informal* remain cheerful, esp. in adversity. **take it on the chin 1** suffer a severe blow from (a misfortune etc.). **2** endure courageously. □ **-chinned** *adjective* (in *combination*). [Old English *cin(n)* from Germanic]

China /ˈtʃaɪnə/ (official name **People's Republic of China**) a country in E Asia, the third largest and most populous in the world; pop. (est. 2002) 1,284,303,705; language, Chinese (of which Mandarin is the official form); capital, Beijing (*see also* TAIWAN).

china /ˈtʃaɪnə/ **●** *noun* **1** a kind of fine white or translucent ceramic or porcelain. **2** things made from ceramic, esp. household tableware or figurines. **3** *Brit. slang* one's husband or wife. **● adjective** made of china. [originally *China ware* (made in China): name from Persian *chīnī*; sense 3 rhyming slang from *china plate* = mate]

China aster *noun* a plant related to the aster, *Callistephus chinensis*, cultivated for its bright and showy flowers.

china·berry *noun* (*pl.* **-berries**) **1** a tree of the mahogany family, *Melia azedarach*, native to Asia and widely planted elsewhere as an ornamental. **2** the ornamental yellow fruit of this tree.

china cabinet *noun* a large piece of furniture with shelves and often glass doors, used for holding or displaying china.

china clay *noun* = KAOLIN.

China·man *noun* (*pl.* **-men**) usu. *offensive* a native of China.

China Sea the part of the Pacific Ocean off the coast of China, divided by the island of Taiwan into the **East China Sea** in the north and the **South China Sea** in the south.

China syndrome *noun* an imaginary sequence of events following the meltdown of a nuclear reactor, in which the core melts through its containment structure and deep into the earth. [*China*, as being on the opposite side of the earth from a reactor in the US]

China tea *noun* smoke-cured tea from a small-leaved tea plant grown in China.

China·town *noun* a district of any non-Chinese city in which the population is predominantly Chinese.

china·ware *noun* ceramic tableware.

China White *noun* a potent form of heroin originating in E Asia.

chinch¹ *noun* (in full **chinch bug**) a small insect of tropical and N America, *Blissus leucopterus*, that destroys the shoots of grasses and grains. [Spanish *chinche* from Latin *cimex -icis*]

chinch² *var. of* CHINSE.

chin·cher·in·chee /ˌtʃɪntʃərɪnˈtʃiː/ *noun* a white-flowered bulbous plant, *Ornithogalum thyrsoides*, native to South Africa. [imitative of the squeaky sound made by rubbing its stalks together]

chin·chilla /tʃɪnˈtʃɪlə/ *noun* **1 a** a small rodent of the genus *Chinchilla*, esp. *C. laniger*, native to S America, having soft silver-grey fur and a bushy tail. **b** its highly valued fur. **2** a breed of cat or rabbit having silver-grey fur resembling that of a chinchilla. [Spanish prob. from S American Aboriginal name]

chin-chin *interjection Brit. informal* a toast; a greeting or farewell. [Chinese *qingqing* (pronounced ch-)]

Chin·dit /ˈtʃɪndɪt/ *noun hist.* a member of the Allied forces behind the Japanese lines in Burma in 1943–5. [Burmese *chinthé*, a mythical creature]

Chind·win River /tʃɪnˈdwɪn/ a river which rises in N Burma (Myanmar) and flows southward for 885 km (550 miles) to meet the Irrawaddy, of which it is the principal tributary.

chine¹ /tʃaɪn/ ● *noun* **1** a backbone, esp. of an animal. **2** a cut of meat containing all or part of this. ● *transitive verb* cut (meat) across or along the backbone. [Old French *eschine* from Latin *spina* SPINE]

chine² /tʃaɪn/ *noun Brit.* (in S England) a deep narrow ravine. [Old English *cinu* chink etc., from Germanic]

chine³ /tʃaɪn/ *noun* the point at which the bottom strakes of a ship meet the sides. [var. of CHINE²]

Chi·nese /tʃaɪˈniːz/ ● *adjective* of or relating to China, its people, or its language. ● *noun* **1** the Sino-Tibetan language of China, having several dialects including Mandarin and Cantonese. **2** (*pl.* same) **a** a native or national of China. **b** a person of Chinese descent.

Chinese boxes *plural noun* a set of nested and usu. decorated boxes, each fitting very closely inside the next larger one.

Chinese burn *noun informal* an act of placing two hands on a person's arm and then twisting it with a wringing motion to produce a burning sensation.

Chinese cabbage *noun* **1** a vegetable, *Brassica pekinensis*, resembling lettuce. **2** = BOK CHOY.

Chinese café *noun Cdn* (*Prairies*) a café in a small town, operated by a Chinese proprietor and serving Chinese and other food.

Chinese checkers *noun* a game for two to six players played with marbles on a star-shaped board, with players attempting to move all of their marbles from one point to the opposite one.

Chinese fire drill *noun slang* a state of disorder or confusion.

Chinese gooseberry *noun* = KIWI 2.

Chinese lantern *noun* **1** a collapsible paper lantern. **2** a solanaceous Eurasian plant, *Physalis alkekengi*, bearing white flowers and globular orange fruits enclosed in an orange-red papery calyx.

Chinese New Year *noun* the celebration of the New Year in the Chinese calendar, observed officially for a month starting in late January or early February.

Chinese puzzle *noun* a very intricate puzzle or problem.

Chinese restaurant syndrome *noun* symptoms, including headache, facial flushing, sweating, etc., caused by dilatation of the blood vessels, and attributed to monosodium glutamate, frequently used in Chinese food.

Chinese skipping *noun Cdn* (*West*) a form of skipping in which a circle of elastic is looped around the ankles of two participants then moved progressively higher while the other participants attempt various jumping manoeuvres.

Chinese wall *noun* an obstacle or barrier, esp. to inhibit the flow of information.

Chinese water chestnut *noun see* WATER CHESTNUT 2.

Chinese water torture *noun* a form of torture in which water is dropped slowly onto the forehead of the victim until insanity ensues.

Chinese white *noun* zinc oxide as a white pigment.

ching *noun* an abrupt ringing sound, esp. one made by a cash register. [imitative]

Ch'ing *var. of* QING.

Chin Hills a range of hills in W Burma (Myanmar), close to the borders with India and Bangladesh.

Chini·quy /ʃiːniːˈkiː/ **Charles (Paschal-Télesphore)** (1809–99), Canadian ecclesiastic. As a Roman Catholic priest he was noted for his temperance crusade in Lower Canada in the 1840s; excommunicated in 1856, he became a Presbyterian minister, and began an international anti-Catholic campaign.

Chink *noun slang offensive* a Chinese person. [abbreviation]

chink¹ ● *noun* **1** a fissure or crack. **2** a narrow opening or slit that admits light. ● *transitive verb* esp. *N Amer.* fill (a crack or opening) with a sealant etc. □ **chink in one's armour** a vulnerability or weakness. □ **chink·ing** *noun* [16th c.: related to CHINE²]

chink² ● *verb* **1** *intransitive* make a slight ringing sound, as of glasses or coins striking together. **2** *transitive* cause to make this sound. ● *noun* this sound. [imitative]

chin·less *adjective* **1** having a receding chin. **2** weak or feeble in character.

chinless wonder *noun Brit. informal* an esp. upper class person lacking firmness of character.

chin music *noun slang* **1** esp. *US* idle talk or chatter. **2** *Baseball* a pitch

thrown near a batter's head. **3** *Cdn (Nfld)* sung or hummed music as accompaniment to a dance.

chino /ˈtʃiːnoː/ *noun* (*pl.* **chinos**) **1** a cotton twill fabric, usu. khaki coloured. **2** (in *pl.*) trousers made from this. [Latin American Spanish, = toasted]

chi·nois·erie /ʃiːnˈwɑːzəˈriː/ *noun* **1** the imitation of Chinese motifs and techniques in painting and in decorating furniture. **2** an object or objects in this style. [French]

Chi·nook /ʃəˈnʊk/ *noun* **1** a member of a Pacific Coast Aboriginal people formerly living along the Columbia River in Oregon and Washington. **2** the language of this people. [Sne Nay Muxw *tsinúk*]

chi·nook /ʃəˈnʊk/ *noun* **1 a** a warm dry wind which blows east of the Rocky Mountains, often causing significant temperature increases in winter. **b** a warm wet southerly wind west of the Rocky Mountains. **2** (in full **chinook salmon**) a large silver-coloured salmon with black spots, *Oncorhynchus tshawytscha*, native to the N Pacific and introduced into the Great Lakes and elsewhere. *Also called* KING SALMON. [CHINOOK]

chinook arch *noun Cdn* a bow-shaped cloud formation bordering an expanse of clear sky, visible on the western Prairies before or during a chinook wind.

Chinook Jargon *noun* a pidgin composed largely of Chinook, Nuu-chah-nulth, English, and French, formerly used by traders on the N Pacific coast of N America.

chin·qua·pin /ˈtʃɪŋkəpɪn/ *noun* **1** any of several N American trees of the beech family: **a** of the deciduous genus *Castanea*, esp. *C. pumila*, resembling the chestnut. **b** of the evergreen genus *Castinopsis*, native to the Pacific coast. **2** the nut of any of these trees. **3** (in full **chinquapin oak**) either of two eastern N American oaks, *Quercus muehlenbergii* or the dwarf *Q. prinoides*. [Algonquian]

chinse /tʃɪns/ *transitive verb* (also **chinch** /tʃɪntʃ/) *N Amer.* (*Maritimes & New England*) fill (the seams or spaces) in a boat, cabin, etc. [dial. var. of CHINK¹]

chin·strap *noun* a strap for fastening a hat or helmet under the chin.

chintz ● *noun* a cotton fabric, usu. multicoloured and often with a flower pattern, with a glazed finish. ● *adjective* made from or upholstered with this fabric. [earlier *chints* (pl.) from Hindi *chint* from Sanskrit *citra* variegated]

chintzy *adjective* (**chintz·i·er**, **chintz·i·est**) **1** resembling, pertaining to, or decorated with chintz. **2** cheap; of poor quality. **3** *N Amer.* contemptible. **4** *N Amer.* stingy, miserly. □ **chintz·i·ly** *adverb* **chintz·i·ness** *noun*

chin-up *noun N Amer.* an exercise involving raising oneself with one's arms by pulling against a horizontal bar fixed above one's head.

chin·wag *informal* ● *noun* a talk or chat. ● *intransitive verb* (**-wagged**, **-wag·ging**) chat or gossip.

chi·ono·doxa /ˌkaɪənəˈdɒksə/ *noun* any liliaceous plant of the Eurasian genus *Chionodoxa*, having early-blooming blue flowers. *Also called* GLORY-OF-THE-SNOW. [modern Latin from Greek *khiōn* snow + *doxa* glory]

Chios /ˈkaɪɒs/ a Greek island in the Aegean Sea; pop. (est. 2002) 52,000.

chip¹ ● *noun* **1 a** a small piece removed by or in the course of chopping, cutting, or breaking, esp. from hard material such as wood or stone. **b** the place from where such a chip has been removed. **2** *N Amer.* **a** (in full **potato chip**) a wafer-thin slice of potato deep-fried until crisp and eaten as a snack. **b** a similarly thin and crisp food (*nacho chips*). **3** a small piece of chocolate etc. used in baking. **4** *Cdn & Brit.* = FRENCH FRY. **5** a piece of dried bovine dung, esp. when used as fuel. **6** a counter used in some gambling games to represent money. **7** = MICROCHIP. **8** (also **chip shot**) *Sport* a short shot, kick, or pass with the ball travelling in an arc. ● *verb* (**chipped**, **chip·ping**) **1** *transitive* (often foll. by *off*, *away*) cut or break (a piece) from a hard material. **2** *intransitive* (often foll. by *at*, *away at*) cut pieces off (a hard material) to alter its shape, break it up, etc. **3** *intransitive* (of stone, china, etc.) be susceptible to being chipped; be apt to break at the edge (*will chip easily*). **4** *transitive & intransitive Sport* strike or kick (the ball) so that it travels in a short arc. **5** *transitive* cut (potatoes) into chips. □ **chip away** gradually and relentlessly make something smaller or weaker. **chip in** *informal* **1** contribute (money, resources, etc.). **2** *Brit.* interrupt or contribute abruptly to a conversation (*chipped in with a reminiscence*). **a chip off the old block** a child who resembles a parent, esp. in character. **a chip on one's shoulder** a disposition or inclination to feel resentful or aggrieved. **have had one's chips** *Brit. informal* be unable to avoid defeat, punishment, etc. **let the chips fall where they may** whatever the consequences. **when the chips are down**

when the situation becomes difficult or critical. [Old English *cipp*, *cyp* beam]

chip² *intransitive verb* (**chipped**, **chip·ping**) (of a bird) chirp, cheep. [imitative]

chip·board *noun* = PARTICLEBOARD.

Chipe·wyan /tʃɪpəˈwaiən/ ● *noun* **1** a member of an Athapaskan people inhabiting much of the northern Prairie provinces and the subarctic NWT. **2** the language of this people. ● *adjective* of or relating to this people or their language. [Cree *ci:pwaya:n*, lit. '(wearing) pointed-skin (garments)' with reference to a style of drying beaver skins that left shirts with points at the bottom]

chip·maker *noun* a manufacturer of microchips. □ **chip·making** *adjective*

chip·munk *noun* any ground squirrel of the genus *Tamias* or *Eutamias*, having alternate light and dark stripes along the back. [Ojibwa *aĉitamon*, = 'red squirrel' from *aĉit-* headfirst, from the manner in which the squirrel climbs down trees]

chipo·lata /ˌtʃɪpəˈlɑtə/ *noun Brit.* a small thin sausage. [French from Italian *cipollata* a dish of onions, from *cipolla* onion]

chi·potle /ˌtʃɪˈpoːtlei/ *noun* a hot red pepper, usu. smoked, commonly used in Mexican cooking. [Mexican Spanish, from Nahuatl *chilli* 'chili pepper' + *poctli* 'smoke']

Chip·pen·dale¹, **Thom·as** (1718–79), English furniture maker and designer. His immensely influential book *The Gentleman and Cabinet-maker's Director* (1754) was the first comprehensive book of furniture designs, many of which are in a neoclassical vein, with elements of the French rococo, chinoiserie, and Gothic revival styles.

Chip·pen·dale² *adjective* **1** (of furniture) designed or made by the English cabinetmaker Thomas Chippendale. **2** in the ornately elegant style of Chippendale's furniture, characterized by curved legs, Chinese or Gothic motifs, and carving.

chip·per¹ *adjective informal* cheerful and lively. [perhaps from Northern English dial. *kipper* lively]

chip·per² *noun* a person or tool that chips timber.

Chip·pe·wa /ˈtʃɪpəˌwɒ/ *noun & adjective* = OJIBWA. ¶ *Chippewa* is normally used to refer only to the Ojibwa living to the east, south, and southwest of the Great Lakes. [alteration of OJIBWA]

chipping sparrow *noun* a widely distributed N American sparrow, *Spizella passerina*, having grey, brown, and black plumage. [CHIP²]

chip·py¹ *adjective* (**chip·pi·er**, **chip·pi·est**) *informal* **1** short-tempered or irritable. **2** *Hockey* characterized by rough or dirty play. □ **chip·pi·ness** *noun* [perhaps from the expression 'have a chip on one's shoulder' (see CHIP¹)]

chip·py² *noun* (*pl.* **-pies**) *N Amer. slang* a promiscuous or delinquent young woman, esp. a prostitute. [CHIP² + -Y¹]

chip·py³ *noun* (*pl.* **-pies**) *Brit. informal* **1** a fish and chip shop. **2** (also **Chips**) a carpenter, esp. on a ship or in the armed services.

chip seal *noun* a type of road surfacing in which asphalt is sprayed on the road surface then coated with stone chips which are rolled into it.

chip set *noun Computing* a set of integrated circuits that when connected together form a single functional block.

chip wagon *noun Cdn* a mobile roadside stand or vehicle selling french fries and sometimes other fast foods.

Chirac /ʃiːrak/ **Jacques (René)** (b.1932), French conservative politician, prime minister 1974–6 and again 1986–8, and mayor of Paris 1977–95, he was elected president in 1995 and again in 2002.

chiral /ˈkairəl/ *adjective Chem.* (of an optically active compound) asymmetric and not superimposable on its mirror image. □ **chiral·ity** /-ˈralɪti/ *noun* [Greek *kheir* hand]

Chiri·aeff /ʃiːriːˈeief/ **Lud·milla** (1924–96), Latvian-born Canadian ballet director, dancer, choreographer, and teacher. She founded Les Grands Ballets Canadiens (1958) in Montreal and served as the company's artistic director (1958–74).

Chi·rico /ˈkiːriːkoː/ **Gior·gio de** (1888–1978), Greek-born Italian painter. His disconnected and unsettling dream images, in a style that became known as 'metaphysical painting', exerted a significant influence on surrealism; his works include *Nostalgia of the Infinite* (1911), and *The Uncertainty of the Poet* (1913).

chiro- /ˈkairoː/ *combining form* of the hand. [Greek *kheir* hand]

chiro·mancy /ˈkairoːˌmansi/ *noun* = PALMISTRY.

Chiron /ˈkairɒn/ **1** *Gk Myth* a learned centaur who acted as teacher to Jason, Achilles, and many other heroes. **2** *Astronomy* asteroid 2060, discovered in 1977; it is believed to have a diameter of 370 km.

chi·ron·omid /kaiˈrɒnəmɪd/ *noun & adjective* ● *noun* an insect of the family Chironomidae, which includes many midges. ● *adjective* of or relating to this family. [modern Latin *Chironomidae* from Greek *kheironomos* pantomime]

chi·rop·ody /ʃɪˈrɒpədi, kɪ-/ *noun esp. Cdn & Brit.* = PODIATRY. □ **chi·rop·odist** *noun* [CHIRO- + Greek *pous podos* foot]

chiro·prac·tic /ˌkairoːˈpraktɪk/ *noun* the diagnosis and manipulative treatment of mechanical disorders of the joints, esp. of the spinal column. □ **chiro·prac·tor** /ˈkairoː-/ *noun* [CHIRO- + Greek *praktikos*: see PRACTICAL]

chir·op·ter·an /ˌkaiˈrɒptərən/ ● *noun* any member of the order Chiroptera, which comprises the bats. ● *adjective* of or pertaining to this order. [CHIRO- + Greek *pteron* wing]

chirp ● *verb* **1** *intransitive* (usu. of small birds, grasshoppers, etc.) emit a short sharp high-pitched note. **2** *transitive & intransitive* speak or utter in a lively or cheerful way. ● *noun* a chirping sound. □ **chirp·er** *noun* [Middle English, earlier *chirk*, *chirt*: imitative]

chirpy *adjective* (**chirp·i·er**, **chirp·i·est**) *informal* cheerful, lively. □ **chirp·i·ly** *adverb* **chirp·i·ness** *noun*

chirr (also **churr**) ● *intransitive verb* (esp. of insects) make a prolonged low trilling sound. ● *noun* this sound. [imitative]

chir·rup ● *intransitive verb* (**chir·ruped**, **chir·rup·ing**) (esp. of small birds) chirp, esp. repeatedly; twitter. ● *noun* a chirruping sound. □ **chir·rupy** *adjective* [trilled form of CHIRP]

chiru /ˈtʃiːruː/ *noun* (*pl.* same) an endangered sandy-coloured gazelle with black horns, *Pantholops hodgsoni*, found on the Tibetan plateau. [probably from Tibetan]

chis·el /ˈtʃɪzəl/ ● *noun* a hand tool with a squared bevelled blade for shaping wood, stone, or metal. ● *transitive & intransitive verb* (**chis·elled**, **chis·el·ling**; also esp. *US* **chis·eled**, **chis·el·ing**) **1** cut or shape with or as if with a chisel. **2** *slang* **a** cheat, swindle. **b** obtain by swindling. □ **chis·el·ler** *noun* (also esp. *US* **chis·el·er**). [Old Northern French, ultimately from Late Latin *cisorium* from Latin *caedere caes-* cut]

chis·elled /ˈtʃɪzəld/ *adjective* (also esp. *US* **chis·eled**) (of facial features, muscles, etc.) well defined.

Chişi·năư /ˌkɪʃɪˈnau/ the capital of Moldova; pop. (est. 2002) 711,700.

chi-square test *noun* a method of comparing observed and theoretical values in statistics.

chit¹ *noun* (usu. **a chit of a girl**) **1** *derogatory* or *jocular* a young and inexperienced girl or woman. **2** a young child. [Middle English, = whelp, cub, kitten, perhaps = dial. *chit* sprout]

chit² *noun* **1** a voucher or note specifying a sum owed, esp. for food or drink. **2** *esp. Brit.* a note or memorandum. [earlier *chitty*: Anglo-Indian from Hindi *citthī* pass, from Sanskrit *citra* mark]

chital /ˈtʃiːtəl/ *noun* = AXIS². [Hindi *cītal*]

chit-chat *informal* ● *noun* light conversation; gossip. ● *intransitive verb* (**-chatted**, **-chatting**) talk informally; gossip. [reduplication of CHAT¹]

chi·tin /ˈkaitɪn/ *noun* a polysaccharide forming the major constituent in the exoskeleton of arthropods and in the cell walls of fungi. □ **chitin·ous** *adjective* [French *chitine* irreg. from Greek *khitōn*: see CHITON]

chit·lin *noun* (also **chit·ling**) *US* (*South*) = CHITTERLING. [contraction]

chi·ton /ˈkaitən/ *noun* **1** a long woollen tunic worn by ancient Greeks. **2** a mollusc of the class Polyplacophora, characterized by a broad oval foot and a symmetrical dorsal shell composed of a series of eight overlapping plates. [Greek *khitōn* tunic]

Chit·ta·gong /ˈtʃɪtəˌgɒŋ/ a seaport in SE Bangladesh, on the Bay of Bengal; pop. (est. 2002) 2,546,400.

chit·ter *esp. N Amer.* ● *intransitive verb* (of a bird, squirrel, etc.) make a twittering or chattering sound. ● *noun* a twittering or chattering sound. [imitative]

chitter·ling /ˈtʃɪtlɪŋ/ *noun* (usu. in *pl.*) the smaller intestines of pigs etc., esp. as cooked for food. [Middle English: origin uncertain]

Chi·tun·gwiza /ˌtʃɪtʊŋˈgwiːzə/ a city in NE Zimbabwe, just south of Harare; pop. (est. 1998) 600,000.

chiv·al·rous /ˈʃɪvəlrəs/ *adjective* **1** (usu. of a male) gallant, honourable, courteous. **2** involving or showing chivalry. □ **chiv·al·rous·ly** *adverb*

chiv·al·ry /ˈʃɪvəlri/ *noun* **1** the medieval knightly system with its religious, moral, and social code. **2** the combination of qualities expected of an ideal knight, esp. courage, honour, courtesy, justice, and readiness to help the weak. **3** a man's courteous behaviour, esp. towards women. **4** *archaic* knights, noblemen, and horsemen collectively. □ **chiv·al·ric** *adjective* [Old French *chevalerie* etc. from medieval Latin *caballerius* for Late Latin *caballarius* horseman: see CAVALIER]

chive *noun* (usu. in *pl.*) a small alliaceous plant, *Allium schoenoprasum*, having purple-pink flowers and dense tufts of long tubular leaves which are used as a herb. [Old French *cive* from Latin *cepa* onion]

chiv·vy *transitive verb* (**-vies, -vied**) (also **chivy, chevy** /'tʃɛvi/) harass, nag. [*chevy* (n. & v.), prob. from a skirmish described in the ballad of *Chevy Chase*, a place on the border of Scotland and England]

Chka·lov /'tʃkɒləf/ the former name (1938–57) for ORENBURG.

chla·myd·ia /klə'mɪdɪə/ *noun* **1** (*pl.* **chla·myd·iae** /-di,iː/) any parasitic bacterium of the genus *Chlamydia*, some of which cause diseases such as trachoma and psittacosis. **2** a sexually transmitted infection caused by *C. trachomatis*, often leading to urethritis or pelvic inflammatory disease. □ **chla·myd·ial** *adjective* [modern Latin from Greek *khlamus -udos* cloak]

chlor- *var. of* CHLORO-.

chlor·acne /klɔr'akni/ *noun* a skin disease resembling severe acne, caused by exposure to chlorinated chemicals. [CHLORINE + ACNE]

chlor·al /'klɔrəl/ *noun* **1** a colourless liquid aldehyde used in making DDT. **2** (in full **chloral hydrate**) a colourless crystalline solid made from chloral and used as a sedative. [French from *chlore* chlorine + *alcool* alcohol]

chlor·am·pheni·col /,klɔram'fenə,kɒl/ *noun* an antibiotic prepared from *Streptomyces venezuelae* or produced synthetically and used against severe infections such as typhoid fever. [CHLORO- + AMIDE + PHENO- + NITRO- + GLYCOL]

chlor·ate /'klɔreit/ *noun* Chem. any salt of chloric acid.

chlor·dane /'klɔrdein/ *noun* a viscous compound of chlorine, carbon, and hydrogen used as an insecticide. [CHLOR- + INDENE + -ANE²]

chlor·ella /klɔr'elə/ *noun* any non-motile unicellular green alga of the genus *Chlorella*. [modern Latin, diminutive of Greek *khlōros* green]

chlor·ic acid /'klɔrɪk/ *noun* Chem. a colourless liquid acid with strong oxidizing properties.

chlor·ide /'klɔraid/ *noun* Chem. any compound of chlorine with another element or group.

chlor·in·ate /'klɔrə,neit/ *transitive verb* **1** treat (esp. water) with chlorine, esp. to disinfect. **2** Chem. cause to react or combine with chlorine. □ **chlor·in·a·tion** *noun* **chlor·in·ator** *noun*

chlor·ine /klɔr'iːn, 'klɔr-/ *noun* Chem. a poisonous greenish-yellow gaseous element of the halogen group occurring naturally esp. as sodium chloride in salt, sea water, rock salt, etc., and used for purifying water, bleaching, and in the manufacture of many organic chemicals. Symbol: **Cl**; at. no.: 17. [Greek *khlōros* green + -INE⁴]

chlor·ite¹ /'klɔraɪt/ *noun* Mineralogy a dark green mineral found in many rocks, consisting of a basic aluminosilicate of magnesium, iron, etc. □ **chlor·itic** /-'rɪtɪk/ *adjective*

chlor·ite² /'klɔraɪt/ *noun* Chem. any salt of chlorous acid.

chloro- /'klɔrɒ/ *combining form* (also **chlor-** esp. before a vowel) **1** Bot. & Mineralogy green. **2** Chem. chlorine. [Greek *khlōros* green: in sense 2 from CHLORINE]

chloro·fluoro·car·bon /,klɔrɒ'fluɔr,kɑːrbən/ *noun* see CFC.

chloro·form /'klɔrə,fɔrm/ ● *noun* a colourless volatile sweet-smelling liquid used as a solvent and formerly used as a general anaesthetic. Chem. formula: $CHCl_3$. ● *transitive verb* render (a person) unconscious with this. [French *chloroforme* formed as CHLORO- + *formyle*: see FORMIC (ACID)]

chloro·phenol /,klɔrɒ'fiːnɒl/ *noun* any phenol derivative in which one or more hydrogen atoms have been replaced by chlorine, such compounds being used in antiseptics, disinfectants, insecticides, herbicides, and dyestuffs.

chloro·phyll /'klɔrəfɪl/ *noun* the green pigment found in most plants, responsible for light absorption to provide energy for photosynthesis. □ **chloro·phyl·lous** /-'fɪləs/ *adjective* [French *chlorophylle* from Greek *phullon* leaf: see CHLORO-]

chloro·plast /'klɔrɒ,plast/ *noun* a plastid containing chlorophyll found in plant cells. [German: (as CHLORO-, PLASTID)]

chloro·quine /'klɔrə,kwiːn/ *noun* a drug related to quinoline used esp. against malaria. [CHLORO- + QUINOLINE]

chlor·osis /klə'rɒsɪs, klɔr-/ *noun* **1** Bot. a reduction or loss of the normal green coloration of plants. **2** hist. a severe form of anemia from iron deficiency esp. in young women, causing a greenish complexion. □ **chlor·otic** /klə'rɒtɪk, klɔr-/ *adjective*

chlor·ous acid /'klɔrəs/ *noun* Chem. a pale yellow liquid acid with oxidizing properties. Chem. formula: $HClO_2$. [CHLOR- + -OUS]

chlor·proma·zine /klɔr'prɒmə,ziːn/ *noun* a drug used as a sedative

and to control nausea and vomiting. [French (as CHLORO-, PROMETHAZINE)]

choc *noun & adjective* Brit. informal chocolate. [abbreviation]

choca·hol·ic *var. of* CHOCOHOLIC.

chock ● *noun* **1** a block or wedge of wood used to prevent a wheel etc. from moving. **2** a strong metal eye or hook on a ship's deck through which a line may be passed or secured. ● *transitive verb* **1** fit or make fast with chocks. **2** (usu. foll. by *up*) Brit. cram full. ● *adverb* as closely or tightly as possible. [prob. from Old French *çouche, çoche*, of unknown origin]

chock·a·block *adjective & adverb* crammed close together; crammed full (*a street chockablock with cars*). [originally Naut., with reference to tackle with the two blocks run close together]

chock full *predicative adjective & adverb* crammed full or close together (*a cupboard chock full of clothes*). [CHOCK + FULL¹: Middle English *chokkefulle* (related to CHOKE) is doubtful]

choco- *combining form* chocolate.

choco·hol·ic *noun* (also **choca·hol·ic**) informal a person very fond of eating chocolate. [blend of CHOCOLATE + ALCOHOLIC]

choc·o·late ● *noun* **1 a** an edible paste or solid made from cacao seeds by roasting, grinding, etc., often combined with flavourings, sugar, cream, etc. **b** a candy made of or coated with this. **c** a drink made by mixing chocolate with (usu. hot) milk or water. **2** (also **chocolate brown**) a dark brown colour. ● *adjective* **1** made from or flavoured with chocolate. **2** (also **chocolate brown**) dark brown in colour. □ **choc·o·latey** *adjective* (also **choc·o·laty**). [French *chocolat* or Spanish *chocolate* from Aztec *chocolatl*]

chocolate bar *noun* a bar of sweetened chocolate or chocolate-coated caramel, nuts, etc.

chocolate-box *attributive adjective* stereotypically pretty or romantic (*chocolate-box art*).

chocolate lily *noun* any of various liliaceous plants of western N America of the genus *Fritillaria*, with brown bell-shaped flowers and edible bulbs that look like cooked rice. *Also called* CHECKER LILY, RICE ROOT, INDIAN RICE.

chocolate milk *noun* milk flavoured with chocolate.

chocolate shot *noun* tiny short strands of chocolate used as a cake decoration.

choc·ola·tier /,ʃɒkɒla'tjei/ *noun* a maker or seller of chocolate, esp. of fine quality. [French]

Choc·taw *noun* **1 a** (*pl.* same or **Choc·taws**) a member of a Muskogean people originally resident in Mississippi and Alabama, and subsequently in Oklahoma. **b** the language spoken by this people and the Chickasaw. **2** Figure Skating a step from one edge of a skate to the other edge of the other skate in the opposite direction (compare MOHAWK 2). [Choctaw *čahta*]

choice ● *noun* **1 a** an act or instance of choosing between alternatives. **b** a thing or person chosen (*not a good choice*). **c** one of two or more possibilities from which one may choose (*you have three choices*). **2** a range from which to choose. **3** the best or preferred item (*the critics' choice*). **4** the power or opportunity to choose (*what choice do I have?*). **5** the right of a woman to choose to have an abortion. ● *adjective* **1** of superior quality; carefully chosen. **2** designating a grade of canned fruits and vegetables between standard and fancy, where slight variation in size, colour, or maturity is allowed but the produce is almost free from blemishes and other defects. □ **by choice** because one has chosen (*I am here by choice*). **of choice** preferred (*our method of choice*). **of one's choice** that one has chosen (*dine at the restaurant of your choice*). □ **choice·ly** *adverb* **choice·ness** *noun* [Old French *chois* from *choisir* CHOOSE]

choir /'kwaɪr/ *noun* **1** a group or company of singers, esp. taking part in church services or performing concerts. **2 a** the part of a church in which the choir sings. **b** in some cathedrals and other (esp. Anglican) churches, the area between the altar and the nave lined on either side with benches, used by the choir and clergy (compare CHANCEL). **3** Christianity = ORDER *noun* 19. **4** Music a group of instruments of one family playing together. [Old French *quer* from Latin *chorus*: see CHORUS]

choir·boy *noun* a young boy who sings in a choir, esp. a church choir.

choir·girl *noun* a young girl who sings in a choir, esp. a church choir.

choir loft *noun* N Amer. a balcony in a church, usu. at the rear, in which the choir sings.

choir·master *noun* the director of a choir, esp. a church choir.

choir school *noun* a school maintained by a cathedral, church, or college, providing general education and voice instruction, usu. for boys.

choir stall *noun* = STALL[1] *noun* 4.

choke ● *verb* **1** *transitive* hinder or impede the breathing of (a person or animal) esp. by constricting the windpipe or (of gas, smoke, etc.) by being unbreathable. **2** *intransitive* suffer a hindrance or stoppage of breath (*choked on a piece of food*). **3** *transitive & intransitive* (often foll. by *up*) make or become speechless from emotion. **4** *transitive* retard the growth of or kill (esp. plants) by the deprivation of light, air, nourishment, etc. **5** *transitive* (often foll. by *back*) suppress (emotions) with difficulty. **6** *transitive & intransitive* (often foll. by *up*) block or clog (a passage, tube, etc.). **7** *intransitive* esp. *Sport informal* fail to perform effectively when under pressure (*the team choked in the playoffs*). **8** *transitive* (often foll. by *up*) *N Amer.* move one's hands up the handle of (a baseball bat etc.) to shorten the swing and improve control. **9** *transitive* enrich the fuel mixture in (an internal combustion engine) by reducing the intake of air. ● *noun* **1** an instance of choking. **2** the valve in the carburetor of an internal combustion engine that controls the intake of air, esp. to enrich the fuel mixture. **3** *Electricity* an inductance coil used to smooth the variations of an alternating current or to alter its phase. **4** the centre part of an artichoke. □ **choke down** swallow with difficulty. **choke off** impede or stop. [Old English *ācēocian* from *cēoce, cēce* CHEEK]

choke·berry *noun* (*pl.* **-berries**) **1** any N American shrub of the genus *Aronia* of the rose family. **2** its scarlet berry-like fruit.

choke chain *noun* (also **choke collar**) a chain looped round a dog's neck to exert control by pressure on its windpipe when the dog pulls.

choke·cherry *noun* (*pl.* **-cher·ries**) **1** any of several N American cherry trees, esp. *Prunus virginiana*. **2** the astringent fruit of this tree.

choked *adjective* clogged or plugged (*a snow-choked country road*). □ **choked up** on the verge of tears and unable to speak.

choke·damp *noun* asphyxiating gas, largely carbon dioxide, accumulated in a mine or underground chamber.

choke·hold *noun* **1** a tight grip around a person's neck, used to restrain them by restricting their breathing. **2** unshakable control.

choke point *noun N Amer.* the point at which the flow of something is constricted; a bottleneck.

chok·er *noun* **1** a close-fitting necklace or ornamental neckband. **2** a clerical or other high collar. **3** *N Amer.* a heavy cable with a hook used for gripping and hauling logs. **4** a competitor that fails to perform effectively under pressure.

choker·man *noun* (*pl.* **-men**) (also **choker·setter**) *N Amer.* a person responsible for attaching chokers to logs.

choky[1] *noun* (also **chok·ey**) (*pl.* **-ies** or **-eys**) *Brit. slang* prison. [originally Anglo-Indian, from Hindi *caukī* shed]

choky[2] *adjective* (**chok·i·er**, **chok·i·est**) tending to choke or to cause choking.

chol·angi·og·raphy /ˌkɒlandʒiˈɒɡrəfi/ *noun Med.* X-ray examination of the bile ducts, used to find the site and nature of any obstruction. [CHOLE- + Greek *aggeion* vessel + -GRAPHY]

chole- /ˈkɒli/ *combining form* (also **chol-** esp. before a vowel) *Med. & Chem.* bile. [Greek *kholē* gall, bile]

chole·cal·cif·er·ol /ˌkɒlɪkalˈsɪfərɒl/ *noun* one of the D vitamins, produced by the action of sunlight on a cholesterol derivative widely distributed in the skin, a deficiency of which results in rickets in children and osteomalacia in adults. *Also called* VITAMIN D$_3$. [CHOLE- + CALCIFEROL]

chole·cyst·ec·tomy /ˌkɒləsɪsˈtektəmi/ *noun Med.* (*pl.* **-ies**) surgical removal of the gallbladder. [CHOLE- + CYSTO- + -ECTOMY]

chole·cyst·og·raphy /ˌkɒləsɪsˈtɒɡrəfi/ *noun Med.* X-ray examination of the gallbladder, esp. used to detect the presence of any gallstones. [CHOLE- + CYSTO- + -GRAPHY]

chole·cys·to·kinin /ˌkɒləsɪstəˈkaɪnɪn/ *noun* a hormone which is secreted by cells in the duodenum and stimulates the release of bile into the intestine and the secretion of enzymes by the pancreas. [CHOLE- + CYSTO- + KININ]

chol·ent /ˈtʃʊlənt/ *noun* a Jewish Sabbath dish of slowly baked meat and vegetables, prepared on a Friday and cooked overnight. [Yiddish *tscholnt*]

choler /ˈkɒlər/ *noun* **1** *hist.* bile regarded as one of the four bodily humours. **2** *literary* or *archaic* anger, irascibility. [Old French *colere* bile, anger, from Latin *cholera* from Greek *kholera* diarrhea, in Late Latin = bile, anger, from Greek *kholē* bile]

chol·era /ˈkɒlərə/ *noun* an infectious and often fatal disease of the small intestine caused by the bacterium *Vibrio cholerae*, resulting in

severe vomiting and diarrhea. □ **chol·er·aic** /-ˈreɪɪk/ *adjective* [see CHOLER]

chol·er·ic /ˈkɒlərɪk/ *adjective* irascible, angry.

chol·es·terol /kəˈlestəˌrɒl/ *noun* a sterol found in most body tissues, including the blood, where high concentrations promote arteriosclerosis. [*cholesterin* from Greek *kholē* bile + *stereos* stiff]

choli /ˈtʃoːli/ *noun* (*pl.* **cholis**) a short-sleeved bodice worn as part of some East Indian women's clothing. [Hindi *colī*]

choli·amb /ˈkoːliˌamb/ *noun Prosody* a Greek or Latin metre of limping character, esp. a trimeter of two iambs and a spondee or trochee. □ **choli·am·bic** /ˌkoːliˈambɪk/ *adjective* [Late Latin *choliambus* from Greek *khōliambos* from *khōlos* lame: see IAMBUS]

cho·line /ˈkoːliːn, -lɪn/ *noun Biochem.* a basic nitrogenous organic compound occurring widely in living matter. [German *Cholin* from Greek *kholē* bile]

cholin·ergic /ˌkoːlɪnˈɜrdʒɪk/ *adjective* releasing or involving acetylcholine as a neurotransmitter. [CHOLINE + -ERGIC]

cholin·ester·ase /ˌkoːlɪnˈestəreɪz/ *noun* an enzyme which hydrolyzes esters of choline.

cholla /ˈtʃɔɪə/ *noun* any of several cacti of the genus *Opuntia*, native to the southern US and Central America. [Latin American Spanish, lit. 'skull, head']

cholo /ˈtʃoːloː/ *noun US often derogatory* a Mexican American, esp. a member of a youth gang. [Latin American Spanish *Cholula* a district of Mexico]

chomp (also **champ**) ● *verb* **1** *transitive & intransitive* munch or chew noisily. **2** *transitive* (of a horse etc.) work (the bit) noisily between the teeth. ● *noun* a chewing noise or motion. [imitative]

Chom·sky, (Avram) Noam (b.1928), US linguist, philosopher, and political activist. His theory of transformational grammar, set out in *Syntactic Structures* (1957), influenced the course of US linguistics in the 1960s and 1970s. He is also an outspoken critic of the US government and the media. □ **Chomsky·an** (also **Chomski·an**) *adjective & noun*

chon /tʃɒn/ *noun* a monetary unit of North and South Korea, equal to one-hundredth of a won. [Korean]

chon·drite /ˈkɒndraɪt/ *noun* a stony meteorite containing small mineral granules. □ **chon·drit·ic** /kɒnˈdrɪtɪk/ *adjective* [German *Chondrit* from Greek *khondros* granule]

chondro- /ˌkɒndrəʊ/ *prefix Anat.* cartilage. [Greek *khondros* grain, cartilage]

Chong·jin /tʃʌŋˈdʒɪn/ a port on the northeast coast of N Korea; pop. (est. 2002) 674,000.

Chong·ju /tʃʌŋˈdʒuː/ a city in central S Korea; pop. (est. 1995) 531,376.

Chong·qing /tʃʊŋˈtʃɪŋ/ (also **Chung·king** /-ˈkɪŋ/) a city in Sichuan province in central China; pop. (est. 2002) 6,974,300. It was the capital of China from 1938 to 1946, a period when the present capital Beijing, and Nanjing, another former capital, were held by the Japanese.

Chon·ju /tʃʌnˈdʒuː/ a town in southwestern S Korea, northeast of Kwangju; pop. (1995) 563,153.

choo-choo *noun informal* (esp. as a child's word) a railway train or locomotive, esp. a steam engine. [imitative]

choose *verb* (*past* **chose**; *past participle* **chosen**) **1** *transitive* select from a number of alternatives. **2** *intransitive* (usu. foll. by *between, from*) take or select one or another. **3** *transitive* (usu. foll. by *to* + infin.) decide, be determined (*chose to stay behind*). **4** *intransitive* like, prefer (*do as you choose*). □ **cannot choose but** must. **nothing** (or **little**) **to choose between** little or no difference between. □ **choos·er** *noun* [Old English *cēosan* from Germanic]

choosy *adjective* (**choos·i·er**, **choos·i·est**) *informal* demanding; fussy. □ **choos·i·ly** *adverb* **choos·i·ness** *noun*

chop[1] ● *transitive verb* (**chopped**, **chop·ping**) **1 a** (usu. foll. by *off, down*, etc.) cut or fell by a blow, usu. with an axe or other blade. **b** make or prepare by cutting into large pieces (*chop firewood*). **2** (often foll. by *up*) cut (esp. meat or vegetables) into small pieces. **3** strike (esp. a ball) with a short downward stroke or blow. **4** *informal* remove; reduce by (*chopped $5,000 from the budget*). ● *noun* **1** a cutting blow, esp. with an axe. **2** a thick slice of meat (esp. pork or lamb) usu. including a rib. **3** a short downward stroke or blow in tennis, baseball, boxing, etc. **4** the broken motion of water, usu. owing to the action of the wind against the tide. **5** *Cdn, Brit., & Austral.* (prec. by *the*) *informal* **a** dismissal from employment. **b** the action of killing or being killed. **6** *N Amer.* chopped animal feed. □ **chop logic** argue pedantically. [Middle English, var. of CHAP[2]]

chop[2] *noun* (usu. in *pl.*) **1** the jaw or mouth. **2** *Music informal* technical facility or virtuosity on an instrument. **3** *informal* talent or skill in any field. □ **bust one's chops** N Amer. slang exert oneself. **bust someone's chops** N Amer. slang nag or criticize. [16th-c. var. (occurring earlier) of CHAP³, of unknown origin]

chop³ intransitive verb (**chopped**, **chop·ping**) □ **chop and change** vacillate; change direction frequently. [Middle English, perhaps related to chap from Old English cēapian (as CHEAP)]

chop block noun N Amer. Football the tackling of an opponent at or below the knees. □ **chop blocking** noun

chop-chop adverb & interjection informal quickly, quick. [pidgin English from Chinese dial. k'wâi-k'wâi]

chop·house noun a restaurant whose specialty is chops of meat.

Cho·pin /ˈʃoːpã/ **1 Fré·dé·ric (Fran·çois)** (Polish name Fryderyk Franciszek Szopen) (1810–49), Polish-born French composer and pianist. A concert pianist from the age of eight, he wrote almost exclusively for the piano: mazurkas and polonaises inspired by Polish folk music, nocturnes, preludes, and two piano concertos (1829; 1830). **2 Kate (O'Flaher·ty)** (1851–1904), American novelist and short-story writer. She is noted for her interpretations of Creole and Cajun life in collections such as Bayou Folk (1894) and A Night in Acidie (1897). Her frank treatment of sexuality in her novel The Awakening (1899) caused a furor. □ **Chopin·esque** adjective

chopped liver noun N Amer. **1** a dish of cooked esp. chicken liver, chopped with onions, hard-boiled eggs, and seasonings. **2** slang a person or thing regarded as of insignificant worth or interest (why didn't they invite us? What are we, chopped liver?).

chop·per ● noun **1** a person, tool, or piece of machinery that chops. **2** informal a helicopter. **3** a device for regularly interrupting an electric current or beam of light. **4** a type of bicycle or motorcycle with high handlebars. **5** Baseball a high-bouncing ground ball. **6** (in pl.) slang teeth. ● transitive & intransitive verb informal transport or travel by helicopter.

chopping block noun a block of wood on which logs etc. are chopped with an axe or on which food is cut with a knife. □ **on the chopping block** vulnerable to imminent removal, elimination, etc. (subsidies to the arts are on the chopping block).

chop·py adjective (**chop·pi·er**, **chop·pi·est**) **1** (of a body of water) with a rough surface of small, irregular waves. **2** disjointed (the movie's editing was choppy). **3** jerky, not fluid (his choppy stride). □ **chop·pi·ly** adverb **chop·pi·ness** noun

chop shop noun N Amer. informal a place where stolen cars are cut up into parts for resale.

chop-socky noun N Amer. informal (usu. attributive) an action film featuring martial arts. [CHOP¹ + SOCK² + -Y, possibly influenced by CHOP SUEY]

chop·stick noun each of a pair of small thin sticks of wood or plastic etc., held in one hand as eating utensils, originally in the Far East. [pidgin English from chop = quick + STICK¹ equivalent of Cantonese k'wâi-tsze nimble ones]

chop suey /tʃɒp ˈsuːi/ noun a Chinese-style dish usu. consisting of meat, bean sprouts, bamboo shoots, and onions, and served with rice. [Cantonese shap sui mixed bits]

chor·al /ˈkɔːrəl/ adjective of, for, or sung by a choir or chorus. □ **chor·al·ly** adverb [medieval Latin choralis from Latin chorus: see CHORUS]

chor·ale /kɔrˈal/ noun (also **choral**) **1 a** a stately and simple hymn tune. **b** a harmonized version of this. **2** esp. US a group of singers; a choir. [German Choral(gesang) from medieval Latin cantus choralis]

choral society noun a choir.

chord¹ /kɔrd/ Music ● noun a group of (usu. three or more) notes sounded together, as a basis of harmony. ● intransitive verb play a chord, esp. on a guitar etc. □ **chord·al** adjective [originally cord from ACCORD: later confused with CHORD²]

chord² /kɔrd/ noun **1** Math. a straight line joining the extremities of an arc. **2** Aviation the width of an airfoil from leading to trailing edge. **3** Anat. var. of CORD. **4** archaic the string of a harp etc. **5** Engin. one of the two principal members, usu. horizontal, of a truss. □ **strike** (or **touch**) **a chord** evoke some reaction in a person, esp. elicit sympathy. [16th-c. refashioning of CORD after Latin chorda]

chord·ate /ˈkɔrdeit/ ● noun any animal of the phylum Chordata, possessing a notochord at some stage during its development. ● adjective of or relating to the chordates. [modern Latin chordata from Latin chorda CHORD² after Vertebrata etc.]

chore noun **1 a** a routine task, esp. a domestic one. **b** N Amer. (in pl.) the routine daily tasks of a farm, such as feeding, milking, gathering eggs, etc. **2** any tedious or unpleasant piece of work. [originally dial. & US form of CHAR³]

chorea /kəˈriə/ noun Med. a disorder characterized by jerky involuntary movements affecting esp. the shoulders, hips, and face. [Latin from Greek khoreia (as CHORUS)]

chore·boy noun N Amer. a boy or man employed to do odd jobs on a farm, ranch, or logging camp.

chore·o·graph /ˈkɔriəˌgraf/ transitive verb **1** compose the choreography for (a ballet etc.). **2** arrange or direct, esp. something involving large numbers of people and complicated interactions. □ **chor·eog·ra·pher** /-iˈɒgrəfər/ noun [back-formation from CHOREOGRAPHY]

chor·eog·ra·phy /ˌkɔriˈɒgrəfi/ noun (pl. **-ies**) **1** the design or arrangement of a staged dance, figure skating, etc. **2** the sequence of steps and movements in dance or figure skating. **3** the written notation for this. □ **choreo·graph·ic** /ˌkɔriəˈgrafɪk/ adjective **choreo·graph·ic·ally** adverb [Greek khoreia dance + -GRAPHY]

chor·eol·ogy /ˌkɔriˈɒlədʒi/ noun the description of dance steps by a system of graphic notation. □ **chor·eol·o·gist** noun

chori·amb /ˈkɔriˌamb/ noun a metrical foot consisting of two short (unstressed) syllables between two long (stressed) ones. □ **chori·am·bic** adjective [Late Latin Greek khoriambos from khoreios of the dance + IAMBUS]

choric /ˈkɔrɪk/ adjective of, like, or for a chorus in drama or recitation.

chor·ine /ˈkɔriːn/ noun a chorus girl. [CHORUS + -INE³]

chor·ion /ˈkɔriən/ noun the outermost membrane surrounding an embryo of a mammal, reptile, or bird (compare AMNION). □ **chori·onic** /-ˈɒnɪk/ adjective [Greek khorion]

chorionic gonadotropin noun see HUMAN CHORIONIC GONADOTROPIN.

chorionic villus sampling noun a procedure for obtaining information about a fetus in which a sample of tissue is taken from the villi of the chorion. Abbr.: **CVS**.

chor·is·ter /ˈkɔrɪstər/ noun **1** a member of a choir. **2** a choirboy. [Middle English, ultimately from Old French cueriste from quer CHOIR]

cho·ri·zo /tʃəˈriːzoʊ/ noun (pl. **-rizos**) a type of sausage containing pork, garlic, and hot spices. [Spanish]

chor·oid /ˈkɔrɔid/ ● adjective like a chorion in shape or vascularity. ● noun (in full **choroid coat** or **choroid membrane**) a layer of the eyeball between the retina and the sclera. [Greek khoroeidēs for khorioeidēs: see CHORION]

chor·tle ● intransitive verb chuckle gleefully. ● noun a gleeful chuckle. [blend coined by Lewis Carroll, prob. from CHUCKLE + SNORT]

chor·us /ˈkɔrəs/ ● noun (pl. **chor·us·es**) **1** a group (esp. a large one) of singers; a choir. **2** a piece of music composed for a choir. **3** the refrain or the recurring part of a popular song, sometimes sung by more than one voice. **4** any simultaneous utterance by many persons etc. (a chorus of disapproval followed; a chorus of barks). **5** a group of singers or dancers performing in concert in a musical comedy, opera, etc. **6** (in Greek tragedy) **a** a group of performers who comment together in voice and movement on the main action. **b** an utterance of the chorus. **7** (in Elizabethan drama) **a** a character who speaks the prologue and other linking parts of the play. **b** the part spoken by this character. ● transitive & intransitive verb (of a group) speak or utter simultaneously. □ **in chorus** (uttered) together; in unison. [Latin from Greek khoros]

chorus boy noun a young man who sings or dances in the chorus of a musical comedy etc.

chorus frog noun any of various frogs of the genus Pseudacris, widespread throughout N America, esp. P. triseriata, the voice of which sounds like a rasping trill.

chorus girl noun a young woman who sings or dances in the chorus of a musical comedy etc.

chorus line noun a group of esp. female singers and dancers performing in a musical comedy, cabaret act, etc., often dancing together in a long line.

chose past of CHOOSE.

chosen ● verb past participle of CHOOSE. ● adjective **1** selected or preferred. **2** destined by God for salvation.

chosen people noun **1** those selected by God for a special relationship with him, esp. the people of Israel; the Jews. **2** those destined to be saved by God; believing Christians.

Chou see ZHOU.

chou·croute /ʃuːˈkruːt/ noun sauerkraut as prepared in Alsace, with bacon and sausages. [French, from German dialect Surkrut 'sauerkraut', influenced by French chou 'cabbage']

Chou En-lai see ZHOU ENLAI.

chough /tʃʌf/ *noun* any corvine bird of the genus *Pyrrhocorax*, with a glossy blue-black plumage and red legs. [Middle English, prob. originally imitative]

choux pastry /ʃuː/ *noun* a pastry made of flour, water, butter, and eggs, which when cooked forms a hollow round puff, used in cream puffs etc. [French, pl. of *chou* cabbage, rosette]

chow *slang* ● *noun* food. ● *intransitive verb* N Amer. (foll. by *down*) eat. [shortened from CHOW CHOW 2]

chow chow *noun* **1** (also **chow**) a breed of dog developed in China, with a thick coat, compact body, and a bluish-black tongue. **2** a relish of pickled chopped mixed vegetables. [pidgin English]

chow·der *noun* N Amer. a thick soup, usu. containing fish, clams, corn, or potatoes. [perhaps French *chaudière* pot: see CAULDRON]

chowder·head *noun* N Amer. informal a stupid person; a blockhead.

chow mein /tʃau 'mein/ *noun* a Chinese-style dish of fried noodles with chopped meat or shrimp etc. and vegetables. [Chinese *chao mian* fried flour]

Chr. *abbreviation Bible* Chronicles.

Chré·tien /kreit'jã/ **(Joseph-Jacques) Jean** (b.1934), Canadian lawyer and politician, Liberal prime minister 1993–2004. He held a series of ministerial posts in the Pearson and Trudeau administrations before serving briefly as deputy prime minister in 1984. As leader of the Liberal Party from 1990, he led the party to victory in the 1993, 1997, and 2000 federal elections.

Chré·tien de Troyes /kreit jã də trwɒ/ (12th c.), French poet. His courtly romances include some of the earliest on Arthurian themes; of his four extant volumes of romances, *Lancelot* (c.1177–81) is the most famous.

chrism /'krizəm/ *noun* a consecrated mixture of oil and balsam used for anointing in rites of the Catholic and Orthodox Churches. [Old English *crisma* from ecclesiastical Latin from Greek *khrisma* anointing]

chris·om /'krizəm/ *noun Christianity* (in full **chrisom cloth**) *hist.* a white robe put on a child at baptism, and used as its shroud if the child died within the month. [Middle English, as popular pronunciation of CHRISM]

Chris·sake /'krəiseik/ *noun & interjection* (also **Chris·sakes** /'krəiseiks/) *informal* (for) Christ's sake (see SAKE¹).

Christ /krəist/ ● *noun* **1** the title, also now treated as a name, given to Jesus of Nazareth, believed by Christians to have fulfilled the Old Testament prophecies of a coming Messiah. **2** the Messiah as prophesied in the Old Testament. **3** an image or picture of Jesus. ● *interjection taboo slang* expressing surprise, anger, etc.□ **Christ·hood** *noun* **Christ·like** *adjective* [Old English *Crīst* from Latin *Christus* from Greek *khristos* anointed one, from *khriō* anoint: translation of Hebrew *māšīah* MESSIAH]

Christ·adelph·ian /,kristə'delfiən/ ● *noun* a member of a Christian denomination founded in the US, rejecting the doctrine of the Trinity and expecting a second coming of Christ on earth. ● *adjective* of or adhering to this denomination and its beliefs. [CHRIST + Greek *adelphos* brother]

Christ child *noun* (prec. by *the*) Jesus as a child, esp. as a baby.

Christ·church a city on South Island, New Zealand; pop. (2001) 234,297.

chris·ten /'krisən/ *transitive verb* **1** admit (a person) to the Christian Church by baptism. **2** give a Christian name to (a person) at baptism. **3** name and dedicate (a ship, a bell, etc.) by a ceremony analogous to baptism. **4** give a name to a thing; call (*discovered a new element which they christened 'radium'*). **5** *informal* use for the first time. □ **chris·ten·er** *noun* **chris·ten·ing** *noun* [Old English *cristnian* make Christian]

Chris·ten·dom /'krisəndəm/ *noun* **1** Christians worldwide, regarded as a collective body. **2** *hist.* the countries occupied by Christians, esp. in the Middle Ages. [Old English *cristendōm* from *cristen* CHRISTIAN² + -DOM]

Chris·tian¹ /'kristiən, 'kristʃən/ **Fletch·er** (c.1764–c.1793), English seaman and mutineer. As master's mate under Captain William Bligh on the HMS *Bounty*, in April 1789 Christian seized the ship and cast Bligh adrift on account of his alleged tyranny. In 1790 the crew settled on Pitcairn Island, where Christian was probably killed by Tahitians.

Chris·tian² /'kristʃən/ ● *adjective* **1** pertaining to Christ or his teachings. **2** believing in or adhering to the teachings of Christianity. **3** showing the qualities associated with Christianity. **4** (of a person) kind, fair, decent. ● *noun* **1 a** a person who has received Christian baptism. **b** an adherent of Christianity. **2** a person exhibiting Christian qualities. □ **Chris·tian·ize** *transitive & intransitive verb* (also esp. Brit. **-ise**).

Chris·tian·iz·a·tion *noun* **Chris·tian·ly** *adverb* [*Christianus* from *Christus* CHRIST]

Christian and Missionary Alliance *noun* an evangelical Protestant movement founded in New York in the late 19th c., stressing Christ as saviour and actively promoting missionary work.

Christian Brothers *plural noun* (in full **Brothers of the Christian Schools**) a Roman Catholic religious congregation involved in education, esp. of the poor.

Christian Democrat *noun* a member of any of various moderate European political parties having a Roman Catholic base. □ **Christian Democratic** *adjective*

Christian era *noun* the era reckoned from the traditional date of Christ's birth.

Chris·ti·ania /,kristi'ɒniə/ (also **Kris·ti·ania**) the former name (1624–1924) for OSLO.

Christian Island an island off the southeastern shore of Georgian Bay in south central Ontario.

Chris·ti·an·ity /,kristʃi'aniti, ,kristi-/ *noun* **1** the religion based on the doctrines of Christ and his disciples, encompassing the Catholic, Protestant, and Orthodox faiths. **2** the state of being a Christian; Christian quality or character. **3** = CHRISTENDOM.

Christian name *noun* esp. Brit. = FIRST NAME.

Christian Reformed *adjective* of or pertaining to a Calvinist denomination whose adherents are primarily of Dutch origin.

Christian Science *noun* the beliefs and practices of the Church of Christ, Scientist, which holds that God and his spiritual creation are the only ultimate reality, and that healing can be effected through prayer. □ **Christian Scientist** *noun*

Chris·tie¹ /'kristi/ **Dame Aga·tha (Mary Clar·issa)** (1890–1976), English writer of detective fiction. Her novels are characterized by ingenious plots, and many feature the Belgian detective Hercule Poirot or the resourceful Miss Marple; her most famous works include *Murder on the Orient Express* (1934), *Death on the Nile* (1937), and the play *The Mousetrap* (1952).

Chris·tie² /'kristi/ *noun* (also **Chris·ty**) (*pl.* **-ties**) *Skiing* a sudden turn in which the skis are kept parallel, used for changing direction or stopping quickly. [abbreviation of *Christiania*, former name of Oslo, Norway]

Christie stiff *noun* (also **Christy stiff**) Cdn hist. a derby hat. [prob. from *Christy* & Co., English hat manufacturer]

Chris·tina /kri'stiːnə/ (1626–89), daughter of Gustavus Adolphus, queen of Sweden 1644–54. She abdicated in 1654 following her secret conversion to Roman Catholicism; living the remainder of her life in Rome, she was noted for her patronage of art, literature, and music.

Christ·ly /'krəistli/ *adjective* **1** Christlike. **2** Cdn & US (New England) *slang* used as an intensifier (*I always hated that Christly goat*).

Christ·mas /'krisməs/ *noun* **1** (also **Christmas Day**) *Christianity* the annual festival of Christ's birth, celebrated by western churches on 25 December, and by most eastern churches on 7 January. **2** the season in which this occurs; the time immediately before and after 25 December. □ **Christ·masy** (also **Christ·mas·sy**) *adjective* [Old English *Crīstes mæsse* (MASS²)]

Christmas box *noun* **1** Brit. a present or gratuity given at Christmas esp. to tradespeople and employees. **2** Cdn (Nfld) a Christmas present.

Christmas cactus *noun* a cactus of the genus *Schlumbergia* with spineless, flattened stems and brilliant pink flowers, frequently grown as a houseplant. [so named because it flowers at about the northern mid-winter]

Christmas cake *noun* Cdn & Brit. a rich fruitcake eaten at Christmas.

Christmas card *noun* a card sent with greetings at Christmas.

Christmas cherry *noun* a plant of the genus *Solanum*, grown as a houseplant and bearing bright red berries which ripen at Christmastime.

Christmas cracker *noun* a small tube wrapped in decorated paper gathered at both ends, usu. containing a paper hat, small toy, etc., which pops when the ends are pulled to open it, usu. at a Christmas dinner.

Christmas Eve *noun* the day or the evening before Christmas Day.

Christmas fern *noun* a fern, *Polystichum acrostichoides*, of rocky places of eastern N America, with dark green fronds.

Christmas Island 1 an island in the Indian Ocean 350 km (200 miles) south of Java, administered as an external territory of Australia since 1958; pop. (est. 2002) 474. **2** the former name (until 1981) for KIRITIMATI.

---

uː mood   ai my   əi pipe   au brown   ʌu house   ei day   ɔi boy   ā franglais   ã Canadien   ɔ̃ Brayon   (*see over for consonants*)

Christmas lights *plural noun* a string of small, usu. coloured light bulbs, used esp. at Christmas to decorate houses, trees, etc.

Christmas list *noun* a list of people and the gifts one intends to buy them at Christmas.

Christmas paper *noun* decorated paper used to wrap gifts at Christmas.

Christmas pepper *noun* an ornamental pepper plant, *Capsicum annuum*, grown as a houseplant for its yellow, orange and red fruit which ripen at Christmastime.

Christmas pudding *noun* a rich steamed pudding eaten at Christmas, made with flour, suet, dried fruit, spices, etc.

Christmas rose *noun* a white-flowered winter-blooming evergreen, *Helleborus niger*.

Christmas spirit *noun* a mood of joy and generosity, held to be prevalent at Christmas.

Christmas stocking *noun* a stocking hung by children at Christmas to be filled with small gifts.

Christ·mas·time *noun* (also **Christ·mas·tide**) the Christmas season.

Christmas tree *noun* **1** an evergreen or artificial tree set up with decorations at Christmas. **2** *Cdn* a Christmas party. **3** a system of pipes and valves which controls the pressure of an oil or natural gas well.

Christo- /'krɪstɔ/ *combining form* Christ.

Christ·ol·ogy /krɪs'tɒlədʒi/ *noun* the branch of Christian theology relating specifically to the nature, acts, and person of Christ. □ **Christ·o·logic·al** *adjective*

Chris·tophe /kriː'stɒf/ **Henri** (1767–1820), Haitian revolutionary leader, president 1807–11, and King 1811–20. A W Indian slave, he joined Toussaint L'Ouverture and became a leader in the war for Haitian independence (1793–1804); in 1811 he set up his own kingdom in N Haiti, proclaiming himself King Henry I.

Chris·to·pher, St. /'krɪstəfər/ legendary Christian martyr, adopted as the patron saint of travellers. He is represented as a giant who carried travellers across a river. His feast day (25 July) was dropped from the Roman calendar in 1969. [Greek, = one who bore Christ]

Christ the King *noun* a feast day observed on the last Sunday before Advent in the Catholic, Anglican, and Lutheran Churches, celebrating the all-embracing authority of Christ.

Christy *var. of* CHRISTIE². [abbreviation]

chroma /'krɔːmə/ *noun* purity or intensity of colour. [Greek *khrōma* colour]

chroma-key /'krɔːmə,kiː/ ● *noun* a technique or process for selectively combining two video images to form a composite picture, in which all areas of the first image that are of a particular colour or chrominance (usually blue) are detected, and are replaced by corresponding parts of the second image. ● *transitive verb* combine (images) using this technique.

chro·mate /'krɔːmeɪt/ *noun Chem.* a salt or ester of chromic acid.

chro·mat·ic /krɔː'matɪk/ *adjective* **1** of or produced by colour; in (esp. bright) colours. **2** *Music* **a** of or having notes not belonging to a diatonic scale (*chromatic chord*). **b** (of a scale) ascending or descending by semitones. **c** (of an instrument) capable of producing all the tones of the chromatic scale (*chromatic harmonica*). □ **chro·mat·ic·ally** *adverb* **chro·mati·cism** /-tɪ,sɪzəm/ *noun* [French *chromatique* or Latin *chromaticus* from Greek *khrōmatikos* from *khrōma -atos* colour]

chromatic aberration *noun Optics* the failure of different wavelengths of electromagnetic radiation to come to the same focus after refraction.

chro·ma·ti·city /,krɔːmə'tɪsɪti/ *noun* the quality of colour regarded independently of brightness.

chro·ma·tid /'krɔːmətɪd/ *noun* either of two threadlike strands into which a chromosome divides longitudinally during cell division. [Greek *khrōma -atos* colour + -ID²]

chro·ma·tin /'krɔːmətɪn/ *noun* the material in a cell nucleus that stains with basic dyes and consists of protein, RNA, and DNA, of which eukaryotic chromosomes are composed. [German: see CHROMATID]

chromato- /'krɔːmətɔ/ *combining form* (also **chromo-** /'krɔːmɔ/) colour. [Greek *khrōma -atos* colour]

chro·ma·tog·raphy /,krɔːmə'tɒɡrəfi/ *noun Chem.* the separation of the components of a mixture by slow passage through or over a material which adsorbs them differently. □ **chro·mato·graph** /-'matə,ɡraf/ *noun* **chro·mato·graph·ic** /-mətɔ'ɡrafɪk/ *adjective* [German *Chromatographie* (as CHROMATO-, -GRAPHY)]

chro·mato·phore /krə'matə,fɔr/ *noun* a cell or plastid containing pigment.

chrome *noun* **1** chromium, esp. as plating on the trimmings of a car etc. **2** (in full **chrome yellow**) a yellow pigment obtained from lead chromate. [French, = chromium, from Greek *khrōma* colour]

chromed *adjective* **1** plated with chromium. **2** trimmed with chrome.

chrome dome *noun N Amer. slang derogatory* a bald person. □ **chrome-domed** *adjective*

chrome-moly /'krɔːm 'mɒli/ *noun* (also **chro·moly**) a strong but light steel alloy of chromium and molybdenum.

chrome steel *noun* a hard fine-grained steel containing much chromium and used for tools etc.

chrom·ic /'krɔːmɪk/ *adjective Chem.* of or containing trivalent chromium.

chromic acid *noun* an acid that exists only in solution or in the form of chromate salts.

chro·min·ance /'krɔːmɪnəns/ *noun* the colorimetric difference between a given colour and a standard colour of equal luminance. [from CHROMO-² after LUMINANCE]

chro·mite /'krɔːmaɪt/ *noun* **1** *Mineralogy* a black mineral of chromium and iron oxides, which is the principal ore of chromium. **2** *Chem.* a salt of bivalent chromium.

chro·mium /'krɔːmiəm/ *noun Chem.* a hard white metallic transition element, occurring naturally as chromite and used in alloys and as a shiny decorative electroplated coating. Symbol: **Cr**; at. no.: 24. [modern Latin from French CHROME]

chromo-¹ /'krɔːmɔ/ *combining form Chem.* chromium.

chromo-² /'krɔːmɔ/ *var. of* CHROMATO-.

chromo·genic /,krɔːmə'dʒenɪk/ *adjective* colour-producing. [CHROMO-² + -GENIC]

chromo·litho·graph /,krɔːmɔ'lɪθə,ɡraf/ ● *noun* a coloured picture printed by lithography. ● *transitive verb* print or produce by this process. □ **chromo·lith·og·raph·er** /-'θɒɡrəfər/ *noun* **chromo·litho·graph·ic** /-,lɪθə'ɡrafɪk/ *adjective* **chromo·litho·graphy** /-lɪ'θɒɡrəfi/ *noun*

chromo·phore /'krɔːmə,fɔr/ *noun* that part of the molecule that is responsible for a compound's colour.

chromo·some /'krɔːmə,sɔːm/ *noun Biochem.* one of the threadlike structures, usu. found in the cell nucleus, that carry the genetic information in the form of genes. □ **chromo·som·al** *adjective* [German *Chromosom* (as CHROMO-², -SOME³)]

chromosome map *noun* a plan showing the relative positions of genes along the length of a chromosome.

chromo·sphere /'krɔːmə,sfɪːr/ *noun* a gaseous layer of the sun's atmosphere between the photosphere and the corona. □ **chromo·spher·ic** /-'sferɪk/ *adjective* [CHROMO-² + SPHERE]

Chron. *abbreviation Bible* Chronicles.

chron·ic /'krɒnɪk/ *adjective* **1** persisting for a long time (usu. of an illness or a personal or social problem). **2** having a chronic complaint. **3** *informal* habitual, inveterate (*a chronic liar*). **4** *Brit. informal* very bad; intense, severe. □ **chron·ic·ally** *adverb* **chron·icity** /krɒ'nɪsɪti/ *noun* [French *chronique* from Latin *chronicus* (in Late Latin of disease), from Greek *khronikos* from *khronos* time]

chronic fatigue syndrome *noun* a disease characterized by extreme fatigue, poor coordination, giddiness, depression, and general malaise, the cause of which is unknown. Abbr.: **CFS**.

chron·icle /'krɒnɪkəl/ ● *noun* **1** a register of events in order of their occurrence. **2** a narrative, a full account. ● *transitive verb* record (events) in the order of their occurrence. □ **chron·ic·ler** *noun* [Anglo-French *cronicle*, ultimately from Latin *chronica* from Greek *khronika* annals: see CHRONIC]

Chron·icles /'krɒnɪkəlz/ either of two books of the Bible, recording the history of Israel and Judah from the Creation until the return from Exile (536 BC).

chrono- /'krɒnɔ/ *combining form* time. [Greek *khronos* time]

chrono·biol·ogy /,krɒnɔbaɪ'ɒlədʒi/ *noun* the branch of biology concerned with natural physiological rhythms and other cyclical phenomena. □ **chrono·biol·o·gist** *noun*

chrono·graph /'krɒnə,ɡraf, 'krɒnɔ-/ *noun* **1** an instrument for recording time with great accuracy. **2** a stopwatch. □ **chrono·graph·ic** *adjective*

chrono·logic·al /,krɒnə'lɒdʒɪkəl/ *adjective* **1** (of a number of events) arranged or regarded in the order of their occurrence. **2** of or relating

---

Consonants: **b** but   **d** *dog*   **f** *few*   **ɡ** *get*   **h** *her*   **j** *yes*   **k** *cat*   **l** *leg*   **m** *man*   **n** *no*   **p** *pen*   **r** *red*   **s** *sit*

to chronology. **3** of or relating to time (*chronological age*).
□ **chrono·logic·al·ly** *adverb*

chron·ol·ogy /krə'nɒlədʒi/ *noun* (*pl.* **-ogies**) **1 a** the arrangement of events, dates, etc. in the order of their occurrence. **b** a table or document displaying this. **2** the study of historical records to establish the dates of past events. □ **chron·ol·o·gist** *noun* **chron·ol·o·gize** *transitive verb* (also esp. *Brit.* **-gise**). [modern Latin *chronologia* (as CHRONO-, -LOGY)]

chron·om·eter /krə'nɒmɪtər/ *noun* a time-measuring instrument, esp. one keeping accurate time at all temperatures and used in navigation.

chron·om·etry /krə'nɒmətri/ *noun* the science of accurate time measurement. □ **chrono·met·ric** *adjective*

chrono·ther·apy *noun* the treatment of an illness or disorder by administering a drug at a time of day believed to be in harmony with the body's natural rhythms.

chrys·alis /'krɪsəlɪs/ *noun* (*pl.* **chrys·alis·es** or **chrys·al·ides** /krɪ'sali,diːz/) **1 a** a quiescent pupa of a butterfly or moth. **b** the hard outer case enclosing it. **2** a preparatory or transitional state. [Latin from Greek *khrusallis -idos* from *khrusos* gold]

chrys·an·the·mum /krɪ'sanθəməm/ *noun* any composite plant of the genus *Chrysanthemum*, having brightly coloured flowers. [Latin from Greek *khrusanthemon* from *khrusos* gold + *anthemon* flower]

chrys·ele·phant·ine /,krɪselə'fantɪn/ *adjective* (of ancient Greek sculpture) overlaid with gold and ivory. [Greek *khruselephantinos* from *khrusos* gold + *elephas* ivory]

chryso·beryl /'krɪsə,berəl/ *noun* a yellowish-green gem consisting of a beryllium salt. [Latin *chrysoberyllus* from Greek *khrusos* gold + *bērullos* beryl]

chryso·lite /'krɪsə,loɪt/ *noun* a precious stone, a yellowish-green or brownish variety of olivine. [Old French *crisolite* from Latin *chrysolithus* from Greek *khrusolithos* from *khrusos* gold + *lithos* stone]

chryso·prase /'krɪsə,preɪz/ *noun* an apple green variety of chalcedony containing nickel and used as a gem. [Latin *chrysoprasus* from Greek *khrusoprasos* from *khrusos* gold + *prason* leek]

Chrys·os·tom, St. John /'krɪsəstəm/ (*c.*347–407), Doctor of the Church, bishop of Constantinople. As patriarch of Constantinople he was given the name Chrysostom (Greek, = golden-mouthed) in tribute to the eloquence of his preaching. Feast day, 27 Jan.

chryso·tile /'krɪsə,taɪl/ *noun* fibrous serpentine, an important asbestos mineral. [Greek *khrūsos* gold + *tilos* fibre]

chthon·ic /'kθɒnɪk, 'θɒnɪk/ (also **chthon·ian** /'kθɔːnɪən, 'θɔː-/) *adjective* of, relating to, or inhabiting the underworld. [Greek *khthōn* earth]

chub¹ *noun* any of various fishes with short, thick, rounded bodies and large heads, esp. any of several species of the carp family in N America, or a River river fish, *Leuciscus cephalus*. [15th c.: origin unknown]

chub² *noun* a short, fat sausage. [abbreviation of CHUBBY]

chubby *adjective* (**chub·bi·er, chub·bi·est**) plump and rounded (esp. of a person or a part of the body). □ **chub·bi·ly** *adverb* **chub·bi·ness** *noun* [from CHUB¹, orig. in the sense 'short and thickset like a chub']

Chubu /'tʃuːbuː/ a mountainous region of Japan, on the island of Honshu; capital, Nagoya.

chuck¹ ● *transitive verb* **1** *informal* **a** fling or throw carelessly or with indifference. **b** discard. **2** *informal* (often foll. by *in*) give up; reject (*chucked my job*). **3** touch playfully, esp. under the chin. ● *noun* a playful touch under the chin. □ **the chuck** *Brit. slang* dismissal (*he got the chuck*). **chuck out** *informal* **1** expel (a person) from a gathering etc. **2** get rid of, discard. [16th c., perhaps from French *chuquer, choquer* to knock]

chuck² *noun* **1** a cut of beef extending from the neck to the sixth rib. **2** a device for holding a workpiece in a lathe or a bit in a drill. [var. of CHOCK]

chuck³ *noun N Amer.* (*BC, Alaska, & US Northwest*) *informal* a large body of water (*compare* SALTCHUCK). [Chinook Jargon, = water]

chuck⁴ *noun N Amer. informal* food, provisions. [19th c.: perhaps from CHUCK²]

chuck driver *noun N Amer.* a driver in a chuckwagon race.

chucker-out *noun informal* a person employed to expel troublesome people from a gathering etc.; a bouncer.

chuck·hole *noun esp. US* a hole in a road surface; a pothole. [CHUCK¹ + HOLE]

chuckle ● *intransitive verb* laugh quietly or inwardly. ● *noun* a quiet or suppressed laugh. □ **chuck·ler** *noun* [*chuck* cluck]

chuckle·head·ed *noun informal* a stupid person; a blockhead.
□ **chuckle·head·ed** *adjective* [*chuckle* clumsy, prob. related to CHUCK²]

chuck·wagon *noun* **1** a wagon carrying provisions, cooking utensils, etc., as used on a ranch, esp. covered with a canvas supported by hoops. **2** a small cart resembling this, used in chuckwagon races. [CHUCK⁴ + WAGON]

chuckwagon dinner *noun N Amer.* an informal meal in the style of those originally served from chuckwagons, usu. consisting of beef, with potatoes, baked beans, etc.

chuckwagon outfit *noun N Amer.* a chuckwagon, driver, and horses entered in a chuckwagon race.

chuckwagon race *noun N Amer.* a rodeo event in which chuckwagons pulled by teams of four horses race on an oval course.

chuck·wal·la /'tʃʌk,wɒlə/ *noun* a large dark-bodied lizard of the iguana family, *Sauromalus obesus*, of Mexico and the southwestern US. When threatened it inflates itself with air to wedge itself into a crevice. [Mexican Spanish *chacahuala*]

chuff *intransitive verb* **1** (of a steam engine etc.) move with a regular sharp puffing sound. **2** make a sound like a puffing steam engine. [imitative]

chuffed *adjective Brit. informal* delighted. [dial. *chuff* pleased]

chug¹ *N Amer.* ● *intransitive verb* (**chugged, chug·ging**) **1** emit a regular muffled explosive sound, as of an engine running slowly. **2** move with this sound. **3** move slowly but steadily. ● *noun* a chugging sound. [imitative]

chug² *transitive & intransitive verb* (**chugged, chug·ging**) (also **chug·a·lug** (**chug·a·lugged, chug·a·lug·ging**) *slang* drink (a beer etc.) in large gulps without pausing. [imitative]

Chu·go·ku /tʃuː'goːkuː/ a region of Japan, on the island of Honshu; capital, Hiroshima.

chu·kar /tʃʌ'kɑːr/ *noun* a Eurasian red-legged partridge, *Alectoris chukar*, introduced into the Rockies and also domesticated. [Hindi *cakor*]

Chuk·chi /'tʃʊktʃi/ ● *noun* **1** (*pl.* same) a member of an Aboriginal people of extreme NE Siberia. **2** the language of this people. ● *adjective* designating, of, or pertaining to this people or their language. [Russian]

Chukchi Sea part of the Arctic Ocean lying between N America and Asia and to the north of the Bering Strait.

chum¹ ● *noun informal* a close friend. ● *intransitive verb* (often foll. by *with, around*) associate with as a friend. [17th c.: prob. short for *chamber fellow*, orig. Oxford University slang designating a roommate]

chum² *N Amer.* ● *noun* **1** refuse from fish. **2** chopped fish used as bait. ● *verb* **1** *intransitive* fish using chum. **2** *transitive* bait (a fishing place) using chum. [19th c.: origin unknown]

chum³ *noun* (also **chum salmon**) a salmon, *Oncorhynchus keta*, of the N American Pacific coast. *Also called* DOG SALMON, KETA. [Chinook Jargon *tzum (samun)* 'spotted salmon']

Chu·mash /'tʃuːmaʃ/ ● *noun* **1** a member of any of several Aboriginal groups formerly inhabiting the California coast near Santa Barbara. **2** (also **Chu·mash·an**) any of the Hokan languages of the Chumash. ● *adjective* of or pertaining to this people or their language.

chummy *informal* ● *adjective* (**chum·mi·er, chum·mi·est**) intimate, friendly, sociable. ● *noun Cdn* (*Nfld*) a person, usu. male, not known to the speaker; 'buddy' (*chummy slipped on the ice*). □ **chum·mi·ly** *adverb* **chum·mi·ness** *noun*

chump *noun* **1** *informal* a gullible or foolish person. **2** the thick end, esp. of a loin of lamb or mutton (*chump chop*). **3** a short thick block of wood. **4** *Brit. slang* the head. □ **off one's chump** *Brit. informal* crazy. [18th c.: blend of CHUNK¹ and LUMP¹]

chump change *noun US informal* an insignificant amount of money.

chun·der *intransitive verb & noun Austral. slang* vomit. [20th c.: origin unknown]

Chung·king see CHONGQING.

chunk¹ ● *noun* **1** a thick solid slice or piece of something firm or hard. **2** a substantial amount or piece. ● *verb* **1 a** *transitive* tear or cut into chunks (*chunked tuna*). **b** *intransitive* break into chunks (*the tires overheated and chunked*). **2** *transitive Psych.* (of the mind) group items of information together to be remembered as a unit. [prob. var. of CHUNK²]

chunk² ● *verb* **1** *intransitive* make a muffled metallic sound. **2** *transitive* cause to make this sound. ● *noun* this sound. [imitative]

chunky *adjective* (**chunk·i·er, chunk·i·est**) **1** containing or consisting of chunks. **2** thick and solid. **3** (of clothes) made of a thick material. **4** (of a person) stocky. □ **chunk·i·ly** *adverb* **chunk·i·ness** *noun*

Chun·nel *noun informal* the Channel Tunnel.

chun·ter *intransitive verb Brit. informal* mutter, grumble. [prob. imitative]

t *top*   v *voice*   w *we*   z *zoo*   ʃ *she*   ʒ *vision*   θ *thin*   ð *this*   ŋ *ring*   x *loch*   tʃ *chip*   dʒ *jar*   (see over for vowels)

chup·pah /'xupə/ *noun* (also **chuppa**) a canopy beneath which Jewish marriage ceremonies are performed. [Hebrew *huppāh* cover, canopy]

Chu·qui·saca /ˌtʃuːkiːˈspkə/ the former name (1539–1840) for SUCRE[1].

church ● *noun* 1 a building for public (usu. Christian) worship. 2 a meeting for public worship in such a building (*go to church*; *met after church*). 3 (**Church**) the body of all Christians. 4 (**Church**) the clergy or clerical profession (*went into the Church*). 5 (also **Church**) an organized Christian group or society of any time, country, or distinct principles of worship (*the medieval Church*; *Church of Scotland*; *High Church*). 6 (also **Church**) institutionalized religion as a political or social force (*Church and State*). ● *transitive verb* bring (esp. a woman after childbirth) to church for a service of thanksgiving. □ **poor as a church mouse** exceedingly poor. □ **church·ly** *adjective* [Old English *cirice*, *circe*, etc. from medieval Greek *kurikon* from Greek *kuriakon* (*dōma*) Lord's (house) from *kurios* Lord: compare KIRK]

church·goer *noun* a person who goes to church, esp. regularly. □ **church·going** *noun & adjective*

Church·ill[1] ▶ a seaport in NE Manitoba, situated at the mouth of the Churchill River and Hudson Bay, 1 600 km north of Winnipeg; pop. (2001) 963. [J. *Churchill*: see MARLBOROUGH]

Church·ill[2] **1 John**, see MARLBOROUGH. **2 Ran·dolph (Henry Spen·cer)** (1849–95), English Conservative politician, who served as secretary of state for India (1885–6) as well as leader of the House of Commons and chancellor of the Exchequer (1886). **3** his son, **Sir Win·ston (Leon·ard Spen·cer)** (1874–1965), English Conservative politician, prime minister 1940–5 and 1951–5. He held several ministerial posts (1911–29), including First Lord of the Admiralty (1911–15), before replacing Neville Chamberlain as prime minister in May 1940. An outstanding orator, he symbolized British resistance during the war. Defeated in the 1945 general election, he served again as prime minister from 1951 to 1955. His writings include *The Second World War* (1948–53) and *A History of the English-Speaking Peoples* (1956–8); he was awarded the Nobel Prize for literature in 1953. □ **Church·ill·ian** /tʃɜrˈtʃɪliən/ *adjective*

Churchill Falls 1 a waterfall in SW central Labrador, 75 m high, situated on the Churchill River, almost 250 km northeast of Labrador City. **2** an unincorporated place situated at the falls; pop. (2001) 645 (with nearby Twin Falls). [Sir W. CHURCHILL]

Churchill River 1 a river, 1 609 km long, which flows generally eastward across central Saskatchewan to Manitoba, then northeastward to Hudson Bay. **2** a river in south central Labrador, 335 km long, which flows first southeastward from Churchill Falls, then northeastward through Happy Valley-Goose Bay into Lake Melville and Hamilton Inlet, before emptying into the Atlantic Ocean. [sense 1 after J. *Churchill* (see MARLBOROUGH); for sense 2 see CHURCHILL FALLS]

church key *noun* N Amer. *slang* a small, rectangular device made of metal with a triangular point at one end for punching holes in cans and a rounded edge at the other end for removing bottle caps.

church·man *noun* (*pl.* **-men**) a male member of the clergy or of a church.

Church Militant *noun* (prec. by *the*) the whole body of Christian believers as striving to combat evil on earth. [contrasted with 'the Church Triumphant' in heaven]

church mode *noun* each of the eight medieval modes used for plainsong and liturgical chant, each beginning on a different note and having a different pattern of tones and semitones.

Church of Christ, Scientist *noun* the official name of the Christian Science Church.

Church of England *noun* an English branch of the Western or Latin Church, which has retained episcopacy but rejected the Pope's supremacy since the Reformation, having the sovereign as its head.

Church of Jesus Christ of Latter-day Saints *noun* the official name of the Mormon Church.

Church of Rome *noun* the Roman Catholic Church.

Church of Scotland *noun* the official (Presbyterian) Christian Church in Scotland.

church planting *noun* the practice of establishing a core of Christian worshippers in an area, with the intention that they should develop into a thriving congregation. □ **church planter** *noun*

church school *noun* **1** a school founded by or associated with a church. **2** = SUNDAY SCHOOL.

church supper *noun* N Amer. a community supper catered by the members of a church and usu. held in the church hall.

church union *noun* Cdn the merger, in 1925, of Canadian Methodist

and Congregationalist Churches together with the majority of Canadian Presbyterians to form the United Church of Canada.

church·warden *noun* **1** Anglicanism either of two elected lay representatives of a parish, assisting with routine administration. **2** a long-stemmed clay pipe.

church·woman *noun* (*pl.* **-women**) a woman member of the clergy or of a church.

churchy *adjective* **1** obtrusively or intolerantly devoted to the Christian Church or opposed to religious dissent. **2** like a church. □ **church·i·ness** *noun*

church·yard *noun* the enclosed ground around a church, esp. as used for burials.

churi·dars /'tʃʊridɑrz/ *plural noun* tight trousers worn by people from the Indian subcontinent, typically with a kameez. [Hindi *cūīdār* 'having a series of gathered rows' (i.e. at the bottom of the trouser leg, traditionally worn too long and tucked up]

chur·inga /tʃʌˈrɪŋgə/ *noun* (*pl.* same or **chur·ingas**) a sacred object, esp. an amulet, among the Australian Aboriginals. [Aranda *jʷerrenge* 'object from the dreaming']

churl *noun* **1** an ill-mannered person. **2** *archaic* a peasant; a person of low birth. **3** *archaic* a surly or mean person. [Old English *ceorl* from a West Germanic root, = man]

churl·ish *adjective* ungrateful or ungracious. □ **churl·ish·ly** *adverb* **churl·ish·ness** *noun*

churn ● *noun* **1** a machine for making butter by agitating milk or cream. **2** Brit. a large milk can. **3** turnover of customers or employees. ● *verb* **1** *transitive* agitate (milk or cream) in a churn. **2** *transitive* produce (butter) in this way. **3** *transitive* (usu. foll. by *up*) cause distress to; upset, agitate. **4** *intransitive* (esp. of a liquid) move about violently (*the churning sea*; *my stomach churned*). **5** *transitive* (often foll. by *up*) agitate or move (liquid, soil, etc.) vigorously. **6** *transitive* (of a broker) buy and sell (a client's investments) frequently in order to earn more commission. □ **churn out** produce routinely or mechanically, esp. in large quantities. [Old English *cyrin* from Germanic]

churn rate *noun* the annual percentage rate at which customers discontinue using a service, in particular cable and satellite television.

churr *var.* of CHIRR.

Chur·ri·guer·esque /ˌtʃʊrɪgəˈresk/ *adjective* Archit. lavishly ornamented in the late Spanish baroque style. [José de *Churriguera*, Spanish architect d.1725]

chur·ro /'tʃʊrəʊ/ *noun* a deep-fried ring-shaped pastry of Latin America, often sugar-coated. [Spanish]

chute[1] /ʃuːt/ *noun* **1** a sloping or vertical channel, tube, or slide, with or without water, for conveying things to a lower level. **2** a slide into a swimming pool. **3** a pen from which an animal is released to begin a race, rodeo event, etc. **b** a narrow passage or enclosure for sheep or cattle. **4** Cdn a rapid. [French *chute* fall (of water etc.), from Old French *cheoite* fem. past participle of *cheoir* fall, from Latin *cadere*; in some senses = SHOOT]

chute[2] /ʃuːt/ *noun* informal a parachute. □ **chut·ist** *noun* [abbreviation]

Chu Teh see ZHU DE.

chut·ney *noun* (*pl.* **-neys**) a spicy, originally Indian, condiment made of fruits or vegetables, vinegar, sugar, etc. [Hindi *caṭnī*]

chutz·pah /'hʊtzpə, hʌts-, xuːts-, -pɒ/ *noun slang* **1** shameless audacity; cheek. **2** boldness. [Yiddish]

Chu·vash·ia /tʃuːˈvɒʃiə/ an autonomous republic in European Russia, east of Nizhni Novgorod; pop. (est. 1995) 1,361,000; capital, Cheboksary.

chyle /kaɪl/ *noun* a milky fluid consisting of lymph and absorbed food materials from the intestine after digestion. □ **chyl·ous** *adjective* [Late Latin *chylus* from Greek *khulos* juice]

chyme /kaɪm/ *noun* the acidic semi-solid and partly digested food produced by the action of gastric secretion. □ **chym·ous** *adjective* [Late Latin *chymus* from Greek *khumos* juice]

chymo·tryp·sin /kaɪmɔːˈtrɪpsɪn/ *noun* a proteolytic enzyme active in the small intestine. [CHYME + TRYPSIN]

chypre /ʃiːprə/ *noun* a heavy perfume made from sandalwood. [French, = Cyprus, perhaps where it was first made]

CI *abbreviation* Cdn Collegiate Institute.

Ci *abbreviation* curie.

CIA *abbreviation* CENTRAL INTELLIGENCE AGENCY.

cia·batta /tʃəˈbɒtə/ *noun* a type of flattish, open-textured Italian bread with a floury crust, made with olive oil. [Italian, lit. 'slipper' (from its shape)]

Ciano /'tʃɑːnəʊ/ **Galeaz·zo** (full name Conte Galeazzo Ciano di

Cortellazzo) (1903–44), Italian fascist politician, minister of foreign affairs 1936-43. In 1943, as ambassador to the Vatican, he was instrumental in the coup that overthrew his father-in-law Mussolini; captured by pro-Mussolini partisans, he was tried and executed for treason.

ciao /tʃau/ *interjection informal* **1** goodbye. **2** hello. [Italian]

CIB *abbreviation* criminal investigation bureau (or branch).

Cib·ber /'sɪbər/ **Col·ley** (1671–1757), English actor, theatre manager, and dramatist. He excelled in comic roles and won recognition as a dramatist with his first comedy, *Love's Last Shift* (1696). He became joint manager of the Drury Lane Theatre in 1711. After his much-ridiculed appointment as Poet Laureate in 1730 he wrote an *Apology for the Life of Mr. Colley Cibber, Comedian* (1740).

ci·bor·ium /sɪ'bɔriəm/ *noun* (*pl.* **ci·boria** /-riə/) **1** a vessel with an arched cover used to hold the Eucharist. **2** *Archit.* **a** a canopy. **b** a shrine with a canopy. [medieval Latin from Greek *kibōrion* seed vessel of the water lily, a cup made from it]

ci·cada /sɪ'keɪdə/ *noun* any transparent-winged large insect of the family Cicadidae, the males of which make a loud, shrill chirping sound. [Latin *cicada*, Italian from Latin *cicala*, Italian *cigala*]

cica·trice /'sɪkətrɪs/ *noun* (also **cica·trix** /'sɪkətrɪks/) (*pl.* **cica·tri·ces** /ˌsɪkə'traɪsiːz/) **1** any mark left by a healed wound; a scar. **2** *Bot.* **a** a mark on a stem etc. left when a leaf or other part becomes detached. **b** a scar on the bark of a tree. □ **cica·tri·cial** /ˌsɪkə'trɪʃəl/ *adjective* [Old French *cicatrice* or Latin *cicatrix -icis*]

cica·trize /'sɪkə.traɪz/ *verb* Brit. **-trise**) **1** *transitive* heal (a wound) by scar formation. **2** *intransitive* (of a wound) heal by scar formation. □ **cica·triz·a·tion** *noun* [French *cicatriser*: see CICATRICE]

ci·cely /'sɪsəli/ *noun* (*pl.* **-ies**) any of various umbelliferous plants, esp. sweet cicely. [apparently from Latin *seselis* from Greek, assimilated to the woman's name]

Ci·cero /'sɪsəˌroː/ **Mar·cus Tul·lius** (106–43 BC), Roman statesman, orator, and writer. His writings are considered a model of classical Latin prose, and include speeches, treatises on rhetoric, philosophical works, and books of letters; he supported Pompey against Julius Caesar, and in the *Philippics* (43 BC) attacked Antony, who had him put to death.

ci·cer·one /ˌsɪsə'roːni/ *noun* (*pl.* **ci·cer·oni** *pronunc.* same) a guide who gives information about antiquities, places of interest, etc. to sightseers. [Italian: see CICERONIAN]

Ci·cero·nian /ˌsɪsə'roːniən/ *adjective* (of language) eloquent, classical, or rhythmical, in the style of Cicero. [Latin *Ciceronianus* from *Cicero -onis*]

cich·lid /'sɪklɪd/ *noun* any tropical freshwater fish of the family Cichlidae, esp. the kinds kept in aquariums. [modern Latin *Cichlidae* from Greek *kikhlē* a kind of fish]

CID *abbreviation* (in the UK) Criminal Investigation Department.

Cid, El /sɪd/ (also **the Cid**) (born Rodrigo Díaz de Vivar) (*c.*1043–99), Spanish soldier. A champion of Christianity against the Moors, he captured Valencia in 1094, and is immortalized in the Spanish *Poema del Cid* (12th c.) and in Corneille's play *Le Cid* (1637).

CIDA /'siːdə/ *abbreviation* Canadian International Development Agency.

-cide /saɪd/ *combining form* forming nouns meaning: **1** a person or substance that kills (*regicide*; *insecticide*). **2** the killing of (*infanticide*; *suicide*). [French from Latin *-cida* (sense 1), *-cidium* (sense 2), *caedere* kill]

cider /'saɪdər/ *noun* **1** *N Amer.* an unfermented drink made from apple juice. **2** (also **hard cider**) an alcoholic drink made from fermented apple juice. [Old French *sidre*, ultimately from Hebrew *šēkār* strong drink]

cider press *noun* a press for crushing apples to make cider. □ **cider pressing** *noun*

cider vinegar *noun* vinegar made from fermented apple juice.

ci-devant /ˌsiːdə'vɑ̃/ *adjective & adverb* that has been (with person's earlier name or status); former or formerly. [French, = heretofore]

c.i.f. *abbreviation* cost, insurance, freight (as being included in a price).

cig *noun informal* a cigarette or cigar. [abbreviation]

cigar *noun* a cylinder of tobacco leaves for smoking. □ **close but no cigar** *N Amer.* (of an attempt etc.) almost but not quite successful. [French *cigare* or Spanish *cigarro*]

ciga·rette *noun* **1** a thin cylinder of finely-cut tobacco rolled in paper for smoking. **2** a similar cylinder containing a narcotic or medicated substance. [French, diminutive of *cigare* CIGAR]

cigarette paper *noun* thin paper used in rolling cigarettes.

ciga·ril·lo /ˌsɪgə'rɪloː/ *noun* (*pl.* **-los**) a small cigar. [Spanish, diminutive of *cigarro* CIGAR]

cigar-store Indian *noun N Amer.* a usu. stern-looking wooden statue of a N American Indian, formerly traditionally placed at the entrance of tobacco shops.

cig·gie *noun* (*pl.* **-gies**) *informal* cigarette. [abbreviation]

cil·an·tro /sɪ'lantroː/ *noun* fresh coriander, used as a herb. [Spanish from Late Latin *coliandrum*, alteration of Latin *coriandrum* coriander]

cilia /'sɪliə/ *plural noun* (*sing.* **cil·ium** /-iəm/) **1** short minute hairlike vibrating structures on the surface of some cells, causing currents in the surrounding fluid. **2** eyelashes. □ **cili·ary** /'sɪlieri/ *adjective* **cili·at·ed** *adjective* **cili·ation** /-'eiʃən/ *noun* [Latin, = eyelash]

cili·ate /'sɪlieit/ ● *adjective* having cilia. ● *noun* a protozoan with cilia, of the phylum Ciliophora.

Cili·cia /sɪ'lɪʃə/ an ancient region on the coast of SE Asia Minor, corresponding to the present-day province of Adana, Turkey. □ **Cili·cian** *adjective*

Cilician Gates a mountain pass in the Taurus Mountains of S Turkey, historically linking Anatolia with the Mediterranean coast.

cil·ium *sing.* of CILIA.

Cima·bue /tʃiːma'buːei/ **Gio·van·ni** (*c.*1240–1302), Italian painter and mosaicist. A painter of the Florentine school, he is often considered to mark the transition between the Byzantine style of art and the naturalism of Giotto; among the works attributed to him is the *Madonna di Sta Trinità*.

cim·ba·lom /'sɪmbələm/ *noun* a dulcimer. [Magyar from Italian *cembalo*]

cimet·idine /sai'metɪdiːn/ *noun* an antihistamine drug that reduces secretion of acid in the stomach, used to treat digestive disorders. [CYANOGEN + METHYL + -IDINE]

Cim·mer·ian /sɪ'mɪriən/ ● *noun* **1** a member of an ancient nomadic people, the earliest known inhabitants of the Crimea, who overran Asia Minor in the 7th century BC. They conquered Phrygia *c.*676 BC and terrorized Ionia, but were gradually destroyed by epidemics and in wars with Lydia and Assyria. **2** *Gk Myth* a member of a people who lived in perpetual mist and darkness, near the land of the dead. ● *adjective* of or relating to the Cimmerians. [via Latin from Greek *Kimmerios*]

C.-in-C. *abbreviation* commander-in-chief.

cinch ● *noun* **1** *informal* **a** a sure thing; a certainty. **b** an easy task. **2** a firm hold. **3** *esp. N Amer.* a girth for a saddle or pack. ● *transitive verb* **1 a** tighten as with a cinch (*cinched at the waist with a belt*). **b** secure a grip on. **2** *slang* make certain of. **3** *esp. N Amer.* put a cinch (sense 3) on. [Spanish *cincha* 'girth']

cinch bug *noun var.* of CHINCH BUG (see CHINCH).

cin·cho·na /sɪŋ'koːnə/ *noun* **1 a** any evergreen tree or shrub of the genus *Cinchona*, native to S America, with fragrant flowers and yielding cinchona bark. **b** the bark of this tree, containing quinine. **2** any drug from this bark formerly used as a tonic and to stimulate the appetite. [modern Latin from Countess of Chinchón d.1641, introducer of drug into Spain]

Cin·cin·nati /ˌsɪnsə'nati/ an industrial city in Ohio, on the Ohio River; pop. (2000) 331,285.

Cin·cin·nat·us /ˌsɪnsə'natəs/ **Lu·cius Quinc·tius** (*c.*519–*c.*438 BC), Roman statesman who, according to tradition, was briefly called from his farm to be dictator of Rome during a moment of crisis (458 BC); he is often referred to as a model of old-fashioned Roman virtue.

cinc·ture /'sɪŋktʃər/ *noun* a girdle, belt, or border. [Latin *cinctura* from *cingere cinct-* gird]

cin·der *noun* **1** the residue of coal or wood etc. that has stopped giving off flames but still has combustible matter in it. **2** slag. **3** (*in pl.*) ashes. □ **burned to a cinder** made useless by burning. □ **cin·dery** *adjective* [Old English *sinder*, assimilated to the unconnected French *cendre* and Latin *cinis* ashes]

cinder block *noun N Amer.* a block made of cinders mixed with sand and cement, the standard block used in building warehouses etc. (also, with hyphen, *attributive*: *cinder-block house*).

cinder cone *noun* a cone formed around the mouth of a volcano by debris cast up during eruption.

Cin·der·ella *noun* **1** (often *attributive*) a person or thing of unrecognized or disregarded merit or beauty, esp. that achieves success in the end (*Cinderella team*). **2** a neglected or despised member of a group. [the name of a girl in a fairy tale]

cine- /'sɪnei, 'sɪni/ *combining form* (also **ciné-**) cinematographic (*cineradiography*; *cinephotography*). [abbreviation]

uː m**oo**d ai m**y** əi p**i**pe au br**ow**n ʌu h**ou**se ei d**ay** ɔi b**oy** ã fr**an**glais ã Canadi**en** ɔ̃ Br**ay**on   (*see over for consonants*)

cine·aste /ˈsɪneɪˌast, ˈsiːni-/ *noun* **1** a person working in professional filmmaking, esp. a director or producer. **2** a film enthusiast. [French *cinéaste* (as CINE-): compare ENTHUSIAST]

cin·ema *noun* **1 a** motion pictures collectively. **b** the production of films as an art or industry. **2** esp. *Brit.* a movie theatre. [French *cinéma*: see CINEMATOGRAPHY]

Cinema·Scope *noun proprietary* a process (now superseded) of motion picture filming and projection involving anamorphic lenses and standard film, producing a picture 2.35 times as wide as it is high.

cine·ma·theque /ˈsɪnəməˌtek/ *noun* **1** a film library or archive. **2** a small cinema, esp. showing art films. [French]

cine·mat·ic /ˌsɪnəˈmatɪk/ *adjective* **1** having the qualities characteristic of the cinema. **2** of or relating to the cinema. □ **cine·mat·ic·ally** *adverb*

cine·ma·tog·raphy /ˌsɪnəməˈtɒɡrəfi/ *noun* the art or technique of shooting motion pictures, involving the choice of film, camera, lens, lighting, camera angle, etc. □ **cine·ma·tog·raph·er** *noun* **cine·mato·graph·ic** /-matəˈɡrafɪk/ *adjective* **cine·mato·graph·ic·ally** *adverb* [*cinematograph* (French *cinématographe*, an early motion picture projector, from Greek *kinēma -atos* movement, from *kineō* move) + -Y³]

cinéma-vérité /ˌsɪneˌmə veriˈteɪ/ *noun Film* **1** the art or process of making realistic (esp. documentary) films which avoid artificiality and artistic effect. **2** such films collectively. [French, = cinema truth]

cine·phile /ˈsɪnəˌfaɪl/ *noun* a person who is fond of films, the history of cinema, etc. [French *cinéphile* (as CINE-, -PHILE)]

Cine·plex /ˈsɪnəˌpleks/ *noun N Amer. proprietary* a movie theatre comprising several separate cinemas. [blend of CINEMA + COMPLEX]

cin·er·aria /ˌsɪnəˈreːriə/ *noun* any of a variety of hybrids of the species *Pericallis cruenta* having bright daisy-like flowers and frequently grown as a houseplant. [modern Latin, fem. of Latin *cinerarius* of ashes, from *cinis -eris* ashes, from the ash-coloured down on the leaves]

cin·er·ar·i·um /ˌsɪnəˈreːriəm/ *noun* (*pl.* **cin·er·ari·ums**) a place where a cinerary urn is deposited. [Late Latin, neuter of *cinerarius*: see CINERARIA]

cin·er·ary /ˈsɪnəreri/ *adjective* of ashes. [Latin *cinerarius*: see CINERARIA]

cinerary urn *noun* an urn for holding the ashes after cremation.

cin·er·eous /sɪˈniːriəs/ *adjective* (esp. of a bird or plumage) ash-grey. [Latin *cinereus* from *cinis -eris* ashes]

cin·gu·lum /ˈsɪŋɡjʊləm/ *noun* (*pl.* **cin·gula** /-lə/) *Anat.* a girdle, belt, or analogous structure, esp. a ridge surrounding the base of the crown of a tooth. □ **cin·gu·late** *adjective* [Latin, = belt]

cin·na·bar /ˈsɪnəˌbɑːr/ *noun* **1** a bright red mineral form of mercuric sulphide from which mercury is obtained. **2** vermilion. **3** a moth, *Tyria jacobaeae*, with bright red wing markings. [Latin *cinnabaris* from Greek *kinnabari*, of oriental origin]

cin·na·mon /ˈsɪnəmən/ *noun* **1** an aromatic spice from the peeled, dried, and rolled bark of a SE Asian tree. **2** any tree of the genus *Cinnamomum*, esp. *C. zeylanicum*, yielding the spice. **3 a** yellowish-brown. **b** reddish-brown. □ **cin·na·mony** *adjective* [Old French *cinnamome* from Greek *kinnamōmon*, and Latin *cinnamon* from Greek *kinnamon*, from Semitic (compare Hebrew *ḳinnāmôn*)]

cinnamon bear *noun* a cinnamon-coloured phase of the N American black bear.

cinnamon bun *noun* (also **cinnamon roll**) *N Amer.* a baked spiral of cinnamon- and sugar-sprinkled dough, often glazed and with raisins.

cinnamon fern *noun* a fern of wet woodlands, *Osmunda cinnamomea*, of eastern N America, with separate spore-bearing stalks.

cinnamon stick *noun* a stick-shaped roll of cinnamon bark.

cinnamon toast *noun* buttered toast sprinkled with sugar and cinnamon.

cin·que·cento /ˌtʃɪŋkwɪˈtʃentoː/ *noun* the style of Italian art and literature of the 16th c., with a reversion to classical forms. □ **cin·que·cen·tist** *noun* [Italian, = 500, used with reference to the years 1500-99]

cinque·foil /ˈsɪŋkfɔɪl/ *noun* **1** any plant of the genus *Potentilla*, with compound leaves of usu. five leaflets. **2** *Archit.* a five-cusped ornament in a circle or arch. [Latin *quinquefolium* from *quinque* five + *folium* leaf]

Cinque Ports /sɪŋk ˈpɔːts/ *plural noun* a group of ports (originally five only) on the southeast coast of England with ancient privileges. [Old French *cink porz*, Latin *quinque portus* five ports]

Cin·sault /sãˈsoː/ *noun* (also **Cin·saut**) a red grape variety originally of the Languedoc region, used in rosé wines and blended with other grapes. [French]

Cin·tra see SINTRA.

CIO *abbreviation* Congress of Industrial Organizations.

ci·paille /siˈpaɪ/ *noun Cdn* a deep pie with alternating layers of meat and pastry. [Canadian French]

ci·pher /ˈsəɪfər/ (also **cy·pher**) ● *noun* **1 a** a secret or disguised system of writing; a code. **b** a message etc. written in this way. **c** the key to it. **2** the arithmetical symbol (0) denoting no amount but used to occupy a vacant place in decimal etc. numeration (as in 12.05). **3** a person or thing of no importance. **4** the interlaced initials of a person or company etc.; a monogram. **5** any Arabic numeral. **6** continuous sounding of an organ pipe, caused by a mechanical defect. ● *verb* **1** *transitive* put into secret writing, encipher. **2 a** *transitive* (usu. foll. by *out*) work out by arithmetic, calculate. **b** *intransitive archaic* do arithmetic. [Old French *cif(f)re*, ultimately from Arabic *ṣifr* ZERO]

circa /ˈsɜːkə/ *preposition* (preceding a date) about, approximately. [Latin]

cir·cad·ian /sɜːˈkeɪdiən/ *adjective* of or pertaining to physiological and psychological processes occurring or recurring about once per day. [irreg. from Latin *circa* about + *dies* day]

Cir·cas·sian /sɜːˈkasiən/ ● *noun* **1** a native or inhabitant of Circassia, a region in the N Caucasus. **2** the Caucasian language of the people of this region. ● *adjective* of or pertaining to Circassia or the Circassians. [*Circassia*, Latinized form of Russian *Cherkes*]

Circe /ˈsɜːsi/ *Gk Myth* a goddess who turned the companions of Odysseus into pigs.

cir·cin·ate /ˈsɜːsɪˌneɪt/ *adjective Bot. & Zool.* rolled up with the apex in the centre, e.g. of young fronds of ferns. [Latin *circinatus* past participle of *circinare* make round, from *circinus* pair of compasses]

cir·cle ● *noun* **1 a** a round plane figure whose circumference is everywhere equidistant from its centre. **b** the line enclosing a circle. **2** a thing, group, etc. shaped or arranged roughly in a circle. **3** a ring. **4** a curved upper tier of seats in a theatre etc. (*dress circle*). **5** a circular route. **6** *Archaeology* a group of (usu. large embedded) stones arranged in a circle. **7** persons grouped round a centre of interest. **8** a group of people having similar interests, characteristics, etc. (*a large circle of friends; known in scientific circles*). **9** a period or cycle (*the circle of the year*). **10** (in full **vicious circle**) **a** an unbroken sequence of reciprocal cause and effect. **b** an action and reaction that intensify each other (compare VIRTUOUS CIRCLE). **c** the fallacy of proving a proposition from another which depends on the first for its own proof. **11** = FACEOFF CIRCLE. **12** (among N American Aboriginal peoples) a meeting for prayer, healing, rendering justice, etc. in which the participants gather in a circle. ● *verb* **1** *intransitive* (often foll. by *round, about*) move in a circle. **2** *transitive* **a** move in or form a circle around. **b** draw a circle around. □ **circle back** move in a wide loop towards the starting point. **circle the wagons** *N Amer.* (of a group) unite in defence of a common interest. **come full circle** return to the starting point. **go round in circles** make no progress despite effort. **run round in circles** *informal* be fussily busy with little result. □ **circ·ler** *noun* [Old French *cercle* from Latin *circulus* diminutive of *circus* ring]

circ·let *noun* **1** a small circle. **2** a circular band made of precious metal, flowers, etc., worn round the head as an ornament.

circs *plural noun Brit. informal* circumstances. [abbreviation]

cir·cuit /ˈsɜːkɪt/ *noun* **1** a line or course enclosing an area; the distance around. **2** a standard series of events or places visited by a judge, group of athletes, preacher, etc. (*US tennis circuit; circuit court; talk-show circuit*). **3** *Electricity* **a** the path of a current. **b** the apparatus through which a current passes. **4** the circular flight pattern of airplanes before approaching an airport. **5** *Brit.* an auto racing track. **6 a** a group of local Methodist churches forming a minor administrative unit. **b** the journey of an itinerant minister within this. [Old French, from Latin *circuitus* from CIRCUM- + *ire it-* go]

circuit board *noun* a thin rigid board containing an electric circuit.

circuit breaker *noun* an automatic device for stopping the flow of current in an electrical circuit, usu. as a safety measure, e.g. when the circuit is overloaded.

circuit court *noun Law* **1** (in Canada) a province's superior court travelling to different communities to sit. **2** (in the US) a Federal court of authority intermediate between a district court and the Supreme Court.

cir·cu·it·ous /sɜːˈkjuːɪtəs/ *adjective* **1** indirect (and usu. long). **2** going a long way around. □ **cir·cu·it·ous·ly** *adverb* **cir·cu·it·ous·ness** *noun* [medieval Latin *circuitosus* from *circuitus* CIRCUIT]

circuit rider *noun N Amer. hist.* a person, esp. a Methodist preacher, who travels from community to community to preach, work, etc.

cir·cuit·ry /'sɜːkɪtri/ noun (pl. **-ries**) **1** a system of electric circuits. **2** the equipment forming this.

circuit training noun a form of athletic training comprising a series of exercises to be performed within a given time.

cir·cu·lar ● adjective **1 a** having the form of a circle. **b** moving or taking place along a circle (circular tour). **2** Logic (of reasoning) depending on the conclusion for proof. **3** (of a letter or advertisement etc.) printed for distribution to a large number of people. ● noun a circular letter, leaflet, etc. □ **circu·lar·ity** noun **cir·cu·lar·ly** adverb [Anglo-French circuler from Late Latin circularis from Latin circulus CIRCLE]

circular saw noun a power saw with a rapidly rotating toothed disc.

cir·cu·late verb **1** intransitive go round from one place or person etc. to the next and so on; be in circulation. **2** intransitive (of blood, sap, etc.) flow through a body, tree, etc. **3** transitive **a** cause to go around; put into circulation. **b** give currency to (a report etc.). **4** intransitive be actively sociable at a party, gathering, etc. □ **circu·la·tor** noun [Latin circulare circulat- from circulus CIRCLE]

circu·la·tion noun **1 a** movement to and fro, or from and back to a starting point, esp. of a fluid in a confined area or circuit. **b** the movement of blood from and to the heart. **c** a similar movement of sap etc. **2 a** the transmission or distribution (of news or information or books etc.). **b** the number of copies sold, esp. of journals and newspapers. **3 a** currency, coin, etc. **b** the movement or exchange of this in a country etc. □ **in** (or **out of**) **circulation** participating (or not participating) in activities etc.

circu·la·tory /'sɜːkjʊlə,tɔːri/ adjective of or relating to the circulation of blood or sap.

circum- combining form around, about (circumscribe; circumfuse; circumlunar). [from or after Latin circum prep. = round, about]

circum·ambi·ent /ˌsɜːkəm'ambiənt/ adjective (esp. of air or another fluid) surrounding.

circum·ambu·late /ˌsɜːkəm'ambjʊ,leɪt/ transitive & intransitive verb formal walk around or about. □ **circum·ambu·la·tion** /-'leɪʃən/ noun **circum·ambu·la·tory** adjective [CIRCUM- + ambulate from Latin ambulare walk]

circum·bor·eal /ˌsɜːkəm'bɔːrɪəl/ adjective of or pertaining to boreal regions around the world.

cir·cum·cise /'sɜːkəm,saɪz/ transitive verb **1** cut off the foreskin of, as a Jewish or Muslim rite or a surgical operation. **2** cut off the clitoris (and sometimes the labia) of, usu. as a religious rite. [Latin circumcidere circumcis- (as CIRCUM-, caedere cut)]

cir·cum·cision /ˌsɜːkəm'sɪʒən/ noun **1** the act or rite of circumcising or being circumcised. **2** (**Circumcision**) Christianity (in the Anglican Church and formerly in the Roman Catholic Church) the feast of the Circumcision of Christ, 1 Jan.

cir·cum·fer·ence /sə'kʌmfərəns/ noun **1** the enclosing boundary, esp. of a circle or other figure enclosed by a curve. **2** the distance around. □ **cir·cum·fer·en·tial** /ˌsɜːkəmfə'renʃəl/ adjective **cir·cum·fer·en·tial·ly** adverb [Old French circonference from Latin circumferentia (as CIRCUM-, ferre bear)]

cir·cum·flex /'sɜːkəm,fleks/ ● noun (in full **circumflex accent**) a mark (ˆ or ˜) placed over a vowel in some languages to indicate a contraction, length, or a special quality. ● adjective Anat. curved, bending around something else (circumflex nerve). [Latin circumflexus (as CIRCUM-, flectere flex- bend), translation of Greek perispōmenos drawn around]

circum·locu·tion /ˌsɜːkəmlə'kjuːʃən/ noun **1 a** a roundabout expression. **b** evasive talk. **2** the use of many words where fewer would do; verbosity. □ **circum·locu·tory** /-'lɒkjʊ,tɔːri/ adjective

circum·lunar /ˌsɜːkəm'luːnɑːr/ adjective moving or situated around the moon.

circum·navi·gate /ˌsɜːkʌm'navɪgeɪt/ transitive verb sail or fly around (esp. the world). □ **circum·navi·ga·tion** /-'geɪʃən/ noun **circum·navi·ga·tor** noun

circum·polar /ˌsɜːkəm'pəʊlɑːr/ adjective **1** around or near one of the earth's poles. **2** Astronomy (of a star or motion etc.) above the horizon at all times in a given latitude.

cir·cum·scribe /'sɜːkəm,skraɪb/ transitive verb **1** (of a line etc.) enclose or outline. **2** lay down the limits of; confine, restrict. **3** Math. draw (a figure) around another, touching it at points but not cutting it (compare INSCRIBE 4). □ **cir·cum·scrip·tion** /-'skrɪpʃən/ noun [Latin circumscribere (as CIRCUM-, scribere script- write)]

circum·solar /ˌsɜːkəm'səʊlɑːr/ adjective moving or situated around or near the sun.

cir·cum·spect /'sɜːkəm,spekt/ adjective wary, cautious; taking everything into account. □ **cir·cum·spec·tion** /-'spekʃən/ noun **cir·cum·spect·ly** adverb [Latin circumspicere circumspect- (as CIRCUM-, specere spect- look)]

cir·cum·stance /'sɜːkəm,stans/ noun **1 a** a fact, occurrence, or condition, esp. (in pl.) the time, place, manner, cause, occasion etc., or surroundings of an act or event. **b** (in pl.) the external conditions that affect or might affect an action. **2** (often foll. by that + clause) an incident, occurrence, or fact, as needing consideration (the circumstance that he left early). **3** (in pl.) one's state of financial or material welfare (in reduced circumstances). **4** ceremony, fuss (pomp and circumstance). **5** full detail in a narrative (told it with much circumstance). □ **in** (or **under**) **the** (or **these**) **circumstances** the state of affairs being what it is. **in** (or **under**) **no circumstances** not at all; never. □ **cir·cum·stanced** adjective [Latin circumstantia (as CIRCUM-, stantia from sto stand)]

cir·cum·stan·tial /ˌsɜːkəm'stanʃəl/ adjective **1** given in full detail (a circumstantial account). **2** (of evidence, a legal case, etc.) tending to establish a conclusion by inference from known facts hard to explain otherwise. **3 a** depending on circumstances. **b** adventitious, incidental. □ **cir·cum·stan·ti·al·ity** /-ʃɪ'alɪti/ noun **cir·cum·stan·tial·ly** adverb

circum·terres·trial /ˌsɜːkəmtə'restrɪəl/ adjective moving or situated around the earth.

circum·val·late /ˌsɜːkəm'valeɪt/ ● transitive verb surround with or as with a rampart. ● adjective surrounded with or as with a rampart. □ **circum·val·la·tion** noun [Latin circumvallare circumvallat- (as CIRCUM-, vallare from vallum rampart)]

cir·cum·vent /ˌsɜːkəm'vent/ transitive verb **1** evade (a difficulty); find a way around. **2** baffle, outwit. □ **cir·cum·ven·tion** noun [Latin circumvenire circumvent- (as CIRCUM-, venire come)]

circum·volu·tion /ˌsɜːkəmvə'luːʃən/ noun **1** rotation. **2** the winding of one thing around another. **3** a sinuous movement. [Latin circumvolvere circumvolut- (as CIRCUM-, volvere roll)]

cir·cus noun (pl. **cir·cus·es**) **1 a** a travelling show of performing animals, acrobats, clowns, etc. **b** a performance given by them. **2** informal a situation characterized by lively and chaotic activity. **3** Brit. an open space in a town, where several streets converge (Piccadilly Circus). **4** a circular hollow surrounded by hills. **5** Rom. Hist. **a** a rounded or oval arena with tiers of seats, for equestrian and other sports and games. **b** a performance given there (bread and circuses). [Latin, = ring]

circus catch noun US (in baseball, football, etc.) a spectacular catch.

ciré /'siːreɪ/ ● noun a fabric with a smooth shiny surface obtained esp. by waxing and heating. ● adjective having such a surface. [French, = waxed]

Ciren·ces·ter /'saɪrən,sestər/ a town in Gloucestershire, SW England; pop. (est. 1998) 16,700. It was a major town in Roman Britain.

cirque /sɜːk/ noun **1** a large bowl-shaped hollow of glacial origin at the head of a valley or on a mountainside. **2** a style of non-traditional circus act combining acrobatics, dance, mime, etc., accompanied by music and light effects. [French from Latin CIRCUS; in sense 2 in reference to the Canadian circus troupe Cirque du Soleil, which originated the style]

cir·rho·sis /sɪ'rəʊsɪs/ noun a chronic disease of the liver caused by alcoholism, hepatitis, etc. in which much of the liver is replaced by fibrous tissue. □ **cir·rhot·ic** /sɪ'rɒtɪk/ adjective [modern Latin from Greek kirrhos tawny]

cir·ri·ped /'sɪrɪ,ped/ noun (also **cir·ri·pede** /'sɪrɪ,piːd/) any marine crustacean of the class Cirripedia, having a valved shell and usu. sessile when adult, e.g. a barnacle. [Latin cirrus curl (from the form of the legs) + pes pedis foot]

cirro- /'sɪrəʊ/ combining form Meteorol. denoting cloud types formed at high altitudes (above 6 km or 20,000 ft.) (cirrostratus).

cirro·cumu·lus /ˌsɪrəʊ'kjuːmjʊləs/ noun Meteorol. cloud forming a broken layer of small fleecy clouds at high altitude, as in a mackerel sky.

cirro·strat·us /ˌsɪrəʊ'stratəs/ noun Meteorol. cloud forming a thin, fairly uniform layer at high altitude.

cir·rus /'sɪrəs/ noun **1** Meteorol. **a** clouds formed at high altitudes as delicate white wisps. **b** a cloud of this type. **2** Bot. a tendril. **3** Zool. a long slender filamentary appendage. [Latin, = curl]

CIS abbreviation COMMONWEALTH OF INDEPENDENT STATES.

cis- /sɪs/ prefix (opp. TRANS- or ULTRA-). **1** on this side of; on the side nearer to the speaker or writer (cisatlantic). **2** Rom. Hist. on the Roman side of (cisalpine). **3** (of time) closer to the present (cis-Elizabethan).

4 *Chem.* (of an isomer) having two atoms or groups on the same side of a given plane in the molecule. [Latin *cis* on this side of]

cis·alpine /sɪs'alˌpaɪn/ *adjective* on the southern side of the Alps.

Cis·alpine Gaul see GAUL[1].

cis·atlan·tic /ˌsɪsətˈlantɪk/ *adjective* on one's own side of the Atlantic.

cisco /ˈsɪskoː/ *noun* (*pl.* **-coes**) any of various freshwater salmonid whitefish of the genus *Coregonus*, native to N America. [Canadian French, back-formation from *ciscoette, ciscaouette*, ultimately from Ojibwa]

Cis·kei /sɪsˈkaɪ/ a former homeland established in South Africa for the Xhosa people, now part of the province of Eastern Cape. (*See also* HOMELAND 2.)

cis·lunar /sɪsˈluːnɜr/ *adjective* between the earth and the moon.

cist[1] /sɪst, kɪst/ *noun Archaeology* a coffin or burial chamber made from stone or a hollowed tree. [Welsh, = CHEST]

cist[2] /sɪst/ *noun Gk Hist.* a box used for sacred utensils. [Latin *cista* from Greek *kistē* box]

Cis·ter·cian /sɪsˈtɜrʃən/ ● *noun* a monk or nun of an order founded in 1098 as a stricter branch of the Benedictines. ● *adjective* of the Cistercians. [French *cistercien* from Latin *Cistercium* Cîteaux near Dijon in France, where the order was founded]

cis·tern /ˈsɪstɜrn/ *noun* **1** a tank or reservoir for storing water. **2** a fluid-filled cavity in an organism or cell. [Old French *cisterne* from Latin *cisterna* (as CIST[2])]

cis·tus /ˈsɪstəs/ *noun* (*pl.* **cis·tus·es**) any shrub of the genus *Cistus*, with large white or red flowers, often cultivated as an ornamental. *Also called* ROCK ROSE. [modern Latin from Greek *kistos*]

cita·del /ˈsɪtədel, -dəl/ *noun* **1** a fortress, usu. on high ground protecting or dominating a city. **2** a meeting hall of the Salvation Army. **3** a position viewed as unassailable (*the citadels of the avant-garde*). [French *citadelle* or Italian *citadella*, ultimately from Latin *civitas -tatis* city]

cit·a·tion /saɪˈteɪʃən/ *noun* **1** the act of citing something from a book or other source. **2** a passage cited. **3** a summons to appear in court. **4** *Military* a commendation in an official dispatch. **5** a descriptive announcement of an award (*received a citation for bravery*).

cite *transitive verb* **1** mention as an example or to support an argument. **2** quote (a passage, book, or author). **3** *Military* commend in an official dispatch. **4** summon to appear in a law court. □ **cit·able** *adjective* [French from Latin *citare* from *ciēre* set moving]

CITES /ˈsaɪtiːz/ *abbreviation* Convention on International Trade in Endangered Species.

citi·fied /ˈsɪtɪˌfaɪd/ *adjective* (also **city·fied**) usu. *derogatory* city-like or urban in appearance or behaviour.

cit·izen /ˈsɪtɪzən/ *noun* **1** a member of a nation or Commonwealth, either native or naturalized (*Canadian citizen*). **2** (usu. foll. by *of*) an inhabitant of a city or town. **3** a member of society, esp. as regards one's contribution to it (*our company wishes to be a good corporate citizen*). [Anglo-French *citesein* ultimately from Latin *civitas -tatis* city: compare DENIZEN]

citizen of the world *noun* a person who is at home anywhere; a cosmopolitan.

cit·izen·ry /ˈsɪtɪzənri/ *noun* citizens collectively.

citizen's arrest *noun* an arrest by an ordinary person without a warrant, allowable in certain cases.

citizens' band *noun* a system of local intercommunication by individuals on special radio frequencies.

cit·izen·ship /ˈsɪtɪzənˌʃɪp/ *noun* **1** the fact of being a citizen of a country (*dual citizenship*). **2** the qualities considered desirable in a person viewed as a member of society (*received our citizenship award*).

Citizenship Court *noun Cdn* a federal court operating under the Department of the Secretary of State, for awarding Canadian citizenship.

Cit·lal·té·petl /ˌsiːtlalˈteipetəl/ (called in Spanish **Pico de Ori·zaba**) the highest peak in Mexico, in the east of the country, north of the city of Orizaba. It rises to a height of 5 699 m (18,503 ft.) and is an extinct volcano. [Aztec, = star mountain]

cit·rate /ˈsɪtreɪt/ *noun* a salt or ester of citric acid. [CITRIC + -ATE[1]]

cit·ric /ˈsɪtrɪk/ *adjective* derived from citrus fruit. [French *citrique* from Latin *citrus* citron]

citric acid *noun* a sharp-tasting water-soluble organic acid found in the juice of lemons and other sour fruits.

cit·rine /ˈsɪtrɪn, ˈsɪtriːn/ ● *noun* a transparent yellow variety of quartz. *Also called* FALSE TOPAZ. ● *adjective* lemon-coloured. [Old French *citrin* (as CITRUS)]

cit·ron /ˈsɪtrən/ *noun* **1** a shrubby tree, *Citrus medica*, bearing large lemon-like fruits with thick fragrant peel. **2** this fruit. **3** the candied peel of this fruit, used in baking etc. [French from Latin CITRUS, after *limon* lemon]

cit·ron·ella /ˌsɪtrəˈnelə/ *noun* **1** any fragrant grass of the genus *Cymbopogon*, native to S Asia. **2** the scented oil from these, used in insect repellent and perfume and soap manufacture. [modern Latin, formed as CITRON + diminutive suffix]

cit·rus /ˈsɪtrəs/ *noun* (*pl.* same) **1** any tree or shrub of the genus *Citrus*, including citron, lemon, lime, orange, and grapefruit. **2** (in full **citrus fruit**) fruit from such a tree. □ **cit·rusy** *adjective* [Latin, = citron tree or thuja]

cit·tern /ˈsɪtɜrn/ *noun hist.* a wire-stringed lute-like instrument usu. played with a plectrum. [Latin *cithara*, Greek *kithara* a kind of harp, assimilated to GITTERN]

city *noun* (*pl.* **-ies**) **1 a** a large town. **b** (in Canada) a municipality with a large population or area or combination of the two. **c** (in the UK) (strictly) a town created a city by charter and containing a cathedral. **d** (in the US) a municipal corporation, chartered by the state, occupying a definite area. **e** the people of a city. **f** the government, administration, or employees of a city. **2** (**the City**) *Brit.* **a** the oldest part of London, situated on the north side of the Thames. **b** London's principal business district. **c** the financial powers of Britain. **3** (*attributive*) of or relating to a city (*city parks*). **4** *informal* (as an intensifier, used after a noun or uninflected verb) a person, place, state of affairs, etc., characterized by the specified quality or action (*when the teacher called out my name, it was panic city!*). [Old French *cité* from Latin *civitas -tatis* from *civis* citizen]

city block *noun* the area bounded by four streets in a city.

city council *noun* the elective governing body of a city. □ **city councillor** *noun*

city desk *noun* **1** *N Amer.* a department of a newspaper dealing with local news. **2** *Brit.* a department of a newspaper dealing with business news.

city editor *noun* **1** *N Amer.* the editor dealing with local news in a newspaper or magazine. **2** *Brit.* the editor dealing with business news.

city father *noun* (usu. in *pl.*) any of the prominent citizens or esp. elected officials of a city.

city·fied *var. of* CITIFIED.

city hall *noun N Amer.* **1** the central administrative offices of a municipality. **2** municipal government. **3** bureaucracy (*you can't fight city hall*).

city manager *noun N Amer.* an official directing the administration of a city.

City of Bridges a nickname for Saskatoon. [with reference to its seven bridges, which span the South Saskatchewan River]

city planner *noun* = URBAN PLANNER. □ **city planning** *noun*

city·scape *noun* **1** a view of a city (actual or depicted). **2** city scenery.

city slicker *noun* usu. *derogatory* **1** a person with a sophistication often attributed to city dwellers. **2** a slick untrustworthy person.

city state *noun* esp. *hist.* a city that with its surrounding territory forms an independent state.

city-wide *adjective* occurring throughout or open to an entire city (*city-wide elections*).

Ciu·dad Bolí·var /sjuːˌdɒd bɒˈliːvar/ a city in SE Venezuela, on the Orinoco River; pop. (est. 2002) 358,500. It was formerly called Angostura. [S. BOLÍVAR]

Ciu·dad Gua·yana /sjuːˌdad gwəˈjɒnə/ a city in E Venezuela, on the Orinoco River; pop. (est. 2000) 704,168.

Ciu·dad Juá·rez /sjuːˌdad ˈhwarəz/ a city in northern Mexico, on the border with Texas and connected by bridge to El Paso; pop. (est. 2000) 1,190,000.

Ciu·dad Tru·jillo /sjuːˌdad truːˈhiːjoː/ the former name (1936–61) for SANTO DOMINGO.

Ciu·dad Vic·toria /sjuːˌdad vɪkˈtɔriə/ a city in NE Mexico, capital of the state of Tamaulipas; pop. (2000) 249,000.

civ·et /ˈsɪvət/ *noun* **1** (in full **civet cat**) any of several carnivorous mammals of the Asian and African family Viverridae (which also includes the genets and mongooses), esp. *Viverra civetta* of central Africa. **2** a strong musky perfume obtained from the anal glands of these animals. [French *civette* from Italian *zibetto* from medieval Latin *zibethum* from Arabic *azzabād* from *al* the + *zabād* this perfume]

Vowels: a *cat* ɑ *arm* e *bed* ɜr *her* ɜː *deux* ə *ago* ɪ *sit* i *cosy* iː *feed* ɒ *hot* ɔ *pore* oː *no* ʌ *run* ʊ *put*

civic /ˈsɪvɪk/ *adjective* **1** of a city; municipal. **2** of or proper to citizens (*civic virtues*). **3** of citizenship; civil. □ **civic·ally** *adverb* [French *civique* or Latin *civicus* from *civis* citizen]

civic centre *noun* **1** a building or building complex containing municipal offices and sometimes other public buildings such as a library, auditorium, etc. **2** a public recreational facility containing an arena, theatre, etc.

civic holiday *noun* Cdn a holiday that is commonly observed but not legislated, esp. the first Monday in August, observed as a holiday in all of Canada except Alberta, Quebec and PEI.

civ·ics /ˈsɪvɪks/ *plural noun* (usu. treated as *sing.*) **1** the study of the rights and duties of citizenship. **2** N Amer. the study of government and political systems, esp. as taught in schools.

civil /ˈsɪvəl/ *adjective* **1** of or belonging to citizens. **2** of ordinary citizens and their concerns, as distinct from military or naval or ecclesiastical matters. **3** polite, obliging, not rude. **4** Law relating to civil law (*civil court; civil lawyer*). **5** of or relating to the state (*civil authorities*). **6** (of the length of a day, year, etc.) fixed by custom or law, not natural or astronomical. **7** Cdn (Nfld) (of the weather or sea) calm. □ **civil·ly** *adverb* [Old French from Latin *civilis* from *civis* citizen]

civil aviation *noun* non-military, esp. commercial aviation.

civil code *noun* a comprehensive legislative enactment of private law, based on Roman and Napoleonic civil law. ¶ In Canada, only Quebec has a civil code.

civil commotion *noun* a riot or similar disturbance.

civil defence *noun* the organization and training of civilians for the protection of lives and property during and after attacks in wartime.

civil disobedience *noun* the refusal to comply with certain laws or to pay taxes etc. as a peaceful form of political protest.

civil engineer *noun* an engineer who designs or maintains roads, bridges, dams, etc. □ **civil engineering** *noun*

civil·ian /sɪˈvɪljən/ ● *noun* a person not in the armed services or the police force. ● *adjective* of or for civilians.

civil·ian·ize /sɪˈvɪljə,naɪz/ *transitive verb* (also esp. *Brit.* **-ise**) make civilian in character or function. □ **civil·ian·iz·a·tion** *noun*

civil·ity /sɪˈvɪlɪti/ *noun* (pl. **-ities**) **1** politeness. **2** an act of politeness.

civil·iz·a·tion /ˌsɪvɪlaɪˈzeɪʃən, ˌsɪvɪlɪ-/ *noun* (also esp. *Brit.* **-isation**) **1** an advanced stage or system of social development. **2** those peoples of the world regarded as having this. **3** a people or nation (esp. of the past) regarded as an element of social evolution (*ancient civilizations; the Inca civilization*). **4** the act or process of making or becoming civilized. **5** *informal* inhabited or usu. urban areas, esp. as opposed to wilderness (*made it back to civilization*).

civil·ize /ˈsɪvɪˌlaɪz/ *transitive verb* (also esp. *Brit.* **-ise**) **1** bring out of a barbarous or primitive stage of society. **2** enlighten; refine and educate. □ **civil·iz·er** *noun*

civil·ized /ˈsɪvɪˌlaɪzd/ *adjective* (also esp. *Brit.* **-ised**) **1** having an advanced and organized state of human social development. **2** having high moral standards (*no civilized country should permit such terrible injustice*). **3** having or showing good behaviour or manners (*they were brought up to behave in a civilized way in public*). **4** having characteristics considered typical of a sophisticated society, esp. comfort, politeness, orderliness, lack of aggression, etc. (*afternoon tea is a very civilized custom*).

civil law *noun* **1** law concerning private rights (*opp.* CRIMINAL LAW). **2** a system of law, based on Roman law, in which laws are codified in statutes (*opp.* COMMON LAW 1). ¶ In Canada, civil law in sense 2 applies only in Quebec.

civil liberty *noun* (often in *pl.*) freedom of action and speech subject to the law. □ **civil libertarian** *noun*

civil list *noun* (in the UK) an annual allowance voted by Parliament for the royal family's household expenses.

civil marriage *noun* a marriage solemnized as a civil contract without religious ceremony.

civil rights *plural noun* the rights of citizens to political and social freedom and equality.

civil servant *noun* a member of the civil service.

civil service *noun* the permanent professional branches of government administration, excluding military and judicial branches and elected politicians.

civil union *noun* a legally recognized union of a same-sex couple, with rights similar to those of marriage.

civil war *noun* **1** a war between citizens of the same country. **2** (Civil War) see AMERICAN CIVIL WAR, ENGLISH CIVIL WAR, RUSSIAN CIVIL WAR, SPANISH CIVIL WAR.

civil year *noun* see YEAR 2.

civ·vies /ˈsɪviːz/ *plural noun* slang civilian clothes. [abbreviation]

civvy /ˈsɪvi/ *adjective* slang civilian. [abbreviation]

civvy street *noun* slang civilian life. [abbreviation]

CJ *abbreviation* chief justice.

CJD *abbreviation* CREUTZFELDT-JAKOB DISEASE.

CKC *abbreviation* Canadian Kennel Club.

Cl *symbol* Chem. the element chlorine.

cl *abbreviation* centilitre(s).

clack ● *verb* **1** *intransitive* make a sharp sound as of hard objects struck together. **2** *transitive* cause (something) to make a clacking sound, as by hitting it on something (*clacked the paddle against the dock*). **3** *intransitive* chatter, esp. loudly. ● *noun* a clacking sound. □ **clack·er** *noun* [Middle English, = to chatter, prob. from Old Norse *klaka*, of imitative origin]

Clack·mannan·shire /klakˈmanənʃɪr/ an administrative region of Scotland. From 1974 to 1996 it was part of Central Region.

clad¹ *adjective* **1** clothed (often in *combination*: *leather-clad; scantily clad*). **2** provided with cladding. [past participle of CLOTHE]

clad² *transitive verb* (**clad·ding**; *past* and *past participle* **clad·ded** or **clad**) provide with cladding. [apparently from CLAD¹]

clad·dagh ring /ˈkladə/ *noun* a ring in the form of two hands clasping a heart, traditionally given in Ireland as a token of love. [from the name of a small fishing village on the edge of Galway city]

clad·ding *noun* a covering or coating on a structure or material etc.; siding.

clade /kleɪd/ *noun* Biol. a group of organisms evolved from a common ancestor. [Greek *klados* branch]

clad·is·tics /kləˈdɪstɪks/ *plural noun* (usu. treated as *sing.*) Biol. a method of classification of animals and plants on the basis of shared characteristics, which are assumed to indicate common ancestry. □ **clad·ism** /ˈkladɪzəm/ *noun* **clad·is·tic** *adjective* [as CLADE + -IST + -ICS]

cla·doceran /kləˈdɒsərən/ *noun* a minute crustacean of an order that includes the water fleas. They typically have a transparent shell enclosing the trunk, and large antennae which are used for swimming. [modern Latin from Greek *klados* 'branch or root' + *keras* 'horn' (because of the branched antennae)]

clad·ode /ˈkleɪdoːd/ *noun* a flattened leaflike stem. [Greek *kladōdēs* having many shoots, from *klados* shoot]

clado·gram /ˈkleɪdəgram/ *noun* Biol. a branching diagram showing the cladistic relationship between a number of species.

cla·fou·tis /klafuːˈtiː/ *noun* (also **cla·fou·ti**) a dessert consisting of fruit, esp. cherries, baked in a dense custard-like batter. [French, from Limousin dialect, from Old French *claufir* 'fasten with nails', whence 'scatter with something']

claim ● *transitive verb* **1** demand as one's due or property. **2** submit a request for payment under an insurance policy. **3 a** represent oneself as having or achieving (*claim victory; claim accuracy*). **b** (foll. by to + infin.) profess (*claimed to be the owner*). **c** assert, contend (*claim that one knows*). **4** have as an achievement or a consequence (*could then claim five wins; the fire claimed many victims*). **5** (of a thing) deserve (one's attention etc.). ● *noun* **1 a** a demand or request for something considered one's due (*lay claim to; put in a claim*). **b** an application for compensation under the terms of an insurance policy. **2** (foll. by to, on) a right or title to a thing (*his only claim to fame; have many claims on my time*). **3** a contention or assertion. **4** a thing claimed. **5** a statement of the novel features in a patent. **6** Mining a piece of land allotted or taken. □ **claim·able** *adjective* [Old French *claime* from *clamer* call out, from Latin *clamare*]

claim·ant *noun* a person making a claim, esp. in a lawsuit or for a government benefit.

claim·er *noun* **1** a person who makes a claim. **2** a claiming race. **3** a horse entered in a claiming race, esp. frequently because the owner no longer wants it.

claiming race *noun* a horse race at which every horse participating is for sale at a stipulated price.

Clair, René (born René Lucien Chomette) (1898–1981), French film director. His silent and sound films typically contain elements of surrealism underpinned by satire, and include *Un Chapeau de paille d'Italie* (1927), *Sous les toits de Paris* (1930), and *Le Silence est d'or* (1947).

Claire, Lake a lake in NE Alberta, situated between the Peace and Athabasca rivers, in Wood Buffalo National Park. [French, lit. 'bright, clear', with reference to the original clarity of its waters]

---

uː mood   aɪ my   əɪ pipe   aʊ brown   ʌʊ house   eɪ day   ɔɪ boy   ā franglais   ã Canadien   ɔ̃ Brayon   (*see over for consonants*)

clair·voy·ance /klerˈvɔɪəns/ noun 1 the supposed faculty of perceiving things or events in the future or beyond normal sensory contact. 2 exceptional insight. [French *clairvoyance* from *clair* CLEAR + *voir* voy-see]

clair·voy·ant /klerˈvɔɪənt/ ● noun a person having clairvoyance. ● adjective having clairvoyance. □ **clair·voy·ant·ly** adverb

clam ● noun any bivalve mollusc, esp. the edible N American hard or round clam (*Venus mercenaria*) or the soft or long clam (*Mya arenaria*). ● intransitive verb (**clammed, clam·ming**) 1 dig for clams. 2 (foll. by *up*) informal refuse to talk. □ **happy as a clam** extremely happy. [16th c.: apparently from *clam* a clamp]

cla·mant /ˈkleɪmənt/ adjective literary noisy; insistent, urgent. □ **cla·mant·ly** adverb [Latin *clamare clamant-* cry out]

Cla·mato /kləˈmatoʊ/ noun N Amer. proprietary a mixture of tomato juice and clam juice.

clam·bake noun N Amer. 1 a seaside picnic at which clams etc. are baked and eaten. 2 informal any social gathering.

clam·ber /ˈklæmbər, ˈklæmər/ ● intransitive verb climb with hands and feet, esp. with difficulty or laboriously. ● noun a difficult climb. [Middle English, prob. from *clamb*, obsolete past tense of CLIMB]

clam digger noun 1 close-fitting women's casual pants hemmed at mid-calf. 2 a person who digs clams for a living.

clam juice noun a stock obtained by boiling clams in water.

clam·mer noun (also **clam digger**) a person who digs for clams, esp. for a living.

clam·my adjective (**clam·mi·er, clam·mi·est**) 1 cold and damp or slimy. 2 (of weather) cold and damp. □ **clam·mi·ly** adverb **clam·mi·ness** noun [Middle English from *clam* to daub]

clam·our (also **clamor**) ● noun 1 loud or vehement shouting or noise. 2 a protest or complaint. 3 an appeal or demand. ● verb 1 intransitive make a clamour. 2 transitive utter with a clamour. □ **clamour for** demand insistently. □ **clam·or·ous** adjective **clam·or·ous·ly** adverb **clam·or·ous·ness** noun [Old French from Latin *clamor -oris* from *clamare* cry out]

clamp¹ ● noun 1 a device, esp. a brace or band of iron etc., for strengthening other materials or holding things together. ● a device for immobilizing an illegally parked car. ● transitive verb 1 strengthen or fasten with a clamp. 2 place or hold firmly. 3 immobilize (an illegally parked car) by fixing a clamp to one of its wheels. □ **clamp down** 1 (often foll. by *on*) be rigid in enforcing a rule etc. 2 (foll. by *on*) try to suppress. □ **clamp·er** noun (in sense 3 of verb). [Middle English prob. from Middle Dutch, Middle Low German *klamp(e)*]

clamp² noun Brit. 1 a heap of potatoes or other root vegetables stored under straw or earth. 2 a pile of bricks for burning. [16th c.: prob. from Dutch *klamp* heap (in sense 2 related to CLUMP)]

clampdown noun severe restriction or suppression.

clam·shell noun 1 the shell of a clam. 2 a thing with hinged parts that open and shut in a manner resembling the parts of such a shell, such as a container for fast food.

clan noun 1 the basic social and political organization of many Aboriginal societies, consisting of a number of related groups and families, often sharing a common symbol or totem. 2 a group of families in the Scottish Highlands with a common ancestor. 3 a large, close-knit family (*the Clarke clan turned out in strength for the family reunion*). 4 a group with a strong common interest. [Gaelic *clann* from Latin *planta* sprout]

Clan·cy, Fran·cis Mi·chael ('King') (1903–86), Canadian hockey player, who played with the Ottawa Senators (1921–30) and the Toronto Maple Leafs (1930–7), leading the Leafs to a Stanley Cup victory in 1932; he later served as a coach and as executive vice-president of the Leafs.

clan·des·tine /klænˈdɛstɪn, -taɪn, ˈklændɛstaɪn/ adjective surreptitious, secret. □ **clan·des·tine·ly** adverb **clan·des·tin·ity** /-ˈtɪnɪti/ noun [French *clandestin* or Latin *clandestinus* from *clam* secretly]

clang ● noun a loud resonant metallic sound as of a bell or hammer etc. ● verb 1 intransitive make a clang. 2 transitive cause to clang. [imitative: influenced by Latin *clangere* resound]

clang·er /ˈklæŋər/ noun esp. Brit. slang a mistake or blunder. □ **drop a clanger** commit a conspicuous indiscretion.

clang·our /ˈklæŋgər/ noun (also **clang·or**) 1 a prolonged or repeated clanging noise. 2 an uproar or commotion. □ **clang·or·ous** adjective **clang·or·ous·ly** adverb [Latin *clangor* noise of trumpets etc.]

clank ● noun a sound as of heavy pieces of metal meeting or a chain rattling. ● verb 1 intransitive make a clanking sound. 2 transitive cause to clank. 3 intransitive move with a clanking sound (*the car clanked down the street*). □ **clank·ing·ly** adverb **clanky** adjective [imitative: compare CLANG, CLINK¹, Dutch *klank*]

clan·nish adjective usu. derogatory 1 (of a family or group) tending to hold together. 2 of or like a clan. □ **clan·nish·ly** adverb **clan·nish·ness** noun

clans·man noun (pl. **-men**) a member or fellow member of a clan. □ **clans·woman** noun (pl. **-women**).

clap¹ ● verb (**clapped, clap·ping**) 1 a intransitive strike the palms of one's hands together as a signal or repeatedly as applause. b transitive strike (the hands) together in this way. 2 transitive applaud or show one's approval of (esp. a person) in this way. 3 transitive (of a bird) flap (its wings) audibly. 4 transitive put or place quickly or with determination (*clapped him in prison; clapped a tax on books*). 5 transitive (foll. by *on*) slap (a person) encouragingly on (the back, shoulder, etc.). ● noun 1 the act of clapping, esp. as applause. 2 an explosive sound, esp. of thunder. 3 a slap, a pat. □ **clap eyes on** informal see. **clap on the back** see BACK. **clap a person on the back** see BACK. [Old English *clappian* throb, beat, of imitative origin]

clap² noun coarse slang venereal disease, esp. gonorrhea. [Old French *clapoir* venereal bubo]

clap·board /ˈklæpbɔrd/ noun N Amer. 1 a siding material consisting of a series of horizontal boards with edges overlapping to keep out the rain etc. (also attributive: *a clapboard house*). 2 one of these boards. □ **clap·board·ed** adjective [anglicized from Low German *klappholt* cask stave]

clapped out adjective Brit. slang worn out (esp. of machinery etc.); exhausted.

clap·per noun the tongue or striker of a bell. □ **like the clappers** Brit. slang very fast or hard.

clapper·board noun Film a device of hinged boards struck together to synchronize the starting of picture and sound machinery in filming.

clapper loader noun Film the second assistant camera operator, who marks the clapperboard and keeps notes on the shooting.

clap skate noun a type of speed-skating skate in which the blade is attached to the toe of the boot by a hinge. [from the sound of the boot reconnecting with the blade]

Clap·ton, Eric (b.1945), English blues and rock guitarist, singer, and songwriter. An influential virtuosic guitarist, he played in the Yardbirds (1963–65), Cream (1966–8), and Derek and the Dominoes (1970), and has pursued a successful solo career; his recordings include 'Layla' (1970) and 'Cocaine' (1977).

clap·trap noun insincere or pretentious talk, nonsense. [orig. designating language used or feelings expressed only to gain applause, from CLAP¹ + TRAP¹]

claque /klæk/ noun a group of people hired to applaud in a theatre etc. □ **cla·queur** /klaˈkɜr/ noun [French from *claquer* to clap]

Clare a county of the Republic of Ireland, on the west coast in the province of Munster; county town, Ennis.

clar·ence /ˈklerəns, klæ-/ noun hist. a four-wheeled closed carriage with seats for four inside and two on the box. [Duke of *Clarence*, afterwards William IV]

Clarence-Rockland a city in E Ontario, extending southward from the Ottawa River NE of Ottawa, incorporating the former town of Rockland and township of Clarence; pop. (2001) 19,612. [as CLARENCE]

Clar·en·don /ˈklerəndən/ **Earl of** (title of Edward Hyde) (1609–74), English statesman and historian. He was adviser to Charles I during the English Civil War, and following the Restoration he served as chief adviser to Charles II 1660–67; exiled to France after 1667, he completed the *History of the Rebellion and Civil Wars in England* (1704–7).

Claren·ville a town in E Newfoundland, just southwest of the Bonavista Peninsula; pop. (2001) 5,104. [orig. *Clarenceville* after the Duke of Clarence, eldest son of the Prince of Wales (1892)]

Clare of Assisi, St. (1194–1253), Italian saint and abbess. She joined St. Francis in 1212 and together they founded the order of Poor Ladies of San Damiano, more commonly known as the 'Poor Clares', of which she was appointed abbess. Feast day, 11 (formerly 12) Aug.

clar·et /ˈklerət, klæ-/ ● noun 1 red wine, esp. from Bordeaux. 2 a deep purplish red. ● adjective claret-coloured. [Old French (*vin*) *claret* from medieval Latin *claratum* (*vinum*) from Latin *clarus* clear]

clarified butter noun butter from which the milk solids have been removed, leaving pure butterfat.

clar·i·fy verb (**-fies, -fied**) 1 transitive & intransitive make or become clearer. 2 transitive **a** free (liquid, butter, etc.) from impurities or solid matter. **b** make transparent. **c** purify. □ **clari·fi·ca·tion** noun **clari·fi·er** noun [Old French *clarifier* from Latin *clarus* clear]

Consonants: b *but* d *dog* f *few* g *get* h *her* j *yes* k *cat* l *leg* m *man* n *no* p *pen* r *red* s *sit*

clari·net /ˌklerɪˈnet, kla-/ *noun* **1 a** a woodwind instrument with a single-reed mouthpiece, a cylindrical tube with a flared end, holes, and keys. **b** its player. **2** an organ stop with a quality resembling a clarinet. □ **clari·net·ist** *noun* (also esp. *Brit.* **clari·net·tist**). [French *clarinette*, diminutive of *clarine* a kind of bell]

Clar·ing·ton a municipality in S Ontario, situated on Lake Ontario, about 15 km east of Oshawa; pop. (2001) 69,834. [blend of the township names *Clarke* and *Darlington*]

clar·ion /ˈklerɪən, kla-/ ● *noun* **1** a clear rousing sound. **2** *hist.* a shrill narrow-tubed war trumpet. **3** an organ stop with the quality of a clarion. ● *adjective* clear, loud, and stimulating (*a clarion call for action*). [medieval Latin *clario -onis* from Latin *clarus* clear]

clar·ity /ˈklerɪti, kla-/ *noun* the state or quality of being clear, esp. of sound or expression. [Latin *claritas* from *clarus* clear]

Clark ▸ 1 Charles Jo·seph ('Joe') (b.1939), Canadian politician, Progressive Conservative prime minister 1979–80. He became leader of the Progressive Conservative Party in 1976, and served as prime minister of a minority government from May to December of 1979, when his government fell on a vote of non-confidence. **2 Paras·keva** (1898–1986), Russian-born Canadian painter. Her works are noted for their complex internal relationship of forms, as in *Self-Portrait* (1933) and the landscape painting *The Pink Cloud* (1937), and often address political and social issues, as in *Petrouschka* (1937). **3 Wil·liam** (1770–1838), US frontiersman and explorer. He jointly commanded the Lewis and Clark expedition (1804–6) to the Pacific Northwest (see M. Lewis[2]).

Clarke ▸ 1 Ar·thur C(harles) (b.1917), English writer of science fiction. A scientific researcher, he conceived the idea of communications satellites, and is the author of such novels as *Earthlight* (1955) and *The Fountains of Paradise* (1979), as well as the screenplay for the film *2001: A Space Odyssey* (1968). **2 Aus·tin Ches·ter·field** (b.1934) Barbadian-born Canadian writer, known for his novels and stories describing Caribbean immigrant life in Canada and his denunciation of Canadian racism. He won the Giller Prize for his novel *The Polished Hoe* in 2002.

clar·kia *noun* any annual herbaceous plant of the genus *Clarkia*, with showy white, pink, or purple flowers. [W. Clark]

Clark·son, Ad·rienne Lou·ise (b.1939), Canadian television personality, diplomat and Governor General since 1999. After a successful career as a television journalist, host and producer, with forays into diplomacy and publishing, she was named Governor General in 1999.

clary /ˈkleri/ *noun* (*pl.* **-ies**) any of various aromatic herbs of the genus *Salvia* of the mint family, esp. *S. sclarea*. [obsolete French *clarie* representing medieval Latin *sclarea*]

clash ● *noun* **1 a** a loud jarring sound as of metal objects being struck together. **b** a collision, esp. with force. **2 a** a conflict or disagreement. **b** a discord of colours etc. ● *verb* **1 a** *intransitive* make a clashing sound. **b** *transitive* cause to clash. **2** *intransitive* collide. **3** *intransitive* (often foll. by *with*) **a** come into conflict or be at variance. **b** (of colours) be discordant. **c** coincide inconveniently. □ **clash·er** *noun* [imitative: compare clack, clang, crack, crash[1]]

clasp ● *noun* **1 a** a device with interlocking parts for fastening. **b** a buckle or brooch. **c** a metal fastening on a book cover. **2 a** an embrace; a person's reach. **b** a grasp or handshake. **3** a bar, star, etc. on a medal ribbon indicating either the occasion for the award or that it was awarded more than once. ● *verb* **1** *transitive* fasten with or as with a clasp. **2** *transitive* **a** grasp, hold closely. **b** embrace, encircle. **3** *intransitive* fasten a clasp. □ **clasp hands** shake hands with fervour or affection. **clasp one's hands** interlace one's fingers. [Middle English: origin unknown]

clasp·er *noun* (in *pl.*) the appendages of some male fish and insects used to hold the female in copulation.

clasp knife *noun* a folding knife, usu. with a catch holding the blade open.

class ● *noun* **1** any set of persons or things grouped together, or graded or differentiated from others (*first class; economy class; Mozart is in a different class from his contemporaries*). **2 a** a division or order of society (*upper class; professional classes*). **b** a caste system, a system of social classes. **3** *informal* distinction or high quality in appearance, behaviour, etc. **4 a** a group of students or pupils taught together. **b** the occasion when they meet. **c** their course of instruction. **5** *N Amer.* all the students of an educational institution graduating in a given year (*the class of 1990*). **6** *Dance* **a** a series of increasingly difficult exercises performed regularly by dancers to warm up their bodies and improve their technique. **b** the group of dancers engaged in this (*wasn't in class this morning*). **7** esp. *Brit.* a division of candidates according to merit in

an examination (*got a second-class in physics*). **8** *Biol.* a grouping of organisms, the next major rank below a division or phylum. ● *transitive verb* assign to a class or category. ● *adjective* excellent; of high quality. □ **in a class of its** (or **one's**) **own** (also **in a class by oneself** (or **itself**)) unequalled. [Latin *classis* assembly]

class act *noun* a person or thing regarded as elegant or first-rate in quality, performance, etc.

class action *noun* *N Amer.* a single legal action brought on behalf of all members of a group with a common interest or grievance.

class-conscious *adjective* aware of and reacting to social divisions or one's place in a system of social class. □ **class-conscious·ness** *noun*

clas·sic ● *adjective* **1 a** of the first class; of acknowledged excellence. **b** remarkably typical; outstandingly important (*a classic case*). **2 a** of ancient Greek and Latin literature, art, or culture. **b** (of style in art, music, etc.) simple, harmonious, well-proportioned; in accordance with established forms (compare romantic *noun* 4a). **3** having literary or historic associations (*classic ground*). **4** (of clothes) made in a simple elegant style not much affected by changes in fashion. ● *noun* **1** a classic writer, artist, work, or example, esp. one of lasting value. **2 a** an ancient Greek or Latin writer. **b** (in *pl.*) the study of ancient Greek and Latin literature and history. **c** *archaic* a scholar of ancient Greek and Latin. **3** a follower of classic models. **4** a garment in classic style. **5** (usu. in *pl.*) a piece of classical music (*the concert featured light classics*). [French *classique* or Latin *classicus* from *classis* class]

clas·sic·al *adjective* **1 a** of ancient Greek or Latin literature or art. **b** (of language) having the form used by the ancient standard authors (*classical Latin; classical Hebrew*). **c** based on the study of ancient Greek and Latin (*a classical education*). **d** learned in classical studies. **2 a** (of music) seen as serious or conventional esp. as opposed to folk, rock, pop, jazz, etc. **b** of the period from *c*.1750–1800 (compare romantic 4b). **3** designating or pertaining to a form or period of an art etc. regarded as representing the height of achievement; in a long established style of acknowledged excellence. **4** established and widely accepted (*classical economic theory*). **5** in or following the restrained style of classical antiquity (compare romantic *noun* 4a). **6** *Physics* relating to the concepts which preceded relativity and quantum theory. □ **clas·sic·al·ly** *adverb*

classical college *noun* *Cdn* (*Que.*) = collège classique.

classical guitar *noun* an acoustic guitar with a hollow waisted body, a 12-fretted neck, and six usu. nylon or gut strings, usu. played by plucking or strumming with the fingers, and used esp. for classical and folk music (compare folk guitar).

clas·si·cism *noun* **1** the following of a classic style. **2 a** classical scholarship. **b** the advocacy of a classical education. **3** an ancient Greek or Latin idiom. □ **clas·si·cist** *noun*

clas·si·cize *verb* (also esp. *Brit.* **-cise**) **1** *transitive* make classic. **2** *intransitive* imitate a classical style. □ **clas·si·ciz·ing** *adjective*

clas·si·fied ● *adjective* **1** arranged in classes or categories. **2** (of information etc.) designated as officially secret. **3** (of newspaper advertisements) arranged in columns according to various categories. ● *noun* (usu. in *pl.*) a classified advertisement.

clas·si·fy *transitive verb* (**-fies, -fied**) **1 a** arrange in classes or categories. **b** assign (a thing) to a class or category. **2** designate as officially secret or not for general disclosure. □ **clas·si·fi·able** *adjective* **clas·si·fi·ca·tion** *noun* **clas·si·fi·ca·tory** /ˌklasɪfɪˈkeitʒri/ *adjective* **clas·si·fi·er** *noun* [back-formation from *classification* from French (as class)]

class·ism *noun* discrimination on the grounds of social class. □ **class·ist** *adjective & noun*

class·less *adjective* making or showing no distinction of classes (*classless society*). □ **class·less·ness** *noun*

class·mate *noun* a fellow member of a class.

class·room *noun* a room in which a class of students is taught.

class struggle *noun* (also **class war, class warfare**) conflict between social classes.

class·work *noun* work done by students in a classroom, esp. as distinguished from homework.

classy *adjective* (**class·i·er, class·i·est**) **1** of high quality; expensive and stylish (*a classy sports car*). **2** distinguished or admirable, esp. by being dignified, gracious, etc. □ **class·i·ly** *adverb* **class·i·ness** *noun*

clas·tic *adjective* *Geol.* designating a rock composed of broken pieces of older rocks. [French *clastique* from Greek *klastos* broken in pieces]

clath·rate /ˈklaθreit/ *noun* *Chem.* a solid in which one component is enclosed in the structure of another. [Latin *clathratus* from *clathri* lattice bars, from Greek *klēthra*]

clat·ter ● *noun* **1** a rattling sound as of many hard objects struck together. **2** noisy talk; chatter. ● *verb* **1** *intransitive* **a** make a clatter. **b** fall or move etc. with a clatter (*the train clattered over the bridge*). **2** *transitive* cause (plates etc.) to clatter. [Old English, of imitative origin]

Claudel /kloː'del/ **1 Ca·mille (Rosa·lie)** (1864–1943), French sculptor. Her work is primarily concerned with the human form. She was the student, collaborator, and lover of Rodin; she was committed to an asylum from 1913. **2** her brother, **Paul (Louis Charles Marie)** (1868–1955), French poet, dramatist, and diplomat. He converted to Roman Catholicism in 1886, and often explores the themes of personal destiny and redemption in his works, which include the poetry collection *Cinq Grandes Odes* (1910), and the plays *L'Annonce faite à Marie* (1910) and *Le Soulier de satin* (1924).

Claude Lor·rain /kloːd lɒrã/ (born Claude Gellée) (1600–82), French landscape painter who worked mainly in Rome. His mature works concentrate on the poetic power of light and atmosphere in idealized Italian landscapes; he was particularly admired in England, where his works inspired Turner and the romantic poets.

claudi·ca·tion /ˌklɒdɪ'keɪʃn/ *noun Med.* **1** limping. **2** = INTERMITTENT CLAUDICATION. [Latin *claudicare* limp, from *claudus* lame]

Claud·ius /'klɒdɪəs/ (full name Tiberius Claudius Nero Germanicus) (10 BC–AD 54), Roman emperor 41–54. He was proclaimed emperor after the murder of Caligula, and his reign was noted for its restoration of order and its expansion of the Roman Empire, in particular his invasion of Britain in 43; he is said to have been poisoned by his fourth wife, Agrippina.

Claudius II /'klɒdɪəs/ (full name Marcus Aurelius Claudius; also called Gothicus) (214–70), Roman emperor 268–70, noted for his defeat of the Goths in 269.

clause *noun* **1** *Grammar* a distinct part of a sentence, including a subject and predicate. **2** a single statement in an accord, law, bill, contract, or insurance policy. □ **claus·al** *adjective* [Old French from Latin *clausula* conclusion, from *claudere claus*- shut]

Clause·witz /'klauzə,vɪts/ **Karl von** (1780–1831), Prussian officer and military theorist. A general in the Prussian army, he wrote the detailed study *On War* (1833), which had a marked influence on strategic studies in the 19th c. □ **Clause·witz·ian** *adjective*

Claus·ius /'klauzɪəs/ **Ru·dolf** (1822–88), German physicist, one of the founders of modern thermodynamics. He was the first to formulate the second law of thermodynamics (1850), and later developed the concept (and coined the term) of entropy, which was his greatest contribution to physics; he also carried out pioneering work on the kinetic theory of gases.

claus·tral /'klɒstrəl/ *adjective* of or associated with the cloister; monastic. [Late Latin *claustralis* from *claustrum* CLOISTER]

claus·tro·phobia /ˌklɒstrə'fəʊbɪə/ *noun* an abnormal fear of confined places. [modern Latin from Latin *claustrum*: see CLOISTER]

claus·tro·phob·ic /ˌklɒstrə'fəʊbɪk/ *adjective* **1** suffering from claustrophobia. **2** inducing claustrophobia. □ **claus·tro·phob·ic·ally** *adverb*

cla·vate /'kleɪveɪt/ *adjective Bot.* club-shaped; thicker at the apex than at the base. [modern Latin *clavatus* from Latin *clava* club]

claves /'klɒveɪz/ *plural noun Music* a pair of hardwood sticks that make a hollow sound when struck together and are used to accompany certain kinds of music, dancing, etc. [Latin American Spanish from Spanish, = keystone, from Latin *clavis* key]

clavi·chord /'klavɪ,kɔːd/ *noun* an early keyboard instrument with strings activated by brass blades fixed upright in the key levers, producing a very soft tone. [medieval Latin *clavichordium* from Latin *clavis* key, *chorda* string: see CHORD²]

clav·icle /'klavɪkəl/ *noun* the collarbone. □ **cla·vic·u·lar** /klə'vɪkjʊlər/ *adjective* [Latin *clavicula* diminutive of *clavis* key (from its shape)]

cla·vier /'klavɪər/ *noun Music* **1** esp. *hist.* any keyboard instrument. **2** its keyboard. [French *clavier* or German *Klavier* from medieval Latin *claviarius*, originally = key bearer, from Latin *clavis* key]

clavi·form /'klavɪ,fɔːm/ *adjective* = CLAVATE. [Latin *clava* club]

claw ● *noun* **1 a** a pointed horny nail on an animal's or bird's foot. **b** a foot armed with claws. **2** the pincers of a shellfish. **3** a device for grappling, holding, etc. ● *verb* **1** *transitive & intransitive* scratch, tear, or pull (a person or thing) with or as with claws. **2** *transitive* proceed by or as if by using one's hands or claws (*clawing her way to the top*). **3** *transitive* make by or as if by clawing (*clawed a hole in the earth*). **4** *intransitive Naut.* beat to windward. □ **claw back** *Cdn & Brit.* **1** regain laboriously or

gradually. **2** recover (money paid out) from another source (e.g. by taxation). □ **clawed** *adjective* (also in *combination*). **claw·less** *adjective* [Old English *clawu, clawian*]

claw·back *noun Cdn & Brit.* **1** the act of clawing back. **2** money recovered in this way.

claw foot *noun* a foot of a table, bathtub, etc., shaped like a bird's or animal's claw. □ **claw-footed** *adjective*

claw hammer *noun* a hammer with one side of the head forked for extracting nails.

Clay ▶ **1 Cas·sius**, see MUHAMMAD ALI 2. **2** Henry (1777–1852), US politician. As speaker of the House of Representatives (1811–14, 1815–20, 1823–5) he helped to initiate the War of 1812, and to pass the Missouri Compromise bill (1820), in an attempt to reconcile the slave states and free states.

clay *noun* **1** a stiff sticky fine-grained earth which can be moulded when wet and is dried and baked to make bricks, pottery, ceramics, etc. **2** *literary* the substance of the human body. **3** = CLAY PIGEON. **4** a hardened clay surface for a tennis court. □ **clay·ey** *adjective* **clay·ish** *adjective* **clay·like** *adjective* [Old English *clæg* from West Germanic]

Clay Belt a region of NE Ontario and NW Quebec, stretching roughly from Hearst to Senneterre, characterized by deposits of clay.

Clay·mation *noun proprietary* a type of animation using clay sculptures rather than drawings. [blend of CLAY + ANIMATION]

clay·more *noun* **1** a type of anti-personnel mine. **2** *hist.* **a** a Scottish two-edged broadsword. **b** a broadsword, often with a single edge, having a hilt with a basketwork design. [Gaelic *claidheamh mór* great sword]

Clayo·quot Sound /'klakwət/ a large inlet of the Pacific Ocean, situated on the west central coast of Vancouver Island. [after the *Clayoquot*, a Nuu-chah-nulth band]

clay-pan *noun Austral.* a natural hollow in clay soil, retaining water after rain.

clay pigeon *noun* a breakable disc thrown up from a trap as a target for shooting.

CLC *abbreviation* Canadian Labour Congress.

-cle *suffix* forming (originally diminutive) nouns (*article; particle*). [as -CULE]

clean ● *adjective* **1** (often foll. by *of*) free from dirt or contaminating matter, unsoiled. **2** clear; unused or unpolluted; preserving what is regarded as the original state (*clean air; clean page*). **3** free from obscenity or indecency. **4** attentive to personal hygiene and cleanliness. **5** even; straight; free from roughness (*a clean edge*). **6** unobstructed; without difficulty (*a clean getaway*). **7 a** (of a ship, aircraft, or car) streamlined, smooth. **b** well-formed, slender and shapely (*clean-limbed; the car has clean lines*). **8** adroit, skilful (*clean fielding*). **9** legible; having few corrections (*clean copy*). **10** *Sport* fair; played without fouls. **11** (of a nuclear weapon) producing relatively little fallout. **12 a** free from ceremonial defilement or from disease. **b** (of food) not prohibited. **13 a** free from any record of a crime, offence, etc. (*a clean driver's licence*). **b** *informal* above suspicion. **c** *informal* not carrying a weapon or incriminating material. **14** faultless (*performed a clean triple Axel*). **15** *informal* free from or cured of addiction to drugs. **16** (of a taste, smell, etc.) sharp, fresh, distinctive. ● *adverb* **1** completely, outright, simply (*cut clean through; clean forgot*). **2** in a clean manner. ● *verb* **1** *transitive* (also foll. by *of*) & *intransitive* make or become clean. **2** *transitive* eat all the food on (one's plate). **3** *transitive Cooking* remove the innards of (fish or fowl). **4** *transitive Weightlifting* raise (a weight) from the floor to shoulder level in a single movement. ● *noun* the act or process of cleaning or being cleaned (*give it a clean*). □ **clean bill of health** see BILL OF HEALTH. **clean down** clean by brushing or wiping. **clean out 1** clean thoroughly. **2** *slang* empty or deprive (esp. of money). **clean up 1** clear (a mess) away. **b** put (things) tidy. **c** make (oneself) clean. **2** restore order or morality to. **3** *slang* **a** acquire as gain or profit. **b** make a gain or profit. **clean up one's act** begin to behave responsibly or soberly. **come clean** *informal* own up; confess everything. **make a clean breast of** see BREAST. **clean hands** freedom from guilt. **make a clean job of** *informal* do thoroughly. **make a clean sweep of** see SWEEP. □ **clean·able** *adjective* **clean·ish** *adjective* **clean·ness** *noun* [Old English *clæne* (adj. & adv.), *clēne* (adv.), from West Germanic]

clean and jerk *noun Weightlifting* an event in which the weightlifter, from a crouching position, lifts the barbell to the shoulders, stands up, then raises it over the head.

clean break *noun* a quick and final separation.

clean-cut *adjective* **1** sharply outlined. **2** (of a person) clean and tidy.

Vowels: a *cat* ɑː *arm* e *bed* ɜː *her* ɜ: *deux* ə *ago* ɪ *sit* i *cosy* iː *feed* ɒ *hot* ɔ *pore* ɔː *no* ʌ *run* ʊ *put*

clean·er *noun* **1** a person employed to clean the interior of a building. **2** (usu. in *pl.*) a commercial establishment for cleaning clothes. **3** a device or substance for cleaning. □ **take to the cleaners** *slang* **1** defraud or rob (a person) of all his or her money. **2** criticize severely.

clean·ing lady *noun* a woman paid to clean the interior of a building.

clean-living *adjective* of upright character.

clean·ly[1] *adverb* **1** in a clean way. **2** efficiently; without difficulty.

clean·ly[2] /ˈklenli/ *adjective* (**clean·li·er**, **clean·li·est**) habitually clean; with clean habits. □ **clean·li·ness** *noun* [Old English *clænlic*: see CLEAN, -LY[1]]

clean·out *noun N Amer.* **1** the act or an instance of cleaning (something) out. **2** an opening for cleaning something out.

clean room *noun* a room free from dust and bacteria, used for medical purposes or the assembly of products such as computer parts.

cleanse /klenz/ *transitive verb* **1** usu. *formal* make clean. **2** (often foll. by *of*) purify from sin or guilt. **3** *archaic* cure (a leper etc.). [Old English *clænsian* (see CLEAN)]

cleans·er /ˈklenzɜr/ *noun* something that cleans, esp. an abrasive or disinfectant product for cleaning the skin, household surfaces, etc.

clean-shaven *adjective* without a beard, whiskers, or moustache.

clean sheet *noun* (also **clean slate**) freedom from commitments or imputations; the removal of these from one's record.

cleans·ing *noun* the purging of 'undesired' social or ethnic groups from an area (*ethnic cleansing*).

clean·skin *noun Austral.* **1** an unbranded animal. **2** *slang* a person free from blame, without a police record, etc.

Cle·an·thes /kliˈænθiːz/ (*c.*331–*c.*232 BC), Greek philosopher who succeeded Zeno of Citium as head of the Stoic school (*c.*261–232 BC).

clean·up *noun* **1** an act of cleaning up. **2** *Baseball* the fourth position in the batting order.

clear ● *adjective* **1** free from dirt or contamination. **2** (of weather, the sky, etc.) not dull or cloudy. **3 a** transparent. **b** lustrous, shining; free from obscurity. **4** (of soup) not containing solid ingredients. **5** (of a fire) burning with little smoke. **6 a** distinct, easily perceived by the senses. **b** unambiguous, easily understood (*make a thing clear*; *make oneself clear*). **c** manifest; not confused or doubtful (*clear evidence*). **7** that discerns or is able to discern readily and accurately (*clear thinking*; *clear-sighted*). **8** (usu. foll. by *about*, *on*, or *that* + clause) confident, convinced, certain. **9** (of a conscience) free from guilt. **10** (of a road etc.) unobstructed, open. **11 a** net, without deduction (*a clear $1000*). **b** complete (*three clear days*). **12** (often foll. by *of*) free, unhampered; unencumbered by debt, commitments, etc. **13** (foll. by *of*) not obstructed by. **14** (of timber) free from knots (*clear pine*). **15** (of skin) not marked by pimples or other blemishes. ● *adverb* **1** clearly (*speak loud and clear*). **2** completely (*he got clear away*). **3** apart, out of contact (*keep clear*; *stand clear of the doors*). **4** (often foll. by *to*) *N Amer.* all the way. ● *verb* **1** *transitive & intransitive* make or become clear. **2 a** *transitive* (often foll. by *of*) free from prohibition or obstruction. **b** *transitive & intransitive* make or become empty or unobstructed. **c** *transitive* free (land) for cultivation or building by cutting down trees etc. **d** *transitive* cause people to leave (a room etc.). **3** *transitive* (often foll. by *of*) show or declare (a person) to be innocent (*cleared them of complicity*). **4** *transitive* approve (a person) for special duty, access to information, etc. **5** *transitive* pass over or by safely or without touching. **6** *transitive* make (an amount of money) as a net gain or to balance expenses. **7** *transitive* pass (a cheque) through a clearing house. **8** *transitive* pass through (a customs office etc.). **9** *transitive* remove (an obstruction, an unwanted object, etc.) (*clear them out of the way*). **10** *transitive & intransitive Sport* send (the ball, puck, etc.) out of one's defensive zone. **11** *intransitive* (often foll. by *away*, *up*) (of physical phenomena) disappear, gradually diminish (*mist cleared by lunchtime*; *my cold has cleared up*). **12** *transitive* (often foll. by *off*) discharge (a debt). □ **clear the air 1** make the air less sultry. **2** disperse an atmosphere of suspicion, tension, etc. **clear away 1** remove completely. **2** remove the remains of a meal from the table. **clear the decks** prepare for action, esp. fighting. **clear off 1** get rid of. **2** *informal* go away. **clear out 1** empty. **2** remove. **3** *informal* go away. **clear one's throat** cough slightly to make one's voice clear. **clear up 1** tidy up. **2** solve (a mystery etc.). **3** (of weather) become fine. **clear the way 1** remove obstacles. **2** stand aside. **clear a thing with** get approval or authorization for a thing from (a person). **in clear** not in cipher or code. **in the clear** free from suspicion or difficulty. **out of a clear blue sky** as a complete surprise. □ **clear·able** *adjective* **clear·er** *noun* **clear·ly** *adverb* **clear·ness** *noun* [Old French *cler* from Latin *clarus*]

clear·ance *noun* **1** the act or an instance of clearing. **2** clear space between two objects or two parts in machinery etc. **3** special

authorization or permission (esp. for an aircraft to take off or land, or for access to information etc.). **4** (also **clearance sale**) a sale to get rid of superfluous stock. **5** the removal of buildings, persons, etc., so as to clear land. *See also* HIGHLAND CLEARANCES. **6 a** the clearing of a person, ship, etc., by customs. **b** a certificate showing this. **7** the clearing of cheques.

clear-cut ● *adjective* **1** sharply defined. **2** completely evident; very clear. **3** of or relating to a method of logging in which all of the trees in an area of forest are harvested at the same time. ● *noun* an area of forest that has been clear-cut. ● *transitive verb* log (an area of forest) by cutting down all of the trees. □ **clear-cutter** *noun* **clear-cutting** *noun*

clear-eyed *adjective* **1** having clear or bright eyes. **2** perceptive; discerning.

Clear Grit *noun Cdn hist.* a member or supporter of the Clear Grit Party, a liberal reform party in Upper Canada during the 1840s and 1850s, which formed the basis of the Liberal Party after Confederation.

clear-headed *adjective* **1** (of a person) able to think clearly. **2** (of an idea, argument, etc.) reasoned, well thought-out.

clear·ing *noun* **1** in senses of CLEAR *verb*. **2 a** an area in a forest cleared of trees. **b** an area of a forest naturally devoid of trees. **3** *Cdn hist.* a settlement in the bush.

clearing bank *noun Brit.* a bank which is a member of a clearing house.

clearing house *noun* **1** a bankers' establishment where cheques and bills from member banks are exchanged, so that only the balances need be paid in cash. **2** an agency for collecting and distributing information, materials, etc.

clearing pass *noun Hockey* a forward pass intended to move the puck out of the defending team's end of the rink.

clear-sighted *adjective* **1** perceptive; having good judgment. **2** having clear vision.

Clear·water River a river in NW Saskatchewan and NE Alberta, 280 km long, rising west of Cree Lake and flowing first southeastward, then generally westward into Alberta to join the Athabasca River at Wood Buffalo. [so called because its waters are clearer than others in the area]

clear·way *noun Brit.* a main road (other than a motorway) on which vehicles are not permitted to stop.

cleat *noun* **1** a metal or wooden fitting with two projecting horns, fastened to a flagpole, boat, etc., around which a rope may be made fast. **2 a** a projecting piece on the bottom or side of a shoe or boot, to improve grip. **b** (in *pl.*) *N Amer.* a pair of shoes or boots equipped with these, esp. for playing field sports. **3** a projecting piece on a spar, gangway, etc., to improve footing. **4** a piece of metal, wood, etc. attached to something to provide strength or hold it in place. **5** a wedge-shaped piece of wood etc. serving as a support. [Old English: compare CLOT]

cleat·ed *adjective* equipped with cleats.

cleav·age *noun* **1** the hollow between a woman's breasts, esp. as exposed by a low-cut garment. **2** a division or splitting. **3** the splitting of rocks, crystals, etc., in a preferred direction.

cleave[1] *verb* (*past* **cleaved** or **clove** or **cleft**; *past participle* **clo·ven** or **cleft** or **cleaved**) **1 a** *transitive* chop or break apart, split, esp. along the grain or the line of cleavage. **b** *intransitive* come apart in this way. **2** *transitive* make one's way through (air or water). □ **cleav·able** *adjective* [Old English *cléofan* from Germanic]

cleave[2] *intransitive verb* (*past* **cleaved**) (foll. by *to*) *literary* stick fast; adhere. [Old English *cleofian*, *clifian* from West Germanic: compare CLAY]

cleav·er *noun* a tool for cleaving, esp. a broad-bladed knife used for cutting meat.

cleav·ers *noun* (also **cliv·ers**) (treated as *sing.* or *pl.*) a plant, *Galium aparine*, having hooked bristles on its stem that catch on clothes etc. Also called GOOSE GRASS. [Old English *clife*, formed as CLEAVE[2]]

Cleese /kliːs/ **John (Mar·wood)** (b.1939), English comic actor and writer. He gained international fame with the television programs *Monty Python's Flying Circus* (1969–74) and *Fawlty Towers* (1975 and 1979), and has also appeared in a number of films.

clef *noun Music* any of several symbols placed at the beginning of a staff, indicating the pitch of the notes written on it. [French from Latin *clavis* key]

cleft[1] *adjective* split, partly divided. [past participle of CLEAVE[1]]

cleft[2] *noun* a split or fissure; a space or division made by cleaving. **2** a vertical indentation in the middle of a person's forehead or chin. [Old English (related to CLEAVE¹): assimilated to CLEFT¹]

cleft lip *noun* a congenital split in the upper lip.

cleft palate *noun* a congenital split in the roof of the mouth.

cleft stick *noun* a difficult position, esp. one allowing neither retreat nor advance.

cleg *noun Brit.* a horsefly. [Old Norse *kleggi*]

Cleis·the·nes /ˈklaɪsθəˌniːz/ (also **Clis·the·nes** /ˈklɪs-/) (c.570–c.508 BC), Athenian statesman, principal archon of Athens 525–524 BC. Democratic reforms he introduced in 508 undermined the power of the nobility, and consolidated the democratic process begun by Solon.

cleis·to·gam·ic /ˌklaɪstəˈɡamɪk/ *adjective Bot.* (of a flower) permanently closed and self-fertilizing. [Greek *kleistos* closed + *gamos* marriage]

clem·atis /kləˈmatɪs, ˈklemətɪs/ *noun* any erect or climbing plant of the genus *Clematis*, bearing white, pink, or purple flowers and feathery seeds, e.g. old man's beard. [Latin from Greek *klēmatis* from *klēma* vine branch]

Cle·men·ceau /klemɑ̃ˈsoː/ **Georges Eu·gène Ben·ja·min** (1841–1929), French journalist and politician, prime minister 1906–9 and 1917–20. A radical, he persistently opposed the government during the early years of the First World War; as prime minister he presided over the negotiation of the Treaty of Versailles (1919).

Clemenceau, Mount /klemˈɒnsoː/ a peak in the Rocky Mountains (3 658 m), situated in eastern BC, just west of Mount Columbia. [G.E.B. CLEMENCEAU]

Clem·ens /ˈklemənz/ **Sam·uel Lang·horne**, see TWAIN.

Clem·ent, St. (also **St. Clement of Rome**) (1st c. AD), pope c.88–c.97, probably the third bishop of Rome after St. Peter. Feast day, 23 Nov.

Clement V (born Bertrand de Got) (c.1260–1314), French pope 1305–14. He chose Avignon as the papal residence in 1309, and it remained the seat of the papacy until 1377.

Clement VII (born Giulio de' Medici) (1478–1534), Italian pope 1523–34. He refused to allow the divorce of Henry VIII from Catherine of Aragon, and was a patron of Cellini, Raphael, and Michelangelo.

clem·ent *adjective* **1** mild, temperate (*clement weather*). **2** merciful. □ **clem·ency** *noun* [Latin *clemens -entis*]

clem·en·tine /ˈklemənˌtaɪn/ *noun* a small citrus fruit, thought to be a hybrid between a tangerine and sweet orange. [French *clémentine*]

Clement of Alexandria, St. (Latin name Titus Flavius Clemens) (c.150–c.215), Greek theologian. Head of the catechetical school of Alexandria (c.190–202), he was the first to apply Greek culture and philosophy to the exposition of Christianity. Feast day, 5 Dec.

clen·but·erol /klenˈbjuːtərɒl/ *noun* a synthetic drug used in the treatment of asthma and respiratory diseases and also in veterinary obstetrics. It also promotes the growth of muscle and has been used illegally by athletes to enhance performance. [*c(h)l(oro-) +(ph)en(yl) + but(yl) + er* -OL]

clench ● *transitive verb* **1** close (the teeth or fingers) tightly. **2** grasp firmly. **3** = CLINCH *verb* 4. ● *noun* **1** a clenching action. **2** a clenched state. [Old English from Germanic: compare CLING]

cle·ome /kliˈoːmi/ *noun* any plant of the genus *Cleome*, with long stamens, esp. spider flower and bee plant.

Cleon /ˈkliːɒn/ (d.422 BC), Athenian politician and military leader prominent during the first part of the Peloponnesian War (431–404 BC).

Cleo·patra /kliːəˈpatrə/ (also **Cleopatra VII**) (69–30 BC), queen of Egypt 47–30 BC. The last Ptolemaic ruler, she was the mistress of Julius Caesar and later of Mark Antony, and both helped her expand the Egyptian Empire. She and Antony were defeated by Octavian at the battle of Actium in 31 BC; following this she committed suicide.

clep·syd·ra /ˈklepsɪdrə/ *noun* an instrument used in antiquity to measure time by the flow of water. [Latin from Greek *klepsudra* from *kleptō* steal + *hudōr* water]

clere·story /ˈkliːrstəri, -ˌstɔri/ *noun* (*pl.* **-ies**) **1 a** an upper row of windows in a cathedral or large church, above the level of the aisle roofs. **b** the section of wall containing such windows. **2** a similar wall or row of windows in other types of buildings. [Middle English from CLEAR + STOREY]

clergy /ˈklɜrdʒi/ *noun* (*pl.* **-gies**) (usu. treated as *pl.*) **1** (usu. prec. by *the*) the body of all persons ordained for religious duties, esp. in the Christian church. **2** a number of such persons (*ten clergy were present*). **3** a member of the clergy. [partly from Old French *clergé* from

ecclesiastical Latin *clericatus*, partly from Old French *clergie* from *clerc* CLERK]

clergy·man *noun* (*pl.* **-men**) an esp. male member of the clergy.

clergy·person *noun* (*pl.* **-persons**) a member of the clergy.

Clergy Reserves *noun Cdn hist.* Crown lands set aside during the settlement of Upper and Lower Canada, the revenue from which was to be used to support Protestant clergy. They caused considerable political debate until the land was secularized in 1854.

clergy·woman *noun* (*pl.* **-women**) a female member of the clergy.

cler·ic /ˈklerɪk/ *noun* a member of the clergy. [(originally adj.) from ecclesiastical Latin from Greek *klērikos* from *klēros* lot, heritage, as in Acts 1:17: 'he was allotted his share in this ministry']

cler·ic·al /ˈklerɪkəl/ *adjective* **1** of the clergy. **2** of or done by an office clerk or secretary. □ **cler·ic·al·ism** *noun* **cler·ic·al·ist** *noun* **cler·ic·al·ly** *adverb*

clerical collar *noun* a stiff upright white collar fastening at the back, worn by the clergy in some Christian denominations.

clerical error *noun* an error made in copying or writing out.

cleri·hew /ˈklerɪˌhju/ *noun* a short comic or nonsensical verse, usu. in two rhyming couplets with lines of unequal length and referring to a famous person. [E. *Clerihew* Bentley, English writer d.1956, its inventor]

cler·isy /ˈklerɪsi/ *noun* a distinct class of learned or literary persons. [apparently after German *Klerisei*, formed as CLERIC]

clerk /klɑrk/ ● *noun* **1** a person employed in an office, bank, store, etc., to keep records, accounts, etc. **2** *N Amer.* a salesperson or assistant in a store or hotel. **3** a secretary, agent, or record-keeper of a municipal government (*town clerk*). **4** *Law* **a** an officer of a court who keeps records, issues subpoenas and other court documents, etc. **b** *Cdn* a judge's research assistant. **c** *see* ARTICLED CLERK. **5** (also /klɑrk/) = CLERK OF SESSION. **6** a senior official in a legislative assembly. **7** *archaic* a clergyman. ● *intransitive verb* work as a clerk. □ **clerk·ish** *adjective* **clerk·ly** *adjective* **clerk·ship** *noun* [Old English *cleric, clerc*, & Old French *clerc*, from ecclesiastical Latin *clericus* CLERIC]

clerk of session *noun* (in Presbyterian and United churches) an elder elected to serve as a congregation's primary officer.

Clerk of the House *noun Cdn & Brit.* the chief administrative officer and procedural adviser of the House of Commons, responsible for all officers and records of the House.

Clerk of the Privy Council *noun Cdn* the senior public servant in charge of the Privy Council Office.

Clermont-Ferrand /klermɔ̃feˈrɑ̃/ an industrial city in central France, capital of the Auvergne region, at the centre of the Massif Central; pop. (1999) 137,140.

Cleve·land¹ 1 a major port and industrial city in NE Ohio, situated on Lake Erie; pop. (2000) 478,403. **2** a former county on the North Sea coast of NE England. It was formed in 1974 from parts of Durham and North Yorkshire, and subdivided in 1996 into four separate jurisdictions. □ **Cleveland·er** *noun*

Cleve·land², (Ste·phen) Gro·ver (1837–1908), US Democratic politician, 22nd and 24th president of the US 1885–9 and 1893–7. His terms were marked by efforts to reverse the heavily protective import tariff, and by his application of the Monroe doctrine to Britain's border dispute with Venezuela (1895).

clev·er *adjective* (**clev·er·er, clev·er·est**) **1** quick to understand and learn. **2** skilful, dexterous. **3** (of the doer or the thing done) ingenious, cunning. **4** witty (*clever dialogue*). □ **clev·er·ly** *adverb* **clev·er·ness** *noun* [Middle English, = adroit: perhaps related to CLEAVE², with sense 'apt to seize']

clever Dick *noun* (also **clever clogs** etc.) esp. *Brit. informal* a person who is or purports to be smart or knowing.

clev·is /ˈklevɪs/ *noun* **1** a U-shaped piece of metal at the end of a beam for attaching tackle etc. **2** a connection in which a bolt holds one part that fits between the forked ends of another. [16th c.: related to CLEAVE¹]

clew /klu/ ● *noun* **1** *Naut.* **a** a lower or after corner of a sail. **b** a set of small cords suspending a hammock. **2** *archaic* **a** a ball of thread or yarn, esp. with reference to the legend of Theseus and the labyrinth. **b** = CLUE. ● *transitive verb Naut.* **1** (foll. by *up*) draw the lower ends of (a sail) to the upper yard or the mast ready for furling. **2** (foll. by *down*) let down (a sail) by the clews in unfurling. [Old English *cliwen, cleowen*]

CLGA *abbreviation* (in Canada) Canadian Ladies' Golf Association.

cli·ché /kliˈʃeɪ, ˈkliː-/ *noun* **1** a hackneyed phrase, opinion, or thing. **2** *Brit.* a metal casting of a stereotype or electrotype. [French from *clicher* to stereotype]

Consonants: b *but*   d *dog*   f *few*   g *get*   h *her*   j *yes*   k *cat*   l *leg*   m *man*   n *no*   p *pen*   r *red*   s *sit*

cli·chéd /kliːˈʃeid, ˈkliː-/ *adjective* hackneyed; full of clichés.

click ● *noun* **1** a slight sharp sound as of a switch being operated. **2** a sharp non-vocal suction, used as a speech sound in some languages. **3** a catch in machinery acting with a slight sharp sound. **4** *Computing* an instance of clicking a button on a mouse. ● *verb* **1 a** *intransitive* make a click. **b** *transitive* cause (one's tongue, heels, etc.) to click. **2** *intransitive informal* **a** become clear or understandable (often prec. by *it* as subject: *when I saw them it all clicked*). **b** be successful, secure one's object. **c** (foll. by *with*) become friendly, esp. with a person of the opposite sex. **d** come to an agreement. **3** *transitive & intransitive Computing* **a** press (one of the buttons on a mouse). **b** select (an item represented on the screen, a particular function, etc.) by so doing. □ **click in** *N Amer. informal* (of a system) become active or effective. □ **click·able** *adjective* (in sense 3 of *verb*). **click·er** *noun* [imitative: compare Dutch *klikken*, French *cliquer*]

click beetle *noun* any of a family of beetles (Elateridae) that make a click in recovering from being overturned.

click-through *noun* **1** the action of clicking on an advertisement or other link on a website to be taken to another site. **2** a measure of the frequency of users doing this.

click track *noun Music* a regular click or beep used to help musicians maintain tempo.

cli·ent /ˈklaiənt/ *noun* **1** a person using the services of a lawyer, architect, social worker, or other professional person. **2** a customer or patron. **3** *Computing* a terminal or workstation that is connected to a server. **4** *Rom. Hist.* a plebeian under the protection of a patrician. [Latin *cliens -entis* from *cluere* hear, obey]

clien·tele /ˌklaiənˈtel/ *noun* **1** clients collectively. **2** the customers or patrons of a store, theatre, etc. [French *clientèle*]

client-server *noun Computing* (*attributive*) designating a type of system in which a server distributes files and databases to clients.

client state *noun* a nation dependent upon a larger one for trade, military protection, etc.

cliff *noun* a steep rock face. □ **cliff·like** *adjective* **cliffy** *adjective* [Old English *clif* from Germanic]

cliff·hanger *noun* **1** a story etc. with a strong element of suspense; a suspenseful ending to an episode of a serial. **2** a game, contest or situation in which the outcome is uncertain until the very end. □ **cliff·hang·ing** *adjective*

cliff·side ● *noun* the face of a cliff. ● *adjective* situated or occurring beside a cliff (*cliffside restaurant*).

cliff swallow *noun* a short-tailed swallow, *Hirunod pyrrhonota*, which builds mud nests on the side of cliffs or buildings.

cliff·top *noun* the top of a cliff.

Clift, (Ed·ward) Mont·gom·ery (1920–66), US actor best known for his roles in the films *Red River* (1948), *A Place in the Sun* (1951), and *From Here to Eternity* (1953).

cli·mac·ter·ic /klaiˈmaktərik, ˌklaimakˈterik/ ● *noun* **1** *Med.* the period of life when fertility and sexual activity are in decline. **2** a supposed critical period in life (esp. occurring at intervals of seven years). ● *adjective* **1** *Med.* occurring at the climacteric. **2** constituting a crisis; critical. [Latin *climactericus* from Greek *klimaktērikos* from *klimaktēr* critical period, from *klimax -akos* ladder]

cli·mac·tic /klaiˈmaktik/ *adjective* of or forming a climax. □ **clim·ac·tic·al·ly** *adverb* [CLIMAX + -IC, perhaps after SYNTACTIC or CLIMACTERIC]

cli·mate /ˈklaimət/ *noun* **1** the prevailing weather conditions of an area. **2** a region with particular weather conditions. **3** the prevailing trend of opinion or public feeling. □ **cli·mat·ic** /-ˈmatik/ *adjective* **cli·mat·ic·al·ly** /-ˈmatikli/ *adverb* [Old French *climat* or Late Latin *clima climat-* from Greek *klima* from *klinō* slope]

climate control *noun* a system for regulating air temperature and humidity by heating and air conditioning. □ **climate-controlled** *adjective*

clima·tol·ogy /ˌklaiməˈtɒlədʒi/ *noun* the scientific study of climate. □ **cli·mato·logic·al** /-təˈlɒdʒikəl/ *adjective* **clima·tol·o·gist** *noun*

cli·max /ˈklaimaks/ ● *noun* **1** the event or point of greatest intensity or interest; a culmination or apex. **2** orgasm. **3** *Rhetoric* **a** a series arranged in order of increasing importance etc. **b** the last term in such a series. **4** (also **climax community, climax vegetation**) *Ecology* the final stage in a succession in a given environment, at which a plant community reaches a state of equilibrium (*a mixed hardwood climax forest*). ● *transitive & intransitive verb informal* bring or come to a climax. [Late Latin from Greek *klimax -akos* ladder, climax]

climb ● *verb* **1** *transitive & intransitive* (often foll. by *up*) ascend, mount, go or come up, esp. by using one's hands. **2** *intransitive* (of a plant) grow up

a wall, tree, trellis, etc. by clinging with tendrils or by twining. **3** *intransitive* make progress from one's own efforts, esp. in social rank, intellectual or moral strength, etc. **4** *intransitive* (of an aircraft, the sun, etc.) go upwards. **5** *intransitive* slope upwards. **6** *intransitive* (of numbers etc.) increase. ● *noun* **1** an ascent by climbing. **2 a** a place, esp. a hill, climbed or to be climbed. **b** a recognized route up a mountain etc. □ **climb down 1** descend with the help of one's hands. **2** withdraw from a stance taken up in argument, negotiation, etc. **climb the walls** *N Amer.* go crazy; become frantic. □ **climb·able** *adjective* [Old English *climban* from West Germanic, related to CLEAVE²]

climb·down *noun* a withdrawal from a position taken up in argument, negotiation, etc.

climb·er *noun* **1** a mountaineer. **2** a climbing plant. **3** a person with strong social etc. aspirations.

climb·ing frame *noun Brit.* = MONKEY BARS.

climb·ing lily *noun* = GLORY LILY.

climb·ing skins *plural noun* strips of fur etc. strapped to the bottom of skis to give traction when climbing slopes.

climb·ing wall *noun* a wall at a sports centre or in a gymnasium fitted with attachments to simulate a rock face for climbing.

climb-out *noun* the part of a flight of an aircraft after takeoff and before it reaches a level altitude.

clime /klaim/ *noun literary* **1** a region. **2** a climate. [as CLIMATE]

clinch ● *verb* **1** *transitive* confirm or settle (an argument, bargain, etc.) conclusively. **2** *transitive Sport* secure (a position on a team, in league standings, etc.). **3** *intransitive Boxing & Wrestling* (of participants) become too closely engaged. **4** *intransitive informal* embrace. **5** *transitive* secure (a nail or rivet) by driving the point sideways when through. **6** *transitive Naut.* fasten (a rope) with a particular half hitch. ● *noun* **1 a** a clinching action. **b** a clinched state. **2** *informal* an (esp. amorous) embrace. **3** *Boxing & Wrestling* an action or state in which participants become too closely engaged. [16th-c. var. of CLENCH]

clinch·er *noun informal* **1** a person or thing that clinches. **2** a remark or argument that settles a matter conclusively. **3** *Sport* a game or match that clinches a player's or team's position in standings etc.

Cline, Patsy (born Virginia Petterson Hensley) (1932–63), US country singer. Discovered in 1957 when she sang 'Walkin' After Midnight' on television, she later had hits with 'Heartaches' and 'Sweet Dreams of You'. Just as she was becoming well known she was killed in a plane crash.

cline *noun* **1** a continuum with an infinite number of gradations. **2** *Biol.* the graded sequence of differences within a species etc. □ **clinal** *adjective* [Greek *klinō* to slope]

cling ● *intransitive verb* (*past* and *past participle* **clung**) **1** (foll. by *to, onto, on*) hold on tightly. **2** (foll. by *to*) become attached to; stick closely to (*the smell of smoke clings to one's clothes*). **3** (foll. by *to*) refuse to abandon; remain persistently or stubbornly attached to (a belief, power, hope, possessions, etc.). **4** be emotionally dependent on (a person); stay too close to (a person) (*he clung to me like a leech all evening*). **5** stay close to (something) (*don't cling to the curb when driving*). ● *noun* **1** the adhering together of separate objects (*static cling*). **2** = CLINGSTONE (also *attributive*: *cling peach*). □ **cling·er** *noun* [Old English *clingan* from Germanic: compare CLENCH]

cling film *noun Brit.* = PLASTIC WRAP.

cling·ing vine *noun N Amer. informal* a person who is emotionally dependent upon others to an excessive degree.

cling·stone *noun* a variety of peach or nectarine in which the flesh adheres to the stone (*compare* FREESTONE 1).

clingy *adjective* (**cling·i·er**, **cling·i·est**) liable to cling. □ **cling·i·ness** *noun*

clin·ic *noun* **1** a place or occasion for giving medical or dental treatment or advice (*fertility clinic*). **2** *N Amer.* a group of doctors or dentists sharing the same building and working together. **3** a gathering at a hospital bedside for the teaching of medicine or surgery. **4** *N Amer.* a conference or short course on a particular subject (*golf clinic*). **5** *see* BLOOD DONOR CLINIC. **6** *see* LEGAL CLINIC. **7** *Brit.* a private or specialized hospital. [French *clinique* from Greek *klinikē (tekhnē)* clinical, lit. 'bedside (art)', from *klinē* 'bed']

clin·ic·al *adjective* **1** *Med.* **a** of or for the treatment of patients. **b** taught or learned at the hospital bedside. **c** based on the observed symptoms. **d** involving the study or care of actual patients (*clinical trials*). **2** dispassionate, coldly detached. **3** (of a room, building, etc.) bare, functional. □ **clin·ic·al·ly** *adverb*

clinical depression *noun* severe depression accompanied by symptoms such as loss of appetite, sleep disturbance, inability to concentrate, etc. □ **clinically depressed** *adjective*

clinical medicine *noun* medicine dealing with the observation and treatment of patients.

clinical psychology *noun* the branch of psychology concerned with the assessment and treatment of mental illness and handicap. □ **clinical psychologist** *noun*

clinical thermometer *noun* a thermometer with a small range, for taking a person's temperature.

clin·ician /klɪˈnɪʃən/ *noun* a doctor having direct contact with and responsibility for patients, as opposed to one doing research.

clink¹ ● *noun* a sharp ringing sound. ● *verb* **1** *intransitive* make a clink. **2** *transitive* cause (glasses etc.) to clink. [prob. from Middle Dutch *klinken*; compare CLANG, CLANK]

clink² *noun* *slang* prison. [16th c.: origin unknown]

clink·er¹ *noun* **1** a mass of slag or lava. **2** a stony residue from burnt coal. [earlier *clincard* etc. from obsolete Dutch *klinkaerd* from *klinken* CLINK¹]

clink·er² *noun* **1** *N Amer. informal* a mistake or blunder. **2** *Brit. slang* something excellent or outstanding. [CLINK¹ + -ER¹]

clinker-built *adjective* (of a boat) having external planks overlapping downwards and secured with clinched copper nails. [*clink* Northern English var. of CLINCH + -ER¹]

clin·om·eter /klaɪˈnɒmɪtər/ *noun* *Surveying* an instrument for measuring slopes. [Greek *klinō* to slope + -METER]

Clin·ton, Wil·liam Jef·fer·son ('Bill') (b.1946), US Democratic politician, 42nd president of the US 1993–2001. His presidency became dominated by contested allegations of financial and sexual misconduct: in 1998 he was impeached on charges of perjury and obstruction of justice, but was acquitted. □ **Clin·ton·ian** /klɪnˈtoːniən/ *adjective*

clin·tonia /klɪnˈtoːniə/ *noun* any liliaceous plant of the chiefly N American genus *Clintonia*, esp. *C. borealis*, with yellow flowers and dark blue berries. *Also called* BLUE-BEAD LILY, CORN LILY, QUEENCUP. [named in honour of DeWitt Clinton, US politician d.1828]

Clio /ˈkliːoː, ˈklaɪoː/ *Gk & Rom. Myth* the Muse of history. [Greek *kleiō* celebrate]

clio·met·rics /ˌklaɪəˈmetrɪks/ *plural noun* (usu. treated as *sing.*) a method of historical research making much use of statistical information and methods. □ **clio·met·ric** *adjective* **clio·met·ri·cian** *noun* **cli·om·etry** *noun* [CLIO + METRIC + -ICS]

clip¹ ● *noun* **1** a device for holding things together or for attachment to an object as a marker, esp. a paper clip or a device worked by a spring. **2** a piece of jewellery fastened by a clip. **3** a set of attached cartridges for a firearm. ● *transitive verb* (**clipped, clip·ping**) **1** attach with a clip. **2** grip tightly. **3** surround closely. [Old English *clyppan* embrace, from West Germanic]

clip² ● *verb* (**clipped, clip·ping**) **1** *transitive* cut with shears or scissors, esp. cut short or trim (hair, wool, fingernails etc.). **2** *transitive* trim or remove the hair or wool of (a person or animal). **3** *transitive informal* hit smartly. **4** *transitive* **a** curtail, diminish, cut short. **b** omit (a letter etc.) from a word; omit letters or syllables of (words pronounced). **c** *Linguistics* shorten (a word) by dropping one or more syllables. **5** *transitive* cut (an article, coupon, etc.) from a newspaper etc. **6** *transitive* cut the wings of (a bird) so that it is unable to fly. **7** *transitive* redeem (coupons on savings bonds etc.). **8** *transitive & intransitive* *Football* block (a member of the opposing team) illegally from behind. **9** *transitive slang* swindle, rob. **10** *transitive* pare the edge of (a coin). ● *noun* **1** an act of clipping, esp. shearing or haircutting. **2** *informal* a smart blow, esp. with the hand. **3** a short sequence from a film, video, etc. **4** the quantity of wool clipped from a sheep, flock, etc. **5** *informal* (in phr. **at a fair clip**, etc.) speed, esp. rapid. □ **clip a person's wings** prevent a person from pursuing ambitions or acting effectively. □ **clip·pable** *adjective* [Old Norse *klippa*, prob. imitative]

clip art *noun* artwork, either published in printed form or included as part of computer software, that can be copied into reports, advertisements, etc.

clip·board *noun* **1** a small board with a spring clip for holding papers etc. and providing support for writing. **2** a feature of some computer programs which allows extracted text to be temporarily stored so that it can be edited etc. before being inserted or saved into another file.

clip-clop ● *noun* a sound such as the beat of a horse's hooves. ● *intransitive verb* (**-clopped, -clopping**) make such a sound. [imitative]

clip joint *noun slang* a nightclub etc. charging exorbitant prices.

clip-on ● *adjective* attached by a clip. ● *noun* a thing (e.g. a necktie, earring, sunglass lenses, etc.) that attaches by a clip.

clip·per *noun* **1** a person or thing that clips. **2** (usu. in *pl.*) any of various instruments for clipping hair, fingernails, hedges, etc. **3** a fast sailing ship, esp. one with raking bows and masts. **4** a fast horse. **5** = ALBERTA CLIPPER.

clip·ping *noun* **1** a short piece clipped or cut from a newspaper, magazine, etc. **2** (usu. in *pl.*) small pieces of grass etc. produced by clipping or mowing.

clique /kliːk/ *noun* a small exclusive group of people. □ **cliquey** *adjective* **cliquish** *adjective* **cliquish·ness** *noun* [French from *cliquer* CLICK]

Clis·the·nes *var. of* CLEISTHENES.

clit *noun coarse slang* = CLITORIS. [abbreviation]

clit·ic /ˈklɪtɪk/ *adjective & noun* (often *attributive*) enclitic or proclitic. □ **cliti·ci·za·tion** /-tɪkaɪˈzeɪʃən/ *noun*

clit·ori·dec·tomy /ˌklɪtərɪˈdektəmɪ/ *noun* surgical removal of all or part of the clitoris.

clit·or·is /ˈklɪtɜrɪs/ *noun* a small erectile part of the female genitals at the upper end of the vulva. □ **clit·oral** *adjective* [modern Latin from Greek *kleitoris*]

Clive, Rob·ert, 1st Baron Clive of Plassey (1725–74), English general and colonial administrator. His victory at the Battle of Plassey (1757) and subsequent term as governor of Bengal (1760–67) helped to establish the British in India; later implicated in corruption scandals involving the East India Company, he committed suicide.

cliv·ers *var. of* CLEAVERS.

clo·aca /kloːˈeɪkə/ *noun* (*pl.* **clo·acae** /-siː/) **1** the genital and excretory cavity at the end of the intestinal canal in birds, reptiles, etc. **2** a sewer. □ **clo·acal** *adjective* [Latin, = sewer]

cloak ● *noun* **1** an outdoor garment, usu. sleeveless, hanging loosely from the shoulders. **2** a covering (*cloak of snow*). **3** something which conceals (*a cloak of secrecy*). ● *transitive verb* **1** cover with a cloak. **2** cover over (*the hills cloaked in trees*). **3** conceal, disguise. □ **under the cloak of** using as a pretext. [Old French *cloke*, dial. var. of *cloche* bell, cloak (from its bell shape), from medieval Latin *clocca* bell: see CLOCK¹]

cloak-and-dagger *adjective* involving or characteristic of plot and intrigue, esp. espionage.

cloak·room *noun* **1** a room where outdoor clothes or luggage may be left by visitors, clients, etc. **2** *Brit. euphemism* a washroom.

clob·ber¹ *transitive verb informal* **1 a** hit repeatedly; beat up. **b** strike with great force. **2** defeat. **3** criticize severely. [20th c.: origin unknown]

clob·ber² *noun Brit. slang* clothing or personal belongings. [19th c.: origin unknown]

cloche /klɒʃ, kloːʃ/ *noun* **1** (in full **cloche hat**) a woman's close-fitting bell-shaped hat. **2** a small translucent cover for protecting or forcing outdoor plants. [French, = bell, from medieval Latin *clocca*: see CLOCK¹]

clock¹ ● *noun* **1** an instrument for measuring time, driven mechanically or electrically and indicating hours, minutes, etc., by hands on a dial or by displayed figures. **2** any measuring device resembling a clock, e.g. a speedometer, taximeter, or stopwatch. **3** *Brit. slang* a person's face. **4** a downy seed head, esp. that of a dandelion. ● *transitive verb* **1 a** (often foll. by *up*) attain or register (a stated time, distance, or speed, esp. in a race). **b** time (a race) with a stopwatch. **c** measure the speed of (*his fastball was clocked at 95 mph*). **2** *Brit. slang* hit, esp. on the head. □ **against the clock 1** against time taken as an element in competitive sports etc. (*ran against the clock*). **2** hurriedly and with time running out (*we're working against the clock on this project*). **clean someone's clock** *N Amer.* beat someone soundly. **clock in** register one's arrival at work, esp. by means of an automatic recording clock. **clock out** register one's departure similarly. **round** (or **around**) **the clock** all day and (usu.) night. **turn** (or **put**) **the clock back** (or **turn back the clock**) return to an earlier time. **watch the clock** be a clock-watcher. □ **clock·er** *noun* [Middle Dutch, Middle Low German *klocke* from medieval Latin *clocca* bell, perhaps from Celtic]

clock² *noun* an ornamental pattern on the side of a stocking or sock near the ankle. [16th c.: origin unknown]

clock·maker *noun* a person who makes and repairs clocks and watches. □ **clock·making** *noun*

clock radio *noun* a combined radio and clock, which can be set so that the radio will come on at a desired time.

clock speed *noun* the operating speed of a computer or its microprocessor, defined as the rate at which it performs internal operations and expressed in cycles per second (megahertz).

Vowels: a cat ɑ arm e bed ɜr her ɜː deux ə ago ɪ sit i cosy iː feed ɒ hot ɔ pore ɔː no ʌ run ʊ put

clock-watcher *noun* a person, esp. an employee, who keeps a close watch on the passage of time, esp. so as not to exceed minimum working hours. □ **clock-watching** *noun*

clock·wise *adjective & adverb* in a curve corresponding in direction to the movement of the hands of a clock.

clock·work *noun* **1** a mechanism like that of a mechanical clock, with a spring and gears. **2** (*attributive*) **a** driven by clockwork. **b** regular, mechanical. □ **like clockwork** smoothly, regularly, automatically.

clod *noun* **1** a lump of earth, clay, etc. **2** *informal* a silly or foolish person. [Middle English: var. of CLOT]

clod·dish *adjective* loutish, foolish, clumsy. □ **clod·dish·ly** *adverb* **clod·dish·ness** *noun*

clod·hop·per *noun* **1** (usu. in *pl.*) *informal* a large heavy shoe. **2** an unsophisticated person.

clod·hop·ping *adjective* = CLODDISH.

clog ● *noun* **1** a shoe with a thick wooden sole. **2** *N Amer.* an encumbrance or impediment (*a clog in the drain*). **3** a block of wood tied to an animal to impede its movement. ● *transitive & intransitive verb* (**clogged**, **clog·ging**) (often foll. by *up*) block or become blocked so as to hinder free passage, action, or function. □ **clog·ger** *noun* [Middle English: origin unknown]

clog dance *noun* a dance performed in clogs. □ **clog dancer** *noun*

cloi·son·né /ˌklwɒzɒˈneɪ/ ● *noun* **1** a type of enamel finish in which the colours in the pattern are separated by thin strips of metal. **2** this process. ● *adjective* (of enamel) made by this process. [French from *cloison* compartment]

clois·ter ● *noun* **1** a covered walk, often with a wall on one side and a colonnade open to a quadrangle on the other, esp. in a convent, monastery, or cathedral. **2 a** a convent or monastery. **b** life in a convent or monastery. **3** a place or the state of seclusion. ● *transitive verb* seclude or shut up in or as if in a convent or monastery. □ **clois·tral** *adjective* [Old French *cloistre* from Latin *claustrum*, *clostrum* lock, enclosed place, from *claudere claus-* CLOSE²]

clois·tered *adjective* **1** secluded, sheltered. **2** living in a convent or monastery, esp. in an order whose members have little or no contact with the outside world.

clomp *var. of* CLUMP *verb* 2.

clone ● *noun* **1 a** a group of organisms produced asexually from one stock or ancestor, to which they are genetically identical. **b** one such organism. **2** a person or thing regarded as identical with another. **3** a microcomputer designed to simulate another, more expensive, model. ● *transitive verb* propagate as a clone. □ **clon·al** *adjective* [Greek *klōn* twig, slip]

clonk ● *noun* an abrupt heavy sound of impact. ● *verb* **1** *intransitive* make such a sound. **2** *transitive informal* hit. [imitative]

Clon·mel /klɒnˈmel/ the county town of Tipperary, in the Republic of Ireland; pop. (est. 2002) 16,700.

clo·nus /ˈkloːnəs/ *noun Physiol.* a spasm with alternate muscular contractions and relaxations. □ **clon·ic** *adjective* [Greek *klonos* turmoil]

clop ● *noun* the sound made by a horse's hooves. ● *intransitive verb* (**clopped**, **clop·ping**) make this sound. [imitative]

close¹ ● *adjective* **1** (often foll. by *to*) situated at only a short distance or interval. **2 a** having a strong or immediate relation or connection (*close friend*; *close relative*). **b** in intimate friendship or association (*we're very close*). **c** corresponding almost exactly (*close resemblance*). **d** fitting tightly (*close cap*). **e** (of hair etc.) short, near the surface. **3** in or almost in contact (*close combat*; *close proximity*). **4** dense, compact, with no or only slight intervals (*close texture*; *close writing*; *close formation*; *close thicket*). **5** in which competitors are almost equal (*close contest*; *close election*). **6** leaving no gaps or weaknesses, rigorous (*close reasoning*). **7** concentrated, searching (*close examination*; *close attention*). **8** (of air etc.) stuffy or humid. **9** closed, shut. **10** limited or restricted to certain persons etc. (*close corporation*). **11 a** hidden, secret, covered. **b** secretive. **12** (of a danger etc.) directly threatening, narrowly avoided (*that was close*). **13** niggardly. **14** (of a vowel) pronounced with a relatively narrow opening of the mouth. **15** narrow, confined, contracted. **16** under prohibition; not readily available. ● *adverb* **1** (often foll. by *on*, *to*, *upon*) at only a short distance or interval (*they live close by*; *close to the church*). **2** closely, in a close manner (*shut close*). ● *noun* **1** an enclosed space, esp. (in Britain) the precinct of a cathedral. **2** *Brit.* a street closed at one end. □ **close to the wind** *see* WIND¹. □ **close·ly** *adverb* **close·ness** *noun* [Old French *clos* from Latin *clausum* enclosure & *clausus* past participle of *claudere* shut]

close² ● *verb* **1 a** *transitive* shut (a lid, box, door, eye, etc.). **b** *intransitive* be shut (*the door closed slowly*). **c** *transitive* prevent access to (a room, region,

border, bridge, etc.) (*closed the border to tourists*). **2 a** *transitive & intransitive* bring or come to an end (*closed the debate*). **b** *intransitive* finish speaking (*closed with an expression of thanks*). **c** *transitive & intransitive* settle or finalize (a deal, offer, etc.). **3 a** *intransitive* (of a business, school, etc.) cease work or business temporarily (*the store closes at six*). **b** *transitive* temporarily cease work or business at (a business, school, etc.). **4** *transitive & intransitive* cease or cause to cease the operation of (an office, business, etc.) (*the police closed the illegal bar*; *the factory closed*). **5** *transitive* withdraw all the money from (a bank account etc.) (*close my account*). **6** *transitive* remove from use or stop using (a room, bed, etc.) (*the hospital closed 100 beds*). **7 a** *intransitive* (of a group of people) come close to or surround someone or something. **b** *transitive & intransitive* draw near to or come within striking distance of (a person or thing). **8** *intransitive* (of stocks, shares, precious metals, etc.) be at a particular price at the close of a day's trading. **9** *transitive* make (an electric circuit etc.) continuous. ● *noun* **1** a conclusion, an end. **2** *Music* a cadence. □ **close down 1** discontinue (or cause to discontinue) business, esp. permanently. **2** (of a broadcasting station) end transmission esp. until the next day. **close one's eyes to** pay no attention to. **close in 1** come nearer. **2** (of days) get successively shorter with the approach of the winter solstice. **close off** prevent access to by covering or blocking the means of entrance. **close out** *N Amer.* discontinue, terminate, dispose of (a business). **close ranks 1** (esp. of soldiers) move closer together. **2** establish or maintain solidarity. **close up 1** shut, esp. temporarily. **2** (of groups of people) move closer. **3** block up. **4** (of an aperture) grow smaller. □ **clos·able** *adjective* [Old French *clos-* stem of *clore* from Latin *claudere* shut]

close call *noun* a narrow escape.

close-cropped *adjective* (of hair, grass, etc.) cut very short.

closed *adjective* **1** not giving access; shut. **2** (of a store etc.) having ceased business temporarily. **3** (of a society, system, etc.) self-contained; not communicating with others. **4** *Cdn* (of a mortgage etc.) that may not be paid off before the stated term without a financial penalty. **5** (of a sport etc.) restricted to specified competitors etc.

closed book *noun* a subject about which one is ignorant.

closed caption ● *noun* one of a series of captions to a television program, accessible through a decoder. ● *transitive verb* provide (a program) with these. □ **closed-captioned** *adjective* **closed-caption·ing** *noun*

closed-circuit *adjective* (of television) transmitted by wires to a restricted set of receivers.

closed custody *noun Cdn* = SECURE CUSTODY.

closed door ● *noun* an obstacle, impasse, or restriction. ● *adjective* (usu. **closed-door**) private; not open to the public (*closed-door meeting*). □ **behind closed doors** privately; in secret.

closed-end *adjective* of or relating to an investment company that offers a fixed number of shares (*compare* OPEN-ENDED).

closed-minded *adjective* not receptive to new or different ideas; prejudiced. □ **closed-minded·ness** *noun*

closed season *noun N Amer.* the season when something, esp. the killing of game etc., is illegal.

closed shop *noun* **1** a place of work etc. where all employees must belong to an agreed labour union (*opp.* OPEN SHOP). **2** this system.

closed syllable *noun* a syllable ending in a consonant.

close-fisted *adjective* stingy.

close-fitting *adjective* (of a garment) fitting close to the body.

close-grained *adjective* (of wood etc.) without gaps between fibres etc.

close harmony *noun* harmony in which the notes of the chord are close together.

close-hauled *adjective* (of a ship) with the sails hauled aft to sail close to the wind.

close-knit *adjective* (also **closely-knit**) tightly bound or interlocked; closely united in friendship.

close-mouthed *adjective* reticent.

close quarters ● *plural noun* a cramped place (*we're living in very close quarters*). ● *adjective* (usu. **close-quarter**; also **close-quarters**) (of battle etc.) involving direct and close combat. □ **at close quarters** very close together.

clos·er *noun* **1** a person or thing that closes. **2** *Baseball* a relief pitcher brought in by a team with a lead to pitch the final innings.

close season *noun Brit.* = CLOSED SEASON.

close-set *adjective* separated only by a small interval or intervals.

close shave *noun informal* a narrow escape.

clos·et ● *noun* **1** a cupboard or recess, esp. one used for hanging clothes. **2** a small or private room. **3** *Brit.* = WATER CLOSET. **4** (*attributive*) secret, covert (*closet homosexual*; *closet leftist*). ● *transitive verb* (**clos·et·ed**, **clos·et·ing**) shut away, esp. in private conference or study. □ **in the closet 1** keeping one's homosexuality from public knowledge. **2** hidden from public scrutiny. **out of the closet 1** into the open; into public scrutiny. **2** having publicly declared one's homosexuality. [Old French, diminutive of *clos*: see CLOSE¹]

closet drama *noun* a play to be read rather than acted.

clos·et·ed *adjective* keeping something secret, esp. the fact of being homosexual (*a closeted lesbian*).

close-up ● *noun* **1** a photograph etc. taken at close range and showing the subject on a large scale. **2** an intimate description. ● *adjective* done, photographed, etc. from close range.

clos·ing *noun* **1** an act or the process of closing. **2** the end or conclusion, e.g. of a speech. **3** the final phase of a transaction, esp. of buying or selling real estate. **4** something that closes; a fastener.

closing time *noun* the time at which a bar, store, etc., ends business.

clos·trid·ial /klɒˈstrɪdɪəl/ *adjective* of, relating to, or caused by rod-shaped bacteria of the genus *Clostridium*, many of which cause disease (e.g. tetanus, botulism). [modern Latin *Clostridium* genus name from Greek *klōstēr* spindle]

clos·ure /ˈkloʒər/ ● *noun* **1** the act or process of closing. **2** a closed condition. **3** something that closes or seals. **4** a procedure for ending a debate and taking a vote, esp. in Parliament. **5** a feeling of conclusion or resolution (*catching her murderer will give her family a sense of closure*). ● *transitive verb* apply closure to (a motion, speakers, etc.) in a legislative assembly. [Old French from Late Latin *clausura* from *claudere* claus- CLOSE²]

clot ● *noun* **1 a** a thick mass of coagulated liquid, esp. of blood. **b** a mass of material stuck together. **2** *Brit. informal* a silly or foolish person. ● *transitive & intransitive verb* (**clot·ted**, **clot·ting**) form into clots. [Old English *clot(t)* from West Germanic: compare CLEAT]

clot·bur *noun* any of various plants with burr-like seeds, such as cocklebur, *Xanthium*, and burdock, *Arctium*.

clot-buster *noun* a substance (esp. a drug) which dissolves or breaks down a blood clot. □ **clot-busting** *adjective*

cloth *noun* (*pl.* **cloths**) **1** woven or felted material. **2** a piece of this. **3** a piece of cloth for a particular purpose; a tablecloth, dishcloth, etc. **4 a** a profession or status, esp. of the clergy, as shown by clothes. **b** (*prec.* by *the*) the clergy (*man of the cloth*). **5** = CLOTH-BOUND. [Old English *clāth*, of unknown origin]

cloth-bound *adjective* (of a book) bound with cloth rather than paper.

cloth-cap *adjective Brit.* relating to or associated with the working class.

clothe *transitive verb* (*past* and *past participle* **clothed** or *formal* **clad**) **1** put clothes on; provide with clothes. **2** cover as with clothes or a cloth. **3** (foll. by *with*) endue (with qualities etc.). [Old English: related to CLOTH]

clothes *plural noun* **1** garments worn to cover the body. **2** bedclothes. [Old English *clāthas* pl. of *clāth* CLOTH]

clothes horse *noun* **1** a frame for airing washed clothes. **2** *informal* a person who has many, esp. fashionable, clothes.

clothes·line *noun* a rope or wire etc. on which washed clothes are hung to dry.

clothes moth *noun* any moth of the family Tineidae, with a larva destructive to wool, fur, etc.

clothes peg *noun* esp. *Brit.* = CLOTHESPIN.

clothes·pin *noun N Amer.* a clip or forked device for securing clothes to a clothesline.

cloth·ier /ˈkloʊðɪər/ *noun* a maker or seller of clothes, esp. men's clothes. [Middle English *clother* from CLOTH]

cloth·ing *noun* clothes collectively.

Clo·tho /ˈkloʊθoʊ/ *Gk Myth* one of the three Fates, the spinner of the thread of human destiny. [Greek, = she who spins]

cloth of gold *noun* fabric made of gold threads interwoven with silk or wool.

clotted cream *noun* esp. *Brit.* thick cream made by scalding milk.

clotting factor *noun* any of a number of blood proteins which are involved in the clotting process.

clo·ture /ˈkloʊtʃər, -tjʊr/ *US* ● *noun* the closure of a debate. ● *transitive verb* closure. [French *clôture* from Old French CLOSURE]

cloud ● *noun* **1** a visible mass of condensed watery vapour floating in the atmosphere high above the general level of the ground. **2** a mass of smoke or dust. **3** *Astronomy* **a** a hazy area in the night sky produced by the light of distant stars. **b** a region of dust, gas, etc., in deep space

appearing lighter or darker owing to the reflection, absorption, etc. of light. **4** (foll. by *of*) a great number of insects, birds, etc., moving together. **5 a** a state of gloom, trouble, or suspicion. **b** a frowning or depressed look (*a cloud on his brow*). **6** a local dimness or a vague patch of colour in or on a liquid or a transparent body. ● *verb* **1** *transitive* cover or darken with clouds or gloom or trouble. **2** *intransitive* (often foll. by *over*, *up*) become overcast or gloomy. **3** *transitive* **a** make unclear (*prejudice clouded the issue*). **b** make unreliable; distort (*alcohol clouded his judgment*). **4** *transitive* variegate with vague patches of colour. □ **in the clouds 1** unreal, imaginary, mystical. **2** (of a person) abstracted, inattentive. **on cloud nine** *informal* extremely happy. **under a cloud** out of favour, discredited, under suspicion. **with one's head in the clouds** daydreaming, unrealistic. □ **cloud·less** *adjective* **cloud·less·ly** *adverb* **cloud·let** *noun* [Old English *clūd* mass of rock or earth, prob. related to CLOD]

cloud base *noun* the lowest level attained by a mass of cloud.

cloud·berry *noun* (*pl.* **-berries**) a low-growing plant of the raspberry family, *Rubus chamaemorus*, with a white flower and an edible amber fruit. *Also called* BAKEAPPLE.

cloud·burst *noun* a sudden violent rainstorm.

cloud chamber *noun* a device containing vapour for tracking the paths of charged particles, X-rays, and gamma rays.

cloud cover *noun* **1** a canopy of clouds. **2** the extent of this canopy.

cloud-cuckoo-land *noun* a fanciful or ideal place. [translation of Greek *Nephelokokkugia* from *nephelē* cloud + *kokkux* cuckoo (in Aristophanes' *Birds*)]

clouded leopard *noun* a mottled arboreal S Asian feline, *Neofelis nebulosa*.

cloud forest *noun* a forest growing at high altitude on a mountain, almost constantly enveloped in mist, characterized by the presence of abundant mosses, lichens, and ferns.

cloud·land *noun* a utopia or fairyland.

cloud·scape *noun* **1** a picturesque grouping of clouds. **2** a picture or view of clouds.

cloudy *adjective* (**cloud·i·er**, **cloud·i·est**) **1 a** (of the sky) covered with clouds, overcast. **b** (of weather) characterized by clouds. **2** not transparent; unclear. □ **cloud·i·ly** *adverb* **cloud·i·ness** *noun*

clout ● *noun* **1** a heavy blow. **2** *informal* influence; power of effective action esp. in politics or business. **3** *archaic* **a** a piece of cloth or clothing. **b** a patch. ● *transitive verb* hit hard. □ **clout·er** *noun* [Old English *clūt*, related to CLEAT, CLOT]

clove¹ ● *noun* **1 a** a dried flower bud of a tropical plant, *Syzygium aromaticum*, used as a pungent aromatic spice. **b** this plant. **2** (in full **clove gillyflower** or **clove pink**) a clove-scented pink, *Dianthus caryophyllus*, the original of the carnation and other double pinks. [Old French *clou* (*de girofle*) nail (of gillyflower), from its shape, GILLYFLOWER being originally the name of the spice; later applied to the similarly scented pink]

clove² *noun* any of the small bulbs making up a compound bulb of garlic, shallot, etc. [Old English *clufu*, related to CLEAVE¹]

clove³ *past* of CLEAVE¹.

clove hitch *noun* a knot by which a rope is secured by passing it twice around a spar or rope that it crosses at right angles. [old past participle of CLEAVE¹, as showing parallel separate lines]

clo·ven *adjective* split, partly divided. [past participle of CLEAVE¹]

cloven hoof *noun* (also **cloven foot**) the divided hoof of ruminant quadrupeds (e.g. oxen, sheep, goats). □ **cloven-footed** *adjective* **cloven-hoofed** *adjective*

clo·ver *noun* any leguminous fodder plant of the genus *Trifolium*, having dense flower heads and leaves each consisting of usu. three leaflets. □ **in clover** in ease and luxury. [Old English *clāfre* from Germanic]

clover·leaf *noun* (*pl.* **clover·leafs**) a junction of roads intersecting at different levels with connecting sections forming the pattern of a four-leaf clover.

Clo·vis¹ /ˈkloʊvɪs/ (c.466–511), king of the Franks 481–511. He extended Merovingian rule to Gaul and Germany after victories at Soissons (486) and Cologne (496).

Clo·vis² *noun Archaeology* a paleo-Indian culture of Central and North America, dated to about 11,500–11,000 years ago and earlier. The culture is distinguished by heavy leaf-shaped stone spearheads (**Clovis points**), often found in conjunction with the bones of mammoths. [first found near *Clovis* in eastern New Mexico]

clown ● *noun* **1** a comic entertainer, esp. in a circus, usu. with traditional costume and makeup. **2** a silly, foolish, or playful person.

3 *archaic* a rustic. ● *verb* **1** *intransitive* (often foll. by *around*) behave like a clown; act foolishly or playfully. **2** *transitive* perform (a part, an action, etc.) like a clown. □ **clown·ery** *noun* **clown·ish** *adjective* **clown·ish·ly** *adverb* **clown·ish·ness** *noun* [16th c.: perhaps of Low German origin]

cloy *transitive verb* (usu. foll. by *with*) satiate or sicken with an excess of sweetness, richness, etc. [Middle English from obsolete *acloy* from Anglo-French *acloyer*, Old French *encloyer* from Romanic: compare ENCLAVE]

cloy·ing *adjective* **1** extremely sweet. **2** excessively sentimental. □ **cloy·ing·ly** *adverb*

clo·za·pine /ˈkloːzəpiːn/ *noun* a sedative of the benzodiazepine group used to treat schizophrenia. [CHLORO- + BENZODIAZEPINE]

cloze *noun* the exercise of supplying a word that has been omitted from a passage as a test of readability or comprehension (usu. *attributive*: *cloze test*). [CLOSURE]

CLSC *noun* *Cdn* (in Quebec) a provincially funded community health care clinic. [abbreviation of *centre local des services communautaires*, lit. 'local centre of community services']

club ● *noun* **1** a heavy stick with a thick end, used as a weapon etc. **2** a stick or bat used in a game to strike a ball, esp. one with a head used in golf. **3 a** a playing card of a suit denoted by a black trefoil. **b** (in *pl.*) this suit. **4** an association of persons united by a common interest, usu. meeting periodically for a shared activity (*bridge club*; *science club*). **5** an organization or premises offering members social amenities, meals, temporary accommodation, etc. **6** an organization or premises having athletic and exercise facilities (*health club*; *curling club*). **7** an organization offering members certain benefits (*travel club*). **8** a group of persons, nations, etc., having something in common. **9** a sports team and its administrative staff. **10** a bar or nightclub. **11** a structure or organ, esp. in a plant, with a knob at the end. ● *verb* (**clubbed**, **club·bing**) **1** *transitive* beat with or as with a club. **2** *intransitive* (foll. by *together*, *with*) combine for joint action, esp. making up a sum of money for a purpose. **3** *transitive* contribute (money etc.) to a common stock. **4** *intransitive* visit nightclubs etc. □ **join** (or **welcome to**) **the club** you're not the only one to feel that way. [Old Norse *klubba* assimilated form of *klumba* club, related to CLUMP]

club·able /ˈklʌbəbəl/ *adjective* esp. *Brit.* sociable; fit for membership in a club. □ **club·abil·ity** *noun* **club·able·ness** *noun*

club·ber *noun* **1** a member of a club. **2** a person who frequents nightclubs.

club·bing *noun* the practice of frequenting nightclubs.

clubby *adjective* (**club·bi·er**, **club·bi·est**) **1** sociable; friendly. **2** cliquish; tending to exclude others. **3** typical of a social club, esp. in sumptuous decor etc. □ **club·bi·ness** *noun*

club car *noun* *N Amer.* a rail car equipped with a lounge and other amenities.

club foot *noun* a congenitally deformed foot, usu. turned downward and inward so that the person walks on the outer edge of the foot. □ **club-footed** *adjective*

club·head *noun* the head of a golf club.

club·house *noun* **1** the premises used by a club. **2** *N Amer.* the dressing room of a sports team, esp. a baseball team.

club·land *noun* **1** nightclubs collectively. **2** *Brit.* an area with many clubs, esp. the vicinity of St. James's in London.

club·man *noun* (*pl.* **-men**) a man who belongs to one or more clubs, esp. socially prestigious ones.

club·mate *noun* a fellow member of a sports club.

club·moss *noun* any pteridophyte of the family Lycopodiaceae, bearing upright spikes of spore cases.

club·root *noun* a fungal disease of cabbages etc. causing swelling at the base of the stem.

club sandwich *noun* (*Cdn* also **clubhouse sandwich**) a sandwich usu. consisting of two layers of bacon, lettuce, tomato, mayonnaise, and chicken or turkey served between three slices of toast or bread.

club seat *noun* *N Amer.* a high-priced luxury seat in a sports stadium intended for corporate subscribers, often including access to amenities.

club soda *noun* *N Amer.* = SODA 2.

club steak *noun* *N Amer.* one of the first three or four steaks on the short loin, with the T-bone removed.

club·woman *noun* (*pl.* **-women**) a woman who belongs to one or more clubs, esp. socially prestigious ones.

cluck ● *noun* **1** a guttural cry like that of a hen. **2** *slang* a silly or foolish person (*dumb cluck*). ● *intransitive verb* **1** (of a hen) emit a cluck or clucks. **2** (of a person) make a clucking sound with the tongue. **3** (also **cluck-cluck**) express annoyance, disapproval, etc. by making a similar noise. [imitative]

cluck·er *noun* *N Amer. informal* a chicken.

clue ● *noun* **1** a fact or idea that serves as a guide, or suggests a line of inquiry, in a problem or investigation. **2** a piece of evidence etc. in the detection of a crime. **3** a verbal formula serving as a hint as to what is to be inserted in a crossword. ● *transitive verb* (**clues**, **clued**, **clu·ing** or **clue·ing**) provide a clue to. □ **clue in** (or *Brit.* **up**) *informal* inform. **not have a clue** *informal* be ignorant or incompetent. [var. of CLEW]

clue·less *adjective* *informal* ignorant, stupid. □ **clue·less·ly** *adverb* **clue·less·ness** *noun*

Cluj-Napoca /ˌkluːʒˈnɒpɒkə/ (also **Cluj**) a city in west central Romania; pop. (est. 2002) 332,200.

clump ● *noun* **1** (foll. by *of*) a cluster or compact group of things or people, esp. of trees or other plants, hair, buildings, etc. **2** an agglutinated mass or lump. **3** a dull thudding sound. ● *verb* **1 a** *intransitive* form a clump. **b** *transitive* heap or plant together. **2** *intransitive* (also **clomp**) walk with heavy steps. **3** *transitive informal* hit. □ **clumpy** *adjective* (**clump·i·er**, **clump·i·est**). [Middle Low German *klumpe*, Middle Dutch *klompe*: see CLUB]

clum·per *noun* (also **clum·pet**) *Cdn* (*Maritimes & Nfld*) a large floating chunk of ice. [obsolete *clumper* lump, mass, from Old English *clympre*]

clumsy *adjective* (**clum·si·er**, **clum·si·est**) **1** not graceful in movement or shape; awkward. **2** done without skill or ease (*a clumsy forgery*; *clumsy sentence construction*). **3** tactless (*a clumsy apology*). **4** (of tools, furniture, etc.) difficult to use or move; not well designed. □ **clum·si·ly** *adverb* **clum·si·ness** *noun* [obsolete *clumse* be numb with cold, (prob. from Scandinavian)]

clung *past and past participle* of CLING.

Clun·iac /ˈkluːniˌak/ ● *adjective* of or relating to a monastic order founded at Cluny in E France in 910. The order was formed with the object of returning to the strict Benedictine rule, and became centralized and influential in the 11th–12th c. ● *noun* a monk of this order.

clunk ● *noun* a dull sound as of thick pieces of metal striking. ● *verb* **1** *intransitive* make such a sound. **2** *intransitive* (often foll. by *along*) move or progress clumsily. **3** *transitive* hit hard so as to make a clunking sound. □ **clunk·ing** *adjective* [imitative]

clunk·er *noun* *N Amer. informal* **1** a dilapidated automobile or machine. **2** a failure; flop.

clunky *adjective* (**clunk·i·er**, **clunk·i·est**) *informal* **1** *N Amer.* awkward or clumsy. **2** *N Amer.* not sleekly designed (*a clunky station wagon*). **3** tending to make clunking sounds (*a clunky transmission*).

clus·ter ● *noun* **1** a close group or bunch of similar things growing together. **2** a close arrangement or group of people, animals, faint stars, gems, etc. **3** a group of successive consonants or vowels. ● *verb* **1** *transitive* bring into a cluster or clusters. **2** *intransitive* be or come into a cluster or clusters. **3** *intransitive* (foll. by *around*) gather, congregate. [Old English *clyster*: compare CLOT]

cluster bomb *noun* an anti-personnel bomb spraying smaller bombs or shrapnel when detonated.

cluster fly *noun* a dipterous fly, *Pollenia rudis*, with larvae parasitic on earthworms, which gathers around buildings in autumn.

cluster headache *noun* a type of headache characterized by a short attack of severe pain on one side of the head and face, occurring several times a day for a number of weeks.

cluster pine *noun* a Mediterranean pine, *Pinus pinaster*, with clustered cones. *Also called* MARITIME PINE.

clutch[1] ● *verb* **1** *transitive* **a** seize eagerly. **b** grasp tightly. **2** *intransitive* (foll. by *at*) snatch suddenly. ● *noun* **1** a tight grasp. **2** (in *pl.*) power or control (*freed from the clutches of the system*). **3 a** (in a motor vehicle) a device for connecting and disconnecting the engine to the transmission. **b** the pedal operating this. **c** an arrangement for connecting or disconnecting working parts of a machine. **4** *N Amer.* a decisive or crucial situation (*came through in the clutch*). **5** = CLUTCH BAG. ● *attributive adjective* *N Amer. Sport slang* **1** occurring at a decisive time (*hit a clutch home run*). **2** (of a person) performing well at decisive or crucial times. □ **clutch at straws** see STRAW. □ **clutch·less** *adjective* [Middle English *clucche*, *clicche* from Old English *clyccan* crook, clench, from Germanic]

clutch[2] *noun* **1 a** a set of eggs to be hatched at one time. **b** the brood resulting from this. **2** a group of people or of similar items. [18th c.:

prob. S English var. of *cletch* from *cleck* to hatch, from Old Norse *klekja*, assoc. with CLUTCH[1]

clutch bag *noun* (also **clutch purse**) a handbag without a handle or strap.

Clutha River /ˈkluːθə/ a gold-bearing river at the southern end of South Island, New Zealand. It flows 338 km (213 miles) to the Pacific Ocean.

clut·ter ● *noun* **1** a crowded and untidy collection of things. **2** an untidy state. ● *transitive verb* (often foll. by *up, with*) crowd untidily, fill with clutter. [partly var. of *clotter* coagulate, partly assoc. with CLUSTER, CLATTER]

clut·tered *adjective* crowded so as to cause confusion, esp. with many small objects.

Clwyd /ˈkluːɪd/ a former county in NE Wales, subdivided in 1996 into Denbighshire, Flintshire, Wrexham, and part of Conwy.

Clyde, Firth of the estuary of the Clyde River in W Scotland. Opening on to the North Channel to the south, the firth separates southern Scotland to the east from the southern extremities of the Highlands to the northwest.

Clyde River a river in western central Scotland which flows 170 km (106 miles) from the Southern Uplands to the Firth of Clyde. It flows through Glasgow, and was formerly famous for the shipbuilding industries along its banks.

Clydes·dale *noun* a draft horse of a heavy powerful breed, usu. dark-coloured with thick white hair on the lower legs. [originally bred near the CLYDE RIVER: see DALE]

clyp·eus /ˈklɪpɪəs/ *noun* (*pl.* **clypei** /-piaɪ/) the hard protective area of an insect's head. [Latin, = round shield]

Clytem·nes·tra /ˌklaɪtəmˈnɛstrə/ *Gk Myth* sister of Helen and the Dioscuri, wife of Agamemnon. She killed Agamemnon on his return from the Trojan War, and was killed in retribution by her son Orestes and her daughter Electra.

CM *abbreviation* Member of the Order of Canada.

Cm *symbol Chem.* the element curium.

cm *abbreviation* centimetre(s).

CMA *abbreviation* **1** Canadian Medical Association. **2** (in Canada) CERTIFIED MANAGEMENT ACCOUNTANT.

Cmdr *abbreviation* COMMANDER.

Cmdre *abbreviation* COMMODORE.

CMG *abbreviation* (in the UK) Companion (of the Order) of St. Michael and St. George.

CMHC *abbreviation* Canada Mortgage and Housing Corporation.

CMM *abbreviation* (in Canada) Commander of the Order of Military Merit.

CMV *abbreviation* CYTOMEGALOVIRUS.

CN *abbreviation* Canadian National.

CNC *abbreviation* computer numerical control, a system by which a manufacturing process is controlled by a computer.

CNE *abbreviation* Canadian National Exhibition.

CNG *abbreviation* compressed natural gas.

CNIB *abbreviation* Canadian National Institute for the Blind.

cni·dar·ian /knaɪˈdɛrɪən/ *noun* an aquatic invertebrate animal of a phylum that includes the coelenterates. [modern Latin from Greek *knidē* 'nettle']

C-note *noun N Amer. slang* a one-hundred-dollar bill.

CNR *abbreviation hist.* Canadian National Railways.

CNS *abbreviation* CENTRAL NERVOUS SYSTEM.

Cnut *var.* of CANUTE.

CO *abbreviation* **1** Commanding Officer. **2** conscientious objector. **3** Colorado (in official postal use).

Co *symbol Chem.* the element cobalt.

Co. *abbreviation* **1** company. **2** county. □ **and Co.** /koʊ/ *informal* and the rest of them; and similar things.

c/o *abbreviation* care of.

co- *prefix* **1** added to: **a** nouns, with the sense 'joint, mutual, common' (*co-editor; co-pilot*). **b** adjectives and adverbs, with the sense 'jointly, mutually' (*codependent; coequally*). **c** verbs, with the sense 'together with another or others' (*co-operate; co-author*). **2** *Math.* **a** of the complement of an angle (*cosine*). **b** the complement of (*co-latitude; coset*). [originally a form of COM-]

co-accused *noun* a person who is accused of a crime jointly with another or others.

coach ● *noun* **1** a four-wheeled carriage, usu. closed and drawn by one or more horses. **2** a bus which is comfortably equipped for longer journeys. **3** a railway car. **4 a** a person who trains or instructs a sports team or athlete. **b** a private tutor. **c** a person who teaches an actor, dancer, singer, etc. in specific aspects of their art. **5** *N Amer.* economy class seating in an aircraft, train, etc. ● *adverb N Amer.* in economy class seating (*we're travelling coach*). ● *verb* **1 a** *transitive* train or instruct (a student, sports team, etc.) as a coach. **b** *intransitive* work as a coach. **c** *transitive* give hints to; prime with facts. **2** *intransitive* travel by coach. □ **coach·able** *adjective* **coach·ing** *noun* [French *coche* from Magyar *kocsi* (adj.) from *Kocs* in Hungary]

coach box *noun Cdn* (*Nfld*) a wooden box fastened to a komatik to carry one or more passengers.

coach house *noun* a building designed to hold horse-drawn coaches or carriages.

coach·man *noun* (*pl.* **-men**) the driver of a horse-drawn carriage.

coach·roof *noun* a raised part of the cabin roof of a yacht.

coach·work *noun* the bodywork of an automobile.

co·adju·tor /koʊˈædʒʊtər/ *noun* an assistant, esp. an assistant bishop. [Old French *coadjuteur* from Late Latin *coadjutor* (as CO-, *adjutor* from *adjuvare* -*jut*- help)]

coady /ˈkoʊdi/ *noun Cdn* (*Nfld*) a thick sweetened sauce, usu. made from boiled molasses. [20th c.: origin unknown]

co·agu·lant /koʊˈæɡjʊlənt/ *noun* a substance that produces coagulation.

co·agu·late /koʊˈæɡjʊˌleɪt/ *transitive & intransitive verb* **1** change from a fluid to a solid or semi-solid state. **2** clot, curdle. **3** set, solidify. □ **co·agu·la·tive** /-lətɪv/ *adjective* **co·agu·la·tor** *noun* [Latin *coagulare* from *coagulum* rennet]

co·agu·la·tion /ˌkoʊæɡjʊˈleɪʃən/ *noun* the process by which a liquid changes to a semi-solid mass. [as COAGULATE]

Coa·huila /ˌkoʊəˈwiːlə/ a state of N Mexico, on the border with the US; capital, Saltillo.

coal ● *noun* **1 a** a hard black or blackish substance, mainly carbonized plant matter, found in underground seams and used as a fuel and as a source of many organic chemicals. **b** a piece or pieces of this for burning. **2** (in *pl.*) burning or charred pieces of coal, wood, etc. in a fire. **3** = CHARCOAL 1. ● *verb* **1** *intransitive* take in a supply of coal. **2** *transitive* put coal into (an engine, fire, etc.). □ **coals to Newcastle** something brought or sent to a place where it is already plentiful. **rake** (or **haul**) **over the coals** reprimand severely. [Old English *col* from Germanic]

coal-black *adjective* completely black.

Coal·dale a town in S Alberta, just east of Lethbridge; pop. (2001) 6,008. [after the Lethbridge residence of E. Galt, general manager of the Alberta Railway and Irrigation Company *c*.1909]

co·alesce /ˌkoʊəˈlɛs/ *intransitive verb* **1** come together and form one whole. **2** combine in a coalition. □ **co·ales·cence** *noun* **co·ales·cent** *adjective* [Latin *coalescere* (as CO-, *alescere alit-* grow, from *alere* nourish)]

coal face *noun* an exposed surface of coal in a mine. □ **at the coal face** *esp. Brit.* engaged in the practical work in a given field.

coal·field *noun* an extensive area with strata containing coal.

coal-fired *adjective* heated or powered by coal.

coal gas *noun* a mixture of gases (chiefly hydrogen and methane) extracted from coal and used for lighting and heating.

coal hole *noun Brit.* a compartment or small cellar for storing coal.

co·ali·tion /ˌkoʊəˈlɪʃən/ *noun* a temporary alliance for combined action, esp. of distinct political parties forming a government. □ **co·ali·tion·ist** *noun* [medieval Latin *coalitio* (as COALESCE)]

coal measure *noun* **1** (**Coal Measures**) *Geol.* the uppermost strata of rock formed during the Carboniferous period, containing rich coal deposits. **2** a stratum of rock containing workable coal seams.

coal oil *noun N Amer. dated* kerosene or petroleum.

Coal·sack *noun Astronomy* a dark nebula of interstellar dust in the Milky Way, esp. the one near the Southern Cross.

coal scuttle *noun* see SCUTTLE[1].

coal seam *noun* a stratum of coal suitable for mining.

coal tar *noun* a thick black viscid liquid distilled from coal and used as a source of benzene and many other organic chemicals.

coam·ing /ˈkoʊmɪŋ/ *noun Naut.* a raised border around the hatches etc. of a ship to keep out water. [17th c.: origin unknown]

co-anchor ● *noun* a person who anchors a broadcast jointly with another. ● *transitive & intransitive verb* act as a co-anchor (for).

coarse *adjective* **1 a** rough or loose in texture or grain; made of large

Vowels: a *cat* ɑ *arm* e *bed* ɜr *her* ɜː *deux* ə *ago* ɪ *sit* i *cosy* iː *feed* ɒ *hot* ɔ *pore* oː *no* ʌ *run* ʊ *put*

particles. **b** (of a person's features) rough or large. **2** lacking refinement or delicacy; crude, obscene (*coarse humour*). □ **coarse·ly** *adverb* **coarse·ness** *noun* [Middle English: origin unknown]

coarse fish *noun Brit.* any freshwater fish other than salmon and trout.

coarse grain *noun* any cereal grain other than wheat.

coarse-grained *adjective* coarse in texture or grain (*coarse-grained mustard*).

coars·en *transitive & intransitive verb* make or become coarse.

coast ● *noun* **1 a** the border of the land near the sea; the seashore. **b** (**the Coast**) *N Amer.* the Pacific coast of N America. **2** a run, usu. downhill, in or on a vehicle without the use of power. ● *intransitive verb* **1** ride or move, usu. downhill, without use of power. **2** make progress without much effort. **3** *US* slide down a hill on a toboggan. **4 a** sail along the coast. **b** trade between ports on the same coast. □ **the coast is clear** there is no danger of being observed or caught. □ **coast·al** *adjective* [Old French *coste*, *costeier* from Latin *costa* rib, flank, side]

coastal boat *noun* (Cdn (*Nfld*) a boat transporting supplies, mail, and some passengers to Newfoundland outports.

coast·er *noun* **1** a small tray or mat for a bottle or glass. **2** *N Amer.* **a** a sled or toboggan. **b** a roller coaster. **3** a ship that travels along the coast from port to port.

coaster brake *noun N Amer.* a brake on the hub of the rear wheel of a bicycle, operated by pedalling backwards.

coast guard *noun* **1** (also **Coast Guard**) **a** (in Canada) a federal government organization whose responsibilities include rescue at sea or on major lakes, icebreaking, maintaining lighthouses and aids to navigation, inspecting ships to enforce regulations, and resupply of remote northern settlements. **b** a similar organization in another country. **2** a member of a coast guard.

coast·land *noun* an expanse of land near the sea.

coast·line *noun* the line of the seashore, esp. with regard to its shape (*a rugged coastline*).

Coast Mountains a mountain range extending along the length of the Pacific coast of BC. Its highest peak, at over 4 000 m, is Mount Waddington.

Coast Salish *noun* = SNE NAY MUXW.

coast-to-coast *adjective & adverb* **1** across a continent or island. **2** *Basketball* from one end of the court to the other while in possession of the ball.

Coast Tsim·shian *noun* **1** a member of a part of the Tsimshian linguistic group living on the NW coast of BC. **2** the language of these people.

coast·ward *adverb & adjective* towards the coast.

coast·wise *adjective & adverb* along, following, or connected with the coast.

coat ● *noun* **1** an outer garment with sleeves and often extending below the hips; an overcoat or jacket. **2 a** an animal's fur, hair, etc. **b** *Physiol.* a structure, esp. a membrane, enclosing or lining an organ. **c** a skin, rind, or husk. **d** *Bot.* a layer of a bulb etc. **3 a** a layer or covering. **b** a covering of paint etc. laid on a surface at one time. ● *transitive verb* **1** (usu. foll. by *with*, *in*) apply a coat of paint etc. to; provide with a layer or covering. **2** (of paint etc.) form a covering over. [Old French *cote* from Romanic from Frankish, of unknown origin]

coat check *noun N Amer.* a place at a theatre, museum, restaurant, etc. where patrons may leave their coats, bags, etc. with an attendant.

coat dress *noun* a woman's tailored dress having buttons up the front, resembling a coat.

coat·ed *adjective* **1** covered with a coat of some substance. **2** (also in *combination*) having a coat of a specified sort. **3** (of paper) treated with a coating of clay to provide a glazed surface.

coat hanger *noun see* HANGER 2.

coati /kəʊˈɑːti/ *noun (pl.* **coatis**) any raccoon-like carnivorous mammal of the genera *Nasua* or *Nasuella*, with a long flexible snout and a long usu. ringed tail, found mainly in Central and South America. [Tupi from *cua* belt + *tim* nose]

Co·ati·cook /kəʊˈætəkʊk/ a town in S Quebec, situated south of Sherbrooke, close to the border with Vermont; pop. (2001) 8,988. [Abenaki, = river of the pine land]

coati·mundi /ˌkəʊɒtəˈmʌndi/ *noun (pl.* **coati·mundis**) = COATI. [as COATI + Tupi *mondi* solitary]

coat·ing *noun* **1** a thin layer or covering. **2** a substance used for covering in a thin layer.

coat of arms *noun* a shield or other arrangement of the heraldic bearings of a person, family, government, or corporation.

coat of mail *noun* a jacket composed of or covered with linked metal rings, chains, or plates, worn as armour. *Also called* HAUBERK.

coat rack *noun N Amer.* (also esp. *Brit.* **coat stand**) a stand with hooks or a long pole on which to hang coats, hats, etc.

coat·room *noun N Amer.* = CLOAKROOM 1.

Coats Island an island at the northern entrance to Hudson Bay, south of Southampton Island. It is administered by Nunavut. [W. Coats, Hudson's Bay Co. supplier d.1752]

Coats Land a region of Antarctica, to the east of the Antarctic Peninsula. Bordering the Weddell Sea, it lies south of South Georgia and the South Sandwich Islands.

coat·tail *noun* each of the flaps extending below the waist from the back of a tailcoat. □ (**riding**) **on the coattails of** undeservedly benefiting from (another's success).

co-author ● *noun* an author who collaborates with another on a book or article. ● *transitive verb* be a co-author of.

coax¹ /kəʊks/ *transitive verb* **1** (usu. foll. by *into*, or *to* + *infin.*) persuade gradually by flattery or by continued patient trial. **2** (foll. by *out of*) obtain by coaxing. **3** manipulate (a thing) carefully or slowly. □ **coax·er** *noun* **coax·ing** *noun* **coax·ing·ly** *adverb* [16th c.: from 'make a *cokes* of' from obsolete *cokes* simpleton, of unknown origin]

coax² /ˈkəʊaks/ ● *adjective* = COAXIAL. ● *noun* coaxial cable. [abbreviation]

co·axial /kəʊˈaksiəl/ *adjective* **1** having a common axis. **2** *Electricity* (of a cable or line) transmitting (telephone, telegraph, television, or radio signals) by means of two concentric conductors separated by an insulator. □ **co·axial·ly** *adverb*

cob¹ *noun* **1** the cylindrical centre of an ear of corn, to which the rows of kernels are attached. **2** a roundish lump of coal etc. **3** a sturdy horse with short legs. **4** a male swan. **5** = COBNUT. **6** *Brit.* a domed loaf of bread. [Middle English: origin unknown]

cob² *noun* a material for walls, made from compressed earth, clay, or chalk reinforced with straw. [17th c.: origin unknown]

Co·bain /kəʊˈbeɪn/ **Kurt (Donald)** (1967–94), US rock singer, songwriter, and guitarist. As lead singer and songwriter of the Seattle-based group Nirvana, he epitomized the grunge sound; he committed suicide in 1994.

Co·balt /ˈkəʊbɒlt/ a former silver-mining town in NE Ontario, about 125 km north of North Bay; pop. (2001) 1,229. [COBALT, so called because traces of the element were found in the silver ore]

co·balt /ˈkəʊbɒlt/ *noun Chem.* a silvery-white magnetic metallic element occurring naturally as a mineral in combination with sulphur and arsenic, and used in many alloys. Symbol: **Co**; at. no.: 27. □ **co·balt·ous** /kəˈbɒltəs/ *adjective* [German *Kobalt* etc., prob. = KOBOLD in mines]

cobalt-60 *noun* a long-lived radioisotope of cobalt, used as a radioactive tracer and in cancer therapy.

cobalt blue ● *noun* **1** a pigment containing a cobalt salt. **2** the deep blue colour of this. ● *adjective* (hyphenated when *attributive*) of this colour.

cobalt bomb *noun* **1** a container of cobalt-60 or other radioisotope used in the treatment of cancer. **2** a hydrogen bomb designed to disperse radioactive cobalt.

Cobb, Ty(rus Ray·mond) (known as 'the Georgia Peach') (1886–1961), US baseball player and manager. He set a number of major-league records during his career (1905–28), and was the first player elected into the Baseball Hall of Fame (1936).

cob·ber *noun Austral. & NZ informal* a companion or friend. [19th c.: perhaps related to Brit. dial. *cob* take a liking to]

Cob·bett /ˈkɒbət/ **Wil·liam** (1763–1835), English writer and political reformer. He founded the periodical *Cobbett's Political Register* in 1802 and was one of the leaders for political and social reform in England after 1815; his numerous writings include *Rural Rides* (1830).

cob·ble¹ ● *noun* a small stone, larger than a pebble, rounded by the action of water. ● *transitive verb* (esp. as **cob·bled** *adjective*) pave with cobblestones. [Middle English *cobel*, from COB¹]

cob·ble² *transitive verb* **1** mend or patch up (esp. shoes). **2** (often foll. by *together*) join or assemble roughly. [back-formation from COBBLER]

cob·bler *noun* **1** a person who mends shoes, esp. professionally. **2** a baked dessert of fruit topped with a tea-biscuit crust. **3** an iced drink of wine etc., sugar, and lemon (*sherry cobbler*). **4** (in *pl.*) *Brit. slang*

---

uː mood aɪ my əɪ pipe au brown ʌu house eɪ day ɔɪ boy ɑ̃ franglais ã Canadien ɔ̃ Brayon   (*see over for consonants*)

a nonsense. **b** the testicles. [Middle English, of unknown origin: sense 4 rhyming slang from *cobbler's awls = balls*]

cobble·stone *noun* a small rounded stone used for paving.
□ **cobble·stoned** *adjective* [as COBBLE¹]

Cobb salad *noun* esp. *US* a large salad of chopped usu. iceberg lettuce, chopped chicken or turkey, crumbled bacon, hard cooked eggs, tomatoes, avocado, and cheddar cheese, with crumbled blue cheese and vinaigrette dressing. [invented by R. *Cobb*, Hollywood restaurateur, in 1926]

Cob·den /ˈkɒbdən/ **Rich·ard** (1804–65), English political reformer. A leading spokesman of the free-trade movement in Britain, after 1838 he led the successful campaign for the repeal of the Corn Laws (1846).

Cobe·quid Mountains /ˈkoːbəkwɪd/ a low-lying mountain range in north central Nova Scotia, extending in an easterly direction north of Minas Basin and Cobequid Bay. [the name of the bay, possibly from Mi'kmaq *wakobetquick* end of flowing water]

cobia /ˈkoːbiə/ *noun* (*pl.* same) a large slender predatory game fish, *Rachycentron canadum*, of the tropical Atlantic, Indian, and western Pacific Oceans. [19th c.: origin unknown]

cob·nut *noun* a hazelnut. [COB¹]

COBOL /ˈkoːbɒl/ *noun Computing* a programming language designed for use in commerce. [common business oriented language]

Co·bourg /ˈkoːbɜrg/ a town in SE Ontario, situated on Lake Ontario, about 50 km east of Oshawa; pop. (2001) 17,172. □ **Co·bourg·er** *noun* [corruption of *Coburg*, in honour of the marriage of Charlotte, daughter of George IV, to Prince Leopold of Saxe-*Coburg*]

cobra /ˈkoːbrə/ *noun* any of a number of venomous Asian and African snakes esp. of the genus *Naja*, which can dilate their necks to form a hood when excited. [Portuguese from Latin *colubra* snake]

cob·web *noun* **1 a** a fine network of threads spun by a spider from a liquid secreted by it, used to trap insects etc. **b** the thread of this. **2** anything compared with a cobweb, esp. in flimsiness of texture. **3** a trap or insidious entanglement. **4** (in *pl.*) a state of mental inertia (*a brisk walk will clear the cobwebs*). □ **cob·webbed** *adjective* **cob·web·by** *adjective* [Middle English *cop(pe)web* from obsolete *coppe* spider]

coca /ˈkoːkə/ *noun* **1** a S American shrub, *Erythroxylum coca*. **2** its dried leaves, chewed as a stimulant. [Spanish from Quechua *cuca*]

co·caine /koːˈkein/ *noun* a white crystalline alkaloid derived from coca leaves, used as a local anaesthetic or in various forms as a narcotic with euphoric effects. [COCA + -INE⁴]

coc·cid·ia /kɒkˈsɪdiə/ *plural noun* parasitic protozoa of a group that includes those that cause diseases such as coccidiosis and toxoplasmosis. □ **coc·cid·ian** *adjective & noun*

coc·ci·di·osis /ˌkɒksɪdiˈoːsɪs/ *noun* a disease of mammals and birds, esp. livestock, caused by any of various parasitic protozoa of the order Coccidia, affecting the intestine. [*coccidium* (modern Latin from Greek *kokkis* diminutive of *kokkos* berry) + -OSIS]

coc·cus /ˈkɒkəs/ *noun* (*pl.* **cocci** /-ki/) **1** *Biol.* any spherical or roughly spherical bacterium (also in *combination*: *streptococcus*). **2** *Bot.* one of the separable round carpels of a fruit, containing one seed. □ **coc·cal** *adjective* **coc·coid** *adjective* [modern Latin from Greek *kokkos* berry]

coc·cyx /ˈkɒksɪks/ *noun* (*pl.* **coc·cy·ges** /-ˌdʒiːz/ or **coc·cyx·es**) the small triangular bone at the base of the spinal column in humans and some apes; the tailbone. □ **coc·cy·geal** /kɒkˈsɪdʒiəl/ *adjective* [Latin from Greek *kokkux -ugos* cuckoo (from being shaped like its bill)]

Cocha·bam·ba /ˌkɒtʃəˈbambə/ a city in Bolivia, situated at the centre of a rich agricultural region; pop. (2001) 516,683.

co-chair ● *noun* (also **co-chairman**, **co-chairperson**) a person who chairs a committee jointly with another or others. ● *transitive verb* act as a co-chair for (a committee etc.).

Co·chin¹ /ˈkoːtʃɪn/ a seaport and naval base on the Malabar Coast of SW India, in the state of Kerala; pop. (2001) 596,500.

Co·chin² /ˈkoːtʃɪn/ *noun* (in full **Cochin China**) a fowl of an Asian breed with feathered legs. [COCHIN-CHINA]

Cochin-China /ˈkoːtʃɪnˈtʃainə/ the former name for the southern region of what is now Vietnam. Part of French Indochina from 1862, in 1946 it became a French overseas territory, then merged officially with Vietnam in 1949.

coch·in·eal /ˈkoːtʃəˌniːl, -ˈniːl/ *noun* **1** a scarlet dye used esp. for colouring food. **2** a Mexican insect, *Dactylopius coccus*, the female of which yields this when dried and crushed. [French *cochenille* or Spanish *cochinilla* from Latin *coccinus* scarlet, from Greek *kokkos* berry]

Co·chise /koːˈtʃiːs, -ˈtʃiːz/ (d.1874), Apache chief, who led Native resistance to white settlement in the southwestern US during the 1860s.

coch·lea /ˈkɒkliə/ *noun* (*pl.* **coch·leae** /-kli,iː/) the spiral cavity of the internal ear, in which the sensory reception of sound occurs.
□ **coch·lear** *adjective* [Latin, = snail shell, from Greek *kokhlias*]

cochlear implant *noun* a device surgically implanted in the cochlea which translates sound into electrical impulses conveyed to the auditory nerve to facilitate hearing.

Coch·rane /ˈkɒkrən/ **1** a town in SW Alberta, about 25 km northwest of Calgary; pop. (2001) 11,798. **2** a town in NE central Ontario, situated about 90 km northeast of Timmins; pop. (2001) 5,690.
□ **Coch·ran·ite** *noun* [sense 1 after M. H. *Cochrane*, senator *c.*1884; sense 2 after F. *Cochrane*, Ontario minister of lands and forests d.1919]

cock¹ ● *noun* **1 a** a male bird, esp. of a domestic fowl; a rooster. **b** the male of certain sea creatures, e.g. the lobster or clam. **2** = WOODCOCK. **3** *coarse slang* the penis. ¶ Usually considered a taboo word. **4 a** a firing lever in a gun which can be raised to be released by the trigger. **b** the cocked position of this (*at full cock*). **5** *Curling* the position at the end of the rink at which rocks are aimed. **6** a tap or valve controlling flow. **7** *Brit. & Cdn* (*Nfld*) *slang* (usu. **old cock** as a form of address) a friend; a fellow. **8** *Brit. slang* nonsense. ● *transitive verb* **1** raise or make upright or erect. **2** turn or move (the eye or ear) attentively or knowingly. **3** set aslant, or turn up the brim of (a hat). **4** raise the cock of (a gun). □ **at half cock** only partly ready. **cock a snook** see SNOOK¹. **cock up** *Brit. slang* bungle; make a mess of. [Old English *cocc* and Old French *coq* prob. from medieval Latin *coccus*]

cock² ● *noun* a small rounded or conical pile of hay, straw, etc. ● *transitive verb* pile into cocks. [Middle English, perhaps of Scandinavian origin]

cock·ade /kɒˈkeid/ *noun* a rosette etc. worn in a hat as a badge of office or party, or as part of a uniform. □ **cock·ad·ed** *adjective* [French *cocarde* originally in *bonnet à la coquarde*, from fem. of obsolete *coquard* saucy, from *coq* COCK¹]

cock-a-doodle-doo *noun* a rooster's crow. [imitative]

cock-a-hoop ● *adjective* exultant; boastfully triumphant. ● *adverb* exultantly. [16th c.: originally in phr. *set cock a hoop* apparently denoting the action of turning on the tap and allowing liquor to flow prior to heavy drinking]

cock-a-leekie *noun* a soup traditionally made in Scotland with chicken and leeks. [COCK¹ + LEEK]

cocka·lorum /ˌkɒkəˈlɔːrəm/ *noun informal* a self-important little man. [18th c.: arbitrary alteration of COCK¹]

cocka·mamie /ˈkɒkəˌmeimi/ *adjective* (also **cocka·mamy**) *N Amer. informal* ridiculous or incredible (*a cockamamie theory*). [origin uncertain]

cock-and-bull story *noun* an absurd or incredible tale or account.

cocka·poo *noun* a breed of dog obtained by crossing a cocker spaniel and a poodle. [blend of COCKER SPANIEL + POODLE]

cocka·tiel /ˈkɒkəˌtiːl/ *noun* a small delicately coloured crested Australian parrot, *Nymphicus hollandicus*. [Dutch *kaketielje*, prob. a diminutive of *kaketoe* 'cockatoo']

cocka·too /ˌkɒkəˈtuː/ *noun* **1** any of several parrots of the subfamily Cacatuinae, having powerful beaks and erectile crests. **2** *Austral. & NZ informal* a farmer with a small holding. [Dutch *kaketoe* from Malay *kakatua*, assimilated to COCK¹]

cocka·trice /ˈkɒkətrɪs, -ˌtriːs/ *noun* **1** = BASILISK 1. **2** *Heraldry* a fabulous animal in the form of a rooster with a serpent's tail. [Old French *cocatris* from Latin *calcare* tread, track, rendering Greek *ikhneumōn* tracker: see ICHNEUMON]

cock·boat *noun* a small boat, esp. one towed behind a larger vessel. [obsolete *cock* small boat (from Old French *coque*) + BOAT]

Cock·burn /ˈkoːbɜrn/ **1 Bruce** (b.1945), Canadian folk and rock singer, songwriter, and guitarist. His songs are influenced by jazz, folk, and rock, and include 'Wondering Where the Lions Are' and 'If I Had a Rocket Launcher'. **2 James** (1819–83), Canadian Conservative politician, Father of Confederation. Elected to the legislative assembly in 1861, he was a delegate to the Quebec Conference (1864) and at Confederation became the first speaker of the House of Commons.

cock·chafer /ˈkɒkˌtʃeifər/ *noun* a large nocturnal beetle, *Melolontha melolontha*, which feeds on leaves and whose larva feeds on roots of crops etc. [perhaps from COCK¹ as expressing size or vigour + CHAFER]

Cock·croft, **Sir John Doug·las** (1897–1967), English physicist. In 1932 he succeeded (with E. T. S. Walton) in 'splitting the atom' by means of artificially accelerated protons, ushering in the whole field of nuclear and particle physics which rely on particle accelerators; the two shared the 1951 Nobel Prize for physics.

cock crow *noun* dawn.

Consonants: b *but* d *dog* f *few* g *get* h *her* j *yes* k *cat* l *leg* m *man* n *no* p *pen* r *red* s *sit*

cocked hat *noun* a hat with the brim permanently turned up in two or usu. three places. □ **knock into a cocked hat** defeat utterly.

cock·erel /ˈkɒkərəl/ *noun* a young rooster. [Middle English: diminutive of COCK¹]

cock·er spaniel *noun* a small breed of spaniel with a silky coat and long drooping ears. [as COCK¹, from use in hunting woodcocks]

cock·eyed *adjective informal* **1** crooked, askew, not level. **2** (of a scheme etc.) absurd, not practical. **3** drunk. **4** squinting. [19th c.: apparently from COCK¹ + EYE]

cock·fight *noun* a fight between pitted gamecocks, often fitted with metal spurs, usu. with spectators betting on the outcome.
□ **cock·fight·ing** *noun*

cock·le¹ *noun* **1 a** any edible mollusc of the genus *Cardium*, having a chubby ribbed bivalve shell. **b** its shell. **2** (in full **cockle·shell**) a small shallow boat. □ **warm the cockles of one's heart** make one contented; be satisfying. [Old French *coquille* shell, ultimately from Greek *kogkhulion* from *kogkhē* CONCH]

cock·le² *noun* **1** any of various plants, esp. the corn cockle, of the genus *Agrostemma*. **2** a disease of wheat that turns the grains black. [Old English *coccul*, perhaps ultimately from Late Latin COCCUS]

cock·le³ ● *verb* **1** *intransitive* pucker, wrinkle. **2** *transitive* cause to cockle. ● *noun* a pucker or wrinkle in paper, glass, etc. [French *coquiller* blister (bread in cooking) from *coquille*: see COCKLE¹]

cockle·bur *noun* any of various plants with fruit covered in hooked bristles, esp. of the genus *Xanthium* of the daisy family. [COCKLE² + BUR]

cock·ney ● *noun* (*pl.* **-neys**) **1** a native of the East End of London. **2** the dialect or accent typical of this area. ● *adjective* of or characteristic of cockneys or their dialect or accent. □ **cock·ney·ism** *noun* [Middle English *cokeney* cock's egg, later derogatory for 'townsman']

cock-of-the-rock *noun* a S American bird, *Rupicola rupicola*, having a crest and bright orange plumage.

cock of the walk *noun* a dominant or arrogant person.

cock·pit *noun* **1 a** a compartment for the pilot (or the pilot and crew) of an aircraft or spacecraft. **b** a similar compartment for the driver in an automobile. **c** a space for the helmsman in some small yachts. **d** the space in which the paddler sits in a kayak. **2** an arena of war or other conflict. **3** a place where cockfights are held. [originally in sense 3, from COCK¹ + PIT¹]

cock·roach *noun* any of various flat brown insects, typically a stout-bodied scavenger resembling a beetle, with hardened forewings; esp. the large dark brown *Blatta orientalis* and *Periplaneta americana*, which infest households, warehouses, etc. [Spanish *cucaracha*, assimilated to COCK¹, ROACH¹]

cocks·comb *noun* **1** the crest or comb of a rooster. **2** a garden plant, *Celosia cristata*, with a terminal plume of tiny white or red flowers.

cocks·foot *noun* any pasture grass of the genus *Dactylis*, with broad leaves and green or purplish spikes.

cock·shy /ˈkɒkʃai/ *noun Brit.* **1** a target at which sticks, stones, etc. are thrown. **2** a throw at this. [COCK¹ + SHY²: originally a game in which objects were thrown at a rooster]

cock·suck·er *noun coarse slang* **1** a person who performs fellatio. **2** a contemptible person. □ **cock·suck·ing** *noun & adjective*

cock·sure *adjective* presumptuously or arrogantly confident.
□ **cock·sure·ness** *noun* [cock = God + SURE]

cock·tail *noun* **1** a usu. alcoholic drink made by mixing various spirits, fruit juices, etc. **2** (*attributive*) **a** denoting a small item of food served as an hors d'oeuvre etc. (*cocktail wiener*). **b** denoting a place or occasion where drinks are served (*cocktail party*). **3** a dish of mixed ingredients (*fruit cocktail*; *shrimp cocktail*). **4** any hybrid mixture. **5** a number of different drugs used together to treat a condition (*a new cocktail of drugs has made life better for many AIDS patients*). [origin unknown: compare earlier sense 'docked horse' from COCK¹: the connection is unclear]

cocktail dress *noun* a usu. short evening dress suitable for wearing on a semi-formal occasion.

cocktail-length *noun* (*attributive*) a skirt or dress length with the hemline halfway between mid-calf and the ankle bone.

cocktail lounge *noun* a room in a restaurant, hotel, etc. where alcoholic drinks are served.

cocktail napkin *noun N Amer.* a small square paper or cloth napkin.

cocktail party *noun* a social event, usu. held in the early evening, at which cocktails and refreshments are served.

cocktail table *noun* a small low table used for holding drinks etc.

cock·teas·er *noun coarse slang* a woman regarded as provocatively refusing sexual intercourse. □ **cock·teas·ing** *noun*

cock-up *noun esp. Brit. slang* a muddle or mistake.

cocky¹ *adjective* (**cock·i·er**, **cock·i·est**) **1** conceited, arrogantly confident. **2** saucy, impudent. □ **cock·i·ly** *adverb* **cock·i·ness** *noun* [COCK¹ + -Y¹]

cocky² *noun* (*pl.* **-ies**) *Austral. & NZ informal* = COCKATOO 2. [abbreviation]

coco *noun* (also **cocoa**, **coconut palm**) (*pl.* **cocos** or **cocoas**) a tall tropical palm tree, *Cocos nucifera*, bearing coconuts. [Portuguese & Spanish *coco* grimace: the base of the shell resembles a face]

cocoa *noun* **1** a powder made from crushed cacao seeds, often with other ingredients. **2** a drink made from this powder and hot water or milk. [alteration of CACAO]

cocoa bean *noun* a cacao seed.

cocoa butter *noun* a fatty substance obtained from cocoa beans and used for confectionery, cosmetics, etc.

coco-de-mer /ˌkoːkoːdəˈmer/ *noun* a tall palm tree, *Lodoicea maldivica*, of the Seychelles. [French, lit. 'coco from the sea' (because the tree was first known from nuts found floating in the sea)]

coco matting *noun N Amer.* (*Brit.* **coconut matting**) a matting made of fibre from coconut husks.

co-conspira·tor *noun* a fellow conspirator.

coco·nut *noun* **1** a large ovate brown seed of the coco, with a hard shell and edible white fleshy lining enclosing a milky juice. **2** (in full **coconut palm**) = COCO. **3** the edible white fleshy lining of a coconut. □ **coco·nut·ty** *adjective* [COCO + NUT]

coconut milk *noun* **1** the white milky liquid found inside the coconut. **2** a coconut-flavoured liquid obtained by soaking grated coconut in water.

coconut oil *noun* the liquid or semi-solid oil obtained from the flesh of the coconut, used as an ointment or in foods.

co·coon /kəˈkuːn/ ● *noun* **1 a** a silky case spun by many insect larvae for protection as pupae. **b** a similar structure made by other animals. **2** anything which encloses or protects like a cocoon. **3** a protective covering sprayed on metal equipment to prevent corrosion. ● *verb* **1** *transitive & intransitive* wrap in or form a cocoon. **2** *transitive* spray with a protective coating. [French *cocon* from modern Provençal *coucoun* diminutive of *coca* shell]

co·coon·ing /kəˈkuːnɪŋ/ *noun N Amer.* the practice of spending one's leisure time in the home rather than by going out. □ **co·coon·er** *noun*

Cocos Islands /ˈkoːkəs/ (also called **Keel·ing Islands**) a group of twenty-seven small coral islands in the Indian Ocean, administered as an external territory of Australia since 1955; pop. (2002) 632. The islands (previously uninhabited) were discovered in 1609 by Captain William Keeling of the East India Company.

co·cotte /kəˈkɒt/ *noun* **1** a small fireproof dish for cooking and serving an individual portion of food. **2** *dated* a fashionable prostitute. [French, from a child's name for a hen]

Coc·teau /kɒkˈtoː/ **Jean** (1889–1963), French poet, dramatist, novelist, and film director. A writer of immense versatility, he is best known for the plays *La Machine infernale* (1934) and *Orphée* (1926), and the novel *Les Enfants terribles* (1929); his films include *Le Sang d'un poète* (1930) and *La Belle et la bête* (1946).

COD *abbreviation* **1** *N Amer.* collect on delivery. **2** cash on delivery.

cod *noun* (*pl.* same) any large marine food fish of the family Gadidae, esp. *Gadus morhua*. [Middle English: origin unknown]

coda /ˈkoːdə/ *noun* **1** *Music* the concluding passage of a piece or movement, usu. forming an addition to the basic structure. **2** the concluding section of a dance, drama, or literary work. **3** a concluding event or series of events. [Italian from Latin *cauda* tail]

cod·dle *transitive verb* **1** treat indulgently or over-attentively. **2** cook (an egg) in water below boiling point. □ **cod·dler** *noun* [prob. dial. var. of *caudle* invalids' gruel, based on Latin *caldum* 'hot drink', from *caldus* 'warm']

code ● *noun* **1 a** a pre-arranged system of words, letters, numbers, signals, or symbols, used to represent others for brevity or to ensure secrecy. **b** any similar system used for conveying specific information with arbitrarily assigned symbols (*area code*; *postal code*). **c** = GENETIC CODE. **2** *Computing* **a** a set of instructions written in a programming language. **b** the language itself. **c** = BAR CODE. **3 a** a systematic collection of statutes; a body of laws so arranged as to avoid inconsistency and overlapping. **b** a set of rules on any subject (*dress code*; *code of ethics*). **4 a** the prevailing morality of a society or class (*code* *of honour.* **b** a person's standard of moral behaviour. ● *verb* **1** *transitive* put (a message, program, etc.) into code. **2** *intransitive* (foll. by *for*) *Biochem.* be the genetic code for (an amino acid etc.). □ **bring up to code** *N Amer.* renovate an older building to make it conform to revised, more stringent building code regulations. □ **coder** *noun* [Old French from Latin CODEX]

codec /ˈkoːdek/ *noun* a device that converts an analog signal into an encoded digital form, and decodes digital signals into analog form, used in telephone systems and in video systems for computers. [blend of *coder-decoder*]

co·defend·ant *noun* a joint defendant.

co·deine /ˈkoːdiːn/ *noun* an alkaloid derived from morphine and used to relieve pain. [Greek *kōdeia* poppy head + -INE⁴]

code name *noun* a name used for secrecy or convenience instead of the usual name. □ **code-name** *transitive verb*

cod end *noun* the narrow-necked bag at the end of a trawl net etc. [Old English *cod* 'bag']

code of silence *noun* an unwritten set of rules enjoining members of a group not to talk about its activities.

co·depend·ent /koːdəˈpendənt/ ● *adjective* emotionally or psychologically dependent on supporting or caring for another person, esp. a person with an addiction or illness. ● *noun* a codependent person. □ **co·depend·ency** *noun*

code-sharing *noun* the practice of two airlines listing certain flights in a reservation system under each other's names. □ **code-share** *intransitive verb*

code-switch·ing *noun* the practice of alternating spontaneously between two or more languages, dialects, or accents.

co·determin·a·tion *noun* co-operation between management and workers in decision-making.

code word *noun* **1** a word used to convey information secretly. **2** a word, esp. a euphemism, the meaning or implication of which is understood only by an in-group.

codex /ˈkoːdeks/ *noun* (*pl.* **co·dices** /ˈkoːdəˌsiːz, ˈkɒd-/) an ancient manuscript text in book form. [Latin, = block of wood, tablet, book]

cod·fish *noun* = COD.

codg·er *noun* (usu. in **old codger**) *informal* a person, esp. an old or strange one. [perhaps var. of *cadger*: see CADGE]

co·dices *pl.* of CODEX.

co·di·cil /ˈkoːdəsɪl, ˈkɒd-/ *noun* an addition explaining, modifying, or revoking a will or part of one. [Latin *codicillus*, diminutive of CODEX]

codi·fy /ˈkoːdəˌfaɪ, ˈkɒd-/ *transitive verb* (**-fies**, **-fied**) arrange (laws etc.) systematically into a code. □ **codi·fi·ca·tion** *noun* **codi·fi·er** *noun*

cod·ling¹ /ˈkɒdlɪŋ/ *noun* (also **cod·lin**) (also **codling moth**) a small moth, *Carpocapsa pomonella*, the larva of which feeds on apples. [orig. a type of apple, from Anglo-French *quer de lion* lion-heart]

cod·ling² /ˈkɒdlɪŋ/ *noun* a small codfish.

cod-liver oil *noun* an oil pressed from the fresh liver of cod or related fishes, which is rich in vitamins D and A.

co·domain *noun* *Math.* a set that includes all the possible expressions of a given function. [CO- 2 + DOMAIN]

codon /ˈkoːdɒn/ *noun* *Biochem.* a sequence of three nucleotides, forming a unit of genetic code in a DNA or RNA molecule. [CODE + -ON]

cod·piece *noun* *hist.* an appendage like a small bag or flap at the front of a man's breeches, covering the genitals. [Middle English, from *cod* scrotum + PIECE]

co·driver *noun* a person who shares the driving of a vehicle with another, esp. in a race or rally.

cods·wallop *noun* *Cdn, Brit.*, & *Austral. slang* nonsense. [20th c.: origin unknown]

cod tongue *noun* *Cdn* (*Nfld*) the tongue of a codfish, fried in pork fat and eaten as a delicacy.

cod trap *noun* *Cdn* a device used for inshore fishing, consisting of a long net along which fish are guided into a box-shaped trap.

Cody /ˈkoːdi/ **Wil·liam Fred·erick**, see BUFFALO BILL.

coe·cil·ian *var.* of CAECILIAN.

coed /ˈkoːed, koːˈed/ *informal* ● *adjective* **1** coeducational. **2** open to both males and females. ● *noun* *N Amer. dated* a female student at a coeducational institution. [abbreviation]

co-edit *transitive verb* edit jointly with another or others. □ **co-editor** *noun*

co·educa·tion *noun* the education of male and female students together. □ **co·educa·tion·al** *adjective*

co·effi·cient /ˌkoːɪˈfɪʃənt/ *noun* **1** *Math.* a quantity placed before and multiplying an algebraic expression (e.g. 4 in 4x^v). **2** *Physics* a multiplier or factor that measures some property (*coefficient of expansion*).

coela·canth /ˈsiːləˌkanθ/ *noun* a large bony marine fish, *Latimeria chalumnae*, formerly thought to be extinct, having a three-lobed tail fin and fleshy pectoral fins. [modern Latin *Coelacanthus* from Greek *koilos* hollow + *akantha* spine]

-coele *var.* of -CELE.

coel·enter·ate /siːˈlentəˌreit/ *noun* any marine animal of the phylum Coelenterata with a simple tube-shaped or cup-shaped body, e.g. jellyfish, corals, and sea anemones. [modern Latin *Coelenterata* from Greek *koilos* hollow + *enteron* intestine]

coel·iac *var.* of CELIAC.

coelom /ˈsiːləm, ˈsiːloːm/ *noun* (also **celom**) (*pl.* **-oms** or **-omata** /-ˈloːmətə/) *Zool.* the principal body cavity in animals, between the intestinal canal and the body wall. □ **coel·om·ate** *adjective & noun* **coel·om·ic** /siˈlemɪk/ *adjective* [Greek *koilōma* cavity]

coeno·bite *var.* of CENOBITE.

co·enzyme /ˈkoːˌenzaɪm/ *noun* *Biochem.* a non-proteinaceous compound that assists in the action of an enzyme.

co·equal ● *adjective* equal to one another. ● *noun* an equal. □ **co·equal·ity** *noun* **co·equal·ly** *adverb*

co·erce /koːˈɜrs/ *transitive verb* (often foll. by *into*) persuade or restrain (an unwilling person) by force (*coerced you into signing*). □ **co·er·cible** *adjective* [Latin *coercēre* restrain (as CO-, *arcēre* restrain)]

co·er·cion /koːˈɜrʃən/ *noun* the act or process of coercing. □ **co·er·cive** /koːˈɜrsɪv/ *adjective* **co·er·cive·ly** *adverb* **co·er·cive·ness** *noun*

co·er·civ·ity /ˌkoːɜrˈsɪvəti/ *noun* *Physics* the resistance of a magnetic material to changes in magnetization, esp. measured as the field intensity required to demagnetize it when fully magnetized.

Coet·zee /ˈkoːtsi/ **J(ohn) M(i·chael)** (b.1940), South African novelist. His major works, such as the two *Dusklands* novellas (1974), *In the Heart of the Country* (1977), and the Booker Prize-winning *The Life and Times of Michael K* (1983), explore the psychology and mythology of colonialism and racial domination. He received his second Booker Prize for *Disgrace* in 1999, and in 2003 was awarded the Nobel Prize for literature.

Coeur de Lion /ˌkɜr də liːˈɒn/ see RICHARD I.

co·eval /koːˈiːvəl/ ● *adjective* **1** having the same age or date of origin. **2** living or existing at the same epoch. **3** having the same duration. ● *noun* a coeval person, a contemporary. [Late Latin *coaevus* (as CO-, Latin *aevum* age)]

co-evolution *noun* a complementary evolution of closely associated species. □ **co-evolve** *intransitive verb*

co·exist *intransitive verb* (often foll. by *with*) **1** exist together (in time or place). **2** (esp. of nations) exist in mutual tolerance though professing different ideologies etc. □ **co·exist·ence** *noun* **co·exist·ent** *adjective*

co-extensive *adjective* extending over the same space, time, or limits.

co·factor *noun* *Biochem.* any substance (other than the substrate) whose presence is essential for the activity of an enzyme.

C. of E. *abbreviation* *Brit.* Church of England.

coffee ● *noun* **1** **a** a drink made from the roasted and ground bean-like seeds of a tropical shrub of the genus *Coffea*. **b** a cup of this. **c** = INSTANT COFFEE. **2** **a** the shrub yielding these seeds, one or more of which are contained in each berry. **b** these seeds raw, or roasted and ground. **3** the pale brown colour of coffee mixed with milk. ● *adjective* **1** of the colour of coffee mixed with milk. **2** flavoured with coffee. □ **wake up and smell the coffee** become aware of (usu. unpleasant) realities. [ultimately from Turkish *kahveh* from Arabic *kahwa*]

coffee bar *noun* a bar or café serving coffee and light refreshments from a counter.

coffee bean *noun* the bean-like seed of the coffee shrub, esp. when roasted but not ground.

coffee break *noun* a short break from work during which food or drink may be consumed.

coffee cake *noun* *N Amer.* a type of cake or sweet bread topped or filled with cinnamon sugar, often containing nuts or raisins.

coffee cream *noun* *Cdn* cream with a 10% (or sometimes 18%) milk fat content.

coffee grinder *noun* (also **coffee mill**) a small machine for grinding roasted coffee beans.

Vowels: a *cat* ɑ *arm* e *bed* ɜr *her* ɜː *deux* ə *ago* ɪ *sit* i *cosy* iː *feed* ɒ *hot* ɔ *pore* oː *no* ʌ *run* ʊ *put*

coffee hour *noun* an occasion for socializing, as after a church service, at which coffee and other refreshments are served.

coffee house *noun* **1** a place serving coffee and other refreshments. **2** (in 17th- and 18th-c. England) an establishment serving coffee and used as a centre for political and literary conversation, circulation of news, etc. **3** a form of entertainment, usu. jazz or folk music or poetry readings etc., performed cabaret-style.

coffee klatch /klatʃ/ *noun* (also **coffee klatsch, kaffeeklatsch**) *N Amer.* an informal gathering for conversation at which coffee is served, esp. one involving only women. [German *Kaffeeklatsch*, lit. 'coffee gossip']

coffee maker *noun* a device for making coffee, esp. an electrical appliance using a drip filter.

coffee morning *noun Brit.* a morning gathering, often in aid of charity, at which coffee is served.

coffee pot *noun* a tall covered pot with a handle and spout, in which coffee is made or served.

coffee row /roː/ *noun Cdn (Sask.)* a regular gathering of people for coffee and gossip at a café etc., esp. in a rural area.

coffee shop *noun* a small informal restaurant, esp. in a hotel or office building, serving simple meals and beverages.

coffee spoon *noun* a spoon, smaller than a teaspoon, for stirring coffee.

coffee table *noun* a small low oblong table.

coffee-table book *noun* a large lavishly illustrated book suitable for prominent display.

coffee whitener *noun* a soluble powder added to coffee as a substitute for cream.

cof·fer *noun* **1** a box, esp. a large strongbox for valuables. **2** (in *pl.*) a treasury or store of funds. **3** *Archit.* a sunken panel in a ceiling, soffit, etc. [Old French *coffre* from Latin *cophinus* from Greek *kophinos* basket]

cof·fer·dam *noun* a watertight enclosure pumped dry to permit work below the waterline on building bridges etc., or for repairing a ship.

cof·fered *adjective* (of a ceiling) having coffers.

cof·fin *noun* **1** a long narrow usu. wooden box in which a corpse is buried or cremated. **2** the part of a horse's hoof below the coronet. □ **cof·fined** *adjective* [Old French *cof(f)in* little basket etc., from Latin *cophinus*: see COFFER]

coffin bone *noun* the terminal phalangeal bone in a horse's hoof.

coffin corner *noun Football* one of the corners formed by the goal line and sideline.

coffin joint *noun* the joint at the top of a horse's hoof.

coffin nail *noun slang* a cigarette.

cof·fle *noun* a line of animals, slaves, etc., fastened together. [Arabic *kāfila* caravan]

co-founder *noun* a person who founds an institution etc. jointly with another or others. □ **co-found** *transitive verb*

cog *noun* **1 a** each of a series of teeth on the edge of a wheel or shaft transferring motion by engaging with another series. **b** (in full **cog·wheel**) a wheel or shaft furnished with these. **2** a person who plays a minor or routine role in an organization. □ **cogged** *adjective* [Middle English: prob. of Scandinavian origin]

co·gener·a·tion /ˌkoːdʒenəˈreiʃən/ *noun* the utilization of otherwise wasted energy for useful heating or for generating electricity.

co·gent /ˈkoːdʒənt/ *adjective* (of arguments, reasons, etc.) convincing, compelling. □ **co·gen·cy** *noun* **co·gent·ly** *adverb* [Latin *cogere* compel (as CO-, *agere act-* drive)]

cogi·tate /ˈkɒdʒəˌteit/ *transitive & intransitive verb* ponder, meditate. □ **cogi·ta·tion** *noun* **cogi·ta·tor** *noun* [Latin *cogitare* think (as CO-, AGITATE)]

cogi·to /ˈkɒdʒɪˌtoː/ *noun Philos.* the principle establishing the existence of a being from the fact of its thinking or awareness. [Latin, = I think, in the French philosopher Descartes's formula (1641) *cogito, ergo sum* 'I think, therefore I exist']

co·gnac /ˈkɒnjak, ˈkoːn-/ *noun* a high-quality brandy, properly that distilled in Cognac in W France.

cog·nate /ˈkɒgneit/ ● *adjective* **1** *Linguistics* (of a word) having the same linguistic family or derivation (as another); representing the same original word or root (e.g. English *father*, German *Vater*, Latin *pater*). **2** related to or descended from a common ancestor (*compare* AGNATE). ● *noun* **1** a cognate word. **2** a relative. [Latin *cognatus* (as CO-, *natus* born)]

cognate object *noun Grammar* an object that is related in origin and sense to the verb governing it (as in *live a good life*).

cog·ni·tion /kɒgˈnɪʃən/ *noun* **1** the mental faculties of perception, thought, reason, and memory, as distinct from emotion and volition. **2** a perception, sensation, notion, or intuition. [Latin *cognitio* (as CO-, *gnoscere gnit-* apprehend)]

cog·ni·tive /ˈkɒgnɪtɪv/ *adjective* **1** of or pertaining to cognition. **2** based on or pertaining to empirical knowledge. □ **cog·ni·tive·ly** *adverb*

cognitive dissonance *noun* the simultaneous holding of incompatible ideas, beliefs, etc.

cog·niz·able /ˈkɒgnɪzəbəl, ˌkɒgˈnaizəbəl/ *adjective Law* within the jurisdiction of a court. □ **cog·niz·ably** *adverb* [COGNIZANCE + -ABLE]

cog·ni·zance /ˈkɒgnɪzəns/ *noun* **1** knowledge or awareness; perception, notice. **2** the sphere of one's observation or concern. **3** *Law* the right of a court to deal with a matter. **4** *Heraldry* a distinctive device or mark. □ **take cognizance of** notice or take account of, esp. officially. [Old French *conoisance*, ultimately from Latin *cognoscent-* from *cognitio*: see COGNITION]

cog·ni·zant /ˈkɒgnɪzənt/ *adjective* (foll. by *of*) having knowledge or being aware of.

cog·nom·en /kɒgˈnoːmen/ *noun* **1** a name, esp. a nickname, epithet, or surname. **2** (in ancient Rome) a citizen's third personal name or nickname, as in Marcus Tullius *Cicero* or Publius Cornelius Scipio *Africanus*. [Latin]

cogno·scen·ti /ˌkɒgnəˈsenti/ *plural noun* people who are considered to be especially well informed about a subject. [Italian, lit. 'people who know']

cog·wheel *noun* = COG 1b.

co·habit *intransitive verb* (**co·habit·ed, co·habit·ing**) **1** live together amicably. **2** live together in a sexual and romantic relationship without marriage. □ **co·habit·ant** *noun* **co·habit·a·tion** *noun* **co·habit·ee** *noun* **co·habit·er** *noun* [Latin *cohabitare* (as CO-, *habitare* dwell)]

Cohen /ˈkoːən/ **1 Leonard** (b.1934), Canadian poet, novelist, singer, and songwriter. His works include the poetry collection *Let us Compare Mythologies* (1956), the novel *Beautiful Losers* (1966), and the album *The Songs of Leonard Cohen* (1968). **2 Matt** (1942–99), Canadian novelist and short-story writer. His novels are often set in the fictitious eastern Ontario town of Salem, and include *The Disinherited* (1974), *The Sweet Second Summer of Kitty Malone* (1979), and *The Bookseller* (1993). His last novel, *Elizabeth and After* (1999), won the Governor General's Award.

co·here /koːˈhir/ *intransitive verb* **1** (of parts or a whole) stick together, remain united. **2** (of reasoning etc.) be logical or consistent. [Latin *cohaerēre cohaes-* (as CO-, *haerēre* stick)]

co·her·ent /koːˈhirənt/ *adjective* **1** (of a person) able to speak intelligibly and articulately. **2** (of speech, an argument, etc.) logical and consistent; easily followed. **3** cohering; sticking together. **4** *Physics* (of waves) having a constant phase relationship. □ **co·her·ence** *noun* **co·her·ency** *noun* **co·her·ent·ly** *adverb* [Latin *cohaerēre cohaerent-* (as COHERE)]

co·hesion /koːˈhiːʒən/ *noun* **1 a** the act or condition of sticking together. **b** a tendency to cohere. **2** *Chem.* the force with which molecules cohere. □ **co·hesive** /-sɪv/ *adjective* **co·hesive·ly** /-sɪvli/ *adverb* **co·hesive·ness** /-sɪvnəs/ *noun* [Latin *cohaes-* (see COHERE) after adhesion]

Cohn /koːn/ **Fer·di·nand (Jul·ius)** (1828–98), German botanist, a founder of bacteriology. Noted for his studies of algae, bacteria, and other micro-organisms, he was the first to devise a systematic classification of bacteria into genera and species.

coho *noun* (in full **coho salmon**) (*pl.* same or **cohos**) a silver salmon, *Oncorhynchus kisutch*, of the N Pacific. [cohose (taken as *pl.*) from Halkomelem]

co·hort *noun* **1** *N Amer.* a companion or colleague. **2 a** a group of persons with a common demographic or statistical characteristic. **b** persons banded or grouped together, esp. in a common cause. **3** (in ancient Rome) a military unit equal to one-tenth of a legion. **4** a band of warriors. [French *cohorte* or Latin *cohors cohort-* enclosure, company]

co·hosh /ˈkoːhɒʃ/ *noun* any of various woodland plants with divided leaves, esp. **black cohosh**, *Cimicifuga racemos*, with a long spike of white flowers, **blue cohosh** *Caulophyllum thalictroides*, with dark blue berries, or **white cohosh** white baneberry, *Actaea pachypoda*, bearing white berries each with a black spot. [Eastern Abenaki *kahas*]

co-host ● *noun* a person who hosts (esp. a broadcast) jointly with another or others. ● *transitive verb* act as a co-host for (a broadcast, competition, conference, etc.).

co-housing *noun* a residential development in which individual households share some common facilities or amenities.

coif¹ /kɔɪf/ ● *noun* **1** a close-fitting cap, esp. as worn by nuns under a veil. **2** *hist.* a protective metal skullcap worn under armour. [Old French *coife* from Late Latin *cofia* helmet]

coif² /kwɒf/ ● *noun* esp. *N Amer.* a hairstyle. ● *transitive verb* (**coiffed**, **coif·fing**, esp. *US* **coifed**, **coif·ing**) (usu. as **coiffed** *adjective*) arrange or style (hair). [abbreviation of COIFFURE]

coif·feur /kwɒˈfɜr/ *noun* a male hairdresser. [French]

coif·fure /kwɒˈfjʊr/ ● *noun* a hairstyle. ● *transitive verb* style (hair), often in a specified way. □ **coif·fured** *adjective* [French]

coign of vantage /kɔɪn/ *noun* a favourable position for observation or action. [earlier spelling of COIN in the sense 'cornerstone']

coil¹ ● *noun* **1** anything arranged in a joined sequence of concentric circles. **2** a length of rope, a spring, etc., arranged in this way. **3** a single turn of something coiled. **4** a lock of hair twisted and coiled. **5** an intrauterine contraceptive device in the form of a coil. **6** *Electricity* **a** = INDUCTION COIL. **b** any helix of wire through which electric current passes, as in a transformer or electromagnet. **7** a length of wire, piping, etc., wound in circles or spirals. **8 a** a roll of postage stamps, usu. with at least one unperforated edge. **b** a stamp from such a roll. **9** *Cdn* a haycock. ● *verb* **1** *transitive* arrange in a series of concentric loops or rings. **2** *transitive & intransitive* twist or be twisted into a circular or spiral shape. **3** *intransitive* move sinuously. [Old French *coillir* from Latin *colligere* COLLECT¹]

coil² *noun* □ **this mortal coil** the difficulties of earthly life (with reference to Shakespeare's *Hamlet* III. i. 67). [16th c.: origin unknown]

coil spring *noun* a helical spring, having the form of a cone or a cylinder.

Co·im·ba·tore /ˌkoɪmbəˈtɔr/ a city in the state of Tamil Nadu, in S India; pop. (2001) 923,100.

Co·im·bra /koˈɪmbrə/ a university city in central Portugal; pop. (est. 2001) 103,000.

coin ● *noun* **1** a piece of flat usu. round metal stamped and issued by a government as money. **2** metal money collectively. **3** *slang* money, wealth (*they've got coin*). ● *transitive verb* **1** invent or devise (esp. a new word or phrase). **2** make (metal) into coins. **3** make (coins) by stamping. □ **coin money** *informal* make a large amount of money quickly. **the other side of the coin 1** the opposite view of the matter. **2** an apparently contrasting aspect of a situation. **to coin a phrase** *ironic* introducing a banal remark or cliché. [Old French, = stamping die, from Latin *cuneus* wedge]

coin·age *noun* **1** the act or process of coining. **2 a** coins collectively. **b** a system or type of coins in use. **3 a** an invention, esp. of a new word or phrase. **b** a newly invented word or phrase.

coin box *noun* **1** a receptacle for receiving coins, as on a bus, pay telephone, etc. **2** *Brit.* = PAY PHONE.

co·incide /ˌkoɪnˈsaɪd/ *intransitive verb* **1** occur at or during the same time. **2** occupy the same portion of space. **3** (often foll. by *with*) be in agreement. [medieval Latin *coincidere* (as CO-, INCIDENT)]

co·inci·dence /koˈɪnsɪdəns/ *noun* **1** a remarkable concurrence of events or circumstances without apparent causal connection. **2 a** the fact of occurring or being together. **b** an instance of this. **3** *Physics* the presence of ionizing particles etc. in two or more detectors simultaneously, or of two or more signals simultaneously in a circuit. [medieval Latin *coincidentia* (as COINCIDE)]

co·inci·dent /koˈɪnsɪdənt/ *adjective* **1** occurring together in space or time. **2** (foll. by *with*) in agreement; harmonious. □ **co·inci·dent·ly** *adverb*

co·inci·dent·al /koˌɪnsɪˈdentəl/ *adjective* **1** in the nature of or resulting from a coincidence. **2** happening or existing at the same time. □ **co·inci·dent·al·ly** *adverb*

coin·er *noun* **1** a person who invents or devises something (esp. a new word or phrase). **2 a** a person who coins money. **b** a counterfeiter.

coin-op *noun* **1** a coin-operated machine, esp. a computer video game. **2** a laundromat.

coin-operated *adjective* (of a machine) automatically activated when the user inserts a coin or coins.

co-instruc·tional *adjective* *Cdn* (*Ont.*) = EXTRACURRICULAR 1.

coin toss *noun* **1** an instance of tossing a coin to decide a question. **2** a situation in which the outcome could as easily go one way as the other.

Coin·treau /ˈkwɒntroʊ/ *noun* *proprietary* a colourless orange-flavoured liqueur. [French]

coir /ˈkɔɪr/ *noun* fibre from the outer husk of the coconut, used for ropes, matting, etc. [Malayalam *kāyar* cord, from *kāyaru* be twisted]

coit·us /ˈkɔɪtəs, ˈkoɪt-/ *noun* (also **co·ition** /koˈɪʃən/) *Med.* sexual intercourse. □ **coit·al** *adjective* **coit·al·ly** *adverb* [Latin *coitio* from *coire coit-* go together]

coit·us inter·rup·tus /ˌɪntəˈrʌptəs/ *noun* sexual intercourse in which the penis is withdrawn before ejaculation.

cojon·es /kəˈhoʊneɪs/ *plural noun* *N Amer. coarse slang* **1** testicles. **2** courage, guts. [Spanish, pl. of *cojón* testicle: compare BALL¹ *noun* 6]

Coke *noun* *proprietary* Coca-Cola, a cola-flavoured soft drink. [abbreviation]

coke¹ ● *noun* **1** a solid substance left after the gases have been extracted from coal, used as fuel and in metallurgy. **2** a residue left after the incomplete combustion of petroleum. ● *transitive verb* convert (coal) into coke. [prob. from Northern English dial. *colk* core, of unknown origin]

coke² *slang* ● *noun* cocaine. ● *transitive verb* (usu. foll. by *up*; usu. in *passive*) drug (esp. oneself) with cocaine. [abbreviation]

Coke-bottle *noun* *N Amer.* (*attributive*) designating very thick eyeglass lenses.

coke·head *noun* *slang* a person addicted to or habitually using cocaine.

coke oven *noun* a furnace in which coke is produced from coal.

Col *abbreviation* **1** (also **Col.**) COLONEL. **2** (also **Col.**) New Testament Colossians.

col /kɒl/ *noun* **1** a depression in a ridge or range of mountains, generally affording a pass from one slope to another. **2** *Meteorol.* a low-pressure region between high-pressure systems. [French, = neck, from Latin *collum*]

col. *abbreviation* column.

col- /kɒl/ *prefix* assimilated form of COM- before l.

COLA /ˈkoʊlə/ *abbreviation* *N Amer.* cost-of-living adjustment.

cola /ˈkoʊlə/ *noun* **1** (also **kola**) any small tree of the genus *Cola*, native to W Africa, bearing seeds containing caffeine. **2** a sweet carbonated drink usu. flavoured with cola seeds. [Temne *k'ola* cola nut]

col·an·der /ˈkɒləndər, ˈkʌl-/ *noun* a perforated metal or plastic container, used to strain off liquids. [Middle English, ultimately from Latin *colare* strain]

cola nut *noun* a seed of the cola tree.

co-latitude *noun* *Astronomy* the complement of the latitude, the difference between it and 90°.

Col·bert /kɒlˈbɛr/ **Jean Bap·tiste** (1619–83), French statesman, chief minister to Louis XIV 1661–83. A vigorous reformer, he reordered the country's finances, boosted industry and commerce, and established the French navy as one of the most formidable in Europe; in New France he established the position of Intendant as an administrator responsible for colonial commerce, finance, and police (1663).

Col·borne /ˈkoʊlbərn/ **Sir John, 1st Baron Sea·ton** (1778–1863), English army officer and colonial administrator. He served as Lieutenant-Governor of Upper Canada (1828–36), commander of British forces (1836–7), during which he suppressed the Rebellion of 1837 in Lower Canada, and Governor General of British North America (1838–39).

colby /ˈkoʊlbi/ *noun* a mild, soft-textured cheese resembling cheddar. [*Colby*, Wisconsin, where it was first made]

col·can·non /kɒlˈkanən/ *noun* **1** an Irish and Scottish dish of cabbage and potatoes boiled and pounded. **2** *Cdn* (*Nfld*) a dish of various vegetables, usu. including cabbage, traditionally eaten on Halloween. [Gaelic *cal ceannan*, lit. 'white-headed cabbage', from Latin *caulis* 'cabbage' + Old Irish *ceann* 'head']

Col·ches·ter /ˈkoʊltʃɛstər/ a town in Essex, E England; pop. (est. 2002) 100,000. A prominent town in Roman Britain, Colchester is noted for its Roman ruins.

col·chi·cine /ˈkɒltʃəˌsiːn, ˈkɒlkə-/ *noun* a yellow alkaloid obtained from colchicum, used in the treatment of gout.

col·chi·cum /ˈkɒltʃɪkəm, ˈkɒlki-/ *noun* any liliaceous plant of the genus *Colchicum*, esp. meadow saffron. *Also called* AUTUMN CROCUS. **2** its dried corm or seed. [Latin from Greek *kolkhikon* of COLCHIS]

Col·chis /ˈkɒlkɪs/ an ancient region south of the Caucasus mountains at the east end of the Black Sea. In classical mythology it was the goal of Jason's expedition for the Golden Fleece.

cold ● *adjective* **1** of or at a low or relatively low temperature. **2** not heated; cooled after being heated. **3** (of a person) feeling cold. **4** lacking ardour, friendliness, or affection; undemonstrative, apathetic. **5** depressing, dispiriting, uninteresting (*cold facts*). **6 a** dead. **b** *informal* unconscious. **7** *informal* at one's mercy (*had me cold*). **8** sexually frigid. **9** (of soil) slow to absorb heat. **10** *N Amer. Sport* not performing well. **11** (of a scent in hunting) having become weak. **12** (in guessing games) far from finding or guessing what is wanted. **13** without preparation or rehearsal. ● *noun* **1 a** the prevalence of a low temperature, esp. in the atmosphere. **b** cold weather; a cold environment (*went out into the cold*). **2** an infection in which the mucous membrane of the nose and throat becomes inflamed, causing runny nose, sneezing, sore throat, coughing, etc. ● *adverb* **1** completely, entirely (*was stopped cold; cold sober*). **2** unrehearsed, without preparation. □ **cold (hard) cash** cash, esp. in large quantities and as opposed to credit. **in cold blood** without feeling or passion; deliberately, ruthlessly. **out in the cold** ignored, neglected. **throw** (or **pour**) **cold water on** be discouraging or depreciatory about. □ **cold·ish** *adjective* **cold·ly** *adverb* **cold·ness** *noun* [Old English *cald* from Germanic, related to Latin *gelu* frost]

cold-blooded *adjective* **1** having a body temperature varying with that of the environment (e.g. of fish); poikilothermic. **2** callous; deliberately cruel. □ **cold-blooded·ly** *adverb* **cold-blooded·ness** *noun*

cold call *noun* an unsolicited sales call to a prospective customer by telephone or in person. □ **cold-call** *transitive & intransitive verb* **cold calling** *noun*

cold case *noun* a police investigation that is unsolved after some time.

cold chisel *noun* a steel chisel suitable for cutting unheated metal.

cold-cock *transitive verb* N *Amer. slang* punch or strike (a person) in the head, esp. to render unconscious.

cold comfort *noun* poor or inadequate consolation.

cold cream *noun* a cream for removing makeup and dirt from the skin, esp. of the face and neck.

cold cuts *plural noun* slices of cold cooked meats.

cold dark matter *noun see* DARK MATTER.

cold deck *noun* N *Amer. Forestry* a pile of logs intended to be moved or processed at a later time.

cold draw *noun* Curling a shot in which a rock is curled into the house without touching another rock.

cold feet *plural noun* informal loss of nerve or confidence.

cold fish *noun* informal a person, little moved by emotions, regarded as hard and unfeeling.

cold frame *noun* a box-shaped frame with a glass top, placed over small plants to protect them from the weather.

cold front *noun* the forward edge of an advancing mass of cold air.

cold fusion *noun* a form of nuclear fusion hypothetically occurring at a much lower temperature than is usually required, esp. as a possible energy source. Claims for its discovery in 1989 are generally held to have been mistaken.

cold-hearted *adjective* lacking affection or warmth; unfriendly. □ **cold-hearted·ly** *adverb* **cold-hearted·ness** *noun*

Cold Lake 1 a lake straddling the border between Alberta and Saskatchewan, situated northeast of Edmonton. **2** a town on its southwestern shore, in east central Alberta; pop. (2001) 11,520. [so called because of the lake's year-round low temperatures]

cold one *noun* N *Amer. slang* a cold beer.

cold-pressed *adjective* (of an oil) obtained by pressing the olives, nuts, etc. without the addition of heat. □ **cold-pressing** *noun*

cold-rolled *adjective* (of steel) flattened into sheets at room temperature.

cold room *noun* a room kept at a cold temperature, esp. for storage of food.

cold shoulder ● *noun* a show of intentional unfriendliness. ● *transitive verb* (**cold-shoulder**) be deliberately unfriendly to.

cold snap *noun* (also **cold spell**) a sudden brief spell of cold weather.

cold sore *noun* inflammation and blisters in and around the mouth, caused by a virus infection.

cold squad *noun* a team of police officers who attempt to solve cold cases.

cold storage *noun* **1** storage in a refrigerator or other cold place for preservation. **2** a state in which something (esp. an idea) is put aside temporarily.

Cold·stream a district municipality in south central BC, southeast of Kamloops; pop. (2001) 9,106. [the name of a ranch, after the cold springs that rise on the creek nearby]

cold sweat *noun* a state of sweating induced by fear or illness.

cold turkey *informal* ● *noun* **1** abrupt withdrawal from addictive drugs. **2** the symptoms of this. ● *adverb* abruptly. □ **go cold turkey** cease (esp. an addictive habit) completely and abruptly.

cold war *noun* **1** a state of prolonged hostility between nations short of armed conflict, often consisting of threats, violent propaganda, and subversive political activities. **2** (**Cold War**) relations of this nature between the Soviet Union and the US and their respective allies in the decades following the Second World War. □ **Cold Warrior** *noun*

cold-water *adjective* (of a dwelling) equipped with cold running water but without central heat.

cold wave *noun* **1** a temporary spell of cold weather over a wide area. **2** a kind of permanent wave for the hair using chemicals and without heat.

Cold·well, Major James Wil·liam ('M.J.') (1888–1974), English-born Canadian educator and politician. A Saskatchewan teacher, he became involved in various farm and labour political organizations in the 1920s and 1930s, helped to found the Co-operative Commonwealth Federation, and succeeded J.S. Woodsworth as leader of the party (1942–60).

Cole ▸ 1 Holly (b.1963), Canadian jazz singer, known for her husky contralto voice, one of the best-selling Canadian jazz artists ever. **2 Nat King** (born Nathaniel Adams) (1917–65), US singer, pianist, and actor. He was known for his relaxed style of ballad singing, and his most popular songs include 'Straighten Up and Fly Right' (1943), 'Mona Lisa' (1950), and 'Unforgettable' (1953).

cole *noun* any of various brassicas, esp. cabbage or rape. [Old Norse *kál* from Latin *caulis* stem, cabbage]

Cole·man, Or·nette (b.1930), US jazz saxophonist, trumpeter, violinist, and composer, known for his development of improvisational 'free jazz' during the late 1950s and early 1960s.

Coleman lamp *noun* (also **Coleman lantern**) N *Amer. proprietary* a portable lantern used esp. for camping, usu. fuelled by naphtha.

Cole·man stove *noun* N *Amer. proprietary* a camp stove.

col·eop·ter·an /ˌkɒliˈɒptərən, ˌkɒli-/ ● *noun* any insect of the order Coleoptera, comprising the beetles and weevils, with front wings modified into sheaths to protect the hindwings, and biting mouthparts. ● *adjective* of or pertaining to the order Coleoptera. □ **col·eop·ter·ist** *noun* **col·eop·ter·ous** *adjective* [modern Latin *Coleoptera* from Greek *koleopteros* from *koleon* sheath + *pteron* wing]

col·eop·tile /ˌkɒliˈɒptail/ *noun* Bot. a hollow organ enclosing the first leaf of a germinating cereal grain. [Greek *koleon* sheath + *ptilon* feather]

Cole·ridge /ˈkoːləˌrɪdʒ/ **Sam·uel Tay·lor** (1772–1834), English poet and critic. His poetry collection *Lyrical Ballads* (1798), co-written with William Wordsworth, marked the beginnings of English Romanticism; his poems include 'The Rime of the Ancient Mariner' (1798), the ballad 'Christabel' (1816) and the opium fantasy 'Kubla Khan' (1816).

Coles, George (1810–75), Canadian politician, premier of PEI 1851–68, Father of Confederation. As leader of the opposition he attended the Quebec Conference (1864), but spoke against PEI joining Confederation, which it did not do until 1873.

cole·slaw *noun* a salad of shredded raw cabbage with a dressing and often other vegetables, esp. carrots. [Dutch *koolsla*: see COLE, SLAW]

Col·ette /kɒˈlet/ (born Sidonie Gabrielle Colette) (1873–1954), French novelist. Her *Claudine* series (1900–3) was published by her husband, the novelist Henri Gauthier-Villars, who caused a scandal by inserting erotic passages; her other novels include *Chéri* (1920) and *La Fin de Chéri* (1926).

co·leus /ˈkoːliəs/ *noun* (pl. **co·leus·es**) any plant of the genus *Coleus*, having variegated coloured leaves, frequently cultivated in gardens and as a houseplant. [modern Latin from Greek *koleon* sheath]

col·ic /ˈkɒlɪk/ *noun* **1** severe spasmodic abdominal pain caused by wind or obstruction in the intestines. **2** a condition in young babies characterized by long, loud crying. □ **col·icky** *adjective* [French *colique* from Late Latin *colicus*]

coli·form /ˈkɒləfɔrm/ ● *adjective* of or pertaining to a group of bacteria typified by *Escherichia coli*, which inhabit the large intestine of humans and animals and when present in water indicate fecal contamination. ● *noun* a bacillus of this group. [modern Latin *coli* 'of the colon' + -FORM]

Co·ligny /ˈkɒliːnjiː/ **Gas·pard de** (1519–1572), French admiral, soldier, and Huguenot leader, who was killed in the massacre on St. Bartholomew's Day (August 24, 1572).

Co·li·ma /kɒˈliːmə/ **1** a state of SW Mexico, on the Pacific coast. **2** the capital city of this state; pop. (2000) 119,600.

coli·seum /ˌkɒləˈsiːəm/ *noun* a large amphitheatre, sports stadium, arena, etc. [medieval Latin *colosseum*, neuter of *colosseus* gigantic (as COLOSSUS)]

col·itis /kəˈlaitɪs/ *noun* inflammation of the lining of the colon.

Coll /kɒl/ an island in the Inner Hebrides, west of Scotland.

coll. *abbreviation* **1** college. **2** collection.

col·lab·or·ate /kəˈlabəˌreɪt/ *intransitive verb* (often foll. by *with*) **1** work jointly, esp. in a literary or artistic production. **2** co-operate traitorously with an enemy. □ **col·lab·or·a·tion** *noun* **col·lab·or·a·tion·ist** *noun & adjective* **col·lab·or·a·tive** /-rətɪv/ *adjective* **col·lab·or·a·tive·ly** *adverb* **col·lab·or·a·tor** *noun* [Latin *collaborare collaborat-* (as COM-, *laborare* work)]

col·lage /kəˈlɒʒ/ ● *noun* **1 a** a form of art in which various materials (e.g. photographs, pieces of paper or cloth) are arranged and assembled or glued to a backing. **b** a work of art done in this way. **2** a literary, musical, or cinematic work involving the juxtaposition of several genres or elements. **3** a collection of unrelated things. ● *transitive verb* (**col·laged**, **col·la·ging**) arrange in a collage. □ **col·la·gist** *noun* [French, = gluing]

col·la·gen /ˈkɒlədʒən/ *noun* a protein found in animal connective tissue which provides support and resiliency, used in injectable form in plastic surgery to eliminate wrinkles and scars, augment lip size, etc. [French *collagène* from Greek *kolla* glue + *-gène* = -GEN]

col·lapse /kəˈlaps/ ● *noun* **1** the tumbling down or falling in of a structure or hollow body; caving in. **2** a sudden failure or breakdown of a plan, undertaking, organization, etc. **3** a physical or mental breakdown. ● *verb* **1 a** *intransitive* undergo or experience a collapse. **b** *transitive* cause to collapse. **2** *intransitive informal* sit or lie down and relax, esp. after prolonged effort (*collapsed into a chair*). **3 a** *intransitive* (of furniture etc.) be foldable and capable of storage in a small space. **b** *transitive* fold (furniture) in this way. □ **col·laps·ible** *adjective* [Latin *collapsus* past participle of *collabi* (as COM-, *labi* slip)]

col·lar ● *noun* **1** the part of a shirt, dress, coat, etc., that goes around the neck, either upright or folded over. **2 a** a band of linen, lace, or other material encircling the neck or forming the upper part of a garment. **b** = CLERICAL COLLAR. **c** a band worn around the neck for a specific purpose (*flea collar; cervical collar*). **3** a band put around the neck of a dog or other animal, esp. in order to control or identify it. **4** a band or ring fastened over a pipe, rod, etc. in order to restrain or connect. **5** a strip of paper, foil, etc. fastened around the rim of a casserole or esp. soufflé dish. **6** a coloured marking resembling a collar around the neck of a bird or animal. **7** a thickly padded part of a harness that goes over the horse's shoulders. **8** *Cdn (Nfld)* a rope or chain with a looped end used to moor a boat. **9** *Brit.* a piece of meat rolled up and tied. ● *transitive verb* **1** seize (a person) by the collar or neck. **2** furnish with a collar. **3** capture, apprehend, arrest. **4** *informal* accost and detain (a reluctant listener etc.). □ **hot under the collar** see HOT. **on (the) collar** *Cdn (Nfld)* (of a boat) moored. □ **col·lared** *adjective* (also in *combination*). **collar·less** *adjective* [Anglo-French *coler* from Latin *collare* from *collum* neck]

collar beam *noun* a horizontal beam connecting two rafters and forming with them an A-shaped roof truss.

collar·bone *noun* either of the two curved bones joining the breastbone and the shoulder blade. Also called CLAVICLE.

col·lard /ˈkɒlərd/ *noun* (also **col·lards**, **collard greens**) *N Amer.* a variety of cabbage without a distinct heart. [reduced form of *colewort*, from COLE + WORT]

col·lared lem·ming *noun* a tailless lemming of the tundra, whose coat turns white in winter.

col·late /ˈkoːleɪt, kəˈleɪt, ˈkɒ-/ *transitive verb* **1** sort or arrange (pages) in the correct order. **2** (in bookbinding) verify the order of (sheets) by their signatures. **3** analyze and compare (texts, statements, etc.) to identify points of agreement and difference. **4** assemble from different sources. **5** (often foll. by *to*) *Christianity* appoint (a clergyman) to a benefice. □ **col·la·tor** *noun* [Latin *collat-* past participle stem of *conferre* compare]

col·lat·er·al /kəˈlatərəl/ ● *noun* **1** security pledged as a guarantee for repayment of a loan. **2** a person having the same ancestry as another but by a different line. ● *adjective* **1** descended from the same ancestors but by a different line. **2** side by side; parallel. **3 a** additional but subordinate. **b** contributory; corroborating. **c** connected but aside from the main subject, course, etc. □ **col·lat·er·al·ize** (also esp. *Brit.* **-ise**) *transitive verb* **col·lat·er·al·ly** *adverb* [medieval Latin *collateralis* (as COM-, LATERAL)]

collateral damage *noun* destruction or injury to civilians as the unintended or unexpected result of a military attack.

col·la·tion /koːˈleɪʃən, kə-, ˈkɒ-/ *noun* **1** the act or an instance of collating. **2** a light informal meal. [Old French from Latin *collatio -onis* (see COLLATE)]

col·league /ˈkɒliːɡ/ *noun* a person with whom one works, esp. in a

profession or business. [French *collègue* from Latin *collega* (as COM-, *legare* depute)]

col·lect¹ ● *verb* **1** *transitive & intransitive* bring or come together; assemble, accumulate. **2** *transitive* systematically seek and acquire (e.g. books, stamps, coins) as a continuing hobby. **3 a** *transitive* demand or obtain (taxes, contributions, payment due, etc.) from a person or persons. **b** *intransitive* (often foll. by *on*) receive a payment. **4** *transitive* come for and take away (*collected her belongings before leaving; garbage is collected once a week*). **5 a** *reflexive* regain control of oneself esp. after a shock. **b** *transitive* concentrate (one's energies, thoughts, etc.). **6** *transitive* receive (an award, prize, etc.) (*collected 14 of 20 nominations*). ● *adjective & adverb N Amer.* (of a telephone call, parcel, etc.) to be paid for by the recipient. [French *collecter* or medieval Latin *collectare* from Latin *collectus* past participle of *colligere* (as COM-, *legere* pick)]

col·lect² /ˈkɒlekt/ *noun* a short prayer of the Anglican and Roman Catholic Churches, esp. one assigned to a particular day or season. [Old French *collecte* from Latin *collecta* fem. past participle of *colligere*: see COLLECT¹]

col·lect·ed *adjective* **1** calm and cool; not perturbed or distracted. **2** (esp. of literary works) gathered together in one place or publication. □ **col·lect·ed·ly** *adverb*

col·lect·ible (also esp. *Brit.* **col·lect·able**) ● *adjective* **1** worth collecting. **2** able to be collected. ● *noun* an item sought by collectors. □ **col·lect·ibil·ity** *noun* (also **col·lect·abil·ity**).

col·lec·tion *noun* **1** the act or process of collecting or being collected. **2** any group of things systematically assembled, esp.: **a** specimens or collectibles acquired by a specialist or hobbyist (*coin collection*). **b** the holdings of a museum, library, etc. **c** a book of short stories, poems, or essays, or a recording including several songs or compositions. **d** a line of fashionable clothes, cosmetics, furniture etc. offered by a designer or retail store. **3** (foll. by *of*) an accumulation; a mass or pile (*a collection of dust*). **4 a** the collecting of money, esp. in church or for a charitable cause. **b** the amount collected. **5** the regular removal of mail, garbage, etc. for dispatch or disposal.

collection agency *noun* a company hired by another to collect accounts receivable from customers who are slow to pay.

col·lect·ive ● *adjective* **1** formed by or constituting a collection. **2** taken as a whole; aggregate (*our collective opinion*). **3** of or from several or many individuals; common (*collective consciousness; collective memory*). **4** of or pertaining to a union of workers (*collective bargaining*). ● *noun* **1 a** a co-operative enterprise. **b** its members. **c** = COLLECTIVE FARM. **2** = COLLECTIVE NOUN. □ **col·lect·ive·ly** *adverb* **col·lect·ive·ness** *noun*

collective agreement *noun* an agreement between a union and an employer arrived at through collective bargaining.

collective bargaining *noun* the process by which wages, terms of employment, etc. for all members of a bargaining unit are negotiated between the union and an employer.

collective farm *noun* (in communist countries) the state-owned holdings of several farmers run as a joint enterprise.

collective memory *noun* the memory of a group of people, often passed from one generation to the next.

collective noun *noun Grammar* a noun that is grammatically singular and denotes a collection or number of individuals (e.g. *assembly, family, troop*).

collective ownership *noun* the ownership of land and means of production by a number of people for their common benefit.

collective unconscious *noun Psych.* (in Jungian theory) the part of the unconscious mind derived from ancestral memory and experience common to all mankind, as distinct from the personal unconscious.

col·lec·tiv·ism *noun* the theory and practice of the collective ownership of land and the means of production. □ **col·lec·tiv·ist** *noun* **col·lec·tiv·is·tic** *adjective*

col·lec·tiv·ity *noun* **1** a group or community of people bound together by common beliefs or interests. **2** collective quality.

col·lec·tiv·ize *transitive verb* (also esp. *Brit.* **-ise**) organize on the basis of collective ownership. □ **col·lec·tiv·iz·a·tion** *noun*

col·lect·or *noun* **1** a person who collects, esp. things of interest as a hobby. **2** a person who collects due payments etc. (*tax collector; ticket collector*). **3** a thing that collects, esp. solar energy or heat. **4** *Electronics* the region in a transistor that absorbs charge carriers. **5** *Cdn* a lane running parallel to the express lanes of a freeway affording access between it and other roads. **6** *Cdn (Nfld)* (in full **collector boat**) a boat which gathers catches of cod from several locations and transports them to a single location for processing.

collector's item *noun* a valuable object, esp. one of interest to collectors.

col·leen *noun* an Irish girl. [Irish *cailín*, diminutive of *caile* country woman]

col·lege *noun* **1** an establishment for further or higher education: **a** an institution within a university, usu. with residence facilities and curricular autonomy but without degree-granting privileges. **b** a faculty within a university. **c** a school for specialized professional education (*business college*). **d** = COMMUNITY COLLEGE. **e** *Cdn* = CEGEP. **f** *N Amer.* post-secondary education in general (*our daughter is saving for college*). **g** (in the US) a post-secondary institution offering a liberal education and granting bachelor's degrees. **h** *Brit.* a private secondary school. **2** the buildings or premises of a college. **3** the students and teachers in a college. **4** an organized body of persons with shared functions and privileges (*College of Physicians; a college of electors*). □ **give a thing the (old) college try** *N Amer.* put forth one's best effort despite the unlikelihood of success. [Old French *college* or Latin *collegium* from *collega* (as COLLEAGUE)]

col·lège clas·sique /kɒˈleʒ klaˈsiːk/ *noun* (*pl.* **col·lèges clas·siques**) *Cdn hist.* (in Quebec) a private school offering a four-year secondary education and a four-year post-secondary program leading to a BA, with the curriculum emphasizing classics, literature, philosophy, and religion. [French, lit. 'classical college']

College of Arms *noun* (in the UK) a corporation recording lineage and granting arms.

College of Cardinals *noun* a body comprising all the cardinals of the Roman Catholic Church, which elects and advises the Pope.

college of education *noun* (esp. in proper names) a training college for schoolteachers.

col·legial /kəˈliːdʒəl, -dʒiəl/ *adjective* **1** characterized by collaboration among colleagues. **2** pertaining to or involving a body of colleagues. **3** of or pertaining to a college. □ **col·legi·al·ity** /kəliːdʒiˈaliti/ *noun* **col·legial·ly** *adverb*

col·legian /kəˈliːdʒən/ *noun* a member of a college.

col·legi·ate /kəˈliːdʒət/ ● *adjective* **1** of or pertaining to colleges or universities (*collegiate sports*). **2** constituted of or belonging to colleges. ● *noun* *Cdn* = COLLEGIATE INSTITUTE. [Late Latin *collegiatus* (as COLLEGE)]

collegiate and vocational institute *noun* *Cdn* (in Ontario) a public secondary school, originally one having academic, vocational, and commercial streams. Abbr.: **CVI**.

collegiate church *noun* **1** a Catholic or Anglican church endowed for a chapter of canons but without a bishop's see. **2** (in the US) one of an association of churches presided over by a joint pastorate. **3** (in Scotland) a church presided over by two or more ministers.

collegiate institute *noun* *Cdn* (in some provinces) a public secondary school, originally one having specialist teachers and a prescribed classical curriculum. Abbr.: **CI**.

col·len·chyma /kɒˈleŋkɪmə/ *noun Bot.* a tissue strengthened by the thickening of cell walls, as in young shoots. [Greek *kolla* glue + *egkhuma* infusion]

col·let /ˈkɒlət/ *noun* **1** a slit sleeve with an external taper which is placed over a shaft and designed to tighten and grip it when pushed into an internally tapered socket. **2** a setting designed to hold a gem in jewellery. [French, diminutive of COL]

col·lide /kəˈlaɪd/ *intransitive verb* (often foll. by *with*) **1** strike together with an abrupt or violent impact. **2** be in conflict. [Latin *collidere collis-* (as COM-, *laedere* strike, damage)]

col·lid·er /kəˈlaɪdər/ *noun Physics* a particle accelerator emitting beams of particles which are made to collide.

col·lie /ˈkɒli, ˈkɔːli/ *noun* a sheepdog of a breed originating in Scotland, with a long pointed nose and usu. dense long hair. [perhaps from *coll* COAL (as being originally black)]

col·lier /ˈkɒliər/ *noun* **1** a coal miner. **2 a** a ship transporting coal. **b** a member of its crew. [Middle English, from COAL + -IER]

col·liery /ˈkɒliəri/ *noun* (*pl.* **-ies**) a coal mine and its associated buildings.

col·li·mate /ˈkɒliˌmeɪt/ *transitive verb* **1** adjust the line of sight of (a telescope etc.). **2** make (telescopes or rays) accurately parallel. □ **col·li·ma·tion** *noun* [Latin *collimare*, erroneous for *collineare* align (as COM-, *linea* line)]

col·li·ma·tor /ˈkɒləˌmeɪtər/ *noun* **1** a device for producing a parallel beam of rays or radiation. **2** a small fixed telescope used for adjusting the line of sight of an astronomical telescope, etc.

col·linear /kəˈlɪniər, kɔː-/ *adjective Geom.* (of points) lying in the same straight line. □ **col·linear·ity** /-ˈɛrɪti/ *noun*

Col·ling·wood a town in south central Ontario, on Nottawasaga Bay; pop. (2001) 16,039. [Baron *Collingwood*, British admiral d.1810]

Col·lins[1] ▸ **1** Joan (Hen·ri·etta) (b.1933), English actress. She established a reputation as a sex symbol in the 1950s in films such as *Our Girl Friday* (1953), and has since appeared in both television and film. **2 Mi·chael** (1890–1922), Irish nationalist leader and politician. Elected to Parliament as a member of Sinn Fein in 1919, he directed the IRA's guerrilla campaign against the British, and was one of the negotiators of the Anglo-Irish treaty of 1921; appointed head of state in 1922, he was assassinated ten days later. **3 (Wil·liam) Wil·kie** (1824–89), English writer of detective fiction, known for the first full-length detective stories in English, notably *The Woman in White* (1860) and *The Moonstone* (1868).

Col·lins[2] *noun* an iced drink made of gin or whisky etc. with soda water, lemon or lime juice, and sugar. [20th c.: origin unknown]

Col·lip /ˈkɒlɪp/ **James Ber·tram** ('Bert') (1892–1965), Canadian biochemist and medical researcher, who was a co-discoverer of insulin with Banting, Best, and J. J. R. Macleod.

col·li·sion /kəˈlɪʒən/ *noun* **1** a violent impact of a moving body, esp. a vehicle, with another or with a fixed object. **2** the clashing of opposed interests or considerations. **3** *Physics* the action of particles striking or coming together. □ **col·li·sion·al** *adjective* [Late Latin *collisio* (as COLLIDE)]

collision course *noun* a course or action that is bound to cause a collision or conflict.

col·lo·cate /ˈkɒləˌkeɪt/ *verb* **1** *transitive* place together or side by side. **2** *transitive* arrange; set in a particular place. **3** *intransitive & transitive* (often foll. by *with*) *Linguistics* (of a word) habitually associate with another ('*miracle' collocates with 'worker'*). [Latin *collocare collocat-* (as COM-, *locare* to place)]

col·lo·ca·tion /ˌkɒləˈkeɪʃən/ *noun* **1** the action of collocating or state of being collocated. **2** *Linguistics* **a** the (esp. habitual) juxtaposition or association of a particular word with other particular words. **b** the words so juxtaposed or associated.

col·lo·dion /kəˈloʊdiən/ *noun* a syrupy solution of pyroxylin in a mixture of alcohol and ether, used in photography and surgery to form a thin flexible film. [Greek *kollōdēs* glue-like, from *kolla* glue]

col·loid /ˈkɒlɔɪd/ *noun* **1** *Chem.* **a** a substance consisting of ultramicroscopic particles. **b** a mixture of such a substance uniformly dispersed through a second substance esp. to form a viscous solution. **2** *Physiol.* a gelatinous substance in the body, esp. present in the thyroid gland or in diseased tissue. □ **col·loid·al** *adjective* [Greek *kolla* glue + -OID]

col·lop /ˈkɒləp/ *noun* a slice of meat. [Middle English, original sense 'bacon and eggs'; compare Old Swedish *kolluppadher* roasted on coals, Swedish *kalops* stewed meat]

col·lo·qui·al /kəˈloʊkwiəl/ *adjective* belonging to or proper to ordinary or familiar conversation, not formal or literary. ¶ *Colloquial* is often understood to mean 'incorrect' or 'vulgar' but in fact it designates words or usages appropriate to a familiar or informal, rather than a formal style of speech or writing. □ **col·lo·qui·al·ly** *adverb* [Latin *colloquium* COLLOQUY]

col·lo·qui·al·ism /kəˈloʊkwiəˌlɪzəm/ *noun* **1** a colloquial word or phrase. **2** the use of colloquialisms.

col·lo·qui·um /kəˈloʊkwiəm/ *noun* (*pl.* **col·lo·quia** /-kwiə/) an academic conference focused on a specific topic. [Latin: see COLLOQUY]

col·lo·quy /ˈkɒləkwi/ *noun* (*pl.* **-quies**) **1** the act of conversing. **2** a conversation. [Latin *colloquium* (as COM-, *loqui* speak)]

col·lo·type /ˈkɒləˌtaɪp/ *noun Printing* **1** a thin sheet of gelatin exposed to light, treated with reagents, and used to make high-quality prints by lithography. **2** a print made by this process. [Greek *kolla* glue + TYPE]

col·lude /kəˈluːd/ *intransitive verb* conspire together for a fraudulent or underhanded purpose; connive, plot. □ **col·lud·er** *noun* [Latin *colludere collus-* (as COM-, *ludere lus-* play)]

col·lu·sion /kəˈluːʒən/ *noun* **1** a secret agreement, esp. for a fraudulent purpose. **2** *Law* such an agreement between ostensible opponents in a lawsuit. □ **col·lu·sive** *adjective*

colly·wobbles /ˈkɒliˌwɒbəlz/ *plural noun informal* **1** a rumbling or pain in the stomach. **2** a feeling of strong apprehension. [fanciful, from COLIC + WOBBLE]

Colo. *abbreviation* Colorado.

colo·bus /ˈkɒləbəs/ *noun* any leaf-eating monkey of the genus *Colobus*, native to Africa, having shortened thumbs. [modern Latin from Greek *kolobos* docked]

---

uː **mood**   aı **my**   əɪ **pipe**   aʊ **brown**   ʌʊ **house**   eı **day**   ɔı **boy**   ɑ̃ **franglais**   ã **Canadien**   ɔ̃ **Brayon**   (*see over for consonants*)

co·locate *transitive verb* share a location or facility with something else. □ **co·lo·ca·tion** *noun*

colo·cynth /ˈkɒləsɪnθ/ *noun* **1 a** a plant of the gourd family, *Citrullus colocynthis*, bearing a pulpy fruit. **b** this fruit. *Also called* BITTER APPLE. **2** a bitter purgative drug obtained from the fruit. [Latin *colocynthis* from Greek *kolokunthis*]

Co·logne /kəˈloːn/ an industrial and university city in western Germany, in North Rhine-Westphalia; pop. (est. 2002) 966,800.

co·logne /kəˈloːn/ *noun* a dilute solution of alcohol and a concentrate of perfume. [abbreviation of EAU DE COLOGNE]

Co·lom·bia /kəˈlʌmbiə/ a country in the extreme northwest of S America, having a coastline on both the Atlantic and the Pacific Ocean; pop. (est. 2002) 41,008,227; capital, Bogotá. □ **Co·lom·bian** *adjective & noun*

Co·lom·bo /kəˈlʌmboː/ the capital and chief port of Sri Lanka; pop. (2001) 642,000.

Colón /kɒˈlɒn/ the chief port of Panama, at the Caribbean end of the Panama Canal; pop. (2000) 42,100. [Spanish form of the surname COLUMBUS]

co·lon[1] /ˈkoːlən/ *noun* a punctuation mark (:) with several uses: **1** to introduce a quotation or a list of items. **2** to separate clauses when the second expands or illustrates the first. **3** between numbers in a statement of proportion (*odds of 10:1*). **4** to separate hour from minutes in rendering the time (*9:30 in the morning*). **5** in Biblical references to separate chapter and verse (*John 3:16*). [Latin from Greek *kōlon* limb, clause]

co·lon[2] /ˈkoːlən/ *noun Anat.* the lower and greater part of the large intestine, from the cecum to the rectum. □ **col·onic** /kəˈlɒnɪk/ *adjective* [Middle English, ultimately from Greek *kolon*]

colón /kɒˈlɒn/ *noun* (*pl.* **colon·es** /-ˈlɒnez/) the basic monetary unit of Costa Rica and El Salvador, equal to 100 centimos in Costa Rica and 100 centavos in El Salvador. [*Colón*, Spanish form of the name *Columbus*: see COLUMBUS]

col·onel /ˈkɜrnəl/ *noun* **1** (also **Colonel**) **a** (in Canada and the US) an officer in the armed forces ranking above a lieutenant colonel and below a brigadier general. Abbr.: **Col** *Cdn* or **Col. b** a lieutenant colonel. **2** (also **Colonel**) (in the UK and *hist.* in the Canadian Army) an officer in the army ranking above a lieutenant colonel and below a brigadier. □ **col·onel·cy** *noun* (*pl.* **-cies**). [obsolete French *coronel* from Italian *colonnello* from *colonna* COLUMN]

Colonel Blimp *noun* see BLIMP *noun* 2.

col·oni·al /kəˈloːniəl/ ● *adjective* **1 a** of, relating to, or characteristic of a colony or colonies. **b** (of mentalities, attitudes etc.) typical of people living in a colony or former colony, esp. in their dependence on and admiration for the mother country or other dominant culture. **2** of or relating to the period of a nation's history during which it was under the rule of a mother country. **3** of or relating to the Thirteen Colonies. **4** (of architecture or furniture) built, designed in, or in a style characteristic of a colonial period. **5** (of plants or animals) living in colonies. ● *noun* **1** a person inhabiting a colony. **2** a house built in colonial style. □ **col·oni·al·ly** *adverb*

col·oni·al·ism /kəˈloːniəˌlɪzəm/ *noun* **1** a policy of acquiring or maintaining colonies. **2** the exploitation or subjugation of a people by a larger or wealthier power. □ **col·oni·al·ist** *noun & adjective*

col·oni·al·ize /kəˈloːniəlaɪz/ *transitive verb* (also esp. *Brit.* **-ise**) make colonial, esp. in attitudes. □ **col·oni·al·iz·a·tion** *noun*

Colonial Office *noun hist.* the British government department in charge of colonies.

Colonial Secretary *noun hist.* the British government minister in charge of the Colonial Office.

colonic irrigation *noun* the application of water via the anus to flush out the colon.

col·onist /ˈkɒlənɪst/ *noun* a settler in or inhabitant of a colony.

colonist car *noun Cdn hist.* a railway car furnished with slatted wooden platforms for sitting or sleeping and equipped with a small stove.

col·onize /ˈkɒləˌnaɪz/ *verb* (also esp. *Brit.* **-onise**) **1** *transitive* **a** establish a colony or colonies in (a country or area). **b** settle as colonists. **2** *intransitive* establish or join a colony. **3** *transitive* (of one country, society, etc.) impose its culture on (another). **4** *transitive* (of plants, animals, and micro-organisms) become established (in an area). □ **col·oniz·a·tion** *noun* **col·oniz·er** *noun*

col·on·nade /ˌkɒləˈneɪd/ *noun* a row of columns, esp. supporting an entablature or roof. □ **col·on·nad·ed** *adjective* [French from *colonne* COLUMN]

colon·o·scope /kəˈlɒnəskoːp/ *noun Med.* an illuminated fibre optic tube introduced through the anus and used to examine the colon, remove polyps, or obtain tissue specimens. □ **colon·o·scop·ic** /kəˌlɒnəˈskɒpɪk/ *adjective* **colon·os·copy** /ˌkɒlənˈɒskəpi/ *noun*

col·ony /ˈkɒləni/ *noun* (*pl.* **-onies**) **1 a** a group of people who settle in a new territory (whether or not already inhabited) and form a community connected with a mother country. **b** the territory of such settlers. **2** any country or area subject to the colonial rule of another. **3** a group of people of common nationality, religion, or (esp. artistic) occupation inhabiting a particular area in a city. **4 a** a group which is segregated from a larger population, either freely or through expulsion (*nudist colony*; *penal colony*). **b** the territory occupied by such a group. **5** a community of Hutterites. **6** *Bot. & Zool.* a collection of plants or animals connected, in contact, or living close together. **7** *Biol.* a group of bacteria, yeasts, etc. that have developed from a single parent cell. [Latin *colonia* from *colonus* farmer, from *colere* cultivate]

colo·phon /ˈkɒlɔˌfɒn, -fən/ *noun* **1** a publisher's emblem or imprint, esp. on the title page of a book. **2** *hist.* a statement at the end of a manuscript or book giving information about its authorship and production. [Late Latin from Greek *kolophōn* summit, finishing touch]

col·or etc. *var.* of COLOUR etc.

Col·o·rado /ˌkɒləˈradoː/ a state in the western central US; pop. (2000) 4,301,261; capital, Denver. □ **Col·o·radan** *noun & adjective*

Colorado beetle *noun* (also **Colorado potato beetle**) a yellow and black striped beetle, *Leptinotarsa decemlineata*, the larva of which is highly destructive to the potato plant.

Colorado River a river which rises in the Rocky Mountains of N Colorado and flows generally southwestward for 2 333 km (1,468 miles) to the Gulf of California. Approximately 447 km (278 miles) of its course is through the Grand Canyon in Arizona.

Colorado spruce *noun* = BLUE SPRUCE.

color·a·tion *noun* (also **colour·a·tion**) **1** colouring; a scheme or method of applying colour. **2** the natural (esp. variegated) colour of living things or animals. [French *coloration* or Late Latin *coloratio* from *colorare* COLOUR]

colo·ra·tura /ˌkʌlərəˈtʊrə, -ˈtjʊrə, kɒl-/ *noun* **1** elaborate ornamentation of a vocal melody with runs and trills. **2** a singer (esp. a soprano) skilled in this method of singing. [Italian from Latin *colorare* COLOUR]

colo·rectal /ˌkoːloːˈrektəl/ *adjective Med.* pertaining to or affecting the colon and the rectum. [COLON[2] + RECTAL]

color·ific /ˌkʌləˈrɪfɪk/ *adjective* **1** producing colour. **2** highly coloured. [French *colorifique* or modern Latin *colorificus* (as COLOUR)]

color·im·eter /ˌkʌləˈrɪmətər/ *noun* an instrument for measuring the intensity of colour by comparison with a standard, used esp. to determine the concentration of a substance in solution. □ **color·im·et·ric** /-ˈmetrɪk/ *adjective* **color·im·et·ric·al·ly** *adverb* **color·im·etry** *noun* [Latin *color* COLOUR + -METER]

col·os·sal /kəˈlɒsəl/ *adjective* of immense size, scope, extent, or amount; huge, gigantic. □ **col·os·sal·ly** *adverb* [French from *colosse* COLOSSUS]

Col·os·seum /ˌkɒləˈsiːəm/ *noun* a large amphitheatre in Rome, begun by Vespasian *c.*75 AD.

Col·os·sians /kəˈlɒʃənz/ a book of the New Testament, an epistle of St. Paul to the Church at Colossae in Phrygia, Asia Minor.

col·os·sus /kəˈlɒsəs/ *noun* (*pl.* **col·os·si** /-saɪ/) **1** a gigantic person, animal, building, etc. **2** a statue much bigger than life-size. **3** an extremely powerful person, country, etc. [Latin from Greek *kolossos*]

col·os·tomy /kəˈlɒstəmi/ *noun* (*pl.* **-mies**) *Med.* an operation on the colon to make an opening in the abdominal wall to provide an artificial anus. [as COLON[2] + Greek *stoma* mouth]

col·os·trum /kəˈlɒstrəm/ *noun* the yellowish fluid secreted from the mammary glands in the first few days after giving birth, rich in protein and antibodies. [Latin]

col·our (also **color**) ● *noun* **1 a** the sensation produced on the eye by rays of light when resolved as by a prism, selective reflection, etc., into different wavelengths. **b** the perception of colour by the eye; a system of colours. **2** one, or any mixture, of the constituents into which light can be separated as in a spectrum or rainbow, sometimes including (loosely) black and white. **3** a colouring substance, e.g. a paint or pigment. **4** the use of all colours, not only black and white, in photography, motion pictures, and television. **5** *N Amer.* (also *attributive*: *colour commentary*; *colour analyst*) analysis, trivia, statistics, etc. provided by a sports broadcaster as a supplement to the play-by-play. **6 a** pigmentation of the skin, esp. as determined by race or ethnicity.

b a skin colour or race other than white (*people of colour*). **7** ruddiness of complexion (*a healthy colour*). **8** quality, mood, or variety in music, literature, speech, etc.; distinctive character or timbre. **9** (in *pl.*) appearance or aspect (*see things in their true colours*). **10** (in *pl.*) **a** a coloured ribbon or uniform etc. worn to signify membership in a particular school, club, team, or group. **b** the flag of a regiment or ship. **c** a national flag. **11** (in *pl.*) coloured clothing (*washed the colours separately*). **12** a show of reason; a pretext (*lend colour to; under colour of*). ● *verb* **1** *transitive & intransitive* apply colour to, esp. by painting or dyeing or with coloured pens or pencils. **2** *transitive* influence (*an attitude coloured by experience*). **3** *transitive* misrepresent, exaggerate, esp. with spurious detail (*a highly coloured account*). **4** *intransitive* take on colour; blush. □ **of colour** not Caucasian. **show one's true colours** reveal one's true character or intentions. **under false colours** falsely, deceitfully. **with flying colours** *see* FLYING. [Old French *color*, *colorer* from Latin *color*, *colorare*]

colour·able *adjective* (also **color·able**) apparently valid or true.

colour·ant *noun* (also **color·ant**) a colouring substance; pigment.

colour·a·tion *var. of* COLORATION.

colour bar *noun* = COLOUR LINE.

colour-blind *adjective* **1** unable to distinguish certain colours. **2** (of a company, group of people, project, etc.) characterized by or displaying freedom from racial bias. □ **colour-blindness** *noun*

colour code ● *noun* the use of colours as a standard means of identification. ● *transitive verb* (**colour-code**) identify by means of a colour code. □ **colour-coded** *adjective* **colour-coding** *noun*

col·oured (also **col·ored**) ● *adjective* **1** having colour(s). **2** (also **Coloured**) *offensive* **a** wholly or partly of non-white descent. **b** *South Africa* of mixed white and non-white descent. **c** of or relating to coloured people (*a coloured audience*). ● *noun* **1** (also **Coloured**) *offensive* **a** a coloured person. **b** *South Africa* a person of mixed descent speaking Afrikaans or English as the mother tongue. **2** (in *pl.*) = COLOUR *noun* 11.

colour·fast *adjective* (also **color·fast**) dyed in colours that will not fade or be washed out. □ **colour·fast·ness** *noun*

colour·ful *adjective* (also **color·ful**) **1** having much or varied colour; bright. **2** full of interest; vivid, lively. □ **colour·ful·ly** *adverb* **colour·ful·ness** *noun*

col·our·ing *noun* (also **col·or·ing**) **1** the act or process of using colour(s). **2** the style in which a thing (e.g. a painting) is coloured. **3 a** facial complexion. **b** natural colour (e.g. of a bird or animal). **4** an artificial colouring agent; a pigment. **5** false appearance; show.

colouring book *noun* a book of outline drawings to be coloured with crayons, pencil crayons, etc., usu. by children.

col·our·ist *noun* (also **col·or·ist**) **1** a person who uses colour, esp. with great skill. **2** a hairdresser who dyes or colours hair. □ **col·our·is·tic** *adjective*

col·our·ize *transitive verb* (also **col·or·ize**; esp. *Brit.* **-ise**) colour (a black and white film etc.) by means of a computer. □ **col·our·iz·a·tion** *noun*

colour·less *adjective* (also **color·less**) **1** without colour. **2** lacking character or interest. **3** dull or pale in hue. **4** neutral, impartial, indifferent. □ **colour·less·ly** *adverb*

colour line *noun* (also **colour bar**) legal, social, or occupational discrimination on the basis of colour.

colour of right *noun Cdn* the right of ownership of a thing.

colour scheme *noun* an arrangement or planned combination of colours, esp. in interior design.

colour sergeant *noun* a sergeant who carries one of the colours in an honour guard etc.

colour supplement *noun Brit.* a magazine with coloured illustrations, issued as a supplement to a newspaper.

colour wash ● *noun* coloured distemper. ● *transitive verb* (**colour-wash**) paint with coloured distemper.

colour·way *noun* (also **color·way**) a coordinated combination of colours; a colour scheme.

col·pos·copy /ˌkɒlˈpɒskəpi/ *noun* (*pl.* **-ies**) examination of the vagina and the neck of the uterus. □ **col·po·scope** *noun* [Greek *kolpos* womb + -SCOPY]

Colt, Sam·uel (1814–62), US inventor and manufacturer, who designed the first revolver (patented in 1835).

colt *noun* **1** a young uncastrated male horse, usu. less than four years old. **2** a young or inexperienced person. □ **colt·hood** *noun* **colt·ish** *adjective* **colt·ish·ly** *adverb* **colt·ish·ness** *noun* [Old English, = young ass or camel]

col·ter *var. of* COULTER.

Col·trane /ˈkoːltreɪn/ **John (Wil·liam)** (1926–67), US jazz saxophonist and composer. One of the most influential and successful figures in avant-garde jazz, he spanned the transition from the harmonically dense jazz of the 1950s to the evolving free jazz of the 1960s.

colts·foot *noun* (*pl.* **colts·foots**) a composite herbaceous plant, *Tussilago farfara*, with large leaves and yellow flowers. *See also* SWEET COLTSFOOT.

colu·brid /ˈkɒljuːbrɪd/ *Zool.* ● *adjective* of or relating to the large family Colubridae to which most non-venomous snakes belong. ● *noun* a snake of this family. [Latin *coluber* 'snake' + -ID³]

colu·brine /ˈkɒljuˌbraɪn/ *adjective* **1** snakelike. **2** of the subfamily Colubrinae of non-poisonous snakes. [Latin *colubrinus* from *coluber* snake]

Col·um·ba, St. /kəˈlʌmbə/ (*c.*521–97), Irish abbot and missionary. After founding several churches and monasteries in Ireland, he established a monastery at Iona (Scotland) in *c.*563, and successfully converted the Picts to Christianity. Feast day, 9 June.

col·um·bar·ium /ˌkɒləmˈbɛriəm/ *noun* a room or building with niches and shelves for cinerary urns to be stored. [Latin, = pigeon house (from *columba* 'pigeon')]

Col·um·bia /kəˈlʌmbiə/ the state capital of S Carolina; pop. (2000) 116,278.

Columbia, Cape /kəˈlʌmbiə/ a cape on the northern shore of Ellesmere Island, the most northerly point of land in Canada. [*Columbia*, a poetic name for America]

Columbia, District of *see* DISTRICT OF COLUMBIA.

Columbia, Mount a peak (3 747 m) in the Rocky Mountains, situated on the BC–Alberta border, at the southern end of Jasper National Park. [*see* COLUMBIA RIVER]

Columbia Mountains a mountainous area of southeastern BC, lying west of the Columbia River and comprising (from east to west) the Purcell, Selkirk and Monashee mountain ranges.

Columbia River a river in northwestern N America which rises in the Rocky Mountains of southeastern BC (north of Kimberley), and flows 2 000 km first northwestward, then generally southward through Revelstoke and Castlegar into the US, where it turns westward to form the Washington–Oregon border and enters the Pacific north of Portland. [the name of a ship captained by R. Gray, Boston trader]

Col·um·bine /ˈkɒləmˌbaɪn/ *noun* the partner of Harlequin in pantomime. [French *Colombine* from Italian *Colombina* from *colombino* dovelike]

col·um·bine /ˈkɒləmˌbaɪn/ *noun* any wild or cultivated plant of the genus *Aquilegia* with flowers said to resemble five clustered doves. *Also called* AQUILEGIA. [Old French *colombine* from medieval Latin *columbina herba* dovelike plant, from Latin *columba* dove]

col·um·bite /kəˈlʌmbaɪt/ *noun* an ore of iron and niobium. [*Columbia*, a poetic name for America, + -ITE¹]

col·um·bium /kəˈlʌmbiəm/ *noun* = NIOBIUM.

Col·um·bus¹ /kəˈlʌmbəs/ the state capital of Ohio; pop. (2000) 711,470.

Col·um·bus² /kəˈlʌmbəs/ **Chris·to·pher** (1451–1506), Italian-born Spanish explorer. He persuaded Ferdinand and Isabella of Spain to sponsor an expedition to sail westwards across the Atlantic in search of Asia; sailing with three small ships in 1492, he reached the New World (in fact various Caribbean islands), and made three further voyages between 1493 and 1504, discovering the S American mainland in 1498.

Columbus Day *noun* (in the US) a holiday commemorating the landing of Columbus in the West Indies on 12 Oct. 1492; observed on either 12 Oct. or the second Monday in October.

col·umn /ˈkɒləm/ *noun* **1** *Archit.* an upright cylindrical pillar often slightly tapering and usu. supporting an entablature or arch, or standing alone as a monument. **2** a structure or part shaped like a column. **3** a vertical cylindrical mass of liquid or vapour. **4 a** a vertical division of a page, chart, etc., containing a sequence of figures or words. **b** the figures or words themselves. **5** a part of a newspaper regularly devoted to a particular subject (*gossip column*). **6 a** *Military* an arrangement of troops in successive lines, with a narrow front. **b** *Naut.* a similar arrangement of ships. □ **col·um·nar** /kəˈlʌmnər/ *adjective* **col·umned** *adjective* [Old French *columpne* & Latin *columna* pillar]

column inch *noun* a quantity of print (esp. newsprint) occupying a one-inch length of a column.

col·um·nist /ˈkɒləmnɪst, -mɪst/ *noun* a journalist contributing a regular column to a newspaper, magazine, etc.

colure /kəˈlʊr/ *noun Astronomy* either of two great circles intersecting at right angles at the celestial poles and passing through the ecliptic at either the equinoxes or the solstices. [Late Latin *colurus* from Greek *kolouros* truncated]

Col·vile /'koːlvɪl/ **Eden** (1819–93), English administrator, who served as deputy governor (1872–80) and governor (1880–89) of Rupert's Land.

Col·vile /'koːlvɪl/ **Alex·an·der** (b.1920), Canadian painter. His realist paintings, with their hazy, sensual texture and meticulous, detailed brushwork, depict people and animals isolated in a frozen moment; they include *Hound in Field* (1958) and *Horse and Train* (1959).

Col·wood /'kɒlwʊd/ a city in BC, located at the southern tip of Vancouver Island, just west of Victoria; pop. (2001) 13,745. [the name of a farm belonging to the Puget Sound Agricultural Company, after a property in Sussex, England]

colza /'kɒlzə/ *noun* = RAPE². [French *kolza(t)* from Low German *kōlsāt* (as COLE, SEED)]

COM *abbreviation* computer output on microfilm or microfiche.

com- *prefix* (also **co-, col-, con-, cor-**) with, together, jointly, altogether. ¶ *com-* is used before *b, m, p,* and occas. before vowels and *f; co-* esp. before vowels, *h,* and *gn; col-* before *l, cor-* before *r,* and *con-* before other consonants. [Latin *com-, cum* with]

coma¹ *noun (pl.* **comas**) a prolonged deep unconsciousness, caused esp. by severe injury or excessive use of drugs. [medieval Latin from Greek *kōma* deep sleep]

coma² *noun (pl.* **comae** /-miː/) **1** *Astronomy* a cloud of gas and dust surrounding the nucleus of a comet. **2** *Bot.* a tuft of silky hairs at the end of some seeds. [Latin from Greek *komē* hair of head]

Com·an·che /kə'mæntʃi/ ● *noun (pl.* same or **-ches**) **1** a member of an American Indian people of the southwestern US. **2** the Uto-Aztecan language of this people, now virtually extinct. ● *adjective* of or relating to this people or their language. [Spanish, from Comanche]

coma·tose /'kəʊmətəʊs/ *adjective* **1** in a coma. **2** drowsy, sleepy, lethargic.

comb ● *noun* **1** a toothed strip of rigid material for tidying and arranging the hair, or for keeping it in place. **2** a device or part of a machine having a similar design or purpose. **3 a** the red fleshy crest of a fowl, esp. a rooster. **b** an analogous growth in other birds. **4** a honeycomb. ● *transitive verb* **1** arrange or tidy (the hair) by drawing a comb through. **2** curry (a horse). **3** dress (wool or flax) with a comb. **4** search (a place) thoroughly. □ **comb out 1** tidy and arrange (hair) with a comb. **2** remove with a comb. □ **combed** *adjective* [Old English *camb* from Germanic]

com·bat ● *noun* **1** a fight, struggle, or contest. **2** an armed encounter with enemy forces (also *attributive: combat aircraft; combat zone*). ● *verb* (**com·bat·ted, com·bat·ting** or **com·bat·ed, com·bat·ing**) **1** *intransitive* engage in combat. **2** *transitive* engage in combat with. **3** *transitive* oppose; strive against. [French *combat* from *combattre* from Late Latin (as COM-, Latin *batuere* fight)]

com·bat·ant /kɒm'bætənt, kəm-/ ● *noun* a person engaged in fighting. ● *adjective* **1** fighting. **2** for fighting.

Combatant Mountain a peak (3 756 m) in the Coast Mountains of SW central BC, east of Mount Waddington. [possibly because it was difficult to climb *c.*1933]

combat boot *noun* a heavy, laced, close-fitting leather boot reaching above the ankle, with a thick sole of hard rubber.

combat dress *noun* = BATTLEDRESS.

combat fatigue *noun* **1** (in *pl.*) = ARMY FATIGUES. **2** = BATTLE FATIGUE.

com·bat·ive /ˌkɒm'bætɪv, ˌkəm-/ *adjective* ready or eager to fight; pugnacious. □ **com·bat·ive·ly** *adverb* **com·bat·ive·ness** *noun*

combe *var. of* COOMB.

comb·er *noun* **1** a person or thing that combs, esp. a machine for combing cotton or wool very fine. **2** a long curling wave; a breaker.

comb filter *noun* a filter (esp. in televisions etc.) that allows only distinctly separated narrow ranges of wavelengths to pass.

comb. form *abbreviation* = COMBINING FORM.

combi *noun* a machine, appliance, aircraft, etc. with a combined function or mode of action (often *attributive*). [abbreviation of COMBINATION]

com·bin·a·tion *noun* **1** the act or an instance of combining; the process of being combined. **2** a combined state (*in combination with*). **3** a combined set of things or people. **4** a sequence of numbers or letters used to open a combination lock. **5** *Boxing* a rapid succession of punches. **6** (in *pl.*) a single undergarment for the body and legs. **7** *Math.* a selection of a given number of elements from a larger number of elements, without regard to the order of the elements chosen (*compare*

PERMUTATION). **8 a** united action. **b** *Chess* a coordinated and effective sequence of moves. **9** *Chem.* a union of substances in a compound with new properties. **10** *Brit.* a motorcycle with sidecar attached. □ **com·bin·a·tive** /'kɒmbɪnətɪv/ *adjective* **com·bin·a·tion·al** *adjective* **com·bin·a·tory** /'kɒmbɪnət(ə)ri/ *adjective*

Combination Act any of the British laws of 1799–1800 making illegal the confederacy of persons to further their own interests, affect the rate of wages, etc. Formulated to prevent revolutionary ideas from spreading to England after the French Revolution, the laws were in fact enforced mainly against workers' unions; most of the legislation was repealed in 1824.

combination lock *noun* a lock that can be opened only by a specific sequence of movements.

combination therapy *noun* medical treatment in which a patient is given two or more drugs (or other therapeutic agents) for a single condition.

com·bin·a·tor·ial /ˌkɒmbɪnə'tɔːriəl/ *adjective Math.* relating to combinations of items.

com·bine ● *verb* /kəm'baɪn/ **1** *transitive & intransitive* join together; unite for a common purpose. **2** *transitive* possess (qualities usually distinct) together (*combines charm and authority*). **3 a** *intransitive* coalesce in one substance. **b** *transitive* cause to do this. **c** *intransitive* form a chemical compound. **4** *intransitive* co-operate. **5** /'kɒmbaɪn/ *transitive & intransitive* harvest (crops etc.) by means of a combine. ● *noun* /'kɒmbaɪn/ **1** a combination of esp. commercial interests to control prices etc. **2** a self-propelled machine that reaps and threshes in one operation. □ **com·bin·able** *adjective* **com·bin·er** *noun* [Old French *combiner* or Late Latin *combinare* (as COM-, Latin *bini* two)]

com·bined /kəm'baɪnd/ *adjective* **1** united; joined together (*combined choirs*). **2** (of an action, etc.) performed by a group acting together (*combined effort*).

combined time *noun Sport* (in an event or competition in which each competitor completes a certain activity more than once) the total of all times taken by a competitor.

combine harvester *noun* = COMBINE *noun* 2.

comb·ings /'kəʊmɪŋz/ *plural noun* hairs combed off.

combining form *noun Grammar* a linguistic element used in combination with another element to form a word, e.g. *Anglo-* = English, *bio-* = life, *-graphy* = writing.

combo *noun (pl.* **-bos**) *informal* **1** a small jazz or dance band. **2** any combination (*seafood combo*). [abbreviation of COMBINATION + -o]

comb-over *noun* a men's hairstyle in which the hair is grown long on the sides then combed over the top of the head to cover a bald spot.

com·bust *verb* **1** *transitive* subject to combustion. **2** *intransitive* undergo combustion. [obsolete *combust* (adj.) from Latin *combustus* past participle of *comburere* 'burn up']

com·bust·ible ● *adjective* **1** capable of or used for burning. **2** excitable; easily irritated. ● *noun* a combustible substance. □ **com·bust·ibil·ity** *noun*

com·bus·tion *noun* **1** burning; consumption by fire. **2** *Chem.* the development of light and heat from the chemical combination of a substance with oxygen. □ **com·bus·tive** *adjective*

combustion chamber *noun* a space in which combustion takes place, e.g. in an internal combustion engine.

come ● *intransitive verb (past* **came***; past participle* **come**) **1** move, be brought towards, or reach a place thought of as near or familiar to the speaker or hearer (*come and see me; shall we come to your house?; the books have come*). **2** reach or be brought to a specified situation or result (*you'll come to no harm; have come to believe it; has come to be used wrongly; came into prominence*). **3** reach or extend to a specified point (*the road comes within a mile of us*). **4** traverse or accomplish (*have come a long way*). **5** occur, happen; become present instead of future (*how did you come to break your leg?*). **6** take or occupy a specified position in space or time (*it comes on the third page; it does not come within the scope of the inquiry*). **7** become perceptible or known (*the church came into sight; the news comes as a surprise; it will come to me*). **8** be available (*this T-shirt comes in three sizes; this model comes with optional features*). **9** (foll. by *of*) **a** be descended from (*comes of a rich family*). **b** be the result of (*that comes of complaining*). **11** (foll. by *from*) **a** originate in; have as its source. **b** have as one's home. **12** *informal* play the part of; behave like (*don't come the bully with me*). **13** *coarse slang* have an orgasm. **14** (in *subjunctive*) *informal* when a specified time is reached (*come the revolution*). **15** (as *interjection*) expressing caution or reserve (*come, it cannot be that bad*). ● *noun coarse slang* ejaculated semen. □ **as ... as they come** typically or supremely so (*is as tough as they come*). **come**

about 1 happen; take place. **2** (of a boat) change direction. **come across 1** be effective or understood. **2** slang (foll. by with) hand over what is wanted. **3** meet or find by chance (came across an old jacket). **4** slang (of a woman) have sexual intercourse with a man. **come again** informal **1** make a further effort. **2** (as imperative) what did you say? **come along 1** arrive, appear. **2** make progress; move forward. **3** (as imperative) hurry up. **come and go 1** pass to and fro; be transitory. **2** pay brief visits. **come apart** fall or break into pieces, disintegrate. **come at 1** reach, discover; get access to. **2** attack (came at me with a knife). **come away 1** become detached or broken off (came away in my hands). **2** (foll. by with) be left with a feeling, impression, etc. (came away with many misgivings). **come back 1** return. **2** recur to one's memory. **3** become fashionable or popular again. **4** N Amer. reply, retort. **come before 1** be dealt with by (a judge etc.). **2** have greater importance than. **come between 1** interfere with the relationship of. **2** separate; prevent contact between. **come by 1** pass; go past. **2** call on a visit (why not come by tomorrow?). **3** acquire, obtain (came by a new bicycle). **come clean** see CLEAN. **come down 1** come to a place or position regarded as lower. **2** lose position or wealth (has come down in the world). **3** be handed down by tradition or inheritance. **4** be reduced; show a downward trend (prices are coming down). **5** (foll. by against, in favour of) reach a decision or recommendation (the report came down against change). **6** (foll. by to) signify or betoken basically; be dependent on (a factor) (it comes down to who is willing to go). **7** (foll. by on) criticize harshly; rebuke, punish. **8** (foll. by with) begin to suffer from (a disease). **9** (of rain) fall heavily. **10** (of a decision, budget, etc.) be announced or delivered. **11** cease to feel the effects of an intoxicating drug. **come for 1** come to collect or receive. **2** attack (came for me with a hammer). **come forward 1** advance. **2** offer one's help, services, etc. **come in 1** enter a house or room. **2** take a specified position in a race etc. (came in third). **3** become fashionable or seasonable. **4 a** have a useful role or function. **b** prove to be (came in very handy). **c** have a part to play (where do I come in?). **5** be received (more news has just come in). **6** begin speaking, esp. in radio transmission. **7** be elected; come to power. **8** (foll. by for) receive; be the object of (usu. something unwelcome) (came in for much criticism). **9** (foll. by on) join (an enterprise etc.). **10** (of a tide) turn to high tide. **11** (of a train, ship, or aircraft) approach its destination. **12** return to base (come in, number 9). **13** (of breast milk) start to flow. **come into 1** see senses 2, 7 of verb. **2** receive, esp. as heir. **come near** see NEAR. **come of age** see AGE. **come off 1** informal (of an action) succeed; be accomplished. **2** fare; turn out (came off badly; came off the winner). **3** coarse slang have an orgasm. **4** be detached or detachable (from). **5** fall (from). **6** be reduced or subtracted from ($5 came off the price). **come off it** (as imperative) informal an expression of disbelief or refusal to accept another's opinion, behaviour, etc. **come on 1** continue to come. **2** advance, esp. to attack. **3** make progress; thrive (is really coming on). **4** begin (I've got a cold coming on). **5** appear on the stage, field of play, etc. **6** be heard or seen on television, on the telephone, etc. **7** arise to be discussed. **8** (as imperative) expressing encouragement. **9** = COME UPON. **10** (foll. by to) make sexual advances to. **11** (of a light, appliance, etc.) start functioning. **come out 1** emerge; become known (it came out that he had left). **2** appear or be published (comes out every Saturday). **3 a** declare oneself; make a decision (came out in favour of joining). **b** openly declare that one is a homosexual. **4** Brit. go on strike. **5 a** be satisfactorily visible in a photograph etc., or present in a specified way (the dog didn't come out; he came out badly). **b** (of a photograph) be produced satisfactorily or in a specified way (only three have come out; they all came out well). **6** attain a specified result in an examination etc. **7** (of a stain etc.) be removed. **8** make one's debut on stage or in society. **9** (foll. by in) be covered with (came out in a rash). **10** (of a problem) be solved. **11** (foll. by with) declare openly; disclose. **come over 1** come from some distance or nearer to the speaker (came over from Paris; come over here a moment). **2** change sides or one's opinion. **3 a** (of a feeling etc.) overtake or affect (a person). **b** informal feel suddenly (came over faint). **4** appear or sound in a specified way (you came over very well; the ideas came over clearly). **5** affect or influence (I don't know what came over me). **come round 1** pay an informal visit. **2** recover consciousness. **3** be converted to another person's opinion. **4** (of a date or regular occurrence) recur; be imminent again. **come through 1** be successful; survive. **2** survive or overcome (a difficulty) (came through the ordeal). **3** provide support, assistance, etc. when needed. **come to 1** recover consciousness. **2** Naut. bring a vessel to a stop. **3** reach in total; amount to. **4** reflexive **a** recover consciousness. **b** stop being foolish. **5** reach a particular (usu. bad) situation or state of affairs (what is the world coming to?). **come to hand** become available; be recovered. **come to light** see LIGHT¹. **come to nothing** have no useful result

in the end; fail. **come to pass** happen, occur. **come to rest** cease moving. **come to one's senses** see SENSE. **come to that** informal in fact; if that is the case. **come under 1** be classified as or among. **2** be subject to (influence or authority). **come up 1** come to a place or position regarded as higher. **2** attain wealth or position (come up in the world). **3 a** (of an issue, problem, etc.) arise; present itself; be mentioned or discussed. **b** (of an event etc.) occur, happen (coming up next on CBC). **4** (often foll. by to) **a** approach a person, esp. to talk. **b** approach or draw near to a specified time, event, etc. (is coming up to eight o'clock). **5** (foll. by to) match (a standard etc.). **6** (foll. by with) produce (an idea etc.), esp. in response to a challenge. **7** (of a plant etc.) spring up out of the ground. **8** become brighter (e.g. with polishing); shine more brightly. **come up against** be faced with or opposed by. **come upon 1** meet or find by chance. **2** attack by surprise. **come what may** no matter what happens. **have it coming to one** informal be about to get one's deserts. **how come?** informal why? **if it comes to that** in that case. **not know if one is coming or going** be confused from being very busy. **to come** future; in the future (the year to come; many problems were still to come). **where a person is coming from** a person's meaning, intention, or personality. [Old English cuman from Germanic]

come·along noun N Amer. a hand-operated winch.

come·back noun **1** a return to a previous (esp. successful) state. **2** informal a retaliation or retort.

Come By Chance a town in SE Newfoundland, situated at the northern end of the Avalon Isthmus, about 150 km southeast of Gander; pop. (2001) 265. [the name of the bay on which it is situated, perhaps because of the risk taken by fishermen while attempting to bring their boats ashore during rough weather]

Com·econ /ˈkɒmiˌkɒn/ noun hist. an economic association of East European countries. [abbreviation of Council for Mutual Economic Assistance]

com·ed·ian /kəˈmiːdiən/ noun **1** a humorous entertainer on stage, television, etc. **2** an actor in comedy. **3** a person who behaves comically.

com·edi·enne /kəˌmiːdiˈen/ noun a female comedian.

com·ed·ist /ˈkɒmɪdɪst/ noun a writer of comedies.

com·edo /ˈkɒmɪˌdoʊ/ noun (pl. **com·edo·nes** /-ˈdoʊniːz/) Med. a blackhead. [Latin, = glutton from comedere eat up]

come·down noun **1** a loss of status; decline or degradation. **2** a disappointment. **3** a lessening of the sensations generated by a narcotic drug as its effects wear off.

com·edy /ˈkɒmədi/ noun (pl. **-ies**) **1 a** a play, film, etc., of an amusing or satirical character, usu. with a happy ending. **b** the dramatic genre consisting of works of this kind (compare TRAGEDY 3). **2** an amusing or farcical incident or series of incidents in everyday life. **3** humour, esp. in a work of art etc. □ **com·ed·ic** /kəˈmiːdɪk/ adjective [Old French comedie from Latin comoedia from Greek kōmōidia from kōmōidos comic poet, from kōmos revel]

comedy of errors noun **1** a comedy in which the humour derives from mistaken identities, misunderstandings, etc. **2** any event made laughable by an accumulation of mistakes.

comedy of manners noun a comedy that presents a satirical portrayal of social life.

come from away noun Cdn (Maritimes & Nfld) a person who is not from the Atlantic region generally (she's a come from away).

come-hither attributive adjective informal (of a look or manner) enticing, flirtatious.

come·ly /ˈkʌmli/ adjective (**come·li·er**, **come·li·est**) (esp. of a person) pleasant to look at. □ **come·li·ness** /ˈkʌmlinəs/ noun [Middle English cumelich, cumli prob. from becumelich from BECOME]

Com·en·ius /kəˈmiːniəs/ **John Amos** (Czech name Jan Komenský) (1592–1670), Czech educational reformer and theologian, who became famous throughout Europe with the publication of his Janua linguarum reserata (1633), an innovative textbook on language instruction.

come-on noun informal **1** a gesture, remark, description, etc. intended to attract or persuade. **2** a remark or behaviour intended to allure someone sexually.

com·er noun **1** a person who comes, esp. as an applicant, participant, etc. (offered the job to the first comer). **2** informal a person likely to be a success. □ **all comers** any applicants (with reference to a position etc. that is unrestricted in entry).

com·est·ible /kəˈmestɪbəl/ noun (usu. in pl.) formal or jocular food. [French from medieval Latin comestibilis from Latin comedere comest- eat up]

uː mood ai my əi pipe au brown ʌu house ei day ɔi boy ã franglais ã Canadien ɔ̃ Brayon (see over for consonants)

comet *noun* a hazy object usu. with a nucleus of ice and dust surrounded by gas and with a tail pointing away from the sun, moving about the sun in an eccentric orbit. □ **comet·ary** *adjective* [Old French *comete* from Latin *cometa* from Greek *komētes* long-haired (star)]

come·uppance /kʌmˈʌpəns/ *noun informal* one's deserved fate or punishment (*got his comeuppance*). [COME + UP + -ANCE]

com·fit /ˈkʌmfɪt/ *noun archaic* a candy consisting of a nut, seed, etc., coated in sugar. [Old French *confit* from Latin *confectum* past participle of *conficere* prepare: see CONFECTION]

Com·fort, Charles (Fraser) (1900–1994), Scottish-born Canadian painter, whose best-known works include the watercolour portrait *Young Canadian* (1932), the landscape painting *Tadoussac* (1935), and his series of murals for the Toronto Stock Exchange (1937).

com·fort ● *noun* **1** consolation; relief in affliction. **2 a** a state of physical well-being; being comfortable (*live in comfort*). **b** (usu. in *pl.*) things that make life easy or pleasant (*has all the comforts*). **3** a cause of satisfaction (*a comfort to me that you are here*). **4** a person who consoles or helps one (*he's a comfort to her in her old age*). ● *transitive verb* **1** soothe in grief; console. **2** make comfortable (*comforted by the warmth of the fire*). □ **com·fort·ing** *adjective* **com·fort·ing·ly** *adverb* [Old French *confort(er)* from Late Latin *confortare* strengthen (as COM-, Latin *fortis* strong)]

com·fort·able /ˈkʌmftərbəl, -fərtəbəl, -frtəbəl/ *adjective* **1** ministering to comfort; giving ease (*a comfortable pair of shoes*). **2** free from discomfort; at ease (*I'm quite comfortable thank you*). **3** *informal* having an adequate standard of living; free from financial worry. **4** having no qualms (*did not feel comfortable about refusing him*). **5** with a wide margin (*a comfortable win*). □ **com·fort·able·ness** *noun* **com·fort·ably** *adverb*

com·fort·er *noun* **1 a** a person who comforts. **b** (**Comforter**) *Christianity* the Holy Spirit. **2** *N Amer.* a warm quilt.

comfort food *noun* food, esp. rich in carbohydrates, which provides psychological comfort as well as nourishment.

com·fort·less *adjective* **1** dreary, cheerless. **2** without comfort.

comfort station *noun N Amer. euphemism* a public washroom.

comfort woman *noun* (in the Second World War) a woman forcibly recruited by the Japanese army to provide sexual services to Japanese soldiers.

comfort zone *noun* **1** the range of temperature and relative humidity within which people, animals, etc. feel comfortable. **2** = PERSONAL SPACE. **3** a range of action, behaviour, etc. with which a person feels comfortable, often complacently so.

com·frey /ˈkʌmfri/ *noun* (*pl.* **-freys**) any of various herbs of the genus *Symphytum*, esp. *S. officinale* having large hairy leaves and clusters of usu. white or purple bell-shaped flowers. [Anglo-French *cumfrie*, ultimately from Latin *conferva* (as COM-, *fervēre* boil)]

comfy *adjective* (**com·fi·er**, **com·fi·est**) *informal* comfortable. □ **com·fi·ly** *adverb* **com·fi·ness** *noun* [abbreviation]

com·ic ● *adjective* **1** (often *attributive*) of, or in the style of, comedy (*a comic actor*; *comic opera*). **2** causing or meant to cause laughter; funny (*comic to see his struggles*). ● *noun* **1** a professional comedian. **2 a** (**com·ics**) a section of a newspaper containing comic strips. **b** = COMIC BOOK. [Latin *comicus* from Greek *komikos* from *komos* revel]

comic·al *adjective* funny; causing laughter. □ **comic·al·ity** *noun* **comic·al·ly** *adverb* [COMIC]

comic book *noun* a book or magazine containing a single narrative told through comic strips.

Com·ice /ˈkɒmɪs/ *noun* a large yellow dessert pear of a late-fruiting variety. [French, lit. = 'association, co-operative', referring to the *Comice Horticole* of Angers, France, where this variety was developed]

comic opera *noun* **1** an opera with much spoken dialogue, usu. with humorous treatment. **2** this genre of opera.

comic relief *noun* **1** comic episodes in a play etc. intended to offset more serious portions. **2** the relaxation of tension etc. provided by such episodes.

comic strip *noun* a horizontal series of drawings in a comic book, newspaper, etc., usu. telling a story.

Co·mines /kɒˈmiːn/ **Phi·lippe de** (also **Com·mines**) (*c.*1447–1511), French diplomat and chronicler, remembered for his *Mémoires* (1524–8) of the reigns of Louis XI (1423–83) and Charles VIII (1470–98) of France.

com·ing ● *attributive adjective* **1** approaching, next (*in the coming week*; *this coming Sunday*). **2** of potential importance (*a coming entrepreneur*). ● *noun* arrival; approach. □ **coming and going** (or **comings and goings**) activity, esp. intense.

co·min·gle *var. of* COMMINGLE.

coming of age *noun* the reaching of adulthood by a young person.

Com·in·tern /ˈkɒmɪnˌtɜːn/ *noun* an association of world communist parties, established by Lenin in 1919 and dissolved in 1943. *Also called* THIRD INTERNATIONAL (*see* INTERNATIONAL *noun* 1a). [Russian *Komintern* from Russian forms of *communist*, *international*]

com·ity /ˈkɒmɪti/ *noun* (*pl.* **-ities**) **1** courtesy, civility; considerate behaviour towards others. **2 a** an association of nations etc. for mutual benefit. **b** (in full **comity of nations**) the mutual recognition by nations of the laws and customs of others. [Latin *comitas* from *comis* courteous]

comm *noun* (also **comms**) communication, especially to and from a computer.

comma *noun* **1** a punctuation mark (,) indicating a pause between parts of a sentence, or dividing items in a list, a string of figures, etc. **2** (in full **comma butterfly**) a butterfly, *Polygonia c-album*, with a white comma-shaped mark on the underside of the hindwing. [Latin from Greek *komma* clause]

comma bacillus *noun* a comma-shaped bacillus causing cholera.

comma fault *noun* any incorrect use of a comma, esp. a comma splice.

com·mand ● *verb* **1** *transitive* (often foll. by to + infin., or *that* + clause) give formal orders or instructions to (*commands us to obey*; *commands that it be done*). **2** *transitive & intransitive* have authority or control over. **3** *transitive* **a** restrain, master. **b** gain the use of; have at one's disposal or within reach (skill, resources, etc.) (*commands an extensive knowledge of history*; *commands a salary of $80,000*). **4** *transitive* deserve and get (sympathy, respect, etc.). **5** *transitive* dominate (a strategic position) from a superior height; look down over. ● *noun* **1** an authoritative order; an instruction. **2** mastery, control, possession (*a good command of languages*; *has command of the resources*). **3** the exercise or tenure of authority, esp. naval or military (*has command of this ship*). **4** *Military* **a** *Cdn* one of the three divisions of the Canadian Forces (*Air Command*). **b** a body of troops etc. (*Bomber Command*). **c** a district under a commander (*Western Command*). **5** *Computing* **a** an instruction causing a computer to perform one of its basic functions. **b** a signal initiating such an operation. □ **at** (or **by**) **a person's command** following a person's request. **in command of** commanding; having under control. **under command of** commanded by. **word of command 1** *Military* an order for a movement in a drill etc. **2** a pre-arranged spoken signal for the start of an operation. [Old French *comander* from Late Latin *commandare* COMMEND]

com·mand·ant /ˌkɒmənˈdant, -ˈdɒnt, ˈkɒm-/ *noun* a commanding officer, esp. of a particular force, military academy, etc. [French *commandant*, or Italian or Spanish *commandante* (as COMMAND)]

command economy *noun* an economy, e.g. that of Cuba, which relies on the direction of a central governing body.

com·man·deer /ˌkɒmənˈdiːr/ *transitive verb* **1** seize (men or goods) for military purposes. **2** take possession of without authority. [South African Dutch *kommanderen* from French *commander* COMMAND]

com·mand·er *noun* **1** a person who commands, esp.: **a** (also **Commander**) a naval officer next in rank below captain. Abbr.: **Cdr**. **b** = WING COMMANDER. **2** (in full **knight commander**) a member of a higher class in some orders of knighthood. □ **com·mand·er·ship** *noun*

commander-in-chief *noun* (*pl.* **commanders-in-chief**) the supreme commander, esp. of a nation's forces.

com·mand·ing *adjective* **1** dignified, exalted, impressive. **2** (of a hill or other high point) giving a wide view. **3** (of an advantage, a position, etc.) controlling; superior (*she has a commanding lead*). □ **com·mand·ing·ly** *adverb*

commanding officer *noun* (also **Commanding Officer**) the officer in command of a military unit, formation, or force. Abbr.: **CO**.

com·mand·ment *noun* a divine command.

command module *noun* the control compartment in a spacecraft.

com·mando *noun* (*pl.* **-dos**) *Military* **1** a group of soldiers specially trained for carrying out quick attacks in enemy areas. **2** a member of such a group. **3** (*attributive*) of or concerning a commando (*a commando operation*). [Portuguese from *commandar* COMMAND]

Command Paper *noun* (in the UK) a paper laid before Parliament by command of the Crown.

command performance *noun* (in the UK) a theatrical or film performance given by royal command.

command post *noun* the headquarters of a military unit.

comma splice *noun* the use of a comma rather than a semicolon to connect two independent clauses.

Consonants: b *but*   d *dog*   f *few*   g *get*   h *her*   j *yes*   k *cat*   l *leg*   m *man*   n *no*   p *pen*   r *red*   s *sit*

comme ci, comme ça /kɒmˌsiː kɒmˈsɑ/ *adverb & adjective* SO-SO; neither good nor bad. [French, = like this, like that]

com·media dell'arte /koˈmeidiə delˈɑrtei/ *noun* an improvised kind of popular comedy in Italian theatres in the 16th–18th c., based on stock characters. [Italian, = comedy of art]

comme il faut /ˌkɒm iːl ˈfoː/ ● *predicative adjective* (esp. of behaviour, etiquette, etc.) proper, correct. ● *adverb* properly, correctly. [French, = as is necessary]

com·mem·or·ate /kəˈmeməˌreit/ *transitive verb* **1 a** preserve in memory by some celebration. **b** (of a stone, plaque, etc.) be a memorial of. **2** celebrate in speech or writing. □ **com·mem·or·a·tive** /kəˈmemərətɪv/ *adjective* **com·mem·or·ator** *noun* [Latin *commemorare* (as COM-, *memorare* relate from *memor* mindful)]

com·mem·or·a·tion /kəˌmeməˈreiʃən/ *noun* **1** an act of commemorating. **2** a service or part of a service in memory of a person, an event, etc.

com·mence /kəˈmens/ *transitive & intransitive verb formal* begin. [Old French *com(m)encier* from Romanic (as COM-, Latin *initiare* INITIATE)]

com·mence·ment /kəˈmensmənt/ *noun formal* **1** a beginning. **2** esp. *N Amer.* a ceremony for the conferment of diplomas.

com·mend /kəˈmend/ *transitive verb* **1** (often foll. by *to*) entrust, commit (*commends his soul to God*). **2** praise (*commends the author for her thorough research*). **3** recommend. **4** (*reflexive*) find favour with (*this approach commended itself to the politicians*). □ **commend me to** *archaic* remember me kindly to. [Latin *commendare* (as COM-, *mendare* = *mandare* entrust: see MANDATE)]

com·mend·able /kəˈmendəbəl/ *adjective* praiseworthy. □ **com·mend·ably** *adverb*

com·men·da·tion /ˌkɒmenˈdeiʃən/ *noun* **1** an act of commending or recommending (esp. a person to another's favour). **2** praise.

com·men·da·tory /kəˈmendətəri/ *adjective* serving to present something as suitable for approval or acceptance. [Late Latin *commendatorius* (as COMMEND)]

com·men·sal /kəˈmensəl/ ● *adjective Biol.* of, relating to, or exhibiting commensalism. ● *noun Biol.* a commensal organism. □ **com·men·sal·ity** /ˌkɒmənˈsalıti/ *noun* [French *commensal* or medieval Latin *commensalis* 'eating at the same table' (as COM-, *mensa* table)]

com·men·sal·ism /kəˈmensəˌlızəm/ *noun Biol.* an association between two organisms in which one benefits and the other derives no benefit or harm.

com·men·sur·able /kəˈmenʃərəbəl, -sjərəbəl/ *adjective* **1** (often foll. by *with, to*) measurable by the same standard. **2** (foll. by *to*) proportionate to. **3** *Math.* (of numbers) in a ratio equal to the ratio of integers. □ **com·men·sur·abil·ity** *noun* **com·men·sur·ably** *adverb* [Late Latin *commensurabilis* (as COM-, MEASURE)]

com·men·sur·ate /kəˈmensərət, -ʃərət, -sjərət/ *adjective* **1** (usu. foll. by *with*) having the same size, duration, etc.; co-extensive. **2** (often foll. by *to, with*) proportionate. **3** at a level appropriate to (*salary commensurate with qualifications*). □ **com·men·sur·ate·ly** *adverb* [Late Latin *commensuratus* (as COM-, MEASURE)]

com·ment ● *noun* **1 a** a remark (*made comments on her work*). **b** criticism; gossip (*his behaviour aroused much comment*). **c** the action of responding to questions (*refused comment*). **d** commentary (*an hour of news and comment*). **2 a** an explanatory note (e.g. on a written text). **b** written criticism or explanation (e.g. of a text). **3** (of a play, book, etc.) a critical illustration; a parable (*her art is a comment on society*). ● *intransitive verb* **1** (often foll. by *on, upon,* or *that* + clause) make (esp. critical) remarks (*commented on her choice of friends*). **2** (often foll. by *on, upon*) write explanatory notes. □ **no comment** *informal* I decline to answer your question. [Latin *commentum* contrivance (in Late Latin also = interpretation), neuter past participle of *comminisci* devise, or French *commenter* (v.)]

com·men·tary *noun* (pl. **-ies**) **1** a set of explanatory or critical notes on a text etc. **2** a descriptive spoken account (esp. on radio or television) of an event or a performance as it happens. **3** something that serves to illustrate or exemplify something (*a sad commentary on our lack of caring*).

com·men·tate *intransitive verb disputed* act as a commentator. [back-formation from COMMENTATOR]

com·men·ta·tor *noun* **1** a person who provides a commentary on an event etc. **2** the writer of a commentary. **3** a person who writes or speaks on current events.

com·merce *noun* **1** financial transactions, esp. the buying and selling of merchandise, on a large scale. **2** social intercourse (*the daily commerce*

of gossip and opinion). **3** *archaic* sexual intercourse. [French *commerce* or Latin *commercium* (as COM-, *mercium* from *merx mercis* merchandise)]

com·mer·cial ● *adjective* **1** of, engaged in, or concerned with, commerce. **2** of or relating to the production of esp. foodstuffs on an industrial scale (*commercial fishery*). **3** (of radio or television broadcasting) funded by the revenue from broadcast advertising. **4** (of an airline, aircraft, vehicle, etc.) engaged in, used by, or suitable for business or commerce; not private or governmental (*commercial flight*). **5** of, relating to, or suitable for office buildings etc. (*commercial land*). **6** usu. *derogatory* having profit as a primary aim rather than artistic etc. value; philistine. **7** (of chemicals) supplied in bulk more or less unpurified. ● *noun* **1** a television or radio advertisement. **2** *archaic* a commercial traveller. □ **com·mer·ci·al·ity** *noun* **com·mer·cial·ly** *adverb*

commercial art *noun* art used in advertising, selling, etc. □ **commercial artist** *noun*

commercial bank *noun* a privately-owned bank that provides a wide range of financial services to businesses and the general public.

commercial break *noun N Amer.* an interruption in a television or radio program for the broadcasting of commercials.

com·mer·cial·ism *noun* **1** the principles and practice of commerce. **2** (esp. excessive) emphasis on financial profit as a measure of worth.

com·mer·cial·ize *transitive verb* (also esp. *Brit.* **-ise**) **1** exploit or spoil for the purpose of gaining profit. **2** make commercial. □ **com·mer·cial·iz·a·tion** *noun* **com·mer·cial·ized** *adjective*

commercial paper *noun* **1** a corporate promissory note, usu. unsecured and for a short term. **2** *N Amer.* any negotiable paper, such as drafts or bills of exchange.

commercial traveller *noun* a travelling salesman or saleswoman who visits stores etc. to get orders.

com·mie *slang derogatory* Communist. [abbreviation]

com·min·a·tion /ˌkɒmɪˈneiʃən/ *noun* the threatening of divine vengeance. [Latin *comminatio* from *comminari* threaten]

com·min·a·tory /ˈkɒmɪnətəri/ *adjective* threatening, punitive, or vengeful. [medieval Latin *comminatorius* (as COMMINATION)]

Com·mines *var. of* COMINES.

com·min·gle *transitive & intransitive verb* (also **co·min·gle**) mingle together.

com·min·ute /ˈkɒmɪˌnjuːt/ *transitive verb* **1** reduce to small fragments. **2** divide (property) into small portions. □ **com·minu·tion** /-ˈnjuːʃən/ *noun* [Latin *comminuere comminut-* (as COM-, *minuere* lessen)]

com·min·uted fracture *noun* a fracture producing multiple bone splinters.

com·mis /ˈkɒmi, ˈkɒmɪs/ *noun* (*pl.* **com·mis** /ˈkɒmi, ˈkɒmɪz/) **1** a junior chef. **2** *Brit.* a junior waiter. [originally = deputy, clerk, from French, past participle of *commettre* entrust (as COMMIT)]

com·miser·ate /kəˈmɪzəˌreit/ *intransitive verb* **1** (usu. foll. by *with*) express or feel sympathy or pity. **2** express sorrows jointly with others (*they would meet at the bar to commiserate*). □ **com·miser·a·tion** *noun* **com·miser·a·tive** (-rətɪv) *adjective* **com·miser·ator** *noun* [Latin *commiserari* (as COM-, *miserari* pity, from *miser* wretched)]

com·mish /kəˈmɪʃ/ *noun N Amer. informal* a commissioner, esp. a commissioner of a professional sports league. [abbreviation]

com·mis·sar /ˈkɒmɪˌsɑr/ *noun hist.* **1** an official of the former Soviet Communist Party responsible for political education and organization. **2** the head of a government department in the former USSR before 1946. [Russian *komissar* from French *commissaire* (as COMMISSARY)]

com·mis·sar·iat /ˌkɒmɪˈseriət/ *noun* **1** *Military* **a** a department for the supply of food etc. **b** the food supplied. **2** *hist.* a government department of the former USSR before 1946. [French *commissariat* & medieval Latin *commissariatus* (as COMMISSARY)]

com·mis·sary /ˈkɒmɪsəri/ *noun* (*pl.* **-ies**) **1** a deputy or delegate. **2** a representative or deputy of a bishop. **3** *hist.* an officer responsible for the supply of food etc. to soldiers. **4** *N Amer.* **a** a restaurant in a film studio etc. **b** the food supplied. **5** *N Amer.* a store for the sale of food and other goods, esp. to soldiers etc. [medieval Latin *commissarius* person in charge (as COMMIT)]

com·mis·sion /kəˈmɪʃən/ ● *noun* **1 a** the authority to perform a task or certain duties. **b** a person or group entrusted esp. by a government with such authority (*set up a commission to look into it*). **c** an instruction, command, or duty given to such a group or person (*their commission was to simplify the procedure; my commission was to find him*). **2** an order for something, esp. a work of art, to be produced specially. **3** *Military* **a** a warrant conferring the rank of officer in the army, navy, or air force. **b** the rank so conferred. **4 a** the authority to act as agent for a company etc. in trade. **b** a percentage paid to the agent or sales representative from the profits of goods etc. sold, or business obtained (*his wages are low, but he gets 20 per cent commission*). **c** the pay of a commissioned agent. **5** the act of committing (a crime, sin, etc.). **6** the office or department of a commissioner. **7** *hist.* the government of Newfoundland, consisting of a governor and six commissioners, that was appointed by the Crown between 1934 and 1949. ● *transitive verb* **1** authorize or empower by a commission. **2 a** give (an artist etc.) a commission for a piece of work. **b** order (a work) to be written (*commissioned a new concerto*). **3 a** *Military* appoint (an officer) by means of a commission. **b** prepare (a ship) for active service. **4** bring (a machine, equipment, etc.) into operation. □ **in commission** (of a warship etc.) manned, armed, and ready for service. **out of commission** not in service, not in working order. [Old French from Latin *commissio -onis* (as COMMIT)]

com·mis·sion·aire /kə,mɪʃəˈnɛr/ *noun* **1** *Cdn* a member of the Corps of Commissionaires. **2** esp. *Brit.* a uniformed door attendant at a theatre, cinema, etc. [French (as COMMISSION)]

com·mis·sion·er /kəˈmɪʃənər/ *noun* **1** a person appointed, esp. by a commission, to perform a specific task. **2** a person appointed as a member of a commission. **3** a representative of the supreme authority in a district, department, etc., e.g. (in Canada) a person appointed to serve in a role analogous to that of Lieutenant Governor in the Northwest Territories, Yukon, and Nunavut. **4 a** (in the Ontario Provincial Police) the highest ranking officer. **b** (in the RCMP) the highest ranking officer. **5** *N Amer.* a person appointed by an athletic league or association to carry out various administrative and judicial functions (*baseball commissioner*). **6** a delegate to a convention.

Commissioner for Oaths *noun* a person, e.g. a lawyer, MP, MLA or MPP, etc., authorized to administer oaths and take affidavits.

com·mis·sure /ˈkɒmɪ,sjʊr/ *noun* **1** a junction, joint, or seam. **2** *Anat.* **a** the joint between two bones. **b** a band of nerve tissue connecting the hemispheres of the brain, the two sides of the spinal cord, etc. **c** the line where the upper and lower lips, or eyelids, meet. **3** *Bot.* any of several joints etc. between different parts of a plant. □ **com·mis·sur·al** /kəmɪˈsjʊrəl/ *adjective* [Latin *commissura* junction (as COMMIT)]

com·mit *verb* (**com·mit·ted**, **com·mit·ting**) **1** *transitive* (usu. foll. by *to*) entrust or consign for: **a** safekeeping (*I commit him to your care*). **b** treatment, usu. destruction (*committed the book to the flames*). **2** *transitive* perpetrate, do (esp. a crime, sin, or blunder) (*commit murder*). **3** *transitive* pledge, involve, or bind (esp. oneself) to a certain course or policy (*does not like committing herself*; *committed by the vow he had made*). **4** *intransitive* (usu. foll. by *to*) pledge or engage oneself firmly (*we expect you to commit to the project for four years*; *she wanted to get married, but he wouldn't commit*). **5** *transitive* consign (a person) to a mental hospital, prison, etc., by or as if by legal authority. **6** *transitive Politics* refer (a bill etc.) to a committee. □ **commit to memory** memorize. □ **com·mit·table** *adjective* **com·mit·ter** *noun* [Latin *committere* join, entrust (as COM-, *mittere* miss- send)]

com·mit·ment *noun* **1** the process or an instance of committing oneself; a pledge or undertaking. **2** an engagement or (esp. financial) obligation that restricts freedom of action. **3** the state of being committed.

commitment ceremony *noun* a ceremony analogous to a wedding in which a same-sex couple proclaim publicly a lifelong commitment to each other.

com·mit·tal *noun* **1** the act of committing a person to an institution, esp. prison or a mental hospital. **2** the burial of a dead body.

com·mit·ted *adjective* **1** having a strong dedication to a cause or belief (*a committed Christian*). **2** obliged (to take a certain action) (*felt committed to staying there*).

com·mit·tee *noun* **1** a body of persons elected or appointed for a specific function by, and usu. out of, a larger body. **2** (also **parliamentary committee**) (in the Commonwealth) such a body drawn from members of the upper or lower houses of a legislature, appointed to consider the details of a proposed bill after its second reading (*the bill has reached committee stage*). **3** = COMMITTEE OF THE WHOLE. **4** /,kɒmɪˈtiː/ *Law* a person entrusted with the charge of another person or another person's property. [COMMIT + -EE]

com·mit·tee·man *noun* (*pl.* **-men**) **1** a person, esp. a man, who serves on a committee or committees, esp. frequently. **2** (in the US) a person, esp. a man, who is the local leader of a political party in a ward etc.

Committee of Public Safety (during the French Revolution) a governing body set up in France in Apr. 1793. It was at first dominated by Danton but later in the year came under the influence of the more

radical Robespierre and initiated the Terror. The Committee's power ended with the fall of Robespierre in 1794, although it was not dissolved until the following year.

committee of the whole *noun* **1** a committee comprising all the members of a legislative body or other organization. **2** (in full **Committee of the Whole House**) (in the Commonwealth) the entire House of Commons when sitting as a committee to discuss the details of a proposed bill.

committee woman *noun* (*pl.* **-women**) **1** a woman who serves on a committee or committees, esp. frequently. **2** (in the US) a woman who is the local leader of a political party in a ward etc.

com·mode /kəˈmoːd/ *noun* **1 a** a chest of drawers. **b** = CHIFFONIER. **2 a** a bedside table with a cupboard containing a chamber pot. **b** a chamber pot concealed in a chair with a hinged cover. **3** *N Amer. informal* a toilet or bathroom (*where is the commode?*). [French, adj. (as noun) from Latin *commodus* convenient (as COM-, *modus* measure)]

com·modi·fi·ca·tion /kə,mɒdɪfɪˈkeɪʃən/ *noun* the action of turning something into or treating something as a (mere) commodity. □ **com·mod·ify** /kəˈmɒdɪfaɪ/ *transitive verb* (**-fies**, **-fied**). [COMMODITY; see -FICATION]

com·modi·ous /kəˈmoːdiəs/ *adjective* roomy and comfortable. □ **com·modi·ous·ly** *adverb* **com·modi·ous·ness** *noun* [French *commodieux* or from medieval Latin *commodiosus* from Latin *commodus* (as COMMODE)]

com·mod·itize /kəˈmɒdətaɪz/ *transitive verb* (also esp. *Brit.* **-itise**) **1** turn into or treat as a mere commodity. **2** (of the market) perceive (goods of different brands) to be essentially the same and interchangeable. □ **com·modi·tiz·a·tion** *noun*

com·mod·ity /kəˈmɒdəti/ *noun* (*pl.* **-ities**) **1** an article that can be bought and sold, esp. a product as opposed to a service. **2** any of several raw or partially processed materials, e.g. grain, coffee, wool, or metals. **3** a useful thing. [Old French *commodité* or from Latin *commoditas* (as COMMODE)]

com·mo·dore /ˈkɒmə,dɔr/ *noun* **1** (also **Commodore**) (in Canada and the UK, and formerly also in the US) a naval officer ranking above captain and below rear admiral. Abbr.: **Cmdre**. **2** the commander of a squadron or other group of vessels smaller than a fleet travelling together. **3** the senior officer of a yacht club. **4** the senior captain of a shipping line. [prob. from Dutch *komandeur* from French *commandeur* COMMANDER]

Com·mo·dus /ˈkɒmədəs/ **Lu·cius Ael·ius Aurel·ius** (161–92), son of Marcus Aurelius, Roman emperor 180–192, noted for his violent and despotic reign.

com·mon ● *adjective* (**com·mon·er**, **com·mon·est**) **1 a** occurring often (*a common mistake*). **b** ordinary; of ordinary qualities; without special rank or position (*common soldier*; *the common people*). **2 a** shared by, coming from, or done by, more than one (*common knowledge*; *by common consent*; *our common benefit*). **b** belonging to, open to, or affecting, the whole community or the public (*common land*). **3** *derogatory* low-class; vulgar; inferior. **4** of the most familiar type (*common cold*; *common nightshade*). **5** *Math.* belonging to two or more quantities (*common denominator*; *common factor*). **6** *Grammar* (of gender) referring to individuals of either sex (e.g. *teacher*). **7** *Prosody* (of a syllable) that may be either short or long. **8** *Law* (of a crime) of lesser importance (compare GRAND 9, PETTY 4). ● *noun* **1** (**the Commons**) = HOUSE OF COMMONS. **2** a piece of land set aside for public use, esp. as a park or recreation area in a city or town. **3** (in *pl.*) **a** the common people as opposed to those in authority. **b** the common people viewed as forming part of a political system, esp. as opposed to those of aristocratic status. **4** *Christianity* a service used for each of a group of occasions for which no individual proper is appointed. **5** (in full **right of common**) *Law* a person's right to use another's property for pasturing animals or for fishing. □ **common or garden** *informal* ordinary. **in common 1** in joint use; shared. **2** of joint interest (*have little in common*). **in common** = IN COMMON. **short commons** *archaic* insufficient food. □ **com·mon·ly** *adverb* **com·mon·ness** *noun* [Old French *comun* from Latin *communis*]

com·mon·age /ˈkɒmənədʒ/ *noun* **1** right of common (see COMMON *noun* 5). **2 a** land held in common. **b** the state of being held in common.

com·mon·al·ity /,kɒməˈnaliti/ *noun* (*pl.* **-ities**) **1** the sharing of an attribute. **2** a shared feature or attribute. **3** = COMMONALTY. [var. of COMMONALTY]

com·mon·alty /ˈkɒmənəlti/ *noun* (*pl.* **-ties**) **1** esp. *hist.* people without special rank or position, usu. viewed as an estate of the realm. **2** the general body of a group. [Old French *comunalté* from medieval Latin *communalitas -tatis* (as COMMON)]

common carrier *noun* **1** a person or company undertaking to transport any goods or person in a specified category (compare PRIVATE CARRIER). **2** *N Amer.* a company providing public telecommunications services.

common chord *noun Music* any note with its major or minor third and perfect fifth.

common council *noun N Amer.* a town council in some communities, e.g. Saint John, New Brunswick.

common denominator *noun* **1** *Math.* a common multiple of the denominators of several fractions. **2** a common feature of members of a group.

common eider *noun see* EIDER 1.

com·mon·er *noun* one of the common people, as opposed to the aristocracy.

Common Era *noun* = CHRISTIAN ERA.

common goldeneye *noun see* GOLDENEYE.

common ground *noun* a point or argument accepted by both sides in a dispute.

common law *noun* (usu. hyphenated when *attributive*) **1** law derived from custom and judicial precedent rather than statutes (compare CASE LAW, STATUTE LAW). **2 a** (usu. *attributive*) denoting a relationship between cohabiting partners, recognized as a marriage in some common law jurisdictions but not brought about by a civil or ecclesiastical ceremony. **b** a common-law spouse.

common logarithm *noun* a logarithm to the base 10.

common loon *noun see* LOON 1.

common market *noun* **1** a group of countries imposing few or no duties on trade with one another and a common tariff on trade with other countries. **2** (**the Common Market**) a name for the European Economic Community used esp. in the 1960s and 1970s.

common merganser *noun see* MERGANSER.

common murre *noun see* MURRE.

common noun *noun* (also **common name**) *Grammar* a name denoting a class of objects or a concept as opposed to a particular individual, e.g. *boy, chocolate, beauty.*

com·mon·place ● *adjective* lacking originality; trite. ● *noun* **1 a** an everyday saying; a platitude. **b** an ordinary topic of conversation. **2** anything usual or trite. **3** a notable passage in a book etc. copied into a commonplace book. □ **com·mon·place·ness** *noun* [translation of Latin *locus communis* = Greek *koinos topos* general theme]

commonplace book *noun* a book into which notable extracts from other works are copied for personal use.

Common Prayer *noun* the Anglican liturgy originally set forth in the *Book of Common Prayer* of Edward VI (1549).

common room *noun* a room in a college, school, etc., which students and staff may use for relaxation or work.

common rorqual *noun* = FINBACK.

common salt *noun see* SALT 1.

common seal *noun* a seal with a mottled grey coat, *Phoca vitulina*, of N Atlantic and N Pacific coasts.

common sense ● *noun* sound practical sense, esp. in everyday matters. ● *adjective* = COMMONSENSICAL.

common·sens·ical *adjective* possessing or marked by common sense.

common share *noun* (also **common stock**) *N Amer.* an ordinary capital share in a company, yielding a flexible dividend (compare PREFERRED SHARE).

common soldier *noun see* SOLDIER 2.

common time *noun Music* a time signature having four beats in a bar with each quarter note receiving one beat.

common touch *noun* an ability to get on with and appeal to people of a lower professional or social status.

com·mon·weal *noun* **1** common well-being; the general good. **2** *archaic* commonwealth.

com·mon·wealth /ˈkɒmən‿welθ/ *noun* **1 a** a community of people viewed as a political entity in which everyone has an interest. **b** any aggregate of persons or nations united by some common factor. **2** (**Commonwealth**) **a** (in full **the Commonwealth of Nations**) an international association comprising members of the former British Empire which acknowledge the British sovereign as their official head of state. ¶ Before 1946, called the *British Commonwealth of Nations*. **b** *hist.* the republican period of government in Britain 1649–60.

c the formal title of Puerto Rico and the states of Kentucky, Massachusetts, Pennsylvania, and Virginia. **d** the formal title of the federated Australian states.

Commonwealth Games *plural noun* a sports competition including teams from all commonwealth countries, held every four years.

Commonwealth of Independent States a confederation of independent states, formerly constituent republics of the Soviet Union, established in 1991 following a meeting in the Belarussian city of Brest at which the USSR was dissolved. The member states are Armenia, Belarus, Kazakhstan, Kyrgyzstan, Moldova, Russia, Tajikistan, Turkmenistan, Ukraine, and Uzbekistan (Azerbaijan left in 1992). The administrative headquarters of the CIS is at Minsk in Belarus. Abbr.: **CIS**.

common year *noun see* YEAR 2.

com·mo·tion *noun* **1 a** a confused and noisy disturbance or outburst. **b** loud and confusing noise. **2** a civil insurrection. [Old French *commotion* or Latin *commotio* (as COM-, MOTION)]

com·mun·al /kəˈmjuːnəl/ *adjective* **1** relating or belonging to a community; for common use (*communal bathroom*). **2** of or relating to a commune. **3** of or relating to ethnic or religious groups within a larger community (*communal violence*). □ **com·mun·al·ity** /ˌkɒmjəˈnaləti/ *noun* **com·mun·al·ly** *adverb*

com·mun·al·ism /kəˈmjuːnəˌlɪzəm/ *noun* **1** a principle of political organization based on federated communes. **2** the principle of communal ownership etc. **3** excessive devotion to one's own ethnic or religious community as opposed to society in general.
□ **com·mun·al·ist** *noun* **com·mun·al·is·tic** *adjective*

com·mu·nard /ˈkɒmjuˌnɑrd/ *noun* **1** a member of a commune. **2** (**Communard**) *hist.* a supporter of the Paris Commune (1871). [French (as COMMUNE¹)]

com·mune¹ /ˈkɒmjuːn/ *noun* **1 a** a group of people, not necessarily related, sharing living accommodation and possessions, esp. as a political act. **b** a communal settlement esp. for the pursuit of shared interests. **2 a** the smallest French territorial division for administrative purposes. **b** a similar division elsewhere. [French from medieval Latin *communia* neuter pl. of Latin *communis* common]

com·mune² /kəˈmjuːn/ *intransitive verb* **1** (usu. foll. by *with*) **a** speak confidentially and intimately (*communed with her friends about their loss*). **b** feel in close touch (*communed with nature*). **2** *N Amer.* Christianity receive Holy Communion. [Old French *comuner* share, from *comun* COMMON]

Commune, the (also **Commune of Paris, Paris Commune**) **1** a group which seized the municipal government of Paris in the French Revolution and in this capacity played a leading part in the Reign of Terror until suppressed in 1794. **2** a communalistic municipal government containing many socialists and revolutionaries, elected in Paris in 1871 after the Franco-Prussian War and the collapse of the Second Empire. It was soon brutally suppressed by government troops from Versailles.

com·munic·able /kəˈmjuːnɪkəbəl/ *adjective* (esp. of a disease) able to be passed on. □ **com·munic·abil·ity** *noun*

com·muni·cant /kəˈmjuːnɪkənt/ *noun* Christianity a person who receives Holy Communion, esp. regularly. [Latin *communicare communicant-* (as COMMON)]

com·muni·cate *verb* **1** *transitive* **a** transmit or pass on (information) by speaking, writing, or other means. **b** transmit (heat, motion, etc.). **c** pass on (an infectious illness). **d** impart (feelings etc.) non-verbally (*communicated his affection*). **2** *intransitive* succeed in conveying information, evoking understanding etc. (*she communicates well*). **3** *intransitive* (often foll. by *with*) share a feeling or understanding; relate socially. **4** *intransitive* (often foll. by *with*) (of a room etc.) have a common connecting door. **5** *Christianity* **a** *transitive* administer Holy Communion to. **b** *intransitive* receive Holy Communion. □ **com·muni·ca·tor** *noun* **com·muni·ca·tory** *adjective* [Latin *communicare communicat-* (as COMMON)]

com·muni·ca·tion *noun* **1 a** the act of communicating, esp. imparting news. **b** an instance of this. **c** the information etc. communicated. **2** a means of connecting different places, such as a door, passage, road, or railway. **3** social contact; routine exchange of information. **4** (in *pl.*) **a** the science and practice of transmitting information esp. by electronic or mechanical means. **b** a field of study encompassing writing and broadcasting skills as they apply to media and business. **c** the function of communicating information to the public by a company, organization, etc. (also *attributive*: *communications officer*). **5** (in *pl.*) *Military* the means of transport between a base and the front. **6** a paper read to a learned society. □ **com·muni·ca·tion·al** *adjective* (in senses 1 and 3).

communications satellite *noun* (also **communication satellite**) an artificial satellite used to relay telephone, television, or radio signals to another (usu. distant) location.

com·mu·ni·ca·tive /kəˈmjuːnɪkətɪv, -ˌkeɪtɪv/ *adjective* **1** open, talkative, informative. **2** ready to communicate. **3** designating styles of teaching, esp. of a second language, that emphasize the communication of meaning in real-life situations rather than the mastery of grammatical forms. □ **com·mu·ni·ca·tive·ly** *adverb*

com·mun·ion /kəˈmjuːnɪən/ *noun* **1** an instance of sharing, esp. thoughts or feelings; fellowship (*their minds were in communion*). **2** participation; a sharing in common (*communion of interests*). **3** (also **Communion**) *Christianity* **a** (in full **Holy Communion**) the Eucharist. **b** participation in the Communion service. **c** (*attributive*) of or used in the Communion service. **4** fellowship, esp. between branches of the Catholic Church. **5** a body or group within the Christian faith (*the Anglican communion*).

communion of saints *noun* *Christianity* fellowship between Christians living and dead.

communion rail *noun* a low railing in front of an altar at which people kneel to receive Holy Communion.

communion table *noun* (in some Protestant denominations) the table used in the celebration of the Communion of the Lord's Supper.

com·mu·ni·qué /kəˈmjuːnɪˌkeɪ, kəmjuːnəˈkeɪ/ *noun* an official communication, esp. a news report. [French, = communicated]

com·mun·ism /ˈkɒmjʊˌnɪzəm/ *noun* **1** a system of society with property vested in the community and each member working for the common benefit according to his or her capacity and receiving according to his or her needs. **2** (usu. **Communism**) **a** the movement or political party advocating such a system, esp. as derived from Marxism and seeking the overthrow of capitalism by a proletarian revolution. **b** the communistic form of society established in the 20th c. in the former USSR and elsewhere. **3** = COMMUNALISM. [French *communisme* from *commun* COMMON]

Communism Peak a former name for ISMAIL SAMANI PEAK.

com·mun·ist /ˈkɒmjʊnɪst/ ● *noun* **1** a person advocating or practising communism. **2** (**Communist**) a member of a Communist Party. ● *adjective* **1** of or relating to communism (*a communist play*). **2** (**Communist**) of or relating to Communism. □ **com·mun·is·tic** /-ˈnɪstɪk/ *adjective*

com·mu·ni·tar·ian /kəˌmjuːnɪˈteriən/ ● *noun* a member of a community practising co-operation and some communism. ● *adjective* of or relating to such a community. □ **com·mu·ni·tar·ian·ism** *noun* [COMMUNITY + -ARIAN after *unitarian* etc.]

com·mun·ity /kəˈmjuːnɪti/ *noun* (pl. **-ities**) **1 a** all the people living in a specific locality. **b** a specific locality, including its inhabitants. **c** *Cdn* (*Nfld & PEI*) a small incorporated municipality. **2** a body of people having a religion, a profession, etc., in common (*the immigrant community*). **3** fellowship of interests etc.; similarity (*community of intellect*). **4** a monastic, socialistic, etc. body practising common ownership. **5** joint ownership or liability (*community of goods*). **6** (prec. by *the*) the public. **7** a body of nations unified by common interests. **8** *Ecology* a group of animals or plants living or growing together in the same area. **9** (*attributive*) = COMMUNITY ACCESS (*community channel*). [Old French *comuneté* from Latin *communitas -tatis* (as COMMON)]

community access *noun* (usu. *attributive*) *Cdn* = PUBLIC ACCESS.

community care *noun* public health care emphasizing the treatment of long-term patients in their communities rather than in hospitals or institutions.

community centre *noun* (also **community club**) a place providing social and recreational facilities for a neighbourhood.

community chest *noun* a fund for charity and welfare work in a community.

community college *noun* esp. *N Amer.* a post-secondary educational institution offering training esp. in specific employment fields.

community garden *noun* a piece of public land which members of the community are allowed to cultivate as a garden.

community hall *noun* *Cdn* a hall maintained by a community for holding suppers, dances, wedding receptions, etc.

community living *noun* the integration into the community of people with developmental disabilities, esp. as opposed to institutionalization.

community policing *noun* policing by officers intended to have personal knowledge of the community which they police.

community service *noun* work, esp. voluntary and unpaid, or stipulated by a community service order, in the community.

community service order *noun* an order for a convicted offender to perform a period of unpaid work in the community.

community spirit *noun* a feeling of belonging to a community, expressed in mutual support etc.

community worker *noun* a person who works in a community to promote its welfare, either as a paid social worker or volunteer. □ **community work** *noun*

com·mut·able /kəˈmjuːtəbəl/ *adjective* **1** convertible into money; exchangeable. **2** within commuting distance. □ **com·mut·abil·ity** *noun* [Latin *commutabilis* (as COMMUTE)]

com·mu·tate /ˈkɒmjuːˌteɪt/ *transitive verb* *Electricity* **1** regulate the direction of (an alternating current), esp. to make it a direct current. **2** reverse the direction (of an electric current).

com·mu·ta·tion /ˌkɒmjuːˈteɪʃən/ *noun* **1** the act or process of commuting or being commuted (in legal and exchange senses). **2** *Electricity* the act or process of commutating or being commutated. **3** *Math.* the reversal of the order of two quantities.

com·mu·ta·tive /kəˈmjuːtətɪv/ *adjective* **1** relating to or involving substitution. **2** *Math.* unchanged in result by the interchange of the order of quantities, e.g. that $a \times b = b \times a$.

com·mu·ta·tor /ˈkɒmjuːˌteɪtər/ *noun* **1** *Electricity* a device for reversing electric current. **2** an attachment connected with the armature of a generator which directs and makes continuous the current produced.

com·mute ● *verb* **1** *intransitive* travel to and from one's daily work, esp. from suburbs to the centre of a city by car or public transit. **2** *transitive* *Law* (often foll. by *to*) change (a judicial sentence etc.) to another less severe. **3** *transitive* (often foll. by *into, for*) **a** change (one kind of payment) for another. **b** make a payment etc. to change (an obligation etc.) for another. **4** *transitive* **a** exchange; interchange (two things). **b** change (to another thing). **5** *transitive Electricity* commutate. **6** *intransitive Math.* have a commutative relation. ● *noun* **1** an act of commuting. **2** a distance travelled by a commuter. [Latin *commutare commutat-* (as COM-, *mutare* change)]

com·mut·er ● *noun* a person who travels some distance to work, esp. from suburbs to the centre of a city by car or public transit. ● *adjective* **1** relating to or for the use of commuters (*commuter train*). **2** of or relating to a flight, aircraft, or airline that flies comparatively short distances, usu. between small communities.

commuter marriage *noun* *N Amer.* a marriage in which the spouses live at considerable distance from one another because of work obligations, and regularly travel to be together.

com·mut·er·shed *noun* *N Amer.* the region from within which it is possible to commute to work in a large, central city.

Como, Lake /ˈkoːmoː/ a lake in the foothills of the Alps in N Italy.

Como·doro Riva·davia /ˌkɒmoˌdɔːroː ˌriːvəˈdɒviə/ a port in Argentina situated on the Atlantic coast of Patagonia; pop. (est. 2002) 157,600.

Com·or·in, Cape /ˈkɒmərɪn/ a cape at the southern tip of India, in the state of Tamil Nadu.

Com·or·os /ˈkɒməˌrɒz/ a country consisting of a group of islands in the Indian Ocean north of Madagascar; pop. (est. 2002) 614,382; capital, Moroni. □ **Com·or·an** *adjective & noun*

co·mose /ˈkoːmoːs/ *adjective Bot.* (of seeds etc.) having hairs, downy. [Latin *comosus* (as COMA²)]

Comox¹ /ˈkoːmɒks/ a town in BC, situated on the east central coast of Vancouver Island, near Courtenay; pop. (2001) 11,172. [COMOX²]

Comox² /ˈkoːmɒks/ *noun* **1** a member of an Aboriginal group, part of the Salishan linguistic group, living on Vancouver Island. **2** the Salishan language of these people. [Comox, = 'land of plenty']

comp *informal* ● *noun* **1** a competition. **2** a complimentary ticket, pass, etc. **3** a comprehensive examination. **4** composition. **5** compensation (*worker's comp*). **6** *Printing etc.* **a** a compositor. **b** a composite. **7** *Music* an accompaniment. ● *verb* **1** play (music) as an accompaniment, esp. in jazz and blues. **2** *Printing* **a** *intransitive* work as a compositor. **b** *transitive* work as a compositor on. **3** *transitive* give (something) away free, esp. as part of a promotion. [abbreviation]

com·pact¹ ● *adjective* /ˈkɒmpakt, kəmˈpakt/ **1** closely or neatly packed together. **2** (of a piece of equipment, a room, etc.) well fitted and practical though small. **3** (of style etc.) condensed; brief. **4** (esp. of the human body) small but well-proportioned. **5** *N Amer.* designating a car that is larger than a subcompact and smaller than a mid-size, usu. having a wheelbase of 85 to 95 inches, and a four-cylinder, 1.5-litre engine. ● *transitive verb* /kəmˈpakt/ **1** join or press firmly together. **2** condense. ● *noun* /ˈkɒmpakt/ **1** a small, flat case for face powder, a mirror, pills, etc. **2** a mass of powdered metal compacted together in

Consonants: b *but*   d *dog*   f *few*   g *get*   h *her*   j *yes*   k *cat*   l *leg*   m *man*   n *no*   p *pen*   r *red*   s *sit*

preparation for sintering. **3** N Amer. a compact car. □ **com·pac·tion** noun **com·pact·ly** adverb **com·pact·ness** noun **com·pact·or** noun (also **com·pact·er**). [Latin compingere compact- (as COM-, pangere fasten)]

com·pact² /ˈkɒmpakt/ noun an agreement or contract between two or more parties. [Latin compactum from compacisci compact- (as COM-, pacisci covenant): compare PACT]

compact disc noun a disc on which information or sound is recorded digitally and reproduced by reflection of laser light.

compact fluorescent noun a low-wattage energy-efficient fluorescent light bulb with a standard screw-in base, designed to replace a regular incandescent bulb.

com·padre /kəmˈpɒdrei/ noun (pl. **com·padres**) esp. N Amer. informal friend, companion. [Spanish, = godfather]

com·pan·ion¹ /kəmˈpanjən/ ● noun **1 a** a person or animal with whom one spends a lot of time or with whom one travels. **b** (often foll. by in, of) a person who shares the experiences of another, esp. when these are unpleasant or unwelcome (a companion in adversity). **c** a person with similar tastes and interests to one's own and with whom one has an enjoyable, friendly relationship. **d** used euphemistically to denote a person's long-term sexual partner outside marriage. **e** a person, esp. an unmarried or widowed woman, employed to live with and assist another. **2** a handbook or reference book on a particular subject (A Companion to Canadian Literature). **3** a thing that matches another (the companion to this bookend is over there). **4** (**Companion**) a member of the highest grade of the Order of Canada. **5** (**Companion**) a member of the lowest grade of some honorary orders etc. **6** Astronomy a star etc. that accompanies another. ● transitive verb accompany. [Old French compaignon, lit. = 'one who breaks bread with another', ultimately from Latin panis bread]

com·pan·ion² /kəmˈpanjən/ noun Naut. **1** a raised frame on a quarterdeck used for lighting the cabins etc. below. **2** = COMPANIONWAY. [obsolete Dutch kompanje quarterdeck, from Old French compagne from Italian (camera della) compagna pantry, prob. ultimately related to COMPANION¹]

com·pan·ion·able adjective agreeable as a companion; sociable. □ **com·pan·ion·abil·ity** noun **com·pan·ion·able·ness** noun **com·pan·ion·ably** adverb

companion animal noun a pet.

companion piece noun a musical composition, literary work, etc. that deals with similar themes to another work.

companion planting noun a method of gardening in which plants are arranged so that they benefit from the properties of the plants adjacent to them.

com·pan·ion·ship noun good fellowship; friendship.

com·pan·ion·way noun Naut. a staircase to a cabin.

com·pany ● noun (pl. **-ies**) **1 a** a number of people assembled; a crowd; an audience (addressed the company). **b** guests or a guest (am expecting company). **2** a state of being a companion or fellow; companionship, esp. of a specific kind (enjoys low company; do not care for their company). **3 a** a commercial business. **b** (usu. **Company**) the partner or partners not named in the title of a firm (Smith and Company). Abbr.: **Co. 4 a** a group of performers. **b** the organization to which they belong, including administrators, fundraisers, etc. **5** Military a subdivision of an infantry battalion usu. commanded by a major or a captain. **6** a group of Guides. **7** Cdn = HUDSON'S BAY COMPANY. **8** (**the Company**) US informal the CIA. ● verb (**-ies**, **-ied**) **1** transitive archaic accompany. **2** intransitive literary (often foll. by with) be a companion. □ **be in good company** discover that one's companions, or better people, have done the same as oneself. **in company** not alone. **in company with** together with. **keep company** (often foll. by with) associate habitually. **keep** (archaic **bear**) **a person company** accompany a person; be sociable. **part company 1** separate (we parted company until the weekend). **2** (often foll. by with) **a** cease to associate. **b** differ, disagree. [Anglo-French compainie, Old French compai(g)nie from Romanic (as COMPANION¹)]

company car noun a car provided by a company for the business and usu. private use of an employee.

company of heaven noun Christianity all the angels and redeemed souls in heaven.

company sergeant major noun Military (in the Commonwealth) the highest non-commissioned officer of a company.

company store noun N Amer. a store operated by a company, esp. in an isolated area, for the sale of commercial goods to its employees, usu. as a monopoly.

company town noun N Amer. a town, esp. in an isolated area, that is dependent upon one company, e.g. a mine or mill, for all or almost all of its employment, housing, etc.

com·par·able /ˈkɒmpərəbəl, kəmˈperəbəl/ adjective (often foll. by to, with) **1** fit to be compared; worth comparing. **2** able to be compared. **3** similar. □ **com·par·abil·ity** /-ˈbɪlɪti/ noun **com·par·ably** adverb

com·para·tive /kəmˈperətɪv/ ● adjective **1** measured or judged by estimating the similarity or dissimilarity between one thing and another; relative (in comparative comfort). **2** of or involving the systematic observation of the similarities or dissimilarities between two or more branches of science or subjects of study (comparative anatomy; comparative literature). **3** Grammar (of an adjective or adverb) expressing a higher degree of a quality, but not the highest possible (e.g. braver, more fiercely) (compare POSITIVE adjective 4b, SUPERLATIVE adjective 2). ● noun Grammar a comparative adjective or adverb. □ **com·para·tive·ly** adverb

com·para·tor /kəmˈperətər/ noun Engin. a device for comparing a product, an output, etc., with a standard, esp. an electronic circuit comparing two signals.

com·pare ● verb **1** transitive (usu. foll. by to) express similarities in; liken (compared the landscape to a painting). **2** transitive (often foll. by to, with) estimate the similarity or dissimilarity of; assess the relation between (compared radio with television; that lacks quality compared to this). ¶ In current use to and with are generally interchangeable, but with often implies a greater element of formal analysis, as in compared my account with yours. **3** intransitive (often foll. by with) bear comparison (compares favourably with the rest). **4** intransitive (often foll. by with) be equal or equivalent to. **5** transitive Grammar form the comparative and superlative degrees of (an adjective or an adverb). ● noun literary comparison (beyond compare; has no compare). □ **compare notes** exchange ideas or opinions. [Old French comparer from Latin comparare (as COM-, parare from par equal)]

com·pari·son /kəmˈperɪsən/ noun **1** the act or an instance of comparing. **2** a simile or semantic illustration. **3** capacity for being likened; similarity (there's no comparison). **4** Grammar the positive, comparative, and superlative forms of adjectives and adverbs. □ **bear** (or **stand**) **comparison** (often foll. by with) be able to be compared favourably. **beyond comparison 1** totally different in quality. **2** greatly superior; excellent. **in comparison** with compared to. [Old French comparesoun from Latin comparatio -onis (as COMPARE)]

comparison shop intransitive verb N Amer. shop around to various providers of goods or services to locate the best value, service, etc. for the same product before buying. □ **comparison shopper** noun **comparison shopping** noun

com·part·ment ● noun **1** a space within a larger space, separated from the rest by partitions, e.g. in a railway carriage, wallet, desk, etc. **2** Naut. a watertight division of a ship. **3** an area of activity etc. kept apart from others in a person's mind. ● transitive verb put into compartments. □ **com·part·men·ta·tion** noun [French compartiment from Italian compartimento from Late Latin compartiri (as COM-, partiri share)]

com·part·ment·al adjective consisting of or relating to compartments or a compartment. □ **com·part·ment·al·ly** adverb

com·part·ment·al·ize transitive verb (also esp. Brit. **-ise**) divide into compartments or categories. □ **com·part·ment·al·iz·a·tion** noun

com·pass /ˈkʌmpəs/ ● noun **1** (in full **magnetic compass**) an instrument showing the direction of magnetic north and bearings from it. **2** (often in pl.) an instrument for taking measurements and describing circles, with two legs connected at one end by a movable joint. **3** a circumference or boundary. **4** area, extent; scope (e.g. of knowledge or experience) (beyond my compass). **5** the range of tones of a voice or a musical instrument. ● transitive verb literary **1** hem in. **2** grasp mentally. **3** contrive, accomplish. **4** go around. [Old French compas, ultimately from Latin passus PACE¹]

compass card noun a circular rotating card showing the 32 principal bearings, forming the indicator of a magnetic compass.

com·pas·sion /kəmˈpasʃən/ noun pity inclining one to help or be merciful. [Old French from ecclesiastical Latin compassio -onis from compati (as COM-, pati pass- suffer)]

com·pas·sion·ate adjective sympathetic, pitying. □ **com·pas·sion·ate·ly** adverb

compassionate leave noun leave granted on grounds of bereavement etc.

compassion club noun Cdn a non-profit organization which sells marijuana for medical use.

compassion fatigue *noun* indifference to charitable appeals resulting from the frequency of such appeals.

compass rose *noun* a graduated circle showing the points of the compass.

compass saw *noun* a saw with a narrow blade, for cutting curves.

com·pat·ible /kəmˈpatəbəl/ ● *adjective* **1** (often foll. by *with*) **a** able to coexist; well-suited; mutually tolerant (*a compatible couple*). **b** consistent (*their views are not compatible with their actions*). **2** (of equipment etc.) capable of being used in combination. ● *noun* (usu. in *combination*) *Computing* a piece of equipment that can use software etc. designed for another brand of the same equipment (*IBM compatibles*). □ **com·pat·ibil·ity** /-ˈbɪlɪti/ *noun* **com·pat·ibly** *adverb* [French from medieval Latin *compatibilis* (as COMPASSION)]

com·patri·ot /kəmˈpeitriət/ *noun* **1** a native or inhabitant of one's own country or region. **2** an associate, colleague, or peer. [French *compatriote* from Late Latin *compatriota* (as COM-, *patriota* PATRIOT)]

com·peer /ˈkɒmpiːr, -ˈpiːr/ *noun* **1** an equal, a peer. **2** a comrade. [Old French *comper* (as COM-, PEER²)]

com·pel /kəmˈpel/ *transitive verb* (**com·pelled**, **com·pel·ling**) **1** (usu. foll. by *to* + infin.) force, oblige (*compelled them to admit it*). **2** bring about (an action) by force (*compel submission*). [Latin *compellere compuls-* (as COM-, *pellere* drive)]

com·pel·lable *adjective Law* (of a witness) able to be made to attend court or give evidence.

com·pel·ling /kəmˈpelɪŋ/ *adjective* arousing strong interest, attention, conviction, or admiration. □ **com·pel·ling·ly** *adverb*

com·pen·di·ous /kəmˈpendiəs/ *adjective* (esp. of a book etc.) comprehensive but fairly brief. □ **com·pen·di·ous·ly** *adverb* **com·pen·di·ous·ness** *noun*

com·pen·dium /kəmˈpendiəm/ *noun* (*pl.* **com·pen·diums** or **com·pen·dia** /-diə/) **1** a collection of detailed items of information, esp. in a book. **2 a** a summary or abstract of a larger work. **b** an abridgement. **3** esp. *Brit.* a usu. one-volume handbook or encyclopedia. [Latin, = what is weighed together, from *compendere* (as COM-, *pendere* weigh)]

com·pen·sate /ˈkɒmpənˌseit/ *verb* (often foll. by *for*) **1** *transitive* recompense (a person) (*compensated her for her loss*). **2** *intransitive* make amends (*compensated for the insult*). **3** *transitive* counterbalance. **4** *transitive Mech.* provide (a pendulum etc.) with extra or less weight etc. to neutralize the effects of temperature etc. **5** *intransitive Psych.* offset a disability or frustration by development in another direction. □ **com·pen·sa·tor** *noun* **com·pen·sa·tory** /-ˈpensətɔri, -ˈseitɔri/ *adjective* [Latin *compensare* (as COM-, *pensare* frequentative of *pendere* *pens-* weigh)]

com·pen·sa·tion /ˌkɒmpenˈseiʃən/ *noun* **1 a** the act of compensating. **b** the process of being compensated. **2** something, esp. money, given as a recompense. **3** *N Amer.* a salary or wages. **4** *Psych.* **a** an act of compensating. **b** the result of compensating.

compensation pendulum *noun Physics* a pendulum designed to neutralize the effects of temperature variation.

com·père /ˈkɒmper/ *Brit.* ● *noun* a master of ceremonies, esp. in a variety show etc. ● *verb* **1** *transitive* act as a compère to. **2** *intransitive* act as compère. [French, = godfather, from Romanic (as COM-, Latin *pater* father)]

com·pete *intransitive verb* **1** (often foll. by *with*, *against* a person, *for* a thing) strive for superiority or supremacy (*competed with his sister*; *compete against the Americans*; *compete for the victory*). **2** (often foll. by *in*) take part (in a contest etc.) (*competed in the hurdles*). [Latin *competere competit-*, in late sense 'strive after or contend for (something)' (as COM-, *petere* seek)]

com·pe·tence /ˈkɒmpətəns/ *noun* (also **com·pe·tency** /ˈkɒmpətənsi/ *pl.* **-cies**) **1 a** (often foll. by *for*, or *to* + infin.) ability; the state of being competent. **b** an area in which a person is competent; a skill. **2** *Law* the legal capacity (of a court, a magistrate, etc.) to deal with a matter.

com·pe·tent /ˈkɒmpətənt/ *adjective* **1 a** (usu. foll. by *to* + infin. or *for*) adequately qualified or capable (*not competent to drive*). **b** effective (*a competent swimmer*). **2** *Law* (of a judge, court, or witness) legally qualified or qualifying. □ **com·pe·tent·ly** *adverb* [Old French *competent* or Latin *competent-* (as COMPETE)]

com·pe·ti·tion /ˌkɒmpəˈtɪʃən/ *noun* **1** (often foll. by *for*) the act or an instance of competing or contending with others (for supremacy, a position, a prize, etc.). **2** an event or contest in which people compete. **3 a** the people competing against a person. **b** the opposition they represent. **c** products in the same category as another sold in the marketplace (*the dictionary was vastly better than the competition*). **4** *Biol.*

interaction between organisms etc. that share a limited environmental resource. [Late Latin *competitio* rivalry (as COMPETITIVE)]

competition bureau *noun* a government agency that enforces laws and regulations aimed at ensuring fair competition in the marketplace.

com·peti·tive /kəmˈpetɪtiv/ *adjective* **1** involving, offered for, or by competition (*competitive contest*). **2** (of prices etc.) low enough to compare well with those of rival products etc. **3** (of a person) having a strong urge to win; keen to compete. □ **com·peti·tive·ly** *adverb* **com·peti·tive·ness** *noun* [*competit-*, past participle stem of Latin *competere* COMPETE]

com·peti·tor /kəmˈpetɪtər/ *noun* **1** a person who competes. **2** a rival, esp. in business or commerce. [French *compétiteur* or Latin *competitor* (as COMPETE)]

com·pil·a·tion /ˌkɒmpəˈleiʃən/ *noun* **1 a** the act of compiling. **b** the process of being compiled. **2** something compiled, esp. a book, CD, etc. that is put together by assembling previously separate articles, stories, musical selections, etc.

com·pile *transitive verb* **1 a** collect (material) into a list, volume, etc. **b** make up (a volume etc.) from such material. **2** *Computing* produce (a machine-coded form of a high-level program). **3** *Sport* accumulate (a large number of) (*compiled a score of 160*). [Old French *compiler* or its apparent source, Latin *compilare* plunder, plagiarize]

com·pil·er *noun* **1** *Computing* a program for translating a high-level programming language into machine code. **2** a person who compiles.

com·pla·cency /kəmˈpleisən,si/ *noun* (also **com·pla·cence**) a feeling of smug self-satisfaction. [medieval Latin *complacentia* from Latin *complacēre* (as COM-, *placēre* please)]

com·pla·cent /kəmˈpleisənt/ *adjective* smugly self-satisfied. □ **com·pla·cent·ly** *adverb* [Latin *complacēre*: see COMPLACENCY]

com·plain *intransitive verb* **1** express dissatisfaction (*complained about the state of the room*; *is always complaining*). **2** (foll. by *of*) announce that one is suffering from (an ailment) (*complained of a headache*). **3** make a mournful sound; groan or creak under a strain. □ **com·plain·er** *noun* **com·plain·ing·ly** *adverb* [Old French *complaindre* (stem *complaign-*) from medieval Latin *complangere* bewail (as COM-, *plangere planct-* lament)]

com·plain·ant *noun Law* a plaintiff in certain lawsuits.

com·plaint *noun* **1** an act of complaining. **2** a grievance. **3** an ailment or illness. **4** *N Amer. Law* the plaintiff's case in a civil action. [Old French *complainte* from *complaint* past participle of *complaindre*: see COMPLAIN]

com·plai·sant /kəmˈpleizənt/ *adjective* **1** politely deferential. **2** willing to please; acquiescent. □ **com·plai·sance** *noun* [French from *complaire* (stem *complais-*) acquiesce to please, from Latin *complacēre*: see COMPLACENCY]

com·pleat /kəmˈpliːt/ *adjective* **1** *jocular* accomplished (*the compleat cook*). **2** *archaic var. of* COMPLETE. [variant spelling of COMPLETE, esp. in 16th and 17th c., revived because of use in I. Walton's *The Compleat Angler*]

com·plec·ted /kəmˈplektəd/ *adjective N Amer. informal* having a (specified) complexion. [apparently from COMPLEXION]

com·ple·ment ● *noun* /ˈkɒmpləmənt/ **1 a** something that completes. **b** one of a pair, or one of two things that go together. **2** (often **full complement**) the full number needed to crew a ship, operate a factory, etc. **3** *Grammar* a word or phrase added to a verb to complete the predicate of a sentence. **4** *Biochem.* a group of proteins in the blood capable of lysing bacteria etc. **5** *Math.* any element not belonging to a specified set or class. **6** *Geom.* the amount by which an angle is less than 90° (*compare* SUPPLEMENT *noun* 5). ● *transitive verb* /ˈkɒmpləˌment/ **1** complete. **2** form a complement to (*the scarf complements her dress*). ¶ Often confused with *compliment*. [Latin *complementum* (as COMPLETE)]

com·ple·men·tar·ity /ˌkɒmplimenˈtærɪti/ *noun* (*pl.* **-ities**) **1** a complementary relationship or situation. **2** *Physics* the concept that a single model may not be adequate to explain atomic systems in different experimental conditions.

com·ple·ment·ary /ˌkɒmpliˈmentəri/ *adjective* **1** completing; forming a complement. **2** (of two or more things) complementing each other. ¶ Often confused with *complimentary*. □ **com·ple·men·tar·i·ly** *adverb*

complementary angle *noun* either of two angles making up 90°.

complementary colour *noun* a colour that combined with a given colour makes white or black.

complementary medicine *noun* any of a range of medical therapies that fall beyond the scope of scientific medicine but may be used alongside it in the treatment of disease and ill health. Examples include acupuncture and osteopathy.

com·plete ● *adjective* **1** having all its parts; entire (*the set is complete*). **2** finished (*my task is complete*). **3** of the maximum extent or degree (*a complete surprise; a complete stranger*). **4** *Football* (of a forward pass) caught by the receiver. **5** = COMPLEAT 1. ● *verb* **1** *transitive* finish. **2** *transitive* **a** make whole or perfect. **b** make up the amount of (*completes the quota*). **3** *transitive* fill in the answers to (a questionnaire etc.). **4** *transitive Football* make or execute (a forward pass) successfully. **5** *transitive & intransitive Brit. Law* = CLOSE² *verb* 2c. □ **complete with** having (as an important accessory) (*comes complete with instructions*). □ **com·plet·ed** *adjective* **com·plete·ly** *adverb* **com·plete·ness** *noun* **com·plet·er** *noun* **com·ple·tion** *noun* [Old French *complet* or Latin *completus* past participle of *complēre* fill up]

com·plet·ist *noun* an obsessive or indiscriminate collector.

com·plex ● *noun* **1** a building, series of rooms, network, etc. made up of related parts (*the arts complex*). **2** *Psych.* a related group of usu. repressed feelings or thoughts which cause abnormal behaviour or mental states (*inferiority complex; Oedipus complex*). **3** (in general use) a preoccupation or obsession (*has a complex about punctuality*). **4** *Chem.* a compound in which molecules or ions form coordinate bonds to a metal atom or ion. ● *adjective* **1** consisting of related parts; composite. **2** complicated (*a complex problem*). **3** *Math.* containing real and imaginary parts (*compare* IMAGINARY). □ **com·plex·ity** *noun* (*pl.* **-ities**) **com·plex·ly** *adverb* [French *complexe* or Latin *complexus* past participle of *complectere* embrace, assoc. with *complexus* braided]

complex carbohydrate *noun* a carbohydrate that is mostly in the polysaccharide form, found in unrefined foods such as whole-grain breads in combination with vitamins, minerals, and fibre.

com·plex·ion /kəmˈplɛkʃən/ *noun* **1** the natural colour, texture, and appearance of the skin, esp. of the face. **2** an aspect; a character (*puts a different complexion on the matter*). □ **com·plex·ioned** *adjective* (also in *combination*) [Old French from Latin *complexio -onis* (as COMPLEX): originally = combination of supposed qualities determining the nature of a body]

complex sentence *noun* a sentence containing a subordinate clause or clauses.

com·pli·ance /kəmˈplaɪəns/ *noun* **1** the act or an instance of complying; obedience to a request, command, etc. **2** *Mech.* **a** the capacity to yield under an applied force. **b** the degree of such yielding. **3** unworthy acquiescence. □ **in compliance with** according to (a wish, command, etc.).

compliance officer *noun* a person who is employed to ensure that statutes or regulations are not contravened.

com·pli·ant /kəmˈplaɪənt/ *adjective* disposed to comply; yielding, obedient. □ **com·pli·ant·ly** *adverb*

com·pli·cate *transitive & intransitive verb* make or become difficult, confused, or complex. [Latin *complicare complicat-* (as COM-, *plicare* fold)]

com·pli·cat·ed *adjective* complex; intricate. □ **com·pli·cat·ed·ly** *adverb* **com·pli·cat·ed·ness** *noun*

com·pli·ca·tion *noun* **1 a** an involved or confused condition or state. **b** a complicating circumstance; a difficulty. **2** *Med.* a secondary disease or condition aggravating a previous one.

com·plic·i·ty /kəmˈplɪsɪti/ *noun* partnership in a crime or wrongdoing. □ **com·plicit** *adjective* **com·plici·tous** *adjective* [*complice* (see ACCOMPLICE) + -ITY]

com·pli·ment ● *noun* /ˈkɒmplɪmənt/ **1 a** a spoken or written expression of praise. **b** an act or circumstance implying praise (*their success was a compliment to their efforts*). **2** (in *pl.*) **a** a formal greetings, esp. as a written accompaniment to a gift etc. (*with the compliments of the management*). **b** praise (*my compliments to the cook*). ● *transitive verb* /ˈkɒmplɪment/ **1** (often foll. by *on*) congratulate; praise (*complimented him on his cooking*). **2** (often foll. by *with*) present as a mark of courtesy (*complimented her with his attention*). ¶ Often confused with *complement*. □ **compliments of 1** given free of charge (*won a book, compliments of OUP*). **2** usu. *ironic* thanks to (*a 75-cent surcharge, compliments of the Minister of Finance*). **pay a compliment to** praise. **return the compliment 1** give a compliment in return for another. **2** retaliate or recompense in kind. [French *complimenter* from Italian *complimento*, ultimately from Latin (as COMPLEMENT)]

com·pli·ment·ary /ˌkɒmpləˈmɛntəri/ *adjective* **1** expressing a compliment; praising. **2** (of a service, goods, theatre ticket, etc.) provided free of charge. ¶ Often confused with *complementary*.

complimentary closing *noun* the formulaic closing of a letter preceding the signature, e.g. 'Yours truly'.

com·pline /ˈkɒmplɪn, -plaɪn/ *noun Christianity* **1** the last of the canonical hours of prayer, said before retiring at night. **2** the service taking place

during this. [Old French *complie*, fem. past participle of obsolete *complir* complete, ultimately from Latin *complēre* fill up]

com·ply /kəmˈplaɪ/ *intransitive verb* (**-plies**, **-plied**) (often foll. by *with*) act in accordance (with a wish, command, regulation, etc.) (*complied with her expectation; had no choice but to comply*). [Italian *complire* from Catalan *complir*, Spanish *cumplir* from Latin *complēre* fill up]

com·pon·ent /kəmˈpoʊnənt/ ● *noun* **1** a part of a larger whole or system. **2** *Math.* one of two or more vectors equivalent to a given vector. ● *adjective* being part of a larger whole (*assembled the component parts*). □ **com·pon·en·tial** /ˌkɒmpəˈnɛnʃəl/ *adjective* **com·pon·en·try** /kəmˈpoʊnəntri/ *noun* [*component component-* (as COM-, *ponere* put)]

com·port /kəmˈpɔrt/ *reflexive verb literary* conduct oneself; behave. □ **com·port·ment** *noun* [Latin *comportare* (as COM-, *portare* carry)]

com·pose *verb* **1 a** *transitive* construct or create (a work of art, esp. literature or music). **b** *intransitive* compose music (*gave up composing in 1917*). **2** *transitive* (often in *passive*) constitute; make up (*the committee is composed of workers and managers*). **3** *transitive* put together to form a whole, esp. artistically; order; arrange (*composed the group for the photographer*). **4** *transitive* (often *reflexive*) calm; settle (*compose your expression; took a deep breath to compose himself*). **5** *transitive* settle (a dispute etc.). **6** *transitive Printing* set up (type) to form words and blocks of words. **b** set up (a manuscript etc.) in type. [French *composer*, from Latin *componere* (as COM-, *ponere* put)]

com·posed *adjective* calm, unruffled.

com·pos·er *noun* a person who composes (esp. music).

com·pos·ite /ˈkɒmpəzɪt/ ● *adjective* **1** made up of various parts; blended. **2** (esp. of a synthetic building material) made up of recognizable constituents. **3** (also **Composite**) *Archit.* of the fifth classical order of architecture, consisting of elements of the Ionic and Corinthian orders. **4** of the plant family Compositae. ● *noun* **1** a thing made up of several parts or elements. **2** a synthetic building material. **3** any plant of the family Compositae, having a head of many small flowers forming one bloom, e.g. the daisy or the dandelion. ● *transitive verb* combine into a composite. □ **com·pos·ite·ly** *adverb* **com·pos·ite·ness** *noun* [French from Latin *compositus* past participle of *componere* (as COM-, *ponere posit-* put)]

composite high school *noun Cdn* (*Alta.*) (also **composite school**) a secondary school offering both vocational and academic courses.

composite index *noun* a stock market index based on the performance of a selection of stocks.

com·pos·ition /ˌkɒmpəˈzɪʃən/ *noun* **1 a** the act of putting together; formation or construction. **b** something so composed; a mixture. **c** the constitution of such a mixture; the nature of its ingredients (*the powers and composition of the Senate*). **2 a** a literary or musical work. **b** the act or art of producing such a work. **c** a piece of writing assigned as an exercise. **d** the craft of writing (*taught grammar and composition*). **e** an artistic arrangement (of parts of a picture, subjects for a photograph, etc.). **3** (often *attributive*) a compound artificial substance, esp. one serving the purpose of a natural one. **4** the setting up of type. **5** *Grammar* the formation of words into a compound word. **6** *Law* **a** a compromise, esp. a legal agreement to pay a sum in lieu of a larger sum, or other obligation (*made a composition with his creditors*). **b** a sum paid in this way. **7** *Math.* the combination of functions in a series. □ **com·pos·ition·al** *adjective* **com·pos·ition·al·ly** *adverb* [Old French, from Latin *compositio -onis* (as COMPOSITE)]

com·pos·itor /kəmˈpɒzɪtər/ *noun* a person who sets up type or text for printing. [Anglo-French *compositour* from Latin *compositor* (as COMPOSITE)]

com·pos men·tis /ˌkɒmpəs ˈmɛntɪs/ *adjective* having control of one's mind; sane. [Latin]

com·post /ˈkɒmpoʊst/ ● *noun* a mixture of decomposing vegetable matter, table scraps, manure, etc., used to fertilize soil. ● *verb* **1** *transitive* treat (soil) with compost. **2** *transitive & intransitive* make (manure, vegetable matter, etc.) into compost. **3** *intransitive* degrade into compost. □ **com·post·able** *adjective & noun* [Old French *composte* from Latin *compos(i)tum* (as COMPOSITE)]

com·post·er *noun* (also **compost bin**) a container for vegetable matter, table scraps, soil, etc., used to create compost.

compost heap *noun* (also **compost pile**) a layered structure of garden refuse, soil, etc., which decays to become compost.

com·po·sure /kəmˈpoʊʒər/ *noun* a tranquil manner; calmness.

com·pote /ˈkɒmpoʊt, -pɒt/ *noun* **1** fruit preserved or cooked in syrup. **2** a bowl supported on a stem for serving this. [French from Old French *composte* (as COMPOSITE)]

com·pound¹ ● *noun* /ˈkɒmpaʊnd/ **1** a mixture of two or more things, qualities, etc. **2** (also **compound word**) a word made up of two or more existing words. **3** *Chem.* a substance formed from two or more elements chemically united in fixed proportions. ● *adjective* /ˈkɒmpaund/ **1 a** made up of several ingredients. **b** consisting of several parts. **2** combined; collective. **3** *Zool.* consisting of individual organisms. **4** *Biol.* consisting of several or many parts. **5 a** (of a noun) that is a compound. **b** (of a verb tense) formed using an auxiliary verb. ● *verb* /kəmˈpaund/ **1** *transitive* mix or combine (ingredients, ideas, motives, etc.) (*grief compounded with fear*). **2** *transitive* increase or complicate (difficulties etc.) (*anxiety compounded by discomfort*). **3** *transitive* make up (a composite whole). **4** *transitive & intransitive* settle (a debt, dispute, etc.) by concession or special arrangement. **5** *transitive Law* **a** condone (a liability or offence) in exchange for money etc. **b** forbear from prosecuting (an indictable offence) from private motives. **6** *intransitive* (usu. foll. by *with*, *for*) *Law* come to terms with a person, for forgoing a claim etc. for an offence. **7** *transitive* combine (words or elements) into a word. **8** *transitive & intransitive* increase by compound interest. □ **com·pound·able** *adjective* [Old French *compondre* from Latin *componere* (as COM-, *ponere* put: *-d* as in *expound*)]

com·pound² /ˈkɒmpaund/ *noun* **1** an enclosed area, as for a school, prison, etc. **2** an enclosure, esp. in India, China, etc., in which a factory or a house stands (*compare* KAMPONG). [Portuguese *campon* or Dutch *kampong* from Malay]

compound eye *noun* an eye consisting of numerous visual units, as found in insects and crustaceans.

compound fracture *noun* a fracture involving the exposure of the bone through a skin wound.

compound interest *noun* interest payable on capital and its accumulated interest (*compare* SIMPLE INTEREST).

compound leaf *noun* a leaf consisting of several or many leaflets.

compound lens *noun* = LENS 2.

compound sentence *noun* a sentence with more than one independent clause, joined by a coordinating conjunction, and having no subordinate clauses.

com·pra·dor /ˌkɒmprəˈdɔr/ *noun* (also **com·pra·dore**) **1** *hist.* a Chinese business agent of a foreign company. **2** an agent of a foreign power. [Portuguese *comprador* buyer, from Late Latin *comparator* from Latin *comparare* purchase]

com·pre·hend /ˌkɒmprɪˈhɛnd/ *transitive verb* **1** grasp mentally; understand (a person or a thing). **2** include; take in. □ **com·pre·hend·er** *noun* [Old French *comprehender* or Latin *comprehendere comprehens-* (as COM-, *prehendere* grasp)]

com·pre·hen·sible /ˌkɒmprɪˈhɛnsɪbəl/ *adjective* **1** that can be understood; intelligible. **2** that can be included or contained. □ **com·pre·hen·si·bil·ity** *noun* **com·pre·hen·sibly** *adverb* [French *compréhensible* or Latin *comprehensibilis* (as COMPREHEND)]

com·pre·hen·sion /ˌkɒmprɪˈhɛnʃən/ *noun* **1** the act or capability of understanding, esp. writing or speech. **2** inclusion.

com·pre·hen·sive /ˌkɒmprɪˈhɛnsɪv/ ● *adjective* **1** complete; including all or nearly all elements, aspects, etc. (*a comprehensive study*). **2** of or relating to understanding (*the comprehensive faculty*). **3** (of motor vehicle insurance) providing complete protection. ● *noun* **1** (in full **comprehensive examination**) a test of one's learning or proficiency in all aspects, elements, etc. of a subject. **2** (in full **comprehensive school**) *Brit.* a secondary school catering to children of all abilities from a given area. □ **com·pre·hen·sive·ly** *adverb* **com·pre·hen·sive·ness** *noun* [French *compréhensif -ive* or Late Latin *comprehensivus* (as COMPREHENSIBLE)]

comprehensive high school *noun Cdn* a secondary school offering both vocational and academic courses.

comprehensive land claim *noun Cdn* an Aboriginal land claim made on a usu. large area of land which was never ceded or surrendered by treaty or purchase.

com·press ● *transitive verb* /kəmˈprɛs/ **1** squeeze together. **2** bring into a smaller space or shorter extent. **3** *Computing* condense (data etc.) for easier handling, storage, etc. ● *noun* /ˈkɒmprɛs/ a cloth or ice pack etc. pressed onto part of the body to relieve inflammation, stop bleeding, etc. □ **com·press·ibil·ity** *noun* **com·press·ible** *adjective* [Late Latin *compressare* frequentative of Latin *comprimere compress-* (as COM-, *premere* press)]

compressed air *noun* air at more than atmospheric pressure.

com·pres·sion *noun* **1** the act of compressing or being compressed. **2** the reduction in volume (causing an increase in pressure) of the fuel mixture in an internal combustion engine before ignition.

compression ratio *noun* the ratio of volume before compression to that after compression, as in an internal combustion engine etc.

com·pres·sive *adjective* tending to compress.

com·pres·sor *noun* an instrument or device for compressing, esp. a machine used for increasing the pressure of air or other gases.

com·prise *transitive verb* **1** include; comprehend. **2** consist of, be composed of (*the book comprises 350 pages*). **3** make up, compose (*the essays comprise his total work*). ¶ Such uses as *The panel is comprised of five individuals* or *Women comprise a large proportion of the sample* have traditionally been criticized and are still strongly opposed by some, who prefer *The panel is composed* (or *made up*) *of five individuals* or *Women constitute* (or *make up*) *a large proportion of the group*. The disputed uses are very common, however, and considered unobjectionable by many. [Old French, fem. past participle of *comprendre* COMPREHEND]

com·prom·ise /ˈkɒmprəˌmaɪz/ ● *noun* **1** the settlement of a dispute by mutual concession (*reached a compromise by bargaining*). **2** (often foll. by *between*) an intermediate state between conflicting opinions, actions, etc., reached by mutual concession or modification (*a compromise between ideals and material necessity*). ● *verb* **1** *intransitive* settle a dispute by mutual concession (*compromised over the terms*). **2** *transitive* bring into disrepute or danger esp. by indiscreet, foolish, or reckless behaviour (*don't compromise our relationship*). **3** *transitive* weaken (a reputation or principle) by accepting standards that are lower than is desirable. **4** *intransitive* expediently accept standards that are lower than desirable. □ **com·prom·is·er** *noun* [Old French *compromis* from Latin *compromissum* neuter past participle of *compromittere* (as COM-, *promittere* PROMISE)]

com·prom·ised *adjective* unable to resist infection (*compromised immune system*).

Comp·ton, Ar·thur Holly (1892–1962), US physicist. He observed that the wavelength of X-rays increased when scattered by electrons (known as the Compton effect), providing evidence for the dual wave-particle nature of radiation; he shared the 1927 Nobel Prize for physics.

comp·trol·ler /kənˈtroʊlər, kɒmp-/ *noun* (also **con·trol·ler**) an official or executive in charge of financial affairs. [var. of CONTROLLER, by erroneous assoc. with COUNT[1], Latin *computus*]

com·pul·sion *noun* **1** the action of compelling; an obligation. **2** *Psych.* an irresistible urge to a form of behaviour, esp. against one's conscious wishes. [French from Late Latin *compulsio -onis* (as COMPEL)]

com·pul·sive *adjective* **1** resulting or acting from, or as if from, compulsion (*a compulsive gambler*). **2** *Psych.* resulting or acting from compulsion against one's conscious wishes. □ **com·pul·sive·ly** *adverb* **com·pul·sive·ness** *noun* [medieval Latin *compulsivus* (as COMPEL)]

com·pul·sory /kəmˈpʌlsəri/ ● *adjective* **1** required by law or a rule (*attendance is compulsory*). **2** essential; necessary. ● *noun* (also **compulsory figure**) one of a number of specified figures that must be performed as a component of a competition, e.g. in figure skating or synchronized swimming. □ **com·pul·sor·i·ly** *adverb* **com·pul·sor·i·ness** *noun* [medieval Latin *compulsorius* (as COMPEL)]

com·punc·tion *noun* (usu. with *neg.*) **1** an uneasy conscience; a feeling of remorse. **2** a slight regret; a scruple (*without compunction; had no compunction about refusing them*). [Old French *componction* from ecclesiastical Latin *compunctio -onis* from Latin *compungere compunct-* (as COM-, *pungere* prick)]

com·pur·ga·tion /ˌkɒmpərˈgeɪʃən/ *noun Law hist.* an acquittal from a charge or accusation obtained by the oaths of witnesses. [medieval Latin *compurgatio* from Latin *compurgare* (as COM-, *purgare* purify)]

com·pur·ga·tor /ˈkɒmpərˌgeɪtər/ *noun Law hist.* a witness who swore to the innocence or good character of an accused person.

com·pu·ta·tion·al /ˌkɒmpjuˈteɪʃənəl/ *adjective* **1** of or pertaining to computing. **2** using computers to assist in analysis (*computational linguistics*).

com·pute /kəmˈpjuːt/ *verb* **1** *transitive* (often foll. by *that* + clause) reckon or calculate (a number, an amount, etc.). **2** *intransitive* make a reckoning, esp. using a computer. **3** *Computing informal* make sense (*their explanation doesn't compute*). □ **com·put·abil·ity** *noun* **com·put·able** *adjective* **com·pu·ta·tion** /ˌkɒmpjuːˈteɪʃən/ *noun* **com·put·ing** *noun* [French *computer* or Latin *computare* (as COM-, *putare* reckon)]

com·put·er *noun* **1** an electronic device for storing and processing data (usu. in binary form), according to instructions given to it in a variable program. **2** a non-electronic device that assists in making calculations. **3** a person who computes or makes calculations.

computer crime *noun* crime involving illegal access to or manipulation of electronic data.

Consonants: b *but*   d *dog*   f *few*   g *get*   h *her*   j *yes*   k *cat*   l *leg*   m *man*   n *no*   p *pen*   r *red*   s *sit*

com·puter·ese /kəm‚pjuːtɜrˈiːz/ *noun* the jargon associated with computers.

computer game *noun* **1** a game played on a computer, esp. one involving graphics and operating in real time. **2** a software package for such a game.

computer graphics *noun* **1** visual images produced or modified by means of a computer. **2** the use of a computer to generate and manipulate these.

com·puter·ize *verb* (also esp. Brit. **-ise**) **1 a** *transitive* equip with a computer; install a computer in. **b** *intransitive* equip oneself with computers (*the business will have to computerize*). **2** *transitive* store, process, perform, or produce by computer. □ **com·puter·i·za·tion** *noun*

com·puter·ized *adjective* controlled, performed, or produced by a computer (*computerized appliances*).

computerized axial tomography *noun* tomography in which the X-ray scanner makes many sweeps of the body and the results are processed by computer to give a cross-sectional image. Abbr.: **CAT**.

computer language *noun* any of numerous systems of rules, words, and symbols for writing computer programs or representing instructions etc.

computer-literate *adjective* able to use computers; familiar with the operation of computers. □ **computer literacy** *noun*

com·puter·phobia *noun* fear or mistrust of computer technology; an aversion to using computers. □ **com·puter·phobe** *noun* **com·puter·phob·ic** *adjective*

computer science *noun* the study of the principles and use of computers.

computer virus *noun* a piece of code which is capable of copying itself and typically has a detrimental effect, such as corrupting a system or destroying data stored in it.

com·rade /ˈkɒmrad/ *noun* **1 a** a workmate, friend, or companion. **b** (also **comrade-in-arms**) a fellow soldier etc. **2** a fellow socialist or communist (often as a form of address). □ **com·rade·ly** *adjective* **com·rade·ship** *noun* [earlier *cama- camerade*, via French *camerade*, *camarade* (originally fem.) and Spanish *camarada* roommate, from Latin CAMERA)]

Comte /kɔ̃t/ **Au·guste** (1798–1857), French philosopher, a founder of sociology. His positivist philosophy attempted to define the laws of social evolution and to found a social science that could be used for social reconstruction; his major works include *Cours de philosophie positive* (1830–42) and *Système de politique positive* (1851–4). □ **Comt·ean** /ˈkɔ̃tiən/ *adjective*

con[1] *informal* ● *noun* **1** a swindle in which the swindler first gains the victim's confidence (also *attributive:* con man). **2** a deceiving comment, action, etc. ● *transitive verb* (**conned**, **con·ning**) **1** swindle (*conned them out of their money*). **2** deceive (*you can't con me; you're not really sick!*). **3** (foll. by *into*) persuade after dishonestly gaining trust (*readers are conned into buying trash*). [abbreviation of CONFIDENCE GAME]

con[2] ● *noun* (usu. in *pl.*) a reason against. ● *preposition & adverb* against (compare PRO[2]). [Latin *contra* against]

con[3] *noun slang* a convict. [abbreviation]

con[4] *transitive verb* (also esp. US **conn**) (**conned**, **con·ning**) *Naut.* direct the steering of (a ship). [apparently weakened form of obsolete *cond*, *condie*, from French *conduire* from Latin *conducere* CONDUCT]

con[5] *transitive verb* (**conned**, **con·ning**) *archaic* (often foll. by *over*) study, learn by heart (*conned his part well*). [Middle English *cunn-*, *con*, forms of CAN[1]]

Con. *abbreviation* Cdn (esp. Ont.) = CONCESSION 4.

con- *prefix* assimilated form of COM- before *c, d, f, g, j, n, q, s, t, v,* and sometimes before vowels.

Con·acher /ˈkɒnəkɜr/ **Lionel (Pre·to·ria)** (known as 'The Big Train') (1902–54), Canadian athlete and politician. Considered the best all-round athlete of his time, he participated in eight sports, excelling in baseball, boxing, football, hockey, and lacrosse; he led the Toronto Argonauts to a Grey Cup victory in 1921 and played in two Stanley Cup championships (1934 and 1935).

Con·akry /ˈkɒnəˌkriː/ the capital and chief port of Guinea; pop. (est. 2002) 1,587,600.

con amore /ˌkɒn əˈmɔreɪ/ *adverb Music* tenderly. [Italian, = with love]

Conan, Laure see ANGERS[2].

Conan Doyle, Sir Ar·thur see DOYLE.

con artist *noun* **1** a swindler. **2** a person skilled at deception.

con brio /kɒn ˈbriːoː/ *adverb Music* with vigour. [Italian]

Conc. *abbreviation* Cdn (esp. Ont.) = CONCESSION 4.

CONCACAF /ˈkɒnkəˌkaf/ *abbreviation* Confederation of North, Central American, and Caribbean Association Football.

con·cat·en·ate /kənˈkatɪˌneɪt/ ● *transitive verb* link together (a chain of events, things, etc.). ● *adjective* joined; linked. □ **con·ca·ten·a·tion** *noun* [Late Latin *concatenare* (as COM-, *catenare* from *catena* chain)]

con·cave /ˈkɒnkeɪv, kɒnˈkeɪv/ *adjective* having an outline or surface curved like the interior of a circle or sphere (compare CONVEX). □ **con·cave·ly** *adverb* **con·cav·ity** /-ˈkavɪti/ *noun* (pl. **-ities**). [Latin *concavus* (as COM-, *cavus* hollow)]

con·ceal *transitive verb* **1** (often foll. by *from*) keep secret (*concealed her motive from him*). **2** not allow to be seen; hide (*concealed the letter in her pocket*). □ **con·ceal·ment** *noun* [Old French *conceler* from Latin *concelare* (as COM-, *celare* hide)]

con·ceal·er *noun* **1** a cosmetic which covers blemishes and dark spots on the skin, esp. the circles under the eyes. **2** a person or thing that conceals.

con·cede /kənˈsiːd/ *transitive verb* **1 a** (often foll. by *that* + clause) admit to be true (*conceded that his work was inadequate*). **b** admit defeat in. **2** (often foll. by *to*) grant, yield, or surrender (a right, a privilege, points or a start in a game, etc.). **3** *Sport* allow an opponent to score (a goal) or to win (a match), etc. □ **con·ced·er** *noun* [French *concéder* or Latin *concedere concess-* (as COM-, *cedere* yield)]

con·ceit /kənˈsiːt/ *noun* **1** excessive pride in oneself or one's powers, abilities, etc. **2 a** a far-fetched comparison, esp. as a stylistic affectation; a convoluted or unlikely metaphor. **b** a fanciful notion. [Middle English from CONCEIVE after *deceit*, *deceive*, etc.]

con·ceit·ed /kənˈsiːtəd/ *adjective* full of conceit; vain. □ **con·ceit·ed·ly** *adverb* **con·ceit·ed·ness** *noun*

con·ceiv·able /kənˈsiːvəbəl/ *adjective* capable of being grasped or imagined; understandable. □ **con·ceiv·abil·ity** *noun* **con·ceiv·ably** *adverb*

con·ceive /kənˈsiːv/ *verb* **1 a** *intransitive* become pregnant. **b** *transitive* become pregnant with (a child). **2** *transitive* (usu. in *passive*) **a** devise, compose, formulate (a plan, scheme, idea, etc.). **b** apprehend, understand, perceive. **3** *transitive* develop (an emotion, feeling, etc.). □ **conceive of** form in the mind; imagine. [Old French *conceiv-* stressed stem of *concevoir* from Latin *concipere concept-* (as COM-, *capere* take)]

con·cele·brate /kənˈseləˌbreɪt, kɒn-/ *intransitive verb & transitive* (of two or more clergy) celebrate the Eucharist together. □ **con·cele·brant** /-brənt/ *noun* **con·cele·bra·tion** *noun* [Latin *concelebrare* (as COM-, *celebrare* CELEBRATE)]

con·cen·trate /ˈkɒnsənˌtreɪt/ ● *verb* **1** *intransitive* (often foll. by *on, upon*) focus all one's attention or mental ability. **2** *transitive* **a** bring towards or collect at a centre (*industry is concentrated in the east*). **b** cause to converge or be focused on (*such things concentrate the mind*). **3** *transitive* increase the strength of (a liquid etc.) by removing water or any other diluting agent. **4** *transitive* bring (ore etc.) to a state of greater purity by mechanical means. ● *noun* **1** a concentrated substance. **2** a concentrated form of esp. food. □ **con·cen·tra·tive** *adjective* **con·cen·tra·tor** *noun* [French *concentrer* (as CON- + CENTRE)]

con·cen·trat·ed /ˈkɒnsənˌtreɪtəd/ *adjective* **1** (of an emotion etc.) intense, strong. **2** increased in strength or value by concentrating (*concentrated orange juice*). **3** wholly directed towards one thing (*a concentrated effort*). □ **con·cen·trat·ed·ly** *adverb*

con·cen·tra·tion *noun* **1 a** the act or power of concentrating (*needs to develop concentration*). **b** an instance of this (*interrupted my concentration*). **2** something concentrated (*a concentration of resources*). **3** something brought together; a gathering. **4** (often in *pl.*) the weight of substance in a given weight or volume of material.

concentration camp *noun* **1** a camp for the detention or extermination of political prisoners, internees, etc., esp. one run by Nazi Germany (with connotations of inhuman privations endured by the inhabitants and systematic genocide). **2** any of the camps (instituted by Lord Kitchener) where non-combatants of a district were accommodated during the Second Boer War of 1899–1902.

con·cen·tric /kənˈsentrɪk/ *adjective* (esp. of circles) having a common centre (compare ECCENTRIC). □ **con·cen·tric·ally** *adverb* **con·cen·tric·ity** /ˌkɒnsənˈtrɪsɪti/ *noun* [medieval Latin *concentricus* (as COM-, *centricus* from CENTRE)]

Con·cep·ción /kɒnˌsepsiˈoːn/ an industrial city in south central Chile; pop. (est. 2002) 404,600.

con·cept *noun* **1** a general notion; an abstract idea (*the concept of evolution*). **2 a** an idea, theme or design, esp. as the basis for development or execution (*the concept for the publication was hers*). **b** the

---

t *top*   v *voice*   w *we*   z *zoo*   ʃ *she*   ʒ *vision*   θ *thin*   ð *this*   ŋ *ring*   x *loch*   tʃ *chip*   dʒ *jar*   (*see over for vowels*)

product of this (*a new concept in swimwear*). **3** an idea or mental picture of a group or class of objects formed by combining all their aspects. [Late Latin *conceptus* from *concept*-: see CONCEIVE]

concept album *noun Music* an album whose songs all treat a common subject.

concept car *noun* a car designed with engineering and styling not yet suitable for mass production.

con·cep·tion *noun* **1** the act or an instance of conceiving; the process of being conceived. **2** an idea or plan, esp. as being new or daring (*the whole conception showed originality*). **3** an understanding (*his conception of God was simplistic*). ☐ **no conception of** an inability to imagine.

Conception Bay an inlet of the N Atlantic Ocean, situated on the northern shore of the Avalon Peninsula, SE Newfoundland. [in honour of the Immaculate *Conception*]

Conception Bay South a town on the Avalon Peninsula in SE Newfoundland, situated on the southeastern shore of Conception Bay; pop. (2001) 19,772.

con·cep·tual /kən'septʃʊəl/ *adjective* of mental conceptions or concepts. ☐ **con·cep·tual·ly** *adverb*

conceptual art *noun* art which emphasizes the process of producing art and the ideas conveyed rather than the art object produced.

con·cep·tual·ism /kən'septʃʊə,lɪzəm/ *noun* **1** *Philos.* the theory that universals exist, but only as concepts in the mind. **2** = CONCEPTUAL ART. ☐ **con·cep·tual·ist** *noun*

con·cep·tual·ize /kən'septʃʊə,laɪz/ *transitive verb* (also esp. *Brit.* **-ise**) form a concept or idea of. ☐ **con·cep·tual·iz·a·tion** *noun*

con·cern ● *transitive verb* **1 a** be relevant or important to (*this concerns you*). **b** relate to; be about. **2** (usu. *reflexive*; often foll. by *with, in, about,* or *to* + infin.) interest or involve oneself (*don't concern yourself with my problems*). **3** worry, affect (*it concerns me that he is always late*). ● *noun* **1 a** anxiety, worry (*growing concern over violence on TV*). **b** solicitude, interest in others' well-being (*known for his honesty, warmth and concern*). **2 a** a matter of interest or importance to one, esp. causing anxiety (*finding a manager was their main concern*). **b** (usu. in *pl.*) affairs, private business (*meddling in my concerns*). **3** a business (*quite a prosperous concern*). ☐ **have a concern in** have an interest or share in. **have no concern with** have nothing to do with. **to whom it may concern** to those who have a proper interest in the matter (as an address to the reader of a testimonial, reference, etc.). [French *concerner* or Late Latin *concernere* (as COM-, *cernere* sift, discern)]

con·cerned *adjective* **1** involved, interested (*the people concerned*; *concerned with proving his innocence*). **2** (often foll. by *that, about, at, for,* or *to* + infin.) troubled, anxious (*concerned about him*; *concerned to hear that*). ☐ **as** (or **so**) **far as I am concerned** as regards my interests. ☐ **con·cern·ed·ly** /-'sɜrnədli/ *adverb*

con·cern·ing *preposition* about, regarding.

con·cert ● *noun* /'kɒnsərt/ **1 a** a musical performance of usu. several separate compositions. **b** a public performance of a variety of entertainments, e.g. music, dancing, comedy skits, etc. **c** (*attributive*) designating a performance (of an opera etc.) without scenery, costumes, or action (*a concert version of Orfeo*). **d** (*attributive*) performing in concerts, esp. as a professional soloist (*a concert pianist*). **2** agreement, accordance, harmony. **3** a combination of voices or sounds. ● *transitive verb* /kən'sɜrt/ arrange (by mutual agreement or coordination). ☐ **in concert 1** (often foll. by *with*) acting jointly and accordingly. **2** (*predicative*) (of a musician) in a performance. [French *concert* (n.), *concerter* (v.) from Italian *concertare* harmonize]

concert band *noun N Amer.* a musical ensemble consisting of a range of brass, woodwind, and percussion instruments, performing esp. on a stage (*compare* MARCHING BAND, STAGE BAND).

con·cert·ed /kən'sɜrtəd/ *adjective* **1** combined together; jointly arranged or planned. **2** serious (*she made a concerted effort to improve*). **3** *Music* arranged in parts for voices or instruments.

con·cert·goer *noun* a person who often goes to concerts.

concert grand *noun* the largest size of grand piano.

concert hall *noun* **1** an auditorium in which concerts are performed. **2** a building enclosing this.

con·cer·tina /ˌkɒnsər'tiːnə/ ● *noun* a musical instrument held in the hands and stretched and squeezed like bellows, having reeds and a set of buttons at each end to control the valves. ● *transitive & intransitive verb* (**con·cer·tinas, con·cer·tinaed** or **con·cer·tina'd, con·cer·tina·ing**) compress or collapse in folds like those of a concertina (*the car concertinaed into the bridge*). [CONCERT + -INA]

concertina wire *noun* barbed wire in coils, placed at the top of fences etc.

con·cer·tino /ˌkɒntʃər'tiːnoʊ/ *noun* (*pl.* **-tinos**) *Music* **1** a simple or short concerto. **2** a solo instrument or solo instruments playing in a concerto. [Italian, diminutive of CONCERTO]

con·cert·ize *intransitive verb* (also esp. *Brit.* **-ise**) perform regularly in concerts.

con·cert·master *noun* esp. *N Amer.* the principal first-violin player in an orchestra.

con·certo /kən'tʃertoʊ/ *noun* (*pl.* **-tos** or **con·certi** /-tiː/) *Music* a composition for a solo instrument or instruments accompanied by an orchestra. [Italian (see CONCERT)]

concerto grosso /'groːsoʊ/ *noun* (*pl.* **concerti grossi** /-siː/ or **concerto grossos**) an esp. baroque concerto characterized by the use of a small group of solo instruments alternately with the full orchestra. [Italian (as CONCERTO): *grosso* big]

concert overture *noun* a piece of music like an operatic overture but intended for independent performance.

concert pitch *noun* **1** *Music* the international pitch standard used for tuning musical instruments, with the A above middle C at 440 Hz. **2** a state of unusual readiness, efficiency, and keenness (for action etc.).

con·ces·sion /kən'sefən/ *noun* **1 a** the act or an instance of conceding (*made the concession that we were right*). **b** a thing conceded. **2 a** a right or privilege granted by a government (*tax concessions*). **b** the right to use land or other property, granted esp. by a government or local authority, esp. for a specific use. **c** the right, given by a company, to sell goods, esp. in a particular territory. **d** the land or property used or given. **3** *N Amer.* a booth or stand in a stadium, theatre, etc., where esp. refreshments and souvenirs are sold. **4** *Cdn a* (*Ont.* & *Que.*) a tract of surveyed farmland, itself further divided into lots. **b** esp. *Ont.* (also **concession road** or **concession line**) a rural road separating concessions. Abbr.: **Con., Conc. 5** *Brit.* a reduction in the price of admission etc. for children, students, senior citizens, etc. ☐ **con·ces·sion·ary** *adjective* (also **concessional**). [French *concession* from Latin *concessio* (as CONCEDE)]

con·ces·sion·aire /kən,sefə'ner/ *noun* the operator or holder of a concession. [French *concessionnaire* (as CONCESSION)]

concession line *noun Cdn* (*Ont.*) **1** a surveying line separating concessions. **2** (also **concession road**) = CONCESSION 4b.

con·ces·sive /kən'sesɪv/ *adjective* **1** of or tending to concession. **2** *Grammar* **a** (of a preposition or conjunction) introducing a phrase or clause which might be expected to preclude the action of the main clause, but does not (e.g. *in spite of, although*). **b** (of a phrase or clause) introduced by a concessive preposition or conjunction. [Late Latin *concessivus* (as CONCEDE)]

conch /kɒntʃ, kɒŋk/ *noun* (*pl.* **conch·es** /'kɒntʃəz/ or **conchs** /kɒŋks/) **1 a** a thick heavy spiral shell, occasionally bearing long projections, of various marine gastropod molluscs of the family Strombidae. **b** any of these gastropods. **2** *Archit.* the domed roof of a semicircular apse. **3** = CONCHA. [Latin *concha* shell, from Greek *kogkhē*]

concha /'kɒŋkə/ *noun* (*pl.* **con·chae** /-kiː/) *Anat.* any part resembling a shell, esp. the depression in the external ear leading to its central cavity. [Latin: see CONCH]

Con·cho·bar /'kɒŋkəwɜr/ *Irish Myth* a king of Ulster (see DEIRDRE).

con·choid·al /kɒŋ'kɔɪdəl/ *adjective Mineralogy* (of a solid fracture etc.) resembling the surface of a bivalve shell.

con·chol·ogy /kɒŋ'kɒlədʒi/ *noun Zool.* the scientific study of the shells of molluscs. ☐ **con·cho·logic·al** *adjective* **con·chol·o·gist** *noun* [Greek *kogkhē* shell + -LOGY]

con·cierge /kõsi'erʒ, kɒn-/ *noun* **1** (esp. in France) a person in charge of the entrance of a building, often also serving as a caretaker, typically living on the premises. **2** a hotel employee responsible for attending to special needs of guests, making taxi reservations, booking theatre tickets, etc. **3** an attendant at the entrance to a condominium building. [French, prob. ultimately from Latin *conservus* fellow slave]

con·cili·ar /kən'sɪliər/ *adjective* of or concerning a council, esp. an ecclesiastical council. [medieval Latin *consiliarius* counsellor]

con·cili·ate /kən'sɪlieɪt/ *verb* **1** *intransitive* attempt to settle an esp. labour dispute by hearing all disputants and recommending solutions. **2** *transitive* make calm and co-operative; pacify. **3** *transitive* gain (esteem or goodwill). ☐ **con·cili·ator** *noun* **con·cili·a·tory** /-'sɪliə,tɔri/ *adjective* [Latin *conciliare* combine, gain (*concilium* COUNCIL)]

con·cili·a·tion /kən,sɪli'eɪʃən/ *noun* **1** *Law* the hearing and attempted resolution of a dispute by an appointed conciliator. **2** the use of conciliating measures; reconcilement. [Latin *conciliatio* (as CONCILIATE)]

con·cise *adjective* (of speech, writing, style, or a person) brief but comprehensive in expression. □ **con·cise·ly** *adverb* **con·cise·ness** *noun* [French *concis* or Latin *concisus* past participle of *concidere* (as COM-, *caedere* cut)]

con·ci·sion /kənˈsɪʒən/ *noun* (esp. of literary style) conciseness.

con·clave *noun* **1** a private meeting. **2** *Catholicism* **a** the assembly of cardinals for the election of a pope. **b** the meeting place for a conclave. [Old French from Latin *conclave* lockable room (as COM-, *clavis* key)]

con·clude *verb* **1** *transitive & intransitive* bring or come to an end. **2** *transitive* (often foll. by *from*, or *that* + clause) infer (from given premises) (*what did you conclude?; concluded from the evidence that he had been mistaken*). **3** *transitive* settle, arrange (a treaty etc.). **4** *transitive* state in conclusion. [Latin *concludere* (as COM-, *claudere* shut)]

con·clu·sion *noun* **1** a final result; a termination. **2** a judgment reached by reasoning. **3** the summing-up of an argument, article, book, etc. **4** a settling; an arrangement (*the conclusion of peace*). **5** *Logic* a proposition that is reached from given premises; the third and last part of a syllogism. □ **in conclusion** lastly, to conclude.

con·clu·sive *adjective* decisive, convincing. □ **con·clu·sive·ly** *adverb* **con·clu·sive·ness** *noun*

con·coct *transitive verb* **1** make by combining elements not usually mixed together, esp. from what is available (*concocted a dessert from peanut butter, whipped cream, and bananas*). **2** invent (a story, a lie, etc.). □ **con·coct·er** *noun* **con·coc·tion** *noun* [Latin *concoquere* concoct- (as COM-, *coquere* cook)]

con·comi·tant /kənˈkɒmɪtənt/ ● *adjective* going together; associated (*concomitant circumstances*). ● *noun* an accompanying thing. □ **con·comi·tant·ly** *adverb* [Late Latin *concomitari* (as COM-, *comitari* from Latin *comes -mitis* companion)]

Con·cord /ˈkɒnkɔrd/ **1** the state capital of New Hampshire; pop. (2000) 40,687. **2** a town in NE Massachusetts, US; pop. (2000) 15,559. Battles there and at Lexington in Apr. 1775 marked the start of the American Revolution.

con·cord /ˈkɒnkɔrd, ˈkɒŋ-/ *noun* **1** agreement or harmony between people or things. **2** a treaty. **3** *Music* a chord that is pleasing or satisfactory in itself, not requiring resolution. **4** *Grammar* agreement between words in gender, number, etc. [Old French *concorde* from Latin *concordia* from *concors* of one mind (as COM-, *cors* from *cor cordis* heart)]

con·cord·ance /kənˈkɔrdəns, kɒŋ-/ ● *noun* **1** agreement. **2 a** a book containing an alphabetical list of the important words used in a book or by an author, usu. with citations of the passages concerned. **b** an alphabetized list of all the words in a text or group of texts, usu. with some accompanying text. ● *transitive verb* (esp. of a computer) make a concordance to (a book etc.). □ **con·cord·an·cer** *noun* **con·cord·an·cing** *noun* [Old French from medieval Latin *concordantia* (as CONCORD)]

con·cord·ant /kənˈkɔrdənt/ *adjective* **1** (often foll. by *with*) agreeing, harmonious. **2** *Music* in harmony. □ **con·cord·ant·ly** *adverb* [Old French from Latin *concordare* from *concors* (as CONCORD)]

con·cordat /kənˈkɔrdæt/ *noun* an agreement, esp. between the Vatican and a secular government relating to matters of mutual interest. [French *concordat* or Latin *concordatum* neuter past participle of *concordare* (as CONCORDANCE)]

Concord grape *noun* a variety of dark purple grape, a cultivated variety of the fox grape, used esp. for making juice, jelly, etc. [CONCORD 2, where it was first developed]

con·cours /kɒŋˈkuːr/ *noun* a competition. [French]

con·course *noun* **1** an open central area in a large public building, airport, etc. **2** *N Amer.* an indoor shopping area, often on the lowest (usu. underground) level of an office building or office complex. **3** a crowd. **4** a coming together; a gathering (*a concourse of ideas*). [Old French *concours* from Latin *concursus* (as CONCUR)]

con·cres·cence /kənˈkrɛsəns/ *noun* *Biol.* coalescence; growing together. □ **con·cres·cent** *adjective* [CON-, after *excrescence* etc.]

con·crete ● *adjective* **1 a** existing in a material form; real. **b** specific, definite (*concrete evidence; a concrete proposal*). **2** *Grammar* (of a noun) denoting a material object as opposed to an abstract quality, state, or action. ● *noun* (often *attributive*) a durable building material made from a mixture of gravel, sand, cement, and water, which forms a stone-like mass on hardening. ● *verb* **1** *transitive* **a** cover with concrete. **b** embed in concrete. **2 a** *transitive & intransitive* form into a mass; solidify. **b** *transitive* make concrete instead of abstract. □ **con·crete·ly** *adverb* **con·crete·ness** *noun* [French *concret* or Latin *concretus* past participle of *concrescere* (as COM-, *crescere* cret- GROW)]

concrete jungle *noun* a heavily urbanized area, esp. one with no green space.

concrete music *noun* music constructed by mixing recorded sounds.

concrete poetry *noun* poetry using unusual typographical layout to enhance the effect on the page.

con·cre·tion *noun* **1 a** a hard solid concreted mass. **b** the forming of this by coalescence. **2** *Med.* a stony mass formed within the body. **3** *Geol.* a small round mass of rock particles embedded in limestone or clay. □ **con·cre·tion·ary** *adjective* [French from Latin *concretio* (as CONCRETE)]

con·cret·ize /ˈkɒnkrɪˌtaɪz, ˈkɒŋ-/ *transitive verb* (also esp. *Brit.* **-ise**) make concrete instead of abstract. □ **con·cret·iz·a·tion** *noun*

con·cu·bin·age /kənˈkjuːbɪnɪdʒ, kɒŋ-/ *noun* **1** *Law* the cohabitation of a man and woman not married to each other. **2** the state of being or having a concubine.

con·cu·bine /ˈkɒnkjuˌbaɪn, ˈkɒŋ-/ *noun* **1** *archaic* a woman who lives with a man as his wife; a kept mistress. **2** (among polygamous peoples) a secondary wife. [Old French from Latin *concubina* (as COM-, *cubina* from *cubare* lie)]

con·cu·pis·cence /kənˈkjuːpɪsəns/ *noun* *formal* sexual desire. □ **con·cu·pis·cent** *adjective* [Old French from Late Latin *concupiscentia* from Latin *concupiscere* begin to desire (as COM-, inceptive of *cupere* desire)]

con·cur *intransitive verb* (**con·curred**, **con·cur·ring**) **1** happen together; coincide. **2** (often foll. by *with*) **a** agree in opinion. **b** express agreement. **3** combine together for a cause; act in combination. [Latin *concurrere* (as COM-, *currere* run)]

con·cur·rent /kənˈkɜrənt/ *adjective* **1** (often foll. by *with*) **a** existing or in operation at the same time (*served two concurrent sentences*). **b** existing or acting together. **2** *Math.* (of three or more lines) meeting at or tending towards one point. **3** agreeing, harmonious. □ **con·cur·rence** *noun* **con·cur·rent·ly** *adverb*

concurrent jurisdiction *noun* *Law* jurisdiction shared by two courts, levels of government, etc., over the same subject matter and geographical area.

con·cuss /kənˈkʌs/ *transitive verb* subject to concussion. □ **con·cus·sive** *adjective* [Latin *concutere* concuss- (as COM-, *cutere* quatere* shake)]

con·cus·sion *noun* **1** *Med.* a violent injury to the brain caused by shaking or jarring, usu. accompanied by loss of consciousness. **2** violent shaking. [Latin *concussio* (as CONCUSS)]

cond. *abbreviation* condition.

Condé /kɔˈdeɪ/ **Prince de** (title of Louis II de Bourbon; known as 'the Great Condé') (1621–86), French general, noted as a commander during the last phase of the Thirty Years War.

con·demn /kənˈdɛm/ *transitive verb* **1** express utter disapproval of; censure (*was condemned for his irresponsible behaviour*). **2 a** find guilty; convict. **b** (usu. foll. by *to*) sentence to (a punishment, esp. death). **c** show or suggest one's guilt (*his looks condemn him*). **3** pronounce (a building etc.) unfit for use or habitation. **4** (usu. foll. by *to*) doom or assign (to something unwelcome or painful) (*condemned to spending hours at the kitchen sink*). **5** pronounce incurable. □ **con·dem·nable** /-ˈdɛmnəbəl/ *adjective* **con·dem·na·tion** /ˌkɒndɛmˈneɪʃən/ *noun* **con·dem·na·tory** /-ˈdɛmnəˌtɔri/ *adjective* **con·demned** *adjective* [Old French *condem(p)ner* from Latin *condemnare* (as COM-, *damnare* DAMN)]

condemned cell *noun* *Brit.* a cell for a prisoner condemned to death.

con·den·sate /kənˈdɛnseɪt, ˈkɒndənˌseɪt/ *noun* a substance produced by condensation.

con·den·sa·tion /ˌkɒndɛnˈseɪʃən/ *noun* **1** the act of condensing. **2** any condensed material (esp. water on a cold surface). **3** an abridgement. **4** *Chem.* the combination of molecules with the elimination of water or other small molecules.

condensation trail *noun* = CONTRAIL.

con·dense /kənˈdɛns/ *verb* **1** *transitive* make denser or more concentrated. **2** *transitive* express in fewer words; make concise. **3** *transitive & intransitive* reduce or be reduced from a gas or solid to a liquid. [French *condenser* or Latin *condensare* (as COM-, *densus* thick)]

condensed milk *noun* milk thickened by evaporation and sweetened, usu. tinned.

con·dens·er *noun* **1** an apparatus or vessel for condensing vapour. **2** *Electricity* = CAPACITOR. **3** a lens or system of lenses for concentrating light. **4** a person or thing that condenses.

con·des·cend /ˌkɒndəˈsɛnd/ *intransitive verb* **1** (usu. foll. by *to* + infin.) usu. *ironic* be gracious enough (to do a thing) esp. while showing one's sense of dignity or superiority (*condescended to attend the meeting*). **2** (foll. by *to*) *derogatory* behave as if one is on equal terms with (an inferior),

---

uː m**oo**d   aɪ m**y**   əi p**i**pe   au br**ow**n   ʌv h**ou**se   ei d**ay**   ɔi b**oy**   ā fr**an**glais   ã Canadien   ɔ̃ Brayon   (*see over for consonants*)

usu. while maintaining an attitude of superiority.
□ **con·des·cend·ing** *adjective* **con·des·cend·ing·ly** *adverb* [Old French *condescendre* from ecclesiastical Latin *condescendere* (as COM-, DESCEND)]

con·des·cen·sion /ˌkɒndə'senʃən/ *noun* **1** a condescending manner. **2** an act or instance of condescending.

con·dign /kən'daɪn/ *adjective* (of a punishment etc.) severe and well-deserved. [Old French *condigne* from Latin *condignus* (as COM-, *dignus* worthy)]

con·di·ment /'kɒndəmənt/ *noun* a spice or foodstuff used in small quantities to enhance the flavour of other foods, e.g. salt and pepper, vinegar, etc. [Latin *condimentum* from *condire* pickle]

con·di·tion /kən'dɪʃən/ ● *noun* **1** a stipulation; something upon the fulfillment of which something else depends. **2 a** the state of being or fitness of a person or thing (*arrived in bad condition; not in a condition to be used*). **b** an ailment or abnormality (*a heart condition*). **3** (in *pl.*) circumstances, esp. those affecting the functioning or existence of something (*working conditions are good*). **4** *archaic* social rank (*all sorts and conditions of men*). **5** *Grammar* a clause expressing a condition. ● *transitive verb* **1 a** bring into a good or desired state or condition. **b** make fit. **2** teach or accustom to adopt certain habits etc. (*conditioned by society*). **3** govern, determine (*his behaviour was conditioned by his drunkenness*). **4 a** impose conditions on. **b** be essential to (*the two things condition each other*). **5** apply conditioner to (hair, the skin, etc.). □ **in** (or **out of**) **condition** in good (or bad) condition. **in no condition to** certainly not fit to. **on condition that** with the stipulation that. □ **con·di·tioned** *adjective* [Latin *condicio -onis* from *condicere* (as COM-, *dicere* say)]

con·di·tion·al ● *adjective* **1** (often foll. by *on, upon*) dependent; not absolute; containing a condition or stipulation (*a conditional offer*). **2** (of a clause, sentence, mood, proposition, etc.) expressing a condition on which something depends, e.g. the first clause in *if she wins, we will be rich*. ● *noun* **1** esp. *Grammar & Logic* a word, clause, proposition, etc., expressing or including a condition. **2** *Grammar* the conditional mood. □ **con·di·tion·al·ity** /kənˌdɪʃə'nalɪti/ *noun* **con·di·tion·al·ly** *adverb*

conditional discharge *noun* an order made by a criminal court whereby an offender will not be sentenced for an offence unless a further offence is committed within a stated period.

conditional sale *noun* a sale of goods, esp. real estate, which is subject to certain conditions being met by the buyer in a specified time period, such as payment of a percentage of the purchase price.

conditional sentence *noun* **1** *Cdn Law* a criminal sentence of up to two years that is served in the community rather than in jail under various conditions imposed by the trial judge, such as house arrest, curfews, community service, etc., the breaching of which may lead to incarceration. **2** *Grammar* a sentence including a conditional clause.

conditioned reflex *noun* (also **conditioned response**) a reflex response to a non-natural stimulus, established by training.

con·di·tion·er *noun* a substance or device that improves the condition of something, esp. a substance applied to the hair.

con·di·tion·ing ● *noun* **1** the act of bringing a person, animal, or thing into good condition. **2** degree of fitness, esp. aerobic capacity. **3** the training or accustoming of a person or animal to give conditioned responses. ● *adjective* that conditions (*conditioning shampoo*).

con·do *noun* (*pl.* **-dos**) *N Amer. informal* = CONDOMINIUM 1. [abbreviation]

con·dole *intransitive verb* (foll. by *with*) express sympathy with a person over a loss, grief, etc. [Late Latin *condolēre* (as COM-, *dolēre* suffer)]

con·dol·ence /kən'dəʊləns/ *noun* (often in *pl.*) an expression of sympathy (*my condolences on the death of your wife*).

con·dom /'kɒndəm/ *noun* **1** a rubber sheath worn on the penis during sexual intercourse as a contraceptive or to prevent infection. **2** (in full **female condom**) a plastic sheath inserted into the vagina prior to intercourse to prevent pregnancy or infection. [18th c.: origin unknown]

con·do·min·ium /ˌkɒndə'mɪniəm/ *noun* **1** *N Amer.* **a** an apartment building, office building or townhouse complex containing units which are individually owned. **b** a unit in such a building or complex. **2** the joint control of a country's affairs by other countries. [modern Latin (as COM-, *dominium* DOMINION)]

con·done *transitive verb* **1** forgive or overlook (an offence or wrongdoing). **2** approve or sanction, usu. reluctantly. **3** (of an action) atone for (an offence); make up for. □ **con·don·ation** /ˌkɒndə'neɪʃən/ *noun* **con·don·er** *noun* [Latin *condonare* (as COM-, *donare* give)]

con·dor /'kɒndɔr/ *noun* **1** (in full **Andean condor**) a large vulture, *Vultur gryphus*, of S America, having black plumage with a white neck

ruff and a fleshy wattle on the forehead. **2** (in full **California condor**) a small vulture, *Gymnogyps californianus*, of California. [Spanish from Quechua *cuntur*]

Con·dor·cet /kɒndɔr'se/ **Marquis de** (title of Marie Jean Antoine Nicolas de Caritat) (1743–94), French philosopher, mathematician, and politician, who is best known for his *Sketch for a Historical Picture of the Progress of the Human Mind* (1795), setting forth his ideas on the progressive perfectibility of the human race.

con·dot·tiere /ˌkɒndɒt'jeri/ *noun* (*pl.* **condottieri** *pronunc.* same) *hist.* a leader or a member of a troop of mercenaries in Italy. [Italian from *condotto* troop under contract (*condotta*) (as CONDUCT)]

con·duce /kən'duːs, -djuːs/ *intransitive verb* (foll. by *to*) (usu. of an event or attribute) lead or contribute to (a result). [Latin *conducere conduct-* (as COM-, *ducere duct-* lead)]

con·du·cive /kən'duːsɪv, -djuːs-/ *adjective* (often foll. by *to*) contributing or helping (towards something) (*not a conducive atmosphere for negotiation; good health is conducive to happiness*).

conduct ● *noun* /'kɒndʌkt/ **1** behaviour; way of acting. **2** the action or manner of directing or managing (business, war, etc.). **3** *archaic* leading, guidance. ● *verb* /kən'dʌkt/ **1** *transitive* direct or manage (business etc.). **2** *transitive* carry out or administer (*conduct an investigation*). **3 a** *transitive & intransitive* be the conductor of (an orchestra, choir, etc.). **b** *transitive* direct the performance (of a piece of music). **4** *transitive* *Physics* transmit (heat, electricity, etc.) by conduction. **5** *reflexive* behave (*conducted himself appropriately*). **6** *transitive* lead or guide (a person or persons). □ **con·duct·ible** /kən'dʌktɪbəl/ *adjective* [Latin *conductus* (as COM-, *ducere duct-* lead): (v.) from Old French *conduite* past participle of *conduire*]

con·duct·ance /kən'dʌktəns/ *noun* *Physics* the power of a specified material to conduct electricity. Symbol: **G**.

conduct disorder *noun* a range of anti-social types of behaviour displayed in childhood or adolescence.

con·duc·tion *noun* **1 a** the transmission of heat through a substance from a region of higher temperature to a region of lower temperature. **b** the transmission of electricity through a substance by the application of an electric field. **2** the transmission of impulses along nerves. **3** the conducting of liquid through a pipe etc.

con·duct·ive *adjective* having the property of conducting (esp. heat, electricity, etc.). □ **con·duct·ive·ly** *adverb*

conductive education *noun* a system of training for people with motor disorders, esp. children, which aims to reduce their dependence on artificial aids and facilitate active participation in society.

con·duc·tiv·ity *noun* the conducting power of a specified material.

con·duct·or *noun* **1** a person who directs the performance of an orchestra or choir etc. **2** *Physics* **a** a thing that conducts or transmits heat or electricity, esp. regarded in terms of its capacity to do this (*a poor conductor*). **b** = LIGHTNING ROD. **3 a** a person who collects fares in a bus etc. **b** *N Amer.* a person in charge of a train. **4** a guide or leader. □ **con·duct·or·ship** *noun*

con·duc·tress *noun* **1** a woman who collects fares in a bus etc. **2** *N Amer.* a woman in charge of a train.

con·duit /'kɒnduɪt, -djuɪt/ *noun* **1** a channel or pipe for conveying liquids. **2** a person, organization, etc. through which anything is conveyed (*the mediator was a conduit for communication between the parties*). **3 a** a tube or trough for protecting insulated electric wires. **b** a length or stretch of this. [Old French *conduit* from medieval Latin *conductus* CONDUCT *noun*]

con·dyle /'kɒndɪl, -daɪl/ *noun* *Anat.* a rounded outgrowth at the end of a bone, forming an articulation with another bone. □ **con·dyl·ar** *adjective* **con·dyl·oid** *adjective* [French from Latin *condylus* from Greek *kondulos* knuckle]

cone ● *noun* **1** a solid figure with a circular (or other curved) plane base, tapering to a point. **2** a thing of a similar shape, solid or hollow, e.g. as used to mark off areas of roads. **3** the reproductive structure of conifers and related plants, often woody and cone-shaped. **4 a** a conical wafer for holding ice cream. **b** = ICE CREAM CONE. **5** any of the minute cone-shaped structures in the retina. **6** a conical mountain esp. of volcanic origin. **7** (in full **cone shell**) any marine gastropod mollusc of the family Conidae and esp. of the genus *Conus*, with a conical, typically intricately patterned shell. ● *transitive verb* shape like a cone. [French *cône* from Latin *conus* from Greek *kōnos*]

cone·flower *noun* any of several N American plants belonging to the genus *Rudbeckia* and related genera of the composite family, having flowers with cone-like centres. *See also* PURPLE CONEFLOWER, PRAIRIE CONEFLOWER.

Consonants: b *but* d *dog* f *few* g *get* h *her* j *yes* k *cat* l *leg* m *man* n *no* p *pen* r *red* s *sit*

Con·eglia·no /kɒˌneˈljɑːnəʊ/ **Em·man·uele**, see DA PONTE.

cone of silence noun jocular an imaginary device which surrounds a speaker or speakers and prevents them from being heard by others.

Con·es·toga wagon /ˌkɒnəˈstoːɡə/ noun N Amer. a large horse-drawn covered wagon used in the 18th and 19th c. [Conestoga, Pennsylvania, where it was first built in 1725]

co·ney var. of CONY.

Coney Island a resort and amusement park on the Atlantic coast in Brooklyn, New York City, on the south shore of Long Island.

con·fab informal ● noun a conversation (see CONFABULATE). ● intransitive verb (**con·fabbed**, **con·fab·bing**) converse, chat. [abbreviation]

con·fabu·late /kənˈfabjʊˌleɪt/ intransitive verb 1 converse, chat. 2 Psych. fabricate imaginary experiences as compensation for the loss of memory. □ **con·fabu·la·tion** noun [Latin confabulari (as COM-, fabulari from fabula tale)]

con·fect transitive verb make by putting together ingredients or materials. [Latin conficere confect- put together (as COM-, facere make)]

con·fec·tion noun 1 a sweet dessert or candy. 2 mixing, compounding. 3 a fashionable or elaborate article of women's clothing. 4 anything regarded as over-elaborate or contrived. [Old French from Latin confectio -onis (as CONFECT)]

con·fec·tion·ary ● noun var. of CONFECTIONERY (in sense 1). ● adjective of or like confections.

con·fec·tion·er noun a maker or retailer of confectionery.

confectioner's sugar noun US icing sugar.

con·fec·tion·ery noun 1 (also **con·fec·tion·ary**) **a** candy and other sweets. **b** a candy factory or store. **c** N Amer. a corner store. 2 the art or business of making candy or sweets.

con·fed·er·acy /kənˈfedərəsi/ noun (pl. **-acies**) **1 a** a league or alliance of persons, states, etc. **b** N Amer. (usu. **Confederacy**) a league or alliance of Aboriginal peoples (the Iroquois Confederacy). **2** a league for an unlawful or evil purpose; a conspiracy. **3** (**the Confederacy**) the Confederate States.

con·fed·er·al /kənˈfedərəl/ adjective of or pertaining to a confederation. □ **con·fed·er·al·ism** noun

con·fed·er·ate /kənˈfedərət/ ● adjective **1** esp. Polit. allied; joined by an agreement or treaty. **2** (**Confederate**) of or relating to the Confederate States. **3** Cdn (Nfld) of or relating to the political movement which supported the union of Newfoundland and Canada. ● noun **1** (**Confederate**) a supporter of the Confederate States. **2** Cdn (Nfld) (**Confederate**) a supporter of the political union of Newfoundland and Canada. **3** an accomplice, esp. in criminal activity. [Late Latin confoederatus (as COM-, FEDERATE)]

con·fed·er·at·ed /kənˈfedəreɪtəd/ adjective (of a person, state, etc.) united or allied with another.

Confederate States (also called **the Confederacy**) the eleven southern states (Alabama, Arkansas, Florida, Georgia, Louisiana, Mississippi, North Carolina, South Carolina, Tennessee, Texas, and Virginia) which seceded from the United States in 1860–1 and formed a confederacy of their own, thus precipitating the American Civil War. The Confederate states were defeated in 1865, after which they were reunited with the US.

con·fed·er·a·tion /kənˌfedəˈreɪʃən/ noun **1 a** a union or alliance of peoples, countries, labour unions, etc. **b** (**Confederation**) (in Canada) the federal union of provinces and territories forming Canada, originally including Ontario, Quebec, New Brunswick and Nova Scotia and subsequently expanded to include the present provinces and territories. **c** (**Confederation**) (in Newfoundland) the political union of Newfoundland and Canada. **2 a** the act or an instance of confederating. **b** (**Confederation**) (in Canada) the date of the creation of the Dominion of Canada, 1 July 1867. **c** (**Confederation**) (in Newfoundland) the date of the political union of Newfoundland and Canada, 31 March 1949. [French confédération (as CONFEDERATE)]

Confederation Day noun **1** (in Canada) the date of the creation of the Dominion of Canada, 1 July 1867. **2** (in Newfoundland) the date of the political union of Newfoundland and Canada, 31 March 1949.

con·fed·er·a·tion·ist /kənˌfedəˈreɪʃənɪst/ Cdn esp. hist. ● noun a supporter of Confederation. ● adjective of or relating to a political movement supporting Confederation.

Confederation poets noun the Canadian poets Charles G.D. Roberts, Bliss Carman, Archibald Lampman, and Duncan Campbell Scott, active shortly after Confederation, who incorporated Canadian themes and the Canadian landscape into their poems.

con·fer /kənˈfɜːr/ verb (**con·ferred**, **con·fer·ring**) **1** transitive (often foll. by on, upon) grant or bestow (a title, degree, favour, etc.). **2** intransitive (often foll. by with) converse, consult. □ **con·fer·ment** or **con·fer·ral** noun [Latin conferre (as COM-, ferre bring)]

con·feree /ˌkɒnfəˈriː/ noun **1** a person on whom something is conferred. **2** a participant in a conference.

con·fer·ence /ˈkɒnfərəns/ ● noun **1** a meeting for discussion or presentation of information, esp. a regular one held by an association or organization. **2** the linking of several telephones, computer terminals, etc., so that each user may communicate with the others simultaneously. **3** a division within a sports league. **4 a** an assembly of clergy or clergy and laity which discusses church issues, formulates policy, etc. **b** a group of churches whose representatives meet regularly in such an assembly. **5** an association of nations etc. for a specified purpose (the Conference on Security and Cooperation in Europe). **6** consultation, discussion. ● intransitive verb (usu. as **con·fer·en·cing** noun) take part in a conference or conference call. □ **in conference** engaged in discussion. [French conférence or medieval Latin conferentia (as CONFER)]

Conference Board of Canada a non-profit research institute which publishes reports and conducts surveys on economic and business issues.

con·fess verb **1** transitive & intransitive acknowledge or admit (a fault, wrongdoing, etc.) (confessed his guilt; confessed to having lied). **2** transitive admit reluctantly; concede (I confess I have my doubts about it). **3 a** transitive & intransitive declare (one's sins) to a priest. **b** transitive (of a priest) hear the confession of. [Old French confesser from Romanic from Latin confessus past participle of confitēri (as COM-, fatēri declare, avow)]

con·fess·ed·ly /kənˈfesədli/ adverb by one's own or general admission.

con·fes·sion noun **1 a** confessing or acknowledgement of a fault, wrongdoing, crime, etc. **b** an instance of this. **c** a thing confessed. **2 a** the act of a penitent declaring sins to a priest to obtain absolution. **b** that part of the public litany in some Christian churches in which a general acknowledgement of sinfulness is made. **3** (in full **confession of faith**) a formal declaration of one's religious beliefs.

con·fes·sion·al ● noun **1** an enclosed stall in a church in which a priest hears confessions. **2** the practice of confession (the secrecy of the confessional). ● adjective **1** (esp. of speech or writing) in which a person reveals or admits to private thoughts or incidents in their past, esp. ones about which they feel ashamed or embarrassed. **2** denominational. ¶ In Canada, confessional is used in the sense denominational primarily in reference to Quebec and Newfoundland and Labrador. **3** of or relating to religious confession. □ **con·fes·sion·al·ism** noun [French from Italian confessionale from medieval Latin, neuter of confessionalis (as CONFESSION)]

con·fes·sor noun **1** a priest who hears confessions and gives spiritual counsel. **2** a person who makes a confession. **3** a person who avows a religion in the face of its suppression, but does not suffer martyrdom.

con·fetti noun small bits of paper, usu. coloured, thrown on festive occasions, esp. at the bride and groom at weddings. [Italian, = sweetmeats, from Latin (as COMFIT)]

con·fi·dant /ˈkɒnfɪˌdɒnt, ˈkɒnfɪˈdɒnt/ noun a person to whom secrets, problems or other private matters are confided. [18th-c. for earlier confident, prob. to represent the pronunciation of French confidente (as CONFIDE)]

con·fi·dante /ˌkɒnfɪˈdɒnt, ˈkɒnfɪˌdɒnt, -dant/ noun a woman to whom secrets, problems or other private matters are confided.

con·fide verb **1** transitive tell (a secret etc.) in confidence. **2** intransitive (foll. by in, to) take (a person) into one's confidence; talk confidentially (she confided in her doctor). **3** transitive literary (foll. by to) entrust (an object of care, a task, etc.) to. □ **con·fid·ing·ly** adverb [Latin confidere (as COM-, fidere trust)]

con·fi·dence /ˈkɒnfɪdəns/ noun **1** firm trust; faith (have confidence in his ability). **2 a** self-reliance; belief in one's own abilities. **b** assurance or certainty. **3 a** something told confidentially; a secret (shared confidences). **b** the telling of private matters with mutual trust. **4** Parl. (often attributive) majority support for a government, policy, etc. expressed by a legislature. □ **in confidence** as a secret. **take into one's confidence** confide in. [(as CONFIDE)]

confidence game noun N Amer. (Brit. **confidence trick**) a swindle in which the victim is persuaded to trust the swindler in some way.

confidence interval noun Statistics a range of values so defined that there is a specified probability that the value of a parameter of a population lies within it.

confidence man noun a con man.

con·fi·dent /ˈkɒnfɪdənt/ adjective **1** feeling or showing confidence; self-assured, bold (spoke with a confident air). **2** (often foll. by of, or that +

clause) assured, trusting (*confident of your support*; *confident that he will come*). □ **con·fi·dent·ly** *adverb* [French from Italian *confidente* (as CONFIDE)]

con·fi·den·tial /ˌkɒnfɪ'denʃəl/ *adjective* **1** spoken, written or kept in confidence. **2** indicating private intimacy (*a confidential tone of voice*). **3** entrusted with secrets (*a confidential secretary*). □ **con·fi·den·ti·al·i·ty** /-ʃi'alɪti/ *noun* **con·fi·den·tial·ly** *adverb*

con·fig·ur·a·tion *noun* **1 a** an arrangement of parts or elements in a particular form or figure. **b** the form, shape, or figure resulting from such an arrangement. **2** *Computing* **a** the interrelating or interconnecting of a computer system or elements of it so that it will accommodate a particular specification. **b** an instance of this. **3** *Chem.* the fixed three-dimensional relationship of the atoms in a molecule. **4** *Physics* the distribution of electrons among the energy levels of an atom, or of nucleons among the energy levels of a nucleus, as specified by quantum numbers. **5** *Psych.* = GESTALT. □ **con·fig·ur·a·tion·al** *adjective*

con·fig·ure *transitive verb* **1** put together in a certain configuration; shape, fashion. **2** *Computing* interconnect or interrelate (a computer system or elements of it) so as to fit it for a designated task. □ **con·fig·ur·able** *adjective* **con·fig·ur·abil·ity** *noun* [Latin *configurare* (as COM-, *figurare* fashion)]

con·fine ● *transitive verb* /kən'faɪn/ (often foll. by *to*) **1** (also *reflexive*) keep or restrict (within certain limits etc.) (*she confined herself to drinking alcohol only on weekends*; *confine your opening remarks to ten minutes*). **2** hold captive; imprison. **3** oblige (a person) to remain indoors, in bed, etc., through illness, bad weather, etc. ● *noun* /'kɒnfaɪn/ (usu. in *pl.*) a limit or boundary (*within the confines of the town*). □ **be confined** *dated* be in childbirth. [(v.) from French *confiner*, (n.) Middle English from French *confins* (pl.), from Latin *confinia* (as COM-, *finia* neuter pl. from *finis* end, limit)]

con·fine·ment *noun* **1** the act or an instance of confining; the state of being confined. **2** *dated* the time of a woman's giving birth.

con·firm *transitive verb* **1** provide support for the truth or correctness of; make definitely valid (*confirmed my suspicions*; *confirmed his arrival time*). **2** establish more firmly (power, possession, etc.). **3** (foll. by *in*) encourage (a person) in (an opinion etc.) (*his conduct confirmed me in my view of him*). **4** ratify (a treaty, possession, title, etc.); make formally valid. **5** administer the religious rite of confirmation to. □ **con·firm·a·tory** *adjective* [Old French *confermer* from Latin *confirmare* (as COM-, FIRM[1])]

con·firm·and /'kɒnfər,mand/ *noun* a person who is to be or has just been confirmed.

con·firm·a·tion *noun* **1** the act or an instance of confirming; the state of being confirmed. **2 a** a religious rite confirming a baptized person as a full member of the Christian Church. **b** a ceremony in which a young person is formally confirmed as an adult member of the Jewish faith.

con·firmed *adjective* **1** firmly settled in some habit or condition (*confirmed in his ways*; *a confirmed bachelor*). **2** genuine; valid (*confirmed reservations*).

con·fis·cate /'kɒnfɪ,skeɪt/ *transitive verb* **1** take or seize by authority. **2** appropriate to the public treasury (by way of a penalty). □ **con·fis·cable** /kən'fɪskəbəl/ *adjective* **con·fis·ca·tion** /-'skeɪʃən/ *noun* **con·fis·ca·tor** *noun* **con·fis·ca·tory** /kən'fɪskə,tɔri/ *adjective* [Latin *confiscare* (as COM-, *fiscare* from *fiscus* treasury)]

con·fit /kɔ'fiː, kən-/ *noun* pork, duck, goose, turkey, etc., cooked slowly in its own fat, and preserved by storing in the fat. [French from Latin *confectum* something prepared]

Con·fit·eor /kən'fiːti,ɔr/ *noun* *Catholicism* a prayer confessing sins, said esp. at the beginning of the Mass. [Latin *confiteor* I confess]

con·fla·gra·tion /ˌkɒnflə'greɪʃən/ *noun* a great and destructive fire. [Latin *conflagratio* from *conflagrare* (as COM-, *flagrare* blaze)]

con·flate *transitive verb* blend or fuse together. □ **con·fla·tion** *noun* [Latin *conflare* (as COM-, *flare* blow)]

con·flict ● *noun* **1 a** a state of opposition or hostilities. **b** a fight or struggle. **2** (often foll. by *of*) **a** the clashing of opposed principles etc. **b** an instance of this. **c** a difficulty caused by the occurrence of two events at the same time. **3** *Psych.* **a** the opposition of incompatible wishes or needs in a person. **b** an instance of this. **c** the distress resulting from this. ● *intransitive verb* **1** clash; be incompatible. **2** (often foll. by *with*) struggle or contend (*in conflict* conflicting). □ **con·flict·ive** *adjective* **con·flic·tual** *adjective* [Latin *confligere* *conflict-* (as COM-, *fligere* strike)]

con·flict·ed *adjective* having or showing confused and mutually inconsistent feelings.

con·flict·ing *adjective* not compatible; contradictory (*conflicting opinions*).

conflict of interest *noun* (*pl.* **conflicts of interest**) the situation of a politician, corporate officer, etc., whose private interests might benefit from his or her public actions or influence.

conflict resolution *noun* the process of solving disputes.

con·flu·ence /'kɒnfluəns/ *noun* **1** the place where two rivers etc. meet. **2** a coming together (*a confluence of ideas*). [Latin *confluere* (as COM-, *fluere* flow)]

con·flu·ent /'kɒnfluənt/ ● *adjective* **1** flowing together, uniting. **2** *Med.* coalescing so as to form one continuous mass or surface (*confluent lesions*). ● *noun* a stream joining another.

con·form *verb* **1** *intransitive* (usu. foll. by *to*) comply in behaviour, actions, dress, etc., with general custom. **2** *intransitive* (foll. by *to*, *with*) be in accordance with; comply with (*conform to safety standards*). **3** *transitive* (often foll. by *to*) form according to a pattern; make similar. **4** *hist.* comply with the practices of an established church, esp. the Church of England. [Old French *conformer* from Latin *conformare* (as COM-, FORM)]

con·form·able *adjective* **1** (often foll. by *to*) similar. **2** (often foll. by *with*) consistent (*conformable with feminist theory*). **3** tractable, submissive. **4** *Geol.* (of strata in contact) lying in the same direction.

con·form·al /kən'fɔrməl/ *adjective* (of a map) showing any small area in its correct shape, but with some distortion of size (*compare* EQUAL AREA PROJECTION).

con·form·ance /kən'fɔrməns/ *noun* (often foll. by *to*, *with*) = CONFORMITY 1, 2.

con·form·a·tion /ˌkɒnfɔr'meɪʃən/ *noun* **1** the way in which a thing is formed; shape, structure (*a horse of good conformation*). **2** *Chem.* any spatial arrangement of atoms in a molecule from the rotation of part of the molecule about a single bond. □ **con·form·a·tion·al** *adjective*

con·form·ist /kən'fɔrmɪst/ ● *noun* **1** a person who conforms to an established practice; a conventional person. **2** a person who conforms to the practices of an established church, esp. the Church of England. ● *adjective* (of a person) conforming to established practices; conventional. □ **con·form·ism** *noun*

con·form·ity /kən'fɔrmɪti/ *noun* **1** (often foll. by *to*, *with*) action or behaviour in accordance with established practice; compliance. **2** (often foll. by *to*, *with*) correspondence in form or manner; likeness, agreement. **3** compliance with the practices of an established church, esp. the Church of England.

con·found *transitive verb* **1** throw into perplexity or confusion (*his bizarre behaviour confounded me*). **2** mix up; confuse (in one's mind) (*she confounded fact with fiction*). **3** *archaic* defeat, overthrow. **4** damn (used in mild imprecations) (*confound it!*). [Anglo-French *conf(o)undre*, Old French *confondre* from Latin *confundere* mix up (as COM-, *fundere* *fus-* pour)]

con·found·ed *adjective* *informal* damned (*a confounded nuisance!*). □ **con·found·ed·ly** *adverb*

con·fra·ter·ni·ty /ˌkɒnfrə'tɜrnɪti/ *noun* (*pl.* **-ties**) **1** a brotherhood devoted to religious or charitable work. **2** an association, esp. of men, united for some purpose, or in some profession. [Old French *confraternité* from medieval Latin *confraternitas* (as COM-, FRATERNITY)]

con·frere /'kɒnfrer/ *noun* a fellow member of a profession, scientific body, etc. [Old French from medieval Latin *confrater* (as COM-, *frater* brother)]

con·front *transitive verb* **1 a** face in hostility or defiance. **b** face up to and deal with (a problem, difficulty, etc.). **2** (of a difficulty etc.) present itself to (*countless obstacles confronted us*). **3** (foll. by *with*) bring (a person) face to face with (a circumstance), esp. by way of accusation (*confronted them with the evidence*). **4** meet or stand facing (*confronted me at the door*). □ **con·fron·ta·tion** *noun* **con·fron·ta·tion·al** *adjective* [French *confronter* from medieval Latin *confrontare* (as COM-, *frontare* from *frons* *frontis* face)]

Con·fu·cian /kən'fjuːʃən/ ● *adjective* of or relating to Confucius or his philosophy. ● *noun* a follower of Confucius.

Con·fu·cian·ism /kən'fjuːʃə,nɪzəm/ *noun* a system of philosophical and ethical teachings founded by Confucius in China in the 6th c. BC and developed by Mencius in the 4th c. BC, one of the two major Chinese ideologies (the other is Taoism). The basic concepts are ethical ones, for example love for one's fellows and filial piety, and the ideal of the superior man; traditional ideas such as yin and yang have also been incorporated into Confucianism. □ **Con·fu·cian·ist** *noun*

Con·fu·cius /kən'fjuːʃəs/ (Latinized name of K'ung Fu-tzu = 'Kong the master') (551–479 BC), Chinese philosopher. He spent much of his life as a moral teacher of a group of disciples, and his ideas about the importance of practical moral values formed the basis of the

Vowels: a *cat* ɑ *arm* e *bed* ɜr *her* ɜː *deux* ə *ago* ɪ *sit* i *cosy* iː *feed* ɒ *hot* ɔ *pore* oː *no* ʌ *run* ʊ *put*

philosophy of Confucianism; his teachings were collected by his pupils after his death in the *Analects*.

con·fus·able ● *adjective* that is able or liable to be confused. ● *noun* a thing, esp. a word, that is liable to be confused with another. □ **con·fus·abil·ity** *noun*

con·fuse *transitive verb* **1** disconcert, perplex, bewilder. **2** mix up in the mind; mistake (one for another). **3** make indistinct (*that point confuses the issue*). **4** throw into disorder. □ **con·fus·ing** *adjective* **con·fus·ing·ly** *adverb* [19th-c. back-formation from *confused* (14th c.) from Old French *confus* from Latin *confusus*: see CONFOUND]

con·fused *adjective* **1** perplexed; bewildered. **2** unclear; indistinct (*confused thinking*). **3** (of elderly persons) mentally infirm. **4** disorderly (*a confused jumble of clothes*). □ **con·fus·ed·ly** *adverb*

con·fu·sion *noun* **1 a** the act of confusing (*the confusion of fact and fiction*). **b** an instance of this; a misunderstanding (*confusions arise from a lack of communication*). **2 a** the result of confusing; a confused state; disorder (*thrown into confusion by his words; trampled in the confusion of battle*). **b** (foll. by *of*) a disorderly jumble (*a confusion of ideas*). **3** civil commotion (*confusion broke out at the announcement*).

con·fute /kənˈfjuːt/ *transitive verb* **1** prove (a person) to be in error. **2** prove (an argument) to be false. □ **con·fu·ta·tion** /ˌkɒnfjuːˈteɪʃən/ *noun* [Latin *confutare* restrain]

conga ● *noun* **1** a Latin-American dance of African origin, usu. performed by people in a single line, one behind another, who take three steps forward and then kick. **2** (also **conga drum**) a tall, narrow, low-toned drum beaten with the hands. ● *intransitive verb* (**congas**, **con·gaed**, **con·ga·ing**) perform the conga. [Latin American Spanish from Spanish feminine form of *congo* of or pertaining to Congo]

con·geal /kənˈdʒiːl/ *transitive & intransitive verb* **1** make or become semi-solid by cooling. **2** (of blood etc.) coagulate. **3** (of ideas etc.) make or become fixed or established. □ **con·gealed** *adjective* [Old French *congeler* from Latin *congelare* (as COM-, *gelare* from *gelu* frost)]

con·gee /ˈkɒndʒiː/ *noun* a thick Oriental soup made of rice. [Tamil *kañci*]

con·gel·a·tion /ˌkɒndʒəˈleɪʃən/ *noun* **1** the process of congealing. **2** a congealed state. **3** a congealed substance. [Old French *congelation* or Latin *congelatio* (as CONGEAL)]

con·gen·er /ˈkɒndʒənər/ *noun* a thing or person of the same kind or category as another, esp. animals or plants of a specified genus (*the goldfinch is a congener of the canary*). [Latin (as CON-, GENUS)]

con·gen·er·ic /ˌkɒndʒəˈnɛrɪk/ *adjective* **1** of the same genus, kind, or race. **2** allied in nature or origin; akin.

con·gen·ial /kənˈdʒiːnɪəl/ *adjective* **1** (of a person, character, etc.) pleasant because akin to oneself in temperament or interests. **2** (of a place, activity, etc.) suited or agreeable. □ **con·geni·al·ity** /-ˈalɪti/ *noun* **con·gen·ial·ly** *adverb* [CON- + GENIAL]

con·gen·ital /kənˈdʒɛnɪtəl/ *adjective* **1** (esp. of a disease, defect, etc.) existing from birth. **2** having a specified nature deeply ingrained as if from birth (*a congenital liar*). □ **con·gen·ital·ly** *adverb* [Latin *congenitus* (as COM-, *genitus* past participle of *gigno* beget)]

con·ger /ˈkɒŋgər/ *noun* (in full **conger eel**) any eel of the family Congridae, comprising scaleless sea eels usu. found in coastal waters, esp. *Conger conger*, a European conger reaching up to 3 metres in length and caught for food. [Greek *goggros*]

con·ger·ies /ˈkɒndʒəriːz, kɒnˈdʒiːriːz/ *noun* (*pl.* same) a disorderly collection; a mass or heap. [Latin, formed as CONGEST]

con·gest /kənˈdʒɛst/ *transitive verb* (esp. as **con·gest·ed** *adjective*) **1** affect with congestion (*congested lungs*). **2** obstruct, block (*congested streets*). □ **con·gest·ive** *adjective* [Latin *congerere congest-* (as COM-, *gerere* bring)]

con·ges·tion /kənˈdʒɛstʃən/ *noun* **1** abnormal accumulation of blood or mucus in a part of the body. **2** crowding or obstruction, esp. of traffic.

con·glom·er·ate /kənˈglɒmərət/ ● *noun* **1** a number of things or parts forming a heterogeneous mass. **2** a group or corporation formed by the merging of separate and diverse firms. **3** *Geol.* a rock made up of small stones held together (*compare* AGGLOMERATE *noun* 2). ● *adjective* **1** gathered into a rounded mass. **2** *Geol.* of or forming a conglomerate. ● *transitive & intransitive verb* /kənˈglɒmə,reɪt/ collect into a coherent mass. □ **con·glom·er·a·tion** *noun* [Latin *conglomeratus* past participle of *conglomerare* (as COM-, *glomerare* from *glomus -eris* ball)]

con·glom·era·teur /kən,glɒmərəˈtɜːr/ *noun* N *Amer.* a person who forms or manages a corporate conglomerate. [CONGLOMERATE + common French suffix *-eur*; compare ENTREPRENEUR]

Congo 1 (in full **the Democratic Republic of the Congo**) a large equatorial country in central Africa with a short coastline on the Atlantic Ocean; pop. (est. 2002) 55,225,478; capital, Kinshasa. Congo is largely a low-lying forested region, encompassing the greater part of the Congo River basin. The area became a Belgian colony and was known as the Congo Free State (1885–1908), the Belgian Congo (1908–60), and Zaire (1960–97). **2** (in full **the Republic of the Congo**) an equatorial country in Africa, with a short Atlantic coastline; pop. (est. 2002) 2,958,448; capital, Brazzaville. The Congo River and its tributary the Ubanghi form most of the country's eastern boundary (with Congo). The region was colonized in the 19th c. by France, and became known as Middle Congo, forming part of the larger territory of French Congo (later, French Equatorial Africa).

Con·go·lese ● *adjective* of or relating to Congo (formerly Zaire), the Republic of the Congo, or the region surrounding the Congo River. ● *noun* **1** a native or resident of any of these regions. **2** any of the Bantu languages spoken by the Congolese people. [French *congolais*]

Congo River (also called **Zaire River**) a major river of central Africa, which rises as the Lualaba, to the south of Kisangani in N Congo (formerly Zaire), and flows 4 630 km (2,880 miles) in a great curve westward, turning southwestward to form the border between the Republic of the Congo and the Democratic Republic of the Congo, before emptying into the Atlantic.

con·grats *plural noun & interjection informal* congratulations. [abbreviation]

con·gratu·late /kənˈgratʃə,leɪt, -ˈgradʒ-/ *transitive verb & reflexive* (often foll. by *on*, *upon*) **1** *transitive* express pleasure at the happiness or good fortune or excellence of (a person) (*congratulated them on their success*). **2** *reflexive* think oneself fortunate or clever. □ **con·gratu·la·tor** *noun* **con·gratu·la·tory** /-lə,tɔːri/ *adjective* [Latin *congratulari* (as COM-, *gratulari* show joy, from *gratus* pleasing)] ¶ Although the second pronunciation is very common, some people look upon its use unfavourably.

con·gratu·la·tion /kən,gratʃəˈleɪʃən, -,gradʒ-/ *noun* **1** the act or an instance of congratulating. **2** (also as *interjection*; usu. in *pl.*) an expression of this (*congratulations on winning!*).

con·gre·gant /ˈkɒŋgrəgənt/ *noun* a member of a congregation (esp. Jewish). [Latin *congregare* (as CONGREGATE)]

con·gre·gate /ˈkɒŋgrə,geɪt/ *transitive & intransitive verb* collect or gather into a crowd or mass. [Latin *congregare* (as COM-, *gregare* from *grex gregis* flock)]

con·gre·ga·tion /ˌkɒŋgrəˈgeɪʃən/ *noun* **1 a** a body assembled for religious worship. **b** a body of persons regularly attending a particular church etc. **2** the process of congregating; collection into a crowd or mass. **3** a crowd or mass gathered together. **4** *Catholicism* **a** a body of persons obeying a common religious rule. **b** any of several permanent committees of the College of Cardinals.

con·gre·ga·tion·al /ˌkɒŋgrəˈgeɪʃənəl/ *adjective* **1** of a congregation. **2** (**Congregational**) of or adhering to Congregationalism.

Con·gre·ga·tion·al·ism /ˌkɒŋgrəˈgeɪʃənə,lizəm/ *noun* a system of ecclesiastical organization whereby individual churches are largely self-governing. □ **Con·gre·ga·tion·al·ist** *noun*

Congregation of the Mission see LAZARIST.

con·gress *noun* **1** (**Congress**) **a** the national legislative body of the US, comprising the House of Representatives and the Senate. **b** this body during any two-year term. **2** the national legislative body in some other countries. **3** a formal meeting of delegates for discussion. **4** a society or organization. **5** the act or an instance of coming together, meeting. □ **con·gres·sion·al** *adjective* [Latin *congressus* from *congredi* (as COM-, *gradi* walk)]

con·gress·man *noun* (*pl.* **-men**) a member of the US Congress, esp. of the House of Representatives.

con·gress·person *noun* (*pl.* **con·gress·persons** or **con·gress·people**) a member of the US Congress, esp. of the House of Representatives.

con·gress·woman *noun* (*pl.* **-women**) a female member of the US Congress, esp. of the House of Representatives.

Con·greve /ˈkɒŋgriːv/ **Wil·liam** (1670–1729), English dramatist whose plays, such as *Love for Love* (1695) and *The Way of the World* (1700), epitomize the wit and satire of Restoration comedy.

con·gru·ence /ˈkɒŋgrʊəns, kənˈgruːəns/ *noun* (also **con·gru·ency** /-ənsi/) **1** agreement, consistency. **2** *Math.* the state of being congruent.

con·gru·ent /ˈkɒŋgrʊənt, kənˈgruːənt/ *adjective* **1** (often foll. by *with*) suitable, agreeing. **2** *Math.* (of figures) coinciding exactly when superimposed. □ **con·gru·ent·ly** *adverb* [Latin *congruere* agree]

con·gru·ous /ˈkɒŋgruːəs/ *adjective* suitable, agreeing; fitting.

con·gru·ity /-'gruːɪti/ *noun* **con·gru·ous·ly** *adverb* [Latin *congruus* (as CONGRUENT)]

Coni·bear /'kɒnəbər/ *noun* (in full **Conibear trap**) N *Amer.* proprietary a trap with a trigger mechanism designed to kill an animal instantly. [F. Conibear d.1988, its Canadian inventor]

con·ic /'kɒnɪk/ ● *adjective* of, pertaining to, or resembling a cone. ● *noun* **1** a conic section. **2** (in *pl.*) the study of conic sections. [modern Latin *conicus* from Greek *kōnikos* (as CONE)]

con·ic·al /'kɒnɪkəl/ *adjective* cone-shaped. □ **con·ic·al·ly** *adverb*

conical projection *noun* (also **conic projection**) a map projection in which a spherical surface is projected on to a cone, usually with its vertex above the pole.

conic section *noun* a figure formed by the intersection of a cone and a plane.

co·nid·ium /kə'nɪdiəm/ *noun* (*pl.* **co·nidia** /-diə/) a spore produced asexually by various fungi. [modern Latin diminutive from Greek *konis* dust]

con·ifer /'kɒnɪfər/ *noun* any evergreen tree of a group usu. bearing cones, including pines, yews, cedars, and redwoods. □ **con·ifer·ous** /kə'nɪfərəs/ *adjective* [Latin (as CONE, -FEROUS)]

coni·ine /'koʊnɪˌiːn, 'koʊniːɪn/ *noun* a poisonous alkaloid found in hemlock, that paralyzes the nerves. [Latin *conium* from Greek *kōneion* hemlock]

conj. *abbreviation* **1** conjunction. **2** conjunctive. **3** conjugation.

con·jec·tur·al /kən'dʒektʃərəl/ *adjective* based on, involving, or given to conjecture. □ **con·jec·tur·al·ly** *adverb*

con·jec·ture /kən'dʒektʃər/ ● *noun* **1** the formation of an opinion on incomplete information; guessing. **2** an opinion or conclusion reached in this way. ● *transitive & intransitive verb* guess. [Old French *conjecture* or Latin *conjectura* from *conjicere* (as COM-, *jacere* throw)]

con·join *transitive & intransitive verb* join, combine. [Old French *conjoign-* pres. stem of *conjoindre* from Latin *conjungere* (as COM-, *jungere* junct- join)]

con·joined twins *plural noun* twins joined at any part of the body and sometimes sharing organs etc.

con·joint *adjective* associated, joint. □ **con·joint·ly** *adverb*

con·ju·gal /'kɒndʒʊgəl/ *adjective* of marriage or the relation between spouses. [Latin *conjugalis* from *conjux* consort (as COM-, *-jux -jugis* from root of *jungere* join)]

conjugal rights *plural noun* the legal rights of each partner in a marriage to companionship, support, and affection (often taken to imply sexual relations) provided by the other.

conjugal visit *noun* a prison visit during which spouses or partners are allowed to be in private to have sexual relations.

con·ju·gate ● *verb* /'kɒndʒʊˌgeɪt/ **1** *transitive Grammar* inflect (a verb) in its various forms of voice, mood, tense, number or person. **2** *intransitive Biol.* **a** unite sexually. **b** (of gametes) become fused. **3** *intransitive Chem.* (of protein) combine with non-protein. ● *adjective* /'kɒndʒʊgət/ **1** joined together, esp. as a pair. **2** *Grammar* derived from the same root. **3** *Biol.* fused. **4** *Chem.* (of an acid or base) related by loss or gain of an electron. **5** *Math.* joined in a reciprocal relation, esp. having the same real parts, and equal magnitudes but opposite signs of imaginary parts. ● *noun* /'kɒndʒʊgət/ a conjugate word or thing. □ **con·ju·ga·tive** *adjective* [Latin *conjugare* yoke together (as COM-, *jugare* from *jugum* yoke)]

con·ju·ga·tion /ˌkɒndʒʊ'geɪʃən/ *noun* **1** *Grammar* a system of verbal inflection. **2** the act or an instance of conjugating. **3** *Biol.* **a** the fusion of two gametes in reproduction. **b** the temporary union of two unicellular organisms for the exchange of genetic material. □ **con·ju·ga·tion·al** *adjective*

con·junct ● *adjective* /kən'dʒʌŋkt/ joined together; combined; associated. ● *noun* /'kɒndʒʌŋkt/ a person or thing conjoined or associated with another. [Latin *conjunctus* (as CONJOIN)]

con·junc·tion /kən'dʒʌŋkʃən/ *noun* **1** *Grammar* a word used to connect clauses or sentences or words in the same clause (e.g. *and*, *but*, *if*). **2 a** the action of joining; the condition of being joined. **b** an instance of this. **3 a** a combination (of events or circumstances). **b** a number of associated persons or things. **4** *Astronomy & Astrology* the alignment of two bodies in the solar system so that they have the same longitude as seen from the earth. □ **in conjunction with** together with. □ **con·junc·tion·al** *adjective* [Old French *conjonction* from Latin *conjunctio -onis* (as CONJUNCT)]

con·junc·tiva /ˌkɒndʒʌŋk'taɪvə, kən'dʒʌŋktɪvə/ *noun* (*pl.* **con·junc·tivas** or **con·junc·tivae** /-viː/) *Anat.* the mucous membrane that covers the front of the eye and lines the inside of the eyelids. □ **con·junc·tival** *adjective* [medieval Latin (*membrana*) *conjunctiva* (as CONJUNCTIVE)]

con·junct·ive /kən'dʒʌŋktɪv/ ● *adjective* **1** serving to join; connective. **2** *Grammar* of the nature of a conjunction. ● *noun Grammar* a conjunctive word. □ **con·junct·ive·ly** *adverb* [Late Latin *conjunctivus* (as CONJOIN)]

con·junc·tiv·itis /kənˌdʒʌŋktɪ'vaɪtɪs/ *noun* inflammation of the conjunctiva.

con·junc·ture /kən'dʒʌŋktʃər/ *noun* a combination of events; a state of affairs. [obsolete French from Italian *congiuntura* (as CONJOIN)]

con·jur·a·tion /ˌkɒndʒʊ'reɪʃən/ *noun* an incantation; a magic spell.

con·jure /'kɒndʒər/ *verb* **1** *transitive* cause to appear or disappear as if by magic (*conjured a rabbit out of a hat*; *conjured visions of a faraway land*). **2** *intransitive* perform tricks which are seemingly magical. **3** *transitive* call upon (a demon, spirit, etc.) to appear. **4** *transitive* /kən'dʒʊər/ (often foll. by *to* + infin.) appeal solemnly to (a person). **5** *transitive* evoke. □ **conjure up 1** bring into existence or cause to appear as if by magic. **2** cause to appear to the eye or mind; evoke. [Old French *conjurer* plot, exorcise, from Latin *conjurare* band together by oath (as COM-, *jurare* swear)]

con·jur·ing *noun* the performance of seemingly magical tricks, esp. by rapid movements of the hands.

con·jur·or *noun* (also **con·jur·er**) a performer of conjuring tricks.

conk[1] *intransitive verb informal* □ **conk out 1** (of a machine etc.) break down. **2** (of a person) become exhausted and give up. **3** (of a person) fall asleep. [20th c.: origin unknown]

conk[2] *slang* ● *noun* **1** the head. **2** a blow, esp. on the nose or head. **3** *Brit.* the nose. ● *transitive verb* hit, esp. on the head. [19th c.: perhaps = CONCH]

conk[3] *noun* N *Amer.* **1** the fruiting body of a bracket fungus, esp. the fungus *Trametes pini*. **2** infestation of timber by such a fungus. [variant of CONCH]

conk·er *noun* **1** *Brit.* the hard fruit of a horse chestnut. **2** (in *pl.*) *Brit. & Cdn* a children's game played with conkers on strings, one hit against another to try to break it. [dial. *conker* snail shell (originally used in the game), assoc. with CONQUER]

con man *noun* a man who robs or cheats someone by first persuading them to trust him.

con moto /kɒn 'moʊtoʊ/ *adverb Music* with movement. [Italian]

Conn. *abbreviation* Connecticut.

conn esp. US var. of CON[4].

Con·nacht /'kɒnɒt/ (also **Con·naught**) a province of the Republic of Ireland, in the west on the Atlantic coast.

con·nate /'kɒneɪt/ *adjective* **1** existing in a person or thing from birth; innate. **2** *Bot.* (of organs) congenitally united so as to form one part. **3** *Geol.* (of water) trapped in sedimentary rock during its deposition. [Late Latin *connatus* past participle of *connasci* (as COM-, *nasci* be born)]

Con·naught see CONNACHT.

Con·naught and Strath·earn /kə'nɒt, straθ'ɜːrn/ **Ar·thur Wil·liam Pat·rick Al·bert, 1st Duke of** (1850–1942), English statesman and field marshal, son of Queen Victoria, Governor General of Canada 1911–16.

con·nect *verb* **1 a** *transitive* (often foll. by *to*, *with*) join (one thing with another) (*connected the hose to the tap*). **b** *transitive* join (two things) (*a bridge connected the two towns*). **c** *intransitive* be joined or joinable (*the two parts do not connect*). **2** *transitive* (often foll. by *with*) associate mentally or practically (*did not connect the two ideas*; *never connected her with the theatre*). **3** *intransitive* (foll. by *with*) (of an airplane etc.) be synchronized at its destination with another airplane etc., so that passengers can transfer. **4** *transitive* put into communication by telephone. **5** *intransitive* meet; establish contact (*let's try to connect next week*). **6** *transitive* **a** join (a house etc.) to a source of electricity, gas, water, etc. (*our hydro hasn't been connected yet*). **b** hook up (a phone, television, etc.) to a telecommunications system (*they won't connect our phone until we pay our outstanding bills*). **7 a** *transitive* (usu. in *passive*; foll. by *with*) unite or associate with others in relationships etc. (*he is connected with the mayor's office*). **b** *intransitive* establish a rapport based on common interests, opinions etc. (*Nicole found it easy to connect with Sally*). **8** *intransitive* form a logical sequence; be meaningful (*the two ideas do not connect*). **9** *intransitive informal* hit or strike effectively (*the batter connected with the ball*). □ **con·nect·able** *adjective* **con·nect·or** *noun* [Latin *connectere connex-* (as COM-, *nectere* bind)]

con·nect·ed *adjective* **1** joined in sequence. **2** (of ideas etc.) coherent. **3** related or associated. □ **con·nect·ed·ly** *adverb* **con·nect·ed·ness** *noun*

Con·necti·cut /kə'netɪkət/ **1** a state in the northeastern US, on the

Atlantic coast; capital, Hartford; pop. (2000) 3,405,565. **2** the longest river in New England, rising in N New Hampshire and flowing south for 655 km (407 miles) to enter Long Island Sound.

connecting rod *noun* the rod between the piston and the crankpin etc. in an internal combustion engine or between the wheels of a locomotive.

con·nec·tion *noun* **1 a** the act of connecting; the state of being connected. **b** an instance of this. **2** the point at which two things are connected (*broke at the connection*). **3 a** a thing or person that connects; a link (*a radio formed the only connection with the outside world; cannot see the connection between the two ideas*). **b** a telephone link (*got a bad connection*). **c** *Computing* an electronic link to computer networks, electronic mail, etc. (*a connection to the Internet*). **4** arrangement or opportunity for catching a connecting airplane etc.; the airplane etc. itself (*missed the connection*). **5** *Electricity* **a** the linking up of an electric current by contact. **b** a device for effecting this. **6** (often in *pl.*) a relative or associate, esp. one with influence (*has connections at city hall; heard it through a business connection*). **7** *slang* a supplier of narcotics. □ **in connection with** with reference to. **in this** (or **that**) **connection** with reference to this (or that). □ **con·nec·tion·al** *adjective*

con·nect·ive ● *adjective* serving or tending to connect. ● *noun* something that connects. □ **con·nec·tiv·ity** *noun*

connective tissue *noun* a fibrous tissue that supports, binds, or separates more specialized tissue and organs of the body.

connect-the-dots *adjective* *N Amer.* (of a children's colouring book etc.) containing pictures which are formed by connecting sequentially numbered dots with straight lines.

Con·ne·mara /ˌkɒnəˈmɑrə/ a mountainous coastal region of Galway, in the west of the Republic of Ireland.

con·ner *noun* (also **con·nor**) *Cdn* (*Nfld*) a saltwater bottom-feeding fish, *Tautogolabrus adspersus*, found commonly around rocks and wharves. [origin unknown]

Con·nery, **Sean** (born Thomas Connery) (b.1930), Scottish actor, chiefly known for his portrayal of Ian Fleming's secret agent James Bond.

con·ning tower *noun* **1** the superstructure of a submarine from which the vessel may be directed when on or near the surface. **2** the armoured pilothouse of a warship. [CON⁴ + -ING¹]

con·nip·tion *noun* *N Amer. informal* (often in *pl.*) (also **conniption fit**) a fit of anger, worry, etc. [19th c.: origin unknown]

con·niv·ance /kəˈnaɪvəns/ *noun* **1** (often foll. by *at, in*) conniving (*connivance in the crime*). **2** tacit permission (*done with his connivance*).

con·nive /kəˈnaɪv/ *intransitive verb* **1** (often foll. by *with*) conspire. **2** (foll. by *at*) disregard or tacitly consent to (a wrongdoing). □ **con·niv·er** *noun* **con·niv·ing** *adjective & noun* [French *conniver* or Latin *connivēre* shut the eyes (to)]

con·nois·seur /ˌkɒnəˈsɜr, -ˈsʊr/ *noun* (often foll. by *of, in*) an expert judge in matters of taste (*a connoisseur of fine wine*). □ **con·nois·seur·ial** *adjective* **con·nois·seur·ship** *noun* [French, obsolete spelling of *connaisseur* from pres. stem of *connaître* know + *-eur* -OR¹: compare *reconnoitre*]

Con·nolly /ˈkɒnəli/ **James** (1868–1916), Irish nationalist and union leader, who was instrumental in bringing about the Easter Rising (April 24–9, 1916) in Dublin; he was executed by the British.

con·nor *var. of* CONNER.

Con·nors /ˈkɒnərz/ **1 James Scott ('Jimmy')** (b.1952), US tennis player who won the US Open men's singles title in 1974, 1976, 1978, 1982, and 1983, and the Wimbledon title in 1974 and 1982. **2 Stompin' Tom** (b.1936), Canadian singer, songwriter, and guitarist, who is known for his trademark stomping foot during performances; his most popular songs include 'Bud the Spud', 'The Hockey Song', and 'Sudbury Saturday Night'.

con·no·ta·tion /ˌkɒnəˈteɪʃən/ *noun* **1** that which is implied by a word etc. in addition to its literal or primary meaning (*a letter with sinister connotations*). **2** the act of connoting or implying.

con·note /kəˈnoʊt/ *transitive verb* **1** (of a word etc.) imply in addition to the literal or primary meaning. **2** (of a fact) imply as a consequence or condition. **3** mean, signify. □ **con·no·ta·tive** /ˈkɒnəˌteɪtɪv, kɒnəˈnoʊtətɪv/ *adjective* [medieval Latin *connotare* mark in addition (as COM-, *notare* from *nota* mark)]

con·nu·bi·al /kəˈnuːbiəl, -ˈnjuːbiəl/ *adjective* of or relating to marriage or the relationship of spouses. [Latin *connubialis* from *connubium* (*nubium* from *nubere* marry)]

con·odont /ˈkoːnədɒnt, ˈkɒn-/ *noun* any of various Paleozoic toothlike fossils of uncertain affinity. [Greek *kōnos* cone + *odont-, odous* tooth]

con·oid /ˈkoːnɔɪd/ ● *adjective* (also **con·oid·al** /-ˈnɔɪdəl/) cone-shaped. ● *noun* a cone-shaped object.

con·quer /ˈkɒŋkər/ *verb* **1** *transitive* **a** overcome and control (an enemy or territory) by military force. **b** *intransitive* be victorious. **2** *transitive* overcome by effort (*conquered his fear; smallpox has been conquered*). **3** *transitive* climb (a mountain) successfully. **4** *transitive* gain the admiration, love, etc. of (*she conquered all hearts*). □ **con·quer·able** *adjective* [Old French *conquerre* from Romanic from Latin *conquirere* (as COM-, *quaerere* seek, get)]

con·quer·or /ˈkɒŋkərər/ *noun* a person who conquers.

con·quest /ˈkɒnkwest, ˈkɒŋ-/ *noun* **1** the act or an instance of conquering; the state of being conquered. **2 a** a conquered territory. **b** something won. **3** a person whose affection or favour has been won. **4 (the Conquest) a** the British conquest of French North America in 1763. **b** = NORMAN CONQUEST. [Old French *conquest(e)* from Romanic (as CONQUER)]

con·quis·ta·dor /kɒnˈkwɪstəˌdɔr, -kɪst-, -kist-/ *noun* (*pl.* **con·quis·ta·dores** /-rez/ or **con·quis·ta·dors**) a conqueror, esp. one of the Spanish conquerors of Mexico and Peru in the 16th c. [Spanish]

Con·rad, **Jo·seph** (born Teodor Jósef Konrad Korzeniowski) (1857–1924), Polish-born English novelist. His long career as a sailor (1874–94) inspired many of his most famous works, such as the novel *Lord Jim* (1900) and the story *Heart of Darkness* (1902). □ **Con·rad·ian** /kɒnˈradiən/ *adjective*

con rod *noun informal* connecting rod. [abbreviation]

Cons. *abbreviation* Conservative.

con·san·guin·ity /ˌkɒnsanˈgwɪnɪti/ *noun* **1** relationship by descent from a common ancestor; blood relationship. **2** close connection or association. □ **con·san·guin·eous** /-ˈgwɪniəs/ *adjective* [Latin *consanguinitas* from CON- + *sanguis* 'blood']

con·science /ˈkɒnʃəns/ *noun* **1** a moral sense of right and wrong esp. as felt by a person and affecting behaviour (*my conscience won't allow me to do that*). **2** an inner feeling as to the goodness or otherwise of one's behaviour (*my conscience is clear; has a guilty conscience*). □ **in all** (or **good** or **all good**) **conscience** honestly; fairly; in such a way that one's conscience is clear. **on one's conscience** causing one feelings of guilt. □ **con·science·less** *adjective* [Old French from Latin *conscientia* from *conscire* be privy to (as COM-, *scire* know)]

conscience clause *noun* a clause in a law exempting those whose conscience does not permit them to comply.

conscience money *noun* a sum paid to relieve one's conscience, esp. about a payment previously evaded.

conscience-stricken *adjective* made uneasy by a guilty conscience.

con·scien·tious /ˌkɒnʃiˈenʃəs/ *adjective* (of a person or conduct) diligent and scrupulous. □ **con·scien·tious·ly** *adverb* **con·scien·tious·ness** *noun* [French *consciencieux* from medieval Latin *conscientiosus* (as CONSCIENCE)]

conscientious objector *noun* a person who for reasons of conscience objects to conforming to a requirement, esp. that of military service.

con·scious /ˈkɒnʃəs/ ● *adjective* **1** awake and aware of one's surroundings and identity. **2** (usu. foll. by *of*, or *that* + clause) aware, knowing (*conscious of his inferiority*). **3** (of actions, emotions, etc.) realized or recognized by the doer; intentional (*made a conscious effort not to laugh*). **4** (in *combination*) aware of; concerned with (*appearance-conscious*). ● *noun* (prec. by *the*) the conscious mind. □ **con·scious·ly** *adverb* [Latin *conscius* knowing with others or in oneself, from *conscire* (as COM-, *scire* know)]

con·scious·ness /ˈkɒnʃəsnəs/ *noun* **1** the state of being conscious (*lost consciousness during the fight*). **2** awareness of one's existence; self-consciousness. **3 a** awareness, perception (*had no consciousness of being ridiculed*). **b** (in *combination*) awareness of, concern with (*class-consciousness; social consciousness*). **4** the totality of the thoughts and feelings of a person or group, esp. relating to a particular sphere (*moral consciousness*).

consciousness-raising *noun* the activity of increasing esp. social or political sensitivity or awareness.

con·script ● *transitive verb* /kənˈskrɪpt/ enlist by conscription. ● *noun* /ˈkɒnskrɪpt/ a person enlisted by conscription. [(v.) back-formation from CONSCRIPTION: (n.) from French *conscrit* from Latin *conscriptus* (as CONSCRIPTION)]

con·scrip·tion /kənˈskrɪpʃən/ *noun* compulsory enlistment for military service. [French from Late Latin *conscriptio* levying of troops, from Latin *conscribere conscript-* enrol (as COM-, *scribere* write)]

con·se·crate /ˈkɒnsəˌkreɪt/ *transitive verb* **1** make or declare sacred; dedicate formally to a religious or divine purpose. **2** (in Christian belief) make (bread and wine) into the body and blood of Christ. **3** (foll. by *to*) devote (one's life etc.) to (a purpose). **4** ordain (esp. a bishop) to a sacred office. □ **con·se·crat·ed** *adjective* **con·se·cra·tion** *noun* **con·se·cra·tor** *noun* **con·se·cra·tory** *adjective* [Latin *consecrare* (as COM-, *secrare* = *sacrare* dedicate, from *sacer* sacred)]

con·secu·tive /kənˈsɛkjʊtɪv/ *adjective* **1 a** following continuously, in uninterrupted sequence. **b** in unbroken or logical order. **2** *Grammar* expressing consequence. □ **con·secu·tive·ly** *adverb* **con·secu·tive·ness** *noun* [French *consécutif* *-ive* from medieval Latin *consecutivus* from *consequi consecut-* overtake (as COM-, *sequi* pursue)]

con·sen·sual /kənˈsɛnʃʊəl/ *adjective* of or by consent or consensus. □ **con·sen·sual·ly** *adverb* [Latin *consensus* (as CONSENSUS) + -AL]

con·sen·sus /kənˈsɛnsəs/ *noun* (often foll. by *of*) **1 a** general agreement (of opinion, testimony, etc.). **b** an instance of this. **2** (*attributive*) majority view, collective opinion (*consensus politics*). [Latin, = agreement (as CONSENT)]

consensus government *noun* *Cdn* a form of government operating in the NWT and Nunavut, in which all the members of each territory's Legislative Assembly are elected as independent candidates rather than as members of political parties, the premier and cabinet are selected by secret-ballot voting in the legislature, and non-cabinet members serve as an unofficial opposition.

con·sent ● *intransitive verb* (often foll. by *to*) express willingness, give permission, agree. ● *noun* voluntary agreement, permission, compliance (*see also* AGE OF CONSENT). [Old French *consentir* from Latin *consentire* (as COM-, *sentire sens-* feel)]

consenting adult *noun* an adult who consents to something, esp. a sexual act.

con·se·quence /ˈkɒnsəkwəns/ *noun* **1** the result or effect of an action or condition. **2 a** importance (*it is of no consequence*). **b** social distinction (*persons of consequence*). □ **in consequence** as a result. **face** (or **take**) **the consequences** accept the results of one's choice or action. [Old French from Latin *consequentia* (as CONSEQUENT)]

con·se·quent /ˈkɒnsəkwənt/ ● *adjective* **1** (often foll. by *on, upon*) following as a result or consequence. **2** logically consistent. ● *noun* **1** a thing that follows another. **2** *Logic* the second part of a conditional proposition, dependent on the antecedent. [Old French from Latin *consequi* (as CONSECUTIVE)]

con·se·quen·tial /ˌkɒnsəˈkwɛnʃəl/ *adjective* **1** following as a result or consequence. **2** resulting indirectly (*consequential damage*). **3** (of a person) self-important. □ **con·se·quen·ti·al·ity** /-ʃɪˈalɪti/ *noun* **con·se·quen·tial·ly** *adverb*

con·se·quen·tial·ism /ˌkɒnsəˈkwɛnʃəˌlɪzm/ *noun* *Philos.* the doctrine that the morality of an action is to be judged solely by its consequences. □ **con·se·quen·tial·ist** *adjective & noun*

con·se·quent·ly /ˈkɒnsəˌkwɛntli/ *adverb & conjunction* as a result; therefore.

con·serv·an·cy /kənˈsɜrvənsi/ *noun* (*pl.* **-cies**) **1** a body concerned with the preservation of natural resources (*Nature Conservancy*). **2** conservation; official preservation (of forests etc.). **3** *Brit.* a commission etc. controlling a port, river, etc. (*Thames Conservancy*). [18th-c. alteration of obsolete *conservancy* from Anglo-French *conservacie* from Anglo-Latin *conservatia* from Latin *conservatio* (as CONSERVE)]

con·serv·a·tion /ˌkɒnsərˈveɪʃən/ *noun* **1** the action of conserving something, esp.: **a** preservation, protection, or restoration of the natural environment and of wildlife. **b** preservation and repair of archaeological, historical, and cultural sites and artifacts. **c** prevention of wasteful use of a resource. **2** *Physics* the principle by which the total value of a physical quantity or parameter (such as energy, mass, linear or angular momentum) remains constant in a system which is not subject to external influence. □ **con·serv·a·tion·al** *adjective*

conservation area *noun* *Cdn & Brit.* an area containing a noteworthy environment and specially protected by law against undesirable changes.

con·serv·a·tion·ist *noun* a supporter or advocate of environmental conservation.

conservation officer *noun* a public employee responsible for wildlife.

con·serv·a·tism /kənˈsɜrvəˌtɪzm/ *noun* **1** any of several political philosophies, esp. one opposing radical reform, placing value in established institutions, and subjugating individual freedom to order,

rank, security, and the good of the community, or one promoting individualism and non-intervention by the State. **2** opposition to change.

con·serv·a·tive /kənˈsɜrvətɪv/ ● *adjective* **1 a** averse to rapid change. **b** (of taste etc.) moderate, avoiding extremes (*conservative in his dress*). **2** (of an estimate etc.) purposely low; moderate, cautious. **3 a** (**Conservative**) of or characteristic of a Conservative party. **b** espousing the tenets of political conservatism. **4** tending to conserve. ● *noun* **1** a conservative person. **2** (**Conservative**) a supporter or member of a Conservative party. □ **con·serv·a·tive·ly** *adverb* [Late Latin *conservativus* (as CONSERVE)]

Conservative Judaism *noun* a branch of Judaism allowing only minor changes in traditional ritual etc.

Conservative Party *noun* **1** a Canadian political party, whose name was changed to Progressive Conservative Party in 1942. In 2003, the Progressive Conservative Party merged with the Canadian Alliance to re-form the Conservative Party. **2** a British political party promoting free enterprise and private ownership. **3** a similar party elsewhere.

con·serv·a·toire /kənˈsɜrvəˌtwɑr/ *noun* a (usu. European) school of music or other arts. [French from Italian *conservatorio* (as CONSERVATORY)]

con·serv·a·tor /kənˈsɜrvətər, ˈkɒnsərˌveɪtər/ *noun* a person who preserves something, esp. in a museum etc.

con·serv·a·tory /kənˈsɜrvəˌtɔri, -triː/ *noun* (*pl.* **-ies**) **1** esp. *N Amer.* a school of esp. classical music or other arts. **2** a greenhouse. **3** a glassed-in sunroom attached to a house. [Late Latin *conservatorium* (as CONSERVE)]

con·serve /kənˈsɜrv/ ● *transitive verb* **1** store up; keep from harm, damage, or depletion, esp. for later use. **2** *Physics* maintain a quantity of (heat etc.). **3** preserve (food, esp. fruit), usu. with sugar. ● *noun* (also /ˈkɒnsɜrv/) a jam-like mixture, often of several fruits. [Old French *conserver* from Latin *conservare* (as COM-, *servare* keep)]

con·sid·er /kənˈsɪdər/ *verb* **1** *transitive & intransitive* contemplate mentally, esp. in order to reach a conclusion. **2** *transitive & intransitive* examine the merits of (a course of action, a candidate, claim, etc.). **3** *transitive* give attention to. **4** *transitive* take into account. **5** *transitive* (foll. by *that* + clause) have the opinion. **6** *transitive* believe; regard as (*consider it to be genuine; consider it settled*). **7** *transitive* show thoughtfulness for (*consider his feelings*). **8** *transitive* look at. □ **all things considered** taking everything into account. [Old French *considerer* from Latin *considerare* examine, perhaps from CON- + *sider-, sidus* constellation, star]

con·sid·er·able /kənˈsɪdərəbəl/ *adjective* **1** enough in amount or extent to need consideration. **2** much; a lot of (*considerable pain*). **3** notable, important. □ **con·sid·er·ably** *adverb*

con·sid·er·ate /kənˈsɪdərət/ *adjective* thoughtful towards other people; careful not to cause hurt or inconvenience. □ **con·sid·er·ate·ly** *adverb*

con·sid·er·a·tion /kənˌsɪdəˈreɪʃən/ *noun* **1** the act of considering; careful thought. **2** thoughtfulness for others; being considerate. **3** a fact or a thing taken into account in deciding or judging something. **4** compensation; a payment or reward. **5** *Law* (in a contractual agreement) anything given or promised or forborne by one party in exchange for the promise or undertaking of another. **6** *archaic* importance or consequence. □ **in consideration of** in return for; on account of. **take into consideration** include as a factor, reason, etc.; make allowance for. **under consideration** being considered.

con·sid·ered /kənˈsɪdərd/ *attributive adjective* formed after careful thought (*a considered opinion*).

con·sid·er·ing /kənˈsɪdərɪŋ/ *preposition* **1** in view of; taking into consideration (*considering their youth; considering that it was snowing*). **2** *informal* all in all; taking everything into account (*not so bad, considering*).

con·si·gliere /ˌkɒnsiˈljɛreɪ/ *noun* (*pl.* **con·si·glieri** /-riː/) a top adviser to an organized crime boss. [Italian, = counsellor]

con·sign /kənˈsaɪn/ *transitive verb* (often foll. by *to*) **1** hand over; deliver to a person's possession or trust. **2** assign; commit decisively or permanently (*consigned it to the dustbin; consigned to years of misery*). **3** transmit or send (goods), usu. by a public carrier. □ **con·sign·ee** /ˌkɒnsaɪˈniː, kənˌsaɪˈniː/ *noun* **con·sign·or** *noun* [French *consigner* or Latin *consignare* mark with a seal (as COM-, SIGN)]

con·sign·ment /kənˈsaɪnmənt/ *noun* **1** the act or an instance of consigning; the process of being consigned. **2** a batch of goods consigned. **3** (*attributive*) designating a store selling goods, esp. second-hand clothes, on consignment. □ **on consignment** (of goods) held in trust to be sold for the owner.

con·sist *intransitive verb* **1** (foll. by *of*) be composed; have specified ingredients or elements. **2** (foll. by *in*, *of*) have its essential features as specified (*its beauty consists in the use of colour*). [Latin *consistere* exist (as COM-, *sistere* stop)]

con·sist·ency *noun* (*pl.* **-cies**) **1** the degree of density, firmness, or viscosity, esp. of thick liquids. **2** the state of being consistent; conformity with other or earlier attitudes, practice, etc. **3** the state or quality of holding or sticking together and retaining shape. [French *consistence* or Late Latin *consistentia* (as CONSIST)]

con·sist·ent /kən'sɪstənt/ *adjective* (usu. foll. by *with*) **1** compatible or in harmony; not contradictory. **2** (of a person) constant to the same principles of thought or action. **3** tending to maintain a constant level of success. □ **con·sist·ent·ly** *adverb* [Latin *consistere* (as CONSIST)]

con·sis·tory /kən'sɪstəri/ *noun* (*pl.* **-ies**) **1** *Catholicism* a council of cardinals presided over by the pope. **2** (in full **consistory court**) (in the Anglican Church) a court presided over by a bishop, for the administration of ecclesiastical law in a diocese. **3** (in other Churches) a local administrative body. □ **con·sis·tor·ial** /ˌkɒnsɪs'tɔːriəl/ *adjective* [Anglo-French *consistorie* from Late Latin *consistorium* (as CONSIST)]

con·so·ci·a·tion /kən‚səʊsi'eɪʃən, kən‚səʊʃi-/ *noun* **1** close association, esp. of Churches or religious communities. **2** *Ecology* a closely related subgroup of plants having one dominant species. □ **con·so·ci·a·tion·al** *adjective* [Latin *consociatio*, *-onis* from *consociare* (as COM-, *socius* fellow)]

con·sol·a·tion /ˌkɒnsə'leɪʃən/ *noun* **1** the act or an instance of consoling; the state of being consoled. **2** a consoling thing, person, or circumstance. □ **con·sol·a·tory** /kən'sɒlə‚tɔri/ *adjective*

consolation final *noun* a contest to determine third place between the losers of semifinals.

consolation prize *noun* a prize given to a competitor who just fails to win a main prize.

con·sole¹ /kən'səʊl/ *transitive verb* comfort, esp. in grief or disappointment. □ **con·sol·able** *adjective* **con·sol·er** *noun* **con·sol·ing·ly** *adverb* [French *consoler* from Latin *consolari*]

con·sole² /'kɒnsəʊl/ *noun* **1 a** a panel or unit accommodating a set of switches, controls, etc. **b** a small machine for playing computerized video games, normally requiring connection to a television set. **2** a cabinet for television or radio equipment etc. **3** *Music* a cabinet with the keyboards, stops, pedals, etc., of an organ. **4** an ornamented bracket supporting a shelf etc. [French, perhaps from *consolider* (as CONSOLIDATE)]

console table *noun* a table supported by a bracket against a wall.

con·soli·date /kən'sɒlɪ‚deɪt/ *verb* **1** *transitive & intransitive* make or become strong or solid. **2** *transitive* reinforce or strengthen (one's position, power, etc.). **3** *transitive* combine (territories, companies, debts, etc.) into one whole. □ **con·soli·dat·ed** *adjective* **con·soli·da·tion** *noun* **con·soli·da·tor** *noun* [Latin *consolidare* (as COM-, *solidare* from *solidus* solid)]

consolidated revenue fund *noun* *Cdn* a federal or provincial government fund into which all revenue (taxes, tariffs, charges, etc.) is paid and from which all government expenditures are made.

consolidated school *noun* *Cdn* a school replacing several smaller schools in a district.

con·som·mé /'kɒnsə‚meɪ/ *noun* a clear soup made with meat stock. [French, past participle of *consommer* from Latin *consummare* (as CONSUMMATE)]

con·son·ance /'kɒnsənəns/ *noun* **1** agreement, harmony. **2** *Prosody* a recurrence of similar-sounding consonants, esp. at the ends of adjacent words. **3** *Music* a harmonious combination of notes; a harmonious interval. [Old French *consonance* (as CONSONANT)]

con·son·ant /'kɒnsənənt/ *noun* **1** a speech sound in which the breath is at least partly obstructed, and which to form a syllable must be combined with a vowel. **2** a letter or letters representing this. ● *adjective* (foll. by *with*, *to*) **1** consistent; in agreement or harmony. **2** similar in sound. **3** *Music* making a concord. □ **con·son·ant·al** /-'nantəl/ *adjective* [French from Latin *consonare* (as COM-, *sonare* sound, from *sonus*)]

con·sort¹ ● *noun* /'kɒnsɔrt/ **1 a** a wife or husband, esp. of royalty (*prince consort*). **b** a partner, companion, associate, etc. **2** a ship sailing with another. ● *verb* /kən'sɔrt/ *intransitive* (usu. foll. by *with*) keep company; associate. [French from Latin *consors* sharer, comrade (as COM-, *sors sortis* lot, destiny)]

con·sort² /'kɒnsɔrt/ *noun* a group of musicians, esp. playing early music (*recorder consort*). [earlier form of CONCERT]

con·sor·tium /kən'sɔrtiəm, -'sɔrʃəm/ *noun* (*pl.* **con·sor·tia** /-tiə/ or

con·sor·tiums) **1** an association, esp. several large companies in a joint venture. **2** *Law* the companionship, affection, and assistance which each spouse in a marriage is entitled to receive from the other. [Latin, = partnership (as CONSORT¹)]

con·specif·ic /ˌkɒnspə'sɪfɪk/ *Biol.* ● *adjective* of the same species. ● *noun* an organism of the same species as another.

con·spec·tus /kən'spektəs/ *noun* **1** a general or comprehensive survey. **2** a summary or synopsis. [Latin from *conspicere conspect-* (as COM-, *spicere* look at)]

con·spicu·ous /kən'spɪkjʊəs/ *adjective* **1** clearly visible; striking to the eye; attracting notice. **2** remarkable of its kind (*conspicuous extravagance*). □ **con·spicu·ity** /ˌkɒnspɪ'kjuːɪti/ *noun* **con·spicu·ous·ly** *adverb* **con·spicu·ous·ness** *noun* [Latin *conspicuus* (as CONSPECTUS)]

conspicuous consumption *noun* ostentatious acquisition and display of expensive goods.

con·spir·acist *noun* a person who supports a conspiracy theory.

con·spir·acy /kən'spɪrəsi/ *noun* (*pl.* **-acies**) **1** a secret plan to commit a crime or do harm, often for political ends; a plot. **2** the act of conspiring. [Anglo-French *conspiracie*, alteration of form of Old French *conspiration* from Latin *conspiratio -onis* (as CONSPIRE)]

conspiracy of silence *noun* an agreement not to mention something.

conspiracy theory *noun* a belief that some covert but influential agency or organization is responsible for an unexplained event. □ **conspiracy theorist** *noun*

con·spir·ator /kən'spɪrətər/ *noun* a person who takes part in a conspiracy. [Anglo-French *conspiratour* (as CONSPIRE)]

con·spira·tor·ial /kənspɪrə'tɔriəl/ *adjective* **1** pertaining to or characteristic of a conspirator or a conspiracy. **2** suggestive of a conspirator (*conspiratorial whispers*). □ **con·spira·tor·ial·ly** *adverb*

con·spire /kən'spaɪr/ *intransitive verb* **1** combine secretly to plan and prepare an unlawful or harmful act. **2** (often foll. by *against*, or to + infin.) (of events or circumstances) seem to be working together, esp. disadvantageously. [Old French *conspirer* from Latin *conspirare* agree, plot (as COM-, *spirare* breathe)]

Const. *abbreviation* constable.

Con·stable /'kɒnstəbəl/ **John** (1776–1837), English landscape painter. He is best known for his detailed paintings of countryside scenes, such as *The Hay Wain* (1821), and for his depiction of the transient effects of cloud and light.

con·stable /'kɒnstəbəl/ *noun* **1** (also **police constable**) (in Canada, the UK, Australia, NZ, etc.) a police officer of the lowest rank. **2** an officer of the peace, as a bailiff etc., with minor judicial duties. **3** the governor of a royal castle. **4** *hist.* the principal officer in a royal household. [Old French *conestable* from Late Latin *comes stabuli* count of the stable]

con·stabu·lary /kən'stabjuː‚leri/ *noun* (*pl.* **-ies**) an organized body of police; a police force (*Royal Newfoundland Constabulary*). [medieval Latin *constabularius* (as CONSTABLE)]

Con·stance, Lake /'kɒnstəns/ a lake in SE Germany on the north side of the Swiss Alps, at the meeting point of Germany, Switzerland, and Austria, forming part of the course of the Rhine River.

con·stancy /'kɒnstənsi/ *noun* **1** the quality of being unchanging and dependable; faithfulness. **2** firmness, endurance. [Latin *constantia* (as CONSTANT)]

Con·stant /kɔ̃stɑ̃/ **Benjamin** (full name Henri-Benjamin Constant de Rebecque) (1767–1830), French novelist and politician, who is known for the psychological novel *Adolphe* (1816), reflecting his affair with Mme de Staël.

con·stant /'kɒnstənt/ ● *adjective* **1** continuous (*needs constant attention*). **2** occurring frequently (*receive constant complaints*). **3** unchanging (*speed remained constant*). **4** faithful, dependable. ● *noun* **1** anything that does not vary. **2** *Math.* a component of a relationship between variables that does not change its value. **3** *Physics* **a** a number expressing a relation, property, etc., and remaining the same in all circumstances. **b** such a number that remains the same for a substance in the same conditions. □ **con·stant·ly** *adverb* [Old French from Latin *constare* (as COM-, *stare* stand)]

Con·stan·ţa /kɒn'stantsə/ (also **Con·stan·za**) the chief port of Romania, on the Black Sea; pop. (est. 2002) 337,800. It was formerly called Tomis. [CONSTANTINE²]

con·stan·tan /'kɒnstən‚tan/ *noun* an alloy of copper and nickel used in electrical equipment. [CONSTANT + -AN]

Con·stan·tine¹ /'kɒnstən‚taɪn/ a city in NE Algeria; pop. (est. 2002)

515,800. In ancient times it was the capital of the Roman province of Numidia. It was destroyed in 311 but rebuilt soon afterwards. [CONSTANTINE²]

Con·stan·tine² /ˈkɒnstənˌtiːn, -ˌtaɪn/ (**'the Great'**) (full name Flavius Valerius Constantinus Augustus) (c.285–337), Roman emperor 306–37. The first Roman emperor to be converted to Christianity, he declared it a state religion in 324; in 330 he moved the capital from Rome to Byzantium, renaming it Constantinople.

Con·stan·tin·ople /ˌkɒnstæntɪˈnoʊpəl/ the former name for Istanbul from AD 330 to the capture of the city by the Turks in 1453. [anglicized form of *Constantinopolis* city of Constantine, from CONSTANTINE² + Greek *polis* city]

Con·stan·za see CONSTANŢA.

con·stel·late /ˈkɒnstəˌleɪt/ *verb* **1** *transitive & intransitive* form into (or as if into) a constellation. **2** *transitive* adorn as with stars.

con·stel·la·tion /ˌkɒnstəˈleɪʃən/ *noun* **1 a** a group of fixed stars whose outline is traditionally regarded as forming a particular figure. **b** one of eighty-eight sections based on these into which the sky has been divided. **2** a group of associated persons, ideas, etc. [Old French from Late Latin *constellatio -onis* (as COM-, *stella* star)]

con·ster·nate /ˈkɒnstərˌneɪt/ *transitive verb* (usu. in *passive*) dismay; fill with anxiety. [Latin *consternare* (as COM-, *sternere* throw down)]

con·ster·na·tion /ˌkɒnstərˈneɪʃən/ *noun* anxiety or dismay causing mental confusion.

con·sti·pate /ˈkɒnstɪˌpeɪt/ *transitive verb* (usu. in *passive*) **1** cause constipation in. **2** hinder or obstruct abnormally. [Latin *constipare* (as COM-, *stipare* press)]

con·sti·pat·ed /ˈkɒnstɪˌpeɪtəd/ *adjective* **1** affected with constipation. **2** restricted, constrained.

con·sti·pa·tion /ˌkɒnstɪˈpeɪʃən/ *noun* **1** irregularity and difficulty in defecating. **2** abnormal lack of efficacy or ease.

con·stit·u·en·cy /kənˈstɪtʃuənsi/ *noun* (*pl.* **-cies**) **1** a body of voters in a specified area who elect a representative member to a legislative body. **2** the area represented in this way. **3** a body of customers, supporters, etc.

con·stit·u·ent /kənˈstɪtʃuənt/ ● *adjective* **1** composing or helping to make up a whole. **2** able to make or change a (political etc.) constitution (*constituent assembly*). **3** appointing or electing. ● *noun* **1** a member of a constituency (esp. political). **2** a component part. **3** *Law* a person who appoints another as agent. [Latin *constituent-* partly through French *-ant* (as CONSTITUTE)]

con·sti·tute /ˈkɒnstɪˌtuːt, -ˌtjuːt/ *transitive verb* **1** be the components or essence of; make up, form. **2 a** be equivalent or tantamount to (*this constitutes an official warning*). **b** formally establish (*does not constitute a precedent*). **3** give legal or constitutional form to; establish by law. [Latin *constituere* (as COM-, *statuere* set up)]

con·sti·tu·tion /ˌkɒnstɪˈtuːʃən, -ˈtjuːʃən/ *noun* **1** the act or method of constituting; the composition (of something). **2 a** the body of fundamental principles or established precedents according to which a state or other organization is acknowledged to be governed. **b** a (usu. written) record of this. **3** a person's physical state as regards vitality, health, strength, etc. **4** a person's mental or psychological makeup. **5** *hist.* a decree or ordinance.

con·sti·tu·tion·al /ˌkɒnstɪˈtuːʃənəl, -ˈtjuː-/ ● *adjective* **1** of, consistent with, authorized by, or limited by a political constitution (*a constitutional monarchy*). **2** inherent in, stemming from, or affecting the physical or mental constitution. ● *noun* a walk taken regularly to maintain or restore good health. □ **con·sti·tu·tion·al·i·ty** /-ˈnalɪti/ *noun* **con·sti·tu·tion·al·ize** *transitive verb* (also esp. *Brit.* **-ise**). **con·sti·tu·tion·al·ly** *adverb*

con·sti·tu·tion·al·ism /ˌkɒnstɪˈtuːʃənəˌlɪzəm, -ˈtjuː-/ *noun* **1** a constitutional system of government. **2** the adherence to or advocacy of such a system.

con·sti·tu·tion·al·ist /ˌkɒnstɪˈtuːʃənəˌlɪst, -ˈtjuː-/ ● *noun* **1** a proponent of constitutional government. **2** an expert in constitutional matters. ● *adjective* of or pertaining to a constitution.

con·sti·tu·tive /ˈkɒnstɪˌtuːtɪv, -ˈtjuː-/ *adjective* **1** having the power to establish or give organized existence to something (*the state began to exercise a new and constitutive function*). **2** forming a part or constituent of something (*poverty is a constitutive element of a particular form of economic growth*). **3** forming an essential element of something (*language is constitutive of thought*). □ **con·sti·tu·tive·ly** *adverb*

con·strain /kənˈstreɪn/ *transitive verb* (usu. in *passive*) **1** restrict severely as regards action, behaviour, etc. **2** compel; urge irresistibly or by

necessity. **3** confine forcibly; imprison. [Old French *constraindre* from Latin *constringere* (as COM-, *stringere* strict- tie)]

con·strained /kənˈstreɪnd/ *adjective* **1** in senses of CONSTRAIN *verb*. **2** forced, not natural (*a constrained manner*).

con·straint /kənˈstreɪnt/ *noun* **1** the act or result of constraining or being constrained; restriction of liberty. **2** something that constrains; a limitation on motion or action. **3** the restraint of natural feelings or their expression; a constrained manner. [Old French *constreinte*, fem. past participle (as CONSTRAIN)]

con·strict /kənˈstrɪkt/ *verb* **1** *transitive & intransitive* make or become narrow or tight. **2** *transitive & intransitive Biol.* contract (*constricts the blood vessels*). **3** *transitive* restrict, obstruct. □ **con·stric·tion** *noun* **con·stric·tive** *adjective* [Latin (as CONSTRAIN)]

con·stric·tor /kənˈstrɪktər/ *noun* **1** any snake (esp. a boa) that kills by coiling around its prey and compressing it. **2** *Anat.* any muscle that compresses or contracts an organ or part of the body.

con·stru·al /kənˈstruːəl/ *noun* an act or the action of construing.

con·struct ● *transitive verb* /kənˈstrʌkt/ **1** make by fitting parts together; build, form (something physical or abstract). **2** *Math.* draw or delineate, esp. accurately to given conditions (*construct a triangle*). ● *noun* /ˈkɒnstrʌkt/ **1** a thing constructed, esp. by the mind. **2** *Linguistics* a group of words forming a phrase. □ **con·struct·or** *noun* [Latin *construere construct-* (as COM-, *struere* pile, build)]

con·struc·tion /kənˈstrʌkʃən/ *noun* **1** the act or a mode of constructing. **2 a** a thing constructed. **b** repair or building work on a stretch of road. **3** the building industry (*works in construction*). **4** an interpretation or explanation (*put a strict construction on the law*). **5** the manner in which something is arranged; structure. **6** *Grammar* an arrangement of words according to syntactical rules. □ **con·struc·tion·al** *adjective*

construction boot *noun* (usu. in *pl.*) a sturdy leather boot, usu. with a steel-encased toe for protection, worn esp. by construction workers.

construction holiday *noun Cdn* (*Que.*) a holiday traditionally taken by construction workers in Quebec during the last two weeks of July, often taken as a holiday by many other Quebecers as well.

con·struc·tion·ism /kənˈstrʌkʃəˌnɪzəm/ *noun* = CONSTRUCTIVISM.

construction paper *noun N Amer.* a heavy, usu. coloured paper used for making posters and crafts.

construction worker *noun* an esp. manual labourer who constructs buildings, roadways, etc.

con·struc·tive /kənˈstrʌktɪv/ *adjective* **1** of construction. **2** helpful, tending to construct (*constructive criticism; a constructive approach*) (opp. DESTRUCTIVE 2). **3** *Law* derived by inference; not expressed (*constructive liability*). □ **con·struc·tive·ly** *adverb* **con·struc·tive·ness** *noun*

constructive dismissal *noun* the changing of an employee's job or working conditions with the aim of forcing resignation.

con·struc·tiv·ism /kənˈstrʌktɪˌvɪzəm/ *noun* an orig. Russian artistic movement in which assorted (usu. mechanical or industrial) objects are combined into non-representational and mobile structural forms. □ **con·struc·tiv·ist** *noun* [Russian *konstruktivizm* (as CONSTRUCT)]

con·strue /kənˈstruː/ *transitive verb* (**con·strues, con·strued, con·stru·ing**) **1** interpret (words or actions) (*their decision can be construed in many ways*). **2** (often foll. by *with*) combine (words) grammatically (*'rely' is construed with 'on'*). **3** analyze the syntax of (a sentence). □ **con·stru·able** *adjective* [Latin *construere* CONSTRUCT]

con·sub·stan·tial /ˌkɒnsəbˈstanʃəl/ *adjective Christianity* of the same substance (esp. of the three persons of the Trinity). □ **con·sub·stan·ti·al·i·ty** /-ʃiˈalɪti/ *noun* [ecclesiastical Latin *consubstantialis*, translation of Greek *homoousios* (as COM-, SUBSTANTIAL)]

con·sub·stan·ti·a·tion /ˌkɒnsəbˌstanʃiˈeɪʃən/ *noun Christianity* the real substantial presence of the body and blood of Christ together with the bread and wine in the Eucharist. [modern Latin *consubstantiatio*, after *transubstantiatio* TRANSUBSTANTIATION]

con·sue·tude /ˈkɒnswɪˌtuːd/ *noun* a custom, esp. one having legal force. □ **con·sue·tud·in·ary** /ˌkɒnswɪˈtjuːdɪnəri/ *adjective* [Old French *consuetude* or Latin *consuetudo -dinis* from *consuetus* accustomed]

con·sul /ˈkɒnsəl/ *noun* **1** an official appointed by a nation to live in a foreign city and protect the interests of the nation's citizens in the region and promote trade. **2** *hist.* either of two annually elected chief magistrates in ancient Rome. **3** any of the three chief magistrates of the French republic (1799–1804). □ **con·su·lar** *adjective* **con·sul·ship** *noun* [Latin, related to *consulere* take counsel]

con·su·late /ˈkɒnsələt, -sjəl-/ *noun* **1** the building officially used by a consul. **2** the office, position, or period of office of a consul. **3** *hist.*

government by consuls. **4** *hist.* (**Consulate**) the government of France by three consuls (1799–1804).

consul general *noun* (*pl.* **consuls general**) a consul of the highest rank.

con·sult /kən'sʌlt/ *verb* **1** *transitive* seek information or advice from (a person, book, watch, etc.). **2** *intransitive* (often foll. by *with*) refer to a person for advice, an opinion, etc. **3** *transitive* seek permission or approval from (a person) for a proposed action. **4** *transitive* take into account; consider (feelings, interests, etc.). □ **con·sul·ta·tive** /-tətɪv, 'kɒnsəl,teitɪv/ *adjective* [French *consulter* from Latin *consultare* frequentative of *consulere consult-* take counsel]

con·sult·an·cy /kən'sʌltənsi/ *noun* (*pl.* **-cies**) the professional practice or position of a consultant.

con·sult·ant /kən'sʌltənt/ *noun* **1** a person who gives professional advice or services in a specialized field, esp. on a freelance basis. **2** *Brit.* a senior specialist in a branch of medicine responsible for patients in a hospital. [prob. French (as CONSULT)]

con·sul·ta·tion /,kɒnsəl'teiʃən/ *noun* **1** a meeting arranged to consult (esp. with a physician). **2** the act or an instance of consulting.

con·sult·ing /kən'sʌltɪŋ/ *attributive adjective* giving professional advice to others working in the same field or subject (*consulting physician*).

con·sum·able ● *adjective* that can be consumed; intended for consumption. ● *noun* (usu. in *pl.*) a commodity that is eventually used up, worn out, or eaten.

con·sume *transitive verb* **1** eat or drink. **2** use up (time, energy, resources, etc.). **3** completely destroy; reduce to nothing or to tiny particles (*fire consumed the building*). **4** (esp. in *passive*) engage the full attention of, engross (*consumed with rage*). [Latin *consumere* (as COM-, *sumere sumpt-* take up): partly through French *consumer*]

con·sum·er ● *noun* **1** a person who consumes, esp. one who uses a product. **2** a purchaser of goods or services. ● *attributive adjective* intended for use by consumers, esp. domestically, rather than in business or manufacturing (*consumer goods; consumer electronics*).

consumer confidence *noun* consumers' willingness to spend.

consumer credit *noun* credit granted, e.g. by a retail store, for the purchase of consumer goods.

consumer durable *noun* a household product with a relatively long useful life (e.g. a radio or washing machine).

consumer goods *plural noun* goods put to use by consumers, not used in producing other goods (*opp.* CAPITAL GOODS).

con·sum·er·ism *noun* **1** the protection or promotion of consumers' interests. **2** preoccupation with consumer goods and their acquisition. **3** the promoting of consumer spending for the economic benefit of society. □ **con·sum·er·ist** *adjective & noun* **con·sum·er·is·tic** *adjective*

consumer price index *noun* esp. *N Amer.* an index of price changes for standard consumer goods and services, expressed as a percentage of the prices in a base year. Abbr.: **CPI**.

consumer research *noun* investigation of purchasers' needs and opinions.

consumer society *noun* (also **consumer culture**) a society in which the marketing and consumption of goods and services is the most important social and economic activity.

con·sum·ing *adjective* that engages one's entire energy and attention (*a consuming passion*). □ **con·sum·ing·ly** *adverb*

con·sum·mate ● *transitive verb* /'kɒnsə,meit, -sjə-/ **1** complete; make perfect. **2 a** make (a marriage) legally complete by having sex. **b** give sexual expression to (love, a non-marital union, etc.). ● *adjective* /'kɒnsəmət/ **1** complete, perfect, of the highest level (*consummate artistry*). **2** perfectly skilled (*a consummate general*). □ **con·sum·mate·ly** *adverb* [Latin *consummare* (as COM-, *summare* complete, from *summus* utmost)]

con·sum·ma·tion /,kɒnsə'meiʃən/ *noun* **1** the action of consummating (esp. a marriage). **2** a desired end or goal; perfection.

con·sump·tion *noun* **1** the using up of a resource (*energy consumption*). **2** the eating, drinking, or ingesting of something (*liquor is sold for consumption off the premises*). **3** an amount of something which is used up or ingested (*a daily consumption of 15 cigarettes*). **4** the purchase and use of goods and services by the public. **5** the reception of information or entertainment, esp. by a mass audience (*his confidential speech was not meant for public consumption*). **6** *hist.* any disease causing wasting of tissues, esp. pulmonary tuberculosis. [Old French *consomption* from Latin *consumptio* (as CONSUME)]

con·sump·tive ● *adjective* **1** of or tending to consumption. **2** *hist.* tending to or affected with pulmonary tuberculosis. ● *noun hist.* a

person suffering from tuberculosis. □ **con·sump·tive·ly** *adverb* [medieval Latin *consumptivus* (as CONSUMPTION)]

cont. *abbreviation* **1** contents. **2** continued.

con·tact ● *noun* **1 a** the state or condition of touching, meeting, or communicating. **b** the first interaction between Europeans and Aboriginal peoples in parts of the world colonized by Europeans. **2** a person who is or may be communicated with for information, supplies, assistance, etc. **3** *Electricity* **a** a connection for the passage of a current. **b** a device for providing this. **4** a person likely to carry a contagious disease through being associated with an infected person. **5** (usu. in *pl.*) *informal* a contact lens. ● *adjective* caused by touching (*contact dermatitis*). ● *transitive verb* **1** get into communication with (a person). **2** begin correspondence or personal dealings with. □ **con·tact·able** *adjective* [Latin *contactus* from *contingere* (as COM-, *tangere* touch)]

contact cement *noun* an instantly-bonding adhesive applied to both surfaces to be bonded.

contact lens *noun* a small glass or plastic lens placed directly on the eyeball to correct vision.

contact print *noun* a photographic print made by placing a negative directly on sensitized paper etc. and illuminating it.

contact sheet *noun* a sheet of contact prints made from a roll of film.

contact sport *noun* a sport in which participants necessarily come into bodily contact with one another.

con·ta·gion /kən'teidʒən/ *noun* **1 a** the communication of disease from one person to another by bodily contact. **b** a contagious disease. **2** a contagious or harmful influence. **3** moral corruption, esp. when tending to be widespread. [Latin *contagio* (as COM-, *tangere* touch)]

con·ta·gious /kən'teidʒəs/ *adjective* **1 a** (of a person) likely to transmit disease by direct or indirect contact. **b** (of a disease) transmitted in this way. **2** (of emotions, reactions, etc.) likely to affect others (*contagious enthusiasm*). □ **con·ta·gious·ly** *adverb* **con·ta·gious·ness** *noun*

con·tain *transitive verb* **1** hold or be capable of holding within itself; include, comprise. **2** (of measures) consist of or be equal to (*a metre contains a hundred centimetres*). **3** prevent (an enemy, difficulty, costs, etc.) from moving, spreading, or increasing. **4** control or restrain (oneself, one's feelings, etc.). **5** (of a number) be divisible by (a factor) without a remainder. □ **con·tain·able** *adjective* [Old French *contenir* from Latin *continēre content-* (as COM-, *tenēre* hold)]

con·tained *adjective* **1** included, enclosed, held. **2** restrained, showing self-restraint, reserved.

con·tain·er *noun* **1** a vessel, box, etc., for holding particular things. **2** a large boxlike receptacle of standard design for the transport of goods, esp. one readily transferable from one form of transport to another (also *attributive*: *container ship*).

container gardening *noun* the maintenance of a garden in containers such as flower boxes rather than in the ground.

container-grown *adjective* (of a plant) grown in a container, e.g. a flower box, rather than in the ground.

con·tain·er·ize *transitive verb* (also esp. *Brit.* **-ise**) **1** pack in or transport by container. **2** adapt to transport by container. □ **con·tain·er·iz·a·tion** *noun*

container port *noun* a port specializing in handling goods stored in containers.

container ship *noun* a ship designed to carry goods stored in containers.

con·tain·ment *noun* **1** in senses of CONTAIN *verb*. **2** the action or policy of preventing the expansion of a hostile country or influence.

con·tam·in·ant /kən'tamɪnənt/ *noun* something which contaminates.

con·tam·in·ate /kən'tamɪ,neit/ *transitive verb* **1** make impure by contact or mixture; pollute. **2** infect. **3** introduce radioactivity into (a substance where it is harmful or undesirable). □ **con·tam·in·a·tion** *noun* [Latin *contaminare* (as COM-, *tamen-* related to *tangere* touch)]

con·tango /kən'taŋgəʊ/ *noun* (*pl.* **-gos**) *Brit. Stock Exch.* **1** the postponement of the transfer of stock from one account day to the next. **2** a percentage paid by the buyer for such a postponement. [19th c.: prob. an arbitrary formation]

cont'd *abbreviation* continued.

Conté /'kɒntei/ *noun* a kind of hard, grease-free crayon used as a medium for artwork. [N.J. *Conté*, French inventor d.1805]

conte /kɔ̃t/ *noun* **1** a short story (as a form of literary composition). **2** a medieval narrative tale. [French]

con·temn /kən'tem/ *transitive verb literary* despise; treat with contempt.

□ **con·tem·ner** /-'temɜr, -'temnɜr/ *noun* [Old French *contemner* or Latin *contemnere* (as COM-, *temnere tempt-* despise)]

con·tem·plate /'kɒntəm,pleit/ *verb* **1** *transitive* look at or consider in a calm, reflective manner. **2** *transitive* regard (an event) as possible. **3** *transitive* intend; have as one's purpose (*we contemplate leaving tomorrow*). **4** *intransitive* meditate. □ **con·tem·pla·tion** *noun*

con·tem·pla·tor *noun* [Latin *contemplari* (as COM-, *templum* place for observations)]

con·tem·pla·tive /kən'templətɪv, 'kɒntəm,pleɪtɪv/ ● *adjective* of or given to (esp. religious) contemplation; meditative. ● *noun* a person whose life is devoted to religious contemplation, esp. a monk or nun of a cloistered order devoted to prayer. □ **con·tem·pla·tive·ly** *adverb*

con·tem·por·an·eous /kən,tempə'reɪnɪəs/ *adjective* (usu. foll. by *with*) **1** existing or occurring at the same time. **2** of the same period. □ **con·tem·por·an·eity** /-'niːɪti, -'neɪɪti/ *noun* **con·tem·por·an·eous·ly** *adverb* **con·tem·por·an·eous·ness** *noun* [Latin *contemporaneus* (as COM-, *temporaneus* from *tempus -oris* time)]

con·tem·por·ary /kən'tempə,reri/ ● *adjective* **1** living or occurring at the same time. **2** approximately equal in age. **3** (of designs, styles, etc.) following the latest ideas or fashion. **4** living or existing at the present. ● *noun* (*pl.* **-ies**) **1** a person or thing living or existing at the same time as another. **2** a person of roughly the same age as another. □ **con·tem·por·ar·i·ness** *noun* [medieval Latin *contemporarius* (as CONTEMPORANEOUS)]

con·tem·por·ize *transitive verb* make up-to-date or fashionable. □ **con·tem·por·iz·a·tion** *noun*

con·tempt *noun* **1** a feeling that a person or a thing is beneath consideration or worthless, or deserving scorn or extreme reproach. **2** the condition of being held in contempt. **3** (in full **contempt of court**) disobedience to or disrespect for a court of law and its officers. □ **beneath contempt** utterly despicable. **hold in contempt** despise. [Latin *contemptus* (as CONTEMN)]

con·tempt·ible *adjective* deserving contempt; despicable. □ **con·tempt·ibly** *adverb*

con·temp·tu·ous *adjective* (often foll. by *of*) showing contempt, scornful; insolent. □ **con·temp·tu·ous·ly** *adverb*

con·tend *verb* **1** *intransitive* (usu. foll. by *with*) strive, fight, vie. **2** *intransitive* compete (*contending emotions*). **3** *transitive* (usu. foll. by *that* + clause) assert, maintain. [Old French *contendre* or Latin *contendere* (as COM-, *tendere tent-* stretch, strive)]

con·tend·er *noun* an esp. serious challenger or competitor.

con·tent¹ /kən'tent/ ● *predicative adjective* **1** (often foll. by *with*) satisfied; adequately happy; in agreement. **2** (foll. by *to* + infin.) willing. ● *verb transitive* (usu. *reflexive* or in *passive*; often foll. by *with*, or *to* + infin.) make content; satisfy. ● *noun* a contented state; satisfaction. □ **to one's heart's content** to the full extent of one's desires. [Old French from Latin *contentus* satisfied, past participle of *continēre* (as CONTAIN)]

con·tent² /'kɒntent/ *noun* **1** (usu. in *pl.*) what is contained in something, esp. in a book, pot, house, etc. **2 a** the amount of a substance contained (*low sodium content*). **b** the proportion of a specified feature present (*Canadian content*). **3** the substance or material dealt with (in a speech, work of art, etc.) as distinct from its form or style. **4** the capacity or volume of a thing. **5** (in *pl.*) (in full **table of contents**) a list of the titles of chapters etc. given at the front of a book, periodical, etc. **6** material (such as writing, music, or art) that is the result of creative or intellectual effort, esp. such material considered in relation to its manner of presentation. **7** information made available by a website or other electronic medium. [medieval Latin *contentum* (as CONTAIN)]

con·tent·ed /kən'tentəd/ *adjective* happy, satisfied. □ **con·tent·ed·ly** *adverb* **con·tent·ed·ness** *noun*

con·ten·tion /kən'tenʃən/ *noun* **1** a point contended for in an argument (*it is my contention that you are wrong*). **2 a** a dispute or argument. **b** rivalry, competition. □ **in contention** competing, esp. with a good chance of success. **out of contention** having lost any chance of succeeding.

con·ten·tious /kən'tenʃəs/ *adjective* **1** argumentative, quarrelsome. **2** likely to cause an argument; disputed, controversial. □ **con·ten·tious·ly** *adverb* **con·ten·tious·ness** *noun*

con·tent·ment /kən'tentmənt/ *noun* a satisfied state; tranquil happiness.

content provider *noun* a company (such as a publisher, a record company, or a film studio) that produces creative material for use by others.

con·ter·min·ous /kɒn'tɜrmɪnəs/ *adjective* (often foll. by *with*) **1** having a

common boundary. **2** co-extensive, coterminous. **3** = CONTIGUOUS 3. □ **con·ter·min·ous·ly** *adverb* [Latin *conterminus* (as COM-, *terminus* boundary)]

con·tes·sa /kɒn'tesə, kən-/ *noun* an Italian countess. [Italian from Late Latin *comitissa*: see COUNTESS]

con·test ● *noun* /'kɒntest/ **1 a** a competition, raffle, draw, etc. **b** a process of contending. **2** a dispute; a controversy. ● *transitive verb* /kən'test/ **1** challenge or dispute (a decision etc.). **2** debate (a point, statement, etc.). **3** contend or compete for (a prize, parliamentary seat, etc.); compete in (an election). □ **no contest 1** *US Law* a plea equivalent to guilty for a criminal matter in question. **2** indicating a clearly undisputed winner in some supposed competition. □ **con·test·able** /kən'testəbəl/ *adjective* **con·test·a·tory** /kən'testə,tɔri/ *adjective* **con·test·ed** /kən'testəd/ *adjective* [Latin *contestari* (as COM-, *testis* witness)]

con·test·ant /kən'testənt/ *noun* a person who takes part in a contest or competition.

con·test·a·tion /,kɒntes'teɪʃən/ *noun* **1** an act or instance of disputation. **2** an assertion contended for.

con·text *noun* **1** the parts of something written or spoken that immediately precede and follow a word or passage and clarify its meaning. **2** the circumstances relevant to something under consideration. □ **in context** with the surrounding words or circumstances (*must be seen in context*). **out of context** without the surrounding words or circumstances and so not fully understandable. □ **con·text·ual** *adjective* **con·text·ual·ize** *transitive verb* (also esp. *Brit.* **-ise**). **con·text·ual·iz·a·tion** *noun* **con·text·ual·ly** *adverb* [Latin *contextus* (as COM-, *texere text-* weave)]

con·text·ual·ism *noun* any theory which emphasizes the importance of the context of inquiry in a particular question. □ **con·text·ual·ist** *adjective & noun*

con·ti·gu·ity /,kɒntɪ'gjuːɪti/ *noun* **1 a** being contiguous. **b** proximity or contact. **2** *Psych.* the proximity of ideas or impressions in place or time as a principle of association.

con·tig·u·ous /kən'tɪgjʊəs/ *adjective* (usu. foll. by *with*, *to*) **1** touching, adjoining, in contact. **2** neighbouring, in close proximity. **3** esp. *US* used in reference to the continental US, excluding Alaska and Hawaii (*the contiguous 48 states*). □ **con·tig·u·ous·ly** *adverb* [Latin *contiguus* (as COM-, *tangere* touch)]

con·ti·nent¹ *noun* **1** any of the main continuous expanses of land (Europe, Asia, Africa, N and S America, Australia, Antarctica). **2** (**the Continent**) the mainland of Europe as distinct from the British Isles. **3** continuous land. [Latin *terra continens* (see CONTAIN) continuous land]

con·ti·nent² *adjective* **1** able to control movements of the bowels and bladder. **2** exercising self-restraint, esp. sexually. □ **con·tin·ence** *noun* [Middle English from Latin (as CONTAIN)]

con·ti·nent·al ● *adjective* **1** of or characteristic of a continent. **2 a** (**Continental**) of, relating to, or characteristic of mainland Europe. **b** (of food, cooking, etc.) reflecting the traditions of various European countries. **3** *hist.* of or pertaining to the colonies or states of America collectively, esp. at the time of the American Revolution. **4** *Meteorol.* of or relating to the climate of continental interiors, esp. as characterized by wide variants of temperature. ● *noun* **1** an inhabitant of mainland Europe. **2** *hist.* a soldier of the Continental Army in the American Revolution. □ **con·tin·ent·al·ly** *adverb*

continental breakfast *noun* a light breakfast of coffee, rolls, etc.

continental crust *noun* the two-layered, hard portion of the earth's surface which underlies and forms the large land masses and continental shelves.

continental divide *noun* **1** the boundary between separate drainage basins on a continent. **2** (**Continental Divide**) the North American watershed formed by the Rocky Mountains which divides waters flowing east from those flowing west.

continental drift *noun* the gradual movement through geological time of the continents over the surface of the earth on a substratum of magma.

con·tin·ent·al·ism *noun* *N Amer.* the belief that Canada and the US should pursue greater economic, political, and cultural co-operation, esp. in contrast to nationalistic policies. □ **con·tin·ent·al·ist** *noun & adjective*

continental quilt *noun* *Brit.* = DUVET.

continental shelf *noun* a gently sloping or near-horizontal, shallow, marine platform between the shore of a continent and the deeper ocean.

continental slope *noun* the slope between the outer edge of the continental shelf and the deep ocean floor.

con·tin·gency /kən'tɪndʒənsi/ *noun* (*pl.* **-cies**) **1** a future event or circumstance which is possible but cannot be predicted with certainty (*a detailed contract which attempts to provide for all possible contingencies*). **2** a provision for such an event or circumstance (*stores were kept as a contingency against a blockade*). **3** an incidental expense (*allow an extra fifteen per cent for contingencies*). **4** the absence of certainty in events.

contingency fund *noun* a fund to cover incidental or unforeseen expenses.

contingency plan *noun* a plan designed to take account of a possible future event or circumstance.

con·tin·gent /kən'tɪndʒənt/ ● *noun* **1** a group with common origins, interests, etc. representing a larger body. **2** a force (of troops, ships, etc.) contributed to form part of an army or navy. ● *adjective* **1** (usu. foll. by *on, upon*) occurring or existing only if certain other circumstances are the case; dependent on. **2** subject to chance. □ **con·tin·gent·ly** *adverb* [Latin *contingere* (as COM-, *tangere* touch)]

con·tin·ual /kən'tɪnjuəl/ *adjective* **1** constantly or frequently recurring. **2** ongoing; always happening. □ **con·tin·u·al·ly** *adverb* ¶ See Usage Note at CONTINUOUS.

con·tin·u·ance /kən'tɪnjuəns/ *noun* **1** a state of continuing in existence or operation. **2** the duration of an event or action. **3** *N Amer. Law* an adjournment or postponement of proceedings to a future date.

con·tin·u·ant /kən'tɪnjuənt/ *Phonetics* ● *noun* a speech sound in which the vocal tract is only partly closed, allowing the breath to pass through and the sound to be prolonged (as with *f, r, s, v*). ● *adjective* of or relating to such a sound.

con·tin·u·a·tion /kən,tɪnju'eɪʃən/ *noun* (often foll. by *of*) **1 a** the act or an instance of continuing. **b** the process of being continued. **2** a part that continues something else.

con·tin·ue /kən'tɪnjuː/ *verb* (**con·tinues, con·tinued, con·tinu·ing**) **1** *transitive* (often foll. by verbal noun, or *to* + infin.) persist in, maintain, not stop (an action etc.). **2 a** *transitive & intransitive* resume or prolong (a narrative, journey, etc.). **b** *intransitive* recommence after a pause (*the concert will continue shortly*). **3** *transitive* be a sequel to. **4** *intransitive* **a** remain in existence or unchanged. **b** remain in a specified state (*the weather will continue cold*). **5** *transitive N Amer. & Scot. Law* adjourn (proceedings) until some future date. [Old French *continuer* from Latin *continuare* make or be CONTINUOUS]

continuing education *noun* **1** instruction intended esp. for adult, part-time students. **2** courses given to update participants in a particular field of study.

con·tinu·ity /,kɒntɪ'nuːɪti -njuːɪti/ *noun* (*pl.* **-ities**) **1 a** the state of being continuous. **b** an unbroken succession. **c** a logical sequence. **2 a** the detailed and self-consistent scenario of a film or broadcast. **b** the maintenance of consistency or of a continuous flow of action in a film sequence. **3 a** the linking of broadcast items. **b** the music, commentary, etc. introducing or providing linkage between items in a broadcast. [French *continuité* from Latin *continuitas -tatis* (as CONTINUOUS)]

con·tinuo /kən'tɪnjuːoʊ/ *noun* (*pl.* **-tinuos**) *Music* **1** an accompaniment consisting of a bass line and harmonies which are indicated by figures, usu. played on a keyboard instrument. **2** the instrument(s) playing this part. [*basso continuo* (Italian, = continuous bass)]

con·tinu·ous /kən'tɪnjuːəs/ *adjective* **1** unbroken, uninterrupted. ¶ *Continuous* refers to something which is non-stop; *continual*, with which it is often confused, refers to something happening repeatedly, but with intervals in between. **2** (often foll. by *with*) connected throughout in time or space. **3** *Grammar* = PROGRESSIVE *adjective* 6. **4** (of paper etc.) designating a folded stack or roll with sheets joined together and perforated to form separate sheets. □ **con·tinu·ous·ly** *adverb* **con·tinu·ous·ness** *noun* [Latin *continuus* uninterrupted, from *continēre* (as COM-, *tenēre* hold)]

continuous assessment *noun* the evaluation of a pupil's progress throughout a course of study, as well as or instead of by examination.

con·tinu·um /kən'tɪnjuəm/ *noun* (*pl.* **con·tinua** /-juə/) anything seen as having a continuous structure without perceptibly distinct parts (*space-time continuum*). [Latin, neuter of *continuus*: see CONTINUOUS]

con·tort /kən'tɔrt/ *verb* **1** *transitive* twist or force out of normal shape. **2** *intransitive* become twisted, distorted, or forced out of shape (*face contorts with pain*). [Latin *contorquēre contort-* (as COM-, *torquēre* twist)]

con·tort·ed /kən'tɔrtəd/ *adjective* distorted, esp. out of shape.

con·tor·tion /kən'tɔrʃən/ *noun* **1** the act or process of twisting. **2** a twisted state, esp. of the face or body. **3** a thing or idea distorted by a

twisting of character, meaning, context, etc. (*the verbal contortions of the politician*). [Latin *contortio* (as CONTORT)]

con·tor·tion·ist /kən'tɔrʃənɪst/ *noun* an entertainer who adopts contorted postures.

con·tour /'kɒntʊr/ ● *noun* **1** an outline, esp. representing or bounding the shape of something with a curving form. **2** the outline of a natural feature, e.g. a coast or mountain mass. **3** = CONTOUR LINE 1. **4** the defining traits of a person's character, of a society, etc., perceived as a linkage of common and delimiting characteristics (*the changing contours of an imaginary character*). ● *transitive verb* **1** mark with contour lines. **2** construct (a road or railway) along and according to the outline of the land. [French from Italian *contorno* from *contornare* draw in outline (as COM-, *tornare* turn)]

con·toured /'kɒntʊrd/ *adjective* **1** designed or shaped to fit a specific form (*contoured seats*). **2** furnished with contour lines.

contour feather *noun* any of the surface feathers which form the outline of an adult bird's plumage.

contour line *noun* **1** a line on a map joining points of equal altitude. **2** a line in a drawing, painting, etc. joining points or enclosing an area of similar colour, texture, etc.

contour map *noun* a map marked with contour lines to depict the relief of the land.

contour plowing *noun* plowing along lines of constant altitude to minimize soil erosion.

Con·tra /'kɒntrə/ *noun* (*pl.* **Con·tras**) a member of a right-wing guerrilla force in Nicaragua which opposed the left-wing Sandinista government 1979–90, supported by the US for much of that time. The Contras were officially disbanded in 1990, after the Sandinistas' electoral defeat. [abbreviation of Spanish *contrarevolucionario* counter-revolutionary]

con·tra *noun Dance* a social form of American folk dance in which double lines of couples face one another as they dance, e.g. Virginia Reel. [French, *contredanses anglaises*]

contra- *combining form* **1** against, opposite (*contradict*). **2** *Music* (of instruments, organ stops, etc.) pitched an octave below (*contrabassoon*). [Latin *contra* against]

con·tra·band ● *noun* **1** anything that has been smuggled, imported, or exported illegally. **2** prohibited trade; smuggling. **3** (in full **contraband of war**) goods forbidden to be supplied by neutrals to belligerents. ● *adjective* **1** forbidden to be imported or exported (at all or without payment of duty). **2** concerning traffic in contraband (*contraband trade*). **3** forbidden. □ **con·tra·band·ist** *noun* [Spanish *contrabanda* from Italian (as CONTRA-, *bando* proclamation)]

con·tra·bass /'kɒntrə,beɪs/ *noun* = DOUBLE BASS. □ **contra·bass·ist** *noun* [Italian (*basso* BASS[1])]

con·tra·cep·tion *noun* the intentional prevention of pregnancy; the use of contraceptives. [CONTRA- + CONCEPTION]

con·tra·cep·tive ● *adjective* preventing pregnancy. ● *noun* a device, drug, etc. preventing conception.

con·tract ● *noun* /'kɒntrakt/ **1** a written or spoken agreement between two or more parties, intended to be enforceable by law. **2** a document recording this. **3** marriage regarded as a legal arrangement. **4** *Bridge etc.* a commitment to win the number of tricks bid. **5** *informal* a criminal arrangement for someone to be killed in exchange for money. ● *verb* /kən'trakt/ **1** *transitive & intransitive* make or become smaller. **b** draw together (muscles, the brow, etc.) or be drawn together. **2 a** *intransitive* (usu. foll. by *with*) make a contract. **b** *intransitive* (usu. foll. by *for*, or *to* + infin.) enter formally into a business or legal arrangement. **c** *transitive* (often foll. by *out*) arrange (work) to be done by contract. **d** *transitive* place under a contract. **3** *transitive* catch or develop (a disease). **4** *transitive* form or develop (a friendship, habit, etc.). **5** *transitive* enter into (marriage). **6** *transitive* incur (a debt etc.). **7** *transitive* shorten (a word) by combination or elision. □ **contract in** (or **out**) (also *reflexive*) esp. *Brit.* choose to be involved in (or withdraw or remain out of) a scheme or commitment. [earlier as adj., = contracted: Old French, from Latin *contractus* (as COM-, *trahere tract-* draw)]

contract bridge *noun* the most common form of bridge, in which only tricks bid and won count towards the game.

con·tract·ile *adjective* capable of or producing contraction. □ **con·tract·ility** /,kɒntrak'tɪlɪti/ *noun*

con·trac·tion *noun* **1** an act or instance of contracting. **2 a** a shortening or tensing of a muscle in response to a nerve impulse. **b** (usu. in *pl.*) the tensing of the uterine muscles esp. during labour. **3** shrinking, diminution. **4 a** a shortening of a word by combination or elision. **b** a contracted word or group of words. □ **con·trac·tion·al** *adjective* **con·tract·ive** *adjective*

con·tract·or /ˈkɒntraktər/ *noun* **1** a person who undertakes a contract, esp. to provide materials, conduct building operations, etc. **2** (also **contracting party**) *Law* a person who enters into a contract or agreement.

con·trac·tual /kənˈtraktʃuːəl/ *adjective* of, in the nature of, or secured by a contract. □ **con·trac·tual·ly** *adverb*

con·tract·ure /kənˈtraktʃər/ *noun Med.* a shortening and hardening of fibrous tissues, esp. muscles and tendons, caused by spasms, scarring, etc.

con·tra·dict /ˌkɒntrəˈdɪkt/ *verb* **1** *transitive* affirm the contrary of (a proposition, statement, etc.). **2 a** *transitive* deny or express the opposite of a statement made by (a person). **b** *intransitive* make a contradictory statement (*our father always told us not to contradict*). **3** *transitive* be in opposition to or in conflict with (*new evidence contradicted our theory*). [Latin *contradicere contradict-* (as CONTRA-, *dicere* say)]

con·tra·dic·tion *noun* **1 a** a denial; statement of the opposite. **b** an instance of this. **2** an inconsistency between statements, qualities, etc. **3** a person or thing characterized by conflicting qualities. □ **contradiction in terms** a self-contradictory statement or group of words.

con·tra·dict·ory *adjective* **1** expressing a denial or opposite statement. **2** (of statements etc.) mutually opposed or inconsistent. **3** (of a person) inclined to contradict. **4** *Logic* (of two propositions) so related that one and only one must be true. □ **con·tra·dic·tor·ily** *adverb* **con·tra·dict·ori·ness** *noun*

contra·dis·tinc·tion /ˌkɒntrədɪˈstɪŋkʃən/ *noun* (esp. in phr. **in contradistinction to**) difference made apparent by contrast.

contra·dis·tin·guish /ˌkɒntrədɪˈstɪŋgwɪʃ/ *transitive verb* (usu. foll. by *from*) distinguish two things by contrasting them.

contra·flow *noun Brit.* a flow (esp. of road traffic) alongside, and in a direction opposite to, an established or usual flow, esp. as a temporary or emergency arrangement.

con·trail *noun* a visible stream of water droplets or ice crystals occurring in the engine exhaust of an aircraft, rocket, etc. *Also called* VAPOUR TRAIL. [abbreviation of CONDENSATION TRAIL]

contra·indi·cate *transitive verb Med.* (usu. in *passive*) cause (a medication, course of treatment, etc.) to be inappropriate. □ **contra·indi·ca·tion** *noun*

con·tral·to /kənˈtraltoː -altoː/ *noun* (pl. **-tos**) **1 a** the lowest female singing voice. **b** a singer with this voice. **2** a part written for contralto. [Italian (as CONTRA-, ALTO)]

contra·pos·ition /ˌkɒntrəpəˈzɪʃən/ *noun* **1** opposition, contrast. **2** *Logic* inferring the opposite of a proposition through negation (e.g. converting *all A is B* to *all not-B is not-A*). □ **contra·posi·tive** /-ˈpɒzɪtɪv/ *adjective & noun* [Late Latin *contrapositio* (as CONTRA-, *ponere posit-* place)]

con·trap·posto /ˌkɒntrəˈpɒstoː/ *noun Sculpture* an asymmetrical arrangement of the human figure in which the line of the arms and shoulders contrast with, while balancing, those of the hips and legs. [Italian, past participle of *contrapporre*, counter, from Latin *contraponere*, place against (as CONTRA-, *ponere posit-* place)]

con·trap·tion *noun* often *derogatory* or *jocular* a machine or device, esp. a strange, improvised, or particularly intricate one. [19th c.: perhaps from CONTRIVE, INVENTION: assoc. with TRAP[1]]

contra·pun·tal /ˌkɒntrəˈpʌntəl/ *adjective Music* of, pertaining to, or of the nature of counterpoint. □ **contra·pun·tal·ly** *adverb* **contra·pun·tist** *noun* [Italian *contrappunto* counterpoint]

con·trar·ian /kɒnˈtreriən/ ● *noun* a person who opposes or rejects majority opinions, attitudes, etc., esp. in economic matters. ● *adjective* going against popular opinion or current practice. □ **con·trar·ian·ism** *noun*

con·trar·iety /ˌkɒntrəˈraɪɪti/ *noun* (pl. **-ieties**) **1** opposition in nature, quality, or action. **2** disagreement, inconsistency. **3** an antagonistic action, fact, or statement.

con·trari·wise /kənˈtreriˌwaɪz/ *adverb* **1** on the other hand. **2** in the opposite way.

con·trary /ˈkɒnˌtreri/ ● *adjective* **1** (usu. foll. by *to*) opposed in nature or tendency. **2** mutually opposed. **3** (of a wind) unfavourable, impeding. **4** opposite in position or direction. **5** /kənˈtreri/ *informal* perverse, wilful. ● *noun* (pl. **-ies**) (usu. prec. by *the*) the opposite. ● *adverb* (foll. by *to*) in opposition or contrast (*contrary to expectations it rained*). □ **on the contrary** intensifying a denial of what has just been implied or stated. **to the contrary** to the opposite effect (*can find no indication to the contrary*). □ **con·trar·i·ly** /kənˈtrerɪli/ *adverb* **con·trar·i·ness**

/kənˈtrerɪnəs/ *noun* [Anglo-French *contrarie*, Old French *contraire*, from Latin *contrarius* from *contra* against]

con·trast ● *noun* /ˈkɒntrast/ **1 a** a juxtaposition or comparison showing striking differences. **b** a difference so revealed. **2** (often foll. by *to*) a thing or person having qualities noticeably different from another. **3** the degree of difference between tones in a television picture or a photograph. **4** the change of apparent brightness or colour of an object caused by the juxtaposition of other objects. ● *verb* /kənˈtrast/ (often foll. by *with*) **1** *transitive* compare or set together so as to reveal a difference. **2** *intransitive* have or show a difference on comparison. □ **con·trast·ing** /ˈkɒntrastɪŋ, kənˈtrastɪŋ/ *adjective* **con·trast·ing·ly** /kənˈtrastɪŋli/ *adverb* **con·trast·ive** /kənˈtrastɪv/ *adjective* **con·trast·ive·ly** /kənˈtrastɪvli/ *adverb* [French *contraste*, *contraster*, from Italian *contrasto* from medieval Latin *contrastare* (as CONTRA-, *stare* stand)]

con·trasty /ˈkɒntrasti/ *adjective* (of photographic negatives, prints, or a television picture) showing a high degree of contrast with few intermediate tones.

con·tra·vene /ˌkɒntrəˈviːn/ *transitive verb* **1** infringe, violate (a law, standards, guidelines, etc.). **2** (of things) conflict with. □ **con·tra·ven·er** *noun* [Late Latin *contravenire* (as CONTRA-, *venire vent-* come)]

con·tra·ven·tion /ˌkɒntrəˈvenʃən/ *noun* **1** infringement, violation, opposition. **2** an instance of this. □ **in contravention of** infringing, violating (a law etc.). [French from medieval Latin *contraventio* (as CONTRAVENE)]

Contre·cœur /kɔ̃trəˈkər/ a municipality in south central Quebec, situated on the south shore of the St. Lawrence, southwest of Sorel-Tracy; pop. (2001) 5,222. [A. Pécaudy de *Contrecœur*, officer and seigneur d.1688]

contre·danse /ˈkɒntrəˌdɒns/ *noun* **1** a quadrille-like variation of the English country dance. **2** music for such a dance, usu. in 2/4 or 6/8 time. [French alteration of COUNTRY DANCE by association with CONTRA-]

contre·temps /ˈkɒntrəˌtɑ̃/ *noun* (pl. **-temps**) **1** an awkward or unfortunate occurrence. **2** an unexpected mishap. **3** a dispute, disagreement, or minor conflict. [French]

con·trib·ute /kənˈtrɪbjuːt/ *verb* (often foll. by *to*) **1** *transitive* give (money, an idea, help, etc.) towards a common purpose (*contributed time to the cause*). **2** *intransitive* help to bring about a result etc. (*his miserliness contributed to his loneliness*). **3** *transitive & intransitive* supply (an article etc.) for publication with others in a journal etc. □ **con·trib·ut·ing** *adjective* **con·tribu·tive** *adjective* **con·tribu·tor** *noun* [Latin *contribuere contribut-* (as COM-, *tribuere* bestow)]

con·tri·bu·tion /ˌkɒntrɪˈbjuːʃən/ *noun* **1** the act of giving or contributing. **2** something given, esp. money. **3** an article etc. furnished to a publication.

con·tribu·tory /kənˈtrɪbjʊtəri, -tɔri/ *adjective* **1** contributing to a result; partly responsible for. **2** operated by means of contributions (*contributory pension scheme*).

contributory negligence *noun* failure on the part of an injured party to take adequate precautions to prevent accident or injury.

con·trite /kənˈtraɪt, ˈkɒntraɪt/ *adjective* **1** penitent; sincerely filled with guilt, regret, etc. and desirous of making amends. **2** *archaic* (of an action) showing a contrite spirit. □ **con·trite·ly** *adverb* **con·trite·ness** *noun* [Old French *contrit* from Latin *contritus* bruised (as COM-, *terere trit-* rub)]

con·tri·tion /kənˈtrɪʃən/ *noun* the condition of being distressed in mind for some fault or injury done, usu. with resolution to make amends.

con·triv·ance /kənˈtraɪvəns/ *noun* **1 a** a device or tool made for a particular purpose. **b** an obviously artificial construction or presentation of parts or details. **2** an elaborate act or plan, esp. a deceitful one.

con·trive /kənˈtraɪv/ *transitive verb* **1 a** devise. **b** plan or make resourcefully or with skill. **2** (often foll. by *to* + infin.) manage (*contrived to make matters worse*). **b** plot or scheme (*contrived to restore her henchmen*). [Old French *controver* find, imagine, from medieval Latin *contropare* compare]

con·trived /kənˈtraɪvd/ *adjective* so obviously planned as to seem unnatural, artificial, or forced (*the plot seemed contrived*).

con·trol ● *noun* **1** the power of directing, command (*under the control of*). **2** the power of restraining, esp. self-restraint. **3 a** a means of restraint; a check. **b** prevention of the spread or proliferation of something (*disease control*). **4** (usu. in *pl.*) a means of regulating prices

Consonants: b but d dog f few g get h her j yes k cat l leg m man n no p pen r red s sit

etc. **5** (also *attributive*: *control panel*; *control room*) **a** a device or switch used to control something, e.g. a television, amplifier, etc. **b** (usu. in *pl.*) the switches etc. by which an aircraft or car is controlled (*the plane crashed with two experienced pilots at the controls*). **6** (in full **control key**) *Computing* a key which is held down while another key is depressed, altering the function of the latter. **7** a person or group that checks, monitors, or controls something. **8 a** a standard of comparison for checking the results of a survey or experiment. **b** a person or thing acting as such a standard. **9** a member of an intelligence organization who personally directs the activities of a spy. ● *transitive verb* (**con·trolled**, **con·trol·ling**) **1** dominate or have command of. **2** regulate or exert control over. **3** curb, restrain, or hold in check (*told him to control himself*). **4** serve as a standard of comparison for a test, study, etc. **5** check, verify. □ **control for** take into account (an extraneous factor that might affect the results of an experiment). **in control** (often foll. by *of*) directing an activity. **out of control** no longer subject to containment, restraint, or guidance. **under control** being controlled; in order. □ **con·trol·lable** *adjective* **con·trol·labil·ity** *noun* [Anglo-French *controller* keep a copy of a roll of accounts, from medieval Latin *contrarotulare* (as CONTRA-, *rotulus* ROLL *noun*): (n.) perhaps from French *contrôle*]

control column *noun* a column, usu. with a wheel-shaped attachment, by which the pilot controls the lateral and longitudinal movements of an aircraft.

control freak *noun informal* a person with a near obsessive desire for order and control of self, others, surroundings, etc.

control group *noun* a group forming the standard of comparison in an experiment.

controlled experiment *noun* (also **controlled trial**) an experiment designed with strictly controlled variables so that the effects of any one factor may be precisely observed.

controlled-release *adjective* (of a substance, esp. a drug) activated gradually or at predetermined intervals over a period of time (*a controlled-release antihistamine*).

controlled substance *noun* (also **controlled drug**) any addictive or behaviour-altering substance the possession of which is restricted by law, e.g. steroids, cocaine.

con·trol·ler *noun* **1** a person or device that regulates, directs, or controls. **2** = COMPTROLLER. **3** *Cdn* (in Ontario) a member of a board of control. [Middle English *counterroller* from Anglo-French *contrerollour* (as CONTROL)]

con·trol·ling *adjective* (of a person) inclined to control the actions, thoughts, etc. of others.

controlling interest *noun* ownership of sufficient stock in a company to enable a shareholder to exert control over policy, management, etc.

controlling shareholder *noun* an individual who owns a sufficient number of shares in a company to have a controlling interest in it.

control rod *noun* a rod of neutron-absorbing material used to vary the output power of a nuclear reactor.

control top *noun* (usu. *attributive*) a spandex-reinforced panty on a pair of pantyhose, designed to make the buttocks and abdomen appear slimmer.

control tower *noun* a tall structure at an airport etc. from which air traffic is controlled.

con·tro·ver·sial /ˌkɒntrə'vɜrʃəl/ *adjective* **1** causing or subject to dispute or debate. **2** fond of debate, argument, or controversy. □ **con·tro·ver·sial·ist** *noun & adjective* **con·tro·ver·sial·ly** *adverb*

con·tro·ver·sy /'kɒntrəˌvɜrsi/ *noun* (*pl.* **-sies**) a prolonged argument or dispute, esp. when conducted publicly and over a matter of opinion. [Latin *controversia* (as CONTROVERT)]

con·tro·vert /'kɒntrəˌvɜrt, -'vɜrt/ *transitive verb* **1** dispute, deny, oppose. **2** argue about; discuss. □ **con·tro·vert·ed** *adjective* **con·tro·vert·ible** *adjective* [originally past participle; from French *controvers(e)* from Latin *controversus* (as CONTRA-, *vertere vers-* turn)]

con·tu·macy /'kɒntjʊməsi/ *noun* stubborn refusal to obey or comply. □ **con·tu·ma·cious** /ˌkɒntjʊ'meɪʃəs/ *adjective* [Latin *contumacia* from *contumax*, perhaps related to *tumēre* swell]

con·tume·ly /'kɒntjuːmli/ *noun* **1** insulting or contemptuous language or treatment. **2** disgrace or insult. □ **con·tu·meli·ous** /ˌkɒntjuː'miːliəs/ *adjective* [Old French *contumelie* from Latin *contumelia* (as COM-, *tumēre* swell)]

con·tu·sion /kən'tuːʃən, -tjuː-/ *noun* a bruise or an injury which does not break the skin. [Late Latin *contusio* from *contundere contus-* (as COM-, *tundere* thump)]

con·un·drum /kə'nʌndrəm/ *noun* **1** a riddle, esp. one with a pun in its answer. **2** a hard or puzzling question or issue. [16th c.: origin unknown]

con·urba·tion /ˌkɒnɜr'beɪʃən/ *noun* an extended urban area, esp. one consisting of several towns and merging suburbs. [CON- + Latin *urbs urbis* city + -ATION]

con·ure /kɒ'njʊr/ *noun* any of numerous Central and S American medium-sized parrots belonging to the genera *Aratinga*, *Pyrrhura*, and related genera, with mainly green plumage and a long gradated tail. [modern Latin *conurus* from Greek *kōnos* cone + *oura* tail]

Conv. *abbreviation* = CONVENTIONAL *adjective* 2.

con·va·lesce /ˌkɒnvə'les/ *intransitive verb* recover one's health after illness or medical treatment. [Latin *convalescere* (as COM-, *valēre* be well)]

con·va·les·cent /ˌkɒnvə'lesənt/ ● *adjective* **1** recovering from an illness. **2** pertaining to convalescents (*convalescent hospital*). ● *noun* a person recovering from an illness or injury. □ **con·va·les·cence** *noun*

con·vec·tion *noun* **1** transference of heat in a gas or liquid by upward movement of the heated and less dense medium. **2** *Meteorol.* the atmospheric process of air transfer, esp. of hot air upward. □ **con·vec·tion·al** *adjective* **con·vec·tive** [Late Latin *convectio* from Latin *convehere convect-* (as COM-, *vehere vect-* carry)]

convection oven *noun* an oven with a fan that continually and uniformly circulates heated air to decrease cooking time.

con·vec·tor *noun* a heating appliance that circulates warm air by convection.

con·vene *verb* **1** *transitive* **a** call or arrange (a meeting etc.). **b** call together (people) for a meeting. **2** *intransitive* assemble or meet together, esp. for a common purpose. **3** *transitive* summon (a person) before a tribunal. □ **con·ven·or** *noun* (also **con·ven·er**). [Latin *convenire convent-* assemble, agree, fit (as COM-, *venire* come)]

con·ven·ience *noun* **1** the quality of being convenient; suitability. **2** freedom from difficulty or trouble. **3** an accommodation or advantage (*your help was a great convenience*). **4** any thing, esp. an installation or device, that saves or simplifies effort. **5** a convenient time or place. **6** esp. *Brit.* a lavatory, esp. a public one. □ **at your convenience** at a time or place that suits you. **at your earliest convenience** as soon as you can. [Middle English from Latin *convenientia* (as CONVENE)]

convenience food *noun* food, esp. complete meals, sold in convenient form and requiring very little preparation.

convenience store *noun* a small, conveniently located store with extended opening hours.

con·ven·ient *adjective* **1** (often foll. by *for, to*) **a** serving one's comfort, interests, or needs. **b** easily accessible. **c** suitable. **d** free of trouble or difficulty. **2** available or occurring at a suitable time or place (*will try to find a convenient moment*). **3** well situated for some purpose (*parking convenient for shoppers*). □ **con·ven·ient·ly** *adverb* [Middle English (as CONVENE)]

con·vent /'kɒnvent, -vənt/ ● *noun* **1** a religious community, esp. of nuns, under vows. **2** the premises occupied by this. **3** (in full **convent school**) a school attached to and run by a convent. ● *adjective* of, pertaining to, or associated with a convent (*convent girls*). [Anglo-French *covent*, Old French *convent* from Latin *conventus* assembly (as CONVENE)]

con·ven·ticle /kən'ventɪkəl/ *noun* esp. *hist.* **1** a secret or unlawful religious meeting, esp. of dissenters. **2** a building used for this. [Latin *conventiculum* (place of) assembly, diminutive of *conventus* (as CONVENE)]

con·ven·tion /kən'venʃən/ *noun* **1 a** a general agreement, esp. on social behaviour etc. by implicit consent of the majority. **b** a custom or customary practice, esp. an artificial or formal one. **2 a** a formal assembly or conference for a common purpose. **b** *N Amer.* an assembly of the delegates of a political party to select candidates for office. **3 a** a formal agreement. **b** an agreement between nations, somewhat less formal than a treaty. **4** *Cards* an accepted method of play (in leading, bidding, etc.) used to convey information to a partner. [Old French from Latin *conventio -onis* (as CONVENE)]

con·ven·tion·al /kən'venʃənəl/ *adjective* **1** depending on or according with convention. **2** (of a person) conforming to social conventions (*her father was a strictly conventional person*). **3 a** usual or of agreed significance (*a suit is conventional office attire*). **b** traditional, normal (in opposition to recent inventions etc.) (*suitable for conventional or microwave ovens*). **4** not spontaneous, sincere, or original. **5** (of weapons or power) non-nuclear. **6** *Art* following accepted models, traditions, etc. instead of directly imitating nature or working out original ideas. □ **con·ven·tion·al·ity** *noun* **con·ven·tion·al·ize** *transitive verb* (also esp. *Brit.* **-ise**). **con·ven·tion·al·ly** *adverb* [French *conventionnel* or Late Latin *conventionalis* (as CONVENTION)]

conventional wisdom *noun* a common body of accumulated opinion, tradition, etc. on a certain subject.

con·ven·tion·eer /kən,venʃəˈniːr/ *noun N Amer.* a person attending a convention.

con·ven·tual /kənˈventʃuəl/ ● *adjective* **1** of or belonging to a convent. **2** of a branch of the Franciscans living in convents. ● *noun* **1** a member of a convent. **2** a conventual Franciscan.

con·verge /kənˈvɜrdʒ/ *intransitive verb* **1 a** (often foll. by *on*) come together from several diverse points towards a common point. **b** (of ideas) move towards a common conclusion, opinion, etc. **2** (of lines) tend to meet at a point. **3** (foll. by *on, upon*) approach from different directions. **4** *Math.* (of a series) have a finite sum or limit at which values eventually close. [Late Latin *convergere* (as COM-, *vergere* incline)]

con·ver·gence /kənˈvɜrdʒəns/ *noun* **1** the action, fact, or property of converging. **2** *Biol.* the tendency of distinct animals and plants to evolve similar structural or physiological characteristics under similar environmental conditions. **3** the progressive integration of previously distinct technologies. □ **con·ver·gent** *adjective*

con·ver·sant /kənˈvɜrsənt/ *adjective* (usu. foll. by *with*) well experienced or acquainted with a subject etc.

con·ver·sa·tion /,kɒnvərˈseiʃən/ *noun* **1** the informal exchange of ideas by spoken words. **2** an instance of this. □ **make conversation** talk politely. [Old French from Latin *conversatio -onis* (as CONVERSE[1])]

con·ver·sa·tion·al *adjective* **1** of conversation. **2** fond of or skilled in conversation. **3** informal in style; typical of conversation. □ **con·ver·sa·tion·al·ly** *adverb*

con·ver·sa·tion·al·ist *noun* a person who is fond of or excels at conversing.

conversation piece *noun* **1** any thing, practice, etc. that serves as a topic of conversation because of its unusualness etc. **2** a small group portrait of people in a domestic or landscape setting.

conversation stopper *noun informal* **1** an unexpected remark, esp. one that cannot readily be answered. **2** something outrageous or startling.

con·ver·sa·zione /,kɒnvər,satsiˈoːni/ *noun* a social gathering usu. held by a learned or art society. [Italian from Latin (as CONVERSATION)]

con·verse[1] ● *intransitive verb* /kənˈvɜrs/ (often foll. by *with*) engage in conversation (*conversed with her about various subjects*). ● *noun* /ˈkɒnvɜrs/ *archaic* conversation. [Old French *converser* from Latin *conversari* keep company (with), frequentative of *convertere* (CONVERT)]

con·verse[2] /ˈkɒnvɜrs/ ● *adjective* opposite, contrary, reversed. ● *noun* **1** something that is opposite or contrary. **2** *Logic* a statement formed from another statement by the transposition of certain words, e.g. *some philosophers are men* from *some men are philosophers*. **3** *Math.* a theorem whose hypothesis and conclusion are the conclusion and hypothesis of another. □ **con·verse·ly** /kənˈvɜrsli/ *adverb* [Latin *conversus*, past participle of *convertere* (CONVERT)]

con·ver·sion /kənˈvɜrʒən/ *noun* **1 a** the act or an instance of changing one's beliefs, opinions, etc. **b** the process of having one's beliefs changed, esp. in religion. **c** the turning of sinners to God. **2** an adaptation of a building for new purposes. **3 a** the changing of funds from one national currency to another. **b** the changing of units, measurements, etc. from one system or expression to another (*conversion of miles to kilometres*). **4** alteration to a car, camera, rifle, etc. to enhance its performance. **5 a** the physical transformation of something from one substance, state, etc. to another (*conversion of food into energy*). **b** the transformation of fertile into fissile material in a nuclear reactor. **6** *Sport* the scoring of additional points in certain sports, e.g. by a successful kick at goal in football or rugby or by a free throw in basketball. **7** *Psych.* the transformation of an unconscious conflict into a physical disorder or disease. **8** *Computing* **a** the adaptation of software designed for one system to another system. **b** the transfer or copying of data from one storage medium to another. [Old French from Latin *conversio -onis* (as CONVERT)]

con·vert ● *verb* /kənˈvɜrt/ **1** *transitive* (usu. foll. by *into*) change in form, character, or function. **2 a** *intransitive* to change beliefs, opinions, etc. **b** *transitive* cause (a person) to change beliefs, opinion, party, etc. **3** *transitive* change (moneys, stocks, units in which a quantity is expressed, etc.) into others of a different kind. **4** *transitive* make structural alterations in (a building) to serve a new purpose. **5** *transitive & intransitive* **a** *Football* complete (a touchdown) by kicking a goal or crossing the goal line. **b** *Rugby* score extra points from (a try) by a successful kick at goal. **6** *intransitive* be converted or convertible (*the sofa converts into a bed*). **7** *transitive* *Computing* **a** adapt (software) from one

system to another. **b** transfer or copy (data) from one storage medium to another. **8** *transitive* *Logic* interchange the terms of (a proposition). ● *noun* /ˈkɒnvɜrt/ **1** (often foll. by *to*) a person who has been converted to a different belief, opinion, etc. **2** *Cdn Football* the scoring of points after a touchdown by kicking the ball between the uprights (for one additional point) or by carrying or passing the ball over the defending team's goal line (for two additional points). □ **convert to one's own use** *Law* wrongfully make use of (another's property). [Old French *convertir* ultimately from Latin *convertere convers-* turn about (as COM-, *vertere* turn)]

con·vert·er /kənˈvɜrtər/ *noun* (also *Brit.* **con·vert·or**) **1** a person or thing that converts. **2** *Electricity* **a** an electrical apparatus for the interconversion of alternating current and direct current. **b** *Electronics* an apparatus for converting a signal from one frequency to another. **c** an auxiliary apparatus that allows a television or radio to pick up channels or frequencies for which it was not originally designed. **3** a reaction vessel used in making steel. **4** = CATALYTIC CONVERTER.

converter reactor *noun* a nuclear reactor that converts fertile material into fissile material.

con·vert·ible ● *adjective* **1** that may be converted. **2** (of currency, bonds, etc.) that may be converted into other forms, esp. into gold or US dollars. **3** (of a car) having a folding or detachable roof. **4** *Cdn* designating a mortgage which may not be paid off before the stated term without a financial penalty, but which may be converted to a longer term without penalty. ● *noun* **1** a car with a folding or detachable roof. **2** bonds or securities which can be readily changed to common stock. □ **con·vert·ibil·ity** *noun*

con·vex /ˈkɒnveks/ *adjective* having an outline or surface curved like the exterior of a circle or sphere (*compare* CONCAVE). □ **con·vex·ity** /-ˈveksɪti/ *noun* **con·vex·ly** *adverb* [Latin *convexus* vaulted, arched]

con·vey *transitive verb* **1** communicate (an idea, meaning, etc.). **2** transport or carry (goods, passengers, etc.). **3** *Law* transfer the title to (property). □ **con·vey·able** *adjective* [Old French *conveier* from medieval Latin *conviare* (as COM-, Latin *via* way)]

con·vey·ance *noun* **1 a** the act or process of carrying. **b** the communication (of ideas etc.). **c** transmission. **2** a means of transport; a vehicle. **3** *Law* **a** the transfer of property from one owner to another. **b** a document effecting this. □ **con·vey·an·cer** *noun* (in sense 3). **con·vey·an·cing** *noun* (in sense 3).

con·vey·or *noun* (also **con·vey·er**) **1** a person or thing that conveys. **2** = CONVEYOR BELT.

conveyor belt *noun* a flexible, endless belt moving on rollers used to convey articles or materials.

con·vict ● *transitive verb* /kənˈvɪkt/ **1** (often foll. by *of*) declare guilty, esp. by the verdict of a jury or the decision of a judge. **2** cause to feel guilt or remorse. ● *noun* /ˈkɒnvɪkt/ **1** a person found guilty of a criminal offence. **2** a person serving a prison sentence. [Latin *convincere convict-* (as COM-, *vincere* conquer): noun from obsolete *convict* convicted]

con·vic·tion *noun* **1 a** the act or process of proving or finding guilty. **b** an instance of this (*has two previous convictions*). **2** a firm belief or opinion. [Latin *convictio* (as CONVICT)]

con·vince *transitive verb* (often foll. by *of*, or *that* + clause) persuade (a person) to believe, realize, or agree. □ **con·vin·cer** *noun* [Latin (as CONVICT)]

con·vinced *adjective* firmly persuaded (*a convinced pacifist*).

con·vin·cing *adjective* **1** persuading by argument or evidence (*a convincing case*). **2 a** plausible or seeming worthy of belief (*a convincing message*). **b** leaving no margin of doubt, substantial (*a convincing victory*). □ **con·vin·cing·ly** *adverb*

con·viv·ial /kənˈvɪviəl/ *adjective* **1 a** (of a person) friendly, fond of good company. **b** sociable and lively (*convivial banter*). **2** festive (*a convivial atmosphere*). □ **con·vivi·al·ity** /-ˈalɪti/ *noun* **con·vivi·al·ly** *adverb* [Latin *convivialis* from *convivium* feast (as COM-, *vivere* live)]

con·vo·ca·tion /,kɒnvəˈkeiʃən/ *noun* **1** *N Amer.* a formal assembly at a university or college for graduation ceremonies. **2** a large, formal gathering of people. **3** *Cdn Law* a meeting of the elected governing officials of a provincial law society. **4** *Brit.* a provincial synod of the Anglican clergy of Canterbury or York. **5** *Brit.* a legislative or deliberative assembly of a university. □ **con·vo·ca·tion·al** *adjective*

con·voke *transitive verb* *formal* call (people) together to a meeting etc.; summon to assemble. [Latin *convocare convocat-* (as COM-, *vocare* call)]

con·vo·lut·ed /ˈkɒnvə,luːtɪd/ *adjective* **1** (of style, meaning, etc.) complicated, involved, difficult to comprehend (*a convoluted plot*). **2** coiled, twisted. □ **con·vo·lut·ed·ly** *adverb* [past participle of *convolute* from Latin *convolutus* (as COM-, *volvere volut-* roll)]

Vowels: a *cat* ɑ *arm* e *bed* ɜr *her* ɜ: *deux* ə *ago* ɪ *sit* i *cosy* iː *feed* ɒ *hot* ɔ *pore* oː *no* ʌ *run* ʊ *put*

con·vo·lu·tion /ˌkɒnvəˈluːʃən/ noun **1** a complex, intricate, or confused condition or issue. **2** coiling or twisting. **3** a coil or twist. **4** a sinuous fold in the surface of the brain. □ **con·vo·lu·tion·al** adjective [medieval Latin convolutio (as CONVOLUTED)]

con·volve /kənˈvɒlv/ transitive & intransitive verb (esp. as **con·volved** adjective) roll together; coil up. [Latin convolvere (as CONVOLUTED)]

con·volvu·lus /kənˈvɒlvjʊləs/ noun (pl. **con·volvu·lus·es** or **con·vol·vu·li** /-laɪ/) any twining plant of the genus Convolvulus, with trumpet-shaped flowers, e.g. bindweed. [Latin]

con·voy /ˈkɒnvɔɪ/ ● noun **1** a group of ships travelling together or under escort. **2** a supply of provisions etc. under escort. **3** a group of vehicles travelling on land together or under escort. **4** the act of travelling or moving in a group or under escort. ● transitive verb **1** (of a warship) escort (a merchant or passenger vessel). **2** escort, esp. with armed force. □ **in convoy** under escort with others; as a group. [Old French convoyer var. of conveier CONVEY]

con·vul·sant /kənˈvʌlsənt/ Pharm. ● adjective producing convulsions. ● noun a drug that may produce convulsions.

con·vulse /kənˈvʌls/ verb **1** intransitive **a** move violently or uncontrollably. **b** contort. **2 a** transitive cause to laugh uproariously. **b** intransitive laugh wildly. **3 a** transitive disturb greatly. **b** intransitive be agitated. **4 a** transitive affect with convulsions; cause to twist or contort. **b** intransitive be affected with convulsions. [Latin convellere convuls- (as COM-, vellere pull)]

con·vul·sion /kənˈvʌlʃən/ noun **1** (usu. in pl.) violent irregular motion of a limb or limbs or the body caused by involuntary contraction of muscles. **2** a violent natural disturbance, esp. an earthquake. **3** violent social or political agitation. **4** (in pl.) uncontrollable laughter.

con·vul·sive /kənˈvʌlsɪv/ adjective **1** of the nature of, characterized by or affected with convulsions. **2** producing convulsions. □ **con·vul·sive·ly** adverb

cony¹ /ˈkəʊni/ noun (also **coney**) (pl. **conies** or **coneys**) **1 a** a rabbit. **b** its fur. **2** Bible a hyrax. [Middle English cunin(g) from Anglo-French coning, Old French conin, from Latin cuniculus]

cony² /ˈkəʊni/ noun Cdn (North) = INCONNU.

COO abbreviation CHIEF OPERATING OFFICER.

coo ● noun a soft murmuring sound like that of a dove or pigeon. ● verb (**coos, cooed**) **1** intransitive make the sound of a coo. **2** intransitive & transitive talk or say in a soft or amorous voice. ● interjection Brit. slang expressing surprise or incredulity. [imitative]

co-occur intransitive verb occur together or simultaneously. □ **co-occur·rence** noun

coochy-coo interjection eliciting response from a baby.

Cook, Captain James (1728–79), English explorer and navigator. He charted the St. Lawrence River and the coasts of Nova Scotia and Newfoundland (1759–67), and conducted three expeditions to the Pacific (1768–71, 1772–5, and 1776–9), charting the coasts of New Zealand and New Guinea as well as exploring the eastern coast of Australia and claiming it for Britain.

Cook, Mount 1 a peak (4 194 m) in the St. Elias Mountains, on the Yukon–Alaska border. **2** (called in Maori **Aor·angi**) the highest peak in New Zealand, in the Southern Alps on South Island, rising to a height of 3 764 m (12,349 ft.). [Captain J. COOK]

cook ● verb **1 a** transitive prepare (food) by heating it. **b** intransitive prepare food for consumption (loves to cook). **2** intransitive (of food) undergo cooking. **3** transitive informal falsify (accounts etc.); alter to produce a desired result (cooked the books). **4** transitive slang ruin, spoil. **5** transitive (esp. as **cooked** adjective) Brit. slang fatigue, exhaust. **6** intransitive N Amer. informal **a** perform music with excitement or inspiration. **b** perform or proceed well. **7** intransitive (as **be cooking**) informal be happening or about to happen (went to find out what was cooking). ● noun a person who cooks, esp. professionally or in a specified way (a good cook). □ **cook a person's goose** ruin a person's chances. **cook up** informal invent or concoct (a story, excuse, etc.). **cook with gas** N Amer. informal proceed rapidly; be on the way to rapid success. **too many cooks (in the kitchen) spoil the broth** if too many people are involved in a task or activity, it will not be done well. □ **cook·able** adjective & noun [Old English cōc from popular Latin cocus for Latin coquus]

cook·book noun N Amer. a book containing recipes and other information about cooking.

cook-chill noun Brit. **1** the process of cooking and refrigerating food ready for reheating at a later time. **2** (attributive) (of food) prepared in this way.

cook·er noun **1** a container or device for cooking food. **2** Brit. an appliance powered by gas, electricity, etc., for cooking food; a range.

cook·ery noun (pl. **-ies**) **1** the art or practice of cooking. **2** N Amer. a place or establishment for cooking.

cookery book noun Brit. a cookbook.

cook·house noun **1** a building used for cooking, esp. at a ranch, logging camp, etc. **2** a ship's galley.

cook·ie¹ noun **1** N Amer. a small sweet biscuit. **2** N Amer. slang a person (one tough cookie; smart cookie). **3** Computing a token or packet of data, passed between computers or programs to allow access or to activate certain features, esp. a packet of data sent by an Internet server to a browser, which is returned by the browser each time it subsequently accesses the same server, thereby identifying the user or monitoring their access to the server. □ **toss** (or **lose**) **one's cookies** N Amer. slang vomit. **the way the cookie crumbles** N Amer. informal how things turn out; the unalterable state of affairs. [Dutch koekje diminutive of koek cake]

cook·ie² noun **1** a cook, esp. in a work camp or in the military. **2** a cook's assistant in a work camp. [COOK noun + -IE]

cookie cutter noun N Amer. **1** a stamp for cutting cookie dough into a particular shape. **2** (often attributive) denoting something mass-produced or lacking any distinguishing characteristics (cookie-cutter novels).

cookie jar noun N Amer. **1** a container for cookies. **2** a reserve of good things, usu. off limits (caught with their hands in the cookie jar).

cookie sheet noun N Amer. a flat metal tray on which cookies etc. are baked.

cook·ing noun **1** the art or process by which food is prepared for consumption. **2** (attributive) suitable for or used in cooking (cooking apple; cooking utensils).

cooking oil noun vegetable oil used in cooking.

Cook Islands a group of fifteen islands in the SW Pacific Ocean between Tonga and French Polynesia, which have the status of a self-governing territory in free association with New Zealand; pop. (est. 2002) 20,811; capital, Avarua, on Rarotonga. [Captain J. COOK]

cook-off noun N Amer. a cooking competition in which competitors assemble to prepare their entries.

cook·out noun N Amer. a gathering with an open-air cooked meal; a barbecue.

cook·shack noun N Amer. a building where meals are prepared and served, esp. in a work camp.

Cook·shire-Eaton /ˈkʊkʃiːr ˈiːtən/ a town in SE Quebec, just east of Sherbrooke; pop. (2001) 5,065. [after the first settler, J. Cook d.1819, and possibly after a place called Eaton in England]

Cook's tour noun **1** a tour or journey in which many places are visited, often briefly. **2** a rapid survey of something. [T. Cook, English travel agent d.1892]

cook·stove noun N Amer. an esp. wood-burning stove used for cooking.

Cook Strait the strait separating the North and South Islands of New Zealand. [Captain J. COOK]

cook tent noun N Amer. a tent reserved for cooking and eating meals when camping out.

cook·top noun N Amer. a cooking unit consisting of burners or elements, esp. built into a countertop.

cook·ware noun utensils for cooking, esp. dishes, pans, etc.

cool ● adjective **1** of or at a fairly low temperature, moderately cold (a cool day; a cool bath). **2** suggesting or achieving coolness (cool colours; cool clothes). **3** calm, unexcited. **4** lacking zeal or enthusiasm. **5** unfriendly; lacking cordiality (got a cool reception). **6** informal **a** excellent, esp. appealing to youth. **b** (of a person, style, etc.) following the latest fashions; hip. **c** considered socially acceptable by a group (esp. youth). **d** used to express acceptance of or agreement with something (if you need to shower first, that's cool). **7** (of jazz playing) restrained, relaxed. **8** calmly audacious (a cool customer). **9** (prec. by a) informal at least; not less than (cost me a cool thousand). ● noun **1** coolness. **2** cool air; a cool place. **3** slang calmness, composure (keep one's cool; lose one's cool). ● transitive & intransitive verb (often foll. by down, off) make or become cool. □ **cool as a cucumber** completely unruffled. **cool one's heels** see HEEL¹. **cool it** informal relax, calm down. **cool one's jets** N Amer. slang be less agitated. **cool out** informal relax, calm down. □ **cool·ish** adjective **cool·ly** adverb **cool·ness** noun [Old English cōl, cōlian, from Germanic: compare COLD]

coola·bah /ˈkuːləbɑː/ noun (also **cooli·bah** /-lɪbɑː/) Austral. any of various gum trees, esp. Eucalyptus microtheca. [Kamilaroi (and related languages) gulaaba]

cool·ant noun **1** a cooling agent, esp. fluid, to remove heat from an engine, nuclear reactor, etc. **2** a fluid used to lessen the friction of a cutting tool. [COOL + -ANT after *lubricant*]

cool-down noun a period during which something cools down, esp. a period of gentle exercise after a session of more vigorous exercise, allowing the body to cool down gradually.

cool·er noun **1** N Amer. an insulated, usu. portable container for keeping drinks etc. cool. **2** a vessel in which a thing is cooled. **3** a mixture of wine or spirits and soda water, often with a fruit flavour. **4** slang prison or a prison cell.

cool-headed adjective not easily excited.

cooli·bah var. of COOLABAH.

Cool·idge, (John) Cal·vin (1872–1933), US Republican politician, 30th president of the US 1923–9. Highly popular personally, he was noted for his policy of non-interference in foreign affairs, which culminated in the signing of the Kellogg Pact (1928).

coo·lie noun (pl. **-lies**) an unskilled, low-paid labourer in or from India, China, or other Asian countries. [perhaps from *Kulī*, an aboriginal tribe of Gujarat, India]

coolie hat noun a broad conical hat as worn by coolies.

cooling-off period noun an interval to allow for a change of mind before commitment to action.

cooling tower noun a tall structure for cooling hot water before reuse, esp. in industry.

coolth noun informal coolness.

coomb /kuːm/ noun (also **combe**) Brit. **1** a valley or hollow on the side of a hill. **2** a short valley running up from the coast. [Old English *cumb*: compare CWM]

coon noun **1** N Amer. a raccoon. **2** slang offensive a black person. □ **a coon's age** a long time. [abbreviation]

coon-can noun a simple card game like rummy (originally Mexican). [Latin American Spanish *con quién* with whom?]

Coon Come, Mat·thew (b.1956), Canadian Cree political leader and activist, Grand Chief of the Grand Council of the Crees 1987–99 and National Chief of the Assembly of First Nations 2000–2003. Known internationally for his work on behalf of aboriginal rights, he has been particularly active in asserting the rights of the Crees of Northern Quebec, especially in the face of hydroelectric megaprojects and threats of Quebec sovereignty.

coon·hound noun (also **coon dog**) a dog of a breed developed for the hunting of raccoons.

coon·shit noun □ **a pinch of coonshit** Cdn coarse slang a negligible or contemptible quantity (*not worth a pinch of coonshit; don't care a pinch of coonshit*).

coon·skin noun **1** the skin of a raccoon. **2** a cap etc. made of this.

coop ● noun **1** a cage or pen for confining poultry. **2** a small place of confinement, esp. a prison. ● transitive verb **1** put or keep (a fowl) in a coop. **2** (often foll. by *up*) confine (a person) in a small space. □ **fly the coop** N Amer. informal leave abruptly. [Middle English *cupe* basket, from Middle Dutch, Middle Low German *kūpe*, ultimately from Latin *cupa* cask]

co-op noun informal **1** a co-operative business or store. **2** N Amer. a co-operative housing complex. **3** esp. Cdn an educational program in which students alternate terms in the classroom with terms in the workforce in a job related to their studies. [abbreviation]

Coop·er ▶ **1 Gary** (born Frank James Cooper) (1901–61), US actor, who is remembered for his roles in westerns such as *The Virginian* (1929) and *High Noon* (1952); his other films include *Sergeant York* (1940), and *For Whom the Bell Tolls* (1943). **2 James Feni·more** (1789–1851), US novelist. He is renowned for his tales of US Aboriginal peoples and frontier life, including *The Last of the Mohicans* (1826), *The Prairie* (1827), and *The Deerslayer* (1841); he also wrote novels inspired by his early career at sea, as well as historical studies.

coop·er ● noun a maker or repairer of casks, barrels, etc. ● transitive verb make or repair (a cask). [Middle English from Middle Dutch, Middle Low German *kūper* from *kūpe* COOP]

coop·er·age noun **1** the work or establishment of a cooper. **2** money payable for a cooper's work. **3** a place where casks and barrels are made.

co-operate intransitive verb (also **cooperate**) **1** (often foll. by *with*) work or act together, esp. agreeably. **2** (of things) concur in producing an effect. □ **co-operant** adjective **co-operator** noun [ecclesiastical Latin *cooperari* (as CO-, *operari* from *opus operis* work)]

co-operation noun (also **cooperation**) **1** working together to the same end. **2** the formation and operation of co-operatives.

co-operative (also **cooperative**) ● adjective **1** characterized by co-operation, esp. rather than competition; joint (*a co-operative venture*). **2** willing to co-operate. **3** (of a farm, store, or other business, or a society owning such businesses) owned and run jointly by its members, with profits shared among them. **4** N Amer. designating a type of non-profit housing where the housing complex is jointly owned by the occupants, who pay rent on their individual unit to cover costs but cannot sell their unit. ● noun a co-operative farm, society, business, or housing complex. □ **co-operative·ly** adverb **co-operative·ness** noun **co-operativ·ism** noun

Co-operative Commonwealth Federation noun hist. (in Canada) a progressive labour party formed in 1932, re-founded as the New Democratic Party in 1961. Abbr.: **CCF**.

co-operative federalism noun Cdn the policy or practice of the federal government consulting with provincial governments and making joint decisions on matters that are of shared or strictly federal jurisdiction.

Cooper's hawk noun a N American bird of prey, *Accipiter cooperii*, resembling but smaller than the goshawk. [W. *Cooper*, US naturalist d.1864]

Coopers·town a resort village in central New York state, on Otseo Lake, site of the Baseball Hall of Fame.

co-opt transitive verb **1 a** divert to or use in a role different from the usual or original one. **b** take over, adopt (an idea or policy) for one's own use. **2** appoint to membership of a body by invitation of the existing members. □ **co-optation** noun **co-option** noun **co-optive** adjective [Latin *cooptare* (as CO-, *optare* choose)]

co·ordin·ate (also **co-ordin·ate**) ● verb /koːˈɔrdɪˌneɪt/ **1** transitive bring (various parts, movements, activities, etc.) into a proper or required relation to ensure harmony or effective operation etc. **2** intransitive work or act together effectively. **3** transitive make coordinate. ● adjective /koːˈɔrdɪnət/ **1** equal in rank or importance. **2** in which the parts are coordinated; involving coordination. **3** Grammar (of parts of a compound sentence) equal in status. **4** Chem. denoting a type of covalent bond in which one atom provides both the shared electrons. ● noun /koːˈɔrdɪnət/ **1** each of a set of numbers or letters used to fix the position of a point on a map or graph. **2** (in pl.) matching items of clothing. □ **co·ordin·ator** noun [CO- + Latin *ordinare ordinat-* from *ordo -inis* order]

co·ordin·at·ed adjective **1** put together so as to ensure efficient functioning (*a coordinated schedule*). **2** matching (*colour-coordinated pumps*). **3** able to move various parts of the body in harmony; graceful (*Katherine wanted to be a dancer, but she's not very coordinated*).

Coordinated Universal Time noun (also **Universal Time Coordinated**) an atomically measured global standard time, calculated from midnight on the zero meridian, and adjusted by a leap second every time it deviates by that amount from universal time. Coordinated Universal Time replaced the use of Greenwich Mean Time in scientific contexts.

coordinate geometry noun = ANALYTIC GEOMETRY.

co·ordin·at·ing conjunction noun any of a number of conjunctions (*and, or, but, nor, yet, for, so, whereas*) which can join independent clauses.

co·ordin·a·tion noun **1** the harmonious or effective working together of different parts. **2** the arrangement of parts etc. into an effective relation. **3** Chem. the formation of a coordinate bond. **4** the ability to control one's movements properly or effectively, esp. of one part of the body in conjunction with another (*hand-eye coordination*).

coot noun **1** any dark grey or black marsh bird of the genus *Fulica*, e.g. the American coot, *F. americana* or the Eurasian coot, *F. atra*, with the upper mandible extended backwards to form a white plate on the forehead. **2** a scoter. **3** derogatory a stupid person, esp. an elderly person. [Middle English, prob. from Low German]

cootie noun slang **1** a body louse. **2** any of various indeterminate bugs. **3** (esp. in the usage of schoolchildren) germs. [perhaps from Malay *kutu* a biting parasite]

co-own transitive verb own (something) jointly. □ **co-owner** noun **co-owner·ship** noun

cop[1] informal ● noun **1** a police officer. **2** Brit. a capture or arrest (*it's a fair cop*). ● transitive verb (**copped**, **cop·ping**) **1** catch or arrest (an offender). **2** receive, suffer. **3** take, seize, win (*copped three medals*). □ **cop an attitude** N Amer. assume an esp. arrogant posture, attitude, etc. **cop a feel** N Amer. slang fondle someone sexually, esp. surreptitiously or without their permission. **cop a plea** N Amer. plea bargain. **cop it** *Brit.* **1** get into trouble; be punished. **2** be killed. **cop out 1** withdraw; give up an attempt. **2** go back on a promise. **3** escape. **not much** (or **no**) **cop** *Brit.* of little or no value or use. [perhaps from obsolete *cap* arrest, from Old French *caper* seize, from Latin *capere*: (n.) compare COPPER[2]]

cop[2] *noun* (in spinning) a conical ball of thread wound on a spindle. [Old English *cop* summit]

Copa·ca·bana Beach /ˌkoːpəkəˈbanə/ a fashionable resort on the Atlantic coast of Brazil near Rio de Janeiro.

copa·cet·ic /ˌkoːpəˈsetɪk/ *adjective N Amer. slang* excellent; in good order. [20th c.: origin unknown]

copal /ˈkoːpəl/ *noun* a resin from any of various tropical trees, used for varnish. [Spanish from Aztec *copalli* incense]

Copán /koːˈpan/ an ancient Mayan city, in W Honduras near the Guatemalan frontier, which flourished from the 4th to the 10th c. AD. It was the southernmost point of the Mayan Empire.

co-parent *transitive verb* (of a divorced couple or a gay man and a lesbian) share parenting duties for (a child). □ **co-parenting** *noun*

co·partner *noun* a partner or associate, esp. when sharing equally. □ **co·partner·ship** *noun*

co·pay·ment *noun N Amer.* (also **copay**) a payment made by a beneficiary (esp. for health services) in addition to that made by an insurer.

cope[1] *intransitive verb* **1** (foll. by *with*) deal effectively or contend successfully with a person or task. **2** manage successfully; deal with a situation or problem (*found they could no longer cope*). [Old French *coper, colper* from *cop, colp* blow, from medieval Latin *colpus* from Latin *colaphus* from Greek *kolaphos* blow with the fist]

cope[2] ● *noun* **1** *Christianity* a long cloak-like vestment worn by a priest or bishop in ceremonies and processions. **2** esp. *poet.* a covering compared with a cope. ● *transitive verb* cover with a cope or coping. [Middle English, ultimately from Late Latin *cappa* CAP, CAPE[1]]

Copen·hagen /ˈkoːpənˌheigən, -hɒg-, -ˈheig-/ the capital and chief port of Denmark, a city occupying the eastern part of Zealand and northern part of the island of Amager; pop. (1998) 487,969.

co·pepod /ˈkoːpəˌpɒd/ *noun* any small aquatic crustacean of the class Copepoda, many of which form the minute components of plankton. [Greek *kōpē* oar handle + *pous podos* foot]

Copernican system /kəˈpɜrnɪkən/ *noun* (also **Copernican theory**) the theory that the planets (including the earth) move round the sun (*compare* PTOLEMAIC SYSTEM). [COPERNICUS]

Coper·ni·cus /kəˈpɜrnɪkəs/ **Nico·laus** (Latinized name of Mikołaj Kopernik) (1473–1543), Polish astronomer. In his *De Revolutionibus Orbium Coelestium* (1543) he rejected Ptolemy's epicyclic theory of planetary motion, proposing a simpler model in which the planets orbited in perfect circles around the sun; his work ultimately led to the overthrow of the established geocentric cosmology. □ **Coper·ni·can** *adj.*

copi·able *adjective* that can or may be copied.

copi·er *noun* a machine or person that copies (esp. documents).

co-pilot *noun* a second pilot in an aircraft.

cop·ing[1] *noun* the action of dealing with difficult circumstances (also *attributive: coping mechanism*).

cop·ing[2] *noun* the top (usu. sloping) course of masonry in a wall or parapet.

coping saw *noun* a D-shaped saw for cutting curves in wood. [*cope* cut wood, from Old French *coper*: see COPE[1]]

copi·ous /ˈkoːpiəs/ *adjective* abundant, plentiful. □ **copi·ous·ly** *adverb* **copi·ous·ness** *noun* [Old French *copieux* from Latin *copiosus* from *copia* plenty]

co·planar /koːˈpleinər/ *adjective Math.* in the same plane. □ **co·planar·ity** /-pləˈnerɪti/ *noun*

Cop·land /ˈkoːplənd/ **Aaron** (1900–90), US composer, pianist, and conductor, who sought to establish a distinctive American style in music, borrowing from jazz in his *Music for the Theater* (1925), from Shaker music in *Appalachian Spring* (1944), and from other folk and traditional songs in the ballet score *Rodeo* (1942).

Cop·ley /ˈkɒpli/ **John Single·ton** (1738–1815), US painter. A distinguished colonial portraitist, he settled in England in 1775, and made his mark with such large-scale historical paintings as *The Death of Chatham* (1779–80).

co·polymer /koːˈpɒlɪmər/ *noun Chem.* a polymer with units of more than one kind. □ **co·polymer·ize** *transitive & intransitive verb* (also esp. *Brit.* **-ise**).

cop-out *noun* a cowardly or feeble evasion.

cop·per[1] ● *noun* **1** *Chem.* a malleable red-brown metallic element of the transition series occurring naturally esp. in cuprite and malachite, and used esp. as an electrical conductor and in alloys. Symbol: **Cu**; at. no.: 29. **2** a copper or bronze coin, esp. a penny. **3** *Brit.* a large metal vessel for boiling esp. laundry. **4** any of various butterflies with copper-coloured wings. ● *adjective* made of or coloured like copper. ● *transitive verb* cover (a ship's bottom, a pan, etc.) with copper. [Old English *copor, coper*, ultimately from Latin *cyprium aes* Cyprus metal]

cop·per[2] *noun slang* a police officer. [COP[1] + -ER[1]]

cop·peras /ˈkɒpərəs/ *noun* green crystals of hydrated ferrous sulphate, esp. as an industrial product. [Middle English *coperose* from Old French *couperose* from medieval Latin *cup(e)rosa*: perhaps originally *aqua cuprosa* copper water]

copper beech *noun* a variety of beech with copper-coloured leaves.

Copper·belt, the a mining region of central Zambia with rich deposits of copper, cobalt, and uranium; chief town, Ndola.

copper-bottomed *adjective* **1** having a bottom sheathed with copper (esp. of a ship or pan). **2** genuine or reliable (esp. financially).

copper·head *noun* **1** a venomous but rarely fatal viper, *Agkistrodon contortrix*, native to N America. **2** a venomous cobra, *Denisonia superba*, native to Australia.

Copper Inuit *plural noun* an Inuit people living along the Coppermine River in Nunavut. [named for the native copper found in their area]

Copper·mine the former name for KUGLUKTUK.

Coppermine River a river in eastern NWT and northwestern Nunavut, 845 km long, flowing northwestward through the hamlet of Kugluktuk, where it empties into Coronation Gulf. [so called because of the presence of copper along its banks]

copper·plate ● *noun* **1 a** a polished copper plate for engraving or etching. **b** a print made from this. **2** an ornate style of handwriting resembling that originally used in engravings. ● *adjective* of or in copperplate writing.

copper pyrites *noun* a double sulphide of copper and iron. *Also called* CHALCOPYRITE.

copper·smith *noun* a person who works in copper.

copper sulphate *noun* a blue crystalline solid used in electroplating, textile dyeing, etc.

cop·pery *adjective* of or like copper, esp. in colour.

cop·pice /ˈkɒpɪs/ esp. *Brit.* ● *noun* an area of undergrowth and small trees, grown for periodic cutting. ● *transitive verb* cut back (young trees) periodically to stimulate growth of shoots. □ **cop·piced** *adjective* [Old French *copeiz*, ultimately from medieval Latin *colpus* blow: see COPE[1]]

Cop·pola /ˈkɒpələ/ **Fran·cis Ford** (b.1939), US film director, writer, and producer, whose reputation was established with *The Godfather* (1972) and its two sequels (1974 and 1990); other notable films include *Apocalypse Now* (1979).

copra /ˈkɒprə/ *noun* the dried kernels of the coconut. [Portuguese from Malayalam *koppara* coconut]

copro- /ˈkɒproː/ *combining form* dung, feces. [Greek *kopros* dung]

co·proces·sor *noun Computing* a microprocessor providing additional functions to supplement a primary processor.

co-produce *transitive verb* produce (a play, film, broadcast, etc.) jointly with another producer. □ **co-producer** *noun* **co-produc·tion** *noun* **co-product** *noun*

copro·lite /ˈkɒprəˌlaɪt/ *noun Archaeology* fossil dung or a piece of it.

cop·roph·agy /kəˈprɒfədʒi/ *noun Zool.* the eating of dung. □ **cop·roph·a·gous** *adjective*

copro·philia /ˌkɒprəˈfɪliə/ *noun* an abnormal interest in feces and defecation.

cops and robbers *noun* a children's game in which the participants stalk, chase, and pretend to shoot each other, impersonating police officers and criminals.

copse *noun* a small wood or thicket. □ **copsy** *adjective* [shortened from COPPICE]

cop shop *noun informal* a police station.

Copt *noun* **1** a native Egyptian in the Hellenic and Roman periods. **2** a Christian of the Coptic Church. [French *Copte* or modern Latin *Coptus* from Arabic *al-ḳibṭ, al-ḳubṭ* Copts, from Coptic *Gyptios* from Greek *Aiguptios* Egyptian]

cop·ter *noun* a helicopter. [abbreviation]

Cop·tic ● *noun* the language of the Copts, now used only in the Coptic Church. ● *adjective* of or relating to the Copts.

Coptic Church *noun* the native Christian Church of Egypt, isolated from the rest of Christendom since 451 when it maintained the Monophysite doctrine condemned by the Council of Chalcedon.

cop·u·la /ˈkɒpjʊlə/ *noun* (*pl.* **cop·u·las**) *Logic & Grammar* a connecting word, esp. parts of the verbs *be*, *seem*, *look*, etc., connecting a subject and predicate. □ **cop·u·lar** *adjective* [Latin (as CO-, *apere* fasten)]

cop·u·late /ˈkɒpjʊˌleɪt/ *intransitive verb* (often foll. by *with*) have sexual intercourse. □ **cop·u·la·tory** *adjective* [Latin *copulare* fasten together (as COPULA)]

cop·u·la·tion /ˌkɒpjʊˈleɪʃən/ *noun* **1** sexual union. **2** a grammatical or logical connection.

cop·u·la·tive /ˈkɒpjʊlətɪv/ *adjective* **1** serving to connect. **2** *Grammar* **a** (of a word) that connects words or clauses linked in sense (compare DISJUNCTIVE *adjective* 2). **b** connecting a subject and predicate. **3** relating to sexual union.

copy ● *noun* (*pl.* **-ies**) **1** a thing made to imitate or be identical to another. **2** a single specimen of a publication or issue (*ordered twenty copies*). **3 a** a matter to be printed. **b** material for a newspaper or magazine article (*scandals make good copy*). **c** the text of an advertisement. **4 a** a model to be copied. **b** a page written after a model (of penmanship). ● *verb* (**-ies, -ied**) **1** *transitive* **a** make a copy of. **b** (often foll. by *out*) transcribe. **2** *intransitive* make a copy, esp. clandestinely. **3** *transitive* (foll. by *to*) send a copy of (a letter) to a third party. **4** *transitive* do the same as; imitate. **5** *intransitive* *Cdn* (*Nfld*) jump from one ice floe to the next in a game of follow-the-leader. [Old French *copie, copier*, ultimately from Latin *copia* abundance (in medieval Latin = transcript)]

copy·book *noun* **1** a book containing models of handwriting for learners to imitate. **2** (*attributive*) **a** tritely conventional. **b** accurate, exemplary.

copy·cat *noun* *informal* a person who copies another, esp. slavishly (often *attrib*: *copycat remark*).

copy desk *noun* the desk at which copy is edited for printing.

copy-edit *transitive verb* edit (copy) for printing.

copy editor *noun* a person who edits copy for printing, esp. to correct grammatical, stylistic, or punctuation errors.

copy·ist *noun* **1** a person who makes (esp. written) copies. **2** an imitator.

copy protection *noun* *Computing* a system intended to prevent software from being copied. □ **copy protected** *adjective*

copy·read·er *noun* a person who reads and edits copy for a newspaper or book. □ **copy·read** *transitive verb*

copy·right ● *noun* the exclusive legal right granted for a specified period to an author, designer, etc., or another appointed person, to print, publish, perform, film, or record original literary, artistic, or musical material. ● *adjective* (of such material) protected by copyright. ● *transitive verb* secure copyright for (material). □ **copy·right·able** *adjective*

copy shop *noun* a shop offering photocopying and other related services.

copy·writer *noun* a person who writes or prepares copy (esp. of advertising material) for publication. □ **copy·writ·ing** *noun*

coq au vin /ˌkɒk oː ˈvã/ *noun* a stew of chicken pieces cooked in red wine with mushrooms, onions, bacon, and carrots. [French]

co·quet·ry /ˈkoːkɪtrɪ/ *noun* (*pl.* **-ries**) **1** coquettish behaviour. **2** a coquettish act. [French *coquetterie* from *coqueter* (as COQUETTE)]

co·quette /koːˈket/ *noun* a woman who flirts. □ **co·quet·tish** *adjective* **co·quet·tish·ly** *adverb* **co·quet·tish·ness** *noun* [French, fem. of *coquet* wanton, diminutive of *coq* cock]

co·quilles St. Jacques /kɒˈkiːˈsãˌzak/ *plural noun* a dish of scallops in a sauce of white wine and cream, usu. served in a scallop shell. [French, = scallop, lit. 'St. James's shell', in reference to the shells being worn by pilgrims to the shrine of Santiago de Compostela]

co·quina /koːˈkiːnə/ *noun* *N Amer.* a soft limestone of broken shells, used in road building. [Spanish, = cockle]

Co·quit·lam /kəˈkwɪtləm/ a district municipality in southwestern BC, situated on the north side of the Fraser River, east of Vancouver; pop. (2001) 112,890. □ **Co·quit·lam·ite** *noun* [after the *Coquitlam*, a Sne Nay Muxw band whose name means 'stinking with fish slime']

co·quito /koːˈkiːtoː/ *noun* (*pl.* **-quitos**) a palm tree, *Jubaea chilensis*, native to Chile, yielding honey from its sap, and fibre. [Spanish, diminutive of *coco* coconut]

Cor. *abbreviation* Corinthians (New Testament).

cor *interjection* *Brit. slang* expressing surprise, alarm, exasperation, etc. □ **cor blimey** *see* BLIMEY. [corruption of *God*]

cor- *prefix* assimilated form of COM- before *r*.

cor·acle /ˈkɒrəkəl, kɒ-/ *noun* *Brit.* a small boat of wickerwork covered with watertight material, used on Welsh and Irish lakes and rivers. [Welsh *corwgl* (*corwg* = Irish *currach* boat: compare CURRACH)]

cora·coid /ˈkɒrəˌkɔɪd, kɒ-/ *noun* (in full **coracoid process**) a short projection from the shoulder blade in vertebrates. [modern Latin *coracoides* from Greek *korakoeidēs* raven-like, from *korax -akos* raven]

coral /ˈkɒrəl, kɒ-/ ● *noun* **1 a** a hard calcareous substance secreted by various marine polyps for support and habitation, and occurring in both single specimens and vast accumulations. **b** any of these usu. colonial organisms. **2** the unfertilized roe of a lobster or scallop, which is used as food and becomes reddish when cooked. **3** a reddish-pink colour. ● *adjective* **1** of a reddish-pink colour. **2** made of coral. [Old French from Latin *corallum* from Greek *korallion*, prob. of Semitic origin]

coral·bells *noun* a herbaceous plant of the saxifrage family, *Heuchera sanguinea*, which has small pink bell-shaped flowers.

coral·berry *noun* (*pl.* **-berries**) a N American shrub, *Symphoricarpos orbiculata*, of the honeysuckle family, with deep red berries.

coral·line /ˈkɒrəˌlaɪn, kɒ-/ ● *noun* **1** any seaweed of the genus *Corallina* having a calcareous jointed stem. **2** (in general use) the name of various plantlike compound organisms. ● *adjective* **1** coral-red. **2** of or like coral. [French *corallin* & Italian *corallina* from Late Latin *corallinus* (as CORAL)]

coral·lite /ˈkɒrəˌlaɪt, kɒ-/ *noun* **1** the coral skeleton of a marine polyp. **2** fossil coral. [Latin *corallum* CORAL]

coral·loid /ˈkɒrəˌlɔɪd, kɒ-/ ● *adjective* like or akin to coral. ● *noun* a coralloid organism.

coral reef *noun* (also **coral island**) a reef (or island) formed by the growth of coral.

coral root *noun* **1** a woodland plant, *Cardamine* or *Dentaria bulbifera* (family Cruciferae), with purple flowers and scaly rhizomes. **2** (in full **coral root orchid**) a brown saprophytic orchid of the genus *Corallorhiza*.

Coral Sea a part of the W Pacific lying between Australia, New Guinea, and Vanuatu. It was the scene of a naval battle between US and Japanese carriers in 1942, in which the US forestalled Japanese moves against Port Moresby and the Solomon Islands.

coral snake *noun* any of various brightly coloured poisonous snakes.

cor an·glais /kɔr ˈɒŋgleɪ, ãˈgleɪ/ *noun* (*pl.* **cors an·glais** *pronunc.* same) *Music* **1** an alto woodwind instrument of the oboe family. **2** a player of this. [French, = English horn]

cor·bel /ˈkɔrbəl/ *Archit.* ● *noun* **1** a projection of stone, timber, etc., jutting out from a wall to support a weight. **2** a short timber laid longitudinally under a beam to help support it. ● *transitive & intransitive verb* (**cor·belled, cor·bel·ling**; esp. *US* **cor·beled, cor·bel·ing**) (foll. by *out, off*) support or project on corbels. [Old French, diminutive of *corp*: see CORBIE]

cor·bie /ˈkɔrbɪ/ *noun* *Scot.* **1** a raven. **2** a carrion crow. [Old French *corb, corp* from Latin *corvus* crow]

corbie steps *plural noun* the step-like projections on the sloping sides of a gable.

Cor·co·vado /ˌkɔrkəˈvɒdoː/ a peak rising to 711 m (2,310 ft.) on the south side of Rio de Janeiro. A gigantic statue of Christ, 40 m (131 ft.) high, named 'Christ the Redeemer', stands on its summit.

Cor·cyra /kɔrˈsaɪrə/ the ancient Greek name for CORFU.

cord ● *noun* **1 a** long thin flexible material made from several twisted strands, esp. thicker than string and finer than rope. **b** a piece of this. **2** *Anat.* a structure in the body resembling a cord (*spinal cord*). **3 a** a ribbed fabric, esp. corduroy. **b** (in *pl.*) corduroy pants. **c** a cordlike rib on fabric. **4** an insulated electric cable bringing power to appliances etc. **5** a measure of cut wood (usu. 128 cu. ft., 3.6 cubic metres). ● *transitive verb* fasten or bind with cord. □ **cord·like** *adjective* [Old French *corde* from Latin *chorda* from Greek *khordē* gut, string of musical instrument]

cord·age *noun* cords or ropes, esp. in the rigging of a ship.

cor·date /ˈkɔrdeɪt/ *adjective* heart-shaped. [modern Latin *cordatus* from Latin *cor cordis* heart]

Cor·day /kɔrˈdeɪ/ **Char·lotte** (full name Marie Anne Charlotte Corday d'Armont) (1768–93), French noblewoman, a supporter of the Girondin party, who assassinated the revolutionary leader Marat in his bath (1793), and was subsequently guillotined.

corded *adjective* **1** (of cloth) ribbed. **2** provided with cords. **3** (of muscles) standing out like taut cords.

cord·grass *noun* = SPARTINA.

cor·dial /ˈkɔrdʒəl, -diəl/ ● *adjective* **1** heartfelt, sincere. **2** warm, friendly. ● *noun* **1** a fruit-flavoured drink. **2** a comforting or pleasant-tasting medicine. □ **cor·di·al·i·ty** /kɔrdiˈaliti/ *noun* **cor·dial·ly** *adverb* [medieval Latin *cordialis* from Latin *cor cordis* heart]

cor·dil·lera /kɔrˈdɪlərə, ˌkɔrdɪˈlerə/ *noun* a system or group of usu. parallel mountain ranges together with intervening plateaux etc., esp. as a major continental feature. □ **cor·dil·ler·an** *adjective* [Spanish from *cordilla* diminutive of *cuerda* CORD]

Cor·dil·leran Region /kɔrˈdɪlərən, ˌkɔrdɪˈljerən/ a physiographic region of W Canada comprising most of BC and Yukon Territory, as well as SW Alberta and the western part of the NWT. It is part of a mountain system extending along the Pacific coast to S America. [CORDILLERA + -AN]

cord·ing *noun* cords collectively.

cord·ite *noun* a smokeless explosive made from nitrocellulose and nitroglycerine. [CORD (from its appearance) + -ITE¹]

cord·less *adjective* (of an electrical appliance, telephone, etc.) working from an internal source of energy etc. (esp. a rechargeable battery).

Cor·doba /ˈkɔrdəbə/ (also **Cor·dova** /-dəvə/) **1** a city in Andalusia, S Spain; pop. (est. 2001) 314,034. As capital of the most powerful of the Arab states in Spain, it was a centre of learning and culture, earning the title of 'the Athens of the West', and was renowned for its architecture, particularly the Great Mosque. **2** a city in central Argentina; pop. (est. 2001) 1,275,585.

cor·doba oro /ˈkɔrdəbə/ *noun* the basic monetary unit of Nicaragua, equal to 100 centavos. [F. de *Córdoba* (fl. 1524), Spanish governor of Nicaragua]

cor·don /ˈkɔrdən/ ● *noun* **1** a line or circle of police, soldiers, guards, etc., esp. preventing access to or from an area. **2 a** an ornamental cord or braid. **b** the ribbon of a knightly order. **3** a fruit tree trained to grow as a single stem. **4** *Archit.* a stringcourse. ● *transitive verb* (often foll. by *off*) enclose or separate with a rope, a cordon of police etc. [Italian *cordone* augmentative of *corda* CORD, & French *cordon* (as CORD)]

cor·don bleu /ˌkɔrdɒn ˈblu, ˌkɔrdɔ̃/ *Cooking* ● *adjective* **1** of the highest class. **2** designating a type of chicken or veal dish consisting of a cutlet of meat stuffed with ham and Swiss cheese, breaded and shallow fried. ● *noun* a cordon bleu cook. [French, = blue ribbon]

cor·don sani·taire /ˌkɔrdɒn ˌsanɪˈter/ *noun* **1** a guarded line surrounding an area infected by disease. **2** any measure designed to prevent communication or the spread of undesirable influences. [French]

cor·do·van /ˈkɔrdəvən/ *noun* a kind of soft leather made originally from goatskin and now from horsehide. [Spanish *cordovan* of Cordova (Cordoba) where it was originally made]

Cor·dura /kɔrˈdʊrə/ *noun proprietary* a tough nylon used in bags, boots, etc.

cor·du·roy /ˈkɔrdəˌrɔɪ/ *noun* **1** a thick cotton fabric with velvety ribs. **2** (in *pl.*) corduroy pants. [18th c.: prob. from CORD ribbed fabric + obsolete *duroy* coarse woollen fabric]

corduroy road *noun* esp. *hist.* a road made of tree trunks laid across muddy or swampy ground.

cord·wood *noun* wood that is or can easily be measured in cords.

-core *combining form* designating types of usu. abrasive popular music (*grindcore*).

core ● *noun* **1** the hard central part of various fruits, containing the seeds. **2** (often *attributive*) the central or most important part of anything (*the city core; core curriculum*). **3** the central part of the earth, esp. that within the mantle, with a radius of 3 500 km (2,200 miles). **4** (in full **core lanes**) *Cdn* the express lanes on a highway, usu. separated by a guardrail from the collector lanes. **5** the central part of a nuclear reactor, containing the fissile material. **6** the inner strand of an electric cable, rope, etc. **7** a piece of soft iron forming the centre of an electromagnet or an induction coil. **8** an internal mould filling a space to be left hollow in a casting. **9** the central part cut out (esp. of rock etc. in boring). **10** *Archaeology* a piece of flint from which flakes or blades have been removed. ● *transitive verb* remove the core from. □ **corer** *noun* [Middle English: origin unknown]

core French *noun Cdn* a program of French-as-a-second-language instruction in English-speaking schools consisting of a few periods of study each week, as opposed to French immersion.

co-religion·ist *noun* an adherent of the same religion.

cor·ella /kəˈrelə/ *noun* either of two small Australian cockatoos of the genus *Cacatua* with pink-tinged white plumage and blue skin around the eye. [Wiradhuri]

Cor·elli /kəˈreli/ **Arc·angelo** (1653–1713), Italian violinist and composer, best known for his concerti grossi (published posthumously in 1714), and his trio and solo sonatas for the violin; his work influenced Purcell, Bach, and Handel.

core·op·sis /ˌkɔriˈɒpsɪs, kɒ-/ *noun* (*pl.* same) any composite plant of the genus *Coreopsis*, having rayed usu. yellow flowers. [modern Latin from Greek *koris* bug + *opsis* appearance, with reference to the shape of the seed]

co-respond·ent /ˌkɔrɪˈspɒndənt/ *noun* a person cited in a divorce case as having committed adultery with the respondent.

Corfu /kɔrˈfuː/ a Greek island, one of the largest of the Ionian Islands, off the west coast of mainland Greece. It was known in ancient times as Corcyra.

corgi /ˈkɔrgi/ *noun* (*pl.* **corgis**) (in full **Welsh corgi**) a short-legged breed of dog with a foxlike head. [Welsh from *cor* dwarf + *ci* dog]

cori·aceous /ˌkɔriˈeɪʃəs/ *adjective* like leather; leathery. [Late Latin *coriaceus* from *corium* leather]

Cor·ian /ˈkɔriˌan/ *noun proprietary* a composite material which looks like marble and can be moulded for use in countertops, vanity tops, etc.

cori·an·der /ˌkɔriˈandər/ *noun* **1** a plant, *Coriandrum sativum*, with leaves used for flavouring and small round aromatic fruits. **2** (also **coriander seed**) the dried fruit used for flavouring curries etc. [Old French *coriandre* from Latin *coriandrum* from Greek *koriannon*]

Cor·inth /ˈkɔrɪnθ/ a city on the north coast of the Peloponnese, Greece; pop. (est. 2002) 32,900. The modern city, built in 1858, is a little to the northeast of the site of an ancient city of the same name, which was a prominent city state in ancient Greece and is associated with the teaching of St. Paul.

Corinth, Gulf of (also called **Gulf of Lepanto**) an inlet of the Ionian Sea extending between the Peloponnese and central Greece.

Corinth, Isthmus of a narrow neck of land linking the Peloponnese with central Greece and separating the Gulf of Corinth from the Saronic Gulf.

Corinth Canal an artificial shipping channel across the narrowest part of the isthmus of Corinth (a distance of 6.4 km, or 4 miles). Opened in 1893, it links the Gulf of Corinth and the Saronic Gulf.

Cor·inth·ian /kəˈrɪnθiən/ ● *adjective* **1** of ancient Corinth in S Greece. **2** *Archit.* of an order characterized by ornate decoration and flared capitals with rows of acanthus leaves. ● *noun* a native of Corinth.

Cor·inth·ians /kəˈrɪnθiənz/ either of two books of the New Testament, epistles of St. Paul to the Church at Corinth.

Corio·lanus /ˌkɔriəˈleɪnəs/ **Gaius** (or **Gnaeus**) **Mar·cius** (5th c. BC), Roman general. According to legend, he led a Volscian army against Rome in 491 BC, and was turned back only by the pleas of his mother Veturia and his wife Volumnia; he was subsequently put to death by the Volscians.

Cori·olis effect /ˌkɔriˈoːlɪs/ *noun* an effect whereby a mass moving in a rotating system experiences a force (the **Coriolis force**) acting perpendicular to the direction of motion and to the axis of rotation. On the earth, the effect tends to deflect moving objects to the right in the northern hemisphere and to the left in the southern hemisphere and is important in the formation of cyclonic weather systems. [G. G. *Coriolis*, French scientist d.1843]

cor·ium /ˈkɔriəm/ *noun Anat.* the dermis. [Latin, = skin]

Cork 1 a county of the Republic of Ireland, on the south coast in the province of Munster. **2** its county town, a port on the Lee River; pop. (est. 2002) 187,600.

cork ● *noun* **1** the buoyant light brown bark of the cork oak. **2** a bottle stopper of cork or other material. **3** a float of cork used in fishing etc. **4** *Bot.* a protective layer of dead cells immediately below the bark of woody plants. **5** (*attributive*) made of cork. ● *transitive verb* (often foll. by *up*) **1** stop or confine. **2** restrain (feelings etc.). **3** *Baseball* hollow out and fill (a bat) with cork illicitly to make it lighter. **4** blacken with burnt cork. □ **put a cork in it** *slang* shut up; be quiet. □ **cork·like** *adjective* [Dutch & Low German *kork* from Spanish *alcorque* cork sole, perhaps from Arabic]

cork·age *noun* a charge made by a restaurant or hotel for serving wine etc. when brought in by customers.

cork·board *noun N Amer.* **1** board made of compressed cork. **2** a piece of this on which bulletins etc. are posted.

cork boot *noun Cdn* (BC) a logger's boot with spiked soles. [pronunciation spelling of CAULK²]

uː mood   ai my   əi pipe   au brown   ʌu house   ei day   ɔi boy   ɑ̃ franglais   ã Canadien   ɔ̃ Brayon   (*see over for consonants*)

corked *adjective* **1** stopped with a cork. **2** (of wine) spoiled by a decayed cork. **3** blackened with burnt cork.

cork·er *noun informal* **1** an excellent or astonishing person or thing. **2** something that puts an end to a discussion etc.

cork·ing *adjective informal* strikingly impressive or excellent.

cork oak *noun* a S European oak, *Quercus suber*, from which cork is obtained.

cork·screw ● *noun* **1** a spirally twisted steel device for extracting corks from bottles. **2** (often *attributive*) a thing with a spiral shape. ● *transitive & intransitive verb* move spirally; twist.

cork·wood *noun* **1** any of various trees or shrubs yielding a light porous wood, e.g. *Leitneria floridana* of the southeastern US. **2** this wood.

corky *adjective* (**cork·i·er, cork·i·est**) **1** corklike. **2** (of wine) corked.

corm *noun* an underground swollen stem base of some plants, e.g. gladiolus. [modern Latin *cormus* from Greek *kormos* trunk with boughs lopped off]

Cor·mier /'kɔrmiːeɪ/ **Er·nest** (1885–1980), Canadian engineer and architect. His works display a fusion of classicism and modernism, and include the neoclassical Palais de Justice in Montreal (1922–6), the main pavilion of the Université de Montréal (1928–43), planned on beaux-arts principles, and the Supreme Court of Canada (1938–9).

cor·mor·ant /'kɔrmərənt/ *noun* any diving, fish-eating water bird of the family Phalacrocoracidae, having lustrous black plumage. [Old French *cormaran* from medieval Latin *corvus marinus* sea crow: for ending *-ant* compare *peasant, tyrant*]

corn¹ ● *noun* **1 a** a cereal plant, *Zea mays*, native to N America, yielding large, edible, usu. yellow grains set in rows on a cob. *Also called* (esp. *Brit.*) MAIZE. **b** the cob or grains of this. **2 a** any cereal before or after harvesting, esp. the chief crop of a region: maize in N America, wheat in England, oats in Scotland. **b** a grain or seed of a cereal plant. **3** *informal* something corny or trite. ● *transitive verb* preserve (meat) with brine. [Old English from Germanic: related to Latin *granum* grain]

corn² *noun* a small area of horny usu. tender skin esp. on the toes, extending into subcutaneous tissue. [Anglo-French from Latin *cornu* horn]

corn·ball *adjective* N Amer. = CORNY 1.

corn belt *noun* (also **Corn Belt**) the major corn growing area of esp. the US (including Indiana, Iowa, and Illinois).

corn boil *noun* N Amer. a social gathering at which corn on the cob is boiled and eaten.

corn·bread *noun* bread, esp. a quick bread, made from cornmeal.

corn broom *noun* Curling a straw broom.

corn chip *noun* N Amer. = TORTILLA CHIP.

corn·cob *noun* the cylindrical centre of an ear of corn, to which rows of grains are attached.

corncob pipe *noun* a tobacco pipe with a bowl made from a hollowed-out corncob.

corn cockle *noun* see COCKLE² 1.

corn·crake *noun* a slender European brown bird of the rail family, *Crex crex*, which has a harsh grating cry and lives in grassland.

corn·crib *noun* a ventilated building for storing ears of corn.

corn dog *noun* N Amer. a cornmeal-covered hot dog fried (or baked) and served on a stick, esp. at fairs etc.

corn dolly *noun* a symbolic or decorative figure made of braided straw.

cor·nea /'kɔrniə/ *noun* the transparent circular part of the front of the eyeball. □ **cor·neal** *adjective* [medieval Latin *cornea tela* horny tissue, from Latin *corneus* horny, from *cornu* horn]

corn ear·worm *noun* **1** a moth, *Heliothis armigera* or *H. zea*, whose larvae are a major pest of cultivated plants, esp. of corn in N America. **2** a larva of this moth.

corned beef *noun* **1** N Amer. beef brisket cured in brine and boiled, often served cold. **2** Brit. low quality beef preserved in brine and saltpetre, chopped and pressed and packaged in tins.

Cor·neille /kɔr'neɪ/ **Pierre** (1606–84), French dramatist, who is generally regarded as the creator of classical French tragedy; his plays include *Le Cid* (1637), *Cinna* (1641), and *Polyeucte* (1643), as well as comedies such as *Mélite* (1629) and *Le Menteur* (1642).

cor·nel /'kɔrnəl/ *noun* = DOGWOOD 1. [Middle English from Latin *cornus*]

cor·nel·ian *var. of* CARNELIAN.

cornelian cherry *noun* a dogwood, *Cornus mas*, with small, yellow flowers and red fruit, frequently planted as an ornamental. [CORNEL + -IAN]

Cor·nell /kɔr'nel/ **Ezra** (1807–1874), US businessman and philanthropist, who formed the Western Union Telegraph Company (1855), and helped to found Cornell University (1865).

cor·ner ● *noun* **1** a place where converging sides or edges meet. **2** a projecting angle, esp. where two streets meet. **3** the internal space or recess formed by the meeting of two sides, esp. of a room. **4** a difficult position, esp. one from which there is no escape (*driven into a corner*). **5** a secluded or remote place. **6** a region or quarter, esp. a remote one (*from the four corners of the earth*). **7** the action or result of buying or controlling the whole available stock of a commodity, thereby dominating the market. **8** Boxing & Wrestling **a** an angle of the ring, esp. one where a contestant rests between rounds. **b** a contestant's supporters offering assistance at the corner between rounds. **9** (also called **corner kick**) Soccer a free kick from a corner of the field after the ball has been kicked over the goal line by a defending player. ● *verb* **1** *transitive* force (a person or animal) into a difficult or inescapable position. **2** *transitive* **a** establish a corner in (a commodity). **b** dominate (dealers or the market) in this way. **3** *intransitive* (esp. of or in a vehicle) go around a corner. □ **in a person's corner** esp. N Amer. supporting a person. **just around the corner** informal very near, imminent. **turn a** (or **the**) **corner** pass from one situation to another, particularly making a decisive change for the better. [Anglo-French, ultimately from Latin *cornu* horn]

corner·back *noun* Football a defensive player or position covering the sideline behind the line of scrimmage.

Corner Brook a city in west central Newfoundland, situated at the mouth of the Humber River, where it empties into an inlet of the Bay of Islands; pop. (2001) 20,103. □ **Corner Brook·er** *noun* [the name of the brook, prob. with reference to the way it turns sharply at its mouth]

corner office *noun* an office in one of the corners of an office building, esp. considered the most prestigious and reserved for the most important employee.

corner·stone *noun* **1 a** a stone in a projecting angle of a wall. **b** a foundation stone. **2** an indispensable part or basis of something.

corner store *noun* a small local convenience store, esp. at a street corner.

cor·net¹ /kɔr'net/ *noun* **1** Music **a** a brass instrument resembling a trumpet but shorter and wider. **b** its player. **c** an organ stop with the quality of a cornet. **d** a cornetto. **2** Brit. an ice cream cone. □ **cor·net·ist** *noun* (also **cor·net·tist**). [Old French, ultimately from Latin *cornu* horn]

cor·net² /'kɔrnət/ *noun* Brit. hist. the fifth commissioned officer in a cavalry troop, who carried the colours. □ **cornet·cy** *noun* (pl. **-cies**) [earlier sense 'pennon, standard' from French *cornette* diminutive of *corne*, ultimately from Latin *cornua* horns]

corn-fed *adjective* **1** fed on corn. **2** plump; well-fed. **3** esp. US informal unsophisticated.

corn·field *noun* a field in which corn is being grown.

corn·flake *noun* (also **corn flake**) **1** (in *pl.*) a breakfast cereal of toasted flakes made from ground corn. **2** a flake of this cereal.

corn flour *noun* **1** flour made from corn. **2** (**corn·flour**) Brit. = CORNSTARCH.

corn·flower *noun* any herbaceous plant of the genus *Centaurea*, esp. *C. cyanus*, with deep-blue flowers.

cor·nice /'kɔrnɪs/ *noun* **1** Archit. **a** an ornamental moulding round the wall of a room just below the ceiling. **b** a horizontal moulded projection crowning a building or structure, esp. the uppermost member of the entablature of an order, surmounting the frieze. **2** Mountaineering an overhanging mass of hardened snow at the edge of a precipice. □ **cor·niced** *adjective* [French *corniche* etc. from Italian *cornice*, perhaps from Latin *cornix -icis* crow]

cor·niche /'kɔrnɪʃ, kɔr'niːʃ/ *noun* (in full **corniche road**) **1** a road cut into the edge of a cliff etc. **2** a coastal road with wide views. [French: see CORNICE]

cor·ni·chon /'kɔrniʃɔ̃/ *noun* a tiny pickled cucumber. [French = pickled cucumber, diminutive of *corne* 'horn']

Cor·nish ● *adjective* of or relating to Cornwall in SW England. ● *noun* **1** the ancient Celtic language of Cornwall. **2** a small, heavy, English breed of chicken used primarily in crossbreeding to produce roasting chickens.

Cornish hen *noun* (also **Cornish game hen**) = ROCK CORNISH.

Cornish pasty *noun* seasoned meat and vegetables baked in a pastry envelope.

Corn Laws various 19th-century laws introduced in an attempt to maintain the prosperity enjoyed by British agriculture during the Napoleonic Wars, but which tended to force bread prices so high that both consumer and producer suffered. After mounting opposition, the Corn Laws were repealed in 1846.

corn lily *noun see* CLINTONIA.

corn·meal *noun* meal made from corn.

corn on the cob *noun* corn cooked and eaten from the corncob.

corn pone *noun US* **1** a simple cornbread. **2** *derogatory* (usu. *attributive*) denoting something rustic or unsophisticated; hick, hillbilly (*a corn-pone enterprise*).

corn roast *noun N Amer.* a party at which corn on the cob is cooked and eaten.

corn·row ● *noun* (usu. in *pl.*) each of a series of small tight braids made close to the head. ● *transitive verb* arrange (hair) in cornrows.

corn salad *noun* = LAMB'S LETTUCE.

corn·silk *noun* (also **corn silk**) the fine threadlike styles on an ear of corn.

corn snow *noun Skiing* a soft surface layer of coarse granular snow, formed during cold nights after warm days.

corn·stalk *noun N Amer.* the stalk of a corn plant.

corn·starch *noun esp. N Amer.* purified starch from corn, a fine white flour used as a thickener and also as an absorbent powder.

corn syrup *noun N Amer.* glucose syrup, esp. when made from corn flour.

cor·nu·co·pia /ˌkɔːnjʊˈkɔːpiə/ *noun* **1 a** a symbol of plenty consisting of a goat's horn overflowing with flowers, fruit, and grain. **b** an ornamental vessel shaped like this. **2** an abundant supply. □ **cor·nu·co·pian** *adjective* [Late Latin from Latin *cornu copiae* horn of plenty]

Corn·wall 1 an industrial city in SE Ontario, situated on the St. Lawrence, about 100 km southwest of Montreal; pop. (2001) 45,640. **2** a county occupying the extreme southwestern peninsula of England; county town, Truro. [sense 1 after Duke of *Cornwall*, George III's eldest son d.1830]

Corn·wal·lis /kɔːnˈwɒlɪs/ **1 Charles, 1st Marquess and 2nd Earl** (1738–1805), English general, whose forces were defeated at Yorktown, Virginia (1781) during the American Revolution; he later served as Governor General of India (1786–93, 1805) and viceroy of Ireland (1798–1801). **2 Ed·ward** (*c.*1712–76), English army officer and colonial administrator, governor of Nova Scotia 1749–52. He founded the settlement of Halifax (1749) and made it the capital of Nova Scotia.

Cornwallis Island one of the Parry Islands in the Canadian High Arctic, situated between Bathurst and Devon islands. [Sir W. *Cornwallis*, British admiral d.1819]

Cornwall Island /ˈkɔːnwɒl/ one of the Sverdrup Islands in the Canadian High Arctic, situated south of Amund Ringnes Island. [Edward, Prince of Wales and Duke of *Cornwall*]

corny *adjective* (**corn·i·er**, **corn·i·est**) **1** *informal* **a** trite. **b** feebly humorous. **c** sentimental. **d** old-fashioned; out of date. **2** of or abounding in corn. □ **corn·i·ly** *adverb* **corn·i·ness** *noun* [CORN¹ + -Y¹: sense 1 from sense 'rustic']

cor·olla /kəˈrɒlə, -rɔːlə/ *noun Bot.* a whorl or whorls of petals forming the inner envelope of a flower. [Latin, diminutive of *corona* crown]

cor·ol·lary /kəˈrɒləri/ ● *noun* (*pl.* **-ies**) **1 a** a proposition that follows from (and is often appended to) one already proved. **b** an immediate deduction. **2** (often foll. by *of*) a natural consequence or result. ● *adjective* **1** supplementary, associated. **2** (often foll. by *to*) forming a corollary. [Latin *corollarium* money paid for a garland, gratuity: neuter adj. from COROLLA]

Coro·man·del Coast /ˌkɒrəˈmandəl/ the southern part of the east coast of India, from Point Calimere to the mouth of the Krishna River.

corona¹ /kəˈrəʊnə/ *noun* (*pl.* **cor·onae** /-niː/ or **cor·onas**) **1 a** a small circle of light round the sun or moon. **b** the rarefied gaseous envelope of the sun, seen as an irregularly shaped area of light around the moon's disc during a total solar eclipse. **2** a circular chandelier hung from a roof. **3** *Anat.* a crown or crown-like structure. **4** *Bot.* a crown-like outgrowth from the inner side of a corolla. **5** *Archit.* a broad vertical face of a cornice, usu. of considerable projection. **6** *Electricity* the glow around a conductor at high potential. [Latin, = crown]

cor·ona² /kəˈrəʊnə/ *noun* a long cigar with straight sides. [Spanish *La Corona* the crown]

cor·ona·graph /kəˈrəʊnəˌɡrɑːf/ *noun* an instrument for observing the sun's corona, esp. other than during a solar eclipse.

cor·on·al¹ /kəˈrəʊnəl, ˈkɒrənəl, ˈkɒ-/ *adjective Astronomy & Bot.* of or relating to a corona.

cor·on·al² /ˈkɒrənəl, ˈkɒ-/ *noun* **1** *literary* a circlet (esp. of gold or gems) for the head. **2** a wreath or garland. [Middle English, apparently from Anglo-French from *corone* CROWN]

cor·on·ary /ˈkɒrəˌneri, ˈkɒ-/ ● *adjective* **1** of or relating to the heart. **2** of or relating to the coronary arteries. **3** (of blood vessels, nerves, etc.) resembling or encircling like a crown. ● *noun* (*pl.* **-aries**) = CORONARY THROMBOSIS. [Latin *coronarius* from *corona* crown]

coronary artery *noun* either of two arteries supplying blood to the heart.

coronary bypass *noun* a surgical procedure to relieve obstruction of the coronary arteries by creating an additional channel connecting the aorta to a point beyond the obstruction.

coronary thrombosis *noun* a blockage of blood flow to the heart caused by a blood clot in a coronary artery.

cor·on·a·tion /ˌkɒrəˈneɪʃən, ˌkɒ-/ *noun* the act or ceremony of crowning a sovereign or a sovereign's consort. [Old French from medieval Latin *coronatio -onis* from *coronare* to crown, from CORONA¹]

Coronation Gulf a gulf in the Canadian Arctic, separating Victoria Island from mainland Nunavut. [in honour of the coronation of George IV]

Coronation stone *see* STONE OF SCONE.

corona·virus /kəˈrəʊnəˌvaɪrəs/ *noun* a virus having a roughly spherical shape with a crown-like appearance, causing respiratory ailments and gastroenteritis in humans.

cor·oner /ˈkɒrənər, ˈkɒ-/ *noun* a public official responsible for investigating violent, suspicious, or accidental deaths, and certifying deaths occurring outside hospital. □ **coroner·ship** *noun* [Anglo-French *cor(o)uner* from *coro(u)ne* CROWN, reflecting the Latin title *custos placitorum coronae* 'guardian of the pleas of the crown']

cor·onet /ˈkɒrənet, ˈkɒ-, '-net/ *noun* **1** a small crown (esp. as worn, or used as a heraldic device, by a peer or peeress). **2** a circlet of precious materials, esp. as a woman's headdress or part of one. **3** the lowest part of a horse's pastern. **4** a ring of bone at the base of a deer's antler. □ **cor·on·et·ed** *adjective* [Old French *coronet(t)e* diminutive of *corone* CROWN]

Corot /ˈkɒrəʊ/ **(Jean-Bap·tiste) Ca·mille** (1796–1875), French landscape painter, whose misty and ethereal landscapes influenced the Impressionists, notably Pissarro; his works include *La Danse des nymphes* (1850) and *Sens Cathedral* (1874).

cor·ozo /kəˈrəʊzəʊ/ *noun* (*pl.* **-ozos**) any of various tropical palm trees yielding palm oil. [Spanish]

corozo-nut *noun* a seed of one species of palm, *Phytelephas macrocarpa*, which when hardened forms vegetable ivory. *Also called* IVORY NUT.

Corp.¹ *abbreviation* **1** *N Amer.* Corporation. **2** Corporal.

Corp.² *noun Cdn informal* = MOTHER CORP.

cor·pora *pl.* of CORPUS.

cor·por·al¹ /ˈkɔːpərəl, -prəl/ *noun* **1 a** (in the Canadian army and air force) a non-commissioned officer ranking above private and below master corporal. **b** (in the UK and *hist.* in Canada) a non-commissioned army or air force officer ranking next below sergeant. **c** (in the US Army) a non-commissioned officer ranking above a private first class. **d** (in the US Marine Corps) a non-commissioned officer ranking above a lance corporal. **2** (in some Canadian municipalities and in the RCMP) a police officer ranking above constable and below sergeant. **3** (in the Sûreté du Québec) an officer ranking below sergeant. [obsolete French, var. of *caporal* from Italian *caporale* prob. from Latin *corporalis* (as CORPORAL²), confused with Italian *capo* head]

cor·por·al² /ˈkɔːpərəl, -prəl/ *adjective* of or relating to the human body (compare CORPOREAL). □ **cor·por·al·ity** /ˌkɔːpəˈralɪti/ *noun* **cor·por·al·ly** *adverb* [Old French from Latin *corporalis* from *corpus -oris* body]

cor·por·al³ /ˈkɔːpərəl, -prəl/ *noun Christianity* a cloth on which the vessels containing the consecrated elements are placed during the celebration of the Eucharist. [Old English from Old French *corporal* or medieval Latin *corporale pallium* body cloth (as CORPORAL²)]

corporal punishment *noun* punishment inflicted on the body, esp. by beating.

corporal's guard *noun N Amer.* a small group of people, esp. a remnant of a larger group.

cor·por·ate /ˈkɔːpərət, -prət/ *adjective* **1** of or relating to business corporations (*corporate responsibility*). **2** forming a corporation (*corporate body*). **3** forming one body of many individuals. □ **cor·por·ate·ly** *adverb* [Latin *corporare corporat-* form into a body (*corpus -oris*)]

corporate citizen *noun* a business corporation considered in terms of its responsibility to society as a whole (*a good corporate citizen*). □ **corporate citizenship** *noun*

corporate culture *noun* **1** the ethos of a particular business or other organization. **2** the ethos of large businesses in general.

corporate identity *noun* the image presented by a company, esp. the use of a distinctive logo and coordinated packaging etc. to aid product recognition.

corporate raider *noun* a person who mounts an unwelcome takeover bid by buying up a company's shares on the stock market, esp. one who makes a practice of doing so.

corporate welfare *noun* government support or subsidy of private businesses, such as by tax incentives.

corporate welfare bum *noun Cdn slang derogatory* **1** a business perceived to be exploiting tax loopholes, capital gains concessions, etc. or to be benefiting unduly from government subsidies or tax breaks. **2** a person who directs such a business. [coined by David Lewis: see LEWIS[2] 3]

cor·por·a·tion /ˌkɔrpəˈreɪʃən/ *noun* **1** a group of people authorized to act as an individual and recognized in law as a single entity, esp. in business. **2** the legal entity established by law which carries on the business of a municipality. [Late Latin *corporatio* (as CORPORATE)]

cor·por·a·tism /ˈkɔrprə,tɪzəm, -pərə,tɪz-/ *noun* a political ideology or system, esp. associated with fascist states, in which business, industry, labour, etc. are organized as corporate entities. □ **cor·por·a·tist** *adjective*

cor·por·a·tive /ˈkɔrpərətɪv, -pərətɪv/ *adjective* **1** of or pertaining to a corporation. **2** (of a state) governed by or organized into corporations. □ **cor·por·a·tiv·ism** *noun*

cor·por·a·tize /ˈkɔrprə,taiz, -pərə,taiz/ *transitive verb* (also esp. *Brit.* **-tise**) to develop or convert (a small business operation) into a corporation. □ **cor·por·a·tiz·a·tion** /-ˈzeiʃən/ *noun*

cor·por·eal /kɔrˈpɔriəl/ *adjective* **1** bodily, physical, material, esp. as distinct from spiritual (*compare* CORPORAL[2]). **2** *Law* consisting of material objects (*corporeal property*). □ **cor·por·eal·ity** /-ˈaliti/ *noun* **cor·por·eal·ly** *adverb* [Late Latin *corporealis* from Latin *corporeus* from *corpus -oris* body]

corps /kɔr/ *noun* (pl. **corps** /kɔrz/) **1** *Military* **a** a body of troops with special duties (*intelligence corps*). **b** a main subdivision of an army in the field, consisting of two or more divisions. **2** a body of people engaged in a special activity (*diplomatic corps; press corps*). **3** = CORPS DE BALLET. [French (as CORPSE)]

corps de ballet /ˌkɔr də baˈlei/ *noun* **1** the group of ensemble dancers in a ballet. **2** the group of dancers belonging to the lowest rank in a ballet company. [French]

corps dip·lo·ma·tique /ˌkɔr dɪpləməˈtiːk/ *noun* a diplomatic corps. [French]

corpse /kɔrps/ *noun* a dead (usu. human) body. [Middle English *corps*, var. spelling of *cors* (CORSE), from Old French *cors* from Latin *corpus* body]

corps·man /ˈkɔrmən/ *noun* (pl. **-men**) *US* an enlisted medical auxiliary in the army or navy.

corps sergeant major *noun* (in the RCMP) an officer ranking above sergeant major and below inspector.

cor·pu·lent /ˈkɔrpjʊlənt/ *adjective* portly; fat. □ **cor·pu·lence** *noun* [Latin *corpulentus* from *corpus* body]

cor·pus /ˈkɔrpəs/ *noun* (pl. **cor·pora** /ˈkɔrpərə/ or **cor·pus·es**) **1** a body or collection of writings, esp. by one author. **2** *Linguistics* a body of spoken or written material taken as a representative sample of a language, on which a linguistic analysis is based. **3** *Anat.* any of various masses of tissue in the body that have a distinct structure or function. [Latin, = body]

cor·pus cal·lo·sum /ˈkɔrpəs kəˈloːsəm/ *noun* (pl. **cor·pora cal·losa**) *Anat.* a broad band of nerve fibres joining the two hemispheres of the brain. [Latin CORPUS + *callosus, -um* tough]

Cor·pus Chris·ti[1] /ˌkɔrpəs ˈkrɪsti/ a city and port in S Texas; pop. (2000) 277,454. It is situated on Corpus Christi Bay, an inlet of the Gulf of Mexico.

Cor·pus Chris·ti[2] /ˌkɔrpəs ˈkrɪsti/ *noun Christianity* a feast commemorating the Eucharist, observed on the Thursday after Trinity Sunday or the following Sunday. *Also called* FEAST OF THE BODY AND BLOOD OF CHRIST. [Latin, = Body of Christ]

cor·puscle /ˈkɔrpʌsəl/ *noun* a minute body or cell in an organism, esp. (in *pl.*) the red or white cells in the blood of vertebrates. □ **cor·pus·cu·lar** /kɔrˈpʌskjʊlər/ *adjective* [Latin *corpusculum* (as CORPUS)]

cor·pus de·licti /ˌkɔrpəs dɪˈlɪktai/ *noun Law* **1** the facts and circumstances constituting a crime. **2** concrete evidence of a crime, esp. a corpse. [Latin, = body of offence]

cor·pus lu·teum /ˌkɔrpəs ˈluːtiəm/ *noun Anat.* a hormone-secreting mass of tissue that develops in the ovary after discharge of an ovum, remaining in existence only if pregnancy has begun. [modern Latin from CORPUS + *luteus, -um* yellow]

cor·ral /kəˈral/ ● *noun N Amer.* **1** a pen for cattle, horses, etc. **2** a trap for capturing wild animals or fish. **3** *hist.* a defensive enclosure of wagons in an encampment. ● *transitive verb* (**cor·ralled, cor·ral·ling**) **1** drive or keep in or as in a corral (*he corralled us into the living room*). **2** *N Amer.* form (wagons) into a corral. **3** *N Amer. informal* capture; get (*corralled some new members for the team*). [Spanish & Old Portuguese (as KRAAL)]

cor·rect ● *adjective* **1** true, right, accurate. **2** (of conduct, manners, etc.) proper, right. **3** in accordance with good standards of taste etc. ● *verb* **1** *transitive* set right; amend (an error, omission, etc., or the person responsible for it). **2** *transitive* mark the errors in (written or printed work etc.). **3** *transitive* substitute the right thing for (the wrong one). **4** *transitive* **a** admonish or rebuke (a person). **b** punish (a person or fault). **5** *transitive* counteract (a harmful quality, ailment, etc.). **6** *transitive* adjust (an instrument etc.) to function accurately or accord with a standard. **7** *intransitive* (of stock prices) stabilize, esp. after a sharp decline or increase. □ **correct for** adjust or recalculate (statistical data etc.) to compensate for a deviant factor. □ **cor·rect·able** *adjective* (also **cor·rect·ible**). **cor·rect·ly** *adverb* **cor·rect·ness** *noun* [Middle English (adj. through French) from Latin *corrigere correct-* (as COM-, *regere* guide)]

cor·rec·tion *noun* **1 a** the act or process of correcting. **b** an instance of this. **2** a thing substituted for what is wrong. **3** *N Amer.* (usu. **cor·rec·tions**) **a** the treatment of convicted offenders through incarceration, parole, etc. **b** the administrative system which oversees such treatment.

cor·rec·tion·al *adjective* **1** *N Amer.* of or pertaining to the corrections system (*correctional facility; correctional officer*). **2** of or pertaining to correction.

correction fluid *noun* a usu. white liquid that is painted over a typed or written error leaving a blank space for typing or writing afresh.

correction line *noun Surveying* **1** *N Amer.* (*West*) one of a set of parallel lines of latitude 24 miles apart along which correction is made for the discrepancy between strictly parallel north-south surveying lines and northward-converging meridians. **2** *Cdn* (*Prairies*) a jog in a road where it intersects one of these lines.

cor·rec·ti·tude *noun* correctness, esp. conscious correctness of conduct. [19th c., from CORRECT + RECTITUDE]

cor·rect·ive ● *adjective* serving or tending to correct or counteract something undesired or harmful. ● *noun* (usu. foll. by *to*) something, e.g. a theory or a practice, that corrects or counteracts a tendency viewed as harmful. □ **cor·rect·ive·ly** *adverb*

cor·rect·or *noun* **1** something that provides a means of correction or prevents error (*spelling corrector*). **2** a person who corrects or points out faults.

Cor·reg·gio /kɒˈredʒiɔː/ **Antonio Al·legri da** (born Antonio Allegri) (1494–1534), Italian painter, who is best known for his dome frescoes in Parma churches, esp. S. Giovanni Evangelista (1520–3) and Parma cathedral (*c.*1526–30); his mythological paintings such as *Jupiter and Io* (*c.*1530) influenced the rococo of the 18th c.

cor·rel·ate ● *verb* /ˈkɔrə,leit, ˈkɒ-/ **1** *intransitive* (foll. by *with, to*) have a mutual relation (*postal codes correlate with geographic locations*). **2** *transitive* (usu. foll. by *with*) bring into a mutual relation; establish the likely relation between. ● *noun* /ˈkɔrə,lət, ˈkɒr-, -leit/ each of two related or complementary things (esp. so related that one implies the other). [back-formation from CORRELATION, CORRELATIVE]

cor·rel·a·tion /ˌkɔrəˈleiʃən, ˌkɒ-/ *noun* **1** a mutual relation between two or more things (*a correlation between smoking and cancer*). **2** the act or process of correlating. **3** *Statistics* **a** interdependence of variable quantities. **b** a quantity measuring the extent of this. □ **cor·rel·a·tion·al** *adjective* [medieval Latin *correlatio* (as CORRELATIVE)]

correlation coefficient *noun Statistics* a number between +1 and -1 calculated so as to represent the degree of correlation of variables or sets of data.

Vowels: a *cat*   ɑ *arm*   e *bed*   ɜr *her*   ɜː *deux*   ə *ago*   ɪ *sit*   i *cosy*   iː *feed*   ɒ *hot*   ɔ *pore*   oː *no*   ʌ *run*   ʊ *put*

cor·rela·tive /kəˈrelətɪv/ ● adjective **1** (often foll. by with, to) having a mutual relation; corresponding. **2** Grammar (of words) corresponding to each other and regularly used together (as neither and nor). ● noun a correlative word or thing. □ **cor·rela·tive·ly** adverb **cor·rela·tiv·ity** /-ˈtɪvɪti/ noun [medieval Latin correlativus (as COM-, RELATIVE)]

correlative conjunction noun either member of a matched pair of words, of which the second is a coordinating conjunction, such as either...or, both...and, etc.

cor·res·pond /ˌkɒrəˈspɒnd, ˌkɔː-/ intransitive verb **1 a** (usu. foll. by to) be analogous or similar. **b** (usu. foll. by to) match; agree in amount, position, etc. (my tally corresponds with yours). **c** (usu. foll. by with, to) be in harmony or agreement. **2** (usu. foll. by with) communicate by interchange of letters. [French correspondre from medieval Latin correspondere (as COM-, RESPOND)]

cor·res·pond·ence /ˌkɔːrəˈspɒndəns, ˌkɒ-/ noun **1** (usu. foll. by with, to, between) agreement, similarity, or harmony. **2 a** communication by letters or email. **b** letters or email sent or received.

correspondence course noun a course of study conducted by mail or online.

correspondence school noun an educational institution conducting correspondence courses.

cor·res·pond·ent /ˌkɔːrəˈspɒndənt, ˌkɒr-/ ● noun **1** a person employed to contribute material for publication in a periodical or for broadcasting (CBC's Moscow correspondent). **2** a person who writes letters to a person or a newspaper, esp. regularly. **3** a person or firm having regular business relations with another, esp. in another country. ● adjective (often foll. by to, with) archaic corresponding.

cor·res·pond·ing /ˌkɔːrəˈspɒndɪŋ, ˌkɒr-/ adjective **1** identical; equivalent (two men of corresponding height). **2** analogous in position, purpose, etc. **3** belonging together as a unit (a skirt with its corresponding jacket). **4** handling correspondence (the club's corresponding secretary). □ **cor·res·pond·ing·ly** adverb

cor·ret·to /kɒˈretoː/ noun espresso laced with brandy or liqueur. [Italian, lit. = 'corrected']

cor·rida /kɒˈriːdə/ noun **1** a bullfight. **2** bullfighting. [Spanish corrida de toros running of bulls]

cor·ri·dor /ˈkɔːrɪˌdɔr, ˈkɒr-, -dər/ noun **1** a passage from which doors lead into rooms; hallway. **2** a passage in a railway car from which doors lead into compartments. **3** a densely populated belt of land with major overland and air transportation routes (the Quebec-Windsor corridor). **4 a** a strip of territory that runs through that of another state and secures access to the sea or some desired part. **b** a right-of-way reserved for utilities (hydro corridor). **5** a route to which aircraft are restricted, esp. over a foreign country. **6** an extent of land characterized by a specific activity, e.g. wildlife migration, passing through an area of a contrasting nature. [French from Italian corridore corridor for corridojo running place, from correre run, by confusion with corridore runner]

corridors of power plural noun the upper echelons of government, business, etc., where power and influence are considered to reside.

cor·rie /ˈkɔri, ˈkɒri/ noun Scot. a circular hollow on a mountainside; a cirque. [Gaelic coire cauldron]

cor·ri·gen·dum /ˌkɔrɪˈdʒendəm, ˌkɒr-/ noun (pl. **cor·ri·gen·da** /-də/) a thing to be corrected, esp. an error in a printed book. [Latin, neuter gerundive of corrigere: see CORRECT]

cor·rob·or·ate /kəˈrɒbəˌreit/ transitive verb confirm or give support to (a statement or belief, or the person holding it), esp. in relation to witnesses in a law court. □ **cor·rob·or·a·tion** noun

cor·rob·ora·tive /-rətɪv/ adjective **cor·rob·or·ator** noun [Latin corroborare strengthen (as COM-, roborare from robur -oris strength)]

cor·rob·oree /kəˈrɒbəri/ noun **1** a dance-drama ceremony of Australian Aboriginals, featuring song and rhythmical musical accompaniment. **2** Austral. a noisy party. [Dharuk garabari a style of dancing]

cor·rode /kəˈroːd/ verb **1 a** transitive wear away, esp. by chemical action. **b** intransitive be worn away; decay. **2** transitive destroy gradually (unemployment corroded his self-esteem). □ **cor·rod·ed** adjective **cor·rod·ible** adjective [Latin corrodere corros- (as COM-, rodere gnaw)]

cor·ro·sion /kəˈroːʒən/ noun **1** the process of corroding, esp. of a rusting metal. **2** damage caused by corroding.

cor·ro·sive /kəˈroːsɪv/ ● adjective **1** tending to corrode or consume. **2** destructive; wearing (the corrosive effects of famine and disease). ● noun a corrosive substance. □ **cor·ro·sive·ly** adverb **cor·ro·sive·ness** noun [Old French corosif -ive (as CORRODE)]

cor·ru·gate /ˈkɔːrʊˌgeit, ˈkɒr-/ verb **1** transitive form into alternate ridges and grooves, esp. to strengthen. **2** transitive & intransitive contract into wrinkles or folds. □ **cor·ru·ga·tion** noun [Latin corrugare (as COM-, rugare from ruga wrinkle)]

cor·ru·gat·ed adjective formed into alternate ridges and grooves, esp. to strengthen (corrugated cardboard; corrugated iron).

cor·rupt /kəˈrʌpt/ ● adjective **1** influenced by or using bribery or fraudulent activity (a corrupt judge). **2** morally depraved; wicked. **3** (of a text, language, etc.) harmed (esp. made suspect or unreliable) by errors or alterations. **4** (of a computer disk or program) contaminated with errors; unusable. **5** archaic rotten. ● verb **1** transitive & intransitive make or become corrupt or depraved. **2** transitive affect or harm by errors or alterations. **3** transitive archaic infect, taint. □ **cor·rupt·er** noun **cor·rupt·ible** adjective **cor·rupt·ibil·ity** noun **cor·rupt·ive** adjective **cor·rupt·ly** adverb **cor·rupt·ness** noun [Old French corrupt or Latin corruptus past participle of corrumpere corrupt- (as COM-, rumpere break)]

cor·rup·tion /kəˈrʌpʃən/ noun **1** use of corrupt practices, esp. bribery or fraud. **2** moral deterioration, esp. widespread. **3 a** irregular alteration (of a text, language, etc.) from its original state. **b** an irregularly altered form of a word. **4** decomposition, esp. of a corpse or other organic matter.

cor·sage /kɔrˈsɒʒ/ noun an arrangement of flowers worn by a woman at the front of a dress below the shoulder, or at the waist or wrist, usu. on formal occasions. [Old French from cors body: see CORPSE]

cor·sair /ˈkɔrser, -ˈser/ noun **1** a pirate ship. **2** hist. a pirate, esp. of the Barbary Coast. [French corsaire from medieval Latin cursarius from cursus inroad from currere run]

corse /kɔrs/ noun archaic a corpse. [var. of CORPSE]

corse·let /ˈkɔrslət, ˈkɔrsəˌlet/ noun hist. a piece of armour covering the trunk but not the limbs. [Old French corselet, diminutive formed as CORSET]

cor·sel·ette /ˌkɔrsəˈlet/ noun a woman's foundation garment combining corset and brassiere.

cor·set /ˈkɔrsət/ ● noun **1** a close-fitting undergarment worn by women to shape and support the torso. **2** a similar garment worn by men and women because of injury, weakness, or deformity. ● transitive verb (**cor·set·ed, cor·set·ing**) provide with a corset. □ **cor·set·ed** adjective **cor·setry** noun [Old French, diminutive of cors body: see CORPSE]

Cor·sica /ˈkɔrsɪkə/ a mountainous island off the west coast of Italy, forming an administrative region of France; pop. (1999) 260,196; chief towns, Bastia (northern department) and Ajaccio (southern department). It was the birthplace of Napoleon I.

Cor·si·can /ˈkɔrsɪkən/ ● adjective of or relating to Corsica. ● noun **1** a native of Corsica. **2** the Italian dialect of Corsica.

cor·tège /kɔrˈteʒ/ noun **1** a procession, esp. for a funeral. **2** a train of attendants. [French, from Italian corteggio, from corteggiare 'attend court', from corte 'court' from Latin cohors cohort- 'yard, retinue']

Cor·tes /ˈkɔrtez/ noun the legislative assembly of Spain and formerly of Portugal. [Spanish & Portuguese, pl. of corte COURT]

Cor·tés /ˈkɔrtez/ **Her·nan·do** (also **Cor·tez**) (1485–1547), Spanish conquistador. He overthrew the Aztec Empire, conquering the capital city, Tenochtitlán, in 1519 and deposing the emperor Montezuma; in 1521 he destroyed Tenochtitlán, rebuilt it as the new capital of Mexico City, and served briefly as governor of the colony of New Spain.

cor·tex noun (pl. **cor·ti·ces** /-tɪˌsiːz/) **1** Anat. the outer part of an organ, esp. of the brain (**cerebral cortex**) or kidneys (**renal cortex**). **2** Bot. **a** an outer layer of tissue immediately below the epidermis. **b** bark. [Latin cortex, -icis bark]

cor·ti·cal /ˈkɔrtɪkəl/ adjective belonging to or forming a cortex.

cor·ti·cate /ˈkɔrtɪˌkət, -ˌkeit/ adjective (also **cor·ti·ca·ted**) having bark or rind. □ **cor·ti·ca·tion** /ˌkɔrtɪˈkeiʃən/ noun [Latin corticatus (as CORTEX)]

cortico- /ˈkɔrtɪˌkoː/ combining form of or relating to a cortex, esp. the adrenal or cerebral.

cor·ti·co·ster·oid /ˌkɔrtɪkoːˈsteroid/ noun (also **cor·ti·coid**) **1** any of a group of steroid hormones produced in the adrenal cortex and concerned with regulation of salts and carbohydrates, inflammation, and sexual physiology. **2** an analogous synthetic steroid.

cor·ti·co·trophin /ˌkɔrtɪkəˈtroːfɪn/ noun (also **cor·ti·co·tropin**) = ADRENOCORTICOTROPHIC HORMONE.

cor·ti·sol /ˈkɔrtəsɒl/ noun = HYDROCORTISONE.

cor·ti·sone /ˈkɔrtəˌzoːn/ noun a steroid hormone produced by the adrenal cortex or synthetically, used medicinally esp. against inflammation and allergy. [abbreviation of 17-hydroxy-11-dehydrocorticosterone]

Cort·land *noun* N Amer. a red variety of apple. [Cortland, New York]

cor·un·dum /kə'rʌndəm/ *noun* Geol. extremely hard crystallized alumina, used esp. as an abrasive, and varieties of which, e.g. ruby and sapphire, are used for gemstones. [Tamil *kurundam* from Sanskrit *kuruvinda* ruby]

Cor·un·na /kə'rʌnə/ (also **La Cor·uña** /lɒ kɒ'ruːnja/) a port in NW Spain; pop. (est. 2002) 241,000. The Armada set sail from Corunna in 1588.

cor·us·cate /'kɒrə,skeit, 'kɒr-/ *intransitive verb* **1** give off flashing light; sparkle. **2** be showy or brilliant. □ **cor·us·cant** *adjective* **cor·us·ca·tion** *noun* [Latin *coruscare* glitter]

cor·vée /'kɔrvei/ *noun* **1** hist. a day's work of unpaid labour due to a feudal lord from a vassal. **2** hist. labour enforced by statute, esp. for the maintenance of roads, etc. [Old French, ultimately from Latin *corrogare* ask for, collect (as COM-, *rogare* ask)]

cor·vette /kɔr'vet/ *noun* **1** a small naval escort vessel. **2** hist. a warship with a flush deck and one tier of guns. [French from Middle Dutch *korf* kind of ship + diminutive -ETTE]

cor·vine /'kɔrvain/ *adjective* of or akin to the raven or crow. [Latin *corvinus* from *corvus* raven]

cory·ban·tic /,kɒrə'bantik, ,kɒr-/ *adjective* wild, frenzied. [*Corybantes* priests of Cybele performing wild dances (Latin from Greek *Korubantes*)]

coryd·alis /kə'ridəlis/ *noun* a plant of the genus *Corydalis* of the poppy family, with tubular flowers. [Greek *korudallis* 'crested lark' (with reference to the flower, likened to the bird's spur)]

cor·ymb /'kɒrimb, 'kɒr-, -im/ *noun* Bot. a flat-topped cluster of flowers with the flower stalks proportionally longer lower down the stem. [French *corymbe* or Latin *corymbus* from Greek *korumbos* cluster]

cory·phée /'kɒrə,fei, 'kɒr-/ *noun* (in some ballet companies) a leading dancer in a corps de ballet. [French from Greek *koruphaios* leader of a chorus, from *koruphē* head]

co·ryza /kə'raizə/ *noun* a catarrhal inflammation of the mucous membrane in the nose; a cold in the head. [Latin from Greek *koruza* running at the nose]

Cos see Kos.

cos¹ /kɒs/ *noun* = ROMAINE. [Latin from Greek *Kōs*, island in the Aegean, where it originated]

cos² /kɒːs/ *abbreviation* cosine.

cos³ /kɒz/ *conjunction & adverb* Brit. informal because. [abbreviation]

Cos. /kɒːz/ *abbreviation* **1** Companies. **2** Counties.

Cosa Nos·tra /,kɒːzə 'nɒstrə/ *noun* a US criminal organization resembling and related to the Mafia. [Italian, = our affair]

cosec /'kɒːsek/ *abbreviation* cosecant.

co·secant /kɒ'siːkənt/ *noun* Math. the ratio of the hypotenuse (in a right-angled triangle) to the side opposite an acute angle; the reciprocal of sine. [CO- + SECANT]

co·set /'kɒːset/ *noun* Math. a subset of a group composed of all the products obtained by multiplying each element of a subgroup in turn by one particular element of the group.

cosh¹ Brit. informal ● *noun* a heavy blunt weapon. ● *transitive verb* hit with a cosh. [19th c.: origin unknown]

cosh² *abbreviation* Math. hyperbolic cosine.

co-sign *transitive & intransitive verb* sign (a document, esp. a cheque, lease, etc.) jointly with another. □ **co-signer** *noun*

Cos·imo de' Med·ici /'kɒsimɔː də 'meditʃi/ (known as 'Cosimo the Elder') (1389–1464), Italian statesman and banker. He laid the foundations of the Medici family's power in Florence, becoming the city's ruler in 1434; he used his considerable wealth to promote the arts and learning.

co·sine /'kɒːsain/ *noun* Math. the ratio of the side adjacent to an acute angle (in a right-angled triangle) to the hypotenuse. [as CO-, SINE]

co-sleep *intransitive verb* (of parents and babies) sleep together in the parents' bed.

cos·met·ic /kɒz'metik/ ● *adjective* **1** intended to adorn or beautify the body, esp. the face. **2** intended to improve only appearances; superficially improving or beneficial (a cosmetic change). **3** (of surgery) aimed at improving, restoring, or modifying the appearance. ● *noun* (often in pl.) a cosmetic preparation, esp. for the face. □ **cos·met·ic·ally** *adverb* [French *cosmétique* from Greek *kosmētikos* from *kosmeō* adorn, from *kosmos* order, adornment]

cosmetic bag *noun* N Amer. a usu. zippered bag with a waterproof lining, for storing cosmetics or other toiletries.

cos·met·ician /,kɒzmə'tɪʃən/ *noun* N Amer. a person who sells or applies cosmetics for a living.

cos·meti·cize /kɒz'metə,saiz/ *transitive verb* (also esp. Brit. **-cise**) **1** treat with cosmetics. **2** make superficially presentable.

cos·met·ol·ogy /,kɒzmə'tɒlədʒi/ *noun* the art or profession of applying cosmetics. □ **cos·met·ol·o·gist** *noun*

cos·mic *adjective* **1** of the universe or cosmos, esp. as distinct from the earth. **2** of or for space travel. **3** immeasurably vast. □ **cos·mic·al** *adjective* **cos·mic·al·ly** *adverb*

cosmic dust *noun* small particles of matter distributed throughout space.

cosmic microwave background radiation *noun* = BACKGROUND RADIATION 2.

cosmic rays *plural noun* (also **cosmic radiation** *noun*) radiation from outer space that reaches the earth from all directions, usu. with high energy and penetrative power.

cosmic string *noun* see STRING noun 11b.

cos·mog·ony /kɒz'mɒgəni/ *noun* (pl. **-ies**) **1** a theory or account of the origin of the universe. **2** the study of the origin of the universe. □ **cosmo·gon·ic** /-mə'gɒnik/ *adjective* **cosmo·gon·ic·al** /-mə'gɒnikəl/ *adjective* **cos·mog·on·ist** *noun* [Greek *kosmogonia* from *kosmos* world + -gonia -begetting]

cos·mog·raphy /kɒz'mɒgrəfi/ *noun* (pl. **-ies**) a description or mapping of general features of the universe. □ **cos·mog·raph·er** *noun*

cos·mol·ogy /kɒz'mɒlədʒi/ *noun* **1** the study of the origin and development of the universe. **2** an account or theory of the origin of the universe. □ **cosmo·logic·al** *adjective* **cosmo·logic·al·ly** *adverb* **cos·mol·o·gist** *noun* [French *cosmologie* or modern Latin *cosmologia* (as COSMOS¹, -LOGY)]

cosmo·naut /'kɒzmə,nɒt/ *noun* an astronaut in the Russian or hist. Soviet space program. [Russian *kosmonavt*, as COSMOS¹, after *astronaut*]

cos·mop·olis /kɒz'mɒpəlis/ *noun* a cosmopolitan city. [Greek *kosmos* world + *polis* city]

cosmo·pol·itan /,kɒzmə'pɒlitən/ ● *adjective* **1 a** of or from or knowing many parts of the world. **b** consisting of people from many or all parts (Toronto is a very cosmopolitan city). **2 a** free from national limitations or prejudices. **b** sophisticated; worldly. **3** Ecology (of a plant, animal, etc.) widely distributed. ● *noun* **1** a cosmopolitan person. **2** a cocktail of vodka, orange liqueur, lime juice, and cranberry juice. □ **cosmo·pol·itan·ism** *noun* **cosmo·pol·itan·ize** *transitive & intransitive verb* (also esp. Brit. **-ise**). [COSMOPOLITE + -AN]

cos·mop·olite /kɒz'mɒpə,ləit/ *noun* **1** a cosmopolitan person. **2** Ecology a widely distributed animal or plant. [French from Greek *kosmopolitēs* from *kosmos* world + *politēs* citizen]

cos·mos¹ /'kɒzmɒs, -məs/ *noun* **1** the universe, esp. as a well-ordered whole. **2** an ordered system of ideas etc. [Greek *kosmos*]

cos·mos² /'kɒzmɒːs, -məs/ *noun* any composite plant of the genus *Cosmos*, bearing single usu. pink or white daisy-like blossoms, frequently grown in gardens. [modern Latin from Greek *kosmos* in sense 'ornament']

Cos·sack ● *noun* **1** a member of a people living on the northern shores of the Black and Caspian seas, originally famous for their military skill. **2** a member of a Cossack military unit. ● *adjective* of, relating to, or characteristic of the Cossacks. [French *cosaque* from Russian *kazak* from Turki *quzzâq* nomad, adventurer]

cos·sack /'kɒsək/ *noun* Cdn (Nfld) a hooded pullover made of animal skin or heavy cotton. [alteration of CASSOCK]

cos·set /'kɒsət/ *transitive verb* (**cos·set·ed, cos·set·ing**) (usu. in passive) pamper. [dial. *cosset* = pet lamb, prob. from Anglo-French *coscet*, *cozet* from Old English *cotsæta* cottager (as COT², SIT)]

cost ● *verb* (past and past participle **cost**) **1** *transitive* be obtainable for (a sum of money); have as a price (what does it cost?; it cost me $50). **2** *transitive* **a** involve as a loss or sacrifice (it cost him his life). **b** necessitate or involve the expenditure of (time, trouble, etc.). **3** *transitive* (past and past participle **cost·ed**) fix or estimate the cost or price of. **4** informal **a** *transitive* be costly to (that ring will cost you). **b** *intransitive* be costly. ● *noun* **1** what a thing costs; the price paid or to be paid. **2** a loss or sacrifice; an expenditure of time, effort, etc. **3** (in pl.) **a** expenses for running a home or business (switched to a cheaper courier to cut costs). **b** legal expenses, esp. those allowed in favour of the winning party or against the losing party in a suit. □ **at all costs** (or **at any cost**) no matter what the cost or risk may be. **at cost** at the initial cost; at cost price. **at the cost of** at the expense of losing or sacrificing. **cost a person dear** (or **dearly**) involve a person in a high cost or a heavy penalty. **to a person's cost** with loss or disadvantage to a person.

[Old French *coster*, *couster*, *coust*, ultimately from Latin *constare* stand firm, stand at a price (as COM-, *stare* stand)]

Costa Blanca /ˌkɒstə ˈblaŋkə/ a resort region on the Mediterranean coast of SE Spain. [Spanish, = white coast]

Costa Brava /ˌkɒstə ˈbrɒvə/ a resort region to the north of Barcelona, on the Mediterranean coast of NE Spain. [Spanish, = wild coast]

cost accounting *noun* the recording and review of all the costs incurred in a business, as an aid to management. □ **cost accountant** *noun*

Costa del Sol /ˌkɒstə del ˈsɒl/ a resort region on the Mediterranean coast of S Spain. Marbella and Torremolinos are the principal resort towns. [Spanish, = coast of the sun]

cos·tal /ˈkɒstəl/ *adjective* of the ribs. [French from modern Latin *costalis* from Latin *costa* rib]

co-star ● *noun* 1 a film, television, or stage star appearing with another or other stars of equal importance. 2 a film, television, or stage star whose status in a production is slightly below that of a star. ● *verb* (**-starred**, **-star·ring**) 1 *intransitive* take part as a co-star. 2 *transitive* (of a production) include as a co-star.

cos·tard /ˈkɒstərd/ *noun Brit.* 1 a large ribbed variety of apple. 2 *archaic jocular* the head. [Anglo-French from *coste* rib from Latin *costa*]

Costa Rica /ˌkɒstə ˈriːkə/ a republic in Central America on the Isthmus of Panama; pop. (est. 2002) 3,834,934; capital, San José. □ **Costa Rican** *adjective & noun*

cost-benefit *adjective* assessing the relation between the cost of an operation and the value of the resulting benefits (*cost-benefit analysis*).

cost-conscious *adjective* aware of cost or costs.

cost-cutting *noun* the cutting of costs (often *attributive*: *cost-cutting measures*).

cost-effect·ive *adjective* effective or productive in relation to its cost. □ **cost-effect·ive·ly** *adverb* **cost-effect·ive·ness** *noun*

cost-efficient *adjective* = COST-EFFECTIVE. □ **cost-efficien·cy** *noun* **cost-efficient·ly** *adverb*

Cos·tel·lo see ABBOTT AND COSTELLO.

coster·monger /ˈkɒstərˌmʌŋgər/ *noun* (also **coster**) *Brit.* a person who sells fruit, vegetables, etc., in the street from a cart. [COSTARD + MONGER]

cost·ing *noun* (often in *pl.*) 1 the determination of the cost of producing or undertaking something. 2 the cost so arrived at.

cos·tive /ˈkɒstɪv/ *adjective* 1 constipated. 2 slow or reluctant in speech or action; unforthcoming. □ **cos·tive·ly** *adverb* **cos·tive·ness** *noun* [Old French *costivé* from Latin *constipatus*: see CONSTIPATE]

cost·ly *adjective* (**cost·li·er**, **cost·li·est**) 1 costing much; expensive. 2 involving great loss or sacrifice (*a costly mistake*). 3 of great value. □ **cost·li·ness** *noun*

cost·mary /ˈkɒstˌmeri/ *noun* (*pl.* **-ies**) an aromatic composite plant, *Balsamita major*, formerly used in medicine and for flavouring ale. [Old English *cost* from Latin *costum* from Greek *kostos* from Arabic *kust* an aromatic plant + (St.) *Mary* (with whom it was associated in medieval times)]

cost of living *noun* the level of prices esp. of the basic necessities of life (often *attributive*: *cost-of-living index*).

cost-plus *adjective* calculated as the basic cost plus a profit factor.

cost price *noun* the price paid for a thing by a person who later sells it.

cost-push inflation *noun* increase in the prices of goods caused by increases in the cost of inputs, esp. wages and raw materials.

cos·tume /ˈkɒstjuːm/ ● *noun* 1 a style or fashion of dress, esp. that of a particular place, time, nationality, or class. 2 an ensemble of unusual or period clothes worn at Halloween etc. (*a pirate costume*) (often *attributive*: *costume party*; *costume ball*). 3 clothing for a particular activity (*riding costume*). 4 a theatrical performer's clothes for a part. ● *transitive verb* (esp. in *passive* or *adj.*) provide with a costume. □ **cos·tum·ing** *noun* [French from Italian from Latin *consuetudo* CUSTOM]

costume drama *noun* a drama, esp. produced for television or film, for which historical costume is worn.

costume jewellery *noun* relatively inexpensive jewellery made of metal, wood, plastic, etc., often set with artificial or semi-precious stones.

cos·tum·er /ˈkɒstjəmər/ *noun* a person who makes or provides costumes, esp. for theatrical use.

cosy *var.* of COZY.

cot¹ *noun* 1 *N Amer.* a small folding or portable bed. 2 *Brit.* a baby's crib. [Anglo-Indian, from Hindi *khāṭ* bedstead, hammock]

cot² *noun* 1 a small shelter; a cote. 2 *literary* a cottage. [Old English from Germanic, related to COTE]

cot³ *abbreviation Math.* cotangent.

co·tan·gent /ˈkoʊˌtandʒənt/ *noun Math.* the ratio of the side adjacent to an acute angle (in a right-angled triangle) to the opposite side.

cot death *noun Brit.* = SUDDEN INFANT DEATH SYNDROME.

cote /koʊt/ *noun archaic* (except in *combination*) a shelter, esp. for animals or birds; a shed or stall (*sheep-cote*). [Old English from Germanic, related to COT²]

co·teau /kəˈtoʊ, ˈkoʊtoʊ/ *noun N Amer.* (*West*) any of various kinds of elevated geographical features, such as a plateau, a divide between valleys, etc. [French *coteau* slope, hillside]

co·terie /ˈkoʊtəri/ *noun* a group of people who associate closely; a clique. [French, originally = association of tenants, ultimately from Middle Low German *kote* COTE]

co·termin·ous /koʊˈtɜrmənəs/ *adjective* (often foll. by *with*) having the same boundaries or extent (in space, time, or meaning). [CO- + TERMINUS + -OUS]

Côte-Saint-Luc /koʊtsã̃ˈluːk/ a former city in south central Quebec, on the southern part of the Island of Montreal, now part of the city of Montreal; pop. (2001) 30,244. [L. de La Corne *Saint-Luc*, military officer and legislative councillor d.1784]

Côtes du Rhône /ˌkoʊtduːˈroʊn/ *noun* a light, fruity red wine produced in the southern Rhone valley in France. [French]

coth /kɒθ/ *abbreviation Math.* hyperbolic cotangent.

co·til·lion /kəˈtɪljən, koʊ-/ *noun* 1 *US* **a** a formal ball, esp. one at which debutantes are presented. **b** a ballroom dance resembling a quadrille. 2 any of various French dances of the 18th and 19th c. with elaborate steps and figures. [French *cotillon* petticoat, diminutive of *cotte* from Old French *cote* COAT]

co·tin·ga /kəˈtɪŋgə/ *noun* a tropical American bird of the passerine family Cotingidae, often with brilliant plumage. [French from Tupi *cutinga*]

coto·ne·as·ter /kəˌtoʊniːˈastər/ *noun* any rosaceous shrub of the genus *Cotoneaster*, bearing usu. bright red berries. [modern Latin from Latin *cotoneum* QUINCE + -ASTER]

Coto·nou /ˌkɒtəˈnuː/ the largest city, chief port, and chief commercial and political centre of Benin, on the coast of West Africa; pop. (est. 2002) 720,100.

Coto·paxi /ˌkɒtəˈpaksi/ the highest active volcano in the world, rising to 5 896 m (19,142 ft.) in the Andes of central Ecuador. [Quechua, = shining peak]

Cots·wold Hills /ˈkɒtswoʊld/ (also **Cots·wolds**) a range of limestone hills in SW England, largely in the county of Gloucestershire.

cot·ta /ˈkɒtə/ *noun Christianity* a short surplice. [Italian, formed as COAT]

cot·tage ● *noun* 1 *N Amer.* a dwelling used for vacation purposes, usu. located in a rural area near a lake or river (also *attributive*: *cottage country*). 2 *Cdn* (*Que.*) a small, two-storey house in the city. 3 *Brit.* a small simple house, esp. in the country. 4 a dwelling forming part of a farm establishment, used by a worker. ● *intransitive verb N Amer.* vacation at a cottage. □ **cot·tagey** *adjective* [Anglo-French, formed as COT², COTE]

cottage cheese *noun* soft white cheese made from skimmed milk curds.

cottage country *noun Cdn* an area in which there are many cottages.

cottage garden *noun* an informal garden well-stocked with colourful traditional hardy plants.

cottage hospital *noun* 1 *Cdn* (*Nfld*) a small hospital with non-specialist medical services, usu. located in outports. 2 *Brit.* a small hospital not having resident medical staff.

cottage industry *noun* a business activity partly or wholly carried on at home.

cottage loaf *noun Brit.* a loaf formed of two round masses, the smaller on top of the larger.

cottage pie *noun Brit.* = SHEPHERD'S PIE.

cottage pudding *noun* plain cake covered with a sweet sauce, often of fruit.

cot·tag·er *noun* 1 *N Amer.* a person vacationing at a cottage. 2 a person who lives in a cottage.

cottage roll *noun Cdn* a pickled, boneless, prepared ham from the pork butt.

cot·tag·ing *noun* 1 spending time in a cottage in the country. 2 *informal* casual gay sex in public washrooms.

t *top*   v *voice*   w *we*   z *zoo*   ʃ *she*   ʒ *vision*   θ *thin*   ð *this*   ŋ *ring*   x *loch*   tʃ *chip*   dʒ *jar*   (*see over for vowels*)

cot·tar /'kɒtɜr/ *noun* (also **cot·ter**) **1** *Scot. & hist.* a farm labourer or tenant occupying a cottage in return for labour as required. **2** *Irish hist.* = COTTIER. [COT² + -ER¹ (Scots -ar)]

cot·ter *noun* **1** a bolt or wedge for securing parts of machinery etc. **2** (in full **cotter pin**) a split pin that opens after passing through a hole. □ **cotter·less** *adjective* [17th c. (related to earlier *cotterel*): origin unknown]

cot·ti·er /'kɒti:ɜr/ *noun hist.* an Irish peasant who rented a small portion of land at a price fixed by competition. [Old French *cotier* from medieval Latin *cotarius*: see COTERIE]

cot·ton ● *noun* **1** a soft white fibrous substance covering the seeds of certain plants. **2 a** (in full **cotton plant**) such a plant, esp. any of the genus *Gossypium*. **b** cotton plants cultivated as a crop for the fibre or the seeds. **3** thread or cloth made from the fibre. ● *intransitive verb* *N Amer.* take a liking to (a person). □ **cotton on** (often foll. by *to*) *informal* begin to understand. □ **cot·tony** *adjective* [Old French *coton* from Arabic *ḳuṭn*]

cotton batting *noun N Amer.* (also **cotton batten**) fluffy cotton wadding used for crafts, first aid, etc.

cotton cake *noun* compressed cotton seed used as food for cattle.

cotton candy *noun N Amer.* candy floss.

cotton gin *noun* a machine for separating cotton from its seeds.

cotton grass *noun* a sedge of the genus *Eriophorum*, with fruiting heads of long white cottony hairs.

cotton-pickin' *adjective* (also **cotton-picking**) esp. *US slang* damned (*you're a cotton-pickin' liar!*).

cotton·seed *noun* the seed of the cotton plant, from which an edible oil is obtained.

cotton·tail *noun* a rabbit of the N American genus *Sylvilagus*, most species of which have a white fluffy underside to the tail.

cotton·wood *noun* **1** any of several poplars, native to N America, having seeds covered in white cottony hairs. **2** any of several trees native to Australia, esp. a downy-leaved tree, *Bedfordia arborescens*.

cotton wool *noun* **1** esp. *Brit.* = COTTON BATTING **2** *US* raw cotton.

CO2 *noun* carbon dioxide.

coty·ledon /ˌkɒtə'li:dən/ *noun* **1** an embryonic leaf in seed-bearing plants. **2** any succulent plant of the chiefly African genus *Cotyledon* and related genera. □ **coty·ledon·ary** *adjective* **coty·ledon·ous** *adjective* [Latin, = pennywort, from Greek *kotulēdōn* cup-shaped cavity, from *kotulē* cup]

couch¹ ● *noun* **1** an upholstered piece of furniture for several people; a sofa. **2** a long padded seat with a headrest at one end, esp. one on which a psychiatrist's or doctor's patient lies during examination. ● *verb* **1** *transitive* (foll. by *in*) (usu. in *passive*) express in words of a specified kind (*couched in simple language*). **2** *transitive* cause (an animal) to lie down. **3** *intransitive archaic* (of an animal) lie in ambush. **4** *transitive archaic* lower (a spear etc.) to the position for attack. [Old French *couche*, *coucher* from Latin *collocare* (as COM-, *locare* place)]

couch² /kʌtʃ, ku:tʃ/ *noun* (in full **couch grass**) any of several grasses of the genus *Agropyron*, esp. *A. repens*, having long creeping roots. *Also called* QUACK GRASS. [var. of QUITCH]

couch·ant /'kʌutʃ ʃənt/ *adjective* (placed after noun) *Heraldry* (of an animal) lying with the body resting on the legs and the head raised. [French, pres. part. of *coucher*: see COUCH¹]

couch·ette /ku:'ʃet/ *noun* **1** a railway car on European trains with seats convertible into sleeping berths. **2** a berth in this. [French, = little bed, diminutive of *couche* COUCH¹]

Cou·chi·ching, Lake /'ku:tʃə,tʃɪŋ/ a small lake in south central Ontario, joining Lake Simcoe with the Severn River. [Ojibwa, = lake source of a river, or water running out]

couch potato *noun slang* a person who spends much of his or her leisure time watching television.

Coué /ku:'ei/ **Émile** (1857–1926), French pharmacist and psychologist, who pioneered psychotherapy through autosuggestion in the 1920s with the phrase 'Every day, and in every way, I am becoming better and better'. □ **Coué·ism** /'ku:ei,ɪzəm/ *noun*

cou·gar *noun N Amer.* **1** a moderately large carnivorous mammal of the cat family, *Felis concolor*, with a tawny or greyish coat and long black-tipped tail, found in parts of N and S America. *Also called* PUMA, PANTHER, MOUNTAIN LION. **2** *slang* an older woman pursuing or dating a younger man. [French, representing Guarani *guaçu ara*]

cough /kɒf/ ● *intransitive verb* **1** expel air from the lungs with a sudden sharp sound produced by abrupt opening of the glottis, to remove an obstruction or congestion. **2** (of an engine, gun, etc.) make a similar sound. ● *noun* **1** an act of coughing. **2** a condition of the respiratory organs causing coughing. **3** a tendency to cough. □ **cough up** (also **cough out**) **1** eject by coughing. **2** *slang* bring out or hand over (money or information) reluctantly. **3** *N Amer. slang* yield or eject (*cough up the puck*). □ **cough·er** *noun* [Middle English *coghe*, *cowhe*, related to Middle Dutch *kuchen*, Middle High German *kūchen*, of imitative origin]

cough drop *noun* a medicated lozenge to relieve a cough.

cough syrup *noun* (also **cough medicine**) a liquid medicine to relieve a cough.

could /kʊd, kəd/ *auxiliary verb* (3rd. sing. **could**) past of CAN¹, used esp.: **1 a** in reported speech (*she said she could come to the party*). **b** to express the conditional mood (*he could have been on time if he had left earlier*). **2** to express a question or polite request (*could you please shut the window?*). **3** to express probability (*that could be the right answer*). **4** to ask permission (*could I leave early?*). **5** to offer a suggestion, advice, etc. (*you could try looking in the encyclopedia for more information*). **6** to express habitual action (*when I was a child, I could not play hockey because of my asthma*).

couldn't /'kʊdənt/ *contraction* could not.

cou·lee /'ku:li/ *noun* **1** *N Amer.* (*West*) a deep ravine with steep sides, formed by heavy rain or melting snow. **2** a stream of molten or solidified lava. [French, fem. past participle of *couler* flow, from Latin *colare* strain, filter]

cou·lis /'ku:li/ *noun* (*pl.* same) a purée of fruit, tomatoes, etc., thin enough to pour. [French from *couler*, as COULEE]

cou·lisse /ku:'li:s/ *noun* (usu. in *pl.*) *Theatre* a piece of side scenery or a space between two of these; the wings. [French from *coulis* sliding: see PORTCULLIS]

coul·oir /'ku:lwar/ *noun* a steep narrow gully on a mountainside. [French from *couler* glide: see COULEE]

Cou·lomb /'ku:lɔ̃/ **Charles-Augustin de** (1736–1806), French physicist. He conducted research on electricity and magnetism, and is best known for **Coulomb's Law**, according to which the forces between two electrical charges are proportional to the product of the charges and inversely proportional to the square of the distance between them.

cou·lomb /'ku:lɒm/ *noun Electricity* the SI unit of electric charge, equal to the quantity of electricity conveyed in one second by a current of one ampere. Symbol: **C**. [COULOMB]

coul·ter /'kɔ:ltɜr/ *noun* (also **col·ter**) a vertical cutting wheel or blade fixed in front of a ploughshare. [Old English from Latin *culter*]

Coul·thard /'ku:ltɑr/ **Jean** (1908–2000), Canadian composer, pianist, and educator. Her work shows the influence of her teacher Vaughan Williams, and reflects her interest in solo and choral vocal music; her compositions include *Spring Rhapsody* (1958) for voice and orchestra, written for Maureen Forrester, *The Pines of Emily Carr* (1969), and *Lyric Sonatinas* (1969, 1971, 1976).

cou·ma·rin /'ku:mɜrɪn/ *noun* an aromatic substance with the smell of new-mown hay, found in many plants and used in perfumery. [French *coumarine* from Tupi *cumarú* tonka bean]

Coun. *abbreviation Cdn & Brit.* Councillor.

coun·cil *noun* **1 a** an advisory, deliberative, or administrative body of people formally constituted and meeting regularly. **b** a meeting of such a body. **2 a** the elected administrative body of a municipality. **b** *Brit.* (*attributive*) (esp. of housing) provided by a local council (*council flat*). **3** a body of persons chosen as advisers (*Privy Council*). **4** an ecclesiastical assembly. **5** = GENERAL COUNCIL. [Anglo-French *cuncile* from Latin *concilium* convocation, assembly, from *calare* summon: compare COUNSEL]

council chamber *noun* a room in which a council meets.

council house *noun Brit.* a house owned and rented out as public housing by a local council.

coun·cil·lor *noun* **1** *Cdn & Brit.* an elected member of a municipal council. Abbr.: **Coun.** **2** a member of a council. **3** *Cdn hist.* (in PEI) one of the two representatives elected to the Legislative Assembly in each riding (*compare* ASSEMBLYMAN 2). □ **coun·cil·lor·ship** *noun*

council·man *noun* (*pl.* **-men**) esp. *US* a member of an esp. municipal council; a councillor.

Council of Trent *see* TRENT, COUNCIL OF.

council tax *noun* (in the UK) a tax levied by local authorities, based on the estimated value of a property and the number of people living in it.

council·woman *noun* (*pl.* **-women**) esp. *US* a female member of an esp. municipal council; a councillor.

coun·sel ● *noun* **1** advice, esp. formally given. **2** consultation, esp. to seek or give advice. **3** (*pl.* same) a lawyer; a body of these advising in a case. **4** a plan of action. ● *transitive verb* (**coun·selled, coun·sel·ling**; esp. *US* **coun·seled, coun·sel·ing**) **1** (often foll. by *to* + infin.) advise (a person). **2 a** give advice to (a person) on social or personal problems, esp. professionally. **b** assist or guide (a person) in resolving personal difficulties. **3** (often foll. by *that*) recommend (a course of action). □ **keep one's own counsel** not confide in others. **take counsel** (usu. foll. by *with*) consult. [Old French *c(o)unseil, conseiller* from Latin *consilium* consultation, advice]

coun·sel·ling *noun* (also esp. *US* **coun·sel·ing**) **1** the act or process of giving counsel. **2** the process of assisting and guiding clients, esp. by a trained person on a professional basis, to resolve esp. personal, social, or psychological problems and difficulties (compare COUNSEL *verb* 2a).

coun·sel·lor *noun* (also **coun·sel·or**) **1** a person who gives counsel; an adviser. **2** a person trained to give guidance on personal, social, or psychological problems (*marriage counsellor; guidance counsellor*). **3** *N Amer.* any of the supervisors of a children's camp. **4** (also **counselor-at-law**) *US* a barrister. **5** a senior officer in the diplomatic service.

count¹ ● *verb* **1** *transitive* determine the total number or amount of (*don't forget to count your change*). **2** *intransitive* repeat numbers in ascending order; conduct a reckoning. **3 a** *transitive* (often foll. by *in*) include in one's reckoning or plan (*you can count me in; fifteen people, counting the guide*). **b** *intransitive* be included in a reckoning or plan. **4** *transitive* consider (a person or thing) to be (lucky etc.) (*count yourself lucky; counted it a blessing*). **5** *intransitive* (often foll. by *for*) have value; matter (*her opinion counts for a great deal; that try doesn't count*). **6** *intransitive* depend or rely on (*I'm counting on you to be on time*). ● *noun* **1 a** the act of counting; a reckoning (*after a count of fifty*). **b** the sum total of a reckoning (*blood count; pollen count*). **2** *Law* each charge in an indictment (*guilty on ten counts*). **3** a count of up to ten seconds by a referee when a boxer is knocked down. **4** *Politics* the act of counting the votes after an election. **5** one of several points under discussion (*you're wrong on three counts*). **6** *Baseball* the number of balls and strikes called against a batter during a single at-bat. **7** the measure of the fineness of a yarn expressed as the weight of a given length or the length of a given weight. **8** (in commercial language) the actual number of items (e.g. fruit, containers, etc.) in a package. **9** *Physics* the number of ionizing particles detected by a counter. □ **count against** be reckoned to the disadvantage of. **count one's blessings** be grateful for what one has. **count one's chickens (before they're hatched)** be over-optimistic or hasty in anticipating good fortune. **count the cost 1** consider the risks before taking action. **2** suffer the consequences of a careless or foolish action. **count the days** (or **hours** etc.) be impatient. **count down** recite numbers backwards to zero, esp. as part of a rocket-launching procedure. **count on** (or **upon**) **1** depend on, rely on; expect confidently. **2** make allowance for. **count on (the fingers of) one hand** reckon as no more than five. **count out 1** count while taking from a stock. **2** complete a count of ten seconds over (a fallen boxer etc.), indicating defeat. **3** (in children's games) select (a player) for dismissal or a special role by use of a counting rhyme etc. **4** *informal* exclude from a plan or reckoning (*I'm too tired, count me out*). **count sheep** imagine sheep jumping over a fence and count them, to combat insomnia. **count to ten** count up to ten under one's breath to prevent oneself from speaking impetuously, esp. in anger or exasperation. **count up** find the sum of. **down** (or **out**) **for the count** *Boxing* defeated by being unable to rise within ten seconds. **2** *informal* **a** defeated or demoralized. **b** soundly asleep. **keep count** take note of how many there have been etc. **lose count** fail to take note of the number etc. **not counting** excluding from the reckoning. **stand up and be counted** state publicly one's support. **take the count** *Boxing* be defeated. [Old French *co(u)nter, co(u)nte* from Late Latin *computus, computare* COMPUTE]

count² *noun* (in some countries) a noble corresponding in rank to an English earl. [Old French *conte* from Latin *comes comitis* companion]

count·able *adjective* **1** that can be counted. **2** *Grammar* (of a noun) that can form a plural or be used with the indefinite article.

count·back *noun Sport* a system of scoring in which the winner of a tied contest is the contestant with the better score in the later part.

count·down *noun* **1 a** the act of counting down, esp. at the launching of a rocket etc. **b** the procedures carried out during this time. **2** the time leading up to any significant event, esp. the final moments.

coun·ten·ance /ˈkaʊntənəns/ ● *noun* **1 a** the face. **b** the facial expression. **2** composure. **3** favour; moral support. ● *transitive verb* give approval to (an act etc.) (*cannot countenance this breach of the rules*).

[Anglo-French *c(o)untenance*, Old French *contenance* bearing from *contenir*: see CONTAIN]

count·er¹ *noun* **1 a** a long flat-topped fixture in a store, bank, etc., across which business is conducted with customers. **b** a similar structure used for serving food etc. in a cafeteria or bar. **c** *N Amer.* a flat surface in a kitchen, usu. on top of a low cabinet, at a height suitable for working standing up, on which food is prepared. **2 a** a small disc or other object used for keeping score etc., esp. in some board games. **b** a token representing a coin. **c** something used in bargaining; a pawn (*a counter in the struggle for power*). **3** an apparatus used for counting. **4** *Physics* an apparatus used for counting individual ionizing particles etc. **5** a person or thing that counts. □ **over the counter** by ordinary retail purchase, without a prescription or permit etc. **under the counter** (esp. of the sale of scarce goods) surreptitiously, esp. illegally. [Anglo-French *count(e)our*, Old French *conteo(i)r*, from medieval Latin *computatorium* (as COMPUTE)]

count·er² ● *verb* **1** *transitive* **a** oppose, contradict (*countered our proposal with their own*). **b** meet by a countermove. **2** *intransitive* make a countermove. **b** make an opposing statement. **3** *intransitive Boxing* give a return blow while parrying. ● *adverb* **1** in the opposite direction. **2** contrary (*her action was counter to my wishes*). ● *adjective* **1** opposed; opposite. **2** duplicate; serving as a check. ● *noun* **1** a parry; a countermove. **2** something opposite or opposed. □ **act** (or **go**) **counter to** disobey (instructions etc.). **run counter to** act contrary to. [Old French *countre* from Latin *contra* against: see COUNTER-]

count·er³ *noun* **1** the part of a horse's breast between the shoulders and under the neck. **2** the curved part of the stern of a ship. **3** *Printing* the white space of a letter such as O. [17th c.: origin unknown]

count·er⁴ *noun* the back part of a shoe or a boot around the heel. [abbreviation of *counterfort* buttress]

counter- *combining form* denoting: **1** retaliation, opposition, or rivalry (*counter-threat*). **2** opposite direction (*countercurrent*). **3** correspondence, duplication, or substitution (*counterpart; countersign*). [from or after Anglo-French *countre*, Old French *contre* from Latin *contra* against]

counter·act *transitive verb* **1** hinder or oppose by contrary action. **2** neutralize. □ **counter·action** *noun* **counter·active** *adjective*

counter-argument *noun* an argument in reply or opposition to another.

counter-attack ● *noun* an attack in reply to an attack by an enemy or opponent. ● *transitive & intransitive verb* attack in reply.

counter-attrac·tion *noun* **1** a rival attraction. **2** the attraction of a contrary tendency.

counter·balance ● *noun* **1** a weight balancing another. **2** an argument, force, etc., balancing another. ● *transitive verb* act as a counterbalance to.

counter·blast *noun* (often foll. by *to*) an energetic or violent verbal or written reply to an argument etc.

counter·charge ● *noun* a charge or accusation made in response to another or against an accuser. ● *transitive verb* make a countercharge against.

counter cheque *noun* a cheque that is not preprinted with an account holder's name, address, and account number.

counter·claim ● *noun* **1** a claim made against another claim. **2** *Law* a claim made by a defendant in a suit against the plaintiff. ● *transitive & intransitive verb* make a counterclaim (for).

counter-clockwise *N Amer.* ● *adverb* in a curve opposite in direction to the movement of the hands of a clock. ● *adjective* moving counter-clockwise.

counter·culture *noun* a culture having values or lifestyles that are in opposition to those of the current accepted culture. □ **counter·cultur·al** *adjective*

counter·current *noun* a current flowing in an opposite direction to another.

counter-cyclical *adjective* of or pertaining to an economic change or trend stimulated, esp. by a government, to mitigate or compensate for the effects of fluctuations in business or in the national economy.

counter-espionage *noun* = COUNTER-INTELLIGENCE.

counter-example *noun* an example serving to counter or contradict another.

counter·fac·tual ● *adjective* relating to or expressing what has not happened or is not the case. ● *noun* a counterfactual conditional statement.

counter·feit /ˈkaʊntərfɪt/ ● *adjective* **1** (of money, documents, recordings, etc.) made in imitation; not genuine; forged. **2** (of a

claimant etc.) pretended. ● *noun* a forgery; an imitation. ● *transitive verb*
1 a imitate fraudulently (money, documents, recordings, etc.); forge.
b make an imitation of. **2** simulate (feelings etc.) (*counterfeited interest*).
3 resemble closely. □ **counter·feit·er** *noun* **counter·feit·ing** *noun*
[Old French *counterfet*, *-fait*, past participle of *contrefaire* from Romanic]

counter·foil *noun* the part of a cheque, receipt, etc., retained by the
payer and containing details of the transaction.

counter·force *noun* a force acting or maintained in opposition to
another.

counter·insurgen·cy *noun* (usu. *attributive*) action against
insurrection (*counter-insurgency operations*).

counter·intelli·gence *noun* action taken to frustrate enemy spying.

counter·intui·tive /ˌkaʊntɜrɪnˈtuːɪtɪv, -ˈtjuːɪtɪv/ *adjective* contrary to
intuition.

counter·irri·tant *noun* **1** *Med.* something used to produce surface
irritation of the skin, thereby counteracting more painful symptoms.
2 anything resembling a counterirritant in its effects.
□ **counter·irri·ta·tion** *noun*

counter·man *noun* (*pl.* **-men**) *N Amer.* a person who works behind a
counter, e.g. in a cafeteria or diner.

counter·mand /ˌkaʊntɜrˈmand/ ● *transitive verb* **1** *Military* **a** revoke (an
order or command). **b** recall (forces etc.) by a contrary order. **2** cancel
an order for (goods etc.); stop (what has been commanded, ordered,
etc.). ● *noun* an order revoking a previous one. [Old French *contremander*
from medieval Latin *contramandare* (as CONTRA-, *mandare* order)]

counter·march ● *transitive & intransitive verb* march or cause to march
in the opposite direction, e.g. with the front marchers turning and
marching back through the ranks. ● *noun* an act of countermarching.

counter·measure *noun* an action taken to counteract a danger,
threat, etc.

counter·move ● *noun* a move or action in opposition to another.
● *intransitive verb* make a countermove.

counter·offen·sive *noun* **1** *Military* an attack made against an
attacking force. **2** any attack made from a defensive position.

counter·offer *noun* an offer made in response to a previous offer.

counter·pane *noun* a bedspread. [alteration (with assimilation to
pane in obsolete sense 'cloth') from obsolete *counterpoint*, via Old
French *contrepointe* (alteration of *cou(l)tepointe*) from medieval Latin
culcita puncta 'quilted mattress']

counter·part *noun* **1 a** a person or thing extremely like another. **b** a
person or thing forming a natural complement or equivalent to
another. **2** one of two copies of a legal document.

counter·party *noun* (*pl.* **-ties**) an opposite party in a contract or
financial transaction.

counter·plot ● *noun* a plot intended to defeat another plot. ● *verb*
(**-plot·ted**, **-plot·ting**) **1** *intransitive* make a counterplot. **2** *transitive*
make a counterplot against.

counter·point ● *noun* **1** *Music* **a** the art or technique of setting,
writing, or playing a melody or melodies in conjunction with another,
according to fixed rules. **b** a melody played in conjunction with
another. **2** a contrasting element, argument, theme, etc. **3** contrast.
● *transitive verb* **1** *Music* add counterpoint to. **2** set (an argument, theme,
etc.) in contrast to (a main element). [Old French *contrepoint* from
medieval Latin *contrapunctum* or marked opposite, i.e. to the
original melody (as CONTRA-, *pungere punct-* prick)]

counter·poise ● *noun* **1** a force etc. equivalent to another on the
opposite side. **2** a state of equilibrium. **3** a counterbalancing weight.
● *transitive verb* **1** counterbalance. **2** compensate. **3** bring into or keep in
equilibrium. [Old French *contrepeis*, *-pois*, *contrepeser* (as COUNTER-, *peis*,
pois from Latin *pensum* weight: compare POISE[1])]

counter·product·ive *adjective* having the opposite of the desired
effect.

counter·punch ● *noun* a punch or attack given in return; a boxer's
counter. ● *intransitive verb* make a counterpunch or counterpunches.
□ **counter·punch·er** *noun*

counter·reform·a·tion *noun* **1** (**Counter-Reformation**) *hist.* the
reform of the Roman Catholic Church in the 16th and 17th c. which
took place in response to the Protestant Reformation. *Also called*
CATHOLIC REFORMATION. **2** a reformation running counter to another.

counter·revolu·tion *noun* a revolution opposing a former one or
reversing its results. □ **counter·revolu·tion·ary** *adjective & noun* (*pl.*
-aries).

counter·shaft *noun* an intermediate shaft driven by a main shaft and
transmitting motion to a particular machine etc.

counter·sign ● *transitive verb* add a signature to (a document
previously signed by oneself or another). ● *noun* a sign or signal used in
response to another, esp. a watchword or password spoken to a person
on guard. □ **counter·signature** *noun* [French *contresigner* (v.),
contresigne (n.) from Italian *contrasegno* (as COUNTER-, SIGN)]

counter·sink ● *transitive verb* (*past* and *past participle* **-sunk**) **1** enlarge
and bevel (the rim of a hole) so that a screw or bolt can be inserted
flush with the surface. **2** sink (a screw etc.) in such a hole. ● *noun* a tool
used to countersink a hole.

counter·suit *noun* a lawsuit undertaken in response to another.

counter·tenor *noun* **1** an adult male alto singing voice. **b** a singer
with this voice. **2** a part written for counter-tenor. [French *contre-teneur*
from obsolete Italian *contratenore* (as CONTRA-, TENOR)]

counter·terror·ism *noun* measures to combat terrorism.

counter·top *noun* esp. *N Amer.* the flat working surface of a counter,
esp. in a kitchen.

counter·transfer·ence *noun* **1** the redirection of childhood
emotions felt by an analyst towards a patient. **2** any emotion felt by an
analyst towards a patient.

counter·vail ● *verb* **1** *transitive* counterbalance. **2** *transitive & intransitive*
(often foll. by *against*) oppose forcefully and usu. successfully. ● *noun Cdn*
a countervailing duty. □ **counter·vail·able** *adjective* [Anglo-French
contrevaloir from Latin *contra valēre* be of worth against]

counter·vail·ing duty *noun* a tax put on imports to offset a subsidy
in the exporting country or a tax on similar goods not from abroad.

counter·weight *noun* a counterbalancing weight.

coun·tess *noun* **1** the wife or widow of a count or an earl. **2** a woman
holding the rank of count or earl.

count·ing house *noun* an office etc. where the financial records of a
business are maintained.

count·less *adjective* too many to be counted.

count noun *noun* a countable noun (*see* COUNTABLE 2).

Count Pala·tine *noun hist.* **1** a count of the imperial palace in the
later Roman Empire having supreme judicial authority in the imperial
court. **2** any of several counts in the German Empire, each having
supreme jurisdiction within his own territory. **3** (**count palatine**)
the earl or lord of a county palatine in England or Ireland.

coun·tri·fied *adjective* (also **coun·try·fied**) often *derogatory* (of
manners, appearance, etc.) rural or rustic. [past participle of *countrify*
from COUNTRY]

coun·try *noun* (*pl.* **-tries**) **1** the territory of a nation with its own
government; a nation. **2** (often *attributive*) **a** rural districts as opposed to
cities or towns (*lives in the country*; *a country girl*). **b** styles of clothing,
fabric, furnishing, etc. supposed to be typically rural, usu. inspired by
historical fashions. **3** the land of a person's birth or citizenship. **4** a
territory marked by some particular characteristic (*maple country*). **5** an
area of interest or knowledge. **6** a region associated with a particular
person, esp. a writer or painter (*Leacock country*). **7** a national
population, esp. as voters (*the country won't stand for it*). **8 a** = COUNTRY
AND WESTERN. **b** = NEW COUNTRY. **9** *Cdn* (*Nfld*) **a** the thin strip of
settlements along the coast. **b** the interior of Newfoundland and
Labrador. □ **across country** not keeping to roads. **by a country
mile** *N Amer. informal* by a great extent (*better by a country mile*). **go** (or
appeal) **to the country** *Cdn & Brit.* test public opinion by dissolving
Parliament and holding a general election. □ **country·ish** *adjective*
[Old French *cuntree*, from medieval Latin *contrata* (*terra*) (land) lying
opposite (CONTRA)]

country and western *noun* a style of music combining elements of
British folk music as preserved in the rural or southern areas of
N America, cowboy songs, and other styles of popular music, usu.
suggesting a rural atmosphere and often dealing with themes of
separation and lost love.

country-born *adjective Cdn hist.* designating English-speaking
Protestants of mixed European and Aboriginal ancestry.

country bumpkin *noun* = BUMPKIN.

country club *noun* a suburban sport and social club, with facilities
for golf and usu. tennis, swimming, etc.

country cousin *noun* often *derogatory* **1** a countrified relation or
other person who is out of place in a city or among urban dwellers. **2** a
person, animal, organization, thing, etc. having some similarities with
another but viewed as rustic or unsophisticated in comparison.

country dance *noun* a traditional English rural dance, with couples
facing each other in long lines.

Consonants: b *but*   d *dog*   f *few*   g *get*   h *her*   j *yes*   k *cat*   l *leg*   m *man*   n *no*   p *pen*   r *red*   s *sit*

country elevator noun Cdn (Prairies) a grain elevator equipped to unload grain from trucks, store it, and load it into rail cars.

country·fied var. of COUNTRIFIED.

country food noun Cdn game, fish, or other foods that can be obtained while in the bush.

country gentleman noun a wealthy man living on a large estate in the country.

country house noun 1 a usu. large house in the country, esp. the residence of a wealthy person. 2 Cdn (Que.) a summer cottage.

country kitchen noun N Amer. a large airy kitchen, usu. with pine or oak kitchen cabinets and room for a large wooden kitchen table.

country·man noun (pl. **-men**) 1 a person living in a rural area. 2 a (also **fellow countryman**) a person of one's own country or region. b (often in combination) a person from a specified country or region.

country marriage noun Cdn hist. a common-law marriage between a fur trader of European descent and an Aboriginal or Metis woman.

country music noun 1 = COUNTRY AND WESTERN. 2 = NEW COUNTRY.

country rock[1] noun a blend of rock music with country and western. [ROCK[2]]

country rock[2] noun the rock which encloses a mineral deposit or an igneous intrusion. [ROCK[1]]

country seat noun a large country estate or mansion.

country·side noun 1 a a rural area. b rural areas in general. 2 the inhabitants of a rural area.

country store noun N Amer. a rural general store.

country·wide adjective extending throughout a nation (a countrywide opinion poll).

country wife noun Cdn hist. the Indian or Metis common-law wife of a fur trader.

country·woman noun (pl. **-women**) 1 a woman living in a rural area. 2 a a person of one's own country or region. b (often in combination) a person from a specified country or region.

coun·ty ● noun (pl. **-ties**) 1 a any of the territorial divisions of some countries or provinces, for electoral, judicial, or local government purposes. b US a political and administrative division of a State. 2 Brit. the people of a county, esp. the leading families. ● adjective Brit. having the social status or characteristics of county families. [Anglo-French counté, Old French conté from Latin comitatus (as COUNT[2])]

county clerk noun (in the US) an elected county official who is responsible for local elections and maintaining public records.

county council noun the elected governing body of an administrative county. □ **county councillor** noun

county palatine noun hist. 1 the territory of a Count Palatine. 2 Brit. a county in which royal privileges and exclusive rights of jurisdiction were held by its earl or lord.

county seat noun (also **county town**) the administrative capital of a county.

coup /kuː/ noun 1 a notable or successful stroke or move. 2 = COUP D'ÉTAT. 3 (among Plains Indian peoples) the act of touching an enemy in battle and escaping, considered a heroic act. □ **count coup** (among Plains Indian peoples) perform a coup or recount having done so. [French from medieval Latin colpus blow: see COPE[1]]

coup de foudre /kuː də ˈfuːdrə/ noun (pl. **coups de foudre** pronunc. same) 1 a sudden unforeseen event. 2 love at first sight. [French, literally 'stroke of lightning']

coup de grâce /ˌkuː də ˈɡras, -ɡrɒs/ noun (pl. **coups de grâce** pronunc. same) a finishing stroke, esp. to kill a wounded animal or person. [French, lit. 'stroke of grace']

coup de main /ˌkuː də ˈmã/ noun (pl. **coups de main** pronunc. same) a sudden vigorous attack. [French, lit. 'stroke of the hand']

coup d'état /ˌkuː deiˈtɒ/ noun (pl. **coups d'état** pronunc. same) a violent or illegal seizure of power. [French, lit. 'stroke of the State']

coup de thé·âtre /ˌkuː də teiˈatrə/ noun (pl. **coups de thé·âtre** pronunc. same) a sensational or dramatically sudden turn of events. [French, lit. 'stroke of the theatre']

coup d'oeil /kuː ˈdɔi/ noun (pl. **coups d'oeil** pronunc. same) 1 a comprehensive glance. 2 a general view. [French, lit. 'stroke of the eye']

coupe[1] /kuːp/ noun 1 a two-door car with a hard roof, esp. one seating only two persons. 2 hist. a four-wheeled enclosed carriage for two passengers and a driver. [French coupé, past participle of couper cut (formed as COUP)]

coupe[2] /kuːp/ noun 1 a shallow glass or dish used for serving fruit, ice cream, etc. 2 fruit, ice cream, etc. served in this. [French, = goblet]

Coupe·rin /ˈkuːpə,rã/ **Fran·çois** (1668–1733), French composer, organist, and harpsichordist. One of Louis XIV's court musicians, he composed more than 230 harpsichord works; his music and treatise L'Art de toucher le clavecin (1716) influenced Bach.

Coup·land /ˈkoːplənd/ **Doug·las** (b.1961), Canadian writer, author of Generation X: Tales for an Accelerated Culture (1991) and other novels focusing on those born in the 1960s and 1970s.

couple ● noun 1 (usu. foll. by of; often treated as sing.) a two (a couple of girls). b about two (a couple of hours). ¶ The use of couple without a following of, as in they'd had a couple beers, is highly informal and should be avoided in writing. 2 (often treated as sing.) a two people who are romantically involved (they make a lovely couple). b a pair of partners in dancing, figure skating, etc. 3 Mech. a pair of equal and parallel forces acting in opposite directions, and tending to cause rotation about an axis perpendicular to the plane containing them. ● verb 1 transitive fasten or link together; connect (esp. railway cars etc.). 2 transitive (often foll. by together, with) associate in thought or speech (couple our congratulations with our best wishes; high unemployment coupled with inflation). 3 transitive & intransitive (often foll. by with, up (with)) bring or come together as companions or partners. 4 intransitive copulate. 5 transitive Physics connect (oscillators) with a coupling. □ **couple·dom** noun [Old French cople, cuple, copler, cupler from Latin copulare, Latin COPULA]

coup·ler noun 1 a person or thing that couples or links things together. 2 = COUPLING 1. 3 a transformer used for connecting electric circuits. 4 Music a a device in an organ for connecting two manuals, or a manual with pedals, so that they both sound when only one is played. b (also **octave coupler**) a similar device for connecting notes with their octaves above or below.

coup·let /ˈkʌplət/ noun Prosody two successive lines of verse, usu. rhyming and of the same length. [French diminutive of couple, formed as COUPLE]

coup·ling noun 1 a a link connecting railway cars etc. b a device for connecting parts of machinery. 2 a thing that couples or links things together. 3 the act of a person that couples. 4 Physics a connection between two systems, causing one to oscillate when the other does so.

cou·pon /ˈkuːpɒn, ˈkjuː-/ noun 1 a certificate entitling the bearer to a discount on a purchase etc. 2 a form in a newspaper, magazine, etc., which may be filled in and sent as an application for a purchase, information, etc. 3 a voucher given with a retail purchase, a certain number of which entitle the holder to a discount, premium, etc. 4 a detachable portion of a bond etc. which is given up in return for a payment of interest. 5 Brit. an entry form for a sports pool or other competition. 6 a detachable ticket entitling the holder to a ration of food, clothes, etc., esp. in wartime. [French, = piece cut off, from couper cut: see COUPE[1]]

cour·age noun the ability to disregard fear; bravery. □ **courage of one's convictions** the courage to act on one's beliefs. **lose courage** become less brave. **pluck up** (or **take**) **courage** muster one's courage. **take one's courage in both hands** nerve oneself to a venture. [Old French corage, from Latin cor heart]

cour·age·ous adjective brave, fearless. □ **cour·age·ous·ly** adverb

cou·rante /kuˈrant/ noun 1 hist. a running or gliding dance. 2 Music the music used for this, esp. as a movement of a suite. [French, fem. pres. part. (as noun) of courir run, from Latin currere]

Cour·bet /kuːrˈbei/ **Gus·tave** (1819–77), French painter. A leader of the 19th-c. realist school of painting, he favoured an unidealized depiction of contemporary life; important works include Burial at Ornans (1850) and The Artist's Studio (1855).

Cour·celle /kuːrˈsel/ **Dan·iel de Rémy de** (1626–98), French army officer and colonial administrator, governor of New France 1665–72. In 1666 he led two expeditions against the Iroquois in retaliation for raids against the settlements of New France.

cour·eur de bois /ˌkuːrər də ˈbwɒ/ noun Cdn hist. (pl. **cour·eurs de bois** pronunc. same) a French or Metis fur trader, esp. one employed by the Hudson's Bay or North West Companies. [French, = 'runner of the woods']

cour·gette /kuːrˈʒet/ noun esp. Brit. = ZUCCHINI. [French, diminutive of courge gourd]

cour·ier /ˈkuːriːɚ/ ● noun 1 a person or company hired to convey documents, packages etc. from sender to recipient. 2 a person who transports drugs, arms, etc. illegally, esp. from one country to another. 3 a special messenger. 4 (also **Courier**) a serif font similar to that traditionally produced by manual typewriters. 5 a tour guide.

---

t top   v voice   w we   z zoo   ʃ she   ʒ vision   θ thin   ð this   ŋ ring   x loch   tʃ chip   dʒ jar   (see over for vowels)

● *transitive verb* ship (a package etc.) by courier. [obsolete French, from Italian *corriere*, & from Old French *coreor*, both from Latin *currere* run]

courier parent *noun Cdn* a person who obtains a visa to immigrate to Canada only so that his or her children may also immigrate.

Cour·règes /kuːˈreʒ/ **André** (b.1923), French fashion designer, who is known for promoting unisex fashion and introducing the miniskirt (1964).

course ● *noun* **1** a continuous onward movement or progression. **2 a** a line along which a person or thing moves; a direction taken (*has changed course; the course of the winding river*). **b** a correct or intended direction or line of movement. **c** the direction taken by a ship or aircraft. **3 a** the ground on which a race (or other sport involving extensive linear movement) takes place. **b** a series of fences, hurdles, or other obstacles to be crossed in a race etc. **c** = GOLF COURSE. **4 a** a series of lectures, lessons, etc., in a particular subject. **b** a book for such a course (*A Modern French Course*). **5** any of the successive parts of a meal. **6** a sequence of medical treatment etc. (*prescribed a course of antibiotics*). **7** a line of conduct (*disappointed by the course he took*). **8** a continuous horizontal layer of brick, stone, shingles, etc., in a building. **9** a channel in which water flows. **10** the pursuit of game (esp. hares) with hounds, esp. greyhounds, by sight rather than scent. **11** *Naut.* a sail on a square-rigged ship (*fore course; main course*). ● *verb* **1** *intransitive* (esp. of liquid) run, esp. fast (*blood coursed through her veins*). **2** *transitive & intransitive* **a** use (hounds) to hunt. **b** pursue (hares etc.) in hunting. □ **the course of nature** ordinary events or procedure. **in the course of** during. **in the course of time** as time goes by; eventually. **of course** naturally; as is or was to be expected; admittedly. **on** (or **off**) **course** following (or deviating from) the desired direction or goal. **run** (or **take**) **its course** (esp. of an illness) complete its natural development. [Old French *cours* from Latin *cursus* from *currere curs-* run]

course·book *noun* a book designed for use on a particular course of study.

cours·er[1] *noun literary* a swift horse. [Old French *corsier* from Romanic]

cours·er[2] *noun* **1** a dog used in coursing. **2** any fast-running plover-like bird of the genus *Cursorius*, native to Africa and Asia, having long legs and a slender bill. [Late Latin *cursorius* adapted for running]

course·ware *noun* material (esp. computer programs) designed for use in an educational or training course.

course·work *noun* the work done during a course of study, esp. when counting towards a student's final assessment.

court ● *noun* **1** (in full **court of law**) **a** an assembly of a judge or judges and other persons acting as a tribunal in civil and criminal cases. **b** a regular session of a court. **c** a courtroom or courthouse. **2 a** a demarcated quadrangular area for playing certain games (*tennis court; basketball court*). **b** a subdivision of this area. **3 a** a small enclosed street adjoining a larger one. **b** (in proper names) a large house, apartment building, street, etc. **c** *Brit.* = COURTYARD. **d** = ATRIUM 1b. **4 a** the establishment, retinue, and courtiers of a sovereign. **b** a sovereign and his or her councillors, constituting a ruling power. **c** a sovereign's residence. **d** an assembly held by a sovereign; a State reception. **5** attention paid to a person whose favour, love, or interest is sought (*paid court to her*). **6** (in some fraternal societies) a local lodge or branch. **7** (in Presbyterian and United churches) any of several governing bodies made up of clergy and elders, e.g. sessions, presbyteries, etc. ● *transitive verb* **1 a** try to win the affection or favour of (a person). **b** pay amorous attention to (*courting couples*). **2** seek to win (applause, fame, etc.). **3** invite (misfortune) by one's actions (*you are courting disaster*). □ **go to court** take legal action. **hold court** preside (esp. pompously) over a group of attendants, admirers, etc. **in court** appearing as a party or an advocate in a court of law. **out of court 1** (of a plaintiff) not entitled to be heard. **2** (of a settlement) arranged before a hearing or judgment can take place. **3** esp. *Brit.* **a** not worthy of consideration (*that suggestion is out of court*). **b** (esp. in phr. **laugh out of court**) so as to ridicule completely. [Old French *cort*, ultimately from Latin *cohors, -hortis* yard, retinue]

court bouil·lon /ˌkuːr buːˈjɔ̃/ *noun* (*pl.* **courts bouil·lons**) stock usu. made from wine, vegetables, etc., often used in fish dishes. [French from *court* short + BOUILLON]

court card *noun Brit.* = FACE CARD. [originally *coat card*, from the decorative dress of the figures depicted]

court circular *noun Brit.* a daily report of royal court affairs, published in some newspapers.

court dress *noun* formal dress worn at a royal court.

Courte·nay /ˈkɔːrtni/ a city on the east central coast of Vancouver

Island, 107 km northwest of Nanaimo; pop. (2001) 18,304. [Capt. G. W. Conway *Courtenay*, commander of HMS *Constance* 1846–9]

cour·te·ous /ˈkɜːrtiːəs/ *adjective* polite, kind, or considerate in manner; well-mannered. □ **cour·te·ous·ly** *adverb* **cour·te·ous·ness** *noun* [Old French *corteis, curteis* from Romanic (as COURT): assimilated to words in -OUS]

cour·tesan /ˈkɔːrtɪˌzan/ *noun hist.* **1** a prostitute, esp. one with wealthy or upper-class clients. **2** the mistress of a wealthy man. [French *courtisane* from Italian *cortigiana*, fem. of *cortigiano* courtier, from *corte* COURT]

cour·tesy /ˈkɜːrtɪsi/ ● *noun* (*pl.* **-ies**) **1** courteous behaviour; good manners. **2** a courteous act. **3** *archaic* = CURTSY. ● *adjective* (esp. of transport) supplied free of charge to people who are already paying for another service (*the autobody repair shop provides a courtesy car; use the courtesy phone to call a cab*). □ **by courtesy** by favour, not by right. **by courtesy of** with the formal permission of (a person etc.). **courtesy of** thanks to. [Old French *curtesie, co(u)rtesie* from *curteis* etc. COURTEOUS]

courtesy light *noun* a small light in a car, automatically switched on when one of the doors is opened.

courtesy title *noun* a title held by courtesy, usu. having no legal validity, e.g. a title given to the heir of a duke etc.

court·house *noun* **1** a building in which a judicial court is held. **2** *US* a building containing the administrative offices of a county.

court·ier /ˈkɔːrtiːər/ *noun* a person who attends or frequents a sovereign's court. [Anglo-French *courte(i)our*, from Old French from *cortoyer* be present at court]

court·ly *adjective* (**court·li·er, court·li·est**) **1** polished or refined in manners. **2** obsequious. □ **court·li·ness** *noun*

courtly love *noun* a highly conventionalized medieval tradition of love between a knight and a married noblewoman, first developed by the troubadours of southern France and extensively employed in European literature of the time. The love of the knight for his lady, characterized by devoted service to her, was regarded as an ennobling passion and the relationship was typically unconsummated.

courtly romance *noun* a conventional work of literature, esp. of the Middle Ages, dealing with courtly love.

court martial ● *noun* (*pl.* **courts martial**) a judicial court for trying members of the armed services. ● *transitive verb* (**court-martial**) (**-martialled**, **-martial·ling**; esp. *US* **-martialed**, **-martial·ing**) try by a court martial.

Court of Appeal *noun* a court of law hearing appeals against judgments in lower courts, esp. (in Canada) the highest appeal court in a province or territory.

court of first instance *noun* a court of primary jurisdiction.

Court of Queen's Bench *noun see* QUEEN'S BENCH.

court of record *noun* a court whose proceedings are recorded and available as evidence of fact.

court of review *noun* a court before which sentences etc. come for revision.

court of summary jurisdiction *noun* a court having the authority to use summary proceedings and arrive at a judgment or conviction.

court order *noun* a direction issued by a court or a judge, usu. requiring a person to do or not do something.

court plaster *noun hist.* an adhesive bandage for cuts etc. [formerly used by ladies at court for face patches]

court reporter *noun N Amer.* **1** an official stenographer in a court of law. **2** a journalist who reports on trials, etc.

court·room *noun* the place or room in which a court of law meets.

court·ship *noun* **1 a** a courting, esp. with intent to marry. **b** the behaviour of male and female animals, birds, etc. prior to and during mating. **c** a period of courtship. **2** an attempt, often protracted, to gain advantage by flattery, attention, etc.

court shoe *noun* **1** *N Amer.* an athletic shoe with a non-marking sole, worn esp. when playing sports on a wooden floor, such as squash or racquetball. **2** *Brit.* = PUMP[2].

court·side ● *noun* the area or seats immediately alongside the edge of a basketball or tennis court. ● *adverb* in this area.

court tennis *noun N Amer.* a type of tennis played on an indoor walled court.

court·yard *noun* an area enclosed by walls or buildings, often opening off a street.

cous·cous /ˈkuːskuːs/ *noun* **1** a type of North African pasta in granules made from crushed durum wheat. **2** a dish of this, often with meat or fruit added. [French from Arabic *kuskus* from *kaskasa* to pound]

cous·in *noun* **1 a** (also **first cousin**) the child of one's uncle or aunt. **b** any other relative with whom one shares a common ancestor; a second cousin, etc. **c** a person who is married to one's cousin. **2 a** person or thing related to another by common features etc. **3** (usu. in *pl.*) applied to the people of kindred races or nations (*our American cousins*). **4** *hist.* a title formerly used by a sovereign in addressing another sovereign or a noble of his or her own country. □ **cousin·hood** *noun* **cousin·ly** *adjective* **cousin·ship** *noun* [Old French *cosin, cusin*, from Latin *consobrinus* mother's sister's child]

cousin-german *noun* esp. *hist.* = COUSIN 1a. [COUSIN + GERMAN]

Cous·teau /kuːˈstoʊ/ **Jacques-Yves** (1910–97), French oceanographer and film director, renowned for his innovative work in undersea exploration, notably his invention of the scuba apparatus; he was also known for his popular television series and commitment to marine conservation issues.

couth /kuːθ/ *jocular* ● *adjective* cultured; well-mannered. ● *noun* good manners; cultured behaviour. [back-formation as antonym of UNCOUTH]

Cou·ture /kuːˈtʊr/ **Guil·laume** (1851–1915), Canadian composer and educator. He was the founder (1894) and director (1894–6) of the Montreal Symphony Orchestra, and his compositions include the oratorio *Jean le Précurseur* (*c.*1907).

cou·ture /kuːˈtʃuːr, -tuːr, -tjuːr/ ● *noun* **1** the design and manufacture of fashionable clothes. **2** = HAUTE COUTURE. ● *adjective* (of clothing) highly fashionable; designed by a couturier. [French, = sewing, dressmaking]

cou·tur·ier /kuːˈtʊriˌei/ *noun* a person who designs and oversees the making of high-fashion clothes. [French]

cou·turi·ère /kuːˌtʊriˈer/ *noun* a woman who designs and oversees the making of high-fashion clothes. [French]

cou·vade /kuːˈvɒd/ *noun* a custom in some cultures by which a father appears to undergo labour and childbirth when his child is being born. [French from *couver* hatch, from Latin *cubare* lie down]

couver·ture /ˌkuːvɜrˈtʃʊr/ *noun* chocolate for covering candies, cakes, etc. [French, = covering]

co·valence /koˈveiləns/ *noun* (also **co·valen·cy** /koˈveilənsi/) *Chem.* **1** the linking of atoms by a covalent bond. **2** the number of pairs of electrons an atom can share with another.

co·valent /koˈveilənt/ *adjective Chem.* **1** relating to, designating, or characterized by chemical bonds. **2** formed by sharing of electrons usu. in pairs by two atoms in a molecule (*covalent bond*). □ **co·valent·ly** *adverb* [CO- + *valent*, after *trivalent* etc.]

cove¹ ● *noun* **1** a small, esp. sheltered, bay or other indentation in the shoreline of an ocean, lake, river, etc. **2** a sheltered recess. **3** *Archit.* a concave arch or arched moulding, esp. one formed at the junction of a wall with a ceiling. ● *transitive verb Archit.* provide (a room, ceiling, etc.) with a cove. [Old English *cofa* chamber, from Germanic]

cove² *noun Brit. slang archaic* a fellow; a chap. [16th-c. cant: origin unknown]

cov·en /ˈkʌvən/ *noun* an assembly of witches. [var. of *covent*; see CONVENT]

coven·ant /ˈkʌvənənt/ ● *noun* **1** an agreement; a contract. **2** *Law* **a** a contract drawn up under a seal. **b** a clause of a covenant. **3** (**Covenant**) *Bible* an agreement between God and a person or nation, etc. *See also* ARK OF THE COVENANT. ● *transitive & intransitive verb* agree, esp. by legal covenant. □ **coven·ant·al** /-ˈnantəl/ *adjective* **coven·ant·or** *noun* (in sense 2). [Old French, pres. part. of *co(n)venir*, formed as CONVENE]

coven·ant·ed /ˈkʌvənəntəd/ *adjective* bound by a covenant.

coven·ant·er /ˈkʌvənəntər/ *noun* **1** a person who covenants. **2** (**Covenanter**) *hist.* an adherent of either the National Covenant or the Solemn League and Covenant in 17th-c. Scotland, in support of Presbyterianism.

Cov·ent Garden /ˈkɒvənt/ a district in central London, originally the convent garden of the Abbey of Westminster. It was the site for 300 years (until 1974) of London's chief fruit and vegetable market. The Royal Opera House (built 1888), home to the Royal Ballet and the Royal Opera, is located there.

Cov·en·try /ˈkɒvəntri/ an industrial city in the West Midlands of central England, east of Birmingham; pop. (2001) 300,844. Its cathedral, built in 1443, was badly damaged during the Second World War and was replaced by a new cathedral, consecrated in 1962.

□ **send a person to Coventry** refuse to associate with or speak to a person.

cov·er ● *transitive & intransitive verb* **1** *transitive* (often foll. by *with*) protect or conceal by means of a cloth, lid, etc. **2** *transitive* **a** extend over; occupy the whole surface of (*covered in dirt; covered with writing*). **b** (often foll. by *with*) strew thickly or thoroughly (*covered the floor with straw*). **c** lie over; be a covering to (*the blanket scarcely covered her*). **3** *transitive* protect; clothe. **4** *transitive* include; comprise; deal with (*the talk covered recent discoveries*). **5** *transitive* travel (a specified distance) (*covered sixty miles*). **6** *transitive Journalism* **a** report (events, a meeting, etc.). **b** investigate as a reporter. **7** *transitive* be enough to defray (expenses, a bill, etc.) (*$20 should cover it*). **8 a** *reflexive* take precautionary measures so as to protect oneself (*had covered myself by saying I might be late*). **b** *intransitive* (foll. by *for*) deputize or stand in for (a colleague etc.) (*will you cover for me?*). **9** *transitive Military* **a** aim a gun etc. at. **b** (of a fortress, guns, etc.) command (a territory). **c** stand behind (a person in the front rank). **d** protect (an exposed person etc.) by being able to return fire. **10** *transitive Sport* **a** esp. *Baseball* stand behind (another player) to stop any missed balls. **b** (in hockey, football, etc.) keep close to so as to prevent the free movement of (a player of the other side). **c** defend (an area of a field or court, a base, etc.). **11** *transitive & intransitive* (in some card games) play a card higher than (one already played to the same trick). **12** *transitive* (of a stallion, bull, etc.) copulate with. **13** *transitive* perform or record a cover (of a song etc.). ● *noun* **1** something that covers or protects, esp.: **a** a lid. **b** the binding of a book, magazine, etc. **c** either board or sheet of this. **d** an envelope or the wrapper of a parcel (*under separate cover*). **e** a stamped envelope of interest to stamp collectors. **f** the outer case of a pneumatic tire. **g** (in *pl.*) bedclothes. **2** a hiding place; a shelter. **3** woods or undergrowth sheltering game or covering the ground. **4 a** a pretense; a screen (*under cover of humility*). **b** a spy's pretended identity or activity, intended as concealment. **c** *Military* a supporting force protecting an advance party from attack. **5 a** funds, esp. obtained by insurance, to meet a liability or secure against a contingent loss. **b** the state of being protected (*third party cover*). **6** a place setting at table, esp. in a restaurant. **7** = COVER CHARGE. **8** a recording or performance of a previously recorded song etc., made esp. to take advantage of the original's success (also *attributive*: *cover version*; *cover song*). □ **break cover** (of an animal, esp. game, or a hunted person) leave a place of shelter, esp. vegetation. **cover in** provide with a roof etc. **cover one's ass** (or **behind** or **butt** or **backside**) foresee and avoid the possibility of attack or criticism. **cover one's tracks** conceal evidence of what one has done. **cover up 1** completely cover or conceal. **2** conceal (circumstances etc., esp. illicitly). **3** assist in a deception (*refused to cover up for them*). **from cover to cover** from beginning to end of a book etc. **take cover** use a natural or prepared shelter against an attack. □ **cover·able** *adjective* **cover·er** *noun* [Old French *covrir, cuvrir* from Latin *cooperire* (as CO-, *operire opert-* cover)]

cover·age *noun* **1** an area or an amount covered. **2** *Journalism* the amount of press, publicity, etc. received by a particular story, person, etc. **3** a risk covered by an insurance policy. **4** an area reached by a particular broadcasting station or advertising medium.

cover·all *noun* esp. *N Amer.* (usu. in *pl.*) a one-piece garment worn over other clothing to protect it.

cover band *noun* a band whose repertoire consists of cover versions rather than original material.

cover boy *noun informal* a man whose picture has appeared on the cover of a magazine.

cover charge *noun* an extra charge levied per head in a restaurant, nightclub, etc.

cover crop *noun* a crop grown between main crops for the protection and enrichment of the soil.

Cov·er·dale, **Miles** (1488–1568), English Protestant Biblical scholar. He translated the first complete printed English Bible (1535), and edited the Great Bible, published in 1539 by the printer Richard Grafton (*c.*1513–*c.*1572).

cov·ered *adjective* **1** provided with a cover or lid (*covered butter dish*). **2** provided with a covering (*covered connector, covered button*). **3 a** enclosed; provided with a roof, top, or cover (*a covered bridge*). **b** (of a ship) decked. **4** thickly laid over or enveloped (*snow-covered hills*). **5** insured. **6** wearing a hat, veil, etc.

covered wagon *noun N Amer.* a large wagon with an arched canvas roof, used by pioneers for travel westward across the prairies.

cover girl *noun* a female model, esp. a beautiful one, whose picture appears on magazine covers etc.

cov·er·ing *noun* anything that covers something else for protection, concealment, etc.

covering letter *noun* (*N Amer.* also **cover letter**) a letter of introduction, explanation, etc. which accompanies a resumé, package, etc.

cov·er·let *noun* a bedspread. [Anglo-French *covrelet, -lit* from Old French *covrir* cover + *lit* bed]

cover plate *noun* a plate, usu. of metal, that covers some opening, electrical outlet, etc.

cover-point *noun* **1** *Hockey hist.* a player who stands just in front of point to prevent the puck from coming near the goal. **2** *Lacrosse* a player positioned just in front of point.

cover price *noun* the retail price indicated on the cover of a book, magazine, etc.

cover slip *noun* a thin sheet of glass that covers slide samples intended for microscopic examination.

cover story *noun* **1** a story in a magazine that is illustrated or advertised on the front cover. **2** an invented story intended to mislead or to conceal one's true actions, motives, etc.

co·vert /ˈkʌvərt, koʊˈvɜːrt, kʌ-/ ● *adjective* secret or disguised (*a covert glance; covert operations*). ● *noun* /ˈkʌvərt/ **1** a shelter, esp. a thicket or wooded area which hides game. **2** a feather covering the base of a bird's flight feather. □ **co·vert·ly** *adverb* [Old French *covert* past participle of *covrir* COVER]

cover-up *noun* **1** an act of concealing circumstances, esp. illicitly. **2** any loose outer garment worn over a bathing suit, exercise clothes, etc.

cover version *noun* see COVER *noun* 8.

cov·et /ˈkʌvət/ *transitive verb* (**cov·et·ed, cov·et·ing**) **1** desire wrongfully or inordinately, esp. something belonging to another person (*she coveted her friend's earrings*). **2** long for or desire greatly, but not inappropriately (*we covet your prayers*). □ **covet·able** *adjective* **cov·et·ed** *adjective* [Old French *coveitier* from Romanic]

cov·et·ous /ˈkʌvətəs/ *adjective* (usu. foll. by *of*) **1** greedy, wrongfully eager to possess something. **2** greatly desirous (of something). □ **cov·et·ous·ly** *adverb* **cov·et·ous·ness** *noun*

covey /ˈkʌvi/ *noun* (*pl.* **-eys**) **1** a brood of game birds, as partridges, ptarmigan, etc. **2** a small party or group of people or things. [Old French *covee* from Romanic from Latin *cubare* lie]

cov·ing *noun* = COVE[1] *noun* 3.

cow[1] *noun* **1 a** a fully grown female of any bovine animal, esp. of the genus *Bos*, used as a source of milk and beef. **b** a domestic bovine animal (regardless of sex or age). ¶ It is considered incorrect by many people to call a male bovine a *cow*. **c** a female domestic bovine animal which has borne a calf (*compare* HEIFER). **2** the female of other large animals, esp. the moose, elephant, whale, and seal. **3** *derogatory slang* a woman, esp. a coarse or unpleasant one. □ **have a cow** *N Amer. slang* become angry, hysterical, excited, etc. **till the cows come home** *informal* an indefinitely long time. □ **cow·like** *adjective* [Old English *cū* from Germanic, related to Latin *bos*, Greek *bous*]

cow[2] *transitive verb* (usu. in *passive*) intimidate, frighten, or browbeat into submission (*cowed by the threats*). [prob. from Old Norse *kúga* oppress]

cowa·bunga *interjection slang* expressing delight or satisfaction, or as a call to action. [prob. fanciful]

cow·age /ˈkaʊɪdʒ/ *noun* (also **cow·hage**) a climbing plant, *Mucuna pruritum*, having hairy pods which cause stinging and itching. [Hindi *kawānch*]

Cow·ans·ville /ˈkaʊənzvɪl/ a town in S Quebec, located southwest of Sherbrooke, near the border with Vermont; pop. (2001) 12,032. [P. Cowan, the town's first postmaster and merchant *c.*1841]

Cow·ard, Sir Noël (Pierce) (1899–1973), English playwright, actor, and composer, who is best known for his witty social comedies such as *Private Lives* (1930) and *Blithe Spirit* (1941); his revues and musicals include *Bitter Sweet* (1929) and *Cavalcade* (1931).

cow·ard *noun* a person with little courage who shows shameful fear in the face of danger, pain, etc. [Old French *cuard, couard*, ultimately from Latin *cauda* tail]

cow·ard·ice /ˈkaʊərdɪs/ *noun* lack of courage.

cow·ard·ly *adjective* **1** of or like a coward; lacking courage. **2** (of an action) done against a person who cannot retaliate (*cowardly attack on innocent tourists*). □ **cow·ard·li·ness** *noun*

cow·bane *noun* any of several marsh umbelliferous plants poisonous to cattle, esp. water hemlock, *Cicuta maculata*, and *Oxypolis rigidior*.

cow·bell *noun* **1** a bell worn round a cow's neck for easy location of the animal. **2** a similar bell used as a percussion instrument.

cow·berry *noun* (*pl.* **-berries**) **1** an evergreen shrub, *Vaccinium vitis-idaea*, bearing dark red berries. **2** the berry of this plant.

cow·bird *noun* any of several N American orioles which often eat insects stirred up by grazing cattle, esp. the brown-plumaged *Molothrus ater*, which lays its eggs in other birds' nests.

cow·boy *noun* **1** a person who herds and tends cattle, esp. in western N America. **2** *informal* **a** a person who acts outside of established rules, conventions, etc. (*cowboy pilot*). **b** an unscrupulous or reckless person, esp. an unqualified one.

cowboy boot *noun* a square-heeled boot with a pointed toe, extending to mid-calf and usu. with decorative tooling or stitching.

cowboy hat *noun* a hat, usu. of felt, with a high crown and broad brim.

cow·boy·ing *noun N Amer.* the job, skills, etc. of a cowboy.

cowboy poetry *noun* a type of folk poetry of the North American West, typically written by cattle ranchers or those associated with the ranching lifestyle, and often performed in public. □ **cowboy poem** *noun* **cowboy poet** *noun*

cowboys and Indians *noun* a children's game in which the participants imitate the supposed actions of cowboys and Indians in conflict.

cow cabbage *noun* = COW PARSNIP.

cow-calf *adjective N Amer.* of or pertaining to a type of beef farming which maintains a breeding herd to produce the heaviest calves possible.

cow camp *noun N Amer.* a seasonal camp apart from the primary buildings of a ranch, used during roundup.

cow·catch·er *noun N Amer.* a triangular metal frame at the front of a locomotive for pushing aside obstacles on the line.

cow·er *intransitive verb* crouch or shrink back, esp. in fear; cringe. [Middle Low German *kūren* lie in wait, of unknown origin]

Cowes /kaʊz/ a town on the Isle of Wight, S England; pop. (est. 1998) 17,700. It is internationally famous as a yachting centre.

cow·fish *noun* **1** any of several small plant-eating cetaceans, e.g. the manatee. **2** a marine fish covered in hard bony plates and having hornlike spines over the eyes and on other parts of the body.

cow flop *noun N Amer.* = COW-PIE.

cow·girl *noun* a woman who herds and tends cattle.

cow·hage *var. of* COWAGE.

cow·hand *noun N Amer.* a person who tends cattle.

cow·herd *noun esp. Brit.* = COWHAND.

cow·hide *noun* **1 a** a cow's hide. **b** leather made from this. **2** a leather whip made from cowhide.

Cowi·chan /ˈkaʊwɪtʃən/ (*pl.* same) ● *noun* **1** a member of a Coast Salish Aboriginal people living on SE Vancouver Island. **2** The language of this people, a dialect of Halkomelem. ● *adjective* of or relating to this people or their culture or language. [*Kawutsun*, the name of a rock]

Cowichan sweater *noun Cdn* a heavy sweater of homespun, undyed wool with various patterns of animals, birds, fish, whales, etc., produced by the Coast Salish of the Cowichan valley.

cowl *noun* **1 a** the hood of a monk's habit. **b** a loose hood. **c** a monk's hooded habit. **d** a cloak with wide sleeves worn by members of Benedictine orders. **2** the hood-shaped covering of a chimney or ventilating shaft. **3** the removable cover of a vehicle or aircraft engine. □ **cowled** *adjective* [Old English *cugele, cūle* from ecclesiastical Latin *cuculla* from Latin *cucullus* hood of a cloak]

cow·lick *noun* a projecting lock of hair, esp. at the crown or forehead.

cowl·ing *noun* = COWL 3.

cowl neck *noun* a neckline on a garment, hanging in draped folds.

co-worker *noun* a person who works with another.

cow parsley *noun* a herbaceous plant, *Anthriscus sylvestris*, having lace-like umbels of flowers.

cow parsnip *noun* any of various umbelliferous herbaceous plants of the genus *Heraculeum* with large divided leaves. *Also called* HOGWEED, COW CABBAGE.

cow·pea *noun* = BLACK-EYED PEA.

Cow·per /ˈkuːpər/ **Wil·liam** (1731–1800), English poet, who is best known for the long poem *The Task* (1785), notable for its intimate sketches of English rural life, and the comic ballad *John Gilpin* (1782).

cow-pie *noun* (also **cow patty, cow pat**) a flat, round piece of cow dung.

Consonants: b *but* d *dog* f *few* g *get* h *her* j *yes* k *cat* l *leg* m *man* n *no* p *pen* r *red* s *sit*

cow·poke noun (also **cow·punch·er**) N Amer. = COWBOY 1.

cow·pox noun a contagious disease of cows, of which the virus was formerly used in vaccination against smallpox.

cow·punk noun **1** a performer of a type of popular music combining elements of country and western with those of punk rock. **2** this type of music.

cow·rie noun (also **cowry**) (pl. **-ries**) **1** any gastropod mollusc of the family Cypraeidae, having a smooth glossy and usu. brightly coloured shell. **2** its shell, formerly used as money in parts of Africa and S Asia. [Urdu & Hindi *kauṛī*]

co-write transitive verb (past **-wrote**; past participle **-written**) write (something) together with another person. □ **co-writer** noun

cow·shed noun **1** a shed for cattle that are not at pasture. **2** a milking shed.

cow·slip noun **1** a primula, *Primula veris*, with fragrant yellow flowers and growing in pastures. **2** US a marsh marigold. **3** (in full **American cowslip**) = SHOOTING STAR 2. **4** (in full **Virginian cowslip**) = VIRGINIA BLUEBELL. [Old English *cūslyppe* from *cū* COW[1] + *slyppe* slimy substance, i.e. cow dung]

Cow·town a nickname for Calgary.

cow·town noun a town or city in a cattle-raising area of western N America, esp. one involved in the cattle industry.

cow-wheat noun any plant of the genus *Melampyrum*, esp. *M. lineare* with tubular flowers, growing across Canada and the northern US.

Cox noun (in full **Cox's orange pippin**) a variety of eating apple with a red-tinged green skin. [R. *Cox*, amateur English fruit grower d.1825]

cox ● noun a coxswain, esp. of a racing boat. ● verb **1** intransitive act as a cox (*coxed for Trent*). **2** transitive act as cox for (*coxed the winning boat*). □ **coxed** adjective **cox·less** adjective [abbreviation]

coxa /ˈkɒksə/ noun (pl. **coxae** /-siː/) **1** Anat. the hip bone or hip joint. **2** Zool. the first segment of an insect's leg. □ **coxal** adjective [Latin]

cox·comb /ˈkɒkskoːm/ noun an ostentatiously conceited man; a dandy or fop. □ **cox·combry** /-kəmri/ noun [= *cock's comb* (see COCK[1]), originally (a cap worn by) a jester]

Cox·sack·ie virus /kɒkˈsaki/ noun any of a group of enteroviruses which cause various respiratory, neurological, and muscular diseases in humans. [named after *Coxsackie, New York State*, where the first cases were diagnosed]

Cox's Bazar a port and resort town on the Bay of Bengal, near Chittagong, S Bangladesh; pop. (est. 2002) 106,600.

cox·swain /ˈkɒksən, -swein/ noun **1** a person who steers, esp. in a rowboat. **2** the senior petty officer in a small ship. □ **cox·swain·ship** noun [Middle English from *cock* (see COCKBOAT) + SWAIN: compare BOATSWAIN]

coy adjective (**coy·er**, **coy·est**) **1** artfully or affectedly shy, esp. in a provocative manner. **2** irritatingly reticent (*always coy about his age*). □ **coyly** adverb **coy·ness** noun [Old French *coi*, *quei* from Latin *quietus* QUIET]

coyau /ˈkɔjɔ/ noun Cdn (Que.) Archit. a steep roof design having wing-like gables to channel runoff snow and ice; a bellcast roof. [French from Old French *coe* from Latin *cauda*, 'tail']

coy·dog noun N Amer. a hybrid between a coyote and a dog. [COYOTE + DOG]

coy·ote /kaiˈoːti, ˈkaiɔt, ˈkaiuːt/ noun **1** a wolflike wild dog, *Canis latrans*, native to N America, noted for its cunning. **2** a hero and trickster figure in N American Aboriginal folklore. **3** US slang a person who smuggles Latin American illegal immigrants into the US. [Latin American Spanish from Aztec *coyotl*]

coyote willow noun = SANDBAR WILLOW.

coy·pu /ˈkɔipuː/ noun (pl. **coy·pus**) an aquatic beaver-like rodent, *Myocastor coypus*, native to S America and kept in captivity for its fur. [Araucanian]

coz¹ /kʌz/ noun (also **cuz**) N Amer. informal cousin. [abbreviation]

coz² /kʌz/ conjunction (also esp. N Amer. **cuz**) slang because. [abbreviation]

coz·en /ˈkʌzən/ transitive & intransitive verb literary cheat, deceive, trick. □ **cozen·age** noun [16th-c. cant, perhaps related to COUSIN]

Cozu·mel /ˌkozəˈmel/ a resort island in the Caribbean, off the northeast coast of the Yucatán Peninsula of Mexico.

cozy (also **cosy**) ● adjective (**cozi·er**, **cozi·est**) **1** comfortable, warm, or snug (*a cozy quilt*). **2** intimate and friendly (*a cozy restaurant*). **3** beneficial or opportune, esp. for insidious purposes (*a cozy contract*). **4** derogatory complacent (*cozy liberal pieties*). ● noun (pl. **-ies**) a cover to keep something hot, esp. a teapot or a boiled egg. □ **cozy up to** (**-ies**, **-ied**) N Amer. informal **1** ingratiate oneself with. **2** snuggle up to.

□ **cozi·ly** adverb **cozi·ness** noun [18th c. from Scots, of unknown origin]

CP abbreviation **1** Canadian Pacific (Railway etc.). **2** The Canadian Press. **3** Med. cerebral palsy. **4** Physics charge parity. **5** Military Command Post. **6** Communist Party.

c.p. abbreviation = CANDLEPOWER.

CPA abbreviation US Certified Public Accountant.

CPI abbreviation CONSUMER PRICE INDEX.

cpi abbreviation characters per inch.

Cpl abbreviation (also **Cpl.**) CORPORAL[1].

CPO abbreviation CHIEF PETTY OFFICER.

CPP abbreviation Canada Pension Plan.

CPR abbreviation **1** CARDIOPULMONARY RESUSCITATION. **2** Canadian Pacific Railway.

CPR strawberries plural noun Cdn informal jocular prunes or dried apples.

CPS abbreviation Canadian Parks Service.

cps abbreviation (also **c.p.s.**) **1** Computing characters per second. **2** cycles per second.

CPU abbreviation Computing CENTRAL PROCESSING UNIT.

Cr symbol Chem. the element chromium.

Cr. abbreviation **1** creditor. **2** credit. **3** Crescent. **4** Creek.

crab¹ ● noun **1 a** a crustacean with a broad carapace, stalked eyes, and five pairs of legs, the first pair of which are modified as pincers. **b** the flesh of a crab, esp. *Cancer pagurus*, as food. **2** (**the Crab**) the zodiacal sign or constellation Cancer. **3** (in full **crab louse**) (often in pl.) a parasitic louse, *Phthirus pubis*, infesting hairy parts of the body and causing extreme irritation. **4** a machine for hoisting heavy weights. ● intransitive verb (**crabbed**, **crab·bing**) **1** fish for crabs. **2** move sideways, esp. with short, abrupt movements. □ **catch a crab** Rowing effect a faulty stroke in which the oar is jammed under water or misses the water altogether. □ **crab·like** adjective [Old English *crabba*, related to Old Norse *krafla* scratch]

crab² noun **1** (in full **crab·apple**) a small, sour apple. **2** (in full **crab tree** or **crabapple tree**) any of several trees of the genus Malus bearing this fruit. **3** a bad-tempered person. [Middle English, perhaps alteration (after CRAB[1] or CRABBED) of earlier *scrab*, prob. of Scandinavian origin]

crab³ transitive & intransitive verb (**crabbed**, **crab·bing**) informal find fault, criticize; grumble. [originally of hawks fighting, from Middle Low German *krabben*]

crabbed adjective **1** (of handwriting) cramped and hard to decipher. **2** = CRABBY. **3** perverse (*crabbed view of democracy*). **4** difficult to understand (*crabbed construction of the law*). □ **crab·bed·ly** adverb [Middle English from CRAB[1], assoc. with CRAB[2]]

crab·ber noun **1** a person who fishes for crabs. **2** a boat used in crab fishing.

crabby adjective (**crab·bi·er**, **crab·bi·est**) surly, irritable, or morose. □ **crab·bi·ly** adverb **crab·bi·ness** noun

crab·grass noun N Amer. any of several creeping grasses infesting lawns, esp. of the genus *Digitaria*.

crab·meat noun = CRAB[1] 1b.

crab pot noun a wicker trap for crabs.

crab·wise adverb & attributive adjective (of movement) sideways or backwards like a crab.

crack ● noun **1 a** a sudden sharp or explosive noise (*the crack of a whip*; *a rifle crack*). **b** (in a voice) a sudden harshness or change in pitch. **2** a sharp blow (*a crack on the head*). **3 a** a narrow opening formed by a break (*entered through a crack in the wall*). **b** a partial fracture, with the parts still joined (*the teacup has a crack in it*). **c** a chink (*looked through the crack formed by the door; a crack of light*). **4** informal a joke or gibe; a witty or cutting remark (*a nasty crack about my age*). **5** informal **a** an attempt (*I'll have a crack at it*). **b** an opportunity (*I'd like a crack at the job*). **6** (in full **crack cocaine**) slang a potent, highly addictive hard crystalline form of cocaine broken into small pieces and inhaled or smoked for its stimulating effect. **7** the exact moment (*the crack of dawn*). **8** dialect informal conversation; good company; fun (*Natasha only went there for the crack*). ● verb **1** transitive & intransitive break without a complete separation of the parts (*cracked the mirror; the cup cracked on hitting the floor*). **2** intransitive & transitive make or cause to make a sudden sharp or explosive sound. **3** transitive & intransitive break or cause to break with a sudden sharp sound. **4** intransitive & transitive break down, esp. under severe pressures, e.g torture; yield. **5** intransitive (of the voice, esp. of an adolescent boy or a person under strain) change tone, break, become harsh. **6** *transitive* **a** decipher, find a solution to (a problem, code, etc.). **b** break into or force open (*they cracked the safe*). **7** *transitive* tell (a joke etc.) in a jocular way. **8** *transitive informal* hit sharply or hard (*cracked her head on the ceiling*). **9** *transitive Chem.* decompose (heavy oils) by heat and pressure with or without a catalyst to produce lighter hydrocarbons (such as gasoline). **10** *transitive* gain access to (*crack the job market*). **11** *transitive* **a** open (a bottle) (*crack a beer; crack open a bottle of champagne*). **b** open slightly (*crack open the car window for air*). **12** *transitive* break (wheat) into coarse pieces. ● *attributive adjective informal* excellent; first-rate (*a crack regiment; a crack shot*). □ **crack a book** *informal N Amer.* study or research. **crack down on** *informal* take severe measures against. **crack a smile** *informal* begin to smile. **crack the whip** *informal* exercise authority. **crack up** *informal* **1** suffer a mental or emotional breakdown. **2** burst into laughter suddenly (*cracked up in hysterics*). **3** cause to break into laughter (*he cracked me up*). **crack wise** *N Amer. informal* to make wisecracks. **get cracking** *informal* begin promptly and vigorously. **have a crack at** *informal* attempt. **not all it's cracked up to be** *informal* not all a thing seems to be (*grandchildren are not all they are cracked up to be*). □ **cracky** *adjective* [Old English *cracian* resound]

crack baby *noun* a baby exposed to crack cocaine in the womb and so at high risk for mental, emotional, and physical disabilities.

crack-brained *adjective* bizarre, foolish, senseless.

crack cocaine *noun* = CRACK *noun* 6.

crack·down *noun informal* enforcement of severe or repressive measures (esp. against lawbreakers, activists, etc.).

cracked *adjective* **1** broken, but without extensive separation of parts; having cracks (*a cracked and leaky foundation*). **2** *informal* (usu. *predicative*) eccentric, mad, or crazy. **3** damaged, injured, or impaired (*cracked hooves; blistered and cracked hands*). **4** varying or broken in tone, e.g. voice or sounds (*a cracked and defiant voice*).

cracked wheat *noun* wheat that has been crushed into small pieces.

crack·er *noun* **1 a** a thin, dry biscuit often eaten with cheese. **b** *N Amer.* a cookie (*a graham cracker*). **2** a paper cylinder both ends of which are pulled, esp. at Christmas, making a sharp noise and releasing a small toy etc. **3** a firework exploding with a sharp noise. **4** *slang* esp. *Brit.* **a** a notable or attractive person. **b** a fine example of something (*a cracker of a match*). **5** *US* (esp. *South*) *offensive* = POOR WHITE. **6** *Computing* a hacker who wilfully damages or destroys the information or systems accessed.

cracker-barrel *adjective US* (of philosophy etc.) homespun; unsophisticated.

cracker·berry *noun* (*pl.* **-berries**) = BUNCHBERRY.

cracker·jack esp. *N Amer. slang* ● *adjective* exceptionally fine or expert. ● *noun* an exceptionally fine thing or person.

crack·ers *predicative adjective slang* **1** crazy. **2** wildly enthusiastic (*crackers over the new film*).

crack·head *noun N Amer. slang* a habitual user of crack cocaine.

crack house *noun N Amer.* a gathering place where crack cocaine is bought, sold, or used.

crack·ie *noun Cdn* (*Nfld*) a small, yappy dog of mixed breed.

crack·ing *Brit. slang* ● *adjective* outstanding; very good (*a cracking performance*). ● *adverb* outstandingly (*a cracking good time*).

crackle ● *intransitive verb* make a repeated slight cracking sound (*radio crackled; fire was crackling*). ● *noun* **1** such a sound. **2 a** paintwork, china, or glass decorated with a pattern of minute surface cracks. **b** the smooth surface of such paintwork etc. □ **crack·ly** *adjective* [CRACK + -LE⁴]

crack·ling *noun* the crisp skin of roast pork.

crack·nel /'kraknəl/ *noun* a light crisp cracker. [Middle English from French *craquelin* from Middle Dutch *krākelinc* from *krāken* CRACK]

crack·pot *slang* ● *noun* an eccentric, impractical, or fanatical person. ● *adjective* mad, bizarre, unworkable (*a crackpot scheme*).

crack the whip *noun N Amer.* a skating game in which participants form a line and, by skating rapidly then changing directions abruptly, attempt to fling the end skaters off.

crack-up *noun informal* **1** a mental breakdown. **2** a car crash. **3** a collapse, disintegration, fragmentation (*the crack-up of the former Soviet Union*).

cracky *noun* □ **by cracky** interjection expressing determination, assertiveness, etc. (*we will go, by cracky*). [corruption of or euphemism for *by Christ*]

Cra·cow /'krakau/ an industrial and university city in S Poland, on the Vistula River; pop. (est. 2000) 741,510. It was the capital of Poland from 1320 until replaced by Warsaw in 1609. The city's many fine medieval buildings survived the Second World War largely unscathed.

-cracy /krəsi/ *combining form* denoting a particular form of government, rule, or influence (*aristocracy; bureaucracy*). [from or after French *-cratie* from medieval Latin *-cratia* from Greek *-kratia* from *kratos* strength, power]

cradle ● *noun* **1 a** a baby's bed with high sides, esp. one mounted on rockers. **b** a place in which a thing begins, esp. a civilization etc., or is nurtured in its infancy (*cradle of Confederation; cradle of democracy*). **2 a** framework resembling a cradle, esp.: **a** one on which a ship, a boat, etc., rests during construction or repairs. **b** one on which a worker is suspended to work on a ceiling, a ship, the vertical side of a building, etc. **c** the part of a telephone on which the receiver rests when not in use. **3** *Mining* a trough on rockers in which gravel and sand are shaken in water to separate and collect gold or other heavy metals. ● *transitive verb* **1 a** hold, contain, or shelter as if in a cradle (*cradled his head in her arms*). **b** support, rock, or move gently as though in a cradle (*cradled on the waves*). **2** *Lacrosse* carry (the ball) in the stick's net, esp. when running with it. **3** place (a telephone receiver in its cradle. ● *adjective* designating a person who was baptized into a specified religion in infancy (*a cradle Catholic*). □ **from the cradle** from infancy (*a socialist from the cradle*). **from (the) cradle to (the) grave** from infancy till death. **revenge of the cradle** *see* REVENGE OF THE CRADLE. **rob the cradle** become romantically involved with someone much younger. [Old English *cradol*, perhaps related to Old High German *kratto* basket]

cradle·board *noun* (among some N American Aboriginal peoples) a thin board to which an infant is strapped so that it can be transported on its mother's back or placed on the ground or against a tree.

cradle cap *noun* a condition common in infants, in which the scalp is inflamed and affected with greasy scales and yellowish crusts.

cradle-hill *noun Cdn* (*Maritimes*) a small hill or mound of earth usu. formed by a fallen or uprooted tree.

Cradle of Confederation an informal name for Charlottetown and/or Prince Edward Island. [because it was a meeting place in 1864 for the Fathers of Confederation]

cradle-robber *noun* (also **cradle-snatcher**) *informal* a person amorously attached to a much younger person.

cradle song *noun* a lullaby.

cradle-to-grave *adjective* from birth to death.

crad·ling *noun Archit.* a wooden or iron framework, esp. one used as a structural support in a ceiling.

craft ● *noun* **1 a** (esp. in *combination*) a trade or an art (*statecraft; handicraft; priestcraft; the craft of pottery*). **b** (usu. in *pl.* or *attributive*) the product of such skill. **2** skill, esp. in practical arts. **3** the activity of producing handiwork (*keep your children entertained with crafts*). **4 a** a trade union, guild or company. **b** the members of such an association. **5** (*pl.* **craft**) **a** a boat or vessel. **b** an aircraft or spacecraft. **6** cunning or deceit. **7** (**the Craft**) the brotherhood of Freemasons. ● *transitive verb* make, fashion, or hone in a skilful way (*crafted a poem; a well-crafted piece of work*). [Old English *cræft*]

craft·er *noun N Amer.* = CRAFTSPERSON.

craft guild *noun* **1** *hist.* a guild of workers of the same trade. **2** (also **crafts guild**) an association, usu. informal, of craftspeople, artists, writers, etc.

craft shop *noun* **1** a small store in which handicrafts, usu. made locally, are sold. **2** (also **craft store**) a store in which craft supplies are sold.

crafts·man *noun* (*pl.* **-men**) **1** a skilled worker who has usu. completed a period of apprenticeship or training. **2** a person who practises a handicraft.

crafts·man·ship *noun* **1** the quality of execution in a thing made. **2** skilled workmanship.

crafts·person *noun* (*pl.* **-people**) a person who practises a handicraft, esp. a highly skilled artisan.

crafts·woman *noun* (*pl.* **-women**) **1** a skilled female worker who has usu. completed a period of apprenticeship or training. **2** a woman who practises a handicraft.

craft·work *noun* **1** the making of things, esp. decorative objects, by hand as a profession or leisure activity. **2** work produced in such a way.

crafty *adjective* (**craft·i·er**, **craft·i·est**) cunning, artful, wily. □ **craft·i·ly** *adverb* **craft·i·ness** *noun* [Old English *cræftig*]

crag *noun* a steep or rugged rock. [Middle English, of Celtic origin]

craggy *adjective* (**crag·gi·er**, **crag·gi·est**) **1** (of a landscape) having crags. **2** (esp. of a person's face) rugged; angular, with sharply defined features, e.g. jutting cheekbones, aquiline nose, etc. □ **crag·gi·ly** adverb **crag·gi·ness** noun

crags·man noun (pl. **-men**) a skilled climber of crags.

Craig ▸ 1 Ed·ward Gor·don (1872–1966), English director and stage designer, whose innovative theories on scenery and lighting had an immense influence on US and European theatre; his writings include *On the Art of the Theatre* (1911). **2 Sir James (Henry)** (1748–1812), English army officer and colonial administrator, governor of Lower Canada and governor-in-chief of British North America 1807–12. He was known for his open hostility to French Canadians, and conducted a ruthless campaign of suppression in Quebec, imprisoning members of the Parti canadien (1810).

Craig, Mount a peak in the St. Elias Mountains of SW Yukon Territory (4 039 m). [J. D. *Craig*, surveyor of the Yukon–Alaska boundary d.1936]

Craig·el·lachie /ˌkreigəˈlaki/ a place in SE central BC, about 30 km west of Revelstoke. It was here that Donald Smith (Lord Strathcona) ceremonially drove the last spike in the construction of the Canadian Pacific Railway. [the name of a prominent crag in Moray, Scotland]

Crai·gie /ˈkreigi/ **Sir Wil·liam Alex·an·der** (1867–1957), Scottish lexicographer, who was co-editor of the *Oxford English Dictionary* (1901–33), and editor of *A Dictionary of American English on Historical Principles* (1938–44), and the *Dictionary of the Older Scottish Tongue* (1925–55).

Craio·va /krɑˈjoːvə/ a city in SW Romania; pop. (est. 2002) 317,600.

crake noun **1** any rail (see RAIL³), esp. a corncrake. **2** the cry of a corncrake. [Old Norse *kráka* (imitative): compare CROAK]

cram verb (**crammed, cram·ming**) **1** transitive **a** fill to bursting; stuff (*the room was crammed*). **b** (foll. by *in, into*) force (a thing) into (*cram the books into the bag*). **2** transitive & intransitive prepare for an examination by intensive study. **3** transitive (often foll. by *with*) feed (poultry etc.) to excess. **4** transitive & intransitive informal eat greedily. □ **cram in** push in to bursting point (*crammed in another five minutes' work*). [Old English *crammian* from Germanic]

cram·mer noun esp. Brit. a person or institution that helps students cram for examinations.

cramp ● noun **1 a** a painful involuntary contraction of a muscle or muscles from the cold, exertion, etc. **b** = WRITER'S CRAMP. **c** esp. N Amer. (usu. in pl.) a painful muscle contraction in the abdomen, uterus, etc., esp. preceding or accompanying menstruation. **2** a metal bar with bent ends for holding masonry etc. together. **3** a portable tool for holding two planks etc. together; a clamp. ● verb **1** transitive affect with a cramp or cramps. **2** transitive confine, restrict, or hamper (energies etc.). **3** transitive fasten with a cramp. **4** intransitive (usu. foll. by *up*) become stiff or incapacitated because of a cramp (*I lost the race because I cramped up*). □ **cramp a person's style** prevent a person from acting freely or naturally. □ **crampy** adjective [Old French *crampe* from Middle Dutch, Middle Low German *krampe*, Old High German *krampfo* from adj. meaning 'bent': compare CRIMP]

cramp bark noun = GUELDER ROSE.

cramped adjective **1** (of handwriting) small, tightly packed, and difficult to read. **2** uncomfortably limited or restricted in space (*cramped quarters*).

cram·pon /ˈkrampɒn/ noun (usu. in pl.) a spiked iron plate fixed to a boot for walking on ice, climbing, etc. [French (as CRAMP)]

Cran·ach /ˈkranək/ **Lucas, 'the Elder'** (1472–1553), German painter, who is noted for his early religious pictures in which landscape plays a prominent part, as in *The Rest on the Flight into Egypt* (1504); he also painted portraits, including several of his friend Martin Luther. His son Lucas, 'the Younger' (1515–86), continued working in the same tradition.

cran·apple adjective **1** (**Cranapple**) proprietary designating a combination of cranberry and apple juices. **2** designating a combination of cranberries and apples (*cranapple muffins*). [blend of CRANBERRY + APPLE]

cran·berry noun (pl. **-berries**) **1** any of several evergreen shrubs of the genus *Vaccinium*, esp. V. *macrocarpon* of eastern N America, grown commercially for its red acid fruit, and V. *oxycoccos* and V. *vitis-idaea*, yielding smaller fruit. See also HIGHBUSH (CRANBERRY), LOWBUSH (CRANBERRY). **2** a berry from this used for a sauce and in cooking. [17th c.: named by American colonists from German *Kranbeere*, Low German *kranebere* crane berry]

cranberry bog noun N Amer. a bog in which cranberry bushes are grown.

cranberry glass noun a red, transparent glassware originally made in England and the US in the 19th c.

Cran·brook a city in southeastern BC, situated in the Kootenay region, 229 km east of Castlegar; pop. (2001) 18,476. □ **Cran·brook·er** noun [*Cranbrook* in Kent, England]

Crane, 1 (Har·old) Hart (1899–1932), US poet. He published two volumes of verse, *White Buildings* (1926) and *The Bridge* (1930), the latter an epic poem uniting a dreamlike perception of US history with a view of modern industrial reality. **2 Ste·phen** (1871–1900), US novelist, poet, and short-story writer. His reputation rests on his novel *The Red Badge of Courage* (1895), a study of an inexperienced soldier and his reactions to the ordeal of battle in the American Civil War.

crane ● noun **1** a machine for moving heavy objects, usu. by suspending them from a projecting arm or beam. **2 a** any tall wading bird of the family Gruidae, with long legs, long neck, and straight bill. **b** = GREAT BLUE HERON. **3** a trolley with a long boom supporting a platform on which a television or motion picture camera can be mounted. ● verb **1** transitive & intransitive stretch out (one's neck) in order to see something. **2** transitive move (an object) by a crane. [Old English *cran*, related to Latin *grus*, Greek *geranos*]

crane fly noun any fly of the family Tipulidae, having two wings and long legs.

cranes·bill noun any of various herbaceous plants of the genus *Geranium*, having beaked fruits.

cra·nial /ˈkreiniəl/ adjective of or relating to the skull. [CRANIUM + -AL]

cranial nerve noun each of twelve pairs of nerves which originate directly in the brain, not from the spinal cord, and which reach the external surface of the body through natural skull apertures.

cra·niate /ˈkreiniət/ ● adjective having a skull. ● noun an animal with a skull. [modern Latin *craniatus* from CRANIUM]

cranio- /ˈkreinioː/ combining form cranium.

crani·ol·ogy /ˌkreiniˈɒlədʒi/ noun the scientific study of the shape and size of the human skull. □ **cra·nio·logic·al** /ˌkreiniəˈlɒdʒikəl/ adjective **crani·ol·o·gist** noun

crani·om·etry /ˌkreiniˈɒmitri/ noun the scientific measurement of skulls for study and comparison (e.g. in anthropology). □ **cra·nio·met·ric** /-niəˈmetrik/ adjective

crani·o·sacral therapy /ˌkreinioːˈseikrəl/ noun a system of alternative medicine intended to relieve pain and tension by gentle manipulations of the skull regarded as harmonizing with a natural rhythm in the central nervous system.

crani·ot·omy /ˌkreiniˈɒtəmi/ noun (pl. **-mies**) **1** surgical removal of a portion of the skull. **2** surgical perforation of the skull of a dead fetus to ease delivery.

cra·nium /ˈkreiniəm/ noun (pl. **cra·niums** or **cra·nia** /-niə/) **1** the skull of a vertebrate. **2** the part of the skeleton that encloses the brain. [medieval Latin from Greek *kranion* skull]

crank¹ ● noun **1** part of an axle or shaft bent at right angles for converting reciprocal into circular motion and vice versa. **2** slang methamphetamine; speed. ● transitive verb **1** cause to move by means of a crank. **2** start (an engine etc.), esp. by turning a crank. □ **crank out** informal produce quickly in a mechanical or mass-produced fashion (*he cranks out pulp novels*). **crank up 1** start, turn on, or power up (a machine, appliance, etc.) (*crank up the engine*). **2** informal increase (speed, sound, etc.) (*crank up the volume*). **3** stimulate, stir up, or produce (*crank up the economy; crank up enthusiasm*). **turn one's crank** slang please, appeal to, or excite one's interest. [Old English *cranc*, apparently from *crincan*, related to *cringan* fall in battle, originally 'curl up']

crank² ● noun **1** an eccentric person, esp. one obsessed by a particular theory (*health food crank*). **2** N Amer. a bad-tempered person. ● adjective of, by, or pertaining to an eccentric or unbalanced person (*crank theories*). [back-formation from CRANKY]

crank³ adjective Naut. liable to capsize. [perhaps from *crank* weak, shaky]

crank·bait noun N Amer. a plug type fishing lure which dives beneath the surface when retrieved.

crank call noun a harassing telephone call usu. made by young people as a prank. □ **crank caller** noun

crank·case noun a metal covering enclosing an engine's crankshaft, connecting rods, and related parts.

Cran·ko, John (1927–73), South African-born British dancer, choreographer, and ballet director, best known for his dramatic ballets such as *Romeo and Juliet* (1962), *The Taming of the Shrew* (1969), and *Onegin* (1965). Under his direction (1961–73) the Stuttgart Ballet became one of the world's major ballet companies.

crank·pin noun a pin by which a connecting rod is attached to a crank.

crank·shaft noun a shaft driven by one or more cranks (see CRANK¹ noun).

cranky *adjective* (**crank·i·er, crank·i·est**) **1** esp. *N Amer.* bad-tempered or crotchety. **2** working badly; shaky. ▭ **crank·i·ly** *adverb* **crank·i·ness** *noun* [perhaps from obsolete *crank* rogue feigning sickness]

Cran·mer, Thom·as (1489–1556), English Protestant cleric and martyr. The first Protestant Archbishop of Canterbury (1533–56), he was largely responsible for English liturgical reform, particularly under Edward VI, and for the compilation of the Book of Common Prayer (1549); he was burned as a heretic by Mary I.

cran·nog /'kranəg/ *noun* an ancient lake-dwelling in Scotland or Ireland. [Irish from *crann* tree, beam]

cranny *noun* (*pl.* **-nies**) (esp. in *nook and cranny*) a small narrow opening or hole; a chink, crevice, or crack. [Old French *crané* past participle of *craner* from *cran* from popular Latin *crena* notch]

Cran·ston, Tol·ler (b.1949), Canadian figure skater and painter. Known for his innovative and individualistic style, he was the Canadian men's figure skating champion (1971–6), and won a bronze medal at the 1976 Winter Olympics.

crap¹ *coarse slang* ● *noun* **1 a** feces. **b** an act of defecation (*take a crap*). **2** nonsense or falsehood (*he talks crap*). **3** something without value (*the poetry was crap*). **4** garbage, litter, refuse (*pick up that crap*). ● *intransitive verb* (**crapped, crap·ping**) defecate. ● *adjective* of extremely poor quality. ▭ **cut the crap** *slang* get to the point; stop evading the issue. **give a crap** *slang* (usu. in *neg.*) care, be concerned about (*I don't give a crap*). [earlier senses 'chaff, refuse from boiling fat': Middle English from Dutch *krappe*]

crap² *noun N Amer.* **1** (in *pl.*) a gambling game in which two dice are thrown with the aim of scoring 7 or 11 on a first throw or any score but 7 on a second throw. **2** a losing score of 2, 3, or 12 on a first throw in craps. ▭ **crap out** *N Amer.* **1** make a losing throw while shooting craps. **2** *informal* **a** fail, be unsuccessful. **b** withdraw from a game, activity, etc. **shoot craps** play craps. [19th c.: perhaps from *crab* lowest throw at dice]

crape *noun* **1** CREPE. **2** a fabric, usu. of black silk or imitation silk, formerly used for mourning clothes. [earlier *crispe, crespe* from French *crespe* CREPE]

crape myrtle *noun* a Chinese ornamental shrub, *Lagerstroemia indica*, of the purple loosestrife family, with pink, white or purplish crinkled petals.

crap·ola *noun N Amer. slang* = CRAP¹ 2. [CRAP¹ 2 + -OLA]

crap·per *noun coarse slang* **1** a toilet. **2** a washroom, outhouse, etc.

crap·pie *noun* a N American freshwater sunfish of the genus *Pomoxis*. [Canadian French *crapet*]

crappy *adjective* (**crap·pier, crap·pi·est**) *slang* **1** markedly inferior (*a crappy production; crappy weather*). **2** disgusting, unfair, nasty (*a crappy comment*).

crap·shoot *noun N Amer. slang* a gamble, risk, or highly uncertain venture. ▭ **crap·shoot·er** *noun* [CRAP²]

crapu·lous /'krapjʊləs/ *adjective* **1** given to indulging in alcohol. **2** resulting from drunkenness. **3** drunk. ▭ **crapu·lence** *noun* **crapu·lent** *adjective* [Late Latin *crapulentus* very drunk, from Latin *crapula* inebriation, from Greek *kraipalē* drunken headache]

craque·lure /'krakə,lʊːr/ *noun* a network of fine cracks in a painting caused by the shrinkage of its pigment or varnish over time. [French]

crash¹ ● *verb* **1** *intransitive & transitive* make or cause to make a loud smashing noise (*the cymbals crashed; crashed the plates together*). **2** *transitive & intransitive* throw, move, drop, or fall with a loud smashing noise. **3** *intransitive & transitive* **a** collide or cause (a vehicle) to collide violently with another vehicle, obstacle, etc. **b** overturn or cause to overturn (a vehicle) at high speed. **4** *intransitive & transitive* fall or cause (an aircraft) to fall violently to the land or water (*crashed the plane; the plane crashed into the sea*). **5** *intransitive* (usu. foll. by *into*) collide violently (*crashed into the window*). **6** *intransitive* undergo financial ruin (*the market crashed*). **7** *transitive informal* enter without permission (*crashed the cocktail party*). **8** *intransitive informal* be heavily defeated (*crashed to a 4–0 defeat*). **9** *intransitive Computing* (of a machine or system) fail suddenly. **10** *transitive informal* pass (a red traffic light etc.). **11** *intransitive* (often foll. by *out*) *slang* **a** sleep, esp. in an improvised setting. **b** stay somewhere temporarily. **12** *intransitive slang* experience depression, exhaustion, etc. as the effects of amphetamines, cocaine, etc. wear off. **13** *transitive* fall drastically (*the deer population will crash*). ● *noun* **1 a** a loud and sudden smashing noise (*a thunder crash; the crash of crockery*). **b** an instance of noisily breaking or falling to pieces (esp. of china, glass, etc.). **2 a** a violent collision, esp. of one vehicle with another or with an object. **b** the violent fall of an aircraft to the land or water. **3** a sudden collapse of the stock market etc. **4** *Computing* a sudden failure which puts a system out of action.

5 (*attributive*) marked by an urgent and concentrated effort, esp. for immediate results etc. (*a crash course in first aid*). **6** a dramatic decrease in numbers, esp. in a specific population. ▭ **crash and burn** *informal* ● *intransitive verb* collapse or fail utterly (*our system crashed and burned*). ● *noun* (usu. *attributive*) a complete and often spectacular failure (*crash and burn programming*). [Middle English: imitative]

crash² *noun* a coarse plain linen, cotton, etc., fabric. [Russian *krashenina* coloured linen]

crash barrier *noun* a barrier intended to prevent a car from leaving the road.

crash-dive ● *verb* **1** *intransitive* **a** (of a submarine or its pilot) dive hastily and steeply in an emergency. **b** (of an aircraft or pilot) plunge steeply downwards at high speed before hitting the ground. **2** *transitive* cause (a submarine or aircraft) to crash-dive. ● *noun* such a dive.

crash helmet *noun* a helmet worn by a motorcyclist etc. to protect the head in a crash.

crash·ing *adjective informal* overwhelming (*a crashing bore*). ▭ **crash·ing·ly** *adverb*

crash-land *verb* **1** *intransitive* (of an aircraft or pilot) make an emergency landing, usu. with damage to the craft. **2** *transitive* cause (an aircraft) to crash-land. ▭ **crash landing** *noun*

crash pad *noun* **1** *slang* a place to sleep, esp. in an emergency. **2** protective padding added to cars, planes, etc. to protect passengers and property in event of a crash.

crash test ● *transitive verb* assess and evaluate (a product, usu. a vehicle) for safety and reliability under severe conditions often including collisions etc. ● *noun* such a test.

crass *adjective* **1** boorish, unsubtle (*crass materialism*). **2** insensitive, rude, vulgar (*what a crass remark*). **3** extreme (*crass stupidity*). ▭ **crass·ly** *adverb* **crass·ness** *noun* [Latin *crassus* solid, thick]

Cras·sus /'krasəs/ **Mar·cus Li·cin·ius** (*c.*115–53 BC), Roman general and politician. He defeated Spartacus in 71 and joined Caesar and Pompey in the first triumvirate in 60; he was defeated and killed while fighting the Parthians in Mesopotamia.

-crat *combining form* a member or supporter of a particular form of government or rule (*autocrat; democrat*). [from or after French *-crate*: see -CRACY]

crate ● *noun* **1** a case or box, often of slatted wood, for packing, shipping, or storing esp. fragile goods for transportation. **2** *slang* an old airplane or other vehicle. ● *transitive verb* pack in a crate. [Middle English, perhaps from Dutch *krat* basket]

cra·ter ● *noun* **1** the mouth of a volcano. **2** a bowl-shaped cavity, esp. that made by the explosion of a shell or bomb. **3** *Astronomy* a hollow with a raised rim on the surface of a planet or moon, caused by the impact of a meteorite. ● *transitive & intransitive verb* **1** make a crater or craters in. **2** *informal* drop dramatically in value. ▭ **cra·tered** *adjective* **crater·ous** *adjective* [Latin from Greek *kratēr* mixing bowl, from Greek *krasis* mixture]

Crater Lake a lake filling a volcanic crater in the Cascade mountains of SW Oregon. With a depth of more than 600 m (1,968 ft.) it is the deepest lake in the US.

-cratic *combining form* denoting a particular kind of government or rule (*autocratic; democratic*). ▭ **-cratically** *combining form*. [from or after French *-cratique*: see -CRACY]

C ration *noun N Amer.* a canned field ration such as was originally used by the US army. [abbreviation of canned ration]

cra·ton /'kreɪtɒn/ *noun Geol.* a large stable block of the earth's crust. ▭ **cra·ton·ic** *adjective* [alteration of *kratogen* from Greek *kratus* strength + -GEN]

cra·vat /krə'vat/ *noun* **1** a scarf worn inside an open-necked shirt, esp. by men. **2** *hist.* a necktie. ▭ **cra·vat·ted** *adjective* [French *cravate* from German *Krawat, Kroat* from Serbo-Croatian *Hrvat* Croat]

crave *verb* **1** *transitive* **a** long for (*craved affection*). **b** beg for (*craves a blessing*). **c** need desperately (*craved water*). **2** *intransitive* (foll. by *for*) long for; beg for (*craved for comfort*). ▭ **crav·er** *noun* [Old English *crafian*, related to Old Norse *krefja*]

cra·ven /'kreɪvən/ ● *adjective* (of a person, behaviour, etc.) cowardly, obsequious. ● *noun* a cowardly person. ▭ **cra·ven·ly** *adverb* **craven·ness** *noun* [Middle English *cravand* etc. perhaps from Old French *cravanté* defeated, past participle of *cravanter*, ultimately from Latin *crepare* burst; assimilated to -EN³]

crav·ing *noun* (usu. foll. by *for*) a strong desire or longing.

craw *noun* the crop of a bird or insect. ▭ **stick in one's craw** *informal* be difficult to accept due to differences of opinion. [Middle

English, related to Middle Dutch *crāghe*, Middle Low German *krage*, Middle High German *krage* neck, throat]

craw·dad noun esp. *US* (also **craw·dad·dy** pl. **-dies**) = CRAYFISH 1. [CRAWFISH + DAD¹].

craw·fish noun (pl. same) a large marine spiny lobster. [var. of CRAYFISH]

Craw·ford ▸ 1 Isa·bel·la Val·ancy (1850–87), Irish-born Canadian poet, novelist, and short-story writer. The dialogue of hope and despair and the purgatorial role of suffering are the central themes of much of her poetry, which includes the pastoral narrative 'Malcolm's Katie', collected in the volume *Old Spookses' Pass, Malcolm's Katie, and Other Poems* (1884). **2 Joan** (born Lucille le Sueur) (1908–77), US actress, who is known for her screen portrayals of ambitious and successful women; her films include *Rain* (1932), *Mildred Pierce* (1945), and *Whatever Happened to Baby Jane?* (1962).

crawl ● *intransitive verb* **1** move slowly, esp. on hands and knees. **2** (of an insect, snake, etc.) move slowly with the body close to the ground etc. **3** move or progress slowly (*the train crawled into the station*). **4** (often foll. by *to*) *informal* behave obsequiously or ingratiatingly in the hope of advantage. **5** (often foll. by *with*) be or seem to be covered or filled with crawling or moving things, people etc. (*the mall was crawling with shoppers*). **6** (esp. of the skin) feel a creepy sensation. **7** swim with a crawl stroke. ● *noun* **1** an act of crawling. **2** a slow rate of movement. **3** a high-speed swimming stroke with alternate overarm movements and rapid straight-legged kicks. **4 a** (usu. in *combination*) *informal* a leisurely journey between places of interest (*culture-crawl*). **b** = PUB-CRAWL. □ **crawly** *adjective* (in senses 5, 6 of verb). [Middle English: origin unknown: compare Swedish *kravla*, Danish *kravle*]

crawl·er noun **1** a person or thing that crawls, esp. a baby or an insect. **2** a tractor moving on an endless chain. **3** *N Amer.* (usu. in pl.) a baby's overall for crawling in; rompers. **4** *N Amer.* (also **night crawler**) *informal* an earthworm.

crawl space noun a low, constricted space, usu. in a house, used for storage or to gain access to the wiring, plumbing, etc.

cray·fish noun (pl. same) **1** a small lobster-like freshwater crustacean. **2** a crawfish. [Old French *crevice, crevis*, ultimately from Old High German *krebiz* CRAB¹: assimilated to FISH¹]

cray·on noun **1** a stick or pencil of coloured wax, charcoal, chalk, etc. used for drawing. **2** a drawing made with this. ● *verb* **1** *transitive* draw or colour (a picture) with crayons. **2** *intransitive* draw or colour with crayons. [French from *craie* from Latin *creta* chalk]

craze ● *verb* **1** *transitive* (usu. in *passive*) make insane (*crazed with grief*). **2 a** *transitive* produce fine surface cracks on (*pottery glaze etc.*). **b** *intransitive* develop such cracks. ● *noun* **1 a** usu. temporary enthusiasm (*a craze for hula hoops*). **2** the object of this (*the dinosaur craze*). □ **craz·ing** noun (in sense 2 of verb). [Middle English, originally = break, shatter, perhaps from Old Norse]

crazed *adjective* **1** mentally impaired, insane. **2** (usu. in *combination*) manic, wildly enthusiastic (*dance-crazed teens*). **3** covered with a pattern of cracks (*a crazed network of fissures*).

crazy ● *adjective* (**craz·i·er, craz·i·est**) **1** *informal* (of a person, an action, etc.) mentally unstable, insane. **b** foolish, impractical. **2** *informal* (usu. foll. by *about*) extremely enthusiastic. **3** *slang* **a** exciting, wild (*a crazy party*). **b** excellent. ● *noun* (pl. **-ies**) *slang* (usu. in pl.) a person who is wild, eccentric, unbalanced, etc. □ **like crazy** *informal* = LIKE MAD (see MAD). □ **craz·i·ly** *adverb* **craz·i·ness** noun

crazy carpet noun *N Amer.* a rectangular piece of flexible plastic used to slide downhill over compacted snow.

crazy eights noun (treated as *sing.*) *N Amer.* a card game, usu. played by children, in which a player plays a card of the same suit or denomination as the preceding one, with eight being a wild card.

crazy glue noun a cyanoacrylate glue that forms an instant and extremely strong bond.

Crazy Horse (Sioux name Ta-Sunko-Witko) (*c.*1842–77), Sioux chief. With Sitting Bull at Little Bighorn he played an important strategic and military role in the defeat of US forces under General Custer; he surrendered in 1877 and was killed in custody a few months later.

crazy paving noun *Cdn & Brit.* a form of cobbling or paving in which stones of various shapes and sizes are joined together to form paths etc.

crazy quilt noun **1** a patchwork quilt made of material of various shapes, sizes, and colours. **2** an apparently random collection (e.g. of laws, districts, etc.).

crazy·weed noun any of several leguminous plants of the genus *Oxytropis* poisonous to cattle.

creak ● noun a harsh scraping or squeaking sound. ● *intransitive verb* **1** make a creak. **2 a** move with a creaking noise. **b** move slowly or stiffly (*creaking economy*). **c** show weakness or frailty under strain. □ **creak·ing·ly** *adverb* [Middle English, imitative: compare CRAKE, CROAK]

creaky *adjective* (**creak·i·er, creak·i·est**) **1** creaking or liable to creak. **2** stiff or frail (*creaky joints*). **b** (of a practice, institution, etc.) decrepit, dilapidated, outmoded. □ **creak·i·ly** *adverb* **creak·i·ness** noun

cream ● noun **1 a** the fatty content of milk which gathers at the top and can be made into butter by churning. **b** this eaten (often whipped) with a dessert, as a cake filling, etc. (*strawberries and cream*). **2** (usu. prec. by *the*) the best or choicest part of something, esp. an elite group of people (*the cream of the nation*). **3** a cream-like preparation, esp. a cosmetic (*hand cream*). **4** a very pale yellow or off-white colour. **5 a** a filling, dessert, etc. with a creamy consistency. **b** a soup or sauce containing milk or cream. **c** a full-bodied mellow sweet sherry. **d** a sandwich cookie with a cream filling. **e** a chocolate-covered, usu. fruit-flavoured, fondant. ● *verb* **1** *transitive* **a** take the cream from (*milk*). **b** (usu. foll. by *off*) take the best or a specified part from. **2** *transitive* work (butter, esp. with sugar etc.) to a creamy consistency. **3** *transitive* treat (the skin etc.) with cosmetic cream. **4** *transitive* add cream to (*coffee etc.*). **5** *intransitive* (of milk or any other liquid) form a cream or scum. **6** *transitive* *N Amer. informal* defeat decisively (esp. in a game etc.). **7** *transitive* esp. *N Amer. slang* a hit (*I creamed him with my purse*). **b** beat thoroughly. **8** *intransitive* *slang* become sexually excited; have an orgasm. ● *adjective* pale yellow; off-white. [Old French *cre(s)me* from Late Latin *cramum* (perhaps from Gaulish) & ecclesiastical Latin *chrisma* CHRISM]

cream cheese noun a soft, rich, spreadable, and unripened cheese made from milk or cream.

cream cracker noun *Brit. & Cdn* a crisp dry unsweetened biscuit usu. eaten with cheese.

creamed *adjective* **1** prepared in a cream sauce (*creamed spinach*). **2** (of honey) whipped or churned. **3** (of cottage cheese) having the curds combined with milk.

cream·er noun **1** esp. *N Amer.* a jug or container for cream. **2 a** a non-dairy product used as a substitute for cream or milk in coffee or tea. **b** a small, single-serving container of this. **3** a small, single-serving container of cream for use in coffee or tea.

cream·ery noun (pl. **-eries**) **1** a factory producing butter and cheese. **2** a shop where milk, cream, etc., are sold; a dairy.

cream of tartar noun purified and crystallized potassium hydrogen tartrate, used esp. in cooking as a leavener.

cream pie noun *N Amer.* a pie with a custard-like filling, often with a whipped cream topping.

cream puff noun **1** a ball-shaped pastry shell filled with whipped cream etc. **2** *informal* a weak, ineffectual person. **3** *slang* (also *attributive*) a car etc. maintained in excellent condition.

cream sauce noun **1** a sauce containing a high proportion of cream. **2** a white sauce made from milk and thickened with butter and flour.

cream soda noun a carbonated vanilla-flavoured soft drink.

cream tea noun esp. *Brit.* afternoon tea with scones, jam, and cream.

cream·ware noun an earthenware of a rich cream colour.

creamy *adjective* (**cream·i·er, cream·i·est**) like cream in taste, colour, or consistency. □ **cream·i·ly** *adverb* **cream·i·ness** noun

crease ● noun **1 a** a line in paper etc. caused by folding etc. **b** a vertical line pressed into trousers with an iron. **c** a fold or wrinkle. **2** a marked area in front of the goal in hockey or lacrosse into which the puck or the ball must precede the players. ● *verb* **1** *transitive* make creases in (*material*). **2** *intransitive* become creased (*linen creases badly*). **3** *transitive* esp. *US slang* graze with a shell and wound slightly (*the bullet creased my head*). [earlier *creast* = CREST ridge in material]

cre·ate *verb* **1** *transitive* **a** cause to exist; make (something) new or original (*God created the world; a ballet created by James Kudelka; the government plans to create new jobs*). **b** have as a result; produce (a feeling, situation, etc.) (*poverty creates resentment; create a good impression*). **2** *transitive* (of a performer) be the first person to perform (a role). **3** *transitive* invest (a person) with a rank (*created him a lord; created eight new peers*). **4** *intransitive* *slang Brit.* make a fuss; grumble. □ **cre·at·able** *adjective* [Latin *creare*]

cre·a·tine /ˈkriːətiːn/ noun a product of protein metabolism found in the muscles of vertebrates. [Greek *kreas* meat + -INE⁴]

cre·ation noun **1 a** the act of creating. **b** an instance of this. **c** something created. **2 a** (usu. **the Creation**) the creating of the universe regarded as an act of God. **b** (usu. **Creation**) everything so created; the universe. **3** a product of human intelligence, esp. of imaginative thought or artistic ability. **4 a** the act of investing with a title or rank. **b** an instance of this.

cre·ation·ism noun Theol. a theory attributing all matter, biological species, etc., to separate acts of creation, esp. according to a literal interpretation of Genesis, rather than to evolution. □ **cre·ation·ist** noun & adjective

creation myth noun a myth explaining the creation of the world.

creation science noun the reinterpretation of scientific knowledge in accord with belief in the literal truth of the Bible, esp. regarding the origin of matter, life, and humankind.

cre·ative adjective **1** of or involving the skilful and imaginative use of something to produce e.g. a work of art (her creative use of colour). **2** able to create things, usu. in an imaginative way. **3** inventive. □ **cre·ative·ly** adverb **cre·ative·ness** noun **crea·tiv·ity** noun

creative accounting noun informal the exploitation of loopholes in financial legislation in order to gain advantage or present figures in a misleadingly favourable light.

creative writing noun the writing of fiction, plays, etc.

cre·ator noun **1** a person who creates. **2** (as **the Creator**) God.

crea·ture noun **1 a** an animal, as distinct from a human being. **b** any living being (we are all God's creatures). **2** a person of a specified kind (poor creature). **3** a person owing nature to and obsequiously subservient to another. **4** anything created; a creation. **5** a person whose character is defined by a specified influence (creatures of our culture). □ **creature of habit** a person set in an unvarying routine. □ **crea·ture·ly** adjective [Old French from Late Latin creatura (as CREATE)]

creature comforts plural noun material comforts such as good food, warmth, etc.

crèche /kreʃ, kreɪʃ/ noun **1** N Amer. = NATIVITY SCENE. **2** Brit. a daycare centre. [French, from Old French creche manger, crib, from Germanic]

Crécy, Battle of /ˈkresi/ a battle between the English and the French in 1346 near the village of Crécy-en-Ponthieu in Picardy in northern France, in which the forces of Edward III defeated those of Philip VI. This was the first great English victory of the Hundred Years War.

cred noun informal credibility (street cred). [abbreviation]

cre·dal /ˈkriːdəl/ adjective (also **creed·al**) pertaining to a creed.

cre·dence /ˈkriːdəns/ noun **1** belief. **2** believability. **3** (in full **credence table**) a small side table, shelf, or niche which holds the elements of the Eucharist before they are consecrated. □ **give credence to 1** believe. **2** (also **lend credence to**) (of a fact etc.) support or reinforce the believability of. [Old French from medieval Latin credentia from credere believe]

cre·den·tial /krəˈdenʃəl/ noun (usu. in pl.) **1** evidence of a person's achievements or trustworthiness, usu. in the form of certificates, references, etc. **2** a letter or letters of introduction. □ **cre·den·tialed** adjective **cre·den·tial·ing** noun [medieval Latin credentialis (as CREDENCE)]

cre·den·za /krəˈdenzə/ noun **1** a sideboard or buffet. **2** a long, low piece of office furniture for storing papers etc., usu. with sliding doors. [Italian from medieval Latin (as CREDENCE)]

cred·ibil·ity /ˌkredɪˈbɪlɪti/ noun **1** the condition of being credible or believable. **2** reputation, status.

credibility gap noun an apparent difference between what is said and what is true.

cred·ible /ˈkredɪbəl/ adjective **1** (of a person or statement) believable or worthy of belief. **2** (of a threat etc.) convincing. □ **cred·ibly** adverb [Latin credibilis from credere believe]

cred·it ● noun **1** (usu. of a person) a source of honour, pride, etc. (is a credit to the school). **2** the acknowledgement of merit. **3** a good reputation. **4 a** acknowledgement of competence (give me some credit!). **b** something believable or trustworthy (that statement has credit). **5 a** a person's financial standing; the sum of money at a person's disposal in a bank etc. **b** the power to obtain goods etc. before payment (based on the trust that payment will be made). **6** (usu. in pl.) **a** an acknowledgement of a contributor's services to a film, television program, etc., usually listed at the beginning or end. **b** a film or television program etc. in which a person has participated (his TV credits include Due South). **7** a reputation for solvency and honesty in business. **8 a** (in bookkeeping) the acknowledgement of being paid by an entry on the credit side of an account. **b** the sum entered. **c** the credit side of an account. **d** = TAX CREDIT. **9** N Amer. **a** official recognition that a student has completed a course meeting the requirements of a diploma or degree (took the course for credit). **b** a value ascribed to a credit course (needed three credits to graduate). ● transitive verb

(cred·it·ed, cred·it·ing) 1 (foll. by with; usu. in passive) ascribe (often without certainty) an accomplishment to (was credited with the discovery). **2** believe (cannot credit it). **3** (usu. foll. by to, with) enter on the credit side of an account (credited $20 to him; credited him with $20). □ **credit where credit is due** praise given when it is deserved, even if one is reluctant to give it. **do credit to** (or **do a person credit**) enhance the reputation of. **get credit for** be given credit for. **give a person credit for 1** enter (a sum) to a person's credit. **2** ascribe (a good quality) to a person. **give credit to** believe. **on credit** with an arrangement to pay later. **take credit (for)** accept praise or commendation, esp. for something one is not responsible for. **to one's credit** in one's praise, commendation, or defence (to his credit, he refused the offer). [French crédit from Italian credito or Latin creditum from credere credit- believe, trust]

credit·able adjective (often foll. by to) **1** bringing credit or honour. **2** that can be credited (tax-creditable). □ **credit·abil·ity** noun **credit·ably** adverb

credit card noun a card issued by a bank or business authorizing the obtaining of goods on credit.

credit course noun N Amer. a course taken for credit towards a degree, diploma, etc.

credit crunch noun a situation in which moneylending bodies make it difficult to obtain loans.

Crédi·tiste /kredɪˈtiːst/ noun Cdn a member or supporter of the Quebec wing of the Social Credit Party. [French]

credit line noun = LINE OF CREDIT.

credit note noun a note given by a store etc. in return for goods returned, stating the value of goods owed to the customer.

credit·or noun **1** a person to whom a debt is owing. **2** a person or company that gives credit for money or goods (compare DEBTOR).

credit rating noun an estimate of one's suitability to receive credit.

credit union noun a banking co-operative offering financial services to members.

credit watch noun the status of an organization, government, etc., whose bond rating is under consideration for downgrading.

credit·worthy adjective considered suitable to receive commercial credit. □ **credit·worthi·ness** noun

credo /ˈkriːdoʊ, ˈkreɪ-/ noun (pl. **credos**) **1** a set of principles held by a specified group, esp. as a philosophy (the environmentalist credo). **2** (**Credo**) a statement of Christian belief; a creed, esp. the Apostles' or Nicene creed beginning in Latin with credo. **3** a musical setting of the Nicene Creed. [Latin, = I believe]

credu·lous /ˈkredjʊləs/ adjective **1** too ready to believe; gullible. **2** (of behaviour) showing such gullibility. □ **credu·lity** /krəˈdjuːlɪti/ noun **credu·lous·ly** adverb **credu·lous·ness** noun [Latin credulus from credere believe]

Cree ● noun (pl. same or **Crees**) **1** a member of a part of the Algonquian linguistic family, living from the east coast to the Rocky Mountains, and forming the largest Aboriginal group in Canada. **2** the language of this people. ● adjective of or relating to the Cree or their language. [Canadian French Cris (earlier Cristinaux) from Algonquian]

creed noun **1** a set of principles or opinions, esp. as a philosophy of life (his creed is moderation in everything). **2 a** (often **the Creed**) a brief formal summary of Christian doctrine (compare APOSTLES' CREED, NICENE CREED, ATHANASIAN CREED). **b** the Creed as part of the Mass. [Old English crēda from Latin CREDO]

creed·al var. of CREDAL.

Creek ● noun **1** a member of a N American Aboriginal confederacy of the Muskogee and some other peoples. **2** the Muskogean language of the Muskogee. ● adjective of or relating to this people or their culture or language. [Creek]

creek /kriːk, krɪk/ noun **1** N Amer., Austral., & NZ a tributary of a river; a stream or brook. **2** Brit. **a** a small bay or harbour on a seacoast. **b** a narrow inlet on a seacoast or in a riverbank. □ **up the creek** slang **1** in difficulties or trouble. **2** crazy. [Old Norse kriki nook or Old French crique, perhaps reinforced by Middle Dutch krēke: ultimate origin unknown]

Creek·er noun a native or resident of Stoney Creek.

creek·side ● adjective alongside a creek. ● noun the bank of a creek.

creel noun **1** a large wicker basket for fish. **2** an angler's fishing basket. [Middle English, originally Scots: ultimate origin unknown]

Cree Lake a lake in north central Saskatchewan, about 600 km north of Saskatoon.

creep ● intransitive verb (past and past participle **crept**) **1** move with the body prone and close to the ground; crawl. **2** (often foll. by in, out, up, etc.) come, go, or move slowly and stealthily or timidly (*crept out without being seen*). **3** enter slowly (into a person's affections, life, awareness, etc.) (*a feeling crept over her*; *crept into her heart*). **4** *informal* act abjectly or obsequiously in the hope of advancement. **5** (of a plant) grow along the ground or up a wall by means of tendrils etc. **6** (as **creep·ing** *adjective*) developing slowly and steadily (*creeping inflation*). **7** (of the flesh) feel as if insects etc. were creeping over it, as a result of fear, horror, etc. **8** (of metals etc.) undergo creep. ● *noun* **1 a** the act of creeping. **b** an instance of this. **2** (in *pl.*; prec. by *the*) *informal* a nervous feeling of revulsion or fear (*gives me the creeps*). **3** *informal* an unpleasant or obnoxious person. **4** the gradual downward movement of disintegrated rock due to gravitational forces etc. **5** (of metals etc.) a gradual change of shape under stress. **6** a feeding enclosure with a long narrow entrance designed to admit only young animals. **7** a phenomenon characterized by a gradual increase (*cost creep*). □ **creep out** (*past* and *past participle* **creeped**) *N Amer. informal* give (someone) a nervous feeling of revulsion or fear. **creep up on** approach (a person) stealthily or unnoticed. [Old English *crēopan* from Germanic]

creep·er *noun* **1** *Bot.* any climbing or creeping plant. **2** any bird that climbs, esp. a treecreeper. **3** *slang* a soft-soled shoe.

creeping char·lie *noun* a common Eurasian plant of the mint family, *Glechoma hederacea*, naturalized in N America, with bluish-purple flowers. *Also called* GROUND IVY.

creeping Jenny *noun* any of various creeping plants, esp. moneywort.

creepy *adjective* (**creep·i·er**, **creep·i·est**) **1** *informal* having or producing a creeping of the flesh (*I feel creepy*; *a creepy film*). **2** given to creeping. □ **creep·i·ly** *adverb* **creep·i·ness** *noun*

creepy-crawly *informal* ● *noun* (*pl.* **-crawlies**) an insect, worm, etc. ● *adjective* creeping and crawling.

cre·mate /ˈkriːmeit, kriːˈmeit, krəˈ-/ *transitive verb* burn (a corpse etc.) to ashes, esp. ceremonially at a funeral. □ **cre·ma·tion** *noun*
     cre·ma·tor *noun* [Latin *cremare* burn]

crema·tor·ium /ˌkriːməˈtɔriəm/ *noun* (*pl.* **crema·tor·ia** or **crema·tor·iums**) a building in which corpses are cremated. [modern Latin (as CREMATE, -ORIUM)]

crema·tory /ˈkriːməˌtɔri/ ● *adjective* of or relating to cremation. ● *noun* (*pl.* **-ies**) *N Amer.* = CREMATORIUM.

Créma·zie /kreimaˈzi/ **Oc·tave** (1827–79), Canadian poet. He has been called 'the father of French-Canadian poetry' for his patriotic verse, often rhetorical in style, celebrating such subjects as Montcalm's defence of Fort Carillon in 'Le drapeau de Carillon' (1858).

creme /kriːm/ *noun* **1** a creamy substance used as a filling etc., not containing real cream (*creme-filled cookies*). **2** a toiletry, cosmetic product, or ointment having the consistency of cream (*tanning creme*).

crème an·glaise /ˌkrem ɑ̃ˈglez/ *noun* a thin vanilla-flavoured custard sauce. [French, = English cream]

crème brû·lée /ˌkrem bruːˈlei/ *noun* a baked custard topped with caramelized sugar. [French, = burnt cream]

crème cara·mel /ˌkrem kerəˈmel, kɑrə-, karə-/ *noun* a baked custard cooked in a caramel-coated dish, usu. served inverted so that the caramel forms a sauce over the custard. [French, = caramel cream]

crème de cacao /ˌkrem də kəˈkau, kəˈkeiɔ/ *noun* a chocolate-flavoured liqueur. [French, = cream of cacao]

crème de cas·sis /ˌkrem də kəˈsiːs/ *noun* a blackcurrant-flavoured liqueur. [French, = cream of blackcurrant]

crème de la crème /ˌkrem də lə ˈkrem/ *noun* the best part; the elite. [French, = cream of the cream]

crème de menthe /ˌkrem də ˈmɑ̃t, ˈmenθ/ *noun* a mint-flavoured liqueur. [French, = cream of mint]

crème fraîche /ˌkrem ˈfreʃ/ *noun* heavy cream thickened by slight fermentation, with a tart taste. [French, = fresh cream]

creme rinse *noun* a conditioner applied to the hair after shampooing and rinsed out, esp. to detangle the hair.

cre·mini /krəˈmiːni/ *noun* (*pl.* same) a brown variety of the common mushroom eaten before the cap has opened and fully matured (*compare* PORTOBELLO). [Italian]

Cre·mona /krɪˈmoːnə/ a city in Lombardy, in N Italy; pop. (2001) 69,444. Between the 16th and the 18th c. the city was home to three renowned families of violin makers: the Amati, the Guarneri, and the Stradivari. □ **Cremon·ese** *noun & adjective*

cre·nate /ˈkriːneit/ *adjective Bot. & Zool.* having a notched edge or rounded teeth. □ **cre·na·tion** *noun* [modern Latin *crenatus* from popular Latin *crena* notch]

crenel /ˈkrenəl/ *noun* (also **cren·elle** /krɪˈnel/) an indentation or gap in the parapet of a tower, castle, etc., originally for shooting through etc. [Old French *crenel*, ultimately from popular Latin *crena* notch]

crenel·late /ˈkrenəˌleit/ *transitive verb* (also **crenel·ate**) (esp. in *passive*) provide (a tower etc.) with battlements or loopholes (*crenellated walls*). □ **crenel·la·tion** /-ˈleiʃən/ *noun* [French *créneler* (as CRENEL)]

Cren·shaw *noun* a variety of melon that is a cross between a Persian and a Casaba melon, the fruit being large and oval-shaped, with a pale yellow rind and salmon-pink coloured flesh.

Cre·ole /ˈkriːoːl/ ● *noun* **1 a** a descendant of European (esp. Spanish) settlers in the W Indies or Central or South America. **b** a white descendant of French settlers in the southern US. **c** a person of mixed European and black descent. **2 a** a language formed from the contact of a European language (esp. English, French, or Portuguese) with another (esp. African) language. **b** (usu. **creole**) a former pidgin language that has become the sole or native language of a community. ● *adjective* **1** of or relating to a Creole or Creoles. **2** (usu. **creole**) of Creole origin or production. [French *créole*, *criole* from Spanish *criollo*, prob. from Portuguese *crioulo* native, from *criar* breed, from Latin *creare* CREATE]

creol·ize /ˈkriːəˌlaiz/ *transitive & intransitive verb* (also esp. *Brit.* **-ise**) transform (a language) into a Creole. □ **creol·iz·a·tion** *noun*

Creon /ˈkriːɒn/ *Gk Myth* the brother of Jocasta, who ruled Thebes after the downfall of Oedipus.

creo·sote /ˈkriːəˌsoːt/ ● *noun* **1** (in full **creosote oil**) a dark brown oil distilled from coal tar, used as a wood preservative. **2** a colourless oily fluid distilled from wood tar, used as an antiseptic. ● *transitive verb* treat with creosote. □ **creo·soted** *adjective* [German *Kreosote* from Greek *kreas* flesh + *sōtēr* preserver, with reference to its antiseptic properties]

creosote bush *noun* a shrub of arid parts of Mexico and the western US, *Larrea tridentata*, with leaves smelling of creosote.

crepe /kreip/ *noun* **1** (also **crape**) a woven or knitted fabric with a wrinkled surface. **2** (also /krep/) a thin pancake, usu. with a savoury or sweet filling. **3** (also **crepe rubber**) a very hard-wearing wrinkled sheet rubber used for the soles of shoes etc. **4** = CREPE PAPER. □ **crepey** *adjective* **crep·i·ness** *noun* [French from Old French *crespe* curled, from Latin *crispus*]

crepe de Chine /kreip də ˈʃiːn/ *noun* a light synthetic or silk crepe. [French, lit. 'crepe of China']

crepe paper *noun* thin crinkled paper.

crêp·erie /ˈkreipəri/ *noun* a restaurant serving crepes. [French]

crepe Su·zette /suːˈzet/ *noun* (*pl.* **crepes Su·zette** *pronunc.* same) a crepe in an orange sauce, flamed in alcohol at the table.

crepi·tate /ˈkrepiˌteit/ *intransitive verb* make a crackling sound. □ **crepi·tant** *adjective* [Latin *crepitare* frequentative of *crepare* creak]

crepi·ta·tion /ˌkrepiˈteiʃən/ *noun* **1** *Med.* a crackling sound made when breathing with an inflamed lung, detected using a stethoscope. **2** the action or sound of crackling or rattling.

crepi·tus /ˈkrepitəs/ *noun Med.* **1** a grating noise from the ends of a fractured bone rubbing together. **2** a similar sound heard from the chest in pneumonia etc. [Latin from *crepare* rattle]

crept *past* and *past participle* of CREEP.

cre·pus·cu·lar /krəˈpʌskjulər/ *adjective* **1 a** of twilight. **b** dim. **2** *Zool.* appearing or active in twilight. [Latin *crepusculum* twilight]

Crerar /krəˈrɑr/ **Henry Dun·can Gra·ham** (1888–1965), Canadian army officer. He served in France and Belgium during the First World War, and during the Second World War was appointed commander-in-chief of the First Canadian Army during the operations in NW Europe (1944–5); he was promoted to the rank of general in 1944.

Cres. *abbreviation* Crescent.

cresc. *abbreviation* (also **cres.**) *Music* = CRESCENDO.

cre·scendo /krəˈʃendoː/ ● *noun* (*pl.* **-dos**, **-scendi** /-iː/) **1** *Music* a passage gradually increasing in loudness. **2 a** progress towards a climax (*a crescendo of emotions*). **b** a climax (*reached a crescendo then died away*). ● *adverb & adjective* with a gradual increase in loudness. ● *intransitive verb* (**-does**, **-doed**) increase gradually in loudness or intensity. [Italian, part. of *crescere* grow (as CRESCENT)]

cres·cent /ˈkresənt/ ● *noun* **1** the curved sickle shape of the waxing or waning moon. **2** anything of this shape. **3** a curving street. **4** a crescent-shaped item of food, esp. a bread roll or cookie. **5 a** the crescent-shaped emblem of Islam or Turkey. **b** (**the Crescent**) the world or power of Islam. ● *adjective* **1** increasing. **2** crescent-shaped.

---

uː m**oo**d   ai m**y**   əi p**i**pe   au br**ow**n   ʌu h**ou**se   ei d**ay**   ɔi b**oy**   ɑ̃ fr**an**glais   ã Canadi**en**   ɔ̃ Bray**on**   (*see over for consonants*)

□ **cres·cent·ic** /-'sɛntɪk/ *adjective* [Old French *creissant*, from Latin *crescere* grow]

crescent wrench *noun* N Amer. a wrench with a crescent-shaped head with jaws which can be adjusted by a screw mechanism.

cresol /'kriːsɒl/ *noun* any of three isomeric phenols present in creosote and used as disinfectants. [CREOSOTE + -OL²]

cress *noun* any of various cruciferous plants usu. with pungent edible leaves, e.g. watercress. [Old English *cresse* from West Germanic]

cres·set /'krɛsɪt/ *noun* hist. a metal container for oil, coal, etc., lighted and usu. mounted on a pole for illumination. [Old French *cresset* from *craisse* = *graisse* GREASE]

Cres·sida /'krɛsɪdə/ (in medieval legends of the Trojan War) the daughter of Calchas, a priest; she was faithless to her lover Troilus, a son of Priam.

crest ● *noun* **1 a** a comb or tuft of feathers, fur, etc. on a bird's or animal's head. **b** something resembling this, esp. a plume of feathers on a helmet. **c** a helmet; the top of a helmet. **2** the top of something, esp. of a mountain, wave, roof, etc. **3** *Heraldry* **a** a device above the shield and helmet of a coat of arms. **b** such a device reproduced on writing paper or on a seal, signifying a family. **4** a shield or coat of arms (*our school crest*). **5 a** a line along the top of the neck of some animals. **b** the hair growing from this; a mane. **6** *Anat.* a ridge along the surface of a bone. **7** the highest level reached by a river in flood. ● *verb* **1** *transitive* reach the crest of (a hill, wave, etc.). **2** *transitive* **a** provide with a crest. **b** serve as a crest to. **3** *intransitive* (of a wave) form into a crest. **4** *intransitive* (of a river in flood) reach its highest level. □ **the crest of a wave** the most favourable moment in one's progress. □ **crest·ed** *adjective* (also in *combination*). **crest·less** *adjective* [Old French *creste* from Latin *crista* tuft]

crest·fallen *adjective* **1** dejected, dispirited. **2** with a fallen or drooping crest.

cre·ta·ceous /krɪ'teiʃəs/ ● *adjective* **1** of the nature of chalk. **2** (**Cretaceous**) *Geol.* of or relating to the last period of the Mesozoic era, lasting from about 144 to 65 million years BP, between the Jurassic and Tertiary periods. The climate was warm, the sea level rose, the first flowering plants emerged, and the domination of the dinosaurs continued, although they died out quite abruptly towards the end of it. ● *noun* (**Cretaceous**) *Geol.* this geological era or system. [Latin *cretaceus* from *creta* chalk]

Crete /kriːt/ a Greek island in the E Mediterranean; pop. (2001) 601,159; capital, Heraklion. It is noted for the remains of the Minoan civilization which flourished there in the 2nd millennium BC. Crete played an important role in the Greek struggle for independence from the Turks in the late 19th and early 20th c., becoming administratively part of an independent Greece in 1913. □ **Cretan** *adjective & noun*

cret·in /'krɛtɪn, 'kriː-/ *noun* **1** a person who is deformed and mentally retarded as the result of a thyroid deficiency. **2** *informal derogatory* a stupid person. □ **cret·in·ism** *noun* **cret·in·ize** *transitive verb* (also esp. Brit. **-ise**). **cret·in·ous** *adjective* [French *crétin* from Swiss French *creitin*, *crestin* from Latin *Christianus* CHRISTIAN²]

cre·tonne /krə'tɒn/ *noun* (often *attributive*) a heavy cotton fabric with a usu. floral pattern printed on one or both sides, used for drapery. [French from *Creton* in Normandy]

cre·tons /krə'tɔ̃/ *plural noun* Cdn (Que.) a spread of shredded pork cooked with onions in pork fat. [Canadian French, probably from Middle Dutch *kerte* 'cut']

Creutzfeldt-Jakob disease /krɔɪtsfɛlt'jakɒb/ *noun* a type of spongiform encephalopathy affecting human beings, characterized by progressive dementia. [H. G. *Creutzfeldt* (d.1964) and A. *Jakob* (d.1931), German physicians]

cre·vasse /krə'vas/ *noun* a deep open crack, esp. in a glacier. [French from Old French *crevace*: see CREVICE]

crev·ice /'krɛvɪs/ *noun* a narrow opening or fissure, esp. in a rock or building etc. [Old French *crevace* from *crever* burst, from Latin *crepare*]

crevice tool *noun* a vacuum cleaner attachment consisting of a long narrow nozzle, used for cleaning in corners.

crew¹ ● *noun* (often treated as *pl.*) **1 a** group of people operating a ship, aircraft, train, etc. **b** such a group as distinguished from the captain or officers. **c** a body of people working together; a team. **2** *informal* a company of people; a gang (*a motley crew*). ● *verb* **1** *transitive* supply or act as a crew or member of a crew for. **2** *intransitive* act as a crew or member of a crew. [Middle English from Old French *creüe* increase, fem. past participle of *croistre* grow, from Latin *crescere*]

crew² *past of* CROW².

crew cab *noun* a four-doored cab on a pickup truck, with rear seats for passengers.

crew·cut *noun* a very short haircut; a brush cut. [apparently first adopted by rowing crews at Harvard and Yale universities]

Crewe a town and major railway junction in Cheshire, west central England; pop. (est. 1993) 109,500 (with Nantwich).

crewel /'kruːəl/ *noun* a thin worsted yarn used for tapestry and embroidery. [Middle English *crule* etc., of unknown origin]

crewel work *noun* an embroidered design worked in crewel.

crew·man *noun* (*pl.* **-men**) a member of a crew.

crew·neck *noun* **1** a close-fitting round neckline, esp. on a sweater. **2** a sweater etc. with a crewneck.

crib ● *noun* **1 a** a bed for a baby or young child, having barred sides. **b** Brit. a model of the Nativity of Christ, with a manger as a bed; a crèche. **2** a barred container or rack for animal fodder. **3** *informal* **a** a sheet of notes, answers to questions, etc. used surreptitiously by students as an aid in an exam etc. **b** plagiarized work etc. **4 a** heavy crossed timbers used in foundations in loose soil, to support a pier, to form a dam, etc. **b** a framework lining the shaft of a mine. **5 a** *informal* cribbage. **b** (in cribbage) a set of cards discarded by the players and used by the dealer. ● *verb* (**cribbed**, **crib·bing**) **1** *transitive & intransitive* *informal* copy (another person's work) unfairly or without acknowledgement. **2** *transitive & intransitive* confine in a small space. **3** *transitive & intransitive* *informal* pilfer, steal. **4** *intransitive* (of a horse) bite a manger or other object while swallowing large amounts of air. □ **crib·ber** *noun* [Old English *crib(b)*]

crib·bage /'krɪbɪdʒ/ *noun* a card game for two, three, or four players, in which the dealer may score from the cards in the crib (see CRIB *noun* 5b), esp. using pegs in a board for keeping score. [17th c.: origin unknown]

cribbage board *noun* a board with pegs and holes, usu. in the shape of a rectangle or the number 29, used for keeping score in cribbage.

crib·bing *noun* **1** = CRIB *noun* 4a. **2** the action by a horse of biting something while swallowing large amounts of air.

crib death *noun* N Amer. = SUDDEN INFANT DEATH SYNDROME.

cribri·form /'krɪbrɪˌfɔrm/ *adjective* Anat. & Bot. having numerous small holes. [Latin *cribrum* sieve + -FORM]

crib sheet *noun* **1** a piece of paper with notes consulted surreptitiously during an exam. **2** a sheet for a child's crib.

Crich·ton /'kraitən/ **James** ('the Admirable Crichton') (1560–82), Scottish adventurer. A skilled swordsman, poet, orator, and scholar who spoke several languages, he gained fame throughout Renaissance Europe for his accomplishments.

Crick, Fran·cis Harry Comp·ton (b.1916), English biophysicist. With J. D. Watson he discovered the double helix structure of the DNA molecule, thus broadly explaining how genetic information is carried in living organisms and how genes replicate; he shared a Nobel Prize with Watson and M. H. F. Wilkins in 1962.

crick ● *noun* a sudden painful stiffness in the neck or the back etc. ● *transitive verb* produce a crick in (the neck etc.). [Middle English: origin unknown]

crick·et¹ *noun* any of various grasshopper-like insects of the family Gryllidae, the males of which produce a characteristic chirping sound. [Old French *criquet* from *criquer* creak etc. (imitative)]

crick·et² ● *noun* a game played on a grass field with two teams of 11 players taking turns to bowl at a wicket defended by a batting player of the other team. ● *intransitive verb* (**crick·et·ed**, **crick·et·ing**) play cricket. □ **not cricket** Brit. *informal* underhand or unfair behaviour. □ **crick·et·er** *noun* [16th c.: origin uncertain]

cri·coid /'kraikɔid/ ● *adjective* ring-shaped. ● *noun* (in full **cricoid cartilage**) Anat. the ring-shaped cartilage of the larynx. [modern Latin *cricoides* from Greek *krikoeidēs* from *krikos* ring]

cri de cœur /ˌkriː də 'kɜr/ *noun* (*pl.* **cris de cœur** *pronunc.* same) a passionate appeal, complaint, or protest. [French, = cry from the heart]

cried *past and past participle of* CRY.

crier *noun* **1** a person who cries. **2** an officer who makes public announcements in a court of justice or in a public place.

crikey *interjection* esp. Brit. *slang* an expression of astonishment, dismay, etc. [euphemism for CHRIST]

crime *noun* **1 a** an offence punishable by law. **b** illegal acts as a whole (*resorted to crime*). **2** an evil act (*a crime against humanity*). **3** a shameful act (*a crime to waste them*). [Old French from Latin *crimen -minis* judgment, offence]

Crimea, the /krai'miːə/ (also **Crimea**) a peninsula of Ukraine lying between the Sea of Azov and the Black Sea. It was the scene of the

Crimean War in the 1850s. The majority of the population is Russian. □ **Cri·mean** *adjective*

Crimean War /kraɪˈmiːən/ a war between Russia and an alliance of Great Britain, France, Sardinia, and Turkey (1853-56). The main theatre of the war was the Crimean peninsula, where, after a lengthy siege and heavy losses, an Anglo-French army captured the fortress city of Sebastopol in 1855.

crime family *noun* N Amer. an organized crime syndicate centred around and controlled by a specific family.

crime fighter *noun* a person who fights crime. □ **crime-fighting** *noun*

crime of passion *noun* a crime, esp. murder, committed in a fit of sexual jealousy.

crime scene *noun* N Amer. the place where a crime has been committed.

Crime Stoppers *noun* a non-profit organization operating a program through which cash rewards are offered to persons who provide information anonymously to the police which leads to the conviction of a criminal.

crime wave *noun* a sudden increase in crime.

crime writer *noun* **1** a writer of detective fiction or thrillers. **2** a print journalist specializing in crime news.

crim·in·al ● *noun* a person who has committed a crime or crimes. ● *adjective* **1** of, involving, or concerning crime (*criminal records*). **2** having committed (and usu. been convicted of) a crime. **3** *Law* relating to or expert in criminal law rather than civil or political matters (*Criminal Code*; *criminal lawyer*). **4** scandalous, deplorable. □ **crim·in·al·ity** *noun* **crim·in·al·ly** *adverb*

Criminal Code *noun* a Canadian federal statute embodying most of Canada's criminal law and specifying criminal procedures and sentencing options.

criminal harassment *noun* Cdn the criminal offence of stalking.

crim·in·al·is·tic *adjective* relating to criminals or their habits.

crim·in·al·ize *transitive verb* (also esp. Brit. **-ise**) **1** turn (an activity) into a criminal offence by making it illegal. **2** turn (a person) into a criminal, esp. by making his or her activities illegal. □ **crim·in·al·iz·a·tion** *noun*

criminal law *noun* law concerned with the prosecution of crime (*opp.* CIVIL LAW 1).

criminal libel *noun* Law a deliberate defamatory statement in a permanent form.

criminal negligence *noun* Cdn Law an offence involving a wanton or reckless disregard for the lives or safety of others.

crim·in·ol·ogy *noun* the scientific study of crime. □ **crim·in·o·logic·al** *adjective* **crim·in·ol·o·gist** *noun* [Latin *crimen -minis* CRIME + -OLOGY]

crimp ● *transitive verb* **1** compress into small folds or ridges. **2** make narrow wrinkles or flutings in; corrugate. **3** make waves in (the hair) with a hot iron. ● *noun* a crimped thing or form. □ **put a crimp in** N Amer. informal thwart; interfere with. □ **crimp·er** *noun* **crimpy** *adjective* [Middle English, prob. ultimately from Old High German *krimphan*]

crim·son ● *adjective* of a rich deep red inclining to purple. ● *noun* this colour. ● *transitive & intransitive verb* make or become crimson. [Middle English *cremesin*, *crimesin*, ultimately from Arabic *ḳirmizi* KERMES]

cringe ● *intransitive verb* **1** contract the muscles of the body involuntarily; shrink back in fear, apprehension, or disgust. **2** feel excessively embarrassed. **3** (often foll. by *to*) behave obsequiously. ● *noun* the act or an instance of cringing. □ **crin·ger** *noun* [Old English *cringan*, *crincan*: see CRANK[1]]

cringe-making *adjective* (also **cringe·worthy**) esp. Brit. causing feelings of embarrassment or awkwardness.

crin·kle ● *noun* **1** a wrinkle or crease in paper, cloth, etc. **2** fabric with a wrinkled surface (also *attributive*: *crinkle cotton*). ● *verb* **1** *intransitive* form crinkles. **2** *transitive* form crinkles in. □ **crink·ly** *adjective* [Old English *crincan*: see CRANK[1]]

crinkle-cut *adjective* (of vegetables) cut with wavy edges.

crinkle·root *noun* = TOOTHWORT 1.

crin·oid /ˈkrɪnɔɪd/ ● *noun* any echinoderm of the class Crinoidea, usu. sedentary with feathery arms, e.g. sea lilies and feather stars. ● *adjective* lily-shaped. □ **crin·oid·al** *adjective* [Greek *krinoeidēs* from *krinon* lily]

crino·line /ˈkrɪnəlɪn/ *noun* **1** a stiffened or hooped petticoat worn to make a skirt stand out. **2** a stiff fabric of horsehair or cotton, used for

linings, hats, etc. □ **crino·lined** *adjective* [French from Latin *crinis* hair + *linum* thread]

cripes *interjection* slang expressing surprise, anger, etc. [alteration of CHRIST]

crip·ple ● *noun* dated or offensive a person who is permanently impaired in movement, esp. one unable to walk normally. ¶ The noun *cripple* has long been in use to refer to 'a person unable to walk through illness or disability' and is recorded (in the *Lindisfarne Gospels*) as early as AD 950. The term has recently acquired offensive connotations and has now been largely replaced by terms such as 'disabled person'. ● *transitive verb* **1** make a cripple of; lame. **2** disable, impair. **3** weaken or damage (an institution, enterprise, etc.) seriously (*crippled by the loss of funding*). □ **crip·pled** *adjective* **crip·pler** *noun* **crip·pling** *adjective* **crip·pling·ly** *adverb* [Old English *crypel*, related to CREEP]

crisis /ˈkraɪsɪs/ *noun* (*pl.* **crises** /-siːz/) **1** a time of danger or great difficulty. **2** the turning point, esp. of a disease. **3** a decisive moment. [Latin from Greek *krisis* decision, from *krinō* decide]

crisis centre *noun* a place offering immediate counselling, treatment, etc. to people who are victims of sexual assault, physical abuse, etc.

crisis management *noun* **1** the practice of taking managerial action only when a crisis has developed. **2** the management of a crisis situation.

crisp ● *adjective* **1** hard but brittle. **2** (of air or weather) dry and cold. **3** (of a style or manner) brisk and decisive, esp. dismissive. **4** (of pictures, designs, etc.) clear and distinct. **5** (of paper or cloth) slightly stiff. **6** (of hair) closely curling. **7** (of fruit or vegetables) firm and fresh. **8** invigorating to the sense of smell or taste. ● *noun* **1** (also **crumble**) a baked dessert made of fruit topped with a crumbly mixture of flour (and sometimes oats), butter, and sugar. **2** (in full **potato crisp**) Brit. = CHIP[1] *noun* 2a. **3** a thing overdone in roasting etc. (*burned to a crisp*). **4** a crisp cookie. ● *transitive & intransitive verb* **1** make or become crisp. **2** curl in short stiff folds or waves. □ **crisp·ly** *adverb* **crisp·ness** *noun* [Old English from Latin *crispus* curled]

crisp·ate /ˈkrɪspeɪt/ *adjective* **1** crisped. **2** Bot. & Zool. having a wavy margin. [Latin *crispare* curl]

crisp·bread *noun* **1** a thin crisp biscuit of crushed rye etc. **2** these collectively.

crisp·er *noun* a compartment in a refrigerator for storing fruit and vegetables.

Cris·pin *noun* a large yellow or greenish-yellow cooking and eating apple. [CRISP *adjective* after the English personal name *Crispin*]

Cris·pin, St. (3rd c. AD), legendary Roman martyr said to have spread Christianity while working as a shoemaker with his brother Crispinian. Feast day, 25 Oct.

crispy *adjective* (**crisp·i·er**, **crisp·i·est**) crisp, brittle. □ **crisp·i·ness** *noun*

criss-cross ● *verb* **1 a** *transitive & intransitive* cross or intersect repeatedly. **b** *intransitive* move crosswise. **2** *transitive* mark or make with a criss-cross pattern. ● *noun* **1** a pattern of crossing lines. **2** the crossing of lines or currents etc. ● *adjective* crossing; in cross lines (*criss-cross marking*). ● *adverb* crosswise; at cross purposes. [15th c., from *Christ's cross*: later treated as reduplication of CROSS]

crista /ˈkrɪstə/ *noun* (*pl.* **cris·tae** /-tiː/) **1** Anat. & Zool. a ridge or crest. **2** Anat. an infold of the inner membrane of a mitochondrion. □ **cris·tate** *adjective* [Latin]

cris·to·bal·ite /krɪˈstɒbəˌlaɪt/ *noun* a principal form of silica, occurring as opal. [German *Cristobalit* from Cerro San Cristóbal in Mexico]

crit *noun* informal **1** = CRITICISM 2. **2** = CRITIQUE. **3** Physics critical mass. [abbreviation]

cri·ter·ion /kraɪˈtiːrɪən/ *noun* (*pl.* **cri·ter·ia** /-rɪə/) a principle or standard that a thing is judged by. ¶ The plural form of *criterion*, *criteria*, is often used incorrectly as the singular. In the singular, *criterion* should always be used. □ **cri·ter·ial** *adjective* [Greek *kritērion* means of judging (compare CRITIC)]

crit·ic *noun* **1** a person who censures. **2 a** a person who reviews, analyzes, or judges the merits of literary, artistic, theatrical, or musical works etc., esp. regularly or professionally. **b** a person who writes or broadcasts reviews of restaurants, wine, etc. **3** a person engaged in textual criticism. **4** Cdn a member of an opposition party monitoring and criticizing a specific government ministry (*finance critic*). [Latin *criticus* from Greek *kritikos* from *kritēs* judge, from *krinō* judge, decide]

crit·ic·al *adjective* **1 a** making or involving adverse or censorious comments or judgments. **b** expressing or involving criticism.

c involving judgment or discernment (*use your critical sense*). **2** skilful in or engaged in criticism. **3** providing textual criticism (*a critical edition of Milton*). **4 a** of or at a crisis; involving risk or suspense (*in critical condition*; *a critical operation*). **b** decisive, crucial (*of critical importance*; *at the critical moment*). **5 a** *Math. & Physics* marking transition from one state etc. to another (*critical angle*). **b** *Physics* (of a nuclear reactor) maintaining a self-sustaining chain reaction. □ **crit·ic·al·ity** *noun* (in sense 5). **crit·ic·al·ly** *adverb* **crit·ic·al·ness** *noun* [Latin *criticus*: see CRITIC]

critical apparatus *noun* = APPARATUS 4.

critical mass *noun* **1** the amount of fissile material needed to maintain a nuclear chain reaction. **2** the amount of anything required to achieve a desired effect (*a critical mass of volunteers*).

critical path *noun* the sequence of stages determining the minimum time needed for an operation.

critical temperature *noun* the temperature above which a gas cannot be liquefied.

criti·cism /ˈkrɪtɪˌsɪzəm/ *noun* **1 a** finding fault; censure. **b** a statement or remark expressing this. **2 a** the work of a critic. **b** an article, essay, etc., expressing or containing an analytical evaluation of something. [CRITIC or Latin *criticus* + -ISM]

criti·cize /ˈkrɪtɪˌsaɪz/ *transitive & intransitive verb* (also esp. *Brit.* **-cise**) **1** find fault with; censure. **2** discuss critically. □ **criti·ciz·able** *adjective* **criti·ciz·er** *noun*

cri·tique /krɪˈtiːk/ *noun* a critical essay or analysis; an instance or the process of formal criticism. ● *transitive verb* (**cri·tiques**, **cri·tiqued**, **cri·tiquing**) discuss critically. [French from Greek *kritikē tekhnē* critical art]

crit·ter *noun informal* an animal, insect, etc. [var. of CREATURE]

CRM *abbreviation* customer relationship management.

croak ● *noun* **1** a deep hoarse sound as of a frog or a raven. **2** a sound resembling this. ● *verb* **1 a** *intransitive* utter a croak. **b** *transitive* utter with a croak or in a dismal manner. **2** *slang* **a** *intransitive* die. **b** *transitive* kill. [Middle English: imitative]

croak·er *noun* **1** an animal that croaks. **2** any fish of the family Sciaenidae, which make sounds using the swim bladder as a resonating chamber.

croaky *adjective* (**croak·i·er**, **croak·i·est**) (of a voice) croaking; hoarse. □ **croak·i·ly** *adverb* **croak·i·ness** *noun*

Croat /ˈkroʊat/ *noun & adjective* = CROATIAN. [modern Latin *Croatae* from Serbo-Croatian *Hrvat*]

Cro·atia /kroʊˈeɪʃə/ a country in SE Europe, formerly a constituent republic of Yugoslavia; pop. (est. 2002) 4,390,751; language, Croatian; capital, Zagreb.

Cro·atian /kroʊˈeɪʃən/ ● *noun* **1 a** a native or inhabitant of Croatia. **b** a person of Croatian descent. **2** the language of the Croatians, a form of Serbo-Croat written in the Roman alphabet (*see also* SERBO-CROAT). ● *adjective* of or relating to Croatia, the Croatians, or their language.

croc *noun informal* a crocodile. [abbreviation]

Croce /ˈkroʊtʃeɪ/ **Bene·detto** (1866–1952), Italian philosopher and politician. His major philosophical work, *Filosofia dello spirito* (1902–17), identifies philosophical endeavour with a methodological approach to history; a leading opponent of Fascism, he helped to rebuild democracy after the fall of Mussolini.

cro·chet /ˈkroʊˌʃeɪ, ˈkroʊ-/ ● *noun* **1** a handicraft in which yarn is made up into a patterned fabric by means of a small slender hooked rod. **2** work made in this way. ● *verb* (**cro·cheted** /-ʃeɪd/, **cro·chet·ing** /-ʃeɪɪŋ/) **1** *transitive* make by crocheting. **2** *intransitive* do crochet. □ **cro·chet·er** /ˈkroʊˌʃeɪər/ *noun* [French, diminutive of *croc* hook]

cro·cido·lite /kroʊˈsɪdəˌlaɪt/ *noun* a fibrous blue or green silicate of iron and sodium; blue asbestos. [Greek *krokis -idos* nap of cloth]

crock¹ *noun informal* an old person. [originally Scots, perhaps from Flemish]

crock² *noun* **1** an earthenware pot or jar. **2** a broken piece of earthenware. **3** esp. *N Amer. informal* (also **crock of shit** *coarse slang*) something untrue, deceitful, etc. (*their story was just a crock*). [Old English *croc(ca)*]

crocked *adjective N Amer. slang* drunk.

crock·ery *noun* earthenware or china dishes, plates, etc. [obsolete *crocker* potter: see CROCK²]

crock·et *noun Archit.* a small carved ornament (usu. a bud or curled leaf) on the inclined side of a pinnacle, gable, etc. [Middle English from var. of Old French *crochet*: see CROCHET]

Crock·ett, **David ('Davy')** (1786–1836), US frontiersman, soldier, and politician. As a member of the House of Representatives (1827–31 and 1833–35) he cultivated the image of a rough backwoods legislator; he joined the Texan revolutionaries and was killed at the battle of the Alamo.

Crock-Pot *noun* proprietary a slow cooker.

croco·dile *noun* **1 a** any of a group of large tropical and subtropical amphibious reptiles with thick scaly skin, long tail, and long jaws (sometimes treated as a family, Crocodylidae) related to alligators. **b** leather from its skin, used to make bags, shoes, etc. **2** *Brit. informal* a line of schoolchildren etc. walking in pairs. [Middle English from Old French *cocodrille* from medieval Latin *cocodrillus* from Latin *crocodilus* from Greek *krokodilos* from *krokē* pebble + *drilos* worm]

crocodile clip *noun* = ALLIGATOR CLIP.

crocodile tears *noun* **1** insincere grief. **2** tears shed without feeling any real sorrow, pain, etc. [with reference to the belief that crocodiles wept while devouring or alluring their prey]

croco·dil·ian /krɒkəˈdɪliən/ ● *noun* a reptile of the group including crocodiles and alligators, esp. one of the order Crocodylia, which also includes the caimans, the gharials, and numerous extinct animals, all large lizard-like semi-aquatic carnivores with a long powerful tail and jaws, short legs, and a covering of horny and bony plates. ● *adjective* **1** of or relating to the crocodilians. **2** like a crocodile (*crocodilian grin*).

cro·cus /ˈkroʊkəs/ *noun* (*pl.* **cro·cus·es**) **1** any dwarf plant of the genus *Crocus*, growing from a corm and having brilliant usu. yellow or purple flowers. **2** *see* PRAIRIE CROCUS. [Middle English, = saffron, from Latin from Greek *krokos* crocus, of Semitic origin]

Croe·sus /ˈkriːsəs/ (6th c. BC), last king of Lydia c.560–546 BC. He subjugated the Greek cities on the coast of Asia Minor, and was renowned for his great wealth; his empire was overthrown by the Persian king Cyrus the Great.

croft *Brit.* ● *noun* **1** an enclosed piece of (usu. arable) land. **2** a small rented farm in Scotland or northern England. ● *intransitive verb* farm a croft; live as a crofter. [Old English: origin unknown]

croft·er *noun Brit.* a person who rents a small holding, esp. a joint tenant of a divided farm in parts of Scotland.

Crohn's disease /ˈkroʊnz/ *noun* a chronic inflammatory disease of the intestines, esp. the colon and ileum, causing ulcers and fistulae. [B. B. *Crohn*, US pathologist d.1983]

crois·sant /krwʌˈsɑ̃, krwɑ-/ *noun* a rich, flaky, crescent-shaped bread roll. [French, formed as CRESCENT]

cro·ki·nole /ˈkroʊkəˌnoʊl/ *noun* esp. *Cdn* a game in which wooden discs are flicked across a round wooden board towards its centre. [French *croquignole* a flip, flick]

Cro-Magnon /kroʊˈmagnɒn, -ˈmagnən/ ● *adjective* of a tall broad-faced European race of late paleolithic times. ● *noun* a Cro-Magnon person. [name of a hill in the Dordogne, France, where remains were found in 1868]

Crom·arty Firth /ˈkrɒmərti/ an inlet of the Moray Firth on the coast of Highland Region, N Scotland.

crom·lech /ˈkrɒmlek/ *noun* **1** a dolmen; a megalithic tomb. **2** a circle of upright prehistoric stones. [Welsh from *crom* fem. of *crwm* bent + *llech* flat stone]

Cromp·ton, **Sam·uel** (1753–1827), English inventor of the spinning mule (1779).

Crom·well ▶ **1 Oli·ver** (1599–1658), English general and political leader. The leader of the Parliamentary forces during the English Civil War, he oversaw the trial and execution of Charles I, and became Lord Protector of the Commonwealth (1653–8); he crushed opposition in Scotland and Ireland with considerable cruelty and imposed puritanical values while ruling as a virtual dictator. **2 Thom·as** (c.1485–1540), English statesman, chief minister to Henry VIII 1532–40. He presided over the king's divorce from Catherine of Aragon (1533) and his break with the Roman Catholic Church, as well as the dissolution of the monasteries and the passage of the Act of Supremacy (1534); he fell from favour and was executed on a charge of treason. □ **Crom·well·ian** *adjective & noun*

crone *noun* a withered old woman. [Middle English, ultimately from Old Northern French *carogne* CARRION]

Cronen·berg, **David** (b.1943), Canadian film director, whose science fiction and horror films include *Scanners* (1980), *The Dead Zone* (1983), *The Fly* (1986), and *Naked Lunch* (1991).

Cro·nin /ˈkroʊnɪn/ **James Wat·son** (b.1931), US physicist. He studied the subatomic particles known as neutral kaons, and discovered that during weak interactions between particles a combination of charge conjugation and parity was not conserved; he shared the Nobel Prize for physics in 1980.

Cro·nus /ˈkroːnəs/ *Gk Myth* the youngest son of Uranus (Heaven) and Gaia (Earth) and leader of his brothers, the Titans. He overthrew and castrated his father, and then married his sister Rhea, who gave birth to many of the future gods, including Zeus. Because he was fated to be overcome by one of his male children, Cronus swallowed all of them as soon as they were born, but when Zeus was born, Rhea deceived him with a stone wrapped in swaddling clothes and hid the baby away in Crete. Cronus swallowed the stone, and Zeus eventually dethroned him as ruler of the universe.

crony *noun* (*pl.* **-ies**) often *derogatory* a close friend or companion. [17th-c. *chrony*, (university slang) from Greek *khronios* long-standing, from *khronos* time]

crony·ism *noun N Amer.* the appointment of friends to political posts without due regard to their qualifications; patronage.

crook ● *noun* **1** *informal* **a** a criminal. **b** a swindler. **2** the hooked staff of a shepherd or bishop. **3 a** a bend, curve, or hook. **b** anything hooked or curved. ● *transitive & intransitive verb* bend, curve. ● *adjective* crooked. □ **crook·ery** *noun* [Old Norse *krókr* hook]

crook-back *noun archaic* a hunchback.

crook·ed *adjective* (**crook·ed·er**, **crook·ed·est**) **1 a** not straight or level; bent, curved, twisted. **b** deformed, bent with age. **2** *informal* dishonest. □ **crook·ed·ly** *adverb* **crook·ed·ness** *noun* [Middle English from CROOK, prob. after Old Norse *krókóttr*]

Crookes, Sir Wil·liam (1832–1919), English physicist and chemist. He discovered the element thallium (1861), invented the radiometer (1875), developed a vacuum tube (the precursor of the X-ray tube), and invented the spinthariscope for detecting alpha particles (1903).

crook·neck squash *noun* a variety of squash with a curved neck.

croon ● *transitive & intransitive verb* hum or sing in a low subdued voice, esp. in a sentimental manner. ● *noun* such singing. □ **croon·er** *noun* **croony** *adjective* [Middle English (originally Scots & Northern English) from Middle Dutch & Middle Low German *krönen* groan, lament]

crop ● *noun* **1 a** the produce of cultivated plants, esp. cereals. **b** the season's total yield of this (*a good crop*). **2** a group or an amount produced or appearing at one time (*this year's crop of students*). **3** the stock or handle of a whip. **4 a** a style of hair cut very short. **b** the cropping of hair. **5** *Zool.* **a** the pouch in a bird's gullet where food is prepared for digestion. **b** a similar organ in other animals. **6** the entire tanned hide of an animal. **7** a piece cut off or out of something. ● *verb* (**cropped**, **crop·ping**) **1** *transitive* **a** cut off. **b** (of animals) bite off (the tops of plants). **2** *transitive* **a** cut (hair, edges of a book, a dog's ears, etc.) short. **b** trim (a photograph) to fit a space. **3** *transitive* gather or reap (produce). **4** *transitive* (foll. by *with*) sow or plant (land) with a crop. **5** *intransitive* (of land) bear a crop. □ **crop out** *Geol.* appear at the surface. **crop up 1** (of a subject, circumstance, etc.) appear or come to one's notice unexpectedly. **2** *Geol.* appear at the surface. [Old English *crop(p)*]

crop circle *noun* a mysterious circular depression in a standing crop, often only visible from the air.

crop-dusting *noun* the sprinkling of powdered insecticide or fertilizer on crops, esp. from the air. □ **crop-duster** *noun*

crop-eared *adjective* having the ears (esp. of animals) cut short.

crop·land *noun* land on which crops are grown.

crop·per *noun* a crop-producing plant of specified quality (*a good cropper; a heavy cropper*). □ **come a cropper** *slang* **1** fail badly. **2** fall heavily.

crop top *noun* a garment, usu. of a stretchy material, covering the upper body only down to the midriff.

crop year *noun* a period of usu. twelve months corresponding to the growing and harvesting season or harvesting and marketing season of an agricultural product.

croque mon·sieur /ˌkrɒkməˈsjə/ *noun* a sandwich of ham and cheese, toasted so that the cheese melts. [French]

cro·quet /kroːˈkei, ˈkroː-/ ● *noun* **1** a game played on a lawn, in which mallets are used to drive wooden balls through a series of hoops. **2** the act of croqueting a ball. ● *transitive verb* (**cro·queted** /-keid/; **cro·quet·ing** /-keiɪŋ/) drive away (one's opponent's ball in croquet) by placing one's own against it and striking one's own. [perhaps dial. form of French CROCHET hook]

cro·quette /kroːˈket/ *noun* a fried, breaded roll or ball of mashed potato or minced meat etc. [French from *croquer* crunch]

crore /krɔr/ *noun Ind.* **1** ten million. **2** one hundred lakhs (of rupees, units of measurement, persons, etc.). [Hindi *k(a)rōr*, ultimately from Sanskrit *koṭi* apex]

Cros·bie /ˈkrɒzbi/ **John (Car·nell)** (b.1931), Canadian lawyer and Progressive Conservative politician. He was minister of finance in the minority government of Joe Clark (1979), introducing the budget which brought about a vote of non-confidence in the House of Commons.

Cros·by /ˈkrɒzbi/ **Bing** (born Harry Lillis Crosby) (1903–77), US singer and actor. A famous crooner, he is best known for songs such as 'Pennies from Heaven' (1936) and 'White Christmas' (from the film *Holiday Inn*, 1942); he also starred in the series of *Road* films (1940–62) with Bob Hope.

cro·sier *var. of* CROZIER.

cross ● *noun* **1** an upright post with a transverse bar, as used in antiquity for crucifixion. **2 a** (**the Cross**) in Christianity, the cross on which Christ was crucified. **b** a representation of this as an emblem of Christianity. **c** = SIGN OF THE CROSS. **3** a staff surmounted by a cross and borne before an archbishop or in a religious procession. **4 a** a thing or mark shaped like a cross, esp. a figure made by two short intersecting lines (+ or x). **b** a monument in the form of a cross, esp. one in the centre of a town or on a tomb. **5** a cross-shaped decoration indicating rank in some orders of knighthood or awarded for personal valour. **6 a** an intermixture of animal breeds or plant varieties. **b** an animal or plant resulting from this. **7** (foll. by *between*) a mixture or compromise of two things (*a cross between jazz and blues*). **8** a crosswise movement, e.g. of an actor on stage. **9 a** *Soccer etc.* a pass of the ball across the direction of play. **b** *Boxing* a blow with a crosswise movement of the fist. **10** a trial or affliction; something to be endured. ● *verb* **1** *transitive & intransitive* (often foll. by *over*) go across or to the other side of (a road, river, sea, etc.). **2 a** *intransitive* intersect or be across one another (*the roads cross near the bridge*). **b** *transitive* cause to do this; place crosswise (*cross one's legs*). **3** *transitive* draw a line or lines across (*dot your i's and cross your t's*). **4** *transitive* (foll. by *off*, *out*) cancel or obliterate or remove from a list with lines drawn across. **5** *transitive* (often *reflexive*) make the sign of the cross on or over. **6** *intransitive* **a** pass in opposite or different directions. **b** (of letters between two correspondents) each be dispatched before receipt of the other. **c** (of telephone lines) become wrongly interconnected so that intrusive calls can be heard. **7** *transitive Soccer etc.* pass (the ball) across the field, esp. towards the centre. **8** *transitive* a cause to interbreed. **b** cross-fertilize (plants). **9** *transitive* thwart or frustrate (*crossed in love*). **10** *transitive slang* cheat; double-cross. ● *adjective* **1** (often foll. by *with*) peevish, angry. **2** (usu. *attributive*) transverse; reaching from side to side. **3** (usu. *attributive*) intersecting. **4** (usu. *attributive*) contrary, opposed, reciprocal. □ **at cross-purposes** misunderstanding or conflicting with one another. **bear one's cross** accept trials and misfortunes stoically. **cross one's fingers** (or **keep one's fingers crossed**) **1** put one finger across another as a sign of hoping for good luck. **2** trust in good luck. **cross the floor** *Cdn & Brit.* join the opposing side in a legislature, leadership convention, etc. **cross one's heart** make a solemn pledge, esp. by crossing one's front. **cross one's mind** (of a thought etc.) occur to one, esp. transiently. **cross over 1** pass over (a street, boundary, etc.). **2** move from one culture or artistic style to another. **cross a person's palm** (usu. foll. by *with*) pay a person for a favour. **cross paths** (or **cross one's path**) encounter or meet. **cross swords** (often foll. by *with*) encounter in opposition; have an argument or dispute. **cross wires** (or **get one's wires crossed**) have a misunderstanding. □ **cross·ly** *adverb* **cross·ness** *noun* [Old English *cros* from Old Norse *kross* from Old Irish *cros* from Latin *crux cruc-*]

cross- *combining form* **1** denoting movement or position across something (*cross-country*). **2** denoting interaction (*crossbreed; cross-cultural; cross-fertilize*). **3 a** passing from side to side; transverse (*crossbar; cross-current*). **b** having a transverse part (*crossbow*). **4** describing the form or figure of a cross (*crossroads*).

cross·bar *noun* a horizontal bar between two upright bars, e.g. on a bicycle or a hockey net.

cross·beam *noun* a transverse beam in a structure.

cross-bedding *noun Geol.* lines of stratification crossing the main rock strata. *Also called* FALSE BEDDING. □ **cross-bedded** *adjective*

cross·bill *noun* any stout finch of the genus *Loxia*, having a bill with crossed mandibles for opening pine cones.

cross·bones *noun* a representation of two crossed thigh bones, usu. under the figure of a skull, as an emblem of piracy or death.

cross-border *adjective* passing, occurring, or performed across a border between two countries (*cross-border shopping*).

cross·bow *noun* a bow fixed across a wooden stock, with a groove for

uː m**oo**d   ai m**y**   əi p**i**pe   au br**ow**n   ʌu h**ou**se   ei d**ay**   ɔi b**oy**   ã fr**an**glais   ã Canadi**en**   ɔ̃ Br**ay**on   (*see over for consonants*)

an arrow and a mechanism for drawing and releasing the string. □ **cross·bow·man** *noun* (*pl.* **-men**).

cross·breed ● *noun* **1** a breed of animals or plants produced by crossing different breeds. **2** an individual animal or plant of a crossbreed. ● *transitive verb* (*past* and *past participle* **-bred**) produce or modify by crossing different breeds.

cross-check ● *transitive verb* **1** check by a second or alternative method, or by several methods. **2** (in hockey and lacrosse) obstruct (an opponent) by holding one's stick horizontally in both hands and thrusting it at the opponent's body. ● *noun* an instance of cross-checking.

cross-contam·ination *noun* the process by which bacteria or other micro-organisms are unintentionally transferred from one substance to another, with harmful effect.

cross-country ● *adjective & adverb* **1** across fields or open country, rather than on roads or tracks (*cross-country running*). **2** across a country (*a cross-country train trip*). ● *adjective* of or designating the sport of skiing across the countryside using long, narrow skis. ● *noun* (*pl.* **-countries**) a cross-country sport or race.

cross-court ● *adjective* (of a stroke in tennis) hit diagonally across the court. ● *adverb* to the opposite or diagonally opposite side of the court.

cross-cultural *adjective* of or relating to different cultures or comparison between them. □ **cross-cultur·al·ly** *adverb*

cross-current *noun* **1** a current in a body of water flowing across the main current. **2** (often in *pl.*) a conflicting tendency or movement (*cross-currents in popular culture*).

cross-curricular *adjective* (of a teaching style, treatment of a topic, etc.) incorporating contributions from several different disciplines (*a cross-curricular approach to media education*).

cross·cut ● *verb* (*past* and *past participle* **cross·cut**) **1** *transitive* cut across (a piece of wood etc). **2** *intransitive* switch back and forth between two or more sequences or shots in a film so they appear to be taking place at the same time. ● *adjective* cut across the main grain or axis. ● *noun* a diagonal cut, path, etc.

cross·cut saw *noun* a saw for cutting across the grain of wood.

cross-dating *noun Archaeology* dating by correlation with another site or level.

cross-dressing *noun* the practice of wearing the clothes of the opposite sex. □ **cross-dress** *intransitive verb* **cross-dresser** *noun*

crosse *noun* (in women's field lacrosse) the stick. [Canadian French from Old French *croce, croc* hook]

cross-examine *transitive verb* **1** examine (a witness in a law court) esp. to check, extend or discredit testimony already given. **2** interrogate with minute and persistent questioning. □ **cross-examin·a·tion** *noun* **cross-examin·er** *noun*

cross-eyed *adjective* (as a disorder) having one or both eyes turned permanently inwards towards the nose.

cross-fade *Radio etc.* ● *intransitive verb* fade in one sound as another is faded out. ● *noun* an act of cross-fading.

cross-fertiliz·a·tion *noun* (also esp. *Brit.* **-isation**) **1** fertilization (of an animal or plant) from one of a different species. **2** fruitful interchange of ideas, information, etc. □ **cross-fertil·ize** *transitive verb*

cross·fire *noun* **1** lines of gunfire crossing one another simultaneously from different positions. **2 a** attack or criticism from several sources at once. **b** a lively or combative exchange of views etc.

cross fox *noun* a yellowish N American variety of the red fox with a cross-shaped patch across the shoulders.

cross-grained *adjective* **1** (of timber) having a grain that runs across the regular grain. **2** perverse, intractable.

cross·hairs *plural noun* **1** a pair of fine wires crossing at right angles at the focus of an optical instrument or gun sight, for use in positioning, aiming, and measuring. **2** a representation of this on a computer screen.

cross-hatch *transitive verb* shade with intersecting sets of parallel lines. □ **cross-hatching** *noun*

cross-head *noun* **1** a bar between the piston rod and connecting rod in a steam engine. **2** = CROSS-HEADING.

cross-heading *noun* a heading to a paragraph printed across a column in the body of an article in a newspaper etc.

cross-ice *adjective* (of a pass in hockey, ringette, etc.) shot from one side of the rink to the other.

cross-index *transitive verb* index under another heading as a cross-reference.

cross·ing *noun* **1** a place where things (esp. roads) cross. **2** a place at which one may cross a street, railway tracks, etc. (*pedestrian crossing*). **3** a journey across water (*had a smooth crossing*). **4** the intersection of a church nave and transepts. **5** *Biol.* mating.

crossing guard *noun N Amer.* a person who escorts pedestrians, usu. children, safely across a busy intersection or crosswalk.

crossing over *noun* an exchange of genes between homologous chromosomes (*compare* RECOMBINATION).

cross-legged *adjective* with one leg crossed over the other.

cross-link *Chem.* ● *noun* (also **cross-linkage**) a bond between chains of atoms in a polymer etc. ● *transitive & intransitive verb* form a cross-link (with).

cross·match *transitive verb Med.* test the compatibility of (a donor's and a recipient's blood). □ **cross·match·ing** *noun*

Cross of Valour *noun* Canada's highest award for bravery, given to civilians and military personnel who perform selfless acts of courage in the face of extreme danger. Abbr.: **CV**. *See also* MEDAL OF BRAVERY, STAR OF COURAGE.

cross·over ● *noun* **1** a point or place of crossing from one side to the other. **2** the process of crossing over, esp. from one style or genre of music etc. to another. ● *adjective* **1** having a part that crosses over. **2** that crosses over, esp. from one style or genre to another.

cross-ownership *noun* ownership of two or more similar or related businesses, esp. media outlets, in the same locality.

cross·patch *noun informal* a bad-tempered person. [CROSS *adjective* 1 + obsolete *patch* fool, clown]

cross·piece *noun* a transverse beam or other component of a structure etc.

cross-platform *adjective Computing* able to be used on different types of computers or with different software packages.

cross·ply *adjective Brit.* = BIAS-PLY.

cross-pollin·ate *transitive & intransitive verb* **1** pollinate (a plant) from another. **2** blend together (styles of music, ideas, etc.) □ **cross-pollin·a·tion** *noun*

cross-post *transitive & intransitive verb* send a message simultaneously to more than one newsgroup or other distribution system on the Internet in such a way that the receiving software at individual sites can detect and ignore duplicates. □ **cross-posting** *noun*

cross-promo·tion *noun* co-operative marketing by two or more companies of one another's products. □ **cross-promote** *transitive verb*

cross-question *transitive verb* = CROSS-EXAMINE.

cross-reaction *noun* the reaction of an antibody with an antigen other than the one which gave rise to it. □ **cross-react** *intransitive verb*

cross-refer *intransitive verb* (**-referred**, **-refer·ring**) refer from one part of a book, article, etc., to another.

cross-reference ● *noun* a reference from one part of a book, article, etc., to another. ● *transitive verb* provide with cross-references.

cross-rhythm *noun* **1** a rhythm used simultaneously with another rhythm or other rhythms. **2** an instance of using two or more rhythms simultaneously.

cross rib *noun* a cut of beef from the front part of the ribs, below the blade.

cross·road *noun* **1** *N Amer.* a road that crosses a main road or connects two main roads. **2** = CROSSROADS.

cross·roads *plural noun* (treated as *sing.*) **1** an intersection of two or more roads. **2** a critical turning point in one's life, a career, history, etc.

cross-ruff *Bridge etc.* ● *noun* the alternate trumping of partners' leads. ● *intransitive verb* play in this way.

cross-section *noun* **1 a** a cutting of a solid at right angles to an axis. **b** a plane surface produced in this way. **c** a representation of this. **2** a representative sample, esp. of people. **3** *Physics* a quantity expressing the probability of interaction between particles. □ **cross-section·al** *adjective*

cross-sell *transitive verb* sell (a different product or service) to an existing customer.

cross-stitch ● *noun* **1** a stitch formed of two stitches crossing each other. **2** needlework done using this stitch. ● *transitive verb* sew or embroider with cross-stitches.

cross street *noun* a street crossing another or connecting two streets (*turn right at the next cross street*).

cross-subsid·ize *transitive verb* (also esp. *Brit.* **-ise**) subsidize out of the profits of another business or activity. □ **cross-subsid·iz·a·tion** *noun* **cross-subsidy** *noun*

Consonants: b *but* d *dog* f *few* g *get* h *her* j *yes* k *cat* l *leg* m *man* n *no* p *pen* r *red* s *sit*

cross·talk *noun* **1** unwanted transfer of signals between communication channels. **2** *Brit.* witty talk; repartee.

cross·town *N Amer.* ● *adjective* **1** extending across or following a route across a town or city (*crosstown traffic*). **2** coming from the other side of a town or city, esp. in reference to two competing sports teams in the same town (*crosstown rivals*). ● *adverb* **1** across a town or city (*we headed crosstown in a taxi*). **2** to a rival team in the same city (*he was traded crosstown to the White Sox*).

cross-train *verb* **1** *transitive* train in two or more sports to improve performance, esp. in one's main sport. **2** *transitive & intransitive* train (an employee etc.) in more than one skill. □ **cross-trainer** *noun* **cross-training** *noun*

cross·walk *noun N Amer. & Austral.* a pedestrian crossing.

cross·ways *adverb* = CROSSWISE.

cross·wind *noun* a wind blowing across one's direction of travel.

cross·wise *adjective & adverb* **1** across; transverse or transversely. **2** in the form of a cross; intersecting.

cross·word *noun* (also **crossword puzzle**) a puzzle of a grid of squares and blanks into which words crossing vertically and horizontally have to be filled from clues.

cros·tata /krɒˈstɑːtə/ *noun* an open-faced fruit tart with a lattice top. [Italian, = pie]

cros·tini /krɒˈstiːni/ *plural noun* small pieces of toasted bread topped with vegetables etc., served as an appetizer. [Italian, pl. of *crostino* 'little crust']

crotch *noun* **1** the place where the legs join the trunk of the human body. **2** the part of a pair of pants, underwear, etc. where the two legs or panels join. **3** a fork of a tree or bough. [perhaps = Middle English & Old French *croc(he)* hook, formed as CROOK]

crotch·et /ˈkrɒtʃət/ *noun* **1** *Brit. Music* = QUARTER NOTE. **2** a whimsical fancy. [Old French *crochet* diminutive of *croc* hook (see CROTCH]

crotch·ety /ˈkrɒtʃəti/ *adjective* peevish, irritable. □ **crotch·et·i·ness** *noun* [CROTCHET + -Y¹]

crotch·less *adjective* (of underwear) having a hole cut so as to leave the genitals uncovered.

cro·ton /ˈkroʊtən/ *noun* **1** any plant of the genus *Croton*, producing a capsule-like fruit. **2** any small tree or shrub of the genus *Codiaeum*, esp. *C. variegatum*, cultivated for its colourful ornamental leaves. [modern Latin from Greek *krotōn* sheep tick, croton (from the shape of its seeds)]

crouch ● *intransitive verb* stoop low with the legs bent close to the body, esp. for concealment, or (of an animal) before pouncing; be in this position. ● *noun* an act of crouching; a crouching position. [perhaps from Old French *crochir* be bent, from *croc* hook: compare CROOK]

croup¹ /kruːp/ *noun* an inflammation of the larynx and trachea in children, with a hard cough and difficulty in breathing. □ **croupy** *adjective* [*croup* to croak (imitative)]

croup² /kruːp/ *noun* the rump or hindquarters esp. of a horse. [Old French *croupe*, related to CROP]

croup·ier /ˈkruːpiːər, -ɪ̩eɪ/ *noun* the person in charge of a gaming table, raking in and paying out money etc. [French, originally = rider on the croup: see CROUP²]

crou·ton /ˈkruːtɒn/ *noun* a small cube of fried or toasted bread used as a garnish for soups, salads, etc. [French from *croûte* CRUST]

Crow ● *noun* (*pl.* same or **Crows**) **1** a member of an Aboriginal people living in southern Montana. **2** the Siouan language of this people. ● *adjective* of or relating to this people or their culture or language. [CROW¹]

crow¹ *noun* **1** any large black bird of the genus *Corvus*, having a powerful black beak, e.g. the omnivorous common crow of N America, *C. brachyrhynchos* or the carrion crow of Europe. **2** any similar bird of the family Corvidae, e.g. the raven or magpie. **3** *slang derogatory* a woman, esp. an old or ugly one. □ **as the crow flies** in a straight line. **eat crow** *N Amer. informal* be forced to admit a mistake; submit to humiliation. [Old English *crāwe* ultimately from West Germanic]

crow² ● *intransitive verb* **1** (*past* **crowed** or **crew**) (of a rooster) utter its characteristic loud cry. **2** (usu. foll. by *over*, *about*) express gleeful satisfaction; swagger; boast. ● *noun* **1** the cry of a rooster. **2** a happy or triumphant cry uttered by a person. [Old English *crāwan*, of imitative origin]

crow·bar *noun* an iron bar with a flattened end, used as a lever.

Crow Benefit *noun Cdn hist.* a subsidy to the Canadian Pacific Railway in return for a reduced rate for shipping grain or flour by rail from Western Canada to Eastern Canada. [as CROW RATE]

crow·berry *noun* (*pl.* **-berries**) **1 a** a heath-like evergreen shrub

Empetrum nigrum, bearing black berries. **b** the flavourless edible berry of this plant. **2** *US* a cranberry.

crowd ● *noun* **1** a large number of people gathered together, usu. without orderly arrangement. **2** a mass of spectators; an audience. **3** *informal* a particular company or set of people (*met the crowd from the sales department*). **4** (prec. by *the*) the mass or multitude of people (*go along with the crowd*). **5** a large number (of things). ● *verb* **1** *intransitive* **a** come together in a crowd (*fans crowded around the hockey player*). **b** force one's way (*we crowded into the bar*). **2** *transitive* **a** (foll. by *into*) force or compress into a confined space (*the teachers crowded the children into the gym.*). **b** (often foll. by *with*; usu. in *passive*) fill or make abundant with (*was crowded with tourists; images crowded the canvas*). **3** *transitive* **a** (of a number of people) come aggressively close to. **b** *informal* harass or pressure (a person). **4** *transitive N Amer. informal* approach (a specified age, time, etc.) closely (*must be crowding fifty*). □ **crowd out** exclude by crowding. □ **crowd·ed** *adjective* **crowded·ness** *noun* [Old English *crūdan* press, drive]

crowd-pleaser *noun informal* an event, person, or thing, esp. a song, movie, poem, etc., that is well received by an audience. □ **crowd-pleasing** *adjective*

crowd-surf *intransitive verb* be passed in a prone position over the heads of the audience at a rock concert, esp. after having jumped from the stage.

crow duck *noun N Amer.* a cormorant, esp. the double-crested cormorant.

Crow·foot (c.1830–90), Blackfoot chief, who was born a Blood. Noted for his scouting abilities and bravery in battle, he rescued Father Lacombe from a band of hostile Cree (1866), and welcomed the arrival of the NWMP on the Prairies (1874); though his adopted son Poundmaker took part in the Northwest Rebellion, Crowfoot did not.

crow·foot *noun* **1** = BUTTERCUP. **2** a grass widely naturalized in N America, *Dactyloctenium aegyptium*.

crown ● *noun* **1** a monarch's ornamental and usu. jewelled headdress. **2** (**the Crown**) **a** the monarch, esp. as head of state. **b** the power or authority residing in the monarchy. **c** *Cdn* the federal or provincial government (often *attributive*: *Crown agencies; Crown assets*). **3 a** a wreath of leaves or flowers etc. worn on the head, esp. as an emblem of victory. **b** an award or distinction gained by a victory or achievement, esp. in sport. **4** a crown-shaped thing, esp. a device or ornament. **5** the top part of a thing, esp. of the head or a hat. **6 a** the highest or central part of an arched or curved thing (*crown of the road*). **b** a thing that completes or forms the summit. **7 a** the part of a plant just above and below the ground. **b** the leaves and upper branches of a tree. **8** the upper part of a cut gem above the girdle. **9 a** the part of a tooth projecting from the gum. **b** an artificial replacement or covering for this. **10** = CROWN ATTORNEY. **11 a** a former British coin equal to five shillings (25p). **b** any of several foreign coins with a name meaning 'crown', esp. the krona or krone. ● *transitive verb* **1** put a crown on (a person or a person's head). **2** invest (a person) with a royal crown or authority. **3** (often in *passive*) be a crown to; encircle or rest on the top of (*the hill was crowned with an oak tree*). **4 a** (often as **crowning** *adjective*) be or cause to be the consummation, reward, or finishing touch to (*the crowning achievement of his career*). **b** bring (efforts) to a happy issue. **c** give an award or distinction gained by a victory or achievement, esp. in sport (*the team was crowned South Shore champion*). **5** fit a crown to (a tooth). **6** *slang* hit on the head. **7** promote (a piece in checkers) to king. **8** (of a baby's head during labour) fully appear in the vaginal opening prior to emerging. [Old French *corone* from Latin *corona*]

crown and anchor *noun* a gambling game played with three dice each bearing a crown, an anchor, and the four card suits, and played on a board similarly marked.

Crown attorney *noun Cdn* a lawyer who conducts prosecutions of indictable offences on behalf of the Crown.

crown colony *noun* a colony controlled by a foreign monarchy.

Crown corporation *noun Cdn* a corporation owned by the federal or provincial governments, e.g. Canadian Broadcasting Corporation, Canada Post, etc.

Crown counsel *noun Cdn* = CROWN ATTORNEY.

Crown Court *noun Brit.* a court of criminal jurisdiction in England and Wales.

crown fire *noun* a forest fire which moves through the tops of trees.

crown imperial *noun* a tall fritillary, *Fritillaria imperialis*, with a flower cluster at the top of the stalk.

crowning glory *noun* **1** the best and most notable aspect of something; a supreme achievement. **2** *informal* the hair on one's head, esp. when luxuriant.

crown jewel *noun* **1** (in *pl.*) the regalia and other jewellery worn by a sovereign on certain state occasions. **2** the most valuable or most beautiful possession, feature, etc. (*the crown jewel of my record collection*).

Crown land *noun* (in Canada and other Commonwealth nations) land owned by federal or provincial or state governments.

crown of thorns *noun* **1** a starfish, *Acanthaster planci*, which has spines on its upper surface and feeds on coral polyps. **2** a plant, *Euphorbia milli*, with very thorny stems and small flowers surrounded by showy bracts, often grown as a houseplant.

crown prince *noun* a male heir to a sovereign throne.

crown princess *noun* **1** the wife of a crown prince. **2** a female heir to a sovereign throne.

Crown prosecutor *noun* (in Canada, England, and Wales) a lawyer who acts for the Crown, esp. a prosecutor in a criminal court. *Also called* CROWN ATTORNEY.

Crown reserve *noun Cdn hist.* a portion of land reserved for the Crown as a source of revenue free from the control of the colonial legislature.

crown roast *noun* a roast of rib pieces of pork, lamb, or veal arranged like a crown.

crown wheel *noun* a wheel with teeth set at right angles to its plane, esp. in the gears of motor vehicles.

Crown witness *noun Cdn* a witness called to testify by the Crown.

Crow rate *noun Cdn hist.* a reduced rate for shipping grain or flour by rail from Western Canada to Eastern Canada. [legislated by the Crow's Nest Pass Agreement in 1897, ensuring a subsidy to the Canadian Pacific Railway in return for the reduced rate]

crow's feet *plural noun* wrinkles at the outer corner of a person's eye.

crow's nest *noun* a barrel or platform fixed at the masthead of a sailing vessel as a shelter for a lookout man.

Crows·nest Pass 1 a mountain pass in SW Alberta (over 1 350 m), situated in the Rocky Mountains on the border with BC, west of Lethbridge. **2** a municipality in SW Alberta, an amalgamation of the towns, villages and adjacent communities to the east of the pass; pop. (2001) 6,262. □ **Crows·nest·er** *noun* (in sense 2) [perhaps after a nearby hill, where Blackfoot and Cree legends place the location of the raven's (or crow's) nest]

crow steps *plural noun* = CORBIE STEPS.

Cro·zet Islands /krɔːˈzeɪ/ a group of five small islands in the S Indian Ocean, under French administration.

cro·zier /ˈkrɔːʒər, -ziər/ *noun* (also **cro·sier**) **1** a hooked staff carried by a bishop as a symbol of pastoral office. **2** the curled tip of a young plant, esp. a fern. [originally = bearer of a crook, from Old French *crocier* & Old French *croisier* from *crois* CROSS]

CRS *abbreviation* computer reservation system.

CRT *abbreviation* cathode ray tube.

CRTC *abbreviation* Canadian Radio-television and Telecommunications Commission.

cru /kruː/ *noun* **1** a French vineyard or wine-producing region. **2** the grade of wine produced from it. [French from *crû* grown]

cru·ces *pl.* of CRUX.

cru·cial /ˈkruːʃəl/ *adjective* **1** decisive, critical. **2** very important. □ **cru·cial·ly** *adverb* [French from Latin *crux crucis* cross]

cru·ciate ligament /ˈkruːʃət/ *noun* either of a pair of ligaments in the knee which cross each other and connect the femur and the tibia. [Latin *cruciatus* from *crux crucis* cross]

cru·cible /ˈkruːsəbəl/ *noun* **1** a container in which metals or other materials are heated. **2** a severe test or trial. [medieval Latin *crucibulum* night lamp, crucible, (perhaps originally a lamp hanging in front of a crucifix), from Latin *crux crucis* cross]

cruci·fer /ˈkruːsəfər/ *noun* **1** a cruciferous plant. **2** a person carrying a processional cross or crucifix.

cru·cifer·ous /kruːˈsɪfərəs/ *adjective* of the family Cruciferae, having flowers with four petals arranged in a cross, e.g. cabbage, mustard, etc. [modern Latin *Cruciferae* from Latin *crux, cruc-* 'cross' + *-fer* 'bearing' (because the flowers have four equal petals arranged crosswise)]

cruci·fix /ˈkruːsəfɪks/ *noun* a model or image of a cross with a figure of Christ on it. [Old French from ecclesiastical Latin *crucifixus* from Latin *cruci fixus* fixed to a cross]

cruci·fix·ion /ˌkruːsəˈfɪkʃən/ *noun* **1 a** a crucifying or being crucified. **b** an instance of this. **2** (**Crucifixion**) **a** the crucifixion of Christ. **b** a representation of this. [ecclesiastical Latin *crucifixio* (as CRUCIFIX)]

cruci·form /ˈkruːsəˌfɔrm/ ● *adjective* cross-shaped (esp. of a church with transepts). ● *noun* a cross. [Latin *crux crucis* cross + -FORM]

cru·cify /ˈkruːsəˌfaɪ/ *transitive verb* (**-fies**, **-fied**) **1** put to death by fastening to a cross. **2 a** cause extreme pain to. **b** persecute; torment. **c** criticize or punish harshly. **3** *slang* defeat thoroughly in an argument, game, etc. □ **cruci·fi·er** *noun* [Old French *crucifier* from Late Latin *crucifigere* (as CRUCIFIX)]

crud *noun slang* **1** a deposit of dirt, grease, encrusted food, etc. **2** an unpleasant person. **3** drivel; something of little value (*who wrote this crud?*). □ **cruddy** *adjective* (**crud·di·er**, **crud·di·est**). [var. of CURD]

crude ● *adjective* **1 a** in the natural or raw state; not refined (*crude oil*). **b** rough, unpolished; lacking finish. **2 a** offensive, indecent (*a crude gesture*). **b** (of an action or statement or manners) rude, blunt. **3 a** *Statistics* (of figures) not adjusted or corrected. **b** rough (*a crude estimate*). ● *noun* unrefined petroleum. □ **crude·ly** *adverb* **crude·ness** *noun* **cru·dity** *noun* (*pl.* **-ties**). [Latin *crudus* raw, rough]

cru·di·tés /ˌkruːdɪˈteɪ, -diː-/ *plural noun* an hors d'oeuvre of mixed raw vegetables often served with a sauce into which they are dipped. [French pl. of *crudité* lit. rawness, from Latin *crudus* raw]

cruel *adjective* (**cruel·ler**, **cruel·lest** or **cruel·er**, **cruel·est**) **1** causing pain or suffering, esp. deliberately (*a cruel remark*). **2** indifferent to or gratified by another's suffering. **3** merciless; harsh; unrelentingly severe (*cruel fate*). □ **cruel·ly** *adverb* [Old French from Latin *crudelis*, related to *crudus* (as CRUDE)]

cruelty *noun* (*pl.* **-ties**) **1** a cruel act or attitude; indifference to another's suffering. **2** a succession of cruel acts; a continued cruel attitude (*suffered much cruelty*). **3** *Law* physical or mental harm inflicted (whether or not intentional), esp. as a ground for divorce.

cruelty-free *adjective* (of cosmetics etc.) produced without involving cruelty to animals in the development or manufacturing process.

cru·et /ˈkruːət/ *noun* **1** a small container for salt, pepper, oil, or vinegar for use at table. **2** (in full **cruet stand**) a stand holding cruets. **3** *Christianity* one of two small containers for the wine and water in the celebration of the Eucharist. [Old French *crue* pot, from Old Saxon *krūka*: related to CROCK[2]]

Cruik·shank /ˈkrʊkʃæŋk/ **George** (1792–1878), English painter, illustrator, and caricaturist. The most eminent political cartoonist of his day, he was known for exposing the private life of the Prince Regent; his later work includes illustrations for Charles Dickens's *Sketches by Boz* (1836) and *Oliver Twist* (1838).

cruise ● *verb* **1** *intransitive* make a journey aboard ship calling at a series of ports usu. according to a predetermined plan, esp. for pleasure. **2** *intransitive* sail about without a precise destination. **3** *intransitive* **a** (of a motor vehicle or aircraft) travel at a moderate or economical speed. **b** (of a vehicle or its driver) travel at random, esp. slowly. **4** *intransitive* achieve an objective, win a race etc., with ease. **5** *intransitive & transitive slang* walk or drive about (the streets etc.) in search of a sexual (esp. homosexual) partner. **6** *transitive & intransitive N Amer.* inspect an area of forest to estimate the volume of timber on it, esp. for a logging company. ● *noun* **1** a cruising voyage on board a ship, esp. as a holiday (also *attributive*: *cruise ship*; *cruise line*). **2** the act or an instance of cruising. **3** *N Amer.* a survey or estimate of the volume of timber in an area. □ **cruisin' for a bruisin'** *N Amer. slang* heading for trouble or a beating. [prob. from Dutch *kruisen* from *kruis* CROSS]

cruise control *noun* a device on some motor vehicles that can be set to maintain a predetermined constant speed without use of the accelerator pedal.

cruise missile *noun* a missile able to fly at a low altitude and guide itself by reference to the features of the region it crosses.

cruis·er *noun* **1** a warship of high speed and medium armament. **2** = CABIN CRUISER. **3** *N Amer.* a police patrol car. **4** *N Amer.* a person who estimates the volume of timber in an area of forest.

cruiser·weight *noun* **1** esp. *Brit.* = LIGHT HEAVYWEIGHT. **2** in professional boxing, a weight between light heavyweight and heavyweight, ranging from 79 to 85 kg.

cruising speed *noun* a comfortable and economical speed for a motor vehicle, airplane or boat, below its maximum speed.

cruisy *adjective* (also **cruis·ey**) (**cruis·i·er**, **cruis·i·est**) *informal* (of a bar, location, etc.) much frequented by gay people cruising for casual partners.

crul·ler /ˈkrʌlər, ˈkruː-, ˈkrʊ-/ *noun N Amer.* a small, sweet cake made of a rich dough twisted or curled and deep-fried. [Dutch *kruller*, from *krullen* curl]

crumb ● *noun* **1 a** a small fragment, esp. of bread. **b** a small particle; bit (*a crumb of sympathy*). **2** the soft inner part of a loaf of bread or a cake. **3** slang an objectionable person. ● *transitive verb* **1** cover with bread crumbs. **2** break into crumbs. [Old English *cruma*]

crum·ble ● *verb* **1** *transitive & intransitive* break or fall into crumbs or fragments. **2** *intransitive* (of power, a reputation, etc.) gradually disintegrate. ● *noun* **1** = CRISP *noun* 1. **2** a crumbly or crumbled substance.

crum·bly ● *adjective* (**crum·bli·er**, **crum·bli·est**) consisting of, or apt to fall into, crumbs or fragments. ● *noun* (*pl.* **-blies**) *Brit. slang* offensive an old person.

crumby *adjective* (**crumb·i·er**, **crumb·i·est**) **1** like or covered in crumbs. **2** = CRUMMY *adjective*.

crum·horn /'krʌmhɔrn/ *noun* a medieval wind instrument with a double reed and a curved end. [German from *krumm* crooked + *Horn* HORN]

crum·my ● *adjective* (**crum·mi·er**, **crum·mi·est**) *informal* **1** dirty, squalid (*a crummy apartment*). **2** inferior, worthless. **3** sick or depressed (*I feel crummy*). ● *noun* (*pl.* **-mies**) *N Amer.* an old or converted vehicle for transporting loggers from their camp to work. □ **crum·mi·ly** *adverb* **crum·mi·ness** *noun* [var. of CRUMBY]

crump *slang* ● *noun* the sound of a bursting bomb or shell. ● *intransitive verb* make this sound. [imitative]

crum·pet *noun* **1** a small, round, sponge-like yeast cake resembling an English muffin, eaten toasted and buttered. **2** *Brit. jocular offensive* **a** a sexually attractive person, esp. a woman. **b** women regarded collectively, esp. as objects of sexual desire. [17th c.: origin uncertain]

crum·ple ● *transitive & intransitive verb* **1** crush or become crushed into a compact mass or irregular creases (*she crumpled the paper into a ball*). **2** *intransitive* collapse, give way (*she crumpled to the floor*). ● *noun* a crease or wrinkle. □ **crum·ply** *adjective* [obsolete *crump* 'make or become curved', from Old English *crump* 'bent, crooked']

crumple zone *noun* a part of a motor vehicle, esp. the extreme front and rear, designed to crumple easily in a crash and absorb impact.

crunch ● *verb* **1** *transitive* **a** crush noisily with the teeth. **b** grind (gravel, dry snow, etc.) under foot, wheels, etc. **2** *intransitive* (often foll. by *along*, *through*) make a crunching sound in walking, moving, etc. **3** *transitive informal* process (large amounts of numbers or data) esp. by computer. ● *noun* **1** crunching; a crunching sound. **2** crunchiness (*nuts add crunch to a salad*). **3** *informal* a shortage or reduction (*a housing crunch*). **4** *informal* a decisive event or moment (also *attributive: crunch time*). **5** *N Amer.* (often in *pl.*) a half sit-up, in which a person raises the upper body a few centimetres off the ground rather than sitting up fully. □ **crunch numbers** do mathematical calculations, esp. to determine profit, affordability, etc. □ **crunch·er** *noun* [earlier *cra(u)nch*, assimilated to *munch*]

crunchy ● *adjective* (**crunch·i·er**, **crunch·i·est**) hard and crispy. ● *noun* (*pl.* **-ies**) something that crunches when eaten. □ **crunch·i·ly** *adverb* **crunch·i·ness** *noun*

crup·per *noun* **1** a strap buckled to the back of a saddle and looped under the horse's tail to hold the harness back. **2** the hindquarters of a horse. [Old French *cropiere* (compare CROUP²)]

crural /'krʊrəl/ *adjective Anat.* of or pertaining to the leg. [French *crural* or Latin *cruralis* from *crus cruris* leg]

cru·sade ● *noun* **1** (usu. **Crusade**) **a** any of several medieval military expeditions made by Europeans to recover the Holy Land from the Muslims. **b** *hist.* a war instigated by the Church for alleged religious ends. **2** a vigorous campaign in favour of a cause (*a crusade for stricter gun laws*). ● *intransitive verb* engage in a crusade. □ **cru·sad·er** *noun* [earlier *croisade* (French from *croix* cross) or *crusado* (Spanish from *cruz* cross)]

crush ● *verb* **1** *transitive* compress with force or violence, so as to break, bruise, etc. **2** *transitive* reduce to powder by pressure. **3** *transitive* crease or crumple by rough handling. **4** *transitive* defeat or subdue completely (*crushed the uprising*). **5** *transitive* (usu. in *passive*) humiliate; disappoint; upset (*I was crushed by his comment*). **6** *intransitive* advance in large numbers; throng (*the crowd crushed into the stadium*). ● *noun* **1** an act of crushing. **2** a crowded mass of people. **3** *informal* **a** (usu. foll. by *on*) a (usu. passing) infatuation. **b** the object of an infatuation (*who is Jessica's latest crush?*). □ **crush·able** *adjective* **crush·er** *noun* **crush·ing** *adjective* (esp. in sense 4 of *verb*). **crush·ing·ly** *adverb* **crush·proof** *adjective* [Anglo-French *crussir*, Old French *croissir*, gnash (teeth), crack, from Romanic]

crushed velvet *noun* a type of velvet in which the pile has been crushed, creating a crinkled, shiny appearance (often *attributive: a crushed-velvet dress*).

crust ● *noun* **1 a** the hard outer part of a loaf of bread. **b** a slice of bread from the end of the loaf. **c** a hard dry scrap of bread. **d** esp.

Austral. slang a livelihood (*what do you do for a crust?*). **2 a** the pastry covering of a pie, tart, etc. **b** the bottom, usu. of pastry, of a pie, tart, pizza, etc. **3** a hard casing of a softer thing, e.g. a harder layer over soft snow. **4** *Geol.* the outer portion of the earth. **5 a** a coating or deposit on the surface of anything. **b** a hard dry formation on the skin, a scab. **6** a deposit of tartar formed in bottles of old wine, esp. port. ● *transitive & intransitive verb* **1** cover or become covered with a crust. **2** form into a crust. □ **crust·al** *adjective* (in sense 4 of *noun*). **crust·less** *adjective* [Old French *crouste* from Latin *crusta* rind, shell]

crus·ta·cean /krʌ'steiʃən/ ● *noun* any arthropod of the class Crustacea, having a hard shell and usu. aquatic, e.g. the crab, lobster, and shrimp. ● *adjective* of or relating to crustaceans. □ **crus·ta·ceol·ogy** /-ʃiː'ɒlədʒi/ *noun* **crus·ta·ceous** /-ʃəs/ *adjective* [modern Latin *crustaceus* from *crusta*: see CRUST]

crust·ed *adjective* **1** having a crust. **2** (of wine, esp. port) having deposited a crust.

crust·ose /krʌ'stoʊs/ *adjective* (esp. of a lichen) forming or resembling a crust. [Latin *crustosus* from *crusta* 'crust']

crusty *adjective* (**crust·i·er**, **crust·i·est**) **1** having a crisp crust (*a crusty loaf*). **2** irritable, curt. **3** hard, crust-like (*a crusty scab*). □ **crust·i·ly** *adverb* **crust·i·ness** *noun*

crutch *noun* **1** a support for a lame person, usu. with a crosspiece at the top fitting under the armpit (*pair of crutches*). **2** any support or prop (*alcohol is a crutch for many people*). **3** *Brit.* the crotch of the human body or garment. [Old English *cryc(c)* from Germanic]

Crutched Friars /krʌtʃt, 'krʌtʃɪd/ an order of mendicant friars established in Italy by 1169, which spread to England, France, and the Low Countries in the 13th c. and was suppressed in 1656. The word *crutched* means 'carrying a cross', and refers to the cross worn on top of their staves, and later on the front of their habits.

crux /krʌks/ *noun* (*pl.* **crux·es** or **cru·ces** /'kruːsiːz/) **1** the decisive point at issue. **2** a difficult matter; a puzzle. **3** (**Crux**) = SOUTHERN CROSS. [Latin, = cross]

cry ● *verb* (**cries**, **cried**) **1** *intransitive* (often foll. by *out*) make a loud or shrill sound, esp. to express pain, grief, etc., or to appeal for help. **2 a** *intransitive* shed tears; weep. **b** *transitive* shed (tears). **3** *transitive* (often foll. by *out*) say or exclaim loudly or excitedly. **4** *intransitive* (of an animal, esp. a bird) make a loud call. **5** *transitive* (of a vendor etc.) proclaim (wares etc.) in the street. ● *noun* (*pl.* **cries**) **1** a loud inarticulate utterance of grief, pain, fear, joy, etc. **2** a loud excited utterance of words. **3** an urgent appeal or entreaty. **4** a period of weeping. **5 a** public demand; a strong movement of opinion. **b** a watchword or rallying call. **6** the natural utterance of an animal, esp. of birds. **7** the call of a street vendor etc. □ **cry one's eyes** (or **heart**) **out** weep bitterly. **cry from the heart** a passionate appeal or protest. **cry off** *informal* withdraw from a promise or undertaking. **cry out for** demand as a self-evident requirement or solution. **cry over spilt milk** see MILK. **cry up** praise, extol. **cry wolf** see WOLF. **a far cry** **1** a long way. **2** a very different thing. **for crying out loud** *informal* an exclamation of surprise or annoyance. **in full cry** (esp. of hounds) in keen pursuit. [Old French *crier*, *cri* from Latin *quiritare* wail]

cry·baby *noun* (*pl.* **-babies**) **1** a person, esp. a child, who sheds tears frequently. **2** a whiny or self-pitying person.

cry·ing *attributive adjective* (of an injustice or other evil) flagrant, demanding redress (*a crying need; a crying shame*).

crying room *noun N Amer.* a soundproofed room at the back of a church etc., with a window and loudspeakers, permitting parents with crying children to follow the service without disturbing the congregation.

cryo- /'kraɪəʊ/ *combining form* (extreme) cold. [Greek *kruos* frost]

cryo·biol·ogy /ˌkraɪəʊbaɪ'ɒlədʒi/ *noun* the branch of biology dealing with the effects of very low temperatures on organisms, tissues, etc. □ **cryo·bio·logic·al** /-baɪə'lɒdʒɪkəl/ *adjective* **cryo·biol·o·gist** *noun*

cryo·gen /'kraɪədʒən/ *noun* a substance used to produce very low temperatures.

cryo·gen·ics /ˌkraɪə'dʒɛnɪks/ *noun* **1** the branch of physics dealing with the production and effects of very low temperatures. **2** = CRYONICS. □ **cryo·gen·ic** *adjective* **cryo·gen·ic·ally** *adverb*

cryo·lite /'kraɪəˌlaɪt/ *noun* a lustrous mineral of sodium-aluminum fluoride, used in the manufacture of aluminum.

cry·on·ics /kraɪ'ɒnɪks/ *noun* the practice or technique of deep-freezing human corpses for possible revival in the future. □ **cry·on·ic** *adjective* **cry·oni·cist** *noun* [contraction of CRYOGENICS]

cryo·pres·er·va·tion /ˌkraɪəʊprɛzɜr'veɪʃən/ *noun* the freezing of

---

uː m**oo**d ai m**y** əi p**i**pe au br**ow**n ʌu h**ou**se ei d**ay** ɔi b**oy** ã fr**an**glais ã Ca**na**dien ɔ̃ Br**ay**on (*see over for consonants*)

living tissue, organs, sperm, etc. for storage and subsequent use. □ **cryo·pre·served** *adjective*

cryo·pro·tect·ant /ˌkraɪoːprəˈtektənt/ *noun Biochem.* a substance that prevents the freezing of tissues, or prevents damage to cells etc. during freezing.

cryo·stat /ˈkraɪoːˌstat/ *noun* **1** an apparatus for maintaining chemical or organic samples at a very low steady temperature. **2** a vessel or chamber in which such samples are stored.

cryo·sur·gery /ˌkraɪoːˈsɜrdʒəri/ *noun* surgery using the local application of intense cold for anaesthesia or therapy.

crypt /krɪpt/ *noun* **1** an underground room or vault, esp. one beneath a church, used usu. as a burial place. **2** *Anat.* a small tubular gland, pit, or recess. [Latin *crypta* from Greek *kruptē* from *kruptos* hidden]

crypt·analy·sis /ˌkrɪptəˈnaləsɪs/ *noun* (also **crypto·analy·sis**) the art or process of deciphering codes and ciphers by analysis. □ **crypt·ana·lyst** /-ˈanəlɪst/ *noun* **crypt·ana·lytic** /-ˌanəˈlɪtɪk/ *adjective* **crypt·ana·lytic·al** /-anəˈlɪtɪkəl/ *adjective* [CRYPTO- + ANALYSIS]

cryp·tic /ˈkrɪptɪk/ *adjective* **1 a** obscure in meaning. **b** (of a crossword clue etc.) indirect; indicating the solution in a way that is not obvious. **c** secret, mysterious, enigmatic. **2** *Zool.* (of coloration etc.) serving to camouflage an animal in its natural environment. □ **cryp·tic·ally** *adverb* [Late Latin *crypticus* from Greek *kruptikos* (as CRYPTO-)]

crypto- /ˈkrɪptoː/ *combining form* concealed, secret (*crypto-communist*). [Greek *kruptos* hidden]

crypto·analy·sis /ˌkrɪptoːəˈnaləsɪs/ *var. of* CRYPTANALYSIS.

crypto·coc·co·sis /ˌkrɪptoːkɒˈkoːsɪs/ *noun* infestation with a yeast-like fungus, *Cryptococcus neoformans*, usu. attacking the lungs and central nervous system. □ **crypto·coc·cal** *adjective* [modern Latin *cryptococcus* + -OSIS]

crypto·crys·tal·line /ˌkrɪptoːˈkrɪstəˌlaɪn/ *adjective* having a crystalline structure visible only when magnified.

crypto·gam /ˈkrɪptəˌgam/ *noun* a plant that has no true flowers or seeds, e.g. ferns, mosses, algae, and fungi. □ **crypto·gam·ic** /-ˈgamɪk/ *adjective* **cryp·tog·am·ous** /-ˈtɒgəməs/ *adjective* [French *cryptogame* from modern Latin *cryptogamae* (*plantae*) formed as CRYPTO- + Greek *gamos* marriage]

crypto·gram /ˈkrɪptəˌgram/ *noun* a text written in code or cipher. □ **crypto·gram·mic** *adjective*

cryp·tog·raphy /krɪpˈtɒɡrəfi/ *noun* the art of writing or solving codes and ciphers. □ **cryp·tog·raph·er** *noun* **crypto·graph·ic** /-təˈɡrafɪk/ *adjective* **crypto·graph·ic·ally** /-təˈɡrafɪkli/ *adverb*

cryp·tol·ogy /krɪpˈtɒlədʒi/ *noun* = CRYPTOGRAPHY. □ **cryp·tol·o·gist** *noun* **crypto·logic·al** /-təˈlɒdʒɪkəl/ *adjective*

crypto·meria /ˌkrɪptəˈmiːriə/ *noun* a tall evergreen tree, *Cryptomeria japonica*, native to China and Japan, with long curved spirally arranged leaves and short cones. *Also called* JAPANESE CEDAR. [CRYPTO- + Greek *meros* part (because the seeds are enclosed by scales)]

crypto·spor·idi·osis /ˌkrɪptoːspɒrˌɪdiˈoːsɪs/ *noun* an intestinal disease caused by infection with cryptosporidium, causing diarrhea and vomiting.

crypto·spor·id·ium /ˌkrɪptoːspɒrˈɪdiəm/ *noun* a parasitic coccidian protozoan found in the intestinal tract of many vertebrates, where it sometimes causes disease. [CRYPTO- + modern Latin *sporidium* 'small spore']

crypto·zo·ology *noun* the search for and study of animals whose existence or survival is disputed or unsubstantiated, such as the Loch Ness monster and the sasquatch. □ **crypto·zo·ologic·al** *adjective* **crypto·zo·olo·gist** *adjective*

Crysler's Farm /ˈkraɪzlərz/ a site along the St. Lawrence, near the present-day village of Morrisburg, Ontario, southeast of Ottawa. It was the scene in 1813 of a battle between a large US invasion force planning an attack on Montreal and a much smaller British force; though both sides suffered hundreds of casualties, the British prevailed, forcing a US retreat. [J. *Crysler*, farmer who owned the land]

crys·tal /ˈkrɪstəl/ ● *noun* **1 a** a clear transparent mineral, esp. rock crystal. **b** a piece of this. **2 a** highly transparent glass, usu. containing lead oxide. **b** articles made of this, such as glassware and ornaments. **3** the glass over a watch face. **4** *Electronics* a crystalline piece of semiconductor. **5** *Chem.* **a** an aggregation of molecules with a definite internal structure and the external form of a solid enclosed by symmetrically arranged plane faces. **b** a solid whose constituent particles are symmetrically arranged. **6** *slang* = CRYSTAL METH. ● *adjective* (usu. *attributive*) made of, like, or clear as crystal. □ **crystal clear 1** unclouded, transparent. **2** readily understood. [Old French *cristal* from Latin *crystallum* from Greek *krustallos* ice, crystal]

crystal ball *noun* a glass globe used in crystal gazing.

crystal class *noun* any of 32 categories of crystals classified according to their symmetry.

crystal gazing *noun* the process of concentrating one's gaze on a crystal ball supposedly in order to obtain a picture of future events etc. □ **crystal gazer** *noun*

crystal lattice *noun* the regular repeating pattern of atoms, ions, or molecules in a crystalline substance.

crys·tal·line /ˈkrɪstəˌlaɪn, -ˌliːn/ *adjective* **1** of, like, or clear as crystal. **2** *Chem.* & *Geol.* having the structure and form of a crystal. □ **crys·tal·lin·ity** /-ˈlɪnɪti/ *noun*

crystalline lens *noun* a transparent lens enclosed in a membranous capsule behind the iris of the eye.

crys·tal·lite /ˈkrɪstəˌlaɪt/ *noun* **1** a small crystal. **2** an individual crystal or grain in a metal etc. **3** *Bot.* a region of cellulose etc. with a crystal-like structure.

crys·tal·lize /ˈkrɪstəˌlaɪz/ *verb* (also esp. *Brit.* **-lise**) **1** *transitive & intransitive* form or cause to form crystals. **2** (often foll. by *out*) **a** *intransitive* (of ideas or plans) become definite. **b** *transitive* make definite. **3** *transitive & intransitive* coat or impregnate or become coated or impregnated with sugar (*crystallized fruit*). □ **crys·tal·liz·able** *adjective* **crys·tal·liz·a·tion** *noun*

crys·tal·log·raphy /ˌkrɪstəˈlɒɡrəfi/ *noun* the science of crystal form and structure. □ **crys·tal·log·raph·er** *noun* **crys·tal·lo·graph·ic** /-ləˈɡrafɪk/ *adjective*

crys·tal·loid /ˈkrɪstəˌlɔɪd/ ● *adjective* **1** crystal-like. **2** having a crystalline structure. ● *noun* a substance that in solution is able to pass through a semi-permeable membrane (*compare* COLLOID).

crystal meth *noun* methamphetamine in a solid form.

crystal set *noun* a simple early form of radio receiving apparatus with a crystal touching a metal wire as the rectifier.

crystal system *noun* any of seven possible unique combinations of unit cells, crystal lattices, and symmetry elements of a crystal class.

crystal therapy *noun* an alternative therapy popular in New Age culture and based on the supposed healing power of crystals.

CS *abbreviation* **1** Civil Service. **2** Christian Science.

Cs *symbol Chem.* the element cesium.

c/s *abbreviation* cycles per second.

CSA *abbreviation* Canadian Standards Association.

CSB *abbreviation* Canada Savings Bond.

CSC *abbreviation* Correctional Service of Canada.

CSCE *abbreviation* Conference for Security and Cooperation in Europe.

C-section *noun N Amer.* = CAESAREAN SECTION. [abbreviation]

CSF *abbreviation Med.* cerebrospinal fluid.

CS gas *noun* a gas causing tears and choking, used to control riots etc. [B. B. *Corson* & R. W. *Stoughton*, US chemists]

CSIS /ˈsiːsɪs/ *abbreviation* Canadian Security Intelligence Service.

CSJ *abbreviation Catholicism* Congregation of St. Joseph.

CSM *abbreviation Military* (in the Commonwealth) Company Sergeant Major.

CSR *abbreviation* customer service representative.

C.SS.R. *abbreviation* Congregationis Sanctissimi Redemptoris (used after the name of a member of the Redemptorist Order).

CST *abbreviation* CENTRAL STANDARD TIME.

Cst. *abbreviation Cdn* Constable.

CT *abbreviation* **1** Connecticut (in official postal use). **2** *Med.* computerized tomography. **3** CENTRAL TIME.

ct. *abbreviation* carat.

CTC *abbreviation* Canadian Transport Commission.

cten·oid /ˈtiːnɔɪd/ *adjective Zool.* (of fish scales) characterized by tiny toothlike processes (*compare* PLACOID). [Greek *kteis ktenos* comb]

cteno·phore /ˈtiːnəˌfɔr, ˈten-/ *noun* any animal of the phylum Ctenophora, comprising pelagic marine creatures resembling jellyfish and moving by means of stiff cilia borne on comb-like plates. [modern Latin *ctenophorus* (as CTENOID)]

Ctesi·phon /ˈtesəfən/ an ancient city on the Tigris near Baghdad, capital of the Parthian kingdom from *c.*224 and then of Persia under the Sassanian dynasty. It was taken by the Arabs in 636 and destroyed in the 8th c.

Ctrl. *abbreviation Computing* Control key.

CT scan *noun* = CAT SCAN.

CTV *abbreviation* Canadian Television Network Limited.

Consonants: b *but* d *dog* f *few* g *get* h *her* j *yes* k *cat* l *leg* m *man* n *no* p *pen* r *red* s *sit*

Cu *symbol Chem.* the element copper.

cu. *abbreviation* cubic.

cub ● *noun* **1** the young of a fox, bear, lion, etc. **2** (**Cub**) a member of the junior level (ages 8, 9, and 10) in Scouting. **3** (in full **cub reporter**) *informal* a young or inexperienced newspaper reporter. **4** *N Amer.* an apprentice. **5** an ill-mannered young man. ● *transitive & intransitive verb* (**cubbed, cub·bing**) give birth to (cubs). [16th c.: origin unknown]

Cuba a Caribbean country, the largest and furthest west of the islands of the W Indies, situated at the mouth of the Gulf of Mexico; pop. (est. 2002) 11,224,321; capital, Havana. Under Communist rule since 1959, Cuba has become increasingly isolated in the international community, having had to bear the loss of Eastern-European backing, a continued US trade embargo, and internal human rights abuses. □ **Cu·ban** *noun & adjective*

Cu·bango River see OKAVANGO RIVER.

Cuban heel *noun* a moderately high straight heel of a man's or woman's shoe.

Cuban Missile Crisis an international crisis in October 1962, the closest approach to nuclear war at any time between the US and the USSR. When the US discovered that Soviet nuclear missiles had been placed on Cuba, President Kennedy demanded their removal and announced a naval blockade of the island; the Soviet leader Khrushchev acceded to the US demands a week later.

cubby *noun* (*pl.* **-bies**) **1** a very small room. **2** a snug or confined space. **3** *N Amer.* an enclosure containing bait and a hidden trap for animals. [dial. *cub* stall, pen, of Low German origin]

cubby·hole *noun* **1** a very small room. **2** a small compartment.

cube¹ ● *noun* **1** a solid contained by six equal squares. **2** a cube-shaped block. **3** *Math.* the product of a number multiplied by its square. ● *transitive verb* **1** find the cube of (a number). **2** cut (food for cooking etc.) into small cubes. [French *cube* or Latin *cubus* from Greek *kubos*]

cube² *noun informal* an office cubicle. [shortening]

cubeb /ˈkjuːbeb/ *noun* **1** a climbing plant, *Piper cubeba*, bearing pungent berries. **2** this berry crushed for use in medicated cigarettes. [Old French *cubebe* ultimately from Arabic *kobāba, kubāba*]

cube farm *noun slang* an office where the work space is divided into cubicles.

cube root *noun* the number which produces a given number when cubed.

cube steak *noun* (also **cubed steak**) *N Amer.* mechanically tenderized beef in the shape of a steak. [from the square marks left on the meat by the tenderizing machine]

cube van *noun* (also **cube truck**) esp. *Cdn* a truck resembling a van at the front, with a taller and wider cube-like storage compartment behind.

cubic /ˈkjuːbɪk/ *adjective* **1** cube-shaped. **2** of three dimensions. **3** involving the cube (and no higher power) of a number (*cubic equation*). **4** *Mineralogy* having three equal axes at right angles. **5** designating a volume equal to that of a cube whose edge is a specified unit of linear measure (*cubic yard*).

cubic·al /ˈkjuːbɪkəl/ *adjective* cube-shaped. □ **cubic·al·ly** *adverb*

cu·bicle /ˈkjuːbɪkəl/ *noun* **1** a small partitioned space, esp. screened for privacy. **2** one of a number of small offices created out of a larger workspace, separated by chest- or shoulder-height partitions. [originally a sleeping compartment, from Latin *cubiculum* from *cubare* lie down]

cubic zirconia *noun* a colourless form of zirconia that is very similar to diamond in refractivity and appearance.

cubi·form /ˈkjuːbɪˌfɔrm/ *adjective* cube-shaped.

cub·ism /ˈkjuːˌbɪzəm/ *noun* a style and movement in art, esp. painting, in which objects are represented as an assemblage of geometrical forms. □ **cub·ist** *noun & adjective* **cub·is·tic** *adjective*

cubit /ˈkjuːbɪt/ *noun* an ancient measure of length, approximately equal to the length of a forearm. [Latin *cubitum* elbow, cubit]

cu·bit·al /ˈkjuːbɪtəl/ *adjective* **1** *Anat.* of the forearm. **2** *Zool.* of the corresponding part in animals.

cu·boid /ˈkjuːbɔɪd/ ● *adjective* cube-shaped; like a cube. ● *noun* **1** *Math.* a rectangular parallelepiped. **2** (in full **cuboid bone**) *Anat.* the outer bone of the tarsus. □ **cu·boid·al** /-ˈbɔɪdəl/ *adjective*

Cu·chul·ain /kuːˈkʌlən/ *Irish Myth* a nephew of Conchobar and hero of Ulster.

cuck·ing stool *noun hist.* a chair on which offenders were ducked in water or exposed to ridicule as a punishment. [Middle English from obsolete *cuck* defecate]

cuck·old /ˈkʌkoʊld/ ● *noun* a man whose wife is unfaithful. ● *transitive verb* make a cuckold of. □ **cuck·old·ry** *noun* [Middle English *cukeweld, cokewold*, from Old French *cucu* cuckoo, with reference to the cuckoo's habit of laying its eggs in other birds' nests]

cuckoo /ˈkuːkuː, ˈkʊkuː/ ● *noun* **1** any of various birds of the family Cuculidae, e.g. the black-billed cuckoo *Coccyzus erythropthalmus* or yellow-billed cuckoo *C. americanus* of N America, with brown backs and white underparts, or the Eurasian grey or brown speckled bird, *Cuculus canorus*, which leaves its eggs in the nests of small birds and has a distinctive two-note call, the first hearing of which is regarded as a harbinger of spring. **2** *informal* a crazy or foolish person. ● *predicative adjective informal* crazy, foolish. □ **cuckoo in the nest** an unwelcome intruder. [Old French *cucu*, imitative]

cuckoo bee *noun* (also **cuckoo wasp**) a bee (or wasp) which lays its eggs in the nest of another species.

cuckoo clock *noun* a clock that strikes the hour with a sound like a cuckoo's call, usu. with the emergence on each note of a mechanical cuckoo.

cuckoo flower *noun* a meadow plant, *Cardamine pratensis*, with pale lilac flowers.

cuckoo pint *noun* an arum, *Arum maculatum*, with arrow-shaped leaves and scarlet berries.

cuckoo-spit *noun* froth exuded by larvae of insects of the family Cercopidae on leaves, stems, etc.

cu·cum·ber *noun* **1** a long green fleshy fruit eaten esp. as a salad vegetable or pickled. **2** the climbing plant, *Cucumis sativus*, yielding this fruit. [Old French *co(u)combre* from Latin *cucumer*]

cucumber beetle *noun N Amer.* any of several beetles which attack cucumbers, corn, and other plants.

cucumber mosaic *noun* a virus disease of the gourd family spread by cucumber beetles and aphids and causing mottling and stunting.

cu·cumber-root *noun* a liliaceous plant of eastern N America, with two whorls of leaves and a white cucumber-flavoured tuber. *Also called* INDIAN CUCUMBER-ROOT.

cucumber tree *noun* (also **cucumber magnolia**) any of several N American magnolias, esp. *Magnolia acuminata*, with small cucumber-like fruit.

cu·cur·bit /kjuːˈkɔrbɪt/ *noun* = GOURD 1b. □ **cu·cur·bit·aceous** /-ˈteɪʃəs/ *adjective* [Latin *cucurbita*]

Cú·cu·ta /ˈkuːkuːtə/ a city in NE Colombia, close to the border with Venezuela; pop. (est. 1999) 606,932.

cud *noun* **1** half-digested food returned from the first stomach of ruminants to the mouth for further chewing. **2** any substance, e.g. tobacco, used by a person to keep in the mouth and chew. □ **chew the cud** reflect meditatively, ruminate. [Old English *cwidu, cudu* what is chewed, corresponding to Old High German *kuti, quiti* glue]

cud·dle ● *verb* **1** *transitive* hold in an affectionate embrace, hug. **2** *intransitive* nestle together, lie close and snug. ● *noun* an instance of cuddling. □ **cud·dler** *noun* **cuddle·some** *adjective* [16th c.: perhaps from dial. *couth* snug]

cud·dly *adjective* (**cud·dli·er, cud·dli·est**) **1** pleasant to cuddle. **2** (of a person) plump. □ **cud·dli·ness** *noun*

cuddy¹ *noun* (*pl.* **-dies**) *Scot.* **1** a donkey. **2** a stupid person. [perhaps a pet form of the name *Cuthbert*]

cuddy² *noun* (*pl.* **-dies**) (in full **cuddy cabin**) a room or cabin in a ship, esp. a shelter or locker in the bow of a small boat. [probably from early modern Dutch *kajute* from Old French *cahute* 'shanty']

cudgel ● *noun* a short thick stick used as a weapon. ● *transitive verb* (**cudg·elled, cudgel·ling**; also esp. *US* **cudg·eled, cudgel·ing**) beat with a cudgel. □ **cudgel one's brains** think hard about a problem. **take up the cudgels** (often foll. by *for*) make a vigorous defence. [Old English *cycgel*, of unknown origin]

cud·weed *noun* any composite plant of the genus *Gnaphalium*, with scales and round flower heads, formerly given to cattle that had lost their cud.

cue¹ ● *noun* **1** something said or done on stage which serves as a signal for another performer or technician to speak, enter, or execute an action. **2 a** a stimulus to perception, understanding, etc. **b** a signal for action. **c** a hint on how to behave in particular circumstances. **3** a facility for or an instance of cueing audio equipment (see sense 2 of *verb*). ● *transitive verb* (**cues, cued, cue·ing** or **cuing**) **1** give a cue to. **2** put (a piece of audio equipment, esp. a record player or tape recorder) in readiness to play a particular part of the recorded material. □ **cue in 1** insert a cue for. **2** give information to. **on cue** at the correct moment. **take one's cue from** follow the example or advice of. [16th c.: origin unknown]

cue² Billiards etc. ● noun a long straight tapering rod for striking the ball. ● verb (**cues, cued, cue·ing** or **cuing**) **1** transitive strike (a ball) with a cue. **2** intransitive use a cue. □ **cue·ist** noun [var. of QUEUE]

cue ball noun Billiards etc. the usu. white ball that is to be struck with the cue.

cue-bid noun Cards (in bridge) an artificial bid to show a particular card etc. in the bidder's hand.

cue card noun a small card from which a person giving a speech, a television presenter, etc. reads lines.

Cuen·ca /ˈkweŋkə/ a city in the Andes in S Ecuador; pop. (est. 2002) 277,000. Founded in 1557, it is known as the 'marble city' because of its many fine buildings.

Cuer·na·vaca /ˌkwernəˈvakə/ a resort town in central Mexico, at an altitude of 1 542 m (5,060 ft.), capital of the state of Morelos; pop. (2000) 327,200.

cues·ta /ˈkwestə/ noun Geog. a gentle slope, esp. one ending in a steep drop. [Spanish, = slope, from Latin costa: see COAST]

cuff¹ ● noun **1 a** the end part of a sleeve. **b** the part of a glove covering the wrist. **2** N Amer. the lower turned-up end of a pant leg. **3** (in pl.) informal handcuffs. **4** the inflatable band which is wound around a limb when blood pressure is measured. **5** a muscle ringing a joint (rotator cuff). ● transitive verb **1** provide (a garment) with a cuff or cuffs. **2** informal put handcuffs on. □ **off-the-cuff** informal without preparation, extempore. **shoot one's cuffs** make the cuffs of one's shirt visible by pulling them out beyond the cuffs of one's jacket. □ **cuffed** adjective (also in combination). [Middle English: origin unknown]

cuff² ● transitive verb strike with an open hand. ● noun such a blow. [16th c.: perhaps imitative]

cuff·able adjective (of socks) intended to be folded down to the ankles.

cuff·link noun a device of two joined studs etc. to fasten the sides of a cuff together.

Cufic var. of KUFIC.

Cuia·bá /ˌkuːjəˈba/ a river port in west central Brazil, on the Cuiabá River; pop. (2000) 475,632.

Cuia·bá River a river of W Brazil, which rises in the Mato Grosso plateau and flows for 483 km (300 miles) to join the São Lourenço River near the border with Bolivia.

cui bono? /kwiː ˈbɒnɔː, ˈboː-/ interjection Law who stands, or stood, to gain? (with the implication that this person is responsible). [Latin, = to whom (is it) a benefit?]

cui·rass /kwɪˈras/ noun hist. a piece of armour consisting of breastplate and backplate fastened together. [Old French cuirace, ultimately from Late Latin coriaceus from corium leather]

cui·ras·sier /ˌkwɪrəˈsiːr/ noun hist. a cavalry soldier wearing a cuirass. [French (as CUIRASS)]

cui·sine /kwɪˈziːn/ noun a style or method of cooking, esp. of a particular country or establishment. [French from Latin coquina from coquere to cook]

cuisse /kwɪs/ noun (usu. in pl.) hist. thigh armour. [Old French cuisseaux pl. of cuissel from Late Latin coxale from coxa hip]

cuke noun N Amer. informal a cucumber. [abbreviation]

cul·chie /ˈkʌltʃi/ (also **cul·shie**) Irish slang derogatory ● noun a country bumpkin. ● adjective provincial, rustic. [perhaps alteration of Kiltimagh, a country town in County Mayo, Ireland]

Cul·dee /kʌlˈdiː/ noun any of various Irish and Scottish monks in the 8th–12th c., who lived as hermits, usu. in groups of thirteen on the analogy of Christ and his Apostles, until they and their Celtic Church were gradually brought under Roman Catholic rule. [from Irish céile Dé client of God]

cul-de-sac /ˈkʌldəˌsak, ˈkʊl-/ noun (pl. **cul-de-sacs**) **1** a street or passage closed at one end. **2** a route or course leading nowhere; a position from which one cannot escape. **3** Anat. = DIVERTICULUM. [French, = bottom of the sack]

-cule suffix forming (originally diminutive) nouns (molecule). [French -cule or Latin -culus]

Culia·cán Ros·ales /ˌkʊljəˈkɒn roːˈzɒles/ a city in NW Mexico, capital of the state of Sinaloa; pop. (2000) 540,800.

culin·ary /ˈkʌlɪˌneri/ adjective of or for cooking. □ **culin·ar·i·ly** adverb [Latin culinarius from culina kitchen]

cull ● transitive verb **1** select, choose, or gather from a large quantity or amount (knowledge culled from books). **2** pick or gather (flowers, fruit, etc.). **3** select (animals) according to quality, esp. poor or surplus specimens for killing. **4** N Amer. remove (timber) as being inferior. ● adjective selected in a cull; rejected as being surplus or inferior (cull apples). ● noun **1** an act of culling. **2** an animal or animals culled. **3** an item picked out as being surplus or inferior. □ **cull·er** noun [Old French coillier etc., ultimately from Latin colligere COLLECT¹]

Cul·len /ˈkʌlən/ **Mau·rice (Gal·braith)** (1866–1934), Canadian painter. He is noted for his Impressionist depiction of snow in brightly coloured Quebec winter landscapes; his works include Logging in Winter, Beaupré (1896) and Winter Evening, Quebec (c.1905).

cul·let /ˈkʌlət/ noun recycled waste or broken glass used in glass-making. [var. of COLLET in sense 'portion of glass left on a blowing iron after removal of finished object']

Cul·loden, Battle of /kəˈlɒdən/ the final engagement of the Jacobite uprising of 1745–6, fought on a moor near Inverness in NE Scotland. The small Jacobite army was crushed by the Hanoverian army, and a ruthless pursuit after the battle effectively prevented any chance of saving the Jacobite cause.

culm¹ /kʌlm/ noun coal dust, esp. of anthracite. [Middle English, prob. related to COAL]

culm² /kʌlm/ noun Bot. the stem of a plant, esp. of grasses. [Latin culmus stalk]

cul·min·ant /ˈkʌlmɪnənt/ adjective **1** at or forming the top. **2** (of a celestial object) at its greatest altitude, on the meridian.

cul·min·ate /ˈkʌlmɪˌneɪt/ verb **1** intransitive (usu. foll. by in) reach its highest or final point (the antagonism culminated in war). **2** transitive bring to its highest or final point. **3** intransitive (of a celestial object) reach its greatest altitude, be on the meridian. □ **cul·min·a·tion** noun [Late Latin culminare culminat- from culmen summit]

cu·lottes /kuːˈlɒts, ˈkuː-/ plural noun a woman's garment that hangs like a skirt but has separate legs, like trousers; a divided skirt. [French, = knee breeches]

culpa /ˈkʌlpə, ˈkʊlpə/ noun Law neglect resulting in damage; negligence. [Latin, = fault, blame]

culp·able /ˈkʌlpəbəl/ adjective deserving blame. □ **culp·abil·ity** noun **culp·ably** adverb [Latin culpabilis from culpare from culpa blame]

cul·prit noun **1** a person accused of or guilty of an offence. **2** a person or thing held responsible for something (smoking is often the culprit in heart disease). [17th c.: originally in the formula Culprit, how will you be tried?, said by the Clerk of the Crown to a prisoner pleading Not Guilty: perhaps abbreviation of Anglo-French Culpable: prest d'averrer etc. (You are) guilty: (I am) ready to prove etc.]

cult noun **1 a** a system of religious worship esp. as expressed in ritual. **b** a religious sect considered to be unorthodox or anti-social. **c** the members of such a sect. **2 a** devotion or homage to a person or thing (the cult of aestheticism). **b** a popular fashion esp. followed by a specific section of society. **3** (attributive) denoting a person or thing popularized in this way (cult film; cult figure). □ **cult·ic** adjective **cult·ish** adjective **cult·ish·ness** noun **cult·ism** noun **cult·ist** noun [French culte or Latin cultus worship, from colere cult- inhabit, till, worship]

cul·ti·gen /ˈkʌltɪdʒən/ noun a plant species or variety known only in cultivation, esp. one with no known wild ancestor. [cultivated + -GEN]

cul·ti·var /ˈkʌltɪˌvar/ noun Bot. a plant variety that has been produced in cultivation by selective breeding (a new tomato cultivar). [CULTIVATE + VARIETY]

cul·ti·vate transitive verb **1 a** prepare and use (soil etc.) for crops or gardening. **b** break up (the ground) with a cultivator. **c** remove weeds using a cultivator or hoe. **2 a** raise or produce (crops). **b** culture (bacteria etc.). **c** raise or produce (mussels, pearls, etc.). **3 a** make (the mind, feelings, etc.) more educated and sensitive. **b** pay attention to or nurture (a person or a person's friendship). **4** try to acquire or develop (a talent, attitude, manner, etc.). □ **cul·tiv·able** adjective **cul·ti·va·tion** noun [medieval Latin cultivare from cultiva (terra) arable (land) (as CULT)]

cul·ti·vat·ed adjective **1** (of a person, manners, etc.) having or showing education and good taste; refined. **2 a** (of land) used for growing crops. **b** (of plants) grown on farms etc. **3** (of mussels, pearls, etc.) grown in farms.

cul·ti·va·tor noun **1 a** a mechanical implement for breaking up the ground and uprooting weeds. **b** a two- or three-pronged hand tool used for weeding and loosening soil. **2** a person or thing that cultivates.

cul·tur·al adjective **1** of or relating to artistic or intellectual activity seen as cultivating the mind. **2** of or pertaining to culture in a society or civilization. □ **cul·tur·al·ly** adverb

Vowels: a cat   ɑ arm   e bed   ɜr her   ɜː deux   ə ago   ɪ sit   i cosy   iː feed   ɒ hot   ɔ pore   oː no   ʌ run   ʊ put

cultural anthropology *noun* the comparative study of peoples through their culture and kinship systems.

cultural attaché *noun* an embassy or consular official whose function is to promote cultural relations.

cultural imperialism *noun* the increasing influence or domination in one country of the culture of another.

Cultural Revolution a political upheaval led by the Red Guard in China, 1966–8, characterized by attacks on intellectuals and what were seen as bourgeois elements, a large-scale purge in party posts, and the appearance of a personality cult around the Chinese leader Mao Zedong. After considerable economic dislocation the movement was gradually brought to a halt by Chou En-lai.

cultural sovereignty *noun Cdn* the power of a country to maintain independence in its cultural activities from another, culturally dominant, nation.

cultural tourism *noun* tourism motivated by a desire to experience the history, folklore, social or artistic culture of another region.

cul·ture ● *noun* **1 a** the arts and other manifestations of human intellectual achievement regarded collectively (*a city lacking in culture*). **b** a refined understanding of this; intellectual development (*a person of culture*). **2 a** the customs, civilization, and achievements of a particular time or people (*studied Chinese culture*). **b** the mode of behaviour within a particular group (*corporate culture; youth culture*). **3** improvement by mental or physical training. **4 a** the cultivation of plants; the rearing of bees, silkworms, etc. **b** the cultivation of the soil. **5** a quantity of micro-organisms and the nutrient material supporting their growth. ● *transitive verb* maintain (bacteria etc.) in conditions suitable for growth. [French *culture* or Latin *cultura* (as CULT): (v.) from obsolete French *culturer* or medieval Latin *culturare*]

cul·tured *adjective* **1** having refined taste and manners and a good education. **2** caused to develop by artificial means or in an artificial nutrient medium.

cultured pearl *noun* a pearl formed by an oyster after the insertion of a foreign body into its shell.

culture jamming *noun* the practice of criticizing and subverting advertising and consumerism in the mass media, by methods such as producing advertisements parodying those of global brands. □ **culture jammer** *noun* [coined by the US band Negativland]

culture shock *noun* the feeling of disorientation experienced by a person suddenly subjected to an unfamiliar culture or way of life.

culture vulture *noun informal* a person who is a voracious consumer of culture.

cul·tus /ˈkʌltəs/ *noun* a system of religious worship; a cult. [Latin: see CULT]

cul·verin /ˈkʌlvərɪn/ *noun hist.* **1** a long cannon. **2** a small firearm. [Old French *coulevrine* from *couleuvre* snake, ultimately from Latin *colubra*]

Cul·ver's root *noun* a herbaceous plant of eastern N America, *Veronicastrum virginicum*, with long spikes of white flowers and whorled leaves. [a Dr. *Culver fl.* before 1716, American physician who used it for medicinal purposes]

cul·vert /ˈkʌlvərt/ *noun* **1** an underground channel carrying water across a road etc. **2** a channel for an electric cable. [18th c.: origin unknown]

cum[1] *preposition* (usu. in *combination*) with, combined with, also used as (*a farmhouse-cum-museum*). [Latin]

cum[2] *coarse slang* ● *noun* = COME *noun*. ● *intransitive verb* (past **came**; past participle **cum**) = COME 13. [corruption]

cum·ber ● *transitive verb literary* hamper, hinder, inconvenience. ● *noun* a hindrance, obstruction, or burden. [Middle English, prob. from ENCUMBER]

Cum·ber·land 1 a former township in E Ontario, now part of Ottawa; pop. (2001) 52,430. **2** a former county in NW England. In 1974 it was united with Westmorland and part of Lancashire to form the county of Cumbria. [sense 1 after Prince E. Augustus, Duke of *Cumberland* and Teviotdale d.1851]

Cumberland Peninsula a large peninsula of the southeastern region of Baffin Island. [see CUMBERLAND SOUND]

Cumberland Sound a large inlet of Davis Strait, almost 300 km in length and over 150 km wide. Carving into the southeastern coast of Baffin Island, it forms the Cumberland and Hall peninsulas. [G. Clifford, 3rd Earl of *Cumberland*, English naval commander d.1605]

cum·ber·some *adjective* inconvenient in size, weight, or shape; unwieldy. □ **cum·ber·some·ly** *adverb* **cum·ber·some·ness** *noun*

cum·bia /ˈkʊmbiə/ *noun* **1** a form of dance music originating in Colombia. **2** a dance resembling the fandango performed to this

music. [Colombian Spanish, perhaps from Spanish *cumbé*, the name of a dance performed by blacks]

Cum·bria /ˈkʌmbriə/ a county of NW England; county town, Carlisle. Cumbria was an ancient British kingdom, and its name continued to be used for the hilly northwestern region of England containing the Lake District and much of the N Pennines. The county of Cumbria was formed in 1974, largely from the former counties of Westmorland and Cumberland. □ **Cum·brian** *adjective & noun*

cum·brous /ˈkʌmbrəs/ *adjective* = CUMBERSOME. □ **cum·brous·ly** *adverb*

cumin /ˈkjuːmɪn/ *noun* **1** an umbelliferous plant, *Cuminum cyminum*, bearing aromatic seeds. **2** these seeds used as flavouring, esp. ground and used in curry powder. [Old French from Latin *cuminum* from Greek *kuminon*, prob. of Semitic origin]

cum laude *adverb & adjective N Amer.* (of a degree, diploma, etc.) with distinction; of a higher standard than average. [Latin, lit. 'with praise']

cummer·bund *noun* a wide, often horizontally pleated sash worn around the waist, esp. with a tuxedo. [Hindustani & Persian *kamar-band* loin band]

Cum·mings ▸ 1 Bur·ton (b.1947), Canadian rock singer and songwriter. He was the lead singer of the Guess Who (1968–75), and as a solo performer his songs have included 'I'm Scared' and 'Stand Tall'. **2 Ed·ward Est·lin** (known as 'e. e. cummings') (1894–1962), US poet. His poems are characterized by their inventive typography (esp. the avoidance of capital letters), and innovative grammar, punctuation, and line breaks; his works include *95 Poems* (1956) and the novel *The Enormous Room* (1922).

cumu·late ● *transitive & intransitive verb* /ˈkjuːmjʊˌleit/ accumulate, amass; combine. ● *noun* /ˈkjuːmjʊlət/ an igneous rock formed by particles in a magma settling to the bottom. ● *adjective* /ˈkjuːmjʊlət/ heaped up, massed. □ **cumu·la·tion** *noun* [Latin *cumulare* from *cumulus* heap]

cumu·la·tive /ˈkjuːmjʊlətɪv/ *adjective* **1 a** increasing or increased in amount, force, etc., by successive additions (*cumulative evidence*). **b** formed by successive additions (*learning is a cumulative process*). **2** *Stock Exch.* (of shares) entitling holders to arrears of interest before any other distribution is made. □ **cumu·la·tive·ly** *adverb* **cumu·la·tive·ness** *noun*

cumulative voting *noun* a system in which each voter has as many votes as there are candidates and may give all to one candidate or divide them among several candidates.

cumu·lo·nim·bus /ˌkjuːmjʊlɔːˈnɪmbəs/ *noun* a cumulus cloud developed to a great height and producing rain or hail; a thundercloud (also *attributive: cumulonimbus cloud*). [as CUMULUS + NIMBUS]

cumu·lus /ˈkjuːmjʊləs/ *noun* **1** clouds formed in rounded masses heaped on each other above a flat base. **2** a cloud of this type (also *attributive: cumulus cloud*). [Latin, = heap]

Cu·nard /kjuːˈnɑːrd/ **Sir Sam·uel** (1787–1865), Canadian-born English shipowner. A pioneer of regular transatlantic passenger service, he founded the steamship company (1839) which still bears his name with the aid of a contract to carry the mail between Canada and Britain.

cune·ate /ˈkjuːniət/ *adjective* wedge-shaped. [Latin *cuneus* wedge]

cu·nei·form /kjuːˈneiəˌfɔrm, -ˈniːə-, ˈkjuːnɪ-/ ● *adjective* **1** wedge-shaped. **2** of, relating to, or using the wedge-shaped writing impressed esp. in clay in ancient Babylonian etc. inscriptions. ● *noun* cuneiform writing. [French *cunéiforme* or modern Latin *cuneiformis* from Latin *cuneus* wedge]

Cu·nene River /kjuːˈneinə/ a river of Angola, which rises near the city of Huambo and flows 250 km (156 miles) southward as far as the frontier with Namibia, which then follows it westward to the Atlantic.

cunit /ˈkjuːnɪt/ *noun Forestry* 100 cubic feet (2.832 cubic metres) of wood. [blend of CUBIC and UNIT]

cunni·lin·gus /ˌkʌnɪˈlɪŋgəs/ *noun* stimulation of the female genitals using the tongue or lips. [Latin from *cunnus* vulva + *lingere* lick]

cun·ning ● *adjective* (**cun·ning·er**, **cun·ning·est**) **1 a** skilled in ingenuity or deceit. **b** selfishly clever or crafty. **2** ingenious (*a cunning device*). **3** *N Amer.* attractive, quaint. ● *noun* **1** craftiness; skill in deceit. **2** skill, ingenuity. □ **cun·ning·ly** *adverb* **cun·ning·ness** *noun* [Old Norse *kunnandi* knowing, from *kunna* know: compare CAN[1]]

Cun·ning·ham /ˈkʌnɪŋhəm/ **Merce** (b.1919), US dancer and choreographer. A dancer with the Martha Graham Dance Company (1939–45), he experimented with choreography and collaborated with the composer John Cage in solo performances in 1944; in 1953 he formed his own company to explore new abstract directions for modern dance, and his works include *Suite for Five* (1956) and *Travelogue* (1977).

Cuno·bel·in·us see CYMBELINE.

cunt *noun coarse slang* **1** the female genitals. **2** *offensive* a woman. **3** *offensive* an unpleasant or stupid person. ¶ A highly taboo word. [Middle English from Germanic]

cup ● *noun* **1** a small bowl-shaped container, often with a handle, for drinking from. **2 a** its contents (*a cup of tea*). **b** *N Amer.* a measure of capacity esp. in cooking, equal to eight fluid ounces (237 ml). **3** a cup-shaped thing, esp. the calyx of a flower or the socket of a bone. **4** flavoured wine, cider, etc., usu. chilled. **5** an ornamental cup-shaped trophy as a prize for victory or prowess, esp. in a sports contest. **6** one's fate or fortune (*a bitter cup*). **7** either of the two cup-shaped parts of a brassiere. **8** the chalice used or the wine taken at the Eucharist. **9** *Golf* the hole on a putting green or the metal container in it. **10** the hard protective triangular shell in a jockstrap. **11** a shallow bowl-shaped cooking utensil (*muffin cups; custard cup*). ● *transitive verb* (**cupped**, **cup·ping**) **1** form (esp. one's hands) into the shape of a cup. **2** take or hold as in a cup. **3** (in alternative medicine) apply to the skin a glass in which a partial vacuum is formed by heating. □ **one's cup of tea** *informal* what interests or suits one. **in one's cups** while drunk; drunk. □ **cup·ful** *noun* (*pl.* **-fuls**). [Old English *cuppe* from medieval Latin *cuppa* cup, prob. differentiated from Latin *cupa* tub]

cup·bear·er *noun* a person who serves wine, esp. an officer of a royal or noble household.

cup·board *noun* a recess or piece of furniture with a door and (usu.) shelves, in which things are stored.

cupboard love *noun* a display of affection meant to secure a gain.

cup·cake *noun* **1** a small cake baked in a cup-shaped mould. **2** a term of endearment.

CUPE /ˈkjuːpi/ *abbreviation* Canadian Union of Public Employees.

cupel /ˈkjuːpəl/ ● *noun* a small flat porous vessel used in assaying gold or silver in the presence of lead. ● *transitive verb* (**cu·pelled**, **cupel·ling**; esp. *US* **cupeled**, **cupel·ing**) assay or refine in a cupel. □ **cupel·la·tion** /-ˈleɪʃən/ *noun* [French *coupelle* from Late Latin *cupella* diminutive of *cupa*: see CUP]

cup·holder *noun* a moulded plastic ring or well designed to hold a cup alongside a seat in a car.

Cu·pid /ˈkjuːpɪd/ *noun* **1** *Rom. Myth* the god of love, identified by the Romans with Eros. He is often pictured as a naked boy with wings, carrying a bow and arrows, with which he wounds his victims. **2** (also **cupid**) a representation of Cupid.

cu·pid·ity /kjuːˈpɪdɪti/ *noun* greed for gain; avarice. [Latin *cupiditas* from *cupidus* desirous]

Cu·pids /ˈkjuːpɪdz/ *noun* a town on the Avalon Peninsula in SE Newfoundland, situated on the west side of Conception Bay; pop. (2001) 775. It was the site of one of the earliest British colonies in the New World. [from its original 17th-c. name *Cuperres coue*, prob. so called because in the fish-packing process, coopers were sent to the nearby forested slopes to cut wood for barrel making]

Cupid's bow *noun* the upper lip etc. shaped like the double-curved bow carried by Cupid.

cu·pola /ˈkjuːpələ/ *noun* **1 a** a rounded dome forming a roof or ceiling. **b** a small rounded dome adorning a roof. **2** a revolving dome protecting mounted guns in a fort or on a warship etc. **3** a furnace for melting metals. □ **cu·po·laed** /-ləd/ *adjective* [Italian from Late Latin *cupula* diminutive of *cupa* cask]

cup·pa *noun* (also **cup·per**) *Brit. informal* **1** a cup of. **2** a cup of tea. [corruption]

cu·pram·mo·nium /ˌkjuːprəˈmoːniəm/ *noun* a complex ion of divalent copper and ammonia, solutions of which dissolve cellulose. [Late Latin *cuprum* + AMMONIUM]

cu·pre·ous /ˈkjuːprias, ˈkuː-/ *adjective* of or like copper. [Late Latin *cupreus* from *cuprum* copper]

cu·pric /ˈkjuːprɪk, ˈkuː-/ *adjective* of copper, esp. divalent copper. □ **cu·prif·er·ous** /-ˈprɪfərəs/ *adjective* [Late Latin *cuprum* copper]

cu·prite /ˈkjuːprʌɪt/ *noun Mineralogy* native cuprous oxide, a red mineral and major copper ore.

cupro- /ˈkjuːproː, ˈkuː-/ *combining form* copper (*cupro-nickel*).

cupro-nickel /ˌkjuːproːˈnɪkəl, ˌkuː-/ *noun* an alloy of copper and nickel, esp. in the proportions 3:1 as used in 'silver' coins.

cu·prous /ˈkjuːprəs, ˈkuː-/ *adjective* of copper, esp. monovalent copper. [Late Latin *cuprum* copper]

cu·pule /ˈkjuːpjuːl/ *noun Bot. & Zool.* a cup-shaped organ, receptacle, etc. [Late Latin *cupula* CUPOLA]

CUPW /ˌkʌpˈdʌbəljuː/ *abbreviation* Canadian Union of Postal Workers.

cur *noun* **1** a worthless or snappy dog. **2** a contemptible person. [Middle English, prob. originally in *cur-dog*, perhaps from Old Norse *kurr* grumbling]

cur·able *adjective* that can be cured. □ **cur·abil·ity** *noun*

Cura·çao /ˌkjʊrəˈsoː, -ˈseɪoː/ the largest island of the Netherlands Antilles, situated in the Caribbean Sea 60 km (37 miles) north of the Venezuelan coast; pop. (est. 2002) 186,300; chief town, Willemstad.

cura·çao /ˌkjʊrəˈsoː, ˌkjʊrə-/ *noun* (also **cura·çoa** /-ˈsoːə/) (*pl.* **-çaos** or **cura·çoas**) a liqueur of spirits flavoured with the peel of bitter oranges. [CURAÇAO, which produces these oranges]

cur·acy /ˈkjʊrəsi, ˈkjʊrə-/ *noun* (*pl.* **-acies**) a curate's office or the tenure of it.

cur·are /kjʊˈrɑri, kʊ-/ *noun* a resinous bitter substance prepared from S American plants of the genera *Strychnos* and *Chondodendron*, paralyzing the motor nerves, formerly used to poison arrows and blowpipe darts by Aboriginals of S America, and as a muscle relaxant in surgery. [Carib]

cur·as·sow /ˈkjʊrəsoː, ˈkjʊrə-/ *noun* any game bird of the family Cracidae, found in Central and S America. [anglicized from CURAÇAO]

cur·ate[1] /ˈkjʊrət, ˈkjɜrət/ *noun* **1** *Catholicism* the priest of a parish in continental Europe. **2** a member of the clergy engaged as assistant to a parish priest. □ **curate's egg** a thing that is partly good and partly bad. [medieval Latin *curatus* from Latin *cura* CURE]

cur·ate[2] /ˈkjʊreɪt, ˈkjɜreɪt/ *verb* **1** *transitive* act as curator of (a museum, exhibits, etc.); look after and preserve. **2** *transitive* select, organize, and present items for (an exhibition, film festival, etc.). **3** *intransitive* perform the duties of a curator. □ **cur·a·tion** *noun* [back-formation from CURATOR]

cur·a·tive /ˈkjʊrətɪv, ˈkjɜrə-/ ● *adjective* tending or able to cure (esp. disease). ● *noun* a curative medicine or agent. [French *curatif -ive* from medieval Latin *curativus* from Latin *curare* CURE]

cur·ator /ˈkjɜreɪtər, ˈkjʊ-, kjʊˈreɪtər/ *noun* **1** an employee of a museum, art gallery, etc., responsible for the collections. **2** a person who curates an exhibition. **3** *Cdn* (*Que.*) = PUBLIC CURATOR. □ **cur·a·tor·ial** /ˌkjɜrəˈtɔːriəl, ˌkjʊrə-/ *adjective* **cur·ator·ship** *noun* [late Middle English (denoting an ecclesiastical pastor) from Old French *curateur* or Latin *curator* (as CURE)]

curb ● *noun* **1** the raised, usu. concrete border along the side of a street etc. **2** a check or restraint. **3** a strap etc. fastened to the bit and passing under a horse's lower jaw, used as a check. **4** an enclosing border or edging such as the frame round the top of a well or a fender round a hearth. ● *transitive verb* **1** restrain. **2** have (one's dog) defecate by the curb rather than on the sidewalk. **3** put a curb on (a horse). [Old French *courber* from Latin *curvare* bend, CURVE]

curb appeal *noun N Amer.* the immediate attractiveness of a property, esp. a house, to someone passing by, esp. a potential buyer.

curb cut *noun N Amer.* a small ramp built into the curb of a sidewalk to make it easier for wheelchairs, strollers, etc. to pass from the sidewalk to the street.

curb·side *noun N Amer.* the area adjacent to a curb, often where garbage etc. is placed for collection (often *attributive: curbside recycling program*).

curb·stone *noun N Amer.* **1** a stone or portion of concrete forming a curb. **2** (*attributive*) **a** denoting a transaction conducted outside an office or usual place of business. **b** denoting an opinion etc. made by an amateur or untrained person (*curbstone comments*).

curb weight *noun* the weight of a vehicle without occupants or baggage.

cur·cuma /ˈkɜrkjuːmə/ *noun* **1** the spice turmeric. **2** any tuberous plant of the genus *Curcuma*, yielding this and other commercial substances. [medieval Latin or modern Latin from Arabic *kurkum* saffron, from Sanskrit *kuṇkuma*ᵐ]

curd *noun* **1** (often in *pl.*) a coagulated substance formed by the action of acids on milk, which may be made into cheese or eaten as food. **2** a fatty substance found between flakes of boiled salmon flesh. **3** the edible head of a cauliflower. □ **curdy** *adjective* [Middle English: origin unknown]

curd cheese *noun* a soft smooth cheese made from skimmed milk curds.

cur·dle *transitive & intransitive verb* make into or become curds. □ **make one's blood curdle** fill one with horror. [frequentative form of CURD (as verb)]

cure ● *verb* **1** *transitive* (often foll. by *of*) restore (a person or animal) to health. **2** *transitive* eliminate (a disease, evil, etc.). **3** *transitive* preserve (meat, fruit, tobacco, or skins) by salting, drying, etc. **4 a** *transitive*

Consonants: b *but*   d *dog*   f *few*   g *get*   h *her*   j *yes*   k *cat*   l *leg*   m *man*   n *no*   p *pen*   r *red*   s *sit*

vulcanize (rubber). **b** *transitive* harden (concrete or plastic). **c** *intransitive* (of glue, caulking, etc.) set, harden. **5** *intransitive* effect a cure. **6** *intransitive* undergo a process of curing. ● *noun* **1** restoration to health. **2** a means of curing a disease. **3** a course of medical or healing treatment. **4 a** the office or function of a curate. **b** a parish or other sphere of spiritual ministration. **5 a** the process of curing rubber or plastic. **b** (with qualifying adj.) the degree of this. **6** the process of curing meat, fruit, tobacco, skins, etc. □ **curer** *noun* [Old French *curer* from Latin *curare* 'take care of', from *cura* care]

curé /kjʊˈreɪ/ *noun* a parish priest in Quebec, France etc. [French from medieval Latin *curatus*: see CURATE¹]

cure-all *noun* a panacea; a universal remedy.

cur·et·tage /kjʊˈretɪdʒ, -rɪˈtɒdʒ/ *noun* the use of or an operation involving the use of a curette. [French (as CURETTE)]

cur·ette /kjʊˈret/ ● *noun* a surgeon's small scraping instrument. ● *transitive & intransitive verb* clean or scrape with a curette. [French, from *curer* cleanse (as CURE)]

cur·few *noun* **1 a** a regulation restricting or forbidding the public circulation of people, esp. requiring people to remain indoors between specified hours, usu. at night. **b** a requirement that one be home, returned to one's hotel etc., or in bed by a certain time. **c** *hist.* a medieval regulation requiring people to extinguish fires at a fixed hour in the evening. **2** the hour designated as the beginning of such a restriction. **3** a daily signal indicating this. **4** the ringing of a bell at a fixed evening hour. □ **break curfew** fail to observe a curfew. [Middle English from Anglo-French *coeverfu*, Old French *cuevrefeu* from the stem of *couvrir* COVER + *feu* fire]

Curia /ˈkjɜːrɪə, ˈkjʊ-/ *noun* (also **curia**) the papal court; the government departments of the Vatican. □ **Cur·ial** *adjective* [Latin: originally a division of an ancient Roman tribe, the senate house at Rome, a feudal court of justice]

Curie /ˈkjʊri, kjʊˈriː/ **Marie** (1867–1934), Polish-born French physicist, and her husband **Pierre** (1859–1906), French physicist, pioneers of radioactivity. They discovered the elements polonium and radium, for which they shared the 1903 Nobel Prize for physics with Becquerel. Marie received another Nobel Prize (for chemistry) in 1911 for her isolation of radium.

curie /ˈkjʊri/ *noun* **1** a unit of radioactivity, corresponding to 3.7×10^{10} disintegrations per second. Abbr.: **Ci**. **2** a quantity of radioactive substance having this activity. [P. and M. CURIE]

curio /ˈkjʊrɪəʊ/ *noun* (*pl.* **curios**) a rare or unusual object or person. [19th-c. abbreviation of CURIOSITY]

curi·osa /ˌkjʊrɪˈəʊsə/ *plural noun* **1** curiosities. **2** erotic or pornographic books. [neuter pl. of Latin *curiosus*: see CURIOUS]

curi·os·ity *noun* (*pl.* **-ities**) **1** an eager desire to know; inquisitiveness. **2** strangeness. **3** a strange, rare, or interesting object or thing.

curi·ous *adjective* **1** eager to learn; inquisitive. **2** strange, surprising, odd. □ **curi·ous·ly** *adverb* **curi·ous·ness** *noun* [Old French *curios* from Latin *curiosus* careful, from *cura* care]

Curi·tiba /ˌkʊrɪˈtiːbə/ a city in S Brazil; pop. (2000) 1,586,898.

cur·ium /ˈkjʊrɪəm/ *noun* an artificially made transuranic radioactive metallic element, first produced by bombarding plutonium with helium ions. Symbol: **Cm**; at. no.: 96. [CURIE]

curl ● *verb* **1** *transitive & intransitive* (often foll. by *up*) **a** bend or coil into a spiral. **b** form or make something form into a curved shape, esp. so that the edges are rolled up. **2** *intransitive* move in a spiral form (*smoke curling upwards*). **3 a** *intransitive* (of the upper lip) be raised slightly on one side as an expression of contempt or disapproval. **b** *transitive* cause (the lip) to do this. **4 a** *intransitive* play curling. **b** *transitive* play (a game of curling). **c** *intransitive* (of a curling rock) slide with a curving motion. ● *noun* **1** a lock of curled hair. **2** anything spiral or curved inwards. **3 a** a curling movement or act. **b** the state of being curled. **4** an exercise in which part of the body (e.g. the arms, legs, or abdomen) is curled and then released. **5** a disease of plants in which the leaves are curled up. □ **curl up** **1** lie or sit with the knees drawn up. **2** *informal* writhe with embarrassment or horror. **make a person's hair curl** *informal* shock or horrify a person. [Middle English; earliest form *crolled*, *crulled* from obsolete adj. *crolle*, *crulle* curly, from Middle Dutch *krul*]

curl·er *noun* **1** a pin or roller etc. for curling the hair. **2** a player in the game of curling.

cur·lew *noun* (*pl.* same) any wading bird of the genus *Numenius*, possessing a usu. long slender down-curved bill. [Old French *courlieu*, *courlis* originally imitative, but assimilated to *courliu* courier, from *courre* run + *lieu* place]

curl·i·cue /ˈkɜːrlɪˌkjuː/ *noun* a decorative curl or twist. [CURLY + CUE² (= pigtail) or Q¹]

curl·ing *noun* **1** in senses of CURL *verb*. **2** a game played on ice, in which large round stones are slid across the surface towards a mark.

curling iron *noun* (also esp. *Brit.* **curling tongs** *plural noun*) a device consisting of a barrel and a hinged clamp, heated so that hair can be twisted into curls around it.

curly *adjective* (**curl·i·er**, **curl·i·est**) **1** having or arranged in curls. **2** moving in curves. □ **curl·i·ness** *noun*

curly endive *noun* = ENDIVE 2.

curly-grass fern *noun* a fern of Newfoundland, Nova Scotia and New Jersey, *Schizaea pusilla*, with wiry, grasslike fronds.

curly kale *noun* see KALE 1.

cur·mudg·eon /kɜːrˈmʌdʒən/ *noun* a bad-tempered person. □ **cur·mudg·eon·ly** *adjective* **cur·mudg·eon·li·ness** *noun* [16th c.: origin unknown]

Cur·noe /ˈkɜːrnəʊ/ **Greg·ory Rich·ard** (**'Greg'**) (1936–92), Canadian painter. His brightly coloured hard-edge compositions embodied elements of pop art, and often drew on his immediate surroundings and experiences for their themes; they include *Family Painting No. 1 – In Labour* (1966) and *Homage to van Dongen (Sheila) No. 1* (1979–80).

cur·rach /ˈkʌrə/ *noun* (also **cur·ragh**) *Irish* a coracle. [Irish: compare CORACLE]

Cur·ragh, the /ˈkʌrə/ a plain in County Kildare in the Republic of Ireland, noted for the breeding of racehorses. The Irish Derby is run annually on its racecourse.

cur·rant *noun* **1** a dried fruit of a small seedless variety of grape grown in California and the Middle East and much used in cooking. **2 a** any of various shrubs of the genus *Ribes* producing red, white, or black berries. **b** a berry of these shrubs. [Middle English *raysons of corance* from Anglo-French, = grapes of Corinth (the original source)]

cur·ren·cy *noun* (*pl.* **-cies**) **1 a** the money in general use in a country. **b** any other commodity used as a medium of exchange. **2** the condition of being current; prevalence, e.g. of words or ideas. **3** the time during which something is current.

cur·rent ● *adjective* **1** belonging to the present time; happening now (*current events; the current week*). **2** (of money, opinion, a rumour, a word, etc.) in general circulation or use. ● *noun* **1** a body of water, air, etc., moving in a definite direction, esp. through a stiller surrounding body. **2 a** an ordered movement of electrically charged particles. **b** a quantity representing the intensity of such movement. **3** (usu. foll. by *of*) a general tendency or course (of events, opinions, etc.). [Old French *corant* from Latin *currere* run]

current account *noun* **1** the part of a country's balance of payments account that records non-capital transactions. **2** a bank account from which money may be drawn without notice.

current affairs *plural noun* esp. *Cdn & Brit.* (also esp. *N Amer.* **current events**) matters of public interest in progress.

cur·rent·ly *adverb* at the present time; now.

current value assessment *noun* assessment of the value of a property for tax purposes based on current or recent market prices for similar properties.

cur·ricle /ˈkɜːrɪkəl/ *noun* *hist.* a light open two-wheeled carriage drawn by two horses abreast. [Latin *curriculum*: see CURRICULUM]

cur·ric·u·lum /kəˈrɪkjʊləm/ *noun* (*pl.* **cur·ric·u·la** /-lə/) the subjects that are studied or prescribed for study in a school, school board, etc. (*not part of the school curriculum*). □ **cur·ric·u·lar** *adjective* [Latin, = course, race chariot, from *currere* run]

curriculum vitae /kəˈrɪkjʊləm ˈviːtaɪ/ *noun* (*pl.* **curricula vitae** or **vitarum**) a brief account of one's education, qualifications, and previous occupations. Abbr.: **c.v.** [Latin, = course of life]

Cur·rie, Sir Ar·thur (Wil·liam) (1875–1933), Canadian army officer and administrator. In the First World War he commanded the 2nd Canadian Infantry Brigade and led the 1st Canadian Infantry Division during the Battles of the Somme and Vimy Ridge; he was promoted to the rank of general in 1919, and after retiring from the army became the principal and vice-chancellor of McGill University (1920–33).

Cur·rier, Na·than·iel (1813–88), US lithographer, who with James Merritt Ives produced lithographs depicting 19th-c. American life.

cur·ri·er *noun* a person who dresses and colours tanned leather. [Old French *corier*, from Latin *coriarius* from *corium* leather]

curry¹ ● *noun* (*pl.* **-ries**) a dish of meat, vegetables, etc., cooked in a highly spiced sauce, usu. served with rice. ● *transitive verb* (**-ries**, **-ried**) prepare or flavour with hot-tasting spices (*curried eggs*). [Tamil]

curry² *transitive verb* (**-ries**, **-ried**) **1** groom (a horse) with a curry comb. **2** *hist.* treat (tanned leather) to improve its properties. □ **curry favour** ingratiate oneself. [Old French *correier*, ultimately from Germanic]

curry comb *noun* a hand-held metal serrated device for grooming horses.

curry powder *noun* a preparation of turmeric, cumin, and other spices for making curry.

curse ● *noun* **1** a solemn utterance intended to invoke a supernatural power to inflict destruction or punishment on a person or thing. **2** the evil supposedly resulting from a curse. **3** a violent exclamation of anger; a profane oath. **4** a thing that causes evil or harm. **5** (prec. by *the*) *slang* menstruation; a menstrual period. ● *verb* **1** *transitive* **a** utter a curse against. **b** (in *imperative*) may God curse. **2** *transitive* (usu. in *passive*; foll. by *with*) afflict with (*cursed with bad luck*). **3 a** *intransitive* utter expletive curses; swear. **b** *transitive* feel or express negative thoughts about (*cursed my luck*). □ **curs·er** *noun* [Old English *curs*, *cursian*, of unknown origin]

cursed /ˈkɜːrsəd, kɜːrst/ *adjective* used to express annoyance or irritation. □ **curs·ed·ly** *adverb*

curs·es *interjection* expressing annoyance.

cur·sillo /kʊrˈsiːoː/ *noun* (*pl.* **-sillos**) a short informal Christian spiritual retreat. [Spanish, = little course]

cur·sive /ˈkɜːrsɪv/ ● *adjective* (of writing) done with joined characters. ● *noun* cursive writing (compare PRINT *verb* 4, UNCIAL). [medieval Latin (*scriptura*) *cursiva* from Latin *currere cars*- run]

cur·sor *noun* **1** *Computing* a movable indicator on a computer screen identifying a particular position in the display, esp. the position that the program will operate on with the next keystroke. **2** *Math.* a transparent slide engraved with a hairline and forming part of a slide rule. [Latin, = runner (as CURSIVE)]

cur·sor·ial /kɜːrˈsɔːriəl/ *adjective* having limbs adapted for running. [as CURSOR + -IAL]

cursor key *noun* one of usu. four keys grouped together on a computer keyboard, used to move the cursor vertically or horizontally.

cur·sory /ˈkɜːrsəri/ *adjective* hasty, hurried; superficial (*a cursory examination*). □ **cur·sor·i·ly** *adverb* **cur·sor·i·ness** *noun* [Latin *cursorius* of a runner (as CURSOR)]

curst *archaic var.* of CURSED.

curt *adjective* noticeably or rudely brief. □ **curt·ly** *adverb* **curt·ness** *noun* [Latin *curtus* cut short, abridged]

cur·tail *transitive verb* cut short; reduce; terminate esp. prematurely (*curtailed his visit to Italy*). □ **cur·tail·ment** *noun* [obsolete *curtal* horse with docked tail, from French *courtault* from *court* short, from Latin *curtus*: assimilated to *tail*]

cur·tain ● *noun* **1** a piece of cloth etc. hung up as a screen, usu. movable sideways or upwards, esp. at a window or between the stage and auditorium of a theatre. **2** *Theatre* the rise or fall of the stage curtain at the beginning or end of an act or scene. **3** a partition or cover. **4** (in *pl.*) *slang* the end. **5** any concentration of something forming a barrier (*curtain of bullets*; *curtain of fog*). ● *transitive verb* **1** furnish or cover with a curtain or curtains. **2** (foll. by *off*) shut off with a curtain or curtains. □ **cur·tained** *adjective* **cur·tain·less** *adjective* [Old French *cortine* from Late Latin *cortina*, translation of Greek *aulaia* from *aulē* court]

curtain call *noun* an appearance by a performer or performers to take a bow at the end of a performance.

curtain raiser *noun* **1** *Theatre* a piece prefaced to the main performance. **2** a preliminary event.

curtain rod *noun* a rod from which a curtain is suspended.

curtain-up *noun* the beginning of a stage performance.

curtain wall *noun* **1** *Fortification* the plain wall of a fortified place, connecting two towers etc. **2** *Archit.* a wall, esp. of glass, which encloses a building but does not support the roof.

cur·tana /kɜːrˈtɒnə/ *noun Brit.* an unpointed sword borne before English sovereigns at their coronation, as an emblem of mercy. [Anglo-Latin *curtana* (*spatha*) 'shortened (sword)' from Old French *cortain* the name of the sword belonging to ROLAND (the point of which was damaged when it was thrust into a block of steel), from *cort* short, from Latin *curtus* 'cut short']

cur·til·age /ˈkɜːrtəlɪdʒ/ *noun esp. Law* a small court, yard, or piece of ground surrounding a house and forming one unit with it. [Old French *co(u)rtillage* from *co(u)rtil* small court, from *cort* COURT]

curt·sy (also **curt·sey**) ● *noun* (*pl.* **-sies** or **-seys**) a woman's or girl's formal greeting or salutation made by bending the knees with one foot in front of the other. ● *intransitive verb* (**-sies**, **-sied** or **-seys**, **-seyed**) make a curtsy. [var. of COURTESY]

cur·ule /ˈkjɜːruːl, ˈkjʊ-/ *adjective Rom. Hist.* designating or relating to the authority exercised by the senior Roman magistrates, chiefly the consul and praetor, who were entitled to use the *sella curulis* ('curule seat' or seat of office). [Latin *curulis* from *currus* chariot (in which the chief magistrate was conveyed to the seat of office)]

curv·aceous /kɜːrˈveɪʃəs/ *adjective informal* (esp. of a woman) having a shapely figure with voluptuous breasts and hips.

curva·ture /ˈkɜːrvətʃər/ *noun* **1** the act or state of curving. **2** a curved form. **3** *Math.* **a** the deviation of a curve from a straight line, or of a curved surface from a plane. **b** the quantity expressing this. [Old French from Latin *curvatura* (as CURVE)]

curve ● *noun* **1** a line or surface having along its length a regular deviation from being straight or flat, as exemplified by the surface of a sphere or lens. **2** a curved form or thing. **3** a curved line on a graph. **4** (also **curve·ball**) **a** *Baseball* a ball pitched so that it curves away from the side from which it was thrown. **b** something unexpected or unsettling. **5 a** a curved line on a graph illustrating a tendency. **b** a tendency which could be plotted on a graph as a curve. ● *transitive & intransitive verb* **1** bend or shape so as to form a curve. **2** move or send along a curved path. □ **throw a person a curve** *see* THROW. □ **curved** *adjective* [originally as adj. (in *curve line*) from Latin *curvus* bent: (v.) from Latin *curvare*]

curvi- *combining form* curved. [Latin *curvus* curved]

curvi·foli·ate /ˌkɜːrvɪˈfoʊliət/ *adjective Bot.* with the leaves bent back.

curvi·form *adjective* having a curved shape.

curvi·linear /ˌkɜːrvɪˈlɪniər/ *adjective* contained by or consisting of curved lines. [CURVI- after *rectilinear*]

curvy *adjective* (**curv·i·er**, **curv·i·est**) **1** having many curves. **2** (of a woman's figure) shapely. □ **curv·i·ness** *noun*

cus·cus¹ /ˈkʌskəs/ *noun* the aromatic fibrous root of an Indian grass, *Vetiveria zizanioides*, used for making fans etc. [Persian *kaškaš*]

cus·cus² /ˈkʌskəs/ *noun* any of several nocturnal, usu. arboreal, marsupial mammals of the genus *Phalanger*, native to New Guinea and N Australia. [French *couscous* from Dutch *koeskoes* from native Moluccas name]

cu·sec /ˈkjuːsek/ *noun* a unit of flow (esp. of water) equal to one cubic foot per second. [abbreviation]

Cush /kʊʃ/ **1** in the Bible, the eldest son of Ham and grandson of Noah (Gen. 10:6). **2** the southern part of ancient Nubia, first mentioned in Egyptian records of the Middle Kingdom (see EGYPT). In the Bible it is the country of the descendants of Cush.

Cush·ing's disease /ˈkʊʃɪŋz/ *noun Med.* Cushing's syndrome as often caused by a tumour of the pituitary gland. [H.W. Cushing, US neurosurgeon d.1939]

Cush·ing's syndrome *noun Med.* a metabolic disorder caused by overactivity of the adrenal cortex, often involving obesity and hypertension and occurring when large doses of steroids are used over an extended period of time. [H.W. Cushing, US neurosurgeon d.1939]

cush·ion /ˈkʊʃən/ ● *noun* **1** a pad or bag of cloth etc. stuffed with a mass of soft material and used as a soft support for sitting etc. **2** a means of protection against shock, jarring, etc. **3** a buffer of savings, time, etc. or (in sports) a comfortable lead in score meant to mitigate the effects of difficulty, possible future distress, etc. (*a financial cushion*). **4** the rubber rim of a billiard table, from which the ball rebounds. **5** a body of air supporting a hovercraft etc. ● *transitive verb* **1** provide or protect with a cushion or cushions. **2** provide with a defence; protect. **3** mitigate the adverse effects of (*cushioned the blow*). □ **cush·ioned** *adjective* **cush·ion·ing** *noun* **cush·iony** *adjective* [Old French *co(i)ssin* from Gallo-Roman from Latin *culcita* mattress, cushion]

Cush·itic /kʊˈʃɪtɪk/ ● *noun* an Afro-Asiatic language family of NE Africa, including Somali, Galla, and other languages of Somalia and Ethiopia. ● *adjective* designating, of, or pertaining to this group. [*Cush* an ancient country in the Nile valley + -ITE¹ + -IC]

cushy /ˈkʊʃi/ *adjective* (**cush·i·er**, **cush·i·est**) *informal* **1** (of a job etc.) easy and pleasant. **2** *N Amer.* (of a seat, surroundings, etc.) soft, comfortable. □ **cush·i·ness** *noun* [Anglo-Indian from Hindustani *khūsh* pleasant]

cusk /kʌsk/ *noun N Amer.* an important food fish of the cod family. [origin unknown]

cusp *noun* **1** an apex or peak. **2** the horn of a crescent moon etc. **3** *Astrology* the zodiacal degree which marks the initial point of an astrological house. **4** *Archit.* a projecting point between adjacent small arcs in Gothic tracery, arches, etc. **5** *Math.* the point at which two arcs meet from the same direction terminating with a common tangent. **6** *Bot.* a pointed end, esp. of a leaf. **7** a cone-shaped prominence on the surface of a tooth esp. a molar or premolar. **8** a pocket or fold in a valve of the heart. □ **on the cusp** (usu. foll. by *of*) at a point marking a change in condition etc. (*on the cusp of burnout*). □ **cus·pate** /ˈkʌspeit/ *adjective* **cusped** *adjective* [Latin *cuspis, -idis* point, apex]

cus·pi·dor /ˈkʌspɪˌdɔr/ *noun* esp. *US* a spittoon. [Portuguese, = spitter, from *cuspir* spit, from Latin *conspuere*]

cuss *informal* ● *noun* **1** an obscene or profane expression; a curse. **2** usu. *derogatory* a strange and obstinate person or creature (*a tenacious cuss*). ● *verb* **1** *intransitive* swear, use profanity; curse. **2** *transitive* swear at, curse. [var. of CURSE]

cuss·ed /ˈkʌsɪd/ *adjective informal* awkward and stubborn. □ **cuss·ed·ly** *adverb* **cuss·ed·ness** *noun* [var. of CURSED]

cuss word *noun* *N Amer. informal* a profane, obscene, or indecent expression; a swear word.

cus·tard *noun* **1** (also **baked custard**) a baked dish made with milk and eggs, usu. sweetened. **2** (*N Amer.* **custard sauce**) a sweet sauce or filling of sweetened, flavoured milk, and thickened with eggs or cornstarch. □ **cus·tardy** *adjective* [Middle English, earlier *crustarde* from Anglo-French from Old French *crouste* CRUST]

custard apple *noun* a W Indian fruit, *Annona reticulata*, with a custard-like pulp.

custard cup *noun* a small heatproof bowl used for baking individual servings of egg custard.

custard pie *noun* **1** a pie with a custard filling. **2** *Brit.* (*attributive*) denoting slapstick comedy.

custard powder *noun* a preparation of cornstarch and flavourings for thickening milk to make a custard sauce.

Cus·ter, George Arm·strong (1839–76), US cavalry general. He served with distinction in the American Civil War, but is remembered for the controversial battle in which he and his forces were killed by the Sioux at Little Bighorn, Montana (1876).

cus·tod·ial /kʌˈstoːdiəl/ *adjective* **1** relating to legal custody or guardianship (*custodial parent*). **2** of or pertaining to the work of a caretaker or janitor. **3** of or pertaining to imprisonment or forcible institutionalization (*a custodial sentence*).

cus·tod·ian /kʌˈstoːdiən/ *noun* **1** a person who has custody of and responsibility for another person, a thing, etc. **2** *N Amer.* a person responsible for maintaining a building etc.; a caretaker, a janitor. □ **cus·tod·ian·ship** *noun* [CUSTODY + -AN, after *guardian*]

cus·tody /ˈkʌstədi/ *noun* **1 a** a legal guardianship, esp. of a minor (*they had joint custody of the child*). **b** safekeeping, protective care. **2** (often prec. by *in* or *into*) the charge or keeping of the police; imprisonment (*the accused remains in custody*). □ **take into custody** arrest. [Latin *custodia* from *custos -odis* guardian]

cus·tom ● *noun* **1 a** the usual way of behaving or acting (*a slave to custom*). **b** a particular, established way of behaving (*our customs seem strange to foreigners*). **2** *Law* established usage having the force of law. **3 a** habitual business patronage (*all the shops wanted our custom*). **b** regular dealings or customers (*lost a lot of custom*). **4** (in *pl.*; also treated as *sing.*) **a** a duty levied on certain imported and exported goods. **b** the official department that administers this. **c** the area at an airport, border, etc. where customs officials deal with incoming goods, baggage, etc. ● *adjective* CUSTOM-MADE. [Old French *custume*, ultimately from Latin *consuetudo -dinis*: see CONSUETUDE]

custom adoption *noun* (among aboriginal peoples) the adoption of a child in accordance with the customs of the native people.

cus·tom·ary *adjective* **1** usual, commonly done; in accordance with custom. **2** *Law* in accordance with custom rather than common law or statute. □ **cus·tom·ar·i·ly** *adverb*

cus·tom·er *noun* **1** a person who buys goods or services from a store or business. **2** a person one has to deal with (*one tough customer*).

custom house *noun* (also **customs house**) esp. *hist.* the office at a port of frontier where customs duty is collected.

cus·tom·ize *transitive verb* (also esp. *Brit.* **-ise**) make to order or modify according to individual requirements. □ **cus·tom·iz·abil·ity** *noun* **cus·tom·iz·able** *adjective* **cus·tom·iz·a·tion** *noun* **cust·om·ized** *adjective*

custom-made *adjective* (also **custom-built** etc.) made to an individual customer's order or specifications.

customs broker *noun* a person or company that clears goods through customs for a shipper or importer.

customs house *noun* (also **custom house**) the government office at an airport, border, etc. at which customs duties are levied.

customs union *noun* a group of countries with an agreed common tariff, and usu. free trade with each other.

cut ● *verb* (**cut·ting**; *past* and *past participle* **cut**) **1** *transitive & intransitive* penetrate or wound with a sharp-edged instrument (*cut his finger*; *the knife won't cut*). **2** *transitive & intransitive* (often foll. by *into*) divide or be divided with a knife etc. (*cut the bread*; *cut the cloth into metre lengths*). **3** *transitive* **a** trim or reduce the length of (hair, a hedge, etc.) by cutting. **b** divide (what grows) with an edged instrument to take the part detached; mow (grass), hew (timber), etc. **4** *transitive* (foll. by *loose, open,* etc.) make loose, open, etc. by cutting. **5** *transitive* (esp. as **cut·ting** *adjective*) cause sharp physical or mental pain to (*a cutting remark*; *was cut to the quick*; *a cutting wind*). **6** *transitive* (often foll. by *back* or *down*) **a** reduce (wages, time, etc.). **b** reduce or cease (services etc.). **7** *transitive* **a** shape or fashion (a gem, key, etc.) by cutting. **b** make (a path, tunnel, etc.) by removing material. **8** *transitive* perform, execute, make (*cut a caper*; *cut a sorry figure*). **9** *transitive & intransitive* cross, intersect (*the line cuts the circle at two points*; *the two lines cut*). **10** *intransitive* (foll. by *across, through,* etc.) pass or traverse, esp. in a hurry or as a shorter way (*cut across the grass*). **11** *transitive* **a** ignore or refuse to recognize (a person). **b** renounce (a connection). **12** *transitive* esp. *N Amer.* deliberately fail to attend (a class etc.). **13** *Cards* **a** *transitive* divide (a pack) into two parts. **b** *intransitive* select a dealer etc. by dividing the pack. **14** *Film* **a** *transitive* edit (a film or tape). **b** *intransitive* (often in *imperative*) stop filming or recording. **c** *intransitive* (foll. by *to*) go quickly to (another shot). **15** *transitive* switch off (an engine etc.). **16** *transitive* hit (a ball) with a chopping or glancing motion, esp. so as to change its direction. **17** *transitive* esp. *N Amer.* dilute, adulterate. **18 a** *transitive* remove (lines etc.) from a text; edit, abridge. **b** *transitive* *Computing* remove (information, esp. text) for placing elsewhere in a file etc. **19** *transitive* dissolve, clean away (*cut the grease*). **20** *intransitive* swerve sharply; make a sudden turn or change in direction (*cut left*). **21** *transitive* (of a performer etc.) make (a recording) (*cut their first album*). **22** *transitive* *Cooking* (usu. foll. by *into*) incorporate (fat into flour) by cutting into increasingly small pieces. **23** *transitive* castrate. **24** *transitive* *slang* slash or stab with a knife. **25** *transitive* *N Amer.* issue (a cheque). ● *adjective* **1** divided or separated into pieces (*cover with cut grass*). **2** *Art* made, fashioned, etc. by cutting, grinding, etc. (*cut glass*). **3** lowered or reduced (*cut-price competitors*). **4** gelded or castrated. **5** esp. *Brit. slang* drunk. **6** *slang* (of a person's body) having well defined musculature. ● *noun* **1** an act of cutting. **2** a division or wound made by cutting. **3** a stroke with a knife, sword, whip, etc. **4 a** a reduction (in prices, wages, etc.). **b** a cessation (of a power supply etc.). **5 a** an excision of part of a play, film, etc. **b** an abrupt transition between film shots, achieved by splicing two distinct shots together. **c** an edited version of a film (*the director's cut*). **d** a single song, piece, etc. on an album, CD, etc. **6** a wounding remark or act. **7** the way or style in which a garment, the hair, etc., is cut. **8** a piece of meat cut from a carcass. **9** *informal* commission; a share of profits. **10 a** *Sport* an exclusion from a team, tournament, etc. (*the final cuts will be made Friday*). **b** *Tennis* etc. a stroke made by cutting. **11** ignoring of or refusal to recognize a person. **12 a** an engraved block for printing. **b** = WOODCUT 1, 2. **13 a** a railway cutting. **b** a passage cut through rock or gravel in building a road, canal, etc. **14** a new channel made for a river. **15** a quantity of a crop, esp. timber, cut in a season. □ **a cut above** *informal* noticeably superior to. **cut a deal** *informal* come to an agreement, esp. in business; make a deal. **cut along** run along. **be cut out** (foll. by *for*, or *to* + infin.) be suited (*was not cut out to be a teacher*). **cut across 1** transcend or take no account of (normal limitations etc.) (*their concerns cut across normal rivalries*). **2** see sense 10 of *verb*. **cut and dried 1** completely decided; pre-arranged; inflexible. **2** (of opinions etc.) ready-made, lacking freshness. **cut and run** *slang* depart hurriedly, esp. irresponsibly. **cut and thrust** a lively interchange of argument etc. **cut back 1** reduce (expenditure etc.). **2** prune (a tree etc.). **3** *Film* repeat part of a previous scene for dramatic effect. **cut both ways 1** serve both sides of an argument etc. **2** (of an action) have both good and bad effects. **cut the cheese** *slang* break wind. **cut one's coat according to one's cloth 1** adapt expenditure to resources. **2** limit ambition to what is feasible. **cut a corner** go across and not around a corner. **cut corners** do a task etc. perfunctorily or incompletely, esp. to save time or money. **cut down 1 a** bring or throw down by cutting. **b** kill, disable; defeat, ruin (*cut down in battle*). **2** see sense 6 of *verb*. **3** reduce the length of (*cut down the trousers to make shorts*). **4** (often foll. by *on*) reduce one's consumption (*try to cut down on beer*). **cut a person down to size** *informal* ruthlessly expose the limitations of a person's importance, ability, etc. **cut one's eye teeth** attain experience and some sophistication. **cut from the same cloth** of the same nature; alike. **cut in 1** interrupt. **2** pull in too closely in front of another vehicle (esp. having passed it). **3** give a share of profits etc. to (a person).

4 connect (a source of electricity, etc.). **5** join in a card game by taking the place of a player who cuts out. **6** interrupt a dancing couple to take over from one partner. **cut into 1 a** make a cut in (*they cut into the cake*). **b** divide (*cut the board into smaller pieces*). **2** interfere with and reduce (*travelling cuts into my free time*). **cut it fine** see FINE[1]. **cut it** *N Amer. informal* function or perform adequately (*couldn't cut it in the big leagues*). **cut it out** (usu. in *imperative*) *informal* stop doing something. **cut the (Gordian) knot** solve a problem in an irregular but efficient way. **cut loose 1** begin to act freely. **2** see sense 4 of *verb*. **cut one's losses** (or **a loss**) abandon an unprofitable enterprise before losses become too great. **cut the mustard** *esp. N Amer. slang* reach the required standard. **cut no ice** *slang* **1** have no influence or importance. **2** achieve little or nothing. **cut off 1** remove (an appendage) by cutting. **2 a** (often in *passive*) bring to an abrupt end or (esp. early) death. **b** intercept, interrupt; prevent from continuing (*cut off supplies; cut off the gas*). **c** interfere with the progress of, esp. by abruptly pulling one's vehicle into another's lane of traffic. **d** disconnect (esp. a person engaged in a telephone conversation). **3 a** prevent from travelling or venturing out (*was cut off by the snow*). **b** (as **cut off** *adjective*) isolated, remote (*felt cut off in the country*). **4** disinherit (*was cut off without a penny*). **cut out 1** remove from the inside by cutting. **2** make by cutting from a larger whole. **3** omit; leave out (*cut him out of our loop*). **4** *informal* stop doing or using (something) (*managed to cut out chocolate; let's cut out the arguing*). **5** cease or cause to cease functioning (*the engine cut out*). **6** *N Amer. informal* leave (*let's cut out of here*). **7** *N Amer.* detach (an animal) from the herd. **cut short 1** interrupt; terminate prematurely (*cut short his visit*). **2** make shorter or more concise. **cut a** (or **the**) **rug** *N Amer. slang* dance, esp. ballroom dance. **cut (a person) some slack** *N Amer. slang* allow an individual some leeway in conduct, performance, etc. **cut one's teeth on** acquire initial practice or experience from (something). **cut a tooth** have it appear through the gum. **cut to the bone 1** reduce (expenditures) to a minimum. **2** chill thoroughly (*the wind cut to the bone*). **cut to the chase** *N Amer.* come to the point. **cut up 1** cut into pieces. **2** slash, wound, etc. (*we were all cut up and bruised*). **3** (usu. in *passive*) distress greatly (*was very cut up about it*). **4** criticize severely. **5** *N Amer.* behave in a comical or unruly manner. **cut up rough** *Brit. slang* show anger or resentment. **have one's work cut out** see WORK. **make the cut** *informal* **1** be selected for a team, short list, etc. **2** achieve a specified status, condition, etc. [Middle English *cutte, kitte, kette,* perhaps from Old English *cyttan* (unrecorded)]

cut-and-paste *noun* the process of assembling text by adding or combining sections from other texts.

cu·ta·neous /kjuːˈteɪniəs/ *adjective* of the skin. [modern Latin *cutaneus* from Latin *cutis* skin]

cut·away ● *adjective* **1** (of a diagram etc.) with some parts left out to reveal the interior. **2** (of a coat) with the front below the waist cut away. **3** *Film* designating a shot filmed separately from the shot to which it is later joined in editing. ● *noun* a cutaway graphic, garment, shot, etc.

cut·back *noun* an instance or the act of cutting back, esp. a reduction in expenditure.

cut·bank *noun* *N Amer.* a steep cliff or riverbank resulting from erosion.

cut·block *noun* **1** an area with defined boundaries authorized for logging. **2** *Football* a tackle at or below the knees.

cut-down *adjective* that has been reduced, esp. in length (*a cut-down raincoat; a cut-down version of the play*).

cute *adjective* *informal* **1** esp. *N Amer.* **a** attractive. **b** quaintly or affectedly attractive. **c** endearing, charming. **2** clever, ingenious, shrewd. □ **cute·ly** *adverb* **cute·ness** *noun* [shortening of ACUTE]

cutesy *adjective* dainty or quaint to an affected degree.

cutesy-poo *adjective* *slang* cutesy. [*poo* perhaps alteration of *pie* (as in CUTIE-PIE) with assimilation to the vowel in *cute*]

cut fastball *noun* *Baseball* a fastball thrown with a slight side spin, causing the ball to move in or out.

cut flowers *noun* flowers that have been cut for use in bouquets etc. but not arranged.

cut glass *noun* glass with patterns and designs cut or ground on it.

cu·ticle /ˈkjuːtɪkəl/ *noun* **1** the dead skin at the base of a fingernail or toenail. **2** the outer cellular layer of a hair. **3** the epidermis. **4** *Bot. & Zool.* the outer layer of an organism, esp. a protective often waxy layer covering the epidermis of a plant or invertebrate. □ **cu·ticu·lar** /-ˈtɪkjʊlər/ *adjective* [Latin *cuticula,* diminutive of *cutis* skin]

cutie *noun* *slang* an attractive person.

cutie-pie *noun* **1** *informal* darling, sweetheart. **2** an attractive person, animal, etc.

cut-in *noun* something that is cut in, esp. an interposed scene in film.

cutis /ˈkjuːtɪs/ *noun* *Anat.* the skin; the dermis. [Latin, = skin]

Cut Knife a town in west central Saskatchewan, northwest of Saskatoon; pop. (2001) 556. It was the site of a battle during the Northwest Rebellion (1885), in which a group of Cree and Assiniboine defeated a force of some 300 soldiers. [after a Sarcee warrior killed there]

cut·lass /ˈkʌtləs/ *noun* a short sword with a slightly curved blade, esp. of the type formerly used by sailors. [French *coutelas,* ultimately from Latin *cultellus* 'small knife': see CUTLER]

cut·ler *noun* a person who makes or deals in knives and similar utensils. [Old French *coutelier* from *coutel* from Latin *cultellus* diminutive of *culter* knife]

cut·lery *noun* knives, forks, and spoons for use at the table. [Old French *coutel(l)erie* (as CUTLER)]

cut·let *noun* **1** a small, thin piece of boneless veal etc. usu. served fried. **2** a flat patty of ground meat or nuts and bread crumbs etc. **3** *Brit.* a chop from the neck of mutton or lamb. [French *côtelette,* Old French *costelet* diminutive of *coste* rib, from Latin *costa*]

cut·lette *noun* *Cdn* a roughly oval-shaped, breaded patty of finely chopped meat.

cut·line *noun* **1** a caption to an illustration. **2** a line marked on wood etc. that indicates where a cut should be made (*score your cutline with a utility knife*). **3** *Cdn* a line cut through the bush, e.g. as a survey line, etc.

cut-off *noun* **1** the point at which something is cut off. **2** a device for stopping a flow. **3** (in *pl.*) esp. *N Amer.* shorts, esp. made from cut-down jeans. **4** (often *attributive*) a time or point of demarcation after which some action is no longer possible, effective, etc. (*the cut-off date for applications*). **5** *Baseball* (usu. *attributive*) the interception by an infielder of a ball thrown from outfield, e.g. to relay the ball to home plate. **6** *N Amer.* a road to a specific town etc. which turns off a larger thoroughfare. **7** *N Amer.* a shortcut.

cut-out ● *noun* **1 a** a figure cut out of paper etc. **b** a person, personality, etc. so little differentiated from the majority that it seems of a piece with it (*the characters in the novel are cardboard cut-outs*). **2** a device for automatic disconnection, the release of exhaust gases, etc. ● *adjective* of or like CUT-OUT 1.

cut·over ● *adjective* (of timberland etc.) having had the saleable timber felled and removed. ● *noun* cutover land.

cut·purse *noun* *archaic* a pickpocket; a thief.

cut-rate *adjective* (also **cut-price**) selling or sold at a reduced price.

cut·ter *noun* **1** a person or thing that cuts, esp. a person who takes measurements and cuts cloth, as a tailor, costumer, etc. **2** *Naut.* **a** a small, fast sailing ship. **b** a small, lightly armed government vessel (*a Coast Guard cutter*). **3** *N Amer.* a light horse-drawn sleigh.

cutter bar *noun* a horizontal bar in a mower or combine on which a sharp blade or blades operate.

cut·throat ● *noun* **1** a murderer. **2** *Brit.* (in full **cutthroat razor**) = STRAIGHT RAZOR. **3** (also **cutthroat trout**) a species of trout, *Salmo clarki,* with an orange or red mark under the jaw. ● *adjective* **1** (of competition) ruthless and intense. **2** (of a card game) having three or more players in which each scores individually (*cutthroat poker*).

cut time *noun* *N Amer. Music* a time signature indicating 2 or 4 half note beats in a bar; alla breve.

cut·ting ● *noun* **1** a piece or section cut from something. **2** a piece cut from a plant for propagation. **3** *Brit.* = CLIPPING 1. **4** an excavated channel through high ground for a railway or road. **5** *N Amer. Forestry* **a** a stand of timber. **b** the site of a logging operation. ● *adjective* causing sharp physical or mental pain (*a cutting remark*). □ **cut·ting·ly** *adverb*

cutting edge ● *noun* **1** an edge that cuts. **2** the forefront of a movement etc. ● *attributive adjective* (**cutting-edge**) pioneering, innovative.

cutting horse *noun* *N Amer.* a saddle horse trained to separate individual cows, calves, etc. from a herd.

cutting room *noun* *Film* a room where film is cut and edited. □ **left on the cutting-room floor** (esp. of film, recorded music, etc.) rejected during the editing process.

cut·tle *noun* = CUTTLEFISH. [Old English *cudele,* Middle English *codel,* related to *cod* bag, with reference to its ink bag]

cuttle·bone *noun* the internal shell of the cuttlefish crushed and used as a supplement to the diet of a cage bird.

cuttle·fish *noun* any of various marine cephalopods of the genus Sepia or order Sepioidea, having an elongated body with an undulating lateral fin, ten arms, a cuttlebone, and the habit of ejecting a black fluid when alarmed.

cut-up *noun* *esp. N Amer.* a person who plays the fool; a prankster.

cut·water *noun* **1** the forward edge of a ship's prow. **2** a wedge-shaped projection from a pier or bridge, serving to divide the current, break up ice, etc.

cut·work *noun* **1** embroidery or lace with parts cut out and the edges oversewn or filled with needlework designs. **2** work produced by cutting or carving.

cut·worm *noun* any of various caterpillars that eat through the stems of young plants level with the ground.

cu·vée /kuː'veɪ/ *noun* a blend or batch of wine. [French, = quantify filling a vat, from *cuve* cask, from Latin *cupa*]

cu·vette /kjuː'vet/ *noun* **1** a shallow vessel for liquid. **2** a straight-sided transparent container for holding a liquid sample in a spectrophotometer etc. [French, diminutive of *cuve* cask, from Latin *cupa*]

Cu·vier /'kuːviˌeɪ/ **Georges, Baron** (1769–1832), French naturalist, who pioneered the sciences of paleontology and comparative anatomy through his study of fossil elephants and classification of the lower invertebrates.

cuz¹ *conjunction* *slang* because.

cuz² *noun* *slang* cousin.

Cuzco /'kuskoː/ a city in the Andes in S Peru; pop. (est. 2002) 282,600. It was the capital of the Inca Empire until the Spanish conquest in 1533.

CV *abbreviation* **1** (in Canada) CROSS OF VALOUR. **2** (*pl.* **CVs**) CURRICULUM VITAE.

CVA *abbreviation* current value assessment.

CVI *abbreviation* *Cdn* = COLLEGIATE AND VOCATIONAL INSTITUTE.

CVS *abbreviation* CHORIONIC VILLUS SAMPLING.

C.V.S.M. *abbreviation* Canadian Volunteer Service Medal.

CWAC /kwak/ *abbreviation* *hist.* **1** Canadian Women's Army Corps. **2** a member of this.

CWB *abbreviation* Canadian Wheat Board (*see* WHEAT BOARD).

CWL *abbreviation* Catholic Women's League.

cwm /kuːm/ *noun* **1** (in Wales) = COOMB. **2** *Geog.* a cirque. [Welsh]

CWO *abbreviation* CHIEF WARRANT OFFICER.

CWS *abbreviation* Canadian Wildlife Service.

cwt. *abbreviation* hundredweight.

-cy *suffix* (*see also* -ACY, -ANCY, -CRACY, -ENCY, -MANCY). **1** denoting state or condition (*bankruptcy*; *idiocy*). **2** denoting rank or status (*captaincy*). [from or after Latin -*cia*, -*tia*, Greek -*k(e)ia*, -*t(e)ia*]

cyan /'saɪan/ ● *adjective* of a greenish-blue. ● *noun* a greenish-blue colour. [Greek *kuan(e)os* dark blue]

cy·ana·mide /saɪ'anəˌmaɪd/ *noun* *Chem.* **1** a colourless crystalline amide of cyanogen; Chem. formula: CH_2N_2. **2** any salt of this, esp. the calcium one which is used as a fertilizer. [CYANOGEN + AMIDE]

cyan·ic acid /saɪ'anɪk/ *noun* an unstable colourless pungent acid gas. Chem. formula: HCNO. [CYANOGEN]

cyan·ide /'saɪəˌnaɪd/ *noun* any of the highly poisonous salts or esters of hydrocyanic acid. [CYANOGEN + -IDE]

cyano- *combining form* **1** relating to the colour blue, esp. dark blue (*cyanosis*). **2** representing CYANIDE. [Greek *kuan(e)os* 'dark blue']

cyano·acryl·ate /ˌsaɪəˌnoːˈakrɪleɪt/ *noun* any of a class of compounds which are cyanide derivatives of acrylates. They are easily polymerized and are used to make quick-setting adhesives.

cyano·bac·teria /ˌsaɪəˌnoːbakˈtɪːriə/ *plural noun* (*sing.* **-bac·terium** /-riəm/) any prokaryotic organisms of the division Cyanobacteria, found in many environments and capable of photosynthesizing. *Also called* BLUE-GREEN ALGAE. □ **cyano·bacter·ial** *adjective*

cyano·co·bal·amin /ˌsaɪəˌnoːkəˈbaləmɪn/ *noun* a vitamin of the B complex, found in foods of animal origin such as liver, fish, and eggs, a deficiency of which can cause pernicious anemia. *Also called* VITAMIN B_{12}. [CYANOGEN + cobalamin from COBALT + VITAMIN]

cy·ano·gen /saɪ'anədʒən/ *noun* *Chem.* a colourless highly poisonous gas intermediate in the preparation of many fertilizers. Chem. formula: C_2N_2. [French *cyanogène* from Greek *kuanos* dark blue mineral, as being a constituent of Prussian blue]

cy·ano·gen·ic /ˌsaɪənoːˈdʒenɪk/ *adjective* capable of providing cyanide.

cyan·o·sis /ˌsaɪə'noːsɪs/ *noun* *Med.* a bluish discoloration of the skin due to the presence of oxygen-deficient blood. □ **cyan·otic** /-'nɒtɪk/ *adjective*

Cybele /'sɪbɪli/ *Myth* a mother goddess worshipped esp. in Phrygia and later in Greece (where she was associated with Demeter), Rome, and the Roman provinces, with her consort Attis.

cyber- /'saɪbər/ *combining form* of computers, esp. pertaining to artificial intelligence, electronic communication, or virtual reality. [back-formation from CYBERNETICS]

cyber·café *noun* = INTERNET CAFÉ.

cyber·crime *noun* crime or a crime committed using computers or the Internet. □ **cyber·crim·in·al** *noun*

cyber·culture *noun* the social conditions brought about by computerization and the Internet; computers and the Internet viewed as a cultural phenomenon.

Cy·ber·ia /ˌsaɪ'bɪːriə/ *noun* the notional environment within which electronic communication occurs; the space of virtual reality, esp. viewed as a 'global village' or sphere of human interaction; cyberspace. □ **Cy·ber·ian** *noun & adjective* [CYBER- + -IA¹, punningly after SIBERIA]

cyber·net·ics /ˌsaɪbər'netɪks/ *plural noun* (usu. treated as *sing.*) the science of communications and automatic control systems in both machines and living things. □ **cyber·net·ic** *adjective* **cyber·net·ic·ally** *adverb* **cyber·net·ician** /-'tɪʃən/ *noun* **cyber·neti·cist** /-sɪst/ *noun* [Greek *kubernētēs* steersman]

cyber·punk /'saɪbərpʌŋk/ *noun* **1** a style of science fiction featuring urban counterculture in a world of high technology and virtual reality. **2** *Computing* *slang* a highly proficient hacker; CRACKER 6. [CYBERNETICS + PUNK]

cyber·sex *noun* sexual arousal or simulated intercourse using computer technology, esp. by wearing virtual reality equipment, or by exchanging messages with another person via the Internet.

cyber·space *noun* **1** the forum in which the global electronic communications network operates. **2** *Computing* the electronic realm in which virtual reality is experienced.

cyber·squat·ter *noun* a person who registers well-known company or brand etc. names as Internet domain names, in the hope of later selling them back to the brand owner at a profit. □ **cyber·squat·ting** *noun*

cyber·stalk·ing *noun* the repeated use of electronic communications to harass or frighten someone, e.g. by sending threatening emails.

cyber·terror·ism *noun* terrorist acts consisting of hacking into a computer network, e.g. one belonging to the armed forces, a government, a utility, etc. to cause widespread havoc. □ **cyber·terror·ist** *noun & adjective*

cyber·war *noun* a conflict in which enemies attempt to hack into each other's computer networks to disrupt communications, shut down systems, steal information, etc.

cy·borg /'saɪbɔrg/ *noun* a person whose physical abilities are extended beyond normal human limitations by machine technology (as yet undeveloped). [CYBERNETIC + ORGANISM]

cycad /'saɪkad/ *noun* any of the palm-like plants of the order Cycadales (including fossil forms) inhabiting tropical and subtropical regions and often growing to a great height. [modern Latin *cycas*, *cycad-* from supposed Greek *kukas*, scribal error for *koîkas*, pl. of *koíx* Egyptian palm]

Cycla·des /'sɪkləˌdiːz/ a large group of islands in the S Aegean Sea, regarded in antiquity as circling around the sacred island of Delos. The Cyclades form a department of modern Greece.

Cy·clad·ic /saɪ'kladɪk, sɪ-/ *adjective* of the Cyclades, esp. of the Bronze Age civilization that flourished there.

cycla·mate /'saɪkləˌmeɪt, 'sɪk-/ *noun* any of various compounds formerly used as artificial sweetening agents. [abbreviation of chemical name *cyclohexylsulphamate*]

cycla·men /'sɪkləmən/ *noun* **1** any plant of the genus *Cyclamen*, originating in Europe, having pink, red, or white flowers with reflexed petals, often grown as a houseplant. **2** the shade of colour of the red or pink cyclamen flower. [medieval Latin from Greek *kuklaminos*, perhaps from *kuklos* circle, with reference to its bulbous roots]

cycle ● *noun* **1 a** a recurrent series or period (of events, phenomena, etc.). **b** the time needed for one such series or period. **2 a** *Physics etc.* a recurrent series of operations or states. **b** *Electricity* = HERTZ. **3** a series of songs, poems, etc., usu. on a single theme. **4** a bicycle, tricycle, or similar machine. **5** *Computing* **a** (in full **cycle time**) the time required for one cycle of the memory system. **b** a set of operations which is repeated regularly and in the same sequence. ● *intransitive verb* **1** ride a bicycle etc. **2** move in cycles. **hit for the cycle** *Baseball* hit a single, a double, a triple, and a home run all in the same game. [Old French from Late Latin *cyclus* from Greek *kuklos* circle]

cyclic /'saɪklɪk, 'sɪk-/ *adjective* **1 a** recurring or revolving in cycles.

b belonging to a chronological cycle. **c** of, pertaining to, or characterized by cycles. **2** *Chem.* with constituent atoms forming a ring. **3** of a cycle of songs, legends, etc. **4** *Bot.* (of a flower) with its parts arranged in whorls. **5** *Math.* **a** of a circle or other closed curve. **b** (of a group) having the property that each element of the group can be expressed as a power of one particular element.

cyclic·al /ˈsaɪklɪkəl, ˈsɪk-/ ● *adjective* = CYCLIC 1. ● *noun* (usu. in *pl.*) industries, companies, etc. that are heavily dependent on global economic circumstances for their success. □ **cyclic·al·ly** *adverb*

cyc·ling *noun* **1** travelling or touring on a bicycle etc. **2** the sport of bicycle racing, usu. on a lightweight bicycle with low handlebars. **3** the act of moving in cycles.

cycling shorts *noun* = BICYCLE SHORTS.

cyc·list *noun* a rider of a bicycle.

cyclo- /ˈsaɪkləʊ/ *combining form* circle, cycle, or cyclic (*cyclometer*; *cyclorama*). [Greek *kuklos* circle]

cyclo·alkane /ˌsaɪkləʊˈalkeɪn/ *noun Chem.* a saturated cyclic hydrocarbon.

cyclo·cross /ˈsaɪkləʊˌkrɒs/ *noun* cross-country racing on bicycles.

cyclo·hex·ane /ˌsaɪkləʊˈhekseɪn/ *noun Chem.* a colourless liquid cycloalkane used as a solvent and paint remover. Chem. formula: C_6H_{12}.

cyc·loid /ˈsaɪklɔɪd/ *noun Math.* the path traced out by a point on a circle when the circle is rolled along a straight line. □ **cyc·loid·al** /-ˈklɔɪdəl/ *adjective*

cyc·lom·eter /saɪˈklɒmɪtər/ *noun* **1** an instrument for measuring circular arcs. **2** an instrument for measuring the distance traversed by a bicycle etc.

cy·clone /ˈsaɪkləʊn/ *noun* **1 a** a system of winds rotating inwards to an area of low barometric pressure; a depression. **b** a tornado. **2 a** (also **tropical cyclone**) a wind system of this kind formed in localized areas over tropical oceans, sometimes developing into a hurricane or typhoon. **b** such a wind system having hurricane-force winds, originating in the Indian Ocean. **3** a centrifugal machine for separating solids. □ **cy·clon·ic** /-ˈklɒnɪk/ *adjective* [prob. representing Greek *kuklōma* wheel, coil of a snake]

cyclo·par·af·fin /ˌsaɪkləʊˈparəfɪn/ *noun Chem.* = CYCLOALKANE.

cyclo·pean /ˌsaɪkləʊˈpiːən, -ˈklɔːpiən/ *adjective* (also **cyclo·pian**) **1** (of ancient masonry) made with massive irregular blocks. **2** (**Cyclopean**) of or resembling a Cyclops.

cyclo·pedia /ˌsaɪkləˈpiːdiə/ *noun* (also **cyclo·paedia**) an encyclopedia. □ **cyclo·ped·ic** *adjective* [shortening of ENCYCLOPEDIA]

cyclo·pro·pane /ˌsaɪkləʊˈprəʊpeɪn/ *noun Chem.* a colourless gaseous cycloalkane used as a general anaesthetic. Chem. formula: C_3H_6.

Cy·clops /ˈsaɪklɒps/ *noun* **1** (*pl.* **Cy·clops** or **Cy·clops·es** or **Cy·clo·pes** /saɪˈkləʊpiːz/) (in Greek mythology) a member of a race of one-eyed giants. **2** (**cyclops**) (*pl.* **cy·clops** or **cy·clo·pes**) a crustacean of the genus *Cyclops*, with a single central eye. [Latin from Greek *Kuklōps* from *kuklos* circle + *ōps* eye]

cyclo·rama /ˌsaɪkləʊˈrɑːmə/ *noun* a circular panorama, curved wall, or cloth at the rear of a stage, esp. one used to represent the sky. □ **cyclo·ram·ic** *adjective*

cyclo·sporin /ˌsaɪkləˈspɔrɪn/ *noun Med.* (also **cyclo·sporine**) a peptide drug used to prevent the rejection of grafts and transplants. [CYCLO- + -*sporum* part of the name of a fungus which produces it + -IN]

cyclo·stome /ˈsaɪkləˌstəʊm/ *noun* a fish of the former taxon Cyclostomata, which includes primitive forms (the lampreys and hagfishes) having a round sucking mouth. □ **cy·clos·tom·ate** /-ˈklɒstəmət/ *adjective* [CYCLO- + Greek *stoma* mouth]

cyclo·tron /ˈsaɪkləˌtrɒn/ *noun Physics* an apparatus in which charged atomic and subatomic particles are accelerated by an alternating electric field while following an outward spiral or circular path in a magnetic field.

cyg·net /ˈsɪɡnət/ *noun* a young swan. [Anglo-French *cignet* diminutive of Old French *cigne* swan, from medieval Latin *cycnus* from Greek *kuknos*]

Cyg·nus /ˈsɪɡnəs/ *noun* the Swan, a large constellation of the northern hemisphere in the Milky Way between Hercules and Pegasus. [Latin *cygnus* swan]

cyl. *abbreviation* CYLINDER.

cylin·der /ˈsɪlɪndər/ *noun* **1 a** a uniform solid or hollow body with straight sides and a circular section. **b** a thing of this shape, e.g. a container for liquefied gas. **2** a cylinder-shaped part of various machines, esp. a piston chamber in an engine. **3** a hollow metal roller used in printing for inking the type, carrying the type or printing surface, etc. **4** the rotating part of a revolver which houses the cartridge chambers. **5** a cylindrical record formerly used for a phonograph. □ **firing (or hitting, etc.) on all cylinders** working at peak efficiency and capacity. □ **cylin·dric·al** /-ˈlɪndrɪkəl/ *adjective* **cylin·dric·al·ly** *adverb* [Latin *cylindrus* from Greek *kulindros* from *kulindō* roll]

cylinder block *noun* esp. *Brit.* = ENGINE BLOCK.

cylinder head *noun* the end cover of a cylinder in an internal combustion engine, against which the piston compresses the cylinder contents.

cylinder saw *noun* a cylinder with a toothed edge for making a circular hole.

cylinder seal *noun* a small barrel-shaped object of stone or baked clay bearing a cuneiform inscription, esp. for use as a seal in Babylon, Assyria, etc.

cyma /ˈsaɪmə/ *noun* **1** *Archit.* an ogee moulding of a cornice. **2** = CYME. [modern Latin from Greek *kuma* wave, wavy moulding]

cym·bal /ˈsɪmbəl/ *noun* a musical instrument consisting of a concave brass or bronze plate, struck with another or with a stick etc. to make a ringing sound. □ **cym·bal·ist** *noun* [Latin *cymbalum* from Greek *kumbalon* from *kumbē* cup]

Cym·bel·ine /ˈsɪmbəˌliːn/ (also called **Cuno·bel·in·us** /ˌkjuːnəʊbəˈlaɪnəs/) (died *c*.42 AD), British chieftain. Ruler of the powerful Catuvellauni tribe of S England, he made Camulodunum (Colchester) his capital.

cym·bid·ium /sɪmˈbɪdiəm/ *noun* any tropical orchid of the genus *Cymbidium*, with a hollow recess in the flower lip. [modern Latin from Greek *kumbē* cup]

cyme /saɪm/ *noun* an inflorescence in which the primary axis bears a single terminal flower that develops first, the system being continued by the axes of secondary and higher orders each with a flower (compare RACEME). □ **cym·ose** *adjective* [French, var. of *cime* summit, ultimately from Greek *kuma* wave]

Cym·ric /ˈkɪmrɪk/ ● *adjective* Welsh in language or culture. ● *noun* the Welsh language. [Welsh *Cymru* Wales]

Cyne·wulf /ˈkɪnɪˌwʊlf/ (late 8th–9th c.), Anglo-Saxon poet, author of four extant poems in Old English, *Juliana*, *Elene*, *The Fates of the Apostles*, and *Christ II*, each of which is inscribed with his name in runes.

cyn·ic /ˈsɪnɪk/ ● *noun* **1** a person with little faith in human goodness who sarcastically doubts or despises sincerity and merit. **2** (**Cynic**) one of a school of ancient Greek philosophers founded by Antisthenes, marked by a belief in self-control as the essence of virtue and an ostentatious contempt for ease and pleasure. ● *adjective* **1** (**Cynic**) of the Cynics. **2** *archaic* = CYNICAL. □ **cyni·cism** /-ˌsɪzəm/ *noun* [Latin *cynicus* from Greek *kunikos* from *kuōn kunos* dog, nickname for a Cynic]

cyn·ic·al /ˈsɪnɪkəl/ *adjective* **1** of or characteristic of a cynic; incredulous of human goodness. **2** (of behaviour etc.) disregarding normal standards, esp. of morality. **3** sneering, mocking, sarcastic. □ **cyn·ic·al·ly** *adverb*

cyno·sure /ˈsɪnəˌʃʊr, ˈsaɪn-/ *noun* **1** a centre of attraction or admiration. **2** something that serves for guidance or direction. [French *cynosure* or Latin *cynosura* from Greek *kunosoura* dog's tail, Ursa Minor, from *kuōn kunos* dog + *oura* tail]

cy·pher *var. of* CIPHER.

cy pres /siː ˈpreɪ/ *Law* ● *noun* the principle of adhering as closely as possible to the testator's or donor's intentions when these cannot be precisely followed. ● *adverb & adjective* following as near as practicable. [Anglo-French, = *si près* so near]

cy·press /ˈsaɪprəs/ *noun* **1** any coniferous tree of the genus *Cupressus* or *Chamaecyparis*, with hard wood and dark foliage. **2** the wood of this tree. [Old French *cipres* from Late Latin *cypressus* from Greek *kuparissos*]

Cypress Hills a region of rolling uplands in SE Alberta and SW Saskatchewan, reaching a maximum elevation of 1 468 m. [so (erroneously) called with reference to its cypress-like trees (actually lodgepole pines)]

Cyp·rian, St. /ˈsɪpriən/ (*c*.200–258), Carthaginian bishop and martyr. The author of a work on the nature of true unity in the Church in its relation to the episcopate, he was martyred in the reign of the emperor Valerian. Feast day, 16 or 26 Sept.

cyp·rin·oid /ˈsɪprɪˌnɔɪd/ ● *adjective* of or like a carp. ● *noun* a carp or related fish. [Latin *cyprinus* from Greek *kuprinos* carp]

Cyp·ri·ot /ˈsɪpriət/ (also **Cyp·ri·ote** /-əʊt/) ● *noun* a native or national of Cyprus. ● *adjective* of Cyprus.

cypri·ped·ium /ˌsɪprɪˈpiːdiəm/ *noun* any orchid of the genus

Cypripedium, esp. the lady's slipper. [modern Latin from Greek *Kupris* Aphrodite + *pedilon* slipper]

Cy·prus /ˈsəiprəs/ an island in the E Mediterranean about 80 km (50 miles) south of the Turkish coast; pop. (est. 2002) 767,314; capital, Nicosia. Tension between Greek Cypriots (some of whom favour enosis or union with Greece) and Turkish Cypriots led to an invasion by Turkish forces of the northern part of the island in 1974. This became the Turkish Federated State of Cyprus in 1975, and proclaimed itself the independent Turkish Republic of Northern Cyprus in 1983, but has only been recognized by Turkey.

cyp·sela /ˈsɪpsələ/ *noun* (*pl.* **cyp·selae** /-ˌliː/) a dry single-seeded fruit formed from a double ovary of which only one develops into a seed, characteristic of the daisy family Compositae. [modern Latin from Greek *kupselē* hollow vessel]

Cyr /siːr/ **Louis** (1863–1912), Canadian strongman. Known as 'the strongest man in the world', he won the world championship in weightlifting (1892) and established several world records for strength and endurance in London, England (1892).

Cyr·ano de Ber·gerac /ˌsɪrənoː də ˈbɛrʒəˌrak/ **Savi·nien** (1619–55), French soldier and writer. He wrote comedies and satire, but is chiefly remembered for his proverbially large nose and the numerous duels that he fought.

Cy·ren·aic /saɪrəˈneɪɪk/ ● *adjective* of or denoting the hedonistic school of philosophy founded *c.* 400 BC by Aristippus the Elder of Cyrene which holds that pleasure is the highest good and that virtue is to be equated with the ability to enjoy. ● *noun* a follower of this school of philosophy.

Cy·rene /saɪˈriːni/ an ancient Greek city in North Africa, near the coast in Cyrenaica. From the 4th c. BC it was a great intellectual centre.

Cyril, St. /ˈsɪrəl/ (*c.*827–69), Greek missionary. The invention of the Cyrillic alphabet is ascribed to him; he and his brother St. Methodius (*c.*815–85) became known as the 'Apostles of the Slavs' for their work in Moravia. Feast day (in the Eastern Church) 11 May; (in the Western Church) 14 Feb.

Cyr·il·lic /ˈsɪˈrɪlɪk/ ● *adjective* denoting the alphabet derived from Greek, adapted by the Slavic peoples, and now used esp. for Russian and Bulgarian. ● *noun* this alphabet. [St. CYRIL]

Cyrus /ˈsaɪrəs/ **1 'the Great'** (d.529 BC), king of Persia 559–529 BC and founder of the Achaemenid dynasty. He became ruler of the Median Empire after the capture of King Astyages in 549 BC, and went on to conquer Asia Minor, Babylonia, Assyria, Syria, and Palestine. **2 Cyrus 'the Younger'** (d.401 BC), Persian prince, son of Darius II (who ruled over Persia 424–405 BC). On the death of his father (405 BC), Cyrus led an army of mercenaries against his elder brother, who had succeeded to the throne as Artaxerxes II; he was killed in battle north of Babylon.

cyst /sɪst/ *noun* **1** *Med.* an abnormal sac containing fluid, pus, etc. **2** *Biol.* **a** a hollow organ, bladder, etc., in an animal or plant, containing a liquid secretion. **b** a cell or cavity enclosing reproductive bodies, an embryo, parasite, micro-organism, etc. [Late Latin *cystis* from Greek *kustis* bladder]

cyst·eine /ˈsɪstɪˌiːn, -tɪɪn/ *noun* *Biochem.* a sulphur-containing amino acid, essential in the human diet and a constituent of many enzymes. [CYSTINE + -*eine* (var. of -INE⁴)]

cyst·ic /ˈsɪstɪk/ *adjective* **1** characterized by, of the nature of, or having a cyst. **2** of the urinary bladder or gallbladder.

cystic fibrosis *noun* a hereditary disease of the exocrine glands characterized by abnormal mucus production which affects esp. the lungs, pancreas, and gastrointestinal tract. Abbr.: **CF**.

cyst·ine /ˈsɪstiːn, -tɪn/ *noun* *Biochem.* an organic base which is a naturally occurring dimer of cysteine. [Greek *kustis* 'bladder' (because first found in urinary calculi) + -INE⁴]

cyst·itis /sɪˈstaɪtɪs/ *noun* an inflammation of the urinary bladder, often caused by infection, and usu. accompanied by frequent painful urination.

cysto- /ˈsɪstoː/ *combining form* urinary bladder, cyst (*cystoscope*). [Greek *kustē, kustis* bladder]

cysto·scope /ˈsɪstəˌskoːp/ *noun* an instrument inserted in the urethra for examining the urinary bladder. □ **cysto·scop·ic** /-ˈskɒpɪk/ *adjective* **cyst·os·copy** /sɪˈstɒskəpi/ *noun*

-cyte /səit/ *combining form* *Biol.* denoting (usu. mature) cells (*leukocyte*) (compare -BLAST). [Greek *kutos* vessel]

Cythe·rea /ˌsɪθəˈriːə/ another name for APHRODITE. □ **Cythe·rean** /ˌsɪθəˈriːən/ *adjective*

cyti·dine /ˈsɪtɪˌdiːn/ *noun* a nucleoside obtained from RNA by hydrolysis. [German *Cytidin* (as -CYTE)]

cyto- /ˈsaitoː/ *combining form* *Biol.* cells or a cell. [as -CYTE]

cyto·chrome /ˈsaitoːˌkroːm/ *noun* *Biochem.* a compound consisting of a protein linked to a heme, which is involved in electron transfer reactions.

cyto·gen·etics /ˌsaitoːdʒəˈnetiks/ *noun* (treated as *sing.*) the study of inheritance in relation to the structure and function of cells. □ **cyto·gen·etic** *adjective* **cyto·gen·eti·cist** /-sɪst/ *noun*

cyto·kine /ˌsaitoːˈkain/ *noun* *Biochem.* any of various hormones secreted by certain cells of the immune system.

cy·tol·ogy /sai·ˈtɒlədʒi/ *noun* the microscopic study of cells, esp. to detect and identify disease. □ **cyto·logic·al** *adjective* **cyto·logic·al·ly** *adverb* **cy·tol·o·gist** *noun*

cyto·meg·alo·virus /ˌsaitoːˈmegaloːˌvairəs/ *noun* *Med.* a kind of herpesvirus which usually produces very mild symptoms in an infected person but may cause severe neurological damage in the newborn and in people with weakened immune systems. Abbr.: **CMV**.

cyto·plasm /ˈsaitoːˌplazəm/ *noun* the protoplasmic content of a cell apart from its nucleus. □ **cyto·plas·mic** *adjective*

cyto·sine /ˈsaitoːˌsiːn/ *noun* one of the principal component bases of the nucleotides and the nucleic acids DNA and RNA, derived from pyrimidine. Symbol: **C**.

cyto·skel·eton /ˈsaitoːˌskelətən/ *noun* *Biol.* a network of protein filaments and tubules giving shape and coherence to a living cell. □ **cyto·skel·etal** *adjective*

cyto·sol /ˈsaitoːˌsɒl/ *noun* the aqueous component of the cytoplasm of a cell, within which various organelles and particles are suspended. □ **cyto·sol·ic** *adjective* [CYTO- + SOL(UBLE)]

cyto·toxic /ˌsaitoːˈtɒksɪk/ *adjective* toxic to living cells. □ **cyto·tox·icity** *noun*

czar /zɑr/ *noun* (also **tsar**) **1** *hist.* the title of the former emperor of Russia. **2** a person with great authority. □ **czar·dom** *noun* **czar·ism** *noun* **czar·ist** *adjective* [Russian *czarʹ*, ultimately from Latin *Caesar*]

czar·das /ˈtʃɑrdas/ *noun* (*pl.* same) a Hungarian dance with a slow start and a quick finish. [Magyar *csárdás* from *csárda* inn]

czar·evich /ˈzɑrəvɪtʃ/ *noun* (also **tsar·evich**) *hist.* the eldest son of an emperor of Russia. [Russian *czarevich* son of a czar]

czar·ina /zɑrˈiːnə/ *noun* (also **tsar·ina**) *hist.* the title of the former empress of Russia. [Italian & Spanish (*c*)*zarina* from German *Czarin, Zarin*, fem. of *Czar, Zar*]

Czech /tʃek/ ● *noun* **1** a native or national of the Czech Republic or *hist.* Czechoslovakia. **2** the Slavic language spoken in the Czech Republic or *hist.* Czechoslovakia. ● *adjective* **1** of or relating to the Czech Republic or *hist.* Czechoslovakia. **2** of or relating to the Czech language. [Polish spelling of Bohemian *Čech*]

Czecho·slo·vakia /ˌtʃekəsloˈvakiə/ a former country in central Europe in the period 1918–1992, now divided between the Czech Republic and Slovakia; capital, Prague. Czechoslovakia was created out of the northern part of the old Austro-Hungarian Empire at the end of the First World War. It incorporated the Czech-speaking Bohemians and Moravians in the west with the Slovaks of Slovakia in the east. In Aug. 1990 the official name of the country was changed to the Czech and Slovak Federal Republic, and the two parts separated on 1 January 1993. □ **Czecho·slo·vak** /-ˈsloːˌvak/ *noun & adjective* **Czecho·slo·vak·ian** *adjective & noun*

Czech Republic a country in central Europe; pop. (est. 2002) 10,256,760; capital, Prague. Formerly one of the two constituent republics of Czechoslovakia, the Czech Republic became independent on the partition of that country on 1 Jan. 1993. It comprises the former provinces of Bohemia, Silesia, and Moravia.

Czerny /ˈtʃerni/ **Karl** (1791–1857), Austrian pianist, teacher, and composer. A pupil of Beethoven and the teacher of Liszt, he is best known for his more than 1,000 exercises and studies for piano.

Często·chowa /ˌtʃenstəˈxoːvə/ an industrial city in south central Poland; pop. (est. 2000) 255,549. It is famous for the statue of the black Madonna in its church.

Dd

D¹ *noun* (also **d**) (*pl.* **Ds** or **D's**) **1** the fourth letter of the alphabet. **2** *Music* the second note of the diatonic scale of C major. **3** the fourth hypothetical person or example in a series etc. **4** the fourth class or category (of academic marks etc.) denoting a barely acceptable quality. **5** *Math.* the fourth known quantity, group, section, etc. **6** = DEE. **7** (as a Roman numeral) 500. **8** a size of battery, having a voltage of 1.5 V.

D² *symbol* **1** *Chem.* the element deuterium. **2** *Physics* density. **3** *Chem.* dextrorotatory.

D³ *abbreviation* (also **D.**) **1** *Politics* a government department (*DND*). **2** Doctor. **3** *US* Democrat. **4** dimension (*3-D*). **5** digital (recording).

d.¹ *abbreviation* **1** died. **2** departs. **3** delete. **4** daughter. **5** diameter. **6** depth. **7** degree.

d.² *symbol* **1** deci-. **2** *Brit.* (pre-decimal) penny. [sense 2 from Latin *denarius* silver coin]

'd *verb* (usu. after pronouns) had, would (*I'd*; *he'd*). [abbreviation]

DA *abbreviation* **1** *US* district attorney. **2** *slang* = DUCK'S ASS.

D/A *abbreviation Computing* digital to analog.

da¹ *abbreviation* deca-.

da² *noun dialect* dad; father. [abbreviation of DAD¹]

dab¹ ● *verb* (**dabbed**, **dab·bing**) **1** *transitive* press (a surface) briefly with a cloth, sponge, etc., without rubbing, esp. in cleaning or to apply a substance. **2** *transitive* press (a cloth etc.) lightly on a surface. **3** *transitive* (foll. by *on*) apply (a substance) by dabbing a surface. **4** *intransitive* (usu. foll. by *at*) pat; tap (*I dabbed at my eyes with a tissue*). ● *noun* **1** a brief application of a cloth, sponge, etc. to a surface without rubbing. **2** a small amount of something (*a dab of paint*). **3** *Brit. informal* (usu. in *pl.*) fingerprints. □ **smack dab** *adverb N Amer. informal* exactly, directly (*smack dab in the middle*). □ **dab·ber** *noun* [Middle English, imitative]

dab² *noun* any of various flatfishes. [15th c.: origin unknown]

dab·ble *verb* **1** *intransitive* (usu. foll. by *in*, *at*) take a casual or superficial interest or part (in a subject or activity). **2** *intransitive* splash, play, move the feet, hands, etc. about in (usu. a small amount of) liquid. **3** *intransitive* (of a duck) feed in shallow water with splashing and quick bill movements. □ **dab·bler** *noun* [16th c.: from Dutch *dabbelen* or DAB¹]

dab·bling duck *noun* any of the tribe Anatini of mostly freshwater ducks that habitually feed in shallow water by dabbling or upending, e.g. the mallard, teal, shoveler, etc.

dab hand *noun informal* (usu. foll. by *at*) a person especially skilled at something (*a dab hand at cooking*). [17th c.: origin unknown]

DAC *abbreviation* = DIGITAL TO ANALOG CONVERTER.

da capo /da ˈkapoː/ *adverb & adjective Music* repeated from the beginning. [Italian, lit. 'from the head']

Dacca see DHAKA.

dace *noun* (*pl.* same) *N Amer.* any of several freshwater fishes of the carp family. [Old French *dars*: see DART]

dacha /ˈdatʃə/ *noun* a country house or cottage in Russia. [Russian, lit. 'gift']

Dachau /ˈdaxau, ˈdakau/ a Nazi concentration camp in southern Bavaria, Germany, from 1933 to 1945.

dachs·hund /ˈdakshənt, dɒk-/ *noun* a breed of dog with short legs and a long body. [German, = badger dog]

Dacia /ˈdeɪʃə, ˈdeɪsɪə/ an ancient country of SE Europe in what is now NW Romania. It was annexed by Trajan in AD 106 as a province of the Roman Empire. □ **Dacian** *adjective*

da·cite /ˈdeɪsəɪt/ *noun Geol.* a volcanic rock similar to andesite but containing free quartz. [from *Dacia*, a Roman province in central Europe + -ITE¹]

da·coit /dəˈkɔɪt/ *noun* (in India or Burma) a member of a band of armed robbers. [Hindi *ḍakait* from *ḍākā* gang robbery]

Dac·ron *noun proprietary* a synthetic polyester used as a textile fabric. [invented word, after NYLON]

dac·tyl /ˈdaktɪl/ *noun* a metrical foot consisting of one long or stressed syllable followed by two short or unstressed syllables. [Latin *dactylus* from Greek *daktulos* finger, the three bones corresponding to the three syllables]

dac·tyl·ic /dakˈtɪlɪk/ ● *adjective* of or using dactyls. ● *noun* (usu. in *pl.*) dactylic verse.

dad¹ *noun informal* father. [perhaps imitative of a child's *da*, *da*]

dad² (usu. in *combination*) *euphemism* = DAMN (*dad-blasted*).

Dada /ˈdɑːdɒ/ *noun* an early 20th-c. international movement in art, literature, music, and film, repudiating and mocking artistic and social conventions. □ **Dada·ism** *noun* **Dada·ist** *noun & adjective* **Dada·is·tic** *adjective* [French (the title of an early 20th-c. review) from *dada* hobby horse]

dada *noun informal* father. [perhaps imitative of a child's *da*, *da*]

daddy *noun* (*pl.* **-dies**) *informal* **1** father. **2** (usu. foll. by *of*) the oldest or supreme example (*had a daddy of a headache*).

daddy-long-legs *noun* **1** *N Amer.* any of various arachnids of the family Opilionidae, with very long thin legs, found in humus and on tree trunks. **2** *Brit.* a crane fly.

dado /ˈdeɪdoː/ *noun* (*pl.* **dados**) **1** the lower part of the wall of a room when visually distinct from the upper part. **2** *N Amer.* a rectangular slot or groove cut into a board etc. **3** the cube of a pedestal between the base and the cornice. [Italian, = DIE²]

Daeda·lus /ˈdiːdələs, ˈded-/ *Gk Myth* a craftsman who is said to have built the labyrinth for Minos, king of Crete. Minos imprisoned him and his son Icarus, but they escaped on wings made by Daedalus.

dae·mon¹ *var. of* DEMON 5.

dae·mon² /ˈdiːmən/ *noun Computing* in some operating systems, an unseen program that controls a peripheral device; a background task. [*disk + and execution monitor*]

dae·mon·ic *var. of* DEMONIC.

daff *noun informal* = DAFFODIL. [abbreviation]

daf·fo·dil *noun* **1 a** a bulbous plant, *Narcissus pseudonarcissus*, with a yellow trumpet-shaped crown. **b** any of various other large-flowered plants of the genus *Narcissus*. **c** a flower of any of these plants. **2** a pale-yellow colour. [earlier *affodill*, as ASPHODEL]

daffy *adjective* (**daf·fi·er**, **daf·fi·est**) *slang* **1** silly, foolish, crazy. **2** (foll. by *about*) fond of; infatuated with. □ **daf·fi·ly** *adverb* **daf·fi·ness** *noun* [*daff* simpleton + -Y²]

daft *adjective* esp. *Brit. informal* = DAFFY. □ **daft·ly** *adverb* [Middle English *daffte* = Old English *gedæfte* mild, meek, from Germanic]

da Gama see GAMA.

Dagan /ˈdaɡən/ a Babylonian and Assyrian god of fertility and the underworld.

Dag·estan /ˌdaɡəˈstan/ an autonomous republic in SW Russia, on the western shore of the Caspian Sea; pop. (est. 2002) 2,184,400; capital, Makhachkala. □ **Dag·estani** *noun & adjective*

dag·ger *noun* **1** a short stabbing weapon with a pointed and edged blade. **2** = OBELUS. □ **at daggers drawn** in bitter enmity. **look daggers at** glare angrily or venomously at. [Middle English, perhaps from obsolete *dag* pierce, influenced by Old French *dague* long dagger]

dagger·board *noun* a kind of centreboard which slides vertically through the keel of a sailing boat.

dago /ˈdeɪɡoʊ/ *noun* (*pl.* **dagos**) *slang offensive* an Italian, Hispanic, Spaniard, etc; any foreigner. [Spanish *Diego* = James]

Dagon /ˈdeɪɡɒn/ in the Bible, a national deity of the ancient Philistines, represented as a fish-tailed man. [Hebrew *Dāgōn*]

Da·guerre /dəˈɡer/ **Louis** (1787-1851), French inventor of the first practical photographic process.

da·guerre·otype /dəˈɡeroʊ,taɪp/ *noun* **1** a photograph taken by an early photographic process employing an iodine-sensitized silvered plate and mercury vapour. **2** this process. [DAGUERRE]

dah *noun* esp. *US* (in the Morse system) = DASH *noun* 7 (*compare* DIT). [imitative]

Dahl /dɒl/ **Roald** (1916-90), British writer, of Norwegian descent. He is noted for his short stories with macabre plots and unexpected outcomes, and for his stories and poems for children, especially *Charlie and the Chocolate Factory* (1964) and *The BFG* (1982).

dahl·ia /ˈdeɪljə/ *noun* any composite garden plant of the genus *Dahlia*, of Mexican origin, cultivated for its many-coloured single or double flowers. [A. *Dahl*, Swedish botanist d.1789]

Da·homey /dəˈhoʊmi/ the former name (until 1975) of BENIN.

dai·kon /ˈdaɪkɒn, -ən/ *noun* a long, thin, white oriental radish. [Japanese from Middle Chinese *dà* 'big' + *gen* 'root']

Dáil /dɔɪl/ *noun* (in full **Dáil Éire·ann** /ˈeɪrən/) the lower house of parliament in the Republic of Ireland. [Irish, = assembly (of Ireland)]

d'Aille·boust /daɪjəˈbuː/ **Louis d'Ailleboust de Cou·longe et d'Ar·gen·te·nay** (*c.*1612-60), French colonial administrator, governor of New France 1648-51. Arriving in Montreal in 1643, he was named governor of all of Canada in 1648, but could not prevent the Iroquois from all but destroying his Huron allies. He remained in the colony until his death, serving as acting governor 1657-8.

daily ● *adjective* **1** done, produced, or occurring every day or every weekday. **2** constant, regular. **3** calculated, measured, etc. by the day (*a daily quota*). ● *adverb* **1** every day; from day to day. **2** constantly. ● *noun* (*pl.* **-lies**) *informal* **1** a daily newspaper. **2** (usu. in *pl.*) the first prints from cinematographic takes, made rapidly for film producers or editors; the rushes. □ **daili·ness** *noun*

daily bread *noun* **1** necessary food. **2** a livelihood.

daily double *noun* a bet on the winning horses or dogs in two usu. consecutive races in one day, usu. the first and second race.

daily dozen *noun informal* regular exercises, esp. on rising.

Daim·ler /ˈdaɪmlər/ **Gott·lieb** (1834-1900), German engineer and car manufacturer. In 1885 he patented one of the first high-speed internal combustion engines, and designed an automobile in 1889. He founded the Daimler motor company in 1890.

dai·mon /ˈdaɪmoʊn/ *noun* = DEMON 5. □ **dai·mon·ic** *adjective* [Greek, = deity]

dai·myo /ˈdaɪmjoʊ, ˈdaɪmioʊ/ *noun* (also **dai·mio**) (*pl.* **-myo** or **-myos**; **-mio** or **-mios**) *hist.* in feudal Japan, any of the chief landowning nobles, vassals of the shogun. [Japanese from *dai*, 'great' + *myō*, 'name']

dainty ● *adjective* (**dain·ti·er**, **dain·ti·est**) **1** delicately pretty. **2** delicate of build or in movement. **3** (of food) delicious or pleasing to the palate. **4** (of a person) possessing delicate taste, perception, and sensibility. ● *noun* (*pl.* **-ties**) **1** a choice morsel; a delicacy. **2** *Cdn* (*Prairies & NW Ont.*) (in *pl.*) fancy cookies, cakes, etc. usu. served at social gatherings. □ **dain·ti·ly** *adverb* **dain·ti·ness** *noun* [Anglo-French *dainté*, Old French *daintié*, *deintié* from Latin *dignitas -tatis* from *dignus* worthy]

dai·quiri /ˈdakəri/ *noun* (*pl.* **dai·quiris**) a cocktail of rum, sugar, and lime or lemon juice, etc. [*Daiquiri* in Cuba]

dairy *noun* (*pl.* **-ies**) **1** a building or room for the storage, processing, and distribution of milk and its products. **2** a store where milk and milk products are sold. **3** milk and milk products (*contains no dairy, meat, or fish*). **4** (*attributive*) **a** of, containing, or concerning milk and its products. **b** compatible with dairy products according to Jewish dietary law. **c** used for or relating to the production of dairy products (*dairy cow*). **5** *Cdn* (*Cape Breton*) a convenience store. [Middle English *deierie* from *deie* maidservant, from Old English *dǣge* kneader of dough]

dairy bar *noun* a small establishment selling ice cream, milkshakes, and other dairy products.

dairy farm *noun* a farm which produces milk or milk products. □ **dairy farmer** *noun* **dairy farming** *noun*

dairy·ing *noun* the business of producing, storing, and distributing milk and its products.

dairy·maid *noun* esp. *hist.* a woman employed in a dairy.

dairy·man *noun* (*pl.* **-men**) **1** a dairy farmer. **2** a person, esp. a man, employed in or operating a dairy.

dairy princess *noun* (in the US and formerly in Canada) a young woman, usu. one who has grown up on a dairy farm, selected through a competition to serve for one year making public appearances to promote dairy farmers and dairy products. In Canada, dairy princesses have been replaced by **dairy educators** and **dairy ambassadors**.

dais /ˈdeɪəs, ˈdeɪɪs/ *noun* a low platform, usu. at the upper end of a room and used to support a table, lectern, throne, etc. [Old French *deis* from Latin *discus* disc, dish, in medieval Latin = table]

daisy *noun* (*pl.* **-ies**) **1** a small composite plant, *Bellis perennis*, bearing flowers each with a yellow disc and white rays. **2** any other plant with daisy-like flowers, esp. the larger ox-eye daisy, the Michaelmas daisy, or the shasta daisy. □ **fresh as a daisy** extremely fresh, clean, or invigorated. **pushing up the daisies** *slang* dead and buried. [Old English *dæges ēage* day's eye, the flower opening in the morning]

daisy chain ● *noun* **1** a string of daisies threaded together. **2** a group of several connected things, events, etc. ● *transitive verb* (**daisy-chain**) esp. *Computing* link (several pieces of hardware, etc.) together in succession. □ **daisy-chained** *adjective*

daisy cutter *noun informal* an immensely powerful aerial thermobaric bomb.

Dak. *abbreviation* Dakota.

Dakar /dəˈkɑr/ the capital of Senegal, a port on the Atlantic coast of West Africa; pop. (est. 2002) 2,384,000.

Da·kota¹ /dəˈkoʊtə/ (*pl.* **-kotas**) **1** a former territory of the US, organized in 1889 into the states of North Dakota and South Dakota. **2** (in *pl.*) North and South Dakota considered together.

Da·kota² /dəˈkoʊtə/ ● *noun* (*pl.* same or **-kotas**) **1** a member of a N American Aboriginal people inhabiting the upper Mississippi and Missouri river valleys. **2** the Siouan language of this people. ● *adjective* of or relating to the Dakota or their language. [Dakota *Dakhóta*, lit. 'allies']

dal /dɒl/ *noun* (also **dhal**) **1** a kind of lentil or split pea, a common foodstuff in India. **2** a dish made with this. [Hindi]

Dalai Lama /ˌdɒlaɪ ˈlɒmə/ the spiritual head of Tibetan Buddhism and, until the establishment of Chinese Communist rule in 1959, the spiritual and temporal ruler of Tibet. The present Dalai Lama, the fourteenth to hold the title, escaped to India in 1959; he was awarded the Nobel Peace Prize in 1989 in recognition of his non-violent opposition to Chinese domination of Tibet. [Mongolian *dalai* ocean; see LAMA]

da·lasi /dɒˈlɒsi/ *noun* (*pl.* same or **da·lasis**) the chief monetary unit of Gambia. [name of an earlier local coin]

Dale, Sir Henry Hal·lett (1875-1968), English physiologist and pharmacologist. He investigated the role of histamine in anaphylactic shock and allergy, and his research on acetylcholine as a natural neurotransmitter led to a clearer understanding of the chemical transmission of nerve impulses. He shared a Nobel Prize in 1936.

dale *noun* a valley, esp. in Northern England. [Old English *dæl* from Germanic]

d'Alem·bert /dalɑ̃ˈber/ **Jean le Rond**, see ALEMBERT.

dales·man *noun* (*pl.* **-men**) an inhabitant of the dales in Northern England.

Dal·housie¹ /dalˈhauzi/ a town in N New Brunswick, situated at the mouth of the Restigouche River, at the head of Chaleur Bay; pop. (2001) 3,975. [G. Ramsay, 9th Earl of DALHOUSIE]

Dal·housie² /dalˈhauzi/ **1 George Ram·say, 9th Earl of** (1770-1838), English army officer and colonial administrator, Lieutenant-Governor of Nova Scotia 1816-20, and governor-in-chief of British North America 1820-8. An authoritarian governor, he dissolved the House of Assembly in 1827 rather than accept Louis-Joseph Papineau as speaker; he founded Dalhousie University at Halifax (1818). **2** his son **James An·drew Broun Ram·say, 1st Marquis of** (1812-60), British colonial administrator. As Governor General of India (1847-56) he oversaw the annexation of Punjab, Pegu, Oudh, and Nagpur, improved communications with the introduction of railways and the telegraph, and was responsible for the drafting of legislation against slavery, suttee, and female infanticide.

Dali /'dɒli/ **Sal·va·dor** (1904–89), Spanish surrealist painter. He was much influenced by Freud, and many of his paintings, such as *The Persistence of Memory* (1931) with its images of melting watches, portray subconscious or dream images painted with almost photographic realism against backgrounds of arid Catalan landscapes. □ **Dali·esque** *adjective*

Dalit /'dɒlɪt/ *noun* (in the traditional Indian caste system) a member of the lowest caste.

Dal·las a city in NE Texas, a centre of the oil industry; pop. (2000) 1,118,580.

dal·li·ance /'dalɪəns/ *noun* **1** a leisurely or frivolous passing of time. **2** a casual love affair.

Dall sheep /dɒl/ *noun* (also **Dall's sheep**) a white thinhorn sheep, *Ovis dalli dalli* of the mountains of NW Canada and Alaska. [W. H. *Dall*, US naturalist d.1927]

dally[1] *intransitive verb* (-**lies**, -**lied**) **1** delay; waste time, esp. frivolously. **2** (often foll. by *with*) play about; flirt, treat frivolously. [Old French *dalier* chat]

dally[2] *N Amer.* (*West*) ● *noun* a loop of rope wound around a saddle horn etc. to act as a brake. ● *transitive & intransitive verb* (-**lies**, -**lied**) loop (a rope) around a saddle horn etc. [abbreviation of *dally welter*, corruption of Spanish *dale vuelta* 'give it a turn']

Dal·ma·tia /dal'meɪʃə/ *noun* a region in what is now SW Croatia, comprising mountains and a narrow coastal plain along the Adriatic, together with offshore islands.

Dal·ma·tian /dal'meɪʃən/ ● *noun* **1** a breed of large dog having white, short hair with dark spots. **2** a native or inhabitant of Dalmatia. ● *adjective* of or relating to Dalmatia.

dal·mat·ic /dal'matɪk/ *noun* a wide-sleeved long loose vestment open at the sides, worn by deacons and bishops, and by English monarchs at their coronations. [Old French *dalmatique* or Late Latin *dalmatica* (*vestis* robe) of Dalmatia]

Dal·ri·ada /dal'riːədə/ an ancient Gaelic kingdom in northern Ireland.

dal segno /dal 'seɪnjoː/ *adverb Music* repeat from the point marked by a sign. Abbr.: **DS**. [Italian, = from the sign]

Dal·ton /'dɒltən/ **John** (1766–1844), English chemist. He formulated modern atomic theory and the law of partial pressures (Dalton's law). He also gave the first detailed description of colour-blindness, based on his own inability to distinguish green from red.

dal·ton /'dɒltən/ *noun Chem.* = ATOMIC MASS UNIT. [DALTON]

dal·ton·ism /'dɒltə,nɪzəm/ *noun* colour-blindness, esp. a congenital inability to distinguish between red and green. [French *daltonisme* from DALTON]

dam[1] ● *noun* **1** a barrier constructed to hold back water and raise its level, forming a reservoir or preventing flooding. **2** = BEAVER DAM. **3** anything functioning as a dam does. **4 a** (in full **rubber dam**) esp. *N Amer.* a rubber sheet used to keep saliva from the teeth during dental operations. **b** (in full **dental dam**) a similar device used to prevent the transmission of disease during oral sex. ● *transitive verb* (**dammed**, **dam·ming**) **1** provide or confine with a dam. **2** (often foll. by *up*) block up; hold back; obstruct. [Middle Low German, Middle Dutch]

dam[2] *noun* the female parent of an esp. four-footed domestic animal. [Middle English: var. of DAME]

dam·age ● *noun* **1** harm or injury impairing the value or usefulness of something, or the health or normal function of a person. **2** (in *pl.*) *Law* a sum of money claimed or awarded in compensation for a loss or an injury. **3** (prec. by *the*) *informal* cost (*what's the damage?*). ● *transitive verb* **1** inflict damage on. **2** (esp. as **dam·ag·ing** *adjective*) detract from the reputation of (*a most damaging admission*). □ **dam·aged** *adjective* **dam·ag·ing·ly** *adverb* [Old French *damage*, from *dam(me)* loss, from Latin *damnum* loss, damage]

damage control *noun* **1** action taken to alleviate the effects of damage after an accident, negative publicity, etc. **2** the taking of such action.

damage deposit *noun* a sum of money given as a deposit against possible future damage to something rented or leased.

damaged goods *noun* **1** merchandise which has deteriorated in quality. **2** a person who is regarded as inadequate or undesirable in some way, esp. a woman considered ineligible for marriage because of her past.

Da·mara /də'mɑːrə/ ● *noun* (*pl.* same or **Da·maras**) a member of a people inhabiting mountainous parts of SW Africa and speaking the Nama language. ● *adjective* of or relating to the Damara. [Nama]

Da·mara·land /də'mɑːrə,land/ a plateau region of central Namibia inhabited chiefly by the Damara and Herero peoples.

dam·as·cene /'damə,siːn, ,damə'siːn/ ● *transitive verb* decorate (metal, esp. iron or steel) by etching or inlaying esp. with gold or silver, or with a watered pattern produced in welding. ● *noun* a design or article produced in this way. ● *adjective* of, relating to, or produced by this process. [*Damascene* of Damascus, from Latin *Damascenus* from Greek *Damaskēnos*]

Da·mas·cus /də'maskəs/ the capital of Syria since the country's independence in 1946; pop. (est. 2002) 1,803,700. The apostle Paul experienced a dramatic conversion to Christianity while on the road to ancient Damascus.

dam·ask /'daməsk/ ● *noun* **1 a** a figured woven fabric (esp. silk or linen) with a pattern visible on both sides. **b** twilled table linen with woven designs shown by the reflection of light. **2** a tablecloth made of this material. **3** *hist.* steel with a watered pattern produced in welding. ● *adjective* **1** made of or resembling damask. **2** coloured like a damask rose, velvety pink or vivid red. ● *transitive verb* **1** weave with figured designs. **2** = DAMASCENE *verb*. **3** ornament. [Middle English, ultimately from Latin DAMASCUS]

damask rose *noun* an old sweet-scented variety of rose, with very soft velvety petals, used to make attar.

dame *noun* **1** (**Dame**) **a** (in the UK) the title given to a woman with the rank of Knight Commander or holder of the Grand Cross in the Orders of Chivalry. **b** a woman holding this title. **2** *N Amer. slang offensive* a woman. **3** *Brit.* a comic middle-aged woman in modern pantomime, usu. played by a man. **4** *archaic* a mature woman. [Old French from Latin *domina* mistress]

dame school *noun hist.* a primary school kept by an elderly woman.

Da·mien /dam'jã/ (1840–89), Belgian missionary who devoted his life to serving lepers in Hawaii, eventually contracting the disease himself.

Dami·etta /,dami'etə/ **1** the eastern branch of the Nile delta. **2** a port at the mouth of this; pop. (est. 2002) 90,200.

dam·mar /'damər/ *noun* **1** any E Asian tree, esp. one of the genus *Agathis* or *Shorea*, yielding a resin used in varnish making. **2** this resin. [Malay *damar*]

dam·mit *interjection* damn it.

damn ● *verb* **1** *transitive & intransitive* curse (a person or thing). **2** *transitive* doom to hell; cause the damnation of. **3** *transitive* condemn, censure (*a review damning the performance*). **4** *transitive* **a** (often as **damn·ing** *adjective*) (of a circumstance, piece of evidence, etc.) show or prove to be guilty; bring condemnation upon (*evidence against them was damning*). **b** be the ruin of. **5** *transitive* used when swearing at a person or thing (*damn you!*). ● *noun* **1** an uttered curse. **2** *slang* a negligible amount (*not worth a damn*). ● *interjection* expressing emphatic annoyance, frustration, approval, etc. (*Damn! I've missed the bus; Damn, I'm good!*) ● *adjective & adverb informal* = DAMNED. □ **damn all** *informal* nothing at all. **damn fool** *informal* foolish, stupid (*that's a damn fool idea*). **damn near** (also **damned near**) *informal* almost (*damn near died*). **damn well** *informal* (as an emphatic) simply (*damn well do as I say*). **damn with faint praise** commend so unenthusiastically as to imply disapproval. **I'll be** (or **I'm**) **damned if** *informal* I certainly do not, will not, etc. **not give a damn** *informal* not care at all. **well I'll be** (or **I'm**) **damned** *informal* exclamation of surprise, dismay, etc. □ **damn·ing·ly** *adverb* [Old French *damner* from Latin *damnare* 'inflict loss on' from *damnum* 'loss']

dam·nable /'damnəbəl/ *adjective* annoying. □ **dam·nably** *adverb*

dam·na·tion /dam'neɪʃən/ ● *noun* condemnation to eternal punishment, esp. in hell. ● *interjection* expressing anger or annoyance.

damned *informal* ● *adjective* damnable, infernal, unwelcome. ● *adverb* extremely (*damned hot; damned lovely*). □ **damned if you do and damned if you don't** unable to win approval no matter what one does.

damned·est *adjective informal* most surprising or extraordinary (*the damnedest thing you ever saw*). □ **do one's damnedest** do one's utmost.

Damo·cles /'damə,kliːz/ a legendary courtier who was forced by Dionysius, ruler of Syracuse (4th c. BC) to sit at a banquet underneath a sword suspended by a single hair, thus demonstrating how precarious the king's happiness was. □ **Damo·clean** /,damə'kliːən/ *adjective*

Damon /'deɪmən/ a legendary Syracusan of the 4th c. BC whose friend Pythias (also spelled Phintias) was sentenced to death by Dionysius I; Damon stood bail for Pythias, who returned from settling his affairs just in time to save him, and Pythias was then reprieved.

damp ● *adjective* slightly wet; moist. ● *noun* **1** diffused moisture in the air, on a surface, or in a solid, esp. as a cause of inconvenience or

danger. **2** dejection; discouragement. **3** = FIREDAMP. ● *transitive verb*
1 make damp; moisten. **2** (often foll. by *down*) **a** take the force or vigour out of (*damp one's enthusiasm*). **b** make flaccid or spiritless. **c** make (a fire) burn less strongly by reducing the flow of air to it. **3** reduce or stop the vibration of (esp. the strings of a musical instrument).
4 quieten. □ **damp off** (of a plant) die from a fungus attack in damp conditions. □ **damp·ish** *adjective* **damp·ly** *adverb* **damp·ness** *noun* [Middle Low German, = vapour etc., Old High German *dampf* steam, from West Germanic]

damp·en *verb* **1** *transitive & intransitive verb* make or become damp. **2** *transitive* make less forceful or vigorous. □ **damp·en·er** *noun*

damp·er *noun* **1** a person or thing that discourages, or tempers enthusiasm. **2** a device that reduces shock or noise. **3** a movable metal plate in a flue to control the draft, and so the rate of combustion. **4** *Cdn* (*Nfld*) a round lid or cover placed over an opening on the cooking surface of a wood or coal etc. stove. **5** *Music* a pad silencing a piano string except when removed by means of a pedal or by the note's being struck. □ **put a damper on** take the vigour or enjoyment out of.

damping off *noun* a plant disease occurring in excessively damp conditions, in particular the collapse and death of young seedlings as a result of a fungal infection.

damp squib *noun Brit.* an unsuccessful attempt to impress etc.

dam·sel *noun archaic* or *jocular* a young unmarried woman. [Old French *dam(e)isele*, ultimately from Latin *domina* mistress]

damsel·fish *noun* (*pl.* same) any of numerous brightly coloured tropical marine fishes of the family Pomacentridae.

damsel·fly *noun* (*pl.* **-flies**) any of various insects of the order Odonata, like a dragonfly but with its wings folded over the body when resting.

dam·son /'damzən/ *noun* **1** a small dark purple plum. **2** the small deciduous tree, *Prunus institia*, bearing this. [Middle English *damacene*, *-scene*, *-sene* from Latin *damascenum* (*prunum* plum) of *Damascus*: see DAMASCENE]

Dan (in the Bible) **1** a Hebrew patriarch, son of Jacob and Bilhah. **2** the tribe of Israel traditionally descended from him. **3** an ancient town in the north of Canaan, where the tribe of Dan settled. It marked the northern limit of the ancient Hebrew kingdom of Israel (Judges 20; *see also* BEERSHEBA).

Dan. *abbreviation Bible* Daniel.

dan¹ *noun* **1** any of twelve degrees of advanced proficiency in judo etc. **2** a person who has achieved any of these. [Japanese]

dan² *noun* (in full **dan buoy**) a small buoy used as a marker in deep-sea fishing, or to mark the limits of an area cleared by minesweepers. [17th c.: origin unknown]

Danae /'danei,iː/ *Gk Myth* the daughter of Acrisius, king of Argos. An oracle foretold that she would bear a son who would kill her father. In an attempt to evade this he imprisoned her in a tower, but Zeus visited her in the form of a shower of gold and she conceived Perseus, who after many adventures killed Acrisius by accident.

Dana·ids /'danei,idz/ *Gk Myth* the daughters of Danaus, king of Argos, who were compelled to marry the sons of his brother Aegyptus but murdered their husbands on the wedding night, except for Hypermnestra, who helped her husband to escape. They were punished in Hades by being set to fill a leaky jar with water.

Dana·kil Depression /'danə,kil/ a long low-lying desert region of NE Ethiopia and N Djibouti, between the Red Sea and the Great Rift Valley.

Da Nang /dɒ 'naŋ/ a port and city (formerly called Tourane) in central Vietnam, on the South China Sea; pop. (est. 2002) 446,000. During the Vietnam War it was used as a US military base.

Dana·us /'danɪəs/ *Gk Myth* a king of Argos, father of the Danaids.

dance ● *verb* **1** *intransitive* move about rhythmically alone or with a partner or in a group, usu. in fixed steps or sequences to music, for pleasure, as entertainment, or as a ritual. **2** *intransitive* move in a lively way; skip or jump about. **3** *transitive* **a** perform (a specified dance or form of dancing). **b** perform (a specified role) in a ballet etc. **4** *intransitive* move up and down (on water, in the field of vision, etc.). **5** *transitive* move (esp. a child) up and down; dandle. ● *noun* **1** a sequence of steps or bodily motions etc., usu. performed to music. **2** the act or an instance of dancing (*may I have this dance?*). **3** a social gathering for dancing. **4** the art of dancing (*I want to study dance*). **5** a piece of music having a rhythm or style that is suitable for a particular dance. **6** a dancing or lively motion. **7** a formal or stylized pattern of movements etc. performed by an animal or bird, esp. as part of a courtship ritual. **8** = ICE DANCING. □ **dance attendance on** follow or wait on (a

person) obsequiously. **dance to a person's tune** accede obsequiously to a person's demands and wishes. **lead a person a dance** (or **merry dance**) *Brit.* cause a person much trouble in following a course one has instigated. □ **dance·able** *adjective* **dan·cey** *adjective* [Old French *dance* from Romanic, of unknown origin]

dance band *noun* a band that plays music that is especially suitable for dancing to.

dance captain *noun* (in musical theatre) a person who rehearses the dancers and watches their performance so as to give suggestions for improvement, often also acting as an understudy able to replace any of several dancers as needed.

dance card *noun* a card bearing the names of (esp. a woman's) partners for specified dances.

dance floor *noun* a usu. uncarpeted area of floor reserved for dancing.

dance hall *noun* **1** a public establishment for dancing. **2** an uptempo usu. electronic style of popular music, originating in the dance halls of Jamaica, derived from reggae and incorporating elements of rap and ragga.

dance·mak·er *noun* **1** a choreographer, esp. of modern dance. **2** a dancer. □ **dance·making** *noun*

dance of death *noun* a medieval dance in which a personified Death is represented as leading all to the grave.

dan·cer *noun* **1** a person who performs a dance. **2** a person whose profession is dancing.

dance·sport *noun* competitive ballroom dancing.

dance·wear *noun* clothing suitable for dance classes, e.g. tights, leotards, bodysuits, etc.

dancing dervish *noun* = WHIRLING DERVISH.

dancing girl *noun* a girl or woman who performs esp. erotic or music hall dances.

dancing master *noun hist.* a person who teaches dancing.

D & C *noun* an operation in which the cervix is dilated and the lining of the uterus scraped off with a curette, performed after a miscarriage or to diagnose the condition of the endometrium. [abbreviation of 'dilatation and curettage']

dan·de·lion *noun* a composite plant, *Taraxacum officinale*, with jagged leaves and a large bright yellow flower on a hollow stalk, followed by a globular head of seeds with downy tufts. [French *dent-de-lion* translation of medieval Latin *dens leonis* lion's tooth]

dan·der¹ *noun informal* temper, anger, indignation. □ **get one's dander up** lose one's temper; become angry. [19th c.: origin uncertain]

dan·der² *noun* dandruff, esp. as found in the hair of animals. [related to DANDRUFF]

dan·di·fy *transitive verb* (**-fies**, **-fied**) cause to resemble a dandy. □ **dan·di·fied** *adjective*

dan·dle *transitive verb* **1** dance (a child) on one's knees or in one's arms. **2** pamper, pet. [16th c.: origin unknown]

Dan·dong /dan'dʊŋ/ a port in Liaoning province, NE China, near the mouth of the Yalu River, on the border with North Korea; pop. (est. 2002) 1,488,300.

dan·druff *noun* **1** dead skin in small scales among the hair. **2** the condition of having this. [16th c.: *-ruff* perhaps related to Middle English *rove* 'scurfiness' from Old Norse *hrufa* or Middle Low German, Middle Dutch *rōve*]

dandy ● *noun* (*pl.* **-dies**) **1** a man unduly devoted to style, smartness, and fashion in dress and appearance. **2** *informal* an excellent thing. ● *adjective* (**dan·di·er**, **dan·di·est**) esp. *N Amer. informal* very good of its kind; splendid, first-rate. □ **dandy·ish** *adjective* **dandy·ism** *noun* [18th c.: perhaps an abbreviation of *Jack-a-dandy*: *dandy* may be a pet form of *Andrew*]

dandy brush *noun* a brush for grooming a horse.

Dane *noun* **1** a native or national of Denmark. **2** *hist.* a Viking invader of England in the 9th–11th c. [Old Norse *Danir* (pl.)]

Dane·geld /'deingeld/ a land tax levied in Anglo-Saxon England to buy off Danish invaders during the reign of King Ethelred (especially 991–1016), the term also applies to taxes collected for national defence by the Norman kings until 1162. [Old English (as DANE + Old Norse *gjald* payment)]

Dane·law the part of northern and eastern England occupied or subjugated by Danes from the late 9th century and administered according to their laws until after the Norman Conquest. [Old English *Dena lagu* Danes' law]

u: m**oo**d   ai m**y**   əi p**i**pe   au br**ow**n   ʌu h**ou**se   ei d**ay**   ɔi b**oy**   ā fr**an**glais   ã Canadi**en**   ɔ̃ Br**ay**on   (*see over for consonants*)

dang *adjective & interjection* N Amer. *informal* = DAMN (in imprecatory senses). [euphemism]

dan·ger *noun* **1** liability or exposure to harm. **2** a thing that causes or is likely to cause harm. **3** an unwelcome possibility (*danger of frost tonight; the danger that people will do nothing about the problem*). □ **in danger of** likely to incur or to suffer from. [earlier sense 'jurisdiction, power', from Old French *dangier*, ultimately from Latin *dominus* lord]

dan·ger·ous *adjective* involving or causing danger. □ **dan·ger·ous·ly** *adverb* **dan·ger·ous·ness** *noun*

dangerous offender *noun* Cdn Law a person who has been convicted of a serious personal injury offence and constitutes a threat to the life, safety, or physical or mental well-being of others, and whose history suggests little hope of reform, who is imprisoned indefinitely.

danger pay *noun* extra payment for dangerous work.

dan·gle *verb* **1** *intransitive* be loosely suspended, so as to be able to sway to and fro. **2** *transitive* hold or carry loosely suspended. **3** *transitive* hold out (a hope, temptation, etc.) enticingly. □ **dan·gler** *noun* **dan·gly** *adjective* [16th c. (imitative): compare Swedish *dangla*, Danish *dangle*]

dan·gling *adjective* (of a participle in an absolute clause or phrase) having no expressed subject, but having an implicit subject that is different than the subject of the clause modified, e.g. *talking* in *while talking on the cellphone, the car ran into the ditch.*

Dan·iel 1 a Hebrew prophet (6th c. BC), who spent his life as a captive at the court of Babylon, interpreted the dreams of Nebuchadnezzar, and was delivered by God from the lions' den into which he had been thrown as the result of a trick. **2** a book of the Bible containing his prophecies. It was probably written at the outbreak of persecution of the Jews under Seleucid rule c.167 BC.

Dan·iell cell /ˈdanjəl/ *noun* Physics & Chem. a primary voltaic cell with a copper anode and a zinc-amalgam cathode giving a standard electromotive force when either copper sulphate or sulphuric acid is used as the electrolyte. [John *Daniell*, English chemist d.1845, its inventor]

Dan·ish ● *adjective* of or relating to Denmark or the Danes. ● *noun* **1** the Danish language. **2** (prec. by *the*; treated as *pl.*) the Danish people. **3** = DANISH PASTRY.

Danish blue *noun* a soft salty white cheese with blue veins.

Danish pastry *noun* a baked good of sweet, flaky bread topped with icing, fruit, nuts, etc.

dank *adjective* disagreeably damp and cold. □ **dank·ly** *adverb* **dank·ness** *noun* [prob. from Scandinavian: compare Swedish *dank* marshy spot]

D'Annun·zio /daˈnʊntsiˌɔː/ **Gab·ri·ele** (1863–1938), Italian novelist, playwright, and poet. His novels, including *The Child of Pleasure* (1890) and *The Triumph of Death* (1894), feature Nietzschean superheroes and an emphasis on sensual gratification.

dan·sak *var. of* DHANSAK.

danse macabre /ˌdãs məˈkɒbr/ *noun* = DANCE OF DEATH. [French (as DANCE, MACABRE)]

dan·seur /dãˈsɜːr/ *noun* a male ballet dancer. [French, = dancer]

dan·seur noble /dãˈsɜːr nɒblə, nɔːbəl/ *noun* a male principal dancer in a ballet company, esp. one who is particularly suited (by physique, bearing, elegance of line, etc.) to princely roles. [French, = noble dancer]

dan·seuse /dãsɜːz/ *noun* a female ballet dancer. [as DANSEUR]

Dante /ˈdɒnteɪ, ˈdanteɪ/ (full name Dante Alighieri) (1265–1321), Italian poet. His early work consisted mainly of courtly love poetry; his first book, *Vita nuova* (c.1290–4), tells of his love for Beatrice Portinari (c.1265–90). *The Divine Comedy* (c.1309–20) is an epic poem recounting allegorically an imagined visit to Hell and Purgatory escorted by Virgil, and finally to Paradise guided by Beatrice, now a blessed spirit. □ **Dan·te·an** *noun & adjective* **Dan·tesque** *adjective*

Dan·ton /dãˈtɔ̃/ **Georges Jacques** (1759–94), French revolutionary. A noted orator, he won great popularity in the early days of the French Revolution. Initially an ally of Robespierre and the Jacobins, he later opposed the Reign of Terror, and was arrested and executed on Robespierre's orders.

Dan·ube River /ˈdanjuːb/ a river which rises in the Black Forest in SW Germany and flows about 2 850 km (1,770 miles) into the Black Sea. It is the second longest river in Europe after the Volga; Vienna, Bratislava, Budapest, and Belgrade are situated on it. □ **Dan·ub·ian** /dəˈnuːbiən, -ˈnjuːbiən/ *adjective*

Danubian principalities the former European principalities of Moldavia and Wallachia. They united in 1861 to form the state of Romania.

Dan·zig see GDAŃSK.

dap *verb* (**dapped, dap·ping**) **1** *intransitive* fish by letting the bait bob on the water. **2** *transitive & intransitive* dip lightly. **3** *transitive & intransitive* bounce on the ground. [compare DAB[1]]

Daph·ne /ˈdafni/ Gk Myth a nymph who was turned into a laurel bush to save her from the amorous pursuit of Apollo.

daph·ne /ˈdafni/ *noun* any flowering shrub of the genus *Daphne*, e.g. the spurge laurel or mezereon. [Middle English, = laurel, from Greek *daphnē*]

daph·nia /ˈdafniə/ *noun* (*pl.* same) a minute semi-transparent freshwater crustacean with long antennae and prominent eyes, often used as food for aquarium fish. *Also called* FRESHWATER FLEA. [modern Latin from DAPHNE]

Daph·nis /ˈdafnis/ Gk Myth a Sicilian shepherd, who, according to one version of the legend, is credited with the invention of pastoral poetry, with which he consoled himself after being blinded for his infidelity to a nymph.

Da Ponte /da ˈpɒnteɪ/ **Lor·enzo** (real name Emmanuele Conegliano) (1749–1838), Italian poet and librettist best known for the libretti of Mozart's *Marriage of Figaro* (1786), *Don Giovanni* (1787), and *Così fan tutte* (1790).

dap·per *adjective* **1** neat and precise, esp. in dress or movement. **2** sprightly. □ **dap·per·ly** *adverb* **dap·per·ness** *noun* [Middle Low German, Middle Dutch *dapper* strong, stout]

dap·ple ● *verb* **1** *transitive* mark with spots or rounded patches of colour or shade. **2** *intransitive* become marked in this way. ● *noun* **1** a dappled effect. **2** a dappled animal, esp. a horse. □ **dap·pled** *adjective* [Middle English *dappled, dappeld*, (adj.), of unknown origin]

dapple grey ● *adjective* (of an animal's coat) grey or white with darker spots. ● *noun* a dapple grey horse.

Dap·sang /dʌpˈsʌŋ/ an alternative name for the mountain K2.

Da·qing /daˈtʃɪŋ/ a major industrial city in NE China, in Heilongjiang province; pop. (est. 2002) 1,231,700.

DAR see DAUGHTERS OF THE AMERICAN REVOLUTION.

Darby, Abra·ham (c. 1687–1717), English iron manufacturer, the first to use coke successfully to produce high-quality iron.

Darby and Joan *noun* informal a devoted old married couple. [18th c.: perhaps from a poem of 1735 in the *Gentleman's Magazine*]

Dar·dan·elles /ˌdɑːdəˈnelz/ a narrow strait between Europe and Asiatic Turkey (called the Hellespont in classical times), linking the Sea of Marmara with the Aegean Sea. It is 60 km (38 miles) long. In 1915, during the First World War, it was the scene of an unsuccessful attack on Turkey by Allied troops, with Australian and New Zealand contingents playing a major part (see GALLIPOLI).

Dar·danus /ˈdɑːdənəs/ Gk Myth the son of Zeus and the Pleiad Electra and legendary founder of the royal house of Troy.

dare ● *transitive verb* **1** (*3rd sing. present* **dares** or sometimes **dare**) (foll. by infin. with or without *to*) venture (to); have the courage or impudence (to) (*dare he do it?; if they dare to come; how dare you?; I dare not speak; I do not dare to jump*). **2** (usu. foll. by *to* + infin.) defy or challenge (a person) (*I dare you to own up*). **3** *literary* attempt; take the risk of (*dare all things; dared their anger*). ● *noun* **1** an act of daring. **2** a challenge, esp. to prove courage. □ **I dare say 1** (often foll. by *that* + clause) it is probable. **2** probably; I grant that much (*I dare say, but you are still wrong*). [Old English *durran* with Germanic cognates: compare Sanskrit *dhrsh*, Greek *tharseō* be bold]

dare·devil ● *noun* a recklessly daring person. ● *adjective* recklessly daring. □ **dare·devil·ry** *noun*

Dar es Sa·laam /ˌdɑr es səˈlɒm/ the chief port and former capital of Tanzania; pop. (est. 2002) 2,421,900. [Arabic, = haven of peace]

Dar·fur /dɑrˈfʊr/ a region in the west of Sudan.

Dari /ˈdɑri/ *noun* the form of Persian spoken in Afghanistan. [Persian]

Dar·ien /ˈderiən/ a sparsely populated province of E Panama. The name was formerly applied to the whole of the Isthmus of Panama.

dar·ing ● *noun* adventurous courage. ● *adjective* adventurous, bold; prepared to take risks. □ **dar·ing·ly** *adverb*

Dario /daˈrioː/ **Ru·bén** (pseudonym of Félix Rubén García Sarmiento) (1867–1916), Nicaraguan writer. His boldly experimental and innovative poetry, typified by *Cantos de vida y esperanza* (Songs of Life and Hope, 1905), made him a leader of the Spanish-American modernist movement.

Consonants: b *but*   d *dog*   f *few*   g *get*   h *her*   j *yes*   k *cat*   l *leg*   m *man*   n *no*   p *pen*   r *red*   s *sit*

dari·ole /'dɛriˌoːl/ *noun* a savoury or sweet dish cooked and served in a small mould usu. shaped like a flowerpot. [Old French]

Darius I /də'raiəs, 'dɛriəs/ 'the Great' (*c*.550–486 BC), king of Persia 521–486 BC. He expanded the Persian Empire and developed commerce. After suppressing a revolt of the Greek cities in Ionia, he was defeated by the mainland Greeks at Marathon (490).

Darius III /də'raiəs, 'dɛriəs/ (died 330 BC) king of Persia 336-330 BC. His defeat by Alexander the Great brought about the end of the Persian Empire.

Dar·jee·ling /dɑr'dʒiːlɪŋ/ **1** (also **Dar·ji·ling**) a hill station at an altitude of 2 150 m (7,054 ft.) in West Bengal, NE India, near the Sikkim border; pop. (2001) 107,500. **2** the high-quality tea grown in the area around Darjeeling.

dark ● *adjective* **1** with little or no light. **2** of a deep or sombre colour. **3** (of a person) with deep brown or black hair, complexion, or skin. **4** gloomy, depressing, dismal (*dark thoughts*). **5** evil, sinister (*dark deeds*). **6** sullen, angry (*a dark mood*). **7** remote, secret, mysterious, little-known (*the dark and distant past*). **8** ignorant, unenlightened. **9** (of a theatre) not offering a performance; closed. ● *noun* **1** absence of light. **2** nightfall (*don't go out after dark*). **3** a dark area or colour, esp. in painting (*the skilled use of lights and darks*). □ **in the dark 1** with little or no light. **2** lacking information. □ **dark·ish** *adjective* **dark·ly** *adverb* **dark·ness** *noun* **dark·some** *adjective literary*. [Old English *deorc* prob. from Germanic]

Dark Ages *plural noun* (also **Dark Age**) (prec. by *the*) **1 a** the period of western European history between the fall of the Roman Empire and the high Middle Ages, *c*.500–1100, so called because it has been judged a time of relative lack of enlightenment. Broadly, the period was characterized by political fragmentation, a hiatus in city life, and, except for isolated monasteries, a lack of major centres of learning. **b** a similar period in the history of Greece and other Aegean countries from the end of the Bronze Age until the beginning of the historical period. **2** any period of supposed unenlightenment.

dark chocolate *noun* esp. *N Amer.* sweet or semi-sweet chocolate made without the addition of milk (*compare* MILK CHOCOLATE).

Dark Continent *noun* (prec. by *the*) a name for Africa, esp. when little known to Europeans.

dark·en *verb* **1** *transitive* make dark or darker. **2** *intransitive* become dark or darker. □ **darken a door** appear at a place (*I'll never darken this door again!*). □ **dark·en·er** *noun*

dark energy *noun Astronomy* a form of energy with largely unknown properties which in some cosmological models is postulated to act in opposition to gravitation and to occupy the entire universe, accounting for most of the energy in it, and causing its expansion to accelerate.

dark glasses *plural noun* eyeglasses with dark-tinted lenses.

dark horse *noun* a little-known person who is unexpectedly successful or prominent.

dark·ie *noun* (also **darky**) (*pl.* **-ies**) *slang offensive* a black person.

dark·ling *adjective & adverb literary* in the dark; in the night.

dark matter *noun Astronomy* (in some cosmological theories) non-luminous material that is postulated to exist in space and that could take any of several forms, including weakly interacting particles (**cold dark matter**) or high-energy randomly moving particles created soon after the big bang (**hot dark matter**).

dark night of the soul *noun* a period of spiritual anguish, esp. one during which one questions one's whole purpose in life.

dark·room *noun* a room for developing photographic work, with normal light excluded.

darky var. of DARKIE.

dar·ling ● *noun* **1** (often as a form of address) a beloved or lovable person or thing. **2** a person etc. who is particularly popular. **3** *informal* a pretty or endearing person or thing. ● *adjective* **1** beloved, lovable. **2** favourite. **3** *informal* charming or pretty. [Old English *dēorling* (as DEAR, -LING[1])]

Darling River a river of SE Australia, flowing 2 757 km (1,712 miles) generally southwestward to join the Murray River.

darn[1] ● *transitive verb* mend (esp. knitted material, or a hole in it) by interweaving yarn across the hole with a needle. ● *noun* a darned area in material. □ **darn·er** *noun* [16th c.: perhaps from obsolete *dern* hide]

darn[2] *transitive verb, interjection, adjective, & adverb informal* = DAMN (in imprecatory senses). [corruption of DAMN]

darndest *adjective* (also **darned·est**) = DAMNEDEST.

darned *adjective & adverb informal* = DAMNED.

dar·nel /'dɑrnəl/ *noun* any of several grasses of the genus *Lolium*, native to Europe and N Africa and naturalized in N America, planted as pasture grasses or to stabilize soil. [Middle English: compare Walloon *darnelle*]

darn·ing *noun* **1** the action of a person who darns. **2** things to be darned.

darning needle *noun* **1** a long needle with a large eye, used in darning. **2** *N Amer.* a dragonfly.

Darn·ley, Lord (title of Henry Stewart or Stuart) (1545-67), Scottish nobleman, second husband of Mary, Queen of Scots and father of James I of England. Implicated in the murder of his wife's secretary Rizzio in 1566, he was killed in a mysterious explosion in Edinburgh.

darn tootin' *N Amer. informal* ● *interjection* indicating fervent agreement. ● *adverb & adjective* used as an intensifier (*a darn tootin' good idea*; *darn tootin' I mind!*). □ **you're darn tootin'** you're darn right.

Dar·row, Clar·ence (1857-1938), US lawyer, remembered for his defence of John T. Scopes, accused of breaking a Tennessee state law by teaching Darwin's theory of evolution.

dar·shan /'dɑrʃən/ *noun Hinduism* an opportunity to see or an occasion of seeing a holy person or the image of a deity. [Hindi from Sanskrit *darśana* 'sight, seeing']

Dart, Ray·mond Ar·thur (1893–1988), Australian-born South African anthropologist and anatomist. He identified a skull found near the Kalahari desert as being that of a hominid, coining the genus name *Australopithecus* for it.

dart ● *noun* **1** a small pointed projectile thrown or fired as a weapon. **2 a** a small pointed projectile with a feather or plastic flight, used in the game of darts. **b** (in *pl.*; usu. treated as *sing.*) an indoor game in which such darts are thrown at a circular target to score points. **3** a sudden rapid movement. **4** *Zool.* a dart-like structure, such as an insect's sting or the calcareous projections of a snail (used during copulation). **5** a stitched tapered tuck for shaping a garment. ● *verb* **1** *intransitive* (often foll. by *out*, *in*, *past*, etc.) move or go suddenly or rapidly (*darted into the road*). **2** *transitive* direct suddenly (*a glance etc.*). **3** *transitive* shoot (an animal) with a dart, typically to administer a drug. [Old French *darz*, *dars*, from Frankish]

dart·board *noun* a circular board marked with numbered segments, used as a target in darts.

dart·er *noun* **1** any large water bird of the genus *Anhinga*, having a narrow head and long thin neck. **2** any of various small quick-moving freshwater fish of the family Percidae, native to N America.

Dart·moor 1 a moorland district in Devon (SW England). **2** a prison near Princetown in this district, originally built to hold French prisoners of war from the Napoleonic Wars.

Dartmoor pony *noun* a breed of small pony with a shaggy coat.

Dart·mouth /'dɑrtməθ/ **1** a former city on the east central coast of Nova Scotia, on the east side of Halifax Harbour, now part of the regional municipality of Halifax; pop. (2001) 65,741. **2** a port in Devon, SW England; pop. (est. 1998) 5,600. It is the site of the Royal Naval College. □ **Dart·mouth·ian** *noun & adjective* [sense 1 prob. after DARTMOUTH 2]

Dar·win[1] the capital of Northern Territory, Australia; pop. (2001) 108,200.

Dar·win[2], Charles Rob·ert (1809–82), English natural historian and geologist, proponent of the theory of evolution by natural selection, expressed in *On the Origin of Species* (1859) and *The Descent of Man* (1871).

Dar·win·ian /dɑr'wɪniən/ ● *adjective* **1** of or relating to Charles Darwin's theory of the evolution of species by the action of natural selection. **2** characterized by ruthless competition for survival. ● *noun* an adherent of Darwin's theory. □ **Dar·win·ism** *noun* **Dar·win·ist** *noun*

dash ● *verb* **1** *intransitive* rush hastily or forcefully (*dashed up the stairs*). **2** *transitive* strike or fling with great force, esp. so as to shatter (*dashed it to the ground*; *the cup was dashed from my hand*). **3** *transitive* frustrate, daunt, dispirit (*dashed their hopes*). **4** *transitive informal* (as **dash it** or **dash it all**) = DAMN *verb* 1. **5** *transitive* splash or splatter. ● *noun* **1** a rushing movement; a sudden advance (*made a dash for shelter*). **2** a horizontal stroke in writing or printing to mark a pause or break in sense or to represent omitted letters or words. **3** a small amount of something (*a dash of salt*). **4** impetuous vigour or the capacity for this. **5** showy appearance or behaviour. **6** esp. *N Amer.* a short race; a sprint. **7** the longer signal of the two used in Morse code (*compare* DOT[1] *noun* 3). **8** = DASHBOARD. □ **cut a dash** make a brilliant show. **dash down** (or **off**) write or finish hurriedly. [Middle English, prob. imitative]

dash·board *noun* **1** the surface below the windshield on the inside of a motor vehicle or aircraft, containing instruments and controls. **2** *hist.* a board of wood or leather in front of a carriage, to keep out mud.

da·sheen *noun* a cultivated variety of taro. [origin unknown]

dash·er *noun* **1** *N Amer.* (in full **dasher board**) one of the boards surrounding a hockey rink. **2** a device for agitating or mixing a liquid or semi-solid, e.g. cream in a churn.

da·shiki /dəˈʃiːki/ *noun* (*pl.* **-shikis**) a loose, usu. brightly coloured and patterned pullover shirt. [West African, prob. Yoruba from Hausa]

dash·ing *adjective* **1** spirited, lively. **2** attractive in a lively or stylish way. □ **dash·ing·ly** *adverb*

das·tard·ly *adjective* despicable. □ **das·tard·li·ness** *noun* [*dastard* base coward, prob. from *dazed* past participle + -ARD, or obsolete *dasart* dullard, DOTARD]

dasy·ure /ˈdasiʊr/ *noun* any of a number of carnivorous arboreal catlike marsupials of the genus *Dasyurus*, native to Australia and New Guinea. [French from modern Latin *dasyurus* from Greek *dasus* hairy + *oura* tail]

DAT *abbreviation* digital audiotape.

data /ˈdatə, ˈdeɪtə/ *noun* **1** quantities or characters operated on by a computer. **2** (treated as *sing.*) a body or series of facts; information. **3** (treated as *pl.*) facts, statistics. **4** *pl.* of DATUM. ¶ In scientific writing, *data* is almost always treated as a plural, but the singular use is standard in all other levels of writing. [pl. of DATUM]

data·base *noun* (also **data bank**) an organized store of data, esp. one that may be accessed and manipulated by a computer.

dat·able *adjective* capable of being dated (to a particular time).

data capture *noun* the action or process of entering data into a computer.

data centre *noun* a facility which provides storage, processing, and transmission services for large amounts of data, often one at a location separate from a business's main operations.

data glove *noun* *Computing* a device worn like a glove and containing sensors linked to a representation of a hand in a computer display, allowing the manual manipulation of images in virtual reality.

data link *noun* a telecommunications link over which data may be transmitted.

data mining *noun* the practice of examining large pre-existing databases in order to generate new information.

data port *noun* a socket, jack, or wireless device by which a computer may connect to a computer network.

data processing *noun* a series of operations on data, esp. by a computer, to retrieve or classify etc. information. □ **data processor** *noun*

data warehouse *noun* a large store of data accumulated from a wide range of sources within a company and used to guide management decisions. □ **data warehousing** *noun*

date¹ ● *noun* **1** a day of the month, esp. specified by a number. **2** a particular day or year, esp. when a given event occurred. **3** a statement (usu. giving the day, month, and year) in a document or inscription etc., of the time of composition or publication. **4 a** a social engagement, often of a romantic nature, with one other person (*Tom has a date with her on Saturday night*). **b** *N Amer.* a person with whom one has a social engagement (*my date is picking me up at eight*). **5** the period to which a work of art etc. belongs. **6** the time when an event happens or is to happen. **7** (in *pl.*) the dates of a person's birth and death, usu. in years (*Laurier's dates are 1841–1919*). **8** a theatrical, musical, etc., engagement or performance. ● *verb* **1** *transitive* mark with a date. **2** *transitive* **a** assign a date to (an object, event, etc.). **b** (foll. by *to*) assign to a particular time, period, etc. **3 a** *transitive* make or go out on a date with (a person). **b** *intransitive* go out on a date or dates (*they are now dating regularly*). **4** *intransitive* (often foll. by *from*, *back to*, etc.) have its origins at a particular time. **5** *intransitive* be recognizable as from a past or particular period; become evidently out of date (*a design that does not date*). **6** *transitive* indicate or expose as being out of date (*that hat really dates you*). □ **to date** until now. **up to date** (*attributive* **up-to-date**) meeting or according to the latest requirements, knowledge, or fashion; modern. □ **dat·ing** *noun* [Old French from medieval Latin *data*, fem. past participle of *dare* give: from the Latin formula used in dating letters, *data* (*epistola*) (letter) given or delivered (at a particular time or place)]

date² *noun* **1** a dark oval single-stoned fruit. **2** (in full **date palm**) the tall tree *Phoenix dactylifera*, native to W Asia and North Africa, bearing this fruit. [Old French from Latin *dactylus* from Greek *daktulos* finger, from the shape of its leaf]

date·book *noun* *N Amer.* a book containing a calendar and usu. an address list etc., used to plan one's activities; an appointment diary.

dated *adjective* **1** old-fashioned. **2** marked with a date.

date·less *adjective* **1** having no date. **2** of immemorial age. **3** not likely to become out of date.

date line ● *noun* **1** (usu. **Date Line**) the line from north to south partly along the meridian 180° from Greenwich, to the east of which the date is a day earlier than it is to the west. **2** (**date·line**) a line at the head of a dispatch or special article in a newspaper showing the date and place of writing. ● *verb transitive* (**dateline**) (usu. in *passive*) provide (a newspaper story) with a dateline.

date rape *noun* the rape of a girl or woman by a person with whom she is on a date.

date-rape drug *noun* a sedative drug causing loss of inhibition and memory that is easily and undetectably slipped into a person's drink, facilitating date rape.

date square *noun* *Cdn* (often in *pl.*) a dessert consisting of date filling spread on an oatmeal base and covered with a crumble topping, served cut into squares or rectangles.

date stamp ● *noun* **1** an adjustable rubber stamp etc. used to record a date. **2** the impression made by this. ● *transitive verb* (**date-stamp**) mark with a date.

dat·ive /ˈdeɪtɪv/ *Grammar* ● *noun* the case of nouns and pronouns (and words in grammatical agreement with them) indicating an indirect object or recipient. ● *adjective* of or in the dative. [Latin (*casus*) *dativus* from *dare dat-* give]

Da·tong /daˈtʊŋ/ a city in northern China in Shanxi province; pop. (est. 2002) 1,368,400.

datum /ˈdatəm, ˈdeɪtəm/ *noun* (*pl.* **data**) **1** a piece of information. **2** a thing known or granted; an assumption or premise from which inferences may be drawn (see SENSE DATUM). **3** a fixed starting point of a scale etc. (*datum line*). **4** see also DATA. [Latin, = thing given, neuter past participle of *dare* give]

da·tura /dəˈtjʊərə/ *noun* any poisonous plant of the genus *Datura*, e.g. the thornapple. [modern Latin from Hindi *dhatura*]

daub ● *verb* **1** *transitive* spread (paint, plaster, or some other thick substance) crudely or roughly on a surface. **2** *transitive* coat or smear (a surface) with paint etc. **3 a** *transitive & intransitive* paint crudely or unskilfully. **b** *transitive* lay (colours) on crudely and clumsily. ● *noun* **1** paint or other substance daubed on a surface. **2** plaster, clay, etc., for coating a surface, esp. mixed with straw and applied to laths or wattles to form a wall. **3** a crude painting. [Old French *dauber* from Latin *dealbare* whitewash, from *albus* white]

daube /dəʊb/ *noun* a stew of braised meat (usu. beef) with wine etc. [French]

daub·er *noun* a person or implement that daubs, esp. in painting.

Dau·bigny /dəʊbiːˈnjiː/ **Charles Fran·çois** (1817–78), French landscape painter. A member of the Barbizon school whose work influenced the Impressionists, he frequently painted stretches of water.

Dau·det /dəʊˈdeɪ/ **Al·phonse** (1840–97), French novelist and playwright. He is best known for his sketches of life in his native Provence, particularly the *Lettres de mon moulin* (1869), and for the comic *Tartarin de Tarascon* (1872), the hero of which is a caricature of the southern Frenchman.

daugh·ter *noun* **1** a girl or woman in relation to either or both of her parents. **2** a female descendant. **3** (foll. by *of*) a female member of a family, nation, etc. **4** (foll. by *of*) a woman who is regarded as the spiritual descendant of, or as spiritually attached to, a person or thing. **5** a product or attribute personified as a daughter in relation to its source (*Truth is the daughter of Time*). **6** *Physics* a nuclide formed by the radioactive decay of another. **7** *Biol.* a cell etc. formed by the division etc. of another. □ **daugh·ter·ly** *adjective* [Old English *dohtor* from Germanic]

daughter-in-law *noun* (*pl.* **daughters-in-law**) the wife of one's son.

Daughters of the American Revolution a US patriotic and benevolent society, first organized in 1890. Membership is limited to female descendants of soldiers and others of the revolutionary period who aided the cause of independence. Abbr.: **DAR**.

Dau·mier /dəʊmˈjeɪ/ **Hon·oré** (1808–78), French painter and lithographer. He produced over 4,000 lithographs sharply satirizing French society and politics. His later oil paintings, such as *Don Quixote* (1868), are powerfully realistic.

daunt *transitive verb* discourage, intimidate. □ **daunt·ing** *adjective* **daunt·ing·ly** *adverb* [Anglo-French *daunter* from Latin *domitare* frequentative of *domare* tame]

Vowels: a *cat* ɑ *arm* e *bed* ɜr *her* ɜ: *deux* ə *ago* ɪ *sit* i *cosy* iː *feed* ɒ *hot* ɔ *pore* ɔː *no* ʌ *run* ʊ *put*

daunt·less *adjective* intrepid, persevering. □ **daunt·less·ly** *adverb* **daunt·less·ness** *noun*

Dau·phin /ˈdɒfɪn/ a city in SW Manitoba, about 150 km north of Brandon; pop. (2001) 8,085. □ **Dau·phin·ite** *noun* [after the *Dauphin*, eldest son of Louis XV]

dau·phin /ˈdɒfɪn, dɔːˈfã/ *noun* the title borne by the eldest son of the king of France from 1349 to 1830. [French, from the family name of the lords of the Dauphiné, ultimately a nickname meaning 'dolphin']

Dau·phiné /ˈdɔːfiˌneɪ/ a region and former province of SE France. Its capital was Grenoble. [see DAUPHIN]

Davao /dɒˈvaʊ/ a seaport in the S Philippines, on the island of Mindanao; pop. (est. 2002) 873,800. It is the largest city on the island and the third largest city in the Philippines.

daven /ˈdɒvən/ *intransitive verb* *Judaism* recite prayers. [Yiddish *davenen* 'pray']

Dav·enant /ˈdavənənt/ **Sir Wil·liam** (1606–1668), English poet and playwright. He was Poet Laureate from 1638 until his death, and played an important role in the revival of theatre after the Restoration.

daven·port /ˈdavənˌpɔːt/ *noun* **1** *N Amer.* a large heavily upholstered sofa. **2** *Brit.* an ornamental writing desk with drawers and a sloping surface for writing. [19th c.: from the name *Davenport*]

David ▶ **1** (died *c*.962 BC), king of Judah and Israel *c*.1000–*c*.962 BC. He was made a military commander by Saul in reward for slaying the Philistine Goliath. On Saul's death he became king of Judah and later of all Israel, making Jerusalem his capital; he is traditionally regarded as the author of the Psalms. **2** /daˈviːd/ **Jacques-Louis** (1748–1825), French painter. A celebrated neoclassicist, he is best known for his paintings recording the events of the Revolutionary and Napoleonic eras; his works include *The Oath of the Horatii* (1784), *The Dead Marat* (1793), and the Napoleonic *Coronation* (1805–07). **3 St.** (also **Dewi** /ˈdewɪ/) (6th c.), Welsh monk. Since the 12th c. he has been regarded as the patron saint of Wales. Feast day, 1 March.

David I /ˈdeɪvɪd/ (*c*.1082–1153), son of Malcolm III, king of Scotland 1124–53. He invaded England in 1136 in support of his niece Matilda, but was defeated at the Battle of the Standard in Yorkshire in 1138; he later reasserted Scottish independence from English feudal domination, drawing up a common law of Scotland.

Davies ▶ **1** /ˈdeɪvɪs/ **Sir Peter Max·well** (b.1934), English composer and conductor. In 1967, with Harrison Birtwistle, he co-founded the Pierrot players (later the Fires of London ensemble), for whom he composed many of his works; these include *Taverner* (1970) and *Eight Songs for a Mad King* (1969). **2** /ˈdeɪviːz/ **(Wil·liam) Rob·ert·son** (1913–1995), Canadian novelist and playwright. He won international recognition with his Deptford trilogy of novels, the first two of these, *Fifth Business* (1970) and *The Manticore* (1972) (winner of the Governor General's Award), show the influence of Jungian psychology; the third novel, *World of Wonders* (1975), also explores psychological and spiritual issues.

da Vinci see LEONARDO DA VINCI.

Davis ▶ **1 Bette** (born Ruth Elizabeth Davis) (1908–89), US actress. She established her Hollywood career with a number of strong, independent female roles in such films as *Dangerous* (1935), *Jezebel* (1938), and *All About Eve* (1950); her other films include *Whatever Happened to Baby Jane?* (1962) and *The Whales of August* (1986). **2 Jef·fer·son** (1808–89), US soldier and political leader, president of the Confederacy 1861–65; following the war he was imprisoned for two years and charged with treason (1866), though never tried. **3 John** (also **Davys**) (*c*.1550–1605), English navigator and explorer, who conducted three Arctic expeditions in an attempt to find the Northwest Passage (1585–87), charting the coasts of Greenland, Baffin Island, and Labrador, and discovering the strait named after him; he also discovered the Falkland Islands (1592). **4 Miles Dewey** (1926–91), US jazz trumpeter, composer, and bandleader. In the 1950s he pioneered the style of music that later became known as 'cool jazz', and in the 1960s he was one of the first to fuse jazz and rock; his albums include *Kind of Blue* (1959), *In a Silent Way* (1969), and *Bitches Brew* (1969). **5 Wil·liam Gren·ville ('Bill')** (b.1929), Canadian lawyer and politician, Progressive Conservative premier of Ontario 1971–85. He was minister of education under John Robarts (1962–71), and as premier introduced moderate reforms, overseeing a period of relative prosperity in Ontario.

Davis·son ▶ **Clin·ton Jo·seph** (1881–1958), US physicist. With L. H. Germer (1896–1971) he discovered electron diffraction, thus confirming de Broglie's theory of the wave nature of electrons; he shared the Nobel Prize for physics for this in 1937.

Davis Strait a sea passage 645 km (400 miles) long separating Greenland from Baffin Island and connecting Baffin Bay with the Atlantic Ocean. [John DAVIS]

davit /ˈdavɪt, ˈdeɪvɪt/ *noun* a small crane on board a ship, esp. one of a pair for suspending or lowering a lifeboat. [Old French *daviot* diminutive of *Davi* David]

Davy¹ ▶ **Sir Hum·phry** (1778–1829), English chemist. A pioneer of electrochemistry, he discovered the elements sodium, potassium, magnesium, calcium, strontium, and barium during 1807–8, and identified and named the element chlorine after he had demonstrated that oxygen was not a necessary constituent of acids.

Davy² *noun* (*pl.* **-ies**) (in full **Davy lamp**) a miner's safety lamp (invented by Sir Humphry Davy) with the flame enclosed by wire gauze to prevent an explosion of gas.

Davy Jones's locker *noun* *slang* the bottom of the sea, esp. regarded as the grave of those drowned at sea. [18th c.: origin unknown]

Davys see DAVIS 3.

daw *noun* = JACKDAW. [Middle English: compare Old High German *tāha*]

daw·dle *intransitive verb* **1** walk or move slowly. **2** delay; waste time. □ **dawd·ler** *noun* [perhaps related to dial. *daddle*, *doddle* idle, dally]

Dawes, Charles Gates (1865–1951), US financier, diplomat, and statesman, vice-president 1925–29. His Dawes Plan (1924) led to the reorganization of Germany's finances after the First World War; he was awarded the Nobel Peace Prize in 1925.

Daw·kins, Rich·ard (b.1941), English zoologist, whose book *The Selfish Gene* (1976) helped to popularize the theory of sociobiology; his other works include *The Blind Watchmaker* (1986).

dawn ● *noun* **1** the first light of day; daybreak. **2** the beginning or incipient appearance of something. ● *intransitive verb* **1** (of a day) begin; grow light. **2** begin to appear or develop; become visible. **3** (often foll. by *on*, *upon*) begin to become evident or understood (by a person). [originally as verb: back-formation from *dawning*, Middle English from earlier *dawing* after Scandinavian (as DAY)]

dawn chorus *noun* the singing of many birds at the break of day.

dawn·ing *noun* **1** daybreak. **2** the first beginning of something.

dawn redwood *noun* a Chinese deciduous coniferous tree, *Metasequoia glyptostroboides*, of a genus first known only from fossils.

Daw·son¹ (also called **Dawson City**) a town in west central Yukon, situated at the junction of the Klondike and Yukon rivers, close to the border with Alaska; pop. (2001) 1,251. □ **Dawson·ite** *noun* [G. M. DAWSON]

Daw·son² ▶ **1 George Mer·cer** (1849–1901), Canadian geologist. He conducted the first survey of northern BC and the Yukon in 1887. **2** his father, **Sir John Wil·liam** (1820–99), Canadian geologist and educator. As principal of McGill University (1855–93) he acquired an international reputation for his work promoting the sciences and research on fossils; he founded the Royal Society of Canada (1882).

Daw·son Creek a city in northeastern BC, situated 406 km northeast of Prince George, near the border with Alberta; pop. (2001) 10,754. [G. M. DAWSON]

Day, Doris (born Doris Kappelhoff) (b.1924), US actress and singer, who became a screen star in the 1950s and 1960s with her roles in musicals and romantic and comedy films; these include *Calamity Jane* (1953) and *Pillow Talk* (1959).

day *noun* **1** the time between sunrise and sunset. **2 a** a period of 24 hours as a unit of time, esp. from midnight to midnight, corresponding to a complete revolution of the earth on its axis. **b** a corresponding period on other planets (*Martian day*). **3** the time in a day during which work or another activity is engaged in (*an eight-hour day; the school day finishes at 3; the day will include a visit to the Falls*). **4** daylight (*clear as day*). **5 a** (also *pl.*) a period of the past or present (*the modern day; the old days*). **b** (prec. by *the*) the present time (*the issues of the day*). **6** the lifetime of a person or thing, esp. regarded as useful or productive (*have had my day; in my day things were different*). **7** a point of time (*will do it one day*). **8 a** the date of a specific festival. **b** a day associated with a particular event or purpose (*graduation day; payday; Christmas day*). **9** a particular date; a date agreed on. □ **all in a (or the) day's work** part of normal routine. **any day** at any time; under any conditions (*my dog can beat yours any day!*). **any day now** in the immediate future (*Rebecca could go into labour any day now*). **at the end of the day** in the final reckoning, when all is said and done. **back in the day** in the past; some time ago. **call it a day** end a period of activity, esp. resting content that enough has been done. **day after day** without respite. **day and night** all the time. **day by day** gradually. **day in court** an opportunity to defend oneself, present one's case, etc. before a legal body. **day in, day out** routinely,

---

uː m**oo**d aɪ m**y** əi p**i**pe aʊ br**ow**n ʌʊ h**ou**se eɪ d**ay** ɔi b**oy** ã fr**an**glais ã Ca**na**dien ɔ̃ Bra**y**on *(see over for consonants)*

constantly. **from day one** from the beginning. **if one is a day** adding emphasis to an estimate of a person's age (*he must be sixty if he's a day*). **not one's day** a day of successive misfortunes for a person. **one of these days** before very long. **one of those days** a day when things go badly. **that will be the day** *informal* that will never happen. **this day and age** the present time or period. **win the day** be successful. [Old English *dæg* from Germanic]

Dayak /ˈdaiak/ *noun* (also **Dyak**) a member of a group of aboriginal peoples inhabiting parts of Borneo or Sarawak. [Malay, = upcountry]

Dayan /daiˈan/ **Moshe** (1915–81), Israeli politician and general, minister of defence (1967–74), and foreign minister (1977–79). He commanded Israeli forces at the time of the Suez crisis (1956), and as minister of defence oversaw Israel's victory in the Six Day War (1967); he later played a prominent role in negotiations toward the Israeli–Egyptian peace treaty (1979).

day·bed *noun* a piece of furniture that can be used as a couch in the daytime and as a bed at night, usu. a single bed with a frame around three sides serving as a back and arms.

day·book *noun* an appointment diary.

day boy *noun Brit.* a boy who is a day student.

day·break *noun* the first appearance of light in the morning.

day camp *noun N Amer.* a camp which children attend during the day, usu. only on summer weekdays.

day·care *noun* **1** the supervision of young children during the working day by people other than their parents. **2** the care provided by a day centre. **3** *N Amer., Austral., & NZ* (in full **daycare centre**) a place where daycare is provided.

day centre *noun* a place providing care for the elderly or handicapped during the day.

day·dream ● *noun* a pleasant fantasy or reverie. ● *intransitive verb* indulge in this. □ **day·dream·er** *noun* **day·dream·ing** *noun & adjective* **day·dreamy** *adjective*

day girl *noun Brit.* a girl who is a day student.

Day-Glo ● *noun proprietary* a make of fluorescent paint or other colouring. ● *adjective* coloured with or like this. [DAY + GLOW]

day job *noun* a job with regular daytime working hours, esp. as opposed to artistic or creative pursuits (*don't give up your day job*).

day labourer *noun* an unskilled labourer hired by the day.

Day-Lewis, Cecil (1904–72), Irish-born English poet and critic. A leftist poet during the 1930s, he became less radical after 1940 and was appointed Poet Laureate 1968–72.

day·light *noun* **1** the light of day. **2** dawn (*before daylight*). **3 a** openness, publicity. **b** open knowledge. **4** a visible gap or interval (*I see daylight around the door frame*). □ **see daylight** begin to understand what was previously obscure.

daylight robbery *noun informal* a blatantly excessive charge.

day·lights *plural noun informal* senses or wits (*scared the daylights out of me; beat the living daylights out of him*). [influenced by LIGHTS]

daylight saving *noun* (also **daylight savings**) the achieving of longer evening daylight, esp. in summer, by setting the time an hour ahead of the standard time.

daylight time *noun* (also **daylight saving time**) esp. *N Amer.* time as adjusted for daylight saving.

day lily *noun* any plant of the genus *Hemerocallis*, whose flowers last only a day.

day·long *adjective* lasting for a day.

day nursery *noun* = DAYCARE 3.

Day of Atonement *noun* = YOM KIPPUR.

day off *noun* a day's holiday from work.

Day of Judgment *noun* = JUDGMENT DAY.

day of reckoning *noun see* RECKONING.

day of rest *noun* a day in the week set aside from normal work or activity, typically Sunday on religious grounds.

day pack *noun* (also *Brit.* **day sack**) a small backpack for use on one-day hikes or for carrying books etc.

day pass *noun* **1** a certificate or ticket entitling a person to unlimited use of a transit system, amusement park, etc. throughout a given day. **2** a permit allowing a jailed offender to leave prison for a day.

day release *noun* **1** *Cdn* release of a jailed offender during the day or for a short period of time, e.g. to attend school or for employment. **2** *Brit.* a system of allowing employees days off work for education.

day return *noun* a fare or ticket at a reduced rate for a journey out and back in one day.

day room *noun* a room, esp. a communal room in an institution, used during the day.

day school *noun* a school not providing boarding for students.

day student *noun N Amer.* a boy or girl who goes daily from home to school, esp. a school that also has boarders.

day surgery *noun* minor surgery that does not require the patient to stay in hospital overnight.

day·time *noun* the part of the day when there is natural light.

Day-timer *noun N Amer. proprietary* an appointment diary, esp. one with loose-leaf sheets.

daytime TV *noun* television programs broadcast during the daytime, esp. soap operas, sensational talk shows, light news, etc.

day-to-day *adjective* **1** involving daily routine. **2** planning for only one day at a time.

Day·ton a city in W Ohio; pop. (2000) 166,179. It was the home of the Wright brothers and is still a centre of aerospace research.

day trader *noun* a person who tries to make quick profits by buying extremely volatile stocks and holding them for a very short time, usu. less than a full day. □ **day trading** *noun*

day trip *noun* a trip or excursion completed in one day. □ **day tripper** *noun*

day·wear *noun* **1** clothing etc. suitable for wearing during the day. **2** underclothing worn during the day as opposed to nightwear, e.g. camisoles, slips, panties.

daze ● *transitive verb* stupefy, bewilder. ● *noun* a state of confusion or bewilderment (*in a daze*). □ **dazed** *adjective* **daz·ed·ly** *adverb* [Middle English *dased* past participle, from Old Norse *dasathr* weary]

daz·zle ● *verb* **1** *transitive* blind temporarily or confuse the sight of by an excess of light. **2** *transitive* impress or overpower (a person) with knowledge, ability, or any brilliant display or prospect. ● *noun* bright confusing light. □ **daz·zled** *adjective* **dazzle·ment** *noun* **daz·zler** *noun* **daz·zling** *adjective* **daz·zling·ly** *adverb* [Middle English, from DAZE + -LE⁴]

dB *abbreviation* decibel(s).

DBS *abbreviation* **1** direct-broadcast satellite. **2** direct broadcasting by satellite.

DC *abbreviation* **1** (also **d.c.**) direct current. **2** District of Columbia. **3** da capo.

DCC *abbreviation* DIGITAL COMPACT CASSETTE.

D.C.L. *abbreviation* Doctor of Civil Law.

D.D. *abbreviation* Doctor of Divinity.

D-Day *noun* **1** the day (6 June 1944) on which Allied forces invaded northern France to begin the liberation of western Europe. **2** the day on which an important operation is to begin or a change to take effect. [D for *day* + DAY (compare H-HOUR)]

DDE *noun Computing* a standard allowing data to be shared between different programs. [abbreviation of *Dynamic Data Exchange*]

ddI *abbreviation* dideoxyinosine, a drug intended for use against HIV.

DDoS *abbreviation* distributed denial of service, denoting the intentional paralyzing of a computer network by flooding it with data sent simultaneously from many individual computers.

D.D.S. *abbreviation* Doctor of Dental Surgery.

DDT *abbreviation* dichlorodiphenyltrichloroethane, a colourless chlorinated hydrocarbon used as an insecticide, now banned in many countries.

DE *abbreviation* Delaware (in official postal use).

de- *prefix* **1** forming verbs and their derivatives: **a** down, away (*descend; deduct*). **b** completely (*declare; denude; deride*). **2** added to verbs and their derivatives to form verbs and nouns implying removal or reversal (*decentralize; de-ice; demoralization*). [from or after Latin *de* (adv. & prep.) = off, from: sense 2 through Old French *des-* from Latin *dis-*]

DEA *abbreviation* **1** (in Canada) Department of External Affairs (until 1994). **2** (in the US) Drug Enforcement Administration.

de·acces·sion /ˌdiːakˈseʃən/ *transitive verb* (of a museum, library, etc.) sell (a work).

dea·con ● *noun* **1** (in churches with a hierarchy) a minister of the third order, below bishop and priest. **2** (in some Protestant Churches) a layperson elected or appointed to assist the minister, manage the congregation's secular affairs, etc. ● *transitive verb* appoint or ordain as a deacon. [Old English *diacon* from ecclesiastical Latin *diaconus* from Greek *diakonos* servant]

deacon·ess /ˈdiːkənes/ *noun* **1** a laywoman with functions similar to a deacon's. **2** = DIACONAL MINISTER.

de·acti·vate *transitive verb* make inactive or less reactive.
□ **de·acti·va·tion** *noun* **de·acti·va·tor** *noun*

dead ● *adjective* **1** no longer alive. **2** *informal* extremely tired or unwell. **3** benumbed; affected by loss of sensation (*my fingers are dead*). **4** (foll. by *to*) unappreciative or unconscious of; insensitive to. **5 a** no longer effective or in use; obsolete, extinct. **b** no longer functioning. **6** (of a fire etc.) no longer burning; extinguished. **7** inanimate. **8 a** lacking force or vigour; dull, lustreless, muffled. **b** (of sound) not resonant. **c** (of sparkling wine etc.) no longer effervescent. **9 a** quiet; lacking activity (*the dead season*). **b** motionless, idle. **10 a** (of a microphone, telephone, etc.) not transmitting any sound, esp. because of a fault. **b** (of a circuit, conductor, etc.) carrying or transmitting no current; not connected to a source of electricity (*a dead battery*). **11 a** (of the ball etc. in a game) out of play. **b** (of play) suspended. **12** abrupt, complete, exact, unqualified, unrelieved (*come to a dead stop; a dead faint; a dead calm; in dead silence; a dead certainty*). **13** without spiritual life or energy. ● *adverb* **1** absolutely, exactly, completely (*dead on target; dead ahead; dead last; dead against; seen from dead on*). **2** *informal* very, extremely (*dead easy; dead broke; dead tired*). ● *noun* (prec. by *the*) **1** (treated as *pl.*) those who have died. **2** a time of silence or inactivity (*the dead of night*). □ **dead as the dodo** *see* DODO. **dead as a doornail** *see* DOORNAIL. **dead drunk** so drunk as to be immobile or insensible. **dead from the neck up** *informal* stupid. **dead in the water** *N Amer.* **1** (of a ship etc.) motionless, esp. as a result of damage, malfunction, etc. **2** not moving, progressing or functioning (*the economy is dead in the water*). **dead to rights** in the act; red-handed. **dead to the world** *informal* fast asleep; unconscious. **play dead** pretend to be dead by lying still. **stop dead in one's tracks** stop abruptly and decisively. **wouldn't be caught** (or **seen**) **dead in** (or **with**) *informal* shall have nothing to do with; shall refuse to wear etc. □ **dead·ness** *noun* [Old English *dēad* from Germanic, related to DIE[1]]

dead air *noun* **1** a pause in a radio etc. transmission, during which nothing is broadcast, the speakers are silent, etc. **2** air trapped for insulating purposes, as in layers of clothing.

dead·beat *noun* **1 a** someone who avoids paying debts. **b** (in full **deadbeat dad** or **deadbeat father**) a man who avoids paying child support. **2** a worthless sponging idler; a loafer.

dead beat *adjective informal* completely exhausted.

dead·bolt *noun* esp. *N Amer.* a bolt engaged by turning a knob or key, rather than by spring action.

dead-cat bounce *noun* a temporary recovery on a stock exchange after a substantial fall, after which the downward trend continues.

dead centre *noun* **1** the exact centre. **2** the position of a crank etc. in line with the connecting rod and not exerting torque.

dead cert *noun see* CERT.

dead duck *noun slang* **1** a person in a hopeless position, unable to elude a crisis. **2** an unsuccessful or useless person or thing.

dead·en *verb* **1** *transitive & intransitive* deprive of or lose vitality, force, brightness, sound, feeling, etc. **2** *transitive* (foll. by *to*) make insensitive. □ **dead·en·er** *noun*

dead end ● *noun* **1 a** a closed end of a road, passage, etc. **b** a street or road with a dead end. **2** (often, with hyphen, *attributive*) a situation offering no prospects of progress or advancement (*dead-end job*). ● *intransitive verb* (**dead-end**) *N Amer.* (of a road or one's progress, development, etc.) come to an end.

dead·eye *noun* **1** *Naut.* a circular wooden block with a groove around the circumference to take a lanyard, used singly or in pairs to tighten a shroud. **2** *informal* (often *attributive*) an expert marksman.

dead·fall *noun* *N Amer.* **1** a trap in which a raised weight is made to fall on and kill esp. large game. **2** a tangled mass of fallen trees, branches, etc. **3** a dead tree that has fallen to the ground.

dead·head ● *noun* **1** a faded flower head. **2** *N Amer.* a sunken or submerged log, esp. one that is a hazard to boats. **3** a useless or unenterprising person. ● *verb* **1** *transitive* remove deadheads from (a plant). **2** *intransitive* *N Amer.* (of a driver etc.) complete a journey with an empty train, bus, etc.

dead heat ● *noun* **1** a race in which two or more competitors finish at exactly the same time. **2** a situation in which all participants, competitors, etc. receive the same number of votes etc. **3** the result of such a competition. ● *intransitive verb* (**dead-heat**) (usu. foll. by *with*) run a dead heat.

dead horse *noun* an unalterable fact or situation which one wastes time attempting to change. □ **flog** (or **beat**) **a dead horse** waste energy on something unalterable.

dead language *noun* a language no longer in everyday spoken use, e.g. Latin.

dead letter *noun* **1** a law or practice no longer observed or recognized. **2** a piece of mail that cannot be delivered.

dead lift ● *noun* **1** the exertion of one's utmost strength to lift something. **2** a powerlifting event in which a weight is lifted from the ground to hip level in one movement. ● *transitive verb* (**dead·lift**) lift (a weight) in a dead lift.

dead·line *noun* **1** a time limit for the completion of an activity etc. **2** *hist.* a line beyond which prisoners were not allowed to go.

dead·lock ● *noun* **1** a situation, esp. one involving opposing parties, in which no progress can be made. **2** a type of lock requiring a key to open or close it. ● *transitive & intransitive verb* bring or come to a standstill. □ **dead·locked** *adjective*

dead loss *noun* **1** *informal* a useless person or thing. **2** a complete loss.

dead·ly ● *adjective* (**dead·li·er**, **dead·li·est**) **1 a** causing or able to cause fatal injury or serious damage. **b** poisonous (*deadly snake*). **2** intense, extreme (*deadly dullness*). **3** (of an aim etc.) extremely accurate or effective. **4** deathlike (*deadly gloom*). **5** *informal* dreary, dull. **6** implacable. ● *adverb* **1** like death; as if dead (*deadly faint*). **2** extremely, intensely (*deadly serious*). □ **dead·li·ness** *noun*

deadly nightshade *noun* = BELLADONNA 1.

deadly sin *noun* a sin regarded as leading to damnation, esp. pride, covetousness, lust, gluttony, envy, anger, or sloth.

dead·man *adjective* (also **dead man's**) designating a safety mechanism which stops a train or other machinery if the operator ceases to engage a switch, pedal, etc. (*deadman feature; dead man's pedal*).

dead man's fingers *noun* **1** a kind of orchis, *Orchis mascula*. **2** the finger-like divisions of a lobster's or crab's gills.

deadman's float *noun* a floating position, often used by beginning swimmers, in which a person lies face down in the water with arms outstretched or extended forward and legs extended backward.

dead march *noun* a funeral march.

dead meat *noun* *N Amer. informal* a person or thing that is doomed or finished (*if they don't arrive soon, we're dead meat*).

dead nettle *noun* any plant of the genus *Lamium*, having nettle-like leaves but without stinging hairs.

dead-on *adjective* **1** exactly right. **2** perfectly on target.

dead·pan ● *adjective & adverb* with a face or manner totally lacking expression or emotion. ● *transitive & intransitive verb* (**dead·panned**, **dead·pan·ning**) say in a deadpan manner. ● *noun* a deadpan countenance.

dead reckoning *noun* calculation of a ship's or aircraft's position from the log, compass, etc., when observations are impossible.

dead ringer *noun see* RINGER.

Dead Sea a salt lake or inland sea in the Jordan valley, on the Israel–Jordan border. Its surface is 400 m (1,300 ft.) below sea level.

Dead Sea scrolls a collection of Hebrew and Aramaic manuscripts discovered in caves near Qumran, at the northwestern end of the Dead Sea, between 1947 and 1956. They include texts of many books of the Old Testament, as well as commentaries, psalms, and other works; they are some 1,000 years older than previously known versions.

dead set *adjective* (foll. by *against*) fiercely opposed.

dead soldier *noun* *N Amer. informal* a bottle after its contents have been drunk.

dead·stick landing *noun* an unpowered landing of an aircraft.

dead time *noun* **1** *Physics* the period after the recording of a pulse etc. when the detector is unable to record another. **2** any period of inactivity between events.

dead·water *noun* a still, smooth section of a river.

dead weight *noun* **1 a** an inert mass. **b** a heavy weight or burden. **2** a debt not covered by assets. **3** the total weight carried on a ship.

dead·wood *noun* *informal* one or more useless or unprofitable people or things.

dead zone *noun* an area of the ocean that is depleted of oxygen, esp. due to pollution.

de-aerate *transitive verb* remove air from. □ **de-aeration** *noun* **de-aerator** *noun*

deaf *adjective* **1** wholly or partly without hearing (*deaf in one ear*). **2** (foll. by *to*) refusing to listen or comply. **3** insensitive to harmony, rhythm, etc. (*tone-deaf*). □ **deaf as a post** completely deaf. **fall on deaf ears** be ignored. **turn a deaf ear** (usu. foll. by *to*) be unresponsive. □ **deaf·ly** *adverb* **deaf·ness** *noun* [Old English *dēaf* from Germanic]

deaf-blind *adjective* (of a person) both deaf and blind.

deaf·en *transitive verb* **1** (often as **deaf·en·ing** *adjective*) overpower with sound. **2** deprive of hearing by noise, esp. temporarily. □ **deaf·en·ing·ly** *adverb*

deaf-mute ● *adjective* (of a person) both deaf and mute. ● *noun* a deaf-mute person.

deal¹ ● *verb* (*past* and *past participle* **dealt**) **1** *intransitive* (foll. by *with*) **a** take measures concerning (a problem, person, etc.), esp. in order to put something right. **b** do business with; associate with. **c** discuss or treat (a subject). **2** *intransitive* (foll. by *in*) sell or be concerned with commercially (*deals in insurance*). **3** *transitive* (often foll. by *out, round*) distribute or apportion to several people etc. **4** *transitive & intransitive* distribute (cards) to players for a game or round. **5** *transitive* cause to be received; administer (*deal a heavy blow*). **6** *transitive* (foll. by *in*) *informal* include (a person) in an activity (*you can deal me in*). ● *noun* **1** (usu. **a good** or **great deal**) *informal* **a** a large amount (*a great deal of trouble*). **b** to a considerable extent (*is a good deal better*). **2** an agreement, esp. in business on certain terms for buying or doing something (*we have a deal; a package deal; the deal fell through*). **3** a specified form of treatment given or received (*gave them a rough deal; got a fair deal*). **4 a** the distribution of cards by dealing. **b** a player's turn to do this (*it's my deal*). **c** the round of play following this. **d** a set of hands dealt to players. □ **it's a deal** *informal* expressing assent to an agreement. [Old English *dǽl, dǽlan*, from Germanic]

deal² *noun* **1** fir or pine timber, esp. sawn into boards of a standard size. **2 a** a board of this timber. **b** such boards collectively. [Middle Low German, Middle Dutch *dele* plank, from Germanic]

de-alcohol·ized *adjective* (also esp. *Brit.* **-ised**) (of an alcoholic drink) having had all or almost all alcohol removed.

deal·er *noun* **1** a person or business dealing in (esp. retail) goods (*contact your dealer; car dealer*). **2** the player dealing at cards. **3** a person who deals in illegal drugs. □ **dealer·ship** *noun* (in sense 1).

deal·ings *plural noun* contacts or transactions, esp. in business.

dealt *past and past participle of* DEAL¹.

Dean ▸ 1 Chris·to·pher, see TORVILL AND DEAN. **2 James (Byron)** (1931–55), US actor who became a cult figure following his early death in a car accident; he starred in three films, *East of Eden* (1955), *Rebel Without a Cause* (1955; released posthumously), and *Giant* (1956).

dean *noun* **1 a** the head of a university faculty or department. **b** a college or university official with disciplinary and advisory functions. **2 a** the head of the chapter of a cathedral or collegiate church. **b** (usu. **rural dean**) *Brit.* a member of the clergy exercising supervision over a group of parish clergy within a division of an archdeaconry. **3** the most senior or most prominent of a particular category or body of people. [Anglo-French *deen*, Old French *deien*, from Late Latin *decanus* from *decem* ten; originally = chief of a group of ten]

dean·ery *noun* (pl. **-eries**) **1** a dean's house or office. **2** *Brit.* the group of parishes presided over by a rural dean.

Dean River a river in west central BC, rising in the Fraser Plateau and flowing northwestward, then westward into Dean Channel, an inlet of the Pacific Ocean.

dean's list *noun N Amer.* a list of students receiving special recognition from the dean of a college or university for academic excellence.

dear ● *adjective* **1 a** beloved or much esteemed. **b** as a merely polite or ironic form (*my dear man*). **2** used as a formula of address, esp. at the beginning of letters (*Dear Rebecca*). **3** (often foll. by *to*) precious; much cherished. **4** (usu. in *superlative*) earnest, deeply felt (*my dearest wish*). **5 a** high-priced relative to its value. **b** having high prices. **c** (of money) available as a loan only at a high rate of interest. ● *noun* (esp. as a form of address) a dear person. ● *adverb* at a high price or great cost (*buy cheap and sell dear; will cost you dear*). ● *interjection* expressing surprise, dismay, pity, etc. (*dear me!; oh dear!; dear, dear!*). □ **dear (only) knows** heaven knows. **for dear life** see LIFE. □ **dear·ness** *noun* [Old English *dēore* from Germanic; compare Dutch *dier* beloved, German *teuer* expensive]

dear·ie *noun* (esp. as a form of address) usu. *jocular* or *ironic* my dear. □ **dearie me!** *interjection* expressing surprise, dismay, etc.

Dear John *noun informal* (also **Dear John letter**) a letter from a woman to an absent boyfriend, husband, etc., notifying him of the end of their relationship and her attachment to another man.

dear·ly *adverb* **1** affectionately, fondly (*loved him dearly*). **2 a** earnestly; keenly. **b** very much, greatly (*would dearly love to go*). **3** at a high price or great cost.

dearth /dɜːθ/ *noun* a scarcity or lack. [Middle English *derthe*, originally in the sense 'shortage and dearness of food']

death *noun* **1** the final cessation of vital functions in an organism; the ending of life. **2** the event that terminates life. **3 a** the fact or process of being killed or killing (*stone to death; fight to the death*). **b** the fact or state of being dead (*eyes closed in death; their deaths caused rioting*). **4 a** the destruction or permanent cessation of something (*was the death of our hopes*). **b** *informal* something terrible or appalling. **5** (usu. **Death**) a personification of death, esp. as a destructive power, usu. represented by a skeleton. **6** a lack of religious faith or spiritual life. □ **at death's door** close to death. **be in at the death 1** be present when an animal is killed, esp. in hunting. **2** witness the (esp. sudden) ending of an enterprise etc. **be the death of 1** cause the death of. **2** be very harmful to. **catch one's death** *informal* catch a serious chill etc. **do to death 1** kill. **2** overdo. **fate worse than death** *informal* a disastrous misfortune or experience. **like death warmed over** *slang* very tired or ill. **put to death** kill or cause to be killed. **to death** to the utmost, extremely (*bored to death; worked to death*). □ **death·less** *adjective* **death·less·ness** *noun* **death·like** *adjective* [Old English *dēath* from Germanic: related to DIE¹]

death adder *noun* any of various venomous snakes of the genus *Acanthopis*, esp. *A. antarcticus* of Australia.

death angel *noun* = DEATH CAP.

death·bed *noun* a bed as the place where a person is dying or has died (also *attributive*: *deathbed conversion*). □ **on one's deathbed** near death.

death blow *noun* **1** a blow or other action that causes death. **2** an event or circumstance that abruptly ends an activity, enterprise, etc.

death camas *noun* any of several poisonous plants of the chiefly N American genus *Zigadenus*, of the lily family.

death camp *noun* a prison camp in which many people die or are put to death.

death cap *noun* a poisonous mushroom, *Amanita phalloides*.

death certificate *noun* an official statement of the cause and date and place of a person's death.

death knell *noun* **1** the tolling of a bell to mark a person's death. **2** an event that heralds the end or destruction of something.

death·ly ● *adjective* (**death·li·er**, **death·li·est**) suggestive of death (*deathly silence*). ● *adverb* **1** in a deathly way (*deathly pale*). **2** extremely (*deathly ill*).

death mask *noun* a cast taken of a dead person's face.

death metal *noun* a form of heavy metal music whose lyrics frequently deal with death, violence, and Satanism.

death penalty *noun* punishment by being put to death.

death rate *noun* the number of deaths per thousand of population per year.

death rattle *noun* a gurgling sound sometimes heard in a dying person's throat.

death row *noun* a prison block or section for prisoners sentenced to death, esp. in the US.

death sentence *noun* **1** a judicial sentence of punishment by death. **2** a situation implying imminent or premature death (*a cancer diagnosis is not a death sentence*).

death's head *noun* a human skull as an emblem of mortality.

death spiral *noun Figure Skating* a move in pairs figure skating where the man pivots on one foot with the other leg extended forward while the woman, stretched out almost parallel to the ice and holding onto his outstretched hand, circles around him with one skate on the ice.

death squad *noun* an armed paramilitary group formed to kill political enemies etc.

death star *noun Cdn* a satellite transmitting television signals directly to consumers' homes, esp. considered as a threat to cable television providers. [recalling a sinister space station in the film *Star Wars* (1977), and perhaps from DTH Direct-To-Home]

death tax *noun N Amer.* a tax on property payable on the owner's death.

death toll *noun* the number of people killed in an accident, battle, etc.

death trap *noun informal* a dangerous or unhealthy building, vehicle, etc.

Death Valley a deep arid desert basin in SE California and SW Nevada, the hottest and driest part of N America and one of the hottest places on earth.

death warrant *noun* **1** an order for the execution of a condemned person. **2** anything that causes the end of an established practice etc.

death watch *noun* a vigil for a dying person.

death-watch beetle *noun* a small beetle (*Xestobium rufovillosum*)

Vowels: a cat ɑ arm e bed ɜr her ɜː deux ə ago ɪ sit i cosy iː feed ɒ hot ɔ pore oː no ʌ run ʊ put

which makes a sound like a watch ticking, once supposed to portend death, and whose larva bores in old wood.

death wish *noun* a desire (usu. unconscious) for the death of oneself or another.

deb *noun informal* a debutante. [abbreviation]

de·ba·cle /də'bɒkəl, -'bakəl/ *noun* **1 a** an utter failure or disaster. **b** a sudden collapse or downfall. **2** a confused rush or rout; a stampede. **3 a** a breakup of ice in a river, with resultant flooding. **b** a sudden rush of water carrying along blocks of stone and other debris. [French from *débâcler* unbar]

debag *transitive verb* (**de·bagged**, **de·bag·ging**) *Brit. slang* remove the trousers of (a person), esp. as a joke.

debar *transitive verb* (**de·barred**, **de·bar·ring**) (foll. by *from*) exclude from admission or from a right; prohibit from an action (*was debarred from entering*). □ **de·bar·ment** *noun* [French *débarrer* unbar]

de·bark¹ *transitive & intransitive verb* = DISEMBARK. □ **de·bark·a·tion** *noun* [French *débarquer*]

de·bark² *transitive verb* remove the bark from (a tree, log, etc.).

de·base *transitive verb* **1** lower in quality, value, or character. **2** depreciate (coin) by alloying etc. □ **de·base·ment** *noun* **de·bas·er** *noun* [DE- + obsolete *base* for ABASE]

de·bat·able *adjective* **1** questionable; subject to dispute. **2** capable of being debated. □ **de·bat·ably** *adverb*

de·bate ● *verb* **1** *transitive & intransitive* discuss or dispute about (an issue, proposal, etc.) esp. formally in a legislative assembly, public meeting, etc. **2** *transitive* consider, ponder (a matter). **b** *intransitive* consider different sides of a question. **3** *transitive* engage in a debate with (someone). ● *noun* **1** a formal discussion on a particular matter, esp. in a legislative assembly etc. **2** argument, discussion (*open to debate*). **3** a contest in which the affirmative and negative sides of a question are presented by opposing speakers. □ **de·bat·er** *noun* [Old French *debatre*, *debat* from Romanic (as DE-, BATTLE)]

de·bauch /də'bɔtʃ/ ● *transitive verb* **1** corrupt morally. **2** cause to indulge in immoral or excessive sexual activity or excessive drinking. **3** seduce (a woman). ● *noun* a bout of excessive indulgence in such activities (*looked utterly unaffected by the previous night's debauch*). □ **de·bauched** *adjective* **de·bauch·er** *noun* [French *débauche(r)*, of unknown origin]

de·bauch·ee /ˌdebɔ'tʃiː, -'ʃiː/ *noun* a person addicted to excessive indulgence in sex, alcohol, drugs, etc.

de·bauch·ery /də'bɒtʃəri/ *noun* (*pl.* **-eries**) excessive indulgence in pleasures of the flesh, esp. sex, alcohol, or drugs.

de Beau·voir see BEAUVOIR.

de·ben·ture /də'bentʃər/ *noun* a sealed bond issued by a corporation or company in respect of a long-term (esp. fixed-interest) loan. [Latin *debentur* are owing, from *debēre* owe: assimilated to -URE]

de·bili·tate /də'bɪlɪˌteɪt/ *transitive verb* enfeeble, enervate. □ **de·bili·tat·ing** *adjective* **de·bili·tat·ing·ly** *adverb* **de·bili·ta·tion** *noun* **de·bili·ta·tive** /-tətɪv/ *adjective* [Latin *debilitare* (as DEBILITY)]

de·bil·ity /də'bɪlɪti/ *noun* (*pl.* **-ities**) **1** feebleness, esp. of health. **2** a disability or handicap. [Old French *debilité* from Latin *debilitas -tatis* from *debilis* weak]

deb·it ● *noun* **1** an entry in an account recording a sum owed or paid out. **2** the sum recorded. **3** the total of such sums. **4** the debit side of an account. ● *transitive verb* (**deb·it·ed**, **deb·it·ing**) **1** (foll. by *against*, *to*) enter (an amount) on the debit side of an account (*debited $500 against me*). **2** (foll. by *with*) enter (a person) on the debit side of an account (*debited me with $500*). [French *débit* from Latin *debitum* DEBT]

debit card *noun* a card enabling the holder to pay for purchases electronically by transferring funds from a bank account.

deb·on·air /ˌdebə'neər/ *adjective* **1** carefree, cheerful. **2** suave, self-assured. **3** having pleasant manners. □ **deb·on·air·ly** *adverb* [Old French *debonaire* = *de bon aire* of good disposition]

de·bone *transitive verb* remove the bones from (poultry etc.).

Deb·or·ah /'debərə, 'debrə/ a Biblical prophet and leader who inspired the Israelite army to defeat the Canaanites (Judges 4–5).

de·bouch /də'baʊtʃ, -'buːʃ/ *intransitive verb* **1** emerge from a narrow or confined place into open ground. **2** emerge from or as from a mouth or outlet. **3** (of a body of water) flow into a larger body of water. □ **de·bouch·ment** *noun* [French *déboucher* (as DE-, *bouche* mouth)]

De·brett /də'bret/ **John** (c.1750–1822), English publisher, who compiled *The Peerage of England, Scotland and Ireland* (first issued in 1803 and until fairly recently issued annually), which is regarded as the authority on the British nobility.

de·bride·ment /də'briːdmənt/ *noun Med.* the removal of damaged tissue or foreign matter from a wound etc. [French, literally 'unbridling']

de·brief *transitive verb* discuss a completed mission, undertaking, or event with (a person). □ **de·brief·ing** *noun*

deb·ris /də'briː, de-/ *noun* **1** scattered fragments, esp. of something wrecked or destroyed. **2** *Geol.* an accumulation of loose material, e.g. from rocks or plants. [French *débris* from obsolete *débriser* break down (as DE-, *briser* break)]

de Brog·lie /də 'broːli/ **Louis-Victor, Prince** (1892–1987), French physicist. He was the first to suggest that subatomic particles can also have the properties of waves, and his name is now applied to such a wave; he further developed the study of wave mechanics, and was awarded the Nobel Prize for physics in 1929.

debt *noun* **1** a sum of money owed. **2** a state of obligation to pay something owed (*in debt; out of debt; get into debt*). **3** gratitude for kindness, help, influence, etc. (*owes a debt to the work of earlier historians*). **4** *archaic* sin (*forgive us our debts*). □ **in a person's debt** under an obligation to a person. [Old French *dette*, ultimately from Latin *debitum* past participle of *debēre* owe]

debt·or *noun* a person, country, etc. that owes a debt, esp. money.

de·bug *transitive verb* (**de·bugged**, **de·bug·ging**) **1** identify and remove defects from (a machine, computer program, etc.). **2** trace and remove concealed listening devices from (a room etc.). □ **de·bug·ging** *noun*

debug·ger *noun Computing* a program for debugging other programs.

de·bunk *transitive verb informal* **1** show the good reputation or aspirations of (a person, institution, etc.) to be spurious. **2** expose the falseness of (a claim etc.). □ **de·bunk·er** *noun*

De·bussy /dəbuː'siː, debju'siː/ (**Achille**) **Claude** (1862–1918), French composer and critic. He carried the ideas of Impressionist art and symbolist poetry into music, and his works include the orchestral tone poem *Prélude à l'après-midi d'un faune* (1894), the opera *Pelléas et Mélisande* (1902), and books of piano preludes and studies.

debut /'deɪbjuː, 'deɪ-/ ● *noun* **1** the first public appearance of a person in a specified role, esp. a performer (*made his debut as Romeo; her coaching debut*). **2** *dated* the first appearance of a young woman of marriageable age in fashionable society. ● *adjective* first; inaugural (*their debut album*). ● *intransitive & transitive verb* make a debut. [French from *débuter* lead off]

debu·tante /'debjuːˌtɒnt, 'deɪ-/ *noun* a (usu. wealthy) young woman making her social debut. [French, fem. part. of *débuter*: see DEBUT]

Debye /dɪ'baɪ/ **Peter (Jo·seph Wil·liam)** (1884–1966), Dutch-born US chemical physicist. He determined the size and shape of numerous molecules by establishing the existence of permanent electric dipole moments, and pioneered the use of X-ray scattering to determine crystal structure; he received the Nobel Prize for chemistry in 1936.

Dec. *abbreviation* December.

dec. *abbreviation* **1** deceased. **2** declared.

deca- *combining form* (also **dec-** before a vowel) **1** having ten. **2** tenfold. **3** ten, esp. of a metric unit (*decagram; decalitre*). [Greek *deka* ten]

dec·ade /'dekeɪd/ *noun* **1** a period of ten years. **2** a set, series, or group of ten. **3** /'dekəd/ *Catholicism* a set of ten Hail Marys as part of the rosary. □ **dec·ad·al** /'dekədəl/ *adjective* [French *décade* from Late Latin *decas -adis* from Greek *deka* ten]

deca·dence /'dekədəns/ *noun* **1** moral or cultural deterioration, esp. after a peak or culmination of achievement. **2** decadent behaviour; a state of decadence. [French *décadence* from medieval Latin *decadentia* from *decadere* DECAY]

deca·dent ● *adjective* **1 a** in a state of moral or cultural deterioration; showing or characterized by decadence. **b** of a period of decadence. **2** self-indulgent. **3** (of food, esp. dessert) very rich or sweet (with the implication that eating it is an act of self-indulgence). ● *noun* a decadent person. □ **deca·dent·ly** *adverb* [French *décadent* (as DECADENCE)]

de·caf /'diːkaf/ *informal* ● *noun* decaffeinated coffee. ● *adjective* decaffeinated.

de·caf·fein·ate /diː'kafɪˌneɪt/ *transitive verb* **1** remove the caffeine from. **2** reduce the quantity of caffeine in (usu. coffee). □ **de·caf·fein·at·ed** *adjective* **de·caf·fein·a·tion** *noun*

deca·gon /'dekəˌgɒn/ *noun* a plane figure with ten sides and angles. □ **dec·ag·on·al** /də'kagənəl/ *adjective* [DECA-, -GON]

deca·he·dron /ˌdekə'hiːdrən/ *noun* (*pl.* **-hed·rons** or **-hedra** /-drə/) a solid figure with ten faces.

dec·al /'diːkal, 'dekəl/ *noun* a picture or design transferred from

u: m**oo**d   ai m**y**   əi p**i**pe   au br**ow**n   ʌu h**ou**se   ei d**ay**   ɔi b**oy**   ã fr**an**glais   ã C**a**nadien   ɔ̃ Br**ay**on   (*see over for consonants*)

specially prepared paper to the surface of glass, plastic, etc. [abbreviation of DECALCOMANIA]

de·cal·ci·fy *transitive verb* (**-fies, -fied**) remove lime or calcareous matter from (a bone, tooth, etc.). □ **de·cal·ci·fi·ca·tion** *noun* **de·cal·ci·fi·er** *noun*

de·cal·co·mania /diːˌkalkəˈmeɪnɪə/ *noun* **1** a process of transferring designs from specially prepared paper to the surface of glass, porcelain, etc. **2** = DECAL. [French *décalcomanie* from *décalquer* transfer]

deca·litre *noun* (also esp. *US* **deca·liter**) a metric unit of capacity, equal to 10 litres.

Deca·logue /ˈdekəˌlɒg/ *noun* the Ten Commandments. [French *décalogue* or ecclesiastical Latin *decalogus* from Greek *dekalogos* (after *hoi deka logoi* the Ten Commandments)]

deca·metre *noun* (also esp. *US* **deca·meter**) a metric unit of length, equal to 10 metres.

de·camp *intransitive verb* **1** depart suddenly. **2** break up or leave a camp. □ **de·camp·ment** *noun* [French *décamper* (as DE-, CAMP¹)]

de·can·al /dɪˈkeɪnəl, ˈdekə-/ *adjective* **1** of a dean or deanery. **2** (in a church with choir stalls facing inward) of the right side of the choir (when facing the front of the church). [medieval Latin *decanalis* from Late Latin *decanus* DEAN]

de·cani /dɪˈkeɪnaɪ, deˈkɑːni/ *adjective Music* to be sung by the decanal side in antiphonal singing (*compare* CANTORIS). [Latin, genitive of *decanus* DEAN]

de·cant /dɪˈkant/ *transitive verb* gradually pour off (liquid, esp. wine or a solution) from one container to another, esp. without disturbing the sediment. [medieval Latin *decanthare* (as DE-, CANTHUS, used for the lip of a beaker)]

de·cant·er *noun* a stoppered glass container into which wine or liquor is decanted.

de·capi·tate *transitive verb* remove the head or top of. □ **de·capi·ta·tion** *noun* [Late Latin *decapitare* (as DE-, *caput -itis* head)]

deca·pod /ˈdekəˌpɒd/ *noun* **1** any crustacean of the chiefly marine order Decapoda, characterized by five pairs of walking legs, e.g. shrimps, crabs, and lobsters. **2** any of various molluscs of the class Cephalopoda, having ten tentacles, e.g. squids and cuttlefish. [French *décapode* from Greek *deka* ten + *pous podos* foot]

de·carbon·ize *transitive verb* (also esp. *Brit.* **-ise**) remove carbon or carbonaceous deposits from (an internal combustion engine etc.). □ **de·carbon·iz·a·tion** *noun*

de·carb·oxyl·ate /ˌdiːkɑːrˈbɒksɪleɪt/ *verb* **1** *transitive* remove a carboxyl group from (a molecule). **2** *intransitive* lose a carboxyl group. □ **de·carb·oxyl·ase** *noun* **de·carb·oxyl·a·tion** *noun*

deca·sylla·ble /ˈdekəˌsɪləbəl/ *noun* a metrical line of ten syllables. □ **deca·syllab·ic** /-sɪˈlabɪk/ *adjective & noun*

dec·ath·lon /dəˈkaθlɒn/ *noun* an athletic contest in which each competitor takes part in ten events. □ **dec·ath·lete** /-liːt/ *noun* [DECA- + Greek *athlon* contest]

De·catur /dəˈkeɪtər/ **Ste·phen** (1779–1820), US naval officer, who was noted for his exploits during the war with Tripoli (1801–5) and the War of 1812.

de·cay ● *verb* **1 a** *intransitive* rot, decompose. **b** *transitive* cause to rot or decompose. **2** *intransitive & transitive* decline or cause to decline in quality, power, wealth, energy, beauty, etc. **3** *intransitive Physics* **a** (of a substance etc.) undergo change by radioactivity. **b** undergo a gradual decrease in magnitude of a physical quantity. ● *noun* **1** the state or process of rotting or decomposition (*hardwood is more resistant to decay than softwood; tooth decay*). **2** structural or physical deterioration (*the old barn rapidly fell into decay*). **3** rotten matter or tissue (*fluoride heals small spots of decay*). **4** the process of declining in quality, power, or vigour (*preachers warning of moral decay*). **5** *Physics* **a** change into another substance etc. by radioactivity. **b** a decrease in the magnitude of a physical quantity, esp. the intensity of radiation or amplitude of oscillation. [Old French *decair* from Romanic (as DE-, Latin *cadere* fall)]

Dec·can /ˈdekən/ a triangular plateau in S India, bounded by the Malabar Coast in the west, by the Coromandel Coast in the east, and by the Vindhaya mountains in the north.

de·cease *formal esp. Law* ● *noun* death. ● *intransitive verb* die. [Old French *deces* from Latin *decessus* from *decedere* (as DE-, *cedere cess-* go)]

de·ceased ● *adjective* dead. ● *noun* (usu. prec. by *the*) a person who has died, esp. recently.

de·ced·ent /dɪˈsiːdənt/ *noun N Amer. Law* a deceased person. [Latin *decedere* die: see DECEASE]

de·ceit *noun* **1** the act or process of deceiving or misleading, esp. by concealing the truth. **2** a dishonest trick or stratagem. **3** willingness to deceive. [Old French from past participle of *deceivir* from Latin *decipere* deceive (as DE-, *capere* take)]

de·ceit·ful *adjective* **1** (of a person) using deceit, esp. habitually. **2** (of an act, practice, etc.) intended to deceive. □ **de·ceit·ful·ly** *adverb* **de·ceit·ful·ness** *noun*

de·ceive *verb* **1** *transitive* make (a person) believe what is false; mislead purposely. **2** *transitive* be unfaithful to, esp. sexually. **3** *intransitive* use deceit. □ **be deceived** be mistaken or deluded. **deceive oneself** persist in a mistaken belief. □ **de·ceiv·able** *adjective* **de·ceiv·er** *noun* [Old French *deceivre* or *deceiv-* stressed, stem of *deceveir* (as DECEIT)]

de·celer·ate *verb* **1** *intransitive* move more slowly, slow down. **2** *transitive* diminish the speed of; cause to go slower. □ **de·celer·a·tion** *noun* **de·celer·ator** *noun* [DE-, after ACCELERATE]

De·cem·ber *noun* the twelfth month of the year. [Old French *decembre* from Latin *December* from *decem* ten: originally the tenth month of the Roman year]

De·cem·brist /dɪˈsembrɪst/ *noun* a member of a group of Russian revolutionaries who in December 1825 led an unsuccessful revolt against Czar Nicholas I. The leaders were executed and later came to be regarded as martyrs by the Left. [translation of Russian *dekabrist*]

de·cency *noun* (pl. **-cies**) **1** correct and tasteful standards of behaviour as generally accepted. **2** conformity with current standards of behaviour or propriety. **3** avoidance of obscenity. **4** (in pl.) the requirements of correct behaviour. [Latin *decentia* from *decēre* be fitting]

de·cen·nial /dɪˈsenɪəl/ *adjective* **1** lasting ten years. **2** recurring every ten years. □ **de·cen·nial·ly** *adverb* [Latin *decennis* of ten years, from *decem* ten + *annus* year]

de·cent *adjective* **1** conforming with current standards of behaviour or propriety. **2** respectable. **3** satisfying a fair standard; acceptable. **4** kind, obliging, generous (*was decent enough to apologize*). **5** *informal* sufficiently clothed to see visitors (*Are you decent? Can we come in?*). □ **de·cent·ly** *adverb* [French *décent* or Latin *decēre* be fitting]

de·cen·tral·ize *transitive verb* (also esp. *Brit.* **-ise**) **1** transfer (powers, functions, etc.) from a central to a regional or local authority, division, etc. **2** reorganize (a centralized institution, organization, etc.) on the basis of greater local or regional autonomy. □ **de·cen·tral·ist** *noun & adjective* **de·cen·tral·iz·a·tion** *noun* **de·cen·tral·ized** *adjective*

de·centre *transitive verb* (also esp. *US* **de·center**) remove the centre from.

de·cep·tion *noun* **1** the act or an instance of deceiving; the process of being deceived. **2** a thing that deceives; a trick or sham. [Old French or Late Latin *deceptio* from *decipere* (as DECEIT)]

de·cep·tive *adjective* giving an appearance or impression different from the true one; misleading (*he put the question with deceptive casualness*). [Old French *deceptif -ive* or Late Latin *deceptivus* (as DECEPTION)]

de·cep·tive·ly *adverb* **1** in a way or to an extent that gives a misleading impression. **2** to a lesser extent than appears the case (*the idea was deceptively simple*). **3** to a greater extent than appears the case (*the airy and deceptively spacious dining room*). ¶ *Deceptively* belongs to a very small set of words whose meaning is genuinely ambiguous in that it can be used in similar contexts to mean both one thing and also its complete opposite. To avoid confusion, use it with caution (or not at all) unless the context makes clear in what way the thing modified is not what it first appears to be.

de·cere·brate /dɪˈserɪbrət/ *adjective* having had the cerebrum removed.

de·certi·fy *transitive & intransitive verb* (**-fies, -fied**) revoke or renounce certification of (a person or thing, esp. a union) (*union members have voted to decertify*). □ **de·certi·fi·ca·tion** *noun*

deci- /ˈdesɪ/ *combining form* one-tenth, esp. of a unit in the metric system (*decilitre; decimetre*). [Latin *decimus* tenth]

deci·bel /ˈdesɪbəl, -ˌbel/ *noun* **1** a unit (one-tenth of a bel) used in the comparison of two power levels relating to electrical signals or sound intensities, one of the pair usually being taken as a standard. Abbr.: **dB**. **2** *informal* a degree of noise (*his voice went up several decibels*).

de·cide *verb* **1 a** *intransitive* (often foll. by *on, about*) come to a resolution as a result of consideration. **b** *transitive* (usu. foll. by *to* + infin., or *that* + clause) have or reach as one's resolution about something (*decided to stay; decided that we should leave*). **2** *transitive* **a** resolve or settle (a question, dispute, etc.). **b** cause (a person) to reach a resolution (*was unsure about going but the weather decided me*). **3** *intransitive* (usu. foll. by *between, for, against, in favour of,* or *that* + clause) give a judgment concerning a matter. □ **de·cid·able** *adjective* [French *décider* from Latin *decidere* (as DE-, *cædere* cut)]

de·cid·ed *adjective* **1** (usu. *attributive*) definite, unquestionable (*a decided difference*). **2** (of a person, esp. as a characteristic) having clear opinions, resolute, not vacillating. □ **de·cid·ed·ness** *noun*

de·cid·ed·ly *adverb* undoubtedly, undeniably.

de·cid·er *noun* **1** a game, race, etc., to decide between competitors finishing equal in a previous contest. **2** any person or thing that decides.

de·cidu·ous /dɪ'sɪdʒʊəs, -djʊəs/ *adjective* **1** (of a tree) shedding its leaves annually. **2** (of leaves, horns, teeth, etc.) shed periodically. **3** (of an ant etc.) shedding its wings after copulation. **4** fleeting, transitory. [Latin *deciduus* from *decidere* from *cadere* fall]

deci·gram *noun* a metric unit of mass, equal to 0.1 gram.

decile /'desaɪl, -səl/ *noun Statistics* any of the nine values of a random variable which divide a frequency distribution into ten groups, each containing one-tenth of the total population. [French *décile*, ultimately from Latin *decem* ten]

deci·litre *noun* (also esp. *US* **deci·liter**) a metric unit of capacity, equal to 0.1 litre.

deci·mal ● *adjective* **1** (of a system of numbers, weights, measures, etc.) based on the number ten, in which the smaller units are related to the principal units as powers of ten (units, tens, hundreds, thousands, etc.). **2** of tenths or ten; reckoning or proceeding by tens. ● *noun* a decimal fraction. □ **deci·mal·ly** *adverb* [modern Latin *decimalis* from Latin *decimus* tenth]

decimal fraction *noun* a fraction whose denominator is a power of ten, esp. when expressed positionally by units to the right of a decimal point.

deci·mal·ize *transitive verb* (also esp. *Brit.* **-ise**) **1** express as a decimal. **2** convert to a decimal system (esp. of coinage). □ **deci·mal·iz·a·tion** *noun*

decimal place *noun* the position of a digit to the right of a decimal point.

decimal point *noun* a period placed before a numerator in a decimal fraction.

decimal scale *noun* a scale with successive places denoting units, tens, hundreds, etc.

deci·mate *transitive verb* **1** destroy a large proportion of. ¶ Now the usual sense, although some still consider this an inappropriate use. **2** kill or remove one in every ten of. □ **deci·ma·tion** *noun* **deci·ma·tor** *noun* [Latin *decimare* take the tenth man, from *decimus* tenth]

deci·metre *noun* (also esp. *US* **deci·meter**) a metric unit of length, equal to 0.1 metre.

de·cipher /dɪ'saɪfər/ *transitive verb* **1** succeed in understanding (anything obscure or unclear). **2** convert (a text written in cipher) into an intelligible script or language. □ **de·cipher·able** *adjective* **de·cipher·ment** *noun*

de·ci·sion *noun* **1** the act or process of deciding. **2** a conclusion or resolution reached, esp. as to future action, after consideration (*Patrick has made his decision*). **3** *Baseball* a win or a loss credited to a pitcher. **4** *Boxing* a victory determined by points. **5 a** the settlement of a question. **b** a formal judgment. **6** a tendency to decide firmly; resoluteness. [Old French *decision* or Latin *decisio* (as DECIDE)]

de·ci·sive *adjective* **1** that decides an issue; conclusive. **2** (of a person, esp. as a characteristic) able to decide quickly and effectively. □ **de·ci·sive·ly** *adverb* **de·ci·sive·ness** *noun* [French *décisif -ive* from medieval Latin *decisivus* (as DECIDE)]

De·cius /'di:siəs/ (full name Gaius Messius Quintus Trajanus (*c.*201–51), Roman emperor 249–51. He was the first Roman emperor to promote systematic persecution of Christians.

deck ● *noun* **1 a** a platform in a ship covering all or part of the hull's area at any level and serving as a floor. **b** the accommodation on a particular deck of a ship. **2** anything compared to a ship's deck. **3** a component that carries a particular recording medium (such as a disc or tape) in sound-reproduction equipment. **4** *N Amer.* **a** a pack of cards. **b** *slang* a packet of narcotics. **5** *slang* the ground. **6** any floor or platform, esp. the floor of a pier or a platform for sunbathing. **7** *N Amer.* a level unroofed area, usu. of wooden planks, adjoining a house to provide an outdoor seating space. **8** the flat, usu. concrete area surrounding a swimming pool. **9** a tier of seats in a ballpark. **10** the flat part of a skateboard or snowboard. **11** a pile of logs ready for hauling, milling, etc. ● *transitive verb* **1** (often foll. by *out*) decorate, adorn. **2** furnish with or cover as a deck. **3** *slang* knock (a

person) to the ground. □ **below deck** (or **decks**) in or into the space below the main deck. **on deck 1** in the open air on a ship's main deck. **2** (esp. of a batter in baseball) next in line. □ **deck·less** *adjective* [Middle English, = covering, from Middle Dutch *dec* roof, cloak]

deck chair *noun* a folding chair of wood and canvas, of a kind used on deck on passenger ships.

-decker *combining form* having a specified number of decks or layers (*double-decker*).

deck·hand *noun* a person employed in cleaning and odd jobs on a ship's deck.

deck·ing *noun* **1** the material of the deck of a ship, floor, or platform. **2** the part of a snowshoe, attached to the frame, that supports the person's weight.

deckle /'dekəl/ *noun* a device in a papermaking machine for limiting the size of the sheet. [German *Deckel* diminutive of *Decke* cover]

deckle edge *noun* the rough uncut edge formed by a deckle. □ **deckle-edged** *adjective*

deck shoe *noun* a shoe resembling a moccasin with rubber soles, leather uppers, and laces, usu. having a second lace looped around the heel.

deck tennis *noun* a game in which a quoit of rope, rubber, etc., is tossed to and fro over a net.

de·claim /dɪ'kleɪm/ *verb* **1** *intransitive & transitive* speak or utter rhetorically or affectedly. **2** *intransitive* practise oratory or recitation. **3** *intransitive* (foll. by *against*) protest forcefully. **4** *intransitive* deliver an impassioned (rather than reasoned) speech. □ **de·claim·er** *noun* [French *déclamer* or from Latin *declamare* (as DE-, CLAIM)]

dec·lam·a·tion /ˌdeklə'meɪʃən/ *noun* **1** the act or art of declaiming. **2** a rhetorical exercise or set speech. **3** an impassioned speech; a harangue. □ **de·clama·tory** /dɪ'klæmə,tɔrɪ/ *adjective* [French *déclamation* or Latin *declamatio* (as DECLAIM)]

de·clar·ant *noun* a person who makes a legal declaration.

dec·lar·a·tion *noun* **1** the act or process of declaring. **2 a** a formal, emphatic, or deliberate statement or announcement. **b** a statement asserting or protecting a legal right. **3** a written public announcement of intentions, terms of an agreement, etc. **4** *Cards* **a** the naming of trumps. **b** an announcement of a combination held. **5** *Law* **a** a plaintiff's statement of claim. **b** an affirmation made instead of taking an oath.

Declaration of Independence a document drawn up by Thomas Jefferson, Benjamin Franklin, John Adams, and others, declaring the US to be independent of the British Crown, signed on 4 July 1776 by the Congressional representatives of eleven states.

Declaration of Rights a statute passed by the English government in 1689, later incorporated in the Bill of Rights, which established the joint monarchy of William and Mary and which was designed to ensure that the Crown would not act without Parliament's consent.

de·clara·tive /dɪ'klerətɪv/ ● *adjective* **1 a** of the nature of, or making, a declaration. **b** *Grammar* (of a sentence) that takes the form of a simple statement. **2** *Computing* designating high-level programming languages that can be used to solve problems without requiring the programmer to specify an exact procedure to be followed. ● *noun Grammar* a declarative sentence. □ **de·clara·tive·ly** *adverb*

de·clare *verb* **1** *transitive* announce openly or formally (*declare war*; *declare a dividend*). **2** *transitive* pronounce (a person or thing) to be something (*declared him to be an imposter*; *declared it invalid*). **3** *transitive* (often foll. by *that* + clause) assert emphatically; state explicitly. **4** *transitive* acknowledge possession of (dutiable goods, taxable income, etc.). **5** *transitive Cards* **a** (also *intransitive*) name (the trump suit, conditions of play, etc.). **b** reveal that one holds (certain combinations of cards etc.) for scoring. **6** *transitive* (of things) make evident, prove. **7** *intransitive* (often foll. by *for*, *against*) take the side of one party or another. **8** *intransitive N Amer.* announce oneself to be a candidate (for an electoral race). □ **declare oneself** reveal one's intentions or identity. **well, I declare** (or **I do declare**) an exclamation of incredulity, surprise, or vexation. □ **de·clara·tory** *adjective* **de·clar·er** *noun* [Latin *declarare* (as DE-, *clarare* from *clarus* clear)]

de·clared *adjective* **1** that has been declared or made known. **2** (of a person) admitted, professed (*a declared atheist*). □ **de·clar·ed·ly** *adverb*

de·class *transitive verb* remove or degrade from one's social class.

dé·classé /deɪkla'seɪ/ *adjective* **1** that has fallen in social status. **2** considered to be of or appropriate to a lower social status, rank, etc. [French]

de·classi·fy *transitive verb* (**-fies, -fied**) declare (information etc.) to be no longer secret. □ **de·classi·fi·ca·tion** *noun*

de·claw *transitive verb* **1** remove the claws from (a cat). **2** remove the force, vigour, influence from (a movement, individual, etc.).

de·clen·sion /dɪˈklenʃən/ *noun* **1** *Grammar* **a** the variation of the form of a noun, pronoun, or adjective, by which its grammatical case, number, and gender are identified. **b** the class in which a noun etc. is put according to the exact form of this variation. **c** the entire set of inflected forms of a noun etc. **2** deterioration, declining. ☐ **de·clen·sion·al** *adjective* [Old French *declinaison* from *decliner* DECLINE, after Latin *declinatio*: assimilated to ASCENSION etc.]

dec·lin·a·tion /ˌdeklɪˈneɪʃən/ *noun* **1** *Astronomy* the angular distance of a star etc. north or south of the celestial equator. **2** *Physics* the angular deviation of a compass needle from true north. **3** a downward bend or turn. **4** *US* a formal refusal. [Latin *declinatio* (as DECLINE)]

de·cline ● *verb* **1** *intransitive* deteriorate; lose strength or vigour. **2 a** *transitive* reply with formal courtesy that one will not accept (an invitation, honour, etc.). **b** *transitive* refuse, esp. formally and courteously (*declined to speak*). **c** *transitive* turn away from (a challenge, battle, discussion, etc.). **d** *intransitive* give or send a refusal. **3 a** *intransitive* slope downwards or bend down. **b** *transitive* bend (something) down. **4** *transitive Grammar* state the forms of (a noun, pronoun, or adjective) corresponding to cases, number, and gender. **5** *intransitive* **a** diminish in numbers or size (*the caribou population declined*). **b** decrease in price etc. ● *noun* **1 a** a decrease in numbers, rates, etc. **b** gradual loss of vigour or excellence. **2** decay, deterioration. **3** a fall in price or value. ☐ **on the decline** in a declining state; falling off. ☐ **de·clin·able** *adjective* **de·clin·er** *noun* [Latin *declinare* (as DE-, *clinare* bend]

de·clin·ing years *noun* the later years of a person's life, often characterized by a falling off of strength etc.

de·cliv·i·ty /dɪˈklɪvɪti/ *noun* (*pl.* **-ities**) a downward slope, esp. a piece of sloping ground (*opp.* ACCLIVITY). [Latin *declivitas* from *declivis* (as DE-, *clivus* slope)]

de·clutch *intransitive verb* disengage the clutch of a motor vehicle.

Deco /ˈdekoʊ/ *noun* (also **deco**) (usu. *attributive*) = ART DECO. [French *décoratif* DECORATIVE]

de·coc·tion /dɪˈkɒkʃən/ *noun* **1** a process of boiling down so as to extract some essence. **2** the extracted liquor resulting from this. [Late Latin *decoctio* (as DE-, Latin *coquere coct-* boil)]

de·code *transitive verb* **1** convert (a coded message) into intelligible language. **2** analyze to extract meaning from (written or spoken communication, an artistic style, etc.) (*I tried to decode the politician's speech*) (*compare* ENCODE 2). **3** *Electronics* convert or unscramble (a coded signal) into an accessible format. ☐ **de·cod·able** *adjective*

de·cod·er *noun* **1** a person or thing that decodes (texts etc.). **2** an electronic device for analyzing stereophonic signals and feeding separate amplifier channels. **3** (in full **decoder box**) an electronic device connected to a television to unscramble encoded transmissions, esp. cable programs and closed-captioning.

dé·col·le·tage /ˌdeɪkɒlˈtɑːʒ, -ɪˈtɒʒ/ *noun* a low neckline of a woman's dress etc. [French (as DE-, *collet* collar of a dress)]

dé·col·le·té /deɪˈkɒltei/ ● *adjective* **1** (of a dress etc.) having a low neckline. **2** (of a woman) wearing a dress with a low neckline. ● *noun* a low neckline. [French (as DÉCOLLETAGE)]

de·col·onize *transitive verb* (also esp. *Brit.* **-onise**) (of a state) withdraw from (a colony), leaving it independent. ☐ **de·col·oniz·a·tion** *noun*

de·color·ize *verb* (also esp. *Brit.* **-ise**, *Cdn* **de·colour·ize**) *transitive* remove the colour from. ☐ **de·color·iz·a·tion** *noun* **de·color·iz·ing** *adjective*

de·com·mis·sion *transitive verb* **1** close down (a nuclear reactor etc.). **2** take (a ship or aircraft) out of service.

de·com·pen·sa·tion *noun Med.* failure of an organ to maintain functioning, esp. after a period of compensation for disease, deficiency, etc.

de·com·pose *verb* **1 a** *intransitive* decay, rot. **b** *transitive* cause to decay. **2** *transitive* separate (a substance, light, etc.) into its elements or simpler constituents. **3** *intransitive* disintegrate; break up. ☐ **de·com·pos·able** *adjective* **de·com·pos·abil·ity** *noun* **de·com·pos·i·tion** *noun*

de·com·pos·er *noun* a thing, esp. a living organism, that performs decomposition.

de·com·press *verb* **1** *transitive* **a** subject to decompression. **b** relieve or reduce the compression on. **2** *transitive Computing* restore (computer files compacted for storage or distribution) to normal size. **3** *intransitive N Amer. informal* calm down, relax. ☐ **de·com·pres·sor** *noun*

de·com·pres·sion *noun* **1** the process of relieving or reducing pressure. **2** a gradual reduction of air pressure on a person who has been subjected to high pressure (esp. underwater). **3** a sudden reduction of air pressure in an aircraft etc. to the ambient external pressure. **4** *Computing* the act or process of restoring compacted computer files to their normal size.

decompression chamber *noun* a steel chamber in which atmospheric pressure can be raised or lowered, e.g. for subjecting a person to decompression.

decompression sickness *noun* a serious disorder, esp. of deep-sea divers, caused by nitrogen bubbles forming in the tissues from a too rapid decompression and characterized by pain, nausea, paralysis, etc. *Also called* CAISSON DISEASE or *informal* THE BENDS (*see* BEND[1] *noun* 4).

de·con·gest·ant /ˌdiːkənˈdʒestənt/ ● *adjective* that relieves (esp. nasal) congestion. ● *noun* a medicinal agent that relieves nasal congestion.

de·con·se·crate *transitive verb* transfer (esp. a building) from sacred to secular use. ☐ **de·con·se·cra·tion** *noun*

de·con·struct *transitive verb* **1** subject to deconstruction. **2** undo the construction of, take to pieces. ☐ **de·con·struct·ive** *adjective* [back-formation from DECONSTRUCTION]

de·con·struc·tion *noun* **1** a method of critical analysis directed towards exposing unquestioned metaphysical assumptions and internal inconsistencies in (esp. philosophical and literary) language and texts. **2** a critical movement begun in the 1960s, associated with Jacques Derrida, and propounding such strategies. ☐ **de·con·struc·tion·ism** *noun* **de·con·struc·tion·ist** *adjective & noun* [French *déconstruction*]

de·con·tam·in·ate *transitive verb* remove contamination or the risk of it from (an area, person, etc.) affected by radioactivity, infectious disease, harmful chemicals, etc. ☐ **de·con·tam·in·a·tion** *noun*

de·context·ual·ize *transitive verb* (also esp. *Brit.* **-ise**) study or treat (a word, text etc.) in isolation from its context. ☐ **de·context·ual·iz·a·tion** *noun* **de·context·ual·ized** *adjective*

de·con·trol ● *transitive verb* (**de·con·trolled**, **de·con·trol·ling**) release (a commodity etc.) from controls or restrictions, esp. those imposed by the state. ● *noun* the removal of (esp. governmental) control or restrictions.

decor /ˈdeɪkɔːr, ˈdeɪkɔːr, dəˈkɔːr/ *noun* **1** the overall effect, style, etc. of the decorations and furnishings of a room, building, etc. **2** the furnishing and decoration of a room etc. **3** the decoration and scenery of a stage. [French from *décorer* (as DECORATE)]

decor·ate *transitive verb* (often foll. by *with*) **1** make (something) more attractive by adding colour, adornments, etc. **2** provide (a room or building) with new paint, wallpaper, etc. **3** invest (a person) with a military or other decoration, medal, etc. ☐ **decor·at·ed** *adjective* [Latin *decorare decorat-* from *decus -oris* beauty]

Decorated style *noun Archit.* the second stage of English Gothic (14th c.), with increasing use of decoration and geometrical tracery.

decor·a·tion *noun* **1** the process or art of decorating. **2** a thing that decorates or serves as an ornament. **3** a medal etc. conferred and worn as an honour.

decor·a·tive /ˈdekrətɪv, ˈdekərə-/ *adjective* **1** serving to decorate. **2** ornamental rather than operational. ☐ **decor·a·tive·ly** *adverb* **decor·a·tive·ness** *noun*

decorative art *noun* (usu. in *pl.*) an art form embracing the applied arts as well as the creation of objects which are purely for decoration, e.g. ceramics, cabinetmaking, tapestry, etc.

decor·ator *noun* **1** an interior decorator. **2** a person who decorates (a cake etc.). **3** (*attributive*) chosen or fashioned to contribute to a plan of interior design (*decorator fabrics*).

dec·or·ous /ˈdekərəs/ *adjective* respecting good taste or propriety; dignified. ☐ **dec·or·ous·ly** *adverb* **dec·or·ous·ness** *noun* [Latin *decorus* seemly]

de·cor·ti·cate /diːˈkɔːrtɪˌkeɪt/ *transitive verb* **1** remove the bark, rind, or husk from. **2** remove the outside layer from a structure or organ, e.g. the kidney, brain, etc. ☐ **de·cor·ti·ca·tion** *noun* [Latin *decorticare decorticat-* (as DE-, *cortex -icis* bark)]

de·cor·um /dɪˈkɔːrəm/ *noun* **1** seemliness, propriety. **2 a** behaviour required by politeness or decency. **b** (usu. in *pl.*) the accepted customs or behaviours of polite society. [Latin, neuter of *decorus* seemly]

De Cos·mos /də ˈkɒsmɒs/ **Amor** (born William Alexander Smith) (1825–97), Canadian politician, premier of BC 1872–4. During his political career he worked toward the union of Vancouver Island and mainland BC, the entry of the united BC into Confederation, and the achievement of responsible government for the province.

de·coup·age /ˌdeɪkuːˈpɑːʒ, -ˈpɑːʒ/ *noun* **1** the decoration of surfaces with paper cut-outs. **2** something so decorated. [French, = the action of cutting out]

Vowels: a cat ɑ arm e bed ɜː her ɜ: deux ə ago ɪ sit i cosy iː feed ɒ hot ɔ pore ɔː no ʌ run ʊ put

de·couple *verb* **1** *transitive* make separate or independent. **2** *transitive* *Electricity* make the interaction between (oscillators etc.) so weak that there is little transfer of energy between them. **3** *intransitive* *Physics* cease to interact (so that the thermal equilibrium is no longer maintained); become differentiated. □ **de·coupled** *adjective* **de·coup·ling** *noun*

de·coy ● *noun* /ˈdiːkɔɪ/ **1 a** a person or thing used to mislead or to lure an animal or person into a trap or danger. **b** a bait or enticement. **2** a bird or animal, or an imitation of one, used to attract others. **3** a pond with narrow netted arms into which wild duck may be tempted in order to catch them. **4** *Military* an aircraft, missile, etc. used to distract the enemy, mislead radar, etc. ● *transitive verb* /dɪˈkɔɪ, ˈdiːkɔɪ/ (often foll. by *into*, *out of*) allure or entice, esp. by means of a decoy. [17th c.: perhaps from Dutch *de kooi* the decoy, from *de* THE + *kooi* from Latin *cavea* cage]

de·crease ● *transitive & intransitive verb* /dɪˈkriːs/ make or become smaller, fewer, weaker, less, etc. ● *noun* /ˈdiːkriːs/ **1** the act or an instance of decreasing. **2** the amount by which a thing decreases. □ **de·creas·ing·ly** *adverb* [ultimately from Latin *decrescere* (as DE-, *crescere* cret- grow)]

de·cree ● *noun* **1** an official order issued by a legal authority. **2** a judgment or decision of certain law courts, esp. in matrimonial cases. ● *transitive & intransitive verb* (**de·crees**, **de·creed**, **de·cree·ing**) order by or as if by decree. [Old French *decré* from Latin *decretum* neuter past participle of *decernere* decide (as DE-, *cernere* sift)]

dec·re·ment /ˈdekrɪmənt/ *noun* **1** the act of decreasing. **2** the amount lost by diminution or waste. □ **dec·re·ment·al** *adjective* [Latin *decrementum* (as DECREASE)]

de·creol·iz·a·tion /diːˌkriːəlaɪˈzeɪʃən/ *noun* the modification of (a language) away from its creole characteristics.

de·crep·it /dɪˈkrepɪt/ *adjective* **1** weakened or worn out by age and infirmity. **2** worn out by long use; dilapidated. □ **de·crep·i·tude** *noun* [Latin *decrepitus* (as DE-, *crepitus* past participle of *crepare* creak)]

de·crescen·do /ˌdiːkreˈʃendəʊ, ˌdeɪkrɪ-/ *adverb, adjective, & noun* (*pl.* **-dos**) = DIMINUENDO. [Italian, part. of *decrescere* DECREASE]

de·cretal /dɪˈkriːtəl/ ● *noun* **1** a papal decree. **2** (in *pl.*) a collection of these, forming part of canon law. ● *adjective* pertaining to, of the nature of, or containing a decree or decrees, esp. papal. [medieval Latin *decretale* from Late Latin (*epistola*) *decretalis* (letter) of decree, from Latin *decernere*: see DECREE]

de·crim·in·al·ize *transitive verb* (also esp. *Brit.* **-ise**) make or treat (an action etc.) as no longer criminal; legalize (esp. a drug, its possession, or use). □ **de·crim·in·al·iz·a·tion** *noun*

de·cry /dɪˈkraɪ/ *transitive verb* (**-cries**, **-cried**) denounce or disparage openly. □ **de·crier** *noun* [after French *décrier*]

de·crypt *transitive verb* decipher or decode. □ **de·cryp·tion** *noun* [DE- + CRYPTOGRAM]

de·cum·bent /dɪˈkʌmbənt/ *adjective* **1** *Bot.* (of a plant, shoot, etc.) lying or trailing on the ground with the extremity ascending. **2** *Zool.* (of hairs or bristles) lying flat on the surface of the body. [Latin *decumbere decumbent-* lie down]

de·cus·sate /diːˈkʌseɪt/ ● *adjective* **1** X-shaped. **2** *Bot.* with pairs of opposite leaves etc. each at right angles to the pair below. ● *transitive & intransitive verb* **1** arrange or be arranged in a decussate form. **2** intersect. □ **de·cus·sa·tion** /-ˈseɪʃən/ *noun* [Latin *decussatus* past participle of *decussare* divide in a cross shape, from *decussis* the numeral ten or the shape X, from *decem* ten]

dedi·cate *transitive verb* **1** (foll. by *to*) **a** devote (esp. oneself) to a noble task or purpose. **b** commit, contribute, or set apart (resources etc.) for a particular cause or effort. **2** (foll. by *to*) **a** inscribe or address (one's own book, music, etc.) to a patron or friend as a compliment, mark of respect, etc. **b** request (a song or video) to be played on the radio or television as a greeting or token of affection for a friend. **3** (often foll. by *to*) consecrate or devote with solemn rites (a building etc.) to a god, saint, sacred purpose, etc. **4 a** formally open (a building etc.) to the public. **b** devote (a monument etc.) to the memory of someone deceased etc. □ **dedi·catee** *noun* **dedi·ca·tory** /ˌdedɪkəˈtɔːri/ *adjective* [Latin *dedicare* (DE-, *dicare* declare, dedicate)]

dedi·cat·ed *adjective* **1** (of a person) devoted to an aim or vocation; having single-minded loyalty or integrity. **2** (of equipment etc.) designed, manufactured, or installed so as to be available only for a particular purpose or a particular category of user. **3** sacredly, solemnly, or formally set apart for a specific use or purpose.

dedi·ca·tion *noun* **1** the act or an instance of dedicating; the process or state of being dedicated. **2** the words or inscription with which a book etc. is dedicated. **3** the devoting (of a person's time etc.) to the pursuit of a purpose. **4** a formal ceremony commemorating a public opening of a building, monument, etc.

de·duce /dɪˈduːs, -ˈdjuːs/ *transitive verb* **1** (often foll. by *from*) infer; draw as a logical conclusion. **2** *archaic* trace the course or derivation of. □ **de·ducible** *adjective* [Latin *deducere* (as DE-, *ducere duct-* lead)]

de·duct *transitive verb* (often foll. by *from*) subtract, take away, withhold (an amount, portion, etc.). [Latin (as DEDUCE)]

de·duct·ible ● *adjective* that may be deducted, esp. from tax to be paid or taxable income. ● *noun* *N Amer.* a sum payable by an insured party in the event of a claim, the insurer paying the amount by which the claim exceeds this sum. □ **de·duct·ibil·ity** *noun*

de·duc·tion *noun* **1 a** the act or process of deducting. **b** an amount deducted. **c** an allowable amount, expense, etc. deducted from taxable income. **2 a** the inferring of particular instances from a general law (compare INDUCTION 3a). **b** a conclusion deduced. [Latin *deductio* (as DEDUCE)]

de·duct·ive *adjective* of or reasoning by deduction. □ **de·duct·ive·ly** *adverb* [medieval Latin *deductivus* (as DEDUCE)]

de Duve /de duːv/ **Chris·tian (René)** (b.1917), English-born Belgian biochemist. A pioneer in the study of cell biology, he discovered lysosomes with the aid of electron microscopy in 1955; he shared a Nobel Prize in 1974.

dee *noun* **1** the letter D. **2** a thing shaped like the letter D, esp. **a** an iron or steel loop for connecting parts of a harness or for fastening articles to a saddle. **b** *Physics* either of two hollow semicircular electrodes in a cyclotron. [the name of the letter]

deed ● *noun* **1** a thing done; an act. **2** a brave, skilful, or conspicuous act; a feat. **3** actual fact or performance, often as contrasted with words (*kind in word and deed*; *in thought, word, and deed*). **4** *Law* a written or printed document under seal often used for a legal transfer of ownership and bearing the disposer's signature. ● *transitive verb* *N Amer.* convey or transfer by legal deed. [Old English *dēd* from Germanic: compare DO¹]

dee·jay *informal* ● *noun* a disc jockey. ● *intransitive verb* act as, or hold a job as, a disc jockey. [abbreviation *DJ*]

deem *transitive verb* regard, consider, judge (*deem it my duty*; *was deemed sufficient*). [Old English *dēman* from Germanic, related to DOOM]

de-emphasize *transitive verb* (also esp. *Brit.* **-emphasise**) reduce emphasis on. □ **de-emphasis** *noun*

deep ● *adjective* **1 a** extending far down from the top (*deep hole*; *deep water*). **b** extending far in from the surface or edge (*deep wound*; *deep plunge*; *deep shelf*). **2** (*predicative*) **a** extending to or lying at a specified depth (*water 6 feet deep*; *ankle-deep in mud*). **b** in a specified number of ranks one behind another (*soldiers drawn up six deep*). **3** situated far down, back, or in (*hands deep in his pockets*; *a cabin deep in the bush*). **4** coming or brought from far down or in (*deep breath*; *deep sigh*). **5** low-pitched, full-toned, not shrill (*deep voice*; *deep note*; *deep bell*). **6 a** (of a condition, quality, state, etc.) intense, profound, extreme (*deep disgrace*; *deep sleep*). **b** (of a colour) vivid, darkly hued (*a deep red*). **c** mysterious or obscure (*a deep secret*). **7** heartfelt, absorbing (*deep affection*; *deep interest*). **8** (*predicative*) fully absorbed or overwhelmed (*deep in a book*; *deep in debt*). **9** profound, penetrating, not superficial; difficult to understand (*deep thinker*; *deep thought*; *deep insight*; *deep learning*). **10** *Baseball* relatively far in or into the outfield (*a line drive into deep right field*). **11** *Sport* far into usu. the opposing team's territory. **12** (of prices, discounts, etc.) significantly larger than customary or expected. **13** cunning or secretive (*a deep one*). **14** (of bows, curtsies, etc.) executed with a marked bending or lowering of the body. ● *noun* **1** (prec. by *the*) *literary* the sea. **2** *Naut.* a deep part of the sea, esp. below 3000 fathoms or approx. 6000 metres. **3** an abyss, pit, or cavity. **4** the most intense part (of the night, winter, etc.), when the cold, dark, etc. are at their most intense. **5** *literary* a mysterious region of thought or feeling. **6** *Naut.* an estimated fathom on a sounding line between marked depths. ● *adverb* **1** deeply (*dig deep*). **2** far down, in, on, or back (*she lived deep in the bush*). **3** for an extended period, long (into) (*read deep into the night*). **4 a** *Baseball* farther than usual in the outfield (*play deep*). **b** *Sport* far into usu. the other team's territory (*fumbled deep in the end zone*). **5** profoundly, intensely, seriously. □ **go off the deep end** *informal* **1** go crazy. **2** lose control and give way to anger or emotion. **3** act without due regard to common sense, moderation, etc. **in deep** inextricably involved in or committed (usu. to something complicated or unpleasant). **jump** (or **be thrown**) **in at the deep end** face (or be made to face) a difficult problem, undertaking, etc., with little experience of it. □ **deep·ly** *adverb* **deep·ness** *noun* [Old English *dēop* (adj.), *dīope*, *dēope* (adv.), from Germanic: related to DIP]

deep-bodied *adjective* (of an animal, especially a fish) having a body which is deeper (from top to belly) than it is wide.

deep breathing *noun* breathing with long breaths, esp. as a relaxation technique.

deep-dish esp. *N Amer.* ● *noun* (usu. *attributive*) **1** a baking pan or dish with high sides and a flat bottom (*deep-dish pizza*). **2** something shaped like this (*a deep-dish satellite*). ● *adjective* **1** (of a pie) not having a bottom crust. **2** serious, staunch, ardent (*a deep-dish conservative*).

deep ecology *noun* an approach to environmentalism that considers humanity and the natural world to be inextricably interconnected and advocates the sacred world view of primal peoples, reverence for all life forms, etc. □ **deep ecologist** *noun*

deep·en *transitive & intransitive verb* **1** make or become deep or deeper. **2** make or become more serious, intense, or severe (*concerns about the economy deepened*).

deep-freeze ● *noun* **1** a refrigerator in which food can be quickly frozen and kept for long periods at a very low temperature. **2** a place or situation in which progress or activity is suspended. **3** *N Amer.* a period of very cold weather. ● *transitive verb* (**-froze**, **-frozen**) freeze or store (food) in a deep-freeze.

deep-fry *transitive verb* (**-fries**, **-fried**) fry (food) in an amount of hot oil or fat sufficient to cover it. □ **deep-fried** *adjective*

deep fryer *noun* (also **deep fat fryer**) a deep, heavy pan or appliance capable of holding 3-4 cm of hot fat in which food is immersed for frying.

deep-laid *adjective* (of a scheme, plot, etc.) secret and elaborate.

deep mourning *noun hist.* mourning expressed by wearing only black clothes.

deep pocket *noun* esp. *N Amer. informal* (usu. in *pl.*) substantial financial resources (*we need backers with deep pockets*). □ **deep-pocket·ed** *adjective*

deep-rooted *adjective* **1** (esp. of convictions) firmly established. **2** having long roots (*deep-rooted grasses*).

deep sea *noun* (often, with hyphen, *attributive*) the deeper parts of the ocean (*deep-sea diving*).

deep-seated *adjective* (of emotion, disease, etc.) firmly established, profound.

deep-set *adjective* **1** (of the eyes) set deeply in the sockets. **2** firmly fixed or established (*deep-set differences*).

deep-six *transitive verb N Amer. slang* **1** defeat thoroughly, destroy completely (*she deep-sixed her opponent*). **2** abandon, dispose of, discard (*the council deep-sixed the proposal*). [originally 'bury at sea']

Deep South *noun* the southeast section of the US, esp. the states of S Carolina, Georgia, Alabama, Mississippi, and Louisiana.

deep space *noun* (often *attributive*) the regions beyond the solar system or the earth's atmosphere (*deep space probe*).

deep structure *noun Linguistics* the fundamental abstract grammatical or semantic relationships of the elements of a phrase or sentence in transformational grammar.

deep throat *noun* a person working within an organization who supplies anonymously information concerning misconduct by other members of the organization. [originally applied to the principal informant in the Watergate scandal, after a 1972 pornographic film so titled]

deep-vein thrombosis *noun* thrombosis in a vein lying deep below the skin, especially in the legs.

deep·water *noun* (often *attributive*) water which is of great depth, esp. with great depressions in the seabed.

deer *noun* (*pl.* same) any four-hoofed grazing animal of the family Cervidae, the males of which usu. have deciduous branching antlers, or of the related families Tragulidae and Moschidae (both lacking horns). □ **deer-like** *adjective* [Old English *dēor* animal, deer]

deer·berry *noun* (*pl.* **-berries**) any of various shrubs of N America, esp. of the genus *Vaccinium*.

Deere, John (1804–86), US inventor and manufacturer, who devised and produced a series of plows suitable for prairie soils.

deer fly *noun* any bloodsucking fly of the genus *Chrysops*.

deer·hound *noun* a large rough-haired greyhound.

Deer Island an island in Passamaquoddy Bay, SW New Brunswick.

Dee River 1 a river in NE Scotland, which rises in the Grampian Mountains and flows eastward past Balmoral Castle to the North Sea at Aberdeen. **2** a river which rises in North Wales and flows past Chester and on into the Irish Sea.

Deer Lake 1 a small narrow lake in west central Newfoundland, northeast of Corner Brook. **2** a town situated at its northern end; pop. (2001) 4,769.

deer mouse *noun* any mouse of the large North and Central American genus *Peromyscus*, esp. *P. maniculatus*, which is common throughout N America.

deer·skin ● *noun* leather from a deer's skin. ● *adjective* made from a deer's skin.

deer·stalk·er *noun* a soft cloth cap with peaks in front and behind and earflaps usu. worn tied together at the crown.

deer tick *noun* a tiny tick of the genus *Ixodida*, found in northeastern N America and known to spread Lyme disease.

deer tongue *noun* a N American plant of the genus *Liatris*, used to flavour tobacco.

deer yard *noun N Amer.* a sheltered area where deer herd in winter and tread the ground down.

de-escalate *transitive verb* reduce the level or intensity of (a crisis etc.). □ **de-escala·tion** *noun*

DEET /diːt/ *noun* esp. *N Amer.* N,N-diethyl-meta-toluamide, the active ingredient in many insect repellents.

def /def/ *adjective* esp. *N Amer. slang* excellent. [corruption of DEATH or shortened from DEFINITIVE]

def. *abbreviation Sport* defeated.

de·face *transitive verb* **1** spoil the appearance of; disfigure. **2** make illegible. □ **de·face·able** *adjective* **de·face·ment** *noun* **de·facer** *noun* [French *défacer*]

de facto /də ˈfaktɔː, diː, dei/ ● *adjective* that exists or is such in fact, whether legally acknowledged or not (*a de facto ruler*). ● *adverb* in fact, whether by right or not (*compare DE JURE*). [Latin]

de·fal·ca·tion /ˌdiːfalˈkeiʃən/ *noun formal Law* **1** a misappropriation of money. **2** an amount misappropriated. □ **de·fal·cate** /ˈdiːfalˌkeit/ *intransitive verb* [medieval Latin *defalcatio* (as DE-, Latin *falx -cis* sickle)]

de Falla see FALLA.

def·am·a·tion /ˌdefəˈmeiʃən/ *noun* **1** the act of defaming or the fact of being defamed. **2** *Law* the offence of bringing a person into undeserved disrepute by making false statements; libel, slander. □ **de·fama·tory** /dɪˈfamətɔːri/ *adjective*

de·fame /dɪˈfeim/ *transitive verb* attack the good reputation of; speak ill of. □ **de·fam·er** *noun* [Latin *diffamare* spread evil report (as DIS-, *fama* report)]

de·famil·iar·ize *transitive verb* (also esp. *Brit.* **-ise**) render (a word etc.) unfamiliar, esp. as a critical technique to revitalize the perception of words and their sounds by differentiation from ordinary language. □ **de·famil·iar·iz·a·tion** *noun*

de·fang *transitive verb* **1** extract the fangs of (a snake etc.). **2** render harmless (*the defeat defanged the militarists*).

de·fat *transitive verb* (**de·fat·ted**, **de·fat·ting**) remove fat or fats from (chicken broth etc.). □ **de·fat·ted** *adjective*

de·fault /ˈdiːfɔlt, dɪˈfɔlt/ ● *noun* **1** a failure to fulfill an obligation, esp. to appear, pay, or act in some way. **b** *Sport* failure to compete in or finish a game, contest, etc. **2** (often *attributive*) a pre-selected option adopted by a computer program when no alternative is specified by the user or programmer. ● *verb* **1 a** *intransitive Law* (often foll. by *on* or *in*) fail to fulfill an obligation, esp. to pay money or to appear in a law court. **b** *intransitive Sport* fail to appear for or complete a game, contest, etc. **2** *transitive Law* declare (a party) in default and give judgment against (that party). **3** *transitive* lose by default. □ **by default 1** because of absence or failure to act. **2** because of a lack of opposition. **in default** guilty of default. **in default of** because of the absence of. **win by default** win because an opponent fails to be present. □ **de·fault·ed** *adjective* **de·fault·er** *noun* [Old French *defaut(e)* from *defaillir* fail, from Romanic (as DE-, Latin *fallere* deceive): compare FAIL]

de·feas·ance /dɪˈfiːzəns/ *noun Law* **1** the act or process of rendering null and void. **2 a** a condition which, if fulfilled, renders an agreement or instruction null and void. **b** a document setting out such a condition. [Old French *defesance* from *de(s)faire* undo (as DE-, *faire* make, from Latin *facere*)]

de·feas·ible /dɪˈfiːzɪbəl/ *adjective* **1** capable of annulment. **2** liable to forfeiture. □ **de·feas·ibil·ity** *noun* **de·feas·ibly** *adverb* [Anglo-French (as DEFEASANCE)]

de·feat ● *transitive verb* **1** overcome in a battle or other contest. **2** frustrate, thwart. **3** reject (a motion etc.) by voting. **4** *Law* render (something) null and void; annul (something). ● *noun* **1** the act or process of defeating or being defeated. **2** a state or instance of being defeated. [Old French *deffait, desfait* past participle of *desfaire* from medieval Latin *disfacere* (as DIS-, Latin *facere* do)]

de·feat·ism *noun* **1** an excessive readiness to accept defeat. **2** conduct conducive to this. □ **de·feat·ist** *noun & adjective*

defe·cate /ˈdefəˌkeit/ *intransitive verb* discharge feces from the body. ☐ **defe·ca·tion** *noun* [earlier as adj., = purified, from Latin *defaecare* (as DE-, *faex faecis* dregs)]

defect ● *noun* /ˈdiːfekt/ **1** a shortcoming, failing, or imperfection. **2** lack of something essential or required. **3** *Physics* a local irregularity or discontinuity in a crystal lattice. ● *intransitive verb* /dəˈfekt, di-/ abandon one's country or cause in favour of another. ☐ **de·fect·or** *noun* [Latin *defectus* from *deficere* desert, fail (as DE-, *facere* do)]

de·fec·tion *noun* **1** the abandonment of one's country or cause. **2** an instance of ceasing in allegiance to a leader, party, religion, or duty.

de·fect·ive ● *adjective* **1** having a defect or defects; incomplete, imperfect, faulty. **2** *offensive* (of a person) having a mental handicap. **3** (usu. foll. by *in*) lacking, deficient. **4** *Grammar* (of a word) not having all the usual inflections. ● *noun offensive* a person who is inadequate or handicapped, esp. a person who has a mental handicap. ☐ **de·fect·ive·ly** *adverb* **de·fect·ive·ness** *noun*

de·fence /dəˈfens/ *noun* (also **de·fense**) **1** the act of defending from or resisting attack. **2 a** a means of resisting attack. **b** (in *pl.*) something that protects, e.g. fortifications. **3** the military resources of a country. **4 a** justification, vindication. **b** a speech or piece of writing used to this end. **c** the act of defending a thesis or dissertation. **5 a** the defendant's case in a lawsuit. **b** the counsel for the defendant. **6** *Sport* (also /ˈdiːfens/) **a** the role of defending one's goal etc. against attack. **b** the plays, moves, or tactics aimed at such resistance. **c** the players in a team who perform this role. **7** DEFENCE MECHANISM. ☐ **de·fence·less** *adjective* **de·fence·less·ness** *noun* [Old French *defens(e)* from Late Latin *defensum, -a,* past participle of *defendere*: see DEFEND]

de·fence·man *noun* (*pl.* **-men**) (esp. *US* **de·fense·man**) a player in a defensive position in hockey or lacrosse.

defence mechanism *noun* **1** a usu. unconscious mental process to avoid conscious conflict or anxiety. **2** the body's reaction against disease organisms.

de·fend /dəˈfend, di-/ *verb* **1** *transitive & intransitive* (often foll. by *against, from*) resist an attack made on; protect (a person or thing) from harm or danger. **2 a** *transitive* support or uphold by argument; speak or write in favour of. **b** *transitive* present (a thesis or dissertation) orally to examiners and answer questions, challenges etc. **c** *intransitive* make such a presentation. **3** *transitive & intransitive* conduct the case for (a defendant in a lawsuit). **4** *Sport* **a** *transitive & intransitive* protect (a goal etc.); resist an attack on (the goal etc.). **b** *transitive* compete to retain (a title) in a contest. ☐ **de·fend·able** *adjective* **de·fend·er** *noun* [Latin *defendere*: compare OFFEND]

de·fend·ant *noun* a person etc. sued or accused in a court of law.

Defender of the Faith a title conferred on Henry VIII by Pope Leo X in 1521 in recognition of his treatise defending the seven sacraments against Luther. It was recognized by Parliament as an official title of the English monarch in 1544, and has been borne by all subsequent sovereigns. [translation of Latin *Fidei Defensor*]

de·fen·es·tra·tion /ˌdiːfenəˈstreiʃən/ *noun formal* or *jocular* the action of throwing (esp. a person) out of a window. ☐ **de·fen·es·trate** *transitive verb* [modern Latin *defenestratio* (as DE-, Latin *fenestra* window)]

de·fense etc. *var. of* DEFENCE etc.

de·fen·si·ble *adjective* **1** justifiable; supportable by argument. **2** that can be easily defended militarily. ☐ **de·fens·ibil·ity** *noun* **de·fens·ibly** *adverb* [Late Latin *defensibilis* (as DEFEND)]

de·fen·sive *adjective* **1** done or intended for defence or to defend. **2** (of a person or attitude) self-protective, ready to reject criticism. **3** *Sport* (of players) primarily concerned with preventing the other team from scoring. ☐ **on the defensive 1** expecting criticism. **2** in an attitude or position of defence. ☐ **de·fen·sive·ly** *adverb* **de·fen·sive·ness** *noun* [French *défensif -ive* from medieval Latin *defensivus* (as DEFEND)]

defensive back *noun Football* **1** a player in charge of covering esp. the receivers in the defensive backfield, usu. a cornerback or safety. **2** this position.

defensive zone *noun Sport* the end of the field, court, or rink in which one's goal, territory, etc. is to be defended.

defer¹ *transitive verb* (**de·ferred, de·fer·ring**) **1** put off to a later time; postpone. **2** *US hist.* postpone the conscription of (a person). ☐ **de·fer·ment** *noun* [Middle English, originally the same as DIFFER]

defer² *intransitive verb* (**de·ferred, de·fer·ring**) (foll. by *to*) yield or make concessions in opinion or action (*he deferred to her superior judgment*). [French *déférer* from Latin *deferre* (as DE-, *ferre* bring)]

def·er·ence /ˈdefərəns/ *noun* **1** courteous regard, respect. **2** respectful compliance with the advice or wishes of another (*pay deference to*). ☐ **in**

deference to out of respect for; in response to. [French *déférence* (as DEFER²)]

def·er·en·tial /ˌdefəˈrenʃəl/ *adjective* showing deference; respectful. ☐ **def·er·en·tial·ly** *adverb*

de·fer·ral *noun* a putting off, postponement, delay.

deferred payment *noun* payment by instalments.

de·fi·ance *noun* **1 a** open disobedience, bold resistance. **b** open disregard, contempt. **2** a challenge to fight or maintain a cause, assertion, etc. ☐ **in defiance of** disregarding; in conflict with. [Old French (as DEFY)]

de·fi·ant *adjective* **1** showing defiance. **2** openly disobedient. ☐ **de·fi·ant·ly** *adverb*

de·fib·ril·la·tion /ˌdiːfɪbrɪˈleiʃən/ *noun Med.* the application of an electric shock to the heart to stop fibrillation and encourage the resumption of coordinated contractions. ☐ **de·fib·ril·la·tor** *noun*

de·fi·cien·cy *noun* (*pl.* **-cies**) **1** the state or condition of being deficient. **2** (usu. foll. by *of*) a lack or shortage. **3** a thing lacking or a defect. **4** the amount by which a thing, esp. revenue, falls short.

deficiency disease *noun* a disease caused by the lack of some essential or important element in the diet.

de·fi·cient *adjective* **1** (usu. foll. by *in*) incomplete; not having enough of a specified quality or ingredient. **2** insufficient in quantity, force, etc. ☐ **de·fi·cient·ly** *adverb* [Latin *deficiens* part. of *deficere* (as DEFECT)]

defi·cit *noun* **1** the amount by which a thing (esp. a sum of money) is too small. **2** an excess of liabilities or expenditures over assets or income in a given period, esp. a fiscal year (*opp.* SURPLUS 2a). **3** a deficiency, esp. a lack or impairment (*sleep deficit; cognitive deficit*). [French *déficit* from Latin *deficit* 3rd sing. pres. of *deficere* (as DEFECT)]

deficit financing *noun* financing of (esp. government) spending by borrowing.

deficit spending *noun* spending, esp. by the government, financed by borrowing.

def·il·ade /ˌdefiˈleid/ ● *transitive verb* shield (a position, troops, etc.) from observation or (enfilading) fire by utilizing natural obstacles or erecting fortifications. ● *noun* **1** protection of troops etc. from enemy observation or fire. **2** an obstacle or fortification giving shelter. [DEFILE² + -ADE¹]

de·file¹ /dəˈfail/ *transitive verb* **1** make dirty or foul; pollute. **2** corrupt morally; taint. **3** desecrate, profane; make unfit for ritual or ceremonial use. **4** violate the chastity of; deflower. ☐ **de·file·ment** *noun* **de·fil·er** *noun* [Middle English *defoul* from Old French *defouler* trample down, outrage (as DE-, *fouler* tread, trample), altered after obsolete *befile* from Old English *befȳlan* (BE-, *fūl* FOUL)]

de·file² /dəˈfail, ˈdiːfail/ *noun* a gorge or narrow passage, esp. one through which people can pass only in single file. [French *défiler* and *défilé* past participle (as DE-, FILE²)]

de·fine *transitive verb* **1** give the exact meaning of (a word etc.). **2** describe or explain the scope, essential qualities, etc. of (something) (*define one's position*). **3** make clear, esp. in outline (*well-defined image*). **4** determine or indicate the boundary or extent of (something). **5** specify, fix with precision; prescribe. **6** *Computing* create (a macro function) by assigning a particular series of commands to a single key. ☐ **de·fin·able** *adjective* **de·fin·er** *noun* [ultimately from Latin *definire* (as DE-, *finire* finish, from *finis* end)]

de·fined *adjective* **1** having a definite or specified outline or form. **2** clearly marked; definite.

def·in·ite ● *adjective* **1** having exact and discernible limits. **2** clearly defined; precise and explicit. ¶ See the note at *definitive*. **3** certain, sure (*a definite offer; are you definite he was there?*). ● *noun* a definite thing, esp. *Grammar* a noun denoting a definite thing or object. ☐ **def·in·ite·ness** *noun* [Latin *definitus* past participle of *definire* (as DEFINE)]

definite article *noun Grammar* the word (*the* in English) preceding a noun and implying a specific or known instance e.g. *the book on the table; the art of government.*

definite integral *noun* an integral expressed as the difference between the values of the integral at specified upper and lower limits of the independent variable.

def·in·ite·ly ● *adverb* **1** in a definite manner. **2** certainly; without doubt (*they were definitely there*). ● *interjection informal* yes, certainly.

def·in·ition *noun* **1 a** the act or process of defining. **b** a statement of the meaning of a word or the nature of a thing. **2 a** the degree of distinctness in outline of an object or image (esp. of an image produced by a lens or shown in a photograph or on a film or television screen). **b** the distinctness of the outline of a muscle. **3 a** making or being distinct in outline. **b** definiteness, precision, exactitude. □ **by definition** self-evidently. □ **def·in·ition·al** *adjective* [Old French from Latin *definitio* (as DEFINE)]

de·fin·itive *adjective* **1** (of an answer, verdict, etc.) conclusive, decisive, final. ¶ Often confused in this sense with *definite*, which does not have connotations of authority and conclusiveness: *a definite no* is a firm refusal, whereas *a definitive no* is an authoritative judgment or decision that something is not the case. **2** (of an edition of a book etc.) most complete, reliable, and authoritative. **3** (of a postage stamp) for regular, standard, or permanent use; not commemorative etc. □ **de·fin·itive·ly** *adverb* [Old French *definitif -ive* from Latin *definitivus* (as DEFINE)]

def·la·grate /ˈdeflə.greit, ˈdiː-/ *transitive & intransitive verb* burn away with sudden flame. □ **def·la·gra·tion** *noun* [Latin *deflagrare* (as DE-, *flagrare* blaze)]

de·flate *verb* **1 a** *transitive* let air or gas out of (a tire, balloon, etc.). **b** *intransitive* be emptied of air or gas. **2 a** *transitive* cause to lose confidence or conceit. **b** *intransitive* lose confidence. **3** *transitive Econ.* subject (a currency or economy) to deflation. **4** *transitive* reduce the importance of, depreciate. □ **de·flat·ed** *adjective* **de·fla·tor** *noun* [DE- + INFLATE]

de·fla·tion *noun* **1** the act, process, or state of deflating or being deflated. **2** a policy or process of reducing economic activity and the inflation of currency. **3** *Geol.* the removal of loose particles of rock etc. by the wind. □ **de·fla·tion·ary** *adjective* **de·fla·tion·ist** *noun*

de·flect *verb* **1** *transitive & intransitive* bend or turn aside from a straight course or intended purpose. **2** *transitive* redirect (criticism, attempts for change, etc.) from the intended target. □ **de·flect·or** *noun* [Latin *deflectere* (as DE-, *flectere flex-* bend)]

de·flec·tion *noun* **1 a** the action of turning, or the state of being turned, from a straight line or course. **b** the amount of such deviation. **2** *Physics* the displacement of a pointer on an instrument from its zero position.

de·flor·a·tion /ˌdiːflɔːˈreiʃən/ *noun* the act of deflowering.

de·flower *transitive verb* **1** deprive (esp. a woman) of virginity. **2** ravage, spoil. **3** strip of flowers.

de·focus *transitive & intransitive verb* (**de·focused, de·focus·ing** or **de·focussed, de·focus·sing**) put or go out of focus.

Defoe /dəˈfoː/ **Dan·iel** (1660–1731), English novelist and journalist. A prolific political journalist, he is best known for *Robinson Crusoe* (1719), which is traditionally considered to be the first English novel; other works include *Moll Flanders* (1722) and *A Journal of the Plague Year* (1722).

de·fog·ger *noun N Amer.* a device in vehicles for clearing condensation, frost, and ice from windshields, mirrors, etc. □ **de·fog** *transitive & intransitive verb* (**de·fogged, de·fog·ging**).

de·foli·ate *transitive verb* remove leaves from, esp. as a military tactic. □ **de·foli·ant** *noun & adjective* **de·foli·a·tion** *noun* [Late Latin *defoliare* from *folium* leaf]

de·forest *transitive verb* clear of forests or trees. □ **de·forest·a·tion** *noun* **de·forest·ed** *adjective*

de·form *verb* **1** *transitive* mar the beauty or excellence of; disfigure, deface. **2** *transitive* spoil the form or shape of; misshape. **3** *intransitive* undergo deformation; be deformed. **4** *transitive* alter the form or configuration of (rocks etc.). □ **de·form·able** *adjective* [ultimately from Latin *deformare* (as DE-, *formare* from *forma* shape)]

de·forma·tion *noun* **1 a** the action or result of marring the appearance, excellence, etc.; disfigurement, defacement. **b** alteration of a form for the worse; the action or result of misshaping. **2** *Physics* **a** (often foll. by *of*) change in shape, configuration, or structure. **b** a quantity representing the amount of this change. **3** an altered form of a word (e.g. *dang* for *damn*). □ **de·forma·tion·al** *adjective*

de·formed *adjective* **1** (of a person or limb) misshapen. **2** that has undergone deformation.

de·form·ity *noun* (pl. **-ities**) **1** the state of being deformed; ugliness, disfigurement. **2** a malformation, esp. of body or limb.

de·frag·ment *transitive verb* (also informal **de·frag** (**de·fragged, de·frag·ging**)) *Computing* (of software) reduce the fragmentation of (a file or data) by concatenating parts stored in separate locations on a disk. □ **de·frag·ment·er** *noun*

de·fraud *transitive verb* (often foll. by *of*) take or withhold rightful property, status, etc. from (a person) by fraud; cheat. □ **de·fraud·er** *noun*

de·fray *transitive verb* provide money to pay (a cost or expense). □ **de·fray·able** *adjective* **de·fray·al** *noun* **de·fray·ment** *noun* [French

défrayer (as DE-, obsolete *frai(t)* cost, from medieval Latin *fredum, -us* fine for breach of the peace)]

de·frock *transitive verb* deprive (a person, esp. a priest) of ecclesiastical status.

de·frost ● *verb* **1** *transitive* **a** free (the interior of a refrigerator) of excess frost. **b** remove frost or ice from (esp. the windshield of a motor vehicle). **2** *transitive* thaw (frozen food). **3** *intransitive* become unfrozen. ● *noun N Amer.* **1** a device for defrosting, esp. one preventing the formation of ice on a windshield. **2** the setting on a refrigerator, microwave, etc., which causes defrosting. □ **de·frost·er** *noun* **de·frost·ing** *noun*

deft *adjective* neatly skilful or dexterous; adroit. □ **deft·ly** *adverb* **deft·ness** *noun* [Middle English, var. of DAFT in obsolete sense 'meek']

de·funct *adjective* **1** no longer existing. **2** no longer used or in fashion. **3** *jocular* dead or extinct. [Latin *defunctus* dead, past participle of *defungi* (as DE-, *fungi* perform)]

de·fuse *transitive verb* **1** remove the fuse from (an explosive device). **2** reduce the tension or potential danger in (a crisis, difficulty, etc.).

defy *transitive verb* (**-fies, -fied**) **1** resist (an authority etc.) openly; refuse to obey. **2** (of a thing) resist completely (*defies solution*). **3** (foll. by *to* + infin.) challenge (a person) to do or prove something. **4** challenge the power of (esp. something immutable) (*death-defying; defying the laws of gravity*). [Old French *defier* from Romanic (as DIS-, Latin *fidus* faithful)]

deg. *abbreviation* degree.

Degas /ˈdeigɒ, dəˈgɒ/ **(Hi·laire Ger·main) Edgar** (1834–1917), French painter and sculptor. He exhibited with the Impressionists, and is best known for his pastels and paintings concentrating on the human form and movement, esp. of ballet dancers and racehorses.

degas /diːˈgas/ *transitive verb* (**de·gassed, de·gas·sing**) remove unwanted gas from.

de Gaulle /də ˈgɒl, də ˈgoːl/ **Charles (André Jo·seph Marie)** (1890–1970), French general and political leader, head of government 1944–6, and president 1959–69. During the Second World War he instigated the resistance and organized the Free French movement; as president he was noted for rebuilding the French economy and for his assertive foreign policy (including withdrawing French forces from NATO).

de·gauss /diːˈgaus/ *transitive verb* neutralize the magnetism in (a thing) by encircling it with a current-carrying conductor. □ **de·gauss·er** *noun* [DE- + GAUSS]

de·gen·er·ate ● *adjective* /dɪˈdʒenərət/ **1 a** degenerated or characterized by degeneration. **b** having lost the qualities that are normal, desirable, or proper to the kind. **c** fallen from former excellence, esp. physical or moral. **2** *Biol.* having changed to a lower type. **3** *Physics* having quantum states with the same energy. ● *noun* /dɪˈdʒenərət/ **1 a** a person of debased physical or mental condition. **b** a sexual deviate. **2 a** a person or thing which has lost, or become degenerate in, the qualities considered proper to its race or kind. **b** a degenerate specimen. ● *intransitive verb* /dɪˈdʒenəˌreit/ (often foll. by *into*) **1** lose, or become deficient in, the qualities proper to one's kind. **2** deteriorate physically, mentally, or morally. **3 a** revert to a lower type; gradually change into something inferior. **b** (of an organ or tissue) deteriorate to a simpler structure or less active form. □ **de·gen·er·acy** *noun* **de·gen·er·ate·ly** *adverb* [Latin *degeneratus* past participle of *degenerare* (as DE-, *genus -eris* race)]

de·gen·er·a·tion *noun* **1 a** the process of becoming degenerate. **b** the state of being degenerate. **2** *Med.* morbid deterioration of tissue or change in its structure.

de·gen·er·a·tive *adjective* **1** of or tending to degeneration. **2** (of disease) characterized by progressive, often irreversible deterioration.

de·glaci·a·tion *noun Geol.* the disappearance of ice from a previously glaciated region.

de·glaze *transitive verb Cooking* make a sauce by adding liquid to the cooking juices and food particles in (a pan in which meat has been cooked).

deg·rad·a·tion *noun* **1 a** an action that humiliates or lowers a person in social position, status, etc. **b** moral or intellectual debasement. **2** reduction in strength, amount, or other measurable property. **3** *Geol.* the wearing down and disintegration of material, esp. rock, by erosion. **4** *Chem.* conversion of matter to simpler substances; chemical breakdown. **5** *Physics* conversion of energy to a form less able to be transformed.

de·grade *verb* **1** *transitive* lower in character or quality; debase. **2** *transitive* reduce to a lower rank, esp. as a punishment. **3** *transitive* bring into dishonour or contempt. **4** *Chem.* **a** *transitive* reduce to a simpler molecular structure. **b** *intransitive* disintegrate. **5** *transitive Physics* reduce (energy) to a less convertible form. **6** *transitive Geol.* wear down (rocks etc.) by disintegration. **7** *intransitive* deteriorate; become weaker or worse. □ **de·grad·abil·ity** *noun* **de·grad·able** *adjective* **de·grad·a·tive** *adjective* [Old French *degrader* from ecclesiastical Latin *degradare* (as DE-, Latin *gradus* step)]

de·grad·ed *adjective* **1 a** lowered in rank, position, reputation, etc.; debased. **b** diminished in quality or value. **2** (of soil etc.) differing from its natural or primary state as a result of cultivation, erosion, etc.

de·grad·ing *adjective* humiliating; causing a loss of self-respect. □ **de·grad·ing·ly** *adverb*

de·grease *transitive verb* remove unwanted grease or fat from. □ **de·greas·er** *noun*

de·gree *noun* **1** a stage in an ascending or descending scale, series, or process. **2** a stage in intensity or amount (*to a high degree; in some degree*). **3** relative condition (*each is good in its degree*). **4** an academic rank conferred by a college or university after examination or after completion of a course, or conferred as an honour on a distinguished person. **5** *Math.* a unit of measurement of angles, one-ninetieth of a right angle or the angle subtended by one-three-hundred-and-sixtieth of the circumference of a circle. Symbol: ° (as in 45°). **6** a unit of latitude or longitude used to define points on the earth's surface. Symbol: °. **7** *Physics* a unit in a scale of temperature, hardness, etc. Symbol: ° (or abbreviation **deg.**, or omitted where the letter indicating the scale being used serves as the symbol). **8** *Med.* any of three grades (first, second, third) used to categorize burns according to their severity. **9** a grade of crime or criminality (*first-degree murder*). **10** a step in direct genealogical descent. **11** *Grammar* any of three stages (positive, comparative, superlative) in the comparison of an adjective or adverb. **12** *Music* the classification of a note by its position in the scale. **13** *Math.* the highest power of unknowns or variables in an equation etc. (*equation of the third degree*). **14** a masonic rank. **15** a unit of measurement of alcohol content. Symbol: °. **16** *archaic* social or official rank. □ **by degrees** a little at a time; gradually. **to a degree** somewhat. □ **degree·less** *adjective* [Old French *degré* from Romanic (as DE-, Latin *gradus* step)]

degree day *noun* a unit used to determine the heating requirements for buildings, representing a fall of one degree below a specified average outdoor temperature for one day.

degree of freedom *noun* **1** *Physics* the independent direction in which motion can occur. **2** *Chem.* the number of independent factors required to specify a system at equilibrium. **3** *Statistics* the number of independent values or quantities which can be assigned to a statistical distribution.

de·gres·sive /dəˈɡrɛsɪv/ *adjective* **1** (of taxation) at successively lower rates on low amounts. **2** reducing in amount. [Latin *degredi* (as DE-, *gradi* walk)]

de·hair *transitive verb* remove the hair from (an animal skin).

de haut en bas /də ˌoːt ɑ̃ ˈbɒ/ *adverb* in a condescending or superior manner. [French, = from above to below]

de Hav·il·land /də ˈhavɪlənd/ **1 Sir Geof·frey** (1882–1965), English aircraft designer and manufacturer, who built many famous light aircraft including the Moth series, the Mosquito of the Second World War, and some of the first jet aircraft. A Canadian branch of his aircraft company established in 1928 built the Otter and Beaver aircraft which were stalwarts of bush flying in Canada, and later designed the DASH-7 and DASH-8 STOL aircraft. **2 Oliv·ia (Mary)** (b.1916), US actress, whose films include *Gone With the Wind* (1939), *To Each His Own* (1946), for which she won an Academy Award, and *Lady in a Cage* (1964).

Deh Cho /dei tʃoː/ ● *noun* **1** a member of a Dene people living in various communities in southern NWT, west of Great Slave Lake. **2** the Athapaskan language of this people. ● *adjective* of or relating to this people or their culture or language. [Dene = 'big river']

de·hisce /diːˈhɪs/ *intransitive verb* gape or burst open (esp. of a pod or seed vessel or of a cut or wound). □ **de·his·cence** *noun* **de·his·cent** *adjective* [Latin *dehiscere* (as DE-, *hiscere* inceptive of *hiare* gape)]

de Hooch /də ˈhuːtʃ/ **Pieter** (also **de Hoogh** /də ˈhuːɡ/) (c.1629–c.1684), Dutch genre painter. His paintings of domestic interior and courtyard scenes are noted for their sensitive handling of light and tranquil atmosphere; they include *Interior with a Woman Peeling Apples* (1663).

de·horn *transitive verb* remove the horns from (an animal).

de·human·ize *transitive verb* (also esp. *Brit.* **-ise**) **1** deprive of human characteristics. **2** make impersonal or machine-like. □ **de·human·iz·a·tion** *noun*

de·humidi·fy *transitive verb* (-fies, -fied) reduce the degree of humidity of; remove moisture from (a gas, esp. air). □ **de·humidi·fi·ca·tion** *noun* **de·humidi·fi·er** *noun*

de·hy·drate *verb* **1** *transitive* **a** remove water from (esp. foods for preservation and storage in bulk). **b** make dry, esp. make (the body) deficient in water. **2** *intransitive* lose water. □ **de·hydrat·ed** *adjective* **de·hydra·tion** *noun* **de·hydra·tor** *noun*

de·hydro·gen·ase /ˌdiːhaiˈdrɒdʒəˌneiz/ *noun Biochem.* an enzyme which abstracts a hydrogen atom or hydrogen atoms from a substrate.

de·hydro·gen·ate /ˌdiːhaiˈdrɒdʒəˌneit/ *transitive verb Chem.* remove a hydrogen atom or atoms from (a compound). □ **de·hydro·gen·a·tion** *noun*

Deia·nira /ˌdiːəˈnairə/ *Gk Myth* the wife of Hercules, who was tricked into smearing poison on a garment, which caused his death.

de-ice *transitive verb* **1** remove ice from. **2** prevent the formation of ice on.

de-icer *noun* a device or substance for removing ice from a windshield, aircraft, etc.

dei·cide /ˈdiːəˌsaid, ˈdeiə-/ *noun* **1** the killing of a god. **2** the killer of a god. [ecclesiastical Latin *deicida* from Latin *deus* god + -CIDE]

deic·tic /ˈdəiktɪk/ *Linguistics* ● *adjective* serving to relate that which is spoken of to the spatial and temporal context of the utterance, as the words *we, you, here, now, then,* and *that*. ● *noun* a deictic word, form, or expression. □ **deic·tic·ally** *adverb* [Greek *deiktikos* from *deiktos* capable of proof, from *deiknumi* show]

deify /ˈdiːəˌfai, ˈdeiə-/ *transitive verb* (-fies, -fied) **1** make a god of. **2** regard or worship as a god. □ **deifi·ca·tion** /-fəˈkeiʃən/ *noun* [Old French *deifier* from ecclesiastical Latin *deificare* from *deus* god]

Deigh·ton /ˈdeitən/ **Len** (b.1929), English writer of spy thrillers including *The Ipcress File* (1962) and the trilogy *Berlin Game, Mexico Set,* and *London Match* (1983–5).

deign /dein/ *verb* **1** *intransitive* (foll. by *to* + infin.) think fit; condescend (*she deigned to grace us with her presence*). **2** *transitive* (usu. with *neg.*) *archaic* condescend to give (an answer etc.). [Old French *degnier, deigner, daigner* from Latin *dignare, -ari* deem worthy, from *dignus* worthy]

Dei gratia /ˌdeiiː ˈɡratiə, ˈɡratsiə/ *adverb* by the grace of God. [Latin]

Dei·mos /ˈdeiːmɔːs, -mɒs/ **1** *Gk Myth* one of the sons of Ares. **2** *Astronomy* the outer of the two small satellites of Mars, discovered in 1877.

de-index *transitive verb* cancel the indexation of (pensions or other benefits). □ **de-indexa·tion** *noun*

de·indus·tri·al·ize *transitive verb* (also esp. *Brit.* **-ise**) make (a region, nation, etc.) less or no longer industrial. □ **de·indus·tri·al·iza·tion** *noun* **de·indus·tri·al·ized** *adjective*

de-ink *transitive verb* remove ink from (paper), esp. as a stage in recycling.

de·insti·tu·tion·al·ize *transitive verb* (also esp. *Brit.* **-ise**) **1** remove from an institution or from the effects of institutional life. **2** make less institutional; reorganize on more individual lines. □ **de·insti·tu·tion·al·iza·tion** *noun* **de·insti·tu·tion·al·ized** *adjective*

de·ionize /diːˈaiəˌnaiz/ *transitive verb* (also esp. *Brit.* **-ionise**) remove the ions or ionic constituents from (water, air, etc.). □ **de·ioniza·tion** *noun* **de·ionized** *adjective* **de·ioniz·er** *noun*

Deir·dre /ˈdiːrdri, -drə/ *Irish Myth* the tragic heroine of the tale of 'The Sons of Usnach'. She was destined to be the wife of King Conchobar, but fell in love with Naoise; when Naoise was slain by Conchobar, Deirdre took her own life.

deism /ˈdiːɪzəm/ *noun* belief in the existence of a supreme being arising from reason rather than revelation (*compare* THEISM). □ **deist** *noun* **deis·tic** *adjective* [Latin *deus* god + -ISM]

deity /ˈdiːti, ˈdeiɪ-/ *noun* (pl. **-ties**) **1** a god or goddess. **2** divine status, quality, or nature. **3** (**the Deity**) the Creator, God. [Old French *deité* from ecclesiastical Latin *deitas -tatis* translation of Greek *theotēs* from *theos* god]

déjà vu /ˌdeiʒɑ ˈvuː, -ʒɒ-/ *noun* **1** an illusory feeling of having already experienced a present situation. **2** something tediously familiar. [French, = already seen]

de·ject *transitive verb* (usu. as **de·ject·ed** *adjective*) make sad or dispirited; depress. □ **de·ject·ed·ly** *adverb* [Latin *dejicere* (DE-, *jacĕre* throw)]

de·jec·tion *noun* a dejected state; low spirits.

de jure /di ˈdʒuːri, dei ˈjuːrei/ ● *adjective* rightful (*compare* DE FACTO). ● *adverb* rightfully; by right. [Latin]

deke *N Amer. esp. Hockey slang* ● *noun* a fake shot or movement done to draw a defensive player out of position and thus create a better opportunity to score. ● *verb* **1** *transitive & intransitive* deceive (a defensive player) with a fake shot or movement. **2** *intransitive* (foll. by *around*) avoid (an obstacle) or evade (an issue) (*ran across the road, deking around the cars*). **3** *intransitive* move or go quickly; dart, dash (*deked in and out of the crowd*). [abbreviation of DECOY]

dek·ko *noun* (*pl.* **-kos**) *Brit. slang* a look or glance (*took a quick dekko*). [Hindi *dekho*, imperative of *dekhnā* look]

de Klerk /də ˈklerk/ **F(red·erik) W(il·lem)** (b.1936), South African National Party politician, president 1989–94. As president, he instigated significant political reforms designed to dismantle apartheid in South Africa, freeing Nelson Mandela (1990), lifting the ban on membership in the ANC, and opening negotiations with black political leaders to bring about the eventual introduction of majority rule; he shared the 1993 Nobel Peace Prize with Mandela.

de Koo·ning /də ˈkuːnɪŋ/ **Wil·lem** (1904–97), Dutch-born US painter. One of the leading exponents of abstract expressionism, his work often retained some figurative elements, as in *Painting* (1948); the female form became a central theme in his later work, notably in the *Women* series (1950–3).

Del. *abbreviation* Delaware.

De·la·croix /ˌdeləˈkrwɑ/ **(Fer·di·nand Vic·tor) Eu·gène** (1798–1863), French painter. The leading painter of the French romantic school, he is known for his use of vivid colour, free drawing, and exotic, violent, or macabre subject matter, as in *The Massacre at Chios* (1824).

de la Mare /ˌdə lə ˈmer/ **Wal·ter (John)** (1873–1956), English poet and novelist. A predominantly lyric poet, he had his first major success with *The Listeners* (1912); his volumes of verse for children include *Peacock Pie* (1913).

de·lam·in·ate *intransitive verb* split into separate layers (*rain caused the plywood to delaminate*). □ **de·lam·in·a·tion** *noun*

De la Roche /də lə ˈrɔːʃ/ **Mazo** (1879–1961), Canadian novelist, who wrote an internationally popular series of novels about the fictional Whiteoak family of S Ontario, including *Jalna* (1927).

de·late /dəˈleit/ *transitive verb archaic* **1** inform against; impeach (a person). **2** report (an offence). □ **de·la·tion** *noun* **de·la·tor** *noun* [Latin *delat-* (as DE-, *lat-* past participle stem of *ferre* carry)]

De·lau·nay /dəˈlɔːnei/ **Rob·ert** (1885–1941), French painter who painted some of the first truly abstract pictures.

Dela·ware[1] a state of the US on the Atlantic coast, one of the original thirteen states of the Union (1787); pop. (2000) 783,600; capital, Dover. □ **Dela·ware·an** *noun*

Dela·ware[2] ● *noun* **1** a member of an Aboriginal people formerly inhabiting the Delaware river basin in the northeastern US, some of whom moved north and now live near London, Ont. **2** the Algonquian language of these people. ● *adjective* of or relating to these people or their language. [DELAWARE[1]]

Delaware River a river of the northeastern US. Rising in the Catskill Mountains in New York State, it flows some 450 km (280 miles) southward to N Delaware, where it meets the Atlantic at Delaware Bay. For much of its length it forms the eastern border of Pennsylvania.

De La Warr /ˈde lə ˌwer/ **Baron** (title of Thomas West) (1577–1618), English-born US colonial administrator, who was the first governor of Virginia (1610); the state of Delaware is named after him.

de·lay ● *verb* **1** *transitive* postpone; defer. **2** *transitive* make late (*was delayed at the doctor's office*). **3** *intransitive* loiter; procrastinate (*don't delay!*). ● *noun* **1** the act or an instance of delaying; the process of being delayed. **2** time lost by inaction or the inability to proceed. □ **de·lay·able** *adjective* **de·lay·er** *noun* [Old French *delayer* (v.), *delai* (n.), prob. from *des-* DIS- + *laier* leave]

delayed-action *attributive adjective* (esp. of a bomb, camera, etc.) operating some time after being primed or set.

delayed penalty *noun Hockey* **1** a penalty which the referee has signalled, but for which play has not yet been stopped. **2** the interval between the signalling of the penalty and the stopping of play (*he scored on the delayed penalty*).

delay line *noun* a device producing a desired delay in the transmission of a signal.

dele /ˈdiːli/ ● *transitive verb* (**deled**, **dele·ing**) delete or mark for deletion (a letter, word, etc.) from typeset material. ● *noun* a proofreader's sign marking something to be deleted; a deletion. [Latin, imperative of *delēre*: see DELETE]

de·lect·able ● *adjective* **1** (of food) delicious. **2** delightful, pleasant.

● *noun N Amer.* (in *pl.*) delicious food or dishes, esp. desserts. □ **de·lect·ably** *adverb* [Latin *delectabilis* from *delectare* DELIGHT]

de·lect·a·tion /ˌdiːlekˈteiʃən/ *noun literary* pleasure; enjoyment (*sang for his delectation*). [Old French (as DELECTABLE)]

del·eg·acy /ˈdeləgəsi/ *noun* (*pl.* **-acies**) **1** a system of delegating. **2 a** an appointment as a delegate. **b** a body of delegates; a delegation.

dele·gate ● *noun* /ˈdeləgət/ **1** a person chosen or elected to represent others at a conference, political convention, etc. **2** a member of a committee. ● *transitive verb* /ˈdeləˌgeit/ **1** (often foll. by *to*) **a** commit (authority, power, etc.) to an agent or deputy. **b** entrust (a task) to another person. **2** send or authorize (a person) as a representative; depute. [Latin *delegatus* (as DE-, *legare* depute)]

delegate-general *noun* (*pl.* **delegates-general**) *Cdn (Que.)* the chief representative of the province of Quebec in a foreign country or region.

dele·ga·tion *noun* **1** a body of delegates; a number of people chosen to act as representatives. **2** the act or process of delegating or being delegated. [Latin *delegatio* (as DELEGATE)]

de·legit·im·ize *transitive verb* (also esp. *Brit.* **-ise**) withdraw legitimate status from (an organization, state, person, etc.). □ **de·legit·im·iz·a·tion** *noun*

de Les·seps see LESSEPS.

de·lete ● *transitive verb* **1** remove or obliterate (written or printed matter). **2** remove (an item) from a catalogue, so that it is no longer offered for sale. **3** (in *passive*) *Genetics* be lost from a chromosome. ● *noun* (in full **delete key**) *Computing* a key which is held down in order to remove characters from a document, screen display, etc. □ **de·letion** *noun* [Latin *delēre delet-* efface]

dele·teri·ous /ˌdeləˈtiːriəs/ *adjective* harmful (to the mind or body) (*deleterious effects of alcohol*). □ **dele·teri·ous·ly** *adverb* [medieval Latin *deleterius* from Greek *dēlētērios* noxious]

Delft /delft/ *noun* **1** a town in the Netherlands, in the province of South Holland; pop. (est. 2002) 97,100. Since the 17th c. the town has been noted for its pottery. **2** (also **Delft·ware**) **a** a glazed, usu. blue and white, earthenware, made in Delft. **b** similar earthenware made in England.

Delhi /ˈdeli/ a Union Territory in north central India, containing the cities of Old and New Delhi; pop. (2001) 9,817,000. **Old Delhi**, a walled city on the Jumna River, was made the capital of the Mogul Empire in 1638 by Shah Jahan (1592–1666), who built within the city the Red Fort containing the imperial palace. **New Delhi**, the capital of India, was built in 1912–29 to replace Calcutta as the capital of British India.

deli *noun* (*pl.* **delis**) *informal* a delicatessen. [abbreviation]

Del·ian /ˈdiːliən/ ● *adjective* of or relating to Delos. ● *noun* a native or inhabitant of Delos.

Delian League the alliance of ancient Greek city states formed in 478–447 BC against the Persians. The league was dominated by Athens (it is also known as the **Athenian Empire**), and when Athens was defeated in the Peloponnesian War (404 BC) the league was disbanded. The league reunited against Sparta 377–338 BC, again under Athens' leadership.

de·liber·ate ● *adjective* /dəˈlibərət/ **1 a** intentional; done on purpose (*a deliberate lie*). **b** fully considered; not impulsive (*made a deliberate choice*). **2** slow in deciding; cautious. **3** (of movement etc.) slow and careful. ● *verb* /dəˈlibəˌreit/ **1** *intransitive* think carefully; take counsel (*the jury deliberated for an hour*). **2** *transitive* consider, discuss carefully (*deliberated the question*). □ **de·liber·ate·ly** *adverb* **de·liber·ate·ness** *noun* [Latin *deliberatus* past participle of *deliberare* (as DE-, *librare* weigh, from *libra* balance)]

de·liber·a·tion *noun* **1** careful consideration. **2** (often in *pl.*) formal debate or discussion, as of a committee, jury, etc. **3 a** caution and care. **b** (of movement) slowness or ponderousness.

de·liber·a·tive /dəˈlibərətiv/ *adjective* of, characterized by, or appointed for the purpose of, deliberation or debate (*a deliberative assembly*).

De·libes /dəˈliːb/ **(Clé·ment Phili·bert) Léo** (1836–91), French composer and organist, best known for the ballets *Coppélia* (1870) and *Sylvia* (1876), and the opera *Lakmé* (1883).

deli·cacy *noun* (*pl.* **-cies**) **1** (esp. in craftsmanship or artistic or natural beauty) fineness or intricacy of structure or texture; gracefulness. **2** a choice or expensive food. **3** the quality of requiring discretion or sensitivity (*a situation of some delicacy*). **4** susceptibility to injury or disease; weakness. **5 a** consideration for the feelings of others. **b** avoidance of immodesty or vulgarity. **6** (esp. in a person, a sense, or an instrument) accuracy of perception; sensitiveness.

deli·cate *adjective* **1 a** fine in texture or structure; soft, slender, or

Consonants: **b** *but* **d** *dog* **f** *few* **g** *get* **h** *her* **j** *yes* **k** *cat* **l** *leg* **m** *man* **n** *no* **p** *pen* **r** *red* **s** *sit*

slight. **b** of exquisite quality or workmanship. **c** (of a colour) subtle or subdued; not bright. **d** (of a flavour or scent) subtle; faint; not overpowering. **2 a** not robust; easily damaged. **b** (of a person) susceptible to illness. **3 a** requiring careful handling; tricky (*a delicate situation; a delicate balance*). **b** (of an instrument) highly sensitive. **4** deft (*a delicate touch*). **5** (of a person) avoiding the immodest or offensive. **6** (esp. of actions) considerate. □ **deli·cate·ly** *adverb* **deli·cate·ness** *noun* [Latin *delicatus*, of unknown origin]

deli·ca·tes·sen *noun* **1** a place selling cooked meats, cheeses, and unusual or foreign prepared foods. **2** (often *attributive*) such foods collectively (*a delicatessen counter*). [German *Delikatessen* or Dutch *delicatessen* from French *délicatesse* from *délicat* (as DELICATE)]

de·li·cious ● *adjective* **1** highly delightful and enjoyable to the taste or sense of smell. **2** entertaining; very enjoyable (*delicious gossip*). ● *noun* (**Delicious**) *N Amer.* a red or yellow variety of eating apple with a sweet flavour and a slightly elongated shape. □ **de·li·cious·ly** *adverb* **de·li·cious·ness** *noun* [Late Latin *deliciosus* from Latin *deliciae* delight]

de·lict /də'lɪkt, 'diː-/ *noun* (in civil law jurisdictions) a civil wrong other than a breach of contract (*compare* TORT). [Latin *delictum* neuter past participle of *delinquere* offend (as DE-, *linquere* leave)]

de·light ● *noun* **1** great pleasure. **2** something giving pleasure (*her singing is a delight*). ● *verb* **1** *transitive* (often foll. by *with*) please greatly (*the gift delighted them; was delighted that you won; delighted with the result*). **2** *intransitive* take great pleasure; be highly pleased (*delighted in her success; they delight in humiliating us*). □ **de·light·ed** *adjective* **de·light·ed·ly** *adverb* [Middle English via Old French *delitier, delit*, from Latin *delectare* frequentative of *delicere*: spelling with -*gh*- influenced by *light* etc.]

de·light·ful *adjective* causing great delight; pleasant, charming. □ **de·light·ful·ly** *adverb* **de·light·ful·ness** *noun*

De·li·lah /də'laɪlə/ a Biblical character who betrayed Samson to the Philistines (Judges 16) by revealing to them that the secret of his strength lay in his long hair.

de·limit /diː'lɪmɪt/ *transitive verb* (**de·limit·ed, de·limit·ing**) **1** determine the limits of. **2** fix the territorial boundary of; demarcate. □ **de·limit·a·tion** *noun*

de·lin·eate /də'lɪni.eit/ *transitive verb* **1** trace out by lines; trace or serve as the outline of. **2** represent by drawing; portray; draw in fine detail. **3** sketch out; outline (something to be constructed, a scheme, etc.). **4** describe or portray in words; express (*delineated her character*). □ **de·lin·ea·tion** *noun* **de·lin·ea·tor** *noun* [Latin *delineare delineat-* (as DE-, *lineare* from *linea* line)]

de·link *transitive verb* break the connection between (something) and something else (*this agreement would delink trade and human rights*).

de·lin·quency /də'lɪŋkwənsi/ *noun* (*pl.* -**cies**) **1** minor crime such as vandalism, esp. when committed by young people (*juvenile delinquency*). **2** wickedness (*moral delinquency; an act of delinquency*). **3** neglect of one's duty. **4** a minor offence or misdeed. [ecclesiastical Latin *delinquentia* from Latin *delinquens* part. of *delinquere* (as DELICT)]

de·lin·quent ● *noun* an offender (*juvenile delinquent*). ● *adjective* **1** guilty of a minor crime or a misdeed. **2** failing in one's duty. **3** *N Amer.* in arrears (*a delinquent loan*). □ **de·lin·quent·ly** *adverb*

deli·quesce /ˌdelə'kwes/ *intransitive verb* **1** become liquid, melt. **2** *Chem.* dissolve in water absorbed from the air. **3** *Bot.* (of a plant) form many new branches or divisions. □ **deli·ques·cence** *noun*

deli·ques·cent *adjective* [Latin *deliquescere* (as DE-, *liquescere* inceptive of *liquēre* be liquid)]

de·liri·ous /də'liːriəs/ *adjective* **1** affected with delirium; temporarily or apparently mad; raving. **2** wildly excited, ecstatic. **3** (of behaviour) betraying delirium or ecstasy. □ **de·liri·ous·ly** *adverb*

de·lir·ium /də'liːriəm/ *noun* **1** an acutely disordered state of mind involving incoherent speech, hallucinations, and frenzied excitement, occurring in metabolic disorders, intoxication, fever, etc. **2** great excitement, ecstasy. [Latin from *delirare* be deranged (as DE-, *lira* ridge between furrows)]

delirium trem·ens /'tremenz/ *noun* a psychosis of chronic alcoholism involving tremors and hallucinations.

de·lish *adjective informal* delicious. [shortening]

de·list *transitive verb* delete from a list, esp. from a list of securities that may be traded on a stock exchange.

De·lius /'diːliəs/ **Fred·erick (Theo·dore Al·bert)** (1862–1934), English composer. He is best known for orchestral works such as *Brigg Fair* (1907).

de·liv·er *verb* **1** *transitive* **a** distribute (letters, parcels, ordered goods, etc.) to the addressee or the purchaser. **b** (often foll. by *to*) hand over (*delivered the boy safely to his teacher*). **2** *transitive* (also *reflexive*) utter or recite (an opinion, verdict, speech, etc.) (*delivered the sermon well; delivered himself of the observation*). **3** *transitive* give forth or produce (*this laser printer delivers high-quality printouts*). **4** *transitive* **a** give birth to (*delivered a girl*). **b** assist at the birth of (*delivered six babies that week*). **c** assist in giving birth (*delivered the patient successfully*). **d** (in *passive*; often foll. by *of*) give birth (*was delivered of a child*). **5** *transitive* launch or aim (a blow, a ball, or an attack). **6** *transitive* (often foll. by *from*) save, rescue, or set free (*delivered from his enemies*). **7** *transitive* (often foll. by *up, over*) abandon; resign; hand over (*delivered his soul up to God*). **8** *intransitive informal* (often foll. by *on*) provide what is expected or what one has promised. **9** *transitive* cause (a substance, data, etc.) to be conveyed (*deliver the medication intravenously*). **10** *transitive* present or render (an account). **11** *transitive Law* hand over formally (esp. a sealed deed to a grantee). **12** *transitive US* cause (voters etc.) to support a candidate. □ **deliver the goods** *informal* carry out one's part of an agreement. □ **de·liv·er·abil·ity** *noun* **de·liv·er·able** *adjective* **de·liv·er·er** *noun* [Old French *delivrer* from Gallo-Roman (as DE-, LIBERATE)]

de·liv·er·ance *noun* the act or an instance of rescuing; the process of being rescued.

de·liv·ery *noun* (*pl.* -**eries**) **1 a** the delivering of letters, goods, etc. (also *attributive*: *delivery man; delivery service*). **b** a regular distribution of letters, goods, etc. (*two deliveries a day*). **c** something delivered. **2 a** the process of childbirth. **b** an act of this. **3 a** the uttering of a speech etc. **b** the manner or style of such a speech (*a measured delivery*). **4 a** an act of throwing, esp. of a baseball. **b** the style of such an act (*a good delivery*). **5** provision, esp. of services (*health care delivery systems*). **6** the act of giving or surrendering (*delivery of the town to the enemy*). **7** *Law* **a** the formal handing over of property. **b** the transfer of a deed to a grantee or a third party. **8** *archaic* deliverance. □ **take delivery of** receive (something purchased).

dell *noun* a small usu. wooded hollow or valley. [Old English from Germanic]

Della Falls a waterfall situated on Vancouver Island, northwest of Port Alberni. With a vertical drop of 440 m, it is the highest waterfall in Canada. [*Della* Drinkwater, wife of a local prospector *c*.1948]

della Rob·bia /ˌdelə 'rɔːbiə/ **Luca** (1400–82), Italian sculptor and ceramicist. He is known for his relief panels in Florence Cathedral, and for inventing vitreous glazes to colour terracotta figures.

de·local·ize *transitive verb* (also esp. *Brit.* -**ise**) **1** (as **de·local·ized** *adjective*) *Chem.* (of electrons) shared among more than two atoms in a molecule. **2** detach or remove (a thing) from its place. □ **de·local·iz·a·tion** *noun*

De·lorme /'dələrm/ **Phili·bert** (also **de l'Orme**) (*c*.1510–70), French architect. He adapted classical architecture to French traditions and materials, as in the palace of the Tuileries in Paris.

Delos /'diːlɒs/ a small Greek island in the Aegean Sea, regarded as the centre of the Cyclades. It is now virtually uninhabited, but thrived in classical times: considered to be sacred to Apollo, it was, according to legend, the birthplace of both Apollo and Artemis.

de los An·gel·es /de lɒs 'andʒəles/ **Vic·toria** (born Victoria López Cima) (b.1923), Spanish operatic soprano, noted for her singing in the operas of Mozart and Puccini, and for her interpretations of Spanish songs.

de·louse *transitive verb* rid (a person or animal) of lice.

Del·phi /'delfi, -fai/ one of the most important religious sanctuaries of the ancient Greek world, dedicated to Apollo and situated on the lower southern slopes of Mount Parnassus above the Gulf of Corinth. Reputedly the navel of the earth, it was the seat of the Delphic Oracle, whose often riddling responses to a wide range of religious, political, and moral questions were delivered in a state of ecstasy by the Pythia, the priestess of Apollo.

Del·phic /'delfik/ *adjective* **1** (of an utterance, prophecy, etc.) obscure, ambiguous, or enigmatic. **2** of or concerning the ancient Greek oracle at Delphi.

del·phin·ium /del'fɪniəm/ *noun* any garden plant of the genus *Delphinium*, of the buttercup family, with tall spikes of usu. blue flowers. [modern Latin from Greek *delphinion* larkspur, from *delphin* dolphin]

del·phin·oid /'delfɪˌnɔid/ ● *adjective* **1** of the family that includes dolphins, porpoises, grampuses, etc. **2** dolphin-like. ● *noun* **1** a member of the delphinoid family of aquatic mammals. **2** a dolphin-like animal. [Greek *delphinoeidēs* from *delphin* dolphin]

del Sarto *see* ANDREA DEL SARTO

Del·son /'delsən/ a town in S Quebec, south of Montreal; pop. (2001) 7,024. [blend of *Dela*ware and Hud*son*, the name of a railway company]

t **top**　v **voice**　w **we**　z **zoo**　ʃ **she**　ʒ **vision**　θ **thin**　ð **this**　ŋ **ring**　x **loch**　tʃ **chip**　dʒ **jar**　　(*see over for vowels*)

delt *noun slang* a deltoid muscle.

Del·ta a district municipality in southwestern BC, situated on the south side of the Fraser River near its mouth, about 20 km southeast of Vancouver; pop. (2001) 96,950. □ **Del·tan** *noun* [so called with reference to the deltaic shape of the land at the mouth of the Fraser]

del·ta *noun* **1** a triangular tract of deposited earth, alluvium, etc., at the mouth of a river, formed by its diverging outlets. **2** the fourth letter of the Greek alphabet (Δ, δ). **3** (*attributive*) designating the fourth of a series or set. **4** *Math.* an increment of a variable. **5** *Astronomy* the fourth brightest star in a constellation. **6** *Brit.* a fourth-class mark given for a piece of work or in an examination. □ **del·taic** /del'teɪɪk/ *adjective* [Greek from Phoenician *daleth*]

delta rays *plural noun* rays of low penetrative power consisting of slow electrons ejected from an atom by the impact of ionizing radiation.

delta rhythm *noun* (also **delta wave**) low-frequency electrical activity of the brain during sleep.

delta wing *noun* a triangular swept-back wing on an aircraft.

del·toid /'deltɔɪd/ ● *noun* (in full **deltoid muscle**) a thick triangular muscle covering the shoulder joint and used for raising the arm away from the body. ● *adjective* triangular; like a river delta. [French *deltoïde* or modern Latin *deltoides* from Greek *deltoeidēs* (as DELTA, -OID)]

de·lude /də'luːd/ *transitive verb* (also *reflexive*) deceive or mislead (*deluded by false optimism*). □ **de·lud·er** *noun* [Latin *deludere* mock (as DE-, *ludere lus-* play)]

del·uge /'deljuːʒ, -juːdʒ/ ● *noun* **1** a great flood. **2** a great outpouring (of words, paper, etc.). **3** a heavy fall of rain. **4** (**the Deluge**) the Biblical Flood (Gen. 6-8). ● *transitive verb* **1** (usu. foll. by *with*) inundate with a great number or amount (*deluged with complaints*). **2** flood. [Latin *diluvium*, related to *lavare* wash]

de·lu·sion /də'luːʒn/ *noun* **1** a false belief or impression. **2** *Psych.* this as a symptom or form of mental disorder. □ **de·lu·sion·al** *adjective* [Late Latin *delusio* (as DELUDE)]

delusions of grandeur *plural noun* a false idea of oneself as being important, noble, famous, etc.

de·lu·sive /də'luːsɪv/ *adjective* **1** deceptive or unreal. **2** disappointing.

de·lu·sory /də'luːsəri/ *adjective* = DELUSIVE. [Late Latin *delusorius* (as DELUSION)]

de·luxe *adjective* **1** of a superior kind. **2** luxurious or sumptuous. [French *de luxe* of luxury]

delve *intransitive verb* **1** (often foll. by *in, into*) **a** make a laborious search in documents etc.; research (*delved into his family history*). **b** search energetically (*delved into his pocket*). **2** *literary* dig. □ **delv·er** *noun* [Old English *delfan* from West Germanic]

Dem. *abbreviation US* **1** Democrat. **2** Democratic.

de·magnet·ize *transitive verb* (also esp. *Brit.* **-ise**) remove the magnetic properties of. □ **de·magnet·iz·a·tion** *noun* **de·magnet·iz·er** *noun*

dema·gogue /'deməˌgɒg/ *noun* (*US* also **-gog**) **1** a leader or orator who tries to win support by inflaming people's emotions and prejudices. **2** *hist.* a leader of the people, esp. in ancient times. □ **dema·gogic** /-'gɒdʒɪk, -'gɒgɪk/ *adjective* **dema·goguery** /-'gɒgəri/ *noun* **dema·gogy** /-'gɒdʒi, -'gɒgi/ *noun* [Greek *dēmagōgos* from *dēmos* the people + *agōgos* leading]

de·mand ● *noun* **1** an insistent and peremptory request. **2** the desire of purchasers or consumers for a commodity (*demand for CD players has increased*). **3** an urgent claim or requirement (*care of her mother makes demands on her; the body's oxygen demand increases with exercise*). ● *transitive verb* **1** (often foll. by *of, from*, or *to* + infin., or *that* + clause) ask for (something) insistently and urgently (*demanded to know the answer; demanded five dollars from him*). **2** require or need (*a task demanding skill*). **3** insist on being told (*demanded her business; 'What do you want?' she demanded*). □ **in demand** sought after. **on demand** as soon as a demand is made (*a cheque payable on demand*). □ **demand·able** *adjective* **de·mand·er** *noun* [Old French *demande* (n.), *demander* (v.) from Latin *demandare* entrust (as DE-, *mandare* order: see MANDATE)]

demand curve *noun* a graph showing how the demand for a commodity or service varies with or depends on some other quantity, esp. one that shows how demand, at any particular time, varies according to the price charged.

demand feeding *noun* the practice of feeding a baby when it cries to be fed rather than at set times.

de·mand·ing *adjective* **1** requiring skill, effort, etc. (*a demanding but worthwhile job*). **2** hard to satisfy; exacting (*a demanding boss*). □ **de·mand·ing·ly** *adverb*

demand loan *noun* a loan repayable upon demand.

demand note *noun* a promissory note payable on demand.

demand-pull inflation *noun* inflation in which rising demand results in an increase in prices.

demand-side *adjective* of or relating to changes in price or output caused by variations in consumer demand (*compare* SUPPLY-SIDE).

de·man·toid /də'mantɔɪd/ *noun* a lustrous green garnet. [German from *Demant* diamond]

de·mar·ca·tion /ˌdiːmɑr'keɪʃən/ *noun* **1** separation or distinction (*a line of demarcation*). **2** a boundary or limit. **3** the act of marking a boundary or limits. □ **de·mar·cate** /'diː-/ *transitive verb*

de·mar·ca·tor /'diː-/ *noun* [Spanish *demarcación* from *demarcar* mark the bounds of (as DE-, MARK¹)]

dé·marche /deɪ'mɑrʃ/ *noun* a political step or initiative. [French from *démarcher* take steps (as DE-, MARCH¹)]

de·materi·al·ize *verb* (also esp. *Brit.* **-ise**) **1** *transitive & intransitive* make or become non-material or spiritual. **2** *intransitive* vanish; disappear. □ **de·materi·al·iz·a·tion** *noun*

deme /diːm/ *noun* **1** a political division of Attica in ancient Greece. **2** a local population of closely related plants or animals. [Greek *dēmos* the people]

de·mean¹ *transitive verb* lower the dignity of; debase (*his behaviour demeaned the profession*). □ **de·mean·ing** *adjective* [DE- + MEAN², after *debase*]

de·mean² *reflexive verb* (with *adv.*) *rare* behave (*demeaned himself well*). [Old French *demener* from Romanic (as DE-, Latin *minare* drive animals, from *minari* threaten)]

de·mean·our /də'miːnər/ *noun* (also **de·mean·or**) outward behaviour or bearing. [DEMEAN², prob. influenced by obsolete *havour* behaviour]

de' Med·ici ▸ **1 Catherine**, see CATHERINE DE' MEDICI. **2 Cosimo**, see COSIMO DE' MEDICI. **3 Giovanni**, see LEO X. **4 Lorenzo**, see LORENZO DE' MEDICI.

de Mé·di·cis see MARIE DE MÉDICIS.

de·men·ted *adjective* **1** mad; crazy. **2** suffering from dementia. □ **de·men·ted·ly** *adverb* **de·men·ted·ness** *noun* [past participle of *dement* verb from Old French *dementer* or from Late Latin *dementare* from *demens* out of one's mind (as DE-, *mens mentis* mind)]

de·men·tia /də'menʃə, -ʃiə/ *noun* *Med.* a chronic or persistent disorder of the mental processes marked by memory disorders, personality changes, impaired reasoning, etc., due to brain disease or injury. [Latin from *demens* (as DEMENTED)]

dementia prae·cox /'priːkɒks/ *noun* *archaic* or *hist.* schizophrenia. [Latin, lit. 'early insanity']

Dem·er·ara /ˌdemə'rerə/ a former Dutch colony in S America, now part of Guyana.

Demerara River a river of N Guyana. Rising in the Guiana Highlands, it flows about 320 km (200 miles) northward to the Atlantic.

demerara sugar /ˌdemə'rerə/ *noun* (also **demerara**) light brown raw sugar coming originally and chiefly from Demerara. [DEMERARA]

de·merge /diː'mɜrdʒ/ *transitive verb* separate (a business) from another.

de·mer·ger *noun* the separation of one business from another.

de·merit *noun* **1** a quality or action deserving blame; a fault. **2** *N Amer.* a mark given to an offender, esp. in a school or the armed forces or for traffic offences. [Latin *demeritum* neuter past participle of *demerēri* deserve]

Dem·er·ol /'demərɒl/ *noun proprietary* a brand of the painkiller meperidine.

de·mer·sal /də'mɜrsəl/ *adjective* (of a fish etc.) being or living near the sea bottom (*compare* PELAGIC 2). [Latin *demersus* past participle of *demergere* (as DE-, *mergere* plunge)]

de·mesne /də'miːn, -'meɪn/ *noun* **1 a** landed property; an estate. **b** a sovereign's or state's territory; a domain. **c** land attached to a mansion etc. **2** (usu. foll. by *of*) a region or sphere. **3** *Law hist.* possession (of real property) as one's own. [Old French *demeine* (later Anglo-French *demesne*) belonging to a lord, from Latin *dominicus* (as DOMINICAL)]

Dem·eter /də'miːtər/ *Gk Myth* the goddess of grain, daughter of Cronus and Rhea and mother of Persephone; she was the patroness of agriculture in general and goddess of the Eleusinian mysteries. [Greek from *mētēr* mother]

demi- /'demi/ *prefix* **1** half; half-size. **2** partially or imperfectly such (*demigod*). [French from medieval Latin *dimedius* half, for Latin *dimidius*]

demi-glace /'demiglas/ *noun* a meat stock from which the liquid has been partially evaporated. [French, = half-glaze]

demi·god *noun* **1 a** a partly divine being. **b** the offspring of a god or goddess and a mortal. **2** *informal* a person of compelling beauty, powers, or personality.

demi·god·dess *noun* **1 a** a partly divine female being. **b** the female offspring of a god or goddess and a mortal. **2** *informal* a woman of compelling beauty, powers, or personality.

demi·john *noun* a bulbous narrow-necked bottle holding from 11 to 38 litres and usu. in a wicker cover. [prob. corruption of French *dame-jeanne* Lady Jane, assimilated to DEMI- + the name *John*]

de·mili·tar·ize *transitive verb* (also esp. *Brit.* **-ise**) remove a military organization or forces from (a frontier, a zone, etc.). □ **de·mili·tar·iz·a·tion** *noun*

de Mille /dəˈmɪl/ **Cecil B(lount)** (1881–1959), US film producer and director. One of the founders of the Hollywood film industry, he is best known for his lavish Biblical spectacles, which include *The Ten Commandments* (1923; remade in 1956) and *Samson and Delilah* (1949).

de Mille /dəˈmɪl/ **Agnes (George)** (1905–93), niece of Cecil B. deMille, US choreographer and dancer, noted for her innovative choreography, which contributed to both plot and character development, for musicals such as *Oklahoma!* (1943) and *Carousel* (1945), and for ballets depicting American themes such as *Rodeo* (1942) and *Fall River Legend* (1948), based on the story of Lizzie Borden.

demi·mon·daine /ˈdemimɒnˌdeɪn, -mɔ̃ˌdeɪn/ *noun* a woman of a demimonde.

demi·monde /ˈdemiˌmɒnd, -ˈmɔ̃d/ *noun* **1** any group considered to be on the fringes of respectable society. **2 a** *hist.* a class of women in 19th-c. France considered to be of doubtful social standing and morality. **b** a similar class of women in any society. [French, = half-world]

de·min·er·al·ize *transitive verb* (also esp. *Brit.* **-ise**) remove minerals from (water etc.). □ **de·min·er·al·iz·a·tion** *noun* **de·min·er·al·ized** *adjective*

de·mining *noun* the action or process of removing mines (esp. land mines). □ **de·miner** *noun*

demi-pension /dəmiˈpɑ̃sjɔ̃/ *noun* (esp. in Europe) hotel accommodation with bed, breakfast, and one main meal per day. [French (as DEMI-, PENSION²)]

de·mise /dəˈmaɪz/ ● *noun* **1** death (*left a will on her demise*). **2** termination or failure (*the demise of the business*). **3** *Law* conveyance or transfer (of property, a title, etc.) by demising. ● *transitive verb Law* **1** convey or grant (an estate) by will or lease. **2** transmit (a title etc.) by death. [Anglo-French use of past participle of Old French *de(s)mettre* DISMISS, in reflexive abdicate]

demi·semi·quaver /ˌdemiˈsemiˌkweɪvər/ *noun Brit. Music* = THIRTY-SECOND NOTE.

de·mist·er /diːˈmɪstər/ *noun* a device for clearing mist from a windshield etc. □ **de·mist** *transitive verb*

demit /dəˈmɪt/ *transitive & intransitive verb* (**de·mit·ted**, **de·mit·ting**) *archaic* resign or abdicate (an office etc.). [French *démettre* from Latin *demittere* (as DE-, *mittere miss-* send)]

demi·tasse /ˈdemiˌtas/ *noun* **1** a small cup used to serve strong black coffee. **2** a serving of coffee in such a cup. [French, = half-cup]

demi·urge /ˈdemiˌɜːdʒ/ *noun* **1** (in the philosophy of Plato) the creator of the universe. **2** (in Gnosticism etc.) a heavenly being subordinate to the Supreme Being. □ **demi·urgic** *adjective* **demi·urgic·al** *adjective* [ecclesiastical Latin from Greek *dēmiourgos* craftsman, from *dēmios* public, from *dēmos* people + *-ergos* working]

demo *informal* ● *noun* (*pl.* **demos**) **1** = DEMONSTRATION 1, 2. **2** (*attributive*) demonstrating the capabilities of a group of musicians, computer software, etc. (*demo tape*; *demo disc*). **3** a demographic group (*this audience really isn't the band's demo*). ● *transitive verb* (**demos**, **demoed**) record (a song) for demonstration purposes (*they've already demoed twelve new songs*). [abbreviation]

demob /diːˈmɒb/ *Cdn, Brit.,* & *Austral. dated* ● *transitive verb* (**de·mobbed**, **de·mob·bing**) demobilize. ● *noun* demobilization. [abbreviation]

de·mobil·ize *transitive verb* (also esp. *Brit.* **-ise**) **1** disband (troops, ships, etc.). **2** release from a mobilized state or from service in the armed forces. □ **de·mobil·iz·a·tion** *noun*

dem·oc·racy *noun* (*pl.* **-cies**) **1 a** a system of government by the whole population or all the eligible members of a state, typically through elected representatives. **b** a state so governed. **2** any organization governed on democratic principles. **3** a classless and tolerant form of society. [French *démocratie* from Late Latin *democratia* from Greek *dēmokratia* from *dēmos* the people + -CRACY]

demo·crat *noun* **1** an advocate of democracy. **2** (**Democrat**) (in the US) a member or supporter of the Democratic Party. **3** (in full

democrat wagon) *N Amer. hist.* a light wagon seating two or more people and usu. drawn by two horses. [French *démocrate* (as DEMOCRACY), after *aristocrate*]

demo·crat·ic *adjective* **1** of, like, practising, advocating, or constituting democracy or a democracy. **2** favouring social equality. **3** (**Democratic**) (in the US) of or pertaining to the Democratic Party (*the Democratic candidate*). □ **demo·crat·ic·ally** *adverb*

democratic centralism *noun* an organizational system in which policy is decided centrally and is binding on all members. □ **democratic centralist** *adjective*

Democratic Party *noun* one of the two main US political parties, considered to support social reform and international commitment (compare REPUBLICAN PARTY).

Democratic Republican Party *hist.* a US political party founded in 1792 by Thomas Jefferson, a forerunner of the modern Democratic Party.

dem·oc·ra·tize *transitive verb* (also esp. *Brit.* **-tise**) make (a state, institution, etc.) democratic. □ **dem·oc·ra·tiz·a·tion** *noun*

De·moc·ri·tus /dɪˈmɒkrɪtəs/ (c.460–c.370 BC), Greek philosopher. He developed the atomic theory originated by his teacher, Leucippus (5th c. BC), which explained natural phenomena in terms of the arrangement and rearrangement of atoms moving in a void.

dé·mo·dé /ˌdeɪmɔˈdeɪ/ *adjective* out of fashion. [French, past participle of *démoder* (as DE-, *mode* fashion)]

de·modu·late *transitive verb Physics* extract (a modulating signal) from its carrier. □ **de·modu·la·tion** *noun* **de·modu·la·tor** *noun*

Demo·gor·gon /ˌdiːmɔˈɡɔrɡən/ a primeval god in ancient mythology, often of the underworld.

demo·graph·ic /ˌdemɔˈɡrafɪk/ ● *adjective* having to do with the structure of populations or population statistics, esp. those showing average age, income, marital status, etc.: *the demographic trend is towards an older population.* ● *noun* a demographic category: *networks are competing for the young female demographic.* □ **demo·graph·ic·al·ly** *adverb*

demo·graph·ics *plural noun* population statistics, esp. those showing average age, income, marital status, etc.

dem·og·raphy /dəˈmɒɡrəfi/ *noun* the study of the statistics of births, deaths, disease, etc., as illustrating the conditions of life in communities. □ **dem·og·raph·er** *noun* [Greek *dēmos* the people + -GRAPHY]

dem·oi·selle /ˌdemwaˈzel/ *noun* **1** a small crane, *Anthropoides virgo*, native to Asia and North Africa. **2 a** a damselfly. **b** a damselfish. **3** *literary* a young woman. [French, = DAMSEL]

de·mol·ish *transitive verb* **1 a** pull down (a building). **b** completely destroy or break. **2** refute (an argument, theory, etc.). **3** overthrow (an institution). **4** *jocular* eat up completely and quickly (*we demolished all the cookies before lunch*). □ **de·mol·ish·er** *noun* **demo·li·tion** *noun*

demo·li·tion·ist *noun* [French *démolir* from Latin *demolīri* (as DE-, *moliri molit-* construct, from *moles* mass)]

demolition derby *noun N Amer.* a competition in which drivers crash old cars into each other, the winner being the last vehicle still running.

de·mon *noun* **1** an evil spirit or devil, esp. one thought to possess a person. **2** (often *attributive*) a forceful, fierce, or skilful performer (*a demon on the tennis court; a demon player*). **3** an evil passion or habit (*the demon drink*). **4** a cruel or destructive person. **5** (also **dae·mon**, **dai·mon**) an inner or attendant spirit; a genius (*the demon of creativity*). □ **a demon for work** *informal* a person who works strenuously. [medieval Latin *demon* from Latin *daemon* from Greek *daimōn* deity]

de·monet·ize /diːˈmɒnɪˌtaɪz/ *transitive verb* (also esp. *Brit.* **-ise**) withdraw (a coin etc.) from use as money. □ **de·monet·iz·a·tion** *noun* [French *démonétiser* (as DE-, Latin *moneta* MONEY)]

de·mon·iac /dəˈmoːnɪˌak, ˈdiːməˌnaiak/ ● *adjective* = DEMONIC. ● *noun* a person possessed by an evil spirit. □ **de·mon·iac·al** /ˌdiːməˈnaiəkəl/ *adjective*

de·mon·ic /dəˈmɒnɪk/ *adjective* (also **dae·mon·ic**) **1** of or like demons. **2 a** supposedly possessed by an evil spirit. **b** of or concerning such possession. **3** fiercely energetic or frenzied. **4** having or seeming to have supernatural genius or power. □ **de·mon·ic·ally** *adverb*

demon·ism *noun* belief in the power of demons.

demon·ize *transitive verb* (also esp. *Brit.* **-ise**) **1** make into or like a demon. **2** represent as a demon. □ **demon·iz·a·tion** *noun*

demon·ol·ogy /ˌdiːmənˈɒlədʒi/ *noun* (*pl.* **-gies**) **1** the study of demons. **2** belief in demons. **3** a group of persons or things regarded as evil (*the *twin demonologies of communism and fascism).* □ **demon·ologic·al** /-əˈlɒdʒɪkəl/ **demon·ol·o·gist** noun

de·mon·strable /dəˈmɒnstrəbl/ adjective capable of being shown or logically proved. □ **de·mon·strably** adverb

dem·on·strate verb **1** transitive describe and explain (a scientific theory, machine, etc.) with the help of examples, experiments, practical use, etc. (*the lifeguard demonstrated how to do the breaststroke*). **2** transitive **a** logically prove the truth of (*our findings demonstrate a link between diet and cancer*). **b** be proof of the existence of. **3** transitive make known by outward indications; show evidence of (feelings etc.) (*demonstrated his affection by giving her a kiss*). **4** intransitive take part in or organize a public demonstration. **5** intransitive act as a demonstrator. [Latin *demonstrare* (as DE-, *monstrare* show)]

dem·on·stra·tion noun **1 a** a practical exhibition or explanation of something by experiment or example in order to teach or inform (*a cooking demonstration*). **b** a practical display of a piece of equipment etc. to show how it works and its capacity. **2** a public meeting, march, etc., for a political or moral purpose. **3** proof provided by logic, argument, etc. **4** (foll. by *of*) **a** the outward showing of feeling etc. **b** an instance of this. **5** Military a show of military force.

de·mon·stra·tive /dəˈmɒnstrətɪv/ ● adjective **1** given to or marked by an open expression of feeling, esp. of affection (*a very demonstrative person*). **2** (usu. foll. by *of*) logically conclusive; giving proof (*the work is demonstrative of their skill*). **3** serving to point out or exhibit; illustrative. **4** Grammar (of an adjective or pronoun) indicating the person or thing referred to, e.g. *this*, *that*, *those*. ● noun Grammar a demonstrative adjective or pronoun. □ **de·mon·stra·tive·ly** adverb **de·mon·stra·tive·ness** noun

dem·on·stra·tor noun **1** a person who takes part in a political demonstration etc. **2 a** a person who demonstrates, esp. machines, equipment, etc., to prospective customers. **b** a machine, etc., esp. a car, used for such demonstrations.

de Monts /dəˈmɔ̃/ **Pierre Du Gua** (1558–1628), French explorer and colonizer. A close associate of Champlain, he established a settlement on the Île Sainte-Croix in 1604; the colony was forced by disease to move to Port-Royal in 1605. He himself returned to France, but in 1608 sent Champlain to found a trading post at Quebec.

de·moral·ize transitive verb (also esp. Brit. **-ise**) **1** destroy (a person's) morale; make hopeless. **2** archaic corrupt (a person's) morals. □ **de·moral·iz·a·tion** noun **de·moral·iz·ing** adjective **de·moral·iz·ing·ly** adverb [French *démoraliser* (as DE-, MORAL)]

De·mos·then·es /dɪˈmɒsθəˌniːz/ (384–322 BC), Athenian orator and statesman, known for the *Philippics*, four political speeches focusing on the need to defend Athens against Philip II of Macedon.

de·mote /diːˈmoʊt, də-/ transitive verb reduce to a lower rank or class. □ **de·mo·tion** noun [DE- + PROMOTE]

dem·otic /dəˈmɒtɪk/ ● noun **1** the popular colloquial form of a language. **2** a popular simplified form of ancient Egyptian writing (*compare* HIERATIC). **3** a popular written or spoken form of modern Greek. ● adjective **1** (esp. of language) popular, colloquial, or vulgar. **2** of or concerning the ancient Egyptian or modern Greek demotic. [Greek *dēmotikos* from *dēmotēs* one of the people (*dēmos*)]

de·motiv·ate transitive verb cause to lose motivation; discourage. □ **de·motiv·at·ing** adjective **de·motiv·a·tion** noun

de·mount transitive verb **1** take (apparatus, a gun, etc.) from its mounting. **2** dismantle for later reassembly. □ **de·mount·able** adjective & noun [French *démonter*: compare DISMOUNT]

Demp·sey /ˈdempsi/ **Wil·liam Har·ri·son ('Jack')** (1895–1983), US boxer. Known as the 'Manassa Mauler', he was world heavyweight champion 1919–26, and helped to popularize the sport.

de·mul·cent /dɪˈmʌlsənt/ ● adjective soothing. ● noun an agent that forms a protective film soothing irritation or inflammation in the mouth. [Latin *demulcēre* (as DE-, *mulcēre* soothe)]

demur /dəˈmɜr/ ● intransitive verb (**de·murred**, **de·mur·ring**) **1** raise scruples or objections. **2** Law put in a demurrer. ● noun (also **de·mur·ral** /dɪˈmʌrəl/) (usu. in neg.) **1** an objection (*agreed without demur*). **2** the act or process of objecting. [Old French *demeure* (n.), *demeurer* (v.) from Romanic (as DE-, Latin *morari* delay)]

de·mure /dəˈmjʊr/ adjective (**de·mur·er**, **de·mur·est**) **1** composed; quiet and reserved. **2** affectedly shy and quiet; coy. **3** modest (*a demure high collar*). □ **de·mure·ly** adverb **de·mure·ness** noun [Middle English, perhaps from Anglo-French *demuré* from Old French *demoré* past participle of *demorer* remain, stay (as DEMUR): influenced by Old French *meür* from Latin *maturus* ripe]

de·mur·rage /dəˈmɜrɪdʒ/ noun **1 a** a rate or amount payable to a

shipowner by a charterer for failure to load or discharge a ship within the time agreed. **b** a charge for the similar detention of railway cars or other goods. **2** such a detention or delay. [Old French *demo(u)rage* from *demorer* (as DEMUR)]

de·mur·rer /dəˈmɜrər/ noun Law an objection raised or exception taken. [Anglo-French (infin. used as a noun), = DEMUR]

de·mutual·ize /diːˈmjuːtʃuəlaɪz/ intransitive verb (of a mutual insurance company etc.) change from being owned by its members to a different type of ownership. □ **de·mutual·iz·a·tion** noun

de·mysti·fy transitive verb (**-fies**, **-fied**) clarify (obscure beliefs or subjects etc.); simplify; explain (*this book attempts to demystify computers*). □ **de·mysti·fi·ca·tion** noun

de·myth·olo·gize transitive verb (also esp. Brit. **-gise**) **1** remove mythical elements from (a legend, famous person's life, etc.). **2** reinterpret what some consider to be the mythological elements in (the Bible).

den ● noun **1** a wild animal's lair. **2** a place of crime or vice (*den of iniquity*; *opium den*). **3** a room in a home serving as an informal place for reading, pursuing a hobby, etc. ● intransitive verb (**denned**, **den·ning**) live in or as if in a den. [Old English *denn* from Germanic, related to DENE]

Den·ali /dəˈnɑli/ another name for Mount MCKINLEY. [Athapaskan, = 'the high one']

denar /ˈdiːnɑr/ noun the basic monetary unit of the former Yugoslav Republic of Macedonia. [Latin *denarius*]

den·ar·ius /dəˈnɛriəs/ noun (pl. **den·arii** /-ri,aɪ/) an ancient Roman silver coin. [Latin, = (coin) worth ten asses (as DENARY: see AS[2])]

den·ary /ˈdiːnəri/ adjective of ten; decimal. [Latin *denarius* containing ten (*deni* by tens)]

de·nation·al·ize transitive verb (also esp. Brit. **-ise**) **1** transfer (a nationalized industry or institution etc.) from public to private ownership. **2 a** deprive (a nation) of its status or characteristics as a nation. **b** deprive (a person) of nationality or national characteristics. □ **de·nation·al·iz·a·tion** noun

de·natur·al·ize transitive verb (also esp. Brit. **-ise**) **1** change the nature or properties of; make unnatural. **2** deprive of the rights of citizenship. **3** = DENATURE 2. □ **de·natur·al·iz·a·tion** noun

de·nature transitive verb **1** change the properties of (a protein etc.) by heat, acidity, etc. **2** make (alcohol) unfit for drinking esp. by the addition of another substance. **3** change the essential nature of (a person, a literary or artistic work, etc.). □ **de·natur·ant** noun **de·natur·a·tion** /diːˌnatʃəˈreɪʃən/ noun **de·natured** adjective

de·nazify /diːˈnatsɪfaɪ/ transitive verb (**-fies**, **-fied**) esp. hist. remove from, or declare to be free from, Nazi allegiance or influence. □ **de·nazifi·ca·tion** noun

Den·bigh·shire /ˈdenbiˌʃɪr/ a county of N Wales. It was divided between Clwyd and Gwynedd in 1974, and was restored (with redrawn borders) in 1996.

Dench /dentʃ/ **Dame Jud·ith Oliv·ia ('Judi')** (b.1934), English actress and theatre director, noted for her performances in Shakespearean roles and in film and television.

den·dri·mer /ˈdendrɪmər/ noun Chem. a synthetic polymer with a branching, treelike structure. [Greek *dendron* tree + -MER]

den·drite /ˈdendraɪt/ noun **1 a** a stone or mineral with natural treelike or mosslike markings. **b** such marks on stones or minerals. **2** Chem. a crystal with branching treelike growth. **3** Zool. & Anat. a branching process of a nerve cell conducting signals to a cell body. [French from Greek *dendritēs* (adj.) from *dendron* tree]

den·drit·ic /denˈdrɪtɪk/ adjective **1** of or like a dendrite. **2** treelike in shape or markings.

den·dro·bium /denˈdroʊbiəm/ noun any epiphytic orchid of the genus *Dendrobium*, frequently cultivated as an ornamental. [Greek *dendron* tree]

den·dro·chron·ol·ogy /ˌdendroʊkrəˈnɒlədʒi/ noun **1** a system of dating using the characteristic patterns of annual growth rings of trees to assign dates to timber. **2** the study of these growth rings. □ **den·dro·chrono·logic·al** adjective **den·dro·chron·ol·o·gist** noun [Greek *dendron* tree + CHRONOLOGY]

den·droid /ˈdendrɔɪd/ adjective tree-shaped. [Greek *dendrōdēs* treelike + -OID]

den·drol·ogy /denˈdrɒlədʒi/ noun the scientific study of trees. □ **den·dro·logic·al** /-drəˈlɒdʒɪkəl/ adjective **den·drol·o·gist** noun [Greek *dendron* tree + -LOGY]

Dene /ˈdeneɪ/ noun a member of a group of Aboriginal peoples of the

Athapaskan linguistic family, living esp. in the Canadian north. [Chipewyan *dene* person]

dene /diːn/ *noun Brit.* **1** a narrow wooded valley. **2** a vale (esp. as the ending of place names). [Old English *denu*, related to DEN]

Deneb /dəˈneb/ a supergiant star, the brightest in the constellation Cygnus. [Arabic, = 'tail']

Denen·deh /dəˈnendə/ a proposed name for the NWT. [Dene, lit. 'land of the Dene']

De·neuve /dəˈnɜːv/ **Cath·er·ine** (born Catherine Dorléac) (b.1943), French actress, known for her classic beauty and for her roles in such films as *Repulsion* (1965) and *Belle de jour* (1967).

den·gue /ˈdeŋɡi/ *noun* an infectious viral disease of the tropics causing a fever and acute pains in the joints. [West Indian Spanish, from Swahili *denga*, *dinga*, assimilated to Spanish *dengue* fastidiousness, with reference to the stiffness of the patient's neck and shoulders]

Deng Xiao·ping /ˌdeŋ ʃaʊˈpɪŋ/ (also **Teng Hsiao-p'ing**) (1904–97), Chinese Communist leader, vice-premier 1973–6 and 1977–80; vice-chairman of the Central Committee of the Chinese Communist Party 1977–80. From 1977 he promoted economic modernization, and improved relations with the West; although officially retired in 1989, he continued to be regarded as the effective leader of China. In 1989 he authorized the massacre of over 2,000 pro-democracy demonstrators in Beijing's Tiananmen Square.

deni·able /dɪˈnaɪəbəl/ *adjective* that may be denied. □ **deni·abil·ity** *noun*

de·nial /dɪˈnaɪəl/ *noun* **1** the act or an instance of denying. **2** a refusal of a request or wish. **3** a statement that a thing is not true; a rejection (*denial of the accusation*). **4** a disavowal or disowning; refusal to recognize. **5** = SELF-ABNEGATION. **6** *Psych.* the usu. subconscious suppression of an unacceptable truth or emotion. □ **in denial** in a state in which one suppresses (usu. unconsciously) a painful or unacceptable wish or experience etc.

denial of service *noun* an interruption in an authorized user's access to a computer system, esp. such an interruption caused by a malicious and organized effort to occupy the computer with useless or unnecessary tasks (also *attributive*: *denial-of-service attacks*).

de·nier[1] /dɪˈnaɪr/ *noun* a person who denies something.

de·nier[2] /ˈdenjər/ *noun* a unit of weight by which the fineness of silk, rayon, or nylon yarn is measured. [originally the name of a small coin: Middle English from Old French from Latin *denarius*]

deni·grate /ˈdenɪˌɡreɪt/ *transitive verb* defame or disparage the reputation of (a person). □ **deni·gra·tion** *noun* **deni·gra·tor** *noun* **deni·gra·tory** /-ˈɡreɪtɜri/ *adjective* [Latin *denigrare* (as DE-, *nigrare* from *niger* black)]

denim *noun* **1** (often *attributive*) a usu. blue hard-wearing cotton twill fabric used for jeans, overalls, etc. (*a denim skirt*). **2** (in *pl.*) *informal* jeans, overalls, etc. made of this. [for *serge de Nim* from Nîmes in S France]

De Niro /də ˈniːroː/ **Rob·ert** (b.1943), US actor and film producer, noted for his portrayal of tough but sensitive characters; his films include *Taxi Driver* (1976), *Raging Bull* (1980), for which he won an Oscar, and *GoodFellas* (1990).

Denis, St. /ˈdenɪs, deˈni/ (also **Denys**) (died *c*.250), Italian-born French bishop and patron saint of France. According to tradition he was sent from Rome to convert Gaul, later became bishop of Paris, and was martyred in the reign of the emperor Valerian (*c*.193–260). Feast day, 9 October.

de·nitri·fy /diːˈnaɪtrɪˌfaɪ/ *transitive verb* (**-fies**, **-fied**) remove the nitrates or nitrites from (soil etc.). □ **de·nitri·fi·ca·tion** /-fɪˈkeɪʃən/ *noun*

deni·zen /ˈdenɪzən/ *noun* **1** (usu. foll. by *of*) an inhabitant or occupant. **2** a person who frequents a certain place. **3** *Brit.* a foreigner admitted to certain rights in his or her adopted country. **4** a naturalized foreign word, animal, or plant. □ **deni·zen·ship** *noun* [Anglo-French *deinzein* from Old French *deinz* within, from Latin *de* from + *intus* within + *-ein* from Latin *-aneus*: see -ANEOUS]

Den·mark a Scandinavian country consisting of the greater part of the Jutland peninsula and several neighbouring islands, between the North Sea and the Baltic; pop. (est. 2002) 5,368,854; capital, Copenhagen.

den mother *noun N Amer.* a person, usu. a woman, who acts as a parent or chaperone to a group of children, students, etc.

de·nomin·ate /dəˈnɒmɪˌneɪt/ *transitive verb* **1** give a name to. **2** call or describe (a person or thing) as. **3** (in *passive*; usu. foll. by *in*) express in a specified monetary unit. [Latin *denominare* (as DE-, NOMINATE)]

de·nomin·a·tion /dəˌnɒmɪˈneɪʃən/ *noun* **1** a religious sect or body with a distinctive name and organization. **2** a class of units within a range

or sequence of numbers, weights, money, etc. (*money of small denominations*). **3 a** a name or designation, esp. a characteristic or class name. **b** a class or kind having a specific name. **4** the rank of a playing card within a suit, or of a suit relative to others.

de·nomin·a·tion·al *adjective* **1** of or relating to a particular denomination. **2** (of education) according to the principles of a religious denomination. □ **de·nomin·a·tion·al·ism** *noun* **de·nomin·a·tion·al·ist** *noun*

de·nomin·a·tive /diːˈnɒmɪnətɪv/ *adjective* serving as or giving a name.

de·nomin·ator /diːˈnɒmɪˌneɪtɜr/ *noun Math.* the number below the line in a vulgar fraction; a divisor (*compare* COMMON DENOMINATOR 1, LOWEST COMMON DENOMINATOR 1).

Denon·ville /dənɔ̃ˈviːl/ **Jacques-René de Brisay, Marquis de** (1642–1710), French colonial administrator, Governor General of New France 1685–9. He supported the fur traders in their efforts to expand to the west and north, and led two expeditions against the Iroquois in retaliation for raids against French settlements.

de·nota·tion *noun* **1** the meaning or signification of a term, as distinct from its implications or connotations. **2** the act of denoting or indicating. **3** a mark, sign, etc. that serves to denote something. **4** a term used to denote something; a designation.

de·note /diːˈnoːt/ *transitive verb* **1** be a sign of; indicate (*the arrow denotes direction*). **2** (usu. foll. by *that* + clause) mean, convey. **3** stand as a name for; signify. □ **de·nota·tive** /diːnoːˈteɪtɪv/ *adjective* [French *dénoter* or from Latin *denotare* (as DE-, *notare* mark, from *nota* NOTE)]

de·noue·ment /ˌdeɪnuːˈmɑ̃/ *noun* (also **dé·noue·ment**) **1** the final unravelling of a plot or complicated situation. **2** the final scene in a play, novel, etc., in which the plot is resolved. [French *dénouement* from *dénouer* unknot (as DE-, Latin *nodare* from *nodus* knot)]

de·nounce *transitive verb* **1** accuse publicly; condemn (*denounced him as a traitor*). **2** inform against (*denounced her to the police*). □ **de·nounce·ment** *noun* **de·noun·cer** *noun* [Old French *denoncier* from Latin *denuntiare* (as DE-, *nuntiare* make known, from *nuntius* messenger)]

de novo /diː ˈnoːvoː, deɪ/ *adverb* starting again; anew. [Latin]

Den·pasar /denˈpɒsar/ the chief city of the island of Bali, a seaport on the south coast; pop. (est. 2002) 491,500.

dense *adjective* (**dens·er**, **dens·est**) **1** closely compacted in substance; thick (*dense fog*). **2** crowded together (*the population is less dense on the outskirts*). **3** *informal* stupid. □ **dense·ly** *adverb* **dense·ness** *noun* [French *dense* or Latin *densus*]

densi·tom·eter /ˌdensɪˈtɒmɪtɜr/ *noun* an instrument for measuring the photographic density of an image on a film or photographic print.

dens·ity *noun* (*pl.* **-ities**) **1** the degree of compactness of a substance. **2** *Physics* degree of consistency measured by the quantity of mass per unit volume. **3** the opacity of a photographic image. **4** a crowded state. **5** stupidity.

dent ● *noun* **1** a slight mark or hollow in a surface made by, or as if by, a blow with a hammer etc. **2** a noticeable effect (*lunch made a dent in our funds*). ● *transitive verb* **1** mark with a dent. **2** have (esp. an adverse) effect on (*the news dented our hopes*). [Middle English, prob. from INDENT[1]]

den·tal *adjective* **1** of or relating to the teeth. **2** of or relating to dentistry. **3** *Phonetics* (of a consonant) produced with the tip of the tongue against the upper front teeth (as *th*) or the ridge of the teeth (as *n*, *s*, *t*). [Late Latin *dentalis* from Latin *dens dentis* tooth]

dental assistant *noun* a person trained and licensed to act as a dentist's assistant, e.g. by mixing amalgam, taking X-rays, etc.

dental dam *noun* = DAM[1] *noun* 4b.

dental floss *noun* a strong, soft thread used to clean between the teeth.

dental hygienist *noun* a person trained and licensed to act as a dentist's assistant, specializing in oral hygiene, cleaning and scaling teeth, etc.

den·tal·ium /denˈteɪliəm/ *noun* (*pl.* **den·tal·ia** /-liə/) **1** any marine mollusc of the genus *Dentalium*, having a conical foot protruding from a tusk-like shell. **2** this shell used as an ornament or as a form of currency. [modern Latin from Late Latin *dentalis*: see DENTAL]

den·tal·ize *transitive verb Phonetics* (also esp. *Brit.* **-ise**) change into a dental sound; make dental.

dental mechanic *noun* a person who makes and repairs artificial teeth.

dental surgeon *noun* a dentist.

dental technician *noun* a person who makes and repairs false teeth.

den·tate /ˈdenteɪt/ *adjective* Bot. & Zool. toothed; with toothlike notches; serrated. [Latin *dentatus* from *dens dentis* tooth]

denti·care /ˈdentəˌker/ *noun* Cdn a plan for providing dental care funded by some provincial governments. [DENTAL, after MEDICARE]

den·ticle /ˈdentɪkəl/ *noun* Zool. a small tooth or toothlike projection, scale, etc. □ **den·ticu·late** /denˈtɪkjʊlət/ *adjective* [Latin *denticulus* diminutive of *dens dentis* tooth]

denti·frice /ˈdentəfrɪs/ *noun* a paste or powder for cleaning the teeth. [French from Latin *dentifricium* from *dens dentis* tooth + *fricare* rub]

den·til /ˈdentɪl/ *noun* Archit. each of a series of small rectangular blocks as a decoration under the moulding of a cornice in classical architecture. [obsolete French *dentille* diminutive of *dent* tooth, from Latin *dens dentis*]

den·tine /ˈdentiːn/ *noun* a hard dense bony tissue forming the bulk of a tooth. □ **den·tin·al** /ˈdentɪnəl/ *adjective* [Latin *dens dentis* tooth + -INE⁴]

den·tist *noun* a person who is qualified to treat the diseases and conditions that affect the mouth, jaws, teeth, and their supporting tissues, esp. the repair and extraction of teeth and the insertion of artificial ones. □ **dent·istry** *noun* [French *dentiste* from *dent* tooth]

den·ti·tion /denˈtɪʃən/ *noun* **1** the type, number, and arrangement of teeth in a species or individual. **2** the cutting of teeth; teething. [Latin *dentitio* from *dentire* to teethe]

den·ture /ˈdentʃər/ *noun* an artificial replacement for one or more teeth carried on a removable plate or frame. [French from *dent* tooth]

den·tur·ist /ˈdentʃərɪst/ *noun* a person who makes dentures. □ **den·tur·ism** *noun*

de·nuclear·ize /diːˈnuːkliːəˌraɪz, diːˈnjuːk-/ *transitive verb* (also esp. Brit. **-ise**) remove nuclear armaments from (a country etc.). □ **de·nuclear·iz·a·tion** *noun*

de·nude /dɪˈnuːd, -ˈnjuːd/ *transitive verb* **1** make naked or bare. **2** (foll. by *of*) **a** strip of clothing, a covering, etc. **b** deprive of a possession or attribute. **3** Geol. lay (rock or a formation etc.) bare by removing what lies above. □ **de·nud·a·tion** /ˌdiːnuːˈdeɪʃən, ˌdiːnjuː-/ *noun* [Latin *denudare* (as DE-, *nudus* naked)]

de·nunci·a·tion /dɪˌnʌnsiˈeɪʃən/ *noun* **1** the act of denouncing (a person, policy, etc.); public condemnation. **2** an instance of this. □ **de·nunci·a·tory** /dɪˈnʌnsiəˌtɔri/ *adjective* [Latin *denunciatio* (as DENOUNCE)]

Den·ver¹ the state capital of Colorado; pop. (2000) 554,636, situated at an altitude of 1 608 m (5,280 ft.) on the eastern side of the Rocky Mountains. □ **Den·ver·ite** *noun*

Den·ver² *noun* (in full **Denver sandwich**) N Amer. (West) a sandwich containing an omelette made with ham, onions, and sometimes green pepper. [DENVER¹]

Denver boot *noun* a metal clamp that may be attached to the wheel of a motor vehicle preventing it from being moved, esp. until a fine is paid. [DENVER¹, where it was first used]

deny /dɪˈnaɪ, dəˈnaɪ/ *transitive verb* (**-nies**, **-nied**) **1** declare untrue or non-existent (*denied the charge; denied that it is so; denied having lied*). **2** repudiate or disclaim (*denied his faith; denied her signature*). **3** (often foll. by *to*) refuse (a person or thing, or something to a person) (*this was denied to me; denied her the satisfaction*). **4** refuse access to (a person sought) (*denied him his daughter*). □ **deny oneself** be abstinent. [Old French *denier* from Latin *denegare* (as DE-, *negare* say no)]

Denys, St. *var. of* DENIS, ST.

deo·dar /ˈdiːəˌdɑr/ *noun* the Himalayan cedar *Cedrus deodara*, the tallest of the cedar family, with drooping branches bearing large barrel-shaped cones. [Hindi *dẽ'odār* from Sanskrit *deva-dāru* divine tree]

de·odor·ant *noun* (often *attributive*) a substance sprayed or rubbed on to the body or sprayed into the air to remove or conceal unpleasant smells (*a roll-on deodorant; has a deodorant effect*). [as DEODORIZE + -ANT]

de·odor·ize *transitive verb* (also esp. Brit. **-ise**) remove or destroy the (usu. unpleasant) smell of. □ **de·odor·iz·a·tion** *noun* **de·odor·iz·er** *noun* [DE- + Latin *odor* smell]

Deo gra·tias /ˌdeɪo ˈɡratsiəs/ *interjection* thanks be to God. [Latin, = (we give) thanks to God]

de·ontic /diːˈɒntɪk/ *adjective* Philos. of or relating to duty and obligation as ethical concepts. [Greek *deont-* part. stem of *dei* it is right]

de·ontol·ogy /ˌdiːɒnˈtɒlədʒi/ *noun* Philos. the study of duty. □ **de·onto·logic·al** *adjective* **de·ontol·o·gist** *noun*

Deo vol·ente /ˌdeɪo vəˈlentei/ *adverb* God willing; if nothing prevents it. [Latin]

de·oxygen·ate *transitive verb* remove oxygen, esp. free oxygen, from. □ **de·oxygen·at·ed** *adjective* **de·oxygen·a·tion** *noun*

de·oxy·ribo·nucleic acid /diːˌɒksiˌraɪboːnuːˈkleɪɪk, -njuːˈkleɪɪk/ *noun* see DNA. [DE- + OXYGEN + RIBONUCLEIC (ACID)]

dep *noun* Cdn (Que.) = DEPANNEUR. [abbreviation]

dep. *abbreviation* **1** departs. **2** deputy.

depan·neur /ˌdepəˈnɜr/ *noun* Cdn (Que.) a convenience store. [Canadian French]

De·par·dieu /ˈdəpɑrˈdjɜ/ **Gé·rard** (b.1948), French actor, whose international reputation is based on his many films, including *The Return of Martin Guerre* (1981), *Jean de Florette* (1986), and *Cyrano de Bergerac* (1990).

de·part *verb* **1** *intransitive* **a** (usu. foll. by *from*) go away; leave (*the train departs from this platform*). **b** (usu. foll. by *for*) start; set out (*buses depart for Hamilton every hour*). **2** *intransitive* (usu. foll. by *from*) diverge; deviate (*departs from standard practice*). **3 a** *intransitive* leave by death; die. **b** *transitive* formal or literary leave by death (*departed this life*). [Old French *departir*, ultimately from Latin *dispertire* divide]

de·part·ed ● *adjective* bygone (*departed greatness*). ● *noun* (prec. by *the*) euphemism a particular dead person or dead people (*we are here to mourn the departed*).

de·part·ment *noun* **1** a separate part of a complex whole, esp.: **a** a branch of municipal, provincial, or federal administration (*Justice Department; Department of Health; the fire department*). **b** a branch of study and its administration at a university, school, etc. (*the physics department*). **c** a specialized section of a large store (*hardware department*). **d** a subdivision of a company or organization (*the marketing department*). **2** *informal* an area of special expertise. **3** *informal* the specified subject under discussion (*I never thought of myself as above average in the looks department*). **4** an administrative district in France and other countries. [French *département* (as DEPART)]

de·part·ment·al *adjective* of or belonging to a department. □ **de·part·ment·al·ism** *noun* **de·part·ment·al·ize** *transitive verb* (also esp. Brit. **-ise**). **de·part·ment·al·iz·a·tion** *noun* **de·part·ment·al·ly** *adverb*

department store *noun* (also Brit. **departmental store**) a large store stocking many varieties of goods in different departments.

de·par·ture *noun* **1** the act or an instance of departing. **2** (often foll. by *from*) a deviation (from the truth, a standard, etc.). **3** (often *attributive*) the starting of a train, an aircraft, etc. on a journey (*the departure was late; departure lounge*). **4** a new course of action or thought (*driving a car is rather a departure for him*). **5** Naut. the amount of a ship's change of longitude.

de·pend *intransitive verb* **1** (often foll. by *on, upon*) be controlled or determined by (*it depends on whether they agree; it depends how you tackle the problem*). **2** (foll. by *on, upon*) **a** be unable to do without (*depends on her mother*). **b** rely on (*I'm depending on you to come*). **3** (foll. by *on, upon*) be grammatically dependent on. □ **depending on** according to. **depend upon it!** you may be sure! **it** (or **it all** or **that**) **depends** expressing uncertainty or qualification in answering a question (*Will they come? It depends*). [Old French *dependre*, ultimately from Latin *dependēre* (as DE-, *pendēre* hang)]

de·pend·able *adjective* reliable. □ **de·pend·abil·ity** *noun* **de·pend·ably** *adverb*

de·pend·ant *noun* (also **de·pend·ent**) a person who relies on another esp. for financial support. [French *dépendant* pres. part. of *dépendre* (as DEPEND)]

de·pend·ence *noun* **1** the state of being dependent, esp. on financial or other support. **2** reliance; trust; confidence (*shows great dependence on my judgment*). **3** the state of being dependent on a drug, physically or psychologically. [French *dépendance* (as DEPEND)]

de·pend·ency *noun* (pl. **-cies**) **1** a country or province controlled by another. **2** anything subordinate or dependent. **3** the fact or condition of being dependent on another for financial or emotional support. **4** the state of being dependent on drugs.

de·pend·ent ● *adjective* **1** (usu. foll. by *on*) depending, conditional. **2** unable to do without (esp. a drug). **3** maintained at another's cost. **4** Math. (of a variable) having a value determined by that of another variable. **5** Grammar (of a clause, phrase, or word) subordinate to a sentence or word. ● *noun var. of* DEPENDANT. □ **de·pend·ent·ly** *adverb* [Middle English, earlier *-ant* = DEPENDANT]

de·person·al·iz·a·tion *noun* (also esp. Brit. **-is·a·tion**) esp. Psych. the loss of one's sense of identity.

de·person·al·ize *transitive verb* (also esp. Brit. **-ise**) **1** make impersonal. **2** deprive of personality.

Vowels: a cat   ɑ arm   e bed   ɜr her   ɜ: deux   ə ago   ɪ sit   i cosy   iː feed   ɒ hot   ɔ pore   oː no   ʌ run   ʊ put

de·pict *transitive verb* **1** represent in a drawing or painting etc. **2** portray in words; describe (*the play depicts him as vain and petty*). □ **de·pict·er** *noun* **de·pic·tion** *noun* [Latin *depingere depict-* (as DE-, *pingere* paint)]

dep·il·ate /'depɪˌleɪt/ *transitive verb* remove the hair from. □ **dep·il·a·tion** *noun* [Latin *depilare* (as DE-, *pilare* from *pilus* hair)]

de·pil·a·tory /dəˈpɪləˌtɔri/ ● *adjective* that removes unwanted hair. ● *noun* (*pl.* **-tories**) a depilatory substance.

de Pisan /də piːˈzɑ̃/ **Chris·tine** (also **de Pizan**) (c.1364–c.1430), Italian-born French writer. The first professional woman writer in France, she is known for her works on women's achievements; these include *Epistre au dieu d'amours* (1399) and *La Cité des dames* (*Book of the City of Ladies*) (1405).

de·plane *verb* esp. *N Amer.* **1** *intransitive* disembark from an airplane. **2** *transitive* remove from an airplane.

de·plete /diːˈpliːt/ *transitive verb* (esp. in *passive*) **1** reduce in numbers or quantity (*depleted forces*). **2** empty out; exhaust (*their energies were depleted*). □ **de·plet·er** *noun* **de·ple·tion** *noun* [Latin *deplēre* (as DE-, *plēre plet-* fill)]

depletion allowance *noun N Amer.* an income tax deduction made after the taxpayer amortizes or deducts exploration or development expenses.

de·plor·able *adjective* **1** exceedingly bad (*a deplorable meal*). **2** that can be deplored. □ **de·plor·ably** *adverb*

de·plore *transitive verb* **1** grieve over; regret. **2** be scandalized by; find exceedingly bad. □ **de·plor·ing·ly** *adverb* [ultimately from Latin *deplorare* (as DE-, *plorare* bewail)]

de·ploy *verb* **1** *transitive* bring or send (armaments, armed forces, etc.) into position for action. **2** *Military* **a** *transitive* cause (troops) to spread out from a column into a line. **b** *intransitive* (of troops) spread out in this way. **3** *transitive & intransitive* move into a position for effective action (*deployed the parachute; the air bags deploy automatically*). **4** *transitive* use (talents, arguments, stylistic devices, etc.) effectively. □ **de·ploy·ment** *noun* [French *déployer* from Latin *displicare* (as DIS-, *plicare* fold) & Late Latin *deplicare* explain]

de·polar·ize *transitive verb* (also esp. *Brit.* **-ise**) *Physics* reduce or remove the polarization of. □ **de·polar·iz·a·tion** *noun*

de·polit·i·cize *transitive verb* (also esp. *Brit.* **-cise**) **1** make (a person, an organization, etc.) non-political. **2** remove from political activity or influence. □ **de·polit·i·ciz·a·tion** *noun*

de·poly·mer·ize *transitive & intransitive verb* (also esp. *Brit.* **-ise**) *Chem.* break down into monomers or other smaller units. □ **de·poly·mer·iz·a·tion** *noun*

de·pon·ent /diːˈpoʊnənt/ ● *adjective* *Grammar* (of a verb, esp. in Latin or Greek) passive or middle in form but active in meaning. ● *noun* **1** *Grammar* a deponent verb. **2** *Law* **a** a person making a deposition under oath. **b** a witness giving written testimony for use in court etc. [Latin *deponere* (as DE-, *ponere posit-* place): adj. from the notion that the verb had laid aside the passive sense]

de·popu·late *verb* **1** *transitive* reduce the population of. **2** *intransitive* decline in population. □ **de·popu·la·tion** *noun*

de·port /diːˈpɔrt/ *transitive verb* **1 a** expel (an immigrant or foreigner) from a country, e.g. for criminal activity. **b** exile (a native) to another country. **2** *reflexive archaic* conduct (oneself) or behave (in a specified manner) (*deported himself well*). □ **de·port·able** *adjective* **de·por·ta·tion** *noun* [Old French *deporter* and (sense 1) French *déporter* (as DE-, Latin *portare* carry)]

de·por·tee /ˌdiːpɔrˈtiː/ *noun* a person who has been or is being deported.

de·port·ment /diːˈpɔrtmənt/ *noun* bearing, demeanour, or manners, esp. of a cultivated kind.

de·pose /diːˈpoʊz/ *verb* **1** *transitive* remove (esp. a ruler) from office. **2** *intransitive Law* (usu. foll. by *to*, or *that* + clause) bear witness, esp. on oath in court. [Old French *deposer* after Latin *deponere*: see DEPONENT, POSE¹]

de·posit ● *noun* **1 a** a sum of money placed or kept in an account in a bank. **b** anything stored or entrusted for safekeeping, usu. in a bank. **2 a** a sum payable as a first instalment on an item bought, or as a pledge for a contract. **b** a returnable sum payable on the short-term rental of a car, boat, etc. **c** a sum payable for a refillable bottle or other container, refunded when the empty container is returned. **d** = DAMAGE DEPOSIT. **3** *Cdn & Brit.* a sum of money deposited by an election candidate and forfeited if he or she fails to receive a certain proportion of the votes. **4 a** a natural layer or accumulation of sand, rock, minerals, etc. **b** a layer of precipitated matter on a surface, e.g. scale in a kettle. ● *transitive verb* (**de·posit·ed, de·posit·ing**) **1** put or lay

down in a (usu. specified) place (*deposited the book on the floor*). **b** (of water, wind, etc.) leave (matter etc.) lying in a displaced position. **2 a** store or entrust for keeping. **b** pay (a sum of money) into a bank account. **3** pay (a sum) as a first instalment or as a pledge for a contract. **4** insert (coins) in a vending machine etc. □ **on deposit** (of money) placed in a bank account. [Latin *depositum* (n.), medieval Latin *depositare* from Latin *deponere deposit-* (as DEPONENT)]

deposit account *noun Brit.* a bank account that pays interest but from which money cannot usu. be withdrawn without notice or loss of interest.

de·posit·ary /diːˈpɒzɪteri/ *noun* (*pl.* **-aries**) a person to whom something is entrusted; a trustee.

depo·si·tion /ˌdepəˈzɪʃən, ˌdiːp-/ *noun* **1** the act or an instance of depositing. **2** *Law* **a** the process of giving sworn evidence; allegation. **b** an instance of this. **c** evidence given under oath; a testimony. **3** the act or an instance of deposing. **4** (**the Deposition**) **a** the taking down of the body of Christ from the Cross. **b** a representation of this. [Latin *depositio -onis* from *deponere*: see DEPOSIT]

de·posit·or *noun* a person who deposits money etc.

de·posi·tory /diːˈpɒzɪˌtɔri/ *noun* (*pl.* **-ies**) **1 a** a place where something is deposited. **b** a storehouse or warehouse etc. **c** a store (of wisdom, knowledge, etc.) (*the book is a depository of wit*). **2** = DEPOSITARY.

depot /'diːpoʊ/ *noun* **1** a storehouse. **2 a** *N Amer.* = BUS DEPOT. **b** esp. *US* a railway station. **c** a building for the servicing, parking, etc. of esp. buses, trains, or trucks. **3** *Military* **a** a storehouse for equipment etc. **b** the headquarters of a regiment. **c** a military establishment at which recruits or other troops are assembled. [French *dépôt* from Latin (as DEPOSIT)]

de·prave *transitive verb* pervert or corrupt, esp. morally. □ **dep·rav·a·tion** *noun* **de·praved** *adjective* [Latin *depravare* (as DE-, *pravare* from *pravus* crooked)]

de·prav·ity /diˈpravɪti/ *noun* (*pl.* **-ities**) **1** moral corruption; wickedness. **2** an instance of this; a wicked act. [DE- + obsolete *pravity* from Latin *pravitas* (as DEPRAVE)]

dep·re·cate /'depriˌkeɪt/ *transitive verb* **1** express disapproval of or a wish against (a plan, proceeding, purpose, etc.); deplore; plead earnestly against (*deprecate hasty action*). **2 a** express disapproval of (a person), reprove. **b** = DEPRECIATE 2. ¶ Although *deprecate* in sense 2b has been traditionally considered incorrect, it is not incorrect in such combinations as *self-deprecating* etc., which are far more common than *self-depreciating* etc. It is rarely used in this sense outside of these combinations, and may be considered incorrect if it is. □ **dep·re·cat·ing·ly** *adverb* **dep·re·ca·tion** *noun* **dep·re·ca·tory** /-ˈkeɪtəri/ *adjective* [Latin *deprecari* (as DE-, *precari* pray)]

de·pre·cia·ble /dɪˈpriːʃəbl/ *adjective N Amer.* **1** capable of depreciating. **2** (of property, an asset, etc.) able to be depreciated for tax purposes.

de·preci·ate /dɪˈpriːʃiˌeɪt/ *verb* **1** *transitive & intransitive* diminish in value (*the car has depreciated*). **2** *transitive* disparage; belittle. ¶ See Usage Note at DEPRECATE. **3** *transitive* reduce the purchasing power of (money). □ **de·preci·a·tory** /dɪˈpriːʃiˌətɔri/ *adjective* [Late Latin *depretiare* (as DE-, *pretiare* from *pretium* price)]

de·preci·a·tion /dɪˌpriːʃiˈeɪʃən, -siˈeɪʃən/ *noun* **1** the amount of wear and tear (of a property etc.) for which a reduction may be made in a valuation, an estimate, or a balance sheet. **2** *Econ.* a decrease in the value of a currency. **3** the act or an instance of depreciating; belittlement.

dep·re·da·tion /ˌdeprəˈdeɪʃən/ *noun* (usu. in *pl.*) **1** the act of despoiling, ravaging, or plundering. **2** an instance or instances of this. [French *déprédation* from Late Latin *depraedatio* (as DE-, *praedatio -onis* from Latin *praedari* plunder)]

de·press *transitive verb* **1** push or pull down; lower (*depressed the lever*). **2** make dispirited or dejected. **3** *Econ.* reduce the activity of (esp. trade). □ **de·press·ible** *adjective* **de·press·ing** *adjective* **de·press·ing·ly** *adverb* [Old French *depresser* from Late Latin *depressare* (as DE-, *pressare* frequentative of *premere* press)]

de·pres·sant ● *adjective* **1** that depresses. **2** *Med.* sedative. ● *noun* **1** *Med.* an agent, esp. a drug, that sedates. **2** an influence that depresses.

de·pressed *adjective* **1** dispirited or miserable. **2** *Psych.* suffering from depression. **3** suffering from economic hardship (*a depressed area of the city*). **4** pressed down; having a flattened or hollowed surface. **5** (of the price of a commodity etc.) persistently lower than normal.

de·pres·sion *noun* **1 a** *Psych.* a state of extreme dejection or morbidly excessive melancholy; a mood of hopelessness and feelings of inadequacy, often with physical symptoms such as loss of appetite,

u: m**oo**d   ai m**y**   əi p**i**pe   au br**ow**n   ʌu h**ou**se   ei d**a**y   ɔi b**oy**   ɑ̃ fr**an**glais   ã Canadi**en**   ɔ̃ Bray**on**   (*see over for consonants*)

insomnia, etc. **b** a reduction in vitality, vigour, or spirits. **2 a** a long period of financial and industrial decline; a slump. **b** (**the Depression**, **the Great Depression**) the depression which began in 1929 and lasted throughout most of the 1930s. **3** *Meteorol.* a lowering of atmospheric pressure, esp. the centre of a region of minimum pressure or the system of winds around it. **4** a sunken place or hollow on a surface. **5 a** a lowering or sinking (often foll. by *of*: *depression of freezing point*). **b** the act or an instance of pressing down. **6** *Astronomy & Geog.* the angular distance of an object below the horizon or a horizontal plane.

Depression glass *noun N Amer. & Austral.* a type of usu. coloured pressed glass produced esp. during the 1930s.

de·pres·sive ● *adjective* **1** tending to depress. **2** *Psych.* involving or characterized by depression. ● *noun Psych.* a person suffering or with a tendency to suffer from depression.

de·pres·sor *noun* **1** *Anat.* **a** (in full **depressor muscle**) a muscle that causes the lowering of some part of the body. **b** a nerve that lowers blood pressure. **2** *Med.* an instrument for pressing down an organ etc. (*tongue depressor*).

de·pres·sur·ize *verb* (also esp. *Brit.* **-ise**) **1** *transitive* cause an appreciable drop in the pressure of the gas inside (a container), esp. to the ambient level. **2** *intransitive* lose air pressure (*the airplane cabin will depressurize*). □ **de·pres·sur·iz·a·tion** *noun*

dep·riv·a·tion /ˌdeprəˈveɪʃən/ *noun* (usu. foll. by *of*) **1** the act or an instance of depriving (*deprivation of liberty*; *suffered many deprivations*). **2** the state of being deprived.

de·prive /diˈpraɪv, də-/ *transitive verb* (usu. foll. by *of*) deny (a person or place) the possession or use of something (*illness deprived her of success*). [Old French *depriver* from medieval Latin *deprivare* (as DE-, Latin *privare* deprive)]

de·prived *adjective* **1** (of a child etc.) suffering from the effects of a poor or loveless home. **2** (of an area) having inadequate housing, facilities, employment, etc. **3** suffering from a deprivation.

de pro·fun·dis /ˌdeɪ prəˈfʊndɪs/ ● *adverb* from the depths (of sorrow etc.). ● *noun* a cry from the depths. [opening Latin words of Ps. 130]

de·pro·gram *transitive verb* (**de·pro·grammed**, **de·pro·gram·ming**) free (a person) from the influence of an experience, cult, etc., by intensive therapy.

Dept. *abbreviation* Department.

depth *noun* **1 a** deepness (*the depth is not great at the edge*). **b** the measurement from the top down, from the surface inwards, or from the front to the back (*the depth of the drawer is 12 inches*). **2** difficulty; abstruseness. **3 a** sagacity; wisdom. **b** intensity of emotion etc. (*the poem has little depth*). **4** an intensity of colour, darkness, etc. **5** the strength of a team, company, etc., not only in its upper ranks but throughout the organization. **6** (in *pl.*) **a** deep water, a deep place; an abyss. **b** a low, depressed state. **c** the lowest or inmost part (*the depths of the country*). **7** the middle (*in the depth of winter*). □ **in depth** comprehensively, thoroughly, or profoundly. **out of one's depth 1** in water over one's head. **2** engaged in a task or on a subject too difficult for one. [Middle English (as DEEP, -TH²)]

depth charge *noun* an explosive device that detonates under water, esp. for dropping on a submerged submarine etc.

depth finder *noun* an instrument used for measuring the depth of water by radar, ultrasound, etc.

depth·less *adjective* **1** extremely deep; fathomless. **2** shallow, superficial.

depth perception *noun* the ability to discern spatial relationships, dimensions, etc.

depth psychology *noun* psychology seeking to explain behaviour in terms of the unconscious. □ **depth psychologist** *noun*

depth sounder *noun* an instrument used for measuring the depth of water under a ship by ultrasound.

dep·ur·ate /ˈdepjuˌreit/ *transitive & intransitive verb* make or become free from impurities. □ **dep·ur·a·tion** *noun* **dep·ur·ative** /diˈpjʊrətɪv/ *adjective & noun* [medieval Latin *depurare* (as DE-, *purus* pure)]

depu·ta·tion /ˌdepjuːˈteɪʃən/ *noun* a group of people appointed to represent others, usu. for a specific purpose; a delegation.

de·pute ● *transitive verb* /diˈpjuːt/ (often foll. by *to*) **1** appoint as a deputy. **2** delegate (a task, authority, etc.) (*deputed the leadership to her*). ● *noun* /ˈdepjuːt/ *Scot.* a deputy. [Old French *député* past participle of *deputer* from Latin *deputare* regard as, allot (as DE-, *putare* think)]

depu·tize *verb* (also esp. *Brit.* **-tise**) **1** *transitive* esp. *N Amer.* appoint (a person) as a deputy. **2** *intransitive* (usu. foll. by *for*) act as a deputy or understudy. □ **depu·tiz·a·tion** *noun*

dep·uty *noun* (*pl.* **-uties**) **1** a person appointed or delegated to act for another or others (also *attributive*: *deputy manager*). **2** a parliamentary representative in certain countries, e.g. France. □ **deputy·ship** *noun* [Middle English var. of DEPUTE *noun*]

deputy chief *noun* **1** (in police municipal forces) an officer ranking above staff superintendent and below chief of police. **2** (in the Royal Newfoundland Constabulary) an officer ranking above superintendent and below chief.

deputy commissioner *noun* **1** (in the Ontario Provincial Police) an officer ranking above chief superintendent and detective chief superintendent, but below commissioner. **2** (in the RCMP) an officer ranking above assistant commissioner and below commissioner.

deputy director *noun* (in Quebec) a municipal police officer ranking above inspector and below director.

deputy minister *noun Cdn* the senior civil servant in a government department or ministry. Abbr.: **DM**.

deputy returning officer *noun* an official in charge of a polling station. Abbr.: **DRO**.

De Quin·cey /də ˈkwɪnsi/ **Thom·as** (1785–1859), English essayist and critic. A lifelong opium addict, he achieved fame with his *Confessions of an English Opium Eater* (1821), a study of his addiction and its psychological effects.

de·racin·ate /diːˈrasɪˌneɪt/ *transitive verb literary* **1** tear up by the roots. **2** obliterate. □ **de·racin·a·tion** *noun* [French *déraciner* (as DE-, *racine* from Late Latin *radicina* diminutive of *radix* root)]

de·rail *verb* **1** *transitive* cause (a train etc.) to leave the rails. **2** *intransitive* (of a train) leave the rails. **3** *transitive* obstruct the progress of (a person, plan, etc.). □ **de·rail·ment** *noun*

de·rail·leur /diːˈreɪlər/ *noun* a bicycle gear-shifting mechanism which switches the line of the chain while pedalling so that it jumps to a different sprocket. [French *dérailleur* (as DE- RAIL¹)]

de·range /diˈreɪndʒ/ *transitive verb* **1** throw into confusion; disorganize; cause to act irregularly. **2** (esp. as **de·ranged** *adjective*) make insane (*deranged by the tragic events*). □ **de·range·ment** *noun* [French *déranger* (as DE-, *rang* RANK¹)]

de·ration /diːˈraʃən/ *transitive verb* free (food etc.) from rationing.

Derby¹ /ˈdɑrbi/ a city on the Derwent River in the Midlands of England, formerly part of Derbyshire; pop. (2001) 221,716.

Derby² /ˈdɑrbi/ **14th Earl of** (title of Edward George Geoffrey Smith Stanley) (1799–1869), English Conservative politician, prime minister 1852, 1858–9, and 1866–8. He led the protectionists in the House of Lords in their opposition to Peel's attempted repeal of the Corn Laws in 1846.

Derby³ /ˈdɑrbi/ *noun* (*pl.* **Derbies**) **1 a** /ˈdɑrbi/ an annual horse race run at Epsom Downs, near London, England. **b** any of several other important annual horse races (*Kentucky Derby*). **2** (**derby**) a sporting contest or race open to all who wish to participate. **3** (**derby**) *N Amer.* a man's hard felt hat with a round dome-shaped crown. [the 12th Earl of *Derby* d.1834, founder of the horse race]

Derby·shire /ˈdɑrbiˌʃɪr/ a county of north central England; county town, Matlock.

de·regis·ter *transitive verb* remove from a register, esp. from a list of government-regulated items (*deregistered their RRSP*).

de·regu·late *transitive verb* remove regulations or restrictions from. □ **de·regu·la·tion** *noun* **de·regu·la·tor** *noun* **de·regu·la·tory** *adjective*

dere·lict /ˈderəlɪkt/ ● *adjective* **1** (esp. of property) ruined; dilapidated. **2** *N Amer.* negligent (of duty etc.). **3** abandoned, ownerless (esp. of a ship at sea or an empty decrepit property). ● *noun* **1** a social outcast; a person without a home, a job, or property. **2** abandoned property, esp. a ship. [Latin *derelictus* past participle of *derelinquere* (as DE-, *relinquere* leave)]

dere·lic·tion /ˌderɪˈlɪkʃən/ *noun* **1** (usu. foll. by *of*) **a** neglect; failure to carry out one's obligations (*dereliction of duty*). **b** an instance of this. **2** the act or an instance of abandoning; the process of being abandoned.

de·ride /dəˈraɪd/ *transitive verb* be scornful of; mock. □ **de·rid·ing·ly** *adverb* [Latin *deridēre* (as DE-, *ridēre ris-* laugh)]

de ri·gueur /də rɪˈɡɜr/ *predicative adjective* required by custom or etiquette (*evening dress is de rigueur*). [French, = 'of strictness']

de·rision /dəˈrɪʒən/ *noun* ridicule; mockery. □ **hold** (or **have**) **in derision** *archaic* mock at. □ **de·ris·ible** /dɪˈrɪzɪbəl/ *adjective* [Old French from Late Latin *derisio -onis* (as DERIDE)]

de·ri·sive /dəˈraɪsɪv/ *adjective* = DERISORY. □ **de·ri·sive·ly** *adverb* **de·ri·sive·ness** *noun*

de·ri·sory /dəˈraɪsəri/ *adjective* **1** scoffing; ironical; scornful (*derisory cheers*). **2** so small or unimportant as to be ridiculous (*derisory offer*; *derisory costs*). [Late Latin *derisorius* (as DERISION)]

der·iv·a·tion *noun* **1** the act or an instance of deriving or obtaining from a source; the process of being derived. **2 a** the formation of a word from another word or from a root. **b** a derivative. **c** the tracing of the origin of a word. **d** a statement or account of this. **3** extraction, descent. **4** *Math.* a sequence of statements showing that a formula, theorem, etc., is a consequence of previously accepted statements. □ **der·iv·a·tion·al** *adjective*

de·riv·a·tive ● *adjective* derived from another source; not original (*their music is derivative and uninteresting*). ● *noun* **1** something derived from another source, esp.: **a** a word derived from another or from a root (e.g. *quickly* from *quick*). **b** *Chem.* a chemical compound that is derived from another. **2** *Math.* a quantity measuring the rate of change of another. **3** *Finance* an arrangement or instrument (such as a future, option, or warrant) whose value derives from and is dependent upon the value of an underlying variable asset, such as a commodity, currency, or security. □ **de·riv·a·tive·ly** *adverb*

de·rive *verb* **1** *transitive* (usu. foll. by *from*) get, obtain, or form (*derived satisfaction from work*). **2** *intransitive* (foll. by *from*) arise from, originate in, be descended or obtained from (*happiness derives from many things*). **3** *transitive* gather or deduce (*derived the information from the clues*). **4** *transitive* **a** trace the descent of (a person). **b** show the origin of (a thing). **5** *transitive* (usu. foll. by *from*) show or state the origin or formation of (a word etc.) (*derived the word from Latin*). **6** *transitive Math.* obtain (a function) by differentiation. □ **de·riv·able** *adjective* [Latin *derivare* (as DE-, *rivus* stream)]

derm·a·bra·sion /ˌdɜrməˈbreɪʒən/ *noun* the surgical removal of superficial layers of skin with a rapidly revolving abrasive tool. [Greek *derma* skin + ABRASION]

derma·titis /ˌdɜrməˈtaɪtɪs/ *noun* inflammation of the skin. [Greek *derma -atos* skin + -ITIS]

derma·to·glyph·ics /ˌdɜrmətoʊˈɡlɪfɪks/ *noun* the science or study of skin markings or patterns, esp. of the fingers, hands, and feet. □ **derma·to·glyph·ic** *adjective* [as DERMATITIS + Greek *gluphē* carving: see GLYPH]

derma·tol·ogy /ˌdɜrməˈtɒlədʒi/ *noun* the study of the diagnosis and treatment of skin disorders. □ **derma·to·logic** *adjective* **derma·to·logic·al** *adjective* **derma·to·logic·al·ly** *adverb* **derma·tol·o·gist** *noun* [as DERMATITIS + -LOGY]

der·mis /ˈdɜrmɪs/ *noun* **1** (in general use) the skin. **2** *Anat.* the thick layer of living tissue below the epidermis. □ **der·mal** *adjective* **der·mic** *adjective* [modern Latin, after EPIDERMIS]

der·nier cri /ˌdɜrnjeɪ ˈkriː/ *noun* the very latest fashion. [French, = last cry]

dero·gate /ˈderəˌɡeɪt/ *intransitive verb* (foll. by *from*) *formal* **1** take away a part from; detract from (a merit, a right, etc.). **2** deviate from (correct behaviour etc.). □ **de·rog·a·tive** /dɪˈrɒɡətɪv/ *adjective* [Latin *derogare* (as DE-, *rogare* ask)]

dero·ga·tion /ˌderəˈɡeɪʃən/ *noun* **1** (foll. by *of*) a lessening or impairment of (a law, authority, position, dignity, etc.). **2** deterioration; debasement.

de·rog·a·tory /dəˈrɒɡətəri/ *adjective* (often foll. by *to*) involving disparagement or discredit; insulting, depreciatory (*made a derogatory remark*; *derogatory to my position*). □ **de·rog·a·tor·i·ly** *adverb*

der·rick /ˈderɪk/ *noun* **1** a kind of crane for moving or lifting heavy weights, having a movable pivoted arm. **2** the framework over an oil well or similar excavation, holding the drilling machinery. [obsolete senses *hangman, gallows*, from the name of a London hangman *c.*1600]

Der·ri·da /ˈderɪdə/ **Jacques** (b.1930), French philosopher and critic. His radical critique of Western philosophy and literary analysis led to the emergence of the school of deconstruction in the late 1960s; his works include *Of Grammatology* (1967) and *Writing and Difference* (1967). □ **Der·rid·ean** /ˈderɪdiən/ *adjective* & *noun*

der·rière /ˌderiˈer/ *noun informal* the buttocks. [French, = behind]

derring-do /ˌderɪŋˈduː/ *noun literary jocular* heroic courage or action. [Middle English, = *daring to do*, misinterpreted by Spenser and by Scott]

der·rin·ger /ˈderɪndʒər/ *noun* a small large-bore pistol. [H. *Deringer*, US inventor d.1868]

der·ris /ˈderɪs/ *noun* **1** any woody tropical climbing leguminous plant of the genus *Derris*, bearing leathery pods. **2** an insecticide made from the powdered root of some kinds of derris. [modern Latin from Greek, = leather covering (with reference to its pod)]

Derry see LONDONDERRY.

der·vish *noun* a Muslim (specifically Sufi) religious man who has taken vows of poverty and austerity (*compare* WHIRLING DERVISH). [Turkish *derviş* from Persian *darvēsh* poor, a mendicant monk]

DES *abbreviation* **1** DIETHYLSTILBESTROL. **2** *Computing* Data Encryption Standard.

de Sade see SADE.

de·salin·ate *transitive verb* remove salt from (esp. sea water). □ **de·salin·a·tion** *noun* **de·salin·ator** *noun*

de·salin·ize *transitive verb US* = DESALINATE. □ **de·salin·iz·a·tion** *noun*

de·salt *transitive verb* = DESALINATE.

des·apare·cido /ˌdesaˌpereˈsiːdoʊ/ *noun* (*pl.* **-cidos**) (usu. in *pl.*) a person, esp. a perceived political activist, abducted by government or other forces in Central or S America, esp. in Argentina. [Spanish, lit. 'disappeared', past participle of *desaparacer* disappear]

Des·Barres /deɪˈbɑr/ **Jo·seph Fred·erick Wallet** (1722–1824), Swiss-born English military engineer and surveyor, Lieutenant-Governor of Cape Breton 1784–7 and governor of PEI 1804–12. Between 1763 and 1773 he surveyed the St. Lawrence River and the eastern coast of N America from Nova Scotia to the Gulf of Mexico for the British Admiralty.

de·scale *transitive verb* remove the scale from (teeth etc.).

des·cant ● *noun* /ˈdeskant/ **1** *Music* an independent soprano melody usu. sung or played above a basic melody, esp. of a hymn tune. **2** *literary* a melody; a song. ● *intransitive verb* /dəsˈkant/ **1** (foll. by *on, upon*) make remarks or observations; comment or talk at length. **2** *Music* sing or play a descant. [Old French *deschant* from medieval Latin *discantus* (as DIS-, *cantus* song, CHANT)]

Des·cartes /ˈdeɪkɑrt/ **René** (1596–1650), French philosopher, mathematician, and scientist. In philosophy, he held that the only things any individual can be certain of are that he thinks, and that therefore he exists; on this he based his theory that the world is composed of mind and matter. In mathematics he developed a system of coordinates for which he is regarded as the founder of analytic geometry.

des·cend *verb* **1** *transitive & intransitive* go or come down (a hill, stairs, etc.). **2** *intransitive* (of a thing) pass from a higher to lower position in space; fall (*rain descended heavily*). **3** *intransitive* slope downwards, lie along a descending slope (*fields descended to the beach*). **4** *intransitive* (usu. foll. by *on*) **a** make a sudden attack. **b** *informal* make an unexpected and usu. unwelcome visit (*I hope they don't descend on us this weekend*). **5** *transitive & intransitive* (usu. foll. by *from, to*) **a** (often in *passive*) originate with or derive from (a progenitor or predecessor) (*are birds descended from the dinosaurs?*). **b** (of property, qualities, rights, etc.) be passed by inheritance. **6** *intransitive* (foll. by *to*) come down mentally or morally; stoop to something unworthy (*descend to violence*). **7** *intransitive Music* (of sound) become lower in pitch; go down (the scale). **8** *intransitive* (usu. foll. by *to*) proceed (in discourse or writing) to what follows, esp. from the general (to the particular). **9** *transitive* move downstream along (a river etc.) to the sea etc. **10** *intransitive* (of the sun etc.) move away from the zenith, esp. down toward the horizon. [Latin *descendere* (as DE-, *scandere* climb)]

des·cend·ant *noun* (often foll. by *of*) **1** a person or animal descended from another (*a descendant of Scottish immigrants*). **2** something deriving from or following after the form, function, or style of another, earlier instance, model, etc. (*the cello is the modern descendant of the viola da gamba*).

des·cend·er *noun* *Typography* a part of a letter that extends below the line.

descending colon *noun* the part of the large intestine that passes downward on the left side of the abdomen toward the rectum.

des·cent *noun* **1 a** the act of descending. **b** an instance of this. **c** a downward movement, esp. of an airplane. **2 a** a way or path etc. by which one may descend. **b** a downward slope. **3 a** lineage, family origin (*traces his descent from William Lyon Mackenzie*). **b** the transmission of qualities, property, privileges, etc. by inheritance. **4** a fall or decline to a lower state or condition. **5** a sudden violent attack. [Old French *descente* from *descendre* DESCEND]

Des·champs /deɪˈʃɑ̃/ **Yvon** (b.1935), Canadian actor and comedian, best known as a comic satirist for his popular monologues.

de·scram·ble *transitive verb* convert or restore (an electronic signal) to intelligible form, esp. through an electronic device. □ **de·scram·bler** *noun*

de·scribe *transitive verb* **1 a** portray in words; give a detailed or graphic account of (*described the landscape*). **b** (foll. by *as*) assert to be; call (*described him as an agitator*). **2 a** mark out or draw (esp. a geometrical figure) (*described a triangle*). **b** move in (a specified way, esp. a curve) (*described a parabola through the air*). □ **de·scrib·able** *adjective* **de·scrib·er** *noun* [Latin *describere* (as DE-, *scribere* *script-* write)]

de·scrip·tion *noun* **1 a** the act or an instance of describing; the process of being described. **b** a spoken or written representation (of a person, object, or event). **2** a sort, kind, or class (*no food of any description*). □ **answers** (or **fits**) **the description** has the qualities specified. [Latin *descriptio -onis* (as DESCRIBE)]

de·scrip·tive *adjective* **1** serving or seeking to describe (*long descriptive paragraphs*). **2** describing or classifying without expressing feelings or judging (*a purely descriptive account*). **3** *Linguistics* describing a language without comparing, endorsing, or condemning particular usage, vocabulary, etc. **4** *Grammar* (of an adjective) describing a quality of the noun, rather than its relation, position, etc., e.g. *blue* as distinct from *few*. □ **de·scrip·tive·ly** *adverb* **de·scrip·tive·ness** *noun* **de·scrip·tiv·ism** *noun* **de·scrip·tiv·ist** *noun & adjective* (both in sense 3). [Late Latin *descriptivus* (as DESCRIBE)]

de·scrip·tor *noun* **1** a word or expression etc. used to describe or identify. **2** *Computing* a data item, or stored information, that describes how other information is stored, e.g. in an array, record, or file. [Latin, = describer (as DESCRIBE)]

des·cry /dəˈskraɪ/ *transitive verb* (**-cries, -cried**) *literary* catch sight of; discern or detect (*descried her in the crowd*; *descries no glimmer of light in his situation*). [Middle English (earlier senses 'proclaim, DECRY') from Old French *descrier*: prob. confused with var. of obsolete *descrive* from Old French *descrivre* DESCRIBE]

dese·crate /ˈdesəˌkreɪt/ *transitive verb* **1** violate (a venerated place or thing) with violence, profanity, etc. **2** deprive (a church, a sacred object, etc.) of sanctity; deconsecrate. □ **dese·cra·tion** *noun* **dese·cra·tor** *noun* [DE- + CONSECRATE]

de·seed *transitive verb Brit.* remove the seeds from (a plant, vegetable, etc.). □ **de·seed·er** *noun*

de·seg·re·gate *transitive verb* abolish racial segregation in (schools etc.) or of (people etc.). □ **de·seg·re·ga·tion** *noun*

de·select *transitive verb Politics* decline to select or retain as a constituency candidate in an election. □ **de·selec·tion** *noun*

de·sensi·tize *transitive verb* (also esp. *Brit.* **-tise**) **1** reduce or destroy the sensitiveness of (photographic materials, an allergic person, etc.). **2** reduce or eliminate emotional responses to, esp. through repeated exposure (*have we become desensitized to violence?*). □ **de·sensi·tiz·a·tion** *noun* **de·sensi·tiz·er** *noun*

de·sert¹ *verb* **1** *transitive* abandon, give up, leave without intention of returning (*deserted the sinking ship*). **2** *transitive* forsake or abandon (a cause, person, etc., esp. one having a claim on a person) (*deserted his wife and children*). **3** *transitive* (of a power or faculty) fail (someone) (*his presence of mind deserted him*). **4** *transitive & intransitive Military* run away from or forsake (one's duty etc.) (*deserted his post*; *deserted to the enemy*). □ **de·sert·er** *noun* (in sense 4). **de·ser·tion** *noun* [French *déserter* from Late Latin *desertare* from Latin *desertus* (as DESERT²)]

des·ert² ● *noun* **1** a dry, barren area of land, often sand-covered, characteristically desolate, with little fresh water and scanty vegetation (also *attributive*: *desert camouflage*; *desert birds*). **2** an uninteresting or intellectually barren place, subject, etc. (*a cultural desert*). ● *adjective* uninhabited, desolate (*desert island*). [Old French from Latin *desertus*, ecclesiastical Latin *desertum* (n.), past participle of *deserere* leave, forsake]

de·sert³ *noun* **1** (usu. in *pl.*) **a** acts or qualities deserving reward or punishment. **b** just reward or punishment (*has got his just deserts*). **2** *archaic* the fact of being worthy of reward or punishment; merit. [Old French from *deservir* DESERVE]

desert boot *noun* a soft-soled, ankle-high suede boot with laces.

desert candle *noun* = FOXTAIL LILY.

de·sert·ed *adjective* empty, abandoned (*a deserted house*).

desert·ifi·ca·tion /dəˌzɜːtɪfɪˈkeɪʃən/ *noun* the transformation of fertile land into a desert or arid waste, esp. as a result of human activity.

desert island *noun* a remote (usu. tropical) island presumed to be uninhabited.

desert rat *noun* **1** *N Amer.* (esp. *West*) a person who lives and works in the desert, e.g. a prospector. **2** *Brit. informal* a soldier of the 7th British armoured division (with the jerboa as a badge) in the N African desert campaign of 1941–2.

Desert Shield *noun* the code name for the US-led military deployment to the Middle East after Iraq attacked Kuwait on 2 August 1990.

Desert Storm *noun* the code name for the multinational military campaign against Iraq, beginning in January 1991, after Iraq had failed to meet the demands of a UN resolution that it withdraw from Kuwait.

de·serve *transitive verb* (often foll. by *to* + infin.) be entitled to or worthy of (a reward, punishment, etc.) (*deserves to be imprisoned*; *deserves a prize*). □ **de·served** *adjective* **de·serv·ed·ly** *adverb* [Latin *deservire* (as DE-, *servire* serve)]

de·serv·ing *adjective* meritorious, worthy. □ **deserving of** showing conduct or qualities worthy of (praise, blame, help, etc.). □ **de·serv·ing·ly** *adverb* **de·serv·ing·ness** *noun*

desex *transitive verb* **1** castrate or spay (an animal). **2** remove, diminish, or minimize the sexual interest, attractions, etc. of (a person). **3** remove qualities, expectations, etc. perceived as distinctively gendered from (a course, job, etc.).

de·sex·ual·ize *transitive verb* (also esp. *Brit.* **-ise**) deprive of sexuality or sexual qualities.

Des Gro·seil·liers /deɪ ɡroˈzeɪjeɪ/ **Mé·dard Chouart** (1618–c.1696), French explorer and fur trader. He journeyed to the fur-trading regions of Lake Michigan (1654–6) and Lake Superior (1659–60) with his brother-in-law Radisson; in 1668 they voyaged to Hudson Bay on behalf of a group of English merchants (the nucleus of the Hudson's Bay Company), and made a number of fur-trading expeditions there until 1675.

des·ha·bille /ˌdezaˈbiːl/ *noun* (also **dis·ha·bille** /ˌdɪsaˈbiːl/) a state of being only partly or carelessly clothed. [French, = undressed]

De Sica /də ˈsiːkə/ **Vit·torio** (1901–74), Italian film director and actor. A key figure in Italian neo-realist cinema, his most celebrated films include *Shoeshine* (1946) and the Oscar-winning *The Bicycle Thief* (1948).

desic·cant /ˈdesɪkənt/ *noun* a drying or desiccating agent.

desic·cate /ˈdesɪˌkeɪt/ *transitive verb* **1** remove the moisture from, dry (esp. food for preservation). **2** deprive (land, plants, etc.) thoroughly of moisture. □ **desic·ca·tion** *noun* [Latin *desiccare* (as DE-, *siccus* dry)]

desic·cat·ed *adjective* **1 a** deprived or freed of moisture. **b** (of food) dried for preservation. **2** (of a person, text, etc.) deprived of energy or feeling.

desic·ca·tor *noun* **1** an apparatus for desiccating fruit, milk, tanbark, etc. **2** a chemical apparatus used to dry substances which are decomposed by heat or exposure to air.

de·sid·era·tive /dəˈzɪdərətɪv, -ˈsɪdərətɪv/ ● *adjective* **1** *Grammar* (of a verb, conjugation, etc.) formed from another verb etc. and denoting a desire to perform the action of that verb etc. **2** having, expressing, or pertaining to desire. ● *noun Grammar* a desiderative verb, conjugation, etc. [Late Latin *desiderativus* (as DESIDERATUM)]

de·sid·er·atum /dəˌzɪdəˈrɑːtəm, dəˌsɪd-/ *noun* (*pl.* **de·sid·er·ata** /-tə/) something lacking but needed and desired. [Latin neuter past participle of *desiderare* (as DE-, *siderare* as in CONSIDER)]

de·sign ● *noun* **1** a preliminary plan or sketch for the making or production of a building, machine, garment, etc. **2 a** the art of planning and creating something in accordance with appropriate functional and aesthetic criteria. **b** the selection and arrangement of artistic or functional elements making up a work of art, machine, etc. **c** INTERIOR DESIGN. **3 a** the general arrangement or layout of a product. **b** an example or a completed version of a sketch, concept, or pattern. **c** an established version of a product (*one of our most popular designs*). **4** a motif or pattern of lines, shapes, etc. **5 a** a plan, purpose, or intention. **b** a plot, scheme, or intrigue. ● *verb* **1** *transitive* **a** make drawings and plans for the construction or production of (a building, machine, garment, etc.). **b** plan and execute (a structure, work of art, etc.), skilfully or artistically. **2** *transitive* **a** intend (something) for a specific purpose (*the remark was designed to offend*; *a course designed for beginners*). **b** form a plan or scheme of; contrive (*designed an attack*). **3** *intransitive* be a designer of works of art, buildings, garments, etc. □ **by design** on purpose. **have designs on 1** have one's sights set on. **2** hope to establish a romantic or sexual relationship with. **3** plan to attack or appropriate. [ultimately from Latin *designare* DESIGNATE]

desig·nate ● *transitive verb* **1** (often foll. by *as*) appoint to an office or function (*designated her own successor*). **2** mark or point out clearly (*designate the boundaries of something*). **3** (often foll. by *as*) give a name or title to (*this year is designated as International Women's Year*; *she was designated Athlete of the Year*). **4** serve as the name or distinctive mark of (*English uses French words to designate ballet steps*). ● *adjective* (placed after noun) appointed to a position but not yet officially occupying it (*bishop designate*). □ **desig·nat·ed** *adjective* **desig·na·tor** *noun* [Latin *designare*, past participle *designatus* (as DE-, *signare* from *signum* mark)]

designated driver *noun N Amer.* a person who abstains from alcohol at a social gathering so as to be fit to drive others home.

designated hitter *noun Baseball* a non-fielding player named before the start of a game to bat for the pitcher anywhere in the batting order. Abbr.: **DH**.

designated import *noun Cdn Football* (formerly) an import player who may enter the game at a position, when the total allowable number of import players is already in the game. Abbr.: **DI**.

desig·na·tion *noun* **1** a name, description, or title. **2** the act or process of designating. **3** the appointment or nomination of (a person, city, etc.) to (a particular office, status, etc.).

de·signed *adjective* **1** planned, purposed, intended. **2** outlined, formed, or framed according to some design.

de·sign·ed·ly *adverb* intentionally, on purpose; by design.

de·sign·er *noun* **1 a** a person who makes artistic designs or plans for construction, e.g. for clothing, machines, theatre sets, etc. **b** an interior designer. **2** (*attributive*) **a** (of clothing etc.) bearing the name or label of a famous designer and so considered prestigious (*designer jeans*). **b** (of ideas, objects, etc.) being or seeming fashionable or trendy (*designer water; designer beers*). **c** (of chemicals etc.) designed for a specific purpose or function (*designer herbicides*).

designer baby *noun* a baby, conceived by in vitro fertilization, selected for certain traits, e.g. gender, hair colour, etc.

designer drug *noun* **1** a drug synthesized to mimic a legally restricted or prohibited drug without being subject to such restriction. **2** a specially formulated drug designed to be highly effective against a precisely targeted disease, chemical process, etc.

de·sign·ing *adjective* crafty, artful, or scheming.

de·sir·able *adjective* **1 a** worth having or doing; choice, excellent (*desirable accommodations*). **b** worthwhile, advisable (*a desirable law*). **2** arousing sexual desire; very attractive. □ **de·sir·abil·ity** *noun* **de·sir·ably** *adverb*

de·sire ● *noun* **1 a** an unsatisfied longing or craving. **b** an expression of this or a request (*expressed a desire to rest*). **2** sexual appetite. **3** something desired (*achieved his heart's desire*). ● *transitive verb* **1 a** (often foll. by *to* + infin., or *that* + clause) long for, crave. **b** feel sexual desire for. **2** request (*desires a cup of tea*). **3** *archaic* pray, entreat, or command (*desire him to wait*). [Old French *desir* from *desirer* from Latin *desiderare*, perhaps from *de-* down + *sidus sider-* star]

de·sir·ous */dəˈzaɪrəs/ predicative adjective* (usu. foll. by *of*) having desire, wishful, wanting (*desirous of doing well*). [Anglo-French *desirous* from Romanic (as DESIRE)]

de·sist *intransitive verb* (often foll. by *from*) stop, cease, or abstain (*please desist from interrupting; when requested, he desisted*). [Old French *desister* from Latin *desistere* (as DE-, *sistere* stop, reduplication from *stare* stand)]

Des·jar·dins */deiʒarˈdã/ **Al·phonse** (1854–1920), Canadian journalist, founder of the caisse populaire movement.

desk *noun* **1** a piece of furniture with a flat or sloped writing surface, often having drawers or compartments for paper, writing materials, etc. **2** a service counter in a library, hotel, etc. at which a specific function is performed (*reference desk; information desk*). **3** a section of an office, e.g. of a newspaper, that handles a particular matter, topic, etc. (*the sports desk; the city desk*). **4** *Music* a music stand, esp. as shared by two players in an orchestra. **b** (in an orchestra) a seating position assigned according to rank (*a second desk violin*). **5** *Brit.* (in a place of worship) a sloping board or rest on which the books used in the service are laid. **6** (*attributive*) **a** designating an item designed for use at a desk (*a desk dictionary*). **b** designating something done or someone working at a desk (*a desk job; a desk cop*). [medieval Latin *desca* from Latin DISCUS disc]

desk-bound *adjective* **1 a** performing sedentary work, usu. exclusively at a desk. **b** obliged to remain working at a desk. **2** better acquainted with theoretical than practical matters (*desk-bound executives*).

desk clerk *noun N Amer.* the person on duty at the reception desk of a hotel.

desk copy *noun* a free copy of a book, esp. one supplied for the personal use of a teacher.

de·skill *transitive verb* **1 a** (of new technology) render (a skilled worker) unskilled. **b** reduce the number of skilled workers in (an industry). **2** remove the need for skill, initiative, or judgment from (a job, production, etc.).

desk jockey *noun N Amer. informal* usu. *derogatory* a person who works at a desk.

desk·top *noun* **1** the working surface of a desk. **2** (*attributive*) of a size and nature suitable for use on a desk, esp. designating or pertaining to a microcomputer. **3** a desktop computer.

desktop publishing *noun* the design and production of high-quality printed matter using a desktop computer and a laser printer. Abbr.: **DTP**.

des·man */ˈdesmən/ noun* (*pl.* **des·mans**) any aquatic flesh-eating shrew-like mammal of two species, one originating in Russia (*Desmana moschata*) and one in the Pyrenees (*Galemys pyrenaicus*). [French & German from Swedish *desman-råtta* muskrat]

des·mid */ˈdesmɪd/ noun* a microscopic unicellular freshwater alga of the family Desmidiaceae. [modern Latin genus name *Desmidium*, from Greek *desmos* 'band, chain']

Des Moines */dəˈmɔɪn/* the capital and largest city of Iowa; pop. (2000) 198,682.

Des·mou·lins */deimuːˈlã/* **(Lucie Sim·plice) Ca·mille (Be·noît)** (1760–94), French journalist, pamphleteer, and revolutionary, who supported Danton and wrote against the Reign of Terror during the French Revolution; he was arrested and executed.

deso·late ● *adjective* */ˈdesələt/* **1** (of a person) forlorn, wretched, and usu. solitary (*was left desolate and weeping*). **2 a** (of a building or place) uninhabited, ruined, neglected, barren, empty (*desolate Arctic wastes*). **b** dreary, dismal, depressing (*desolate prospects*). ● *transitive verb* */ˈdesəˌleit/* depopulate or devastate, lay waste to. □ **deso·late·ly** *adverb* **deso·late·ness** *noun* [Latin *desolatus* past participle of *desolare* (as DE-, *solare* from *solus* alone)]

deso·lat·ed *adjective* **1** made wretched or forlorn (*desolated by grief; inconsolable and desolated*). **2** made barren or uninhabitable; devastated.

deso·la·tion *noun* **1** loneliness, grief, or wretchedness, esp. caused by desertion. **2 a** the act of desolating. **b** the process or act of being desolated. **3** a neglected, ruined, barren, or empty region, place, etc.

de·sorb */diːˈzɔrb/ verb* **1** *transitive* remove (a substance etc.) from a surface upon which it is adsorbed. **2** *intransitive* (of a substance) leave a surface upon which it is adsorbed. □ **de·sorp·tion** *noun* [DE-, after ADSORB]

De Soto */dəˈsoːtoː/ **Her·nan·do** (c.1500–42), Spanish explorer. He landed on the Florida coast in 1539 and explored much of what is now the southeastern US, as far west as Oklahoma.

de·spair ● *noun* the complete loss or absence of hope. ● *intransitive verb* (often foll. by *of*) lose or be without hope (*despaired of ever seeing her again*). □ **be the despair of** be the cause of despair by badness or unapproachable excellence (*he's the despair of his parents*). □ **de·spair·ing** *adjective* **de·spair·ing·ly** *adverb* [Old French *desespeir*, *desperer* from Latin *desperare* (as DE-, *sperare* hope)]

des·patch esp. *Brit.* var. of DISPATCH.

des·per·ado */ˌdespəˈrɒdoː, -ˈradoː/ noun* (*pl.* **-adoes** or *N Amer.* **-ados**) esp. *hist.* a desperate or reckless person, esp. a person ready for any deed of lawlessness or violence. [after DESPERATE (obsolete n.) & words in -ADO]

des·per·ate *adjective* **1** reckless from despair, esp. to the point of violence or lawlessness. **2 a** extremely grave, critical, or serious (*a desperate situation*). **b** undertaken as a last resort, esp. as staking all on a small chance (*a desperate remedy*). **3** extreme, excessive, awful (*a desperate night; desperate poverty*). **4** (usu. foll. by *for*) needing or desiring very much (*desperate for recognition*). □ **des·per·ate·ly** *adverb* **des·per·a·tion** *noun* [Latin *desperatus* past participle of *desperare* (as DE-, *sperare* hope)]

des·pic·able */dəˈspɪkəbəl, ˈdespɪk-/ adjective* vile, deserving to be despised, morally contemptible. □ **des·pic·ably** *adverb* [Late Latin *despicabilis* from *despicari* (as DE-, *specere* look at)]

des·pise *transitive verb* look down on (someone etc.) as inferior, worthless, or contemptible. □ **de·spised** *adjective* **de·spis·er** *noun* [*despis-* pres. stem of Old French *despire* from Latin *despicere* (as DE-, *specere* look at)]

de·spite ● *preposition* notwithstanding; in spite of. ● *noun archaic* or *literary* **1** outrage, injury. **2** malice, hatred (*died of mere despite*). □ **despite** (or **in despite**) **of** *archaic* in spite of. [Old French *despit* from Latin *despectus* noun from *despicere* (as DESPISE)]

de·spoil *transitive verb* **1** spoil, destroy, make useless (*rivers despoiled by industry and untreated sewage*). **2** *literary* plunder, rob, deprive by force or violence (*despoiled her of her inheritance*). □ **de·spoil·er** *noun* **de·spoli·a·tion** *noun* [Old French *despoill(i)er* from Latin *despoliare* (as DE-, *spoliare* SPOIL)]

de·spond */dəˈspɒnd/* ● *noun archaic* (except in phr. **slough of despond**) despondency. ● *intransitive verb archaic* lose heart or hope; be dejected, depressed. [Latin *despondēre* give up, abandon (as DE-, *spondēre* promise)]

de·spond·ent *adjective* characterized by loss of courage or enthusiasm; dejected. □ **de·spond·ence** noun **de·spond·ency** noun **de·spond·ent·ly** adverb

des·pot /'despɒt/ noun **1** an absolute ruler. **2** a tyrant or oppressor. **3** any person in authority who acts like a tyrant. □ **des·pot·ic** /-'spɒtɪk/ adjective **des·pot·ic·ally** adverb [French despote from medieval Latin despota from Greek despotēs master, lord]

despot·ism /'despə,tɪzəm/ noun **1 a** the exercise of absolute political authority or rule, esp. by a despot. **b** a political system under the control of a despot. **2** absolute power or control; tyranny.

des Prez see JOSQUIN DES PREZ.

des·qua·mate /'deskwə,meɪt/ intransitive verb Med. (esp. of the skin in some diseases) come off in scales. □ **des·qua·ma·tion** noun [Latin desquamare (as DE-, squama scale)]

des res /dez 'rez/ noun Brit. (in advertisement and ironic) a desirable residence. [abbreviation]

Des·ro·siers /deɪ'rɒzjeɪ/ **Rob·ert Guy** (b.1953), Canadian dancer, choreographer, and director. He founded the Robert Desrosiers Dance Company in 1980, and his productions include The Blue Snake (1985, for the National Ballet of Canada).

Des·sa·lines /desɑ'liːn/ **Jean Jacques** (c.1758–1806), Haitian emperor, 1804–6. Brought to Haiti as a slave, he expelled the French, proclaimed Haiti's independence, and proclaimed himself emperor (1804).

des·sert noun **1** a sweet food, esp. as eaten at the end of a meal, e.g. cake, fruit, ice cream, etc. **2** the sweet course of a meal served after the main course. [French, past participle of desservir clear the table (as DIS-, servir SERVE)]

dessert spoon noun **1** a spoon used for dessert, smaller than a tablespoon and larger than a teaspoon. **2** the amount held by this.

dessert wine noun a sweet wine usu. served with or following a dessert.

de·stabil·ize transitive verb (also esp. Brit. -ise) **1** deprive of stability, render unstable. **2** subvert or undermine (a government, economy, etc.), so as to make it politically unstable. □ **de·stabil·iz·a·tion** noun

de Staël see STAËL.

de-Stalin·iz·a·tion noun the removal or counteracting of the influence of Stalin or Stalinism on (a nation etc.).

de Stijl /də 'staɪl/ noun an early 20th-c. Dutch movement in art and architecture characterized by the use of geometric shapes and primary colours. [Dutch, lit. 'the Style', name of a Dutch art periodical 1917-1932]

des·tin·a·tion noun **1** a place to which a person or thing is going, the intended end of a journey. **2** the end or purpose for which a person or thing is destined. **3** (attributive) denoting a place that people will make a special trip to visit (a destination restaurant). [Old French destination or Latin destinatio (as DESTINE)]

des·tine /'destɪn/ transitive verb (in passive, often foll. by to, for, or to + infin.) set apart for or devote to a particular purpose, activity, etc. [French destiner from Latin destinare (as DE-, stanare (unrecorded) settle, from stare stand)]

des·tined adjective (often foll. by to, for, or to + infin.) **1** having a future decided or planned beforehand, esp. by fate or as if by fate (she is destined for greatness; the project was destined to fail). **2** (foll. by for) bound (for a certain place) (the shipment was destined for Mexico).

des·tiny noun (pl. -ies) **1 a** fate or the predetermined course of events. **b** (often **Destiny**) the power or agency that supposedly predetermines events etc. **2** what is destined to happen to a particular person etc. (it was their destiny to be rejected). [Old French destinée from Romanic, past participle of destinare: see DESTINE]

des·ti·tute /'destɪ,tjuːt, -tuːt/ adjective **1** completely impoverished; without food, shelter, etc. **2** archaic (usu. foll. by of) deprived, lacking, or bereft. □ **des·ti·tu·tion** noun [Latin destitutus past participle of destituere forsake (as DE-, statuere place)]

de·stream·ing noun Cdn the reversal of the practice of categorizing students into formal academic divisions based on their perceived ability. □ **de·stream** transitive verb

de-stress verb **1** intransitive become less stressed. **2** transitive remove stress from (one's life etc.).

des·trier /'destriːər/ noun hist. a warhorse. [Old French destrier, ultimately from Latin DEXTER right (as the knight's horse was led by the squire with the right hand)]

de·stroy transitive verb **1** demolish, pull or break down; shatter, smash to pieces (destroyed the bridge). **2** put an end to or do away with (the accident destroyed his confidence). **3** kill (esp. a sick or savage animal). **4** make useless, spoil utterly. **5** utterly discredit or ruin financially,

professionally, or in reputation. **6** defeat, annihilate, wipe out (destroyed the enemy). [Old French destruire, ultimately from Latin destruere (as DE-, struere struct- build)]

de·stroy·er noun **1** a person or thing that destroys. **2** Naut. a small, fast, lightly armoured and heavily armed warship used to protect other ships, destroy torpedo boats, etc.

destroying angel noun a poisonous white toadstool, Amanita virosa.

de·struct ● transitive verb destroy (one's own rocket etc.) deliberately, esp. for safety reasons. ● noun **1** an act of destructing. **2** (attributive) designating something capable of causing the destruction of itself, some other object, etc. (destruct mechanism). [Latin destruere (as DESTROY) or as back-formation from DESTRUCTION]

de·struct·ible adjective able or liable to be destroyed. □ **de·struct·ibil·ity** noun

de·struc·tion noun **1** the act or an instance of destroying; the process of being destroyed. **2** the fact or condition of being destroyed; ruin. **3** a cause of ruin; something that destroys (greed was their destruction). [Old French from Latin destructio -onis (as DESTROY)]

de·struc·tive adjective **1** (often foll. by to, of) destroying or tending to destroy (is destructive to organisms; destructive behaviour; destructive of human life). **2** negative in attitude or criticism; refuting without suggesting, helping, amending, etc. (opp. CONSTRUCTIVE 2) (has only destructive criticism to offer). □ **de·struc·tive·ly** adverb **de·struc·tive·ness** noun

de·sue·tude /də'sjuːɪ,tuːd, -tjuːd/ noun the condition or state into which anything falls when one ceases to use or practise it; a state of disuse (the custom fell into desuetude). [French désuétude or Latin desuetudo (as DE-, suescere suet- be accustomed)]

de·sulphur·ize /diː'sʌlfəraɪz/ transitive verb (also esp. Brit. -ise, US **de·sulfur·ize**) remove sulphur or sulphur compounds from. □ **de·sulphur·iz·a·tion** noun

des·ul·tory /'desəl,tɔːri/ adjective **1** going constantly from one subject to another, esp. digressively and unmethodically. **2** disconnected, random, or occasional. □ **des·ul·tor·i·ly** adverb [Latin desultorius superficial, from desultor vaulter, from desult- (as DE-, salt- past participle stem of salire leap)]

Det. abbreviation Detective.

det. abbreviation **1** Math. determinant. **2** detonator. **3** detachment.

de·tach transitive verb **1** (often foll. by from) unfasten and remove; disconnect or disengage (detached the buttons; detached himself from the group). **2** Military separate and send off (a part from a main body, e.g. a ship, regiment, officer, etc.) for a particular purpose, separate mission, etc. □ **de·tach·abil·ity** noun **de·tach·able** adjective [French détacher (as DE-, ATTACH)]

de·tached adjective **1** impartial, unemotional (a detached viewpoint). **2** esp. Cdn & Brit. (esp. of a house) separate, not joined to another or others (compare SEMI-DETACHED). □ **de·tach·ed·ly** adverb

detached retina noun a retina that has become detached from the underlying tissue, causing partial or total blindness.

de·tach·ment noun **1 a** a state of aloofness from or indifference to other people, public opinion, etc. **b** disinterested independence of judgment; impartiality, objectivity. **2 a** the act or process of detaching or being detached. **b** an instance of this. **3** Military **a** the action of separating a number of troops etc. from a main military body for a particular purpose. **b** a separate group or unit of an army etc. used for such a purpose. **4** Cdn the office or headquarters of a police district, esp. one patrolled by the RCMP, OPP, etc.

de·tail ● noun **1 a** a small or subordinate particular; an item. **b** such a particular, considered (ironically) to be unimportant (the truth of the statement is just a detail). **2 a** small items or particulars (esp. in an artistic work) regarded collectively (has an eye for detail). **b** the treatment of them (the detail was insufficient and unconvincing). **3** (often in pl.) a number of particulars or an aggregate of small details (filled in the details on the form). **4 a** a minor decoration on a building, in a picture, etc. **b** a small part of a picture etc. shown alone or considered in isolation. **5** Military **a** the distribution of detailed orders for the day, ranging from general to specific directives. **b** a small detachment of soldiers etc. for special duty. **c** this special duty (kitchen detail). ● transitive verb **1** relate or describe minutely, give particulars of (detailed the plans). **2** Military assign for special duty. **3** decorate (a carving, car, etc.) with intricate drawings or designs. □ **go into detail** give all the items or particulars in turn, minutely. **in detail** item by item, minutely. [French détail, détailler (as DE-, tailler cut, formed as TAIL²)]

de·tailed adjective **1** (of a picture, story, etc.) having many details.

2 related or described minutely, itemized (*a detailed list*). **3** thorough in handling of details (*a detailed analysis*).

de·tail·ing *noun* the treatment of detail in a work of art, building, design, etc.

de·tain *transitive verb* **1** keep in confinement or under restraint as a prisoner, esp. without charge. **2** delay or keep (someone) waiting. □ **de·tain·ment** *noun* [Old French *detenir*, ultimately from Latin *detinēre detent-* (as DE-, *tenēre* hold)]

de·tain·ee *noun* a person detained in custody, esp. for political reasons.

de·tain·er *noun* Law **1** the wrongful detaining of goods taken from the owner for distraint etc. **2** the detention of a person in prison etc. **3** an order authorizing the continued detention of a person in custody who would otherwise be released. [Anglo-French *detener* from Old French *detenir* (as DETAIN)]

de·tan·gle *transitive verb* remove tangles from (the hair). □ **de·tan·gler** *noun*

de·tect *transitive verb* **1** discover or perceive the existence or presence of (*detecting cancer before the symptoms appear*; *do I detect a note of sarcasm?*). **2** *Physics* use an instrument to observe (a signal, radiation, etc.). **3 a** discover the real (esp. hidden or disguised) character of. **b** discover (crime etc.). □ **de·tect·able** *adjective* **de·tect·ably** *adverb* [Latin *detegere detect-* (as DE-, *tegere* cover)]

de·tec·tion *noun* **1 a** the act or an instance of detecting. **b** the process of being detected. **2** the work of a detective. **3** *Physics* the extraction of a desired signal; a demodulation.

de·tec·tive *noun* **1** (often *attributive*) a person, esp. a member of a police force, employed to investigate crime (*police detective*; *detective agency*) (compare PRIVATE INVESTIGATOR). **2** (in Canadian police forces with a detective branch) an officer ranking above constable and below detective sergeant. **3** (*attributive*) designating a type of fiction describing crime and the detection of criminals (compare MYSTERY¹ 5).

detective chief superintendent *noun* (in the Ontario Provincial Police) an officer ranking above detective superintendent and below deputy commissioner.

detective inspector *noun* (in the Ontario Provincial Police) an officer ranking above sergeant major and below superintendent.

detective sergeant *noun* **1** (in Canadian police forces with a detective branch) an officer ranking above detective and below inspector with the equivalent rank of staff sergeant. **2** (in the Ontario Provincial Police) an officer ranking above senior constable and below detective staff sergeant.

detective staff sergeant *noun* (in the Ontario Provincial Police) an officer ranking above detective sergeant and below sergeant major.

detective superintendent *noun* (in the Ontario Provincial Police) an officer ranking above detective inspector and below detective chief superintendent.

de·tec·tor *noun* **1** a device which detects something liable to escape observation or indicates something out of the ordinary (*smoke detector*; *lie detector*). **2** *Physics* a device for the detection or demodulation of signals.

de·tent /dəˈtent/ *noun* **1** any stop or catch in a machine which, until released, prevents a motion. **2** (in a clock etc.) a catch that regulates striking. [French *détente* from Old French *destente* from *destendre* slacken (as DE-, Latin *tendere*)]

dé·tente /deiˈtɑ̃t/ *noun* an easing of strained relations esp. between nations. [French, = relaxation]

de·ten·tion *noun* **1** an act or instance of detaining or being detained. **2 a** the fact of being kept in school after hours as a punishment. **b** an instance of this. **3** the state of imprisonment or confinement, esp. of a criminal or political offender. **4** (*attributive*) designating a place where people are held in detention (*detention camp*). [French *détention* or Late Latin *detentio* (as DETAIN)]

detention centre *noun* **1** an institution for the short-term detention of criminals, esp. young offenders. **2** a camp or centre, esp. one established during or after a war, to house refugees, prisoners of war, etc. (compare CONCENTRATION CAMP).

deter *transitive verb* (**de·terred**, **de·ter·ring**) **1** (often foll. by *from*) discourage or prevent (a person) through fear or dislike of the consequences. **2** discourage, check, or prevent (a thing, process, etc.). □ **deter·ment** *noun* [Latin *deterrēre* (as DE-, *terrēre* frighten)]

de·ter·gent ● *noun* a water-soluble cleansing agent which combines with impurities and dirt to make them more soluble, and differs from soap in not forming a scum with the salts in hard water. **2** any additive with a similar action, e.g. holding dirt in suspension in lubricating oil. ● *adjective* cleansing, esp. in the manner of a detergent. [Latin *detergēre* (as DE-, *tergēre ters-* wipe)]

de·teri·or·ate *transitive & intransitive verb* make or become worse or lower in quality, character, etc. (*food deteriorates in hot weather*; *his condition deteriorated after the operation*). □ **de·teri·or·a·tion** *noun* [Late Latin *deteriorare deteriorat-* from Latin *deterior* worse]

de·ter·min·ant ● *noun* **1** a factor which decisively affects the nature or outcome of something (*the single most important determinant of church membership was gender*). **2** *Math.* a quantity obtained by the addition of products of the elements of a square matrix according to a given rule. ● *adjective* serving to determine or decide something (*a determinant factor*).

de·ter·min·ate *adjective* **1** limited in time, space, or character. **2** of definite scope or nature. **3** (of inflorescence) having the terminal flower bud open first, followed by those on the lateral branches. **4** (of a plant) producing a single crop all at once (*determinate tomatoes*). □ **de·ter·min·acy** *noun* **de·ter·min·ate·ly** *adverb* **de·ter·min·ate·ness** *noun* [Latin *determinatus* past participle (as DETERMINE)]

de·ter·min·a·tion *noun* **1** firmness of purpose; resoluteness. **2 a** the process of deciding, determining, or calculating. **b** the result of such consideration. **3 a** the conclusion of a dispute by the decision of a judge or an arbitrator. **b** the authoritative decision so reached. **4** *Biol.* the fixing of the future of embryonic cells at a stage when they can develop only as a certain kind of tissue rather than as any kind. **5** *archaic* a tendency to move in a fixed direction.

de·ter·mina·tive ● *adjective* serving to define, qualify, or direct. ● *noun* a determinative thing or circumstance. □ **de·ter·mina·tive·ly** *adverb*

de·ter·mine *verb* **1** *transitive* find out or establish precisely (*determine the extent of the problem*). **2** *transitive* decide or settle (*determined who should go*). **3** *transitive* be a decisive factor in regard to (*demand determines supply*). **4** *intransitive & transitive* make or cause (a person) to make a decision (*we determined to go at once*). **5** *transitive & intransitive* esp. *Law* bring or come to an end. **6** *transitive* fix or define the position of. □ **de·ter·min·able** *adjective* [Old French *determiner* from Latin *determinare* (as DE-, *terminus* end)]

de·ter·mined *adjective* showing determination; resolute, unflinching. □ **de·ter·min·ed·ly** *adverb*

de·ter·min·er *noun* **1** a person or thing that determines. **2** *Grammar* any of a class of words that determine the kind of reference a noun or noun substitute has, e.g. *a*, *the*, *every*.

de·ter·min·ism *noun* *Philos.* the doctrine that all events, including human action, are determined by causes regarded as external to the will. □ **de·ter·min·ist** *noun* **de·ter·min·is·tic** *adjective* **de·ter·min·is·tic·ally** *adverb*

de·ter·rent ● *noun* **1** a thing or factor that deters (someone). **2** military strength or combat capability, esp. nuclear, intended to deter an enemy from attack. ● *adjective* tending to deter. □ **de·ter·rence** *noun*

de·test *transitive verb* hate, loathe. [Latin *detestari* (as DE-, *testari* call to witness, from *testis* witness)]

de·test·able *adjective* deserving to be detested; intensely hateful. □ **de·test·ably** *adverb*

de·test·ation *noun* intense dislike, hatred.

de·thatch *transitive & intransitive verb* remove thatch from (a lawn). □ **de·thatch·er** *noun*

de·throne *transitive verb* **1** remove from a position of authority or influence. **2** remove from the throne, depose. □ **de·throned** *adjective* **de·throne·ment** *noun*

deton·ate *verb* **1** *transitive* set off (an explosive charge). **2** *intransitive* (of an explosive charge) be set off, explode. □ **deton·a·tive** *adjective* [Latin *detonare detonat-* (as DE-, *tonare* thunder)]

deton·a·tion *noun* **1** the act or process of detonating. **2** a violent explosion.

deton·ator *noun* a device for detonating an explosive.

de·tour ● *noun* a divergence from a direct or intended route, esp. one that avoids a blocked road etc. ● *transitive & intransitive verb* make or cause to make a detour. [French *détour* change of direction, from *détourner* turn away (as DE-, TURN)]

detox esp. *N Amer. informal* ● *noun* **1** = DETOXIFICATION. **2 a** a detoxification clinic, program, etc. **b** = DRUNK TANK. ● *verb* **1** *transitive* subject (an alcoholic or drug addict) to detoxification. **2** *intransitive* **a** (of a person) subject oneself to detoxification; undergo treatment to overcome addiction to drugs or alcohol. **b** recover temporarily from the effects of alcohol or drugs. [abbreviation]

de·tox·i·fi·ca·tion *noun* **1 a** the act of depriving of poisonous qualities, esp. the elimination of poison from the body. **b** the state of being detoxified. **2** the supervised withdrawal of drugs or alcohol from an addict.

detoxification centre *noun* (also **detox centre**) a (usu. residential) centre for the treatment of alcoholism or drug abuse.

de·tox·i·fy *transitive verb* (**-fies**, **-fied**) **1** subject (an alcoholic or drug addict) to detoxification. **2** remove the poison from (something). [DE- + Latin *toxicum* poison]

de·tract *verb* **1** *intransitive* (foll. by *from*) **a** take something away from. **b** diminish or belittle. **2** *transitive* (foll. by *from*) take away (something) so as to diminish the whole, esp. an achievement. ¶ *Detract* does not mean *distract*; uses such as *Nothing will detract their attention from the issue* are incorrect. □ **de·trac·tion** *noun* [Latin *detrahere detract-* (as DE-, *trahere* draw)]

de·tract·or *noun* a person who disparages or belittles another's achievements, merits, etc.

de·train *transitive & intransitive verb* alight or cause to alight from a train. □ **de·train·ment** *noun*

de·tribal·ize *transitive verb* (also esp. *Brit.* **-ise**) (usu. in *passive*) **1** make (a person) no longer a member of a tribe. **2** remove the tribal social structure from. □ **de·tribal·iz·a·tion** *noun*

detri·ment *noun* **1** harm, damage, disadvantage. **2** something causing this. □ **to the detriment of** to the disadvantage of; harming (*pursues his own interests to the detriment of others'*). [Latin *detrimentum* (as DE-, *terere trit-* rub, wear)]

detri·ment·al *adjective* harmful, damaging, or causing loss. □ **detri·ment·al·ly** *adverb*

detri·ti·vore /dəˈtrɪtɪˌvɔr/ *noun* an animal that feeds on dead organic material, esp. plant detritus. □ **detri·tiv·or·ous** /ˌdetrəˈtɪvərəs/ *adjective*

de·tritus /dəˈtraɪtəs, ˈdetˌrɪtəs/ *noun* **1** matter produced by erosion, such as gravel, silt, etc. **2** debris of any kind. **3** the organic litter produced by decomposing leaves etc. □ **de·trital** /dəˈtraɪtəl/ *adjective* [after French *détritus* from Latin *detritus* (n.) = wearing down (as DETRIMENT)]

De·troit /dəˈtrɔɪt/ a major industrial city and Great Lakes shipping centre in SE Michigan; pop. (2000) 951,270. It is the centre of the US automobile industry, whence its nickname 'Motown' (short for 'motor town'). In the 1960s it was also an important centre for rock and soul music.

Detroit·er *noun* **1** a person from Detroit. **2** *Figure Skating* a lift in pairs skating in which the female partner is held overhead in a horizontal position with one arm by the male partner, who spins around.

de trop /də ˈtroʊ/ *predicative adjective* **1** excessive. **2** not wanted, unwelcome, in the way. [French, = excessive]

de·tumes·cence /ˌdiːtuːˈmesəns, -tjuː-/ *noun* subsidence from a swollen state, esp. subsidence of the penis or clitoris from erection. □ **de·tumes·cent** *adjective* [Latin *detumescere* (as DE-, *tumescere* swell)]

de·tune *transitive verb* adjust (a mechanism, musical instrument, etc.) so that it is no longer tuned.

Deu·ca·lion /duːˈkeɪliən, djuː-/ *Gk Myth* son of Prometheus. He and his wife Pyrrha were the only survivors of a flood sent by Zeus; to repopulate the world they were advised to throw stones over their shoulders, with those thrown by Deucalion becoming men, and those thrown by Pyrrha women.

deuce¹ /duːs, djuːs/ *noun* **1** the two in dice or playing cards. **2 a** *Sport* two points, goals, runs, etc. **b** *Tennis* the score of 40 all, at which two consecutive points are needed to win. **3 a** *informal* the number two as an identifying feature for various items (*a double deuce is a .22-calibre gun*). **b** *N Amer. slang* a two-year jail sentence. **4** *slang* **a** *Cdn hist.* a two-dollar bill. **b** *N Amer.* two dollars. **c** *N Amer.* a two-dollar bet. [Old French *deus* from Latin *duo* (accusative *duos*) two]

deuce² /duːs, djuːs/ *noun* misfortune, the Devil, used esp. *informal* as an exclamation of surprise or annoyance (*who the deuce are you?*). □ **a** (or **the) deuce of a** a very bad or remarkable (*a deuce of a problem*; *a deuce of a fellow*). **the deuce to pay** trouble is to be expected. [Low German *duus*, formed as DEUCE¹, two aces at dice being the worst throw]

deuced /djuːsd, duːst/ *adjective & adverb* dated or jocular damned, confounded (*a deuced liar*). □ **deuced·ly** /ˈdjuːsədli/ *adverb*

deus ex mach·ina /ˌdeɪus eks ˈmakɪnə, ˌdiːəs/ *noun* **1** a power, event, or person arriving in the nick of time to solve a difficulty or save a

seemingly hopeless situation. **2** a providential, often rather contrived, interposition, esp. in a novel or a play. [modern Latin translation of Greek *theos ek mēkhanēs*, = god from the machinery (by which in the Greek theatre the gods were suspended above the stage)]

Deut. *abbreviation Bible* Deuteronomy.

deu·ter·ate /ˈduːtəˌreit, ˌdjuː-/ *transitive verb* replace the usual isotope of hydrogen in (a substance) by deuterium. □ **deu·ter·at·ed** *adjective* **deu·ter·a·tion** *noun*

deu·ter·ium /duːˈtɪːriəm, ˌdjuː-/ *noun* a stable isotope of hydrogen with a mass about double that of the usual isotope. *Also called* HEAVY HYDROGEN. Symbol: **D** or **²H**; at. no.: 1. [modern Latin, formed as DEUTERO- + -IUM]

deutero- /ˈduːtɔːrəʊ, ˌdjuː-/ *combining form* **1** second, secondary. **2** *Chem.* forming names of deuterated compounds. [Greek *deuteros* second]

deu·tero·canon·ical /ˌduːtərəʊkəˈnɒnɪkəl, ˌdjuː-/ *adjective* of or forming a secondary canon (of sacred writings), used esp. to designate those books of the Old Testament accepted as part of the canon by the Roman Catholic and Orthodox Churches but not by Protestants.

deu·ter·on /ˈduːtəˌrɒn, ˌdjuː-/ *noun Physics* the nucleus of a deuterium atom, consisting of a proton and a neutron. [DEUTERIUM + -ON]

Deu·ter·on·omy /ˌduːtəˈrɒnəmiː, ˌdjuː-/ *noun* the fifth book of the Pentateuch, containing a repetition of and commentary on most of the laws in Exodus. [ecclesiastical Latin *Deuteronomium* from Greek *Deuteronómion* from Greek *deúteros* second + *nómos* law]

Deutsch·mark /ˈdɔɪtʃmɑrk/ *noun* (also **Deutsche Mark** /ˈdɔɪtʃə mɑrk/) *hist.* the chief monetary unit of Germany, equal to 100 pfennigs. [German, = German mark (see MARK²)]

deut·zia /ˈdjuːtsiə, ˈdɔɪtsiə/ *noun* any ornamental shrub of the genus *Deutzia*, with usu. white flowers. [J. *Deutz* 18th-c. Dutch patron of botany]

Deux Montagnes, Lac des see LAC DES DEUX MONTAGNES.

Deux-Montagnes /dəmõtaiɲə/ a town in south central Quebec, on the northwest shore of the Rivière des Mille-Îles across from Laval and Île Bizard; pop. (2001) 17,080.

deva /ˈdeɪvə/ *noun* a member of a class of divine beings in the Vedic period, which in Indian mythology are benevolent (opposed to the asuras) and in Zoroastrianism are evil. (*Compare* ASURA.) [Sanskrit, = god]

de Va·lera /ˌdə vəˈlerə/ **Eamon** (1882–1975), US-born Irish nationalist, prime minister of Ireland 1937–48, 1951–4, 1957–9, and president 1959–73. One of the leaders of the Easter rising (1916), he became president of the Irish Free State in 1932, and subsequently prime minister and president of the Irish Republic.

de Val·ois /də ˈvalwɒ/ **Dame Nin·ette** (born Edris Stannus) (1898–2001), Irish-born English choreographer and ballet dancer. A founder and director (1931–63) of the Vic-Wells Ballet Company, which eventually became the Royal Ballet (1956), she choreographed numerous works.

de·value *transitive verb* (**de·val·ues**, **de·val·ued**, **de·valu·ing**) **1** reduce the value of (a person, thing, etc.). **2** *Econ.* reduce the value of (a currency) in relation to other currencies or to gold (*opp.* REVALUE 2). □ **de·valu·a·tion** *noun*

Deva·nag·ari /ˌdeɪvəˈnagəri/ *noun* the alphabet used for Sanskrit, Hindi, and other Indian languages. [Sanskrit, = divine town script]

dev·as·tate *transitive verb* **1** lay waste; cause great destruction to. **2** (often in *passive*) overwhelm with shock or grief; upset deeply. □ **dev·as·ta·tion** *noun* **dev·as·ta·tor** *noun* [Latin *devastare devastat-* (as DE-, *vastare* lay waste)]

dev·as·tat·ing *adjective* crushingly effective; overwhelming. □ **dev·as·tat·ing·ly** *adverb*

de·vein /diːˈveɪn/ *transitive verb* remove the main central vein from (a shrimp).

de·velop *verb* (**de·veloped**, **de·velop·ing**) **1** *transitive & intransitive* **a** make or become bigger or fuller. **b** bring or come to an active or visible state (*developed a plan of action*; *symptoms developed rapidly*). **c** bring or come into existence (*a crisis developed*). **2 a** *transitive* elaborate more fully and systematically the details of (a thought, argument, plot, etc.) **b** *intransitive* (of a thought, argument, plot, etc.) unfold in this way. **3** *transitive & intransitive* **a** grow or cause to grow to maturity or to a more advanced state (*develop a child's potential*; *some teens develop early*). **b** (of organisms) evolve or progress from a simpler or lower to a higher or more complex type. **4** *transitive* begin to exhibit or suffer from (*developed an infection*). **5** *transitive* **a** make (a tract of land) suitable for new purposes, esp. residential, industrial, etc. **b** realize the resource potential of (a site or property) by mining etc. **6** *transitive* create or

Vowels: a cat ɑ arm e bed ɜr her ɜː deux ə ago ɪ sit i cosy iː feed ɒ hot ɔ pore ɔː no ʌ run ʊ put

design (a program, product, etc.). **7** *transitive* process (photographic film etc.) chemically to make the latent image visible. **8** *transitive Music* elaborate (a theme) by modification of the melody, harmony, rhythm, etc. **9** *transitive Math.* **a** convert (a curved surface) conceptually into a plane or figure as if by unrolling. **b** expand (a function etc.) in the form of a series. **10** *transitive Chess* bring (a piece) into position for effective use. □ **de·vel·op·able** *adjective* [French *développer* from Romanic (as DIS-, origin of second element unknown)]

de·vel·op·er *noun* **1** a person or company that develops land, esp. a speculative builder. **2** a chemical agent for developing photographs. **3** a person or thing that develops (a product etc.).

developing country *noun* a country that is becoming economically more advanced and more industrialized.

de·vel·op·ment *noun* **1 a** the act or an instance of developing; the process of being developed. **b** *Business* the process of working up (an idea, product, etc.) for marketing etc. **2 a** a stage of growth or advancement. **b** a full-grown state. **3** a significant change in a course of action, events, circumstances, etc. (*the latest developments*). **4** the process of developing a photograph. **5** a developed tract of land, esp. a new housing area. **6** industrialization or economic advancement of a country or area. **7** *Music* the elaboration of a theme or themes, esp. in the middle section of a sonata movement. **8** *Chess* the developing of pieces from their original position.

de·vel·op·ment·al *adjective* **1** pertaining to the process of achieving physical, mental, or social maturity (*developmental delays*). **2** of or pertaining to development (*the project is in the developmental stage*). □ **de·vel·op·ment·al·ly** *adverb*

development bank *noun* *Politics* a regional multilateral organization designed to contribute to the economic development and social progress of its member states through loans at low or no interest, equity investment, etc.

Dev·er·eux /ˈdevərə/ **Rob·ert**, see ESSEX².

Devi /ˈdeivi/ *Hinduism* the supreme goddess, often identified with Parvati and Sakti. [Sanskrit, = goddess]

de·vi·ant /ˈdiːviənt/ ● *adjective* deviating or divergent, esp. from normal social standards. ● *noun* a person who or thing which deviates from the normal, esp. from normal social or sexual practices. □ **devi·ance** *noun* **devi·ancy** *noun* [as DEVIATE]

de·vi·ate ● *intransitive verb* /ˈdiːvi.eit/ (often foll. by *from*) **1** turn aside or diverge (from a course of action, rule, truth, norm, etc.). **2** digress. ● *noun* /-viət/ a deviant, esp. a sexual pervert. ● *adjective* /ˈdiːviət/ = DEVIANT *adjective*. [Late Latin *deviare deviat-* (as DE-, *via* way)]

de·vi·a·tion *noun* **1** divergence from a course, method, rule, or norm. **b** an instance of this. **2** *Statistics* the amount by which a single measurement differs from the mean. **3** the deflection of a compass needle caused by local deposits of iron, regional magnetic disturbances, etc. □ **devi·a·tion·ism** *noun* **devi·a·tion·ist** *noun* [as DEVIATE]

de·vice *noun* **1 a** a thing made or adapted for a particular purpose, esp. a mechanical contrivance. **b** an explosive contrivance, esp. a nuclear bomb. **2** a plan, scheme, or trick. **3 a** an emblematic or heraldic design. **b** an artistic drawing, design, pattern, etc. **4** any literary technique deliberately employed to achieve a specific effect, e.g. figures of speech etc. **5** *archaic* the design (of something) or manner in which a thing is devised or framed (*things of rare device*). □ **leave a person to his or her own devices** leave a person to do as he or she wishes. [Old French *devis*, ultimately from Latin (as DIVIDE)]

devil ● *noun* **1** (usu. **the Devil**) (in Christian and Jewish belief) the supreme spirit of evil; Satan. **2** an evil spirit; a demon; a superhuman malignant being. **3 a** a wicked or cruel person. **b** a mischievously energetic, clever, or self-willed person. **4** *informal* a person or animal (*lucky devil; frisky devil*). **5** fighting spirit, mischievousness (*the devil is in him tonight*). **6** *informal* something difficult or awkward (*this door is a devil to open*). **7** (**the devil, the Devil**) *informal* used as an exclamation of surprise or annoyance (*who the devil are you?*). **8** any of various instruments or machines, esp. ones fitted with sharp teeth or spikes. ● *verb* (**dev·illed, devil·ling**; *US* **dev·iled, devil·ing**) *transitive N Amer.* harass; worry. □ **between the devil and the deep blue sea** in a dilemma. **a devil of** *informal* a considerable, difficult, or remarkable. **the devil to pay** serious trouble to be dealt with. **go to the devil 1** be damned. **2** (in *imperative*) used to express anger or annoyance. **like the devil** with great energy. **play the devil with** cause severe damage to. **speak of the devil** said when a person appears just after being mentioned.

devil's own *informal* very difficult or unusual (*the devil's own job*). **devil take the hindmost** everyone should (or does) look after their own interests rather than considering those of others.

[Old English *dēofol* from Late Latin *diabolus* from Greek *diabolos* accuser, slanderer, from *dia* across + *ballō* to throw]

devil·fish *noun* (*pl.* same or **-fishes**) **1** a manta ray. **2** any of various large or deadly fish. **3** *hist.* an octopus.

devil·ish *adjective* **1** of or like a devil; wicked. **2** mischievous. **3** *informal* very great; extreme (*a devilish din*). □ **devil·ish·ly** *adverb* **devil·ish·ness** *noun*

dev·illed *adjective* (also esp. *US* **dev·iled**) (of eggs, ham, etc.) prepared with spicy seasonings.

devil-may-care *adjective* cheerful and reckless (*a devil-may-care manner*).

devil·ment *noun* mischief; wild spirits.

devil·ry *noun* (also **devil·try**) (*pl.* **-ries**) **1 a** wickedness; reckless mischief. **b** an instance of this. **2 a** black magic. **b** diabolism.

devil's advocate *noun* **1** a person who supports an opposing or unpopular view in order to provoke argument or discussion. **2** *Catholicism* the official whose function is to argue the case against beatification or canonization of a candidate.

devil's bit *noun* a N American plant of the lily family, *Chamaelirium luteum*, bearing tightly packed spikes of white flowers.

devil's claw *noun* **1** any of several plants whose seed pods have the appearance of a claw and can harm livestock, esp. *Harpagophytum procumbens* of Africa and various plants of the genus *Proboscidea* of the warm regions of America. **2** an extract from *Harpagophytum procumbens* used to treat arthritis etc.

devil's club *noun* *N Amer.* a prickly shrub, *Oplopanax horridus*.

devil's darning needle *noun* a dragonfly or damselfly.

devil's food cake *noun* *N Amer.* a chocolate cake with a reddish tinge.

Devil's Island a rocky island, now chiefly a tourist attraction, off the coast of French Guiana. From 1852 until 1953 it was part of a penal settlement and was notorious for its harsh conditions.

devil's ivy *noun* a climbing plant, *Epipremium aureum* (also *Scindapsus aureum*), with usu. shiny yellow and green leaves, frequently grown as a houseplant. *Also called* GOLDEN POTHOS.

devil's paintbrush *noun* *N Amer.* an orange-flowered hawkweed, *Hieracium aurantiacum*.

devil's walking stick *noun* a shrub of eastern N America, *Aralia spinosa*, of the ginseng family.

De·vine /dəˈvain/ **(Don·ald) Grant** (b.1944), Canadian politician, Progressive Conservative premier of Saskatchewan 1982–91.

de·vi·ous *adjective* **1** (of a person, plan etc.) not straightforward or sincere; underhand. **2** winding; circuitous (*a devious passageway*). □ **de·vi·ous·ly** *adverb* **de·vi·ous·ness** *noun* [Latin *devius* from DE- + *via* way]

de·vise /dəˈvaiz/ ● *transitive verb* **1** plan or invent by careful thought. **2** *Law* leave (real estate) by the terms of a will (*compare* BEQUEATH). ● *noun Law* **1** the act or an instance of devising real estate. **2** a devising clause in a will. □ **de·vis·able** *adjective* **de·visee** /-ˈziː/ *noun* (in sense 2 of *verb*). **de·vis·er** *noun* **de·vis·or** *noun* (in sense 2 of *verb*). [Old French *deviser* ultimately from Latin *dividere divis-* DIVIDE: (n.) from Old French *devise* from medieval Latin *divisa* fem. past participle of *dividere*]

de·vital·ize *transitive verb* (also esp. *Brit.* **-ise**) take away strength and vigour from. □ **de·vital·iz·a·tion** *noun*

de·void *predicative adjective* (foll. by *of*) totally lacking or free from (*a book devoid of all interest*). [late Middle English: past participle of obsolete *devoid* cast out, from Old French *devoidier*]

de·voir /dəˈvwar/ *noun archaic* **1** duty; one's best (*do one's devoir*). **2** (in *pl.*) courteous or formal attentions; respects (*pay one's devoirs to*). [Old French *devoir* from Latin *debēre* owe]

devo·lu·tion /ˌdevəˈluːʃən, ˌdiː-/ *noun* **1** the delegation of power, esp. by central government to local or regional administration. **2 a** a descent or passing on through a series of stages. **b** descent by natural or due succession from one to another of property or qualities. **3** the transfer of an unexercised right to an ultimate owner. **4** *Biol.* degeneration. □ **devo·lu·tion·ary** *adjective* **devo·lu·tion·ism** *noun* **devo·lu·tion·ist** *noun* [Late Latin *devolutio* (as DEVOLVE)]

de·volve /dəˈvolv/ *verb* **1** (foll. by *on, upon*, etc.) **a** *transitive* pass (work or duties) to (a deputy etc.). **b** *intransitive* (of work or duties) pass to (a deputy etc.). **2** *intransitive* (foll. by *on, to, upon*) *Law* (of property etc.) descend or fall by succession to. [Latin *devolvere devolut-* (as DE-, *volvere* roll)]

Devon /ˈdevən/ **1** a town in Alberta, about 45 km southwest of Edmonton; (pop. (2001) 4,969. **2** (also **Devon·shire** /-ˌʃiːr/) a county of

uː m**oo**d   ai m**y**   əi p**i**pe   au br**ow**n   ʌu h**ou**se   ei d**ay**   ɔi b**oy**   ɑ̃ fr**an**glais   ã C**an**adien   ɔ̃ Br**ay**on   (*see over for consonants*)

SW England; county town, Exeter. [sense 1 in reference to the layer of Devonian rock underlying the area]

Devon·ian /dəˈvoːnɪən/ ● *adjective* **1** *Geol.* of or relating to the fourth period of the Paleozoic era, from about 408 to 360 million years BP, between the Silurian and Carboniferous periods. During this period, amphibians and forests first appeared. **2** of or relating to Devon. ● *noun* **1** the Devonian period or the system of rocks dating from this time. **2** a resident of Devon, Alberta. [medieval Latin *Devonia* Devonshire]

Devon Island an island in the Canadian Arctic, the second largest among the Queen Elizabeth Islands. It lies between Ellesmere and Baffin islands. [DEVON]

Devon·shire /ˈdevənʃɪr/ **Vic·tor Chris·tian Wil·liam Cav·en·dish, 9th Duke of** (1868–1938), English statesman, Governor General of Canada 1916–21.

Devonshire cream *noun* = CLOTTED CREAM.

de·vote *transitive verb & reflexive* (foll. by *to*) apply or give over (resources etc. or oneself) to (a particular activity or purpose or person) (*devoted their time to reading*; *devoted himself to his guests*). [Latin *devovēre* *devot-* (as DE-, *vovēre* vow)]

de·vot·ed *adjective* very loving or loyal (*a devoted husband*). □ **de·vot·ed·ly** *adverb*

de·votee /ˌdevoˈtiː, devˈoːtiː, ˌdevoːˈteɪ/ *noun* **1** (usu. foll. by *of*) a zealous enthusiast or supporter. **2** a zealously pious or fanatical person.

de·vo·tion *noun* **1** (usu. foll. by *to*) enthusiastic attachment or loyalty (to a person or cause); great love. **2 a** religious worship. **b** (in *pl.*) prayers. **c** devoutness; religious fervour.

de·vo·tion·al ● *adjective* of, pertaining to, or characterized by (esp. religious) devotion. ● *noun* (often in *pl.*) a short religious service or text. □ **de·vo·tion·al·ism** *noun*

de·vour *transitive verb* **1** eat hungrily or greedily. **2** consume destructively; waste; destroy (*the West devours a disproportionate share of the world's resources*). **3** take in greedily with the eyes or ears (*devoured book after book*). **4** (usu. in *passive*) absorb the attention of (*devoured by anxiety*). □ **de·vour·er** *noun* [Latin *devorare* (as DE-, *vorare* swallow)]

de·vout *adjective* **1** earnestly religious. **2** earnestly sincere (*devout hope*). □ **de·vout·ly** *adverb* **de·vout·ness** *noun* [Old French *devot* from Latin *devotus* past participle (as DEVOTE)]

de Vries /də ˈvriːs/ **Hugo (Marie)** (1848–1935), Dutch botanist and geneticist. His plant-breeding experiments on heredity and variation contributed substantially to the chromosome theory of heredity.

dew /duː, djuː/ ● *noun* **1** atmospheric vapour condensing in small drops on cool surfaces at night. **2** beaded or glistening moisture resembling this, e.g. tears. ● *transitive verb* (usu. in *passive*) wet with or as with dew (*her forehead was dewed with sweat*). [Old English *dēaw* from Germanic]

dewan /dəˈwɒn/ *noun* (also **diwan**) *hist.* a chief treasury official, finance minister, or prime minister of an Indian state. [Arabic & Persian *diwān* fiscal register]

Dewar /ˈduːər, ˈdjuːər/ **Sir James** (1842–1923), Scottish chemist and physicist. He is chiefly remembered for his work in cryogenics; he devised the vacuum flask, achieved temperatures close to absolute zero, and was the first to produce liquid oxygen and hydrogen in quantity.

dewar /ˈduːər, ˈdjuːər/ *noun* (in full **dewar vessel** or **dewar flask**) a double-walled vessel with a vacuum between the walls to reduce the transfer of heat, used for storing hot or cold liquids. [DEWAR]

de·water /diːˈwɒtər/ *transitive verb* remove water from (sludge, a mine, etc.); drain.

dew·berry *noun* (*pl.* **-berries**) **1** a bluish fruit like the blackberry. **2** any of various shrubs of the genus *Rubus* bearing this.

dew·claw *noun* **1** a rudimentary inner toe found on some dogs. **2** a false hoof on a deer etc.

dew·drop *noun* a drop of dew.

Dewey /ˈduːi, ˈdjuːi/ **John** (1859–1952), US philosopher and educator. His pragmatic philosophy defined knowledge as successful practice, and argued that children learn best by doing.

Dewey Decimal Classification *noun* (also **Dewey system** *informal*) a decimal system of library classification. [M. *Dewey*, American librarian d.1931, its deviser]

dew·lap *noun* **1** a loose fold of skin hanging from the throat of cattle, dogs, etc. **2** similar loose skin round the throat of an elderly person.

DEW Line /duː, djuː/ *noun* N Amer. a network of radar stations stretching along the Arctic coast from Alaska to Baffin Island, built in the 1950s to provide advance warning of an aircraft or missile attack. [acronym from Distant Early Warning]

de·worm *transitive verb* rid (a dog, cat, etc.) of worms. □ **de·worm·er** *noun*

dew point *noun* the temperature at which dew forms.

dew worm *noun* = EARTHWORM.

dewy *adjective* (**dew·i·er, dew·i·est**) **1 a** wet with dew. **b** moist as if with dew (*a dewy complexion*). **2** = DEWY-EYED. **3** of or like dew. □ **dew·i·ly** *adverb* **dew·i·ness** *noun*

dewy-eyed *adjective* innocently trusting; naively sentimental.

dexa·metha·sone /ˌdeksəˈmeθozoːn/ *noun* a synthetic corticosteroid used esp. as an anti-inflammatory agent. [from *dexa-* (blend of HEXA- + DECA-) + METHYL + *-a* + CORTISONE]

Dexe·drine /ˈdeksədriːn, -drɪn/ *noun proprietary* **1** a brand of dextroamphetamine. **2** a tablet of this. [DEXTRO- + BENZEDRINE]

Dex·ter, Colin (b.1930), British mystery writer. He is noted for his Inspector Morse stories, set in Oxford.

dex·ter /ˈdekstər/ *adjective* esp. *Heraldry* on or of the right-hand side (the observer's left) of a shield etc. [Latin, = on the right]

dex·ter·ity /dekˈsterəti/ *noun* **1** manual or manipulative skill or adroitness; good physical coordination. **2** mental adroitness or skill; cleverness. [originally = 'right-handedness': French *dextérité* from Latin *dexteritas* (as DEXTER)]

dex·ter·ous /ˈdekstrəs/ *adjective* (also **dex·trous**) having or showing dexterity. □ **dex·ter·ous·ly** *adverb*

dex·tral /ˈdekstrəl/ ● *adjective* **1** (of a person) right-handed. **2** of or on the right. **3** *Zool.* (of a spiral shell) with whorls rising to the right and coiling in a counter-clockwise direction. ● *noun* a right-handed person. [medieval Latin *dextralis* from Latin *dextra* right hand]

dex·tran /ˈdekstran/ *noun Chem.* **1** an amorphous gum formed by the fermentation of sucrose etc. **2** a degraded form of this used as a substitute for blood plasma. [German (as DEXTRO- + -*an* as in chemical names)]

dextro- /ˈdekstroː/ *combining form* on or to the right (*dextrorotatory*; *dextrose*). [Latin *dexter*, *dextra*]

dextro·ampheta·mine /ˌdekstroːamˈfetəˌmiːn, -ˌmɪn/ *noun* an amphetamine used as a central nervous system stimulant.

dextro·meth·or·phan /ˌdekstroːˈmeθorfən/ *noun* (also **dextromethorphan hydro·bro·mide**) a cough suppressant acting by making the cough centre in the brain less sensitive to incoming stimuli. Abbr.: **DM**. [DEXTRO- + methoxy- + methylmorphinan]

dextro·rota·tory /ˌdekstroːroːˈteɪtəri/ *adjective Chem.* having the property of rotating the plane of a polarized light ray to the right (*compare* LEVOROTATORY). □ **dextro·rota·tion** *noun*

dex·trose /ˈdekstroːs, -oːz/ *noun* a dextrorotatory form of glucose. [formed as DEXTRO- + -OSE²]

dex·trous *var. of* DEXTEROUS.

DF *abbreviation Brit.* Defender of the Faith. [Latin *Defensor Fidei*]

df *abbreviation Statistics* degree of freedom.

DFC *abbreviation Brit.* Distinguished Flying Cross.

DFM *abbreviation Brit.* Distinguished Flying Medal.

DFO *abbreviation* (in Canada) Department of Fisheries and Oceans.

DG *abbreviation* **1** DEI GRATIA. **2** director general.

DH ● *noun Baseball* DESIGNATED HITTER. ● *verb Baseball* (**DHs, DHed**) **1** *intransitive* act as a designated hitter. **2** *transitive* use (a player) as a designated hitter (*the Jays DHed him last night*). ● *abbreviation Skiing* DOWNHILL.

Dhaka /ˈdakə/ (also **Dacca**) the capital of Bangladesh, on the Ganges delta; pop. (est. 2002) 8,539,500.

dhal /dɒl/ *var. of* DAL.

Dhan·bad /ˈdanbad/ a city in Bihar, NE India; pop. (2001) 1,064,357.

dhan·sak /ˈdansak/ *noun* (also **dan·sak**) a casserole of various meats and vegetables, a specialty of Parsi cuisine from western India. [Gujarati, from *dhan* 'wealth']

dhar·ma /ˈdarmə/ *noun* **1** (in Hinduism) the eternal law of the cosmos, inherent in the very nature of things, upheld (but neither created nor controlled) by the gods; in the context of individual action, it denotes the social rules codified in the law books. **2** (in Buddhism) the true doctrine as preached by the Buddha. **3** (in Jainism) **a** virtue. **b** a fundamental substance, the medium of motion. [Sanskrit, = decree, custom]

dhar·na /ˈdarnə, ˈdar-/ *noun* (also **dhur·na**) (in India) a method of compelling payment or compliance by sitting at the debtor's or offender's door without eating until the demand is complied with. [Hindi *dharnā* placing, act of sitting in restraint]

Dhar·uk /ˈdɑːrʊk/ noun an Aboriginal language of the area around Sydney, Australia, now extinct.

Dhaula·giri /ˌdaʊləˈɡiːri/ a mountain massif in the Himalayas, in Nepal, with six peaks, rising to 8 172 m (26,810 ft.) at its highest point.

dhobi /ˈdoːbi/ noun (pl. **dhobis**) (in the Indian subcontinent) a washerman or washerwoman. [Hindi *dhobī* from *dhob* washing]

dho·lak /ˈdoːlək/ noun a medium-sized barrel-shaped or cylindrical drum, usu. with two heads, used in the Indian subcontinent. [Hindi *dholak*]

dhoti /ˈdoːti/ noun (pl. **dhotis**) the loincloth worn by male Hindus. [Hindi *dhotī*]

dhow /daʊ/ noun a lateen-rigged Arab ship used on the E African, Arabian, and Indian coasts. [19th c.: origin unknown]

DHS abbreviation Cdn District High School.

dhur·ra var. of DURRA.

dhur·rie /ˈdʌri/ noun a rug of heavy cotton cloth, originally used in the Indian subcontinent. [Hindi *darī*]

DI abbreviation 1 Cdn Football DESIGNATED IMPORT. 2 US drill instructor. 3 Brit. Detective Inspector.

di-[1] combining form 1 twice, two-, double. 2 Chem. containing two atoms, molecules, or groups of a specified kind (*dichromatic*; *dioxide*). [Greek from *dis* twice]

di-[2] prefix form of DIS- occurring before *l*, *m*, *n*, *r*, *s* (foll. by a consonant), *v*, usu. *g*, and sometimes *j*. [Latin var. of *dis-*]

di-[3] prefix form of DIA- before a vowel.

DIA abbreviation (in the US) Defense Intelligence Agency.

dia. abbreviation diameter.

dia- /ˈdaɪə/ prefix (also **di-** before a vowel) 1 through (*diaphanous*). 2 apart (*diacritical*). 3 across (*diameter*). [Greek from *dia* through]

dia·base /ˈdaɪəbeɪs/ noun Geol. dolerite. [French, as if from DI-[1] + BASE[1], but associated with Greek *diabasis* 'transition']

dia·betes /ˌdaɪəˈbiːtiːz, -tɪs/ noun 1 any disorder of the metabolism characterized by excessive thirst and the production of large amounts of urine. 2 (in full **diabetes mel·li·tus**) the most common form of diabetes in which sugar and starch are not properly absorbed from the blood, characterized by thirst, emaciation, and excessive excretion of urine with glucose. [originally = siphon: Latin from Greek from *diabainō* go through]

diabetes in·sip·idus noun a metabolic disorder due to a pituitary deficiency, characterized by excessive urination and thirst.

dia·bet·ic /ˌdaɪəˈbetɪk/ ● adjective 1 of or relating to or having diabetes. 2 for use by diabetics. ● noun a person suffering from diabetes.

diab·lerie /diːˈɑːbləri, daɪ-/ noun 1 sorcery; witchcraft. 2 wild recklessness. 3 demonology. [French from *diable* from Latin *diabolus* DEVIL]

dia·bol·ic·al /ˌdaɪəˈbɒlɪkəl/ adjective (also **dia·bol·ic**) 1 of the Devil. 2 devilish; inhumanly cruel or wicked. 3 fiendishly clever or cunning or annoying. □ **dia·bol·ic·al·ly** adverb [Latin *diabolus* (as DEVIL)]

diab·ol·ism /daɪˈabəˌlɪzəm/ noun 1 a belief in or worship of the Devil. b sorcery. 2 devilish conduct or character. □ **diab·ol·ist** noun [Greek *diabolos* DEVIL]

diab·ol·ize /daɪˈabəˌlaɪz/ transitive verb (also esp. Brit. **-ise**) make into or represent as a devil.

diab·olo /diːˈabəloː, daɪ-/ noun (pl. **-olos**) 1 a game in which a two-headed top is thrown up and caught with a string stretched between two sticks. 2 the top itself. [Italian, = DEVIL: formerly called *devil on two sticks*]

dia·chron·ic /ˌdaɪəˈkrɒnɪk/ adjective Linguistics concerned with the historical development of a subject (esp. a language) (opp. SYNCHRONIC). □ **dia·chron·ic·ally** adverb **dia·chron·ous** /daɪˈakrənəs/ adjective **di·achrony** /daɪˈakrəni/ noun [French *diachronique* (as DIA-, CHRONIC)]

di·ac·onal /daɪˈakənəl, diː-/ adjective 1 of or pertaining to a deacon or deaconess. 2 of or relating to a diaconal minister. [ecclesiastical Latin *diaconalis* from *diaconus* DEACON]

diaconal minister noun Cdn (in Presbyterian and United churches) a layperson belonging to a religious order who is employed by a congregation or presbytery etc. to work with children, youth, the elderly, etc.

di·ac·on·ate /daɪˈakəˌneɪt, diː-, -ˌnət/ noun 1 a the office of deacon. b a person's time as deacon. 2 a body of deacons. [ecclesiastical Latin *diaconatus* (as DIACONAL)]

dia·crit·ic /ˌdaɪəˈkrɪtɪk/ ● noun a sign, e.g. an accent, diaeresis, cedilla, used to indicate different sounds or values of a letter. ● adjective = DIACRITICAL. [Greek *diakritikos* (as DIA-, CRITIC)]

dia·crit·ic·al noun (in full **diacritical mark** or **diacritical sign**) = DIACRITIC.

dia·dem /ˈdaɪəˌdem/ noun a crown or headband worn as a sign of sovereignty. [Latin *diadema* from Greek *diadēma* (as DIA-, *deō* bind)]

di·aer·esis /daɪˈɛrəsɪs/ noun (US **di·er·esis** /-ˌsiːz/) (pl. **-eses** /-ˌsiːz/) 1 a mark (¨) over a vowel to indicate that it is sounded separately. 2 Prosody a break where a foot ends at the end of a word. [Latin from Greek, = separation]

dia·gen·esis /ˌdaɪəˈdʒenəsɪs/ noun Geol. the transformation occurring during the conversion of sedimentation to sedimentary rock. □ **dia·gen·etic** adjective

Di·aghi·lev /diˈagɪˌlef/ **Ser·gei (Pav·lo·vich)** (1872–1929), Russian ballet impresario. Through his company the Ballets Russes (1909–29), he introduced Russian ballet to the West, transforming the European ballet scene into a creative centre for a large and varied array of artists.

diag·nose /ˌdaɪəɡˈnoːs, -ˈnoːz, ˈdaɪəɡˌnoːs, -ˌnoːz/ verb 1 transitive make a diagnosis of (a disease, a mechanical fault, etc.) from its symptoms. 2 intransitive identify or distinguish by diagnosis. □ **diag·nos·able** adjective

diag·no·sis noun (pl. **-ses**) 1 a the identification of an illness or disease by means of a patient's symptoms. b an instance or formal statement of this. 2 a conclusion reached from analysis of a problem or situation. 3 a the distinctive characterization in precise terms of a genus, species, etc. b an instance of this. [modern Latin from Greek (as DIA-, *gignōskō* recognize)]

diag·nos·tic ● adjective of or assisting diagnosis. ● noun a distinctive symptom or characteristic; a specific trait. □ **diag·nos·tic·ally** adverb **diag·nos·ti·cian** /-nɒˈstɪʃən/ noun [Greek *diagnōstikos* (as DIAGNOSIS)]

diag·nos·tics noun 1 (treated as pl.) Computing programs and other mechanisms used to detect and identify faults in hardware or software. 2 (treated as sing.) the science or study of diagnosing disease.

di·ag·on·al /daɪˈaɡənəl, -ˈaɡnəl/ ● adjective 1 crossing a straight-sided figure from corner to corner. 2 slanting; oblique. ● noun 1 a straight line joining two non-adjacent corners. 2 Chess a diagonal row of squares. □ **di·ag·on·al·ly** adverb [Latin *diagonalis* from Greek *diagōnios* (as DIA-, *gōnia* angle)]

dia·gram ● noun 1 a drawing showing the general scheme or outline of an object and its parts. 2 a graphic representation of the course or results of an action or process. 3 Math. a figure made of lines used in proving a theorem etc. ● transitive verb (**dia·grammed**, **dia·gram·ming**; US **dia·gramed**, **dia·gram·ing**) represent by means of a diagram. □ **dia·gram·mat·ic** adjective **dia·gram·mat·ic·ally** adverb [Latin *diagramma* from Greek (as DIA-, -GRAM)]

dia·kin·esis /ˌdaɪəkəˈniːsɪs, -kaɪ-/ noun (pl. **-eses** /-ˌsiːz/) Biol. a stage during the prophase of meiosis when the separation of homologous chromosomes is complete and crossing over has occurred. [modern Latin (as DIA-, Greek *kinēsis* motion)]

dial ● noun 1 the face of a clock or watch, marked to show the hours etc. 2 a similar flat plate marked with a scale for measuring weight, volume, pressure, consumption, etc., indicated by a pointer. 3 a movable disc on a telephone which is rotated for each digit of a number being called. 4 a a rotating knob or button on a radio or television set for selecting wavelength or channel. b a similar selecting device on other equipment, e.g. a washing machine. 5 television or radio broadcasting (*on the dial*). 6 Brit. slang a person's face. ● verb (**dialed**, **dial·ing**; **dialled**, **dial·ling**) 1 transitive & intransitive make a telephone call to (a person or number) (*dialled 911*). 2 transitive (often foll. by *up*) (of a modem) connect with (another modem). 3 transitive measure, indicate, or regulate by means of a dial. [Middle English, = sundial, from medieval Latin *diale* clock dial, ultimately from Latin *dies* day]

dia·lect noun 1 a form of speech peculiar to a particular region. 2 a subordinate variety of a language with non-standard vocabulary, pronunciation, or grammar. □ **dia·lect·al** adjective **dia·lect·o·logic·al** adjective **dia·lect·ol·ogy** noun **dia·lect·ol·o·gist** noun [Latin *dialectus* from Greek *dialektos* discourse, from *dialegomai* converse]

dia·lect·ic Philos. ● noun 1 a the art of critically investigating the truth of opinions; the testing of truth by discussion. b logical disputation or argument. 2 a the philosophy of metaphysical contradictions and their solutions, esp. in the thought of Kant and Hegel. b the existence or action of opposing forces or tendencies in

---

t top   v voice   w we   z zoo   ʃ she   ʒ vision   θ thin   ð this   ŋ ring   x loch   tʃ chip   dʒ jar   (see over for vowels)

society etc. ● *adjective* **1** of, pertaining to or of the nature of logical disputation. **2** fond of or skilled in logical disputation. [Latin *dialectica* from Greek *dialektikē (tekhnē)* (art) of debate (as DIALECT)]

dia·lect·ic·al *adjective* of dialectic or dialectics. □ **dia·lect·ic·al·ly** *adverb*

dialectical materialism *noun* the Marxist theory that political and historical events are due to a conflict of social forces caused by man's material needs.

dia·lect·ician *noun* a person skilled in dialectic.

dia·lect·ics *noun* (treated as *sing.* or *pl.*) = DIALECTIC *noun* 1.

dial·er *noun* (also **dial·ler**) **1** an electronic device which dials phone numbers automatically. **2** a person who dials a telephone.

dia·logic /ˌdaɪəˈlɒdʒɪk/ *adjective* (also **dia·logic·al**) of, pertaining to, or of the nature of dialogue.

dialo·gist /daɪˈæˈlədʒɪst/ *noun* a speaker in or writer of dialogue.

dia·logue (*US* also **dia·log**) ● *noun* **1 a** conversation between two or more people. **b** conversation in written form, esp. between characters in a novel, play etc. **2 a** discussion or diplomatic contact between representatives of different nations, blocs, etc. **b** the exchange of proposals, valuable or constructive communication, etc. between different groups (*dialogue between health care activists and the medical profession*). **3** a conversation; a talk (*long dialogues between the two main characters*). **4** a literary form in prose or verse based on a debate or discussion, usu. between two speakers. ● *intransitive verb* take part in a dialogue; converse. [Old French *dialoge* from Latin *dialogus* from Greek *dialogos* from *dialegomai* converse]

dialogue box *noun* (*US* also **dialog box**) a small area on a computer screen, usu. temporarily displayed, in which the user is prompted to provide information, select commands, etc.

dial tone *noun* (*Brit.* **dialling tone**) an uninterrupted telephone tone indicating that a caller may start to dial.

dial-up *adjective* pertaining to or designating a data transmission link that uses the telephone system (*dial-up access*).

di·aly·sis /daɪˈæləsɪs/ *noun* (*pl.* **-ses** /-ˌsiːz/) **1** *Chem.* the separation of particles in a liquid by differences in their ability to pass through a membrane into another liquid. **2** *Med.* the clinical purification of blood, e.g. of a person without adequately functioning kidneys, by this technique. □ **dia·lyt·ic** /ˌdaɪəˈlɪtɪk/ *adjective* [Latin from Greek *dialusis* (as DIA-, *luō* set free)]

dia·lyze /ˈdaɪəˌlaɪz/ *transitive verb* (also esp. *Brit.* **-lyse**) (usu. in *passive*) subject to dialysis. □ **dia·lyz·able** *adjective* **dia·lyz·er** *noun*

diam. *abbreviation* diameter.

dia·mag·net·ic /ˌdaɪəmæɡˈnetɪk/ *adjective* tending to become magnetized in a direction at right angles to the applied magnetic field. □ **dia·mag·net·ism** *noun*

dia·manté /ˌdiːəmɒnˈteɪ, ˌdaɪ-/ ● *adjective* decorated with powdered crystal, sequins, or another sparkling substance. ● *noun* fabric so decorated. [French, past participle of *diamanter* set with diamonds, from *diamant* DIAMOND]

dia·man·tine /ˌdaɪəˈmæntaɪn/ *adjective* of or like diamonds. [French *diamantin* from *diamant* DIAMOND)]

diam·eter *noun* **1 a** a straight line passing from side to side through the centre of a body or figure, esp. a circle or sphere. **b** the length of this line. **2** a transverse measurement; width, thickness. **3** a unit of linear measurement of magnifying power (*a lens magnifying 2000 diameters*). □ **diam·etral** *adjective* [Old French *diametre* from Latin *diametrus* from Greek *diametros (grammē)* (line) measuring across, from *metron* measure]

dia·met·ric·al *adjective* (also **dia·met·ric**) **1** of or along a diameter. **2** (of opposition, difference, etc.) complete, like that between opposite ends of a diameter. □ **dia·met·ric·al·ly** *adverb*

dia·mine /ˈdaɪəmiːn, daɪˈæmiːn/ *noun* a compound whose molecule contains two amino groups, esp. when joined to radicals other than acid radicals. [DI-¹ + AMINE]

dia·mond /ˈdaɪmənd, ˈdaɪə-/ ● *noun* **1 a** a usu. colourless or lightly tinted precious stone of great brilliance and hardness, used in jewellery and for cutting and abrading. **b** a piece of jewellery set with one or more diamonds (*wore her diamonds to the opera*). **2** a rhombus placed with its diagonals horizontal and vertical. **3** *Baseball* **a** the space delimited by the bases. **b** the entire field. **4 a** a playing card of a suit denoted by a red rhombus. **b** (in *pl.*) this suit. **5** a tool with a small diamond for glass cutting. ● *adjective* **1** made of or set with diamonds or a diamond. **2** rhombus-shaped. [Old French *diamant* from medieval Latin *diamas diamant-* var. of Latin *adamas* ADAMANT, from Greek]

diamond anniversary *noun* the 60th (or 75th) anniversary of a wedding, graduation, etc.

dia·mond·back *noun* **1** an edible freshwater terrapin, *Malaclemys terrapin*, native to N America, with diamond-shaped markings on its shell. **2** any rattlesnake of the genus *Crotalus*, native to N America, with diamond-shaped markings.

diamond drill ● *noun* a drill set with diamonds, used for boring rock and other hard surfaces. ● *transitive verb* excavate (an area) using a diamond drill. □ **diamond driller** *noun*

Diamond Head a volcanic crater overlooking the port of Honolulu on the Hawaiian island of Oahu.

dia·mond·if·er·ous /ˌdaɪmənˈdɪfərəs, ˌdaɪə-/ *adjective* yielding diamonds.

diamond in the rough *noun* N *Amer.* (also **rough diamond**) **1** an uncut diamond. **2** a person, place or thing of intrinsic but unrefined worth.

diamond jubilee *noun* the 60th (or 75th) anniversary of an event, esp. (**Diamond Jubilee**) the 60th anniversary of Queen Victoria's accession to the throne, in 1897.

diamond lane *noun* N *Amer.* a traffic lane reserved for buses or vehicles with several occupants and marked with large diamond shapes on the pavement.

diamond point *noun* **1** a bas-relief diamond motif often used to ornament furniture (also *attributive*: *diamond-point armoire*). **2** a diamond-tipped stylus used in engraving.

diamond willow *noun* N *Amer.* **1** a willow found across Canada with a diamond pattern in the bark and wood caused by fungi. **2** (often *attributive*) the timber from such a willow, used to make walking sticks, furniture, etc. *Also called* BEBB WILLOW, BEAKED WILLOW.

Diana ▸ **1** *Rom. Myth* an early Italian goddess identified with Artemis and associated with hunting, virginity, and, in later literature, with the moon. **2 Diana, Princess of Wales** (born Lady Diana Frances Spencer) (1961–97), wife of Prince Charles 1981–1996.

Dia·net·ics /ˌdaɪəˈnetɪks/ *noun* a system developed by the American founder of the Church of Scientology L. Ron Hubbard (1911–86) which aims to relieve psychosomatic disorder by a process of cleansing the mind of harmful mental images. [Greek *dianoētikos* from *dianoeisthai* think (as DIA- + *noein* think, suppose) + -ICS]

dian·thus /daɪˈænθəs/ *noun* any flowering plant of the genus *Dianthus*, e.g. a carnation or pink. [Greek *Dios* of Zeus + *anthos* flower]

dia·pa·son /ˌdaɪəˈpeɪzən, -ˈpeɪsən/ *noun Music* **1 a** a combination of notes or parts in a harmonious whole. **b** a melodious succession of notes, esp. a grand swelling burst of harmony. **2** the compass of a voice or musical instrument. **3** a fixed standard of musical pitch. **4** (in full **open diapason** or **stopped diapason**) either of two main organ stops extending through the organ's whole compass. [Middle English in sense 'octave' from Latin *diapason* from Greek *dia pasōn (khordōn)* through all (notes)]

dia·pause /ˈdaɪəˌpɔːz/ ● *noun* a period of retarded or suspended development in some insects. ● *intransitive verb* undergo or be in diapause.

dia·per /ˈdaɪpər, ˈdaɪə-/ ● *noun* **1** N *Amer.* a piece of folded cloth or disposable absorbent material wrapped around a baby's bottom to absorb and retain urine and feces. **2 a** a linen or cotton fabric with a small diamond pattern. **b** this pattern. **3** a similar ornamental design of diamonds etc. for panels, walls, etc. ● *transitive verb* **1** N *Amer.* put a diaper on (a baby). **2** decorate with a diaper pattern. [Old French *diapre* from medieval Latin *diasprum* from medieval Greek *diaspros* (adj.) (as DIA-, *aspros* white)]

diaper bag *noun* N *Amer.* a lightweight, usu. fabric bag for carrying diapers, baby clothes, bottles, ointment, etc.

diaper pail *noun* N *Amer.* a plastic pail for storing soiled cloth diapers until they can be laundered.

diaper rash *noun* N *Amer.* redness and irritation of a baby's skin around the genitals or buttocks, caused by persistent contact with wet diapers.

diaper service *noun* N *Amer.* a business which supplies and launders diapers.

di·aph·an·ous /daɪˈæfənəs/ *adjective* **1** (of fabric etc.) light and delicate, and almost transparent. **2** vague; amorphous. [medieval Latin *diaphanus* from Greek *diaphanes* (as DIA-, *phainō* show)]

dia·phor·esis /ˌdaɪəfəˈriːsɪs/ *noun Med.* sweating, esp. artificially induced. [Late Latin from Greek from *diaphoreō* carry through]

dia·phor·et·ic /ˌdaɪəfəˈretɪk/ ● *adjective* relating to or inducing perspiration. ● *noun* an agent inducing perspiration. [Late Latin *diaphoreticus* from Greek *diaphorētikos* (formed as DIAPHORESIS)]

dia·phragm /'daɪəˌfram/ *noun* **1** (in mammals) a muscular, dome-shaped partition which separates the thorax from the abdomen, and whose contraction leads to expansion of the lungs in respiration. **2** a thin, dome-shaped device of rubber placed over the cervix before intercourse to prevent conception. **3** a vibrating disc or cone producing sound waves, e.g. in telephone receivers, loudspeakers, etc. **4** a thin sheet of material used as a partition, esp. in a tube or pipe. **5** a device for varying the effective aperture of the lens in a camera etc. **6** a partition in animal and plant tissues. □ **dia·phrag·mat·ic** /-frag'matɪk/ *adjective* [Late Latin *diaphragma* from Greek (as DIA-, *phragma -atos* from *phrassō* fence in)]

diaphragm pump *noun* a pump using a flexible diaphragm in place of a piston.

dia·pir /'daɪəpiːr/ *noun* Geol. an anticline in which the upper strata are pierced by a rock core from below. □ **dia·pir·ic** /-'pɪːrɪk/ *adjective* **dia·pir·ism** *noun* [Greek *diapeirainein* 'pierce through']

di·archy /'daɪɑrki/ *noun* (also **dy·archy**) (*pl.* **-ies**) **1** government by two independent authorities (esp. in India 1921–37). **2** an instance of this. [DI-1 + Greek *-arkhia* rule, after *monarchy*]

diar·ist /'daɪərɪst/ *noun* a person who keeps a diary. □ **diar·is·tic** *adjective*

diar·rhea /ˌdaɪə'riːə/ *noun* (also esp. Brit. **diar·rhoea**) **1** a condition of excessively frequent and loose bowel movements. **2** watery or semi-liquid feces characteristic of this condition. □ **diar·rheal** *adjective* [Late Latin from Greek *diarrhoia* (as DIA-, *rheō* flow)]

diary *noun* (*pl.* **-ies**) **1** a daily written record of events, feelings, or thoughts. **2** a book for this or for noting future engagements, usu. printed and with a calendar and other information. [Latin *diarium* from *dies* day]

Dias /'diːəs/ **Bar·tolo·meu** (also **Díaz**) (c.1450–1500), Portuguese navigator and explorer, the first European to discover the sea route from the Atlantic to Asia via the Cape of Good Hope (1488).

Di·as·pora /daɪ'asporə/ *noun* (also **Dispersion**; prec. by *the*) **a** the dispersion of the Jews among the Gentiles mainly in the 8th–6th c. BC. **b** Jews dispersed in this way. **c** (also *attributive*) Jews or Jewish communities outside the state of Israel. **2** (also **diaspora**) **a** any group of people similarly dispersed. **b** their dispersion. □ **dias·poric** /daɪə'sporɪk/ *adjective* **di·as·por·ist** *noun* [Greek from *diaspeirō* (as DIA-, *speirō* scatter)]

dia·stase /'daɪəˌsteɪz/ *noun* Biochem. an amylase, esp. one that breaks down starch into maltose and is present in seeds and the pancreas. □ **dia·stat·ic** /-'statɪk/ *adjective* [French from Greek *diastasis* separation (as DIA-, *stasis* placing)]

dia·stole /'daɪˈastəli/ *noun* Physiol. the period between two contractions of the heart when the heart muscle relaxes and allows the chambers to fill with blood (compare SYSTOLE). □ **dia·stol·ic** /ˌdaɪə'stɒlɪk/ *adjective* [Late Latin from Greek *diastellō* (as DIA-, *stellō* place)]

dia·thermy /'daɪəˌθɜrmi/ *noun* the application of high-frequency electric currents to produce heat in the deeper tissues of the body, used during some surgical procedures and to treat arthritis, bursitis, fractures, etc. [German *Diathermie* from Greek *dia* through + *thermon* heat]

diath·esis /daɪ'aθəsɪs/ *noun* Med. a constitutional predisposition to a particular disease or condition. [modern Latin from Greek from *diatithēmi* arrange]

dia·tom /'daɪətəm/ *noun* a microscopic unicellular alga with a siliceous cell wall, found as plankton and forming fossil deposits. [modern Latin *Diatoma* (genus name) from Greek *diatomos* (as DIA-, *temnō* cut)]

dia·tom·aceous earth /daɪətə'meɪʃəs/ *noun* a soft, fine-grained deposit composed of fossil diatoms, used as a filter, filler, insulator, etc., in various manufacturing processes, and as an insecticide in gardening applications. [DIATOM + -ACEOUS]

dia·tom·ic /ˌdaɪə'tɒmɪk/ *adjective* consisting of two atoms.

di·atom·ite /daɪ'atəˌmaɪt/ *noun* a sedimentary rock composed of the siliceous skeletons of diatoms.

dia·ton·ic /ˌdaɪə'tɒnɪk/ *adjective* Music **1** (of a scale, interval, etc.) involving only notes proper to the prevailing key without chromatic alteration. **2** (of a melody or harmony) constructed from such a scale. [Late Latin *diatonicus* from Greek *diatonikos* at intervals of a tone (as DIA-, TONIC)]

dia·tribe /'daɪəˌtraɪb/ *noun* a forceful verbal attack; a piece of bitter criticism. [French from Latin *diatriba* from Greek *diatribē* spending of time, discourse, from *diatribō* (as DIA-, *tribō* rub)]

Díaz /'diːəs/ **1 Bar·tolo·meu**, var. of DIAS. **2 Por·firio** (1830–1915), Mexican general and political leader, president 1877–80 and 1884–1911, who promoted the development of Mexico's infrastructure and industry.

Díaz de Vivar /'diːɒθ de viː'vɑr/ **Rod·rigo**, see CID, EL.

di·aze·pam /daɪ'azəˌpam/ *noun* a tranquilizing muscle-relaxant drug with anticonvulsant properties used to relieve anxiety, tension, etc. (compare VALIUM). [benzodiazepine + am]

di·az·inon /daɪ'azɪnɒn/ *noun* an organophosphorous insecticide derived from pyrimidine. [DI-1 + AZINE + -ON]

diazo /daɪ'azo/ *noun* a copying or colouring process using a diazo compound decomposed by light. [DI-1 + AZO-]

diazo- /daɪ'azo/ *combining form* indicating the presence of two nitrogen atoms joined to one carbon atom. [DI-1 + AZO-]

diazo compound *noun* a chemical compound containing two usu. multiply-bonded nitrogen atoms, often highly coloured and used as dyes.

di·basic /daɪ'beɪsɪk/ *adjective* Chem. having two replaceable hydrogen atoms. [DI-1 + BASE1 6]

dib·ber *noun* a hand-held tool with a pointed end, used for making holes in the ground for seeds or young plants. [Middle English *dib*, var. of DAB1]

dib·ble *noun* = DIBBER.

d'Iber·ville /'diːbervɪl/ **Pierre Le Moyne** (full surname d'Iberville et d'Ardillières) (1661–1706), French-Canadian soldier, explorer, and colonial administrator. He made numerous successful raids against English forts and trading posts, esp. on James Bay and Hudson Bay (1686–97), and established settlements in Louisiana (1699–1702).

dibs *plural noun* N Amer. slang a first claim or option to use or have something (*I have dibs on that book when it is returned*). [earlier sense 'pebbles for game', also *dib-stones*]

dice ● *plural noun* **1 a** small cubes usu. made of plastic or wood, marked on each side with 1–6 spots, used in games and gambling. **b** (treated as *sing.*) one of these cubes (see DIE2). **2** a game played with one or more such cubes. **3** food cut into small cubes for cooking. ● *verb* **1** transitive cut (food) into small cubes. **2 a** intransitive play or gamble with dice. **b** intransitive take great risks, gamble (*dicing with death*). □ **no dice** slang no success or luck (*I tried to make him talk, but no dice*). [pl. of DIE2]

dicer *noun* **1** a manual or electrical appliance for dicing vegetables etc. **2** a person who plays or gambles with dice.

dicey *adjective* (**dicier**, **diciest**) slang risky; uncertain. [DICE + -Y1]

di·chot·omy /daɪ'kɒtəmi/ *noun* (*pl.* **-ies**) **1 a** a division into two, esp. a sharply defined one. **b** the result of such a division (*the dichotomy between the rich and the poor*). **2** binary classification. **3** Bot. & Zool. repeated bifurcation. □ **di·chot·om·ize** *verb*

di·chot·om·ous *adjective* [modern Latin *dichotomia* from Greek *dikhotomia* from *dikho-* apart + -TOMY]

di·chro·ic /daɪ'kroːɪk/ *adjective* (esp. of doubly refracting crystals) showing two colours. □ **di·chro·ism** *noun* [Greek *dikhroos* (as DI-1, *khrōs* colour)]

di·chro·matic /ˌdaɪkroː'matɪk/ *adjective* **1** two-coloured. **2** (of animal species) having individuals that show different colorations. **3** having vision sensitive to only two of the three primary colours.

□ **di·chro·ma·tism** /daɪ'kroːməˌtɪzəm/ *noun* [DI-1 + Greek *khrōmatikos* from *khrōma -atos* colour]

dick1 ● *noun* **1** coarse slang **a** the penis. ¶ Usually considered a taboo word. **b** a stupid, annoying boy or man; a jerk. **2** coarse slang very little; nothing (*I know dick about that*). **3** Brit. informal (in certain set phrases) fellow; person (*clever dick*). ● *intransitive verb* N Amer. coarse slang (often foll. by *around*) waste time; fool around. [pet form of the name *Richard*]

dick2 *noun* esp. N Amer. slang a detective. [perhaps abbreviation]

Dick·ens, Charles (John Huf·fam) (pseudonym 'Boz') (1812–70), English novelist. His novels are broad in scope and particularly notable for their treatment of contemporary social injustices; they include *Oliver Twist* (1837–8), *Bleak House* (1852–3), *A Tale of Two Cities* (1859), and *Great Expectations* (1860–1).

dick·ens *noun* (usu. prec. by *how, what, why*, etc., *the*) informal (esp. in exclamations) deuce; the Devil (*what the dickens are you doing here?*). [16th c.: prob. a use of the surname *Dickens*]

Dick·ens·ian /də'kenziən/ ● *adjective* **1** of or relating to Charles Dickens or his work. **2** resembling or reminiscent of the situations, poor social conditions, or comically repulsive characters described in Dickens's work. ● *noun* an admirer or student of Dickens or his work. □ **Dick·ens·ian·ly** *adverb*

dick·er esp. *N Amer.* ● *intransitive verb* bargain; haggle (*dickered with the saleswoman for a better price*). ● *noun* a deal, a barter. [perhaps from *dicker* set of ten (hides), as a unit of trade]

Dick·ey, Rob·ert Barry (1811–1903), Canadian politician, Father of Confederation. He sat on the legislative council of Nova Scotia (1858–67), and was a delegate to the Charlottetown and Quebec Conferences.

dick·ey *noun* **1** (also **dicky**) a small extra folding seat at the back of some old-fashioned two-seater cars. **2** *var. of* DICKIE 1. [from *Dicky* (as DICK[1])]

dick·head *noun coarse slang* a stupid or obnoxious person, esp. a man; an idiot. [DICK[1]]

dick·ie *noun* (*pl.* **-ies** or **-eys**) **1** (also **dick·ey**) a false shirt front. **2** (in full **dickie-bow**) *Brit.* a bow tie.

Dick·in·son /ˈdɪkənsən/ **Emily (Eliza·beth)** (1830–86), US poet, a recluse from the age of 24. Her withdrawal and inner struggle are reflected in her mystical lyric poems, expressed in her own elliptical language.

dicky *adjective* (**dick·i·er**, **dick·i·est**) *Brit. slang* unsound; likely to collapse or fail. [19th c.: perhaps from 'as queer as Dick's hatband']

dicky-bird *noun* (also **dickey-bird**, **dickie-bird**) **1** a child's word for a little bird. **2** *Brit. rhyming slang* a word (*I haven't heard a dicky-bird from anyone*).

dicot /ˈdaɪkɒt/ *noun* = DICOTYLEDON. [abbreviation]

di·coty·ledon /ˌdaɪkɒtəˈliːdən/ *noun* any flowering plant having two cotyledons. □ **di·coty·ledon·ous** *adjective*

dicta *pl.* of DICTUM.

Dicta·phone /ˈdɪktəˌfoʊn/ *noun proprietary* a machine for recording and playing back dictated words. [DICTATE + PHONE[1]]

dic·tate ● *verb* **1** *transitive* say or read aloud (words to be written down or recorded). **2** tell someone what to do, esp. with no consideration for their wishes (*the czar's attempts to dictate policy; I will not be dictated to*). **3** control or influence how something happens (*it's generally your job that dictates where you live; we can make changes as circumstances dictate*). ● *noun* (usu. in *pl.*) an order, rule, or command that must be obeyed (*dictates of conscience; the dictates of fashion*). [Latin *dictare dictat-* frequentative of *dicere dict-* say]

dic·ta·tion *noun* **1 a** the saying of words to be written down or recorded (*does your secretary take dictation?*). **b** the activity of taking down a passage that is read aloud by a teacher as a test of spelling, writing, or language skills (*always hated French dictations*). **c** the material that is dictated. **2** the action of giving orders authoritatively or categorically.

dic·ta·tor *noun* **1** a ruler with unrestricted authority, esp. one who suppresses or succeeds a democratic government. **2** a person with supreme authority in any sphere. **3** a domineering person. **4** *Rom. Hist.* a chief magistrate with absolute power, appointed in an emergency.

dic·ta·tor·ial /ˌdɪktəˈtɔːriəl/ *adjective* **1** of or like a dictator. **2** imperious; overbearing. □ **dic·ta·tor·ial·ly** *adverb*

dic·ta·tor·ship *noun* **1** a state ruled by a dictator. **2 a** the position, rule, or period of rule of a dictator. **b** rule by a dictator.

dic·tion *noun* **1** the manner of enunciation in speaking or singing. **2** the choice of words or phrases in speech or writing. [French *diction* or Latin *dictio* from *dicere dict-* say]

dic·tion·ary *noun* (*pl.* **-ies**) **1 a** a book that lists (usu. in alphabetical order) and explains the words of a language or gives equivalent words in another language. **b** a similar reference published online or on CD-ROM or loaded onto the hard drive of a computer. **2** a reference book on any subject, the items of which are arranged in alphabetical order (*dictionary of architecture*). **3** an ordered list stored in and used by a computer, esp. a list of words acceptable to a spell-checker, against which each word of a text is checked. [medieval Latin *dictionarium* (*manuale* manual) & *dictionarius* (*liber* book) from Latin *dictio* (as DICTION)]

dic·tum /ˈdɪktəm/ *noun* (*pl.* **dicta** /-tə/ or **dic·tums**) **1** a formal utterance or pronouncement. **2** a saying or maxim. **3** *Law* = OBITER DICTUM. [Latin, = neuter past participle of *dicere* say]

dicty *adjective US Black slang* **1** conceited; snobbish. **2** elegant; stylish (*a dicty neighbourhood*). [20th c.: origin unknown]

did *past of* DO[1].

di·dac·tic /daɪˈdaktɪk, də-/ *adjective* **1** meant to instruct (*didactic poetry*). **2** (of a person) tediously pedantic. □ **di·dac·tic·ally** *adverb* **di·dac·ti·cism** *noun* [Greek *didaktikos* from *didaskō* teach]

did·dle *verb informal* **1** *transitive* cheat, swindle. **2** *transitive* have sexual intercourse with (a person). **3** *intransitive* (often foll. by *with*) adjust; toy with (*diddled with the controls*). **4** *intransitive N Amer.* waste time. □ **did·dler** *noun* [19th c.: probably from the name of Jeremy *Diddler*, a character in the farce *Raising the Wind* (1803) by Irish dramatist James Kenney (d.1849), who constantly borrowed and failed to pay small sums of money: the name may have been based on an earlier verb *diddle* walk unsteadily, swerve]

did·dly *noun* (also **did·dley**) = DIDDLY-SQUAT.

diddly-squat *noun* (also **diddley-squat**, **doodly-squat**) *N Amer. slang* **1** (with *neg.*) anything, the least bit (*doesn't mean diddly-squat to me*). **2** nothing at all. [variant of DOODLY-SQUAT, prob. from US slang *doodle* 'excrement' + *squat* 'to void excrement']

did·dums *interjection Brit.* expressing commiseration esp. to a child. [= *did 'em*, i.e. did they (tease you etc.)?]

Di·derot /ˈdiːdəˌroʊ/ **Denis** (1713–84), French philosopher, writer, and critic. A leading figure of the Enlightenment, he was chief editor (1745–72) of the *Encyclopédie* (1751–76), through which he disseminated and popularized philosophy and scientific knowledge.

didger·idoo /ˌdɪdʒəriˈduː/ *noun* (also **didjer·idoo**) a tubular wooden wind instrument of Australian Aboriginal origin, producing a low-pitched, resonant sound. [imitative]

didn't *contraction* did not.

Dido /ˈdaɪdoʊ/ (in Virgil's *Aeneid*) the founder and queen of Carthage, who fell in love with the shipwrecked Aeneas and killed herself when he deserted her.

dido /ˈdaɪdoʊ/ *noun* (*pl.* **didoes** or **didos**) *N Amer. informal* an antic, a caper, a prank. □ **cut** (or **cut up**) **didoes** play pranks. [19th c.: origin unknown]

didst *archaic 2nd sing. past of* DO[1].

Didy·ma /ˈdɪdɪmə/ an ancient sanctuary of Apollo, site of one of the most famous oracles of the Aegean region, close to the west coast of Asia Minor.

di·dym·ium /dɪˈdɪmiəm/ *noun* a mixture of praseodymium and neodymium, originally regarded as an element. [modern Latin from Greek *didumos* twin (from being closely associated with lanthanum)]

die[1] *verb* (**dies**, **died**, **dying**) **1** *intransitive* (often foll. by *of*) (of a person, animal, or plant) cease to live; expire, lose vital force (*died of hunger*). **2** *intransitive* **a** come to an end, cease to exist, fade away (*the project died within six months*). **b** cease to function; break down (*the engine died*). **c** (of a flame) go out. **3** *intransitive* (foll. by *on*) die or cease to function while in the presence or charge of (a person). **4** *intransitive* (usu. foll. by *of, from, with*) be exhausted or tormented (*nearly died of boredom; was dying from the heat*). **5** *intransitive informal* be overcome with embarrassment, laughter, etc. (*nearly died when she said that*). **6** *transitive* suffer (a specified death) (*died a natural death*). □ **be dying** (foll. by *for*, or *to* + infin.) wish for longingly or intently (*was dying for a drink; am dying to see you*). **die away** become weaker or fainter to the point of extinction. **die back** (of a plant) decay from the tip towards the root. **died and gone to heaven** *informal* having reached a state of supreme bliss. **die down** become less loud or strong. **die hard** die reluctantly, not without a struggle (*old habits die hard*). **die off 1** die one after another until few or none are left. **2** fade away gradually. **die out** become extinct, cease to exist. **never say die** keep up courage, not give in. **to die for** (*predicative*) *informal* extremely good or desirable (*chocolate to die for*). [prob. from Old Norse *deyja* from Germanic]

die[2] *noun* **1** *sing.* of DICE *noun* 1a. ¶ *Dice* is now standard in general use in this sense. **2** (*pl.* **dies**) **a** an engraved device for stamping a design on coins, medals, etc. **b** a device for stamping, cutting, or moulding material into a particular shape. **c** an internally threaded hollow tool for cutting a screw thread. **3** (*pl.* **dice**) *Archit.* the cubical part of a pedestal between the base and the cornice; a dado or plinth. □ **as straight** (or **true**) **as a die 1** quite straight. **2** entirely honest or loyal. **the die is cast** an irrevocable step has been taken. [Old French *de* from Latin *datum* neuter past participle of *dare* give, play]

die·back *noun* the progressive dying back of a shrub or tree shoot owing to disease or unfavourable conditions.

die-casting *noun* the process or product of casting from metal moulds. □ **die-cast** *transitive verb*

Dief·en·baker /ˈdiːfənˌbeɪkər/ **John (George)** (1895–1979), Canadian lawyer and politician, Progressive Conservative prime minister 1957–63. Known as an impassioned orator, populist, and champion of civil liberties, he introduced the Canadian Bill of Rights (1960).

Diefenbaker, Lake a reservoir in south central Saskatchewan, a widening of the South Saskatchewan River, situated south of Saskatoon. Created in 1958 as a result of the construction of two dams,

---

Consonants: b *but*   d *dog*   f *few*   g *get*   h *her*   j *yes*   k *cat*   l *leg*   m *man*   n *no*   p *pen*   r *red*   s *sit*

its waters are used for hydroelectric power, irrigation, and recreation. [DIEFENBAKER]

dief·fen·bachia /ˌdiːfənˈbakiə/ *noun* any tropical American evergreen plant of the genus *Dieffenbachia*, of the arum family, often grown as a houseplant and having poisonous sap which can cause loss of the power of speech or death. *Also called* DUMB CANE. [E. *Dieffenbach*, German naturalist d.1855]

Diego Gar·cia /diˌeigoː ɡɑrˈsiːə/ the largest island of the Chagos Archipelago in the middle of the Indian Ocean, site of a strategic Anglo-American naval base established in 1973.

die·hard ● *noun* a conservative or stubborn person. ● *adjective* **1** resolutely opposing change. **2** staunchly loyal (*a diehard fan*).

die-in *noun informal* a demonstration in which people lie down as if dead (*held a die-in to protest the arms race*).

di·el·drin /diˈeldrɪn/ *noun* a crystalline insecticide produced by the oxidation of aldrin. [O. *Diels*, German chemist d.1954 + ALDRIN]

di·elec·tric /ˌdaiəˈlektrɪk/ *Electricity* ● *noun* an insulating medium or substance. [DI-³ + ELECTRIC = through which electricity is transmitted (without conduction)]

dielectric constant *noun Electricity* permittivity.

Dien Bien Phu /ˌdjen bjen ˈfuː/ a village in NW Vietnam, in 1954 the site of a French military post which was captured by the Vietminh after a 55-day siege.

di·ene /ˈdaiiːn/ *noun* any organic compound possessing two double bonds between carbon atoms. [DI-¹ + -ENE]

die-off *noun* a sudden, sharp decline in a natural population, due to some factor other than human intervention.

Di·eppe /diˈep/ **1** a channel port in N France; pop. (1999) 34,700. In August 1942, during the Second World War, it was the scene of an amphibious raid by a joint force of 5,000 Canadian and 1,000 British troops to destroy the German-held port and airfield. The raid ended disastrously, with two-thirds of the Allied troops being killed, wounded, or taken prisoner. **2** a town in E New Brunswick, just outside Moncton; pop. (2001) 14,951.

di·er·esis *US var. of* DIAERESIS.

Diesel /ˈdiːzəl/ **Ru·dolf (Chris·tian Karl)** (1858–1913), German engineer, who invented and patented (1892) the internal combustion engine named after him.

diesel /ˈdiːzəl/ *noun* **1** (in full **diesel engine**) an internal combustion engine in which the heat produced by the compression of air in the cylinder ignites the fuel. **2** a vehicle driven by a diesel engine. **3** = DIESEL FUEL. □ **diesel·ize** *transitive verb* (also esp. *Brit.* **-ise**).

diesel·iz·a·tion *noun* [DIESEL]

diesel-electric ● *noun* a vehicle driven by the electric current produced by a diesel-engined generator. ● *adjective* of or powered by this means.

diesel fuel *noun* (also **diesel oil**) a heavy petroleum fraction used as fuel in diesel engines.

diesel·ling *noun N Amer.* (also **diesel·ing**) the continued operation of an internal combustion engine after the ignition has been shut off.

Dies irae /ˌdiːes ˈiːrei/ *noun* a Latin hymn frequently sung as part of a Requiem Mass. [Latin (its first words), = day of wrath]

die stamp·ing *noun* embossing paper etc. with a die. □ **die stamped** *adjective*

diet¹ *noun* **1** the kinds of food that a person or animal habitually eats. **2** a special course of food to which a person is restricted, esp. for medical reasons or to control weight. **3** a regular occupation or series of activities to which one is restricted or which form one's main concern, for a purpose (*a diet of light reading and fresh air*). ● *verb* (**diet·ed, diet·ing**) **1** *intransitive* restrict oneself to small amounts or special kinds of food, esp. to control one's weight. **2** *transitive* restrict (a person or animal) to a special diet. ● *adjective* suitable for consumption by someone on a special (esp. calorie-reduced) diet (*bought some diet pop*). □ **diet·er** *noun* [Old French *diete* (n.), *dieter* (v.) from Latin *diaeta* from Greek *diaita* a way of life]

diet² *noun* **1** a legislative assembly in certain countries, e.g. Japan. **2** *hist.* a national or international conference, esp. of a federation or confederation. [medieval Latin *dieta* day's work, wages, etc.]

diet·ary *adjective* of, relating to, or provided by diet. [medieval Latin *dietarium* (as DIET¹)]

dietary fibre *noun* the part of a foodstuff that cannot be digested or absorbed; roughage.

diet·etic /ˌdaiəˈtetɪk/ *adjective* **1** of or relating to diet. **2** (of foodstuffs, etc.) suitable for a specific (esp. calorie-reduced) diet (*dietetic candies*).

□ **diet·etic·ally** *adverb* [Latin *dieteticus* from Greek *diaitētikos* (as DIET¹)]

diet·et·ics *plural noun* (usu. treated as *sing.*) the scientific study of diet and nutrition.

di·ethyl ether /daiˈeθəl, daiˈiːθail/ *noun Chem.* = ETHER 1.

di·ethyl·stil·bes·trol /daiˈeθəlstɪlˌbestrɒl/ *noun* a powerful synthetic estrogen formerly used to prevent miscarriage, withdrawn from use because of carcinogenic effects on offspring. Abbr.: **DES**.

diet·itian /ˌdaiəˈtɪʃən/ *noun* (also **diet·ician**) an expert in dietetics.

Diet of Worms a meeting of Charles V's imperial Diet at Worms in 1521, at which Martin Luther committed himself to the cause of Protestant reform; on the last day of the Diet his teaching was formally condemned in the **Edict of Worms**.

diet pill *noun* a medication prescribed as an aid in weight loss, esp. an amphetamine which acts as an appetite suppressant.

Diet·rich /ˈdiːtrɪx/ **Mar·lene** (born Maria Magdelene von Losch) (1901–92), German-born US actress and singer, known for her glamorous roles in film and as an international cabaret star; her films include *The Blue Angel* (1930), *The Devil is a Woman* (1935), and *Judgment at Nuremberg* (1961).

dif- /dɪf/ *prefix* assimilated form of DIS- before *f*. [Latin var. of DIS-]

diff *noun N Amer. informal* difference (*what's the diff?*). [abbreviation]

dif·fer *intransitive verb* **1** (often foll. by *from*) be unlike or distinguishable. **2** (often foll. by *with*) disagree; be at variance (with a person). □ **dif·fer·ing** *adjective* [Old French *differer* from Latin *differre*, differ, DEFER¹, (as DIS-, *ferre* bear, tend)]

dif·fer·ence *noun* **1** the state or condition of being different or unlike. **2** a point in which things differ; a distinction. **3** a degree of unlikeness. **4 a** the quantity by which amounts differ; a deficit (*will have to make up the difference*). **b** the remainder left after subtraction. **5 a** a disagreement, quarrel, or dispute. **b** the grounds of disagreement (*put aside their differences*). **6** *Heraldry* an alteration in a coat of arms distinguishing members of a family. □ **make a** (or **all the** etc.) **difference** (often foll. by *to*) have a significant effect or influence (on a person, situation, etc.). **make no difference** (often foll. by *to*) have no effect (on a person, situation, etc.). **split the difference** *see* SPLIT. **with a difference** having a new or unusual feature.

dif·fer·ent *adjective* **1** (often foll. by *from, than*) unlike, distinguishable in nature, form, or quality (from another). ¶ *Different from* is generally regarded as the most acceptable collocation, but *than* is well established, esp. when followed by a clause, e.g. *I am a different person than I was a year ago*. The usage *different to*, though common in the UK, is found infrequently in Canadian English. **2** distinct, separate; not the same one (as another). **3** *informal* unusual (*wanted to do something different*). □ **dif·fer·ent·ly** *adverb* **dif·fer·ent·ness** *noun*

dif·fer·en·tia /ˌdɪfəˈrenʃiə/ *noun* (*pl.* **dif·fer·en·tiae** /-ʃɪˌiː/) a distinguishing mark, esp. between species within a genus. [Latin: see DIFFERENCE]

dif·fer·en·tial ● *adjective* **1** of, showing, or depending on a difference; varying according to circumstances or relevant factors (*the differential achievements of boys and girls*). **2** *Math.* relating to infinitesimal differences. **3** constituting a specific difference; distinctive; relating to specific differences (*differential diagnosis*). **4** *Physics & Mech.* concerning the difference of two or more motions, pressures, etc. ● *noun* **1** a difference between individuals or examples of the same kind. **2** a difference in wage or salary between industries or categories of employees in the same industry. **3** a difference between rates of interest etc. **4** *Math.* **a** an infinitesimal difference between successive values of a variable. **b** a function expressing this as a rate of change with respect to another variable. **5** (in full **differential gear**) a gear allowing power to be divided between two axles in line with one another and able to rotate at different speeds, e.g. when a vehicle corners. □ **dif·fer·en·tial·ly** *adverb* [medieval & modern Latin *differentialis* (as DIFFERENCE)]

differential calculus *noun* the part of calculus that deals with derivatives and differentiation (*compare* INTEGRAL CALCULUS).

differential equation *noun* an equation involving differentials among its quantities.

dif·fer·en·ti·ate *verb* **1** *transitive* constitute a difference between or in. **2 a** *transitive* find differences (between). **b** *intransitive* (often foll. by *between*) find differences; discriminate. **3** *transitive & intransitive* make or become different in the process of growth or development. **4** *transitive Math.* transform (a function) into its derivative. □ **dif·fer·en·ti·able** *adjective* **dif·fer·en·ti·at·ed** *adjective* **dif·fer·en·ti·a·tion** *noun*

t top   v voice   w we   z zoo   ʃ she   ʒ vision   θ thin   ð this   ŋ ring   x loch   tʃ chip   dʒ jar   (see over for vowels)

dif·fer·en·ti·ator noun [medieval Latin differentiare differentiat- (as DIFFERENCE)]

differently abled adjective euphemism disabled.

dif·fi·cult adjective **1 a** needing much effort or skill. **b** troublesome, perplexing. **2 a** not easy to please or satisfy. **b** uncooperative, troublesome. **3** characterized by hardships or problems (a difficult period in her life). □ **dif·fi·cult·ly** adverb **dif·fi·cult·ness** noun [Middle English, back-formation from DIFFICULTY]

dif·fi·culty noun (pl. **-ties**) **1** the state or condition of being difficult. **2 a** a difficult thing; a problem or hindrance. **b** (often in pl.) a cause of distress or hardship (in financial difficulties). □ **make difficulties** be intransigent or unaccommodating. **with difficulty** not easily. [Latin difficultas (as DIS-, facultas FACULTY)]

dif·fi·dent adjective **1** shy, lacking self-confidence. **2** hesitant or reserved. □ **dif·fi·dence** noun **dif·fi·dent·ly** adverb [Latin diffidere (as DIS-, fidere trust)]

dif·fract /dɪˈfrakt/ transitive verb Physics (of the edge of an opaque body, a narrow slit, etc.) break up (a beam of light) into a series of dark or light bands or coloured spectra, or (a beam of radiation or particles) into a series of alternately high and low intensities. □ **dif·frac·tion** noun **dif·frac·tive** adjective [Latin diffringere diffract- (as DIS-, frangere break)]

dif·fract·om·eter /ˌdɪfrakˈtɒmətər/ noun an instrument for measuring diffraction, esp. in crystallographic work.

dif·fuse ● adjective /dɪˈfjuːs/ **1** (of light, inflammation, etc.) spread out, diffused, not concentrated. **2** (of prose, speech, etc.) not concise; long-winded, verbose. ● transitive & intransitive verb /dɪˈfjuːz/ **1** disperse or be dispersed from a centre. **2** spread or be spread widely; reach a large area. **3** Physics (esp. of fluids) intermingle by diffusion. □ **dif·fused** adjective **dif·fuse·ly** /dɪˈfjuːsli/ adverb **dif·fuse·ness** /dɪˈfjuːsnəs/ noun **dif·fus·ible** /dɪˈfjuːzɪbəl/ adjective **dif·fu·sive** /dɪˈfjuːsɪv/ adjective [Latin diffusus extensive (as DIS-, fusus past participle of fundere pour)]

dif·fus·er /dɪˈfjuːzər/ noun (also **dif·fus·or**) **1** a person or thing that diffuses, esp. a device for diffusing light. **2** a duct for broadening an airflow and reducing its speed.

dif·fu·sion /dɪˈfjuːʒən/ noun **1** the act or an instance of diffusing; the process of being diffused. **2** Physics & Chem. the interpenetration of substances by the natural movement of their particles. **3** the spread of elements of culture etc. to another region or people. [Latin diffusio (as DIFFUSE)]

dif·fu·sion·ism noun Anthropology the theory that all or most cultural similarities are due to diffusion. □ **dif·fu·sion·ist** noun

dig ● verb (**dig·ging**; past and past participle **dug**) **1** intransitive break up and remove or turn over soil, ground, etc., with a tool, one's hands, (of an animal) claws, etc. **2** transitive **a** break up and displace (the ground etc.) in this way. **b** (foll. by up) break up the soil of (a piece of land) (dug up the lawn and planted flowers). **3** transitive make (a hole, grave, tunnel, etc.) by digging. **4** transitive (often foll. by up, out) **a** obtain or remove by digging or by an action similar to digging (dug the puck out of the corner; dug a lipstick out of her purse). **b** find or discover after searching. **5** transitive & intransitive excavate (an archaeological site). **6** transitive dated slang like, appreciate, or understand. **7** transitive & intransitive (often foll. by in, into) thrust or poke into or down into (dig the manure into the soil; the collar dug into my neck; dug its teeth into my leg). **8** intransitive make one's way by digging (dug through the mountainside). ● noun **1** the act or an instance of digging. **2** a thrust or poke (a dig in the ribs). **3** informal (often foll. by at) a pointed or critical remark. **4** an archaeological excavation. **5** (in pl.) informal lodgings. □ **dig deep 1** draw on one's innermost resources (dug deep to finish the race). **2** give generously from one's financial resources (dug deep to help the flood victims). **dig in one's heels** be obstinate. **dig in** informal begin eating. **dig (oneself) in 1** prepare a defensive trench or pit. **2** establish one's position. **dig one's own grave** do something which causes one's own failure or ruin. [Middle English: perhaps from Old English dīc ditch]

Digam·bara /dɪˈɡʌmbərə/ noun one of two principal sects of Jainism (the other is Svetambara), which was formed as a result of doctrinal schism in about AD 80 and continues today in parts of S India. Its adherents reject property ownership and usu. do not wear clothes. [Sanskrit, = sky-clad]

di·gamma /daiˈɡamə/ noun the sixth letter (F, ϝ) of the early Greek alphabet (prob. pronounced /w/), later disused. [Latin from Greek (as DI-¹, GAMMA)]

Digby a town in W Nova Scotia, southwest of Annapolis Royal; pop. (2001) 2,111. □ **Digby·ite** noun [R. Digby, British rear admiral and commander of HMS Atlanta d.1815]

Digby chicken noun (also **Digby chick**) Cdn (Maritimes) a dried or cured herring. [DIGBY]

diger·ati /dɪdʒəˈrɒti/ plural noun people with expertise or professional involvement in information technology. [blend of DIGITAL + LITERATI]

di·gest ● verb /daiˈdʒɛst, də-/ **1** transitive & intransitive assimilate (food) in the stomach and bowels. **2** intransitive (of food) undergo digestion. **3** transitive understand and assimilate mentally. **4** transitive Chem. treat (a substance) with heat, enzymes, or a solvent in order to decompose it, extract the essence, etc. **5** transitive **a** reduce to a systematic or convenient form; classify; summarize. **b** think over; arrange in the mind. ● noun /ˈdaidʒɛst/ **1** a regular or occasional synopsis of current literature or news. **2 a** a methodical summary esp. of a body of laws. **b** (**the Digest**) the compendium of Roman law compiled in the reign of Justinian (6th c. AD). □ **di·gest·ant** noun **di·gest·er** noun **di·gest·ible** adjective **di·gest·ibil·ity** noun [Latin digerere digest- distribute, dissolve, digest (as DI-², gerere carry)]

di·ges·tif /ˌdiːʒɛsˈtiːf/ noun something which promotes good digestion, esp. a drink taken after a meal, e.g. a liqueur or brandy. [French: see DIGESTIVE]

di·ges·tion noun **1** the process of digesting. **2** the capacity to digest food (has weak digestion). **3** digesting a substance by means of heat, enzymes, or a solvent.

di·ges·tive /dəˈdʒɛstɪv, dai-/ ● adjective **1** of or relating to digestion. **2** aiding or promoting digestion. ● noun **1** a substance that aids digestion. **2** (in full **digestive cookie** or **digestive biscuit**) Cdn & Brit. a usu. round semi-sweet whole wheat cookie. □ **di·gest·ive·ly** adverb [Old French digestif -ive or Latin digestivus (as DIGEST)]

dig·ger noun **1** a person who digs. **2** a tool or machine for digging, e.g. a mechanical excavator. **3** a miner. **4** N Amer. informal a person who works diligently, esp. a hockey player etc. **5** (**Digger**) a member of a group of radical dissenters formed in England in 1649 as an offshoot of the Levellers, advocating a form of agrarian communism in which common land would be made available to the poor. **6** informal an Australian or New Zealander, esp. a private soldier. **7** Austral. & NZ informal (as a form of address) mate, fellow.

dig·gings plural noun **1 a** a mine or goldfield. **b** material dug out of a mine etc. **2** Brit. informal lodgings, accommodation.

dight /dait/ adjective archaic clothed, arrayed. [past participle of dight (v.) from Old English dihtan from Latin dictare DICTATE]

digi·cam /ˈdɪdʒiˌkam/ noun informal a digital camera. [blend]

digit noun **1** any numeral from 0 to 9, esp. when forming part of a number. **2** each of a series of these representing increasingly higher powers of ten in a decimal-based numeral (a six-digit income). **3** a finger, thumb, or toe. [Latin digitus]

digit·al ● adjective **1** of or relating to a numerical digit or digits. **2** (of a clock, watch, etc.) that gives a reading by means of displayed digits instead of hands. **3 a** (of a computer) operating on data represented as a series of usu. binary digits or in similar discrete form. **b** of or relating to computers (the digital age). **4 a** (of a recording) with sound information represented in digits for more reliable transmission. **b** (of a recording medium) using this process. **5** of or relating to a finger or fingers. ● noun a digital device, esp. a watch or clock (bought a digital). □ **digit·al·ize** transitive verb (also esp. Brit. **-ise**). **digit·al·ly** adverb [Latin digitalis (as DIGIT)]

digital audiotape noun magnetic tape on which sound is recorded digitally. Abbr.: **DAT**.

digital camera noun a camera that records images digitally rather than on photographic film.

digital cash noun (also **digital money**) money that may be transferred electronically from one party to another during a transaction.

digital compact cassette noun **1** a format for tape cassettes similar to ordinary audio cassettes but with digital rather than analog recording. Abbr.: **DCC**. **2** a cassette in this format.

digital divide noun the gulf between those who have ready access to computers and the Internet and those who do not.

digi·talin /ˌdɪdʒiˈtalɪn/ noun the pharmacologically active constituent(s) of the foxglove. [DIGITALIS + -IN]

digi·talis /ˌdɪdʒiˈtalɪs/ noun a drug prepared from the dried leaves of foxgloves and containing substances that stimulate the heart muscle. [modern Latin, = pertaining to the finger, genus name of foxglove, influenced by German Fingerhut 'foxglove, thimble': see DIGITAL]

digital money noun = DIGITAL CASH.

digital signature noun a digital code (generated and authenticated by public key encryption) that is attached to an electronically transmitted document to verify its contents and the sender's identity.

Vowels: a cat ɑ arm e bed ɜr her ɜː deux ə ago ɪ sit i cosy iː feed ɒ hot ɔ pore oː no ʌ run ʊ put

digital to analog converter noun a device for converting digital values to analog form.

digi·tate /'dɪdʒɪˌteɪt/ adjective **1** Zool. having separate fingers or toes. **2** Bot. having deep radiating divisions. [Latin digitatus (as DIGIT)]

digi·ti·grade /'dɪdʒɪtɪˌgreɪd/ Zool. ● adjective (of an animal, e.g. dogs, cats, and rodents) walking on its toes and not touching the ground with its heels. ● noun a digitigrade animal (compare PLANTIGRADE). [French from Latin digitus + -gradus -walking]

digit·ize transitive verb (also esp. Brit. **-ise**) convert (pictures or sound etc.) into a digital form that can be processed by a computer. □ **digit·iz·a·tion** noun **digit·iz·er** noun

digni·fied adjective **1** having or expressing dignity. **2** noble or stately in appearance or manner.

dig·nify transitive verb (**-fies, -fied**) **1** give dignity or distinction to. **2** give a high-sounding name to (something unworthy or unimportant) (it is a misnomer to dignify such works with the term Art). **3** represent or treat as worthy (will not dignify your proposal with an answer). [Old French dignefier from Late Latin dignificare from dignus worthy]

digni·tary noun (pl. **-ies**) a person holding high rank or office. [DIGNITY + -ARY[1], after PROPRIETARY]

dig·nity noun (pl. **-ties**) **1** a composed and serious manner or style. **2** the state of being worthy of honour or respect. **3** worthiness, excellence (the dignity of work). **4** a high or honourable rank or position. **5** high regard or estimation. □ **beneath one's dignity** not considered worthy enough for one to do. **stand on one's dignity** insist (esp. by one's manner) on being treated with due respect. [Old French digneté, dignité from Latin dignitas -tatis from dignus worthy]

digox·in /dɪ'dʒɒksɪn/ noun a potentially poisonous steroid glycoside that is present in the foxglove etc. and is commonly used as a cardiac stimulant. [contraction of digitoxin (a similar, less widely used drug), blend of DIGITALIS + TOXIN]

di·graph /'daɪgrɑːf/ noun a group of two letters representing one sound, as in ph and ey. □ **di·graph·ic** adjective

di·gress /daɪ'grɛs/ intransitive verb depart from the main subject temporarily in speech or writing. □ **di·gres·sion** noun **di·gres·sive** adjective **di·gres·sive·ly** adverb **di·gres·sive·ness** noun [Latin digredi digress- (as DI-[2], gradi walk)]

digs plural noun see DIG noun 5.

di·hed·ral /daɪ'hiːdrəl/ ● adjective having or contained by two plane faces. ● noun (in full **dihedral angle**) an angle formed by two plane surfaces, esp. an upward inclination of an aircraft wing. [dihedron from DI-[1] + -HEDRON]

di·hyd·ric /daɪ'haɪdrɪk/ adjective Chem. containing two hydroxyl groups. [DI-[1] + HYDROGEN + -IC]

Dijon /diː'ʒɔ̃/ an industrial city in east central France, the former capital of Burgundy; pop. (1999) 149,867.

Dijon mustard /'diːʒɔ̃, 'diːʒɒn, diː'ʒɔ̃, diː'ʒɒn/ noun a mild mustard paste using brown and black varieties of seed and blended with white wine. [DIJON]

dik-dik noun any of several very small African antelopes constituting the genus Madoqua. [name in East Africa and in Afrikaans]

dike[1] (also **dyke**) ● noun **1** a long wall or embankment built to prevent flooding. **2 a** a ditch or artificial watercourse. **b** Brit. a natural watercourse. **3 a** a low wall, esp. of turf. **b** a causeway. **4** a barrier or obstacle; a defence. **5** Geol. an intrusion of igneous rock across sedimentary strata. **6** esp. Austral. informal a lavatory. ● transitive verb provide or defend with a dike or dikes. [Old Norse dík or Middle Low German dīk dam, Middle Dutch dijc ditch, dam: compare DITCH]

dike[2] var. of DYKE[2].

dik·tat /'dɪktat/ noun a categorical statement or decree, esp. terms imposed after a war by a victor. [German, = DICTATE]

di·lapi·date /dɪ'lapɪˌdeɪt/ transitive & intransitive verb fall or cause to fall into disrepair or ruin. [Latin dilapidare demolish, squander (as DI-[2], lapis lapid- stone)]

di·lapi·dat·ed adjective in a state of disrepair or ruin, esp. as a result of age or neglect.

di·lapi·da·tion noun a state of disrepair or ruin.

dila·ta·tion noun **1** the widening or expansion of a hollow organ or cavity. **2** the process of dilating. □ **dila·ta·tion·al** adjective

dilatation and curettage noun = D & C

di·late /'daɪleɪt, daɪ'laɪt/ verb **1** transitive & intransitive make or become wider or larger (esp. of an opening in the body) (dilated pupils). **2** intransitive (often foll. by on, upon) speak or write at length.

di·la·tion noun [Old French dilater from Latin dilatare spread out (as DI-[2], latus wide)]

di·la·tor noun **1** Anat. a muscle that dilates an organ. **2** Med. an instrument for dilating a tube or cavity in the body.

dila·tory /'dɪlətɔri/ adjective given to or causing delay. □ **dila·tor·i·ly** adverb **dila·tor·i·ness** noun [Late Latin dilatorius (as DI-[2], dilat- past participle stem of differre DEFER[1])]

dil·do noun (pl. **-dos**) an object shaped like an erect penis and used for sexual stimulation. [16th c.: origin unknown]

di·lem·ma /dɪ'lɛmə/ noun **1** a situation in which a choice has to be made between two equally undesirable alternatives. **2** a state of indecision between two alternatives. **3** a difficult situation. **4** an argument forcing an opponent to choose either of two unfavourable alternatives. [Latin from Greek (as DI-[1], lēmma premise)]

dil·et·tante /ˌdɪlə'tɒnt, -'tɒnt/ ● noun (pl. **dil·et·tantes** or **dil·et·tanti** /-tiː/) **1** a person who studies a subject or area of knowledge superficially. **2** a person who enjoys the arts. ● adjective trifling, not thorough; amateurish. □ **dil·et·tant·ish** adjective **dil·et·tant·ism** noun [Italian from pres. part. of dilettare delight, from Latin delectare]

Dili /'diːliː/ the capital of East Timor, situated on the north coast of the island; pop. (2000) 48,200.

dili·gence[1] noun **1** careful and persistent application or effort. **2** (as a characteristic) industriousness. [as DILIGENT]

dili·gence[2] /'dɪlɪdʒəns, ˌdiːliː'ʒɑ̃s/ noun hist. a public stagecoach, esp. in France. [French, for carrosse de diligence coach of speed]

dili·gent adjective **1** careful and steady in application to one's work or duties. **2** showing care and effort. □ **dili·gent·ly** adverb [Old French from Latin diligens assiduous, part. of diligere love, take delight in (as DI-[2], legere choose)]

dill noun **1** an umbelliferous herb, Anethum graveolens, with yellow flowers and aromatic seeds. **2** the leaves or seeds of this plant used for flavouring and medicinal purposes. [Old English dile]

dill pickle noun a pickled cucumber flavoured with dill.

dill·weed noun the leaves of the dill plant used as a seasoning.

dilly[1] noun (pl. **-lies**) esp. N Amer. informal a remarkable or excellent person or thing. [dilly (adj.) from DELIGHTFUL or DELICIOUS]

dilly[2] adjective Austral. & NZ informal **1** odd or eccentric. **2** foolish, stupid, mad. [perhaps from DAFT, SILLY]

dilly-dally intransitive verb (**-dallies, -dallied**) informal **1** dawdle, loiter. **2** vacillate. [reduplication of DALLY[1]]

dilu·ent /'dɪljʊənt/ Chem. & Biochem. ● adjective that serves to dilute. ● noun a diluting agent. [Latin diluere diluent- DILUTE]

di·lute /daɪ'luːt, dɪ-/ ● transitive verb **1** reduce the strength of (a fluid) by adding water or another solvent. **2** weaken or reduce the strength or forcefulness of, esp. by adding something. ● adjective (also /'daɪ-/) **1** (esp. of a fluid) diluted, weakened. **2** (of a colour) washed out; low in saturation. **3** Chem. **a** (of a solution) having relatively low concentration of solute. **b** (of a substance) in solution (dilute sulphuric acid). □ **di·lut·ed** adjective **di·lut·er** noun **di·lu·tion** noun [Latin diluere dilut- (as DI-[2], luere wash)]

di·lu·vial /daɪ'luːvɪəl, də-/ adjective **1** of or relating to a flood, esp. the Flood described in Genesis. **2** Geol. of or consisting of diluvium. [Late Latin diluvialis from diluvium DELUGE]

di·lu·vi·um /daɪ'luːvɪəm, də-/ (pl. **di·lu·via** /-vɪə/) Geol. = DRIFT noun 8. [Latin: see DILUVIAL]

dim ● adjective (**dim·mer, dim·mest**) **1 a** only faintly luminous or visible; not bright. **b** obscure; ill-defined. **2** not clearly perceived or remembered. **3** informal stupid; slow to understand. **4** (of the eyes) not seeing clearly. **5** N Amer. not likely to succeed or happen (there's only a dim chance of that). ● verb (**dimmed, dim·ming**) **1** transitive & intransitive make or become dim or less bright. **2** transitive N Amer. lower the beam of (a vehicle's headlights) to reduce dazzle. □ **take a dim view of** informal **1** disapprove of. **2** feel gloomy about. □ **dimly** adverb **dim·mish** adjective **dim·ness** noun [Old English dim, dimm, of unknown origin]

dim. abbreviation diminuendo.

Di·Maggio /də'madʒioː/ **Jo·seph Paul** (1914–99), US baseball player. Star of the New York Yankees 1936–51, he gained renown as an outstanding batter and outfielder.

dim-bulb N Amer. informal ● noun a stupid person. ● adjective stupid, senseless (what a dim-bulb idea).

dime noun N Amer. **1** a ten-cent coin. **2** a small amount of money. □ **a dime a dozen** very cheap or commonplace. **it's your dime** see

NICKEL. **on a dime** *N Amer. informal* **1** within a small area or short distance. **2** quickly, instantly. [Middle English (originally = tithe) from Old French *disme* from Latin *decima pars* tenth part]

dime bag *noun N Amer. slang* a package of an illegal drug selling for ten dollars.

di·men·hy·drin·ate /ˌdaimen'haidrineit/ *noun* a medication used to counter nausea and vomiting and prevent motion sickness, the active ingredient in Gravol. [DI-¹ + METHYL + HYDRO- + AMINE + -ATE¹]

dime novel *noun* a cheap popular novel.

di·men·sion /dɪ'menʃən, dai-/ ● *noun* **1** a measurable extent of any kind, as length, breadth, depth, area, and volume. **2** (in *pl.*) size, scope, extent. **3** an aspect or facet of a situation, problem, etc. **4** *Algebra* one of a number of unknown or variable quantities contained as factors in a product (x^3, x^2y, xyz, are all of three dimensions). **5** *Physics* the product of mass, length, time, etc., raised to the appropriate power, in a derived physical quantity. ● *transitive verb* (usu. as **di·men·sioned** *adjective*) mark the dimensions on (a diagram etc.). □ **di·men·sion·al** *adjective* (also in *combination*). **di·men·sion·al·ity** *noun* (*pl.* **-ities**). **di·men·sion·al·ly** *adverb* **di·men·sion·less** *adjective* [Latin *dimensio -onis* (as DI-², *metiri mensus* measure)]

dimer /'daimər/ *noun Chem.* a compound consisting of two identical molecules linked together (compare MONOMER). □ **di·meric** /-'merɪk/ *adjective* [DI-¹ + -*mer* after POLYMER]

di·mer·ous /'daimərəs/ *adjective* (of a plant) having two parts in a whorl etc. [modern Latin *dimerus* from Greek *dimerēs* bipartite]

dime store *noun N Amer.* **1** = FIVE-AND-DIME STORE. **2** (**dime-store**) (*attributive*) **a** bought at a dime store. **b** cheap, of poor quality (*dime-store psychology*).

dim·eter /'dimitər/ *noun* a line of verse consisting of two metrical feet. [Late Latin *dimetrus* from Greek *dimetros* (as DI-¹, METER³)]

dimin·ish *verb* **1** *transitive & intransitive* make or become smaller or less. **2** *transitive* lessen the reputation or influence of (a person). □ **law of diminishing returns** the fact that an increase in expenditure, investment, taxation, etc., beyond a certain point ceases to produce a proportionate yield. □ **dimin·ish·able** *adjective* **dimin·ish·ment** *noun* [Middle English, blending of earlier *minish* from Old French *menusier* (formed as MINCE) and *diminue* from Old French *diminuer* from Latin *diminuere diminut-* break up small]

dimin·ished *adjective* **1** reduced; made smaller or less. **2** *Music* (of an interval, usu. a seventh or fifth) less by a semitone than the corresponding minor or perfect interval.

diminished responsibility *noun Brit.* the limitation of criminal responsibility on the ground of mental weakness or abnormality.

di·minu·endo /dɪˌminju'endoʊ/ *Music* ● *noun* (*pl.* **-endos**) **1** a gradual decrease in loudness. **2** a passage to be performed with such a decrease. ● *adverb & adjective* with a gradual decrease in loudness. [Italian, part. of *diminuire* DIMINISH]

dim·in·u·tion /ˌdimɪ'njuːʃən/ *noun* **1 a** the act or an instance of diminishing. **b** the amount by which something diminishes. **2** *Music* the repetition of a passage in notes shorter than those originally used. [Old French from Latin *diminutio -onis* (as DIMINISH)]

di·minu·tive /dɪ'mɪnjʊtɪv/ ● *adjective* **1** remarkably small; tiny. **2** *Grammar* (of a word or suffix) implying smallness, either actual or imputed in token of affection, scorn, etc. (e.g. *-let*, *-kins*). ● *noun Grammar* a diminutive word or suffix. □ **di·minu·tive·ness** *noun* [Old French *diminutif*, *-ive* from Late Latin *diminutivus* (as DIMINISH)]

dim·ity /'dimiti/ *noun* (*pl.* **-ties**) a fairly sheer lightweight fabric of cotton or artificial fibres, often woven with fine stripes, checks, or printed patterns. [ultimately from Greek *dimitos* (as DI-¹, *mitos* warp thread)]

dim·mer *noun* (in full **dimmer switch**) a device for varying the brightness of an electric light.

di·morph·ic /dai'mɔrfɪk/ *adjective* (also **di·morph·ous** /dai'mɔrfəs/) *Biol., Chem., & Geol.* exhibiting, or occurring in, two distinct forms. □ **di·morph·ism** *noun* [Greek *dimorphos* (as DI-¹, *morphē* form)]

dim·ple ● *noun* **1** a small hollow or dent in the flesh, esp. in the cheeks or chin. **2** a round depression, e.g. in a golf ball. ● *verb* **1** *intransitive* produce or show dimples. **2** *transitive* produce dimples in (a cheek etc.). **3** *transitive* make a dent or depression in (a piece of sheet metal, the surface of a body of water, etc.). □ **dim·pled** *adjective* **dim·ply** *adjective* [ultimately from a Germanic word related to German *Tümpel* pond]

dim sum /dim 'sʌm/ *noun* an assortment of small steamed or fried Chinese dumplings with various savoury fillings. [Cantonese *dim-sām*, lit. 'dot of the heart']

dim-wit *noun informal* a stupid person. □ **dim-witted** *adjective*

din ● *noun* a prolonged loud and distracting noise. ● *verb* (**dinned**, **din·ning**) **1** *transitive* (foll. by *into*) instill (something to be learned) by constant repetition. **2** *intransitive* make a din. [Old English *dyne*, *dynn*, *dynian* from Germanic]

di·nar /'diːnɑr/ *noun* **1** a former monetary unit of Yugoslavia and Bosnia-Herzegovina. **2** the chief monetary unit of Serbia and Montenegro, equal to 100 paras. **3** the chief monetary unit of certain countries of the Middle East and North Africa. [Arabic & Persian *dīnār* from Greek *dēnarion* from Latin *denarius*: see DENIER²]

Di·nar·ic Alps /dɪ'nerɪk/ a mountain range in the Balkans, running parallel to the Adriatic coast from Slovenia in the northwest, through Croatia, Bosnia, and Montenegro, to Albania in the southeast.

din-din *noun* (also **din-dins**) *informal* a jocular or child's word for dinner. [reduplication of first syllable of DINNER]

d'Indy /dã'di/ **(Paul Marie Théo·dore) Vin·cent** (1851–1931), French composer and teacher. He was a founder (1894) and director of the Schola Cantorum in Paris, and his compositions include *Symphony on a French Mountaineer's Chant* (1886) and *Istar* (1896).

dine *verb* **1** *intransitive* eat dinner. **2** *transitive* give dinner to. □ **dine out** **1** dine away from home. **2** (foll. by *on*) be entertained to dinner etc. on account of (one's ability to relate an interesting event, story, etc.). □ **din·ing** *noun* [Old French *diner*, *disner*, ultimately from DIS- + Late Latin *jejunare* from *jejunus* fasting]

diner *noun* **1** a person who is eating, esp. in a restaurant. **2** *N Amer.* a small restaurant. **3** = DINING CAR.

di·nero /diː'neroʊ/ *noun slang* money; cash. [Spanish]

Din·esen /'dɪnəsən/ **Isak** (pseudonym of Baroness Karen Blixen) (1885–1962), Danish short-story writer, best known for her memoir *Out of Africa* (1937), about her experiences in Kenya (1914–31).

din·ette /dai'net/ *noun* **1** a small room or part of a room used for eating meals. **2** *N Amer.* a set of a table and chairs for this.

ding¹ ● *intransitive verb* make a ringing sound. ● *noun* a ringing sound, as of a bell. [imitative: influenced by DIN]

ding² *N Amer. informal* ● *noun* a dent (*has a ding in the fender*). ● *transitive verb* **1** make a dent in (*dinged my car*). **2** hit. **3** charge (esp. an excessive amount). [prob. of Scandinavian origin: compare Old Norse *dengja* 'to hammer, whet a scythe']

ding-a-ling ● *noun* **1** the sound of a bell or bells. **2** *N Amer. informal* a crazy or stupid person (*he's a real ding-a-ling*). ● *adjective* crazy, eccentric (*what a ding-a-ling idea*). [imitative]

Ding an sich /ˌdɪŋ an 'zɪx/ *noun Philos.* a thing in itself. [German]

ding·bat *noun informal* **1** *N Amer. & Austral.* a stupid or eccentric person. **2** a typographical device other than a letter or numeral (such as an asterisk), used to signal divisions in text or to replace letters in a euphemistically presented vulgar word. [19th c.: perhaps from *ding* to beat + BAT¹]

ding-dong ● *noun* **1** the sound of alternate chimes, as of two bells. **2** *N Amer.* a crazy or stupid person. ● *adjective* crazy (*a ding-dong idea*). [16th c.: imitative]

ding·er *noun Baseball slang* a home run.

din·ghy /'dɪŋi, 'dɪŋgi/ *noun* (*pl.* **-ghies**) **1** a small boat carried by a ship. **2** a small pleasure boat. **3** a small inflatable rubber boat (esp. for emergency use). [originally a rowboat used on Indian rivers, from Hindi *dīngī*]

din·gle *noun* a deep wooded valley or dell. [Middle English: origin unknown]

dingo *noun* (*pl.* **-goes**) **1** a wild or half-domesticated Australian dog, *Canis dingo*. **2** *Austral. slang* a coward or scoundrel. [Dharuk *din-gu* or *dayn-gu* 'domesticated dingo']

din·gus /'dɪŋgəs/ *noun N Amer.* **1** *informal* a gadget or contraption. **2** *coarse slang* the penis. [Dutch *ding* thing]

dingy /'dɪndʒi/ *adjective* (**din·gi·er**, **din·gi·est**) **1** dirty-looking. **2** drab, dull-coloured. **3** not bright; lacking light. □ **din·gi·ly** *adverb* **din·gi·ness** *noun* [perhaps ultimately from Old English *dynge* DUNG]

din·ing car *noun* a railway car equipped as a restaurant.

din·ing hall *noun* a hall in which meals are eaten.

din·ing room *noun* a room in which meals are eaten.

din·ing table *noun* (also **dining-room table**) a table on which meals are served or eaten.

dink¹ *noun N Amer. slang* **1** the penis. **2** a foolish or stupid person. [prob. from earlier *dinkus*, var of DINGUS, influenced by DICK¹]

dink² *Sport* ● *noun* a drop shot in tennis. ● *transitive verb* hit (a ball) softly so that it falls just over the net. [imitative]

dink³ noun (also **dinky**) slang **1** a well-off young working couple with no children. **2** either partner of this. [acronym from double income no kids]

Dinka /'dɪŋkə/ ● noun **1** a member of a Sudanese people of the Nile basin. **2** the language of this people. ● adjective of or relating to the Dinkas or Dinka. [Dinka jieng people]

din·kum /'dɪŋkəm/ Austral. & NZ informal ● adjective genuine, right. ● noun work, toil. [19th c.: origin unknown]

dinkum oil noun Austral. & NZ informal the honest truth.

dinky¹ adjective (**dink·i·er**, **dink·i·est**) informal **1** N Amer. trifling, insignificant. **2** Brit. (esp. of a thing) neat and attractive; small, dainty. [Scots dink neat, trim, of unknown origin]

dinky² noun (pl. **-ies**) var. of DINK³. [DINK³ + -Y²]

din·ner noun **1** the main meal of the day, eaten either at midday or in the evening. **2** a formal meal, often in honour of a person or event. □ **done like dinner** Cdn informal utterly defeated. [Old French diner, disner: see DINE]

dinner dance noun a formal dinner followed by dancing.

dinner guest noun a person invited to dinner as a guest.

dinner jacket noun a man's short usu. black formal jacket for evening wear. □ **dinner-jacketed** adjective

dinner party noun a party to which guests are invited to eat dinner together.

dinner plate noun a large plate used for eating the main course of a dinner.

dinner service noun a set of usu. matching china for serving a meal.

dinner theatre noun N Amer. **1** a theatre in which dinner, included in the price of the ticket, is served usu. before the performance. **2** the type of theatre performed in such a place.

dinner·time noun the time at which dinner is customarily eaten.

dinner·ware noun dishes used for eating from, e.g. plates, bowls, etc.

dino /'daino/ noun (pl. **dinos**) informal a dinosaur (also attributive: dino tracks). [abbreviation]

dino·flagel·late /daino'fladʒəleit/ noun a unicellular aquatic organism with two flagella, of a group variously classed as algae and protozoa. [modern Latin Dinoflagellata, from Greek dinos 'whirling' + Latin FLAGELLUM]

dino·saur noun **1** an extinct reptile of the Mesozoic era, often of enormous size. **2 a** a person or thing that has not adapted to new conditions. **b** a person or thing that is large or unwieldy.
□ **dino·saur·ian** /,dainə'sɔriən/ adjective & noun [modern Latin dinosaurus from Greek deinos terrible + sauros lizard]

Dinosaur Provincial Park a UNESCO World Heritage Site in the badlands of Alberta, east of Calgary. The park contains fossil evidence of about 35 species of dinosaur, dating back 75 million years.

dino·there /'dainə,θiːr/ noun any elephant-like animal of the extinct genus Deinotherium, having downward curving tusks. [modern Latin dinotherium from Greek deinos terrible + thērion wild beast]

dint ● noun **1** a dent. **2** archaic a blow or stroke. ● transitive verb mark with dints. □ **by dint of** by force or means of. [Old English dynt, and partly from cognate Old Norse dyntr: ultimate origin unknown]

dio·ces·an /dai'ɒsɪsən, -zən/ ● adjective of or concerning a diocese. ● noun the bishop of a diocese. [as DIOCESE]

dio·cese /'daiəsiːz, -sɪs, -siːs/ noun a district under the pastoral care of a bishop. [Old French diocise from Late Latin diocesis from Latin dioecesis from Greek dioikēsis administration (as DI-², oikeō inhabit)]

Dio·cle·tian /,daiə'kliːʃən/ (full name Gaius Aurelius Valerius Diocletianus) (245–313), Roman emperor 284–305. He divided the empire between himself in the east and Maximian (d.310) in the west (293), and launched the final persecution of the Christians (303).

di·ode /'daioʊd/ noun **1** a semiconductor allowing the flow of current in one direction only and having two terminals. **2** a thermionic valve having two electrodes. [DI-¹ + ELECTRODE]

di·oe·cious /dai'iːʃəs/ adjective **1** Bot. having male and female organs on separate plants. **2** Zool. having the two sexes in separate individuals (compare MONOECIOUS). [DI-¹ + Greek -oikos -housed]

Di·og·enes /dai'ɒdʒə,niːz/ (c.400–c.325 BC), Greek philosopher. The most famous of the Cynics, he lived in Athens in extreme poverty and asceticism, emphasizing the need for self-sufficiency and natural, uninhibited behaviour.

diol /'daiɒl/ noun Chem. any alcohol containing two hydroxyl groups in each molecule. [DI-¹ + -OL¹]

Dio·medes /daiə'miːdiːz/ Gk Myth one of the Greek leaders of the Trojan War.

Dion /diː'ɒn, diː'ɔ̃/ **Cé·line** (b.1968), Canadian singer and actress. She released her first hit single at 13, and was French Canada's most popular chanteuse within 5 years. Her album The Colour of My Love (1994) sold 11 million copies worldwide to become the most successful album ever released by a female Canadian pop singer.

Dione /dai'oːni/ **1** Gk Myth a Titan, the mother of Aphrodite. **2** Astronomy satellite IV of Saturn, the twelfth closest to the planet, discovered by Cassini in 1684 (diameter 1 120 km).

-dione combining form used to form the names of compounds containing two carbonyl groups.

Di·onne Quintuplets /diː'ɒn/ **Cé·cile**, **Yvonne** (d.2001), **Émi·lie** (d.1954), **An·nette**, and **Marie** (d.1970), five daughters born to Oliva and Elzire Dionne on May 28th, 1934 at Corbeil, Ontario. The quintuplets created a sensation at their birth, and were known as 'the world's most famous youngsters' during the 1930s.

Dio·nys·iac /,daiə'niːsi,ak/ adjective (also **Dio·nys·ian** /-siən/) **1** wildly sensual; unrestrained. **2** (in Greek mythology) of or relating to Dionysus or his worship. [DIONYSUS]

Dio·nys·ius I /,daiə'nisiəs/ (**'the Elder'**) (c.430–367 BC), ruler of Syracuse 405–367 BC. A tyrannical ruler, he waged three wars against the Carthaginians for control of Sicily, the third of which (383–c.375) resulted in his defeat at Cronium.

Dio·nys·ius Ex·ig·u·us /eg'zɪgjuːəs/ (died c.556), Scythian monk and scholar. He introduced the system of dates BC and AD that is still in use today, and accepted (mistakenly) 753 AUC as the year of the Incarnation.

Dio·nys·ius of Hali·car·nas·sus (1st c. BC), Greek historian, literary critic, and rhetorician, best known for his detailed history of Rome from earliest times until the outbreak of the First Punic War (264 BC).

Dio·nys·us /,daiə'naisəs/ Gk Myth a Greek god, son of Zeus and Semele, also called Bacchus. Originally a god of fertility, associated with wild and ecstatic religious rites, in later traditions he is a god of wine who loosens inhibitions and inspires creativity in music and poetry.

di·optre /dai'ɒptɜr/ noun (also **di·opter**) Optics a unit of refractive power of a lens, equal to the reciprocal of its focal length in metres. [see DIOPTRIC]

di·op·tric /dai'ɒptrɪk/ adjective Optics **1** serving as a medium for sight; assisting sight by refraction (dioptric glass; dioptric lens). **2** of refraction; refractive. [Greek dioptrikos from dioptra a kind of theodolite]

di·op·trics /dai'ɒptrɪks/ noun the part of optics dealing with refraction.

Dior /diː'ɔr/ **Chris·tian** (1905–57), French fashion designer, noted for introducing the 'New Look' of narrow-waisted tightly fitted bodices and full pleated skirts in 1947.

dio·rama /,daiə'ramə/ noun **1** a scenic painting in which changes in colour and direction of illumination simulate a sunrise etc. **2** a representation of a scene with three-dimensional figures, often against a painted background. **3** a small-scale model or film set.
□ **dio·ram·ic** adjective [DI-³ + Greek horama -atos from horaō see]

dio·rite /'daiə,rɔit/ noun a coarse-grained plutonic igneous rock containing quartz. [French from Greek diorizō distinguish]

Dios·curi /,daiə'skjuri/ Gk & Rom. Myth the twins Castor and Pollux (also called Polydeuces), born to Leda after her seduction by Zeus; they are often identified with the constellation Gemini, and were the patrons of mariners. [Greek, = sons of Zeus]

di·ox·an /dai'ɒksən/ noun (also **di·ox·ane** /-ein/) Chem. a colourless toxic liquid used as a solvent. Chem. formula: $C_4H_8O_2$.

di·ox·ide /dai'ɒksaid/ noun Chem. an oxide containing two atoms of oxygen which are not linked together (carbon dioxide).

di·ox·in /dai'ɒksɪn/ noun Chem. any of a class of cyclic compounds produced as chemical by-products, esp. the highly toxic tetrachlorodibenzoparadioxin (TCDD).

DIP /dɪp/ noun Computing a form of integrated circuit consisting of a small plastic or ceramic slab with two parallel rows of pins. [abbreviation of dual in-line package]

dip ● verb (**dipped**, **dip·ping**) **1** transitive put or let down briefly into liquid etc.; immerse. **2** intransitive go below a surface or level (the sun dipped below the horizon). **b** (of a level of income, activity, etc.) decline slightly, esp. briefly (profits dipped in May). **3** intransitive extend downwards; take or have a downward slope (the road dips after the bend). **4** intransitive go under water and emerge quickly. **5** intransitive (foll. by into) **a** read briefly from (a book etc.). **b** take a cursory interest in (a subject). **6** (foll. by into) **a** intransitive put a hand, ladle, etc., into a container to take something out. **b** transitive put (a hand etc.) into a container, pocket, etc. to do this. **c** intransitive spend from or make use of one's

---

t top   v voice   w we   z zoo   ʃ she   ʒ vision   θ thin   ð this   ŋ ring   x loch   tʃ chip   dʒ jar   (see over for vowels)

resources (*dipped into our savings*). **7** *transitive & intransitive* lower or be lowered, esp. in salute. **8** *transitive* colour (a fabric) by immersing it in dye. **9** *transitive* wash (sheep etc.) by immersion in a vermin-killing liquid. **10** *transitive* make (a candle) by immersing a wick repeatedly in hot tallow or wax. **11** *transitive jocular* baptize by immersion. **12** *transitive* **a** (often foll. by *up, out of*) remove or scoop up (liquid, grain, etc., or something from liquid). **b** *Cdn (Nfld)* use a dip net to transfer (cod) from a large net etc. to another net, boat etc. **13** *transitive Brit.* dim (headlights). ● *noun* **1** an act of dipping or being dipped. **2** a liquid into which something is dipped. **3** a brief swim. **4** a brief downward slope, followed by an upward one, in a road etc. **5** a usu. thick sauce into which food, esp. raw vegetables, chips, etc., is dipped before eating. **6** *N Amer.* an item of food, esp. a sandwich, served with a dipping sauce (*beef dip*). **7** *N Amer.* an ice cream cone dipped in melted chocolate etc. **8** a depression or hollow. **9** *Astronomy & Surveying* the apparent depression of the horizon from the line of observation, due to the curvature of the earth. **10 a** the angle made with the horizontal at any point by the earth's magnetic field. **b** the downward inclination of a magnetic needle. **11** *Geol.* the angle a stratum makes with the horizon. **12** *N Amer. slang* a foolish or bumbling person. **13** *slang* a pickpocket. [Old English *dyppan* from Germanic: related to DEEP]

di·pep·tide /daɪˈpeptaɪd/ *noun* a peptide formed by the combination of two amino acids.

di·phen·hydra·mine /daɪfenˈhaɪdrəmiːn/ *noun* an antihistamine compound used for the symptomatic relief of allergies. [DI-[1] + PHENO- + HYDRO- + AMINE]

di·phos·phate /daɪˈfɒsfeɪt/ *noun* a compound with two phosphate groups in the molecule, or a salt with two phosphate anions per cation.

diph·ther·ia /dɪpˈθɪəriə, dɪf-/ *noun* an acute infectious bacterial disease with inflammation of a mucous membrane esp. of the throat, resulting in the formation of a false membrane causing difficulty in breathing and swallowing. □ **diph·ther·ial** *adjective* **diph·ther·it·ic** /-θəˈrɪtɪk/ *adjective* [French *diphthérie*, earlier *diphthérite* from Greek *diphthera* skin, hide]

diph·thong /ˈdɪfθɒŋ, dɪp-/ *noun* **1** a speech sound in one syllable in which the articulation begins as for one vowel and moves as for another (as in *coin, loud,* and *side*). **2 a** a digraph representing the sound of a diphthong or single vowel (as in *feat*). **b** a compound vowel character; a ligature (as æ). □ **diph·thong·al** /-ˈθɒŋgəl/ *adjective* [French *diphtongue* from Late Latin *diphthongus* from Greek *diphthoggos* (as DI-[1], *phthoggos* voice)]

diph·thong·ize *transitive verb* (also esp. *Brit.* **-ise**) pronounce as a diphthong. □ **diph·thong·iz·a·tion** *noun*

Dipl. *abbreviation* Diploma.

diplo- /ˈdɪploʊ/ *combining form* double. [Greek *diplous* double]

diplo·coc·cus /ˌdɪpləˈkɒkəs/ *noun* (pl. **diplo·cocci** /-kaɪ, -ksaɪ, -kiː, -ksiː/) any of various spherical bacteria that occur mainly in pairs. [DIPLO- + COCCUS]

dip·lod·ocus /dɪˈplɒdəkəs, ˌdɪploʊˈdoʊkəs/ *noun* (pl. **dip·lod·ocus·es**) a huge plant-eating dinosaur of the genus *Diplodocus*, of the Jurassic period, with a long neck and long slender tail. [DIPLO- + Greek *dokos* wooden beam]

dip·loid /ˈdɪplɔɪd/ *Biol.* ● *adjective* (of an organism or cell) having two complete sets of chromosomes per cell. ● *noun* a diploid cell or organism. [German (as DIPLO-, -OID)]

dip·loidy /ˈdɪplɔɪdi/ *noun* the condition of being diploid.

dip·lo·ma *noun* **1 a** a certificate awarded for passing an examination, completing a course of study, etc. **b** the qualification conferred with a diploma. **2** *hist.* a document conferring an honour or privilege. [Latin *diplōma*, letter of recommendation, from Greek *diplōma -atos* folded paper, from *diploō* to fold, from *diplous* double]

dip·lo·macy *noun* **1 a** the management of international relations by negotiation. **b** expertise in this. **2** skill or tact in handling negotiations, dealing with people, etc. [French *diplomatie* from *diplomatique* DIPLOMATIC after *aristocratic*]

dip·lo·mat *noun* **1** a person engaged by a government to conduct official negotiations with other countries; a member of a diplomatic service. **2** a tactful person. [French *diplomate*, back-formation from *diplomatique*: see DIPLOMATIC]

dip·lo·mate /ˈdɪpləmeɪt/ *noun* esp. *US* a person who holds a diploma, esp. in medicine.

dip·lo·mat·ic *adjective* **1 a** of or involved in diplomacy. **b** skilled in diplomacy. **2** tactful; skilful in personal relations. □ **dip·lo·mat·ic·ally** *adverb* [French *diplomatique* from Latin DIPLOMA]

diplomatic bag *noun* *Cdn, Brit., & Austral.* (*US* **diplomatic pouch**) a container, not usu. subject to customs inspection, in which official mail etc. is dispatched to or from an embassy, consulate, etc.

diplomatic corps *noun* the body of diplomats representing other countries at a seat of government.

diplomatic immunity *noun* the exemption of diplomatic staff abroad from arrest, taxation, etc.

diplomatic recognition *noun* see RECOGNITION 5.

diplomatic service *noun* the branch of a national government concerned with the official representation of a country abroad.

dip·lo·mat·ist /dɪˈploʊmətɪst/ *noun* = DIPLOMAT.

dip·lont /ˈdɪplɒnt/ *noun* an animal or plant which has a diploid number of chromosomes in its cells (other than gametes). [DIPLO- + Greek *ont-* stem of *ōn* being]

dip·lo·pia /dɪˈploʊpiə/ *noun* *Med.* double vision.

dip·lo·tene /ˈdɪploʊˌtiːn/ *noun* a stage during the prophase of meiosis where paired chromosomes begin to separate. [DIPLO- + Greek *tainia* band]

dip net *noun* a fishing net with a long handle, used to scoop fish out of the water.

di·pole /ˈdaɪpoʊl/ *noun* **1** *Physics* two equal and oppositely charged or magnetized poles separated by a distance. **2** *Chem.* a molecule in which a concentration of positive charges is separated from a concentration of negative charges. **3** (also **dipole antenna**) an antenna composed of two equal straight rods mounted in line with one another and having an electrical connection in the centre. □ **di·polar** /daɪˈpoʊlər/ *adjective*

dipole moment *noun* *Physics* the product of the separation of the charges etc. of a dipole and their magnitudes.

dip·per *noun* **1** any of several stocky short-tailed songbirds constituting the genus *Cinclus* and family Cinclidae, which habitually bob up and down, frequent fast-flowing streams, and swim and walk under water to feed, esp. *C. mexicanus* of western N America, or *C. cinclus* of Eurasia. Also called WATER OUZEL. **2** a ladle. **3** = BIG DIPPER or LITTLE DIPPER. **4** *N Amer.* an item of food suitable for dipping, e.g. a potato chip, a raw vegetable, etc. **5** *Cdn* (esp. *Nfld & PEI*) a small, lidless saucepan with a long handle. □ **dipper·ful** *noun* (pl. **-fuls**).

dippy *adjective* (**dip·pi·er**, **dip·pi·est**) *informal* foolish or unintelligent. □ **dip·pi·ness** *noun* [20th c.: origin uncertain]

dip·shit *noun* esp. *N Amer. coarse slang* a contemptible or inept person. [perhaps from DIPPY + SHIT]

dip·so *noun* (pl. **-sos**) *slang* a dipsomaniac. [abbreviation]

dip·so·mania /ˌdɪpsəˈmeɪniə/ *noun* an abnormal craving for alcohol. □ **dip·so·maniac** *noun* [Greek *dipso-* from *dipsa* thirst + -MANIA]

dip·stick *noun* **1** a graduated rod for measuring the depth of a liquid, esp. in a vehicle's engine. **2** a chemically sensitive stick or strip of paper etc. dipped into a liquid (esp. a urine sample) for diagnostic purposes. **3** *slang* a foolish or inept person; an idiot.

DIP switch *noun* an arrangement of switches on a printer for selecting a printing mode.

dipsy-doodle esp. *Cdn slang* ● *intransitive verb* esp. *Hockey* evade the defending team by using feints, dekes, swerving motions, and finesse in stickhandling etc. ● *noun* **1** an evasive movement of this type. **2** a tactic designed to confuse, evade, or outwit opponents or competitors (*the redrawing of the electoral boundaries is a dipsy-doodle*). [DIP + DOODLE]

dip·teran /ˈdɪptərən/ ● *noun* a dipterous insect. ● *adjective* = DIPTEROUS 1. [modern Latin *diptera* from Greek *diptera* neuter pl. of *dipterous* two-winged (as DI-[2], *pteron* wing)]

dip·ter·ous /ˈdɪptərəs/ *adjective* **1** of or relating to the insect order Diptera, whose members (the 'true' flies) have two membranous wings, the hindwings being reduced to halteres or balancing organs, e.g. houseflies, mosquitoes, etc. **2** *Bot.* having two wing-like appendages. [modern Latin *diptera* from Greek *dipteros*: see DIPTERAN]

dip·tych /ˈdɪptɪk/ *noun* **1** a pair of thematically linked paintings, photographs, sculptures, etc. on two panels. **2** two films, books, etc. considered as a thematically linked pair. **3** an ancient writing tablet consisting of two hinged leaves with waxed inner sides. [Late Latin *diptycha* from Greek *diptukha* (as DI-[1], *ptukhē* fold)]

Dirac /dɪˈræk/ **Paul Ad·rian Mau·rice** (1902–84), English theoretical physicist. He applied Einstein's theory of relativity to quantum mechanics in order to describe the behaviour of the electron, and later predicted the existence of the positron; he was also the co-inventor of Fermi-Dirac statistics, and shared the Nobel Prize for physics in 1933.

Vowels:　a *cat*　ɑ *arm*　e *bed*　ɜr *her*　ɜ: *deux*　ə *ago*　ɪ *sit*　i *cosy*　iː *feed*　ɒ *hot*　ɔ *pore*　oː *no*　ʌ *run*　ʊ *put*

diram /'diːrəm/ *noun* a monetary unit of Tajikistan, equal to one-hundredth of a somoni. [Tajik]

dire *adjective* **1 a** calamitous, dreadful (*in dire straits*). **b** ominous (*dire warnings*). **2** urgent (*in dire need*). □ **dire·ly** *adverb* **dire·ness** *noun* [Latin *dirus* fearful, threatening evil]

dir·ect ● *adjective* **1 a** extending or moving in a straight line or by the shortest route; not crooked or circuitous. **b** (of a journey) not involving any changes of airplane, train, etc. **2 a** straightforward; going straight to the point. **b** frank; not ambiguous. **3** without intermediaries or the intervention of other factors (*direct rule*; *the direct result*; *made a direct approach*; *this plant prefers direct sunlight*). **4** (of descent) lineal, not collateral. **5** exact, complete, greatest possible (esp. where contrast is implied) (*the direct opposite*). **6** (of a quotation, translation, etc.) literal; word for word. **7** *Astronomy* (of planetary etc. motion) proceeding from west to east; not retrograde. ● *adverb* **1** in a direct way or manner; without an intermediary or intervening factor (*dealt with them direct*; *you can dial direct to most points in Canada*; *buy direct from the manufacturer*). **2** by a direct route (*send it direct to head office*). ● *verb* **1** *transitive* guide, esp. with advice. **2** *transitive* control the movement of (*the police officer was directing traffic*; *the output will be directed to whichever printer you select*). **3** *transitive* administer, oversee. **4** *transitive* (foll. by *to* + infin., or *that* + clause) give a formal order or command to. **5** *transitive* (foll. by *to*) **a** address or give indications for the delivery of (a letter etc.). **b** tell or show (a person) the way to a destination. **6** *transitive* (foll. by *at, to, toward*) **a** point, aim, or cause (a blow or missile) to move in a certain direction. **b** aim or address (one's attention, energies, communication, etc.). **7 a** *transitive & intransitive* supervise the performing, staging, etc., of (a film, play, etc.). **b** *transitive* supervise the performance of (an actor etc.). **8** *transitive & intransitive Music* **a** conduct (a group of musicians, esp. singers). **b** guide the performance of (a group of musicians), esp. while performing oneself. □ **dir·ect·ness** *noun* [Latin *directus* past participle of *dirigere direct*- (as DI-², *regere* put straight)]

direct access *noun* the facility of retrieving data immediately from any part of a computer file without searching through the file sequentially. *Also called* RANDOM ACCESS.

direct action *noun* action such as a strike or sabotage directly affecting the community and meant to reinforce demands on a government, employer, etc.

direct cinema *noun* a style of documentary filmmaking in which the subjects are filmed without special planning, lighting, staging, or intervention by the director.

direct current *noun* an electric current flowing in one direction only. Abbr.: **DC, d.c.**

direct debit *noun Cdn & Brit.* an arrangement, authorized by the holder of an account in a bank etc., for the regular debiting of the account at the request of the payee.

direct deposit *noun N Amer.* the electronic transfer of money from one bank account to another.

direct dialing *noun* the facility of dialing a long-distance telephone number without making use of the operator. □ **direct-dial** *transitive & intransitive verb & attributive adjective*

direct discourse *noun esp. N Amer.* = DIRECT SPEECH.

direct drive *noun* (usu. (with hyphen) *attributive*) a method of driving a mechanism, e.g. a turntable, directly by a motor, without an intervening belt.

dir·ec·tion *noun* **1** the act or process of directing. **2** (usu. in *pl.*) an order or instruction, esp. each of a set guiding use of equipment etc. **3 a** the course or line along which a person or thing moves or looks, or which must be taken to reach a destination. **b** (in *pl.*) guidance on how to reach a destination. **c** the point to or from which a person or thing moves or looks. **4** the tendency taken by events, research, etc. □ **sense of direction** the ability to know without guidance the direction in which one is or should be moving. □ **dir·ec·tion·less** *adjective* [French *direction* or Latin *directio* (as DIRECT)]

dir·ec·tion·al *adjective* **1** of or indicating direction. **2** *Electronics* **a** concerned with the transmission of radio or sound waves in a particular direction. **b** (of equipment) designed to receive radio or sound waves most effectively from a particular direction or directions and not others. □ **dir·ec·tion·al·ity** *noun* **dir·ec·tion·al·ly** *adverb*

direction finder *noun* a device for determining the source of radio waves, esp. as an aid in navigation.

dir·ec·tive ● *noun* a general instruction from an authority. ● *adjective* serving to direct. [medieval Latin *directivus* (as DIRECT)]

dir·ect·ly ● *adverb* **1 a** at once; without delay. **b** presently, shortly. **2** exactly, immediately (*directly opposite*; *directly after lunch*). **3** in a direct manner. ● *conjunction Brit. informal* as soon as (*will tell you directly they come*).

direct mail *noun* advertising or fundraising material sent unsolicited through the mail to usu. large numbers of prospective customers or donors. □ **direct mailing** *noun*

direct marketing *noun* selling goods or services by dealing directly with consumers rather than through retailers, usu. by mail order, direct mail, telemarketing, etc. □ **direct marketer** *noun*

direct method *noun* a system of teaching a second language using only that language and without the study of formal grammar.

direct object *noun* the primary object of the action of a transitive verb.

Di·rec·toire /dɪrek'twɒr/ *adjective* designating styles of clothing, furniture, etc. typical of the neoclassical style of the late 18th c. in France, characterized by simple lines and the use of antique ornamental motifs. [French (as DIRECTORY)]

dir·ec·tor /dɪ'rektər, dai-/ *noun* **1** a person who directs, controls, or manages something, esp. an institution or a major division of a company. **2** a member of the board which governs the affairs of a company, corporation, charitable institution, etc. **3** a person who directs a film etc., esp. professionally. **4** a conductor, esp. of a choir, band, or small chamber ensemble of which the director is a performing instrumentalist. **5** (in Quebec municipal police forces) the highest ranking officer. □ **dir·ec·tor·ial** *adjective* **dir·ec·tor·ship** *noun* (esp. in sense 2). [Anglo-French *directour* from Late Latin *director* governor (as DIRECT)]

dir·ec·tor·ate /dɪ'rektərət, dai-/ *noun* **1** a government agency or subdivision of a ministry with a specific responsibility (*Agriculture Canada's pesticides directorate*). **2** a board of directors. **3** the office of director.

director general *noun* (*pl.* **directors general**) **1** the chief executive of an organization, especially a public one. **2** *Cdn* **a** a rank in the civil service immediately below assistant deputy minister. **b** a person holding this rank. **3** (in the Sûreté du Québec) the highest ranking officer.

director's chair *noun* a collapsible chair with a canvas seat and back and legs crossed in the shape of an X.

Dir·ec·tory /dɪ'rektəri, dai-/ the French revolutionary government constituted in 1795, led by an executive of five members to avoid the one-man dictatorship previously achieved by Robespierre. Too weak to control events, it was overthrown by Napoleon in 1799. [translation of French *Directoire*]

dir·ec·tory /dɪ'rektəri, dai-/ *noun* (*pl.* **-ies**) **1 a** a book listing alphabetically or thematically a particular group of individuals (e.g. telephone subscribers) or organizations with various details. **b** *N Amer.* a large board listing names of departments, individuals, etc. and giving their location, esp. in a building complex, department store, etc. **2** a computer file listing other files or programs etc. [Late Latin *directorium* (as DIRECT)]

directory assistance *noun N Amer.* a telephone service providing a subscriber's number on request.

direct payment *noun* payment by means of a debit card, in which funds are transferred electronically from the cardholder's bank account to the account of a merchant etc.

direct proportion *noun* a relation between quantities whose ratio is constant.

dir·ec·trix /dɪ'rektrɪks, dai-/ *noun* (*pl.* **dir·ec·tri·ces** /-trɪˌsiːz/) *Math.* a fixed line used in describing a curve or surface. [medieval Latin from Late Latin *director*: see DIRECTOR, -TRIX]

direct speech *noun* (esp. *N Amer.* also **direct discourse**) words actually spoken, not reported in the third person.

direct tax *noun* a tax paid directly to the government, e.g. income tax or property tax, rather than through an intermediary, e.g. the seller of goods who collects and passes on sales tax.

dire·ful *adjective literary* terrible, dreadful. □ **dire·ful·ly** *adverb*

dirge /dɜrdʒ/ *noun* **1** a lament for the dead, esp. forming part of a funeral service. **2** any mournful song or lament. [Latin *dirige* (imperative) 'direct', the first word in the Latin antiphon (from Ps. 5:8) in the Matins part of the Office for the Dead]

dir·ham /'dɜrham/ *noun* **1** the principal monetary unit of Morocco and the United Arab Emirates, equal to 100 francs in Morocco and 100 fils in the United Arab Emirates. **2** a monetary unit of Libya, Iraq, and Qatar, equal to one-thousandth of a dinar in Libya, one-twentieth of a dinar in Iraq, and one-hundredth of a riyal in Qatar. [Arabic from Latin DRACHMA]

diri·gible /'dɪrɪdʒɪbəl, dɪ'rɪdʒ-/ ● *noun* an airship. ● *adjective* capable of being steered or guided. [Latin *dirigere* arrange, direct: see DIRECT]

uː mood ai my əi pipe au brown ʌu house ei day ɔi boy ɑ̃ franglais ã Canadien ɔ̃ Brayon (*see over for consonants*)

di·ri·gisme /ˌdiːriːˈʒiːzəm/ *noun* state control of economic and social matters. □ **di·ri·giste** *adjective* [French from *diriger* DIRECT]

dirk *noun* a long dagger, esp. as formerly worn by Scottish Highlanders. [17th-c. *durk*, of unknown origin]

dirndl /ˈdərndəl/ *noun* **1** a woman's dress styled in imitation of Alpine peasant costume, with close-fitting bodice, tight waistband, and full skirt. **2** (also **dirndl skirt**) a full skirt of this kind. [German dial., diminutive of *Dirne* girl]

dirt *noun* **1** a substance, such as mud or dust, that soils someone or something (*his face was covered in dirt*). **2 a** earth, soil. **b** earth, cinders, etc., used to make a surface for a road etc. (usu. *attributive*: *dirt track*). **3 a** obscene or foul language. **b** information, especially of a scandalous nature; gossip (*what's the dirt on the people down the street?*). **4** excrement (*dog dirt*). **5** a person or thing considered worthless. □ **do a person dirt** *slang* harm or injure a person's reputation maliciously. **eat dirt** suffer insults, humiliation, etc. without retaliating. **hit the dirt** *N Amer.* **1** drop to the floor, ground, etc. **2** *Baseball slang* slide into base. **treat like dirt** treat (a person) contemptuously; abuse. [Old Norse *drit* excrement]

dirt·bag *noun* (also **dirt·ball**) *slang* a contemptible, despicable, or disgusting person.

dirt bike *noun* a motorcycle designed for use on dirt roads and in cross-country racing.

dirt cheap *adjective & adverb informal* extremely cheap.

dirt farmer *noun N Amer.* a farmer who ekes out a living from a farm, usu. without the help of hired labour. □ **dirt farming** *noun*

dirt poor *adjective* very poor.

dirt road *noun N Amer.* a road of packed earth, gravel, etc. with an unsealed surface.

dirt track *noun* **1** a rudimentary road or trail made of packed earth. **2** a course made of rolled cinders, soil, etc., for motorcycle racing or horse racing. □ **dirt tracker** *noun*

dirty ● *adjective* (**dirt·i·er**, **dirt·i·est**) **1** soiled, unclean. **2** causing one to become dirty; producing dirt (*a dirty job*). **3** pertaining to or obsessed with sexual activity; obscene (*dirty joke*; *dirty mind*). **4** unpleasant, nasty. **5** dishonest, dishonourable, unfair (*dirty play*). **6** (of weather) rough, squally. **7** (of a colour) not pure or clear, dingy. **8** *informal* (of a nuclear weapon) producing considerable radioactive fallout. **9** *Cdn (Nfld)* (of sea water) clear due to a lack of the plankton which attract fish but rich in marine organisms which clog fishing nets. **10** *Cdn (Nfld)* bad-tempered. ● *adverb* **1** *informal* in a malicious, unfair, or underhanded manner (*fight dirty*). **2** *Brit. slang* (with adjectives expressing magnitude) very (*a dirty great diamond*). ● *transitive & intransitive verb* (**-ies**, **-ied**) make or become dirty. □ **dirty one's hands** (or **get one's hands dirty**) *informal* acquire practical experience, esp. as opposed to theoretical knowledge. **do the dirty on** *informal* play a mean trick on. **talk dirty** *informal* use obscene language. □ **dirt·i·ly** *adverb* **dirt·i·ness** *noun*

dirty bomb *noun informal* a conventional weapon containing radioactive material.

dirty laundry *noun* (also **dirty linen**) intimate secrets, esp. of a scandalous nature. □ **wash** (or **air**) **one's dirty laundry** (or **linen**) **in public** be indiscreet about one's domestic quarrels etc.

dirty look *noun informal* a look of disapproval, anger, or disgust.

dirty money *noun* money obtained through illicit or disreputable activity.

dirty old man *noun informal* a lecherous older man.

dirty pool *noun N Amer. informal* dishonest, unfair, or unsportsmanlike conduct.

dirty thirties *noun esp. Cdn informal* **1** the Great Depression of the 1930s. **2** the years of drought coinciding with this on the Prairies, accompanied by vast dust storms.

dirty trick *noun* **1** a spiteful and underhanded act. **2** (in *pl.*) underhanded political activity, esp. to discredit an opponent. □ **dirty trickster** *noun*

dirty weekend *noun informal esp. Brit.* a weekend spent clandestinely with a lover.

dirty word *noun* **1** an offensive or indecent word. **2** a word for something which is disapproved of (*profit is a dirty word*).

dirty work *noun* unpleasant, difficult, or illegal activity, esp. if delegated by someone wishing to avoid it.

dis /dɪs/ (also **diss**) *US slang* ● *transitive verb* (**dissed**, **dis·sing**) put (a person etc.) down; badmouth. ● *noun* a disrespectful attitude. [abbreviation of DISRESPECT]

dis- *prefix* forming nouns, adjectives, and verbs: **1** expressing negation (*dishonest*). **2** indicating reversal or absence of an action or state (*disengage*; *disbelieve*). **3** indicating removal of a thing or quality (*dismember*; *disable*). **4** indicating separation (*distinguish*; *dispose*). **5** indicating completeness or intensification of the action (*disembowel*). **6** indicating expulsion from (*disbar*). [Latin *dis-*, sometimes through Old French *des-*]

dis·abil·ity *noun* (pl. **-ities**) **1 a** a physical or mental handicap, either congenital or caused by injury, disease, etc. **b** the condition of having such a handicap. **2** a lack of some asset, quality, or attribute, that prevents one's doing something. **3** incapacity created or recognized by the law.

dis·able *transitive verb* **1** render unable to function. **2** deprive of an ability. □ **dis·able·ment** *noun*

dis·abled *adjective* **1** having reduced physical or mental abilities, esp. through injury or disease. **2** for the use of people with physical disabilities (*disabled parking space*). **3** made incapable of action or use (*the disabled ships were towed into harbour*).

disabled list *noun Baseball* a list of injured players who are unable to play, usu. for a specified length of time. Abbr.: **DL**.

dis·abuse /ˌdɪsəˈbjuːz/ *transitive verb* **1** (foll. by *of*) free from a mistaken idea. **2** disillusion, undeceive.

di·sac·char·ide /daiˈsakəraid/ *noun* a sugar whose molecule contains two linked monosaccharides.

dis·advan·tage ● *noun* **1** an unfavourable circumstance or condition. **2** damage to one's interest or reputation. ● *transitive verb* cause disadvantage to. □ **at a disadvantage** in an unfavourable position or aspect.

dis·advan·taged *adjective* suffering from social or economic deprivation or discrimination.

dis·advan·ta·geous *adjective* involving disadvantage or discredit. □ **dis·advan·ta·geous·ly** *adverb*

dis·affect·ed *adjective* **1** alienated and discontented, esp. with regard to authority. **2** disloyal. [past participle of *disaffect* (v.), originally = dislike, disorder (as DIS-, AFFECT[2])]

dis·affec·tion *noun* **1** discontentedness, esp. with political or social structures. **2** disloyalty. **3** (usu. foll. by *with*) disenchantment; loss of affection or respect.

dis·af·fili·ate *verb* **1** *transitive* end the affiliation of. **2** *intransitive* end one's affiliation. □ **dis·af·fili·a·tion** *noun*

dis·aggre·gate *transitive verb* separate into component parts; cease to treat as aggregated. □ **dis·aggre·ga·tion** *noun*

dis·agree *intransitive verb* (**-agrees**, **-agreed**, **-agree·ing**) (often foll. by *with*) **1** hold a different opinion. **2** quarrel. **3** (of factors or circumstances) not correspond. **4** have an adverse effect upon (a person's health, digestion, etc.). □ **dis·agree·ment** *noun*

dis·agree·able *adjective* **1** unpleasant, not to one's liking. **2** quarrelsome; rude or bad-tempered. □ **dis·agree·able·ness** *noun* **dis·agree·ably** *adverb*

dis·allow *transitive verb* **1** refuse to allow or accept as valid; prohibit. **2** annul (a statute) passed by a lower legislative body. □ **dis·allow·ance** *noun*

dis·am·bigu·ate *transitive verb* make unambiguous, esp. distinguish the various senses of (words in context). □ **dis·am·bigu·a·tion** *noun*

dis·appear *intransitive verb* **1** cease to be visible; pass from sight. **2** cease to exist or be in circulation or use (*the problem has disappeared*). **3** (of a person or thing) go missing. □ **dis·appear·ance** *noun*

disappearing act *noun* an instance of vanishing as if by magic, esp. to avoid unpleasantness.

dis·appoint *verb* **1 a** *transitive* fail to fulfill a desire or expectation of (a person). **b** *intransitive* fail to live up to expectations (*we had great hopes of the team and they did not disappoint*). **2** *transitive* frustrate (hopes etc.). □ **dis·appoint·ing** *adjective* **dis·appoint·ing·ly** *adverb* [French *désappointer* (as DIS-, APPOINT)]

dis·appoint·ed *adjective* (often foll. by *with*, *at*, *by*, *in*, or *to* + infin., or *that* + clause) frustrated or saddened by not having one's expectation etc. fulfilled in some regard (*disappointed job applicants*; *was disappointed with you*; *disappointed at the result*; *am disappointed to find so little interest in Canada*). □ **dis·appoint·ed·ly** *adverb*

dis·appoint·ment *noun* **1** an event, thing, or person that disappoints. **2** a feeling of distress, vexation, etc., resulting from this (*I cannot hide my disappointment*).

dis·ap·pro·ba·tion /ˌdɪsaprəˈbeɪʃən/ *noun* strong (esp. moral) disapproval.

dis·ap·prove *verb* **1** *intransitive* (usu. foll. by *of*) have or express an unfavourable opinion. **2** *transitive* withhold approval from (an action, etc.); express disfavour of. □ **dis·ap·prov·al** *noun* **dis·ap·prov·ing** *adjective* **dis·ap·prov·ing·ly** *adverb*

dis·arm *verb* **1** *transitive* deprive of a weapon or weapons. **2 a** *intransitive* (of a nation) reduce the size, armament, etc. of one's armed forces. **b** *transitive* cause (a nation) to do this. **3** *transitive* remove the fuse from (a bomb etc.). **4** *transitive* deprive of the power to injure. **5** *transitive* pacify or allay the hostility or suspicions of; mollify; placate. **6** *transitive* deactivate (an alarm system etc.). □ **dis·arm·er** *noun*

dis·arma·ment *noun* the reduction by a nation of its military forces and weapons.

dis·arm·ing *adjective* reducing suspicion, anger, hostility, distrust, etc. (*a disarming smile*). □ **dis·arm·ing·ly** *adverb*

dis·arrange *transitive verb* bring into disorder. □ **dis·arrange·ment** *noun*

dis·array ● *noun* (often prec. by *in*, *into*) disorder, confusion. ● *transitive verb literary* throw into disorder.

dis·arti·cu·late *transitive & intransitive verb* separate (a skeleton etc.) at the joints. □ **dis·arti·cu·la·tion** *noun*

dis·assem·ble *transitive verb* take (a machine etc.) to pieces. □ **dis·assem·bly** *noun*

dis·assem·bler *noun* Computing a program for converting machine code into assembly language.

dis·associ·ate *transitive & intransitive verb* = DISSOCIATE. □ **dis·associ·a·tion** *noun*

dis·as·ter *noun* **1** a great or sudden misfortune. **2 a** a complete failure. **b** a person or enterprise ending in failure. □ **dis·as·trous** *adjective* **dis·as·trous·ly** *adverb* [originally 'unfavourable aspect of a star', from French *désastre* or Italian *disastro* (as DIS-, *astro* from Latin *astrum* star)]

disaster area *noun* **1 a** an area affected by a natural disaster, e.g. earthquake, flooding, etc. **b** *US* such an area that is officially declared eligible for emergency relief funds and services from the government. **2** a place characterized by extreme disorderliness or misfortune.

disaster movie *noun* a film whose plot centres on a major disaster such as a flood, fire, airplane crash, etc.

dis·avow /ˌdɪsəˈvaʊ/ *transitive verb* disclaim knowledge of, responsibility or support for, or belief in. □ **dis·avow·al** *noun*

dis·band /dɪsˈbænd/ *verb* **1** *transitive* break up the organization of (a group etc.). **2** *intransitive* (of an organization) cease to work or act together; disperse. □ **dis·band·ment** *noun*

dis·bar *transitive verb* (**dis·barred**, **dis·bar·ring**) deprive (a lawyer) of the right to practise. □ **dis·bar·ment** *noun*

dis·belief *noun* **1** lack of belief; failure to believe. **2** astonishment.

dis·believe *verb* **1** *transitive* be unable or unwilling to believe (a person or statement). **2** *intransitive* have no faith. □ **dis·believ·er** *noun* **dis·believ·ing·ly** *adverb*

dis·bud *transitive verb* (**dis·bud·ded**, **dis·bud·ding**) remove (esp. superfluous) buds from.

dis·burden *transitive verb* **1** relieve (a person, one's mind, etc.) of a burden. **2** get rid of, remove (a load etc.).

dis·burse /dɪsˈbɜrs/ *verb transitive* expend (money). □ **dis·burse·ment** *noun* **dis·burs·er** *noun* [Old French *desbourser* (as DIS-, BOURSE)]

disc *noun* (also **disk**) **1 a** a flat thin circular object. **b** a round flat or apparently flat surface (*the sun's disc*). **2** (in full **intervertebral disc**) a layer of cartilage between vertebrae. **3** a sound or video recording in the form of a disc. **4** the close-packed cluster of tubular florets in the centre of a composite flower. **5** esp. *Brit.* var. of DISK 1. **6** var. of DISK 3. [French *disque* or Latin *discus*: see DISCUS]

dis·calced /dɪsˈkælst/ *adjective* denoting or belonging to one of several strict orders of Catholic friars or nuns who go barefoot or wear only sandals. [var. of *discalceated* (after French *déchaux*) from Latin *discalceatus* (as DIS-, *calceatus* from *calceus* shoe)]

dis·card ● *verb* /dɪsˈkɑrd/ **1** *transitive* reject or get rid of as unwanted or superfluous. **2 a** *transitive* remove or put aside (a playing card) from one's hand. **b** *transitive* play (a card) from a remaining suit when not following suit or trumping. **c** *intransitive* discard a playing card. ● *noun* /ˈdɪskɑrd/ **1** a rejected or abandoned item or person. **2** a discarded playing card. □ **dis·card·able** /-ˈkɑrdəbəl/ *adjective* [DIS- + CARD¹]

dis·car·nate /dɪsˈkɑrnət/ *adjective* having no physical body; separated from the flesh. □ **discar·na·tion** /dɪskɑrˈneɪʃən/ *noun* [DIS-, Latin *caro carnis* flesh]

disc brake *noun* a brake employing the friction of pads against a disc which is attached to the wheel.

dis·cern /dɪˈsɜrn/ *transitive verb* **1** perceive through the senses, esp. by sight. **2** distinguish (one thing or fact) by the intellect; recognize or detect (*her drama teacher failed to discern her potential*). □ **dis·cern·er** *noun* **dis·cern·ible** *adjective* **dis·cern·ibly** *adverb* [Old French *discerner* from Latin DIS-, *cernere cret-* separate)]

dis·cern·ing *adjective* having or showing good judgment, taste, or insight. □ **dis·cern·ing·ly** *adverb*

dis·cern·ment *noun* **1** good judgment or insight. **2** the act or an instance of discerning.

dis·charge ● *verb* /dɪsˈtʃɑrdʒ/ **1** *transitive* **a** let go, release, esp. from a duty, commitment, or period of confinement. **b** relieve (a bankrupt) of residual liability. **2** *transitive* dismiss from office, employment, army commission, etc. **3** *transitive* **a** fire (a gun etc.). **b** (of a gun etc.) fire (a bullet etc.). **4 a** *transitive & intransitive* pour out or cause to pour out; emit (pus, liquid, etc.) (*the abscess burst and discharged pus; raw sewage is discharged into the lake*). **b** *intransitive* (foll. by *into*) (of a river etc.) flow into (esp. a large body of water). **5** *transitive* **a** carry out, perform (a duty or obligation). **b** relieve oneself of (a financial commitment) (*discharged his debt*). **6** *transitive* *Physics* release an electrical charge from. **7** *transitive* **a** remove cargo from (a ship etc.). **b** unload (a cargo) from a ship. ● *noun* /ˈdɪstʃɑrdʒ/ **1** the act or an instance of discharging; the process of being discharged. **2** a dismissal, esp. from the armed services. **3 a** a release, exemption, acquittal, etc. **b** a written certificate of release etc. **4** an act of firing a gun etc. **5 a** an emission (of pus, liquid, etc.). **b** the liquid or matter so discharged. **6** (usu. foll. by *of*) **a** the payment (of a debt). **b** the performance (of a duty etc.). **7** *Physics* **a** the release of a quantity of electric charge from an object. **b** a flow of electricity through the air or other gas esp. when accompanied by the emission of light. **c** the conversion of chemical energy in a cell into electrical energy. **8** the unloading (of a ship or a cargo). □ **dis·charge·able** *adjective* **dis·char·ger** *noun* (in sense 7 of *verb*).

dis·ciple /dɪˈsaɪpəl/ *noun* **1** a follower or pupil of a leader, teacher, philosophy, etc. (*a disciple of Zen Buddhism*). **2 a** one of the personal followers of Jesus during his lifetime, esp. one of the twelve Apostles. **b** a professed Christian. □ **dis·ciple·ship** *noun* [Old English *discipul* from Latin *discipulus* from *discere* learn]

disci·plin·ar·ian /ˌdɪsɪplɪˈnɛriən/ *noun* a person who practises or upholds firm discipline (*a strict disciplinarian*).

disci·plin·ary /ˈdɪsɪplɪnˌɛri/ *adjective* of, promoting, or enforcing discipline.

disci·pline /ˈdɪsɪplɪn/ ● *noun* **1 a** a training, esp. of the mind and character, aimed at producing self-control, obedience, orderly conduct, etc. **b** the result of such training; ordered behaviour, e.g. of schoolchildren, soldiers, etc. (*poor discipline in the ranks; university professors do not expect to have to deal with discipline problems*). **2** a system of rules used to maintain control over people, e.g. prisoners, military personnel, etc. **3** a branch of instruction or learning (*the scientific disciplines*). **4** a subcategory of a sporting activity (*ice dancing is an Olympic discipline*). **5** punishment. ● *transitive verb* **1** punish, reprimand. **2** train to be obedient, self-controlled, skilful, etc. [Late Latin *disciplinare, disciplina* from *discipulus* DISCIPLE]

disc jockey *noun* a person who introduces and/or plays recorded music on a radio program, at a dance, etc.

dis·claim *transitive verb* deny or disown (*disclaim all responsibility*).

dis·claim·er *noun* **1** a renunciation or disavowal, esp. of responsibility. **2** *Law* an act of repudiating another's claim or renouncing one's own. [Anglo-French (= DISCLAIM as noun)]

dis·close *transitive verb* **1** make known; reveal (*disclosed the truth*). **2** expose to view. □ **dis·clos·er** *noun* [Old French *desclos-* stem of *desclore* from Gallo-Roman (as DIS-, CLOSE²)]

dis·clos·ing *adjective* (of a tablet, solution, etc.) revealing, by means of a special dye, any plaque on the teeth.

dis·clo·sure *noun* **1** the act or an instance of disclosing; the process of being disclosed. **2** something disclosed; a revelation.

disc number *noun* *Cdn hist.* a number used in an identification system introduced in 1940 by the federal government in order to identify individual Inuit.

disco *informal* ● *noun* (pl. **-cos**) **1** a place or event at which recorded popular music is played for dancing, often with elaborate lighting and other special effects. **2** = DISCO MUSIC. ● *intransitive verb* (**-coes**, **-coed**) dance to disco music. [abbreviation]

disc·ob·olus /dɪsˈkɒbələs/ *noun* (pl. **disc·ob·oli** /-ˌlaɪ/) **1** a discus thrower in ancient Greece. **2** a statue of a discobolus. [Latin from Greek *diskobolos* from *diskos* DISCUS + *-bolos* -throwing, from *ballō* to throw]

t top v voice w we z zoo ʃ she ʒ vision θ thin ð this ŋ ring x loch tʃ chip dʒ jar *(see over for vowels)*

disc·og·raphy /dɪsˈkɒgrəfi/ *noun* (*pl.* **-ies**) **1** a descriptive catalogue of sound recordings, esp. of a particular performer or composer. **2** a musician's recordings considered collectively. □ **disc·og·raph·er** *noun* **disc·o·graph·ic·al** *adjective* [DISC + -GRAPHY after *biography*]

disc·oid /ˈdɪskɔɪd/ *adjective* disc-shaped. [Greek *diskoeidēs* (as DISCUS, -OID)]

dis·colour *transitive & intransitive verb* (also **dis·color**) spoil or cause to spoil the colour of; stain; tarnish. □ **dis·color·a·tion** *noun* (also **dis·colour·a·tion**).

dis·com·bobu·late /ˌdɪskəmˈbɒbjuˌleɪt/ *transitive verb* N Amer. jocular disturb; disconcert. □ **dis·com·bobu·la·tion** *noun* [prob. based on *discompose* or *discomfit*]

dis·com·fit /dɪsˈkʌmfɪt/ *transitive verb* (**dis·com·fit·ed**, **dis·com·fit·ing**) **1** disconcert, embarrass, or throw into confusion. **2** *archaic* defeat in battle. □ **dis·com·fi·ture** *noun* [*disconfit* from Old French past participle of *desconfire* from Romanic (as DIS-, Latin *conficere* put together: see CONFECTION)]

dis·com·fort ● *noun* **1 a** a lack of ease; slight pain (*you may experience some discomfort after the extraction*). **b** mental uneasiness (*she felt some discomfort about taking drugs*). **2** a lack of comfort. ● *transitive verb* make uneasy, disturb.

dis·com·mode /ˌdɪskəˈmoʊd/ *transitive verb* inconvenience (a person etc.). [obsolete French *discommoder* var. of *incommoder* (as DIS-, INCOMMODE)]

dis·com·pose *transitive verb* disturb the composure of; agitate; disturb. □ **dis·com·po·sure** *noun*

disco music *noun* a style of dance music characterized by a strong, repetitive rhythm, and the use of electronic instrumentation, popular esp. in the 1970s.

dis·con·cert /ˌdɪskənˈsɜrt/ *transitive verb* **1** (esp. in *passive*) disturb the composure of; agitate; fluster (*disconcerted by his expression*). **2** *archaic* spoil or upset (plans etc.). □ **dis·con·cert·ed·ly** *adverb* **dis·con·cert·ing** *adjective* **dis·con·cert·ing·ly** *adverb* [obsolete French *desconcerter* (as DIS-, CONCERT)]

dis·con·firm *transitive verb* formal disprove or tend to disprove (a hypothesis etc.). □ **dis·con·firm·a·tion** *noun*

dis·con·form·ity *noun* (*pl.* **-ities**) *Geol.* an unconformity in which the strata above and below are more or less parallel, the lower set having been eroded but not deformed. **2** lack of conformity.

dis·con·nect ● *verb* **1 a** *transitive* detach or separate something connected (*when I want to watch television, I disconnect my phone; disconnect the hose from the dishwasher*). **b** *intransitive* become detached. **2** *transitive* detach (a customer) from a network of services, e.g. telephone, cable television, electricity, etc. **3** *transitive* interrupt (a telephone connection) (*I was on hold for five minutes and then I was disconnected*). **4** *transitive* (usu. in *passive*; often foll. by *from*) break a connection between (people, actions, etc.). ● *noun* **1** an act or instance of disconnecting (*schedule disconnect dates with the hydro and gas companies before you move*). **2** a lack of connection; a discrepancy (*a disconnect between what they say and what they do*). □ **dis·con·nec·tion** *noun*

dis·con·nect·ed *adjective* **1** (of speech, writing, argument, etc.) incoherent and illogical. **2** not connected. □ **dis·con·nect·ed·ly** *adverb* **dis·con·nect·ed·ness** *noun*

dis·con·so·late /dɪsˈkɒnsələt/ *adjective* **1** without consolation or comfort; unhappy. **2** (of a place, thing, etc.) causing or showing a complete lack of comfort; cheerless, miserable. □ **dis·con·so·late·ly** *adverb* **dis·con·so·la·tion** *noun* [medieval Latin *disconsolatus* (as DIS-, *consolatus* past participle of Latin *consolari* console)]

dis·con·tent ● *noun* lack of contentment; restlessness, dissatisfaction. ● *adjective* dissatisfied (*was discontent with his lot*). □ **dis·con·tent·ment** *noun*

dis·con·tent·ed *adjective* dissatisfied. □ **dis·con·tent·ed·ly** *adverb* **dis·con·tent·ed·ness** *noun*

dis·con·tinue *verb* (**-tinues**, **-tinued**, **-tinu·ing**) **1** *intransitive & transitive* cease or cause to cease to exist or be made (*that model has been discontinued*). **2** *transitive* give up, cease from (*the doctor recommended discontinuing antidepressants*). **3** *transitive* cease subscribing to or paying for (a newspaper, service, etc.). □ **dis·con·tinu·ance** *noun* **dis·con·tinu·a·tion** *noun*

dis·con·tinu·ous *adjective* lacking continuity in space or time; intermittent. □ **dis·con·tinu·ity** *noun* (*pl.* **-ities**). **dis·con·tinu·ous·ly** *adverb*

dis·cord ● *noun* /ˈdɪskɔrd/ **1** disagreement; strife. **2** a harsh or unpleasing clashing of sounds; a confused noise. **3** *Music* **a** a lack of harmony between notes sounding together. **b** an unpleasing or

unfinished chord needing to be completed by another. **c** any interval except unison, an octave, a perfect fifth and fourth, a major and minor third and sixth, and their octaves. **d** a single note dissonant with another. ● *intransitive verb* /dɪˈskɔrd/ (usu. foll. by *with*) *archaic* disagree or quarrel. [Old French *descord* (n.), *descorder* (v.) from Latin *discordare* from *discors* discordant (as DIS-, *cor* cord- heart)]

dis·cord·ant /dɪˈskɔrdənt/ *adjective* **1** not in accord; incongruous. **2** (of sounds) not in harmony; dissonant. □ **dis·cord·ance** *noun* **dis·cord·ancy** *noun* **dis·cord·ant·ly** *adverb* [Old French, part. of *discorder*: see DISCORD]

disco·theque /ˈdɪskəˌtek/ *noun* = DISCO 1. [French, = record library]

dis·count ● *noun* /ˈdɪskaʊnt/ **1** a deduction from a bill or amount due given esp. for prompt or advance payment or to a special category of buyers. **2** a deduction from the face value of a bond, treasury bill, promissory note, or other bill of exchange when it is purchased before its maturity date. ● *transitive verb* /dɪˈskaʊnt/ **1** disregard as being unreliable or unimportant (*discounted his story*). **2** /ˈdɪskaʊnt/ **a** detract from; lessen; deduct (esp. an amount from a bill etc.). **b** reduce in price. **3** /ˈdɪskaʊnt/ buy or sell (a bill of exchange before its maturity date) at a price less than its face value. ● *adjective* /ˈdɪskaʊnt/ **1** selling goods at less than the normal retail price (*discount store*). **2** sold at less than the normal retail price (*discount fares*). □ **at a discount** below the nominal or usual price (compare PREMIUM). □ **dis·count·able** *adjective* **dis·count·er** *noun* [obsolete French *descompte*, *-conte*, *descompter* or Italian (*di*)*scontare* (as DIS-, COUNT[1])]

discount broker *noun* esp. N Amer. a stockbroker who charges reduced fees, commissions, etc. □ **discount brokerage** *noun*

dis·coun·ten·ance /dɪˈskaʊntənəns/ *transitive verb* **1** disconcert. **2** *archaic* show disapproval of; discourage.

discount house *noun* **1** N Amer. a discount store. **2** Brit. a company that specializes in discounting bills of exchange, esp. treasury bills.

discount rate *noun* esp. US the interest rate set by the central bank on short-term loans to banks etc. Compare BANK RATE.

dis·cour·age *transitive verb* **1** deprive of courage, confidence, or enthusiasm. **2** (usu. foll. by *from*) dissuade (*discouraged him from going*). **3** oppose or deter (*the police presence is designed to discourage drug use in the neighbourhood; companion planting discourages weed growth*). □ **dis·cour·age·ment** *noun* **dis·cour·aging** *adjective* **dis·cour·aging·ly** *adverb* [Old French *descouragier* (as DIS-, COURAGE)]

dis·course ● *noun* /ˈdɪskɔrs/ **1** conversation; talk. **2** a formal discussion of a subject in speech or writing. **3** the body of statements, analysis, etc., both written and spoken, concerning a specific subject, esp. as typified by recurring terms and concepts (*feminist discourse*). **4** *Linguistics* a connected series of utterances; a text. ● *verb* /dɪˈskɔrs/ **1** *intransitive* talk; converse. **2** *intransitive* (usu. foll. by *of*, *on*, *upon*) speak or write learnedly or at length (on a subject). [Latin *discursus* (as DIS-, COURSE); (v.) partly after French *discourir*]

discourse analysis *noun* a method of analyzing the structure of texts or utterances longer than one sentence, taking into account both their linguistic content and their sociolinguistic context.

dis·cour·te·ous *adjective* impolite; rude. □ **dis·cour·te·ous·ly** *adverb* **dis·cour·te·ous·ness** *noun*

dis·cour·tesy *noun* (*pl.* **-ies**) **1** bad manners; rudeness. **2** an impolite act or remark.

dis·cov·er *transitive verb* **1** (often foll. by *that* + clause) **a** find out or become aware of, whether by research or searching or by chance (*discovered a new entrance; discovered that they had been overpaid*). **b** be the first to find or find out (*Banting and Best discovered insulin*). ¶ The use of the words *discover* and *discovery* in reference to Europeans' first contact with Aboriginal peoples in other continents is widely considered to be offensive to Aboriginal peoples. **2** (in show business) find and promote as a new singer, actor, etc. **3** *archaic* **a** make known. **b** exhibit; manifest. **c** disclose; betray. □ **dis·cov·er·able** *adjective* **dis·cov·er·er** *noun* [Old French *descovrir* from Late Latin *discooperire* (as DIS-, COVER)]

dis·cov·ery *noun* (*pl.* **-ies**) **1 a** the act or process of discovering or being discovered. **b** an instance of this (*the discovery of a new planet*). **2** a person or thing discovered. **3** *Law* the compulsory disclosure, by a party to an action, of facts or documents on which the other party wishes to rely. [DISCOVER after *recover*, *recovery*]

Discovery Day *noun* **1** (in the Yukon) a statutory holiday observed on the third Monday in August, commemorating the discovery of gold in the Klondike on August 17, 1896. **2** (in Newfoundland prior to 1993) a statutory holiday observed on the Monday nearest June 24, the date on which John Cabot landed in Newfoundland in 1497.

discovery well *noun* the first productive well drilled in an oil exploration area.

dis·cred·it ● *noun* **1** harm to reputation (*brought discredit on the enterprise*). **2** a person or thing causing such harm (*he is a discredit to his family*). **3** lack of credibility or doubt (*the notion has fallen into discredit*). ● *transitive verb* (**dis·cred·it·ed, dis·cred·it·ing**) **1** harm the good reputation of. **2** take away the credibility of or destroy confidence in (an effort, a person, etc.). □ **dis·cred·it·ed** *adjective*

dis·cred·it·able *adjective* shameful; bringing discredit. □ **dis·cred·it·ably** *adverb*

dis·creet *adjective* (**dis·creet·er, dis·creet·est**) **1 a** circumspect in speech or action, esp. to avoid social disgrace or embarrassment. **b** tactful, trustworthy. **2** unobtrusive (*discreet camerawork*). □ **dis·creet·ly** *adverb* **dis·creet·ness** *noun* [Old French *discret -ete* from Latin *discretus* separate (as DIS-, *cretus* past participle of *cernere* sift), with Late Latin sense from its derivative *discretio* discernment]

dis·crep·ancy *noun* (*pl.* **-cies**) (often foll. by *between*) an illogical or surprising lack of compatibility or similarity between two or more facts (*there's a discrepancy between Mary's account and Bernard's; pointed out the discrepancies in the statement*). □ **dis·crep·ant** *adjective* [Latin *discrepare* be discordant (as DIS-, *crepare* creak)]

dis·crete *adjective* **1** separate or individually distinct (*a series of discrete events*). **2** discontinuous; consisting of distinct or individual parts. **3** *Math.* specified only for a distinct set of points (*discrete variables*). □ **dis·crete·ly** *adverb* **dis·crete·ness** *noun* [Latin *discretus*: see DISCREET]

dis·cre·tion *noun* **1** the quality of being discreet; tact, circumspection (*treats confidences with discretion*). **2** ability to discern what is right, advisable, etc., esp. as regards a person's own conduct. **3** the freedom to act and think as one wishes, usu. within legal limits (*it is within his discretion to leave*) (see also AGE OF DISCRETION). **4** *Law* a court's freedom to decide a sentence etc. □ **at one's discretion** as one pleases. **at the discretion of** (to be settled or disposed of) according to the judgment or choice of (a person). **discretion is the better part of valour** wise caution is better than brave foolhardiness. **use one's discretion** act according to one's own judgment. [Old French from Latin *discretio -onis* (as DISCREET)]

dis·cre·tion·ary *adjective* (usu. *attributive*) used, adopted, etc. when considered necessary (*discretionary powers; discretionary spending*).

dis·crim·in·ant ● *adjective* *Statistics* designating a function of several variates that is used to give the best classification of items for which values of the variates are available. ● *noun* *Math.* a function derived from another function and providing information about its behaviour.

dis·crim·in·ate /dɪˈskrɪmɪˌneɪt/ *verb* **1** *intransitive* (often foll. by *between*) make or see a distinction; differentiate (*cannot discriminate between right and wrong*). **2** *intransitive* (usu. foll. by *against*) make a distinction, esp. unjustly and on the basis of race, age, sex, etc. **3** *transitive* (usu. foll. by *from*) make, discern, or constitute a difference in or between (*many things discriminate one person from another*). **4** *intransitive* observe distinctions carefully; have good judgment. **5** *transitive* mark as distinctive; be a distinguishing feature of. □ **dis·crim·in·ate·ly** /-nətli/ *adverb* **dis·crim·in·a·tive** /-nətɪv/ *adjective* **dis·crim·in·ator** *noun* **dis·crim·in·a·tory** /-nətɔri/ *adjective* [Latin *discriminare* from *discrimen -minis* distinction, from *discernere* DISCERN]

dis·crim·in·at·ing *adjective* **1** able to discern, esp. distinctions. **2** having good taste. **3** (usu. in *predicative*) practising or demonstrating racial, sexual, etc. discrimination. □ **dis·crim·in·at·ing·ly** *adverb*

dis·crim·in·a·tion *noun* **1** (often foll. by *against*) an act, instance, policy, etc. of unfavourable treatment based on prejudice, esp. regarding race, age, or sex. **2** good taste or judgment in artistic matters etc. **3** the power of discriminating or observing differences. **4** a distinction made with the mind or in action.

dis·cur·sive *adjective* **1** rambling, digressive; passing indiscriminately from subject to subject. **2** *Philos.* proceeding by argument or reasoning (*opp.* INTUITIVE). □ **dis·cur·sive·ly** *adverb* **dis·cur·sive·ness** *noun* [medieval Latin *discursivus* from Latin *discurrere discurs-* (as DIS-, *currere* run)]

dis·cus /ˈdɪskəs/ *noun* (*pl.* **dis·cuses**) **1** a heavy thick-centred disc thrown in ancient Greek games. **2** a similar disc thrown in modern field events. **3** the sport of discus throwing. [Latin from Greek *diskos*]

dis·cuss *transitive verb* **1** hold a conversation about (*discussed their holidays*). **2** debate or examine by argument. □ **dis·cuss·able** *adjective* **dis·cuss·ant** *noun* **dis·cuss·er** *noun* [Latin *discutere discuss-* disperse (as DIS-, *quatere* shake)]

dis·cus·sion *noun* **1** a conversation or exchange of views, esp. on specific subjects; informal debate (*had a discussion about what they should do*). **2** an examination by argument, written or spoken.

dis·dain ● *noun* (often foll. by *for*) a feeling or attitude of scorn or contempt. ● *transitive verb* **1** treat or regard (a person, idea, etc.) with scorn or contempt. **2** think oneself superior to; reject (*disdained his offer; disdained answering*). [Old French *desdeign(ier)*, ultimately from Latin *dedignari* (as DE-, *dignari* from *dignus* worthy)]

dis·dain·ful *adjective* showing disdain or contempt. □ **dis·dain·ful·ly** *adverb*

dis·ease *noun* **1 a** an unhealthy condition of the body or mind; illness, sickness. **b** a particular kind of disease with special symptoms or location (*Crohn's disease*). **2** a corresponding physical condition of plants (*Dutch elm disease*). **3** a deranged, depraved, or morbid condition (of society etc.) (*disease of materialism*). [Old French *desaise*]

dis·eased *adjective* **1** affected with disease. **2** abnormal, disordered.

dis·econ·omy *noun* *Econ.* (*pl.* **-ies**) **1** a lack or absence of economy. **2** something that increases costs, esp. in a large-scale operation.

dis·em·bark *transitive & intransitive verb* leave or remove from a ship, aircraft, train, etc. □ **dis·em·bark·a·tion** *noun*

dis·em·body *transitive verb* (**-ies, -ied**) (esp. as **dis·em·bod·ied** *adjective*) separate or free from the body or a concrete form (*disembodied voices*). □ **dis·em·bodi·ment** *noun*

dis·em·bogue /ˌdɪsɪmˈboɡ/ *transitive & intransitive verb* (**dis·em·bogues, dis·em·bogued, dis·em·boguing**) (of a river etc.) pour forth (waters) at the mouth. [Spanish *desembocar* (as DIS-, *en* in, *boca* mouth)]

dis·em·bowel *transitive verb* (**-bowelled, -bowel·ling**; also esp. *US* **-boweled, -bowel·ing**) remove the bowels or entrails of. □ **dis·em·bow·elled** *adjective* **dis·em·bowel·ment** *noun*

dis·em·power *transitive verb* remove the power to act from (a person, group, etc.). □ **dis·em·powered** *adjective* **dis·em·power·ment** *noun*

dis·en·chant *transitive verb* disillusion; free from enchantment. □ **dis·en·chant·ed** *adjective*

dis·en·cum·ber *transitive verb* free from encumbrance.

dis·en·fran·chise *transitive verb* (also **dis·fran·chise**) **1** deprive (a person) of the right to vote. **2** deprive of or exclude from anything viewed as a right or privilege. □ **dis·en·fran·chise·ment** *noun*

dis·en·fran·chised *adjective* deprived of (esp. social) rights and privileges deemed normative in a society.

dis·en·gage *verb* **1 a** *transitive* detach, free, loosen, or separate (parts etc.) (*disengaged the clutch*). **b** *reflexive* detach oneself; get loose (*disengaged ourselves from their company*). **c** *intransitive* become detached. **2** *transitive Military* remove (troops) from a battle or a battle area. **3** *intransitive Fencing* pass the point of one's sword over or under one's opponent's sword to change the line of attack.

dis·en·gaged *adjective* detached, uncommitted, withdrawn.

dis·en·gage·ment *noun* **1** the action or process of withdrawing from involvement in a particular activity, situation, or group. **2** emotional detachment; objectivity. **3** the withdrawal of military forces or the renunciation of military or political influence in a particular area. **4** the process of separating or releasing something or of becoming separated or released (*the mechanism prevents accidental disengagement*).

dis·en·tangle *verb* **1** *transitive* **a** extricate; free from complications, difficulties, etc. **b** unravel, untwist; bring out of a tangled state. **2** *intransitive* become disentangled. □ **dis·en·tangle·ment** *noun*

dis·en·title *transitive verb* (usu. foll. by *to*) deprive of any rightful claim.

dis·equi·lib·rium *noun* (*pl.* **-ria**) a lack or loss of equilibrium, stability, or balance.

dis·estab·lish *transitive verb* deprive (a Church) of a state connection and support; remove from a position as the national or state Church. □ **dis·estab·lish·ment** *noun*

dis·esteem *noun* low esteem or regard.

dis·fa·vour (also **dis·fa·vor**) ● *noun* **1** disapproval or dislike. **2** the state of being disliked (*fell into disfavour*). ● *transitive verb* regard or treat with disfavour.

dis·fig·ure *transitive verb* spoil the appearance or beauty of; deface, deform. □ **dis·fig·ur·a·tion** *noun* **dis·fig·ured** *adjective* **dis·figure·ment** *noun*

dis·fran·chise *var. of* DISENFRANCHISE.

dis·gorge *transitive verb* **1** vomit or eject (matter) from the throat or stomach. **2** discharge the contents of; empty (*the boat disgorged a crowd of passengers onto the pier*). **3** surrender, esp. what has been wrongly appropriated. □ **dis·gorge·ment** *noun* [Old French *desgorger* (as DIS-, GORGE)]

dis·grace ● *noun* **1** the loss of reputation; shame, ignominy (*brought disgrace on his family*). **2** a person or thing that brings dishonour or shame (*the bus service is a disgrace; a disgrace to her profession*). ● *transitive verb* **1** bring shame or discredit on or be a disgrace to. **2** degrade from a position of honour; dismiss from favour. □ **in disgrace** having lost respect or reputation; out of favour. [French *disgrâce*, *disgracier* from Italian *disgrazia*, *disgraziare* (as DIS-, GRACE)]

dis·grace·ful *adjective* shameful, dishonourable, degrading.
□ **dis·grace·ful·ly** *adverb*

dis·grun·tled *adjective* discontented; irritated, annoyed.
□ **dis·gruntle·ment** *noun* [DIS- + *gruntle* obsolete frequentative of GRUNT]

dis·guise ● *transitive verb* **1 a** (often foll. by *as*) alter the appearance, dress, mannerisms, etc. of (a person) so as to conceal true identity (*disguised herself as a police officer*). **b** alter so as to make unrecognizable (*disguised his voice; disguised the taste by adding sugar*). **2** misrepresent or cover up (*disguised the truth; disguised their intentions*). ● *noun* **1 a** garment, style, manner, etc. assumed as a means of concealment or deception. **2** the act, practice, or an instance of concealing reality under a false appearance. □ **in disguise 1** wearing a concealing costume etc. **2** appearing to be the opposite (*a blessing in disguise*). □ **dis·guised** *adjective* [Old French *desguis(i)er* (as DIS-, GUISE)]

dis·gust ● *noun* (usu. foll. by *at*, *for*) **1** repugnance; strong and instinctive aversion to something that is physically loathsome, morally offensive, etc. **2** a strong distaste for a food, drink, medicine, etc.; nausea. ● *transitive verb* **1** offend the sensibilities or principles of (*their behaviour disgusts me*). **2** excite physical nausea and loathing in (*finding a slug disgusted me*). □ **in disgust** as a result of disgust (*left in disgust*). □ **dis·gust·ed·ly** *adverb* [Old French *degoust*, *desgouster*, or Italian *disgusto*, *disgustare* (as DIS-, GUSTO)]

dis·gust·ing *adjective* arousing disgust; sickening, repulsive (*disgusting behaviour*). □ **dis·gust·ing·ly** *adverb* **dis·gust·ing·ness** *noun*

dish ● *noun* **1 a** a shallow, usu. flat-bottomed container made of glass, ceramic, metal, etc., used for holding or serving food. **b** the food served in a dish (*a dish of ice cream*). **c** food prepared in a particular way (*an Italian dish*). **2** (in *pl.*) dirty plates, cutlery, pots, etc. after a meal. **3 a** a dish-shaped receptacle, object, or cavity. **b** = SATELLITE DISH. **4** *slang* a sexually attractive person. ● *verb* **1** *transitive* put (food) into a dish for serving. **2** *transitive* make concave or dish-shaped. **3** *informal* **a** *transitive* gossip about (someone). **b** *intransitive* gossip. □ **dish it out** *N Amer.* *informal* deal out punishment, criticism, etc. **dish out** *informal* deal out, distribute, esp. roughly or indiscriminately. **dish up 1** serve or prepare to serve (food). **2** *informal* seek to present (facts, argument, etc.) attractively. **dish the dirt** (often foll. by *on*) *informal* spread scandal or gossip. □ **dish·like** *adjective* [Old English *disc* plate, bowl (with Germanic and Old Norse cognates), from Latin *discus* DISC]

dis·ha·bille *var.* of DESHABILLE.

dish antenna *noun* = SATELLITE DISH.

dis·har·mony *noun* (*pl.* **-ies**) **1** a lack of harmony or agreement; discord. **2** something discordant. □ **dis·har·moni·ous** *adjective* **dis·har·moni·ous·ly** *adverb*

dish·cloth *noun* a usu. open-weave cloth for washing dishes etc.

dishcloth gourd *noun* = LOOFAH.

dish drainer *noun* = DISH RACK.

dis·heart·en *transitive verb* cause to lose courage, confidence, hope, etc.; make despondent. □ **dis·heart·en·ing** *adjective* **dis·heart·en·ing·ly** *adverb* **dis·heart·en·ment** *noun*

dished *adjective* **1** dishlike or concave (*a dished face*). **2** (of vehicle wheels) angled so as to be closer to each other at the bottom than at the top.

di·shev·elled /dɪˈʃevəld/ *adjective* (also esp. *US* **di·shev·eled**) (of the hair, clothes, appearance, etc.) disordered, unkempt, untidy.
□ **di·shevel·ment** *noun* [Middle English *dischevelee* from Old French *deschevelé* past participle (as DIS-, *chevel* hair, from Latin *capillus*)]

dis·hon·est *adjective* (of a person, act, or statement) fraudulent or insincere. □ **dis·hon·est·ly** *adverb*

dis·hon·esty *noun* (*pl.* **-ies**) **1** a lack of honesty, esp. a willingness to cheat, steal, lie, or act fraudulently. **2** a dishonest or fraudulent act.

dis·hon·our (also **dis·hon·or**) ● *noun* **1** a state of shame, disgrace, or ignominy. **2** something that causes shame or disgrace (*a dishonour to his profession*). ● *transitive verb* **1** disgrace (*dishonoured his name*). **2** treat without honour or respect. **3** (often in *passive*) refuse to accept or pay a cheque or a bill of exchange. **4** *archaic* rape or seduce.

dis·honour·able *adjective* (also **dis·honor·able**) **1** ignominious; causing disgrace (*a dishonourable discharge from the army*). **2** (of a person) unprincipled; having no sense of honour. □ **dis·honour·able·ness** *noun* **dis·honour·ably** *adverb*

dish·pan *noun* esp. *N Amer.* a large usu. plastic pan in which dishes are washed.

dishpan hands *noun* hands roughened by frequent washing of dishes, use of detergents, etc.

dish rack *noun* a rack in which dishes are placed to drain after being washed.

dish·rag *noun* *N Amer.* = DISHCLOTH.

dish soap *noun* *Cdn* = DISHWASHING LIQUID.

dish·towel *noun* a thin cotton or linen towel for drying dishes, cutlery, etc.

dish·wash·er *noun* **1** a machine for automatically washing dishes. **2** a person who washes dishes. □ **dish·wash·ing** *noun*

dishwashing liquid *noun* *N Amer.* (also **dishwashing detergent**) a liquid detergent used for washing dishes by hand.

dish·water *noun* **1** water in which dishes have been washed. **2** *informal* (often *attributive*) something weak, diluted, or resembling dishwater.

dishy *adjective* (**dish·i·er**, **dish·i·est**) *informal* **1** esp. *Brit.* attractive, esp. sexually. **2** *N Amer.* gossipy (*a dishy biography*).

dis·illu·sion ● *noun* disenchantment, freedom from illusions.
● *transitive verb* deprive of belief in an illusion or ideal; disenchant.
□ **dis·illu·sion·ment** *noun*

dis·in·cen·tive ● *noun* **1** something that tends to discourage a particular action etc. **2** *Econ.* a source of discouragement to productivity or progress. ● *adjective* tending to discourage.

dis·inclin·a·tion *noun* (usu. foll. by *for*, or *to* + infin.) unwillingness or reluctance (*a disinclination for work; disinclination to go*).

dis·in·cline *transitive verb* (usu. foll. by *to* + infin. or *for*) make unwilling or reluctant. □ **dis·in·clined** *adjective*

dis·in·fect *transitive verb* clean (something) by destroying germs, esp. with a disinfectant. □ **dis·infec·tion** *noun*

dis·infect·ant ● *noun* a usu. commercially produced chemical liquid or spray that destroys germs etc. ● *adjective* of disinfectants or causing disinfection.

dis·in·fla·tion *noun* *Econ.* a policy designed to counteract inflation without causing deflation, including such measures as restricting consumer spending by raising the interest rate and introducing price controls on commodities in short supply. □ **dis·in·fla·tion·ary** *adjective*

dis·infor·ma·tion *noun* deliberately false information, esp. as supplied by governments, the military, etc.

dis·in·genu·ous /ˌdɪsɪnˈdʒenjʊəs/ *adjective* insincere; lacking in frankness or honesty. □ **dis·in·genu·ous·ly** *adverb* **dis·in·genu·ous·ness** *noun*

dis·in·herit *transitive verb* (**dis·in·herit·ed**, **dis·in·herit·ing**) reject as one's heir; deprive of the right of inheritance. □ **dis·in·herit·ance** *noun* [Middle English from DIS- + INHERIT in obsolete sense 'make heir']

dis·in·te·grate *verb* **1** *transitive & intransitive* **a** separate into component parts or fragments. **b** lose or cause to lose cohesion or unity. **2** *Physics* **a** *intransitive* (of a nucleus, particle, or radioactive substance) undergo disintegration. **b** *transitive* cause (a substance, atom, or nucleus) to undergo disintegration. **3** *intransitive* *informal* deteriorate mentally or physically. □ **dis·in·te·gra·tor** *noun*

dis·in·te·gra·tion *noun* **1** the act, process, or an instance of disintegrating. **2** *Physics* the process in which an atomic nucleus emits one or more particles or splits into smaller nuclei.

dis·in·ter *transitive verb* (**dis·in·terred**, **dis·in·ter·ring**) **1** exhume; remove or dig up from the ground. **2** bring (a secret, artifact, etc.) out of obscurity or concealment. □ **dis·in·ter·ment** *noun*

dis·in·ter·est *noun* **1** impartiality. **2** *disputed* lack of interest; unconcern. ¶ The use of *disinterest* to mean 'lack of interest' is sometimes objected to, but it is in this sense that it is most commonly found, and the alternative *uninterest* is rare. The phrase *lack of interest* avoids both ambiguity and accusations of incorrect usage.

dis·in·ter·est·ed *adjective* **1** unbiased, impartial; not influenced by one's own advantage (*a disinterested critic*). **2** *disputed* uninterested, unconcerned. ¶ *Disinterested* is commonly used informally to mean 'uninterested', but this is regarded by some as incorrect.
□ **dis·in·ter·est·ed·ly** *adverb* **dis·in·ter·est·ed·ness** *noun* [past participle of *disinterest* (v.) divest of interest]

dis·in·vest *verb* **1** *intransitive* (often foll. by *from*) reduce or withdraw financial investment from a place, company, etc. **2** *transitive* reduce or withdraw (investments or assets). □ **dis·in·vest·ment** *noun*

dis·invite *transitive verb* withdraw or cancel an invitation to (someone) (*called to disinvite him from the party*).

dis·join *transitive & intransitive verb* separate or part.

dis·joint ● *transitive verb* **1** take apart at the joints. **2 a** disturb the

---

Consonants: b *but*   d *dog*   f *few*   g *get*   h *her*   j *yes*   k *cat*   l *leg*   m *man*   n *no*   p *pen*   r *red*   s *sit*

working, connection, or arrangement of (a system etc.). **b** dislocate or disturb (a pattern etc.). ● *adjective Math.* (of two or more sets) having no elements in common.

dis·joint·ed *adjective* (of speech, writing, etc.) incoherent, rambling; not properly connected. □ **dis·joint·ed·ly** *adverb* **dis·joint·ed·ness** *noun*

dis·junct ● *noun* **1** *Logic* each of the terms of a disjunctive proposition. **2** *Grammar* an adverb or adverbial phrase that expresses a writer's or speaker's attitude to the content of the sentence in which it occurs. ● *adjective* disconnected, separate, distinct.

dis·junc·tion *noun* **1 a** the process of disjoining; separation. **b** an instance of this. **2** *Logic* **a** the relation of two mutually incompatible alternatives. **b** a statement expressing this, esp. one using the word 'or'.

dis·junc·tive ● *adjective* **1** characterized by or involving separation. **2** *Grammar* (esp. of a conjunction) expressing a choice between two words or connected clauses, e.g. *or* in *asked if he was going or staying* (compare COPULATIVE 2a). **3** *Logic* involving a choice between two or more things, propositions, etc. ● *noun* **1** *Grammar* a disjunctive conjunction or other word. **2** *Logic* a disjunctive proposition. □ **dis·junc·tive·ly** *adverb*

dis·junc·ture *noun* a disjointed state; a separation, a disconnection.

disk ● *noun* **1** (also esp. *Brit.* **disc**) **a** (in full **magnetic disk**) a computer storage device consisting of a rotatable disc or discs with a magnetic coating. **b** (in full **optical disk**) a smooth non-magnetic disc with large storage capacity for data recorded and read by laser, esp. a CD-ROM. **2** *var. of* DISC. **3** (also **disc**) *N Amer. & NZ* **a** = DISKER. **b** a circular steel blade on a disker. ● *transitive verb* till (soil) with a disker. □ **disk·less** *adjective* [as DISC]

disk drive *noun Computing* a device that can store and retrieve data from rotating magnetic or optical disks.

disk·er *noun* (also **disk harrow**) *N Amer.* a harrow using sharp, curved disks to till the land, remove weeds, etc.

disk·ette *noun* = FLOPPY *noun*.

disk jockey *var. of* DISC JOCKEY.

dis·like ● *transitive verb* have an aversion or objection to; not like. ● *noun* **1** a feeling that something is distasteful, unpleasant, objectionable, etc. **2** an object of dislike (*reveals his likes and dislikes*). □ **dis·lik·able** *adjective* (also **dis·like·able**).

dis·lo·cate *transitive verb* **1** disturb the normal connection of (esp. a joint in the body) (*she dislocated her shoulder*). **2** disorder or disrupt (affairs etc.) from their natural course. **3** displace or put (a thing) out of its proper relative position.

dis·lo·ca·tion *noun* **1** the act or result of dislocating, esp. the displacement of a bone from its natural position. **2** a disordered state or disarrangement of parts. **3** *Geol.* the fracture of strata with upheaval or subsidence. **4** the displacement of rows of atoms in a crystal lattice structure.

dis·lodge *transitive & intransitive verb* remove from or leave an established or fixed position (*was dislodged from her directorship*). □ **dis·lodge·able** *adjective* **dis·lodge·ment** *noun*

dis·loy·al *adjective* (often foll. by *to*) **1** not loyal; unfaithful. **2** untrue to one's allegiances; treacherous to one's government etc. □ **dis·loy·al·ist** *noun* **dis·loy·al·ly** *adverb* **dis·loy·al·ty** *noun*

dis·mal *adjective* **1** causing or showing gloom; cheerless, miserable. **2** dreary or sombre (*dismal brown walls*). **3** *informal* feeble or inept (*a dismal performance*). □ **dis·mal·ly** *adverb* **dis·mal·ness** *noun* [originally noun = unlucky days: Anglo-French *dis mal* from medieval Latin *dies mali* two days in each month held to be unpropitious]

dismal science *noun* (prec. by *the*) *jocular* economics. [coined by T. CARLYLE]

Dismal Swamp see GREAT DISMAL SWAMP.

dis·man·tle *transitive verb* **1 a** take apart; disassemble (*dismantle a faulty motor*). **b** end (a system, organization, etc.) in a gradual and planned way (*dismantled apartheid*). **2** deprive of defences or equipment. **3** (often foll. by *of*) strip of covering or protection. □ **dis·mantle·ment** *noun* **dis·mant·ler** *noun* [Old French *desmanteler* (as DIS-, MANTLE)]

dis·mast *transitive verb* deprive (a ship) of masts; break down the mast or masts of.

dis·may ● *noun* **1** keenly felt disappointment. **2** discouragement, despair, or faintness of heart. **3** consternation or anxiety. ● *transitive verb* **1** discourage, depress, or reduce to despair. **2** fill with consternation or anxiety. □ **dis·may·ing** *adjective* **dis·may·ing·ly** *adverb* [Old French *desmaiier* (unrecorded), ultimately from a Germanic root = deprive of power (as DIS-, MAY)]

dis·mem·ber *transitive verb* **1** tear or cut the limbs from. **2** divide up (a country, organization, etc.). □ **dis·mem·ber·ment** *noun* [Old French *desmembrer* from Romanic (as DIS-, Latin *membrum* limb)]

dis·miss *verb* **1 a** *transitive* send away; cause (a person) to leave one's presence. **b** *transitive* disband (an assembly or army). **c** *intransitive* (of an assembly etc.) disperse; break ranks. **2** *transitive* discharge from employment, office, etc., esp. dishonourably. **3** *transitive* banish (a thought, feeling, etc.) from the mind; treat as unworthy of consideration (*dismissed it from memory*). **4** *transitive* treat (a subject) summarily (*dismissed his application*). **5** *transitive Law* refuse further hearing to (a case); send out of court. **6** *intransitive* (in *imperative*) *Military* a word of command at the end of drilling. □ **dis·miss·al** *noun* **dis·miss·ible** *adjective* [Middle English, originally as past participle after Old French *desmis* from medieval Latin *dismissus* (as DIS-, Latin *mittere miss-* send)]

dis·mis·sive *adjective* disdainful; tending to dismiss from consideration. □ **dis·mis·sive·ly** *adverb* **dis·mis·sive·ness** *noun*

dis·mount ● *verb* /dɪsˈmaʊnt/ **1 a** *intransitive* alight from a horse, bicycle, etc. **b** *transitive* (usu. in *passive*) throw from a horse; unseat. **2** *transitive* take (a mechanism) from its framework; take apart. **3** *transitive Computing* make (a disk or disk drive) unavailable for use. ● *noun* /ˈdɪsmaʊnt/ an act or method of dismounting (from a horse, parallel bars, etc.).

Dis·ney, Wal·ter Elias ('Walt') (1901–66), US animator and film producer, who pioneered animated cartoon films and created characters such as Mickey Mouse and Donald Duck; his animated films include *Snow White and the Seven Dwarfs* (1937), *Fantasia* (1940), and *Bambi* (1942). □ **Disney·esque** *adjective*

Disney·fi·ca·tion *noun* often *derogatory* the action or process of making something resemble Disney cartoons, movies, or theme parks, esp. by idealizing, simplifying, or prettifying it. □ **Disney·fied** *adjective*

dis·obedi·ent *adjective* disobeying; rebellious, rule-breaking. □ **dis·obedi·ence** *noun* **dis·obedi·ent·ly** *adverb*

dis·obey *verb* **1** *transitive* fail or refuse to obey (orders, rules, a person, etc.); disregard (*disobeyed his mother*). **2** *intransitive* be disobedient or show disobedience (*how dare you disobey!*).

dis·oblige *transitive verb* refuse to consider the convenience or wishes of.

dis·obli·ging *adjective* uncooperative.

dis·or·der ● *noun* **1** confusion, disarray; lack of order or regular arrangement. **2** a disturbance or commotion, esp. a breach of public order. **3** *Med.* an ailment or disturbance of the normal state of body or mind. ● *transitive verb* **1** disarrange; throw (a situation etc.) into confusion. **2** *Med.* upset the health or proper function of the body or mind. □ **dis·or·dered** *adjective* [Middle English, alteration (influenced by ORDER *verb*) of earlier *disordain* from Old French *desordener* (as DIS-, ORDAIN)]

dis·or·der·ly *adjective* **1** unruly, riotous. **2** *Law* contrary to public order or morality. **3** marked by lack of order or regularity; untidy (*a disorderly heap of clothes*). □ **dis·or·der·li·ness** *noun*

disorderly conduct *noun Law* unruly or offensive behaviour constituting a minor offence.

disorderly house *noun Law* a common bawdy house, common betting house, or common gaming house.

dis·or·gan·ize *transitive verb* (also esp. *Brit.* **-ise**) destroy the system, order, or organization of; throw into confusion. □ **dis·or·gan·iz·a·tion** *noun*

dis·or·gan·ized *adjective* (also esp. *Brit.* **-ised**) lacking organization or system.

dis·ori·ent *transitive verb* **1** confuse (a person) as to his or her whereabouts or bearings. **2** confuse (a person) as to what is true, correct, etc. (*disoriented by his unexpected behaviour*). □ **dis·orien·ta·tion** *noun*

dis·orien·tate *transitive verb* esp. *Brit.* = DISORIENT.

dis·own *transitive verb* **1** refuse to acknowledge (a person) as one's own or as connected with oneself (*disowned her son*). **2** repudiate or disclaim (an idea, intention, result, etc.).

dis·par·age /dɪˈsperɪdʒ/ *transitive verb* **1** vilify or speak slightingly or critically of (a person, idea, etc.). **2** bring discredit or reproach upon (a person). □ **dis·par·age·ment** *noun* **dis·para·ging** *adjective*

dis·para·ging·ly *adverb* [Old French *desparagier* marry unequally (as DIS-, *parage* equality of rank, ultimately from Latin *par* equal)]

dis·par·ate /ˈdɪsparət/ *adjective* essentially different in kind; without comparison or relation. □ **dis·par·ate·ly** *adverb* **dis·par·ate·ness**

noun [Latin *disparatus* separated (as DIS-, *paratus* past participle of *parare* prepare), influenced in sense by Latin *dispar* unequal]

dis·par·i·ty /dɪˈspɛrɪti/ noun (pl. **-ities**) (often foll. by *between*) a great difference or gap, esp. one regarded as unfair (*economic disparities between the East and West*). [French *disparité* from Late Latin *disparitas -tatis* (as DIS-, PARITY[1])]

dis·pas·sion·ate adjective calm, impartial; free from the influence or effect of strong emotion. □ **dis·pas·sion** noun **dis·pas·sion·ate·ly** adverb **dis·pas·sion·ate·ness** noun

dis·patch (also esp. *Brit.* **des·patch**) ● *transitive verb* **1** send off to a destination or for a purpose (*dispatched him with the message; dispatched the letter yesterday*). **2** kill, execute. **3** perform (business, a task, etc.) promptly; finish off. **4** *informal* eat (food, a meal, etc.) quickly. ● noun **1** the act or an instance of sending (a messenger, letter, etc.). **2** the act or an instance of killing; execution. **3 a** an official written message on state or esp. military affairs. **b** a report sent in by a newspaper's correspondent, usu. from a foreign country. **c** any written message requiring fast delivery. **4** promptness, efficiency (*done with dispatch*). [Italian *dispacciare* or Spanish *despachar* expedite (as DIS-, Italian *impacciare* and Spanish *empachar* hinder, of uncertain origin)]

dispatch box noun (also **dispatch case**) a container or attaché case for carrying documents, esp. official state or military dispatches.

dis·patch·er noun a person who coordinates the departure of taxis, buses, trains, etc.

dispatch rider noun esp. *Brit.* a motorcyclist or rider on horseback carrying dispatches.

dis·pel transitive verb (**dis·pelled**, **dis·pel·ling**) dissipate; disperse; scatter (*the dawn dispelled their fears*). [Latin *dispellere* (as DIS-, *pellere* drive)]

dis·pens·able adjective **1** unnecessary or expendable. **2** capable of being dispensed or administered. **3** (of a law etc.) able to be relaxed in special cases. □ **dis·pens·abil·ity** noun

dis·pens·ary noun (pl. **-ies**) **1** a place in a clinic, pharmacy, etc. where medicines are dispensed. **2** a public or charitable institution offering medical advice and the dispensing of medicines. **3** a place from which something is dispensed.

dis·pen·sa·tion noun **1** the act or an instance of dispensing or distributing. **2 a** (usu. foll. by *from*) an exemption from a religious or legal observance, penalty, etc. **b** an instance of this. **3 a** the ordering or management of the world by Providence. **b** a specific example of such ordering (of a community, a person, etc.). **4** any established or prevailing system (of administration, government, etc.) under which one lives or works. □ **dis·pen·sa·tion·al** adjective

dis·pense verb **1** *transitive* **a** distribute or provide (a service or information) to a number of people. **b** (of a machine) supply (a product or cash) (*the machines dispense a range of drinks and snacks*). **2** *transitive* administer (a sacrament, justice, etc.). **3** *transitive* make up and give out (medicine etc.) according to a doctor's prescription. **4** *transitive* (usu. foll. by *from*) grant (a person) a dispensation from an esp. religious obligation. **5** *intransitive* (foll. by *with*) **a** do without; render needless (*dispense with formalities*). **b** give exemption from (a rule). [Latin *dispensare* frequentative of *dispendere* weigh or pay out (as DIS-, *pendere pens-* weigh)]

dis·pens·er noun **1** an automatic machine that dispenses an item or a specific amount of something, e.g. money, soap, etc. **2** a person who dispenses something.

dis·per·sant /dɪˈspɜrsənt/ noun a liquid or gas used to disperse small particles in a medium.

dis·perse verb **1 a** *transitive* drive, throw, send, or scatter in different directions. **b** *intransitive* become scattered, dispelled, or dissipated (*the clouds dispersed*). **2 a** *intransitive* (of people in a crowd etc.) separate and go different ways. **b** *transitive* cause to do this. **3** *transitive* (usu. in *passive*) place or station at widely separated points. **4** *transitive* distribute or put (books, currency, etc.) into circulation, esp. from a main source or centre. **5** *transitive Chem.* distribute (small particles) uniformly in a medium. **6** *transitive Physics* separate (white light) into its coloured constituents. □ **dis·per·sal** noun **dis·pers·er** noun **dis·pers·ible** adjective **dis·per·sive** adjective [Latin *dispergere dispers-* (as DIS-, *spargere* scatter)]

dis·per·sion noun **1** the act or an instance of dispersing; the process of being dispersed. **2** *Physics* **a** the separation of white light into colours, or of any radiation according to wavelength. **b** the degree of this. **3** *Statistics* the degree to which a set of observed values are spread over a range. **4** *Chem.* a mixture of one substance dispersed in another. **5** *Ecology* the pattern of distribution of individuals within the habitat. **6** (**the Dispersion**) = DIASPORA 1.

dispir·it *transitive verb* discourage; lower the morale of. □ **dispir·it·ing** adjective **dispir·it·ing·ly** adverb

dispir·it·ed adjective dejected; discouraged. □ **dispir·it·ed·ly** adverb **dispir·it·ed·ness** noun

dis·place *transitive verb* **1 a** replace (a thing) with another. **b** supplant or take the place of (a person), esp. in some official capacity (*moderates have displaced the extremists on the committee*). **2** move or shift from its accustomed place. **3** force (a person) to leave his or her home, country, etc., esp. because of military or political pressures. □ **dis·place·able** adjective **dis·pla·cer** noun [DIS- + PLACE: partly from French *desplacer*]

displaced person noun esp. *hist.* a refugee or person forced to leave his or her home country because of war, persecution, etc. Abbr.: **DP**.

dis·place·ment noun **1 a** the act of displacing or the process of being displaced. **b** an instance of this. **2** *Physics* the amount by which anything is displaced, esp. the amount of a fluid displaced by a solid floating or immersed in it (*a ship with a displacement of 11,000 tons*). **3** *Psych.* **a** the substitution of one idea or impulse for another. **b** the unconscious transfer of strong unacceptable emotions from one object to another. **4** *Geol.* the relative movement on either side of a fault plane. **5** *Mech.* the volume swept by a reciprocating piston, as in a pump or engine.

dis·play ● *transitive verb* **1** expose to view; show, exhibit. **2** show ostentatiously. **3** allow to appear; reveal, betray (*displayed his ignorance*). **4** unfurl, spread out; unfold to view (*the Canadian flag should be properly displayed*). **5** show (data, images, etc.) on a computer screen etc. ● noun **1** the act or an instance of displaying. **2 a** an exhibition or show. **b** a presentation (of merchandise etc.) designed to show the product to advantage. **3** ostentation; flashiness. **4** the distinct behaviour of some birds and fish, used esp. to attract a mate. **5 a** the presentation of data, images, etc. on a computer screen etc. **b** the information so presented. **6** *Typography* the arrangement and choice of type in order to attract attention. [Old French *despleier* from Latin *displicare* (as DIS-, *plicare* fold): compare DEPLOY]

display case noun (also **display cabinet**) a usu. clear glass case for displaying items for observation or inspection.

display home noun = MODEL HOME.

dis·please *transitive verb* make indignant or angry; offend; annoy. □ **be displeased** (often foll. by *at, with*) be indignant or dissatisfied; disapprove. □ **dis·pleas·ing** adjective **dis·pleas·ing·ly** adverb

dis·pleas·ure noun disapproval; dissatisfaction; anger.

dis·port /dɪˈspɔrt/ verb **1** *transitive & intransitive* cavort, frolic, or enjoy oneself (*disported on the sand; disported themselves in the sea*). **2** *reflexive* show or display (oneself) in a playful manner (*the seals disport themselves close to shore*). [Old French *desporter* (as DIS-, *porter* carry, from Latin *portare*)]

dis·pos·able ● adjective **1** intended to be used once and then thrown away (*disposable diapers*). **2** that can be thrown away or disposed of safely (*disposable alkaline batteries*). **3** (esp. of financial assets) accessible; available for use; at the owner's disposal. ● noun a thing designed to be thrown away after one use. □ **dis·pos·abil·ity** noun

disposable income noun **1** income available after taxes, expenses, etc. for spending, saving, or investment. **2** the total amount of money at the disposal of consumers in a country, community, etc.

dis·pos·al noun **1** the act or an instance of getting rid of something. **2** the arrangement, disposition, or placing of something. **3** control or management (of a person, business, etc.). **4** (esp. as **waste disposal**) the disposing of garbage. **5** *US informal* an electrical device fitted to the waste pipe of a kitchen sink etc. for grinding up waste. □ **at one's disposal 1** available for one's use. **2** subject to one's orders or decisions.

dis·pose verb **1** *transitive* (usu. foll. by *to*, or *to* + infin.) make willing; incline (*disposed him to the idea; was disposed to release them*). **2** *transitive* place suitably or in order (*disposed the pictures in sequence*). **3** *intransitive* determine the course of events (*man proposes, God disposes*). □ **dispose of 1 a** settle or deal conclusively with (an issue, opponent, etc.). **b** get rid of. **c** finish (a task etc.). **d** kill. **2** sell (property etc.). **3** prove (a claim, argument, opponent, etc.) to be incorrect. **4** *informal* consume (food). □ **dis·pos·er** noun [Old French *disposer* (as DIS-, POSE[1]) after Latin *disponere disposit-*]

dis·posed adjective (usu. foll. by *to*, or *to* + infin.) **1** inclined, prepared, or in the mood (to do something etc.). **2** having a specified mental inclination (usu. in *combination*: *ill-disposed*). **3** subject, liable, or having a physical inclination to (*the wheel was disposed to buckle*).

dis·po·si·tion noun **1 a** temperament or character, esp. as displayed in dealings with others (*a gentle disposition*). **b** (often foll. by *to*) a natural tendency or inclination (*a disposition to overeat*). **2 a** a condition or

Vowels: a cat ɑ arm e bed ɜr her ɜː deux ə ago ɪ sit i cosy iː feed ɒ hot ɔ pore ɔː no ʌ run ʊ put

arrangement of affairs, esp. for a particular purpose. **b** spatial arrangement or relative position, esp. of constituent parts. ¶ *Disposition* is the noun corresponding to the verb *dispose* 'arrange', whereas *disposal* corresponds to the verb *dispose of* 'get rid of'. **3** (usu. in *pl.*) **a** *Military* the stationing of troops ready for attack or defence. **b** preparations, plans. **4 a** a bestowal by deed or will (*the disposition of the estate*). **b** control; the power of disposing. **5** the action of ordering or regulating by esp. divine right or power. □ **dis·pos·i·tion·al** *adjective* [Old French from Latin *dispositio* (as DIS-, *ponere posit-* place)]

dis·pos·sess *transitive verb* **1** dislodge; oust (a person) from a dwelling etc. **2** (usu. foll. by *of*) deprive of possessions, status, rights, etc. **3** alienate, disenfranchise, or estrange. □ **dis·pos·sessed** *adjective* **dis·pos·ses·sion** *noun* **dis·pos·ses·sor** *noun*

dis·praise ● *transitive verb* express disapproval or censure of. ● *noun* disapproval, censure. [Old French *despreisier*, ultimately from Late Latin *depretiare* DEPRECIATE]

dis·proof *noun* **1** a fact, piece of evidence, etc. that disproves. **2 a** refutation. **b** an instance of this.

dis·pro·por·tion *noun* **1** a lack of proportion. **2** an instance of this. □ **dis·pro·por·tion·al** *adjective* **dis·pro·por·tion·al·ly** *adverb*

dis·pro·por·tion·ate *adjective* **1** lacking proportion. **2** relatively too large or small, long or short, etc. □ **dis·pro·por·tion·ate·ly** *adverb*

dis·prove *transitive verb* prove false; refute. □ **dis·prov·able** *adjective*

Dis·pur /ˈdɪsˈpʊr/ a city in NE India, capital of the state of Assam.

dis·put·able *adjective* open to question; contentious (*a disputable win*). □ **dis·put·ably** *adverb*

dis·put·ant *noun* a person who disputes or argues, esp. one who engages in public debate or disputation.

dis·pu·ta·tion *noun* **1 a** the act or an instance of disputing or debating. **b** an argument; a controversy. **2** a formal debate.

dis·pu·ta·tious *adjective* fond of or inclined to argument. □ **dis·pu·ta·tious·ly** *adverb* **dis·pu·ta·tious·ness** *noun*

dis·pute ● *verb* **1** *intransitive* (usu. foll. by *with*, *against*) **a** debate, argue (*was disputing with them about the meaning of life*). **b** quarrel. **2** *transitive* discuss, esp. heatedly (*disputed whether it was true*). **3** *transitive* question the truth, correctness, or validity of (a statement, alleged fact, etc.) (*I dispute that number*). **4** *transitive* contend for; strive to win (*disputed the crown; disputed the lead*). **5** *transitive* resist (a landing, advance, etc.). ● *noun* **1** a controversy; a debate. **2** a quarrel. **3** a disagreement between management and employees, esp. one leading to job action. □ **beyond** (or **without**) **dispute** certainly; indisputably. **in dispute** being argued about. □ **dis·put·ed** *adjective* **dis·put·er** *noun* [Old French *desputer* from Latin *disputare* estimate (as DIS-, *putare* reckon)]

dis·quali·fi·ca·tion *noun* **1 a** the act or an instance of disqualifying. **b** the state of being disqualified. **2** something that disqualifies.

dis·qual·ify *transitive verb* (**-fies**, **-fied**) **1** (often foll. by *from*) debar from a competition or pronounce ineligible as a winner because of an infringement of the rules etc. (*disqualified from the race for taking drugs*). **2** (often foll. by *for*, *from*) make or pronounce ineligible or unsuitable (*his age disqualifies him for the job; a criminal record disqualified her from applying*). **3** (often foll. by *from*) deprive of legal capacity, power, or right (*disqualified from practising as a doctor*).

dis·quiet ● *transitive verb* worry; trouble; deprive of peace. ● *noun* anxiety, unrest. □ **dis·quiet·ing** *adjective* **dis·quiet·ing·ly** *adverb*

dis·quiet·ude *noun* a state of uneasiness; anxiety.

dis·quisi·tion /ˌdɪskwɪˈzɪʃən/ *noun* a long or elaborate treatise or discourse on a subject. [French from Latin *disquisitio* (as DIS-, *quaerere quaesit-* seek)]

Dis·raeli /dɪzˈreɪli/ **Ben·ja·min, 1st Earl of Beacons·field** (1804–81), English Tory politician and novelist; prime minister 1868 and 1874–80. He introduced the second Reform Act (1867), which doubled the electorate, and ensured that Britain bought a controlling interest in the Suez Canal; his novels include *Coningsby* (1844) and *Sybil* (1845).

dis·regard ● *transitive verb* **1** pay no attention to; ignore. **2** treat as of no importance. ● *noun* (often foll. by *of*, *for*) **1** indifference; neglect. **2** lack of regard or respect.

dis·remem·ber *transitive & intransitive verb* esp. *US informal* forget; fail to remember.

dis·repair *noun* the state of being in poor condition, esp. due to neglect (*in disrepair*).

dis·rep·ut·able *adjective* **1** discreditable; of bad reputation. **2** not respectable in appearance; shabby; untidy. □ **dis·rep·ut·ably** *adverb*

dis·re·pute *noun* a lack of good reputation or respectability; discredit (*fall into disrepute*).

dis·re·spect ● *noun* a lack of respect or courtesy. ● *transitive verb informal* have or show no respect or reverence for; treat with disrespect. □ **dis·re·spect·ful** *adjective* **dis·re·spect·ful·ly** *adverb*

dis·robe *transitive & intransitive verb* undress; divest of a robe or garment.

dis·rupt *transitive verb* **1** interrupt the flow or continuity of (a meeting, speech, etc.); bring disorder to. **2** separate forcibly; shatter. □ **dis·rupt·er** *noun* (also **dis·rupt·or**). **dis·rup·tion** *noun* **dis·rupt·ive** *adjective* **dis·rupt·ive·ly** *adverb* **dis·rupt·ive·ness** *noun* [Latin *disrumpere disrupt-* (as DIS-, *rumpere* break)]

diss *var. of* DIS.

dis·satis·fy *transitive verb* (**-fies**, **-fied**) make discontented; fail to satisfy (*dissatisfied with the accommodation*). □ **dis·satis·fac·tion** *noun* **dis·satis·fac·tory** *adjective*

dis·sav·ing *noun* **1** the action of spending more than one has earned in a given period. **2** (**dis·sav·ings**) the excess amount spent.

dis·sect *transitive verb* **1** cut into pieces. **2** cut up (a plant or animal) to examine its parts, structure, etc., or (a corpse) for a post-mortem. **3** analyze; criticize or examine in detail. □ **dis·sec·tion** *noun* **dis·sect·or** *noun* [Latin *dissecare dissect-* (as DIS-, *secare* cut)]

dis·sem·ble /dɪˈsembəl/ *verb* **1** *intransitive* conceal one's motives; talk or act hypocritically. **2** *transitive* **a** disguise or conceal (a feeling, intention, act, etc.). **b** simulate (*dissembled grief in public*). □ **dis·sem·blance** *noun* **dis·sem·bler** *noun* [Middle English, alteration (suggested by *semblance*) of obsolete *dissimule*, via Old French *dissimuler* from Latin *dissimulare* (as DIS-, SIMULATE)]

dis·semin·ate /dɪˈsemɪˌneɪt/ *transitive verb* scatter about, spread (esp. ideas) widely. □ **dis·semin·a·tion** *noun* **dis·semin·ator** *noun* [Latin *disseminare* (as DIS-, *semen -inis* seed)]

dis·semin·ated *adjective Med.* spread through an organ or the body.

dis·sen·sion *noun* disagreement giving rise to discord. [Old French from Latin *dissensio* (as DIS-, *sentire sens-* feel)]

dis·sent ● *intransitive verb* (often foll. by *from*) **1** think differently, disagree; express disagreement. **2** differ in religious opinion, esp. from the doctrine of an established or orthodox church. ● *noun* **1 a** a difference of opinion. **b** an expression of this. **2** the refusal to accept the doctrines of an established or orthodox church; nonconformity. □ **dis·sent·ing** *adjective* [Latin *dissentire* (as DIS-, *sentire* feel)]

dis·sent·er *noun* **1** a person who dissents. **2** (**Dissenter**) *Brit. hist.* a member of a non-established church; a Nonconformist.

dis·sen·tient /dɪˈsenʃənt/ *adjective* disagreeing with a majority or official view.

dis·ser·ta·tion *noun* a detailed discourse on a subject, esp. one submitted in partial fulfillment of the requirements of a doctorate. [Latin *dissertatio* from *dissertare* discuss, frequentative of *disserere dissert-* examine (as DIS-, *serere* join)]

dis·ser·vice *noun* an unhelpful or injurious act, esp. done when trying to help.

dis·sever /dɪˈsevər/ *transitive & intransitive verb* sever; divide into parts. [Anglo-French *dis(c)everer* from Late Latin *disseparare* (as DIS-, SEPARATE)]

dis·si·dence *noun* disagreement; political or religious dissent.

dis·si·dent ● *adjective* disagreeing, esp. with an established government, system, etc. ● *noun* a dissident person. [Latin *dissidēre* disagree (as DIS-, *sedēre* sit)]

dis·sim·i·lar *adjective* (often foll. by *to*) unlike, not similar. □ **dis·sim·i·lar·ity** *noun* (*pl.* **-ities**). **dis·sim·i·lar·ly** *adverb*

dis·simi·late /dɪˈsɪmɪˌleɪt/ *verb* (often foll. by *to*) *Phonetics* **1** *transitive* change (a sound or sounds in a word) to another when the word originally had the same sound repeated, as in *purple*, originally *purpuran*. **2** *intransitive* (of a sound) be changed in this way. □ **dis·simi·la·tion** *noun* [Latin *dissimilis* (as DIS-, *similis* like), after *assimilate*]

dis·simu·late /dɪˈsɪmjʊˌleɪt/ *transitive & intransitive verb* dissemble. □ **dis·simu·la·tion** *noun*

dis·si·pate /ˈdɪsɪˌpeɪt/ *verb* **1 a** *transitive* cause (a cloud, vapour, fear, darkness, etc.) to disappear or disperse. **b** *intransitive* disperse, scatter, disappear. **2** *intransitive & transitive* break up; bring or come to nothing. **3** *transitive* squander or fritter away (money, energy, etc.). □ **dis·si·pa·tive** *adjective* **dis·si·pa·tor** *noun* [Latin *dissipare dissipat-* (as DIS-, *sipare* (unrecorded) throw)]

dis·si·pat·ed *adjective* (of a person or way of life) overindulging in sensual pleasures (*dissipated behaviour*).

dis·si·pa·tion *noun* **1** intemperate, dissolute, or debauched living.

2 (usu. foll. by of) wasteful expenditure (dissipation of resources). **3** scattering, dispersion, or disintegration.

dis·so·ci·ate /dɪˈsoːsɪˌeɪt, -ʃɪˌeɪt/ verb **1** transitive & intransitive (usu. foll. by from) disconnect or become disconnected; separate (dissociated her from their guilt). **2** transitive Chem. decompose, esp. reversibly. **3** transitive Psych. cause (a person's mind) to develop more than one centre of consciousness. □ **dissociate oneself from 1** declare oneself unconnected with. **2** decline to support or agree with (a proposal etc.). □ **dis·so·ci·ative** /-ətɪv/ adjective [Latin dissociare (as DIS-, socius companion)]

dis·so·ci·a·tion noun **1** the act or an instance of dissociating. **2** Psych. the state of suffering from multiple personality disorder.

dis·sol·u·ble /dɪˈsɒljʊbəl/ adjective able to be disintegrated, loosened, or disconnected; soluble. □ **dis·sol·u·bil·ity** noun **dis·sol·u·bly** adverb [French dissoluble or Latin dissolubilis (as DIS-, SOLUBLE)]

dis·so·lute /ˈdɪsəˌluːt/ adjective lax in morals; licentious. □ **dis·so·lute·ly** adverb [Latin dissolutus past participle of dissolvere DISSOLVE]

dis·so·lu·tion noun **1** disintegration; decomposition. **2** (usu. foll. by of) the undoing or relaxing of a bond, esp.: **a** a marriage. **b** a partnership. **c** an alliance. **3** the dismissal or dispersal of an assembly, esp. of a parliament at the end of its term. **4** death. **5** bringing or coming to an end; fading away; disappearance. **6** dissipation; debauchery.

dissolution of the monasteries the abolition of monasteries in England by Henry VIII under two Acts (1536 and 1539) by which they were suppressed and their assets vested in the Crown. The dissolution served to replenish the treasury and to establish royal supremacy in ecclesiastical affairs.

dis·solve ● verb **1** transitive & intransitive make or become liquid, esp. by immersion or dispersion in a liquid. **2** intransitive & transitive disappear or cause to disappear gradually. **3 a** transitive dismiss or disperse (an assembly, esp. parliament). **b** intransitive (of an assembly) be dissolved (compare DISSOLUTION). **4** transitive annul or put an end to (a partnership, marriage, etc.). **5** intransitive (of a person) become enfeebled or emotionally overcome (completely dissolved when he saw her; dissolved into tears). **6** intransitive (often foll. by into) change gradually (from one film or video image into another). ● noun the act or process of dissolving a film or video image. □ **dis·solv·able** adjective [Latin dissolvere dissolut- (as DIS-, solvere loosen)]

dis·so·nant /ˈdɪsənənt/ adjective **1** discordant; not harmonious. **2** incongruous; clashing. □ **dis·so·nance** noun [Old French dissonant or Latin dissonare (as DIS-, sonare sound)]

dis·suade /dɪˈsweɪd/ transitive verb (often foll. by from) discourage (a person); persuade against (dissuaded him from continuing; was dissuaded from his belief). □ **dis·sua·sion** /-ˈsweɪʒən/ noun **dis·sua·sive** /-ˈsweɪsɪv/ adjective [Latin dissuadēre (as DIS-, suadēre suas- persuade)]

dis·sym·me·try /dɪˈsɪmɪtri/ noun (pl. -ries) **1 a** lack of symmetry. **b** an instance of this. **2** symmetry as of mirror images or the left and right hands (esp. of crystals with two corresponding forms). □ **dis·sym·met·ric** adjective **dis·sym·met·ric·al** adjective

dis·taff /ˈdɪstɑːf/ ● noun **1** a cleft stick holding wool or flax wound for spinning by hand. **2** the corresponding part of a spinning wheel. ● adjective female; of or pertaining to women. [Old English distæf (as STAFF[1]), the first element being apparently related to Middle Low German dise, disene bunch of flax]

distaff side noun the female side of a family.

dis·tal /ˈdɪstəl/ adjective situated away from the centre of the body or point of attachment; terminal. □ **dis·tal·ly** adverb [DISTANT + -AL]

dis·tance ● noun **1** the condition of being far off; remoteness. **2 a** a space or interval between two things. **b** the length of this (a distance of twenty kilometres). **3** a distant point or place (came from a distance). **4** the avoidance of familiarity; aloofness; reserve (there was a certain distance between them). **5** a remoter field of vision (saw him in the distance). **6** an interval of time (can't remember what happened at this distance). **7 a** the full length of a race etc. **b** Boxing the scheduled length of a fight. ● transitive verb (often reflexive) **1** place far off (distanced herself from them; distanced the painful memory). **2** leave far behind in a race or competition. □ **at a distance** far off. **go the distance 1** Boxing complete a fight without being knocked out. **2** complete, esp. a hard task; endure an ordeal. **keep one's distance** maintain one's reserve. **within hailing distance** not far; close enough to be called to. **within walking distance** near enough to walk to. [Old French from Latin distantia from distare stand apart (as DI[2], stare stand)]

distance education noun (also **distance learning**) education by correspondence course or from broadcasts, telephone tutorials, etc.

distance runner noun an athlete who competes in long- or middle-distance races.

dis·tant adjective **1 a** far away in space or time. **b** (usu. predicative; often foll. by from) at a specified distance (three miles distant from them). **2** remote or far apart in position, time, resemblance, etc. (a distant prospect; a distant relative; a distant likeness; finished a distant second). **3** not intimate; reserved; cool (a distant bow). **4** remote; abstracted (a distant stare). **5** faint, vague (he was a distant memory to her). □ **dis·tant·ly** adverb [Old French distant or Latin distant- part. stem of distare: see DISTANCE]

Distant Early Warning noun N Amer. see DEW LINE.

dis·taste noun (usu. foll. by for) dislike; repugnance; aversion (a distaste for prunes; a distaste for polite company). □ **dis·taste·ful** adjective **dis·taste·ful·ly** adverb **dis·taste·ful·ness** noun

Di Stef·ano /diː ˈstefəˌnoː/ **Al·fredo** (b.1926), Argentinian-born Spanish soccer player. Considered to be one of the greatest soccer players ever; with his club Real Madrid he won the European Cup in each of its first five seasons.

dis·tel·fink /ˈdɪstəlˌfɪŋk/ noun a bird feeder, esp. for finches, consisting of a seed-filled tube suspended vertically, with perches and small feeding holes throughout. [German spelling of Pennsylvania Dutch dischdelfink 'goldfinch', from dischdel 'thistle' + fink 'finch']

dis·tem·per[1] ● noun **1** a kind of paint using glue or size instead of an oil base, for use on walls or for scene painting. **2** a method of mural and poster painting using this. ● transitive verb paint (walls etc.) with distemper. [earlier as verb, from Late Latin distemperare soak, macerate: see DISTEMPER[2]]

dis·tem·per[2] noun **1 a** (also **canine distemper**) a disease of dogs, causing fever, coughing, and catarrh. **b** (also **feline distemper**) a usu. fatal viral disease of cats, causing fever, vomiting, and diarrhea. **c** a disease of various other animals. **2** disorder; uneasiness. [earlier as verb, = upset, derange: Middle English from Late Latin distemperare (as DIS-, temperare mingle correctly)]

dis·tem·pered adjective disordered, disturbed; uneasy.

dis·tend transitive & intransitive verb swell out by pressure from within (distended stomach). □ **dis·ten·si·ble** adjective **dis·ten·si·bil·ity** noun **dis·ten·sion** noun [Latin distendere (as DIS-, tendere tens- stretch)]

dis·tich /ˈdɪstɪk/ noun Prosody a pair of verse lines; a couplet. [Latin distichon from Greek distikhon (as DI[1], stikhos line)]

dis·tich·ous /ˈdɪstɪkəs/ adjective Bot. arranged in two opposite vertical rows. □ **dis·tich·ous·ly** adverb [Latin distichus (as DISTICH)]

dis·till verb (also **dis·til**) (**dis·tilled, dis·till·ing**) **1** transitive Chem. purify (a liquid) by vaporizing it with heat, then condensing it with cold and collecting the result. **2** transitive **a** Chem. extract the essence of (a plant etc.) usu. by heating it in a solvent. **b** extract the essential meaning or implications of (an idea etc.). **3** transitive make (whisky, essence, etc.) by distilling raw materials. **4** transitive (foll. by off, out) Chem. drive (the volatile constituent) off or out by heat. **5** transitive & intransitive come as or give forth in drops; exude. [Latin distillare from destillare (as DE-, stilla drop)]

dis·til·late /ˈdɪstɪlət, -leɪt, -ˈstɪl-/ noun a product of distillation.

dis·til·la·tion noun **1** the process of distilling or being distilled (in various senses). **2** something distilled.

dis·til·ler noun a person who distills, esp. a manufacturer of alcoholic liquor.

dis·til·lery noun (pl. -ies) a place where alcoholic liquor is distilled.

dis·tinct adjective (often foll. by from) **a** not identical; separate; individual. **b** different in kind or quality; unlike. **2 a** clearly perceptible; plain. **b** clearly understandable; definite. **3** unmistakable, decided (had a distinct impression of being watched). □ **dis·tinct·ly** adverb **dis·tinct·ness** noun [Latin distinctus past participle of distinguere DISTINGUISH]

dis·tinc·tion noun **1 a** the act or an instance of discriminating or distinguishing. **b** the difference made by distinguishing. **2 a** something that differentiates, e.g. a mark, name, or title. **b** the fact of being different. **3** special consideration or honour. **4** distinguished character; excellence; eminence (a film of distinction; show distinction in their bearing). **5** a grade in an examination etc. denoting great excellence (passed with distinction).

dis·tinc·tive adjective distinguishing, characteristic. □ **dis·tinc·tive·ly** adverb **dis·tinc·tive·ness** noun

dis·tin·guish verb **1** transitive (often foll. by from) **a** see or point out the difference of; draw distinctions (cannot distinguish one from the other). **b** constitute such a difference (the mole distinguishes him from his twin). **c** draw distinctions between; differentiate. **2** transitive be a mark or

Consonants: b but   d dog   f few   g get   h her   j yes   k cat   l leg   m man   n no   p pen   r red   s sit

property of; characterize (*distinguished by his greed*). **3** *transitive* discover by listening, looking, etc. (*could distinguish two voices*). **4** *transitive* (usu. *reflexive*; often foll. by *by*) make prominent or noteworthy (*distinguished herself by winning first prize*). **5** *intransitive* (foll. by *between*) make or point out a difference between. □ **dis·tin·guish·able** *adjective* [Latin *distinguere* (as DIS-, *stinguere stinct*- extinguish): compare EXTINGUISH]

dis·tin·guished *adjective* **1 a** of high standing. **b** eminent; famous. **2** having a distinguished air, features, manner, etc.

dis·tort *verb* **1 a** *transitive & intransitive* put out of shape; make or become crooked or unshapely. **b** *transitive* warp the appearance of, esp. by curved mirrors, imperfect lenses, etc. **2** *transitive* misrepresent (*motives, facts, statements*, etc.). **3** *transitive* Electronics change the form of (a signal) during transmission or amplification. □ **dis·tort·ed** *adjective* **dis·tort·ed·ly** *adverb* [Latin *distorquēre distort-* (as DIS-, *torquēre* twist)]

dis·tor·tion *noun* **1** the act or an instance of distorting; the process of being distorted. **2** *Electronics* a change in the form of a signal during transmission etc. usu. with some impairment of quality. **3** the characteristic fuzzy sound of electric guitars in some forms of popular music, e.g. heavy metal, rock, etc. □ **dis·tor·tion·al** *adjective* **dis·tor·tion·less** *adjective*

dis·tract *transitive verb* **1** (often foll. by *from*) draw away the attention of (a person, the mind, etc.). **2** bewilder, perplex. **3** amuse, esp. in order to take the attention from pain or worry. □ **dis·tract·ibil·ity** *noun* **dis·tract·ible** *adjective* [Latin *distrahere distract-* (as DIS-, *trahere* draw)]

dis·tract·ed *adjective* **1** mad or angry (*distracted by grief; distracted with worry*). **2** inattentive. □ **dis·tract·ed·ly** *adverb*

dis·trac·tion *noun* **1 a** the act of distracting, esp. the mind. **b** something that distracts; an interruption. **2** a relaxation from work; an amusement. **3** a lack of concentration. **4** confusion; perplexity. **5** frenzy; madness. □ **to distraction** almost to a state of madness.

dis·train /dɪˈstreɪn/ *intransitive verb* Law (usu. foll. by *upon*) impose distraint (on a person, goods, etc.). [Old French *destreindre* from Latin *distringere* (as DIS-, *stringere strict*- draw tight)]

dis·traint /dɪˈstreɪnt/ *noun* Law the seizure of chattels to make a person pay rent etc. or meet an obligation, or to obtain satisfaction by their sale.

dis·trait /dɪˈstreɪ/ *adjective* not paying attention, absent-minded. [Old French *destrait* past participle of *destraire* (as DISTRACT)]

dis·traught /dɪˈstrɔt/ *adjective* extremely worried, upset, fearful, etc. [Middle English, alteration of obsolete *distract* (adj.) (as DISTRACT), after *straught*, obsolete past participle of STRETCH]

dis·tress ● *noun* **1** severe trouble, anxiety, sorrow, anguish, etc. **2** Law = DISTRAINT. **3** *Med.* the state of an organ etc. that is not functioning normally or adequately. ● *transitive verb* **1** subject to distress; exhaust, afflict. **2** cause anxiety to; make unhappy; vex. **3** scratch or mark (clothing, furniture, etc.) to simulate the effects of age and wear. □ **in distress 1** suffering or in danger. **2** (of a ship, aircraft, etc.) in danger or damaged. □ **dis·tress·ful** *adjective* **dis·tress·ing** *adjective* **dis·tress·ing·ly** *adverb* [Old French *destresse* etc., from Gallo-Roman (as DISTRAIN)]

dis·tressed *adjective* **1** suffering from distress. **2** impoverished (*in distressed circumstances*). **3** (of furniture, leather, etc.) having simulated marks of age and wear.

distress signal *noun* (also **distress call**) a signal from a ship etc. in danger.

dis·tribu·tary *noun* (pl. **-ies**) a branch of a river or glacier that does not return to the main stream after leaving it (as in a delta).

dis·trib·ute *transitive verb* **1** give shares of; deal out. **2** spread or disperse throughout a region; scatter (*distributed the seeds evenly over the garden*). **3** divide into parts; arrange; classify. **4** supply (goods etc.) to customers. **5** *Logic* use (a term) to include every individual of the class to which it refers. □ **dis·trib·ut·able** *adjective* [Latin *distribuere distribut*- (as DIS-, *tribuere* assign)]

dis·trib·ut·ed *adjective* designating a computer system, process, etc. involving a number of independent interconnected computers (*distributed computing*).

dis·tri·bu·tion *noun* **1** the act or an instance of distributing; the process or state of being distributed. **2 a** the dispersal of goods etc. among consumers, brought about by commerce. **b** the extent to which different groups, classes, or individuals share in the total production or wealth of a community. **3** *Statistics* the way in which a characteristic is spread over members of a class. □ **dis·tri·bu·tion·al** *adjective*

dis·tribu·tive ● *adjective* **1** of, concerned with, or produced by distribution. **2** *Logic & Grammar* (of a pronoun etc.) referring to each individual of a class, not to the class collectively, e.g. *each, either*. **3** *Math.*

governed by or stating the condition that when an operation is performed on two or more quantities already combined by a second operation, the result is the same as when it is performed on each quantity individually and the products then combined. ● *noun* Grammar a distributive word. □ **dis·tribu·tive·ly** *adverb*

dis·tribu·tor *noun* **1** a person or thing that distributes. **2** an agent who supplies goods. **3** *Electricity* a device in an internal combustion engine for passing the current to each spark plug in turn. □ **dis·tribu·tor·ship** *noun*

dis·trict ● *noun* **1 a** (often *attributive*) a territory marked off for special administrative purposes. **2** an area which has common characteristics; a region (*the wine-growing district*). ● *transitive verb* N Amer. divide into districts. [French from medieval Latin *districtus* (territory of) jurisdiction (as DISTRAIN)]

district attorney *noun* (in the US) the prosecuting officer of a district. Abbr.: **DA**.

district court *noun* (in the US) the Federal court of first instance.

district heating *noun* a supply of heat from one source to a district or a group of buildings.

district municipality *noun* Cdn (BC) a municipality having more than 800 hectares of land and an average population density of less than five people per hectare.

district nurse *noun* Brit. a nurse who visits and treats patients in their homes, operating in an assigned area.

District of Columbia a Federal district of the US, co-extensive with the city of Washington, situated on the Potomac River with boundaries on the states of Virginia and Maryland. Abbr.: **DC**.

dis·trust ● *noun* a lack of trust; doubt; suspicion. ● *transitive verb* have no trust or confidence in; doubt. □ **dis·trust·ful** *adjective* **dis·trust·ful·ly** *adverb*

dis·turb *transitive verb* **1** break the rest, calm, order, or quiet of; interrupt. **2** agitate; worry, unsettle (*your story disturbs me*). **3** move from a settled position, disarrange (*the papers had been disturbed*). □ **dis·turb·er** *noun* **dis·turb·ing** *adjective* **dis·turb·ing·ly** *adverb* [Latin *disturbare* (as DIS-, *turbare* from *turba* tumult)]

dis·turb·ance *noun* **1** the act or an instance of disturbing; the process of being disturbed. **2** a tumult; an uproar. **3** agitation; worry. **4** an interruption. **5** *Meteorol.* a low-pressure feature, e.g. a depression or trough. **6** Law interference with rights or property.

dis·turbed *adjective* **1** in senses of DISTURB. **2** *Psych.* emotionally or mentally unstable or abnormal.

di·sulfi·ram /daɪˈsʌlfɪram/ *noun* a synthetic compound used in the treatment of alcoholics to make drinking alcohol produce unpleasant after-effects, such as nausea. *Also called* ANTABUSE. [blend of *disulfide* and *thiuram* (from THIO- + UREA + AMMONIUM)]

di·sul·phide /daɪˈsʌlfaɪd/ *noun* (N Amer. also **di·sul·fide**) *Chem.* a binary chemical containing two atoms of sulphur in each molecule.

dis·union *noun* a lack of union; separation; dissension.

dis·unit·ed *adjective* not united.

dis·unity *noun* lack of unity.

dis·use ● *noun* **1** lack of use or practice; discontinuance. **2** a disused state. ● *transitive verb* cease to use. □ **fall into disuse** cease to be used.

di·sylla·ble /daɪˈsɪləbəl/ *noun* Prosody a word or metrical foot of two syllables. □ **di·syllab·ic** /-ˈlabɪk/ *adjective*

dit *noun* (in Morse code) = DOT[1] 3 (compare DAH, DASH *noun* 7). [imitative]

ditch ● *noun* **1** a long narrow excavated channel esp. for drainage, defence, or to mark a boundary. **2** a watercourse, stream, etc. ● *verb* **1** *intransitive* make or repair ditches (*hedging and ditching*). **2** *transitive* provide with ditches; drain. **3** *transitive informal* **a** get rid of. **b** cease consorting with (esp. a lover etc.). **c** abandon. **4** *transitive* **a** bring (an aircraft) down on water in an emergency. **b** drive (a vehicle) into a ditch. **5** *intransitive* (of an aircraft) make a forced landing on water. □ **ditch·er** *noun* [Old English *dīc*, of unknown origin: compare DIKE[1]]

ditch·digger *noun* a person who digs ditches, esp. as representative of hard menial labour.

ditch·water *noun* stagnant water in a ditch. □ **dull as ditchwater** extremely dull.

dith·er /ˈdɪðər/ ● *intransitive verb* hesitate; be indecisive. ● *noun informal* **1** a state of agitation or apprehension. **2** a state of hesitation; indecisiveness. □ **dith·er·er** *noun* **dith·ery** *adjective* [var. of *didder*, DODDER[1]]

dith·er·ing *noun* **1** in senses of DITHER *verb*. **2** *Computing* a method of creating apparently smooth gradations of shade or continuous tones

by gradually spacing single-tone pixels (compare GREY-SCALE).
□ **dith·ered** adjective

dithio- /'daɪθaɪɒ/ combining form Chem. containing two sulphur atoms in the molecule, esp. in place of two oxygen atoms or joined together. [DI-¹ + THIO-]

dithy·ramb /'dɪθɪˌram, -ˌramb/ noun **1 a** a wild choral hymn in ancient Greece, esp. to Dionysus. **b** a Bacchanalian song. **2** any passionate or inflated poem, speech, etc. □ **dithy·ram·bic** /-'rambɪk/ adjective [Latin dithyrambus from Greek dithurambos, of unknown origin]

Diti·daht /'dɪtidat/ noun **1** a member of an Aboriginal people, part of the Nuu-chah-nulth, living on southern Vancouver Island. **2** the Wakashan language of this people. [Ditidaht, self-designation]

ditsy var. of DITZY.

dit·tany /'dɪtəni/ noun (pl. **-ies**) any herb of the genus Dictamnus, formerly used medicinally. [Old French dita(i)n from medieval Latin dictamus from Latin dictamnus from Greek diktamnon perhaps from Diktē, a mountain in Crete]

ditto noun (pl. **-tos**) **1** (in accounts, inventories, lists, etc.) the aforesaid, the same. ¶ Often represented by double quotation marks under the word or sum to be repeated. **2** informal (replacing a word or phrase to avoid repetition) the same (came in late last night and ditto the night before). **3** a similar thing; a duplicate. **4** (**Ditto**) proprietary a small duplicating machine using an alcoholic solution to reproduce copies from a master. [Italian dial. from Latin dictus past participle of dicere say]

dit·tog·raphy /dɪ'tɒɡrəfi/ noun (pl. **-ies**) **1** a copyist's mistaken repetition of a letter, word, or phrase. **2** an example of this. □ **ditto·graph·ic** adjective [Greek dittos double + -GRAPHY]

ditto marks plural noun double quotation marks etc. representing 'ditto'.

ditty noun (pl. **-ties**) a short simple song. [Old French dité composition, from Latin dictatum neuter past participle of dictare DICTATE]

ditty bag noun (also **ditty box**) a sailor's or fisherman's receptacle for odds and ends. [19th c.: origin unknown]

ditz noun N Amer. a ditzy person.

ditzy adjective (also **ditsy**) N Amer. informal (usu. of a woman) silly or foolish. □ **ditz·i·ness** noun [20th c.: origin unknown]

di·ur·esis /ˌdaɪjʊ'riːsɪs/ noun Med. an increased excretion of urine. [modern Latin from Greek (as DI-², ourēsis urination)]

di·ur·et·ic /ˌdaɪjʊ'retɪk/ ● adjective causing increased output of urine. ● noun a diuretic drug or substance. [Late Latin diureticus from Greek diourētikos from dioureō urinate]

di·ur·nal /daɪ'ɜːnəl/ adjective **1** of or during the day; not nocturnal. **2** daily; of each day. **3** Astronomy occupying one day. **4** (of animals) active in the daytime. **5** (of plants) open only during the day. □ **di·ur·nal·ly** adverb [Late Latin diurnalis from Latin diurnus from dies day]

Div. abbreviation **1** Division. **2** Divinity.

diva /'diːvə/ noun (pl. **divas**) **1** a famous female opera singer. **2** a female singer who has enjoyed great popular success. **3** an admired, glamorous, or distinguished woman (the former director of the association is still a downtown diva). **4** a haughty, spoiled woman. [Italian from Latin, = goddess]

di·vagate /'daɪvəˌɡeɪt/ intransitive verb literary stray; digress. □ **di·va·ga·tion** noun [Latin divagari (as DI-², vagari wander)]

di·valent /daɪ'veɪlənt/ adjective Chem. having a valence of two; bivalent. □ **di·valence** noun **di·valen·cy** noun [DI-¹ + valent- part. stem (as VALENCE)]

Di·vali noun var. of DIWALI.

divan /dɪ'van/ noun **1 a** a long, low, padded seat set against the wall of a room; a backless sofa. **b** a bed consisting of a base and mattress, usu. with no board at either end. **2** an esp. Middle Eastern state legislative body, council chamber, or court of justice. [French divan or Italian divano from Turkish dīvān from Arabic dīwān from Persian dīvān anthology, register, court, bench]

di·vari·cate /daɪ'verɪˌkeɪt, dɪ-/ intransitive verb diverge, branch; separate widely. □ **di·vari·cate** /-kət/ adjective **di·vari·ca·tion** noun [Latin divaricare (as DI-², varicus straddling)]

dive verb (past **dived**; N Amer. also **dove** /doːv/) **1** intransitive plunge (esp. headfirst) into water. **2** intransitive **a** Aviation (of an aircraft) plunge steeply downwards at speed. **b** Naut. (of a submarine) submerge. **c** plunge downwards, drop. **3** intransitive (foll. by into) informal **a** put one's hand into (a pocket, handbag, vessel, etc.) quickly and deeply. **b** occupy oneself suddenly and enthusiastically with (a subject, meal, etc.). **4** transitive (foll. by into) plunge (a hand etc.) into. **5 a** intransitive swim

underwater, esp. with scuba equipment. **b** transitive swim underwater to explore (a body of water, sunken ship, etc.). **6** (in hockey, soccer, etc.) fall deliberately in an attempt to draw a penalty on one's opponent. ● noun **1** an act or instance of diving; a plunge. **2 a** the submerging of a submarine. **b** the steep descent of an aircraft. **3** a sudden darting movement. **4** informal a seedy, rundown nightclub, bar, etc. (this place is a real dive). **5 a** Boxing slang a pretended knockout (took a dive in the second round). **b** (in hockey, soccer, etc.) a deliberate fall in an attempt to draw a penalty on one's opponent. □ **dive in** informal help oneself (to food). [Old English verbs dūfan (intransitive) dive, sink, and dȳfan (transitive) immerse, from Germanic: related to DEEP, DIP]

dive-bomb transitive verb **1** (of an aircraft) bomb (a target) while diving towards it. **2** (of a bird, insect, etc.) descend rapidly from a height to attack something. □ **dive-bomber** noun

dive·master noun the leader of a diving expedition.

diver noun **1** a person who dives. **2** any of various diving birds, esp. large water birds of the family Gaviidae; a loon.

di·verge verb **1** intransitive **a** proceed in a different direction or in different directions from a point (diverging rays; the path diverges here). **b** take a different course or different courses (their interests diverged). **2** intransitive **a** (often foll. by from) depart from a set course (diverged from the track; diverged from his parents' wishes). **b** differ markedly in opinion. **3** transitive cause to diverge; deflect. **4** intransitive Math. (of a series) increase indefinitely as more of its terms are added (compare CONVERGE 4). [medieval Latin divergere (as DI-², Latin vergere incline)]

di·ver·gent adjective **1** diverging. **2** Psych. (of thought) tending to reach a variety of possible solutions when analyzing a problem. **3** Math. (of a series) increasing indefinitely as more of its terms are added; not convergent. □ **di·ver·gence** noun **di·ver·gency** noun **di·ver·gent·ly** adverb

divers /'daɪvəz/ adjective archaic or literary more than one; various; several. [Old French from Latin diversus DIVERSE (as DI-², versus past participle of vertere turn)]

di·verse /daɪ'vɜːs, 'daɪ-, dɪ-/ adjective unlike in nature or qualities; varied. □ **di·verse·ly** adverb [Middle English (as DIVERS)]

di·vers·ify /daɪ'vɜːsɪˌfaɪ, dɪ-/ verb (**-fies**, **-fied**) **1** transitive make diverse; vary; modify. **2** transitive spread (investment, efforts, etc.) over several enterprises or products, esp. to reduce the risk of loss. **3** intransitive (often foll. by into) esp. Business (of a company etc.) expand the range of products handled. □ **di·vers·ifi·ca·tion** noun [Old French diversifier from medieval Latin diversificare (as DIVERS)]

di·ver·sion /daɪ'vɜːʒən, dɪ-/ noun **1 a** the act of diverting; deviation. **b** an instance of this. **2 a** the diverting of attention deliberately. **b** a stratagem for this purpose (created a diversion to secure their escape). **3** a recreation or pastime, esp. as diverting the mind from preoccupation or boredom. **4** an artificial watercourse created to divert the flow of water from one body to another or to provide drainage. **5** Brit. = DETOUR. □ **di·ver·sion·al** adjective **di·ver·sion·ary** adjective [Late Latin diversio (as DIVERT)]

di·vers·ity /daɪ'vɜːsɪti, dɪ-/ noun (pl. **-ities**) **1** the state of being diverse; variety (there was considerable diversity in the style of the reports). **2** a range of different things (newspapers were obliged to allow a diversity of views to be printed). **3** ethnic, social, or gender variety in a group, culture, or institution (the festival is a celebration of our city's diversity).

di·vert /daɪ'vɜːt, dɪ-/ transitive verb **1** (often foll. by from, to) **a** turn aside from a direction or course; deflect. **b** draw the attention of; distract. **2** (often as **di·vert·ing** adjective) entertain; amuse. [French divertir from Latin divertere (as DI-², vertere turn)]

di·ver·ticu·lar /ˌdaɪvɜː'tɪkjʊlər/ adjective Med. of or relating to a diverticulum.

diverticular disease noun a condition with abdominal pain as a result of muscle spasms in the presence of diverticula.

di·ver·ticu·litis /ˌdaɪvɜːˌtɪkjʊ'laɪtɪs/ noun inflammation of a diverticulum.

di·ver·ticu·losis /ˌdaɪvɜːˌtɪkjʊ'ləʊsɪs/ noun the presence of abnormal diverticula, esp. in the intestine.

di·ver·ticu·lum /ˌdaɪvɜː'tɪkjʊləm/ noun (pl. **di·ver·tic·ula** /-lə/) Anat. a blind tube or sac forming at weak points in the wall of a cavity or passage, esp. of the alimentary tract. [medieval Latin, var. of Latin deverticulum byway, from devertere (as DE-, vertere turn)]

di·ver·ti·mento /dɪˌvɜːtɪ'mentoː, dɪˌver-/ noun (pl. **di·ver·ti·menti** /-ti/ or **-tos**) Music a light and entertaining composition, often in the form of a suite for chamber orchestra. [Italian, = diversion]

di·ver·tisse·ment /diːˌvɜːtiːs'mɑ̃/ noun **1** a diversion; an entertainment. **2** a short ballet in an opera etc. or a dance within a

Vowels: a cat   ɑ arm   e bed   ɜr her   ɜː deux   ə ago   ɪ sit   i cosy   iː feed   ɒ hot   ɔ pore   oː no   ʌ run   ʊ put

larger narrative ballet that does not advance the plot. [French, from *divertiss-* stem of *divertir* DIVERT]

di·vest /daɪˈvɛst/ *verb* **1** *transitive & intransitive* sell off (a subsidiary company, investments, etc.). **2** *transitive* (usu. foll. by *of*; often *reflexive*) unclothe; strip (*divested himself of his jacket*). **3** *transitive* deprive, dispossess; free, rid (*we must divest ourselves of such prejudices; divested the RCMP of some of its powers*). □ **di·vesti·ture** *noun* **di·vest·ment** *noun* [earlier *devest* from Old French *desvestir* etc. (as DIS-, Latin *vestire* from *vestis* garment)]

div·ide ● *verb* **1** *transitive & intransitive* (often foll. by *in*, *into*, *up*) separate or be separated into parts; break up; split (*the river divides in two; the road divides; divided them into three groups*). **2** *transitive & intransitive* (often foll. by *up*) distribute; deal; share (*divided it up between them*). **3** *transitive* **a** cut off; separate; part (*divide the sheep from the goats*). **b** mark out into parts (*a ruler divided into centimetres*). **c** specify different kinds of, classify (*people can be divided into two types*). **4** *transitive* cause to disagree; set at variance (*opinions are divided*). **5** *Math.* **a** *transitive* find how many times (a number) contains another (*divide 20 by 4*). **b** *intransitive* (of a number) be contained in (a number) without a remainder (*4 divides into 20*). **c** *intransitive* be susceptible of division (*10 divides by 2 and 5*). **d** *transitive* find how many times (a number) is contained in another (*divide 4 into 20*). **6** *intransitive Math.* do division (*can divide well*). **7** *Parl.* **a** *intransitive* (of a legislative assembly etc.) part into two groups for voting (*the House divided*). **b** *transitive* so divide (a Parliament etc.) for voting. ● *noun* **1 a** a dividing or boundary line; a gulf (*the divide between rich and poor*). **b** a separation (*the cultural divide*). **2** (also **Divide**; usu. prec. by *the*) an esp. continental watershed. □ **divided against itself** consisting of opposing factions. [Latin *dividere divis-* (as DI-², *vid-* separate)]

divided highway *noun N Amer.* a highway with a median strip or guardrail separating opposing traffic.

divided skirt *noun* culottes.

divi·dend *noun* **1 a** a sum of money to be divided among a number of persons, esp. that paid by a company to shareholders. **b** a similar sum payable to members of a co-operative, to creditors of an insolvent estate, etc. **c** an individual's share of a dividend. **2** *Math.* a number to be divided by a divisor. **3** a benefit from any action (*their long training paid dividends*). [Anglo-French *dividende* from Latin *dividendum* (as DIVIDE)]

dividend yield *noun* a dividend expressed as a percentage of a current share price.

div·id·er *noun* **1** anything which divides a whole into sections, esp. an insert in a binder, notebook, etc., or a screen, piece of furniture, etc., dividing a room into two parts. **2** (in *pl.*) a measuring compass, esp. with a screw for setting small intervals.

div·id·ing line *noun* a real or notional line between sharply contrasted things, characteristics, etc.

divi-divi /ˈdɪvɪˌdɪvɪ/ *noun* (*pl.* **divi-divis**) **1** a small tree, *Caesalpinia coriaria*, native to tropical America, bearing curved pods. **2** this pod used as a source of tannin. [Carib]

div·in·a·tion /ˌdɪvɪˈneɪʃən/ *noun* **1** supposed insight into the future or the unknown gained by supernatural means. **2 a** a skilful and accurate forecast. **b** a good guess. □ **divi·na·tory** *adjective* [Latin *divinatio* (as DIVINE)]

div·ine ● *adjective* (**divin·er**, **divin·est**) **1 a** of, from, or like God or a god. **b** devoted to God; sacred (*divine service*). **2 a** more than humanly excellent, gifted, or beautiful. **b** *informal* excellent; delightful. ● *verb* **1** *transitive* discover by guessing, intuition, inspiration, or magic. **2** *transitive* foresee, predict, conjecture. **3** *intransitive* practise divination. ● *noun* **1** a cleric, usu. an expert in theology. **2** (**the Divine**) providence or God. □ **divine·ly** *adverb* **divine·ness** *noun* **divin·er** *noun* [Old French *devin -ine* from Latin *divinus* from *divus* godlike]

divine office *noun see* OFFICE 10b.

divine right of kings the doctrine that a monarch in the hereditary line of succession has authority derived directly from God, independently of the subjects' will. It is often associated with the Stuart kings of 16th-c. Great Britain and esp. with the absolutism of Louis XIV of France.

div·ing *noun* **1** in senses of DIVE. **2** the sport of performing dives, esp. with elaborate twists and turns of the body.

diving beetle *noun* a predatory water beetle of the family Dytiscidae which stores air under the elytra while diving.

diving bell *noun* an open-bottomed box or bell, supplied with air, in which a person can descend into deep water.

diving board *noun* an elevated board projecting over water, used for diving from.

diving duck *noun* a duck that habitually dives for food, esp. one of the tribe *Aythyini*, which includes the canvasback, scaup, etc.

diving suit *noun* a suit worn while diving, esp. a watertight one with a helmet and an air supply, worn for working under water.

div·ing rod *noun* = DOWSING ROD.

divin·ity *noun* (*pl.* **-ities**) **1** the state or quality of being divine. **2 a** a god; a divine being. **b** (as **the Divinity**) God. **3** the study of religion; theology. **4** *N Amer.* (also **divinity fudge**) a type of fudge made with beaten egg whites and nuts. [Old French *divinité* from Latin *divinitas -tatis* (as DIVINE)]

divinity school *noun N Amer.* a place where students are trained for ordination as ministers.

divin·ize /ˈdɪvɪnaɪz/ *transitive verb* (also esp. *Brit.* **-ise**) make divine; deify. □ **divin·iz·a·tion** *noun*

div·is·ible /dɪˈvɪzəbəl/ *adjective* **1** capable of being divided, physically or mentally. **2** (foll. by *by*) *Math.* containing (a number) a number of times without a remainder (*15 is divisible by 3 and 5*). □ **div·is·ibil·ity** *noun* [Late Latin *divisibilis* (as DIVIDE)]

div·ision *noun* **1** the act or an instance of dividing; the process of being divided. **2** *Math.* the process of dividing one number by another (*see also* LONG DIVISION, SHORT DIVISION). **3** disagreement or discord (*division of opinion*). **4** *Parl.* the separation of members of a legislative body into two sets for counting votes for and against. **5** one of two or more parts into which a thing is divided. **6** a major unit of administration or organization, esp.: **a** a group of army brigades or regiments. **b** *Cdn* an administrative unit of a police force. **c** *Sport* a grouping of teams or athletes within a league etc. **d** = SCHOOL DIVISION. **7 a** a district defined for administrative purposes. **b** *Brit.* a part of a county or borough returning a Member of Parliament. **8 a** *Bot.* a major taxonomic grouping. **b** *Zool.* a subsidiary category between major levels of classification. **9** *Logic* a classification of kinds, parts, or senses. □ **div·ision·al** *adjective* **div·ision·al·ly** *adverb* [Old French *divisiun* from Latin *divisio -onis* (as DIVIDE)]

Divisional Court *noun Cdn* (in Ontario) a court consisting of tribunals of three judges of the Ontario Court, which hears appeals from lower provincial courts and provincial administrative tribunals.

div·ision·al·ize *transitive & intransitive verb* (also esp. *Brit.* **-ise**) organize (a company etc.) into separate divisions. □ **div·ision·al·iz·a·tion** *noun*

divisional point *noun* one of several points along a railway at a distance from each other determined by the range of the locomotive, providing maintenance and repair facilities.

division bell *noun* (usu. in *pl.*) a bell rung to signal the taking of a vote in a parliament.

division of labour *noun* the specialization of workers in the process of production or any other economic, domestic, etc. activity.

division of powers *noun* (in Canada) the separation of governmental responsibilities and privileges into federal and provincial jurisdictions.

division sign *noun* the sign (÷), placed between two numbers to indicate that the one preceding the sign is to be divided by the one following it.

div·isive /dɪˈvɪsɪv, dɪˈvaɪsɪv, -zɪv/ *adjective* tending to divide, esp. in opinion; causing disagreement. □ **div·isive·ly** *adverb* **div·isive·ness** *noun* [Late Latin *divisivus* (as DIVIDE)]

div·isor /dɪˈvaɪzər/ *noun* **1** a number by which another is to be divided. **2** a number that divides another without a remainder. [Latin *divisor* (as DIVIDE)]

di·vorce ● *noun* **1 a** the legal dissolution of a marriage (also *attributive*: *divorce court*). **b** a legal decree of this. **2** a severance or separation (*a divorce between thought and feeling*). ● *verb* **1 a** *transitive* (usu. as **di·vorced** *adjective*) (often foll. by *from*) legally dissolve the marriage of (*a divorced couple; he wants to get divorced from her*). **b** *intransitive* separate by divorce (*they divorced last year*). **c** *transitive* end one's marriage with (*divorced him for neglect*). **2** *transitive* (often foll. by *from*) detach, separate (*divorced from reality*). [Old French *divorce* (n.), *divorcer* (v.) from Late Latin *divortiare* from Latin *divortium* from *divortere* (as DI-², *vertere* turn)]

di·vor·cee /ˌdɪvɔrˈseɪ, -ˈsiː/ *noun* a divorced person, esp. a divorced woman.

div·ot /ˈdɪvət/ *noun* a piece of turf cut out by a golf club in making a stroke. [16th c.: origin unknown]

di·vulge /daɪˈvʌldʒ, dɪ-/ *transitive verb* disclose; reveal (a secret etc.). □ **di·vul·gence** *noun* [Latin *divulgare* (as DI-², *vulgare* publish, from *vulgus* common people)]

divvy /ˈdɪvɪ/ *informal* ● *transitive verb* (**-vies**, **-vied**) (often foll. by *up*) share out; divide. ● *noun* (*pl.* **-vies**) **1** a distribution. **2** *Brit.* a dividend; a share of profits. [abbreviation of DIVIDEND]

Di·wali /dɪ'wɒlɪ/ *noun* (also **Di·vali**) a major Hindu festival held in October or November, honouring Lakshmi, the goddess of prosperity, during which gifts are exchanged and lamps lit. [Hindustani *dīwālī* from Sanskrit *dīpāvalī* row of lights, from *dīpa* lamp]

Dixie *noun* the southern states of the US. □ **whistle Dixie** *see* WHISTLE. [19th c.: origin uncertain]

Dixie cup *noun* N *Amer. proprietary* a small, waxed paper cup for water, ice cream, etc.

Dixie·land *noun* **1** = DIXIE. **2** a kind of jazz with a strong two-beat rhythm and collective improvisation.

Dixon Entrance a passage of the N Pacific, separating the Queen Charlotte Islands (BC) from Prince of Wales Island (Alaska). [G. Dixon, English explorer and navigator d. *c.*1800]

DIY *abbreviation* do-it-yourself. □ **DIY·er** *noun*

Di·yar·ba·kir /dɪ'jɑrbə,kɪːr/ a city in SE Turkey, capital of a province of the same name; pop. (est. 2002) 570,900.

dizzy ● *adjective* (**diz·zi·er**, **diz·zi·est**) **1 a** giddy, unsteady. **b** feeling confused. **c** *informal* scatterbrained. **2** causing giddiness (*dizzy heights*; *dizzy speed*). ● *transitive verb* (**-zies**, **-zied**) **1** make dizzy. **2** bewilder. □ **diz·zi·ly** *adverb* **diz·zi·ness** *noun* **dizzy·ing** *adjective* **dizzy·ing·ly** *adverb* [Old English *dysig* from West Germanic]

DJ ● *noun* **1** a disc jockey. **2** *Brit.* a dinner jacket. ● *intransitive verb* (**DJed**, **DJing**) act as a disc jockey. [abbreviation]

Dja·kar·ta *see* JAKARTA.

djel·la·ba /'dʒɛləbə/ *noun* (also **djel·la·bah**, **jel·la·ba**) a loose, long-sleeved, hooded woollen cloak of a type originally worn by Arab men in North Africa. [Arabic *jallaba*, *jallābīya*]

djem·be /'ʒɛmbə, 'ʒembeɪ/ *noun* a kind of goblet-shaped hand drum originating in West Africa. [French *djembé*, from Mande (a West African language) *jembe*]

DJIA *abbreviation* Dow Jones Industrial Average.

djib·ba (also **djib·bah**) *var. of* JIBBA.

Dji·bou·ti /dʒɪ'buːtɪ/ (also **Ji·bu·ti**) **1** a country on the northeast coast of Africa; pop. (est. 2002) 820,600. **2** the capital of Djibouti, a port at the western end of the Gulf of Aden; pop. (est. 2002) 547,100. □ **Dji·bou·tian** *adjective & noun*

Djilas /'dʒiːlɒs/ **Milo·van** (1911–95), Yugoslav politician and writer, vice-president 1953–54, whose increasing criticism of communism led to his dismissal and imprisonment 1956–61 and 1962–66; his writings include *The New Class* (1957) and *Conversations with Stalin* (1962).

djinn *var. of* JINNI.

DL *abbreviation* Baseball DISABLED LIST.

dl *abbreviation* decilitre(s).

D.Litt. *abbreviation* Doctor of Letters. [Latin *Doctor Litterarum*]

DM *abbreviation* **1** Cdn Deputy Minister. **2** (also **D-mark**) Deutschmark. **3** dextromethorphan.

dm *abbreviation* decimetre(s).

DMA *abbreviation* **1** *Computing* direct memory access. **2** (**D.M.A.**) Doctor of Musical Arts.

DMD *abbreviation* **1** (**D.M.D.**) Doctor of Dental Medicine. **2** DUCHENNE MUSCULAR DYSTROPHY.

DME *abbreviation* distance measuring equipment.

D.Min. *abbreviation* Doctor of Ministry.

DMs *abbreviation* DOCTOR MARTENS.

DMT *abbreviation* dimethyltryptamine, a hallucinogenic drug.

D.Mus. *abbreviation* Doctor of Music.

DMZ *abbreviation* demilitarized zone.

DNA *abbreviation* deoxyribonucleic acid, the self-replicating material which is present in nearly all living organisms, esp. as a constituent of chromosomes, and is the carrier of genetic information.

DNA fingerprinting *noun* = GENETIC FINGERPRINTING.

DND *abbreviation* (in Canada) Department of National Defence.

DNF *abbreviation* did not finish.

Dnie·per River /'dniːpɜr/ a river of E Europe, rising in Russia west of Moscow and flowing southward some 2 200 km (1,370 miles) through Belarus and Ukraine to the Black Sea.

Dnies·ter River /'dniːstɜr/ a river of E Europe, rising in the Carpathian Mountains in W Ukraine and flowing 1 410 km (876 miles) through Ukraine and Moldova to the Black Sea near Odessa.

Dni·pro·dzer·zhinsk /,dniːprədzɜr'ʒɪnsk/ (Russian

Dne·pro·dzer·zhinsk) an industrial city and port in Ukraine, on the Dnieper River; pop. (est. 2001) 256,000.

Dni·pro·pe·trovsk /,dniːprəpə'trɒfsk/ (Russian **Dne·pro·pe·trovsk**) an industrial city and port in Ukraine, on the Dnieper River; pop. (est. 2001) 1,064,000.

DNR *abbreviation* do not resuscitate.

DNS *abbreviation* *Computing* **1** domain name server, the system that automatically translates Internet addresses to the numeric machine addresses that computers use. **2** domain name system, the hierarchical method by which Internet addresses are constructed.

do¹ ● *verb* (*3rd sing. present* **does**; *past* **did**; *past participle* **done**) **1** *transitive* perform, carry out, achieve, complete (work etc.) (*did her homework*; *there's a lot to do*; *we can do anything*). **2** *transitive* **a** produce, make (*she was doing a painting*; *Frank did a translation*; *decided to do a casserole*). **b** provide (*do you do lunches?*). **3** *transitive* bestow, grant; have a specified effect on (*a walk would do you good*; *do me a favour*). **4** *intransitive* act, behave, proceed (*do as I do*; *she would do well to accept the offer*). **5** *transitive* work at, study; be occupied with (*what does your mother do?*; *I did chemistry at university*; *we're doing Chaucer next term*). **6 a** *intransitive* be suitable or acceptable; suffice (*this dress won't do for a wedding*; *a sandwich will do until we get home*; *that will never do*). **b** *transitive* satisfy; be suitable for (*that hotel will do me nicely*). **7** *transitive* deal with; put in order (*the garden needs doing*; *the barber will do you next*; *I must do my hair before we go*). **8** *intransitive* **a** fare; get on (*the patients were doing excellently*; *he did badly in the test*). **b** perform, work (*could do better*). **9** *transitive* **a** solve; work out (*we did the puzzle*). **b** (*prec. by* can *or be able to*) be competent at (*can you do cartwheels?*; *I never could do grammar*). **10** *transitive* **a** traverse (a certain distance) (*we did fifty miles today*). **b** travel at a specified speed (*he overtook us doing about eighty*). **11** *transitive informal* **a** act or behave like (*did a Houdini*). **b** play the part of (*she was asked to do hostess*). **12** *intransitive informal* finish (*I'm done in the bathroom*). **13** *transitive* produce or give a performance of (*the school does many plays and concerts*; *we've never done 'Pygmalion'*). **14** *transitive* cook (*the potatoes aren't done yet*; *let's do the chicken on the barbecue*). **15** *intransitive* be in progress (*what's doing?*). **16** *transitive informal* visit; see the sights of (*we did all the art galleries*). **17** *transitive informal* **a** (often as **done** *adjective*) exhaust; tire out (*the climb has completely done me*). **b** beat up, defeat, kill. **c** ruin (*now you've done it*). **18** *transitive* (foll. by *into*) translate or transform (*the book was done into French*). **19** *transitive slang* **a** rob (*they did a bank in Sarnia*). **b** swindle (*I was done at the market*). **20** *transitive Brit. slang* prosecute, convict (*they were done for shoplifting*). **21** *transitive slang* undergo (a specified term of imprisonment) (*he did two years for fraud*). **22** *transitive coarse slang* have sexual intercourse with. **23** *transitive slang* take (a drug). **24** have (a meal) as a social or business engagement (*let's do lunch!*). ● *auxiliary verb* **1 a** (except with *be, can, may, ought, shall, will*) in questions and negative statements (*do you understand?*; *I don't smoke*). **b** (except with *can, may, ought, shall, will*) in negative commands (*don't be silly*; *do not come tomorrow*). **2** *ellipt.* or in place of verb or verb and object (*you know her better than I do*; *I wanted to go and I did so*; *tell me, do!*). **3** forming emphatic present and past tenses (*I do want to*; *do tell me*; *they did go but she was out*). **4** in inversion for emphasis (*rarely does it happen*; *did she but know it*). ● *noun* (*pl.* **dos** or **do's**) **1** *informal* an elaborate event, party, or operation. **2** *informal* a hairdo. **3** *euphemism* excrement. □ **be done with** *see* DONE. **be to do with** be concerned or connected with (*the argument was to do with money*). **do about** *see* ABOUT *preposition* 1d. **do away with** *informal* **1** abolish. **2** kill. **do battle** enter into combat. **do one's best** *see* BEST. **do one's bit** *see* BIT. **do by** treat or deal with in a specified way (*do as you would be done by*). **do credit to** *see* CREDIT. **do down** *informal* **1** cheat, swindle. **2** get the better of; overcome. **do for 1** be satisfactory or sufficient for. **2** *informal* (esp. as **done for** *adjective*) destroy, ruin, kill (*he knew he was done for*). **3** *informal* act as housekeeper for. **do one's head** (or **nut**) *Brit. slang* be extremely angry or agitated. **do the honours** *see* HONOUR. **do in 1** *slang* **a** kill. **b** ruin, do injury to. **2** *informal* exhaust, tire out. **do it** *informal* have sexual intercourse. **do justice to** *see* JUSTICE. **do nothing for** *informal* **1** detract from the appearance or quality of (*such behaviour does nothing for our reputation*). **2** fail to impress or excite (*people think he's great but he does nothing for me*). **do or die** persist regardless of danger. **do out** *Brit. informal* clean or redecorate (a room). **do a person out of** *informal* unjustly deprive a person of; swindle out of (*she was done out of her holiday*). **do over 1** *N Amer. informal* do again. **2** *slang* attack; beat up. **3** *informal* redecorate, refurbish. **do proud** *see* PROUD. **dos and don'ts** rules of behaviour. **do something for** (or **to**) *informal* enhance the appearance or quality of (*that carpet does something for the room*). **do one's stuff** *see* STUFF. **do to** (*archaic* **unto**) = DO BY. **do to death** *see* DEATH. **do the trick** *see* TRICK. **do up 1** fasten, secure. **2** *informal* **a** refurbish, renovate. **b** adorn, dress up. **3** *slang* **a** ruin, get the better of. **b** beat up. **do well for oneself** prosper. **do well out of** profit by. **do with** (prec. by *could*) would be glad to have; would profit by (*I could do with a rest; you could do with a wash*). **do without** manage without; forgo (*did without supper; we shall just have to do without*). **have** (or **be**) **nothing to do with 1** have no connection or dealings with (*our problem has nothing to do with the latest news; after the disagreement she had nothing to do with her father*). **2** be no business or concern of (*the decision has nothing to do with him*). **have to do** (or **something to do**) **with** be connected with (*what on earth does that have to do with this problem?*). [Old English *dōn* from Germanic: related to Sanskrit *dádhami* put, Greek *tithemi* place, Latin *facere* do]

do² /doː/ *noun* (also **doh**) *Music* **1** (in tonic sol-fa) the first and eighth note of a major scale. **2** the note C in the fixed-do system. [18th c.: from Italian *do*]

DOA *abbreviation* dead on arrival (at hospital etc.).

do·able /'duːəbəl/ *adjective* able to be done; practical.

D.O.B. *abbreviation* date of birth.

dob·bin /'dɒbɪn/ *noun* a draft or farm horse. [pet form of the name *Robert*]

Dober·man /'dəʊbərmən/ *noun* (in full **Doberman pinscher** /'pɪnʃʒr/) a breed of large dog with a smooth coat, frequently used as a guard dog. [L. *Dobermann*, 19th-c. German dog breeder + German *Pinscher* terrier]

Dobos torte /'doːbɒʃ ˌtɔrt/ *noun* a rich cake made of alternate layers of sponge cake and chocolate buttercream, with a crisp caramel topping. [German *Dobostorte* from Hungarian *dobostorta*, from J.C. *Dobós*, Hungarian cook d.1924 + TORTE]

dobra /'dɒbrə/ *noun* the basic monetary unit of São Tomé and Principe, equal to 100 centavos. [Portuguese *dóbra*, 'doubloon']

do·bro /'dɒbroː/ *noun* a type of acoustic guitar with steel resonating discs inside the body under the bridge, used in country and bluegrass music. [from the *Do(pěra) Bro(thers)*, its Czech-American inventors]

DOC *abbreviation* Denominazione di Origine Controllata or Denominação de Origem Controlada; a guarantee of the origin of an Italian or Portuguese wine (or other item of food) in conformity with statutory regulations.

doc *noun informal* **1** doctor. **2** (as a form of address) buddy, fellow (*what's up, doc?*). **3** documentary. **4** *Computing* document. [abbreviation]

do·cent /'doːsənt/ *noun* **1** *N Amer.* a usu. voluntary guide in a museum, art gallery, zoo, etc. **2** *US* (in some colleges and universities) a member of the teaching staff below professorial rank. [German *Docent, Dozent*, from Latin *docent-* pres. part. stem of *docere* teach]

do·cile /'dɒsail, 'doː-/ *adjective* submissive, easily managed. □ **do·cile·ly** *adverb* **do·cil·ity** /-'sɪlɪti/ *noun* [Latin *docilis* from *docēre* teach]

dock¹ ● *noun* **1** *N Amer.* a ship's berth, a wharf. **2** an artificially enclosed body of water for the loading, unloading, and repair of ships. **3** (in *pl.*) a range of docks with wharves and offices; a dockyard. **4** *N Amer.* = LOADING DOCK. **5** = DRY DOCK. ● *verb* **1** *transitive & intransitive* bring or come into a dock. **2 a** *transitive* join (spacecraft) together in space. **b** *intransitive* (of spacecraft) be joined. **3** *transitive* attach (a piece of equipment) to another (*the user wants to dock a portable into a desktop computer*). **4** *transitive* provide with a dock or docks. [Middle Dutch *docke*, of unknown origin]

dock² *noun* the enclosure for the accused in a criminal court. □ **in the dock** on trial. [16th c.: prob. originally cant = Flemish *dok* cage, of unknown origin]

dock³ *noun* any of various plants of the genus *Rumex*, with a spike of many small, green flowers. [Old English *docce*]

dock⁴ ● *transitive verb* **1 a** cut short (an animal's tail). **b** cut short the tail of (an animal). **2 a** (often foll. by *from*) deduct (a part) from wages, supplies, etc. **b** reduce (wages etc.) in this way. ● *noun* the solid bony part of an animal's tail. [Middle English, of uncertain origin]

dock·age *noun* **1** the charge made for using docks. **2** dock accommodation. **3** the berthing of vessels in docks.

dock·er *noun Brit.* = LONGSHOREMAN.

dock·et /'dɒkət/ ● *noun* **1** *N Amer.* a list of causes for trial or persons having causes pending. **2** *N Amer.* a list of things to be done. **3** *Brit.* **a** a document or label listing goods delivered or the contents of a package, or recording payment of customs dues etc. **b** a voucher; an order form. ● *transitive verb* (**dock·et·ed**, **dock·et·ing**) label with a docket. [15th c.: origin unknown]

dock·ing station *noun* a device to which a portable computer is connected so that it can be used like a desktop computer, with an external power supply, monitor, data transfer capability, etc.

dock·land *noun* a district near docks.

dock·side *noun* (often *attributive*) the area immediately adjacent to a dock.

dock-tailed *adjective* having a docked tail.

dock·work·er *noun* = LONGSHOREMAN.

dock·yard *noun* an area with docks and equipment for building and repairing ships.

Doc Mar·tens *var.* of DOCTOR MARTENS.

doc·tor ● *noun* **1 a** a qualified practitioner of medicine; a physician or surgeon. **b** *N Amer.* (esp. as an honorific) a qualified dentist, veterinarian, optometrist, or chiropractor. **2** a person who holds a doctorate (*Doctor of Civil Law*). **3** *informal* a person who carries out repairs. **4** *archaic* a teacher or learned person. **5** an artificial fishing fly. ● *verb informal* **1 a** *transitive* treat medically. **b** *intransitive* (esp. as **doctor·ing** *noun*) practise as a physician. **2** *transitive* castrate or spay. **3** *transitive* patch up (machinery etc.); mend. **4** *transitive* adulterate. **5** *transitive* tamper with, falsify. **6** *transitive* confer a degree of doctor on. □ **what the doctor ordered** *informal* something beneficial or desirable. □ **doc·tor·ial** /dɒk'tɔːriəl/ *adjective* **doc·tor·ly** *adjective* [Old French *doctour* from Latin *doctor* from *docēre doct-* teach]

doc·tor·al *adjective* of or relating to a doctorate.

doctor-assisted suicide *noun* suicide as committed with the help of a doctor.

doc·tor·ate *noun* the highest university degree in any faculty.

Doctor Mar·tens *plural noun* (also **Doc Martens, Dr. Martens**) *proprietary* a type of heavy usu. laced boot or shoe with a cushioned sole. [from *Dr K. Maertens*, the name of the German inventor of the sole]

Doctor of Philosophy *noun* **1** a doctorate awarded in the humanities, social sciences, pure sciences, etc. **2** a person holding such a degree. Abbr.: **Ph.D.**

Doctor of the Church *noun* any of several early Christian and later Catholic theologians (originally Gregory the Great, Ambrose, Augustine, and Jerome).

doc·trin·aire /ˌdɒktrɪ'ner/ ● *adjective* seeking to apply a theory or doctrine in all circumstances without regard to practical considerations; theoretical and impractical. ● *noun* a doctrinaire person; a pedantic theorist. [French from *doctrine* DOCTRINE + *-aire* -ARY¹]

doc·trin·al /dɒk'trainəl, 'dɒktrɪnəl/ *adjective* of, relating to, or concerned with a doctrine or doctrines. □ **doc·trin·al·ly** *adverb*

doc·trine /'dɒktrɪn/ *noun* **1** what is taught; a body of instruction. **2 a** a principle of religious or political etc. belief. **b** a set of such principles; dogma. [Old French from Latin *doctrina* teaching (as DOCTOR)]

docu·drama /'dɒkjʊˌdramə/ *noun* a dramatized television film based on real events. □ **docu·drama·tist** *noun* [DOCUMENTARY + DRAMA]

docu·ment ● *noun* **1** a piece of written or printed matter that provides or evidence of events, an agreement, ownership, identification, etc. **2** *Computing* a file, esp. a text file. ● *transitive verb* **1** prove by or provide with documents or evidence. **2** record (something) in written, photographic, or other form. **3** provide (a monograph etc.) with citations or references to support statements made. □ **docu·ment·able** *adjective* **docu·ment·al** *adjective* **docu·ment·er** *noun* [Old French from Latin *documentum* proof, from *docēre* teach]

docu·men·tar·ian /ˌdɒkjumen'teriən/ *noun* **1 a** a director or producer of documentaries. **b** a photographer specializing in producing a factual record. **2** an expert analyst of historical documents.

docu·men·tar·ist /dɒkjʊ'mentarɪst/ *noun* = DOCUMENTARIAN 1a.

docu·men·tary /ˌdɒkjʊ'mentəri/ ● *noun* (*pl.* **-ies**) a film or broadcast program based on real events, places, or circumstances and usu. intended primarily to record or inform. ● *adjective* **1** consisting of documents (*documentary evidence*). **2** providing a factual record or report.

docu·men·ta·tion *noun* **1** the provision of documents. **2** the preparation or use of documentary evidence or authorities. **3** documents produced as evidence or proof of something (*we don't have enough documentation to process your application*). **4** a collection of documents relating to a process or event, esp. the written specification and instructions accompanying a computer program.

DOD *abbreviation* (in the US) Department of Defense.

dod·der¹ *intransitive verb* tremble or totter, esp. from age. □ **dod·der·er** *noun* **dod·der·ing** *adjective* [17th c.: var. of obsolete dial. *dadder*]

dod·der² *noun* any climbing parasitic plant of the genus *Cuscuta*, with slender leafless threadlike stems. [Germanic]

dod·dery *adjective* tending to tremble or totter, esp. from age.

dod·dle *noun Brit. informal* an easy task. [perhaps from *doddle* = TODDLE]

dodeca- /ˈdɒːdekə/ *combining form* twelve. [Greek *dōdeka* twelve]

do·deca·gon /dɒˈdekəgɒn/ *noun* a plane figure with twelve sides.

do·deca·hed·ron /ˌdɒːdekəˈhiːdrən/ *noun* (*pl.* **-hed·rons** or **-hedra** /-drə/) a solid figure with twelve faces. □ **do·deca·hed·ral** *adjective*

Do·deca·nese /ˌdɒːdekəˈniːz/ a group of twelve Greek islands in the SE Aegean, of which the largest is Rhodes. [Greek, from *dōdeka* twelve, *nēsos* island]

do·deca·phon·ic /ˌdɒːdekəˈfɒnɪk/ *adjective Music* = TWELVE-TONE.

dodge ● *verb* **1** *intransitive* (often foll. by *about*, *around*) move quickly to one side or quickly change position, to elude a pursuer, blow, etc. (*dodged behind the chair*). **2** *transitive* **a** evade by cunning or trickery (*dodged paying the fare*). **b** elude (a pursuer, opponent, blow, etc.) by a sideward movement etc. ● *noun* **1** a quick movement to avoid or evade something. **2** a clever trick or expedient. □ **dodge the draft** *N Amer.* illegally evade military conscription, esp. in the US. [16th c.: origin unknown]

dodge ball *noun* a game in which players attempt to avoid being eliminated by being hit with a large ball.

Dodge City a city in SW Kansas; pop. (2000) 25,200. Established in 1872 as a railhead on the Santa Fe Trail, it rapidly gained a reputation as a rowdy frontier town.

dodg·em /ˈdɒdʒəm/ *noun* (in full **dodgem car**) esp. *Brit.* = BUMPER CAR. [DODGE + ˈEM]

dodg·er *noun* **1** a person who dodges, esp. an artful or elusive person. **2** a screen on a ship's bridge etc. as protection from spray etc.

Dodg·son /ˈdɒdʒsən/ **Charles Lut·widge**, see CARROLL.

dodgy *adjective* (**dod·gi·er**, **dod·gi·est**) **1** esp. *Brit. informal* awkward, unreliable, tricky. **2** *Brit.* cunning, artful.

dodo *noun* (*pl.* **dodos** or **dodoes**) **1** any large flightless bird of the extinct family Raphidae, formerly native to Mauritius. **2** an old-fashioned, stupid, or inactive person. □ **as dead as the** (*or* **a**) **dodo 1** completely or unmistakably dead. **2** entirely obsolete. [Portuguese *doudo* simpleton]

Do·doma /dɒːˈdoːmə/ the capital of Tanzania, in the centre of the country; pop. (est. 2002) 157,300.

DOE *abbreviation* (in the US) Department of Energy.

doe *noun* a female deer, caribou, hare, or rabbit. [Old English *dā*]

doe-eyed *adjective* (esp. of a woman) having large gentle dark eyes.

Doen·itz *var. of* DÖNITZ.

doer /ˈduːər/ *noun* **1** a person who does something. **2** a person who acts rather than merely talking or thinking.

does 3rd *sing. present of* DO[1].

doe·skin *noun* **1 a** the skin of a doe fallow deer. **b** leather made from this. **2** a fine cloth resembling it.

doesn't *contraction* does not.

doest /ˈduːəst/ *archaic* 2nd *sing. present of* DO[1].

doeth /ˈduːəθ/ *archaic* = DOTH.

doff *transitive verb literary* **1** tip (one's hat) as a greeting or token of respect. **2** *dated* remove (an item of clothing). [Middle English, = *do off*]

dog ● *noun* **1** any four-legged flesh-eating animal of the genus *Canis*, of many breeds domesticated and wild, kept as pets or for work or sport. **2** the male of any of these animals. **3** *informal* **a** a despicable person. **b** a person of a specified kind (*a lucky dog*). **c** *slang* an unattractive person, esp. a woman. **d** *slang* a horse that is difficult to handle. **4** a mechanical device for gripping. **5** *N Amer. slang* something of poor quality, e.g. an ill-performing stock, a bad movie, etc. **6** (in full **firedog**) = ANDIRON. **7** (in *pl.*; prec. by *the*) *Brit. informal* greyhound racing. **8** *N Amer. euphemism* God (*dog knows we've seen enough of that lately*). **9** *slang* (usu. in *pl.*) a foot (*my dogs are aching*). **10** = HOT DOG *noun* 1. ● *transitive verb* (**dogged**, **dog·ging**) **1** follow closely and persistently; pursue, track. **2** *Mech.* grip with a dog. □ **die like a dog** die miserably or shamefully. **dog in the manger** a person who prevents others from using something, although that person has no use for it. **dog it** esp. *N Amer. informal* act lazily; idle, shirk. **dog's age** *N Amer. informal* a long time (*haven't been there for a dog's age*). **dog's breakfast** *informal* a mess. **dog's dinner** *Brit. informal* **1** = DOG'S BREAKFAST. **2** (**like a dog's dinner**) over-elaborately or vulgarly (*she was dressed up like a dog's dinner*). **a dog's life** a miserable or wretched existence (*it's a dog's life*). **the dogs of war** *literary* the havoc accompanying war. **everyone** (*or* **everybody**) **and their** (*or* **his**) **dog** absolutely everyone. **go to the dogs** *informal* deteriorate, be ruined. **let sleeping dogs lie** *see* SLEEP. **not a dog's chance** *informal* no chance at all. **put on the dog** *N Amer. informal* behave pretentiously. **sick as a dog** *N Amer.* very

ill. **work like a dog** *N Amer.* work very hard. □ **dog·like** *adjective* [Old English *docga*, of unknown origin]

do·gan /ˈdɒːgən/ *noun Cdn slang offensive* a Roman Catholic, esp. an Irish Roman Catholic. [19th c.: origin uncertain: perhaps from *Dogan*, an Irish surname]

dog-and-pony show *noun N Amer.* an elaborate ostentatious display, presentation, event, etc., esp. for public relations purposes.

dog·bane *noun* any of various herbaceous plants of the genus *Apocynum*, with small bell-shaped flowers. *Also called* INDIAN HEMP.

dog·berry *noun* (*pl.* **-berries**) **1** = MOUNTAIN ASH. **2** any of various other shrubs or small trees bearing fruit of poor eating quality.

dog biscuit *noun* a hard thick biscuit for feeding dogs.

dog·cart *noun* **1** a two-wheeled open carriage with cross seats back to back. **2** a cart pulled by a dog or dogs.

dog collar *noun* **1** a collar for a dog. **2 a** *informal* a clerical collar. **b** a straight high collar. **3** a jewelled band worn around the neck; a choker.

dog daisy *noun* = OX-EYE DAISY.

dog days *plural noun* **1** the hottest period of the year (reckoned in antiquity from the heliacal rising of the Dog Star). **2** *informal* a period of inactivity, lethargy, etc.

doge /doːdʒ/ *noun hist.* the chief magistrate of Venice or Genoa. [French from Italian from Venetian *doze* from Latin *dux ducis* leader]

dog-eared *adjective* (of a book etc.) with the corners worn or battered with use.

dog-eat-dog *adjective informal* (usu. *attributive*; not hyphenated when *predicative*) ruthlessly competitive (*the dog-eat-dog world of business*; *it's dog eat dog out there*).

dog·fight ● *noun* **1** a fight between dogs. **2** a close combat between fighter aircraft. **3** a violent and confused fight. ● *intransitive verb* take part in a dogfight.

dog·fish *noun* (*pl.* same or **dog·fish·es**) any of various small sharks esp. of the families Scyliorhinidae, Squalidae, and Triakidae.

dog·ged /ˈdɒgɪd/ *adjective* tenacious; grimly persistent. □ **dog·ged·ly** *adverb* **dog·ged·ness** *noun* [DOG + -ED[1]]

Dog·ger Bank a submerged sandbank in the North Sea, about 115 km (70 miles) off the northeast coast of England.

dog·ger·el /ˈdɒgərəl/ *noun* poor or trivial verse. [Middle English, apparently from DOG: compare -REL]

dog·gie *var. of* DOGGY *noun*.

dog·gish *adjective* of or like a dog.

doggo /ˈdɒgoː/ *adverb* □ **lie doggo** *slang* lie motionless or hidden, making no sign. [prob. from DOG: compare -O]

dog·gone esp. *N Amer. slang* ● *adjective & adverb* damned. ● *interjection* expressing annoyance. [prob. from *dog on it* = *God damn it*]

doggy ● *adjective* **1** of or like a dog. **2** devoted to dogs. ● *noun* (also **dog·gie**) (*pl.* **-gies**) a little dog; a pet name for a dog. □ **dog·gi·ness** *noun*

doggy bag *noun* a bag given to a customer in a restaurant or to a guest at a party etc. for putting leftovers in to take home.

dog handler *noun* a person, esp. a police officer, in charge of a dog or dogs. □ **dog-handling** *noun*

dog·house *noun N Amer.* a shelter for a dog. □ **in the doghouse** *informal* in disgrace or disfavour.

dogie /ˈdoːgi/ *noun N Amer.* (*West*) a motherless or neglected calf. [19th c.: origin unknown]

dog·leg ● *noun* **1** a sharp bend like that in a dog's hind leg. **2** a hole at which a golf player cannot aim directly at the green from the tee. ● *adjective* (also **dog·legged**) bent sharply. ● *intransitive verb* (**dog·legged**, **dog·leg·ging**) bend sharply.

dog lot *noun N Amer.* (*North*) = DOG YARD.

dog·ma /ˈdɒgmə/ *noun* **1** a belief or set of beliefs held by an authority or group, which others are expected to accept without argument. **2** an arrogant declaration of opinion. [Latin from Greek *dogma -matos* opinion, from *dokeō* seem]

dog·mat·ic /dɒgˈmatɪk/ *adjective* **1 a** (of a person) given to asserting or imposing personal opinions; arrogant. **b** intolerantly authoritative. **2 a** of or in the nature of dogma; doctrinal. **b** based on a priori principles, not on induction. □ **dog·mat·ic·ally** *adverb*

dog·mat·ics *noun* **1** the study of religious dogmas; dogmatic theology. **2** a system of dogma.

dog·ma·tism /ˈdɒgmə,tɪzəm/ *noun* a tendency to be dogmatic. □ **dogma·tist** *noun*

dogma·tize /ˈdɒgmə,taɪz/ *verb* (also esp. *Brit.* **-tise**) **1** *intransitive* make positive unsupported assertions; speak dogmatically. **2** *transitive* express (a principle etc.) as a dogma.

dog meat *noun* **1** the flesh of a dog. **2** meat to be used as food for dogs. **3** *N Amer. informal* a person who is defeated, overwhelmed, etc. (*touch that again and you're dog meat!*).

dog·nap *transitive verb* (**-napped**, **-nap·ping**) steal (a dog), esp. in order to sell it. □ **dog·nap·per** *noun* **dog·nap·ping** *noun* [DOG + *-nap*, after KIDNAP]

do-gooder *noun* a person who actively tries to help other people, esp. one regarded as unrealistic or officious. □ **do-good** *adjective & noun* **do-goodery** *noun* **do-goodism** *noun*

dog-paddle ● *noun* an elementary swimming stroke with short quick movements of the arms and legs beneath the body. ● *intransitive verb* swim using this stroke.

Dogrib ● *noun* **1** a member of a Dene Aboriginal people living along the north shore of Great Slave Lake. **2** the Athapaskan language of this people. ● *adjective* of or relating to this people or their language. [translation of Dogrib *Thlingchadinne* 'dog's flank', from their legend that they are descended from a dog]

dog rose *noun* a wild hedge rose, *Rosa canina*. *Also called* BRIER ROSE.

dog salmon *noun* = CHUM³.

dogs·body /ˈdɒgzˌbɒdi/ *noun* (*pl.* **-ies**) esp. *Brit.* **1** *informal* a drudge. **2** *Naut. slang* a junior officer.

dog·skin *noun* leather made of or imitating dog's skin, used for gloves etc.

dog·sled ● *noun* a sled designed to be pulled by dogs. ● *intransitive verb* travel by dogsled. □ **dog·sled·ding** *noun*

Dog Star *noun* = SIRIUS. [so called because it appears to follow at the heels of Orion, the hunter]

dog's tooth violet *noun var. of* DOGTOOTH VIOLET.

dog tag *noun* **1** a tag attached to a dog's collar, giving an identification number, the dog's name, the owner's phone number, or vaccination information. **2** *N Amer. slang* a soldier's metal identity tag.

dog team *noun* *N Amer.* a team of dogs for pulling a dogsled.

dog-tired *adjective* utterly exhausted.

dog·tooth *noun* **1** a small pointed ornament or moulding esp. in Norman and Early English architecture. **2** a broken check pattern used esp. in cloth for suits.

dogtooth violet *noun* (also **dogtoothed violet**, **dog's tooth violet**) any liliaceous plant of the genus *Erythronium*, often with speckled leaves, esp. *E. americanum* of eastern N America (*also called* TROUT LILY), and *E. grandiflorum* of western N America (*also called* AVALANCHE LILY).

dog·trot *noun* a gentle easy trot.

dog violet *noun* any of various scentless wild violets, esp. *Viola riviniana* and *Viola canina*.

dog·watch *noun* *Naut.* either of two short watches (4–6 or 6–8 p.m.).

dog·wood *noun* **1** any of various shrubs and small trees of the genus *Cornus*, including the flowering dogwoods, *C. florida* of eastern N America and *C. nuttallii* of western N America, and the low-growing bunchberry *C. canadensis*. **2** any of various similar trees. **3** the wood of the dogwood.

dog yard *noun* *N Amer.* (*North*) a usu. fenced area in which a sled dog team is tied up.

DoH *abbreviation* (in the UK) Department of Health.

doh *var. of* DO².

Doha /ˈdoːhɒ/ the capital of Qatar; pop. (est. 2002) 308,800.

DOHC *abbreviation* (of an automobile engine etc.) double overhead camshaft.

doily *noun* (*pl.* **doilies**) a small ornamental mat of paper, lace, etc., e.g. on a table, or on a plate for cookies, sandwiches, etc. □ **doilied** *adjective* [originally the name of a fabric: from *Doiley*, the name of a draper]

do·ing *noun* **1 a** an action; the performance of a deed (*famous for his doings*; *it was my doing*). **b** activity, effort (*it takes a lot of doing*). **2** *Brit. informal* a scolding; a beating. **3** (in *pl.*) *Brit. slang* things needed; things whose names are not known (*have we got all the doings?*).

Dois·neau /dwʊˈnoː/ **Rob·ert** (1912–1994), French photographer, best known for his photographs portraying Paris and its inhabitants; one of his most famous images is 'The Kiss at the Hôtel de Ville' (1950).

do-it-yourself ● *adjective* (of work, esp. building, painting, decorating, etc.) done or to be done by an amateur at home. ● *noun* such work. □ **do-it-yourself·er** *noun*

DOJ *abbreviation* (in the US) Department of Justice.

dojo /ˈdoːdʒoː/ *noun* (*pl.* **dojos**) **1** a room or hall in which judo and other martial arts are practised. **2** a mat on which judo etc. is practised. [Japanese, from *dō* 'way, pursuit' + *jō* 'a place']

dol. *abbreviation* dollar(s).

Dolbeau-Mistas·sini /dɒlˈboː miːstaˈsiːniː/ a town in NE central Quebec, just north of Lac Saint-Jean; pop. (2001) 14,879. [J. *Dolbeau*, Récollet missionary d.1652]

Dolby /ˈdoːlbi/ *noun proprietary* **1** an electronic noise reduction system used esp. in tape recording to reduce hiss. **2** an electronic system used to provide stereophonic sound for movie theatres and television sets. [R. M. *Dolby*, US inventor b.1933]

dolce /ˈdɒltʃeɪ/ *Music* ● *adverb* sweetly and softly. ● *adjective* performed in this manner. [Italian, = sweet]

dolce far niente /ˌdɒltʃeɪ ˌfɑr niˈenti/ *noun* pleasant idleness. [Italian, = sweet doing nothing]

dolce vita /ˌdɒltʃeɪ ˈviːtə/ *noun* a life of pleasure and luxury. [Italian, lit. 'sweet life']

dol·drums /ˈdoːldrəmz, dɒl-/ *plural noun* (usu. prec. by *the*) **1** low spirits; a feeling of boredom or depression. **2** a period of inactivity or state of stagnation. **3** an equatorial ocean region of calms, sudden storms, and light unpredictable winds. [prob. from *dull* and *tantrum*]

dole¹ ● *noun* **1** (usu. prec. by *the*) *informal* benefits claimable by the unemployed from the government. **2 a** a charitable distribution. **b** a charitable (esp. sparing or niggardly) gift of food, clothes, or money. ● *transitive verb* (usu. foll. by *out*) deal out sparingly. □ **on the dole** *informal* receiving government unemployment benefits. [Old English *dāl* from Germanic]

dole² *noun archaic* grief, woe; lamentation. [Old French *do(e)l* etc. from popular Latin *dolus* from Latin *dolēre* grieve]

dole·ful *adjective* **1** mournful, sad. **2** dreary, dismal. □ **dole·ful·ly** *adverb* **dole·ful·ness** *noun* [DOLE² + -FUL]

doler·ite /ˈdɒləˌraɪt/ *noun* a coarse basaltic rock. [French *dolérite* from Greek *doleros* deceptive (because it is difficult to distinguish from diorite)]

doli·cho·ceph·alic /ˌdɒlɪˌkoːsɪˈfalɪk/ *adjective* (also **doli·cho·ceph·alous** /-ˈsefələs/) having a long or narrow head. [Greek *dolikhos* long + -CEPHALIC, -CEPHALOUS]

doll ● *noun* **1** a usu. small model of a human figure, usu. a child or woman, esp. for use as a toy. **2** *informal* **a** a pretty but silly young woman. **b** a young woman. **c** an attractive person. **d** a helpful or kind person. **e** an affectionate or familiar form of address. ● *transitive & intransitive verb* (foll. by *up*) dress up smartly. □ **doll-like** *adjective* [pet form of the name *Dorothy*]

dol·lar *noun* **1** the chief monetary unit of Canada, the US, and Australia. **2** the chief monetary unit of certain countries in the Pacific, W Indies, SE Asia, Africa, and S America. **3** money available to be spent (*a grab for the spectator dollar*). □ **bet dollars to doughnuts** *N Amer.* maintain as a certainty (*I'll bet you dollars to doughnuts he cheated on the exam*). [Low German *daler* from German *Taler*, short for *Joachimstaler*, a coin from the silver mine of *Joachimstal*, now *Jáchymov* in the Czech Republic]

dollar amount *noun* the cost or value of something in dollars.

Dollard-des-Ormeaux /dɒˈlɑrdeɪzɔrˌmoː/ a former city in south central Quebec, in the western part of the Island of Montreal, now part of the city of Montreal; pop. (2001) 48,206. [DOLLARD DES ORMEAUX]

Dol·lard des Or·meaux /dɒˈlɑr deiz ɔrˈmoː/ **Adam** (1635–60), French soldier, commander of the garrison at Ville-Marie (Montreal), he led a small group of settlers, Hurons and Algonquins to lay an ambush for the Iroquois in an abandoned fort at the Long Sault on the Ottawa River; under siege from 500 Iroquois, Dollard and his companions held out for eight days before they were overwhelmed and killed.

dollar diplomacy *noun* diplomatic activity aimed at advancing a country's international influence by furthering its financial and commercial interests abroad.

dollar·iz·a·tion *noun* (also esp. *Brit.* **-isation**) a dominating effect of the US on the economy of a country, esp. the linkage of a currency to the US dollar.

dollar sign *noun* the sign $, representing a dollar.

dollar store *noun* *N Amer.* a store selling low-priced, often discontinued or remaindered, items.

Doll·fuss /ˈdɒlfuːs/ **Engel·bert** (1892–1934), Austrian Christian Socialist politician, Chancellor of Austria 1932–4. He established an

---

uː mood   aɪ my   əi pipe   au brown   ʌu house   ei day   ɔi boy   ã franglais   ã Canadien   ɔ̃ Brayon   (*see over for consonants*)

authoritarian regime (1934), and was assassinated by Austrian Nazis in an abortive coup.

doll·house *noun N Amer.* (also **doll's house**) **1** a miniature toy house for dolls. **2** a very small house.

dol·lop ● *noun* **1** a shapeless lump of something soft, esp. food (*a dollop of mashed potato*). **2** something added as if in dollops (*a dollop of morality*). ● *transitive verb* (**dol·loped, dol·lop·ing**) (usu. foll. by *out*) serve out in large shapeless quantities. [perhaps from Scandinavian]

doll's eyes *noun* = BANEBERRY.

dolly ● *noun* (*pl.* **-lies**) **1** a child's name for a doll. **2** a small four-wheeled cart for moving appliances, boxes, etc. **3** a movable platform for a movie or video camera. **4** = CORN DOLLY. **5** *Brit. informal* = DOLLY BIRD. ● *verb* (**-lies, -lied**) **1** *transitive* (foll. by *up*) dress up smartly. **2** *intransitive* (foll. by *in, up*) move a motion picture camera in or up to a subject, or out from it.

dolly bird *noun Brit. informal* an attractive and stylish young woman.

dolly grip *noun* the member of a film crew who moves the dolly around.

dolly mixture *noun Brit.* any of a mixture of small variously shaped and coloured candies.

Dolly Var·den /ˌdɒlɪ ˈvɑːdən/ *noun* **1** a brightly spotted char, *Salvelinus malma*, of western N America. **2** a woman's large hat with one side drooping and floral trim. [a character in Dickens's *Barnaby Rudge*, who wore a similar hat]

dolma /ˈdɒlmə/ *noun* (*pl.* **dol·mas** or **dol·ma·des** /-ˈmɒðez/) an E European delicacy of spiced rice or meat etc. wrapped in vine or cabbage leaves. [Turkish from *dolmak* fill, be filled: *dolmades* from modern Greek]

dol·man /ˈdɒlmən/ *noun* **1** a long Turkish robe open in front. **2** a hussar's jacket worn with the sleeves hanging loose. **3** a woman's mantle with capelike or dolman sleeves. [ultimately from Turkish *dolama*]

dolman sleeve *noun* a loose sleeve cut in one piece with the body of the coat etc.

dol·men /ˈdɒlmən/ *noun* a megalithic tomb with a large flat stone laid on upright ones. [French, perhaps from Cornish *tolmên* hole of stone]

dolo·mite /ˈdɒləˌmaɪt/ *noun* a mineral or rock of calcium magnesium carbonate. □ **dolo·mit·ic** /ˌdɒləˈmɪtɪk/ *adjective* [French from D. de Dolomieu, French geologist d.1801]

Dolo·mite Mountains (also **Dolo·mites**) a range of the Alps in N Italy.

dolor·ous /ˈdɒlərəs/ *adjective literary* **1** distressing, painful; doleful; dismal. **2** distressed, sad. □ **dolor·ous·ly** *adverb*

dolour /ˈdɒlər/ *noun* (also **dolor**) *literary* sorrow, distress. [Old French from Latin *dolor -oris* pain, grief]

dol·phin *noun* **1** any of various porpoise-like sea mammals of the family Delphinidae having a slender beaklike snout. **2** (in general use) = DORADO 1. **3** a bollard, pile, or buoy for mooring. **4** a structure for protecting the pier of a bridge. **5** a curved fish in heraldry, sculpture, etc. [Latin *delphinus* from Greek *delphis -inos*]

dolphin·arium /ˌdɒlfɪˈneriəm/ *noun* (*pl.* **-ariums**) an aquarium for dolphins, esp. one open to the public.

dolt *noun* a stupid person. □ **dolt·ish** *adjective* **dolt·ish·ly** *adverb* **dolt·ish·ness** *noun* [apparently related to *dol, dold,* obsolete var. of DULL]

Dom /dɒm/ *noun* **1** a title prefixed to the names of some Roman Catholic dignitaries, and Benedictine and Carthusian monks. **2** the Portuguese equivalent of Don (see DON[1] 1). [Latin *dominus* master: sense 2 through Portuguese]

-dom *combining form* forming nouns denoting: **1** state or condition (*freedom*). **2** rank or status (*earldom*). **3** domain (*kingdom*). **4** a class of people (or the attitudes etc. associated with them) regarded collectively (*officialdom*). [Old English *-dōm*, originally = DOOM]

do·main /dəˈmeɪn/ *noun* **1** an area under one rule; a realm. **2** an estate or lands under one control. **3** a sphere of control or influence. **4** *Math.* the set of possible values of an independent variable. **5** *Physics* a discrete region of magnetism in ferromagnetic material. **6** (also **domain name**) the parts of an email address following the @ symbol; a URL. [French *domaine*, Old French *demeine* DEMESNE, assoc. with Latin *dominus* lord]

do·maine /dəˈmeɪn/ *noun* a vineyard. [French: see DOMAIN]

dome ● *noun* **1 a** a rounded vault as a roof, with a circular, elliptical, or polygonal base; a large cupola. **b** the revolving openable hemispherical roof of an observatory. **2** *N Amer.* a stadium with a

domed roof. **3 a** a natural vault or canopy (of the sky, trees, etc.). **b** the rounded summit of a hill etc. **4** *Geol.* a dome-shaped landform or underground structure. **5** *N Amer.* a raised, glassed-in area of the roof of a railway car, allowing passengers a full view of surrounding scenery. **6** *slang* the head. ● *transitive verb* (usu. as **domed** *adjective*) cover with or shape as a dome. □ **dome-like** *adjective* [French *dôme* from Italian *duomo* cathedral, dome, from Latin *domus* house]

dome fastener *noun* a small fastener used on clothing etc., consisting of a rounded portion which snaps into a socket; a snap fastener.

Dome of the Rock an Islamic shrine in Jerusalem, surrounding the sacred rock on which, according to tradition, Abraham prepared to sacrifice his son, and from which the prophet Muhammad made his miraculous midnight ascent into heaven (see NIGHT JOURNEY). Built in the area of Solomon's temple and dating from the end of the 7th c., for Muslims it is the third most holy place, after Mecca and Medina.

Domes·day /ˈduːmzdeɪ/ *noun* (in full **Domesday Book**) a record of the lands of England made in 1086 by order of William I. [Middle English var. of *doomsday,* as being a book of final authority]

do·mes·tic ● *adjective* **1** of the home, household, or family affairs. **2 a** of or within one's own country, not foreign or international. **b** homegrown or homemade. **3** (of an animal) kept by or living with human beings. **4** fond of home life. ● *noun* a household servant. □ **do·mes·tic·ally** *adverb* [French *domestique* from Latin *domesticus* from *domus* home]

do·mes·ti·cate /dəˈmestɪˌkeɪt/ *transitive verb* **1** tame (an animal) and keep it as a pet or for farm produce (*mammals were first domesticated for their milk*). **2** accustom to home life and management. **3** naturalize (a plant or animal). □ **do·mes·tic·able** /-kəbəl/ *adjective*

do·mes·ti·ca·tion *noun* [medieval Latin *domesticare* (as DOMESTIC)]

do·mes·ti·cat·ed *adjective* **1** (of an animal or plant) kept by humans for work, food, or companionship; not wild. **2** (of a person) skilled at and fond of household tasks such as cooking, cleaning, sewing, etc.

do·mes·ti·city /ˌdɒməˈstɪsɪti, ˌdɒm-/ *noun* **1** the state of being domestic. **2** domestic or home life.

domestic partner *noun* a person who shares a residence with a sexual partner, esp. without a legally recognized union. □ **domestic partnership** *noun*

domestic science *noun* the study of household management; home economics.

domestic violence *noun* violent acts occurring within a household.

domi·cile /ˈdɒməˌsaɪl, -sɪl/ ● *noun* **1** a dwelling place; one's home. **2** *Law* **a** a place of permanent residence. **b** the fact of residing. **3** the place at which a bill of exchange is made payable. ● *transitive verb* **1** (usu. as **domi·ciled** *adjective*) (usu. foll. by *at, in*) establish or settle in a place. **2** (usu. foll. by *at*) make (a bill of exchange) payable at a certain place. [Old French from Latin *domicilium* from *domus* home]

domi·cil·iary /ˌdɒmɪˈsɪliəri/ *adjective* (esp. of medical care, etc.) of, relating to, or occurring at a person's home (*domiciliary care*).

dom·in·ance *noun* **1** the state of being dominant. **2** control, authority.

dom·in·ant ● *adjective* **1** dominating, prevailing, most influential. **2** (of a high place) prominent, overlooking others. **3 a** (of an allele) expressed even when inherited from only one parent. **b** (of an inherited characteristic) appearing in an individual even when its allelic counterpart is also inherited (compare RECESSIVE *adjective* 1). **4 a** *Ecology* designating the predominant species in a plant or animal community. **b** (of an animal) allowed priority in access to food, mates, etc. by others of its species because of success in previous aggressive encounters. **5** *Music* based on or pertaining to the dominant. ● *noun* **1 a** a dominant trait or gene. **b** an individual having such a trait or gene. **2** *Ecology* a predominant species in a plant or animal community. **3** a dominating feature, individual, group, etc. (*cultural dominants*). **4** *Music* the fifth note of the diatonic scale of any key. □ **dom·in·ant·ly** *adverb* [French from Latin *dominari* (as DOMINATE)]

dom·in·ate *transitive & intransitive verb* **1** have a commanding influence on; exercise control over (*dominated the meeting by sheer force of character; has authority but doesn't dominate*). **2** (of a person, sound, event, etc.) be the most influential or conspicuous factor in (*the election dominated the news for over a month*). **3** (of a building etc.) have a commanding position over; overlook. □ **dom·in·at·ing** *adjective* **dom·in·ator** *noun* [Latin *dominari dominat-* from *dominus* lord]

dom·in·a·tion *noun* **1** command, control. **2 a** the act or an instance of dominating. **b** the process of being dominated. **3** *Christianity* (in *pl.*) angelic beings of the fourth order of the celestial hierarchy (see ORDER *noun* 19).

Consonants: b *but*   d *dog*   f *few*   g *get*   h *her*   j *yes*   k *cat*   l *leg*   m *man*   n *no*   p *pen*   r *red*   s *sit*

dom·in·atrix /ˌdɒmə'neitrɪks/ *noun* (*pl.* **dom·in·atri·ces** /-trɪsiːz/ or **dom·in·atrix·es**) a woman who is domineering, esp. a woman who takes the dominant or sadistic role in sado-masochistic sexual activities. [Latin]

dom·in·eer *intransitive verb* (often foll. by *over*) behave in an arrogant and overbearing way. [Dutch *dominieren* from French *dominer*]

dom·in·eer·ing *adjective* overbearing; offensively assertive or dictatorial. □ **dom·in·eer·ing·ly** *adverb*

Do·min·go /də'mɪŋgoː/ **Plá·cido** (b.1941), Spanish-born Mexican tenor, who established his reputation as one of the world's leading operatic tenors in the 1970s with his performances in operas by Verdi and Puccini.

Dom·inic, St. /'dɒmənɪk/ (*c.*1170–1221), Spanish priest and friar. He established a number of religious communities, and in 1215 founded the Order of Friars Preachers (see DOMINICAN[1]). Feast day, 8 Aug.

Do·min·ica /ˌdɒmə'niːkə, də'mɪnɪkə/ a mountainous island in the W Indies, the loftiest of the Lesser Antilles and the northernmost and largest of the Windward Islands; pop. (est. 2002) 70,158; capital, Roseau. [Latin *Dominica* from *dies domenica*, lit. 'the Lord's day', so called by Columbus because he arrived there on a Sunday]

do·min·ic·al /də'mɪnɪkəl/ *adjective* **1** of the Lord's Day; of Sunday. **2** of the Lord (Jesus Christ). [Latin *dominicalis* from Latin *dominicus* from *dominus* lord]

Do·min·ic·an[1] /də'mɪnɪkən/ ● *adjective* **1** of or relating to the mendicant Order of Friars Preaching, founded in 1215 by St. Dominic and devoted to preaching and the study of theology. **2** of or relating to either of the two orders of female religious founded on Dominican principles. ● *noun* a Dominican friar, nun, or sister (*see also* BLACK FRIAR). [medieval Latin *Dominicanus* from *Dominicus* DOMINIC]

Do·min·ic·an[2] /də'mɪnɪkən/ ● *noun* **1** a native or inhabitant of the island of Dominica. **2** a native or inhabitant of the Dominican Republic. ● *adjective* **1** of, designating, or pertaining to Dominica. **2** of, designating, or pertaining to the Dominican Republic.

Dominican Republic a country in the Caribbean occupying the eastern part of the island of Hispaniola; pop. (est. 2002) 8,721,594; capital, Santo Domingo.

dom·inie /'dɒmɪni/ *noun Scot.* a schoolmaster. [later spelling of *domine* sir, vocative of Latin *dominus* lord]

Dominion an urban community on Cape Breton Island, part of the regional municipality of Cape Breton. It is situated on the Atlantic coast between New Waterford and Glace Bay. [after the *Dominion* No. 1 coal shaft]

do·min·ion *noun* **1** sovereign authority; control. **2** the territory of a sovereign or government; a domain. **3** the title of each of the self-governing territories of the Commonwealth. **4 a** (**the Dominion**) *hist. informal* Canada. **b** *Cdn* (*Nfld*) *hist.* Newfoundland as a self-governing part of the Commonwealth prior to its entry into the Canadian Confederation in 1949. [Old French from medieval Latin *dominio -onis* from *dominium* from *dominus* lord]

Dominion Day *noun hist.* = CANADA DAY.

Dom·ino, 'Fats' (born Antoine Domino) (b.1928), US rhythm-and-blues and rock pianist, singer, and songwriter, whose popular songs of the 1950s and early 1960s include 'Ain't That a Shame' (1955) and 'Blueberry Hill' (1956).

dom·ino *noun* (*pl.* **-inoes**) **1 a** any of 28 small oblong tiles, marked with 0–6 dots on each half. **b** (in *pl.*, usu. treated as *sing.*) a game played with these. **2** a country etc. perceived as being one in a series and so likely to succumb to circumstances or crises affecting a similar country etc. **3** a loose cloak with a mask for the upper part of the face, worn at masquerades. [French, prob. from Latin *dominus* lord, but unexplained]

domino effect *noun* the effect of one event triggering a succession of other, often similar events, like a falling domino at the beginning of a line of upended dominoes.

domino theory *noun Politics* the theory that a domino effect will occur, esp. that a political event etc. in one country will cause similar events in neighbouring countries.

Dom·itian /də'mɪʃən/ (full name Titus Flavius Domitianus) (AD 51–96), Roman emperor 81–96, son of Vespasian. He embarked on a large building program and was assassinated following a reign of terror 93–96.

don[1] *noun* **1** (**Don**) **a** a Spanish title prefixed to a man's forename. **b** a Spanish gentleman; a Spaniard. **2** an Italian title of respectful address, esp. to a priest. **3 a** *Brit.* a head, fellow, or tutor of a college at a British university, esp. Oxford or Cambridge. **b** *Cdn* a senior person in a

university residence, usu. responsible for the students and community life. **4** *N Amer.* a high-ranking member of the Mafia. □ **don·ship** *noun* [Italian and Spanish from Latin *dominus* lord]

don[2] *transitive verb* (**donned, don·ning**) put on (clothing). [= *do on*]

dona /'dɒnə/ *noun* (also **doña** /'dɒnjə/) used as a courtesy title preceding the name of a Portuguese or Spanish lady. [Portuguese *dona*, Spanish *doña* from Latin (as DONNA)]

do·nair /doː'ner/ *noun N Amer.* spiced lamb cooked on a spit, served in slices, and usu. rolled in pita bread. [Turkish *döner* 'rotating']

do·nate /'doːneit, -'neit/ *transitive verb* **1** give or contribute (money, time, or goods) for a good cause, e.g. to a charity. **2** allow the removal of (blood or an organ) from one's body for transplantation, transfusion, or other use. [back-formation from DONATION]

Dona·tello /ˌdɒnə'teloː/ (born Donato di Betto Bardi) (*c.*1386–1466), Italian sculptor. A pioneer of perspective, he is famous for the bronze *David* (*c.*1430–60) and the bronze equestrian statue *Gattamelata* (1447–53).

do·na·tion *noun* **1** the act or an instance of donating. **2** something, esp. an amount of money, donated. [Old French from Latin *donatio -onis* from *donare* give, from *donum* gift]

Donat·ist /'doːnətist/ *noun* a member of a schismatic Christian group in North Africa, formed in 311. The Donatists held that only those living a blameless life belonged in the Church. They survived until the 7th c. □ **Donat·ism** *noun* [Late Latin *Donatista* follower of Donatus, 4th-c. Roman grammarian]

done ● *verb past participle of* DO[1]. ● *adjective* **1** finished, completed (*is the washing done?; a done deal*). **2** *informal* socially acceptable (*the done thing; it isn't done*). **3 a** (often with *in*) *informal* tired out. **b** (often with *up*) fixed up or made more attractive (*the motel was newly done up*). **4** (of food) cooked sufficiently (*is the turkey done yet?*). □ **be done with** have or be finished with. **done for** *informal* **1** in serious trouble. **2** finished, destroyed. **have done with** be rid of or have finished dealing with.

donee /doː'niː/ *noun* the recipient of a gift. [DONOR + -EE]

Don·egal /ˌdɒnə'gɒl/ a county in the extreme northwest of the Republic of Ireland, part of the old province of Ulster; capital, Lifford.

done·ness *noun* the degree to which food is done or cooked; the state of being sufficiently cooked.

doner kebab /'dɒner/ *noun esp. Brit.* = DONAIR.

Don·ets Basin /dɒ'njets/ a coal-mining and industrial region of SE Ukraine, stretching between the valley of the Donets and lower Dnieper rivers.

Don·etsk /dɒ'njetsk/ the leading city of the Donets Basin in Ukraine; pop. (est. 2001) 1,016,000.

Don·ets River /dɒ'njets/ a river in E Europe, rising near Belgorod in S Russia and flowing southeastward for some 1000 km (630 miles) through Ukraine before re-entering Russia and joining the Don near Rostov.

dong[1] ● *noun* **1** the deep sound of a large bell. **2** esp. *N Amer. coarse slang* the penis. ● *intransitive verb* make the deep sound of a large bell. [imitative]

dong[2] *noun* the chief monetary unit of Vietnam, equal to 100 xu. [Vietnamese]

donga /'dɒŋgə/ *noun South Africa & Austral.* a ravine or watercourse with steep sides caused by erosion. [Nguni]

don·gle /'dɒŋgəl/ *noun Computing* a software protection device which must be plugged into a computer to enable protected software to be used on it. [arbitrary formation]

Dön·itz /'dɜːnɪts/ **Karl** (also **Doen·itz**) (1891–1980), German naval officer. He was commander-in-chief of the German navy (1943–45), and briefly served as head of state following Hitler's death (1945).

Doni·zetti /ˌdɒnɪ'zeti/ (**Domen·ico**) **Gae·tano** (**Maria**) (1797–1848), Italian composer, who wrote 75 operas, including the tragedies *Anna Bolena* (1830) and *Lucia di Lammermoor* (1835), and the comedies *L'Elisir d'amore* (1832) and *Don Pasquale* (1843).

don·jon /'dʌndʒən, 'dɒn-/ *noun* the great tower or innermost keep of a castle. [archaic spelling of DUNGEON]

Don Juan[1] /dɒn 'wɒn, 'hwɒn, 'dʒuən/ a legendary Spanish nobleman of dissolute life, famous for seducing women; according to a Spanish story first dramatized by Gabriel Téllez (see TIRSO DE MOLINA) he was Don Juan Tenorio of Seville. Molière, Byron, and Mozart (in *Don Giovanni*) have all based works on the legend.

Don Juan[2] /dɒn 'wɒn, 'hwɒn/ *noun* a man with a reputation for seducing women; a rake, a libertine. □ **Don Juan·ism** *noun*

don·key *noun* (*pl.* **-keys**) **1** a domestic ass. **2** *informal* a stupid or foolish person. **3** = DONKEY ENGINE. [earlier with pronunciation as *monkey*: perhaps from DUN[1], or the man's name *Duncan*]

donkey engine *noun* a small auxiliary engine.

donkey jacket *noun Brit.* a thick weatherproof jacket worn by workers and as a fashion garment.

donkey·man *noun* (*pl.* **-men**) a person in charge of a donkey engine.

donkey's years *plural noun informal* a very long time.

donkey work *noun* drudgery or the hard, unattractive part of an undertaking.

donna *noun* **1** an Italian, Spanish, or Portuguese lady. **2** (**Donna**) the courtesy title of such a lady. [Italian from Latin *domina* mistress, fem. of *dominus*: compare DON[1]]

Donna·cona[1] /ˌdɒnəˈkɔːnə/ a town in SE central Quebec, situated on the north shore of the St. Lawrence, about 40 km southwest of Quebec City; pop. (2001) 5,479. [DONNACONA[2]]

Donna·cona[2] (d. *c.*1539), Iroquois chief of the village of Stadacona. In 1534 Jacques Cartier persuaded Donnacona to allow his two sons, Domagaya and Taignoagny, to travel to France; Cartier returned with them in 1535, and in 1536 seized Donnacona, his sons, and eight others and took them to France, where Donnacona later died.

Donne /dʌn/ **John** (1572–1631), English poet, dean of St. Paul's Cathedral, London 1621–31. One of the leading metaphysical poets, he is known for his love poems, religious poems, satires, elegies, and sermons.

don·née /dɒˈneɪ/ *noun* **1** the subject, theme, or primary motif of a literary work, opera, etc. **2** a basic fact or assumption. [French, fem. past participle of *donner* give]

Don·nelly /ˈdɒnəliː/ **James**, his wife **Johan·nah**, their sons **Thom·as** and **John**, and their niece **Bridget**, who were murdered on the family farm near London, Ontario on February 4th, 1880, as a result of an Irish feud introduced into Canada from Tipperary, Ireland; six men were subsequently charged with murder, tried, and found not guilty.

don·nish /ˈdɒnɪʃ/ *adjective* resembling or characteristic of a college don; having a pedantic stiffness or gravity of manner. □ **don·nish·ly** *adverb* **don·nish·ness** *noun*

donny·brook *noun* a scene of uproar and disorder; a brawl. [suburb of Dublin, Ireland, once famous for its annual fair]

donor *noun* **1** a person who gives or donates something, e.g. to a charity. **2** a person who provides blood for a transfusion, semen for insemination, or an organ or tissue for transplant. **3** *Chem.* an atom or molecule that provides a pair of electrons in forming a coordinate bond. **4** *Physics* an impurity atom in a semiconductor which contributes a conducting electron to the material. [Anglo-French *donour* from Latin *donator -oris* from *donare* give]

donor card *noun* a card which a person carries to authorize use of body organs for transplant after death.

donor fatigue *noun* a diminishing public willingness to donate to charitable causes, typically attributed to the frequency of appeals for money, or a feeling that such contributions have no real or lasting effect.

do-nothing ● *noun* a person who does little or nothing. ● *adjective* characterized by doing or accomplishing little or nothing (*the do-nothing governments of the Depression*).

Don Qui·xote /dɒn kiːˈhoːteɪ, -ˈɒtɪ, -ˈɔːteɪ/ the hero of a romance (1605–15) by Cervantes, a satirical account of chivalric beliefs and conduct; the character of Don Quixote is typified by a romantic vision and naive idealism. [Spanish, DON[1] + *quixote* thigh armour]

Don River /dɒn/ **1** a river in Russia which rises near Tula, southeast of Moscow, and flows for a distance of 1 958 km (1,224 miles) to the Sea of Azov. **2** a river in S Ontario, rising just west of Richmond Hill and flowing generally southward through Toronto into Lake Ontario. **3** a river in Scotland which rises in the Grampians and flows 131 km (82 miles) eastward to the North Sea at Aberdeen. **4** a river in South Yorkshire which rises in the Peak District and flows 112 km (70 miles) eastward to join the Ouse shortly before it, in turn, joins the Humber.

don't ● *contraction* do not. ● *noun* a prohibition; an injunction not to do something (*dos and don'ts*).

donut esp. *N Amer.* var. of DOUGHNUT.

doob *noun slang* **1** (also **doob·ie** /ˈduːbiː/) *N Amer.* a marijuana cigarette. **2** *Cdn* (*West*) a condom. [origin unknown]

doo·dad *noun N Amer.* something not readily nameable, esp. a gadget or fancy ornament of an unnecessary kind. [20th c.: origin unknown]

doo·dle ● *verb* **1** *intransitive & transitive* scribble or draw, esp. absent-mindedly. **2** *intransitive & transitive* play idly on a musical

instrument. **3** *intransitive N Amer.* waste time; fool around. ● *noun* an idle scrawl or figure drawn absent-mindedly. □ **dood·ler** *noun* **dood·ling** *adjective* [originally = foolish person; compare Low German *dudelkopf*]

doodle·bug *noun* **1** *N Amer.* any of various insects, esp. the larva of an ant-lion. **2** esp. *US* a person looking for oil, water, etc., usu. by other than scientific means. **3** *informal* a flying bomb, esp. one used in World War II.

doodly-squat esp. *US* var. of DIDDLY-SQUAT.

doo-doo *noun slang* **1** excrement. **2** serious trouble (*we're in deep doo-doo*). [reduplication of DO[1] *noun* 3]

doof·us *noun* (also **dufus**) (*pl.* **-us·es**) a stupid or inept person; an idiot. [origin obscure: perhaps alteration of *goofus* 'foolish person'; compare German *doof*, stupid, dopey]

doo·hickey *noun* (*pl.* **-hickeys**) *N Amer. informal* an unspecified object or small device, esp. a mechanical one. [DOODAD + HICKEY 2]

Doo·little, Hilda (known as 'H.D.') (1886–1961), US poet and novelist. Her early imagist poetry gave way to a feminist rewriting of Greek mythology; her works include the verse collection *Sea Garden* (1916), the epic poem *Helen in Egypt* (1961), and the short story collection *Hermione*, published posthumously (1981).

doom ● *noun* **1 a** a grim fate or destiny. **b** impending death, disaster, or ruin. **2** the Last Judgment. ● *transitive verb* (usu. foll. by *to*) condemn or destine to some fate (*a city doomed to destruction*). [Old English *dōm* statute, judgment, from Germanic: related to DO[1]]

doom and gloom *noun* (also **gloom and doom**) a general feeling of despair and pessimism.

doomed *adjective* consigned to misfortune or destruction.

doom-laden *adjective* portending, suggesting, or predicting doom.

doom·say·er *noun* a person who predicts disaster, esp. of a political or economic nature. □ **doom·say·ing** *noun*

dooms·day *noun* **1** the day of the Last Judgment. **2** any day of decisive judgment or final dissolution. **3** (also *attributive*) a projected time of destruction of the world, esp. by nuclear means (*doomsday weapons*). □ **till doomsday** forever (*compare* DOMESDAY). [Old English *dōmes dæg*: see DOOM]

doomsday clock *noun* **1** a symbolic clock created in 1947 to measure the world's proximity to the final midnight of nuclear destruction, the hands being adjusted forward or back as the perceived threat grows or diminishes. **2** this image applied to an imminent crisis of significant proportion.

doomsday cult *noun* a religious cult which believes that the end of the world is imminent, esp. one whose members commit mass suicide on a chosen date.

doom·ster *noun* = DOOMSAYER.

doomy *adjective* **1** portending, suggesting, or predicting doom. **2** ominous, gloomy (*doomy music*).

door *noun* **1 a** a hinged, sliding, or revolving barrier for closing and opening an entrance to a building, room, cupboard, etc. **b** this as representing a house etc. (*lives two doors away*). **2 a** an entrance or exit; a doorway. **b** a means of access or approach. **c** (prec. by *the*) the entrance to a theatre, club, etc. at which admission must be paid or tickets shown (*tickets available at the door*). **3** something resembling a door in its movement or function, e.g. a lid, valve, or cover. **4** either of the two boards or metal plates attached to the ends of a trawl net. □ **close** (or **shut**) **the door to** (or **on**) exclude the opportunity for. **lay something at a person's door** impute something reprehensible etc. to a person. **leave the door open** ensure that an option remains available. **open the door to** create an opportunity for. **out of doors** outside the house, esp. in or into the open air. □ **door·less** *adjective* [Old English *duru, dor*, from Germanic]

door·bell *noun* a bell or buzzer connected to a door, rung by visitors to signal their arrival.

door·case *noun* = DOOR FRAME.

do-or-die *attributive adjective* denoting a determination not to be deterred by any danger or difficulty, esp. in a desperate situation or circumstance.

doored *adjective* (also in *combination*) having a door or doors (*a glass-doored cupboard*).

door frame *noun* the structure into which a door is fitted.

door jamb *noun* = DOORPOST.

door·keep·er *noun* = DOORMAN.

door·knob *noun* **1** a usu. round handle on a door which is turned to open or close the door. **2** *N Amer. slang* an idiot; a stupid person.

Vowels: a *cat* ɑ *arm* e *bed* ɜr *her* ɜː *deux* ə *ago* ɪ *sit* i *cosy* iː *feed* ɒ *hot* ɔ *pore* ɔː *no* ʌ *run* ʊ *put*

door knocker *noun* a metal or wooden instrument hinged to a door to allow visitors to signal their arrival by knocking.

door·man *noun* (*pl.* **-men**) an attendant at the entrance to a hotel, office, etc. who assists those entering or leaving.

door·mat *noun* **1** a mat at an entrance to a building for wiping mud etc. from the shoes. **2** *informal* a passive, submissive person.

door·nail *noun* a nail with which doors were formerly studded for strength or ornament. □ **dead as a doornail** completely or unmistakably dead.

door·plate *noun* a plate on the door of a house or room bearing the name of the occupant.

door·post *noun* each of the uprights of a door frame.

door prize *noun N Amer.* something awarded as a prize at a gathering, usu. through a draw.

door·sill *noun* the horizontal piece of wood forming the threshold of a door frame.

door·step *noun* **1** a step leading up to the outer door of a house etc. **2** *Brit. slang* a thick slice of bread. □ **on one's** (or **the**) **doorstep** very close.

door·stop *noun* **1** a weight or wedge placed under a door to keep it open. **2** a device fixed to the ground or wall to prevent a door from opening too widely, striking a wall, etc., when opened.

door-to-door ● *adjective* **1 a** (of selling, canvassing, etc.) done systematically, covering each house on a street, in an area, etc. **b** (of a salesperson or canvasser) working in this manner. **2** (of journeys, deliveries, etc.) direct. ● *adverb* (**door to door**) calling at each house in turn (*travelled door to door*).

door·way *noun* **1** an entryway to a room, building, etc., esp. one closed or opened by a door. **2** a means or medium of approach or access (*a doorway to freedom*).

door·yard *noun N Amer.* a yard or garden near the door of a house.

doo-wop *noun* (often *attributive*) a style of singing, originated by American rhythm-and-blues groups of the 1950s, in which nonsense phrases are used as the main line or as harmony. □ **doo-wopper** *noun* [imitative]

doozy *noun* (*pl.* **-ies**) (also **dooz·ie**, **dooz·er**) *N Amer. slang* something amazing, remarkable, or incredible. [20th c.: origin uncertain]

dopa *noun Biochem.* an amino acid derivative which is a precursor of dopamine. *See also* L-DOPA. [German from D*i*oxyphenylalanine, former name of the compound]

dopa·mine /ˈdoːpəmiːn/ *noun Biochem.* an amine present in the body as a neurotransmitter and a precursor of other substances including adrenalin. □ **dopa·min·er·gic** /ˌdoːpəmɪˈnɜrdʒɪk/ *adjective* [DOPA + AMINE]

dop·ant /ˈdoːpənt/ *noun Electronics* a substance used in doping a semiconductor.

dope ● *noun* **1 a** *slang* a narcotic drug. **b** a drug taken by an athlete or given to a horse etc. to affect performance. **2** *slang* a silly or stupid person. **3** *slang* essential facts, details, or information about a subject, esp. of a kind not generally divulged (*the inside dope*). **4** *N Amer.* a thick liquid, cream, or gel used as a lubricant, repellent, etc. (*brought sunscreen and bug dope; pipe dope*). **5** a varnish applied to the cloth surface of airplane parts to strengthen them, keep them airtight, etc. **6** a substance added to gasoline etc. to increase its effectiveness. ● *verb* **1 a** *transitive* administer stimulating or stupefying drugs to (an athlete, horse, etc.). **b** *intransitive* take addictive drugs. **2** *transitive* a doctor or treat (a substance) with an adulterant. **b** *Electronics* add an impurity to (a semiconductor) to produce a desired electrical characteristic. **3** *transitive* smear, daub; apply dope to. **4** *transitive informal* (foll. by *out*) work out, infer, or find out by calculation or surmise (*we doped out the plans*). ● *adjective slang* excellent, outstanding. □ **doped up** *slang* heavily under the influence of drugs. □ **doper** *noun* [Dutch *doop* sauce, from *doopen* to dip]

dope fiend *noun slang* a drug addict.

dope pusher *noun* a person who sells illegal drugs.

dope·ster *noun N Amer. slang* a person who collects information on and forecasts the results of sporting events, elections, etc. [DOPE *noun* 3 + -STER]

dopey *adjective* (also **dopy**) (**dop·i·er**, **dop·i·est**) *informal* **1** stupid, silly. **2 a** half asleep. **b** stupefied by or as if by a drug. □ **dop·i·ly** *adverb* **dop·i·ness** *noun*

dop·ing *noun* **1** *Sport* the use of any substance, foreign or natural to the body, to artificially enhance competition performance. **2** *Electronics* the addition of minute amounts of an element to a semiconducting element in order to change its electrical properties.

doppel·gäng·er /ˈdɒpəl.geŋər/ *noun* a ghostly likeness or double of a living person. [German, = double-goer]

Dop·pler¹, **Chris·tian** (1803–1853), Austrian physicist, who described the effect named after him.

Dop·pler² *noun* (also *attributive*) a device, gauge, system, etc. operating on the principles of the Doppler effect, esp. ultrasonic scanning machines. [C. DOPPLER¹]

Doppler effect *noun Physics* an increase (or decrease) in the frequency of sound, light, or other waves as the source and observer move towards (or away) from each other. [C. DOPPLER¹]

Doppler radar *noun* a radar tracking system that determines the velocity of a moving object by measuring the Doppler shift of the frequency of a radar signal reflected by the object. [C. DOPPLER¹]

Doppler shift *noun Physics* the change in frequency of waves caused by the Doppler effect. [C. DOPPLER¹]

dopy *var. of* DOPY.

dor·ado /dəˈradoː/ *noun* (*pl.* **-ados**) **1** a blue and silver marine fish, *Coryphaena hippurus*, showing brilliant colours when dying out of water. **2** a brightly coloured freshwater fish, *Salminus maxillosus*, native to S America. [Spanish from Late Latin *deauratus* gilt, from *aurum* gold]

do-rag *noun US* a scarf or cloth worn on the head to protect one's hairstyle. [from HAIRDO]

Dor·áti /dəˈrati/ **Antal** (1906–88), Hungarian-born US conductor, noted for his performances of the works of Haydn and Bartók.

Dor·ches·ter¹ /ˈdɔrtʃestər, -tʃɑstər/ **1** a town in S England, the county town of Dorset; pop. (est. 1998) 15,700. **2** a town in E New Brunswick, situated near the border with Nova Scotia; pop. (2001) 964. It is the site of a major penitentiary. [sense 2 after Sir Guy CARLETON, 1st Baron *Dorchester*]

Dor·ches·ter² *see* CARLETON 1.

Dor·dogne /dɔrˈdɔɪn/ an inland department of SW France. It contains numerous caves and rock shelters that have yielded abundant remains of early humans and their artifacts and art.

Dordogne River a river of W France which rises in the Auvergne and flows 472 km (297 miles) westward to meet the Garonne and form the Gironde estuary.

Dor·drecht /ˈdɔrdrext/ (also **Dort** /dɔrt/) an industrial city and river port in the Netherlands, near the mouth of the Rhine, 20 km (12 miles) southeast of Rotterdam; pop. (est. 2002) 122,600.

Doré /doːˈrei/ **(Paul) Gus·tave** (1832–83), French illustrator, best known for his dark, detailed woodcut illustrations of books such as Dante's *Inferno* (1861), Cervantes' *Don Quixote* (1863), and the Bible (1865–6).

doré /dɔrˈei/ *noun Cdn* the walleye, *Stizostedion vitreum*. [French, = 'golden']

Doré Lake /ˈdɔrei/ a small lake in central Saskatchewan, situated about 200 km northwest of Prince Albert.

Dor·ian /ˈdɔriən/ ● *noun* a member of an ancient Hellenic people speaking the Doric dialect of Greek, inhabiting the Peloponnese and elsewhere. ● *adjective* of or relating to the Dorians or to Doris in central Greece. [Latin *Dorius* from Greek *Dōrios* from *Dōros*, the mythical ancestor]

Dorian mode *noun Music* a church mode represented by the natural diatonic scale D–D, with D as the final and A as the dominant.

Doric /ˈdɔrɪk/ ● *adjective* **1** relating to or denoting a classical order of architecture characterized by a plain, sturdy column and a thick square abacus resting on a rounded moulding. **2** of or relating to Dorians or their ancient Greek dialect. ● *noun* **1** *Archit.* the Doric order. **2** the dialect of the Dorians in ancient Greece. [Latin *Doricus* from Greek *Dōrikos* (as DORIAN)]

Dor·ion /ˈdɔriɔ̃/ an urban community in south central Quebec, part of the city of Vaudreuil-Dorion. [Sir A.-A. *Dorion*, Canadian politician d.1891]

dork *noun* **1** *informal derogatory* a dull, slow-witted, or socially inept person. **2** *slang* the penis. □ **dorky** *adjective* [20th c.: origin unknown]

dorm *noun informal* dormitory. [abbreviation]

dor·mant *adjective* **1 a** lying inactive as in sleep; sleeping. **b** *Biology* alive but with development suspended; not actively growing (*dormant fruit trees; a dormant virus*). **2** (of a volcano etc.) temporarily inactive. **3** (of potential faculties etc.) latent or not in current operation (*dormant talent*). **4** *Heraldry* (of a beast) lying with its head on its paws and its eyes closed. □ **dor·mancy** *noun* [Old French, pres. part. of *dormir* from Latin *dormire* sleep]

dormant oil noun N Amer. a thin petroleum oil laced with sulphur, used to kill overwintering pests such as aphids, thrips, mites, etc.

dor·mer noun 1 (in full **dormer window**) a projecting upright window in a sloping roof. 2 the projecting construction which supports the window. [Old French dormëor (as DORMANT)]

dor·mie adjective (also **dormy**) Golf (of a player or side) ahead by as many holes as there are holes left to play (dormie five). [19th c.: origin unknown]

dormi·tory /ˈdɔrmɪtɔri/ noun (pl. **-ies**) 1 N Amer. a university or college residence. 2 a large room containing beds, esp. in a school, monastery, or other institution. 3 a small town or suburb from which people travel to work in a city etc. (also attributive: dormitory suburb). [Latin dormitorium from dormire dormit- sleep]

dor·mouse noun (pl. **dor·mice**) any small mouselike hibernating rodent of the family Gliridae, having a long bushy tail. [Middle English: origin unknown]

do·ron·icum /dəˈrɒnɪkəm/ noun = LEOPARD'S BANE. [modern Latin (Linnaeus), ultimately from Arabic darānaj]

dor·sal adjective Anat., Zool., & Bot. 1 of, on, or near the back (dorsal fin) (compare VENTRAL 1). 2 ridge-shaped. 3 = ABAXIAL. □ **dor·sal·ly** adverb [Late Latin dorsalis from Latin dorsum back]

Dor·set[1] a county of SW England; county town, Dorchester.

Dor·set[2] noun a member of an Aboriginal people living in the eastern Arctic c.1000 BC–AD 1000, whose culture was displaced by that of the Inuit. [CAPE DORSET]

Dor·sey, Thom·as Fran·cis ('Tommy') (1905–56), US bandleader, trombonist, and composer, who, both on his own and with his brother Jimmy (1904–57) led a succession of popular swing bands from the 1930s to the 1950s.

dorsi- combining form (also **dorso-**) of, to, or on the back. [as DORSUM]

dor·sum noun (pl. **dorsa**) Anat. & Zool. the dorsal part of an organism or structure. [Latin = back]

Dort see DORDRECHT.

Dort·mund /ˈdɔrtmʊnd/ an industrial city in NW Germany, in North Rhine-Westphalia; pop. (est. 2002) 588,300.

Dor·val /dɔrˈval/ a former city in south central Quebec, in the southern part of the Island of Montreal, now part of the city of Montreal; pop. (2001) 17,706. Dorval is the location of Montreal's principal international airport, renamed Pierre Elliott Trudeau Airport in 2003. [J.-B. Bouchard d'Orval, property owner d.1724]

dory[1] noun (pl. **-ies**) any of various marine fish having a compressed body and flat head, esp. the John Dory, used as food. [French dorée, fem. past participle of dorer gild (as DORADO)]

dory[2] noun (pl. **-ies**) N Amer. a small flat-bottomed fishing boat with high sides. [Miskito dóri dugout]

dory·man noun (pl. **-men**) Cdn a person who fishes from a dory.

DOS /dɒs/ noun Computing an operating system for microcomputers. [abbreviation of disk operating system]

dosa /ˈdoːsə/ noun (pl. **dosas** or **dosai** /ˈdoːsaɪ/) (in southern Indian cooking) a pancake made from rice flour, typically served with a spiced vegetable filling. [Tamil tōcai]

dos·age /ˈdoːsɪdʒ/ noun 1 the size of a dose of medicine etc. 2 the giving of medicine in doses. 3 a small amount of sugar added to some wines before the final corking to make them sweet.

dose ● noun 1 an amount of a medicine or drug taken or recommended to be taken at one time. 2 a quantity of something administered or allocated, e.g. work, praise, punishment, etc. 3 the amount of ionizing radiation to which a person or thing is exposed. 4 slang a bout of gonorrhea or syphilis. 5 = DOSAGE 3. ● transitive verb 1 treat (a person or animal) with doses of medicine. 2 divide into, or administer in, doses. 3 adulterate or blend (esp. wine with sugar). □ **like a dose of salts** Brit. informal very fast and efficiently. [French from Late Latin dosis from Greek dosis gift, from didōmi give]

dosh noun Brit. slang money. [20th c.: origin unknown]

dosha /ˈdoʃə, ˈdoːʃə/ noun (in Ayurvedic medicine) each of the three humours circulating in the body and governing physiological activity, their differing proportions determining individual temperament, physical constitution, and (when imbalanced) giving rise to a disposition to particular physical and mental disorders. [Sanskrit doṣa, fault, disease, used by extension to refer to the three humours themselves]

do-si-do /ˌdoʊsiˈdoː/ (also **do-se-do**) (pl. **-dos**) ● noun a square dance figure in which two dancers pass around each other back to back and return to their original positions. ● intransitive verb perform a do-si-do. [corruption of French dos-à-dos, back to back]

dos·im·eter /doˈsɪmɪtər/ noun a device used to measure an absorbed dose of ionizing radiation. □ **dosi·met·ric** /-ˈmetrɪk/ adjective **dos·im·et·rist** noun **dos·im·etry** noun

Dos Pas·sos /dɒs ˈpasoːs/ **John (Roder·igo)** (1896–1970), US novelist, best known for his portrayal of the diversity of early 20th-c. American life in novels such as Manhattan Transfer (1925) and the trilogy collected as U.S.A. (1938).

doss esp. Brit. slang ● intransitive verb 1 (often foll. by down) sleep, esp. roughly or in cheap lodgings. 2 (often foll. by around, about) spend time idly. ● noun a bed, esp. in cheap lodgings. [prob. = doss ornamental covering for a seat back etc., from Old French dos, ultimately from Latin dorsum back]

dos·sal /ˈdɒsəl/ noun an ornamental cloth hanging behind an altar or around a chancel. [medieval Latin dossale from Late Latin dorsalis DORSAL]

doss·er noun Brit. slang 1 a person who dosses. 2 = DOSS-HOUSE.

doss-house noun Brit. = FLOPHOUSE.

dos·si·er /ˈdɒsɪˌeɪ/ noun a set of documents, esp. a collection of information about a person, event, or subject. [French, so called from the label on the back, from dos back, from Latin dorsum]

dost /dʌst/ archaic 2nd sing. present of DO[1].

Dos·to·ev·sky /ˌdɒstɔɪˈefski/ **Fyodor (Mik·hail·ovich)** (1821–81), Russian novelist. His influential novels are noted for their psychological insight and concern with religious and political issues; they include Crime and Punishment (1866), The Idiot (1868), The Possessed (1871), and The Brothers Karamazov (1880). □ **Dos·to·ev·skian** adjective

DoT abbreviation (also **DOT**) 1 (in Canada and the UK) Department of Transport. 2 (in the US) Department of Transportation.

dot[1] ● noun 1 a a small spot, speck, or mark. b such a mark written or printed as part of an i or j, as a diacritical mark, as one of a series of marks to signify omission, or as a period. c a decimal point. d a period used in an electronic mail address or filename. 2 Music a a point placed after a note or rest to lengthen it by half as much again. b a point placed over or under a note to indicate that it is to be performed staccato. 3 the shorter signal of the two used in Morse code (compare DASH noun 7). 4 a tiny or apparently tiny object (a dot on the horizon). 5 a small amount (a dot of icing). 6 a a point-like element of a television picture. b the area of phosphor on the inside of a television tube corresponding to this. ● transitive verb (**dot·ted, dot·ting**) 1 a mark with a dot or dots. b place a dot over (a letter). 2 Music mark (a note or rest) to show that the time value is increased by half. 3 occur singly throughout (an area) or over (a surface) (sailboats dotted the lake). 4 Brit. slang hit (dotted him one in the eye). □ **dot the i's and cross the t's** informal 1 be minutely accurate or emphasize details. 2 add the final touches to a task, exercise, etc. **on the dot** exactly on time. **the year dot** esp. Brit. informal far in the past. [Old English dott head of a boil, perhaps influenced by Dutch dot knot]

dot[2] noun a woman's dowry. □ **dot·al** /ˈdoːtəl/ adjective [French from Latin dos dotis]

dot·age /ˈdoːtɪdʒ/ noun the state of having the intellect impaired, esp. through old age; senility (in his dotage). [from obsolete sense of DOTE, 'be silly or feeble-minded']

dot·ard /ˈdoːtərd/ noun a senile person. [DOTE + -ARD]

dot-bomb noun a bankrupt, failed, or unsuccessful Internet company. [after DOT-COM]

dot-com noun (also **dot.com**) 1 designating an email address ending in .com. 2 a company or website that conducts business on the Internet. □ **dot-commer** noun

dote intransitive verb (foll. by on, upon) be foolishly or excessively fond of. □ **doter** noun **dot·ing** adjective **dot·ing·ly** adverb [Middle English, corresponding to Middle Dutch doten be silly]

doth /dʌθ/ archaic 3rd sing. present of DO[1].

dot matrix Computing ● noun a regular array of positions that are filled selectively to create a character or graphics (on a screen or paper). ● adjective of or denoting such an array.

dot matrix printer noun Computing a printer that creates each character from an array of dots that are usu. formed by transferring ink by mechanical impact.

dotted line noun a line of dots or small dashes on a document, esp. to indicate the space left for a signature. □ **sign on the dotted line** agree fully or formally.

dot·ter·el /ˈdɒtərəl/ noun a small migrant plover, Eudromias morinellus.

Consonants: b but   d dog   f few   g get   h her   j yes   k cat   l leg   m man   n no   p pen   r red   s sit

[DOTE + -REL, named from the ease with which it is caught, taken to indicate stupidity]

dot·tle *noun* a remnant of unburned tobacco in a pipe. [DOT¹ + -LE¹]

dot-to-dot *adjective* = CONNECT-THE-DOTS.

dotty *adjective* (**dot·ti·er**, **dot·ti·est**) *informal* **1** silly or confused, esp. due to old age. **2** eccentric. **3** absurd. **4** (foll. by *about*, *over*) infatuated with; obsessed by. □ **dot·ti·ly** *adverb* **dot·ti·ness** *noun* [earlier = unsteady: from DOT¹ + -Y¹]

Dou /daʊ/ **Ger·ard** (also **Ger·rit**) (1613–75), Dutch painter, noted for his precise and detailed portraits and domestic scenes, such as *The Young Mother* (1658).

Dou·ala /duːˈɑːlə/ the chief port and largest city of Cameroon; pop. (est. 2002) 1,239,100.

Douay Bible /ˈduːeɪ/ *noun* (also **Douay version**) an English translation of the Bible completed in France in 1609 and formerly used in the Catholic Church.

double ● *adjective* **1 a** consisting of two usu. equal parts or things; twofold. **b** consisting of two identical parts. **2** twice as much or many (*double the amount; double the number; double thickness*). **3** having twice the usual size, quantity, strength, value, etc. (*double whisky*). **4 a** designed or suitable for two people (*double bed*). **b** (of blankets, sheets, etc.) full size or suitable for a double bed. **5 a** having some essential part double (*double-axle trailer*). **b** (of a flower) having more than one circle of petals. **6 a** having two different roles, interpretations, applications, etc. (*double meaning*). **b** characterized by duplicity, falsity, or deceitfulness (*leads a double life*). **7 a** *Music* lower in pitch by an octave (*double bassoon*). **b** referring to a rapid pace in marching. **8** bent, stooping forward. **9** *Figure Skating & Dance* (of a jump, pirouette, etc.) involving two revolutions (*double lutz; double tour en l'air*). ● *adverb* **1** at or to twice the amount, extent, etc. (*counts double*). **2** two at once or two together (*sleep double*). ● *noun* **1 a** a double quantity or thing; twice as much or many. **b** *informal* an alcoholic drink with a double measure of liquor. **2 a** a counterpart of a person or thing. **b** a person who looks exactly like another. **c** a wraith or ghostly image of a person seen shortly before or after his or her death. **3** (in *pl.*) *Sport* (in tennis, badminton, etc.) a game between two pairs of players. **4** *Baseball* a successful hit which allows a player to get to second base safely. **5** *Figure Skating & Dance* a double jump, pirouette, etc. **6** a system of betting in which the winnings and stake from the first bet are transferred to a second. **7** *Bridge* a call that doubles the value of the points to be won or lost on an opponent's bid. **8** *Darts* **a** a hit on the narrow ring enclosed by the two outer circles of a dartboard, scoring double. **b** the ring itself. **9** a sharp turn, esp. of the tracks of a hunted animal, or the course of a river. **10 a** = UNDERSTUDY. **b** an actor who takes two parts in the same performance. **c** = BODY DOUBLE. **11** a double room in a hotel, residence, etc. **12** *Bowling* two strikes in a row. ● *verb* **1** *transitive & intransitive* make, become, or amount to twice as much or many. **2 a** *transitive* fold or bend (paper, cloth, etc.) over on itself so as to bring the two parts into contact. **b** *intransitive* become folded. **3 a** *transitive* (of an actor) play (two parts) in the same piece. **b** *intransitive* (often foll. by *for*) be an understudy, body double, etc. **c** *intransitive* (usu. foll. by *as*) perform or function in an additional capacity (*the student doubled as a house-sitter*). **4** *intransitive* turn sharply in flight or pursuit; take a tortuous course. **5** *transitive Naut.* sail around or to the other side of (a cape or headland). **6** *transitive Bridge* make a call increasing the value of the points to be won or lost on (an opponent's bid). **7** *Music* **a** *intransitive* (often foll. by *on*) play two or more musical instruments (*the clarinetist doubles on tenor sax*). **b** *transitive* add the same note in a higher or lower octave to (a note). **8** *intransitive* move at twice the usual speed, esp. march at double time. **9** *Billiards* **a** *intransitive* (of a ball) rebound from a cushion, esp. into a pocket. **b** *transitive* (of a player) cause (a ball) to rebound. **10** *transitive & intransitive* carry (a person) as a second rider on a bicycle. **11** *Baseball* **a** *intransitive* make a double. **b** *transitive* cause (a baserunner) to advance through a double. **c** *transitive* (usu. foll. by *in*) cause (a run) to score by hitting a double. **d** *transitive* (usu. foll. by *up*) tag out (a baserunner) as the second action of a double play. **12** *intransitive informal* double date. **13** (foll. by *up*) **a** *intransitive* bend or curl up. **b** *transitive* cause to do this, esp. by a blow. **c** *intransitive* be overcome with pain or laughter. **d** *transitive* share or assign to a room, quarters, etc., with another or others. **e** *intransitive* use winnings from a bet as stake for another. □ **on** (or **at**) **the double** running, hurrying, or in double time. **bent double** folded, stooping. **double back** take a new direction opposite to the previous one. **double or nothing** a gamble in which the player either gains twice the bet or loses everything. **see double** perceive or seem to perceive two images of one object. □ **double·ness** *noun* **doub·ler** *noun* **doub·ly** *adverb* [Old French *doble, duble* (n.), *dobler, dubler* (v.) from Latin *duplus* DUPLE]

Double-A = AA 2, 3, 4.

double-acting *adjective* **1** acting in two ways or directions, by two methods, etc. **2** (of an engine) worked by application of power on both sides of the pistons alternately.

double-action *adjective* **1** (of a firearm) needing only a single pull of the trigger to cock and fire the weapon. **2** (of a fishing reel) having a spool that turns twice for every turn of the handle. **3** having twice the normal or expected strength, power, or effectiveness.

double agent *noun* a person who purports to spy for one country or organization while actually working for a hostile or rival one.

double album *noun* two long playing records, cassettes, etc. sold as a set.

double bar *noun Music* a pair of closely spaced bar lines marking the end of a work or a section.

double-barrelled *adjective* (esp. *US* **double-barreled**) **1** (of a gun) having two barrels. **2** very powerful, persuasive, or vehement (*a double-barrelled reputation*). **3** (of a surname) having two parts, usu. joined by a hyphen. **4** twofold or serving a double purpose.

double bass *noun* **1** the largest and lowest-pitched instrument of the violin family. **2** a player of this instrument.

double bed *noun* a bed suitable for two people, esp. one measuring 137 × 190 cm (53 ¹/₂ × 75 inches).

double bill *noun* two films, plays, etc. presented to an audience one after the other in the same program.

double bind *noun* **1** a dilemma; a situation in which either of two possible courses will be wrong. **2** *Psych.* a situation in which contradictory attitudes are expressed towards a person, or contradictory demands are made of him or her, so that he or she cannot avoid being at fault.

double-bitted *adjective* (of an axe) having two cutting blades, one stubbed for chopping knots and the other tapered for cutting heartwood.

double-blind ● *adjective* designating a test or experiment in which neither the tester nor the subject has knowledge of identities or other factors that might lead to bias. ● *noun* such a test or experiment.

double-bogey *Golf* ● *noun* (*pl.* **-bogeys**) a score of two strokes over par on a hole. ● *transitive & intransitive verb* (**-bogeys**, **-bogeyed**) complete (a hole) in two strokes over par.

double boiler *noun* a saucepan with a detachable upper compartment heated by boiling water in the lower one.

double bond *noun* a pair of bonds between two atoms in a molecule.

double-book *transitive verb* **1** accept two reservations simultaneously for (the same seat, room, etc.), esp. to ensure that at least one will be used. **2** inadvertently schedule two appointments (for a person) at the same time.

double-breast·ed *adjective* (of a coat etc.) having a substantial overlap of material at the front which crosses the body and is usu. fastened with two rows of buttons.

double-check *transitive verb* verify twice or in two ways.

double chin *noun* a chin with a fold of fat or loose flesh below it. □ **double-chinned** *adjective*

double-click *verb Computing* **1** *intransitive* press and release the button of a mouse twice in quick succession to activate a program etc. **2** *transitive* click on (an icon etc.) in this way.

double clutch *intransitive verb N Amer.* **1** release and re-engage the clutch twice when changing gears in a car etc. **2** *Sport* begin to throw a ball but hesitate briefly before completing the throw, esp. impairing the pitch.

double cream *noun Brit.* thick cream with a high fat content.

double-crested cormorant *noun* a shiny greenish-black cormorant, *Phalacrocorax auritus*, with an inconspicuous tuft of feathers on either side of the head, found in Canada from Alberta east to the Atlantic coast.

double-cross ● *transitive verb* deceive or betray (a person one is supposedly helping). ● *noun* an act of doing this. □ **double-crosser** *noun*

double dagger *noun* = DOUBLE OBELUS.

double date ● *noun* a date on which two couples go together. ● *intransitive verb* go on a double date.

double day *noun N Amer.* (often in *pl.*) the twofold day of labour put in by many people, esp. women, encompassing both a full-time paid job and their own domestic work.

double-dealing ● *noun* deceit, esp. in business. ● *adjective* deceitful or practising deceit. □ **double-deal** *intransitive verb* **double-dealer** *noun*

double-deck *adjective* (also **double-decked**) having two decks or layers.

double-decker *noun* **1** a bus having an upper and lower deck. **2** *informal* anything consisting of two layers, e.g. a sandwich.

double decomposition *noun Chem.* a reaction in which two compounds exchange radicals or ions. *Also called* METATHESIS 2.

double density *adjective Computing* designating a storage device, esp. a disk, having twice the basic capacity.

double digging *noun* digging in which one spadeful of soil is taken off and the underlying second spadeful broken up before being covered again.

double-digit *adjective* equal in quantity, rate, etc. to a number, esp. a percentage, between 10 and 99 (*double-digit unemployment*).

double-dip ● *adjective* having two downward movements, each followed by an upward one (*double-dip recession*). ● *noun N Amer.* an ice cream cone with two scoops of ice cream.

double-dipping *noun N Amer.* **1** the practice of commuting an occupational pension to a lump sum and then drawing a government pension that would not otherwise be due. **2** the practice of receiving an income from two jobs, esp. a pension from a former job and a salary from a current one. □ **double-dipper** *noun*

double door *noun* (usu. in *pl.*) **1** a pair of doors side by side in one opening, meeting in the middle. **2** two doors situated one close behind the other.

double-double *noun* esp. *Cdn* a cup of coffee with a double serving of both sugar and cream.

double dutch *noun* **1** a children's game in which two people hold the ends of two long skipping ropes and swing the ropes inwards in opposite directions for one or two people to jump over. **2** *Brit. informal* incomprehensible talk.

double duty *noun* a twofold function or role.

double-dyed *adjective* confirmed, long established, deep-rooted (*a double-dyed liberal*).

double eagle *noun* **1** *N Amer. Golf* a score of three strokes under par at any hole. **2** *US hist.* a gold coin, issued from 1849 to 1933, worth twenty dollars.

double-edged *adjective* **1** having two functions or (often contradictory) applications, interpretations, etc. **2** (of a knife etc.) having two cutting edges.

double en·tendre /ɒnˈtɒndrə/ *noun* **1** a word or phrase open to two interpretations, one usu. risqué or indecent. **2** humour using such words or phrases. [obsolete French, = double understanding]

double entry *noun* (also *attributive*) a system of bookkeeping in which each transaction is entered twice, once to the credit of one account and once to the debit of another.

double exposure *noun Photog.* the action or result of exposing the same frame, plate, etc. on two separate occasions, either accidentally or deliberately.

double-faced *adjective* **1** insincere, hypocritical, two-faced. **2** (of a fabric or material) finished on both sides so that either may be used as the right side.

double fault ● *noun Tennis* two consecutive faults in serving, together resulting in the loss of a point. ● *intransitive verb* (also **double-fault**) serve a double fault.

double feature *noun* a motion picture program with two full-length films shown for a single admission price.

double figures *plural noun* the numbers from 10 to 99.

double first *noun Brit.* **1** first-class honours in two subjects or examinations at a university. **2** a person achieving this.

double garage *noun* a garage in which two vehicles can be parked side by side.

double glazing *noun* glazing consisting of two layers of glass with a space between them, designed to reduce loss of heat and exclude noise. □ **double-glazed** *adjective*

double-headed *adjective* having a double head or two heads.

double·head·er *noun* **1** *N Amer.* **a** two games etc. in succession between the same or different opponents, esp. on the same day. **b** two events, occurrences, etc. happening one after the other. **2** a train pulled by two locomotives coupled together.

double helix *noun* a pair of parallel helices with a common axis, esp. in the structure of a DNA molecule.

double-hung *adjective* (of a window) having two vertically sliding sashes, allowing the window to be opened from the top or bottom.

double indemnity *noun N Amer.* the provision for payment of double the face amount of an insurance policy when death occurs as the result of an accident.

double jeopardy *noun* esp. *N Amer.* the immunity which prevents the prosecution of a person twice for the same offence.

double-jointed *adjective* having very flexible joints that allow the fingers, arms or legs to bend backwards as well as forwards.

double-knit *adjective* (of an item of clothing) knitted on a machine with two sets of needles, thereby having a double thickness and the same type of ribbing on the front and back.

double majority *noun* a majority vote from two different groups, required for the approval of a law, proposal, etc.

double minor *noun Hockey* two minor penalties, imposed for a single offence considered to be severe but accidental, served sequentially.

double negative *noun* a negative statement containing two negative elements, e.g. *didn't say nothing*. ¶ The use of the double negative is considered ungrammatical in standard English.

double obelus *noun* (also **double obelisk**) a sign (‡) used in printing to introduce a reference.

double occupancy *noun N Amer.* a type of accommodation in a hotel etc. where two people share the same room.

double-paned *adjective* (of a window) having two panes slightly separated to trap air between them as an insulating barrier.

double-park *transitive & intransitive verb* park (a vehicle) alongside one that is already parked parallel to a curb etc.

double play *noun Baseball* a play in which two runners are put out.

double pneumonia *noun* pneumonia affecting both lungs.

double-quick *adjective & adverb* very quick or quickly.

double refraction *noun* the refraction of unpolarized light into two separate rays or beams going in different directions, producing a double image of an object.

double room *noun* a room in a hotel with two beds, usu. double or queen size.

double-sided *adjective* **1** that can be used on both sides. **2** having two sides. **3** (of a text) typed, printed, etc. on both sides of a sheet of paper. □ **double-sidedness** *noun*

double-sided tape *noun* tape with adhesive on both sides.

double space *transitive & intransitive verb* type or format (a text) with a line left empty between successive lines. □ **double-spaced** *adjective*

double·speak *noun* = DOUBLE-TALK.

double standard *noun* a rule or principle applied more strictly to some people than to others (or to oneself).

double star *noun* two stars actually or apparently very close together.

double steal *noun Baseball* a play in which two baserunners each steal a base.

double-stopping *noun* the sounding of two strings at once on a violin etc. □ **double stop** *noun*

doub·let /ˈdʌblət/ *noun* **1** *hist.* a man's short close-fitting jacket, with or without sleeves. **2** either of a pair of similar things, esp. either of two words in a language that have the same derivation but different sense, e.g. *fashion* and *faction*, *cloak* and *clock*. **3** a historical or biblical account occurring twice in differing contexts, usu. traceable to different sources. **4** (in *pl.*) the same number on two dice thrown at once. **5** a pair of associated lines close together in a spectrum. **6** a combination of two simple lenses. **7** a counterfeit or simulated jewel usu. composed of two pieces of crystal or glass cemented together with a layer of colour between them. [Old French from *double*: see DOUBLE]

double take *noun* a delayed and usu. contradictory reaction to an occurrence or situation immediately after one's first reaction.

double takeout *noun Curling* a shot which hits and knocks out of the house two of an opponent's rocks.

double-talk ● *noun* **1** language or talk that is usu. deliberately ambiguous or misleading. **2** meaningless gibberish. ● *verb* **1** *transitive* persuade (a person) through double-talk. **2** *intransitive* engage in double-talk. □ **double-talking** *adjective*

double-team *verb N Amer.* **1** *transitive Basketball etc.* block (an opposing player) with two players. **2** *intransitive* bring double pressure to bear on a person. □ **double-teaming** *noun*

double·think *noun* **1** the mental capacity to accept as equally valid two entirely contradictory opinions or beliefs, esp. as a result of political indoctrination. **2** the practice of doing this. [coined by George Orwell in *Nineteen Eighty-Four* (1949)]

double time ● *noun* **1** a rate of pay equal to twice the standard rate, usu. given for working extra on holidays etc. **2** *Military* a marching pace

Vowels: a cat ɑ arm e bed ɜr her ɜː deux ə ago ɪ sit i cosy iː feed ɒ hot ɔ pore ɔː no ʌ run ʊ put

in which approximately twice as many steps per minute are made as in slow time. ● *intransitive verb* (also **double-time**) march in double time.

double-tonguing *noun* a method of tonguing using two alternate tongue movements, usu. made by sounding *t* and *k* alternately, in order to facilitate rapid playing of a wind instrument.

double·tree *noun* a crossbar of a wagon with a swingletree at each end, enabling two horses to be harnassed.

double vision *noun* the simultaneous perception of two images of one object.

double whammy *noun informal* a twofold blow or setback.

double-wide *noun N Amer.* a semi-permanent mobile home consisting of two separate units connected on site.

double-wishbone suspension *noun* a suspension system for a vehicle on a chassis resembling two wishbones joined at the open ends.

doub·loon /dʌˈbluːn/ *noun* **1** *hist.* a Spanish gold coin. **2** (in *pl.*) *slang* money. [French *doublon* or Spanish *doblón* (as DOUBLE)]

doub·lure /duːˈblʊr/ *noun* an ornamental lining, usu. leather, inside a book cover. [French, = lining (*doubler* to line)]

doubt ● *noun* **1** a feeling of uncertainty; an undecided state of mind (*be in doubt about*; *have no doubt that*). **2** (often foll. by *of*, *about*) an inclination to disbelieve (*have one's doubts about*). **3** an uncertain state of affairs. **4** a lack of full proof or clear indication (*benefit of the doubt*). ● *verb* **1** *transitive* feel uncertain or undecided about (*I doubt that you are right*; *I doubt that is wise*). **2** *transitive* hesitate to believe or trust (a person, claim, etc.). **3** *intransitive* have doubts or be undecided in opinion or belief. □ **beyond (a) doubt** certainly. **beyond a shadow of a doubt** definitely, absolutely. **give (a person) the benefit of the doubt 1** assume innocence rather than guilt, esp. when the evidence is conflicting. **2** incline to a more favourable or kindly decision, estimate, etc. **in doubt 1** (of a person) in a state of mental uncertainty or indecision. **2** (of an issue etc.) open to question, not certainly known or decided. **no doubt 1** in all likelihood, certainly. **without (a) doubt** certainly, unquestionably. □ **doubt·er** *noun* **doubt·ing·ly** *adverb* [Old French *doute* (n.), *douter* (v.) from Latin *dubitare* hesitate; modern spelling after Latin]

doubt·ful *adjective* **1** feeling doubt, uncertainty, or misgivings; unsure or guarded in one's opinion. **2** causing doubt; ambiguous; uncertain in meaning etc. **3** (of a person) unreliable, of dubious character (*a doubtful ally*). □ **doubt·ful·ly** *adverb* **doubt·ful·ness** *noun*

doubt·ing Thom·as *noun* an incredulous or skeptical person. [see THOMAS 3]

doubt·less *adverb* (often qualifying a sentence) **1** certainly, without doubt. **2** probably, in all likelihood. □ **doubt·less·ly** *adverb*

douce /duːs/ *adjective Scot.* sober, gentle, sedate. [Old French *dous douce* from Latin *dulcis* sweet]

douche /duːʃ/ ● *noun* **1 a** a jet of liquid applied to part of the body, esp. the vagina, for cleansing or medicinal purposes. **b** the application of this. **2** a device for producing such a jet. ● *verb* **1** *transitive* treat with a douche. **2** *intransitive* use a douche. □ **douch·ing** *noun* [French from Italian *doccia* pipe, from *docciare* pour by drops, ultimately from Latin *ductus*: see DUCT]

dough *noun* **1 a** a thick mixture of flour, water, etc. for baking into bread, pastry, etc. **b** any soft, pasty mass. **2** *slang* money. [Old English *dāg* from Germanic]

dough·boy *noun* **1** *US informal* a United States infantryman, esp. in World War I. **2** a boiled or deep-fried dumpling.

dough·nut *noun* (also esp. *N Amer.* **donut**) **1** a small spongy cake of sweetened and deep-fried dough, usu. ring-shaped, or spherical with a jam or cream filling. **2** any of various circular objects with a hole in the middle, esp.: **a** a weighted ring placed around a baseball bat and used by a player to practise his or her swing. **b** *Physics* a toroidal vacuum chamber for acceleration of particles in a betatron or synchrotron. □ **do doughnuts** *N Amer. slang* (of a driver) cause a car to spin in wide circles by slamming on the brakes, esp. for fun (*did doughnuts in the parking lot*).

doughty /ˈdaʊti, ˈdaʊ-/ *adjective* (**dought·i·er**, **dought·i·est**) fearless, valiant, stout-hearted. □ **dought·i·ly** *adverb* **dought·i·ness** *noun* [Old English *dohtig* var. of *dyhtig* from Germanic]

doughy *adjective* (**dough·i·er**, **dough·i·est**) **1** having the form or consistency of dough. **2** pale and sickly in colour. □ **dough·i·ness** *noun*

Doug·las¹ the capital of the Isle of Man; pop. (2001) 25,347.

Doug·las² ▶ **1 Sir James** (1803–77), British fur trader, governor of Vancouver Island 1851–63 and of BC 1858–64. He entered the service of the North West Company in 1819, and of the Hudson's Bay Company in 1821, and founded Fort Victoria on Vancouver Island in 1843 as the Hudson's Bay Company's western headquarters. **2 Thom·as Clem·ent** ('**Tommy**') (1904–86), Scottish-born Canadian politician, CCF premier of Saskatchewan 1944–61. A Baptist minister, he was one of the founders of the CCF (1932), and as premier formed N America's first socialist government, introducing innovative social reforms such as hospital insurance; he later led the newly formed NDP (1961–71).

Douglas fir *noun* (also **Douglas pine** or **Douglas spruce**) **1** any large conifer of the genus *Pseudotsuga*, of western N America. **2** the wood of this tree. [D. *Douglas*, Scottish botanist d.1834]

Douglas-Home /ˌdʌɡləsˈhjuːm/ **Sir Alec, Baron Home of the Hirsel of Coldstream** (born Alexander Frederick Douglas-Home) (1903–95), British Conservative politician, prime minister 1963–4.

Douglas maple *noun* a maple shrub or tree of western N America, *Acer glabrum* var. *douglasii*, planted as an ornamental. [as DOUGLAS FIR]

Doukh·obor /ˈduːkəbɔr/ *noun* a member of a Russian Christian sect similar to the Society of Friends, many members of which migrated to Canada in 1899 after persecution for refusing military service. [Russian *Dukhobor*, from *dukh* spirit + *borets* wrestler]

doula /ˈduːlə/ *noun* a person, esp. an experienced mother, who gives emotional support, practical help, and advice to a woman during pregnancy and childbirth and for the first few weeks after birth, esp. one who is hired to do so. [modern Greek from Greek *doulē* female slave]

doum /daʊm, duːm/ *noun* (in full **doum palm**) a palm tree, *Hyphaene thebaica*, with edible fruit. [Arabic *dawm*, *dūm*]

dour /daʊr, dʊr/ *adjective* severe, stern, or sullenly obstinate in manner or appearance. □ **dour·ly** *adverb* **dour·ness** *noun* [Middle English (originally Scots), prob. from Gaelic *dúr* dull, obstinate, perhaps from Latin *durus* hard]

Douro River /ˈdʊrɔː/ a river of the Iberian peninsula, rising in central Spain and flowing west for 900 km (556 miles) through Portugal to the Atlantic Ocean near Porto. In its valley in Portugal grow the grapes from which port wine is made.

dou·rou·couli /ˌdʊrəˈkuːli/ *noun* (*pl.* **dou·rou·cou·lis**) any nocturnal monkey of the genus *Aotus*, native to S America, having large staring eyes. [Indian name]

douse /daʊs/ *transitive verb* (also **dowse**) **1 a** (often foll. by *with*) drench or wet thoroughly with a liquid. **b** immerse or plunge (a person, thing, etc.) vigorously into water or other liquid. **2 a** extinguish (a light, fire, etc.). **b** suppress (a feeling) or put an end to (an activity). **3** *Naut.* **a** lower (a sail). **b** close (a porthole). [16th c.: perhaps related to Middle Dutch, Low German *dossen* strike]

dout *transitive verb Cdn* (*Nfld*) *dialect* turn off or extinguish (a light, fire, cigarette, etc.). [coalesced form of *do out*]

dove¹ *noun* **1** any bird of the family Columbidae, with short legs, small head, and large breast. **2** a gentle or innocent person. **3 a** *Politics* a person who believes in a policy of negotiation and conciliation rather than warfare or confrontation (compare HAWK¹ 2). **b** a symbol of innocence, harmlessness, or peace. **4** (**Dove**) *Christianity* a representation of the Holy Spirit. **5** a soft grey colour. □ **dove·like** *adjective* **dov·ish** *adjective* [Old Norse *dúfa* from Germanic]

dove² *N Amer.* past and past participle of DIVE.

dove·cote /ˈdʌvkɔːt/ *noun* (also **dove·cot** /-kɒt/) a structure with nesting holes for domesticated pigeons.

dove·kie /ˈdʌvkiː/ *noun N Amer. & Scot.* = LITTLE AUK. [Scots, diminutive of DOVE¹]

Dover¹ a ferry port in Kent, on the coast of the English Channel; pop. (est. 2002) 34,500. It is mainland Britain's nearest point to the Continent, being only 35 km (22 miles) from Calais. **2** the state capital of Delaware; pop. (2000) 32,135.

Dover, Strait of a sea passage between England and France, connecting the English Channel with the North Sea. At its narrowest it is 35 km (22 miles) wide.

Dover sole *noun* **1** a European sole much prized as a food fish. **2** a mottled brown flatfish, *Microstomus pacificus*, of the N Pacific.

dove·tail ● *noun* **1** a joint formed by one or more tenons in the shape of a dove's spread tail, fitting into the mortises of corresponding shape. **2** a tenon or mortise of such a joint. ● *verb* **1** *transitive* join together by means of a dovetail. **2** *transitive & intransitive* (often foll. by *into*, *with*) fit together or become adjusted perfectly, so as to form a compact or harmonious whole.

dow·ager /ˈdaʊədʒɜr/ *noun* **1** a widow with a title or property derived from her late husband (*Queen dowager*; *dowager duchess*). **2** *informal* a dignified elderly woman. [Old French *douag(i)ere* from *douage* (as DOWER)]

dowager's hump *noun* a skeletal deformity, caused by osteoporosis and common in older women, in which the shoulders become rounded and the upper back develops a hump.

dow·dy ● *adjective* (**dow·di·er, dow·di·est**) **1** (of clothes) unfashionable; unattractively dull. **2** (of a person, esp. a woman) frumpy; unattractively dressed. ● *noun* (*pl.* **-ies**) a dowdy woman. □ **dow·di·ly** *adverb* **dow·di·ness** *noun* [Middle English *dowd* slut, of unknown origin]

dowel /ˈdauəl/ ● *noun* a headless peg of wood, metal, or plastic for holding together components of a structure without the peg itself showing. ● *transitive verb* (**dow·elled, dowel·ling**; US **dow·eled, dowel·ing**) fasten with a dowel or dowels. □ **dow·elled** *adjective* [Middle Low German *dovel*: compare THOLE[1]]

Dow·ell /ˈdauəl/ **Sir An·thony** (b.1943) English ballet dancer and ballet director. A principal dancer with the Royal Ballet (1966–86) noted for his elegant style, he created many roles in ballets by Sir Frederick Ashton and Sir Kenneth MacMillan, especially in partnership with Antoinette Sibley. He was artistic director of the Royal Ballet 1986–2001.

dowel·ling *noun* (also **dowel·ing**) cylindrical rods for cutting into dowels.

dower /ˈdauər/ ● *noun* **1** a widow's share for life of her husband's estate. **2** *archaic* a dowry. **3** a natural gift or talent. ● *transitive verb* **1** *archaic* give a dowry to. **2** (foll. by *with*) endow with talent etc. □ **dower·less** *adjective* [Old French *douaire* from medieval Latin *dotarium* from Latin *dos dotis*]

dower house *noun Brit.* a smaller house near a big one, forming part of a widow's dower.

dow·itch·er /ˈdauɪtʃər/ *noun* any N American wading bird of the genus *Limnodromus*, related to sandpipers and having a long, straight bill. [Iroquoian]

Dow Jones Average *noun proprietary* an index of the average level of share prices on the New York Stock Exchange at any time, based on the daily price of a selection of representative stocks. [C. H. *Dow* d.1902 & E. D. *Jones* d.1920, US economists]

Dow·land /ˈdauland/ **John** (c.1562–1626), English lutenist and composer, who wrote lute songs and works for solo lute.

Down one of the Six Counties of Northern Ireland, also an administrative area; chief town, Downpatrick.

down¹ ● *adverb* **1** into or toward a lower place, esp. to the ground (*fall down; knelt down*). **2** in a lower place or position (*blinds were down*). **3 a** to or in a more southerly place (*drove down from Ottawa to Toronto*). **b** *Brit.* away from a major city or university (*down from Oxford*). **4 a** in or into a lower or weaker position or condition (*hit a man when he's down; down with a cold*). **b** in a position of lagging or loss (*our team was down by three; started with $100, but now I'm down $10*). **c** (of a computer system) out of action or unavailable for use (esp. temporarily). **5** from an earlier to a later time (*a tradition that has been handed down; down to 1600*). **6** to a finer or thinner consistency or a smaller amount or size (*grind down; water down; boil down*). **7** cheaper; lower in price or value (*gas is down; shares are down*). **8** into a more settled state (*calm down*). **9** in writing; in or into recorded or listed form (*copy it down; I got it down on tape; you are down to speak next*). **10** (of part of a larger whole) paid; dealt with (*no money down; three down, six to go*). **11** inclusively of the lower limit in a series (*read down to the third paragraph*). **12** (as *interjection*) lie down, put (something) down, etc. **13** (of a crossword clue or answer) read vertically (*cannot go five down*). **14** downstairs, esp. after rising (*is not down yet*). **15** swallowed (*could not get the pill down*). **16** *Football* (of the ball) not in play. **17** *Naut.* **a** with the current or wind. **b** (of a ship's helm) with the rudder to windward. **18** *Cdn* (*Nfld*) heading north along the coast of Newfoundland and Labrador. ● *preposition* **1** downwards along, through, or into. **2** from top to bottom of. **3** along (*walk down the road; cut down the middle*). **4** at or in a lower part of (*situated down the river*). ● *adjective* **1** directed downwards. **2** depressed; in low spirits. **3** *Brit.* of travel away from a capital or centre (*the down train; the down platform*). ● *transitive verb informal* **1** knock, shoot or bring down (*the wrestler downed his opponent; the Americans downed the fighter jet*). **2** defeat (a team, player, etc.) (*the Leafs downed the Canadiens in overtime*). **3** swallow (a drink), esp. quickly. ● *noun* **1** *Football* any of a fixed number of attempts (3 in Canadian football, 4 in American football) to advance the ball a total of 10 yards. **2** an act of putting down (esp. an opponent in wrestling). **3** a reverse of fortune (*ups and downs*). □ **be down on** *informal* disapprove of; show animosity toward. **be down to 1** be attributable to. **2** be the responsibility of. **3** have

used up everything except (*down to their last nickel*). **be down with** *slang* respect, have regard for; be okay with. **down for the count 1** (of a boxer) knocked unconscious. **2** completely defeated. **down in the dumps** depressed; in low spirits. **down on one's luck** *informal* **1** temporarily unfortunate. **2** dispirited by misfortune. **down the road** (or **line**) esp. *N Amer. informal* in the future; later on. **down tools** *informal* cease work, esp. to go on strike. **down to the wire** *informal* right up to the very last minute or the very end. **down with** *interjection* expressing strong disapproval or rejection of a specified person or thing. **when you get** (or **come**) (**right**) **down to it** in the final analysis. [Old English *dūn(e)* from *adūne* downward]

down² *noun* **1 a** small soft feathers that cover and insulate the entire body of a young bird. **b** small soft feathers that lie between and beneath the contour feathers of an adult bird. **c** such feathers, usu. from ducks and geese, used to fill pillows, quilts, etc. **2** fine soft hair esp. on the face. **3** short soft hairs on some leaves, fruit, seeds, etc. **4** a fluffy substance, e.g. thistledown. [Old Norse *dúnn*]

down³ *noun* **1** (usu. in *pl.*) an area of open rolling land. **2** (usu. **the Downs**) undulating chalk and limestone uplands esp. in S England, with few trees and used mainly for pasture. **3** (in *pl.*) *N Amer.* often used in the names of racetracks (*Assiniboia Downs*). □ **downy** *adjective* (in senses 1, 2). [Old English *dūn*, perhaps from Old Celtic]

down-and-dirty *adjective* esp. *N Amer. informal* **1** nasty; unprincipled (*down-and-dirty campaign tactics*). **2** unpretentious; natural (*a down-and-dirty singer*).

down-and-out ● *adjective* **1** penniless; destitute. **2 a** *Boxing* unable to resume the fight. **b** (of a team, business etc.) out of the running; no longer successful. ● *noun* (also **down-and-outer**) a destitute and often homeless person; a vagrant.

down-at-the-heels *adjective* (also **down-at-the-heel, down-at-heel(s)**) **1 a** (of a person) shabby; slovenly. **b** (of a neighbourhood, building, etc.) rundown; dilapidated. **2** (**down-at-heel**) (of shoes) with the heels worn down.

down·beat ● *noun Music* **1** an accented beat, usu. the first of the bar. **2** a downward movement of a conductor's stick or hand indicating such a beat. ● *adjective* pessimistic; gloomy.

down·bound *adjective* heading in a southerly direction (*a downbound train*).

down·cast ● *adjective* **1** (of eyes) looking downwards. **2** (of a person) dejected. ● *noun* a shaft dug in a mine for extra ventilation.

down·court *Basketball* ● *adverb* into or toward the opposite end of the court (*sprinted downcourt*). ● *adjective* directed into or toward the opposite end of the court (*a downcourt pass*).

down·draft *noun* a downward current of air (*a powerful downdraft near the office tower*).

down·er *noun slang* **1** a depressant or tranquilizing drug, esp. a barbiturate. **2 a** a depressing person or experience. **b** a depressed mood or state. **3** an old, diseased, or crippled animal in a shipping load that has fallen and cannot get up under its own power.

down·fall *noun* **1 a** a fall from prosperity or power. **b** the cause of this. **2** a sudden heavy fall of rain, snow, etc.

down·field *adverb* esp. *N Amer.* in or to a position nearer to the opponents' end of a football, soccer, etc. field.

down-filled *adjective* stuffed or insulated with down (*a down-filled sleeping bag*).

down·grade ● *transitive verb* **1** make lower in rank or status (*downgraded the company's credit rating*). **2** speak disparagingly of. ● *noun* **1** an instance of downgrading or being downgraded (in sense 1 of *verb*). **2** esp. *N Amer.* a downward gradient, esp. on a railway or road. ● *adverb* downhill (*the car rolled downgrade*). □ **on the downgrade** *N Amer.* in decline.

down·heart·ed *adjective* dejected; in low spirits. □ **down·heart·ed·ly** *adverb* **down·heart·ed·ness** *noun*

down·hill ● *adverb* /daun'hil/ in a descending direction, esp. toward the bottom of an incline. ● *attributive adjective* /'daunhil/ **1** sloping down; descending. **2** declining; deteriorating. **3 a** designating skiing performed on a mountain or steep slope as distinct from cross-country skiing. **b** of or pertaining to downhill racing (*Canada's downhill champion*). ● *noun* /'daunhil/ *Skiing* a downhill race on a steep track marked by poles set at least 8 m apart, through which the skier has to pass. □ **go downhill** *informal* decline, deteriorate (in health, state of repair, moral state, etc.). □ **down·hill·er** *noun Skiing*.

down·hole ● *adjective* used, occurring, or performed down or in an oil well (*downhole drilling equipment*). ● *adverb* down or in an oil well.

down-home *attributive adjective* esp. *N Amer.* unpretentious; unaffected (*down-home hospitality*).

down in the mouth *adjective informal* unhappy; dejected.

down-island *Cdn* (*BC*) ● *adverb* to or in a more southerly part of Vancouver Island. ● *adjective* directed southwards on Vancouver Island (*a down-island tour*).

down·land *noun Brit.* = DOWN³ 1, 2.

down·light *noun* a light placed or designed to throw illumination downwards.

down·link ● *noun* a communications link for signals coming from a satellite to earth. ● *transitive verb* provide with or send by a downlink.

down·load ● *transitive verb* 1 *Computing* copy or transfer (software or data) from one storage device or computer to another (esp. a smaller remote one). 2 *Cdn* shift or relegate responsibilities or costs for (a program) from one level of government to a lower one (*Queen's Park has downloaded welfare onto the municipalities*). ● *noun* 1 the act or process of copying data in such a way (often *attributive*: *download utilities*). 2 a computer file transferred in such a way (*a popular download from bulletin boards*). □ **down·load·able** *adjective*

down-market *adjective & adverb informal* relating to or directed toward the cheaper or less affluent sector of the market.

down payment *noun* a partial payment made at the time of purchase.

down·pipe *noun Brit.* = DOWNSPOUT.

down·play *transitive verb* play down; minimize the importance of.

down·pour *noun* a heavy fall of rain.

down·range *adverb & adjective* 1 away from a shooter and toward the intended target. 2 *Aviation* away from the launching pad and along the flight path of a missile, rocket, etc.

down·rate *transitive verb* make lower in value, standard, importance, etc.; downgrade.

down·rig·ger *noun* a trolling rig consisting of a cable attached underneath a boat to a fishing line, used to troll live bait at or near the bottom of a body of water.

down·right ● *adverb* thoroughly; completely; positively (*downright rude*). ● *adjective* 1 utter; complete (*a downright lie; downright nonsense*). 2 (of a person's speech or behaviour) straightforward; blunt.

down·river ● *adverb* at or toward a point nearer the mouth of a river. ● *adjective* situated or occurring downriver.

down·scale *N Amer.* ● *adjective* at the lower end of a scale, esp. a social or economic scale (*a downscale neighbourhood*). ● *transitive verb* reduce or restrict in size, scale, or extent.

down·shift ● *intransitive verb* 1 change to a lower gear in a motor vehicle or bicycle. 2 slow down; become less busy (*business is downshifting because of the recession*). 3 change a financially rewarding but stressful career or lifestyle for a less pressured and less highly paid but more fulfilling one (*they want to downshift from full-time work*). ● *noun* an act or instance of downshifting.

down·side *noun* 1 the negative aspect of something; a disadvantage or drawback. 2 a downward movement of share prices etc. (also *attributive*: *downside risk*).

down·size *transitive & intransitive verb* 1 esp. *N Amer.* reduce in size (*downsize the deficit*). 2 esp. *N Amer.* (often euphemistic) lay off or fire (workers). 3 *Computing* replace (a mainframe or minicomputer) by a network of microcomputers. □ **down·siz·ing** *noun*

down·slope ● *adverb* at or toward a lower point on a slope. ● *adjective* caused by, occurring, or acting on a downward slope; descending (*downslope winds*). ● *noun* a downward slope.

down·spout *noun N Amer.* a pipe to carry rainwater from an eavestrough to a drain or to ground level.

Down's syndrome *noun* (also **Down syndrome**) a congenital form of mental retardation due to a chromosome defect, in which the affected individual has a flattened facial profile, weak muscles, etc. [J. L. H. *Down*, English physician d.1896]

down·stage *adjective & adverb* at or to the front of the stage.

down·stairs ● *adverb* 1 down a flight of stairs. 2 to or on a lower floor. ● *adjective* situated downstairs. ● *noun* the main floor or basement of a house etc.

down·state *US* ● *adjective* of, pertaining to, or characteristic of the southern part of a state. ● *noun* a downstate area. ● *adverb* in or to a downstate area. □ **down·stat·er** *noun*

down·stream ● *adverb* in the direction of the flow of a stream, river, etc. ● *adjective* 1 situated or occurring downstream. 2 (in the oil

industry) pertaining to, involved in, or designating activities other than exploration and extraction.

down street *adverb N Amer. dialect* down the street; to or into the central part of a town or city; downtown.

down·stroke *noun* a downward stroke, esp. of a machine part or a pen on paper.

down·swing *noun* 1 a downward trend, esp. in economic conditions. 2 the downward movement of a golf club, baseball bat, etc. when a player is about to hit the ball.

down timber *noun N Amer. Forestry* timber from fallen trees brought down by wind, storm, or other natural causes.

down·time *noun* 1 time during which a machine, esp. a computer, is unavailable for use, usu. as a result of malfunction or regular preventive maintenance. 2 time not spent working; rest, leisure or recovery time.

down-to-earth *adjective* practical; realistic.

down·town *N Amer.* ● *adjective* being or located in the central part of a town or city, esp. the business district (*downtown Victoria; a downtown hotel*). ● *noun* a downtown area. ● *adverb* in or into a downtown area. □ **down·town·er** *noun*

down·trend *noun* a downward or declining trend, esp. in economic or business matters.

down·trod·den *adjective* oppressed; badly treated; kept under.

down·turn *noun* a decline, esp. in economic or business activity.

down under (also **Down Under**) *informal* ● *adverb* in or to Australia or New Zealand. ● *noun* Australia or New Zealand.

down·ward ● *adverb* (also **down·wards**) 1 toward a lower place or position. 2 toward something which is lower in order, inferior, or less important. 3 onward from an earlier to a later time. ● *adjective* directed, moving, extending, pointing, or leading downward. □ **down·ward·ly** *adverb*

down·warp /ˈdaunwɔrp/ *noun Geol.* a broad surface depression; a syncline.

down·wash *noun Aviation* the downward deflection of an airstream by a helicopter rotor etc.

down·wind ● *adverb* in the direction toward which the wind is blowing. ● *adjective* occurring or situated downwind.

downy *adjective* (**down·i·er, down·i·est**) 1 of, like, or covered with down. 2 soft and fluffy. □ **down·i·ness** *noun*

downy mildew *noun* 1 a fungus of the family Peronosporaceae. 2 a plant disease caused by this fungus, characterized by fuzzy whitish patches of spores on the undersurface of the leaves.

downy woodpecker *noun* a small black and white N American woodpecker, *Picoides pubescens*.

down·zone *transitive verb N Amer.* assign (property) a lower zoning designation in order to reduce high-density development.

dowry /ˈdauri/ *noun* (*pl.* **-ries**) property or money brought by a bride to her husband at marriage. [Anglo-French *dowarie* DOWER]

dowse¹ /dauz/ *intransitive verb* search for underground water or minerals by holding a Y-shaped stick or rod which dips abruptly when over the right spot. □ **dows·er** *noun* **dows·ing** *noun* [17th c.: origin unknown]

dowse² *var. of* DOUSE.

dowsing rod *noun* a stick or rod used in dowsing.

dox·ol·ogy /dɒkˈsɒlədʒi/ *noun* (*pl.* **-gies**) a liturgical formula of praise to God. [medieval Latin *doxologia* from Greek *doxologia* from *doxa* glory + -LOGY]

doxo·rubi·cin /ˌdɒksəˈruːbəsɪn/ *noun* an antibiotic drug used to treat leukemia and other cancers. [d(e)ox(y) + -o- + Latin *rubus* red + -i- + -(MY)CIN]

doxy /ˈdɒksi/ *noun* (*pl.* **-ies**) *slang* 1 a lover or mistress. 2 a prostitute. [16th-c. cant: origin unknown]

doxy·cy·cline /ˌdɒksiˈsaɪkliːn, -klɪn/ *noun* a broad spectrum antibiotic of the tetracycline group used to treat some infections. [d(e)ox(y) + (TETRA)CYCLINE]

doy·en /ˈdɔɪən, dɔɪˈen, ˈdwɒnjɑ̃/ *noun* the most senior or most prominent male member of a particular category or body of people. [French (as DEAN)]

doy·enne /dɔɪˈen, dwɒˈjen/ *noun* the most senior or most prominent female member of a particular category or body of people.

Doyle /dɔɪl/ **Sir Ar·thur Conan** (1859–1930), Scottish novelist. He is chiefly remembered as the creator of the detective Sherlock Holmes, who appeared in collections such as *The Adventures of Sherlock Holmes* (1892) and *The Hound of the Baskervilles* (1902).

---

t top   v voice   w we   z zoo   ʃ she   ʒ vision   θ thin   ð this   ŋ ring   x loch   tʃ chip   dʒ jar   (see over for vowels)

D'Oyly Carte /ˌdɔili ˈkɑːt/ **Rich·ard** (1844–1901), English impresario and producer. He commissioned and produced the first operettas of Gilbert and Sullivan for his Savoy Theatre in London.

doz. *abbreviation* dozen.

doze ● *intransitive verb* sleep lightly; be half asleep. ● *noun* a short light sleep. □ **doze off** fall lightly asleep. [17th c.: compare Danish *døse* make drowsy]

dozen *noun* 1 (prec. by *a* or a number) (*pl.* **dozen**) twelve, regarded collectively (*a dozen eggs; ordered three dozen*). 2 a set or group of twelve (*packed in dozens*). 3 *informal* about twelve; a fairly large indefinite number (*several dozen people attended the meeting*). 4 (in *pl.*; usu. foll. by *of*) *informal* very many (*made dozens of mistakes*). 5 (**the dozens**) a Black American game or ritualized exchange of verbal insults. □ **by the dozen** in large quantities. **nineteen to the dozen** *Brit.* incessantly (*talked nineteen to the dozen*). □ **doz·enth** *adjective* [Old French *dozeine*, ultimately from Latin *duodecim* twelve]

doz·er *noun informal* = BULLDOZER. [abbreviation]

dozy *adjective* (**doz·i·er**, **doz·i·est**) 1 drowsy; tending to doze. 2 *Brit.* & *Cdn informal* slow-witted or lazy. □ **doz·i·ly** *adverb* **doz·i·ness** *noun*

DP *abbreviation* 1 DATA PROCESSING. 2 *hist.* DISPLACED PERSON. 3 *Baseball* double play.

D.Phil. *abbreviation* Doctor of Philosophy.

dpi *abbreviation Computing* dots per inch.

DPT *abbreviation* diphtheria, pertussis, tetanus.

Dr. *abbreviation* 1 Doctor. 2 Drive.

dr. *abbreviation* 1 drachm(s). 2 drachma(s). 3 dram(s).

drab[1] ● *adjective* (**drab·ber**, **drab·best**) 1 of a dull brownish colour. 2 lacking brightness or colour; dreary (*drab surroundings*). 3 dull; uninteresting (*a drab novel*). ● *noun* drab colour. □ **drab·ly** *adverb* **drab·ness** *noun* [prob. from obsolete *drap* cloth, from Old French from Late Latin *drappus*, perhaps of Celtic origin]

drab[2] *noun* 1 a dirty untidy woman; a slattern. 2 *archaic* a prostitute. [perhaps related to Low German *drabbe* mire, Dutch *drab* dregs]

Drab·ble /ˈdrabəl/ **Mar·ga·ret** (b.1939), English novelist and editor. Her novels include *The Ice Age* (1977), *The Radiant Way* (1987), and *The Gates of Ivory* (1992), and she has edited *The Oxford Companion to English Literature* (1985); she is the younger sister of novelist A.S. Byatt.

drab·ble *transitive & intransitive verb* become or make dirty and wet with water or mud. [Low German *drabbelen* paddle in water or mire]

dra·caena /drəˈsiːnə/ *noun* any of various shrubs and trees of the genera *Dracaena* and *Cordyline* (agave family) grown for their foliage. [modern Latin from Greek *drakaina*, fem. of *drakōn* 'dragon']

drachm /dram/ *noun Brit.* 1 a weight or measure formerly used by apothecaries, equivalent to 60 grains or one eighth of an ounce (3.89 grams), or (in full **fluid drachm**) 60 minims, one eighth of a fluid ounce. 2 = DRACHMA 2. [Latin *drachma* from Greek *drakhmē* Attic weight and coin]

drach·ma /ˈdrakmə/ *noun* (*pl.* **drach·mas** or **drach·mae** /-miː/) 1 the former chief monetary unit of Greece, now replaced by the euro. 2 a silver coin of ancient Greece. [Latin from Greek *drakhmē*]

Draco[1] /ˈdreikɔː/ (7th c. BC), Athenian legislator, whose codification of Athenian law was notorious for its severity, with nearly all offences punishable by death.

Draco[2] /ˈdreikɔː/ an extensive but rather faint constellation stretching partway around the north celestial pole. [Latin *dracō* snake]

dra·co·nian /drəˈkoːniən, drɔ-/ *adjective* (also **dra·con·ic** /-ˈkɒnɪk/) very harsh or severe (esp. of laws and their application). □ **dra·co·nian·ism** *noun* [DRACO[1]]

drae·ger·man /ˈdreigərmən/ *noun* (*pl.* **-men**) *N Amer.* a member of a crew trained for underground rescue work. [A.B. *Dräger*, German scientist d.1928]

draft ● *noun* 1 a a preliminary written version of a speech, document, book, etc. (also *attributive*: *draft proposal; draft statement*). b a sketch or drawing of something to be constructed. 2 a current of air in a confined space, e.g. a room or chimney. 3 *N Amer.* a system of selection by which sports teams acquire the rights to esp. unsigned players (also *attributive*: *draft pick*). 4 esp. *US* compulsory military service. 5 = DRAFT BEER. 6 a a single act of drinking (*finished the beer in one draft*). b the amount drunk in this. c a dose of liquid medicine. 7 a a written order for payment of money by a bank. b the drawing of money by means of this. 8 *Naut.* the depth of water needed to float a ship. 9 an act or the action of pulling something along, esp. a vehicle or farm implement; traction. 10 a the drawing in of a fishing net. b the fish taken at one drawing. c *Cdn* (*Nfld*) a measure of dried cod equalling two quintals

(101.6 kg). ● *transitive verb* 1 prepare a draft of (a speech, document, etc.). 2 (usu. in *passive*) a *N Amer.* acquire the rights to esp. unsigned sports players. b esp. *US* conscript for military service. 3 select for any special duty or purpose. ● *adjective* (of an animal) used for pulling a cart, plow, etc. (*a team of draft horses*). □ **on draft** (of beer etc.) ready to be drawn from a keg; not bottled or canned. □ **draft·able** *adjective* **draft·ee** *noun* (in senses 3 and 4 of *noun*). **draft·er** *noun* (in senses 1 and 4 of *noun*). **draft·ing** *noun* [phonetic spelling of DRAUGHT]

draft beer *noun* (also esp. *Brit.* **draught beer**) beer drawn from a keg, not bottled or canned.

draft board *noun US* a board of civilians responsible for the selection of personnel for compulsory military service.

draft card *noun US* a card summoning a person to serve in the armed forces.

draft dodger *noun* a person who illegally evades compulsory military service, esp. in the US. □ **draft dodging** *noun*

draft·ing table *noun* a table with an adjustable sloped surface, used by draftsmen, artists, etc.

drafts·man *noun* (also esp. *Brit.* **draughts·man**) (*pl.* **-men**) 1 a person who makes drawings, plans, or sketches. 2 a person who drafts documents, esp. legal or parliamentary ones. □ **drafts·man·ship** *noun*

drafty *adjective* (also esp. *Brit.* **draughty**) (**draft·i·er**, **draft·i·est**) (of a room etc.) letting in sharp currents of air. □ **draft·i·ly** *adverb* **draft·i·ness** *noun*

drag ● *verb* (**dragged**, **drag·ging**) 1 *transitive* pull along with effort or difficulty. 2 a *transitive* allow (one's feet etc.) to trail along the ground. b *intransitive* trail along the ground (*your coat is dragging in the mud*). c *intransitive* (of time etc.) go or pass slowly or tediously. 3 a *intransitive* (usu. foll. by *for*) use grapnels, nets or drags (to find a drowned person or lost object). b *transitive* search the bottom of (a river etc.) with grapnels, nets, or drags. 4 *transitive informal* persuade (a person) to come or go somewhere unwillingly (*tried to drag him away from the office early*). 5 *intransitive* (often foll. by *on*) continue at tedious length. 6 *transitive Computing* move (a window, icon, etc.) from one place to another on a screen, esp. by using a mouse. 7 *intransitive* (foll. by *on, at*) draw on (a cigarette etc.). 8 *transitive* break up the surface of (land) with a drag or heavy harrow. ● *noun* 1 *Physics* the force resisting the motion of a body through a liquid or gas. 2 *informal* a boring or dreary person, duty, performance, etc. 3 *slang* clothes usually worn by the opposite sex (*went to the party in drag*). 4 *slang* a draw on a cigarette etc. 5 *N Amer. slang* a street or road (*the main drag*). 6 *N Amer. slang* influence, pull. 7 an obstruction to progress (*his family has been a drag on his career*). 8 an apparatus for dredging or recovering drowned persons etc. from under water. 9 any of several instruments, such as a harrow, with prongs or claws. 10 = DRAGNET. 11 an act of dragging. 12 slow motion; impeded progress. □ **drag anchor** (of a ship) move from a moored position when the anchor fails to hold. **drag one's feet** (or **heels**) be deliberately slow or reluctant to act. **drag in** introduce (a subject) irrelevantly. **drag out** protract. **drag up** *informal* deliberately mention (an unwelcome subject). [Old English *dragan* or Old Norse *draga* DRAW]

drag and drop *noun* a software technique for moving objects on the screen using a mouse.

drag bunt *noun Baseball* a bunt, usu. by a left-handed batter, that is hit down the first baseline.

drag coefficient *noun Physics* the ratio of the drag on an object moving through air to the product of the velocity and surface area of the object.

dra·gée /ˈdraʒei/ *noun* 1 a sugar-coated almond, candy, etc. 2 a small silver ball for decorating a cake. [French: see DREDGE[2]]

drag end *noun Cdn* (*West*) the end of a moving herd of cattle etc.

drag·ger *noun N Amer.* a fishing boat equipped with dragnets; a trawler. □ **dragger·man** *noun*

drag·gle /ˈdragəl/ *verb* 1 *transitive* make dirty or wet or limp by trailing. 2 *intransitive* hang trailing. 3 *intransitive* lag; straggle in the rear. [DRAG + -LE[4]]

draggy *adjective* (**drag·gi·er**, **drag·gi·est**) *informal* 1 sluggish; lacking liveliness. 2 tedious; boring.

drag·line *noun* a mechanical excavator with a bucket pulled in by a cable.

drag·net *noun* 1 a net drawn through water or across ground to trap fish or game. 2 a systematic hunt for criminals etc.

drago·man /ˈdragəmən/ *noun* (*pl.* **drago·mans** or **drago·men**) *hist.* an interpreter or guide, esp. in countries speaking Arabic, Turkish, or Persian. [French from Italian *dragomano* from medieval Greek *dragomanos* from Arabic *tarjumān* from *tarjama* interpret, from Aramaic *targēm* from Assyrian *targumânu* interpreter]

drag·on *noun* **1** a mythical monster like a reptile, usu. with wings and claws and able to breathe out fire. **2** a fierce person, esp. a woman. **3** (in full **flying dragon**) a lizard, *Draco volans*, with a long tail and membranous wing-like structures. *Also called* FLYING LIZARD. **4** an esp. newly industrialized Asian country with a powerful economy. □ **chase the dragon** *slang* take heroin by inhalation. [Old French from Latin *draco -onis* from Greek *drakōn* serpent]

dragon boat *noun* a long wooden boat with a carved dragon's head on its prow and dragon's tail at its stern, propelled by a crew of 22 paddlers and used in races.

drag·on·et /ˈdragənət/ *noun* any marine spiny fish of the family Callionymidae, the males of which are brightly coloured. [French, diminutive of DRAGON]

dragon·fly *noun* (pl. **-flies**) any of various insects of the order Odonata, having a long slender body and two unequal pairs of large transparent wings usu. spread while resting.

dragon lady *noun* a ruthless and domineering woman.

dragon mouth *noun* an orchid of wet places of N America east of the Rockies, *Arethusa bulbosa*, with a showy pink flower.

dragon's blood *noun* any of various red plant resins obtained from the fruit of some palms and the dragon tree, used as a colouring in varnishes.

dragon tree *noun* a large tree, *Dracaena draco*, native to the Canary Islands, often grown as a houseplant.

drag·oon /drəˈguːn/ ● *noun* **1** hist. a mounted infantryman armed with a carbine. **2** (often **Dragoon**) a member of any of several cavalry (now armoured) regiments (*Royal Canadian Dragoons*). ● *transitive verb* **1** (foll. by *into*) coerce into doing something, esp. by use of strong force. **2** persecute, esp. with troops. [originally = carbine (thought of as breathing fire), from French *dragon* DRAGON]

drag queen *noun* *slang* a man who ostentatiously dresses in women's clothing.

drag race *noun* an acceleration race between cars starting from a standstill. □ **drag racer** *noun* **drag racing** *noun*

drag·ster *noun* a car built or modified to take part in drag races.

drag strip *noun* *N Amer.* a straight stretch of road built or used for drag races.

drail /dreɪl/ *noun* a weighted fish hook for dragging below the surface of the water. [apparently var. of TRAIL]

drain ● *verb* **1** *transitive* draw off liquid from, esp.: **a** make (land etc.) dry by providing an outflow for moisture. **b** (of a river) carry off the superfluous water of (a district). **c** remove purulent matter from (an abscess). **2** *transitive* **a** draw off (liquid) esp. by a pipe (*drain the sink*). **b** remove liquid from (*drain the vegetables*). **3** *intransitive* (often foll. by *away*, *off*, *through*) flow or trickle away. **4** *intransitive* (of dishes, cutlery, etc.) become dry as liquid flows away (*put it there to drain*). **5** *transitive* (often foll. by *of*) exhaust or deprive (a person or thing) of strength, resources, property, etc. **6** *intransitive* gradually disappear or fade (*all hope has drained away*). **7** *transitive* **a** drink (liquid) to the dregs. **b** empty (a glass etc.) by drinking the contents. ● *noun* **1 a** a channel, conduit, or pipe carrying off liquid, esp. an artificial conduit for water or sewage. **b** a tube for drawing off the discharge from an abscess etc. **2** a constant outflow, withdrawal, or expenditure (*a great drain on my resources*). □ **down the drain** *informal* lost, wasted. [Old English *drē(a)hnian* from Germanic]

drain·age *noun* **1** the process or means of draining (*the land has poor drainage*). **2** a system of drains, artificial or natural. **3** what is drained off, esp. sewage.

drainage basin *noun* the area of land drained by a river and its tributaries.

drain·board *noun* *N Amer.* a sloping usu. grooved surface beside a sink, on which washed dishes etc. are left to drain.

drain·er *noun* a device for draining; anything on which things are put to drain.

drain·ing board *noun* = DRAINBOARD.

drain·pipe *noun* a pipe for carrying off water, sewage, etc., from a building.

Draize test /dreɪz/ *noun* a test in which drugs, cosmetics, or other commercial products are injected into a rabbit's eye or applied to a bare patch of skin to determine their potential irritancy to human skin and membranes. [J.H. *Draize*, American pharmacologist d.1992]

Drake, Sir Fran·cis (*c.*1540–96), English sailor and explorer. He was the first Englishman to circumnavigate the globe (1577–80), and as vice

admiral he played an important part in the defeat of the Spanish Armada (1588).

drake *noun* a male duck. [Middle English prob. from Germanic]

Drak·ens·berg Mountains /ˈdrɒkənz,bɜrg/ a range of mountains in southern Africa, stretching northeast to southwest for 1 126 km (700 miles) through Lesotho and the South African provinces of KwaZulu-Natal, Free State, Mpumalanga, and Limpopo. The highest peak is Thabana Ntlenyana (3 482 m, 11,425 ft.).

Drake Passage an area of ocean connecting the S Atlantic with the S Pacific and separating the southern tip of S America (Cape Horn) from the Antarctic Peninsula. [Sir F. DRAKE]

DRAM *abbreviation Computing* dynamic random access memory, a memory chip that depends upon an applied voltage to keep the stored data.

dram[1] *noun* **1** a small drink of spirits. **2** = DRACHM 1. **3** one-sixteenth of an ounce in avoirdupois weight (27.34 grains; 1.77 grams). [Old French *drame* or medieval Latin *drama*, *dragma*: compare DRACHM]

dram[2] *noun* the basic monetary unit of Armenia, equal to 100 luma. [Armenian, lit. = 'coin, money' from Greek *drakhmē* DRACHMA]

drama /ˈdramə, ˈdrɒmə/ *noun* **1** a play for acting on stage or for broadcasting. **2 a** plays as a branch of literature and as a performing art (*a masterpiece of Elizabethan drama*). **b** the art of acting. **3** an exciting or emotional event, set of circumstances, etc. **4** dramatic quality (*the drama of the situation*). [Late Latin from Greek *drama -atos* from *draō* do]

dra·mat·ic /drəˈmatɪk/ *adjective* **1 a** of drama or the study of drama. **b** of acting. **2** (of an event, circumstance, etc.) sudden and exciting or unexpected. **3** vividly striking. **4** (of a gesture etc.) theatrical; overdone; absurd. □ **dra·mat·ic·al·ly** *adverb*

dramatic irony *noun* a device used in drama by which the audience understands the implications of words or actions better than the characters do themselves.

dramatic monologue *noun* a type of poem in which a single character speaks to an implied audience of one or more persons, revealing his or her personality in the process.

dra·mat·ics *plural noun* (often treated as *sing.*) **1** the production and performance of plays. **2** exaggerated or showy behaviour.

dram·atis per·so·nae /ˌdramətɪs pərˈsoːnaɪ, -niː/ *plural noun* (often treated as *sing.*) **1** the characters in a literary work, esp. a play. **2** a list of these. [Latin, = persons of the drama]

drama·tist /ˈdramətɪst/ *noun* a person who writes dramas; a playwright.

drama·tize /ˈdramə,taɪz/ *verb* (also esp. *Brit.* **-tise**) **1** *transitive* adapt (a novel, incident, etc.) to form a dramatic work, esp. a play or film. **2** *transitive & intransitive* express or react to (something) in a dramatic way (*called a press conference to dramatize the issue*). □ **drama·tiz·a·tion** *noun*

drama·turge /ˈdramə,tɜrdʒ/ *noun* (also **drama·turg** /ˈdramətɜrg/) a consultant to a theatre company whose duties may involve the development of new works through script editing etc., historical research to assist in the mounting of older works, advising the artistic director on repertoire, etc. [French or German from Greek *dramatourgos* (as DRAMA, *-ergos* worker)]

drama·turgy /ˈdramə,tɜrdʒi/ *noun* **1** the art of theatrical production; the theory of dramatics. **2** the application of this. □ **drama·tur·gic·al** /-ˈtɜrdʒɪkəl/ *adjective* **drama·tur·gic·al·ly** *adverb*

Dram·buie /dramˈbuːi/ *noun proprietary* a sweet Scotch whisky liqueur. [Scottish Gaelic *dram buidheach* satisfying drink]

dram·edy /ˈdramədi/ *noun slang* (pl. **-ies**) a movie or television program which has both dramatic and comedic elements.

drank *past of* DRINK.

drape ● *transitive verb* **1** hang, cover loosely, or adorn with cloth etc. **2** arrange (clothes or hangings) carefully in folds. **3** place or hang loosely or casually (*draped her arms around his neck*). ● *noun* **1** esp. *N Amer.* (often in *pl.*) a curtain or drapery. **2** a piece of drapery. **3** the way in which a garment or fabric hangs. [Old French *draper* from *drap* from Late Latin *drappus* cloth]

Dra·peau /draˈpoː/ **Jean** (1916–99), Canadian lawyer and politician, mayor of Montreal 1954–7 and 1960–86. During his tenure as mayor he was responsible for the construction of the Place des Arts concert hall, for conceiving Expo 67, and for securing the Olympics in 1976.

Drap·er /ˈdreɪpɜr/ **1 Henry** (1837–82), US astronomer, who made the first photographs of a stellar spectrum (Vega, 1872) and a nebula (Orion nebula, 1880). **2 Wil·liam Henry** (1801–77), English-born Canadian politician and jurist. He supported Sir Charles Metcalfe against the LaFontaine-Baldwin ministry which had claimed the right to control political appointments as an essential tenet of responsible government, and became chief justice of Canada West (1863–7) and of Ontario (1867–9).

drap·er *noun Brit.* a retailer of textile fabrics.

drap·ery *noun (pl.* **-ies)** **1** clothing or hangings arranged in folds. **2** (often in *pl.*) a curtain or hanging. **3** the arrangement of clothing in sculpture or painting. **4** *Brit.* cloth; textile fabrics. **5** *Brit.* the trade or store of a draper. [Old French *draperie* from *drap* cloth]

dras·tic *adjective* having a strong or far-reaching effect; severe. □ **dras·tic·al·ly** *adverb* [Greek *drastikos* from *draō* do]

drat *informal* ● *transitive verb* (**drat·ted, drat·ting**) (usu. as an exclamation) curse, confound (*drat the thing!*). ● *interjection* expressing anger or annoyance. □ **drat·ted** *adjective* [for *'od* (= God) *rot*]

draught /draft/ *noun* **1** esp. *Brit.* var. of DRAFT 2, 6, 8, 9, 10. **2** (in *pl.*; treated as *sing.*) *Brit.* the game of checkers. [Middle English *draht*, perhaps from Old Norse *drahtr*, *dráttr* from Germanic, related to DRAW]

draught beer *noun* esp. *Brit.* var. of DRAFT BEER.

draught·board /'draftbɔrd/ *noun Brit.* = CHECKERBOARD.

draught horse *noun* esp. *Brit.* a draft horse.

draughts·man /'draftsmən/ *noun (pl.* **-men)** **1** esp. *Brit.* var. of DRAFTSMAN. **2** *Brit.* = CHECKER[2] 2b.

draughty /'drafti/ esp. *Brit.* var. of DRAFTY.

Dra·vid·i·an /drə'vɪdiːən/ ● *noun* **1** a member of a dark-skinned aboriginal people of S India and Sri Lanka (including the Tamils and Kanarese). **2** any of the group of languages spoken by this people. ● *adjective* of or relating to this people or group of languages. [Sanskrit *Dravida*, a province of S India]

draw ● *verb (past* **drew**; *past participle* **drawn**) **1** *transitive* pull or cause to move toward or after one. **2** *transitive* pull (a thing) up, over, or across. **3** *transitive* pull (curtains etc.) open or shut. **4** *transitive* take (a person) aside, esp. to talk to. **5** *transitive* attract; bring to oneself or to something; take in (*drew a deep breath; I felt drawn to her; drew my attention to the matter; draw him into conversation; the game drew large crowds*). **6** *transitive* trace (a line, mark, or figure). **7 a** *transitive* produce (a picture) by tracing lines and marks. **b** *transitive* represent (a thing) by this means. **c** *intransitive* make a drawing. **8** *transitive* frame (a document) in due form; compose (*drew up a new will*). **9** *intransitive* make one's or its way, proceed, move, come (*drew near the bridge; draw to a close; the time draws near*). **10** *intransitive* (foll. by *at, on*) inhale smoke from (a cigarette, pipe, etc.). **11** *transitive* take out; remove (a gun from a holster, etc.) **12** *transitive* obtain or take from a source (*draw a salary; draw inspiration; drew $100 from my account*). **13** *transitive & intransitive* finish (a contest or game) with neither side winning. **14** *transitive* infer, deduce (a conclusion). **15** *transitive* **a** elicit, evoke. **b** bring about, entail (*draw criticism; drew a high-sticking penalty*). **c** induce (a person) to reveal facts, feelings, or talent (*refused to be drawn*). **d** (foll. by *to* + infin.) induce (a person) to do something. **e** *Cards* cause to be played (*drew all the trumps*). **16** *transitive* haul up (water) from a well. **17** *transitive* cause (blood) to flow from an incision. **18** *transitive* obtain (beer etc.) from a keg. **19** *transitive* extract a liquid essence from. **20** *intransitive* (of a chimney or pipe) promote or allow a draft. **21** *intransitive* (of tea) infuse. **22 a** *transitive* obtain by lot (*drew the winner*). **b** *intransitive* draw lots. **23** *intransitive* (foll. by *on*) make a demand on a person, a person's skill, memory, imagination, etc. **24** *transitive* write out (a bill, cheque, or draft) (*drew a cheque on the bank*). **25** *transitive* formulate or perceive (a comparison or distinction). **26** *transitive* (of a ship) require (a specified depth of water) to float in. **27** *transitive* disembowel (*hang, draw, and quarter; draw the turkey before cooking it*). **28** *transitive Hunting* search (cover) for game. **29** *transitive* make (wire) by pulling a piece of metal through successively smaller holes. **30** *transitive* **a** *Golf* drive (the ball) to the left (or, of a left-handed player, the right) esp. purposely. **b** *Curling* slide (a rock) so that it stops in the house without striking another rock. **31** *intransitive* (of a sail) swell tightly in the wind. ● *noun* **1** an act of drawing. **2 a** a person or thing that draws customers, attention, etc. **b** the power to attract attention. **3** the drawing of lots, esp. a raffle or lottery. **4** a drawn game; a tie. **5** a suck on a cigarette etc. **6** the act of removing a gun from its holster in order to shoot. **7** *Football* (in full **draw play**) a play in which the quarterback hands the ball off to a running back who is running toward the line of scrimmage. **8** *Curling* a shot in which the rock stops within the target area without striking another rock. **9** *N Amer.* (*West*) a shallow valley; ravine. **10** *N Amer.* the movable part of a drawbridge. □ **draw back** withdraw from an undertaking. **draw a bead on** see BEAD. **draw a blank** see BLANK. **draw fire** (also **draw heat**) attract hostility, criticism, etc. **draw in 1 a** (of successive days) become shorter because of the changing seasons. **b** (of a day) approach its end. **c** (of successive evenings or nights) start earlier because of the changing seasons. **2** persuade to

join, entice (*was drawn into their circle*). **3** (of a train, bus, etc.) arrive at a station. **draw in one's horns** see HORN. **draw the line** set a limit (of tolerance etc.). **draw lots** see LOT. **draw off 1** drain away (liquid). **2** withdraw (troops). **draw on 1** utilize (*drew on her expertise*). **2** approach, come near. **3** put (gloves, boots, etc.) on. **draw out 1** remove; pull out (*drew out a gun*). **2** prolong. **3** elicit. **4** induce to talk. **5** (of successive days) become longer because of the changing seasons. **6** (of a train, bus, etc.) leave a station etc. **draw up 1** compose or draft (a document etc.). **2** (of troops etc.) bring or come into regular order. **3** (of a vehicle) come to a halt. **4** make (oneself) stand straight. **5** (foll. by *with, to*) gain on or overtake. **quick on the draw** quick to act or react. [Old English *dragan* from Germanic]

draw·back *noun* **1** a thing that impairs satisfaction; a disadvantage. **2** an amount of excise or import duty paid back or remitted on goods exported.

draw·bar *noun* **1** a heavy metal bar on the rear of a locomotive, tractor, etc. used as a hitch to pull railway cars, machinery, etc. **2** any of a number of bars on an electric organ that may be pulled out to control harmonics.

draw·bridge *noun* a bridge, esp. over water, hinged at one end so that it may be raised to prevent passage or to allow ships etc. to pass.

draw·cord *noun* a cord on clothing etc. that can be drawn tight.

draw·down *noun* **1** a lowering of the water level in a lake, pond, etc. **2** a withdrawal of oil from a reservoir. **3** an act of raising money through loans; borrowing. **4** a reduction or withdrawal, esp. of military troops.

draw·ee /drɔ'iː/ *noun* the person or financial institution on whom a cheque or bill is drawn.

draw·er /drɔr/ *noun* **1** a boxlike storage compartment without a lid, sliding in and out of a frame, table, etc. (*chest of drawers*). **2** (in *pl.*) **a** *hist.* or *jocular* underpants. **b** *slang* pants or trousers (*pull up your drawers!*). **3** /'drɔ·ər/ a person or thing that draws, esp.: **a** a person who draws a cheque etc. **b** a person who draws pictures. □ **drawer·ful** *noun (pl.* **-fuls)**.

draw·ing *noun* **1 a** the art of representing objects by line, using pencil, pen, etc., rather than paint. **b** a picture produced in this way. **2** a sketch, diagram, or representation.

drawing board *noun* a board on which paper is placed for drawing plans etc. □ **back to the drawing board** back to begin afresh (after the failure of an enterprise).

drawing card *noun N Amer.* a performer, show, attraction, etc. that draws a large audience.

drawing pin *noun Brit.* = THUMBTACK.

drawing power *noun N Amer.* the ability to attract customers, attention, etc. (*a movie star with tremendous drawing power*).

drawing-room *noun* **1** a room, esp. in a large private house, in which people relax and guests are received and entertained. **2** (*attributive*) restrained; observing social proprieties (*drawing-room conversation*). **3** *US* a private compartment in a train. **4** *hist.* a levee, a formal reception esp. at court. [earlier *withdrawing-room*, because originally used for women to withdraw to after dinner]

draw·knife *noun* a knife with a handle at each end at right angles to the blade, drawn toward the user to remove wood from a surface.

drawl /drɔl/ ● *verb* **1** *intransitive* speak with drawn-out vowel sounds. **2** *transitive* utter in this way. ● *noun* a drawling utterance or way of speaking. □ **drawl·er** *noun* [16th c.: prob. originally cant, from Low German, Dutch *dralen* delay, linger]

drawn ● *verb past participle of* DRAW. ● *adjective* **1** looking strained from fear, anxiety, or pain. **2** (of butter) melted. **3** (of a position in chess etc.) that will result in a draw if both players make the best moves available.

drawn-out *adjective* = LONG-DRAWN-OUT.

drawn·work *noun* (also **drawn threadwork**) ornamental work on linen etc., done by drawing out threads, usu. with additional needlework.

draw play *noun* see DRAW *noun* 7.

draw·string *noun* a string that can be pulled to tighten the mouth of a bag, the waist of a garment, etc.

dray *noun* **1** a low cart without sides used esp. formerly by brewers for carrying heavy loads. **2** *Austral. & NZ* a two-wheeled cart. [Old English *dræge* dragnet, *dragan* DRAW]

dray horse *noun* a large, powerful horse used for pulling a dray.

dray man *noun* the driver of a dray, esp. a brewer's driver.

Dray·ton Valley /'dreitən/ a town in central Alberta, about 135 km

---

Consonants: b *but*   d *dog*   f *few*   g *get*   h *her*   j *yes*   k *cat*   l *leg*   m *man*   n *no*   p *pen*   r *red*   s *sit*

southwest of Edmonton; pop. (2001) 5,801. [after the hometown of the postmaster's wife, a town in Hampshire, England]

dread ● *transitive verb* **1** fear greatly. **2** shrink from; look forward to with great apprehension or fear (*I dread going to the dentist*). **3** *archaic* be in great awe of. ● *noun* **1 a** great fear or apprehension. **b** an object of fear or apprehension. **2** *archaic* great awe or reverence. **3 a** *slang* a Rastafarian. **b** (in *pl.*) = DREADLOCKS. ● *adjective* **1** dreaded (*a dread disease*). **2** *archaic* awe-inspiring; revered. [Old English *ādrædan*, *ondrædan*]

dread·ed *adjective* **1** regarded with fear, apprehension, or awe. **2** *informal* regarded with mock fear (*the dreaded fax machine*).

dread·ful *adjective* **1** terrible; causing great fear or suffering (*a dreadful accident*). **2** troublesome, disagreeable; very bad (*dreadful weather; a dreadful movie*). □ **dread·ful·ly** *adverb* **dread·ful·ness** *noun*

dread·locks *plural noun* **1** a Rastafarian hairstyle in which the hair is twisted into tight braids or ringlets hanging down on all sides. **2** hair dressed in this way. □ **dread·locked** *adjective*

dread·nought *noun hist.* a type of battleship whose main armament was entirely big guns of the same calibre. [from the name of the first, launched in 1906]

dream ● *noun* **1 a** a series of pictures or events occurring in the mind during sleep. **b** the act or time of seeing this. **c** (in full **waking dream**) a similar experience while awake. **2** a daydream or fantasy. **3** an ideal, aspiration, or ambition. **4** a beautiful or ideal person or thing. **5** a state of mind without proper perception of reality (*goes about in a dream*). ● *verb* (*past* and *past participle* **dreamt** or **dreamed**) **1** *intransitive* experience a dream. **2** *transitive* imagine in or as if in a dream. **3** (usu. with *neg.*) **a** *intransitive* (foll. by *of*) contemplate the possibility of, have any conception or intention of (*would not dream of upsetting them*). **b** *transitive* (often foll. by *that* + clause) think of as a possibility (*never dreamt that he would come*). **4** *transitive* (foll. by *away*) spend (time) unprofitably. **5** *intransitive* be unrealistic or unpractical. **6** *intransitive* fall into a reverie. ● *adjective* ideal; perfect (*dream home*). □ **a dream come true** an ideal or desired situation or thing (*getting the job was a dream come true*). **dream in colour** (or **Technicolor**) *Cdn* be wildly unrealistic. **dream up** imagine, invent. **like a dream** *informal* easily, effortlessly. □ **dream·ful** *adjective* **dream·ful·ly** *adverb* **dream·less** *adjective* **dream·less·ly** *adverb* **dream·like** *adjective* [Old English *drēam* joy, music]

dream·boat *noun informal* a very attractive or ideal person, esp. of the opposite sex.

dream catcher *noun* a webbed hoop used by some woodland Aboriginal groups to protect a person from bad dreams; good dreams are held to pass through the webbing, while bad dreams get caught and perish at dawn.

dream·er *noun* **1** a person who dreams. **2** a romantic or unpractical person.

dream·land *noun* **1** an ideal or imaginary land. **2** sleep.

dream·scape *noun* a dreamed or dreamlike landscape or scene.

dreamt *past* and *past. part.* of DREAM.

dream team *noun N Amer. slang* **1** a team, real or hypothetical, composed of the top players in a given sport. **2** a group of people considered to be the stars of their field, discipline, etc. (*the dream team of the Canadian literary world*).

dream ticket *noun* an ideal pair of candidates standing together for esp. political office.

dream·time *noun* (in the belief of some Australian Aboriginals) a mythical golden age when the first ancestors were created.

dream world *noun* a state of mind distanced from reality.

dreamy *adjective* (**dream·i·er**, **dream·i·est**) **1** given to daydreaming; fanciful; unpractical. **2** dreamlike; vague; misty. **3** *informal* very attractive or ideal, esp. to the opposite sex (*a dreamy movie star; dreamy eyes*). **4** *informal* delightful; marvellous (*a dreamy little house*). **5** full of dreams. □ **dream·i·ly** *adverb* **dream·i·ness** *noun*

drear /driːr/ *adjective literary* = DREARY. [abbreviation]

dreary *adjective* (**drear·i·er**, **drear·i·est**) dismal, dull, gloomy. □ **drear·i·ly** *adverb* **drear·i·ness** *noun* [Old English *drēorig* from *drēor* gore: related to *drēosan* to drop, from Germanic]

dreck /drek/ *noun slang* **1** garbage; worthless junk. **2** a person or thing having no redeeming qualities (*his latest play was pure dreck*). □ **drecky** *adjective* [Yiddish *drek* filth, dregs, dung]

dredge¹ /dredʒ/ ● *verb* **1** *transitive* **a** (often foll. by *up*) bring up (lost or hidden material) as if with a dredge (*don't dredge all that up again*). **b** (often foll. by *up*, *out*) bring up or clear (mud etc.) from a river, harbour, etc. with a dredge. **2** *transitive* clean (a harbour, river, etc.) with

a dredge. **3** *intransitive* use a dredge. ● *noun* an apparatus used to scoop up objects or to clear mud etc. from a river or sea floor. [15th-c. Scots *dreg*, perhaps related to Middle Dutch *dregghe*]

dredge² *transitive verb* coat (food) with flour, sugar, etc. [obsolete *dredge* sweetmeat, from Old French *dragie, dragee*, perhaps from Latin *tragemata* from Greek *tragēmata* spices]

dredg·er *noun* **1** a machine used for dredging rivers etc.; a dredge. **2** a boat containing this.

dree /driː/ *transitive verb* (**drees**, **dreed**, **dree·ing**) *Scot.* or *archaic* endure. □ **dree one's weird** submit to one's destiny. [Old English *drēogan* from Germanic]

dreg /dreg/ *noun* **1** (usu. in *pl.*) **a** a sediment; grounds, lees, etc. **b** a worthless part; refuse (*the dregs of humanity*). **2** a small remnant (*not a dreg*). □ **drink to the dregs** consume leaving nothing (*drank life to the dregs*). [prob. from Old Norse *dreggjar*]

drei·del /ˈdreidəl/ *noun* (also **dreidl**) **1** a four-sided spinning top with a Hebrew letter on each side. **2** a gambling game played with this, esp. during Hanukkah. [Yiddish *dreydl* from Middle High German *drae(je)n* (German *drehen*) turn]

Drei·ser /ˈdraisər, -zər/ **Theo·dore (Her·man Al·bert)** (1871–1945), US novelist, who is perhaps best known for his novel *Sister Carrie* (1900); his later works express his faith in socialism, and include *An American Tragedy* (1925) and *America is Worth Saving* (1941).

drench ● *transitive verb* **1 a** wet thoroughly (*was drenched by the rain*). **b** saturate; soak (in liquid). **c** cover thoroughly all over (*sunlight drenched the garden*). **2** force (an animal) to take medicine. ● *noun* **1** a soaking; a downpour. **2** medicine administered to an animal. [Old English *drencan, drenc* from Germanic: related to DRINK]

Dres·den /ˈdrezdən/ a city in eastern Germany, the capital of Saxony, on the Elbe River; pop. (est. 2002) 413,600. Once famous for its baroque architecture, it was almost totally destroyed by Allied bombing on the night of 13 Feb. 1945.

Dresden china *noun* **1** delicate and elaborate porcelain originally made at Dresden, made at nearby Meissen since 1710. **2** (*attributive*) delicately pretty.

dress ● *verb* **1** *transitive* clothe; array (*dressed in rags; dressed her quickly*). **b** *intransitive* wear clothes of a specified kind or in a specified way (*dresses well*). **2** *intransitive* **a** put on clothes. **b** put on formal or evening clothes, esp. for dinner. **3** *transitive* decorate or adorn. **4** *transitive* **a** treat (a wound) with ointment etc. **b** apply a dressing to (a wound). **5** *transitive* trim, comb, brush, or smooth (the hair). **6** *transitive* **a** add a dressing to (a salad etc.). **b** clean and prepare (poultry, shellfish, etc.) for cooking or eating. **7** *transitive* apply manure etc. to a field, garden, etc. **8** *transitive* prepare and finish the surface of (fabric, stone, pelts, etc.). **9** *transitive* groom (a horse). **10** *transitive* curry (leather etc.). **11** *Military* **a** *transitive* correct the alignment of (troops etc.). **b** *intransitive* (of troops) come into alignment. **12** *transitive* make (an artificial fly) for use in fishing. ● *noun* **1** a one-piece woman's garment consisting of a bodice and skirt. **2** clothing, esp. a whole outfit etc. (*fussy about his dress*). **3** formal or ceremonial costume (*evening dress; military dress*). **4** an external covering; the outward form (*birds in their winter dress*). □ **dress down** *informal* **1** dress informally. **2** reprimand or scold. **dress for success** wear expensive, tailored clothes in the workplace in order to cultivate a professional image (also *attributive: a dress-for-success suit*). **dress up** **1** dress (oneself or another) in good clothes, esp. for a special occasion. **2** (esp. of a child) dress in a costume or in special clothes for entertainment. **3** decorate; make more attractive (*fancy wrapping paper helps to dress up a modest gift*). **4** disguise (unwelcome facts) by embellishment. [Old French *dresser*, ultimately from Latin *directus* DIRECT]

dres·sage /drəˈsɑːʒ/ *noun* **1** the training of a horse in obedience and deportment, esp. for competition. **2** the execution by a horse of precise movements in response to its rider. [French from *dresser* to train]

dress circle *noun* the first balcony in a theatre etc., in which evening dress was formerly required.

dress coat *noun* = TAILCOAT.

dress code *noun* a set of rules specifying the required manner of dress at a school, office, club, etc.

dress·er¹ *noun* **1** *N Amer.* a chest of drawers. **2** a kitchen sideboard with shelves above for displaying plates etc. [Old French *dresseur* from *dresser* prepare: compare medieval Latin *directorium*]

dress·er² *noun* **1** a person who assists theatrical performers to put on and remove costumes. **2** a person who dresses elegantly or in a specified way (*a snappy dresser*). **3** *Brit.* a surgeon's assistant in operations.

dresser set noun N Amer. a toiletry set usu. consisting of a brush, comb, and mirror, often displayed on a dresser.

dress·ing noun **1** in senses of DRESS verb. **2 a** a sauce for salads, esp. a mixture of oil, vinegar etc. (French dressing). **b** N Amer. = STUFFING 2. **3 a** a bandage for a wound. **b** ointment etc. used to dress a wound. **4** compost etc. spread over land (a top dressing of fertilizer).

dressing case noun dated a case containing toiletries etc.

dressing-down noun informal a scolding; a severe reprimand.

dressing gown noun a loose usu. belted robe worn over nightwear or while resting.

dressing room noun **1** a room in a sports stadium, theatre, etc. where athletes or performers change into their uniforms or stage clothes. **2** a small room attached to a bedroom, containing clothes.

dressing table noun a piece of furniture with a flat top, an upright mirror, and usu. drawers underneath, for use while applying makeup etc.

dress·maker noun a person who makes clothes professionally. □ **dress·making** noun

dress pants noun trousers, usu. of wool or linen.

dress rehearsal noun the final rehearsal of a play etc., with the performers in costume.

dress shield noun a piece of waterproof material fastened in the armpit of a garment to protect it from sweat.

dress shirt noun **1** N Amer. a man's long-sleeved shirt, usu. worn with a tie. **2** a man's usu. starched white shirt worn with evening dress.

dress shoe noun any type of shoe, e.g. an oxford, pump, etc., usu. worn with dressy or formal clothes.

dress suit noun **1** a suit appropriate for professional or formal social occasions. **2** a man's formal evening suit, esp. tails.

dress uniform noun formal military dress worn by members of the armed forces on ceremonial occasions.

dress-up noun the action of dressing up, either more formally or in costume (also attributive: dress-up clothes).

dressy adjective (**dress·i·er**, **dress·i·est**) **1** (of clothes or accessories) suitable for a formal occasion. **2** (of an occasion or place) requiring formal dress or one's best clothes (a dressy restaurant). **3** stylish; elegant (a dressy audience; a dressy main course). □ **dress·i·ness** noun

Drew, **George Alex·an·der** (1894–1973), Canadian politician, Progressive Conservative premier of Ontario 1943–8, leader of the federal Progressive Conservative party (1948–56).

drew past of DRAW.

Drey·fus /ˈdreifəs, ˈdrai-/ **Al·fred** (1859–1935), French army officer. Falsely accused of espionage and imprisoned (1894), he was later exonerated (1906). The controversy caused by the army's attempt to cover up his innocence, known as the 'Dreyfus Affair', polarized French society and revealed deep-set anti-militarist and anti-Semitic attitudes.

drib·ble ● verb **1** intransitive allow saliva to flow from the mouth. **2** intransitive & transitive flow or allow to flow in drops or a trickling stream. **3** transitive & intransitive **a** (in basketball) bounce (the ball), either to move forward or to prepare for a pass. **b** (esp. in soccer and field hockey) advance (the ball) with slight touches of the feet or stick. **4** intransitive move with little momentum (the puck dribbled into the net). ● noun **1** the act or an instance of dribbling. **2** a small trickling stream. **3** a small amount. □ **drib·bler** noun **drib·bly** adjective [frequentative of obsolete drib, var. of DRIP]

drib·let noun (also **drib·blet**) **1 a** a small quantity. **b** a petty sum. **2 a** thin stream; a dribble. [as DRIBBLE + -LET]

dribs and drabs plural noun informal small scattered amounts (did the work in dribs and drabs). [as DRIBBLE + drab reduplication]

dried past and past participle of DRY.

drier¹ comparative of DRY.

drier² var. of DRYER.

dri·est superlative of DRY.

drift ● noun **1 a** slow movement or variation. **b** such movement caused by a slow current. **2** the intention, meaning, scope, etc. of what is said etc. (didn't understand her drift). **3** a large mass of snow, sand, etc., accumulated by the wind. **4** esp. derogatory a state of inaction. **5 a** Naut. a ship's deviation from its course, due to currents. **b** Aviation an aircraft's deviation due to side winds. **c** a projectile's deviation due to its rotation. **d** a controlled slide of a race car etc. **6** Mining a horizontal passage following a mineral vein. **7** a large mass of esp. flowering plants (a drift of bluebells). **8** Geol. **a** material deposited by the wind, a current of water, etc. **b** (**Drift**) Pleistocene ice detritus, e.g. boulder

clay. **9** = CONTINENTAL DRIFT. ● verb **1** intransitive be carried by or as if by a current of air or water. **2** intransitive move or progress passively, casually, or aimlessly (drifted into teaching; the old friends had drifted apart; drifting in and out of consciousness). **3 a** transitive & intransitive pile or be piled by the wind into drifts. **b** transitive cover (a field, a road, etc.) with drifts. **4** transitive (of a current) carry. □ **drift off** fall asleep, esp. gradually. [Old Norse drift 'snowdrift, something driven'; in later use from Middle Dutch drift 'course, current'; related to DRIVE]

drift·er noun **1** an aimless or rootless person. **2** a boat used for drift net fishing.

drift ice noun ice driven or deposited by water.

drift net noun a large net for herrings etc., kept upright by weights at the bottom and floats at the top, and allowed to drift with the tide. □ **drift netter** noun **drift netting** noun

drift·wood noun wood floating on, or driven ashore by, water.

drill¹ ● noun **1 a** a tool or machine with a usu. detachable revolving pointed end, used for boring cylindrical holes, sinking wells, etc. **b** a dentist's rotary tool for cutting away part of a tooth etc. **2 a** instruction or training in military exercises. **b** rigorous discipline or methodical instruction, esp. when learning or performing tasks. **c** a rehearsal of the routine procedure to be followed in an emergency (fire drill; this is not just a drill). **d** a routine or exercise (drills in irregular verb patterns). **3** informal a recognized procedure (I expect you know the drill). **4** any of various predatory molluscs, esp. Urosalpinx cinera, that bore into the shells of young oysters. ● verb **1** transitive & intransitive **a** (of a person or a tool) make a hole with a drill through or into (wood, metal, etc.). **b** make (a hole) with a drill. **2** transitive & intransitive esp. Military subject to or undergo discipline by drill. **3** transitive impart (knowledge etc.) by a strict method or by repetition, etc. **4** transitive slang **a** shoot with a gun (drilled him full of holes). **b** punch or hit (a person) sharply (drilled me one in the stomach). **c** cause (a ball etc.) to move rapidly (drilled the puck down the ice). □ **drill·er** noun [earlier as verb, from Middle Dutch drillen bore, of unknown origin]

drill² ● noun **1** a machine used for making furrows, sowing, and covering seed. **2** a small furrow for sowing seed in. **3** a ridge with such furrows on top. **4** a row of plants so sown. ● transitive verb **1** sow (seed) with a drill. **2** plant (the ground) in drills. [perhaps from obsolete drill rill (17th c., of unknown origin)]

drill³ noun a West African baboon, Papio leucophaeus, related to the mandrill. [prob. of African origin: compare MANDRILL]

drill⁴ noun a coarse twilled cotton or linen fabric. [earlier drilling from German Drillich from Latin trilix -licis from tri- three + licium thread]

drill·ing platform noun = PLATFORM 9.

drill·ing rig noun a structure with equipment for drilling an oil well etc.

drill press noun an upright drilling machine which uses a hand lever or other force to press the bit into the material to be drilled.

drily var. of DRYLY.

drink ● verb (past **drank**; past participle **drunk**) **1 a** transitive swallow (a liquid). **b** transitive swallow the liquid contents of (a vessel). **c** intransitive swallow liquid, take drafts (drank from the stream). **2** intransitive take alcohol, esp. to excess (don't drink and drive). **3** transitive (of a plant, porous material, etc.) absorb (moisture). **4** reflexive bring (oneself etc.) to a specified condition by drinking (drank herself into a stupor). **5** transitive (usu. foll. by away) spend (wages etc.) on drink (drank away her money). **6** transitive wish (a person's good health, luck, etc.) by drinking (drank his health). ● noun **1 a** a liquid for drinking (milk is a nourishing drink). **b** a draft or specified amount of this (had a drink of milk). **2 a** alcoholic liquor (got the drink in for Christmas). **b** a portion, glass, etc. of this (have a drink). **c** excessive indulgence in alcohol (drink is his vice). **3** (as **the drink**) informal a body of water. □ **drink deep** take a large draft or drafts. **drink in** listen to or watch closely or eagerly (drank in her every word; drink in the breathtaking view). **drink off** drink the whole (contents) of at once. **drink to** toast; wish success to. **drink a person under the table** remain sober longer than one's drinking companion. **drink up** drink the whole of; empty. **in drink** drunk. □ **drink·ing** noun **drink·able** adjective [Old English drincan (v.), drinc(a) (n.) from Germanic]

drink driving noun Brit. = DRUNK DRIVING. □ **drink driver** noun

drink·er noun **1** a person who drinks (something). **2** a person who drinks alcohol, esp. to excess.

drink·ing age noun the age at which it is legal to consume alcohol.

drink·ing box noun Cdn a small plasticized cardboard carton of juice etc. packaged with a straw that can be inserted through a foil-covered hole in the top.

Vowels: a cat ɑ arm e bed ɜr her ɜː deux ə ago ɪ sit i cosy iː feed ɒ hot ɔ pore oː no ʌ run ʊ put

drink·ing fountain *noun* a device that releases a small jet of water for drinking from.

drink·ing song *noun* a song sung while drinking, usu. concerning drink.

drinking-up time *noun Brit.* a short period legally allowed for finishing drinks bought before closing time in a bar etc.

drink·ing water *noun* water pure enough for drinking.

drip ● *verb* (**dripped**, **drip·ping**) **1** *intransitive & transitive* fall or let fall in drops. **2** *intransitive* (often foll. by *with*) be so wet as to shed drops (*dripped with blood*). ● *noun* **1 a** the act or an instance of dripping. **b** a drop of liquid (*a drip of paint*). **c** a sound of dripping. **2** *informal* a stupid, dull, or ineffective person. **3** *Med.* = DRIP-FEED *noun*. **4** *Archit.* a projection, esp. from a windowsill, keeping rain off the walls. **5** (*attributive*) pertaining to coffee made by pouring boiling water through ground coffee in a paper or mesh filter. □ **dripping wet** very wet. **dripping with** full of or covered with (*dripping with pearls*). [Middle Danish *drippe* from Germanic (compare DROP)]

drip-dry ● *verb* (**-dries**, **-dried**) **1** *intransitive* (of fabric etc.) dry crease-free when hung up to drip. **2** *transitive* leave (a garment etc.) hanging up to dry. ● *adjective* able to be drip-dried.

drip-feed ● *transitive verb* (*past* and *past participle* **-fed**) feed intravenously in drops. ● *noun* **1** the continuous intravenous introduction of fluid into the body. **2** the fluid so introduced. **3** the apparatus used to do this.

drip filter *noun* a device for making coffee in which boiling water is allowed to drip through a filter basket containing ground coffee.

drip·less *adjective* (of a candle, etc.) designed so as not to drip.

drip·ping *noun* (often in *pl.*) **1** fat melted from roasted meat and used for cooking. **2** water, oil, wax, etc., dripping from anything.

drippy *adjective* (**drip·pi·er**, **drip·pi·est**) **1** tending to drip. **2** *informal* (of a song etc.) sloppily sentimental. **3** (of a person) ineffectual; lacking character.

drive ● *verb* (*past* **drove**; *past participle* **driv·en**) **1** *transitive* (usu. foll. by *away*, *back*, *in*, *out*, *to*, etc.) urge in some direction, esp. forcibly (*drove back the wolves*). **2** *transitive* **a** (usu. foll. by *to* + infin., or *to* + verbal noun) compel or constrain forcibly (*was driven to complain*; *drove her to stealing*). **b** (often foll. by *to*) force into a specified state (*drove him mad*; *driven to despair*). **c** (often *reflexive*) urge to overwork (*drives herself too hard*). **3** *transitive & intransitive* **a** operate and direct the course of (a vehicle, a locomotive, etc.) (*drove a sports car*; *drives well*). **b** convey or be conveyed in a vehicle (*drove them to the station*; *drove to the station in a bus*) (compare RIDE). **c** be licensed or competent to drive (a vehicle) (*do you drive?*). **d** urge and direct the course of (an animal drawing a vehicle, plow, etc.). **4** *transitive* (of wind, water, etc.) carry along, propel, send, or cause to go in some direction. **5** *transitive* (often foll. by *into*) force (a stake, nail, etc.) into place by blows (*drove the nail home*). **6** *transitive* effect or conclude forcibly (*drove a hard bargain*; *drove her point home*). **7** *transitive* (of steam or other power) set or keep (machinery) going. **8** *intransitive* (usu. foll. by *at*) work hard; dash, rush, or hasten. **9** *transitive Sport* hit or kick (the ball, puck, etc.) forcefully. **10** *transitive Baseball* (often foll. by *in*) **a** cause the advance of (a baserunner) by a base hit or sacrifice fly. **b** cause (a run) to be scored by a base hit or sacrifice fly. **11** *transitive & intransitive Golf* strike (a ball) with a driver from the tee. **12** *transitive N Amer. & NZ* float (timber) down a river etc. **13** *transitive* chase or frighten (game, wild beasts, an enemy in warfare, etc.) from a large area to a smaller, to kill or capture; corner. **14** *transitive Mining* bore (a tunnel, horizontal cavity, etc.). ● *noun* **1** an act of driving in a motor vehicle; a journey or excursion in such a vehicle (*went for a pleasant drive*; *lives an hour's drive from us*). **2 a** the capacity for achievement; motivation and energy (*lacks the drive needed to succeed*). **b** *Psych.* an inner urge to attain a goal or satisfy a need (*sex drive*). **3 a** a street or road, esp. a curving one. Abbr.: **Dr. b** = DRIVEWAY. **4** *Military* a forceful advance or attack. **5** an organized effort to achieve a usu. charitable purpose (*a famine-relief drive*). **6 a** the act or an instance of driving a puck, ball, etc. **b** the flight of the puck or ball etc. so driven. **c** *Football* a series of plays that advances the ball towards the opposing end of the field, often resulting in a touchdown or field goal. **d** *Golf* a shot, made esp. from the tee with a driver, intended to travel a great distance. **7 a** the transmission of power to machinery, the wheels of a motor vehicle, etc. (*belt drive*; *front-wheel drive*). **b** the position of a steering wheel in a motor vehicle (*left-hand drive*). **c** the gear position or function in an automatic transmission which imparts forward motion. **8** *Computing* a device that can store and retrieve data on disks or tape. **9** an act of impelling along (cattle, game, etc.) (*cattle drive*). **10** *Cdn* = LOG DRIVE. **11** *Brit.* an organized competition, for many players, of whist, bingo, etc. □ **drive at** seek, intend, or mean (*what is she driving at?*). **drive**

out take the place of; oust; exorcise, cast out (*evil spirits etc.*). □ **drive·abil·ity** *noun* (also **driv·abil·ity**). **drive·able** *adjective* (also **driv·able**). [Old English *drīfan* from Germanic]

drive bay *noun* a space inside a computer in which a floppy disk, hard disk, or disk drive can be accommodated.

drive-by *adjective & noun* ● *attributive adjective* (of a crime etc.) carried out from a moving vehicle. ● *noun* (*pl.* **-bys**) a drive-by shooting.

drive-in ● *attributive adjective* (of a movie theatre, restaurant, etc.) that can be visited without getting out of one's car. ● *noun* such a movie theatre, restaurant, etc.

driv·el /ˈdrɪvl/ ● *noun* silly nonsense; twaddle. ● *verb* (**driv·elled**, **driv·el·ling**; also esp. *US* **driv·eled**, **driv·el·ing**) **1** *intransitive* talk foolishly or idiotically. **2** *intransitive archaic* run at the mouth or nose; dribble. □ **driv·el·ler** *noun* (also esp. *US* **driv·el·er**). **driv·el·ling** *adjective* (also esp. *US* **driv·el·ing**). [Old English *dreflian* (v.)]

drive·line *noun* the parts of a vehicle's powertrain that lie between the transmission and the differential, usu. consisting of the driveshaft and universal joint.

driv·en ● *verb past participle of* DRIVE. ● *adjective* **1** (of snow) piled into drifts or made smooth by the wind. **2** urged onward, impelled, forced. **3** (of a person) showing intensity or compulsion in behaviour. **4** (in *combination*) having as the chief reason or determinant the thing specified (*market-driven*; *event-driven*). **5** (in *combination*) controlled by the means specified (*menu-driven*). □ **white** (or **pure**) **as driven snow** immaculately white or pure. □ **driven·ness** *noun*

drive-on *adjective* (of a ship) on to which motor vehicles may be driven.

driv·er *noun* **1** (often in *combination*) a person who drives a vehicle (*bus driver*). **2** *Golf* a club with a flat face and wooden head, used for driving from the tee. **3** *Electricity* a device or part of a circuit providing power for output. **4** *Mech.* a wheel etc. receiving power directly and transmitting motion to other parts. **5** *Computing* a program that controls the operation of a device. **6** a person who herds or drives a usu. specified type of animal (*cattle driver*). □ **in the driver's seat** in charge. □ **driv·er·less** *adjective*

driver's licence *noun N Amer.* a licence permitting a person to drive a motor vehicle.

driver's test *N Amer. var. of* DRIVING TEST.

drive·shaft *noun* a rotating shaft that transmits power to the differential in a motor vehicle or to a propeller in a ship or aircraft.

drive shed *noun Cdn* (esp. *Ont.*) a large shed used for storing farm machinery, vehicles, etc.

drive-through (also *informal* **drive-thru**) esp. *N Amer.* ● *attributive adjective* **1** designating a restaurant etc. which has a window at which customers are served without leaving their cars. **2** (of a place, facility, etc.) suitable for driving through (*a drive-through tunnel*). ● *noun* a place where drive-through service is offered.

drive-time *noun* (often *attributive*) the parts of the day when many people commute by car (*a drive-time radio show*).

drive·train *noun* the powertrain of an automobile, consisting of all the components between the engine and the wheels, e.g. the clutch, driveline, axle, etc.

drive·way *noun* **1** a paved or gravelled parking area leading to a garage or house. **2** a private road or lane leading to a house, barn, etc.

driv·ing ● *noun* the control and operation of a motor vehicle (*she was convicted of reckless driving*; *his driving is terrible*). ● *adjective* **1** moving rapidly, esp. before the wind (*a driving rain*). **2** energetic (*a driving rhythm*). **3** having a strong and controlling influence (*she was the driving force behind the plan*; *a driving ambition*). **4** used when driving a motor vehicle (*driving gloves*).

driving licence esp. *Brit. var. of* DRIVER'S LICENCE.

driving range *noun Golf* an area for practising drives.

driving shed *noun Cdn* (esp. *Ont.*) = DRIVE SHED.

driving test *noun* an official test of a motorist's competence which must be passed to obtain a driver's licence.

driz·zle ● *noun* **1** very fine rain. **2** esp. *Cooking* fine drops; a fine trickle. ● *verb* **1** *intransitive* (esp. of rain) fall in very fine drops (*it's drizzling again*). **2** *transitive* esp. *Cooking* **a** sprinkle in fine drops or a thin trickle. **b** pour a liquid in a fine stream over (a food). □ **driz·zly** *adjective* [prob. from Old English *drēosan* fall]

Dr. Mar·tens *var. of* DOCTOR MARTENS.

DRO *abbreviation* DEPUTY RETURNING OFFICER.

drogue /droːg/ *noun* **1** *Naut.* **a** a sea anchor. **b** a buoy at the end of a harpoon line. **2** *Aviation* a fabric cone or cylinder open at both ends and towed behind an aircraft to serve as a brake or target. **3** a similar device used as an auxiliary parachute. **4** a funnel-shaped device at the end of the supply line from a tanker aircraft, which receives the probe from an aircraft to be refuelled in flight. [18th c.: origin unknown]

droid /drɔɪd/ *noun* an android. [abbreviation]

droit /drɔɪt/ *noun Law* a right or due. [Old French from Latin *directum* (n.) from *directus* DIRECT]

droit de seigneur /ˌdrwɒ də senˈjɜr/ *noun hist.* the alleged right of a feudal lord to have sexual intercourse with a vassal's bride on her wedding night. [French, = lord's right]

droke /droʊk/ *noun Cdn* (*Nfld & Maritimes*) **1** a grove of trees. **2** a steep-sided valley. [origin unknown]

droll /droʊl/ ● *adjective* **1** quaintly amusing. **2** strange; odd; surprising. ● *noun archaic* **1** a jester; an entertainer. **2** a quaintly amusing person. □ **droll·ery** *noun* (*pl.* **-eries**) **droll·ness** *noun* **drolly** /ˈdroʊlli/ *adverb* [French *drôle*, perhaps from Middle Dutch *drolle* little man]

-drome /droʊm/ *combining form* forming nouns denoting: **1** a place for running, racing, or other forms of movement (*aerodrome; hippodrome*). **2** a thing that runs or proceeds in a certain way (*palindrome; syndrome*). [Greek *dromos* course, running]

drom·ed·ary /ˈdrɒmədɛri/ *noun* (*pl.* **-ies**) = ARABIAN CAMEL. [Late Latin *dromedarius*, ultimately from Greek *dromas -ados* runner]

drone ● *noun* **1** a non-working male of the honeybee, whose sole function is to mate with fertile females. **2** an idler. **3** a deep humming sound. **4** a monotonous speech or speaker. **5 a** a pipe, esp. of a bagpipe, sounding a continuous note of fixed low pitch. **b** the note emitted by this. **6** a remote-controlled pilotless aircraft or missile. ● *verb* **1** *intransitive* make a deep humming sound. **2** *intransitive & transitive* speak or utter monotonously. **3 a** *intransitive* be idle. **b** *transitive* (often foll. by *away*) idle away (one's time etc.). □ **dron·er** *noun* [Old English *drān, drǣn*, prob. from West Germanic]

dron·go /ˈdrɒŋɡoʊ/ *noun* (*pl.* **-gos** or **-goes**) **1** any black bird of the family Dicruridae, native to India, Africa, and Australia, having a long forked tail. **2** *Austral. & NZ slang derogatory* a simpleton. [Malagasy]

drool ● *intransitive verb* **1** have saliva coming out of the mouth; slobber. **2** (often foll. by *over*) show much pleasure or infatuation. ● *noun* saliva. [contraction of *drivel*]

droop ● *verb* **1** *intransitive & transitive* hang or allow to hang down; languish, decline, or sag, esp. from weariness. **2** *intransitive* **a** (of the eyes) look downwards. **b** (of the sun) sink. **3** *intransitive* lose heart; be dejected; flag. ● *noun* **1** an instance of drooping. **2** a loss of spirit or enthusiasm. □ **droop·ing** *adjective* **droop·ing·ly** *adverb* [Old Norse *drúpa* 'hang the head', from Germanic: compare DROP]

droopy *adjective* (**droop·i·er, droop·i·est**) **1** drooping. **2** dejected, gloomy. □ **droop·i·ly** *adverb* **droop·i·ness** *noun*

drop ● *noun* **1 a** a small round or pear-shaped portion of liquid that hangs or falls or adheres to a surface (*drops of dew; tears fell in large drops*). **b** a very small amount of usu. drinkable liquid (*just a drop left in the glass*). **c** a glass etc. of alcoholic liquor (*take a drop with us*). **2 a** an abrupt fall or slope. **b** the amount of this (*a drop of fifteen feet*). **c** an act of falling or dropping (*had a nasty drop*). **d** a reduction in prices, temperature, etc. **e** a deterioration or worsening (*a drop in status*). **3** something resembling a drop, esp.: **a** a pendant or earring. **b** a crystal ornament on a chandelier etc. **c** (often in *combination*) a candy or lozenge (*cough drop*). **4** something that drops or is dropped, esp.: **a** *Theatre* a painted curtain or scenery. **b** a platform or trap door on a gallows, the opening of which causes the victim to fall. **5** *Med.* **a** the smallest separable quantity of a liquid. **b** (in *pl.*) liquid medicine to be measured in drops (*eye drops*). **6** a minute quantity (*not a drop of pity*). **7 a** the act of dropping people, supplies, etc. by parachute. **b** a descent by parachute. **c** the persons or supplies dropped. **8** *informal* a delivery. **9** *slang* **a** a hiding place for stolen or illicit goods. **b** a secret place where documents etc. may be left or passed on in espionage. **10** (*attributive*) (of a part of a garment) set lower than normal (*drop waist*). **11** *US informal* a mailbox. ● *verb* (**dropped, drop·ping**) **1** *intransitive & transitive* fall or let fall in drops (*tears dropped onto the book; dropped the soup down his shirt*). **2** *intransitive & transitive* fall or allow to fall; relinquish; let go (*dropped the box; the egg dropped from my hand*). **3 a** *intransitive & transitive* sink or cause to sink or fall to the ground, onto a chair etc., from exhaustion, a blow, a wound, etc. **b** *intransitive* die. **4 a** *intransitive & transitive* cease or cause to cease; lapse or let lapse; abandon (*the connection dropped; dropped the friendship; drop everything and come at once; the Crown dropped the charges*). **b** *transitive informal* cease to associate with. **5** *transitive* set down (a passenger etc.) (*drop me at the station*). **6** *transitive & intransitive* utter or be uttered casually (*dropped a hint; the remark dropped into the conversation*). **7** *transitive* send casually (*drop me a postcard*). **8 a** *intransitive & transitive* fall or allow to fall in direction, amount,

condition, degree, pitch, etc. (*dropped her voice; the wind dropped; we dropped the price by $20; the road dropped southwards*). **b** *intransitive* (of a person) jump down lightly; let oneself fall. **c** *transitive* remove (clothes, esp. trousers) rapidly, allowing them to fall to the ground. **9** *transitive informal* **a** lose (money). **b** spend (money) (*dropped $200 on ballet tickets*). **10** *transitive* esp. *N Amer.* dismiss (a person) from employment, a team, etc. **11** *transitive slang* take (a drug, esp. an illegal drug) orally. **12** *transitive* omit (a letter, syllable, etc.) in speech. **13** *transitive* (of a female animal) give birth to (esp. a lamb, kitten, etc.). **14 a** *intransitive* (of a card) be played in the same trick as a higher card. **b** *transitive* play or cause (a card) to be played in this way. **15** *transitive Sport* lose (a game, point, contest, match, etc.). **16** *transitive* deliver (supplies etc.) by parachute. **17** *transitive Football* **a** send (a ball) by a drop kick. **b** score (a goal) by a drop kick. **18** *transitive* set (a part of a garment) in a lower position than is normal. □ **at the drop of a hat** given the slightest excuse. **drop anchor** anchor ship. **drop asleep** fall gently asleep. **drop away** decrease or depart gradually. **drop back** (or **behind** or **to the rear**) fall back; get left behind. **drop back into** return to (a habit etc.). **drop the ball** *N Amer.* make a mess of something; fumble. **drop a brick** *informal* make an indiscreet or embarrassing remark. **drop a curtsy** make a curtsy. **drop dead 1** die suddenly, usu. from a heart attack or stroke. **2** *slang* an exclamation of intense scorn. **drop in** (or **by**) *informal* call casually as a visitor. **a drop in the ocean** (or **a bucket**) a very small amount, esp. compared with what is needed or expected. **drop into** *informal* **1** call casually at (a place). **2** fall into (a habit etc.). **drop it!** *slang* stop that! **drop names** = NAME-DROP (see NAME-DROPPING). **drop off 1** decline gradually. **2** *informal* fall asleep. **3** = sense 5 of *verb*. **4** leave or deposit (something) at an assigned place. **drop out** *informal* cease to participate, esp. in a race, a course of study, or in conventional society. **drop a stitch** let a stitch fall off the end of a knitting needle. **fit** (or **ready**) **to drop** extremely tired. **have the drop on** *informal* have the advantage over. **have had a drop too much** *informal* be slightly drunk. **one's jaw drops** one shows sudden surprise, dismay, or disappointment. □ **drop·let** *noun* [Old English *dropa* (n.), *drop(p)ian* (v.), ultimately from Germanic: compare DRIP, DROOP]

drop cloth *noun N Amer.* a sheet of cloth or plastic used to protect furniture, floors, etc. when painting.

drop cookie *noun* a cookie made by dropping a small quantity of dough from a spoon onto a cookie sheet before baking.

drop-dead *attributive adjective* (also **drop-dead gorgeous** *attributive & predicative adjective*) *slang* stunningly beautiful.

drop-down *adjective Computing* designating a menu or list that appears below a heading when the heading is selected with a mouse.

drop-forging *noun* a method of forcing white-hot metal through an open-ended die by a heavy weight. □ **drop-forge** *transitive verb* **drop-forged** *adjective*

drop goal *noun Rugby* a goal scored from a drop kick during play.

drop-in ● *adjective* **1** (of a place or function) at which one can turn up informally, without prior appointment or referral (*drop-in centre*). **2** designed to drop into position. ● *noun informal* **1** esp. *N Amer.* a place or function at which one can turn up informally, without prior appointment or referral. **2** an unexpected visitor or visit.

drop kick ● *noun* **1** *Football etc.* a kick made by dropping the ball and kicking it on the bounce. **2** *Wrestling* a movement in which a wrestler jumps into the air and kicks his or her opponent with both feet simultaneously, then drops onto one side. ● *verb* (**drop-kick**) **1** *transitive* kick (a ball, a field goal, etc.) by means of a drop kick. **2** *intransitive* make a drop kick.

drop-leaf *adjective* (of a table etc.) having a hinged flap.

drop-off *noun* **1 a** an act of dropping off or delivering something or someone. **b** a place where this can be done. **2** a decline, a decrease (*a drop-off in CD sales*). **3** *N Amer.* a sheer downward slope.

drop·out *noun* **1** *informal* a person who has dropped out of society. **2** a person who leaves school before completing the program. **3** *Rugby* the restarting of a game by a drop kick.

drop pass *noun* a backwards pass of a ball or puck, often executed without the passer turning or looking around.

dropped *adjective* in a lower position than usual (*dropped handlebars; dropped waist*).

drop·per *noun* **1** a device for administering liquid, esp. medicine, in drops. **2** a person or thing that drops.

drop·pings *plural noun* **1** the dung of animals or birds. **2** something that falls or has fallen in drops, e.g. wax from candles.

drop·seed *noun* any of various grasses of the genus *Sporobolus*.

Consonants: **b** *but*   **d** *dog*   **f** *few*   **g** *get*   **h** *her*   **j** *yes*   **k** *cat*   **l** *leg*   **m** *man*   **n** *no*   **p** *pen*   **r** *red*   **s** *sit*

drop shot *noun* (in tennis, badminton, etc.) a shot dropping abruptly over the net.

drop·sy *noun* (*pl.* **-sies**) **1** = EDEMA. **2** *Brit. slang* a tip or bribe. □ **drop·si·cal** *adjective* (in sense 1). [Old French *idropesie*, ultimately from Latin *hydropisis* from Greek *hudrōps* dropsy (as HYDRO-)]

drop test *Engin.* ● *noun* a test done by dropping under standard conditions. ● *transitive verb* carry out a drop test on.

drop·top *noun* informal a convertible car (also *attributive*: *droptop model*).

drop·wort *noun* a plant, *Filipendula vulgaris*, with tuberous root fibres.

drosh·ky /ˈdrɒʃki/ *noun* (*pl.* **-kies**) a Russian low four-wheeled open carriage. [Russian *drozhki*, diminutive of *drogi* wagon, from *droga* shaft]

dro·soph·i·la /drəˈsɒfɪlə/ *noun* any fruit fly of the genus *Drosophila*, used extensively in genetic research. [modern Latin from Greek *drosos* dew, moisture + *philos* loving]

dross /drɒs/ *noun* **1** material without value or worth. **2 a** the scum separated from metals in melting. **b** foreign matter mixed with anything; impurities. □ **drossy** *adjective* [Old English *drōs*: compare Middle Low German *drōsem*, Old High German *truosana*]

Drott·ning·holm /ˈdrɒtnɪŋˌhɒlm/ the winter palace of the Swedish royal family, on an island to the west of Stockholm. [Swedish, lit. 'queen's island']

drought /draʊt/ *noun* **1** the continuous absence of rain; dry weather. **2** the prolonged lack of something. **3** *archaic* a lack of moisture; thirst; dryness. □ **droughty** *adjective* [Old English *drūgath* from *drȳge* DRY]

drouth /draʊθ/ *dialect* or *archaic* var. of DROUGHT.

drove¹ *past of* DRIVE.

drove² *noun* **1 a** a large number (of people etc.) moving together; a crowd; a multitude. **b** (*in pl.*) a great number (*people arrived in droves*). **2** a herd or flock being driven or moving together. [Old English *drāf* from *drīfan* DRIVE]

drov·er /ˈdroʊvər/ *noun* a person who drives herds to market; a cattle dealer. □ **drove** *transitive verb* **drov·ing** *noun*

drove road *noun* esp. *Scot.* an ancient cattle track.

drown *verb* **1** *transitive & intransitive* kill or be killed by submersion in liquid. **2** *transitive* submerge; flood; drench (*drowned the fields in six feet of water*). **3** *transitive* (often foll. by *in*) deaden (grief etc.) with drink (*drowned his sorrows in beer*). **4** *transitive* **a** (often foll. by *out*) make (a sound) inaudible by means of a louder sound. **b** overcome by superior strength. □ **like a drowned rat** *informal* extremely wet and bedraggled. [Middle English (originally northern) *drun(e)*, *droun(e)*, related to Old Norse *drukkna* 'be drowned', from the Germanic base of DRINK]

drowse ● *verb* **1** *intransitive* be dull and sleepy or half asleep. **2** *transitive* (often foll. by *away*) pass (the time) in drowsing. ● *noun* a condition of sleepiness. [back-formation from DROWSY]

drowsy *adjective* (**drows·i·er**, **drows·i·est**) **1** half asleep; dozing. **2** making one feel sleepy. **3** sluggish. □ **drows·i·ly** *adverb* **drows·i·ness** *noun* [prob. related to Old English *drūsian* be languid or slow, *drēosan* fall: compare DREARY]

drub /drʌb/ *transitive verb* (**drubbed**, **drub·bing**) **1** thump; belabour. **2** beat in a fight. **3** (usu. foll. by *into*, *out of*) beat (an idea, attitude, etc.) into or out of a person. **4** defeat soundly. **5** criticize or reprimand harshly. □ **drub·bing** *noun* [ultimately from Arabic *ḍaraba* beat]

drudge ● *noun* a person who does heavy, unpleasant, or menial work. ● *intransitive verb* (often foll. by *at*) work slavishly at heavy, unpleasant, or menial tasks. □ **drudg·ery** *noun* [15th c.: perhaps related to DRAG]

drug ● *noun* **1** a medicinal substance. **2** a narcotic, hallucinogen, or stimulant, esp. one causing addiction. ● *verb* (**drugged**, **drug·ging**) **1** *transitive* add a drug to (food or drink). **2** *transitive* **a** administer a drug to. **b** stupefy with a drug. □ **drug·less** *adjective* [Old French *drogue*, of unknown origin]

drug addict *noun* a person who is addicted to a narcotic drug.

drug·get /ˈdrʌɡɪt/ *noun* a coarse woven fabric used as a floor or table covering. [French *droguet*, of unknown origin]

drug·gie *noun* informal a drug addict.

drug·gist *noun* esp. *N Amer.* a pharmacist. [French *droguiste* (as DRUG)]

drug·gy *adjective* (**drug·gi·er**, **drug·gi·est**) informal of or associated with narcotic drugs.

drug squad *noun* a division of a police force investigating crimes involving illegal drugs.

drug·store *noun* *N Amer.* a pharmacy that also sells cosmetics, household items, soft drinks, snacks, etc.

drugstore cowboy *noun* *N Amer. informal* **1** a person who loafs on

street corners or near drugstores etc. **2** a person who is not a cowboy but dresses like one.

Druid /ˈdruːɪd/ *noun* **1** an ancient Celtic priest, magician, or soothsayer of Gaul, Britain, or Ireland. **2** a member of a Welsh etc. Druidic order, esp. the Gorsedd. □ **Druid·ic** /-ˈɪdɪk/ *adjective* **Druid·ic·al** *adjective* **Druid·ism** *noun* [French *druide* or Latin pl. *druidae*, *-des*, Greek *druidai* from Gaulish *druides*]

drum¹ ● *noun* **1 a** a percussion instrument made of a hollow cylinder or hemisphere covered at one or both ends and sounded by striking (*bass drum*; *kettledrum*). **b** (often in *pl.*) a drummer or a percussion section (*the drums are playing too loud*). **c** a sound made by or resembling that of a drum. **2** something resembling a drum in shape, esp.: **a** a cylindrical container or receptacle for oil, etc. **b** a cylinder or barrel in machinery on which something is wound etc. **c** *Archit.* the solid part of a Corinthian or composite capital. **d** *Archit.* a stone block forming a section of a shaft. **3** *Zool. & Anat.* the membrane of the middle ear; the eardrum. **4** (*pl.* **drum** or **drums**) (in full **drum fish**) any marine fish of the family Sciaenidae, having a swim bladder that produces a drumming sound. ● *verb* (**drummed**, **drum·ming**) **1** *intransitive & transitive* play on a drum. **2** *transitive & intransitive* beat, tap, or thump (knuckles, feet, etc.) continuously (on something) (*drummed on the table*; *drummed her feet*; *drumming at the window*). **3** *intransitive* (of a bird or an insect) make a loud, hollow noise with quivering wings. □ **drum into** drive (a lesson) into (a person) by persistence. **drum out** *Military* cashier (a soldier) by the beat of a drum; dismiss with ignominy. **drum up** summon, gather, or call up (*needs to drum up more support*). [Middle Dutch or Low German *tromme* drum, of imitative origin]

drum² *noun* esp. *Scot. Geol.* a long narrow hill often separating two parallel valleys. [Scottish Gaelic & Irish *druim* ridge]

drum·beat *noun* a stroke or the sound of a stroke on a drum.

drum brake *noun* a brake in which shoes on a vehicle press against the drum on a wheel.

drum dance *noun* a dance, performed to an accompaniment of drumming, combining traditional Inuit dancing with Scottish and French-Canadian jigs and reels. □ **drum dancing** *noun & adjective*

drum·fire *noun* **1** *Military* heavy continuous rapid artillery fire, usu. heralding an infantry attack. **2** a barrage of criticism etc.

drum·head *noun* **1** the skin or membrane of a drum. **2** an eardrum. **3** the circular top of a capstan. **4** (*attributive*) improvised (*drumhead court martial*).

Drum·hel·ler /ˌdrʌmˈhɛlər/ a city in south central Alberta, situated on the Red Deer River, northeast of Calgary; pop. (2001) 7,785. [S. *Drumheller*, town developer d.1925]

drum kit *noun* a set of drums, cymbals, etc.

drum·lin /ˈdrʌmlɪn/ *noun* *Geol.* a long oval mound of boulder clay moulded by glacial action. [DRUM² + *-lin* (perhaps for -LING¹)]

drum machine *noun* an electronic device that imitates the sound of percussion instruments.

drum major *noun* **1** the leader of a marching band. **2** *archaic* an NCO commanding the drummers of a regiment.

drum majorette *noun* esp. *N Amer.* a member of a female baton-twirling parading group.

drum·mer *noun* **1** a person who plays a drum or drums. **2** esp. *N Amer. informal* a sales representative.

Drum·mond /ˈdrʌmənd/ **Wil·liam Henry** (1854–1907), Irish-born Canadian physician and poet. He is best known for his distinctive dialect verse about French-Canadian habitant life, collected in works such as *The Habitant and other French-Canadian Poems* (1897) and *Johnny Courteau and other Poems* (1901).

Drum·mond·ville /ˈdrʌməndˌvɪl/ a city in south central Quebec, situated on the Rivière Saint-François, about 100 km northeast of Montreal; pop. (2001) 46,599. [General Sir G. *Drummond*, colonial administrator d.1854]

drum roll *noun* a rapid succession of notes sounded on a drum.

drum·stick *noun* **1** a stick used for beating a drum. **2** the lower joint of the leg of a cooked chicken, turkey, etc.

drunk ● *adjective* **1** rendered incapable by alcohol (*dead drunk*). **2** (often foll. by *with*) overcome or elated with joy, success, power, etc. ● *noun* **1** a habitually drunk person. **2** *slang* a drinking bout; a period of drunkenness. □ **drunk as a skunk** *informal* extremely drunk. □ **drunk·ish** *adjective* [past participle of DRINK]

drunk·ard /ˈdrʌŋkərd/ *noun* a person who is drunk, esp. habitually.

drunk driving *noun* the act of driving a vehicle with an excess of alcohol in the blood. □ **drunk driver** *noun*

drunk·en *adjective* (usu. *attributive*) **1** = DRUNK. **2** caused by or exhibiting drunkenness (*a drunken brawl*). **3** fond of drinking; often drunk. □ **drunk·en·ly** *adverb* **drunk·en·ness** *noun*

drunken driving *noun* = DRUNK DRIVING. □ **drunken driver** *noun*

drunk tank *noun N Amer. slang* a large prison cell where persons arrested for drunkenness are detained, esp. overnight.

drupe /druːp/ *noun* any fleshy or pulpy fruit enclosing a stone containing one or a few seeds, e.g. an olive, plum, or peach. [Latin *drupa* from Greek *druppa* olive]

drupe·let /ˈdruːplət/ *noun* (also **drup·el** /ˈdruːpəl/) a small drupe usu. in an aggregate fruit, e.g. a blackberry or raspberry.

druse /druːz/ *noun* **1** a crust of crystals lining a rock cavity. **2** a cavity lined with this. [French from German, = weathered ore]

druth·ers /ˈdrʌðərz/ *noun N Amer. informal* preference, choice; one's way (*if I had my druthers*). [from a dialect pronunciation of *would rather*]

Druze /druːz/ *noun* (often *attributive*) a member of a political or religious sect linked with Islam and living near Mt. Lebanon (*Druze militia*). [French from Arabic *durūz* (pl.), prob. from the name of their founder, Muhammad ibn Ismail *al-Darazi* (d.1019)]

dry ● *adjective* (**drier**; **dri·est**) **1** free from moisture, not wet, esp.: **a** with any moisture having evaporated, drained, or been wiped away (*the clothes are not dry yet*). **b** (of the eyes) free from tears. **c** (of a climate etc.) with insufficient rainfall; not rainy (*a dry spell*). **d** (of a river, well, etc.) dried up; not yielding water. **e** (of a liquid) having disappeared by evaporation etc. **f** not connected with or for use without moisture (*dry shampoo*). **g** (of a shave) with an electric razor. **2** (of wine etc.) not sweet (*dry sherry*). **3 a** meagre, plain, or bare (*dry facts*). **b** uninteresting; dull (*dry as dust*). **4** (of a sense of humour, a joke, etc.) subtle, ironic, and quietly expressed; not obvious. **5 a** (of a country, legislation, etc.) prohibiting the sale of alcoholic drink. **b** (of a person) abstaining from alcohol or drugs. **6 a** (of toast, bread, etc.) without butter, margarine, etc. **b** (of bread, rolls, etc.) stale. **7** (of provisions, groceries, etc.) solid, not liquid. **8** (of a person etc.) impassive, unsympathetic; hard; cold. **9** (of a cow etc.) not yielding milk. **10** *informal* **a** thirsty (*feel dry*). **b** causing thirst (*this is dry work*). **11** *N Amer.* (of beer) having little or no aftertaste, due to longer brewing. **12** (of weather, a climate, etc.) not humid (*40 below, but it's a dry cold*). **13** (of ingredients in a recipe) not liquid, as flour, salt, baking powder, spices, etc. **14** *Brit. Politics informal* of or being a political 'dry' (see sense 3 of *noun*). ● *verb* (**dries**, **dried**) **1** *transitive & intransitive* make or become dry by wiping, evaporation, draining, etc. **2** *transitive* (usu. as **dried** *adjective*) preserve (food etc.) by removing the moisture (*dried egg; dried fruit; dried flowers*). **3** *intransitive* (often foll. by *up*) *Theatre informal* forget one's lines. **4** *transitive & intransitive* (often foll. by *off*) cease or cause (a cow etc.) to cease yielding milk. ● *noun* (*pl.* **dries**) **1** the process or an instance of drying. **2** (prec. by *the*) a dry place (*come into the dry*). **3** *Brit. slang* a politician, esp. a Conservative, who advocates individual responsibility, free trade, and economic stringency, and opposes high government spending. **4 a** (prec. by *the*) esp. *Austral. informal* the dry season. **b** *Austral.* a desert area; waterless country. **5 a** a dry ginger ale. **b** dry wine, sherry, etc. □ **come up dry** *N Amer.* be unsuccessful. **dry out 1** become fully dry. **2** (of a drug addict, alcoholic, etc.) undergo treatment to cure addiction. **dry up 1** make utterly dry. **2** *Brit.* dry dishes. **3** (of moisture) disappear utterly. **4** (of a well etc.) cease to yield water. **5** *informal* (esp. in *imperative*) cease talking. **6** disappear or cease (*had a good business until the market dried up*). **go dry** enact legislation for the prohibition of alcohol. **hang a person out to dry** see HANG. □ **dry·able** *adjective* **dry·ish** *adjective* **dry·ness** *noun* [Old English *drȳge, drygan*, related to Middle Low German *drȫge*, Middle Dutch *drȫghe*, from Germanic]

dryad /ˈdraɪad, ˈdraɪəd/ *noun Myth* a nymph inhabiting a tree; a wood nymph. [Old French *dryade* from Latin from Greek *druas -ados* from *drus* tree]

dryas /ˈdraɪəs/ *noun* (*pl.* **dryas**) = MOUNTAIN AVENS. [Greek *druas* from *drus* tree]

dry battery *noun* an electric battery consisting of dry cells.

dry cell *noun* a voltaic cell in which the electrolyte is absorbed in a solid and cannot be spilled.

dry clean *transitive & intransitive verb* clean (clothes etc.), or be cleanable, with organic solvents without using water. □ **dry cleaner** *noun* **dry cleaning** *noun*

dry cough *noun* a cough not producing phlegm.

dry-cure *transitive verb* cure (meat etc.) without pickling in liquid. □ **dry-cured** *adjective*

Dry·den[1] /ˈdraɪdən/ a city in NW Ontario, about 150 km north of Fort Frances; pop. (2001) 8,198. [J. *Dryden*, minister of agriculture and founder of the town d.1909]

Dry·den[2] ▸ **1 John** (1631–1700), English poet, dramatist, and critic. He established the heroic couplet as the favoured verse form, and his works include the plays *Marriage à la mode* (1672) and *All for Love* (1677), and the verse satire *Absalom and Achitophel* (1681). **2 Ken·neth Wayne** (**'Ken'**) (b.1947), Canadian hockey player, executive, author, and lawyer. A goalie with the Montreal Canadiens (1970–3 and 1974–9), he was awarded numerous league trophies. In 1997 he became president and general manager of the Toronto Maple Leafs.

dry dock *noun* an enclosure for the building or repairing of ships, from which water can be pumped out.

dryer *noun* (also **drier**) **1** a machine or apparatus for drying the hair, laundry, etc. **2** a substance mixed with oil paint or ink to promote drying.

dry-erase *adjective* designating a whiteboard, or felt-tip pens for use with one, which can be erased without being sprayed with liquid.

dry-eyed *adjective* not weeping.

dry farming *noun* esp. *N Amer.* a method of farming without irrigation, used in semi-arid areas.

dry fly ● *noun* an artificial fly which floats on the water (often hyphenated when *attributive*: *dry-fly anglers*). ● *intransitive verb* (usu. **dry-fly**) (**-flies**, **-flied**) fish by such a method.

dry goods *plural noun* **1** *N Amer.* fabrics, clothing, etc. **2** *Cdn & Brit.* solid as opposed to liquid foodstuffs.

dry ice *noun* **1** solid carbon dioxide, which passes directly from solid to vapour at −78.5°C and is used as a refrigerant and to create theatrical effects of fog, which it produces when water is poured onto it. **2** the fog produced in this way.

dry land *noun* **1** land as opposed to the sea, a river, etc. **2** (**dry·land**) (also in *pl.*) esp. *N Amer.* an area or land where rainfall is low (also *attributive*: *dryland farming*). **3** (**dry·land**) (also in *pl.*) esp. *N Amer.* a surface not covered by snow or ice as used for training by skiers, skaters, etc. (also *attributive*: *dryland training*).

dryly *adverb* (also **drily**) **1** (said) in a dry manner; humorously. **2** in a dry way or condition.

dry measure *noun* a measure of capacity for dry products such as grains etc.

dry-mount *transitive verb* mount (a print etc.) on a backing with shellac or shellac-coated paper in between, the whole then being pressed between hot plates to produce bonding. □ **dry-mounting** *noun*

dry·point *noun* **1** a needle for engraving on a bare copper plate without acid. **2** an engraving produced with this.

dry-roasted *adjective* (esp. of nuts, spices, etc.) roasted by a process using little or no oil or liquid. □ **dry-roast** *transitive verb*

dry rot *noun* **1** a decayed state of wood in poorly ventilated conditions, caused by certain fungi. **2** these fungi.

dry run *noun informal* a rehearsal.

dry-salt *transitive verb* = DRY-CURE.

dry-shod *adjective & adverb* without wetting the shoes.

dry sink *noun N Amer.* an antique usu. wooden kitchen cabinet with an inset sink not connected to a supply of running water.

dry spell *noun* **1** a period of dry weather. **2** a period of unproductiveness.

dry·stone *attributive adjective Brit.* (of a wall etc.) built without mortar.

dry suit *noun* a close-fitting waterproof rubber suit worn esp. when skin diving (*compare* WETSUIT).

dry·wall esp. *N Amer.* ● *noun* prefabricated sheets of plaster sandwiched between heavy paper, used for interior walls. ● *transitive verb* install drywall (on a wall etc.). □ **dry·wall·er** *noun* **dry·wall·ing** *noun*

dry well *noun* **1** a well, drilled for oil, water, gas, etc., that is unproductive. **2** *N Amer.* an underground chamber used for draining off excess surface water, grey water, etc.

DS *abbreviation* DAL SEGNO.

DSC *abbreviation* Distinguished Service Cross.

D.Sc. *abbreviation* Doctor of Science.

DSL *abbreviation Computing* digital subscriber line, a technology for high-speed transmission of digital information over standard telephone lines.

DSM *abbreviation* Distinguished Service Medal.

DSO *abbreviation* (in the UK) Distinguished Service Order.

DSP *abbreviation* **1** digital signal processing. **2** digital signal processor.

DSS *abbreviation* (in the UK) Department of Social Security.

DTH *abbreviation* (of a satellite television transmission) direct-to-home.

DTI *abbreviation* (in the UK) Department of Trade and Industry.

Vowels: a cat ɑ arm e bed ɜr her ɜː deux ə ago ɪ sit i cosy iː feed ɒ hot ɔ pore ɔː no ʌ run ʊ put

DTP *abbreviation* DESKTOP PUBLISHING.

DT's *abbreviation* DELIRIUM TREMENS.

DU *abbreviation* depleted uranium.

dual /'duːəl, 'djuːəl/ ● *adjective* **1** of two; twofold. **2** divided in two; double (*dual ownership*). **3** *Grammar* (in some languages) denoting two persons or things (in addition to singular and plural). ● *noun* (also **dual number**) *Grammar* a dual form of a noun, verb, etc. □ **dual·ity** /-'alɪti/ *noun* **dual·ize** *transitive verb* (also esp. *Brit.* **-ise**) [Latin *dualis* from *duo* two]

dual carriageway *noun Brit.* = DIVIDED HIGHWAY.

dual citizenship *noun* the status of a person who is a citizen of more than one country concurrently.

dual control *adjective* (of a vehicle or an aircraft) having two sets of controls, one of which is used by the instructor.

dual in-line package *noun Computing* see DIP.

dual·ism /'djuːəˌlɪzəm/ *noun* **1** the state of being twofold; duality. **2** *Philos.* the theory that in any domain of reality there are two independent underlying principles, e.g. mind and matter, form and content (*compare* IDEALISM 4, MATERIALISM 2). **3** *Theol.* **a** the theory that the forces of good and evil are equally balanced in the universe. **b** the theory of the dual (human and divine) personality of Christ. □ **dual·ist** *noun* **dual·is·tic** *adjective* **dual·is·tic·ally** *adverb*

dual·ly ● *adverb* in a dual or twofold capacity. ● *noun* (also **dual·lie**) *informal* a pickup truck with double rear wheels.

dual-purpose *adjective* **1** (of a vehicle) usable for passengers or goods. **2** (of a farm animal) able to be used for two purposes, e.g. (of a cow) providing both meat and milk.

du·ath·lon /duːˈaθlɒn/ *noun* a sporting event combining two disciplines, e.g. running and swimming, running and biking, etc. □ **du·ath·lete** *noun* [DUAL, after PENTATHLON]

dub[1] *transitive verb* (**dubbed**, **dub·bing**) **1** confer an order of knighthood upon (a person) by the ritual touching of the shoulder with a sword. **2** give (a person or thing) a name, nickname, or title (*dubbed it an exercise in futility*). **3** dress (an artificial fishing fly). **4** smear (leather) with grease. [Old English from Old French *adober* 'equip with armour, repair,' of unknown origin]

dub[2] (**dubbed**, **dub·bing**) ● *transitive verb* **1** provide (a film etc.) with an alternative soundtrack, esp. in a different language. **2** add (sound effects or music) to a film or a broadcast. **3** combine (soundtracks) into one. **4** transfer or make a copy of (a tape or disc). ● *noun* **1** (also **dub music**) a remixed version of a piece of recorded (esp. reggae) music, usu. with the melodic line removed and special effects added. **2** (also **dub poetry**) a kind of performance poetry in Jamaican (or black English) vernacular, orig. accompanied by dub music. **3** a dubbed tape etc. [abbreviation of DOUBLE]

dub[3] *noun* esp. *US slang* an inexperienced or unskilful person. [perhaps from DUB[1] in obsolete sense 'beat flat']

Dubai /duːˈbaɪ/ a port in the United Arab Emirates, on the Persian Gulf; pop. (est. 2002) 912,700.

du Barry /duː ˈbari/ **Com·tesse** (title of Marie Jeanne Bécu) (*c.*1743–93), French courtier. The mistress of Louis XV, she was executed during the French Revolution.

Du·bawnt Lake /duːˈbɒnt/ a lake in southwestern Nunavut, on the border with the NWT, over 300 km east of Great Slave Lake. [Chipewyan *tobutua* water shore, perhaps because the lake thaws only along the shoreline in summer]

Du·bawnt River a river in southwestern NWT and southeastern Nunavut, rising north of Lake Athabasca and flowing 842 km generally northeastward through Dubawnt Lake to join the Thelon River just west of Aberdeen Lake. [see DUBAWNT LAKE]

dub·bin /'dʌbɪn/ ● *noun* (also **dub·bing** /'dʌbɪŋ/) prepared grease for softening and waterproofing leather. ● *transitive verb* (**dub·bined**, **dub·bin·ing**) apply dubbin to (boots etc.). [see DUB[1] 4]

dub·bing *noun* an alternative soundtrack to a film etc.

Dub·ček /'duːbtʃek/ **Alex·an·der** (1921–92), Czechoslovak Communist leader, first secretary of the Czechoslovak Communist Party 1968–9. His attempt to increase civil liberties led to the invasion of Czechoslovakia by Warsaw Pact forces (1968) and his removal from office (1969); with the abandonment of Communism he was appointed speaker of the Federal Assembly (1989–92).

Dubé /duːˈbei/ **Mar·cel** (b.1930), Canadian playwright. He is noted for his highly poetic prose style, classic sense of dramatic structure, and tragic vision of life applied to contemporary situations in Quebec society.

Dubhe /duːˈbei/ a giant star in the constellation Ursa Major. [Arabic, lit. 'the bear']

dubi·ety /duːˈbaiəti, djuːˈbaiəti/ *noun* (pl. **-eties**) *literary* **1** a feeling of doubt. **2** a doubtful matter. [Late Latin *dubietas* from *dubium* doubt]

dubi·ous /'duːbiəs, 'djuːbiəs/ *adjective* **1** hesitating or doubting (*dubious about going*). **2** of questionable value or truth (*a dubious claim*). **3** unreliable; suspicious (*dubious company*). **4** of doubtful result (*a dubious undertaking*). □ **dubi·ous·ly** *adverb* **dubi·ous·ness** *noun* [Latin *dubiosus* from *dubium* doubt]

Dub·lin /'dʌblɪn/ **1** the capital city of the Republic of Ireland, situated on the Irish Sea at the mouth of the Liffey River; pop. (2002) 495,101. **2** a county of the Republic of Ireland, in the province of Leinster; county town, Dublin. □ **Dub·lin·er** *noun*

dub·nium *noun* a very unstable chemical element made by high-energy atomic collisions. Symbol: **Du**; at. no. 105. [modern Latin, from *Dubna* in Russia, site of the Joint Nuclear Institute]

Du Bois /duː ˈbɔis/ **W(il·liam) E(d·ward) B(urg·hardt)** (1868–1963), US sociologist, writer, and political activist. A leading advocate of racial equality through black organization, he co-founded the NAACP and worked as the editor of its magazine *Crisis* from 1910 to 1934.

Du·brov·nik /dʊˈbrɒvnɪk/ a port and resort on the Adriatic coast of Croatia; pop. (2001) 43,770.

Du·buf·fet /duːbuːˈfei/ **Jean (Phi·lippe Ar·thur)** (1901–85), French painter and sculptor, who developed 'art brut' (raw art) from his study of graffiti and the artwork of children and psychotics.

ducal /'duːkəl, 'djuː-/ *adjective* of, like, or pertaining to a duke or dukedom. [French from *duc* DUKE]

ducat /'dʌkət/ *noun* **1** *hist.* any of various gold or silver coins, formerly current in most European countries. **2 a** a coin. **b** (in *pl.*) money. **3** a ticket, esp. an admission ticket or one for the train, bus, etc. [medieval Latin *ducatus* DUCHY]

Duce /'duːtʃei/ *noun* a leader, esp. (**Il Duce**) the title assumed by Mussolini. [Italian, = leader]

Du·champ /duːˈʃɑ̃/ **Mar·cel** (1887–1968), French-born US painter and sculptor. A leading figure of the Dada movement and originator of conceptual art, he invented 'ready-mades', mass-produced articles selected at random and displayed as works of art.

Du·chenne muscular dystrophy /duːˈʃein/ *noun* a severe form of muscular dystrophy caused by a genetic defect and usually affecting boys. Abbr.: **DMD**. [named after G.B.A. *Duchenne*, French neurologist d.1875]

duch·ess /'dʌtʃəs/ *noun* (as a title usu. **Duchess**) **1** a duke's wife or widow. **2** a woman holding the rank of duke in her own right. [Old French *duchesse* from medieval Latin *ducissa* (as DUKE)]

du·chesse potatoes /duːˈʃes/ *plural noun* mashed potatoes formed into croquettes or small cakes, or piped into fancy shapes, and then baked or fried to acquire a crisp surface. [French, = DUCHESS]

duchy /'dʌtʃi/ *noun* (pl. **-ies**) **1** a dukedom or the territory of a duke or duchess. **2** (often as **the Duchy**) the royal dukedom of Cornwall or Lancaster, each with certain estates, revenues, and jurisdiction of its own. [Old French *duché(e)* from medieval Latin *ducatus* from Latin *dux ducis* leader]

duck[1] *noun* **1 a** any of various swimming birds of the family Anatidae, esp. the domesticated form of the mallard or wild duck. **b** the female of this (*opp.* DRAKE). **c** the flesh of a duck as food. **2** (also **ducks**) *Brit. informal* (esp. as a form of address) dear, darling. **3** esp. *N Amer.* a fellow, individual, etc., esp. a somewhat eccentric one (*he's an odd duck*). □ **get** (or **have**) **one's ducks in a row** *N Amer.* get (or have) all one's facts, details, etc. straight, together, and organized. **like a duck to water** adapting very readily. **like water off a duck's back** *informal* (of remonstrances etc.) producing no effect. [Old English *duce*, *dūce*: related to DUCK[2]]

duck[2] ● *verb* **1** *intransitive & transitive* plunge, dive, or dip under water and emerge (*ducked him in the pond*). **2 a** *intransitive* stoop suddenly or move quickly and unobtrusively, esp. as an evasive measure (*ducked out of sight*). **b** *transitive* bob, jerk down, or lower (esp. the head) momentarily (*ducked his head under the beam*). **3** *transitive & intransitive* *informal* (often foll. by *out*) avoid or dodge; withdraw (from) (*ducked out of the engagement; ducked the meeting*). **4** *intransitive* *Bridge* play a low card to a trick rather than attempt to win with a high card. ● *noun* **1** a quick swim or plunge into water etc. **2** a quick lowering of the head, rapid evasive movement, etc. □ **duck·er** *noun* [Old English *dūcan* (unrecorded) from Germanic]

duck[3] *noun* **1** a strong untwilled linen or cotton fabric used for the outer clothing of sailors, small sails, etc. **2** (in *pl.*) trousers made of this (*white ducks*). [Middle Dutch *doek*, of unknown origin]

duck⁴ *noun informal* an amphibious landing craft, esp. as used in World War II. [*DUKW*, its official designation]

duck·bill *noun* **1** (also **duck-billed platypus**) = PLATYPUS. **2** (also **duck-billed dinosaur**) = HADROSAUR. ● *adjective* = DUCK-BILLED.

duck-billed *adjective* having the spatulate shape of the bill of a duck.

duck·board *noun* (usu. in *pl.*) a path of wooden slats placed over soft or muddy ground, fragile surfaces, etc. to facilitate movement.

duck boot *noun* a low cut waterproof boot with a moulded rubber upper and laces at the tongue.

duck-dive ● *noun* a vertical dive down into the water. ● *intransitive verb* make such a dive.

duck, duck, goose *noun N Amer.* a children's game in which a player walks around a circle of participants, tapping each and saying 'duck' until, selecting another child to be it and saying 'goose', he or she runs around the circle one way as the chosen child runs the other way, each trying to reach the empty spot first.

ducking-stool *noun hist.* a chair fastened to the end of a pole, on which offenders were ducked in water as a punishment.

duck·ish *noun Cdn* (*Nfld*) (also *attributive*) dusk, twilight, or the time between sunset and dark (*duckish times*).

Duck Lake a town in central Saskatchewan, southwest of Prince Albert; pop. (2001) 624. It was the site in 1885 of a battle marking the beginning of the Northwest Rebellion. [the name of a lake to the west, so called because of the multitude of ducks in the area]

duck·ling *noun* **1** a young duck. **2** its flesh as food.

ducks and drakes *noun* **1** a game of making a flat stone skim along the surface of water. **2** idle play. □ **play ducks and drakes with** *informal* squander, trifle with, or use recklessly.

duck's ass *noun* (also esp. *Brit.* **duck's arse**) = DUCKTAIL. Abbr.: **DA**.

duck soup *noun N Amer. slang* **1** an easy task. **2** an easily or thoroughly beaten or defeated person.

duck·tail *noun esp. N Amer. slang* a haircut with the hair on the nape of the head shaped like a duck's tail. □ **duck·tailed** *adjective*

duck·walk ● *noun* a waddle or a walk in a squatting position. ● *intransitive verb* walk in a squatting position.

duck·weed *noun* any of various aquatic plants, esp. of the genus *Lemna*, growing on the surface of still water.

ducky ● *noun* (pl. **-ies**) **1** *Brit. informal* (esp. as a term of endearment) darling, dear. **2** *N Amer.* (usu. in *pl.*) = DUCK BOOT. **3** *N Amer.* a small, inflatable water craft, e.g. a rubber dinghy, kayak, etc. **4** (in full **rubber ducky**) a toy duck made of plastic, rubber, etc. ● *adjective* sweet, fine, splendid.

duct *noun* **1** a channel or tube for conveying air, fluid, cable, etc. **2 a** a tube or passage in the body conveying fluids or secretions such as tears, lymph, etc. **b** *Bot.* any of the vessels of the vascular tissue of plants, containing air, water, etc. □ **duct·al** *adjective* **duct·ed** *adjective* [Latin *ductus* leading, aqueduct, from *ducere duct-* lead]

duc·tile /ˈdʌktaɪl/ *adjective* **1** (of a substance) flexible, pliant, malleable. **2** (of a material, esp. metal) pliable or capable of being drawn into wire. **3** (of a person) docile, tractable, open to persuasion. □ **duc·til·ity** /-ˈtɪlɪti/ *noun* [Latin *ductilis* from *ducere duct-* lead]

duct·ing *noun* **1** a system of ducts. **2** material, esp. tubing or piping, in the form of a duct or ducts.

duct·less *adjective* lacking or not using a duct or ducts, esp. of a gland secreting directly into the bloodstream.

duct tape *noun N Amer.* tape, of plastic-backed webbed cloth, used for household repairs etc. □ **duct-tape** *transitive verb*

duct·work *noun* a system of ducts for conveying gases, liquids, etc.

dud *slang* ● *noun* **1** a thing that fails to work properly or is otherwise unsatisfactory or worthless (*a box office dud; all three bombs are duds*). **2** an ineffectual person (*a complete dud, incapable of even hitting the ball*). **3** (in *pl.*) clothes. ● *adjective* **1** not working or meeting standards; faulty (*a dud ignition switch*). **2** counterfeit (*charged with issuing dud cheques*). [Middle English: origin unknown]

dude *N Amer. slang* ● *noun* **1** a fellow or person. **2** a person, usu. male, fastidiously concerned with clothes, appearance, etc. **3** a city dweller, esp. one vacationing on a ranch in western Canada or the US; a tenderfoot. ● *reflexive verb & transitive* (usu. foll. by *up*, usu. in *passive*) dress or fix up (oneself, another, a thing), esp. ostentatiously. □ **duded up** dressed or fixed up, esp. ostentatiously. □ **dude·ness** *noun* **dud·ette** *noun* [19th c.: prob. from German dial. *dude* fool]

Dudek /ˈduːdek/ **Louis** (1918–2001), Canadian poet, known for poems such as *East of the City* (1946), *Continuation !* (1981), and *Continuation !!* (1990).

dude ranch *noun N Amer.* a cattle ranch converted to a vacation resort for tourists, featuring riding, camping, barbecues, etc.

dudg·eon /ˈdʌdʒən/ *noun* a feeling of anger, offence, or resentment. □ **in high dudgeon** very angry or angrily. [16th c.: origin unknown]

Dud·ley¹ an industrial town in the west Midlands of England, near Birmingham; pop. (est. 2002) 195,900.

Dudley², **Rob·ert**, **Earl of Leicester** (*c.*1532–88), English courtier during the reign of Elizabeth I. He remained in favour with the Queen throughout his life, receiving two military appointments.

due /duː, djuː/ ● *adjective* **1** (*predicative*) owing or payable as a debt or an obligation, whether immediately or at some future date (*our thanks are due to him; $500 was due on the 15th*). **2** (often foll. by *to*) belonging to or incumbent upon (a person) by right, by duty, or as a necessity (*his due reward; received the applause due to a hero*). **3** proper, sufficient, or adequate (*after due consideration*). **4** (*predicative*; foll. by *to*) attributable or ascribable to (a cause, an agent, etc.) (*death was due to cardiac arrest*). **5** (*predicative*) expected or intended to arrive or appear at a certain time (*a train is due at 7:30*). **6** (foll. by *to* + infin.) scheduled or under an obligation or agreement to do something (*due to speak tonight*). ● *noun* **1** a thing which is owed to a person legally or morally (*a fair hearing is my due*). **2** (in *pl.*) **a** what a person owes, esp. obligations, responsibilities, etc. **b** an obligatory and legally demandable payment, toll, or charge, esp. the membership fees for a club etc. (*union dues*). ● *adverb* (of a point of the compass) exactly, directly (*went due east*). □ **due to** because of, owing to (*was late due to an accident*) (*compare sense 4 of adjective*). **fall** (or **become**) **due** (of a bill etc.) be immediately payable. **give a person his or her due** treat a person fairly or with justice. **in due course** (or **time**) **1** at about the appropriate time. **2** in the natural order. **pay one's dues 1** fulfill one's obligations. **2** undergo hardships to succeed or gain experience. [Old French *deü*, ultimately from Latin *debitus* past participle of *debēre* owe]

due date *noun* **1** the date on which payment of a bill etc. falls due. **2** the date, in a pregnancy, on which a child is predicted to be born. **3** the date on which a library book, rented item, etc. must be returned.

due diligence *noun Law* reasonable steps taken by a person in order to satisfy a legal requirement, esp. in buying or selling something.

duel /ˈduːəl, ˈdjuːəl/ ● *noun* **1** *hist.* a contest with deadly weapons arranged between two people in order to settle a point of honour. **2** any contest between two people, parties, causes, animals, etc. (*a duel of wits*). ● *intransitive verb* (**duelled, duel·ling**; *US* **dueled, duel·ing**) fight a duel or duels. □ **duel·ler** *noun* (*US* **duel·er**). **duel·list** *noun* (*US* **duel·ist**). [Italian *duello* or Latin *duellum* (archaic form of *bellum* war), in medieval Latin = single combat]

duen·na /duːˈenə, djuːˈenə/ *noun* an older woman acting as a governess, companion, or chaperone in charge of girls, esp. in a Spanish family. [Spanish *dueña* from Latin *domina* mistress]

due process *noun* (in full **due process of the law**) the administration of justice through the courts in accordance with established rules and principles, esp. to enforce and protect private rights.

duet /duːˈet, djuːˈet/ ● *noun* **1** *Music* a performance by two voices, instrumentalists, etc. **2** a composition for two performers. ● *intransitive verb* (usu. foll. by *with*) (**duet·ted, duet·ting**) perform a duet. □ **duet·tist** *noun* [German *Duett* or Italian *duetto* diminutive of *duo* duet, from Latin *duo* two]

duff¹ /dʌf/ *noun Brit., Cdn* (*Maritimes & Nfld*), *& US* (*New England*) a boiled pudding. [Northern English form of DOUGH]

duff² ● *noun N Amer.* decaying vegetable matter, such as leaves or bits of wood, which covers forest ground. ● *adjective Brit. slang* **1** worthless, counterfeit. **2** useless, broken. [orig. Scots; ultimate origin uncertain]

duff³ *noun N Amer. & Scot.* buttocks (*get off your duff and get a job*). [origin unknown]

duff⁴ *transitive verb slang* **1** esp. *Brit. Golf* bungle or mis-hit (a shot, a ball). **2** *Brit.* (foll. by *up*) beat or thrash (a person). [perhaps back-formation from DUFFER]

duf·fel /ˈdʌfəl/ *var. of* DUFFLE.

duf·fer /ˈdʌfər/ *noun informal* **1** an incompetent or stupid person, esp. an elderly one. **2** a person inexperienced at something, esp. at playing golf. [perhaps from Scots *doofart* stupid person, from *douf* spiritless]

Duf·fer·in and Ava /ˈdʌfrən, ˈeivə/ **Fred·erick Tem·ple Black·wood, 1st Marquess of** (1826–1902), English statesman, Governor General of Canada 1872–8.

Consonants: b *but* d *dog* f *few* g *get* h *her* j *yes* k *cat* l *leg* m *man* n *no* p *pen* r *red* s *sit*

duf·fle /ˈdʌfəl/ *noun* (also **duf·fel**) **1** a coarse, closely woven, woollen cloth with a thick nap. **2** *N Amer.* a sportsman's or camper's equipment, food, clothing, etc. **3** = DUFFLE BAG. [*Duffel* in Belgium, where the cloth was originally made]

duffle bag *noun* (also **duffel bag**) a large, cylindrical canvas bag closed by a drawstring and carried over the shoulder.

duffle coat *noun* (also **duffel coat**) a hooded overcoat of duffle, usu. fastened with toggles.

Du·fresne /duːˈfren/ **Diane** (b.1944), Canadian singer and actress, whose songs include 'J'ai rencontré l'homme de ma vie'.

dufus /ˈduːfəs/ var. of DOOFUS.

Dufy /duːfiː/ **Raoul** (1877–1953), French painter and textile designer, noted for his paintings of racecourses, boating scenes, and French society life which employ calligraphic outlines sketched over bright background washes.

dug[1] *past and past participle of* DIG.

dug[2] *noun* **1** the udder, breast, teat, or nipple of a female animal. **2** *slang* (usu. in *pl.*) the breast of a woman. [16th c.: possibly of Old Norse origin and related to Swedish *dägga*, Danish *dægge* suckle]

du·gong /ˈduːgɒŋ/ *noun* (*pl.* same or **du·gongs**) a marine mammal, *Dugong dugon*, of Asian seas and coasts. *Also called* SEA COW. [ultimately from Malay *dūyong*]

dug·out *noun* **1 a** *N Amer. Sport* a low shelter at the side of a baseball diamond etc. with seating for the team manager, trainer, players, etc. **b** a roofed shelter, esp. for troops in trenches. **2 a** *esp. N Amer.* a rough shelter hollowed out in a bank or hillside, usu. roofed with turf, canvas, etc. **b** *Cdn* (*Prairies*) a large hole, either shallow or with steep sides, used as a reservoir to catch and hold rain, spring runoff, etc. **3** a canoe made from a hollowed out tree trunk, used by many Aboriginal groups.

duh /də/ *interjection* indicating stupidity or mental slowness.

DUI *abbreviation US* driving under the influence (of drugs or alcohol).

dui·ker /ˈdəɪkər/ *noun* (also **duy·ker**) any of various small African antelopes of the genera *Cephalophus* and *Silvicapra*, esp. *S. grimmia*, usu. having a crest of long hair between its horns, widespread in southern African savannah and bush. [Dutch *duiker* diver, with reference to its habit of plunging through bushes when pursued]

Duis·burg /ˈduːsbɜrg/ an industrial city in NW Germany, in North Rhine-Westphalia; pop. (est. 2002) 517,000.

du jour /duː ˈʒʊr/ *adjective* (placed after noun) of the day; trendy or fashionable. [French, after PLAT DU JOUR]

Dukas /duːˈkɒ/ **Paul (Abra·ham)** (1865–1935), French composer, best known for the orchestral work *The Sorcerer's Apprentice* (1897).

duke /duːk, djuːk/ ● *noun* **1** (as a title usu. **Duke**) **a** a person holding the highest hereditary title of the nobility and ranking next below a prince, esp. in Britain. **b** a sovereign prince ruling a duchy or small nation, esp. in certain European countries. **2** (usu. in *pl.*) *slang* **a** the hand or fist (*put up your dukes!*). **b** the verdict in a boxing match (*won a unanimous duke in a lively four rounds*). **3** a kind of cherry that is a hybrid between the mazard and the morello, neither very sweet nor very sour. ● *transitive verb N Amer. slang* (usu. foll. by *out*) fight, esp. with the fists (*they decided to duke it out*). [Old French *duc* from Latin *dux ducis* leader; in sense 'fist' from *Duke of Yorks*, rhyming slang for *forks* fingers]

duke·dom *noun* **1** a duchy or the territory ruled by a duke. **2** the rank of duke.

Dul·bec·co /dʌlˈbekoʊ/ **Ren·ato** (b.1914), Italian-born US virologist, who conducted research into the genetic material of cancer-causing viruses; he shared a Nobel Prize in 1975.

dul·cet /ˈdʌlsət/ *adjective* (esp. of sound) sweet and soothing (*dulcet tones*). [Middle English, earlier *doucet* from Old French diminutive of *doux* from Latin *dulcis* sweet]

dul·ci·mer /ˈdʌlsɪmər/ *noun* **1** a musical instrument with strings of graduated length stretched over a trapezoidal sounding board or box, played by being struck with hammers. **2** a zither-like folk instrument with three or four strings, played by plucking or strumming. [Old French *doulcemer*, said to represent Latin *dulce* sweet, *melos* song]

dull ● *adjective* **1** uninteresting, tedious, or boring. **2** (of the weather) cloudy, overcast, gloomy. **3 a** (esp. of a knife-edge etc.) blunt. **b** (of colour, light, or taste) not bright, vivid, or keen. **4** (of a pain etc.) prolonged and indistinct, not acute (*a dull ache*). **5** slow to understand, not quick-witted. **6** (of a trade, goods, etc.) sluggish or stagnant, slow-moving or not easily saleable. **7** (of a person, animal, etc.) listless, depressed, not lively or cheerful (*he's a dull fellow since the accident*). **8** (of the ears, eyes, etc.) without keen perception. **9** (of sound) indistinct, muffled, not clear or loud (*a dull thud*). ● *transitive & intransitive verb* make

or become dull. □ **dull the edge of** blunt or make less sensitive, interesting, effective, amusing, etc. □ **dulled** *adjective* **dull·ish** *adjective*

dull·ness *noun* **dully** /ˈdʌlli, ˈdʌli/ *adverb* [Middle Low German, Middle Dutch *dul*, corresponding to Old English *dol* stupid]

dull·ard /ˈdʌlərd/ *noun* a slow, dull, or stupid person.

Dul·les /ˈdʌləs/ **John Fos·ter** (1888–1959), US Republican politician, lawyer, and diplomat. He was the US adviser at the creation of the United Nations (1945) and negotiated the Peace Treaty with Japan (1951); as secretary of state (1953–9) he urged the US buildup of nuclear weapons during the Cold War.

dulls·ville *noun* an extremely dull place or situation.

dulse /dʌls/ *noun* an edible seaweed, *Rhodymenia palmata*, with red wedge-shaped fronds. [Irish & Gaelic *duileasg*]

duly /ˈduːli, ˈdjuːli/ *adverb* **1** in due manner, order, form, or time. **2** correctly, properly, fitly, or sufficiently.

Duma /ˈduːmə/ **1** a legislative body in the ruling assembly of Russia and of some other republics of the former USSR. **2** any of four elected legislative bodies existing in Russia between 1905 and 1917. Introduced by Tsar Nicholas II in response to popular unrest, they in fact had little effective power. [Russian: originally an elective municipal council]

Dumas /duːˈmɒ/ **1 Alex·andre** (known as 'Dumas *père*') (1802–70), French novelist and dramatist, noted for his historical adventure novels, which include *The Three Musketeers* (1844–5) and *The Count of Monte Cristo* (1844–5). **2** his son, **Alex·andre** (1824–95) (also called 'Dumas *fils*'), French dramatist and novelist, who wrote the novel and play *La Dame aux camélias* (1848), which formed the basis of Verdi's opera *La Traviata* (1853).

Du Maur·ier /duː ˈmɔriˌeɪ/ **1 Dame Daphne** (1907–89), English novelist, known for her popular novels and period romances, which include *Rebecca* (1938). **2** her grandfather, **George (Louis Pal·mel·la Bus·son)** (1834–96), French-born English cartoonist, illustrator, and novelist, chiefly remembered for his novel *Trilby* (1894), which included the character Svengali.

dumb ● *adjective* **1 a** (of a person) unable to speak, usu. because of a congenital defect or deafness; mute. **b** (of an animal) naturally unable to speak (*our dumb friends*). **2** temporarily silenced by surprise, shyness, grief, etc. (*struck dumb by this revelation*). **3** persistently taciturn or reticent, esp. insultingly (*dumb insolence*). **4** (of an action, expression, etc.) performed or made without speech. **5** *informal esp. N Amer.* stupid, ignorant, foolish. **6** (usu. of a class, population, etc.) having no voice in government (*the dumb masses*). **7** (of a computer terminal etc.) not programmable, able only to transmit data to or receive data from a computer (*opp.* INTELLIGENT 3b.) **8** (of missiles etc.) not guided after being launched (*opp.* SMART 7b.) ● *transitive verb N Amer. slang* (usu. foll. by *down*) reduce or adapt (a text etc.) to a lower level of understanding. □ **dumb as (or dumber than) a sack of hammers** *N Amer. informal* very stupid. □ **dumb·ly** *adverb* **dumb·ness** *noun* [Old English: origin unknown: sense 6 from German *dumm*]

dumb animals *plural noun* animals, esp. as objects of pity.

dumb-ass *noun N Amer. slang* (also *attributive*) a thoroughly stupid or foolish person.

dumb·bell *noun* **1** a short bar with a weight at each end, used for exercise, muscle building, etc. **2** *slang* a stupid person; a fool.

dumb blond *noun informal derogatory* (as a stereotype) a pretty but stupid blond person, usu. a woman.

dumb cane *noun see* DIEFFENBACHIA.

dumb cluck *noun slang* a foolish or stupid person.

dumb·found *transitive verb* (also **dum·found**) (usu. in *passive*) astonish, strike dumb, or confound. [blend of DUMB + CONFOUND]

dumb·head *noun esp. N Amer. slang* a stupid person.

dumbo *noun* (*pl.* **dumbos**) *slang* a stupid person; a fool.

dumb show *noun* **1** significant gestures or mime, used when words are inappropriate. **2** a part of a play acted in mime in early drama.

dumb·struck *adjective* greatly shocked or surprised and so lost for words.

dumb waiter *noun* **1** a small elevator for carrying food, plates, etc. between floors. **2** *Brit.* a movable table, esp. with revolving shelves, used in a dining room (*compare* LAZY SUSAN).

dum·dum[1] *noun* a foolish person. [DUMB]

dum·dum[2] *noun* (in full **dumdum bullet**) a kind of soft-nosed or hollow-nosed bullet that expands on impact to inflict extensive injuries. [*Dum-Dum* in India, where it was first produced]

Dum·fries /dʌmˈfriːs/ a market town in SW Scotland, administrative centre of Dumfries and Galloway region; pop. (est. 2002) 32,400.

Dumfries and Galloway a local government region in SW Scotland; administrative centre, Dumfries.

Dum·fries·shire /dʌmˈfriːʃiːr/ a former county of SW Scotland. It became part of Dumfries and Galloway region in 1975.

dummy ● *noun* (*pl.* **-mies**) **1** a model of a human being, esp.: **a** a ventriloquist's doll. **b** a figure used to model clothes in a store window etc. **c** a target used for firearms practice. **d** a mannequin used in crash tests for vehicles etc. **2** (often *attributive*) **a** an imitation, representation, or counterfeit of an object used to replace or resemble a real or normal one, as in a display etc. **b** a prototype, esp. in publishing. **3** *informal* **a** a stupid person. **b** *derogatory* a mute person. **4 a** a figurehead present only for appearances or a person taking no significant part in an activity. **b** a person who is merely a tool for another, buying etc. on another's behalf. **5** *Cdn & Brit.* a soother, pacifier, or rubber nipple for a baby to suck on. **6** an imaginary fourth player at whist, whose hand is turned up and played by a partner. **7** *Bridge* **a** the partner of the declarer, whose cards are exposed after the first lead. **b** this player's hand. **8** *Military* a blank round of ammunition. **9** *Rugby & Soccer* a pretended pass. **10** (in full **dummy instruction**) *Computing* a sequence of data inserted into an instruction stream that merely occupies space and is not intended for execution. ● *adjective* **1** of or pertaining to a dummy, imitation, or copy. **2** sham, counterfeit, or fictitious (*a dummy corporation*). ● *intransitive verb* (**-mies, -mied**) *Soccer* make a pretended pass or swerve etc. □ **dummy up** *N Amer. slang* refuse to talk, keep quiet, give no information. [DUMB + -Y²]

dummy run *noun* a practice, trial run, or rehearsal.

Du·mont /duːˈmɔ̃/ **Gab·riel** (1837–1906), Canadian Metis leader. A member of the group that invited Louis Riel to the Saskatchewan valley to organize the movement for the constitutional expression of Metis grievances, he commanded military operations during the Northwest Rebellion (1885), gaining victories at Duck Lake and Fish Creek, and defending Batoche before fleeing to the US.

dump ● *noun* **1 a** (in full **garbage dump**) a place for depositing garbage. **b** a heap or pile of garbage, waste material, etc. **c** *N Amer. informal* a large deposit of something (*a fresh dump of snow*). **2** *informal* a shabby, unpleasant, or dreary place. **3** *Military* a temporary store of ammunition, provisions, etc. deposited for later use. **4 a** an accumulated pile of ore, earth, etc. from mining operations. **b** the place where this is deposited. **5** *Computing* **a** a printout or listing of stored data, esp. of the complete contents of a computer memory. **b** a periodic record of the state of a disk, made on magnetic tape in order to protect against accidental overwriting or mechanical failure. **6** (in full **log dump**) a place where logs are piled such as on a riverbank, near a road or railway, etc., in preparation for being moved to the mill. **7** *esp. N Amer. slang* an act of defecation. **8** *esp. N Amer. informal* a swamping of a water craft or a sudden depositing of its occupants into the water. ● *verb* **1** *transitive* **a** throw (a thing) down carelessly, clumsily, or unceremoniously (*dumped the groceries on the table*). **b** throw down in or as in a lump or mass (*the storm dumped 15 cm of snow on the city*). **c** fling abruptly out of a craft, esp. into water (*the wind came up and dumped us into the drink*). **2** *transitive* **a** empty or tip out (garbage etc.), esp. from a container. **b** discard or dispose of (garbage, hazardous waste, etc.). **3** *transitive informal* **a** abandon or desert (a person, issue, etc.) (*they dumped their grandmother at the hospital and left*). **b** cast aside or transfer (difficulties etc.), usu. hastily and irresponsibly (*he dumped his work on me when he went on vacation*). **c** abruptly end a relationship with (a person), usu. less than amicably (*the company dumped him for absenteeism; she dumped him on their honeymoon*). **4** *transitive Econ.* **a** put (goods) on the market in large quantities and at low prices. **b** send (goods unsaleable at a high price in the home market) to a foreign market for sale at a low price, to keep up the price at home, and to capture a new market. **5** *transitive Computing* **a** copy (stored data) to a different location, esp. to an external storage medium from an internal one, e.g. to check a program or safeguard data. **b** reproduce the contents of (a store) externally. **6** *transitive* **a** *Sport* beat (another team etc.) decisively. **b** *Boxing* lose (a match) intentionally. **7** *intransitive N Amer. slang* defecate. □ **dump on** *esp. N Amer.* **1** criticize severely, treat with scorn or contempt, or defeat heavily. **2** thwart (*fate dumped on my plans*). **take a dump** *N Amer. slang* defecate. [Middle English perhaps from Old Norse; compare Danish *dumpe*, Norwegian *dumpa* fall suddenly]

dump-and-chase *adjective Cdn Hockey* designating a strategy of play in which a player shoots the puck far down the ice and then chases after it.

dump·er *noun* **1** *N Amer.* a large metal bin for garbage. **2 a** a person or company that dumps garbage etc., esp. one that disposes of toxic waste covertly or illegally. **b** a thing that dumps or disposes of garbage etc.

□ **into the dumper** *N Amer. informal* into a dire state or condition (*the market has gone right into the dumper*).

dump·ing *noun* **1** the practice of discarding garbage, hazardous waste, etc., esp. covertly or illegally (*No dumping!*). **2 a** the practice of putting goods on the market in large quantities and at low prices. **b** the practice of sending goods unsaleable at a high price on the home market to a foreign market for sale at a low price, esp. to keep up the price at home and to capture new markets. **3** *esp. US* the act of abandoning a person, esp. one considered burdensome, at a hospital etc. (*granny dumping*).

dumping ground *noun* **1** = DUMP 1a. **2** a catch-all category, institution, etc. used for something unclassified or as a place of last resort for those considered socially undesirable (*a dumping ground for criminals*).

dump·ling *noun* **1 a** a small piece of dough, sometimes with a filling, boiled in water or in stew. **b** a dessert consisting of apple or other fruit enclosed in dough and baked. **2** *informal* a small fat person. [apparently diminutive of *dump* small round object, but recorded much earlier]

dumps *plural noun informal* a state of depression, melancholy, or low spirits (*down in the dumps*). [prob. from Low German or Dutch, fig. use of Middle Dutch *domp* exhalation, haze, mist: related to DAMP]

Dump·ster *noun proprietary* a very large container for garbage, usu. emptied by being mechanically lifted onto trucks. [originally *Dempster Dumpster*, proprietary name (based on DUMP) given by the US manufacturers, Dempster Brothers of Knoxville, Tennessee]

Dumpster diver *noun slang* a person, usu. poor or homeless, who searches for food, clothing, etc. in dumpsters. □ **Dump·ster dive** *intransitive verb* **Dump·ster div·ing** *noun*

dump truck *noun* a usu. open-topped truck with a body that tilts or opens at the back for unloading.

dumpy *adjective* (**dump·i·er, dump·i·est**) short, rounded, and stout. □ **dump·i·ness** *noun*

dun¹ ● *adjective* dull greyish-brown. ● *noun* **1** a dun colour. **2** a dun horse. **3 a** any of various dusky coloured flies, esp. mayflies. **b** a dark fishing fly resembling this. [Old English *dun, dunn*]

dun² ● *noun* **1** a debt collector or an importunate creditor. **2** a demand for money, esp. in payment of a debt. ● *transitive verb* (**dunned, dun·ning**) **1** make repeated and persistent demands upon, esp. for money owed. **2** bother, pester, assail constantly. [abbreviation of obsolete *dunkirk* privateer, from DUNKIRK]

Du·nant /duːˈnɑ̃/ **Jean Henri** (1828–1910), Swiss philanthropist. He founded the International Red Cross (1864), and shared the first Nobel Peace Prize in 1901.

Dun·bar /dʌnˈbɑr/ **Wil·liam** (*c.*1460–*c.*1520), Scottish poet and priest, known for the political allegory 'The Thrissill and the Rois' (1503), satires, and elegies.

Dun·bar·ton·shire /dʌnˈbɑrtənˌʃiːr/ a former county of west central Scotland, on the Clyde, which became part of Strathclyde region in 1975, and is now divided among East Dunbartonshire, West Dunbartonshire, and Argyll and Bute.

Dun·can¹ /ˈdʌŋkən/ a city in BC, located on the east coast of Vancouver Island, southeast of Nanaimo; pop. (2001) 4,699. □ **Dun·can·ite** *noun* [W. C. *Duncan*, a farmer who settled there in 1862]

Dun·can², **Isa·dora** (1877–1927), US dancer and teacher. A pioneer of modern dance, she developed a form of 'free' barefoot dancing based on instinctive movements and inspired by classical Greek art.

Duncan I (*c.*1010–40), king of Scotland 1034–40, who was killed by Macbeth, his rival to the throne.

dunce /dʌns/ *noun* a person slow at learning; a stupid person. [DUNS SCOTUS, whose followers were ridiculed by 16th-c. humanists and reformers as enemies of learning]

dunce cap *noun* (also **dunce's cap**) a conical paper hat formerly put on the head of a slow or lazy student as a mark of disgrace.

Dun·dalk /dʌnˈdɔk/ the county town of Louth, in the Republic of Ireland, a port on the east coast; pop. (est. 2002) 31,500.

Dun·das /ˈdʌndəs/ a former town in S Ontario, situated at the west end of Hamilton, now part of the city of Hamilton; pop. (2001) 24,394. [H. *Dundas*, 1st Viscount Melville, British politician d.1811]

Dundas Peninsula a peninsula of the southern coast of Melville Island, NWT. [R. S. *Dundas*, 2nd Viscount Melville, English statesman d.1851]

Dun·dee /dʌnˈdiː/ a city in E Scotland, on the north side of the Firth of Tay, formerly in Tayside region; pop. (est. 2002) 148,500.

dunder·head /ˈdʌndərˌhed/ *noun* a ponderously stupid person.

Vowels: a *cat* ɑ *arm* e *bed* ɜr *her* ɜ: *deux* ə *ago* ɪ *sit* i *cosy* iː *feed* ɒ *hot* ɔ *pore* ɔː *no* ʌ *run* ʊ *put*

□ **dun·der·head·ed** *adjective* [17th c.: perhaps related to dial. *dunner* resounding noise]

dune /duːn, djuːn/ *noun* a mound or ridge of loose sand etc. formed by the wind, esp. beside the sea or in a desert. [French from Middle Dutch *dūne*: compare DOWN³]

dune buggy *noun* a low, lightweight motor vehicle with wide, low pressure tires for recreational driving on sand.

Dun·edin /dʌnˈiːdɪn/ a city and port in South Island, New Zealand; pop. (2001) 118,038. [Gaelic *Duneideann* Edinburgh]

dune grass *noun* = MARRAM.

Dun·ferm·line /dʌnˈfɜrmlɪn/ an industrial city in Fife, Scotland, near the Firth of Forth; pop. (est. 2002) 56,500. A number of Scottish kings, including Robert the Bruce, are buried in its Benedictine abbey.

dung *noun* the excrement of animals; manure. [Old English, related to Old High German *tunga*, Icelandic *dyngja*, of unknown origin]

dun·ga·ree /ˌdʌŋgəˈriː/ *noun* **1** a coarse, hard-wearing cotton fabric, often blue. **2** (in *pl.*) trousers, esp. jeans, made of dungaree or similar material. **3** trousers with a bib, esp. as worn by children or as a fashion garment. [Hindi *dungrī*]

dung beetle *noun* any of various beetles which lay their eggs in dung or roll up balls of dung for their larvae to feed on.

Dun·gen·ess crab /ˈdʌŋgənəs/ *noun* N Amer. **1** a Pacific coast crab, *Cancer magister*. **2** the flesh of this crab eaten as food. [after *Dungeness*, a village in Washington state]

dun·geon /ˈdʌndʒən/ ● *noun* **1** a strong underground cell for prisoners. **2** *archaic* a donjon. ● *transitive verb archaic* imprison in a dungeon. [originally = *donjon*: Middle English from Old French *donjon*, ultimately from Latin *dominus* lord]

Dungeons and Dragons *noun proprietary* a fantasy role-playing game set in a supposed medieval world of wizards, goblins, etc. Abbr.: **D&D**.

dung·heap *noun* (also **dung·hill**) **1** a heap of dung or refuse, esp. in a farmyard. **2** a disgusting place or situation.

dunk ● *transitive verb* **1** dip (bread, a biscuit, etc.) into soup, coffee, etc. while eating. **2 a** immerse, dip (*was dunked in the river*). **b** *Christianity slang* baptize. **3** *Basketball* shoot (the ball) down through the hoop by jumping so that the hands are above the ring. ● *noun* **1** (in full **dunk shot** or **slam dunk**) *Basketball* a shot made by jumping and pushing the ball down through the basket from above. **2** *N Amer.* an act or instance of dipping or immersing oneself in a lake etc. □ **dunk·er** *noun* [Pennsylvania Dutch *dunke* to dip, from German *tunken*]

Dun·kirk /dʌnˈkɜrk/ a French port on the English Channel; pop. (1999) 70,850. In 1940, over 300,000 troops of the British Expeditionary Force and other Allied forces, trapped by the German breakthrough at Sedan, were evacuated from Dunkirk between May 27 and June 2 by warships, requisitioned civilian ships, and a host of small boats, under constant attack from the air.

dunk tank *noun* a pitching game, often used to raise funds for charity, in which a person sits suspended over a tank of water and is dropped into it when a nearby target is hit by a baseball etc. thrown by another person who has paid for the chance.

Dun Laoghaire /dʌn ˈliːri, ˈlerə/ a ferry port and resort town in Ireland, near Dublin; pop. (1998) 58,839.

dun·lin /ˈdʌnlɪn/ *noun* a long-billed Holarctic sandpiper, *Calidris alpina*, the male of which has a reddish back and a black patch on the front. [prob. from DUN¹ + -LING¹]

Dun·lop /ˈdʌnlɒp/ **John Boyd** (1840–1921), Scottish veterinarian, who invented the first successful pneumatic bicycle tire (1888), which was later manufactured by the company named after him.

dun·nage /ˈdʌnɪdʒ/ *noun Naut.* **1** loose material, such as mats etc., stowed under or among cargo to prevent wetting or chafing. **2** *informal dated* miscellaneous baggage. [Anglo-Latin *dennagium*, of unknown origin]

Dunne-Za /ˌdʌnəˈzɒ/ ● *noun* **1** a member of an Aboriginal people of the Peace River area of Alberta and BC. **2** the Athapaskan language of this people. ● *adjective* of or relating to the Beaver or their culture or language. ¶ Formerly called BEAVER. [Dunne-Za, = 'real people']

dunno /dəˈnoː/ *interjection informal* (I) do not know. [corruption]

Dunn·ville /ˈdʌnvɪl/ a former town in S Ontario, situated on the Grand River near its mouth on Lake Erie, southeast of Brantford, now part of the city of Haldimand; pop. (2001) 12,581. [J. H. *Dunn*, receiver general of Upper Canada d.1854]

Duns Sco·tus /dʌnz ˈskoːtəs/ **John** (known as 'the Subtle Doctor') (c.1266–1308), Scottish theologian and scholar. In opposition to Aquinas he argued that faith was a matter of will, not dependent on logical proofs; his system was accepted by the Franciscans as their doctrinal basis and exercised a profound influence on the Middle Ages.

Dun·stan, St. /ˈdʌnstən/ (924–988), Anglo-Saxon clergyman, archbishop of Canterbury 959–988. He introduced the Benedictine rule into England and was a zealous supporter of education. Feast day, 19 May.

duo /ˈduːo, ˈdjuːoː/ *noun* (*pl.* **duos**) **1** a pair of actors, entertainers, singers, etc. (*a comedy duo*). **2** *Music* a duet. [Italian from Latin, = two]

duo- /ˈduːo-/ *combining form* two. [Latin *duo*, two]

duo·deci·mal /ˌduːoˈdesɪməl/ *adjective* relating to or using a system of numerical notation that has 12 as a base. □ **duo·deci·mal·ly** *adverb* [Latin *duodecimus* twelfth, from *duodecim* twelve]

duo·deci·mo /ˌduːoˈdesɪˌmoː, ˌdjuːoː-/ *noun* (*pl.* **-mos**) *Books* **1** a size of book or paper in which each leaf is one-twelfth of the size of a standard printing sheet. Abbr.: **12mo. 2** a book of this size. [Latin (*in*) *duodecimo* in a twelfth (as DUODECIMAL)]

duo·den·um /ˌduːoˈdiːnəm, ˌdjuːoː-, duˈɒdnəm/ *noun Anat.* the first part of the small intestine immediately below the stomach. □ **duo·denal** *adjective* [medieval Latin from *duodeni* from its length of about 12 fingers' breadth]

duo·logue /ˈduːəˌlɒg, ˈdjuːə-/ *noun* **1** a conversation between two people. **2** a dramatic piece for two actors, voices, etc. [irreg. from Latin *duo* or Greek *duo* two, after *monologue*]

duomo /ˈdwoːmoː/ *noun* (*pl.* **duomos**) an Italian cathedral. [Italian, = DOME]

du·op·oly /duːˈɒpəli, dju-/ *noun* (*pl.* **-ies**) *Econ.* a condition in which a particular market is controlled or dominated by only two suppliers, individuals, etc. □ **du·op·ol·ist** *noun* **du·op·o·lis·tic** *adjective* [Greek *duo* two + *pōleō* sell, after *monopoly*]

Duo-Tang /ˈduːoːtaŋ, dju-/ *noun Cdn proprietary* a report folder of light coloured cardboard, having three flexible metal fasteners to insert through the holes of loose-leaf paper.

duo·tone /ˈduːəˌtoːn, ˈdjuː-/ *Books* ● *noun* **1** a halftone illustration in two colours from the same original with different screen angles. **2** the process of making a duotone. ● *adjective* **1** made by this process. **2** of or in two colours. [Latin *duo* two + TONE]

Du·parc /duːpark/ **(Marie Eu·gène) Henri** (born Henri Fouques-Duparc) (1848–1933), French composer, remembered for his songs on poems of Baudelaire and others.

du·pat·ta /dəˈpʌtə/ *noun* a length of cloth worn as a scarf or head covering, typically with a shalwar, by women from the Indian subcontinent. [Hindi *dupaṭṭa*]

dupe¹ /duːp, djuːp/ ● *noun* a person who is deluded or deceived by another. ● *transitive verb* deceive, mislead, make a dupe of, or gull (a person). □ **dup·ery** *noun* [dial. French *dupe* hoopoe, from the bird's supposedly stupid appearance]

dupe² *slang* ● *noun* a duplicate, esp. a duplicate negative made from a positive print. ● *adjective* duplicate (*dupe transparencies*). □ **dup·er** *noun* **dup·ing** *noun*

du·pion /ˈduːpiən, ˈdjuːp-/ *noun* **1** a rough silk fabric woven from the threads of double cocoons. **2** an imitation of this with other fibres. [French *doupion* from Italian *doppione* from *doppio* double]

duple /ˈduːpəl, ˈdjuːpəl/ *adjective* double, twofold, or of two parts. [Latin *duplus* from *duo* two]

Du·ples·sis /duːpleˈsiː/ **Mau·rice Le Nob·let** (1890–1959), Canadian politician, Union Nationale premier of Quebec 1936–9 and 1944–59. A conservative and strong supporter of provincial rights, he was a founder of the Union Nationale (1935); his governments were characterized by the lavish use of patronage, anti-communism and strong-arm methods, and effective electoral campaigning.

duple time *noun* rhythm consisting of two beats to the bar.

du·plex /ˈduːpleks, ˈdjuːpleks/ ● *noun* **1** esp. *N Amer.* (also *attributive*) **a** = SEMI-DETACHED. **b** a residential building divided into two apartments, esp. a two-storey dwelling with a separate apartment on each floor. **2** *Biochem.* a double-stranded polynucleotide molecule. **3** the capacity of a computer etc. to send and receive data simultaneously along a communications link such as a telephone etc. (*set the parameter at full duplex*). ● *adjective* **1** twofold, having two parts, or combining two elements, esp. with similar functions. **2** *Computing* (of a circuit) allowing the transmission or reception of signals in opposite directions simultaneously over a single channel etc. (*opp.* SIMPLEX 2). **3** *Metallurgy* designating or made by a steelmaking process employing successive treatment in two furnaces or by two methods. **4** designating a manner of printing both sides of a document on a single pass through a copying machine. **5** *Biochem.* (of a molecule or structure) having two polynucleotide strands linked side by side. ● *transitive verb* **1** make (a cable, system, etc.) capable of transmitting in two directions simultaneously. **2** print both sides of a document in a single pass through a copying machine, esp. to conserve paper. **3** make (a building etc.) duplex. □ **du·plexed** *adjective* **du·plex·ing** *noun* [Latin *duplex duplicis* from *duo* two + *plic-* fold]

dupli·cate ● *adjective* /'duːplɪkət, 'djuːplɪkət/ **1** copied or exactly like something already existing (in any number of copies). **2 a** paired, double, or having two corresponding parts, examples, etc. **b** doubled or consisting of twice the number or quantity. ● *noun* /'duːplɪkət, 'djuːplɪkət/ **1** one of two or more things exactly alike, so that each is a double of some original. **2** *Law* a second copy of a letter or document, having equal legal force of the original. **3** (in full **duplicate bridge** or **whist**) a form of bridge or whist in which the same hands are played successively by different players. ● *transitive verb* /'duːplɪˌkeit, 'djuːplɪˌkeit/ **1** multiply by two; double. **2 a** make or be an exact copy of. **b** make or supply copies of (*duplicated the leaflet for distribution*). **3** repeat (an action etc.), esp. unnecessarily. □ **in duplicate** consisting of two exact copies. □ **du·plic·able** /-kəbəl/ *adjective* **dupli·ca·tion** *noun* **dupli·ca·tive** /-ˈkeitɪv/ *adjective* [Latin *duplicatus* past participle of *duplicare* (as DUPLEX)]

dupli·ca·tor *noun* a thing that duplicates, esp. a machine for making copies of a document, leaflet, slide, etc.

du·pli·city /duːˈplɪsɪti, djuː-/ *noun* (*pl.* **-ties**) **1** the quality or practice of being two-faced, deceitful in manner or conduct, or double-dealing. **2** the state or quality of being double or twofold, esp. physically, psychologically, etc. □ **du·pli·ci·tous** *adjective* [Late Latin *duplicitas* (as DUPLEX)]

Dupré /duːˈprei/ **Mar·cel** (1886–1971), French organist and composer, noted for his improvisational abilities.

du Pré /duː ˈprei, djuː-/ **Jacque·line** (1945–87), English cellist, known for her interpretations of cello concertos, esp. that of Elgar.

Dupuy /duːˈpwiː/ **Claude-Thomas** (1678–1738), French lawyer, intendant of New France 1725–8, who was noted for his opposition to Governor Beauharnois.

Duque de Ca·xias /ˌduːkei də kəˈfiːəs/ a city in SE Brazil, a suburb of Rio de Janeiro; pop. (est. 2000) 767,724.

Du·quesne /duːˈken/ **Ange Du·quesne de Menne·ville, Marquis** (*c.*1700–78), French naval officer, Governor General of New France 1752–5. Instructed to maintain French control over the Ohio valley, he established a series of forts (1753–4).

dura /'duːrə/ *noun* = DURA MATER.

dur·able /'duːrəbəl, 'djuːrəbəl/ ● *adjective* capable of lasting or able to withstand change, decay, or wear. ● *noun* (in *pl.*) = DURABLE GOODS. □ **dur·abil·ity** /-ˈbɪlɪti/ *noun* **dur·ably** *adverb* [Old French from Latin *durabilis* from *durare* endure, from *durus* hard]

durable goods *plural noun* (also **dur·ables**) goods which remain useful over a period of time, such as automobiles, machinery, etc., as opposed to those produced for immediate consumption.

dura mater /ˌduːrə ˈmeitər/ *noun* *Anat.* (also **dura**) the tough outermost membrane enveloping the brain and spinal cord (see MENINGES). [medieval Latin = hard mother, translation of Arabic *al-'umm al-jāfiya* ('mother' in Arabic indicating the relationship of things)]

du·ra·men /duːˈreimen, djuː-/ *noun* = HEARTWOOD. [Latin from *durare* harden]

dur·ance /'duːrəns, 'djuːr-/ *noun* *archaic* imprisonment or forced confinement (*in durance vile*). [French from *durer* last, from Latin *durare*: see DURABLE]

Du·ran·go /duːˈrangoʊ/ **1** a state of north central Mexico. **2** (in full **Vic·toria de Durango**) its capital city; pop. (2000) 1,448,700.

Du·rante /dəˈranti/ **James Fran·cis ('Jimmy')** (1893–1980), US comedian, remembered for his trademark large nose, worn felt hat, and hoarse voice.

Duras /duːˈrɒs/ **Mar·guer·ite** (pseudonym of Marguerite Donnadieu) (1914–1996), French novelist, filmmaker, and dramatist. She is known for novels such as *L'Amant* (1984), and the screenplay for the film *Hiroshima mon amour* (1960).

dur·ation /duˈreiʃən, djʊ-/ *noun* the time during which something lasts or continues (*the severity and duration of the attacks increased; the runs were of short duration; the concert is 90 minutes in duration*). □ **for the duration 1** for a very long time. **2** until the end of a particular activity (*we're in the war for the duration*). □ **dur·ation·al** *adjective* [Old French from medieval Latin *duratio -onis* (as DURANCE)]

dura·tive /'duːrətɪv, 'djuːrətɪv/ *adjective* *Grammar* denoting continuing action.

Dur·ban /'dɜrbən/ a seaport and resort in South Africa, on the coast of KwaZulu-Natal; pop. (est. 2002) 2,354,900. It was formerly known as Port Natal.

dur·bar /'dɜrbɑr/ *noun* *hist.* **1** the court of an Indian ruler. **2** a public levee of an Indian prince or an Anglo-Indian governor or viceroy. [Urdu from Persian *darbār* court]

durch·kom·pon·iert /'dʊrx,kɒmpɒˌniːrt/ *adjective* *Music* (of a composition) having a formal design which does not rely on repeated sections, esp. having different music for each verse. [German from *durch* through + *komponiert* composed]

Dürer /'dʊrər/ **Al·brecht** (1471–1528), German painter and engraver. Generally regarded as the leading figure of German Renaissance art, he is noted for his woodcuts such as *Apocalypse* (1498) and his copper engravings, which include *Knight, Death and the Devil* (1513) and *Melancholia I* (1514).

dur·ess /dʊˈres, djʊ-/ *noun* **1 a** a compulsion, constraint, esp. imprisonment, threats, or violence (*under duress*). **b** *Law* such constraint illegally used to force a person to act against his or her will. **2** *archaic* forcible restraint, confinement, or imprisonment. [Old French *duresse* from Latin *duritia* from *durus* hard]

Durga /'dɜrgə/ *Hinduism* a fierce goddess, the wife of Shiva, often identified with Kali. She is usually depicted riding a tiger or lion and slaying the buffalo demon, and with eight or ten arms. [Sanskrit, = inaccessible]

Dur·ham¹ /'dʌrəm/ **1** a county of NE England. **2** a city in NE England on the Wear River. It is the county town of Durham; pop. (est. 1998) 90,300.

Dur·ham² /'dʌrəm/ **John George Lamb·ton, Earl of** (1792–1840), British colonial administrator, Governor General and high commissioner of British North America 1838. He was sent to Quebec in 1838 to investigate the circumstances surrounding the Rebellion of 1837, and his detailed and famous *Report on the Affairs of British North America* (1839) recommended a modified form of responsible government and a legislative union of Canada and the Maritime provinces.

dur·ian /'dʊriən/ *noun* **1** a large tree, *Durio zibethinus*, native to SE Asia, bearing oval spiny fruits containing a creamy pulp with a fetid smell and an agreeable taste. **2** this fruit. [Malay *durian* from *dūri* thorn]

duri·crust /'dʊrɪkrʌst, 'djʊrɪkrʌst/ *noun* *Geol.* a hard mineral crust formed near the surface of soil in semi-arid regions by evaporation of groundwater. [Latin *durus* 'hard' + CRUST]

dur·ing *preposition* **1** throughout the whole continuance, course, or duration of (an activity, event, etc.) (*read during the meal*). **2** within, in the course of, or at some point in the duration of (a specified period of time) (*came in during the evening*). [Old French *durant*, ultimately from Latin *durare* last, continue]

Durk·heim /'dɜrkhaim/ **Émile** (1858–1917), French sociologist. One of the founders of modern sociology, he examined the influence of social structures on the behaviour of individuals in *The Division of Labour in Society* (1893), and formalized a methodology for sociological investigation.

dur·mast /'dɜrmast/ *noun* a Eurasian oak tree, *Quercus petraea*, having sessile flowers. [*dur-* (perhaps erroneous for DUN¹) + MAST²]

Dur·nan /'dɜrnən/ **Wil·liam Ar·nold ('Bill')** (1915–72), Canadian hockey player. A goalie with the Montreal Canadiens (1943–50), he won the Vezina Trophy six times.

Du·ro·cher /dəˈroʊˌʃei/ **Leo (Er·nest)** (1906–91), US baseball player and manager, known for the saying 'Nice guys finish last'.

dur·ra /'dʌrə/ *noun* (also **dhur·ra**) a variety of sorghum, *Sorghum bicolor*, grown esp. in N Africa and the Indian subcontinent. [Arabic *dura, durra*]

Dur·rell /'dʌrəl/ **Law·rence (George)** (1912–90), English novelist, poet, and travel writer. He is best known for *The Alexandria Quartet* (1957–1960), a series of novels set in Alexandria before World War II.

durst /dɜrst/ *archaic* past of DARE.

durum /'duːrəm, 'djʊərəm/ *noun* a kind of wheat, *Triticum durum*, having hard seeds and yielding a flour used in the manufacture of pasta. [Latin, neuter of *durus* hard]

Duse /'duːze/ **Eleo·nora** (1858–1924), Italian actress, acclaimed for her roles in the plays of D'Annunzio and Ibsen.

Du·shan·be /duːˈʃanbei/ the capital of Tajikistan; pop. (2000) 562,000.

dusk /dʌsk/ *noun* **1** the darker stage of twilight in the evening. **2** = NIGHTFALL. **3** shade, shadow, gloom. [Middle English *dosk, dusk* from Old English *dox* dark, swarthy, *doxian* darken in colour]

dusky *adjective* (**dusk·i·er, dusk·i·est**) **1** shady, shadowy, dim.

Consonants: b *but*   d *dog*   f *few*   g *get*   h *her*   j *yes*   k *cat*   l *leg*   m *man*   n *no*   p *pen*   r *red*   s *sit*

2 somewhat dark in colour. **3** (of a complexion) swarthy, dark hued. □ **dusk·i·ly** *adverb* **dusk·i·ness** *noun*

Düs·sel·dorf /ˈdʊsəlˌdɔrf/ an industrial city of NW Germany, on the Rhine; pop. (est. 2002) 568,300. It is the capital of North Rhine-Westphalia.

dust ● *noun* **1 a** finely powdered earth, dirt, etc., lying on the ground or on surfaces and blown about by the wind. **b** fine powder of any material (*pollen dust*; *sawdust*). **c** any substance pulverized. **d** a cloud of finely powdered earth or of other fine particles floating in the air. **2 a** that to which anything is reduced by disintegration or decay, esp. a dead person's remains. **b** *archaic* or *poet.* the mortal human body (*we are all dust*). **3** an act of dusting (*give the table a dust*). ● *verb* **1** *transitive & intransitive* clear (furniture etc.) of dust etc. by wiping, brushing, etc. **2** *transitive* **a** sprinkle (the skin, a plant, a cake, etc.) with powder, dust, sugar, etc. **b** sprinkle or strew (sugar, powder, etc.). **3** *transitive* make dusty. **4 a** *transitive slang* beat, vanquish, win a victory over (*we'll dust him in the third race*). **b** *transitive* esp. *US slang* kill. **5** *transitive* apply a dust-like chemical to an object, esp. as a means of discovering fingerprints (*the police dusted the window for prints*). □ **dust and ashes** something very disappointing. **dust off 1** remove the dust from (an object on which it has long been allowed to settle). **2** use, apply, or enjoy again after a long period of neglect. **eat (a person's) dust 1** fall far behind. **2** an expression of contempt or dismissal (*Eat my dust!*). **in the dust 1** humiliated. **2** far behind or much inferior. **3** abandoned. **not see a person for dust** find that a person has made a hasty departure. **shake the dust off** (or **from**) **one's feet** depart indignantly or disdainfully. **throw dust in a person's eyes** mislead a person by misrepresentation or by diverting attention from a point. **when the dust settles** when things quieten down or clear. □ **dust·less** *adjective* [Old English *dūst*: compare Low German *dunst* vapour]

dust·ball *noun N Amer. informal* a clump of dust, lint, etc. found indoors, esp. in corners, under furniture, etc.

dust bath *noun* a bird's rolling in or sprinkling itself with dust to freshen its feathers.

dust·bin *noun esp. Brit.* a garbage can, esp. one kept outside.

dust bowl *noun* an arid or unproductive dry region, specifically an area in the US prairie states, esp. Oklahoma, where drought, overgrazing, and poor land management in the 1930s resulted in a large part of the topsoil blowing away, causing great hardship as thousands were forced to leave.

dust bunny *noun N Amer. informal* = DUSTBALL.

Dust·bust·er *noun proprietary* a small, hand-held vacuum cleaner, usu. running on rechargeable batteries.

dust cover *noun* **1** = DUST SHEET. **2** = DUST JACKET.

dust devil *noun* a small whirlwind common in dry regions which becomes visible as it whips up dust, debris, leaves, etc.

dust·er *noun* **1 a** a cloth, brush, etc. for dusting surfaces. **b** a person who dusts. **c** a device for sifting or applying dust. **2** a short, light, usu. cotton bathrobe or item of sleepwear, esp. for women. **3** *N Amer. informal Mining* a dry oil well or a promising well that produces nothing. **4** *Baseball* = BEANBALL. **5** (also **duster coat**) a woman's light, loose, full-length coat.

dust·ing *noun* **1** the action of removing dust (*having one's heating vents cleaned cuts down on dusting*). **2** the action of sprinkling with dust, powder, etc. (*the aircraft is particularly suitable for crop-dusting*). **3** a very thin layer of dust, powder, snow, etc.

dusting powder *noun* powder for dusting over something, esp. talcum powder.

dust jacket *noun* a removable, usu. decorated paper cover used to protect a book from dirt or damage.

dust·man *noun* (*pl.* **-men**) *Brit.* a garbage collector.

dust·pan *noun* a small pan into which dust etc. is brushed from the floor.

dust ruffle *noun N Amer.* = BEDSKIRT.

dust sheet *noun esp. Brit.* a cloth put over furniture to protect it from dust.

dust storm *noun* a strong wind storm, raising and carrying clouds of dust or sand.

dust-up *noun informal* a fight, quarrel, or disturbance.

dusty *adjective* (**dust·i·er**, **dust·i·est**) **1 a** full of or covered with dust. **b** of the nature of or resembling dust. **2** staid and uninteresting (*a dusty old bore*). **3** (of a colour) dull or muted (*dusty rose*). □ **dust·i·ly** *adverb* **dust·i·ness** *noun* [Old English *dūstig* (as DUST)]

dusty miller *noun* any of various plants grown for their silvery foliage, esp. *Senecio cineraria*.

Dutch /dʌtʃ/ ● *adjective* **1** of, relating to, or associated with the Netherlands. **2** *N Amer.* German (*compare* PENNSYLVANIA DUTCH). ● *noun* **1** the language of the Netherlands. **2** (prec. by *the*; treated as *pl.*) the people of the Netherlands or their descendants. □ **go Dutch** share expenses equally. [Middle Dutch *dutsch* etc. 'Netherlandish, German,' Old High German *diutisc* national]

Dutch apple cake *noun* a plain cake topped with sliced apples and sugar or streusel topping before baking.

Dutch apple pie *noun* an apple pie with a single bottom crust and a streusel topping over the apple filling.

Dutch auction *noun* a usu. public sale of goods, in which the price is reduced by the auctioneer until a buyer is found.

Dutch clover *noun* white clover, *Trifolium repens.*

Dutch courage *noun informal* often *offensive* **1** false courage gained from alcohol. **2** liquor.

Dutch door *noun N Amer.* a door divided into two parts horizontally, allowing one part to be shut and the other open.

Dutch East India Company a Dutch trading company (1602–1799) founded to protect Dutch trading interests in the Indian Ocean.

Dutch East Indies the former name (until 1949) of INDONESIA.

Dutch elm disease *noun* a disease affecting elms caused by the fungus *Ceratocystis ulmi*, first found in the Netherlands.

Dutch Guiana the former name (until 1948) of SURINAME.

Dutch hoe *noun* a hoe used with a pushing action just under the surface of the soil so as to kill weeds at this level.

Dutch·ie *noun Cdn* a usu. square, raised, glazed doughnut containing raisins.

Dutch·man *noun* (*pl.* **-men**) **1 a** a native or national of the Netherlands. **b** a person of Dutch descent. **2** a Dutch ship. **3** *N Amer. slang* a German. **4** esp. *N Amer.* a piece of wood or stone used to repair a flaw or fault or to patch up bad workmanship.

Dutchman's breeches *noun N Amer.* (usu. treated as *sing.*) a plant, *Dicentra cucullaria*, with white flowers and finely divided leaves.

Dutchman's pipe *noun* a climbing vine of eastern N America, *Aristolochia durior*, with hooked tubular flowers.

Dutch New Guinea a former name (until 1963) for IRIAN JAYA.

Dutch oven *noun* **1** a covered container, casserole, or cooking pot for braising etc. **2** *hist.* a small metal cooking utensil with an open side which is turned towards a fire.

Dutch Reformed Church *noun* a Christian denomination based upon the teachings of Dutch Calvinists.

Dutch treat *noun* a party, outing, meal, etc. to which each person makes a contribution or for which each person pays his or her own share of the expenses.

Dutch uncle *noun* a well-disposed authoritative person, often a mentor or adviser, who lectures, gives advice, etc. with benevolent firmness and unrelenting frankness.

Dutch West India Company a Dutch trading company (1621–1794) founded to develop Dutch trading interests in competition with Spain and Portugal and their colonies in western India, South America, and West Africa.

Dutch·woman *noun* (*pl.* **-women**) **1** a woman who is a native or national of the Netherlands. **2** a woman of Dutch descent.

dut·eous /ˈdjuːtiːəs, ˈdjuː-/ *adjective literary* (of a person or conduct) dutiful, obedient. □ **dut·eous·ly** *adverb* **dut·eous·ness** *noun* [DUTY + -OUS: compare *beauteous*]

duti·able /ˈdjuːtiːəbl, ˈdjuː-/ *adjective* liable to customs taxes or other duties.

duti·ful /ˈdjuːtɪful, ˈdjuː-/ *adjective* **1** doing or observant of one's duty. **2** (of a response, action, etc.) characteristic of, resulting from, or expressing a sense of duty. □ **duti·ful·ly** *adverb* **duti·ful·ness** *noun*

Du·toit /djuˈtwɒ/ **Charles Édouard** (b.1936), Swiss conductor and violist. He was the conductor of the Montreal Symphony Orchestra 1978–2002, and has been the chief conductor of the Orchestre National de Paris since 1990.

duty /ˈdjuːti, ˈdjuː-/ *noun* (*pl.* **-ies**) **1 a** a moral or legal obligation or responsibility (*his duty to report it*). **b** the binding force of what is morally right (*strong sense of duty*). **c** the action or behaviour due by moral or legal obligation (*do one's duty*). **2** payment due to the public revenue and enforced by law or custom, esp.: **a** that levied on the import, export, manufacture, or sale of goods (*customs duty*). **b** that levied on the transfer of property, licences, the legal recognition of documents, etc. (*death duty*; *probate duty*). **3 a** an action required by a person's business, occupation, or function (*his duties as caretaker*). **b** the performance of or engagement in the activities required by a person's occupation etc. **c** *Military* active service in armed forces of one's country (*reservists were called up for duty*). **4** (*attributive*) **a** (of a person) having specific duties or being on duty (*duty officer*). **b** (of an accessory, post, etc.) for use by an individual while on duty (*duty holster*; *duty station*). **c** (of a visit, call, or other undertaking) done as a duty rather than as a pleasure. **5** *archaic* deference, respect, or the behaviour due to a superior. **6** the measure of an engine's effectiveness in units of work done per unit of fuel. □ (**above and**) **beyond the call of duty** much more than expected by obligation. **do duty for** serve as or pass for (something else). **duty bound** morally or legally obliged by duty. **on** (or **off**) **duty** engaged (or not engaged) in one's work. [Anglo-French *deweté*, *dueté* (as DUE)]

duty cycle *noun* **1** the cycle of operation of a device acting intermittently. **2** the time occupied by this, esp. as a fraction of available time.

duty-free ● *adjective* (of goods, shopping, etc.) exempt from payment of customs and excise duties, esp. as a small personal allowance on entering or re-entering a country. ● *noun* = DUTY-FREE SHOP.

duty-free shop *noun* a shop at an airport etc. at which duty-free goods can be bought. □ **duty-free shopping** *noun*

duty of care *noun Law* the legal duty of a person to take reasonable care in any given circumstance in order to avoid injuries, damages to others, and charges of negligence.

du·um·vir /duːˈʌmvər, ˈduːəm-, djuˈʌmvər, ˈdjuːəm-/ *noun Rom. Hist.* one of two coequal magistrates or officials. [Latin from *duum virum* of the two men]

du·um·vir·ate /duːˈʌmvɪrət/ *noun* **1** a coalition of two people. **2** either of two people with joint authority.

Du·va·lier /duːˈvaljeɪ/ **1 Fran·çois** (known as 'Papa Doc') (1907–71), Haitian leader, president 1957–71. He proclaimed himself president for life in 1964, and was noted for his authoritarian and oppressive regime. **2** his son, **Jean-Claude** (known as 'Baby Doc', b.1951), Haitian leader, president 1971–86. He was forced to flee the country after a mass uprising in 1986.

du·vet /duːˈveɪ, ˈduːveɪ/ *noun* a quilt, filled with down or a synthetic fibre with a high loft, used instead of an upper sheet and blankets. [French, lit. 'down']

Du Vi·gneaud /duː ˈviːnjoː/ **Vin·cent** (1901–78), US biochemist, who was awarded the 1955 Nobel Prize for chemistry for isolating and synthesizing the pituitary hormones oxytocin and vasopressin.

dux·elles /duːkˈsel/ *noun* a seasoning or sauce of mushrooms, shallots, parsley, and onions. [French, possibly after the 17th-c. Marquis d'Uxelles, whose chef is said to have invented the recipe]

duy·ker *var. of* DUIKER.

DV *abbreviation* **1** digital video. **2** *Deo volente*.

DVA *abbreviation* (in Canada) Department of Veterans Affairs.

DVD *noun proprietary* a digital recording medium similar in appearance to a CD but with much increased storage capacity, capable of storing a full-length feature film. [abbreviation of *digital video disc* or *digital versatile disc*]

DVD-audio *noun* (also **DVD-A**) a format for audio recording, offering better sound reproduction than CDs.

DVD-RAM *noun* a DVD that can be recorded many times; a rewritable DVD.

DVD-ROM *noun* a DVD that is played through a computer but cannot be re-recorded.

DVE *abbreviation* digital video effects.

DVI *abbreviation* digital video interaction.

D.V.M. *abbreviation* Doctor of Veterinary Medicine.

Dvoř·ák /ˈdvɔrʒak/ **An·tonin (Leo·pold)** (1841–1904), Czech composer. He combined ethnic folk elements with the Viennese musical tradition from Haydn to Brahms, and is best known for his ninth symphony ('From the New World', 1893) and *Slavonic Dances* (1878); he also wrote chamber music, operas, and songs.

dwale /dweɪl/ *noun* = BELLADONNA 1. [prob. from Scandinavian]

dwarf ● *noun* (*pl.* **dwarfs** or **dwarves** /dwɔrvz/) **1 a** a person of abnormally small stature, esp. one with a normal-sized head and body but short limbs. **b** (also *attributive*) an animal or plant much below the ordinary size for the species. **2** any of a mythological race of short, stocky human-like creatures, figuring esp. in Scandinavian folklore, who are typically skilled in mining and metalworking and often possess magical powers. **3** (in full **dwarf star**) a small, dense star with low to average luminosity. ● *transitive verb* **1** stunt or restrict the growth or development of (a thing etc.). **2** cause (something similar or

comparable) to seem small or insignificant (*efforts dwarfed by their rivals' achievements*). □ **dwarfed** *adjective* **dwarf·ish** *adjective* **dwarf·ish·ness** *noun* **dwarf-like** *adjective* [Old English *dweorg* from Germanic]

dwarf birch *noun* any of several shrubby birches of N America, esp. *Betula pumila*, growing in wet places across Canada and the northern US.

dwarf dogwood *noun* = BUNCHBERRY.

dwarf·ism /ˈdwɔrfɪzəm/ *noun* the condition of being a dwarf.

dweeb *noun informal* a nerd, esp. a studious or boring person. □ **dweeb·ish** *adjective* **dweeby** *adjective* (**dweeb·i·er**, **dweeb·i·est**).

dwell ● *intransitive verb* (*past* and *past participle* **dwelt** or **dwelled**) **1 a** *literary* (usu. foll. by *in*, *at*, *near*, *on*, etc.) live, reside (*dwelt in the forest*). **b** continue for a time in a place, state, or condition. **2** (of a machine part) pause slightly during the working of the machine. ● *noun* (also *attributive*) a slight, regular pause in the motion of a machine, allowing time for its own or another part's operation (*dwell time*). □ **dwell on** (or **upon**) **1** spend time on, linger over; write, brood, or speak at length on (a specified subject) (*always dwells on his grievances*). **2** prolong (a note, syllable, etc.). □ **dwell·er** *noun* [Old English *dwellan* lead astray, later 'continue in a place', from Germanic]

dwell·ing *noun* (also **dwelling place**) a house or place of residence.

DWI *abbreviation US Law* driving while intoxicated, a criminal offence.

dwin·dle /ˈdwɪndəl/ *intransitive verb* **1** waste away or become gradually reduced in size or quantity. **2** degenerate, decline, or diminish in quality, value, or importance. □ **dwin·dling** *adjective* [*dwine* fade away, from Old English *dwīnan*, Old Norse *dvína*]

dwt. *abbreviation* **1** *hist.* pennyweight. **2** dead-weight tonnage.

DX *abbreviation* distance, esp. used for shortwave radio reception.

DX coding *noun proprietary* an electronic system which uses optical, electrical, and mechanical encoding to read the pattern on film and automatically select the appropriate film type, speed, etc.

Dy *symbol Chem.* the element dysprosium.

dyad /ˈdaɪad/ *noun* **1** two, a group of two, a pair, or a twofold entity. **2** *Math.* an operator which is a combination of two vectors. [Late Latin *dyas dyad-* from Greek *duas duados* from *duo* two]

dy·ad·ic /daɪˈadɪk/ *adjective* **1** double, twofold, or of the nature of a dyad. **2** *Philos.* designating or pertaining to a relationship between exactly two entities. **3** *Math. & Computing* designating an expression, operator, etc. which requires or acts on two arguments.

Dyak *var. of* DAYAK.

dy·archy *var. of* DIARCHY.

dyb·buk /ˈdɪbʊk/ *noun* (*pl.* **dyb·buk·im** /-kɪm/ or **dyb·buks**) (in Jewish folklore) a wandering malevolent spirit that enters and possesses the body of a living person until exorcised. [Hebrew *dibbūk* from *dādak* cling]

dye ● *noun* **1 a** a substance used to change the colour of hair, fabric, wood, etc. **b** a colour produced by this. **2** (in full **dye·stuff**) a substance yielding a dye, esp. for colouring materials in solution. ● *verb* (**dye·ing**) **1** *transitive* impregnate with dye. **2** *transitive* make (a thing) a specified colour with dye (*dyed it yellow*). **3** *intransitive* take colour in the process of dyeing. □ **dye·able** *adjective* [Old English *deag*, *deagian*]

dyed-in-the-wool *adjective* **1** out-and-out; unchangeable, inveterate. **2** (of a fabric) made of yarn dyed in its raw state.

dyer /ˈdaɪr/ *noun* a person who dyes cloth etc.

dyer's greenweed *noun* (also **dyer's broom**) a bushy yellow-flowered leguminous plant, *Genista tinctoria*, formerly used to make a green dye.

dyer's oak *noun* an E Mediterranean oak, *Quercus infectoria*, bearing galls formerly used to make a yellow dye.

Dyfed /ˈdʌvɪd/ a former county of SW Wales, comprising Cardiganshire, Carmarthenshire, and Pembroke from 1974 to 1996; administrative centre, Carmarthen.

dying ● *adjective* **1** connected with, or at the time of, death (*her dying words*). **2** about to die (*a dying art*). **3** coming to an end (*the dying days of the age of sail*). ● *noun* the act or process of ceasing to live, function, etc. □ **to one's dying day** for the rest of one's life.

dying breed *noun informal* something that is about to disappear or cease to exist (*the family farm is a dying breed*).

dyke¹ *var. of* DIKE¹.

dyke² /daɪk/ *noun* (also **dike**) *slang* a lesbian. □ **dykey** *adjective* [20th c.: origin unknown]

Dylan /ˈdɪlən/ **Bob** (born Robert Allen Zimmerman) (b.1941), US folk

---

Vowels: a cat   ɑ arm   e bed   ɜr her   ɜ: deux   ə ago   ɪ sit   i cosy   iː feed   ɒ hot   ɔ pore   oː no   ʌ run   ʊ put

and rock singer and songwriter. A leader of the urban folk-music revival in the 1960s, he became known for his anti-war protest songs, such as 'The Times They are a-Changin'' (1964), and for his complex and poetic lyrics set to simple melodies.

dyn *abbreviation* dyne.

dy·nam·ic /dai'namɪk/ ● *adjective* **1** energetic; active. **2** (also **dy·nam·i·cal**) *Physics* **a** concerning motive force (*opp.* STATIC 3). **b** concerning force in actual operation. **3** (also **dy·nam·i·cal**) of or concerning dynamics. **4** *Music* relating to the volume of sound. **5** *Philos.* relating to dynamism. **6** *Computing* (of memory, etc.) depending on an applied voltage to refresh it periodically. ● *noun* **1** an energizing or motive force. **2** *Music* = DYNAMICS 3. □ **dy·nam·i·cal·ly** *adverb* [French *dynamique* from Greek *dunamikos* from *dunamis* power]

dynamic equilibrium *noun* a state of balance between continuing processes.

dy·nam·ics /dai'namɪks/ *plural noun* **1** (usu. treated as *sing.*) **a** *Mech.* the branch of mechanics concerned with the motion of bodies under the action of forces (*compare* STATICS). **b** the branch of any science in which forces or changes are considered (*aerodynamics*; *population dynamics*). **2** the motive forces, physical or moral, affecting behaviour and change in any sphere. **3** *Music* the varying degree of volume of sound in musical performance. □ **dy·nam·i·cist** /dai'namɪsɪst/ *noun* (in sense 1a).

dyna·mism /'dainə,mɪzəm/ *noun* **1** energizing or dynamic action or power. **2** *Philos.* the theory that phenomena of matter or mind are due to the action of forces (rather than to motion or matter). [Greek *dunamis* power + -ISM]

dyna·mite ● *noun* **1** a high explosive consisting of nitroglycerine mixed with an absorbent. **2** a potentially dangerous person, thing, or situation. **3** *slang* a narcotic, esp. heroin. **4** *informal* a powerful or impressive person or thing. ● *transitive verb* charge or shatter with dynamite. ● *adjective informal* excellent or powerful. □ **dyna·mit·er** *noun* [formed as DYNAMISM + -ITE¹]

dy·namo /'dainə,moʊ/ *noun* (*pl.* **-mos**) **1** a machine converting mechanical into electrical energy, esp. by rotating coils of copper wire in a magnetic field. **2** *informal* an energetic person. [abbreviation of *dynamo-electric machine* from Greek *dunamis* power, force]

dyna·mom·eter /,dainə'mɒmɪtər/ *noun* an instrument that measures the power output of an engine. [French *dynamomètre* from Greek *dunamis* power, force]

dy·nast /'dainast/ *noun* a member of a powerful family, esp. a hereditary ruler. [Latin from Greek *dunastēs* from *dunamai* be able]

dy·nasty /'dainəsti/ *noun* (*pl.* **-ties**) **1** a line of hereditary rulers. **2** a succession of leaders in any field. □ **dy·nas·tic** /-'nastɪk/ *adjective* **dy·nas·tic·ally** *adverb* [French *dynastie* or Late Latin *dynastia* from Greek *dunasteia* lordship (as DYNAST)]

dyne /dain/ *noun* *Physics* a unit of force that, acting on a mass of one gram, increases its velocity by one centimetre per second every second along the direction that it acts. Abbr.: **dyn**. [French from Greek *dunamis* force, power]

dys- /dɪs/ *combining form* esp. *Med.* bad, difficult. [Greek *dus-* bad]

Dysart /dɪ'sɑrt/ **(Al·bert) Al·li·son** (1880–1962), Canadian lawyer and politician, Liberal premier of New Brunswick 1935–40. He introduced a number of reforms, including the first Landlord and Tenants Act (1938).

dys·en·tery /'dɪsənteri, -tri/ *noun* a disease with inflammation of the intestines, causing severe diarrhea with blood and mucus.

dys·en·ter·ic /-'terɪk/ *adjective* [Latin *dysenteria* from Greek *dusenteria* (as DYS-, *enteria* from *entera* bowels)]

dys·func·tion /dɪs'fʌŋkʃən/ *noun* **1** an abnormality or impairment of function. **2** disruption of normal social relations (*inner-city dysfunction*).

dys·func·tion·al *adjective* **1** not operating normally or properly (*dysfunctional gut syndrome*). **2** unable to deal adequately with normal social relations (*a dysfunctional family*).

dys·kin·esia /dɪskɪn'iːʃiə/ *noun* abnormality or impairment of voluntary movement. [Greek]

dys·lexia /dɪs'leksiə/ *noun* a general term for disorders that involve difficulty in learning to read or interpret words, letters, and other symbols, but that do not affect general intelligence. □ **dys·lexic** *adjective & noun* [German *Dyslexie* (as DYS-, Greek *lexis* speech)]

dys·men·or·rhea /,dɪsmenə'riːə/ *noun* (also **dys·men·or·rhoea**) painful menstruation.

dys·pep·sia /dɪs'pepsiə/ *noun* indigestion. [Latin *dyspepsia* from Greek *duspepsia* (as DYS-, *peptos* cooked, digested)]

dys·pep·tic /dɪs'peptɪk/ ● *adjective* **1** of or relating to dyspepsia. **2** ill-tempered, depressed. ● *noun* a person suffering from dyspepsia.

dys·pha·sia /,dɪs'feizə, -ziə/ *noun* *Med.* lack of coordination in speech, owing to brain damage. [Greek *dusphatos* hard to utter (as DYS-, PHATIC)]

dys·phor·ia /dɪs'fɔriə/ *noun* a state of unease or mental discomfort. □ **dys·pho·ric** *adjective* [Greek *dusphoria* from *dusphoros* hard to bear (as DYS-, *pherō* bear)]

dys·pla·sia /dɪs'pleizə, -ziə/ *noun* *Med.* abnormal growth of tissues etc. □ **dys·plas·tic** /-'plastɪk/ *adjective* [modern Latin, formed as DYS- + Greek *plasis* formation]

dys·pnea /dɪsp'niːə/ *noun* (also esp. *Brit.* **dys·pnoea**) *Med.* difficult or laboured breathing. [Latin from Greek *duspnoia* (as DYS-, *pneō* breathe)]

dys·pro·sium /dɪs'proːziəm/ *noun* *Chem.* a naturally occurring soft metallic element of the lanthanide series, used as a component in certain magnetic alloys. Symbol: **Dy**; at. no.: 66. [modern Latin from Greek *dusprositos* 'hard to get at' + -IUM]

dys·to·cia /dɪs'toːʃə/ *noun* *Med.* difficult or prolonged childbirth. [DYS- + Greek *tokos* childbirth]

dys·to·nia /dɪs'toːniə/ *noun* a state of abnormal muscle tone, esp. a postural disorder marked by spasm of the trunk, neck, shoulders or limbs and due to disease of the basal ganglia of the brain. □ **dys·ton·ic** *adjective* [DYS- + TONE + -IA¹]

dys·to·pia /dɪs'toːpiə/ *noun* a nightmare vision of society, often as one dominated by a totalitarian state (*opp.* UTOPIA). □ **dys·to·pian** *adjective & noun* [DYS- + UTOPIA]

dys·troph·ic /dɪs'trɒfɪk, -'troːf-/ *adjective* **1** *Med.* relating to or affected by dystrophy. **2** *Ecology* (of a lake etc.) containing much dissolved organic matter and little oxygen.

dys·trophy /'dɪstrəfi/ *noun* impaired nourishment of an organ or part of the body. *See also* MUSCULAR DYSTROPHY. [modern Latin *dystrophia* formed as DYS- + Greek *-trophia* nourishment]

dys·uria /dɪs'juriə/ *noun* painful or difficult urination. [Late Latin from Greek *dusouria* (as DYS-, *ouron* urine)]

Dzer·zhinsk /dzɜr'ʒɪnsk/ a city in west central Russia, west of Nizhni Novgorod; pop. (est. 2002) 277,000.

Dzong·kha /'zɒŋkə/ *noun* the official language of Bhutan, closely related to Tibetan. [Tibetan]

Ee

E¹ *noun* (also **e**) (*pl.* **Es** or **E's**) **1** the fifth letter of the alphabet. **2** *Music* the third note of the diatonic scale of C major.

E² *abbreviation* (also **E.**) **1** East, Eastern. **2** (also **e**) *slang* **a** the drug ecstasy. **b** a tablet of this. **3** emissivity. **4** electronic.

E³ *symbol Physics* energy ($E = mc^2$).

e¹ *abbreviation* euro or euros.

e² *symbol Math.* the base of natural logarithms, equal to approx. 2.71828.

e-¹ /i, e/ *prefix* form of EX-¹ 1 before some consonants.

e-² *prefix* denoting anything in an electronic state, esp. the use of electronic data transfer in cyberspace for information exchange and financial transactions, esp. through the Internet (*e-zine*; *e-commerce*; *e-cash*).

ea. *abbreviation* each.

each ● *adjective* every one of two or more persons or things, regarded separately (*each person*; *five in each class*). ● *pronoun* each person or thing (*each of us*; *have two books each*; *cost five cents each*). □ **each and every** every single. [Old English *ǽlc* from West Germanic phrase = 'ever alike', formed as AYE² + ALIKE]

each other *pronoun* one another (*they hate each other*; *they wore each other's hats*).

eager *adjective* **1 a** full of keen desire, enthusiastic. **b** (of passions etc.) keen, impatient. **2** keen, impatient, strongly desirous (*eager to learn*; *eager for news*). □ **eager·ly** *adverb* **eager·ness** *noun* [Anglo-French *egre* keen, ultimately from Latin *acer acris*]

eager beaver *noun informal* a very or excessively diligent person.

eagle ● *noun* **1 a** any of various large birds of prey of the family Accipitridae, with keen vision and powerful flight. **b** a figure of an eagle, e.g. as a symbol of the US, or formerly as a Roman or French ensign. **2** *Golf* a score of two strokes under par at any hole. **3** *US* a former gold coin worth ten dollars. ● *transitive verb Golf* play (a hole) in two strokes less than par. [Anglo-French *egle* from Latin *aquila*]

eagle eye *noun* keen sight, watchfulness. □ **eagle-eyed** *adjective*

eagle owl *noun* any large owl of the genus *Bubo*, with long ear tufts.

Eagle Pass a pass (over 560 m) through the Monashee Mountains of SE central BC, between Revelstoke and Craigellachie.

eag·let /ˈiːɡlət/ *noun* a young eagle.

Ea·kins /ˈiːkənz/ **Thom·as** (1844–1916), US painter. A dominant figure in American realist painting of the 19th c., he was noted for his portraits and scenes of boating and swimming.

-ean /ˈiːən, iən/ *var. of* -AN.

E. & O. E. *abbreviation* errors and omissions excepted.

ear¹ *noun* **1 a** the organ of hearing and balance in humans and vertebrates, esp. the external part of this. **b** an organ sensitive to sound in other animals. **2** the faculty for discriminating sounds (*an ear for music*; *plays by ear*). **3** an ear-shaped thing, esp. the handle of a jug. **4** listening, attention. □ **all ears** listening attentively. **bring about one's ears** bring down upon oneself. **give ear to** listen to. **have a person's ear** receive a favourable hearing. **have (or keep) an ear to the ground** be alert to rumours or the trend of opinion. **have something coming out of one's ears** have something in abundance. **in one ear and out the other** heard but disregarded or quickly forgotten. **out on one's ear** dismissed ignominiously. **up to one's ears** (often foll. by *in*) *informal* deeply involved or occupied. □ **eared** *adjective* (also in *combination*). **ear·less** *adjective* [Old English *ēare* from Germanic: related to Latin *auris*, Greek *ous*]

ear² *noun* the seed-bearing head of a cereal plant. [Old English *ēar* from Germanic]

ear·ache *noun* a (usu. prolonged) pain in the ear.

ear·bud *noun* a small earphone that fits inside the ear.

ear·drops *plural noun* **1** medicinal drops for the ear. **2** hanging earrings.

ear·drum *noun* the membrane separating the outer ear and middle ear and transmitting vibrations resulting from sound waves to the inner ear. *Also called* TYMPANIC MEMBRANE.

ear·flap *noun* a flap attached to the side of a hat or cap, used for covering the ear in cold weather.

ear·ful *noun* (*pl.* **-fuls**) *informal* **1** a copious or prolonged amount of talking. **2** a strong reprimand.

Ear·hart /ˈerhɑrt/ **Amelia** (1897–1937), US aviator. In 1932 she became the first woman to make a solo transatlantic flight, flying from Newfoundland to Londonderry; she disappeared over the Pacific Ocean during a subsequent around-the-world flight.

ear·hole *noun* the orifice of the ear.

earl *noun* a British nobleman ranking between a marquess and a viscount (*compare* COUNT²). □ **earl·dom** *noun* [Old English *eorl*, of unknown origin]

Earle /ˈɜrl/ **David** (b.1939), Canadian dancer and choreographer, whose works include *Baroque Suite* and *Sacra Conversazione* (1986). In 1968 he helped to found Toronto Dance Theatre, with which he was involved variously as choreographer and artistic director until 1996.

Earl Grey *noun* a type of tea flavoured with bergamot. [after Charles, 2nd Earl GREY, to whom the recipe was given]

Earl Marshal *noun* (in the UK) the officer presiding over the College of Heralds, with ceremonial duties on various royal occasions.

ear·lobe *noun* the lower soft pendulous external part of the ear.

early ● *adjective* (**earli·er**, **earli·est**) **1** happening before the due, usual, or expected time (*was early for my appointment*). **2 a** not far on in the day or night, or in time (*early evening*; *at the earliest opportunity*). **b** prompt (*early payment appreciated*; *at your earliest convenience*). **3 a** not far on in a period, development, or process of evolution; being the first stage (*early Canadian painting*; *in her early thirties*; *early spring*). **b** of the distant past (*early man*). **c** not far on in a sequence or serial order (*the early chapters*; *appears early in the list*). **4 a** of childhood, esp. the preschool years (*early learning*). **b** (of a piece of writing, music, etc.) immature, youthful (*an early work*). **5** flowering, ripening, etc., before other varieties (*early peaches*). ● *adverb* before the due, usual, or expected time (*please arrive early*). □ **at the earliest** (often placed after a specified time) not before (*will arrive on Monday at the earliest*). **early days yet** (or **still early days**) early in time for something to happen (*should save for my retirement, but it's early days yet*). **early** (or **earlier**) **on** at an early (or earlier) stage. □ **ear·li·ness** *noun* [originally as *adv.*, Old English *ǽrlīce*, *ārlīce*, from *ǽr* ERE]

early bird *noun informal* a person who arrives, gets up, etc. early or earlier than others. □ **the early bird gets the worm** *informal* the person who seizes the earliest opportunity will be successful.

early grave *noun* an untimely or premature death.

early immersion *noun Cdn* a French immersion program started when the child is in grade 1.

early music *noun* medieval, Renaissance, and baroque music, esp. as revived and played on period instruments.

Consonants: b *but*   d *dog*   f *few*   g *get*   h *her*   j *yes*   k *cat*   l *leg*   m *man*   n *no*   p *pen*   r *red*   s *sit*

early night *noun* an occasion on which a person goes to bed early.

early retirement *noun* retirement from one's occupation before the statutory retirement age, esp. on advantageous financial terms.

early warning *noun* advance warning of an imminent (esp. nuclear) attack.

ear·mark ● *noun* **1** an identifying mark or distinguishing characteristic. **2** an owner's mark on the ear of an animal. ● *transitive verb* **1** set aside (money etc.) for a special purpose. **2** mark (an animal) with an earmark.

ear·muff *noun* (usu. in *pl.*) either of a pair of ear coverings connected by a band across the top of the head, and worn to protect the ears, esp. from the cold.

earn *verb* **1** *transitive & intransitive* **a** (of a person) obtain (income) in the form of money in return for labour or services (*earn a weekly wage*; *happy to be earning at last*). **b** (of capital invested) bring in as interest or profit. **2** *transitive* **a** deserve; be entitled to; obtain as the reward for hard work or merit (*have earned a holiday*; *earned our admiration*; *earn one's keep*). **b** incur (a reproach, reputation, etc.). **3** *transitive Baseball* score (a run) without any error on the fielding side. □ **earned** *adjective* [Old English *earnian* from West Germanic, related to Germanic roots assoc. with reaping]

earned income *noun* income derived from wages etc.

earned run *noun Baseball* a run that is not the result of an error or passed ball.

earned run average *noun Baseball* a figure used to demonstrate the effectiveness of a pitcher, obtained by calculating the average number of earned runs scored against the pitcher in every nine innings pitched. Abbr.: **ERA**.

earn·er *noun* **1** a person who obtains money in return for labour or services. **2** an activity or product that brings in income of a specified kind. **3** *Brit. informal* a lucrative job or enterprise.

earn·est[1] ● *adjective* **1** serious in intention; not trifling. **2** zealous or intense. **3** resulting from or displaying sincere conviction. ● *noun* seriousness. □ **in earnest** serious(ly), not joking(ly); with determination. □ **earn·est·ly** *adverb* **earn·est·ness** *noun* [Old English *eornust*, *eornost* (with Germanic cognates): compare Old Norse *ern* vigorous]

earn·est[2] *noun* **1** money paid as an instalment, esp. to confirm a contract etc. **2** a token or foretaste (*in earnest of what is to come*). [Middle English *ernes*, prob. via Old French and medieval Latin from Latin *arr(h)a* 'pledge']

earn·ings *plural noun* money earned.

earnings-related *adjective* (of benefits, a pension, etc.) calculated on the basis of past or present income.

EARP *abbreviation* (in Canada) Environmental Assessment and Review Process.

Earp /ɜrp/ **Wyatt (Berry Stapp)** (1848–1929), US frontiersman and marshal, who was involved in the legendary gunfight at the O.K. Corral in Tombstone, Arizona (October 26, 1881).

ear·phone *noun* **1** each of a pair of receivers attached to each other so that they fit over the ears, used for listening to a radio, stereo, etc. **2** a similar device with only one receiver that fits inside one ear.

ear·piece *noun* **1** the part of a telephone etc. held to the ear during use. **2** the part of a pair of glasses, a helmet, etc., that fits over the wearer's ear.

ear-piercing ● *adjective* loud and shrill. ● *noun* the piercing of the ears to allow the wearing of earrings.

ear·plug *noun* either of two pieces of soft material placed in the ears to keep out cold air, water, or noise.

ear·ring *noun* a piece of jewellery worn in or on (esp. the lobe of) the ear.

ear·shot *noun* the distance over which something can be heard (*within earshot*; *out of earshot*).

ear-splitting *adjective* excessively loud.

earth ● *noun* **1** (also **Earth**) one of the planets of the solar system orbiting around the sun between Venus and Mars; the planet on which we live. **2** the inhabitants of this planet (*the earth is rejoicing*). **3 a** dry land; the ground (*fell to earth*). **b** the material that makes up the earth's surface; dirt, soil. **c** bodily matter (*earth to earth*). **4** the present abode of mankind, as distinct from heaven or hell; the world. **5** *Brit. Electricity* = GROUND[1] *noun* 11. **6** the hole of a badger, fox, etc. **7** (*prec. by the*) *informal* a huge amount; everything (*cost the earth*; *want the earth*). **8** any of several metallic oxides that are stable, dry, and lacking in taste and odour, e.g. alumina, zirconia, etc. ● *verb* **1** *transitive* (foll. by *up*) cover (the roots and lower stems of plants) with heaped-up earth. **2 a** *transitive*

drive (a fox) to its earth. **b** *intransitive* (of a fox etc.) run to its earth. **3** *transitive Brit. Electricity* = GROUND[1] *verb* 5. □ **come back** (or **down**) **to earth** return to realities. **gone to earth** in hiding. **on earth** *informal* **1** existing anywhere (*the happiest person on earth*; *looked like nothing on earth*). **2** as an intensifier (*what on earth?*). [Old English *eorthe* from Germanic]

earth·bound *adjective* **1** attached to the earth or earthly things. **2** moving toward the earth.

earth·en /ˈɜrθən/ *adjective* **1** made of earth. **2** made of baked clay.

earthen·ware ● *noun* pottery, vessels, etc., made of clay fired to a porous state which can be made impervious to liquids by the use of a glaze (*compare* PORCELAIN, STONEWARE). ● *adjective* made of fired clay.

earth·ling *noun* an inhabitant of the earth, esp. as regarded in fiction by outsiders.

earth·ly *adjective* **1** of the earth or human life on earth; terrestrial. **2** (usu. with *neg.*) *informal* remotely possible or conceivable (*is no earthly use*; *there wasn't an earthly reason*). □ **earth·li·ness** *noun*

earthly paradise *noun* see PARADISE 3.

earth mother *noun* **1** *Myth* a spirit or deity symbolizing the earth. **2** a sensual and maternal woman.

earth·mov·er *noun* a vehicle or machine for moving earth. □ **earth·mov·ing** *noun*

earth·quake *noun* **1** a convulsion of the superficial parts of the earth due to the release of accumulated stress as a result of faults in strata or volcanic action. **2** a severe disturbance, disruption, or upheaval.

earth science *noun* any of various sciences concerned with the earth or part of it, or its atmosphere (e.g. geology, oceanography, meteorology). □ **earth scientist** *noun*

earth-shatter·ing *adjective* (also **earth-shaking**) having a traumatic or devastating effect. □ **earth-shatter·ing·ly** *adverb*

earth·shine *noun Astronomy* the glow caused by sunlight reflected by the earth, esp. on the darker portion of a crescent moon.

earth·star *noun* any woodland fungus of the genus *Geastrum*, esp. *G. triplex*, with a spherical spore-containing fruit body surrounded by a fleshy star-shaped structure.

earth station *noun* a station which receives or retransmits signals received from satellites.

earth tone *noun* any of several rich brown colours.

earth tremor *noun* see TREMOR *noun* 3.

earth·ward ● *adverb* (also **earth·wards**) toward the earth. ● *adjective* moving or directed toward the earth.

earth·work *noun* **1** an artificial bank of earth in fortification or road-building etc. **2** the process of excavating soil in civil engineering work.

earth·worm *noun* any of various annelid worms, esp. of the genus *Lumbricus* or *Allolobophora*, living and burrowing in the ground.

earthy *adjective* (**earth·i·er**, **earth·i·est**) **1** of or like earth or soil. **2** somewhat coarse or crude; unrefined (*earthy humour*). □ **earth·i·ly** *adverb* **earth·i·ness** *noun*

ear trumpet *noun* a trumpet-shaped device formerly used as a hearing aid.

ear·wax *noun* a yellow waxy secretion produced by the ear. *Also called* CERUMEN.

ear·wig *noun* any small elongate insect of the order Dermaptera, with a pair of terminal appendages in the shape of forceps. [Old English *ēarwicga* from *ēare* EAR[1] + *wicga* earwig, prob. related to *wiggle*: the insect was once thought to crawl into the human ear]

ease ● *noun* **1** absence of difficulty; facility, effortlessness (*did it with ease*). **2 a** freedom or relief from pain, anxiety, or trouble. **b** freedom from embarrassment or awkwardness. **c** freedom or relief from constraint or formality. **3** freedom from toil; leisure (*a life of ease*). ● *verb* **1** *transitive* (often foll. by *of*) relieve from pain or anxiety etc. (*eased my mind*; *eased me of the burden*). **2** *intransitive* (often foll. by *off*, *up*) **a** become less painful or burdensome. **b** relax; begin to take it easy. **c** slow down; moderate one's behaviour, habits, etc. **3** *transitive jocular* rob or extract money etc. from (*let me ease you of your loose change*). **4** *intransitive Meteorol.* become less severe (*the wind will ease tonight*). **5 a** *transitive* relax; slacken; make a less tight fit. **b** *transitive & intransitive* (foll. by *through*, *into*, etc.) move or be moved carefully into place (*eased it into the hole*). **6** *intransitive* (often foll. by *off*) *Stock Exch.* (of shares etc.) descend in price or value. □ **at ease 1** free from anxiety or constraint. **2** *Military* **a** in a relaxed attitude, with the feet apart. **b** the order to stand in this way. **at one's ease** free from embarrassment, awkwardness, or undue formality. **ease away** (or **down** or **off**) *Naut.*

slacken (a rope, sail, etc.). [Anglo-French *ese*, ultimately from Latin *adjacens* ADJACENT]

easel /'iːzəl/ *noun* a standing frame, usu. of wood, for supporting an artist's work, a blackboard, etc. [Dutch *ezel* = German *Esel* ASS¹]

ease·ment *noun Law* a right-of-way or a similar right over another's land. [Old French *aisement*]

eas·i·ly *adverb* **1** without difficulty. **2** by far (*easily the best*). **3** very probably (*it could easily snow*).

east ● *noun* **1 a** the point of the horizon where the sun rises at the equinoxes (cardinal point 90° to the right of north). **b** the compass point corresponding to this. **c** the direction in which this lies. **2** (usu. **the East**) **a** the regions or countries lying to the east of Europe. **b** *hist.* the former Communist States of E Europe. **3** the eastern part of a country, town, etc. **4** (**East**) *Bridge* a player occupying the position designated 'east'. ● *adjective* **1** toward, at, near, or facing east. **2** coming from the east (*east wind*). ● *adverb* **1** toward, at, or near the east. **2** (foll. by *of*) further east than. [Old English *ēast-* from Germanic]

East An·glia /'ængliə/ a region of E England consisting of the counties of Norfolk, Suffolk, and parts of Essex and Cambridgeshire.

East Bengal the part of the former Indian province of Bengal that was ceded to Pakistan in 1947, forming the greater part of the province of East Pakistan. It gained independence as Bangladesh in 1971.

east·bound *adjective & adverb* travelling or leading eastwards.

East Cape a peninsular region of North Island, New Zealand. Its tip forms the most easterly point of the island.

East China Sea see CHINA SEA.

East End *noun* **1** the eastern part of London to the north of the Thames, noted for its converted docklands and its cockney culture. **2** (also **east end**) the eastern part of any city or town. □ **East Ender** *noun*

Eas·ter *noun* **1** (also **Easter Day** or **Easter Sunday**) a Christian festival (held on a variable Sunday in March or April) commemorating Christ's resurrection. **2** the season in which this occurs, esp. the weekend from Good Friday to Easter Monday. [Old English *ēastre* apparently from *Ēostre*, a goddess associated with spring, from Germanic]

Easter Bunny *noun* a rabbit popularly said to bring candy to children at Easter.

Easter cactus *noun* a succulent plant of the cactus family *Rhipsalidopsis gaertneri*, with flat, jointed stems and bright red flowers, grown as a houseplant.

Easter egg *noun* **1** an artificial (usu. chocolate) or decorated egg given at Easter, esp. to children. **2** *Computing* a message, graphic, sound effect, etc. hidden within a program or on a CD-ROM etc., and revealed in response to an undocumented combination of keystrokes or commands.

Easter Island an island in the SE Pacific west of Chile; pop. (est. 2002) 2,100. It has been administered by Chile since 1888. The island, first settled by Polynesians in about AD 400, is famous for its large monolithic statues of human heads, believed to date from the period 1000–1600.

Easter lily *noun* esp. *N Amer.* **1** a cultivated variety of *Lilium longiflorum*, a white-flowered lily native to Japan, sold as a houseplant in Canada and the US at Easter. **2** any of various spring-flowering lilies or similar plants, esp. species of the dog's tooth violet *Erythronium*.

east·er·ly ● *adjective & adverb* **1** in an eastern position or direction. **2** (of a wind) blowing from the east. ● *noun* (*pl.* **-lies**) a wind blowing from the east.

Easter Monday *noun* the Monday after Easter.

east·ern *adjective* **1** of or in the east; inhabiting the east. **2** lying or directed toward the east. **3** (**Eastern**) of or in the Far East or Middle East. **4** (**Eastern**) of or pertaining to that branch of the Christian Church which developed in the territories formerly part of the Eastern Roman Empire. □ **east·ern·most** *adjective* [Old English *ēasterne* (as EAST, -ERN)]

Eastern bloc the countries of eastern and central Europe which were under Soviet domination from the end of World War II until the collapse of the Russian Communist system in 1989–91.

Eastern Cape a province of SE South Africa, formerly part of Cape Province; capital, Bisho.

Eastern Church *noun* **1** the Orthodox Church. **2** any other Christian Church observing a liturgical rite based on that of the Orthodox Church, but in communion with the Catholic Church.

Eastern Daylight Time *noun* daylight time in the Eastern Time zone. Abbr.: **EDT**.

Eastern Desert an alternative name for the ARABIAN DESERT.

Eastern Empire see ROMAN EMPIRE, BYZANTINE EMPIRE.

east·ern·er *noun* a native or inhabitant of the east.

Eastern Ghats see GHATS, THE.

eastern hemisphere *noun* the half of the earth containing Europe, Asia, Africa, and Australia.

Eastern rite *noun* a Christian Church observing a liturgical rite based on the Eastern tradition, esp. one in communion with the Catholic Church, e.g. the Ukrainian Catholic Church.

Eastern Roman Empire see ROMAN EMPIRE, BYZANTINE EMPIRE.

Eastern Standard Time *noun* standard time in the Eastern Time zone. Abbr.: **EST**.

Eastern Star *noun see* ORDER OF THE EASTERN STAR.

Eastern Time *noun* the time in a zone including most of Ontario and Quebec as well as the eastern US. Eastern Standard Time is five hours behind Greenwich Mean Time; Eastern Daylight Time is four hours behind Greenwich Mean Time. Abbr.: **ET**.

Eastern Townships a region of south central Quebec, lying between the St. Lawrence and the US border, and Montreal and Quebec City.

Eastern Transvaal a former province of NE South Africa, now called MPUMALANGA.

Easter rising the insurrection in Dublin and other cities in Ireland against British rule, Easter 1916. It ended with the surrender of the insurgents, but was a contributory factor in the establishment of the Irish Free State (1921).

Easter·tide *noun* the period including Easter.

Easter week *noun* the week beginning on Easter Sunday.

East Germanic ● *noun* the extinct eastern group of Germanic languages, including Gothic. ● *adjective* of or relating to this group.

East Germany *hist.* the German Democratic Republic (see GERMANY).

East Gwil·lim·bury a town in S central Ontario, situated north of Newmarket; pop. (2001) 20,555. [as (BRADFORD) WEST GWILLIMBURY]

East India Company a British trading company formed in 1600 to develop commerce in the newly colonized East Indies, and which administered the colony from the second half of the 18th c. to 1858, maintaining its own army and political service.

East Indian ● *adjective N Amer.* of or pertaining to the Indian subcontinent or its indigenous peoples or their descendants. ● *noun* a person descended from the indigenous peoples of the Indian subcontinent. ¶ The term *South Asian* is now often preferred.

East Indies 1 the islands of SE Asia, esp. the Malay Archipelago. **2** *hist.* (also **East India**) the whole of SE Asia to the east of and including India.

east·ing *noun* the distance travelled or the angle of longitude measured eastward from either a defined north–south grid line or a meridian.

East Lothian a former county of east central Scotland. It became a district of Lothian region in 1975.

East·main Cree *noun* a member of a part of the Algonquian linguistic family, living at the mouth of the Eastmain River on the eastern shore of James Bay. [EASTMAIN RIVER]

East·main River a river in west central Quebec, which flows 756 km westward from the central part of the province to the eastern shore of James Bay. [so called because it was considered the bay's east shore main (water body)]

East·man, George (1854–1932), US inventor and manufacturer of photographic equipment. He invented flexible roll-film coated with light-sensitive emulsion, and the Kodak camera (1888) to use it, and later developed colour photography.

east-northeast *noun* the direction or compass point midway between east and northeast.

East Prussia the northeastern part of the former kingdom of Prussia, on the Baltic coast from the Vistula in the west to beyond the town of Klaipeda, now in Lithuania. Its capital was Königsberg (now Kaliningrad). Reduced in size after World War I, when it was separated from the rest of Germany by the Polish Corridor, it was divided after World War II between the USSR and Poland.

East River an arm of the Hudson River in New York City, separating Manhattan and the Bronx from Brooklyn and Queens.

East Side a part of Manhattan in New York City, lying between the East River and Fifth Avenue.

Vowels: a cat ɑ arm e bed ɜr her ɜː deux ə ago ɪ sit i cosy iː feed ɒ hot ɔ pore ɔː no ʌ run ʊ put

east-southeast *noun* the direction or compass point midway between east and southeast.

East Sussex a county of SE England; county town, Lewes.

East Timor the eastern part of the island of Timor in the southern Malay Archipelago; chief town, Dili. Formerly a Portuguese colony, the region declared itself independent in 1975. In 1976 it was invaded by Indonesia, which annexed and claimed it, although the claim was never recognized by the United Nations. The region became the scene of bitter fighting and of alleged mass killings by the Indonesian government and military forces. East Timor gained full independence following a referendum in 1999 and a formal declaration by the United Nations in 2002. □ **East Timor·ese** *noun* & *adjective*

east·ward ● *adjective* & *adverb* (also **east·wards**) toward the east. ● *noun* an eastward direction or region. □ **east·wardly** *adjective* & *adverb*

East-West *attributive adjective* of or relating to countries of the East and the West (*East–West relations*).

East·wood, Clint (full name Clinton Eastwood, Jr.) (b.1930), US film actor and director. He first appeared in the spaghetti western *A Fistful of Dollars* (1964), and has gone on to star in and/or direct many successful films, including *Dirty Harry* (1971), *Bird* (1988), and *Unforgiven* (1992).

East York a former borough in S Ontario, now part of east central Toronto; pop. (2001) 115,185. [ultimately after YORK in England]

easy ● *adjective* (**easi·er, easi·est**) **1** not difficult; achieved without great effort. **2 a** free from pain, discomfort, anxiety, etc. **b** comfortably off, affluent (*easy circumstances*). **3** free from embarrassment, awkwardness, constraint, etc.; relaxed and pleasant (*an easy manner*). **4** compliant, obliging; easily persuaded (*easy prey*). **5** (of a person) promiscuous; sexually available. **6** moderate, relaxed (*an easy pace*). **7** (of a slope) gentle, gradual; not steep. **8** loosely fitting; not tight (*an easy fit*). **9** *Stock Exch.* (of goods, money on loan, etc.) not much in demand. **10** (of credit) obtainable without stringent requirements of the borrower. ● *adverb* with ease; in an effortless or relaxed manner. ¶ The use of *easy* as an adverb is usually restricted to set phrases such as *easy does it* and *take it easy*. Outside of such expressions, the adverb *easily* is more standard, e.g. *I can do it easily* rather than *I can do it easy*. ● *interjection* go carefully; move gently. □ **easy as pie** *see* PIE[1]. **easy come easy go** *informal* what is easily got is soon lost or spent. **easy does it** *informal* go carefully. **easy on the eye** (or **ear** etc.) *informal* pleasant to look at (or listen to etc.). **go easy** (foll. by *with, on*) be sparing or cautious. **I'm easy** *informal* I have no preference. **of easy virtue** (of a woman) sexually promiscuous. **stand easy!** *Cdn* & *Brit. Military* permission to a squad standing at ease to relax their attitude further. **take it easy 1** proceed gently or carefully. **2** relax; avoid overwork. **3** (often as *interjection*) calm down. □ **eas·i·ness** *noun* [Old French *aisié* past participle of *aisier* EASE]

easy-care *adjective* (esp. of synthetic fabrics) simple to wash, dry, etc.; serviceable.

easy chair *noun* a large comfortable chair, usu. an armchair.

easy·going *adjective* placid and tolerant; relaxed in manner; accepting things as they are.

easy listening *noun* (often *attributive*) music that appeals to conventional tastes and is not loud, raucous, discordant, unmelodious, etc.

easy money *noun* money got without effort (esp. of dubious legality).

easy street *noun informal* comfortable circumstances, affluence.

eat *verb* (past **ate**; past participle **eaten**) **1 a** *transitive* take into the mouth, chew, and swallow (food). **b** *intransitive* consume food; take a meal. **c** *transitive* devour; feed destructively on (*the mosquitoes will eat you alive*). **2** *intransitive* (foll. by (*away*) *at, into*) **a** destroy gradually, esp. by corrosion, erosion, disease, etc. **b** begin to consume or diminish (*resources etc.*). **3** *transitive informal* trouble, vex (*what's eating you?*). **4** *transitive informal* (of a machine etc.) cause (something) to disappear or be destroyed by absorbing it into its workings (*the bank machine ate my card; the printer's eaten the paper*). **5** *transitive N Amer. slang* perform cunnilingus or fellatio on (a person). □ **eat crow** *see* CROW[1]. **eat dirt** *see* DIRT. **eat one's hat** *informal* admit one's surprise in being wrong (only as a proposition unlikely to be fulfilled: *I'll eat my hat if that's true*). **eat one's heart out** suffer from excessive longing or envy. **eat humble pie** *see* HUMBLE. **eat out** have a meal away from home, esp. in a restaurant. **eat out of a person's hand** be entirely submissive to a person. **eat up 1** eat or consume completely. **2** use or deal with rapidly or wastefully (*eats up gasoline; eats up the miles*). **3** encroach upon or annex (*eating up the neighbouring municipalities*). **4** absorb, preoccupy (*eaten up with pride*). **5** *informal* receive (something presented) with vigorous

enjoyment. **6** consume; use up (*this project is eating up a lot of my time*). **eat one's words** admit that one was wrong. **good enough to eat** very attractive (*looked good enough to eat*). [Old English *etan* from Germanic]

eat·able ● *adjective* that is in a condition to be eaten (compare EDIBLE). ● *noun* (usu. in *pl.*) food.

eater *noun* **1** a person who eats (*a big eater*). **2** *Brit.* an eating apple etc.

eat·ery *noun* esp. *N Amer.* (*pl.* **-eries**) *informal* a restaurant.

eat·ing *adjective* **1** suitable for eating (*an eating apple*). **2** used for eating (*eating place*). **3** of or relating to the process of eating (*eating habits; eating disorders*).

eat-in kitchen *noun* esp. *N Amer.* a kitchen large enough to accommodate a table and chairs so that meals may be eaten in it.

Eaton, Tim·othy (1834–1907), Irish-born Canadian merchant. He established the T. Eaton Company in Toronto in 1869 to sell goods for cash at fixed prices, and in 1884 revolutionized mail-order sales with the introduction of the Eaton's Catalogue (published until 1976).

eats *plural noun informal* food.

eau de co·logne /ˌoː də kəˈloːn/ *noun* = COLOGNE. [French, lit. 'water of Cologne']

eau de toi·lette /ˌoː də twɒˈlet/ *noun* (*pl.* **eaux de toi·lette**) a dilute form of perfume that is somewhat stronger than eau de cologne. [French]

eau-de-vie /ˌoːdəˈviː/ *noun* (*pl.* **eaux-de-vie**) spirits, esp. brandy. [French, lit. 'water of life']

eaves *plural noun* the underside of a projecting roof. [originally sing., from Old English *efes*; prob. related to OVER]

eaves·drop *intransitive verb* (**-dropped, -drop·ping**) listen secretly to a private conversation. □ **eaves·drop·per** *noun* [from an earlier noun *eavesdrop* 'the ground onto which water drips from the eaves', prob. from Old Norse *upsardropi*; *eavesdropper* originally 'a person who listens by the wall (in the eavesdrop)': the modern verb by back-formation from 'eavesdropper']

eaves·trough *noun* (also **eaves·trough·ing**) *N Amer.* (esp. *Cdn*) a shallow trough attached to the eaves of a building to collect runoff from the roof.

Ebadi /eˈbɒdiː/ **Shi·rin** (b.1947), Iranian lawyer and human rights activist who was awarded the Nobel Peace Prize in 2003 for her work.

ebb ● *noun* **1** the movement of the tide out to sea (also *attributive*: *ebb tide*) (opp. FLOOD *noun* 3). **2** a flowing away; decline or decay. ● *intransitive verb* (often foll. by *away*) **1** (of tidewater) flow out to sea; recede; drain away. **2** decline; run low (*his life was ebbing away*). □ **at a low ebb** in a poor condition or state of decline. **ebb and flow** a continuing process of decline and upturn in circumstances. **on the ebb** in decline. [Old English *ebba, ebbian*]

EBITDA /ˈebɪtdə/ *abbreviation* earnings before interest, taxes, depreciation, and amortization.

Ebla /ˈeblə/ a city of ancient Syria, situated southwest of Aleppo. In the mid-third millennium BC, it dominated a region corresponding to modern Lebanon, N Syria, and SE Turkey. It was a thriving trading city and centre of scholarship, as testified in some 15,000 cuneiform tablets discovered among the city's ruins in 1975.

Ebola /ɪˈboːlə/ *noun* a tropical African virus that causes a severe, infectious, generally fatal hemorrhagic disease in humans (also *attributive*: *Ebola virus; Ebola fever*). [the name of a river and district in Congo (formerly Zaire), where the disease was first observed in 1976]

Ebon·ics /iːˈbɒnɪks/ *plural noun* (treated as *sing.*) American black English regarded as a language in its own right rather than as a dialect of standard English. [blend of EBONY + PHONICS]

ebon·ite /ˈebəˌnaɪt/ *noun* = VULCANITE. [EBONY + -ITE[1]]

ebony /ˈebəni/ ● *noun* (*pl.* **-ies**) **1** a heavy hard dark wood used for furniture. **2** any of various trees of the genus *Diospyros* producing this. ● *adjective* **1** made of ebony. **2** black like ebony. [ultimately from Latin *ebenus*, Greek *ebenos* 'ebony tree', perhaps on the pattern of *ivory*]

e-book *noun* an electronic version of a printed book which can be read on a personal computer or hand-held device designed specifically for this purpose.

Ebro /ˈiːbroː, ˈeb-/ the principal river of NE Spain, rising in the mountains of Cantabria and flowing 910 km (570 miles) southeastward into the Mediterranean Sea.

ebul·li·ent /ɪˈbʌliənt, ɪˈbʊliənt/ *adjective* **1** exuberant, high-spirited. **2** *Chem.* boiling. □ **ebul·li·ence** *noun* **ebul·li·ent·ly** *adverb* [Latin *ebullire ebullient-* bubble out (as E-[1], *bullire* boil)]

e-business *noun* = E-COMMERCE.

EBV *abbreviation* EPSTEIN-BARR VIRUS.

EC *abbreviation* **1 a** European Community. ¶ Replaced by *EU* ('European Union') in November 1993. **b** European Commission. **2** executive committee.

écarté /ei'kɑːtei/ *noun* **1** a card game for two persons in which cards from a player's hand may be exchanged for others from the pack. **2** a position in classical ballet with one arm and leg extended, the body being at an oblique angle to the audience. [French, past participle of *écarter* discard]

Eca·tepec /ei'katəpek/ (in full **Eca·tepec de Mor·elos** /mɒ'reloːs/) an industrial centre in central Mexico, just north of Mexico City; pop. (est. 2000) 1,619,000.

Ecce Homo /,ekei 'hoːmoː/ *noun* (in Renaissance painting) a depiction of Christ wearing the crown of thorns. [Latin, = 'behold the man', the words of Pilate after the crowning with thorns (John 19:5)]

ec·cen·tric /ɪk'sentrɪk, ek-/ ● *adjective* **1** odd or capricious in behaviour or appearance; whimsical. **2 a** not placed or not having its axis etc. placed centrally (*compare* CONCENTRIC). **b** (often foll. by *to*) (of a circle) not concentric (to another). **c** (of an orbit) not circular. ● *noun* **1** an eccentric person. **2** *Mech.* an eccentric contrivance for changing rotatory into backward-and-forward motion, e.g. the cam used in an internal combustion engine. □ **ec·cen·tric·ally** *adverb* **ec·cen·tri·city** /-'trɪsɪti/ *noun* (*pl.* **-ties**). [Late Latin *eccentricus* from Greek *ekkentros* from *ek* out of + *kentros* CENTRE]

Ec·cles /'ekəlz/ **1 Sir John Carew** (1903–1997), Australian physiologist. His work on the chemical means by which nerve impulses are conducted greatly influenced physiological research and the treatment of nervous diseases; he was awarded a Nobel Prize in 1963. **2 Wil·liam John** (1917–98), English-born Canadian historian. He is noted as a leading social historian of New France, and his best-known works include *Frontenac: The Courtier Governor* (1959), *Canada Under Louis XIV: 1663–1701* (1964), and *Essays on New France* (1987).

Eccles. *abbreviation* (also **Eccl.**) *Bible* Ecclesiastes.

ec·cle·sial /ɪ'kliːzjəl/ *adjective* = ECCLESIASTICAL. [Greek *ekklesia* assembly, church, from *ekklētos* summoned out from *ek* out + *kaleō* call]

Ec·clesi·as·tes /ɪ,kliːzi'astiːz/ a book of the Bible traditionally attributed to Solomon, consisting largely of reflections on the vanity of human life.

ec·clesi·as·tic /ɪ,kliːzi'astɪk/ ● *noun* a member of the Christian clergy. ● *adjective* = ECCLESIASTICAL. [French *ecclésiastique* or Late Latin *ecclesiasticus* from Greek *ekklēsiastikos* from *ekklēsia* assembly, church: see ECCLESIAL]

ec·clesi·as·tic·al /ɪ,kliːzi'astɪkəl/ *adjective* of or relating to the Christian Church or the clergy. □ **ec·clesi·as·tic·al·ly** *adverb*

Ec·clesi·as·ti·cus /ɪ,kliːzi'astikəs/ a book of the Apocrypha containing moral and practical maxims, probably composed or compiled in the early 2nd c. BC.

ec·clesi·ol·ogy /ɪ,kliːzi'ɒlədʒi/ *noun* **1** the study of churches, esp. church building and decoration. **2** theology as applied to the nature and structure of the Christian Church. □ **ec·clesi·o·logic·al** /-ziə'lɒdʒɪkəl/ *adjective* **ec·clesi·ol·o·gist** *noun* [Greek *ekklēsia* assembly, church (see ECCLESIAL) + -LOGY]

Ecclus. *abbreviation* Ecclesiasticus.

ec·crine /'ekriːn/ *adjective* *Biol.* designating or pertaining to those sweat glands which lose none of their cytoplasm during secretion (*compare* APOCRINE). [Greek *ek* out of + *krinō* sift]

ec·dy·sis /ek'daisɪs/ *noun* the action of casting off skin or shedding an exoskeleton etc. [modern Latin from Greek *ekdusis* from *ekduō* put off]

ECE *abbreviation* **1** early childhood education. **2** early childhood educator.

ECG *abbreviation* **1** electrocardiogram. **2** electrocardiograph. **3** electrocardiographic. **4** electrocardiographically. **5** electrocardiography.

ech·elon /'eʃə,lɒn/ ● *noun* **1** (often in *pl.*) a level or rank in an organization, in society, etc.; those occupying it (*the upper echelons*). **2** *Military* a formation of troops, ships, aircraft, etc., in parallel rows with the end of each row projecting further than the one in front (*in echelon*). ● *transitive verb* arrange in an echelon. [French *échelon* from *échelle* ladder, from Latin *scala*]

eche·veria /,etʃə'viːriə/ *noun* any succulent plant of the genus *Echeveria*, native to Central and S America, and grown in gardens and as a houseplant. [M. *Echeveri*, 19th-c. Mexican botanical illustrator]

ech·idna /ɪ'kɪdnə/ *noun* any of several egg-laying pouch-bearing mammals native to Australia and New Guinea, with a covering of spines, and having a long snout and long claws. *Also called* SPINY ANTEATER. [modern Latin from Greek *ekhidna* viper]

echin·acea /,ekɪ'neiʃə/ *noun* **1** a composite plant of the genus *Echinacea*, of eastern N America, esp. the purple coneflower, *E. purpurea*, cultivated as an ornamental. **2** a preparation made from the roots of an echinacea plant, used as a herbal remedy esp. for its wound-healing properties and to boost the immune system. [as ECHINUS + Latin *-acea* 'of the nature of']

ech·ino·derm /ɪ'kaina,dɜːm, 'ekɪn-/ *noun* any marine invertebrate of the phylum Echinodermata, usu. having a spiny skin, e.g. starfish and sea urchins. [ECHINUS + Greek *derma -atos* skin]

echi·noid /ɪ'kainɔid/ *noun* a sea urchin.

echi·nus /ɪ'kainəs/ *noun* **1** any sea urchin of the genus *Echinus*. **2** *Archit.* a rounded moulding below an abacus on a Doric or Ionic capital. [Latin from Greek *ekhinos* hedgehog, sea urchin]

Echo *Gk Myth* a nymph deprived of speech by Hera, and left able only to repeat what others had said; on being repulsed by Narcissus she wasted away with grief until there was nothing left but her voice.

echo ● *noun* (*pl.* **echoes**) **1 a** the repetition of a sound by the reflection of sound waves. **b** the secondary sound produced. **2** a reflected radio or radar beam. **3** a close imitation or repetition of something already done. **4** a person who slavishly repeats the words or opinions of another. **5** (often in *pl.*) circumstances or events reminiscent of or remotely connected with earlier ones. **6** *Bridge etc.* a conventional mode of play to show the number of cards held in the suit led etc. ● *verb* (**echoes**, **echoed**) **1** *intransitive* **a** (of a place) resound with an echo. **b** (of a sound) be repeated; resound. **2** *transitive* repeat (a sound) by an echo. **3** *transitive* **a** repeat (another's words). **b** imitate the words, opinions, or actions of (a person). **4** *transitive & intransitive* (of a computer system) send a copy of (an input signal) back to its source for display; cause (a keyed character) to appear on a monitor screen as it is keyed. □ **echo·er** *noun* **echo·less** *adjective* [Latin from Greek *ēkhō*, related to *ēkhē* a sound]

echo boomer *noun* a child born to a baby boomer.

echo·cardio·gram /,ekoː'kɑːdiə,gram/ *noun* a tracing or image obtained by echocardiography. Abbr.: **ECG**.

echo·cardi·og·raphy /,ekoː,kɑːdi'ɒgrəfi/ *noun* the use of ultrasound waves to investigate the action of the heart. □ **echo·cardio·graph** *noun* **echo·cardi·og·raph·er** *noun* **echo·cardio·graph·ic** *adjective*

echo chamber *noun* an enclosure with sound-reflecting walls.

echo·en·ceph·alo·gram /,ekoːen'sefələ:,gram/ *noun* *Med.* a tracing or image obtained by echoencephalography.

echo·en·cephal·og·raphy /,ekoːen,sefə'lɒgrəfi/ *noun* *Med.* the examination of the inside or contents of the skull by means of ultrasound.

echo·ey /'ekoːi/ *adjective* of or like an echo; resounding with echoes.

echo·gram *noun* a record produced by an echograph.

echo·graph *noun* **1** a device for measuring and recording ocean depths using sonic waves. **2** a similar device using ultrasound to examine internal body structures or monitor fetal development.

echo·ic /e'koːɪk/ *adjective* *Phonetics* (of a word) imitating the sound it represents; onomatopoeic. □ **echo·ic·ally** *adverb*

echo·la·lia /,ekoː'leiliə/ *noun* **1** the meaningless repetition of another person's spoken words. **2** the repetition of speech by a child learning to talk. [modern Latin from Greek *ēkhō* echo + *lalia* talk]

echo·loca·tion *noun* the location of objects by reflected sound. □ **echo·locate** *transitive verb*

echo sounder *noun* a sounding apparatus for determining the depth of water beneath a ship by measuring the time taken for an echo to be received. □ **echo-sounding** *noun*

echo·virus *noun* (also **ECHO virus**) any of a group of enteroviruses sometimes causing mild meningitis, encephalitis, etc. [from *enteric cytopathogenic human orphan* (because not originally assignable to any known disease) + VIRUS]

echt /ext/ *adjective* authentic, genuine, typical. [German]

Eck·hart /'ekhɑrt/ **Jo·han·nes** (known as 'Meister Eckhart') (c.1260–c.1328), German Dominican theologian, who is considered the founder of German mysticism.

eclair /ei'kler, ɪ'kler/ *noun* a small elongated cream puff filled with cream or custard and iced with chocolate or coffee icing. [French, lit. 'lightning flash']

eclamp·sia /ɪ'klampsiə/ *noun* a condition involving convulsions leading to coma, occurring esp. in pregnant women. □ **eclamp·tic**

adjective [modern Latin from French *eclampsie* from Greek *eklampsis* sudden development, from *eklampō* shine forth]

éclat /eɪˈklɒ/ *noun* **1** brilliant display; dazzling effect. **2** social distinction; conspicuous success; universal approbation (*with great éclat*). [French from *éclater* burst out]

eclec·tic /ɪˈklektɪk/ ● *adjective* **1** deriving ideas, tastes, style, etc., from various sources. **2** *Philos.* & *Art* selecting one's beliefs etc. from various sources; attached to no particular school of philosophy. ● *noun* an eclectic person. □ **eclec·tic·ally** *adverb* **eclec·ti·cism** *noun* [Greek *eklektikos* from *eklegō* pick out]

eclipse /ɪˈklɪps/ ● *noun* **1** the obscuring of the reflected light from one celestial body by the passage of another between it and the eye or between it and its source of illumination. **2** a deprivation of light or the period of this. **3** a rapid or sudden loss of importance or prominence, esp. in relation to another or a newly-arrived person or thing. ● *transitive verb* **1** (of a celestial body) obscure the light from or to (another). **2** deprive of prominence or importance; outshine; surpass. □ **in eclipse 1** surpassed; in decline. **2** (of a bird) having lost its courting plumage. □ **eclips·er** *noun* [Old French from Latin from Greek *ekleipsis* from *ekleipō* fail to appear, be eclipsed, from *leipō* leave]

eclipsing binary *noun* a binary star whose brightness varies periodically as the two components pass one in front of the other.

eclip·tic /ɪˈklɪptɪk/ ● *noun* the sun's apparent path among the stars during the year. ● *adjective* of an eclipse or the ecliptic. [Latin from Greek *ekleiptikos* (as ECLIPSE)]

ec·logue /ˈeklɒg/ *noun* a short poem, esp. a pastoral dialogue. [Latin *ecloga* from Greek *eklogē* selection, from *eklegō* pick out]

eclo·sion /ɪˈkloʊʒən/ *noun* the emergence of an insect from a pupa case or of a larva from an egg. [French *éclosion* from *éclore* hatch (as EX-1, Latin *claudere* to close)]

Eco /ˈekoʊ/ **Um·ber·to** (b.1932), Italian novelist and semiotician. He is known for his extensive writings on semiotics, such as *Travels in Hyperreality* (1986), and for the novels *The Name of the Rose* (1981) and *Foucault's Pendulum* (1988).

eco /ˈiːkoʊ/ *noun informal* ecology (also *attributive*: *eco freak*). [abbreviation]

eco- /ˈiːkoʊ/ *combining form* ecology, ecological.

eco·cide /ˈiːkoʊsaɪd/ *noun* destruction of the natural environment.

eco-freak *noun* a person who is unusually enthusiastic about the protection and preservation of the environment.

eco-friend·ly *adjective* not harmful to the environment.

eco·gift *noun Cdn* a donation to the federal, provincial, or municipal government, or to a charitable organization, of land or of an interest in land that has been designated as environmentally sensitive, e.g. wetlands, forests, grasslands, etc.

ecol. *abbreviation* **1** ecology. **2** ecological.

eco-label *noun* a label identifying manufactured products that satisfy certain environmental conditions. □ **eco-labelling** *noun*

E. coli *var. of* ESCHERICHIA COLI.

ecological integrity *noun* the maintenance of an ecological region's natural components, such as plants, animals, and other organisms, in an unimpaired or uncorrupted condition.

ecol·ogy /ɪˈkɒlədʒi/ *noun* **1 a** the relations of organisms to one another and to their physical surroundings. **b** the branch of biology dealing with this. **2** (in full **human ecology**) the study of the interaction of people with their environment. □ **eco·logic** *adjective* **eco·logic·al** /ˌiːkəˈlɒdʒɪkəl/ *adjective* **eco·logic·al·ly** /ˌiːkəˈlɒdʒɪkli/ *adverb* **ecol·o·gist** *noun* [German *Ökologie* from Greek *oíkos* house]

e-commerce *noun* business transactions conducted over the Internet.

eco·museum /ˈekoʊmjuːˌziːəm/ *noun* an area designated as a living museum which preserves and promotes the natural and human activities traditionally carried on there, and seeks to explain the relationship between the inhabitants and their environment. [French *écomusée*, as ECO- + MUSEUM]

econ. *abbreviation* **1** economics. **2** economic.

econo- *combining form* economy, economical. [as ECONOMIC]

econo·box *noun N Amer. informal* a small car or truck designed for economical operation rather than comfort or style. [blend of ECONOMY + BOX1]

econo·met·rics *plural noun* (usu. treated as *sing.*) the branch of economics that deals with the application of mathematics, esp. statistics, to economic data. □ **econo·met·ric** *adjective* **econo·met·ric·al** *adjective* **econo·met·ri·cian** *noun* **econo·met·rist** *noun* [ECONOMY + METRIC]

eco·nom·ic /ˌekəˈnɒmɪk, ˌiːk-/ *adjective* **1 a** of, pertaining to, or concerned with economics. **b** relating to the wealth of a community or nation. **c** relating to the management of private or domestic finances. **2 a** maintained for profit or on a business footing (*an economic rent*). **b** paying at least the expenses of its operation or use (*not economic to run buses on Sunday*). **3** (of a subject etc.) practical or studied from a utilitarian or material standpoint (*economic geography*). **4** = ECONOMICAL.

eco·nom·ical /ˌekəˈnɒmɪkəl, ˌiːk-/ *adjective* **1** thrifty, careful in the use of resources, not wasteful. **2** inexpensive. **3** = ECONOMIC. □ **economical with the truth** discreditably reticent. □ **eco·nom·ic·al·ly** *adverb*

economic growth *noun* the rate of expansion of the national income, esp. the growth of output of goods and services per head of the population over a stated period of time, this output being measured by the Gross National Product.

economic indicator *noun* a statistical measure indicating the relative strength or weakness of selected economic variables such as output, inflation, debt burden, foreign investment, etc. in a given nation or region.

eco·nom·ics /ˌiːkəˈnɒmɪks, ˌek-/ *plural noun* (treated as *sing.*) **1 a** the social science of the production and distribution of wealth in theory and practice. **b** the application of this discipline to a particular subject or sphere (*the economics of publishing*). **2 a** the condition of a country etc. as regards material prosperity. **b** the financial considerations attaching to a particular activity, commodity, etc.

econo·mist /iːˈkɒnəmɪst/ *noun* **1** an expert in or student of economics. **2** a person who manages financial or economic matters.

econo·mize /ɪˈkɒnəˌmaɪz/ *verb* (also esp. *Brit.* **-mise**) **1** *intransitive* practice economy, reduce expenses, or make savings in or on a commodity etc. **2** *transitive* (foll. by *on*) use sparingly, make a saving in, or spend less on (a thing). □ **econo·miz·er** *noun* **econo·miz·ing** *noun*

Econo·museum *noun Cdn proprietary* a small business which practises a traditional craft or skill (e.g. paper making, cheese making, apple growing, etc.) and also acts as a museum by allowing visitors to observe the work and learn more about its history through displays and other interpretive materials.

econ·omy /ɪˈkɒnəmi/ *noun* (pl. **-omies**) **1 a** the wealth and resources of a community, esp. in terms of the production and consumption of goods and services. **b** a particular kind of this (*a capitalist economy*). **c** the administration or condition of an economy. **2 a** frugality or the careful management of, esp. financial, resources. **b** (often in *pl.*) an act, instance, or means of saving or reducing expenditure (*fuel economy*). **3** sparing or careful use of resources etc. (*economy of language*; *economy of movement*). **4** the cheapest class of some service or product, esp. of air travel. **5** (*attributive*) (of a product) offering the customer the best value for money spent, esp. a large quantity for a proportionally lower cost. [French *économie* or Latin *oeconomia* from Greek *oikonomia* household management, from *oíkos* house + *nemō* manage]

economy class *noun* (also *attributive*) the cheapest class of air travel, hotel accommodation, etc.

economy-class syndrome *noun* deep-vein thrombosis said to be caused by periods of prolonged immobility on long-haul flights.

economies of scale *plural noun* proportionate savings gained by using larger quantities.

economy size *noun* a size, usu. the largest in a range, in which goods are sold to offer a customer the best value for the money. □ **economy-sized** *adjective*

eco·region *noun* a local ecosystem.

eco·sphere *noun* **1** the region of space around the sun or a star within which conditions compatible with the existence of life, esp. on planets, may theoretically occur. **2** = BIOSPHERE.

eco·system *noun* a biological community of interacting organisms and their physical environment.

eco·tage /ˈiːkoʊˌtɒʒ/ *noun N Amer.* acts of sabotage perpetrated in the name of environmental protection against individuals or companies perceived to be polluters, destroyers of natural resources, etc. [blend of ECOLOGICAL (*see* ECOLOGY) + SABOTAGE]

eco-terror·ism *noun* **1** violence carried out to further environmentalist ends. **2** politically motivated damage to the natural environment. □ **eco-terror·ist** *noun*

eco·tone *noun* a region of transition between two ecological communities. □ **eco·tonal** *adjective* [ECO- + Greek *tonos*, lit. = 'tension']

eco·tour·ism *noun* tourism to exotic or wild, often threatened, natural environments, esp. intended to support conservation efforts. □ **eco·tour** *noun* **eco·tour·ist** *noun*

eco·toxi·col·ogy *noun* the branch of science that deals with the nature, effects, and interactions of substances that are harmful to the environment.

eco·type *noun* a distinct form of a species occupying a particular habitat. □ **eco·typ·ic** *adjective*

eco-warrior *noun* a person actively involved in preventing damage to the environment.

eco·zone *noun* a regional ecosystem.

ecru /'eikru:/ ● *noun* light brown or the colour of unbleached linen. ● *adjective* of this colour. [French *écru* unbleached]

ec·stasy *noun* (*pl.* **-sies**) **1** an overwhelming feeling of joy or rapture. **2 a** *Psych.* a pathological state of absorption and unresponsiveness. **b** a sort of trance or rapture such as is supposed to accompany religious, prophetic, or mystical inspiration. **c** a frenzy of poetic inspiration. **3** *slang* methylenedioxymethamphetamine, a powerful stimulant and hallucinatory drug (*see* MDMA). □ **in ecstasies** extremely delighted, filled with pleasure. [Old French *extasie* from Late Latin *extasis* from Greek *ekstasis* standing outside oneself, from *ek* out + *histēmi* to place]

ec·stat·ic ● *adjective* **1** in a state of ecstasy. **2** very enthusiastic or excited (*was ecstatic about her new job*). **3** of the nature of, characterized by, or producing ecstasy; sublime (*an ecstatic embrace*). ● *noun* a person subject to spells of usu. mystical ecstasy. □ **ec·stat·ic·ally** *adverb* [French *extatique* from Greek *ekstatikos* (as ECSTASY)]

ECT *abbreviation* ELECTROCONVULSIVE THERAPY.

ecto- *combining form* outside, external. [Greek *ekto-* stem of *ektos* outside]

ecto·blast *noun* = ECTODERM. □ **ecto·blas·tic** *adjective*

ecto·derm *noun Biol.* the outermost layer of an embryo in early development, giving rise to epidermis and neural tissue. □ **ecto·derm·al** *adjective* **ecto·derm·ic** *adjective*

ecto·gen·esis /,ektɔ'dʒɛnɪsɪs/ *noun Biol.* reproduction occurring outside the body. □ **ecto·gen·etic** /-dʒə'netɪk/ *adjective* **ecto·gen·etic·ally** *adverb*

ecto·morph *noun* a person with a lean and delicate build of body and with a large skin surface in comparison with weight (*compare* ENDOMORPH 1, MESOMORPH). □ **ecto·morph·ic** *adjective* **ecto·morphy** *noun* [ECTO- + Greek *morphē* form]

-ectomy *combining form* (*pl.* **-ies**) denoting a surgical operation in which a part of the body is removed (*appendectomy*). [Greek *ektomē* excision, from *ek* out + *temnō* cut]

ecto·para·site *noun Biol.* a parasite that lives on the outside of its host. □ **ecto·para·sit·ic** *adjective*

ec·top·ic /'ektɒpɪk/ *adjective Med.* occurring in an abnormal place or position. [modern Latin *ectopia* from Greek *ektopos* out of place]

ectopic pregnancy *noun* a pregnancy in which the fertilized ovum is implanted somewhere other than in the uterus, e.g. in a Fallopian tube.

ecto·plasm *noun* **1** the dense, clear, outer layer of the cytoplasm in some cells (*compare* ENDOPLASM). **2** the viscous substance supposed to exude from the body of a medium during a spiritualistic trance. □ **ecto·plas·mic** *adjective*

ECU /'eikju:/ *noun* (also **ecu, Ecu**) (*pl.* same or **-s**) = EUROPEAN CURRENCY UNIT.

Ecua·dor /'ekwə,dɔr/ an equatorial republic in S America, on the Pacific coast; pop. (est. 2002) 13,447,494; capital, Quito. □ **Ecua·dor·ean** /,ekwə'dɔrɪən/ *adjective & noun*

ec·u·mene /'ekju,mi:n/ *noun Geog.* an inhabited area. [Greek *oikoumenē* the inhabited earth]

ecu·men·ical /,ekju:'menɪkəl, ,i:k-/ *adjective* **1 a** of or representing the whole Christian world. **b** of or representing Christians of several denominations; inter-denominational. **2** seeking or promoting worldwide Christian unity that transcends doctrinal differences. □ **ecu·men·ical·ly** *adverb* [Late Latin *oecumenicus* from Greek *oikoumenikos* of the inhabited earth (*oikoumenē*)]

ecumenical council *noun* any of the various general councils of the early church or, in modern times, of the Roman Catholic Church, whose decisions are considered authoritative.

ecu·men·ism /e'kju:mə,nɪzəm, 'ekju:mə,nɪzəm/ *noun* the belief in or striving for the unity of Christians worldwide, transcending differences of doctrine.

ec·zema /ek'zi:mə, 'eksɪmə/ *noun* non-infectious, superficial inflammation of the skin, usu. with itching and discharge from blisters. □ **ec·zema·tous** /ek'zi:mətəs, ek'zem-/ *adjective* [modern Latin from Greek *ekzema -atos* from *ek* out + *zeō* boil]

ed *noun informal* education (*driver ed*).

ed. *abbreviation* **1** edited by. **2** (*pl.* **eds.**) edition. **3** (*pl.* **eds.**) editor. **4** education (*B.Ed.*). **5** educated.

-ed¹ *suffix* forming adjectives: **1** from nouns, meaning: **a** 'having, wearing, affected or characterized by, etc.' (*talented; diseased*). **b** 'having the character of' (*bigoted*). **2** from phrases of adjective and noun (*good-humoured; three-cornered*). [Old English *-ede*]

-ed² *suffix* forming: **1** the past tense and past participle of weak verbs (*needed; risked*). **2** participial adjectives (*escaped prisoner; a pained look*). [Old English *-ed, -ad, -od*]

Edam /'i:dæm, -dam/ *noun* a mild, round, pressed Dutch cheese, usu. pale yellow with a red rind. [*Edam*, a town in the NE Netherlands]

eda·mame /,edə'mɒmeɪ/ *noun* a Japanese dish of salted green soybeans boiled in their pods, typically served as a snack or appetizer. [Japanese, literally 'beans on a branch']

ed·aph·ic /ɪ'dafɪk/ *adjective Bot.* of, pertaining to, produced, or influenced by the soil. [German *edaphisch* from Greek *edaphos* floor]

EDC *abbreviation* (in Canada) Export Development Corporation.

Ed.D. *abbreviation N Amer.* Doctor of Education.

Edda *noun* **1** (also **Elder Edda, Poetic Edda**) a collection, made c. 1200, of medieval Icelandic poems on Old Norse myths, legends, and traditional subjects. **2** (also **Younger Edda, Prose Edda**) a miscellaneous handbook to Old Norse poetry, written c. 1230. □ **Eddaic** /e'deiɪk/ *adjective* **Eddic** /e'dɪk/ *adjective* [perhaps a name in a Norse poem or from Old Norse *óthr* poetry]

Ed·ding·ton, Sir Ar·thur Stan·ley (1882–1944), English astronomer, founder of the science of astrophysics. He established the fundamental principles of stellar structure, discovered the mass-luminosity relationship, and suggested possible sources of the energy within stars.

eddo /'edɔ/ *noun* (*pl.* **-does**) = TARO. [West African word]

Eddy ▸ **1** Ezra But·ler (1827–1906), US-born Canadian manufacturer. He established the friction-match factory named after him at Hull in 1851 and later expanded his operations to include lumber and paper products. **2** Mary Baker (1821–1910), US religious leader and founder of the Christian Science movement. Her book *Science and Health* (1875) set out her beliefs concerning spiritual healing.

eddy ● *noun* (*pl.* **-dies**) **1** a circular or contrary movement of water causing a small whirlpool. **2** a movement of wind, fog, or smoke resembling this. **3** a usu. relatively insignificant trend, opinion, mood, etc. going contrary to the prevailing currents of thought, attitudes, etc. ● *transitive & intransitive verb* (**-dies, -died**) whirl around in an eddy or eddies. [prob. Old English *ed-* again, back, perhaps of Scandinavian origin]

edel·weiss /'eidəl,vais/ *noun* an alpine plant, *Leontopodium alpinum*, with woolly white bracts around the flower heads, growing in rocky places. [German from *edel* noble + *weiss* white]

edema /ɪ'di:mə/ *noun* (*Brit.* **oedema**) a condition characterized by an excess of watery fluid collecting in the cavities or tissues of the body. □ **ede·ma·tous** /ɪ'demətəs, ɪ'di:-/ *adjective* [modern Latin, from Greek *oidēma*, from *oidein* 'to swell']

Eden¹ /'i:dən/ *noun* (also **Garden of Eden**) **1** a paradise or a delightful abode. **2** a state of supreme happiness. **3** the abode of Adam and Eve in the Biblical account of the Creation, from which they were expelled for their disobedience in eating the forbidden fruit of the tree of knowledge. □ **Eden·ic** /ɪ'denɪk/ *adjective* [Late Latin from Greek *ēdēn* from Hebrew *'ēden*, originally = delight]

Eden² /'i:dən/ (**Rob·ert**) **An·thony, 1st Earl of Avon** (1897–1977), English Conservative politician, prime minister 1955–7. He joined the French and Israelis in a secret pact, and launched an Anglo-French offensive on Egypt (1956) after President Nasser nationalized the Suez Canal; widespread opposition led to his resignation.

edent·ate /ɪ'denteit/ ● *adjective* **1** having no or few teeth. **2** *Zool.* of or belonging to the order *Edentata* (or *Xenarthra*) of mammals lacking incisor and canine teeth, including anteaters, sloths, and armadillos. ● *noun* an edentate mammal. [Latin *edentatus* (as E-¹, *dens dentis* tooth)]

edge ● *noun* **1** a boundary line or margin of an area or surface (*the outside edge of the road*). **2 a** the edging of a garment, curtain, etc. **b** a narrow surface or side of a thin object, esp. each of the three surfaces of a book not protected by the binding (*a gilt-edge notebook*). **3** a line along which two surfaces of a solid intersect. **4 a** the sharpened side of the blade of a cutting instrument etc. **b** the sharpness given a blade by whetting (*the knife has lost its edge*). **5 a** the area close to a steep drop (*along the edge of the cliff*). **b** the brink, verge, or crest of a bank, precipice, or sharply pointed ridge. **6** the inner or outer side of the blade of a skate. **7 a** (as a personal attribute) incisiveness, excitement. **b** an advantage, superiority. **8** the beginning of a period of time (*at the edge of night*). ● *verb* **1** *transitive & intransitive* (often foll. by *in, into, out,* etc.) move gradually or furtively towards an objective (*edged it into the corner; they all edged towards the door*). **2** *transitive* **a** provide with an edge or border. **b** form a border to. **c** trim the edge of. **3** *transitive* sharpen or give an edge to (a knife, tool, etc.). **4** *transitive N Amer.* defeat by a small margin. **5** *transitive Sport* tilt or incline (a ski or skate) sideways to make one edge dig into the snow or ice. □ **have the** (or **an**) **edge on** (or **over**) have a slight advantage over. **on edge 1** tense and restless or irritable. **2** eager, excited. **on the edge of** almost involved in or affected by. **set a person's teeth on edge** (esp. of a taste or sound) cause a person acute irritation or discomfort, as if eating sour fruit. **take the edge off** dull, weaken; make less effective or intense. □ **edge·less** *adjective* [Old English *ecg* from Germanic]

edge city *noun* esp. *N Amer.* a relatively large urban area situated on the outskirts of a city, typically beside a major road.

edged *adjective* **1** (usu. in *combination*) **a** having an edge or border, esp. of a specified kind. **b** having a cutting edge. **2** (of a tone, comment, etc.) sarcastic, acerbic.

Edge·hill the first pitched battle of the English Civil War (1642), fought at the village of Edgehill southeast of Birmingham. Though victorious, the royal army failed to exploit its position, leaving the parliamentary army stationed between the king and London.

edg·er *noun* a tool for making, trimming, or finishing an edge, e.g. of a flower bed.

edge·wise *adverb* (also esp. *Brit.* **edge·ways**) **1** with the edge forward, uppermost, or towards the viewer. **2 a** sideways. **b** edge to edge. □ **get a word in edgewise** contribute to a conversation when the dominant speaker pauses briefly.

Edge·worth, **Maria** (1767–1849), Anglo-Irish novelist. She is best known for works such as *Castle Rackrent* (1800), a novel of Irish life, and *Belinda* (1801).

edg·ing *noun* **1** something forming an edge, border, or fringe on a garment, curtain, flower bed, etc. **2** the process of making an edge. **3** *Skiing* the tilting or angling of a ski so that it cuts into the snow.

edgy *adjective* (**edg·i·er, edg·i·est**) **1** irritable, nervously anxious. **2 a** sharp-edged, not smooth. **b** (of humour, writing, etc.) characterized by sharp observation or wit. **3** *slang* unconventional, on the cutting edge. □ **edg·i·ly** *adverb* **edg·i·ness** *noun*

edh *var. of* ETH.

EDI *abbreviation* ELECTRONIC DATA INTERCHANGE.

ed·ible /ˈɛdɪbəl/ ● *adjective* fit or suitable to be eaten (*compare* EATABLE). ● *noun* (in *pl.*) things that may be eaten, food. □ **ed·ibil·ity** /-ˈbɪlɪti/ *noun* [Late Latin *edibilis* from *edere* eat]

edict /ˈiːdɪkt/ *noun* an order proclaimed by authority, esp. an ordinance or proclamation having the force of law. [Latin *edictum* from *edicere* proclaim]

Edict of Nantes *noun* an edict issued by Henry IV of France in 1598 and revoked by Louis XIV in 1685, granting toleration to Protestants.

edi·fi·ca·tion /ˌɛdɪfɪˈkeɪʃən/ *noun* mental or moral improvement, enlightenment, or instruction.

edi·fice /ˈɛdɪfɪs/ *noun* **1** a building, esp. a large, imposing, or stately one. **2** a complex organizational or conceptual structure. [Old French from Latin *aedificium* from *aedis* dwelling + *-ficium* from *facere* make]

edify /ˈɛdɪˌfaɪ/ *transitive verb* (**-fies, -fied**) (of a circumstance, experience, etc.) instruct and improve morally or intellectually. □ **edi·fy·ing** *adjective* **edi·fy·ing·ly** *adverb* [Old French *edifier* from Latin *aedificare* (as EDIFICE)]

Edin·burgh /ˈɛdɪnbərə/ the capital of Scotland, lying on the southern shore of the Firth of Forth; pop. (est. 2002) 380,500.

Edinburgh, Duke of, see PHILIP 2.

Edi·son, **Thom·as Alva** (1847–1931), US inventor. He devised systems for generating and distributing electricity, and patented more than a thousand inventions, including automatic telegraph systems, the mimeograph, the carbon microphone for telephones, the phonograph, and the carbon filament lamp. □ **Edi·son·ian** /ˌɛdɪˈsoːniən/ *adjective*

edit ● *transitive verb* (**edit·ed, edit·ing**) **1 a** assemble, prepare, or modify (written material, esp. the work of another or others) for publication. **b** prepare an edition of (an author's work, a musical score, etc.), esp. by researching manuscripts. **2** be in overall charge of the content and arrangement of (a newspaper, journal, etc.). **3** prepare (a film, tape, etc.) by rearrangement, cutting, or collation of recorded material to form a unified sequence. **4 a** prepare (data) for processing

by a computer. **b** alter (a text entered in a word processor etc.). **5 a** reword, revise, or alter (a text etc.) to correct, alter the emphasis, etc. **b** (foll. by *out*) remove (part) from a text etc. ● *noun* **1 a** the action or process of editing. **b** an act, instance, or piece of editing. **2** an edited item. □ **edit·able** *adjective* [French *éditer* (as EDITION): partly a back-formation from EDITOR]

Edith Cavell, Mount /ˈiːdɪθ ˌkavəl, kaˈvɛl/ a mountain (3 363 m) in W Alberta, situated in the Rocky Mountains, south of Jasper. [E. CAVELL]

edi·tion *noun* **1 a** a form or version of a book etc. at its first publication and after each revision, enlargement, abridgement, or change of format (*paperback edition; pocket edition; electronic edition*). **b** one copy of a book in a particular form (*a first edition*). **2 a** a whole number of similar copies of a book, newspaper, etc. issued at one time. **b** the whole number of any product, esp. an artwork, issued at one time. **3** a particular version or instance of a broadcast, esp. of a regular program or feature. **4** a person or thing similar to or resembling another (*a miniature edition of her mother*). [French *édition* from Latin *editio -onis* from *edere edit-* put out (as E-¹, *dare* give)]

edi·tio prin·ceps /ɪˌdɪʃɪoː ˈprɪnseps/ *noun* (*pl.* **editiones principes** /-ˌoːniːz -sɪˌpiːz/) the first printed edition of a book, text, etc. [Latin]

edi·tor *noun* **1 a** a person who edits material for publication or broadcasting. **b** the head of a department at a publishing house. **2** a person who selects or commissions material for publication. **3 a** a person in charge of the running and contents of a newspaper, periodical, etc. **b** a person who directs the preparation of one particular section of a newspaper etc. (*sports editor*). **4** a person who cuts and edits film, videotape, sound tracks, etc. **5** a computer program enabling the user to write or alter programs, text, or other information. **6** a machine used to edit film, videotape, etc. □ **editor·ship** *noun* [Late Latin, = producer (of games), publisher (as EDIT)]

edi·tor·ial ● *adjective* **1 a** of or concerned with editing or editors. **b** of or pertaining to an editorial. **2** written or approved by an editor. **3** distinguished from news and advertising matter (*the editorial content is shallow*). ● *noun* **1** a newspaper article written by, on behalf of, or under the direct responsibility of an editor, esp. one giving an opinion on a topical issue. **2** a statement broadcast on radio, television, etc. expressing the opinions of a station owner, manager, etc. □ **edi·tor·ial·ist** *noun* **edi·tor·ial·ly** *adverb*

editorial cartoon *noun* a cartoon in a newspaper offering comment on some news story.

edi·tor·ial·ize *verb* (also esp. *Brit.* **-ise**) **1** *intransitive* write editorials or comment editorially. **2** *transitive* add editorial comment to.

editor-in-chief *noun* (*pl.* **editors-in-chief**) the chief editor of a publication in a publishing house, magazine, etc.

Ed·mon·chuk a nickname for Edmonton. [blend of *Edmonton* + *-chuk*, a common suffix in Ukrainian surnames]

Ed·mon·ton the capital city of Alberta, located near the geographical centre of the province; pop. (2001) 666,104. □ **Ed·mon·ton·ian** /ˌɛdmənˈtoːniən/ *noun & adjective* [prob. after *Edmonton* in London, England, birthplace of J. P. Pruden, a Hudson's Bay Co. clerk]

Ed·mund I (921–46), king of England 939–46. Early in his reign a Norse army took control of York and its dependent territories; Edmund recovered these northern territories after 941, but with his death York fell again to a Norse king.

Ed·mund II (known as 'Edmund Ironside') (*c*.993–1016), son of Ethelred the Unready, king of England 1016. He was forced to divide the kingdom with Canute, retaining only Wessex; on Edmund's death Canute became king of all England.

Ed·mund Campion, St. see CAMPION 1.

Ed·munds·ton a city in NW New Brunswick, situated on the Saint John River where it forms part of the border with Maine, 275 km (171 miles) northwest of Fredericton; pop. (2001) 17,373. [Sir *Edmund* Walker Head, Lieutenant-Governor of New Brunswick d.1868]

Edo /ˈɛdoː/ *noun* = TOKUGAWA.

EDP *abbreviation* electronic data processing.

Edson a town in central Alberta, about 200 km west of Edmonton; pop. (2001) 7,585. □ **Edson·ite** *noun* [*Edson* J. Chamberlain, vice-president and general manager of the Grand Trunk Pacific Railway d.1924]

EDT *abbreviation* EASTERN DAYLIGHT TIME.

EDTA *abbreviation Chem.* ethylenediamine tetra-acetic acid, a common chelating agent.

edu·cate *transitive & intransitive verb* **1** give intellectual, moral, and social instruction to (a pupil, a child), esp. as a formal and prolonged process. **2** provide education for. **3** (often foll. by *in*, or *to* + infin.) train or instruct for a particular purpose. **4** instruct, advise, or give information to. □ **educ·able** *adjective* **educ·abil·ity** *noun* **edu·cat·able** *adjective* **edu·ca·tive** *adjective* [Latin *educare educat-*, related to *educere* EDUCE]

edu·cat·ed *adjective* **1** having had an education, esp. to a higher level than average. **2** characterized by or displaying cultivated taste, learning, culture, etc. **3** based on experience or study (*an educated guess*).

edu·ca·tion *noun* **1 a** the act or process of educating or being educated. **b** systematic instruction, schooling, or training, including the whole course of such instruction received by a person. **2** a particular kind of or stage in education (*further education; a classical education*). **3** pedagogical theory or the art and science of teaching (*a master's degree in education*).

edu·ca·tion·al *adjective* **1** of, pertaining to, or concerned with education. **2** conducive to education or having the power to educate (*educational television*). □ **edu·ca·tion·al·ly** *adverb*

edu·ca·tion·ist *noun* (also **edu·ca·tion·al·ist**) **1** an expert in the methods of education. **2** an advocate of education.

edu·ca·tor *noun* **1** a person who teaches, educates, or is in the business of education, e.g. a principal, educational administrator, etc. **2** an educational specialist.

educe /ɪˈdjuːs/ *transitive verb archaic* **1** evoke or bring out or develop from latent or potential existence. **2** infer or elicit a principle, number, etc. from data. [Latin *educere educt-* lead out (as E-¹, *ducere* lead)]

edu·tain·ment *noun* entertainment with an educational aspect. [EDUCATION + ENTERTAINMENT]

Edw. *abbreviation* Edward.

Ed·ward ▸ **1** (known as 'the Black Prince') (1330–1376), Prince of Wales, the son of Edward III. An acclaimed commander during the Hundred Years War, he fought at the battles of Crécy (1346) and Poitiers (1356). **2 Prince**, Edward Antony Richard Louis (b.1964), Duke of York, third son of Elizabeth II.

Edward I (known as 'the Hammer of the Scots') (1239–1307), son of Henry III, king of England 1272–1307. His campaign against the Welsh Prince Llewelyn (d.1282) ended with the annexation of Wales in 1284, but he failed in his attempt to conquer Scotland.

Edward II (1284–1327), son of Edward I, king of England 1307–27. He invaded Scotland in 1314 and was defeated by Robert the Bruce at Bannockburn; in 1326 Edward's wife, Isabella of France (1292–1358), allied herself with the exiled Roger de Mortimer to invade England, and Edward was deposed in favour of his son and murdered.

Edward III (1312–77), son of Edward II, king of England 1327–77. In 1330 he ended his mother Isabella's four-year regency, banishing her and executing her lover Roger de Mortimer; he started the Hundred Years War with France by claiming the French throne in right of his mother (1337).

Edward IV (1442–83), son of Richard, Duke of York, king of England 1461–70 and 1471–83. He became king after defeating the Lancastrian king Henry VI in battle (1461), and as a result of Lancastrian plots he was briefly forced into exile (1470–71).

Edward V (1470–c.1483), son of Edward IV, king of England 1483, but not crowned. Following his father's death, he was declared illegitimate on debatable evidence of the illegality of Edward IV's marriage; his throne was taken by his uncle, Richard III. (See PRINCES IN THE TOWER.)

Edward VI (1537–53), son of Henry VIII, king of England 1547–53. During his brief reign as a minor, England was effectively ruled by two protectors, the Duke of Somerset and the Duke of Northumberland; he was succeeded by his elder sister, Mary I.

Edward VII (1841–1910), son of Queen Victoria, king of the United Kingdom 1901–10, whose popularity and interest in public appearances helped to revitalize the monarchy.

Edward VIII (1894–1972), son of George V, king of the United Kingdom 1936, but not crowned. He abdicated 11 months after coming to the throne in order to marry Wallis Simpson, a US divorcee; he was created Duke of Windsor (1936).

Edward, Lake a lake on the border between Uganda and the Democratic Republic of the Congo (formerly Zaire). It is linked to Lake Albert by the Semliki River. [Albert *Edward*, Prince of Wales *c.*1888–9]

Ed·ward·ian /edˈwordiən, -ˈwɔr-/ ● *adjective* of, characteristic of, or associated with the reign of Edward VII of England (1901–10). ● *noun* a person belonging to this period.

Ed·wards, Hen·ri·etta Lou·ise (1849–1931), Canadian feminist and

women's rights activist. An outspoken advocate of women's legal and political rights, she was a founder of the National Council of Women (1893) and the Victorian Order of Nurses (1897), and was one of the five women involved in the successful Persons Case (1929).

Edward the Confessor, St. (*c.*1003–66), son of Ethelred the Unready, king of England 1042–66. Famed for his piety, Edward founded Westminster Abbey, where he was eventually buried; he was canonized in 1161. Feast day, 13 Oct.

-ee *suffix* forming nouns denoting: **1** the person affected directly or indirectly by the verbal action (*addressee; employee; lessee*). **2** a person concerned with or described as (*absentee; refugee*). **3** an object of smaller size (*bootee*). [from or after Anglo-French past participle in *-é* from Latin *-atus*]

EEC *abbreviation* European Economic Community. ¶ See Usage Note at EUROPEAN COMMUNITY.

eeew *interjection* (also **eew**) *N Amer.* expressing disgust, squeamishness, etc.

EEG *abbreviation* **1** ELECTROENCEPHALOGRAM. **2** ELECTROENCEPHALOGRAPH(Y); ELECTROENCEPHALOGRAPHIC.

eejit *noun* Scottish and Irish form of IDIOT.

eek *interjection* expressing surprise, mild alarm, etc. [imitative]

eel *noun* any of various snakelike fishes with slender bodies and poorly developed fins of the genus *Anguilla*, members of which spend most of their lives in fresh water but breed in warm deep oceans. □ **eel-like** *adjective* **eely** *adjective* [Old English *æl* from Germanic]

Eelam /ˈiːləm/ the proposed homeland of the Tamil people of Sri Lanka. Since the early 1980s Tamil separatists have been fighting for control of provinces in the north and east of the country, where there is a Tamil majority. [*Elara*, the last Tamil king of Anuradhapura]

eel·grass *noun* **1** any marine plant of the genus *Zostera*, esp. *Z. marina*, with long ribbon-like leaves. **2** any submerged freshwater plant of the genus *Vallisneria*.

eel·pout *noun* **1** = BURBOT. **2** any fish of the family Zoarcidae, with slender body and dorsal and anal fins meeting to fuse with the tail. *Also called* POUT². [Old English *ælepūta* (as EEL, POUT²)]

eel·worm *noun* any of various small nematode worms infesting plant roots.

e'en *archaic* or *poet. var. of* EVEN¹.

eensy *adjective* (also **eensy-weensy**) esp. *N Amer. informal* tiny. [alteration of TEENSY]

e'er /er/ *poet. var. of* EVER.

-eer *suffix* forming: **1** nouns meaning 'person concerned with or engaged in' (*auctioneer; mountaineer; profiteer*). **2** verbs meaning 'be concerned with' (*electioneer*). [from or after French *-ier* from Latin *-arius*: compare -IER, -ARY¹]

eerie *adjective* (**eer·i·er, eer·i·est**) gloomy, strange, or weird, esp. inspiring unease or fear (*an eerie silence*). □ **eer·i·ly** *adverb* **eer·i·ness** *noun* [originally Northern English and Scots *eri*, of obscure origin: compare Old English *earg* cowardly]

ef- *prefix assimilated form of* EX-¹ before *f* (*efface*).

EFA *abbreviation* essential fatty acid.

eff *slang euphemism* (often foll. by *off*) = FUCK (in expletive use). □ **ef·fing** *adjective*

ef·face /ɪˈfeɪs/ *verb* **1** *transitive* rub or wipe out (a mark etc.). **2** *transitive* **a** cause (a thing) to disappear entirely or remove all traces of (a thing). **b** (in abstract senses) obliterate or wipe out (a memory, mental impression, etc.). **3** *transitive* utterly surpass, outshine, or eclipse (*success has effaced all previous attempts*). □ **ef·face·ment** *noun* [French *effacer* (as EX-¹, FACE)]

ef·fect ● *noun* **1** (often foll. by *on*) the result or consequence of an action etc. **2** efficacy (*the drug had little effect*). **3** an impression produced on a spectator, hearer, etc. (*lights had a pretty effect; my words had no effect*). **4** (in *pl.*) (in full **personal effects**) property, luggage, etc. **5** (in *pl.*) (in full **special effects**) the lighting, sound, etc. used to enhance a play, film, broadcast, etc. **6** a scientific phenomenon, often named after its discoverer (*Doppler effect; greenhouse effect*). **7** the state of being operative (*the seat belt law came into effect last year*). ● *transitive verb* **1** bring about (an event or result) or accomplish (an intention or desire). **2** cause to exist or occur. □ **bring into effect** accomplish, realize. **for effect** for the sake of making an impression. **give effect to** make operative or put into force. **in effect 1** virtually, for practical purposes. **2** in fact, in reality. **take effect** prove successful, come into force, or become operative. **to the effect that** to that end, with that significance, or the general substance or gist being. **to that effect**

having that result or implication. [Old French *effect* or Latin *effectus* (as EX-[1], *facere* make)] ¶ See Usage Note at AFFECT[1].

ef·fect·ive ● *adjective* **1 a** having a definite or desired effect. **b** efficient. **2** impressively powerful in effect. **3 a** actual, existing in fact rather than officially or theoretically (*took effective control in their absence*). **b** actually usable, realizable, or equivalent in its effect (*effective money; effective demand*). **4** coming into operation (*effective May 1st*). **5** (of manpower) fit for work or service. **●** *noun* a soldier available for service. □ **ef·fect·ive·ly** *adverb* **ef·fect·ive·ness** *noun* **ef·fec·tiv·ity** *noun*

ef·fect·or *noun* Biol. (often *attributive*) an organ or cell acting in response to a stimulus.

ef·fec·tual *adjective* **1** effective, efficacious, or capable of producing the intended result or effect. **2** (of a legal document) valid, binding. □ **ef·fec·tual·ity** *noun* **ef·fec·tual·ly** *adverb*

ef·fec·tu·ate /ɪˈfektʃuˌeit/ *transitive verb* cause to happen, put into effect, accomplish. [medieval Latin *effectuare* (as EFFECT)]

ef·fem·in·ate /ɪˈfemɪnət/ *adjective* **1** (of a man) feminine in appearance or manner; unmasculine. **2** characterized by or proceeding from weakness, delicacy, etc. □ **ef·fem·in·acy** *noun* **ef·fem·in·ate·ly** *adverb* [Latin *effeminatus* past participle of *effeminare* (as EX-[1], *femina* woman)]

ef·fen·di /eˈfendi/ *noun* (pl. **ef·fen·dis**) **1** a man of education or standing in E Mediterranean or Arab countries. **2** a former title of respect or courtesy in Turkey. [Turkish *efendi* from modern Greek *afentēs* from Greek *authentēs* lord, master: see AUTHENTIC]

ef·fer·ent /ˈefərənt/ *adjective* Physiol. conducting outwards away from the central nervous system, an organ, etc. (*efferent nerves; efferent vessels*) (opp. AFFERENT). [Latin *efferre* (as EX-[1], *ferre* carry)]

ef·fer·vesce /ˌefərˈves/ *intransitive verb* bubble or give off bubbles of gas, e.g. as a result of chemical reaction. [Latin *effervescere* (as EX-[1], *fervēre* be hot)]

ef·fer·ves·cent /ˌefərˈvesənt/ *adjective* **1** bubbly, fizzy. **2** (of a person) showing great enthusiasm, excitement, etc.; lively, energetic, and vivacious. □ **ef·fer·ves·cence** *noun*

ef·fete /ɪˈfiːt/ *adjective* **1** decadent, degenerate, ineffectual, esp. as a result of overrefinement. **2** *archaic* worn out, exhausted of its essential quality or vitality. □ **ef·fete·ly** *adverb* **ef·fete·ness** *noun* [Latin *effetus* worn out by bearing young (as EX-[1], FETUS)]

ef·fi·ca·cious /ˌefɪˈkeiʃəs/ *adjective* (of a thing) producing or sure to produce the desired effect; effective. □ **ef·fi·ca·cious·ly** *adverb* **ef·fi·ca·cious·ness** *noun* **ef·fi·ca·cy** /ˈefɪkəsi/ *noun* [Latin *efficax* (as EFFICIENT)]

ef·fi·cien·cy /ɪˈfiʃənsi/ *noun* (pl. **-cies**) **1 a** the state or quality of being efficient. **b** effectiveness, competence, or the ability to accomplish or fulfill what is intended. **c** an action aimed at achieving greater efficiency (*this allows a variety of administrative efficiencies*). **2** Mech. & Physics the ratio of useful work performed to the total energy expended or heat taken in. **3** = EFFICIENCY UNIT.

efficiency expert *noun* a person who studies the methods and procedures used in a company or organization and advises on ways to improve efficiency, production, etc.

efficiency unit *noun* Cdn (esp. US **efficiency apartment**) a hotel room or small apartment with limited washing and cooking facilities.

ef·fi·cient /ɪˈfiʃənt/ *adjective* **1** productive with minimum waste or effort. **2** (of a person) capable, competent, acting effectively. **3** characterized by high or specified efficiency (*energy-efficient appliances*). □ **ef·fi·cient·ly** *adverb* [Middle English from Latin *efficere* (as EX-[1], *facere* make, accomplish)]

ef·fi·gy /ˈefɪdʒi/ *noun* (pl. **-gies**) **1** (also *attributive*) a representation of a person in the form of a sculptured figure, dummy, etc. **2** a crude representation of a person, esp. for ridicule, scorn, derision, etc. □ **burn in effigy** subject a usu. crude image of a person to a punishment desired for the person represented, e.g. burning. [Latin *effigies* from *effingere* to fashion]

ef·fleur·age /ˌefləˈrɑːʒ/ **●** *noun* a form of massage involving a circular inward stroking movement made with the flat or heel of the hand, used esp. during childbirth. **●** *intransitive verb* massage with a circular stroking movement. [French from *effleurer* to skim, touch lightly]

ef·flor·esce /ˌefləˈres/ *intransitive verb* **1** bloom or burst out into flower. **2** Chem. **a** (of a substance) turn to a fine powder through loss of water or exposure to air. **b** (of salts) be carried in solution to the surface of the ground etc. and crystallize there. **c** (of a surface) become covered with salt particles. **3** reach an optimum stage of development. □ **ef·flor·es·cence** *noun* **ef·flor·es·cent** *adjective* [Latin *efflorescere* (as EX-[1], *florēre* to bloom, from *flos floris* flower)]

ef·flu·ence /ˈefluːəns/ *noun* literary **1** a flowing out. **2** something that flows out. [French *effluence* or medieval Latin *effluentia* from Latin *effluere efflux-* flow out (as EX-[1], *fluere* flow)]

ef·flu·ent /ˈefluːənt/ *noun* sewage or industrial waste discharged into a body of water.

ef·flu·vium /ɪˈfluːviəm/ *noun* (pl. **ef·flu·via** /-viə/) **1** (usu. in *pl.*) waste material or refuse, esp. when transported by water. **2** an unpleasant or noxious odour or exhaled substance. [Latin, from *effluere* 'flow out']

ef·flux /ˈeflʌks/ *noun* the action of flowing out or of emanating, e.g. of ions. □ **ef·flux·ion** /eˈflʌkʃən/ *noun* [medieval Latin *effluxus* from *effluere* 'flow out']

ef·fort *noun* **1** strenuous physical or mental exertion. **2** a vigorous or determined attempt. **3** Mech. a force applied to a thing in motion along the direction of motion. **4** *informal* an achievement, accomplishment, or result of any concentrated or special activity (*not bad for a first effort*). **5** an undertaking engaged in by a group to support some specific action, end, goal, etc. (*the war effort*). □ **ef·fort·ful** *adjective* **ef·fort·ful·ly** *adverb* [French from Old French *esforcier*, ultimately from Latin *fortis* strong]

ef·fort·less *adjective* easy, requiring no effort. □ **ef·fort·less·ly** *adverb* **ef·fort·less·ness** *noun*

ef·front·ery /ɪˈfrʌntəri/ *noun* (pl. **-eries**) shameless insolence or impudent audacity (*he had the effrontery to tell her how to do her job*). [French *effronterie* from *effronté*, ultimately from Late Latin *effrons -ontis* shameless (as EX-[1], *frons* forehead)]

ef·ful·gent /ɪˈfʌldʒənt/ *adjective* often *literary* radiant, resplendent, or shining out brilliantly. □ **ef·ful·gence** *noun* **ef·ful·gent·ly** *adverb* [Latin *effulgēre* shine forth (as EX-[1], *fulgēre* shine)]

ef·fu·sion /ɪˈfjuːʒən/ *noun* **1 a** a copious outpouring. **b** something poured forth. **2** usu. *derogatory* **a** an unrestrained flow of speech or writing. **b** a literary composition or speech regarded as an excessive outpouring of emotion etc. **3 a** an escape of blood, pus, etc. into a body cavity. **b** accumulation of fluid in a body cavity. [Latin *effusio* from *effundere effus-* pour out (as EX-[1], *fundere* pour)]

ef·fu·sive /ɪˈfjuːsɪv/ *adjective* **1** gushing, demonstrative, exuberant (*effusive praise*). **2** Geol. **a** (of rock) poured out when molten and later solidified, volcanic. **b** marked by outpouring of igneous rock. □ **ef·fu·sive·ly** *adverb* **ef·fu·sive·ness** *noun*

e-file *transitive & intransitive verb* file (an income tax return) electronically.

EFL *abbreviation* English as a foreign language.

EFT *abbreviation* electronic funds transfer.

eft *noun* a newt. [Old English *efeta*, of unknown origin]

EFTPOS /ˈeftpɒz/ *abbreviation* esp. Austral. & NZ electronic funds transfer at point-of-sale; direct debit.

e.g. *abbreviation* for example. [Latin *exempli gratia*]

egad /iːˈɡad/ *interjection* archaic or jocular a mild oath meaning 'by God'. [prob. originally *a* ah + GOD]

egali·tar·ian /ɪˌɡaliˈteriən/ **●** *adjective* **1** of or relating to the principle of equal rights and opportunities for all (*an egalitarian society*). **2** advocating this principle. **●** *noun* a person who advocates or supports egalitarian principles. □ **egali·tar·ian·ism** *noun* [French *égalitaire* from *égal* EQUAL]

Egas Moniz /ˌiːɡas ˈmɒniz/ **An·tónio (Cae·tano de Abreu Freire)** (1874–1955), Portuguese neurologist. He developed cerebral angiography as a diagnostic technique, and pioneered the treatment of certain psychotic disorders by the use of prefrontal leucotomy; he shared a Nobel Prize for this in 1949.

Eg·bert (d.839), king of Wessex 802–39. He created a powerful kingdom around Wessex, and his reign foreshadowed the supremacy that Wessex would later secure over all England.

egg[1] **●** *noun* **1 a** the more or less spheroidal reproductive body produced by females of animals such as birds, reptiles, fish, etc. and enclosed in a protective layer, shell, or firm membrane. **b** the egg of a domestic fowl, esp. of a hen, used for food. **c** material from inside an egg, esp. in or as food. **2** (also **egg cell**) Biol. an ovum, female gamete, or reproductive cell in animals and plants. **3** *informal* a person, usu. of a specified character (*a bad egg*). **4** anything resembling or imitating an egg, esp. in shape or appearance. **●** *verb* **1** *transitive* Cooking cover with egg, or dip in beaten egg. **2** *transitive* pelt with eggs. **3** *intransitive* collect or go looking for eggs. □ **go suck an egg** *slang* get lost. **have** (or **put**) **all one's eggs in one basket** *informal* risk everything on a single venture. **lay an egg** N Amer. (of a performer, performance, etc.) fail badly. **teach one's grandmother to suck eggs** (usu. in *neg.*) presume to instruct a person in something already known. **walk on eggs** or **eggshells** see EGGSHELL. **with egg on one's face** *informal* in a condition of looking foolish or being embarrassed or humiliated by the turn of events. □ **egg·less** *adjective* **eggy** *adjective* (**egg·i·er**, **egg·i·est**). [Old Norse, related to Old English *æg*]

egg² *transitive verb* (foll. by *on*) urge, incite, provoke, or tempt (*egged us on to it*; *egged them on to do it*). [Old Norse *eggja* = EDGE]

egg and dart *noun* a type of moulding with alternating egg-shaped and triangular figures.

egg and spoon race *noun* a race in which runners must balance an egg in a spoon as they run.

egg beater *noun* **1** a small hand-operated, rotary beater, used for beating eggs, whipping cream, etc. **2** *N Amer. slang* a helicopter.

egg case *noun Biol.* a hollow, usu. rigid protective structure secreted by various invertebrates, in which eggs develop.

egg cream *noun US* a cold drink composed of milk, soda water, and flavoured syrup, usu. chocolate.

egg cup *noun* a small, cup-like container for holding a boiled egg while it is eaten.

egg custard *noun* = CUSTARD 2.

egg drop soup *noun* a Chinese soup made by trailing beaten egg into a simmering meat broth.

egg·head *noun informal* a person regarded as intellectual or highbrow.

egg money *noun N Amer. informal* money earned usu. by farm wives, and reserved for their use, by selling eggs to neighbours etc.

egg·nog *noun* a thick drink, served hot or cold, consisting of beaten eggs, milk or cream, sugar, flavourings, and usu. rum or brandy.

egg·plant *noun esp. N Amer.* **1** a tropical plant, *Solanum melongena*, having erect or spreading branches bearing white or purple egg-shaped fruit. **2** this fruit eaten as a vegetable.

egg roll *noun* a deep-fried appetizer consisting of a thin shell of egg dough filled with a mixture of bean sprouts, minced meat, bamboo shoots, etc.

eggs and bacon *noun* (also **egg and bacon**) any of various yellow- and orange- or red-flowered plants, esp. bird's-foot trefoil, *Lotus corniculatus*.

eggs Benedict *noun* a dish consisting of poached eggs on a slice of ham on toast, covered with hollandaise sauce.

egg·shell ● *noun* **1** the thin shell or external covering of a bird's egg. **2** anything very fragile. ● *adjective* **1 a** having a delicacy like that of an eggshell. **b** (of china) of extreme thinness, fragility, and delicacy. **2** (of paint or finish) having the slight sheen or pale colour of a bird's egg. □ **walk on eggshells** walk warily or proceed cautiously.

egg timer *noun* a device for timing the cooking of an egg, e.g. a miniature hourglass.

egg tooth *noun* a hard, white projection on the beak or jaw of an embryonic bird or reptile which is used to break out of its egg and which is discarded after birth.

egg white *noun* albumen or the translucent viscous fluid surrounding the yolk of an egg, which turns white when cooked.

egg yolk *noun* the yellow, internal part of a bird's egg which, surrounded by egg white, is rich in protein and fat to nourish the embryo.

eglan·tine /ˈeɡlənˌtain/ *noun* sweet-brier. [French *églantine* from Old French *aiglent*, ultimately from Latin *acus* needle]

Eg·mont, Mount /ˈeɡmɒnt/ (called in Maori **Taranaki**) a volcanic peak in North Island, New Zealand, rising to a height of 2 518 m (8,260 ft.). [Sir J. Perceval, 2nd Earl of *Egmont*, British politician d.1770]

ego /ˈiːɡoː/ *noun* (pl. **egos**) **1** *Metaphysics* oneself or the conscious, thinking subject. **2** *Psych.* **a** that part of the mind which has a sense of individuality and is most conscious of self. **b** the part of the mind which, according to Freud, mediates between the id and the superego and deals with external reality. **3 a** a person's self-esteem. **b** self-importance, egotism, conceit. □ **ego·less** *adjective* [Latin, = I]

ego·cen·tric /ˌiːɡoːˈsentrik/ ● *adjective* **1** *Psych. & Philos.* understanding the self as the centre of all experience with everything being considered only in relation to the self. **2** self-centred, egoistic, little considering the needs, interests, ideas, etc. of others. ● *noun* an egocentric person. □ **ego·cen·tric·al·ly** *adverb* **ego·cen·tri·city** /-ˈtrɪsɪti/ *noun* **ego·cen·trism** *noun* [EGO + -CENTRIC after geocentric etc.]

ego-ideal *noun* **1** *Psych.* the superego or the part of the mind that is evolved from the ego through an awareness of social standards and that tries to impose concepts of ideal behaviour upon the ego. **2** (in general use) a person's ideal conception of him or herself.

ego·ism /ˈiːɡoːˌɪzəm/ *noun* **1** an ethical theory that regards self-interest as the foundation of morality. **2** systematic self-centredness. **3** =

EGOTISM. □ **ego·ist** *noun* **ego·is·tic** *adjective* **ego·is·tic·al** *adjective* **ego·is·tic·al·ly** *adverb* [French *égoisme*, ultimately from modern Latin *egoismus* (as EGO)] ¶ The senses of *egoism* and *egotism* overlap, but *egoism* alone is a term used in philosophy and psychology to mean 'self-interest' (often contrasted with *altruism*).

ego·mania /ˌiːɡoːˈmeiniə/ *noun* obsessive self-love or self-centredness. □ **ego·maniac** /-ˈmeiniˌak/ *noun* **ego·man·iacal** /-məˈnaiəkəl/ *adjective*

ego·tism /ˈiːɡəˌtɪzəm/ *noun* **1** the practice of continually talking about oneself. **2** an exaggerated opinion of oneself. **3** extreme selfishness. □ **ego·tist** *noun* **ego·tis·tic** /-ˈtɪstɪk/ *adjective* **ego·tis·tic·al** /-ˈtɪstɪkəl/ *adjective* **ego·tis·tic·al·ly** /-ˈtɪstɪkəli/ *adverb* [EGO + -ISM with intrusive -t-]

ego trip *informal* ● *noun* an action or activity performed or indulged in to draw attention to one's abilities, for vanity's sake, etc. ● *intransitive verb* (**ego-trip**) (**ego-tripped**, **ego-trip·ping**) indulge in an ego trip. □ **ego-tripper** *noun*

Egoy·an /eˈɡɔijən/ **Atom** (b.1960), Canadian filmmaker of Armenian descent. His films usually depict tragic characters with compassion, and have won three first prizes at the Toronto Film Festival. His film *The Sweet Hereafter* won the 1997 Grand Prix at the Cannes Film Festival.

egre·gious /ɪˈɡriːdʒəs/ *adjective* gross, flagrant, shocking, or outstandingly bad (*egregious folly*; *an egregious ass*). □ **egre·gious·ly** *adverb* **egre·gious·ness** *noun* [Latin *egregius* illustrious, lit. 'standing out from the flock' from *grex gregis* flock]

egress /ˈiːɡres/ *noun* **1 a** the action of going out or coming in. **b** *Law* the right or freedom to do this. **2** an exit or a way out. **3** *Astronomy* the end of an eclipse or transit. [Latin *egressus* from *egredi egress-* (as E-¹, *gradi* to step)]

egret /ˈiːɡrət/ *noun* any of various herons of the genus *Egretta* or *Bulbulcus*, usu. having long white feathers in the breeding season. [Middle English, var. of AIGRETTE]

Egypt /ˈiːdʒɪpt/ a country in NE Africa bordering on the Mediterranean Sea; pop. (est. 2002) 70,712,345; capital, Cairo. The population of Egypt is concentrated chiefly along the fertile valley of the Nile, the rest of the country being largely desert.

Egyp·tian /ɪˈdʒɪpʃən/ ● *adjective* of or relating to ancient or modern Egypt, Egyptian, or Egyptians. ● *noun* **1** a native of modern Egypt or a national of the Arab Republic of Egypt. **2** the Hamitic language used in ancient Egypt until the 3rd c. AD. *Compare* COPTIC.

Egypt·ol·ogy /ˌiːdʒɪpˈtɒlədʒi/ *noun* the study of the language, history, and culture of ancient Egypt, esp. the branch of archaeology that deals with Egyptian antiquities. □ **Egypt·o·logic·al** /ˌiːˌdʒɪptəˈlɒdʒikəl/ *adjective* **Egypt·ol·o·gist** *noun*

eh *interjection informal* **1** inviting assent (*nice day, eh?*). **2** *Cdn* ascertaining the comprehension, continued interest, agreement, etc. of the person or persons addressed (*it's way out in the suburbs, eh, so I can't get there by bike*). ¶ This is the only usage of *eh* that can be categorized as peculiarly Canadian, all other uses being common amongst speakers in other Commonwealth countries and to a lesser extent in the United States. **3** expressing inquiry or surprise. **4** asking for something to be repeated or explained. [Middle English *ey*]

Ehren·burg /ˈeːrənˌbɜːrɡ/ **Ilya Grig·ori·evich** (1891–1967), Russian novelist and journalist. His novels include *The Thaw* (1954), a work openly critical of Stalinism and dealing with the temporary period of liberalization following Stalin's death.

Ehr·lich /ˈerlɪx/ **Paul** (1854–1915), German bacteriologist. One of the founders of modern immunology, he also pioneered the study of chemotherapy and developed an effective treatment for syphilis (1911); he shared a Nobel Prize in 1908.

EI *abbreviation Cdn* employment insurance.

EIA *abbreviation* environmental impact assessment.

Eich·mann /ˈaixmən/ **(Karl) Adolf** (1906–62), German Nazi administrator. He was responsible for the introduction of concentration camps in which millions died; he was traced to Argentina by Israeli agents (1960), abducted, and executed after trial in Israel.

eicosa·penta·enoic acid /ˌaikɒsəˌpentəˈiːnoːik/ *noun* a polyunsaturated fatty acid found esp. in fish oils. In humans it is a metabolic precursor of prostaglandins. [Greek *eicosa-* 'twenty' (the number of carbon atoms in the molecule) + PENTA- + -ENE + -*oic* on the pattern of *methanoic*]

Eid *var.* of ID.

eider /ˈaidər/ *noun* **1** (in full **eider duck**) any large northern sea duck of the genera *Somateria* and *Polysticta*, esp. the common eider, *S. mollisima*, the male of which is largely black and white and the female dull brown, and which is the source of eiderdown, or the king eider. **2** = EIDERDOWN 2. [Icelandic *aethr*]

eider·down /ˈaidərˌdaun/ *noun* esp. *Brit.* **1** a quilt, sleeping bag, etc. stuffed with down (originally from the eider) or some other soft material, esp. as the upper layer of bedclothes. **2** the soft feathers from the breast of the eider, with which it lines its nest.

eid·etic /aiˈdetik/ ● *adjective Psych.* of, pertaining to, or designating a recollected mental image having unusual vividness and detail, as if actually visible. ● *noun* a person able to perceive eidetic images. [German *eidetisch* from Greek *eidētikos* from *eidos* form]

eido·lon /aiˈdoːlɒn/ *noun* (*pl.* **eido·lons** or **eido·la** /-lə/) **1** a spectre or phantom. **2** an idealized figure. [Greek *eidōlon*: see IDOL]

Eif·fel /ˈaifəl/ **(Alex·andre) Gus·tave** (1832–1923), French engineer who designed and built the Eiffel Tower in Paris and designed the inner structure of the Statue of Liberty in New York harbour.

Eigen /ˈaigən/ **Man·fred** (b.1927), German physical chemist, noted for his study of high-speed chemical reactions; he shared a Nobel Prize in 1967.

eigen- /ˈaigən/ *combining form Math. & Physics* proper, characteristic. [German *eigen* OWN]

eigen·frequen·cy /ˈaigənˌfriːkwənsi/ *noun* (*pl.* **-cies**) *Math. & Physics* any of the natural resonant frequencies of a system.

eigen·func·tion /ˈaigənˌfʌŋkʃən/ *noun Math. & Physics* each of a set of independent functions which are solutions to a given differential equation.

eigen·value /ˈaigənˌvaljuː/ *noun Math. & Physics* **1** each of a set of values of a parameter for which a differential equation has a non-zero solution, or eigenfunction, under given conditions. **2** any of the numbers such that a given matrix minus that number times the identity matrix has zero determinant.

Eiger /ˈaigər/ a mountain peak in the Bernese Alps in central Switzerland, which rises to 3 970 m (13,101 ft.).

eight ● *noun* **1 a** one more than seven, or two less than ten; the product of two units and four units. **b** a symbol or figuring representing this (8, viii, VIII). **2** the eighth of a set or series with numbered members, esp. the one designated eight (*chapter eight*; *exercise eight*). **3** (in full **figure eight**) a figure resembling the form of 8, esp. in skating or folk dancing. **4 a** a size etc. denoted by eight. **b** a shoe, garment, etc. of such a size. **5 a** a crew of eight in a rowboat. **b** an eight-oared rowboat. **6** eight o'clock. **7** a playing card with eight pips or spots. **8** an engine or motor vehicle with eight cylinders. **9** *Music* the number eight in a time signature indicating that an eighth note counts for a beat. ● *adjective* one more than seven. [Old English *ehta, eahta*]

eight ball *noun N Amer.* **1** a variety of pool in which the winner is the first side to sink all seven of its own balls (either the striped ones or those in solid colours) and then sink the eight ball. **2** the black ball, numbered eight, in this. **3** *slang* a portion of an illegal drug weighing an eighth of an ounce (3.54 grams). □ **behind the eight ball 1** in a difficult situation, at a disadvantage. **2** baffled, stymied.

eight·een ● *noun* **1 a** one more than seventeen, or eight more than ten; the product of two units and nine units. **b** a symbol for this (18, xviii, XVIII). **2** the eighteenth of a set or series with numbered members, esp. the one designated eighteen (*chapter eighteen*; *exercise eighteen*). **3** a size etc. denoted by eighteen. **4** a set or team of eighteen individuals. ● *adjective* one more than seventeen. □ **eight·eenth** *adjective, noun, & adverb* [Old English *ehtatēne, eaht-*]

eight·een·mo /eiˈtiːnmoː/ *noun* = OCTODECIMO.

eighteen-wheeler *noun N Amer. informal* a large transport truck having eighteen wheels.

eight·fold *adjective & adverb* **1** eight times as much or as many. **2** consisting of eight parts, divisions, units, etc. **3** amounting to eight.

Eightfold Path *noun Buddhism* the path to nirvana, comprising the eight aspects in which an aspirant must become practised, these being right views, intentions, speech, conduct, livelihood, effort, mindfulness, and meditation.

eighth ● *noun* **1 a** the position in a sequence corresponding to the number 8 in the sequence 1–8. **b** something occupying this position, usu. identified contextually as the day of the month or, following a proper name, a person, esp. a monarch or pope. **2** one of eight equal parts of a thing. **3** *Baseball* the eighth inning. ● *adjective* (also **8th**) next in order after the seventh, being number eight in a series. ● *adverb* in the eighth place; eighthly. □ **eighth·ly** *adverb*

eighth note *noun esp. N Amer. Music* a note having the time value of an eighth of a whole note or half a quarter note and represented by a large dot with a hooked stem.

eighth rest *noun N Amer. Music* a rest having the time value of an eighth note.

800 number *noun N Amer.* a toll-free telephone number, with 800 in place of an area code, used esp. for business etc. to encourage customers at a distance to call or order.

eight·some reel *noun* a lively Scottish reel for eight dancers.

eight-track *noun* (often *attributive*) **1** a type of magnetic sound recording with four stereo tracks, any of which can be selected as the tape loops. **2** a tape player for this type of recording.

eighty ● *noun* (*pl.* **-ies**) **1 a** the product of eight and ten. **b** a symbol for this (80, lxxx, LXXX). **2** (in *pl.*) the numbers from 80 to 89, esp. the years of a century or of a person's life. ● *adjective* that amount to eighty. □ **eighty-first, -second**, etc. the ordinal numbers between eightieth and ninetieth. **eighty-one, -two**, etc. the cardinal numbers between eighty and ninety. □ **eight·i·eth** *adjective, noun, & adverb* [Old English *-eahtatig* (as EIGHT, -TY²)]

eighty-six *transitive verb N Amer. slang* reject, discard, dismiss or destroy (a thing, person, idea, etc.). [possibly rhyming slang for *nix*]

Eijk·man /ˈeikmən/ **Chris·tiaan** (1858–1930), Dutch physician. He discovered the cause of beriberi to be dietary rather than bacteriological, and his work resulted in a cure for the disease; he shared the Nobel Prize for medicine in 1929.

Eilat /eiˈlat/ (also **Elat**) the southernmost town in Israel, a port and resort at the head of the Gulf of Aqaba; pop. (2000) 41,100. Founded in 1949 near the ruins of biblical Elath, it is Israel's only outlet to the Red Sea.

Eind·hoven /ˈaintˌhoːvən/ a city in the south of the Netherlands; pop. (est. 2002) 201,300. The city is a major producer of electrical and electronic goods.

ein·korn /ˈainkɔrn/ *noun* a kind of wheat (*Triticum monococcum*). [German from *ein* one + *Korn* seed]

Ein·stein /ˈainstain/ **Al·bert** (1879–1955), German-born US theoretical physicist and mathematician. Generally considered the greatest scientist of the 20th c., he formulated the special and general theories of relativity (1905 and 1916), and searched for a unified field theory embracing electromagnetism, gravitation, and quantum mechanics; he was awarded the Nobel Prize for physics in 1921, and in later life became a campaigning pacifist. □ **Ein·stein·ian** *adjective*

ein·stein·ium /ainˈstainiəm/ *noun Chem.* a transuranic radioactive metallic element produced artificially from plutonium. Symbol: **Es**; at. no.: 99. [A. EINSTEIN]

Eint·hoven /ˈeintˌhoːvən/ **Wil·lem** (1860–1927), Dutch physiologist. He devised the first electrocardiograph and diagnosed various heart diseases; he was awarded a Nobel Prize in 1924.

Eire /ˈerə/ the Gaelic name for Ireland. It was the official name of the former Irish Free State from 1937 to 1949, when the country became a republic, and is often used loosely to refer to the Republic of Ireland.

eir·en·ic *var. of* IRENIC.

Eisen·hower /ˈaizənˌhauər/ **Dwight David** (known as 'Ike') (1890–1969), US general and Republican politician, 34th president of the US 1953–61. He was commander-in-chief of Allied forces in N Africa and Italy 1942–3 and supreme commander of Allied Expeditionary Forces in W Europe 1943–51; as president, he adopted a stern attitude towards Communism both in his domestic and foreign policy.

Eisen·staedt /ˈaizənˌstat/ **Al·fred** (1898–1995), German-born US photographer, noted as a pioneering photojournalist for his documentary photographs of the 1930s.

Eisen·stein /ˈaizənˌstain/ **Ser·gei (Mik·hail·ovich)** (1898–1948), Soviet film director. He made his name with *The Battleship Potemkin* (1925), a film commemorating the Revolution of 1905; his other films include *Alexander Nevsky* (1938), and *Ivan the Terrible* (1944 and 1946).

eis·tedd·fod /aiˈsteðvɒd, -ˈstedfəd/ *noun* (*pl.* **eis·tedd·fods** or **eis·tedd·fodau** /-ˌdai/) **1** a congress of Welsh bards. **2** a national or local gathering (in Wales, or in other places with a strong Welsh influence) for competitions of literature, music, folk dance, etc. □ **eis·tedd·fod·ic** /-ˈfɒdik/ *adjective* [Welsh, lit. = 'session' from *eistedd* sit]

either /ˈaiðər, ˈiːðər/ ● *adjective & pronoun* **1** one or the other of two (*either of you can go; you may have either book*). **2** each of two (*houses on either side of the road; either will do*). ● *adverb & conjunction* **1** as one possibility (*is either black or white*). **2** as one choice or alternative (*either come in or go out*). **3** (with *neg.* or *interrogative*) **a** any more than the other (*I didn't like it either; if I do not go, she will not either*). **b** moreover (*there is no time to lose,* *either*). □ **either way** in either case or event. [Old English *ǣgther* from Germanic]

either-or ● *noun* an unavoidable choice between alternatives. ● *adjective* involving such a choice.

ejac·u·late ● *verb* /ɪˈdʒakjʊˌleɪt/ **1** *intransitive* forcefully eject semen on achieving orgasm. **2** *transitive* **a** forcefully eject (semen). **b** suddenly eject (any matter) from the human, animal, or plant body. **3** *transitive* utter (words) suddenly; exclaim. ● *noun* /ɪˈdʒakjʊlət/ semen that has been ejaculated from the body. □ **ejac·u·la·tion** *noun* **ejac·u·la·tor** *noun* **ejac·u·la·tory** /ɪˈdʒakjʊləˌtɔːri/ *adjective* [Latin *ejaculari* to dart (as E-¹, *jaculum* javelin)]

eject ● *verb* **1** *transitive* **a** send or drive out precipitately or by force. **b** compel to leave, esp. a place or sporting event. **2 a** *transitive* cause (the pilot etc.) to be propelled from an aircraft or spacecraft in an emergency. **b** *intransitive* (of the pilot etc.) be ejected in this way (*they both ejected safely before the plane crashed*). **3** *transitive* cause to be removed or drop out, e.g. a disk or tape from a machine, a spent cartridge from a gun. ● *noun* (often *attributive*) a device, computer command, etc. which causes something to be ejected (*eject button*). □ **eject·able** *adjective* [Latin *ejicere eject-* (as E-¹, *jacere* throw)]

ejecta /ɪˈdʒɛktə/ *plural noun* (also treated as *sing.*) material that is thrown out, esp. from a volcano or a star. [Latin from *ejicere eject-* EJECT]

ejec·tion *noun* **1 a** the act or an instance of ejecting. **b** the process of being ejected. **2** an emergency procedure in which a pilot is catapulted out of and away from an aircraft. **3** = EJECTA.

ejection seat *noun* (also **ejector seat**) a device for the automatic ejection of the pilot etc. of an aircraft or spacecraft in an emergency.

eject·or *noun* (also *attributive*) an appliance or mechanical part that serves to eject something, e.g. a cartridge from a gun.

ejido /eˈhiːdoʊ/ *noun* (in Mexico) a piece of land farmed communally under a system supported by the state. [Mexican Spanish, from Spanish, denoting common land on the road leading out of a village]

Ekat·er·ino·dar /jəˌkatəˈriːnəˌdar/ (also **Yekat·er·ino·dar**) a former name (until 1922) for KRASNODAR 2.

Ekat·er·ino·slav /jəˌkatəˈriːnəˌslaf/ (also **Yekat·er·ino·slav**) a former name (1787–1926) for DNIPROPETROVSK.

eke *transitive verb* □ **eke out 1** contrive to make (a livelihood) or support (an existence). **2** (foll. by *with*, *by*) **a** supplement, make up for deficiencies in. **b** cause to last longer by economical use or by expedients. [Old English *ēacan*, related to Latin *augēre* increase]

EKG *abbreviation* N Amer. **1** electrocardiogram. **2** electrocardiograph.

ekka *noun* a small one-horse vehicle used in the Indian subcontinent. [Hindi *ekkā* unit]

Ekman, V(agn) Wal·frid (1874–1954), Swedish oceanographer. He recognized that the Coriolis effect on ocean currents can be responsible for surface water moving at an angle to the prevailing wind direction.

el *noun* US an elevated railway as part of a city's subway system. [abbreviation]

-el *var. of* -LE².

elab·or·ate ● *adjective* /ɪˈlabərət/ **1** carefully or minutely worked out. **2** highly developed or complicated. **3** ostentatious, showy. ● *verb* /ɪˈlabəˌreɪt/ **1 a** *transitive* work out or explain in detail. **b** *transitive & intransitive* go into the specifics or details of a situation, matter, etc. (*I need not elaborate*). **c** *intransitive* (foll. by *on*) explain in detail. **2** *transitive* produce or develop (a thing) by effort or labour, esp. fashion (a product of art, craft, etc.) from raw material. **3** *transitive* (of nature or a natural agency) produce (a substance etc.) from its elements or sources. □ **elab·or·ate·ly** *adverb* **elab·or·ate·ness** *noun* **elab·or·a·tion** /-ˈreɪʃən/ *noun* [Latin *elaboratus* past participle of *elaborare* (as E-¹, *labor* work)]

elae·agnus /ˌeliagnəs/ *noun* = OLEASTER. [Modern Latin from Greek *elaiagnos* a kind of willow, from *elaia* olive tree + *agnos* chaste tree]

Ela·gab·alus see HELIOGABALUS.

El Ala·mein, Battle of /el ˌaləˈmeɪn/ a decisive battle in 1942 at El Alamein in Egypt, 90 km (60 miles) west of Alexandria, in which the German Afrika Korps under Rommel was checked in its advance towards the Nile by the British 8th Army under Montgomery.

El Alto /el ˈaltoʊ/ a city in western Bolivia, adjoining Le Paz; pop. (est. 2000) 568,919.

Elam /ˈiːlam/ an ancient kingdom east of the Tigris, established in the 4th millennium BC. Its capital was at Susa. □ **Elam·ite** *adjective & noun*

élan /eɪˈlɑ̃/ *noun* style, vivacity, energy arising from enthusiasm. [French from *élancer* launch]

eland /ˈiːlənd/ *noun* any antelope of the genus *Tragelaphus*, native to Africa, having spirally twisted horns, esp. the largest of living antelopes, *T. derbianus*. [Dutch,= moose]

elapse /ɪˈlaps/ ● *intransitive verb* (of time) pass by. ● *noun* a lapse or period of time passing. [Latin *elabor elaps-* slip away]

elas·mo·branch /ɪˈlazməˌbraŋk/ *noun* any cartilaginous fish of the subclass Chondrichthyes, e.g. sharks, skates, rays. [modern Latin *elasmobranchii* from Greek *elasmos* beaten metal + *bragkhia* gills]

elas·mo·saur /ɪˌlazməˈsɔːr/ *noun* (also **elas·mo·saur·us** /ɪˌlazməˈsɔːrəs/) a large extinct marine reptile with paddle-like limbs and tough crocodile-like skin. [modern Latin from Greek *elasmos* beaten metal + *sauros* lizard]

elas·tane *noun* Brit. = SPANDEX.

elas·tase /ɪˈlasteɪz, i-/ *noun* a pancreatic enzyme which digests elastin.

elas·tic ● *adjective* **1** able to resume its normal bulk or shape spontaneously after contraction, dilatation, or distortion. **2** flexible; adaptable (*elastic rules*). **3** springy. **4** (of a person or feelings) not permanently or easily depressed; buoyant. **5** *Econ.* (of demand) variable according to price. **6** *Physics* (of a collision) involving no decrease of kinetic energy. ● *noun* **1** elastic cord or fabric, usu. woven with strips of rubber. **2** esp. N Amer. = RUBBER BAND. □ **elas·tic·ally** *adverb* **elas·ti·city** /ˌɪlasˈtɪsɪti, ˌiː-/ *noun* [modern Latin *elasticus* from Greek *elastikos* propulsive, from *elaunō* drive]

elas·ti·cated *adjective* Brit. = ELASTICIZED.

elastic band *noun* = RUBBER BAND.

elas·ti·cized *adjective* (also esp. Brit. **-cised**) **1** (of a fabric) made elastic by weaving with rubber thread. **2** (of part of a garment, esp. a waistline, neckline, or cuff) made stretchy by the insertion of elastic in a casing.

elas·tin /ɪˈlastɪn, i-/ *noun* an elastic fibrous glycoprotein found in connective tissue. [ELASTIC + -IN]

elas·to·mer /ɪˈlastəmər, i-/ *noun* a natural or synthetic rubber or rubber-like plastic. □ **elas·to·mer·ic** /-ˈmɛrɪk/ *adjective* [ELASTIC, after *isomer*]

Elat see EILAT.

elate /ɪˈleɪt, i-/ *transitive verb* make very happy or proud; fill with joy. □ **ela·tion** *noun* [Middle English from Latin *efferre elat-* raise]

elat·ed /ɪˈleɪtɪd, i-/ *adjective* very happy or proud; overjoyed. □ **elat·ed·ly** *adverb* **elat·ed·ness** *noun*

elat·er /ˈelətər/ *noun* a click beetle. [modern Latin from Greek *elatēr* driver, from *elaunō* drive]

E-layer *noun* a layer of the ionosphere at about 100 km height able to reflect medium-frequency radio waves. [E (arbitrary) + LAYER]

Ela·zig /ˌeləˈziːg/ a city in east central Turkey; pop. (est. 1997) 250,534.

Elba a small island off the west coast of Italy, famous as the place of Napoleon's first exile (1814–15).

Elbe River /elb/ a river of central Europe, flowing 1 159 km (720 miles) from the Czech Republic through Dresden, Magdeburg, and Hamburg, to the North Sea.

El·bert, Mount /ˈelbərt/ a mountain in Colorado, to the east of the resort town of Aspen. Rising to 4 399 m (14,431 ft.), it is the highest peak in the Rocky Mountains.

elbow ● *noun* **1 a** the joint between the forearm and the upper arm. **b** the part of the sleeve of a garment covering the elbow. **2** an elbow-shaped bend or corner. **3** a short piece of pipe bent at a right angle. **4** a push with an elbow. ● *transitive verb* (foll. by *aside*, *out*, etc.) **1** thrust or jostle (a person or oneself). **2** make (one's way) by thrusting or jostling. **3** get rid of or disregard (a person or idea) in a cursory and dismissive way. □ **at one's elbow** close at hand. **bend one's elbow** see BEND¹. **elbow to elbow** sitting or standing close together. **give a person the elbow** *informal* send a person away; dismiss or reject a person. **out at (the) elbows 1** (of a coat, sweater, etc.) worn out; shabby. **2** (of a person) ragged, poor. **up to the elbows** *informal* busily engaged (in). [Old English *elboga*, *elnboga*, from Germanic (as ELL¹, BOW¹)]

elbow grease *noun informal* hard manual work, esp. vigorous polishing or cleaning.

elbow·ing *noun* Hockey the illegal action of fouling an opponent with an elbow.

elbow macaroni *noun* N Amer. a small, curved, tubular variety of pasta.

elbow pad *noun* a protective pad for the elbows, worn when playing hockey etc.

Elbow River a river in SW Alberta, which flows eastward about 60 km from the Rocky Mountains to join the Bow River at Calgary.

elbow room *noun* **1** adequate space to move or work in. **2** freedom from restriction; opportunity (*we have more elbow room than our parents did*).

El·brus /el'bruːs/ a peak in the Caucasus mountains, on the border between Russia and Georgia. At 5 642 m (18,481 ft.), it is the highest mountain in Europe.

El·burz Mountains /el'bʊrz/ a mountain range in NW Iran, close to the southern shore of the Caspian Sea. Damavand is the highest peak, at 5 604 m (18,386 ft.).

Elche /'eltʃi/ a town in the province of Alicante in SE Spain; pop. (est. 2002) 199,800. A 13th-c. mystery play is performed every August in the church of Santa María.

el cheapo *N Amer. & Austral. slang* ● *adjective* **1** cheap; inexpensive. **2** of inferior quality. **3** stingy. ● *noun* **1** something cheap or inferior. **2** a stingy person. [CHEAP after Spanish such as *El Dorado*]

ELCIC *abbreviation* Evangelical Lutheran Church in Canada.

El Cid see CID, EL.

eld *noun archaic* or *literary* **1** old age. **2** olden time. [Old English (*i*)*eldu* from Germanic: compare OLD]

elder[1] ● *attributive adjective* (of two indicated persons, esp. when related) senior; of a greater age (*my elder brother*). ● *noun* (often prec. by *the*) **1 a** the older or more senior of two indicated (esp. related) persons (*who is the elder?; is my elder by ten years*). **b** (**Elder**) a title to distinguish between related persons of renown (*Pliny the Elder*). **2** (in *pl.*) **a** persons of greater age or seniority (*respect your elders*). **b** persons venerable because of age and wisdom (*consulted with the village elders*). **c** a leader or senior figure in an aboriginal group etc. **3** *hist.* a member of a senate or governing body. **4** an official in the Presbyterian, United, or Mormon Churches who assists in the administration and government of the Church. □ **elder·ship** *noun* [Old English *eldra*, related to OLD]

elder[2] *noun* any shrub or tree of the genus *Sambucus*, with white flowers and usu. blue-black or red berries. [Old English *ellærn*]

elder abuse *noun* maltreatment of an elderly person, esp. by family members, friends or caregivers.

elder·berry *noun* (*pl.* **-berries**) the berry of the elder, esp. common elder (*Sambucus nigra*) used for making jelly, wine, etc.

elder·care *noun* care of the elderly or infirm, provided by residential institutions or family members.

elder·flower *noun* the flower of the elder.

Elder·hos·tel *noun proprietary* an international non-profit organization offering short-term educational programs for esp. retired adults and those fifty-five years of age and older. □ **Elder·hostel·er** *noun*

elder·ly *adjective* (of a person) rather old; past middle age.

elder statesman *noun* an older experienced person, esp. a politician, whose advice is often sought.

eld·est ● *adjective* first-born or oldest surviving (member of a family, son, daughter, etc.). ● *noun* (often prec. by *the*) the eldest of three or more indicated (*who is the eldest?*). [Old English (as ELDER[1])]

El Djem /el 'dʒem/ a town in eastern Tunisia, noted for its well-preserved Roman amphitheatre.

El Dor·ado /ˌeldə'rɑːdoʊ/ *noun* (*pl.* **-ados**) **1** a fabled city or country abounding in gold, believed by the Spanish and Sir Walter Raleigh to exist upon the Amazon. **2** (**El·dor·ado**) a place of great abundance or opportunity. [Spanish *el dorado* the gilded]

el·dritch /'eldrɪtʃ/ *adjective N Amer. & Scot.* **1** weird; spooky (*an eldritch cry in the night*). **2** hideous. [16th c.: perhaps related to ELF]

Elea·nor of Aquitaine /'elənər/ (c.1122–1204), daughter of the Duke of Aquitaine, queen of France as wife of Louis VII 1137–52 and of England as wife of Henry II 1154–89. She intrigued with her sons, the future kings Richard I and John, against their father and was imprisoned for the last 15 years of her life.

Elea·nor of Castile /'elə,nɔr/ (1246–90), wife of Edward I of England, daughter of Ferdinand III of Castile. She accompanied Edward on a crusade (1270–73).

ele·cam·pane /ˌeləkam'peɪn/ *noun* a sunflower-like plant, *Inula helenium*, with bitter aromatic leaves and roots, used in herbal medicine and cookery. [corruption of medieval Latin *enula* (for Latin *inula* from Greek *helenion*) *campana* (prob. = of the fields)]

elect ● *transitive verb* **1** choose (a person) by vote (*elected a new chairman*). **2** (usu. foll. by *to* + infin.) choose (a thing, a course of action, etc.) in preference to an alternative (*the principles they elected to follow*). **3** *Theol.* (of God) choose (persons) in preference to others for salvation.

● *adjective* **1** chosen. **2** select, choice. **3** *Theol.* chosen by God. **4** (in *combination*, after a noun designating office) chosen but not yet in office (*president-elect*). ● *noun* (prec. by *the*; treated as *pl.*) **1** a specially chosen group of people; an elite. **2** *Theol.* those chosen by God for salvation. □ **elect·abil·ity** *noun* **elect·able** *adjective* [Latin *electus* past participle of *eligere elect-* (as E-[1], *legere* pick)]

elec·tion *noun* **1** selection by vote (of candidates for a position, esp. a political office). **2** the act or an instance of electing. **3** *Theol.* the doctrine of Calvin that God chooses some people for salvation without relation to their faith or good works.

election day *noun* **1** any day set aside for the election of public officials. **2** (**Election Day**) (in the US) the first Tuesday after the first Monday in November, on which voting for national elections takes place in even years.

elec·tion·eer *intransitive verb* **1** take part in an election campaign. **2** seek election by currying favour with voters. □ **elec·tion·eer·ing** *noun*

elect·ive ● *adjective* **1** (of an office or its holder) filled or appointed by election. **2** (of a body of people) having the power to elect (*an elective assembly*). **3** (of a surgical operation etc.) optional; not urgently necessary. **4** (of a course of study etc.) chosen by the student; optional. ● *noun esp. N Amer.* an elective course of study.

elec·tor *noun* **1** a person who has the right to vote in an election. **2** (**Elector**) *hist.* a German prince entitled to take part in the election of the Holy Roman Emperor. **3** *US* a member of the Electoral College. □ **elec·tor·ship** *noun*

elec·tor·al /ɪ'lektərəl, -lek'tɔrəl/ *adjective* relating to electors or elections. □ **elec·tor·al·ly** *adverb*

electoral college *noun* **1** (**Electoral College**) *US* the group of electors from within each state who officially elect the President and Vice-President. **2** any body of electors.

elec·tor·ate *noun* **1** the body of persons entitled to vote in a country or constituency. **2** *Austral. & NZ* an area represented by one Member of Parliament. **3** *hist.* the office or territories of a German Elector.

Elec·tra *Gk Myth* the daughter of Agamemnon and Clytemnestra. She persuaded her brother Orestes to kill Clytemnestra and her lover Aegisthus in revenge for the murder of Agamemnon.

Electra complex *noun Psych.* a daughter's subconscious sexual attraction to her father and hostility towards her mother, corresponding to the Oedipus complex in a son. [ELECTRA]

elec·tret /ɪ'lektrɪt, i-/ *noun Physics* a permanently polarized piece of dielectric material, analogous to a permanent magnet. [ELECTRICITY + MAGNET]

elec·tric ● *adjective* **1** of, worked by, or charged with electricity (*an electric frying pan*). **2** producing or capable of generating electricity. **3 a** (of a musical instrument) amplified electronically. **b** (of an album, show, etc.) performed using electronically amplified instruments. **4** causing or charged with sudden and dramatic excitement (*the news had an electric effect; the atmosphere was electric*). ● *noun* **1** an electric car, train, etc. **2** (in *pl.*) electrical appliances or circuitry. [modern Latin *electricus* from Latin *electrum* from Greek *ēlektron* amber, the rubbing of which causes electrostatic phenomena]

elec·tric·al *adjective* **1** of or concerned with or of the nature of electricity. **2** operating by electricity. □ **elec·tric·al·ly** *adverb*

electrical conductivity *noun* a measure of the rate at which electricity can pass through a body, the reciprocal of resistivity.

electrical engineering *noun* the branch of engineering that deals with the utilization of electricity, esp. electric power. □ **electrical engineer** *noun*

electrical storm *noun* (also **electric storm**) a violent disturbance of the electrical condition of the atmosphere; a thunderstorm.

electrical tape *noun* (also **electrician's tape**) *N Amer.* an adhesive tape used to cover exposed electrical wires etc.

electric blanket *noun* an electrically wired blanket used to heat a bed.

electric blue ● *noun* a steely or brilliant light blue. ● *adjective* of this colour.

electric broom *noun* a lightweight upright vacuum cleaner.

electric chair *noun* **1** a chair used for capital punishment by electrocution in certain judicial systems. **2** (usu. prec. by *the*) execution by this method.

electric charge *noun* (also **electrical charge**) = CHARGE *noun* 6.

electric circuit *noun* (also **electrical circuit**) = CIRCUIT *noun* 3a.

electric current *noun* (also **electrical current**) = CURRENT *noun* 2.

electric eel *noun* an eel-like freshwater fish, *Electrophorus electricus*, native to S America, which possesses electric organs and can give a severe electric shock.

electric eye *noun* a photoelectric cell that operates a relay when the beam of light illuminating it is interrupted.

electric fence *noun* (also **electric fencing**) a fence (often consisting of a single strand of wire) which gives a mild electric shock to an animal touching it.

electric field *noun* a region in which an electric charge experiences a force, usu. because of a distribution of other charges.

electric guitar *noun* a guitar in which the vibrations of the strings are not amplified by the body of the instrument but are converted by a pickup into electrical signals and amplified by an independent amplifier and speaker.

elec·tri·cian /ˌelek'trɪʃən, ˌiːl-/ *noun* a person who installs or maintains electrical equipment, esp. professionally.

electrician's tape *noun* N Amer. = ELECTRICAL TAPE.

elec·tri·city /ˌelek'trɪsiti, ˌiːl-, ˌɪl,ek-/ *noun* **1** a form of energy resulting from the existence of charged particles (electrons, protons, etc.), either statically as an accumulation of charge or dynamically as a current. **2** a supply of electric current for heating, lighting, etc. **3** a state of heightened emotion; excitement, tension.

electric organ *noun* **1** *Music* an organ in which the sound is made electrically rather than by pipes. **2** an organ in certain fishes able to produce an electrical discharge for stunning prey or sensing the surroundings, or as a defence.

electric ray *noun* any ray of the family Torpedinidae, as the Atlantic torpedo ray, *Torpedo nobiliana*, which possess electric organs and can give an electric shock (see RAY²).

electric shaver *noun* (also **electric razor**) an electrical device for shaving, with oscillating or rotating blades behind a metal guard.

electric shock *noun* **1** the effect of a sudden discharge of electricity on a person or animal, usually with stimulation of the nerves and contraction of the muscles. **2** = SHOCK TREATMENT 1.

electric storm *var. of* ELECTRICAL STORM.

elec·tri·fy *transitive verb* (**-fies, -fied**) **1** charge with electricity; pass an electric current through. **2** convert (machinery or the place or system employing it) to the use of electric power. **3** cause dramatic or sudden excitement in. □ **elec·tri·fi·ca·tion** *noun* **elec·tri·fi·er** *noun*

elec·tro *noun* (*pl.* **-tros**) **1** = ELECTROTYPE *noun*. **2** = ELECTROPLATE *noun*. **3** (also *attributive*) a style of dance music with a fast electronic beat backed by a synthesizer. [abbreviation]

electro- *combining form* of, relating to, or caused by electricity (*electrocute; electromagnet*). [Greek *ēlektron* amber: see ELECTRIC]

elec·tro·acous·tic *adjective* **1** involving the direct conversion of electrical into acoustic energy or vice versa. **2** (of music) performed or composed with the creative use of electronic equipment.

elec·tro·cardio·gram *noun* a chart or record produced by an electrocardiograph, used in the diagnosis of heart disease. Abbr.: **ECG, EKG**.

elec·tro·cardio·graph *noun* an instrument that records or displays the electric activity of the heart by means of electrodes attached to the skin. Abbr.: **ECG, EKG**. □ **elec·tro·cardio·graph·ic** *adjective* **elec·tro·cardio·graph·ic·ally** *adverb* **elec·tro·cardi·og·raphy** *noun*

elec·tro·chem·istry *adjective* the branch of science that deals with the relations between electrical and chemical phenomena. □ **elec·tro·chem·ical** *adjective* **elec·tro·chem·ical·ly** *adverb* **elec·tro·chem·ist** *noun*

elec·tro·chromic *adjective* changing colour when placed in an electric field. □ **elec·tro·chrom·ism** *noun*

elec·tro·con·vul·sive therapy *noun* a method of treating certain mental illnesses in which an electric current is passed through the brain so as to produce a convulsion. Abbr.: **ECT**.

elec·tro·cute *transitive verb* (usu. in *passive*) **1** cause the death of (a person or animal) by means of an electric current (*electrocuted during a thunderstorm*). **2** execute (a criminal) in the electric chair. **3** give a serious but not fatal electric shock to (a person). □ **elec·tro·cu·tion** *noun* [ELECTRO-, after EXECUTE]

elec·trode *noun* a conductor through which electricity enters or leaves an electrolyte, gas, vacuum, etc. [ELECTRIC + Greek *hodos* way]

elec·tro·di·aly·sis /ɪˌlektrəʊ·daɪˈaləsɪs, i-/ *noun* dialysis in which the movement of ions is aided by electrodes placed on either side of a semi-permeable membrane.

elec·tro·dy·nam·ics *plural noun* (usu. treated as *sing.*) the study of electric charges in motion, the forces created by electric and magnetic fields, and the relationship between them. □ **elec·tro·dy·nam·ic** *adjective*

elec·tro·enceph·alo·gram /ɪˌlektrəʊen'sefələˌgram, i-/ *noun* a chart or record produced by an electroencephalograph. Abbr.: **EEG**.

elec·tro·enceph·alo·graph /ɪˌlektrəʊen'sefələˌgraf, i-/ *noun* an instrument that records or displays the electrical activity of the brain, using electrodes attached to the scalp. Abbr.: **EEG**. □ **elec·tro·enceph·alo·graph·ic** /-'grafɪk/ *adjective* **elec·tro·enceph·al·og·raphy** /-'ɒgrəfi/ *noun*

elec·trol·o·gist /ɪlek'trɒlədʒɪst/ *noun* N Amer. a person trained to remove excess body or facial hair using electrolysis.

elec·tro·lumin·es·cence /ɪˌlektrəʊˌluːmɪ'nesəns, i-/ *noun* luminescence produced electrically, esp. by the application of a voltage. □ **elec·tro·lumin·es·cent** *adjective*

elec·troly·sis /ɪˌlek'trɒləsɪs, ˌiː-, ˌel-/ *noun* **1** chemical decomposition produced by passing an electric current through an electrolyte. **2** the removal of excess body or facial hair by passing an electric current through the root. □ **elec·tro·lytic** /ɪˌlektrəʊ'lɪtɪk/ *adjective* **elec·tro·lytic·al** /-'lɪtɪkəl/ *adjective* **elec·tro·lytic·al·ly** /-'lɪtɪkli/ *adverb* [ELECTRO- + -LYSIS]

elec·tro·lyte /ɪ'lektrəˌlaɪt, i-/ *noun* **1** a liquid, esp. that present in a battery, which contains ions and can be decomposed by electrolysis. **2** (usu. in *pl.*) the ionized or ionizable constituents of a living cell, blood, etc. [ELECTRO- + Greek *luō* loosen]

elec·tro·lyze /ɪ'lektrəˌlaɪz, i-/ *transitive verb* (esp. *Brit.* **-lyse**) subject to or treat by electrolysis. □ **elec·tro·lyz·er** *noun* [ELECTROLYSIS after *analyze*]

elec·tro·magnet *noun* a piece of soft iron that becomes magnetic when an electric current is passed through the coil surrounding it.

elec·tro·magnet·ic *adjective* having both an electrical and a magnetic character or properties. □ **elec·tro·magnet·ic·ally** *adverb*

electromagnetic field *noun* a field of force created by changing electric and magnetic fields. Abbr.: **EMF**.

electromagnetic pulse *noun* a burst of electromagnetic energy generated by a nuclear explosion in the atmosphere, capable of disrupting or destroying telecommunications and electronic systems. Abbr.: **EMP**.

electromagnetic radiation *noun* a kind of radiation including visible light, radio waves, gamma rays, X-rays, etc., in which electric and magnetic fields vary simultaneously.

electromagnetic spectrum *noun* the range of wavelengths over which electromagnetic radiation extends.

elec·tro·magnet·ism *noun* **1** the magnetic forces produced by electricity. **2** the study of this.

elec·tro·mechan·ical *adjective* relating to the application of electricity to mechanical processes, devices, etc.

elec·trom·eter /ˌɪlek'trɒmɪtər, ˌiː-/ *noun* an instrument for measuring small voltages without drawing any current from the circuit. □ **elec·tro·met·ric** /-'metrɪk/ *adjective* **elec·trom·etry** *noun*

elec·tro·motive *adjective* producing or tending to produce an electric current.

electromotive force *noun* a difference in potential that tends to give rise to an electric current. Abbr.: **emf, EMF**.

elec·tro·myo·gram /ɪˌlektrəʊ'maɪəgram, i-/ *noun* a chart or record produced by an electromyograph. Abbr.: **EMG**. [ELECTRO- + MYO- + -GRAM]]

elec·tro·myo·graph /ɪˌlektrəʊ'maɪəgraf, i-/ *noun* an instrument that records or displays or converts into sound the electrical activity of muscle, using electrodes attached to the skin or inserted into the muscle. Abbr.: **EMG**. □ **elec·tro·myo·graph·ic** /-'grafɪk/ *adjective* **elec·tro·myog·raphy** /-'ɒgrəfi/ *noun*

elec·tron *noun* a stable subatomic particle with a charge of negative electricity, found in all atoms and acting as the primary carrier of electricity in solids. [ELECTRIC + -ON]

electron diffraction *noun* the diffraction of a beam of electrons by atoms or molecules, used for determining crystal structures etc.

elec·tro·nega·tive *adjective* (of an element) tending to acquire electrons in chemical reactions. □ **elec·tro·nega·tiv·ity** *noun*

electron gun *noun* a device for producing a narrow stream of electrons from a heated cathode.

elec·tron·ic /ˌɪlek'trɒnɪk, ˌiː-, ˌel-/ *adjective* **1 a** produced by or involving the flow of electrons. **b** of or relating to electrons or electronics. **2** (of a device) using electronic components. **3** using the electronic transmission or storage of information, as by computer (*electronic text*). **4 a** (of music) produced by electronic means and usu. recorded on tape. **b** (of a musical instrument) producing sounds by electronic means. □ **elec·tron·ic·ally** *adverb*

elec·tron·ica *noun* **1** any of various kinds of electronically-generated music. **2** any of various popular styles of electronic music deriving from techno and rave music, esp. those having a more ambient, esoteric, or cerebral quality.

electronic age *noun* the period in human history since computers, electronic communication, the Internet, etc. have become dominant phenomena in most aspects of life.

electronic book *noun* = E-BOOK.

electronic bulletin board *noun* = BBS.

electronic data interchange *noun* a computer protocol for the exchange of electronic information, used by banks, businesses, etc. for invoicing, ordering, etc. Abbr.: **EDI**.

electronic engineering *noun* the branch of engineering that deals with the design of devices that rely on the movement of electrons in circuits containing semiconductors, resistors, capacitors, etc. □ **electronic engineer** *noun*

electronic flash *noun* a flash lamp used in high-speed photography that produces a brilliant flash of light by discharging a capacitor through a gas-filled tube.

electronic funds transfer *noun* the transfer of money from one bank account to another by means of computers and communications links. Abbr.: **EFT**.

electronic mail *noun* = EMAIL *noun* 1, 2.

electronic point-of-sale *noun* a computerized method of recording sales in retail outlets, using a laser scanner at the checkout to read bar codes printed on the items' packages. Abbr.: **EPOS**.

electronic publishing *noun* the publishing of books etc. in machine-readable form rather than on paper.

elec·tron·ics *plural noun* **1** (treated as *sing.*) a branch of physics and technology concerned with the behaviour and movement of electrons in a vacuum, gas, semiconductor, etc. **2** the circuits used in this. **3** (treated as *pl.*) electronic devices.

electronic warfare *noun Military* the use of electronic technology to block or decrease an enemy's use and to safeguard friendly use of electromagnetic radiation equipment.

electron lens *noun* a device for focusing a stream of electrons by means of electric or magnetic fields.

electron micrograph *noun* a magnified image obtained with an electron microscope.

electron microscope *noun* a microscope with high magnification and resolution, employing electron beams in place of light and using electron lenses (*compare* OPTICAL MICROSCOPE). □ **electron microscopy** *noun*

electron pair *noun* **1** *Chem.* two electrons in the same orbital in an atom or molecule. **2** *Physics* an electron and a positron produced in a high-energy reaction.

electron spin resonance *noun* a spectroscopic method of locating electrons within the molecules of a paramagnetic substance. Abbr.: **ESR**.

electron volt *noun* a unit of energy equal to the work done on an electron in moving it through a potential difference of one volt. Abbr.: **eV**.

electro-optics *noun* the branch of science that deals with the effect of electric fields on light and on the optical properties of substances. □ **electro-optic** *adjective* **electro-optical** *adjective*

elec·tro·phil·ic /ɪˌlektroˈfɪlɪk, i-/ *adjective Chem.* having or involving an affinity for electrons. □ **elec·tro·phile** /ɪˈlektroˌfaɪl/ *noun*

elec·tro·phor·esis /ɪˌlektrofəˈriːsɪs, i-/ *noun Physics & Chem.* the movement of charged particles in a fluid or gel under the influence of an electric field. □ **elec·tro·phor·et·ic** /-fəˈrɛtɪk/ *adjective* **elec·tro·phor·et·ic·ally** /-fəˈrɛtɪkli/ *adverb* [ELECTRO- + Greek *phorēsis* being carried]

elec·tro·phor·us /ɪlekˈtrɒfərəs, ˌiː-/ *noun* a device for repeatedly generating static electricity by induction. [modern Latin from ELECTRO- + Greek *-phoros* bearing]

elec·tro·physi·ol·ogy /ɪˌlektroːfɪziˈɒlədʒi, i-/ *noun* the branch of physiology that deals with the electrical phenomena associated with bodily processes. □ **elec·tro·physio·logic·al** /-ziəˈlɒdʒɪkəl/ *adjective* **elec·tro·physio·logic·al·ly** /-ziəˈlɒdʒɪkli/ *adverb*

elec·tro·plate ● *transitive verb* coat (a utensil etc.) by electrolytic deposition with chromium, silver, etc. ● *noun* electroplated articles. □ **elec·tro·plat·er** *noun*

elec·tro·pora·tion /ɪˌlektroːpəˈreɪʃən, i-/ *noun Biol.* the action or process of introducing DNA or chromosomes into the cells of bacteria etc. using a pulse of electricity to open the pores in the cell membranes briefly. [ELECTRO- + PORE¹ -ATION]

elec·tro·posi·tive *adjective* **1** electrically positive. **2** (of an element) tending to lose electrons in chemical reactions.

elec·tro·scope *noun* an instrument for detecting and measuring electricity, esp. as an indication of the ionization of air by radioactivity. □ **elec·tro·scop·ic** *adjective*

elec·tro·shock ● *noun* = ELECTROCONVULSIVE THERAPY. ● *adjective* (of medical treatment) by means of electric shocks. ● *transitive verb* **1** treat (a patient) with electroconvulsive therapy. **2** kill (an animal) with an electric current.

elec·tro·stat·ic *adjective* of or relating to stationary electric charges or electrostatics. □ **elec·tro·stat·ic·ally** *adverb* [ELECTRO- + STATIC after *hydrostatic*]

elec·tro·stat·ics *plural noun* (treated as *sing.*) the study of stationary electric charges or fields as opposed to electric currents.

elec·tro·ther·apy *noun* the treatment of diseases by the use of electricity.

elec·tro·ther·mal *adjective* relating to heat electrically derived.

elec·tro·type ● *transitive verb* copy by the electrolytic deposition of copper on a mould, esp. for printing. ● *noun* a copy so formed. □ **elec·tro·typ·er** *noun*

elec·tro·valent /ɪˌlektroˈveɪlənt, i-/ *adjective Chem.* (of bonding) resulting from electrostatic attraction between ions. □ **elec·tro·valence** *noun* **elec·tro·valen·cy** *noun* [ELECTRO- + *-valent* after *trivalent* etc.]

elec·tro·weak *adjective Physics* relating to or denoting electromagnetic and weak interactions regarded as manifestations of the same interaction.

elec·trum /ɪˈlektrəm, i-/ *noun* **1** an alloy of silver and gold used in ancient times. **2** an alloy of copper, nickel, and zinc. [Latin from Greek *ēlektron* amber, electrum]

elec·tu·ary /ɪˈlektʃuːeri, i-/ *noun* (*pl.* **-aries**) a medicinal substance mixed with honey or syrup. [Late Latin *electuarium*, prob. from Greek *ekleikton* from *ekleikhō* lick up]

ele·emosyn·ary /ˌeləˈmɒsəneri, ˌeliə-, -ˈmɒz-/ *adjective* **1** dependent on or supported by charity (*an eleemosynary organization*). **2** charitable. [medieval Latin *eleemosynarius* from Late Latin *eleemosyna*: see ALMS]

ele·gant *adjective* **1** tasteful, stylish, and refined in appearance (*elegant clothes*; *an elegant apartment*). **2** showing refined grace in movement (*an elegant dancer*). **3** (of a mode of life etc.) of refined luxury. **4** ingeniously simple and satisfying (*an elegant solution*). □ **ele·gance** *noun* **ele·gan·cy** *noun* **ele·gant·ly** *adverb* [French *élégant* or Latin *elegant-*, related to *eligere*: see ELECT]

ele·giac /ˌeləˈdʒaɪək/ ● *adjective* **1** (esp. of a work of art) having a pleasing quality of gentle and wistful mournfulness (*haunting and elegiac music*). **2** (of a poetic metre) used for an elegy. ● *noun* (in *pl.*) verses in an elegiac metre. □ **ele·giac·ally** *adverb* [French *élégiaque*: see ELEGY]

elegiac couplet *noun* a pair of lines consisting of a dactylic hexameter and a pentameter, esp. in Greek and Latin verse.

elegy /ˈelədʒi/ *noun* (*pl.* **-gies**) **1** a song or poem of lamentation, esp. for the dead. **2** a poem in elegiac metre. □ **ele·gist** *noun* **ele·gize** *transitive & intransitive verb* (also esp. *Brit.* **-gise**). [French *élégie* or Latin *elegia* from Greek *elegeia* from *elegos* mournful poem]

ele·ment *noun* **1** a component part or group; a contributing factor or thing. **2** *Chem. & Physics* any of the hundred or so substances that cannot be resolved by chemical means into simpler substances, each consisting of atoms with the same atomic number. **3** a resistance wire that heats up in an electric heater, stove, kettle, etc.; an electrode. **4** (in *pl.*) weather, esp. wind and storm. **5 a** any of the four substances (earth, water, air, and fire) in ancient and medieval philosophy. **b** any of these as a being's natural environment or habitat. **6** (in *pl.*) the rudiments of learning or of a branch of knowledge. **7** (in *pl.*) the bread and wine of the Eucharist. **8** *Math. & Logic* an entity that is a single member of a set. □ **in** (or **out of**) **one's element** in (or out of) one's accustomed or preferred surroundings. **reduced to its elements** analyzed. [Old French from Latin *elementum*]

ele·men·tal ● *adjective* **1** essential; basic (*elemental truths*). **2** of the forces of nature, esp. seen as powerful and uncontrolled (*the elemental* *fury of the storm*). **3** pertaining to chemical elements. **4** (of a chemical element) uncompounded (*elemental oxygen*). **5** of the four elements. ● *noun* an entity or force thought to be physically manifested by occult means.

ele·men·tary ● *adjective* **1 a** dealing with or arising from the simplest facts of a subject; rudimentary, introductory (*elementary mathematics*). **b** simple. **2** *N Amer.* of or pertaining to elementary school (*elementary education*). **3** *Chem.* not decomposable. ● *noun N Amer.* an elementary school. □ **ele·men·tar·i·ly** *adverb*

elementary backstroke *noun N Amer.* a swimming stroke performed on the back in which the arms are extended in the water above the head, then swept down along the sides of the body, while the legs execute a frog kick or whip kick.

elementary particle *noun* a subatomic particle, esp. one not known to be decomposable into simpler particles.

elementary school *noun* **1** *N Amer.* a school offering primary education, usu. for the first six or eight grades and also usu. including kindergarten. **2** *Brit. hist.* a school in which elementary subjects were taught to young children.

ele·phant *noun* (*pl.* **ele·phants** or same) the largest living land animal, of which two species survive, the larger African (*Loxodonta africana*) and the smaller Indian (*Elephas maximus*), both with a trunk and long curved ivory tusks. □ **ele·phant·oid** /ˌeləˈfantɔɪd/ *adjective* [Old French *elefant*, ultimately from Latin *elephantus*, *elephans* from Greek *elephas -antos* ivory, elephant]

elephant bird *noun* an extinct, heavily built, giant flightless bird of Madagascar.

elephant ear *noun* any of various ornamental plants, esp. species of begonia, with large heart-shaped leaves.

elephant grass *noun* any of various tall African grasses, esp. *Pennisetum purpureum*.

elephant head *noun* a lousewort of wet places of northern Canada and mountainous areas of western N America, *Pedicularis groenlandica*, with a spike of reddish flowers which look like elephants' heads.

ele·phant·ia·sis /ˌeləfənˈtaɪəsɪs/ *noun* gross enlargement of the body, esp. the limbs, due to lymphatic obstruction by a nematode parasite transmitted by mosquitoes. [Latin from Greek (as ELEPHANT)]

ele·phant·ine /ˈeləfənˌtaɪn, ˌeləˈfantaɪn, -tiːn/ *adjective* **1** of or pertaining to elephants. **2 a** huge. **b** clumsy, unwieldy (*elephantine movements; elephantine humour*).

Elephant Pass a narrow strip of land at the north end of Sri Lanka, linking the Jaffna peninsula with the rest of the island.

elephant seal *noun* either of two very large seals of the genus *Mirounga*, of which the males have inflatable snouts.

elephant shrew *noun* any small insect-eating mammal of the order Macroscelidea, native to Africa, having a long snout and long hind limbs.

Eleu·sin·ian /ˌeljuːˈsɪnɪən/ *adjective* of or relating to Eleusis near Athens. [Latin *Eleusinius* from Greek *Eleusinios*]

Eleusinian mysteries *plural noun Gk Hist.* the annual celebrations held at ancient Eleusis in honour of Demeter.

elev. *abbreviation* elevation.

ele·vate *transitive verb* **1** raise above the usual level or position (*elevate your heart rate with exercise*). **2** raise in status, rank or importance; promote. **3** turn or direct upwards (*one's eyes, a gun, etc.*). **4** raise morally or intellectually (*elevate the level of discussion*). **5** raise the spirits of; elate, exhilarate. **6** raise (a railway, highway, etc.) above ground level. **7** *Christianity* hold up (the Host or the chalice) after consecration. [Latin *elevare* raise (as E-¹, *levis* light)]

ele·va·tion *noun* **1** the process, state, or fact of elevating or being elevated. **2** the height above a given level, esp. sea level. **3** a high place or position. **4 a** a drawing or diagram made by projection on a vertical plane (*compare* PLAN *noun* 2a). **b** an exterior face of a building or structure. **5** *Dance* **a** the capacity of a dancer to attain height in jumps. **b** the height attained in a jump. **6** *Christianity* the lifting of the Host and chalice in turn by the celebrant immediately after consecration. **7** the angle with the horizontal, esp. of a gun or of the direction of a celestial object. □ **ele·va·tion·al** *adjective*

ele·va·tor *noun* **1** *N Amer.* a platform or compartment housed in a shaft for raising and lowering persons or things to different floors of a building etc. **2** *N Amer.* (in full **grain elevator**) a tall building, typically one having several concrete silos or (on the prairies) a box-shaped wooden construction with a pitched roof, incorporating an elevating device, usu. a vertical conveyor belt of buckets, which conveys grain from an unloading platform to bins

where it is sorted, stored and cleaned before onward shipment. *See also* COUNTRY ELEVATOR, PRIMARY ELEVATOR, TERMINAL ELEVATOR. **3** *Aviation* the movable part of a tailplane for changing the pitch of an aircraft. **4** a device for hoisting or raising something from a lower level to a higher one. **5** something which elevates, esp. a muscle that raises a limb.

elevator manager *noun Cdn* (also esp. *hist.* **elevator agent**) an employee of a grain-handling company who receives, grades, and ships grain at a grain elevator and issues to the farmer a ticket negotiable for payment.

elevator music *noun N Amer.* recorded light background music, usu. in a very conventional style.

elevator shoes *plural noun N Amer.* shoes with a raised insole intended to make a person appear taller.

elev·en ● *noun* **1 a** one more than ten; the sum of six units and five units. **b** a symbol for this (11, xi, XI). **2 a** a group of eleven persons or things. **b** the eleventh of a set or series (*page eleven*). **3 a** a size etc. denoted by eleven. **b** a shoe, garment, etc. of such a size. **4** eleven o'clock. ● *adjective* that amount to eleven. [Old English *endleofon* from Germanic]

eleven·fold *adjective & adverb* **1** eleven times as much or as many. **2** consisting of eleven parts.

eleven-plus *noun* esp. *hist.* (in the UK) an examination taken at the age of 11–12 to determine the type of secondary school a child should enter.

elev·ens·es /ɪˈlevənzɪz/ *plural noun Brit. informal* light refreshment, usu. with tea or coffee, taken about 11 a.m.

elev·enth ● *noun* **1** the position in a sequence corresponding to the number 11 in the sequence 1–11. **2** the eleventh person or thing of a category, series, etc. **3** one of eleven equal parts of a thing. **4** *Music* **a** an interval or chord spanning an octave and a third in the diatonic scale. **b** a note separated from another by this interval. ● *adjective* that is the eleventh. ● *adverb* in the eleventh place. □ **the eleventh hour** the last possible moment.

ELF *abbreviation* extremely low frequency.

elf *noun* (*pl.* **elves**) **1** a mythological being, esp. one that is small and mischievous. **2** a small person. □ **elf·ish** *adjective* **elv·ish** *adjective* [Old English from Germanic]

elf·in *adjective* **1** of elves; elf-like. **2** diminutive, delicate, and full of strange charm.

elf-locks *plural noun* a tangled mass of hair.

Elgar /ˈelɡɑr/ **Sir Ed·ward (Wil·liam)** (1857–1934), English composer. A self-taught musician, he is best known for his 14 orchestral *Enigma Variations* (1899), a cello concerto (1919), and *Pomp and Circumstance* marches (1901–30), one of which provides the tune for 'Land of Hope and Glory'. □ **Elgar·ian** *adjective*

Elgin /ˈelɡɪn/ **1 7th Earl of** (title of Thomas Bruce) (1766–1841), English diplomat and art collector, remembered for his controversial acquisition of Greek sculptures from the Parthenon (Athens) now known as the 'Elgin Marbles'; they are housed in the British Museum. **2** his son, **8th Earl of** (title of James Bruce) (1811–63), Governor General of Canada (1847–54). Instructed by the colonial secretary, Earl Grey, to concede responsible government, Elgin accepted the Baldwin-LaFontaine ministry and signed the Rebellion Losses Act (1849), which provided funds for those in Canada East who had sustained losses in the suppression of the Rebellion of 1837.

El Giza see GIZA.

Elgon, Mount /ˈelɡɒn/ an extinct volcano on the border between Kenya and Uganda, rising to 4 321 m (14,178 ft.).

El Greco /el ˈɡrekoː/ (Spanish, = the Greek; born Domenikos Theotokopoulos) (1541–1614), Cretan-born Spanish painter. His portraits and religious works are characterized by distorted perspective, elongated figures, and strident use of colour, and include the altarpiece *The Assumption of the Virgin* (1577–9) and the painting *The Burial of Count Orgaz* (1586).

Eli /ˈiːlaɪ/ *Bible* a priest who acted as a teacher to the prophet Samuel (1 Sam. 1–3).

Elia /ˈiːlɪə/ the pseudonym adopted by Charles Lamb in his *Essays of Elia* (1823) and *Last Essays of Elia* (1833).

elicit /ɪˈlɪsɪt, i-/ *transitive verb* (**elicit·ed**, **elicit·ing**) draw out or forth; evoke (an admission, response, etc.). □ **elicit·a·tion** /-ˈteɪʃən/ *noun* **elicit·or** *noun* [Latin *elicere elicit-* (as E-¹, *lacere* entice)]

elide /ɪˈlaɪd, i-/ *transitive verb* **1** omit (a vowel, consonant, or syllable) by elision. **2** pass over in silence; ignore. [Latin *elidere elis-* crush out (as E-¹, *laedere* knock)]

eli·gible /ˈelɪdʒəbəl/ *adjective* **1** (often foll. by *for*) fit or entitled to be chosen for a position, award, etc. **2** meeting specified preconditions (*eligible to receive EI benefits*). **3** desirable or suitable, esp. as a partner in marriage. □ **eli·gi·bil·ity** /-ˈbɪlɪti/ *noun* **eli·gibly** *adverb* [French *éligible* from Late Latin *eligibilis* (as ELECT)]

Eli·jah /ɪˈlaɪdʒə/ (9th c. BC) a Hebrew prophet in the time of Jezebel, who maintained the worship of Jehovah against that of Baal and other pagan gods (1 Kings 17–2 Kings 2).

elim·in·ate /ɪˈlɪmɪˌneɪt, i-/ *transitive verb* **1** remove, get rid of. **2** exclude from consideration; ignore as irrelevant. **3** exclude from further participation in a competition etc. by defeat. **4** *slang* murder cold-bloodedly. **5** discharge (waste matter) from the body. **6** *Chem.* remove (a simpler substance) from a compound. **7** *Algebra* remove (a quantity in an equation) by combining equations. □ **elim·in·a·tion** *noun* **elim·in·a·tive** *adjective* **elim·in·a·tor** *noun* [Latin *eliminare* (as E-¹, *limen liminis* threshold)]

Eliot /ˈeliət/ **1 George** (pseudonym of Mary Ann Evans) (1819–80), English novelist. Famed for her intellect, scholarly style, and moral sensibility, she is regarded as one of the great English novelists; her novels include *Adam Bede* (1859), *The Mill on the Floss* (1860), and *Middlemarch* (1871–2). **2 T(hom·as) S(tearns)** (1888–1965), US-born English poet, critic, and dramatist. Works like *The Waste Land* (1922) and *Four Quartets* (1943) express his disillusioned but deeply religious view of the world, and his verse dramas include *Murder in the Cathedral* (1935); he was awarded the Nobel Prize for literature in 1948.

ELISA /ɪˈlaɪzə/ *noun* a diagnostic technique for determining the amount of protein or other antigen in a blood sample by means of an enzyme-catalyzed colour change. [acronym from enzyme-linked immunosorbent assay]

Elisa·beth·ville the former name (until 1966) of Lubumbashi in SE Congo (formerly Zaire).

Eli·sha /ɪˈlaɪʃə/ (9th c. BC) a Hebrew prophet, disciple and successor of Elijah.

eli·sion /ɪˈlɪʒən, i-/ *noun* **1** the omission of a vowel, consonant, or syllable in pronouncing (as in *I'm, let's, e'en*). **2** the omission of a passage in a book etc. [Late Latin *elisio* (as ELIDE)]

El·ista /eˈlɪstə/ a city in SW Russia, capital of the autonomous republic of Kalmykia; pop. (est. 2002) 105,000.

elite /ɪˈliːt, ei-/ ● *noun* **1** (prec. by *the*) the best or choice part of a larger body or group. **2** a class or group of persons possessing wealth, power, prestige, etc. (*a member of the ruling elite*). **3** a size of type used in typewriters and some computer printers, having twelve characters to the inch. ● *adjective* of or belonging to an elite; exclusive. [French from past participle of *élire* from Romanic: related to ELECT]

elit·ism /ɪˈliːtɪzəm, ei-/ *noun* **1** the advocacy or existence of an elite as a dominating element in a system or society. **2** the attitude or behaviour of a person or group who regard themselves as belonging to an elite. □ **elit·ist** *noun & adjective*

elix·ir /ɪˈlɪksər, i-/ *noun* **1 a** a preparation supposedly able to change metals into gold. **b** (in full **elixir of life**) a preparation supposedly able to prolong life indefinitely. **2** a supposed remedy for all ills; a panacea. **3** *Pharm.* an aromatic solution used as a medicine or flavouring. [medieval Latin from Arabic *al-iksīr* from *al* the + *iksīr*, prob. from Greek *xērion* powder for drying wounds, from *xēros* dry]

Eliza·beth ▶ **1** (Russian name Yelizaveta Petrovna) (1709–62), daughter of Peter I the Great, empress of Russia 1741–62. Her reign was notable for educational and cultural development, and saw Russia's entry into the Seven Years War (1756–63). **2** (1843–1916), queen of Romania 1881–1916. A poet, she wrote under the pen name 'Carmen Sylva'. **3** (title 'the Queen Mother'; originally Lady Elizabeth Angela Marguerite Bowes-Lyon) (1900–2002), wife of George VI, mother of Elizabeth II and Princess Margaret (1930–2002). **4 St.** *New Testament* a relative of the Virgin Mary, the wife of Zacharias and mother of John the Baptist.

Elizabeth I (1533–1603), daughter of Henry VIII, queen of England and Ireland 1558–1603. Succeeding her Catholic sister Mary I, Elizabeth re-established Protestantism as the state religion, and her reign was characterized by a flowering of national culture, particularly in the field of literature with Shakespeare, Marlowe, and Spenser.

Elizabeth II (originally Princess Elizabeth Alexandra Mary) (b.1926), daughter of George VI, queen of the United Kingdom since 1952. One of the most travelled contemporary monarchs, she has made extensive royal tours both in the UK and abroad.

Eliza·beth·an /ɪˌlɪzəˈbiːθən, i-/ ● *adjective* **1** of, belonging to, or characteristic of the period of Elizabeth I (*Elizabethan drama*). **2** of or belonging to the United Kingdom during the reign of Elizabeth II.

● *noun* **1** (usu. in *pl.*) a person, esp. a poet or dramatist, of the time of Elizabeth I. **2** a person of the time of Elizabeth II.

Eliza·vet·pol /jəˌliːzəˈvjetpɒl/ (also **Yeliza·vet·pol**) the former Russian name (1804–1918) for GÄNCÄ.

elk *noun* (*pl.* same or **elks**) **1** *N Amer.* a wapiti. **2** esp. *Brit.* a moose. **3** (**Elk**) a member of the Benevolent and Protective Order of Elks, a social and charitable organization. [Middle English, prob. representing Old English *elh, eolh*]

elk·hound *noun* a large Scandinavian hunting dog with a shaggy coat.

Elk Island National Park a small park in central Alberta, just east of Edmonton. A fenced 'island', it was established in 1913 as a wildlife preserve for elk, bison, deer, etc.

ell¹ *noun hist.* a measure of length, varying in different countries; in England equal to about 114 cm (45 inches). [Old English *eln*, related to Latin *ulna*: see ULNA]

ell² *noun* **1** an extension of a building etc. which is at right angles to the main part. **2** a short piece of pipe bent at a right angle. [representing the pronunciation of *L, l*, as the letter's name]

el·la·gic acid /eˈladʒɪk/ *noun* a compound extracted from oak galls and various fruits and nuts. It has some ability to inhibit blood flow and retard the growth of cancer cells. [French *ellagique* (an anagram of *galle* 'gall nut' + -*ique*), thus avoiding the form *gallique*, already in use]

Ellef Ringnes Island /ˈelef ˈrɪŋnes/ the most westerly of the Sverdrup Islands in the Canadian High Arctic, situated north of Bathurst Island. [*Ellef Ringnes*, Norwegian promoter of Arctic exploration *c*.1900]

Elles·mere Island /ˈelzmiːr/ the northernmost island in the Canadian Arctic, the largest among the Queen Elizabeth Islands, separated from Greenland by Nares Strait. With an area of 196 236 sq. km, it is the third largest island in Canada. [F. Egerton, Earl of *Ellesmere*, British statesman d.1857]

Ellesmere Island National Park a former name for Quttinirpaaq National Park.

El·lice Islands /ˈelɪs/ the former name for TUVALU.

El·ling·ton, Ed·ward Ken·nedy ('Duke') (1899–1974), US jazz pianist, composer, and bandleader. One of the most influential figures in the history of jazz, he wrote hundreds of compositions, including 'Creole Love Call' (1928) and 'Mood Indigo' (1930).

El·liot Lake a city in north central Ontario, about 160 km west of Sudbury; pop. (2001) 11,956. □ **El·liot Laker** *noun* [after the name of the lake, prob. named by a geologist in the late 19th c.]

el·lipse /ɪˈlɪps, i-/ *noun* a regular oval, traced by a point moving in a plane so that the sum of its distances from two other points is constant, or resulting when a cone is cut by an oblique plane which does not intersect the base (*compare* HYPERBOLA). [French from Latin *ellipsus* from Greek *elleipsis* from *elleipō* come short, from *en* in + *leipō* leave]

el·lip·sis /ɪˈlɪpsɪs, i-/ *noun* (*pl.* **el·lip·ses** /-siːz/) **1** the omission from a sentence of words not needed to complete the construction or sense. **2** the omission of a sentence at the end of a paragraph. **3** a set of three dots etc. indicating an omission.

el·lips·oid /ɪˈlɪpsɔɪd, i-/ ● *noun* a solid of which all the plane sections normal to one axis are circles and all the other plane sections are ellipses. ● *adjective* = ELLIPSOIDAL.

el·lips·oid·al /ˌelɪpˈsɔɪdəl, ˌi-/ *adjective* having the nature or shape of an ellipsoid.

el·lip·tic /ɪˈlɪptɪk, i-/ *adjective* (also **el·lip·tic·al**) **1** of, relating to, or having the form of an ellipse or ellipsis. **2** (of writing or speech) very concise, often so as to be obscure or cryptic. □ **el·lip·tic·al·ly** *adverb* **el·lip·ti·city** /ˌelɪpˈtɪsɪti/ *noun* [Greek *elleiptikos* defective, from *elleipō* (as ELLIPSE)]

Ellis, (Henry) Have·lock (1859–1939), English writer and physician, who studied the psychology of human sexual behaviour; his major work is the seven-volume *Studies in the Psychology of Sex* (1897–1928).

Ellis Island an island in the bay of New York. From 1892 until 1943 the island served as an entry point for immigrants to the US, and later (until 1954) as a detention centre for people awaiting deportation. In 1965 it became part of the Statue of Liberty National Monument.

Ells·worth Land a plateau region of Antarctica between the Walgreen Coast and Palmer Land. It rises at the Vinson Massif, the highest mountain in Antarctica, to 5 140 m (16,863 ft.). Parts of the region are the subject of rival claims by the UK and Chile.

elm *noun* **1** any tree of the genus *Ulmus*, esp. the American elm, *U. americana*, with asymmetrical toothed leaves. **2** (in full **elm·wood**) the wood of the elm. [Old English, related to Latin *ulmus*]

El·nath /ˈelnaθ/ the second-brightest star in the constellation Taurus, marking the tip of one of the bull's horns. [Arabic, lit. 'the one butting with horns']

El Niño /elˈniːnjoː/ *noun* an irregularly occurring and complex series of climatic changes affecting the equatorial Pacific region and beyond every few years, characterized by the appearance of unusually warm, nutrient-poor water off northern Peru and Ecuador. [Spanish, = the (Christ) child, as commonly appearing around Christmas]

el·o·cu·tion /ˌeləˈkjuːʃən/ *noun* **1** the art of clear and expressive speech, esp. of distinct pronunciation and articulation. **2** a particular style of speaking. □ **el·o·cu·tion·ary** *adjective* **el·o·cu·tion·ist** *noun* [Latin *elocutio* from *eloqui elocut-* speak out (as E-¹, *loqui* speak)]

El·o·him /eˈloːhɪm, ˈeloˌhiːm/ in the Bible, a name used frequently for God. Compare JEHOVAH, YAHWEH. [Hebrew *ĕlōhîm* god(s)]

El·o·hist /eˈloːhɪst/ the postulated author or authors of parts of the Hexateuch, in which God is regularly named Elohim.

elon·gate /ˈiːlɒŋˌgeit, ˈiːlɒŋˌgeit/ ● *verb* **1** lengthen, prolong. **2** *intransitive Bot.* grow, become longer; have a slender or tapering form. ● *adjective Bot. & Zool.* long in proportion to width. [Late Latin *elongare* (as E-¹, Latin *longus* long)]

elon·gat·ed /ˈiːlɒŋˌgeitɪd, ˈiːlɒŋgeitɪd/ *adjective* **1** long in relation to its width. **2** that has been made longer.

elon·ga·tion /ˌiːlɒŋˈgeiʃən/ *noun* **1** the act or an instance of lengthening; the process of being lengthened. **2** a part of a line etc. formed by lengthening. **3** *Mech.* the amount of extension under stress. **4** *Astronomy* the difference in celestial longitude between a planet and the sun or between a moon and its planet.

elope *intransitive verb* run away secretly with a lover, esp. to get married. □ **elope·ment** *noun* [Anglo-French *aloper* perhaps from a Middle English form *alope*, related to LEAP]

elo·quence /ˈeləkwəns/ *noun* fluent and effective use of language or persuasive speaking or writing. [Old French from Latin *eloquentia* from *eloqui* speak out (as E-¹, *loqui* speak)]

elo·quent /ˈeləkwənt/ *adjective* **1** possessing or showing eloquence. **2** clearly expressive or indicative (*an eloquent performance from the lead actor*). □ **elo·quent·ly** *adverb*

El Paso /el ˈpasoː/ a city in W Texas on the Rio Grande, on the border with Mexico; pop. (2000) 563,662.

El Sal·va·dor /el ˈsalvəˌdɔr/ a country in Central America, on the Pacific coast; pop. (est. 2002) 6,353,681; capital, San Salvador. □ **Sal·va·doran** (also **Sal·va·dor·ean** /ˌsalvəˈdɔriən/) *adjective & noun*

else *adverb* **1** (prec. by indefinite or interrogative pron.) besides; in addition (*someone else; nowhere else; who else*). **2** instead; other, different (*what else could I say?; he did not love her, but someone else*). ● **or else 1** otherwise; if not (*run, or else you will be late*). **2** *informal* a warning or threat of the consequences should a previously expressed order, expectation, etc. not be carried out or realized (*clean up your room, or else!*). [Old English *elles*]

else·where *adverb* in or to some other place.

Elsi·nore a port on the northeast coast of the island of Zealand, Denmark; pop. (1998) 44,860. It is the site of the 16th-c. Kronborg Castle, which is the setting for Shakespeare's *Hamlet*.

ELT *abbreviation* **1** English Language Teaching. **2** EMERGENCY LOCATOR TRANSMITTER.

Élu·ard /ˌeiluːˈar/ **Paul** (pseudonym of Eugène Grindel) (1895–1952), French poet. A leading figure of the surrealist movement, he joined the French resistance during the Second World War and secretly circulated his poetry denouncing the German occupation, such as the collection *Poésie et vérité* (1942).

elu·ate /ˈeljuːˌeit/ *noun Chem.* a solution or gas mixture obtained by elution.

elu·ci·date /ɪˈluːsɪˌdeit, i-/ *transitive verb* throw light on; explain, clarify. □ **elu·ci·da·tion** /-ˈdeiʃən/ *noun* **elu·ci·da·tive** *adjective* **elu·ci·da·tor** *noun* [Late Latin *elucidare* (as E-¹, LUCID)]

elude *transitive verb* **1** escape adroitly from (a danger, difficulty, pursuer, etc.); dodge. **2** avoid compliance with (a law, request, etc.) or fulfillment of (an obligation). **3** (of a fact, solution, etc.) escape from or baffle (a person's memory or understanding). [Latin *eludere elus-* (as E-¹, *ludere* play)]

elu·sive /ɪˈluːsɪv, i-/ *adjective* **1** difficult to find or catch; tending to elude. **2** difficult to remember or recall. **3** (of an answer etc.) avoiding the point raised; seeking to elude. □ **elu·sive·ly** *adverb* **elu·sive·ness** *noun*

elute /iˈluːt, ɪ-/ *transitive verb Chem.* remove (an adsorbed substance) by washing with a solvent, esp. as a chromatographic technique. □ **elu·tion** *noun* [Latin *eluere* wash out (as E-¹, *luere lut-* wash)]

elu·tri·ate /ɪˈluːtriˌeit, i-/ *transitive verb Chem.* separate (lighter and heavier particles in a mixture) by suspension in an upward flow of liquid or gas. □ **elu·tri·a·tion** /-ˈeiʃən/ *noun* [Latin *elutriare elutriat-* (as E-¹, *lutriare* wash)]

elver *noun* a young eel. [var. of *eel-fare* (see FARE) = a brood of young eels]

elves *pl. of* ELF.

elv·ish *see* ELF.

ELW *abbreviation* (in Canada) Evangelical Lutheran Women.

Ely /ˈiːli/ a cathedral city in the fenland of Cambridgeshire, on the Ouse River; pop. (1998) 10,500.

Ely, Isle of a former county of England extending over the northern part of present-day Cambridgeshire. Before widespread drainage it formed a fertile 'island' in the surrounding fenland.

Elys·ium /ɪˈlɪziəm, ɪˈlɪʒ-, ɪˈliːi-/ *noun* **1** (also **Elys·ian Fields**) (in Greek mythology) the abode of the blessed after death. **2** a place or state of ideal happiness. □ **Elys·ian** *adjective* [Latin from Greek *Elusion (pedion* plain)]

ely·tron /ˈeləˌtrɒn/ *noun* (*pl.* **ely·tra** /-trə/) each of the two hard, often coloured wing-cases of a beetle or earwig. [Greek *elutron* sheath]

EM *abbreviation* ELECTROMAGNETIC.

em *noun* **1** a unit of horizontal measurement in typesetting, usually equal to the nominal width of capital M. **2** a unit of measurement equal to 12 points. [name of the letter M]

em- *prefix* assimilated form of EN-¹, EN-² before *b, p*.

'em *pronoun informal* them (*let 'em all come*). [originally a form of Middle English *hem*, dative and accusative 3rd person plural pronoun: now regarded as an abbreviation of THEM]

ema·ci·ate /ɪˈmeisiˌeit, i-/ *transitive verb* (esp. as **ema·ci·at·ed** *adjective*) make abnormally thin or feeble. □ **ema·ci·a·tion** /-ˈeiʃən/ *noun* [Latin *emaciare emaciat-* (as E-¹, *macies* leanness)]

email ● *noun* **1** messages distributed by electronic means esp. from one computer system to one or more recipients. **2** the electronic mail system. **3** a message sent by email (*received 5 emails*). ● *transitive verb* **1** send email to (a person). **2** send by email. □ **email·able** *adjective*

ema·lan·geni *pl. of* LILANGENI.

eman·ate /ˈeməˌneit/ *verb* **1** *intransitive* (usu. foll. by *from*) issue, originate (from a source) (*the idea originally emanated from her sister*). **2** *transitive* emit; send forth. [Latin *emanare* flow out]

eman·a·tion /ˌeməˈneiʃən/ *noun* **1** the act or process of emanating. **2** something that emanates from a source (esp. of virtues, qualities, etc.). □ **eman·a·tive** /ˈeməˌneitɪv/ *adjective*

eman·ci·pate /ɪˈmansəˌpeit, i-/ *transitive verb* **1** free from restraint, esp. legal, social, or political. **2** free from slavery. □ **eman·ci·pa·tion** *noun* **eman·ci·pa·tor** *noun* **eman·ci·pa·tory** /ɪˈmansəpəˌtɔri/ *adjective* [Latin *emancipare* transfer property (as E-¹, *manus* hand + *capere* take)]

eman·ci·pat·ed *adjective* **1** not inhibited by moral or social convention. **2** liberated, as from slavery.

Emancipation Proclamation (in the American Civil War) the announcement made by President Lincoln on 22 Sept. 1862 that from the beginning of 1863 all black slaves would be emancipated. The declaration turned the war into a crusade against slavery and led to the recruitment of many thousands of black soldiers.

emas·cu·late ● *transitive verb* /ɪˈmaskjʊˌleit, i-/ **1** deprive of force or vigour; make feeble or ineffective. **2** castrate. ● *adjective* /ɪˈmaskjʊlət/ **1** deprived of force or vigour. **2** castrated. □ **emas·cu·la·tion** *noun* **emas·cu·la·tor** *noun* **emas·cu·la·tory** /-lətɔri/ *adjective* [Latin *emasculatus* past participle of *emasculare* (as E-¹, *masculus* diminutive of *mas* male)]

em·balm /emˈbɒm, ɪm-/ *transitive verb* **1** preserve (a corpse) from decay by means of arterial injection of a preservative, e.g. formaldehyde. **2** preserve (someone or something) in an unaltered state. □ **em·balm·er** *noun* [Old French *embaumer* (as EN-¹, BALM)]

em·bank *transitive verb* shut in or confine (a river etc.) with an artificial bank.

em·bank·ment *noun* an earth or stone bank for keeping back water, or for carrying a road or railway.

em·bargo /emˈbargoː, ɪm-/ ● *noun* (*pl.* **-goes**) **1** an order prohibiting ships from entering or leaving a country's ports, usu. issued in anticipation of war. **2** an official, usu. temporary, suspension of commerce or other activity (*be under an embargo*). **3** a prohibition (*an embargo on discussion*). ● *transitive verb* (**-goes, -goed**) **1** place (ships, trade, etc.) under embargo. **2** seize (a ship, goods) for state service. [Spanish from *embargar* arrest, from Romanic (as IN-², BAR¹)]

em·bark *verb* **1** *transitive & intransitive* (often foll. by *for*) put or go on board a ship or aircraft (to a destination) (*they embarked for the Caribbean yesterday*). **2** *intransitive* (foll. by *on, upon*) engage in an activity or undertaking. □ **em·bark·a·tion** *noun* (in sense 1). [French *embarquer* (as IN-², BARK³)]

em·bar·ras de ri·chesses /ˌɑ̃baˌra də riːˈʃes/ *noun* (also **embarras de choix** /ʃwɒ/) = EMBARRASSMENT OF RICHES. [French]

em·bar·rass /ɛmˈberəs, ɪm-/ *transitive verb* **1** cause (a person) to feel awkward or self-conscious or ashamed. **2** (as **em·bar·rassed** *adjective*) encumbered with debts. □ **em·bar·rassed·ly** *adverb* **em·bar·rass·ing·ly** *adverb* [French *embarrasser* (originally = hamper) from Spanish *embarazar* from Italian *imbarrare* bar in (as IN-², BAR¹)]

em·bar·rass·ment /ɛmˈberəsmənt, ɪm-/ *noun* **1 a** a feeling of awkward confusion, shame, or self-consciousness. **b** a cause of this (*their behaviour is an embarrassment*). **2** a state of financial difficulty; shortage of money.

embarrassment of riches *noun* more choices or resources than one needs or can deal with.

em·bassy /ˈɛmbəsi/ *noun* (*pl.* **-sies**) **a** the residence or offices of an ambassador. **b** the ambassador and staff attached to an embassy. [earlier *ambassy* from Old French *ambassée* etc. from medieval Latin *ambasciata* from Romanic (as AMBASSADOR)]

em·bat·tled *adjective* **1** involved in a conflict or difficult undertaking. **2** involved in or prepared for war, esp. because surrounded by enemy forces.

em·bay·ment /ɛmˈbeɪmənt, ɪm-/ *noun* **1** a bay. **2** a recess like a bay.

embed *transitive verb* (also **imbed**) (**-bed·ded, -bed·ding**) (usu. in *passive*) **1** fix firmly in a surrounding mass (*embedded in concrete*). **2** fix (an idea, attitude, etc.) firmly within a structure. **3** *Linguistics* place (a clause etc.) within a larger unit of meaning, e.g. another clause, a sentence, etc. **4** *Math.* incorporate (a structured set) into a larger structure while preserving the main features. **5** *Computing* represent (a graph) in a given surface so that no two edges intersect. □ **em·bed·ded·ness** *noun* **em·bed·ment** *noun*

em·bel·lish /ɛmˈbɛlɪʃ, ɪm-/ *transitive verb* **1** beautify, adorn. **2** add interest to (a narrative) with fictitious additions. □ **em·bel·lish·er** *noun* **em·bel·lish·ment** *noun* [Old French *embellir* (as EN-¹, *bel* handsome, from Latin *bellus*)]

em·ber *noun* (usu. in *pl.*) **1** a small piece of glowing coal or wood in a dying fire. **2** an almost extinct residue of a past activity, feeling, etc. [Old English *ǣmyrge* from Germanic]

ember day *noun* a Wednesday, Friday, or Saturday immediately following the first Sunday in Lent, Pentecost, September 14, and December 13, traditionally days of fasting and prayer in some Western Churches. [Old English *ymbren* (n.), perhaps from *ymbryne* period, from *ymb* about + *ryne* course]

em·bez·zle *transitive & intransitive verb* divert (money etc.) fraudulently to one's own use in violation of trust. □ **em·bez·zle·ment** *noun* **em·bez·zler** *noun* [Anglo-French *embesiler* (as EN-¹, Old French *besillier* maltreat, ravage, of unknown origin)]

em·bit·ter *transitive verb* **1** (usu. as **em·bit·tered** *adjective*) make (a person or feeling) intensely hostile, bitter, or discontented. **2** make more bitter or painful. □ **em·bit·ter·ment** *noun*

em·bla·zon /ɛmˈbleɪzən, ɪm-/ *transitive verb* **1** (usu. in *passive*) **a** (foll. by *with*) inscribe a conspicuous design, logo, slogan, etc. on (a surface). **b** (foll. by *on*) inscribe (such a design) on a surface. **2 a** portray conspicuously on a heraldic shield. **b** adorn (a shield) with heraldic devices.

em·blem *noun* **1** a symbol or representation typifying or identifying an institution, quality, etc. **2** a heraldic device or symbolic object as a distinctive badge. □ **em·blem·atic** *adjective* **em·blem·atic·al·ly** *adverb* [Latin *emblema* from Greek *emblēma -matos* insertion, from *emballō* throw in (as EN-¹, *ballō* throw)]

em·blem·a·tize /ɛmˈblɛməˌtaɪz, ɪm-/ *transitive verb* (also esp. *Brit.* **-tise**) **1** serve as an emblem of. **2** represent by an emblem.

em·bodi·ment *noun* a tangible or visible form of an idea, quality, or feeling (*women were viewed as the embodiment of domestic virtue*).

em·body *transitive verb* (**-ies, -ied**) **1** give a concrete or discernible form to (an idea, concept, etc.). **2** (of a thing or person) be an expression of (an idea etc.). **3** express tangibly (*courage embodied in heroic actions*). **4** include, comprise (*the changes in law embodied in the Act*). **5** provide (a spirit) with bodily form.

em·bold·en *transitive verb* (usu. in *passive*) make bold; encourage.

em·bol·ism /ˈɛmbəˌlɪzəm/ *noun* an obstruction of any artery by a clot of blood, air bubble, etc. [EMBOLUS + -ISM]

em·bol·us /ˈɛmbələs/ *noun* (*pl.* **em·boli** /-ˌlaɪ/) an object causing an embolism. □ **em·bol·ic** /-ˈbɒlɪk/ *adjective* [Latin, = piston, from Greek *embolos* peg, stopper]

em·bon·point /ˌɑ̃bɔ̃ˈpwæ̃/ *noun* plumpness (of a person). [French *en bon point* in good condition]

em·boss *transitive verb* (usu. as **em·bossed** *adjective*) **1** carve or mould in relief. **2** form figures etc. so that they stand out on (a surface). □ **em·boss·er** *noun* **em·boss·ing** *noun* [Old French (as EN-¹, BOSS²)]

em·bouch·ure /ˈɒmbʊˌʃʊr/ *noun* **1** *Music* the mode of applying the mouth to the mouthpiece of a brass or woodwind instrument. **2** the mouthpiece of some instruments. [French from *emboucher* put in or to the mouth (as EN-¹, *bouche* mouth)]

em·bour·geoise·ment /ɑ̃ˌbʊrʒwɒzˈmɑ̃/ *noun* conversion to a bourgeois outlook or way of life.

em·bow·er /ɛmˈbaʊər, ɪm-/ *transitive verb* *literary* enclose as in a bower.

em·brace ● *verb* **1 a** *transitive* hold (a person) closely in the arms, esp. as a sign of affection. **b** *intransitive* (of two people) hold each other closely. **2** *transitive* clasp, enclose. **3** *transitive* accept eagerly (an offer, opportunity, etc.). **4** *transitive* adopt (a course of action, doctrine, cause, etc.). **5** *transitive* include, comprise. **6** *transitive* take in with the eye or mind. ● *noun* **1** an act of embracing. **2** the act of holding someone in one's arms. □ **em·brace·able** *adjective* **em·bra·cer** *noun* [Old French *embracer*, ultimately from Latin *in- IN-¹ + bracchium* arm]

em·bras·ure /ɛmˈbreɪʒər, ɪm-/ *noun* **1** the bevelling of a wall at the sides of a door or window; splaying. **2** a small opening in a parapet of a fortified building, splayed on the inside, made to fire a weapon through. [French from *embraser* splay, of unknown origin]

em·brit·tle *transitive & intransitive verb* make or become brittle. □ **em·brittle·ment** *noun*

em·bro·ca·tion /ˌɛmbroːˈkeɪʃən/ *noun* a liquid used for rubbing on the body to relieve muscular pain etc. [medieval Latin *embrocatio*, ultimately from Greek *embrokhē* lotion]

em·broid·er *verb* **1 a** *transitive & intransitive* decorate (cloth etc.) with needlework. **b** *transitive* create (a design) in this way. **2** *transitive* embellish (a narrative etc.) with fictitious additions. □ **em·broid·er·er** *noun* [Anglo-French *enbrouder* (as EN-¹, Old French *brouder, broisder* from Germanic]

em·broid·ery *noun* (*pl.* **-eries**) **1** the art of embroidering. **2** embroidered work; a piece of this. **3** unnecessary or extravagant ornament. **4** fictitious additions to a story etc.).

em·broil *transitive verb* **1** (often foll. by *in*) involve (a person, company, etc.) in conflict or difficulties. **2** bring (affairs) into a state of confusion. □ **em·broil·ment** *noun* [French *embrouiller* (as EN-¹, BROIL²)]

em·bryo /ˈɛmbrioː/ *noun* (*pl.* **-bryos**) **1 a** an unborn or unhatched offspring. **b** a human offspring in the first eight or twelve weeks from conception. **2** a rudimentary plant contained in a seed. **3** a thing in a rudimentary stage. □ **in embryo** undeveloped. □ **embry·oid** *adjective* **embry·on·al** /ɛmˈbraɪənəl/ *adjective* **embry·on·ic** /ˌɛmbriˈɒnɪk/ *adjective* **embry·on·ic·al·ly** /-ˈɒnɪkli/ *adverb* [Late Latin *embryo -onis* from Greek *embruon* fetus (as EN-², *bruō* swell, grow)]

embryo- /ˈɛmbrioː/ *combining form* embryo.

embryo·gen·esis /ˌɛmbrioːˈdʒɛnəsɪs/ *noun* the formation of an embryo.

embry·ol·ogy /ˌɛmbriˈɒlədʒi/ *noun* the study of embryos. □ **embryo·logic** *adjective* **embryo·logic·al** *adjective* **embryo·logic·al·ly** *adverb* **embryo·l·o·gist** *noun*

embryo transfer *noun* **1** *Agriculture* the removal of an embryo from a superior cow, sow, etc. and its replacement inside an inferior one, performed to increase the potential number of offspring from superior livestock. **2** the transfer of a human embryo from one female, or from storage, to another for gestation.

emcee *informal* ● *noun* a master of ceremonies. ● *verb* (**em·cees, em·ceed**) **1** *intransitive* act as master of ceremonies. **2** *transitive* act as master of ceremonies for. [the letters *MC*]

em dash *noun* a long dash (—) used in punctuation.

-eme *suffix Linguistics* forming nouns denoting units of structure etc. (*grapheme; morpheme*). [French *-ème* unit, from Greek *-ēma*]

emend /iˈmɛnd, ɪ-/ *transitive verb* edit (a text etc.) to remove errors and corruptions. □ **emend·a·tion** *noun* [Latin *emendare* (as E-¹, *menda* fault)]

em·er·ald /ˈɛmrəld, ˈɛmərəld/ ● *noun* **1** a bright green precious stone, a variety of beryl. **2** (in full **emerald green**) the colour of this.

● *adjective* (in full **emerald green**; sometimes hyphenated when *attributive*) bright green. [Old French *emeraude*, *esm-*, ultimately from Greek *smaragdos*]

Emerald Isle *noun informal* Ireland.

emerg /iː'mɜrdʒ/ *noun Cdn slang* = EMERGENCY 4. [abbreviation]

emerge *intransitive verb* (often foll. by *from*) **1** come up or out into view, esp. when formerly concealed. **2** come up out of a liquid. **3** (of facts, circumstances, etc.) come to light, become known, esp. as a result of inquiry etc. **4** become recognized or prominent (*emerged as a leading contender*). **5** (of a question, difficulty, etc.) become apparent. **6** survive an ordeal etc. with a specified result (*emerged unscathed*). □ **emer·gence** *noun* [Latin *emergere emers-* (as E-¹, *mergere* dip)]

emer·gency *noun* (*pl.* **-cies**) **1** a sudden state of danger, conflict, etc., requiring immediate action. **2 a** a medical condition requiring immediate treatment. **b** a patient with such a condition. **3** (*attributive*) characterized by or for use in an emergency. **4** *N Amer.* (often *attributive*) a section of a hospital for handling emergencies (*emergency room*; *emergency ward*). [medieval Latin *emergentia* (as EMERGE)]

emergency brake *noun N Amer.* a brake on a car etc., usually operated by hand, used to stop it if the main brakes fail, and to prevent it from rolling while parked.

emergency contraception *noun* the morning-after pill, or its use.

emergency locator transmitter *noun* a radio transmitter on an aircraft activated automatically by the inertia of impact and serving as a homing beacon for searching aircraft. Abbr.: **ELT**.

emergency room *noun N Amer.* (also **emergency department**) = EMERGENCY 4. Abbr.: **ER**.

emergency services *plural noun* the public organizations that respond to and deal with emergencies when they occur, esp. the ambulance service, the police, and the fire department.

emer·gent *adjective* **1** becoming apparent; emerging. **2** (of a nation) newly formed or made independent.

emerging market *noun* a country with a low- to middle- income GNP as defined by the World Bank which is pursuing measures to liberalize its economy and open its market to international investment and trade.

emeri·tus /ɪ'merɪtəs/ *adjective* retired and retaining one's title as an honour (*emeritus professor*; *professor emeritus*). [Latin, past participle of *emerēri* (as E-¹, *merēri* earn)]

emerse /ɪ'mɜrs/ *adjective Bot.* (of part of an aquatic plant) reaching above the surface of the water (*opp.* SUBMERSE). □ **emersed** *adjective*

emer·sion /ɪ'mɜrʒən/ *noun* **1** the act or an instance of emerging. **2** *Astronomy* the reappearance of a celestial body after its eclipse or occultation. [Late Latin *emersio* (as EMERGE)]

Emer·son /'emərsən/ **Ralph Waldo** (1803–82), US philosopher and poet. He and Thoreau are regarded as the central figures of New England transcendentalism, which, in its reverence for nature, foreshadowed the ecological movement of the 20th c.; among his best-known works is the essay *Nature* (1836). □ **Emer·son·ian** /ˌemər'soːniən/ *adjective*

emery /'eməri/ *noun* **1** a coarse rock of corundum and magnetite or hematite used for polishing metal or other hard materials. **2** (*attributive*) covered with emery. [French *émeri(l)* from Italian *smeriglio*, ultimately from Greek *smuris*, *smēris* polishing powder]

emery board *noun* a strip of thin wood or board coated with emery or another abrasive, used as a nail file.

emery cloth *noun* (also **emery paper**) cloth or paper covered with emery, used for polishing or cleaning metals etc.

eme·sis /'eməsɪs/ *noun Med.* vomiting. [Greek, from *emein* to vomit]

emet·ic /ɪ'metɪk/ ● *adjective* that causes vomiting. ● *noun* an emetic medicine. [Greek *emetikos* from *emeō* vomit]

EMF *abbreviation* **1** (usu. **emf**) electromotive force. **2** electromagnetic field(s).

EMG *abbreviation* **1** electromyogram. **2** electromyograph. **3** electromyography. **4** electromyographic. **5** electromyographically.

-emia *combining form* (also **-aemia**, **-hemia**, **-haemia**) forming nouns denoting that a substance is (esp. excessively) present in the blood (*leukemia*). [modern Latin from Greek *-aimia* from *haima* blood]

emic /'iːmɪk/ *adjective* describing the structure of a particular language or culture in terms of its internal elements and their functioning, rather than in terms of any existing external scheme (*compare* ETIC). [from PHONEMIC (see PHONEME)]

emi·grant /'emɪɡrənt/ ● *noun* a person who emigrates. ● *adjective* emigrating.

emi·grate /'emɪˌɡreɪt/ *intransitive verb* leave one's own country to settle in another. □ **emi·gra·tion** *noun* [Latin *emigrare emigrat-* (as E-¹, *migrare* depart)]

émi·gré /'emɪˌɡreɪ/ *noun* an emigrant, esp. a political exile. [French, past participle of *émigrer* EMIGRATE]

Emi Kous·si /ˌeimi 'kuːsə/ a volcanic mountain in the Sahara, in N Chad. Rising to 3 415 m (11,202 ft.), it is the highest peak in the Tibesti Mountains.

Emilia-Romagna /eˌmiːljaroˈmɒnja/ a region of N Italy; capital, Bologna.

emi·nence /'emɪnəns/ *noun* **1** distinction; recognized superiority. **2** a piece of rising ground. **3** (**Eminence**) a title used in addressing or referring to a cardinal (*Your Eminence*; *His Eminence*). **4** an important person. **5** a rounded projection, esp. on a bone. [Latin *eminentia* (as EMINENT)]

émi·nence grise /ˌeimiːˌnɑːs 'ɡriːz/ *noun* (*pl.* **émi·nences grises** *pronunc.* same) a person who exercises power or influence without holding office. [French, = grey cardinal (see EMINENCE): originally applied to Cardinal Richelieu's private secretary, Père Joseph d.1638]

emi·nent /'emɪnənt/ *adjective* **1** distinguished, notable. **2** (of qualities) remarkable in degree. □ **emi·nent·ly** *adverb* [Latin *eminēre eminent-jut*]

eminent domain *noun* sovereign control over all property in a country, with the right of expropriation.

emir /e'miːr/ *noun* a title of various Muslim rulers, esp. in the Middle East. [French *émir* from Arabic *'amīr*: compare AMIR]

emir·ate /'emərət, -ˌreɪt/ *noun* the rank, domain, or reign of an emir.

emis·sary /'emɪˌseri/ *noun* (*pl.* **-ies**) a person sent as a diplomatic representative on a special mission. [Latin *emissarius* scout, spy (as EMIT)]

emis·sion /ɪ'mɪʃən, i-/ *noun* **1** (often foll. by *of*) the process or an act of emitting. **2** a thing emitted, as exhaust, radiation, fluid, etc. [Latin *emissio* (as EMIT)]

emission spectrum *noun* a spectrum of the electromagnetic radiation emitted by a source.

emis·sive /ɪ'mɪsɪv, i-/ *adjective* having the power to radiate light, heat, etc. □ **emis·siv·ity** /ˌiːmɪ'sɪvɪti/ *noun*

emit /ɪ'mɪt, i-/ *transitive verb* (**emit·ted**, **emit·ting**) **1 a** send out (heat, light, exhaust, etc.). **b** discharge from the body. **2** give forth (a sound). [Latin *emittere emiss-* (as E-¹, *mittere* send)]

emit·ter /ɪ'mɪtər, i-/ *noun* something which emits, esp. a region in a transistor producing carriers of current.

Em·man·uel /ɪ'manjuːəl/ (also **Im·man·uel**) the name given to Christ as the deliverer of Judea prophesied by Isaiah (Isa. 7:14, 8:8; Matt. 1:23). [Hebrew, = God with us]

Em·men·thal /'emənˌtɒl/ *noun* (also **-tal**, **-taler** /-ˈtɒlər/, **-thaler**) a kind of hard yellow Swiss cheese with many large holes in it, similar to Gruyère. [German *Emmentaler* from *Emmental* in Switzerland]

emmer *noun* a kind of wheat, *Triticum dicoccum*, grown mainly for fodder. [German dial.]

em·met *noun archaic* or *dialect* an ant. ¶ In Canada, this word is common in Newfoundland. [Old English *æmete*: see ANT]

Emmy *noun* (*pl.* **Emmys**) (in the US) a statuette awarded annually to an outstanding television program or performer. [perhaps from *Immy* = *image orthicon* (a kind of television camera tube)]

emo *noun* (also **emo·core**) a style of rock music resembling punk but having more complex arrangements and lyrics that deal with more emotional subjects. [shortening of *emotional hardcore*]

emol·li·ent /ɪ'mɒliənt, e-/ ● *adjective* **1** that softens or soothes the skin. **2** soothing. ● *noun* an emollient agent. □ **emol·li·ence** *noun* [Latin *emollire* (as E-¹, *mollis* soft)]

emolu·ment /ɪ'mɒljʊmənt, e-/ *noun* a salary, fee, or profit from employment or office. [Old French *emolument* or Latin *emolumentum*, originally prob. 'payment for wheat grinding', from *emolere* (as E-¹, *molere* grind)]

emote *intransitive verb informal* show excessive emotion. □ **emot·er** *noun* [back-formation from EMOTION]

emoti·con /ɪ'moːtɪˌkɒn, i-/ *noun* a (usu. sideways) representation of a facial expression constructed out of keyboard characters, added to an esp. email message to help establish the tone, e.g. ;-) representing a winking face or :-(representing a sad face. [blend of EMOTION + ICON]

emo·tion *noun* **1** a strong mental or instinctive feeling such as love, sorrow, or fear. **2** emotional intensity or sensibility (*he spoke with* *emotion*). □ **emo·tion·less** *adjective* [earlier = agitation, disturbance of the mind, from French *émotion* from *émouvoir* excite]

emo·tion·al *adjective* **1** of or relating to the emotions. **2 a** (of a person) liable to excessive emotion. **b** showing strong emotion, esp. by weeping. **3** expressing or based on emotion (*an emotional appeal*). **4** likely to excite emotion (*an emotional issue*). □ **emo·tion·al·ism** *noun* **emo·tion·al·ist** *noun* **emo·tion·al·ity** *noun* **emo·tion·al·ize** *transitive verb* (also esp. *Brit.* **-ise**). **emo·tion·al·ly** *adverb*

emotional intelligence *noun* the ability to feel or display appropriate emotion; emotional maturity.

emo·tive *adjective* **1** of or characterized by emotion. **2** tending to excite emotion. **3** arousing feeling; not purely descriptive. □ **emo·tive·ly** *adverb* **emo·tive·ness** *noun* **emo·tiv·ity** *noun* [Latin *emovēre emot-* (as E-¹, *movēre* move)]

EMP *abbreviation* ELECTROMAGNETIC PULSE.

em·pan·ada /empəˈnɑdə/ *noun* a baked or fried Spanish or Latin American turnover with a filling of meat, fish, cheese, fruit, or vegetables. [Spanish, fem. past. part. of *empanar* bake or roll in pastry]

em·panel *transitive verb* (also **im·panel**) (**-panelled**, **-panel·ling**; also esp. *US* **-paneled**, **-panel·ing**) enrol or enter on a panel (those eligible for jury service). □ **em·panel·ment** *noun* [Anglo-French *empaneller* (as EN-¹, PANEL)]

em·pa·thize *intransitive verb* (also esp. *Brit.* **-thise**) *Psych.* (usu. foll. by *with*) exercise empathy.

em·pathy *noun Psych.* the power of identifying oneself mentally with (and so fully comprehending) a person or object of contemplation. □ **em·pa·thet·ic** *adjective* **em·pa·thet·ic·ally** *adverb* **em·path·ic** /emˈpaθɪk/ *adjective* **em·path·ic·ally** /emˈpaθ-/ *adverb* [translation of German *Einfühlung* from *ein* in + *Fühlung* feeling, after Greek *empatheia*: see SYMPATHY]

Em·pedo·cles /emˈpedəˌkliːz/ (*c.*490–*c.*430 BC), Greek philosopher. His poem *On Nature* teaches that the universe is composed of four elements, fire, air, water, and earth, which mingle and separate under the influence of the opposing principles of Love and Strife.

em·pen·nage /ˌemˈpenɪdʒ/ *noun* the rear assembly of an aircraft, consisting of the stabilizer, elevators, fin, and rudder. [French from *empenner* to feather (an arrow)]

em·per·or *noun* **1** the male sovereign of an empire. **2** a male sovereign of higher rank than a king. □ **em·peror·ship** *noun* [Old French *emperere*, *empereor* from Latin *imperator -oris* from *imperare* command]

emperor penguin *noun* the largest known penguin, *Aptenodytes forsteri*, of the Antarctic.

em·pha·sis *noun* (*pl.* **em·pha·ses** /-ˌsiːz/) **1** special importance or prominence attached to a thing, fact, idea, etc. (*emphasis on economy*). **2** stress laid on a word or words to indicate special meaning or importance. **3** vigour or intensity of expression, feeling, action, etc. **4** prominence, sharpness of contour. [Latin from Greek from *emphainō* exhibit (as EN-², *phainō* show)]

em·pha·size /ˈemfəˌsaiz/ *transitive verb* (also esp. *Brit.* **-sise**) **1** bring (a thing, fact, etc.) into special prominence; put emphasis or stress on. **2** lay stress on (a word in speaking).

em·phat·ic /emˈfatɪk, ɪm-/ *adjective* **1** (of language, tone, or gesture) forcibly expressive. **2** of words: **a** bearing the stress. **b** used to give emphasis. **3** expressing oneself with emphasis. **4** (of an action or process) forcible, significant. □ **em·phat·ic·ally** *adverb* [Late Latin *emphaticus* from Greek *emphatikos* (as EMPHASIS)]

em·phy·sema /ˌemfɪˈziːmə, -ˈsiː-/ *noun* **1** enlargement of the air sacs of the lungs causing breathlessness. **2** a swelling caused by the presence of air in the connective tissues of the body. □ **em·phy·sema·tous** /ˌemfɪˈsiːmətəs, -ˈsem-, -ˈziː-, -ˈzem-/ *adjective* [Late Latin from Greek *emphusēma* from *emphusaō* puff up]

em·pire *noun* **1** an extensive group of states or countries under a single supreme authority, esp. an emperor. **2 a** supreme dominion. **b** (often foll. by *over*) *archaic* absolute control. **3** a large commercial organization etc. owned or directed by one person or group. **4** (**the Empire**) *hist.* **a** the British Empire. **b** the Holy Roman Empire. **5** a type or period of government in which the sovereign is called emperor. **6** (*attributive*) **a** denoting a style of dress with a waistline under the bust and often a low neckline, originally popular during the first French Empire (1804–14) (*empire waist*). **b** (**Empire**) denoting a neoclassical style of furniture fashionable during the first French Empire (1804–14), often with Egyptian motifs. **7** (**Empire**) a red, sweet and tart eating apple, with characteristics of both McIntosh and Red Delicious apples. [Old French from Latin *imperium* related to *imperare*: see EMPEROR]

empire builder *noun* a person who deliberately acquires extra territory, authority, etc. esp. unnecessarily. □ **empire building** *noun*

Empire State *noun* an informal name for the state of New York.

em·pir·ic /emˈpɪrɪk, ɪm-/ ● *adjective* = EMPIRICAL. ● *noun archaic* **1** a person relying solely on experiment. **2** a quack doctor. [Latin *empiricus* from Greek *empeirikos* from *empeiria* experience, from *empeiros* skilled]

em·pir·ic·al /emˈpɪrɪkəl, ɪm-/ *adjective* **1** based on or acting on observation or experiment, not on theory. **2** *Philos.* regarding sense data as valid information. **3** deriving knowledge from experience alone. □ **em·pir·ic·al·ly** *adverb*

empirical formula *noun Chem.* a formula showing the constituents of a compound but not their configuration.

em·piri·cism /emˈpɪrɪsɪzəm, ɪm-/ *noun Philos.* the theory that all knowledge is derived from sense-experience. □ **em·piri·cist** *noun & adjective*

em·place *transitive verb* put into a specified position; situate. [back-formation from EMPLACEMENT]

em·place·ment *noun* **1** the act or an instance of putting in position. **2** a platform or defended position where a gun is placed for firing. **3** situation, position.

em·plane *transitive & intransitive verb* (also **en·plane**) go or put on board an airplane.

em·ploy ● *transitive verb* **1** use the services of (a person) in return for payment. **2** (often foll. by *for, in, on*) use (a thing, time, energy, strategy, etc.) esp. to good effect. **3** (often foll. by *in*) keep (a person) occupied. ● *noun* the state of being employed, esp. for wages. □ **in the employ of** employed by. □ **em·ploy·er** *noun* [Old French *employer*, ultimately from Latin *implicari* be involved, from *implicare* enfold: see IMPLICATE]

em·ploy·able ● *adjective* **1** qualified for employment and available for work. **2** usable. ● *noun* an employable person. □ **em·ploy·abil·ity** *noun*

em·ploy·ee *noun* a person employed for wages or salary.

em·ploy·ment *noun* **1** the act of employing or the state of being employed. **2** the prevalence or proportion of this in a given area (*startling employment statistics; politicians promising full employment*). **3** a person's regular trade or profession.

employment agency *noun* a business etc. that finds employers or employees for those seeking them.

employment equity *noun Cdn & S Africa* a hiring policy encouraging fair representation of women, visible minorities, native people, handicapped people, etc. in the work force.

employment insurance *noun Cdn* a federal government program providing payments to eligible unemployed people, funded by tax revenues and contributions by employers and workers. Abbr.: **EI**. ¶ Formerly called UNEMPLOYMENT INSURANCE.

employment office *noun* an esp. government office concerned with advising and finding work for the unemployed.

em·por·ium /emˈpɔriəm, ɪm-/ *noun* (*pl.* **em·poria** /-riə/ or **-iums**) **1** a specialized retail store etc. (*trading card emporium; bodybuilding emporium*). **2** a large retail store selling a wide variety of goods. **3** a centre of commerce, a market. [Latin from Greek *emporion* from *emporos* merchant]

em·pow·er *transitive verb* (foll. by *to* + infin.) **1** authorize, license. **2** give power to; make able. **3** provide with the means, opportunity, etc. necessary for independence, self-assertion, etc. □ **em·power·ment** *noun*

em·press /ˈemprəs/ *noun* **1** the wife or widow of an emperor. **2** a female sovereign of an empire. **3** a female sovereign of higher rank than a queen. [Old French *emperesse* fem. of *emperere* EMPEROR]

empty ● *adjective* (**emp·ti·er**, **emp·ti·est**) **1** containing nothing. **2** (of a house etc.) unoccupied or unfurnished. **3** (of a transport vehicle etc.) without a load, passengers, etc. **4 a** meaningless, hollow, insincere (*empty threats; an empty gesture*). **b** without substance or purpose (*an empty existence*). **5** *informal* hungry. **6** (foll. by *of*) devoid, lacking. **7** *Math. & Logic* (of a class or set) containing no members or elements. **8** (of a piece of land) without structures, crops, etc. (*empty lot; empty field*). **9** *Hockey* (of a net) left unguarded while a team substitutes an extra attacker for its goaltender. ● *verb* (**-ties**, **-tied**) **1** *transitive* **a** make empty; remove the contents of. **b** (foll. by *of*) deprive of certain contents (*emptied the room of its chairs*). **2** *transitive* (often foll. by *into*) transfer (the contents of a container). **3** *intransitive* become empty. **4** *intransitive* (usu. foll. by *into*) (of a river) discharge itself (into the sea etc.). ● *noun* (*pl.* **-ties**) *informal* a container (esp. a bottle) left empty of its contents. □ **on an empty stomach** see STOMACH. **run on empty** continue to function though having exhausted all one's resources, sustenance, etc. □ **emp·ti·ly** *adverb* **emp·ti·ness** *noun* [Old English *æmtig, æmetig* from *æmetta* leisure]

empty calorie *noun* a calorie from food containing no or few nutrients.

empty-handed *adjective* (usu. *predicative*) **1** bringing or taking nothing. **2** having achieved or obtained nothing. □ **empty-handed·ly** *adverb*

empty-headed *adjective* foolish; lacking common sense. □ **empty-headed·ness** *noun*

empty nest *noun* esp. *N Amer.* a household where the parents alone remain after the children have grown up and left home.

empty nester *noun* esp. *N Amer.* either of a couple whose children have grown up and left home.

empty-netter *noun* (in full **empty-net goal**) *Hockey* a goal scored into an empty net.

Empty Quarter an alternative name for the RUB' AL KHALI.

em·pur·ple *transitive verb* **1** make purple or red. **2** make angry.

em·py·ema /ˌempaɪˈiːmə, ˌempi-/ *noun* a collection of pus in a cavity, esp. in the pleura. [Late Latin from Greek *empuēma* from *empueō* suppurate (as EN-², *puon* pus)]

em·pyr·ean /ˌemˈpɪriːən/ ● *noun* **1** the highest heaven, as the sphere of fire in ancient cosmology or as the abode of God in early Christianity. **2** the visible heavens. ● *adjective* of the empyrean. □ **em·pyr·eal** *adjective* [medieval Latin *empyreus* from Greek *empurios* (as EN-², *pur* fire)]

EMS *abbreviation* **1** EUROPEAN MONETARY SYSTEM. **2** *Computing* Expanded Memory Specification. **3** emergency medical services.

EMU /ˈiːmˈjuː, ˈiːmjuː/ *abbreviation* economic and monetary union (of the EC); European monetary union.

emu /ˈiːmjuː, ˈiːmuː/ *noun* a large shaggy flightless Australian bird, *Dromaius novaehollandiae*, related to the ostrich and capable of running at high speed. [earlier *emia, eme* from Portuguese *ema*]

emu·late /ˈemjʊˌleɪt/ *transitive verb* **1** try to equal or excel. **2** imitate zealously. **3** rival. **4** *Computing* reproduce the function or action of (a different computer or software system). □ **emu·la·tion** *noun* **emu·la·tive** /-lətɪv/ *adjective* **emu·la·tor** *noun* [Latin *aemulat-* 'rivalled, equalled', from *aemulari* from *aemulus* rival]

emul·si·fi·er /ɪˈmʌlsɪˌfaɪər/ *noun* **1** any substance that stabilizes an emulsion, esp. a food additive used to stabilize processed foods. **2** an apparatus used for producing an emulsion.

emul·si·fy /ɪˈmʌlsɪˌfaɪ/ *transitive verb* (**-fies, -fied**) convert into an emulsion. □ **emul·si·fi·able** *adjective* **emul·si·fi·ca·tion** /-fɪˈkeɪʃən/ *noun*

emul·sion /ɪˈmʌlʃən/ *noun* **1 a** a fine dispersion of one liquid in another, esp. as paint, medicine, etc. **b** (in full **emulsion paint**) a paint consisting of an emulsion of resin in water. **2** a mixture of a silver compound suspended in gelatin etc. for coating plates or films. [French *émulsion* or modern Latin *emulsio* from *emulgēre* (as E-¹, *mulgēre* muls- to milk)]

en *noun* *Typography* a unit of measurement equal to half an em. [name of the letter N]

en-¹ *prefix* (also **em-** before *b, p*) forming verbs, = IN-¹: **1** from nouns, meaning 'put into or on' (*engulf*; *entrust*; *embed*). **2** from nouns or adjectives, meaning 'bring into the condition of' (*enslave*); often with the suffix *-en* (*enlighten*). **3** from verbs: **a** in the sense 'in, into, on' (*enfold*). **b** as an intensive (*entangle*). [from or after French *en-* from Latin *in-*]

en-² *prefix* (also **em-** before *b, p*) in, inside (*energy*; *enthusiasm*). [Greek]

-en¹ *suffix* forming verbs: **1** from adjectives, usu. meaning 'make or become so or more so' (*deepen*; *fasten*; *moisten*). **2** from nouns (*happen*; *strengthen*). [Old English *-nian* from Germanic]

-en² *suffix* (also **-n**) forming adjectives from nouns, meaning: **1** made or consisting of (often with extended and figurative senses) (*wooden*). **2** resembling; of the nature of (*golden*; *silvern*). [Old English from Germanic]

-en³ *suffix* (also **-n**) forming past participles of strong verbs: **1** as a regular inflection (*spoken*; *sworn*). **2** with restricted sense (*drunken*). [Old English from Germanic]

-en⁴ *suffix* forming the plural of a few nouns (*children*; *brethren*; *oxen*). [Middle English reduction of Old English *-an*]

-en⁵ *suffix* forming diminutives of nouns (*chicken*; *maiden*). [Old English from Germanic]

-en⁶ *suffix* **1** forming feminine nouns (*vixen*). **2** forming abstract nouns (*burden*). [Old English from Germanic]

en·able *transitive verb* **1** (foll. by *to* + infin.) give (a person etc.) the means

or authority to do something. **2** make possible. **3** esp. *Computing* make (a device, a function, etc.) operational; switch on.

en·abler *noun* **1** a person or thing which enables, esp. a person who helps others to achieve their potential or develop skills. **2** a person who, through action, financial support, silence, etc., supports, often unconsciously, another person's addictions, bad habits, etc.

en·abling *adjective* (of legislation) empowering a person or body to take certain action.

en·act *transitive verb* **1 a** establish (a law, legal penalty, etc.). **b** make (a bill etc.) law. **2** play (a part or scene on stage or in life). □ **en·ac·tion** *noun* **en·act·ive** *adjective*

en·act·ment *noun* **1** a law enacted. **2** the process of enacting.

en·amel ● *noun* **1** a glasslike opaque or semi-transparent coating on metallic or other hard surfaces for ornament or as a preservative lining. **2 a** a smooth hard coating. **b** (in full **enamel paint**) a paint that dries to give a smooth hard coat. **3** the hard glossy natural coating over the crown of a tooth. **4** painting done in enamel. ● *transitive verb* (**en·am·elled, en·am·el·ling; en·am·eled, en·am·el·ing**) **1** inlay or encrust (a metal etc.) with enamel. **2** portray (figures etc.) with enamel. □ **en·amel·ler** *noun* **enamel·work** *noun* [Anglo-French *enameler, enamailler* (as EN-¹, Old French *esmail* from Germanic)]

en·am·our /ɪˈnamər, e-/ *transitive verb* (also **en·am·or**) (usu. in *passive*; foll. by *of*) **1** inspire with love or liking. **2** charm, delight. [Old French *enamourer* from *amourer* (as EN-¹, AMOUR)]

en·antio·dro·mia /eˌnantɪəˈdrəːmiə/ *noun* the process by which something becomes its opposite, and the effects of this. [Greek, = running in contrary ways, from *enantio* opposite + *dromos* running]

en·antio·mer /enˈantɪəmər/ *noun Chem.* a molecule that is the mirror image of another. □ **en·antio·mer·ic** /-ˈmerɪk/ *adjective* **en·antio·mer·ic·ally** /-ˈmerɪkli/ *adverb* [Greek *enantios* opposite + -MER]

en·antio·morph /enˈantɪəˌmɔrf/ *noun* a mirror image; a form (esp. of a crystal structure etc.) related to another as an object is to its mirror image. □ **en·antio·morph·ic** *adjective* **en·antio·morph·ism** *noun* **en·antio·morph·ous** *adjective* [German from Greek *enantios* opposite + *morphē* form]

en·arth·ro·sis /ˌenɑrˈθrəːsɪs/ *noun* (pl. **en·arth·ro·ses** /-siːz/) *Anat.* a ball-and-socket joint. [Greek from *enarthros* jointed (as EN-², *arthron* joint)]

en banc /ɑ̃ bɑ̃k/ *adverb Law* (of a court) sitting with several judges presiding. [French, lit. 'at bench']

en bloc /ɑ̃ ˈblɒk/ *adverb* in a block; all at the same time. [French]

enc. *abbreviation* **1** enclosed. **2** enclosure.

en·cae·nia /enˈsiːniə/ *noun* **1** *Cdn* (at the University of New Brunswick and the University of King's College in Halifax) graduation ceremonies. **2** (at Oxford University) an annual celebration in memory of founders and benefactors. **3** a dedication festival. [Latin from Greek *egkainia* (as EN-², *kainos* new)]

en·camp *transitive & intransitive verb* **1** settle in a military camp. **2** lodge in the open in tents.

en·camp·ment *noun* **1** a place where troops etc. are encamped. **2** the process of setting up a camp.

en·capsu·late /enˈkapsʊˌleɪt, -ˈkapsjʊ-/ *transitive verb* **1** enclose in or as in a capsule. **2** summarize; express the essential features of. □ **en·capsu·la·tion** *noun* **en·capsu·la·tor** *noun* [EN-¹ + Latin *capsula* CAPSULE]

en·case *transitive verb* **1** put into a case. **2** surround as with a case. □ **en·case·ment** *noun*

en·caus·tic /enˈkɒstɪk/ ● *adjective* **1** (in painting, ceramics, etc.) using pigments mixed with hot wax, which are burned in as an inlay. **2** (of bricks and tiles) inlaid with differently coloured clays burned in. ● *noun* **1** the art of encaustic painting. **2** a painting done with this technique. [Latin *encausticus* from Greek *egkaustikos* (as EN-², CAUSTIC)]

-ence *suffix* forming nouns expressing: **1** a quality or state or an instance of one (*patience*; *an impertinence*). **2** an action (*reference*; *reminiscence*). [from or after French *-ence* from Latin *-entia, -antia* (compare -ANCE) from pres. part. stem *-ent-, -ant-*]

en·ceinte /ɑ̃ˈsãt/ ● *noun* an enclosure, esp. in fortification. ● *adjective* pregnant. [French, ultimately from Latin *cingere cinct-* gird: see CINCTURE]

En·cela·dus /enˈseladəs/ **1** *Gk Myth* a giant who rebelled against the gods, was killed by Athena, and buried under Mount Etna. **2** a satellite of Saturn (diameter 500 km).

en·ceph·alic /ˌensəˈfalɪk, ˌenk-/ *adjective* of or relating to the brain. [Greek *egkephalos* brain (as EN-², *kephalē* head)]

Vowels: a *cat* ɑ *arm* e *bed* ɜr *her* ɜ: *deux* ə *ago* ɪ *sit* i *cosy* iː *feed* ɒ *hot* ɔ *pore* oː *no* ʌ *run* ʊ *put*

en·ceph·al·itis /ˌenˌsefəˈlaɪtɪs/ noun inflammation of the brain. □ **en·ceph·al·itic** /-ˈlɪtɪk/ adjective

encephalitis le·thar·gica /ləˈθɑrdʒɪkə/ noun an infectious encephalitis caused by a virus, with headache and drowsiness leading to coma; sleeping sickness.

encephalo- /enˈsefəlo/ combining form brain. [Greek egkephalos brain]

en·ceph·alo·gram /enˈsefəloˌgram/ noun an X-ray photograph of the brain.

en·ceph·alo·graph /enˈsefəloˌgraf/ noun = ELECTROENCEPHALOGRAPH.

en·ceph·alo·myel·itis /enˌsefəloˌmaɪəˈlaɪtɪs/ noun inflammation of the brain and spinal cord, esp. due to viral infection.

en·ceph·alon /enˈsefəˌlɒn/ noun Anat. the brain.

en·ceph·al·op·athy /enˌsefəˈlɒpəθi/ noun (pl. **-athies**) disease of the brain. □ **en·ceph·alo·path·ic** /-ˈpaθɪk/ adjective

en·chant transitive verb (usu. in passive) **1** charm, delight. **2** bewitch. □ **en·chant·ed·ly** adverb **en·chant·ing** adjective **en·chant·ing·ly** adverb **en·chant·ment** noun [French enchanter from Latin incantare (as IN-², canere cant- sing)]

en·chant·er noun a person who enchants, esp. by supposed use of magic. □ **en·chant·ress** noun

enchanter's nightshade noun any plant of the genus Circaea, with small white flowers.

en·chase /enˈtʃeɪs/ transitive verb **1** (foll. by in) place (a jewel) in a setting. **2** (foll. by with) set (gold etc.) with gems. **3** inlay with gold etc. **4** adorn with figures in relief. **5** engrave. [French enchâsser (as EN-¹, CHASE²)]

en·chil·ada /ˌentʃɪˈlɒdə/ noun a tortilla with chili sauce and usu. a filling, esp. meat. □ **big enchilada** N Amer. a person or thing of great importance. **the whole enchilada** N Amer. a thing in its entirety. [Latin American Spanish, fem. past participle of enchilar season with chili]

en·ci·pher /enˈsaɪfər/ transitive verb **1** write (a message etc.) in cipher. **2** convert into coded form using a cipher. □ **en·ci·pher·ment** noun

en·cir·cle transitive verb **1** (usu. foll. by with) surround, encompass. **2** form a circle around. □ **en·cir·cle·ment** noun

encl. abbreviation **1** enclosed. **2** enclosure.

en·clave /ˈɒnkleɪv, ˈen-/ noun **1** a portion of territory of one state surrounded by territory of another or others, as viewed by the surrounding territory (compare EXCLAVE). **2** a group of people who are culturally, intellectually, or socially distinct from those surrounding them. **3** N Amer. a gated community. [French from enclaver, ultimately from Latin clavis key]

en·clit·ic /enˈklɪtɪk/ Grammar ● adjective (of a word) pronounced with very little emphasis and usually shortened and forming part of the preceding word. ● noun such a word, e.g. 's in let's. □ **en·clit·ic·ally** adverb [Late Latin encliticus from Greek egklitikos (as EN-², klinō lean)]

en·close transitive verb **1** (often foll. by with, in) **a** surround with a wall, fence, etc. **b** shut in on all sides. **2** fence in (common land) so as to make it private property. **3** put in a receptacle (esp. in an envelope together with a letter). **4** (usu. as **en·closed** adjective) seclude (a religious community) from the outside world. **5** esp. Math. bound on all sides; contain. **6** hem in on all sides. [Old French enclos past participle of enclore, ultimately from Latin includere (as INCLUDE)]

en·clos·ure noun **1** the act of enclosing, esp. of common land. **2** an enclosed space or area. **3** a thing enclosed with a letter. **4** an enclosing fence etc.

en·code transitive verb **1** put (a message etc.) into code or cipher. **2** Linguistics convert ideas into linguistic expression (compare DECODE 2). **3** (of a gene or stretch of nucleic acid) specify the genetic code for (a protein or peptide). □ **en·cod·er** noun

en·comi·as·tic /enkoˈmiˈastɪk/ adjective highly flattering. [Greek egkōmiastēs (as ENCOMIUM)]

en·comi·um /enˈkoːmiəm/ noun (pl. **en·comi·ums** or **en·comia** /-miə/) a formal or high-flown expression of praise. [Latin from Greek egkōmion (as EN-², kōmos revelry)]

en·com·pass /enˈkʌmpəs, ɪn-/ transitive verb **1** surround or form a circle about. **2** contain, include comprehensively.

en·core /ˈɒŋkɔr, ˈɒn-/ ● noun **1** a call by an audience or spectators for the repetition of an item, or for a further item. **2** such an item. **3** a repetition of an event. ● interjection (also /-ˈkɔr/) again, once more. [French, = once again]

en·coun·ter ● transitive verb **1** meet, come across, esp. by chance or unexpectedly. **2** meet as an adversary. ● noun **1** a meeting by chance. **2** a meeting in conflict. **3** a sexual liaison or meeting. **4** an instance of

exposure to something, esp. for the first time (my first encounter with opera). **5** participation in an encounter group. [Old French encontrer, encontre, ultimately from Latin contra against]

encounter group noun a group of persons seeking psychological benefit through close contact with one another.

en·cour·age transitive verb **1** give courage, confidence, or hope to. **2** (foll. by to + infin.) urge, advise. **3** stimulate by help, reward, etc. **4** promote or assist (an enterprise, opinion, etc.). □ **en·cour·age·ment** noun **en·cour·ager** noun **en·cour·aging** adjective **en·cour·aging·ly** adverb [French encourager (as EN-¹, COURAGE)]

en·croach intransitive verb **1** (foll. by on, upon) intrude, esp. on another's territory or rights. **2** advance gradually beyond due limits. □ **en·croach·er** noun **en·croach·ment** noun [Old French encrochier (as EN-¹, crochier from croc hook: see CROOK)]

en croûte adverb in a pastry crust. [French]

en·crust verb **1** transitive cover with a crust. **2** transitive overlay with an ornamental crust of precious material. **3** intransitive form a crust.

en·crust·a·tion noun (also **in·crust·a·tion**) **1** the process of encrusting or state of being encrusted. **2** a crust or hard coating, esp. of fine material. **3** a concretion or deposit on a surface. **4** a facing of marble etc. on a building.

en·crypt /enˈkrɪpt/ transitive verb **1** convert (data) into code, esp. to prevent unauthorized access. **2** conceal by this means. □ **en·cryp·tion** noun [EN-¹ + Greek kruptos hidden]

en·cul·tur·a·tion /ɪnˌkʌltʃʌˈreɪʃən, en-/ noun the process by which the values and norms of a society are passed on to or acquired by its members. □ **en·cul·tur·ate** transitive verb

en·cum·ber transitive verb **1** be a burden to. **2** hamper, impede. **3** burden (a person or estate) with debts, esp. mortgages. **4** fill or block (a place). □ **en·cum·ber·ment** noun [Old French encombrer block up, from Romanic]

en·cum·brance noun **1** a burden. **2** an impediment. **3** a mortgage or other charge on property. **4** an annoyance.

-ency suffix forming nouns denoting a quality (efficiency; fluency) or state (presidency) but not action (compare -ENCE). [Latin -entia (compare -ANCY)]

en·cyc·lic·al /enˈsɪklɪkəl/ ● noun a papal letter addressed to bishops and all members of the Roman Catholic Church. ● adjective (of a letter) for wide circulation. [Late Latin encyclicus from Greek egkuklios (as EN-², kuklos circle)]

en·cyclo·pedia /enˌsaɪkləˈpiːdiə, ɪn-, ən-/ noun (also **en·cyclo·paedia**) a book or set of books, usu. arranged alphabetically, giving information on many subjects or on many aspects of one subject. [modern Latin from spurious Greek egkuklopaideia for egkuklios paideia all-round education: compare ENCYCLICAL]

en·cyclo·ped·ic /enˌsaɪkləˈpiːdɪk, ɪn-, ən-/ adjective (also **en·cyclo·paed·ic**) **1** of, pertaining to, or resembling an encyclopedia, esp. in embracing all branches of learning. **2** (of knowledge or information) comprehensive.

en·cyclo·ped·ist /enˌsaɪkləˈpiːdɪst, ɪn-, ən-/ noun (also **en·cyclo·paed·ist**) **1** a person who writes, edits, compiles, or contributes to an encyclopedia. **2** (**Encyclopedist**) one of the collaborators on the French Encyclopédie (1751-1765) written by Diderot, d'Alembert, etc. and presenting the views of the Enlightenment.

en·cyst /ɪnˈsɪst, en-, ən-/ transitive & intransitive verb Biol. enclose or become enclosed in a cyst. □ **en·cyst·ed** adjective **en·cyst·ment** noun

end ● noun **1 a** the extreme limit or the point beyond which a thing does not continue (the north end of town). **b** either of the two extremities of a line or of the greatest dimension of any object. **c** the furthest, most remote point imaginable (to the ends of the earth). **d** a part of a town originally situated on the outskirts (grew up in the North End). **2** an extreme part of a thing or the surface bounding a thing at either extremity (a strip of wood with a nail in one end). **3 a** the conclusion, finish, or termination of an action, state, process, etc. (no end to his misery). **b** the latter or final part. **c** death, destruction, downfall (met an untimely end). **d** a result or outcome. **e** an ultimate state or condition. **4 a** an aim or thing one seeks to attain (will do anything to achieve his ends; to what end?). **b** the purpose or object for which a thing exists. **5** a remnant, fragment, or piece left over (cigarette end). **6** (prec. by the) informal the limit of endurability. **7** the part or share, esp. of an enterprise or activity, with which a person is concerned (no problem at my end). **8** one half or side of a rink, court, or playing field, esp. the part occupied by either of two opposing teams or players. **9** Curling one of the frames of a game during which each player on both teams delivers two rocks. **10** *N Amer. Football* **a** the lineman positioned furthest from centre. **b** the position occupied by this player. **11** *N Amer.* = END OF STEEL. ● *verb* **1** *transitive & intransitive* bring or come to an end. **2** *transitive* conclude, destroy, put an end to, cause to cease. **3** *intransitive* (foll. by *in*) lead to, have as a result or conclusion (*will end in tears*). **4** *intransitive* (foll. by *by* or *up*) do, achieve, or come eventually to, esp. some specified state (*ended by marrying money*; *ended up making a fortune*). **5** *intransitive* (of a portion of space, an object, etc.) terminate or have its end or extremity. **6** *transitive* (usu. in *infinitive*) surpass, outdo, epitomize (*war to end all wars*). □ **at an end** exhausted or completed. **at the end of one's rope** (or **tether**) having reached the limits of one's patience, resources, abilities, etc. **change ends** *Sport* switch from occupying one half of a rink, field, or court to the other, and change the direction of play. **come to a bad end** meet with ruin or disgrace. **come to an end** cease to exist. **end it** (**all**) *informal* commit suicide. **end of the road** **1** the terminus of a road, path, etc. **2** the point at which a hope or endeavour has been abandoned. **end of the world 1** a calamitous matter or situation. **2** the cessation of life on earth. **end-on** with the end facing one, or with the end adjoining the end of the next object. **end to end 1** lengthwise, with the ends in contact. **2** from one end to another. **from end to end** from one end to the other or throughout the length of something. **in the end** finally, ultimately, in the long run. **keep one's end up** do one's part, hold one's own, or sustain one's part in an undertaking or performance, esp. despite difficulties. **make ends meet** live within one's income. **no end** *informal* to a great extent, very much (*pleased his parents no end*). **no end of** *informal* much or many of (*no end of trouble*; *no end of worries*). **on end 1** in an upright position (*hair stood on end*). **2** consecutively or continuously (*for three weeks on end*). **put an end to 1** stop (an activity etc.). **2** abolish, destroy. [Old English *ende, endian*, from Germanic]

-end *suffix* forming nouns in the sense 'person or thing to be treated in a specified way' (*dividend*; *reverend*). [Latin gerundive ending *-endus*]

en·dan·ger *transitive verb* **1** place in danger. **2** jeopardize the continuance of (a species etc.). □ **en·dan·ger·ment** *noun*

endangered species *noun* **1** a species in danger of extinction, esp. when formally designated as such by a government, environmental protection agency, etc. **2** a category of person, phenomenon, etc., which is in danger of disappearing (*unskilled labourers are an endangered species*).

en·dear *transitive verb* (usu. foll. by *to*) make dear to or beloved by.

en·dear·ing *adjective* inspiring or manifesting affection. □ **en·dear·ing·ly** *adverb*

en·dear·ment *noun* **1** an expression of love, affection, or fondness such as a pet name, caress, etc. **2** fondness, affection.

en·deav·our /ɪnˈdɛvər, en-, ən-/ (also **en·deav·or**) ● *intransitive verb* (foll. by *to* + infin.) try earnestly. ● *noun* (often foll. by *at*, or *to* + infin.) **1** an undertaking or effort directed to attain an object. **2** an earnest or strenuous attempt. [Middle English from *put oneself in devoir* 'do one's utmost': see DEVOIR]

en·dem·ic /enˈdɛmɪk, ɪn-, ən-/ ● *adjective* **1** (of a disease, condition, etc.) of common occurrence or habitually present in a certain area as a result of permanent local factors. **2** (of a plant or animal) native and usu. restricted to a certain country or area. ● *noun* an endemic disease, plant, or animal. □ **en·dem·ic·ally** *adverb* **en·dem·ic·ity** /ˌɛndɪˈmɪsɪti/ *noun* **en·dem·ism** /ˈɛndəˌmɪzəm/ *noun* [modern Latin *endemicus* from Greek *endēmos* native (as EN-², *dēmos* the people)]

En·der·by Land /ˈɛndərbi/ a part of Antarctica, claimed by Australia. Its coast was discovered in 1831–2 by the English navigator John Biscoe.

En·ders, **John Frank·lin** (1897–1985), US virologist. With F. C. Robbins (1916–2003) and T. H. Weller (b.1915) he developed a method of growing viruses in tissue cultures; this eventually led to the development of vaccines against mumps, polio, and measles, and the three scientists shared a Nobel Prize in 1954.

end·game *noun* **1** the final stage of a game (esp. chess), when few pieces remain. **2 a** the penultimate stage, usu. of critical importance, of an effort or process. **b** a strategy of last resort, esp. one played out in a military, political, or economic sphere.

end·ing *noun* **1** an instance of termination, conclusion, or completion. **2** an end or final part, esp. of a literary work, metrical line, or piece of music. **3** an inflected final part of a word.

en·dive /ˈɛndaɪv/ *noun* **1** *N Amer.* = BELGIAN ENDIVE. **2** a curly-leaved plant, *Cichorium endivia*, used in salads. [Old French from Late Latin *endivia*, ultimately from Greek *entubon*]

end·less *adjective* **1** infinite, without end, eternal. **2** continual, incessant (*tired of their endless complaints*). **3** *informal* (of a number, quality, etc.) innumerable, unlimited (*drank endless cups of coffee*). **4** (of a belt, chain, etc.) made in the form of a loop, having the ends joined, for continuous action over wheels etc. □ **end·less·ly** *adverb* **end·less·ness** *noun*

end line *noun* **1** a boundary line marking the end of the field, court, etc. in various sports. **2** a line forming a conclusion.

end·most *adjective* nearest the end, furthest, most distant.

end·note *noun* a note, similar to a footnote, printed at the end of a book, chapter, article, etc.

endo- *combining form* internal, inner, inside. [Greek *endon* within]

endo·card·itis /ˌɛndəʊkɑrˈdaɪtɪs/ *noun* inflammation of the endocardium.

endo·card·ium /ˌɛndəʊˈkɑrdɪəm/ *noun* (pl. **-ia**) the smooth membrane lining the cavities and valves of the heart. [ENDO- + Greek *kardia* heart]

endo·carp /ˈɛndəʊˌkɑrp/ *noun* the innermost layer of the pericarp of a fruit, which lines the seed chamber. □ **endo·carp·al** *adjective* [ENDO- + PERICARP]

endo·crine /ˈɛndəʊˌkraɪn, -ˌkrɪn/ ● *adjective* **1** (of a gland) secreting directly into the blood; ductless. **2** of or pertaining to such glands or their secretions. ● *noun* an endocrine gland, e.g. the thyroid, adrenal, or pituitary gland (*compare* EXOCRINE). [ENDO- + Greek *krinō* sift]

endocrine disrupter *noun* a chemical compound which is believed to disrupt the normal metabolic action of hormones in humans and other animals, causing developmental and reproductive abnormalities, esp. one present as an environmental pollutant.

endo·crin·ol·ogy /ˌɛndəʊkrɪˈnɒlədʒi/ *noun* the branch of medicine that deals with the structure and physiology of endocrine glands and hormones. □ **endo·crino·logic·al** /-nəˈlɒdʒɪkəl/ *adjective* **endo·crin·ol·o·gist** *noun*

endo·cyt·osis /ˌɛndəʊsaɪˈtəʊsɪs/ *noun Biol.* the taking in of matter by a living cell by invagination of its membrane.

endo·derm /ˈɛndəʊˌdɜrm/ *noun Biol.* **1** the innermost layer of an animal embryo in early development. **2** cells or tissues derived from this. □ **endo·derm·al** /-ˈdɜrməl/ *adjective* [ENDO- + Greek *derma* skin]

endo·don·tics /ˌɛndəʊˈdɒntɪks/ *noun* the branch of dentistry that deals with the prevention, diagnosis, and treatment of diseases of tooth pulp and the surrounding tissues, e.g. root canals. □ **endo·don·tist** *noun*

end of steel *noun* (also **end of the steel**) *N Amer.* **1** a terminus or the limit to which a railway extends. **2** the farthest extent to which tracks have been laid, including the most recent tracks of a railway under construction.

endog·amy /enˈdɒɡəmi/ *noun* **1** *Anthropology* the custom of marrying only within the same tribe, clan, community, etc. (*compare* EXOGAMY). **2** the fusion of reproductive cells from the same or related plants. □ **endo·gamic** /ˌɛndəʊˈɡamɪk/ *adjective* **endog·am·ous** *adjective* [ENDO- + Greek *gamos* marriage]

en·dogen·ous /enˈdɒdʒɪnəs/ *adjective* **1** growing or originating from within. **2 a** having a cause inside the body or self. **b** not attributable to any external or environmental factor. □ **en·dogen·ous·ly** *adverb*

endo·lymph /ˈɛndəʊˌlɪmf/ *noun* the fluid in the membranous labyrinth of the ear. □ **endo·lymph·at·ic** /ˌɛndəʊlɪmˈfatɪk/ *adjective*

endo·metri·osis /ˌɛndəʊmiːtriˈəʊsɪs/ *noun* a condition in which endometrial tissue grows in the pelvic cavity, resulting in pelvic pain and the formation of cysts.

endo·met·rium /ˌɛndəʊˈmiːtrɪəm/ *noun* (pl. **-ria**) the mucous membrane lining the uterus. □ **endo·met·rial** *adjective* **endo·met·ri·tis** /ˌɛndəʊmɪˈtraɪtɪs/ *noun* [ENDO- + Greek *mētra* womb]

endo·morph /ˈɛndəʊˌmɔrf/ *noun* **1** a person with a soft round build of body and a high proportion of fat tissue (*compare* ECTOMORPH, MESOMORPH). **2** *Geol.* a mineral enclosed within another. □ **endo·morph·ic** /-ˈmɔrfɪk/ *adjective* **endo·morphy** *noun* [ENDO- + Greek *morphē* form]

endo·morph·ism /ˌɛndəʊˈmɔrfɪzəm/ *noun Geol.* a change in cooling molten rock caused by reaction with the surrounding rock mass or assimilation of fragments of it.

endo·para·site /ˌɛndəʊˈpɛrəˌsaɪt/ *noun* a parasite that lives on the inside of its host. *Also called* ENTOPARASITE. □ **endo·para·sit·ic** *adjective*

endo·phyte /ˈɛndəʊˌfaɪt/ *noun* a plant growing inside a plant or animal.

endo·plasm /ˈɛndəʊˌplazəm/ *noun* the inner, usu. granular, fluid of the cytoplasm of some cells, e.g. amoebae (*compare* ECTOPLASM 1). □ **endo·plas·mic** /ˌɛndəʊˈplazmɪk/ *adjective*

endoplasmic reticulum *noun Biol.* a system of tubular membranes

Consonants: **b** *but* **d** *dog* **f** *few* **g** *get* **h** *her* **j** *yes* **k** *cat* **l** *leg* **m** *man* **n** *no* **p** *pen* **r** *red* **s** *sit*

within the cytoplasm of a eukaryotic cell that forms a link between the cell and nuclear membranes and usu. has ribosomes attached to its surface.

end organ *noun* *Anat.* a specialized, encapsulated ending of a sensory or motor nerve.

en·dor·phin /ɛnˈdɔrfɪn/ *noun* *Biochem.* any of a group of peptide neurotransmitters occurring naturally in the brain and having pain-relieving properties. [French *endorphine* from *endogène* endogenous + MORPHINE]

en·dorse *transitive verb* **1 a** declare one's approval of (a candidate etc.). **b** confirm (a statement or opinion). **2 a** sign on the back of (a cheque) either as payee or to make (it) payable to someone other than the stated payee. **b** sign (a bill) to accept responsibility for paying it. **3** write (a supplementary or official explanation, comment, or instruction) on a document, often to extend or limit its provisions. □ **en·dors·able** *adjective* **en·dor·see** *noun* **en·dors·er** *noun* [medieval Latin *indorsare* (as IN-2, Latin *dorsum* back)]

en·dorse·ment *noun* **1** (*Cdn* also **en·dors·a·tion**) **a** the act or an instance of endorsing. **b** approval, acceptance, support. **2** (in full **product endorsement**) a recommendation of a product or service, esp. in exchange for remuneration, which can be cited in advertising material. **3** *Aviation* an acknowledgement and accreditation for a stated number of hours of experience in certain flying skills. **4** something with which a document etc. is endorsed, esp. a signature or comment.

endo·scope *noun* *Med.* a flexible instrument, consisting of illuminated optical tubes, designed for viewing the internal cavities or hollow organs of the body, such as the lungs, stomach, or bowel. □ **endo·scop·ic** *adjective* **endo·scop·ic·ally** *adverb* **endos·cop·ist** /ɛnˈdɒskəpɪst/ *noun* **endos·copy** /ɛnˈdɒskəpi/ *noun*

endo·skel·eton *noun* an internal skeleton as found in vertebrates (opp. EXOSKELETON). □ **endo·skel·etal** *adjective*

endo·sperm *noun* nutritive material surrounding the germ in some plant seeds.

endo·spore *noun* **1** a resistant, asexual spore that develops inside a vegetative bacterial cell. **2** the inner layer of the membrane or wall of some spores.

endo·thel·ium /ˌɛndoʊˈθiːliəm/ *noun* (*pl.* **-ia**) *Anat.* a layer of cells lining the blood vessels, heart, and lymphatic vessels. □ **endo·thel·ial** *adjective* [ENDO- + Greek *thēlē* teat]

endo·ther·mic *adjective* **1** occurring or formed with the absorption of heat. **2** dependent on or capable of internal generation of heat. □ **endo·thermy** *noun* (in sense 2).

endo·toxin *noun* a toxin present inside a bacterial cell and released when the cell disintegrates. □ **endo·toxic** *adjective*

en·dow *transitive verb* **1 a** bequeath or give a permanent income to (a person, institution, etc.). **b** establish (an academic chair, annual prize, etc.) by providing the funds needed to maintain it. **2** (usu. foll. by *with*) enrich, provide, or invest with (a quality, ability, talent, etc.). □ **en·dowed** *adjective* [Anglo-French *endouer* (as EN-1, Old French *douer* from Latin *dotare* from *dos dotis* DOWER)]

en·dow·ment *noun* **1** the act or an instance of endowing. **2** assets, esp. property or income, with which a person or organization is endowed, esp. a fund the capital of which is never used but which generates interest to cover operating expenses. **3** (usu. in *pl.*) a skill, talent, quality, etc. with which a person or place is endowed.

end·paper *noun* a usu. blank leaf of paper at the beginning and end of a book, fixed to the inside cover.

end plate *noun* **1** a usu. flat, plate-like piece at the end of a thing. **2** *Anat.* a specialized structure forming the junction between a motor nerve fibre and a muscle fibre.

end·play *Bridge* ● *noun* a method of play in the last few tricks to force an opponent to make a disadvantageous lead. ● *transitive verb* force (an opponent's hand) by an endplay.

end point *noun* **1** a point at the end of a line. **2** the final stage of a process, esp. the point at which an effect is observed in titration, dilution, etc.

end product *noun* the final product, esp. of a manufacturing process, radioactive decay series, etc.

end result *noun* the final outcome.

end run *noun* *N Amer.* **1** *Football* an attempt by a player to run with the ball round the flank of his own team. **2** an evasive tactic, esp. in war or politics.

end-stopped *adjective* (of verse) having both a logical and syntactic pause at the end of each line.

end table *noun* a small, low table usu. placed at an end of a couch, beside a chair, etc.

end time *noun* (also **end times**) the time leading up to the end of the world and of human history.

endue /ɛnˈdjuː, ɛn-, ən-/ *transitive verb* (foll. by *with*) invest or provide (a person) with qualities, powers, etc. [earlier = induct, put on clothes: Middle English from Old French *enduire* from Latin *inducere* lead in, assoc. in sense with Latin *induere* put on (clothes)]

en·dur·ance /ɪnˈdjʊərəns, ɛn-, ən-/ *noun* **1** the fact, habit, or power of enduring something unpleasant (*beyond endurance*). **2 a** the ability of a person or thing to last, hold out, or withstand prolonged strain (*endurance test*). **b** the ability of a metal or other substance to withstand the repeated applications of stress. **3** the act of enduring. **4** a thing which is endured. [Old French from *endurer*: see ENDURE]

en·dure /ɪnˈdjʊr, ɛn-, ən-, -ˈdjɜr, -dʊr/ *verb* **1** *transitive* **a** (of a person) undergo (a difficulty, hardship, etc.), esp. without giving way. **b** (of a thing) withstand (strain, pressure, etc.) without being damaged, compromised, etc. **2** *transitive* **a** tolerate (a person) (*cannot endure him*). **b** (esp. with *neg.*; foll. by *to* + infin.) bear. **3** *intransitive* remain in existence, last, persist. **4** *transitive* submit to, experience without resisting. □ **en·dur·abil·ity** *noun* **en·dur·able** *adjective* **en·dur·ing** *adjective* **en·dur·ing·ly** *adverb* [Old French *endurer* from Latin *indurare* harden (as IN-2, *durus* hard)]

en·duro /ɪnˈdjʊəroʊ, ɛn-, ən-/ *noun* (*pl.* **-duros**) a long-distance race for motor vehicles, designed to test endurance rather than speed.

end use *noun* the final or intended use to which a thing is put or for which it is made.

end-user *noun* (often *attributive*) **1** the person, customer, etc. who is the intended ultimate recipient or user of a product. **2** *Computing* the final destination of information transferred within a system, e.g. an operator, program, etc.

end·ways *adverb* (also **end·wise**) **1** with its end uppermost, foremost, or towards the viewer. **2** end to end. **3** lengthwise.

En·dym·ion /ɛnˈdɪmiən/ *Gk Myth* a handsome youth, loved by the Moon (Selene), who caused him to sleep everlastingly so that she could enjoy his beauty for ever.

end zone *noun* *N Amer.* *Football* the rectangular area between the goal line and the end line at the end of the field into which the ball must be carried or passed to score a touchdown.

ENE *abbreviation* east-northeast.

-ene *suffix* **1** forming names of inhabitants of places (*Nazarene*). **2** *Chem.* forming names of unsaturated hydrocarbons containing a double bond (*benzene*; *ethylene*). [from or after Greek *-ēnos*]

enema /ˈɛnɪmə/ *noun* (*pl.* **enemas**) **1** the injection of liquid or gas into the rectum or colon, esp. to expel the contents. **2** a fluid so injected. **3** a syringe or other appliance used for this purpose. [Late Latin from Greek *enema* from *eniēmi* inject (as EN-2, *hiēmi* send)]

enemy *noun* (*pl.* **-emies**) **1 a** a person or group actively nursing hatred for or seeking to harm another person, group, or cause. **b** (usu. foll. by *of*, *to*) an adversary or opponent. **2 a** an armed foe, esp. another nation. **b** the hostile army or military force of a nation opposing or at war with one's own. **c** a member of such a force. **d** a hostile ship, aircraft, etc. **3** a thing that harms, injures, or is prejudicial to another. **4** (*attributive*) of or belonging to an enemy (*destroyed by enemy action*). □ **be one's own worst enemy** have the habit of bringing trouble upon oneself by one's own actions or behaviour. **enemy of the people** a person considered to be a negative influence in society. [Old French *enemi* from Latin *inimicus* (as IN-1, *amicus* friend)]

enemy alien *noun* esp. *hist.* a national of a country at war with the nation in which the person resides.

ener·get·ic *adjective* **1** having much energy or being strenuously active. **2** forcible, vigorous. **3** powerfully operative or effective. □ **ener·get·ic·ally** *adverb* [Greek *energētikos* from *energeō* (as EN-2, *ergon* work)]

ener·get·ics *plural noun* (usu. treated as *sing.*) **1** the branch of science that deals with energy. **2** the properties of a system as they concern its energy and its energy flow and changes.

ener·gize *transitive verb* (also esp. *Brit.* **-gise**) **1** infuse energy or vigour into (a person, work, movement, etc.). **2** provide energy for the operation of (a device), esp. by means of an electrical current. □ **ener·gized** *adjective* **ener·giz·er** *noun*

Ener·Guide *noun* *Cdn* (*attributive*) designating a rating of an appliance indicating its typical annual energy consumption. [blend of ENERGY + GUIDE]

ener·gumen /ˌɛnərˈɡjuːmɛn/ *noun* an enthusiast or fanatic. [Late Latin *energumenus* from Greek *energoumenos* passive part. of *energeō*: see ENERGETIC]

en·er·gy *noun* (*pl.* **-gies**) **1 a** a person's force, vigour, or capacity for and tendency to strenuous activity. **b** force or vigour of expression. **2** (in *pl.*) individual powers in use (*devote your energies to this*). **3** *Physics* **a** the quantity of work a system is capable of doing, usu. measured in joules. **b** this ability provided in a readily utilized form, such as an electric current or piped gas. **c** resources that can be drawn on for this purpose. **4** a latent ability or capacity to produce an effect. [French *énergie* or Late Latin *energia* from Greek *energeia* from *ergon* work]

energy drink *noun* a carbonated beverage containing high levels of usu. caffeine or other stimulants.

ener·vate /ˈenərˌveɪt/ *transitive verb* deprive of vigour, vitality, or strength, mentally, morally, or physically. □ **ener·vated** *adjective* **ener·vat·ing** *adjective* **ener·va·tion** *noun* [Latin *enervatus* past participle of *enervare* (as E-[1], *nervus* sinew)]

En·esco /eˈnesko/ **Georges** (1881–1955), Romanian violinist, composer, and conductor, noted for his use of Romanian folk song and dance rhythms in many of his works, which include the *Poème roumain* (1898) and the opera *Oedipus* (1936).

Ene·wetak see ENIWETOK.

en fa·mille /ˌɑ̃ faˈmiːj/ *adverb* **1** in or with one's family. **2** at home. **3** casually, informally. [French, = in family]

en·fant ter·rible /ˌɑ̃fɑ̃ teˈriːbl/ *noun* (*pl.* **enfants terribles** *pronunc.* same) a person whose behaviour, ideas, etc. annoy, shock, or embarrass those with more conventional attitudes or opinions. [French, = terrible child]

en·fee·ble *transitive verb* weaken, make feeble. □ **en·fee·bled** *adjective* **en·feeble·ment** *noun*

en fête /ˌɑ̃ ˈfet/ *adverb & predicative adjective* holding or ready for a holiday or celebration. [French, = in festival]

En·field *noun* (in full **Enfield rifle**) any of various bolt action rifles made at the Royal Small Arms Factory, Enfield, or designed in imitation of them. [after *Enfield*, an area of Greater London]

en·fil·ade /ˌenfiˈleɪd/ ● *noun* **1** a suite of rooms with doorways in line with each other. **2** gunfire directed along a line from end to end. ● *transitive verb* **1** subject (troops, a road, etc.) to an enfilade. **2** cover the whole length of (a target) with a gun or guns. [French from *enfiler* (as EN-[1], *fil* thread)]

en·fold *transitive verb* **1** (usu. foll. by *in, with*) wrap up, envelop, or enclose. **2** clasp, embrace, encompass, or encircle.

en·force *transitive verb* **1** compel performance or observance of (a law etc.). **2** (foll. by *on, upon*) produce or impose (an action, conduct, one's will) by force. **3** urge, press home, or persist in (a demand or argument). □ **en·force·able** *adjective* **en·force·abil·ity** *noun* [Old French *enforcir, -ier*, ultimately from Latin *fortis* strong]

en·force·ment *noun* the act or an instance of enforcing, esp. the process of compelling observance of a law, regulation, etc.

en·for·cer *noun* **1** a person, organization, etc. that enforces something. **2** *N Amer. Hockey* a highly aggressive player whose fighting and intimidation skills serve to protect other players on his team. **3** *slang* a person who imposes his will on others by violence and intimidation, esp. as a member of a criminal group.

en·fran·chise /ɪnˈfræntʃaɪz, en-, ən-/ *verb* **1** *transitive* grant (a person) the rights of a citizen, esp. the right to vote. **2** *intransitive Cdn* give up one's status as an Indian. **3** *transitive hist.* free (a slave, villein, etc.). □ **en·fran·chise·ment** /-aɪzmənt/, /-ɪzmənt/ *noun* [Old French *enfranchir* (as EN-[1], *franc franche* FRANK[1])]

ENG *abbreviation* electronic news gathering, a system of obtaining and reporting television news, esp. from the field and on location, through the use of portable cameras, sound equipment, etc.

Eng. *abbreviation* **1 a** English. **b** England. **2 a** Engineering. **b** Engineer.

en·gage *verb* **1** *transitive* arrange to employ or hire (a person). **2** *transitive* **a** (usu. in *passive*) be occupied or have a social or business engagement arranged (*sorry, I'm otherwise engaged tomorrow*). **b** attract and hold fast (a person's attention, interest, etc.). **c** draw (a person) into a conversation. **3 a** *transitive* (usu. foll. by *to* + infin.) bind by a legal or moral obligation, esp. by promise or contract. **b** *transitive* (usu. in *passive*) betroth or bind by a promise of marriage. **c** *intransitive* (foll. by *that* + clause or *to* + infin.) enter into a contract or pledge oneself. **4** *transitive* book, reserve, or secure for one's own use (a room, seat, etc.). **5** *Mech.* **a** *transitive* bring (a component) into operation (*engage the clutch*). **b** *transitive & intransitive* (usu. foll. by *with*) (of parts of a machine etc.) interlock or fit together to prevent or transmit movement (*one cogwheel engages with the other; the two cogwheels engaged and the machine started*).

c *transitive* cause (gears, cogs, etc.) to do this. **6 a** *transitive* enter into combat with or attack (an enemy etc.). **b** *transitive* bring (forces) into battle. **c** *intransitive* (usu. foll. by *with*) (of troops etc.) come into combat. **7** *intransitive* take part in or be occupied by (a thing) (*engage in politics*). **8** *transitive* (of combatants) bring (weapons) together in preparation for fighting. □ **en·gager** *noun* [French *engager*, related to GAGE[1]]

en·ga·gé /ɑ̃ˈɡazei/ ● *adjective* (of a writer, artist, etc.) showing social, moral, or political commitment. ● *noun Cdn hist.* (also **en·ga·ge**) a boatman, originally usu. French-Canadian, hired by a trader, explorer, or fur company to work the inland trade. [French, past participle of *engager*: see ENGAGE]

en·gaged *adjective* **1** under a promise to marry. **2** (of a person) occupied, busy. **3** *Brit.* (of a telephone line, toilet, etc.) unavailable because already in use. **4** *Archit.* (of a column) partly attached to a wall. **5** concerned, committed, actively participating in issues etc. (*an engaged, professional historian*). **6** (of gears etc.) in operation. **7** (of a baby's head) descended into the mother's pelvic area in the final weeks of pregnancy.

en·gage·ment *noun* **1** the act or state of engaging or being engaged. **2** an appointment with another person. **3** a betrothal. **4** an encounter between hostile forces. **5** a moral commitment or obligation. **6** a period or position of employment, esp. for a set term. **7** the period during which a theatrical performance is being produced at a given location.

engagement ring *noun* a usu. diamond ring given by a man to a woman when they promise to marry.

en·gaging *adjective* **1** pleasing, attractive, charming. **2** interesting. □ **en·gaging·ly** *adverb*

Engel /ˈeŋɡəl/ **Mar·ian** (1933–85), Canadian novelist and short-story writer. Her novels are centrally concerned with the situation of women in society, and include *No Clouds of Glory* (1968), *The Honeyman Festival* (1970), and *Bear* (1976), about the erotic relationship between a woman and a pet bear.

Engel·mann spruce /ˈeŋɡəlmən/ *noun* a spruce of the Rocky Mountains, *Picea engelmannii*, used for lumber and wood pulp. [G. *Engelmann*, botanist and physician, d.1884]

En·gels /ˈeŋɡəlz/ **Frie·drich** (1820–95), German socialist and political philosopher. The founder of modern communism with Marx, he collaborated with him on the *Communist Manifesto* (1848) and completed the second and third volumes of Marx's *Das Kapital* (1885; 1894); his own writings include *The Condition of the Working Classes in England in 1844* (1845).

en·gen·der /ɪnˈdʒendər, en-, ən-/ *transitive verb* give rise to; bring about (a feeling etc.). [Old French *engendrer* from Latin *ingenerare* (as IN-[2], *generare* GENERATE)]

en·gine *noun* **1** a machine for producing energy of motion from some other form of energy, esp. heat that the machine itself generates. **2 a** a railway locomotive. **b** = FIRE ENGINE. **c** a stationary steam engine. **3** (foll. by *of*) a thing that is an agent or instrument of a desired end or achievement (*drive the engine of progress faster*). **4** *archaic* a machine or instrument, esp. a contrivance used in warfare or torture. □ **en·gined** *adjective* (also in *combination*). **en·gine·less** *adjective* [Old French *engin* from Latin *ingenium* talent, device: compare INGENIOUS]

engine block *noun* (also esp. *Brit.* **cylinder block**) *N Amer.* the metal casting housing the cylinders etc. of an internal combustion engine.

en·gin·eer ● *noun* **1** a person qualified in any branch of engineering, esp. as a qualified professional. **2** = CIVIL ENGINEER. **3 a** a person who designs or makes engines. **b** a technician, mechanic, or other person who is in charge of or maintains an engine or other machine (*stationary engineer*). **4** *N Amer.* a person who drives an engine, esp. a railway locomotive. **5** a soldier in a division of an army that specializes in engineering and the design as well as construction of military works. **6** (foll. by *of*) a skilful or artful plotter or contriver. ● *verb* **1** *transitive* arrange, contrive, or bring about, esp. artfully. **2** *transitive* design, make, or build as an engineer. **3** *transitive* deliberately alter or modify some specific aspect of a particular model, substance, etc., e.g. genes.

en·gin·eer·ing *noun* **1** the application of science for directly useful purposes, as construction, propulsion, communication, or manufacture. **2** the work done by or the occupation of an engineer. **3** the action of working artfully to bring something about. **4** a field of study or activity concerned with deliberate alteration or modification in some particular area (*genetic engineering*).

engine house *noun* a building in which an engine is kept or maintained.

engine room *noun* a room containing engines, esp. a ship's engines.

Eng·land a part of Great Britain and the UK, largely made up of the area south of the Tweed River, and containing the capital, London; pop. (2001) 49,138,831. (*See also* GREAT BRITAIN.)

Eng·lish ● *adjective* **1** of or relating to England, its language, its people or their descendants. **2** *Cdn* of or relating to English-speaking Canadians. ● *noun* **1 a** the language descended from that of the Germanic invaders of England in the 5th c. **b** (*pl.* **-es**) a regional variety of this. **2** (prec. by *the*; treated as *pl.*) **a** the people of England. **b** English-speaking people. **3** English language or literature as a subject to be studied. **4** *N Amer.* Billiards a spinning motion given to a ball by hitting it on one side rather than centrally. □ **Eng·lish·ness** *noun* [Old English *englisc*, *ænglisc* (as ANGLE, -ISH¹)]

English bond *noun* a bond of brickwork arranged in alternate courses of stretchers and headers.

English breakfast *noun* **1** a substantial breakfast usu. including bacon or sausages, eggs, toast and condiments, and tea or coffee. **2** (usu. **English Breakfast**) a blend of tea originally made of black teas from Northern China but now more commonly made of blends of Ceylon or Indian teas.

English Canada *noun Cdn* the areas of Canada where English-speaking Canadians predominate, as distinct from French Canada and esp. Quebec.

English Canadian ● *noun* **1** an English-speaking Canadian. **2** a Canadian of English descent. ● *adjective* (**English-Canadian**) of, by, or pertaining to English Canada or English Canadians.

English Channel the sea channel separating S England from N France. It is 35 km (22 miles) wide at its narrowest point. A railway tunnel beneath it linking England and France was opened in 1994.

English Church 1 the Anglican Church. **2** an Anglican church.

English Civil War the war between the supporters of Charles I (the Royalists, or Cavaliers) and his Parliamentary opponents (the Roundheads), 1642–9. After several years of warfare, the better-organized Parliamentary forces gained the upper hand in 1644–5, with Royalist resistance collapsing in 1646. An attempt by Charles to regain power in alliance with the Scots was defeated at Preston in 1648, Charles himself being tried and executed by Parliament in 1649. The war dramatically changed the nature of English society and government, even though the attempt to find an alternative to the monarchy eventually ended with the restoration of Charles II after the death of Oliver Cromwell, the Parliamentary leader.

English cucumber *noun N Amer.* a long, thin-skinned, seedless variety of cucumber.

English garden *noun* a garden typically having a large proportion of perennial flowers and flowering shrubs laid out in a fairly informal design.

English horn *noun* = COR ANGLAIS.

English ivy *noun* an ivy with many cultivated varieties, *Hedera helix*, grown both in gardens as climbers and ground cover and as houseplants.

Eng·lish·man *noun* (*pl.* **-men**) a man who is English by birth, descent, or naturalization.

English muffin *noun N Amer.* a small, round, flat, yeast bread, usu. served split and toasted.

English Pale 1 the small area round Calais, the only part of France remaining in English hands after the Hundred Years War. It was recaptured by France in 1558. **2** (also **the Pale**) that part of Ireland centred on Dublin over which England exercised jurisdiction from the reign of Henry II until the full conquest of Ireland under Elizabeth I. [PALE²]

English River a river in NW Ontario, which rises in Lac Seul and flows westward to join the Winnipeg River at the border with Manitoba. [so called because it formed part of the British fur trade route]

English walnut *noun* the common walnut tree, *Juglans regia*, native to Europe and Asia, grown commercially for its nuts and timber.

Eng·lish·woman *noun* (*pl.* **-women**) a woman who is English by birth, descent, or naturalization.

en·gorge *transitive verb* cause to swell with blood, water, breast milk, or another fluid. □ **en·gorged** *adjective* **en·gorge·ment** *noun* [French *engorger* (as EN-¹, GORGE)]

en·grain *var. of* INGRAIN.

en·grained *var. of* INGRAINED.

en·gram /ˈɛŋɡram/ *noun* a supposed permanent and physical change in the brain accounting for the existence of memory.

en·gram·mat·ic /-ɡrəˈmatɪk/ *adjective* [German *Engramm* from Greek *en* in + *gramma* letter of the alphabet]

en·grave *transitive verb* **1** (often foll. by *on*) inscribe, cut, or carve (a text or design) on a hard surface. **2** (often foll. by *with*) inscribe or ornament (a surface) with incised marks. **3 a** cut or produce (a design) for printing by removing parts of the surface of a plate or block. **b** produce (a representation of such a picture, lettering, etc.) from such a surface. **4** (often foll. by *on*) impress deeply or indelibly on a person's memory etc. □ **en·graved** *adjective* **en·grav·er** *noun* [EN-¹ + GRAVE³]

en·grav·ing *noun* **1** a print made from an engraved plate. **2** the process or art of cutting a design etc. on metal, stone, etc. **3** an engraved figure, design, or inscription.

en·gross /ɪnˈɡroːs, en-, ən-/ *transitive verb* **1 a** (of an object of thought or feeling) fully occupy (the mind, affections, etc.). **b** (usu. in *passive*; usu. foll. by *with*) absorb the whole attention of (a person) (*was engrossed in studying*). **2** make a fair copy of, esp. produce (a legal document) in its final or definitive form. **3** *hist.* reproduce (a document etc.) in larger letters or larger format, esp. in a particular script derived from an ancient court hand. **4** monopolize (a market etc.) or concentrate (property, privileges, functions, etc.) in one's own possessions. □ **en·gross·ed·ly** *adverb* **en·gross·ing** *adjective* (in sense 1). **en·gross·ment** *noun* [Anglo-French *engrosser*: senses 2 and 3 from *en* in + *grosse* large writing: senses 1 and 4 from *en gros* wholesale]

en·gulf *transitive verb* **1** flow over and swamp or swallow up as in a gulf, abyss, etc. **2** overwhelm, engross, or affect powerfully. □ **en·gulf·ment** *noun*

en·hance *transitive verb* **1 a** heighten or intensify (qualities, powers, value, etc.). **b** exaggerate or make (a colour etc.) appear greater or brighter, esp. by contrast. **c** raise (a price) or increase (a cost). **2 a** improve (a thing), esp. in quality or utility. **b** add on to or provide (a computer etc.) with more advanced, complex, or sophisticated features. □ **en·hance·ment** *noun* **en·han·cer** *noun* [Anglo-French *enhauncer*, prob. alteration from Old French *enhaucier*, ultimately from Latin *altus* high]

en·har·mon·ic /ˌɛnhɑrˈmɒnɪk/ *adjective* Music of or having intervals smaller than a semitone (esp. such intervals as that between G sharp and A flat, these notes being made the same in a scale of equal temperament). □ **en·har·mon·ic·ally** *adverb* [Late Latin *enharmonicus* from Greek *enarmonikos* (as EN-², *harmonia* HARMONY)]

en·ig·ma /ɪˈnɪɡmə, en-, ən-/ *noun* **1 a** a puzzling, perplexing, or unexplained thing. **b** a person who baffles others' conjecture as to his or her character, identity, etc. **2** a riddle or paradox, usu. involving metaphor. □ **en·ig·mat·ic** /ˌenɪɡˈmatɪk/ *adjective* **en·ig·mat·ic·al** /ˌenɪɡˈmatɪkəl/ *adjective* **en·ig·mat·ic·al·ly** /ˌenɪɡˈmatɪkli/ *adverb* [Latin *aenigma* from Greek *ainigma* -*matos* from *ainissomai* speak allusively, from *ainos* fable]

Eni·wetok /eˈniːwəˌtɒk, ˌenəˈwiːtɒk/ (also **Ene·wetak**) an uninhabited island in the N Pacific, one of the Marshall Islands. Cleared of its Aboriginal population, it was used by the US as a testing ground for atomic bombs from 1948 to 1954.

en·jamb·ment /enˈdʒambmənt, enˈdʒamənt/ *noun* (also **en·jambe·ment**) *Prosody* the continuation of a sentence without a pause beyond the end of a line, couplet, or stanza. □ **en·jamb** *transitive verb* **en·jambed** *adjective* [French *enjambement* from *enjamber* (as EN-¹, *jambe* leg)]

en·join *transitive verb* **1** (foll. by *to* + infin.) command, order, or call upon (a person). **2** (often foll. by *on*) impose or prescribe (an action or conduct). **3** *Law* (usu. foll. by *from*) prohibit or restrain (a person) by an injunction. [Old French *enjoindre* from Latin *injungere* (as IN-², *jungere* join)]

en·joy *verb* **1** *transitive* take delight or pleasure in. **2** *transitive* have the use or benefit of (something pleasant or advantageous). **3** *transitive* experience (*enjoy good health*). **4** *intransitive* esp. *N Amer.* have an enjoyable experience. □ **enjoy oneself** experience pleasure. □ **en·joy·ment** *noun* [Old French *enjoier* give joy to or *enjoïr* enjoy, ultimately from Latin *gaudēre* rejoice]

en·joy·able *adjective* pleasant, giving enjoyment, able to be enjoyed. □ **en·joy·able·ness** *noun* **en·joy·ably** *adverb*

en·keph·alin /enˈkefəlɪn/ *noun Biochem.* either of two morphine-like peptides occurring naturally in the brain and thought to control levels of pain (*compare* ENDORPHIN). [Greek *egkephalos* brain]

en·kindle /ɪnˈkɪndəl, en-, ən-/ *transitive verb literary* **1** cause (flames) to flare up. **2** excite, arouse, or inflame (strong feelings, passion, etc.).

en·lace *transitive verb* **1** encircle tightly. **2** interlace, entangle, or entwine. [Old French *enlacier*, ultimately from Latin *laqueus* noose]

en·large *verb* **1 a** *transitive & intransitive* make or become larger or wider.

---

uː m**oo**d   aɪ m**y**   əɪ p**i**pe   au br**ow**n   ʌu h**ou**se   ei d**ay**   ɔi b**oy**   ã fr**an**glais   ã Cana**di**en   ɔ̃ Br**ay**on   (*see over for consonants*)

b *transitive* make more comprehensive or increase in range or scope. **2 a** *transitive* describe in greater detail. **b** *intransitive* (usu. foll. by *upon*) write or speak at great length or in detail. **3** *transitive* produce an enlargement of (a photographic negative). □ **en·larged** *adjective*

en·large·ment *noun* **1 a** an act or instance of increasing in size, extent, or scope. **b** the state of being enlarged. **2** *Photog.* a print that is larger than the negative from which it is produced.

en·larg·er *noun* an apparatus for producing photographic enlargements.

en·light·en *transitive verb* **1** (often foll. by *on*) instruct or inform (about a subject). **2** free from prejudice or superstition. **3** *literary* illuminate or shed light on (an object). **4** give spiritual knowledge or insight to (a person). □ **en·light·en·ing** *adjective*

en·light·ened *adjective* having or showing an understanding of people's needs, a situation, etc. that is not based on old-fashioned attitudes and prejudice (*enlightened opinions; an enlightened approach to teaching; people often act out of enlightened self-interest; for instance, an employer who improves working conditions may improve profits*).

en·light·en·ment *noun* **1 a** the act or an instance of enlightening. **b** the state of being enlightened. **2** (**the Enlightenment**) the 18th-c. philosophical movement in Europe in which reason and individualism were emphasized at the expense of tradition. **3** *Buddhism* a state of pure and unqualified knowledge and intuitive insight, of perfect clarity of mind in which things are seen as they truly are.

en·list *verb* **1** *intransitive & transitive* enrol in the armed forces. **2** *transitive* engage or secure (a person etc.) as a means of help or support. □ **en·list·er** *noun* **en·list·ment** *noun*

en·list·ed man *noun* US a soldier or sailor below the rank of commissioned or warrant officer, esp. one below a non-commissioned or petty officer.

en·liven /ɪnˈlaɪvən/ *transitive verb* **1** animate, invigorate, give fuller life or spirit to. **2** brighten, make cheerful, or relieve the monotony or dreariness of (a picture, scene, etc.). □ **en·liven·er** *noun* **en·liven·ing** *adjective* **en·liven·ment** *noun*

en masse /ɑ̃ ˈmas/ *adverb* in a mass, all together, or as a group. [French]

en·mesh *transitive verb* catch or entangle in or as in a net. □ **en·mesh·ment** *noun*

en·mity /ˈenmɪti/ *noun* (pl. **-ties**) **1** the condition of being an enemy or a state of mutual hostility. **2** a feeling of hostility, hatred, or ill-will. [Old French *enemitié* from Romanic (as ENEMY)]

en·nead /ˈeniˌad/ *noun* a group of nine. [Greek *enneas enneados* from *ennea* nine]

Ennis /ˈenɪs/ the county town of Clare, in the Republic of Ireland; pop. (2002) 18,977.

en·noble *transitive verb* **1** refine, dignify, or elevate in nature, character etc. **2** give the rank of noble to (a person). □ **en·noble·ment** *noun* **en·nob·ling** *adjective*

ennui /ɒˈnwiː/ *noun* boredom or mental weariness from lack of occupation or interest. [French from Latin *in odio*: compare ODIUM]

Enoch /ˈiːnɒk/ *Bible* **1** the eldest son of Cain. **2** the first city, built by Cain and named after Enoch (Gen. 4:17). **3** a Hebrew patriarch, father of Methuselah. Two works ascribed to him, the *Book of Enoch* and the *Book of the Secrets of Enoch*, date from the 2nd–1st c. BC and 1st c. AD respectively.

enoki /iˈnɒkiː/ *noun* a long-stemmed edible white Japanese mushroom with a tiny cap. [Japanese *enoki(-take)* Chinese nettle tree (mushroom)]

enol·ogy N Amer. var. of OENOLOGY.

enor·mity *noun* (pl. **-ties**) **1** monstrous wickedness (*recognized the enormity of his crime*). **2** an act of extreme wickedness. **3** *disputed* great size, enormousness, or daunting magnitude. **4** a serious irregularity or a gross error. [French *énormité* from Latin *enormitas -tatis* from *enormis* (as ENORMOUS)] ¶ Though regarded as incorrect by many people, the use of *enormity* in sense 3, e.g. *the enormity of the problem*, is well established and has been in continuous use since the 18th c.

enor·mous *adjective* huge, very great, excessive in size or intensity (*enormous animals; an enormous difference*). □ **enor·mous·ly** *adverb* **enor·mous·ness** *noun* [Latin *enormis* (as E-¹, *norma* pattern, standard)]

eno·sis /ˈenɒsɪs/ *noun* political union as an ideal or proposal, esp. that between Cyprus and Greece. [modern Greek *enōsis* from *ena* one]

enough ● *adjective* as much or as many as required (*we have enough apples; we do not have enough sugar; earned enough money to buy a house*). ● *noun* as much as is needed or that which is sufficient (*we have enough of everything now; enough is as good as a feast*). ● *adverb* **1** sufficiently, adequately, or to the required degree (*are you warm enough?*). **2** fairly,

tolerably, or passably (*she sings well enough*). **3** very, fully, quite (*you know well enough what I mean; oddly enough*). ● *interjection* that is enough (in various senses, esp. to put an end to an action, thing said, etc.). □ **enough is enough** stop, no more. **enough said** no more need be said. **have enough to do** (**to achieve something**) have no easy task. **have had enough of** be satiated with, tired of, or want no more of. [Old English *genog* from Germanic]

en pas·sant /ˌã paˈsã/ *adverb* in passing, by the way. □ **take a pawn en passant** *Chess* with one's own pawn on the fifth rank, take an opponent's pawn that has just made an initial move of two squares as if it had advanced only one square. [French, = in passing]

en·plane var. of EMPLANE.

en·quire var. of INQUIRE.

en·quiry var. of INQUIRY.

en·rage *transitive verb* (often foll. by *at, by, with*) make furious or very angry. □ **en·raged** *adjective*

en·rap·ture *transitive verb* give intense pleasure or joy to.

en·rich *transitive verb* **1 a** make wealthy or wealthier. **b** endow with mental or spiritual wealth. **2 a** enhance, heighten or make (a thing) richer in quality, colour, flavour, etc. **b** fertilize or make (soil or land) more productive. **c** improve the nutritive quality of (food) by adding vitamins etc. **3** add something valuable or worthwhile to the contents of (a collection, museum, book, etc.). **4** N Amer. make (a course or program of study) more challenging, esp. by adding activities, coursework, etc., which is not part of the standard curriculum. **5** increase the proportion of a particular constituent in (a substance), esp. enrich uranium with isotope U-235. □ **en·riched** *adjective* **en·rich·ing** *adjective* **en·rich·ment** *noun*

en·robe *transitive verb* **1** cover with a coating. **2** dress in a robe, vestment, etc. □ **en·rober** *noun*

en·rol *verb* (also **en·roll**) (**en·rolled, en·rol·ling**) **1** *intransitive* **a** enter one's name on a list or register, esp. as a commitment to membership of a society, class, etc. **b** join, esp. as a member, student, etc. **2** *transitive* **a** write the name of (a person) on a list for membership etc. **b** (usu. foll. by *in*) incorporate (a person) as a member of a society etc. **3** *transitive hist.* enter (a deed etc.) among the rolls of a court of justice. □ **en·rol·lee** *noun* [Old French *enroller* (as EN-¹, *rolle* ROLL)]

en·rol·ment *noun* (also **en·roll·ment**) **1 a** the act or an instance of enrolling. **b** the state of being enrolled. **2** N Amer. the number of persons enrolled, esp. at a school, university, etc.

en route /ã ˈruːt/ *adverb* (usu. foll. by *to, for*) on or along the way. [French]

en·sconce *transitive verb* (usu. *reflexive* or in *passive*) establish or settle comfortably, safely, or secretly.

en·sem·ble /ɒnˈsɒmbəl/ *noun* **1 a** a thing viewed as the sum of its parts. **b** the general effect of this. **2** an outfit or a set of clothes that harmonizes and is worn together. **3** a group of actors, dancers, musicians, etc. who perform together in a production, esp. the supporting members as opposed to the stars or principals. **4** *Music* **a** a group of singers or musicians, esp. a small group of soloists, who perform together. **b** a piece of music sung or played by the whole group of musicians rather than by soloists. **c** the manner in which this is performed (*good ensemble*). **5** *Math.* a group of systems with the same constitution but possibly in different states. [French, ultimately from Latin *insimul* (as IN-², *simul* at the same time)]

en·shrine *transitive verb* **1** enclose in or as in a shrine. **2** integrate (a right, principle, etc.) into a law, constitution, etc. so as to preserve it perpetually. **3** contain or embody in a way that preserves, protects, or cherishes. □ **en·shrine·ment** *noun*

en·shroud *transitive verb* **1** cover with or as with a shroud. **2** cover completely or hide from view.

en·sign /ˈensaɪn, -sən/ *noun* **1 a** a military or naval standard, esp. a flag flown at the stern of a vessel to show its nationality. **b** each of three such standards with the union flag in the corner (*see also* BLUE ENSIGN, RED ENSIGN, WHITE ENSIGN). **2** US the lowest commissioned officer in the navy or coast guard. [Old French *enseigne* from Latin *insignia*: see INSIGNIA]

en·sil·age /ˈensɪlɪdʒ, ˈɪn-/ ● *noun* **1** the process of preserving green crops in a silo or pit without having previously dried them. **2** the material resulting from this process. *Also called* SILAGE. ● *transitive verb* = ENSILE.

en·sile /ɪnˈsaɪl, en-/ *transitive verb* **1** put (fodder) into a silo or closed pit for preservation. **2** convert (fodder) into ensilage. [French *ensiler* from Spanish *ensilar* (as EN-¹, SILO)]

en·slave *transitive verb* **1** make (a person) completely subject to or

Consonants: b *but*   d *dog*   f *few*   g *get*   h *her*   j *yes*   k *cat*   l *leg*   m *man*   n *no*   p *pen*   r *red*   s *sit*

dominated by habit, superstition, passion, etc. **2** reduce (a person) to slavery or deprive (a person) of political freedom. □ **en·slave·ment** noun **en·slav·er** noun

en·snare transitive verb entrap, entangle in difficulties, or catch in or as in a snare.

en·soul transitive verb endow with a soul. □ **en·soul·ment** noun

ensue intransitive verb **1** be subsequent or happen afterwards. **2** (often foll. by from) occur as a result or consequence. □ **en·su·ing** adjective [Old French ensuivre, ultimately from Latin sequi follow]

en·suite /ɑ̃ˈswiːt/ Cdn & Brit. ● adverb forming a single unit, with one room leading into another (bedroom with bathroom ensuite). ● adjective (of a room) immediately adjoining or forming part of the same set. ● noun an ensuite room, esp. an ensuite bathroom. [French, = in sequence]

en·sure transitive verb **1** (often foll. by that + clause) make certain the occurrence of (an event, situation, outcome, etc.). **2** (usu. foll. by to, for) secure (a thing for a person etc.). **3** (usu. foll. by against) make safe from a risk etc. **4** esp. N Amer. = INSURE 1-3. [Anglo-French enseürer from Old French aseürer ASSURE]

ENT abbreviation Med. ear, nose, and throat.

-ent suffix **1** forming adjectives denoting existence of an action (consequent) or state (existent). **2** forming nouns denoting an agent (coefficient; president). [from or after French -ent or Latin -ent- pres. part. stem of verbs (compare -ANT)]

en·tabla·ture /ɪnˈtablətʃər, en-/ noun Archit. the upper part of a classical building supported by columns or a colonnade, comprising architrave, frieze, and cornice. [Italian intavolatura from intavolare board up (as IN-², tavola table)]

en·table·ment /ɪnˈteibəlmənt, en-/ noun a platform supporting a statue, above the dado and base. [French, from entabler (as EN-¹, TABLE)]

en·tail ● transitive verb **1** necessitate as a consequence, have as an inevitable accompaniment, or involve unavoidably (the work entails much effort). **2** Law bequeath (property etc.) so that it remains within a family. ● noun Law **1** the settlement of the succession of land or other property so that it cannot subsequently be bequeathed or sold, but must pass to a designated class of descendants. **2** the line of succession so prescribed. □ **en·tail·ment** noun [Middle English, from EN-¹ + Anglo-French taile TAIL²]

en·tan·gle transitive verb **1** cause to get caught in something that is tangled or that impedes movement or extrication. **2** interlace or cause to become tangled so that separation is difficult. **3 a** involve (a person) in difficulties, doubtful undertakings, etc. **b** involve (a person) in a compromising relationship etc. **4** make (a thing) tangled, complicated, or intricate.

en·tangle·ment noun **1** the act or condition of entangling or being entangled. **2 a** a thing that entangles. **b** a complication or embarrassment. **3** Military an extensive barrier, esp. one made of stakes and interlaced barbed wire, designed to obstruct an enemy's movements. **4** a compromising, esp. amorous, relationship.

en·tasis /ˈentəsɪs/ noun Archit. a slight convex curve in a column shaft to correct the visual illusion that straight sides give of curving inwards. [modern Latin from Greek enteinō to stretch]

En·tebbe /enˈtebi/ a town in S Uganda, on the north shore of Lake Victoria; pop. (est. 2002) 57,400. It was the capital of Uganda during the period of British rule, from 1894 to 1962.

en·tel·echy /enˈteləki, ɪn-/ noun (pl. **-echies**) Philos. **1 a** (in Aristotle's use) the condition in which a potentiality has become an actuality, esp. the soul, essential nature, or informing principle of a living thing. **b** (in Leibniz's use) a monad. **2** a supposed vital principle that guides the development and functioning of an organism. [Late Latin entelechia from Greek entelekheia, from telos 'end, perfection' + ekhein 'be in a state']

en·tente /ɒnˈtɒnt/ noun **1** = ENTENTE CORDIALE. **2** a group of nations in such a relation. **3** an agreement to co-operate between esp. opposing parties. [French, = understanding (as INTENT)]

entente cor·di·ale /ɑ̃,tɑ̃t kɔrdiˈal/ noun (pl. **ententes cor·di·ales**) a friendly understanding between nations, esp. (often **Entente Cordiale**) that reached in 1904 between Britain and France settling outstanding colonial disputes. [French, = cordial understanding: see ENTENTE]

en·ter ● verb **1 a** intransitive (often foll. by into) go or come in. **b** transitive go or come into (a place etc.). **c** transitive come or pass into (a certain condition). **2 a** transitive pierce, penetrate, or go through (a bullet entered his chest). **b** transitive (of a male) have sexual intercourse with. **3** transitive **a** write or record (particulars) in a list, register, account book, etc. **b** input (data) into a computer or issue (a command) to a computer

program. **4 a** intransitive register or announce oneself as a competitor (entered for the long jump). **b** transitive become a competitor in (an event). **c** transitive submit (an animal, inanimate object) for judging in a competition (entered Bathsheba in the cat show). **5** transitive **a** enrol as or become a member or prospective member of (a society, school, etc.). **b** procure admission into a society etc. for (a person). **6** transitive introduce, make known, or present (a matter etc.) for consideration (entered a protest). **7** transitive put into an official record, esp. record in due form in a court of law, deliberative body, etc. **8** intransitive (foll. by into) **a** engage in (conversation, relations, an undertaking, etc.). **b** subscribe to or bind oneself by (an agreement etc.). **c** form part of (one's calculations, plans, etc.). **d** sympathize with (feelings etc.). **9** intransitive (foll. by on, upon) **a** begin, undertake, or begin to deal with (a subject). **b** assume the functions of (an office). **10** transitive assume possession of (property), esp. as an assertion of ownership. **11** intransitive come on stage (as a direction: enter Macbeth). ● noun the key on a computer keyboard or button on a computer window which when pressed or clicked instructs the computer to execute a command or enters a blank line into a text. □ **en·ter·er** noun [Old French entrer from Latin intrare]

en·ter·ic /enˈterɪk/ adjective of, pertaining to, or occurring in the intestines. [Greek enterikos (as ENTERO-)]

enteric-coated adjective (of a capsule) coated so that the contents are released in the intestine after passing, unaltered, through the stomach so as to minimize stomach upset.

enteric fever noun typhoid.

en·ter·itis /entəˈraitɪs/ noun inflammation of the small intestine, often causing diarrhea.

entero- /ˈentərɔ/ combining form intestine. [Greek enteron intestine]

entero·bac·teria /,entərɔˈbaktɪriə/ noun (sing. **entero·bac·ter·ium** /-riəm/) a class of rod-like, Gram-negative bacteria that occur either normally or pathologically in the intestine, e.g. salmonella.

entero·col·itis /,entərɔkəˈlaitɪs/ noun inflammation of the small intestine and the colon.

enter·os·tomy /,entəˈrɒstəmi/ noun (pl. **-mies**) Surgery a surgical operation in which the small intestine is brought through the abdominal wall and opened, in order to bypass the stomach or the colon.

entero·virus /,entərɔˈvairəs/ noun a genus of small RNA viruses which typically occur in the gastrointestinal tract, but include the poliovirus and the virus of hepatitis A.

Enter·phone noun esp. Cdn proprietary an intercom device at an entrance to a building by which callers may identify themselves to gain admission.

en·ter·prise noun **1** an undertaking, esp. a bold or difficult one. **2** (as a personal attribute) readiness to engage in such undertakings (discouraged individual enterprise). **3** a business. **4** businesses collectively. **5** activity undertaken with an economic or commercial end in view. See also FREE ENTERPRISE, PRIVATE ENTERPRISE. □ **en·ter·pris·er** noun [Old French entreprise fem. past participle of entreprendre var. of emprendre, ultimately from Latin prendere, prehendere take]

enterprise zone noun Brit. & US a depressed (usu. urban) area where government incentives such as tax concessions are designed to encourage investment.

en·ter·pris·ing adjective **1** ready to engage in enterprises. **2** resourceful, imaginative, energetic. □ **en·ter·pris·ing·ly** adverb

en·ter·tain verb **1** transitive amuse; occupy agreeably. **2 a** transitive receive or treat as a guest. **b** intransitive receive guests (they entertain a great deal). **3** transitive give attention or consideration to (an idea, feeling, or proposal). [French entretenir, ultimately from Latin tenēre hold]

en·ter·tain·er noun a person who entertains, esp. professionally on stage etc.

en·ter·tain·ing adjective amusing, diverting. □ **en·ter·tain·ing·ly** adverb

en·ter·tain·ment noun **1** the act or an instance of entertaining; the process of being entertained. **2** a public performance or show. **3** diversions or amusements for guests etc. **4** amusement (much to my entertainment). **5** hospitality.

entertainment centre noun **1 a** a combination of components such as a television, VCR, stereo console, etc. **b** a large shelving unit used to hold these. **2** a place offering entertainment.

en·thalpy /ˈenθalpi, enˈθalpi/ noun Physics the total thermodynamic heat content of a system. [Greek enthalpō warm in (as EN-¹, thalpō to heat)]

en·thrall *transitive verb* (also **en·thral**) (**-thralled, -thrall·ing**) **1** captivate, please greatly. **2** enslave. □ **en·thrall·ing** *adjective* **en·thrall·ment** *noun* (also **en·thral·ment**).

en·throne *transitive verb* (usu. in *passive*) **1** install (a king, bishop, etc.) on a throne, esp. ceremonially. **2** exalt. □ **en·throne·ment** *noun*

en·thuse /ɪnˈθuːz, -ˈθjuːz, en-, ən-/ *transitive & intransitive verb informal* **1** be or make enthusiastic. **2** (often foll. by *about*) speak enthusiastically. [back-formation from ENTHUSIASM]

en·thusi·asm /ɪnˈθuːziˌazəm, -ˈθjuːziˌazəm, en-, ən-/ *noun* **1** (often foll. by *for, about*) **a** strong interest or admiration. **b** great eagerness. **2** an object of enthusiasm. [French *enthousiasme* or Late Latin *enthusiasmus* from Greek *enthousiasmos* from *entheos* 'possessed by a god, inspired' (as EN-², *theos* god)]

en·thusi·ast /ɪnˈθuːziˌast, -ˈθjuːziˌast, en-, ən-, -iəst/ *noun* **1** a person who is full of enthusiasm. **2** *archaic* a person of intense and visionary Christian views.

en·thusi·astic /ɪnˌθuːziˈastɪk, -ˌθjuːziˈastɪk, en-, ən-/ *adjective* having or showing enthusiasm. □ **en·thusi·astic·ally** *adverb*

en·thy·meme /ˈenθɪˌmiːm/ *noun Logic* a syllogism in which one premise is not explicitly stated. [Latin *enthymema* from Greek *enthumēma* from *enthumeomai* consider (as EN-², *thumos* mind)]

en·tice *transitive verb* (often foll. by *from, into,* or *to* + infin.) lure or attract by the offer of pleasure or reward. □ **en·tice·ment** *noun* **en·ticer** *noun* **en·ticing** *adjective* **en·ticing·ly** *adverb* [Old French *enticier* prob. from Romanic]

en·tire ● *attributive adjective* **1** whole, complete. **2** not broken or decayed. **3** unqualified, absolute (*an entire success*). **4** in one piece; continuous. **5** (esp. of a horse) not castrated. **6** *Bot.* without indentation. ● *noun* an uncastrated animal, esp. a horse. [Old French *entier* from Latin *integer* (as IN-², *tangere* touch)]

en·tire·ly *adverb* **1** wholly, completely (*the stock is entirely exhausted*). **2** solely, exclusively (*did it entirely for my benefit*).

en·tire·ty /ɪnˈtaɪrəti, ɪnˈtaɪrti, enˈtaɪrti, ən-/ *noun* **1** completeness. **2** (usu. foll. by *of*) the sum total. □ **in its entirety** in its complete form; completely.

en·title *transitive verb* **1 a** (usu. foll. by *to*) give (a person etc.) a just claim. **b** (foll. by *to* + infin.) give (a person etc.) a right. **2** give (a book etc.) the title of.

en·title·ment *noun* **1** something to which a person is entitled, esp. a social benefit. **2** the fact of being entitled or qualified.

en·tity /ˈentɪti/ *noun* (pl. **-ties**) **1** a thing with distinct and independent existence. **2** existence; being. [French *entité* or medieval Latin *entitas* from Late Latin *ens* being]

ento- *combining form* within. [Greek *entos* within]

en·tomb /ɪnˈtuːm, en-, ən-/ *transitive verb* **1** place in or as in a tomb. **2** serve as a tomb for. □ **en·tomb·ment** *noun*

entomo- /ˈentəmoʊ/ *combining form* insect. [Greek *entomos* cut up (in neuter = INSECT) from EN-² + *temnō* cut]

ento·mol·ogy /ˌentəˈmɒlədʒi/ *noun* the study of the forms and behaviour of insects. □ **ento·mo·logic·al** *adjective* **ento·mol·o·gist** *noun*

ento·moph·a·gous /ˌentəˈmɒfəgəs/ *adjective Zool.* insect-eating.

ento·moph·il·ous /ˌentəˈmɒfɪləs/ *adjective Biol.* pollinated by insects.

ento·para·site /ˌentoʊˈperəˌsaɪt/ *noun Biol.* = ENDOPARASITE.

ento·phyte /ˈentoʊˌfaɪt/ *Bot.* var. of ENDOPHYTE.

en·tour·age /ˈɒntʊˌrɒʒ/ *noun* **1** people attending an esp. important person. **2** surroundings. [French from *entourer* surround]

entr'acte /ˈɒntrakt/ *noun* **1** an interval between two acts of a play. **2** a piece of music or a dance performed during this. [French from *entre* 'between' + *acte* 'act']

en·trails /ˈentreɪlz/ *plural noun* **1** the intestines of a person or animal. **2** the internal organs. **3** the innermost parts (*entrails of the earth*). [Old French *entrailles* from medieval Latin *intralia* alteration of Latin *interaneus* internal, from *inter* among]

en·train¹ /ɪnˈtreɪn, en-, ən-/ *transitive verb* **1** (of a fluid) carry (particles etc.) along in its flow. **2** incorporate or trap (air) in concrete etc. **3** bring on as a consequence. □ **en·train·ment** *noun* [French *entraîner* (as EN-¹, *traîner* drag, formed as TRAIN)]

en·train² /ɪnˈtreɪn, en-, ən-/ *verb* **1** *intransitive* go on board a train. **2** *transitive* put (a person or thing) on board a train.

en·trance¹ /ˈentrəns/ *noun* **1** the act or an instance of coming or going in. **2 a** a door, passage, etc., by which one enters. **b** a point of entering something (*the entrance to the harbour*). **3** the right or privilege of admission (also *attributive*: *university entrance exam*). **4** the moment, or

point in the script, when an actor, dancer, etc. comes on stage. **5** *Music* = ENTRY 8. **6** *Brit.* = ENTRANCE FEE. [Old French (as ENTER, -ANCE)]

en·trance² /ɪnˈtrans/ *transitive verb* (usu. in *passive*) **1** fill someone with wonder and delight, holding their entire attention. **2** put into a trance. □ **en·trance·ment** *noun* **en·tran·cing** *adjective* **en·tran·cing·ly** *adverb*

entrance fee *noun* a fee paid for admission to an exhibition, park, attraction, club, etc.

en·trance·way *noun* a passage or hallway at the entrance to a building etc.

en·trant *noun* **1** a person who enters a competition; a candidate in an examination etc. **2** a person who enters a school, profession, etc. or becomes a member of an organization etc. **3** a company, product, etc. which enters a new market, field, etc. [French, pres. part. of *entrer*: see ENTER]

en·trap *transitive verb* (**en·trapped, en·trap·ping**) **1** catch in or as in a trap. **2** (often foll. by *into* + verbal noun) beguile or trick (a person).

en·trap·ment *noun* **1** the act or an instance of entrapping; the process of being entrapped. **2** *Law* inducement to commit a crime, esp. by the authorities to secure a prosecution.

en·treat *transitive verb* **1** (foll. by *to* + infin.) ask (a person) earnestly. **2** ask earnestly for (a thing). □ **en·treat·ing·ly** *adverb* [Old French *entraiter* (as EN-¹, *traiter* TREAT)]

en·treaty *noun* (pl. **-ies**) an earnest request; a supplication.

entre·chat /ˌɒntrəˈʃɒ/ *noun* a jump in ballet, in which the dancer beats the legs in the air and criss-crosses them at least once. [French from Italian (*capriola*) *intrecciata* complicated (caper)]

entre·côte /ˈɒntrəˌkoʊt/ *noun* a boned steak cut off the sirloin. [French from *entre* between + *côte* rib]

Entre-Deux-Mers /ˌɒntrədəˈmer/ *noun* a dry white wine from a region of Bordeaux between the Dordogne and Garonne rivers. [French, lit. 'between two seas']

en·tree /ˈɒntreɪ, ˈɑːtreɪ/ *noun* **1 a** esp. *N Amer.* the main dish of a meal. **b** *Brit.* a dish served between the fish and meat courses. **2** the right or privilege of admission, esp. to an exclusive group. [French, = ENTRY]

entre·mets /ˌɒntrəˈmeɪ/ *noun* **1** a sweet dish. **2** any light dish served between two courses. [French from *entre* between + *mets* dish]

en·trench *verb* **1** *transitive* establish firmly (in a defensible position, in office, etc.). **2** *transitive* surround (a post, army, town, etc.) with a trench as a fortification. **3** *transitive* safeguard (rights etc.) by constitutional provision; provide for the legal or political perpetuation of. □ **en·trench·ment** *noun*

en·trenched *adjective* (of an attitude, etc.) not easily modified.

entre·pôt /ˈɒntrəˌpoʊ/ *noun* **1** a warehouse for temporary storage of goods in transit. **2** a commercial centre for import and export, and for collection and distribution. [French from *entreposer* store, from *entre*- INTER- + *poser* place]

entre·pre·neur /ˌɒntrəprəˈnɜːr/ *noun* a person who starts or organizes a commercial enterprise, esp. one involving financial risk. □ **entre·pre·neur·ial** *adjective* **entre·pre·neur·ial·ism** *noun* (also **entre·pre·neur·ism**). **entre·pre·neur·ial·ly** *adverb* **entre·pre·neur·ship** *noun* [French from *entreprendre* 'undertake': see ENTERPRISE]

entre·sol /ˈɒntrəˌsɒl/ *noun* a low storey between the ground floor and the floor above; a mezzanine floor. [French from *entre* 'between' + *sol* 'ground']

en·tropy /ˈentrəpi/ *noun* **1** *Physics* a measure of the unavailability of a system's thermal energy for conversion into mechanical work. Symbol: **S**. **2** *Physics* a measure of the disorganization or degradation of the universe. **3** a measure of the rate of transfer of information in a message etc. **4** lack of order or predictability; gradual decline into disorder. □ **en·trop·ic** /-ˈtrɒpɪk/ *adjective* **en·trop·ic·ally** /-ˈtrɒpɪkli/ *adverb* [German *Entropie* (as EN-², Greek *tropē* transformation)]

en·trust *transitive verb* **1** (foll. by *to*) give responsibility for (a person or a thing) to a person in whom one has confidence. **2** (foll. by *with*) assign responsibility for a thing to (a person).

entry *noun* (pl. **-tries**) **1** the act or an instance of coming or going in. **2 a** a place of entrance; a door, gate, etc. **b** *Brit.* a lobby. **3** liberty to go or come in. **4** an actor's entrance on stage. **5** an item entered in a diary, list, account book, etc. **6 a** a word, phrase, abbreviation, etc. entered in a dictionary, encyclopedia, etc. **b** this and its accompanying definition or explanation. **7 a** a person or thing competing in a race, contest, etc. **b** a list of competitors. **8** the start or resumption of a performer's part in a musical composition. **9** the act of entering (data etc.) into a file, database, etc. **10** *Law* the act of taking possession.

11 *Bridge* **a** the transfer of the lead to one's partner's hand. **b** a card providing this. [Old French *entree*, ultimately from Latin *intrare* ENTER]

entry draft *noun N Amer.* a draft of players, esp. juniors, whose rights are not owned by any team.

entry form *noun* an application form for a competition.

entry-level *attributive adjective* **1** (of employment) suitable for inexperienced applicants (*entry-level position in sales*). **2** relatively unsophisticated and low in cost (*entry-level computers*).

Entry·phone *noun Brit. proprietary* = ENTERPHONE.

entry·way *N Amer.* = ENTRANCEWAY.

en·twine *transitive verb* **1** (foll. by *with, about, around*) twine together (a thing with or around another). **2** interweave.

enu·cle·ate /ɪˈnjuːkliˌeit, ɪˈnuːk-/ *transitive verb Surgery* extract (a tumour, eyeball, etc.). □ **enu·cle·a·tion** /-ˈeiʃən/ *noun* [Latin *enucleare* (as E-¹, NUCLEUS)]

enum·er·ate /ɪˈnjuːməˌreit, ɪˈnuː-/ *verb* **1** *transitive* specify (items); mention one by one. **2** *Cdn* **a** *transitive* enter (a person's name) on a list of voters for an election. **b** *transitive* prepare the voters list for (an area), usu. by conducting a house-to-house survey. **c** *intransitive* conduct such a survey. **3** *transitive* count; establish the number of. □ **enum·er·able** *adjective* **enum·er·a·tion** /-ˈreiʃən/ *noun* **enum·er·a·tive** /-rətɪv/ *adjective* [Latin *enumerare* (as E-¹, NUMBER)]

enum·er·ator /ɪˈnjuːməˌreitər, ɪˈnuː-/ *noun* **1** a person who enumerates. **2** a person employed in census taking. **3** *Cdn* a person employed to conduct a survey to register voters for a voters list.

enun·ci·ate /ɪˈnʌnsiˌeit/ *verb* **1** *transitive & intransitive* pronounce (words) clearly. **2** *transitive* express (a proposition or theory) in definite terms. **3** *transitive* proclaim. □ **enun·ci·a·tion** *noun* [Latin *enuntiare* (as E-¹, *nuntiare* announce, from *nuntius* messenger)]

enure /ɪˈnjʊr/ *intransitive verb Law* = INURE 2. [var. of INURE]

en·ur·esis /ˌenjʊˈriːsɪs/ *noun Med.* involuntary urination. □ **en·ur·etic** /-ˈretɪk/ *adjective & noun* [modern Latin from Greek *enoureō* urinate in (as EN-², *ouron* urine)]

en·vel·op /ɪnˈveləp/ *transitive verb* (**en·vel·oped**, **en·vel·op·ing**) **1** (often foll. by *in*) **a** wrap up or cover completely. **b** obscure; conceal (*was enveloped in mystery*). **2** *Military* completely surround (an enemy). □ **en·vel·op·ment** *noun* [Old French *envoluper* (as EN-¹; compare DEVELOP)]

en·vel·ope /ˈenvəˌloʊp, ˈɒn-/ *noun* **1** a folded paper container, usu. with a sealable flap, for a letter etc. **2** a wrapper or covering. **3** the structure within a balloon or airship containing the gas. **4** the outer metal or glass housing of a vacuum tube, electric light, etc. **5** *Electricity* a curve joining the successive peaks of a modulated wave. **6** *Bot.* any enveloping structure esp. the calyx or corolla (or both). **7** *Math.* a line or curve tangent to each line or curve of a given family. □ **back of the envelope** (of a calculation) carried out or arrived at quickly, roughly, or simply, as though scribbled on the back of an envelope. **push** (or **push the edge of**) **the envelope** *N Amer.* go to the greatest length that an activity allows. [French *enveloppe* (as ENVELOP), *push the envelope* from FLIGHT ENVELOPE]

en·ven·om *transitive verb* **1** put poison on or into; make poisonous. **2** infuse venom or bitterness into (feelings, words, or actions).

envi·able *adjective* (of a person or thing) exciting or likely to excite envy. □ **envi·ably** *adverb*

envi·ous *adjective* (often foll. by *of*) feeling or showing envy. □ **envi·ous·ly** *adverb*

enviro- *combining form* **1** environment. **2** environmental. **3** environmentally.

en·vir·on /ɪnˈvairən, en-, ən-/ *transitive verb* encircle, surround (esp. hostilely or protectively). [Old French *environer* from *environ* surroundings, from *en* in + *viron* circuit from *virer* turn, VEER¹]

en·viron·ment /ɪnˈvairənmənt, en-, ən-/ *noun* **1** the physical surroundings, conditions, circumstances, etc., in which a person lives, works, etc. (*poor home environment; a smoke-free work environment*). **2** the area surrounding a place. **3 a** external conditions as affecting plant and animal life. **b** (usu. **the environment**) the totality of the physical conditions on the earth or a part of it, esp. as affected by human activity. **4** *Computing* the overall structure within which a user, computer, or program operates. **5** a large artistic creation intended to be experienced with several senses while one is surrounded by it. □ **en·viron·ment·al** *adjective* **en·viron·ment·al·ly** *adverb*

environmental audit *noun* an assessment of the extent to which an organization is observing practices which seek to minimize harm to the environment.

environmental engineering *noun* a branch of civil engineering concerned with the environmental impact of proposed projects.

en·viron·ment·al·ist /ɪnˌvairənˈmentəlɪst, en-, ən-/ *noun* **1** a person who is concerned with or advocates the protection of the environment. **2** a person who considers that environment has the primary influence on the development of a person or group. □ **en·viron·ment·al·ism** *noun*

environmentally friendly *adjective* (also **environment-friendly**) not harmful to the environment.

en·vir·ons /ɪnˈvairənz/ *plural noun* a surrounding district, esp. around an urban area.

en·vis·age /ɪnˈvɪzɪdʒ, en-, ən-/ *transitive verb* **1** have a mental picture of (a thing or conditions not yet existing). **2** contemplate or conceive, esp. as possible or desirable. □ **en·visage·ment** *noun* [French *envisager* (as EN-¹, VISAGE)]

en·vision *transitive verb* envisage, visualize.

en·voi /ˈenvɔi/ *noun* (also **envoy**) **1** a short stanza concluding a ballade etc. **2** *archaic* an author's concluding words. [Old French *envoi*, from *envoyer* (as ENVOY)]

en·voy /ˈɒnvɔi, ˈen-/ *noun* **1** a messenger or representative, esp. on a diplomatic mission. **2** (in full **envoy extraordinary**) a minister plenipotentiary, ranking below ambassador and above chargé d'affaires. [French *envoyé*, past participle of *envoyer* send, from *en voie* on the way, from Latin *via*]

envy ● *noun* (pl. **-vies**) **1** a feeling of discontented or resentful longing aroused by another's better fortune etc. **2** the object or ground of this feeling (*their house is the envy of the neighbourhood*). ● *transitive verb* (**-vies**, **-vied**) feel envy of (a person, circumstances, etc.) (*I envy you your position*). □ **envi·er** *noun* [Old French *envie* from Latin *invidia* from *invidēre* envy (as IN-¹, *vidēre* see)]

en·wrap *transitive verb* (also **in·wrap**) (**-wrapped**, **-wrap·ping**) (often foll. by *in*) *literary* wrap or enfold.

en·zo·otic /ˌenzoʊˈɒtɪk/ ● *adjective* (of a disease etc.) regularly affecting animals in a particular district (*compare* ENDEMIC, EPIZOOTIC). ● *noun* an enzootic disease. [Greek *en* in + *zōion* animal]

en·zyme /ˈenzaim/ *noun Biochem.* a protein produced by living cells and functioning as a catalyst in a specific biochemical reaction. □ **en·zym·atic** /-ˈmatɪk/ *adjective* **en·zym·atic·ally** *adverb* **en·zym·ic** /-ˈzaimɪk/ *adjective* **en·zym·ol·ogy** /-ˈmɒlədʒi/ *noun* [German *Enzym* from medieval Greek *enzumos* leavened, from Greek *en* in + *zumē* leaven]

Eocene /ˈiːoʊˌsiːn/ *Geol.* ● *adjective* of, relating to, or denoting the second epoch of the Tertiary period, between the Paleocene and the Oligocene, lasting from about 54.9 to 38 million years BP and having evidence of an abundance of mammals. ● *noun* this epoch or geological system. [Greek *ēōs* dawn + *kainos* new]

eolian *var. of* AEOLIAN.

eolith /ˈiːəliθ/ *noun Archaeology* any of various roughly chipped flint objects found in Tertiary strata and originally thought to be early artifacts. [Greek *ēōs* dawn + *lithos* stone]

eon /ˈiːɒn/ *noun* (also **aeon**) **1** a very long or indefinite period. **2** an eternity. **3** *Astronomy* a billion years. **4** the largest division of geological time, composed of two or more eras. **5** *Philos.* (in Neoplatonism, Platonism, and Gnosticism) a power existing from eternity; an emanation or phase of the supreme deity. [ecclesiastical Latin from Greek *aiōn* 'age']

Eos /ˈiːɒs/ *Gk Myth* the Greek goddess of the dawn, corresponding to the Roman Aurora. [Greek, = dawn]

eosin /ˈiːoʊsɪn/ *noun* a red fluorescent dye used esp. as a stain in optical microscopy. [Greek *ēōs* dawn + -IN]

eosin·o·phil /ˌiːoʊˈsɪnəfɪl/ *noun* a white blood cell readily stained by eosin.

eosin·o·philia /ˌiːoʊˌsɪnəˈfɪliə/ *noun* an increased number of eosinophils in the blood, as in some allergic disorders and parasitic infections. □ **eosin·o·phil·ic** *adjective* [EOSINOPHIL + -IA¹]

-eous *suffix* forming adjectives meaning 'of the nature of' (*erroneous; gaseous*).

EP *abbreviation* **1** an extended play record (one that plays for longer than most singles, usu. at 45 rpm). **2** (used of the speed of a videotape) extended play, allowing six hours of material to be recorded on a standard tape. **3** electroplate. **4** *N Amer.* EUROPEAN PLAN. **5** extreme pressure (used in grading lubricants). **6** European Parliament.

Ep. *abbreviation* Epistle.

e.p. *abbreviation Chess* EN PASSANT.

ep- *prefix* form of EPI- before a vowel or *h*.

EPA *abbreviation* (in the US) Environmental Protection Agency.

epact /'iːpakt/ *noun* the number of days by which the solar year exceeds the lunar year. [French *épacte* from Late Latin *epactae* from Greek *epaktai (hēmerai)* intercalated (days), from *epagō* intercalate (as EPI-, *agō* bring)]

ep·arch /'epɑːk/ *noun* the chief bishop of an eparchy. [Greek *eparkhos* (as EPI-, *arkhos* ruler)]

ep·archy /'epɑːki/ *noun* (*pl.* -ies) a diocese in an Eastern-rite church.

epaul·ette /,epə'let, 'epə,let/ *noun* (also **epaul·et**) a decoration on the shoulder of a coat, jacket, etc., esp. on a uniform. [French *épaulette* diminutive of *épaule* shoulder, from Latin *spatula*: see SPATULA]

épée /ei'pei/ *noun* Fencing a sharp-pointed duelling sword, often used with the end blunted. □ **épée·ist** *noun* [French, = sword, from Old French *espee*: see SPAY]

epeir·ogeny /e,pai'rɒdʒəni/ *noun* (also **epeiro·gen·esis** /-rɒ'dʒenəsɪs/) Geol. the regional uplift of extensive areas of the earth's crust. □ **epeiro·gen·ic** /-'dʒenɪk/ *adjective* [Greek *ēpeiros* mainland + GENESIS, -GENY]

epen·thesis /e'penθɪsɪs, -ɪ-/ *noun* (*pl.* **epen·theses** /-siːz/) the insertion of a letter or sound within a word, e.g. the sound /ə/ inserted by some people in the pronunciation of *biathlon*. □ **epen·thet·ic** /,epen'θetɪk/ *adjective* [Late Latin from Greek from *epentithēmi* insert (as EPI- + EN-² + *tithēmi* place)]

ep·ergne /ɪ'pɜːn/ *noun* an ornament (esp. in branched form) for the centre of a dinner table, holding flowers or fruit. [18th c.: perhaps a corruption of French *épargne* 'saving, economy', in the phrase *taille* or *gravure d'épargne*, metal or etching in which parts are 'spared', i.e. left in relief]

Eph. *abbreviation* New Testament Ephesians.

ephah /'iːfə/ *noun* Bible an ancient Hebrew unit of dry measure, approximately equal to a bushel or 33 litres. [Hebrew *'ēpāh*, prob. from Egyptian]

eph·ebe /'efiːb/ *noun* Gk Hist. a young man of 18–20 undergoing military training. □ **epheb·ic** /e'fiːbɪk/ *adjective* [Latin *ephebus* from Greek *ephēbos* (as EPI-, *hēbē* early manhood)]

ephed·ra /ɪ'fedrə/ *noun* any evergreen shrub of the genus *Ephedra*, with trailing stems and scale-like leaves. Some kinds are a source of ephedrine and are used medicinally. [modern Latin from Greek *ephedra* sitting upon]

ephed·rine /ɪ'fedrɪn/ *noun* an alkaloid drug found in some ephedras, causing constriction of the blood vessels and widening of the bronchial passages, used to relieve asthma, hay fever, colds, etc. [EPHEDRA + -INE⁴]

ephem·era /ɪ'femrə, ɪ'fiːm-/ *noun* (*pl.* **ephem·er·as** or **ephem·erae** /-,riː/) **1** a winged insect of the genus *Ephemera* or the order Ephemeroptera, a mayfly. **2** = EPHEMERON. [modern Latin from Greek *ephēmeros* lasting only a day (as EPI-, *hēmera* day)]

ephem·er·al /ɪ'femrəl/ *adjective* **1** lasting or of use for only a short time; transitory. **2** (of an insect, flower, etc.) lasting a day or a few days. □ **ephem·er·al·ity** /-'ralɪti/ *noun* **ephem·er·al·ly** *adverb* [Greek *ephēmeros*: see EPHEMERA]

ephem·er·is /ɪ'femərɪs, ɪ'fiːm-/ *noun* (*pl.* **ephem·er·ides** /,efɪ'merɪ,diːz/) Astronomy **1** a table of the predicted positions of a celestial body. **2** a book of such tables. [Latin from Greek *ephēmeris* diary (as EPHEMERAL)]

ephem·er·on /ɪ'femərən, ɪ'fiːm-/ *noun* **1** (*pl.* **ephem·era** /-rə/) (usu. in *pl.*) **a** a thing (esp. a printed item) of short-lived interest or usefulness. **b** a short-lived thing. **2** (*pl.* **ephem·er·ons**) = EPHEMERA 1. [as EPHEMERA]

Ephe·sians /ɪ'fiːʒənz/ a book of the New Testament ascribed to St. Paul, an epistle to the Church at Ephesus.

Eph·esus /'efəsəs/ an ancient Greek city on the west coast of Asia Minor, in present-day Turkey, site of the temple of Diana, one of the Seven Wonders of the World. It was an important centre of early Christianity; St. Paul preached there and St. John is traditionally said to have lived there.

eph·od /'iːfɒd, 'efɒd/ *noun* a vestment, resembling an embroidered apron, worn by priests in ancient Israel. [Hebrew *'ēpōd*]

eph·or /'efɔr/ *noun* Gk Hist. any of five senior magistrates in ancient Sparta. □ **ephor·ate** *noun* [Greek *ephoros* overseer (as EPI-, *horaō* see)]

epi- *prefix* (usu. **ep-** before a vowel or h) **1** upon (*epicycle*). **2** above (*epicotyl*). **3** in addition (*epiphenomenon*). [Greek *epi* 'upon, near to, in addition']

epi·blast *noun* Biol. the outermost layer of a young embryo.

epic ● *noun* **1 a** a long poem, typically one derived from ancient oral tradition, narrating the adventures or deeds of one or more heroic or legendary figures, e.g. the *Iliad*, *Paradise Lost*. **b** the genre of such poems. **2** an imaginative work of any form, embodying a nation's conception of its past history. **3** a book or film based on an epic narrative or heroic in type or scale. **4** an exceptionally long and arduous task or activity. ● *adjective* **1** of or like an epic. **2** grand, heroic. **3** impressive in scope, grandeur, etc. □ **epical·ly** *adverb* [Latin *epicus* from Greek *epikos* from *epos* word, song]

epi·car·di·um /,epɪ'kɑːdiəm/ *noun* the visceral part of the serous pericardium, covering the heart. □ **epi·car·di·al** *adjective* [EPI- + -cardium, after PERICARDIUM]

epi·cene /'epɪ,siːn/ ● *adjective* **1** Grammar denoting either sex without change of gender. **2** of, for, or used by both sexes. **3** having characteristics of both sexes. **4** having no characteristics of either sex. **5** effete, effeminate. ● *noun* an epicene person. [Late Latin *epicoenus* from Greek *epikoinos* (as EPI-, *koinos* common)]

epi·centre *noun* (also esp. *US* **epi·center**) **1** Geol. the point at which an earthquake reaches the earth's surface. **2** the centre or heart of something. □ **epi·cen·tral** *adjective* [Greek *epikentros* (adj.) (as EPI-, CENTRE)]

epi·con·tin·en·tal *adjective* (of a sea) situated on a continental shelf.

epi·cotyl /,epɪ'kɒtɪl/ *noun* Bot. the region of an embryo or seedling stem above the cotyledon(s).

Epic·tetus /,epɪk'tiːtəs/ (c.55–c.135 AD), Greek Stoic philosopher, who preached the obligation of moral perfection, to be attained by resignation and renunciation; his teachings were published posthumously in the *Enchiridion*.

epi·cure /'epɪ,kjʊr/ *noun* a person who takes particular pleasure in fine food and drink. □ **epi·cur·ism** *noun* [medieval Latin *epicurus* one preferring sensual enjoyment, from EPICURUS]

epi·cur·ean /,epɪ'kjʊriːən/ ● *noun* **1** = EPICURE. **2** (**Epicurean**) a disciple or student of Epicurus. ● *adjective* **1** characteristic of an epicure. **2** (**Epicurean**) of or concerning Epicurus or his ideas.

Epi·cur·ean·ism /,epɪ'kjʊriːənɪzəm/ *noun* an ancient school of philosophy, founded in Athens by Epicurus. The school rejected determinism and advocated hedonism (pleasure as the highest good), but of a restrained kind: mental pleasure was regarded more highly than physical, and the ultimate pleasure was held to be freedom from anxiety and mental pain, esp. that arising from needless fear of death and of the gods.

Epi·curus /,epɪ'kjʊrəs/ (341–270 BC), Greek philosopher. He proposed a materialist theory of the universe, with atoms moving in a void, and a related moral theory which stressed the avoidance of pain and freedom from disturbance.

epi·cycle *noun* Geom. **1** a small circle moving around the circumference of a larger one. **2** hist. any such circle used to describe planetary orbits in the Ptolemaic system. □ **epi·cyc·lic** /-'saiklɪk, -'sɪklɪk/ *adjective*

epi·cyc·loid /,epɪ'saikloid/ *noun* Math. a curve traced by a point on the circumference of a circle rolling on the exterior of another circle. □ **epi·cyc·loid·al** /-'klɔidəl/ *adjective*

Epi·daur·us /,epɪ'dɔrəs/ an ancient Greek city and port on the northeast coast of the Peloponnese, site of a temple dedicated to Asclepius and a well-preserved Greek theatre dating from the 4th c. BC.

epi·dem·ic /,epɪ'demɪk/ ● *noun* **1** a widespread occurrence of a disease in a community at a particular time. **2** a wide prevalence of something usu. undesirable. ● *adjective* **1** in the nature of an epidemic (compare ENDEMIC). **2** widespread; prevalent. [ultimately from Greek *epidēmia* prevalence of disease, from *epidēmios* (adj.) (as EPI-, *dēmos* the people)]

epi·demi·ol·ogy /,epɪdiːmi'ɒlədʒi/ *noun* the study of the incidence and distribution of diseases, and of their control and prevention. □ **epi·demi·o·logic** /-miə'lɒdʒɪk/ *adjective* **epi·demi·o·logic·al** *adjective* **epi·demi·o·logic·al·ly** *adverb* **epi·demi·ol·o·gist** *noun*

epi·der·mis /,epɪ'dɜːmɪs/ *noun* **1** the outer cellular layer of the skin. **2** Bot. the outer layer of cells of leaves, stems, roots, etc. □ **epi·der·mal** *adjective* **epi·der·mic** *adjective* **epi·derm·oid** *adjective* [Late Latin from Greek (as EPI-, DERMIS)]

epi·didy·mis /,epɪ'dɪdɪmɪs/ *noun* (*pl.* **epi·didy·mi·des** /-'dɪmɪ,diːz/) Anat. a convoluted duct behind the testis, along which sperm passes to the vas deferens. [Greek *epididumis* (as EPI-, *didumoi* testicles)]

epi·dote /'epɪ,dɒt/ *noun* any of several rock-forming silicates of calcium, aluminum, and iron that occur as monoclinic usu. green crystals in many metamorphic rocks. [French *épidote* from Greek *epiddidonai*, as EPI- + *didonai* 'give', with reference to the great length of the crystals]

epi·dur·al /ˌepɪˈdʒərəl, -ˈdʊərəl, -ˈdj-/ ● *adjective* **1** *Anat.* on or around the dura mater. **2** (of an anaesthetic) introduced into the space around the dura mater of the spinal cord. ● *noun* an epidural anaesthetic, used esp. in childbirth to produce loss of sensation below the waist. [EPI- + DURA (MATER)]

epi·gas·tri·um /ˌepɪˈgastriəm/ *noun* (*pl.* **epi·gas·tria** /-riə/) *Anat.* the part of the abdomen immediately over the stomach. □ **epi·gas·tric** *adjective* [Late Latin from Greek *epigastrion* (neuter adj.) (as EPI-, *gastēr* belly)]

epi·geal /ˌepɪˈdʒiːəl/ *adjective* *Bot.* **1** having one or more cotyledons above the ground. **2** growing above the ground. [Greek *epigeios* (as EPI-, *gē* earth)]

epi·gene /ˈepɪˌdʒiːn/ *adjective* *Geol.* produced on the surface of the earth. [French *épigène* from Greek *epigenēs* (as EPI-, *genēs* born)]

epi·glot·tis /ˌepɪˈɡlɒtəs/ *noun* *Anat.* a flap of cartilage at the root of the tongue, which is depressed during swallowing to cover the windpipe. □ **epi·glot·tal** *adjective* **epi·glot·tic** *adjective* [Greek *epiglōttis* (as EPI-, *glōtta* tongue)]

epi·gone /ˈepɪˌɡoːn/ *noun* (*pl.* **epi·gones** or **epi·goni** /eˈpɪɡəˌnaɪ/) a less distinguished follower or imitator of someone, esp. an artist or philosopher. □ **epi·gon·ic** *adjective* [Greek *epigonoi* those born afterwards (as EPI-, root of *gignomai* be born)]

epi·gram *noun* **1** a pithy saying or remark expressing an idea in a clever and amusing way. **2** a short witty poem. □ **epi·gram·mat·ic** *adjective* **epi·gram·mat·ic·ally** *adverb* **epi·gram·ma·tist** *noun* [French *épigramme* or Latin *epigramma* from Greek *epigramma -atos* (as EPI-, -GRAM)]

epi·graph *noun* **1** a quotation at the beginning of a chapter, book, etc. **2** an inscription on a statue, building, tomb, coin, etc. [Greek *epigraphē* from *epigraphō* (as EPI-, *graphō* write)]

epig·raphy /eˈpɪɡrəfi/ *noun* **1** the study of (esp. ancient) inscriptions. **2** epigraphs collectively. □ **epig·raph·er** *noun* **epig·raph·ic** *adjective* **epig·raph·ic·al** *adjective* **epig·raph·ic·al·ly** /-ˈɡrafɪkli/ *adverb* **epig·raph·ist** *noun*

epi·la·tion /ˌepɪˈleɪʃən/ *noun* the removal of hair. □ **epi·la·tor** *noun* [French *épiler* (compare DEPILATE)]

epi·lepsy /ˈepɪˌlepsi/ *noun* a condition in which a person has intermittent attacks of disordered brain function, usu. causing loss of awareness or consciousness and sometimes convulsions (compare GRAND MAL, PETIT MAL). [Greek *epilēpsia* from *epilambanō* attack (as EPI-, *lambanō* take)]

epi·lep·tic /ˌepɪˈleptɪk/ ● *adjective* of or relating to epilepsy. ● *noun* a person with epilepsy.

epi·lim·nion /ˌepɪˈlɪmniən/ *noun* (*pl.* **epi·lim·nia** /-niə/) the upper layer of water in a stratified lake. [EPI- + Greek *limnion* diminutive of *limnē* lake]

epi·logue /ˈepəˌlɒɡ/ *noun* **1** the concluding part of a literary work. **2** a speech or short poem addressed to the audience by an actor at the end of a play. Compare PROLOGUE. [Greek *epilogos* (as EPI-, *logos* speech)]

epi·mer /ˈepɪmɜr/ *noun* *Chem.* either of two isomers with different configurations of atoms about one of several asymmetric carbon atoms present. □ **epi·mer·ic** /-ˈmerɪk/ *adjective* **epi·mer·ism** /eˈpɪm-/ *noun* [German (as EPI-, -MER)]

epi·mer·ize /eˈpɪməˌraɪz/ *transitive verb* (also esp. *Brit.* **-ise**) *Chem.* convert (one epimer) into the other.

-epine /əˈpiːn/ *combining form* occurring in the names of compounds whose molecule includes an unsaturated seven-membered ring containing nitrogen. [EPI- + -INE[4]]

epi·neph·rine /ˌepɪˈnefrɪn/ *Biochem.* = ADRENALIN. [Greek *epi* upon + *nephros* kidney]

Epi·Pen /ˈepɪˌpen/ *noun* proprietary a pen-like device with a spring-activated concealed needle used to self-administer a dose of epinephrine (adrenalin) in an allergic emergency. [blend of EPINEPHRINE + PEN[1]]

epiph·any /eˈpɪfəni, ɪˈpɪf-/ *noun* (*pl.* **-ies**) **1** (**Epiphany**) a Christian festival observed on 6 January or the following Sunday in the Western Church and on 19 January in Eastern-rite churches. In the Western Church it commemorates the manifestation of Jesus to the Magi; in Eastern Churches the baptism of Jesus. **2** a manifestation of a god or demigod. **3** a sudden and important manifestation or realization. □ **epi·phan·ic** /ˌepɪˈfanɪk/ *adjective* **epiph·an·ous** *adjective* [Greek *epiphaneia* manifestation, from *epiphainō* reveal (as EPI-, *phainō* show)]

epi·phenom·enon /ˌepɪfɪˈnɒmɪnən/ *noun* (*pl.* **epi·phenom·ena** /-nə/)

1 a secondary symptom, which may occur simultaneously with a disease etc. but is not regarded as its cause or result. **2** *Psych.* consciousness regarded as a by-product of brain activity. □ **epi·phenom·enal** *adjective*

epiphy·sis /eˈpɪfɪsɪs/ *noun* (*pl.* **epiphy·ses** /-ˌsiːz/) *Anat.* **1** the end part of a long bone, initially growing separately from the shaft. **2** = PINEAL GLAND. [modern Latin from Greek *epiphusis* (as EPI-, *phusis* growth)]

epi·phyte /ˈepɪˌfaɪt/ *noun* a plant growing but not parasitic on another, e.g. a moss. □ **epi·phyt·ic** /ˌepɪˈfɪtɪk/ *adjective* [EPI- + Greek *phuton* plant]

EPIRB /ˈiːpɜrb/ *abbreviation* Emergency Position Indicating Radio Beacon.

Epirus /ɪˈpaɪrəs/ **1** a coastal region of NW Greece; capital, Ioánnina. **2** an ancient country of which the modern region of Epirus corresponds to the southwestern part, extending northward to Illyria and eastward to Macedonia and Thessaly.

epis·co·pacy /ɪˈpɪskəpəsi/ *noun* (*pl.* **-cies**) **1** government of a Church by bishops. **2** = EPISCOPATE.

epis·co·pal /ɪˈpɪskəpəl/ *adjective* **1** of a bishop or bishops. **2** (of a Church) constituted on the principle of government by bishops. **3** (**Episcopal**) of or relating to the Episcopal Church. □ **epis·co·pal·ism** *noun* **epis·co·pal·ly** *adverb* [ecclesiastical Latin *episcopalis* from *episcopus* BISHOP]

Episcopal Church *noun* the Anglican Church in the US and Scotland.

epis·co·pal·ian /ɪˌpɪskəˈpeɪliən/ ● *adjective* **1** of or advocating government of a Church by bishops. **2** of or belonging to an episcopal Church or (**Episcopalian**) the Episcopal Church. ● *noun* **1** an adherent of episcopacy. **2** (**Episcopalian**) a member of the Episcopal Church. □ **epis·co·pal·ian·ism** *noun*

epis·co·pate /ɪˈpɪskəpət/ *noun* **1** the office or tenure of a bishop. **2** (prec. by *the*) the bishops collectively. [ecclesiastical Latin *episcopatus* from *episcopus* BISHOP]

epi·sem·atic /ˌepɪsɪˈmatɪk/ *adjective* *Zool.* (of coloration, markings, etc.) serving to help recognition by animals of the same species. [EPI- + Greek *sēma sēmatos* sign]

episi·ot·omy /eˌpiːziˈɒtəmi, eˌpɪz-/ *noun* (*pl.* **-mies**) a surgical cut made at the opening of the vagina during childbirth, to aid delivery. [Greek *epision* pubic region]

epi·sode *noun* **1** one event or a group of events as part of a sequence. **2** each of the parts of a serial story or broadcast. **3** an incident or set of incidents in a narrative. **4** an incident that is distinct but contributes to a whole (*a romantic episode in her life*). **5** *Music* a passage containing distinct material or introducing a new subject. **6** the part between two choric songs in Greek tragedy. [Greek *epeisodion* (as EPI- + *eisodos* entry, from *eis* into + *hodos* way)]

epi·sod·ic /ˌepɪˈsɒdɪk/ *adjective* **1** in the nature of an episode. **2** sporadic; occurring at irregular intervals. **3** (of a novel, play, film, etc.) made up of unconnected episodes. □ **epi·sod·ic·ally** *adverb*

epi·stax·is /ˌepɪˈstaksɪs/ *noun* *Med.* a nosebleed. [modern Latin from Greek (as EPI-, *stazō* drip)]

epi·stem·ic /ˌepɪˈstiːmɪk, -ˈstemɪk/ *adjective* *Philos.* relating to knowledge or to the degree of its validation. □ **epi·stem·ic·ally** *adverb* [Greek *epistēmē* knowledge]

epis·tem·ol·ogy /ɪˌpɪstɪˈmɒlədʒi/ *noun* the theory of knowledge, esp. with regard to its methods and validation. □ **epis·temo·logic·al** *adjective* **epis·temo·logic·al·ly** *adverb* **epis·tem·ol·o·gist** *noun*

epis·tle /ɪˈpɪsəl/ *noun* **1** *formal* or *jocular* a letter, esp. a long one on a serious subject. **2** (**Epistle**) **a** any of the letters of the apostles in the New Testament. **b** an extract from an Epistle read in a church service. **3** a poem or other literary work in the form of a letter or series of letters. [Old French from Latin *epistola* from Greek *epistolē* from *epistellō* send news (as EPI-, *stellō* send)]

epis·tol·ary /ɪˈpɪstəˌleri/ *adjective* **1** in the style or form of a letter or letters. **2** of, carried by, or suited to letters. [French *épistolaire* or Latin *epistolaris* (as EPISTLE)]

epis·tro·phe /ɪˈpɪstrəfi/ *noun* the repetition of a word at the end of successive clauses. [Greek (as EPI-, *strophē* turning)]

epi·style /ˈepɪˌstaɪl/ *noun* *Archit.* = ARCHITRAVE. [French *épistyle* or Latin *epistylium* from Greek *epistulion* (as EPI-, *stulos* pillar)]

epi·taph /ˈepɪˌtaf/ *noun* words written in memory of a person who has died, esp. as a tomb inscription. [Old French *epitaphe* from Latin *epitaphium* from Greek *epitaphion* funeral oration (as EPI-, *taphos* tomb)]

epi·taxy /ˈepɪˌtaksi/ *noun* *Crystallog.* the growth of crystals on a crystalline substrate that determines their orientation. □ **epi·tax·ial** /-ˈtaksiəl/ *adjective* [French *épitaxie* (as EPI-, Greek *taxis* arrangement)]

---

t top   v voice   w we   z zoo   ʃ she   ʒ vision   θ thin   ð this   ŋ ring   x loch   tʃ chip   dʒ jar   (*see over for vowels*)

epi·thal·ami·um /ˌɛpɪθəˈleimiəm/ *noun* (*pl.* **epi·thal·amia** /-miə/) a song or poem celebrating a marriage. [Latin from Greek *epithalamion* (as EPI-, *thalamos* bridal chamber)]

epi·thel·ium /ˌɛpɪˈθiːliəm/ *noun* (*pl.* **epi·the·liums** or **epi·the·lia** /-liə/) the tissue forming the outer layer of the body surface and lining many hollow structures. □ **epi·thel·ial** *adjective* [modern Latin from EPI- + Greek *thēlē* teat]

epi·thet /ˈɛpɪˌθet/ *noun* **1** an adjective or other descriptive word expressing a quality or attribute, esp. used with or as a name. **2** such a word as a term of abuse. □ **epi·thet·ic** /-ˈθetɪk/ *adjective* [Greek *epitheton* from *epitithēmi* add (as EPI-, *tithēmi* place)]

epit·ome /ɪˈpɪtəmi/ *noun* **1** a typical example of a person or thing embodying a particular quality, class, etc. **2** a summary, abstract, or condensed account of a written work. [Latin from Greek *epitomē* from *epitemnō* abridge (as EPI-, *temnō* cut)]

epit·om·ize /ɪˈpɪtəˌmaiz/ *transitive verb* (also esp. *Brit.* **-ise**) typify or be a perfect example of (a quality etc.). □ **epit·om·iz·a·tion** /-ˈzeiʃən/ *noun*

epi·zo·on /ˌɛpɪˈzoːɒn/ *noun* (*pl.* **epi·zoa** /-ˈzoːə/) an animal that lives on the surface of another, esp. a parasite. [modern Latin (as EPI-, Greek *zōion* animal)]

epi·zo·otic /ˌɛpɪzoːˈɒtɪk/ ● *adjective* (of an animal disease) normally absent or infrequent in a population, but liable to become temporarily widespread (*compare* ENZOOTIC). ● *noun* a temporary but widespread outbreak of a particular disease among animals. [French *épizootique* from *épizootie* (as EPIZOON)]

EPO *abbreviation* erythropoietin.

epoch /ˈiːpɒk, ˈɛpɒk, ˈepək/ *noun* **1** a period of history or of a person's life marked by notable events. **2** the beginning of an era. **3** *Geol.* a division of geological time, esp. a subdivision of a period corresponding to a set of strata. **4** *Astronomy* the point in time at which a particular phenomenon takes place, esp. an arbitrarily fixed date relative to which planetary or stellar measurements are expressed. □ **epoch·al** /ˈepəkəl/ *adjective* [modern Latin *epocha* from Greek *epokhē* stoppage]

epoch-making *adjective* remarkable, historic, of major importance, or marking the beginning of a new epoch.

epode /ˈepoːd/ *noun* **1** a serious lyric poem composed of couplets in which a long line is followed by a shorter one. **2** the third section of an ancient Greek choral ode, following the strophe and antistrophe. [French *épode* or Latin *epodos* from Greek *epōidos* (as EPI-, ODE)]

epo·nym /ˈepənɪm/ *noun* **1** a person (real or imaginary) after whom a discovery, invention, place, institution, etc. is named or thought to be named. **2** the name given. [Greek *epōnumos* (as EPI-, *-ōnumos* from *onoma* name)]

eponym·ous /ɪˈpɒnɪməs/ *adjective* **1** (of a person) giving their name to something (*the eponymous hero of the novel*). **2** (of a thing) named after a particular person (*their eponymous debut LP*). □ **eponym·ous·ly** *adverb*

ep·ox·ide /ɪˈpɒksaid/ *noun Chem.* a compound containing an oxygen atom bonded in a triangular arrangement to two carbon atoms. [EPI- + OXIDE]

epoxy /ɪˈpɒksi/ *Chem.* ● *adjective* relating to or derived from an epoxide, esp. designating epoxy resins and the substances made from them. ● *noun* (*pl.* **-ies**) (in full **epoxy resin**) a synthetic thermosetting resin containing epoxy groups or a substance made from them and used as a coating, adhesive, etc. ● *transitive verb* (**-ies, -ied**) secure (two materials) with epoxy glue or cement. [EPI- + OXY-²]

ep·si·lon /ˈepsɪˌlɒn/ *noun* the fifth letter of the Greek alphabet (Ε, ε). [Greek, = 'bare E' from *psilos* bare]

Epsom salts /ˈepsəm/ *noun* (as *sing.* or *pl.*) a preparation of hydrated magnesium sulphate used as a laxative and in bath salts. [Epsom in SE England, where it was first found occurring naturally]

Ep·stein /ˈepstain/ **1 Brian** (1934–67), English manager of the Beatles. Epstein replaced drummer Pete Best with Ringo Starr and arranged the group's contract with Parlophone. He died suddenly, probably of an accidental drug overdose. **2 Sir Jacob** (1880–1959), US-born English sculptor. A founding member of the vorticist group, he is best known for his religious and allegorical works such as *Genesis* (1930), and his portraits of the famous, in particular *Einstein* (1933).

Epstein-Barr virus /ˌepstainˈbɑr, ˌepstiːn-/ *noun* a DNA herpesvirus which causes infectious mononucleosis and is associated with certain cancers, e.g. Burkitt's lymphoma. Abbr.: **EBV**. [M.A. *Epstein*, British virologist b.1921, and Y.M. *Barr*, Irish-born virologist b.1932]

EQ *abbreviation Electronics* equalization.

equable /ˈekwəbəl/ *adjective* **1** (of a person) not easily disturbed or angered. **2** (of motion, temperature, etc.) uniform, moderate, free from

fluctuation or variation (*an equable climate*). □ **equa·bil·ity** /-ˈbɪlɪti/ *noun* **equably** *adverb* [Latin *aequabilis* (as EQUATE)]

equal ● *adjective* **1** (often foll. by *to, with*) **a** identical in amount, size, number, value, intensity, etc. **b** on the same level in rank, power, excellence, etc. **2** evenly proportioned or balanced (*an equal contest*). **3** having the same rights or status (*human beings are essentially equal*). **4** uniform in operation, application, or effect. ● *noun* a person or thing equal to another, esp. in rank, status, or characteristic quality (*their treatment of the subject has no equal; is the equal of anyone*). ● *transitive verb* (**equalled, equal·ling**; esp. *US* **equaled, equal·ing**) **1** be equal to in number, quality, etc. **2** match, rival, or achieve something that is equal to (an achievement) or to the achievement of (a person). □ **be equal to** have the ability or resources for. [Latin *aequalis* from *aequus* even]

equal area projection *noun* a map projection in which equal areas on the earth's surface are represented by equal areas on the map, but with some distortion of shape (*compare* CONFORMAL).

equal·ity /iːˈkwɒlɪti/ *noun* (*pl.* **-ities**) **1** the condition of being equal in quantity, magnitude, value, intensity, etc. **2** the condition of having equal rank, power, excellence, etc. with others. **3** *Math.* an equation or symbolic expression of the fact that two quantities are equal.

equality rights *plural noun Cdn Politics* the rights guaranteed in section 15 of the Canadian Charter of Rights and Freedoms to equal treatment for all before and under the law regardless of race, national or ethnic origin, colour, religion, sex, age, or disability.

equal·iz·a·tion *noun* (also esp. *Brit.* **-isation**) the act or an instance of equalizing.

equalization payment *noun* (also **equalization grant**) *Cdn* an unconditional transfer by the federal government of funds from general revenues to a poorer province to ensure that all provincial governments provide comparable levels of service and taxation.

equal·ize *verb* (also esp. *Brit.* **-ise**) **1** *transitive & intransitive* make or become equal. **2** *transitive* render (a process, condition, etc.) uniform, esp. by compensating for (an inequality, imbalance, etc.). **3** *Electricity* **a** *transitive* correct or modify (a signal) with an equalizer. **b** *intransitive* compensate for (an imbalance) by means of an equalizer. **4** *intransitive* reach one's opponent's score in a game after being behind.

equal·iz·er *noun* **1** a thing that makes disparities equal. **2** *Electricity* a passive network designed to modify a frequency response, esp. in such a way as to compensate for distortion. **3** a goal, run, etc. that equalizes the score in a game. **4** *slang* a weapon, esp. a gun.

equal·ly *adverb* **1** in an equal manner (*treated them all equally*). **2** to an equal degree (*is equally important*). ¶ In sense 2, construction with *as* (*equally as important*) is often found, but is considered incorrect by some people. **3** in equal shares or amounts.

equal opportunity *noun* **1** the opportunity or right to be considered for employment or promotion without discrimination on the grounds of race, gender, disability, etc. **2** (often *attributive*) the practice or policy of not discriminating in this way.

equal pay *noun* the policy of giving the same rate of pay for a particular job, similar work, or work of equal value, regardless of the gender of the person doing it.

equal sign *noun* (also **equals sign**) the symbol =, used to indicate mathematical or other equality.

equa·nim·ity /ˌekwəˈnɪmɪti/ *noun* mental composure, evenness of temper, esp. in misfortune. [Latin *aequanimitas* from *aequanimis* from *aequus* even + *animus* mind]

equate *verb* **1** *transitive* (usu. foll. by *to, with*) **a** treat or regard as equal or equivalent. **b** associate strongly; establish a clear link between. **2** *intransitive* (foll. by *with*) **a** be equal or equivalent to. **b** agree or correspond. **3** *transitive* esp. *Math.* state the equality of (a thing) with or to another. □ **equat·able** *adjective* [Latin *aequare aequat-* from *aequus* equal]

equa·tion /ɪˈkweiʒən/ *noun* **1 a** the action of making equal or equating. **b** the state of being equal or in equilibrium. **2 a** a statement that two mathematical expressions are equal (indicated by the sign =). **b** the relationship between factors to be taken into account when considering a matter. **3** a formula indicating a chemical reaction by means of the symbols for the elements or compounds involved in it. **4** *Astronomy* **a** a numerical quantity added to or subtracted from an observed or calculated one to compensate for an irregularity or error. **b** the action of making such an adjustment.

equa·tor *noun* **1 a** an imaginary line round the earth or other body, equidistant from the poles and marking the division between the northern and southern hemispheres. **b** the irregular line, passing round the earth near the geographical equator, on which the earth's

Vowels: a *cat* ɑ *arm* e *bed* ɜr *her* ɜː *deux* ə *ago* ɪ *sit* i *cosy* iː *feed* ɒ *hot* ɔ *pore* oː *no* ʌ *run* ʊ *put*

magnetic field is horizontal. *Also called* MAGNETIC EQUATOR. **2** *Astronomy* = CELESTIAL EQUATOR. **3** a circle on any spherical body that divides it into two equal parts, esp. one equidistant from the two poles of rotation. **4** the plane of division of a cell or nucleus which lies midway between the poles and at right angles to a line joining them. □ **equa·tor·ward** *adverb & adjective*

equa·tor·ial /ˌɛkwəˈtɔːriəl/ *adjective* **1 a** of or pertaining to an equator, esp. that of the earth. **b** situated on, occurring near, or being characteristic of the earth's equator or equatorial regions. **2** (of the orbit of a satellite) lying in the plane of the equator. **3** (of an astronomical telescope or its mounting) such that the telescope can be rotated about one axis in the plane of the equator and another parallel to the earth's axis, so that the diurnal motion of a celestial object anywhere in the sky can be followed by rotation about the latter axis only. □ **equa·tor·ial·ly** *adverb*

Equatorial Guinea a small country of West Africa on the Gulf of Guinea, comprising several offshore islands and a coastal settlement between Cameroon and Gabon; pop. (est. 2002) 498,144; capital, Malabo (on the island of Bioko). □ **Equa·tor·ial Guin·ean** *adjective & noun*

equer·ry /ˈɛkwəri, ɪˈkweri/ *noun* (*pl.* **-ries**) **1** an officer of the British royal household attending members of the royal family. **2** *hist.* an officer of a prince's or noble's household having charge over the horses. [earlier *esquiry* from Old French *esquierie* company of squires, prince's stables, from Old French *esquier* ESQUIRE: perhaps assoc. with Latin *equus* horse]

eques·trian /ɪˈkwestriən/ ● *adjective* **1 a** of or relating to horses and horseback riding. **b** (of a person, team, etc.) skilled in horseback riding. **2 a** on horseback. **b** (of a portrait or statue) representing a person on horseback. ● *noun* a person who is skilled at horseback riding. [Latin *equestris* from *eques* horseman, knight, from *equus* horse]

eques·tri·enne /ɪˌkwestriˈen/ *noun* a female skilled at horseback riding.

equi- /ˈiːkwi, ˈɛkwi/ *combining form* equal, equally, in an equal degree. [Latin *aequi-* from *aequus* equal]

equi·angu·lar /ˌiːkwiˈaŋɡjʊlər, ˈɛkwi-/ *adjective* having all angles equal.

equi·dis·tant /ˌiːkwiˈdɪstənt, ˈɛkwi-/ *adjective* separated by an equal distance or equal distances. □ **equi·dis·tance** *noun* **equi·dis·tant·ly** *adverb*

equi·lat·eral /ˌiːkwiˈlatərəl, ˈɛkwi-/ *adjective* having all its sides equal in length.

equili·brate /ɪˈkwɪlɪˌbreit/ *verb* **1** *transitive* cause (two things) to balance or to come or stay in equilibrium. **2** *intransitive & transitive* balance or be in equilibrium. **3** *intransitive* approach a state of equilibrium. □ **equili·bra·tion** *noun* **equili·bra·tor** *noun* [Late Latin *aequilibrare aequilibrat-* (as EQUI-, *libra* balance)]

equili·brist /ɪˈkwɪlɪbrɪst/ *noun* a person who performs feats of balancing, esp. on a tightrope.

equi·lib·rium /ˌiːkwɪˈlɪbriəm, ˈɛkwi-/ *noun* (*pl.* **equi·lib·ria** /-riə/ or **equi·lib·riums**) **1** a condition of balance between opposing physical forces. **2** a state of mental or emotional equanimity. **3** a state in which the influences or processes to which a thing is subject cancel one another and produce no overall change or variation. **4** *Econ.* a situation in which supply and demand are matched and prices stable. [Latin (as EQUI-, *libra* balance)]

equine /ˈɛkwain/ ● *adjective* of, like, or affecting a horse or horses. ● *noun* a horse. [Latin *equinus* from *equus* horse]

equine encephalitis *noun* a viral infection of horses which is spread to humans by mosquitoes, its symptoms including inflammation of the brain, headache, high fever, nausea, vision problems, etc.

equi·noc·tial /ˌɛkwɪˈnɒkʃəl, ˌiːk-/ ● *adjective* **1** happening at or near the time of either equinox (*equinoctial gales*). **2** of or relating to equal day and night. **3** at or near the (terrestrial) equator. ● *noun* (in full **equinoctial line**) = CELESTIAL EQUATOR. [Old French *equinoctial* or Latin *aequinoctialis* (as EQUINOX)]

equinoctial point *noun Astronomy* the point at which the ecliptic cuts the celestial equator (twice each year at an equinox).

equi·nox /ˈiːkwiˌnɒks, ˈek-/ *noun* **1** either of the two occasions in the year when the sun crosses the celestial equator and day and night are of equal length throughout the world. **2** = EQUINOCTIAL POINT. [Old French *equinoxe* or medieval Latin *equinoxium* for Latin *aequinoctium* (as EQUI-, *nox noctis* night)]

equip *transitive verb* (**equipped**, **equip·ping**) **1** supply, fit out, or provide with what is needed. **2** (usu. in *passive*) provide with the mental, emotional, or physical abilities or resources needed for a task

etc. □ **equip·per** *noun* [French *équiper*, prob. from Old Norse *skipa* to man (a ship) from *skip* SHIP]

equip·age *noun* **1** personal items, equipment, tackle, etc. necessary for a particular undertaking. **2** a carriage and horses with attendants. [French *équipage* (as EQUIP)]

equip·ment *noun* **1** tools, articles, clothing, etc. used or required for a particular purpose. **2** intellectual or physical resources. **3** the process of equipping or being equipped.

equi·poise /ˈekwɪˌpɔiz, ˈiːkwi-/ ● *noun* **1** a balanced state or equilibrium, esp. of intellectual, moral, or social forces or interests. **2** a counterbalancing force or thing. ● *transitive verb* counterbalance or serve as an equipoise to.

equi·poten·tial /ˌekwɪpəˈtenʃəl, ˈiːkwi-/ *Physics* ● *adjective* (of a surface or line) composed of points having the same or constant potential. ● *noun* an equipotential line or surface.

equit·able /ˈekwɪtəbəl/ *adjective* **1** just or characterized by fairness or equity. **2** *Law* **a** (of a right, claim, etc.) valid or recognized in equity as distinct from common law. **b** pertaining to equity. □ **equit·able·ness** *noun* **equit·ably** *adverb* [French *équitable* (as EQUITY)]

equi·ta·tion /ˌekwɪˈteiʃən/ *noun* the art and practice of horsemanship and horseback riding. [French *équitation* or Latin *equitatio* from *equitare* ride a horse, from *eques equitis* horseman from *equus* horse]

equity /ˈekwɪti/ *noun* (*pl.* **-ties**) **1** fairness, impartiality, even-handedness. **2** the recourse to general principles of justice to correct or supplement common and statute law, esp. to provide remedies not otherwise available. **3 a** (in full **equity capital**) the issued share capital of a company. **b** the shareholders' interest in a company. **c** (in *pl.*) the common shares of a company which pay relatively low, profit-related dividends rather than fixed interest. **4 a** the excess of assets over financial liabilities. **b** (in full **equity of redemption**) the net value of a mortgaged property after deducting any charges and claims against it. **5** (**Equity**) (in full **Actors' Equity Association**) a union for actors, musicians, dancers and other performers. [Old French *equité* from Latin *aequitas -tatis* from *aequus* fair]

equiva·lent /ɪˈkwɪvələnt/ ● *adjective* **1** (often foll. by *to*) equal in value, amount, importance, etc. **2** corresponding or having the same relative position or function. **3** (of words) having the same meaning. **4** having the same result or effect. **5** *Chem.* (of a quantity of a substance) being just sufficient to combine with or displace a specified quantity of another substance. ● *noun* **1** an equivalent thing, amount, word, etc. **2** *Chem.* **a** (in full **equivalent weight**) the weight of a substance that can combine with or displace 1.0079 grams of hydrogen or 8 grams of oxygen. **b** an amount of a substance whose weight is the equivalent weight of the substance. □ **equiva·lence** *noun* **equiva·lency** *noun* **equiva·lent·ly** *adverb* [Old French from Late Latin *aequivalēre* (as EQUI-, *valēre* be worth)]

equivo·cal /ɪˈkwɪvəkəl/ *adjective* **1** (of a word, expression, etc.) ambiguous or capable of more than one interpretation. **2** (of evidence, signs, etc.) of uncertain or doubtful significance. **3** (of a person) using ambiguous or evasive language. □ **equivo·cal·ity** /-ˈkalɪti/ *noun* **equivo·cal·ly** *adverb* **equivo·cal·ness** *noun* [Late Latin *aequivocus* (as EQUI-, *vocare* call)]

equivo·cate /ɪˈkwɪvəˌkeit/ *intransitive verb* hedge, prevaricate, or use ambiguous words and expressions to mislead. □ **equivo·ca·tion** *noun* **equivo·ca·tor** *noun* [Late Latin *aequivocare* (as EQUIVOCAL)]

ER¹ *abbreviation N Amer.* EMERGENCY ROOM (*see* EMERGENCY 4).

ER² *abbreviation* **1** Queen Elizabeth. **2** King Edward. [Latin *Elizabetha Regina, Edwardus Rex*]

Er *symbol Chem.* the element erbium.

er *interjection* expressing the inarticulate sound made by a speaker who hesitates or is uncertain what to say. [imitative]

-er¹ *suffix* forming nouns from nouns, adjectives, and many verbs, denoting: **1 a** a person involved with or in something, esp. as an occupation or profession (*executioner*; *cobbler*; *lover*). **b** an animal or thing that does a specified action or activity (*poker*; *computer*; *eye-opener*). **2 a** a person who or thing which has or is, esp. a specified attribute, form, or nature (*foreigner*; *four-wheeler*; *second-rater*). **b** a thing suitable for a specified function (*broiler*). **3** a person or thing belonging to or connected with (*airliner*; *old-timer*; *whaler*). **4** a person belonging to, originating from, or resident in a specified place or group (*villager*; *Newfoundlander*; *fifth-grader*). [originally 'one who has to do with': Old English *-ere* from Germanic]

-er² *suffix* forming the comparative of adjectives (*wider*; *hotter*) and adverbs (*faster*). [Old English *-ra* (adj.), *-or* (adv.) from Germanic]

-er³ *suffix* esp. *Brit.* added to shortened forms of words to form slang and informal equivalents, usu. distorting the root word (*brekker; rugger; soccer*). [prob. an extension of -ER¹]

-er⁴ *suffix* forming verbs or verbals that express frequent repetition or intensity of action (*blunder; glimmer; twitter*). [Old English *-erian, -rian* from Germanic]

-er⁵ *suffix* **1** forming nouns and adjectives through Old French or Anglo-Norman, corresponding to: **a** Latin *-aris* (*sampler*) (compare -AR¹). **b** Latin *-arius, -arium* (*butler; carpenter; danger*). **c** (through Old French *-eüre*) Latin *-atura* or (through Old French *-eör*) Latin *-atorium* (see COUNTER¹). **2** = -OR¹.

-er⁶ *suffix* esp. *Law* forming nouns denoting verbal action or a document effecting this (*disclaimer; misnomer*). ¶ The same ending occurs in *dinner* and *supper*. [Anglo-French infin. ending of verbs]

ERA *abbreviation* **1** (also **era**) *Baseball* EARNED RUN AVERAGE. **2** *US* Equal Rights Amendment, a proposed constitutional amendment prohibiting discrimination on the basis of gender.

era /ˈɪərə, ˈiːrə/ *noun* **1 a** a system of numbering years from a particular, noteworthy event. **b** a period of years so numbered (*the Christian era*). **2 a** usu. lengthy period of history characterized by a particular state of affairs, series of events, etc. (*the pre-Roman era*). **b** a date or period to which an event, item, etc. is assigned. **3** a date or event marking the beginning of a distinctive period. **4** *Geol.* a major division of geological time that is a subdivision of an eon and is itself divided into periods. [Late Latin *aera* number expressed in figures (pl. of *aes aeris* money, treated as fem. sing.)]

erad·i·cate /ɪˈrædɪˌkeɪt/ *transitive verb* **1** get rid of, remove or destroy completely. **2** uproot, root out, or pull out by the roots. □ **erad·ic·able** *adjective* **eradi·cant** *noun* **eradi·ca·tion** *noun* **eradi·ca·tor** *noun* [Latin *eradicare* tear up by the roots (as E-¹, *radix -icis* root)]

erase /ɪˈreɪs/ *transitive verb* **1** rub out or obliterate (something written, typed, drawn, etc.). **2** remove all traces of, esp. from one's memory or mind. **3** remove recorded material from (a magnetic tape or medium). **4** *Computing* overwrite selected data with input representing an absence of data to give the impression that the original material has been removed. □ **eras·able** *adjective* **eras·abil·ity** *noun* [Latin *eradere eras-* (as E-¹, *radere* scrape)]

eras·er /ɪˈreɪsər/ *noun* a thing that erases, esp. a piece of rubber or plastic used for removing pencil and ink marks.

Eras·mus /ɪˈræzməs/ **1 Desi·der·ius** (Dutch name Gerhard Gerhards) (*c.*1469–1536), Dutch humanist and scholar. During his lifetime he was the most famous scholar in Europe, and his numerous works include the *Encomium Moriae* (*The Praise of Folly*, 1509), an edition of the New Testament in Greek (1516), and the *Colloquia Familiaria* (1519). **2 Georges** (b.1948), Canadian politician. President of the Dene Nation (1976–83), he was national chief of the Assembly of First Nations in 1985–91, and co-chair of the Royal Commission on Aboriginal Peoples (1991).

era·sure /ɪˈreɪʒər/ *noun* **1** an act or instance of erasing. **2 a** a word etc. that has been erased. **b** a place or mark where a letter, word, recording, etc. has been erased.

Erato /ˈerəˌtoʊ/ *Gk & Rom. Myth* the Muse of lyric poetry and hymns. [Greek, = lovely]

Era·tos·thenes /ˌerəˈtɒsθəˌniːz/ (*c.*275–*c.*194 BC), Greek scholar, geographer, and astronomer. Head of the library at Alexandria, he calculated the circumference of the earth by measuring the angle of the sun's rays at different places at the same time.

er·bium *noun Chem.* a soft, silvery metallic element of the lanthanide series. Symbol: **Er**; at. no.: 68. [modern Latin from *Ytterby* in Sweden, where it was first found]

ere /eər/ *preposition & conjunction archaic* before (of time) (*ere noon; ere they come*). [Old English *ær* from Germanic]

Ere·bus /ˈerəbəs/ *Gk Myth* the primeval god of darkness, son of Chaos.

Erebus, Mount a volcanic peak on Ross Island, Antarctica. Rising to 3 794 m (12,452 ft.), it is the world's most southerly active volcano. [*Erebus*, ship of Sir J. Ross's expedition to the Antarctic]

Erech·theus /ɪˈrekθiːəs/ *Gk Myth* a king of Athens, who, following the oracle at Delphi, sacrificed one of his daughters in order to defeat the invading Eleusinians.

erect ● *adjective* **1 a** upright, vertical, not bending or stooping. **b** (of an optical image) having the same orientation as the subject, not inverted. **2** (of the penis, clitoris, or nipples) enlarged and firm, esp. in sexual excitement. **3 a** (of hair) bristling, standing up from the skin. **b** (of an animal's tail or ears) standing out stiffly from the body.

● *transitive verb* **1** raise or set in an upright position. **2** build, construct, set up. **3** establish, devise, or form (a theory, conclusion, etc.). □ **erect·able** *adjective* **erect·ly** *adverb* **erect·ness** *noun* **erect·or** *noun* [Latin *erigere erect-* set up (as E-¹, *regere* direct)]

erec·tile /ɪˈrektaɪl/ *adjective* **1** that can be erected or become erect. **2** (of tissue or an organ) able to become erect when suitably stimulated.

erectile dysfunction *noun* inability to achieve an erection; impotence.

erec·tion *noun* **1 a** the act or an instance of erecting. **b** the state of being erected. **2** a thing that is erected or built, esp. a building or structure. **3** *Physiol.* **a** an erect state of an organ, esp. of the penis. **b** an occurrence of this.

erector set *noun* a construction toy consisting of components for making model buildings and vehicles.

ere·mite /ˈerəmaɪt/ *noun* a hermit or recluse, esp. one under religious vows. □ **ere·mit·ic** /-ˈmɪtɪk/ *adjective* **ere·mit·ic·al** /-ˈmɪtɪkəl/ *adjective* **ere·mit·ism** *noun* [Old French, var. of *hermite, ermite* HERMIT]

Er·furt /ˈerfʊrt/ an industrial city in central Germany, capital of Thuringia; pop. (est. 2002) 195,100.

erg¹ /ɜrg/ *noun Physics* a unit of work or energy, equal to the amount of work done by a force of one dyne when its point of application moves one centimetre in the direction of action of the force. [Greek *ergon* work]

erg² /ɜrg/ *noun* (pl. **ergs** or **areg** /ˈɑreg/) an area of shifting desert sand dunes, esp. in the Sahara. [French from Arabic *'irj*]

erga·tive /ˈɜrgətɪv/ *Grammar* ● *noun* a case of noun in some languages, such as Inuktitut or Basque, that identifies the doer of an action as the object rather than the subject of a verb. ● *adjective* **1** of or in this case. **2** denoting a language in which the object of a verb is typically the doer of an action and the subject is typically the recipient of the action. **3** functioning as such a case although not distinctively inflected as one. □ **erga·tiv·ity** /ˌɜrgəˈtɪvɪtiː/ *noun* [Greek *ergatē* worker + -IVE]

-ergic /ˈɜrdʒɪk/ *combining form* releasing, involving, or mimicking a specified substance as a neurotransmitter (*cholinergic*). [Greek *ergon* 'work' + -IC]

ergo /ˈergoʊ, ˈɜr-/ *adverb* therefore. [Latin]

er·gom·eter /erˈgɒmɪtər/ *noun* an instrument or machine which measures work or energy, esp. the work done during a period of exercise. [Greek *ergon* work + -METER]

ergo·nom·ics /ˌɜrgəˈnɒmɪks/ *noun* (treated as *sing.* or *pl.*) the field of study that deals with the relationship between people and their working environment, esp. as it affects efficiency, safety, and ease of action. □ **ergo·nom·ic** *adjective* **ergo·nom·ic·ally** *adverb* **er·gono·mist** /ɜrˈgɒnəmɪst/ *noun* [Greek *ergon* work: compare ECONOMICS]

er·gos·terol /ɜrˈgɒstəˌrɒl/ *noun Biochem.* a plant sterol, found in ergot and other fungi, that is converted to vitamin D_2 when irradiated with ultraviolet light. [ERGOT, after CHOLESTEROL]

ergot /ˈɜrgət/ *noun* **1** a disease of rye and other cereals caused by the fungus *Claviceps purpurea*. **2 a** this fungus. **b** a preparation or extract of this fungus, used medicinally for the alkaloids they contain, esp. to induce labour. [French from Old French *argot* cock's spur, from the appearance produced]

er·gota·mine /erˈgɒtəmiːn/ *noun* the pharmacologically active isomer of an alkaloid present in some kinds of ergot, used chiefly to treat migraine.

er·got·ism /ˈɜrgəˌtɪzəm/ *noun* poisoning produced by eating food affected by ergot.

erica /ˈerɪkə/ *noun* any shrub or heath of the genus *Erica*, with small leathery leaves and bell-like flowers. [Latin from Greek *ereikē* heath]

eri·ca·ceous /ˌerɪˈkeɪʃəs/ *adjective* **1** of or relating to the plant family Ericaceae, which includes heathers, azaleas, and rhododendrons. **2** (of compost) suitable for ericaceous and other lime-hating plants. [modern Latin *Ericaceae* from ERICA]

Erick·son, Ar·thur Charles (b.1924), Canadian architect. His designs are often characterized by dramatic siting and the interpenetration of exterior and interior spaces within a post-and-beam framework; they include the Central Mall of Simon Fraser University in Burnaby (1963–5), the Law Courts in Vancouver (1974–9), and Roy Thomson Hall in Toronto (1982).

Erics·son ▶ 1 John (1803–89), Swedish engineer. He invented the marine screw propeller (1836) and built the first ship to have a revolving armoured turret, the ironclad *Monitor* (1862), which was used by the Union in the American Civil War. **2 Leif** (also **Eric·son,**

Consonants: b *but* d *dog* f *few* g *get* h *her* j *yes* k *cat* l *leg* m *man* n *no* p *pen* r *red* s *sit*

Eriks·son) (970–1020), Norse explorer, son of Eric the Red. He sailed westward from Greenland (c.1000) and reputedly discovered land (variously identified as Labrador, Newfoundland, or New England), which he named Vinland because of the vines he found growing there.

Eric the Red (c.940–c.1010), Norse explorer. He left Iceland in 982 in search of land to the west, exploring Greenland and establishing a Norse settlement there in 986.

Eri·danus /e'rɪdənəs/ the River, a winding constellation of the southern hemisphere, spanning sixty degrees in delineation, from near Orion to near Hydrus. [Latin from Greek, name of river in which Phaethon drowned in Greek mythology]

Erie, Lake the most southerly of the Great Lakes (25 812 sq. km), situated on the border between Canada and the US. It is linked to Lake Huron by the Detroit River and to Lake Ontario by the Welland Canal and the Niagara River, which is its only natural outlet. [the *Erie*, a native people absorbed after 1650 into the Iroquois, from *erihon* 'wildcat']

erig·eron /ɪ'rɪgə,rɒn/ *noun* any composite herb of the genus *Erigeron*, with daisy-like flowers. [Greek *ērigerōn* from *ēri* early + *gerōn* old man, because some species bear grey down]

Eriks·son see ERICSSON 2.

Erin /'ɛrɪn, 'iːrɪn/ *noun* **1** *archaic* or *poet.* Ireland. **2** a town in S central Ontario, NW of Brampton; pop. (2001) 11,052. [Irish]

Erinys /e'rɪnəs/ *noun* (*pl.* **Erinyes** /e'rɪnɪ,iːz/) *Myth* any of the Furies. [Greek]

Eris /'ɛrəs/ *Gk Myth* the goddess of discord.

eris·tic /e'rɪstɪk/ ● *adjective* **1** of, characterized by, or pertaining to disputation. **2** (of an argument or arguer) aiming at winning rather than at reaching the truth. ● *noun* **1** the art or practice of disputation. **2** a person given to disputation. [Greek *eristikos* from *erizō* wrangle from *eris* strife]

Eri·trea /,ɛrɪ'triːə, -treɪə/ an independent state in NE Africa, on the Red Sea; pop. (est. 2002) 4,465,651; language, Tigre and other Cushitic languages; capital, Asmara. □ **Eri·trean** *adjective* & *noun*

Er·langer /'ɜːrlæŋər/ **Jo·seph** (1874–1965), US physiologist. With H. Gasser he developed techniques for recording nerve impulses, and demonstrated that different fibres in the same nerve cord can have different functions; they shared a Nobel Prize for this in 1944.

erl-king *noun* (in Germanic mythology) a bearded giant or goblin who lures little children to the land of death. [German *Erlkönig* alder-king, a mistranslation of Danish *ellerkonge* king of the elves]

ERM *abbreviation* EXCHANGE RATE MECHANISM.

er·mine /'ɜːmɪn/ *noun* (*pl.* same or **er·mines**) **1** a flesh-eating mammal, *Mustela erminea*, of the weasel family, having brown fur in the summer turning mainly white in the winter, with the tail remaining black-tipped. **2 a** the white fur of an ermine as used in clothing, often with the black tails displayed for the sake of effect. **b** a symbol of purity or honour, esp. with reference to the use of ermine in the robes of judges and peers. **3** *Heraldry* one of the two chief furs, consisting of a white field covered with distinctive black markings. □ **er·mined** *adjective* [Old French (h)*ermine* prob. from medieval Latin (*mus*) *Armenius* Armenian (mouse)]

Er·mite /er'miːt/ *noun* a creamy, semi-soft, and salty blue veined cheese made in Quebec. [French *ermite* hermit]

-ern *suffix* forming adjectives from the names of the directions (*northern*; *western*). [Old English -*erne* from Germanic]

Ernst, Max (1891–1976), German artist. A leading member of the dada and surrealist movements, he is best known for paintings such as *L'Éléphant de Célèbes* (1921); in 1925 he developed the technique of frottage, using such surfaces as leaves and wood grain, as in *Habit of Leaves* (1925).

erode *verb* **1** *transitive* & *intransitive* wear away (esp. soil or rock), destroy or be destroyed gradually. **2** *transitive* & *intransitive* make or become gradually diminished in value, strength, etc. □ **eroded** *adjective* **erod·ible** *adjective* [French *éroder* or Latin *erodere* (as E-¹, *rodere* ros- gnaw)]

er·ogen·ous /ɪ'rɒdʒɪnəs/ *adjective* (esp. of a part of the body) sensitive to sexual stimulation (*erogenous zone*). [as EROTIC + -GENOUS]

-eroo *suffix* esp. *N Amer.*, *Austral.*, & *NZ* forming nouns from verbs with the senses 'large of the type or class', 'overwhelming', 'remarkable', 'unexpected' (*switcheroo*; *smackeroo*). [fanciful]

Eros /'ɛrɒs, 'iːr-/ **1** *Gk Myth* the god of love (see CUPID). **2** *Astronomy* asteroid 433, discovered in 1898, which comes at times nearer to earth than any celestial body except the moon. [Greek *erōs*, = sexual love]

eros /'ɛrɒs, iːrɒs/ *noun* **1** earthly, romantic, or sexual love. *Compare*

AGAPE². **2** *Psych.* **a** the libido. **b** the urge towards self-preservation (opp. THANATOS). [Greek]

ero·sion /ɪ'rəʊʒən/ *noun* **1** *Geol.* the wearing away of the earth's surface by wind, water, or glacial action. **2 a** the act or an instance of eroding. **b** the process of being eroded. □ **ero·sion·al** *adjective* **ero·sive** *adjective* [French *érosion* from Latin *erosio* (as ERODE)]

erot·ic /ɪ'rɒtɪk/ *adjective* **1** of or pertaining to sexual love. **2** tending to arouse sexual desire or excitement. □ **erot·ic·ally** *adverb* [French *érotique* from Greek *erōtikos* from *erōs erōtos* sexual love]

erot·ica /ɪ'rɒtɪkə/ *noun* intentionally erotic literature or art.

eroti·cism /ɪ'rɒtɪ,sɪzəm/ *noun* **1 a** erotic nature or character. **b** sexual excitement. **2** the use of or response to erotic images or stimulation.

eroti·cize /ɪ'rɒtɪsaɪz/ *transitive verb* (also esp. *Brit.* **-cise**) **1** make erotic or endow with an erotic quality. **2** stimulate sexually.
□ **eroti·ciz·a·tion** *noun* **eroti·cized** *adjective*

eroto- /ɪ,rɒtɒ/ *combining form* erotic, eroticism. [Greek *erōs erōtos* sexual love]

eroto·mania /ɪ,rɒtə'meɪnɪə/ *noun* **1** an obsessive erotic desire, esp. with fantasies, delusions, etc. **2** an excessive, but not pathological, preoccupation with sexual passion. □ **eroto·maniac** *noun*

err /er/ *intransitive verb* **1** be mistaken or incorrect. **2** do wrong, go morally astray, sin. □ **err on the side of** act with a specified bias (*errs on the side of generosity*). [Old French *errer* from Latin *errare* stray]

er·rand *noun* **1** a short trip, often on another's behalf, to buy or deliver something, take a message, etc. **2** the object of such a journey.
□ **errand of mercy** a journey to give help, relieve suffering, etc. [Old English *ærende* from Germanic]

er·rant /'erənt/ *adjective* **1 a** erring, doing wrong, deviating from an accepted standard. **b** erratic or breaking with the dominant pattern, movement, etc. (*soaked by an errant wave*). **2** *literary* or *archaic* travelling in search of adventure (*knight errant*). □ **er·rancy** *noun* (in sense 1).
er·rant·ry *noun* (in sense 2). [Middle English: sense 1 formed as ERR: sense 2 from Old French *errer*, ultimately from Late Latin *itinerare* from *iter* journey]

er·rat·ic /ɪ'ratɪk/ ● *adjective* **1** inconsistently variable in conduct, opinions, etc. **2** irregular or uncertain in movement, esp. having no fixed course or direction. **3** (of a boulder etc.) differing from surrounding rock and believed to have been brought from a distance by glacial action. ● *noun* a large block of rock carried by a glacier and deposited some distance from where it was formed. □ **er·rat·ic·ally** *adverb* [Old French *erratique* from Latin *erraticus* (as ERR)]

er·ratum /ɪ'ratəm/ *noun* (*pl.* **er·rata** /-tə/) **1** an error in a printed or written text, esp. one noted in a list appended to a book or published in a subsequent issue of a journal. **2** (in *pl.*) a list of corrected errors attached to a book etc. [Latin, neuter past participle (as ERR)]

Er Rif see RIF MOUNTAINS.

er·ro·ne·ous /ɪ'rəʊnɪəs/ *adjective* incorrect, containing or arising from an error. □ **er·ro·ne·ous·ly** *adverb* **er·ro·ne·ous·ness** *noun* [Latin *erroneus* from *erro -onis* vagabond (as ERR)]

er·ror *noun* **1** a mistake. **2** the condition of being wrong in conduct or judgment (*led into error*). **3** a wrong opinion or judgment. **4** the amount by which something is incorrect or inaccurate in a calculation or measurement. **5** *Baseball* a fielder's misplay, such as a fumble or wild throw, allowing a batter to reach base, a runner to advance, etc. **6** a postage stamp which contains a misprint or other irregularity, such as incorrect colour or paper. □ **error·less** *adjective* [Old French *errour* from Latin *error -oris* (as ERR)]

error message *noun* *Computing* a message occurring on a computer screen or printout, reporting an error usu. in the commands given to the computer.

er·satz /'erzats, 'ɜr-/ ● *adjective* imitation (esp. of inferior quality). ● *noun* an ersatz thing. [German, = replacement]

Erse /ɜrs/ ● *adjective* Irish or Highland Gaelic. ● *noun* the Gaelic language. [early Scots form of IRISH]

erst /ɜrst/ *adverb* archaic formerly; of old. [Old English *ærest* superlative of *ær*: see ERE]

erst·while /'ɜrstwaɪl/ ● *adjective* former, previous. ● *adverb* archaic = ERST.

ERT *abbreviation* emergency response team.

eru·cic acid /ɪ'ruːsɪk/ *noun* a solid, unsaturated fatty acid present in mustard seeds and rape seeds. [Latin *eruca* rocket (the plant), caterpillar]

eruc·ta·tion /iːrʌk'teɪʃən, ɪ-/ *noun* the act or an instance of belching. [Latin *eructatio* from *eructare* (as E-¹, *ructare* 'belch')]

eru·dite /ˈerjuːˌdəɪt, ˈeroˌdəɪt/ *adjective* **1** (of a person) learned, scholarly. **2** (of writing etc.) showing great learning. □ **eru·dite·ly** *adverb* **eru·di·tion** /-ˈdɪʃən/ *noun* [Latin *eruditus* past participle of *erudire* instruct, train (as E-¹, *rudis* untrained)]

erupt *intransitive verb* **1** break out or burst forth suddenly or dramatically. **2** (of a volcano) become active and eject lava etc. **3 a** (of a rash, boil, etc.) appear on the skin. **b** (of the skin) produce a rash, pimples, etc. **4** (of the teeth) break through the gums in normal development. □ **erup·tion** *noun* **erup·tive** *adjective* [Latin *erumpere erupt-* (as E-¹, *rumpere* break)]

-ery *suffix* forming nouns denoting: **1** a class or kind of thing (*greenery*; *machinery*; *citizenry*). **2 a** employment or an occupation (*dentistry*; *midwifery*). **b** a state or condition (*slavery*; *bravery*). **3** a place of work or where things can be bought (*brewery*; *bakery*; *eatery*). **4** often *derogatory* characteristic qualities, ideas, or actions (*knavery*; *tomfoolery*). **5** a place where plants or animals live or are reared (*rookery*; *pinery*). [French *-erie*, *-ere*, ultimately from Latin *-ario-*, *-ator*]

ery·sip·elas /ˌerɪˈsɪpɪləs/ *noun Med.* an acute, sometimes recurrent, streptococcal infection characterized by large raised patches on the skin, esp. of the face and legs, with fever and severe general illness. [Latin from Greek *erusipelas*, perhaps related to *eruthros* red + a root *pel-* skin]

ery·thema /ˌerɪˈθiːmə/ *noun* a superficial reddening of the skin, usu. in patches, as a result of injury or irritation. □ **ery·thema·tous** /ˌerɪˈθiːmətəs/ *adjective* [modern Latin from Greek *eruthēma* from *eruthainō* be red, from *eruthros* red]

erythro- /əˈrɪθrɔː/ *combining form* red. [Greek *eruthros* red]

eryth·ro·blast /ɪˈrɪθrɔːˌblast/ *noun* a nucleated cell which develops into an erythrocyte. [German]

eryth·ro·cyte /ɪˈrɪθrɔːˌsəɪt/ *noun* one of the principal cells in the blood of vertebrates, containing the pigment hemoglobin and transporting oxygen and carbon dioxide to and from the tissues. *Also called* RED BLOOD CELL. □ **eryth·ro·cyt·ic** /-ˈsɪtɪk/ *adjective*

eryth·roid /ˈerɪˌθrɔɪd/ *adjective* of or relating to erythrocytes.

eryth·ro·mycin /ɪˌrɪθrɔːˈməɪsɪn/ *noun* an antibiotic isolated from *Streptomyces erythreus*, similar in its effects to penicillin. [ERYTHRO- + -MYCIN]

eryth·ro·poi·esis /ɪˌrɪθrɔːpɔɪˈiːsɪs/ *noun* the formation of red blood cells. □ **eryth·ro·poi·etic** /-pɔɪˈetɪk/ *adjective* [ERYTHRO- + Greek *poiesis* creation]

eryth·ro·poi·etin /ɪˌrɪθrɔːpɔɪˈiːtɪn/ *noun* a hormone, secreted by the kidneys, that increases the rate of formation of red blood cells, often used as a performance-enhancing drug. Abbr.: **EPO**. [ERYTHROPOIESIS + -IN]

Erz·ge·birge /ˈertsgəˌbirgə/ (also called the **Ore Mountains**) a range of mountains on the border between Germany and the Czech Republic.

Erzu·rum /ˈerzuˌrum/ a city in NE Turkey, capital of a mountainous province of the same name; pop. (est. 2002) 333,300.

Es *symbol Chem.* the element einsteinium.

-es¹ *suffix* forming plurals of nouns ending in sibilant sounds (such words in *-e* dropping the *e*) (*kisses*; *cases*; *boxes*; *churches*). [var. of -S¹]

-es² *suffix* forming the 3rd person sing. present of verbs ending in sibilant sounds (such words in *-e* dropping the *e*) and ending in *-o* (but not *-oo*) (*goes*; *places*; *pushes*). [var. of -S²]

ESA *abbreviation* **1** European Space Agency. **2** *Brit.* Environmentally Sensitive Area.

Esaki /ɪˈsɒki/ **Leo** (born Esaki Reiona) (b.1925), Japanese physicist. He pioneered the development of quantum-mechanical tunnelling of electrons in semiconductor devices, and his tunnel diodes (also known as Esaki diodes) are now widespread in electronic devices; he shared the Nobel Prize for physics in 1973.

Esau /ˈiːsɒ/ *Bible* the elder of the twin sons of Isaac and Rebecca, who sold his birthright to his brother Jacob and was tricked out of his father's blessing by his brother (Gen. 25, 27).

Esc *abbreviation Computing* escape (key).

es·cal·ate /ˈeskəˌleɪt/ *verb* **1** *intransitive & transitive* increase or develop (usu. rapidly) by stages. **2** *transitive* cause (an action, activity, or process) to become more intense. □ **es·cal·at·ing** *adjective* **es·cal·a·tion** /-ˈleɪʃən/ *noun* [back-formation from ESCALATOR]

es·cal·ator /ˈeskəˌleɪtɚ/ *noun* a moving staircase consisting of an endless chain of steps on a circulating belt driven by a motor. [from the stem of *escalade* 'climb a wall by ladder' + -ATOR]

escalator clause *noun* (also **escalation clause**) a clause in a contract etc. providing for changes in prices, wages etc. under certain conditions.

es·cal·lon·ia /ˌeskəˈlɔːniə/ *noun* any evergreen shrub of the genus *Escallonia*, bearing pink, red, or white flowers. [*Escallon*, 18th-c. Spanish traveller]

es·cal·ope /ˈeskəˌlɒp/ *noun* a thin, boneless slice of meat, esp. veal or turkey. [French (in Old French = shell): see SCALLOP]

es·cap·ade /ˈeskəˌpeɪd, ˌeskəˈpeɪd/ *noun* a daring, reckless, or adventurous act. [French from Provençal or Spanish *escapada* (as ESCAPE)]

es·cape ● *verb* **1** *intransitive* (often foll. by *from*) break free or free oneself by fleeing or struggling. **2** *intransitive* (of a gas, liquid, etc.) leak or seep out from a container or pipe etc. **3** *intransitive* get off safely or succeed in avoiding danger, punishment, etc. **4** *transitive* get completely free of (a person, grasp, etc.). **5** *transitive* avoid or elude (a commitment, danger, etc.). **6** *transitive* elude the notice or memory of (*nothing escapes you*; *the name escaped me*). **7** *transitive* (of words etc.) be uttered inadvertently by. ● *noun* **1** the act or an instance of escaping or avoiding danger, injury, etc. **2** the state or fact of having escaped (*was a narrow escape*). **3** (often *attributive*) a possibility or means of escaping (*a trap with no escape*; *escape hatch*). **4** a leakage of gas etc. **5** a temporary relief from reality or worry. **6** (in full **escape key**) *Computing* a key which either ends the current operation or changes the function of other keys pressed subsequently. **7 a** a garden plant running wild. **b** an animal or bird which has escaped captivity. □ **es·cap·able** *adjective* **es·cap·er** *noun* [Old Northern French *escaper*, ultimately from medieval Latin (as EX-¹, *cappa* cloak)]

escape artist *noun* **1** a person proficient at escaping from handcuffs, chains, etc., esp. for entertainment purposes. **2** a person, esp. a prisoner, adept at escaping confinement.

escape clause *noun* a clause in a law, contract, etc. specifying the conditions under which a party is free from an obligation.

es·capee /ɪskeɪˈpiː, ɪˈskeɪpiː, ˌeskeɪˈpiː/ *noun* a person, esp. a prisoner, who has escaped.

es·cape·ment *noun* **1 a** a mechanism in a clock or watch that alternately checks or releases the train by a fixed amount and transmits a periodic impulse from the spring or weight to the balance wheel or pendulum. **b** the mechanism in a typewriter which controls the regular, leftward movement of the carriage between key strokes. **2** the part of the mechanism in a piano that enables the hammer to fall back as soon as it has struck the string. [French *échappement* from *échapper* ESCAPE]

escape velocity *noun* the minimum velocity at which a body must be projected into space if it is not eventually to return to a planet etc. by gravitational attraction.

escape wheel *noun* a toothed wheel in the escapement of a watch or clock.

es·cap·ism *noun* the tendency to seek distraction and relief from reality, esp. in the arts or through fantasy. □ **es·cap·ist** *noun & adjective*

es·cap·ol·ogy /ˌeskəˈpɒlədʒi/ *noun* the methods and techniques of escaping from confinement, esp. as a form of entertainment. □ **es·cap·ol·o·gist** *noun*

es·car·got /eskarˈgoː/ *noun* (*pl.* **es·car·gots** *pronunc.* same) a snail as an item of food. [French]

es·car·ole /ˈeskərɔːl/ *noun N Amer.* a variety of chicory with broad, crisp, undivided, and bitter-tasting leaves used in salads.

es·carp·ment *noun Geol.* a long, steep-sided ridge, esp. one at the edge of a plateau or separating areas of land at different heights. [French *escarpement* from *escarpe* SCARP]

-esce /es/ *suffix* forming verbs, usu. initiating action (*effervesce*; *fluoresce*). [from or after Latin *-escere*]

-escent /ˈesənt/ *suffix* forming adjectives denoting the beginning of a state or action (*effervescent*; *fluorescent*). □ **-escence** *suffix*. [from or after French *-escent* or Latin *-escent-*, pres. part. stem of verbs in *-escere*]

es·char /ˈeskɑr/ *noun* a dry, dark scab, esp. one caused by burning.

es·chat·ol·ogy /ˌeskəˈtɒlədʒi/ *noun* (*pl.* **-gies**) **1** the branch of theology concerned with last things, e.g. death, judgment, heaven, and hell. **2** a belief or beliefs about the destiny of humankind and the world. □ **es·chato·logic·al** /-təˈlɒdʒɪkəl/ *adjective* **es·chat·ol·o·gist** *noun* [Greek *eskhatos* last + -LOGY]

es·cheat /ɪsˈtʃiːt/ ● *noun* **1** the reversion of property to the state, or (in feudal law) to a lord, on the owner's dying without legal heirs. **2** property affected by this. ● *verb* **1** *transitive* hand over (property) as an escheat. **2** *intransitive* revert by escheat. [Old French *eschete*, ultimately from Latin *excidere* (as EX-¹, *cadere* fall)]

Escher /ˈeʃɚ/ **Maur·its Cor·neille** (1898-1972), Dutch graphic artist. His prints make sophisticated use of visual illusion. From the 1940s his work became more surrealist, with, for example, staircases that appear to lead both up and down in the same direction.

Esche·rich·ia coli /ˌeʃəˈrɪkiːə ˈkoːlaɪ/ *noun* (also **E. coli**) a species of Gram-negative bacillus which normally inhabits the large intestine and, under certain conditions, becomes pathogenic, esp. when transferred to other sites such as the urinary tract. [Theodor *Escherich*, German pediatrician d.1911 + *coli* see COLIFORM]

es·chew /esˈtʃuː/ *transitive verb literary* carefully or deliberately avoid, abstain from, or shun. □ **es·chew·al** *noun* [Middle English from Old French *eschiver*, ultimately from Germanic: related to SHY¹]

Es·cof·fier /eˈskɒfieɪ/ **(Georges) Au·guste** (1846–1935), French chef, who gained an international reputation while working at the Savoy Hotel, London (1890–9).

es·cort ● *noun* /ˈeskɔrt/ **1 a** one or more persons, vehicles, ships, etc. accompanying another, esp. for protection, security, or as a mark of rank or status. **b** the protection or company of an escort. **2** a person accompanying a person of the opposite sex socially. **3** (also *attributive*) **a** a usu. young, attractive person legitimately employed to provide another with entertainment etc. (*escort agency*). **b** *euphemism* a prostitute. ● *transitive verb* /esˈkɔrt/ accompany for protection, guidance, courtesy, etc. [French *escorte, escorter* from Italian *scorta* fem. past participle of *scorgere* conduct]

es·cri·toire /ˌeskriˈtwɒr/ *noun* a writing desk with drawers for papers, envelopes, etc. and usu. a hinged flap to conceal these. [French from Latin *scriptorium* writing room: see SCRIPTORIUM]

es·crow /eˈskroʊ/ *Law* ● *noun* **1** money, property, or a written bond, kept in the custody of a third party until a specified condition has been fulfilled. **2** the status of this (*in escrow*). ● *transitive verb* place in escrow. [Anglo-French *escrowe*, Old French *escroe* scrap, scroll, from medieval Latin *scroda* from Germanic]

es·cudo /eˈskuːdoʊ/ *noun* (*pl.* **-cudos**) the former principal monetary unit of Portugal (equal to 100 centavos) and, formerly, of some other countries that were or had been Portuguese or Spanish territories, e.g. Chile. [Spanish & Portuguese from Latin *scutum* shield]

es·cut·cheon /ɪˈskʌtʃən/ *noun* **1** a shield or emblem bearing a coat of arms. **2** the protective plate around a keyhole, door handle, tap, etc. **3** the middle part of a ship's stern where the name is placed. □ **es·cut·cheoned** *adjective* [Anglo-French & Old Northern French *escuchon*, ultimately from Latin *scutum* shield]

Esd. *abbreviation* Esdras (Apocrypha).

Es·dras /ˈezdrəs/ **1** either of two books of the Apocrypha, of which the first is mainly a compilation from Chronicles, Nehemiah, and Ezra, and the second is a record of angelic revelation. **2** (in the Vulgate) the books of Ezra and Nehemiah.

ESE *abbreviation* east-southeast.

-ese *suffix* forming adjectives and nouns denoting: **1** an inhabitant or language of a country or city (*Japanese; Milanese; Viennese*). ¶ Plural forms are the same. **2** often *derogatory* character or style, esp. of language (*officialese*). [Old French *-eis*, ultimately from Latin *-ensis*]

Esfa·han see ISFAHAN.

es·ker *noun Geomorph.* a long, narrow ridge, usu. of sand and gravel, deposited in a river valley by a stream flowing under a former glacier or ice sheet. [Irish *eiscir*]

Es·kimo ● *noun* (*pl.* same or **-kimos**) **1** a member of an Aboriginal people inhabiting N Canada, Alaska, Greenland, and E Siberia. **2** the language of this people. ● *adjective* of or relating to the Eskimos or their language. ¶ In Canada, the word *Eskimo* has been superseded by *Inuit* with reference to the people and *Inuktitut* with reference to their language. [Danish from French *Esquimaux* (pl.) from Algonquian]

Eskimo dog *noun N Amer.* a sturdy dog with webbed feet and slanting eyes, used in the north for pulling sleds, hunting, etc.

Eskimo roll *noun* a complete revolution in a kayak, from upright to capsized to upright.

Es·ki·şe·hir /esˌkiʃəˈhiːr/ a city in W Turkey, approximately 200 km west of Ankara; pop. (est. 1997) 454,536.

ESL *abbreviation* English as a second language.

ESN *abbreviation* electronic serial number, a unique number programmed into a cellphone which identifies it.

esoph·a·gus /iːˈsɒfəgəs/ *noun* (*pl.* **esoph·agi** /-dʒaɪ/ or **-gus·es**) (also esp. *Brit.* **oesoph·a·gus**) the gullet or the part of the alimentary canal from the mouth to the stomach. □ **esopha·geal** /iːˌsɒfəˈdʒiːəl, ˌiːsəˈfadʒiəl/ *adjective* [var. of OESOPHAGUS]

eso·ter·ic /ˌesoʊˈterɪk/ *adjective* (of a doctrine, field of study, mode of speech, etc.) intended only for, or intelligible only to, the initiated or those with special knowledge. □ **eso·ter·ic·ally** *adverb*

eso·ter·icism /-ˌsɪzəm/ *noun* **eso·ter·icist** /-sɪst/ *noun* [Greek *esōterikos* from *esōterō* comparative of *esō* within]

eso·ter·ica /esəˈterɪkə, iːs-/ *noun* esoteric details, items, or publications.

ESP *abbreviation* extrasensory perception.

esp. *abbreviation* especially.

es·pa·drille /ˌespəˈdrɪl/ *noun* a light canvas shoe with a braided fibre sole. [French from Provençal *espardillo* from *espart* ESPARTO]

es·pal·ier /əˈspaljər/ ● *noun* **1** a latticework or framework of stakes along which the branches of a tree or shrub are trained to grow flat against a wall etc. **2** a tree or shrub trained in this way. ● *transitive verb* train (a plant, shrub, etc.) as an espalier. □ **es·pal·iered** *adjective* [French from Italian *spalliera* from *spalla* shoulder]

Es·pan·ola /espəˈnoːlə/ a town in north central Ontario, situated on the Spanish River, about 60 km southwest of Sudbury; pop. (2001) 5,449. □ **Es·pan·olian** *noun* [Spanish, feminine form of adjective *español* Spanish, after the Spanish River]

es·parto /eˈspɑrtoʊ/ *noun* (*pl.* **-tos**) (in full **esparto grass**) a coarse grass, *Stipa tenacissima*, native to Spain and N Africa, with tough narrow leaves, used to make ropes, wickerwork, and high-quality paper. [Spanish from Latin *spartum* from Greek *sparton* rope]

es·pe·cial *adjective* **1** notable, pre-eminent, or exceptional. **2** particular, individual, or attributed or belonging chiefly to one person or thing (*your especial charm*). [Old French from Latin *specialis* special]

es·pe·cial·ly *adverb* **1** chiefly, pre-eminently. **2** particularly or much more than in other cases.

Es·per·anto /ˌespəˈrantoʊ/ *noun* an artificial language invented in 1887 and based on roots common to the chief European languages with endings standardized. □ **Es·per·an·tist** *noun* [the pen name (from Latin *sperare* hope) of its inventor, L. L. Zamenhof, Polish physician d.1917]

es·pial /ɪˈspaɪəl/ *noun* the act or an instance of catching sight of or of being seen. [Old French *espiaille* from *espier*: see ESPY]

es·pion·age /ˈespiəˌnɒʒ/ *noun* the practice of spying or of using spies, esp. to obtain secret information. [French *espionnage* from *espionner* from *espion* SPY]

es·plan·ade /ˌespləˈnɒd, -ˈneɪd, ˈesp-/ *noun* **1** a level, open space along a waterfront, where people may walk or drive. **2** a level space separating a fortress from the town that it commands. [French from Spanish *esplanada* from *esplanar* make level, from Latin *explanare* (as EX-¹, *planus* level)]

Es·poir, Bay d' /əˈsper/ a long, narrow inlet of the N Atlantic, situated on the south central coast of Newfoundland. [French, lit. 'bay of hope']

es·poir /ˈespwɑr/ *noun* **1** *Wrestling* a category of competition for wrestlers between 17 and 20 years old. **2** *Cdn* (in other amateur sports) a junior elite athlete potentially of national team calibre. [French, lit. 'hope']

Espoo /ˈespoʊ/ a city in S Finland, just west of Helsinki; pop. (est. 2000) 209,667.

Es·po·sito /ˌespəˈziːtoʊ/ **Phil·ip An·thony ('Phil')** (b.1942), Canadian hockey player. During his NHL career (1963–82), he was a centre with the Boston Bruins (1967–75), leading the team to two Stanley Cup victories (1970 and 1972), played for Team Canada during the Canada-Soviet hockey series (1972), and played for the New York Rangers (1975–82).

es·pous·al *noun* (foll. by *of*) the action or an act of espousing a cause.

es·pouse /ɪˈspaʊz/ *transitive verb* adopt or support (a cause, doctrine, etc.). □ **es·pous·er** *noun* [Old French *espouser* from Latin *sponsare* from *sponsus* past participle of *spondēre* betroth]

es·presso *noun* (also **ex·presso** /ekˈspresoʊ/) (*pl.* **-sos**) strong, concentrated, black coffee made by forcing steam through ground coffee beans. [Italian, = pressed out]

es·prit /eˈspriː/ *noun* **1** wit. **2** spirit, liveliness. [French from Latin *spiritus* SPIRIT]

esprit de corps /eˈspriː də ˈkɔr/ *noun* loyalty and devotion to, as well as regard for the honour and interests of, a group to which one belongs. [French from Latin *spiritus* SPIRIT + *corps* body]

espy /ɪˈspaɪ/ *transitive verb* (**-ies, -ied**) *literary* catch sight of or perceive, esp. at a distance. [Old French *espier*: see SPY]

Esq. *abbreviation* Esquire.

-esque *suffix* forming adjectives meaning 'resembling in style or characteristics' (*romanesque*; *Schumannesque*; *statuesque*). [French from Italian *-esco* from medieval Latin *-iscus*]

Es·qui·malt[1] /esˈkwaimɒlt/ a district municipality in BC, situated at the southern tip of Vancouver Island, just west of Victoria; pop. (2001) 16,127. [Straits, = 'place of gradual shoaling']

Es·qui·malt[2] /esˈkwaimɒlt/ *noun* a member of a Salishan Aboriginal group living near Esquimalt. [ESQUIMALT[1]]

Es·qui·mau /ˈeskɪˌmoː/ *noun* (*pl.* **-maux** /-oːz/) *archaic var. of* ESKIMO. [French]

Es·qui·pu·las /ˌeskiːˈpuːlas/ a town in SE Guatemala, near the border with Honduras; pop. (est. 2002) 16,800. Noted for the image of the 'Black Christ of Esquipulas' in its church, the town is a centre of religious pilgrimage.

es·quire /ɪˈskwair, ˈeskwair/ *noun* **1** (usu. as abbr. **Esq.**) *Brit.* a title appended to a man's surname when no other form of address is used, esp. as a formal form of address for letters. **2** *archaic* = SQUIRE. [Old French *esquier* from Latin *scutarius* shield bearer, from *scutum* shield]

ESR *abbreviation* *Physics* electron spin resonance.

ess *noun* the letter S, s. [representing pronunciation of the letter]

-ess[1] *suffix* forming nouns denoting females (*actress*; *lioness*; *goddess*). [from or after French *-esse* from Late Latin *-issa* from Greek *-issa*] ¶ For nouns designating women, those ending in *-er*, *-or*, etc. which are not gender specific, where such exist, are now often preferred.

-ess[2] *suffix* forming abstract nouns from adjectives (*duress*). [French *-esse* from Latin *-itia*; compare -ICE]

es·say ● *noun* /ˈesei/ **1 a** a written composition, usu. short and in prose, on any subject. **b** a short, coherent composition in any medium (*photo essay*). **2** (often foll. by *at*, *in*) *formal* an attempt. ● *transitive verb* /eˈsei/ *formal* attempt, try. □ **essay·ist** *noun* **essay·is·tic** *adjective* [Middle English from ASSAY, assimilated to French *essayer*, ultimately from Late Latin *exagium* weighing, from *exigere* weigh: see EXACT]

Essen /ˈesən/ an industrial city in the Ruhr valley, in NW Germany; pop. (est. 2002) 589,900.

es·sence *noun* **1 a** the indispensable quality or element identifying a thing or determining its character. **b** the intrinsic nature or quality of something. **2 a** an extract of a plant, drug, etc. usu. obtained by distillation and containing all the source's important qualities in concentrated form. **b** a perfume or scent, esp. as an alcoholic solution of volatile substances. **3** *Philos.* an abstract reality underlying a phenomenon or all phenomena. □ **in essence** fundamentally, essentially. **of the essence** very important, indispensable, vital. [Old French from Latin *essentia* from *esse* be]

Es·sene /ˈesiːn, eˈsiːn/ *noun* a member of an ancient Jewish ascetic sect who lived communally and are widely regarded as the authors of the Dead Sea Scrolls. [Latin pl. *Esseni* from Greek pl. *Essēnoi*]

es·sen·tial /ɪˈsenʃəl, i-/ ● *adjective* **1** absolutely necessary; indispensable. **2** fundamental, basic (*essential principles*). **3** of or constituting the essence of a person or thing. **4** (of an amino acid or a fatty acid) required by a living organism for normal growth, but not produced by the organism and therefore required in the diet. **5** (of a disease) with no known external stimulus or cause; idiopathic. ● *noun* (esp. in *pl.*) a basic or indispensable element or thing. □ **es·sen·ti·al·ity** /-ʃiˈalɪti/ *noun* **es·sen·tial·ly** *adverb* [Late Latin *essentialis* (as ESSENCE)]

essential element *noun* any of various chemical elements, such as calcium, magnesium, etc., required by living organisms for normal growth.

es·sen·tial·ism /ɪˈsenʃəlɪzəm, i-/ *noun* *Philos.* the belief that things have a set of characteristics which make them what they are, and that the task of science and philosophy is their discovery and expression. □ **es·sen·tial·ist** *noun & adjective*

es·sen·tial·ize /ɪˈsenʃəlaiz, i-/ *transitive verb* (also esp. *Brit.* **-ise**) formulate in essential form; express the essential form of. □ **es·sen·tial·iz·a·tion** *noun* (also esp. *Brit.* **-isation**).

essential oil *noun* a natural oil typically obtained by distillation and having the characteristic odour of the plant etc. from which it is extracted.

Esse·quibo River /ˌesiˈkiːboː/ a river in Guyana, rising in the Guiana Highlands and flowing about 965 km (600 miles) northward to the Atlantic.

Essex[1] /ˈesiks/ **1** a county of E England; county town, Chelmsford. **2** a town in SW Ontario, about 20 km southeast of Windsor; pop. (2001) 20,085. [sense 2 after sense 1]

Essex[2] /ˈesiks/ **2nd Earl of** (title of Robert Devereux) (1567–1601), English soldier and courtier. A favourite of Elizabeth I, he was executed

for treason after organizing an unsuccessful rebellion in London (1601).

EST *abbreviation* **1** EASTERN STANDARD TIME. **2** electroshock treatment.

est /est/ *noun* a group technique for raising self-awareness using motivational theories from the business world. [acronym from Erhard Seminars Training, from the name of W. *Erhard*, American businessman (b.1935), who devised the technique]

est. *abbreviation* **1** established. **2** estimate. **3** estimated.

-est[1] /ɪst/ *suffix* forming the superlative of adjectives (*widest*; *nicest*; *happiest*) and adverbs (*soonest*). [Old English *-ost-*, *-ust-*, *-ast-*]

-est[2] /ɪst/ *suffix* (also **-st**) *archaic* forming the 2nd person sing. of verbs (*canst*; *findest*; *gavest*). [Old English *-est*, *-ast*, *-st*]

es·tab·lish /ɪˈstablɪʃ/ *transitive verb* **1** found or consolidate (a business, system, etc.) on a permanent basis. **2** (foll. by *in*) settle (a person or oneself) in some capacity (*we are now established in our new house*). **3** (esp. as **es·tab·lished** *adjective*) achieve permanent acceptance for (a custom, belief, practice, institution, etc.). **4 a** validate; place beyond dispute (a fact etc.). **b** find out; ascertain. **5** (of a person) gain recognition and acceptance (*established herself as an expert on Renaissance painting*). **6** bring about; achieve (*establish contact with extraterrestrials*). **7** enact; decree in law (*establish reprography legislation*). **8** (in a novel, film, etc.) make a (character, setting, etc.) plausible and convincing (*the first soliloquy establishes him as an evil character*). □ **es·tab·lished** *adjective* **es·tab·lish·er** *noun* [Old French *establir* (stem *establiss-*) from Latin *stabilire* from *stabilis* STABLE[1]]

established church *noun* a religious denomination recognized by a national government as its nation's official church.

es·tab·lish·ment /ɪˈstablɪʃmənt/ *noun* **1** the act or an instance of establishing; the process of being established. **2 a** a business organization or public institution. **b** a place of business. **3 a** the staff or equipment of an organization. **b** a household. **4** any organized body permanently maintained for a purpose. **5** a church system organized by law. **6 a** (also **Establishment**) the group in a society exercising authority or influence, and seen as resisting change. **b** any influential or controlling group (*the literary establishment*).

estab·lish·men·tar·ian /ɪˌstablɪʃmənˈteriən/ ● *adjective* **1** adhering to or advocating the principle of an established church. **2** of, relating to, or supporting the Establishment. ● *noun* **1** a person adhering to or advocating the principle of an established church. **2** a person belonging to or supporting the Establishment. □ **estab·lish·men·tar·ian·ism** *noun*

es·tami·net /eˈstamiˌnei/ *noun* a small French café or bistro selling alcoholic drinks. [French from Walloon *staminé* 'cowshed' from *stamo* a pole for tethering a cow, prob. from German *Stamm* stem]

estan·cia /eˈstansiːa/ *noun* a cattle ranch in Latin America or the southern US. [Spanish, lit. 'station', from medieval Latin *stancia* from Latin *stant-* pres. part. stem of *stare* to stand]

es·tate /əˈsteit/ *noun* **1** a property consisting of an extensive area of land usu. with a large house. **2** *Brit.* a modern residential or industrial area with integrated design or purpose. **3** *Law* **a** the interest that a person has in land or other property. **b** all of a person's assets and liabilities, esp. at death. **4** a property where grapes, rubber, tea, etc., are cultivated. **5** (in full **estate of the realm**) esp. *hist.* an order or class forming (or regarded as) a part of the body politic, consisting of the first estate (the clergy), the second estate (the aristocracy), and the third estate (the commons). **6** *archaic* or *literary* a state or position in life (*the estate of holy matrimony*; *poor man's estate*). **7** *Brit. informal* = ESTATE CAR. [Old French *estat* (as STATUS)]

estate agent *noun* *Brit.* **1** = REAL ESTATE AGENT. **2** the steward of an estate.

estate car *noun* *Brit.* = STATION WAGON.

Estates General *noun* the legislative body in France before 1789, representing the three estates of the realm (i.e. the clergy, the nobility, and the commons). It met occasionally from 1302 to 1614, but then not again until 1789, when it was urgently summoned to push through much-needed financial and administrative reforms. The same voting methods as in 1614 were used and as a result the radical Third Estate (the commons) gained control and formed themselves into a National Assembly, helping to precipitate the French Revolution. [French *états généraux*]

estate tax *noun* a tax levied on the estate of a dead person.

Este /ˈestei/ an Italian princely family, founded by Alberto Azzo II (d.1097), which prospered from the 13th to the 18th c. and greatly influenced the cultural life of medieval and Renaissance Italy.

es·teem /ɪˈstiːm/ ● *transitive verb* **1** (usu. in *passive*) have a high regard

Consonants: b *but* d *dog* f *few* g *get* h *her* j *yes* k *cat* l *leg* m *man* n *no* p *pen* r *red* s *sit*

for; greatly respect; think favourably of. **2** *formal* consider, deem (*esteemed it an honour*). ● *noun* high regard; respect; favour (*held them in esteem*). □ **es·teemed** *adjective* [Old French *estimer* from Latin *aestimare* fix the price of]

es·ter /ˈestər/ *noun Chem.* any of a class of organic compounds produced by replacing the hydrogen of an acid by an alkyl, aryl, etc. group, many of which occur naturally as oils and fats. □ **es·teri·fi·ca·tion** /eˌsterɪfəˈkeɪʃən/ *noun* **es·teri·fy** /eˈsterɪˌfaɪ/ *transitive verb* (**-fies, -fied**). [German, prob. from *Essig* vinegar + *Äther* ether]

es·ter·ase /ˈestəreɪs, -reɪz/ *noun Chem.* an enzyme which hydrolyzes an ester into an acid and an alcohol, phenol, etc. [ESTER + -ASE]

Es·te·van /ˈestəvən/ a city in SE Saskatchewan, 204 km southeast of Regina, close to the border with N Dakota; pop. (2001) 10,242. □ **Estevan·ite** *noun* [alteration of *Esther Van Horne*, daughter of Sir W. Van Horne, 2nd president of the CPR *c.*1892]

Esth. *abbreviation* Esther (Old Testament & Apocrypha).

Es·ther /ˈestər/ **1** *Bible* a beautiful Jewish woman chosen to be the queen of the Persian king Ahasuerus (generally supposed to be Xerxes I) who used her influence with him to save the Jews in captivity from persecution. **2** the book of the Bible containing an account of these events.

es·thete *var. of* AESTHETE.

es·thet·ic *var. of* AESTHETIC.

es·thet·ician *var. of* AESTHETICIAN.

Es·tienne /eɪˈtjɛn/ (also **Étienne**) **1** Henri (*c.*1460–1520), French scholar and printer, who founded his family printing house in Paris (*c.*1502). **2** his son, **Rob·ert** (1503–59), French scholar and printer, noted for his Latin dictionary (1531) and editions of works by Greek and Roman authors. **3** his son, **Henri** (1528–98), French scholar and printer, noted for his 5-volume Greek dictionary *Thesaurus graecae linguae* (1572).

es·tim·able /ˈestɪməbəl/ *adjective* worthy of esteem. □ **es·tim·ably** *adverb* [French from Latin *aestimabilis* (as ESTEEM)]

es·ti·mate ● *noun* /ˈestəmət/ **1** a judgment or calculation of the approximate cost, value, size, etc. of something. **2** an appraisal of the character or qualities of a person or thing. **3** a price specified as that likely to be charged for work to be undertaken. ● *transitive verb* /ˈestəˌmeɪt/ **1** form an approximate idea or rough calculation of (a number, size, etc.). **2** fix (a price etc.) by estimate. **3** form an opinion of. □ **es·ti·mated** *adjective* **es·ti·ma·tive** *adjective* **es·ti·ma·tor** /-ˌmeɪtər/ *noun* [Latin *aestimare aestimat-* fix the price of]

es·ti·ma·tion /ˌestəˈmeɪʃən/ *noun* **1** the process or result of estimating. **2** judgment or opinion of worth (*in my estimation*).

es·tival *var. of* AESTIVAL.

es·tiv·ate *var. of* AESTIVATE.

es·tiv·a·tion *var. of* AESTIVATION.

Es·tonia /eˈstoʊniə/ a Baltic country on the south coast of the Gulf of Finland; pop. (est. 2002) 1,415,681; capital, Tallinn.

Es·ton·ian ● *noun* **1 a** a native of Estonia. **b** a person of Estonian descent. **2** the Finno-Ugric language of Estonia. ● *adjective* of or relating to Estonia or its people or language.

estop /eˈstɒp/ *transitive verb* (**estopped, estop·ping**) (foll. by *from*) *Law* bar or preclude, esp. by estoppel. [Old French *estoper* from Late Latin *stuppare* stop up, from Latin *stuppa* tow: compare STOP, STUFF]

es·top·pel /eˈstɒpəl/ *noun Law* the principle which precludes a person from asserting something contrary to what is implied by a previous action or statement of that person or by a previous pertinent judicial determination. [Old French *estouppail* bung, from *estoper* (as ESTOP)]

es·tra·diol /ˌestrəˈdaɪɒl/ *noun* (*Brit.* also **oes·tra·diol**) *Biochem.* a major estrogen produced in the ovarian follicles of female mammals. [ESTRUS + DI-² + -OL¹]

es·trange /ɪˈstreɪndʒ/ *transitive verb* (usu. in *passive*; often foll. by *from*) cause (a person or group) to become unfriendly or distant; alienate. □ **es·trange·ment** *noun* [Old French *estranger* from Latin *extraneare* treat as a stranger, from *extraneus* stranger]

es·tranged /ɪˈstreɪndʒd/ *adjective* (of a spouse) no longer living with his or her spouse.

es·treat /ɪˈstriːt/ *Law* ● *noun* **1** *hist.* a copy of a court record of a fine etc. for use in prosecution. **2** the enforcement of a fine or forfeiture of a recognizance. ● *transitive verb* enforce the forfeit of (a fine etc., esp. surety for bail). [Anglo-French *estrete*, Old French *estraite* from *estraire* from Latin *extrahere* EXTRACT]

Estre·ma·dura /ˌestrəmaˈdʊrə/ a coastal region and former province of west central Portugal.

Est·rie /esˈtriː/ *noun* (also **l'Est·rie**) EASTERN TOWNSHIPS.

es·tro·gen /ˈestrədʒən/ *noun* (*Brit.* **oes·tro·gen**) **1** any of various steroid hormones developing and maintaining female characteristics of the body. **2** this hormone produced artificially for use in oral contraceptives etc. □ **es·tro·gen·ic** /-ˈdʒenɪk/ *adjective* **es·tro·gen·ic·ally** *adverb* [ESTRUS + -GEN]

es·trus /ˈestrəs/ *noun* (*Brit.* **oes·trus**) a recurring period of sexual receptivity in many female mammals; heat. □ **es·trous** *adjective* [Greek *oistros* gadfly, frenzy]

es·tu·ary /ˈestʃuːˌeri/ *noun* (*pl.* **-aries**) the tidal mouth of a large river, where the tide meets the stream. □ **es·tu·ar·ial** /-ˈeriəl/ *adjective* **es·tu·ar·ine** /-ˌraɪn/ *adjective* [Latin *aestuarium* tidal channel, from *aestus* tide]

Estuary English *noun* a type of accent identified as spreading outwards from London and the Thames Estuary, containing features of both upper- and middle-class southern British English and London accents such as Cockney.

esuri·ent /ɪˈsurɪənt/ *adjective archaic* or *jocular* **1** hungry. **2** greedy. □ **esuri·ent·ly** *adverb* [Latin *esurire* ' to hunger' from *edere* es- eat]

ET *abbreviation* **1** EASTERN TIME. **2** extraterrestrial.

-et¹ /ət/ *suffix* forming nouns (originally diminutives) (*bullet*; *sonnet*). [Old French *-et* *-ete*]

-et² /ət/ *suffix* (also **-ete** /iːt/) forming nouns usu. denoting persons (*comet*; *poet*; *athlete*). [Greek *-ētēs*]

ETA¹ *abbreviation* estimated time of arrival.

ETA² /ˈetə/ *noun* a Basque separatist organization active in Spain from the 1960s. [Basque abbreviation, from *Euzkadi ta Azkatasuna* Basque homeland and liberty]

eta /ˈeɪtə, ˈiːtə/ *noun* the seventh letter of the Greek alphabet (Η, η). [Greek]

éta·gère /eɪtaˈʒer/ *noun* a piece of furniture with a number of open shelves on which to display ornaments etc. [French, from *étage* shelf]

e-tailer /ˈiːˌteɪlər/ *noun* a company etc. selling products or services through the Internet. □ **e-tailing** *noun* [blend of E-² + RETAILER]

et al. /et ˈal/ *abbreviation* and others. [Latin *et alii, et alia,* etc.]

eta·lon /ˈetəˌlɒn/ *noun Physics* a device consisting of two reflecting plates, for producing interfering light beams. [French *étalon* standard]

etc. *abbreviation* = ET CETERA.

et cet·era /et ˈsetərə, ˈsetrə/ (also **et·cet·era**) ● *adverb* **1 a** and the rest; and similar things or people. **b** or similar things or people. **2** and so on. ● *noun* (in *pl.*) the usual sundries or extras. [Latin]

etch ● *verb* **1 a** *transitive* engrave (metal, glass, or stone) by coating it with a protective layer, drawing on this with a needle, and then covering it with acid or other corrosive that attacks the parts the needle has exposed. **b** *transitive* engrave (a plate) in this way in order to print from it. **2** *intransitive* practise this craft. **3** *transitive* engrave by any method (*etched her name in the snow*). **4** *transitive* (foll. by *on, upon*) impress deeply (esp. on the mind). ● *noun* the action or process of etching. □ **etch·er** *noun* [Dutch *etsen* from German *ätzen* etch, from Old High German *azzen* cause to eat or to be eaten, from Germanic]

etch·ant /ˈetʃənt/ *noun* a corrosive used in etching.

etch·ing *noun* **1** a print made from an etched plate. **2** the art of producing these plates.

-ete *var. of* -ET².

eter·nal /ɪˈtɜrnəl, i-/ *adjective* **1** existing always; without an end or beginning in time. **2** essentially unchanging; enduring (*eternal truths*). **3** *informal* constant; seeming not to cease (*your eternal nagging*). □ **the Eternal** God. □ **eter·nal·ity** /-ˈnalɪti/ *noun* **eter·nal·ize** *transitive verb* (also esp. *Brit.* **-ise**). **eter·nal·ly** *adverb* **eter·nal·ness** *noun* **eter·nize** *transitive verb* (also esp. *Brit.* **-nise**). [Old French from Late Latin *aeternalis* from Latin *aeternus* from *aevum* age]

Eternal City *noun* Rome.

eternal triangle *noun* a relationship between three people, usu. two of one sex and one of the other, involving sexual rivalry.

eter·nity /ɪˈtɜrnɪti, i-/ *noun* (*pl.* **-ties**) **1** infinite or unending (esp. future) time. **2** *Theol.* the condition into which the soul enters at death; the afterlife. **3** the quality, condition, or fact of being eternal. **4** (often prec. by *an*) a very long time. **5** (in *pl.*) eternal truths. [Old French *eternité* from Latin *aeternitas -tatis* from *aeternus*: see ETERNAL]

eternity ring *noun* a finger ring set with gems all around, usu. given as a token of eternal love.

Etes·ian /ɪˈtiːʒən/ *adjective* designating a dry NW wind blowing each summer in the eastern Mediterranean. [Latin *etesius* from Greek *etēsios* annual, from *etos* year]

---

t *top*   v *voice*   w *we*   z *zoo*   ʃ *she*   ʒ *vision*   θ *thin*   ð *this*   ŋ *ring*   x *loch*   tʃ *chip*   dʒ *jar*   (*see over for vowels*)

eth /eθ/ *noun* (also **edh** /eð/) the name of an Old English and Icelandic letter, = th. [Icelandic]

-eth[1] *var. of* -TH[1].

-eth[2] *suffix* (also **-th**) *archaic* forming the 3rd person sing. present of verbs (*doeth; saith*). [Old English *-eth, -ath, -th*]

etha·nal /'eθə,nal/ *noun Chem.* = ACETALDEHYDE. [ETHANE + ALDEHYDE]

eth·ane /'eθeɪn/ *noun Chem.* a colourless odourless gaseous hydrocarbon of the alkane series, occurring in natural gas. Chem. formula: C_2H_6. [ETHER + -ANE[2]]

eth·ane·diol /'eθeɪn,daɪɒl/ *noun Chem.* = ETHYLENE GLYCOL. [ETHANE + DIOL]

etha·nol /'eθə,nɒl/ *noun Chem.* = ALCOHOL 1. [ETHANE + ALCOHOL]

Ethel·bert /'eθəl,bɜːt/ **St.** (also **Æthel·bert** /'aθəl-/) (d.616), king of Kent 560–616. He was converted to Christianity by St. Augustine of Canterbury in 597, and codified Anglo-Saxon law in 604.

Ethel·red I /'eθəl,red/ (also **Æthel·red** /'aθəl,red/) (d.871), king of Wessex and Kent 865–71, elder brother of Alfred. His reign was marked by the continuing struggle against the invading Danes. Alfred joined Ethelred's campaigns and succeeded him on his death.

Ethel·red II /'eθəl,red/ **'the Unready'** (also **Æthel·red** /'aθəl,red/) (*c.*968–1016), king of England 978–1013 and 1014–1016. His inability to confront the Danes after he succeeded his murdered half-brother St. Edward the Martyr led to his payment of tribute (Danegeld) to prevent their attacks. His nickname meant 'lacking good advice; rash' in Old English.

eth·ene /'eθiːn/ *noun Chem.* = ETHYLENE. [ETHER + -ENE]

ether /'iːθər/ *noun* **1** *Chem.* **a** a colourless volatile organic liquid used as an anaesthetic or solvent. *Also called* DIETHYL ETHER. Chem. formula: $C_2H_5OC_2H_5$. **b** any of a class of organic compounds with a similar structure to this, having an oxygen joined to two alkyl etc. groups. **2** (also **aether**) the clear sky; the upper regions of air beyond the clouds. **3** (also **aether**) *hist.* **a** a medium formerly assumed to permeate space and fill the interstices between particles of matter. **b** a medium through which electromagnetic waves were formerly thought to be transmitted. □ **ether·ic** /iːˈθerɪk, 'iːθerɪk/ *adjective* [Old French *ether* or Latin *aether* from Greek *aithēr* from root of *aithō* burn, shine]

ether·eal /iːˈθiːriəl/ *adjective* **1** light, airy. **2** of unearthly delicacy and refinement (*ethereal music, ethereal beauty*). **3** heavenly, celestial. **4** *Chem.* of or relating to ether. □ **ether·eal·ity** /-'alɪti/ *noun* **ether·eal·ly** *adverb* [Latin *aethereus, -ius* from Greek *aitherios* (as ETHER)]

ether·ize /'iːθə,raɪz/ *transitive verb* (also esp. *Brit.* **-ise**) **1** *hist.* treat or anaesthetize with ether. **2** deaden; dull (feelings, thoughts, etc.) as if by anaesthetic.

Ether·net /'iːθərnet/ *noun Computing* a system of communication for local area networks by coaxial cable that prevents simultaneous transmission by more than one station. [ETHER + NETWORK]

eth·ic /'eθɪk/ **•** *noun* a set of moral principles, esp. those of a specified religion, school of thought, etc. (*the Puritan ethic*). **•** *adjective* = ETHICAL. [Old French *éthique* or Latin *ethicus* from Greek *ēthikos* (as ETHOS)]

eth·ic·al /'eθɪkəl/ *adjective* **1** relating to morals, esp. as concerning human conduct. **2** morally correct; honourable. □ **eth·ic·al·ity** /-'kalɪti/ *noun* **eth·ic·al·ly** *adverb*

ethical investment *noun* (also **ethical investing**) investment in companies that meet ethical and moral criteria specified by the investor.

ethi·cist /'eθɪsɪst/ *noun* a person who studies ethics and makes recommendations about ethical dilemmas.

eth·ics /'eθɪks/ *plural noun* **1** (usu. treated as *sing.*) the science of morals in human conduct; moral philosophy. **2 a** (treated as *pl.*) moral principles; rules of conduct. **b** (often treated as *pl.*) a set of these (*medical ethics*). **3** (treated as *pl.*) moral correctness (*the ethics of his decision are doubtful*).

ethi·nyl estradiol /'eθɪnɪl/ *noun* an artificial estrogen used in oral contraceptives. [*ethine* (var. of ETHYNE) + -YL + ESTRADIOL]

Ethi·opia /,iːθɪˈoːpɪə/ a country in NE Africa, on the Red Sea; pop. (est. 2002) 67,673,031; capital, Addis Ababa. Formerly known as Abyssinia, Ethiopia is the oldest independent country in Africa. Its earliest recorded civilization, known to the ancient Egyptians as Punt, dates from the 2nd millennium BC.

Ethi·op·ian /,iːθɪˈoːpɪən/ **•** *noun* **1 a** a native or national of Ethiopia. **b** a person of Ethiopian descent. **2** *archaic* a black person. **•** *adjective* **1** of or relating to Ethiopia. **2** *Biol.* of or designating a biogeographical region comprising Africa south of the Sahara. [*Ethiopia* from Latin *Aethiops* from Greek *Aithiops* from *aithō* burn + *ōps* face]

Ethi·opic /,iːθɪˈɒpɪk, -'oːpɪk/ **•** *noun* **1** any of several Semitic languages related to Arabic and spoken in Ethiopia and neighbouring areas. **2** the Christian liturgical language of Ethiopia. **•** *adjective* of or in one of these languages.

eth·moid /'eθmɔɪd/ **•** *adjective* of, pertaining to, or designating a square bone at the root of the nose forming part of the cranium, with perforations through which pass the olfactory nerves. **•** *noun* the ethmoid bone. □ **eth·moid·al** /-'mɔɪdəl/ *adjective* [Greek *ēthmoeidēs* from *ēthmos* sieve]

eth·nic /'eθnɪk/ **•** *adjective* **1** (of a population group) sharing a distinctive cultural and historical tradition, often associated with race, nationality, or religion. **2** relating to race or culture (*ethnic group; ethnic origins*). **3** (of clothes, music, etc.) characteristic of or influenced by the traditions of a particular people or culture, esp. a minority within another culture or one regarded as exotic. **4** denoting origin by birth or descent rather than nationality (*ethnic Turks*). **•** *noun* esp. *N Amer.* & *Austral.* a member of an (esp. minority) ethnic group. □ **eth·nic·al·ly** *adverb* **eth·ni·city** /-'nɪsɪti/ *noun* [ecclesiastical Latin *ethnicus* from Greek *ethnikos* heathen, from *ethnos* nation]

ethnic cleansing *noun euphemism* the mass expulsion or extermination of people from opposing ethnic or religious groups within a certain area.

ethnic minority *noun* a (usu. identifiable) group differentiated from the main population of a community by racial origin or cultural background.

ethno- /'eθnoː/ *combining form* ethnic, ethnological. [Greek *ethnos* nation]

ethno·archae·ol·ogy /,eθnoː,ɑːkɪˈɒlədʒi/ *noun* the study of a society's institutions and organization based on examination of its material remains. □ **ethno·archae·o·logic·al** *adjective* **ethno·archae·ol·o·gist** *noun*

ethno·botany /,eθnoːˈbɒtəni/ *noun* **1** the traditional knowledge of a people concerning plants and their uses. **2** the study of such knowledge. □ **ethno·botan·ical** /bəˈtanɪkəl/ *adjective* **ethno·botan·ist** *noun*

ethno·centric /,eθnoːˈsentrɪk/ *adjective* **1** evaluating other races and cultures by criteria specific to one's own. **2** believing in the inherent superiority of one's own race or culture. □ **ethno·centric·ally** *adverb* **ethno·centri·city** /-'trɪsɪti/ *noun* **ethno·centrism** *noun*

ethno·cide /,eθnoːˈsaɪd/ *noun* the deliberate and systematic destruction of the culture of an ethnic group, esp. within a larger community.

ethno·cultur·al *adjective* pertaining to or having a particular ethnic group.

eth·nog·raphy *noun* the scientific description of human races and cultures. □ **eth·nog·raph·er** *noun* **ethno·graph·ic** *adjective* **ethno·graph·ic·al·ly** *adverb*

ethno·hist·ory *noun* the branch of knowledge that deals with the history of races and cultures, esp. non-Western ones. □ **ethno·histor·ian** *noun* **ethno·histor·ic** *adjective* **ethno·histor·ic·al** *adjective* **ethno·histor·ic·al·ly** *adverb*

eth·nol·ogy /eθˈnɒlədʒi/ *noun* the branch of knowledge that deals with the characteristics of different peoples and the differences and relationships between them. □ **ethno·logic** /-nəˈlɒdʒɪk/ *adjective* **ethno·logic·al** /-nəˈlɒdʒɪkəl/ *adjective* **ethno·logic·al·ly** /-nəˈlɒdʒɪkli/ *adverb* **eth·nol·o·gist** *noun*

ethno·method·ol·ogy *noun* a method of sociological analysis that examines how individuals in everyday situations construct and maintain the social order of those situations. □ **ethno·method·o·logic·al** *adjective* **ethno·method·ol·o·gist** *noun*

ethno·music·ol·ogy *noun* the study of the music of one or more (esp. non-European) cultures. □ **ethno·music·o·logic·al** *adjective* **ethno·music·ol·o·gist** *noun*

etho·gram /'iːθə,gram/ *noun Zool.* a list of the kinds of behaviour or activity observed in an animal. [Greek *ētho-* (see ETHOS) + -GRAM]

eth·ol·ogy /iːˈθɒlədʒi/ *noun* **1** the science of animal behaviour. **2** the science of character formation in human behaviour. □ **etho·logic·al** *adjective* **etho·logic·al·ly** *adverb* **eth·ol·o·gist** *noun* [Latin *ethologia* from Greek *ēthologia* (as ETHOS)]

ethos /'iːθɒs, 'iːθoːs/ *noun* the characteristic spirit or attitudes of a community, people, or system, or of a literary work etc. [modern Latin from Greek *ēthos* nature, disposition]

ethyl /'eθaɪl/ *noun* (*attributive*) *Chem.* the monovalent radical derived from ethane by removal of a hydrogen atom (*ethyl alcohol*). [German (as ETHER, -YL)]

Vowels: a cat ɑ arm e bed ɜr her ɜː *deux* ə ago ɪ sit i cosy iː feed ɒ hot ɔ pore ɔː no ʌ run ʊ put

ethyl·ene /ˈeθəˌliːn/ noun Chem. a gaseous hydrocarbon of the alkene series, occurring in natural gas and crude oil, and used in the manufacture of polyethylene. Also called ETHENE. Chem. formula: C_2H_4.

ethylene glycol noun Chem. a colourless viscous hygroscopic liquid used as an antifreeze and in the manufacture of polyesters. Also called ETHANEDIOL. Chem. formula: $C_2H_6O_2$.

ethyne /ˈiːθaɪn, ˈeθ-/ noun Chem. = ACETYLENE.

etic /ˈetɪk/ adjective designating a generalized non-structural approach to the description of a particular language or culture (compare EMIC). [abbreviation of PHONETIC]

-etic /ˈetɪk/ suffix forming adjectives and nouns (ascetic; emetic; genetic; synthetic). [Greek -ētikos or -ětikos: compare -IC]

e-ticket noun (also **electronic ticket**) a reservation for an airline flight for which the details are stored electronically in the airline's computers rather than printed on a paper ticket.

Étienne /eˈtjen/ var. of ESTIENNE.

etio·late /ˈiːtiəˌleɪt/ transitive verb (usu. as **etio·lat·ed** adjective) **1** make (a plant) pale by excluding light. **2** cause to lose vigour or substance. □ **etio·la·tion** noun [French étioler from Norman French étieuler grow into a stem, from éteule, ultimately from Latin stipula straw]

eti·ol·ogy /ˌiːtiˈɒlədʒi/ noun (Brit. also **aeti·ol·ogy**) **1** Med. the causation of diseases and disorders, esp. of a specific disease, as a subject of investigation. **2** the study of causation. **3** the assignment of a cause or reason. □ **etio·logic** adjective **etio·logic·al** adjective **etio·logic·al·ly** adverb [Late Latin aetiologia from Greek aitiologia from aitia cause]

eti·quette /ˈetɪˌkət, -ˌket/ noun **1** the conventional rules of social or official behaviour (party etiquette; parliamentary etiquette). **2 a** the customary behaviour of members of a profession, sports team, etc. towards each other. **b** the unwritten code governing this (medical etiquette). [French étiquette label, etiquette]

Etna, Mount /ˈetnə/ a volcano in E Sicily, rising to 3 323 m (10,902 ft.). It is the highest and most active volcano in Europe.

Etobi·coke /ɪˈtoːbəˌkoː, eˈtoː-/ a former city in S Ontario, now the western part of the city of Toronto; pop. (2001) 338,117. [Mississauga wah-do-be-kaung place where the black alders grow]

Eton collar /ˈiːtən/ noun a broad stiff collar worn outside the coat collar, esp. of an Eton jacket.

Eton·ian /iːˈtoːniən/ ● noun a past or present member of Eton College, an exclusive private school in S England. ● adjective of or relating to Eton College.

Eton jacket /ˈiːtən/ noun a short black jacket reaching only to the waist, formerly worn by pupils of Eton College.

Etosha Pan /ɪˈtɒʃə/ a depression in the plateau of N Namibia, filled with salt water and having no outlets, extending over an area of 4 800 sq. km (1,854 sq. miles). The wetlands are home to a large population of flamingos.

étouf·fée /ˌeituˈfeɪ/ noun a spicy Cajun stew made with vegetables and seafood.

etrier /ˈeitriˌei/ noun Mountaineering a short rope ladder with a few rungs of wood or metal. [French, = stirrup]

Etrog¹ /ˈiːtrɒg/ **Sorel** (b.1933), Romanian-born Canadian sculptor. His mainly large curvilinear sculptures in bronze and marble show the influence of Sumerian, Aztec, and Egyptian art, and are often suggestive of heavy machinery; they include Ritual Head (1976).

Etrog² /ˈiːtrɒg/ noun hist. **1** any one of the Canadian Film Awards, presented annually between 1968 and 1978, for excellence in Canadian filmmaking. **2** a statuette designed by Sorel Etrog, commemorating the award (compare GENIE 2). [S. ETROG¹]

Etru·ria /ɪˈtrʊriə/ an ancient state of W Italy, situated between the rivers Arno and Tiber and corresponding approximately to modern Tuscany and parts of Umbria. It was the centre of the Etruscan civilization, which flourished in the middle centuries of the first millennium BC.

Etrus·can /ɪˈtrʌskən/ ● adjective of ancient Etruria, esp. its pre-Roman civilization and physical remains. ● noun **1** a native of Etruria. **2** the language of Etruria. [Latin Etruscus]

et seq. abbreviation (also **et seqq.**) and the following (pages etc.). [Latin et sequentia]

-ette /et/ combining form forming nouns meaning: **1** small (kitchenette; cigarette). **2** imitation or substitute (leatherette; flannelette). **3** female (usherette; suffragette). ¶ The use of the suffix -ette to indicate a feminine role or identity may be considered offensive. [from or after Old French -ette, fem. of -ET]

étude /eiˈtuːd, -ˈtjuːd, ˈei-/ noun a short musical composition or exercise, usu. for one instrument, designed to improve the technique of the player. [French, = study]

etui /eˈtwiː/ noun a small case for needles etc. [French étui from Old French estui prison]

-etum /ˈiːtəm/ suffix forming nouns denoting a collection of trees or other plants (arboretum; pinetum). [Latin]

ety·mol·o·gize /ˌetɪˈmɒləˌdʒaɪz/ transitive verb (also esp. Brit. **-gise**) give or trace the etymology of (a word).

ety·mol·ogy /ˌetɪˈmɒlədʒi/ noun (pl. **-gies**) **1 a** the historically verifiable sources of the formation of a word and the development of its meaning. **b** an account of these. **2** the branch of linguistics concerned with etymologies. □ **etymo·logic·al** adjective **etymo·logic·al·ly** adverb **ety·mol·o·gist** noun [Greek etumologia (as ETYMON, -LOGY)]

ety·mon /ˈetɪmɒn/ noun (pl. **etyma** /-mə/) the word that gives rise to a derivative or a borrowed or later form. [Latin from Greek etumon (neuter of etumos true), the literal sense or original form of a word]

Etzel /ˈetsəl/ a legendary king of Germany, who in the Nibelungenlied is the second husband of Kriemhild.

EU abbreviation European Union. ¶ See Usage Note at EUROPEAN COMMUNITY.

Eu symbol Chem. the element europium.

eu- /juː/ combining form well, easily. [Greek]

Eu·boea /juːˈbiːə/ an island of Greece in the W Aegean Sea, separated from the mainland by only a narrow channel at its capital, Chalcis.

euca·lyp·tus /ˌjuːkəˈlɪptəs/ noun (also **euca·lypt** /ˈjuːkəlɪpt/) (pl. **euca·lyp·tus·es** or **euca·lyp·ti** /-taɪ/ or **euca·lypts**) **1** any tree of the genus Eucalyptus, native to Australasia, cultivated for its timber and for the oil from its leaves. **2** (in full **eucalyptus oil**) the essential oil from eucalyptus leaves, used esp. in medicinal preparations, perfumes, etc. [modern Latin from EU- + Greek kaluptos covered, from kaluptō to cover, the unopened flower being protected by a cap]

eu·cary·ote var. of EUKARYOTE.

eucha·ris /ˈjuːkərɪs/ noun any bulbous plant of the genus Eucharis, native to S America, with white umbellate flowers. [Greek eukharis pleasing (as EU-, kharis grace)]

Eucha·rist /ˈjuːkərɪst/ noun **1** (in the Catholic, Anglican and Orthodox churches) the sacrament commemorating the Last Supper, in which bread and wine are consecrated and consumed. Also called (HOLY) COMMUNION, (esp. Catholicism) the Mass (see MASS²). **2** the consecrated elements, esp. the bread (receive the Eucharist). □ **Eucha·ris·tic** /-ˈrɪstɪk/ adjective **Eucha·ris·tic·al·ly** /-ˈrɪstɪkli/ adverb [ultimately from ecclesiastical Greek eukharistia thanksgiving, from Greek eukharistos grateful (as EU-, kharizomai offer willingly)]

Eucharistic minister noun Catholicism a lay person appointed to assist in the distribution of the Eucharist during Mass, during home visitations to the sick, etc.

eu·chre /ˈjuːkər/ ● noun **1** a card game for two to four players in which the highest cards are the joker (if used), the jack of trumps, and the other jack of the same colour in a pack with the lower cards removed, the aim being to win at least three of the five tricks played. **2** an instance of euchring or being euchred. ● transitive verb **1** (in euchre) prevent (a bidder) from winning three or more tricks, thereby scoring points oneself. **2** N Amer., Austral., & NZ slang deceive, outwit. **3** Cdn, Austral., & NZ slang (usu. in passive) ruin, finish, foil (if we miss the bus, we're euchred!). [19th c.: German dialect Jucker(spiel)]

Euck·en /ˈɔɪkən/ **Ru·dolf Chris·toph** (1846–1926), German idealist philosopher, whose works include Socialism: An Analysis (1920), and Individual and Society (1923); he was awarded the Nobel Prize for literature in 1908.

Euclid /ˈjuːklɪd/ (c.300 BC), Greek mathematician. He taught at Alexandria, and is famous for his great work Elements of Geometry, which covered plane geometry, the theory of numbers, irrational numbers, and solid geometry; this remained the standard work into the 19th c.

Euclid·ean /juːˈklɪdiən/ adjective (also **Euclid·ian**) of or relating to Euclid, esp. the system of geometry based on his principles (compare NON-EUCLIDEAN).

Euclidean geometry noun the geometry of ordinary experience, based on the principles of Euclid, esp. the one stating that parallel lines do not meet.

Euclidean space noun space for which Euclidean geometry is valid.

Eud·ist /ˈjuːdɪst/ noun a member of the Congregation of Jesus and Mary, an esp. teaching order of Roman Catholic priests. [St. John Eudes, d.1680]

Eu·gène /juːˈdʒiːn/ **Prince** (title of François Eugène de Savoie-Carignan) (1663–1736), French-born Austrian general, noted for his many victories on behalf of the Holy Roman Empire during the War of the Spanish Succession (1701–14).

eu·gen·ics /juːˈdʒenɪks/ *plural noun* (treated as *sing.*) the science of improving the (esp. human) population by controlled breeding for desirable inherited characteristics. □ **eu·gen·ic** *adjective* **eu·gen·ic·ally** *adverb* **eu·gen·cist** /-sɪst/ *noun* **eu·gen·ist** /ˈjuːdʒenɪst/ *noun* [EU- + GENIC]

Eu·gé·nie /ɜːˈɡeɪniː/ (born Eugénia María de Montijo de Guzmán) (1826–1920), Spanish empress of France 1853–71 and wife of Napoleon III. She influenced her husband's foreign policy, esp. against Mexico and Prussia, and acted as regent on three occasions (1859; 1865; 1870).

eu·glena /juːˈɡliːnə/ *noun* a single-celled freshwater flagellate of the genus *Euglena*, which can form a green scum on stagnant water. [modern Latin genus name, from EU- + Greek *glēnē* 'eyeball, socket of joint']

eu·kary·ote /juːˈkæriˌoːt/ *noun* (also **eu·cary·ote**) *Biol.* an organism consisting of a cell or cells in which the genetic material is DNA in the form of chromosomes contained within a distinct nucleus (*compare* PROKARYOTE). □ **eu·kary·otic** /-ˈɒtɪk/ *adjective* [EU- + KARYO- + -*ote* as in ZYGOTE]

eula·chon /ˈjuːləkɒn/ *noun* (also **ooli·chan**) a small oily food fish, *Thaleichthys pacificus*, of the Pacific coast of N America, belonging to the smelt family. *Also called* CANDLEFISH. [Lower Chinook *úlxan*]

Euler /ˈɔɪlər/ **1 Leon·hard** (1707–83), Swiss mathematician. A prolific and original contributor to all branches of mathematics, he attempted to elucidate the nature of functions and his study of infinite series led his successors, notably Abel and Cauchy, to introduce ideas of convergence and rigorous argument into mathematics. **2 Ulf (Svante) von** (1905–83), Swedish physiologist, the son of H. Euler-Chelpin. He identified noradrenalin as the principal chemical neurotransmitter of the sympathetic nervous system, and was awarded a Nobel Prize in 1970.

Euler-Chelpin /ˌɔɪlərˈkelpən/ **Hans (Karl Au·gust Simon) von** (1873–1964), German-born Swedish biochemist. He worked mainly on enzymes and vitamins, and explained the role of enzymes in the alcoholic fermentation of sugar; he shared the Nobel Prize for chemistry in 1929.

eulo·gize /ˈjuːləˌdʒaɪz/ *transitive verb* (also esp. *Brit.* **-gise**) **1** praise in speech or writing. **2** compose or deliver a funeral oration in praise of a person. □ **eulo·gist** *noun* **eulo·gis·tic** /-ˈdʒɪstɪk/ *adjective*

eu·logy /ˈjuːlədʒi/ *noun* (pl. **-gies**) **1 a** speech or writing in praise of a person, esp. a person who has recently died. **b** *N Amer.* a funeral oration in praise of a person. **2** an expression of praise. [medieval Latin *eulogium* from (apparently by confusion with Latin *elogium* epitaph) Late Latin *eulogia* praise, from Greek]

Eu·meni·des /juːˈmeniˌdiːz/ *Gk Myth* a group of goddesses or spirits, identified from an early date with the Furies; they probably originated as well-disposed deities of fertility, whose name was given to the Furies euphemistically. [Greek, = kindly ones]

eun·uch /ˈjuːnək/ *noun* **1** a castrated man, esp. (*hist.*) one employed at an oriental harem or court. **2** a person lacking effectiveness (*political eunuch*). [Latin *eunuchus* from Greek *eunoukhos* lit. bedchamber attendant, from *eunē* bed + second element related to *ekhō* hold]

eu·ony·mus /juːˈɒnɪməs/ *noun* any tree or shrub of the genus *Euonymus*, e.g. the spindle tree and burning bush. [Latin from Greek *euōnumos* of lucky name (as EU-, *onoma* name)]

eu·pep·tic /juːˈpeptɪk/ *adjective* **1** of or having good digestion. **2** cheerful, well-disposed, optimistic. [Greek *eupeptos* (as EU-, *peptō* digest)]

eu·phem·ism /ˈjuːfəˌmɪzəm/ *noun* **1** a mild or vague expression substituted for one thought to be too harsh or direct e.g. *pass away* for *die*. **2** the use of such expressions. □ **eu·phem·is·tic** *adjective* **eu·phem·is·tic·ally** *adverb* **eu·phem·ize** *transitive & intransitive verb* (also esp. *Brit.* **-ise**). [Greek *euphēmismos* from *euphēmos* (as EU-, *phēmē* speaking)]

eu·phoni·ous /juːˈfoːniəs/ *adjective* **1** sounding pleasant, harmonious. **2** concerning euphony. □ **eu·phoni·ous·ly** *adverb*

eu·phoni·um /juːˈfoːniəm/ *noun* a brass wind instrument of the tuba family, used esp. in brass and military bands. [modern Latin from Greek *euphōnos* (as EUPHONY)]

eu·phony /ˈjuːfəni/ *noun* (pl. **-ies**) **1 a** pleasantness of sound, esp. of a word or phrase; harmony. **b** a pleasant sound. **2** the tendency to make a phonetic change for ease of pronunciation. □ **eu·phon·ic** /-ˈfɒnɪk/ *adjective* [French *euphonie* from Late Latin *euphonia* from Greek *euphōnia* (as EU-, *phōnē* sound)]

eu·phor·bia /juːˈfɔːbiə/ *noun* any plant of the genus *Euphorbia*, including spurges and poinsettia. [Latin *euphorbea* from *Euphorbus*, 1st-c. Greek physician]

eu·phoria /juːˈfɔːriə/ *noun* a feeling or state of intense excitement and happiness. □ **eu·phor·ic** *adjective* **eu·phor·ic·ally** *adverb* [Greek from *euphoros* well-bearing (as EU-, *pherō* bear)]

eu·phori·ant /juːˈfɔːriənt/ ● *adjective* inducing euphoria. ● *noun* a euphoriant drug.

Eu·phra·tes River /juːˈfreɪtiːz/ a river of SW Asia which rises in the mountains of E Turkey and flows through Syria and Iraq to join the Tigris, forming the Shatt al-Arab waterway.

Eu·phro·syne /juːˈfrɒzəˌni/ *Gk Myth* one of the three Graces. [Greek, = mirth]

eu·phu·ism /ˈjuːfjuːˌɪzəm/ *noun* an affected style of writing or speaking. □ **eu·phu·is·tic** *adjective* **eu·phu·is·tic·ally** *adverb* [Greek *euphuēs* well endowed by nature: originally of writing imitating Lyly's *Euphues* (1578–80)]

Eur·asia *noun* a term used to describe the total continental land mass of Europe and Asia combined.

Eur·asian /juːˈreɪʒən, jə-/ ● *adjective* **1** of mixed European and Asian parentage. **2** of Europe and Asia. ● *noun* a Eurasian person.

eur·eka /jʊˈriːkə, jə-/ ● *interjection* I have found it! (announcing a discovery etc.). ● *noun* a fortunate discovery. [Greek *heurēka* 1st person singular perfect of *heuriskō* find: attributed to Archimedes]

eureka moment *noun* a moment at which one makes a significant discovery.

eu·rhyth·mic *var.* of EURYTHMIC.

eu·rhyth·mics *var.* of EURYTHMICS.

eu·rhyth·my *var.* of EURYTHMY.

Eu·ripi·des /jʊˈrɪpɪˌdiːz/ (c.480–406 BC), Greek dramatist. His nineteen surviving plays show important innovations in the handling of traditional myths, such as the introduction of realism, an interest in feminine psychology, and the portrayal of abnormal and irrational states of mind; they include *Trojan Women*, *Medea*, and the *Bacchae*.

euro *noun* (pl. **euros**) the European currency unit adopted by the European Union, used in most of the EU countries.

Euro- /ˈjʊrɔː, ˈjɜr-/ *combining form* Europe, European. [abbreviation]

Euro-American ● *noun* a North or South American of European ethnic origin. ● *adjective* of or pertaining to Euro-Americans.

Euro·bond /ˈjʊrɔːbɒnd, ˈjɜr-/ *noun* an international bond issued outside the country in whose currency its value is stated.

Euro-Canadian ● *adjective* pertaining to Canadians of European origin or descent. ● *noun* a Canadian of European origin or descent.

Euro·cen·tric *adjective* **1** having or regarding Europe as its centre. **2** presupposing the supremacy of Europe and Europeans. □ **Euro·cen·tri·city** /-ˈtrɪsɪti/ *noun* **Euro·cen·trism** *noun*

Euro·com·mun·ism *noun* *hist.* a form of Communism in Western European countries emphasizing acceptance of democratic institutions and independence of Soviet influence. □ **Euro·com·mun·ist** *adjective & noun*

Euro·crat *noun* a bureaucrat in the administration of the European Union.

Euro·cur·rency *noun* currency, usu. American or Japanese, held in a European country and used for short and medium-term lending and borrowing.

Euro·dollar *noun* a dollar deposited in a financial institution outside the US, originally in Europe but now in any country.

Euro·market *noun* **1** a market that emerged in the 1950s for financing international trade, backed by the commercial banks, large companies, and central banks of members of the European Union. **2** the European Union, regarded as one large market for goods.

Eur·opa /jʊˈroːpə, jɜr-/ **1** *Gk Myth* the daughter of Agenor, king of Tyre. Wooed by Zeus in the form of a bull, she was carried off to Crete, where she bore him three sons (Minos, Rhadamanthus, and Sarpedon). **2** *Astronomy* satellite II of Jupiter, the sixth closest to the planet, and one of the Galilean moons (diameter 3 138 km).

Eur·ope 1 a continent of the northern hemisphere, consisting of the western part of the land mass of which Asia forms the eastern (and greater) part, and including Scandinavia and the British Isles. **2** *informal* the European Union.

Euro·pean ● *adjective* **1** of or in Europe. **2 a** descended from natives of Europe. **b** originating in or characteristic of Europe. **3 a** happening in

Consonants: b *but* d *dog* f *few* g *get* h *her* j *yes* k *cat* l *leg* m *man* n *no* p *pen* r *red* s *sit*

or extending over Europe. **b** concerning Europe as a whole rather than its individual countries. **4** of or relating to the European Union. ● *noun* **1 a** a native or inhabitant of Europe. **b** a person descended from natives of Europe. **c** a white person, esp. in a country with a predominantly non-white population. **2** a person concerned with Europe as a whole, esp. an advocate of membership in the European Union. □ **Euro·pean·ism** *noun* **Euro·pean·ist** *adjective* & *noun* **Euro·pean·ize** *transitive & intransitive verb* (also esp. *Brit.* **-ise**). **Euro·pean·iz·a·tion** *noun* (also esp. *Brit.* **-isation**).

European Community *noun* an economic and political association of certain European countries as a unit with internal free trade and common external tariffs. ¶ The European Community (EC) was formed in 1967 from the European Coal and Steel Community (ECSC), the European Economic Community (EEC), and the European Atomic Energy Community (Euratom). In November 1993 the EC became known as the European Union (EU).

European Currency Unit *noun* a notional unit of currency formerly used to evaluate the exchange rates and reserves of members of the European Monetary System and in trading Eurobonds. Abbr.: **ECU**.

European Economic Community *see note at* EUROPEAN COMMUNITY.

European Monetary System *noun* a monetary system inaugurated by the European Community in 1979 to coordinate and stabilize the exchange rates of the currencies of member countries, as a prelude to monetary union. Abbr.: **EMS**.

European Parliament *noun* the principal representative and consultative body of the European Union.

European plan *noun N Amer.* a system of charging for a hotel room only without meals (*compare* AMERICAN PLAN, MODIFIED AMERICAN PLAN). Abbr.: **EP**.

European Recovery Program *see* MARSHALL PLAN.

European Union *noun see* EUROPEAN COMMUNITY. Abbr.: **EU**.

Euro·phile *noun* **1** a person who admires and likes Europe, its culture, etc. **2** a person who is in favour of participation in the European Union. □ **Euro·phil·ia** *noun* **Euro·phil·iac** *adjective* **Euro·phil·ic** *adjective*

Euro·phobe *noun* a person who opposes participation in the European Union. □ **Euro·phob·ia** *noun* **Euro·phob·ic** *adjective*

euro·pium /jʊˈroːpiəm/ *noun Chem.* a soft silvery metallic element of the lanthanide series, occurring naturally in small quantities. Symbol: **Eu**; at. no.: 63. [modern Latin from *Europe*]

Euro·poort /ˈjuːroːˌpɔrt/ a major European port facility in the Netherlands, near Rotterdam.

Euro·trash *noun* rich European socialites, esp. those living or working in the US.

euro·zone *noun* (also **euro·land**) the economic region formed by those member countries of the European Union that have adopted the euro.

Eu·ry·ale /jʊˈraiəli/ *Gk Myth* one of the three Gorgons.

Eu·ry·dice /jʊˈrɪdisi/ *Gk Myth* the wife of Orpheus. He secured her release from the underworld on the condition that he not look back at her on their return to the world of the living; Orpheus did look back, whereupon Eurydice disappeared.

eu·ryth·mic /jʊˈrɪðmɪk, jəˈ-/ *adjective* (also **eu·rhyth·mic**) **1** of or in harmonious proportion (esp. of architecture). **2** involving eurythmics (*eurythmic dancing*). [*eurhythmy* harmony of proportions, from Latin *eur(h)ythmia* from Greek *eurhuthmia* (as EU-, *rhuthmos* proportion, rhythm)]

eu·ryth·mics /jʊˈrɪðmɪks/ *plural noun* (also treated as *sing.*) (also **eu·rhyth·mics**) harmony of bodily movement, esp. as developed with music and dance into a system of education.

eu·ryth·my /jʊˈrɪðmi/ *noun* (also **eu·rhyth·my**) = EURYTHMICS.

Euse·bio /juːˈseibioː/ (born Ferraira da Silva Eusebio) (b.1942), Mozambican-born Portuguese soccer player. He was the top scorer in the 1966 World Cup and the top scorer in European soccer in 1968 and 1973.

Euse·bius /juːˈsiːbiəs/ **of Caesaria** (*c*.260–*c*.340 AD), bishop and Church historian. His *Ecclesiastical History* is the principal source for the history of Christianity (esp. in the Eastern Church) from the age of the Apostles until 324.

Eus·tach·ian tube /juːˈsteiʃən, -ʃiən/ *noun* a tube leading from the pharynx to the cavity of the middle ear and equalizing the pressure on each side of the eardrum. [Latin *Eustachius* = B. *Eustachio*, Italian anatomist d.1574]

eu·stasy /ˈjuːstəsi/ *noun* a change in sea level throughout the world caused by tectonic movements, melting of glaciers, etc. □ **eu·stat·ic** /-ˈstatɪk/ *adjective* [back-formation from German *eustatisch* (adj.) (as EU-, STATIC)]

eu·tec·tic /juːˈtektɪk/ *Chem.* ● *adjective* (of a mixture, alloy, etc.) having the lowest freezing point of any possible proportions of its constituents. ● *noun* a eutectic mixture. [Greek *eutēktos* (as EU-, *tēkō* melt)]

eutectic point *noun* (also **eutectic temperature**) the minimum freezing point for a eutectic mixture.

Eu·terpe /juːˈtɜrpi/ *Gk & Rom. Myth* the Muse of flute playing. [Greek, = well-pleasing]

eutha·nasia /ˌjuːθəˈneizə/ *noun* an act of painlessly killing, esp. at the patient's request, a person or animal suffering from an incurable condition. □ **eutha·nize** *transitive verb* [Greek (as EU-, *thanatos* death)]

eu·ther·ian /juːˈθiːriən/ ● *noun* a mammal of the infraclass Eutheria, giving nourishment to its unborn young through a placenta (as in humans). ● *adjective* of or relating to this infraclass, which includes all mammals except marsupials and monotremes. [EU- + Greek *thēr* 'wild beast']

eu·troph·ic /juːˈtrɒfɪk, -ˈtroːfɪk/ *adjective* (of a lake etc.) rich in nutrients and therefore supporting a dense plant population, which kills animal life by depriving it of oxygen. □ **eu·trophi·cate** *transitive verb* **eu·trophi·ca·tion** *noun* **eu·tro·phy** /ˈjuːtrəfi/ *noun* [*eutrophy* from Greek *eutrophia* (as EU-, *trephō* nourish)]

eV *abbreviation* electron volt.

EVA *abbreviation* **1** (in space) extravehicular activity. **2** ethyl vinyl acetate, a material used as cushioning in running shoes, consisting of a rubbery copolymer of ethylene and vinyl acetate.

evacu·ate /ɪˈvakjuːˌeit, i-/ *verb* **1** *transitive* **a** remove (people) from a place of danger to stay elsewhere for the duration of the danger. **b** *transitive* empty (a place) in this way. **c** *intransitive* depart, leave. **2** *transitive* produce a vacuum in (a vessel etc.). **3** *transitive* (of troops) withdraw from (a place). **4** *transitive* **a** empty (the bowels or other bodily organ). **b** discharge (feces etc.). □ **evacu·ant** *noun & adjective* **evacu·a·tion** *noun* [Latin *evacuare* (as E-[1], *vacuus* empty)]

evac·uee /i,vakjuːˈiː, i-/ *noun* a person evacuated from a place of danger.

evade /ɪˈveid, i-/ *transitive verb* **1 a** escape from, avoid (pursuers, arrest, etc.) esp. by guile or trickery. **b** avoid doing (one's duty etc.). **c** avoid giving a direct answer to (a question, questioner, etc.). **2 a** fail to pay (tax due). **b** defeat the intention of (a law etc.), esp. while complying with its letter. **3** (of a thing) elude or baffle (a person). □ **evad·able** *adjective* **evad·er** *noun* [French *évader* from Latin *evadere* (as E-[1], *vadere* vas- go)]

evagin·ate /ɪˈvadʒɪˌneit, i-/ *transitive verb* turn (a tubular organ) inside out. □ **evagin·a·tion** *noun* [Latin *evaginare* (as E-[1], *vaginare* as VAGINA)]

evalu·ate /ɪˈvaljuːˌeit, i-/ *transitive verb* **1** assess, appraise (*evaluate the situation*). **2 a** find or state the number or amount of. **b** find a numerical expression for. □ **evalu·able** /-əbəl/ *adjective* **evalu·a·tion** *noun* **evalu·a·tive** *adjective* **evalu·ator** *noun* [back-formation from *evaluation* from French *évaluation* from *évaluer* (as E-[1], VALUE)]

evan·esce /ˌevəˈnes/ *intransitive verb* fade from sight or existence; disappear. [Latin *evanescere* (as E-[1], *vanus* empty)]

evan·es·cent /ˌevəˈnesənt/ *adjective* (of an impression or appearance etc.) quickly fading; having no permanence. □ **evan·es·cence** *noun* **evan·es·cent·ly** *adverb*

evan·gel /ɪˈvandʒəl, i-/ *noun* **1** *archaic* **a** the Christian gospel. **b** any of the four Gospels. **2** a basic doctrine or set of principles. **3** *N Amer.* (*attributive*) (used in the names of churches) = EVANGELICAL *adjective* 2. [Old French *evangile* from ecclesiastical Latin *evangelium* from Greek *euaggelion* good news (as EU-, ANGEL)]

evan·gel·ic /ˌiːvanˈdʒelɪk, ˌev-/ *adjective* = EVANGELICAL.

evan·gel·ic·al /ˌiːvanˈdʒelɪkəl, ˌev-/ ● *adjective* **1** of or according to the teaching of the gospel or the Christian religion. **2** of or denoting a branch of Protestant Christianity emphasizing the authority of Scripture, personal conversion, and the doctrine of faith in the Atonement. **3** zealously advocating a cause. ● *noun* a person who believes in evangelical doctrines or belongs to an evangelical church. □ **evan·gel·ic·al·ism** *noun* **evan·gel·ic·al·ly** *adverb* [ecclesiastical Latin *evangelicus* from ecclesiastical Greek *euaggelikos* (as EVANGEL)]

evan·gel·ism /ɪˈvandʒəˌlɪzəm, i-/ *noun* **1** the preaching or promulgation of the Christian gospel. **2** zealous advocacy of a cause or doctrine.

evan·gel·ist /ɪˈvandʒəlɪst, i-/ *noun* **1** a preacher of the Christian gospel.

2 a person, esp. a lay person, engaged in itinerant Christian missionary work. **3** a zealous advocate or promulgator of a cause or doctrine. **4** (**Evangelist**) any of the writers of the four Gospels (Matthew, Mark, Luke, John).

evan·gel·is·tic /ɪˌvandʒəˈlɪstɪk, i-/ *adjective* **1** of or relating to evangelism or evangelism. **2** of or relating to the four Evangelists.

evan·gel·ize /ɪˈvandʒəˌlaɪz, i-/ *verb* (also esp. *Brit.* **-ise**) **1** *transitive & intransitive* preach the Christian gospel to. **2** *transitive* convert (a person) to Christianity. **3** *intransitive* try to win support for a cause (*evangelize about forest conservation*). □ **evan·gel·iz·a·tion** *noun* **evan·gel·iz·er** *noun* [ecclesiastical Latin *evangelizare* from Greek *euaggelizomai* (as EVANGEL)]

Evans /ˈevənz/ **1 Sir Ar·thur (John)** (1851–1941), English archaeologist. His excavations at Knossos (1899–1935) resulted in the discovery of the Bronze Age civilization of Crete, which he named Minoan. **2 Gil** (born Ian Ernest Gilmore Green) (1912–88), Canadian jazz pianist, composer, and arranger. In 1947 he began a long association with Miles Davis, producing albums such as *Porgy and Bess* (1958) and *Sketches of Spain* (1959–60). He later experimented with more improvised electronic and synthesized sound. **3 Her·bert Mc·Lean** (1882–1971), US anatomist, noted for his discovery of vitamin E in 1922. **4 James** (1801–46), English-born Canadian minister and linguist. A Methodist minister who became superintendent of the missions in the Northwest, he published an Ojibwa grammar (1837), invented a Cree syllabic alphabet, and hand-printed the *Cree Syllabic Hymn Book* (1841). **5 Mary Ann**, see ELIOT 1. **6 Walk·er** (1903–75), US photographer, best known for his images of rural poverty in the southern US during the Great Depression, collected as *American Photographs* (1938).

evap·or·ate /ɪˈvapəˌreɪt, i-/ *verb* **1** *intransitive* turn from solid or liquid into vapour. **2** *intransitive & transitive* lose or cause to lose moisture by evaporation. **3** *intransitive & transitive* disappear or cause to disappear (*our courage evaporated*). □ **evap·or·able** *adjective* **evap·or·a·tion** *noun* **evap·or·a·tive** /-rətɪv/ *adjective* **evap·or·a·tor** *noun* [Latin *evaporare* (as E-[1], *vaporare* as VAPOUR)]

evaporated milk *noun* thick unsweetened milk, usu. bought in tins, which has had some of its liquid removed by evaporation.

evap·or·ite /ɪˈvapəraɪt, i-/ *noun* *Geol.* a natural salt or mineral deposit formed by evaporation of water. [EVAPORATE + -ITE[1]]

evapo·tran·spir·a·tion *noun* the process by which water is transferred from the land to the atmosphere by evaporation from the soil and other surfaces and by transpiration from plants.

eva·sion /ɪˈveɪʒən, i-/ *noun* **1** the act or a means of evading a duty, question, etc. **2 a** a subterfuge or prevaricating excuse. **b** an evasive answer. [Latin *evasio -onis* (as EVADE)]

evas·ive /ɪˈveɪsɪv, i-/ *adjective* **1** seeking to evade something. **2** not direct in one's answers etc. **3** enabling or effecting evasion (*evasive action*). **4** (of a person) tending to evasion; habitually practising evasion. □ **evas·ive·ly** *adverb* **evas·ive·ness** *noun*

Eve *Bible* the first woman, wife of Adam, who was fashioned by God from Adam's rib.

eve *noun* **1** the evening or day before a church festival or any date or event (*Christmas Eve; the eve of the funeral*). **2** the time just before anything (*the eve of the election*). **3** evening. [Middle English, = EVEN[2]]

evec·tion /ɪˈvekʃən, i-/ *noun* *Astronomy* a perturbation of the moon's motion caused by the sun's attraction. [Latin *evectio* (as E-[1], *vehere vect-* carry)]

Evelyn /ˈiːvlɪn/ **John** (1620–1706), English diarist and writer. His *Diary*, which covers most of his life, is an invaluable record of the 17th c.; he is also known as a pioneer of English forestry and gardening.

even[1] ● *adjective* (**even·er**, **even·est**) **1** level; flat and smooth. **2 a** (of an action, movement, etc.) uniform; constant; free from fluctuations (*ran at an even pace*). **b** equal in number, amount, value, score, etc. **c** equally balanced. **3** (usu. foll. by *with*) in the same plane or line. **4 a** (of a person's temper etc.) equable, calm. **b** (of conduct, laws, etc.) equal, just, impartial. **5 a** (of a number such as 4, 6) divisible by two without a remainder. **b** bearing such a number (*no parking on even dates*). **c** not involving fractions; exact (*in even dozens*). **6 a** (of a person) neither owing money nor owed (*give me $10 and we're even*). **b** (of accounts, affairs, etc.) having no balance of debt on either side. **7** (of a chance, bet, etc.) as likely to succeed as not; fifty-fifty. ● *adverb* **1** used to invite comparison of the stated assertion, negation, etc., with an implied one that is less strong or remarkable (*never even opened [let alone read] the letter; does he even suspect [not to say realize] the danger?; ran even faster [not just as fast as before]; even if my watch is right we will be late [later if it is slow]*). **2** used to introduce an extreme case (*even you must realize it; it might even cost $100*). **3** used to add force to a more exact or precise

version of a word, phrase, etc. (*it's an unattractive building, even ugly*). ● *transitive & intransitive verb* (often foll. by *up*) make or become even. □ **even as** at the very moment that. **even now 1** now as well as before. **2** at this very moment. **even out 1** become level or regular (*house prices should even out shortly*). **2** spread (payments, work, etc.) evenly over a period of time or among a number of people. **even so 1** notwithstanding that; nevertheless. **2** quite so. **3** in that case as well as in others. **even though** despite the fact that. **even up** cause (an account, score, etc.) to become even or equal. **get** (or **be**) **even with** have one's revenge on. □ **even·ly** *adverb* **even·ness** *noun* [Old English *efen, efne*]

even[2] *noun* archaic or literary evening. [Old English *æfen*]

even break *noun* informal an equal chance.

even-handed *adjective* impartial, fair. □ **even-handed·ly** *adverb* **even-handed·ness** *noun*

even·ing ● *noun* **1** the end part of the day, esp. from about 6 p.m., or sunset if earlier, to bedtime (*this evening; during the evening; evening meal*). **2** an outing or party of a specified type, happening in the evening (*a theatre evening has been arranged*). **3** *literary* a time compared with this, esp. the last part of a person's life. ● *interjection* = GOOD EVENING. [Old English *æfnung*, related to EVEN[2]]

evening bag *noun* a very small handbag, usu. made of fabric such as velvet or satin and decorated with beading etc., carried by women as part of evening dress.

evening dress *noun* **1** (also **evening clothes**, **evening wear**) clothes worn for formal occasions in the evening. **2** = EVENING GOWN.

evening gown *noun* a woman's long formal dress.

evening grosbeak *noun* a N American bird, *Coccothraustes vespertinus*, with yellow colouring.

evening paper *noun* a newspaper published after about midday.

evening primrose *noun* any plant of the genus *Oenothera*, esp. the eastern N American *O. biennis*, with yellow flowers, from whose seeds an oil is extracted for medicinal use.

evening star *noun* the planet Venus, and occasionally Mercury, when visible in the western sky at dusk and in the early evening.

even money *noun* betting odds offering the gambler the chance of winning the amount he or she staked (also *attributive: even-money favourite*).

even·song *noun* a service of evening prayer, esp. that of Anglican churches. [EVEN[2] + SONG]

even-steven *adjective* (also **even-Steven**) *informal* **1** having no balance of debt on either side. **2** (of a game etc.) equal; tied. [rhyming compound from EVEN[1]]

even strength *noun* *Hockey* a situation where both teams have the same number of players on the ice (also *attributive: even-strength goal*).

event *noun* **1** a thing that happens or takes place, esp. one of importance. **2 a** the fact of a thing's occurring. **b** a result or outcome. **3** an item in a sports program, or the program as a whole (*the giant slalom event*). **4** *Physics* a single occurrence of a process, e.g. the ionization of one atom. □ **in any event** (or **at all events**) whatever happens. **in the event** as it turns (or turned) out. **in the event of** if (a specified thing) happens. **in the event that** if it happens that. [Latin *eventus* from *evenire event-* happen (as E-[1], *venire* come)]

even-tempered *adjective* not easily annoyed or angered; equable.

event·er *noun* a horse or rider who takes part in horse trials. [EVENT 3 as in *three-day event*]

event·ful *adjective* marked by many events or incidents, esp. noteworthy ones (*an eventful career*). □ **event·ful·ly** *adverb* **event·ful·ness** *noun*

event horizon *noun* the gravitational boundary enclosing a black hole, from which no light escapes.

even·tide *noun* archaic or literary = EVENING. [Old English *æfentíd* (as EVEN[2], TIDE)]

event·ing *noun* participation in horse trials, esp. cross-country, dressage, and show jumping. [EVENT 3, as in *three-day event*]

event·less *adjective* without noteworthy or remarkable events.

even·tu·al *adjective* occurring or existing in due course or at last; ultimate. □ **even·tu·al·ly** *adverb* [as EVENT, after *actual*]

even·tu·al·ity /ɪˌventʃuˈalɪti/ *noun* (*pl.* **-ities**) a possible event or outcome.

even·tu·ate /ɪˈventʃuˌeɪt/ *intransitive verb* formal **1** turn out in a specified way as the result. **2** (often foll. by *in*) result. □ **even·tu·a·tion** *noun* [as EVENT, after *actuate*]

ever *adverb* **1** at all times; always (*ever hopeful; ever after*). **2** at any time (*have you ever been to Paris?*; *nothing ever happens*; *as good as ever*). **3** as an emphatic word: **a** in any way; at all (*how ever did you do it?*; *when will they ever learn?*). **b** (prec. by *as*) in any manner possible (*be as quick as ever you can*). **c** *N Amer. informal* really (*did she ever feel like an idiot*). **4** (in *combination*) constantly (*ever-present*; *ever-recurring*). **5** (foll. by *so, such*) very; very much (*is ever so easy*; *was ever such a nice man*; *thanks ever so much*). **6** (foll. by comparative) constantly, increasingly (*grew ever larger*). □ **did you ever?** *informal* did you ever hear or see the like? **ever since** throughout the period since. [Old English *æfre*]

ever·bear·ing *adjective* (of a plant) bearing (fruit) continuously throughout the growing season.

Ever·est, Mount a mountain in the Himalayas, on the border between Nepal and Tibet. Rising to 8 848 m (29,028 ft.), it is the highest mountain in the world. It was first climbed in 1953 by Sir Edmund Hillary and Tenzing Norgay. [Sir G. *Everest*, British military engineer d.1866]

Ever·glades, the a vast area of marshland and coastal mangrove in S Florida. A national park protects endangered species.

ever·green ● *adjective* **1** always green or fresh. **2** (of a plant) retaining green leaves or needles throughout the year. ● *noun* an evergreen plant (*compare* DECIDUOUS 1).

ever·last·ing ● *adjective* **1** lasting forever. **2** lasting for a long time, esp. so as to become unwelcome. **3** (of flowers) keeping their shape and colour when dried. ● *noun* **1** eternity. **2 a** any of various plants, chiefly of the composite family, with flowers of papery texture that retain their shape and colour after being dried, esp. a helichrysum. **b** (in full **everlasting pea**) a leguminous plant, *Lathyrus latifolius*, with large flowers, naturalized in N America. □ **ever·last·ing·ly** *adverb* **ever·last·ing·ness** *noun*

ever·more *adverb* forever; always.

ever-present *adjective* always present.

Evert /'ɛvərt/ **Chris·tine Marie ('Chris')** (b.1954), US tennis player, who won both the US and French Open championships six times and the Wimbledon title in 1974, 1975, and 1981.

evert /ɪ'vɜːt/ *transitive verb Physiol.* turn (an organ etc.) outwards or inside out. □ **evers·ible** *adjective* **ever·sion** *noun* [Latin *evertere* (as E-¹, *vertere* *vers-* turn)]

every *adjective* **1** each single (*heard every word*; *watched her every movement*). **2** each at a specified interval in a series (*take every third one*; *comes every four days*). **3** all possible: the utmost degree of (*there is every prospect of success*). □ **every bit as** *informal* (in comparisons) quite as (*every bit as good*). **every now and again** (or **now and then**) from time to time. **every other** each second in a series (*every other day*). **every so often** at intervals; occasionally. **every time** *informal* **1** without exception. **2** without hesitation. **every which way** *informal* **1** in all directions. **2** in a disorderly manner. [Old English *æfre ælc* ever each]

every·body *pronoun* every person.

every·day *adjective* **1** occurring every day. **2** suitable for or used on ordinary days (*everyday dishes*). **3** commonplace, usual (*everyday life*). □ **every·day·ness** *noun*

Every·man *noun* the ordinary or typical man or human being. [the principal character in an early 16th-c. morality play]

every·one *pronoun* every person; everybody. □ **everyone who is anyone** (also **everybody who is anybody**) every person who is important, fashionable, etc. ¶ Note that *every one* is used to refer to each person or thing in a given group, as in *every one of them has arrived*.

every·place *adverb N Amer. informal* everywhere.

every·thing *pronoun* **1** all things; all the things of a group or class. **2** a great deal (*he owes her everything*). **3** the essential consideration (*speed is everything*). □ **and everything** *informal* used to refer vaguely to other things associated with what has been mentioned (*you'll still get paid and everything*). **have everything** *informal* possess every attraction, advantage, etc.

every·where *adverb* in every place.

Every·woman *noun* the ordinary or typical woman. [after EVERYMAN]

evict *transitive verb* expel (a tenant) from a property by legal process. □ **evic·tion** *noun* **evict·or** *noun* [Latin *evincere evict-* (as E-¹, *vincere* conquer)]

evi·dence /'ɛvɪdəns/ ● *noun* **1** (often foll. by *for, of*) the available facts, circumstances, etc. supporting or otherwise a belief, proposition, etc., or indicating whether or not a thing is true or valid. **2** *Law* **a** information given personally or drawn from a document etc. and tending to prove a fact or proposition. **b** statements or proofs admissible as testimony in a law court. **3** a sign or indication (*evidence*

of hard work). ● *transitive verb* (usu. in *passive*) be evidence of; demonstrate (*is very popular, as evidenced by the large turnout*). □ **call in evidence** *Law* summon (a person) as a witness. **in evidence** noticeable, conspicuous. [Old French from Latin *evidentia* (as EVIDENT)]

evi·dent /'ɛvɪdənt/ *adjective* plain or obvious (visually or intellectually). [Old French *evident* or Latin *evidēre evident-* (as E-¹, *vidēre* see)]

evi·den·tial /ˌɛvɪ'dɛnʃəl/ *adjective* of or providing evidence. □ **evi·den·tial·ly** *adverb*

evi·den·tiary /ˌɛvɪ'dɛnʃəri/ *adjective* = EVIDENTIAL.

evi·dent·ly /'ɛvɪdəntli/ *adverb* **1** plainly, obviously. **2** (qualifying a whole sentence) it is plain that; it would seem that (*evidently, we're too late*). **3** (said in reply) so it appears.

evil ● *adjective* **1** morally bad; wicked. **2** harmful or tending to harm, esp. intentionally or characteristically. **3** disagreeable or unpleasant (*has an evil temper*; *an evil smell emanated from the sewer*). **4** unlucky; causing misfortune (*evil days*). ● *noun* **1** a moral force regarded as the source of harm or human wickedness, esp. as opposed to goodness. **2** a manifestation of this, esp. in people's actions; wickedness. **3** something that is morally wrong, harmful, or (esp. in the expressions **lesser evil, necessary evil**) undesirable. □ **speak evil of** slander. □ **evil·ly** *adverb* **evil·ness** *noun* [Old English *yfel* from Germanic]

evil·doer *noun* a person who does evil. □ **evil·doing** *noun*

evil eye *noun* a gaze or stare superstitiously believed to be able to cause material harm.

evil one *noun* the embodiment of evil in certain religious beliefs, esp. (in Christianity) Satan.

evince /ɪ'vɪns/ *transitive verb* **1** indicate or make evident. **2** show that one has (a quality). [Latin *evincere*: see EVICT]

evis·cer·ate /ɪ'vɪsəˌreɪt/ *transitive verb formal* **1** disembowel. **2** empty or deprive of essential contents. □ **evis·cer·a·tion** *noun* [Latin *eviscerare eviscerat-* (as E-¹, VISCERA)]

evo·ca·tion /ˌɛvə'keɪʃən/ *noun* **1** the act or an instance of evoking. **2** (esp. in civil law systems) the transfer of a legal case to a higher court.

evoc·a·tive /ɪ'vɒkətɪv/ *adjective* tending to evoke (esp. feelings or memories). □ **evoc·a·tive·ly** *adverb* **evoc·a·tive·ness** *noun*

evoke /ɪ'vəʊk/ *transitive verb* **1** inspire or draw forth (memories, an image, feelings, a response, etc.). **2** summon, call up (a spirit etc.). □ **evok·er** *noun* [Latin *evocare* (as E-¹, *vocare* call)]

evo·lute /'ɛvəˌluːt, 'iːv-, -ˌljuːt/ *noun* (in full **evolute curve**) *Geom.* a curve which is the locus of the centres of curvature of another curve that is its involute. [Latin *evolutus* past participle (as EVOLVE)]

evo·lu·tion /ˌɛvə'luːʃən, ˌiːvə-/ *noun* **1** gradual development, esp. from a simple to a more complex form. **2 a** the development of an animal or plant, or part of one, from a rudimentary to a mature state. **b** a process by which different kinds of organism come into being by the differentiation and genetic mutation of earlier forms over successive generations, viewed as an explanation of their origins. **3** the appearance or presentation of events etc. in due succession (*the evolution of the plot*). **4** the giving off or evolving of gas, heat, etc. **5** an opening out. **6** the unfolding of a curve. **7** a change in the disposition of troops or ships. □ **evo·lu·tion·ar·ily** *adverb* **evo·lu·tion·ary** *adjective* [Latin *evolutio* unrolling (as EVOLVE)]

evo·lu·tion·ist *noun* a person who believes in evolution as explaining the origin of species. □ **evo·lu·tion·ism** *noun* **evo·lu·tion·is·tic** *adjective*

evolve *verb* **1 a** *intransitive & transitive* develop or come forth gradually. **b** *intransitive* (of an organism, part or feature) come into being through evolutionary development. **c** *transitive* (usu. in *passive*) produce or develop in the course of evolution. **2** *transitive* work out or devise (a theory, plan, etc.). **3** *intransitive & transitive* unfold; open out. **4** *transitive* give off (gas, heat, etc.). □ **evolv·abil·ity** *noun* **evolv·able** *adjective* [Latin *evolvere evolut-* (as E-¹, *volvere* roll)]

ev·zone /'ɛvzoʊn/ *noun* a member of a select Greek infantry regiment. [modern Greek *euzōnos* from Greek, = dressed for exercise (as EU-, *zōnē* belt)]

Ewe /'eɪweɪ/ *adjective & noun* ● *adjective* **1** of or relating to a Kwa language of Ghana, Togo, and Benin. **2** of or relating to the people who speak this language. ● *noun* (*pl.* same) **1** the Ewe language. **2** a member of this people. [Ewe]

ewe /juː/ *noun* a female sheep. [Old English *ēowu* from Germanic]

Ewen /'juːən/ **(Wil·liam) Pat·er·son** (1925–2002), Canadian painter. He is perhaps best known for his large panels of painted, routed

u: m**oo**d ai m**y** əi p**i**pe au br**ow**n ʌu h**ou**se ei d**ay** ɔi b**oy** ā fr**an**glais ã C**an**adien ɔ̃ Br**ay**on (*see over for consonants*)

plywood and metal based on landscapes and natural phenomena, as in *The Great Wave: Homage to Hokusai* (1974).

ewe neck *noun* a horse's neck whose upper outline curves inwards instead of outwards. □ **ewe-necked** *adjective*

ewer /ˈjuːər/ *noun* a large pitcher or water jug with a wide mouth. [Old Northern French *eviere*, Old French *aiguiere*, ultimately from Latin *aquarius* of water, from *aqua* water]

Ex. *abbreviation* Bible Exodus.

ex¹ *noun informal* a former spouse, lover, etc. [shortening of *ex-wife*, *ex-husband*, etc.]

ex² *noun Cdn* exhibition.

ex³ *preposition* **1** (of goods) without charges to the purchaser until removed from (*ex warehouse*). **2** (of stocks or shares) without, excluding (*ex dividend*). [Latin, = out of]

ex-¹ *prefix* (also **e-** before some consonants, **ef-** before *f*) **1** forming verbs meaning: **a** out, forth (*exclude*; *exit*). **b** upward (*extol*). **c** thoroughly. **d** bring into a state (*exasperate*). **e** remove or free from (*expatriate*; *exonerate*). **2** forming nouns from titles of office, status, etc., meaning 'formerly' (*ex-convict*; *ex-president*; *ex-wife*). [Latin from *ex* out of]

ex-² *prefix* out (*exodus*). [Greek from *ex* out of]

exa- *combining form* denoting a factor of 10^{18}. [perhaps from HEXA-]

ex·acer·bate /ɛkˈsasərˌbeɪt, ɪɡ-/ *transitive verb* **1** make (pain, a situation, etc.) worse. **2** irritate (a person). □ **ex·acer·ba·tion** *noun* [Latin *exacerbare* (as EX-¹, *acerbus* bitter)]

ex·act ● *adjective* **1** accurate; correct in all details (*an exact description*). **2** precise. **3** rigorous; strict. **4** (of a scientific method, instrument, etc.) not allowing vagueness or uncertainty. ● *transitive verb* **1** demand and obtain (something, esp. payment) from a person. **2** inflict (revenge) on someone. □ **ex·act·able** *adjective* **ex·act·itude** *noun* **exact·ness** *noun* [Latin *exigere exact-* (as EX-¹, *agere* drive)]

ex·acta *noun* esp. *US* = EXACTOR. [Latin American Spanish *quiniela exacta* ' exact quinella']

exact·ing *adjective* **1** making great demands. **2** calling for much effort. □ **exact·ing·ly** *adverb* **exact·ing·ness** *noun*

exac·tion *noun* **1** the act or an instance of exacting; the process of being exacted. **2 a** an illegal or exorbitant demand; an extortion. **b** a sum or thing exacted.

exact·ly *adverb* **1** accurately, precisely; in an exact manner (*worked it out exactly*). **2** in exact terms (*exactly when did it happen?*). **3** (said in reply) quite so; I agree completely. □ **not exactly** *informal* by no means.

ex·acto knife *noun N Amer.* a small knife with a fine fixed or retractable blade, used for crafts, hobbies, etc.

exact·or *noun Cdn* a bet on the first- and second-place finishers in a race, specifying their order of finish (*compare* TRIACTOR). [alteration of EXACTA]

exactor box *noun Cdn* a bet on three or more horses in one race, specifying the first- and second-place finishers, which does not specify which order they will finish in.

exact science *noun* a science admitting of absolute or quantitative precision.

ex·ag·ger·ate /ɪɡˈzadʒəˌreɪt/ *verb* **1** *transitive & intransitive* give an impression of (a thing), esp. in speech or writing, that makes it seem larger or greater etc. than it really is. **2** *transitive* enlarge or alter beyond normal or due proportions (*spoke with exaggerated politeness*). □ **ex·ag·ger·at·ed** *adjective* **ex·ag·ger·at·ed·ly** *adverb* **ex·ag·ger·a·tion** *noun* **ex·ag·ger·ator** *noun* [Latin *exaggerare* (as EX-¹, *aggerare* heap up, from *agger* heap)]

exalt /ɪɡˈzɒlt/ *transitive verb* **1** raise in rank or power etc. **2** praise highly. **3** (usu. as **exalt·ed** *adjective*) make lofty or noble (*exalted aims; an exalted style*). □ **exalt·ed·ly** *adverb* **exalt·ed·ness** *noun* [Latin *exaltare* (as EX-¹, *altus* high)]

exal·ta·tion /ˌɛɡzɒlˈteɪʃən/ *noun* **1** the act or an instance of exalting; the state of being exalted. **2** elation; rapturous emotion.

exam *noun* = EXAMINATION 3, 4.

exam·in·a·tion *noun* **1** the act or an instance of examining; the state of being examined. **2** a detailed inspection. **3 a** the testing of the proficiency or knowledge of students or other candidates for a qualification by oral or written questions. **b** a test of this kind. **4** an instance of examining or being examined medically. **5** *Law* the formal questioning of the accused or of a witness in court.

examination for discovery *noun* (*pl.* **examinations for discovery**) *Cdn Law* a pretrial meeting to disclose the evidence that will be presented at a civil trial.

examination-in-chief *noun* (*pl.* **examinations-in-chief**) *Cdn & Brit.*

Law an examination in a court made by the party that called the person to give evidence (*opp.* CROSS-EXAMINATION, *see* CROSS-EXAMINE).

examination paper *noun* **1** the printed questions in an examination. **2** a candidate's set of answers.

exam·ine *transitive verb* **1** inquire into the nature or condition etc. of. **2** look closely or analytically at. **3** test the proficiency of, esp. by examination (*see* EXAMINATION 3). **4** check the health of (a patient) by inspection or experiment. **5** *Law* formally question (the accused or a witness) in court. □ **exam·in·able** *adjective* **exam·inee** *noun* **exam·in·er** *noun* [Old French *examiner* from Latin *examinare* weigh, test, from *examen* tongue of a balance, ultimately from *exigere* examine, weigh: see EXACT]

ex·ample *noun* **1** a thing characteristic of its kind or illustrating a general rule. **2** a person, thing, or piece of conduct, regarded in terms of its fitness to be imitated (*must set an example; you are a bad example*). **3** a circumstance or treatment seen as a warning to others; a person so treated (*shall make an example of you*). **4** a problem or exercise designed to illustrate a rule. □ **for example** by way of illustration. [Old French from Latin *exemplum* (as EXEMPT)]

ex ante /ɛks ˈanti/ *adjective Econ.* based on expected results; forecast (*compare* EX POST). [modern Latin, = 'from before']

exan·thema /ˌɛksanˈθiːmə/ *noun Med.* a skin rash accompanying a disease such as scarlet fever or measles. [Late Latin from Greek *exanthēma* eruption, from *exantheō* (as EX-², *anthos* blossom)]

ex·arch /ˈɛksɑːk/ *noun* (in Eastern-rite churches) a bishop lower in rank than a patriarch and having jurisdiction wider than the metropolitan of a diocese. □ **ex·arch·ate** *noun* [ecclesiastical Latin from Greek *exarkhos* (as EX-², *arkhos* ruler)]

ex·asper·ate /ɪɡˈzaspəˌreɪt/ *transitive verb* (often as **ex·as·per·at·ed** *adjective* or **ex·as·per·at·ing** *adjective*) irritate intensely. □ **ex·as·per·at·ed·ly** *adverb* **ex·as·per·at·ing·ly** *adverb* **ex·as·per·a·tion** *noun* [Latin *exasperare exasperat-* (as EX-¹, *asper* rough)]

ex cath·edra /ˌɛks kəˈθiːdrə/ *adjective & adverb* with full authority (esp. of a papal pronouncement, implying infallibility as doctrinally defined). [Latin, = from the (teacher's) chair]

ex·cav·ate /ˈɛkskəˌveɪt/ *transitive verb* **1 a** make (a hole or channel) by digging. **b** dig out material from (the ground). **2** reveal or extract by digging. **3** *Archaeology* dig systematically into the ground to explore (a site). □ **ex·cav·a·tion** *noun* **ex·cav·ator** *noun* [Latin *excavare* (as EX-¹, *cavus* hollow)]

ex·ceed *verb* **1** *transitive* be greater or more numerous than (*the price must not exceed $20*; *exceeded all expectations*). **2** *transitive* go beyond what is allowed, necessary, or advisable (*exceeded the speed limit by 20 km/h*). **3** *transitive* surpass, excel (a person or achievement). **4** *intransitive* be pre-eminent; be greater or better. [Old French *exceder* from Latin *excedere* (as EX-¹, *cedere cess-* go)]

exceed·ance *noun* the exceeding of limits set by standards regulating pollution, etc.

ex·ceed·ing ● *adjective* **1** surpassing in amount or degree. **2** pre-eminent. ● *adverb archaic* = EXCEEDINGLY 2.

ex·ceed·ing·ly *adverb* **1** very; to a great extent. **2** surpassingly, pre-eminently.

excel *verb* (**ex·celled**, **ex·cel·ling**) (often foll. by *in*, *at*) **1** *transitive* be superior to. **2** *intransitive* be pre-eminent or the most outstanding (*excels at games*). □ **excel oneself** surpass one's previous performance. [Latin *excellere* (as EX-¹, *celsus* lofty)]

ex·cel·lence *noun* **1** the quality of being excellent; great merit. **2** the activity etc. in which a person excels. [Old French *excellence* or Latin *excellentia* (as EXCEL)]

Ex·cel·lency *noun* (*pl.* **-cies**) (usu. prec. by *Your, His, Her, Their*) a title used in addressing or referring to certain high officials, e.g. governors general, ambassadors, governors, and (in some countries) senior Church dignitaries. [Latin *excellentia* (as EXCEL)]

ex·cel·lent *adjective* extremely good; pre-eminent. □ **ex·cel·lent·ly** *adverb* [Old French (as EXCEL)]

ex·cel·sior /ɪkˈsɛlsiˌɔr, ɛk-/ ● *noun* soft wood shavings used for stuffing, packing, etc. ● *interjection* higher, outstanding (esp. as a motto or trademark). [Latin, comparative of *excelsus* lofty]

ex·cept ● *transitive verb* (often as **ex·cept·ed** *adjective* placed after object) exclude from a general statement, condition, etc. (*excepted her from the amnesty; present company excepted*). ● *preposition* (often foll. by *for*) not including; other than (*all failed except him; all here except for Liz; is all right except that it is too long*). ● *conjunction* **1** (usu. foll. by *that*) with the exception; only. **2** *archaic* unless. [Latin *excipere except-* (as EX-¹, *capere* take)]

ex·cept·ing ● *preposition* = EXCEPT preposition. ● *conjunction archaic* = EXCEPT conjunction.

ex·cep·tion *noun* **1** the act or an instance of excepting; the state of being excepted (*made an exception in my case*). **2** a thing that has been or will be excepted. **3** an instance that does not follow a rule. □ **take exception** (often foll. by *to*) **1** object; make objections to. **2** be offended (by); be resentful (about). **with the exception of** except; not including. □ **excep·tion·less** *adjective*

ex·cep·tion·able *adjective* open to objection. ¶ See Usage Note at UNEXCEPTIONABLE. □ **ex·cep·tion·ably** *adverb*

ex·cep·tion·al *adjective* **1** forming an exception. **2** unusual; not typical (*exceptional circumstances*). **3** unusually good; outstanding. ¶ See Usage Note at UNEXCEPTIONABLE. **4** (of a schoolchild) having mental or physical disabilities. □ **ex·cep·tion·al·ity** *noun* **ex·cep·tion·al·ly** *adverb*

ex·cep·tion·al·ism *noun* **1** the belief that a certain thing is an exception in relation to others in its class. **2** the belief that the peaceful capitalism of the US is an exception to the Marxist law of the inevitability of violent class struggle.

ex·cerpt /ˈeksɜrpt, ˈegz-/ ● *noun* a short extract from a book, film, piece of music, etc. ● *transitive verb* (also /ɪkˈsɜrpt/) **1** take an excerpt or excerpts from (a book etc.). **2** take (an extract) from a book etc. □ **ex·cerpt·ible** /-ˈsɜrptəbəl/ *adjective* **ex·cerp·tion** /-ˈsɜrpʃən/ *noun* [Latin *excerpere excerpt-* (as EX-¹, *carpere* pluck)]

ex·cess /ɪkˈses, ˈekses/ ● *noun* **1** the state or an instance of exceeding. **2** the amount by which one quantity or number exceeds another. **3** exceeding a proper or permitted limit. **4 a** the overstepping of the accepted limits of moderation, esp. intemperance in eating or drinking. **b** (in *pl.*) outrageous or immoderate behaviour. **5** an extreme or improper degree or extent (*an excess of cruelty*). **6** *Brit.* = DEDUCTIBLE *noun*. ● *attributive adjective* (usu. /ˈekses/) exceeding a set or limited amount or number; extra (*excess weight*; *excess time*). □ **in** (or **to**) **excess** exceeding the proper amount or degree. **in excess of** more than; exceeding. [Old French *exces* from Latin *excessus* (as EXCEED)]

excess baggage *noun* **1** baggage exceeding a weight allowance and liable to an extra charge. **2** something perceived as superfluous and burdensome.

ex·ces·sive /ɪkˈsesəv/ *adjective* **1** too much or too great. **2** more than what is normal or necessary. □ **ex·ces·sive·ly** *adverb* **ex·ces·sive·ness** *noun*

exch. *abbreviation* exchange.

ex·change ● *noun* **1** the act or an instance of giving one thing and receiving another in its place. **2 a** the giving of money for its equivalent in the money of the same or another country. **b** the fee or percentage charged for this. **3** a place where telephone calls are connected between different lines. **4** a place where commodities, securities, etc. are bought and sold. **5** a place where an item may be exchanged for another similar item (*needle exchange*). **6** a system of settling debts between persons (esp. in different countries) without the use of money, by bills of exchange. **7 a** a short conversation, esp. a disagreement or quarrel. **b** a sequence of letters between correspondents. **8** *Chess* the capture of an important piece (esp. a rook) by one player at the loss of a minor piece to the opposing player. **9** a reciprocal visit between two people or groups from different regions or countries (also *attributive*: *exchange student*). ● *verb* **1** *transitive* (often foll. by *for*) give or receive (one thing) in place of another. **2** *transitive* give and receive as equivalents (e.g. things or people, blows, information, etc.); give one and receive another of. **3** *transitive* substitute an equivalent item for (one purchased and returned). **4** *intransitive* (often foll. by *with*) make an exchange. □ **in exchange** (often foll. by *for*) as a thing exchanged (for). □ **ex·change·abil·ity** *noun* **ex·change·able** *adjective* **ex·chan·ger** *noun* [Old French *eschangier* from Romanic (as EX-¹, CHANGE)]

exchange rate *noun* the value of one currency in terms of another.

Exchange Rate Mechanism *noun* a system for allowing the value of participating currencies to fluctuate to a defined degree in relation to each other so as to control exchange rates within the European Monetary System.

ex·chequer /eksˈtʃekər/ *noun* **1** *Brit.* the former government department in charge of national revenue. ¶ Its functions now belong to the Treasury, although the name formally survives, esp. in the title *Chancellor of the Exchequer*. **2** a royal or national treasury. **3** *Brit. informal* the money of a private individual or group. [Old French *eschequier* from

medieval Latin *scaccarium* chessboard (its original sense, with reference to keeping accounts on a checkered cloth)]

ex·cimer /ˈeksɪmər/ *noun* *Chem.* & *Physics* a dimer existing only in an excited state, used in some lasers. [*excited* + DIMER]

ex·cise¹ /ˈeksaɪz/ ● *noun* **1** a duty or tax levied on goods and commodities produced or sold within the country of origin. **2** a tax levied on certain licences. ● *transitive verb* **1** charge excise on (goods). **2** force (a person) to pay excise. [Middle Dutch *excijs, accijs*, perhaps from Romanic: related to CENSUS]

ex·cise² /ekˈsaɪz/ *transitive verb* **1** remove (a passage of a book etc.). **2** cut out (an organ etc.) by surgery. □ **ex·ci·sion** /ekˈsɪʒən/ *noun* [Latin *excidere excis-* (as EX-¹, *caedere* cut)]

ex·cise·man /ˈeksaɪzˌman/ *noun* (*pl.* **-men**) *Brit. hist.* an officer responsible for collecting excise duty.

ex·cit·able *adjective* **1** (esp. of a person) easily excited. **2** (of an organism, tissue, etc.) responding to a stimulus, or susceptible to stimulation. □ **ex·cit·abil·ity** *noun* **ex·cit·ably** *adverb*

ex·cit·a·tion /ˌeksaɪˈteɪʃən, -sɪ-/ *noun* **1 a** the act or an instance of exciting. **b** the state of being excited; excitement. **2** the action of an organism, tissue, etc., resulting from stimulation. **3** *Electricity* **a** the process of applying current to the winding of an electromagnet to produce a magnetic field. **b** the process of applying a signal voltage to the control electrode of an electron tube or the base of a transistor. **4** *Physics* the process in which an atom etc. acquires a higher energy state.

ex·cite *transitive verb* **1 a** rouse the feelings or emotions of (a person). **b** bring into play; rouse up (feelings, faculties, etc.). **c** arouse sexually. **2** provoke; bring about (an action or active condition). **3** promote the activity of (an organism, tissue, etc.) by stimulus. **4** *Electricity* cause (a current) to flow in the winding of an electromagnet. **b** supply a signal. **5** *Physics* **a** cause the emission of (a spectrum). **b** cause (a substance) to emit radiation. **c** put (an atom etc.) into a state of higher energy. □ **ex·cit·ant** /ˈeksɪtənt, ɪkˈsaɪtənt/ *adjective* & *noun* **ex·cit·a·tory** /-təˌtɔri/ *adjective* **ex·cit·ed·ly** *adverb* **ex·cit·ed·ness** *noun* **ex·cite·ment** *noun* **ex·cit·er** *noun* (esp. in senses 4, 5). [Old French *exciter* or Latin *excitare* frequentative of *exciēre* (as EX-¹, *ciēre* set in motion)]

ex·cit·ing *adjective* arousing great interest or enthusiasm. □ **ex·cit·ing·ly** *adverb*

ex·citon /ekˈsaɪtɒn, ˈeksɪˌtɒn/ *noun* *Physics* a mobile concentration of energy in a crystal formed by an excited electron and an associated hole. [EXCITATION + -ON]

excl. *abbreviation* **1** excluding. **2** exclusive. **3** exclamation.

ex·claim *transitive & intransitive verb* cry out suddenly, esp. in anger, surprise, pain, etc. [French *exclamer* or Latin *exclamare* (as EX-¹: compare CLAIM)]

ex·clam·a·tion *noun* **1** the act or an instance of exclaiming. **2** a sudden impassioned or emphatic utterance; a cry. [Old French *exclamation* or Latin *exclamatio* (as EXCLAIM)]

exclamation mark *noun* (*N Amer.* also **exclamation point**) a punctuation mark (!) indicating an exclamation.

ex·clam·a·tory /ɪkˈsklaməˌtɔri/ *adjective* of or serving as an exclamation.

ex·clave *noun* a portion of territory of one nation completely surrounded by territory of another or others, as viewed by the home territory (compare ENCLAVE 1). [EX-¹ + ENCLAVE]

ex·clo·sure *noun* an area from which unwanted animals are excluded. [EX-¹ + ENCLOSURE]

ex·clude *transitive verb* **1** shut or keep out (a person or thing) from a place, group, privilege, etc. **2** expel and shut out. **3** remove from consideration (*no theory can be excluded*). **4** prevent the occurrence of; make impossible (*excluded all doubt*). □ **ex·clud·able** *adjective* **ex·clud·er** *noun* [Latin *excludere exclus-* (as EX-¹, *claudere* shut)]

ex·clud·ed middle *noun* *Logic* the principle that of two contradictory propositions one must be true.

ex·clu·sion *noun* **1** the act or an instance of excluding. **2** the state of being excluded. □ **to the exclusion of** so as to exclude. □ **ex·clu·sion·ary** *adjective* [Latin *exclusio* (as EXCLUDE)]

ex·clu·sion·ist ● *adjective* favouring exclusion, esp. from rights or privileges. ● *noun* a person favouring exclusion. □ **ex·clu·sion·ism** *noun*

exclusion order *noun* **1** *Cdn* & *Brit.* an official order preventing a person (esp. a criminal) from entering a country. **2** *Cdn* an order made by a judge to clear spectators, reporters, etc. from a courtroom.

exclusion principle *noun* *Physics see* PAULI EXCLUSION PRINCIPLE.

t *top*   v *voice*   w *we*   z *zoo*   ʃ *she*   ʒ *vision*   θ *thin*   ð *this*   ŋ *ring*   x *loch*   tʃ *chip*   dʒ *jar*   (*see over for vowels*)

exclusion zone *noun* an area into which entry is forbidden, esp. by ships or aircraft of particular nationalities.

ex·clu·sive ● *adjective* **1** excluding other things. **2** (*predicative*; foll. by *of*) not including; except for. **3** tending to exclude others, esp. socially; select. **4** catering for few or select customers; high-class. **5 a** (foll. by *to*) (of a commodity) not obtainable elsewhere. **b** (of a newspaper article) not published elsewhere. **6** (*predicative*; foll. by *to*) restricted or limited to; existing or available only in. **7** (of terms etc.) excluding all but what is specified. **8** employed or followed or held to the exclusion of all else (*my exclusive occupation; exclusive rights*). ● *noun* **1** an article or story published by only one newspaper or periodical. **2** an item available for sale from only one supplier. □ **ex·clu·sive·ly** *adverb* **ex·clu·sive·ness** *noun* **ex·clu·siv·ity** *noun* [medieval Latin *exclusivus* (as EXCLUDE)]

ex·clu·siv·ism *noun* a policy or doctrine of (esp. national, racial, or religious) exclusiveness. □ **ex·clu·siv·ist** *adjective & noun*

ex·cogi·tate /ɛksˈkɒdʒɪˌteɪt/ *transitive verb* think out; contrive. □ **ex·cogi·ta·tion** *noun* [Latin *excogitare excogitat-* (as EX-¹, *cogitare* COGITATE)]

ex·com·mu·ni·cate *Christianity* ● *transitive verb* /ˌɛkskəˈmjuːnɪˌkeɪt/ officially exclude (a person) from participation in the sacraments, or from formal communion with the Church. ● *adjective* /ˌɛkskəˈmjuːnɪkət/ excommunicated. ● *noun* /ˌɛkskəˈmjuːnɪkət/ an excommunicated person. □ **ex·com·mu·ni·ca·tion** *noun* [Latin *excommunicare -atus* (as EX-¹, *communis* COMMON)]

ex-con *noun informal* an ex-convict; a former inmate of a prison.

ex·cori·ate /ɛksˈkɔriˌeɪt/ *transitive verb* **1** censure severely. **2 a** remove part of the skin of (a person etc.) by abrasion. **b** strip or peel off (skin). □ **ex·cori·a·tion** *noun* [Latin *excoriare excoriat-* (as EX-¹, *corium* hide)]

ex·cre·ment /ˈɛkskrəmənt/ *noun* feces. □ **ex·cre·men·tal** /-ˈmɛntəl/ *adjective* [French *excrément* or Latin *excrementum* (as EXCRETE)]

ex·cres·cence /ɪkˈskrɛsəns/ *noun* **1** an abnormal or morbid outgrowth on the body or a plant. **2** an ugly addition. □ **ex·cres·cent** *adjective* [Latin *excrescentia* (as EX-¹, *crescere* grow)]

ex·creta /ɛkˈskriːtə, ɪk-/ *plural noun* waste discharged from the body, esp. feces and urine. [Latin neuter pl.: see EXCRETE]

ex·crete *transitive verb* (of an animal or plant) separate and expel waste matter as a result of metabolism. □ **ex·cret·er** *noun* **ex·cre·tion** *noun* **ex·cre·tory** *adjective* [Latin *excernere excret-* (as EX-¹, *cernere* sift)]

ex·cru·ci·at·ing /ɪkˈskruːʃiˌeɪtɪŋ/ *adjective* (of physical or mental pain) intense, acute (*she has an excruciating headache*). □ **ex·cru·ci·at·ing·ly** *adverb* **ex·cru·ci·a·tion** /-ˈeɪʃən/ *noun* [Latin *excruciare excruciat-* (as EX-¹, *cruciare* torment from *crux crucis* cross)]

ex·cul·pate /ˈɛkskʌlˌpeɪt/ *transitive verb formal* **1** free from blame. **2** (foll. by *from*) clear (a person) of a charge. □ **ex·cul·pa·tion** *noun* **ex·cul·pa·tory** /-ˈkʌlpəˌtɔri/ *adjective* [medieval Latin *exculpare exculpat-* (as EX-¹, *culpa* blame)]

ex·cur·sion /ɪkˈskɜrʒən/ *noun* **1** a short journey, esp. one made by a group of people together for pleasure (*took an excursion to the island*). **2** a group of people making such a trip. **3** a trip at a reduced rate, e.g. on a train, ship, etc. (also *attributive: excursion fare*). **4** a digression, deviation, or diversion. **5** *archaic* a sortie (*see* ALARUM). □ **ex·cur·sion·ist** *noun* [Latin *excursio* from *excurrere excurs-* (as EX-¹, *currere* run)]

ex·cur·sus /ɛkˈskɜrsəs, ɪk-/ *noun* (pl. **ex·cur·sus·es** or same) **1** a detailed discussion of a special point in a book, usu. in an appendix. **2** a digression in a narrative. [Latin, verbal noun formed as EXCURSION]

ex·cuse ● *transitive verb* /ɪkˈskjuːz/ **1** attempt to lessen the blame attaching to (a person, act, or fault). **2** (of a fact or circumstance) serve in mitigation of (a person or act). **3** obtain exemption for (a person or oneself). **4 a** (foll. by *from*) release (a person) from a duty etc. (*excused from supervision duties*). **b** allow (a person) to leave. **5** overlook or forgive (a fault or offence). **6** (foll. by *for*) forgive (a person) for a fault. **7** not insist upon (what is due). **8** *reflexive* apologize for leaving (*excused herself and went to bed*). ● *noun* /ɪkˈskjuːs, ek-/ **1** a reason put forward to mitigate or justify an offence, fault, etc. **2** an apology (*made my excuses*). **3** *informal* (foll. by *for*) a poor or inadequate example of (*a poor excuse for a novel*). □ **be excused** be allowed to leave a room etc., e.g. to go to the lavatory. **excuse me** a polite apology for an interruption etc., or for disagreeing. **2** a polite formula used when trying to make one's way through a crowd etc. **3** implying that one cannot believe what one has just heard. **excuse me for living** a sarcastic formula of apology. □ **ex·cus·able** /-ˈkjuːzəbəl/ *adjective* **ex·cus·ably** *adverb* [Old French *escuser* from Latin *excusare* (as EX-¹, *causa* CAUSE, accusation)]

ex-direc·tory *adjective* Brit. (of a telephone number) unlisted.

ex div. *abbreviation* ex dividend.

ex dividend *adjective & adverb* (of stocks or shares) not including the next dividend.

exec *informal* ● *noun* an executive. ● *adjective* executive. [abbreviation]

exe·crable /ˈɛksɪkrəbəl/ *adjective* **1** abominable, detestable. **2** of very poor quality. □ **exe·crably** *adverb* [Old French from Latin *execrabilis* (as EXECRATE)]

exe·crate /ˈɛksɪˌkreɪt/ *verb* **1** *transitive* express or feel abhorrence for. **2** *transitive* curse (a person or thing). **3** *intransitive* utter curses. □ **exe·cra·tion** *noun* [Latin *exsecrare* (as EX-¹, *sacrare* devote, from *sacer* sacred, accursed)]

exec·u·tant /ɪɡˈzɛkjʊtənt/ *noun formal* **1** a performer, esp. of music. **2** a person who carries something into effect. [French *exécutant* pres. part. (as EXECUTE)]

exe·cute *transitive verb* **1 a** carry out a sentence of death on (a condemned person). **b** kill as a political act. **2** carry into effect, perform (a plan, duty, command, operation, etc.). **3 a** carry out a design for (a product of art or skill). **b** perform (a musical composition, dance, etc.). **4** make (a legal instrument) valid by signing, sealing, etc. **5** put into effect (a judicial sentence, the terms of a will, etc.). **6** *Computing* run or process (a command, program, file, etc.). □ **exe·cut·able** *adjective* [Old French *executer* from medieval Latin *executare* from Latin *exsequi exsecut-* (as EX-¹, *sequi* follow)]

exe·cu·tion *noun* **1** the carrying out of a sentence of death. **2** the act or an instance of carrying out or performing something. **3** technique or style of performance in the arts, esp. music. **4 a** seizure of the property or person of a debtor in default of payment. **b** a judicial writ enforcing a judgment. □ **exe·cu·tion·ary** *adjective*

exe·cu·tion·er *noun* an official who carries out a sentence of death.

exec·u·tive /ɪɡˈzɛkjʊtɪv/ ● *noun* **1** a person or body with managerial or administrative responsibility in a business organization etc.; a senior business person. **2** the branch of a government concerned with executing laws. **3** the person or persons in whom is vested the supreme executive authority of a country or state. ● *adjective* **1 a** designating the branch of government that deals with putting into effect laws and judicial sentences. **b** of or pertaining to the executive of a government. **2 a** concerned with administration or management. **b** relating to, designed for, or used by executives (*executive suite*). **3** *informal* exclusive; of the finest quality (*executive homes*). □ **exec·u·tive·ly** *adverb* [medieval Latin *executivus* (as EXECUTE)]

executive assistant *noun* a clerical assistant to an executive of a corporation etc.

executive council *noun Cdn* **1** the members of a provincial or territorial cabinet. **2** *hist.* (in colonial government) a body of advisers appointed by the governor.

executive director *noun N Amer.* a person employed by a non-profit organization to oversee operations and management and implement the policy decisions of the board of directors.

executive federalism *noun Cdn* the practice of establishing Canadian constitutional, social, and economic policy at meetings of first ministers and cabinet ministers, esp. behind closed doors.

executive officer *noun* **1** the second-in-command in naval units and some military units. **2** a senior executive in a corporation etc.

executive order *noun US* a regulation or rule issued by the president, governor, etc., and having the force of law.

executive privilege *noun* (in the US) the privilege, claimed by the president for the executive branch of the US government, of withholding information in the public interest.

executive producer *noun* the person who oversees the financial aspects of the production of a film. □ **executive-produce** *transitive verb*

executive secretary *noun* a secretary to a business executive.

executive session *noun US* a usu. private meeting of a legislative body for executive business.

exec·u·tor /ɪɡˈzɛkjʊtər/ *noun* a person appointed by a testator to carry out the terms of his or her will. □ **exec·u·tor·ship** *noun* **exec·u·tory** *adjective*

exec·u·trix /ɪɡˈzɛkjʊtrɪks/ *noun* (pl. **exec·u·tri·ces** /ɪɡˌzɛkjʊˈtraɪsiːz/ or **exec·u·trix·es**) a woman appointed by a testator to carry out the terms of his or her will.

exe·gesis /ˌɛksɪˈdʒiːsɪs/ *noun* (pl. **exe·geses** /-siːz/) critical explanation of a text, esp. of Scripture. □ **exe·get·ic** /-ˈdʒɛtɪk/ *adjective* **exe·get·ic·al** /-ˈdʒɛtɪkəl/ *adjective* [Greek *exēgēsis* from *exēgeomai* interpret (as EX-², *hēgeomai* lead)]

exe·gete /ˈeksɪˌdʒiːt/ *noun* a person skilled at exegesis. [Greek *exēgētēs* (as EXEGESIS)]

exem·plar /ɪgˈzemplɜr, -plɑr/ *noun* **1** a model or pattern. **2** a typical instance of a class of things. [Old French *exemplaire* from Late Latin *exemplarium* (as EXAMPLE)]

exem·plary /ɪgˈzemplɜri/ *adjective* **1** fit to be imitated; outstandingly good. **2 a** serving as a warning. **b** *Law* (of damages) exceeding the amount needed for simple compensation. **3** illustrative, representative. □ **exem·plar·i·ly** *adverb* **exem·plar·i·ness** *noun* **exem·plar·ity** *noun* [Late Latin *exemplaris* (as EXAMPLE)]

exem·pli·fy /ɪgˈzemplɪˌfaɪ/ *transitive verb* (**-fies**, **-fied**) **1** illustrate by example. **2** be an example of. **3** *Law* make an attested copy of (a document) under an official seal. □ **exem·pli·fi·ca·tion** /-fɪˈkeɪʃən/ *noun* [medieval Latin *exemplificare* (as EXAMPLE)]

exem·plum /ɪgˈzempləm/ *noun* (*pl.* **exem·pla** /-plə/) an example or model, esp. a moralizing or illustrative story. [Latin: see EXAMPLE]

ex·empt /ɪgˈzempt/ ● *adjective* **1** free from an obligation or liability etc. imposed on others. **2** (foll. by *from*) not liable to. ● *noun* a person who is exempt, esp. from payment of tax. ● *transitive verb* (foll. by *from*) free from an obligation, esp. one imposed on others. □ **exemp·tion** *noun* [Latin *exemptus* past participle of *eximere* exempt- (as EX-¹, *emere* take)]

exe·quies /ˈeksɪkwɪz/ *plural noun* *formal* funeral rites. [Old French from Latin *exsequiae* (as EX-¹, *sequi* follow)]

exer·cise ● *noun* **1** activity requiring physical effort, done esp. as training or to sustain or improve health. **2** mental or spiritual activity, esp. as practice to develop a skill. **3** (often in *pl.*) a particular task or set of tasks devised as exercise, practice in a technique, etc. **4 a** the use or application of a mental faculty, right, etc. **b** practice of an ability, quality, etc. **5** (often in *pl.*) military drill or manoeuvres. **6** (foll. by *in*) a process directed at or concerned with something specified (*was an exercise in public relations*). **7** *N Amer.* (usu. in *pl.*) a formal or traditional routine or ceremony (*graduation exercises; opening exercises*). ● *verb* **1** *transitive* use or apply (a faculty, right, influence, restraint, etc.). **2** *transitive* perform (a function). **3 a** *intransitive* take (esp. physical) exercise; do exercises. **b** *transitive* provide (an animal) with exercise. **c** *transitive* train (a person). **4** *transitive* **a** tax the powers of. **b** perplex, worry. □ **exercise in futility** an activity which proves to be absolutely futile. **the object** (or **point**) **of the exercise** the essential purpose of an action or procedure. □ **exer·cis·able** *adjective* **exer·cis·er** *noun* [Old French *exercice* from Latin *exercitium* from *exercere* exercit- keep at work (as EX-¹, *arcēre* restrain)]

exercise bike *noun* a stationary apparatus used for physical exercise, in which a person can sit and pedal against resistance, like a cyclist.

exercise book *noun* **1** a book containing exercises. **2** esp. *Cdn & Brit.* a book for writing school work, notes, etc., in.

exercise yard *noun* a fenced-in but uncovered area in a prison, used for physical exercise.

exer·cycle *noun* = EXERCISE BIKE.

ex·ergue /egˈzɜrg, ˈek-/ *noun* a small space usu. on the reverse of a coin or medal, below the principal device. [French from medieval Latin *exergum* from Greek *ex-* (as EX-²) + *ergon* work]

ex·ert *transitive verb* **1** bring to bear (a quality, force, influence, etc.). **2** *reflexive* (often foll. by *for*, or *to* + infin.) use one's efforts or endeavours; strive. [Latin *exserere* exsert- put forth (as EX-¹, *serere* bind)]

exer·tion *noun* **1** the act of exerting. **2** strenuous physical activity.

Exe·ter /ˈeksətɜr/ the county town of Devon, on the Exe River; pop. (2001) 111,078.

exe·unt /ˈeksɪˌʌnt/ *intransitive verb* (as a stage direction) (actors) leave the stage. □ **exeunt omnes** all leave the stage. [Latin, = they go out: 3rd pl. pres. of *exire* go out: see EXIT]

ex·fil·trate /ˈeksfɪlˌtreɪt/ *transitive & intransitive verb* withdraw (troops, spies, etc.) surreptitiously, esp. from danger. □ **ex·fil·tra·tion** /-ˈtreɪʃən/ *noun*

ex·foli·ant /eksˈfoːliənt/ *noun* a cosmetic product designed to remove dead cells from the surface of the skin.

ex·foli·ate /eksˈfoːliˌeɪt/ *verb* **1** *intransitive* (of bone, the skin, a mineral, etc.) come off in scales or layers. **2 a** *transitive* shed (material) in scales or layers. **b** *transitive & intransitive* cause (the skin etc.) to shed flakes or scales. **3** *intransitive* (of a tree) throw off layers of bark. □ **ex·foli·ation** *noun* **ex·foli·a·tive** /-liətɪv/ *adjective* [Late Latin *exfoliare* exfoliat- (as EX-¹, *folium* leaf)]

ex gra·tia /eks ˈgreɪʃə/ ● *adverb* as a favour rather than from an (esp. legal) obligation. ● *adjective* granted on this basis. [Latin, = from favour]

ex·hal·a·tion /ˌeksəˈleɪʃən/ *noun* **1 a** an expiration of air. **b** a puff of breath. **2** a mist, vapour. **3** an emanation or effluvium.

ex·hale /eksˈheil, ɪgz-/ *transitive & intransitive verb* **1** breathe out (esp. air or smoke) from the lungs. **2** give off or be given off in vapour. □ **ex·hal·able** *adjective* [Old French *exhaler* from Latin *exhalare* (as EX-¹, *halare* breathe)]

ex·haust /ɪgˈzɒst, eg-/ ● *transitive verb* **1** consume or use up the whole of. **2 a** (often as **ex·haust·ed** *adjective* or **ex·haust·ing** *adjective*) use up the strength or energy of; tire out. **b** drain (soil) of nutritive ingredients. **3** study or expound on (a subject) completely. **4** (often foll. by *of*) empty (a vessel etc.) of its contents. **5** draw out (a gas etc.). ● *noun* **1 a** expelled waste air or other gases etc., esp. those produced by an engine after combustion. **b** (also **exhaust pipe**) the pipe or system by which these are expelled. **c** the process of expulsion of these gases. **2 a** the production of an outward current of air by the creation of a partial vacuum. **b** an apparatus for this. □ **ex·haust·er** *noun* **ex·haust·ible** *adjective* **ex·haust·ing·ly** *adverb* [Latin *exhaurire* exhaust- (as EX-¹, *haurire* draw (water), drain)]

ex·haus·tion /ɪgˈzɒstʃən, eg-/ *noun* **1** a state of extreme physical or mental fatigue. **2** the action or state of using something up or of being used up.

ex·haus·tive /ɪgˈzɒstɪv, eg-/ *adjective* **1** thorough, comprehensive. **2** tending to exhaust a resource. □ **ex·haust·ive·ly** *adverb* **ex·haus·tiv·ity** *noun* **ex·haust·ive·ness** *noun*

ex·hib·it /ɪgˈzɪbɪt, eg-/ *transitive verb* (**ex·hib·it·ed**, **ex·hib·it·ing**) **1** show or reveal publicly (for amusement, in competition, etc.). **2 a** show, display. **b** manifest (a quality). **3** submit for consideration. ● *noun* **1** a thing or collection of things forming part or all of an exhibition. **2** a document or other item or object produced in a law court as evidence. [Latin *exhibēre* exhibit- (as EX-¹, *habēre* hold)]

Exhibit A *noun* **1** *Law* the first exhibit in a case. **2** something regarded as evidence or the most important evidence.

ex·hib·ition /ˌeksɪˈbɪʃən/ *noun* **1** a display (esp. public) of works of art, industrial products, etc. **2** *Cdn* a large regional fair, esp. with amusements, agricultural exhibits, and craft displays, usu. lasting for an extended period. **3** a world's fair. **4** the act or an instance of exhibiting; the state of being exhibited. **5** *N Amer. Sport* (*attributive*) denoting games whose outcomes do not affect the teams' standings, esp. those played before the start of a regular season (*exhibition game; exhibition season*). **6** *Brit.* a scholarship, esp. from the funds of a school, college, etc. □ **make an exhibition of oneself** behave so as to appear ridiculous or foolish.

ex·hib·ition·er /ˌeksɪˈbɪʃənɜr/ *noun* *Brit.* a student who has been awarded an exhibition.

ex·hib·ition·ism /ˌeksɪˈbɪʃəˌnɪzəm/ *noun* **1** a tendency towards display or extravagant behaviour. **2** *Psych.* a mental condition characterized by the compulsion to display one's genitals indecently in public. □ **ex·hib·ition·ist** *noun* **ex·hib·ition·is·tic** *adjective* **ex·hib·ition·is·tic·ally** *adverb*

ex·hib·itor /ɪgˈzɪbɪtɜr, eg-/ *noun* **1** a person, company, etc. displaying their wares, art works, animals, etc. at a trade show, art exhibition, animal show, etc. **2** a person, company, etc. that shows movies for the general public; a movie theatre operator.

ex·hila·rate /ɪgˈzɪləˌreɪt, eg-/ *transitive verb* (often as **ex·hila·rat·ing** *adjective* or **ex·hila·rat·ed** *adjective*) make (someone) feel very happy, elated, or excited. □ **ex·hila·rat·ing·ly** *adverb* **ex·hila·ra·tion** /-ˈreɪʃən/ *noun* [Latin *exhilarare* (as EX-¹, *hilaris* cheerful)]

ex·hort /ɪgˈzɔrt, eg-/ *transitive verb* (often foll. by *to* + infin.) urge or advise strongly or earnestly. □ **ex·horta·tory** *adjective* **ex·hort·er** *noun* [Latin *exhortari* (as EX-¹, *hortari* exhort)]

ex·hort·a·tion /ˌegzɔrˈteɪʃən, ˌeks-/ *noun* the act or an instance of exhorting.

ex·hume /eksˈjuːm, egz-, -ˈuːm, -ˈhjuːm/ *transitive verb* **1** dig out, unearth (esp. a buried corpse). **2** disinter, bring to light (esp. something lost). □ **ex·hum·a·tion** /-ˈmeɪʃən/ *noun* [medieval Latin *exhumare* (as EX-¹, *humus* ground)]

ex hy·poth·esi /ˌeks haiˈpɒθəsi/ *adverb* according to the hypothesis proposed. [modern Latin]

exi·gency /ˈeksɪdʒənsi, ɪgˈzɪdʒ-, eg-/ *noun* (*pl.* **-cies**) (also **exi·gence** /ˈeksɪdʒəns, eg-/) (usu. in *pl.*) an urgent need or demand. [Late Latin *exigentia* (as EXIGENT)]

exi·gent /ˈegzɪdʒənt, eks-/ *adjective* **1** requiring much; exacting. **2** urgent, pressing. [Latin *exigent-* 'completing, ascertaining', from the verb *exigere* (see EXACT)]

exig·u·ous /egˈzɪgjʊəs, ɪg-/ *adjective* scanty, small. □ **exi·gu·ity** /-ˈgjuːɪti/ *noun* **exigu·ous·ly** *adverb* **exigu·ous·ness** *noun* [Latin *exiguus* scanty, from *exigere* weigh exactly: see EXACT]

exile /ˈegzaɪl, ˈeks-/ ● *noun* **1** expulsion, or the state of being expelled, from one's native land or home, esp. for political reasons. **2 a** long absence from home, esp. as constrained by circumstances (*scholars living in academic exile*). **b** exclusion from a group, accustomed place, etc. **3** a person expelled or long absent from his or her native country, home, etc. **4** (also **Babylonian exile, Exile**) the captivity of the Jews in Babylon in the 6th c. BC. ● *transitive verb* (foll. by *from*) **1** officially expel (a person) from his or her native country or town etc. **2** exclude (a person or thing) from a group etc. □ **exilic** /-ˈzɪlɪk, -ˈsɪlɪk/ *adjective* (esp. in sense 4 of *noun*). [Old French *exil, exiler* from Latin *exilium* banishment]

exist *intransitive verb* **1** be real or actual; have being. **2 a** have being under specified conditions. **b** (foll. by *as*) exist in the form of (*sports teams exist solely as public relations vehicles*). **3** (of circumstances etc.) occur; be found. **4** live with no pleasure under adverse conditions (*felt he was merely existing*). **5** continue in being; maintain life (*can hardly exist on this salary*). **6** be alive, live. □ **exist·ing** *adjective* [prob. back-formation from EXISTENCE; compare Late Latin *existere*]

exist·ence *noun* **1** the fact or condition of being or existing. **2** the manner of one's existing or living, esp. under adverse conditions (*a wretched existence*). **3** all that exists. [Old French *existence* or Late Latin *existentia* from Latin *existere* (as EX-¹, *stare* stand)]

exist·ent ● *adjective* existing, actual, current. ● *noun* a person who or thing which exists.

exis·ten·tial /ˌegzɪˈstenʃəl, eks-/ *adjective* **1** of or relating to existence. **2** *Logic* (of a proposition etc.) affirming or implying the existence of a thing. **3** concerned with existence, esp. with human existence as viewed by existentialism. □ **exis·ten·tial·ly** *adverb*

exis·ten·tial·ism /ˌegzɪˈstenʃəˌlɪzəm, eks-/ *noun* a philosophical theory emphasizing the existence of the individual person as a free and responsible agent isolated in an otherwise deterministic world. □ **exis·ten·tial·ist** *noun & adjective*

exit /ˈeksɪt, ˈegzɪt/ ● *noun* **1** a passage or door by which to leave a room, building, etc. **2** the act of going out. **3** the act of departing from or ceasing to participate or engage in. **4** a place where vehicles can leave a highway or major road. **5** the departure of an actor from the stage. **6** death. ● *verb* (**exit·ed, exit·ing**) **1 a** *intransitive* go out of a room, building, etc. **b** *transitive* leave (a building, room, etc.). **2** *transitive & intransitive* esp. *N Amer.* (of a vehicle) leave (a highway or major road). **3** *intransitive* (as a stage direction) (an actor) leaves the stage (*exit Macbeth*). **4** *transitive & intransitive Computing* terminate (a computer session, program, etc.). [Latin, 3rd sing. pres. of *exire* go out (as EX-¹, *ire* go): compare Latin *exitus* going out]

exit permit *noun* (also **exit visa** etc.) authorization to leave a particular country.

exit poll *noun* an unofficial poll, esp. for the media, in which voters leaving a polling station are asked how they voted.

exit strategy *noun* a detailed plan for quitting a job or retiring, or abandoning a business venture or investment.

exit wound *noun* a wound made by a bullet etc. passing out of the body.

ex lib·ris /eksˈliːbriːs/ ● *noun* (*pl.* same) a usu. decorated bookplate or label bearing the owner's name, pasted into the front of a book. ● *adverb* (also **ex libris**) from the books of. [Latin]

Ex·moor /ˈeksmʊr, -mɔr/ an area of moorland in north Devon and west Somerset, SW England.

ex nihi·lo /eks ˈniːhɪˌloː/ *adverb* out of nothing (*creation ex nihilo*). [Latin]

exo- *combining form* external. [Greek *exō* outside]

exo·biol·ogy *noun* the branch of science that deals with the possibility of life on other planets or in space. □ **exo·bio·logic·al** *adjective* **exo·biol·o·gist** *noun*

Exo·cet /ˈeksəˌset/ *noun* a French-made short-range guided missile used esp. in tactical sea warfare. [French *exocet* flying fish]

exo·crine /ˈeksəˌkraɪn/ *adjective* (of a gland) secreting through a duct (*compare* ENDOCRINE 1). [EXO- + Greek *krinō* sift]

exo·cyt·o·sis /ˌeksəsaɪˈtoːsɪs/ *noun* the release of matter by a living cell. □ **exo·cyt·otic** /-ˈtɒtɪk/ *adjective* [EXO- + -CYTE + -OSIS]

Exod. *abbreviation Bible* Exodus.

exo·dus /ˈeksədəs, ˈegz-/ *noun* **1** a mass departure of people. **2** (**Exodus**) *Bible* the departure of the Israelites from Egypt. **b** the book of the Old Testament relating this. [ecclesiastical Latin from Greek *exodos* (as EX-², *hodos* way)]

ex of·fi·cio /ˌeks əˈfɪʃioː, -ˈfɪsioː/ *adverb & adjective* by virtue of one's office or status. [Latin]

ex·og·amy /ekˈsɒgəmi/ *noun* **1** *Anthropology* marriage outside one's own community, clan, or tribe. **2** *Biol.* the fusion of reproductive cells from distantly related or unrelated individuals. □ **exo·gam·ic** /-ˈgamɪk/ *adjective* **ex·og·am·ous** *adjective*

ex·ogen·ous /ekˈsɒdʒənəs/ *adjective* growing or originating from outside. □ **ex·ogen·ous·ly** *adverb*

exon /ˈeksɒn/ *noun Genetics* a segment of a DNA or RNA molecule that contains coding information for a protein (*compare* INTRON). [from EXPRESS¹ 5 + -ON]

ex·on·er·ate /ɪgˈzɒnəˌreɪt/ *transitive verb* (often foll. by *from*) **1** free or declare free from guilt, blame, etc. **2** release from a duty etc. □ **ex·on·er·a·tion** *noun* **ex·on·era·tive** *adjective* [Latin *exonerare exonerat-* (as EX-¹, *onus, oneris* burden)]

ex·oph·thal·mic /eksɒfˈθalmɪk/ *adjective* characterized by protruding eyes.

exophthalmic goitre *noun* = GRAVES' DISEASE.

ex·oph·thal·mos /ˌeksɒfˈθalmɒs/ *noun Med.* abnormal protrusion of the eyeball. [modern Latin from Greek *exophthalmos* having prominent eyes (as EX-², *ophthalmos* eye)]

ex·orbi·tant /ɪgˈzɔrbɪtənt/ *adjective* (of a price, demand, etc.) grossly excessive. □ **ex·orbi·tance** *noun* **ex·orbi·tant·ly** *adverb* [Late Latin *exorbitare* (as EX-¹, *orbita* ORBIT)]

exor·cise /ˈeksɔrˌsaɪz, -ɜr-/ *transitive verb* (also **-ize**) **1 a** endeavour to expel (a supposed evil spirit) by religious ceremonies, prayers, etc. **b** free (a person or place) of a supposed evil spirit. **2 a** remove (a malignant influence). **b** free (a person or place) of a malignant influence. □ **exor·cism** *noun* **exor·cist** *noun* [French *exorciser* or ecclesiastical Latin *exorcizare* from Greek *exorkizō* (as EX-², *horkos* oath)]

ex·ord·ium /ekˈsɔrdiəm/ *noun* (*pl.* **ex·or·diums** or **ex·or·dia** /-diə/) the beginning or introductory part, esp. of a discourse or treatise. □ **ex·or·dial** *adjective* [Latin from *exordiri* (as EX-¹, *ordiri* begin)]

exo·skel·eton /ˌeksoʊˈskelətən/ *noun* a rigid external covering for the body in certain animals, esp. arthropods, providing support and protection (*opp.* ENDOSKELETON). □ **exo·skel·etal** *adjective*

exo·sphere /ˈeksoʊˌsfɪr/ *noun* the outermost part of the atmosphere of a planet etc. □ **exo·spher·ic** /-ˈsferɪk/ *adjective*

exo·ter·ic /eksoʊˈterɪk/ *adjective* **1** (of a doctrine, mode of speech, etc.) intended for, or intelligible to, those outside a select group (*opp.* ESOTERIC). **2** current among the general public; popular, ordinary. [Greek *exōterikos* from *exōterō*, comparative of *exō* 'outside': compare ESOTERIC]

exo·ther·mic /ˌeksoʊˈθɜrmɪk/ *adjective* (also **exo·ther·mal** /-məl/) esp. *Chem.* (of a reaction) accompanied by, or (of a compound) formed with the liberation of heat. □ **exo·ther·mal·ly** *adverb* **exo·ther·mic·ally** *adverb*

exot·ic /ɪgˈzɒtɪk, eg-/ ● *adjective* **1** introduced from or originating in or existing in a foreign or distant place (*exotic birds*). **2** attractively or remarkably strange or unusual; bizarre. **3** (of a fuel, metal, etc.) of a kind newly brought into use. ● *noun* an exotic person or thing. □ **exot·ic·al·ly** *adverb* **exoti·cism** /-ˌtɪˌsɪzəm/ *noun* **exoti·cize** /-tɪˌsaɪz/ *transitive verb* **exotic·ness** *noun* [Latin *exoticus* from Greek *exōtikos* from *exō* outside]

exot·ica /ɪgˈzɒtɪkə, eg-/ *plural noun* remarkably strange or rare things. [Latin, neuter pl. of *exoticus*: see EXOTIC]

exotic dancer *noun* = STRIPPER 1.

exo·toxin *noun* a toxin released by a living bacterial cell into its surroundings.

exp. *abbreviation* **1** expiry. **2** experience(d). **3** *Computing* expansion. **4** experimental. **5** *Photography* exposure.

ex·pand *verb* **1** *transitive & intransitive* increase in size, scope, or importance. **2** *intransitive* (often foll. by *on*) give a fuller description or account. **3** *intransitive* become more genial or effusive; discard one's reserve. **4** *transitive* **a** set or write out in full (something condensed or abbreviated). **b** *Math.* rewrite (a product, power, or function) as a sum. **5** *transitive & intransitive* spread out flat. □ **ex·pand·abil·ity** *noun* **ex·pand·able** *adjective* **ex·pand·er** *noun* **ex·pand·ing** *adjective* **ex·pan·sible** *adjective* **ex·pan·si·bil·ity** *noun* [Latin *expandere expans-* spread out (as EX-¹, *pandere* spread)]

expanded metal *noun* sheet metal slit and stretched into a lattice, used to reinforce concrete and other brittle materials.

expanding universe theory *noun* the hypothesis, based on the observation of red shifts, that galaxies are moving farther apart at a rate proportional to their distance from each other.

ex·panse *noun* **1** a wide continuous area or extent of land, space, etc. **2** an amount of expansion. [modern Latin *expansum* neuter past participle (as EXPAND)]

ex·pan·sile /ɪkˈspansail, ek-/ *adjective* **1** of expansion. **2** capable of expansion.

ex·pan·sion *noun* **1** the act or an instance of expanding; the state of being expanded. **2** enlargement of the scale or scope of (esp. commercial) operations. **3** increase in the amount of a state's territory or area of control. **4** an increase in the volume of fuel etc. on combustion in the cylinder of an engine. **5** *Math.* **a** the process of working out a product, power, or function and expressing it in simpler terms as a sum. **b** the sum. **6 a** an enlarged portion. **b** something formed by the expansion of a thing. **7** *N Amer. Sport* (often *attributive*) the addition of new teams to a league (*expansion team; in favour of expansion*). □ **ex·pan·sion·ary** *adjective* [Late Latin *expansio* (as EXPAND)]

expansion card *noun* (also **expansion board**) *Computing* a circuit board that can be inserted in a computer to give extra facilities.

expansion draft *noun N Amer. Sport* a draft in which expansion teams select available players from existing teams' rosters.

ex·pan·sion·ism *noun* a policy or theory advocating esp. territorial or economic expansion. □ **ex·pan·sion·ist** *noun* **ex·pan·sion·is·tic** *adjective*

expansion joint *noun Engin.* a joint that allows for the thermal expansion of the parts joined.

expansion slot *noun Computing* a place in a computer where an expansion card can be added.

ex·pan·sive *adjective* **1** able or tending to expand. **2** extensive, wide-ranging. **3** (of a person, feelings, or speech) effusive, open. □ **ex·pan·sive·ly** *adverb* **ex·pan·sive·ness** *noun*

ex parte /eks ˈpɑːti/ *adjective & adverb Law* in the interests of one side only (and without notice to the adverse party) or of an interested outside party. [Latin]

ex·pat *noun & adjective informal* = EXPATRIATE. [abbreviation]

ex·pati·ate /ɪkˈspeɪʃi,eɪt, ek-/ *intransitive verb* (usu. foll. by *on, upon*) speak or write at length or in detail. □ **ex·pati·a·tion** *noun* [Latin *exspatiari* digress (as EX-¹, *spatium* SPACE)]

ex·patri·ate ● *adjective* /eksˈpeitriət/ living abroad, esp. for a long period. ● *noun* /eksˈpeitriət/ an expatriate person. ● *transitive verb* /eksˈpeitri,eit/ expel or remove (a person) from his or her native country, home, etc. □ **ex·patri·a·tion** *noun* [medieval Latin *expatriare* (as EX-¹, *patria* native country)]

ex·pect *transitive verb* **1** (often foll. by *to* + infin., or *that* + clause) **a** regard as likely; assume as a future event or occurrence. **b** (often foll. by *of*) look for as appropriate or one's due (from a person) (*I expect co-operation; expect you to be here; expected better of you*). **c** foresee or look forward to the arrival of (*expecting guests*). **2** *informal* (often foll. by *that* + clause) think, suppose (*I expect we'll be on time*). **3** be pregnant with (*expecting twins*). □ **be expecting** *informal* be pregnant. □ **ex·pect·able** *adjective* **ex·pect·ably** *adverb* [Latin *exspectare* (as EX-¹, *spectare* look, frequentative of *specere* see)]

ex·pect·ancy *noun* (*pl.* **-cies**) **1** a state of expectation. **2** what can reasonably be expected (*life expectancy*). [Latin *exspectantia, exp-* (as EXPECT)]

ex·pect·ant *adjective* **1** revealing expectation. **2** (of a mother or father) expecting the birth of a child. □ **ex·pect·ant·ly** *adverb*

ex·pect·a·tion *noun* **1** the state or an instance of expecting or looking forward. **2** something expected or hoped for. **3** (in *pl.*) *archaic* one's prospects of inheritance.

ex·pec·tor·ant /ekˈspektərənt/ ● *adjective* causing the coughing out of phlegm etc. ● *noun* an expectorant medicine.

ex·pec·tor·ate /ekˈspektə,reit/ *transitive & intransitive verb* **1** cough or spit out (phlegm etc.) from the chest or lungs. **2** spit (saliva, tobacco juice, etc.) □ **ex·pec·tor·a·tion** *noun* **ex·pec·tor·ator** *noun* [Latin *expectorare expectorat-* (as EX-¹, *pectus -oris* breast)]

ex·pedi·ent /ɪkˈspiːdɪənt, ek-/ ● *adjective* **1** (of an action) convenient and practical although possibly improper or immoral. **2** suitable, appropriate. ● *noun* a means of attaining an end. □ **ex·pedi·ence** *noun* **ex·pedi·ency** *noun* **ex·pedi·ent·ly** *adverb* [Latin *expedire*: see EXPEDITE]

ex·ped·ite /ˈekspə,dait/ *transitive verb* **1** assist the progress of; hasten (an action, process, etc.). **2** accomplish (esp. business) quickly. [Latin *expedire expedit-* extricate, put in order (as EX-¹, *pes pedis* foot)]

ex·ped·it·er /ˈekspə,daitər/ *noun* (also **ex·ped·it·or**) **1** an employee responsible for ensuring that work is done efficiently and on schedule. **2** *Cdn* = OUTFITTER 1.

ex·ped·ition /ˌekspəˈdiʃən/ *noun* **1** a journey or voyage for a particular purpose, esp. tourism, exploration, or scientific research. **2** the personnel or ships etc. undertaking this. **3** promptness, speed.

□ **ex·ped·ition·er** *noun* **ex·ped·ition·ist** *noun* [Old French from Latin *expeditio -onis* (as EXPEDITE)]

ex·ped·ition·ary /ˌekspəˈdiʃə,neri/ *adjective* of or used in an expedition, esp. a military expedition to a foreign country.

ex·ped·itious /ˌekspəˈdiʃəs/ *adjective* **1** acting or done with speed and efficiency. **2** conducive to speedy performance. □ **ex·ped·itious·ly** *adverb* **ex·ped·itious·ness** *noun*

expel *transitive verb* (**ex·pelled, ex·pel·ling**) (often foll. by *from*) **1** compel the departure of (a person) from a school, community, etc. **2** force out or eject (a substance from the body, a gas from a cavity, etc.). **3** order or force to leave a building etc. □ **ex·pel·lee** /-ˈliː/ *noun* [Latin *expellere expuls-* (as EX-¹, *pellere* drive)]

ex·pend *transitive verb* spend or use up (money, time, energy, etc.). [Latin *expendere expens-* (as EX-¹, *pendere* weigh)]

ex·pend·able ● *adjective* **1** that may be sacrificed or dispensed with, esp. to achieve a purpose. **2 a** not regarded as worth preserving or saving. **b** unimportant, insignificant. **3** not normally reused. ● *noun* an expendable person or thing. □ **ex·pend·abil·ity** *noun* **ex·pend·ably** *adverb*

ex·pendi·ture *noun* **1** the process or an instance of spending or using up. **2** a thing (esp. a sum of money) expended.

ex·pense ● *noun* **1** cost incurred; payment of money. **2** (usu. in *pl.*) **a** costs incurred in doing a particular job etc. (*will pay your expenses*). **b** an amount paid to reimburse this (*offered me $40 per day expenses*). **3** a thing that is a cause of much expense (*the house is a real expense to run*). ● *transitive verb* **1** write off (an expense, loss, etc.) for tax purposes. **2** *informal* charge (an expenditure) to an expense account. □ **at the expense of** so as to cause loss or damage or discredit to (something). **at a person's expense 1** causing a person to suffer injury, ridicule, etc. **2** with costs paid by a person. [Late Latin *expensa* (money) spent, past participle of Latin *expendere* EXPEND]

expense account *noun* an arrangement by which sums of money spent in the course of business by an employee are later reimbursed by the employer.

ex·pen·sive *adjective* **1** costing much. **2** charging high prices (*an expensive store*). **3** causing much expense (*has expensive tastes*). □ **ex·pen·sive·ly** *adverb* **ex·pen·sive·ness** *noun*

ex·peri·ence ● *noun* **1** actual observation of or practical acquaintance with facts or events. **2** knowledge or skill resulting from this. **3 a** an event regarded as affecting one (*an unpleasant experience*). **b** the fact or process of being so affected (*learned by experience*). **4** the events that have taken place within the knowledge of an individual, a community, etc. (*the Canadian experience*). ● *transitive verb* **1** have experience of; undergo. **2** feel or be affected by (an emotion etc.). □ **ex·peri·ence·able** *adjective* **ex·peri·en·cer** *noun* [Old French from Latin *experientia* from *experiri expert-* try]

ex·peri·enced *adjective* **1** having had much experience. **2** skilled from experience (*an experienced driver*).

ex·peri·en·tial /ɪkˌspiːriˈenʃəl, ek-/ *adjective* **1** involving or based on experience. **2** denoting a philosophical view that treats all knowledge as based on experience. □ **ex·peri·en·tial·ism** *noun* **ex·peri·en·tial·ist** *noun* **ex·peri·en·tial·ly** *adverb*

ex·peri·ment ● *noun* **1** a procedure undertaken to make a discovery, test a hypothesis etc., or demonstrate a known fact. **2** (often foll. by *in, with*) a procedure or course of action tentatively adopted without being sure that it will achieve its purpose. ● *intransitive verb* (often foll. by *on, with*) make an experiment. □ **ex·peri·men·ta·tion** *noun* **ex·peri·ment·er** *noun* [Old French *experiment* or Latin *experimentum* (as EXPERIENCE)]

ex·peri·ment·al *adjective* **1** based on or making use of experiment (*experimental psychology; experimental theatre*). **2 a** used in experiments (*experimental animal*). **b** serving or resulting from (esp. incomplete) experiment; tentative, provisional. **3** based on experience, not on authority or conjecture. □ **ex·peri·ment·al·ly** *adverb*

experimental farm *noun* (also **experimental station**) an agricultural research centre, in Canada esp. one established by the federal government through Agriculture and Agri-Food Canada.

ex·peri·ment·al·ism *noun* **1** the empirical approach in philosophy or science. **2** the use of experiment or innovation in the arts. □ **ex·peri·ment·al·ist** *noun*

ex·pert ● *adjective* **1** (often foll. by *at, in, on*) having special knowledge or skill in a subject. **2** involving or resulting from this (*expert advice; an expert piece of work*). ● *noun* (often foll. by *at, in*) a person having special knowledge or skill. □ **ex·pert·ly** *adverb* **ex·pert·ness** *noun* [Old French from Latin *expertus* past participle of *experiri*: see EXPERIENCE]

ex·per·tise /ˌekspərˈtiːz/ *noun* expert skill, knowledge, or judgment. [French (as EXPERT)]

ex·pert·ize /ˈekspərˌtaɪz/ *verb* (also esp. *Brit.* **-ise**) **1** *intransitive* give an expert opinion. **2** *transitive* **a** give an expert opinion concerning. **b** authenticate (*expertized rare stamps*).

expert system *noun Computing* a computer program into which has been incorporated the knowledge of experts on a particular subject so that non-experts can use it for making decisions, evaluations, or inferences.

expert witness *noun* an expert called on to provide specialized information at a trial, inquest, etc.

ex·pi·ate /ˈekspiˌeɪt/ *transitive verb* atone for (guilt or sin). □ **ex·pi·a·tory** /-əˌtɔri/ *adjective* **expi·a·tion** *noun* **expi·a·tor** *noun* [Latin *expiare expiat-* (as EX-[1], *pius* devout)]

ex·pir·a·tion *noun* **1** expiry. **2** breathing out.

ex·pire *verb* **1** *intransitive* (of a period of time, validity, etc.) come to an end. **2** *intransitive* (of a document, authorization, etc.) cease to be valid; become void. **3** *intransitive* (of a person) die. **4** *transitive & intransitive* exhale (air etc.) from the lungs. □ **ex·pir·a·tory** *adjective* (in sense 4). [Old French *expirer* from Latin *exspirare* (as EX-[1], *spirare* breathe)]

ex·pi·ry *noun* (*pl.* **-ies**) **1** the end of the validity or duration of something. **2** death.

ex·plain *verb* **1** *transitive & intransitive* make (something) clear or intelligible with detailed information etc. (*let me explain; they explained nuclear fusion*). **2** *transitive* (foll. by *that* + clause) say by way of explanation. **3** *transitive* account for (one's conduct, a phenomenon, etc.). □ **explain away** minimize the significance of (a difficulty or mistake) by providing reasons for it. **explain oneself 1** make one's meaning clear. **2** give an account of one's motives or conduct. □ **ex·plain·able** *adjective* **ex·plain·er** *noun* [Latin *explanare* (as EX-[1], *planus* flat, assimilated to PLAIN[1])]

ex·plan·a·tion *noun* **1** the act or an instance of explaining. **2** a statement or circumstance that explains something. **3** a declaration made with a view to mutual understanding or reconciliation. [Latin *explanatio* (as EXPLAIN)]

ex·plana·tory /eksˈplanətɔri/ *adjective* serving to explain. □ **ex·plana·tor·i·ly** *adverb* [Late Latin *explanatorius* (as EXPLAIN)]

ex·plant *Biol.* ● *transitive verb* transfer (living cells, tissues, or organs) from animals or plants to a nutrient medium. ● *noun* /ˈeksplant/ a piece of explanted tissue etc. □ **ex·plan·ta·tion** *noun*

ex·ple·tive /ˈekspliːtɪv, ɪkˈspliːtəv, ek-/ ● *noun* **1** an oath, swear word, or other expression, used in an exclamation. **2** a word used to fill out a sentence etc., esp. in verse, without adding anything to the sense. ● *adjective* serving to fill out (esp. a sentence, line of verse, etc.). [Late Latin *expletivus* (as EX-[1], *plēre plet-* fill)]

ex·pli·cable /ekˈsplɪkəbəl, ɪk-, ˈek-/ *adjective* that can be explained.

ex·pli·cate /ˈekspliˌkeɪt/ *transitive verb* **1** make clear, explain. **2** develop the meaning or implication of (an idea, principle, etc.). □ **ex·pli·ca·tion** *noun* **ex·pli·ca·tive** /ekˈsplɪkətɪv, ɪk-, ˈeksplɪˌkeɪtɪv/ *adjective* **ex·pli·ca·tor** *noun* [Latin *explicare explicat-* unfold (as EX-[1], *plicare plicat-* fold)]

ex·plicit /ɪkˈsplɪsɪt, ek-/ *adjective* **1** expressly stated or conveyed, leaving nothing merely implied; stated in detail. **2** (of knowledge, a notion, etc.) definite, clear. **3** expressing views unreservedly; outspoken. **4** describing or representing nudity or intimate sexual activity. □ **ex·plicit·ly** *adverb* **ex·plicit·ness** *noun* [French *explicite* or Latin *explicitus* (as EXPLICATE)]

ex·plode *verb* **1 a** *intransitive* (of gas, gunpowder, a bomb, etc.) expand suddenly, burst, or fly into pieces with a loud noise owing to a release of internal energy. **b** *transitive* cause (a bomb etc.) to explode. **2** *intransitive* give vent suddenly to emotion, esp. anger. **3** *intransitive* increase suddenly or rapidly, esp. in size, numbers, amount, etc. **4** *intransitive* appear suddenly and with great impact. **5** *transitive* show (a theory etc.) to be false or baseless. □ **ex·plod·able** *adjective* **ex·plod·er** *noun* [earliest in sense 5: Latin *explodere* hiss off the stage (as EX-[1], *plodere plos-* = *plaudere* clap)]

ex·plod·ed *adjective* (of a drawing etc.) showing the components of a mechanism separated but in their normal relative positions.

ex·ploit ● *noun* /ˈeksplɔɪt/ a bold or daring feat. ● *transitive verb* /ɪkˈsplɔɪt, ek-/ **1** make use of (a resource etc.); derive benefit from. **2** usu. *derogatory* utilize or take advantage of (esp. a person) for one's own ends. □ **ex·ploit·abil·ity** *noun* **ex·ploit·able** *adjective* **ex·ploit·a·tion** *noun* **ex·ploit·a·tive** *adjective* **ex·ploit·er** *noun* **ex·ploit·ive** *adjective* [Old French *esploit*, *exploiter*, ultimately from Latin *explicare*: see EXPLICATE]

exploitation film *noun* (also **exploitation flick**) a film pandering

to the public's interest or curiosity in a given subject, esp. sex or violence.

Ex·ploits River a river in north central Newfoundland, 246 km long, which flows from Red Indian Lake, in the central part of the island, generally northeastward through Grand Falls-Windsor to the Bay of Exploits, an inlet of Notre Dame Bay. [origin unknown]

ex·plor·a·tion *noun* **1** an act or instance of exploring. **2** the process of exploring. □ **ex·plor·a·tion·al** *adjective*

ex·plora·tory *adjective* **1** (of discussion etc.) preliminary, serving to establish procedure etc. **2** involving exploration or investigation (*exploratory surgery; exploratory wells*).

ex·plore *verb* **1** *transitive & intransitive* travel extensively (through a country etc.) in order to learn or discover about it. **2 a** *transitive & intransitive* inquire (into); investigate thoroughly. **b** *intransitive* experiment, try something new (in music etc.). **3** *transitive Surgery* examine (a part of the body) in detail. **4** *intransitive* search for new deposits of minerals, oil, etc. □ **ex·plora·tive** *adjective* [French *explorer* from Latin *explorare* 'search out', from *ex-* 'out' + *plorare* 'cry']

ex·plor·er *noun* a person who explores, esp. a traveller in undiscovered or uninvestigated territory.

ex·plo·sion *noun* **1** the act or an instance of exploding. **2** a loud noise caused by something exploding. **3 a** a sudden outburst of noise. **b** a sudden outbreak of feeling, esp. anger. **4** a rapid or sudden increase in numbers, size, or amount. [Latin *explosio* scornful rejection (as EXPLODE)]

ex·plo·sive ● *adjective* **1** able or tending or likely to explode. **2 a** highly controversial. **b** (of a situation etc.) dangerously tense. **3** rapid, sudden; violent (*explosive growth*). **4** (of an athlete) characterized by bursts of energy. ● *noun* an explosive substance. □ **ex·plo·sive·ly** *adverb* **ex·plo·sive·ness** *noun*

Expo *noun* (also **expo**) (*pl.* **Expos**) **1** a large international exhibition. **2** an exhibition for a specific industry or with a specific theme (*bridal expo*). [abbreviation of EXPOSITION 4]

ex·po·nent /ɪkˈspoːnənt, ek-/ *noun* **1** a person who favours or promotes an idea etc. **2** a representative or practitioner of an activity, profession, etc. **3** a person who explains or interprets something. **4** *Math.* a raised symbol or expression beside a numeral indicating how many times it is to be multiplied by itself, e.g. $2^3 = 2 \times 2 \times 2$. [Latin *exponere* (as EX-[1], *ponere posit-* put)]

ex·po·nen·tial /ˌekspəˈnentʃəl/ ● *adjective* **1** *Math.* of or indicated by a mathematical exponent. **2** (of an increase etc.) more and more rapid. ● *noun Math.* an exponential quantity. □ **ex·po·nen·tial·ly** *adverb*

exponential growth *noun* growth whose rate becomes ever more rapid in proportion to the growing total number or size.

ex·port ● *transitive verb* /ˈeksport, ɪkˈsport, ek-/ **1** send out (goods, services, etc.) to another country, esp. for sale. **2** disseminate (a trend, ideology, etc.) into another country. **3** *Computing* transmit (data) from a system for use elsewhere. ● *noun* /ˈeksport/ **1** the process of exporting. **2 a** an exported article or service. **b** (in *pl.*) an amount exported (*exports exceeded $50m.*). **3** (*attributive*) suitable for export, esp. of better quality. □ **ex·port·able** *adjective* **ex·port·abil·ity** *noun* **ex·port·a·tion** /-ˈteɪʃən/ *noun* **ex·port·er** *noun* [Latin *exportare* (as EX-[1], *portare* carry)]

ex·pose *transitive verb* **1** remove the covering from or leave uncovered or unprotected. **2** (foll. by *to*) **a** cause to be liable to or in danger of (*was exposed to great danger*). **b** subject, introduce, or lay open to (an influence etc.). **3** *Photog.* subject (a film) to light, esp. by operation of a camera. **4** reveal the identity or fact of (esp. a person or thing disapproved of or guilty of crime etc.). **5** disclose; make public. **6** exhibit, display. **7** leave (a person) in the open to die. □ **expose oneself** display one's body, esp. the genitals, publicly and indecently. □ **ex·pos·er** *noun* [Old French *exposer* after Latin *exponere*: see EXPONENT, POSE[1]]

ex·po·sé /ˌekspoːˈzeɪ/ *noun* **1** the act or an instance of revealing something discreditable. **2** an orderly statement of facts. [French, past participle of *exposer* (as EXPOSE)]

ex·posed *adjective* **1** (foll. by *to*) open to; unprotected from (*exposed to the east*). **2** vulnerable, risky.

ex·pos·i·tion /ˌekspəˈzɪʃən/ *noun* **1** the action or process of stating or describing, in speech or writing; a detailed statement or description. **2** an explanation or commentary. **3** *Music* the part of a movement, esp. in sonata form, in which the principal themes are first presented. **4** a large public exhibition. **5 a** the act or an instance of exposing or being exposed. **b** *Catholicism* the act or an instance of exposing the Host or a relic. □ **ex·pos·i·tion·al** *adjective* [Old French *exposition*, or Latin *expositio* (as EXPONENT)]

ex·posi·tor /ɪkˈspɒzɪtɜr, ek-/ *noun* **1** an expounder or interpreter. **2** someone who describes something in detail; a narrator.

ex·posi·tory *adjective* intended to explain or describe something (*expository prose*).

ex post /eks ˈpoːst/ *adjective Econ.* based on actual results (*compare* EX ANTE). [modern Latin, = from after]

ex post facto /ˌeks poːst ˈfaktoː/ *adjective & adverb* with retroactive action or force. [Latin *ex postfacto* in the light of subsequent events]

ex·pos·tu·late /ekˈspɒstʃəˌleit, ɪk-, -tjʊ-/ *intransitive verb* make a protest; remonstrate earnestly. □ **ex·pos·tu·la·tion** *noun* **ex·pos·tu·la·tory** *adjective* [Latin *expostulare expostulat-* (as EX-¹, *postulare* demand)]

ex·pos·ure *noun* **1** (foll. by *to*) **a** the act or condition of exposing or being exposed (to cold, danger, radiation, an influence, etc.). **b** the duration or extent of this condition. **2** the physical condition resulting from being exposed to the elements, esp. in severe conditions (*died from exposure*). **3** the revelation of an identity or fact, esp. when concealed or likely to find disapproval. **4** *Photog.* **a** the action of exposing a film etc. to the light. **b** the duration of this action. **c** the extent to which the film is exposed (dependent on shutter speed and aperture). **d** an area of film etc. so exposed. **5** the way in which something is situated in relation to compass direction, wind, sunshine, etc. (*has a fine southern exposure*). **6** publicity; presence in the public eye.

exposure meter *noun Photog.* = LIGHT METER.

ex·pound *verb* **1 a** *transitive* set out in detail (a doctrine, theory, etc.). **b** *intransitive* (foll. by *on*) explain, discuss at length. **2** *transitive* explain or interpret (esp. a religious text). □ **ex·pound·er** *noun* [Old French *espondre* (as EXPONENT)]

ex·press¹ *transitive verb* **1 a** represent or make known (thought, feelings, etc.) in words or by gestures, conduct, etc. **b** manifest, indicate, betoken. **2** *reflexive* say what one thinks or means. **3** esp. *Math.* represent by symbols. **4** squeeze out (liquid or air). **5** *Genetics* (usu. as **ex·pressed** *adjective*) cause (an inherited characteristic, a gene) to appear in a phenotype. □ **ex·press·er** *noun* **ex·press·ible** *adjective* [Old French *expresser* from Romanic (as EX-¹, PRESS¹)]

ex·press² ● *attributive adjective* **1 a** operating at high speed. **b** (of a train, bus, elevator, etc.) making relatively few stops before reaching its destination. **c** (of a road, lane, etc.) designed for express traffic. **2** definitely stated, not merely implied. **3** done, made, or sent for a special purpose. **4** (of messages or goods) delivered immediately or rapidly. ● *adverb* **1** at high speed. **2** by express courier or train. ● *noun* **1** an express train, bus, etc. **2** (in company names) a courier. ● *transitive verb* send by express courier or delivery. □ **ex·press·ly** *adverb* (in sense 2 of *adjective*). [Old French *expres* from Latin *expressus* distinctly shown, past participle of *exprimere* (as EX-¹, *premere* press)]

express canoe *noun Cdn hist.* a relatively small, light canoe of the fur trade, usu. lightly burdened to increase speed of important deliveries.

ex·pres·sion *noun* **1** the act or an instance of expressing. **2** a word or phrase expressed, esp. a common saying or figure of speech. **3** *Math.* a collection of symbols expressing a quantity. **4** a person's facial appearance or intonation of voice, esp. as indicating feeling. **5** depiction of feeling, movement, etc., in art. **6** conveying of feeling in the performance of a piece of music. **7** *Genetics* the appearance in a phenotype of a character or effect attributed to a particular gene. □ **ex·pres·sion·al** *adjective* **ex·pres·sion·less** *adjective* **ex·pres·sion·less·ly** *adverb* **ex·pres·sion·less·ness** *noun*

ex·pres·sion·ism *noun* (also **Expressionism**) a style of painting, music, drama, etc., in which an artist or writer seeks to express emotional experience rather than impressions of the external world. □ **ex·pres·sion·ist** *noun & adjective* **ex·pres·sion·is·tic** *adjective* **ex·pres·sion·is·tic·ally** *adverb*

ex·pres·sive *adjective* **1** full of expression (*an expressive look*). **2** (foll. by *of*) serving to express (*words expressive of contempt*). □ **ex·pres·sive·ly** *adverb* **ex·pres·sive·ness** *noun* **ex·pres·siv·ity** *noun*

ex·pres·so *var. of* ESPRESSO.

express train *noun* a fast train, stopping at few intermediate stations.

ex·press·way *noun N Amer. & Austral.* a highway for fast-moving traffic, esp. in urban areas, with limited access and a median dividing opposing traffic.

ex·pro·pri·ate /eksˈproːpriˌeit/ *transitive verb* **1** (esp. of the state) **a** take away (property) from its owner. **b** deprive (a person) of property. **2** use or claim (another's ideas etc.) as one's own. □ **ex·pro·pri·a·tion** *noun* **ex·pro·pri·ator** *noun* [medieval Latin *expropriare expropriat-* (as EX-¹, *proprium* property: see PROPER)]

ex·pul·sion *noun* **1** the act or an instance of expelling; the process of being expelled. **2** (**Expulsion**) the eviction of the francophone Acadians in 1755. □ **ex·pul·sive** *adjective* [Latin *expulsio* (as EXPEL)]

ex·punge /ɪkˈspʌndʒ, ek-/ *transitive verb* **1** erase, remove (esp. a passage from a book or a name from a list). **2** wipe out, annihilate, destroy. [Latin *expungere expunct-* (as EX-¹, *pungere* prick)]

ex·pur·gate /ˈekspərˌgeit/ *transitive verb* **1** remove matter thought to be objectionable from (a book etc.). **2** remove (such matter). □ **ex·pur·ga·tion** *noun* **ex·pur·ga·tor** *noun* [Latin *expurgare expurgat-* (as EX-¹, *purgare* cleanse)]

ex·quis·ite /ekˈskwɪzɪt/ ● *adjective* **1** extremely beautiful or pleasing. **2** acute; keenly felt (*exquisite pleasure; exquisite pain*). **3** keen; highly sensitive or discriminating (*exquisite taste*). ● *noun archaic* a person of refined (esp. affected) tastes. □ **ex·quis·ite·ly** *adverb* **ex·quis·ite·ness** *noun* [Latin *exquirere exquisit-* (as EX-¹, *quaerere* seek)]

ex·san·guin·ate /ekˈsaŋgwɪˌneit/ *transitive verb Med.* drain of blood. □ **ex·san·guin·a·tion** *noun* [Latin *exsanguinatus* (as EX-¹, *sanguis -inis* blood)]

ex-service *adjective* **1** having formerly been a member of the armed forces. **2** relating to former members of the armed forces. □ **ex-service·man** *noun* (*pl.* **-men**). **ex-service·woman** *noun* (*pl.* **-men**).

ext. *abbreviation* **1** extension. **2** exterior. **3** external. **4** extra. **5** extract.

ex·tant /ekˈstant, ɪkˈst-/ *adjective* (esp. of a document, species, etc.) still existing, surviving. [Latin *exstare exstant-* (as EX-¹, *stare* stand)]

ex·tem·por·an·eous /ɪkˌstempəˈreiniəs, ek-/ *adjective* spoken or done without preparation; improvised. □ **ex·tem·por·an·eous·ly** *adverb* [EXTEMPORE + -ANEOUS]

ex·tem·por·ary /ɪkˈstempəˌreri, ek-/ *adjective* = EXTEMPORANEOUS. □ **ex·tem·por·ar·i·ly** /-ˈrerəli/ *adverb*

ex·tem·pore /ɪkˈstempəri, ek-/ *adjective & adverb* without preparation. [Latin *ex tempore* on the spur of the moment, lit. 'out of the time' from *tempus* time]

ex·tem·por·ize /ɪkˈstempəˌraiz, ek-/ *transitive & intransitive verb* (also esp. *Brit.* **-ise**) compose or produce (music, a speech, etc.) without preparation; improvise. □ **ex·tem·por·iz·a·tion** *noun*

ex·tend *verb* **1** *transitive & intransitive* lengthen or make larger in space or time. **2** *transitive* stretch or lay out at full length. **3** *intransitive & transitive* (foll. by *to, over*) reach or be or make continuous over a certain area. **4 a** *intransitive* (often foll. by *over, to*) have a certain scope (*the permit does not extend to camping*). **b** *transitive* increase the scope or range of application of (*extend their control over the region; extend educational opportunity*). **5** *transitive* **a** offer (an invitation, hospitality, kindness, etc.). **b** accord, grant (financial credit). **6** *transitive* (usu. *reflexive* or in *passive*) tax the powers of (an athlete, student, performer, etc.) to the utmost. □ **ex·tend·able** *adjective* **ex·tend·abil·ity** *noun* **ex·tend·ible** *adjective* **ex·tend·ibil·ity** *noun* **ex·ten·sible** *adjective* **ex·ten·si·bil·ity** *noun* [Latin *extendere extens-* or *extent-* stretch out (as EX-¹, *tendere* stretch)]

extended family *noun* **1** one's family including or esp. one's grandparents, aunts, uncles, cousins, etc. **2** such a group living in the same household or near each other.

ex·tend·er *noun* **1** a person or thing that extends. **2** a substance added to paint, ink, glue, etc., to dilute its colour or increase its bulk.

ex·ten·sion *noun* **1** the act or an instance of extending; the process of being extended. **2** prolongation; enlargement. **3** a part enlarging or added on to a main structure, building, room, etc. **4** an additional part of anything. **5 a** a subsidiary telephone on the same line as the main one. **b** its number. **6** an additional period of time, esp. extending allowance for a project etc. **7** extramural instruction by a university or college (*extension course*). **8** extent, range. **9** *Logic* a group of things denoted by a term. **10** *N Amer.* an extension cord. **11** *Computing* a string of letters after a period in a filename, often identifying the file as belonging to a certain category. **12** the action of moving a limb from a bent to a straight position. **13** the ability of a dancer to raise one leg above the waist, esp. to the side. **14** (**ex·ten·sions**) lengths of artificial hair woven into a person's own hair to create a very long hairstyle. □ **ex·ten·sion·al** *adjective* **ex·ten·sion·al·ly** *adverb* [Late Latin *extensio* (as EXTEND)]

extension cord *noun N Amer.* an electrical cable attached to the cord of an appliance etc., so that it can be plugged into a distant outlet.

extension ladder *noun* a ladder with two or more parallel sections which slide against each other to increase the ladder's reach.

ex·ten·sive *adjective* **1** covering a large area in space or time. **2** having a wide scope; far-reaching, comprehensive (*an extensive knowledge of music*). **3** *Agriculture* involving cultivation from a large area, with a

minimum of special resources (compare INTENSIVE adjective 3).
□ **ex·ten·sive·ly** adverb **ex·ten·sive·ness** noun [French extensif -ive or Late Latin extensivus (as EXTENSION)]

ex·ten·som·eter /ˌekstenˈsɒmɪtər/ noun 1 an instrument for measuring deformation of metal under stress. 2 an instrument using such deformation to record elastic strains in other materials. [Latin extensus (as EXTEND) + -METER]

ex·ten·sor /ɪkˈstensər, ek-/ noun (in full **extensor muscle**) Anat. a muscle that extends or straightens out part of the body (compare FLEXOR). [modern Latin (as EXTEND)]

ex·tent noun 1 the space over which a thing extends. 2 the width or limits of application; scope (to a great extent; to the full extent of their power). 3 the whole of a space or area of a specified kind (the extent of the ocean). [Anglo-French extente from medieval Latin extenta past participle of Latin extendere: see EXTEND]

ex·tenu·at·ed /ɪkˈstenjʊˌeɪtəd, ek-/ adjective very thin. [Latin extenuare extenuat- (as EX-1, tenuis thin)]

ex·tenu·at·ing /ɪkˈstenjʊˌeɪtɪŋ, ek-/ adjective showing reasons why a wrong or illegal act, or a bad situation, should be judged less seriously or excused (extenuating circumstances). □ **ex·tenu·a·tion** noun

ex·teri·or ● adjective 1 a of or on the outer side (opp. INTERIOR). b (foll. by to) situated on the outside of (a building etc.). c coming from without. d intended for the outside or outer surfaces. 2 Film outdoor. ● noun 1 the outward aspect or surface of a building etc. 2 the outward or apparent behaviour or demeanour of a person. 3 Film an outdoor scene. □ **ex·teri·or·ity** noun **ex·teri·or·ly** adverb [Latin, comparative of exterus outside]

exterior angle noun the angle between the side of a polygon and the outward extension of an adjacent side.

ex·teri·or·ize transitive verb (also esp. Brit. **-ise**) 1 attribute an external existence to (states of consciousness) (exteriorized their anger violently). 2 Med. bring to the surface of the body or outside it.

ex·ter·min·ate transitive verb 1 destroy utterly (esp. something living). 2 get rid of; eliminate (a pest, disease, etc.). □ **ex·ter·min·a·tion** noun **ex·ter·min·ator** noun **ex·ter·mina·tory** adjective [Latin exterminare exterminat- (as EX-1, terminus boundary)]

ex·ter·nal ● adjective 1 a of or situated on the outside or visible part (opp. INTERNAL). b coming or derived from the outside or an outside source. 2 relating to a country's foreign affairs. 3 outside the conscious subject (the external world). 4 (of medicine etc.) for use on the outside of the body. 5 pertaining to or consisting of outward acts or observances. 6 Computing pertaining to a device that is subsidiary or peripheral to a computer system (external modem). ● noun (in pl.) 1 the outward features or aspect. 2 external circumstances. 3 inessentials. □ **ex·ter·nal·ly** adverb [medieval Latin from Latin externus from exterus outside]

external affairs plural noun 1 a country's international affairs. 2 (treated as sing.) the government department concerned with international affairs.

external evidence noun evidence derived from a source independent of the thing discussed.

ex·ter·nal·ity /ekstərˈnalɪti/ noun (pl. **-ities**) 1 a the quality of being external. b Philos. the fact of existing outside the perceiving subject. 2 an external or outward object, feature, characteristic, circumstance, etc. 3 Econ. a side effect or consequence, esp. of an industrial or commercial activity, which affects other parties without this being reflected in the cost or price of the goods or services involved.

ex·ter·nal·ize transitive verb (also esp. Brit. **-ise**) 1 treat (a fact, responsibility, etc.) as existing or occurring outside of oneself or in the external world. 2 Psych. attribute (one's own emotions, feelings, etc.) to others, the external environment, etc. 3 give external form to. □ **ex·ter·nal·iz·a·tion** noun

external relations plural noun 1 = EXTERNAL AFFAIRS. 2 = PUBLIC RELATIONS.

ex·tero·cep·tive /ˌekstərəʊˈseptɪv/ adjective Biol. relating to stimuli produced outside an organism. □ **ex·tero·cep·tiv·ity** noun **ex·tero·cep·tor** noun [irreg. from Latin externus exterior + RECEPTIVE]

ex·tinct adjective 1 a (of a species, language, etc.) no longer surviving in the world at large or in a specific locale. b (of a family) having no living descendant. 2 a (of fire etc.) extinguished or no longer burning. b (of a volcano) no longer erupting. 3 (of life, hope, etc.) terminated, quenched. 4 no longer in existence or used. [Latin exstinguere exstinct- (as EX-1, stinguere quench)]

ex·tinc·tion noun 1 the act or process of making or becoming extinct. 2 the state or fact of being extinct. 3 total destruction or annihilation.

4 Physics a reduction in the intensity of light or other radiation by absorption, scattering, etc. as it passes through a medium or object.

ex·tin·guish transitive verb 1 quench, put out, or cause (a flame, light, etc.) to die out. 2 exterminate, annihilate, make extinct (a program to extinguish disease). 3 terminate, put an end to, or obscure utterly (a feeling, quality, etc.). 4 a abolish or wipe out (a debt), esp. by full payment. b Law nullify or render void (a right, claim, etc.). □ **ex·tin·guish·able** adjective **ex·tin·guish·ment** noun [irreg. from Latin extinguere (as EXTINCT): compare distinguish]

ex·tin·guish·er noun a device used for extinguishing, esp. a fire extinguisher.

ex·tir·pate /ˈekstərˌpeɪt/ transitive verb 1 kill all the members of (a race, nation, etc.) or make (a species) extinct locally, but not globally. 2 do away with as such (a specified category or grouping of people). 3 root out or destroy completely (a vice or other immaterial thing). □ **ex·tir·pa·tion** noun [Latin exstirpare exstirpat- (as EX-1, stirps stem)]

extol /ɪkˈstəʊl/ transitive verb (**ex·tolled**, **ex·tol·ling**) praise enthusiastically. □ **ex·tol·ler** noun [Latin extollere (as EX-1, tollere raise)]

ex·tort transitive verb obtain (esp. money) by force, threats, persistent demands, etc. □ **ex·tort·er** noun **ex·tort·ive** adjective [Latin extorquēre extort- (as EX-1, torquēre twist)]

ex·tor·tion noun the act or an instance of extorting, esp. money. □ **ex·tor·tion·ist** noun

ex·tor·tion·ate adjective 1 (of a price etc.) exorbitant or grossly excessive. 2 using or given to extortion (extortionate methods). □ **ex·tor·tion·ate·ly** adverb

ex·tra ● adjective additional; more than is usual or necessary or expected. ● adverb 1 more than the usual, specified, or expected amount. 2 additionally (was charged extra). ● noun 1 an extra or additional thing. 2 a thing for which an extra charge is made. 3 a person engaged temporarily to fill out a scene in a film or play, esp. as one of a crowd. 4 a special issue of a newspaper etc. [prob. a shortening of EXTRAORDINARY]

extra- combining form 1 outside, beyond (extragalactic). 2 beyond the scope of (extracurricular). [medieval Latin from Latin extra outside]

extra-base hit noun Baseball a base hit that allows a batter safely to reach more than one base.

extra-billing noun Cdn the practice of a doctor charging patients fees in excess of what provincial health insurance will pay.

extra·cellu·lar /ˌekstrəˈseljʊlər/ adjective situated or taking place outside a cell or cells. □ **extra·cellu·lar·ly** adverb

extra·cor·por·eal /ˌekstrəkɔːrˈpɔːriəl/ adjective involving something situated or occurring outside the body. □ **extra·cor·por·eal·ly** adverb

ex·tract ● transitive verb /ɪkˈstrakt/ 1 remove or take out (a tooth etc.) from a containing body or cavity, usu. with some degree of effort, force, dexterity, etc. 2 obtain (money, information, etc.) with difficulty or against a person's will. 3 obtain (a natural resource) from the earth. 4 take (a part) from a whole, esp. select or reproduce (a passage of writing, music, etc.) for quotation or performance. 5 obtain (constituent elements, juices, etc.) from a thing or substance by chemical or physical means such as pressure, distillation, etc. 6 derive (happiness, pleasure, amusement, etc.) from a specified source or situation. 7 Math. calculate (the root of a number). 8 draw out (the sense of something), deduce (a principle) etc. ● noun /ˈekstrakt/ 1 an excerpt or short passage taken from a book, piece of music, etc. 2 a preparation containing the active principle of a substance in concentrated form (vanilla extract). □ **ex·tract·able** adjective **ex·tract·abil·ity** noun [Latin extrahere extract- (as EX-1, trahere draw)]

ex·trac·tion noun 1 the act or process of extracting or being extracted. 2 an instance of extracting, esp. the removal of a tooth. 3 origin, lineage, descent (of Finnish extraction).

ex·tract·ive ● adjective of, involving, or concerned with the extraction of natural resources or products, esp. non-renewable ones. ● noun a substance that can be extracted.

ex·tract·or noun 1 a machine that extracts one thing from another, e.g. juice from fruit, water from wet laundry, etc. 2 Brit. (attributive) (of a device) that extracts bad air etc. or ventilates a room (extractor fan). 3 the part of a breech-loading firearm which removes the cartridge. 4 a tool or instrument for loosening or removing tight-fitting parts, components, etc.

extra·curricu·lar /ˌekstrəkəˈrɪkjʊlər/ adjective 1 (of an activity or subject of study) not included in the normal curriculum. 2 outside the normal routine, job expectations, etc. 3 extramarital. □ **extra·curricu·lar·ly** adverb

extra·dit·able /ˈekstrəˌdaɪtəbəl/ adjective **1** (of a person) liable to extradition. **2** (of a crime) warranting extradition.

extra·dite /ˈekstrəˌdaɪt/ transitive verb **1** hand over (a person accused or convicted of a crime) to the foreign country etc. in which the crime was committed. **2** obtain the extradition of (a person) from another country. [back-formation from EXTRADITION]

extra·di·tion /ˌekstrəˈdɪʃən/ noun the surrender or delivery of a person into the jurisdiction of another country in order that he or she may be tried by that country for crimes committed there. [French, from ex- 'out, from' + tradition 'delivery']

ex·tra·dos /ekˈstreɪdɒs/ noun Archit. the upper or outer curve of an arch, esp. the upper curve of the voussoirs which form the arch (opp. INTRADOS). [EXTRA- + dos back, from Latin dorsum]

extra end noun Curling an additional end played to break a tie at the completion of regular play.

extra·galac·tic /ˌekstrəgəˈlæktɪk/ adjective occurring or existing outside our galaxy, the Milky Way.

extra·judi·cial /ˌekstrədʒuˈdɪʃəl/ adjective **1** not legally authorized or outside the ordinary course of law or justice. **2** (of an opinion, confession, etc.) informal, not made in court, or not part of the proceedings in court or of the case before a court. □ **extra·judi·cial·ly** adverb

extra·limit·al adjective esp. Biology situated, occurring, or derived from outside a particular area.

extra·lin·guis·tic /ˌekstrəlɪŋˈgwɪstɪk/ adjective outside the field of linguistics or the bounds of language.

extra·mari·tal /ˌekstrəˈmerɪtəl/ adjective involving or constituting a usu. sexual relationship between a married person and someone other than his or her spouse.

extra·mun·dane /ˌekstrəˈmʌndeɪn/ adjective outside or beyond the earth, material world, or physical universe.

extra·mural /ˌekstrəˈmjʊrəl/ adjective **1 a** (of courses etc.) taught or conducted off the premises of a university, college, or school. **b** (of instructors, researchers, etc.) working or located off the premises of a university, college, etc. **2** (of activities, work, etc.) additional to normal teaching or studies, esp. for non-resident students, or not done as part of one's official, paid duties. **3** outside the walls or boundaries of a town or city. □ **extra·mural·ly** adverb [Latin extra muros outside the walls]

extra·neous /ɪkˈstreɪniəs/ adjective **1** of external origin or added from without. **2** (often foll. by to) separate from or foreign to the object or body to which it is attached or which contains it. **3** irrelevant, unnecessary, or not part of the matter at hand. □ **ex·tra·neous·ly** adverb **ex·tra·neous·ness** noun [Latin extraneus]

extra·net noun an Intranet that can be partially accessed by authorized outside users, enabling businesses to exchange information over the Internet in a secure way.

extra·ordin·aire /ˌekstrɔrdɪˈner, ˌekstrə-/ adjective (placed after noun) **1** remarkable, outstanding. **2** (of a person) unusually active or successful in a specified respect.

extra·ordin·ary /ekˈstrɔrdineri, ˌekstrəˈɔrdineri/ adjective **1** unusual, remarkable, or out of the regular course or order. **2** exceeding what is usual in amount, degree, extent, or size, esp. to the point of provoking astonishment, admiration, or disapproval (an extraordinary talent). **3 a** (of an official etc.) additional to regular staff or specially employed (envoy extraordinary). **b** (of a meeting) specially convened, usu. for a very particular purpose. □ **extra·ordin·ar·i·ly** adverb **extra·ordin·ar·i·ness** noun [Latin extraordinarius from extra ordinem outside the usual order]

ex·trapo·late /ekˈstræpəˌleɪt/ transitive & intransitive verb **1 a** infer more widely from a limited range of known facts. **b** predict on the basis of known facts or observed events. **2** Math. & Philos. **a** assume the continuance of a known trend in inferring or estimating an unknown value. **b** extend (a range of values, a curve, etc.) on the assumption that the trend exhibited inside the given part is maintained outside of it (compare INTERPOLATE 3). □ **ex·trapo·la·tion** noun **ex·trapo·la·tive** /-lətɪv/ adjective **ex·trapo·la·tor** noun [EXTRA- + INTERPOLATE]

extra·pyram·id·al /ˌekstrəpɪrɪˈmɪdəl/ adjective Anat. involving or designating nerves concerned with motor activity that descend from the cortex to the spine, e.g. the basal ganglia.

extra·sen·sory /ˌekstrəˈsensəri/ adjective regarded as derived by means other than the known senses, e.g. by telepathy, clairvoyance, etc.

extrasensory perception noun the supposed ability to perceive outside, past, or future events without the use of known senses. Abbr.: **ESP**.

extra·solar adjective outside the solar system.

extra·terres·trial /ˌekstrətəˈrestriəl/ ● adjective **1** existing or occurring beyond the earth or its atmosphere. **2** (in science fiction) from outer space. ● noun (in science fiction) a being, esp. an intelligent one, from outer space.

extra·terri·tor·ial /ˌekstrəˌterɪˈtɔriəl/ adjective **1** situated or (of laws etc.) valid outside a country's territory. **2** (of an ambassador etc.) free from the jurisdiction of the territory of residence. □ **extra·terri·tor·ial·ity** noun [Latin extra territorium outside the territory]

ex·trava·gance /ekˈstrævəgəns/ noun **1 a** prodigality, wastefulness, or excessive spending or use of resources. **b** a purchase or payment difficult to justify except as a whim or indulgence. **2 a** lack of moderation in behaviour. **b** an immoderate statement, action, or quality.

ex·trava·gant /ɪkˈstrævəgənt/ adjective **1** immoderate, excessive, or wasteful in use of resources, esp. money. **2** exorbitant or costing much. **3 a** (of ideas, speech, or behaviour) going beyond what is reasonable, usual, or justifiable (extravagant claims). **b** astonishingly elaborate or ostentatious. □ **ex·trava·gant·ly** adverb [medieval Latin extravagari (as EXTRA-, vagari wander)]

ex·trava·ganza /ɪkˌstrævəˈgænzə/ noun **1** an event, festival, etc. featuring elaborate and colourful spectacle, massive participation, lavish expenditure, etc. **2** a fanciful literary, musical, or dramatic composition. [Italian estravaganza extravagance]

ex·trava·sate /ɪkˈstrævəˌseɪt/ verb **1** transitive let or force out (a fluid, esp. blood) from its proper vessel. **2** intransitive (of blood, lava, etc.) flow out. □ **extra·va·sa·tion** /-ˈseɪʃən/ noun [Latin extra outside + vas vessel]

extra·vascu·lar /ˌɪkstrəˈvæskjuːlər/ adjective Anat. situated or occurring outside the vascular system.

extra·vehicu·lar /ˌekstrəviˈhɪkjulər/ adjective occurring outside a spacecraft in space.

extra·virgin adjective (of olive oil) made from the first pressing, cold pressed, and thus of high quality and low in acid.

Ex·trema·dura /ˌestrəməˈdʊrə/ an autonomous region of W Spain, on the border with Portugal; capital, Mérida.

ex·treme ● adjective **1 a** reaching a high or the highest degree or being exceedingly great or intense (extreme old age; in extreme danger). **b** (of a case, circumstance, etc.) having some feature or characteristic in the utmost degree. **2 a** severe, stringent, lacking restraint or moderation (take extreme measures; an extreme reaction). **b** (of a person, opinion, etc.) going to great lengths, advocating severe and drastic measures, or being immoderate in opinion. **3 a** outermost, furthest from the centre (the extreme edge). **b** endmost, situated at either end. **c** last, utmost, very far advanced in any direction. **4** Politics radical or being on the far left or right of a party. **5** designating sports performed in a hazardous environment, involving a high physical risk (extreme skiing). ● noun **1** (often in pl.) one or other of two things as remote or as different as possible in position, nature, or condition. **2** a thing at either end of anything. **3** the highest degree, the greatest length, or the most extreme measure of anything. □ **go to extremes** take an extreme course of action. **go to the other extreme** take a diametrically opposite course of action. **in the extreme** to an extreme degree. □ **ex·treme·ly** adverb **ex·treme·ness** noun [Old French from Latin extremus superlative of exterus outward]

extreme unction noun the former name for the sacrament of anointing the sick, esp. those thought to be near death.

ex·trem·ist ● noun **1** a person who holds extreme opinions and advocates extreme measures. **2** a person who tends to go to extremes. ● adjective of or pertaining to extremists or extremism. □ **ex·trem·ism** noun

ex·trem·ity /ɪkˈstremɪti/ noun (pl. **-ities**) **1** the very end or terminal portion of anything. **2** (in pl.) the outermost parts of the body, esp. the hands and feet. **3** a condition of extreme adversity or difficulty. **4** extremeness.

ex·tremo·phile /ɪkˈstreməfaɪl/ noun a micro-organism, esp. an archaean, that lives in conditions of extreme temperature, acidity, alkalinity, or chemical concentration.

ex·tri·cate /ˈekstrɪˌkeɪt/ transitive verb (often foll. by from) free or disentangle (esp. a person) from a constraint or difficulty. □ **ex·tri·ca·tion** noun [Latin extricare extricat- (as EX-1, tricae perplexities)]

ex·trin·sic /ekˈstrɪnsɪk/ adjective **1** not inherent, intrinsic, or essential (opp. INTRINSIC). **2** (often foll. by to) (of a cause or influence) extraneous, lying outside, not part of. **3** due to external circumstances (*extrinsic asthma is triggered by exposure to irritants such as smoke*).

□ **ex·trin·sic·al·ly** *adverb* [Late Latin *extrinsicus* outward, from Latin *extrinsecus* (adv.) from *exter* outside + *secus* beside]

ex·tropy /'ekstrəpi/ *noun* the pseudo-scientific principle that life will expand indefinitely and in an orderly, progressive way throughout the entire universe by the means of human intelligence and technology.

□ **ex·trop·ian** /ek'stro:piən/ *adjective & noun*

extro·vert /'ekstrə,vɜrt/ ● *noun* **1** *Psych.* a person whose thoughts and interests are predominantly concerned with things outside the self. **2** an outgoing or sociable person (*compare* INTROVERT). ● *adjective* typical or characteristic of an extrovert. □ **extro·ver·sion** /-'vɜrʒən/ *noun* **extro·vert·ed** *adjective* [*extro-* = EXTRA- (after *intro-*) + Latin *vertere* turn]

ex·trude *verb* **1** *transitive* (foll. by *from*) thrust, force out, or expel. **2** *transitive* shape (metal, plastics, etc.) by forcing through a die. **3** *intransitive* protrude. □ **ex·trud·ed** *adjective* **ex·trud·er** *noun* **ex·tru·sion** *noun* **ex·tru·sive** *adjective* [Latin *extrudere extrus-* (as EX-¹, *trudere* thrust)]

ex·uber·ant /ɪg'zu:bərənt, -ju:/ *adjective* **1** (of people or their actions) lively, high-spirited, effusive in display of feelings. **2** (of speech, writing, etc.) copious, diffuse, lavishly ornamented. **3** (of a plant etc.) prolific, growing luxuriously. □ **ex·uber·ance** *noun* **ex·uber·ant·ly** *adverb* [French *exubérant* from Latin *exuberare* (as EX-¹, *uberare* be fruitful, from *uber* fertile)]

exu·date /'egzjʊ,deit/ *noun* an exuded substance, esp. a mass of cells and fluid that has seeped out of blood vessels or an organ, e.g. in inflammation or malignancy. □ **ex·uda·tive** /ɪg'zju:dətɪv/ *adjective*

exude /ɪg'zu:d, -zju:d/ *verb* **1** *transitive & intransitive* (of a liquid, moisture, etc.) ooze out, escape or cause to escape gradually. **2** *transitive* give off (moisture, a smell, etc.) in this way. **3** *transitive* **a** (of a person) display (a quality, emotion etc.) freely or abundantly (*exuded charm*). **b** (of a place) have a strong atmosphere of. □ **exu·da·tion** *noun* [Latin *exsudare* (as EX-¹, *sudare* sweat)]

exult /ɪg'zʌlt/ *verb* (often foll. by *at, in, over,* or *to* + infin.) **1** *intransitive* (often foll. by *over*) have a feeling of triumph (over a person). **2** *intransitive* be elated or greatly joyful. **3** *transitive* say exultingly. □ **exult·ancy** *noun* **exul·ta·tion** *noun* **exult·ant** *adjective* **exult·ant·ly** *adverb* **exul·ting·ly** *adverb* [Latin *exsultare* (as EX-¹, *saltare* frequentative of *salire* salt- leap)]

Exuma Cays /ɪk'su:mə/ a group of some 350 small islands in the Bahamas.

ex·urb /'eksɜrb/ *noun* a town or community beyond the suburbs of a large city. □ **ex·urban** *adjective* **ex·urban·ite** *noun* [Latin *ex* out of + *urbs* city, or back-formation from *exurban* (as EX-¹ + URBAN, after *suburban*)]

ex·urbia /eks'ɜrbiə/ *noun* the generalized area of the exurbs. [EX-¹, after *suburbia*]

ex·uviae /ɪg'zu:vi,i:/ *plural noun* (also treated as *sing.*) an animal's sloughed skin or covering. [Latin, = 'animal's skins', spoils of the enemy, from *exuere* divest oneself of]

ex voto /eks'vo:to:/ (*pl.* **ex votos**) ● *noun* something offered in fulfillment of a vow previously taken. ● *adjective* designating such an offering. [Latin, = out of a vow]

-ey *suffix var.* of -Y¹, ².

eyas /'aɪəs/ *noun* a young hawk, esp. one taken from the nest for training in falconry. [originally *nyas* from French *niais* ultimately from Latin *nidus* nest: for loss of *n-* compare ADDER]

Eyck see VAN EYCK.

eye ● *noun* **1 a** the organ of sight in humans and other animals. **b** the light-detecting organ in some invertebrates. **2** the eye characterized by the colour of the iris (*has blue eyes*). **3** the region of the face round the eye (*eyes red from weeping*). **4** a glass or plastic ball resembling an eye or serving as an artificial eye. **5** (in *sing.* or *pl.*) **a** sight or the faculty of sight (*demonstrate to the eye; need perfect eyes to be a pilot*). **b** perception (*see it through a woman's eyes*). **6** a particular visual faculty or talent for appreciation, judgment, etc., either in general or with some specific reference (*cast an expert eye over; an accountant's eye for detail*). **7** (in *sing.* or *pl.*) a look, gaze, or glance, esp. as indicating the disposition of the viewer (*a jaundiced eye*). **8 a** close attention, regard, observation, or supervision. **b** the imagined organ of sight as attributed to the heart, mind, or other quasi-personified things (*in my mind's eye*). **9** a person or animal etc. that sees on behalf of another (*you will have to be my eyes*). **10** = ELECTRIC EYE. **11 a** a thing resembling the eye in appearance, shape, function, or relative position. **b** a mark or spot resembling an eye, occurring on eggs, insect wings, near the end of the tail feathers of a peacock, etc. (*compare* EYELET *noun* 3). **c** the leaf bud of a potato.

12 the centre of something circular. **13** the centre of a vortex or eddy, esp. the relatively calm region at the centre of a storm or hurricane. **14** an aperture in an implement, esp. a needle, for the insertion of something, e.g. thread. **15** a ring or loop for a bolt or hook etc. to pass through. **16** the main mass of lean meat in a cut of meat, esp. beef (*eye of round*). ● *transitive verb* (**eyes**, **eyed**, **eye·ing** or **eying**) **1** watch or observe closely, esp. admiringly or with curiosity or suspicion. **2** ogle or look at (a person) amorously or with sexual interest. □ **all eyes 1** watching intently. **2** general attention (*all eyes were on us*). **all my eye (and Betty Martin)** *Brit. slang* all nonsense. **before a person's** (or **a person's very**) **eyes** right in front of a person. **catch a person's eye** attract a person's attention or interest. **close one's eyes to** ignore, refuse to recognize or consider. **an eye for an eye** retaliation in kind (Exodus 21:24). **eyes front** (or **left** or **right**) *Military* a command to turn the head in the direction stated. **eye view** denoting what is seen from the viewpoint of the person or thing specified (*bird's-eye view*). **have an eye for** be capable of perceiving or appreciating. **have one's eye on** wish or plan to procure. **have eyes bigger than one's stomach** wish or expect to eat more than one can. **have eyes for** be interested in (*had eyes for no other*). **have an eye to** have as one's objective or prudently consider. **hit a person (right) between the eyes** *informal* be very obvious or impressive. **in the eyes** (or **eye**) **of** in the view or opinion of (*in the eye of the beholder; in the eyes of the law*). **keep an eye on 1** pay close attention to (a person). **2** look after or take care of (a child etc.). **keep an eye open** (or **out**) (often foll. by *for*) watch carefully. **keep one's eyes open** (or **peeled** or **skinned**) watch out or be on the alert. **lower one's eyes** look modestly or sheepishly down or away. **make eyes** (or **sheep's eyes**) (foll. by *at*) look amorously or flirtatiously at. **my eye** *slang* nonsense. **one in the eye** (foll. by *for*) a disappointment or setback, esp. for someone regarded as deserving it. **open a person's eyes** be enlightening or revealing to a person. **raise one's eyes** look upwards. **see eye to eye** (often foll. by *with*) be in full agreement. **set eyes on** see or catch sight of (a person etc.). **take one's eyes off** (usu. in *neg.*) stop watching or stop paying attention to (*I can't take my eyes off you*). **under the eye of** under the supervision or observation of. **up to the** (or **one's**) **eyes in 1** inundated with or deeply engaged or involved in (a thing) (*up to the eyes in work*). **2** to the utmost limit (*mortgaged up to the eyes*). **with one's eyes open** deliberately or with full awareness. **with one's eyes shut** (or **closed**) **1** easily or with little effort. **2** unobservant or without awareness (*goes around with his eyes shut*). **with an eye to** with a view to or prudently considering. **with one eye on** directing one's attention partly to. □ **eye·less** *adjective* **eye·like** *adjective* [Old English *éage* from Germanic]

eye-appeal *noun* *N Amer.* visual attractiveness; features or qualities to attract the eye.

eye·ball ● *noun* **1** the firm white sphere of the eye within the eyelids and socket that is formed by the sclera and the cornea. **2** (in *pl.*) *informal* the audience of a visual medium, as a television program or a website; viewers, esp. as regarded as a source of potential revenue. ● *transitive verb* *slang* look or stare at. □ **eyeball-to-eyeball** *informal* confronting or encountering closely. **to** (or **up to**) **the eyeballs** *informal* to a great extent.

eye bath *noun* *Cdn & Brit.* = EYECUP 1.

eye·blink *noun* **1** the act or an instance of blinking an eye. **2** a very brief unit of time such as that which it takes to blink an eye.

eye·bolt *noun* a bolt or bar with an eye at the end for a hook, ring, etc.

eye·bright *noun* any plant of the genus *Euphrasia*, formerly used as a remedy for weak eyes.

eye·brow *noun* **1** the line, usu. arched, of short hair growing along the ridge above each eye socket. **2** (in full **eyebrow dormer**) *Archit.* a low dormer over which the roof curves upward in a continuous, shallow arch. □ **raise eyebrows** cause surprise, disbelief, or disapproval. **raise one's eyebrows** (or **an eyebrow**) show surprise, disbelief, or mild disapproval.

eyebrow pencil *noun* a cosmetic pencil for drawing lines to accentuate the eyebrows.

eye candy *noun* **1** visual images that are superficially attractive and entertaining but intellectually undemanding. **2** a person or thing that is pleasing to look at.

eye-catcher *noun* a person or thing which catches the eye, through attractiveness, uniqueness, etc. □ **eye-catching** *adjective*

eye contact *noun* the state or practice of looking directly into another person's eyes while he or she is looking into one's own.

eye·cup *noun* **1** a small glass or vessel for applying lotion etc. to the eye. **2** the usu. plastic or rubber cup-shaped section of the eyepiece on a microscope, telescope, etc.

eyed *adjective* **1** (usu. in *combination*) having an eye or eyes of a particular nature, kind, etc. (*bright-eyed child*; *dreamy-eyed cattle*). **2** (of a needle, implement, etc.) having a hole or holes.

eye doctor *noun* **1** = OPHTHALMOLOGIST (*see* OPHTHALMOLOGY). **2** = OPTOMETRIST.

eye·drop·per *noun* = DROPPER 1.

eye·ful *noun* (*pl.* **-fuls**) *informal* **1** a complete view or a good look at something. **2** a visually striking scene or thing, esp. an attractive person. □ **get an eyeful** take a good, long look.

eye·glass *noun* **1** (in *pl.*) esp. *N Amer.* a pair of lenses, in a frame resting on the nose and ears, used to correct defective eyesight or protect the eyes. **2 a** a lens for correcting or assisting defective sight. **b** *hist.* (in *pl.*) a pair of these held in the hand or kept in position on the nose by means of a frame or a spring. **3** a small glass vessel for applying lotion etc. to the eye.

eye·hole *noun* **1** a hole to look through. **2** a usu. circular opening in a metal bar, anchor, etc. through which a bar, rope, etc. is passed.

eye·lash *noun* a hair, or one of the rows of hairs, growing on the edge of the eyelid. □ **by an eyelash** by a very small margin.

eye·let ● *noun* **1** a small hole in paper, leather, cloth, etc., for string or rope etc. to pass through. **2** a metal ring reinforcement for this. **3** a small eye, esp. the ocellus on a butterfly's wing (*compare* EYE *noun* 11b). **4 a** a form of decoration in embroidery, composed of usu. round eyelets finished along the edge, which produces an open work effect. **b** a lightweight fabric having numerous small embroidered holes in a decorative pattern. **5** a small hole, e.g. in a wall, for observation, shooting through, etc. ● *transitive verb* (**eye·leted**, **eye·let·ing**) provide with eyelets. [Old French *oillet* diminutive of *oil* eye, from Latin *oculus*]

eye level *noun* (often *attributive*) the height of the eyes or the level seen by the eyes looking straight ahead (*eye-level grill*).

eye·lid *noun* either of the upper or lower folds of skin that meet when the eye is closed.

eye lift *noun* = BLEPHAROPLASTY.

eye·liner *noun* a cosmetic applied as a line round the eye, usu. next to the lashes, to accentuate the eyes.

eye mask *noun* **1** a covering of soft material saturated with a lotion for refreshing the eyes. **2** a covering for the eyes.

eye-opener *noun* *informal* **1** a thing or experience that enlightens, surprises, etc. **2** *N Amer.* an alcoholic drink taken on waking up. □ **eye-opening** *adjective*

eye patch *noun* a pad or piece of material worn to shield or protect an injured eye.

eye·piece *noun* the lens or lenses at the end of a telescope etc. to which the eye is applied and through which an image is viewed or magnified.

eye-popping *adjective* surprising, astonishing, esp. visually spectacular. □ **eye-popper** *noun*

eye-rhyme *noun* a correspondence of words, esp. in a poem, in spelling but not in pronunciation (e.g. *love* and *move*).

eye·shade *noun* a visor for protecting the eyes from strong light.

eye·shadow *noun* a coloured cosmetic applied to the eyelids, around the eyes, etc. to enhance the eyes.

eye·shot *noun* range of sight, the distance a person can see (*out of eyeshot*).

eye·sight *noun* the faculty or power of seeing.

eye socket *noun* the orbit of the eye.

eye·sore *noun* a visually offensive or ugly thing, esp. a building.

eye-spot *noun* **1 a** a light-sensitive area on the bodies of some invertebrate animals, such as flatworms or starfish, that serves in place of an eye. **b** an ocellus or other spot resembling an eye, esp. on a plant or animal. **2** *Bot.* an area of light-sensitive pigment found in some algae etc. **3** any of several fungus diseases of plants characterized by yellowish oval spots on the leaves and stems.

eye-stalk *noun* a movable stalk carrying the eye in some animals, esp. in crabs, shrimps, etc.

eye strain *noun* fatigue of the (internal or external) muscles of the eyes, esp. from excessive or incorrect use.

Eye·tie /ˈəitai/ *noun & adjective slang offensive* Italian. [jocular pronunciation of *Italian*]

eye tooth *noun* one of the canine teeth just under or next to the eye, esp. in the upper jaw. □ **would give one's eye teeth for** would make any sacrifice to obtain.

eye·wash *noun* **1** a liquid or lotion for bathing the eyes. **2** *informal* nonsense; a thing said or done to deceive or create a false impression.

eye·wear *noun* glasses, contact lenses, goggles, etc. worn on the eyes.

eye·wit·ness ● *noun* a person who has personally seen a thing done or happen and can testify to it from his or her own observation. ● *transitive verb* be an eyewitness to (an event).

eyra /ˈerə/ *noun* a red form of jaguarundi. [Tupi (*e*)*irara*]

Eyre /ˈer/ **Ivan (Ken·neth)** (b.1935), Canadian painter. He is noted for his prairie and bush landscapes, such as *Mythopoeic Prairie II* (1965) and *Highwater* (1978), as well as crowded tabletop still lifes, often containing mysterious distorted figures in the background.

Eyre, Lake a lake in South Australia. It is Australia's largest salt lake. [E. J. *Eyre*, British-born Australian explorer d.1901]

eyrie *var.* of AERIE.

eyrir /ˈeiriːr/ *noun* (*pl.* **aurar** /ˈoirɑr/) a monetary unit of Iceland, equal to one-hundredth of a krona. [Icelandic, from Old Norse, literally 'ounce (of silver etc.) money', prob. from Latin *aureus* 'golden, a golden coin']

Ez. *abbreviation Bible* (also **Ezr.**) Ezra.

Ezek. *abbreviation Bible* Ezekiel.

Ezek·iel /ɪˈziːkiəl/ **1** a Hebrew prophet of the 6th c. BC who prophesied the forthcoming destruction of Jerusalem and the Jewish nation and inspired hope for the future well-being of a restored state. **2** a book of the Bible containing his prophecies.

e-zine *noun* a magazine or fanzine published in electronic format.

Ezra ▶ **1** a Jewish priest and scribe who played a central part in the reform of Judaism in the 5th or 4th c. BC. **2** a book of the Bible dealing with Ezra, the return of the Jews from Babylon, and the rebuilding of the Temple.

Ff

F¹ *noun* (also **f**) (*pl.* **Fs** or **F's**) **1** the sixth letter of the alphabet. **2** *Music* the fourth note of the diatonic scale of C major. **3** the lowest category of academic mark, denoting a failing grade.

F² *abbreviation* (also **F.**) **1** Fahrenheit. **2** farad(s). **3** female. **4** a fine, moderately soft pencil lead, between B and H. **5** *Biol.* filial generation (as F_1 for the first filial generation, F_2 for the second, etc.). **6** *Physics* force. **7** (in Ontario) FAMILY 9.

F³ *symbol Chem.* the element fluorine.

F *abbreviation Electricity* faraday.

f *abbreviation* (also **f.**) **1** female. **2** *Grammar* feminine. **3** (*pl. ff.*) following page etc. **4** *Music* forte. **5** (*pl. ff.*) folio. **6** focal length (*compare* F-NUMBER). **7** femto-. **8** filly. **9** frequency. **10** *Math.* function. **11** *Metallurgy* fine. **12** fathom. **13** from. **14** *Currency* franc.

FA *abbreviation* **1** *slang* = FUCK ALL. **2** fine arts. **3** (in the UK) Football Association. **4** forced air (heating).

fa *noun* (also **fah**) *Music* **1** (in tonic sol-fa) the fourth note of a major scale. **2** the note F in the fixed-do system. [Middle English *fa* from Latin *famuli*: see GAMUT]

FAA *abbreviation* **1** (in the US) Federal Aviation Administration. **2** (in the UK) Fleet Air Arm.

fab¹ *adjective informal* fabulous, marvellous. [abbreviation]

fab² *noun informal* a computer chip fabrication plant. [abbreviation]

faba bean *var. of* FAVA BEAN. [Latin *faba* bean]

Fab·er·gé /ˈfabɜrˌʒeɪ/ **Peter Carl** (1846–1920), Russian goldsmith and jeweller, famous for the enameled Easter eggs and other intricate and imaginative ornaments he made for Czar Alexander III's family and European royalty.

Fa·bian /ˈfeɪbiən/ ● *noun* a member or supporter of the Fabian Society, a socialist organization founded in England in 1884 to promote cautious and gradual political change. ● *adjective* **1** relating to or characteristic of the Fabians. **2** employing a cautiously persistent and dilatory strategy to wear out an enemy (*Fabian tactics*). □ **Fa·bian·ism** *noun* **Fa·bian·ist** *noun* [Latin *Fabianus* from the name of FABIUS]

Fa·bius /ˈfeɪbiəs/ (full name Quintus Fabius Maximus Verrucosus, known as 'Cunctator' = 'delayer') (d.203 BC), Roman general and statesman. After Hannibal's defeat of the Romans at Cannae (216), Fabius successfully pursued a strategy of caution and delay in order to wear down the Carthaginian invaders.

fable *noun* **1 a** a tale, esp. with animals as characters, conveying a moral. **b** a fictitious narrative, esp. a supernatural one. **2** (*collective*) myths and legendary tales (*in fable*). **3** a fiction, false statement, or lie intended to deceive. **4** a thing falsely claimed to exist or having no existence outside popular legend etc. [Old French *fabler* from Latin *fabulari* from *fabula* discourse, from *fari* speak]

fabled *adjective* **1** famous, legendary. **2** celebrated in fable.

fab·liau /ˈfabliəʊ/ *noun* (*pl.* **fab·liaux** /-oːz/) a coarsely humorous short story in verse, popular in early French poetry, with Chaucer, etc. [French from Old French dialect *fabliaux, -ax* pl. of *fablel* diminutive (as FABLE)]

fab·ric *noun* **1 a** a woven, knitted, or felted material; a textile. **b** the texture of this. **c** something resembling this. **2** a structure or framework, esp. the walls, floor, and roof of a building. **3** (in abstract senses) the essential structure or essence of a thing (*the fabric of society*). [French *fabrique* from Latin *fabrica* from *faber* metalworker etc.]

fabric art *noun* art created using textiles, e.g. wall hangings, weaving, quilts, etc. □ **fabric artist** *noun*

fab·ri·cate *transitive verb* **1** construct or manufacture, esp. from prepared components. **2** invent or concoct (a story, evidence, etc.). **3** forge (a document). □ **fab·ri·ca·tion** *noun* **fab·ri·ca·tor** *noun* [Latin *fabricare fabricat-* (as FABRIC)]

fabric softener *noun N Amer.* a liquid added to the wash or a sheet placed in the dryer when doing laundry to soften clothes, reduce static, etc.

fab·rique /faˈbriːk/ *noun Cdn* (*Que.*) *hist.* a vestry or local parish body responsible for the maintenance, management, etc. of church property.

fabu·list /ˈfabjʊlɪst/ *noun* **1** a person who relates or composes fables or legends. **2** a liar. □ **fabu·lism** *noun* [French *fabuliste* from Latin *fabula*: see FABLE]

fabu·lous *adjective* **1** incredible, exaggerated, astonishing (*fabulous wealth*). **2** excellent, marvellous, terrific (*a fabulous dancer*). **3 a** celebrated in fable. **b** legendary, mythical. □ **fabu·lous·ly** *adverb* **fabu·lous·ness** *noun* [French *fabuleux* or Latin *fabulosus* (as FABLE)]

FAC *abbreviation Cdn* Firearms Acquisition Certificate.

fa·cade /fəˈsɒd/ *noun* **1** the face of a building, esp. its principal front. **2** an outward appearance or front, esp. a deceptive one. [French (as FACE)]

face ● *noun* **1** the front of the head from the forehead to the chin. **2 a** the expression of the facial features (*had a happy face*). **b** a distorted look, grimace, etc. intended to express a usu. negative emotion (*don't make a face!*). **3** calm, cool audacity or effrontery. **4** the surface of a thing, esp. as regarded or approached, esp.: **a** the visible part of the earth, a celestial body, etc. **b** a principal side, often vertical or steeply sloping, presented by an object, esp. the front of a mountain or cliff etc. (*the north face*). **c** *Mining* the end of a tunnel at which work is progressing or the principal surface from which coal etc. is being removed. **d** *Math.* each surface of a solid. **e** the facade of a building. **f** the plate of a clock or watch bearing the digits, hands, etc. **g** the physical conformation of a country. **5 a** the acting, striking, or working surface of an implement, tool etc. **b** the marked or picture side of a playing card. **c** either side of a coin, but esp. the side bearing the effigy. **6** = TYPEFACE. **7 a** the outward appearance, aspect, or semblance, esp. of an immaterial thing (*the unacceptable face of capitalism*). **b** pretense, outward show (*try to put a good face on the matter*). **8** a person, conveying some quality or association (*a face from the past*; *some young faces for a change*). **9** esteem, respectable reputation (*defeat would entail a loss of face*). **10** makeup, cosmetics (*I have to put on my face*). **11** the inscribed side of a document etc. ● *verb* **1** *transitive & intransitive* look or be positioned towards or in a certain direction (*face towards the window*; *facing the window*; *the room faces north*). **2** *transitive* (of an engraving, illustration, etc.) stand on the opposite page to (*facing page 20*). **3** *transitive* **a** (often foll. by *down*) confront, meet resolutely or defiantly (*face one's critics*). **b** meet bravely and boldly or not shrink from. **c** recognize, consider seriously, or accept the inevitability of (an idea etc.) (*face the facts*). **4** *transitive* confront, present itself to (a person etc.) (*the problem that faces us*; *faces us with a problem*). **5** *transitive* **a** cover the surface of (a thing) with a coating, extra layer, etc. **b** put a facing on (a garment). **6** *intransitive & transitive* turn or cause to turn in a certain direction (*right face*). **7** *Lacrosse* **a** *intransitive* start or restart play by placing the ball between the sticks of the two opposing players. **b** *transitive* place (the ball) in this way to start or restart play. □ **face a**

charge (or **charges**) be forced to appear in court accused of something. **face down** (or **downwards**) with the face or surface turned towards the ground, floor, etc. **face off 1** *Hockey & Lacrosse* start or restart play by a faceoff. **2** assume a confrontational attitude; contend or compete against. **face up** (or **upwards**) with the face or surface turned upwards to view. **face up to** confront, accept bravely, or stand up to. **in one's** (or **the**) **face 1** directly at or straight against one. **2** confronting or irritatingly present. **in face** (or **the face**) **of 1** despite. **2** when confronted by. **3** in the presence of. **let's face it** *informal* we must be honest or realistic about it. **look a person in the face** confront a person with a steady gaze, implying courage, defiance, etc. **on the face of it** apparently, superficially, or obviously. **set one's face against** oppose or resist with determination. **the face of the earth 1** the surface of the earth. **2** anywhere. **to a person's face** openly in a person's presence. □ **fa·cing** *adjective* (also in *combination*). [Old French ultimately from Latin *facies*]

face card *noun* a playing card, other than a joker or a tarot, bearing the representation of a human figure, e.g. the king, queen, or jack.

face cloth *noun* *Cdn & Brit.* a small cloth, usu. of terry, for washing one's face, hands, etc.

face cord *noun* *N Amer.* a measure of cut wood that would form a pile eight feet long by four feet high by one piece deep.

face cream *noun* a cosmetic cream applied to the face to improve the complexion.

faced *adjective* (also in *combination*) **1** having a face or expression of a specified kind (*a sweet-faced doll*). **2** having a surface of a specified kind (*marble-faced houses*).

face flannel *noun* *Brit.* = FACE CLOTH.

face·less *adjective* **1** anonymous or purposely not identifiable. **2** without an individual identity, lacking an individualized character. **3** without a face. □ **face·less·ness** *noun*

face·lift *noun* **1** cosmetic surgery to remove wrinkles etc. by tightening the skin of the face. **2** a procedure to improve the appearance of a thing, esp. the refacing or redecoration of a building. □ **face-lifted** *adjective* **face-lifting** *noun*

face mask *noun* **1** any covering or device to shield or protect the face, usu. covering the whole face, nose and mouth, or nose and eyes. **2** (also **facial mask**) a preparation beneficial to the complexion, spread over the face and removed when dry.

face·off *noun* **1** *Hockey & Lacrosse* the action of starting or restarting play by dropping or placing the puck or ball between two opposing players' sticks. **2** a direct confrontation.

faceoff circle *noun* each of five circles on a hockey rink, roughly 9 m in diameter, where faceoffs may be taken, including one at centre ice and two in each end situated to the left and right of the net.

face pack *noun* esp. *Brit.* = FACE MASK 2.

face paint *noun* bold coloured paint used to decorate the face. □ **face painter** *noun* **face painting** *noun*

face plant *noun* *slang* an instance of falling face first into or onto something.

face·plate *noun* **1** an enlarged end or attachment on the end of a mandrel of a lathe to which work may be attached for being faced or made flat. **2** a plate protecting a piece of machinery. **3** the transparent window corresponding to the visor in protective headgear, esp. of a diving or space suit.

face powder *noun* a cosmetic powder for reducing the shine on the face.

facer *noun* *informal* esp. *Brit.* a sudden difficulty or obstacle.

face-saving *noun* (usu. *attributive*) the preserving of one's dignity, reputation, credibility, etc. (*a face-saving resignation*). □ **face-saver** *noun*

facet /ˈfasɪt/ *noun* **1** a particular aspect of a thing. **2 a** one side of a many-sided body, esp. when flat and smooth. **b** any of the cut and polished faces of a cut gem. **3** one segment of a compound eye. □ **facet·ed** *adjective* (also in *combination*). **facet·ing** *noun* [French *facette* diminutive (as FACE, -ETTE)]

face time *noun* **1** time spent being filmed or photographed by the media; a photo opportunity; media exposure. **2** time spent face-to-face with another person.

fa·cetious /fəˈsiːʃəs/ *adjective* **1** not intended seriously or literally; ironic. **2** characterized by flippant or inopportune humour. **3** (of a person) intending to be amusing, esp. inopportunely. □ **fa·cetious·ly** *adverb* **fa·cetious·ness** *noun* [Latin *facetia* jest]

face to face ● *adverb* closely or directly viewing, confronting, etc. ● *attributive adjective* (**face-to-face**) with the people involved facing each other or in each other's presence (*face-to-face discussions*).

face value *noun* **1** the value printed or stamped on money or postage stamps. **2** the superficial appearance or implication of a thing. □ **take at face value** assume (a thing, person, etc.) is genuinely what it, he, she, etc. appears to be.

facia *var.* of FASCIA 3.

fa·cial /ˈfeiʃəl/ ● *adjective* of or for the face. ● *noun* a beauty treatment for the face. □ **fa·cial·ly** *adverb*

-facient /ˈfeiʃənt/ *combining form* forming adjectives and nouns indicating an action or state produced (*abortifacient*). [from or after Latin *-faciens -entis* part. of *facere* make]

fa·cies /ˈfeiʃiːz/ *noun* (*pl.* same) **1** *Med.* the appearance or facial expression of an individual, esp. when characteristic of a particular disease. **2** *Geol.* the character of a rock formation etc. as expressed by its composition, texture, fossil content, etc. [Latin, = FACE]

fa·cile /ˈfasail, ˈfasɪl/ *adjective* **1** usu. *derogatory* **a** easily obtained or achieved and so not highly valued. **b** (of speech, writing, etc.) easily produced, but superficial or of poor quality. **2** (of a person) fluent, glib, saying or doing things easily. □ **fa·cile·ly** *adverb* **fa·cile·ness** *noun* [French *facile* 'easy' or Latin *facilis* from *facere* do]

fa·cili·tate /fəˈsɪlɪˌteit/ *transitive verb* **1** make (an action, result, etc.) easier, less difficult, or more easily achieved. **2** *Physiol.* strengthen, bring about, or increase the likelihood of (a response, transmission of an impulse, etc.). □ **fa·cili·ta·tion** *noun* **fa·cili·ta·tive** *adjective* [French *faciliter* from Italian *facilitare* from *facile* easy, from Latin *facilis*]

fa·cili·ta·tor /fəˈsɪlɪˌteitər/ *noun* **1** a person or thing that facilitates. **2** a person who, as part of a group, encourages discussion and other activity without directing it or controlling it actively.

fa·cil·ity /fəˈsɪlɪti/ *noun* (*pl.* **-ities**) **1 a** fluency, dexterity, or ease of speech, action, etc. (*facility of expression*). **b** absence of difficulty or the fact or condition of being easy or easily done. **2** (esp. in *pl.*) the physical means, equipment, resources, or opportunity required to do something. **3** *N Amer.* a building designed for a specific purpose. **4** *euphemism* (*pl.*) a toilet or washroom. [French *facilité* or Latin *facilitas* (as FACILE)]

fa·cing *noun* **1 a** an esp. interior layer of material covering part of a garment etc. for contrast or strength. **b** (in *pl.*) the contrasting cuffs, collar, etc. of a military or military-style jacket. **2** an outer layer of stone or brick which forms the face of a building, wall, etc.

fac·simile /fakˈsɪmɪli/ *noun* **1** (often *attributive*) an exact copy, esp. of writing, printing, a picture, etc. (*facsimile edition*). **2** = FAX *noun* 1. **3** something that resembles something else strongly (*the sweatshops were a reasonable facsimile of hell*). □ **in facsimile** as an exact copy. [modern Latin from Latin *fac* imperative of *facere* make + *simile* neuter of *similis* like]

fact *noun* **1** a thing that is known to have occurred, to exist, or to be true. **2** a thing that is believed or claimed to be true. **3** *Law* (usu. in *pl.*) a piece of evidence, an item of verified information, or events and circumstances as distinct from their legal interpretation (*the facts of the case*). **4** truth, reality. **5** *Philos.* a thing assumed as the basis for argument or inference. □ **before** (or **after**) **the fact** before (or after) the occurrence of a pertinent event. **facts and figures** precise information, details, etc. **hard fact** (or **facts**) **1** inescapable truth (or truths). **2** concrete evidence. **in** (or **in point of**) **fact 1** in reality. **2** (in summarizing) in short. **the fact of the matter** the truth. [Latin *factum* from *facere* do]

fact-finding ● *noun* the discovery and establishment of the facts of an issue. ● *adjective* **1** engaged in the finding out of facts. **2** (of a committee etc.) set up to discover and establish the facts of an issue. □ **fact-finder** *noun*

fac·tion[1] *noun* **1** a small, organized, and self-interested or turbulent group or class of people within a larger one, esp. in politics. **2** a state of dissension within an organization. [French from Latin *factio -onis* from *facere fact-* do, make]

fac·tion[2] *noun* a book, film, etc., using real events as a basis for a fictional narrative or dramatization. [blend of FACT and FICTION]

-faction *combining form* forming nouns of action from verbs in *-fy* (*petrifaction*; *satisfaction*). [from or after Latin *-factio -factionis* from *-facere* do, make]

fac·tion·al *adjective* **1** characterized by dissent. **2** relating or belonging to a faction. □ **fac·tion·al·ism** *noun*

fac·tious *adjective* relating or inclined to dissension. □ **fac·tious·ly** *adverb* **fac·tious·ness** *noun*

fac·ti·tious /fak'tɪʃəs/ *adjective* **1** specially contrived, not genuine (*factitious value*). **2** artificial, not natural (*factitious joy*).
□ **fac·ti·tious·ly** *adverb* **fac·ti·tious·ness** *noun* [Latin *facticius* from *facere fact-* do, make]

fac·ti·tive /'faktɪtɪv/ *adjective* Grammar (of a verb) expressing the notion of making a thing to be of a certain character, e.g. *paint* the door green, and designating the object, complement, etc. of such a verb. [modern Latin *factitivus*, irreg. from Latin *factitare* frequentative of *facere fact-* do, make]

fact of life *noun* **1** something, esp. unpleasant, that cannot be ignored and must be accepted. **2** (in *pl.*; usu. prec. by *the*) information about sexual functions and practices, esp. as given to children and teenagers.

fact·oid ● *noun* **1** an assumption or speculation that is reported and repeated so often that it becomes accepted as fact; a simulated or imagined fact. **2** N Amer. a brief or trivial item of news or information. ● *adjective* being or having the character of a factoid; containing factoids.

Fac·tor, Max (born Francis Factor) (1904–1996), US cosmetics manufacturer. He turned women's cosmetics into a mass-market industry and among his innovations were lipstick, waterproof mascara, body paint, and Pan-Cake makeup, a matte, water-soluble disk of makeup applied with a sponge which replaced greasepaint for actors.

fac·tor ● *noun* **1** a circumstance, fact, or influence contributing to a result. **2** Math. a whole number etc. that when multiplied with another produces a given number or expression. **3** Biol. a gene etc. determining hereditary character. **4** (foll. by identifying number) Med. any of several substances in the blood, identified by numerals, which contribute to coagulation (*factor VIII*). **5 a** a business agent or a merchant buying and selling on commission. **b** an agent or a deputy. **6** a company that buys a manufacturer's invoices and takes responsibility for collecting the payments due on them. **7** Cdn hist. an employee of the Hudson's Bay Company, ranking higher than a chief trader, in charge of a trading post. ● *transitive verb* **1** Math. resolve into factors or express as a product of factors. **2** sell (one's receivable debts) to a factor. □ **factor in** introduce as a factor. **factor out** exclude from an assessment. □ **fac·tor·able** *adjective* [French *facteur* or Latin *factor* from *facere fact-* do, make]

fac·tor·age /'faktərɪdʒ/ *noun* commission or charges payable to a factor.

factor analysis *noun* a statistical calculation of the relative importance of a number of factors regarded as influencing a set of values.

factor VIII *noun* (also **factor eight**) Med. a blood protein involved in clotting, the deficiency of which causes hemophilia.

fac·tor·ial /fak'tɔrɪəl/ Math. ● *noun* the product of a number and all the whole numbers below it (*factorial four* = 4 × 3 × 2 × 1). Symbol: **!** (as in 4!). ● *adjective* of a factor or factorial. □ **fac·tor·ial·ly** *adverb*

fac·tor·ize *transitive verb* (also esp. Brit. **-ise**) Math. resolve into factors or express as a product of factors. □ **fac·tor·iz·a·tion** *noun*

fac·tory *noun* (pl. **-ies**) **1** a building or buildings containing equipment for manufacturing or processing. **2** hist. a merchant company's foreign trading station. **3** Cdn hist. a main trading post, esp. a large centre for the transshipment of furs (*York Factory*). [Portuguese *feitoria* and Late Latin *factorium*]

factory farming *noun* an intensive system of rearing livestock, organized on industrial lines and usu. in an artificial environment. □ **factory farm** *noun*

factory floor *noun* **1** the workplace of, or a forum for, industrial workers. **2** workers in industry as distinct from management etc.

factory outlet *noun* a store in which factory-made goods, often surplus stock, are sold directly by the manufacturer to consumers at discount prices.

factory ship *noun* a fishing ship with facilities for immediate processing of the catch.

fac·totum /fak'toːtəm/ *noun* (pl. **fac·totums**) an employee who does all kinds of work, esp. as support staff. [medieval Latin from Latin *fac* imperative of *facere* do, make + *totum* neuter of *totus* whole]

fact sheet *noun* a paper on which facts relevant to an issue are set out briefly.

fac·tual *adjective* **1** based on, concerned with, or of the nature of fact or facts. **2** actual, true. □ **fac·tual·ity** *noun* **fac·tual·ly** *adverb* [FACT, after *actual*]

fac·tum *noun* (pl. **fac·tums** or **fac·ta**) Law Cdn a statement of the facts

of a case and the legal arguments which will be made, filed by each party in an appeal. [French from Latin: see FACT]

fac·ture /'faktʃər/ *noun* the quality of execution, esp. of the surface of a painting. [Old French from Latin *factura* from *facere fact-* do, make]

fac·ula /'fakjʊlə/ *noun* (pl. **fac·ulae** /-ˌliː/) Astronomy a bright spot or streak on the sun associated with sunspots and solar activity in general. □ **facu·lar** *adjective* [Latin, diminutive of *fax facis* torch]

fac·ul·ta·tive /'fakəltətɪv/ *adjective* **1** (of actions, conditions, etc.) optional or permissive as opposed to compulsory. **2** Philos. that may or may not take place, have a specific character, etc. **3** Biol. capable of, but not restricted to, a particular, specified function, mode of life, etc. □ **fac·ul·ta·tive·ly** *adverb* [French *facultatif -ive* (as FACULTY)]

fac·ulty /'fakəlti/ *noun* (pl. **-ties**) **1** an aptitude or ability for a particular activity. **2** (often in *pl.*) an inherent mental or physical power. **3 a** a group of university departments concerned with a major division of knowledge (*faculty of arts*). **b** N Amer. the teaching staff of a university or college. **4** authorization, esp. by a Church authority. [Old French *faculté* from Latin *facultas -tatis* from *facilis* easy]

FAD *abbreviation* FLAVIN ADENINE DINUCLEOTIDE.

fad *noun* a craze or something briefly but enthusiastically taken up, esp. by a group. □ **fad·dish** *adjective* **fad·dish·ly** *adverb* **fad·dish·ness** *noun* **fad·dism** *noun* **fad·dist** *noun* **faddy** *adjective* [19th c. (originally dial.): prob. from *fidfad* from FIDDLE-FADDLE]

fade ● *verb* **1** intransitive & transitive lose or cause to lose colour. **2** intransitive lose freshness or strength; (of flowers etc.) droop, wither. **3** intransitive **a** (of colour, light, etc.) disappear gradually; grow pale or dim. **b** (of sound) grow faint. **4** intransitive (of a feeling etc.) diminish. **5** intransitive (foll. by *away, out*) (of a person etc.) disappear or depart gradually. **6** transitive (foll. by *in, out*) Film & Broadcasting **a** cause (a picture) to come gradually in or out of view on a screen, or to merge into another shot. **b** make (the sound) more or less audible. **7** intransitive (of a radio signal) vary irregularly in intensity. **8** intransitive (of a brake) temporarily lose effectiveness. **9** Golf **a** intransitive (of a ball) deviate from a straight course, esp. in a deliberate slice. **b** transitive cause (a ball) to fade. ● *noun* the action or an instance of fading. □ **do a fade** slang depart. **fade away** informal languish, grow thin. □ **fade·less** *adjective* **fader** *noun* (in sense 6 of verb). [Old French *fader* from *fade* dull, insipid, prob. ultimately from Latin *fatuus* silly + *vapidus* VAPID]

fade·away *noun* **1** Baseball = SCREWBALL 1. **2** Basketball a shot made while the shooter jumps or falls away from the basket (also *attributive*: *fadeaway jump shot*).

fade-in *noun* Film & Broadcasting the action or an instance of fading in a picture or sound.

fade-out *noun* **1** Film & Broadcasting the action or an instance of fading out a picture or sound. **2** informal a gradual reduction, disappearance, etc.

fado /'fɑːdoː/ *noun* (pl. **fados**) a type of Portuguese folk song, usu. with guitar accompaniment, and often doleful or plaintive in tone. [Portuguese, lit. 'fate']

faecal var. of FECAL (see FECES).

faeces var. of FECES. [Latin, pl. of *faex* dregs]

faer·ie /'feɪəri/ (also **faery**) archaic ● *noun* **1** the land of the fairies; fairyland. **2** a fairy. ● *adjective* fairy. [var. of FAIRY]

Faer·oe Islands /'feroː/ (also **Faer·oes**) a group of islands in the N Atlantic between Iceland and the Shetland Islands, belonging to Denmark but partly autonomous; pop. (est. 2002) 46,011; capital, Tórshavn.

Faero·ese /ˌferoːˈiːz/ (also **Faro·ese**) ● *adjective* of or relating to the Faeroes. ● *noun* (pl. same) **1** a native of the Faeroes; a person of Faeroese descent. **2** the Norse language of this people.

Fa·fard /fəˈfɑrd/ **Jo·seph** (b.1942), Canadian sculptor. His works include ceramic portraits and folk-art animals, as well as large-scale sculptural installations such as the bronze cows of *The Pasture* in Toronto (1985).

faff Brit. informal ● *intransitive verb* (often foll. by *about, around*) dither. ● *noun* a fuss. [imitative]

Faf·nir /'favniːr/ (also **Faf·ner** /'fafnər/ in the Nibelungenlied) Scand. Myth a dragon guarding a treasure, who was slain by Sigurd.

fag[1] *noun* N Amer. slang offensive a male homosexual. □ **faggy** *adjective* (**fag·gi·er, fag·gi·est**). [abbreviation of FAGGOT]

fag[2] ● *noun* **1** esp. Brit. informal a piece of drudgery; a wearisome or unwelcome task. **2** esp. Brit. informal a cigarette. **3** Brit. (at boarding schools) a junior pupil who runs errands for a senior. ● *verb* (**fagged, fag·ging**) **1** informal **a** transitive (often foll. by *out*) tire out; exhaust.

b *intransitive Brit.* toil. **2** *intransitive Brit.* (in boarding schools) act as a fag. [origin unknown: compare FLAG¹]

Faga·togo /ˌfaɡəˈtoːɡoː/ the legislative and judicial capital of American Samoa, pop. (1990) 2,323.

fag-end *noun slang* **1** the last part or tail end of something, esp. what remains after the best part has been used up. **2** *Brit.* a cigarette butt.

fag·got *noun* **1** *slang* **a** *N Amer. offensive* a male homosexual. **b** *Brit. derogatory* an unpleasant woman. **2** (also **fag·ot**) **a** a bundle of sticks or twigs bound together as fuel. **b** a bundle of iron rods for heat treatment. **c** a bunch of herbs. **d** *Cdn* (*Nfld*) a stack of salted codfish. **3** *Brit.* (usu. in *pl.*) a ball or roll of seasoned chopped liver etc., baked or fried. □ **fag·goty** *adjective* [Old French *fagot*, of uncertain origin]

fag·got·ing *noun* a type of embroidery in which some vertical threads are bound together so as to create a pattern of open rectangles alternating with cords of thread.

fag hag *noun slang* a woman who consorts habitually with homosexual men.

fah *var. of* FA.

Fahd /ˈfɒd/ (full name Fahd ibn Abdul Aziz al-Saud) (b.1923), king of Saudi Arabia from 1982.

Fahr. *abbreviation* Fahrenheit.

Fahren·heit¹ /ˈferənˌhaɪt/ **Gab·riel Dan·iel** (1686–1736), German physicist. He invented the alcohol thermometer (1709) and mercury thermometer (1714), and devised the temperature scale that is named after him.

Fahren·heit² /ˈferənˌhaɪt/ *adjective* of or measured on a scale of temperature on which water freezes at 32° and boils at 212° under standard conditions. Abbr.: **F, Fahr.**

fai·ence /ˈfaɪɑ̃s/ *noun* decorated and glazed earthenware and porcelain, e.g. Delft or majolica. [French *faïence* from Faenza in Italy, where first produced]

fail ● *verb* **1** *intransitive* not succeed (*failed in persuading; failed to qualify; tried but failed*). **2 a** *transitive & intransitive* be unsuccessful in (an examination, test, course, interview, etc.); be rejected as a candidate. **b** *transitive* (of a commodity etc.) not pass (a test of quality). **c** *transitive* reject (a candidate etc.); declare unsuccessful. **3** *intransitive* be unable to; neglect to; choose not to (*I fail to see the reason; he failed to appear*). **4** *transitive* disappoint; let down; not serve when needed. **5** *intransitive* (of supplies, crops, etc.) be or become lacking or insufficient. **6** *intransitive* become weaker; cease functioning; break down (*her health is failing; the engine has failed*). **7** *intransitive* **a** (of an enterprise) collapse; come to nothing. **b** become bankrupt. ● *noun* a failure in an examination or test. □ **without fail** for certain, whatever happens. [Old French *faillir* (v.), *fail(l)e* (n.), ultimately from Latin *fallere* deceive]

failed *adjective* **1** unsuccessful; not good enough (*a failed actor*). **2** weak, deficient; broken down (*a failed crop; a failed battery*).

fail·ing ● *noun* a fault or shortcoming; a weakness, esp. in character. ● *preposition* in default of; in the absence of (*failing a reconciliation, they will divorce*).

faille /faɪl, feɪl/ *noun* a soft ribbed fabric of silk, rayon, etc. [French]

fail-safe *adjective* **1** reverting to a safe condition in the event of a breakdown etc. **2** totally reliable or safe.

fail·ure *noun* **1** lack of success; failing. **2** an unsuccessful person, thing, or attempt. **3** non-performance, non-occurrence. **4** breaking down or ceasing to function (*heart failure; engine failure*). **5** a cessation in the existence or availability of something. **6** bankruptcy, collapse. [earlier *failer* from Anglo-French, = Old French *faillir* FAIL]

fain /feɪn/ *archaic* ● *predicative adjective* (foll. by *to* + infin.) **1** willing under the circumstances. **2** left with no alternative but to. ● *adverb* gladly (*would fain have turned back*). [Old English *fægen* from Germanic]

fai·né·ant /ˈfeɪniˌɑ̃/ ● *noun* an idle or ineffective person. ● *adjective* idle, inactive. [French from *fait* does + *néant* nothing]

faint ● *adjective* **1 a** indistinct, pale, dim. **b** (of a sound) not clearly perceived. **2** (of a person) weak or giddy; inclined to faint. **3** slight, remote, inadequate (*a faint chance*). **4** feeble, half-hearted (*faint praise*). **5** timid (*a faint heart*). ● *intransitive verb* **1** lose consciousness. **2** become faint. ● *noun* a sudden loss of consciousness. □ **not have the faintest** *informal* have no idea. □ **faint·ness** *noun* [Old French, past participle of *faindre* FEIGN]

faint-hearted *adjective* cowardly, timid. □ **faint-hearted·ly** *adverb* **faint-hearted·ness** *noun*

faint·ly *adverb* **1** very slightly (*faintly amused*). **2** indistinctly, feebly.

fair¹ ● *adjective* **1** just, unbiased, equitable; in accordance with the rules. **2** blond; light or pale in colour or complexion. **3 a** of (only) moderate quality or amount; average. **b** considerable, satisfactory (*a*

fair chance of success). **4 a** (of weather) fine and dry. **b** (of the wind) favourable. **c** (of the sky) clear; cloudless. **5** clean, clear, unblemished (*fair copy*). **6** beautiful, attractive. **7** *Baseball* (of a batted ball) that lands or is caught within the legal area of play. **8** *archaic* kind, gentle. **9 a** specious (*fair speeches*). **b** complimentary (*fair words*). **10** *Austral. & NZ* complete, unquestionable. ● *adverb* **1** in a fair manner (*play fair*). **2** exactly, completely (*was hit fair on the jaw*). **3** *dialect* really; thoroughly (*was fair exhausted*). ● *verb transitive* make (the surface of a ship, aircraft, etc.) smooth and streamlined. □ **fair and square 1** exactly. **2** straightforward, honest, above board. **a fair deal** equitable treatment. **fair enough** *informal* that is reasonable or acceptable. **fair name** a good reputation. **the fair sex** *dated or jocular* women. **fair's fair** *informal* all involved should act fairly. **fair shake** *informal* a fair opportunity; an equal chance. **for fair** *US slang* completely. **in a fair way to** likely to. **no fair** *N Amer. informal* (that is) unfair. □ **fair·ness** *noun* [Old English *fæger* from Germanic]

fair² *noun* **1** a usu. annual exhibition of produce, livestock, crafts, etc., held esp. in rural areas in conjunction with a travelling midway (*fall fair*). **2** an exhibition, esp. to promote particular products (*trade fair*). **3** a periodical gathering for the sale of goods, often with entertainments. [Old French *feire* from Late Latin *feria* sing. from Latin *feriae* holiday]

Fair·banks ▸ 1 Doug·las (Elton) (born Julius Ullman) (1883–1939), US actor and producer. He co-founded the United Artists Corporation in 1919 and embarked on the series of swashbuckling films for which he is best known, including *The Mark of Zorro* (1920) and *The Thief of Bagdad* (1924). **2** his son, **Doug·las Jr.** (1909–2000), US actor and producer, noted for playing roles similar to those of his father in films such as *The Prisoner of Zenda* (1937).

fair catch *noun Amer. Football* a catch of a kicked ball made by a player who has signalled that he or she will not attempt to advance the ball, and therefore cannot be tackled.

fair comment *noun* a comment or criticism made without intent of malice and based on correct factual information.

Fair·fax, Thom·as, 3rd Baron Fair·fax of Cam·eron (1612–71), English Parliamentary general. As commander of the New Model Army (1645–71) he helped to lead the Parliamentary forces to victory in the English Civil War; he later helped to secure the restoration of Charles II (1660).

fair game *noun* a thing or person one may legitimately pursue, exploit, etc.

fair·goer *noun* a person who attends a fair.

fair·ground *noun* (usu. in *pl.*) a place where a fair is held, usu. containing some permanent exhibition buildings and barns as well as an open area for amusements etc.

fair-haired *adjective* **1** having fair hair. **2** *N Amer.* favoured; favourite (*he's her fair-haired boy now*).

fair·ing *noun* a streamlining structure added to a ship, aircraft, vehicle, etc. [FAIR¹ *verb* 1 + -ING¹]

Fair Isle¹ an island lying about halfway between Orkney and Shetland.

Fair Isle² *noun* (also *attributive*) a knitwear design with multicoloured stitches usu. radiating outward from the neckline. [FAIR ISLE¹]

fair·lead /ˈferliːd/ *noun Naut.* a device to guide rope etc., e.g. to prevent cutting or chafing.

fair·ly *adverb* **1** in a fair manner; justly. **2** moderately, acceptably (*fairly good*). **3** to a noticeable degree (*fairly narrow*). **4** used as an intensifier (*fairly glowed with excitement; the house fairly rang with laughter*). □ **fairly and squarely** = FAIR AND SQUARE (*see* FAIR¹).

fair-minded *adjective* just, impartial. □ **fair-minded·ly** *adverb* **fair-minded·ness** *noun*

fair play *noun* reasonable treatment or behaviour.

fair trade *noun* **1** trade carried on legally. **2** trade in which fair prices are paid to producers in developing countries.

fair·way *noun* **1** the part of a golf course between a tee and its green, kept free of rough grass. **2** a navigable channel; a regular course or track of a ship.

fair-weather *adjective* (of a person) tending to be unreliable in times of difficulty (*fair-weather friend*).

Fair·weather Mountain a peak at the southern end of the St. Elias Mountains, in northwestern BC. Situated on the border with Alaska, it rises to a height of 4 663 m, making it the highest mountain in the province.

fairy ● *noun* (pl. **-ies**) **1** a small imaginary being with magical powers. **2** *slang derogatory* a male homosexual. ● *adjective* **1** of or relating to fairies. **2** fairy-like; delicate, small. □ **fairy-like** *adjective* [Old French *faerie* from *fae* FAY]

fairy godmother *noun* a person who provides unexpected help.

fairy·land *noun* **1** the imaginary home of fairies. **2** an enchanted region.

fairy lights *plural noun* small coloured lights, used esp. for outdoor decoration or on Christmas trees etc.

fairy ring *noun* a ring of darker grass caused by fungi, esp. the fairy ring mushroom *Marasmius areades.*

fairy slipper *noun* = CALYPSO 3.

fairy tale ● *noun* (also **fairy story**) **1** a tale about fairies. **2** an incredible story; a fabrication. ● *adjective* (**fairy-tale**) **1** of or relating to fairy tales. **2** resembling a fairy tale (*a fairy-tale romance*). **3** highly unlikely (*a fairy-tale description of the accident*).

Fai·sal /ˈfaɪsəl/ (full name Faisal Ibn Abdul Aziz al-Saud) (also **Fei·sal**) (1905–75), king of Saudi Arabia 1964–75. His reign was marked by increased oil production and economic development in Saudi Arabia.

Faisal·abad /ˈfaɪsələˌbad/ an industrial city in Punjab, Pakistan; pop. (1998) 1,977,200. Until 1979 it was known as Lyallpur.

fait ac·com·pli /ˌfet əkɒmˈpliː, feit-/ *noun* a thing that has been done and is past arguing against or altering. [French]

faith *noun* **1** complete trust or confidence. **2** firm belief, esp. without logical proof. **3 a** a system of religious belief (*the Christian faith*). **b** belief in God or religious doctrines. **c** spiritual apprehension of divine truth apart from proof. **d** things believed or to be believed. **4** duty or commitment to fulfill a trust, promise, etc. (*keep faith*). **5** (*attributive*) concerned with a supposed ability to cure by faith rather than treatment (*faith healing*). [Old French *feid* from Latin *fides*]

faith·ful *adjective* **1** showing faith. **2** loyal, trustworthy, constant. **3** remaining sexually loyal to one's spouse, lover, etc. **4** accurate; true to fact (*a faithful account*). **5 a** (**the Faithful**) the believers in a religion, esp. Muslims and Christians. **b** (**the faithful**) the loyal adherents of a political party. □ **faith·ful·ness** *noun*

faith·ful·ly *adverb* in a faithful manner. □ **yours faithfully** a formula for ending a business or formal letter.

faith healing *noun* healing achieved by faith and prayer as opposed to conventional medicine. □ **faith healer** *noun*

faith·less *adjective* **1** false, unreliable, disloyal. **2** without religious faith. □ **faith·less·ly** *adverb* **faith·less·ness** *noun*

faji·ta /fəˈhiːtə/ *noun* (usu. in *pl.*) a dish consisting of small strips of grilled spiced beef or chicken rolled in a tortilla and garnished with fried chopped vegetables and grated cheese and usu. guacamole, salsa, and sour cream. [Latin American Spanish, lit. 'little strip or belt']

fake¹ ● *noun* **1** a thing or person that is not genuine. **2** a trick. **3** *Sport* a misleading movement intended to deceive an opponent; a feint. ● *adjective* counterfeit; not genuine. ● *verb* **1** *transitive* make (a false thing) appear genuine; forge, counterfeit. **2** *transitive* make a pretense of having (a feeling, illness, etc.). **3** *intransitive* pretend; fake something. **4** *transitive & intransitive Sport* deceive (an opponent) by a misleading movement. □ **fake out** *N Amer. slang* deceive or trick (a person etc.). □ **fak·er** *noun* **fak·ery** *noun* **fakey** *adjective* [obsolete *feak, feague* thrash, from German *fegen* sweep, thrash]

fake² *Naut.* ● *noun* one round of a coil of rope. ● *transitive verb* coil (rope). [Middle English: compare Scottish *faik* fold]

fakie ● *noun* (pl. **-ies**) (in skateboarding or snowboarding) a movement in which the board is ridden backwards. ● *adverb* with such a movement.

fa·kir /ˈfeɪkiːr, fəˈkiːr/ *noun* a Muslim or (rarely) Hindu religious mendicant or ascetic. [Arabic *faḳīr* needy man]

fa·la·fel /feˈlɒfəl/ *noun* (also **fe·la·fel**) **1** a spicy fried patty made of ground chickpeas or beans. **2** these served in a pita as a sandwich. [Arabic *falāfil*]

Fa·lange /faˈlandʒ/ a Spanish political group founded in 1933 as a Fascist movement and merged in 1937 with traditional right-wing elements to form the ruling party, the Falange Española Tradicionalista, under General Franco. It was formally abolished in 1977. □ **Fa·lan·gism** *noun* **Fa·lan·gist** *noun* [Spanish, = PHALANX]

Fa·lasha /fəˈlaʃə/ *noun* (pl. same or **Fa·lashas**) (also **Black Jew**) an Ethiopian holding the Jewish faith. [Amharic, = exile, immigrant]

fal·cate /ˈfalkeɪt/ *adjective Anat.* curved like a sickle. [Latin *falcatus* from *falx falcis* sickle]

fal·chion /ˈfɒltʃən/ *noun hist.* a broad curved sword with a convex edge. [Old French *fauchon*, ultimately from Latin *falx falcis* sickle]

fal·ci·form /ˈfalsɪˌfɔrm/ *adjective Anat.* curved like a sickle. [Latin *falcis* sickle]

fal·con /ˈfɒlkən, ˈfal-/ *noun* **1** any diurnal bird of prey of the family Falconidae, having long pointed wings, and sometimes trained to hunt small game for sport. **2** (in falconry) a female falcon (*compare* TERCEL). [Old French *faucon* from Late Latin *falco -onis*, perhaps from Latin *falx* scythe, or from Germanic]

fal·con·er /ˈfɒlkənər, ˈfal-/ *noun* **1** a keeper and trainer of hawks. **2** a person who hunts with hawks.

fal·con·et /ˈfɒlkənət, ˈfal-/ *noun* **1** *hist.* a light cannon. **2** a small falcon. [sense 1 from Italian *falconetto* diminutive of *falcone* FALCON: sense 2 from FALCON + -ET¹]

fal·conry /ˈfɒlkənri, ˈfal-/ *noun* the breeding and training of hawks; the sport of hawking. [French *fauconnerie* (as FALCON)]

Falk·land Islands /ˈfɔlklənd/ (also **Falk·lands**) a group of islands in the S Atlantic, forming a British Crown Colony; pop. (est. 2002) 2,967; capital, Stanley (on East Falkland). The group consists of two main islands and over a hundred smaller ones, about 500 km (300 miles) east of the Strait of Magellan. Argentina has refused to recognize British sovereignty and has continued to refer to the islands by their old Spanish name, the Malvinas (see FALKLANDS WAR).

Falkland Islands Dependencies an overseas territory of the UK in the S Atlantic, consisting of the South Sandwich Islands and South Georgia. The territory is administered from the Falkland Islands.

Falklands War a war between Britain and Argentina in 1982, in which Argentinian forces invaded the Falkland Islands in support of their claim to sovereignty. They were forced to surrender to British forces six weeks later.

Falk·ner *var.* of FAULKNER.

fall ● *verb* (past **fell**; past participle **fal·len**) **1** *intransitive* **a** go or come down freely; descend rapidly from a higher to a lower level (*fell from the top floor; rain was falling*). **b** drop or be dropped (*supplies fell by parachute; the curtain fell*). **2** *intransitive* **a** (often foll. by *over*) cease to stand; come suddenly to the ground from loss of balance etc. **b** collapse forwards or downwards esp. of one's own volition (*fell into my arms; fell over the chair*). **3** *intransitive* become detached and descend or disappear. **4** *intransitive* take a downward direction: **a** (of hair, clothing, etc.) hang down. **b** (of ground etc.) slope. **c** (foll. by *into*) (of a river etc.) discharge into. **5** *intransitive* **a** find a lower level; sink lower. **b** subside, abate. **6** *intransitive* (of the voice, a musical note, etc.) become lower or quieter. **7** *intransitive* (of a barometer, thermometer, etc.) show a lower reading. **8** *intransitive* occur; become apparent or present (*darkness fell*). **9** *intransitive* decline, diminish (*demand is falling; standards have fallen*). **10** *transitive N Amer., Austral., & NZ* cut down (a tree etc.). **11** *intransitive* **a** (of the face) show dismay or disappointment. **b** (of the eyes or a glance) look downwards. **12** *intransitive* **a** lose power or status (*the government will fall*). **b** lose esteem, moral integrity, etc. **13** *intransitive* commit sin; yield to temptation. **14** *intransitive* take or have a particular direction or place (*his eye fell on me; the accent falls on the first syllable*). **15** *intransitive* (of speech) issue forth; proceed from (*the bad news fell from her lips*). **16** *intransitive* find a place; be naturally divisible (*the subject falls into three parts*). **b** (foll. by *under, within*) be classed among. **17** *intransitive* occur at a specified time (*Easter falls early this year*). **18** *intransitive* come by chance or duty (*it fell to me to answer*). **19** *intransitive* **a** pass into a specified condition (*fall into decay; fell ill*). **b** become (*fall asleep*). **20** *intransitive* **a** (of a position etc.) be overthrown or captured; succumb to attack. **b** be defeated; fail. **21** *intransitive* die (*fall in battle*). **22** *intransitive* (foll. by *on, upon*) **a** attack. **b** meet with. **c** embrace or embark on avidly. **23** *intransitive* (foll. by *to* + verbal noun) begin (*fell to wondering*). **24** *intransitive* collapse or sink (*too much sugar will make the cake fall*). **25** *intransitive* (foll. by *to*) lapse, revert (*revenues fall to the Crown*). ● *noun* **1** the act or an instance of falling; a sudden rapid descent. **2** (also **Fall**) *N Amer.* autumn. **3** that which falls or has fallen, e.g. snow, rocks, etc. **4** the recorded amount of rainfall etc. **5** a decline or diminution. **6** overthrow, downfall (*the fall of Rome*). **7 a** a succumbing to temptation. **b** (**the Fall**; also **the Fall of Man**) in Christian and Jewish theology, the lapse into a sinful state and the origin of the human condition (of suffering, toil, death, and sinfulness) resulting from the first act of disobedience by Adam and Eve (Gen. 2 ff.). **8 a** (of material, land, light, etc.) a downward direction; a slope. **b** a downward difference in height (*a fall of 3 inches from back to front*). **9** (esp. in *pl.*) a waterfall, cataract, or cascade. **10** *Music* a cadence. **11 a** *Wrestling* a match or part of a match. **b** *Wrestling* a throw which keeps the opponent on the ground for a specified time. **c** a controlled act of falling, esp. as a stunt or in judo etc. **12 a** an esp. ornamental or decorative item of material that hangs from something (*pulpit fall*). **b** a long hairpiece that is attached to the natural hair at the crown and usu. hangs down the back of the head.

13 a the birth of young of certain animals. **b** the number of young born. **14** a rope of a hoisting tackle. □ **fall about** Brit. informal be helpless, esp. with laughter. **fall apart** (or **to pieces**) **1** break into pieces. **2** (of a situation etc.) disintegrate; be reduced to chaos. **3** lose one's capacity to cope. **fall away 1** (of a surface) drop abruptly. **2** become few or thin; gradually vanish. **3** desert, revolt; abandon one's principles. **fall back** retreat. **fall back on** have recourse to in difficulty. **fall behind 1** be outstripped by one's competitors etc.; lag. **2** be in arrears. **fall down** (often foll. by on) informal fail; perform poorly; fail to deliver (payment etc.). **fall for** informal **1** be captivated or deceived by. **2** admire; yield to the charms or merits of. **fall afoul** (or **foul**) **of** come into conflict with; quarrel with. **fall in 1 a** take one's place in military formation. **b** (as interjection) the order to do this. **2** collapse inwards. **fall in love** see LOVE. **fall into line 1** take one's place in the ranks. **2** conform or collaborate with others. **fall into place** begin to make sense or cohere. **fall in with 1** meet by chance. **2** agree with; accede to; humour. **3** coincide with. **fall off 1** (of demand etc.) decrease, deteriorate. **2** withdraw. **fall out 1** quarrel. **2** (of the hair, teeth, etc.) become detached. **3** Military come out of formation. **4** result; come to pass; occur. **fall out of** gradually discontinue (a habit etc.). **fall over oneself** informal **1** be eager or competitive. **2** be awkward, stumble through haste, confusion, etc. **fall short 1** be or become deficient or inadequate. **2** (of a missile etc.) not reach its target. **fall short of** fail to reach or obtain. **fall through** fail; come to nothing. **fall to** begin an activity, e.g. eating or working. **take the fall** N Amer. informal receive blame or punishment, esp. in the place of someone else (it was Katherine's idea, but I took the fall for it). [Old English fallan, feallan from Germanic]

Falla /ˈfɒjə, ˈfɒljə/ **Man·uel de** (1876–1946), Spanish composer and pianist. A leading exponent of the new nationalism in 20th-c. Spanish music, he is known for works such as the opera La vida breve (1913) and the ballet The Three-Cornered Hat (1919).

fal·lacy /ˈfaləsi/ noun (pl. **-cies**) **1** a mistaken belief, esp. based on unsound argument. **2** faulty reasoning; misleading or unsound argument. **3** Logic a flaw that vitiates an argument. □ **fal·la·cious** /fəˈleɪʃəs/ adjective **fal·la·cious·ly** adverb **fal·la·cious·ness** noun [Latin fallacia from fallax -acis deceiving, from fallere deceive]

fall·away noun Basketball = FADEAWAY 2.

fall·back ● noun **1** a reserve; something that may be used in an emergency. **2** a falling back or reduction. ● attributive adjective reserve, emergency (fallback plan).

fall·en ● verb past participle of FALL. ● adjective **1** having fallen or dropped from a higher place, value, etc. (fallen leaves). **2** (attributive) having lost one's honour or reputation. **3** killed in war. □ **fallen·ness** noun

fall·er noun **1** a person, animal, or thing that falls, esp. a person or animal in a race. **2** N Amer., Austral., & NZ a logger who cuts down trees.

fall·fish noun a N American freshwater fish of the carp family, Semotilus corporalis, similar to the chub.

fall guy noun slang **1** an easy victim. **2** a scapegoat.

fal·li·ble /ˈfalɪbəl/ adjective **1** capable of making mistakes. **2** liable to be erroneous. □ **fal·li·bil·ity** /-ˈbɪlɪti/ noun **fal·li·bly** adverb [medieval Latin fallibilis from Latin fallere deceive]

fall·ing noun the felling of trees for timber.

falling-out noun a quarrel.

falling star noun = SHOOTING STAR 1.

fall-off noun a decrease, deterioration, withdrawal, etc.

Fal·lo·pian tube /fəˈloːpiən/ noun Anat. either of two tubes in female mammals along which ova travel from the ovaries to the uterus. [Fallopius, Latinized name of G. Fallopio, Italian anatomist d.1562]

fall·out noun **1** radioactive debris caused by a nuclear explosion or accident. **2** the adverse side effects of a situation etc.

fal·low[1] /ˈfaloː/ ● adjective **1 a** (of land) plowed and harrowed but left unsown for a year. **b** uncultivated. **2** (of an idea etc.) potentially useful but not yet in use. **3** inactive. **4** (of a sow) not pregnant. ● noun fallow or uncultivated land. ● transitive verb break up (land) for sowing or to destroy weeds. [Old English fealh (n.), fealgian (v.)]

fal·low[2] /ˈfaloː/ adjective of a pale brownish or reddish yellow. [Old English falu, fealu from Germanic]

fallow deer noun a small Mediterranean deer, Cervus dama, widely naturalized in European parks and forests, which has a dappled fawn summer coat.

Falls, the /fɔlz/ an informal name for Niagara Falls.

fall supper noun Cdn = FOWL SUPPER.

false ● adjective **1** not according with fact; wrong, incorrect (a false

idea). **2 a** spurious, sham, artificial (false gods; false teeth; false modesty). **b** acting as such; appearing to be such, esp. deceptively (a false lining). **3** illusory; not actually so (a false economy). **4** used in names of plants, animals, and gems that superficially resemble the thing properly so called (false acacia). **5** deceptive (false advertising). **6** (foll. by to) deceitful, treacherous, or unfaithful. **7** fictitious or assumed (gave a false name). **8** unlawful (false imprisonment). ● adverb in a false manner (play someone false). □ **false·ly** adverb **false·ness** noun **fals·ity** noun (pl. **-ities**). [Old English fals and Old French fals, faus from Latin falsus past participle of fallere deceive]

false acacia noun = LOCUST 4b.

false alarm noun **1** an alarm given needlessly, either intentionally or in error. **2** a situation in which danger threatens but never materializes.

false bedding noun Geol. = CROSS-BEDDING.

false colours plural noun deceitful pretense.

false cypress noun any evergreen tree of the genus Chamaecyparis of the cypress family, used for timber and often cultivated as an ornamental.

false dawn noun **1** a transient light in the east before dawn. **2** a promising sign which comes to nothing.

False Face noun **1** (among the Iroquois) a grimacing mask carved from a living tree and adorned with hair and feathers, used in curing ceremonies. **2** a member of the secret society using these masks.

false front noun a facade extending above the roof of a building to make the building look more imposing. □ **false-fronted** adjective

false hellebore noun = INDIAN POKE.

false·hood noun **1** the state of being false or untrue. **2** a false or untrue thing. **3** the act of lying.

false indigo noun any leguminous plant of the genus Baptisia of the eastern US, formerly used as a dye plant.

false memory syndrome noun apparent memory of an event, esp. childhood sexual abuse, that did not occur, created by psychological techniques such as hypnosis, dream interpretation, etc. Abbr.: **FMS**.

false move noun an imprudent or careless act.

false positive noun a result of a diagnostic test or procedure that incorrectly shows the presence of a disease, condition, etc.

false pretenses plural noun misrepresentations made with intent to deceive (sold under false pretenses).

false rib noun = FLOATING RIB.

false Solomon's seal noun any of various liliaceous plants of the genus Smilacina, with a terminal cluster of white flowers.

false start noun **1** an invalid or disallowed start in a race. **2** an unsuccessful attempt to begin something.

false step noun a slip; a mistake.

false topaz noun = CITRINE.

fal·setto /fɒlˈsetoː/ noun (pl. **-tos**) **1** a method of voice production used by male singers, esp. tenors, to sing notes higher than their normal range. **2** a singer using this method. **3** a voice or sound that is unusually or unnaturally high. [Italian, diminutive of falso FALSE]

false·work noun a temporary framework or support used during building to form arches etc.

fals·ies plural noun informal padded material to increase the apparent size of the breasts.

fals·ify transitive verb (**-fies, -fied**) **1** fraudulently alter or make false (a document, evidence, etc.). **2** misrepresent. **3** show to be false. **4** disappoint (a hope, fear, etc.). □ **falsi·fi·able** adjective **falsi·fi·abil·ity** noun **falsi·fi·ca·tion** noun **falsi·fi·er** noun

Fal·staff·ian /fɒlˈstafiən/ adjective fat, jolly, or dissipated like Shakespeare's character Sir John Falstaff.

Fal·ster /ˈfɒlstər/ a Danish island in the Baltic Sea, south of Zealand. Its southern tip is the most southerly point of Denmark.

fal·ter /ˈfɒltər/ verb **1** intransitive stumble, stagger; go unsteadily. **2** intransitive waver; lose courage. **3** transitive & intransitive stammer; speak hesitatingly. **4** intransitive show loss of momentum, energy, or functioning (the economy was faltering). □ **fal·ter·ing** adjective **fal·ter·ing·ly** adverb [Middle English: origin uncertain]

Falun Gong /ˈfalʊn ˌɡɒŋ/ noun (also **Falun Dafa**) **1** a form of qigong which combines meditation and exercises similar to tai chi with Buddhist and Taoist principles. **2** the adherents of this spiritual movement collectively. [Chinese, lit. 'law wheel qigong']

fame noun **1** renown; the state of being famous. **2** reputation. **3** archaic public report; rumour. [Old French from Latin fama]

---

t top　v voice　w we　z zoo　ʃ she　ʒ vision　θ thin　ð this　ŋ ring　x loch　tʃ chip　dʒ jar　(see over for vowels)

famed *adjective* (foll. by *for*) famous; much spoken of (*famed for its good food*).

Fa·meuse /fə'muz/ *noun* Cdn = SNOW APPLE. [Canadian French from French, lit. 'famous']

fam·il·ial /fə'mɪliəl/ *adjective* of, occurring in, or characteristic of a family or its members. [French from Latin *familia* FAMILY]

fam·il·iar /fə'mɪljər/ ● *adjective* **1 a** (often foll. by *to*) well known; no longer novel. **b** common, usual; often encountered or experienced. **2** (foll. by *with*) knowing a thing well or in detail (*am familiar with all the problems*). **3** (often foll. by *with*) well acquainted (with a person); in close friendship; intimate. **4** excessively informal; impertinent. **5** unceremonious, informal. ● *noun* **1** a close friend or associate. **2** (in full **familiar spirit**) a demon supposedly attending and obeying a witch etc. **3** *Catholicism* a person rendering certain services in a pope's or bishop's household. □ **fam·il·iar·ly** *adverb* [Old French *familier* from Latin *familiaris* (as FAMILY)]

fam·il·iar·ity /fə,mɪli'ɛrɪti/ *noun* (pl. **-ities**) **1** the state of being well known (*the familiarity of the scene*). **2** (foll. by *with*) close acquaintance. **3** a close relationship. **4** familiar or informal behaviour, esp. excessively so. □ **familiarity breeds contempt** extensive knowledge of or close association with someone or something leads to a loss of respect for them or it.

famil·iar·ize /fə'mɪliə,raiz/ *transitive verb* (also esp. *Brit.* **-ise**) **1** (foll. by *with*) make (a person) conversant or well acquainted. **2** make (a thing) well known. □ **famil·iar·iz·a·tion** *noun*

fam·ily *noun* (pl. **-ilies**) **1** a group of people related by blood, legal or common-law marriage, or adoption. **2 a** the members of a household, esp. parents and their children. **b** a person's children. **c** a person's spouse and children. **d** (*attributive*) serving the needs of families (*family entertainment*). **3 a** all the descendants of a common ancestor. **b** a race or group of peoples from a common stock. **4** all the languages ultimately derived from a particular early language, regarded as a group. **5** a brotherhood of persons or nations united by political or religious ties. **6** a group of objects distinguished by common features. **7** *Math.* a group of curves etc. obtained by varying one quantity. **8** *Biol.* a group of related genera of organisms within an order in taxonomic classification. **9** *Cdn* (*Ont.*) a classification code indicating that a film is considered appropriate for viewing by people of all ages. Abbr.: **F**. □ **in the family way** *informal* pregnant. [Latin *familia* household, from *famulus* servant]

family allowance *noun* **1** *Cdn hist.* a universal monthly payment made by the federal government to mothers of children under 18. ¶ Now replaced by the CHILD TAX BENEFIT. **2** *Brit.* a former name for CHILD BENEFIT.

family bible *noun* a large bible including pages for recording births, deaths, and marriages in a family.

Family Compact *noun* Cdn **1** a name given to the ruling class in Upper Canada in the early 19th c., esp. to the members of the legislative and executive councils (*compare* CHÂTEAU CLIQUE). This governing Tory elite was held together by ties of family, patronage, and social and political beliefs, and promoted British institutions such as a social hierarchy and an established Church. **2** any influential clique or faction.

Family Court *noun* Cdn (in Nova Scotia) a court which has jurisdiction over some aspects of family law, including custody and support payments etc., and also serves as a youth court.

Family Day *noun* (in full **Alberta Family Day**) the third Monday in February, a statutory holiday in Alberta.

family doctor *noun* (also **family physician**) a general practitioner.

family farm *noun* a farm that is owned and operated by a family, esp. one that has been handed down from one generation to another. □ **family farmer** *noun*

family-friendly *adjective* **1** (of a workplace, employment policy, etc.) accommodating to the needs of workers with family responsibilities. **2** (of lodging, entertainment, etc.) suited to the needs of young families.

family jewels *plural noun* *informal* the testicles.

family law *noun* the part of the legal system that deals with matters affecting families, e.g. divorce, child custody, etc.

family man *noun* a man having a wife and children, esp. one fond of family life.

family name *noun* a surname.

family planning *noun* the planning of the number of children, intervals between births, etc. in a family by using birth control.

family practice *noun* a medical specialization in general practice. □ **family practitioner** *noun*

family ring *noun* a ring with birthstones representing each of the wearer's children or grandchildren.

family room *noun* N *Amer.* a room in a house used by family members for relaxation etc.

family therapy *noun* a form of psychotherapy for the members of a family, aimed at improving communication and relationships. □ **family therapist** *noun*

family tree *noun* a chart showing relationships and lines of descent.

family values *plural noun* values supposedly learned or reinforced within a traditional, close, family unit, typically those of high moral standards and discipline.

fam·ine /'famɪn/ *noun* **1** extreme scarcity of food. **2** a shortage of something specified (*a labour famine*). [Old French from *faim* from Latin *fames* hunger]

fam·ish *transitive & intransitive verb* (usu. in *passive*) **1** reduce or be reduced to extreme hunger. **2** *informal* feel very hungry. □ **fam·ished** *adjective* [Middle English from obsolete *fame* from Old French *afamer*, ultimately from Latin *fames* hunger]

fam·ous *adjective* **1** (often foll. by *for*) celebrated; well known. **2** *informal* excellent. **3** notorious. □ **famous last words** (an ironic comment on or rejoinder to) an overconfident or boastful assumption that may well be proved wrong by events. □ **famous·ness** *noun*

fam·ous·ly *adverb* **1** *informal* excellently (*got on famously*). **2** notably.

fan¹ ● *noun* **1** an apparatus, usu. with rotating blades, giving a current of air for ventilation etc. **2** a device, usu. folding and forming a semicircle when spread out, for agitating the air to cool oneself. **3** anything spread out like a fan, e.g. a bird's tail or kind of ornamental vaulting (*fan tracery*). **4** a device for winnowing grain. **5** = ALLUVIAL FAN. **6** a small sail for keeping the head of a windmill towards the wind. ● *verb* (**fanned**, **fan·ning**) **1** *transitive* **a** blow a current of air on, with or as with a fan. **b** agitate (the air) with a fan. **2** *transitive* (of a breeze) blow gently on; cool. **3** *transitive* **a** winnow (grain). **b** winnow away (chaff). **4** *transitive* sweep away by or as by the wind from a fan. **5** *intransitive & transitive* (usu. foll. by *out*) spread out in the shape of a fan. **6** *intransitive* (often foll. by *on*) *Hockey* miss or make only partial contact with the puck while attempting to pass or shoot etc. (*he might have scored but he fanned on the shot*). **7** *Baseball* **a** *transitive* (of a pitcher) strike out (a batter). **b** *intransitive* (of a batter) strike out. **8** *transitive* incite; make more ardent (*fanned her desire*). □ **fan the flames of** increase the intensity of (*fanned the flames of nationalism*). □ **fan-like** *adjective* [Old English *fann* (in sense 4 of *n.*) from Latin *vannus* winnowing fan]

fan² *noun* a devotee or admirer of a particular activity, performer, etc. (*hockey fan*; *Jessica is his biggest fan*). [abbreviation of FANATIC]

fan·atic /fə'natɪk/ ● *noun* **1** a person filled with excessive and often misguided enthusiasm for something. **2** *informal* a person who is devoted to a hobby, pastime, sport, etc. (*curling fanatic*). ● *adjective* excessively enthusiastic. □ **fan·at·ic·al** *adjective* **fan·at·ic·al·ly** *adverb* **fan·ati·cism** /-tɪ,sɪzəm/ *noun* [French *fanatique* or Latin *fanaticus* from *fanum* temple (originally in religious sense)]

fan belt *noun* a belt that drives a fan to cool the radiator in a motor vehicle.

fan·ci·er *noun* **1** a connoisseur or follower of some activity or thing. **2** a breeder of a certain type of animal or plant.

fan·ci·ful *adjective* **1** existing only in the imagination or fancy. **2** indulging in fancies; whimsical, capricious. **3** (of things) designed or decorated in an odd but creative manner. □ **fan·ci·ful·ly** *adverb* **fan·ci·ful·ness** *noun*

fan club *noun* an organized group of a person's admirers.

fancy ● *noun* (pl. **-cies**) **1** an individual taste or inclination. **2** a caprice or whim. **3** a thing favoured, e.g. a horse to win a race. **4** an arbitrary supposition. **5 a** the faculty of using imagination or of inventing imagery. **b** a mental image. **6** delusion; unfounded belief. **7** *archaic* (prec. by *the*) those who have a certain hobby; fanciers, esp. patrons of boxing. ● *adjective* (usu. *attributive*) (**fan·ci·er**, **fan·ci·est**) **1 a** elaborate; not plain. **b** of high quality or very expensive. **2** capricious, whimsical, extravagant. **3** based on imagination, not fact. **4 a** (of foods etc.) of fine quality. **b** designating a grade of canned fruits and vegetables that are of the highest quality, as nearly perfect as possible and uniform in colour and size. **5** (of an animal) bred for particular points of beauty etc. ● *transitive verb* (**-cies**, **-cied**) **1** (foll. by *that* + clause) be inclined to suppose; rather think. **2** *Brit. informal* feel a desire for (*do you fancy a drink?*). **3** *Brit. informal* find sexually attractive. **4** *informal* have an unduly high opinion of (oneself, one's ability, etc.). **5** select (a horse, team, etc.).

as the likely winner. **6** (in *imperative*) an exclamation of surprise (*fancy their doing that!*). **7** picture to oneself; conceive, imagine. □ **catch** (or **take**) **the fancy of** please; appeal to. **fancy up** *informal* make more fancy, elegant, etc. **take a fancy to** become (esp. inexplicably) fond of. □ **fan·ci·able** *adjective* (in sense 3 of *verb*). **fan·ci·ly** *adverb* **fan·ci·ness** *noun* [contraction of FANTASY]

fancy-dancy *adjective N Amer. slang* = FANCY-SCHMANCY.

fancy dress *noun* esp. *Brit.* = COSTUME *noun* 2.

fancy footwork *noun* **1** skilful or agile use of the feet, esp. in sports, dancing, etc. **2** agility in negotiation, evasion, etc.

fancy-free *adjective* (often in phr. **footloose and fancy-free**) without (esp. emotional) commitments.

fancy man *noun slang derogatory* **1** a woman's lover. **2** a pimp.

fancy-pants *adjective N Amer. informal* hotshot (*a fancy-pants lawyer*).

fancy-schmancy *adjective derogatory slang* overly fancy.

fancy woman *noun* (also **fancy lady**) *slang derogatory* **1** a man's mistress. **2** a prostitute.

fan dance *noun* a dance in which the dancer is (apparently) nude and partly concealed by fans. □ **fan dancer** *noun*

fan·dangle /ˈfanˈdaŋɡəl/ *noun* **1** a fantastic ornament. **2** nonsense, tomfoolery. [perhaps from FANDANGO after *newfangle*]

fan·dan·go /fanˈdaŋɡoː/ *noun* (pl. **-goes** or **-gos**) **1 a** a lively Spanish dance for two in triple time, usu. accompanied by castanets and guitars. **b** the music for this. **2** nonsense, tomfoolery. [Spanish: origin unknown]

fan·dom *noun* the world of fans and enthusiasts, esp. of fans of science fiction magazines and conventions.

fan·fare *noun* **1** a short showy or ceremonious sounding of trumpets, bugles, etc. **2** an elaborate display; a burst of publicity. [French, imitative]

fan·faro·nade /ˌfanferəˈneɪd/ *noun* **1** arrogant talk; bragging. **2** a fanfare. [French *fanfaronnade* from *fanfaron* braggart (as FANFARE)]

fan·fold *adjective* = CONTINUOUS 4.

fang *noun* **1** a sharply pointed canine tooth, e.g. of a dog or wolf. **2 a** the tooth of a venomous snake, by which poison is injected. **b** the biting mouthpart of a spider. **3** the root of a tooth or its prong. □ **bare one's fangs** show oneself ready for confrontation. □ **fanged** *adjective* (also in *combination*). **fang·less** *adjective* **fang-like** *adjective* [Old English from Old Norse *fang* from a Germanic root = to catch]

fan heater *noun* an electric heater in which a fan drives air over an element.

fan hitch *noun Cdn* (*North*) a method of harnessing sled dogs, with the lead dog on a long trace and the other dogs arranged in a fan-shaped pattern on either side.

fan jet *noun* = TURBOFAN.

fan·light *noun* a small, originally semicircular window over a door or another window.

fan mail *noun* letters from fans to the person they admire.

fanny *noun* (pl. **-nies**) **1** *N Amer. slang* the buttocks. **2** *Brit. coarse slang* the female genitals. [20th c.: origin unknown]

Fanny Adams *noun esp. Brit. slang* (also **sweet Fanny Adams**) nothing at all. ¶ Sometimes understood as a euphemism for *fuck all*. [name of a murder victim *c*.1870]

fanny pack *noun N Amer.* a small pouch for money or other valuables, worn on a belt around the waist or hips.

fan palm *noun* a palm tree with fan-shaped leaves.

fan·tail *noun* **1** a pigeon with a broad fan-shaped tail. **2** a fan-shaped tail or end. **3** the fan of a windmill. **4** the projecting part of a boat's stern. □ **fan·tailed** *adjective*

fan-tan *noun* **1** a Chinese gambling game in which players try to guess the remainder, after division by four, of a number of coins etc. hidden under a bowl. **2** a card game in which players build on sequences of sevens, with the winner being the first person to run out of cards. [Chinese, = repeated divisions]

fan·ta·sia /fanˈteɪʒə, -ziə/ *noun* a musical or other composition free in form and often in improvisatory style, or which is based on several familiar tunes. [Italian, = FANTASY]

fan·ta·sist /ˈfantəˌsɪst/ *noun* **1** a writer of fantasies. **2** a person who fantasizes.

fan·ta·size *verb* (also esp. *Brit.* **-sise**) **1** *intransitive* **a** daydream about something one wishes to happen. **b** indulge in a sexual fantasy. **2** *transitive* imagine; create a fantasy about. □ **fan·ta·siz·er** *noun*

fan·tast /ˈfantast/ *noun* a visionary; a dreamer. [medieval Latin from Greek *phantastēs* boaster, from *phantazomai* make a show, from *phainō* show]

fan·tas·tic *adjective* (also **fan·tas·tic·al**) **1** *informal* excellent, extraordinary. **2** *informal* very large; lavish (*a fantastic increase in salary*). **3** extravagantly fanciful. **4** capricious, eccentric. **5** grotesque or quaint in design etc. **6** existing only in the imagination; unreal or impossible (*fantastic elements in medieval romance*). □ **trip the light fantastic** *see* TRIP. □ **fan·tas·tic·al·ly** *adverb* [orig. in sense 'existing only in the imagination, unreal', from Old French *fantastique* via medieval Latin from Greek *phantastikos* from *phatazein* 'make visible']

fan·tas·ti·cate *transitive verb* make something seem fanciful or fantastic. □ **fan·tas·ti·ca·tion** *noun*

fan·tasy /ˈfantəsi, -zi/ ● *noun* (pl. **-sies**) **1** the faculty of inventing images, esp. extravagant or visionary ones. **2** a sequence of mental images developed in the imagination and arising from conscious or unconscious wishes or attitudes, esp. involving sexual relations. **3** a whimsical speculation. **4** a fantastic invention or composition; a fantasia. **5** a genre of imaginative fiction involving fantastic stories, often in a magical pseudo-historical setting. ● *transitive verb* (**-sies**, **-sied**) imagine in a visionary manner. [Old French *fantasie* from Latin *phantasia* appearance, from Greek (as FANTAST)]

fantasy camp *noun* a sports camp in which members of the general public pay to participate with current or former professional athletes.

fantasy·land *noun* an imaginary world where all fantasies are fulfilled.

Fanti /ˈfanti/ *noun* (also **Fante** /ˈfanti/) (pl. same or **Fan·tis**) **1** a member of a people inhabiting southern Ghana. **2** the language of this people. [Fanti]

fan·tods *plural noun* a state or attack of uneasiness or unreasonableness. [19th c.: origin unknown]

fan·zine /ˈfanziːn/ *noun* a magazine for fans, esp. those of science fiction, sport, or popular music. [FAN² + MAGAZINE]

FAO *abbreviation* Food and Agriculture Organization (of the United Nations).

FAQ /ef ei kjuː, fak/ *noun* a list of questions and answers relating to a particular subject, esp. a text file giving basic information on a topic to users of a website. [acronym from *frequently asked questions*]

far (**fur·ther**, **fur·thest** or **far·ther**, **far·thest**) ● *adverb* **1** at or to or by a great distance (*far away; far off; far out*). **2** a long way (off) in space or time (*are you travelling far?; we talked far into the night*). **3** to a great extent or degree; by much (*far better; far the best; far too early*). **4** much or many (*we need far more than that*). ● *adjective* **1** situated at or extending over a great distance in space or time; remote (*a far country*). **2** more distant (*the far end of the hall*). **3** extreme (*far left*). □ **as far as 1** to the distance of (a place). **2** to the extent that (*as far as I'm concerned*). **by far** by a great amount. **far and away** by a very large amount. **far and near** everywhere. **far and wide** over a large area. **far be it from me** (foll. by *to* + infin.) I am reluctant to (esp. express criticism etc.). **far from** very different from being; tending to the opposite of (*the problem is far from being solved*). **go far 1** achieve much. **2** contribute greatly. **3** be adequate. **go too far** go beyond the limits of what is reasonable, polite, etc. **how far** to what extent. **so far 1** to such an extent or distance; to this point. **2** until now. **so** (or **in so**) **far as** (or **that**) to the extent that. **so far so good** progress has been satisfactory up to now. [Old English *feorr*]

far·ad /ˈferəd/ *noun Electricity* the SI unit of capacitance, such that one coulomb of charge causes a potential difference of one volt. Abbr.: **F**. [shortening of FARADAY]

Fara·day /ˈferəˌdeɪ/ **Mi·chael** (1791–1867), English physicist and chemist. He demonstrated electromagnetic rotation, and discovered electromagnetic induction (the key to the development of the electric dynamo and motor); he also discovered the two laws of electrolysis named after him.

fara·day /ˈferəˌdeɪ/ *noun Chem.* a unit of electric charge equal to Faraday's constant. Abbr.: **F**. [M. FARADAY]

Faraday cage *noun Electricity* a grounded metal screen used for excluding electrostatic influences. [M. FARADAY]

Faraday's constant *noun* the quantity of electric charge carried by one mole of electrons (equal to 96.49 coulombs). [M. FARADAY]

far·ad·ic /fəˈradɪk/ *adjective* (also **fara·daic** /ˌferəˈdeɪɪk/) *Electricity* inductive, induced. [see FARADAY]

far·an·dole /ˌferənˈdɒl/ *noun* **1** a Provençal communal dance, usu. in 6/8 time. **2** the music for this. [French from modern Provençal *farandoulo*]

far·away *adjective* **1** remote; long-past. **2** (of a look) dreamy. **3** (of a voice) sounding as if from a distance.

farce *noun* **1 a** a coarsely comic dramatic work based on ludicrously improbable events. **b** this branch of drama. **2** absurdly futile proceedings; pretense, mockery. [French, originally = stuffing, from Old French *farsir* from Latin *farcire* to stuff, used metaphorically of interludes etc.]

far·ceur /farˈsɜr/ *noun* **1** an actor or writer of farces. **2** a joker or comedian. [French from *farcer* act farces]

far·ci·cal /ˈfɑrsɪkəl/ *adjective* **1** extremely ludicrous or futile. **2** of or like farce. □ **far·ci·cal·ity** /-ˈkalɪti/ *noun* **far·ci·cal·ly** *adverb*

farcy /ˈfɑrsi/ *noun* a bacterial disease of cattle, marked by swelling and inflammation of lymph nodes. [Old French *farcin* from Late Latin *farciminum* from *farcire* 'to stuff']

fare ● *noun* **1 a** the price a passenger has to pay to be conveyed by bus, airplane, etc. **b** a passenger paying to travel in a public vehicle, esp. a taxi. **2** a range of food provided by a restaurant etc. **3** something presented to the public, esp. for entertainment (*typical Hollywood fare*). ● *intransitive verb* **1** progress; get on (*how did you fare?*). **2** happen; turn out. **3** *archaic* journey, go, travel. [Old English *fær, faru* journeying, *faran* (v.), from Germanic]

Far East *noun* China, Japan, and other countries of E Asia. □ **Far Eastern** *adjective*

fare box *noun* a locked receptacle on a bus or other public vehicle into which passengers drop their fares.

fare-thee-well *noun* (also **fare-you-well**) **1** *US informal* the utmost degree (*worked his students to a fare-thee-well*). **2** = FAREWELL.

fare war *noun* a period of intense competition between airlines, bus companies, etc., with each cutting fares to match the other.

fare·well ● *interjection* goodbye, adieu. ● *noun* **1** leave-taking, departure (also *attributive: a farewell kiss; farewell party*). **2** parting good wishes.

Farewell, Cape **1** the southernmost point of Greenland. **2** the northernmost point of South Island, New Zealand.

far·falle /fɑrˈfɒlei/ *plural noun* bow-shaped pasta. [Italian, from *farfalla* 'butterfly']

far-fetched *adjective* (of an idea, explanation, etc.) contrived and unconvincing; improbable.

far-flung *adjective* **1** extending far; widely distributed. **2** remote; isolated (*far-flung northern communities*).

far gone *adjective* **1** *informal* in an advanced state of drunkenness, illness, etc. **2** long ago; past (*those days are far gone*).

Fa·rid·abad /fəˈriːdəbad/ an industrial city in northern India, south of Delhi, in the state of Haryana; pop. (2001) 1,055,000.

far·ina /fəˈriːnə/ *noun* **1** the flour or meal of cereal, nuts, or starchy roots. **2** *Brit.* starch. □ **far·in·aceous** /ˌferəˈneiʃəs/ *adjective* [Latin from *far corn*]

farl *noun* esp. *Scot.* a thin cake, originally quadrant-shaped, of oatmeal or flour. [obsolete *fardel* quarter (as FOURTH, DEAL[1] *noun* (= portion))]

farm ● *noun* **1** an area of land, and the buildings on it, used for growing crops, rearing animals, etc. (also *attributive: farm machinery; farm workers*). **2** a place or establishment for breeding a particular type of animal, growing fruit, etc. (*fish farm; mink farm*). **3** a place for the storage of oil or oil products. ● *verb* **1 a** *transitive* use (land) for growing crops, rearing animals, etc. **b** *intransitive* be a farmer; work on a farm. **2** *transitive* breed (fish etc.) commercially. **3** *transitive* (often foll. by *out*) **a** delegate or subcontract (work) to others. **b** contract (the collection of taxes) to another for a fee. **c** arrange for (a person, esp. a child) to be looked after by another, with payment. □ **buy the farm** see BUY. □ **farm·able** *adjective* **farm·ing** *noun* [Old French *ferme* from medieval Latin *firma* fixed payment, from Latin *firmus* FIRM[1]: originally applied only to leased land]

farm·er *noun* **1** a person who farms land or rears certain animals (usu. of a specified kind). **2** *hist.* a person to whom the collection of taxes is contracted for a fee.

farmers' market *noun* a market where produce of local farmers and growers is sold directly to the public.

farmer's sausage *noun* *Cdn* seasoned raw pork sausage in a casing but not in links, esp. of German origin.

farm gate *noun* the point at which farm produce leaves the farm to be sold, esp. to individuals.

farm·hand *noun* **1** a worker on a farm. **2** *N Amer. informal* a player on a farm team, esp. one who has just been called up to the major leagues.

farm·house *noun* a dwelling (esp. the main one) attached to a farm.

farm·land *noun* land used or suitable for farming.

farm·stead *noun* a farm and its buildings regarded as a unit.

farm system *noun* a system of farm teams.

farm team *noun* *N Amer.* (also **farm club**) a minor-league sports team affiliated with and serving as a source of players for a major-league team.

farm wife *noun* a farmer's wife.

farm·yard *noun* a yard or enclosure attached to a farmhouse.

Farn·bor·ough /ˈfɑrnbərə/ a town in S England, in Hampshire; pop. (est. 2002) 54,700. Noted as a centre of aviation.

Far·nese /fɑrˈneisi/ **1 Ales·san·dro**, see PAUL III. **2 Ales·san·dro, Duke of Parma** (1545–92), Italian general. While in the service of Philip II of Spain, he acted as Governor General of the Netherlands (1578–92); he captured Antwerp in 1585, securing the southern Netherlands for Spain.

Farn·ham /ˈfɑrnəm/ a town in south central Quebec, located on the Rivière Yamaska, southeast of Montreal; pop. (2001) 7,747. [*Farnham* in Surrey, England]

Far North *noun* (in Canada) the Arctic and sub-Arctic regions of the country.

faro /ˈferoʊ/ *noun* a gambling card game in which bets are placed on the order of appearance of the cards. [French *pharaon* PHARAOH (said to have been the name of the king of hearts)]

Faroe Islands *var. of* FAEROE ISLANDS.

Faro·ese *var. of* FAEROESE.

far-off *adjective* remote; distant (*a far-off battlefield*).

fa·rouche /fəˈruːʃ/ *adjective* sullen, shy. □ **fa·rouche·ly** *adverb* [French from Old French *faroche, forache* from medieval Latin *forasticus* from Latin *foras* out of doors]

Far·ouk I /fɑˈruːk/ (also **Far·uk I**) (1920–65), king of Egypt 1936–52. His defeat in the Arab–Israeli conflict of 1948, together with the general corruption of his reign, led to a military coup and his forced abdication in 1952.

far-out *adjective* *slang* **1** unconventional; avant-garde. **2** excellent.

far·rago /fəˈrɒgoʊ/ *noun* (*pl.* **-ragos** or **-ragoes**) a medley or hodgepodge. □ **far·ra·gin·ous** /-ˈradʒənəs/ *adjective* [Latin *farrago farraginis* mixed, fodder from *far* grain]

far-reaching *adjective* **1** extending widely. **2** having important consequences or implications.

Far·rell /ˈferəl/ **James Thom·as** (1904–79), US novelist, best known for his naturalistic *Studs Lonigan* trilogy, recounting the story of a young Catholic man in Chicago after the First World War.

far·rier /ˈferiər/ *noun* **1** a smith who shoes horses. **2** a person who treats the disease and injuries of horses. □ **far·ri·ery** *noun* [Old French *ferrier* from Latin *ferrarius* from *ferrum* iron, horseshoe]

far·row ● *noun* a litter of pigs. ● *transitive & intransitive verb* (of a sow) give birth to (pigs). □ **far·row·ing** *noun* [Old English *fearh, færh* pig]

far-seeing *adjective* having shrewd judgment and an ability to predict and plan for future eventualities.

Farsi /ˈfɑrsi/ *noun* the modern Persian language. [Persian: compare PARSI]

far-sighted *adjective* **1** having foresight, prudent. **2** esp. *N Amer.* able to see distant things more clearly than those close by. □ **far-sighted·ness** *noun*

fart *coarse slang* ● *intransitive verb* **1** emit intestinal gas from the anus. **2** (foll. by *about, around*) waste time on silly or trivial things. ● *noun* **1** an emission of intestinal gas from the anus. **2** an annoying or unpleasant person. [Old English (recorded in *feorting* verbal noun) from Germanic]

far·ther *var. of* FURTHER *adverb* 1, *adjective* 1.

far·thest *var. of* FURTHEST.

far·thing /ˈfɑrðɪŋ/ *noun* **1** *hist.* (in the UK) a coin and monetary unit worth a quarter of an old penny. **2** the least possible amount (*it doesn't matter a farthing*). [Old English *feorthing* from *feortha* fourth]

far·thin·gale /ˈfɑrðɪŋˌgeil/ *noun* *hist.* a framework of hoops or a hooped petticoat worn to expand a woman's skirt. [earlier *vardingale, verd-* from French *verdugale* from Spanish *verdugado* from *verdugo* rod]

fart·lek /ˈfɑrtlek/ *noun* *Athletics* a method of training for middle- and long-distance running, mixing fast with slow work. [Swedish from *fart* speed + *lek* play]

Far·uk I *var. of* FAROUK I.

Far West *noun* **1** *hist.* (in Canada) the regions west of Upper Canada, sequentially Manitoba, Saskatchewan, Alberta, and British Columbia, as settlement advanced westward. **2** (in Canada) the area west of the

Prairies. **3** the region of the United States from the Great Plains to the Rockies and West Coast.

FAS *abbreviation* FETAL ALCOHOL SYNDROME.

fas·ces /ˈfasiːz/ *plural noun* **1** *Rom. Hist.* a bundle of elm or birch rods with a projecting axe blade, carried by a lictor as a symbol of a magistrate's power. **2** *hist.* such an object adopted by Mussolini as an emblem of the Italian Fascist Party. [Latin, pl. of *fascis* bundle]

fas·cia /ˈfeɪʃə, ˈfa-, ˈfaʃiə/ *noun* (*pl.* **fas·cias**) **1** *Archit.* **a** a flat horizontal band of wood, aluminum, etc. around the edge of a roof, to which eavestroughs are attached. **b** a long flat surface between mouldings on the architrave in classical architecture. **2** *Brit.* the upper part of a shopfront on which is written the proprietor's name etc. **3** (also **facia**) *esp. Brit.* **a** the instrument panel or dashboard of a motor vehicle. **b** any similar panel or plate for operating machinery. **4** /ˈfaʃə/ (*pl.* **fas·ciae** /-ʃiiː/) *Anat.* a thin sheath of fibrous tissue. □ **fa·scial** *adjective* [Latin, = band, door frame, etc.]

fas·ci·at·ed /ˈfaʃiˌeɪtəd/ *adjective Bot.* (of contiguous parts) compressed or growing into one. □ **fas·ci·a·tion** /-ˈeɪʃən/ *noun* [Latin *fasciatus* past participle of *fasciare* swathe (as FASCIA)]

fas·cicle /ˈfasɪkəl/ *noun* **1** (also **fas·ci·cule** /-ˌkjuːl/) a separately published instalment of a book, usu. not complete in itself. **2** (also **fas·ci·cu·lus** /faˈsɪkjʊləs/ (*pl.* **-li**)) *Anat. & Biol.* a bundle of structures, such as nerve or muscle fibres or conducting vessels in plants. □ **fas·cicu·late** /-ˈsɪkjʊlət/ *adjective* **fas·cicu·la·tion** /-ˈleɪʃən/ *noun* [Latin *fasciculus* bundle, diminutive of *fascis*: see FASCES]

fasci·itis /faʃiˈaɪtɪs/ *noun Med.* inflammation of the fascia of a muscle etc.

fas·cin·ate /ˈfasəˌneɪt/ *transitive verb* **1** capture the interest of; attract irresistibly. **2** deprive of the power of escape or resistance; transfix. □ **fas·cin·at·ed** *adjective* **fas·cin·at·ing** *adjective* **fas·cin·at·ing·ly** *adverb* **fas·cin·a·tion** *noun* **fas·cin·ator** *noun* [Latin *fascinare* from *fascinum* spell]

fas·cine /faˈsiːn, fə-/ *noun* a bundle of rods, sticks, or plastic pipes bound together, used in construction or military operations for filling in marshy ground or other obstacles and for strengthening the sides of embankments, trenches, or ditches, etc. [French from Latin *fascina* from *fascis* bundle: see FASCES]

Fas·cism /ˈfaʃɪzəm/ *noun* **1** *hist.* the totalitarian principles and organization of the extreme right-wing nationalist movement in Italy (1922–43). **2** (also **fascism**) any similar nationalist and authoritarian movement, esp. German National Socialism. **3** (also **fascism**) *derogatory* extreme right-wing, authoritarian, or intolerant views or practices. □ **Fas·cist** *noun & adjective* (also **fascist**). **Fas·cis·tic** /-ˈʃɪstɪk/ *adjective* (also **fascistic**) [Italian *fascismo* from *fascio* bundle, political group, from Latin *fascis* bundle: see FASCES]

fash·ion /ˈfaʃən/ ● *noun* **1** the current popular custom or style, esp. in dress or social conduct (also *attributive*: *fashion designer*; *fashion show*). **2** a manner or style of doing something (*in a peculiar fashion*). **3** (in *combination*) in a specified manner (*walk crab-fashion*). **4** shape; appearance; characteristic form. **5** fashionable society (*a woman of fashion*). ● *transitive verb* make into a particular or the required form. □ **after** (or **in**) **a fashion** as well as is practicable, though not satisfactorily. **in** (or **out of**) **fashion** fashionable (or not fashionable) at the time in question. □ **fash·ion·er** *noun* **fash·iony** *adjective* [Old French *façon*, from Latin *factio -onis* from *facere* fact- do, make]

fash·ion·able *adjective* **1** following, suited to, or influenced by the current fashion. **2** characteristic of or favoured by those who are leaders of social fashion (*a fashionable resort*). □ **fash·ion·abil·ity** *noun* **fash·ion·able·ness** *noun* **fash·ion·ably** *adverb*

fashion-forward *adjective* on the cutting edge of fashion.

fashion house *noun* a business establishment where high-quality clothes are designed, displayed, and sold.

fashion·ista /faʃənˈiːstə/ *noun* (*pl.* **-istas**) **1** a person employed in the creation or promotion of haute couture, as a designer, photographer, model, etc. **2** a devotee of the fashion industry and its events; a person who wears high-fashion clothing. [FASHION + *ista*, apparently after SANDINISTA etc.]

fashion plate *noun* **1** a person who consistently dresses in the current fashion. **2** a picture, esp. in a magazine, showing a fashion in clothes.

fashion statement *noun* **1** an item of clothing etc. worn to make a conscious impression that one is fashionable. **2** an act of doing this.

fashion victim *noun* a slavish follower of trends in fashion.

Fass·bin·der /ˈfas₁bɪndər/ **Rai·ner Wer·ner** (1946–82), German film director. He was influenced by Brecht, Marx, and Freud, and is remembered for his films about postwar West German society, such as *The Bitter Tears of Petra von Kant* (1972) and the allegorical *The Marriage of Maria Braun* (1979).

fast¹ /fast/ ● *adjective* **1 a** rapid, quick-moving. **b** happening quickly (*a fast trip*). **2** capable of high speed (*a fast car*). **3** enabling or causing or intended for high speed (*a fast road*; *fast lane*). **4** (of a clock etc.) showing a time ahead of the correct time. **5** *Sport* (of a racetrack, ice surface, tennis court, field, etc.) producing or allowing quick movement. **6 a** (of a photographic film) very sensitive to light; needing only a short exposure. **b** (of a lens) having a large aperture. **7 a** firmly fixed or attached. **b** secure; firmly established (*a fast friendship*). **8** (of a colour) not fading in light or when washed. **9** (of a person, lifestyle, etc.) immoral, dissipated. ● *adverb* **1** quickly; in quick succession. **2** firmly, fixedly, tightly, securely (*stand fast*; *eyes fast shut*). **3** soundly, completely (*fast asleep*). **4** in a dissipated manner; extravagantly, unconventionally (*live fast, die young*). **5** close, immediately (*fast on their heels*). □ **pull a fast one** *informal* try to deceive or gain an unfair advantage. [Old English *fæst* from Germanic]

fast² /fast/ ● *intransitive verb* abstain from all or some kinds of food or drink, esp. as a religious observance or in preparation for medical tests, surgery, etc. ● *noun* an act or period of fasting. [Old Norse *fasta* from Germanic (as FAST¹)]

fast and furious ● *adverb* **1** rapidly. **2** eagerly, uproariously. ● *adjective* **1** rapid, fast-paced (*a fast and furious hockey game*). **2** (of a party, music, etc.) lively, energetic.

fast·back *noun* **1** a car with the rear sloping continuously down to the bumper. **2** such a rear.

fast·ball *noun* **1** a baseball pitch thrown at or near a pitcher's maximum speed. **2** *Cdn* = FAST PITCH.

fast break *noun* (in basketball, football, etc.) a swift attack from a defensive position (often *attributive*: *fast-break offence*).

fast-breeder *noun* (also **fast-breeder reactor**) a reactor using fast neutrons to produce the same fissile material as it uses.

fast buck *noun* see BUCK².

fas·ten /ˈfasən/ *verb* **1** *transitive* **a** make or become fixed or secure. **b** secure as a means of connection (a clasp, button, tie, etc.). **2** *transitive* lock securely; shut in. **3** *transitive* (foll. by *on*, *upon*) direct (a look, thoughts, etc.) fixedly or intently. **4** *transitive* (foll. by *on*, *upon*) fix (a nickname or imputation etc.). **5** *intransitive* (foll. by *on*, *upon*) **a** take hold of (*fasten on an idea*). **b** single out (*looking for someone to blame, he fastened on me*). **6** *intransitive* become closed or attached (*this dress fastens in the back*). □ **fas·ten·er** *noun* [Old English *fæstnian* from Germanic]

fas·ten·ing /ˈfasənɪŋ/ *noun* a device that fastens something; a fastener.

fast food *noun* food that is wholly or partially prepared for quick sale or serving, esp. in a snack bar or restaurant (also *attributive*: *fast-food chain*).

fast-forward ● *noun* **1** a control on a tape or video player for advancing the tape rapidly. **2** = CUE¹ *noun* 3. ● *adjective* designating such a control. ● *verb* **1** *transitive* advance (a tape) rapidly, sometimes while simultaneously playing it at high speed. **2** *intransitive* move speedily forward in time when considering or dealing with something over a period (*the text fast-forwards to 1990*).

fas·tidi·ous /faˈstɪdiəs/ *adjective* **1** scrupulous or over-scrupulous in matters of taste, cleanliness, propriety, etc.; fussy. **2** easily disgusted; squeamish. □ **fas·tidi·ous·ly** *adverb* **fas·tidi·ous·ness** *noun* [Latin *fastidiosus* from *fastidium* loathing]

fas·tigi·ate /faˈstɪdʒiət/ *adjective Bot.* (of a tree etc.) having the branches more or less parallel to the main stem. [Latin *fastigium* gable top]

fast lane *noun* **1** a traffic lane on a highway etc. used by high-speed vehicles as a driving lane and by other vehicles as a passing lane. **2** a means or route of rapid progress. **3** a hectic, highly pressured lifestyle.

fast·ness *noun* **1** a stronghold or fortress. **2** the state of being secure. **3** the capacity of a dye to remain permanent and not fade or wash out.

fast neutron *noun* a neutron with high kinetic energy, esp. one released in nuclear fission and not slowed by a moderator etc.

fast-paced *adjective* occurring or led at a rapid pace.

fast pitch *noun* N Amer. a variety of the game of softball, featuring fast underhand pitching.

fast reactor *noun* a nuclear reactor in which fission is caused mainly by fast neutrons.

fast-talk *verb* esp. N Amer. informal ● *transitive verb* persuade by rapid or deceitful talk. ● *noun* (**fast talk**) such talk. □ **fast talker** *noun* **fast-talking** *adjective*

fast track ● *noun* a route, course, method, etc., which provides for more rapid results than usual (*on the fast track for promotion*) (also attributive: *fast-track executive*). ● *verb* (**fast-track**) **1** *transitive* give priority to; treat as urgent (*fast-track the proposal*). **2** *intransitive* advance quickly (*fast-track through the ranks*). ☐ **fast-tracker** *noun*

fast-twitch *adjective* (of a muscle fibre) contracting rapidly, thereby providing strength rather than endurance (*compare* SLOW-TWITCH).

fast water *noun N Amer.* quick-moving river water flowing over rapids.

fat ● *noun* **1 a** any of a group of natural esters of glycerol and various fatty acids found in the adipose tissue of animals and in some plants. **b** animal or vegetable tissue containing this. **c** fat from animals or plants, purified and used for cooking. **2** excessive presence of fat in a person or animal; corpulence. **3** excess; surplus (*trim the fat in the budget*). **4** *Cdn* (*Nfld*) sealskins and the attached blubber. ● *adjective* (**fat·ter**, **fat·test**) **1** (of a person or animal) having excessive fat; corpulent. **2** (of an animal) plump; well-fed. **3** containing much fat. **4** greasy, oily. **5** (of land or resources) fertile, rich; yielding abundantly. **6 a** thick (*a fat book; fat tires*). **b** substantial as an asset or opportunity (*a fat cheque; a fat job in the civil service*). **7 a** (of coal) bituminous. **b** (of clay etc.) sticky. **8** *informal ironic* very little; not much (*fat chance; a fat lot*). ● *transitive & intransitive verb* (**fat·ted**, **fat·ting**) make or become fat. ☐ **the fat is in the fire** trouble is imminent. **kill the fatted calf** celebrate, esp. at a prodigal's return (Luke 15). **live off** (or **on**) **the fat of the land** have the best of everything. ☐ **fat·less** *adjective* **fatly** *adverb* **fat·ness** *noun* **fat·tish** *adjective* [Old English *fæt* (adj.), *fættian* (v.) from Germanic]

Fatah /ˈfatə/ *noun* (also **Al Fatah**) a Palestinian political organization, founded in Cairo in 1957 by Yasser Arafat and fellow Palestinians, which defined its goal as the liberation of Palestine by armed struggle, now the dominant faction of the P.L.O. [Arabic, lit. = 'victory']

fatal /ˈfeitəl/ *adjective* **1** causing or ending in death (*a fatal accident*). **2** (often foll. by *to*) destructive; ruinous; ending in disaster (*was fatal to their chances; made a fatal mistake*). **3** fateful, decisive. ☐ **fatal·ly** *adverb* [Old French *fatal* or Latin *fatalis* (as FATE)]

fatal·ism /ˈfeitəˌlizəm/ *noun* **1** the belief that all events are predetermined and therefore inevitable. **2** a submissive attitude to events as being inevitable. ☐ **fatal·ist** *noun* **fatal·is·tic** *adjective* **fatal·is·tic·ally** *adverb*

fatal·ity /feiˈtaliti, fə-/ *noun* (*pl.* **-ities**) **1 a** an occurrence of death by accident or in war etc. **b** a person killed in this way. **2** deadliness (*this disease has a high fatality*).

Fata Morgana /ˈfatə mɔrˈganə/ *noun* a mirage. [Italian, lit. 'fairy Morgan', orig. referring to a mirage seen in the Strait of Messina between Italy and Sicily and attributed to MORGAN LE FAY, whose legend and reputation were carried to Sicily by Norman settlers]

fat·back *noun N Amer.* a strip of fat and fat meat, usu. salt-cured, from the upper part of a side of pork.

fat cat *noun slang derogatory* a wealthy person, esp. a complacent one who lives off the proceeds of other people's labour (also *attributive: fat-cat lawyers*).

Fat City a derogatory nickname for Ottawa. [with reference to its cushy and stable bureaucratic economy: see FAT *adjective* 6b]

fate ● *noun* **1** a power regarded as predetermining events unalterably. **2 a** the future regarded as determined by such a power. **b** an individual's appointed lot. **c** the ultimate condition or end of a person or thing (*that sealed our fate*). **3** death, destruction. ● *transitive verb* (usu. in *passive*) preordain (*was fated to win*). ☐ **fate worse than death** see DEATH. [Italian *fato* & Latin *fatum* that which is spoken, from *fari* speak]

fated *adjective* **1** decreed, determined or controlled by fate. **2** doomed to destruction.

fate·ful *adjective* having far-reaching and typically disastrous consequences or implications. ☐ **fate·ful·ly** *adverb* **fate·ful·ness** *noun*

Fates, the *Gk Myth* the three goddesses who presided over the birth and life of humankind. Each person was thought of as a spindle, around which the three Fates (Clotho, Lachesis, and Atropos) would spin the thread of human destiny.

fat farm *noun informal esp. N Amer.* a residential establishment offering overweight people a program of dieting and exercise.

fat-free *adjective* (of a food) not containing animal or vegetable fats.

fat·head *noun informal* a stupid person. ☐ **fat·head·ed** *adjective* **fat·head·ed·ness** *noun*

fat hen *noun* the white goosefoot, *Chenopodium album*.

fath·er ● *noun* **1 a** a man in relation to a child or children born from his fertilization of an ovum. **b** a man who has continuous care of a child, esp. by adoption or remarriage. **2** any male animal in relation to its offspring. **3** (usu. in *pl.*) a progenitor or forefather. **4** (also **Father**) an originator, designer, or early leader. **5** (**Fathers**) (also **Fathers of**

the Church) early Christian theologians whose writings are regarded as especially authoritative. **6** (also **Father**) (often as a title or form of address) a priest. **7** (**the Father**) (in Christian belief) the first person of the Trinity. **8** (**Father**) a venerable person, esp. as a title in personifications (*Father Time*). **9** (usu. in *pl.*) the leading men or elders in a city or state (*city fathers*). ● *transitive verb* **1** beget; be the father of. **2** behave as a father towards. **3** bring into existence; originate (a scheme etc.). **4** appear as or admit that one is the father or originator of. ☐ **father·hood** *noun* **father·less** *adjective* **father·less·ness** *noun* **father·like** *adjective & adverb* [Old English *fæder* with many Germanic cognates: related to Latin *pater*, Greek *patēr*]

Father Christmas *noun Brit.* = SANTA CLAUS.

father figure *noun* an older man who is respected like a father; a trusted leader.

father-in-law *noun* (*pl.* **fathers-in-law**) the father of one's spouse.

father·land *noun* one's native country.

father·ly *adjective* **1** like or characteristic of a father in affection, care, etc. (*fatherly concern*). **2** of or proper to a father. ☐ **father·li·ness** *noun*

Father of Confederation *noun Cdn* any of the delegates who represented colonies of British North America at the Charlottetown and Quebec Conferences or the London Conference, which led to Confederation in 1867.

Father's Day *noun* a day (usu. the third Sunday in June) established for a special tribute to fathers.

Father Time *noun* see TIME *noun* 3b.

fathom /ˈfaðəm/ ● *noun* (*pl.* often **fathom** when prec. by a number) a measure of six feet (1.8 m), esp. used in taking depth soundings. ● *transitive verb* **1** grasp or comprehend (a problem or difficulty). **2** measure the depth of (water) with a sounding line. ☐ **fathom·able** *adjective* **fathom·less** *adjective* **fathom·less·ly** *adverb* [Old English *fæthm* outstretched arms, from Germanic]

Fathom Five National Marine Park a marine park in SW Ontario, situated in Georgian Bay, off the tip of the Bruce Peninsula. [so called with reference to its depth of *five fathoms* (9 m)]

fa·tigue /fəˈtiːg/ ● *noun* **1 a** extreme tiredness after physical or mental exertion. **b** an activity that causes fatigue. **c** a state of inurement or indifference brought about by excessive appeals to one's generosity, compassion, etc. (*donor fatigue*). **2** weakness in materials, esp. metal, caused by repeated variations of stress. **3** a reduction in the efficiency of a muscle, organ, etc., after prolonged activity. **4** (in *pl.*) = ARMY FATIGUES. **5 a** a non-military duty in the army, often as a punishment. **b** (in full **fatigue-party**) a group of soldiers ordered to do fatigues. **c** (in *pl.*) clothing worn for such a duty. ● *transitive verb* (**fa·tigues**, **fa·tigued**, **fa·tiguing**) cause fatigue in; tire, exhaust. [French *fatigue*, *fatiguer* from Latin *fatigare* tire out]

Fat·iha /ˈfatiːˌhə/ *noun* (also **Fat·ihah**) the short first sura of the Quran, used by Muslims as a prayer. [Arabic *fātiha* opening, from *fataha* to open]

Fat·ima[1] /ˈfatimə/ (AD *c.*606–32), youngest daughter of the prophet Muhammad, and wife of the fourth caliph, Ali (d.661). The descendants of Muhammad trace their lineage through her, and she is revered esp. by Shiite Muslims as the mother of the imams Hasan (624–80) and Husayn (626–80).

Fat·ima[2] /ˈfatimə/ a village in west central Portugal, northeast of Lisbon; pop. (est. 2002) 10,400. It became a centre of Roman Catholic pilgrimage after the reported sighting in the village in 1917 of the Virgin Mary.

Fat·imid /ˈfatimid/ ● *noun* a descendant of Fatima, the daughter of Muhammad; in particular, a member of an Arabian dynasty claiming descent from her which ruled in parts of northern Africa, Egypt, and Syria from 909 to 1171. ● *adjective* of or relating to the Fatimids.

fat·ling *noun archaic* a calf, lamb, or other young animal fattened for slaughter.

fat lip *noun* a lip swollen from being punched.

fats *noun slang offensive* (as a term of address) a fat person.

fatso *noun* (*pl.* **-sos**) *slang offensive* a fat person. [prob. from FAT or FATS]

fat-soluble *adjective* soluble in fats or oils.

fat·stock *noun Brit.* livestock fattened for slaughter.

fat·ten *verb* **1** *transitive* make fat (esp. animals for slaughter). **2** *intransitive* grow or become fat. ☐ **fat·ten·er** *noun*

fat·ten·ing *adjective* (of foods) high in calories.

fatty ● *adjective* (**fat·ti·er**, **fat·ti·est**) **1** consisting of or containing fat; adipose. **2** marked by abnormal deposition of fat, esp. in fatty degeneration. **3** like fat; oily, greasy. ● *noun* (*pl.* **-ties**) *slang offensive* a fat person (esp. as a nickname). □ **fat·ti·ness** *noun*

fatty acid *noun* any of a class of organic compounds consisting of a hydrocarbon chain and a terminal carboxyl group, esp. those occurring as constituents of lipids.

fatty degeneration *noun* tissue degeneration, e.g. of the liver or heart, marked by the deposition of fat in the cells of the tissue.

fatu·ous /ˈfatʃʊəs/ *adjective* vacantly silly; idiotic. □ **fatu·ity** /fəˈtʃuːɪti/ *noun* (*pl.* **-ities**). **fatu·ous·ly** *adverb* **fatu·ous·ness** *noun* [Latin *fatuus* foolish]

fatwa /ˈfatwə/ *noun* (in Islamic countries) an authoritative ruling on a religious matter given by a mufti. [Arabic *fatwa*]

fau·bourg /ˈfoːbʊr, -bʊrg/ *noun* a suburb, esp. of Paris. [French: compare medieval Latin *falsus burgus* not the city proper]

fau·ces /ˈfɔːsiːz/ *plural noun* the cavity at the back of the mouth from which the larynx and the pharynx open out. □ **fau·cial** /ˈfɔːʃəl/ *adjective* [Latin, = throat]

fau·cet *noun N Amer.* = TAP¹ 1. □ **fau·cet·ry** *noun* [Old French *fausset* (denoting a tap for drawing liquor from a container) from Provençal *falset* from *falsar* to bore]

Faulk·ner /ˈfɔknr/ **Wil·liam (Cuth·bert)** (also **Falk·ner**) (1897–1962), US novelist. His works deal with the history and legends of the southern US, depicting a society in decline; they include *The Sound and the Fury* (1929), *Light in August* (1932) and *Absalom! Absalom!* (1936); he was awarded the Nobel Prize for literature in 1949. □ **Faulk·ner·ian** *noun & adjective*

fault ● *noun* **1** a defect or imperfection of character or of structure, appearance, etc. **2** a transgression, offence, or thing wrongly done. **3** responsibility for wrongdoing, error, etc. (*it will be your own fault*). **4** a defect regarded as the cause of something wrong (*the fault lies in the teaching methods*). **5** a break or other defect in an electric circuit. **6** *Geol.* an extended break in the continuity of strata or a vein. **7 a** *Tennis etc.* a service of the ball not in accordance with the rules, esp. one which falls outside prescribed limits. **b** (in show jumping) a penalty point incurred for an error in performance. ● *verb* **1** *transitive* find fault with; blame. **2** *transitive Geol.* break the continuity of (strata or a vein). **3** *intransitive* commit a fault. **4** *intransitive Geol.* show a fault. □ **at fault** guilty; to blame. **find fault** (often foll. by *with*) make an adverse criticism; complain. **to a fault** (usu. of a commendable quality etc.) excessively (*generous to a fault*). [Middle English *faut(e)* from Old French, ultimately from Latin *fallere* FAIL]

fault-finding *noun* continual criticism. □ **fault-finder** *noun*

fault·less *adjective* without fault; free from defect or error. □ **fault·less·ly** *adverb* **fault·less·ness** *noun*

fault line *noun Geol.* **1** the line of intersection of a fault with the earth's surface or with a horizontal plane. **2** a point where two strongly opposed forces, ideologies, etc. conflict, with the potential for great divisiveness and damage (*trials often reveal fault lines in the social order*).

fault plane *noun Geol.* the surface of a fault fracture along which the rock masses on either side have been displaced.

fault-tolerant *adjective Computing* of or relating to a computer system that is capable of providing either full functionality or reduced functionality after a failure has occurred. □ **fault tolerance** *noun*

faulty *adjective* (**fault·i·er**, **fault·i·est**) having faults; imperfect, defective. □ **fault·i·ly** *adverb* **fault·i·ness** *noun*

fault zone *noun Geol.* a region bounded by major faults, within which subordinate faults may be arranged variably or systematically.

faun *noun* one of a class of Latin rural deities with a human face and torso and a goat's horns, legs, and tail, identified with the Greek satyrs. [Old French *faune* or Latin FAUNUS]

fauna *noun* **1** the animal life of a particular region, geological period, or environment. **2** a treatise on or list of this. □ **faun·al** *adjective* **faun·ist** *noun* **faun·is·tic** *adjective* [modern Latin from the name of a rural goddess, sister of Faunus]

Fau·nus *Rom. Myth* an ancient Italian pastoral god, grandson of Saturn. His association with wooded places caused him to be identified with Pan.

Fauré /ˈfɔreɪ/ **Gab·riel (Ur·bain)** (1845–1924), French composer and organist. He is best known for his lyrical songs, some incorporated in cycles such as *La Bonne chanson* (1891–2), and for his *Messe de requiem* (1887) for solo voices, choir, orchestra, and organ.

Faust /ˈfaʊst/ (also **Faust·us** /ˈfaʊstəs/) (died *c.*1540), German astronomer and necromancer. Reputed to have sold his soul to the

Devil, he became the subject of many legends, and is the hero of works by Goethe, Gounod, and Mann. □ **Faust·ian** *adjective*

Faustian bargain /ˈfaʊstɪən/ *noun* (also **Faustian pact**) an arrangement in which one party sacrifices its values in return for material gain, knowledge, or power.

faute de mieux /ˌfoːt də ˈmjuː/ *adverb* for lack of a better alternative. [French]

Fauve /fəʊv/ *noun* (also **fauve**) any of a group of French artists, active between 1905 and 1910, who painted in very bright colours mainly as a reaction against Impressionism. □ **Fauv·ism** *noun* **Fauv·ist** *noun & adjective* [French *fauve* wild beast]

faux /fəʊ/ *adjective* false, imitation (*a faux fur hood*). [French, = false]

faux pas /fəʊ ˈpɒ/ *noun* (*pl.* same /ˈpɒz/) **1** a tactless mistake; a blunder. **2** a social indiscretion. [French, = false step]

fava bean /ˈfaːvə/ *noun* (also **faba bean** /ˈfabə/) a kind of bean, *Vicia faba*, with pods containing large edible flat seeds. [Italian from Latin *faba* bean]

fave *noun & adjective slang* = FAVOURITE. [abbreviation]

fa·vela /fəˈvelə/ *noun* a Brazilian shack, slum, or shantytown. [Portuguese]

fa·vour (also **favor**) ● *noun* **1** an act of kindness beyond what is due or usual (*did it as a favour*). **2** esteem, liking, approval, goodwill; friendly regard (*gained their favour*; *look with favour on*). **3** partiality; too lenient or generous treatment. **4** a small gift, such as a noisemaker or paper hat, often given to guests at a party. **5** a thing given or worn as a mark of favour or support, e.g. a badge or a knot of ribbons. **6** (usu. in *pl.*) sexual relations, esp. as offered by a woman. ● *transitive verb* **1** regard or treat with favour or partiality. **2** give support or approval to; promote, prefer. **3** facilitate, help (a process etc.) (*the wind favoured their sailing at dawn*). **4** tend to confirm (an idea or theory). **5** (foll. by *with*) oblige (*favour me with a reply*). **6** avoid putting too much strain on (an injured limb etc.) **7** resemble in features (*she favours her mother*). □ **find favour** be liked; prove acceptable. **in favour 1** meeting with approval. **2** (foll. by *of*) **a** in support of. **b** to the advantage of. **in one's favour** to a person's advantage. **out of favour** lacking approval. [Old French from Latin *favor -oris* from *favēre* show kindness to]

fa·vour·able *adjective* (also **fa·vor·able**) **1** commendatory, approving. **2** giving consent (*a favourable answer*). **3** promising, auspicious, satisfactory (*a favourable recovery*). **4** (often foll. by *to*) helpful, suitable (*legislation favourable to our interests*). **5** well-disposed; propitious. □ **fa·vour·able·ness** *noun* **fa·vour·ably** *adverb*

fa·voured *adjective* (also **fa·vored**) **1** treated with preference or partiality (*the favoured daughter*). **2** having special advantages (*the favoured caste*).

fa·vour·ite (also **fa·vor·ite**) ● *adjective* preferred to all others (*my favourite book*). ● *noun* **1** a specially favoured person or thing. **2** *Sport* a competitor thought most likely to win. [obsolete French *favorit* from Italian *favorito* past participle of *favorire* favour]

favourite son *noun* **1** *N Amer.* a person in the public eye who has endeared himself particularly to his province or state, or hometown. **2** *US* a person preferred as the presidential candidate by delegates from the candidate's home state.

fa·vour·it·ism *noun* (also **fa·vor·it·ism**) the unfair favouring of one person or group at the expense of another.

Fawkes, Guy (1570–1606), English conspirator, who was hanged for his part in the Gunpowder Plot.

fawn¹ ● *noun* **1** a young deer in its first year. **2** a light yellowish brown. ● *adjective* of a light yellowish-brown colour. ● *intransitive verb* (of a deer) bring forth (young). □ **in fawn** (of a deer) pregnant. [Old French *faon* etc., ultimately from Latin *fetus* offspring: compare FETUS]

fawn² *intransitive verb* **1** (often foll. by *on, over, upon*) (of a person) behave in an obsequious manner; affect a cringing pleasure or fondness. **2** (of an animal, esp. a dog) show affection or pleasure. □ **fawn·ing** *adjective* **fawn·ing·ly** *adverb* [Old English *fagnian, fægnian* (as FAIN)]

fax ● *noun* **1** (often *attributive*) production of an exact copy of a document etc. by electronic scanning and transmission of the resulting data. **2 a** a copy produced or message sent by this. **b** (also **fax machine**) a machine for transmitting and receiving these. ● *transitive verb* **1** transmit (a document) in this way. **2** contact (someone) by such means. □ **fax·able** *adjective* [abbreviation of FACSIMILE]

fax-back *noun* a service which faxes a document automatically to a user who enters a fax number into a database by telephone or email.

fay *noun literary* a fairy. [Old French *fae, faie* from Latin *fata* (pl.) the Fates]

faze *transitive verb* (often as **fazed** *adjective*) *informal* disconcert, perturb, disorientate. [var. of *feeze* drive off, from Old English *fēsian*, of unknown origin]

FBI *abbreviation* (in the US) Federal Bureau of Investigation.

FC *abbreviation* (in British names) Football Club.

FCC *abbreviation* 1 (in Canada) Farm Credit Corporation. 2 (in the US) Federal Communications Commission.

FD *abbreviation* 1 *Cdn* forest district. 2 Defender of the Faith. [sense 2 from Latin *Fidei Defensor*]

FDA *abbreviation* (in the US) Food and Drug Administration.

FDDI *abbreviation* fibre distributed data interface, a communications, cabling, and hardware standard for high-speed optical-fibre networks.

Fe *symbol Chem.* the element iron.

feal·ty /ˈfiːəlti/ *noun* (*pl.* **-ties**) 1 *hist.* **a** a feudal tenant's or vassal's fidelity to a lord. **b** an acknowledgement of this. 2 allegiance. [Old French *feaulté* from Latin *fidelitas -tatis* from *fidelis* faithful, from *fides* faith]

fear ● *noun* 1 an unpleasant emotion caused by exposure to danger, expectation of pain, etc. 2 a cause of fear (*all fears removed*). 3 (often foll. by *of*) dread or fearful respect (towards) (*had a fear of God*). 4 anxiety for the safety of (*in fear of their lives*). 5 danger; likelihood (of something unwelcome) (*there is little fear of failure*). ● *verb* 1 **a** *transitive* feel fear about or towards (a person or thing). **b** *intransitive* feel fear. 2 *intransitive* (foll. by *for*) feel anxiety or apprehension about (*feared for my life*). 3 *transitive* apprehend; have uneasy expectation of (*fear the worst*). 4 *transitive* (usu. foll. by *that* + clause) apprehend with fear or regret (*I fear that you are wrong*). 5 *transitive* **a** (foll. by *to* + infin.) hesitate. **b** (foll. by verbal noun) shrink from; be apprehensive about (*he feared meeting his ex-wife*). 6 *transitive* show reverence towards. □ **for fear of** (or **that**) to avoid the risk of (or that). **never fear** there is no danger of that. **without fear or favour** impartially. [Old English from Germanic]

fear·ful *adjective* 1 (usu. foll. by *of*, or *that* + clause) afraid. 2 terrible, awful. 3 *informal* extremely unwelcome or unpleasant (*a fearful fight*). □ **fear·ful·ly** *adverb* **fear·ful·ness** *noun*

fear·less *adjective* without fear; courageous, brave. □ **fear·less·ly** *adverb* **fear·less·ness** *noun*

fear·some *adjective* 1 frightening, dreadful. 2 inspiring awe or admiration (*fearsome dedication*). □ **fear·some·ly** *adverb* **fear·some·ness** *noun*

feas·ibil·ity /ˌfiːzəˈbɪlɪti/ *noun* the state or degree of being feasible.

feasibility study *noun* a study of the practicability of a proposed project.

feas·ible /ˈfiːzəbəl/ *adjective* 1 practicable; easily or conveniently done. 2 likely, probable (*a feasible explanation*). ¶ Although there is a tradition of opposition to sense 2, it is widely used and is considered acceptable. □ **feas·ibly** *adverb* [Old French *faisible* from *fais-* stem of *faire* from Latin *facere* do, make]

feast ● *noun* 1 **a** a large or sumptuous meal. **b** a banquet for many guests, often with entertainment (*a wedding feast*). 2 a gratification to the senses or mind. 3 **a** an annual religious celebration. **b** a day dedicated to a particular saint. ● *verb* 1 *intransitive* **a** partake of a feast; eat and drink sumptuously (*feasted on seafood*). **b** enjoy; take pleasure in (*feast on movies*). 2 *transitive* **a** regale. **b** pass (time) in feasting. □ **feast one's eyes on** take pleasure in beholding. **feast or famine** either too much or too little. □ **feast·er** *noun* [Old French *feste*, *fester* from Latin *festus* joyous]

feast day *noun* a day on which a feast (esp. a religious one) is held.

Feast of Tabernacles *noun* = SUKKOT.

Feast of the Body and Blood of Christ *noun* = CORPUS CHRISTI[2].

feat *noun* a noteworthy act or achievement. [Old French *fait*, *fet* (as FACT)]

feath·er ● *noun* 1 any of the appendages growing from a bird's skin, consisting of a partly hollow horny stem fringed with fine strands. 2 one or more of these as decoration etc. (also *attributive*: *a feather boa*). 3 a piece or pieces of feather attached to the base of an arrow to direct its flight. 4 something resembling a feather, as a tuft of hair standing upright on a person's head or growing in a different direction to the rest of a horse's coat. 5 (*collective*) game birds. 6 the wake left by a submarine periscope. ● *verb* 1 *transitive* cover or line with feathers. 2 *transitive Rowing* turn (an oar) so that it passes through the air edgewise. 3 *transitive Aviation & Naut.* **a** cause (the propeller blades) to rotate in such a way as to lessen the air or water resistance. **b** vary the angle of incidence of (helicopter blades). 4 *intransitive* float, move, or wave like feathers. 5 *transitive* = FEATHER-CUT. 6 *transitive* blend in delicate strokes (*carefully feather the paint into the corners*). 7 *intransitive* (of ink,

lipstick, etc.) break into tiny feather-like lines when applied to a surface. 8 *transitive* execute (a pass) or pass (a puck, ball, etc.) lightly or gracefully. □ **a feather in one's cap** an achievement to be proud of. **feather one's nest** make oneself richer, more comfortable, etc. usu. at someone else's expense. **in fine** (or **high**) **feather** *informal* in good spirits. **ruffle** (**a person's**) **feathers** disturb or annoy (a person). □ **feath·ered** *adjective* (also in *combination*). **feather·less** *adjective* **feath·ery** *adjective* [Old English *fether*, *gefithrian*, from Germanic]

feather·bed ● *noun* 1 a bed with a mattress stuffed with feathers. 2 something (esp. a job, situation, etc.) comfortable or easy. ● *transitive verb* (**feather·bed**) (**-bedded**, **-bedding**) provide with advantageous economic or working conditions.

feather·bed·ding *noun* the deliberate limitation of production or retention of excess staff in a business in order to create jobs or prevent unemployment, typically as a result of a union contract.

feather·brain *noun* (also **feather·head**) a silly or absent-minded person. □ **feather·brained** *adjective* (also **feather·headed**).

feather-cut *transitive verb* cut (hair) into wispy feather-like points.

feather duster *noun* a long-handled brush with a head made of feathers, used for dusting.

feathered friend *noun jocular* a bird.

feather-edge *noun* a fine tapered edge, esp. of a board or plank. □ **feather-edged** *adjective*

feather·ing *noun* 1 bird's plumage. 2 the feathers of an arrow. 3 fringes of hairs on the appendages or body of a dog.

feather·light *adjective* extremely light.

feather·stick *noun Cdn* a stick of wood of which one end is cut into thin strips in a fan shape, to make more effective kindling.

feather stitch ● *noun* ornamental zigzag sewing. ● *transitive verb* (**feather-stitch**) sew with this stitch.

feather·weight *noun* 1 **a** a weight in certain sports intermediate between bantamweight and lightweight, in the amateur boxing scale 54–57 kg, but differing for professionals and wrestlers (also *attributive*: *featherweight championship*). **b** a boxer etc. of this weight. 2 (also *attributive*) a very light person or thing. 3 (usu. *attributive*) trifling or unimportant.

fea·ture ● *noun* 1 a distinctive or characteristic part of a thing. 2 (usu. in *pl.*) a distinctive part of the face, esp. with regard to shape and visual effect. 3 something offered for sale as a special (*this week's feature is sirloin steak*). 4 a lengthy article devoted to a particular topic in a newspaper or magazine. 5 **a** (in full **feature film**) a full-length film intended as the main item in a movie theatre program. **b** a broadcast or part of a broadcast devoted to a particular topic. ● *verb* 1 *transitive* **a** make a special display or attraction of; give special prominence to. **b** include as a characteristic part (*the dictionary features clear definitions*). 2 *transitive & intransitive* have as or be an important actor, participant, or topic in a film, broadcast, etc. 3 *intransitive* be a feature or special attraction. □ **fea·tured** *adjective* (also in *combination*). **fea·ture·less** *adjective* [Old French *faiture* form, from Latin *factura* formation: see FACTURE]

feature-length *adjective* of the length of a typical feature film or program, usu. at least an hour long.

featur·ette *noun* 1 a short feature film. 2 a short documentary on some aspect of a film, included on the DVD of the film.

Feb. *abbreviation* February.

feb·ri·fuge /ˈfebrəˌfjuːdʒ/ *noun* a medicine or treatment that reduces fever. [French *fébrifuge* from Latin *febris* fever + -FUGE]

fe·brile /ˈfebrail, ˈfiːb-/ *adjective* 1 of or relating to fever; feverish. 2 nervous or excited as if by fever. □ **fe·bril·ity** /fɪˈbrɪlɪti/ *noun* [French *fébrile* or medieval Latin *febrilis* from Latin *febris* fever]

Feb·ru·ary /ˈfebjuːeri, ˈfebru-/ *noun* (*pl.* **-ies**) the second month of the year, containing 28 days, except in a leap year when it has 29. ¶ Although there is a tradition of opposition to the first pronunciation, it is used by educated speakers. [ultimately from Latin *februarius* from *februa* a purification feast held in this month]

February Revolution *see* RUSSIAN REVOLUTION.

feces /ˈfiːsiːz/ *noun* (also **faeces**) waste matter discharged from the bowels. □ **fecal** /ˈfiːkəl/ *adjective*

Fech·ner /ˈfexnər/ **Gus·tav Theo·dor** (1801–87), German physicist and psychologist, who sought to define the quantitative relationship between degrees of physical stimulation and the resulting sensation, the study of which he termed *psychophysics*.

feck·less *adjective* 1 lacking in efficiency or vitality (*a feckless bunch of layabouts*). 2 unthinking, irresponsible (*the feckless exploitation of the* earth's resources). □ **feck·less·ly** adverb **feck·less·ness** noun [Scots feck from effeck var. of EFFECT]

fec·u·lent /ˈfɛkjʊlənt/ adjective **1** murky; filthy. **2** containing sediments or dregs. □ **fecu·lence** noun [French féculent or Latin faeculentus (as FECES)]

fe·cund /ˈfɛkənd, ˈfiːk-/ adjective **1** fertile; highly productive of offspring, fruit, etc. **2** intellectually prolific or creative (a fecund imagination). □ **fe·cund·ity** /fɪˈkʌndɪti/ noun [French fécond or Latin fecundus]

fe·cund·ate /ˈfiːkənˌdeɪt, ˈfɛk-/ transitive verb **1** make fruitful. **2** = FERTILIZE 2. □ **fe·cund·a·tion** noun [Latin fecundare from fecundus fruitful]

fed[1] past and past participle of FEED.

fed[2] noun slang **1** Cdn & Austral. (in pl.) the federal government. **2** US (also **Fed**) a federal official, esp. a member of the FBI. **3** US (**Fed**) (prec. by the) **a** = FEDERAL RESERVE SYSTEM. **b** = FEDERAL RESERVE BOARD. [abbreviation of FEDERAL]

fed·ay·ee /ˌfɛdəˈjiː/ noun (pl. **fed·ay·een** /-jiːn/ an Arab guerrilla operating esp. against Israel. [informal Arabic fidā'iyīn pl. from Arabic fidā'ī adventurer]

fed·er·al adjective **1** of a system of government in which power is divided between a central government and several regional ones. **2** relating to or affecting such a federation. **3** of or relating to the central government as distinguished from the separate units constituting a federation (federal laws). **4** (**Federal**) of the Northern States in the American Civil War. **5** comprising an association of largely independent units. □ **fed·er·al·ize** transitive verb (also esp. Brit. **-ise**). **fed·er·al·iz·a·tion** noun **fed·er·al·ly** adverb [Latin foedus -eris league, covenant]

federal case noun **1** Law (in the US) a criminal case that falls under the jurisdiction of a federal court. **2** esp. US a matter of great concern or with dire consequences (don't make a federal case out of it).

Federal Court of Canada noun Cdn a court with jurisdiction to hear civil and criminal cases referred by federal boards, commissions, or tribunals, and to rule on constitutional questions referred by the Attorney General.

federal funds rate noun (in the US) the interest rate that banks charge each other for overnight loans.

fed·er·al·ism noun **1** a federal system of government. **2** advocacy of a federal system of government; in Canada esp. support of Confederation in opposition to Quebec separatism. □ **fed·er·al·ist** noun & adjective

Federalist Party an early political party in the US, which held power 1789–1801, and which by the 1820s had been superseded by the then Republican Party.

Federal Republic of Germany see GERMANY.

Federal Reserve Bank noun (in the US) each of twelve regional banks which regulate and serve the member banks of the Federal Reserve System.

Federal Reserve Board noun (in the US) the board regulating the Federal Reserve System and consisting of governors appointed by the US President with Senate approval.

Federal Reserve System noun (in the US) the national banking system with central cash reserves available to twelve major regional banks.

Federal Union, the noun see UNION 3.

fed·er·ate transitive & intransitive verb (esp. as **fed·er·at·ed**) organize or be organized on a federal basis. □ **fed·er·a·tive** /ˈfɛdərətɪv/ adjective

Federated States of Micronesia see MICRONESIA 2.

fed·er·a·tion noun **1** a federal group of provinces, states, etc. **2** a federated society or group (Canadian Federation of Students). **3** the act or an instance of federating.

fe·dora /fəˈdɔːrə/ noun a low soft felt hat with a crown creased lengthwise. [Fédora, drama by V. Sardou (1882)]

fed up adjective informal (often foll. by with) discontented or bored, esp. from a surfeit of something (am fed up with the rain).

fee noun **1** a payment made to a professional person or to a professional or public body in exchange for advice or services. **2** money paid as part of a special transaction, for a privilege, admission to a society, etc. (enrolment fee). **3** (in pl.) money paid (esp. to a school or university) for tuition. **4** Law an inherited estate, unlimited (**fee simple**) or limited (**fee tail**) as to the category of heir. **5** hist. a fief; a feudal benefice. [Old French fieu, etc. from medieval Latin feodum, feudum, perhaps from Frankish: compare FEUD[2], FIEF]

feeb noun N Amer. slang a stupid or feeble-minded person. [abbreviation]

feeble adjective **1** weak, infirm. **2** lacking energy, force, or effectiveness (a feeble argument). **3** dim, indistinct. **4** deficient in character or intelligence. □ **feeble·ness** noun **feebly** adverb [Old French feble, fleible from Latin flebilis lamentable, from flēre weep]

feeble-minded adjective **1** unintelligent. **2** mentally deficient. □ **feeble-mind·ed·ly** adverb **feeble-mind·ed·ness** noun

feed ● verb (past and past participle **fed**) **1** transitive **a** supply with food. **b** put food into the mouth of. **2** transitive give as food, esp. to animals. **3** transitive serve as food for. **4** intransitive (usu. foll. by on) (esp. of animals, or informal of people) take food; eat. **5** transitive nourish; make grow. **6** **a** transitive maintain a supply of raw material, fuel, etc., to (a fire, machine, etc.). **b** transitive (foll. by into) supply (material) to a machine etc. **c** intransitive (often foll. by into) (of a river, road etc.) flow or merge into another (smaller highways feed into the Trans-Canada). **d** transitive insert further coins into (a meter) to continue its function, validity, etc. **7** intransitive (foll. by on) **a** be nourished by. **b** derive benefit from. **8** transitive use (land) as pasture. **9** transitive relay or supply electrical signals or power to, esp. as part of a larger network or system. **10** transitive Theatre slang supply (an actor etc.) with cues. **11** transitive Sport send a pass to (a player). **12** transitive gratify, seek to satisfy (an appetite, passion, etc.). **13** transitive provide (advice, information, etc.) to. **14** intransitive (of plants) take nutrients from the soil. ● noun **1 a** food, esp. for farm animals; fodder. **b** an amount of such food. **2** the act or an instance of feeding; the giving of food (when is the baby's next feed?). **3** informal a meal. **4 a** a supply of raw material to a machine etc. **b** the provision of this or a device for it. **5** a locally broadcast radio or television program transmitted by satellite or network to a larger audience. **6** the charge of a gun. **7** Theatre slang an actor who supplies another with cues. □ **off one's feed** slang having no appetite. [Old English fēdan from Germanic]

feed·back noun **1** information about the result of an experiment, performance, etc.; response. **2** Electronics **a** the return of a fraction of the output signal from one stage of a circuit, amplifier, etc., to the input of the same or a preceding stage. **b** a signal so returned. **3** Biol. etc. the modification or control of a process or system by its results or effects, esp. in a biochemical pathway or behavioural response.

feedback loop noun **1** the path by which some of the output of a system is returned to the input. **2** a situation in which information etc. is passed back and forth.

feed bag noun N Amer. a bag containing fodder and grain, hung on a horse's head.

feed dog noun the mechanism in a sewing machine which feeds the material under the needle.

feed·er noun **1** a person who supplies food for another person, an animal, etc. **2** a person, plant, or animal that eats in a specified manner (the baby is a good feeder). **3** a receptacle from which animals may feed. **4** N Amer. an animal being fattened for market (usu. attributive: feeder steers). **5** Brit. a child's feeding bottle. **b** a bib for an infant. **6** a tributary stream. **7** a branch road, bus route, airline, etc., linking outlying districts with a main transportation system. **8** a school, sports team, etc. which supplies students, players, etc. to a larger or more senior school or team. **9** Electricity **a** a main carrying electricity to a distribution point. **b** an electrical connection between an antenna and a transmitter or receiver of electromagnetic waves. **10** a person or apparatus which supplies material to a machine in regulated quantities (an automatic paper feeder).

feed grain noun barley, wheat, etc. grown for animal food.

feed·ing bottle noun esp. Brit. a bottle with a teat for feeding infants.

feed·ing frenzy noun **1** an instance of ravenous eating by a group of animals. **2** informal competitive, unscrupulous behaviour, esp. as exhibited by journalists covering a sensational or scandalous story.

feed·lot noun a farming operation where livestock are fed or fattened.

feed·stock noun raw material to supply a machine or industrial process.

feed·stuff noun fodder.

fee-for-service adjective of or designating an approach to the delivery of medical services in which physicians are paid a designated amount for each service provided rather than by salary.

feel ● verb (past and past participle **felt**) **1 a** transitive examine or search by touch. **b** intransitive have the sensation of touch (is unable to feel). **2 a** transitive perceive, discover, or ascertain by handling or touching (could feel the heat through the door). **b** transitive have a sensation of (felt that it was cold). **c** intransitive (often foll. by for) grope about, search in, esp. by touch (felt in her purse for a loonie). **3 a** transitive undergo, experience (shall feel my anger). **b** exhibit or be conscious of (an emotion, sensation, conviction, etc.). **4 a** intransitive have a specified feeling or reaction (felt strongly about it). **b** *transitive* be physically or emotionally affected or injured by (*felt the rebuke deeply*). **5** *transitive* (foll. by *that* + clause) have a vague impression or conviction of (*I feel that I am right*). **6** *transitive* consider, think (*I feel it useful to go*). **7** *intransitive* seem, give an impression of being, or be perceived as (*the air feels chilly*). **8** *intransitive* be conscious of being, regard oneself as (*I feel happy; do not feel well*). **9** *intransitive* (foll. by *for*) have pity or compassion for. **10** *transitive* (often foll. by *up*) *slang* fondle for sexual gratification. ● *noun* **1** the act or an instance of feeling or testing by touch. **2 a** a physical or mental sensation. **b** the sensation characteristically produced by an object, situation, etc. **3 a** a sensitive appreciation or an easy understanding of something (*Jeremy has a good feel for languages*). **b** a sense of familiarity, competence, or comfort with something (*haven't got the feel of this car yet*). **4** *coarse slang* an instance of feeling up (*cop a feel*). □ **feel free** (often foll. by *to* + infin.) not be reluctant or hesitant (*do feel free to criticize*). **feel like 1** feel as though or similar to. **2** desire (a thing) or have an inclination towards (doing a thing). **feel no pain** *slang* be very drunk. **feel one's oats** see OAT. **feel out** investigate cautiously. **feel up to** feel capable or be ready to face or deal with. **feel one's way** proceed carefully or act cautiously. **make one's influence** (or **presence** etc.) **felt** use one's authority, power, or strong personality for visible effect or to assert one's influence over others, proceedings, etc. [Old English *fēlan* from West Gothic]

feel·er *noun* **1** an organ in certain animals for testing things by touch or for searching for food. **2** a tentative proposal or suggestion, esp. to elicit a response or test opinion (*put out feelers*). **3** a person or thing that feels, tries, or tests.

feeler gauge *noun* a gauge equipped with thin, usu. metal strips of a known thickness, used to measure narrow gaps or clearances.

feel-good *adjective informal* caused, causing, or characterized by happy, positive, or self-satisfied feelings or responses.

feel·ing ● *noun* **1 a** a sense of touch or the capacity to feel (*lost all feeling in his arm*). **b** a physical sensation. **2 a** (often foll. by *of*) a particular emotional reaction (*a feeling of despair*). **b** (in *pl.*) emotional susceptibilities or sympathies (*hurt my feelings; had strong feelings about it*). **3** a particular and usu. intuitive sensitivity, aptitude, or appreciation (*had a feeling for literature*). **4 a** an opinion, notion, or belief not based solely on reason (*my feelings on the subject; had a feeling she would be there*). **b** a vague, often irrational, awareness or sensation (*had a feeling of safety*). **c** attitude or sentiment (*the general feeling was against it*). **5** the capacity or readiness to feel, esp. sympathy or compassion. **6 a** the general emotional effect produced on a hearer, spectator, etc. by a work of art, piece of music, etc. **b** emotional commitment or sensibility in artistic execution (*played with feeling*). ● *adjective* **1** sensitive, sympathetic, compassionate. **2** showing emotion. **3** sentient or capable of sensation. □ **feel·ing·ly** *adverb*

fee simple *noun* (*pl.* **fees simple**) a permanent and absolute tenure of an estate in land with freedom to dispose of it at will, esp. (in full **fee simple absolute in possession**) a freehold tenure.

feet *pl.* of FOOT.

feign /fein/ *verb transitive* simulate or pretend to be affected by (*feign madness*). □ **feigned** *adjective* [Middle English from *feign-* stem of Old French *feindre* from Latin *fingere* mould, contrive]

feint /feint/ ● *noun* **1** a sham move, attack, blow, etc. to divert attention or fool an opponent or enemy. **2** an assumed appearance or pretense. ● *intransitive verb* make a feint. [French *feinte*, fem. past participle of *feindre* FEIGN]

Fei·sal *var.* of FAISAL.

feisty /ˈfaisti/ *adjective* (**feist·i·er**, **feist·i·est**) *N Amer. informal* **1** spirited, energetic, forceful, or exuberant, esp. when faced with opposition. **2** touchy, irritable, quarrelsome. □ **feist·i·ly** *adverb* **feist·i·ness** *noun* [*feist* (= fist) small dog]

fe·la·fel /feˈlɒfəl/ *var.* of FALAFEL.

Fel·den·krais method /ˈfeldənkraɪs/ *noun* a system designed to promote bodily and mental efficiency and well-being by conscious analysis of neuromuscular activity via exercises which improve flexibility and coordination and increase ease and range of motion. [M. *Feldenkrais*, Russian-born physicist and mechanical engineer d.1984]

feld·spar *noun* any of a group of aluminum silicates of potassium, sodium, or calcium, which are the most abundant minerals in the earth's crust. □ **feld·spath·ic** /feldˈspaθɪk/ *adjective* [German *Feldspat*, *-spath* from *Feld* FIELD + *Spat*, *Spath* SPAR³]

fe·lic·i·tate /fəˈlɪsɪˌteɪt/ *transitive verb formal* (usu. foll. by *on*) congratulate (a person). □ **fe·lic·i·ta·tion** *noun* (usu. in *pl.*). [Late Latin *felicitare* make happy, from Latin *felix -icis* happy]

fe·lic·i·tous /fəˈlɪsɪtəs/ *adjective* **1** (of a name, expression, etc.) strikingly apt. **2 a** pleasing, delightful. **b** happy, showing or marked by great happiness. □ **fe·lic·i·tous·ly** *adverb* **fe·lic·i·tous·ness** *noun*

fe·lic·i·ty /fəˈlɪsɪti/ *noun* (*pl.* **-ties**) **1** happiness, bliss. **2** a cause or source of happiness. **3 a** a capacity for appropriate expression. **b** an appropriate or well-chosen phrase. **4** a stroke of fortune or a fortunate trait. [Old French *félicité* from Latin *felicitas -tatis* from *felix -icis* happy]

fe·line /ˈfiːlaɪn/ ● *adjective* **1** of or relating to the cat family Felidae. **2** catlike in any respect, but esp. in beauty or slyness. ● *noun* any member of the cat family. □ **fe·lin·ity** /fɪˈlɪnɪti/ *noun* [Latin *felinus* from *feles* cat]

feline distemper *noun* see DISTEMPER² 1a.

feline leukemia virus *noun* a retrovirus that suppresses a cat's immune system, allowing for opportunistic infections and causing various disorders including cancer. Abbr.: **FLV** or **FeLV**.

feline urological syndrome *noun* a disorder caused by deposits of mineral crystals, as from foods with a high magnesium content, within a cat's urinary tract. Abbr.: **FUS**.

Felix·stowe /ˈfiːlɪkˌstoʊ/ a port on the east coast of England, in Suffolk; pop. (est. 2002) 32,600.

fell¹ *past of* FALL *verb*.

fell² ● *transitive verb* **1** cut down (esp. a tree). **2** strike or knock down (a person or animal). **3** stitch down (the edge of a seam) so that it lies flat over the outer edge, leaving a smooth surface. ● *noun* an amount of timber cut in one season. [Old English *fellan* from Germanic, related to FALL]

fell³ *noun Northern England & Scot.* **1** a hill or mountain. **2** a ridge, down, or stretch of hills or high moorland. [Old Norse *fjall, fell* hill]

fell⁴ *adjective literary* **1** fierce, ruthless, cruel. **2** terrible, destructive. □ **at** (or **in**) **one fell swoop** in a single (originally deadly) action or effort. [Old French *fel* from Romanic FELON]

fel·la *noun* (also **fel·lah**) *informal* = FELLOW 1, 2. [representing an affected or slang pronunciation]

fel·lah *noun* (*pl.* **fel·la·hin**, **fel·la·heen** /feləˈhiːn/) a peasant in an Arabic-speaking country, esp. Egypt. [Arabic *fallāḥ* husbandman, from *falaḥa* till the soil]

fel·la·tio /fəˈleɪʃɪoʊ/ *noun* oral stimulation of the penis. □ **fel·late** /fəˈleɪt/ *transitive verb* **fel·la·tor** /fəˈleɪtɜr/ *noun* [modern Latin from Latin *fellare* suck]

fel·ler¹ *noun* = FELLOW 1, 2. [representing an affected or slang pronunciation]

fel·ler² *noun* a person or thing that fells something, esp. trees as timber.

feller-buncher *noun* a large machine used to shear trees just above ground level and pile them for later transport.

fell·field *noun Ecology* a tundra area of frost-shattered stony debris with fine interstitial particles which supports sparse vegetation, usu. algae, lichens, and mosses.

Fel·lini /fəˈliːni/ **Fede·rico** (1920–93), Italian film director, who rose to international fame in the 1950s with neo-realist films before turning to unconventional works employing fantasy and symbolism; his films include *La Strada* (1954), *La Dolce vita* (1960) and *Satyricon* (1969). □ **Fel·lini·esque** *adjective*

fel·low *noun* **1** *informal* a man or boy (*poor fellow!; my dear fellow*). **2** (usu. in *pl.*) **a** a companion, associate, or comrade (*were separated from their fellows*). **b** a contemporary. **3** a partner, counterpart, or match; the other of a pair. **4** one of the same class or an equal in rank, ability, or kind. **5 a** an elected graduate receiving a stipend for a period of research. **b** a member of the governing body in some universities. **c** *Brit.* an incorporated senior member of a college. **6** a member of a learned society (*a fellow of the Royal Society of Canada*). **7** (*attributive*) belonging to the same class or activity (*fellow soldier; fellow Canadian*). **8** *derogatory* a person regarded with contempt. **9** *informal* a boyfriend or husband. [Old English *fēolaga* from Old Norse *félagi* from *fé* cattle, property, money]

fellow feeling *noun* sympathy from common experiences, interests, etc.

fellow·ship *noun* **1** companionship or friendly association with others. **2 a** a group of people or a society sharing a common interest or aim, e.g. a religious group, fraternity, or guild. **b** membership in such a group or society. **3 a** an award of money to a graduate student in return for some research, teaching, etc. **b** a post as a fellow in a college etc.

fellow-travel·ler *noun* **1** a person who travels with another. **2** a person who sympathizes with, but is not a member of, a particular party or movement, esp. the Communist party.

fel·on /ˈfelən/ *noun* a person who has been convicted of a felony. [Old French from medieval Latin *felo -onis*, of unknown origin]

fe·lo·ni·ous /fəˈloːnɪəs/ *adjective* **1** *Law* of or involving a felony. **2** (of a person) that has committed a felony. □ **fe·lo·ni·ous·ly** *adverb*

fel·o·ny /ˈfeləni/ *noun* (*pl.* **-onies**) a usu. violent crime, (in the US) one classified as graver than a misdemeanour, usu. punishable by a prison term of more than one year.

fel·quiste /felˈkiːst/ *noun Cdn hist.* a member of the FLQ. [Canadian French]

fel·sic /ˈfelsɪk/ *adjective Geol.* **1** of, pertaining to, or designating a group of light coloured minerals including feldspar, quartz, and muscovite. **2** (of rock) containing a high proportion of such minerals. [contraction of FELDSPAR + SILICA + -IC]

felt[1] *noun* **1** a fabric made of wool, fur, or other fibrous material consolidated by heat and mechanical action so that the fibres are matted together. **2 a** a piece of felt. **b** a thing made of felt, e.g. a hat, blotter, etc. **3** a heavy layer of material, usu. matted and fibrous, used in construction for roofing, insulation, etc. ● *verb* **1** *transitive* **a** make into felt or bring to a felt-like consistency. **b** mat or press together. **2** *transitive* cover with felt. **3** *intransitive* become matted. □ **felt·ed** *adjective* **felt·ing** *noun* **felty** *adjective* [Old English from West Germanic]

felt[2] *past and past participle of* FEEL.

felt pen *noun* a pen with a writing tip made of felt or fibre.

felt tip *noun* (often *attributive*) **1** the writing point of a felt pen. **2** a felt pen. □ **felt-tipped** *adjective*

fe·luc·ca /fəˈlʌkə, -ˈluːkə/ *noun* a small vessel propelled by lateen sails, oars, or both, formerly used along the Mediterranean coast and still in use on rivers, esp. the Nile. [Italian *felucca* from obsolete Spanish *faluca* from Arabic *fulk*, perhaps from Greek *epholkion* sloop]

FeLV *abbreviation* = FELINE LEUKEMIA VIRUS.

fem. *abbreviation* feminine.

fe·male ● *adjective* **1** of the sex that can bear offspring or produce eggs. **2** (of a plant, flower, etc.) bearing fruit or having pistils, but lacking a stamen. **3** of or consisting of women, girls, or female animals. **4** (of a screw, socket, etc.) manufactured hollow or moulded to receive a corresponding, inserted, male part. ● *noun* a female person, animal, or plant. □ **fe·male·ness** *noun* [Old French *femelle* (n.) from Latin *femella* diminutive of *femina* a woman, assimilated to *male*]

female condom *noun* = CONDOM 2.

female genital mutilation *noun* (also **female circumcision**) (among some peoples) the action or traditional practice of cutting off the clitoris and sometimes the labia of girls or young women.

female impersonator *noun* a male performer dressed and acting as a woman.

femi·nazi /ˈfemɪˌnɒtsi, -ˌnatsi/ *noun esp. US derogatory* a radical feminist.

fem·in·ine ● *adjective* **1** of, pertaining to, or characteristic of women. **2** having qualities associated with women. **3** womanly, effeminate. **4** *Grammar* of or denoting the gender to which belong words classified as female on the basis of sex or some arbitrary distinction, such as form. ● *noun* **1** *Grammar* a feminine gender or word. **2** feminine qualities collectively. □ **fem·in·ine·ly** *adverb* **fem·in·ine·ness** *noun* **fem·in·in·ity** *noun* [Old French *feminin -ine* or Latin *femininus* from *femina* woman]

feminine hygiene *noun* practices, products, etc. related to menstruation and other functions of the female reproductive system.

feminine rhyme *noun Prosody* a rhyme on two or more syllables, the first stressed and the others unstressed, e.g. *stocking/shocking, glamorous/amorous* (compare MASCULINE RHYME).

fem·in·ism *noun* **1** the advocacy of equality of the sexes, esp. through the establishment of the political, social, and economic rights of women. **2** the movement associated with this. □ **fem·in·ist** *noun & adjective* [Latin *femina* woman (in sense 1 after French *féminisme*)]

fem·in·ize *verb* (also esp. *Brit.* **-ise**) **1** *transitive & intransitive* make or become feminine or female. **2** *transitive* make characteristic of or associated with women. **3** *transitive Med.* induce female physiological characteristics in. □ **fem·in·iz·a·tion** *noun* **fem·in·ized** *adjective*

femme /fem/ *noun slang* a lesbian taking a traditionally feminine role in a relationship.

femme fa·tale /ˌfem faˈtal/ *noun* (*pl.* **femmes fa·tales** *pronunc.* same) a woman to whom a person feels irresistibly attracted, usu. with dangerous or unhappy results. [French]

femto- *combining form* used in names of units of measurement to denote

a factor of 10⁻¹⁵ (*femtometre*). Symbol: **f**. [Danish or Norwegian *femten* fifteen]

femur /ˈfiːmər/ *noun* (*pl.* **fe·murs** or **fe·mora** /ˈfemərə/) **1** *Anat.* the thigh bone in vertebrates, the thick bone between the hip and the knee. **2** the third articulated segment of the leg in insects and some other arthropods. □ **fem·oral** /ˈfemərəl/ *adjective* [Latin *femur femoris* thigh]

fen[1] *noun* **1** a tract of low land covered wholly or partially with shallow water or subject to frequent flooding. **2** wet land with alkaline, neutral, or only slightly acid peaty soil. **3** (**the Fens**) flat low-lying areas in and around Cambridgeshire in E England, formerly marshland but drained for agriculture since the 17th c. □ **fenny** *adjective* [Old English *fenn* from Germanic]

fen[2] /fʌn/ *noun* (*pl.* same) a coin and monetary unit of the People's Republic of China, worth one-hundredth of a yuan. [Chinese *fēn* 'a hundredth part']

fence ● *noun* **1** a barrier, railing, or other upright structure enclosing an area of ground, esp. to control access to or from a field, yard, etc. **2** a large, upright obstacle for a horse to jump over in a competition, race, etc. **3** a person who or an establishment which deals in stolen goods. **4** a guard, guide, or gauge designed to regulate the movements of a tool, machine, etc. ● *verb* **1 a** *transitive* surround, divide, etc. (a thing) with a fence (*farmers fence their fields*). **b** *intransitive* build a fence or fences. **2** *transitive* **a** (foll. by *in*) surround or enclose (a person, thing, etc.) with a fence. **b** (foll. by *off*) separate (one area from another) (*fenced off one end of the garden for the chickens*). **3** *transitive* (foll. by *out*) keep out or exclude with or as with a fence. **4** *transitive & intransitive* deal in (stolen goods). **5** *intransitive* practise the art or sport of fencing. **6** *intransitive* **a** engage in skilful argument. **b** (foll. by *with*) evade answering (a person or question). □ (**sit**) **on the fence** (remain) neutral or undecided in a dispute etc; (be) uncommitted. □ **fen·cer** *noun* [Middle English from DEFENCE]

fence·line *noun N Amer.* **1** the continuous extent of fence encompassing a tract of land, esp. on a ranch. **2** the line or boundary marked by a fence.

fence-mending *noun* an act of appeasement or reconciliation.

fence post *noun* a post that supports a fence.

fence·row *noun N Amer.* an unused strip of land surrounding a field, farm, etc., usu. containing a fence and sometimes also trees or shrubs etc.

fence-sitter *noun* a person who remains neutral or uncommitted on an issue. □ **fence-sitting** *noun & adjective*

fence·wire *noun* the wire used in making fences on farms, ranches, etc.

fen·cible /ˈfensɪbəl/ *noun hist.* a soldier liable only for defensive military service at home. [Middle English from DEFENSIBLE]

fen·cing *noun* **1** a set or extent of fences. **2** material for making fences. **3** the action of putting up a fence. **4** the practice or sport of engaging in combat with swords, esp. according to a set of rules using foils, épées, or sabres to score points.

fend *verb* **1** *intransitive* (foll. by *for*) support, take care of, or look after (esp. oneself). **2** *transitive* (usu. foll. by *off*) ward off (an attack), keep (a thing) away, or defend from (a threat etc.). [Middle English from DEFEND]

Fen·der, Leo (1907–1991), US guitar maker. He designed and marketed several electric guitars under the name Fender; these include the Broadcaster (1948, later called the Telecaster), the Stratocaster (1956), and electric bass guitars.

fen·der *noun* **1** *N Amer.* **a** the mudguard or area around the wheel well of a motor vehicle. **b** *disputed* the bumper of a motor vehicle. **c** the mudguard of a bicycle etc. **2** *Naut.* a piece of old cable, rubber, etc. hung over a vessel's side to protect it against chafing or impact. **3** a low frame bordering a fireplace to keep in falling coals etc. **4** any thing used to keep something off, prevent a collision, etc. □ **fender·less** *adjective*

fender-bender *noun N Amer. slang* a usu. minor collision between vehicles.

Fé·ne·lon /feinəˈlɔ̃/ **Fran·çois de Sa·lignac de La Mothe** (1651–1715), French theologian, educator, and writer, who is best known for the didactic work he wrote for the grandson of Louis XIV, *Les Aventures de Télémaque* (1699).

fen·es·tra /fəˈnestrə/ *noun* (*pl.* **fen·es·trae** /-triː/) *Anat.* a small hole or opening in a bone etc., esp. one of two (**fenestra oval·is, fenestra ro·tun·da**) in the inner ear. [Latin, = window]

fen·es·trat·ed /ˈfenəstreitəd, fəˈnestreitəd/ *adjective* **1** *Archit.* having windows or openings. **2** (also **fen·es·trate** /ˈfenəstreit, fəˈnestreit/) *Bot. & Zool.* having small, window-like perforations or transparent areas.

fen·es·tra·tion /ˌfenəˈstreiʃən/ *noun* **1** *Archit.* the arrangement of windows in a building. **2** *Bot. & Zool.* the condition of being fenestrated or perforated. **3** a surgical operation in which a new opening is formed in an anatomical structure, esp. in the bony labyrinth of the inner ear as a form of treatment in some causes of deafness.

feng shui /fen ˈʃuːi, ˈfʌŋ ˈʃwei/ *noun* (in Chinese thought) a system of good and evil influences in the natural surroundings, considered when siting or designing buildings etc. [Chinese, from *feng* 'wind' + *shui* 'water']

Fe·ni·an /ˈfiːniən/ ● *noun* a member of the Irish Republican Brotherhood, a militant 19th-c. nationalist organization founded among the Irish in the US, whose members encouraged revolutionary activity and aimed for the overthrow of the British government in Ireland. The Fenians staged an unsuccessful revolt in Ireland in 1867 and were responsible for isolated revolutionary acts against the British, including raids from the US into Canada, until they were gradually eclipsed by the IRA early in the 20th c. ● *adjective* of or relating to the Fenians. □ **Fenian·ism** *noun* [Old Irish *féne* name of an ancient Irish people, confused with *fiann* guard of legendary kings]

fen·land *noun* an area of fens. [FEN[1]]

fen·nec /ˈfenɪk/ *noun* a small fox, *Vulpes zerda*, native to N Africa, having large pointed ears. [Arabic *fanak*]

fen·nel /ˈfenəl/ *noun* **1** a yellow-flowered fragrant umbelliferous plant, *Foeniculum vulgare*, with fragrant seeds and fine leaves used as flavouring. **2** the seeds of this. **3** (in full **Florence** or **sweet fennel**) a variety of this, *azoricum*, with swollen leaf bases eaten as a vegetable. [Old English *finugl* etc. & Old French *fenoil* from Latin *feniculum* from *fenum* hay]

fen·ning *noun* (*pl.* same) a monetary unit of Bosnia and Herzegovina, equal to one-hundredth of a marka. [Bosnian]

Fenno·scan·dia /ˌfenoˈskandiə/ the land mass in NW Europe comprising Scandinavia, Finland, and the adjacent area of NE Russia.

fenu·greek /ˈfenjuˌɡriːk/ *noun* **1** a leguminous plant, *Trigonella foenum-graecum*, having aromatic seeds. **2** these seeds used as flavouring, esp. ground and used in curry powder. [Old English *fenogrecum*, superseded in Middle English from Old French *fenugrec* from Latin *faenugraecum* (*fenum graecum* Greek hay), used by the Romans as fodder]

feoff·ment /ˈfefmənt/ *noun hist.* a mode of conveying a freehold estate by a formal transfer of possession. □ **feof·fee** /feˈfiː/ *noun* **feof·for** *noun* [Anglo-French *feoffement*, related to FEE]

feral /ˈfiːrəl, ˈferəl/ *adjective* **1 a** (of animals) belonging to or forming a wild population ultimately descended from individuals which escaped from captivity or domestication. **b** born in the wild of such an animal. **2** (of an animal or plant) wild, untamed, uncultivated. **3** brutal, savage, fierce. [Latin *ferus* wild]

Fer·ber·ize *transitive verb* train (a baby) to fall asleep on its own by leaving it to cry for successively longer periods and returning only to speak comfortingly to it but not pick it up, feed it, or cuddle it. [R. *Ferber*, US pediatrician]

fer-de-lance /ˌfer də ˈlɒns/ *noun* a large highly venomous snake, *Bothrops atrox*, native to Central and South America. [French, = iron (head) of a lance]

Fer·di·nand I /ˈfɜrdinand/ **1** (known as 'Ferdinand the Great') (*c.*1016–65), king of Castile 1035–65 and León 1037–65, who subjugated the Muslim rulers of Toledo, Seville, and Saragossa (1062). **2** (1503–64), king of Bohemia and Hungary 1526–64 and Holy Roman emperor 1558–64, whose Peace of Augsburg (1555) brought an end to years of religious warfare.

Fer·di·nand II /ˈfɜrdinand/ (1578–1637), Holy Roman emperor 1619–37, king of Bohemia 1617–19; 1620–27 and Hungary 1618–25, who is known for his suppression of Protestantism during the Counter-Reformation.

Fer·di·nand III /ˈfɜrdinand/ (1608–57), Holy Roman emperor 1637–57, king of Hungary 1625–57 and Bohemia 1627–56, whose Peace of Westphalia (1648) ended the Thirty Years War.

Fer·di·nand V /ˈfɜrdinand/ (known as 'Ferdinand the Catholic') (1452–1516), king of Castile 1474–1504, and as Ferdinand II, king of Aragon 1479–1516, who ruled jointly with his wife Isabella I of Castile. He instituted the Spanish Inquisition (1478), captured Granada from the Moors and effectively united Spain (1492), and funded Columbus's expedition to the New World (1492).

Fer·gus a former town in south central Ontario, about 30 km north of Guelph, now part of Centre Wellington township; pop. (2001) 10,017. [A. *Fergusson*, member of the Legislative Council of Upper Canada d.1862]

Fer·gus·on, **George How·ard** (1870–1946), Canadian lawyer and politician, Conservative premier of Ontario 1923–30.

feria /ˈfiːriə, ˈfer-/ *noun Christianity* a weekday which is not a feast day. □ **feri·al** *adjective* [Latin, = 'holiday': see FAIR[2]]

Fer·land /ferˈlɑ̃/ **Jean-Pierre** (b.1934), Canadian singer and songwriter. His songs include 'Les Fleurs de macadam', 'Un Peu plus haut, un peu plus loin', and 'Quand on aime on a toujours vingt ans'.

Fer·lin·ghet·ti /ˌfɑrlɪŋˈɡeti/ **Law·rence (Mon·santo)** (born Lawrence Ferling) (b.1919), US poet and publisher. Identified with San Francisco's beat movement, in 1952 he founded a bookshop and the publishing house City Lights, which produced works such as Allen Ginsberg's *Howl* (1957). Notable works are *A Coney Island of the Mind* (poetry, 1958) and *Her* (novel, 1960).

Fer·man·agh /fərˈmanə/ one of the Six Counties of Northern Ireland, also an administrative area; chief town, Enniskillen.

Fer·mat /ˈfɜrmɒ/ **Pierre de** (1601–65), French lawyer and mathematician. His study of the problems of finding tangents to curves, finding areas under curves, and maxima and minima, led directly to the general methods of calculus introduced by Newton and Leibniz. Fermat is seen as the founder of the theory of numbers. His most famous assertion, known as Fermat's last theorem, is that if n is greater than 2 then there is no integer whose nth power can be expressed as the sum of two smaller nth powers.

fer·mata /ferˈmɒtə/ *noun Music* **1** a prolongation, of unspecified length, of a note or rest. **2** a sign indicating this. [Italian, 'stop, pause']

fer·ment ● *noun* /ˈfɜrment/ social, political, etc. excitement, tumult, or unrest. ● *verb* /fərˈment/ **1** *intransitive & transitive* undergo or subject to fermentation. **2** *transitive* stir up, foment (trouble or disorder). □ **fer·ment·able** *adjective* **fer·ment·ed** *adjective* **fer·ment·er** *noun* [Old French *ferment* or Latin *fermentum* from Latin *fervēre* boil]

fer·men·ta·tion *noun* the anaerobic breakdown of a substance by micro-organisms such as yeasts and bacteria, esp. of sugar to ethyl alcohol in making beers, wines, and spirits. □ **fer·ment·a·tive** /-ˈmentətɪv/ *adjective*

Fermi /ˈfermi/ **En·rico** (1901–54), Italian-born US atomic physicist. He co-invented Fermi-Dirac statistics, predicted the existence of the neutrino, produced radioactive isotopes by bombarding atomic nuclei with neutrons, and joined the Manhattan Project to work on the atomic bomb; he was awarded the Nobel Prize for physics in 1938.

fer·mi /ˈfermi/ *noun* (*pl.* **fer·mis**) a unit of length equal to 10^{-15} metre, formerly used in nuclear physics. [FERMI]

Fermi-Dirac statistics /ˌfermidɪˈrak/ *noun Physics* a type of quantum statistics introduced by Fermi and Dirac and used to describe systems of identical particles which obey the exclusion principle. [FERMI + DIRAC]

fer·mi·on /ˈfermiˌɒn/ *noun Physics* a subatomic particle, such as a nucleon, with half-integral spin. [as FERMI + -ON]

fer·mi·um /ˈfermiəm/ *noun Chem.* a transuranic radioactive metallic element produced artificially. Symbol: **Fm**; at. no.: 100. [as FERMI + -IUM]

fern *noun* any flowerless plant of the order Filicales, reproducing by spores and usu. having feathery fronds. □ **fern·ery** *noun* (*pl.* **-eries**). **ferny** *adjective* [Old English *fearn* from West Germanic]

Fer·nan·do Póo /fɜr ˈnandoː ˈpoː/ the former name (until 1973) of BIOKO.

fern bar *noun N Amer.* a usu. chic restaurant or bar decorated abundantly with ferns or other potted plants.

Fer·nie a city located in the southeastern corner of BC, southwest of Crowsnest Pass; pop. (2001) 4,611. □ **Fernie·ite** *noun* [W. *Fernie*, former gold commissioner in the Kootenay district d.1921]

fe·ro·cious /fəˈroːʃəs/ *adjective* **1** fierce, savage, or wildly cruel or destructive. **2** esp. *N Amer. informal* (as an intensifier) very great, extreme. □ **fe·ro·cious·ly** *adverb* **fe·ro·cious·ness** *noun* [Latin *ferox -ocis*]

fe·roci·ty /fəˈrɒsɪti/ *noun* (*pl.* **-ties**) the quality or state of being ferocious.

-ferous /fərəs/ *combining form* (usu. **-iferous**) forming adjectives with the sense 'bearing', 'having' (*auriferous; odoriferous*). □ **-ferously** *suffix*. **-ferousness** *suffix*. [from or after French *-fère* or Latin *-fer* producing, from *ferre* bear]

Fer·rara /fəˈrarə/ a city in N Italy, capital of a province of the same name; pop. (2001) 130,461.

Fer·rari /fəˈrari/ **Enzo** (1898–1988), Italian racing car designer and

---

Consonants: b *but*   d *dog*   f *few*   ɡ *get*   h *her*   j *yes*   k *cat*   l *leg*   m *man*   n *no*   p *pen*   r *red*   s *sit*

manufacturer. Originally a racing driver and car designer for Alfa Romeo, he founded the company named after him in 1929.

fer·rate /ˈfereɪt/ *noun Chem.* a salt formed from or as from ferric oxide and a base. [Latin *ferrum* iron]

fer·ret ● *noun* a small half-domesticated animal of the weasel family, *Mustela putorius furo*, kept as a pet or (in Europe) used to catch rabbits, rats, etc. ● *verb* **1 a** *transitive* (foll. by *out*) search out (secrets, criminals, etc.). **b** *intransitive* search or rummage about. **2** *intransitive & transitive* hunt with ferrets. □ **fer·ret·er** *noun* **fer·rety** *adjective* [Old French *fu(i)ret* alteration of *fu(i)ron* from Late Latin *furo -onis* from Latin *fur* thief]

ferri- *combining form Chem.* containing iron, esp. in ferric compounds. [Latin *ferrum* iron]

fer·ric *adjective* **1** of or containing iron. **2** *Chem.* of or containing iron in a trivalent form (compare FERROUS).

Fer·ris wheel *noun* a fairground ride consisting of a large, upright wheel revolving on a fixed axle, with seats suspended from its rims. [G. W. G. *Ferris*, US engineer d.1896]

fer·rite *noun Chem.* **1** a compound, often with magnetic properties, formed from ferric oxide and a basic oxide or from ferric hydroxide and a base. **2** an allotrope of pure iron occurring in low carbon steel. □ **fer·rit·ic** /feˈrɪtɪk/ *adjective* [Latin *ferrum* iron]

fer·ri·tin /ˈferɪtɪn/ *noun Biochem.* a water-soluble protein containing ferric iron, involved in storing iron in mammalian metabolism. [FERRIC + -t- + -IN]

ferro- *combining form Chem.* **1** of iron, esp. in ferrous compounds (*ferrocyanide*). **2** (of alloys) containing iron (*ferromanganese*). [Latin *ferrum* iron]

ferro·con·crete ● *noun* concrete reinforced with steel. ● *adjective* made of reinforced concrete.

ferro·elec·tric *Physics* ● *adjective* exhibiting permanent electric polarization which varies in strength with the applied electric field. ● *noun* a ferroelectric body or substance. □ **ferro·elec·tri·city** *noun*

ferro·mag·nes·ian /feroˈmaɡniːʒən/ *adjective* (of a rock or mineral) containing iron and magnesium as major components.

ferro·mag·net·ism *noun Physics* a phenomenon, evidenced by metallic iron, cobalt, and nickel, in which there is a high susceptibility to magnetization, the strength of which varies with the applied magnetizing field, and which may persist after removal of the applied field. □ **ferro·mag·net·ic** *adjective*

Fer·ron /ferˈɒ̃/ **Jacques** (1921–85), Canadian physician and writer. Well known for his political and social activities, he founded the Rhinoceros Party in 1963; his works take as their themes justice, social concepts of love, and the creation of new myths related to Quebec history and politics, and include the play *Les grands soleils* (1958) and the novels *Contes du pays incertain* (1962) and *La nuit* (1965, translated as *Quince Jam*, 1977).

fer·rous *adjective* **1** (of an alloy etc.) containing iron in significant quantities (*ferrous and non-ferrous metals*). **2** *Chem.* of or containing iron in a divalent form (compare FERRIC). [Latin *ferrum* iron]

ferrous sulphate *noun* a pale green iron salt used in inks, tanning, water purification, and treating anemia.

fer·rugin·ous /fəˈruːdʒɪnəs/ *adjective* **1** (of rocks, minerals, etc.) of the nature of or containing iron or its compounds. **2** rust-coloured or reddish brown. [Latin *ferrugo -ginis* rust, from *ferrum* iron]

fer·rule /ˈferuːl/ *noun* **1** a usu. metal ring or cap strengthening the end of a stick or tube, used esp. to prevent splitting or wearing. **2** a band strengthening or forming a joint. [earlier *verrel* etc. from Old French *virelle, virol(e)*, from Latin *viriola* diminutive of *viriae* bracelet: assimilated to Latin *ferrum* iron]

ferry ● *noun* (pl. **-ries**) **1** a boat which conveys passengers, vehicles, etc. across water as a regular service. **2** the service itself or the place where it operates. ● *verb* (**-ries, -ried**) **1** *transitive & intransitive* convey or go in a boat etc. across water. **2** *transitive* transport from one place to another, esp. as a regular service. □ **ferry·man** *noun* (pl. **-men**). [Old Norse *ferja* from Germanic]

ferry boat *noun* = FERRY 1.

fer·tile /ˈfɜrtaɪl/ *adjective* **1** (of soil) fruitful or rich in the materials needed to produce and support vegetation. **2 a** (of a human being, animal, or plant) able to produce offspring. **b** producing many offspring. **c** (of a seed, egg, etc.) capable of becoming a new individual. **3 a** (of the mind) inventive, full of or able to produce new ideas. **b** conducive to creativity, productivity, etc. (*a fertile field for research*). **4** (of nuclear material) able to become fissile by the capture of neutrons. [French from Latin *fertilis*]

Fertile Crescent a crescent-shaped area of fertile land in the Middle East extending from the E Mediterranean coast through the valley of the Tigris and Euphrates rivers to the Persian Gulf. This formed the cradle of the Assyrian, Sumerian, Phoenician, and Babylonian civilizations.

fer·til·ity /fɜrˈtɪlɪti/ *noun* **1** fruitfulness, productiveness, or the quality of being fertile. **2** the actual number of live births.

fer·til·iz·a·tion *noun* (also esp. *Brit.* **-isation**) **1** *Biol.* the fusion of male and female gametes during sexual reproduction to form a zygote. **2 a** the act or an instance of fertilizing. **b** the state or process of being fertilized.

fer·til·ize *transitive verb* (also esp. *Brit.* **-ise**) **1 a** make fertile or productive. **b** enrich (soil, plants, etc.), esp. with minerals, nutrients, etc. **2** cause (an egg, female animal, or plant) to develop a new individual by introducing male reproductive material. □ **fer·til·iz·able** *adjective*

fer·til·iz·er *noun* a chemical or natural substance added to soil to make it more fertile.

fer·ula /ˈferulə/ *noun* **1** any plant of the genus *Ferula*, esp. the giant fennel (*F. communis*), having a tall stick-like stem and thick roots. **2** = FERULE. [Latin, = giant fennel, rod]

fer·ule /ˈferuːl/ *noun* a flat ruler with a widened end formerly used for beating children. [Middle English (as FERULA)]

fer·vent /ˈfɜrvənt/ *adjective* **1** ardent, impassioned, intense (*fervent admirer; fervent hatred*). **2** *archaic* hot, glowing. □ **fer·vency** *noun* **fer·vent·ly** *adverb* [Old French from Latin *fervēre* boil]

fer·vid /ˈfɜrvɪd/ *adjective* **1** ardent, intense. **2** *archaic* hot, glowing. □ **fer·vid·ly** *adverb* [Latin *fervidus* from *fervēre*]

fer·vour /ˈfɜrvər/ *noun* (also **fer·vor**) **1** vehemence, passion, zeal. **2** *archaic* a glowing condition; intense heat. [Latin *fervor -oris* (as FERVENT)]

Fès see FEZ.

fes·cue /ˈfeskjuː/ *noun* any grass of the genus *Festuca*, valuable for lawns, pasture, and fodder. [Old French *festu*, ultimately from Latin *festuca* stalk, straw]

fess¹ *noun* (also **fesse**) *Heraldry* a horizontal stripe across the middle of a shield, usu. occupying one-third of the shield. [Old French from Latin *fascia* band]

fess² *intransitive verb* (usu. foll. by *up*) *informal* confess. [contraction of CONFESS]

Fes·sen·den /ˈfesən,dən/ **Reg·in·ald Aub·rey** (1866–1932), Canadian-born US physicist and radio engineer. He pioneered radio transmission, devising the amplitude modulation of radio waves for carrying audio signals, and inventing the heterodyne receiver; in 1906 he made the first sound broadcast in the US.

fess point *noun Heraldry* a point at the exact centre of a shield.

fest *noun* **1** a festival or special occasion. **2** (in *combination*) an activity of a specified type engaged in by a group of people (*gabfest; slugfest*).

fes·tal *adjective* of, like, or pertaining to a feast or festival. [Old French from Late Latin *festalis* (as FEAST)]

fes·ter *verb* **1** *transitive & intransitive* make or become infected and filled with pus. **2** *intransitive* (of feelings, thoughts, etc.) become more bitter and angry. **3** *intransitive* (of food or garbage) become rotten and offensive to the senses. [Middle English from obsolete *fester* (n.) or Old French *festrir*, from Old French *festre* from Latin *fistula*: see FISTULA]

fes·ti·val ● *noun* **1** a day or period of celebration, religious or secular. **2** a series of performances of music, drama, films, etc. given regularly (*film festival*). ● *attributive adjective* of or concerning a festival.

festival of lights *noun* **1** = HANUKKAH. **2** = Diwali.

fes·tive *adjective* **1** of or characteristic of a feast or festival. **2** joyous, cheerful. □ **fes·tive·ly** *adverb* **fes·tive·ness** *noun* [Latin *festivus* from *festum* (as FEAST)]

festive season *noun* (usu. prec. by *the*) a designated time for festivities and celebration, esp. Christmastime.

fes·tiv·ity *noun* (pl. **-ities**) **1** (often in *pl.*) a celebration. **2** rejoicing, merriment.

fes·toon ● *noun* **1** a garland of flowers, leaves, ribbons, etc. hung in a curve as a decoration. **2** a carved or moulded ornament representing this. **3** something hanging in a downward curve. ● *transitive verb* (often foll. by *with*) **1** adorn with or form into festoons. **2** decorate elaborately. **3** drape with cloth, wires, etc. hanging in festoon-like curves. [French *feston* from Italian *festone* from *festa* FEAST]

Fest·schrift /ˈfestʃrɪft/ *noun* (also **fest·schrift**) (pl. **-schrift·en** or **-schrifts**) a volume of writings collected and published in honour of a scholar, writer, etc., usu. presented to mark a specific occasion in his or her life. [German from *Fest* celebration + *Schrift* writing]

feta /ˈfetə/ *noun* a very soft, white cheese made from ewe's milk or goat's milk, originally from Greece. [modern Greek *pheta*]

fetal /ˈfiːtəl/ *adjective* (also esp. *Brit.* **foetal**) **1** of or pertaining to a fetus. **2** being a fetus (*fetal lambs*).

fetal alcohol syndrome *noun* a syndrome of birth defects caused by alcohol consumption during pregnancy, including facial abnormalities, impaired mental and physical development, etc. Abbr.: **FAS**.

fetal distress *noun* evidence of deteriorating condition of a fetus during labour.

fetal position *noun* a curled position of the body, with the head and legs pulled in towards the torso, resembling that of a fetus in the uterus.

fetch ● *transitive verb* **1 a** go for and bring back (a person or thing) (*fetch a doctor*). **b** cause to come (*the concert fetched a crowd of 15,000*). **c** *Computing* retrieve (a file etc.) (*fetches data from an external database*). **2** sell for (a price); realize (a profit) (*fetched $10*). **3** *informal* (usu. with recipient stated) give (a blow, slap, etc.) (*fetched him a slap on the face*). ● *noun* **1** an act of fetching, retrieving, bringing from a distance, etc. **2** *Naut.* the expanse of open water over which the wind can blow or waves travel continuously without obstruction. **3** a game, usu. played with a dog, in which a person throws a ball, stick, etc. and the dog retrieves it. □ **fetch and carry** run backwards and forwards with things or be a mere servant. **fetch up** *informal* arrive, come to rest. □ **fetch·er** *noun* [Old English *fecc(e)an* var. of *fetian*, prob. related to a Germanic root = grasp]

fetch·ing *adjective* attractive. □ **fetch·ing·ly** *adverb*

fete /feit/ ● *noun* **1** a festival, fair, or great entertainment. **2** *Brit.* an outdoor function with the sale of goods, amusements, etc., esp. to raise funds for charity. **3** a saint's day. ● *transitive verb* honour or entertain (a person) lavishly and in a special way. [French *fête* (as FEAST)]

fête cham·pêtre /fet ʃɑ̃ˈpetr/ *noun* a rural or outdoor festival. [French (as FETE, *champêtre* rural)]

Fête na·tio·nale /fet nasjɒˈnal/ *noun* (in full **Fête nationale du Québec**) (in Quebec) the official name for the holiday celebrated on June 24, formerly (and commonly still) called St. Jean Baptiste Day. [French (as FETE, *nationale* national)]

fetid /ˈfetɪd, ˈfiː-/ *adjective* stinking or foul smelling. □ **fetid·ly** *adverb* [Latin *fetidus* from *fetēre* stink]

fet·ish /ˈfetɪʃ/ *noun* **1** *Psych.* a form of sexual desire in which gratification is linked to an abnormal degree to a particular object, item of clothing, part of the body, etc. **2 a** an inanimate object reverenced as having inherent magical powers or as being inhabited by a spirit. **b** an object, principle, etc. evoking irrational, even obsessive, devotion or respect. □ **fetish·ism** *noun* **fetish·ist** *noun* **fetish·is·tic** /-ˈɪstɪk/ *adjective* [French *fétiche* from Portuguese *feitiço* charm: originally adj. = made by art, from Latin *factitius* FACTITIOUS]

fetish·ize /ˈfetɪʃaɪz/ *transitive verb* (also esp. *Brit.* **-ise**) **1** make a fetish of. **2** overvalue or pay undue respect to. □ **fetish·iz·a·tion** /-zeɪʃən/ *noun*

fet·lock *noun* the part of a horse's leg between the cannon bone and the pastern, forming a projection above and behind the hoof where a tuft of hair often grows. [Middle English *fetlak* etc. related to German *Fessel* fetlock, from Germanic]

fetor /ˈfiːtər/ *noun* an offensive smell. [Latin (as FETID)]

fet·ter ● *noun* **1** a shackle or bond, esp. one put on the feet to limit movement. **2** (in *pl.*) captivity or bondage. **3** a restraint, check, or anything that confines, impedes, etc. ● *transitive verb* **1** bind with fetters etc. **2** restrict, impede, or hinder in any way. [Old English *feter* from Germanic]

fet·tle ● *noun* condition, state, or form (*in fine fettle*). ● *transitive verb* trim or clean (the rough edge of a metal casting, pottery before firing, etc.). □ **fet·tler** *noun* [earlier as verb, from dial. *fettle* (n.) = girdle, from Old English *fetel* from Germanic]

fet·tuc·cine /fetʊˈtʃiːni/ *noun* (also **fet·tu·cini**) pasta made in ribbons. [Italian, pl. of diminutive of *fetta* 'slice, ribbon']

fetus /ˈfiːtəs/ *noun* (also esp. *Brit.* **foetus**) (*pl.* **fetus·es**) the unborn offspring of a mammal from the stage of development where the main features of an adult can be recognized, e.g. for a human, from eight weeks after conception. [Latin, = 'offspring']

feud¹ /fjuːd/ ● *noun* **1** a prolonged mutual hostility, esp. between two families, tribes, etc., with murderous assaults in revenge for a previous injury (*a family feud*). **2** a prolonged or bitter quarrel or dispute.

● *intransitive verb* conduct or participate in a feud. [Old French *fede* from Middle Dutch, Middle Low German *vēde* from Germanic, related to FOE]

feud² /fjuːd/ *noun hist.* a fief or piece of land held under the feudal system in return for homage and service to a superior lord by whom it is granted. [medieval Latin *feudum*: see FEE]

feud·al /ˈfjuːdəl/ *adjective* **1** of, according to, or resembling the feudal system. **2** of or pertaining to a fief or the holding of land in feud. □ **feud·al·ism** *noun* **feud·al·ist** *noun* **feud·al·is·tic** /-ˈlɪstɪk/ *adjective* [medieval Latin *feudalis*, *feodalis* from *feudum*, *feodum* FEE, perhaps from Germanic]

feudal system *noun* a medieval European politico-economic system of landholding which was based on a reciprocal arrangement between vassal (or peasant) and lord. The nobility held lands from the Crown in exchange for a specified amount of military service; the peasantry lived on their lord's land, and had to provide him with labour or a share of their produce in exchange for military protection.

feu de joie /ˌfɜ də ˈʒwɒ/ *noun* (*pl.* **feux de joie** *pronunc.* same) a salute by firing rifles etc. on a ceremonial occasion. [French, = fire of joy]

Feuer·bach /ˈfɔɪərˌbɒx/ **Lud·wig (An·dreas)** (1804–72), German materialist philosopher. In his best-known work, *The Essence of Christianity* (1841), he argued that the dogmas and beliefs of Christianity are figments of human imagination, fulfilling a need inherent in human nature.

Feuilles, Ri·vière aux /fɜj/ a river in N Quebec, 480 km long, flowing northeastward to the western shore of Ungava Bay. [French, = leaf river, prob. with reference to the dwarf willow and birch trees found in this tundra region]

feuil·le·té /fɜjəˈtei/ *noun* a filled puff pastry shell. [French, 'flaky']

feuil·le·ton /ˌfɜjəˈtɔ̃/ *noun* **1** a part of a European newspaper etc. devoted to fiction, criticism, light literature, etc. **2** an article or work suitable for or printed in that part. [French, 'leaflet']

fe·ver *noun* **1 a** an abnormally high body temperature, often as a sign of illness. **b** any of various diseases characterized by this (*scarlet fever*; *typhoid fever*). **2** intense nervous excitement or agitation. [Old English *fēfor* & Anglo-French *fevre*, Old French *fievre* from Latin *febris*]

fever blister *noun* = COLD SORE.

fe·vered *adjective* **1** affected by or suffering from a fever. **2** highly excited (*a fevered imagination*).

fever·few *noun* an aromatic bushy plant, *Tanacetum parthenium*, with feathery leaves and white daisy-like flowers, formerly used to reduce fever, now often used to prevent migraines. [Old English *feferfuge* from Latin *febrifuga* (as FEBRIFUGE)]

fever·ish *adjective* **1 a** having symptoms resembling those of a fever. **b** of the nature or indicative of a fever. **2** excited, hectic, or restless. **3** (of a place) infested by or conducive to fever. □ **fever·ish·ly** *adverb* **fever·ish·ness** *noun*

fever pitch *noun* a state of extreme excitement.

fèves au lard /ˈfevɒlɑr/ *noun* *Cdn* (*Que.*) baked beans with pork. [Canadian French]

few ● *adjective* not many (*few doctors smoke*; *visitors are few*). ¶ See Usage Note at LESS. ● *pronoun* (as *pl.*) **1** (prec. by *a*) some, but not many (*a few of his friends were there*). **2** a small number, not many (*many are called but few are chosen*). **3** (prec. by *the*) **a** the minority. **b** the elect. □ **every few** once in every small group of (*every few days*). **few and far between** neither numerous nor frequent. **a good few** esp. *Brit. informal* a fairly large number. **have a few** *informal* take several alcoholic drinks. **no fewer than** as many as (a specified number). **quite** (or **not**) **a few** a considerable number. **some few** some but not at all many. [Old English *fēawe*, *fēawa* from Germanic]

fey /fei/ *adjective* **1 a** having a strange, almost otherworldly, whimsical charm. **b** clairvoyant. **2** usu. *ironic* or *derogatory* (of a person, behaviour, etc.) affected. □ **fey·ness** *noun* [Old English *fæge* from Germanic]

Fey·deau /ˈfeidoʊ/ **Georges (Léon Jules Marie)** (1862–1921), French dramatist, who is known for his farces, such as *La Dame de chez Maxim* (1899) and *La Puce à l'oreille* (1907).

Feyn·man /ˈfeinmən/ **Rich·ard Phil·lips** (1918–88), US theoretical physicist. He worked in quantum electrodynamics, and introduced important new techniques for studying the electromagnetic interactions between subatomic particles; he shared the Nobel Prize for physics in 1965.

Fez (also **Fès**) a city in N Morocco, founded in 808; pop. (est. 2002) 921,200.

fez *noun* (*pl.* **fez·zes**) a red felt cap with a flat top and tassel but no brim, worn by men in some Muslim countries and formerly the national headdress of Turkey. [Turkish, perhaps from FEZ]

Vowels: a *cat* ɑ *arm* e *bed* ɜr *her* ɜː *deux* ə *ago* ɪ *sit* i *cosy* iː *feed* ɒ *hot* ɔ *pore* ɔː *no* ʌ *run* ʊ *put*

ff *abbreviation* Music fortissimo.

ff. *abbreviation* **1** and the following (pages, lines, etc.). **2** folios.

FFr *abbreviation* French franc.

FGM *abbreviation* FEMALE GENITAL MUTILATION.

f-hole *noun* either of a pair of sound holes resembling an ʃ and a reversed ʃ in shape, cut in the front of musical instruments of the violin family, and some other stringed instruments such as semi-acoustic electric guitars or mandolins.

fi·acre /fiˈakr/ *noun* a small, horse-drawn, four-wheeled carriage. [named after the Hôtel de St. *Fiacre*, Paris, where such vehicles were first hired out]

fi·an·cé /ˌfiˈɒnseɪ, fiɒnˈseɪ, -ɑ̃-/ *noun* a man to whom one is engaged to be married. [French, past participle of *fiancer* betroth, from Old French *fiance* a promise, ultimately from Latin *fidere* to trust]

fi·an·cée /fiˈɒnseɪ, fiˈɑ̃seɪ/ *noun* a woman to whom one is engaged to be married. [as FIANCÉ]

fian·chet·to /ˌfiɑːnˈtʃetoː/ *Chess* ● *noun* (pl. **-toes**) the development of a bishop by moving it one square to a long diagonal of the board. ● *transitive verb* (**-toes, -toed**) develop (a bishop) in this way. [Italian, diminutive of *fianco* FLANK]

Fi·an·na Fáil /fiˌanə ˈfɔɪl/ *noun* one of the two main political parties of the Republic of Ireland. [Irish, from *fianna* 'band of warriors' + *Fáil* an ancient name for Ireland]

fi·as·co /fiˈaskoː/ *noun* (pl. **-cos**) a complete and ridiculous failure. [Italian, 'bottle' (with unexplained allusion): see FLASK]

fiat /ˈfiːat, ˈfaɪat/ *noun* **1** a formal authorization. **2** a decree or order. [Latin, 'let it be done']

fiat money *noun* US paper money that has been authorized as legal tender by a government decree but cannot be exchanged for its value in ordinary coin.

fib ● *noun* a trivial lie, esp. about something unimportant. ● *intransitive verb* (**fibbed, fib·bing**) tell a fib. □ **fib·ber** *noun* [perhaps from obsolete *fible-fable* nonsense, reduplication of FABLE]

fiber *esp. US* var. of FIBRE.

Fibo·nacci /ˌfiːbəˈnɒtʃi/ (also called **Leo·nar·do Pi·sano**) (*c*.1170–*c*.1250), Italian mathematician. He did significant work on Euclidean geometry, but is best remembered for his sequence of 'Fibonacci numbers'.

Fibonacci series /ˌfibəˈnɒtʃi/ *noun* Math. a series of numbers in which each number (**Fibonacci number**) is the sum of the two preceding numbers, e.g. 1, 1, 2, 3, 5, 8, etc. [FIBONACCI]

fibre *noun* (also esp. US **fiber**) **1** Biol. **a** a thread-like element in plant tissue, esp. an elongated cell with thick walls and no protoplasm. **b** any thread-like structure forming part of the muscular, nervous, connective, or other tissue in an animal body. **2 a** a thread or filament forming part of a textile. **b** any material consisting of animal, vegetable, or synthetic fibres, esp. a substance that can be spun, woven, or felted. **3** a thread formed from glass, metal, etc. **4 a** the texture or structure of a thing. **b** the essence of a person's character (*lacks moral fibre*). **5** = DIETARY FIBRE. □ **fibred** *adjective* (also in combination). **fibre·less** *adjective* **fibri·form** /ˈfaɪbrɪˌfɔrm/ *adjective* [French from Latin *fibra*]

fibre·board *noun* (also esp. US **fiber·board**) a building material made of wood or other plant fibres compressed into boards.

fibre·fill *noun* (also esp. US **fiber·fill**) a synthetic material used for insulating or padding garments, cushions, etc.

fibre·glass *noun* (also esp. US **fiber·glass**) any material consisting of glass filaments woven into a textile or paper, or embedded in plastic etc., for use as a construction or insulation material.

fibre optics *plural noun* **1** transmission of information, by means of infrared light signals, along a thin glass fibre. **2** (treated as *pl.*) the fibres etc. so used. □ **fibre optic** *adjective*

fi·bril /ˈfaɪbrɪl/ *noun* **1** a small or delicate fibre, esp. a constituent strand of an animal, vegetable, or synthetic fibre. **2** the ultimate subdivision of a fibre. □ **fi·bril·lar** *adjective* [modern Latin *fibrilla* diminutive of Latin *fibra* fibre]

fi·bril·late /ˈfaɪbrɪˌleɪt/ *intransitive verb* **1** (of a muscle, esp. in the heart) undergo a quivering movement or contract irregularly fibril by fibril. **2** (of a fibre) split up into fibrils. □ **fi·bril·la·tion** *noun*

fib·rin /ˈfaɪbrɪn/ *noun* an insoluble protein formed during blood clotting from fibrinogen. □ **fib·rin·oid** *adjective* **fib·rin·ous** *adjective* [FIBRE + -IN]

fib·rino·gen /faɪˈbrɪnədʒən/ *noun* a soluble blood plasma protein which produces fibrin when acted upon by the enzyme thrombin.

fibro- /ˈfaɪbroː/ *combining form* fibre.

fibro·blast /ˈfaɪbroːblast/ *noun* Anat. a cell producing collagen fibres in connective tissue.

fi·broid /ˈfaɪbrɔɪd/ ● *adjective* **1** of or characterized by fibrous tissue. **2** resembling or containing fibres. ● *noun* a benign tumour of muscular and fibrous tissues, one or more of which may develop in the wall of the uterus.

fi·bro·in /ˈfaɪbroːɪn/ *noun* a protein which is the chief constituent of silk and spider webs. [FIBRO- + -IN]

fi·broma /faɪˈbroːmə/ *noun* (pl. **fi·bro·mas** or **fi·bro·mata** /-mətə/) a fibrous tumour. [modern Latin from Latin *fibra* fibre + -OMA]

fibro·myal·gia /ˌfaɪbroːmaɪˈaldʒə/ *noun* a rheumatic disorder of uncertain origin, characterized by chronic, diffuse muscular or musculo-skeletal pain, with stiffness (esp. on waking) and localized tenderness at specific points on the body.

fi·bro·sis /faɪˈbroːsɪs/ *noun* Med. a thickening and scarring of connective tissue, usu. as a result of injury. □ **fi·brot·ic** /-ˈbrɒtɪk/ *adjective* [modern Latin from Latin *fibra* fibre + -OSIS]

fi·brous /ˈfaɪbrəs/ *adjective* consisting of or like fibres.

fib·ula /ˈfɪbjulə/ *noun* (pl. **fib·ulae** /-ˌliː/ or **fib·ulas**) **1** Anat. the smaller and outer of the two bones between the knee and the ankle in terrestrial vertebrates. **2** Gk & Rom. Hist. a brooch or clasp. □ **fibu·lar** *adjective* [Latin, perhaps related to *figere* fix]

-fic *suffix* (usu. as **-ific**) forming adjectives meaning 'producing', 'making' (*prolific; pacific*). □ **-fically** *suffix*. [from or after French *-fique* or Latin *-ficus* from *facere* do, make]

-fication *suffix* (usu. as **-ification**) forming nouns of action from verbs in *-fy* (*acidification; purification; simplification*). [from or after French *-fication* or Latin *-ficatio -onis* from *-ficare*: see -FY]

fiche /fiːʃ/ *noun* (pl. same or **fiches**) a microfiche. [French, = slip of paper]

Fichte /ˈfɪxtə/ **Jo·hann Gott·lieb** (1762–1814), German Idealist philosopher. His principal work, *Doctrine of Knowledge* (1794), postulated that the ego is the only basic reality, and that the world around it (the 'non-ego') is posited by the ego in defining and delimiting itself; he is known for preaching moral virtues and encouraging patriotic values.

fichu /ˈfiːʃuː/ *noun* a woman's small triangular shawl of lace etc. for the shoulders and neck. [French]

fickle *adjective* inconstant, changeable, esp. in loyalty. □ **fickle·ness** *noun* [Old English *ficol*: compare *befician* deceive, *fǣcne* deceitful]

fic·tion *noun* **1** an invented idea or statement or narrative; an imaginary thing. **2** literature, esp. novels, describing imaginary events and people. **3** a conventionally accepted falsehood (*polite fiction*). **4** the act or process of inventing imaginary things. **5** = LEGAL FICTION. □ **fic·tion·al** *adjective* **fic·tion·al·ity** *noun* **fic·tion·al·ly** *adverb* **fic·tion·ist** *noun* [Old French from Latin *fictio -onis* from *fingere* 'form, contrive']

fic·tion·al·ize *transitive verb* (also esp. Brit. **-ise**) make into fiction; give a fictional quality to. □ **fic·tion·al·iz·a·tion** *noun* **fic·tion·al·izer** *noun*

fic·ti·tious *adjective* **1** imaginary, unreal. **2** counterfeit; not genuine. **3** (of a name or character) assumed. **4** of or in novels. **5** regarded as what it is called by a legal or conventional fiction. □ **fic·ti·tious·ly** *adverb* **fic·ti·tious·ness** *noun* [Latin *ficticius* from *fingere* 'form, contrive']

fic·tive *adjective* **1** creating or created by imagination. **2** not genuine. □ **fic·tive·ness** *noun* [French *fictif -ive* or medieval Latin *fictivus* from *fingere* 'form, contrive']

ficus /ˈfiːkəs, ˈfaɪkəs/ *noun* (pl. same) a tree or shrub of the large genus *Ficus* (mulberry family), including the fig and the rubber plant. Also called WEEPING FIG. [Latin, = fig, fig tree]

Ficus ben·ja·mina /bendʒəˈmiːnə/ *noun* (pl. same) a tropical tree with drooping branches, frequently grown as a houseplant.

fid·dle ● *noun* **1** a stringed instrument played with a bow, esp. a violin. **2** *informal* an instance of cheating or fraud. **3** Naut. a contrivance for stopping things from rolling or sliding off a table in bad weather. ● *verb* **1** *intransitive* **a** (often foll. by *with, at*) play restlessly. **b** (often foll. by *about*) move aimlessly. **c** act idly or frivolously. **d** (usu. foll. by *with*) make minor adjustments; tinker (esp. in an attempt to make improvements). **2** *transitive* *slang* **a** a cheat, swindle. **b** falsify. **c** get by cheating. **3 a** *intransitive* play the fiddle. **b** *transitive* play (a tune etc.) on the fiddle. □ **fiddle while Rome burns** be concerned with relatively trivial matters while ignoring the serious or disastrous events going on around one. **as fit as a fiddle** in very good health. **play second fiddle** take a subordinate role. [Old English *fithele* from Germanic from a Romanic root related to VIOL]

fiddle·back *noun* (also *attributive*) something, e.g. the back of a chair, that is shaped like the back of a fiddle.

fiddle-de-dee *interjection* expressing contempt, dismissiveness, etc.

fiddle-faddle ● *noun* trivial matters. ● *intransitive verb* fuss, trifle. ● *interjection* nonsense! [reduplication of FIDDLE]

fiddle·head *noun* **1** *N Amer.* the young, curled, edible frond of certain ferns. **2** a scroll-like carving at a ship's bows.

fiddlehead green *noun Cdn* (usu. in *pl.*) = FIDDLEHEAD 1.

fid·dler *noun* **1** a person who plays a fiddle. **2** any small N American crab of the genus *Uca*, the male having one of its claws held in a position like a violinist's arm. **3** *Brit. slang* a swindler, a cheat.

fiddle·sticks *interjection* expressing exasperation, scorn, etc.

fid·dling ● *noun* **1** the action of playing a fiddle, esp. in folk music. **2** the action of tinkering or playing with something. ● *adjective* **1** petty, trivial. **2** that fiddles.

fid·dly *adjective* (**fid·dli·er, fid·dli·est**) *informal* intricate, awkward, or tiresome to do or use.

Fidei Defen·sor /ˌfaidɪˌai drˈfensɔr, ˌfiːdeiiː/ *noun see* DEFENDER OF THE FAITH.

fide·ism /ˈfaidɪˌɪzəm, ˈfiːdei-/ *noun* the doctrine that knowledge depends on faith or revelation rather than reason. □ **fide·ist** *noun* **fide·is·tic** *adjective* [Latin *fides* faith + -ISM]

Fi·del·is·ta /fɪdeˈliːstə/ *noun* an adherent of Fidel Castro.

fi·del·ity /fɪˈdeliti/ *noun* **1** (often foll. by *to*) faithfulness, loyalty. **2** sexual faithfulness to one's spouse, lover, etc. **3** strict conformity to truth or fact. **4** exact correspondence to the original. **5** precision in reproduction of sound (*high fidelity*). [French *fidélité* or Latin *fidelitas* (as FEALTY)]

fidelity insurance *noun* insurance taken out by an employer against losses incurred through an employee's dishonesty etc.

fidget ● *verb* (**fidget·ed, fidget·ing**) **1** *intransitive* move or act restlessly or nervously, usu. while maintaining basically the same posture. **2** *intransitive* be uneasy, worry. **3** *transitive* make (a person) uneasy or uncomfortable. ● *noun* **1** a person who fidgets. **2** (usu. in *pl.*) **a** a bodily uneasiness seeking relief in spasmodic movements; such movements. **b** a restless mood. □ **fidget·i·ness** *noun* **fidgety** *adjective* [obsolete or dial. *fidge* to twitch]

fi·du·cial /fɪˈduːʃəl, fɪˈdjuː-/ *adjective* (of a line, point, etc.) assumed as a fixed basis of comparison. [Late Latin *fiducialis* from *fiducia* trust from *fidere* to trust]

fi·du·ci·ary /fɪˈduːʃəri, fɪˈdjuː-/ ● *adjective* **1 a** of or relating to a trust, trustee, or trusteeship. **b** held or given in trust. **2** (of a paper currency) depending for its value on public confidence or securities. ● *noun* (*pl.* **-aries**) a trustee. [Latin *fiduciarius* (as FIDUCIAL)]

fie *interjection archaic* expressing disgust, shame, or a pretense of outraged propriety. [Old French from Latin *fi*, an exclamation of disgust at a stench]

fief /fiːf/ *noun* **1** a piece of land held under the feudal system or in fee. **2** a person's sphere of operation or control. [French (as FEE)]

fief·dom /ˈfiːfdəm/ *noun* a fief.

field ● *noun* **1 a** an area of open land, esp. one used for pasture or crops. **b** (*attributive*) grown in a field, as opposed to in a greenhouse etc. (*field tomatoes*). **2** a piece of land marked out for a specified purpose, esp. an area marked out for games (*football field*). **3 a** the participants in a contest or sport. **b** all the competitors in a race or all except those specified. **4** an area rich in some natural product (*gas field*). **5** an expanse of ice, snow, sea, sky, etc. **6 a** the ground on which a battle is fought; a battlefield (*left his rival in possession of the field*). **b** the scene of a campaign. **c** (*attributive*) (of artillery etc.) light and mobile for use on campaign. **d** *archaic* a battle. **7** an area of operation or activity; a subject of study (*each supreme in her own field*). **8 a** the region in which a force is effective (*gravitational field; magnetic field*). **b** the force exerted in such an area. **9** a range of perception (*field of view; wide field of vision; filled the field of the telescope*). **10** *Math.* a system subject to two operations analogous to those for the multiplication and addition of real numbers. **11** (*attributive*) **a** (of an animal or plant) found in the countryside, wild (*field mouse*). **b** carried out or working in the natural environment, not in a laboratory etc. (*field test*). **12 a** the background of a picture, coin, flag, etc. **b** *Heraldry* the surface of an escutcheon or of one of its divisions. **13** *Computing* a part of a record, representing an item of data. **14** *N Amer.* = FIELD ICE. ● *verb* **1** *Baseball* **a** *intransitive* act as a fielder. **b** *transitive* stop (and return) (the ball). **2** *transitive* **a** select (a team or individual) to play in a game. **b** deploy (an army). **c** propose (a candidate). **3** *transitive* deal with (a succession of questions etc.). □ **in the field 1** on a military campaign. **2** working etc. away from one's laboratory, headquarters, etc. **play the field** *informal* avoid exclusive attachment to one person or activity etc. **take the field 1** begin a campaign. **2** (of a sports team) go on to a playing field to begin a game. [Old English *feld* from West Germanic]

field book *noun* a book used in the field by a botanist, zoologist, etc. for technical notes.

field corn *noun N Amer.* corn grown for use as a grain or animal feed.

field day *noun* **1** wide scope for action or success; a time occupied with exciting events (*anglers are having a field day with the salmon run*). **2** *Military* an exercise, esp. in manoeuvring; a review. **3** a day spent in exploration, scientific investigation, etc., in the natural environment. **4** *N Amer.* a day at which an entire school competes in outdoor track and field events.

field dress *transitive verb* remove the viscera of (an animal that has been killed in a hunt).

field effect transistor *noun* a semiconductor device with current flowing through a channel controlled by a transverse electric field.

field·er *noun Baseball etc.* **1** a player who fields the ball. **2** a member (other than the pitcher) of the side that is fielding, esp. an outfielder.

fielder's choice *noun Baseball* a fielder's attempt to put out a baserunner rather than the batter, thus allowing the batter to reach base safely.

field event *noun* (usu. in *pl.*) an athletic event that involves jumping or throwing something (e.g. a shot or javelin), and is not performed on a running track.

field·fare *noun* a thrush, *Turdus pilaris*, of northern Eurasia, having grey plumage with a speckled breast. [Middle English *feldefare*, perhaps as FIELD + FARE]

field glasses *plural noun* binoculars for outdoor use.

field goal *noun* **1** *Football* a goal scored by a drop kick or place kick from the field. **2** *Basketball* a goal scored when the ball is in normal play.

field guide *noun* a book for the identification of birds, flowers, etc., in the field.

field hand *noun* a farm worker; a person who works in a field or fields.

field hockey *noun* a game played between two teams on a field with curved sticks and a small hard ball.

field hospital *noun* a temporary hospital near a battlefield.

field house *noun N Amer.* a building used for indoor athletic events, e.g. track and field.

field ice *noun N Amer.* a large flat area of floating ice.

Field·ing ▸ 1 Henry (1707–54), English novelist. His works are generally considered the first modern novels in English, and include *Joseph Andrews* (1742), which begins as a parody of his rival Richardson's *Pamela*, and the picaresque novel *Tom Jones* (1749). **2 Wil·liam Ste·vens** (1848–1929), Canadian journalist and politician, Liberal premier of Nova Scotia 1884–96. Initially determined to withdraw Nova Scotia from Confederation, he later concentrated on encouraging economic growth in the province, and resigned in 1896 to become finance minister in Laurier's government.

field lacrosse *noun* a type of lacrosse played on an open field with teams of ten men or twelve women.

field marshal *noun Brit.* an army officer of the highest rank.

field mouse *noun* any of various mice inhabiting fields.

field mushroom *noun* the edible fungus *Agaricus campestris*.

field mustard *noun* charlock.

field notes *plural noun* notes made by a person while engaged in fieldwork.

field officer *noun* an army officer of field rank.

field of honour *noun* the place where a duel or battle is fought.

Field of the Cloth of Gold a meeting between Henry VIII of England and Francis I of France held near Calais in 1520, for which both monarchs erected elaborate temporary palaces and pavilions, including a sumptuous display of golden cloth. Little of importance was achieved.

field of vision *noun* all that comes into view when the eyes are turned in some direction.

field party *noun* (*pl.* **-ties**) *Cdn* a large outdoor party held in an open field.

field rank *noun* any rank in the army above captain and below general.

Fields, W. C. (born William Claude Dukenfield) (1880–1946), US

Consonants: **b** but **d** dog **f** few **g** get **h** her **j** yes **k** cat **l** leg **m** man **n** no **p** pen **r** red **s** sit

comedian, who is known for his bulbous nose, grating voice, and sardonic humour; his films include *The Bank Dick* and *My Little Chickadee* (both 1940).

field sports *plural noun Brit.* outdoor sports, esp. hunting, shooting, and fishing.

field·stone *noun* unfinished stone, esp. when used as a building material.

field test ● *transitive verb* test (a device) in the environment in which it is to be used. ● *noun* a test of a device etc. in the environment in which it is to be used. □ **field tester** *noun*

field trial *noun* **1** a test or competition between gun dogs to determine their ability to perform in actual hunting conditions. **2** = FIELD TEST *noun*.

field trip *noun* **1** a school trip, e.g. to a museum, a park, etc., to gain knowledge or experience away from the classroom. **2** a research trip to study something at first hand.

field·work *noun* **1** the practical work of a surveyor, collector of scientific data, sociologist, etc., conducted in the natural environment rather than a laboratory, office, etc. **2** a temporary fortification. □ **field·work·er** *noun*

fiend /fiːnd/ *noun* **1 a** an evil spirit, a demon. **b** (prec. by *the*) the Devil. **2 a** a very wicked or cruel person. **b** a person causing mischief or annoyance. **3** (with a qualifying word) *informal* **a** a devotee (*a fitness fiend*). **b** an addict (*a dope fiend*). □ **fiend·like** *adjective* [Old English *fēond* from Germanic]

fiend·ish /ˈfiːndɪʃ/ *adjective* **1** like a fiend; extremely cruel or unpleasant. **2** extremely difficult. □ **fiend·ish·ly** *adverb* **fiend·ish·ness** *noun*

fierce *adjective* (**fier·cer**, **fier·cest**) **1** vehemently aggressive or frightening in temper or action, violent. **2** eager, intense, ardent. **3** unpleasantly strong or intense; uncontrolled (*fierce heat*). □ **something fierce** *slang* to a great degree (*I miss him something fierce*). □ **fierce·ly** *adverb* **fierce·ness** *noun* [Old French *fiers fier* proud, from Latin *ferus* savage]

fiery /ˈfaɪəri/ *adjective* (**fier·i·er**, **fier·i·est**) **1** consisting of or flaming with fire. **2** like fire in appearance, bright red. **3 a** hot as fire. **b** acting like fire; producing a burning sensation. **4 a** flashing, ardent (*fiery eyes*). **b** eager, pugnacious, spirited, irritable (*fiery temper*). **5** (of gas, a mine, etc.) inflammable; liable to explosions. □ **fier·i·ly** *adverb* **fier·i·ness** *noun*

Fies·ole /ˈfjezoːlei/ **Gio·van·ni da**, see ANGELICO.

fies·ta /fiˈestə/ *noun* **1** a holiday or festivity. **2** a religious festival in Spanish-speaking countries. [Spanish, = feast]

Fife[1] a local government region and former county (until 1975) of east central Scotland; capital, Glenrothes.

Fife[2] see PHYFE.

fife ● *noun* a kind of small shrill flute used with the drum in military music. ● *verb* **1** *intransitive* play the fife. **2** *transitive* play (an air etc.) on the fife. □ **fifer** *noun* [German *Pfeife* PIPE, or French *fifre* from Swiss German *Pfifre* piper]

fife rail *noun Naut. hist.* a rail round the mainmast of a sailing ship, holding belaying pins. [18th c.: origin unknown]

FIFO /ˈfaɪfoː/ *abbreviation* FIRST IN, FIRST OUT.

fif·teen ● *noun* **1** one more than fourteen, or five more than ten; the product of three units and five units. **2** a symbol for this (15, xv, XV). **3** a size etc. denoted by fifteen. **4** a team of fifteen players, esp. in rugby. **5** (**the Fifteen**) *Brit. Hist.* the Jacobite rebellion of 1715. ● *adjective* that amount to fifteen. □ **fif·teenth** *adjective & noun* [Old English *fīftēne* (as FIVE, -TEEN)]

fifth ● *noun* **1** the position in a sequence corresponding to that of the number 5 in the sequence 1–5. **2** something occupying this position. **3** the fifth person etc. in a race or competition. **4** any of five equal parts of a thing. **5** *Music* **a** an interval or chord spanning five consecutive notes in the diatonic scale (e.g. C to G). **b** a note separated from another by this interval. **6** *US informal* **a** a fifth of a gallon of liquor. **b** a bottle containing this. **7** *Baseball* the fifth inning. **8** *Dance* = FIFTH POSITION. ● *adjective* that is the fifth. ● *adverb* in the fifth place; fifthly. □ **take the Fifth** (in the US) exercise the right guaranteed by the Fifth Amendment. □ **fifth·ly** *adverb* [earlier and dial. *fift* from Old English *fīfta* from Germanic, assimilated to FOURTH]

Fifth Amendment *noun* an amendment to the US constitution which states that no person may be compelled to give testimony that might incriminate himself or herself.

fifth column *noun* a group working for an enemy within a country at war etc. □ **fifth columnist** *noun* [originally with reference to an extra

body of supporters claimed by General Mola as being within Madrid when he besieged the city with four columns of Nationalist forces in 1936]

fifth estate *noun* any group viewed as being separate from the traditional four estates of the nobility, clergy, commons, and the press, e.g. the electronic media, labour unions, etc.

fifth-genera·tion *adjective* denoting a proposed new class of computer employing artificial intelligence.

fifth position *noun Dance* **1** a position of the feet in which they are placed turned outwards one immediately in front of but touching the other so that the toe of the back foot just protrudes beyond the heel of the front foot. **2** a position of the arms in which both are held curved in front of the hips or waist or above the head with the palms of the hands facing towards the body and slightly separated.

Fifth Republic *noun* the French republic established in 1958.

fifth wheel *noun* **1** an extra wheel for a four-wheeled vehicle. **2** a superfluous person or thing. **3** *N Amer.* a coupling between a vehicle used for towing and a trailer. **4** (in full **fifth wheel trailer**) *N Amer.* a camper-trailer towed by a pickup truck. **5** a horizontal turntable over the front axle of a carriage as an extra support to prevent its tipping.

fifty ● *noun* (*pl.* **-ties**) **1** the product of five and ten. **2** a symbol for this (50, l, L). **3** (in *pl.*) the numbers from 50 to 59, esp. the years of a century or of a person's life. **4** a set of fifty persons or things. **5** a fifty-dollar bill, fifty-pound note, etc. ● *adjective* that amount to fifty. □ **fifty-first, -second**, etc. the ordinal numbers between fiftieth and sixtieth. **fifty-one, -two**, etc. the cardinal numbers between fifty and sixty. □ **fif·ti·eth** *adjective, noun, & adverb* **fifty·fold** *adjective & adverb* [Old English *fīftig* (as FIVE, -TY[2])]

fifty-fifty ● *adjective* equal, with equal shares or chances (*on a fifty-fifty basis*). ● *adverb* equally, half and half (*go fifty-fifty*).

50/50 draw *noun* esp. *Cdn* a fundraiser in which participants buy tickets, with the winner taking half of the total take, and the other half going to the charity etc.

fig[1] *noun* **1** a soft pear-shaped fruit with many seeds, eaten fresh or dried. **2** (in full **fig tree**) any deciduous tree of the genus *Ficus*, esp. *F. carica*, having broad leaves and bearing figs. □ **not care** (or **give**) **a fig** not care at all. [Old French *figue* from Provençal *fig(u)a*, ultimately from Latin *ficus*]

fig[2] *Brit.* ● *noun* **1** dress or equipment (*in full fig*). **2** condition or form (*in good fig*). ● *transitive verb* (**figged**, **fig·ging**) **1** (foll. by *out*) dress up (a person). **2** (foll. by *out, up*) make (a horse) lively. [var. of obsolete *feague* (v.) from German *fegen*: see FAKE[1]]

fig. *abbreviation* **1** figure. **2** figurative. **3** figuratively.

figgy duff *noun Cdn* (*Nfld*) a type of boiled pudding containing raisins. [*fig*, English dial. 'raisin', + DUFF[1]]

fight ● *verb* (*past and past participle* **fought**) **1** *intransitive* (often foll. by *against, with*) **a** contend or struggle in war, battle, single combat, fisticuffs, etc. **b** argue or quarrel. **2** *transitive* contend with (an opponent) in this way. **3** *transitive* take part or engage in (a battle, war, duel, etc.). **4** *transitive* contend about (an issue, an election); maintain (a lawsuit, cause, etc.) against an opponent. **5** *intransitive* campaign or strive determinedly to achieve something. **6** *transitive* strive to overcome (disease, fire, fear, etc.). **7** *transitive* make (one's way) by fighting. **8** *transitive* cause (cocks or dogs) to fight. **9** *transitive* handle (troops, a ship, etc.) in battle. ● *noun* **1 a** a combat between two or more persons, animals, or parties. **b** a boxing match. **c** a battle. **d** an argument. **2** a conflict or struggle; a vigorous effort in the face of difficulty. **3** power or inclination to fight (*has no fight left*; *showed fight*). □ **fight back 1** counterattack. **2** suppress (one's feelings, tears, etc.). **fight down** suppress (one's feelings, tears, etc.). **fight for 1** fight on behalf of. **2** fight to secure (a thing). **fight the good fight** act with strong commitment to a worthy cause. **fight off** repel with effort. **fight out** (usu. **fight it out**) settle (a dispute etc.) by fighting. **fight shy of** avoid; be unwilling to approach (a person, task, etc.). **make a fight of it** (or **put up a fight**) offer resistance. [Old English *feohtan, feoht(e)*, from West Germanic]

fight·er *noun* **1** a person or animal that fights. **2** a fast military aircraft designed for attacking other aircraft. **3** a person with great determination, persistence, etc.

fighter bomber *noun* an aircraft serving as both fighter and bomber.

fighting chair *noun N Amer.* a fixed chair on a boat for use when catching large fish.

fighting chance *noun* an opportunity of succeeding by great effort.

fighting fish *noun* (in full **Siamese fighting fish**) a freshwater fish, *Betta splendens*, native to Thailand, the male of which is highly aggressive.

fighting fit *adjective* fit enough to fight; at the peak of fitness.

fighting top *noun* a circular gun platform high on a warship's mast.

fighting trim *noun* excellent health or condition; readiness for action.

fighting words *plural noun informal* words likely to provoke a fight or indicating a willingness to fight.

fight-or-flight *noun* (usu. *attributive*) a response of the sympathetic nervous system to stress, characterized by the release of adrenalin, an increase in heart rate, and other physiological changes.

fig leaf *noun* **1** a leaf of a fig tree. **2** a representation of a leaf used to cover the genitals in sculpture, painting, etc. **3** a means of concealing something shameful or indecorous. [senses 2 & 3 from Gen. 3:7]

fig·ment *noun* a thing invented or existing only in the imagination. [Latin *figmentum*, related to *fingere* fashion]

Fig Newton *noun N Amer. proprietary* a small rectangular plain cookie with a filling of mashed figs, raisins, etc.

fig·ur·al /ˈfɪgjʊrəl/ *adjective* **1** figurative. **2** consisting of figures or shapes.

fig·ur·a·tion *noun* **1 a** ornamentation by designs. **b** *Music* ornamental patterns of scales, arpeggios, etc., often derived from an earlier motif. **2** allegorical representation.

fig·ura·tive /ˈfɪgjʊrətɪv, ˈfɪgɜr-/ *adjective* **1 a** metaphorical, not literal. **b** metaphorically so called. **2** containing or using many figures of speech. **3** of pictorial or sculptural representation. **4** emblematic, serving as a type. □ **fig·ura·tive·ly** *adverb* **fig·ura·tive·ness** *noun*

fig·ure /ˈfɪgjʊr, ˈfɪgɜr/ ● *noun* **1 a** the external form or shape of a thing. **b** bodily shape, esp. of a woman (*has a very nice figure*). **2** a person as seen in outline but not identified (*saw a figure leaning against the door*). **3** a character or personage, esp. an important or well-known one (*a public figure*). **4** appearance as giving a certain impression (*cut a poor figure*). **5 a** a representation of the human form in drawing, sculpture, etc. **b** an image or likeness. **c** an emblem or type. **6 a** a numerical symbol, esp. any of the ten in Arabic notation. **b** a number so expressed. **c** an amount of money, a value (*cannot put a figure on it*). **d** (in *pl.*) arithmetical calculations. **e** = DIGIT 2. **7** any printed or written character that is not a letter. **8** *Geom.* a two-dimensional space enclosed by a line or lines, or a three-dimensional space enclosed by a surface or surfaces; any of the classes of these, e.g. the triangle, the sphere. **9** a diagram or illustrative drawing. **10** a decorative pattern. **11 a** a division of a set dance, an evolution. **b** (in skating) a prescribed pattern of movements from a stationary position. **12** *Music* a short succession of notes producing a single impression, a brief melodic or rhythmic formula out of which longer passages are developed. **13** (in full **figure of speech**) a recognized form of rhetorical expression giving variety, force, etc., esp. metaphor or hyperbole. **14** *Grammar* a permitted deviation from the usual rules of construction, e.g. ellipsis. **15** *Logic* the form of a syllogism, classified according to the position of the middle term. **16** a horoscope. ● *verb* **1** *intransitive* appear or be mentioned, esp. prominently (*she figures significantly in the book*). **2** *transitive* represent in a diagram or picture. **3** *transitive* imagine; picture mentally. **4** *transitive* **a** embellish with a pattern (*figured satin*). **b** *Music* embellish with figures. **5** *transitive* mark with numbers (*figured bass*) or prices. **6 a** *transitive* calculate. **b** *intransitive* do arithmetic. **7** *transitive* be a symbol of, represent typically. **8** esp. *N Amer.* **a** *transitive* understand, ascertain, consider. **b** *intransitive informal* be likely or understandable (*that figures*). □ **figure on** *N Amer.* count on, expect. **figure out 1** work out by arithmetic or logic. **2** estimate. **3** understand. **go figure** *N Amer.* it escapes explanation. □ **figure·less** *adjective* [Old French from Latin *figura*, *figurare*, related to *fingere* fashion]

figured bass *noun* = THOROUGH BASS.

figure eight *noun* (usu. hyphenated when *attributive*) **1** the shape of the number eight. **2** something that has this shape.

figure·head *noun* **1** a nominal leader or head without real power. **2** a carving, usu. a bust or a full-length figure, at a ship's prow.

figure of fun *noun* a ridiculous person.

figure of speech *noun see* FIGURE *noun* 13.

figure skate *noun* a type of skate having a fairly long, narrow blade with toe picks, used in figure skating.

figure skating *noun* a type of ice skating in which the skater combines a number of movements including steps, jumps, turns, etc. □ **figure skater** *noun*

figur·ine /ˌfɪgjʊˈriːn/ *noun* a small moulded or carved figure; a statuette. [French from Italian *figurina* diminutive of *figura* FIGURE]

fig·wort /ˈfɪgwɜrt, -wɔrt/ *noun* any plant of the genus *Scrophularia*

(family Scrophulariaceae), with dull purplish-brown flowers, once believed to be useful against scrofula.

Fiji /ˈfiːdʒi/ a country in the S Pacific consisting of a group of some 840 islands, of which about 100 are inhabited; pop. (est. 2002) 856,436; capital, Suva. The population contains an almost equal mix of indigenous Pacific islanders and Indians descended from those brought in to work the sugar plantations in the 19th c.

Fiji·an /fiːˈdʒiːən/ ● *adjective* of or relating to Fiji, its people, or language. ● *noun* **1** a native or national of Fiji. **2** the Austronesian language of this people.

fil *noun* a monetary unit of Jordan and Iraq, equal to one-thousandth of a dinar.

fila·ment /ˈfɪləmənt/ *noun* **1** a slender threadlike body or fibre (esp. in animal or vegetable structures). **2** a conducting wire or thread with a high melting point in an electric bulb or thermionic valve, heated or made incandescent by an electric current. **3** *Bot.* the part of the stamen that supports the anther. □ **fila·ment·ary** /-ˈmentəri/ *adjective* **fila·ment·ous** /-ˈmentəs/ *adjective* [French *filament* or modern Latin *filamentum* from Late Latin *filare* spin, from Latin *filum* thread]

fil·aria /fɪˈleriə/ *noun* (*pl.* **fil·ariae** /-rɪˌiː/) any threadlike parasitic nematode worm of the family Filariidae introduced into the blood by certain biting flies and mosquitoes. □ **fil·ar·ial** *adjective* [modern Latin from Latin *filum* thread]

fil·ar·iasis /ˌfɪləˈraɪəsɪs, fɪˌlerɪˈeɪsɪs/ *noun* (*pl.* **fil·ar·iases** /-siːz/) a disease common in the tropics, caused by the presence of filarial worms in the lymph vessels.

fil·bert *noun* **1** any of various shrubs or small trees of the genus *Corylus*, esp. the cultivated hazel, *Corylus maxima*, bearing edible ovoid nuts. **2** this nut. [Middle English *philliberd* etc. from Anglo-French *philbert*, dial. French *noix de filbert*, a nut ripe around St. Philibert's day (20 Aug.)]

filch *transitive verb* pilfer, steal. □ **filch·er** *noun* [Middle English: origin unknown]

file¹ ● *noun* **1** a folder, box, etc., for holding loose papers, esp. arranged for reference. **2** a set of papers kept in this. **3** *Computing* a collection of (usu. related) data stored under one name. **4** *Cdn* issues and responsibilities in a specified area, considered collectively (*what progress has the prime minister made on the unity file?*). ● *verb* **1** *transitive* place (papers) in a file or among (esp. public) records. **2** *transitive* submit (a petition for divorce, an application for a patent, etc.) to the appropriate authority. **3** *transitive* (of a reporter) send (a story, information, etc.) to a newspaper. **4** *intransitive Cdn hist.* register one's claim for a homestead. □ **file away** place in a file, or make a mental note of, for future reference. **on file** in a file or filing system. □ **filer** *noun* [French *fil* from Latin *filum* thread]

file² ● *noun* **1** a line of persons or things one behind another. **2** *Chess* a line of squares from player to player (compare RANK¹ *noun* 5). ● *intransitive verb* walk in a file. □ **file off** (or **away**) *Military* go off by files. [French *file* from Late Latin *filare* spin or Latin *filum* thread]

file³ ● *noun* a tool with a roughened surface or surfaces, usu. of steel, for smoothing or shaping wood, fingernails, etc. ● *transitive verb* smooth or shape with a file. □ **file away** remove (roughness etc.) with a file. □ **filer** *noun* [Old English *fíl* from West Germanic]

filé /ˈfiːleɪ, ˈfiːleɪ/ *noun* pounded or powdered sassafras leaves used to flavour and thicken soup, esp. gumbo. [French, past participle of *filer* twist]

file·name *noun Computing* a string of characters that is used to identify a file to the operating system of a computer.

file server *noun Computing* a device which manages shared access to centralized files in a network.

file sharing *noun Computing* the activity of using a network to transfer files between hard drives, e.g. by downloading MP3 files stored on another computer connected to the Internet.

filet /fɪˈleɪ, ˈfɪlət/ *noun* **1** a kind of net or lace with a square mesh. **2** a fillet of meat or fish. [French, = thread]

filet mi·gnon /fɪˈleɪ mɪnˈjɔ̃/ *noun* a small tender piece of beef from the end of the tenderloin. [French, lit. 'dainty fillet']

file transfer protocol *noun* = FTP *noun*.

fil·ial /ˈfɪliəl/ *adjective* **1** of or due from a son or daughter. **2** *Biol.* bearing the relation of offspring (compare F² 5). [Old French *filial* or Late Latin *filialis* from *filius* son, *filia* daughter]

fili·ation /ˌfɪliˈeɪʃən/ *noun* **1** the fact of being the child of one or two specified parents. **2** (often foll. by *from*) descent or transmission. **3** the formation of offshoots. **4** a branch of a society or language. **5** a

Vowels: a *cat* ɑ *arm* e *bed* ɜr *her* ɜː *deux* ə *ago* ɪ *sit* i *cosy* iː *feed* ɒ *hot* ɔ *pore* oː *no* ʌ *run* ʊ *put*

genealogical relation or arrangement. [French from Late Latin *filiatio -onis* from Latin *filius* son]

fil·i·beg /ˈfɪlɪˌbeg/ *noun Scot.* a kilt. [Gaelic *feileadh-beag* little fold]

fili·bus·ter /ˈfɪlɪˌbʌstər/ ● *noun* **1** *esp. N Amer.* the obstruction of progress in a legislative assembly, esp. by prolonged speaking. **2** *esp. hist.* a person engaging in unauthorized warfare against a foreign nation. ● *verb* **1** *intransitive* act as a filibuster. **2** *transitive* act in this way against (a motion etc.). □ **fili·buster·er** *noun* [ultimately from Dutch *vrijbuiter* FREEBOOTER, influenced by French *flibustier*, Spanish *filibustero*]

fili·gree /ˈfɪlɪˌgriː/ *noun* **1** ornamental work of gold or silver or copper as fine wire formed into delicate tracery; fine metal openwork. **2** anything delicate resembling this. □ **fili·greed** *adjective* [earlier *filigreen, filigrane* from French *filigrane* from Italian *filigrana* from Latin *filum* thread + *granum* seed]

fil·ing¹ *noun* (usu. in *pl.*) a particle rubbed off by a file.

fil·ing² *noun* **1** the act of placing something in a file. **2** the act of submitting a petition, application, etc.

filing cabinet *noun* (*N Amer.* also **file cabinet**) a piece of furniture with deep drawers for storing documents.

Fili·pina /ˌfɪlɪˈpiːnə/ ● *noun* a woman or girl who is a native or national of the Philippines. ● *adjective* who is a Filipina.

Fili·pino /ˌfɪlɪˈpiːnəʊ/ ● *noun* (*pl.* **-os**) a native or national of the Philippines. ● *adjective* of or relating to the Philippines or the Filipinos. [Spanish, = Philippine]

filk *noun* (among science fiction and fantasy fans) a type of popular music characterized by the use of familiar or traditional songs whose lyrics have been rewritten or parodied. [from a typographical error in the title of an essay 'The Influence of Science Fiction on Modern American Filk Music']

fill ● *verb* **1 a** *transitive & intransitive* (often foll. by *with*) make or become full. **b** *intransitive* (of the eyes) brim with tears. **2** *transitive* occupy completely; spread over or through; pervade. **3** *transitive* **a** block up (a cavity or hole in a tooth) with cement, amalgam, gold, etc. **b** drill and put a filling into (a decayed tooth). **4** *transitive* appoint a person to hold (a vacant post). **5** *transitive* hold (a position); discharge the duties of (an office). **6** *transitive esp. N Amer.* supply (a prescription, order for goods, etc.). **7** *transitive* occupy (vacant time). **8** *intransitive* (of a sail) be distended by wind. **9** *transitive* (usu. as **fill·ing** *adjective*) (esp. of food) satisfy, satiate. **10** *transitive* satisfy, fulfill (a need or requirement). **11** *transitive* insert a filling into (a doughnut etc.). **12** *transitive Cards* complete (a holding) by drawing the necessary cards. ● *noun* **1** (prec. by possessive) as much as one wants or can bear (*eat your fill*). **2** material used for filling something, esp. earth etc. used to fill a hole or raise the level of the ground. **3** (in popular music) a short interjected phrase on a particular instrument. □ **fill the bill** = FIT THE BILL (see FIT¹). **fill in 1** add information to complete (a form, document, blank cheque, etc.). **2 a** complete (a drawing etc.) within an outline. **b** fill (an outline) in this way. **3** fill (a hole etc.) completely. **4** (often foll. by *for*) act as a substitute. **5** occupy oneself during (time between other activities). **6** *informal* inform (a person) more fully. **7** *Brit. slang* thrash, beat. **fill out 1** enlarge to the required size. **2** become enlarged or plump. **3** *N Amer.* fill in (a document etc.). **fill up 1** make or become completely full. **2** fill the fuel tank of (a car etc.). **3** provide what is needed to occupy vacant parts or places or deal with deficiencies in. **4** do away with (a pond etc.) by filling. **5** *Brit.* fill in (a document etc.). [Old English *fyllan* from Germanic, related to FULL¹]

fille de joie /ˌfiː də ˈʒwɒ/ *noun* (*pl.* **filles de joie** *pronunc.* same) a prostitute. [French, lit. 'girl of pleasure']

fill·er¹ *noun* **1** material or an object used to fill a cavity or increase bulk. **2** an item filling space in a newspaper etc. **3** a person or thing that fills.

fill·er² *noun* (*pl.* same) a monetary unit of Hungary, equal to one-hundredth of a forint. [Hungarian *fillér*]

filles du roi /ˌfiː dʊ ˈrwa/ *plural noun Cdn hist.* women of marriageable age sent from France to New France under royal direction between 1663–73 to be married to the disproportionately large number of men then living in the colony. [French, lit. 'daughters of the king']

fil·let /ˈfɪlət/ ● *noun* **1** (also /ˈfɪleɪ/) **a** a fleshy boneless piece of meat from near the loins or the ribs. **b** (in full **fillet steak**) the undercut of a sirloin. **c** a boned longitudinal section of a fish. **2 a** a headband, ribbon, string, or narrow band, for binding the hair or worn round the head. **b** a band or bandage. **3 a** a thin narrow strip of anything. **b** a raised rim or ridge on any surface. **4** *Archit.* **a** a narrow flat band separating two mouldings. **b** a small band between the flutes of a column. **5** *Carpentry* an added triangular piece of wood to round off an interior angle. **6 a** a plain line impressed on the cover of a book. **b** a roller used to impress this. **7** *Heraldry* a horizontal division of a shield, a quarter of the depth of a chief. ● *transitive verb* (**fil·let·ed, fil·let·ing**) **1** (also /ˈfɪleɪ/) **a** remove bones from (fish or meat). **b** divide (fish or meat) into fillets. **2** bind or provide with a fillet or fillets. **3** encircle with an ornamental band. [Old French *filet* from Romanic diminutive of Latin *filum* thread]

fill-in *noun* a person or thing put in as a substitute or to fill a vacancy.

fill·ing *noun* **1** any material that fills or is used to fill, esp.: **a** a piece of material used to fill a cavity in a tooth. **b** the edible substance between the slices of bread in a sandwich or the layers in a cake, or enclosed by pastry in a pie. **2** weft.

filling station *noun* = GAS STATION.

fil·lip *noun* **1** something that adds interest or excitement. **2** a stimulus or incentive. **3 a** a sudden release of a finger or thumb when it has been bent and checked by a thumb or finger. **b** a slight smart stroke given in this way. [imitative]

Fill·more, Mil·lard (1800–74), US Whig politician, 13th president of the US 1850–3. His unpopular enforcement of the 1850 Fugitive Slave Act hastened the end of the Whig Party.

fill-up *noun* **1** a thing that fills something up. **2** the act of filling up a fuel tank etc.

filly *noun* (*pl.* **-lies**) **1** a young female horse, usu. before it is four years old. **2** *informal offensive* a girl or young woman. [Middle English, prob. from Old Norse *fylja* from Germanic (as FOAL)]

film ● *noun* **1** a thin coating or covering layer. **2** *Photog.* a strip or sheet of plastic or other flexible base coated with light-sensitive emulsion for exposure in a camera, either as individual visual representations or as a sequence of images which form the illusion of movement when shown in rapid succession. **3 a** a representation of a story, episode, etc., on a film, with the illusion of movement. **b** a story represented in this way. **c** (in *pl.*) the cinema industry. **4** a slight veil or haze etc. **5** a dimness or morbid growth affecting the eyes. **6** a fine thread or filament. ● *verb* **1 a** *transitive* make a photographic film of (a scene, person, etc.). **b** *transitive & intransitive* make a cinema or television film of (a book etc.). **c** *intransitive* be (well or ill) suited for reproduction on film. **2** *transitive & intransitive* cover or become covered with or as with a film. □ **film·able** *adjective* [Old English *filmen* membrane, from West Germanic]

film clip *noun* = CLIP² *noun* 3.

film·fest *noun* a festival at which many films are shown.

film·goer *noun* a person who frequents the cinema.

film·ic *adjective* of or relating to films or cinematography.

film·maker *noun* a director or producer of films. □ **film·making** *noun*

film noir /fɪlm ˈnwɑr/ *noun* (*pl.* **films noir** *pronunc.* same) a film genre, popular esp. in the 1940s, characterized by urban gangster settings and contrasty photography. [French, lit. 'black film']

film·og·raphy /fɪlˈmɒgrəfi/ *noun* (*pl.* **-ies**) a list of films by one director etc. or on one subject. [FILM + -GRAPHY after *bibliography*]

Fil·mon /ˈfɪlmən/ **Gary** (b.1942), Canadian politician, Progressive Conservative premier of Manitoba 1988–99.

film star *noun* a celebrated actor or actress in films.

film strip *noun* a series of transparencies in a strip for projection.

filmy *adjective* (**film·i·er, film·i·est**) **1** thin and translucent. **2** covered with or as with a film. □ **film·i·ly** *adverb* **film·i·ness** *noun*

filo *var.* of PHYLLO.

Filo·fax /ˈfaɪloʊˌfaks/ *noun proprietary* a portable loose-leaf datebook including pages for addresses, notes, etc. [FILE¹ + *facts* pl. of FACT]

filo·virus /ˈfiːloʊˌvaɪrəs/ *noun* a filamentous RNA virus of a genus which causes severe hemorrhagic fevers in humans and primates, and which includes the Ebola and Marburg viruses.

fils /fɪls/ *noun* (*pl.* same) a monetary unit of Iraq, Bahrain, Jordan, Kuwait, and Yemen. [informal pronunciation of Arabic *fals*, a small copper coin]

fils /fiːs/ *noun* (added to a surname to distinguish a son from a father) the son, junior (compare PÈRE). [French, = son]

fil·ter ● *noun* **1** a porous device for removing impurities or solid particles from a liquid or gas passed through it. **2** = FILTER TIP. **3** a screen or attachment for absorbing or modifying light, X-rays, etc. **4** a device for suppressing electrical or sound waves of frequencies not required. **5** *Brit.* **a** an arrangement for filtering traffic. **b** a traffic light signalling this. **6** *Computing* a piece of software that processes text, for example to remove unwanted spaces or to format it for use in another application. **7** *Computing* a functionality in email or Internet searching that automatically sorts email into folders or blocks access to pornographic etc. sites. ● *transitive & intransitive verb* **1** pass or cause to pass through a filter. **2** (foll. by *through*, *into*, etc.) make way gradually. **3** (foll. by *out*) leak or cause to leak. **4** *Brit.* allow (traffic) or (of traffic) be allowed to pass to the left or right at an intersection while traffic going straight ahead is halted (esp. at traffic lights). ☐ **filter out** remove (impurities etc.) by means of a filter. [French *filtre* from medieval Latin *filtrum* felt used as a filter, from West Germanic]

filter·able *adjective* (also **fil·trable**) **1** *Med.* (of a virus) able to pass through a filter that retains bacteria. **2** that can be filtered.

filter bed *noun* a tank or pond containing a layer of sand etc. for filtering large quantities of liquid.

filter-feeder *noun Zool.* an animal that feeds by filtering out plankton or nutrients suspended in water. ☐ **filter-feeding** *noun & adjective*

filter paper *noun* porous paper for filtering.

filter tip *noun* **1** a filter attached to a cigarette for removing impurities from the inhaled smoke. **2** a cigarette with this. ☐ **filter-tipped** *adjective*

filth *noun* **1** repugnant or extreme dirt. **2** vileness, corruption, obscenity. **3** foul or obscene language. **4** (prec. by *the*) *Brit. slang* the police. [Old English *fylth* (as FOUL, -TH²)]

filthy ● *adjective* (**filth·i·er**, **filth·i·est**) **1** extremely or disgustingly dirty. **2** obscene. **3** esp. *Brit. informal* (of weather) very unpleasant. **4** vile. ● *adverb* **1** filthily (*filthy dirty*). **2** *informal* extremely (*filthy rich*). ☐ **filth·i·ly** *adverb* **filth·i·ness** *noun*

filthy lucre *noun* **1** dishonourable gain. **2** *jocular* money.

fil·trable *var.* of FILTERABLE.

fil·trate ● *noun* filtered liquid. ● *transitive verb* filter. ☐ **fil·tra·tion** *noun* [modern Latin *filtrare* (as FILTER)]

fim·bri·ate /ˈfɪmbrɪˌeɪt/ *adjective* (also **fim·bri·at·ed**) **1** *Bot. & Zool.* fringed or bordered with hairs etc. **2** *Heraldry* having a narrow border. [Latin *fimbriatus* from *fimbriae* fringe]

fin¹ ● *noun* **1** an organ on various parts of the body of many aquatic vertebrates and some invertebrates, including fish and cetaceans, for propelling, steering, and balancing (*dorsal fin; anal fin*). **2** a small projecting surface or attachment on an aircraft, rocket, or car for ensuring aerodynamic stability. **3** an underwater swimmer's flipper. **4** a fin-like projection on the keel of a boat etc., used to increase stability. **5** a fin-like projection on any device, for improving heat transfer etc. ● *verb* (**finned**, **fin·ning**) **1** *transitive* (usu. as **finned** *adjective*) provide with fins. **2** *intransitive* swim under water. ☐ **fin·less** *adjective* **finned** *adjective* (also in *combination*). [Old English *fin(n)*]

fin² *noun slang* a five-dollar bill or five-pound note. [abbreviation of *finnip*, perhaps representing Yiddish *finef* five]

fin·agle /fɪˈneɪɡəl/ *transitive & intransitive verb informal* act or obtain dishonestly. ☐ **fin·agler** *noun* [dial. *fainaigue* cheat]

final ● *adjective* **1** situated at the end, coming last. **2** conclusive, decisive, unalterable, putting an end to doubt. **3** concerned with the purpose or end aimed at. ● *noun* **1** (usu. in *pl.*) the last or deciding heat or game in sports or in a competition. **2** the edition of a newspaper published latest in the day. **3** (usu. in *pl.*) the last examination in an academic course. **4** *Music* the principal note in any mode. ☐ **final·ly** *adverb* [Old French or from Latin *finalis* from *finis* end]

final cause *noun Philos.* the end towards which a thing naturally develops or at which an action aims.

final drive *noun* the last part of the transmission system in a motor vehicle.

fi·nale /fɪˈnɑːli/ *noun* **1 a** the last movement of an instrumental composition. **b** a piece of music closing an act in an opera. **2** the close of a drama etc. **3** a conclusion. [Italian (as FINAL)]

final·ism /ˈfaɪnəˌlɪzəm/ *noun* the doctrine that natural processes (e.g. evolution) are directed towards some goal. ☐ **final·is·tic** *adjective*

final·ist /ˈfaɪnəlɪst/ *noun* a competitor in the final of a competition etc.

fi·nal·ity /faɪˈnælɪti/ *noun* (*pl.* **-ities**) **1** the quality or fact of being final. **2** the belief that something is final. **3** a final act, state, or utterance. **4** the principle of final cause viewed as operative in the universe.

final·ize *transitive verb* (also esp. *Brit.* **-ise**) **1** put into final form. **2** complete; bring to an end. **3** approve the final form or details of. ☐ **final·iz·a·tion** *noun*

final solution *noun* the policy under the German Nazi regime of exterminating European Jews. Six million Jews were murdered in concentration camps between 1941 and 1945.

fi·nance /ˈfaɪnæns/ ● *noun* **1** the management of large amounts of money, esp. by governments or large companies. **2** monetary support for an enterprise. **3** (in *pl.*) the money resources of a country, company, or person. ● *transitive verb* provide capital for (a person, purchase, or enterprise), esp. as a loan. ☐ **fi·nance·able** *adjective* [Old French from *finer* settle a debt, from *fin* end: see FINE²]

finance company *noun* (also *Brit.* **finance house**) a company that provides money to consumers for purchasing goods on credit.

fi·nan·cial /faɪˈnænʃəl, fɪ-/ ● *adjective* of or pertaining to revenue or money matters. ● *noun* **1** (in *pl.*) shares in companies dealing in money. **2** (in *pl.*) the finances or financial situation of an organization or individual (*they struggle with their financials, particularly cash flow*). ☐ **fi·nan·cial·ly** *adverb*

financial district *noun* the area of a city where the head offices of banks and other financial institutions are concentrated.

financial futures *plural noun* futures in currencies or interest rates.

financial institution *noun* an organization, e.g. a bank or finance company, that collects funds from individuals, other organizations, or government agencies and invests these funds or lends them on to borrowers.

financial instrument *noun* a formal financial document.

financial statement *noun* an official statement of the assets and liabilities, profit or loss of a company etc. over a given year.

financial year *noun Cdn & Brit.* = FISCAL YEAR.

fi·nan·cier /faɪnænˈsɪər, ˌfɪ-/ *noun* a person who is concerned with or skilled in finance, esp. on a large scale. [French (as FINANCE)]

fi·nan·cing /ˈfaɪnænsɪŋ, faɪˈnænsɪŋ/ *noun* an act, instance, or the process of obtaining or providing funds, capital, etc. for an investment, purchase, etc.

fin·back *noun* (also **finback whale**, **fin whale**) a large baleen whale, *Balaenoptera physalus*, which has a prominent dorsal fin. *Also called* COMMON RORQUAL.

finca *noun* (in Spain and Spanish-speaking countries) a country estate; a ranch.

finch *noun* any small seed-eating passerine bird of the family Fringillidae (esp. one of the genus *Fringilla*), including crossbills, canaries, and chaffinches. [Old English *finc* from West Germanic]

find ● *verb* (*past* and *past participle* **found**) **1 a** *transitive* discover or attain by or as if by search or effort (*found a key*). **b** *transitive* become aware of. **c** *transitive* gain or recover the use of (*I found my tongue*). **d** *transitive* discover (a scent etc.), esp. in hunting. **2** *transitive* **a** get possession of by chance (*found a treasure*). **b** obtain, receive (*idea found acceptance*). **c** make up, arrange to have, or succeed in obtaining (*cannot find the money; can't find time to read*). **d** summon up (*found courage to protest*). **3** *transitive* **a** seek out and provide (*will find you a book*). **b** supply, furnish (*each finds his own equipment*). **4** *transitive* ascertain by study, calculation, or inquiry (*could not find the answer*). **5** *transitive* **a** perceive or experience (*find no sense in it; find difficulty in breathing*). **b** (often in *passive*) discover to be present (*the word is not found in Shakespeare*). **c** learn or prove (a thing) to be through experience, trial, etc. (*finds England too cold; you'll find it pays; find it impossible to reply*). **6** *transitive Law* (of a jury, judge, etc.) authoritatively decide and declare (a person) to be innocent, guilty, etc., or (an issue, offence, etc.) to be that specified (*found him guilty; found that he had done it*). **7** *transitive* reach by a natural or normal process (*water finds its own level*). ● *noun* **1** a discovery of treasure, minerals, etc. **2** a thing or person discovered, esp. when of value. ☐ **all found** (of an employee's wages) with board and lodging provided free. **find against** *Law* decide against (a person), judge to be guilty. **find for** *Law* decide in favour of (a person), judge to be innocent. **find God** experience religious conversion. **find one's feet 1** become able to walk or get the use of one's feet. **2** grow in ability or confidence, develop one's powers, acquire knowledge or capability in a new job, etc. **find it in one's heart** (foll. by *to* + infin.) prevail upon oneself, be willing. **find oneself 1** discover that one is (*woke to find myself in hospital; found herself agreeing*). **2** discover and attain one's special place, power, or vocation. **find out 1** discover or detect (a wrongdoer etc.). **2** (often foll. by *about*) get information (*find out about airfares to Winnipeg*). **3** discover (*find out where we are*). **4** (often foll. by *about*) discover the truth, a fact, etc. (*he never found out*). **5** devise. **6** solve. **find one's way 1** (often foll. by *to*) manage to reach a place. **2** (often foll. by *into*) be brought or get. ☐ **find·able** *adjective* [Old English *findan* from Germanic]

find·er *noun* **1 a** a person who finds. **b** a device which finds something, esp. an instrument for determining or discerning something (*rangefinder; fish finder*). **2** a small telescope attached to a large one to locate an object for observation. **3** the viewfinder of a camera. ☐ **finders keepers** *informal* whoever finds a thing is entitled to keep it.

Consonants: b *but*   d *dog*   f *few*   g *get*   h *her*   j *yes*   k *cat*   l *leg*   m *man*   n *no*   p *pen*   r *red*   s *sit*

finder's fee *noun* a sum of money paid to a person who finds something of value for a client, usu. calculated as a percentage of the value of the contract, investment, etc.

fin de siècle /ˌfã də 'sjekl/ ● *noun* the end of a century or the moods, attitudes, etc. characteristic of such a time. ● *adjective* **1** characteristic of the end of the 19th c., esp. in world-weariness, decadence, or sophistication. **2** decadent. **3** designating or characteristic of the end of a century. [French, = end of century]

find·ing *noun* **1 a** (often in *pl.*) a result or conclusion of an official inquiry. **b** a decision or verdict of a court or jury. **2** (in *pl.*) N Amer. small parts or tools.

Find·ley /ˈfɪndli/ **Tim·othy** (1930–2002), Canadian writer. His fiction often uses metaphors derived from film and structural devices resembling camerawork in addressing the themes of madness, violence, and power; his novels include *The Wars* (1977), *The Telling of Lies* (1986), and *Headhunter* (1993).

fine¹ ● *adjective* **1** of superior quality. **2 a** excellent, admirable, or of striking merit (*a fine painting*). **b** highly accomplished or very skilful (*a fine skier*). **c** honourable, noble, virtuous, or morally upright (*a fine young man*). **d** good, enjoyable, satisfactory, or acceptable (*that will be fine*). **e** fortunate (*has been a fine thing for him*). **f** well conceived or expressed (*a fine saying*). **3 a** clear, pure, refined, or free from dross or impurity. **b** (of gold or silver) containing a high, usu. specified proportion of pure metal. **4 a** handsome, beautiful, or remarkably good-looking (*a fine horse*). **b** imposing, dignified (*a fine figure of a man*). **c** large, of a good size (*fine buildings*). **5** well, in good health or spirits (*I'm fine, thank you*). **6** (of weather, a day, etc.) free from rain or fog, esp. bright and clear with sunshine. **7 a** extremely thin or slender (*a fine thread*). **b** (of a weapon, tool, etc.) having a sharp point or edge (*a fine blade*). **c** in small particles. **d** worked in thin, delicate thread. **e** (esp. of print) small. **f** (of a pen) having a narrow point or tip. **8** flattering, complimentary, or euphemistic (*say fine things about a person*). **9** (of a dress etc.) ornate, showy, smart. **10** (of a person) fastidious, dainty, characterized by or affecting refinement. **11** (of speech, writing, etc.) elegant, ornate, or affected. **12 a** capable of delicate perception or discrimination (*a fine eye for detail*). **b** subtle or perceptible only with difficulty (*a fine distinction*). **13 a** delicately beautiful or exquisitely fashioned (*fine crystal*). **b** (of feelings) refined, elevated. **14** *ironic* difficult, inopportune, inconvenient, etc. (*another fine mess; a fine time to leave*). ● *noun* (in *pl.*) very small particles in mining, milling, etc. ● *adverb* *informal* very well (*suits me fine*). ● *verb* **1** *transitive* (often foll. by *down*) refine or make (beer or wine) clear or pure. **2** *transitive & intransitive* (often foll. by *away, down, off*) make or become finer, thinner, less coarse, etc. □ **cut** (or **run**) **it fine** allow very little margin of time, room for error, etc. **fine and dandy** *informal* **1** great, first-rate. **2** (of a person) very well. **a fine line** a distinction that is difficult to make. **not to put too fine a point on it** to speak bluntly. **one fine day 1** (in story-telling) once upon a time or on a certain day, esp. in the past. **2** at some distant time in the future, esp. of a thing unlikely to occur. □ **fine·ly** *adverb* **fine·ness** *noun* [Old French *fin* ultimately from Latin *finire* finish]

fine² ● *noun* a sum of money exacted as a penalty for an offence. ● *transitive verb* impose a fine upon or punish (a person) by a fine (*fined him $50*). □ **in fine** to sum up; in short. [Old French *fin* from medieval Latin *finis* sum paid on settling a lawsuit, from Latin *finis* end]

fine art *noun* **1 a** (in *pl.*) those arts appealing to the intellect or the sense of beauty, as literature, music, and esp. painting, sculpture, and architecture. **b** any one of these arts. **2** a high accomplishment or a thing requiring a high degree of skill.

fine champagne /ˌfiːn ʃã'panj/ *noun* old liqueur brandy from the Grande Champagne and Petite Champagne vineyards in the Charente, France. [French, = fine (brandy from) Champagne]

fine cut ● *noun* a kind of finely shredded tobacco. ● *adjective* finely cut or shredded.

fine-drawn *adjective* slight, subtle, or indefinite (*fine-drawn distinction*).

Fine Gael /ˌfiːnə 'geil/ *noun* one of the two major political parties of the Republic of Ireland, having entered the Dáil in 1937 in succession to the United Ireland Party. [Irish, lit. 'tribe of Gaels']

fine-grain *adjective* **1** *Photog.* of or capable of producing an image which may be consistently enlarged without appearing grainy. **2** = FINE-GRAINED.

fine-grained *adjective* **1** having a fine grain. **2** consisting of very small particles.

fine print *noun* the information in legal documents, contracts, etc. which is often printed in small type and contains important details that are easy to overlook.

finer points *plural noun* details or aspects recognized and appreciated only by those who are very familiar with a thing, field, etc.

fin·ery /ˈfaɪnəri/ *noun* showy or elegant dress or decoration. [FINE¹ + -ERY, after BRAVERY]

fines herbes /fiːnz 'erb/ *plural noun* mixed herbs used in cooking, esp. chopped for flavouring omelettes. [French, = fine herbs]

fi·nesse /fɪˈnes/ ● *noun* **1** skill in dealing with people or situations cleverly or tactfully. **2** delicacy, refinement, or discrimination. **3** subtle or delicate manipulation. **4** artfulness or cunning, esp. in strategy etc. **5** *Bridge* an attempt to win a trick with a card that is not the highest held. ● *verb* **1** *intransitive & transitive* use or achieve by finesse. **2** *Bridge* **a** *intransitive* make a finesse. **b** *transitive* play (a card) by way of finesse. **3** *transitive* evade or trick by finesse. [French, related to FINE¹]

fin·est ● *adjective* superlative of FINE¹ *adjective*. ● *noun* N Amer. the police of a specified city (*was hauled off to jail by Ottawa's finest*).

finest hour *noun* a time of greatest success.

fine structure *noun* **1** small-scale or detailed variation in structure, texture, appearance, etc. **2** *Physics* the presence of closely spaced lines in spectra.

fine-tooth comb *noun* (also **fine-toothed comb**) a comb with narrow, close-set teeth. □ **go over with a fine-tooth** (or **fine-toothed**) **comb** examine, check, or search thoroughly.

fine-tune *transitive verb* make small adjustments to (a mechanism etc.) in order to obtain the best possible results. □ **fine tuning** *noun*

fin·fish *noun* fish with fins, as opposed to shellfish, crustaceans, etc.

Fingal's Cave /ˈfɪŋgəlz/ a cave on the island of Staffa in the Inner Hebrides, noted for the clustered basaltic pillars that form its cliffs. [*Fingal*, a character in an epic poem by J. Macpherson, based on the legendary Irish hero Finn MacCool]

fin·ger ● *noun* **1** any of the terminal members of the hand, including or excluding the thumb. **2** the part of a glove etc. intended to cover a finger. **3** an object, structure, stretch of land, item of food, etc. similar to a finger in shape. **4** any small projecting rod, piece, etc. brought into contact with another object in order to initiate, direct, or arrest motion. **5 a** the breadth or length of a finger as a rough unit of measurement. **b** *informal* a measure of liquor in a glass, based on the breadth of a finger. **6** (in full **finger man**) *slang* **a** an informer. **b** a pickpocket. ● *transitive verb* **1** touch, feel, or turn about with the fingers. **2** *Music* **a** play (a passage) with fingers used in a particular way. **b** play upon (an instrument) with the fingers. **c** mark (music) with signs showing which fingers are to be used. **3** select, identify, or indicate (a person or thing) for a specific purpose etc. **4** *slang* **a** inform on or identify (a criminal) to the police. **b** indicate (a victim) or supply (information) to criminals. □ **get** (or **pull**) **one's finger out** *Brit. slang* cease prevaricating and start to act. **give** (**a person**) **the finger** *slang* make an obscene gesture with the middle finger raised as a sign of contempt. **have a finger in the pie** be concerned, esp. officiously, in a matter. **have** (or **keep**) **one's finger on the pulse of an issue etc.** keep well-informed on or have up-to-date knowledge of (a matter etc.). **lay a finger on** touch however slightly. **point a** (or **the**) **finger at** (**someone**) **1** accuse or identify as responsible. **2** throw scorn on. **put one's finger on** point to or identify with precision (a cause of trouble etc.). **one's fingers itch** (often foll. by *to* + infin.) one is longing or impatient. **put the finger on** *slang* inform against (a person), identify (an intended victim), etc. **twist** (or **wrap**) **around one's finger** (or **little finger**) **1** persuade (a person) without difficulty. **2** dominate (a person) completely. **work one's fingers to the bone** see BONE. □ **finger·less** *adjective* [Old English from Germanic]

finger·board *noun* a piece of wood on a guitar, violin, etc. where the strings are pressed against the neck of the instrument with the fingers to vary the tone.

finger bowl *noun* a small bowl of water etc. for rinsing the fingers during a meal.

finger-dry *transitive verb* dry and style (the hair) by repeatedly running one's fingers through it.

fin·gered *adjective* (usu. in *combination*) having fingers of a specified description or number.

finger food *noun* food so served that it can be eaten conveniently without cutlery.

finger hole *noun* one of a series of holes in a wind instrument which are opened and closed by the fingers in playing to alter the pitch.

fin·ger·ing¹ *noun* **1** a manner or technique of using the fingers in playing a musical instrument, in typing, etc. **2** the marking or numbers on a musical score indicating this.

fin·ger·ing² *noun* a kind of fine wool or yarn used for knitting. [earlier *fingram*, perhaps from French *fin grain*, as GROGRAM from *gros grain*]

finger·ling *noun* **1** a parr or any very young fish. **2** a very small thing. [FINGER + -LING¹]

finger·mark *noun* a mark left on a surface by the touch, esp. from a dirty finger.

finger·nail *noun* the nail at the tip of each finger.

finger·paint ● *noun* a thick, jellylike paint that can be applied with the fingers, esp. for use by children. ● *intransitive verb* apply such paint with the fingers. □ **finger·paint·ing** *noun* **finger·paint·er** *noun*

finger·pick ● *transitive & intransitive verb* play (a guitar etc.) using fingerpicks. ● *noun* any of a set of guitar picks worn on the fingers. □ **finger·pick·er** *noun*

finger·play *noun* a short, usu. rhyming verse with accompanying hand and finger actions, used to entertain young children.

finger pointing *noun* an act of accusing or blaming.

finger·print ● *noun* **1** an impression made on a surface by the fingertips, esp. as used for identifying individuals. **2** any distinctive characteristic, sign, pattern, etc. definitively identifying a particular person, substance, action, etc. ● *transitive verb* record the fingerprints, DNA pattern, etc. of (a person).

finger puppet *noun* a small puppet made to fit on and be worked by a finger.

finger spelling *noun* communication in sign language using a manual alphabet. □ **finger-spell** *transitive verb*

finger·tip ● *noun* the tip of a finger. ● *adjective* **1** (of controls etc.) that can be controlled by a light movement of the fingers. **2** (of a garment) reaching to the fingertips. □ **at one's fingertips** readily accessible. **by one's fingertips** barely. **to the fingertips** completely, in every way, or through and through.

finger weaving *noun* a weaving technique not using a loom, in which long strands of yarn are braided with the fingers. □ **finger-woven** *adjective*

fin·ial /ˈfɪnɪəl/ *noun Archit.* **1** an ornament finishing off the apex of a roof, pediment, gable, etc. **2** an ornamental knob on the top of a piece of furniture, stair post, etc. [Old French *fin* from Latin *finis* end]

fin·icky *adjective* **1** over-particular, fastidious, or too fussy. **2** needing much attention to detail. [earlier *finical* (prob. originally university slang) from FINE¹ + -ICAL + -Y¹]

finis /ˈfiːniː, ˈfɪnɪs/ *noun* **1** (at the end of a book, film, etc.) the end. **2** the end of anything, esp. of life. [Latin]

fin·ish ● *verb* **1 a** *transitive* (often foll. by *off*) complete, come or bring to an end. **b** *intransitive* cease or come to an end of a task, activity, etc. **c** *transitive* (often foll. by *off*) provide with an ending. **2** *transitive* **a** (usu. foll. by *off*) *informal* kill, destroy, or reduce to utter exhaustion or helplessness. **b** (often foll. by *off*, *up*) consume, or get through the whole or the remainder of (food, drink, paint, etc.) (*finish up your dinner*). **3** *intransitive* **a** *Sport* come to the end of a course or race, esp. in a particular condition or place. **b** (foll. by *up + in, by*) end in something, end by doing something (*he finished up last in the race; the plan finished up in the garbage; finished up by apologizing*). **4** *transitive* **a** complete the manufacture of (cloth, woodwork, etc.) by surface treatment. **b** apply varnish, paint, etc. to (wood). **c** put the final touches to. **5** *transitive* **a** make perfect or highly accomplished (*finished manners*). **b** complete or perfect the education of a person, esp. a girl and esp. in the social graces. **6 a** *transitive* complete the fattening of (cattle etc.) for sale or slaughter. **b** *intransitive* (of cattle etc.) reach an intended market weight. **7** *transitive* (foll. by *with*) **a** have no more to do with, be no longer busy with or using (a thing) (*I'm finished with the phone*). **b** end one's association or connection with (a person, organization, etc.). **8** *intransitive* (of wine etc.) leave a particular flavour in the mouth. ● *noun* **1 a** the end, last part, or last stage of a thing. **b** the point at which a race, hunt, or other contest or event ends. **c** a conclusive defeat of one person or party by another (*fight to the finish*). **d** the final taste impression of a wine etc. **2** a method, material, or texture used for surface treatment of wood, cloth, etc. **3** a thing which finishes or gives completeness or perfection to something. [Old French *fenir* from Latin *finire* from *finis* end]

fin·ished *adjective* **1 a** ended, completed, or brought to a conclusion. **b** having passed through the final stage of manufacture or elaboration (*the finished product*). **2** ruined, doomed, or no longer effective (*finished as a politician*). **3** consummate, accomplished, or highly proficient. **4** (of cattle) appropriately fattened for market or slaughter. **5** (of part of a building, esp. a basement) having the walls and ceiling covered with drywall, panelling, etc.

fin·ish·er *noun* **1** a person who finishes something, esp. a race, contest, or similar event. **2** a worker or machine performing the final operation in a process.

finishing nail *noun N Amer.* a thin nail with a small, round head that can be smoothly countersunk.

finishing school *noun* a private, usu. expensive school esp. for girls, for completing a student's education with a strong emphasis on the social graces.

finishing stroke *noun* a final and usu. fatal stroke.

finishing touch *noun* (usu. in *pl.*) a last action, added effect, or final detail completing and enhancing a piece of work, production, etc.

finish line *noun* a line which indicates the end of a race.

Finis·terre, Cape /ˌfɪnɪˈster/ a promontory of NW Spain, forming the westernmost point of the mainland.

fi·nite /ˈfaɪnaɪt/ *adjective* **1 a** having bounds, ends, or limits. **b** having an existence subject to limitations and conditions. **2** *Math.* **a** (of a line) having two ends. **b** (of a numerical quality) neither infinitely large nor infinitesimally small. **c** corresponding to and represented by a finite number or a finite number of items. **3** *Grammar* (of a part of a verb) limited by number and person. □ **finite·ly** *adverb* **finite·ness** *noun* **fini·tude** /ˈfɪnɪˌtuːd, -ˌtjuːd/ *noun* [Latin *finitus* past participle of *finire* FINISH]

finit·ism /ˈfaɪnaɪˌtɪzəm/ *noun* **1** belief in the finiteness of the world, God, etc. **2** a view of mathematics that rejects the validity of actual infinities, esp. the doctrine that every proof should involve only a finite number of steps.

fin·ito /fɪˈniːtoː/ *adjective slang* finished, ended. [Italian]

fink *N Amer. slang* ● *noun* **1** an unpleasant person. **2** an informer. ● *intransitive verb* **1** (foll. by *on*) inform on. **2** (foll. by *out*) back out of something or let a person down. [20th c.: origin unknown]

Fin·land a country on the Baltic Sea, between Sweden and Russia; pop. (est. 2002) 5,183,545; capital, Helsinki.

Finland, Gulf of an arm of the Baltic Sea between Finland and Estonia, extending eastward to St. Petersburg in Russia.

Fin·land·iz·a·tion *noun* (also esp. *Brit.* **-isation**) *hist.* **1** the process or result of becoming obliged for economic reasons to favour, or refrain from opposing, the interests of the former Soviet Union despite not being formally allied to it politically, as happened to Finland after 1944. **2** the process or result of similar influence by other powers on a neighbouring state. □ **Fin·land·ize** *transitive verb* (also esp. *Brit.* **-ise**)

Finn ● *noun* **1** a native or national of Finland. **2** a person of Finnish descent. ● *adjective* Finnish. [Old English *Finnas* pl.]

fin·nan had·die *noun* **1** a haddock cured with the smoke of green wood, turf, or peat. **2** this cooked in a white sauce. [*Findon*, a fishing village near Aberdeen in Scotland + *haddie*, Scots variant of haddock]

Fin·nic *adjective* of or pertaining to the Finns, the group of people ethnically allied to the Finns, or the group of languages allied to Finnish.

Fin·nish ● *adjective* of, pertaining to, or characteristic of Finland, the Finns, or their language. ● *noun* the language of the Finns.

Finno-Ugric /ˌfɪnoˈuːɡrɪk, -ˈjuːɡrɪk/ (also **Finno-Ugrian** /-ˈuːɡriən/) ● *adjective* belonging to the group of Uralic languages including Finnish, Estonian, Lappish, and Hungarian. ● *noun* this group of languages.

finny *adjective* **1 a** having a fin or fins. **b** like a fin. **2** *literary* pertaining to or teeming with fish.

fino /ˈfiːnoː/ *noun* (*pl.* **finos**) a light-coloured dry sherry. [Spanish, = fine]

fin whale *noun* = FINBACK.

fiord *noun* var. of FJORD.

fiori·tura /ˌfiːˌɔrɪˈtʊrə/ *noun* (*pl.* **fiori·ture** *pronunc.* same) *Music* the usu. improvised decoration or elaboration of a melody by a performer. [Italian, = flowering, from *fiorire* tò flower]

fip·ple *noun* a complete or partial plug at the mouth end of a wind instrument, esp. a partial plug at the head of a recorder, whistle, etc. that leaves a narrow channel for air. [17th c.: origin unknown]

fir *noun* **1** (in full **fir tree**) any evergreen coniferous tree, esp. of the genus *Abies*, with needles borne singly on the stems (compare PINE¹ 1). **2** the wood of the fir. [Middle English, prob. from Old Norse *fyri-* from Germanic]

Fir·dausi /fɪrˈdausi/ (also **Fir·dusi** /fɪrˈduːsi/) (pseudonym of Abul Qasim Mansur) (*c.*935–*c.*1020), Persian poet. His *Book of Kings* (1010), recounting Persian history, is considered the national epic of Persia.

fire ● *noun* **1 a** the state or process of combustion, in which substances combine chemically with oxygen from the air, manifested as a hot, bright, shifting body of gas or as incandescence. **b** the flame or incandescence so produced. **2** a conflagration or destructive burning, esp. of a large area or mass (*forest fire*). **3 a** fuel in a state of combustion or a mass of burning material in a grate, furnace, etc. **b** *Brit.* = GAS FIRE. **4** the action of firing guns etc. **5 a** zeal, fervour, enthusiasm. **b** liveliness of imagination or poetic inspiration. **c** a vehement or burning passion or emotion. **6** burning heat, fever. **7** luminosity or a glowing or flashing appearance resembling that of fire (*St. Elmo's fire*). **8** trial, torment, or difficulty. ● *verb* **1 a** *transitive* discharge (a gun etc.). **b** *transitive* throw, eject, or propel (a projectile) from or as from a gun etc. **c** *intransitive* (often foll. by *at, into, on*) shoot or discharge a gun or other firearm. **d** *intransitive* (of a gun etc.) go off. **e** *transitive* produce or deliver (a broadside, salute, etc.) by discharge of guns. **2** *transitive* light (gunpowder), let off (a firework), or explode (a mine). **3** *transitive* (often foll. by *off*) deliver or utter (a speech, questions, etc.) in rapid succession or in a sharp, explosive manner (*fired insults at us; fired off letters to the mayor*). **4** *transitive* dismiss (an employee) from a job. **5** *transitive* set fire to with the intention of damaging or destroying. **6** *intransitive* (of an explosive etc.) catch fire or be ignited. **7** *intransitive* (of an internal combustion engine, or a cylinder in one) undergo ignition of its fuel. **8** *transitive* supply (a furnace, engine, boiler, or power station) with fuel. **9** *transitive* **a** inspire, inflame, or stimulate (the imagination). **b** fill (a person) with enthusiasm. **10** *transitive* **a** subject to the action or effect of fire. **b** bake or dry (pottery, bricks, etc.). **c** dry or cure (tea or tobacco) by artificial heat. **11** *intransitive* become heated or excited. **12** *transitive & intransitive* glow or cause to glow or redden as if on fire. **13** (in *imperative*) begin shooting weapons. □ **catch fire 1** begin to burn. **2 a** (of an idea, trend, etc.) become popular. **b** (of an individual) become motivated, enthusiastic. **fight fire with fire** use similar strategies, methods, etc. as one's opponent does. **fire and brimstone 1** the torments of hell. **2** preaching etc. emphasizing eternal damnation. **fire away** *informal* begin or go ahead. **fire in the belly** a powerful sense of ambition or determination. **fire up 1** *informal* **a** stimulate, fill with enthusiasm, or excite. **b** start up (an engine etc.). **2** show sudden anger. **fired-up 1** (of an engine etc.) started. **2** (of a person) highly motivated or enthused. **hang fire** *see* HANG. **light a fire under** *N Amer.* cause to work faster, decide rapidly, etc. **on fire 1** burning. **2** excited. **set fire to** (or **set on fire**) ignite, kindle, cause to burn. **set the world on fire** do something remarkable or sensational. **take fire 1** catch fire. **2** become enthused, dynamic, energetic, etc. **under fire 1** being shot at. **2** being rigorously criticized or questioned. □ **fire·less** *adjective* **firer** *noun* [Old English *fȳr, fȳrian*, from West Germanic]

fire alarm *noun* a device for giving warning of fire.

fire ant *noun* a tropical American ant of the genus *Solenopsis*, which has a painful and sometimes dangerous sting.

fire·arm *noun* (usu. in *pl.*) a portable gun of any sort, e.g. a pistol, rifle, etc.

fire·back *noun* **1** the back wall of a fireplace. **2** a metal plate for this.

fire·ball *noun* **1** a large, bright meteor. **2 a** a ball of flame or fire. **b** a ball of flame resulting from a nuclear explosion. **3 a** a very energetic person. **b** a person with a fiery temper. **4** lightning appearing as a glowing ball. **5** *Military hist.* a ball filled with combustibles or explosives, used as a projectile to damage an enemy or enemy fortifications.

fire·ball·er *noun* *Baseball slang* a pitcher known for throwing hard fastballs. □ **fire·ball·ing** *adjective*

fire blight *noun* a disease of plants, esp. hops and fruit trees, causing a scorched appearance.

fire·bomb ● *noun* an incendiary bomb, esp. a Molotov cocktail. ● *transitive verb* attack or destroy with a firebomb.

fire boss *noun* the person in charge of a crew of forest fire fighters.

fire·box *noun* **1** an enclosed space in which a fire is made, in a fireplace, stove, etc. **2** the fuel chamber of a steam engine or boiler.

fire·brand *noun* **1** a person who or a thing which kindles strife, inflames passion, causes trouble, etc. **2** a piece of burning wood.

fire·break *noun* an obstacle, usu. a strip of land cleared or plowed, designed to stop fire from spreading in a forest, on grasslands, etc.

fire-breath·ing *adjective* **1** (of a person) having a hotly passionate zeal and aggressive manner. **2** (of a dragon etc.) capable of breathing fire.

fire·brick *noun* a brick capable of standing intense heat without burning, used in grates etc.

fire brigade *noun* esp. *Brit.* an organized body of firefighters.

fire·bug *noun* *informal* an arsonist or pyromaniac.

fire·cherry *noun* = PIN CHERRY.

fire chief *noun* *N Amer.* the officer responsible for and in charge of a municipality's fire department.

fire·clay *noun* clay capable of withstanding high temperatures, often used to make firebricks.

fire company *noun* = FIRE BRIGADE.

fire control *noun* **1** a system of regulating the firing of weapons on a ship, aircraft, etc. **2** the prevention and monitoring of forest fires, grass fires, etc.

fire·crack·er *noun* esp. *N Amer.* a small firework that explodes with a cracking noise.

fire crew *noun* a firefighting team.

fire·damp *noun* a mixture of methane and other combustible gases found in coal mines, which is explosive when mixed in certain proportions with air.

fire department *noun* *N Amer.* the department of a local or municipal authority in charge of preventing, controlling, and fighting fires.

fire·dog *noun* = ANDIRON.

fire door *noun* **1** a fire resistant door to prevent the spread of fire. **2** such a door opening to the outside as an emergency exit.

fire-drake *noun* (in Germanic mythology) a fiery dragon.

fire drill *noun* **1** a rehearsal of the procedures to be used in case of fire. **2** a simple device for kindling fire, consisting of a pointed stick and piece of wood.

fire-eater *noun* **1** an entertainer who appears to swallow fire. **2** a person fond of quarrelling or fighting.

fire engine *noun* = FIRE TRUCK.

fire-engine red ● *adjective* of a deep vibrant red. ● *noun* this colour.

fire escape *noun* an emergency staircase or other apparatus, esp. on the outside of a building, for use during a fire.

fire exit *noun* a passage or door to go through to escape from fire.

fire extinguisher *noun* a portable device that discharges a jet of liquid chemicals, water, or foam to extinguish a fire.

fire·fight *noun* a skirmish or battle involving the exchange of gunfire.

fire·fight·er *noun* a person whose job is to extinguish fires, esp. a member of a fire department. □ **fire·fight·ing** *noun & adjective*

fire·fly *noun* (*pl.* **-flies**) any soft-bodied beetle of the family Lampyridae, emitting phosphorescent light, including glow-worms.

fire·guard *noun* **1** a protective screen or grid placed in front of a fireplace. **2** *N Amer.* a firebreak.

fire hall *noun* esp. *Cdn* a fire station.

fire·hose *noun* a heavy-duty hose used esp. by firefighters in extinguishing fires.

fire·house *noun* esp. *US* a fire station.

fire hydrant *noun* a pipe, usu. on the side of the street, with a valve for drawing water from a main to which a firehose can be attached.

fire insurance *noun* insurance against losses by fire.

fire irons *plural noun* tools for tending a fire in a fireplace, e.g. tongs, poker, shovel, etc.

fire lane *noun* a traffic lane in which parking is not permitted, to allow access for fire trucks, esp. near the entrance to a shopping centre.

fire·light *noun* light from a fire or fires.

fire·light·er *noun* *Brit.* = FIRE STARTER.

fire line *noun* **1** the most forward line of a forest fire. **2** = FIREBREAK.

fire·lock *noun* *hist.* a musket having a gunlock in which sparks are produced by friction or percussion to ignite the priming.

fire·man *noun* (*pl.* **-men**) **1** a firefighter. **2** a stoker or person who tends a furnace or the fire of a steam engine, steamship, etc.

fire marshal *noun* *N Amer.* **1** a public official charged with investigating suspicious fires, enforcing fire regulations, etc. **2** a person responsible for evacuating people from a building in case of fire.

Fire of London (also called **Great Fire**) a huge and devastating fire which destroyed some 13,000 houses over 400 acres in London between 2 and 6 Sept. 1666.

fire·pit *noun* a pit dug into the ground or made from stones etc. in which a fire is made and maintained.

fire·place *noun* **1** a place for a domestic fire, esp. a partially enclosed place at the base of a chimney. **2** a structure surrounding this or the area in front of it.

fire plug *noun* **1** *US* = FIRE HYDRANT. **2** *N Amer.* a short stocky person, esp. an athlete.

u: m**oo**d   ai m**y**   əi p**i**pe   au br**ow**n   ʌu h**ou**se   ei d**ay**   ɔi b**oy**   ã fr**an**glais   ã Canadi**en**   ɔ Brayon   (*see over for consonants*)

fire·power *noun* **1** the destructive capacity of guns, missiles, a military force, etc. **2** financial, intellectual, physical, or emotional strength.

fire·proof ● *adjective* able to resist fire or great heat. ● *transitive verb* make fireproof. □ **fire·proof·ing** *noun*

fire ranger *noun* a person whose job is to prevent and detect forest fires.

fire-resist·ant *adjective* **1** almost completely non-flammable. **2** = FIRE-RETARDANT. □ **fire-resist·ance** *noun*

fire-retard·ant *adjective* capable of slowing or stopping the spread of fire.

fire ring *noun* a small, cleared, usu. circular area, often surrounded with rocks, in which a fire is made while camping etc.

fire road *noun* a rudimentary road providing access for firefighters into a forest.

fire sale *noun* **1** a sale, usu. at low prices, of goods remaining after a fire. **2** a sale of anything at a remarkably low price.

fire screen *noun* **1** a screen to deflect the direct heat of a fire, protect against sparks, etc. **2** an ornamental screen placed in front of a fireplace when the fire is unlit.

fire ship *noun hist.* a ship loaded with explosives and set adrift among enemy ships where it could be ignited and explode, destroying the enemy.

fire·side ● *noun* **1** the area around a fireplace. **2** a person's home or home life. ● *adjective* **1** situated beside or pertaining to a domestic fire or fireplace. **2** intimate or relaxed, esp. designating an informal political talk broadcast to the nation (*fireside chat*).

fire stairs *plural noun* a staircase, usu. inside a building, for use as an emergency exit in event of a fire etc.

fire starter *noun N Amer.* a piece of inflammable material to help start a fire in a barbecue, fireplace, etc.

fire station *noun* a building where fire trucks and firefighters are housed.

fire·storm *noun* **1** an intense conflagration into which surrounding air is drawn with great force, esp. resulting from incendiary or nuclear bombing. **2** an intense and forceful response (*ignited a political firestorm in Canada*).

fire·thorn *noun* = PYRACANTHA.

fire tower *noun N Amer.* a tower, usu. on a high point in the forest or on a mountain, from which forestry officials etc. watch for signs of fire.

fire trap *noun* a building without proper provision for escape in case of fire and which, once a fire started, would burn quickly.

fire truck *noun N Amer.* a heavy vehicle carrying equipment for fighting fires, e.g. hoses, ladders, pumps for shooting water or chemicals, etc.

fire-wagon *noun* **1** esp. *hist.* a wagon, usu. red and formerly pulled by horses, carrying firefighting equipment, firefighters, etc. **2** *Sport slang* (*attributive*) (in hockey) a dramatic manner of play which emphasizes offensive teamwork, heavy checking, hard passing, and speed.

fire-walking *noun* the practice of walking barefoot over white-hot stones, wood ashes, etc. as a religious rite or ordeal.

fire·wall *noun* **1** a fireproof wall to prevent the spread of fire. **2** *Computing* a system designed to control the passage of information between networks.

fire warden *noun N Amer.* a person employed to prevent or extinguish fires, esp. in towns, camps, forest areas, etc.

fire-watcher *noun* a person keeping watch for fires, esp. forest fires.

fire·water *noun informal* strong alcoholic liquor.

fire·weed *noun* any of several plants that spring up on burnt land, esp. the willow herb, *Epilobium angustifolium*, the floral emblem of Yukon.

Fire·Wire *noun Proprietary* a standard high-performance serial bus for connecting devices to a personal computer.

fire·wood *noun* wood prepared or suitable for use as fuel.

fire·work *noun* **1 a** a device containing chemicals that burn or explode spectacularly. **b** (in *pl.*) a colourful and spectacular display of such devices. **2** (in *pl.*) **a** an outburst of passion, esp. anger. **b** an impressive display of wit, brilliance, or skill.

firing *noun* **1** the discharge of guns etc. **2** the action of subjecting something to heat or fire, esp. the process which hardens clay into pottery etc. **3** the action of supplying a furnace etc. with fire or fuel.

firing line *noun* **1** the front line in a battle, nearest the enemy. **2** the forefront of or leading part in an activity, controversy, etc. □ **on the**

firing line subject to challenge, criticism, blame, etc. because of one's responsibilities or position.

firing party *noun* a group of soldiers detailed to fire the salute at a military funeral.

firing pin *noun* the piece of metal in the firing mechanism of a rifle etc. that strikes the primer, igniting the charge.

firing range *noun* = RANGE 5.

firing squad *noun* a group of soldiers detailed to shoot a condemned person.

fir·kin *noun* **1** a small cask for liquids, butter, fish, etc. **2** *Brit.* (as a measure of beer etc.) half a kilderkin (usu. 9 imperial gallons or about 41 litres). [Middle English *ferdekyn*, prob. from Middle Dutch *vierdekijn* (unrecorded) diminutive of *vierde* fourth]

firm¹ ● *adjective* **1 a** hard, resistant to pressure or impact, or of solid or compact structure. **b** securely fixed, stable, steady, not easily moved. **c** steady or controlled, not shaking or wavering (*a firm voice*). **2 a** (of a person, opinion, etc.) resolute, determined, not easily swayed or shaken (*firm belief*). **b** steadfast, constant (*a firm friend*). **c** unassailable (*firm evidence*). **3 a** (of an offer etc.) not liable to cancellation after acceptance. **b** (of a decree, law, etc.) established, immutable. **4** *Commerce* (of prices or goods) maintaining their level or value. ● *adverb* firmly (*stand firm; hold firm to*). ● *verb transitive & intransitive* make or become firm, secure, compact, or solid. □ **a firm hand** strong discipline or control. **firm up 1** work to tone and improve the condition of the muscles, voice, etc. **2** put (a thing) in final, fixed form, tidying up details etc. **3** strengthen, reinforce (standing, credibility, etc.). **4** become firm. □ **firm·ly** *adverb* **firm·ness** *noun* [Old French *ferme* from Latin *firmus*]

firm² *noun* **1** a partnership or company for carrying on a business. **2** the name under which the business of a commercial enterprise is transacted. [earlier = signature, style: Spanish & Italian *firma* from medieval Latin, from Latin *firmare* confirm, from *firmus* FIRM¹]

firma·ment /ˈfɜrməmənt/ *noun literary* the arch or vault of the skies. [Old French from Latin *firmamentum* from *firmare* (as FIRM²)]

fir·man /fɜrˈman, ˈfɜrmən/ *noun* an edict or order issued by a Near Eastern ruler or official, esp. a grant, licence, passport, or permit. [Persian *fermān*, Sanskrit *pramāṇam* right measure]

firm·ware *noun Computing* a permanent kind of software programmed into the read-only memory in certain types of computers.

first ● *adjective* **1 a** earliest or preceding all others in time, order, or experience. **b** coming next after a specified or implied time (*shall take the first train; the first robin*). **2** foremost in position, rank, or importance (*first mate*). **3** *Music* denoting one of two or more parts for the same instrument or voice, often the highest or more prominent of the two. **4** most willing or likely (*should be the first to admit the difficulty*). **5** basic or evident (*first principles*). ● *noun* **1** (prec. by *the*) the first part, the beginning, or the person or thing first mentioned or occurring. **2** the first occurrence of something notable. **3** the first day of a month. **4** first gear. **5 a** first place in a race. **b** the winner of this. **c** *Football* = FIRST DOWN. **d** *Baseball* the first inning. **e** *Baseball* = FIRST BASE. **6** (in *pl.*) goods of the best quality. **7** esp. *Brit.* **a** a place in the first class in an examination. **b** a person having this. ● *adverb* **1** before any other person or thing in time, rank, serial order, etc. (*first of all; first and foremost*). **2** before another specified or implied thing, time, event, etc. (*must get this done first*). **3** for the first time (*when did you first see her?*). **4** rather or in preference to something else (*I'd rather die first*). □ **at first** at the beginning. **at first hand** gained or coming directly from the original source. **first among equals** the person or thing having the highest status in a group. **first and foremost** most important or coming before all other things. **first and last** taking one thing with another, on the whole. **first off** *N Amer. informal* at first, first of all. **first things first** the most important things before any others (*we must do first things first*). **from the first** from the beginning. **from first to last** throughout. **in the first place** as the first consideration. [Old English *fyrst* from Germanic]

first aid *noun* help given to a sick or injured person until proper medical treatment is available. □ **first-aider** *noun*

First Amendment *noun* the amendment to the US constitution which prohibits Congress from infringing on Americans' rights to freedom of religion, speech, assembly, and petition.

first base *noun Baseball* **1** the first of the bases that must be touched to score a run. **2** the position of the player covering this base and the area of the infield surrounding it. □ **get to first base** *N Amer. informal* make a successful start or achieve the first step of an undertaking. □ **first baseman** *noun*

first blood *noun see* BLOOD.

first-born ● *adjective* eldest. ● *noun* the eldest child of a person.

first call *noun* the right of first opportunity at or demand for a benefit, response, etc. (*a first call on the partnership profits*).

First Cause *noun* God considered as the Cause or Creator of the universe.

first class ● *noun* **1** a set of persons grouped together as the best. **2** the most comfortable and costly seating in an airplane, train, etc. **3** the class of mail given priority in handling. **4** esp. *Brit.* **a** the highest division in an examination list. **b** a place in this. ● *adjective* (**first-class**) **1** belonging to, achieving, or travelling by, etc. the first class. **2** very good, of the best quality or highest order. ● *adverb* by the best or quickest form of transport or mail (*send the parcel first class*).

first-come, first-served *noun* a system of providing service to people strictly in the order in which they arrive, apply, etc.

First Communion *noun* *Catholicism* the occasion on which a child first receives Holy Communion, usu. in conjunction with others of the same age.

first contact *noun* the first interaction between colonizers and an Aboriginal people.

first cousin *noun* see COUSIN.

first-day cover *noun* an envelope with a special set of stamps postmarked on their first day of issue.

first-degree *adjective* **1 a** designating the most serious category of crime. **b** (of murder) premeditated and without mitigating circumstances. **2** denoting the least serious category of burn, those that affect only the surface of the skin, causing reddening. **3** (of a relative) designating a sibling, parent, or offspring.

first down *noun* *Football* **1** the first of three attempts (four attempts in American football) to advance the ball ten yards. **2** the achievement of an advance of ten or more yards, by which the offensive team is entitled to a new series of downs.

first edition *noun* **1** the first printed form in which a book etc. is published. **2** the whole number of copies in this form. **3** one copy in this form.

first·er *combining form* *informal* a person, group, nation, etc. that aggressively promotes its own rights, privileges, advancement, etc., usu. with little regard for others (*me-firster*).

first finger *noun* the finger next to the thumb.

first floor *noun* **1** *N Amer.* the floor on the ground level. **2** esp. *Brit.* the floor above the ground floor.

first-foot *Scot.* ● *noun* the first person to cross a threshold in the New Year. ● *intransitive verb* be a first-foot.

first fruit *noun* (usu. in *pl.*) **1** the first results of work etc. **2** the first agricultural produce of a season, esp. as offered to God.

first gear *noun* the lowest gear on a car, bicycle, etc.

first generation *adjective* **1 a** designating the offspring born to immigrants once they have settled in their adopted country. **b** designating the immigrants themselves. **2** of or belonging to an initial model, program, period, etc.

first-hand *adjective & adverb* direct, from the original source or personal experience.

first in, first out *noun* **1** *Computing* a procedure by which the first item in a list of data items is the first to be removed. **2** a method of valuing stock at a homogeneous price regardless of cost at time of acquisition, assuming that material obtained first will be sold first.

First International see INTERNATIONAL *noun* 1.

first lady *noun* **1** the leading woman in some specified activity or profession (*the first lady of Canadian theatre*). **2** (**First Lady**) (in the US) the wife of the President.

first language *noun* a person's native language or mother tongue.

first lieutenant *noun* *US* a military officer next above a second lieutenant and next below captain.

first light *noun* the time when light first appears in the morning; daybreak.

first line *noun* **1** the preliminary effort, resources, etc. ready for immediate use or action (*first line of defence*). **2** (often *attributive*) the thing, treatment, group of people, etc. which is most advanced or of the highest quality.

first·ling *noun* (usu. in *pl.*) the first result or product of anything, esp. the first offspring of a season.

first love *noun* **1 a** the first time one falls in love. **b** the emotion felt then. **2** the first person with whom one falls in love. **3** a person's favourite occupation, possession, etc. (*her first love is the theatre*).

first·ly *adverb* (in enumerating topics, arguments, etc.) in the first place, first (*compare* FIRST *adverb*).

first mate *noun* (on a merchant ship) the officer second-in-command to the master.

First Meridian *noun* *Cdn* the north-south line, 97 degrees 27 minutes west, from which land in the prairies is surveyed.

first minister *noun* *Cdn* **1** the prime minister of Canada. **2** the premier of a province.

first mortgage *noun* the mortgage having priority over all other similar mortgages on the same property.

first name *noun* a person's personal or given name (*opp.* SURNAME).

First Nation *noun* *Cdn* **1** (usu. in *pl.*) the Aboriginal peoples of Canada, not including the Inuit or Metis. **2** an Indian band, or an Indian community functioning as a band but not having official band status.

first night *noun* **1** the first public performance of a play etc. **2** (**First Night**) *N Amer. proprietary* a family-oriented celebration of New Year's Eve without alcohol, usu. featuring inexpensive entertainment such as local artists and performers. □ **first-nighter** *noun*

first offender *noun* a person who is convicted of a criminal offence for the first time.

first officer *noun* **1** the mate on a merchant ship. **2** the second-in-command to the captain on an aircraft.

first past the post *adjective* *Cdn & Brit.* **1** winning a race etc. by being the first to reach the finish line. **2** designating an electoral system in which the winning candidate from each constituency is the one receiving more votes than any other single candidate, and usu. in which parties are allotted a number of seats equal to the number of their candidates so winning (*see also* PROPORTIONAL REPRESENTATION, TRANSFERABLE VOTE).

First Peoples *plural noun* the Aboriginal peoples of a particular country or region etc. ¶ In Canada, the term *First Peoples* includes Indians, Inuit, and Metis.

first person *noun* *Grammar* see PERSON.

first position *noun* **1** *Ballet* **a** a position of the feet in which the legs are turned outwards with the backs of the heels touching so that the feet form a straight line. **b** a position of the arms in which they are curved and held in front of the body at waist height. **2** *Music* the lowest possible position of the hand on the fingerboard of a stringed instrument, i.e. furthest from the body.

first principle *noun* a fundamental axiom, assumption, etc. seen as underlying a given theory or procedure, esp. in mathematics, science, philosophy, etc.

first-rate *adjective* **1** of the highest class, excellent. **2** *informal* very well (*feeling first-rate*).

first reading *noun* the first of three successive occasions on which a bill must have been presented to a legislature before it becomes law, permitting its introduction.

first refusal *noun* see REFUSAL.

First Republic *hist.* **1** the republican regime in France from the abolition of the monarchy in 1792 until Napoleon's accession as emperor (1804). **2** this period in France.

first-rounder *noun* *N Amer. Sport informal* a player obtained by a team in the first round of a draft.

first-run *adjective* designating the initial period in which a film, movie, etc. is first shown publicly.

first school *noun* *Brit.* a primary school for children from 5 to 9 years old.

first sergeant *noun* *US* **1** (in the Army) **a** a non-commissioned officer ranking above master sergeant. **b** the highest-ranking non-commissioned officer in a company. **2** (in the Marine Corps) a non-commissioned officer ranking above gunnery sergeant.

first strike ● *noun* an aggressive attack with nuclear weapons before their use by the enemy. ● *adjective* (**first-strike**) denoting such an attack.

first-string ● *noun* *Sport* the primary and usu. starting line of a team, composed of the best players. ● *adjective* first class, of or like the best of a series, team, etc. □ **first-string·er** *noun*

first team ● *noun* a lineup of first-string players. ● *adjective* **1** belonging or relating to the first team. **2** first-rate.

first thing *informal* ● *noun* (usu. prec. by *the*) the most elementary or rudimentary thing, aspect, etc. of something (*don't know the first thing about surfing*). ● *adverb* **1** before anything else (*first thing, we must establish a budget*). **2** very early in the morning (*shall do it first thing tomorrow*).

first-time buyer *noun* a person seeking to buy a home who has not previously owned one and so has none to sell.

first-timer *noun* a person who does or is something for the first time.

First World *noun* the developed countries apart from the former Communist bloc.

First World War (also **World War I, the Great War**) (1914–18), a war between the Central Powers (Germany and Austria-Hungary, joined later by Turkey and Bulgaria) and the Allies (Britain, Canada, Australia, New Zealand, France, Russia, and other European nations, joined later by Italy and the US). With political tensions rising in central Europe, the assassination of the heir to the Austrian throne, Archduke Franz Ferdinand, in Sarajevo on 28 June 1914 sparked off armed conflict. Most of the fighting took place on land, characterized by a long and bloody entrenched stalemate in the west, and the eventual collapse of Russia in the east. An estimated total of 10 million lives were lost. After the retreat of German forces, the war was finally ended by a series of armistices in late 1918, and peace terms were settled at Versailles in 1919. The war resulted in the collapse of the German, Austro-Hungarian, and Russian Empires.

firth *noun* (also **frith**) an estuary or narrow inlet of the sea. [Middle English (originally Scots) from Old Norse *fjörthr* FJORD]

fisc *noun* the public treasury. [French *fisc* or Latin *fiscus* rush basket, purse, treasury]

fis·cal ● *adjective* **1** of or related to public revenue, usu. taxes. **2** esp. *N Amer.* pertaining to financial matters. **3** *N Amer.* designating a fiscal year (*fiscal 1995*). ● *noun* a legal official in some countries. □ **fis·cal·ly** *adverb* [French *fiscal* or Latin *fiscalis* (as FISC)]

fiscal year *noun* a period of twelve months over which annual accounts and taxes are calculated (*the fiscal year ends 31 March*).

Fisch·er ▶ **1 Emil (Her·mann)** (1852–1919), German organic chemist. He studied the structure of sugars, other carbohydrates, and purines, and synthesized many of them; he was awarded the Nobel Prize for chemistry in 1902. **2 Hans** (1881–1945), German organic chemist. He studied the porphyrin group of pigmented compounds, determining the complex structure of the red oxygen-carrying part of hemoglobin and the green chlorophyll pigments found in plants; he was awarded the Nobel Prize for chemistry in 1930. **3 Rob·ert James (‘Bobby’)** (b.1943), US chess player, who was world champion 1972–5; in 1992 he emerged from seclusion to win a non-sanctioned match against Boris Spassky in Montenegro and Serbia.

Fischer-Dieskau /ˈfɪʃɜrˈdiːskaʊ/ **Diet·rich** (b.1925), German baritone, noted for his interpretations of German lieder, in particular Schubert's song cycles.

fish¹ ● *noun* (*pl.* same or **fish·es**) **1** a vertebrate cold-blooded animal with gills and fins living wholly in water. **2** any animal living wholly in water, e.g. cuttlefish, shellfish, jellyfish. **3** the flesh of fish as food. **4** *informal* a person remarkable in some, usu. unfavourable, way (*an odd fish*). **5** (**the Fish** or **Fishes**) the zodiacal sign or constellation Pisces. **6** *Naut. slang* **a** a torpedo. **b** a submarine. **7** *N Amer. slang* a new inmate in a prison. **8** *Cdn* (*Nfld*) cod. ● *verb* **1** *intransitive* **a** try to catch fish, esp. with a line or net. **b** *Cdn* (*Nfld*) engage in sea fishery, esp. for cod, as opposed to freshwater angling. **2** *transitive* fish for (a certain kind of fish) or in (a certain stretch of water). **3** *intransitive* (foll. by *for*) **a** search, grope, or feel for in water or a concealed place. **b** try to obtain or elicit by indirect means or artifice (*Dominic was fishing for compliments*). **4** *transitive* (foll. by *up, out,* etc.) retrieve with careful or awkward searching. □ **a big fish in a small** (or **little**) **pond** a comparatively significant figure in a small unit, group, community, company, etc. **drink like a fish** drink excessively. **fish or cut bait** *N Amer.* act on or disengage from a matter, an issue, etc. **fish out** depopulate (a lake, area of ocean, etc.) through excessive fishing. **fish out of water** a person in an unfamiliar, unsuitable, or unwelcome environment or situation. **neither fish nor fowl** of indefinite character and difficult to identify or classify. **other** (or **plenty more** etc.) **fish in the sea** other people or things as good as the one that has failed or been lost. **other fish to fry** other matters to attend to. □ **fish·abil·ity** *noun* **fish·able** *adjective* **fish·like** *adjective* [Old English *fisc, fiscian* from Germanic]

fish² ● *noun* **1** a flat plate of iron, wood, etc. laid on a beam, rail, etc. or across a joint to protect or strengthen it. **2** *Naut.* a piece of wood, concave on one side and convex on the other, lashed to a spar that has fractured or been weakened in order to strengthen it. ● *transitive verb* **1** mend or strengthen (a spar etc.) with a fish or fishes. **2** join (rails) with a fish or fishes. [originally as verb: from French *ficher* fix, ultimately from Latin *figere*]

fish and brewis *noun Cdn* (*Nfld*) a dish of salt cod and hardtack soaked in water and then fried and garnished with fried salt pork.

fish and chips *plural noun* fish fried in batter and served with french fries.

fish·boat *noun Cdn* (*esp. BC*) = FISHING BOAT.

fish·bone *noun* a bone from a fish.

fish·bowl *noun* **1** a usu. round glass bowl for keeping pet fish in. **2** a place, situation, etc. in which one's life and activities are carefully and usu. publicly observed, commented upon, etc.

fish·burger *noun N Amer.* a hamburger-like sandwich having a patty made of fish.

fish cake *noun* a small patty of flaked or minced fish and mashed potato, usu. coated in batter or bread crumbs and fried.

fish camp *noun N Amer.* (esp. *North*) a camp used as a base by a group engaged in fishing, sometimes run as a business with rudimentary lodging, supplies, etc.

fish dive *noun Ballet* a diagonal face-down pose in which a female dancer is held by her partner.

fish eagle *noun* **1** any large eagle of the genus *Haliaeetus*, with long broad wings, strong legs, and a strong tail. **2** any of several other eagles catching and feeding on fish.

Fish·er, Charles (1808–80), Canadian lawyer and politician, Liberal premier of New Brunswick 1851–6 and 1857–61, Father of Confederation. He resigned as premier in 1861 when he became involved in a Crown lands scandal, but retained his seat in the House of Assembly and was one of the delegates to the Quebec Conference (1864) and the London Conference (1866) on Confederation.

fish·er *noun* **1 a** a large N American arboreal carnivore of the weasel family, *Martes pennanti*, valued for its fur. **b** the pelt of such an animal. **2** a fisherman, either professional or recreational.

fisher·folk *plural noun* people who make their living by fishing.

fisher·man *noun* (*pl.* **-men**) a person who catches fish as a livelihood or for sport.

fisherman knit *noun* (also **fisherman's knit**) **1** a type of thick, ribbed knitting done primarily with heavy yarn in cable stitches. **2** a garment, esp. a sweater, made in this way.

fish·ery *noun* (*pl.* **-eries**) **1 a** a fish hatchery or place where fish are reared. **b** a fishing ground or area where fish are caught. **2** the occupation or industry of catching or rearing fish.

fish eye *noun* **1** FISH-EYE LENS. **2** an eye of or like that of a fish.

fish-eye lens *noun* a very wide-angle lens with a field of vision covering up to 180°, the scale being reduced towards the edges.

fish farm *noun* a place where fish are bred for food. □ **fish farmer** *noun* **fish farming** *noun*

fish finder *noun* a device equipped with sonar to locate schools of fish in a body of water.

fish finger *noun esp. Brit.* = FISH STICK.

fish flake *noun Cdn* (*Nfld*) a rack on which to dry fish, usu. consisting of a framework of poles covered with spruce boughs to allow free air circulation.

fish fry *noun N Amer.* a usu. outdoor social gathering at which fish are cooked and eaten.

fish hawk *noun* = OSPREY.

fish hook *noun* a barbed hook for catching fish.

fish house *noun N Amer.* **1** a building where fish are stored, processed, etc. **2** a restaurant whose specialty is fish.

fish hut *noun Cdn* a small, portable shack placed over a hole in the ice of a lake to protect a person ice fishing.

fish·ing *noun* the catching of fish as food or as a job, sport, or hobby.

fishing admiral *noun Cdn* (*Nfld*) *hist.* a title given the captain of the first fishing vessel to arrive on the Newfoundland coast each spring, conferring upon him the authority of magistrate for that area.

fishing boat *noun* any water craft used for fishing.

fishing camp *noun N Amer.* **1** = FISHING LODGE. **2** FISH CAMP.

fishing derby *noun N Amer.* a fishing competition, usu. for money or prizes, in which participants try for the largest catch in a variety of fish categories.

fishing expedition *noun* **1** a usu. extended fishing trip. **2** a search or investigation undertaken with the hope, though not the stated purpose, of discovering information.

fishing hole *noun* **1** a favoured spot in a lake, on a river, etc. for catching fish. **2** an opening cut in lake or river ice for ice fishing.

fishing line *noun* a long thread of nylon etc. to which a baited hook, sinker, float, etc., are attached, used with a fishing rod for catching fish.

fishing lodge *noun N Amer.* an establishment, usu. by a lake, providing accommodation, equipment, etc. for sport fishermen.

fishing rod *noun* (also **fishing pole**) a long, tapering, usu. jointed rod to which a fishing line and usu. a reel are attached.

fishing room *noun Cdn* (*Nfld*) a lot on the beach used as a base by a fisherman where he sets up flakes, stages, etc.

fishing stage *noun Cdn* (esp. *Nfld*) a shed near the shoreline for gutting, heading, salting, etc. fish before they are dried on flakes.

fishing station *noun Cdn* a small sheltered cove from which fishing is undertaken on a seasonal basis, esp. in Newfoundland.

fishing trip *noun* a vacation with sport fishing as the primary intended activity.

fish kill *noun* a sudden, dramatic, and simultaneous die-off in a fish population.

fish knife *noun* a knife for eating or serving fish.

fish ladder *noun* a series of pools built like steps to enable fish to ascend a fall or dam to reach their spawning grounds.

fish meal *noun* ground, dried fish used as fertilizer or animal feed.

fish·monger /ˈfɪʃˌmʌŋgɜr, -mʌŋgɜr/ *noun* a person who sells fish.

fish·net *noun* **1** (often *attributive*) an open, meshed fabric or a garment made of it (*fishnet stockings*). **2** a net for catching fish.

fish plant *noun* a factory for cleaning, filleting, processing, freezing etc. fish.

fish·plate *noun* **1** a flat piece of iron etc. connecting railway rails. **2** a flat piece of metal with ends like a fish's tail, used to position masonry.

fish pond *noun* **1** a pond or pool in which fish are kept. **2** *N Amer.* an attraction at a fair etc. where contestants use a rod and line to attempt to extract a prize, or a token (often in the shape of a fish) representing a prize, from a pool, enclosure, etc.

fish sauce *noun* a spicy condiment made from fermented anchovies, used in oriental cuisine.

fish shed *noun Cdn* (*Maritimes*) = FISH HOUSE 1.

fish stick *noun* (also esp. *Brit.* **fish finger**) a small, oblong piece of flaked or minced fish coated in batter or bread crumbs and fried.

fish store *noun* **1** a store selling fish. **2** *Cdn* (*Nfld & Maritimes*) a building where offshore fisherman store dried cod ready for collection or export.

fish story *noun* (also **fish tale**) a vastly exaggerated account of an incident, catch, etc.

fish·tail ● *intransitive verb* move the tail of a vehicle from side to side. ● *noun* a device etc. shaped like a fish's tail.

fish tank *noun* a tank in which to keep and display living, esp. ornamental, pet fish.

fish·way *noun Cdn* a lock built to aid fish in passing a waterfall etc. on their way upstream to spawn.

fish·wife *noun* (pl. **-wives**) **1** a foul-mouthed, coarse-mannered, abusive woman. **2** a woman who sells fish.

fishy *adjective* (**fish·i·er**, **fish·i·est**) **1 a** of or like fish, esp. in smell or taste. **b** (of an eye) dull, vacant looking. **c** consisting of fish (*a fishy repast*). **d** *jocular* or *literary* abounding in fish. **2** *slang* of dubious character, questionable, suspect. □ **fish·i·ly** *adverb* **fish·i·ness** *noun*

fis·sile /ˈfɪsail/ *adjective* **1** capable of undergoing nuclear fission. **2** cleavable, inclined or tending to split. [Latin *fissilis* (as FISSURE)]

fis·sion /ˈfɪʒən, fɪʃ-/ ● *noun* **1** *Physics* the spontaneous or impact-induced splitting of a heavy atomic nucleus, accompanied by a release of energy. **2** *Biol.* the division of a cell or organism into new cells or organisms as a mode of reproduction. **3** the action of splitting or dividing into pieces. ● *transitive & intransitive verb* undergo or cause to undergo fission. □ **fis·sion·able** *adjective* [Latin *fissio* (as FISSURE)]

fission bomb *noun* an atomic bomb.

fis·sip·ar·ous /fɪˈsɪpərəs/ *adjective* **1** *Biol.* reproducing by fission. **2** tending to split or divide. □ **fis·sip·ar·ous·ness** *noun* [Latin *fissus* past participle (as FISSURE) after *viviparous*]

fis·sure /ˈfɪʃɜr, fɪʒ-/ ● *noun* **1** an opening, usu. long and narrow, made by cracking, splitting, or separation of esp. rock or ice. **2** *Bot. & Anat.* a narrow opening in an organ etc., esp. a depression between convolutions of the brain. **3** a division or split (*fissures in the alliance*). ● *transitive & intransitive verb* split or crack. [Old French or Latin *fissura* from *findere fiss-* cleave]

fist ● *noun* a tightly closed hand. ● *transitive verb* **1** strike with the fist.

2 clench (the hand, the fingers) into a fist. □ **make a good** (or **poor** etc.) **fist** (foll. by *at, of*) *informal* make a good (or poor etc.) attempt at. □ **fist·ed** *adjective* (also in *combination*) [Old English *fȳst* from West Germanic]

fist fight *noun* a fight with bare fists. □ **fist fighting** *noun*

fist-fucking *noun coarse slang* (also **fist·ing**) a sexual practice (esp. amongst male homosexuals) in which the fist is inserted into another's anus or vagina for sexual stimulation. □ **fist-fuck** *transitive & intransitive verb* **fist-fucker** *noun*

fist·ful *noun* (pl. **-fuls**) **1** a quantity held in a fist. **2** a large quantity.

fist·ic *adjective* relating to boxing.

fisti·cuffs *noun* fighting with the fists. [prob. obsolete *fisty* adj. = FISTIC, + CUFF[2]]

fis·tula /ˈfɪstjʊlə/ *noun* (pl. **fis·tu·las** or **fis·tu·lae** /-ˌliː/) an abnormal or surgically made passage between a hollow organ and the body surface or between two hollow organs. □ **fis·tu·lous** *adjective* [Latin, = pipe, flute]

fit[1] ● *adjective* (**fit·ter**, **fit·test**) **1 a** (usu. foll. by *for*, or *to* + infin.) well adapted or suited. **b** (foll. by *to* + infin.) qualified, competent, worthy. **c** (foll. by *for*, or *to* + infin.) in a suitable condition, ready. **d** (foll. by *for*) good enough (*a dinner fit for a king*). **2** in good health or athletic condition, esp. having excellent cardiovascular function. **3** proper, becoming, right (*it is fit that*). ● *verb* **1** (**fit** or **fit·ted**, **fit·ting**) **a** *transitive & intransitive* be of the right shape and size for (*the dress fits her*; *the key doesn't fit the lock*; *these shoes don't fit*). **b** *transitive* adjust (an object) to the contours of its receptacle or counterpart (*fitted shelves into the alcove*). **c** *intransitive* (often foll. by *in, into*) (of a component) be correctly positioned (*that piece fits here*). **d** *transitive* find room for (*can't fit another person on the bench*). **2** *transitive* (**fit·ted**, **fit·ting**) (foll. by *for*, or *to* + infin.) **a** make suitable; adapt. **b** make ready or competent (*her education fitted her for the diplomatic service*). **3** *transitive* (**fit·ted**, **fit·ting**) (usu. foll. by *with*) supply, furnish (*fitted the boat with a new rudder*). **4** *transitive* (**fit·ted**, **fit·ting**) fix in place (*fit a lock on the door*). **5** *transitive* (**fit·ted**, **fit·ting**) try clothing on (a person) in order to adjust it to the right size and shape (*the tailor fitted me for a new suit*). **6** *transitive* (**fit** or **fit·ted**, **fit·ting**) be in harmony with, befit, become (*it fits the occasion*; *the punishment fits the crime*). **7** *transitive* (**fit** or **fit·ted**, **fit·ting**) be suitable for (*this fits our needs*). ● *noun* **1** the way in which a garment, component, etc., fits (*a bad fit*; *a tight fit*). **2** suitability, compatibility (*there must be a perfect fit between the employee and the job*). ● *adverb* (foll. by *to* + infin.) *informal* in a suitable manner, appropriately (*was laughing fit to bust*). □ **fit the bill** be suitable or adequate. **fit in 1** (often foll. by *with*) be (esp. socially) compatible or accommodating (*doesn't fit in with the rest of the group*; *tried to fit in with their plans*). **2** find space or time for (an object, engagement, etc.) (*the dentist fitted me in at the last minute*). **fit out** (or **up**) (often foll. by *with*) equip. **see** (or **think**) **fit** (often foll. by *to* + infin.) decide or choose (a specified course of action). □ **fitly** *adverb* [Middle English: origin unknown]

fit[2] *noun* **1** a sudden seizure of epilepsy, hysteria, apoplexy, fainting, or paralysis, with unconsciousness or convulsions. **2** a sudden brief attack of an illness or of symptoms (*fit of coughing*). **3** a sudden short bout or burst (*fit of energy*; *fit of giggles*). **4** an attack of strong feeling (*fit of rage*). **5** a capricious impulse; a mood (*a fit of generosity*). □ **by** (or **in**) **fits and starts** spasmodically. **give a person a fit** *informal* surprise or outrage him or her. **have** (or **throw**) **a fit** *informal* be greatly surprised or outraged. [Middle English, = position of danger, perhaps = Old English *fitt* conflict]

fit[3] *noun archaic* a section of a poem. [Old English *fitt*]

fitch *noun* **1** the European polecat. **2** the hair of a polecat. [Middle Dutch *fisse* etc.]

fit·ful *adjective* active or occurring spasmodically or intermittently. □ **fit·ful·ly** *adverb* **fit·ful·ness** *noun*

fit·ness *noun* **1 a** the quality or state of being physically fit (also *attributive*: *fitness program*). **b** the quality of being suitable, qualified, or morally fit for something (*his fitness for the job was questioned*). **2** *Biol.* a numerical measure of ability to survive and reproduce in a particular environment.

fit·ted *adjective* **1** made or shaped to fill a space or cover something closely or exactly (*fitted sheet*). **2** esp. *Brit.* provided with appropriate equipment, fittings, etc. (*fitted kitchen*). **3** esp. *Brit.* built-in; filling an alcove etc. (*fitted cupboards*).

fit·ter *noun* **1** a person who supervises the cutting, fitting, altering, etc. of garments or shoes. **2** a person who fits together and adjusts machine or engine parts (*a gas fitter*).

fit·ting ● *noun* **1** the process or an instance of having a garment etc. fitted (*needed several fittings*). **2** (usu. in *pl.*) **a** decorative metal handles, corners, etc., on furniture, bathtubs, etc. (*brass fittings*). **b** esp. *Brit.* the furnishings and fixtures of a building. **3** a small standard part or component (*a valve with a compression fitting*). ● *adjective* proper, becoming, right. □ **fit·ting·ly** *adverb* **fit·ting·ness** *noun*

fitting room *noun* a room in a clothing store or in a dressmaker's premises etc. where garments are tried on.

Fit·ti·pal·di /ˌfɪtɪˈpaldi/ **Emer·son** (b.1946), Brazilian racing driver. He entered Formula One with the Lotus team in 1970. He became the youngest-ever world champion in 1972, winning again, with McLaren, in 1974. He retired in 1980, but came back to win the Indianapolis 500 in 1989.

Fitz·ger·ald ▶ **1 Ed·ward** (1809–83), English scholar and poet, who is remembered for his free poetic translation of *The Rubáiyát of Omar Khayyám* (1859). **2 Ella** (1918–1996), US jazz singer. In the 1940s she evolved a distinctive style of scat singing, and from the mid-1950s she made a successful series of recordings of songs by George Gershwin and Cole Porter. **3 Fran·cis Scott (Key)** (1896–1940), US novelist. His novels, particularly *The Great Gatsby* (1925), provide a vivid portrait of the US during the 1920s; his affluent lifestyle with his wife, the writer Zelda Sayre (1900–47), is reflected in the semi-autobiographical novel *Tender is the Night* (1934).

Fitz·Ger·ald ▶ **1 George Fran·cis** (1851–1901), Irish physicist. He suggested that length, time, and mass depend on the relative motion of the observer, while the speed of light is constant; this hypothesis, postulated independently by Lorentz, prepared the way for Einstein's special theory of relativity. **2 (Lionel) Le·Moine** (1890–1956), Canadian artist. A late member of the Group of Seven, he is known for the quiet reverence and carefully arranged and sculpturally modelled forms of his landscapes and still lifes; his works include *Doc Snider's House* (1931), *The Jar* (1938), *The Little Plant* (1947), and *From an Upstairs Window* (c.1949).

FitzGerald contraction *noun Physics* = LORENTZ-FITZGERALD CONTRACTION.

Fiume /ˈfjuːmɛ/ the Italian name for RIJEKA.

five ● *noun* **1** one more than four or one half of ten; the sum of three units and two units. **2** a symbol for this (5, v, V). **3** a size etc. denoted by five. **4** a set or team of five persons or things. **5** five o'clock. **6** a five-dollar bill, five-pound note, etc. **7** a card with five pips. ● *adjective* that amount to five. [Old English *fíf* from Germanic]

five-and-a-half *noun Cdn* (*Que.*) an apartment having three bedrooms, a kitchen, a living room, and a bathroom.

five-and-dime store *noun* (also **five-and-dime**, **five-and-ten**) *N Amer.* **1** *hist.* a store where all the articles were originally priced at five or ten cents. **2** a store selling a wide variety of inexpensive household and personal goods.

five-a-side ● *adverb Hockey* with one player short on each side as a result of penalties. ● *adjective* designating soccer played with five players in each team. ● *noun* a game of five-a-side soccer.

five-finger discount *N Amer. slang* ● *noun* **1** an act of stealing, esp. shoplifting. **2** an item obtained by stealing or shoplifting. ● *transitive verb* steal, shoplift (an item). □ **five-finger discounter** *noun*

five-finger exercise *noun* **1** an exercise on the piano involving all the fingers. **2** an easy task.

five·fold *adjective & adverb* **1** five times as much or as many. **2** consisting of five parts. **3** amounting to five.

five-hole *noun Hockey slang* a gap between a goaltender's parted legs through which a puck can pass.

five hundred *noun* a form of euchre or rummy in which 500 points make a game.

Five Nations *plural noun hist.* the Seneca, Cayuga, Onondaga, Oneida, and Mohawk, who formed the League of the Iroquois in the mid to late 16th c.

five-o *noun* the age of fifty.

five o'clock shadow *noun* beard growth visible on a man's face in the latter part of the day.

Five Pillars of Islam the five duties expected of every Muslim, including profession of the faith in a prescribed form, observance of ritual prayer, giving alms to the poor, fasting during the month of Ramadan, and performing the pilgrimage to Mecca (see HAJJ).

five-pin bowling *noun Cdn* a variety of bowling in which players have three chances to knock down five pins, each of different scoring value, using a smaller ball than in 10-pin bowling.

fiver *noun informal* **1** *N Amer.* a five-dollar bill. **2** *Brit.* a five-pound note.

five senses *plural noun* (prec. by *the*) sight, hearing, smell, taste, and touch.

five-spice powder *noun* a blend of five powdered spices, usu. fennel seeds, cinnamon, cloves, star anise, and Szechwan peppercorns, used in Chinese cuisine.

five-star *adjective* **1** (of a hotel, restaurant, alcoholic beverage, etc.) given five stars in a grading, esp. where this indicates the highest quality. **2** *US* having or being a military rank that is distinguished by five stars on the epaulette of the uniform.

five-year plan *noun* **1** (in the former USSR) a government plan for economic development over five years, inaugurated in 1928. **2** a similar plan in another country, or a company, university, etc.

fix ● *verb* **1** *transitive* mend, repair. **2** *transitive* put in order, adjust (*fix your tie*). **3** *transitive* make firm or stable; fasten, secure (*fixed a picture to the wall*). **4** *transitive* decide, settle, specify (a price, date, etc.). **5** *transitive* implant (an idea or memory) in the mind (*couldn't get the rules fixed in his head*). **6** *transitive* **a** (foll. by *on, upon*) direct steadily, set (one's eyes, gaze, attention, or affection). **b** attract and hold (a person's attention, eyes, etc.). **c** (foll. by *with*) single out with one's eyes etc. **7** *transitive* place definitely or permanently, establish, station. **8** *transitive* determine the exact nature, position, etc., of; refer (a thing or person) to a definite place or time; identify, locate. **9 a** *transitive* make (eyes, features, etc.) rigid. **b** *intransitive* (of eyes, features, etc.) become rigid. **10** *transitive N Amer. informal* prepare (food or drink) (*fixed me a drink*). **11 a** *transitive* deprive of fluidity or volatility; congeal. **b** *intransitive* lose fluidity or volatility, become congealed. **12** *transitive informal* punish, kill, silence, deal with (a person). **13** *transitive informal* **a** secure the support of (a person) fraudulently, esp. by bribery. **b** arrange the result of (a race, match, etc.) fraudulently (*the competition was fixed*). **14** *transitive* **a** make (a pigment, photographic image, etc.) fast or permanent. **b** *Biol.* preserve or stabilize (a specimen) prior to treatment or microscopic examination. **15** *transitive* (of a plant or micro-organism) assimilate (nitrogen or carbon dioxide) by forming a non-gaseous compound. **16** *transitive* castrate or spay (an animal). **17** *transitive* arrest changes or development in (a language or literature). **18** *transitive* allocate or determine the incidence of (a responsibility, liability etc.). **19** *intransitive N Amer.* (foll. by *to* + infin.) prepare; plan. ● *noun* **1** *informal* a position hard to escape from; a dilemma or predicament. **2** *informal* a repair, esp. to a computer program. **3 a** the act of finding one's position by bearings or astronomical observations. **b** a position found in this way. **4** *slang* **a** a dose of a narcotic drug to which one is addicted. **b** anything which one craves and enjoys immensely (*went to the video store to get my movie fix*). **5** *informal* a clear understanding (*I can't get a fix on her mood*). **6** *slang* bribery; an illicit arrangement. □ **be fixed** (usu. foll. by *for*) be disposed or affected (regarding) (*how is he fixed for money?*; *how are you fixed for Friday?*). **fix up 1** arrange, organize, prepare. **2** upgrade, improve (*bought an old cottage to fix up*). **3** (often foll. by *with*) provide (a person) (*fixed me up with a job*). □ **fix·able** *adjective* **fix·ed·ly** *adverb* **fix·ed·ness** *noun* [Old French *fix* or Latin *fixus* past participle of *figere* fix, fasten]

fix·ate /fɪkˈseɪt/ *verb* **1** *intransitive* (foll. by *on, upon*) be or become obsessed with. **2** *transitive Psych.* **a** (usu. in *passive*; often foll. by *on, upon*) cause (a person) to acquire an abnormal attachment to persons or things (*was fixated on his son*). **b** arrest (part of the libido) at an immature stage, causing such attachment. **3** *transitive & intransitive* direct one's gaze on. **4** *transitive* be or become fixed. [Latin *fixus* (see FIX) + -ATE[3]]

fix·a·tion *noun* **1** *Psych.* the act or an instance of being fixated. **2** an obsession; concentration on a single idea. **3** fixing or being fixed. **4** the process of rendering solid; coagulation. **5** the process of assimilating a gas to form a solid compound.

fixa·tive /ˈfɪksətɪv/ ● *noun* a substance used to set or fix colours, hair, biological specimens, etc. ● *adjective* tending to fix or secure.

fixed assets *plural noun* permanent business assets, e.g. buildings and equipment.

fixed costs *plural noun* business costs that do not vary with the amount of work produced.

fixed-do *attributive adjective* applied to a system of sight-singing in which C is called 'do', D is called 're', etc., irrespective of the key in which they occur (*compare* MOVABLE-DO).

fixed focus *noun* a camera focus that cannot be adjusted, typically used with a small aperture lens having a large depth of field.

fixed income *noun* income from a pension, investment, etc. that is set at a particular figure and does not rise with the rate of inflation (also *attributive*: *fixed-income securities*).

fixed link *noun Cdn & Brit.* a permanent means of transit (e.g. a bridge or tunnel) between two geographical areas separated by water.

fixed oil *noun* a non-volatile oil of animal or plant origin used in varnishes, lubricants, soaps, etc.

Consonants: b *but*   d *dog*   f *few*   g *get*   h *her*   j *yes*   k *cat*   l *leg*   m *man*   n *no*   p *pen*   r *red*   s *sit*

fixed point *noun* Physics a well-defined reproducible temperature, usu. that of a change of phase, used for calibration or for defining a temperature scale.

fixed star *noun* a star so far from the earth that it appears motionless.

fixed-wing *adjective* designating aircraft of the conventional type, as opposed to rotating-wing aircraft such as helicopters.

fixer *noun* **1** a person or thing that fixes. **2** Photog. a substance used for fixing a photographic image etc. **3** *informal* a person who makes arrangements, esp. of an illicit kind.

fixer-upper *noun* N Amer. informal a house in need of repairs, often bought at a reduced price.

fix·ing *noun* **1** (in pl.) N Amer. **a** the necessary ingredients for a dish, meal, etc. **b** appropriate trimmings, condiments, etc. for a dish. **2** apparatus or equipment. **3** Brit. something which serves to fasten or affix.

fix-it *noun* **1** the action or an act of fixing something (usu. *attributive: fix-it project*). **2** a handyperson (esp. as a pseudo-surname: *Mr. Fix-It*).

fix·ity *noun* **1** a fixed state. **2** stability; permanence.

fix·ture *noun* **1 a** something fixed or fastened in position (*a light fixture*). **b** (usu. predicative) informal a person or thing confined to or established in one place (*he's a permanent fixture at this restaurant*). **2** Brit. **a** a sporting event, esp. a match, race, etc. **b** the date agreed for this. **3** (in pl.) Law articles attached to a house or land and regarded as legally part of it. [alteration of obsolete *fixure* from Late Latin *fixura* from Latin *figere fix-* fix]

fizz ● *intransitive verb* **1** make a hissing or spluttering sound. **2** (of a drink) make bubbles; effervesce. ● *noun* **1** a hissing or spluttering sound. **2** effervescence. **3** informal an effervescent drink (*a gin fizz*). **4** informal excitement, energy (*the band's live set lacked fizz*). [imitative]

fiz·zle ● *intransitive verb* **1** make a feeble hissing or spluttering sound. **2** (often foll. by *out*) end feebly (*the party fizzled out at 10 o'clock*). ● *noun* **1** a feeble hissing or spluttering sound. **2** a failure, a fiasco. [formed as FIZZ + -LE⁴]

fizzy *adjective* (**fizz·i·er**, **fizz·i·est**) effervescent. □ **fizz·i·ness** *noun*

fjord /fjɔːrd, ˈfiːɔrd, fiːˈɔrd/ *noun* (also **fiord**) a long, narrow, and deep inlet of sea between high cliffs. [Norwegian from Old Norse *fjǫrthr* from Germanic: compare FIRTH, FORD]

FL *abbreviation* Florida (in official postal use).

fl. *abbreviation* **1** floor. **2** floruit. **3** fluid.

Fla. *abbreviation* Florida.

flab *noun* informal fat; flabbiness. [imitative, or back-formation from FLABBY]

flab·ber·gast *transitive verb* (esp. as **flab·ber·gast·ed** *adjective*) overwhelm with astonishment; dumbfound. [18th c.: perhaps from FLABBY + AGHAST]

flabby *adjective* (**flab·bi·er**, **flab·bi·est**) **1** (of flesh etc.) hanging down; limp; flaccid. **2** (of a person) having soft loose fatty flesh; overweight. **3** (of character etc.) feeble; lacking vigour. □ **flab·bi·ly** *adverb* **flab·bi·ness** *noun* [alteration of earlier *flappy* from FLAP]

flac·cid /ˈflasɪd/ *adjective* **1** (of flesh etc.) lacking stiffness; hanging or lying loose; limp, flabby. **2** relaxed, drooping. **3** lacking vigour; feeble (*flaccid prose*). □ **flac·cid·ity** /flaˈsɪdɪti/ *noun* **flac·cid·ly** *adverb* [French *flaccide* or Latin *flaccidus* from *flaccus* flabby]

flack¹ N Amer. slang ● *noun* a publicist. ● *verb* **1** *intransitive* act as a publicist. **2** *transitive* promote (a product, event, etc.). □ **flack·ery** *noun* [20th c.: origin unknown]

flack² *var. of* FLAK.

flag¹ ● *noun* **1 a** a piece of cloth, usu. oblong or square, attachable by one edge to a pole or rope and used as a country's emblem or as a standard, signal, etc. **b** a small toy, device, etc., resembling a flag. **c** a piece of cloth raised, dropped, waved, etc., to indicate the start or finish of a race, to signal a penalty, etc. **2** a device that is raised to indicate that a taxi is for hire. **3** Naut. a flag carried by a flagship as an emblem of an admiral's rank afloat. **4** the tail of an animal, esp. a deer or setter. ● *verb* (**flagged**, **flag·ging**) **1** *intransitive* **a** grow tired; lose vigour; lag (*his energy flagged after the first lap*). **b** hang down; droop; become limp. **2** *transitive* **a** place a flag on or over. **b** mark out with or as if with a flag or flags. **3** *transitive* (often foll. by *that*) **a** inform (a person) by flag signals. **b** communicate (information) by flagging. □ **flag down** signal to (a vehicle or driver) to stop. **keep the flag flying** continue the fight. **put the flag out** celebrate victory, success, etc. **show the flag 1** make an official visit to a foreign port etc. **2** ensure that notice is taken of one's country, oneself, etc.; make a patriotic display. **wave the flag 1** make a display of one's patriotism. **2** (foll. by *for*) assert one's allegiance to (a cause etc.). **wrap oneself in the**

flag assert one's allegiance to one's country. □ **flag·ger** *noun* [16th c.: perhaps from obsolete *flag* drooping]

flag² ● *noun* = FLAGSTONE. ● *transitive verb* (**flagged**, **flag·ging**) pave with flagstones. [Middle English, = sod: compare Icelandic *flag* spot from which a sod has been cut out, Old Norse *flaga* slab of stone, and FLAKE¹]

flag³ *noun* **1** any plant with a bladed leaf (esp. several of the genus *Iris*) growing on moist ground. **2** the long slender leaf of such a plant. [Middle English: compare Middle Dutch *flag*, Danish *flæg*]

flag-bearer *noun* **1** a person who carries a flag in a parade etc. **2** a person who supports a certain cause, ideology, etc.

Flag Day *noun* **1** Cdn 15 February, the anniversary of the adoption of the Maple Leaf flag in 1965. **2** US 14 June, the anniversary of the adoption of the Stars and Stripes in 1777.

flag day *noun* Brit. = TAG DAY.

fla·gel·lant /ˈfladʒələnt, fləˈdʒɛlənt/ ● *noun* **1** a person who scourges himself or herself or others as a religious discipline. **2** a person who engages in flogging as a sexual stimulus. ● *adjective* of or concerning flagellation. [Latin *flagellare* to whip, from FLAGELLUM]

fla·gel·late¹ /ˈfladʒəˌleɪt/ *transitive verb* scourge, flog (*compare* FLAGELLANT). □ **fla·gel·la·tor** *noun* **fla·gel·la·tory** /-ləˌtɔri/ *adjective* [Latin *flagellat-* past participle stem of *flagellare*]

fla·gel·late² /ˈfladʒələt, -ˌleɪt/ ● *adjective* (also **fla·gel·lat·ed**) having flagella (*see* FLAGELLUM). ● *noun* a protozoan having one or more flagella. [FLAGELLUM + -ATE¹]

fla·gel·la·tion /ˌfladʒəˈleɪʃən/ *noun* the act or practice of flagellating others or esp. oneself, as a sexual stimulus or religious discipline.

fla·gel·lum /fləˈdʒɛləm/ *noun* (pl. **fla·gel·la** /-lə/) **1** Biol. a long lash-like appendage found esp. on microscopic organisms. **2** Bot. a runner; a creeping shoot. □ **fla·gel·lar** *adjective* **fla·gel·li·form** *adjective* [Latin, = whip, diminutive of *flagrum* scourge]

fla·geo·let¹ /ˌfladʒəˈlɛt, ˈfladʒ-, ˌfladʒəˈleɪ/ *noun* **1** a small wind instrument resembling the recorder, having six principal holes, including two for the thumb, and sometimes keys. **2** an organ stop having a tone similar to that of this instrument. [French, diminutive of Old French *flag(e)ol* from Provençal *flajol*, of unknown origin]

fla·geo·let² /ˌfladʒəˈleɪ, -ˈlɛt/ *noun* a kind of French kidney bean. [French, based on Latin *phaseolus* 'bean']

flag football *noun* N Amer. a form of touch football in which the ball carrier's advance is halted when a member of the opposite team snatches a flag from the ball carrier's pocket or belt.

flag·ging¹ *adjective* losing vigour, vitality, etc.

flag·ging² *noun* paving of flagstones.

fla·gi·tious /fləˈdʒɪʃəs/ *adjective* deeply criminal; utterly villainous. □ **fla·gi·tious·ness** *noun* [Latin *flagitiosus* from *flagitium* shameful crime]

flag lieutenant *noun* an admiral's aide-de-camp.

flag·man *noun* (pl. **-men**) a person who has charge of, carries, or signals with or as with a flag, e.g. on railway lines, construction sites on roadways, etc.

flag of convenience *noun* a foreign flag under which a ship is registered, usu. to avoid financial charges etc.

flag officer *noun* an admiral, vice admiral, rear admiral, or commodore.

flag of truce *noun* a white flag used to signal the desire for a truce.

flag·on /ˈflagən/ *noun* **1** a large bottle in which wine etc., is sold. **2 a** a large vessel usu. with a handle, spout, and lid, to hold wine etc. **b** a similar vessel used to hold the wine of the Eucharist. [Old French *flacon*, ultimately from Late Latin *flasco -onis* FLASK]

flag·pole *noun* a pole on which a flag may be hoisted. □ **run something up the flagpole** test, try (an idea, proposal, etc.).

flag rank *noun* the rank attained by flag officers.

fla·grant /ˈfleɪɡrənt/ *adjective* (of an offence or an offender) glaring; notorious; scandalous. □ **fla·gran·cy** *noun* **fla·grant·ly** *adverb* [French *flagrant* or Latin *flagrant-* part. stem of *flagrare* blaze]

fla·grante de·lic·to *see* IN FLAGRANTE DELICTO.

flagrant foul *noun* Basketball an instance of excessive or violent physical contact with an opponent.

flag·ship *noun* **1** a ship, esp. in a fleet or squadron, having an admiral on board. **2** something considered a leader or superior example of its kind; the major product, model, etc. in a company's range.

Flag·stad /ˈflagstad/ **Kirs·ten** (1895–1962), Norwegian operatic soprano, who is considered by many to be the outstanding singer of Wagnerian roles in the 20th c.

flag·staff *noun* = FLAGPOLE.

flag·stone *noun* (also **flag**) **1** a flat usu. rectangular stone slab used for paving. **2** (in *pl.*) a pavement made of these. □ **flag·stoned** *adjective*

flag-waving ● *noun* an excessive display of patriotism. ● *adjective* behaving in this manner. □ **flag-waver** *noun*

Fla·her·ty /ˈflahɜrti/ **Rob·ert (Jo·seph)** (1884–1951), US explorer and film director. A pioneer of documentary films, his works include *Nanook of the North* (1922), *Moana* (1926), and *The Land* (1942).

flail ● *noun* a threshing tool consisting of a wooden staff with a short heavy stick swinging from it. ● *verb* **1** *transitive* beat or strike with or as if with a flail. **2** *transitive & intransitive* wave or swing wildly or erratically (*went into the fight with arms flailing*). **3** *intransitive* (often foll. by *about, around*) **a** move with one's limbs swinging wildly, usu. in desperation. **b** attempt desperately but unsuccessfully to find a direction to follow. [Old English prob. from Latin FLAGELLUM]

flair *noun* **1** special talent, aptitude, or ability (*has a flair for languages*). **2** an instinct for selecting or performing what is excellent, useful, etc.; instinctive discernment (*has a flair for knowing what the public wants*). **3** originality, stylishness of dress, manner, etc. [French *flairer* to smell, ultimately from Latin *fragrare*: see FRAGRANT]

flak *noun* (also **flack**) **1** anti-aircraft fire. **2** adverse criticism; hostile reaction. [German, abbreviation of *Flug(zeug)abwehrkanone*, anti-aircraft gun]

flake[1] ● *noun* **1 a** a small thin light piece of snow. **b** a similar piece of another material, esp. one that has peeled or split off a surface or object (*paint flakes*). **2** a thin stratum or lamina. **3** *Archaeology* a piece of hard stone chipped off and used as a tool. **4** (in *pl.*) any of various kinds of flaked breakfast cereal, esp. cornflakes. **5** a natural division of the flesh of some fish. **6** the dogfish or other shark as food. **7** *N Amer. slang* a foolish or unreliable person. ● *transitive & intransitive verb* **1** (often foll. by *away, off*) take off, shed, or come away in flakes. **2** separate or form into flakes (*flake the fish and blend with the mayonnaise*). □ **flake out** *informal* fall asleep or drop from exhaustion. [Middle English: origin unknown: compare Old Norse *flakna* flake off]

flake[2] *noun* a stage for drying fish etc. [Middle English, perhaps from Old Norse *flaki, fleki* wicker shield]

flak jacket *noun* a protective jacket of heavy fabric reinforced with metal, worn by soldiers etc.

flak·y *adjective* (**flak·i·er, flak·i·est**) (also **flak·ey**) **1** of or like flakes; separating easily into flakes. **2** *N Amer. slang* foolish, silly. **3** *slang* unreliable. □ **flak·i·ly** *adverb* **flak·i·ness** *noun*

flaky pastry *noun* pastry consisting of thin light layers.

flam·bé /ˈflɒmˈbeɪ/ *adjective* (of food) covered with alcohol and set alight briefly. ● *transitive verb* /flɒmˈbeɪ/ (**flam·bés, flam·béed, flam·bé·ing**) cover (food) with alcohol and set alight briefly. [French, past participle of *flamber* singe (as FLAMBEAU)]

flam·beau /ˈflɒmboː/ *noun* (*pl.* **flam·beaux** or **flam·beaus** /-oːz/) **1** a flaming torch, esp. composed of several thick waxed wicks. **2** a branched candlestick. [French from *flambe* from Latin *flammula* diminutive of *flamma* flame]

Flam·bor·ough /ˈflamˌbɜroː, -brə/ a former town in S Ontario, now part of the city of Hamilton; pop. (2001) 37,796. [FLAMBOROUGH HEAD]

Flamborough Head /ˈflambrə/ a rocky promontory on the east coast of England, in the former East Riding of Yorkshire.

flam·boy·ant /flamˈbɔɪənt/ *adjective* **1** (of a person, behaviour, etc.) ostentatious; showy. **2** floridly decorated. **3** gorgeously coloured. **4** *Archit.* (of decoration) marked by wavy flamelike lines. □ **flam·boy·ance** *noun* **flam·boy·ant·ly** *adverb* [French (in Archit. sense), pres. part. of *flamboyer* from *flambe*: see FLAMBEAU]

flame ● *noun* **1 a** ignited gas (*the fire burned with a steady flame*). **b** one portion of this (*the flame flickered and died*). **c** (usu. in *pl.*) visible combustion (*burst into flames*). **2 a** a bright light; brilliant colouring. **b** a brilliant orange-red colour. **3 a** strong passion, esp. love (*fan the flame*). **b** *informal* a boyfriend or girlfriend. **4** *slang* an angry message of censure or disparagement sent by one user of a computer network to another. **5** a cause which generates passionate feelings (*a keeper of the flame of public broadcasting*). ● *verb* **1** *intransitive & transitive* (often foll. by *out, up*) emit or cause to emit flames. **2** *intransitive* (often foll. by *out, up*) **a** (of passion, anger, etc.) break out. **b** (of a person) become angry. **3** *intransitive* shine or glow like flame (*leaves flamed in the autumn sun*). **4 a** *transitive* censure or disparage (a user of a computer network) via electronic mail. **b** *intransitive* engage in such behaviour. **5** *transitive* subject to the action of flame. □ **flame out 1** (of a jet engine) lose power through the extinction of the flame in the combustion chamber. **2** esp. *N Amer.* fail, esp. conspicuously. **go up in flames** be consumed

by fire. □ **flame·less** *adjective* **flame·like** *adjective* **flam·er** *noun* (in sense 4 of v.). [Old French *flame, flam(m)er* from Latin *flamma*]

fla·men /ˈfleɪmən/ *noun Rom. Hist.* a priest serving a particular deity. [Latin]

fla·men·co /fləˈmɛŋkoː/ *noun* (*pl.* **-cos**) **1** a style of music played (esp. on the guitar) and sung by Spanish gypsies. **2** a strongly rhythmical dance performed to this music. [Spanish, 'like a gypsy', lit. = 'a Flemish person', from Middle Dutch *Vlaminc*]

flame-out *noun* **1** extinction of the flame in a jet engine causing loss of power. **2** esp. *N Amer.* a complete or conspicuous failure.

flame-proof *adjective* **1** (esp. of a fabric) treated so as to be non-flammable. **2** (of cookware) that can be used in the oven or on a cooking element.

flame·stitch *noun* a multicoloured woven pattern which resembles flickering flames, used esp. in upholstery fabric.

flame-thrower *noun* a weapon that projects a stream of burning fuel.

flame tree *noun* any of various trees with brilliant red flowers.

flame war *noun* an acrimonious and prolonged exchange of emails or postings.

flam·ing *adjective* **1** emitting flames. **2** very hot; fiery. **3** *informal* **a** passionate; intense (*a flaming argument*). **b** expressing annoyance, or as an intensifier (*that flaming dog*). **4** bright-coloured (*flaming red hair*). **5** *slang* (of a homosexual, esp. a man) flamboyant; conspicuously effeminate.

fla·mingo /fləˈmɪŋɡoː/ *noun* (*pl.* **-gos** or **-goes**) any tall long-necked web-footed wading bird of the family Phoenicopteridae, with a crooked bill and pink, scarlet, and black plumage. [Portuguese *flamengo* from Provençal *flamenc* from *flama* flame + *-enc* = -ING[3]]

flam·mable *adjective* easily set on fire; highly combustible. ¶ *Flammable* is often preferred in official use because *inflammable* can be mistaken for a negative (the true negative being *non-flammable*). □ **flam·mabil·ity** *noun* [Latin *flammare* from *flamma* flame]

flam·mu·lat·ed owl /ˈflamjuːleɪtəd/ *noun* (also **flammulated screech owl**) a small reddish-grey owl of North America, *Otus flammeolus*. [modern Latin *flammulatus* from Latin *flammula*, diminutive of *flamma* FLAME]

Flam·steed, John (1646–1719), English astronomer. The first Astronomer Royal at the Royal Greenwich Observatory, he produced the first star catalogue, *Historia Coelestis Britannica* (1725), which gave the positions of nearly 3,000 stars.

flan *noun* **1** an open pastry or sponge pie case containing a fruit, jam or savoury filling. **2** a disc of metal from which a coin etc. is made. [French (originally = round cake) from Old French *flaon* from medieval Latin *flado -onis* from Frankish]

Flan·ders a region in the southwestern part of the Low Countries, now divided between Belgium (where it forms the provinces of East and West Flanders), France, and the Netherlands. It was a powerful medieval principality. The area was the scene of prolonged fighting during the First World War, when Allied troops held the sector of the Western Front around the town of Ypres.

flâ·neur /flaˈnɜr/ *noun* an idler; a lounger. [French from *flâner* lounge, loiter]

flange /flandʒ/ ● *noun* a projecting flat rim, collar, or rib, used for strengthening or attachment, or (on a wheel) maintaining position on a rail. ● *transitive verb* **1** (esp. as **flanged**) provide with a flange. **2** alter (a sound recording) by removing sound of a particular but varying frequency. □ **flange·less** *noun* [17th c.: perhaps from *flange* widen out, from Old French *flangir*, from *flanche, flanc* FLANK]

flan·ger /ˈflandʒɜr/ *noun* **1** *N Amer.* a vertical scraper for clearing snow from railway tracks to allow room for the wheel flanges. **2** a device that alters a sound signal by introducing a cyclically varying phase shift into one of two identical copies of the signal and recombining them.

flank ● *noun* **1 a** the fleshy or muscular part of the side of a person or animal between the ribs and the hip. **b** a cut of meat, esp. beef, from the underside of an animal between the ribs and the hind legs (*flank steak*). **2** the side of a mountain, building, etc. **3** the right or left side of an army or other body of persons. ● *transitive verb* **1** (often in *passive*) be situated at both sides of (*a road flanked by mountains*). **2** *Military* **a** guard, strengthen, or defend on the flank. **b** menace or attack the flank of. [Old French *flanc* from Frankish]

flank·er *noun* **1** *Military* **a** a fortification for protecting or menacing the flank. **b** one of a detachment of soldiers sent to guard the flanks of a military formation. **2** anything that flanks another thing. **3 a** (in football) an offensive player who lines up to the outside of an end. **b** (in rugby) a wing forward. **4** *Cdn* (*Nfld*) a spark from a chimney or fire.

flan·nel ● *noun* **1 a** any of various loose-textured soft woollen or synthetic fabrics of plain or twilled weave and slightly napped on one side. **b** = FLANNELETTE. **c** (in *pl.*) flannel garments, esp. trousers. **2** *Brit.* = FACE CLOTH. **3** *Brit. slang* nonsense; flattery. ● *verb Brit. slang* (**flan·nelled, flan·nel·ling**; also **flan·neled, flan·nel·ing**) **1** *transitive* flatter. **2** *intransitive* use flattery. [perhaps from Welsh *gwlanen* from *gwlân* wool]

flan·nel·board *noun* a piece of flannel as a base for paper or cloth cut-outs, used as a toy or a teaching aid.

flan·nel·ette *noun* a napped cotton fabric imitating the texture of flannel, used for sheets, pyjamas, etc. [FLANNEL]

flan·nel·graph *noun* = FLANNELBOARD.

flap ● *verb* (**flapped, flap·ping**) **1 a** *transitive* move (wings, the arms, etc.) up and down when flying, or as if flying. **b** *intransitive* (of wings, the arms, etc.) move up and down; beat. **2 a** *intransitive* (esp. of curtains, loose cloth, etc.) swing or sway about; flutter, esp. with accompanying noise. **b** *transitive* cause to swing or sway about, flutter or flop, esp. with accompanying noise (*he flapped the lid on the garbage can*). **3** *transitive* (usu. foll. by *away, off*) strike at (a thing) loosely esp. to drive it away (*she flapped his hand away*). **4** *intransitive informal* be agitated or panicky (*she is not easily flapped*). ● *noun* **1** a piece of cloth, wood, paper, etc. hinged or attached by one side only and often used to cover a gap, e.g. the folded part of an envelope or book jacket, the cover of a pocket, a table leaf, etc. **2** one up-and-down motion of a wing, an arm, etc. **3** *informal* **a** a state of agitation; panic (*don't get into a flap*). **b** trouble, confrontation. **4** a hinged or sliding section of an aircraft wing used to control lift. **5** a light blow with something broad. □ **flap·less** *adjective* **flappy** *adjective* [Middle English, prob. imitative]

flap·doodle *noun informal* nonsense. [19th c.: origin unknown]

flap·jack *noun* **1** *N Amer.* a pancake. **2** *Brit.* a sweet dense cake, served in rectangles, made with oats, syrup, and melted butter. [FLAP + JACK¹]

flap·per *noun* **1** a person or thing that flaps. **2** *hist.* a fashionable and unconventional young woman of the 1920s. **3** a young bird.

flare ● *verb* **1** *intransitive & transitive* burn or cause to burn suddenly with a bright unsteady flame. **2** *intransitive* burst into anger etc.; burst forth. **3** *intransitive & transitive* widen or cause to widen gradually towards the top or bottom (*flared trousers*). ● *noun* **1 a** a dazzling irregular flame or light, esp. in the open air. **b** a sudden outburst of flame. **2 a** a bright flame used as a signal of distress etc. **b** a device that produces such a flame. **c** a flame dropped from an aircraft to illuminate a target etc. **3** *Astronomy* a sudden burst of radiation from a star. **4** a sudden outburst of emotion etc. (*a flare of temper*). **5 a** a gradual widening, esp. of a skirt or trousers. **b** (in *pl.*) wide-bottomed pants, esp. popular during the late 1960s and 1970s. **c** (also **flare-out**) a lessening of the steepness of the glide path of an aircraft about to land. **6** an upward and outward curve of a ship's bows. **7** *Photog.* extraneous illumination on film caused by internal reflection in the lens etc. □ **flare up 1** burst into a sudden blaze. **2** become suddenly angry or active. [16th c.: origin unknown]

flare-up *noun* an outburst of flame, anger, activity, a disease, etc.

flash ● *verb* **1** *intransitive & transitive* emit or reflect or cause to emit or reflect light briefly, suddenly, or intermittently; gleam or cause to gleam. **2** *intransitive* break suddenly into flame; give out flame or sparks. **3** *transitive* send or reflect like a sudden flame or blaze (*his eyes flashed fire*). **4** *intransitive* **a** burst suddenly into view or perception (*the explanation flashed into my mind*). **b** move swiftly (*the train flashed through the station*). **5 a** *transitive* send (news etc.) by radio, television, etc. (*the bulletin was flashed to stations across the country*). **b** *intransitive & transitive* (of a message, image, etc.) show or be shown briefly on a television or movie screen. **c** *transitive* signal to (a person) by shining lights or headlights briefly. **6** *transitive informal* **a** show or display briefly (*flashed an identification card*). **b** show or display ostentatiously (*flashed her engagement ring*). **7** *intransitive slang* (esp. of a man) expose one's genitals briefly and indecently. ● *noun* **1** a sudden bright light or flame, e.g. of lightning. **2** a very brief time; an instant (*all over in a flash*). **3 a** a brief, sudden burst of feeling (*a flash of hope*). **b** a sudden display (of wit, understanding, etc.). **4** = NEWS FLASH. **5** *Photog.* a device producing a flash of intense light, used for photographing by night, indoors, etc. **6 a** a rush of water, esp. down a weir to take a boat over shallows. **b** a contrivance for producing this. **7** *Cdn & Brit.* a coloured patch of cloth on a uniform etc. as a distinguishing emblem. **8** vulgar display; ostentation. **9** a bright patch of colour. **10** *Film* the momentary exposure of a scene. **11** excess plastic or metal oozing from a mould during moulding. **12** = HOT FLASH. **13** (**Flash**) *Proprietary* a computer

application used to produce animation sequences that can be viewed by a web browser. ● *adjective informal* **1** gaudy; showy; vulgar (*a flash car*). **2** counterfeit (*flash notes*). **3** connected with thieves, the underworld, etc. □ **flash back** (of a person's thoughts or mind) briefly and suddenly recall a previous time or incident (*flash back to 1950*). **flash in the pan** a promising start followed by failure. **flash over 1** *Electricity* make an (accidental) electric circuit by sparking across a gap. **2** (of a room, building, etc.) burst into flames suddenly. [Middle English originally with reference to the rushing of water: compare SPLASH]

flash·back *noun* **1** a scene in a film, novel, etc. set in a time earlier than the main action. **2** *Psych.* a vivid, often recurrent remembrance of a usu. distressing event from the past.

flash·bulb *noun* a bulb producing a flash of light used for photography under conditions of low light.

flash burn *noun* a burn caused by sudden intense heat, esp. from a nuclear explosion.

flash card *noun* a card printed with words, numerals, etc., shown to children briefly as an aid to learning.

flash·er *noun* **1** *slang* a person, esp. a man, who indecently exposes himself. **2 a** an automatic device for switching lights rapidly on and off. **b** a sign or signal, e.g. hazard lights on a vehicle, using this device. **3** a person or thing that flashes.

flash fire *noun* a fire in which a sudden influx of oxygen causes everything within a burning room, building, etc. to burst into flames.

flash flood *noun* a sudden local flood due to heavy rain etc.

flash-freeze *transitive verb* freeze (food or other material) very rapidly so as to prevent the formation of ice crystals.

flash-fry *transitive verb* (**-fries, -fried**) fry (food) at a high temperature for a short time.

flash gun *noun* = FLASH *noun* 5.

flash·ing *noun* a usu. metallic strip used to prevent water penetration at the junction of a roof with a wall etc. [dial. *flash* seal with lead sheets, or obsolete *flash flashing*]

flash·lamp *noun* a portable flashing electric lamp.

flash·light *noun* **1** a portable, battery-powered light. **2** a flashing light used for signals and in lighthouses.

flash memory *noun Computing* a type of memory device that retains data in the absence of a power supply.

flash·over *noun* **1** an accidental electrical discharge across a gap, esp. where the voltage is too great for the insulation on a conductor. **2** a phenomenon in which an influx of oxygen causes everything within a burning room, building, etc. to burst into flames at the same time.

flash·point *noun* **1** the temperature at which vapour from oil etc. will ignite in air. **2** the point at which anger, indignation, etc. becomes uncontrollable. **3** a place or situation which has the potential to explode into sudden violence.

flash unit *noun* = FLASH GUN.

flashy *adjective* (**flash·i·er, flash·i·est**) showy; gaudy; cheaply attractive. □ **flash·i·ly** *adverb* **flash·i·ness** *noun*

flask *noun* **1 a** a narrow-necked bulbous bottle used in chemistry. **b** a similarly shaped bottle used for storing oil, wine, etc. **2** = HIP FLASK. **3** = VACUUM FLASK. [French *flasque* & (prob.) Italian *fiasco* from medieval Latin *flasca, flasco*: compare FLAGON]

flat¹ ● *adjective* (**flat·ter, flat·test**) **1 a** horizontally level (*a flat roof*). **b** even; smooth; unbroken; without projection or indentation (*a flat stomach*). **c** with a level surface and little depth; shallow (*a flat cap; a flat heel*). **d** spread out on a single plane; extending at full length. **2** unqualified; plain; downright (*a flat refusal; a flat denial*). **3 a** dull; lifeless; monotonous (*spoke in a flat tone*). **b** without energy; dejected. **c** (of a joke etc.) trite; not funny. **4** (of a drink etc.) lacking in flavour, stale; esp. having lost effervescence. **5** (of a tire) punctured; deflated. **6** esp. *Brit.* (of a battery, etc.) having exhausted its charge. **7** *Music* **a** below true or normal pitch (*the violins are flat*). **b** (of a key) having a flat or flats in the signature. **c** (as **B flat, E flat,** etc.) a semitone lower than B, E, etc. **8** not proportional or variable (*flat fee; flat rate*). **9** (of a painting, photograph, etc.): **a** lacking contrast. **b** lacking perspective. **10 a** (of paint etc.) not glossy; matte. **b** (of a tint) of uniform depth and shade. **11** (of a market, prices, etc.) inactive; sluggish. **12** of or relating to flat racing. **13** = FLAT-CHESTED. ● *adverb* **1** lying at full length; spread out, esp. on another surface (*lay flat on the floor; the ladder was flat against the wall*). **2** *informal* **a** completely, absolutely (*turned it down flat; flat broke*). **b** exactly (*in five minutes flat*). **3** *Music* below the true or normal pitch (*always sings flat*). ● *noun* **1** the flat part of anything; something flat (*the flat of the hand*). **2** (usu. in *pl.*) **a** level ground, esp. a plain or swamp. **b** nearly level ground over which the tide flows or which is covered by shallow water (*mud flats*). **3** *Music* **a** a note lowered a semitone below natural pitch. **b** the sign (♭) indicating this. **4** *informal* a flat tire, a puncture. **5** a woman's shoe with a low heel or no heel. **6** = FLATBOAT. **7 a** *N Amer.* a shallow box or container for growing seedlings or shipping produce etc. (*bought a flat of strawberries*). **b** *Cdn* (esp. *West*) a cardboard tray holding 24 cans of beer, etc. **8** *Theatre* a flat section of scenery mounted on a frame. **9** (as **the flat**) *Brit.* **a** flat racing. **b** the flat racing season. ● *transitive verb* (**flat·ted**, **flat·ting**) **1** make flat, flatten (esp. in technical use). **2** *N Amer. Music* make (a note) flat. □ **fall flat** fail to live up to expectations; not win applause. **flat out 1** at top speed. **2** using all one's strength, energy, or resources. **3** directly, bluntly (*told me flat out that he wasn't interested*). □ **flat·ly** *adverb* **flat·ness** *noun* **flat·tish** *adjective* [Middle English from Old Norse *flatr* from Germanic]

flat² *noun* **1** *Brit.* an apartment. **2** *Cdn* (*S Ont.*) an apartment in a house. □ **flat·let** *noun* [alteration of obsolete *flet* floor, dwelling, from Germanic (as FLAT¹)]

flat·bed *noun* **1** (in full **flatbed trailer** or **flatbed truck**) a trailer or truck, the body of which is an open platform without raised sides or ends. **2** *Computing* a scanner, plotter, or other device which keeps paper flat during use.

flatbed press *noun* a printing machine in which the printing surface is carried on a flat bed and pressure is applied by a revolving cylinder.

flat·boat *noun* (also **flat-bottomed boat**) a boat with a flat bottom for transport in shallow water.

flat·bread *noun* any of various flat, thin, often unleavened breads.

flat calm *adjective* (of a body of water) very still; completely calm.

flat·car *noun* a railway car without a roof or raised sides, used for carrying freight.

flat-chested *adjective* (of a woman) having small breasts.

flat file *noun* *Computing* a file having no internal hierarchy.

flat·fish *noun* (*pl.* same or **-es**) any marine fish of various families having an asymmetric appearance with both eyes on one side of a flattened body, including sole, turbot, plaice, etc.

flat foot *noun* **1** (usu. in *pl.*) a foot with a less than normal arch. **2** (**flat·foot**) (*pl.* **-foots** or **-feet**) *dated slang* a police officer.

flat-footed *adjective* **1** having flat feet. **2** *informal* clumsy, awkward (*flat-footed prose*). **3** *informal* unprepared; off guard (*was caught flat-footed*). **4** *informal* downright, positive. □ **flat-footed·ly** *adverb*

flat-four ● *adjective* (of an engine) having four cylinders all horizontal, two on each side of the crankshaft. ● *noun* such an engine.

flat·head ● *noun* **1** any marine fish of the family Platycephalidae, having a flattened body with both eyes on the top side. **2** (**Flathead**) a member of certain North American Indian peoples such as Chinook, Choctaw, and Salish, named from their supposed practice of flattening their children's heads artificially. ● *adjective* (of a screw or nail) having a flat head. □ **flat-headed** *adjective*

flat·iron *noun* **1** *hist.* an iron for pressing clothes etc., heated by external means and usu. triangular in shape. **2** something shaped like a flatiron, esp. a building constructed to fit a triangular intersection.

flat·land *noun* (often in *pl.*) a region of flat land. □ **flat·land·er** *noun*

flat·line *intransitive verb slang* **1** *Med.* (of a patient) die. **2** (of a project, proposal, etc.) stall, fizzle. □ **flat·lin·er** *noun* [from the straight line that registers on an EEG, indicating brain death]

flat·mate *noun* esp. *Brit.* a person in relation to one or more persons living in the same flat.

flat·pick·ing *noun* the technique of playing an esp. acoustic guitar with a plectrum rather than with fingerpicks or the fingers. □ **flat·pick·er** *noun*

flat race *noun* a horse race over level ground, as opposed to a steeplechase or hurdles. □ **flat racing** *noun*

flat screen *noun* (also **flat panel**) electronic display equipment (as television screens, computer monitors, etc.) which is thin in relation to its two visible dimensions.

flat·ten *verb* **1** *transitive & intransitive* make or become flat. **2** *transitive informal* knock down. □ **flatten out** bring an aircraft parallel to the ground. □ **flat·ten·er** *noun*

flat·ter *verb* **1** *transitive* compliment unduly, esp. for gain or advantage. **2** *transitive* (usu. *reflexive*; usu. foll. by *that* + clause) please, congratulate, or delude (oneself etc.) (*I flatter myself that I can sing*). **3** *transitive* **a** (of a colour, a style, etc.) make (a person) appear to the best advantage (*that blouse flatters you*). **b** (esp. of a portrait, a painter, etc.) represent too favourably. **4** *transitive* gratify the vanity of; make (a person) feel honoured. **5** *transitive* inspire (a person) with hope, esp. unduly (*was flattered into thinking himself invulnerable*). **6** *intransitive* use flattery.

□ **flat·ter·er** *noun* **flat·ter·ing** *adjective* **flat·ter·ing·ly** *adverb* [Middle English, perhaps related to Old French *flater* to smooth]

flat·tery *noun* (*pl.* **-ies**) **1** exaggerated or insincere praise. **2** the act or an instance of flattering.

flat·tie *noun* (*pl.* **-ties**) *Brit. informal* a flat-heeled shoe.

flat-top *noun* **1** *US Aviation slang* an aircraft carrier. **2** *slang* a man's short flat haircut.

flatu·lent /ˈflatjʊlənt/ *adjective* **1 a** causing formation of gas in the alimentary canal. **b** caused by or suffering from this. **2** (of speech etc.) inflated, pretentious. □ **flatu·lence** *noun* **flatu·lent·ly** *adverb* [French from modern Latin *flatulentus* (as FLATUS)]

fla·tus /ˈfleɪtəs/ *noun* gas in or from the stomach or bowels. [Latin, = blowing, from *flare* blow]

flat·ware *noun* **1** *N Amer.* domestic cutlery. **2** esp. *Brit.* plates, saucers, etc. (opp. HOLLOWWARE).

flat·water *noun* *N Amer.* slowly moving water, as in a river etc. (also *attributive*: *flatwater canoeing*).

flat·worm *noun* any worm of the phylum Platyhelminthes, having a flattened body and no body cavity or blood vessels, including tapeworms, flukes, etc.

Flau·bert /floːˈbɛr/ **Gus·tave** (1821–80), French novelist and short-story writer. A dominant figure in the French realist school, he achieved fame with the novel *Madame Bovary* (1857), portraying the adulteries and suicide of a provincial doctor's wife.

flaunt *transitive verb* **1** display ostentatiously (oneself or one's finery); show off; parade (*liked to flaunt his gold cufflinks*). ¶ Flaunt should not be confused with *flout*, which means 'to disobey contemptuously'. **2** wave or cause to wave proudly (*flaunted the banner*). □ **if you've got it, flaunt it** *informal* one should make a conspicuous and confident show of one's wealth or attributes rather than be modest about them. [16th c.: origin unknown]

flaut·ist /ˈflɔːtɪst, ˈflaʊ-/ *noun* a flute player. ¶ Although some people believe that this is the only correct form of the noun, *flutist* is in fact more common in N American English and is perfectly acceptable. [Italian *flautista* from *flauto* FLUTE]

flava /ˈfleɪvə/ *noun slang* (in hip hop etc.) a musical style. [black English pronunciation of FLAVOUR]

Fla·velle /fləˈvɛl/ **Sir Jo·seph Wes·ley** (1858–1939), Canadian business executive, financier, and philanthropist. President of the leading meat-packing firm William Davies Company from 1900, he served as the chairman of several other companies, and became known for his philanthropic endeavours.

Fla·vian /ˈfleɪvɪən/ of, relating to, or denoting a dynasty of Roman emperors including Vespasian and his sons Titus and Domitian. [Latin *Flavianus* from *Flavius* name of family]

fla·vin /ˈfleɪvɪn/ *noun* **1** the chemical compound forming the nucleus of various natural yellow pigments. **2** a yellow dye formerly obtained from dyer's oak. [Latin *flavus* yellow + -IN]

fla·vin ad·en·ine di·nucleo·tide *noun* a coenzyme derived from riboflavin, important in various biochemical reactions. Abbr.: **FAD**.

fla·vone /ˈfleɪvəʊn/ *noun Biochem.* any of a group of naturally occurring white or yellow pigments found in plants. [as FLAVIN + -ONE]

fla·von·oid /ˈfleɪvən,ɔɪd/ *noun* any of a large class of plant pigments having a structure based on or similar to flavone, including anthocyanins, flavones, etc. [FLAVONE + -OID]

flavo·pro·tein /ˌfleɪvəʊˈprɔːtiːn/ *noun Biochem.* any of a group of conjugated proteins containing flavin that are involved in oxidation reactions in cells. [FLAVIN + PROTEIN]

fla·vour (also **fla·vor**) ● *noun* **1** a distinctive or characteristic taste (*has a cheesy flavour*). **2** an indefinable characteristic quality (*music with a romantic flavour*). **3** (usu. foll. by *of*) a slight admixture of a quality. **4** esp. *N Amer.* = FLAVOURING. **5** a type or kind (*you can swap files among various flavours of computers*). **6** *Physics* a quantized property of quarks which differentiates them into at least six varieties (up, down, charmed, strange, top, bottom). ● *transitive verb* give flavour to; season. □ **flavour of the month** (or **week**) a temporary trend or fashion. □ **flavour·ful** *adjective* **flavour·less** *adjective* **flavour·some** *adjective* [Old French *flaor* perhaps from Latin *flatus* blowing & *foetor* stench: assimilated to *savour*]

fla·vour·ing *noun* (also **fla·vor·ing**) a substance used to flavour food or drink.

flaw¹ ● *noun* **1** an imperfection; a weakness (*pride was his tragic flaw*). **2** a crack or chip in china, weaving defect in cloth, or similar defect. **3** *Law* an invalidating defect in a legal matter. ● *transitive & intransitive verb* crack; damage; spoil. □ **flawed** *adjective* **flaw·less** *adjective*

flaw·less·ly *adverb* **flaw·less·ness** *noun* [Middle English perhaps from Old Norse *flaga* slab, from Germanic: compare FLAKE¹, FLAG²]

flaw² *noun* a squall of wind; a short storm. [prob. from Middle Dutch *vlâghe*, Middle Low German *vlâge*, perhaps = stroke]

flax *noun* **1 a** any of various plants of the genus *Linum*, esp. the blue-flowered *L. usitatissimum*, cultivated for its textile fibre and its seeds (*see* LINSEED). **b** a plant resembling this. **2** dressed or undressed flax fibres. [Old English *flæx* from West Germanic]

flax·en *adjective* **1** of flax. **2** (of hair) coloured like dressed flax; pale yellow.

flax·seed *noun* the seed of flax; linseed.

flay *transitive verb* **1** strip the skin or hide off, esp. by beating. **2** criticize severely (*the play was flayed by the critics*). **3** peel off (skin, bark, peel, etc.). **4** strip (a person) of wealth by extortion or exaction. □ **flay·er** *noun* [Old English *flēan* from Germanic]

F-layer *noun* the highest and most strongly ionized region of the ionosphere. [F (arbitrary) + LAYER]

flea *noun* a small wingless jumping insect of the order Siphonaptera, feeding on human and other blood. □ **a flea in one's ear** a sharp reproof. [Old English *flēa*, *flēah* from Germanic]

flea·bag *noun slang* **1** N Amer. a cheap, rundown hotel. **2** a shabby or unattractive person or thing, esp. a worthless animal.

flea·bane *noun* any of various composite plants of the genus *Inula* or *Erigeron*, supposed to drive away fleas.

flea beetle *noun* a small jumping leaf beetle of the genus *Phyllotreta* that can be a pest of plants such as crucifers.

flea bite *noun* **1** the bite of a flea. **2** a trivial injury or inconvenience.

flea-bitten *adjective* **1** bitten by or infested with fleas. **2** shabby.

flea circus *noun* an entertainment that claims to consist of trained fleas.

flea collar *noun* an insecticidal collar for pets.

flea-flicker *noun Football* any of several plays in which the ball is quickly passed from one player to another before or after a forward pass.

flea market *noun* a usu. outdoor market with individual vendors selling second-hand goods, antiques, discontinued merchandise, produce, etc.

flea·pit *noun Brit.* a dingy dirty place, esp. a rundown cinema.

flea·wort /ˈfliːwɔːt/ *noun* a plant of the genus *Senecio* of the daisy family, formerly thought to drive away fleas.

flèche /fleʃ/ *noun* a slender spire, often perforated with windows, esp. at the intersection of the nave and the transept of a church. [French, originally = arrow]

flech·ette /fleʃˈet/ *noun* a type of ammunition resembling a small dart, shot from a gun. [French *fléchette*, diminutive of *flèche* 'arrow']

fleck ● *noun* **1** a small patch of colour or light (*eyes with green flecks*). **2** a small particle or speck, esp. of dust. ● *transitive verb* mark with flecks. [perhaps from Old Norse *flekkr* (n.), *flekka* (v.), or Middle Low German, Middle Dutch *vlecke*, Old High German *flec*, *fleccho*]

flec·tion *var. of* FLEXION.

fled *past and past participle of* FLEE.

fledge *verb* **1** *intransitive* (of a bird) grow feathers. **2** *transitive* bring up (a young bird) until it can fly. **3** *transitive* deck or provide with feathers or down. **4** *transitive* provide (an arrow) with feathers. [obsolete *fledge* (adj.) 'fit to fly', from Old English *flycge* (recorded in *unfligge*) from a Germanic root related to FLY¹]

fledged *adjective* **1** able to fly. **2** independent; mature.

fledg·ling ● *noun* a young bird. ● *adjective* young or new; inexperienced (*a fledgling democracy*). [FLEDGE + -LING¹]

flee *verb* (*past and past participle* **fled**) **1** *intransitive* (often foll. by *from*, *before*) run or hurry away; escape (esp. from danger, threat, etc.). **2** *transitive* run away from; leave abruptly; shun (*fled the room*; *fled her advances*). **3** *intransitive* vanish; pass away (*all hope had fled*). [Old English *flēon* from Germanic]

fleece ● *noun* **1 a** the woolly covering of a sheep or a similar animal. **b** the amount of wool sheared from a sheep at one time. **2** a soft warm fabric with a pile, used in nightwear and athletic wear and for lining coats etc. **3** something resembling a fleece. **4** *Heraldry* a representation of a fleece suspended from a ring. ● *transitive verb* **1** (often foll. by *of*) strip (a person) of money, valuables, etc.; swindle. **2** remove the fleece from (a sheep etc.); shear. □ **fleece·able** *adjective* **fleeced** *adjective* (also in *combination*). [Old English *flēos*, *flēs* from West Germanic]

fleecy *adjective* (**flee·ci·er**, **flee·ci·est**) of or like a fleece. □ **flee·ci·ly** *adverb* **flee·ci·ness** *noun*

fleer *intransitive verb* laugh impudently or mockingly; sneer; jeer. [Middle English, prob. from Scandinavian: compare Norwegian & Swedish dial. *flira* to grin]

fleet¹ *noun* **1 a** a number of warships under one commander-in-chief. **b** (prec. by *the*) all the warships and merchant ships of a nation. **2** a number of ships, aircraft, buses, trucks, taxis, etc. operating together or owned by one proprietor. [Old English *flēot* ship, shipping, from *flēotan* float, FLEET⁴]

fleet² *adjective literary* swift; nimble. □ **fleet·ly** *adverb* **fleet·ness** *noun* [prob. from Old Norse *fljótr* from Germanic: compare FLEET⁴]

fleet³ *noun Brit. dialect* a creek; an inlet. [Old English *flēot* from Germanic: compare FLEET⁴]

fleet⁴ *intransitive verb archaic* **1** glide away; vanish; be transitory. **2** (usu. foll. by *away*) (of time) pass rapidly; slip away. **3** move swiftly; fly. [Old English *flēotan* float, swim, from Germanic]

Fleet Admiral *noun US* = ADMIRAL OF THE FLEET.

Fleet Air Arm *noun hist.* the aviation service of the Royal Navy.

fleet-footed *adjective* nimble; fast on one's feet. [FLEET²]

fleet·ing *adjective* transitory; brief. □ **fleet·ing·ly** *adverb* [FLEET⁴ + -ING²]

Fleet Street *noun* **1** the London press. **2** British journalism or journalists. ['the Fleet', a covered stream flowing into the Thames near Fleet Street (see FLEET³)]

Flem·ing¹ ▶ **1 Sir Alex·an·der** (1881–1955), Scottish bacteriologist. In 1928 he accidentally discovered the effect of penicillin on bacteria, and 12 years later Florey and Chain established its therapeutic use as an antibiotic; Fleming was jointly awarded the Nobel Prize for medicine in 1945. **2 Ian (Lan·cas·ter)** (1908–64), English novelist. He is known for his spy novels about the suave secret agent James Bond. **3 Sir John Am·brose** (1849–1945), English electrical engineer, chiefly remembered for his invention of the thermionic valve (1900), which was the basis for all electronic devices until the transistor began to supersede it more than 50 years later. **4 Sir Sand·ford** (1827–1915), Scottish-born Canadian civil engineer. Chief engineer for the construction of the Intercolonial Railway, he was appointed chief engineer for construction of the CPR in 1871 and surveyed a northerly route and a southerly route through the Kicking Horse Pass; Canada's adoption of international standard time in 1884 grew out of his papers on time reckoning, and he also designed the first Canadian stamp, the threepenny beaver, issued in 1851.

Flem·ing² *noun* **1** a native of medieval Flanders. **2** a member of a Flemish-speaking people inhabiting N and W Belgium (*see also* WALLOON). [Old English from Old Norse *Flæmingi* & Middle Dutch *Vlâming* from root of *Vlaanderen* Flanders]

Flem·ish ● *adjective* of or relating to Flanders. ● *noun* **1** the West Germanic language of Flanders, comprising a group of Dutch dialects, now one of the two official languages of Belgium. **2** (**the Flemish**) (*pl.*) Flemings. [Middle Dutch *Vlâmisch* (as FLEMING²)]

Flemish bond *noun* a pattern of bricks in a wall in which each course consists of alternate headers and stretchers.

Flem·ming, Hugh John (1899–1982), Canadian politician, Progressive Conservative premier of New Brunswick 1952–60.

flense *transitive verb* **1** remove the blubber or skin from (a whale or seal). **2** strip off (skin). □ **flens·er** *noun* [Danish *flense*: compare Norwegian *flinsa*, *flunsa* flay]

flesh ● *noun* **1 a** the soft, esp. muscular, substance between the skin and bones of an animal or a human. **b** plumpness; fat (*has put on flesh*). **c** *archaic* meat, esp. excluding poultry, game, and offal. **2** the body as opposed to the mind or the soul, esp. considered as sinful. **3** the pulpy substance of a fruit or a plant. **4 a** the visible surface of the human body with reference to its colour or appearance. **b** = FLESH COLOUR. **5** animal or human life. ● *transitive verb* **1** embody in flesh. **2** incite (a hound etc.) by the taste of blood. **3** remove the flesh adhering to (a skin or hide). **4** initiate (someone) in bloodshed or warfare. □ **flesh out** make or become substantial. **go the way of all flesh** die or come to an end. **in the flesh** in bodily form, in person. **lose** (or **put on**) **flesh** grow thinner or fatter. **make a person's flesh creep** frighten or horrify a person, esp. with tales of the supernatural etc. **sins of the flesh** unchastity. □ **flesh·less** *adjective* [Old English *flæsc* from Germanic]

flesh and blood ● *noun* **1** the body or its substance. **2** humankind. **3** human nature, esp. as being fallible. ● *adjective* actually living, not imaginary or supernatural. □ **one's own flesh and blood** near relatives; descendants.

flesh colour *noun* a light brownish pink. □ **flesh-coloured** *adjective*

flesh-eating disease *noun* a disease in which bodily tissue is rapidly destroyed by streptococcal bacteria.

fleshed *adjective* (usu. in *combination*) having flesh of a usu. specified kind (*an orange-fleshed melon*).

flesh fly *noun* any fly that deposits eggs or larvae in dead flesh.

flesh·ly *adjective* (**flesh·li·er**, **flesh·li·est**) **1** (of desire etc.) bodily; lascivious; sensual. **2** mortal, not divine. **3** worldly.

flesh·pots *plural noun* places providing luxurious or hedonistic living. [Exod. 16:3]

flesh side *noun* the side of a hide that adjoined the flesh.

flesh tone *noun* (usu. in *pl.*) the colour of human skin, esp. as depicted in paintings, photographs, film and television, etc.

flesh wound *noun* a wound not reaching a bone or a vital organ.

fleshy *adjective* (**flesh·i·er**, **flesh·i·est**) **1** plump, fat. **2** (of plant or fruit tissue) pulpy. **3** like flesh. □ **flesh·i·ness** *noun*

fletch *transitive verb* provide (an arrow) with feathers or vanes for flight. [alteration of FLEDGE, prob. influenced by FLETCHER]

Fletch·er, John (1579–1625), English dramatist. A writer of Jacobean tragicomedies, he co-authored some fifteen plays with Francis Beaumont, including *Philaster* (1609) and *The Maid's Tragedy* (1610–11).

fletch·er *noun* a maker or seller of arrows. [Old French *flech(i)er* from *fleche* arrow]

fletch·ing *noun* (also **fletch·ings**) the feathers or vanes of an arrow.

fleur-de-lys /ˌflɜrdəˈliː, ˌflɜrdəˈliːs/ *noun* (also **fleur-de-lis**) (*pl.* **fleurs-** *pronunc.* same) **1** a figure of a lily composed of three petals bound together near their bases, used as a symbol of Quebec and in the former royal arms of France. **2** the flag of the province of Quebec. **3** the iris flower. [Old French *flour de lys* 'flower of the lily']

Fleuri·mont /flɜriˈmɔ̃/ a former town in S Quebec, now part of Sherbrooke; pop. (2001) 16,521. [N.-J. de Noyelles de *Fleurimont*, French settler d.1761]

fleu·ron /flɜːˈrɔ̃/ *noun* a flower-shaped ornament on a building, a coin, a book, etc. [Old French *floron* from *flour* FLOWER]

Fleury /fləˈri/ **An·dré Her·cule de** (1653–1743), French cardinal and politician, who served as Louis XV's chief adviser (1726–43).

Flevo·land /ˈfleɪvəˌlɒnt/ a province of the Netherlands, created in 1986, comprising an area reclaimed from the Zuider Zee during the 1950s and 1960s.

flew *past of* FLY¹.

flews /fluːz/ *plural noun* the hanging lips of a bloodhound etc. [16th c.: origin unknown]

flex ● *verb* **1** *transitive & intransitive* bend (a joint, limb, etc.) or be bent. **2** *transitive & intransitive* move (a muscle) or (of a muscle) be moved to bend a joint. **3** *transitive Geol.* bend (strata). **4** *transitive Archaeology* place (a corpse) with the legs drawn up under the chin. ● *noun* **1** the act or an instance of flexing. **2** flexibility; pliableness (*has a great deal of flex*). **3** *Brit.* = CORD *noun* 4. □ **flex one's muscle(s)** assert one's strength or power. [Latin *flectere flex-* bend]

flex·ible *adjective* **1** able to bend without breaking; pliable; pliant. **2** willing or disposed to yield to influence or persuasion or to adapt to circumstances; not rigid. **3** adaptable; versatile; variable (*works flexible hours*). **4** (of a person) able to bend, twist, and contort the limbs and torso easily and to a greater degree than average. □ **flex·ibil·ity** *noun* **flex·ibly** *adverb*

flex·ion /ˈflɛkʃən/ *noun* (also **flec·tion**) **1 a** the act of bending or the condition of being bent, esp. of a limb or joint. **b** a bent part; a curve. **2** *Grammar* inflection. **3** *Math.* = FLEXURE 2. □ **flex·ion·al** *adjective* (in sense 2). **flex·ion·less** *adjective* (in sense 2). [Latin *flexio* (as FLEX)]

flex·og·raphy /flɛkˈsɒgrəfi/ *noun Printing* a rotary letterpress technique using rubber or plastic plates and synthetic inks or dyes for printing on fabrics, plastics, etc., as well as on paper. □ **flexo·graph·ic** /-səˈgrafɪk/ *adjective*

flex·or /ˈflɛksər/ *noun* (in full **flexor muscle**) a muscle that bends part of the body (*compare* EXTENSOR).

flex·time *noun* (also *Brit.* **flex·i·time**) **1** a system of working a set number of hours with the starting and finishing times chosen within agreed limits by the employee. **2** the hours worked in this way.

flexu·ous /ˈflɛksjʊəs/ *adjective* full of bends; winding. [Latin *flexuosus* from *flexus* bending, formed as FLEX]

flex·ure /ˈflɛkʃər/ *noun* **1 a** the act of bending or the condition of being bent. **b** a bend, curve, or turn. **2** *Math.* the curving of a line, surface, or solid, esp. from a straight line, plane, etc. **3** *Geol.* the bending of strata under pressure. □ **flex·ur·al** *adjective*

flib·ber·ti·gib·bet /ˈflɪbərtiˌdʒɪbət/ *noun* a gossiping, frivolous, or restless person. [imitative of chatter]

flick ● *noun* **1 a** a light, sharp, quickly retracted blow with a whip etc. **b** the sudden release of a bent finger or thumb, esp. to propel a small object. **2** a sudden movement or jerk. **3** a quick turn of the wrist in playing games, esp. in throwing or striking a ball. **4** a slight, sharp sound. **5** *informal* a movie. ● *verb* **1** *transitive* strike, move, or remove with a rapid action of the fingers (*flicked away the dust; flicked the switch*). **2** *transitive* give a flick with (a whip, towel, etc.). **3** *transitive* activate (a light, electrical appliance, etc.) by flicking a switch (*flicked on the lights*). **4** *intransitive & transitive* move rapidly, esp. back and forth. □ **flick through 1** turn over (cards, pages, etc.). **2 a** turn over the pages etc. of, by a rapid movement of the fingers. **b** look cursorily through (a book etc.). [Middle English, imitative]

flick·er¹ ● *intransitive verb* **1** (of light) shine unsteadily or fitfully. **2** (of a flame) burn unsteadily, alternately flaring and dying down. **3 a** (of an eyelid, a video image, etc.) move or wave to and fro; quiver; vibrate. **b** (of the wind) blow lightly and unsteadily. **4** (of hope etc.) increase and decrease unsteadily and intermittently. ● *noun* **1** a flickering movement or light. **2** a brief period of hope, recognition, etc. □ **flicker out** die away after a final flicker. □ **flick·ery** *adjective* [Old English *flicorian, flycerian*]

flick·er² *noun* any woodpecker of the genus *Colaptes*, native to N America. [imitative of its note]

flick knife *noun* = SWITCHBLADE.

fli·er *var. of* FLYER.

flight¹ ● *noun* **1 a** the act or manner of flying through the air (*studied swallows' flight*). **b** the swift movement or passage of a projectile etc. through the air (*the flight of an arrow*). **2 a** a journey made through the air or in space. **b** a scheduled journey made by an airline. **c** a unit of two or more military aircraft. **3 a** a flock or large body of birds, insects, etc., esp. when migrating. **b** a migration. **4** (usu. foll. by *of*) a series, esp. of stairs between floors, or of hurdles across a race track (*lives up six flights*). **5** an extravagant soaring, a mental or verbal excursion or sally (of wit etc.) (*a flight of fancy; a flight of ambition*). **6** the trajectory and pace of a ball in games. **7** the distance that a bird, aircraft, or missile can fly. **8** (usu. foll. by *of*) a volley (*a flight of arrows*). **9** the tail of a dart. **10** the pursuit of game by a hawk. **11** swift passage (of time). **12** a selection of wines for a wine tasting, either a number of wines from the same vintage or the same wine from several vintages. ● *transitive verb* **1** provide (an arrow) with feathers. **2** shoot (wildfowl etc.) in flight. □ **in the first** (or **top**) **flight** taking a leading place. **take** (or **wing**) **one's flight** fly. [Old English *flyht* from West Germanic: related to FLY¹]

flight² *noun* **1 a** the act or manner of fleeing. **b** a hasty retreat. **2** *Econ.* the selling of currency, investments, etc. in anticipation of a fall in value (*capital flight*). □ **put to flight** cause to flee. **take** (or **take to**) **flight** flee. [Old English from Germanic: related to FLEE]

flight attendant *noun* an airline employee trained in safety procedures who also serves meals etc. during a flight.

flight bag *noun* a small, zipped, shoulder bag carried by air travellers.

flight control *noun* an internal or external system directing the movement of aircraft.

flight crew *noun* a team of people who ensure the effective operation and safety of an aircraft during a flight.

flight deck *noun* **1** the deck of an aircraft carrier used for takeoff and landing. **2** the part of an aircraft where the pilot, navigator, etc. perform their duties.

flight engineer *noun* a member of a flight crew responsible for the engines and other mechanical systems of the aircraft in flight.

flight envelope *noun* the possible combinations of speed and altitude, speed and range, etc. of a particular kind of aircraft or aircraft engine.

flight feather *noun* any of the large primary or secondary feathers in a bird's wing, supporting it in flight.

flight·less *adjective* (of a bird etc.) naturally unable to fly.

flight lieutenant *noun* (also **Flight Lieutenant**) (in the RAF and *hist.* in the RCAF) an officer next in rank below squadron leader and above flying officer. Abbr.: **Flt. Lt.**

flight line *noun* a general area in an airfield including hangars, ramps, etc., where aircraft are parked and serviced.

flight officer *noun* (also **Flight Officer**) an officer in the WRAF, corresponding in rank to flight lieutenant. Abbr.: **Flt. Off.**

flight path *noun* the planned course of an aircraft or spacecraft.

Vowels: a *cat* ɑ *arm* e *bed* ɜr *her* ɜː *deux* ə *ago* ɪ *sit* i *cosy* iː *feed* ɒ *hot* ɔ *pore* oː *no* ʌ *run* ʊ *put*

flight plan *noun* the pre-arranged plan for a particular flight, specifying the route, estimated time of arrival, etc.

flight recorder *noun* a device in an aircraft to record technical details during a flight, that may be used in the event of an accident to discover its cause.

flight·seeing *noun N Amer.* viewing places of interest, esp. natural ones, from an airplane (also *attributive: flightseeing tour*).

flight sergeant *noun* (in the RAF and *hist.* in the RCAF) a non-commissioned officer ranking next above sergeant. Abbr.: **Flt. Sgt.**

flight test ● *transitive verb* test (an aircraft, rocket, etc.) during flight. ● *noun* **1** such a test. **2** an official test of competence at flying which must be passed to obtain a pilot's licence. □ **flight testing** *noun*

flighty *adjective* (**flight·i·er**, **flight·i·est**) **1** frivolous, fickle, changeable. **2** crazy. □ **flight·i·ly** *adverb* **flight·i·ness** *noun*

flim-flam ● *noun* **1** a trifle; nonsense; idle talk. **2** a deception or swindle. ● *transitive verb* (**flim-flammed**, **flim-flamming**) cheat; deceive. □ **flim-flammer** *noun* **flim-flammery** *noun* (*pl.* **-ies**). [imitative reduplication]

flim·sy ● *adjective* (**flim·si·er**, **flim·si·est**) **1** lightly or carelessly assembled; insubstantial, easily damaged (*a flimsy structure*). **2** (of an excuse etc.) unconvincing (*a flimsy pretext*). **3** (of clothing) thin (*a flimsy blouse*). ● *noun* (*pl.* **-ies**) **1** very thin paper. **2** a document, esp. a copy, made on this. □ **flim·si·ly** *adverb* **flim·si·ness** *noun* [17th c.: prob. from FLIM-FLAM: compare TIPSY]

flinch ● *intransitive verb* **1** draw back in pain or expectation of a blow etc.; wince. **2** (often foll. by *from*) give way; shrink, turn aside (*flinched from your duty*). ● *noun* an act or instance of flinching. [Old French *flenchir, flainchir* from West Germanic]

flin·ders /ˈflɪndərz/ *plural noun* fragments; splinters. [Middle English, prob. from Scandinavian]

Flinders Island the largest island in the Furneaux group, situated in the Bass Strait between Tasmania and mainland Australia.

Flin Flon a city in NW Manitoba, situated on the border with Saskatchewan, about 350 km northeast of Prince Albert; pop. (2001) 6,267. [named by a prospector upon his discovery of gold after Professor J. *Flintabbatey Flonatin*, a character in J. Muddock's novel *The Sunless City*, a story about the discovery of a strange world paved with gold lying beneath the Rocky Mountains]

fling ● *verb* (*past* and *past participle* **flung**) **1** *transitive* throw or hurl (an object) forcefully. **2** *reflexive* **a** (usu. foll. by *into*) rush headlong (into a person's arms etc.). **b** (usu. foll. by *into*) embark wholeheartedly (on an enterprise). **c** (usu. foll. by *on*) throw (oneself) on a person's mercy etc. **3** *transitive* utter (words) forcefully. **4** *transitive* (usu. foll. by *out*) suddenly spread (the arms). **5** *transitive* (foll. by *on, off*) put on or take off (clothes) carelessly or rapidly. **6** *intransitive* go angrily or violently; rush (*flung out of the room*). **7** *transitive* put or send suddenly or violently (*was flung into jail*). **8** *transitive* (foll. by *away*) discard or put aside thoughtlessly or rashly (*flung away their reputation*). **9** *intransitive* (usu. foll. by *out*) (of a horse etc.) kick and plunge. ● *noun* **1** an act or instance of flinging; a throw; a plunge. **2** a period of indulgence or wild behaviour (*one last fling before the baby is born*). **3** any of various energetic, whirling, Scottish dances, esp. the Highland fling. **4** an attempt or trial (*have a fling at writing a novel*). □ **fling·er** *noun* [Middle English, perhaps from Old Norse]

flint *noun* **1 a** a hard grey stone of nearly pure silica occurring naturally as nodules or bands in chalk. **b** a piece of this esp. as flaked or ground to form a primitive tool or weapon. **2** a piece of hard alloy of rare-earth metals used to give an igniting spark in a lighter etc. **3** a piece of flint used with steel to produce fire, esp. in a flintlock gun. **4** anything hard and unyielding. □ **flinty** *adjective* (**flint·i·er**, **flint·i·est**). **flint·i·ly** *adverb* **flint·i·ness** *noun* [Old English]

flint glass *noun* a pure lustrous kind of glass originally made with flint.

flint·lock *noun hist.* **1** an old type of gun fired by a spark from a flint. **2** the lock producing such a spark.

Flint·shire a county of NE Wales. It was made part of Clwyd in 1974 and restored (with redrawn borders) in 1996.

flip[1] ● *verb* (**flipped**, **flip·ping**) **1 a** *transitive* flick or toss (a coin etc.) with a quick movement so that it spins in the air. **b** *intransitive* decide or settle a question, tie, etc. by flipping a coin (*flipped to see who went first*). **c** *intransitive* (often foll. by *for*) settle a question with (a person) in this way. **2 a** *transitive* turn (a small object) over. **b** *intransitive* (of an object) turn over (*the car hit the shoulder and flipped*). **c** *intransitive* perform a somersault. **3** *transitive* cause (something) to move with a flick of the fingers (*flipped her hair off her forehead*). **4 a** *transitive* turn (a page in a

book) with a flick of the fingers. **b** *intransitive* move through a book etc. by flipping (*flip to page 86; flip through the brochure*). **c** *intransitive* (of pages) flip over (*pages flipping in the breeze*). **d** *transitive* open (a book, box, etc.) with a brisk movement of the fingers. **5** *N Amer.* **a** *transitive* change or switch (the channel on a television etc.), esp. by using a remote control. **b** *intransitive* (often foll. by *through, past,* etc.) move from one channel to another (*flip past the commercials*). **6** *transitive* **a** move (a switch etc.) with a flick of the fingers. **b** (usu. foll. by *on, off*) turn (a light, an appliance, etc.) on or off by flipping a switch (*flip on the television*). **7** *transitive N Amer.* resell (real estate, stocks, etc.), esp. to make a large profit. **8** *intransitive slang* **a** become suddenly excited or enthusiastic. **b** = FLIP OUT. **9** *intransitive* move about with sudden jerks. **10** *intransitive* **a** make a fillip or flicking noise with the fingers. **b** (foll. by *at*) strike smartly at. **11** *transitive* **a** strike or flick (a person's ear, cheek, etc.) lightly or smartly. **b** move (a fan, whip, etc.) with a sudden jerk. ● *noun* **1** an act of flipping over. **2 a** a smart light blow; a flick. **b** the action or an instance of activating a switch etc. with a flip. **3** a somersault. **4** *informal* **a** an esp. short flight in an aircraft. **b** a quick tour etc. **5** *Figure Skating* a jump in which the skater takes off from the back inside edge of one skate, using the toe of the second foot to provide momentum, goes through one or more counter-clockwise rotations, and lands on the second foot. **6** *N Amer.* the act or an instance of flipping real estate, stocks, etc. **7** = FLIP SIDE. **8** (*attributive*) *Hockey* designating a type of pass or shot in which the puck is propelled a few inches above the surface of the ice so as to be above the blade of an opponent's stick (*flip shot*). ● *adjective informal* glib; flippant. □ **flip burgers** work in a fast-food restaurant. **flip one's lid** (*N Amer.* also **wig**) slang = FLIP OUT. **flip out** *N Amer.* **1** lose self-control; become enraged. **2** become insane. **flip someone the bird** *N Amer. slang* make an obscene and offensive gesture of contempt to someone by raising the middle finger of one hand. □ **flip·py** *adjective* [prob. from FILLIP]

flip[2] *noun* = EGGNOG. [perhaps from FLIP[1] in the sense *whip up*]

flip chart *noun* a large writing pad erected on a stand and bound so that one page can be turned over at the top to reveal the next.

flip-flop ● *noun* **1** esp. *N Amer.* an abrupt reversal of policy. **2** a usu. rubber sandal with a thong between the big and second toe. **3** esp. *N Amer.* a backward somersault. **4** a repeated flapping sound. **5** an electronic switching circuit changed from one stable state to another, or through an unstable state back to its stable state, by a triggering pulse. ● *intransitive verb* (**-flopped**, **-flopping**) make a flip-flop. ● *adverb* in a flapping manner. [imitative]

flip·pant *adjective* lacking in seriousness; treating serious things lightly; disrespectful. □ **flip·pancy** *noun* **flip·pant·ly** *adverb* [FLIP[1] + -ANT]

flip·per *noun* **1** a broadened limb of a seal, penguin, etc., used in swimming. **2** a flat rubber etc. attachment worn on the foot for underwater swimming. **3** a person or thing that flips. **4** *N Amer.* = SPATULA 1c. **5** a remote control for a television etc.

flipper pie *noun Cdn (Nfld)* = SEAL FLIPPER PIE.

flip·ping *adjective & adverb Brit. slang* expressing annoyance, or as an intensifier (*where's the flipping towel?; she flipping beat me*).

flip side *noun informal* **1** = B-SIDE. **2** the reverse or opposite of a person or thing.

flip-top *noun* a top or lid that opens with a flip of the fingers.

flirt ● *verb* **1** *intransitive* (usu. foll. by *with*) show sexual interest in (a person) without any serious intent. **2** *intransitive* (usu. foll. by *with*) **a** superficially interest oneself (with an idea etc.). **b** come close to; have a brush with (danger etc.) (*flirting with disaster*). **3** *intransitive & transitive* move or cause to move with a jerk. ● *noun* **1** a person who indulges in flirting. **2** a quick movement; a sudden jerk. □ **flir·ta·tion** *noun* **flir·ta·tious** *adjective* **flir·ta·tious·ly** *adverb* **flir·ta·tious·ness** *noun* **flirty** *adjective* (**flirt·i·er**, **flirt·i·est**). [apparently symbolic, the elements *fl-* and *-irt* both suggesting sudden movement; compare with FLICK and SPURT. The original verb senses were 'give someone a sharp blow' and 'sneer at'; the earliest noun senses were 'joke, gibe' and 'flighty girl' (defined by Samuel Johnson as 'a pert young hussey') with a notion originally of cheeky behaviour, later of playfully amorous behaviour]

flit ● *intransitive verb* (**flit·ted**, **flit·ting**) **1** move lightly, softly, or rapidly (*flitted from one room to another*). **2** fly lightly; make short flights (*flitted from branch to branch*). **3** *Brit. informal* leave one's house etc. secretly to escape creditors or obligations. **4** esp. *Scot. & Northern England* change one's home; move. ● *noun* **1** an act of flitting. **2** *Brit. informal* a secret, hurried departure in order to escape creditors etc. □ **flit·ter** *noun* [Old Norse *flytja*: related to FLEET[4]]

flitch *noun* **1** a side of bacon. **2** a slab of timber from a tree trunk, usu. from the outside. [Old English *flicce* from Germanic]

flit·ter *intransitive verb* flit about; flutter. [FLIT + -ER⁴]

fliv·ver *noun N Amer. slang* a cheap car or aircraft. [20th c.: origin uncertain]

flix·weed *noun* a cruciferous plant, *Descurainia sophia*, formerly thought to cure dysentery. [earlier *fluxweed*]

float ● *verb* **1** *intransitive & transitive* **a** rest or move or cause (a buoyant object) to rest or move on the surface of a liquid without sinking. **b** get afloat or set (a stranded ship) afloat. **2** *intransitive* move with a liquid or current of air; drift (*the clouds floated high up*). **3** *intransitive informal* **a** move in a leisurely or casual way (*floated about humming quietly*). **b** (often foll. by *before*) hover before the eye or mind (*the prospect of lunch floated before them*). **4** *intransitive* (often foll. by *in*) move or be suspended freely in a liquid or a gas. **5** *intransitive* be free from attachment, commitment, etc. **6** *transitive* **a** bring (a company, scheme, etc.) into being; launch. **b** offer (stock, shares, etc.) on the stock market. **7** *Business* **a** *intransitive* (of currency) be allowed to have a fluctuating exchange rate. **b** *transitive* cause (currency) to float. **c** *intransitive* (of an acceptance) be in circulation. **d** *transitive & intransitive* (of an interest rate) fluctuate or be allowed to fluctuate according to market conditions. **8** *transitive* arrange (a loan); arrange a loan for (someone). **9** *transitive* (of water etc.) support; bear along (a buoyant object). **10** *intransitive & transitive* put forward (an idea, proposal, etc.); circulate. **11** *transitive* waft (a buoyant object) through the air. **12** *transitive* drift downstream on (a river) in an inflatable boat, for recreation. ● *noun* **1** a thing that floats, esp. **a** a raft. **b** a buoyant piece of cork or plastic attached to a fishing line as an indicator of a fish biting. **c** a buoyant object supporting the edge of a fishing net. **d** the hollow or inflated part or organ supporting a fish etc. in the water; an air bladder. **e** a hollow structure fixed underneath an aircraft enabling it to float on water. **f** a floating device on the surface of water, fuel, etc., controlling the flow. **g** *N Amer.* a floating platform attached to a bank, dock, etc., and used as a landing for boats or float planes. **2** a vehicle carrying a display in a parade etc. **3 a** *Cdn & Brit.* a sum of money used to provide change at the beginning of a period of selling in a store etc. **b** a small sum of money for minor expenditure; petty cash. **4** a soft drink with a scoop of ice cream floating in it. **5** a tool used for smoothing plaster etc. **6** the act or an instance of floating. **7** *Brit.* a small vehicle or cart, esp. one powered by electricity (*milk float*). □ **float someone's boat** *informal* appeal to or excite someone. **one's back teeth are floating** *informal* have an urgent need to urinate. [Old English *flot, flotian* float, Old English *flota* ship, Old Norse *flota, floti* related to FLEET⁴: in Middle English influenced by Old French *floter*]

float·a·tion *var. of* FLOTATION.

float·base *noun Cdn* a place on a river, lake, etc. where float planes dock.

float camp *noun Cdn* (*BC*) a log raft supporting the living quarters etc. of a coastal logging crew.

float·er *noun* **1** a person or thing that floats. **2** a voter who is undecided or may change allegiance from one party to another. **3** a person who frequently changes occupation etc. **4** a loose particle within the eyeball which is apparent in one's field of vision. **5** *N Amer.* an insurance policy covering loss of articles without specifying a location.

Floater coat *noun* (also **Floater jacket**, **Floater suit**, etc.) *proprietary* a coat, jacket, or suit for use by boaters and snowmobilers, designed to prevent hypothermia and provide flotation.

float glass *noun* a kind of glass made by drawing the molten glass continuously on to a surface of molten metal for hardening.

float·house *noun N Amer.* (*BC, US Northwest, & Alaska*) a house constructed on a log raft, usu. built so that it can be towed from one mooring to another.

float·ing *adjective* **1 a** supported on water. **b** in or on a ship or boat (*a floating disco*). **2 a** not settled in a definite place. **b** fluctuating; variable (*floating interest rates*). **3** (of an internal organ) not in its proper position (*floating kidney*). **4** (of a floor) not attached to the subfloor, e.g. laminated sheets resting on a concrete floor.

floating debt *noun* a debt repayable on demand, or at a stated time.

floating dock *noun* a floating structure usable as a dry dock.

floating island *noun* a dessert consisting of a custard or other sauce in a bowl with a scoop of meringue floating on top.

floating point *noun Computing* a decimal etc. point that does not occupy a fixed position in the numbers processed.

floating rib *noun* any of the lower ribs, which are not attached to the breastbone.

float plane *noun* an airplane equipped with floats instead of wheels, so that it can land on water.

float tube *noun N Amer.* an air-filled inner tube, usu. with supports for the back and arms, used to support a person's weight in the water while fishing.

floaty *adjective* (esp. of a woman's garment or a fabric) light and airy.

floc *noun* a flocculent mass of fine particles. [abbreviation of FLOCCULUS]

floc·cu·late /ˈflɒkjʊˌleɪt/ *transitive & intransitive verb* form into flocculent masses. □ **floc·cu·la·tion** *noun*

floc·cu·lent /ˈflɒkjʊlənt/ *adjective* **1** like tufts of wool. **2** consisting of or showing tufts, downy. **3** *Chem.* (of precipitates) loosely massed. □ **floc·cu·lence** *noun* [as FLOCCULUS]

floc·cu·lus /ˈflɒkjʊləs/ *noun* (*pl.* **floc·cu·li** /-ˌlaɪ/) **1** *Anat.* a small ovoid lobe in the undersurface of the cerebellum. **2** *Astronomy* a small cloudy wisp on the sun's surface. [modern Latin, diminutive of *floccus*, see FLOCK²]

flock¹ ● *noun* **1 a** a number of animals of one kind, esp. birds, feeding or travelling together. **b** a number of domestic animals, esp. sheep, goats, or geese, kept together. **2** a large crowd of people. **3 a** a Christian congregation or body of believers, esp. in relation to one priest or minister. **b** a family of children, a number of pupils, etc. ● *intransitive verb* **1** congregate; mass. **2** (usu. foll. by *to*) move in great numbers; troop (*thousands flocked to the beach*). [Old English *flocc*]

flock² *noun* **1** a lock or tuft of wool, cotton, etc. **2 a** (also in *pl.*; often *attributive*) material for quilting and stuffing made of wool refuse or torn-up cloth (*a flock mattress*). **b** powdered wool or cloth, applied to wallpaper, fabrics etc. to form a raised velvet-like pattern. □ **flocked** *adjective* **flock·ing** *noun* [Old French *floc* from Latin *floccus*]

Flod·den, Battle of a decisive battle of the Anglo-Scottish war of 1513, which took place near the Northumbrian village of Branxton. A Scottish army under James IV was defeated by a smaller but better-led English force under the Earl of Surrey. The Scottish side suffered heavy losses, including the king and most of his nobles.

floe *noun* a sheet of floating ice. [prob. from Norwegian *flo* from Old Norse *fló* layer]

floe edge *noun N Amer.* the limit of landfast ice.

flog *verb* (**flogged, flog·ging**) **1** *transitive* **a** beat with a whip, stick, etc. (as a punishment or to urge on). **b** make work through violent effort (*flogged the engine*). **2** *transitive slang* **a** sell, esp. by aggressive effort. **b** publicize; promote. **3** *intransitive & reflexive Brit. slang* proceed by violent or painful effort. □ **flog a dead horse** *see* DEAD HORSE. **flog to death** *informal* talk about or promote at tedious length. □ **flog·ger** *noun* **flog·ging** *noun* [17th-c. cant: prob. imitative or from Latin *flagellare* to whip]

flood ● *noun* **1 a** an overflowing or influx of water beyond its normal confines, esp. over land; an inundation. **b** the water that overflows. **2 a** an outpouring of water; a torrent (*a flood of rain*). **b** something resembling a torrent (*a flood of tears; a flood of memories*). **3** the inflow of the tide (also *attributive: flood tide*) (*opp.* EBB *noun* 1). **4** *informal* a floodlight. **5** (**the Flood**) any universal flood as described by various ancient religious traditions, esp. the one recorded in the Bible as occurring in the time of Noah (Gen. 7). **6** *archaic* a river; a stream; a sea. ● *verb* **1** *transitive* **a** cover with or overflow in a flood (*rain flooded the basement*). **b** overflow as if with a flood (*the market was flooded with foreign goods*). **2** *transitive* irrigate (*flooded the paddy fields*). **3** *transitive* deluge (a burning house, a mine, etc.) with water. **4** *intransitive* (often foll. by *in, through*) arrive in great quantities (*complaints flooded in; fear flooded through them*). **5** *intransitive* become inundated (*the bathroom flooded*). **6** *transitive* overfill (a carburetor) with fuel. **7** *intransitive* experience a uterine hemorrhage. **8** *transitive* (of rain etc.) fill (a river) to overflowing. **9** *transitive N Amer.* build up (the surface of a skating rink etc.) by covering it with water and allowing it to freeze. □ **flood·ing** *noun* [Old English *flōd* from Germanic]

flood control *noun* the technique or an act of preventing or controlling floods by means of dams, artificial channels, dikes, etc.

flood·gate *noun* **1** a gate opened or closed to admit or exclude water, esp. the lower gate of a lock. **2** (usu. in *pl.*) a restraint, barrier, or check holding back tears, rain, anger, etc.

flood·light ● *noun* **1** a large powerful light (usu. one of several) to illuminate a building, playing field, stage, etc. **2** the illumination so provided. ● *transitive verb* (*past* and *past participle* **flood·lit**) illuminate with floodlights.

flood plain *noun* a relatively flat plain along the bank of a river etc., that is naturally subject to flooding.

flood tide *noun* **1** the inflow or rising of the tide. **2** a sudden influx of something (*the flood tide of immigration*).

flood water *noun* the water left by flooding.

flood·way *noun* N Amer. a channel for diverting flood waters away from a city etc.

floor ● *noun* **1 a** the lower surface of a room. **b** the boards etc. of which it is made. **2 a** the bottom of the sea, a lake, a cave, a cavity, etc. **b** any level area. **3** all the rooms etc. on the same level of a building; a storey (*lives on the ground floor; walked up to the sixth floor*). **4 a** (in a legislative assembly) the part of the house in which members sit and from which they speak. **b** the right to speak next in debate (*gave her the floor*). **5** *Stock Exch.* the large central hall where trading takes place. **6** the minimum of prices, wages, etc. ● *transitive verb* **1** furnish with a floor. **2** bring to the ground; knock (a person) down. **3** *informal* confound, baffle (*was floored by the puzzle*). **4** *informal* get the better of; overcome. **5** N Amer. push (the accelerator pedal of a motor vehicle) all the way to the floor, to gain maximum power or speed. □ **cross the floor** see CROSS. **from the floor** (of a speech etc.) given by a member of the audience, not by those on the platform etc. **take the floor 1** begin to dance on a dance floor etc. **2** speak in a debate. □ **floor·less** *adjective* [Old English *flōr* from Germanic]

floor·board *noun* **1** (usu. in *pl.*) a long wooden board used for flooring. **2** N Amer. the floor of a car etc.

floor cloth *noun* N Amer. an esp. canvas cloth, usu. painted or stencilled, for use as a rug.

floor covering *noun* carpeting, tiles, linoleum, etc. used for covering floors.

floor exercises *plural noun* (in gymnastics) a routine of tumbling exercises without equipment.

floor hockey *noun* N Amer. a form of hockey played on an indoor floor, usu. using plastic sticks and a plastic puck or ball.

floor·ing *noun* the materials with which a floor is made or covered.

floor lamp *noun* N Amer. a lamp set on a tall upright with its base standing on the floor.

floor leader *noun* US the leader of a party in a legislative assembly.

floor-length *adjective* (esp. of clothing) reaching to the floor.

floor manager *noun* **1** the stage manager of a television production. **2** = FLOORWALKER.

floor model *noun* N Amer. an item for sale, esp. a car or appliance, used for displaying or demonstrating others of its kind, often later offered for sale at a reduced price.

floor·pan *noun* the lower part of the body of a motor vehicle, that forms the floor of the passenger compartment.

floor plan *noun* **1** a diagram of the rooms etc. on one storey of a building. **2** the arrangement of rooms in a house, apartment, etc.

floor polish *noun* a substance used for polishing floors. □ **floor polisher** *noun*

floor price *noun* a minimum price for a commodity set by a government to protect producers from losses to market fluctuations.

floor show *noun* an entertainment presented at a nightclub, usu. including singing, dancing, stand-up comedy, etc.

floor·walk·er *noun* N Amer. an employee in a large store who directs customers, supervises assistants, etc.

floo·zie *noun* (also **floo·zy**) (*pl.* **-zies**) *informal* a disreputable or promiscuous girl or woman. [20th c.: compare FLOSSY and dial. *floosy* fluffy]

flop ● *intransitive verb* (**flopped, flop·ping**) **1** sway about heavily or loosely (*hair flopped over her face*). **2** move in an ungainly way (*flopped along the beach in flippers*). **3** (often foll. by *down, on, into*) sit, kneel, lie, or fall awkwardly or suddenly (*flopped down on to the bench*). **4** *slang* (esp. of a play, film, book, etc.) fail; collapse (*flopped on Broadway*). **5** *slang* sleep. **6** make a dull sound as of a soft body landing, or of a flat thing slapping water. ● *noun* **1 a** a flopping movement. **b** the sound made by it. **2** *informal* a failure. **3** *slang* esp. US a bed. [var. of FLAP]

-flop *combining form Computing* floating-point operations per second, used as a measure of computing power (*megaflop*). [acronym, originally as *-flops*, but s for 'second' was taken as indicating a plural]

flop·house *noun* esp. N Amer. *informal* a cheap boarding house, esp. one used by vagrants, transients, etc.

floppy ● *adjective* (**flop·pi·er, flop·pi·est**) tending to flop; not firm or rigid. ● *noun* (*pl.* **-pies**) (in full **floppy disk**) *Computing* a flexible

removable magnetic disk for the storage of data. □ **flop·pi·ly** *adverb* **flop·pi·ness** *noun*

flop sweat *noun* *slang* perspiration caused by a fear of failure, esp. when performing before an audience.

flor. *abbreviation* floruit.

Flora *Rom. Myth* the goddess of flowering plants. [from Latin *flos floris* flower]

flora *noun* **1** the plants of a particular region, geological period, or environment. **2** a catalogue of the plants of a defined area, with descriptions of them, comments on the more unusual species, etc. **3** (in full **intestinal flora**) symbiotic bacteria normally present in the gut. [modern Latin from FLORA]

flor·al /ˈflɔrəl/ ● *adjective* **1** of, made of, or pertaining to flowers (*floral arrangement; floral tribute*). **2** decorated with or depicting flowers (*floral print*). **3** of flora or floras. ● *noun* **1** a print, pattern, fabric, etc. with a floral design. **2** a perfume scent of or like that of flowers. □ **flor·al·ly** *adverb* [Latin *floralis* or *flos floris* flower]

flor·eat /ˈflɔriˌat/ *intransitive verb* may (he, she, or it) flourish. [Latin, 3rd sing. present subjunctive of *florēre* flourish]

Flor·ence a city in west central Italy, the capital of Tuscany, on the Arno River; pop. (2001) 352,227. Florence was a leading centre of the Italian Renaissance from the 14th to the 16th c., esp. under the rule of the Medici family during the 15th c.

Florence fennel *noun* see FENNEL 3.

Flor·en·tine /ˈflɔrənˌtiːn/ ● *adjective* **1 a** of or relating to Florence in Italy. **b** denoting the art, styles, etc. developed in Renaissance Florence. **2** (**florentine** /-ˌtiːn/) (of a dish) served on a bed of spinach. ● *noun* **1** a native or inhabitant of Florence. **2** /-ˌtiːn/ a thin cookie containing nuts and candied fruit and coated on one side with chocolate. [French *Florentin -ine* or Latin *Florentinus* from *Florentia* Florence]

Flor·es /ˈflɔrɛs/ the largest of the Lesser Sunda Islands in Indonesia.

flor·es·cence /flɔˈrɛsəns, flɒ-/ *noun* the process, state, or time of flowering. [modern Latin *florescentia* from Latin *florescere* from *florēre* bloom]

flor·et /ˈflɔrɪt/ *noun* **1** each of the small flowers making up a composite flower head. **2** /ˈflɔrˈet/ any of the segments into which a head of cauliflower, broccoli, etc. may be divided. **3** a tiny blossom or flowering plant. [Latin *flos floris* flower]

Flor·ey, How·ard Wal·ter, Baron (1898–1968), Australian pathologist. With Sir Ernst Chain he isolated and purified penicillin, developed techniques for its large-scale production, and performed the first clinical trials; they shared the 1945 Nobel Prize for medicine with Sir Alexander Fleming.

Flor·ian·óp·olis /ˌflɔriəˈnɒpəlɪs/ a city in S Brazil, on the Atlantic coast; pop. (2000) 321,778.

flori·bun·da /ˌflɔriˈbʌndə, ˌflɒr-/ *noun* a plant, esp. a rose, bearing dense clusters of flowers. [modern Latin from *floribundus* freely flowering, from Latin *flos floris* flower, influenced by Latin *abundus* copious]

flori·cul·ture *noun* the cultivation of esp. ornamental flowers. □ **flori·cul·tur·al** *adjective* **flori·cul·tur·ist** *noun* [Latin *flos floris* flower + CULTURE, after *horticulture*]

flor·id *adjective* **1** (of a person's complexion) ruddy or flushed. **2** (of a book, a picture, music, architecture, etc.) elaborately ornate, ostentatious, or showy. □ **flor·id·ity** **flor·id·ly** *adverb* **flor·id·ness** *noun* [French *floride* or Latin *floridus* from *flos floris* flower]

Flor·ida a state forming a peninsula of the southeastern US; pop. (2000) 15,982,378; capital, Tallahassee. □ **Flor·id·ian** /flɒˈrɪdiən/ *noun & adjective*

Florida Keys a chain of small islands off the tip of the Florida peninsula. Linked to each other and to the mainland by a series of causeways and bridges forming the Overseas Highway, the islands extend southwestward over a distance of 160 km (100 miles). Key Largo, the longest island, is closest to the mainland.

Florida room *noun* N Amer. a sunroom, usu. only partly insulated, enclosed in glass on three sides.

flor·if·er·ous /flɒˈrɪfərəs, flɒ-/ *adjective* (of a seed or plant) producing many flowers. [Latin *florifer* from *flos floris* flower]

flori·legium /ˌflɔrɪˈliːdʒiəm/ *noun* (*pl.* **flori·legia** /-ˈliːdʒiə/ or **flori·legiums**) an anthology of choice extracts from literature. [modern Latin from Latin *flos floris* flower + *legere* gather, translation of Greek *anthologion* ANTHOLOGY]

flor·in /ˈflɔrɪn/ *noun* **1** *hist.* a former British coin worth two shillings. **2 a** *hist.* any of various, usu. gold or silver, coins current at various times on the Continent. **b** a guilder, the former monetary unit of the Netherlands. **3** the basic monetary unit of Aruba, equal to 100 cents. [Old French from Italian *fiorino* diminutive of *fiore* flower, from Latin *flos floris*, the original coin having a figure of a lily on it]

Flor·io /ˈflɔːrɪəʊ/ **John** (*c*.1553–*c*.1625), English lexicographer and translator. He produced an Italian dictionary entitled *A Worlde of Wordes* (1598) and wrote the first translation into English of Montaigne's essays (1603).

flor·ist *noun* **1** a person who retails flowers and ornamental plants. **2** a person who grows flowers. □ **flor·is·try** *noun* [Latin *flos floris* flower + -IST]

flor·is·tic *adjective* relating to the study of the distribution of plants. □ **flor·is·tic·ally** *adverb* **flor·is·tics** *noun*

flor·uit /ˈflɔːruːɪt, ˈflɒr-/ ● *intransitive verb* (he or she) was alive and working; flourished (used of a person, esp. a painter, writer, etc., whose exact dates are unknown). ● *noun* the period or date at which a person lived or worked. Abbr.: **fl.** [Latin, = he or she flourished]

floss ● *noun* **1 a** the rough silk enveloping a silkworm's cocoon. **b** the silk down in corn and certain other plants. **2** untwisted silk or fine cotton thread used in embroidery. **3** = DENTAL FLOSS. ● *transitive & intransitive verb* clean between (the teeth) with dental floss. □ **floss·ing** *noun* [French (*soie*) *floche* floss(-silk), from Old French *flosche* down, nap of velvet]

flossy *adjective* (**floss·i·er**, **floss·i·est**) **1** resembling or consisting of floss. **2** *informal* fancy, showy.

flo·ta·tion *noun* (also **float·a·tion**) **1** the process of launching or financing a commercial enterprise, esp. by selling shares in it to the public. **2** the separation of the components of crushed ore etc. by their different capacities to float on a given liquid. **3** capacity to float. **4 a** the action or process of floating in a liquid etc. **b** the condition of keeping afloat. [alteration of *floatation* from FLOAT, after *rotation* etc.]

flotation tank *noun* a lightproof, soundproof tank of salt water in which a person floats as a form of deep relaxation.

flo·til·la /fləˈtɪlə/ *noun* **1** a fleet of boats or small ships. **2** a small fleet of warships. [Spanish, diminutive of *flota* fleet, Old French *flote* multitude]

flot·sam /ˈflɒtsəm/ *noun* **1** wreckage of a ship or its cargo found floating on the surface of the sea, a lake, etc. **2** (in full **flotsam and jetsam**) **a** odds and ends, bits and pieces, various unimportant items. **b** people who have been rejected by society. [Anglo-French *floteson* from *floter* FLOAT]

flounce¹ ● *intransitive verb* (often foll. by *away*, *about*, *off*, *out*) go or move in an agitated or exaggerated manner, usu. in impatience or anger (*flounced out in a huff*). ● *noun* a sudden fling, jerk, or movement of the body or limbs, usu. as an expression of annoyance, impatience, or disdain. [16th c.: origin unknown: perhaps imitative, as *bounce*, *pounce*]

flounce² *noun* a frill or wide ornamental strip of material gathered and sewn to a skirt, dress, etc., so that its lower edge hangs full and free. □ **flounced** *adjective* **flouncy** *adjective* [alteration of earlier *frounce* fold, pleat, from Old French *fronce* from *froncir* wrinkle]

floun·der¹ ● *intransitive verb* **1** struggle or show confusion in thoughts, words, or actions. **2** manage something badly or with difficulty. **3** move or struggle clumsily or with difficulty through mud, snow, etc. ● *noun* an act or instance of floundering. [imitative: perhaps assoc. with *founder*, *blunder*]

floun·der² *noun* (*pl.* same or **floun·ders**) any flatfish of the family Pleuronectidae or Bothidae, esp. those caught for food, including plaices, soles, and turbot. [Anglo-French *floundre*, Old French *flondre*, prob. of Scandinavian origin]

flour ● *noun* **1** a fine powder obtained by grinding grain, esp. wheat, used for making bread, cakes, etc. **2** a fine powder made from other foodstuffs, e.g. potatoes, nuts, etc. ● *transitive verb* sprinkle or cover with flour. □ **floured** *adjective* **flour·less** *adjective* **floury** *adjective* (**flour·i·er**, **flour·i·est**). [Middle English, different spelling of FLOWER in the sense 'finest part']

flour·ish /ˈflɜːrɪʃ, ˈflʌrɪʃ/ ● *verb* **1** *intransitive* **a** (of a plant, tree, etc.) grow vigorously, thrive. **b** prosper, be successful. **c** be in one's prime or at the height of one's fame or excellence. **d** be in good health. **2** *intransitive* (usu. foll. by *in*, *at*, *about*) spend one's life or be active during a specified period (*flourished in the Middle Ages*). **3** *transitive* show ostentatiously (*flourished his chequebook*). **4** *transitive* wave (a weapon, one's limbs, etc.) vigorously. ● *noun* **1** an ostentatious gesture with a weapon, a hand, etc. (*removed his hat with a flourish*). **2** an ornamental curving decoration of handwriting. **3** a florid verbal expression or rhetorical embellishment. **4** *Music* **a** a fanfare played by brass instruments. **b** an ornate musical passage. **c** an extemporized addition played esp. at the

beginning or end of a composition. **5** scrollwork, tracery, etc. □ **flour·ish·ing** *adjective* [Middle English from Old French *florir*, ultimately from Latin *florēre* from *flos floris* flower]

flour tortilla *noun* *N Amer.* a soft, white, round tortilla made from wheat flour, used in burritos etc.

flout *transitive verb* express contempt or disrespect for (the law, rules, etc.) by openly refusing to heed or obey (*flouted convention by shaving her head*). ¶ *Flout* should not be confused with *flaunt*, which means 'to display proudly, show off'. [perhaps from Dutch *fluiten* whistle, hiss: compare FLUTE]

flow ● *intransitive verb* **1** glide along as a stream (*the Red River flows through Winnipeg*). **2 a** (of a liquid, esp. water) spring or well up, gush out. **b** (of blood, tears, etc.) be spilled. **3** (of blood, money, electric current, etc.) circulate. **4** (of people or things) move freely and continuously (*traffic flowed down the hill*). **5** (of talk, literary style, etc.) proceed easily and smoothly. **6** (of a garment, hair, etc.) hang easily or gracefully, or lie in undulating folds. **7** (often foll. by *from*) result from or be caused by (*his failure flows from his diffidence*). **8** (esp. of the tide) come in, rise and advance. **9** (of wine etc.) be poured out copiously or unstintingly. **10** (of a rock or metal) undergo a permanent change of shape under stress, without fracture or loss of cohesion. **11** (foll. by *with*) *archaic* abound in or be plentifully supplied with (*land flowing with milk and honey*). ● *noun* **1 a** a flowing movement in a stream. **b** the quantity that flows; the rate of flowing (*a sluggish flow*). **c** a flowing liquid (*couldn't stop the flow*). **d** the act or fact of flowing. **2** any continuous movement, outpouring, etc. that resembles the flow of a river and denotes a copious supply (*a continuous flow of complaints*). **3** the incoming or rise of a tide or a tidal river (*ebb and flow*). **4** the gradual deformation of a rock or metal under stress, without fracture or loss of cohesion. □ **go with the flow** *informal* be relaxed and not resist the tide of events. □ **flow·able** *adjective* [Old English *flōwan* from Germanic, related to FLOOD]

flow·age /ˈfloʊədʒ/ *noun* **1** *Cdn* (*Maritimes*) a shallow pond. **2** = FLOW *noun* 4.

flow chart *noun* (also **flow diagram** or **sheet**) **1** a diagram showing the movement, development, or action of things or persons through the different stages or processes of a series, esp. in a complex activity. **2** a graphic representation of a computer program in relation to its sequence of functions (as distinct from the data it processes).

flower ● *noun* **1** the part of a plant from which the fruit or seed is developed, esp. the reproductive organ containing one or more pistils or stamens or both, and usu. a corolla and calyx. **2** a blossom and usu. its stem considered independently of the growing plant, esp. as used in groups for decoration or as a mark of honour or respect. **3** a flowering plant, esp. one cultivated for its flowers. **4 a** the prime or most active or vigorous period in a person's life. **b** the finest embodiment of a quality etc. **c** the pick or choicest person, thing, etc. of a number of persons, things, etc. **5** (of a plant) the state of being in bloom (*the milkweed was in flower*). ● *verb* **1** *intransitive* (of a plant) produce flowers; bloom or blossom. **2** *intransitive* **a** develop into. **b** reach a peak, be in or attain one's fullest perfection, highest stage of development, etc. **3** *transitive* cause or allow (a plant) to flower. □ **flower·less** *adjective* **flower·like** *adjective* [Old French *flour* from Latin *flos floris*]

flower arrangement *noun* **1** the art of arranging flowers in vases etc. for artistic effect. **2** a bouquet of flowers so arranged. □ **flower arranger** *noun* **flower arranging** *noun*

flower·bear·er *noun* *N Amer.* a person, often a child, who follows the pallbearers in a funeral procession, carrying wreaths of flowers.

flower bed *noun* a plot of soil in which flowers are grown.

flower box *noun* a rectangular container filled with soil in which flowers, herbs, etc. are grown, usu. on a balcony or windowsill.

flower child *noun* a hippie, esp. in the late 1960s, who advocated a simple idealistic lifestyle based on love and peace.

flow·ered *adjective* **1** (usu. in *combination*) having flowers of a specified quality. **2** decorated with flowers or a flower pattern.

flower·er *noun* a plant that flowers at a specified time (*a late flowerer*).

flow·er·et /ˈflaʊrət, flaʊrˈet/ *noun* = FLORET.

flower girl *noun* **1** a child bridesmaid. **2** *Brit.* a woman who sells flowers, esp. in the street.

flower head *noun* = HEAD *noun* 4d.

flow·er·ing *adjective* **1** (of a plant) capable of producing flowers, esp. having showy flowers in contrast to a similar plant with the flowers inconspicuous or absent (*flowering dogwood*). **2** (of a plant) in bloom.

flowering plant *noun* an angiosperm.

flower·pot *noun* **1** a container made of clay or plastic for growing plants in. **2** *Cdn* a tall column or island of rock formed by water erosion, often with vegetation on the top, found esp. in the Bay of Fundy and Georgian Bay.

flower power *noun* the ideas of the flower children regarded as an instrument for changing the world.

flowers of sulphur *plural noun* a fine powder produced when sulphur evaporates and condenses.

flow·ery *adjective* **1** decorated with flowers or floral designs. **2** (of literary style, manner of speech, etc.) high-flown, ornate. **3** full of flowers (*a flowery meadow*). **4** of, like, or reminiscent of flowers (*a flowery scent*). □ **flower·i·ness** *noun*

flow·ing *adjective* **1 a** (of language, style, etc.) fluent, coming easily and smoothly. **b** (of manner or demeanour) easy, graceful, smooth. **2** (of a line, a curve, or a contour) smoothly continuous, not rigid or abrupt. **3** (of hair, a garment, a sail, etc.) unconfined, streaming, hanging loosely, easily, and gracefully. **4 a** gliding or running along. **b** brimming, abundant, or copious.

flow·meter *noun* an instrument for measuring the rate of flow of gas, liquid, fuel, etc., esp. in a pipe. □ **flow·meter·ing** *noun*

flown *past participle of* FLY¹.

flow·stone *noun* calcium carbonate rock deposited esp. in caves in thin sheets by flowing water.

fl. oz. *abbreviation* fluid ounce.

FLQ *abbreviation* (in Canada) FRONT DE LIBÉRATION DU QUÉBEC.

FLQ crisis *noun* = OCTOBER CRISIS.

Flt. Lt. *abbreviation* FLIGHT LIEUTENANT.

Flt. Off. *abbreviation* FLIGHT OFFICER.

Flt. Sgt. *abbreviation* FLIGHT SERGEANT.

flu *noun* influenza. □ **flu-like** *adjective* [abbreviation]

flub *N Amer. informal* ● *transitive & intransitive verb* (**flubbed**, **flub·bing**) botch, bungle, or perform badly. ● *noun* a slip-up or something badly or clumsily done. [20th c.: origin unknown]

fluc·tu·ate /ˈflʌktʃuˌeɪt/ *intransitive verb* **1** (of a price, number, rate, etc.) rise and fall or change irregularly. **2** (of an attitude or a state) waver, vacillate, or change continually. □ **fluc·tu·a·tion** *noun* [Latin *fluctuare* from *fluctus* flow, wave, from *fluere fluct-* flow]

flue *noun* **1** a duct for the passage of smoke, waste gases, etc. in a chimney. **2 a** a channel for conveying heat, esp. a hot-air passage in a wall. **b** a tube for heating water in some kinds of boiler. **3** the airway of a flue pipe in an organ. [16th c.: origin unknown]

flue-cure *transitive verb* cure (tobacco) by artificial heat from flues.

flue gas *noun* (*also attributive*) any mixture of gases from flues, esp. of chemical or smelting factories.

flu·ency /ˈfluːənsi/ *noun* (*pl.* **-cies**) **1** a ready command of words or of a specified foreign language. **2** a smooth, easy flow of words, wit, etc., esp. in speech or writing.

flu·ent /ˈfluːənt/ *adjective* **1 a** (of speech or literary style) flowing naturally and readily. **b** able to speak a language easily and without hesitation (*is fluent in German*). **c** articulate, able to speak quickly and easily. **2** (of movement, etc.) easy and graceful, not rigid or stiff (*a dancer in fluent motion*). □ **flu·ent·ly** *adverb* [Latin *fluere* flow]

flue pipe *noun* **1** an organ pipe into which the air enters directly, not striking a reed. **2** a pipe in or connected to a flue.

fluff ● *noun* **1** soft, light, feathery material coming off blankets etc. **2** a piece of downy material, esp. a soft mass of fur or feathers. **3** *informal* a mistake or error made in speaking, delivering theatrical lines, playing music or a game, etc. **4** a trifle; something unimportant, insubstantial, or insignificant. **5** *slang offensive* (esp. in phr. **bit of fluff** or **piece of fluff**) a woman regarded as an object of sexual desire. ● *verb* **1** *transitive & intransitive* (often foll. by *up*) make or become fluffy; shake into or become a soft, fluffy mass. **2** *transitive & intransitive informal* blunder or make a mistake, esp. in a game or performance (*fluffed his opening line*). [prob. dial. alteration of *flue* fluff]

fluff·ball *noun* **1** a ball of fluff. **2** something, e.g. a bird or small animal, resembling a ball of fluff. **3** a vacuous person, film, etc.

fluffy *adjective* (**fluff·i·er**, **fluff·i·est**) **1** of or like fluff. **2** covered in fluff; downy. **3** soft, light and airy (*fluffy mashed potatoes*). **4** lacking depth, seriousness, or substance. □ **fluff·i·ly** *adverb* **fluff·i·ness** *noun*

flugel·horn /ˈfluːɡəlˌhɔrn/ *noun* a valved brass wind instrument with a cup-shaped mouthpiece and a wide conical bore, like a cornet but with a broader tone. □ **flugel·horn·ist** *noun* [German *Flügelhorn* from *Flügel* wing + *Horn* horn]

flu·id ● *noun* **1** a substance, esp. a gas or liquid, lacking definite shape and capable of flowing and yielding to the slightest pressure. **2** a

liquid constituent or secretion of a living organism. ● *adjective* **1** able to flow and alter shape freely. **2** changing readily, not settled or stable (*the situation is fluid*). **3** (of a clutch, coupling, etc.) operating by means of a liquid, esp. using a liquid to transmit power. **4** (of speech etc.) fluent. **5** (of movement) smoothly flowing. □ **flu·id·ity** *noun* **fluid·ly** *adverb* **fluid·ness** *noun* [French *fluide* or Latin *fluidus* from *fluere* flow]

flu·id·ics /fluːˈɪdɪks/ *plural noun* (usu. treated as *sing.*) the study and technique of using small interacting flows and fluid jets for functions usu. performed by electronic devices. □ **flu·id·ic** *adjective*

fluid·ize /ˈfluːɪˌdaɪz/ *transitive verb* (also esp. *Brit.* **-ise**) cause (a finely divided solid) to acquire the characteristics of a fluid by the upward passage of a gas etc. □ **fluid·iz·a·tion** *noun* **fluid·ized** *adjective*

fluidized bed *noun* (also esp. *Brit.* **-ised**) a layer of a fluidized solid, used in chemical processes and in efficient burning of coal for power generation.

fluid mechanics *noun* the branch of mechanics that deals with the flow of fluids and the way they respond to and exert forces.

fluid ounce *noun* **1** a unit of capacity equal to one-twentieth of an imperial pint (approx. 28.4 ml). **2** (in the US) a unit of capacity equal to one-sixteenth of a pint (approx. 29.6 ml). Abbr.: **fl. oz.**

flui·dram /ˈfluːɪˌdram/ *noun US* a fluid drachm (*see* DRACHM).

fluke¹ *informal* ● *noun* a piece of luck, an unexpected success, or an unlikely but usu. fortunate chance occurrence (*won by a fluke*). ● *transitive verb* do, get, achieve etc. by luck rather than skill (*fluked that shot*). [19th c.: perhaps from dial. *fluke* guess]

fluke² *noun* **1** any parasitic flatworm of the class Digenea or Monogenea, including liver flukes and blood flukes. **2** a flatfish, esp. a flounder. [Old English *flōc*]

fluke³ *noun* **1** *Naut.* a broad triangular plate on the arm of an anchor. **2** the barbed head of a lance, harpoon, etc. **3** either of the two lobes of a whale's tail. [16th c.: perhaps from FLUKE²]

fluky *adjective* (also **fluk·ey**) (**fluk·i·er**, **fluk·i·est**) **1** lucky, obtained more by chance than skill. **2** (of wind etc.) erratic, uncertain. □ **fluk·i·ly** *adverb* **fluk·i·ness** *noun*

flume *noun* **1** an artificial channel conveying water etc. for industrial use, esp. for the transport of logs or timber. **2** a deep, narrow channel or ravine with a stream running through it. **3** a water chute or waterslide at an amusement park or swimming pool. [Old French *flum* from Latin *flumen* river, from *fluere* flow]

flum·mery *noun* (*pl.* **-ies**) **1** empty compliments, nonsense, humbug. **2** trifles, useless trappings or ornaments. [Welsh *llymru*, of unknown origin]

flum·mox *transitive verb informal* bewilder, confound, disconcert. [19th c.: prob. from dialect *flummock* 'make untidy, confuse']

flump ● *verb* (often foll. by *down*) **1** *intransitive* fall or move heavily with a dull noise. **2** *transitive* set or throw down with a heavy thud. ● *noun* the action or sound of flumping. [imitative]

flung *past and past participle of* FLING.

flunk *verb N Amer. informal* **1** *transitive* **a** (of a student) fail (an examination, course, etc.). **b** (of a teacher) fail (a student etc.). **2** *intransitive* (often foll. by *out*) fail utterly and quit or be dismissed from school etc. [compare FUNK¹ and obsolete *flink* be a coward]

flun·ky *noun* (also **flun·key**) (*pl.* **-kies** or **-keys**) usu. *derogatory* **1** an obsequious, fawning person. **2** a liveried servant; a footman. **3** a person who performs relatively menial tasks for someone else. □ **flunky·ism** *noun* [18th c. (originally Scots): perhaps from FLANK with the sense 'sidesman, flanker']

fluor·esce /fləˈrɛs/ *intransitive verb* be or become fluorescent or exhibit fluorescence.

fluor·es·cein /ˈflɔrəsiɪn, -sɪn/ *noun Chem.* an orange dye with a yellowish-green fluorescence, used in solution as an indicator in biochemistry and medicine. [FLUORESCENCE + -IN]

fluor·es·cence /fləˈrɛsəns/ *noun* **1** the visible or invisible radiation produced from certain substances as a result of incident radiation of a shorter wavelength as X-rays, ultraviolet light, etc. **2** the property of absorbing light of short (invisible) wavelength and emitting light of longer (visible) wavelength. [FLUORSPAR (which fluoresces) after *opalescence*]

fluor·es·cent /fləˈrɛsənt/ ● *adjective* **1** (of a substance) of, having, or showing fluorescence. **2** (of colours) very bright and glowing, similar to colours produced by fluorescence. ● *noun* (in full, **fluorescent light**, **fluorescent bulb**, etc.) a light or bulb radiating largely by fluorescence, esp. a tubular lamp in which phosphor on the inside surface of the tube is made to fluoresce by ultraviolet radiation from mercury vapour.

uː mood   aɪ my   əɪ pipe   au brown   ʌu house   ei day   ɔi boy   ã franglais   ã Canadien   ɔ̃ Brayon   (*see over for consonants*)

fluorescent screen *noun* a screen coated with fluorescent material to show images from X-rays etc.

fluor·idate /ˈflɔrɪˌdeɪt, flʊ-/ *transitive verb* add traces of fluoride to (drinking water etc.) to reduce or prevent tooth decay.
□ **fluor·id·at·ed** *adjective* **fluor·id·a·tion** *noun*

fluor·ide /ˈflɔraɪd, flʊ-/ *noun* a binary compound of fluorine, esp. as used to prevent tooth decay.

fluor·in·ate /ˈflɔrɪˌneɪt, flʊ-/ *transitive verb* (usu. as **fluor·in·at·ed** *adjective*) introduce one or more fluorine atoms into (a compound or molecule), usu. in place of hydrogen (*fluorinated hydrocarbons*).
□ **fluor·in·a·tion** *noun*

fluor·ine /ˈflɔriːn, flʊ-/ *noun* a poisonous, pale yellow gaseous element of the halogen group occurring naturally in fluorite and cryolite, and the most reactive of all elements. Symbol: **F**; at. no.: 9. [French (as FLUORSPAR)]

fluor·ite /ˈflɔraɪt, flʊ-/ *noun* a mineral form of calcium fluoride. [Italian (as FLUORSPAR)]

fluoro- /ˈflɔroː, flʊ-/ *combining form* **1** fluorine (*fluorocarbon*). **2** fluorescence (*fluoroscope*). [FLUORINE, FLUORESCENCE]

fluoro·carbon /ˌflɔrohˈkɑrbən, flʊ-/ *noun* a synthetic, chemically stable compound formed by replacing one or more of the hydrogen atoms in a hydrocarbon with fluorine atoms.

fluoro·scope /ˈflɔrəˌskoːp, flʊ-/ ● *noun* an instrument with a fluorescent screen on which X-ray images may be viewed without taking and developing X-ray photographs. ● *transitive verb* examine with or by means of a fluoroscope. □ **fluoro·scop·ic** /-ˈskɒpɪk/ *adjective* **fluoro·scop·ic·ally** *adverb* **fluor·os·copy** /-ˈɒskəpi/ *noun*

fluor·osis /flɔˈroːsɪs, flʊ-/ *noun* poisoning by fluorine or its compounds characterized by mottling of dental enamel and by skeletal changes. [French *fluorose* (as FLUORO- 1)]

fluor·spar /ˈfluːərspɑr/ *noun* = FLUORITE. [*fluor* 'a flow, a mineral used as a flux, fluorspar' from Latin *fluor* from *fluere* flow + SPAR³]

fluox·etine /fluˈɒksətiːn/ *noun* an organic compound believed to inhibit the uptake of serotonin into the brain, used (orally, as the hydrochloride) as an antidepressant (compare PROZAC). [FLUORINE + OXYGEN + *etine* perhaps from *e* + a blend of TOLUENE + AMINE]

flurry ● *noun* (pl. **-ries**) **1 a** a short, usu. localized shower of snow. **b** *Brit.* a sudden squall of wind or rain. **2** a sudden burst of intense activity. **3** a number of things happening or arriving at once (*a flurry of penalties*). ● *verb* (**-ries, -ried**) **1** *transitive* agitate or confuse by haste or noise. **2** *intransitive* move in a flustered, agitated manner. □ **flur·ried** *adjective* [imitative: compare obsolete *flurr* ruffle, *hurry*]

flush¹ ● *verb* **1** *intransitive* **a** (of the face) redden because of a rush of blood to the skin (*he flushed with embarrassment*). **b** glow with a warm colour, light, etc. (*sky flushed pink*). **2** *transitive* **a** cleanse (a toilet, drain, etc.) by a rushing flow of water. **b** (often foll. by *away, down*) dispose of (an object) in this way (*flushed away the cigarette*). **c** (often foll. by *out*) remove by a sudden rush of water or other liquid. **3** *Computing* cleanse, dump, or erase (a buffer etc.). **4** *intransitive* rush out, spurt. **5** *intransitive* (of a plant) throw out fresh shoots. ● *noun* **1 a** a flow of blood to the face, neck, etc. that causes red colouring. **b** a glow of light or colour. **2 a** a sudden rush of water, esp. as caused for a specific purpose. **b** the cleansing of a toilet, drain, etc. by flushing. **3** a rush of emotion, elation, etc., esp. as produced by victory, success, etc. (*the flush of triumph*). **4** a sudden abundance or rush (*a flush of interest in outdoor vacations*). **5** the freshness and vigour of youth or a beginning, or the best and most fully developed stage (*in the full flush of success*). **6 a** *Brit.* (also **hot flush**) = HOT FLASH. **b** facial redness, esp. caused by fever, alcohol, etc. **7** a fresh growth of grass etc. □ **flush·able** *adjective* **flush·er** *noun* **flush·ing** *noun* [Middle English, perhaps = FLUSH⁴ influenced by *flash* and *blush*]

flush² ● *adjective* **1 a** (often foll. by *with*) completely level, even, or continuous with another surface (*the sink is flush with the counter; fitted it flush with the wall*). **b** (of a vessel's deck) continued on one level from stem to stern. **2** (usu. *predicative*) *informal* **a** having plenty of something, esp. money. **b** (of money) abundant, plentiful. **3** (of text) even or level with the margin, neither indented nor protruding. ● *transitive verb* **1** make (surfaces) level. **2** fill in (a joint) level with a surface.
□ **flush·ness** *noun* [prob. from FLUSH¹]

flush³ *noun* a hand of cards all of one suit, esp. in poker. [Old French *flus, flux* from Latin *fluxus* FLUX]

flush⁴ *verb* **1** *transitive* cause (esp. a game bird) to fly up suddenly, esp. from undergrowth. **2** *intransitive* (of a bird) fly up and away, esp. from undergrowth. □ **flush out** force or drive (a person) out of a hiding place etc. [Middle English, imitative: compare *fly, rush*]

flushed *adjective* (often foll. by *with*) glowing or blushing, esp. with emotion, excitement, etc. (*flushed with pride*).

flush toilet *noun* a toilet that operates by the flushing of water.

flus·ter ● *transitive verb* **1** make or become nervous, confused, agitated, etc. (*was flustered by the noise*). **2** *intransitive* bustle. ● *noun* a nervous or agitated state (*always in a fluster*). □ **flus·tered** *adjective* [Middle English: origin unknown: compare Icelandic *flaustr(a)* hurry, bustle]

flute ● *noun* **1 a** a high-pitched woodwind instrument of metal or wood, having holes along it, stopped by the fingers or keys. **b** an organ stop having a similar sound. **c** any of various wind instruments resembling a flute. **d** a flute player. **2 a** *Archit.* an ornamental vertical groove in a column. **b** a narrow, furrow-like frill on a dress etc. **c** any similar cylindrical groove. **3** a tall narrow wineglass, used esp. for sparkling wine. ● *verb* **1** *transitive* make, shape, or carve flutes or grooves in a thing as decoration. **2** *intransitive* play the flute. **3** *intransitive* speak, sing, or whistle in a flutelike way. □ **flut·ed** *adjective* **flute·like** *adjective* **flut·ing** *noun* [Old French *fläute*, prob. from Provençal *flaut*, perhaps a blend of *flaujol* 'flageolet' + *laüt* 'lute']

flut·ist *noun N Amer.* a flute player. ¶ See Usage Note at FLAUTIST.

flut·ter ● *verb* **1 a** *intransitive* flap the wings lightly and quickly in flying or trying to fly (*butterflies fluttered in the sunshine*). **b** *transitive* flap (the wings) in this way. **2** *intransitive* fall with a quivering motion (*leaves fluttered to the ground*). **3** *intransitive & transitive* move or cause to move in a quick, irregular way (*the wind fluttered the flag*). **4** *intransitive* hover or move about aimlessly and restlessly. **5** *intransitive* (of a pulse or heartbeat) beat feebly or irregularly, esp. because of nervous excitement. **6** *intransitive* tremble with excitement or agitation. ● *noun* **1 a** the act of fluttering. **b** an instance of this. **2** tremulous excitement or agitation (*was in a flutter; caused a flutter with his behaviour*). **3** *Brit. slang* a small bet, esp. on a horse. **4** an abnormally rapid but regular heartbeat. **5** *Aviation* an undesired oscillation in a part of an aircraft etc. under stress. **6** *Music* a rapid movement of the tongue (as when rolling one's rs) in playing a wind instrument. **7** *Electronics* a rapid variation in the pitch or loudness of a sound, not audible as such, but heard as distortion, esp. in a recording (compare wow²). **8** a vibration. □ **flut·ter·ing** *adjective & noun* **flut·tery** *adjective* [Old English *floterian, flotorian*, frequentative form related to FLEET⁴]

flutter board *noun N Amer.* an elongated piece of polystyrene plastic used as a swimming aid in training or practice.

flutter kick *noun* a type of kick used in the crawl and other swimming strokes in which the legs are held rigid and rapidly moved up and down alternately.

fluty *adjective* (also **flut·ey**) (**-ier** or **-eyer, -iest** or **-eyest**) (of a sound, esp. someone's voice) high-pitched and clear, like a flute.

flu·vial /ˈfluːviəl/ *adjective* **1** of or pertaining to a river or rivers. **2** found or living in rivers. [Latin *fluvialis* from *fluvius* river, from *fluere* flow]

flu·via·tile /ˈfluːviəˌtaɪl/ *adjective* of, found in, or produced by a river or rivers. [French from Latin *fluviatilis* from *fluviatus* moistened, from *fluvius*]

fluvio- /ˈfluːvioː/ *combining form* river (*fluviometer*). [Latin *fluvius* river, from *fluere* flow]

flu·vio·gla·cial /ˌfluːvioːˈgleɪʃəl, -siəl/ *adjective* of or caused by streams from glacial ice, or the combined action of rivers and glaciers.

flux ● *noun* **1 a** a process of flowing or flowing out. **b** the flowing in of the tide (*flux and reflux*). **2** a stream or flood, esp. of people, talk, etc. **3** continuous change (*in a state of flux*). **4 a** *Metallurgy* a substance mixed with a metal etc. to promote fusion. **b** a substance used to make colour fusible in enamelling, pottery, etc. **5** *Physics* **a** the rate of flow of any fluid across a given area. **b** the amount of fluid crossing an area in a given time. **6** *Physics* the amount of radiation or particles incident on an area in a given time. **7** *Electricity* the total electric or magnetic field passing through a surface. **8** *Med.* an abnormal discharge of fluids, esp. blood or excrement, from the body. ● *verb* **1** *transitive & intransitive* make or become fluid. **2** *transitive* treat or heat with a fusing flux.

flux density *noun* the quantity of magnetic, electric, etc. flux passing through a unit of area.

flux·gate *noun* a kind of magnetometer used esp. in aerial surveys and consisting of one or more soft iron cores each surrounded by primary and secondary windings, the characteristics of the external magnetic field being determined from the signals produced in the secondary windings.

flux·ion /ˈflʌkʃən/ *noun Math.* **1** the rate at which a variable quantity changes; a derivative. **2** FLUX. □ **flux·ion·al** *adjective* [French *fluxion* or Latin *fluxio* (as FLUX)]

FLV *abbreviation* = FELINE LEUKEMIA VIRUS.

Consonants: b *but*   d *dog*   f *few*   g *get*   h *her*   j *yes*   k *cat*   l *leg*   m *man*   n *no*   p *pen*   r *red*   s *sit*

fly¹ ● *verb* (**flies**; *past* **flew**; *past participle* **flown**) **1** *intransitive* move through the air with wings. **2** (of an aircraft or its occupants): **a** *intransitive* travel through the air or through space. **b** *transitive* traverse (a region or distance) by flying (*flew the Vancouver-Victoria route*). **3** *a transitive & intransitive* control or pilot the flight of (esp. an aircraft). **b** *transitive* transport in an aircraft. **4 a** *transitive* cause to fly or remain aloft (*build and fly a model plane*). **b** *intransitive* (of a flag, hair, etc.) wave or flutter. **c** *transitive* set or keep (a flag) flying. **5** *intransitive* pass or rise quickly through the air or over an obstacle. **6** *intransitive* **a** go, move, or travel quickly. **b** (of time) pass swiftly, rush by. **7** *intransitive* **a** flee. **b** *informal* depart hastily. **8** *intransitive* **a** be forced or driven off or away suddenly and quickly (*sent me flying*). **b** (of a door, window, etc.) be thrown suddenly (open, up, etc.) (*the door flew open*). **9** *intransitive* (foll. by *at*) **a** hasten or spring violently. **b** attack or criticize fiercely. **10** *transitive* flee from, escape in haste. **11** *intransitive Baseball* (*past & past participle* **flied**) hit a fly ball. **12** *intransitive N Amer. informal* meet with approval, acceptance, success, etc. (*don't think the plan will fly*). **13** *intransitive* levitate. **14** *intransitive* (of snow) fall, esp. for the first time in the winter (*weatherstrip your windows before the snow flies*). ● *noun* (*pl.* **flies**) **1 a** a zippered or buttoned opening, esp. from the waist to the crotch at the front of a pair of trousers. **b** a flap on a garment, esp. trousers, to contain or cover such a fastening. **2 a** a flap of material at the entrance of a tent. **b** an extra layer of fabric placed on top of a tent to repel moisture. **3** (in *pl.*) the space above a theatre stage which is behind the proscenium, into which scenery is raised. **4** the act or an instance of flying. **5** (*pl. usu.* **flys**) *Brit. hist.* a lightweight covered carriage drawn by one horse. **6** a flywheel or other similar speed-regulating device in clockwork and machinery. **7** *Baseball* a fly ball. **8 a** the breadth of a flag from the staff to the end (*compare* HOIST *noun* 3a). **b** the part of the flag which is furthest from the staff (*compare* HOIST *noun* 3b). □ **fly high 1** be happy, enthusiastic, etc. **2** excel, prosper. **3** pursue a high ambition. **fly in the face of** disregard, defy, or oppose rashly something that is generally accepted, e.g. an opinion, decision, facts, etc. **fly into a rage** or **temper** (or **temper**) become suddenly or violently angry. **fly off the handle** *informal* lose one's temper suddenly and unexpectedly. **fly the coop** *informal* escape or leave without warning, esp. a domestic or work situation, one's responsibilities or obligations, etc. **on the fly 1** quickly, esp. while on the go or in the midst of doing something else. **2** (of something hit or thrown) while still flying through the air, before touching the ground (*caught it on the fly*). □ **fly·able** *adjective* [Old English *flēogan* from Germanic]

fly² *noun* (*pl.* **flies**) **1** any insect of the order Diptera with two usu. transparent wings. **2** any other winged insect, e.g. a firefly or mayfly. **3** a natural fly or an imitation of this consisting of a hook with silk and feathers etc., used as bait in fishing. **4** tiny bumps or imperfections in cloth. □ **catch flies** *informal* have one's mouth open for a prolonged time for no reason; breathe with one's mouth open. **fly in the ointment** a minor irritation that spoils an otherwise satisfactory situation or occasion. **fly on the wall** an unnoticed observer. **like flies** in large numbers or quantities. **no flies on** *informal* nothing to diminish (a person's) astuteness. **not hurt a fly** be kind, gentle, and unwilling to injure, offend, or cause unhappiness. [Old English *flȳge*, *flēoge* from West Germanic]

fly³ *adjective* **1** *N Amer.* fine, stylish, or good-looking. **2** *Brit. slang* knowing, clever, alert. [19th c.: origin unknown]

fly agaric *noun* a poisonous fungus, *Amanita muscaria*, forming bright red mushrooms with white flecks.

fly ash *noun* fine ash from a solid combustible fuel, carried with waste gases into the air.

fly-away *adjective* **1** (of hair, a garment, etc.) loose, streaming, or tending to fly out or up. **2** (of a person, action, etc.) sudden, impulsive, volatile, or flighty. **3** (of an aircraft) prepared for or capable of flight.

fly ball *noun Baseball* a ball hit up into the air with the result that it is easily caught.

fly-blow *noun* a fly's egg deposited in and contaminating meat etc. or a maggot hatched from this.

fly-blown *adjective* **1** contaminated, esp. by fly-blows. **2** tainted, impure, corrupt.

fly boy *noun N Amer. slang* a member of the air force, esp. a pilot.

fly·bridge *noun* a bridge or an open deck with duplicate controls, situated above the main bridge of a ship.

flyby *noun* (*pl.* **-bys**) **1** a flight past a position, esp. the approach of a spacecraft to a planet etc. for observation. **2** an often low-level, ceremonial procession, usu. in formation, of aircraft.

fly-by-night ● *adjective* **1** unreliable or dishonest. **2** superficial,

short-lived. ● *noun* (also **fly-by-nighter**) an untrustworthy, dishonest, or unreliable person, esp. one who shirks debts.

fly-by-wire *noun* a semi-automatic and usu. computer-regulated system for controlling the flight of an aircraft, spacecraft, etc.

fly cast *intransitive verb N Amer.* fish recreationally with a rod and artificial flies rather than live bait, using a whip-like motion to cast the line. □ **fly caster** *noun* **fly casting** *noun*

fly·catch·er *noun* any of various passerine birds catching flying insects esp. in short flights from a perch, esp. of the families Muscicapidae, Tyrannidae (**tyrant flycatcher**), and Monarchidae (**monarch flycatcher**).

fly-drive ● *attributive adjective* designating a holiday which combines the cost of the flight and of car rental. ● *noun* such a holiday. ● *intransitive verb* take such a holiday.

flyer *noun* (also **flier**) *informal* **1 a** a pilot or aviator. **b** a person who flies in an aircraft as a passenger, esp. on a commercial carrier (*frequent flyer*). **2** *N Amer.* a small advertising leaflet that is widely distributed. **3** a thing, creature, etc. that flies or is carried through the air. **4** *N Amer.* a risk, esp. a speculative investment. **5** a fast-moving animal or vehicle. **6** an ambitious or outstanding person (*high flyer*). **7** a flying jump or leap.

fly-fish *intransitive verb* fish with an artificial fly as bait. □ **fly·fish·er** *noun* **fly fisherman** *noun* **fly-fishing** *noun*

fly-half *noun Rugby* = STANDOFF 2.

fly-in ● *noun* **1** the action or an act of travelling or delivering goods etc. by air to a specific and usu. remote place. **2** a service, entertainment, etc. provided for people who arrive by air. ● *adjective* **1** of or for people arriving by air, esp. in a remote region (*fly-in canoe trips*). **2** accessible only by plane, helicopter, etc. (*fly-in hunting lodge*).

fly·ing ● *adjective* **1** that flies or flies about (*flying saucer*). **2** fluttering, waving, or hanging loose in the air etc. **3** hasty, brief (*a flying visit*). **4** designed for rapid movement. **5** passing or travelling swiftly (*a flying puck*). **6** (of an animal) able to make very long leaps by using wing-like membranes etc. **7** *Figure Skating* designating a spin which the skater commences with a vigorous leap through the air. ● *noun* the action of guiding, piloting, or travelling in an aircraft or spacecraft. □ **not give a flying fuck** *coarse slang* not care in the least. **with flying colours** with distinction.

flying boat *noun* a seaplane the fuselage of which resembles a boat and is adapted for floating.

flying bomb *noun* esp. *hist.* an unmanned aircraft with an explosive warhead.

flying buttress *noun* a buttress, usu. on an arch, which slants upwards to a wall from a pier or other support.

flying camp *noun* a temporary camp, esp. one easily moved from place to place.

flying circus *noun* a stunt flying show.

Flying Dutchman *noun* **1** a ghostly ship supposedly doomed to sail the seas forever and said to appear around the Cape of Good Hope when a disaster is about to occur. **2** the captain of this vessel.

flying erase head *noun* an editing feature on camcorders etc. that eliminates interference patterns etc. between scenes cut together.

flying fish *noun* any of various tropical fishes of the family Exocoetidae, capable of gliding considerable distances above the water by means of wing-like pectoral fins.

flying fox *noun* any of various fruit-eating bats esp. of the genus *Pteropus*, with a fox-like head, found in India, Madagascar, SE Asia, and Australia.

flying lemur *noun* either of two SE Asian nocturnal arboreal mammals of the genus *Cynocephalus*, which resemble lemurs and can glide hundreds of feet by means of a membrane between the fore and hind limbs and the tail.

flying lizard *noun* any lizard of the genus *Draco*, having membranes on elongated ribs for gliding.

flying machine *noun dated* an aircraft.

flying officer *noun* (also **Flying Officer**) (in the RAF and *hist.* in the RCAF) an officer ranking above pilot officer and below flight lieutenant. Abbr.: **FO**.

flying phalanger *noun* any of various phalangers having a membrane between the fore and hind limbs for gliding.

flying picket *noun* a group of striking workers, or one of its members, who can move rapidly from one site to another, esp. to reinforce local pickets.

flying saucer *noun* any unidentified, esp. circular, flying object, popularly supposed to have come from outer space.

flying school *noun* a place where people are taught to fly aircraft.

flying squad *noun* a police detachment or other body organized and prepared at all times for rapid deployment, e.g. when a crime has occurred.

flying squirrel *noun* any of various squirrels with skin joining the fore and hind limbs for gliding from tree to tree.

flying start *noun* **1** a start (of a race etc.) in which the starting point is passed at full speed. **2** a vigorous start giving an initial advantage.

flying suit *noun* a snug, one-piece suit with many pockets usu. worn by military aircrew.

flying wing *noun* an aircraft with little or no fuselage and no tailplane.

fly-leaf *noun* (*pl.* **-leaves**) a blank page at the beginning or end of a book.

fly·line *noun* **1** a type of line used in fly fishing. **2** *Cdn* a point or height above which flies do not normally fly.

fly net *noun* a net for keeping flies away.

Flynn, **Errol** (born Leslie Thomas Flynn) (1909–59), Australian or Irish-born US actor, best known as the swashbuckling hero of films such as *Captain Blood* (1935) and *The Adventures of Robin Hood* (1938).

fly-out *adjective N Amer.* indicating services etc. that require flying out of a relatively easily accessible area into a remote region (*fly-out Arctic char fishing*).

fly·over *noun* **1** *N Amer.* a flight of aircraft, usu. at low level, for observation, as part of a military display, etc. **2** *Brit.* an overpass. **3** = FLYPAST.

fly·paper *noun* a strip of sticky paper treated with a substance for catching and poisoning flies.

fly·past *noun* a ceremonial flight of aircraft past a person or a place.

fly rod *noun* a very light, flexible rod designed for use in fly casting. □ **fly rod·der** *noun* **fly rod·ding** *noun*

fly·sheet *noun* **1** a tract, circular, instruction sheet, etc. of two or four pages. **2** a canvas cover pitched outside and over a tent to give extra protection against bad weather.

fly·speck ● *noun* **1** a small stain produced by the excrement of a fly. **2** any tiny spot, stain, defect, etc. ● *transitive verb* mark with flyspecks. □ **fly·specked** *adjective*

fly swatter *noun* a device for killing flies by hitting them, usu. a piece of plastic attached to a long, thin handle.

fly-tip *transitive verb Brit.* illegally dump (waste). □ **fly-tipper** *noun* **fly-tipping** *noun*

fly tower *noun* a tall structure above a stage allowing for scenery, backdrops, etc. to be lifted completely out of the view of the audience.

fly·trap *noun* **1** any of various plants that catch flies, esp. the Venus flytrap. **2** a trap in which to catch flies.

fly·way *noun* **1** the regular line of flight followed by a migrating bird. **2** a vast area occupied by bird populations containing both winter and breeding grounds linked by migratory routes.

fly·weight *noun* **1** a weight in certain sports intermediate between light flyweight and bantamweight, in the amateur boxing scale 48-51 kg but differing for professionals and wrestlers. **2** a sportsman of this weight.

fly·wheel *noun* a heavy wheel on a revolving shaft used to regulate machinery or accumulate power.

FM *abbreviation* **1 a** FREQUENCY MODULATION. **b** radio stations broadcast using this. **2** *hist.* Field Marshal.

Fm *symbol Chem.* the element fermium.

fm. *abbreviation* (also **fm**) fathom(s).

FMS *abbreviation* FALSE MEMORY SYNDROME.

FN *abbreviation Cdn* FIRST NATION.

f-number *noun Photog.* the ratio of the focal length to the effective diameter of a lens, e.g. *f* 5, indicating that the focal length is five times the diameter. [*f* (denoting focal length) + NUMBER]

FO *abbreviation* **1** *Military* **a** FLYING OFFICER. **b** field officer. **c** forward observer. **2** *hist.* (in the UK) Foreign Office.

Fo, **Dario** (b.1926), Italian playwright and actor. His work is mainly satirical and often blasphemous, from a left-wing perspective. He was awarded the Nobel Prize for literature in 1997.

fo. *abbreviation* folio.

foal ● *noun* the young of a horse or related animal. ● *intransitive verb* (of a mare etc.) give birth to a foal. □ **in** (or **with**) **foal** (of a mare etc.)

pregnant. □ **foal·ing** *noun* [Old English *fola* from Germanic: compare FILLY]

foam ● *noun* **1** a mass of small bubbles formed on or in liquid by agitation, fermentation, etc. **2** a froth of saliva or sweat. **3** rubber (in full **foam rubber**) or plastic (in full **foam plastic**) solidified in a lightweight cellular mass with many small gas bubbles. **4** any of various chemical substances forming a thick mass of bubbles and used for various purposes (*shaving foam*). **5** *literary* water, the sea (*foam-born Aphrodite*). ● *intransitive verb* **1** emit foam; froth. **2** be very angry, rage. **3** (of a vessel) be filled and overflow with foam. □ **foam at the mouth** be very angry. □ **foam·ing** *adjective* **foam·less** *adjective* **foam-like** *adjective* **foamy** *adjective* (**foam·i·er**, **foam·i·est**). [Old English *fām* from West Germanic]

foam bath *noun* a scented, foaming preparation added to bathwater.

foam board *noun* a thin, pliable polystyrene board used for insulation, in arts and crafts, etc.

foam·flower *noun* a woodland plant of eastern N America, *Tiarella cordifolia*, with a mass of small white flowers.

fob[1] ● *noun* **1** (in full **fob chain**) a chain attached to a watch for carrying in a waistcoat or waistband pocket. **2** a small pocket for carrying a watch. **3** a tab or ornament on a key ring. ● *transitive verb* (**fobbed**, **fob·bing**) put in one's fob; pocket. [originally cant, prob. from German]

fob[2] *transitive verb* (**fobbed**, **fob·bing**) □ **fob off 1** (often foll. by *with* a thing) deceive into accepting something inferior. **2** (often foll. by *on* to a person) palm or pass off (an inferior thing). [16th c.: compare obsolete *fop* to dupe, German *foppen* to banter]

f.o.b. *abbreviation* free on board, i.e. transported to the ship and loaded without the buyer paying extra.

fo·cac·cia /fəˈkatʃə/ *noun* a type of flat Italian bread usu. topped with herbs etc. [Italian from medieval Latin *focacius*, short for *panis focacius*, lit. 'bread cooked in the oven']

focal /ˈfoːkəl/ *adjective* **1** of, at, or in terms of a focus. **2** *Med.* (of a disease etc.) localized or occurring at discrete foci.

focal·ize /ˈfoːkə,laiz/ *transitive verb* (also esp. *Brit.* **-ise**) = FOCUS *verb*. □ **focal·iz·a·tion** *noun*

focal length *noun* (also **focal distance**) **1** the distance between the centre of a mirror or lens and its focus. **2** the equivalent distance in a compound lens or telescope.

focal plane *noun* the plane perpendicular to the axis of a mirror or lens and containing the focus.

focal point *noun* = FOCUS *noun* 1a, 3.

Foch /fɒʃ/ **Fer·di·nand** (1851–1929), French general, who served as the supreme commander of all Allied Forces on the Western Front (1918) in the First World War, and as the senior French representative at the Armistice negotiations.

fo'c'sle *var. of* FORECASTLE.

focus ● *noun* (*pl.* **fo·cus·es** or **foci** /ˈfoːkai, -sai/) **1** *Physics* **a** the point at which rays or waves (of light, heat, sound, etc.) meet after reflection or refraction, or from which divergent rays or waves appear to proceed. Also called FOCAL POINT. **b** the distance from a lens etc. to this point (compare FOCAL LENGTH). **2 a** *Optics* the point at which an object must be situated for an image of it given by a lens or mirror to be well defined (*bring into focus*). **b** the adjustment of the eye or a lens necessary to produce a clear image (*the binoculars were not in focus*). **c** a state of clear definition (*the photograph was out of focus*). **3** the centre of interest, activity, or greatest energy (*focus of attention*). **4** *Math.* one of a number of points from which the distances to any point of a given curve or solid obey a simple arithmetic relation. **5** *Med.* the primary or principal site of an infection, malignant growth, or other disease. **6** *Geol.* the place of origin of an earthquake, storm, volcanic eruption, etc. ● *verb* (**fo·cused**, **fo·cus·ing** or **fo·cussed**, **fo·cus·sing**) **1** *transitive* bring into focus, etc. **2 a** *transitive* adjust the focus of (a lens, the eye, etc.). **b** *intransitive* focus the eye, a lens, etc. **3** *transitive & intransitive* (often foll. by *on*) concentrate or be concentrated on. **4** *intransitive & transitive* converge or make converge to a focus. □ **focus·er** *noun* [Latin, = hearth]

focus group *noun* a representative selection of people surveyed for their opinions on politics, commercial products, etc.

focus puller *noun* an assistant camera operator for a film production, who adjusts the focus while the camera operator views the image to be filmed.

fod·der ● *noun* **1** food, esp. dried hay or straw etc. for cattle, horses, etc. **2 a** something that feeds or stimulates (the imagination, creativity, etc.). **b** people viewed as dispensable commodities. ● *transitive verb* give fodder to. [Old English *fōdor* from Germanic, related to FOOD]

Vowels: a *cat* ɑ *arm* e *bed* ɜr *her* ɜː *deux* ə *ago* ɪ *sit* i *cosy* iː *feed* ɒ *hot* ɔ *pore* oː *no* ʌ *run* ʊ *put*

FOE *abbreviation* Friends of the Earth.

foe *noun* an enemy or opponent. [Old English *fāh* hostile, related to FEUD[1]]

foehn *var. of* FÖHN.

foetid *var. of* FETID.

foetus *esp. Brit. var. of* FETUS. □ **foetal** *adjective*

fog ● *noun* **1 a** a thick cloud of water droplets or smoke suspended in the atmosphere at or near the earth's surface restricting or obscuring visibility. **b** any abnormal darkened state or obscurity in the atmosphere. **c** an opaque mass of smoke (*insecticide fog*). **2** *Photog.* cloudiness on a developed negative etc. obscuring the image. **3** a state of confusion, uncertainty, perplexity, etc. ● *verb* (**fogged**, **fog·ging**) **1** *transitive* **a** envelop or cover with fog or condensed vapour. **b** bewilder (a person), confuse (an idea), etc. **2** *intransitive* become covered with fog or condensed vapour. **3** *transitive* *Photog.* cause cloudiness on (a negative etc.). **4** *intransitive* treat with something in the form of a spray, esp. an insecticide. □ **in a fog** puzzled; at a loss. □ **fogged** *adjective* **fog·ger** *noun* **fog·ging** *noun* [perhaps back-formation from FOGGY]

fog bank *noun* a mass of fog or dense haze over water.

fog·bound *adjective* **1** (of a place) completely shrouded in dense fog. **2** (of a person, aircraft, etc.) unable to leave a place because of fog.

fog-bow *noun* a manifestation like a rainbow, produced by light on fog.

fogey *noun* (also **fogy**) (*pl.* **-eys** or **-ies**) a person with old-fashioned ideas which he or she is unwilling to change (*old fogey*). □ **fogey·dom** *noun* **fogey·ish** *adjective* **fogey·ism** *noun* [18th c.: related to slang *fogram*, of unknown origin]

Foggia /ˈfɒdʒə/ a town in SE Italy, in Apulia; pop. (2001) 146,072.

foggy *adjective* (**fog·gi·er**, **fog·gi·est**) **1** (of the atmosphere) thick or obscured with fog. **2** vague, confused, unclear. **3** (of a photograph) cloudy, obscured by a deposit of silver etc. □ **not have the foggiest** *informal* have no idea at all. □ **fog·gi·ly** *adverb* **fog·gi·ness** *noun*

fog·horn *noun* **1** a deep sounding instrument for warning ships in fog. **2** *informal* a loud penetrating voice.

fog lamp *noun* (also **fog light**) a headlight used to improve visibility in fog.

Fogo Island an island off the northeastern coast of Newfoundland, 78 km north of Gander. [Portuguese, lit. 'fire', possibly with reference to forest fires or smoke-like fog; perhaps also after the island of *Fogo*, one of the Cape Verde Islands]

fogy *noun var. of* FOGEY. □ **fogy·dom** *noun* **fogy·ish** *adjective*

föhn /fɜːn/ *noun* (also **foehn**) **1** a hot southerly wind on the northern slopes of the Alps. **2** a warm dry wind on the lee side of mountains (*compare* CHINOOK 1). [German, ultimately from Latin *Favonius* mild west wind]

FOI *abbreviation* freedom of information.

foi·ble *noun* **1** a minor weakness or idiosyncrasy. **2** *Fencing* the part of a sword's blade from the middle to the point. [French, obsolete form of *faible* (as FEEBLE)]

foie gras /fwɒ ˈɡrɒ/ *noun* the liver of fattened geese or ducks eaten as a delicacy, esp. in the form of a pâté. [French, lit. 'fat liver']

foil[1] ● *transitive verb* **1** frustrate, baffle, defeat. **2** *Hunting* run over or cross (ground or a scent) to confuse the hounds. ● *noun* **1** *Hunting* the track of a hunted animal. **2** *archaic* a repulse or defeat. [Middle English, = trample down, perhaps from Old French *fouler* to full cloth, trample, ultimately from Latin *fullo* FULLER[1]]

foil[2] *noun* **1 a** metal hammered or rolled into a thin sheet (*gold foil*). **b** a sheet of this, or of tin amalgam, attached to mirror glass as a reflector. **c** aluminum foil (*cover with foil and bake*). **d** a leaf of foil placed under a precious stone etc. to brighten or colour it. **2** a person or thing that enhances the qualities of another by contrast. [Old French from Latin *folium* leaf]

foil[3] *noun* a light blunt-edged sword with a button on its point used in fencing. [16th c.: origin unknown]

foil[4] *noun* each of the structures fitted to a hydrofoil's hull to lift it clear of the water at speed. [abbreviation]

foist *transitive verb* **1** (foll. by *off*) on, (*off*) upon) impose (an unwelcome person or thing) on. **2** (foll. by *in*, *into*) introduce surreptitiously or unwarrantably. [originally of palming a false die, from Dutch dial. *vuisten* 'take in the hand' from *vuist* FIST]

Fo·kine /fɒˈkiːn/ **Mi·chel** (born Mikhail Mikhailovich Fokin) (1880–1942), Russian-born US dancer and choreographer. A reformer of ballet, he strove for greater dramatic effect and the integration of music, decor, choreography, and costumes. From 1909 he choreographed many ballets for Diaghilev, including the premieres of Stravinsky's The

Firebird (1910) and Ravel's *Daphnis and Chloë* (1912). His most famous ballet is *Les Sylphides* (original version 1907).

Fok·ker /ˈfɒkər/ **An·thony Her·man Ger·ard** (1890–1939), Dutch pioneer aircraft designer and pilot. He built his first aircraft in 1908, and designed a number of fighter aircraft used by Germany in the First World War; he later designed the successful Trimotor F-7 airliners.

fol. *abbreviation* folio.

fol·acin /ˈfɒləsɪn, ˈfɒl-/ = FOLIC ACID. [*folic acid* + -IN]

fol·ate /ˈfoʊleɪt/ *noun* a salt or ester of folic acid. [*folic acid* + -ATE[1]]

fold[1] ● *verb* **1** *transitive* **a** bend or close (a flexible thing) over upon itself. **b** (foll. by *back*, *over*, *down*) bend a part of (a flexible thing) in the manner specified (*fold down the flap*). **2** *intransitive* become or be able to be folded. **3** *transitive* (foll. by *away*, *up*) make compact by folding. **4** *transitive* **a** bring together and cross or intertwine (the arms, legs, etc.). **b** (of a bird, insect, etc.) bring (the wings) together from an extended position. **5** *intransitive informal* (often foll. by *up*) **a** collapse, disintegrate. **b** (of an enterprise) fail; go bankrupt. **c** close. **6** *transitive & intransitive* lay (one's cards) face down on the table etc., so as to withdraw from play. **7** *transitive* (foll. by *in*) mix (an ingredient with others) using a gentle cutting and turning motion. **8** *transitive literary* embrace (*folded him to her breast*). **9** *transitive* (foll. by *about*, *around*) clasp (the arms). **10** *transitive* (often foll. by *in etc.*) wrap, envelop. ● *noun* **1** the act or an instance of folding. **2** a line made by or for folding. **3** a folded part. **4** a hollow among hills. **5** *Geol.* a curvature of strata. □ **fold·able** *adjective* **fold·ing** *adjective* [Old English *falden*, *fealden* from Germanic]

fold[2] ● *noun* **1** = SHEEPFOLD. **2** a body of believers or members of a church. **3** a community or group of people sharing a way of life, values, etc. (*welcomed her back into the fold*). ● *transitive verb* enclose (sheep) in a fold. [Old English *fald*]

-fold *suffix* forming adjectives and adverbs from cardinal numbers, meaning: **1** in an amount multiplied by (*repaid tenfold*). **2** consisting of so many parts (*threefold blessing*). [Old English *-fald*, *-feald*, related to FOLD[1]: original sense 'folded in so many layers']

fold·away *adjective* adapted or designed to be folded away.

fold-down *adjective* designed to be folded down for use (*fold-down airplane table*).

fold·er *noun* **1** a folding cover or holder for loose papers. **2** a folded leaflet. **3** *Computing* a directory in a computer system in which files may be accumulated.

fol·der·ol /ˈfɒldəˌrɒl/ *noun* **1** foolish chatter or ideas; nonsense. **2** a gewgaw or trifle. [originally as a nonsensical refrain in songs: perhaps from *falbala* trimming on a dress]

folding door *noun* a door with jointed sections, folding on itself when opened.

folding money *esp. N Amer. informal* = PAPER MONEY.

fold-out ● *noun* an oversize page in a book etc. to be unfolded by the reader. ● *attributive adjective* designed to be unfolded for use (*a fold-out bed*).

foley /ˈfoʊli/ *noun* (*attributive*) designating sound effects in a motion picture etc. recorded separately from the shooting of the image and subsequently matched with it on the sound track (*foley artist*; *foley mixer*). [J. Foley, US sound technician d.1967]

foli·aceous /ˌfoʊliˈeɪʃəs/ *adjective* **1** of or like leaves. **2** *esp. Geol.* laminated. [Latin *foliaceus* leafy from *folium* leaf]

foli·age /ˈfoʊliədʒ/ *noun* **1** leaves. **2** a design in art resembling leaves. □ **foli·aged** *adjective* [French *feuillage* from *feuille* leaf, from Old French *foille*: see FOIL[2]]

foliage plant *noun* a plant grown for its attractive leaves, esp. as opposed to one grown for its flowers etc.

foli·ar /ˈfoʊliər/ *adjective* of or relating to leaves. [modern Latin *foliaris* from Latin *folium* leaf]

foliar feed *noun* feed supplied to leaves of plants. □ **foliar feeding** *noun*

foli·ate ● *adjective* /ˈfoʊliət/ **1** decorated with foils or depictions of leaves. **2** leaflike. **3** having leaves. **4** (in combination) having a specified number of leaflets (*trifoliate*). ● *verb* /ˈfoʊlieɪt/ **1** *intransitive Geol.* (usu. as **foli·at·ed** *adjective*) split into laminae. **2** *transitive* decorate (an arch, furniture, etc.) with foils or leaves. **3** *transitive* number leaves (not pages) of (a volume) consecutively. □ **foli·ation** /-ˈeɪʃən/ *noun* [Latin *foliatus* leaved from *folium* leaf]

folic acid /ˈfoʊlɪk, ˈfɒlɪk/ *noun* a vitamin of the B complex, found in leafy green vegetables, liver, and kidney, a deficiency of which causes pernicious anemia. *Also called* FOLACIN, VITAMIN M. [Latin *folium* leaf (because it is found esp. in green leaves) + -IC]

folie à deux /ˌfɒli ɑː ˈdɜː/ *noun* (*pl.* **fo·lies à deux**) an identical delusion or mental disorder affecting two people living in close association. [French, lit. 'madness involving two']

folie de gran·deur /fɒˈliː də grãˈdɜːr/ *noun* (pl. **fo·lies de gran·deur**) a delusion of grandeur. [French]

fo·lio /ˈfəʊlɪəʊ/ ● *noun* (pl. **-lios**) **1** a leaf of paper etc., esp. one numbered only on the front. **2** a page number of a book. **3** a sheet of paper folded once making two leaves of a book. **4** a book made of such sheets. ● *adjective* (of a book) made of folios, of the largest size. □ **in folio** made of folios. [Latin, ablative of *folium* leaf, = *on leaf* (as specified)]

folk *noun* (pl. **folk** or **folks**) **1** (treated as *pl.*) people in general or of a specified class (*few folk about*; *townsfolk*; *just regular folks*). **2** (in *pl.*) (usu. **folks**) one's parents or relatives. **3** (treated as *sing.*) a people. **4** (treated as *sing.*) *informal* = FOLK MUSIC. **5** (*attributive*) of popular origin; traditional (*folk art*). [Old English *folc* from Germanic]

folk dance *noun* **1** any of various traditional dances, often originally derived from festivals etc. **2** these collectively as a genre of dance. **3** the music for such a dance. □ **folk dancer** *noun* **folk dancing** *noun*

Folke·stone /ˈfəʊkstən/ a seaport and resort in Kent, on the southeast coast of England; pop. (est. 2002) 47,020.

folk etymology *noun* **1** a popular modifying of the form of a word or phrase to make it seem to be derived from a more familiar word (e.g. *greyhound*, where Old English *grieg*, bitch, was replaced with the more familiar 'grey', although the dog is not grey in colour). **2** a commonly held but false explanation of the origin of a word.

folk fest *noun* *N Amer.* a cultural festival featuring folk music etc.

folk guitar *noun* an acoustic guitar with a hollow, waisted body, a 14-fretted neck, and six metal strings, usu. played by plucking or strumming with a plectrum, and used esp. for folk and country music (*compare* CLASSICAL GUITAR).

folk hero *noun* a person perceived as a hero by the common people.

folk·ie *informal* ● *noun* a devotee of folk music; a folksinger. ● *attributive adjective* of or relating to folk music (*folkie bands*).

folk·ish *adjective* of the common people; traditional, unsophisticated.

folk·lore *noun* **1** the traditional beliefs, stories, customs, etc. of a people. **2** the study of these. **3** popular fantasy or belief. □ **folk·lor·ic** *adjective* **folk·lor·ist** *noun* **folk·lor·is·tic** *adjective*

folk mass *noun* a Mass in which traditional liturgical music is replaced by folk music, usu. with guitar accompaniment.

folk medicine *noun* medicine of a traditional kind, employing herbal remedies etc.

folk memory *noun* recollection of the past persisting among a people.

folk music *noun* **1** traditional music as made by the common people of a region, community, etc. and transmitted orally. **2** contemporary music composed in this style.

folk-rock *noun* folk music incorporating the stronger beat of rock music and using electric instruments. □ **folk-rocker** *noun*

folk·sing·er *noun* a singer of folk songs. □ **folk·sing·ing** *noun*

folk song *noun* **1** a song having a tune and lyrics that have been handed down esp. orally from one generation to the next in a particular region. **2** a song written in this style.

folksy *adjective* (**folk·si·er**, **folk·si·est**) **1** friendly, sociable, informal. **2 a** having the characteristics of folk art, culture, etc. **b** ostensibly or artificially folkish. □ **folk·si·ness** *noun*

folk tale *noun* a traditional story or legend.

folk·ways *plural noun* the traditional behaviour of a people.

folky *adjective* (**folk·i·er**, **folk·i·est**) **1** = FOLKSY 2. **2** = FOLKISH. □ **folk·i·ness** *noun*

fol·licle /ˈfɒlɪkəl/ *noun* **1** *Anat.* a small secretory cavity, sac, or gland, esp. **a** (in full **hair follicle**) the gland or cavity at the root of a hair. **b** = GRAAFIAN FOLLICLE. **2** *Bot.* a dry fruit with a single carpel opening on one side only to release its seeds. □ **fol·licu·lar** /fɒˈlɪkjʊlər/ *adjective* [Latin *folliculus* diminutive of *follis* bellows]

follicle-stimulating hormone *noun* a pituitary hormone which promotes the formation of ova or sperm. Abbr. **FSH**.

fol·low *verb* **1** *transitive* (or, foll. by *after*, *intransitive*) go or come after (a person or thing proceeding ahead). **2** *transitive* go along (a route, path, etc.). **3** *transitive & intransitive* come after in order or time (*Pearson followed Diefenbaker*; *dessert followed*; *my reasons are as follows*). **4** *transitive* take as a guide or leader. **5** *transitive* conform to (*follow your example*). **6** *transitive* practise (a trade or profession). **7** *transitive* undertake (a course of study etc.). **8** *transitive* understand the meaning or tendency of (a speaker or argument). **9** *transitive* maintain awareness of the current state or progress of (events etc. in a particular sphere). **10** *transitive* (foll. by *with*)

provide with a sequel or successor. **11** *intransitive* happen after something else; ensue. **12** *intransitive* **a** be necessarily true as a result of something else. **b** (foll. by *from*) be a result of. **13** *transitive* strive after; aim at; pursue (*followed fame and fortune*). □ **follow one's nose** trust to instinct. **follow on** continue. **follow out** carry out; adhere precisely to (instructions etc.). **follow suit 1** *Cards* play a card of the suit led. **2** conform to another person's actions. **follow through 1** continue (an action etc.) to its conclusion. **2** *Sport* continue the movement of a stroke after the ball etc. has been struck or thrown. **follow up 1** (foll. by *with*) pursue, develop, supplement. **2** make further investigation of. [Old English *folgian* from Germanic]

fol·low·er *noun* **1** an adherent or devotee. **2** a person or thing that follows. **3** a mechanical part whose motion or action is derived from that of another part to which force is applied.

fol·low·ing ● *preposition* coming after in time; as a sequel to. ● *noun* **1** a body of adherents or devotees. **2** that which follows (*see the following for details*). ● *adjective* that follows or comes after.

follow-on *adjective* **1** following or coming after as the next step in a progression (*follow-on question*). **2** continuing (*follow-on maintenance*).

follow spot *noun* a spotlight which follows a performer on the stage.

follow-the-leader *noun* (also *Brit.* **follow-my-leader**) a game in which players must do as the leader does.

follow-through *noun* the act or an instance of following through.

follow-up *noun* a subsequent or continued action, measure, experience, etc.

folly *noun* (pl. **-lies**) **1** foolishness; lack of good sense. **2** a foolish act, behaviour, idea, etc. **3** an ornamental building, usu. a tower or mock Gothic ruin. **4** (in *pl.*) *Theatre* **a** a revue with glamorous female performers, esp. scantily clad. **b** the performers in such a revue. [Old French *folie* from *fol* mad, FOOL¹]

Fom·al·haut /ˈfɒməlˌhaʊt/ the brightest star in the constellation Piscis Austrinus. [Arabic, lit. 'the fish's mouth']

fo·ment /fəˈment/ *transitive verb* instigate or stir up (trouble, sedition, etc.). □ **fo·men·ta·tion** *noun* **fo·ment·er** *noun* [French *fomenter* from Late Latin *fomentare* from Latin *fomentum* poultice, lotion, from *fovēre* heat, cherish]

Fon /fɒn/ *noun* **1** a member of a W African people inhabiting the southern part of Benin. **2** the Kwa language of these people, a close relative of Ewe. [Fon]

fond *adjective* **1** (foll. by *of*) having affection or a liking for. **2** affectionate, loving (*a fond look*; *a fond farewell*). **3** doting; indulgent (*a fond parent*). **4** (of hopes, dreams, etc.) cherished but not likely to be realized (*has fond hopes of becoming prime minister*). **5** *archaic* foolish. □ **fond·ly** *adverb* **fond·ness** *noun* [Middle English from obsolete *fon* fool, be foolish]

Fonda ▶ **1 Henry (Jaynes)** (1905–82), US actor, noted for his roles in a variety of films, including *The Grapes of Wrath* (1940), *Twelve Angry Men* (1957), and *On Golden Pond* (1981), for which he won an Oscar. **2** his daughter, **Jane (Sey·mour)** (b.1937), US actress, whose films include *Klute* (1971) and *Coming Home* (1978), for both of which she won an Oscar, and *On Golden Pond* (1981).

fon·dant /ˈfɒndənt/ *noun* **1** a creamy, thick paste made of sugar and water, used as an icing or filling. **2** a candy made of or filled with this paste. [French, pres. part. of *fondre* melt, from Latin *fundere* pour]

fon·dle *transitive verb* **1** touch or stroke lovingly; caress. **2** sexually molest (a person) by touching etc. **3** touch (a person's genitals) erotically. □ **fond·ler** *noun* [back-formation from *fondling* fondled person (as FOND, -LING¹)]

fon·due /fɒnˈduː/ *noun* **1** a dish of flavoured melted cheese into which cubes of bread are dipped. **2** any other dish in which small pieces of food are dipped into hot oil or sauce. [French, fem. past participle of *fondre* melt, from Latin *fundere* pour]

font¹ *noun* **1** a receptacle in a church for baptismal water. **2** the reservoir for oil in a lamp. [Old English from Latin *fons fontis* fountain, baptismal water]

font² *noun* (also *Brit.* **fount**) **1** a selection of type of one face and size. **2** a set of letters, numbers, and symbols of a unified design and given size that may be displayed on a computer screen or printed out. [French *fonte* from *fondre* FOUND³]

Fon·taine /fɒnˈteɪn/ **Larry Phil·lip** ('Phil', b.1944), Aboriginal Canadian politician and activist, national chief of the Assembly of First Nations 1997–2000, and again from 2003. He was also chief commissioner of the Indian Claims Commission, 2002–3.

Fon·taine·bleau /ˈfɔ̃tɛnbloʊ/ a town in northern France, about 65 km

SE of Paris, site of a famous royal château built in the 16th century and surrounded by spacious gardens and a forest.

fon·ta·nelle /ˌfɒntəˈnel/ *noun* (*US* also **fon·ta·nel**) a membranous space in an infant's skull at the angles of the parietal bones. [French *fontanelle* from modern Latin *fontanella* from Old French *fontenelle* diminutive of *fontaine* fountain]

Fon·teyn /fɒnˈteɪn/ **Dame Mar·got** (born Margaret Hookham) (1919–91), English ballerina. She danced all the classical ballerina roles and created many new ones for the Royal Ballet; in 1962 she began a celebrated partnership with Rudolf Nureyev. In 1979 she was named *prima ballerina assoluta*, a title given only three times in the history of ballet.

fon·tina /ˌfɒnˈtiːnə/ *noun* a mild, semi-soft to firm, pale yellow cow's milk cheese. [Italian]

Fonyo, Ste·phen Charles ('**Steve**') (b.1965), Canadian runner and activist. Having lost most of his left leg to bone cancer in his youth, he was inspired by Terry Fox's Marathon of Hope to undertake a run across Canada to raise money for cancer research, leaving St. John's in March, 1984 and arriving in Victoria in May, 1985; this 'Journey for Lives' raised $13 million, and Fonyo later undertook a second run from northern to southern Britain (1986–7).

foo *noun* esp. *Computing* used to name temporary, hypothetical, or representative variables or files. [origin uncertain]

Foo·chow see Fuzhou.

food *noun* **1** any substance that can be taken into the body to maintain life and growth; nourishment. **2** solid nourishment, as opposed to drink. **3** nutriment absorbed by a plant from the earth or air. **4** a particular kind of food (*cat food; snack food*). **5** ideas as a resource for or stimulus to mental work (*food for thought*). □ **food·less** *adjective* [Old English *fōda* from Germanic: compare FEED]

food bank *noun N Amer.* a charitable institution which provides food to the needy.

food-borne *adjective* (of an illness, bacteria, etc.) communicated or propagated in food.

food chain *noun* **1** a hierarchy of organisms in which each feeds on those below and is the source of food for those above. **2** any hierarchy.

food colouring *noun* any of various edible dyes used to colour food.

food court *noun* an area, esp. in a shopping mall, with a variety of fast-food stalls surrounding a shared area with tables and chairs.

food·ery *noun* (*pl.* -**eries**) *N Amer. informal* a restaurant.

food fair *noun N Amer.* **1** = FOOD COURT. **2** an exposition with displays relating to various aspects of food.

food fight *noun* **1** an exchange of food items thrown at one another esp. by children. **2** a nasty or petty and childish squabble.

food fish *noun* any fish that is used as food by humans.

food grain *noun* (usu. in *pl.*) any of a variety of grains that are used for human consumption.

food group *noun* any of a number of categories (usu. four or five) into which foods can be classified for nutritional purposes.

foodie *noun informal* a person who is interested in esp. exotic or trendy food; a gourmet.

food·land *noun Cdn* farmland; land that is or may be used for the production of food.

food poisoning *noun* illness due to bacteria or other toxins in food.

food processor *noun* a domestic kitchen appliance for chopping, grating, slicing, blending, or mixing foods.

food stamp *noun* esp. *US* a stamp that is exchangeable for food, sold cheaply to poor or needy people etc.

food·stuff *noun* any substance suitable as food.

food value *noun* the relative nourishing power of a food.

food web *noun Ecology* the system of interdependent food chains in a community.

foo·fa·raw /ˈfuːfərɔː/ *noun N Amer.* a fuss, commotion, or disturbance. [origin unknown]

fool¹ ● *noun* **1** a person who acts unwisely or imprudently; a stupid person. **2** *hist.* a jester; a clown. **3** a dupe. ● *verb* **1** *transitive* deceive so as to cause to appear foolish. **2** *transitive* (foll. by *into* + verbal noun, or *out of*) trick; cause to do something foolish. **3** *transitive* play tricks on; dupe. **4** *intransitive* act in a joking, frivolous, or teasing way. ● *adjective N Amer. informal* foolish, silly. □ **act** (or **play**) **the fool** behave in a silly way. **fool around 1** behave in a playful or silly way. **2 a** engage in sexual activity. **b** engage in adulterous sexual activity. **3** waste time. **fool with** handle idly; play with carelessly. **make a fool of** make (a person or oneself) look foolish; trick. **no** (or **nobody's**) **fool** a shrewd

or prudent person. [Old French *fol* from Latin *follis* bellows, empty-headed person]

fool² *noun* esp. *Brit.* a dessert of usu. stewed fruit crushed and mixed with cream, custard, etc. [16th c.: perhaps from FOOL¹]

fool·ery *noun* (*pl.* -**eries**) **1** foolish behaviour. **2** a foolish act.

fool·hardy *adjective* rashly or foolishly bold; reckless. □ **fool·hard·i·ly** *adverb* **fool·hard·i·ness** *noun* [Old French *folhardi* from *fol* foolish + *hardi* bold]

fool hen *noun N Amer.* the spruce grouse, known for its lack of fear of humans.

fool·ish *adjective* (of a person, action, etc.) lacking good sense or judgment; unwise. □ **fool·ish·ly** *adverb* **fool·ish·ness** *noun*

fool·proof *adjective* (of a procedure, mechanism, etc.) so straightforward or simple as to be incapable of misuse or mistake.

fools·cap /ˈfʊlskap, ˈfuːl-/ *noun* a type of legal-sized writing paper, usu. lined. [named from the former watermark representing a fool's cap]

fool's errand *noun* a fruitless venture.

fool's gold *noun* iron pyrites.

fool's paradise *noun* happiness founded on an illusion.

fool's parsley *noun* a poisonous, umbelliferous plant, *Aethusa cynapium*, resembling parsley.

foos·ball /ˈfuːsbɒl/ *noun* a game played using a table resembling a miniature soccer field, with toy players which can be made to 'kick' the ball by rotating rods extending from the sides. [representing the pronunciation of German *Fussball* football]

foot ● *noun* (*pl.* **feet**) **1 a** the lower extremity of the leg below the ankle. **b** the part of a sock etc. covering the foot. **2 a** the lower or lowest part of anything, e.g. a mountain, a page, stairs, etc. **b** the lower end of a table. **c** the end of a bed where the user's feet normally rest. **d** a part of a chair, appliance, etc. on which it rests. **3** the base, often projecting, of anything extending vertically. **4** a step, pace, or tread; a manner of walking (*fleet of foot*). **5** (*pl.* **feet** or **foot**) a unit of linear measure equal to 12 inches (30.48 cm). **6** *Prosody* **a** a group of syllables (one usu. stressed) constituting a metrical unit. **b** a similar unit of speech etc. **7** *Brit. hist.* infantry (*a regiment of foot*). **8** *Zool.* the locomotive or adhesive organ of invertebrates. **9** *Bot.* the part by which a petal is attached. **10** a device on a sewing machine for holding the material steady as it is sewn. **11** (*pl.* **foots**) **a** dregs; oil refuse. **b** coarse sugar. ● *transitive verb* **1** (usu. as **foot it**) a traverse (esp. a long distance) by foot. **b** dance. **2** pay (a bill). □ **at a person's feet** as a person's disciple or subject. **feet of clay** a fundamental weakness in a person otherwise revered. **get off on the wrong** (or **right**) **foot** make a bad (or good) start. **get one's feet wet** begin to participate. **have one's** (or **both**) **feet on the ground** be practical. **have a foot in the door** have a prospect of success. **have one foot in the grave** be near death or very old. **my foot!** *interjection* expressing strong contradiction. **not put a foot wrong** make no mistakes. **off one's feet** so as to be unable to stand, or in a state compared with this (*was rushed off my feet*). **on foot** walking, not driving or riding etc. **on one's feet 1** standing. **2** completely recovered from an illness or time of trouble. **3** in motion (*fast on one's feet; light on one's feet*). **put one's best foot forward** make every effort; proceed with determination. **put one's feet up** *informal* take a rest. **put one's foot down** *informal* **1** be firmly insistent or repressive. **2** accelerate a motor vehicle. **put one's foot in one's mouth** (also **put one's foot in it**) *informal* commit a blunder or indiscretion. **set foot in** (or **on**) enter; go into. **think on one's feet** think or react rapidly under stress etc. **under foot 1** on the ground. **2** in the way. □ **foot·ed** *adjective* (also in *combination*). **foot·less** *adjective* [Old English *fōt* from Germanic]

foot·age *noun* **1** length or distance in feet. **2** an amount of film made for showing, broadcasting, etc.

foot-and-mouth disease *noun* a contagious viral disease of cattle etc., characterized by ulceration of the hoofs and around the mouth.

foot·ball ● *noun* **1** any of several games in which each of two teams attempts to move a ball across the other's goal line, esp.: **a** *Cdn* = CANADIAN FOOTBALL. **b** *US* = AMERICAN FOOTBALL. **c** *Brit.* = SOCCER. **2** a large inflated ball of a kind used in these. **3** a topical issue or problem that is the subject of continued argument or controversy. ● *intransitive verb* play football. □ **foot·ball·er** *noun*

football pools *plural noun Brit.* an organized nationwide gambling pool on the results of professional soccer games, conducted principally by mail.

foot·bath *noun* **1** an act of washing the feet. **2** a small shallow bath used for this. **3** a preparation added to the water for this.

foot·bed *noun* an insole in a boot, shoe, skate, etc., used for cushioning or to provide a better fit.

foot·board *noun* **1** a board to support the feet or a foot. **2** an upright board at the foot of a bed.

foot·bridge *noun* a bridge for use by pedestrians.

foot-dragging *noun* deliberate slowness or reluctance to act or proceed. □ **foot-dragger** *noun*

foot·er *noun* **1** (in *combination*) a person or thing of so many feet in length or height (*six-footer*). **2** a line or block of text appearing at the foot of each page of a document etc. (*compare* HEADER 3).

foot·fall *noun* the sound of a footstep.

foot-fault *noun* (in tennis etc.) incorrect placement of the feet while serving.

foot·gear *noun* = FOOTWEAR.

foot guard *noun* (often in *pl.*) (usu. **Foot Guard**) (in Canada and the UK) an infantry soldier with a special guarding function, e.g. the Governor General's Foot Guards, who act as ceremonial guards at the Governor General's residence and the Parliament Buildings.

foot·hill *noun* (often in *pl.*) any of the low hills at the base of a mountain or mountain range.

foot·hold *noun* **1** a place, esp. in climbing, where a foot can be supported securely. **2** a secure initial position or advantage.

foot·ing *noun* **1** a foothold; a secure position (*lost her footing*). **2** the basis on which an enterprise is established or operates; the position or status of a person in relation to others (*on an equal footing*). **3** (usu. in *pl.*) the part of a foundation resting directly on the earth.

foot-in-mouth disease *noun jocular* a tendency to put one's foot in one's mouth; indiscretion.

foo·tle /ˈfuːtəl/ *intransitive verb* (usu. foll. by *about*) *informal* behave foolishly or trivially. [19th c.: perhaps from dial. *footer* idle]

foot·lights *plural noun* a row of lights along the front of a stage at the level of the performers' feet.

foot·ling /ˈfuːtlɪŋ/ *adjective informal* trivial, silly.

foot·lock·er *noun N Amer.* a small chest or trunk, esp. one kept at the foot of a bed.

foot-long *noun* a wiener or hot dog containing one which is about a foot long.

foot·loose *adjective* (often in phr. **footloose and fancy-free**) free to go where or act as one pleases.

foot·man *noun* (*pl.* **-men**) **1** a liveried servant attending at the door, at table, or on a carriage. **2** *hist.* an infantryman.

foot·mark *noun* a footprint.

foot·note ● *noun* **1** a note printed at the foot of a page referring to a marked part of the text on the page. **2** an event, comment, etc. that is added or subordinated to something more central or important (*a footnote to history*). ● *transitive verb* supply with a footnote or footnotes.

foot·pad *noun* **1** *hist.* an unmounted highwayman. **2** one of the pads on the sole of an animal's foot.

foot passenger *noun* a passenger on a ferry who is not travelling with a car, bus, etc.

foot·path *noun* **1** a path for walking along through woods, fields, etc. **2** *Brit.* a path for pedestrians, esp. an alley between buildings or a sidewalk.

foot·plate *noun* esp. *Brit.* the platform in the cab of a locomotive for the crew.

foot-pound *noun* (*pl.* **foot-pounds**) the amount of energy required to raise 1 lb. a distance of 1 foot.

foot-pound-second *adjective* of or relating to a system of measurement with these as basic units. Abbr.: **fps**.

foot·print *noun* **1** the impression left by a foot or shoe. **2** the area over which an aircraft is audible, a broadcast can be received, etc. **3** the surface area taken up by something, such as a computer, vehicle, etc.

foot race *noun* a race run between competitors on foot.

foot·rest *noun* a support for the feet or a foot.

foot rot *noun* a bacterial disease of the feet in sheep and cattle.

Foot·sie *noun* (in the UK) *informal* the Financial Times–Stock Exchange 100 share index (based on the share values of Britain's hundred largest public companies). [fanciful acronym, influenced by FOOTSIE]

foot·sie *noun informal* □ **play footsie with a person** touch or caress a person's feet lightly with one's own feet, usu. under a table, as a playful expression of affection or sexual interest. [jocular diminutive of FOOT]

foot·slog *intransitive verb* (**-slogged**, **-slog·ging**) walk or march, esp. laboriously for a long distance. □ **foot·slog·ger** *noun*

foot soldier *noun* **1** a soldier who fights on foot; an infantry soldier. **2** a person who works for a cause at the basic level rather than in the leadership.

foot·sore *adjective* having sore feet, esp. from walking.

foot·stalk *noun* **1** *Bot.* a stalk of a leaf or peduncle of a flower. **2** *Zool.* an attachment of a barnacle etc.

foot·step *noun* **1** a step taken in walking. **2** the sound of this. **3** a footprint. □ **follow** (or **tread**) **in a person's footsteps** do as another person did before.

foot·stool *noun* a stool for resting the feet on when sitting.

foot-tapping *adjective* having or creating a strong rhythmical musical beat (*foot-tapping gospel hymns*).

foot traffic *noun* **1** passage of people on foot over an area (*the carpet can withstand heavy foot traffic*). **2** pedestrians who patronize a business.

foot·way *noun Brit.* a path or way for pedestrians.

foot·wear *noun* anything worn on the feet, e.g. shoes, boots, etc.

foot·well *noun* a space for the feet in front of a seat in a car etc. [FOOT + WELL² (in the sense 'a depression in the floor')]

foot·work *noun* the use of the feet, esp. skilfully, in sports, dancing, etc.

foo yong /fuː ˈjɒŋ/ *noun* a Chinese dish or sauce made with eggs mixed and cooked with other ingredients. [Cantonese *foō yung*, lit. 'hibiscus']

fop *noun* an affectedly elegant or fashionable man; a dandy. □ **fop·pery** *noun* (*pl.* **-ies**). **fop·pish** *adjective* **fop·pish·ly** *adverb* **fop·pish·ness** *noun* [17th c.: perhaps from earlier *fop* fool]

for ● *preposition* **1** in the interest or to the benefit of; intended to go to (*these flowers are for you*; *wish to see it for myself*; *did it all for my country*; *silly for you to go*). **2** in defence, support, or favour of (*fight for one's rights*). **3** suitable or appropriate to (*a dance for beginners*; *not for me to say*). **4** with reference to; regarding; so far as concerns (*usual for ties to be worn*; *don't care for him at all*; *ready for bed*; *MP for Winnipeg North*). **5** representing or in place of (*here for my uncle*). **6** in exchange against (*swapped it for a bigger one*). **7 a** as the price of (*give me $5 for it*). **b** at the price of (*bought it for $20*). **c** to the amount of (*a bill for $100*). **8** as the penalty of (*fined them heavily for it*). **9** in requital of (*that's for upsetting my sister*). **10** as a reward for (*here's $10 for your trouble*). **11 a** with a view to; in the hope or quest of; in order to get (*go for a walk*; *run for a doctor*; *did it for the money*). **b** on account of (*could not speak for laughing*). **12** corresponding to (*word for word*). **13** to reach; in the direction of; towards (*left for Fredericton*; *ran for the end of the road*). **14** in order to achieve (*take the pills for a sound night's sleep*). **15** so as to start promptly at (*the meeting is at seven-thirty for eight*). **16** through or over (a distance or period); during (*walked for miles*; *sang for two hours*). **17** in the character of; as being (*for the last time*; *know it for a lie*; *I for one refuse*). **18** because of; on account of (*could not see for tears*). **19** in spite of; notwithstanding (*for all we know*; *for all your fine words*). **20** considering or making due allowance with regard to (*good for a beginner*). **21** in order to be (*gone for a soldier*). ● *conjunction* because, since, seeing that. □ **be for it** *Brit. informal* be in imminent danger of punishment or other trouble. **o** (or **oh**) **for** I wish I had. [Old English, prob. a reduction of Germanic *fora* (unrecorded) BEFORE (of place and time)]

for- *prefix* forming verbs and their derivatives meaning: **1** away, off, apart (*forget*; *forgive*). **2** prohibition (*forbid*). **3** abstention or neglect (*forgo*; *forsake*). **4** excess or intensity (*forlorn*). [Old English *for-*, *fær-*]

for·age /ˈfɒrədʒ, ˈfɒr-/ ● *noun* **1** food for horses, cattle, etc., esp. hay or grass. **2** the act or an instance of searching for food. ● *verb* **1** *intransitive* go searching; rummage (esp. for food). **2** *transitive* collect food from; ravage. **3** *transitive* **a** get (*here for my uncle*). **b** supply with food. □ **for·ager** *noun* [Old French *fourrage*, *fourrager*, related to FODDER]

forage cap *noun* a peaked cap forming part of a soldier's uniform.

forage fish *noun* a fish that is of interest to humans mainly as food for other fish.

fo·ra·men /fəˈreimen/ *noun* (*pl.* **fo·ra·mi·na** /-ˈramɪnə/ or **fo·ra·mens**) *Anat.* an opening, hole, or passage, esp. in a bone. □ **fo·ram·in·ate** /-ˈramɪnət/ *adjective* [Latin *foramen -minis* from *forare* bore a hole]

foramen magnum /ˈmagnəm/ *noun Anat.* the hole in the base of the skull through which the spinal cord passes. [Latin, = large opening]

fora·mini·fer /ˌfɒrəˈmɪnɪfər/ *noun* (also **fora·mi·nif·er·an** /-ˈnɪfərən/) any protozoan of the order Foraminifera, having a perforated shell through which amoeba-like pseudopodia emerge. □ **fora·mi·nif·er·ous** /-ˈnɪfərəs/ *adjective*

fora·mi·nif·er·an (*pl.* **-fera**) *var.* of FORAMINIFER.

for·as·much as *conjunction archaic* because, since. [= for as much]

Vowels: a cat ɑ arm e bed ɜr her ɜː deux ə ago ɪ sit i cosy iː feed ɒ hot ɔ pore ɔː no ʌ run ʊ put

for·ay /ˈfɔreɪ/ ● *noun* **1** a sudden attack; a raid or incursion. **2** a brief, vigorous attempt to be involved in a different activity, profession, etc. (*made a brief foray into computer science*). ● *intransitive verb* make or go on a foray. [Middle English, prob. earlier as verb: back-formation from *forayer* from Old French *forrier* forager, related to FODDER]

forb *noun* any herbaceous plant other than a grass. [Greek *phorbē* 'fodder, forage', from *ferbein* 'to feed']

for·bade past of FORBID.

for·bear¹ *transitive & intransitive verb* (*past* **for·bore**; *past participle* **for·borne**) (often foll. by *from*, or *to* + infin.) *literary* abstain or desist (from) (*could not forbear (from) speaking out; forbore to mention it*). [Old English *forberan* (as FOR-, BEAR¹)]

for·bear² *var. of* FOREBEAR.

for·bear·ance *noun* patient self-control; tolerance.

Forbes, Mount a peak (3 612 m) in the Rocky Mountains of W Alberta, northwest of Lake Louise. [E. *Forbes*, British naturalist d.1854]

for·bid *transitive verb* (**for·bid·ding**; *past* **for·bade** /-ˈbeɪd, -ˈbad/; *past participle* **for·bid·den**) **1** (foll. by *to* + infin.) order not (*I forbid you to go*). **2** refuse to allow (a thing, or a person to have a thing) (*I forbid it; was forbidden any wine*). **3** refuse a person entry to (*the gardens are forbidden to children*). □ **God** (or **heaven**) **forbid** (sometimes foll. by *that* + clause) may it not happen! □ **for·bid·den** *adjective* [Old English *forbēodan* (as FOR-, BID)]

Forbidden City 1 see LHASA¹. **2** see BEIJING.

forbidden fruit *noun* something desired or enjoyed all the more because not allowed. [from the fruit of the tree forbidden to Adam and Eve in the garden of Eden (Gen. 2:17)]

for·bid·ding *adjective* uninviting, repellent, stern. □ **for·bid·ding·ly** *adverb*

for·bore past of FORBEAR¹.

for·borne *past participle of* FORBEAR¹.

force ● *noun* **1** power; exerted strength or impetus; intense effort. **2** coercion or compulsion, esp. with the use or threat of violence. **3 a** military strength. **b** (in *pl.*) troops; fighting resources. **c** (**Forces**) = CANADIAN FORCES (also *attributive*: *Forces lawyer*). **d** an organized body of people, esp. soldiers, police, or workers. **4** binding power; validity. **5** effect; precise significance (*the force of their words*). **6 a** mental or moral strength; influence, efficacy (*force of habit*). **b** vividness of effect (*described with much force*). **7** *Physics* **a** an influence tending to cause the motion of a body. **b** the intensity of this equal to the mass of the body and its acceleration. **8** a person or thing regarded as exerting influence (*is a force for good*). **9** *Baseball* = FORCEOUT. ● *verb* **1** *transitive* constrain (a person) by force or against his or her will. **2** *transitive* make a way through or into by force; break open by force. **3** *transitive* (usu. with prep. or adv.) drive or propel violently or against resistance (*forced it into the hole; the wind forced them back*). **4** *transitive* (foll. by *on*, *upon*) impose or press (on a person) (*forced their views on us*). **5** *transitive* **a** cause or produce by effort (*forced a smile*). **b** attain by strength or effort (*forced an entry; must force a decision*). **c** make (a way) by force. **6** *transitive* strain or increase to the utmost; overstrain. **7** *transitive* artificially hasten the development or maturity of (a plant). **8** *transitive* seek or demand quick results from; accelerate the process of (*force the pace*). **9** *reflexive* rape (*forced himself on her*). **10** *transitive* *Baseball* **a** cause (a runner) to be put out in a forceout. **b** cause (a runner or run) to score or be scored, esp. by walking a batter with the bases full. **11** *transitive* *Cards* **a** compel (a player) to trump or reveal the strength of a hand. **b** compel a player to play (a certain card). ● **by force of** by means of. **force the bidding** (at an auction) make bids to raise the price rapidly. **force a person's hand** make a person act prematurely or unwillingly. **force the issue** render an immediate decision necessary. **in force 1** valid, effective. **2** in great strength or numbers. **join forces** combine efforts. □ **force·able** *adjective* **force·ably** *adverb* **for·cer** *noun* [Old French *force*, *forcer*, ultimately from Latin *fortis* strong]

forced *adjective* **1** compelled, imposed, or obtained by force; compulsory (*forced labour; a forced march*). **2** produced or maintained with effort; strained, unnatural (*a forced smile*). **3** required by emergency or necessity (*a forced landing*). **4** produced or supplied by artificial means (*forced air*). **5** (of a plant, crop, etc.) made to bear, or produced, out of the proper season.

forced landing *noun* the unavoidable landing of an aircraft in an emergency. □ **force-land** *transitive & intransitive verb*

force-feed *transitive verb* (*past* and *past participle* **-fed**) **1** force (a person or animal) to take food. **2** compel (a person) to absorb or assimilate propaganda, opinions, etc.

force feedback *noun* *Computing* the simulating of physical attributes such as weight in virtual reality, allowing the user to interact directly with virtual objects using touch.

force field *noun* (in science fiction) an invisible barrier of force.

force·ful *adjective* **1** vigorous, powerful. **2** (of speech) compelling, impressive. □ **force·ful·ly** *adverb* **force·ful·ness** *noun*

force ma·jeure /ˌfɔrs maˈʒɜːr/ *noun* **1** irresistible compulsion or coercion. **2** an unforeseeable course of events excusing a person from the fulfillment of a contract. [French, = superior strength]

force·meat *noun* meat or vegetables etc. chopped and seasoned for use as a stuffing or a garnish. [obsolete *force*, *farce* stuff, from Old French *farsir*: see FARCE]

force·out *noun* *Baseball* (also **force play**) a play in which a runner is put out after being forced (by another runner) to advance when he or she is unable to do so safely.

for·ceps /ˈfɔrseps/ *noun* (*pl.* same) **1** surgical pincers, used for grasping and holding. **2** *Bot. & Zool.* an organ or structure resembling forceps. [Latin *forceps forcipis*]

for·cible /ˈfɔrsəbəl/ *adjective* **1** done by or involving force (*forcible confinement*). **2** forceful. □ **for·cibly** *adverb*

Ford ▸ 1 Ford Madox (pseudonym of Ford Hermann Hueffer) (1873–1939), English novelist, editor, and critic, chiefly remembered as the author of the novel *The Good Soldier* (1915) and the tetralogy *Parade's End* (1924–28). **2 Ger·ald Ru·dolph**, US Republican politician, 38th president of the US 1974–77. Vice-President (1973–4), he became president on the resignation of Richard Nixon in the wake of the Watergate affair. **3 Glenn** (born Gwyllyn Samuel Newton Ford) (b.1916), Canadian-born US actor, whose films include *The Big Heat* (1953), and *The Blackboard Jungle* (1955). **4 Har·ri·son** (b.1942), US actor, who became internationally famous with his leading roles in the science fiction film *Star Wars* (1977) and its two sequels, and in the adventure film *Raiders of the Lost Ark* (1981) and its two sequels; other films include *Witness* (1985). **5 Henry** (1863–1947), US industrialist, car designer, and manufacturer. He founded the automobile firm named after him in 1903 and pioneered assembly-line mass production, producing 15 million copies of his famous Model T between 1908 and 1927; he also endowed the Ford Foundation, a major charitable trust. **6 John** (1586–c.1639), English dramatist, noted for his revenge tragedies such as *'Tis Pity She's a Whore* (1633) and *Perkin Warbeck* (1634). **7 John** (born Sean O'Feeney) (1895–1973), US film director. He is chiefly known for his westerns, which include *Stagecoach* (1939) and *Rio Grande* (1950); other notable films include *The Grapes of Wrath* (1940) and *How Green Was My Valley* (1941).

ford ● *noun* a shallow place where a river or stream may be crossed by wading or in a vehicle. ● *transitive verb* cross (water) at a ford. □ **ford·able** *adjective* [Old English from West Germanic]

Ford·ism *noun* the use in manufacturing industry of the methods pioneered by Henry Ford, typified by large-scale mechanized mass production. □ **Ford·ist** *adjective*

fore ● *adjective* situated in front. ● *noun* the front part, esp. of a ship; the bow. ● *interjection* *Golf* a warning to a person in the path of a ball. □ **come to the fore** take a leading part. **to the fore** in front; conspicuous. [Old English from Germanic]

fore- *prefix* forming: **1** verbs meaning: **a** in front (*foreshorten*). **b** beforehand; in advance (*beforedain; forewarn*). **2** nouns meaning: **a** situated in front of (*forecourt*). **b** the front part of (*forehead*). **c** of or near the bow of a ship (*forecastle*). **d** preceding (*forerunner*).

fore and aft ● *adverb* at both front and rear; going from front to rear. ● *adjective* (**fore-and-aft**) **1** (of a sail or rigging) set lengthwise, not on the yards. **2** backwards and forwards. **3** *N Amer.* (*BC & US Northwest*) designating a logging road constructed of logs laid end to end.

fore-and-aft rigged *adjective* (of a vessel) having fore-and-aft rigging (opp. SQUARE-RIGGED).

fore·arm¹ *noun* **1** the part of the arm from the elbow to the wrist or the fingertips. **2** the corresponding part in a foreleg or wing.

fore·arm² /fɔrˈɑrm/ *transitive verb* prepare or arm beforehand.

fore·bear *noun* (also **for·bear**) (usu. in *pl.*) an ancestor. [FORE + obsolete *bear*, *beer* (as BE, -ER¹)]

fore·bode *transitive verb* **1** betoken; be an advance warning of (an evil or unwelcome event). **2** have a presentiment of (usu. evil).

fore·bod·ing ● *noun* an expectation of trouble or evil; a presage or omen. ● *adjective* threatening, esp. evil. □ **fore·bod·ing·ly** *adverb*

fore·brain *noun* the anterior part of the brain, including the cerebrum, thalamus, and hypothalamus.

fore·cast ● *transitive verb* (*past* and *past participle* **-cast** or **-casted**) predict; estimate or calculate beforehand. ● *noun* a calculation or estimate of something future, esp. coming weather. □ **fore·cast·er** *noun*

fore·cast·ing *noun* the art or practice of predicting, esp. the weather.

fore·castle /ˈfoːksəl/ *noun* (also **fo'c'sle**) *Naut.* **1** the forward part of a ship where the crew has quarters. **2** *hist.* a short raised deck at the bow.

fore·check *intransitive verb Hockey* (of a player or team) attempt to gain control of the puck by attacking aggressively in the opposing side's defensive zone before it can organize an attack. □ **fore·check·er** *noun* **fore·check·ing** *noun*

fore·close *verb* **1** *transitive & intransitive* (foll. by *on*) stop (a mortgage) from being redeemable or (a mortgagor) from redeeming, esp. as a result of defaults in payment. **2** *transitive* exclude, prevent. **3** *transitive* shut out; bar. □ **fore·clos·ure** *noun* [Old French *forclos* past participle of *forclore* from *for-* out, from Latin *foras* + CLOSE²]

fore·court *noun* **1** an enclosed space in front of a building. **2** *Tennis* the part of a tennis court between the service line and the net.

fore·deck *noun* **1** the deck at the forward part of a ship. **2** the forward part of the deck.

fore·doom *transitive verb* (often foll. by *to*) doom or condemn beforehand.

fore·father *noun* (usu. in *pl.*) **1** an ancestor. **2** a member of a past generation of a family or people.

fore·finger *noun* the finger next to the thumb.

fore·foot *noun* (*pl.* **-feet**) **1** either of the front feet of a four-footed animal. **2** the front part of the human foot. **3** *Naut.* the foremost section of a ship's keel.

fore·front *noun* **1** the foremost part. **2** the leading position.

fore·gather *intransitive verb* (also **for·gather**) assemble; meet together; associate. [16th-c. Scots from Dutch *vergaderen*, assimilated to FOR-, GATHER]

fore·go¹ *transitive & intransitive verb* (**-goes**; *past* **-went**; *past participle* **-gone**) precede in place or time. [Old English *foregān*]

fore·go² *var. of* FORGO.

fore·go·ing *adjective* preceding; previously mentioned.

fore·gone ● *verb past participle of* FOREGO¹. ● *attributive adjective* previous, preceding, completed.

foregone conclusion *noun* an easily foreseen or predictable result.

fore·ground ● *noun* **1** the part of a view, esp. in a picture, that is nearest the observer. **2** the most conspicuous position. ● *transitive verb* place in the foreground; make prominent.

fore·hand *noun* **1** *Tennis etc.* **a** a stroke played with the palm of the hand facing the opponent. **b** (*attributive*) (also **fore·hand·ed**) of or made with a forehand. **2** the part of a horse in front of the seated rider.

fore·head *noun* the part of the face above the eyebrows.

for·eign /ˈfɔrən, ˈforən/ *adjective* **1** of or from or situated in or characteristic of a country or a language other than one's own. **2** dealing with other countries (*foreign service*). **3** of another district, society, etc. **4** (often foll. by *to*) unfamiliar, strange, uncharacteristic (*her behaviour is foreign to me*). **5** coming from outside (*a foreign body lodged in my eye*). □ **foreign·ness** *noun* [Old French *forein*, *forain*, ultimately from Latin *foras*, *-is* outside: for *-g-* compare *sovereign*]

foreign affairs *plural noun* the activities and interests of a nation that involve its relations with other nations.

foreign aid *noun* money, food, etc. given or lent by one country to another.

Foreign and Commonwealth Office *noun* (in the UK) the government department dealing with foreign affairs.

for·eign·er *noun* **1** a person born in or coming from a foreign country or place. **2** *dialect* a non-native of a place. **3 a** a foreign ship. **b** an imported animal or article.

foreign exchange *noun* **1** the currency of other countries. **2** dealings in these.

foreign-going *adjective* (of a ship) used for overseas trade.

foreign legion *noun* a body of foreign volunteers in a modern, esp. the French, army.

foreign minister *noun* (also **foreign secretary**) esp. *Brit.* a government minister in charge of his or her country's relations with other countries.

Foreign Office *noun Brit.* = FOREIGN AND COMMONWEALTH OFFICE.

foreign service *noun N Amer.* = DIPLOMATIC SERVICE.

foreign trade *noun* international trade.

fore·judge *transitive verb* judge or determine before knowing the evidence.

fore·know *transitive verb* (*past* **-knew**; *past participle* **-known**) know beforehand; have prescience of. □ **fore·know·able** *adjective* **fore·know·ledge** *noun*

fore·land *noun* **1** a cape or promontory. **2** a piece of land in front of something.

fore·leg *noun* each of the front legs of a quadruped.

fore·limb *noun* any of the front limbs of an animal.

fore·lock *noun* a lock of hair growing just above the forehead. □ **touch** (or **tug** etc.) **one's forelock** defer to a person of higher social rank.

Fore·man, George (b.1948), US boxer, who was the world heavyweight boxing champion (1973–74).

fore·man *noun* (*pl.* **-men**) **1** a worker with supervisory responsibilities. **2** the member of a jury who presides over its deliberations and speaks on its behalf.

fore·mast *noun* the forward (lower) mast of a ship.

fore·most ● *adjective* **1** the chief or most notable. **2** the most advanced in position; the front. ● *adverb* before anything else in position; in the first place (*first and foremost*). [earlier *formost*, *formest*, superlative of Old English *forma* first, assimilated to FORE, MOST]

fore·mother *noun* (usu. in *pl.*) a female ancestor or predecessor.

fore·name *noun* a first name.

fore·noon *noun* esp. *N Amer.* the part of the day before noon; the morning.

for·en·sic /fəˈrenzɪk/ ● *adjective* **1** of or used in connection with courts of law, esp. in relation to crime detection (*forensic evidence*). **2** of or employing forensic science. ● *noun* (usu. in *pl.*) **1** forensic science. **2** a forensic science department, esp. as part of a police force. □ **for·en·sic·al·ly** *adverb* [Latin *forensis* from FORUM]

forensic accounting *noun* the use of accounting skills to investigate fraud, embezzlement, etc. and to prepare an analysis of financial information suitable for use in litigation. □ **forensic accountant** *noun*

forensic medicine *noun* the application of medical knowledge to legal problems.

forensic science *noun* the application of biochemical and other scientific techniques to the investigation of crime.

fore·ordain *transitive verb* predestinate; ordain beforehand. □ **fore·ordi·na·tion** *noun*

fore·part *noun* the foremost part; the front.

fore·paw *noun* either of the front paws of a quadruped.

fore·peak *noun Naut.* the front end of a hold or cabin in the angle of the bows of a ship.

fore·person *noun* **1** a worker with supervisory responsibilities. **2** the member of a jury who presides over its deliberations and speaks on its behalf.

fore·play *noun* stimulation preceding sexual intercourse.

fore·quarters *plural noun* the front legs and adjoining parts of a quadruped.

fore·run *transitive verb* (**-run·ning**; *past* **-ran**; *past participle* **-run**) **1** go before. **2** indicate the coming of; foreshadow.

fore·run·ner *noun* **1** a predecessor. **2** an advance messenger.

fore·sail /ˈfɔrseil, -səl/ *noun Naut.* the principal sail on a foremast (the lowest square sail, or the fore-and-aft bent on the mast, or the triangular before the mast).

fore·see *transitive verb* (*past* **-saw**; *past participle* **-seen**) (often foll. by *that* + *clause*) see or be aware of beforehand. □ **fore·see·able** *adjective* **fore·see·ably** *adverb* **fore·see·abil·ity** *noun* **fore·seer** *noun*

fore·shadow *transitive verb* be a warning or indication of (a future event). □ **fore·shadow·ing** *noun*

fore·sheets *plural noun Naut.* the inner part of the bows of a boat with gratings for the bowman to stand on.

fore·shock *noun* a lesser shock preceding the main shock of an earthquake.

fore·shore *noun* the part of the shore between high- and low-water marks, or between the water and cultivated or developed land.

fore·short·en *transitive verb* show or portray (an object) with the apparent shortening due to visual perspective. □ **fore·short·en·ing** *noun*

fore·show *transitive verb* (*past participle* **-shown**) **1** foretell. **2** foreshadow, portend, prefigure.

Consonants:　b *but*　　d *dog*　f *few*　g *get*　h *her*　j *yes*　k *cat*　l *leg*　m *man*　　n *no*　　p *pen*　r *red*　s *sit*

fore·sight *noun* **1** regard or provision for the future. **2** the process of foreseeing. **3** the front sight of a gun. **4** *Surveying* a sight taken forwards. □ **fore·sight·ed** *adjective* **fore·sight·ed·ly** *adverb* **fore·sight·ed·ness** *noun* **fore·sight·ful** *adjective*

fore·skin *noun* the fold of skin covering the end of the penis. *Also called* PREPUCE.

for·est ● *noun* **1 a** a large area covered chiefly with trees and undergrowth. **b** the trees growing in such an area. **2** *Brit. hist.* an area usu. owned by the sovereign and kept for hunting. **3** a large number or dense mass of vertical objects (*a forest of tall buildings*). ● *transitive verb* **1** plant with trees. **2** convert into a forest. □ **not see the forest for the trees** be unable to perceive or understand the overall situation because one is preoccupied with details. □ **for·est·ed** *adjective*

forest·land *noun* [Old French from Late Latin *forestis silva* wood outside the walls of a park, from Latin *foris* outside]

fore·stall /fɔrˈstɔl/ *transitive verb* **1** act in advance of in order to prevent. **2** anticipate (the action of another, or an event). [Old English *foresteall* an ambush (as FORE-, STALL¹)]

fore·stay *noun Naut.* a stay from the head of the foremast to the ship's deck to support the foremast.

Forest City an informal name for London, Ontario. [because it was heavily forested when first settled]

For·est·er, Cecil Scott (pseudonym of Cecil Lewis Troughton Smith) (1899–1966), English novelist, remembered for his 12 seafaring novels set during the Napoleonic Wars and featuring Captain Horatio Hornblower; his other works include *The African Queen* (1935).

for·est·er *noun* **1** a person in charge of a forest or skilled in forestry. **2** a person or animal living in a forest. **3** (**Forester**) a member of the Independent Order of Foresters, a fraternal organization.

forest fire *noun* an uncontrolled fire in a forest.

forest floor *noun* the ground in a forest, specifically the layer of more or less decayed organic debris forming the upper soil of a forest.

forest green ● *noun* a dark green colour. ● *adjective* of this colour.

forest ranger *noun esp. N Amer.* an official who patrols, manages, and protects a public forest.

for·est·ry *noun* the science and practice of planting, caring for, and managing forests.

forest tree *noun* a large tree suitable for a forest.

fore·taste *noun* a small experience of something before it actually happens; a sample in anticipation.

fore·tell *transitive verb* (*past* and *past participle* **-told**) tell of or presage (an event etc.) before it takes place; predict, prophesy.

fore·thought *noun* **1** care or provision for the future. **2** previous thinking or devising.

fore·token ● *noun* a sign of something to come. ● *transitive verb* portend; indicate beforehand.

fore·told *past* and *past participle of* FORETELL.

fore·top *noun Naut.* a platform at the top of a foremast (*see* TOP¹ *noun* 12).

fore-topmast *noun Naut.* the second section of a sailing ship's foremast.

fore-topsail /fɔrˈtɒpseil, -səl/ *noun* the sail above a sailing ship's foresail.

for·ever ● *adverb* **1** for all future time; in perpetuity. **2** continually, persistently (*is forever complaining*). **3** *informal* for an extremely long time (*talked on the phone forever*). ● *noun informal* an extremely long time (*it takes him forever to get dressed*).

for·ever·more *adverb* an emphatic form of FOREVER *adverb* 1.

fore·warn *transitive verb* warn beforehand.

fore·went *past of* FOREGO¹, ².

fore·wing *noun* either of the two front wings of a four-winged insect.

fore·woman *noun* (*pl.* **-women**) **1** a female worker with supervisory responsibilities. **2** a woman who presides over a jury's deliberations and speaks on its behalf.

fore·word *noun* introductory remarks at the beginning of a book, often by a person other than the author.

forex *noun* foreign exchange.

fore·yard *noun Naut.* the lowest yard on a foremast.

for·feit /ˈfɔrfət/ ● *noun* **1** a penalty for a breach of contract or neglect; a fine. **2 a** a trivial fine for a breach of rules in clubs etc. or in games. **b** (*in pl.*) a game in which forfeits are exacted. **3** something surrendered as a penalty. **4** the process of forfeiting. **5** *Law* property or a right or privilege lost as a legal penalty. ● *adjective* lost or surrendered

as a penalty. ● *transitive verb* (**for·feit·ed, for·feit·ing**) lose the right to, be deprived of, or have to pay as a penalty (*forfeited their deposit*; *had to forfeit the game because they didn't have enough players*). □ **for·feit·able** *adjective* **for·feit·er** *noun* **for·feit·ure** *noun* [Middle English (= crime) from Old French *forfet*, *forfait* past participle of *forfaire* transgress (from Latin *foris* outside) + *faire* from Latin *facere* do]

for·fend /fɔrˈfend/ *transitive verb literary* avert; keep off; prevent (*Heaven forfend!*).

for·gather *var. of* FOREGATHER.

for·gave *past of* FORGIVE.

forge¹ ● *transitive verb* **1 a** write (a document or signature) in order to pass it off as written by another. **b** *Brit.* make (money etc.) in fraudulent imitation. **2** create or devise (an alliance, bond, etc.) **3** shape (esp. metal) by heating in a fire and hammering. ● *noun* **1** a blacksmith's workshop; a smithy. **2** a furnace or hearth for melting or refining metal. □ **forge·able** *adjective* **for·ger** *noun* [Old French *forge* (n.), *forger* (v.) from Latin *fabricare* FABRICATE]

forge² *intransitive verb* move forward gradually or steadily. □ **forge ahead 1** take the lead in a race. **2** move forward or make progress rapidly. [18th c.: perhaps an aberrant pronunciation of FORCE]

for·gery *noun* (*pl.* **-ies**) **1 a** the act or an instance of forging, counterfeiting, or falsifying a document etc. **b** the crime of forgery. **2** a forged or spurious thing, esp. a document or signature.

for·get *verb* (**for·get·ting**; *past* **for·got**; *past participle* **for·got·ten**) **1** *transitive & intransitive* lose the remembrance of; not remember (a person or thing). **2** *transitive* (foll. by clause or to + infin.) not remember; neglect (*forgot to come*; *forgot how to do it*). **3** *transitive* inadvertently omit to bring or mention or attend to. **4** *transitive & intransitive* put out of mind; cease to think of (*forgive and forget*). □ **forget** (**about**) **it!** *informal* take no more notice of it; there is no need for apology or thanks. **forget oneself 1** neglect one's own interests. **2** act unbecomingly or unworthily. □ **for·get·table** *adjective* [Old English *forgietan* from West Germanic (as FOR-, GET)]

for·get·ful *adjective* **1** apt to forget; absent-minded. **2** (often foll. by *of*) forgetting, neglectful. □ **for·get·ful·ly** *adverb* **for·get·ful·ness** *noun*

forget-me-not *noun* **1** any plant of the genus *Myosotis*, esp. *M. sylvatica* with small yellow-eyed bright blue flowers. **2** *N Amer.* any of several plants of the Rocky Mountains of the genus *Eritrichium* of the borage family.

for·ging *noun* **1** an act or instance of forging (*see* FORGE¹). **2** the process of forging metal. **3** a product of forging; a forged piece of metal etc.

for·give *transitive & intransitive verb* (*past* **for·gave**; *past participle* **for·given**) **1** cease to feel angry or resentful towards; pardon (an offender or offence). **2** remit or let off (a debt or debtor). □ **for·giv·able** *adjective* **for·giv·ably** *adverb* [Old English *forgiefan* (as FOR-, GIVE)]

for·give·ness *noun* **1** the act of forgiving; the state of being forgiven. **2** readiness to forgive.

for·giv·ing *adjective* **1** inclined readily to forgive. **2** tolerant; accepting of differences in ability etc. (*an aerobics class that is forgiving of beginners*). □ **for·giv·ing·ly** *adverb*

forgo *transitive verb* (also **fore·go**) (**-goes**) *past* **-went**; *past participle* **-gone**) **1** abstain from; go without; relinquish. **2** omit or decline to take or use (a pleasure, advantage, etc.). [Old English *forgān* (as FOR-, GO¹)]

for·got *past of* FORGET.

for·got·ten *past participle of* FORGET.

Foril·lon National Park /fɔriˈjõ/ a small park in E Quebec, situated at the tip of the Gaspé Peninsula, north of the town of Gaspé. [French *forillon* rocky point]

for·int /ˈfɔrint/ *noun* the chief monetary unit of Hungary. [Magyar from Italian *fiorino*: see FLORIN]

fork ● *noun* **1** a (usu. metal) implement with two or more prongs used for holding food while it is cut, conveying food to the mouth or plate, and as a cooking utensil. **2** a similar much larger instrument used for digging, lifting, etc. **3** any pronged device or component (*tuning fork*). **4** a forked support for a bicycle wheel. **5 a** a divergence of anything, e.g. a stick or road, or *N Amer.* a river, into two parts. **b** the place where this occurs. **c** either of the two parts (*take the left fork*). **d** *N Amer.* a major tributary of a river. **e** *N Amer.* (*in pl.*) the confluence of two rivers and the surrounding area (*the forks of the Red and the Assiniboine*). **6** a flash of forked lightning. **7** *Chess* a simultaneous attack on two pieces by one. ● *verb* **1** *intransitive* form a fork or branch by separating into two parts. **2** *intransitive* take one or other road etc. at a fork. **3** *transitive* dig or lift etc. with a fork. **4** *transitive Chess* attack (two pieces) simultaneously with one. □ **fork out** (or **up**) *informal* hand over or pay, usu. reluctantly. **fork over 1** *informal* = FORK OUT. **2** turn over (soil etc.) with a fork. □ **fork·ful** *noun* [Old English *forca, force* from Latin *furca*]

fork·ball *noun Baseball* a pitch in which the ball is held with the thumb, index finger, and middle finger spread.

forked *adjective* **1** having a fork or fork-like end or branches. **2** divergent, cleft. **3** (*in combination*) having so many prongs (*three-forked*).

forked lightning *noun* a lightning flash in the form of a zigzag or branching line.

forked tongue *noun* a lying or deceitful tongue (*he speaks with a forked tongue*).

fork·lift (in full **forklift truck**) ● *noun* a vehicle with a horizontal fork in front for lifting and carrying loads. ● *transitive verb* pile or move (loads) with a forklift.

fork-tender *adjective N Amer.* (of meat etc.) cooked until tender enough to be pierced by a fork.

for·lorn *adjective* **1** sad and abandoned or lonely. **2** in a pitiful state; of wretched appearance. **3** desperate, hopeless, forsaken. □ **for·lorn·ly** *adverb* **for·lorn·ness** *noun* [past participle of obsolete *forlese* from Old English *forlēosan* (as FOR-, LOSE)]

forlorn hope *noun* a persistent or desperate hope that is unlikely to be fulfilled. [Dutch *verloren hoop* lost troop, originally of a raiding party etc.]

form ● *noun* **1 a** a shape; an arrangement of parts. **b** the outward aspect (esp. apart from colour) or shape of a body. **2** a person or animal as visible or tangible (*the familiar form of the mailman*). **3** the mode in which a thing exists or manifests itself (*detergent in powder or liquid form*). **4 a** a species, kind, or variety (*different forms of government*). **b** an artistic or literary genre (*sonnet form*). **5** a printed document with blank spaces for information to be inserted. **6** esp. *Brit.* a class in a school. **7** a customary method; what is usually done (*common form*). **8** a set order of words; a formula. **9** behaviour according to a rule or custom. **10** (prec. by *the*) correct procedure (*knows the form*). **11 a** (of an athlete, horse, etc.) condition of health and training (*is in top form*). **b** *Racing* details of previous performances. **12** general state or disposition (*was in great form*). **13** *Brit. slang* a criminal record. **14** formality or mere ceremony. **15** *Grammar* **a** one of the ways in which a word may be spelled or pronounced or inflected. **b** the external characteristics of words apart from meaning. **16 a** arrangement and expression of ideas esp. in the arts. **b** style in literary or musical composition. **17** *Philos.* the essential nature of a species or thing. **18** *Brit.* a long bench without a back. **19** *Books* = FORME. **20** a hare's lair. **21** a mould, frame or block in or on which something is shaped. ● *verb* **1** *transitive* make or fashion into a certain shape or form. **2** *intransitive* take a certain shape; be formed. **3** *transitive* be the material of; make up or constitute (*together form a unit; forms part of the structure*). **4** *transitive* train or instruct. **5** *transitive* develop or establish as a concept, institution, or practice (*form an idea; formed an alliance; form a habit*). **6** *transitive* (foll. by *into*) embody, organize. **7** *intransitive* come into existence; take shape or develop (*thunderclouds formed in the distance*). **8** *transitive & intransitive* (often foll. by *up*) esp. *Military* bring or be brought into a certain arrangement or formation. **9** *transitive* construct (a new word) by derivation, inflection, etc. □ **in form** fit for racing etc. **off form** not playing or performing well. **on form** playing or performing well. **out of form** not fit for racing etc. □ **form·able** *adjective* [Old French *forme* from Latin *forma* mould, form]

-form *combining form* (usu. as **-iform**) forming adjectives meaning: **1** having the form of (*cruciform; cuneiform*). **2** having such a number of (*uniform; multiform*). [from or after French *-forme* from Latin *-formis* from *forma* FORM]

for·mal ● *adjective* **1** used or done or held in accordance with rules, convention, or ceremony (*formal dress; a formal occasion*). **2** ceremonial; required by convention (*a formal call*). **3** precise or symmetrical (*a formal garden*). **4** prim or stiff in manner. **5** perfunctory, having the form without the spirit. **6** valid or correctly so called because of its form; explicit and definite (*a formal agreement*). **7** in accordance with recognized forms or rules. **8** (of education) officially given at a school, university, etc. **9** of or concerned with (outward) form or appearance, esp. as distinct from content or matter. **10** *Logic* concerned with the form and not the matter of reasoning. **11** *Philos.* of the essence of a thing; essential not material. ● *noun N Amer.* **1** a dance or other social occasion to which evening dress is worn. **2** an evening gown. □ **for·mal·ly** *adverb* **for·mal·ness** *noun*

for·mal·de·hyde /fɔrˈmaldəˌhaɪd, fər-/ *noun* a colourless, pungent, toxic gas used as a disinfectant and preservative and in the manufacture of synthetic resins. Chem. formula: CH_2O. [FORMIC (ACID) + ALDEHYDE]

for·ma·lin /ˈfɔrmələn/ *noun* a colourless solution of formaldehyde in water used as a preservative for biological specimens etc.

for·mal·ism *noun* **1 a** excessive adherence to prescribed forms. **b** the use of forms without regard to inner significance. **2** *derogatory* an artist's concentration on form at the expense of content. **3** the treatment of mathematics as a manipulation of meaningless symbols. **4** *Theatre* a symbolic and stylized manner of production. **5** *Physics & Math.* the mathematical description of a physical situation etc. □ **for·mal·ist** *noun* **for·mal·is·tic** *adjective* **for·mal·is·tic·ally** *adverb*

for·mal·ity *noun* (*pl.* **-ies**) **1 a** a formal or ceremonial act, requirement of etiquette, regulation, or custom (often with an implied lack of real significance). **b** a thing done simply to comply with a rule. **2** the rigid observance of rules or convention. **3** ceremony; elaborate procedure. **4** being formal; precision of manners.

for·mal·ize *transitive verb* (also esp. *Brit.* **-ise**) **1** give definite shape or legal formality to. **2** make ceremonious, precise, or rigid; imbue with formalism. □ **for·mal·iz·a·tion** *noun*

formal wear *noun* clothes customarily worn on formal occasions, e.g. tails, tuxedos or evening dresses.

For·man, Milos (b.1932), Czech-born US film director. He directed *One Flew Over the Cuckoo's Nest* (1975), which won five Oscars, and *Amadeus* (1983), which won eight Oscars, including that for best director.

for·mat ● *noun* **1** the shape, size, and presentation of a page, book, periodical, etc. **2** the way in which something is arranged, set out, or organized. **3** *Computing* a defined structure for holding data etc. in a record for processing or storage. **4** the medium in which a recording is available (*available in VHS and DVD formats*). ● *transitive verb* (**for·mat·ted, for·mat·ting**) **1** arrange or put into a format. **2** *Computing* prepare (a storage medium) to receive data. □ **for·mat·ter** *noun* [French from German from Latin *formatus (liber)* shaped (book), past participle of *formare* FORM]

for·mate /ˈfɔrmeɪt/ *noun Chem.* a salt or ester of formic acid.

for·ma·tion *noun* **1** the act or an instance of forming; the process of being formed. **2** a thing formed. **3** a structure or arrangement of parts. **4** a particular arrangement, e.g. of troops, aircraft in flight, etc. **5** *Geol.* an assemblage of rocks or series of strata having some common characteristic. □ **for·ma·tion·al** *adjective*

form·a·tive /ˈfɔrmətɪv/ ● *adjective* **1** serving to form or fashion; of formation. **2** having an important and lasting influence upon (a person's character etc.) (*a child's formative years*). **3** *Grammar* (of a flexional or derivative suffix or prefix) used in forming words. **4** (of tissue) capable of growth and development. ● *noun Grammar* a formative element. □ **form·a·tive·ly** *adverb*

forme /fɔrm/ *noun* (also **form**) a body of type secured in a chase for printing. [var. of FORM]

for·mer[1] *attributive adjective* **1** of or occurring in the past or an earlier period (*in former times*). **2** having been previously (*her former husband*). ● *noun* (prec. by *the*) the first or first mentioned of two (*opp.* LATTER *noun*). [Middle English from *forme* first, after FOREMOST]

for·mer[2] *noun* **1** a person or thing that forms. **2** *Electricity* a frame or core for winding a coil on. **3** (*in combination*) *Brit.* a pupil of a specified form in a school (*fourth-former*).

for·mer·ly *adverb* in the past; in former times.

form-fitting *adjective* = CLOSE-FITTING.

For·mi·ca /fɔrˈmaɪkə/ *noun* proprietary a hard durable plastic laminate used for working surfaces, cupboard doors, etc. [20th c.: origin uncertain]

for·mic acid /ˈfɔrmɪk/ *noun* a colourless irritant volatile acid used in textile finishing etc., originally obtained from ants but now produced synthetically. *Also called* METHANOIC ACID. Chem. formula: $HCOOH$. [Latin *formica* ant]

for·mi·ca·tion /ˌfɔrmɪˈkeɪʃən/ *noun* a sensation as of ants crawling over the skin. [Latin *formicatio* from *formica* ant]

for·mid·able /fɔrˈmɪdəbəl, ˈfɔrmɪd-/ *adjective* **1** inspiring fear or dread. **2** inspiring respect or awe. **3** likely to be hard to overcome, resist, or deal with. □ **for·mid·able·ness** *noun* **for·mid·ably** *adverb* [French *formidable* or Latin *formidabilis* from *formidare* fear]

form·less *adjective* shapeless; without determinate or regular form. □ **form·less·ly** *adverb* **form·less·ness** *noun*

form letter *noun* a standardized letter to deal with frequently occurring matters.

For·mosa /fɔrˈmoʊsə/ the former name for TAIWAN. [Portuguese *formosa* beautiful]

for·mu·la /ˈfɔrmjʊlə/ *noun* (*pl.* **for·mu·las** or (esp. in senses 1, 2) **for·mu·lae** /-ˌliː/) **1** *Chem.* a set of chemical symbols showing the constituents of a substance and their relative proportions. **2** *Math.* a mathematical rule expressed in symbols. **3 a** a fixed form of words, esp. one used on social or ceremonial occasions. **b** a rule unintelligently or slavishly followed; an established or conventional usage (also *attributive*: *formula fiction*). **c** a fixed form of words as a definition or an enunciation of a principle or religious doctrine, esp. a statement or method intended to reconcile different aims or opinions. **4 a** a method, plan, or set of principles by which parties involved in negotiation arrive at a solution (*compare* AMENDING FORMULA). **b** a means by which something is calculated (*the funding formula for schools*). **5 a** a list of ingredients; a recipe (*formula for a new drug*). **b** *N Amer.* an infant's liquid food preparation, given as a substitute for breast milk. **6** a classification of race car, esp. by the engine capacity. □ **for·mu·la·ic** /-ˈleɪɪk/ *adjective* **for·mu·la·ic·al·ly** *adverb* [Latin, diminutive of *forma* FORM]

Formula One *noun* the form of motor racing on the Grand Prix circuit, for open-wheeled, single-seater cars.

for·mu·lary /ˈfɔrmjʊˌleri/ ● *noun* (*pl.* **-ies**) **1** a collection of formulas or set forms, esp. for religious use. **2** *Pharm.* a compendium of formulae used in the preparation of medicinal drugs. ● *adjective* **1** using formulae. **2** in or of formulae. [noun from French *formulaire* or from medieval Latin *formularius* (*liber* book) from Latin (as FORMULA): the adjective from FORMULA]

for·mu·late /ˈfɔrmjʊˌleɪt/ *transitive verb* **1** express in a formula. **2** express clearly and precisely. **3** devise, create (*formulate a plan*). □ **for·mu·la·tion** *noun* **for·mu·la·tor** *noun*

for·mu·lis·tic /fɔrmjʊˈlɪstɪk/ *adjective* adhering to or depending on conventional formulas.

form·work *noun* a temporary structure for holding fresh concrete in shape while it sets.

for·ni·cate /ˈfɔrnɪˌkeɪt/ *intransitive verb* (of people not married or not married to each other) have sexual intercourse. □ **for·ni·ca·tion** *noun* **for·ni·ca·tor** *noun* [ecclesiastical Latin *fornicari* from Latin *fornix -icis* brothel]

for-profit ● *adjective* denoting an organization operated to make a profit, esp. one (such as a hospital or school) which would more usually be non-profit-making. ● *noun* a for-profit organization.

For·res·ter, Mau·reen (Kath·er·ine Stew·art) (b.1930), Canadian contralto and teacher. One of the foremost lieder singers and recitalists in the world, she is esp. noted as an interpreter of Mahler.

for·sake *transitive verb* (*past* **for·sook**; *past participle* **for·sak·en**) **1** give up; break off from; renounce. **2** withdraw one's help, friendship, or companionship from; desert, abandon. □ **for·saken·ness** *noun* [Old English *forsacan* deny, renounce, refuse, from West Germanic; compare Old English *sacan* quarrel]

For·sey, Eu·gene (Al·fred) (1904–1991), Canadian politician. An authority on constitutional law, he was one of the authors of the Regina Manifesto of the CCF (1933), and was director of research for the Canadian Congress of Labour (1942–56) and the Canadian Labour Congress (1956–66); in 1970 he was appointed to the senate.

for·sooth *adverb archaic* or *jocular* truly; in truth; no doubt. [Old English *forsōth* (as FOR, SOOTH)]

For·ster, Ed·ward Mor·gan (1879–1970), English novelist and literary critic. His fiction examines the social and cultural values of the English middle classes; his novels include *A Room with a View* (1908), *Howards End* (1910), and *A Passage to India* (1924).

for·swear *transitive verb* (*past* **for·swore**; *past participle* **for·sworn**) **1** abjure; renounce under oath. **2** deny or repudiate on oath or with strong protestation. **3** (*reflexive* or in *passive*) swear falsely; commit perjury. [Old English *forswerian* (as FOR-, SWEAR)]

For·sythe, Wil·liam (b.1949) US-born choreographer and ballet director. Director of the Frankfurt Ballet since 1984, he is noted for his highly innovative and energetic ballet style which defies classical ballet conventions.

for·sythia /fɔrˈsɪθiə/ *noun* any ornamental shrub of the genus *Forsythia* bearing bright yellow flowers in early spring. [modern Latin from W. *Forsyth*, English botanist d.1804]

fort *noun* **1** a fortified building or position. **2** *N Amer. hist.* a trading post, originally fortified. □ **hold the fort** see HOLD[1]. [French *fort* or Italian *forte* from Latin *fortis* strong]

Forta·leza /fɔrtəˈleɪzə/ a port in NE Brazil, on the Atlantic coast; pop. (2000) 2,138,234.

Fort Amherst /ˈamərst/ a historic site in south central PEI, on the

shore of Charlottetown Harbour. Built by the British in 1758, it was formerly known by the French as Port La Joie, capital of the colony of Île Saint-Jean.

Fort Anne a historic site in W Nova Scotia, located at present-day Annapolis Royal. Founded as the French-Acadian community of Port-Royal, it was captured by the British in 1710; shortly thereafter it became the capital of peninsular Nova Scotia. [Queen ANNE]

Fort Battle·ford /ˈbatəlfərd/ a historic site in west central Saskatchewan, just south of North Battleford. It was established in 1876 as a headquarters for the North West Mounted Police. [as NORTH BATTLEFORD]

Fort Beau·sé·jour /boːseɪˈʒʊr/ a historic site in E New Brunswick, near Sackville. Built by the French in 1751 to protect the land route to Acadia, it was taken by the British in 1755 and renamed Fort Cumberland. [named after Laurent Chatillon, Sieur de *Beauséjour*]

Fort Chambly /ʃɑˈblɪ/ a historic site in south central Quebec, located on the Richelieu near present-day Chambly. Established by the French in 1665 as Fort Saint-Louis, it developed into a military supply depot for other forts in the area. It was taken by the British in 1760. [J. de *Chambly*, who built the original fort d.1687]

Fort-de-France /ˌfɔrdəˈfrɑns/ the capital of Martinique; pop. (est. 2002) 95,800.

forte[1] /ˈfɔrteɪ/ *noun* **1** a person's strong point; a thing in which a person excels. **2** *Fencing* the part of a sword blade from the hilt to the middle (*compare* FOIBLE 2). [French *fort* strong, from Latin *fortis*]

forte[2] /ˈfɔrteɪ/ *Music* ● *adjective* performed loudly. ● *adverb* loudly. ● *noun* a passage to be performed loudly. [Italian, = strong, loud]

forte·piano /ˌfɔrtəpiˈɑnoː, -ˈpjɑnoː/ *noun* (*pl.* **pianos**) *Music* = PIANOFORTE (esp. with reference to an instrument of the 18th to early 19th c.) [FORTE[2] + PIANO[2]]

forte-piano *adjective & adverb* loud and then immediately soft.

Fort Erie a town in S Ontario, situated on the Niagara River near Lake Erie, across from Buffalo, New York; pop. (2001) 28,143. □ **Fort Erian** *noun*

Fort Fran·ces a town in NW Ontario, situated on the border with Minnesota, about 325 km west of Thunder Bay; pop. (2001) 8,315. □ **Fort Fran·cian** *noun* [Lady *Frances* Simpson d.1853, wife of Sir G. Simpson, Hudson's Bay Co. governor-in-chief]

Fort Garry the former name (1870–1873) for Winnipeg. [the name of a Hudson's Bay Co. fort *c.*1821]

Fort George a historic site in S Ontario, on the Niagara River at Niagara-on-the-Lake. Built by the British at the end of the 18th-c., it was used as a safeguard against American invasion.

Forth a river of central Scotland, rising on Ben Lomond and flowing eastward through Stirling into the North Sea.

forth *adverb* (only in set phrases and after certain verbs, esp. *bring*, *come*, *go*, and *set*) **1** forward; into view. **2** onward in time (*from this time forth*; *henceforth*). **3** forwards. **4** out from a starting point (*set forth*). □ **and so forth** and so on; and the like. [Old English from Germanic]

Forth, Firth of the estuary of the Forth River in Scotland, separating the regions of Fife and Lothian. It is spanned by a cantilever railway bridge (opened 1890) and a road suspension bridge (1964).

forth·com·ing *adjective* **1 a** about or likely to appear or become available. **b** approaching. **2** produced when wanted (*no reply was forthcoming*). **3** (of a person) informative, responsive.

forth·right ● *adjective* **1** direct and outspoken; straightforward. **2** decisive, unhesitating. ● *adverb* in a direct manner; bluntly. □ **forth·right·ly** *adverb* **forth·right·ness** *noun*

forth·with *adverb* immediately; without delay. [earlier *forthwithal* (as FORTH, WITH, ALL)]

For·ties (prec. by *the*) the central North Sea between Scotland and S Norway, so called from its prevailing depth of forty fathoms or more (*compare* ROARING FORTIES). The area is an important centre of North Sea oil production.

for·ti·fi·ca·tion /ˌfɔrtəfɪˈkeɪʃən/ *noun* **1** the act or an instance of fortifying; the process of being fortified. **2** *Military* **a** the art or science of fortifying. **b** (usu. in *pl.*) defensive works fortifying a position.

for·ti·fy *transitive verb* (**-fies, -fied**) **1** provide or equip with defensive works so as to strengthen against attack. **2** strengthen or invigorate mentally or morally; encourage. **3** strengthen the structure of. **4** strengthen (wine) with alcohol. **5** increase the nutritive value of (food, esp. with vitamins). □ **for·ti·fi·er** *noun* [Old French *fortifier* from Late Latin *fortificare* from Latin *fortis* strong]

for·tis·simo /fɔrˈtɪsəˌmoː/ *Music* ● *adjective* performed very loudly.

● *adverb* very loudly. ● *noun* (*pl.* **-mos** or **for·tis·simi** /-ˌmiː/) a passage to be performed very loudly. [Italian, superlative of FORTE²]

for·ti·tude /ˈfɔrtɪˌtuːd, -ˌtjuːd/ *noun* moral strength or courage, esp. in the endurance of pain or adversity. [French from Latin *fortitudo -dinis* from *fortis* strong]

Fort Knox /nɒks/ a US military reservation in Kentucky, famous as the site of the depository which holds the bulk of the nation's gold bullion in its vaults.

Fort Lamy /ˈlami/ the former name (until 1973) for N'DJAMENA.

Fort Langley a historic site in southwestern BC, located on the Fraser River, about 30 km east of Vancouver. Built in 1827 by the Hudson's Bay Co., it served mainly as an administrative and supply centre for the area. [T. *Langley*, HBC director *c.*1827]

Fort Mal·den /ˈmɒldən/ a historic site in SW Ontario, located at present-day Amherstburg. Built in the late 1790s, it served as a British army headquarters during the War of 1812.

Fort Mc·Murray the former name for WOOD BUFFALO.

fort·night *noun* **1** a period of two weeks. **2** *Brit.* (prec. by a specified day) two weeks after (that day) (*Tuesday fortnight*). [Old English *fēowertīene niht* fourteen nights]

fort·night·ly esp. *Brit.* ● *adjective* done, produced, or occurring once a fortnight. ● *adverb* every fortnight. ● *noun* (*pl.* **-lies**) a magazine etc. issued every fortnight.

Fort Prince of Wales (also **Prince of Wales' Fort**) a remote historic site in NE Manitoba, located at the mouth of the Churchill River, opposite the port of Churchill. Established in 1717, this Hudson's Bay Co. fort was significantly enlarged and fortified from 1731 to 1771; it was taken without incident by the French in 1782.

Fort Qu'Appelle /kəˈpel/ a town in SE central Saskatchewan, situated in the valley of the Qu'Appelle River, northeast of Regina; pop. (2001) 1,940. [see QU'APPELLE RIVER]

For·tran /ˈfɔrtran/ *noun* (also **FORTRAN**) *Computing* a high-level programming language used esp. for scientific calculations. [*formula translation*]

fort·ress *noun* **1** a military stronghold, esp. a strongly fortified town fit for a large garrison. **2** any place or source of refuge or protection. **3** (placed before noun) a country or continent viewed as impenetrable to trade, immigration, invasion, etc. (*fears of a protectionist 'Fortress Europe'*). □ **fortress-like** *adjective* [Old French *forteresse*, ultimately from Latin *fortis* strong]

Fort Rodd Hill a historic site at the southern tip of Vancouver Island, about 15 km west of Victoria. Built in 1895, this coastal artillery fort was manned until 1956, though never attacked.

Fort St. James a historic site in central BC, located on Stuart Lake, northwest of Prince George. Founded as a North West Co. post in 1806, it served as an administrative centre for New Caledonia until 1857.

Fort St. John a city in northeastern BC, about 65 km northwest of Dawson Creek; pop. (2001) 16,034.

Fort St. Joseph a historic site in north central Ontario, located on St. Joseph Island in Lake Huron's North Channel. Established as a fur-trading post by the British in 1796, it was destroyed at the onset of the War of 1812.

Fort Saskatchewan a city in central Alberta, just northeast of Edmonton; pop. (2001) 13,121.

Fort Simpson a village in the SW central NWT, situated at the junction of the Liard and Mackenzie rivers, southwest of Yellowknife; pop. (2001) 1,163. [G. *Simpson*, governor of the Hudson's Bay Co. *c.*1821]

Fort Smith a town in the southern NWT, situated on the Slave River, immediately north of the border with Alberta; pop. (2001) 2,186. □ **Fort Smith·er** *noun* [Donald SMITH]

for·tuit·ous /fɔrˈtuːɪtəs, -ˈtjuː-/ *adjective* due to or characterized by chance, esp. lucky chance. □ **for·tuit·ous·ly** *adverb* **for·tuit·ous·ness** *noun* [Latin *fortuitus* from *forte* by chance]

for·tu·ity /fɔrˈtuːɪti, -ˈtjuː-/ *noun* (*pl.* **-ies**) **1** a chance occurrence. **2** accident or chance; fortuitousness.

For·tuna /fɔrˈtuːnə, fɔrˈtjuː-/ *Rom. Myth* the goddess of fortune.

for·tun·ate *adjective* **1** favoured by fortune; lucky, prosperous. **2** auspicious, favourable.

for·tun·ate·ly *adverb* **1** luckily, successfully. **2** (qualifying a whole sentence) it is fortunate that.

for·tune *noun* **1 a** chance or luck as a force in human affairs. **b** a person's destiny or future; fate. **2** (**Fortune**) this force personified, often as a deity. **3** (in *sing.* or *pl.*) luck (esp. favourable) that befalls a person or enterprise. **4** good luck. **5** prosperity; a prosperous condition. **6** great wealth; a huge sum of money. □ **make a** (or **one's**) **fortune** acquire wealth or prosperity. **tell a person's fortune** make predictions about a person's future. [Old French from Latin *fortuna* luck, chance]

Fortune 500 *attributive adjective US* designating the five hundred most profitable US industrial corporations.

Fortune Bay an inlet of the N Atlantic, indenting the southern coast of Newfoundland. [from Portuguese *fortuna* (good) luck]

fortune cookie *noun N Amer.* a small cookie containing a slip of paper printed with a prediction, joke, etc., served esp. in Chinese restaurants.

fortune hunter *noun informal* a person seeking wealth, esp. by marriage. □ **fortune-hunting** *noun & adjective*

fortune teller *noun* a person who claims to predict future events in a person's life. □ **fortune-telling** *noun*

Fort William part of the city of Thunder Bay; it was amalgamated with Port Arthur in 1970. [*William McGillivray, principal director of the North West Co. d.1825*]

Fort Worth a city in N Texas, near Dallas; pop. (2000) 534,694.

forty ● *noun* (*pl.* **-ies**) **1** the product of four and ten. **2** a symbol for this (40, xl, XL). **3** (in *pl.*) the numbers from 40 to 49, esp. the years of a century or of a person's life. ● *adjective* that amount to forty. □ **forty-first, -second**, etc. the ordinal numbers between fortieth and fiftieth. **forty-one, -two**, etc. the cardinal numbers between forty and fifty. □ **for·ti·eth** *adjective, adverb & noun* **forty·fold** *adjective & adverb* **forty·ish** *adjective* [Old English *fēowertig* (as FOUR, -TY²)]

forty-five *noun* **1** (also **45**) a small phonograph record played at 45 rpm. **2** (also **.45**) *N Amer.* a .45 calibre revolver. **3** *N Amer.* (*Maritimes & New England*) a card game for two to six players in which the player or side first reaching forty-five points wins.

forty-niner *noun* a seeker for gold etc. in the Californian gold rush of 1849.

forty-ninth parallel *noun* the parallel of latitude 49° north of the equator, esp. as forming the boundary between Canada and the US west of Lake of the Woods.

forty-ouncer *noun* (also *Cdn slang* **forty-pounder**) a forty-ounce bottle of liquor.

forty winks *plural noun informal* a short sleep.

forum *noun* **1** a place of or meeting for public discussion. **2** a periodical, television program, etc. giving an opportunity for discussion. **3** a court or tribunal. **4** *hist.* a public square or marketplace in an ancient Roman city used for judicial and other business. [Latin, in sense 4]

for·ward ● *adjective* **1** directed or moving towards a point in advance, onward, towards the front (*a forward movement*). **2 a** situated in front; near or at the front. **b** *Naut.* belonging to the forepart of a ship. **3** bold in manner; presumptuous. **4** *Business* **a** relating to future produce, delivery, exchange rates, etc. (*forward contract*). **b** prospective; advanced; with a view to the future (*forward planning*). **5** advanced; progressing towards or approaching maturity or completion. **6** positioned near the front line in a battle, forest fire, etc. (*forward observation*). ● *noun* an attacking player positioned near the front of a team in hockey, soccer, etc. ● *adverb* **1 a** to the front; into prominence (*come forward; move forward*). **b** into a position for consideration or discussion (*brought forward a proposal*). **2** in advance; ahead (*sent them forward*). **3** onward so as to make progress (*not getting any further forward*). **4** towards the future; continuously onward (*from this time forward*). **5** (also **for·wards**) **a** towards the front in the direction one is facing. **b** in the normal direction of motion or of traversal. **c** with continuous forward motion (*backwards and forwards; rushing forward*). **6** *Naut. & Aviation* in, near, or towards the bow or nose. **7** ahead of time (esp. in reference to purchasing currencies etc. for delivery at some future date at the price agreed at the time the contract is made) (*buy forward*). ● *transitive verb* **1** send (a letter, email message, etc.) on to a further destination or recipient. **2** help to advance; promote. **3** advance (a videotape etc.) forward. □ **for·ward·er** *noun* **for·ward·ly** *adverb* **for·ward·ness** *noun* (esp. in sense 3 of *adjective*). [Old English *foreweard*, var. of *forthweard* (as FORTH, -WARD)]

for·ward·ing address *noun* an address to which one has one's mail forwarded.

forward line *noun* an arrangement of forwards in hockey, soccer, etc.

forward-looking *adjective* progressive; favouring change.

forward pass *noun* **1** *Football* a pass thrown from behind the line of scrimmage towards the opponent's goal. **2** *Hockey etc.* a pass towards the opponent's goal. □ **forward passing** *noun*

for·wards var. of FORWARD *adverb* 5.

Consonants:　b *but*　d *dog*　f *few*　g *get*　h *her*　j *yes*　k *cat*　l *leg*　m *man*　n *no*　p *pen*　r *red*　s *sit*

forward slash *noun* an oblique stroke (/), esp. in reference to websites and other computing uses.

forward-thinking *adjective* = FORWARD-LOOKING.

for·went *past of* FORGO.

Fos·bury /ˈfɒzbəri/ **Rich·ard** (b.1947), American high jumper. He originated the now standard style of jumping known as the 'Fosbury flop', in which the jumper clears the bar head first and backwards. In 1968 he won the Olympic gold medal using this technique.

Fo·sheim Peninsula /ˈfoːʃaim/ a large peninsula of the west central coast of Ellesmere Island. [I. *Fosheim*, Norwegian Arctic explorer *c.*1900]

fossa /ˈfɒsə/ *noun* (*pl.* **fos·sae** /-siː/) *Anat.* a shallow depression or cavity. [Latin, = ditch, fem. past participle of *fodere* dig]

fosse /fɒs/ *noun* a long narrow trench or excavation, esp. in a fortification. [Old French from Latin *fossa*: see FOSSA]

Fosse Way an ancient road in Britain, so called from the fosse or ditch that used to run along each side of it. It ran from Axminster to Lincoln, via Bath and Leicester (about 300 km, 200 miles), and marked the limit of the first stage of the Roman occupation (mid-1st c. AD).

fos·sick /ˈfɒsɪk/ *intransitive verb Austral.* & *NZ informal* **1** (foll. by *about, around*) rummage, search. **2** search for gold etc. in abandoned mines. □ **fos·sick·er** *noun* [19th c.: compare dialect *fossick* bustle about]

fos·sil *noun* **1** the remains or impression of a prehistoric plant or animal, usu. petrified while embedded in rock, amber, etc. (often *attributive*: *fossil bones*; *fossil shells*). **2** *informal* an antiquated or unchanging person or thing. **3** a word that has become obsolete except in set phrases or forms, e.g. *hue* in *hue and cry*. □ **fos·sil·ize** *transitive & intransitive verb* (also esp. *Brit.* **-ise**). **fos·sil·i·za·tion** *noun* [French *fossile* from Latin *fossilis* from *fodere foss-* dig]

fossil fuel *noun* a natural fuel such as coal or gas formed in the geological past from the remains of living organisms.

fos·sil·if·er·ous /ˌfɒsɪˈlɪfərəs/ *adjective* (of a rock or stratum) containing fossils or organic remains.

fossil record *noun* information about the geological past as recorded in and deduced from fossils.

fos·sor·ial /fɒˈsɔːriəl/ *adjective* **1** (of animals) burrowing. **2** (of limbs etc. of burrowing animals) used in burrowing. [medieval Latin *fossorius* from *fossor* digger (as FOSSIL)]

Fos·ter, 1 David (b.1949), Canadian musician, composer, and producer. He has won 12 Grammy awards, as well as several Juno and Gemini awards, and has produced records for many artists, including Celine Dion, Michael Jackson, and Whitney Houston. **2 Jodie** (b.1962), US film actress. She has won Oscar nominations for her performances in *Taxi Driver* (1976) and *Nell* (1994), and Oscars for *The Accused* (1988) and *Silence of the Lambs* (1991). **3 Ste·phen (Col·lins)** (1826–64), US composer. He wrote more than 200 songs, including his best-known minstrel songs 'Oh! Susannah' (1848), 'Camptown Races' (1850), and 'Old Folks at Home' (also called 'Swanee River', 1851). **4 Wal·ter (Ed·ward)** (1873–1947), Canadian politician, Liberal premier of New Brunswick 1917–23.

fos·ter ● *transitive verb* **1 a** promote the growth or development of. **b** encourage or harbour (a feeling). **2** bring up (a child that is not one's own by birth). **3** cherish; have affectionate regard for (an idea, scheme, etc.). **4** take care of (a domestic animal) for a humane society etc. before a permanent home is found. ● *adjective* **1** having a family connection by fostering and not by birth (*foster brother*; *foster child*; *foster parent*). **2** involving or concerned with fostering a child (*foster care*; *foster home*). □ **fos·ter·age** *noun* (esp. in sense 2 of *verb*). **fos·ter·er** *noun* [Old English *fōstrian*, *fōster*, related to FOOD]

fos·ter·ling *noun* a foster child; a nursling or protege.

Fou·cault /ˈfuːkoː/ **1 Jean Ber·nard Léon** (1819–68), French physicist. He is chiefly remembered for the huge pendulum which he hung from the roof of the Panthéon (Paris) in 1851: as the pendulum swung, the path of its oscillations slowly rotated, demonstrating the rotation of the earth; he also obtained the first reasonably accurate determination of the velocity of light, and invented the gyroscope. **2 Mi·chel (Paul)** (1926–84), French philosopher. He was mainly concerned with exploring how society defines categories of abnormality such as insanity, sexuality, and criminality, and the manipulation of social attitudes towards such things by those in power. □ **Fou·cauld·ian** *adjective* (also **Fou·cault·ian**).

Fouc·quet *var. of* FOUQUET 2.

fouet·té /ˈfweteɪ/ *noun Ballet* **1** a pirouette performed with a quick circular whipping movement of the raised leg. **2** a quick shift of direction of the upper body. [French, past participle of *fouetter* whip]

fought *past and past participle of* FIGHT.

Fou-hsin see FUXIN.

foul ● *adjective* **1** offensive to the senses; loathsome, stinking. **2** dirty, soiled, filthy. **3 a** revolting, disgusting. **b** angry or disagreeable (*in a foul mood*). **4 a** containing or charged with noxious matter (*foul air*). **b** clogged, choked. **5** morally offensive (*foul language*; *foul deeds*). **6 a** unfair; against the rules of a game etc. (*by fair means or foul*). **b** *Baseball* of or relating to a foul ball or foul line. **7** (of the weather) wet, rough, stormy. **8** (of a rope etc.) entangled. **9** (of a ship's bottom) overgrown with weeds, barnacles, etc. ● *noun* **1** *Sport* an illegal play, esp. one involving illegal physical contact with an opponent. **2** a collision or entanglement, esp. in riding, rowing, or running. **3** a foul thing. ● *adverb* **1** unfairly; contrary to the rules. **2** *Baseball* outside the foul lines (*hit the ball foul*). ● *verb* **1** *transitive & intransitive* make or become foul or dirty. **2** *transitive* (of an animal) make dirty with excrement. **3** *Baseball* **a** *transitive* hit (a pitched ball) foul. **b** *intransitive* hit a foul ball. **4** *Sport* **a** *transitive* commit a foul against (a player). **b** *intransitive* commit a foul. **5 a** *transitive* (often foll. by *up*) cause (an anchor, cable, etc.) to become entangled or muddled. **b** *intransitive* become entangled. **6** *transitive & intransitive* be or become jammed or clogged (*a fouled musket*). **7** *transitive* (usu. foll. by *up*) *informal* spoil or bungle. **8** *transitive* run foul of; collide with. **9** *transitive* dishonour. □ **cry foul** protest. **foul off** hit (a pitch or the ball) foul. **foul one's (own) nest 1** bring discredit on one's family etc. by one's actions. **2** speak disparagingly of one's family etc. **foul out 1** *Baseball* (of a batter) be made out by hitting a foul ball which is caught on the fly by a member of the opposing team. **2** *Basketball* be put out of the game for exceeding the permitted number of fouls. □ **foul·ly** *adverb* **foul·ness** *noun* [Old English *fūl* from Germanic]

fou·lard /fuːˈlɑrd/ *noun* **1** a thin soft material of silk or silk and cotton. **2** an article made of this. [French]

foul ball *noun Baseball* a ball struck so that it falls outside the foul lines.

foul line *noun* **1** *Baseball* either of the straight lines extending from home plate and marking the limit of the playing area within which a ball is deemed to be fair. **2** *Basketball* a line on the court 15 ft. (4.6 m) from the backboard, from which foul shots are made.

foul-mouthed *adjective* using obscene and offensive language.

foul play *noun* **1** unfair play in a sports game. **2** treacherous or violent activity, esp. murder.

foul shot *noun Basketball* = FREE THROW 2.

foul tip *noun Baseball* a pitched ball that glances off the bat and is caught by the catcher.

foul-up *noun* a muddled or bungled situation.

found¹ ● *verb past and past participle of* FIND. ● *adjective* **1** having been discovered by chance or unexpectedly. **2** (of an object or sound) collected in its natural state and presented in a new context as part of a work of art or piece of music (*collages of found objects*). **3** (of art) comprising or making use of such objects. **4** (of poetry) formed by taking a piece of text and reinterpreting its structure metrically.

found² *verb* **1** *transitive* **a** establish (esp. with an endowment). **b** originate or initiate (an institution, society, etc.). **2** *transitive* be the original builder or begin the building of (a town etc.). **3** *transitive* lay the base of (a building etc.). **4** (foll. by *on*, *upon*) **a** *transitive* construct or base (a story, theory, rule, etc.) according to a specified principle or ground. **b** *intransitive* have a basis in. [Old French *fonder* from Latin *fundare* from *fundus* bottom]

found³ *transitive verb* **1** melt and mould (metal or glass). **2** make by founding. □ **found·er** *noun* [Old French *fondre* from Latin *fundere fus-* pour]

foun·da·tion *noun* **1 a** the solid ground or base, natural or artificial, on which a building rests. **b** (usu. in *pl.*) the lowest load-bearing part of a building, usu. below ground level. **2** a body or ground on which other parts are overlaid. **3** a basis or underlying principle; groundwork (*the report has no foundation*). **4 a** the act or an instance of establishing or constituting (esp. an endowed institution) on a permanent basis. **b** an institution, e.g. a monastery, college, or hospital, maintained by an endowment. **c** an organization with a permanent fund devoted to financing research, the arts, and other charitable causes. **d** a fund devoted to the permanent maintenance of an institution or organization; an endowment. **5** (in full **foundation garment**) a woman's supporting undergarment, e.g. a bra, girdle, etc. **6** a cosmetic in liquid or powdered form applied to the face as a base for other makeup and to even out skin tone. □ **foun·da·tion·al** *adjective*

foundation stone *noun* **1** a stone laid with ceremony to celebrate the founding of a building. **2** the main ground or basis of something.

found·er¹ *noun* a person who founds an institution etc.

found·er² ● *verb* **1** *intransitive* (of a ship) fill with water and sink. **2** *intransitive* (of a plan etc.) fail. **3** *intransitive* (of earth, a building, etc.) fall down or in, give way. **4 a** *intransitive* (of a horse or its rider) fall to the ground, fall from lameness, stick fast in mud etc. **b** *transitive* cause (a horse) to break down, esp. with founder. ● *noun* **1** inflammation of a horse's foot from overwork. **2** rheumatism of the chest muscles in horses. [Old French *fondrer*, *esfondrer* submerge, collapse, ultimately from Latin *fundus* bottom]

found-in *noun Cdn* a person arrested for being discovered in a bawdy house or an illegal bar or gambling establishment.

found·ing father *noun* (also **Founding Father**) a person associated with a founding, esp. a member of the US Federal Constitutional Convention of 1787.

found·ling *noun* an abandoned infant of unknown parentage. [Middle English, perhaps from obsolete *funding* (as FIND, -ING³), assimilated to -LING¹]

found object *noun* an object found or picked up at random and presented as a rarity or a work of art.

foun·dry *noun* (*pl.* **-dries**) **1** a factory where metal is melted and moulded into various objects. **2** the art or business of casting metal.

fount¹ *noun* a spring or fountain; a source (*a fount of knowledge*). [back-formation from FOUNTAIN after MOUNT²]

fount² *Brit. var. of* FONT².

foun·tain ● *noun* **1 a** a jet or jets of water made to spout for ornamental purposes. **b** a structure built for such a jet or jets to rise and fall in. **2** a structure for the constant public supply of drinking water. **3** a natural spring of water. **4** a source (in physical or abstract senses). **5** = SODA FOUNTAIN. **6** a reservoir for oil, ink, etc. ● *intransitive verb* rise like the waters of a fountain. □ **foun·tained** *adjective* (also in *combination*). [Old French *fontaine* from Late Latin *fontana* fem. of Latin *fontanus* (adj.) from *fons fontis* a spring]

fountain grass *noun* an ornamental grass of the genus *Pennisetum*.

foun·tain·head *noun* **1** the headwaters or source of a stream etc. **2** an original source, esp. of information.

fountain of youth *noun* a legendary spring said to restore the health and youth of anyone who drank from it.

fountain pen *noun* a pen with a reservoir or cartridge holding ink.

Fou·quet /fuːˈkei/ **1 Jean** (*c.*1420–81), French painter. Regarded as the leading French painter of the 15th c., he is known for a *Book of Hours* (1450–60) and a monumental *Pietà* altarpiece. **2 Nico·las** (also **Fouc·quet**) (1615–80), French finance minister 1653–61 under Louis XIV. He was tried for embezzlement and sentenced to life imprisonment (1664).

four ● *noun* **1** one more than three, or six less than ten; the product of two units and two units. **2** a symbol for this (4, iv, IV, rarely iiii, IIII). **3** a size etc. denoted by four. **4** a set or team of four persons or things. **5** a four-oared rowboat or its crew. **6** four o'clock. **7** a card with four pips. ● *adjective* that amount to four. □ **on all fours** on hands and knees. [Old English *fēower* from Germanic]

four-and-a-half *noun Cdn* (*Que.*) an apartment having two bedrooms, a kitchen, a living room, and a bathroom.

four-by-four *noun* (also **4 × 4**) **1** a four-wheeled automotive vehicle, esp. a truck, with four-wheel drive. **2** a piece of wood measuring four inches by four in cross-section.

Four Can·tons, Lake of the an alternative name for Lake Lucerne (see LUCERNE, LAKE).

four·chette /fuːrˈʃet/ *noun Anat.* a thin fold of skin at the back of the vulva. [French, diminutive of *fourche* (as FORK)]

four-colour *adjective* (of a printing or photographic process) involving the principle in which three primary colours and black are used in combination to produce almost any other colour.

four-eyes *noun slang* a person wearing glasses. □ **four-eyed** *adjective*

four-flush *N Amer.* ● *noun* a poker hand of little value, having four cards of the same suit and one of another. ● *intransitive verb* bluff, brag.

four-flusher *noun N Amer.* a bluffer or humbug.

four·fold *adjective & adverb* **1** four times as much or as many. **2** consisting of four parts. **3** amounting to four.

4-H club *noun N Amer.* a club for the instruction of young people in citizenry and agriculture. [from the aim of the organization to improve head, heart, hands and health]

Four Horsemen of the Apocalypse *noun* four horsemen representing war, destruction, famine and plague (Revelation 6:2-8).

Four Hundred *noun* (*prec. by the*) *US* the social elite of a community.

Fou·rier /ˈfʊriei/ **1 (François Marie) Charles** (1772–1837), French social reformer, who advocated a system of social reorganization known as Fourierism, which proposed the regrouping of society into co-operative communities, or *phalanges*. **2 (Jean Bap·tiste) Jo·seph** (1768–1830), French mathematician. His theory that a wide class of periodic phenomena could be described by means of Fourier series now provides one of the most important methods for solving many partial differential equations that occur in physics and engineering. □ **Fou·rier·ist** *adjective & noun* (in sense 1).

Fourier analysis *noun Math.* the resolution of periodic data into harmonic functions using a Fourier series. [J. FOURIER]

Fourier series *noun Math.* an expansion of a periodic function as a series of trigonometric functions. [J. FOURIER]

four-in-hand *noun* **1 a** a coach or carriage pulled by four horses and driven by one person. **b** a team of four horses pulling such a vehicle. **2** a necktie worn tied in a loose knot with two hanging ends.

four-laning *noun* the widening of a two-lane highway into four lanes.

four-leaf clover *noun* (also **four-leaved clover**) a clover leaf with four leaflets, thought to bring good luck.

four-letter word *noun* any of several short words referring to sexual or excretory functions, regarded as coarse or offensive.

Four Noble Truths *noun* the four central beliefs containing the essence of Buddhist teaching.

four o'clock *noun* = MARVEL OF PERU.

411 /ˌfɔrwʌnˈwʌn/ *noun* (as the *411 on*) the relevant information about. [from the telephone dial code for directory assistance]

four on the floor *noun N Amer. slang* a four-speed manual gearshift mounted on the floor of an automobile etc.

four-part *adjective* arranged for four voices to sing or instruments to play.

four·pence /ˈfɔrpəns/ *noun Brit. hist.* the sum of four pence.

four·plex *noun N Amer.* a residential building divided into four self-contained apartments.

four-poster *noun* (in full **four-poster bed**) a bed with a post at each corner supporting a canopy.

four·score *noun archaic* eighty.

four·some *noun* **1** a group of four persons. **2** a golf match between two pairs with partners playing the same ball.

four-square ● *adjective* **1** solidly based. **2** steady, resolute; forthright. **3** square-shaped. ● *adverb* steadily, resolutely. ● *noun N Amer.* a children's game played with a large ball on a square subdivided into four smaller squares.

four-star *adjective* **1** (of a hotel, restaurant, etc.) given four stars in a grading in which this denotes the highest standard or the next standard to the highest; excellent. **2** *US & Brit.* having or designating a military rank distinguished by four stars on the epaulette of the uniform.

four-stroke ● *attributive adjective* **1** (of an internal combustion engine) having a cycle of four strokes (intake, compression, combustion, and exhaust). **2** (of a vehicle) having a four-stroke engine. ● *noun* a four-stroke engine or vehicle.

four·teen ● *noun* **1** one more than thirteen, or four more than ten; the product of two units and seven units. **2** a symbol for this (14, xiv, XIV). **3** a size etc. denoted by fourteen. **4** a set of fourteen persons or things. ● *adjective* that amount to fourteen. □ **four·teenth** *adjective, adverb & noun*

fourth ● *noun* **1** the position in a sequence corresponding to that of the number 4 in the sequence 1–4. **2** something occupying this position. **3** the fourth person etc. in a race or competition. **4** each of four equal parts of a thing; a quarter. **5** the fourth (and often highest) in a sequence of gears. **6** *Music* **a** an interval or chord spanning four consecutive notes in the diatonic scale, e.g. C to F. **b** a note separated from another by this interval. **7** *Baseball* the fourth inning. **8** *American Football* the fourth down. **9** *Dance* = FOURTH POSITION. ● *adjective* that is the fourth. ● *adverb* in the fourth place; fourthly. □ **fourth·ly** *adverb* [Old English *fēortha, fēowertha* from Germanic]

fourth dimension *noun* **1** a postulated dimension additional to those determining area and volume. **2** time regarded as equivalent to linear dimensions.

fourth estate *noun* (also **Fourth Estate**) the press; journalists or the profession of journalism.

fourth-genera·tion *adjective* (of a computer) distinguished by large-scale integrated-circuit technology and very large rapid-access memory and belonging essentially to the post-1970 period.

Fourth of July *noun* (also called **Independence Day**) in the US, a national holiday celebrating the anniversary of the adoption of the Declaration of Independence in 1776.

fourth position *noun Dance* **1** a position of the feet in which they are placed turned outwards one in front of the other, separated by the length of one foot. **2** a position of the arms in which one is held above the head and the other is curved in front of the waist.

Fourth Republic *hist.* **1** the republican regime in France between the end of the Second World War (1945) and the introduction of a new constitution by de Gaulle in 1958. **2** this period in France.

fourth wall *noun Theatre* the imaginary wall of a box set, through which the audience sees the performance.

Fourth World *noun* the poorest nations in the least developed parts of the world, esp. in Africa and Asia.

four-wheel ● *adjective* **1** having four wheels. **2** acting on all four wheels of a vehicle. ● *intransitive verb* travel in or on a four-wheeler.

four-wheel drive *noun* a system in a motor vehicle which supplies power to all wheels in order to improve traction, cornering, etc.

four-wheeler *noun slang* **1** = ALL-TERRAIN VEHICLE 2. **2** = FOUR-BY-FOUR 1.

fous·ty /ˈfausti/ *adjective Cdn* (*Nfld*) mouldy, musty. [SW England dialect]

fovea /ˈfoːviə/ *noun* (*pl.* **fo·veae** /-viˌiː/) *Anat.* a small depression or pit, esp. the pit in the retina of the eye for focusing images. □ **fo·veal** *adjective* **fo·veate** /-viˌeit/ *adjective* [Latin]

fowl (*pl.* same or **fowls**) ● *noun* **1** any domestic cock or hen of various gallinaceous birds, kept for eggs and flesh. **2** the flesh of birds, esp. a domestic cock or hen, as food. **3** (in *combination* or *collective*) a bird (*wildfowl*). ● *intransitive verb* catch or hunt wildfowl. □ **fowl·er** *noun* **fowl·ing** *noun* [Old English *fugol* from Germanic]

fowl cholera *noun* = CHICKEN CHOLERA.

Fow·ler, Henry Wat·son (1858–1933), English lexicographer and grammarian, who is best known for his guide to style and idiom, *Modern English Usage* (1926); with his brother F(rancis) G(eorge) Fowler (1870–1918), he compiled the first *Concise Oxford Dictionary* (1911).

Fowles, John (Rob·ert) (b.1926), English novelist. His works include the psychological thriller *The Collector* (1963), the magic realist novel *The Magus* (1966), and the semi-historical novel *The French Lieutenant's Woman* (1969).

fowl pest *noun* an infectious virus disease of fowls.

fowl supper *noun* (also **fall supper**) *Cdn* a fundraising dinner at which turkey or other fowl is served, held in the autumn by a church or community group.

Fox¹ ▸ **1 Charles James** (1749–1806), English Whig politician and orator, noted for his advocacy of social and political reforms, and for his work in bringing about the abolition of the English slave trade. **2 George** (1624–91), English preacher, who founded the Society of Friends (Quakers), teaching that truth is the inner voice of God speaking to the soul, and rejecting priesthood and ritual. **3 Mi·chael J.** (born Michael Andrew Fox, b.1961), Canadian actor. His roles have included leading parts in the television series *Family Ties* and the film *Back to the Future* (1985). **4 Ter·rance Stan·ley** (**'Terry'**) (1958–81), Canadian runner and activist. He lost his right leg to bone cancer in 1977; his 1980 'Marathon of Hope' run across Canada, which he was forced to abandon due to the spread of cancer to his lungs after running from St. John's to Thunder Bay, eventually raised $23 million for cancer research.

Fox² ● *noun* **1** a member of a N American Aboriginal people formerly inhabiting parts of Michigan and Wisconsin and, from the 18th c., Iowa. **2** the Algonquian language of this people. ● *adjective* of or relating to this people or their language or culture. [translation of French *Renard* in the same sense, from Huron *Skenchiohronon*, lit. 'people of the red fox']

fox ● *noun* **1 a** any of various wild flesh-eating mammals of the dog family, esp. of the genus *Vulpes*, with a sharp snout, bushy tail, and usu. red or grey fur, proverbial for cunning. **b** the fur of a fox. **2** a cunning or sly person. **3** *N Amer. slang* an attractive young woman. ● *verb* **1** *transitive* deceive, baffle, trick. **2** *transitive* (usu. as **foxed** *adjective*) discolour (the leaves of a book, engraving, etc.) with brownish marks. □ **fox·ing** *noun* (in sense 2 of *verb*). **fox·like** *adjective* [Old English from West Germanic]

fox·berry *noun* (*pl.* **-berries**) the cowberry, *Vaccinium vitis-idaea*.

Foxe Basin a large, shallow basin in NE Canada, separating Baffin Island from the Melville Peninsula of Nunavut. It is connected to the Arctic Ocean via Fury and Hecla Strait and to the Labrador Sea via Hudson Strait. [L. *Fox*, English navigator and Arctic explorer d.1635]

Foxe Peninsula a peninsula of the southwestern coast of Baffin Island. [see FOXE BASIN]

fox·fire *noun N Amer.* the phosphorescent light emitted by certain fungi on decaying timber.

fox·glove *noun* any tall plant of the genus *Digitalis*, with erect spikes of purple or white flowers like the fingers of a glove.

fox grape *noun* a wild grape, *Vitis labrusca*, of the northeastern US and southern Ontario, from which many cultivated varieties are derived.

fox·hole *noun Military* a hole in the ground used as a shelter against enemy fire.

fox·hound *noun* a kind of hound bred and trained to hunt foxes.

fox hunt ● *noun* **1** the hunting of foxes with hounds. **2** a particular group of people engaged in this. ● *intransitive verb* engage in a fox hunt. □ **fox hunter** *noun* **fox hunting** *noun & adjective*

fox snake *noun* a non-venomous snake, *Elaphe vulpina*, of central North America, with a yellow body marked by dark brown blotches.

fox·tail *noun* any of several grasses esp. of the genera *Alopecurus* and *Setaria*, with brushlike spikes.

foxtail lily *noun* any liliaceous plant of the genus *Eremurus*, with flowers in tall spikes, grown as an ornamental. *Also called* DESERT CANDLE.

fox terrier *noun* a short-haired breed of terrier originally used for unearthing foxes.

fox·trot ● *noun* **1** a ballroom dance characterized by varied combinations of slow and quick steps. **2** the music for this. ● *intransitive verb* (**fox·trot·ted, fox·trot·ting**) perform this dance.

foxy *adjective* (**fox·i·er, fox·i·est**) **1** of or like a fox. **2** sly or cunning. **3** reddish brown. **4** (of paper) damaged, esp. by mildew. **5** *N Amer. slang* (of a woman) sexually attractive. □ **fox·i·ly** *adverb* **fox·i·ness** *noun*

foy·er /ˈfɔiei/ *noun* an entrance hall or other large area in a hotel, theatre, apartment building, etc. [French, = hearth, home, ultimately from Latin *focus* fire]

FP *abbreviation* freezing point.

fp *abbreviation* forte-piano.

fps *abbreviation* (also **f.p.s.**) **1** feet per second. **2** FOOT-POUND-SECOND.

FR *abbreviation Cdn* Forest Region.

Fr *symbol Chem.* the element francium.

Fr. *abbreviation* (also **Fr**) **1** Father. **2** French.

fr. *abbreviation* **1** franc(s). **2** from. **3** fragment.

Fra *noun* a prefixed title given to an Italian monk or friar. [Italian, abbreviation of *frate* brother]

frac·as /ˈfrakəs/ *noun* a noisy disturbance or quarrel. [French from *fracasser* from Italian *fracassare* make an uproar]

frac·tal *Math.* ● *noun* a curve or geometrical figure, each part of which has the same statistical character as the whole. ● *adjective* of or relating to a fractal. [FRACTION + -AL]

frac·tion *noun* **1** a numerical quantity that is not a whole number (e.g. $1/2$, 0.5). **2** a small, esp. very small, part, piece, or amount. **3** a part or subdivision of a whole (*a large fraction of the population*). **4** a portion of a mixture separated by distillation etc. **5** the division of the Eucharistic bread. [Old French from Late Latin *fractio -onis* from Latin *frangere fract-* break]

frac·tion·al *adjective* **1** of or relating to or being a fraction. **2** very slight; incomplete. **3** *Chem.* relating to the separation of parts of a mixture by making use of their different physical properties (*fractional crystallization; fractional distillation*). □ **frac·tion·al·iz·a·tion** *noun* (also esp. *Brit.* **-isation**). **frac·tion·al·ize** *transitive verb* (also esp. *Brit.* **-ise**). **frac·tion·al·ly** *adverb* (esp. in sense 2).

frac·tion·ate *transitive verb* **1** break up into parts. **2** separate (a mixture) by fractional distillation etc. □ **frac·tion·a·tion** *noun* **frac·tion·a·tor** *noun*

frac·tious *adjective* **1** irritable, bad-tempered. **2** unruly. □ **frac·tious·ly** *adverb* **frac·tious·ness** *noun* [FRACTION in obsolete sense 'brawling', prob. after *factious* etc.]

frac·ture ● *noun* **1 a** a breakage or breaking, esp. of a bone or cartilage. **b** the result of breaking; a crack or split. **2** the surface appearance of a freshly broken rock or mineral. **3** *Linguistics* **a** the substitution of a diphthong for a simple vowel owing to an influence esp. of a following consonant. **b** a diphthong substituted in this way. ● *transitive & intransitive verb* **1** undergo or cause to undergo a fracture. **2** break or cause to break. **3** (with reference to an organization or other abstract thing) split or fragment so as to no longer function or exist (*the movement had been fractured without her leadership*). [French *fracture* or from Latin *fractura* (as FRACTION)]

frac·tured *adjective* **1** having sustained a fracture. **2** divided or split metaphorically. **3** (of language or syntax) broken, not fluent.

frae·num *var. of* FRENUM.

frag *N Amer. Military slang* ● *noun* a fragmentation grenade. ● *transitive verb* (**fragged, frag·ging**) attack or kill (esp. a superior officer) with a fragmentation grenade. [abbreviation]

fra·gile /ˈfradʒail/ *adjective* **1** easily broken. **2** (of a person) not strong, sturdy or resilient. **3** vulnerable, easily destroyed (*fragile ecosystem*). □ **fra·gile·ly** *adverb* **fra·gil·ity** /frəˈdʒɪlɪti/ *noun* [French *fragile* or Latin *fragilis* from *frangere* break]

fragile X syndrome *noun* an inherited form of mental retardation, caused by a faulty or damaged X chromosome.

frag·ment ● *noun* /ˈfragmənt/ **1** a part broken off; a detached piece. **2** an isolated or incomplete part. **3** the remains of an otherwise lost or destroyed whole, esp. the extant remains or unfinished portion of a book or work of art. **4** a scrap; a leftover piece. ● *transitive & intransitive verb* /fragˈment/ break or separate into fragments. □ **frag·ment·al** /-ˈmentl/ *adjective* **frag·ment·ed** /-ˈmentəd/ *adjective* [French *fragment* or Latin *fragmentum* (as FRAGILE)]

frag·men·tary /ˈfragmənˌteri/ *adjective* **1** consisting of fragments. **2** disconnected. **3** *Geol.* composed of fragments of previously existing rocks. □ **frag·men·tar·i·ly** *adverb* **frag·men·tar·i·ness** *noun*

frag·men·ta·tion /ˌfragmənˈteiʃən/ *noun* **1** the process or an instance of breaking into fragments. **2** (*attributive*) designating a weapon that is designed to break up into small rapidly-moving fragments (*fragmentation bomb; fragmentation grenade*).

Fra·go·nard /ˈfragoˌnar/ **Jean-Honoré** (1732–1806), French rococo painter, who is most famous for erotic canvases such as *The Swing* (*c.*1766) and *The Progress of Love* (1771).

fra·grance /ˈfreigrəns/ *noun* **1** sweetness of smell. **2** a sweet scent. **3** something scented, esp. a perfume, eau de cologne, etc. □ **fra·granced** *adjective*

fra·grant /ˈfreigrənt/ *adjective* pleasant smelling. □ **fra·grant·ly** *adverb* [French *fragrant* or Latin *fragrare* smell sweet]

frail *adjective* **1** (of a person) physically weak or delicate. **2** easily damaged or broken. **3** morally weak; unable to resist temptation. □ **frail·ly** *adverb* **frail·ness** *noun* [Old French *fraile, frele* from Latin *fragilis* FRAGILE]

frail·ty *noun* (*pl.* **-ties**) **1** the condition of being frail. **2** liability to err or yield to temptation. **3** a fault, weakness, or foible.

Frak·tur /ˈfraktʊr/ *noun* a German style of black-letter type, the normal type used for printing German from the 16th to the mid 20th c. [German]

frame ● *noun* **1** a case or border enclosing a picture, window, door, etc. **2** the basic rigid supporting structure of anything, e.g. of a building, motor vehicle, or aircraft. **3** (in *pl.*) a structure of metal, plastic, etc. holding the lenses of a pair of eyeglasses. **4** a human or animal body, esp. with reference to its size or structure (*her frame shook with laughter*). **5** a framed work or structure (*the frame of heaven*). **6 a** an established order, plan, or system (*the frame of society*). **b** construction, constitution, build. **7** a temporary state (esp. in **frame of mind**). **8 a** a single complete image or picture on a movie or transmitted in a series of lines by television. **b** one of the separate drawings of a comic strip. **9** *Sport informal* an inning, period, etc. **10** *Bowling* **a** any of the ten divisions of a bowling game. **b** one of the compartments on a scorecard where the score from a single frame is recorded. **11 a** esp. *Brit.* = RACK¹ 4. **b** a round of play in pool etc. **12** *Hort.* a boxlike structure of glass etc. for protecting plants. **13** a removable box of slats for the building of a honeycomb in a beehive. **14** *N Amer. slang* = FRAME-UP. ● *transitive verb* **1 a** set in or provide with a frame. **b** serve as a frame for. **2** construct by a combination of parts or in accordance with a design or plan. **3** formulate or devise the essentials of (a complex thing, idea, theory, etc.). **4** (foll. by *to, into*) adapt or fit. **5** *informal* concoct a false charge or evidence against; devise a plot with regard to. **6** articulate (words). ● *adjective* (of a building) made of a wooden frame covered with boards, siding, etc. (*frame house; frame bungalow*). □ **frame·able** *adjective* (also **fram·able**). **frame·less** *adjective* **fram·er** *noun* [Old English *framian* be of service, from *fram* forward: see FROM]

frame of reference *noun* **1** a set of standards or principles governing behaviour, thought, etc. **2** *Geom.* a system of geometrical axes for defining position.

frame-up *noun informal* a conspiracy, esp. to make an innocent person appear guilty.

frame·work *noun* **1** an essential supporting structure. **2** a basic system.

fram·ing *noun* **1** a framework; a system of frames. **2** the act or process of framing or constructing something.

franc /fraŋk/ *noun* **1** the former chief monetary unit of France, Belgium, and Luxembourg. **2** the chief monetary unit of Switzerland, Liechtenstein, Madagascar, New Caledonia, and Rwanda. **3** a monetary unit of Morocco, equal to one-hundredth of a dirham. [Old French from *Francorum Rex* 'king of the Franks', the legend on the earliest gold coins so called (14th c.): see FRANK³]

Franca /ˈfraŋkə/ **Celia** (born Celia Franks) (b.1921), English-born Canadian ballet dancer, choreographer, and director. She was the founder (1951) and artistic director (1951–74) of the National Ballet of Canada.

France¹ a country in W Europe; pop. (est. 2002) 59,765,983; capital, Paris.

France² /frãs/ **Anatole** (pseudonym of Jacques-Anatole-François Thibault) (1844–1924), French writer, whose novels are often characterized by social and political satire, and include *Les Dieux ont soif* (1912); he was awarded the Nobel Prize for literature in 1921.

Fran·ces·ca see PIERO DELLA FRANCESCA.

Franche-Comté /ˌfrãʃkɔ̃ˈtei/ a region of E France, in the northern foothills of the Jura mountains.

fran·chise /ˈfrantʃaiz/ ● *noun* **1** the right to vote in elections. **2 a** authorization granted to an individual or group by a company to sell its goods or services. **b** the store, restaurant, etc., granted such authorization. **3 a** authorization granted to an individual or group by a professional sports league to own and operate a team as a member of the league. **b** the team granted such authorization. **4** *hist.* legal immunity or exemption from a burden or jurisdiction. **5** a right or privilege granted to a person or corporation. **6** a series of films featuring one or more of the same characters and similar formulaic plots, usually accompanied by various marketing spinoffs (*the James Bond franchise*). ● *transitive verb* grant a franchise to. □ **fran·chis·ee** *noun* **fran·chis·or** *noun* (also **fran·chis·er**). [Old French from *franc, franche* free: see FRANK¹]

Fran·cis I (1494–1547), king of France 1515–47, who is remembered as a patron of the arts and for his wars against the Holy Roman Empire (1521–44).

Fran·cis II (1768–1835), the last Holy Roman emperor 1792–1806, and as Francis I, emperor of Austria 1804–35. He was defeated by Napoleon at Austerlitz (1805) and abdicated as Holy Roman emperor (1806).

Fran·cis·can /franˈsɪskən/ ● *noun* a monk or nun of an order founded in 1209 by St. Francis of Assisi (*see also* GREY FRIAR). ● *adjective* of St. Francis or his order. [French *franciscain* from modern Latin *Franciscanus* from *Franciscus* Francis]

Fran·cis of Assisi, St. (born Giovanni di Bernardone) (*c.*1181–1226), Italian monk, founder of the Franciscan order (1209). Born into a wealthy family, he renounced his inheritance in favour of a life of poverty, and is remembered for his generosity and love of nature. Feast day, 4 Oct.

Fran·cis of Sales, St. (1567–1622), French bishop. One of the leaders of the Counter-Reformation, he was Bishop of Geneva (1602–22), and co-founder of the Order of the Visitation, an order of nuns (1610). Feast day, 24 Jan.

Francis Xavier, St. see XAVIER, ST. FRANCIS.

fran·cium /ˈfransiəm/ *noun Chem.* a radioactive metallic element occurring naturally in uranium and thorium ores. Symbol: **Fr**; at. no.: 87. [modern Latin from *France* (the discoverer's country)]

fran·ciz·a·tion /ˌfransaiˈzeiʃən/ *noun* (also **fran·cis·a·tion**) *Cdn* (*Que.*) the establishment or adoption of French as the official or working language of business, education, etc. (also *attributive: francization program*).

francization certificate *noun Cdn* (*Que.*) a certificate stating that a business etc. has adopted a program of francization.

fran·cize /ˈfransaiz/ *transitive verb* (also **fran·cise**) *Cdn* (*Que.*) cause (a person, business, etc.) to adopt French as an official or working language. [French *franciser*]

Franck ▶ 1 /ˈfrãk/ **César (Auguste)** (1822–90), Belgian-born French organist and composer. He is known for his organ music and for his *Symphonic Variations* for piano and orchestra (1885), D minor Symphony (1886–8), and String Quartet (1889). **2** /fraŋk/ **James** (1882–1964), German-born US physicist. He worked on the bombardment of atoms by electrons, and found that the atoms absorb and lose energy in discrete increments or quanta; he later worked on the atomic bomb project.

Fran·co¹, **Fran·cis·co** (1892–1975), Spanish general and dictator, head of state 1939–75. He became leader of the Falange (Fascist) Party (1937) which defeated the republican government in the Spanish Civil War (1939); he then established a dictatorship that ruled Spain until his death.

Fran·co² (*pl.* **-cos**) *Cdn* francophone. [abbreviation]

Franco- *combining form* **1** French; French and (*Franco-German*). **2** (also **franco-**) regarding France, the French, or French-speakers (*francophile*). [medieval Latin *Francus* FRANK³]

Franco-Albertan *Cdn* ● *noun* a francophone Albertan. ● *adjective* of or relating to Franco-Albertans.

Franco-American ● *noun* an American of French-Canadian or French descent, esp. one resident in the New England States. ● *adjective* of or relating to France and the US.

Franco-Canadian *Cdn* ● *noun* = FRENCH CANADIAN *noun*. ● *adjective* **1** = FRENCH CANADIAN *adjective*. **2** of or relating to Canada and France.

Franco-Columbian *Cdn* ● *noun* a francophone British Columbian. ● *adjective* of or relating to Franco-Columbians.

fran·co·lin /'fraŋkoːlɪn/ *noun* any medium-sized Eurasian or African partridge of the genus *Francolinus*. [French from Italian *francolino*]

Franco-Manitoban *Cdn* ● *noun* a francophone Manitoban. ● *adjective* of or relating to Franco-Manitobans.

Fran·conia /fraŋˈkoːniə/ a medieval duchy of S Germany, inhabited by the Franks. It was partitioned in 939 into Western, or Rhenish, Franconia and Eastern Franconia. The region now falls mainly within Bavaria, Hesse, and Baden-Württemberg.

Franco-Ontarian *Cdn* ● *noun* a francophone Ontarian. ● *adjective* of or relating to Franco-Ontarians.

franco·phile *noun* a person who admires French or francophone culture. □ **franco·philia** *noun*

franco·phobe *noun* a person who dislikes francophones, or French or francophone culture. □ **franco·phobia** *noun*

franco·phone esp. *Cdn* ● *noun* a French-speaking person. ● *adjective* French-speaking. [FRANCO- + Greek *phōnē* voice]

Franco·phonie /frãkoˈniː, fraŋkə-/ *noun Cdn* **1** (also **la Francophonie, the Francophonie**) a loosely united group of nations in which French is a first, official, or culturally significant language. **2** (also **francophonie**) francophones within Canada. [French]

Franco-Prussian War the war of 1870–1 between France (under Napoleon III) and Prussia, in which Prussian troops advanced into France and decisively defeated the French at Sedan. The French defeat marked the end of the Second Empire, while the Prussian victory led to the proclamation of the new German Empire, the climax of Bismarck's ambitions to unite Germany (see REICH²).

fran·gible /'frandʒɪbəl/ *adjective* breakable, fragile. □ **fran·gi·bil·ity** *noun* [Old French *frangible* or medieval Latin *frangibilis* from Latin *frangere* to break]

fran·gi·pane /'frandʒɪ,peɪn/ *noun* **1** a custard or cream flavoured with almonds and used as a filling. **2** = FRANGIPANI. [French, earlier meaning a perfume resembling jasmine (as FRANGIPANI)]

fran·gi·pani /,frandʒɪˈpaːni/ *noun* (*pl.* **fran·gi·panis**) **1** any tree or shrub of the genus *Plumeria*, native to tropical America, esp. *P. rubra* with clusters of fragrant white, pink, or yellow flowers. **2** the perfume from this plant. [named after M. *Frangipani*, 16th-c. Italian marquis, inventor of a perfume for scenting gloves]

fran·glais /'frãgleɪ/ *noun* often *derogatory* **1** those elements of the French language that have been recently borrowed from English. **2** broken French as spoken by anglophones. [French from *français* French + *anglais* English]

Frank¹ a coal-mining community that is part of the municipality of Crowsnest Pass in SW Alberta. It was the site in 1903 of the Frank Slide, a rock slide disaster in which approx. 74 million tonnes of rock plummeted down from neighbouring Turtle Mountain, burying a coal-mine entrance and killing at least 70 people. [A. L. *Frank*, coal-mining partner in the Canadian American Co. *c.*1901]

Frank², **Anne** (full name Annelies Marie Frank) (1929–45), German Jewish girl, whose *Diary* (1947) records the experiences of her family while living in hiding from the Nazis in occupied Amsterdam (1942–4); they were eventually betrayed and sent to concentration camps, and she died in Belsen.

Frank³ *noun* a member of the Germanic nation or coalition that conquered Gaul in the 6th c. [Old English *Franca*, Old High German *Franko*, perhaps from the name of a weapon: compare Old English *franca* javelin]

frank¹ ● *adjective* **1** candid, outspoken (*a frank opinion*). **2** undisguised, avowed (*frank admiration*). **3** ingenuous, open (*a frank face*). **4** *Med.* unmistakable. ● *transitive verb* stamp (a letter) with an official mark (esp. other than a normal postage stamp) to record the payment of postage. ● *noun* **1** a franking signature or mark. **2** a franked cover. □ **frank·ness** *noun* [Old French *franc* from medieval Latin *francus* free, from FRANK³ (since only Franks had full freedom in Frankish Gaul)]

frank² *N Amer.* = FRANKFURTER. [abbreviation]

Franken·food *noun* a genetically modified food. [blend of FRANKENSTEIN + FOOD]

Frank·en·stein /'fraŋkən,staɪn/ *noun* a thing that becomes terrifying to its maker; a monster. □ **Frank·en·stein·ian** *adjective* [Baron *Frankenstein*, a character in and the title of a novel (1818) by Mary Shelley]

Frank·fort /'fraŋkfərt/ the state capital of Kentucky; pop. (2000) 27,741.

Frank·furt /'fraŋkfərt/ (in full **Frankfurt am Main** /am 'maɪn/) a city in SW Germany, a leading commercial, financial, and transportation centre; pop. (est. 2002) 645,500.

frank·furt·er *noun* a seasoned smoked sausage made of beef and pork. [German *Frankfurter Wurst* Frankfurt sausage]

frank·in·cense /'fraŋkɪn,sens/ *noun* an aromatic gum resin obtained from trees of the genus *Boswellia*, used for burning as incense. [Old French *franc encens* pure incense]

Frank·ish ● *adjective* of or relating to the Franks or their language. ● *noun* any of the West Germanic dialects spoken by the Franks. [Frank]

Frank·lin ▸ **1 Ar·etha** (b.1942), US soul and gospel singer, who is noted for the albums *I Never Loved a Man (the Way I Love You)* (1967) and *Amazing Grace* (1972). **2 Ben·ja·min** (1706–90), US statesman, inventor, and scientist. A wealthy printer and publisher, he was one of the signatories to the Declaration of Independence (1776); his main scientific achievement was the formulation of a theory of electricity; his inventions include the lightning rod and bifocal eyeglasses. **3 Sir John** (1786–1847), English Arctic explorer. He made three expeditions to the Arctic (1819–22, 1825–7, and 1845–7), disappearing on the third voyage in search of the Northwest Passage; it was later discovered that he and his crew had died off King William Island. **4 Rosa·lind Elsie** (1920–58), English physical chemist and molecular biologist. She investigated the various forms of carbon by means of X-ray crystallography, and later used this technique on DNA, thus contributing to the discovery of its structure. **5 (Stel·la Maria Sarah) Miles** (1879–1954), Australian novelist. She wrote the first true Australian novel, *My Brilliant Career* (1901).

Franklin, District of a former district (est. 1895) of the NWT, roughly occupying the Arctic Archipelago. [as FRANKLIN MOUNTAINS]

frank·lin *noun hist.* a landowner of free but not noble birth in the 14th and 15th c. in England. [Middle English *francoleyn* etc. from Anglo-Latin *francalanus* from *francalis* held without dues, from *francus* free: see FRANK¹]

Franklin Mountains a mountain range in the western NWT, situated along the east side of the Mackenzie River. [Sir J. FRANKLIN]

Franklin's gull *noun* a small N American gull, *Larus pipixcan*, with a black head, red bill, and grey tail, breeding in the Prairies.

Franklin stove *noun N Amer.* a cast iron wood stove of the same general shape as a fireplace, usu. having doors on the front. [B. FRANKLIN]

frank·ly *adverb* **1** in a frank manner. **2** (qualifying a whole sentence) to be frank.

frank·um *noun Cdn* (*Nfld*) the hardened resin of a spruce tree, often used as chewing gum. [shortening of *fran(c)kumsence*, 16th–17th c. var. of FRANKINCENSE, in sense 'spruce or fir resin']

Fran·sas·kois /frãsasˈkwɒ/ *noun Cdn* a francophone resident of Saskatchewan. [Canadian French]

fran·tic *adjective* **1** wildly excited; frenzied. **2** characterized by great hurry or anxiety; desperate, violent. **3** *informal* extreme; very great. □ **fran·tic·ally** *adverb* **fran·tic·ness** *noun* [Middle English *frentik*, *frantik* from Old French *frenetique* from Latin *phreneticus*: see FRENETIC]

Franz Fer·di·nand /frants 'fərdɪnənd/ (English name Francis Ferdinand) (1863–1914), archduke of Austria, nephew of Franz Josef I. His assassination in Sarajevo by a Serb nationalist prompted Austria's attack on Serbia and precipitated the First World War.

Franz Josef I /frants 'joːzef/ (English name Francis Joseph) (1830–1916), emperor of Austria 1848–1916 and king of Hungary 1867–1916. He granted Austria a parliamentary constitution (1861), and gave Hungary equal status with Austria; his annexation of Bosnia and

t top   v voice   w we   z zoo   ʃ she   ʒ vision   θ thin   ð this   ŋ ring   x loch   tʃ chip   dʒ jar   (*see over for vowels*)

Herzegovina (1908) contributed to European political tensions, and resulted in the assassination of his nephew and heir apparent, Franz Ferdinand.

Franz Josef Land a group of islands in the Arctic Ocean, discovered in 1873 by an Austrian expedition. [FRANZ JOSEF I]

frap *transitive verb* (**frapped, frap·ping**) *Naut.* bind tightly. [French *frapper* bind, strike]

frap·pé /ˈfrapei/ ● *adjective* (esp. of wine) iced, cooled. ● *noun* **1** an iced drink. **2** a soft sherbet. [French, past participle of *frapper* strike, ice (drinks)]

fras·cati /frəˈskɒti/ *noun* (*pl.* **fras·catis**) a usu. white wine produced in the Frascati region of Italy.

Fraser ▸ **1** (**John**) **Mal·colm** (b.1930), Australian Liberal politician, prime minister 1975–83. He became the youngest-ever Australian MP in 1955, becoming leader of the Liberal Party in 1975. He was appointed prime minister with the dissolution of the previous administration by the Governor General and was elected a month later. **2 Simon** (1776–1862), US-born Canadian fur trader and explorer. He joined the North West Company in 1792, and was sent in 1805 to the Rocky Mountains, where he established several fur-trading posts; in 1808 he explored the Fraser River, mistakenly believing it to be the Columbia River.

Fraser River a river in BC, 1 370 km long, rising in the east central part of the province, just north of Kinbasket Lake, and flowing northwestward to Prince George, then turning sharply southward and flowing through Quesnel and Chilliwack, before turning westward into the Strait of Georgia, just south of Vancouver. [S. FRASER]

frass *noun* **1** a fine refuse left by insects boring. **2** the excrement of insect larvae. [German from *fressen* devour (as FRET[1])]

frat *noun* N Amer. informal a fraternity. [abbreviation]

fra·ter·nal /frəˈtɜrnəl/ *adjective* **1** of a brother or brothers. **2** suitable to a brother; brotherly. **3** (of twins) developed from separate ova and not necessarily closely similar. **4** N Amer. of or concerning a fraternity or other male society or lodge. □ **fra·ter·nal·ism** *noun* **fra·ter·nal·ly** *adverb* [medieval Latin *fraternalis* from Latin *fraternus* from *frater* brother]

fraternal society *noun* an association, usu. of men, devoted to philanthropic, religious, or social activities.

fra·ter·nity /frəˈtɜrnɪti/ *noun* (*pl.* **-ties**) **1** N Amer. a male students' society in a university or college. **2** a religious brotherhood. **3** a group or company with common interests, or of the same professional class. **4** being fraternal; brotherliness. [Old French *fraternité* from Latin *fraternitas -tatis* (as FRATERNAL)]

fra·ter·nize /ˈfratɜrnaiz/ *intransitive verb* (also esp. *Brit.* **-nise**) (often foll. by *with*) **1** associate; make friends; behave as intimates. **2** (of troops) enter into friendly relations with enemy troops or the inhabitants of an occupied country. □ **frater·niz·a·tion** *noun* [French *fraterniser* & medieval Latin *fraternizare* from Latin *fraternus*: see FRATERNAL]

frat house *noun* N Amer. a house where members of a fraternity live or hold meetings or parties etc.

fratri·cide /ˈfratrɪˌsaid/ *noun* **1** the killing of one's brother or sister. **2** a person who does this. **3** the killing of a member of one's own ethnic group, culture, etc. □ **fratri·cid·al** *adjective* [French *fratricide* or Late Latin *fratricidium*, Latin *fratricida*, from *frater fratris* brother]

Frau /frau/ *noun* (*pl.* **Frauen** /ˈfrauən/) (often as a title) a married or widowed German woman. [German]

fraud *noun* **1** the action or an instance of deceiving someone in order to make money or obtain an advantage illegally. **2** a person or thing that is not what it is claimed or expected to be. **3** a dishonest trick or stratagem. [Old French *fraude* from Latin *fraus fraudis* 'deceit, injury']

fraud·ster *noun* a person who commits fraud, esp. in business dealings.

fraudu·lent /ˈfrɒdjʊlənt/ *adjective* **1** characterized or achieved by fraud. **2** guilty of fraud; intending to deceive. □ **fraudu·lence** *noun* **fraudu·lent·ly** *adverb*

fraught *adjective* **1** (foll. by *with*) filled or attended with (*fraught with danger*). **2** *informal* causing or affected by great anxiety or distress. [Middle English, past participle of obsolete *fraught* (v.) load with cargo, from Middle Dutch *vrachten* from *vracht* FREIGHT]

Fräu·lein /ˈfrɔilain/ *noun* (often as a title or form of address) an unmarried (esp. young) German woman. [German, diminutive of FRAU]

Fraun·hofer /ˈfraunˌhoːfɜr/ **Jo·seph von** (1787–1826), German optician and pioneer in spectroscopy. He observed a large number of fine dark lines in the solar spectrum and plotted their wavelengths;

these (**Fraunhofer lines**) were later used to determine the chemical elements present in the spectra of the sun and stars.

fraxi·nella /ˌfraksɪˈnelə/ *noun* an aromatic plant, *Dictamnus albus*, having foliage that emits an ethereal inflammable oil. Also called DITTANY, GAS PLANT, BURNING BUSH. [modern Latin, diminutive of Latin *fraxinus* ash tree]

fray[1] *verb* **1** *transitive & intransitive* wear through or become worn, esp. (of fabric, rope, etc.) become unwoven as a result of frequent use or abrasion. **2** *intransitive* (of nerves, temper, etc.) become strained; deteriorate. [French *frayer* from Latin *fricare* rub]

fray[2] *noun* a situation of intense activity, typically one incorporating an element of aggression or competition (*nineteen companies intend to bid for the contract, with three more expected to enter the fray*). [Middle English from *fray* to quarrel, from *affray* 'startle', from Anglo-Norman French *afrayer see* AFFRAY]

Frazer, Sir James George (1854–1941), Scottish anthropologist. His famous series of essays, *The Golden Bough* (1890–1915), proposed an evolutionary theory of the development of human thought, from the magical and religious to the scientific.

Frazier /ˈfreizɜr/ **Jo·seph ('Joe')** (b.1944), US boxer. He was world heavyweight champion (1970–73) before losing the title to George Foreman.

fraz·il /ˈfrazɪl/ *noun* N Amer. (also **frazil ice**) slush consisting of small ice crystals formed in water too turbulent to freeze over. [Canadian French *frasil* snow floating in the water; compare French *fraisil* cinders]

fraz·zle *informal* ● *noun* a worn or exhausted state. ● *transitive verb* (usu. as **fraz·zled** *adjective*) **1** wear out; exhaust, esp. from stress. **2** char; shrivel up with burning. □ **to a frazzle** completely; absolutely (*worn to a frazzle*). [19th c.: origin uncertain]

FRCPC *abbreviation* Fellow of the Royal College of Physicians of Canada.

FRCS(C) *abbreviation* Fellow of the Royal College of Surgeons (Canada).

freak ● *noun* **1** (also **freak of nature**) a monstrosity; an abnormally developed individual or thing. **2** (often *attributive*) an abnormal, irregular, or bizarre occurrence (*a freak storm*). **3** *informal* **a** an unconventional person. **b** a person with a specified enthusiasm or interest (*health freak*). **c** a person who undergoes hallucinations; a drug addict (see sense 2 of *verb*). **4** a caprice or vagary. ● *verb* (often foll. by *out*) *informal* **1** *intransitive & transitive* become or make very angry, frightened, excited, etc. **2** *intransitive & transitive* undergo or cause to undergo hallucinations or a strong emotional experience, esp. from use of narcotics. **3** *intransitive* adopt a wildly unconventional lifestyle. [16th c.: prob. from dial.]

freak·ing *adjective* N Amer. euphemism expressing annoyance, or as an intensifier (*going out of his freaking mind*).

freak·ish *adjective* **1** of or like a freak. **2** bizarre, unconventional. □ **freak·ish·ly** *adverb* **freak·ish·ness** *noun*

freak-out *noun* informal an act of freaking out; a hallucinatory or strong emotional experience.

freak show *noun* a sideshow at a fair, featuring people or animals with abnormal physical features.

freaky *adjective* (**freak·i·er, freak·i·est**) = FREAKISH. □ **freak·i·ly** *adverb* **freak·i·ness** *noun*

Fré·chette /freiˈʃet/ **Louis-Honoré** (1839–1908), Canadian poet. His verse collections include *Les Fleurs boréales* (1879), and *La Légende d'un peuple* (1887), a cycle of patriotic poems celebrating historical figures and events in French-Canadian history; his prose works include *Christmas in French Canada* (1899).

freckle ● *noun* (often in *pl.*) any of a number of light brown spots on the skin, often caused by exposure to the sun. ● *verb* **1** *transitive* (usu. as **freckled** *adjective*) spot with freckles. **2** *intransitive* be spotted with freckles. □ **freck·ly** *adjective* [Old Norse *freknur* (pl.)]

freckle-faced *adjective* having a freckled face.

Fred·erick I (known as 'Frederick Barbarossa' = 'Redbeard') (c.1123–90), king of Germany and Holy Roman emperor 1152–90. He made a sustained attempt to subdue Italy and the papacy, but was eventually defeated at the Battle of Legnano in 1176.

Fred·erick II 1 (known as 'Frederick the Great') (1712–86), king of Prussia 1740–86. On his succession, Frederick promptly claimed Silesia, launching Europe into the War of the Austrian Succession (1740–8); during the Seven Years War (1756–63), he fought against a coalition of France, Russia, Austria, Sweden, and Saxony, and succeeded in considerably strengthening Prussia's position. **2** (1194–1250), Holy Roman emperor 1220–1250, king of Sicily 1197–1250, and king of Germany 1212–50. He led the Sixth Crusade (1228–29) and had himself crowned king of Jerusalem (1229–43).

Fred·erick IX (1899–1972), king of Denmark 1947–72. As crown prince he was imprisoned during the German occupation of Denmark (1943–45) in the Second World War.

Fred·erick Wil·liam (known as 'the Great Elector') (1620–88), Elector of Brandenburg 1640–88. His program of reconstruction and reorganization following the Thirty Years War brought stability to his country and laid the basis for the expansion of Prussian power in the 18th c.

Fred·erick Wil·liam I (1688–1740), king of Prussia 1713–40, whose reign was notable for the strengthening of the Prussian army.

Fred·erick Wil·liam II (1744–97), king of Prussia 1787–97. He fought in the early campaigns against the French Revolutionary armies, and his reign saw a flourishing of the arts, esp. in music.

Fred·erick Wil·liam III (1770–1840), king of Prussia 1797–1840. In 1811 he joined Napoleon in the war against Russia, later signing a military alliance with Russia and Austria; he became progressively reactionary during the last years of his reign.

Fred·erick Wil·liam IV (1795–1861), king of Prussia 1840–61. He championed a united Germany, but refused the offer of a constitutional monarchy for the German confederation in 1849.

Fred·eric·ton the capital city of New Brunswick, located in the central part of the province, on the Saint John River; pop. (2001) 47,560. The city was founded in 1785 by the United Empire Loyalists. □ **Fred·eric·ton·ian** *noun* [Prince *Frederick*, second son of George III]

free ● *adjective* (**freer**; **freest**) **1** not in bondage to or under the control of another; having personal rights and social and political liberty. **2** (of a nation, or its citizens or institutions) subject neither to foreign domination nor to despotic government; having national and civil liberty (*a free press*; *a free society*). **3 a** unrestricted, unimpeded; not restrained or fixed. **b** at liberty; not confined or imprisoned. **c** released from ties or duties; unimpeded. **d** unrestrained as to action; independent (*set free*). **4** (foll. by *of*, *from*) **a** not subject to; exempt from (*free of tax*). **b** not containing or subject to a specified (usu. undesirable) thing (*free of preservatives*; *free from disease*). **5** (foll. by *to* + infin.) able or permitted to take a specified action (*you are free to choose*). **6** unconstrained (*free gestures*). **7 a** available without charge; costing nothing. **b** not subject to tax, duty, trade restraint, or fees. **8 a** clear of engagements or obligations (*are you free tomorrow?*). **b** not occupied or in use (*the bathroom is free now*). **c** clear of obstructions. **9** spontaneous, unforced (*free compliments*). **10** open to all comers. **11** lavish, profuse; using or used without restraint (*very free with their money*). **12** frank, unreserved. **13** (of a literary style) not observing the strict laws of form. **14** (of a translation) conveying the broad sense; not literal. **15** forward, familiar, impudent. **16** (of talk, stories, etc.) slightly indecent. **17** (of movement) under no force other than that of gravity or inertia (*free flight*). **18** *Physics* **a** not modified by an external force. **b** not bound in an atom or molecule. **19** *Chem.* not combined (*free oxygen*). **20** (of power or energy) disengaged or available. **21** *Linguistics* designating a form that can occur in isolation, e.g. *fire*. **22** *Phonetics* (of a vowel) occurring in a syllable not ended by a consonant. ● *adverb* **1** in a free manner. **2** without cost or payment. **3** *Naut.* not close-hauled. ● *transitive verb* **1** make free; set at liberty. **2** (foll. by *of*, *from*) relieve from (something undesirable). **3** disengage, disentangle. □ **for free** *informal* free of charge, gratis. **free and easy** informal, unceremonious. **free on board** (or **rail**) without charge for delivery to a ship or railway car. **free up** *informal* **1** make available. **2** make less restricted. **it's a free country** *informal* the action proposed is not illegal or forbidden. **make free with 1** take liberties with. **2** use as one's own. □ **free·ly** *adverb* **free·ness** *noun* [Old English *frēo*, *frēon* from Germanic]

-free *combining form* free of or from (*duty-free*; *cruelty-free*).

free agent *noun* **1** a person with freedom of action. **2** a professional athlete who is not under contract, and may sell his or her services to any team. □ **free agency** *noun* (in sense 2). **free agentry** *noun* (in sense 2).

free association *noun* **1** *Psych.* a method of investigating a person's unconscious by eliciting from him or her spontaneous associations with ideas proposed by the examiner. **2** any process in which one thought, word, image, etc. suggests the next without following a logical or conscious direction. □ **free-associ·ate** *intransitive verb*

free·base *slang* ● *noun* cocaine that has been purified by heating with ether, and is taken by inhaling the fumes or smoking the residue. ● *verb* **1** *transitive* purify (cocaine) for smoking or inhaling. **2** *transitive & intransitive* smoke or inhale (freebased cocaine). □ **free·bas·er** *noun*

free·bie *informal* ● *noun* a thing provided free of charge. ● *adjective* free; provided without charge (*a freebie trip*). [arbitrary from FREE]

free·board *noun* the part of a ship's side between the waterline and the deck.

free·boot·er *noun* a pirate or lawless adventurer. □ **free·boot** *intransitive verb* [Dutch *vrijbuiter* (as FREE, BOOTY): compare FILIBUSTER 2]

free·born *adjective* not born in slavery or bondage.

Free Church *noun* a Church dissenting or seceding from an established church (*compare* ESTABLISHED CHURCH).

freed·man *noun* (pl. **-men**) an emancipated slave.

free·dom *noun* **1** the condition of being free or unrestricted. **2 a** personal or civic liberty. **b** absence of slave status. **3** the power of self-determination; independence of fate or necessity. **4** the state of being free to act (often foll. by *to* + infin.: *we have the freedom to leave*). **5** the esp. political right to act, speak, etc. as one pleases without interference (*freedom of speech*; *freedom of religion*; *freedom of association*). **6** frankness, outspokenness; undue familiarity. **7** (foll. by *from*) the condition of being exempt from or not subject to (a defect, burden, etc.). **8** (foll. by *of*) **a** full or honorary participation in (membership, privileges, etc.). **b** unrestricted use of (facilities etc.). **9** a privilege possessed by a city or corporation. **10** facility or ease in action. **11** boldness of conception. [Old English *frēodōm* (as FREE, -DOM)]

freedom fighter *noun* a person who takes part in violent resistance to an established political system etc.

freedom of information *noun* = ACCESS TO INFORMATION.

free enterprise *noun* a system in which private business operates in competition and largely free of governmental control. □ **free enterpriser** *noun N Amer.*

free fall ● *noun* (usu. hyphenated when *attributive*) **1** movement under the force of gravity only, esp.: **a** the part of a parachute descent before the parachute opens. **b** the movement of a spacecraft in space without thrust from the engines. **2** any state of falling rapidly (*prices were in free fall*). ● *intransitive verb* (**free-fall**) move in a free fall.

free-fire zone *noun* an area where shooting, artillery bombardment, etc. is carried on constantly and where all intruders are liable to be shot.

free-floating *adjective* **1** (of an emotion) having no particular focus or cause (*free-floating anxiety*). **2** (of people) not attached or committed to any particular cause, political party, etc. (*the free-floating middle class*). **3** able to move relatively freely.

free-for-all *noun* a fight, competition, or argument in which many people take part, usu. having no rules.

free-form *attributive adjective* of an irregular shape or structure; not constrained by conventional rules etc.

Free French a group of French troops and volunteers organized under General de Gaulle in 1940, who continued fighting against the Axis powers after the surrender of France.

free·hand ● *adjective* (of a drawing or plan etc.) done by hand without special instruments or guides. ● *adverb* in a freehand manner.

free hand *noun* freedom to act at one's own discretion (*gave her a free hand in designing the building*).

free·hold ● *noun* **1** permanent and absolute tenure of land or property with freedom to dispose of it at will. **2** land or property held by such tenure. ● *adjective* held by or having the status of freehold. □ **free·hold·er** *noun*

free house *noun Brit.* an inn or pub not controlled by a brewery and therefore not restricted to selling particular brands of beer or liquor.

free kick *noun Soccer* a set kick allowed to be taken by one side without interference from the other.

free·lance ● *noun* **1** (also **free·lanc·er**) a person, usu. self-employed, offering services on a temporary basis, e.g. to several businesses etc. for particular assignments (also *attributive*: *a freelance editor*). **2** (usu. **free lance**) *hist.* a medieval mercenary. ● *intransitive verb* act as a freelance. ● *adverb* as a freelance. [19th c.: originally in sense 2 of *noun*]

free-living *adjective Biol.* living freely and independently; not attached to a substrate.

free·load·er *noun* esp. *N Amer. slang* a person who eats or drinks at others' expense; a sponger. □ **free·load** *intransitive verb* **free·load·ing** *noun*

free love *noun* sexual relations according to choice and unrestricted by marriage.

free lunch *noun* **1** a lunch provided free of charge. **2** something provided with no obligation on the part of the receiver. □ **there's no (such thing as a) free lunch** nothing is without cost. [from the former practice of bartenders giving out free lunches to attract customers]

uː m**oo**d   ai m**y**   əi p**i**pe   au br**ow**n   ʌ h**ou**se   ei d**ay**   ɔi b**oy**   ã fr**an**glais   ã Canadi**en**   ɔ̃ Br**ay**on   (*see over for consonants*)

free·man noun (pl. **-men**) **1** a person who has the freedom of a city, company, etc. **2** a person who is not a slave or serf.

free market noun a market in which prices are determined by unrestricted competition.

free marketeer noun a supporter or advocate of free market economics.

free·mar·tin noun a female calf born as a twin to a male and sterile, probably as a result of exposure to male hormones in the uterus. [17th c.: origin unknown]

Free·mason noun a member of an international fraternity for mutual help and fellowship (the *Free and Accepted Masons*), with elaborate secret rituals.

Free·mason·ry noun **1** the system and institutions of the Freemasons. **2** (**freemasonry**) instinctive sympathy or understanding.

free port noun **1** a port area where goods in transit are exempt from customs duty. **2** a port open to all traders.

freer comparative of FREE.

free radical noun an uncharged atom or group of atoms with one or more unpaired electrons.

free-range adjective **1** (of hens etc.) kept in natural conditions with freedom of movement. **2** (of eggs) produced by such birds.

free rein see REIN.

free ride noun **1** something obtained at no cost or with no effort. **2** (**free·ride**) a type of snowboard designed for all-round use on and off piste. ● intransitive verb snowboard, esp. off the major runs, for fun rather than competition. □ **free rider** noun

free safety noun Football a secondary defensive player who has no assigned position at the snap of the ball but may roam the field behind the line of scrimmage.

free school noun usu. hist. **1** a school for which no fees are charged. **2** a school run on the basis of freedom from restriction for the pupils.

free·sia /ˈfriːʒə/ noun any bulbous plant of the genus *Freesia*, native to Africa, having fragrant coloured flowers. [modern Latin from F. H. T. *Freese*, German physician d.1876]

free skate noun Figure Skating (in full **free skating program**) a part of a figure skating competition consisting of a program skated to music chosen by the skater, with the number and type of jumps and other elements chosen freely by the skater.

free speech noun the right to express opinions freely.

free-spending adjective spending money liberally or extravagantly. □ **free-spender** noun

free spirit noun an independent or uninhibited person. □ **free-spirit·ed** adjective

freest superlative of FREE.

free-standing adjective **1** not supported by another structure. **2** not affiliated with a larger organization; autonomous (*a free-standing clinic*).

Free State a province in central South Africa, to the north of the Orange River, formerly called Orange Free State; capital, Bloemfontein.

free·stone noun **1** a peach or other fruit having a stone which is loose when the fruit is ripe (*compare* CLINGSTONE). **2** any fine-grained stone which can be cut easily, esp. sandstone or limestone.

free·style ● adjective (of a race or contest) in which all styles are allowed, esp.: **1** Swimming in which any stroke may be used. **2** Wrestling with few restrictions on the holds permitted. ● noun **1** freestyle swimming or wrestling. **2** the front crawl. ● intransitive verb rap, dance, or perform in an improvised or unrestricted fashion (*the hip-hop poet freestyled over the classical music*). □ **free·styl·er** noun

free-swimming adjective (of an aquatic organism) capable of swimming around freely; not sessile or attached to any object.

free·think·er noun a person who rejects dogma or authority, esp. in religious belief. □ **free·think·ing** noun & adjective

free throw noun **1** Sport an unimpeded throw awarded to a player following a foul etc. **2** Basketball such a throw allowing a shot at the basket, taken from behind a marked line.

Free·town the capital and chief port of Sierra Leone; pop. (est. 2002) 1,032,100.

free trade noun international trade free from protectionist tariffs, quotas, export subsidies, and other government intervention.

free trader noun **1** an advocate of free trade. **2** Cdn hist. a fur trader who was not affiliated with any of the large fur-trading companies.

free verse noun irregular or unrhymed verse in which the traditional rules of prosody are disregarded.

free vote noun a Parliamentary vote in which MPs are not constrained to vote along party lines.

free·ware noun Computing software that is available without charge.

free·way noun N Amer. **1** = EXPRESSWAY. **2** a toll-free highway.

free weight noun a barbell, dumbbell, or other weight not attached to a machine, used in weightlifting exercises.

free·wheel ● noun **1** the driving wheel of a bicycle, able to revolve with the pedals at rest. **2** a device in a vehicle's transmission that automatically disengages the drive shaft whenever it begins to move more quickly than the engine. ● intransitive verb (usu. **free-wheel**) **1** coast on a bicycle or in a vehicle. **2** move or act without constraint or effort. □ **free·wheel·er** noun

free·wheel·ing adjective **1** moving freely. **2** (of a person) unconcerned or unconstrained by rules, responsibilities, or conventions. **3** (of actions, speech, etc.) irresponsible.

free will ● noun **1** the power of acting without the constraint of necessity or fate. **2** the ability to act at one's own discretion (*I did it of my own free will*). ● adjective (usu. **free-will**) (of a donation etc.) voluntary (*a free-will collection will be taken*).

free world noun esp. N Amer. the non-Communist countries.

freeze ● verb (past **froze**; past participle **fro·zen**) **1** transitive & intransitive **a** turn or be turned into ice or another solid by cold. **b** (often foll. by *over, up*) make or become rigid or solid as a result of the cold. **2** intransitive be or feel very cold. **3** transitive & intransitive cover or become covered with ice. **4** intransitive (foll. by *to, together*) adhere or be fastened by frost (*the curtains froze to the window*). **5** transitive & intransitive be or become obstructed or closed by the formation of ice (*the pipes froze; cold weather often freezes the water pipes*). **6** transitive preserve (food) by refrigeration below freezing point. **7** transitive & intransitive **a** make or become motionless or powerless through fear, surprise, etc., or when ordered to do so. **b** react or cause to react with sudden aloofness or detachment. **8** transitive stiffen or harden, injure or kill, by chilling (*frozen to death*). **9** transitive informal make (part of the body) insensitive to pain, esp. by injection of a local anaesthetic. **10** transitive make (credits, assets, etc.) temporarily or permanently unrealizable. **11** transitive fix or stabilize (prices, wages, etc.) at a certain level. **12** transitive prohibit the manufacture, sale, use, or development of (a nuclear weapon, etc.). **13** transitive arrest (an action) at a certain stage of development. **14** transitive = FREEZE-FRAME verb. **15** intransitive Computing (of a computer screen) cease to respond to input from the keyboard or mouse. **16** intransitive Curling draw a rock up against a stationary rock without causing the second rock to move. **17** transitive Sport keep possession of (the ball, puck, etc.) for an extended period of time, esp. without attempting to score. ● noun **1** a state of frost; a period or the coming of frost or very cold weather. **2** the fixing or stabilization of prices, wages, etc. **3** = FREEZE-FRAME noun. **4** a decision by one or more nations to stop or limit the manufacture or development of (esp. nuclear) weapons. □ **freeze out** N Amer. informal exclude from business, society, etc. by competition or boycott etc. **freeze up** obstruct or be obstructed by the formation of ice. □ **freez·able** adjective [Old English *frēosan* from Germanic]

freeze-dry transitive verb (**-dries**, **-dried**) preserve (esp. food) by freezing it and then drying it by the sublimation of ice in a vacuum.

freeze-frame ● noun (also *attributive*) the facility of stopping a film or videotape in order to view a motionless image. ● transitive verb use freeze-frame on (an image, a recording, etc.).

freez·er noun a refrigerated cabinet or room for preserving food at very low temperatures; = DEEP-FREEZE noun 1.

freezer bag noun a bag of heavy plastic used for freezing foods etc.

freezer burn noun uneven discoloration of frozen meat or other frozen foods that have been inadequately packaged to prevent surface evaporation.

freeze-up noun esp. Cdn the freezing up of a river, lake, etc., esp. in the fall.

freez·ing adjective **1** (of temperatures) at or near the freezing point. **2** informal (also **freezing cold**) very cold.

freezing point noun **1** the temperature at which a liquid freezes. **2** the freezing point of water, 0°C (32°F) (*the temperature will drop below the freezing point tonight*).

freezing rain noun rain composed of drops which freeze on impact with the ground or other solid objects.

Frege /ˈfreigə/ (**Frie·drich Lud·wig**) **Gott·lob** (1848–1925), German philosopher and mathematician, founder of modern logic. He developed a logical system for the expression of mathematics which was a great improvement on the syllogistic logic which it replaced, and he also worked on general questions of philosophical logic and semantics.

Frei·burg /'fraibɜrg/ (in full **Frei·burg im Breis·gau** /ɪm 'breɪsgau/) a university town in SW Germany, in Baden-Württemberg, on the edge of the Black Forest; pop. (est. 2002) 203,000.

freight /freit/ ● *noun* **1** goods transported by water, air, or land. **2** the transportation of such goods. **3** a charge for transportation of goods. **4** a freight train. **5** the hire of a ship or aircraft for transporting goods. **6** a load or burden. ● *transitive verb* **1** transport (goods) as freight. **2** load with freight. **3** hire or let out (a ship) for the carriage of goods and passengers. **4** load, burden (*freighted with sentiment*). [Middle Dutch, Middle Low German *vrecht* var. of *vracht*: compare FRAUGHT]

freight canoe *noun* (also **freighter canoe**) *Cdn hist.* a large canoe used for transporting freight.

freight car *noun* a railway car for carrying freight.

freight·er /'freitɜr/ *noun* **1** a ship or aircraft designed to carry freight. **2** a person who loads or charters and loads a ship. **3** a person whose business is to receive and forward freight.

freight ton *noun see* TON 4b.

freight train *noun* a train transporting freight rather than passengers.

Fre·man·tle /'fri:mantəl/ the principal port of Western Australia; pop. (2001) 25,199. The city is part of the Perth metropolitan area.

French ● *adjective* **1** of or relating to France or its people or language. **2** of or relating to French Canada or French Canadians. **3** having the characteristics attributed to the French people. ● *noun* **1** the Romance language of France, also used in Canada, Belgium, Switzerland, and elsewhere. **2** (**the French**) (treated as *pl.*) **a** the people of France. **b** the people of French Canada. ● *transitive verb* cut (green beans, etc.) into long thin strips before cooking. □ **pardon** (or **excuse**) **my French** *informal* excuse my use of coarse language. □ **French·ness** *noun* [Old English *frencisc* from Germanic]

French and Indian War a name given to the Seven Years War as fought in N America (1754–63), in which the British defeated the French and their Aboriginal allies and conquered New France.

French bean *noun Brit.* **1** a bean plant, *Phaseolus vulgaris*, having many varieties cultivated for their pods and seeds. **2 a** the pod used as food. **b** the seed used as food: *also called* HARICOT, KIDNEY BEAN.

French braid *N Amer.* ● *noun* a type of braid in which only a small portion of the hair is braided at first, with more strands added gradually as the hair is braided. ● *transitive verb* braid (hair etc.) into a French braid.

French bread *noun* white, yeast-raised bread, usu. in a long loaf with a crisp crust.

French Canada *noun* **1** the part of Canada inhabited primarily by francophones, esp. the province of Quebec. **2** French Canadians collectively.

French Canadian ● *noun* a Canadian whose principal language is French. ● *adjective* (**French-Canadian**) of or relating to French-speaking Canadians.

French Community a political union established by France in 1958 and lasting informally until the late 1970s (its formal operations ceased in the 1960s). Comprising metropolitan France, its overseas departments and territories, and several former French colonies, it coordinated matters of foreign and economic policy, currency, and defence.

French Congo the name (until 1910) for FRENCH EQUATORIAL AFRICA.

French cuff *noun* a cuff designed to be folded back before fastening, usu. fastened with a cufflink.

French curve *noun* a template used for drawing curved lines.

French door *noun* (also **French window**) a long glass door, often one of a pair, and usu. opening onto a patio or balcony.

French dressing *noun* **1** *N Amer.* a creamy, sweet salad dressing, usu. orange in colour. **2** a salad dressing of vinegar and oil, usu. seasoned.

French Equatorial Africa a former federation of French territories in west central Africa (1910–58). Originally called French Congo, its constituent territories were Chad, Ubanghi Shari (now the Central African Republic), Gabon, and Middle Congo (now the Republic of the Congo).

French fact *noun Cdn* (prec. by *the*) francophone culture as a distinct component of Canadian society.

French French *Cdn* ● *noun* the French language as spoken in France, esp. as opposed to that spoken in Quebec. ● *adjective* (**French-French**)

of or relating to the French people or language of France, esp. as opposed to those of Quebec.

french fry esp. *N Amer.* ● *noun* (*pl.* **fries**) a strip of potato which has been deep-fried. ● *transitive verb* (usu. **french-fry**) (**-fried**, **-frying**) fry (food) in deep fat. □ **french-fried** *adjective*

French Guiana an overseas department of France, in northern South America; pop. (est. 2002) 182,333; capital, Cayenne.

French horn *noun* a valved, brass wind instrument with a long, coiled tube and a wide bell.

French·ie *var. of* FRENCHY *noun.*

French·ify *transitive verb* (**-fies**, **-fied**) (usu. as **French·i·fied** *adjective*) make French in form, character, or manners.

French immersion *noun Cdn* an educational program in which anglophone students are taught entirely in French.

French kiss *noun* a kiss with one partner's tongue inserted in the other's mouth. ● **French kiss** *transitive & intransitive verb*

French knickers *plural noun Brit.* loose-fitting and usu. lace-trimmed ladies' underpants with a short, full leg, usu. made in a satiny fabric.

French knot *noun* an embroidery stitch in which the thread is wound around the needle, which is then passed back through the fabric at almost the same point to form a small dot.

French leave *noun* absence without permission.

French letter *noun* esp. *Brit. informal* a condom.

French loaf *noun* a loaf of French bread.

French·man *noun* (*pl.* **-men**) **1** a native or national of France. **2** a francophone.

Frenchman's Butte a prominent hill located almost 50 km northwest of present-day Lloydminster, the scene of an indecisive battle fought between Cree and the Alberta Field Force during the Northwest Rebellion (1885).

French polish ● *noun* shellac polish for wood. ● *transitive verb* polish with this.

French Polynesia an overseas territory of France in the S Pacific; pop. (est. 2002) 257,847; capital, Papeete (on Tahiti). French Polynesia comprises the Society Islands, the Gambier Islands, the Tuamotu Archipelago, the Tubuai Islands, and the Marquesas.

French regime *noun* the period of French rule in Canadian history, until 1763.

French Revolution the overthrow of the Bourbon monarchy in France (1789–99), uniting various groups in French society against the feudal structure of the state, with its privileged Establishment and discredited monarchy. It began with the meeting of the legislative assembly (the Estates General) in May 1789, when the French government was already in crisis; the Bastille was stormed in July of the same year. As the Revolution became steadily more radical and ruthless, figures such as Danton were eclipsed, and the Jacobins and Robespierre dominated: Louis XVI's execution in Jan. 1793 was followed by Robespierre's Reign of Terror (Sept. 1793–July 1794). The Revolution failed to produce a stable form of republican government, and after several different forms of administration, the last, the Directory, was overthrown by Napoleon in 1799.

French River a river in north central Ontario, flowing from the south central shore of Lake Nipissing southwestward to Georgian Bay.

French roll *noun* = FRENCH TWIST.

French safe *noun* esp. *Cdn slang* a condom.

French seam *noun* a seam with the raw edges enclosed.

French Shore 1 an informal name for the district of Clare, a French-Acadian area along the rocky southwestern coast of Nova Scotia, north of Yarmouth. **2** *hist.* that part of the coastline of the island of Newfoundland where the French were granted fishing rights until 1904. It stretched around the island from Cape Bonavista to Cape Ray.

French So·mali·land /sə'mɒli,land/ the former name (until 1967) for DJIBOUTI.

French Southern and Antarctic Territories an overseas territory of France, comprising Adélie Land in Antarctica, and the Kerguelen and Crozet archipelagos and the islands of Amsterdam and St. Paul in the S Indian Ocean.

French Sudan the former name for MALI.

French toast *noun* **1** bread dipped in egg and milk and fried. **2** *Brit.* bread buttered on one side and toasted on the other.

French twist *noun N Amer.* a women's hairstyle in which the hair is gathered at the back of the head into an upswept, shell-shaped bun.

French Wars of Religion a series of religious and political conflicts in France (1562–98) between Catholic groups and the Protestant Huguenots, with interventions from Spain, Rome, England, the Netherlands, and others. The wars ended with the defeat of the Holy League and the settlement of the Edict of Nantes (1598).

French West Africa a former federation of French territories in NW Africa (1895–1959). Its constituent territories were Senegal, Mauritania, French Sudan (now Mali), Upper Volta (now Burkina), Niger, French Guinea (now Guinea), the Ivory Coast, and Dahomey (now Benin).

French window *noun* = FRENCH DOOR.

French·woman *noun* (*pl.* **-women**) **1** a female native or national of France. **2** a francophone woman.

Frenchy usu. *derogatory* ● *noun* (also **French·ie**) (*pl.* **-ies**) a francophone. ● *adjective* *informal* French (*a Frenchy restaurant*).

fren·etic /frəˈnetɪk/ *adjective* frantic, frenzied. □ **fren·etic·ally** *adverb* [Old French *frenetique* from Latin *phreneticus* from Greek *phrenitikos* from *phrenitis* delirium, from *phrēn phrenos* mind]

frenu·lum /ˈfriːnjuːləm/ *noun* (*pl.* **-la** /-lə/) *Anat.* a small frenum. [modern Latin, diminutive of FRENUM]

fre·num /ˈfriːnəm/ *noun* (also **frae·num**) (*pl.* **-na** /-nə/) *Anat.* a fold of mucous membrane or skin esp. under the tongue, checking the motion of an organ. [Latin, = bridle]

fren·zied *adjective* **1** enthusiastic; very excited. **2** frantic; uncontrollably agitated. □ **fren·zied·ly** *adverb*

frenzy ● *noun* (*pl.* **-zies**) **1** mental derangement; wild excitement or agitation. **2** delirious fury. **3** frantic or agitated activity. ● *transitive verb* (**-zies**, **-zied**) drive to frenzy; infuriate. [Old French *frenesie* from medieval Latin *phrenesia* from Latin *phrenesis* from Greek *phrēn* mind]

Freon /ˈfriːɒn/ *noun* *proprietary* any of a group of halogenated hydrocarbons containing fluorine, chlorine, and sometimes bromine, used in aerosols, refrigerants, etc. (*see also* CFC).

fre·quency /ˈfriːkwənsi/ *noun* (*pl.* **-cies**) **1** commonness of occurrence. **2 a** the state of being frequent; frequent occurrence. **b** the process of being repeated at short intervals. **3 a** *Physics* the rate of recurrence of a vibration, oscillation, cycle, etc.; the number of repetitions in a given time, esp. per second. Abbr.: *f.* **b** the number of cycles per second of a carrier wave used for radio transmission. **c** a waveband; a channel. **4** *Statistics* the ratio of the number of actual to possible occurrences of an event.

frequency band *noun* *Electronics* = BAND¹ 5a.

frequency distribution *noun* *Statistics* a measurement of the frequency of occurrence of the values of a variable.

frequency modulation *noun* **1** variation of the frequency of a radio or other wave as a means of carrying information such as an audio signal (*compare* AMPLITUDE MODULATION). **2** the system using such modulation. Abbr.: **FM**.

frequency response *noun* *Electronics* the dependence on signal frequency of the output–input ratio of an amplifier etc.

fre·quent ● *adjective* /ˈfriːkwənt/ **1** occurring often or in close succession. **2** habitual, constant (*a frequent caller*). **3** found near together; numerous, abundant. ● *transitive verb* /frɪˈkwɒnt, frɪˈkwent/ attend or go to habitually. □ **fre·quent·er** /frɪˈkwentər/ *noun* **fre·quent·ly** *adverb* [French *fréquent* or Latin *frequens -entis* crowded]

fre·quen·ta·tive /frɪˈkwentətɪv/ *Grammar* ● *adjective* expressing frequent repetition or intensity of action. ● *noun* a verb or verbal form or conjugation expressing this (e.g. *chatter*, *twinkle*).

frequent flyer *noun* **1** a person who travels by air frequently. **2** (*attributive*) designating programs of rewards offered by airlines to their passengers, or the points accumulated for the rewards.

fres·co ● *noun* (*pl.* **-coes**) **1** a painting done in watercolour on a wall or ceiling while the plaster is still wet. **2** this method of painting. ● *transitive verb* (**-coed**, **-co·ing**) paint in fresco. □ **fres·coed** *adjective* [Italian, = cool, fresh]

fresco secco *noun* = SECCO *noun* 1.

fresh ● *adjective* **1 a** newly made or obtained (*fresh sandwiches*). **b** (of snow) newly fallen. **2 a** other, different; not previously known or used (*start a fresh page*; *we need fresh ideas*; *make a fresh start*). **b** additional (*fresh supplies*). **3** (foll. by *from*) lately arrived from (a specified place or situation). **4** not stale or musty or faded (*fresh flowers*; *fresh eggs*; *fresh memories*). **5 a** (of food) not preserved by drying, salting, canning, freezing, etc. **b** (of fruit) not cooked. **c** not salty (*fresh water*). **7 a** pure, untainted, refreshing, invigorating (*fresh air*). **b** bright and pure in colour (*a fresh complexion*). **8** (of the wind) brisk; of fair strength. **9** alert, vigorous, fit (*never felt fresher*). **10** *informal* impudent or presumptuous, esp. in a sexual way. **11** young and inexperienced. **12** *N Amer.* (esp. of a cow) having just given birth and giving a renewed supply of milk. ● *adverb* newly, recently (esp. in *combination*: *fresh-baked*; *fresh-cut*). □ **fresh out of 1** recently out of (*fresh out of school*). **2** *N Amer.* having just run out of (*fresh out of bread*). □ **fresh·ly** *adverb* **fresh·ness** *noun* [Old French *freis fresche*, ultimately from Germanic]

fresh·en *verb* **1** *transitive & intransitive* make or become fresh or fresher. **2** *intransitive* *N Amer.* (esp. of a cow) begin to yield new milk after giving birth. **3** *transitive* add fresh wine, spirits, etc., to (a drink which has been standing for some time); top up. □ **freshen up 1** wash, change one's clothes, etc. **2** revive, refresh, renew. □ **fresh·en·er** *noun*

fresh·er *noun* *Brit. informal* = FRESHMAN *noun* 1.

fresh·et /ˈfreʃət/ *noun* **1** a rush of fresh water flowing into the sea. **2** the flood of a river from heavy rain or melted snow. [prob. from Old French *freschete* from *frais* FRESH]

fresh-faced *adjective* having a clear and young-looking complexion.

Fresh·ie *noun* *Cdn proprietary dated* a fruit-flavoured powder mixed with water and sugar to make a drink.

fresh·man ● *noun* (*pl.* **-men**) **1** a first-year student at university or college. **2** *N Amer.* a first-year student in high school or junior high school. ● *adjective* **1** of or relating to a freshman. **2** (of a course, etc.) requisite or suitable for first-year students (*freshman biology*). **3** inexperienced; doing something for the first time (*a freshman MP*). **4** first (*her freshman year with the force*). **5** (of a level of school sports competition) for younger, less experienced players.

fresh·water *adjective* **1** of or found in fresh water; not of the sea. **2** *US* (esp. of a school or college) small or provincial.

freshwater flea *noun* = DAPHNIA.

Fres·nel /freɪˈnel/ **Au·gus·tin Jean** (1788–1827), French physicist and civil engineer. Theorizing that light moves in a wavelike motion, with the waves vibrating transversely to the direction of propagation, he explained the phenomenon of double refraction, and invented the lens that is named after him.

fres·nel /freɪˈnel/ *noun* (also **F-**) (in full **fresnel lens**) *Photog.* a flat lens made of a number of concentric rings, to reduce spherical aberration.

Fres·no /ˈfreznoʊ/ a city in central California, in the San Joaquin valley; pop. (2000) 427,652.

fret¹ ● *verb* (**fret·ted**, **fret·ting**) **1** *intransitive* **a** feel or express anxiety, worry, unhappiness, etc. **b** (of a baby) express unhappiness, discomfort, etc., esp. by intermittent whimpering. **2** *transitive* **a** cause anxiety or distress to. **b** irritate, annoy. **3** *transitive* **a** destroy gradually or insidiously by corrosion, erosion, disease, etc. **b** wear or consume by gnawing or rubbing. **4** *transitive* form (a hole, channel, passage, etc.) by corrosion, erosion, etc. **5** *intransitive* (of a stream, the sea, etc.) move in agitation or flow or rise in little waves. ● *noun* irritation, vexation, or agitation of mind (esp. *in a fret*). [Old English *fretan* from Germanic, related to EAT]

fret² ● *noun* **1** an ornamental pattern made of continuous combinations of straight lines joined usu. at right angles. **2** = FRETWORK. ● *transitive verb* (**fret·ted**, **fret·ting**) **1** embellish or decorate with a fret. **2** adorn (esp. a ceiling) with carved or embossed work. □ **fret·ted** *adjective* [Old French *frete* trellis]

fret³ ● *noun* each of a sequence of bars or ridges on the fingerboard of some stringed musical instruments (esp. the guitar) for fixing the positions of the fingers to produce the desired notes. ● *transitive verb* finger a fretted instrument. □ **fret·less** *adjective* **fret·ted** *adjective* [15th c.: origin unknown]

fret·board *noun* a fretted fingerboard on a guitar etc.

fret·ful *adjective* anxious, distressed, or irritated. □ **fret·ful·ly** *adverb* **fret·ful·ness** *noun*

fret·saw *noun* a saw consisting of a narrow vertical blade stretched on a frame, for cutting thin wood in patterns to form ornamental designs.

fret·work *noun* **1** ornamental work in wood, esp. of intersecting straight lines and usu. done with a fretsaw. **2 a** the cutting of wood with a fretsaw to form ornamental designs. **b** wood so cut.

Freud /frɔɪd/ **1 Anna** (1895–1982), Austrian-born English psychiatrist, daughter of Sigmund Freud, who is considered the founder of child psychoanalysis; her works include *Normality and Pathology in Childhood* (1968). **2** her nephew, **Lucian** (b.1922), German-born English painter. His subjects, esp. his portraits and nudes, are painted in a meticulously detailed style based on firm draftsmanship, often using striking angles. **3** his grandfather, **Sigmund** (1856–1939), Austrian neurologist and psychotherapist. The first to draw attention to the significance of unconscious processes in normal and neurotic behaviour, he was the founder of psychoanalysis, and his theory of the sexual origins of neuroses aroused great controversy; his works include *The Interpretation of Dreams* (1899), *Totem and Taboo* (1913), and *The Ego and the Id* (1923).

Freud·ian /ˈfrɔɪdiən/ *Psych.* ● *adjective* **1** of or relating to Sigmund Freud, his theories, or his methods of psychoanalysis, esp. with reference to the importance of sexuality in human behaviour. **2** (of a person's speech or behaviour) possibly revealing one's subconscious thoughts or feelings. ● *noun* a follower of Freud or his methods.
□ **Freud·ian·ism** *noun*

Freudian slip *noun* an unintentional, esp. spoken error that seems to reveal subconscious feelings.

Frey /ˈfreɪ/ (also **Freyr** /ˈfreɪər/) *Scand. Myth* the god of fertility and dispenser of rain and sunshine.

Freya /ˈfreɪə/ *Scand. Myth* the goddess of love and of the night, sister of Frey; she is often identified with Frigga.

FRG *abbreviation* Federal Republic of Germany.

Fri. *abbreviation* Friday.

fri·able /ˈfraɪəbəl/ *adjective* able to be easily crumbled or reduced to powder. □ **fri·abil·ity** /-ˈbɪlɪti/ *noun* [French *friable* or Latin *friabilis* from *friare* crumble]

friar /ˈfraɪr/ *noun Christianity* a member of any of certain religious orders of men, esp. the four mendicant orders (Augustinians, Carmelites, Dominicans, and Franciscans). [Old French *frere* from Latin *frater fratris* brother]

friar's balsam *noun* (also **friars' balsam**) a tincture of benzoin etc. used as an expectorant.

fri·ary /ˈfraɪri/ *noun* (*pl.* **-ies**) a house or building in which a community of friars live.

fric·as·see /ˈfrɪkəˌsiː, -ˈsiː/ ● *noun* a dish of white meat such as chicken, veal, or rabbit, cut up, stewed in stock, and served in a thick white sauce. ● *transitive verb* (**fric·as·sees**, **fric·as·seed**) make a fricassee of. [French, fem. past participle of *fricasser* (v.), 'cut up and cook in a sauce']

frica·tive /ˈfrɪkətɪv/ *Phonetics* ● *adjective* (of a consonant sound) produced by the friction of the airstream through a narrow opening in the mouth. ● *noun* a consonant made in this way, e.g. *f* and *th*. [modern Latin *fricativus* from Latin *fricare* rub]

fri·cot /friːˈkoː/ *noun Cdn* (*Maritimes*) a hearty Acadian stew containing potatoes and meat, fish, or seafood. [French, 'stew']

fric·tion *noun* **1** the action of one surface or object rubbing against another. **2** the resistance an object or surface encounters in moving over another. **3** a clash of wills, temperaments, or opinions; mutual animosity arising from disagreement. **4** (*attributive*) of devices that work or transmit motion by frictional contact (*friction clutch*; *friction disc*). □ **fric·tion·al** *adjective* **fric·tion·less** *adjective* [French from Latin *frictio -onis* from *fricare frict-* rub]

Fri·day ● *noun* the sixth day of the week, following Thursday. ● *adverb* **1** on Friday. **2** (**Fridays**) on Fridays; each Friday. [Old English *frigedæg* from Germanic (named after *Frigg* the wife of Odin)]

fridge *noun informal* = REFRIGERATOR. [abbreviation]

fridge magnet *noun* a usu. decorative trinket with a magnet attached to the back, used esp. for affixing papers etc. to the doors or side of a fridge.

fried ● *adjective* **1** cooked by frying. **2** *N Amer. informal* thoroughly worn out, exhausted, etc. **3** *slang* intoxicated. ● *verb* past and past participle of FRY[1].

Frie·dan /frɪˈdæn/ **Betty (Naomi)** (b.1921), US feminist and writer, best known for *The Feminine Mystique* (1963), which presented femininity as artificial and traced the ways in which US women are socialized to become mothers and housewives; she founded the National Organization for Women (1966) and served as its president until 1970.

Fried·man /ˈfriːdmən/ **Mil·ton** (b.1912), US economist. A leading conservative economist and principal exponent of monetarism, he was awarded the Nobel Prize for economics in 1976.

Frie·drich /ˈfriːdrɪx/ **Cas·par David** (1774–1840), German landscape painter. Noted for his romantic landscapes, he caused controversy with his altarpiece *The Cross in the Mountains* (1808), which lacked a specifically religious subject.

friend *noun* **1** a person with whom one enjoys mutual affection and regard (usu. exclusive of sexual or family bonds) (*Miriam is a true friend*). **2** a sympathizer (*no friend to virtue*; *a friend of order*). **3 a** a person who is an ally, on the same side, or not an enemy (*friend or foe?*). **b** a patron or supporter of a cause etc. (*Friends of the Oldman River*; *Friends of the Canadian Opera Company*). **4** *euphemism* a romantic or sexual partner; a lover. **5 a** a person already mentioned or under discussion (*my friend at*

the next table then left the room). **b** an acquaintance, associate, or person known casually. **c** used as a polite or ironic form of address. **6** (usu. in *pl.*) a regular contributor of money or other assistance to an institution etc. **7** (**Friend**) a member of the Society of Friends, a Quaker. **8** a helpful thing or quality. □ **be friends** (**with**) be on good or intimate terms (with). **friends in high places** highly placed people able or ready to use their influence on one's behalf. **make friends** (**with**) get on good or intimate terms (with). **my honourable friend** *Cdn & Brit.* used in the House of Commons to refer to another member of one's own party. **my learned friend** used by a lawyer in court to refer to another lawyer. □ **friend·less** *adjective* [Old English *frēond* from Germanic]

friend at court *noun* a person in a position to influence others on one's behalf.

friend·ly ● *adjective* (**friend·li·er**, **friend·li·est**) **1** acting as or like a friend, well-disposed, kindly. **2 a** (often foll. by *with*) on amicable terms. **b** not hostile or in opposition. **c** not seriously competitive (*a friendly rivalry*). **3** characteristic of friends, showing or prompted by kindness. **4** favourably disposed, inclined to approve or help. **5 a** (of a thing) serviceable, convenient, opportune. **b** = USER-FRIENDLY. **6** (esp. in *combination*) adapted for or not harmful to (*ozone-friendly*; *reader-friendly*). ● *noun* (*pl.* **-lies**) **1** (usu. in *pl.*) a person, thing, force, etc. which poses no threat, esp. a member of an indigenous people or tribe which is not hostile to invaders. **2** esp. *Soccer* (in full **friendly match**) a game played for enjoyment and not in competition for a cup etc. □ **friend·li·ly** *adverb* **friend·li·ness** *noun*

friendly fire *noun Mil.* gunfire etc. coming from one's own side, esp. as the cause of accidental injury or death to one's own forces.

Friendly Islands an alternative name for TONGA.

friend of the court *noun* = AMICUS CURIAE.

friend·ship *noun* **1 a** the feeling or relationship that friends have. **b** an instance of this (*our friendship is very important to me*). **2** a friendly disposition felt or shown.

friendship bracelet *noun* a frequently brightly coloured bracelet of woven wool, thread, etc., chiefly worn by young people, esp. as a token of friendship.

friendship centre *noun Cdn* an institution established in a predominantly non-Aboriginal community to provide counselling and social services etc. to Aboriginal people.

Frie·sian /ˈfriːʒən, -ziən/ ● *noun* **1** var. of FRISIAN. **2** *Brit.* = HOLSTEIN. ● *adjective* **1** var. of FRISIAN. **2** of or concerning Holsteins.

Fries·land /ˈfriːzlənd/ **1** the western part of the ancient region of Frisia. **2** a northern province of the Netherlands, bounded to the west and north by the IJsselmeer and the North Sea; capital, Leeuwarden.

frieze[1] /friːz/ *noun* **1 a** any broad, horizontal band of sculpted, painted, or other decoration, esp. along a wall near the ceiling. **b** a horizontal paper strip bearing pictures, decorations, etc. for mounting on a wall. **2** (in classical architecture) the part of an entablature between the architrave and the cornice. **3** a horizontal band of sculpture filling this. [French *frise* from medieval Latin *frisium*, *frigium* from Latin *Phrygium* (*opus*) (work) of Phrygia]

frieze[2] /friːz/ *noun* coarse woollen cloth with a nap, usu. on one side only. [French *frise*, prob. related to FRISIAN]

frig[1] *coarse slang* ● *transitive & intransitive verb* (**frigged**, **frig·ging**) **1** = FUCK *verb*. **2** masturbate. **3** *intransitive* (foll. by *about*, *around*) mess about, fool around. ● *noun* = FUCK *noun* 1a, 2. [perhaps imitative: original senses 'move about, rub']

frig[2] /frɪdʒ/ *noun esp. Brit. informal* = REFRIGERATOR. [abbreviation]

frig·ate /ˈfrɪɡət/ *noun* **1 a** *Cdn & Brit.* a naval escort vessel between a corvette and a destroyer in size. **b** *US* a similar ship between a destroyer and a cruiser in size. **2** *hist.* a sailing warship, esp. next in size to a ship of the line and carrying 28-60 guns. [French *frégate* from Italian *fregata*, of unknown origin]

frigate bird *noun* any marine bird of the family Fregatidae, found in tropical seas, with a wide wingspan and deeply forked tail.

Frig·ga /ˈfrɪɡə/ *Scand. Myth* the wife of Odin and goddess of married love and of the hearth, often identified with Freya; Friday is named after her.

frig·ging *coarse slang* = FUCKING.

fright ● *noun* **1** a sudden or extreme fear. **b** an instance of this (*gave me a fright*). **2** a person or thing looking grotesque or ridiculous. ● *transitive verb literary* frighten. □ **take fright** become frightened. [Old English *fryhto*, metathetic form of *fyrhto*, from Germanic]

fright·en *verb* **1** *transitive* scare, terrify, or fill with fright (*was frightened at the bang*; *is frightened of dogs*). **2** *transitive* (foll. by *away*, *off*, *out of*, *into*) drive or force by fright (*frightened it out of the room; frightened them into submission; frightened me into agreeing*). **3** *intransitive* become scared, frightened, or terrified (*he doesn't frighten easily*). □ **fright·en·er** *noun* **fright·en·ing** *adjective* **fright·en·ing·ly** *adverb*

fright·ful *adjective* **1 a** dreadful, shocking, revolting. **b** ugly, hideous. **2** *informal* extremely bad (*a frightful idea*). **3** *informal* very great, extreme. □ **fright·ful·ly** *adverb* **fright·ful·ness** *noun*

fright wig *noun* an outrageous wig with hair standing on end, usu. worn for comic effect etc.

fri·gid /ˈfrɪdʒɪd/ *adjective* **1** extremely cold. **2** (of a woman) **a** unable to achieve orgasm or experience sexual excitement during intercourse. **b** not showing any sexual desire or responsiveness. **3 a** lacking friendliness or enthusiasm; forced, formal. **b** dull, flat, apathetic, or insipid. **c** (of a thing) chilling, depressing. □ **fri·gid·ity** /-ˈdʒɪdɪti/ *noun* **frigid·ly** *adverb* **frigid·ness** *noun* [Latin *frigidus* from *frigēre* be cold, from *frigus* (n.) cold]

frigid zone *noun* each of two parts of the earth's surface, lying north of the Arctic Circle and south of the Antarctic Circle.

fri·jo·les /friːˈhoːleɪs/ *plural noun* **1** (esp. in Mexican cooking) beans, esp. kidney beans. **2** = REFRIED BEANS. [Spanish, pl. of *frijol* bean, ultimately from Latin *phaseolus*]

frill ● *noun* **1 a** an ornamental edging of material, having one side gathered or pleated and the other left loose so as to have a fluted or wavy appearance. **b** a natural fringe of hair, feathers, etc. resembling this on an animal, esp. a bird. **2** an optional or additional extra that is not necessary or essential, but serves for embellishment, decoration, etc. ● *transitive verb* **1** decorate with a frill. **2** form into a frill. □ **frilled** *adjective* [16th c.: origin unknown]

frill lizard *noun* (also **frilled lizard**) a large N Australian lizard, *Chlamydosaurus kingii*, with an erectile membrane around the neck.

frilly ● *adjective* (**frill·i·er**, **frill·i·est**) **1** having a frill or frills. **2** resembling a frill. ● *noun* (pl. **-ies**) (in *pl.*) *informal* women's underwear. □ **frill·i·ness** *noun*

fringe ● *noun* **1 a** an ornamental bordering of threads left loose or formed into tassels or twists. **b** such a bordering made separately. **c** any border or edging. **2 a** esp. *Brit.* a portion of the front hair hanging over the forehead; bangs. **b** a natural border of hair etc. in an animal or plant. **3** (often *attributive*) **a** the outer edge or margin of an area etc. (*in the northern fringes of Saskatchewan*). **b** an unofficial, unconventional, and often extreme approach, opinion, etc. (*fringe theatre*). **4** a thing, part, or area of secondary or minor importance. **5 a** a band of contrasting brightness or darkness produced by diffraction or interference of light. **b** a strip of false colour in an optical image. **6** *US* a fringe benefit. **7** = FRINGE FESTIVAL. ● *transitive verb* **1** make into or provide, decorate, or encircle with a fringe. **2** serve as a fringe to. □ **fringed** *adjective* **fringe·less** *adjective* **fringy** *adjective* [Old French *frenge*, ultimately from Late Latin *fimbria* (earlier only in pl.) fibres, fringe]

fringe benefit *noun* an extra benefit given to an employee in addition to salary or wages, e.g. health insurance, a company car, etc.

fringe festival *noun* an arts festival featuring non-mainstream, alternative music, theatre, poetry, etc.

fringe·tree *noun* a shrub of eastern N America, *Chionanthus virginicus*, with white flowers and plumed seeds.

frin·ging *noun* **1** fringes. **2** the formation or appearance of optical fringes.

fringing reef *noun* a coral reef forming a ring around an island or along a shore.

frip·pery *noun* (pl. **-ies**) **1** unnecessary items of ornament or decoration, e.g. in clothing. **2** empty display or ostentation in speech, writing, etc. [French *friperie* from Old French *freperie* from *frepe* rag]

Fris·bee *noun* *proprietary* a concave plastic disc for skimming through the air as an outdoor game. [perhaps from *Frisbie* bakery (Bridgeport, Conn.), whose pie plates could be used similarly]

Frisch /frɪʃ/ **1 Karl von** (1886–1982), Austrian zoologist. He studied the behaviour and communication of the honeybee, and expounded the theory that they perform an elaborate dance in the hive to show other bees the direction and distance of a food source; he shared a Nobel Prize in 1973. **2 Otto Rob·ert** (1904–79), Austrian-born English physicist. He was the co-discoverer, with his aunt, Lise Meitner, of nuclear fission; during the Second World War he worked on nuclear weapons in the US at Los Alamos. **3 Rag·nar (Anton Kit·til)** (1895–1973), Norwegian economist. A pioneer of econometrics, he shared the first Nobel Prize for economics with Jan Tinbergen (1969).

Fris·co *noun* a nickname for SAN FRANCISCO.

frisée /friːˈzeɪ/ *noun* = ENDIVE 2. [French, from *chicorée frisée* 'curly endive']

Frisia /ˈfriːʒə, ˈfrɪziə/ an ancient region of NW Europe. It consisted of the Frisian Islands and parts of the mainland corresponding to the modern provinces of Friesland and Groningen in the Netherlands and the regions of Ostfriesland and Nordfriesland in NW Germany.

Fri·sian /ˈfriːʒən, ˈfrɪziən/ (also **Frie·sian**) ● *adjective* of Friesland, the Frisians, or the Frisian language. ● *noun* **1** a native or inhabitant of Friesland. **2** the W Germanic language of Friesland, the closest relative of English.

Frisian Islands a chain of islands lying off the coast of NW Europe, extending from the IJsselmeer in the Netherlands to Jutland. The islands consist of three groups: the **West Frisian Islands**, which form part of the Netherlands, the **East Frisian Islands**, which form part of Germany, and the **North Frisian Islands**, which are divided between Germany and Denmark.

frisk ● *verb* **1** *transitive* search (a person) by feeling quickly over the body in search of a concealed weapon etc. **2** *intransitive* leap, skip, or frolic playfully. ● *noun* **1** the act of frisking a person. **2** a playful leap or skip. □ **frisk·er** *noun* [obsolete *frisk* (adj.) from Old French *frisque* lively, of unknown origin]

frisky *adjective* (**frisk·i·er**, **frisk·i·est**) **1** lively, playful. **2** *informal* amorous, sexually excited. □ **frisk·i·ly** *adverb* **frisk·i·ness** *noun*

fris·son /ˈfriːsɒn, -sɔ̃/ *noun* an emotional thrill, esp. a shiver of excitement. [French, = shiver]

frit ● *noun* **1** a calcined mixture of silica and fluxes, which can be melted to make glass. **2** a vitreous composition from which soft porcelain, enamel, etc., are made. ● *transitive verb* (**frit·ted**, **frit·ting**) make into frit, partially fuse, calcine. [Italian *fritta* fem. past participle of *friggere* FRY¹]

frites /friːt/ *plural noun* french fries, esp. very thinly sliced ones. [French, short for *pommes frites* 'fried potatoes']

frit fly *noun* a small European fly, *Oscinella frit*, of which the larvae are destructive to cereals. [19th c.: origin unknown]

frith *var.* of FIRTH.

fri·til·lary /frɪˈtɪləri, ˈfrɪtɪlˌeri/ *noun* (pl. **-ies**) **1** any liliaceous plant of the genus *Fritillaria*, having pendent bell-like flowers. **2** any of various butterflies having red-brown wings checkered with black. [modern Latin *fritillaria* from Latin *fritillus* dice box]

frit·tata /frɪˈtɑtə/ *noun* a type of omelette in which chopped vegetables, meat, etc. are incorporated into the beaten eggs before they are fried. [Italian]

frit·ter¹ *transitive verb* **1** (usu. foll. by *away*) waste (money, time, energy, etc.) triflingly, indiscriminately, etc. **2** *archaic* break or separate into minute pieces. [obsolete n. *fritter(s)* fragments = obsolete *fitters* (n.pl.), perhaps related to Middle High German *vetze* rag]

frit·ter² *noun* a piece of fruit, meat, etc., coated in batter and deep-fried (*apple fritter*). [Old French *friture*, ultimately from Latin *frigere frict-* FRY¹]

frit·to misto /ˌfriːtoː ˈmiːstoː/ *noun* a dish of various foods, usu. types of seafood, deep-fried in batter. [Italian, = mixed fry]

fritz *noun* □ **on the fritz** N Amer. *slang* out of order, broken, defective. [20th c.: origin unknown]

friul·ano /friːuːˈlɑnoː/ *noun* Cdn a mild, pale yellow firm cow's milk cheese of a kind made orig. in Friuli. [Italian, = 'Friulian']

Fri·uli /friːˈuːli/ a historic region of NE Italy between the Alps and the Adriatic and Venice and present-day Slovenia.

Fri·ul·ian /friːˈuːliən/ ● *adjective* of or pertaining to Friuli or Friuli-Venezia Giulia, or the dialect spoken in Friuli. ● *noun* **1** a native or inhabitant of Friuli or Friuli-Venezia Giulia. **2** the Rhaeto-Romance dialect spoken in much of Friuli.

Friuli-Venezia Giu·lia /friˌuːli veˌnetsiə ˈdʒuːliə/ a region in NE Italy, on the border with Slovenia and Austria; capital, Trieste.

frivo·lous /ˈfrɪvələs/ *adjective* **1 a** (of activities) silly or wasteful. **b** (of a claim, charge, etc.) having no reasonable grounds. **2** (of people, their character, etc.) foolish, lighthearted, not sensible or serious. □ **friv·ol·ity** /-ˈvɒlɪti/ *noun* (pl. **-ities**). **frivo·lous·ly** *adverb* **frivo·lous·ness** *noun* [Latin *frivolus* silly, trifling]

frizz ● *verb* **1** *transitive* form (hair) into tight curls. **2** *intransitive* (of hair etc.) curl tightly, esp. so as to be difficult to style. ● *noun* frizzy hair. [French *friser*, perhaps from the stem of *frire* FRY¹]

frizz·ies *plural noun* frizzy, uncontrollable hair.

friz·zle¹ *transitive & intransitive verb* **1** fry, toast, or grill, with a sputtering noise. **2** (often foll. by *up*) burn or shrivel. [*frizz* (in the same sense) from FRY¹, with imitative ending + -LE⁴]

Consonants: b *but* d *dog* f *few* g *get* h *her* j *yes* k *cat* l *leg* m *man* n *no* p *pen* r *red* s *sit*

friz·zle² ● *verb* **1** *transitive* form (hair) into tight curls. **2** *intransitive* (of hair etc.) curl tightly. ● *noun* frizzled hair. [16th c.: origin unknown (earlier than FRIZZ)]

frizz·ly *adjective* in tight curls.

frizzy *adjective* (**frizz·i·er, frizz·i·est**) **1** consisting of small, crisp curls. **2** resembling a frizz. □ **frizz·i·ness** *noun*

fro *adverb* back or from (only in *to and fro*: *see* TO AND FRO). [Old Norse *frá* FROM]

Fro·bi·sher /ˈfroʊbɪʃər/ **Sir Mar·tin** (*c.*1535–94), English explorer. He led an unsuccessful expedition in search of the Northwest Passage (1576), discovering the bay named after him and landing in Labrador; he made two further voyages to the northeast coast of Canada in search of gold (1577 and 1578), and later played a prominent part in the defeat of the Spanish Armada (1588).

Frobisher Bay /ˈfroʊbɪʃər/ **1** a long inlet of the southeastern coast of Baffin Island, forming the Hall and Meta Incognita peninsulas. **2** the former name for IQALUIT. [FROBISHER]

frock ● *noun* **1** *Brit.* a woman's or girl's dress. **2 a** a monk's or priest's long gown with loose sleeves. **b** priestly office. **3** *hist.* a smock worn by shepherds etc. ● *transitive verb* invest with priestly office (*compare* DEFROCK). [Old French *froc* from Frankish]

frock coat *noun* a usu. double-breasted coat with skirts extending almost to the knees and not cut away, but of the same length in front as behind.

froe /froʊ/ *noun* (also **frow**) a wedge-shaped cleaving tool with a handle set at right angles to the blade. [abbreviation of *frower* from FROWARD 'turned away']

Froe·bel /ˈfroʊbəl/ **Frie·drich (Wil·helm Aug·ust)** (also **Fröbel**) (1782–1852), German educator, who founded the kindergarten system. □ **Froe·bel·ian** /froʊˈbiːliən/ *adjective* **Froe·bel·ism** *noun*

frog¹ *noun* **1** any of various small amphibians of the order Anura, having a tailless smooth-skinned body with legs developed for jumping, esp. (as distinct from toads) any of those which have a smooth skin and leap rather than walk. **2** (**Frog**) *slang offensive* a French or francophone person. **3** the nut of a violin bow etc. □ **frog in the** (or **one's**) **throat** *informal* hoarseness. [Old English *frogga* from Germanic]

frog² *noun* a piece of elastic, horny substance growing in the middle of the sole of a horse's hoof. [17th c.: origin uncertain (perhaps a use of FROG¹)]

frog³ *noun* **1** an ornamental coat fastener consisting of a spindle-shaped button covered with silk or similar material and a loop through which it is passed. **2** an attachment to a waist belt to support a sword, bayonet, etc. □ **frogged** *adjective* **frog·ging** *noun* [18th c.: origin unknown]

frog⁴ *noun* a grooved piece of iron placed at the junction of the rails where one railway track crosses another. [19th c.: origin unknown]

frog·fish *noun* **1** = ANGLERFISH. **2** any of numerous fishes of the families Antennariidae and Brachionichthyidae, resembling anglerfishes esp. in attracting prey by means of a lure.

frog·gy ● *adjective* **1** of or like a frog or frogs. **2** abounding in frogs. **3** (also **Frog·gie**) *slang offensive* French or francophone. ● *noun* (**Froggy**) (*pl.* **-gies**) *slang offensive* a French or French-Canadian person.

frog·hop·per *noun* any jumping insect of the family Cercopidae, sucking sap and as larvae producing a protective mass of froth (*see* CUCKOO-SPIT).

frog kick *noun* *Swimming* a type of kick in which the legs are pulled towards the body, then thrust outward, before being brought together again quickly.

frog·man *noun* (*pl.* **-men**) a scuba diver engaged in police or military operations.

frog·march ● *transitive verb* **1** hustle (a person) forward holding and pinning the arms from behind. **2** carry (a person) in a frogmarch. ● *noun* the action or an act of carrying a person face downwards with each of four people holding a limb.

frog·mouth *noun* any of various birds of Australia and SE Asia, esp. of the family Podargidae, having large wide mouths.

frog·spawn *noun* the soft, almost transparent jellylike mass of eggs of a frog.

froid·eur /frwɑˈdɜr/ *noun* coolness or reserve (between people). [French, = 'coldness']

Frois·sart /ˈfrwɑsɑr/ **Jean** (*c.*1333–*c.*1400), French historian and poet, whose *Chronicles* record the chivalric exploits of the French and English nobility from 1325 to 1400.

frolic /ˈfrɒlɪk/ ● *intransitive verb* (**frol·icked, frolick·ing**) **1** play and move about cheerfully, excitedly, or energetically. **2** play about with someone in a flirtatious or sexual way. ● *noun* **1** a lively and enjoyable activity. **2** fun, gaiety, or merriment. □ **frol·ick·er** *noun* [Dutch *vrolijk* (adj.) from *vro* glad + *-lijk* -LY¹]

frolic·some /ˈfrɒlɪksəm/ *adjective* merry, playful. □ **frolic·some·ly** *adverb* **frolic·some·ness** *noun*

from *preposition* expressing separation or origin, followed by: **1 a** a person, place, time, etc. that is the starting point of motion or action (*rain comes from the clouds; repeated from mouth to mouth*). **b** the starting point of an extent in time (*dinner is served from 8; from start to finish*). **2** a place, object, etc. whose distance or remoteness is reckoned or stated (*ten miles from Tuktoyaktuk; I am far from admitting it; absent from home; apart from its moral aspect*). **3 a** a source (*dig gravel from a pit; a man from Saskatoon; draw a conclusion from premises; quotations from Leacock*). **b** a giver or sender (*presents from their parents; have not heard from her*). **4 a** a thing or person avoided, escaped, lost, etc. (*released him from prison; cannot refrain from laughing; dissuaded from folly*). **b** a person or thing deprived (*took his gun from him*). **5** a reason, cause, or motive (*died from fatigue; suffering from mumps; did it from jealousy; from his looks you might not believe it*). **6** a thing or person distinguished or unlike (*know good from bad*). **7** a lower limit (*saw from 10 to 20 boats; tickets from $5*). **8** a state changed for another (*from being the victim he became the attacker; raised the penalty from a fine to imprisonment*). **9** an adverb or preposition of time or place (*from long ago; from abroad; from under the bed*). **10** the position of a person who observes or considers (*saw it from the roof; from his point of view*). **11** a model (*painted it from nature*). □ **from day to day** (or **hour to hour** etc.) daily (or hourly etc.); as the days (or hours etc.) pass. **from home** out, away. **from now on** henceforward, from now and in the future. **from time to time** occasionally or intermittently. **from year to year** each year; as the years pass. [Old English *fram*, *from*, of Germanic origin]

fro·mage blanc /frɒmɒʒ ˈblɑ̃/ *noun* a type of soft French cheese made from cow's milk and having a creamy sour taste. [French, lit. 'white cheese']

fro·mage frais /frɒmɒʒ ˈfreɪ/ *noun* a type of smooth soft fresh cheese, with the consistency of thick yogourt, used esp. as a dessert, with or without added flavouring. [French, lit. 'fresh cheese']

Fromm /ˈfrɒm/ **Erich** (1900–80), German-born US psychoanalyst and social philosopher, whose works investigate emotional problems in free societies and advocate psychoanalysis as a cure for cultural ills and an aid to the development of a sane society.

frond *noun* **1** *Bot.* **a** a leaflike organ formed by the union of stem and foliage in certain flowerless plants, esp. ferns and palms. **b** any large compound leaf, e.g. of the palm, banana, etc. **2** *Zool.* a leaflike structure, e.g. the leaflike thallus of some algae. [Latin *frons frondis* leaf]

Fronde /frɒnd/ a series of civil wars in France 1648–53, in which French nobles, whose power had been weakened by the policies of Cardinal Richelieu, rose in rebellion against Mazarin and the Court during the minority of Louis XIV. Although some concessions were obtained, the nobles were not successful in curbing the power of the monarchy. [French, a type of sling used in a children's game played in the streets of Paris at the time.]

front ● *noun* **1 a** the side or part of a thing normally nearer or towards the spectator (*the front of the car*). **b** the side or part of a thing facing forward (*the front of the chair*). **c** a position or place situated directly before or ahead of a thing, observer, etc. (*the front of the mouth*). **2** any face of a building, esp. that of the main entrance. **3** *Military* **a** the foremost line or part of an army, battalion, etc. **b** the line of battle. **c** the foremost part of an occupied territory, area of operations, etc., or the ground next to an enemy. **d** (usu. prec. by *the*) the foremost part of a position or a scene of actual fighting (*go to the front*) (opp. REAR¹ 4). **e** the direction towards which a line of troops faces when formed (*change front*). **4 a** a sector of activity regarded as resembling a military front. **b** a political group organized to pursue a particular objective or set of objectives. **5** bearing, demeanour, or degree of composure or confidence while under threat or in danger (*show a bold front*). **6 a** the most forward or conspicuous position (*come to the front*). **b** a leading position in a race or contest. **7 a** an outward appearance or show, esp. used as a cover for another trait, motive, etc. **b** a pretext, premise, etc. (*the arguments are false on several fronts*). **8** a person or organization serving as a cover for subversive or illegal activities. **9** (prec. by *the*) frontage or the land facing a road or alongside a body of water. **10** *Meteorol.* the forward edge of an advancing mass of cold or warm air. **11** the auditorium of a theatre. **12** *literary* the forehead. **13 a** the part of a garment, esp. of a dress or shirt, which covers the upper part of the front of the body. **b** a dickie or false shirt front. **14** impudence. ● *attributive adjective* **1** of or pertaining to the front. **2** situated in front. **3** *Phonetics* (of a sound) formed at the front of the mouth, esp. by raising the front part of the tongue, excluding the blade and tip, towards the hard palate. ● *verb* **1** *intransitive* (foll. by *on, to, towards, upon*) have the front facing or directed in a specific direction. **2** *intransitive* (foll. by *for*) *slang* act as a front or cover for. **3** *transitive* furnish with a specific front, material, etc. (*fronted with stone*). **4** *transitive* lead or be the most prominent member of (a band, organization, etc.). **5** *transitive* **a** stand opposite to, have the front towards. **b** (of a building) have its front on the side of (a street etc.). **6** *transitive Broadcasting* act as presenter, promoter, or host of (a television program etc.). **7** *Phonetics* **a** *transitive* articulate (a sound) with the tongue further forward. **b** *intransitive* (of a sound) be or become formed with the tongue further forward. □ **in front 1** in the lead or in an advanced position. **2** in a position exactly ahead, facing the spectator. **in front of 1** ahead of, in advance of. **2** in the presence of, confronting. **out front 1** esp. *N Amer.* in front of a building etc. **2** in the auditorium of a theatre. □ **front·ed** (in *combination*) *adjective* **front·less** *adjective* **front·ward** *adjective & adverb* **front·wards** *adverb* [Old French *front* (n.), *fronter* (v.) from Latin *frons frontis*]

front·age *noun* **1 a** the front of a building or lot. **b** the lineal extent of this. **2 a** land abutting on a street or on water. **b** the land between the front of a building and the road. **3** the way a thing faces.

frontage road *noun N Amer.* a service road.

front·al[1] *adjective* **1 a** of, at, or on the front (*a frontal attack*). **b** of the front as seen by an onlooker (*a frontal view*). **2** of the forehead or front part of the skull (*frontal bone*). □ **front·al·ly** *adverb*

front·al[2] *noun* a covering for the front of an altar.

frontal lobe *noun* each of the paired lobes of the brain lying immediately behind the forehead, including areas concerned with behaviour, learning, and voluntary movement.

front bench *noun Cdn, Brit., Austral., & NZ* the foremost seats in Parliament, occupied by the leading members of the government and opposition.

front-bencher *noun Cdn, Brit., Austral., & NZ* a leading Member of Parliament entitled to sit on the front bench, e.g. a party leader, cabinet member, an opposition critic, etc.

front burner *noun* **1** a position receiving much attention or high priority (*the project has been brought to the front burner*). **2** a heating element at the front of a stove.

front·court *noun Sport* **1** the part of the court closest to the front wall in games such as squash, racquetball, etc. **2** *Basketball* **a** the offensive half of a court for a given team. **b** the centre and two forwards who play offensively in that half of the court. □ **front·court·man** *noun (pl.* **-men***)*

Front de Li·bé·ra·tion du Qué·bec /frɔ̃ də liːbeiraˈsjɔ̃ duː keiˈbek/ *noun* (in Canada) a Quebec separatist terrorist organization esp. active in the 1960s and early 1970s. *Abbr.:* **FLQ**. *See also* Oᴄᴛᴏʙᴇʀ Cʀɪsɪs.

front desk *noun* the registration and reception desk in a hotel etc.

front door *noun* **1** the chief entrance of a house. **2** a chief means of approach or access to a place, situation, opportunity, etc.

front-drive *adjective* (of a car, truck, etc.) having front-wheel drive. □ **front-driver** *noun*

Fron·te·nac /ˈfrɒntəˌnak/ **Comte de** (title of Louis de Buade) (1622–98), Governor General of New France 1672–82 and 1689–98. He established a number of forts on the Great Lakes, and engaged in a series of battles against the British and the Iroquois.

front end *noun* **1** the forward part of a motor vehicle, train, etc. **2** *Electronics* the tuner, local oscillator, and mixer of a superheterodyne receiver. **3** (**front-end**) (often *attributive*) that part of a computer system that a user deals with directly, esp. a device providing input or access to a central computer or other parts of a network. **4** (**front-end**) (*attributive*) designating money paid or charged at the beginning of a transaction (*front-end commission*).

front-end loader *noun* **1** a machine with a scoop or bucket on an articulated arm at the front for digging and loading dirt etc. **2** a hydraulic bucket or scoop that fits onto the front of a tractor.

fron·tier /frʌnˈtiːr, frɒn-/ ● *noun* **1 a** the border between two countries. **b** the district on each side of this. **2** the limits of attainment or knowledge in a subject. **3** *N Amer.* the part of a country held to form the furthest limit of its settled or inhabited regions. ● *adjective* **1** of, belonging to, or situated on the frontier. **2** characteristic of life on a frontier, esp. being remote from the comforts of civilization.

□ **fron·tier·less** *adjective* [Anglo-French *frounter*, Old French *frontiere*, ultimately from Latin *frons frontis* FRONT]

fron·tiers·man *noun (pl.* **-men***)* a man living on a frontier, or on or beyond the borders of civilization.

fron·tiers·woman *noun (pl.* **-women***)* a woman living on a frontier, or on or beyond the borders of civilization.

fron·tis·piece /ˈfrʌntɪsˌpiːs/ *noun* **1** an illustration facing the title page of a book or of one of its divisions. **2** *Archit.* **a** the principal face of a building, esp. a decorated entrance. **b** a pediment over a door etc. [French *frontispice* or Late Latin *frontispicium* facade, from Latin *frons frontis* FRONT + *-spicium* from *specere* look: assimilated to PIECE]

front·let /ˈfrʌntlət/ *noun* **1** a piece of cloth hanging over the upper part of an altar frontal. **2** ornament, band of cloth, etc. worn on the forehead. **3** a phylactery worn on the forehead. **4** an animal's forehead.

front line *noun* **1 a** *Military* the line of fighting closest to the enemy. **b** a role or position of immediate involvement with crises, social problems, etc. (*working on the front lines against AIDS*). **2** the most important, advanced, or responsible position (*on the front line of interactive television*). **3** *Music* the players in a jazz band other than the rhythm section. **4** a role or position of immediate contact with customers etc.

front-load *transitive verb* distribute or allocate (costs, effort, etc.) unevenly, with the greater proportion at the beginning of the process.

front-loading *adjective* (of a washing machine etc.) being loaded through a door in the front of the machine rather than through the top. □ **front-loader** *noun*

front man *noun* **1** a person who leads or represents a group or organization. **2** the leader of a group of musicians, esp. the lead singer of a pop group.

front matter *noun* the title page, preface, explanatory notes, etc. preceding the text of a book.

front nine *noun Golf* the initial nine holes of an 18-hole course.

front office *noun* a main executive or administrative office of a business, organization, etc.

front of house *noun* the areas used by the audience in a theatre, as opposed to the stage and backstage.

fron·ton /ˈfrʌntɒn/ *noun* a building in which pelota or jai alai is played. [French from Italian *frontone* from *fronte* forehead]

front page *noun* (also *attributive*) the first page of a newspaper, esp. as containing important or remarkable news. □ **front-pager** *noun*

front·person *noun (pl.* **-people***)* a person acting as a front or cover (*see* FRONT *noun* 8).

front room *noun* a room, esp. a sitting room, situated at the front of a house.

front-row seat *noun* **1** a seat in the front row of a theatre etc. **2** a central and prominent position, esp. as an observer or participant.

front-runner *noun* **1** the candidate, contestant, etc. most likely to succeed. **2** an athlete or horse running best when in the lead. □ **front-running** *adjective*

front-wheel drive *noun* a drive system in a car etc. in which engine power operates through the front wheels alone.

front·woman *noun* **1** a woman acting as a front or cover (*see* FRONT *noun* 8). **2** the female leader or most prominent member of a group of musicians, an organization, etc.

front yard *noun N Amer.* a piece of ground, usu. with a lawn or flowers etc., in front of a house.

frosh *noun (pl.* **frosh***) N Amer. slang* = FRESHMAN *noun* [alteration of FRESHMAN, perhaps influenced by German *Frosch*, lit. = 'frog', in dialectal use = 'grammar school student']

Frost ▸ 1 Les·lie (Mis·camp·bell) (1895–1973), Canadian politician, Progressive Conservative premier of Ontario 1949–61. **2 Rob·ert (Lee)** (1874–1963), US poet. Considered one of the most accessible of modern poets, he is best known for poems such as 'Mending Wall' (1914), 'The Road Not Taken' (1916), 'Birches' (1916), and 'Stopping by Woods on a Snowy Evening' (1923), which are characterized by simple language and a conversational tone.

frost ● *noun* **1 a** a dew or water vapour frozen into tiny white crystals that cover the ground etc. when the temperature falls below the freezing point (*windows covered with frost*). **b** a consistent temperature below freezing point causing frost to form (*frost warning in effect for low-lying areas*). **2** an influence that chills or depresses, esp. coolness of behaviour or temperament. **3** (of colours of lipstick, eyeshadow, etc.) a silvery, pearlized shade. **4** *slang* a failure. ● *verb* **1** *intransitive* (usu. foll. by *over, up*) become covered with frost. **2** *transitive* **a** cover with or as if with frost, powder, etc. **b** freeze and usu. kill or injure (a plant etc.) with frost. **3** *transitive* give an opaque, roughened, or finely granulated surface to (glass, metal) (*frosted glass*). **4** *transitive N Amer.* **a** cover or decorate (a cake etc.) with icing. **b** coat with sugar. **5** *transitive N Amer.* annoy or anger. **6** *transitive* chemically treat selected strands of hair to produce highlights etc. □ **degrees of frost** *Brit.* degrees below freezing point (*ten degrees of frost tonight*). □ **frost·ed** *adjective* **frost·less** *adjective* [Old English from Germanic]

frost·bite ● *noun* injury to body tissues, esp. the nose, ears, fingers, or toes, caused by intense cold, in extreme cases resulting in gangrene. ● *transitive verb* (usu. as **frost·bit·ten** *adjective*) affect with frostbite.

frost boil *noun* = FROST HEAVE.

Frost fence *noun Cdn proprietary* a chain-link fence.

frost-free *adjective* **1** (of a region, period, etc.) experiencing no frost. **2** (of a freezer etc.) self-defrosting.

frost heave *noun* **1** (also **frost heaving**) the uplift of soil or other surface deposits, esp. on a road, due to expansion of groundwater on freezing. **2** an uneven area caused by this.

frost·ing *noun* **1** *N Amer.* icing for a cake etc. **2** a rough surface on glass etc. **3** *N Amer.* a process of treating hair to produce highlights chemically.

frost line *noun* **1** the maximum ground depth below which frost does not penetrate. **2** the lower limit of permafrost.

frosty *adjective* (**frost·i·er**, **frost·i·est**) **1** very cold, esp. cold with frost. **2** covered with or as with hoarfrost. **3** unfriendly in manner, or lacking in warmth of feeling. **4** like frost in appearance. □ **it'll be a frosty Friday** (**in July**) *Cdn informal* it is unlikely to happen. □ **frost·i·ly** *adverb* **frost·i·ness** *noun*

froth ● *noun* **1 a** a collection of small bubbles in liquid, caused by shaking, fermenting, etc.; foam. **b** impure matter on liquid; scum. **2 a** idle talk or ideas. **b** anything unsubstantial or of little worth. **3** foaming saliva, esp. as in rabies etc. ● *verb* **1** *intransitive* **a** emit froth (*frothing at the mouth*). **b** (of liquid) gather froth or run foaming over etc. **2** *transitive* cause (beer, steamed milk, etc.) to foam. □ **froth·i·ly** *adverb* **froth·i·ness** *noun* **froth·ing** *adjective & noun* **frothy** *adjective* (**froth·i·er**, **froth·i·est**). [Old Norse *frotha*, *frauth* from Germanic]

frot·tage /frɒˈtɒʒ/ *noun* **1** *Art* the technique or process of taking a rubbing from an uneven surface, such as grained wood, as a basis of a work of art. **2** the practice of touching or rubbing one's body against the clothed body of another person usu. in a crowd, as a means of obtaining sexual gratification. [French, = rubbing, from *frotter* rub]

frou-frou /ˈfruːfruː/ *noun* **1** frills, frippery. **2** a trivial or insubstantial thing, person, etc. [French, imitative]

frow *var. of* FROE.

fro·ward /ˈfroʊwərd/ *adjective archaic* perverse, difficult to deal with, ungovernable. □ **fro·ward·ly** *adverb* **fro·ward·ness** *noun*

frown ● *verb* **1** *intransitive* **a** contract the eyebrows and wrinkle the forehead, esp. in anger, worry, or deep thought. **b** make a glum expression, esp. with the corners of the mouth turned down. **2** *intransitive* (foll. by *at*, *on*, *upon*) express disapproval. **3** *intransitive* (of a thing) present a gloomy aspect. **4** *transitive* compel or produce with a frown (*frowned them into silence*). **5** *transitive* express (defiance etc.) with a frown. ● *noun* **1** an act of frowning. **2** a look expressing severity, disapproval, or deep thought. □ **frown·er** *noun* **frown·ing** *adjective* **frown·ing·ly** *adverb* [Old French *frongner*, *froignier* from *froigne* surly look, from Celtic]

frowst /fraʊst/ *noun Brit. informal* stuffy warmth in a room. [back-formation from FROWSTY]

frow·sty /ˈfraʊsti/ *adjective* (**frow·sti·er**, **frow·sti·est**) *esp. Brit.* (of air in a room etc.) stale, stuffy, etc. (var. of FROWZY)

frowzy *adjective* (also **frowsy**) (**-zi·er**, **-zi·est**) **1** musty, ill-smelling, close. **2** slatternly, unkempt, dingy. □ **frow·zi·ness** *noun* [17th c.: origin unknown: compare earlier *frowy*]

froze *past of* FREEZE.

fro·zen ● *verb past participle of* FREEZE. ● *adjective* **1 a** exposed or subject to extreme cold. **b** solidified by exposure to cold. **2** (of food) preserved by refrigeration to below freezing point. **3** emotionally frigid, unfriendly, or unresponsive. **4 a** (of a mechanism etc.) fixed, immobile, e.g. with rust, cold, etc. **b** (of a joint etc.) stiffened or immobile from an injury etc. **5** (of a credit or asset) impossible to liquidate or realize at maturity or some other given time.

frozen yogourt *noun* a dessert of yogourt frozen like ice cream.

FRS *abbreviation* (in the UK) Fellow of the Royal Society.

fruc·tif·er·ous /frʌkˈtɪfərəs/ *adjective* bearing or producing fruit. [Latin *fructifer* from *fructus* FRUIT]

fruc·ti·fi·ca·tion /ˌfrʌktɪfɪˈkeɪʃən/ *noun Bot.* **1** the process of bearing fruit. **2** any spore-bearing structure esp. in ferns, fungi, and mosses. [Late Latin *fructificatio* (as FRUCTIFY)]

fruc·ti·fy /ˈfrʌktɪˌfaɪ/ *verb* (**-fies**, **-fied**) **1** *intransitive* bear fruit or become fruitful. **2** *transitive* cause to bear fruit, or make fruitful, fertile, or productive. [Old French *fructifier* from Latin *fructificare* from *fructus* FRUIT]

fruc·tose /ˈfrʌktoːs, -oːz, ˈfrʌk-/ *noun Chem.* a simple sugar found in honey and fruits. *Also called* LEVULOSE, FRUIT SUGAR. [Latin *fructus* FRUIT + -OSE 2]

frug ● *noun* a vigorous dance to pop music, popular in the mid-1960s. ● *intransitive verb* (**frugged**, **frug·ging**) perform such a dance. [20th c.: origin unknown]

fru·gal /ˈfruːɡəl/ *adjective* **1** (often foll. by *of*) sparing or economical; thrifty. **2** (of things, esp. food) plain, simple, or provided in small quantity and with avoidance of excess. □ **fru·gal·ity** /-ˈɡalɪti/ *noun* **fru·gal·ly** *adverb* **fru·gal·ness** *noun* [Latin *frugalis* from *frugi* economical]

fru·giv·or·ous /fruːˈdʒɪvərəs/ *adjective* (of an animal) feeding on fruit. [Latin *frux frugis* fruit + -VOROUS]

fruit ● *noun* **1 a** the usu. sweet and fleshy edible product of a plant or tree, containing seed. **b** (in *sing.*) these in quantity (*eats fruit*). **2** the seed-bearing structure with its covering of a plant or tree, as a means of reproduction, e.g. an acorn, pea pod, cherry, etc. **3** (usu. in *pl.*) any plant product used as food, e.g. vegetables, grains, etc. (*fruits of the earth*). **4** (usu. in *pl.*) a product, outcome, or anything, concrete or abstract, produced by an activity, process, etc. (*fruits of his labours*). **5** *esp. N Amer. slang derogatory* a male homosexual. **6** *archaic* an offspring (*the fruit of the womb*; *the fruit of his loins*). ● *transitive & intransitive verb* bear or cause to bear fruit. □ **fruit·ed** *adjective* (also in *combination*). **fruit·ing** *adjective* [Old French from Latin *fructus* fruit, enjoyment, from *frui* enjoy]

fruit·ar·ian *noun* a person who eats only fruit. □ **fruit·ar·ian·ism** *noun* [FRUIT, after *vegetarian*]

fruit bat *noun* any large bat of the suborder Megachiroptera, feeding on fruit.

fruit body *noun* (also esp. *Brit.* **fruiting body**) (*pl.* **-ies**) the spore-bearing part of a fungus.

fruit·cake *noun* **1** a cake containing a high proportion of mixed dried fruit and often nuts. **2** *slang* an eccentric or mad person.

fruit cocktail *noun* = FRUIT SALAD.

fruit cup *noun N Amer.* = FRUIT SALAD.

fruit·er·er *noun esp. Brit.* a person who sells fruit.

fruit fly *noun* **1** any of various dipteran flies of the families Tephritidae, whose larvae infest cultivated fruit. **2** any of various dipteran flies of the family Drosophilidae, which feed on rotting or fermenting fruit, much used in genetic research.

fruit·ful *adjective* **1 a** (of a tree etc.) producing much fruit. **b** (of soil etc.) fertile, inducing fertility in plants etc. **2 a** producing good results; beneficial, successful, rewarding. **b** abundantly productive of ideas or some other immaterial thing. **3** producing offspring, esp. prolifically. □ **fruit·ful·ly** *adverb* **fruit·ful·ness** *noun*

fru·i·tion /fruːˈɪʃən/ *noun* **1 a** the bearing of fruit. **b** the production of results. **2** the realization or successful outcome of aims, hopes, plans, etc. [Old French from Late Latin *fruitio -onis* from *frui* enjoy, erroneously associated with FRUIT]

fruit·less *adjective* **1** useless, unsuccessful, unprofitable. **2** not bearing fruit. □ **fruit·less·ly** *adverb* **fruit·less·ness** *noun*

fruit·let *noun* = DRUPELET.

fruit loop *noun slang* a crazy person. [after *Froot Loops*, a brand of breakfast cereal]

fruit machine *noun esp. Brit.* = SLOT MACHINE.

fruit nappy *noun* = NAPPY[2].

fruit salad *noun* various fruits cut up and served in syrup, juice, etc.

fruit sugar *noun* fructose.

fruit tree *noun* a tree grown for its fruit.

fruit·wood *noun* the wood of a fruit tree, esp. when used in furniture.

fruity *adjective* (**fruit·i·er**, **fruit·i·est**) **1 a** of, relating to, or resembling fruit, esp. in taste or smell. **b** (of wine) tasting of the grape. **2** (of a voice etc.) mellow, deep, or of a full rich quality. **3** *slang derogatory* homosexual. □ **fruit·i·ness** *noun*

Frum, Bar·bara (1937–92), Canadian journalist and broadcaster. She was renowned as a persistent and incisive interviewer on CBC Radio's

'As It Happens' (1971–81), and as the host of the CBC television current-affairs program 'The Journal' (1982–92).

fru·menty /ˈfruːmənti/ *noun* (also **furmety** /ˈfɜrmɪti/) *Brit. hist.* hulled wheat boiled in milk and seasoned with cinnamon, sugar, etc. [Old French *frumentee* from *frument* from Latin *frumentum* corn]

frump *noun* a dowdy, unattractive woman. □ **frump·ish** *adjective* **frump·ish·ly** *adverb* [16th c.: perhaps from dial. *frumple* (v.) wrinkle, from Middle Dutch *verrompelen* (as FOR-, RUMPLE)]

frum·py *adjective* (**frump·i·er**, **frump·i·est**) dowdy and unattractive. □ **frump·i·ly** *adverb* **frump·i·ness** *noun*

Frunze /ˈfruːnzi/ a former name (1926–91) for BISHKEK.

frus·trate ● *transitive verb* **1** upset or discourage (a person). **2** make (efforts) ineffective (*parliament frustrated his reforms*). **3** prevent (a person) from achieving a purpose. **4** disappoint (a hope). □ **frus·trat·er** *noun* **frus·trat·ing** *adjective* **frus·trat·ing·ly** *adverb* **frus·tra·tion** *noun* [Latin *frustrari frustrat-* from *frustra* in vain]

frus·trat·ed *adjective* **1** discontented because unable to achieve one's desire. **2** sexually unfulfilled. □ **frus·trat·ed·ly** *adverb*

frus·tule /ˈfrʌstjuːl/ *noun Bot.* the siliceous cell wall of a diatom. [French from Latin *frustulum* (as FRUSTUM)]

frus·tum /ˈfrʌstəm/ *noun* (*pl.* **frusta** /-tə/ or **frus·tums**) *Math.* **1** the remainder of a cone or pyramid whose upper part has been cut off by a plane parallel to its base. **2** the part of a cone or pyramid intercepted between two planes. [Latin, = piece cut off]

fru·ti·cose /ˈfruːtɪˌkoːs, -ˌkoːz/ *adjective Bot.* resembling a shrub. [Latin *fruticosus* from *frutex fruticis* bush]

Fry, Eliza·beth (1780–1845), English Quaker prison reformer. In the forefront of the early 19th-c. campaign for penal reform, she concerned herself particularly with conditions in prisons such as Newgate (London).

fry[1] ● *verb* (**fries, fried**) **1** *transitive & intransitive* cook or be cooked in hot fat. **2** *transitive & intransitive informal* overload, burn out, etc. (electronic components etc.). **3** *transitive & intransitive slang* electrocute or be electrocuted. **4** *transitive & intransitive informal* **a** burn or overheat, esp. with effects analogous to those of frying food. **b** (of the sun) scorch (a person etc.). **5** *N Amer. slang* **a** destroy (*drugs fry the brain*). **b** *transitive* upset or annoy intensely. ● *noun* (*pl.* **fries**) **1** (usu. in *pl.*) *N Amer.* = FRENCH FRY. **2** a dish of fried food, esp. meat. **3** *N Amer.* a party at which fried food is eaten. **4** *Brit.* any of various types of offal usu. eaten fried (*lamb's fry*). □ **fry up** heat or reheat (food) in a frying pan. [Old French *frire* from Latin *frigere*]

fry[2] *plural noun* **1** young or newly hatched fish. **2** the young of other creatures produced in large numbers, e.g. bees or frogs. **3** young or insignificant people. [Middle English from Old Norse *frjó*]

Frye, (Her·man) Nor·throp (1912–91), Canadian literary critic. One of the most influential literary theorists of the 20th c., he is known for his study of the recurring myths and archetypal symbols in literature; his works include *Fearful Symmetry* (1947), *The Anatomy of Criticism* (1957), and *The Great Code: The Bible and Literature* (1982).

fryer *noun* **1** a pot etc. for frying food, esp. in deep fat. **2** *N Amer.* a chicken suitable for frying.

fry·ing pan *noun* (*N Amer.* also **fry pan**) a flat, shallow pan with a long handle, used for frying food. □ **out of the frying pan into the fire** from a bad situation to a worse one.

fry-up *noun Brit. informal* **1** a dish of miscellaneous fried food. **2** the preparation of such a dish.

FSH *abbreviation* = FOLLICLE-STIMULATING HORMONE.

f-stop *noun* an f-number setting on a camera.

Ft. *abbreviation* Fort.

ft. *abbreviation* foot, feet.

FTA *abbreviation* Free Trade Agreement.

FTAA *abbreviation* Free Trade Area of the Americas.

FTP *Computing* ● *abbreviation* file transfer protocol, a standard for the exchange of program and data files across a network. ● *transitive verb* (**FTP's, FTP'd, FTP'ing**) transfer (a file) from one computer or system to another using this protocol, esp. across the Internet.

FTSE *abbreviation* (in the UK) Financial Times Exchange index (*see also* FOOTSIE).

Fuchs /fʊks/ **(Emil) Klaus (Jul·ius)** (1911–88), German-born English physicist. A Communist who had fled Nazi persecution, he conveyed secret details of the Anglo-US atomic program to the USSR in the 1940s, and was imprisoned (1950–59).

fuchsia /ˈfjuːʃə/ *noun* **1** any shrub of the genus *Fuchsia*, with drooping red or purple or white flowers. **2** a bright purple-pink shade of red like that of the fuchsia flower. [modern Latin from L. *Fuchs*, German botanist d.1566]

fuch·sin /ˈfuːksɪn/ *noun* (also **fuch·sine** /ˈfuːksiːn/) a deep red aniline dye used in the pharmaceutical and textile processing industries. [FUCHSIA (from its resemblance to the colour of the flower)]

fuck *coarse slang* ● *verb* **1** *transitive & intransitive* have sexual intercourse (with). **2** *transitive* (usu. as an exclamation) curse, confound (*fuck the thing!*). **3 a** *transitive* (often foll. by *over*) deal with (a person) unfairly, unjustly, etc. **b** ruin, spoil, exhaust, or wear out (a thing). **4** *intransitive* (foll. by *about, around*) **a** mess about, fool around, or involve oneself in. **b** be sexually promiscuous. ● *interjection* expressing anger or annoyance, contempt, impatience, or surprise, or simply for emphasis. ● *noun* **1 a** an act of sexual intercourse. **b** a partner in sexual intercourse. **2** the slightest amount (*don't give a fuck*). **3** a person who is stupid, annoying, hapless, etc. **4** (usu. as *the fuck*) an intensifier (*What the fuck are you doing?*). □ **fuck off** (also **fuck you**) go to hell, drop dead, etc. **fuck that** (or **this**) *noise N Amer.* expressing total dismissiveness of a suggestion, comment etc. **fuck up 1** blunder, fail, make a serious error. **2** ruin, spoil, mess up. **3** disturb emotionally. **fuck with** mess with. □ **fuck·er** *noun* (often as a term of abuse). [16th c.: origin unknown] ¶ Although widely used in many sections of society, *fuck* is still generally considered to be one of the most offensive words in the English language. In discussions about bad language it is sometimes referred to euphemistically as *the F-word*.

fuck all *noun coarse slang* absolutely nothing.

fuck·head *noun coarse slang* (also **fuck·face**) a person considered with contempt.

fuckin' A *interjection coarse slang* expressing agreement, approval, etc.

fuck·ing *adjective & adverb coarse slang* used as an intensive to express annoyance etc.

fuck-up *noun coarse slang* **1** a mess or disastrously bungled matter. **2** a person who is a chronic loser or failure.

fuck·wit *noun coarse slang* a stupid or contemptible person.

fucus /ˈfjuːkəs/ *noun* (*pl.* **fuci** /ˈfjuːsaɪ/) any seaweed of the genus *Fucus*, with flat leathery fronds. □ **fu·coid** *adjective* [Latin, = rock lichen, from Greek *phukos*, of Semitic origin]

fud·dle *transitive verb* confuse or stupefy, esp. with alcoholic liquor. [16th c.: origin unknown]

fud·dle dud·dle *interjection Cdn euphemism* go to hell; drop dead. [what Prime Minister Pierre Trudeau claimed he said in Parliament rather than 'fuck off']

fuddy-duddy *slang* ● *noun* (*pl.* **-duddies**) an old-fashioned or quaintly fussy person. ● *adjective* old-fashioned; quaintly fussy. [20th c.: origin unknown]

fudge ● *noun* **1** a soft crumbly or chewy kind of candy made with milk, sugar, butter, etc. **2** (*attributive*) esp. *N Amer.* designating rich chocolate cakes, cookies, sauces, etc. **3** nonsense. **4** a piece of dishonesty or faking. ● *verb* **1** *transitive* put together in a makeshift or dishonest way; fake (*fudged the budget figures*). **2** *transitive* deal with vaguely or inadequately, usu. deliberately, so as to mislead or avoid making a definite choice. **3** *intransitive* practise such methods (*fudged on the issue of pay raises*). ● *interjection* expressing disbelief or annoyance. [perhaps from obsolete *fadge* (v.) fit]

fudge factor *noun* a figure included in a calculation to account for some unquantified but significant phenomenon or to ensure a desired result.

fueh·rer *var. of* FÜHRER.

fuel ● *noun* **1** material, esp. oil, gas, wood, coal, etc., burned or used as a source of heat or power. **2** food as a source of energy. **3** material used as a source of nuclear energy. **4** anything that sustains or inflames emotion or passion. ● *verb* (**fuelled, fuel·ling**; esp. *US* **fueled, fuel·ing**) **1** *transitive* supply with fuel. **2** *transitive* sustain or inflame (an argument, feeling, etc.) (*drink fuelled his anger*). **3** *transitive* give impetus to (*low interest rates fuelled the recovery*). **4** *intransitive* take in or get fuel. [Old French *fouaille*, ultimately from Latin *focus* hearth]

fuel cell *noun* a cell producing an electric current directly from a chemical reaction, developed e.g. for use in non-polluting motor vehicles.

fuel efficiency *noun* the efficient use of fuel in an engine or other system. □ **fuel-efficient** *adjective*

fuel element *noun* a can of nuclear fuel etc. for use in a reactor.

fuel injection *noun* the direct introduction of fuel under pressure into the combustion chamber of an internal combustion engine. □ **fuel-injected** *adjective*

fuel oil *noun* oil used as fuel in an engine or furnace.

Consonants: b *but* d *dog* f *few* g *get* h *her* j *yes* k *cat* l *leg* m *man* n *no* p *pen* r *red* s *sit*

fuel rod *noun* a rod-shaped fuel element, esp. one used in a nuclear reactor.

fuel·wood *noun* wood burned to provide heat etc.

Fuen·la·brada /ˌfwenlaˈvradə/ a city in Spain, just south of Madrid; pop. (est. 1998) 167,458.

Fuen·tes /ˈfwentes/ **Car·los** (b.1928), Mexican novelist and writer. His first novel, *Where the Air is Clear* (1958), took Mexico City as its theme and was an immediate success; other novels include *Terra nostra* (1975), which explores the Spanish heritage in Mexico.

fug *noun* esp. *Brit.* stuffiness or fustiness of the air in a room. □ **fuggy** *adjective* [19th c.: origin unknown]

fu·ga·cious /fjuːˈgeiʃəs/ *adjective* **1** *literary* fleeting, evanescent, hard to capture or keep. **2** *Bot. & Zool.* falling or fading early; soon cast off. [Latin *fugax fugacis* from *fugere* flee]

fugal /ˈfjuːgəl/ *adjective* of the nature of a fugue.

Fu·gard /ˈfuːgɑrd/ **Athol (Har·old Lan·ni·gan)** (b.1932), South African dramatist. His plays, including *Blood Knot* (1961) and *The Road to Mecca* (1985), are mostly concerned with racial tension and inequality under South African apartheid.

-fuge /fjuːdʒ/ *combining form* forming adjectives and nouns denoting expelling or dispelling (*vermifuge*). [from or after modern Latin *-fugus* from Latin *fugare* put to flight]

Fug·ger /ˈfʊgər/ a German mercantile and banking family which greatly influenced European business during the 15th and 16th c.

fugi·tive /ˈfjuːdʒɪtɪv/ ● *noun* (often foll. by *from*) a person who has escaped from a place or is in hiding, esp. to avoid arrest or persecution. ● *adjective* **1** fleeing; that runs or has run away. **2** quick to disappear; fleeting. [Old French *fugitif -ive* from Latin *fugitivus* from *fugere fugit-* flee]

fugle·man /ˈfjuːgəlmən/ *noun* (*pl.* **-men**) **1** *hist.* a soldier placed in front of a regiment etc. while drilling to show the motions and time. **2** a leader, organizer, or spokesman. [German *Flügelmann* from *Flügel* wing + *Mann* man]

fugu /ˈfuːguː/ *noun* a pufferfish that is eaten as a Japanese delicacy after some highly poisonous parts have been removed. [Japanese]

fugue /fjuːg/ *noun* **1** *Music* a contrapuntal composition in which a short melody or phrase (the subject) is introduced by one part and successively taken up by others and developed by interweaving the parts. **2** *Psych.* (in full **fugue state**) loss of awareness of one's identity, often coupled with flight from one's usual environment. □ **fu·guist** *noun* [French or Italian from Latin *fuga* flight]

füh·rer /ˈfjʊrər/ *noun* (also **fueh·rer**) a leader, esp. a tyrannical one. [German, = leader: part of the title assumed in 1934 by Hitler (see HITLER[1])]

Fu·jai·rah /fuːˈdʒaɪɪrə/ (also **Al Fu·jay·rah**) **1** one of the seven member states of the United Arab Emirates; pop. (est. 2002) 99,400. **2** its capital city.

Fuji *noun* a large firm-fleshed greenish apple with red highlights. [Mount FUJI]

Fuji, Mount /ˈfuːdʒi/ (also **Fuji·yama** /ˌfuːdʒiˈjɒmə/) a dormant volcano in the Chubu region of Japan. Rising to 3 776 m (12,385 ft.), it is Japan's highest mountain. Mount Fuji, regarded by the Japanese as sacred, has been celebrated in art and literature for centuries.

Fu·jian /ˌfuːdʒˈjan/ (also **Fu·kien** /fuːˈkjen/) a province of SE China, on the China Sea; capital, Fuzhou. □ **Fu·jian·ese** *noun & adjective*

Fu·ku·oka /ˌfuːkuːˈoːkə/ an industrial city and port in S Japan, capital of Kyushu island; pop. (est. 2002) 1,361,400.

-ful *suffix* forming: **1** adjectives from nouns, meaning: **a** full of (*beautiful*). **b** having the qualities of (*masterful*). **2** adjectives from adjectives or Latin stems with little change of sense (*direful*; *grateful*). **3** adjectives from verbs, meaning 'apt to', 'able to', 'accustomed to' (*forgetful*; *mournful*; *useful*). **4** nouns (*pl.* **-fuls**) meaning 'the amount needed to fill' (*handful*; *spoonful*).

Fu·lani /ˈfuːlani, ˈfuːlani/ *noun* (*pl.* **Fulanis**) **1** a member of an African people of northern Nigeria and adjacent territories. **2** the language of this people. [Hausa]

Ful·bright (James) Wil·liam (1905–95), US senator 1944–74, who initiated the grants awarded under the Fulbright Act (1946) to finance exchange programs of students and teachers between the US and other countries.

ful·crum /ˈfʊlkrəm/ *noun* (*pl.* **ful·crums** or **ful·cra** /-rə/) **1** the point against which a lever is placed to get a purchase or on which it turns or is supported. **2** the means by which influence etc. is brought to bear. [Latin, = post of a couch, from *fulcire* to prop]

ful·fill *transitive verb* (also **ful·fil**) (**ful·filled**, **ful·fill·ing**) **1** bring to consummation, carry out (a prophecy or promise). **2** satisfy (a desire or prayer). **3 a** execute, obey (a command or law). **b** perform, carry out (a task). **4** comply with (conditions). **5** answer (a purpose). **6** bring to an end, finish, complete (a period or piece of work). □ **fulfill oneself** develop one's gifts and character to the full. □ **ful·fill·ment** *noun* (also **ful·fil·ment**). [Old English *fullfyllan* (as FULL[1], FILL)]

ful·filled *adjective* completely happy; satisfied.

ful·fill·ing *adjective* deeply satisfying.

Ful·ford /ˈfʊlfərd/ **Rob·ert (Mar·shall Blount)** (b.1932), Canadian editor and journalist. He was the editor of Saturday Night magazine (1968–87), and has written for *The Globe and Mail*, *Toronto Life*, and *The National Post*.

ful·gent /ˈfʌldʒənt/ *adjective literary* shining, brilliant. [Middle English from Latin *fulgēre* shine]

ful·gur·ite /ˈfʌlgjuˌraɪt/ *noun* *Geol.* a rocky substance of sand fused or vitrified by lightning. [Latin *fulgur* lightning]

ful·ligin·ous /fjuːˈlɪdʒɪnəs/ *adjective literary* sooty, dusky. [Late Latin *fuliginosus* from *fuligo -ginis* soot]

full[1] ● *adjective* **1** (often foll. by *of*) holding all its limits will allow (*the bucket is full*; *full of water*). **2** having eaten to one's limits or satisfaction. **3** abundant, copious, satisfying, sufficient (*a full program of events*; *led a full life*; *give full details*). **4** (foll. by *of*) having or holding an abundance of, showing marked signs of (*full of vitality*; *full of interest*; *full of mistakes*). **5** (foll. by *of*) **a** engrossed in thinking about (*full of his work*). **b** unable to refrain from talking about (*full of the news*). **6** complete, perfect, reaching the specified or usual or utmost limit (*full membership*; *full daylight*; *waited a full hour*; *in full bloom*). **7 a** (of tone or colour) deep and rich; intense. **b** (of light) intense. **c** (of motion etc.) vigorous (*at full gallop*). **d** (of sound) strong, resonant. **e** (of wine etc.) rich in quality or tone. **8** plump, rounded, protuberant (*a full figure*). **9** (of clothes) amply cut; made of much material arranged in folds or gathers. **10** (of the heart etc.) overcharged with emotion. **11** having all the qualifications or privileges of a designation; of the highest rank (*full professor*; *full lieutenant*). ● *adverb* **1** very (*you know full well*). **2** quite, fully (*full six miles*; *full ripe*). **3** exactly (*hit him full on the nose*). ● *noun* the state or time of full moon. ● *transitive & intransitive verb* be or become or make (esp. clothes) full. □ **be full of it** (or **crap** or **shit**) *coarse slang* talk nonsense. **come full circle** *see* CIRCLE. **full of oneself** conceited. **full speed** (or **steam**) **ahead!** an order to proceed at maximum speed or to pursue a course of action energetically. **full up** completely full. **in full 1** without abridgement. **2** to or for the full amount (*paid in full*). **in full swing** at the height of activity. **in full view** entirely visible. **on a full stomach** *see* STOMACH. **to the full** to the utmost extent. [Old English from Germanic]

full[2] *transitive verb* cleanse and thicken (cloth). [Middle English, back-formation from FULLER[1]: compare Old French *fouler* (FOIL[1])]

full age *noun* *Cdn & Brit.* adult status (esp. with reference to legal rights and duties).

full·back *noun* **1** *Football* a running back who lines up behind the rest of his team at the scrimmage. **2** *Soccer etc.* a defensive player, or a position near the goal.

full bath *noun* *N Amer.* a bathroom containing a sink, toilet, and bathtub (*compare* HALF BATH).

full blood *noun* **1** pure descent; unmixed ancestry. **2** (**full-blood**) a person or animal of unmixed ancestry.

full-blooded *adjective* **1** vigorous, hearty, sensual. **2** not hybrid. **3** of unmixed ancestry.

full-blown *adjective* **1** fully developed, complete (*full-blown AIDS*). **2** (of flowers) very open.

full board *noun* *Brit.* provision of accommodation and all meals at a hotel etc.

full-bodied *adjective* rich in quality, tone, flavour, etc.

full bore esp. *N Amer. informal* ● *adverb* at maximum power, speed, etc. (*ran full bore down the street*). ● *adjective* with maximum power, activity, etc.

full-bottomed *adjective* (of a wig) long at the back.

full breakfast *noun* a substantial breakfast of juice, tea or coffee, cereal, bacon and eggs, etc. (*compare* CONTINENTAL BREAKFAST).

full brother *noun* a brother born of the same parents.

full colour *noun* the full range of colours (often *attributive*: *full-colour brochure*).

full count *noun* *Baseball* a count of three balls and two strikes against a batter (also *attributive*: *full-count pitch*).

full course *noun* N Amer. a university course extending over the entire academic year or one equivalent to it in credits acquired.

full-course *adjective* N Amer. (of a meal) consisting of a number of courses, e.g. soup, salad, entree, and dessert.

full-court press *noun* **1** Basketball an aggressive defence tactic in which the team without the ball harasses the opposing team the whole length of the court. **2** N Amer. an attack; an offensive campaign.

full deck *noun* N Amer. a complete set of playing cards. □ **not playing with a full deck** slang not of normal intelligence or sanity.

full dress ● *noun* clothes worn on ceremonial or formal occasions. ● *adjective* (**full-dress**) thorough, complete (a full-dress investigation).

full dress uniform *noun* military uniform worn for ceremonial parades etc.

full duplex *adjective* Computing (of a circuit) allowing the transmission of signals in both directions simultaneously.

full employment *noun* **1** the condition in which there is no idle capital or labour of any kind that is in demand. **2** the condition in which virtually all who are able and willing to work are employed.

Ful·ler, Rich·ard Buck·min·ster (1895–1983), US designer and architect. An advocate of the use of technology to produce efficiency in many aspects of life, he is best known for his postwar invention of the geodesic dome.

ful·ler[1] *noun* a person who fulls cloth. [Old English fullere from Latin fullo]

ful·ler[2] ● *noun* **1** a grooved or rounded tool on which iron is shaped. **2** a groove made by this esp. in a horseshoe. ● *transitive verb* stamp with a fuller. [19th c.: origin unknown]

ful·ler·ene /ˈfʊləriːn/ *noun* Chem. any of several forms of carbon in which atoms are joined in a hollow structure. [BUCKMINSTERFULLERENE]

fuller's earth *noun* a type of clay used in fulling cloth and as an adsorbent.

full-face *adverb & adjective* with all the face visible to the observer (a full-face portrait).

full-featured *adjective* (of computers, software, electronic equipment, etc.) having many features; technologically up-to-date (a full-featured fax machine).

full-figure *adjective* **1** (of a painting, statue, etc. of a person) representing the entire body. **2** (also **full-figured**) **a** plump, stout. **b** large, oversize (ladies' full-figure blouses).

full-flavoured *adjective* (also **full-flavored**) (of food, wine, etc.) strong and distinct in taste.

full-fledged *adjective* (also **fully-fledged**) **1** of full rank or status (a full-fledged political party). **2** fully developed; mature.

full-frontal *attributive adjective* **1** (of nudity or a nude figure) with full exposure at the front. **2** unrestrained, explicit; with nothing concealed.

full-grain *adjective* (of leather) having all the layers intact.

full-grown *adjective* having reached maturity.

full growth *noun* the size ultimately attained; maturity.

full house *noun* **1** a maximum or large attendance at a theatre, stadium, etc. **2** Cards a poker hand with three of a kind and a pair.

full-length *adjective* **1** of normal, standard, or maximum length; not shortened or abbreviated. **2** (of a mirror, portrait, etc.) showing the whole height of the human figure.

full marks *plural noun* Cdn & Brit. **1** the maximum award in an examination, competition, etc. **2** full credit (I give her full marks for thoughtfulness).

full moon *noun* **1** the moon in its fullest phase, with its whole disc illuminated. **2** the time when this occurs.

full motion video *noun* digital video data that is transmitted or stored (on videodisc etc.) for real-time reproduction esp. on a computer (or other multimedia system) at a rate of not less than 25 frames per second.

full·ness *noun* **1** the state of being full. **2** (of sound, colour, etc.) richness, volume, body. □ **in the fullness of time** after a due length of time has elapsed.

full on ● *adverb* **1** (of a heat or light source, a mechanical device, etc.) running at maximum power; providing maximum capacity. **2** from directly in front; directly; head-on. **3** without reservation or restraint; unambiguously or uninhibitedly. ● *adjective* unrestrained or unqualified in action, nature, or impact.

full out ● *adverb* at full power, speed, etc. ● *adjective* (**full-out**) complete (full-out drunkenness).

full page *noun* an entire page of a newspaper etc. (also *attributive*: full-page spread).

full-scale *adjective* **1** not reduced in size; having the same size as the original. **2** utilizing all available resources; all-out (a full-scale investigation).

full score *noun* Music a score giving the parts for all performers.

full-service *adjective* **1** designating a gas station, restaurant, etc. where service is provided entirely by staff (compare SELF-SERVE 1). **2** providing a wide range of products or services (a full-service gym).

full sister *noun* a sister born of the same parents.

full-size ● *adjective* (also **full-sized**) **1** of the standard size of its kind (a full-size washing machine). **2** N Amer. (of a car) of the largest size, usu. having a wheelbase over 105 inches and a 4-litre engine. ● *noun* N Amer. a full-size car.

full stop *noun* **1** Brit. & Cdn (Nfld) = PERIOD 8. **2** a complete cessation.

full term *noun* the completion of a normal pregnancy.

full-throat·ed *adjective* **1** strong and rich in sound (a full-throated baritone). **2** vociferous.

full throttle *noun* maximum speed, strength, etc.

full tilt *noun* see TILT[1].

full-time ● *adjective* occupying or using the whole of the available working time (a full-time job). ● *adverb* on a full-time basis (works full-time). ● *noun* (**full time**) **1** the total normal duration of work etc. **2** the end of a soccer etc. game.

full-timer *noun* a person who works a full-time job.

fully *adverb* **1** completely, entirely (am fully aware). **2** no less or fewer than (fully 60).

-fully *combining form* forming adverbs corresponding to adjectives in -ful.

fully-fledged var. of FULL-FLEDGED.

ful·mar /ˈfʊlmər/ *noun* any medium-sized seabird of the genus Fulmarus, with a stout body, robust bill, and rounded tail. [originally Hebridean dial.: perhaps from Old Norse fúll FOUL (with reference to its smell) + már gull (compare MEW[2])]

ful·min·ant /ˈfʌlmɪnənt, ˈfʊl-/ *adjective* Med. (of a disease or symptom) developing suddenly.

ful·min·ate /ˈfʊlmɪˌneɪt, ˈfʌl-/ ● *intransitive verb* **1** (often foll. by against) express censure loudly and forcefully. **2** explode violently; flash like lightning (fulminating mercury). **3** Med. (of a disease or symptom) develop suddenly and rapidly. ● *noun* Chem. a salt or ester of fulminic acid. □ **ful·min·a·tion** *noun* [Latin fulminare fulminat- from fulmen -minis lightning]

ful·ness rare var. of FULLNESS.

ful·some /ˈfʊlsəm/ *adjective* **1** (of praise etc.) excessively complimentary or flattering; effusive, overdone. **2** abundant. ¶ Since fulsome may have negative connotations to some people and neutral connotations to others, it is advisable to make clear, when using this word, which connotations are intended. □ **ful·some·ly** *adverb* **ful·some·ness** *noun* [Middle English from FULL[1] + -SOME[1]]

ful·vous /ˈfʌlvəs/ *adjective* brownish yellow, tawny. [Latin fulvus]

fuma·role /ˈfjuːməˌroʊl/ *noun* an opening in or near a volcano, through which hot vapours emerge. □ **fuma·rol·ic** /-ˈrɒlɪk/ *adjective* [from obsolete Italian fumaruolo, from late Latin fumariolum 'vent for smoke', a diminutive based on Latin fumus 'smoke']

fum·ble ● *verb* **1** *intransitive* (often foll. by at, with, for, after) use the hands awkwardly, grope about (fumbled in her pockets for change). **2** *transitive* handle or deal with clumsily or nervously. **3** *transitive & intransitive* Football etc. fail to keep hold of a ball after having touched it or transported it. **4** *transitive* make one's way clumsily (fumbled his way across the garden). ● *noun* an act of fumbling. □ **fum·bler** *noun* **fum·bling·ly** *adverb* [Low German fummeln, fommeln, Dutch fommelen]

fume ● *noun* (usu. in pl.) exuded gas or smoke or vapour, esp. when harmful or unpleasant. ● *verb* **1 a** *intransitive* emit fumes. **b** *transitive* give off as fumes. **2** *intransitive* (often foll. by at) be affected by (esp. suppressed) anger (was fuming at their inefficiency). **3** *transitive* subject to fumes, esp. those of ammonia (to darken tints in oak, photographic film, etc.). □ **fume·less** *adjective* **fumy** *adjective* [Old French fum from Latin fumus smoke]

fu·met /fjuːˈmeɪ/ *noun* a concentrated stock, usu. of game or fish, used as flavouring. [French from fumer FUME v.]

fumi·gate /ˈfjuːmɪˌgeɪt/ *transitive & intransitive verb* disinfect (something contaminated or infested) with the fumes of certain chemicals. □ **fumi·gant** *noun* **fumi·ga·tion** *noun* **fumi·ga·tor** *noun* [Latin fumigare fumigat- from fumus smoke]

fumi·tory /ˈfjuːmɪtɔri/ *noun* an Old World plant of the genus Fumaria, with spikes of small tubular pink or white flowers. [Old French *fumeterre* from medieval Latin *fumus terrae* 'smoke from the earth' (because of its greyish leaves)]

fun ● *noun* **1** amusement, esp. lively or playful. **2** a source of this. **3** playfulness; good humour (*she's very lively and full of fun*). **4** (in full **fun and games**) lighthearted or amusing activities. ● *adjective informal* amusing, entertaining, enjoyable (*a fun thing to do*). ● *intransitive verb informal* have fun; fool, joke. □ **be great** (or **good**) **fun** be very amusing. **for fun** (or **for the fun of it**) not for a serious purpose. **have fun** enjoy oneself. **in fun** as a joke, not seriously. **like fun** *ironic* not at all. **make fun of** (or **poke fun at**) mock; ridicule. **what fun!** how amusing! [obsolete *fun* (v.) var. of *fon* befool: compare FOND]

Funa·bashi /ˌfuːnəˈbaʃi/ a city on the south coast of central Japan, just east of Tokyo; pop. (est. 1995) 540,817.

Funa·futi /ˌfuːnəˈfuːti/ the capital of Tuvalu, situated on an island of the same name; pop. (est. 2002) 5,100.

fu·nam·bu·list /fjuːˈnambjʊlɪst/ *noun* a tightrope walker. [French *funambule* or Latin *funambulus* from *funis* rope + *ambulare* walk]

Fun·chal /fʊnˈʃʊl/ the capital and chief port of Madeira, on the south coast of the island; pop. (2001) 102,521.

func·tion ● *noun* **1 a** an activity proper to a person or institution. **b** a mode of action or activity by which a thing fulfills its purpose. **c** an official or professional duty; an employment, profession, or calling. **2 a** a public ceremony or occasion. **b** a social gathering, esp. a large, formal, or important one. **3** *Math.* a variable quantity regarded in relation to another or others in terms of which it may be expressed or on which its value depends (*x is a function of y and z*). **4** something dependent on another factor or factors (*university attendance as a function of family income*). **5** *Computing* a part of a program that corresponds to a single value. ● *intransitive verb* **1** fulfill a function. **2** operate; be in working order. □ **func·tion·less** *adjective* [French *fonction* from Latin *functio -onis* from *fungi funct-* perform]

func·tion·al *adjective* **1** of or serving a function. **2** functioning; able to work (*is this machine functional?*). **3** (esp. of buildings) designed or intended to be practical rather than attractive; utilitarian. **4** *Physiol.* **a** (esp. of disease) of or affecting only the functions of an organ etc., not structural or organic. **b** (of mental disorder) having no discernible organic cause. **5** *Math.* of a function. □ **func·tion·al·ity** *noun* **func·tion·al·ly** *adverb*

functional food *noun* a foodstuff containing chemical or biological additives intended to have beneficial physiological effects on the consumer; a nutraceutical. [after Japanese *kinōsei-shokuhin* from *kinōsei* functionality + *shokuhin* food]

functional group *noun* *Chem.* a group of atoms that determine the reactions of a compound containing the group.

functional illiterate *noun* a person who cannot read or write well enough to complete everyday tasks, such as reading a menu, filling out a job application, etc. □ **functional illiteracy** *noun* **functionally illiterate** *adjective*

func·tion·al·ism *noun* **1** (in the arts) the doctrine that the design of an object should be determined solely by its function, rather than by aesthetic considerations. **2** (in the social sciences) the theory that all aspects of a society serve a function and are necessary for the survival of that society. **3** belief in or stress on the practical application of a thing. □ **func·tion·al·ist** *noun & adjective*

func·tion·ary *noun* (*pl.* **-aries**) a person who performs official functions or duties; an official.

function key *noun* *Computing* a button on a keyboard, distinct from the alphanumeric keys, to which software can assign a particular function.

function room *noun* a room suitable for meetings, banquets, parties, etc. in a hotel etc.

function word *noun* *Linguistics* a word whose purpose is to contribute to the syntax rather than the meaning of a sentence, e.g. *do* in *we do not live here*.

fund ● *noun* **1** a permanent stock of something ready to be drawn upon (*a fund of knowledge*). **2 a** a reserve of money or investments, esp. one set apart for a purpose. **b** an organization which manages such a reserve (*International Monetary Fund*). **3** (in *pl.*) money resources. ● *transitive verb* **1** provide with money. **2** convert (a floating debt) into a more or less permanent debt at fixed interest. **3** put into a fund. □ **fund·able** *adjective* **fund·ed** *adjective* (usu. in *combination*). **fund·er** *noun* **fund·ing** *noun* [Latin *fundus* bottom, piece of land]

fun·da·ment /ˈfʌndəmənt/ *noun* **1** *jocular* the buttocks or anus. **2** the basis or principle upon which anything is founded. [Old French *fondement* from Latin *fundamentum* (as FOUND²)]

fun·da·men·tal /ˌfʌndəˈmentəl/ ● *adjective* of, affecting, or serving as a base or foundation, essential, primary, original (*a fundamental change; the fundamental rules; the fundamental form*). ● *noun* (usu. in *pl.*) a fundamental rule, principle, or article. □ **fun·da·men·tal·ity** /-ˈtalɪti/ *noun* **fun·da·men·tal·ly** *adverb*

fun·da·men·tal·ism /ˌfʌndəˈmentəˌlɪzəm/ *noun* **1** strict maintenance of traditional Protestant beliefs such as the inerrancy of Scripture and literal acceptance of the creeds as fundamentals of Christianity. **2** strict maintenance of ancient or fundamental doctrines of any religion, esp. Islam. □ **fun·da·men·tal·ist** *noun & adjective*

fundamental particle *noun* a subatomic particle.

fund manager *noun* a person who manages an investment fund at an insurance company, mutual fund company etc. □ **fund management** *noun*

fund·rais·er *noun* **1** a person who seeks financial support for a cause, enterprise, etc. **2** a social function held to raise money for a cause, enterprise, etc. □ **fund·rais·ing** *noun*

fun·dus /ˈfʌndəs/ *noun* (*pl.* **fundi** /-dai/) *Anat.* the base of a hollow organ; the part furthest from the opening. [Latin, = bottom]

Fundy, Bay of an arm of the Atlantic Ocean extending between New Brunswick and Nova Scotia. It is subject to fast-running tides, the highest in the world, which reach 12–15 m (40–48 ft.) and are now used to generate electricity, [possibly from French *fendu* split: *see* SPLIT, CAPE]

Fundy National Park a small park on the southern shore of E New Brunswick, bordering Chignecto Bay. It was established in 1948.

fu·ner·al ● *noun* **1 a** a ceremony or service held shortly after a person's death, usu. including the person's burial or cremation. **b** a burial or cremation procession. **2** *informal* one's (usu. unpleasant) concern (*that's your funeral*). ● *attributive adjective* of or used etc. at a funeral (*funeral oration*). [Old French *funeraille* from medieval Latin *funeralia* neuter pl. of Late Latin *funeralis* from Latin *funus -eris* funeral]

funeral director *noun* an undertaker.

funeral home *noun* N Amer. (also **funeral parlour** or N Amer. **funeral chapel**) an establishment where the dead are prepared for burial or cremation, usu. also having rooms for visitation or funeral services.

funeral urn *noun* an urn holding the ashes of a cremated body.

fu·ner·ary *adjective* of or used at a funeral or funerals. [Late Latin *funerarius* (as FUNERAL)]

fu·ner·eal /fjuːˈnɪːrɪəl/ *adjective* **1** of or appropriate to a funeral. **2** gloomy, dismal, dark. □ **fu·ner·eal·ly** *adverb* [Latin *funereus* (as FUNERAL)]

fun fair *noun* **1** a fair consisting of amusements and sideshows. **2** a fundraising event at a school etc. involving games, auctions, raffles, bake sales, etc.

fun fur *noun* an artificial fabric with a texture resembling fur, often in bright colours.

fun·gal *adjective* of or pertaining to a fungus.

fungi *pl. of* FUNGUS.

fun·gible /ˈfʌndʒəbəl/ *adjective* esp. *Law* precisely or acceptably replacing or replaceable by another item, mutually interchangeable, esp. of goods etc. contracted for, when a particular item is not specified. □ **fun·gi·bil·ity** /-ˈbɪlɪti/ *noun* [medieval Latin *fungibilis* from *fungi* (*vice*) serve (in place of)]

fun·gi·cide /ˈfʌngɪˌsaɪd, ˈfʌndʒ-/ *noun* a fungus-destroying substance. □ **fun·gi·cid·al** *adjective*

fun·gi·stat·ic /ˌfʌndʒəˈstatɪk/ *adjective* inhibiting the growth of fungi.

fungo *noun* *Baseball* (*pl.* **-goes**) **1** a fly ball hit in the air for practice. **2** (in full **fungo bat**) a lightweight practice bat. [origin unknown]

fun·goid ● *adjective* **1** resembling a fungus in texture or in rapid growth. **2** of a fungus or fungi. ● *noun* a fungoid plant.

fun·gous *adjective* of, like, or caused by fungus.

fun·gus *noun* (*pl.* **fungi** /ˈfʌngai, ˈfʌndʒai/ or **fun·gus·es**) **1** any of a group of unicellular, multicellular, or syncytial spore-producing organisms feeding on organic matter, including moulds, yeast, mushrooms, and toadstools. **2** anything similar usu. growing suddenly and rapidly. □ **fun·gi·form** /ˈfʌndʒəˌfɔrm/ *adjective* **fun·giv·or·ous** /-ˈdʒɪvərəs/ *adjective* [Latin, perhaps from Greek *sp(h)oggos* SPONGE]

fun·house *noun* esp. N Amer. (in an amusement park) a building equipped with trick mirrors, shifting floors, etc., designed to scare or amuse patrons as they walk through.

fu·nicu·lar /fəˈnɪkjʊlər/ ● *adjective* **1** (of a railway, esp. on a mountainside) operating by cable with ascending and descending cars counterbalanced. **2** of a rope or its tension. ● *noun* a funicular railway. [Latin *funiculus* from *funis* rope]

Funk, Ca·si·mir (1884–1967), Polish-born US biochemist, who showed that a number of diseases, including scurvy, rickets, and beriberi, were each caused by the deficiency of a particular dietary component; he coined the term *vitamins* for the chemicals concerned.

funk¹ ● *noun informal* **1** *N Amer.* a dejected state of mind (*in a funk*). **2** fear, panic. **3** *Brit.* a coward. ● *verb* **1** *intransitive* flinch, shrink, show cowardice. **2** *transitive* try to evade (an undertaking), shirk. **3** *transitive* be afraid of. [18th-c. Oxford slang: perhaps from slang FUNK² = tobacco smoke]

funk² *noun* **1** a style of popular dance music of US black origin, based on elements of blues and soul and having a strong rhythm. **2** *N Amer.* a strong, unpleasant smell. [*funk* blow smoke on, perhaps from French dial. *funkier* from Latin (as FUMIGATE)]

funk·a·delic *adjective* **1** designating a type of popular music which combines funk with elements derived from soul and psychedelic and rock (such as the use of highly amplified guitars and a heavy drum beat). **2** *slang* funky. [from *Funkadelic*, the name of a rock group formed 1968 by George Clinton (b.1940), after FUNK² + PSYCHEDELIC]

Funk Island an island in the N Atlantic, situated well off the northeastern coast of Newfoundland, about 60 km east of Fogo Island. It is the site of an ecological reserve. [origin unknown]

funkster *noun* a performer or fan of funky music.

funky *adjective* (**funk·i·er, funk·i·est**) **1** (esp. of jazz or rock music) earthy, bluesy, with a heavy rhythmical beat. **2** *informal* **a** fashionable, trendy. **b** unconventional, striking. **3** *N Amer.* having a strong, unpleasant smell. □ **funk·i·ly** *adverb* **funk·i·ness** *noun*

fun·nel ● *noun* **1** a narrow tube or pipe widening at the top, for pouring liquid, powder, etc., into a small opening. **2 a** a metal chimney on a steam engine or ship. **b** *Cdn (Nfld)* a stovepipe. **3** something resembling a funnel in shape or use. ● *verb* (**fun·nelled, fun·nel·ling**; esp. *US* **fun·neled, fun·nel·ing**) **1** *transitive & intransitive* guide or move through or as through a funnel. **2** *transitive* direct, channel (*funnel money to local charities*). □ **funnel-like** *adjective* [Provençal *fonilh* from Late Latin *fundibulum* from Latin *infundibulum* from *infundere* (as IN-², *fundere* pour)]

funnel cloud *noun* a cloud produced in a low-pressure vortex in the centre of a spiral storm, e.g. a tornado or waterspout.

funnel-neck *noun* a neck on a sweater similar to a turtleneck but wider and higher.

funny ● *adjective* (**fun·ni·er, fun·ni·est**) **1** amusing, comical. **2** strange, perplexing, hard to account for. **3** *informal* slightly unwell, nauseous. **4** eccentric, odd (*a funny old man*). **5** underhand, tricky, deceitful. ● *noun* (*pl.* **-nies**) (usu. in *pl.*) *informal* **1** *N Amer.* a comic strip in a newspaper. **2** a joke. □ **fun·ni·ly** *adverb* **fun·ni·ness** *noun* [FUN + -Y¹]

funny bone *noun* **1** the part of the elbow over which the ulnar nerve passes, which, when struck, causes a tingling sensation in the arm and hand. **2** a sense of humour.

funny business *noun* **1** *slang* misbehaviour or deception. **2** comic behaviour, comedy.

funny farm *noun slang* a psychiatric hospital.

funny ha-ha *adjective informal* = FUNNY *adjective* 1.

funny·man *noun* (*pl.* **-men**) a clown or comedian, esp. a professional.

funny money *noun informal* **1** inflated or counterfeit currency. **2** *Cdn hist.* twenty-five-dollar certificates issued to Albertans in 1937 by the Social Credit government of Premier William Aberhart.

funny paper *noun* (usu. in *pl.*) *N Amer.* a section of a newspaper etc. containing comic strips, puzzles, etc.

funny-peculiar *adjective informal* = FUNNY *adjective* 2, 3, 4.

fun park *noun* an amusement park.

fun run *noun informal* an uncompetitive run, esp. for sponsored runners in support of a charity.

fun·ster *noun slang* a person who makes fun; a joker.

fur ● *noun* **1 a** the fine, soft, thick hair of certain animals. **b** the skin of such an animal with the fur on it; a pelt. **2 a** the coat of certain animals as material for making, trimming, or lining clothes. **b** a trimming or lining made of the dressed coat of such animals, or of material imitating this. **c** a garment made of or trimmed or lined with fur. **3** (*collective*) furred animals. **4 a** a coating formed on the tongue in sickness. **b** *Brit.* a coating formed on the inside surface of a pipe, kettle, etc., by hard water. ● *transitive verb* (**furred, fur·ring**) fix timber strips to (uneven joists, walls, etc.) to make a flat surface. □ **the fur is**

flying *informal* there is trouble or a disturbance. □ **fur·less** *adjective* [Old French *forrer* from *forre, fuerre* sheath, from Germanic]

fur. *abbreviation* furlong(s).

furan /ˈfjʊərən, fjʊˈran/ *noun Chem.* a colourless liquid compound which has a planar five-membered ring in its molecule. Chem. formula: C_4H_4O. [abbreviation of German *Furfuran*, from *furfurol*, a volatile oil obtained by distilling bran, from Latin *furfur* 'bran']

fur·ball *noun N Amer.* **1** an accumulation of fur ingested by a cat etc. during self-grooming and then regurgitated. **2** *jocular* a small furry animal, esp. a pet.

fur-bearer *noun* a furred animal, esp. one whose fur is of value in the marketplace. □ **fur-bearing** *adjective*

fur·be·low /ˈfɜrbəˌloʊ/ *noun* **1** a gathered strip or pleated border of a skirt or petticoat. **2** (in *pl.*; esp. in phr. **frills and furbelows**) showy ornamentation. □ **fur·be·lowed** *adjective* [18th-c. var. of *falbala* flounce, trimming]

fur·bish *transitive verb* (often foll. by *up*) **1** remove rust from, polish, burnish. **2** give a new look to, renovate, revive (something antiquated). [Old French *forbir* from Germanic]

fur brigade *noun Cdn hist.* a convoy of Red River carts, York boats, canoes, etc. which transported furs and other commodities to and from isolated trading posts.

fur·cu·la /ˈfɜrkjʊlə/ *noun Zool. & Anat.* a forked organ or structure, esp. the wishbone of a bird. □ **fur·cu·lar** *adjective* [Latin, diminutive of *furca* fork]

fur farm *noun* an establishment on which fur-bearing animals, e.g. mink, are raised in captivity. □ **fur farmer** *noun*

fur·fur·aceous /ˌfɜrfəˈreɪʃəs/ *adjective* **1** *Med.* (of skin) resembling bran or dandruff; scaly. **2** *Bot.* covered with bran-like scales. [*furfur* scurf, from Latin *furfur* bran]

Fur·ies, the *Gk Myth* the spirits of punishment, often represented as three goddesses (Allecto, Megaera, and Tisiphone) with hair composed of snakes.

furi·ous *adjective* **1** extremely angry. **2** raging, violent, intense. **3** rapid, requiring intense energy (*a furious schedule of editing, revising, proofreading*). □ **furi·ous·ly** *adverb* **furi·ous·ness** *noun*

furl *verb* **1** *transitive* roll up and secure (a sail, umbrella, flag, etc.). **2** *intransitive* become furled. □ **furl·able** *adjective* [French *ferler* from Old French *fer(m)* FIRM¹ + *lier* bind, from Latin *ligare*]

fur·long *noun* an eighth of a mile, 220 yards (201.168 metres). [Old English *furlang* from *furh* FURROW + *lang* LONG¹: originally = length of a furrow in a common field]

fur·lough /ˈfɜrloʊ/ ● *noun* **1** leave of absence, esp. granted to a soldier, missionary, or *US* an inmate of a penitentiary. **2** *US* a short-term layoff of employees. ● *verb US* **1** *transitive* grant furlough to. **2** *intransitive* spend furlough. [Dutch *verlof* after German *Verlaub* (as FOR-, LEAVE²)]

fur·mety *var. of* FRUMENTY.

fur·nace *noun* **1** an appliance fired by gas or oil in which air or water is heated to be circulated throughout a building to heat it. **2** an enclosed structure for intense heating by fire, esp. of metals or water. **3** a very hot place. [Old French *fornais* from Latin *fornax -acis* from *fornus* oven]

Fur·neaux Islands /ˈfɜrnoʊ/ a group of islands off the coast of NE Tasmania, in the Bass Strait. The largest island is Flinders Island.

fur·nish *transitive verb* **1** provide (a house, room, etc.) with all necessary contents, esp. movable furniture. **2** (foll. by *with*) cause to have possession or use of. **3** provide, afford, yield. □ **fur·nish·er** *noun* [Old French *furnir*, ultimately from West Germanic]

fur·nished *adjective* (of a house, apartment, etc.) rented with furniture.

fur·nish·ings *plural noun* the furniture, carpets, draperies, etc. in a house, room, etc.

fur·ni·ture *noun* **1** the movable equipment of a house, room, etc., e.g. tables, chairs, and beds. **2** *Naut.* a ship's equipment, esp. tackle etc. **3** accessories, e.g. the handles and lock of a door. □ **part of the furniture** *informal* a person or thing taken for granted. [French *fourniture* from *fournir* (as FURNISH)]

furniture beetle *noun* a beetle, *Anobium punctatum*, the larvae of which bore into wood (*see* WOODWORM).

Fur·ni·vall /ˈfɜrnɪvəl/ **Fred·erick James** (1825–1910), English philologist. He founded the Early English Text Society (1864), and as secretary of the Philological Society (1853–1910) initiated and edited the work that would eventually become the *Oxford English Dictionary*.

fur·or /ˈfjʊərɔr, ˈfjɜr-, -ər/ *noun* (*Brit.* **fur·ore**) an outbreak of public anger or excitement. [Italian *furore* from Latin *furor -oris* from *furere* be mad]

Consonants: b *but*   d *dog*   f *few*   g *get*   h *her*   j *yes*   k *cat*   l *leg*   m *man*   n *no*   p *pen*   r *red*   s *sit*

furo·sem·ide /fʌˈrɒːsəmaɪd/ noun Pharm. a strong diuretic, used esp. in the treatment of edema. [ultimately from Latin *furfur* bran + *sem-* of unknown origin + -IDE]

fur·piece noun an item of clothing, such as a stole or jacket, made out of fur.

furred adjective **1** (of a garment) lined or trimmed with fur. **2** (of an animal) with fur. **3** (of a person) clothed in fur. **4** coated with a fur-like substance.

fur·ri·er noun **1** a person who makes, cleans, and repairs fur garments. **2** a person who buys and sells furs. **3** Cdn (Nfld) a person engaged in hunting or trapping fur-bearing animals. [Middle English *furrour* from Old French *forreor* from *forrer* trim with fur, assimilated to -IER]

fur·row ● noun **1** a narrow trench made in the ground by a plow. **2** a rut, groove, or deep wrinkle. ● verb **1** transitive plow. **2** transitive **a** make furrows, grooves, etc. in. **b** mark with wrinkles. **3** intransitive (esp. of the brow) become furrowed. [Old English *furh* from Germanic]

furry adjective (**fur·ri·er**, **fur·ri·est**) **1** of or like fur. **2** covered with or wearing fur. □ **fur·ri·ness** noun

fur seal noun any of several eared seals constituting the genera *Arctocephalus* and *Callorhinus*, with thick fur on the underside.

fur·ther ● adverb **1** (also **far·ther**) **a** to or at a more advanced point in space or time (*unsafe to proceed further*). **b** at a greater distance (*nothing was further from his thoughts*). **2** to a greater extent, more (*will inquire further*). **3** in addition; furthermore (*I may add further*). ● adjective **1** (also **far·ther**) more distant or advanced (*on the further side*). **2** more, additional, going beyond what exists or has been dealt with (*threats of further punishment*). ● transitive verb promote, favour, help on (a scheme, undertaking, movement, or cause). □ **further to** formal following on from (esp. an earlier letter etc.). **till further notice** (or **orders**) to continue until explicitly changed. □ **further·most** adjective [Old English *furthor* (adv.), *furthra* (adj.), *fyrthrian* (v.), formed as FORTH, -ER²] ¶ The form *farther* is used especially with reference to physical distance, although *further* is preferred by many people even in this sense.

further·ance noun the action of furthering or the state of being furthered; the advancement of a scheme etc.

further education noun Brit. education for persons above school age but usu. below degree level.

further·more adverb in addition, besides (esp. introducing a fresh consideration in an argument).

fur·thest (also **far·thest**) ● adjective **1** most distant in space, direction, or time; most remote. **2** longest; most extended in space. ● adverb **1** to or at the greatest distance in space or time; most remote. **2** to the highest degree or extent; most (*she is the furthest advanced of all my students*). [Middle English, superlative from FURTHER] ¶ The form *farthest* is used especially with reference to physical distance, although *furthest* is preferred by many people even in this sense.

fur·tive /ˈfɜrtɪv/ adjective **1** done by stealth, clandestine, meant to escape notice. **2** sly, stealthy. **3** stolen, taken secretly. □ **fur·tive·ly** adverb **fur·tive·ness** noun [French *furtif -ive* or Latin *furtivus* from *furtum* theft]

fur trade noun esp. hist. the business of trapping, transporting, and selling furs, esp. as carried on between European traders and Aboriginal peoples in N America from the 17th to the 19th c. □ **fur trader** noun **fur-trading** adjective

fu·run·cle /ˈfjʊrʌŋkəl/ noun Med. = BOIL². [Latin *furunculus*, lit. 'petty thief', also 'knob on a vine' (regarded as stealing the sap) from *fur* thief]

fu·run·cu·lo·sis /fjʊˌrʌŋkjʊˈloːsɪs/ noun **1** a diseased condition in which boils appear. **2** a bacterial disease of salmon and trout. [modern Latin (as FURUNCLE)]

fury noun (pl. **-ies**) **1 a** wild and passionate anger, rage. **b** a fit of rage (*in a blind fury*). **2** violence of a storm, disease, etc. **3** an angry or malignant woman. **4** (**Fury**) see FURIES, THE. □ **like fury** informal with great force or effect. [Old French *furie* from Latin *furia* from *furere* be mad]

Fury and Hecla Strait a narrow passage of the Canadian Arctic, connecting Foxe Basin with the Gulf of Boothia. It is usu. jammed with ice. [HMS *Fury* + HMS *Hecla*, the two vessels under the command of William Parry, who discovered the strait in 1822]

furze /fɜrz/ noun Brit. = GORSE. □ **furzy** adjective [Old English *fyrs*, of unknown origin]

FUS abbreviation FELINE UROLOGICAL SYNDROME.

fu·sar·ium /fjuːˈzɛriəm/ noun **1** a mould of a large genus which includes a number that cause plant diseases, esp. wilting. **2** infestation with any of these or related moulds. [modern Latin, from Latin *fusus* 'spindle']

fuse¹ ● verb **1** transitive & intransitive melt with intense heat; liquefy. **2** transitive & intransitive blend or amalgamate into one whole by or as by melting. **3** transitive provide (a circuit, plug, etc.) with a fuse. **4** Brit. **a** intransitive (of an appliance) cease to function when a fuse blows. **b** transitive cause (an appliance) to do this. **5** transitive spell (a hyphenated or open compound) as one word. **6** intransitive (of anatomical structures, groups of atoms, etc.) coalesce, join. ● noun a device or component for protecting an electric circuit, containing a strip of wire or easily melted metal and placed in the circuit so as to break it by melting when an excessive current passes through. □ **blow a fuse** informal **1** cause a fuse to melt by passing excessive current through it. **2** lose one's temper. [Latin *fundere fus-* pour, melt]

fuse² (also **fuze**) ● noun **1** a device for igniting a bomb or explosive charge, consisting of a tube or cord etc. filled or saturated with combustible matter. **2** a component in a shell, mine, etc., designed to detonate an explosive charge on impact, after an interval, or when subjected to a magnetic or vibratory stimulation. ● transitive verb fit a fuse to. □ **have a short fuse** anger easily. □ **fuse·less** adjective [Italian *fuso* from Latin *fusus* spindle]

fuse box noun a box housing the fuses for circuits in a building.

fusee /fjuːˈziː/ noun (also **fuzee**) **1** a conical pulley or wheel esp. in a watch or clock. **2** a large-headed match for lighting a cigar or pipe in a wind. **3** N Amer. a railway signal flare. [French *fusée* spindle, ultimately from Latin *fusus*]

fusel·age /ˈfjuːsəˌlɒʒ, ˈfjuːz-, -lɪdʒ/ noun the body of an airplane, to which the wings and tail are fitted. [French from *fuseler* cut into a spindle, from *fuseau* spindle, from Old French *fusel*, ultimately from Latin *fusus*]

Fu·seli /ˈfjuːzəli/ **Henry** (born Johann Heinrich Füssli) (1741–1825), Swiss-born English romantic painter, who is known for his imaginative and fantastic works, such as *The Nightmare* (1781).

fusel oil /ˈfjuːzəl, -səl/ noun a mixture of several alcohols, chiefly amyl alcohol, produced usu. in small amounts during alcoholic fermentation. [German *Fusel* bad brandy etc.: compare *fuseln* to bungle]

Fu·shun /fuːˈʃʌn/ a coal-mining city in NE China, in the province of Liaoning; pop. (est. 2002) 1,383,900.

fus·ible /ˈfjuːzəbəl/ adjective that can be easily fused or melted. □ **fusi·bil·ity** noun

fusi·form /ˈfjuːzəˌfɔrm/ adjective Bot. & Zool. shaped like a spindle or cigar, tapering at both ends. [Latin *fusus* spindle + -FORM]

fu·sil /ˈfjuːzəl/ noun hist. a light musket. [French, ultimately from Latin *focus* hearth, fire]

fusil·ier /ˌfjuːzəˈliːr/ noun **1** a member of any of several regiments formerly armed with fusils. **2** hist. a soldier armed with a fusil. [French (as FUSIL)]

fusil·lade /ˌfjuːzəˈleid, -ˌlɒd, -sə-/ noun **1** a continuous discharge of firearms. **2** a sustained outburst of criticism etc. [French from *fusiller* shoot]

fu·sil·li /fuːˈsɪli, fjuː-, fuːˈziːli/ plural noun pasta in the form of short spirals. [Italian, literally 'little spindles', diminutive of *fuso* spindle]

fu·sion /ˈfjuːʒən/ noun **1** the act or an instance of fusing or melting. **2** a fused mass. **3** the blending of different things into one. **4** a coalition. **5** Physics = NUCLEAR FUSION. **6** a kind of music in which elements of more than one popular style are combined, esp. jazz and rock. **7** = FUSION CUISINE. □ **fusion·ist** adjective [French *fusion* or Latin *fusio* (as FUSE¹)]

fusion bomb noun a bomb deriving its energy from nuclear fusion, esp. a hydrogen bomb.

fusion cuisine noun a style of cuisine combining ingredients and cooking methods from different countries.

fuss ● noun **1** nervous excitement or activity, esp. of an unnecessary kind; commotion. **2** a display of excitement, worry, or enthusiasm, esp. over something unimportant. **3** a sustained protest or dispute. ● verb **1** intransitive **a** make a fuss. **b** busy oneself restlessly with trivial things. **c** (often foll. by *about*) move fussily. **d** (of a baby) express discomfort or unhappiness by whimpering etc. **2** transitive agitate, worry. □ **make a fuss** complain vigorously. **make a fuss over** (or Brit. **of**) treat (a person or animal) with great or excessive attention. □ **fuss·er** noun [18th c.: perhaps Anglo-Irish]

fuss-budget noun N Amer. informal (also **fuss·pot**) a person given to fussing.

fussy adjective (**fuss·i·er**, **fuss·i·est**) **1** inclined to fuss. **2** full of unnecessary detail or decoration. **3** difficult to please. □ **be not**

fussy about 1 be indifferent about. **2** not like particularly. □ **fuss·i·ly** adverb **fuss·i·ness** noun

fus·tian /ˈfʌstiən, -tʃən/ noun **1** thick twilled cotton cloth with a short nap, usu. dyed in dark colours. **2** turgid speech or writing, bombast. [Old French fustaigne from medieval Latin fustaneus (adj.) relating to cloth from Fostat a suburb of Cairo]

fusty adjective (**fust·i·er**, **fust·i·est**) **1** stale-smelling, musty, mouldy. **2** stuffy, close. **3** antiquated, old-fashioned. □ **fust·i·ly** adverb **fust·i·ness** noun [Old French fusté smelling of the cask, from fust cask, tree trunk, from Latin fustis cudgel]

fu·thorc /ˈfuːθɔrk/ noun the Scandinavian runic alphabet. [its first six letters f, u, th, ö, r, k]

fu·tile /ˈfjuːtaɪl/ adjective useless, ineffectual. □ **fu·tile·ly** adverb **fu·til·i·ty** /-ˈtɪlɪti/ noun [Latin futilis leaky, futile, related to fundere pour]

fu·ton /ˈfuːtɒn/ noun **1** a mattress rolled out or unfolded for use as a bed. **2** a type of low wooden sofa bed having such a mattress. [Japanese]

fut·tock /ˈfʌtək/ noun each of the middle timbers of a ship's frame, between the floor and the top timbers. [Middle English votekes etc. pl. from Middle Low German from fōt FOOT + -ken -KIN]

fu·ture ● adjective **1 a** going or expected to happen or be or become (his future career). **b** that will be something specified (my future wife). **c** that will be after death (a future life). **2 a** of time to come (future years). **b** Grammar (of a tense or participle) describing an event yet to happen. ● noun **1** time to come (past, present, and future). **2** what will happen in the future (the future is uncertain). **3** the future condition of a person, country, etc. **4** a prospect of success etc. (there's no future in it). **5** Grammar the future tense. **6** (in pl.) Stock Exch. **a** goods and stocks sold for future delivery. **b** contracts for these. □ **for the future** = IN FUTURE. **in future** from now onward. □ **future·less** adjective [Old French futur -ure from Latin futurus future part. of esse be, from stem fu- be]

future considerations plural noun Hockey unspecified future compensation (e.g. another player or draft pick) promised to a traded player's former team by the new team.

future perfect noun Grammar a tense giving the sense will have done.

future-proof ● adjective (of a product) unlikely to become obsolete. ● transitive verb make (something) future-proof.

future shock noun a state of distress or disorientation due to rapid social or technological change.

futur·ism noun (also **Futur·ism**) an early 20th-c. movement in art, literature, music, etc., concerned with celebrating and incorporating into art the energy and dynamism of modern technology.

futur·ist noun (often attributive) **1** (also **Futurist**) an adherent of futurism. **2** a person who is concerned with or studies the future.

futur·is·tic adjective **1** suitable for the future; ultra-modern (futuristic design). **2** (also **Futuristic**) of futurism. **3** relating to the future. □ **futur·is·tic·ally** adverb

futur·ity /fjuːˈtʃɜrɪti, -ˈtʃʊr-/ noun (pl. **-ities**) **1** future time. **2** (in sing. or pl.) future events. **3** future condition; existence after death.

futur·ol·ogy noun systematic forecasting of the future esp. from present trends in society. □ **futur·o·logic·al** adjective **futur·ol·o·gist** noun

futz intransitive verb N Amer. slang (usu. foll. by around) spend time unproductively. [20th c.: origin uncertain, perhaps alteration of Yiddish arumfartzen fart around]

Fuxin /fuːˈʃɪn/ (also **Fou-hsin**) an industrial city in NE China, in Liaoning province; pop. (est. 2002) 964,800.

fuze var. of FUSE².

fuzee var. of FUSEE.

Fu·zhou /fuːˈdʒoː/ (also **Foo·chow** /fuːˈtʃau/) a port in SE China, capital of Fujian province; pop. (est. 2002) 1,527,300.

fuzz ● noun **1** a fluffy or frizzy mass of hair or fibre. **2** slang **a** the police. **b** a police officer. **3** an indistinct sound, image, etc. ● transitive & intransitive verb make or become fluffy or blurred. [17th c.: prob. from Low German or Dutch: sense 3 perhaps a different word]

fuzz·ball noun **1** a ball of fuzz. **2** something that looks like this.

fuzz-box noun a device which adds a buzzing quality to the sound of an electric guitar or other instrument.

fuzzy adjective (**fuzz·i·er**, **fuzz·i·est**) **1 a** like fuzz. **b** frayed, fluffy. **c** frizzy. **2 a** blurred, indistinct, esp. in shape or outline. **b** imprecise, vague (fuzzy thinking). **c** (of a guitar sound etc.) buzzing, not crisp or distinct. **3** Computing & Logic of or relating to a form of set theory and logic in which predicates may have degrees of applicability, rather than simply being true or false. It has important uses in artificial intelligence and the design of control systems. □ **fuzz·i·ly** adverb **fuzz·i·ness** noun

fwd abbreviation forward.

f.w.d. abbreviation **1** four-wheel drive. **2** front-wheel drive.

F-word noun informal used instead of or in reference to the word 'fuck' because of its taboo nature.

FX abbreviation = SPECIAL EFFECTS.

-fy suffix forming: **1** verbs from nouns, meaning: **a** make, produce (pacify; speechify). **b** make into (deify; petrify). **2** verbs from adjectives, meaning 'bring or come into such a state' (Frenchify; solidify). **3** verbs in causative sense (horrify; stupefy). [from or after French -fier from Latin -ficare, -facere from facere do, make]

FYI abbreviation for your information.

fyl·fot /ˈfɪlfət/ noun a swastika. [perhaps from fill-foot, pattern to fill the foot of a painted window]

Gg

G¹ *noun* (also **g**) (*pl.* **Gs** or **G's**) **1** the seventh letter of the alphabet. **2** *Music* the fifth note in the diatonic scale of C major.

G² *abbreviation* (also **G.**) **1** *N Amer. informal* = GRAND *noun* 2. **2** good. **3** Gulf. **4** ground level. **5** (in Manitoba) = GENERAL *adjective* 11. **6** group (as in G7 'Group of Seven').

G³ *symbol* **1** gauss. **2** giga-. **3** gravitational constant. **4** conductance. **5** guanine.

g¹ *abbreviation* (also **g.**) **1** gelding. **2** gas. **3** gauge.

g² *symbol* **1** gram(s). **2 a** gravity. **b** acceleration due to gravity.

G7 *abbreviation* (also esp. *US* **G-7**) = GROUP OF SEVEN 2.

G77 *abbreviation* (also esp. *US* **G-77**) = GROUP OF SEVENTY-SEVEN.

G8 *abbreviation* (also esp. *US* **G-8**) = GROUP OF EIGHT.

GA *abbreviation* Georgia (US) (in official postal use).

Ga *symbol Chem.* the element gallium.

Ga. *abbreviation* Georgia (US).

GAA *abbreviation* = GOALS-AGAINST AVERAGE.

GAAP *abbreviation* generally accepted accounting principles.

gab *informal* ● *noun* talk, chatter. ● *intransitive verb* (**gabbed**, **gab·bing**) talk, chatter. □ **gift of the gab** the facility of speaking eloquently or profusely. [17th-c. var. of GOB¹]

GABA /ˈɡabə/ *abbreviation* gamma-aminobutyric acid, an inhibitory neurotransmitter. [acronym]

gab·ar·dine /ˈɡabɑrˌdiːn, -ˈdiːn/ *noun* (also **gab·er·dine**) **1** a smooth durable twill-woven cloth esp. of worsted or cotton. **2** a garment made of this, esp. a raincoat. [var. of GABERDINE]

gabba *noun* a harsh, aggressive type of house music originating in Rotterdam, characterized by its extremely fast dance beat. [Dutch *gabber*]

Gab·beh /ˈɡabei/ *noun* (*pl.* same) a hand-woven and knotted woollen rug with a very thick pile and geometric or symbolic designs, made by nomads in southern Iran. [Farsi, = 'raw, natural']

gab·ble ● *verb* **1 a** *intransitive* speak incoherently or inarticulately; chatter. **b** *transitive* utter rapidly and unintelligibly. **2** *intransitive* (of geese, chickens, etc.) cackle, etc. ● *noun* **1** voluble confused unintelligible talk. **2** the inarticulate noises made by some animals, e.g. chickens, geese, etc. □ **gab·bler** *noun* [Middle Dutch *gabbelen* (imitative)]

gab·bro /ˈɡabro/ *noun* (*pl.* **-bros**) a dark granular plutonic rock of crystalline texture. □ **gab·bro·ic** /-ˈbroːɪk/ *adjective* **gab·broid** *adverb* [Italian from *Gabbro* in Tuscany]

gabby *adjective* (**gab·bi·er**, **gab·bi·est**) *informal* talkative.

gab·er·dine *noun* **1** var. of GABARDINE. **2** *hist.* a loose long upper garment worn esp. by Jews and beggars in the Middle Ages. [Old French *gauvardine* perhaps from Middle High German *wallevart* pilgrimage]

gab·fest *noun* esp. *N Amer. informal* **1** a gathering in which there is much talking or chattering. **2** a prolonged conversation, esp. with chattering.

ga·bion /ˈɡeibiən/ *noun* a rectangular or cylindrical metal basket for filling with earth or stones, used in engineering or (formerly) in fortification. [French from Italian *gabbione* from *gabbia* CAGE]

Gable, (Wil·liam) Clark (1901–60), US actor. He became famous through his numerous roles as a romantic leading man in Hollywood films of the 1930s; they include *It Happened One Night* (1934), for which he won an Oscar, and *Gone with the Wind* (1939).

gable *noun* **1 a** the triangular upper part of a wall enclosed by the two sloping planes of a ridged roof. **b** (in full **gable end**) a gable-topped wall. **2** a gable-shaped canopy over a window or door. □ **gabled** *adjective* (also in *combination*). [Middle English *gable* from Old Norse *gafl*]

Gabo /ˈɡɒboː/ **Naum** (born Naum Neemia Pevsner) (1890–1977), Russian-born US sculptor. A founder of Russian constructivism, he introduced time and movement into sculpture through his kinetic works powered by electric motors.

Gabon /ɡəˈbɒn/ an equatorial country in West Africa, on the Atlantic coast; pop. (est. 2002) 1,233,353; capital, Libreville. □ **Gabon·ese** /ˌɡabəˈniːz/ *adjective & noun*

Gabor /ɡəˈbɔr/ **Den·nis** (1900–79), Hungarian-born English electrical engineer. He invented holography, originally as a microscopic technique, greatly improving it after the invention of lasers (1960); he was awarded the Nobel Prize for physics in 1971.

Gab·or·one /ˌɡabəˈroːni/ the capital of Botswana, in the south of the country near the border with South Africa; pop. (est. 2002) 223,000.

Gab·riel one of the chief angels mentioned in both the Bible and the Quran as a messenger from God. In the New Testament he appears to the Virgin Mary (Luke 1:26–38), telling her that she will be the mother of Jesus; he also appears to Zacharias, father of John the Baptist, and to Daniel. In Islam, Gabriel reveals the Quran to Muhammad.

Gab·rieli /ɡabriˈeliː/ **1 An·drea** (*c*.1510–86), Italian organist and composer, who was organist at St. Mark's Cathedral in Venice (1566–86); his compositions include masses, motets, secular madrigals, and organ works. **2** his nephew, **Gio·van·ni** (*c*.1556–1612), Italian organist and composer, who was noted for his motets and secular madrigals.

Gab·ri·ola Island /ˌɡeibriːˈoːlə/ a small island off the southeastern coast of Vancouver Island, opposite Nanaimo. It is one of the Gulf Islands. [originally Spanish *Punta de Gaviota* seagull point, the name of its eastern point *c*.1791]

Gad ▸ 1 *Bible* a Hebrew patriarch, son of Jacob and Zilpah. **2** the tribe of Israel traditionally descended from him.

gad¹ *intransitive verb* (**gad·ded**, **gad·ding**) (foll. by *about*, *around*) go about idly or in search of pleasure. [back-formation from obsolete *gadling* companion, from Old English *gædeling* from *gæd* fellowship]

gad² *interjection* (also **Gad**) an expression of surprise or emphatic assertion. [= *God*]

gad³ *noun Cdn* (*Maritimes & Nfld*) a pliable twig used as a rope for fastening, carrying, etc. [Old Norse *gaddr* goad, spike, related to YARD¹ or Irish and Gaelic *gad* band or rope made of twisted twigs]

gad·about *noun* a person who gads about; an idle pleasure-seeker.

Gad·ar·ene /ˈɡadəˌriːn/ *adjective* involving or engaged in headlong or suicidal rush or flight. [Late Latin *Gadarenus* from Greek *Gadarēnos* of Gadara in ancient Palestine, with reference to Matthew 8:28–32]

gad·fly *noun* (*pl.* **-flies**) **1** a cattle-biting fly, esp. a warble fly, horsefly, or botfly. **2** a person who repeatedly criticizes or harasses others, esp. those in authority. [obsolete *gad* goad, spike, from Old Norse *gaddr*, related to YARD¹]

gadg·et *noun* an ingenious mechanical or electronic device or tool, esp. a non-essential one designed for a specific purpose. □ **gadg·ety** *adjective* [19th-c. Naut.: origin unknown]

gadg·et·eer *noun* a person who enjoys using or inventing gadgets.

gadg·et·ry *noun* gadgets collectively.

Gad·ha·fi /ɡəˈdafi/ **Moam·mar Muham·mad al** (also **Qad·dafi**) (b.1942), Libyan colonel, head of state since 1970; president since 1977. In 1969 he led the coup which established the Libyan Arab Republic; as head of state he has sought to establish an Islamic Socialist regime, and has been involved in a number of conflicts with the West.

gad·oid /ˈɡeidɔid/ ● *noun* any marine fish of the cod family Gadidae, including haddock and whiting. ● *adjective* belonging to or resembling the Gadidae. [modern Latin *gadus* from Greek *gados* cod + -OID]

gado·lin·ite /ˈɡadəlɪˌnait/ *noun* a dark crystalline mineral consisting of ferrous silicate of beryllium. [J. *Gadolin*, Finnish mineralogist d.1852]

gado·lin·ium /ˌɡadəˈlɪniəm/ *noun Chem.* a soft silvery metallic element of the lanthanide series, occurring naturally in gadolinite. Symbol: **Gd**; at. no.: 64. [modern Latin from GADOLINITE]

gad·roon /ɡəˈdruːn/ *noun* a decoration on silverware etc., consisting of convex curves in a series forming an ornamental edge like inverted fluting. □ **gad·rooned** *adjective* [French *godron*: prob. related to *goder* pucker]

Gads·den Purchase /ˈɡadzdən/ an area in New Mexico and Arizona, near the Rio Grande. Extending over 77 700 sq. km (30,000 sq. miles), it was purchased from Mexico in 1853 with the intention of ensuring a southern railroad route to the Pacific. [J. *Gadsden*, US diplomat who purchased it d.1858]

gad·wall *noun* (*pl.* same or **-walls**) a brownish-grey freshwater duck, *Anas strepera*. [17th c.: origin unknown]

gad·zooks /ɡadˈzuːks/ *interjection archaic* an expression of surprise, annoyance, asseveration, etc. [perhaps from *God's hooks*, i.e. God's nails; see GAD[2]]

Gaea *var. of* GAIA.

Gael /ɡeil/ *noun* a Gaelic Celt, formerly esp. a Scottish Celt. □ **Gael·dom** *noun* [Gaelic *Gaidheal*]

Gael·ic /ˈɡeilɪk/ ● *noun* any of the Celtic languages spoken in Ireland and Scotland. ● *adjective* of or relating to the Celts of Ireland or Scotland, or their languages.

Gael·tacht /ˈɡeiltəxt/ *noun* any or all of the regions in Ireland where the vernacular language is Irish. [Irish]

gaff[1] *noun* **1 a** a stick with an iron hook for landing large fish, seals, etc. **b** a barbed fishing spear. **2** a spar to which the head of a fore-and-aft sail is bent. ● *transitive verb* seize (a fish etc.) with a gaff. [Middle English from Provençal *gaf* hook]

gaff[2] *noun slang N Amer.* rough treatment; criticism (*stand the gaff; take the gaff*). □ **blow the gaff** *esp. Brit.* let out a plot or secret. [19th c., = nonsense: origin unknown]

gaffe *noun* a blunder; an indiscreet act or remark. [French]

gaf·fer *noun* **1** the chief electrician in a film or television production unit. **2** an old man; an elderly rustic. **3** *Cdn* (*Nfld*) a boy or youth at work with adults. **4** *Brit. informal* a foreman or boss. [prob. contraction of GODFATHER]

gaffer tape *noun* wide adhesive tape used esp. on film sets to secure cables, lights, etc.

gag ● *noun* **1** a piece of cloth etc. thrust into or held over the mouth to prevent speaking or crying out. **2** a thing or circumstance restricting free speech. **3** *Parl.* a closure of a debate in a legislative assembly. **4** a joke or comic scene in a play, film, etc., or as part of a comedian's act. **5** an actor's interpolation in a dramatic dialogue. **6 a** a joke or hoax. **b** a humorous action or situation. **7** a device for keeping the jaws separated during a surgical procedure. ● *verb* (**gagged, gag·ging**) **1** *transitive* apply a gag to. **2** *transitive* silence; deprive of free speech. **3 a** *intransitive* choke or retch. **b** *transitive* cause to do this. **4** *intransitive* *Theatre* make gags. ● *interjection* expressing disgust. □ **gag me (with a spoon)** expressing disgust. [Middle English, originally as verb: origin uncertain]

gaga *adjective slang* **1** senile, doting. **2** slightly crazy; fatuous. **3** (often foll. by *about, over*) exceedingly or fatuously enthusiastic or infatuated (*goes gaga over the model*). [French, = senile, reduplication based on *gâteux*, variant of *gâteur*, hospital slang in the sense 'bedwetter']

Ga·gar·in /ɡəˈɡarɪn/ **Yuri Alek·sey·evich** (1934–68), Russian cosmonaut. In 1961 he made the first manned space flight, completing a single orbit of the earth in 108 minutes.

Gage, Thom·as (1721–87), English general. He served as governor of Montreal (1760), commander-in-chief of British forces in N America (1763–75), and governor of Massachusetts (1774–75); his attempts to quell dissent in Massachusetts contributed to the outbreak of the American Revolution.

gage[1] ● *noun* **1** a pledge; a thing deposited as security. **2 a** a challenge to fight. **b** a symbol of this, esp. a glove thrown down. ● *transitive verb archaic* stake, pledge; offer as a guarantee. [Old French *gage* (n.), French *gager* (v.), ultimately from Germanic, related to WED]

gage[2] *esp. US var. of* GAUGE.

gage[3] *noun* = GREENGAGE. [abbreviation]

gag·gle *noun* **1** a flock of geese. **2** *informal* a disorderly, noisy group of people or things. [Middle English, imitative: compare *gabble, cackle*]

gag man *noun* a deviser or performer of theatrical gags.

Ga·gnon /ɡaˈnjõ/ **Clar·ence** (1881–1942), Canadian painter, engraver, and illustrator. He is known for his scenes of rural life, esp. his misty atmospheric paintings of Quebec villages, such as *La Croix du chemin, l'automne* (c.1915).

gag order *noun N Amer. informal* **1** a court order banning the publication of information disclosed at a trial etc. **2** (also **gag rule**) any order, law, etc. banning the disclosure of information.

gag·ster *noun* = GAG MAN.

Gaia /ˈɡaiə, ˈɡeiə/ **1** (also **Gaea** /ˈdʒiːə/, **Ge** /ɡeɪ/) *Gk Myth* the Earth personified as a goddess, daughter of Chaos. She was the mother and wife of Uranus (Heaven); their offspring included the Titans and the Cyclops. **2** the earth viewed as a vast self-regulating organism (*Gaia hypothesis; Gaia theory*). □ **Gaian** *adjective & noun* [Greek, = Earth]

gai·ety /ˈɡeiəti/ *noun* **1** the state of being lighthearted or merry; mirth. **2** merrymaking, amusement. **3** a bright appearance. [French *gaieté* (as GAY)]

gai·jin /ɡaiˈdʒin/ ● *noun* (*pl.* same) (in Japan) a foreigner; an alien. ● *adjective* foreign, alien. [Japanese, contraction of *gaikoku-jin* (*gaikaku* 'foreign country', *jin* 'person')]

gail·lar·dia /ɡeiˈlɑːdiə/ *noun* any composite plant of the genus *Gaillardia*, with showy flowers. Also called BLANKET FLOWER. [modern Latin from *Gaillard* de Marentoneau, 18th-c. French botanist]

gaily *adverb* **1** in a gay or lighthearted manner. **2** with a bright or colourful appearance.

gain ● *verb* **1** *transitive* obtain or secure (usu. something desired or favourable) (*gain an advantage; gain recognition*). **2** *transitive* acquire (a sum) as profits or as a result of changed conditions; earn. **3** *transitive* obtain as an increment or addition (*gain momentum; gain weight*). **4** *transitive* win (a victory). **5** *intransitive* (foll. by *in*) make a specified advance or improvement (*gained in stature*). **6 a** *intransitive* (of a clock etc.) have the fault of becoming fast. **b** *transitive* be or become fast by (a specified amount of time). **7** *intransitive* (often foll. by *on, upon*) come closer to a person or thing pursued. **8** *transitive* bring over to one's interest or views. **9** *transitive* reach or arrive at (a desired place). ● *noun* **1** something gained, achieved, etc. **2** an increase of possessions etc.; a profit, advance, or improvement. **3** the acquisition of wealth. **4** (in *pl.*) sums of money acquired. **5** an increase in amount, weight, etc. **6** *Electronics* **a** the factor by which power etc. is increased. **b** the logarithm of this. □ **gain ground** *see* GROUND[1]. **gain time** improve one's chances by causing or exploiting a delay. □ **gain·able** *adjective* **gain·er** *noun* [Old French *gaigner, gaaignier* to till, acquire, ultimately from Germanic]

gain·ful *adjective* **1** (of employment) paid. **2** lucrative, remunerative. □ **gain·ful·ly** *adverb* **gain·ful·ness** *noun*

gain·say /ˈɡeinsei/ *transitive verb* (*past* and *past participle* **gain·said** /-ˈsed/) deny, contradict. □ **gain·say·er** *noun* [Middle English from obsolete *gain-* against, from Old Norse *gegn* straight, from Germanic + SAY]

Gains·bor·ough /ˈɡeinzbərə/ **Thom·as** (1727–88), English painter. He is known for his portraits, such as *Mr. and Mrs. Andrews* (c.1748) and *The Blue Boy* (c.1770), and his naturalistic landscapes, which include *The Harvest Wagon* (c.1770).

Gai·seric *var. of* GENSERIC.

gait *noun* **1** a manner of walking; one's bearing as one walks. **2** the manner of forward motion of esp. a horse, e.g. walk, gallop. [var. of GATE[2]]

gait·ed *adjective* having a specified gait or number of gaits (*slow-gaited; four-gaited*).

gait·er *noun* a covering of cloth, leather, etc. for the ankle, or ankle and lower leg, and often extending to the instep, worn over the shoe. □ **gait·ered** *adjective* [French *guêtre*, prob. related to WRIST]

Gaius /ˈɡaiəs/ (also **Caius** /ˈkaiəs/) (*fl.* c.130–180 AD), Roman jurist, whose best-known legal work, the *Institutes* (c.161), was used by the emperor Justinian as the basis for his own *Institutes* (533).

Gal. *abbreviation* Galatians (New Testament).

gal[1] *noun esp. N Amer. slang* a girl or woman. [representing a variant pronunciation]

gal[2] *noun Physics* a unit of gravitational acceleration equal to one centimetre per second per second. [abbreviation of GALILEO]

gal. *abbreviation* gallon(s).

gala /ˈɡɑːlə/ *noun* **1** (often *attributive*) a festive or special occasion (*a gala*

Consonants: b *but*   d *dog*   f *few*   g *get*   h *her*   j *yes*   k *cat*   l *leg*   m *man*   n *no*   p *pen*   r *red*   s *sit*

performance). **2** a heart-shaped type of crisp, sweet apple with a yellow-orange skin with red streaks. [French or Italian from Spanish from Old French *gale* rejoicing, from Germanic]

gal·ac·tic /gə'laktɪk/ *adjective* of or relating to a galaxy or galaxies, esp. the Milky Way. [Greek *galaktias*, var. of *galaxias*: see GALAXY]

galacto- /gə'laktoː/ *combining form* **1** milk. **2** galactose. **3** of the Milky Way or a galaxy. [Greek *gala galaktos* milk]

gal·ac·tose /gə'laktoːs/ *noun* a hexose sugar present in many polysaccharides, notably lactose. [Greek *gala galaktos* 'milk' + -OSE²]

gal·ago /gə'leigoː/ *noun* (*pl.* **-agos**) any small tree-climbing primate of the genus *Galago*, found in southern Africa, with large eyes and ears and a long tail. *Also called* BUSH BABY. [modern Latin]

Gala·had /'galə,had/ **1 Sir** (in Arthurian legend) a knight of immaculate purity, destined to retrieve the Holy Grail. **2** (also **Sir Galahad**) a person characterized by nobility, integrity, courtesy, etc.

ga·lakto·bour·eko /gə,laktoː'bʊrəkoː/ *noun* a Greek dessert consisting of vanilla custard enclosed in phyllo pastry which is then soaked in flavoured syrup. [Greek *galakto* 'of milk' + *boureko* 'pie']

gal·an·gal /gə'laŋgəl/ *noun* an aromatic rhizome of an E Asian plant of the genus *Alpinia* of the ginger family, used in cooking and medicine.

gal·an·tine /'galən,tiːn/ *noun* white meat or fish boned, cooked, pressed, and served cold in aspic etc. [Old French, alteration of *galatine* jellied meat, from medieval Latin *galatina*]

Gal·apa·gos Islands /gə'lapəgəs/ a Pacific archipelago on the equator, about 1 045 km (650 miles) west of Ecuador, to which it belongs; pop. (est. 2002) 15,700. It is noted for its abundant wildlife, including giant turtles, flightless cormorants, and many other endemic species. It is the site of Charles Darwin's observations of 1835, which helped him to form his theory of natural selection. [Spanish, = turtles]

Gala·tea /,galə'tiːə/ *Gk Myth* **1** a sea nymph courted by the Cyclops Polyphemus, who in jealousy killed his rival Acis. **2** the name given to the statue fashioned by Pygmalion and brought to life.

Gal·ați /ga'lats/ an industrial city in E Romania, a river port on the lower Danube; pop. (est. 2002) 342,400.

Gal·atia /gə'leiʃə/ an ancient region in the centre of what is now Turkey, settled by invading Gauls (the Galatians) in the 3rd c. BC. In 64 BC it became a protectorate of Rome and, in 25 BC, with the addition of some further territories, was made a province of the Roman Empire. □ **Gal·atian** *adjective & noun*

Gal·atians /gə'leiʃənz/ a book of the New Testament, an epistle of St. Paul to the Church in Galatia.

gal·axy /'galəksi/ *noun* (*pl.* **-axies**) **1** any of many independent systems of stars, gas, dust, etc., held together by gravitational attraction. **2** (**Galaxy**) = MILKY WAY. **3** (foll. by *of*) a brilliant company or gathering. [Old French *galaxie* from medieval Latin *galaxia*, Late Latin *galaxias* from Greek from *gala galaktos* milk]

Galba /'galbə/ (full name Servius Sulpicius Galba) (*c*.3 BC–AD 69), Roman emperor AD 68–9. As emperor he aroused hostility by his severity and parsimony, and he was murdered in a conspiracy organized by Otho.

gal·ba·num /'galbənəm/ *noun* a bitter aromatic gum resin produced from kinds of ferula, used in perfumery. [Latin from Greek *khalbanē*, prob. of Semitic origin]

Gal·braith /gal'breiθ/ **John Ken·neth** (b.1908), Canadian-born US economist. He is well known for his criticism of consumerism and Western society's preoccupation with economic growth for its own sake; his books include *The Affluent Society* (1958) and *The Anatomy of Power* (1983).

gale¹ ● *noun* **1 a** a very strong wind. **b** *Meteorol.* a wind of force 8 on the Beaufort scale, or 34–40 knots. **2** *Naut.* a storm. **3** an outburst, esp. of laughter. ● *intransitive verb* *Cdn* (*Nfld*) (of a child or animal) frolic or scamper playfully. [16th c.: origin unknown]

gale² *noun* (in full **sweet gale**) = BOG MYRTLE. [Old English *gagel(le)*, Middle Dutch *gaghel*]

galea /'geiliə/ *noun* (*pl.* **ga·leae** /-liː/ or **ga·leas**) *Bot. & Zool.* a structure like a helmet in shape, form, or function. □ **gale·ate** /-i,eit/ *adjective* **gale·at·ed** /-i,eitəd/ *adjective* [Latin, = helmet]

Galen /'geilən/ (129–199), Greek physician, anatomist, and physiologist. His works attempting to systematize the whole of medicine were widely influential in Europe from the 12th c. onward. □ **Gal·en·ic** *adjective*

ga·lena /gə'liːnə/ *noun* lead sulphide, PbS, the principal ore of lead, found as grey, usu. cubic crystals with a metallic lustre. [Latin, = lead ore (in a partly purified state)]

gal·ette /gə'let/ *noun* a usu. savoury pancake, esp. one made of grated potatoes etc. or of a buckwheat batter. [French]

Gali·ano Island /,gali'anoː/ one of the Gulf Islands in the Strait of Georgia, BC, situated northeast of Saltspring Island. [D. A. *Galiano*, Spanish explorer d.1805]

Gal·ibi /gə'liːbi/ ● *noun* **1** (*pl.* same or **Gal·ibis**) a member of a S American Aboriginal people inhabiting French Guiana. **2** the Carib language of this people. ● *adjective* of or relating to this people or their language. [Carib, = strong man]

Gal·icia /gə'lɪsiə, -'lɪʃə/ **1** an autonomous region and former kingdom of NW Spain; capital, Santiago de Compostela. **2** a region of east central Europe, north of the Carpathian Mountains. A former province of Austria (until 1918–20), it now forms part of SE Poland and W Ukraine.

Gal·ician¹ /gə'lɪʃən/ *hist.* ● *noun* **1** a Slavic immigrant to W Canada, esp. a Ukrainian. **2** the language of Galicians. ● *adjective* of or pertaining to Galicians. [GALICIA 2]

Gal·ician² /gə'lɪʃən/ ● *noun* **1** a native or inhabitant of Galicia, a medieval Castilian kingdom, subsequently a Spanish province. **2** the language of Galicia, closely related to Portuguese. ● *adjective* of or pertaining to Galicia or its inhabitants. [GALICIA 1]

Gali·lee /'galə,liː/ a northern region of ancient Palestine, west of the Jordan River, associated with the ministry of Jesus. The region is now part of Israel. □ **Gali·lean** *noun & adjective*

Galilee, Sea of (also called **Lake Tiberias**) a lake in N Israel. The Jordan River flows through it from north to south.

Gali·leo Gali·lei /,galɪ'leioː ,galɪ'leii/ (1564–1642), Italian astronomer and physicist. He discovered the constancy of a pendulum's swing, formulated the law of uniform acceleration of falling bodies, and applied the telescope to astronomy, observing craters on the moon, sunspots, and Jupiter's satellites; his acceptance of the Copernican system was rejected by the Catholic Church, and under threat of torture from the Inquisition he publicly recanted his heretical views. □ **Gali·lean** *noun & adjective*

gal·in·gale /'galɪŋ,geil/ *noun* **1** = GALANGAL. **2** (in full **English galingale**) a sedge, *Cyperus longus*, having an aromatic root. [Old English *gallengar* Old French *galingal* from Arabic *kalanjān* from Chinese *ge-liang-jiang* mild ginger from Ge in Canton]

gall¹ *noun* **1** impudence; audacity. **2** bitterness; anything bitter (*gall and wormwood*). **3** the gallbladder, esp. of an animal. [Old Norse, corresponding to Old English *gealla*, from Germanic]

gall² ● *noun* **1** a sore on the skin made by chafing. **2 a** mental soreness or vexation. **b** a cause of this. ● *transitive verb* **1** vex, annoy, humiliate. **2** rub sore; injure by rubbing. □ **gall·ing** *adjective* **gall·ing·ly** *adverb* [Low German or Dutch *galle*, corresponding to Old English *gealla* sore on a horse]

gall³ *noun* **1** a growth produced by insects or fungus etc. on plants and trees, esp. on oak. **2** (*attributive*) of insects producing galls (*gall wasp*). [Old French *galle* from Latin *galla*]

gall. *abbreviation* gallon(s).

Galla /'galə/ ● *noun* **1** (*pl.* same or **Gal·las**) a member of a Hamitic people inhabiting mainly parts of Ethiopia and Kenya. **2** the Cushitic language of this people. ● *adjective* of or relating to this people or their language. [origin unknown]

Gal·lant /gə'lant/ **Mavis Les·lie** (b.1922), Canadian short-story writer and novelist, resident in Paris since 1951. Her fiction is noted for its penetrating examination of character, lifestyles, and human relationships, and often addresses the difficulty of entering an alien culture; her works include the short-story collections *The Other Paris* (1956), *The Pegnitz Junction* (1973), *From the Fifteenth District* (1979), and *Home Truths* (1981), and the novels *Green Water, Green Sky* (1959) and *A Fairly Good Time* (1970).

gal·lant ● *adjective* /'galənt/ **1** brave, noble. **2** /'galənt, gə'lant/ markedly attentive or polite, esp. to women. **3 a** (of a ship, horse, etc.) grand, fine, stately. **b** *archaic* finely dressed. ● *noun* /'galənt, gə'lant/ **1** a ladies' man; a lover or paramour. **2** *archaic* a man of fashion; a fine gentleman. □ **gal·lant·ly** *adverb* [Old French *galant* part. of *galer* make merry]

gal·lant·ry /'galəntri/ *noun* (*pl.* **-ries**) **1** bravery; dashing courage. **2** courtliness; devotion to women. **3** a polite act or speech.

gall·blad·der *noun* the vessel storing bile after its secretion by the liver and before release into the intestine.

gal·leon /'galiən/ *noun* *hist.* a square-rigged ship with three or more decks and masts, having a high forecastle and poop, used chiefly by Spain from the 15th to the 18th c., originally as a warship and later as a trader. [Middle Dutch *galjoen* from French *galion* from *galie* galley, or from Spanish *galeón*]

gal·le·ria /galə'riːə/ *noun* a collection of stores under one often high glass roof. [Italian]

gal·lery *noun* (*pl.* **-ies**) **1** a room or building for showing works of art. **2** a balcony, esp. a platform projecting from the inner wall of a church, hall, legislative assembly, etc., providing extra room for spectators etc. or reserved for musicians, the press, etc. (*press gallery*). **3 a** the highest balcony in a theatre, usu. with the cheapest seats. **b** its occupants. **4 a** a covered space for walking in, partly open at the side; a portico or colonnade. **b** a long narrow passage in the thickness of a wall or supported on corbels, open towards the interior of the building. **5** *N Amer.* (esp. *Que.*, *Nfld.*, & *Gulf States*) a veranda, esp. one surrounding a building on all sides. **6** a long narrow room, passage, or corridor. **7** *Military & Mining* a horizontal underground passage. **8** a group of spectators at a golf tournament etc. **9** a collection or assembly, esp. on display (*a gallery of celebrities*). □ **play to the gallery** seek to win approval by appealing to popular taste. □ **gal·ler·ied** *adjective* [French *galerie* from Italian *galleria* from medieval Latin *galeria*]

gal·ley *noun* (*pl.* **-leys**) **1** *hist.* **a** a low flat single-decked vessel using sails and oars, and usu. rowed by slaves or criminals. **b** an ancient Greek or Roman warship with one or more banks of oars. **c** a large open rowboat, e.g. that used by the captain of a man-of-war. **2** the kitchen in a ship, aircraft, camper, etc. **3 a** esp. *hist.* an oblong tray for set type. **b** the corresponding part of a composing machine. **c** (in full **galley proof**) a proof in the form of long single-column strips (as originally from type in a galley), not in sheets or pages. [Old French *galie* from medieval Latin *galea*, medieval Greek *galaia*]

galley kitchen *noun* a long narrow kitchen with counters and cupboards around three sides.

galley slave *noun* **1** *hist.* a person condemned to row in a galley. **2** a drudge.

Gal·lia Nar·bon·en·sis /'galiə ˌnɑːbə'nensɪs/ the southern province of Transalpine Gaul (see GAUL[1]).

Gal·li·ano *noun proprietary* a sweet, yellow, Italian herbal liqueur.

gal·li·ard /'galiˌɑːd/ *noun hist.* **1** a lively dance usu. in triple time for two persons, popular in the 16th–17th. c. **2** the music for this. [Old French *gaillard* valiant]

Gal·lic /'galɪk/ *adjective* **1** French or typically French. **2** of the Gauls; Gaulish. □ **Gal·li·cize** /-ˌsaɪz/ *transitive & intransitive verb* (also esp. *Brit.* **-cise**). [Latin *Gallicus* from *Gallus* a Gaul]

Gal·li·can /'galɪkən/ *Catholicism hist.* ● *adjective* asserting the right of esp. the French Church to be in certain respects free from papal control. ● *noun* an advocate or supporter of Gallican views (*compare* ULTRAMONTANE). □ **Gal·li·can·ism** *noun* [Latin *Gallicanus*, from *Gallic-us* Gaulish, from *Gallus* Gaul]

Gal·li·cism /'galɪˌsɪzəm/ *noun* a French word or usage, esp. one adopted in another language.

Gallic Wars Julius Caesar's campaigns 58–51 BC, which established Roman control over Gaul north of the Alps and west of the Rhine (Transalpine Gaul). Largely disunited, the Gauls combined in 53–52 BC under the chieftain Vercingetorix but were eventually defeated.

galli·gas·kins /ˌgalɪ'gaskɪnz/ *plural noun hist.* or *jocular* breeches, trousers. [originally wide hose of the 16th–17th c., from obsolete French *garguesque* for *greguesque* from Italian *grechesca* fem. of *grechesco* Greek]

galli·maufry /ˌgalɪ'mɔːfri/ *noun* (*pl.* **-ries**) a heterogeneous mixture; a jumble or medley. [French *galimafrée*, of unknown origin]

gal·lin·aceous /ˌgalɪ'neɪʃəs/ *adjective* of or relating to the order Galliformes, which includes domestic poultry, pheasants, partridges, etc. [Latin *gallinaceus* from *gallina* hen, from *gallus* cock]

gal·li·nule /'galɪˌnjuːl/ *noun* **1** a moorhen. **2** any of various similar birds of the genus *Porphyrula* or *Porphyrio*. [modern Latin *gallinula*, diminutive of Latin *gallina* hen, from *gallus* cock]

Gal·lip·oli /gə'lɪpəli/ a major campaign of the First World War in which the Allies (with heavy involvement of troops from Australia and New Zealand) invaded the Gallipoli peninsula on the European side of the Dardanelles, hoping to remove Turkey from the war and open supply lines to Russia's Black Sea ports. Beginning early in 1915, the campaign quickly became bogged down in trench warfare, and after each side had suffered a quarter of a million casualties, the Allies evacuated the peninsula in Jan. 1916.

gal·li·pot /'galɪˌpɒt/ *noun hist.* a small pot of earthenware, metal, etc., used for ointments etc. [prob. GALLEY + POT[1], because brought in galleys from the Mediterranean]

gal·lium /'galɪəm/ *noun Chem.* a soft bluish-white metallic element which melts just above room temperature, used in high-temperature thermometers and semiconductors. Symbol: **Ga**; at. no.: 31. [modern Latin from Latin *Gallia* France (so named patriotically by its discoverer Lecoq de Boisbaudran d.1912)]

gal·li·vant /'galɪˌvant/ *intransitive verb* **1** (often foll. by *around*) idly search for pleasure; gad about. **2** flirt. [origin uncertain]

gal·li·wasp /'galɪˌwɒsp/ *noun* any of various lizards of the Central American genus *Diploglossus*, esp. *D. monotropis* of the W Indies. [18th c.: origin unknown]

Gallo- /'galəʊ/ *combining form* **1** French; French and. **2** Gaul (*Gallo-Roman*). [Latin *Gallus* a Gaul]

gal·lon *noun* **1 a** (in full **imperial gallon**) (in Britain and other Commonwealth countries and formerly in Canada) a measure of capacity equal to eight pints and equivalent to 4.55 litres, used esp. for liquids. **b** (in full **US gallon**) (in the US) a measure of capacity equivalent to 3.79 litres, used for liquids. **2** (usu. in *pl.*) *informal* a large amount. [Old Northern French *galon* from base of medieval Latin *gallēta*, *gallētum*, perhaps of Celtic origin]

gal·lon·age *noun* the quantity in gallons of a liquid produced or sold.

gal·loon /gə'luːn/ *noun* a narrow close-woven braid of gold, silver, silk, cotton, nylon, etc., for binding dresses etc. [French *galon* from *galonner* trim with braid, of unknown origin]

gal·lop ● *noun* **1** the fastest pace of a horse or other quadruped, with all the feet off the ground together in each stride. **2** a ride at this pace. ● *verb* (**gal·loped**, **gallop·ing**) **1 a** *intransitive* (of a horse etc. or its rider) go at the pace of a gallop. **b** *transitive* make (a horse etc.) gallop. **2** *intransitive* **a** run with leaping strides, as in a gallop. **b** move or progress rapidly (*galloping inflation*). □ **at a gallop** at the pace of a gallop. □ **gal·lop·er** *noun* [Old French *galop*, *galoper*: see WALLOP]

Gal·lo·way /'galəˌweɪ/ an area of SW Scotland consisting of the two former counties of Kirkcudbrightshire and Wigtownshire, and now part of Dumfries and Galloway region. The area is noted for its western peninsula, called the Rhinns, of which the southern tip, the Mull of Galloway, is the most southerly point of Scotland.

gal·lo·way /'galəˌweɪ/ *noun* a breed of hornless black beef cattle. [GALLOWAY]

gal·lows *plural noun* (usu. treated as *sing.*) **1** a structure, usu. of two uprights and a crosspiece, for the hanging of criminals. **2** (prec. by *the*) execution by hanging. [Old English *gealga*, reinforced by Old Norse *gálgi*]

gallows humour *noun* grim and ironic humour.

gall·stone *noun* a small hard mass forming in the gallbladder or bile ducts from bile pigments, cholesterol, and calcium salts.

Gal·lup, George (Hor·ace) (1901–84), US statistician, who founded the American Institute of Public Opinion (1935) and devised the poll named after him.

gal·lus·es /'galəsɪz/ *plural noun N Amer. dated* suspenders. [pl. of *gallus* var. of GALLOWS]

gall wasp *noun* a gall-forming insect of the hymenopteran superfamily *Cynipoidea*. [GALL[3]]

Gal·ois /'galwɒ/ **Éva·riste** (1811–32), French mathematician. His memoir on the conditions for solubility of polynomial equations was highly innovative but was not published until after his early death.

ga·loot *noun N Amer. informal* a person, esp. a strange or clumsy one. [19th-c. Naut. slang: origin unknown]

galop /'galəp/ *noun* **1** a lively ballroom dance in duple time. **2** the music for this. [French: see GALLOP]

ga·lore *adverb* in abundance (placed after noun: *flowers galore*). [Irish *go leór* to sufficiency]

ga·losh *noun* (usu. in *pl.*) a waterproof overshoe, usu. of rubber. [Old French *galoche* from Late Latin *gallicula* small Gallic shoe]

gal pal *noun slang* a female friend.

Gals·worthy /'gɒlz,wɜːðɪ/ **John** (1867–1933), English novelist and dramatist. His sequence of novels known collectively as *The Forsyte Saga* (1906–28) traced the declining fortunes of an affluent family; he was awarded the Nobel Prize for literature in 1932.

Galt[1] part of the city of Cambridge, Ontario; it was amalgamated with the towns of Preston and Hespeler in 1973. [J. *Galt*, novelist and founder of Guelph d.1839]

Galt[2], **Sir Alex·an·der Til·loch** (1817–93), English-born Canadian politician, Father of Confederation. He was a member of the coalition ministry that secured Confederation between 1864 and 1867, and attended the Charlottetown, Quebec, and London conferences; he served as minister of finance (1867) and was the first Canadian High Commissioner in London (1880–3).

Gal·ton /ˈɡɒltən/ **Sir Fran·cis** (1822–1911), English scientist, the founder and advocate of eugenics; he introduced methods of measuring human mental and physical abilities, and developed statistical techniques to analyze his data.

ga·lumph /ɡəˈlʌmf/ *intransitive verb informal* **1** move noisily or clumsily. **2** go prancing in triumph. [coined by Lewis Carroll (in sense 2), perhaps from GALLOP + TRIUMPH]

Gal·vani /ɡælˈvani/ **Luigi** (1737–98), Italian anatomist. Observing the twitching of frogs' legs in an electric field, he concluded that these convulsions were caused by what is now known as galvanic electricity found in the body; this work led to Volta's invention of the electrochemical cell and eventually to an understanding of neuromuscular processes.

gal·van·ic /ɡælˈvanɪk/ *adjective* **1** of or producing an electric current by chemical action. **2 a** sudden and remarkable; convulsive (*a galvanic response*). **b** stimulating; full of energy; electrifying (*a galvanic speech*). □ **gal·van·ic·ally** *adverb*

gal·van·ism /ˈɡælvəˌnɪzəm/ *noun hist.* **1** electricity produced by chemical action. **2** the use of electricity for medical purposes. [French *galvanisme* from GALVANI]

gal·van·ize /ˈɡælvəˌnaɪz/ *transitive verb* (also esp. *Brit.* **-ise**) **1** (often foll. by *into*) rouse forcefully, esp. by shock or excitement (*was galvanized into action*). **2** stimulate by or as if by electricity. **3** coat (metal, esp. iron or steel) with zinc (usu. without the use of electricity) as a protection against rust. □ **gal·van·iz·a·tion** *noun* **gal·van·iz·er** *noun* [French *galvaniser*: see GALVANISM]

gal·van·om·eter /ˌɡælvəˈnɒmətər/ *noun* an instrument for detecting and measuring small electric currents. □ **gal·van·o·met·ric** /-nəˈmetrɪk/ *adjective*

Gal·ves·ton /ˈɡælvəstən/ a port in Texas, southeast of Houston; pop. (2000) 57,247. It is situated on Galveston Bay, an inlet of the Gulf of Mexico.

Gal·way /ˈɡɔlweɪ/ **1** a county of the Republic of Ireland, on the west coast in the province of Connacht. **2** its county town, a seaport at the head of Galway Bay; pop. (est. 2002) 59,800.

Galway Bay an inlet of the Atlantic Ocean on the west coast of Ireland.

gam¹ *noun informal* (usu in *pl.*) a leg, esp. a woman's attractive leg. [prob. from Old French *gambe*, northern form of *jambe* leg]

gam² ● *noun* **1** a school of whales, dolphins, etc. **2** a social meeting or chat, originally of whalers at sea. ● *intransitive verb* (**gammed**, **gam·ming**) **1** (of whales, dolphins, etc.) gather together, form a school. **2** (originally of whalers at sea) meet socially, exchange gossip, chat. [origin unknown]

Gama /ˈɡamə/ **Vasco da** (*c.*1469–1524), Portuguese explorer. He led the first European expedition around the Cape of Good Hope in 1497, arriving in Calicut, India in 1498; he led a second expedition to Calicut in 1502.

Gamay /ɡaˈmeɪ/ *noun* **1** a variety of black wine grape native to the Beaujolais district of France. **2** a fruity red wine made from this grape. [*Gamay*, a hamlet in Burgundy, France]

gam·bade /ɡamˈbɒd/ *noun* (also **gam·bado** /-ˈbɒdoː/) (*pl.* **gam·bades**; **-bados** or **-badoes**) **1** a horse's leap or bound. **2** an escapade or caper. [French *gambade* & Spanish *gambado* from Italian & Spanish *gamba* leg]

Gam·bia (also **the Gambia**) a country on the coast of West Africa; pop. (est. 2002) 1,455,842; capital, Banjul. Gambia consists of a narrow strip of territory on either side of the Gambia River extending upstream from its mouth, forming an enclave in Senegal. □ **Gam·bian** *adjective & noun*

Gambia River a river of West Africa, which rises near Labé in Guinea and flows 800 km (500 miles) through Senegal and Gambia to meet the Atlantic at Banjul.

gam·bier /ˈɡambiər, ˈɡambiːr/ *noun* an astringent extract of a tropical Asiatic plant used in tanning etc. [Malay *gambir* name of the plant]

Gam·bier Islands /ˈɡambiər, ˈɡambiːr/ a group of coral islands in the S Pacific, forming part of French Polynesia; pop. (est. 2002) 1,200.

gam·bit *noun* **1** a chess opening in which a player sacrifices a piece or pawn to secure an advantage. **2** an opening move in a discussion etc. **3** a trick or device, esp. to secure an advantage. [earlier *gambett* from Italian *gambetto* tripping up, from *gamba* leg]

gam·ble ● *verb* **1** *intransitive* play games of chance for money, esp. for high stakes. **2** *transitive* **a** bet (a sum of money) in gambling. **b** (often foll. by *away*) lose (assets) by gambling. **3** *intransitive* take great risks in the hope of substantial gain. **4** *intransitive* (foll. by *on*) act in the hope or expectation of (*gambled on fine weather*). ● *noun* **1** a risky undertaking or attempt, esp. in the hope of substantial gain. **2** an act of gambling. □ **gam·bler** *noun* [obsolete *gamel* to sport, *gamene* GAME¹]

gam·boge /ɡamˈboːdʒ, -ˈbuːʒ/ *noun* a gum resin produced by various E Asian trees and used as a yellow pigment. [modern Latin *gambaugium* from CAMBODIA]

gam·bol ● *intransitive verb* (**gam·bolled**, **gambol·ling**; *US* **gam·boled**, **gambol·ing**) skip or frolic playfully. ● *noun* a playful frolic. [GAMBADE]

gam·brel /ˈɡambrəl/ *noun* (in full **gambrel roof**) *N Amer.* a roof with two sides, each of which has a shallower slope above a steeper one, as in many traditional barns. [Old Northern French *gamberel* from *gambier* forked stick, from *gambe* leg (from the resemblance to the shape of a horse's hind leg)]

game¹ ● *noun* **1 a** an amusement, diversion, pastime, etc. **b** a form of contest played according to rules and decided by skill, strength, or luck. **2** a single portion of play forming a scoring unit in some contests, e.g. bridge or tennis. **3** (in *pl.*) a meeting for athletic etc. contests (*Olympic Games*). **4** a winning score in a game; the state of the score in a game (*the game is two all*). **5** the apparatus necessary to play a game, esp. a board game or computer game. **6** one's level of achievement in, or style of playing a game, as specified (*played a good game; improving their game; theirs is a running game*). **7 a** a piece of fun; a jest (*was only playing a game with you*). **b** (in *pl.*) dodges, tricks (*none of your games!*). **c** an instance of deception or psychological manipulation (*she loathed office politics and game-playing*). **8** a scheme or undertaking etc. regarded as a game (*so that's your game*). **9 a** a policy or plan of action. **b** = GAME PLAN. **10 a** wild animals or birds hunted for sport or food. **b** the flesh of these. **11** a hunted animal; a quarry or object of pursuit or attack. ● *adjective* **1** spirited; eager and willing. **2** (foll. by *for*, or *to* + infin.) having the spirit or energy; eagerly prepared. ● *verb* **1** *intransitive* play at games of chance for money; gamble. **2** *transitive & intransitive* = WAR GAME. **3** *intransitive* play video or computer games. □ **the game is up** the scheme is revealed or foiled. **give the game away** reveal something one would rather keep hidden, esp. inadvertently. **game over** *slang* all is lost; there is no more hope. **game, set, and match** it is completely finished. **make game** (or **a game**) **of** mock, taunt. **off** (or **on**) **one's game** playing badly (or well). **on the game** *Brit. slang* involved in prostitution or thieving. **play the game** behave fairly or according to the rules. □ **game·ly** *adverb* **game·ness** *noun* **game·ster** *noun* [Old English *gamen*]

game² *adjective* (of a leg, arm, etc.) lame, crippled. [18th-c. dial.: origin unknown]

game bird *noun* **1** a bird shot for sport or food. **2** a bird of the order Galliformes, which includes pheasants, grouse, etc.

game·book *noun* **1** *N Amer.* a book containing strategies to be learned or adopted esp. by members of a sports team. **2** a book for recording game killed by a sportsman.

Game Boy *noun proprietary* a hand-held electronic device with a small screen, used to play cartridge computer games.

game-breaking *adjective N Amer.* (of a play etc.) turning a close game decisively and dramatically in one's favour (*a game-breaking touchdown*). □ **game-breaker** *noun*

game·cock *noun* (also **game·fowl**) a cock bred and trained for cockfighting.

game face *noun N Amer.* the focused, intense, determined countenance of an athlete during a competition, match, etc. (*put on his game face during the warm-up*).

game farm *noun* (also **game ranch**) an esp. public farm where wild animals are kept.

game fish *noun* a kind of fish caught for sport.

game·keeper *noun* a person employed to breed and protect game.

gam·elan /ˈɡaməˌlan/ *noun* **1** an Indonesian, esp. Javanese or Balinese, orchestra with a wide range of metal percussion instruments. **2** a kind of xylophone used in this. [Javanese]

game misconduct *noun Hockey* a penalty banishing a player for the rest of the current game.

game of chance *noun* a game decided by luck, not skill.

game plan *noun esp. N Amer.* **1** a winning strategy worked out in advance for a particular match. **2** a plan of campaign, esp. in politics.

game·play *noun* the features of a computer game, such as its plot and the way it is played, as distinct from the graphics and sound effects.

game point *noun* (in tennis etc.) a point which, if won, would win the game.

gamer *noun* **1** *N Amer. informal* an athlete known for consistently making a strong effort. **2** a person who plays a game or games, esp. a participant in a computer or role-playing game.

game show *noun* a television program in which people compete in a game or quiz, usu. for prizes.

games·man *noun* (*pl.* **-men**) an exponent of gamesmanship.

games·man·ship *noun* the art or practice of defeating an opponent by psychological or other questionable (but not strictly illegal) means.

game·some *adjective* playful, merry, sportive. □ **game·some·ly** *adverb* **game·some·ness** *noun*

games room *noun* (also **game room**) a room, esp. in a hotel, student residence, etc., equipped for playing games, e.g. table tennis, billiards, darts, etc.

gamet·an·gium /ˌgamɪˈtandʒiəm/ *noun* (*pl.* **gamet·an·gia** /-dʒiə/) *Bot.* an organ in which gametes are formed. [as GAMETE + Greek *aggeion* vessel]

gam·ete /ˈgamiːt, gəˈmiːt/ *noun Biol.* a mature haploid reproductive cell (male or female) which unites with another of the opposite sex in sexual reproduction to form a zygote. □ **gam·et·ic** /gəˈmɛtɪk/ *adjective* [modern Latin *gameta* from Greek *gametē* wife, from *gamos* marriage]

game theory *noun* (also **games theory**) the mathematical analysis of competitive strategies where choices depend on the actions of others, e.g. in war, economics, games of skill, etc.

gameto- /gəˈmiːtəʊ/ *combining form Biol.* gamete.

gam·eto·cyte /gəˈmiːtəʊˌsəɪt/ *noun Biol.* any cell that is in the process of developing into one or more gametes.

gam·eto·gen·esis /gəˌmiːtəʊˈdʒɛnɪsɪs, ˌgami-/ *noun Biol.* the process by which cells undergo meiosis to form gametes.

gam·eto·phyte /gəˈmiːtəʊˌfəɪt/ *noun* the gamete-producing form of a plant that alternates with the asexual form in a plant that has alternation of generations. □ **gam·eto·phyt·ic** /-ˈfɪtɪk/ *adjective*

game warden *noun* an official locally supervising game, hunting and fishing, etc.

game-winner *noun* the goal, run, etc. that puts one team ahead of the other by the end of the game.

gamey *adjective* = GAMY.

gamin /ˈgamɪn/ *noun* **1** a street urchin. **2** an impudent child. [French]

gam·ine /ˈgamiːn, gaˈmiːn/ ● *noun* **1** a girl with mischievous or boyish charm. **2** a girl street urchin. ● *adjective* of or like a gamine (*a short, gamine haircut*). [French]

gaming *noun* **1** gambling, esp. with cards or dice. **2** the playing of war games or computer role-playing games.

gaming house *noun* a place frequented for gambling; a casino.

gaming table *noun* a table used for gambling.

gamma *noun* **1** the third letter of the Greek alphabet (Γ, γ). **2** (*attributive*) designating the third member of a series or set. **3** *Astronomy* the third brightest star in a constellation. **4** (*attributive*) designating high-energy electromagnetic radiation of wavelengths shorter than those of X-rays, emitted by some radioactive substances (*gamma rays*). **5** *Brit.* a third-class mark given for a piece of work or in an examination. [Greek]

gamma-amino·butyric acid /ˌgamə əˌmiːnəʊbjuːˈtɪrɪk/ *noun Biochemistry* an amino acid which acts to inhibit the transmission of nerve impulses in the central nervous system. [*gamma* indicating the relative position of amino on the third carbon away from the acid group]

gamma globulin *noun* a mixture of blood plasma proteins, mainly immunoglobulins, of relatively low electrophoretic mobility, often given to boost immunity.

gamma knife *noun* a device which focuses gamma rays on an area in the brain to destroy tumours and other lesions without an incision.

gamma-linolenic acid *noun* one of the three known forms of linolenic acid, found e.g. in evening primrose oil, which is a biochemical precursor of prostaglandins, and has been used in the treatment of various disorders including atopic eczema, multiple sclerosis, arthritis, and premenstrual syndrome.

gam·mer *noun archaic* an old woman, esp. as a rustic name. [prob. contraction of GODMOTHER: compare GAFFER 2]

gam·mon¹ *noun Brit.* **1** the bottom piece of a flitch of bacon including a hind leg. **2** the ham of a pig cured like bacon. [Old Northern French *gambon* from *gambe* leg: compare JAMB]

gam·mon² ● *noun* a kind of victory in backgammon (scoring two games) in which all the winner's pieces are removed before any of the loser's. ● *transitive verb* defeat in this way. [apparently = Middle English *gamen* GAME¹]

gammy *adjective* (**gam·mi·er**, **gam·mi·est**) *Brit. informal* (esp. of a leg) lame; permanently injured. [dial. form of GAME²]

Gamow /ˈgeɪmɒf/ **George** (1904–68), Russian-born US physicist, who worked on the theoretical background to the big bang theory and the nature of the genetic code.

gamp *noun Brit. informal* an umbrella, esp. a large unwieldy one. [Mrs. *Gamp* in Dickens's *Martin Chuzzlewit*]

gamut /ˈgamət/ *noun* **1** the whole series or range or scope of anything (*the whole gamut of crime*). **2** *Music* **a** the whole series of notes used in medieval or modern music. **b** a major diatonic scale. **c** a people's or a period's recognized scale. **d** a voice's or instrument's compass. **3** *Music* the lowest note in the medieval sequence of hexachords, = modern G on the lowest line of the bass staff. □ **run the gamut** experience, include, or perform the complete range. [medieval Latin *gamma ut* from GAMMA taken as the name for a note one tone lower than A of the classical scale + *ut* the first of six arbitrary names of notes forming the hexachord, being syllables (*ut, re, mi, fa, so, la*) of the Latin hymn beginning *Ut queant laxis*)]

gamy *adjective* (**gam·i·er**, **gam·i·est**) (also **gamey**) **1** having the strong flavour or scent of game kept until it is high. **2** *N Amer.* scandalous, sensational. **3** = GAME¹ *adjective*. □ **gam·i·ly** *adverb* **gam·i·ness** *noun*

ga·nache /gəˈnaʃ, -nɒʃ/ *noun* a whipped filling of chocolate and cream, used in cakes, truffles, etc. [French]

Gan·an·oque /ˌganəˈnɒkweɪ/ a town in SE Ontario, situated on the St. Lawrence, about 30 km east of Kingston; pop. (2001) 5,167. □ **Gan·an·oque·an** *noun* [Onondaga *ganonocouy* flint at the mountain]

Gana·pati /ˌgʌnəˈpɒti/ *Hinduism* = GANESH. [as GANESH]

Gäncä /ˈgɒndʒə/ an industrial city in Azerbaijan; pop. (est. 2002) 294,700. The city was formerly called Yelizavetpol (Elizavetpol) (1804–1918) and Kirovabad (1935–89).

Gance /gɑ̃s/ **Abel** (1889–1981), French film director. An early pioneer of technical experimentation in film, he is best known for *Napoléon* (1926), in which he made use of a split-screen, hand-held camera, and wide-angle photography.

Gand see GHENT.

Gan·der a town in east central Newfoundland, situated on Gander Lake, 331 km northwest of St. John's; pop. (2001) 9,651. Its airport served the first regular transatlantic flights during the Second World War. □ **Gan·der·ite** *noun* [see GANDER RIVER]

gan·der *noun* **1** a male goose. **2** *informal* a look, a glance (*take a gander*). [Old English *gandra*, related to GANNET]

Gander Bay boat *noun Cdn* (*Nfld*) a large canoe-like boat used on the lower stretches of the Gander River.

Gander River a river in NE Newfoundland, 156 km long, rising in the central part of the island as the Northwest Gander River and flowing northeastward through Gander Lake to empty into Gander Bay on Hamilton Sound, an inlet of the Atlantic Ocean. [prob. so called because of the area's abundance of wild geese]

Gan·dhi /ˈgandi/ **1 In·dira (Priya·dar·shini)** (1917–84), Indian stateswoman, prime minister 1966–77 and 1980–4, daughter of Jawaharlal Nehru. Her second term of office was marked by prolonged religious disturbance, during which she alienated many Sikhs by ordering troops to storm the Golden Temple at Amritsar (1984); she was assassinated by her Sikh bodyguards. **2 Ma·hat·ma** (born Mohandas Karamchand Gandhi) (1869–1948), Indian nationalist and spiritual leader. Prominent in the opposition to British rule, he advocated a policy of passive resistance and non-violent civil disobedience, and although he never held government office, he was regarded as the country's supreme political and spiritual leader and the principal force in achieving India's independence; he was assassinated by a Hindu extremist. **3 Rajiv (Ratna)** (1944–91), Indian politician, prime minister 1984–9, son of Indira Gandhi. He became prime minister after his mother's assassination, and his premiership was marked by continuing unrest; he resigned in 1989 and was assassinated during the election campaign of 1991.

Gan·dhi·nagar /ˌgandiˈnʌgər/ a city in W India, capital of the state of Gujarat; pop. (2001) 195,900.

G and T *noun informal* a gin and tonic.

Consonants: b *but*   d *dog*   f *few*   g *get*   h *her*   j *yes*   k *cat*   l *leg*   m *man*   n *no*   p *pen*   r *red*   s *sit*

gandy dancer *noun* N Amer. a railway maintenance worker. [origin uncertain]

Ganesh /gəˈneɪʃə/ (also called **Ga·nesha**, **Gana·pati**) Hinduism an elephant-headed deity, son of Shiva and Parvati. Worshipped as the remover of obstacles and patron of learning, he is invoked at the beginning of literary works, rituals, or any new undertaking. [Sanskrit, = lord of ganas (Siva's attendants)]

gang[1] ● *noun* **1 a** an organized group of criminals. **b** *informal* a group of people who regularly associate together. **c** an organized territorial group of esp. urban youth demanding loyalty from members, engaging in various criminal activities, and often violently rivalling other groups. **2** a set of workers, slaves, or prisoners. **3** a set of tools etc. arranged to work simultaneously. ● *transitive verb* arrange (tools etc.) to work in coordination. □ **gang up** *informal* **1** (foll. by *on*) combine against. **2** (often foll. by *with*) act in concert. [originally = going, journey, from Old Norse *gangr*, *ganga* GOING, corresponding to Old English *gang*]

gang[2] *intransitive verb* Scot. go. □ **gang agley** (of a plan etc.) go wrong. [Old English *gangan*: compare GANG[1]]

gang·bang *slang* ● *transitive & intransitive verb* **1** (of several men) have sexual intercourse successively with the same person, esp. violently. **2** (of a gang) attack members of a rival gang. ● *noun* an instance of gangbanging. □ **gang·bang·er** *noun*

gang-board *noun* Cdn (Nfld) one of several loose planks placed across the top of the fish storage compartment on a deckless fishing boat, for shielding the fish from the sun. □ **gang-boarded** *attributive adjective*

gang·bust·er N Amer. informal ● *noun* a person who takes part in the aggressive breakup of criminal gangs. ● *adjective* (often as **gang·bust·ers**) outstandingly successful (*a gangbuster year; monthly sales are gangbusters*). □ **go gangbusters** be vigorously successful. **like gangbusters** energetically, vigorously; successfully.

Gan·ges River /ˈɡandʒiːz/ a river of N India and Bangladesh, which rises in the Himalayas and flows some 2 700 km (1,678 miles) southeast to the Bay of Bengal, where it forms the world's largest delta. The river is regarded by Hindus as sacred.

gang·land *noun* (often *attributive*) the world of gangs and gangsters (*a gangland killing*).

gan·gle *intransitive verb* move ungracefully. [back-formation from GANGLING]

gan·gling *adjective* (of a person) loosely built; lanky. [frequentative of GANG[2]]

gan·glion /ˈɡanɡlɪən/ *noun* (pl. **gan·glia** or **gan·glions**) **1 a** an enlargement or knot on a nerve etc. containing an assemblage of nerve cells. **b** a mass of grey matter in the central nervous system forming a nerve nucleus. **2** a cyst, esp. on a tendon sheath. □ **gan·gliar** *adjective* **gan·gli·on·at·ed** *adjective* **gan·gli·on·ic** /-ˈɒnɪk/ *adjective* [Greek *gagglion*]

gan·gly *adjective* (**gan·gli·er**, **gan·gli·est**) = GANGLING.

Gang of Four a group of four Chinese associates involved in implementing many of Mao Zedong's policies during the Cultural Revolution; the four (Wang Hongwen, Zhang Chunjao, Yao Wenyuan, and Mao's wife Jiang Qing) were among the groups competing for power on Mao's death in 1976, but were arrested and imprisoned.

gang·plank *noun* a movable plank usu. with cleats nailed on it for boarding or disembarking from a ship etc.

gang rape *noun* the successive rape of a person by a group of people. □ **gang-rape** *transitive verb*

gan·grene /ˈɡanɡriːn, ɡanˈɡriːn/ ● *noun* **1** Med. death and decomposition of a part of the body tissue, usu. resulting from obstructed circulation or bacterial infection. **2** moral corruption. ● *transitive & intransitive verb* affect or become affected with gangrene. □ **gan·gren·ous** /ˈɡanɡrɪnəs/ *adjective* [French *gangrène* from Latin *gangraena* from Greek *gaggraina*]

gang saw *noun* several saw blades working in unison in a sawmill.

gang·sta *noun* **1** *slang* a member of a street gang. **2** (in full **gangsta rap**) a style of rap music, chiefly from the Los Angeles area, the lyrics of which centre on the violence of gang culture, racism, police brutality, etc. [corruption of GANGSTER]

gang·ster *noun* a member of a gang of violent criminals. □ **gang·ster·ish** *adjective* **gang·ster·ism** *noun*

Gang·tok /ɡanˈtɒk/ a city in N India, in the foothills of the Kanchenjunga mountain range, capital of the state of Sikkim; pop. (2001) 29,200.

gangue /ɡaŋ/ *noun* valueless earth etc. in which ore is found. [French from German *Gang* lode = GANG[1]]

gang·way ● *noun* **1 a** an opening in the bulwarks by which a ship is entered or left. **b** a bridge laid from ship to shore or to another ship. **c** a passage on a ship, esp. a platform connecting the quarterdeck and forecastle. **2** a temporary arrangement of planks for crossing muddy or difficult ground on a construction site etc. **3** a sloped mound of earth with stone walls built against the outer side of a barn so as to provide a ramp leading to the second storey. **4** Brit. a passage, esp. between rows of seats. ● *interjection* make way!

gan·ja /ˈɡandʒə, ˈɡɒn-/ *noun* a potent form of marijuana for smoking. [Hindi *gānjhā*]

gan·net /ˈɡanət/ *noun* **1** any seabird of the genus *Sula*, esp. the northern gannet, *Sula bassana*, catching fish by plunge-diving, and nesting in large colonies on ledges of coastal islands. **2** Brit. informal a greedy person. [Old English *ganot* from Germanic, related to GANDER]

gan·net·ry /ˈɡanətri/ *noun* (pl. **-ries**) a place where gannets breed; a gannet colony.

gan·oid /ˈɡanɔɪd/ ● *adjective* **1** (of fish scales) enamelled; smooth and bright. **2** having ganoid scales. ● *noun* a fish having ganoid scales, e.g. the sturgeon. [French *ganoïde* from Greek *ganos* brightness]

Gan·ong, Gil·bert White (1851–1917) Canadian chocolate and confectionery manufacturer, founder of the New Brunswick chocolate and candy manufacturing company that still bears his name.

Gansu /ɡanˈsuː/ (also **Kansu** /kan-/) a province of NW central China, between Mongolia and Tibet; capital, Lanzhou. This narrow, mountainous province, traversed by the valleys of the upper Yellow River, forms a corridor through which passed, in ancient times, the route to the west known as the Silk Road.

gant·let N Amer. var. of GAUNTLET[2].

gan·try /ˈɡantri/ *noun* (pl. **-tries**) **1** a bridge-like overhead structure whose span supports a suspended travelling crane, railway or road signals, etc. **2** a structure supporting a space rocket prior to launching. [prob. from *gawn*, dial. form of GALLON + TREE]

Gany·mede /ˈɡanɪˌmiːd/ **1** Gk Myth a Trojan youth who was so beautiful that he was carried off (in one version, by an eagle) to be Zeus' cupbearer. **2** Astronomy satellite III of Jupiter, the seventh closest to the planet, and one of the Galilean moons; with a diameter of 5 262 km it is the largest satellite in the solar system.

GAO *abbreviation* (in the US) General Accounting Office.

gaol /dʒeɪl/ *noun* esp. Brit. var. of JAIL. □ **gaol·er** *noun*

gap *noun* **1** an unfilled space or interval; a blank; a break in continuity. **2** a breach in a hedge, fence, or wall. **3** a wide (usu. undesirable) divergence in views, sympathies, development, etc. (*generation gap*). **4** a gorge or pass. □ **fill** (or **close** etc.) **the gap** make up a deficiency. □ **gap·ped** *adjective* **gappy** *adjective* [Old Norse, = chasm, related to GAPE]

gape ● *intransitive verb* **1 a** open one's mouth wide, esp. in amazement or wonder. **b** be or become wide open. **2** (foll. by *at*) gaze curiously or wondrously. **3** split; break apart. **4** yawn. ● *noun* **1** an open-mouthed stare. **2** a yawn. **3** (in *pl.*; prec. by *the*) **a** a disease of birds with gaping as a symptom, caused by infestation with gapeworm. **b** *jocular* a fit of yawning. **4 a** the expanse of an open mouth or beak. **b** the part of a beak that opens. **5** a rent or opening. □ **gaping·ly** *adverb* [Old Norse *gapa*]

gaper *noun* **1** any bivalve mollusc of the genus *Mya*, with the shell open at one or both ends. **2** a person who gapes.

gape·worm *noun* a parasitic nematode worm of the family Syngamidae which infests the respiratory tract of birds, causing the gapes.

gap-toothed *adjective* having gaps between the teeth.

gap year *noun* esp. Brit. a year of travel etc. between secondary school and university.

gar *noun* any freshwater fish of the family Lepisosteidae of eastern N America, having long beaklike jaws with sharp teeth and ganoid scales. Also called GARPIKE. [as GARFISH]

gar·age /ɡəˈrɒʒ, -ˈrɒdʒ, -ˈrɑdʒ, -ˈrɑʒ, esp. Brit. ˈɡarɒdʒ, -rɒʒ, -rɪdʒ/ ● *noun* **1** a building or shed for the storage of a motor vehicle or vehicles. **2 a** an establishment that sells gasoline, repairs motor vehicles, etc. **b** the area at such an establishment where vehicles are serviced. **3** (*attributive*) denoting raw, unpolished, usu. energetic guitar-based rock music, esp. as played by amateurs in suburban garages or basements (*garage band; garage rock*). **4** esp. Brit. soul-influenced house music. ● *transitive verb* put or keep (a motor vehicle) in a garage. [French from *garer* shelter]

garage sale *noun* N Amer. a sale of used household goods, clothes, books, etc. held in the garage or on the lawn of a private house.

garam ma·sa·la /ˌgerəm məˈsɑːlə/ *noun* a spice mixture used in Indian cooking. [Urdu *garam maṣālaḥ* from *garam* 'hot, pungent' and *maṣālaḥ* 'spice']

Gara·mond /ˈgerəmɒnd/ **Claude** (1499–1561), French type designer, whose elegant roman forms were a major factor in establishing this type of lettering as the standard in place of black letter or Gothic.

Ga·rant /gɑˈrɑ̃/ **Serge** (1929–86), Canadian pianist, composer, and conductor. His serial compositions include *Trois Pièces* (1958) for string quartet, *Anerca* (1961) for voice and instrumental ensemble, and three *Offrandes* (1969–71) for orchestra.

garb ● *noun* **1** clothing, esp. of a distinctive kind. **2** the way a person is dressed. ● *transitive verb* **1** (usu. in *passive* or *reflexive*) put (esp. distinctive) clothes on (a person). **2** attire. [obsolete French *garbe* from Italian *garbo* from Germanic, related to GEAR]

gar·bage *noun* **1 a** refuse, filth. **b** household waste. **2** anything worthless. **3** nonsense. **4** *Computing* incorrect or useless data (*garbage in, garbage out*). □ **gar·bagey** *adjective* [Anglo-French: origin unknown]

garbage bag *noun* *N Amer.* a large, often black or dark green plastic bag for holding garbage.

garbage bear *noun* *N Amer.* a wild bear that has become accustomed to scavenging from garbage cans.

garbage can *noun* (also **garbage bin**, **garbage pail**) *N Amer.* a container for household refuse.

garbage disposal *noun* (also **garbage disposer**) *N Amer.* a system installed in a kitchen sink, with blades in the drain to mulch refuse.

garbage·man *noun* *N Amer.* a person employed to remove garbage, esp. from the curbside, and transport it to a dump.

garbage mitt *noun* *Cdn* (*Man.*) *slang* a thickly padded deerskin mitt. [so called because typically worn by garbagemen in the winter]

garbage truck *noun* *N Amer.* a truck, usu. with a powerful compactor, used to collect garbage and bring it to a dump.

gar·ban·zo /gɑrˈbɒnzoː/ *noun* = CHICKPEA. [Spanish]

gar·ble ● *transitive verb* **1** unintentionally distort or confuse (facts, messages, etc.). **2 a** mutilate in order to misrepresent. **b** make (usu. unfair or malicious) selections from (facts, statements, etc.). ● *noun* garbled speech or sounds. □ **gar·bler** *noun* [Italian *garbellare* from Arabic *ġarbala* sift, perhaps from Late Latin *cribellare* to sieve, from Latin *cribrum* sieve]

Garbo, Greta (born Greta Lovisa Gustafsson) (1905–90), Swedish-born US actress, renowned for her beauty. She starred in films such as *Anna Karenina* (1935) and *Camille* (1936), but retired from acting in 1941 to a secluded private life.

gar·board *noun* (in full **garboard strake**) the first range of planks or plates laid on a ship's bottom next to the keel. [Dutch *gaarboord*, perhaps from *garen* GATHER + *boord* BOARD]

gar·bol·o·gist /gɑrˈbɒlədʒɪst/ *noun* a person who studies the discarded rubbish of society. □ **gar·bol·ogy** *noun* [GARBAGE + -LOGIST]

gar·bur·ator /ˈgɑrbəˌreɪtər/ *noun* *Cdn* a garbage disposal unit. [initial element from GARBAGE, perhaps punningly after CARBURETOR or influenced by INCINERATOR]

Gar·cía Lorca see LORCA.

Gar·cía Már·quez /gɑrˌsiə ˈmɑrkes/ **Gab·riel** (b.1928), Colombian novelist, considered one of the founding figures of modern South American literature; his novels include *One Hundred Years of Solitude* (1967), regarded as a classic example of magic realism, in which fantastic material is introduced into a realistic portrayal of political and social issues, and *The General in His Labyrinth* (1990). He was awarded the Nobel Prize for literature in 1982.

gar·çon /gɑrˈsɔ̃/ *noun* (*pl.* **gar·çons** *pronunc.* same) a waiter in a French restaurant, hotel, etc. [French, = 'waiter', lit. 'boy']

Garda /ˈgɑrdə/ *noun* **1** the state police force of the Irish Republic. **2** (also **garda**) (*pl.* **-dai** /-diː/) a member of this. [Irish *Garda Síochána* Civic Guard]

Garda, Lake /ˈgɑrdə/ a lake in NE Italy, lying between Lombardy and Venetia.

gar·den ● *noun* **1 a** esp. *N Amer.* a piece of ground adjoining a private house, used for growing flowers, vegetables, etc. **b** a backyard or front yard adjoining a private house, usu. including a lawn and vegetable or flower garden. **c** flowers and vegetables etc. growing on a patio, balcony, etc. (*a container garden*). **2** (often in *pl.*) ornamental grounds laid out for public enjoyment (*botanical gardens; rock garden*). **3** (*attributive*) **a** (of plants) cultivated, not wild. **b** for use in a garden (*garden tools*). **4** (usu. in *pl.* prec. by a name) *Brit.* a street, square, etc. (*Onslow Gardens*). **5** an especially fertile region (*the Garden of the Gulf*). **6** *N Amer.* (often in

pl.) a large hall or sports arena (*Maple Leaf Gardens*). ● *intransitive verb* cultivate or work in a garden. □ **gar·dened** *adjective* **gar·den·ing** *noun* [Old Northern French *gardin* (Old French *jardin*), ultimately from Germanic: compare YARD²]

garden apartment *noun* *N Amer.* a low-rise apartment complex with plenty of garden space.

garden centre *noun* a store where plants and garden equipment etc. are sold.

garden city *noun* a community laid out systematically with spacious surroundings, parks, etc.

gar·den·er *noun* a person who gardens or is employed to tend a garden.

gar·denia /gɑrˈdiːniə/ *noun* any tree or shrub of the genus *Gardenia*, with large white or yellow flowers and usu. a fragrant scent. [modern Latin from Dr. A. *Garden*, Scottish naturalist d.1791]

garden party *noun* a social event held on a lawn or in a garden.

garden path *noun* a path through a garden. □ **lead a person down** (or **up**) **the garden path** mislead a person into error, folly, etc.

garden salad *noun* *N Amer.* a salad made with common garden vegetables, e.g. lettuce, tomatoes, cucumbers.

garden suburb *noun* esp. *Brit.* a suburb laid out spaciously with open spaces, parks, etc.

garden-variety *attributive adjective* unremarkable, commonplace.

garden warbler *noun* a European woodland songbird, *Sylvia borin*.

Gar·din·er, Sir John Eliot (b.1943), British conductor. His interest in early music led him to revive a number of neglected Baroque works, including several Rameau operas (1973–75), and to form the Monteverdi Choir (1964) and the Monteverdi Orchestra (1968). In 1978, he pioneered the use of period instruments to perform early music when he formed the English Baroque Soloists.

Gard·ner ▶ 1 Ava (La·vinia) (1922–90), US actress. She received praise for her performances in *Bhowani Junction* (1956) and *The Night of the Iguana* (1964). **2 Earle Stan·ley** (1899–1970) US novelist and short-story writer, creator of the lawyer-detective Perry Mason.

Gar·field, James Abram (1831–81), US Republican politician, 20th president of the US 1881. He was assassinated within months of taking presidential office.

gar·fish *noun* (*pl.* same) **1** any mainly marine fish of the family Belonidae, esp. *Belone belone* of the N Atlantic Ocean and Mediterranean and Black Seas. Also called NEEDLEFISH. **2** *NZ & Austral.* either of two marine fish of the genus *Hemiramphus*. Also called HALFBEAK. [apparently from Old English *gār* spear + *fisc* FISH¹]

gar·gan·tuan /gɑrˈgantʃuən/ *adjective* enormous, gigantic. [the name of a giant in Rabelais' book *Gargantua* (1534)]

gar·get /ˈgɑrgət/ *noun* inflammation of a cow's or ewe's udder. [perhaps from obsolete *garget* throat, from Old French *gargate*, *-guete*]

gar·gle ● *verb* **1 a** *intransitive* wash one's mouth and throat, esp. for medicinal purposes, with a liquid kept in motion by a stream of air which is breathed out. **b** *transitive* take (a liquid) in this way. **2** *intransitive* make a sound as when doing this. **3** *transitive* utter with a gargle. ● *noun* **1** a liquid used for gargling. **2** the sound of gargling. **3** *Brit. slang* an alcoholic drink. [French *gargouiller* from *gargouille*: see GARGOYLE]

gar·goyle *noun* **1** a grotesque carved human or animal face or figure projecting from the edge of a roof of (esp. a Gothic) building usu. as a spout to carry water clear of a wall. **2** any grotesque figure of a human or animal. □ **gar·goyled** *adjective* **gar·goyl·ish** *adjective* [Old French *gargouille* throat, gargoyle]

Gari·baldi /ˌgerɪˈbɒldi, ˌgɑr-/ **Giu·seppe** (1807–82), Italian patriot and military leader. A hero of the Risorgimento, he successfully led his volunteer force of 'Red Shirts' to victory against French and Austrian forces in Sicily and southern Italy in 1860–1, thus playing a vital part in the establishment of a united kingdom of Italy.

gari·bal·di /ˌgerɪˈbɒldi, ˌgɑr-/ *noun* (*pl.* **garibaldis**) **1** a kind of loose blouse formerly worn by women or children, originally of bright red material imitating the shirts worn by Garibaldi and his followers. **2** *Brit.* a cookie containing a layer of currants. **3** *US* a small red Californian fish, *Hypsypops rubicundus*. [GARIBALDI]

gar·ish /ˈgerɪʃ, ˈga-/ *adjective* **1** obtrusively bright; showy. **2** gaudy; over-decorated. □ **gar·ish·ly** *adverb* **gar·ish·ness** *noun* [16th-c. *gaurish* apparently from obsolete *gaure* stare]

Gar·land /ˈgɑrlənd/ **Judy** (born Frances Gumm) (1922–69), US singer and actress. Her most famous early film role was as Dorothy in *The*

Wizard of Oz (1939); later successful films included *Meet Me in St. Louis* (1944) and *A Star is Born* (1954).

gar·land ● *noun* **1** a wreath of flowers, leaves, etc., worn on the head or around the neck, or hung as a decoration. **2** a prize or distinction. **3** a literary anthology or miscellany. ● *transitive verb* **1** adorn with garlands. **2** crown with a garland. [Old French *garlande*, of unknown origin]

gar·lic *noun* **1** any of various alliaceous plants, esp. *Allium sativum*. **2** the strong-smelling pungent-tasting bulb of this plant, divided into cloves, used as a flavouring in cooking. □ **gar·licky** *adjective* [Old English *gārleac* from *gār* spear + *lēac* LEEK]

garlic bread *noun* bread, usu. served hot, spread with butter flavoured with garlic.

garlic mustard *noun* a European plant of the mustard family, *Alliaria officinalis*, with white flowers, naturalized in N America.

garlic powder *noun* pulverized dried garlic used as a seasoning.

garlic salt *noun* garlic powder mixed with salt, used as a seasoning.

gar·ment *noun* **1** an article of clothing. **2** the outward and visible covering of anything. [Old French *garnement* (as GARNISH)]

garment bag *noun* a large zippered bag incorporating a hanger on which garments are hung for travel or storage to prevent wrinkling.

garment district *noun* an area of a city where businesses involved in the garment trade such as fashion houses, clothing factories, etc. are concentrated.

Gar·neau /ɡɑrˈnoː/ **1 François-Xavier** (1809–66), Canadian historian and poet. His monumental three-volume *Histoire du Canada* (1845–8) is written from an essentially secular, liberal, and nationalist viewpoint. **2 Marc** (b.1949), Canadian astronaut. He became the first Canadian in space when he joined a NASA mission in 1984, and then joined further space missions in 1996 and 2000.

Gar·ner, Hugh (1913–79), English-born Canadian novelist and short-story writer. His novels include *Storm Below* (1949), *Cabbagetown* (1950, enlarged 1968), describing working-class life in Toronto in the 1930s, *The Silence on the Shore* (1962), and *Death in Don Mills* (1975).

gar·ner ● *transitive verb* **1** collect. **2** earn, get (*garnered 40 per cent of the vote*; *garnered international attention*). **3** *archaic* store, deposit. ● *noun* *literary* a storehouse or granary. [Old French *gernier* from Latin *granarium* GRANARY]

gar·net ● *noun* **1** a vitreous silicate mineral, esp. a transparent, deep red kind used as a gem. **2** a deep red colour. ● *adjective* of this colour. [Old French *grenat* from medieval Latin *granatum* POMEGRANATE, from its resemblance to the fruit's pulp]

gar·nish ● *transitive verb* **1** decorate or embellish (esp. food). **2** *Law* **a** serve notice on (a person) for the purpose of legally seizing money belonging to a debtor or defendant. **b** summon (a person) as a party to litigation started between others. ● *noun* a decoration or embellishment, esp. to food. [earlier 'to equip or arm': Old French *garnir* from a Germanic verb, possibly related to WARN]

gar·nish·ee *Law* ● *noun* a third party required to surrender money belonging to a debtor or defendant in compliance with a court order obtained by the creditor or plaintiff. ● *transitive verb* (**gar·nish·ees**, **gar·nish·eed**) recover a debt from (a person, his or her wages) by garnishee proceedings.

garnishee order *noun* (also **garnishee proceedings**) a legal order requiring a garnishee to surrender money that he or she holds on behalf of or owes to a debtor.

gar·nish·ment *noun* *Law* a legal notice, esp. one seizing the money owed by a debtor and in the keeping of a third party.

gar·ni·ture /ˈɡɑrnɪtʃər/ *noun* decoration or trimmings. [French (as GARNISH)]

Ga·ronne River /ɡaˈrɒn/ a river of SW France, which rises in the Pyrenees and flows 645 km (400 miles) northwest through Toulouse and Bordeaux to join the Dordogne at the Gironde estuary.

gar·otte *var.* of GARROTTE.

Ga·roua /ɡaˈruːə/ a river port in N Cameroon, on the Bénoué River; pop. (est. 2002) 185,800.

gar·pike *noun* = GAR. [Old English *gār* spear + PIKE[1]]

gar·ret *noun* **1** a top-floor or attic room, esp. a dismal one. **2** an attic. [Old French *garite* watchtower, from Germanic]

Gar·rick, David (1717–79), English actor, manager, and dramatist. Acclaimed for his roles in Shakespearean and contemporary plays, he is also remembered as the manager of the Drury Lane Theatre, London.

gar·ri·son ● *noun* **1** the troops stationed in a fortress, town, etc., to

defend it. **2** the building occupied by them. ● *transitive verb* **1** provide (a place) with or occupy as a garrison. **2** place on garrison duty. [Old French *garison* from *garir* defend, furnish, from Germanic]

gar·rotte /ɡəˈrɒt/ (also **garotte**; *US* **gar·rote**) ● *noun* **1** a wire or cord, esp. one with handles attached at each end, used for strangling a person. **2** a method of execution by strangulation, of Spanish origin, in which an iron or wire collar is tightened around the neck. **3** the apparatus used for this. ● *transitive verb* **1** strangle or throttle by means of a wire, cord, etc. **2** execute by means of a garrotte. [French *garrotter* or Spanish *garrotear* from *garrote* a cudgel, of unknown origin]

gar·ru·lous /ˈɡerʊləs/ *adjective* **1** talkative, esp. on trivial matters. **2** loquacious, wordy. □ **gar·ru·lity** /ɡəˈruːlɪti/ *noun* **gar·ru·lous·ly** *adverb* **gar·ru·lous·ness** *noun* [Latin *garrulus* from *garrire* chatter]

Garry oak *noun* an oak native to the Pacific coast of N America, *Quercus garryana*, with a short trunk and furrowed bark. [N. *Garry*, officer of the Hudson's Bay Co. d.1856]

gar·ter ● *noun* **1 a** a band worn to keep a sock or stocking up. **b** a similar band for keeping a shirt sleeve up. **2** *N Amer.* a suspender for a sock or stocking, attached to a garter belt. **3** (**the Garter**) *Brit.* **a** the highest order of English knighthood. **b** the badge of this. **c** membership of this. ● *transitive verb* fasten (a stocking) or encircle (a leg) with a garter. [Old French *gartier* from *garet* bend of the knee]

garter belt *noun* *N Amer.* an undergarment with suspenders for holding up socks or stockings by the top.

garter snake *noun* any of several harmless viviparous, largely semi-aquatic colubrid snakes of the genus *Thamnophis*, often with more or less distinct lengthwise stripes on the back, widespread in N America.

garter stitch *noun* the simplest plain knitting stitch or pattern, forming ridges in alternate rows.

Ga·ruda /ɡaˈruːdə/ *Hinduism* an eagle-like being that serves as the mount of the god Vishnu.

Gar·vey, Mar·cus (Mo·siah) (1887–1940), Jamaican political activist and black nationalist leader. He led the Back to Africa Movement, which advocated the establishment of an African homeland for black Americans, and was the founder of the Universal Negro Improvement Association (1914).

Gary an industrial city in NW Indiana, on Lake Michigan southeast of Chicago; pop. (2000) 102,746.

gas ● *noun* (*pl.* **gases**) **1** any air-like substance which moves freely to fill any space available, irrespective of its quantity, esp. one that does not become liquid or solid at ordinary temperatures. **2** (often *attributive*) such a substance (esp. found naturally or extracted from coal) used as a domestic or industrial fuel, e.g. natural gas, propane (*gas stove*; *gas barbecue*). **3** *N Amer.* **a** gasoline. **b** the accelerator of an automotive vehicle. **4** an explosive mixture of firedamp with air. **5** nitrous oxide or another gas used as an anaesthetic (esp. in dentistry). **6** a gas or vapour used as a poisonous agent to disable an enemy in warfare. **7** *informal* pointless idle talk; boasting. **8** *slang* an enjoyable, attractive, or amusing thing or person (*the party was a gas*). **9** *N Amer.* intestinal gas. ● *verb* (**gases**, **gassed**, **gas·sing**) **1** *transitive* expose to gas, esp. to kill or make unconscious. **2** *transitive* (usu. foll. by *up*) *N Amer. informal* fill (the tank of a motor vehicle) with gasoline. **3** *intransitive* give off gas. **4** *intransitive informal* talk idly or boastfully. □ **run out of gas** (or **steam**) lose one's impetus or energy. [invented by J. B. van Helmont, Belgian chemist d.1644, after Greek *khaos* chaos]

gas·bag *noun* **1** a container of gas, esp. for holding the gas for a balloon or airship. **2** *slang* an idle talker; a windbag.

gas bar *noun* *Cdn* a gas station, esp. one without a garage, consisting of a kiosk and pumps only.

gas chamber *noun* an airtight chamber that can be filled with poisonous gas to kill people or animals.

gas chromatography *noun* chromatography employing a gas as the moving carrier medium. □ **gas chromatograph** *noun* **gas chromatographic** *adjective*

Gas·con[1] /ɡasˈkɔ̃/ **Jean** (1921–88), Canadian actor and theatre director. A renowned performer in both French and English productions, he was a founder of the National Theatre School in Montreal (1960) and artistic director of the Stratford Festival (1968–74).

Gas·con[2] /ˈɡaskən/ ● *noun* **1** a native of Gascony. **2** the dialect of Gascony. ● *adjective* of or relating to Gascony or its people or dialect. [French from Latin *Vasco -onis*]

Gas·cony /ˈɡaskəni/ a region and former province of SW France, in the northern foothills of the Pyrenees.

gas-cooled *adjective* (of a nuclear reactor etc.) cooled by a current of gas.

gas·eous /ˈɡasɪəs, ˈɡaʃəs/ *adjective* **1** of or like gas. **2** *informal* vague, not definite (*a gaseous speech*).

gas field *noun* an area yielding natural gas.

gas fire *noun Brit.* a small space heater using gas as its fuel.

gas-fired *adjective* using natural gas as the fuel.

gas fireplace *noun* a fireplace burning natural gas, esp. one simulating a wood-burning fireplace.

gas fitter *noun* a person trained to connect, disconnect, and service gas fittings and appliances in buildings.

gas gangrene *noun* a rapidly spreading gangrene of injured tissue infected by a soil bacterium and accompanied by the generation of foul-smelling gas.

gas giant *noun Astronomy* a large planet of relatively low density consisting predominantly of hydrogen and helium, such as Jupiter, Saturn, Uranus, or Neptune.

gas guzzler *noun N Amer.* an esp. large, heavy car which consumes much gas. □ **gas-guzzling** *adjective*

gash ● *noun* **1** a long and deep slash, cut, or wound. **2** a cleft such as might be made by a slashing cut. **3** the act of making such a slash or cut. ● *transitive verb* make a gash in; cut. [var. of Middle English *garse* from Old French *garcer* scarify, perhaps ultimately from Greek *kharassō*]

gas·ify /ˈɡasɪ,faɪ/ *transitive & intransitive verb* (**-fies**, **-fied**) convert or be converted into gas. □ **gasi·fi·ca·tion** *noun* **gasi·fi·er** *noun*

gas jet *noun* a jet of burning gas.

gas jockey *noun N Amer.* a person who pumps gas at a gas station.

Gas·kell /ˈɡaskəl/ **Mrs. Eliza·beth (Cleg·horn)** (1810–65), English novelist. Her works reflect her interest in social concerns, and include *Mary Barton* (1848), *North and South* (1855), and *Wives and Daughters* (1864–66); she is also known for her biography, *The Life of Charlotte Brontë* (1857).

gas·ket *noun* **1** a sheet or ring of rubber etc., shaped to seal the junction of metal surfaces. **2** a small cord securing a furled sail to a yard. □ **blow a gasket** *slang* lose one's temper. □ **gas·ket·ed** *adjective* [perhaps from French *garcette* thin rope (originally little girl)]

gas·kin *noun* the hinder part of a horse's thigh. [perhaps erroneously from GALLIGASKINS]

gas·light *noun* **1** a jet of burning gas, usu. heating a mantle, to provide light. **2** light emanating from this. □ **gas·lit** *adjective*

gas·man *noun* (*pl.* **-men**) a man who installs or services gas appliances, or reads gas meters.

gas mask *noun* a respirator used as a defence against noxious gas.

gas meter *noun* an apparatus recording the amount of natural gas consumed by a household etc.

gas·o·hol *noun* a mixture of gasoline and ethyl alcohol used as fuel. [GAS + ALCOHOL]

gas oil *noun* a type of fuel oil distilled from petroleum and heavier than kerosene.

gas·o·line *noun N Amer.* a volatile inflammable liquid obtained from petroleum and used as fuel in motor vehicles etc. [GAS + -OL² + -INE⁴, -ENE]

gasoline station *noun N Amer.* = GAS STATION.

gas·om·eter /ɡaˈsɒmɪtər/ *noun* a large tank in which gas is stored for distribution by pipes to users. [French *gazomètre* from *gaz* gas + *-mètre* -METER]

gasp ● *verb* **1** *intransitive* catch one's breath with an open mouth as in exhaustion or astonishment. **2** *intransitive* (foll. by *for*) strain to obtain by gasping (*gasped for air*). **3** *transitive* (often foll. by *out*) utter with gasps. ● *noun* a convulsive catching of breath. □ **gasp·ing·ly** *adverb* [Old Norse *geispa*: compare *geip* idle talk]

Gaspé /ɡasˈpeɪ/ a town in E Quebec, at the eastern end of the Gaspé Peninsula; pop. (2001) 14,932. [see GASPÉ, CAP DE]

Gaspé, Cap de the easternmost point of the Gaspé Peninsula, situated in Forillon National Park. [origin uncertain: perhaps from Mi'kmaq root *kesp(i)-/gesp(i)-* end]

gas pedal *noun* the accelerator pedal on a motor vehicle.

Gaspé Peninsula a broad extension of the eastern coast of Quebec, stretching into the Gulf of St. Lawrence. It is formed by the St. Lawrence River to the north and Chaleur Bay to the south. [see GASPÉ, CAP DE]

gasp·er *noun* **1** a person who gasps. **2** *Brit. slang* a cigarette.

gas·per·eau /ˈɡaspərɔ/ *noun* (*pl.* **-eaux**) *Cdn* = ALEWIFE 1. [Canadian French *gaspareau*]

gas-permeable *adjective* (esp. of a contact lens) allowing the diffusion of gases into and out of the cornea.

Gas·pe·sian /ɡasˈpeɪʒən/ *Cdn* ● *noun* a native or resident of the Gaspé Peninsula. ● *adjective* of or pertaining to the Gaspé Peninsula.

gas plant *noun* fraxinella.

gas pump *noun N Amer.* a pump with a hose and nozzle for transferring gasoline from a gas station's reservoir to a motor vehicle etc.

gas ring *noun* a hollow ring perforated with gas jets, used esp. for cooking.

gassed *adjective* **1** in senses of GAS *verb.* **2** *informal* drunk.

Gas·sendi /ɡaˈsendi/ **Pierre** (1592–1655), French astronomer and philosopher. He based his atomic theory of matter on his interpretation of the works of Epicurus; he observed a new comet, a lunar eclipse, and a transit of Mercury (confirming Kepler's theories), and coined the term *aurora borealis*.

Gas·ser, Her·bert Spen·cer (1888–1963), US physiologist. Collaborating with Joseph Erlanger, he showed that the velocity of a nerve impulse is proportional to the diameter of the fibre, and demonstrated the differences between sensory and motor nerves; they shared a Nobel Prize in 1944.

gas·ser *noun* **1** *informal* an idle talker. **2** *slang* a very attractive or impressive person or thing.

gas station *noun N Amer.* an establishment selling gasoline etc. for refuelling motor vehicles, often including a garage.

gassy *adjective* (**gas·si·er**, **gas·si·est**) **1 a** of or like gas. **b** full of gas. **2** *informal* (of talk etc.) pointless, verbose. □ **gas·si·ness** *noun*

Gast·arbeit·er /ˈɡastarbaɪtər/ *noun* (*pl.* **Gast·arbeit·ers** or same) a person with temporary permission to work in another country (esp. in W Europe). [German, from *Gast* GUEST + *Arbeiter* 'worker']

gast·haus /ˈɡasthaus/ *noun* a small inn or hotel in German-speaking countries. [German from *Gast* GUEST + *Haus* HOUSE]

gas-tight *adjective* not allowing the leakage of gas.

Gas·town one of several former communities around which the city of Vancouver eventually grew. Gastown is today a restored heritage area within Vancouver's east end. [John 'Gassy Jack' Deighton, hotelier and saloon keeper *c.*1867]

gas·trec·tomy /ɡaˈstrektəmi/ *noun* (*pl.* **-mies**) a surgical operation in which the whole or part of the stomach is removed.

gas·tric *adjective* of the stomach. [modern Latin *gastricus* from Greek *gastēr gast(e)ros* stomach]

gastric acid *noun* **1** acid secreted by the stomach as a component of gastric juice. **2** gastric juice considered with respect to its acidic properties.

gastric juice *noun* a thin clear virtually colourless acid fluid secreted by the stomach glands and active in promoting digestion.

gas·trin *noun* a polypeptide hormone, secreted by the stomach in response to the presence of food, which stimulates the secretion of gastric juice. [GASTRIC + -IN]

gas·tri·tis /ɡaˈstraɪtɪs/ *noun* inflammation of the lining of the stomach.

gastro- /ˈɡastrɔ/ *combining form* (also **gastr-** before a vowel) stomach. [Greek *gastēr gast(e)ros* stomach]

gastro·enter·itis /ˌɡastrɔˌentəˈraɪtɪs/ *noun Med.* inflammation of the stomach and intestines.

gastro·enter·ol·ogy /ˌɡastrɔˌentəˈrɒlədʒi/ *noun* the branch of medicine which deals with disorders of the stomach and intestines. □ **gastro·enter·o·logic·al** *adjective* **gastro·enter·ol·o·gist** *noun*

gastro·intes·tin·al /ˌɡastrɔɪnˈtestɪnəl, -ɪntesˈtaɪnəl/ *adjective* of or relating to the stomach and the intestines.

gas·tro·lith /ˈɡastrɔlɪθ/ *noun* **1** *Zool.* a small stone swallowed by a bird, reptile, or fish, to aid digestion in the gizzard. **2** *Med.* a hard concretion in the stomach. [GASTRO- + -LITH]

gas·tro·nome /ˈɡastrə,nɔːm/ *noun* a gourmet. [French from *gastronomie* GASTRONOMY]

gas·tron·omy /ɡaˈstrɒnəmi/ *noun* **1** the practice, study, or art of eating and drinking well. **2** = CUISINE. □ **gas·tro·nom·ic** /ˌɡastrəˈnɒmɪk/ *adjective* **gas·tro·nom·ic·al** *adjective* **gas·tro·nom·ic·al·ly** *adverb* [French *gastronomie* from Greek *gastronomia* (as GASTRO-, -nomia from *nomos* law)]

gas·tro·pod /ˈɡastrə,pɒd/ *noun* any mollusc of the class Gastropoda that moves along by means of a large muscular foot, e.g. a snail, slug, etc. □ **gas·tro·po·dous** /gaˈstrɒpədəs/ *adjective* [French *gastéropode* from modern Latin *gasteropoda* (as GASTRO-, Greek *pous podos* foot)]

gas·tro·scope /ˈɡastrəˌskoːp/ *noun* an optical instrument used for inspecting the interior of the stomach. □ **gas·tro·scop·ic** /-ˈskɒpɪk/ *adjective*

gas·trula /ˈɡastrʊlə/ *noun* (*pl.* **gas·tru·lae** /-ˌliː/) *Biol.* an embryonic stage developing from the blastula. [modern Latin from Greek *gastēr gast(e)ros* belly]

gas·tru·la·tion /ˌɡastrʊˈleɪʃən/ *noun Biol.* the process of formation of a gastrula from a blastula.

gas turbine *noun* a turbine driven by a flow of gas or by gas from combustion.

gas·works *noun* (usu. treated as *sing.*) a place where gas for heating and lighting is manufactured and processed.

gat[1] *noun slang* a revolver or other firearm. [abbreviation of GATLING]

gat[2] *archaic past of* GET *verb.*

gatch (also **gach**; **gauch**) *Cdn (Nfld)* ● *intransitive verb* behave boastfully or pompously; show off. ● *noun* **1** boastful or pompous behaviour. **2** a person displaying such behaviour. □ **gatch·er** *noun* [origin unknown]

gate[1] ● *noun* **1** a barrier, usu. hinged, used to close an opening made for entrance and exit through a wall, fence, etc. **2 a** such an opening, esp. in the wall of a city, enclosure, or large building. **b** a monument resembling a gate or gateway, esp. adorning the entrance to a park etc. **3** a means of entrance or exit. **4** a numbered place of access to aircraft at an airport or trains at a train station. **5** a mountain pass. **6** an arrangement of slots into which the gear lever of a motor vehicle moves to engage the required gear. **7** a device for holding the frame of a motion picture film momentarily in position behind the lens of a camera or projector. **8 a** an electrical signal that causes or controls the passage of other signals. **b** an electrical circuit with an output which depends on the combination of several inputs. **9** a device regulating the passage of water in a lock etc. **10 a** the number of people entering by payment at the gates of a sporting event etc. **b** (in full **gate money**) the proceeds taken for admission. **11** *N Amer. slang* dismissal. **12** = STARTING GATE. **13** a barrier at a level crossing or at a toll booth. **14** *Skiing* an arrangement of two flexible poles implanted in the snow of a slalom course between which a skier must pass. ● *transitive verb* **1** *Electricity* subject (a signal) to the action of a gate. **2** *esp. Brit.* confine to college or school entirely or after certain hours as a punishment. **3** *Cdn* retain (an inmate, esp. a dangerous offender) in prison for the full length of a sentence, by arresting the inmate as soon as he or she is released under mandatory supervision. □ **get** (or **be given**) **the gate** *N Amer. slang* be dismissed. [Old English *gæt, geat,* pl. *gatu,* from Germanic]

gate[2] *noun* **1** (prec. or prefixed by a name) a street (*Westgate*). **2** *Cdn (PEI)* a lane or driveway. [Old Norse *gata,* from Germanic]

-gate *combining form* forming nouns denoting an actual or alleged scandal (and usu. an attempted cover-up) (*Shawinigate*). [after *Watergate*, from the 1972 US political scandal]

ga·teau /ɡaˈtoː/ *noun* (*pl.* **ga·teaus** or **ga·teaux** /-oːz/) *esp. Brit.* any of various rich layer cakes, usu. containing cream or fruit. [French *gâteau* cake]

gate·crash·er *noun* an uninvited guest at a party etc. □ **gate·crash** *transitive & intransitive verb*

gated *adjective* **1** (of a road, fence, enclosed area, etc.) having a gate or gates to control the movement of traffic or animals. **2** (of a subdivision, community, etc.) enclosed by walls or fences with access controlled by security guards.

gate·fold *noun* = FOLD-OUT.

gate·house *noun* **1** a house standing by a gateway, esp. to a large house or park. **2** *hist.* a room over a city gate, often used as a jail.

gate·keep·er *noun* **1** an attendant at a gate, controlling entrance and exit. **2** a thing or person that controls access to or availability of resources, information, etc.

gate·leg *noun* (in full **gateleg table**) a table with folding flaps supported by legs swung open like a gate. □ **gate·legged** *adjective*

gate·man *noun* (*pl.* **-men**) = GATEKEEPER 1.

gate money (also **gate receipts**) *see* GATE[1] *noun* 10b.

gate·post *noun* a post on which a gate is hung or against which it shuts. □ **between you and me and the gatepost** *informal* in strict confidence.

Gates ▸ 1 Hor·atio (1728–1826), English-born US general, who is noted for his defeat of the British at Saratoga (1777) during the American Revolution. **2 Wil·liam (Henry) ('Bill')** (b.1955), US computer entrepreneur. The co-founder of Microsoft (1975), a leading multinational computer company, he became the youngest multi-billionaire in US history by the late 1980s.

Gates·head an industrial town in NE England, on the south bank of the Tyne River opposite Newcastle; pop. (est. 2002) 81,000.

gate valve *noun* a valve in which a sliding part controls the extent of the aperture.

gate·way *noun* **1** an entrance with or opening for a gate. **2** a frame or structure built over a gate. **3** a means of access or entry (*gateway to the Prairies; gateway to success*). **4** *Computing* a device or software used to connect two different networks.

gateway drug *noun* a drug such as alcohol, tobacco, or marijuana, the use of which is perceived as making subsequent use of harder drugs more likely.

Gateway to the North an informal name for Edmonton. [because of its status as a transportation hub]

gath·er ● *verb* **1** *transitive & intransitive* bring or come together; assemble, accumulate. **2** *transitive* (usu. foll. by *up*) **a** bring together from scattered places or sources. **b** take up together from the ground, a surface, etc. **c** draw together or into a smaller compass (*gathered her scarf around her*). **d** take (a person) into one's embrace (*gathered him into her arms*). **3** *transitive* acquire by gradually collecting; amass. **4** *transitive* **a** pick a quantity (of flowers etc.). **b** collect (grain etc.) as a harvest. **5** *transitive* (often foll. by *that* + clause) infer or understand. **6** *transitive* be subjected to or affected by the accumulation or increase of (*unread books gathering dust; gather speed; gather strength*). **7** *transitive* (often foll. by *up*) summon up (one's thoughts, energy, etc.) for a purpose. **8** *transitive* gain or recover (one's breath). **9** *transitive* **a** draw (material) together in folds or wrinkles. **b** pucker or draw together (part of a dress) by running a thread through. **10** *intransitive* come to a head; develop a purulent swelling. **11** *transitive* collect and put in order (the leaves or sheets of a book). ● *noun* **1** an act or instance of gathering. **2** (in *pl.*) a part of a garment that is gathered or drawn in. □ **gather way** (of a ship) begin to move. □ **gath·er·er** *noun* [Old English *gaderian* from West Germanic]

gath·er·ing ● *noun* **1** an assembly or meeting. **2** a purulent swelling. **3** a group of leaves taken together in bookbinding. **4** the gathers formed by drawing up a fabric. ● *adjective* increasing in intensity etc. (*the gathering storm*).

Gati·neau /ˈɡatənˌoː, ɡatiːˈnoː/ a city in SW Quebec, situated at the junction of the Ottawa and Gatineau rivers; pop. (2001) 102,898. [see GATINEAU RIVER]

Gatineau River a river in SW central Quebec, rising south of Réservoir Gouin and flowing over 380 km southward to join the Ottawa River at Gatineau. [N. *Gatineau dit Duplessis,* 17th-c. fur trader]

Gat·ling *noun* (in full **Gatling gun**) a machine gun with clustered barrels. [R. J. *Gatling,* US inventor d.1903]

ga·tor *noun* (also **'gator**) *esp. N Amer. informal* an alligator. [abbreviation]

Gatsby·esque *adjective* resembling F. Scott Fitzgerald's novel *The Great Gatsby,* esp. in its depiction of the 1920s and of lavish wealth, glamour, and parties, or of its title character's ultimate discovery that his life is hollow.

GATT /ɡat/ *abbreviation* General Agreement on Tariffs and Trade.

Gat·wick an international airport in SE England, to the south of London.

gauche /ɡoːʃ/ *adjective* **1** lacking ease or grace; socially awkward. **2** tactless. □ **gauche·ly** *adverb* **gauche·ness** *noun* [French, = left-handed, awkward]

gauche·rie /ˌɡoːʃəˈriː, ˈɡoːʃəˌriː/ *noun* **1** gauche manners. **2** a gauche action. [French]

gau·cho /ˈɡaʊtʃoː/ *noun* (*pl.* **-chos**) **1** a cowboy from the S American pampas. **2** *N Amer.* (in *pl.*) (in full **gaucho pants**) wide, calf-length pants, similar to ones worn by gauchos. [Spanish from Quechua]

gaud /ɡɒd/ *noun* a gaudy thing; a showy ornament. [perhaps through Anglo-French from Old French *gaudir* rejoice, from Latin *gaudēre*]

Gau·daur /ɡəˈdar/ **Jacob Gill, Jr. ('Jake')** (b.1920), Canadian football player and commissioner. He played for the Hamilton Tigers (1948–50) and the Hamilton Tiger-Cats (1950–4); he also served as president and general manager of the Tiger-Cats (1954–68) and as a CFL commissioner (1968–84).

Gaudí /ɡauˈdiː/ **An·tonio** (full surname Gaudí y Cornet) (1852–1926), Spanish architect. His idiosyncratic art nouveau buildings, chiefly in Barcelona, are notable for their ceramics, wrought-iron work, flowing lines, and organic forms; his most ambitious project, the church of the Sagrada Familia, was begun in 1884.

gaudy[1] *adjective* (**gaud·i·er**, **gaud·i·est**) tastelessly or extravagantly bright or showy. □ **gaud·i·ly** *adverb* **gaud·i·ness** *noun* [prob. from GAUD + -Y[1]]

gaudy[2] *noun* (*pl.* **-ies**) *Brit.* an annual feast or entertainment, esp. a college dinner for old members etc. [Latin *gaudium* joy or *gaude* imperative of *gaudēre* rejoice]

gauge /geidʒ/ (*US* **gage**: see also sense 7) ● *noun* **1** a standard measure to which certain things must conform, esp.: **a** the measure of the inner diameter of an esp. shotgun barrel, representing the number of lead balls of that diameter required to make one pound. **b** the fineness of a textile. **c** the thickness of sheet metal, wire, or other usu. thin materials or objects. **2** any of various instruments for measuring or determining this, or for measuring length, thickness, or other dimensions or properties. **3** the distance between a pair of rails or the wheels on one axle. **4** the capacity, extent, or scope of something. **5** a means of estimating; a criterion or test. **6** a graduated instrument measuring the force or quantity of rainfall, pressure, fuel, wind, etc. **7** (usu. **gage**) *Naut.* a relative position with respect to the wind. ● *transitive verb* **1** measure exactly (esp. objects of standard size). **2** determine the capacity of. **3** estimate or form a judgment of (a person, temperament, situation, etc.). **4** make uniform; bring to a standard size or shape. □ **gauge·able** *adjective* [Old Northern French *gauge, gauger,* of unknown origin]

gauge pressure *noun* the amount by which the pressure measured in a fluid exceeds that of the atmosphere.

gauge theory *noun* *Physics* a form of quantum theory using mathematical functions to describe subatomic interactions in terms of particles not directly detectable.

Gau·guin /ɡoːˈɡã/ (**Eu·gène Henri) Paul** (1848–1903), French painter. His post-Impressionist painting was influenced by primitive art, using colour in flat contrasting areas to achieve decorative or emotional effects; many of his paintings depict the people of the South Sea Islands, esp. Tahiti.

Gau·hati /ɡauˈhɒti/ an industrial city in NE India, in Assam, a river port on the Brahmaputra; pop. (2001) 808,000.

Gaul[1] an ancient region of Europe, corresponding to modern France, Belgium, the south Netherlands, SW Germany, and N Italy. The area was settled by groups of Celts, who had begun migration across the Rhine in 900 BC, spreading further south beyond the Alps from 400 BC. The area south of the Alps was conquered in 222 BC by the Romans, who called it **Cisalpine Gaul**. The area north of the Alps, known to the Romans as **Transalpine Gaul**, was taken by Julius Caesar between 58 and 51 BC. Within Transalpine Gaul the southern province became known as **Gallia Narbonensis**.

Gaul[2] *noun* a native or inhabitant of ancient Gaul. [GAUL[1]; from French *Gaule* from Germanic = foreigners]

gau·leiter /ˈɡau͜ˌlaɪtɜr/ *noun* **1** an official governing a district under Nazi rule. **2** a local or petty tyrant. [German from *Gau* administrative district + *Leiter* leader]

Gaul·ish ● *adjective* of or relating to the ancient Gauls. ● *noun* their language.

Gaulle see DE GAULLE.

Gaull·ism /ˈɡoːlɪzəm/ *noun* **1** the principles and policies of Charles de Gaulle, characterized by their conservatism, nationalism, and advocacy of centralized government with strong executive authority vested in the French Presidency. **2** adherence to these. □ **Gaull·ist** *noun* [French *Gaullisme*]

gaunch *noun* *Cdn* (esp. *BC & Alta.*) *slang* underwear. [alteration of GOTCH]

Gaunt /ɡɒnt/ a former name for GHENT.

gaunt *adjective* **1** lean, haggard. **2** grim or desolate in appearance. □ **gaunt·ly** *adverb* **gaunt·ness** *noun* [Middle English: origin unknown]

gaunt·let[1] *noun* **1** a sturdy glove long enough to cover the wrist and part of the forearm. **2** *hist.* an armoured glove. **3** the part of a glove covering the wrist. □ **take** (or **pick) up the gauntlet** *see* TAKE. **throw down the gauntlet** *see* THROW. □ **gaunt·let·ed** *adjective* [Old French *gantelet* diminutive of *gant* glove, from Germanic]

gaunt·let[2] *noun* (*US* also **gant·let**) **1** a former esp. military punishment in which the offender was required to pass between two rows of people and receive blows from them. **2** the rows of people inflicting this punishment. **3** an ordeal or series of ordeals (*the gauntlet of entrance exams*). □ **run the gauntlet 1** be subjected to harsh criticism. **2** pass between the two rows of a gauntlet as a punishment. [earlier *gantlope* from Swedish *gatlopp* from *gata* lane, *lopp* course, assimilated to GAUNTLET[1]]

gaur /ˈɡaʊr/ *noun* a large wild ox, *Bos gaurus,* found in forests from India to Malaysia. [Hindustani]

Gauss /ɡaus/ **Karl Frie·drich** (1777–1855), German mathematician, astronomer, and physicist. He laid the foundations of number theory, contributed to many areas of mathematics, and applied rigorous mathematical analysis to such subjects as geometry, geodesy, electrostatics, and electromagnetism.

gauss /ɡaus/ *noun* (*pl.* same or **gausses**) a unit of magnetic induction, equal to one ten-thousandth of a tesla. Abbr.: **G**. [GAUSS]

Gauss·ian distribution /ˈɡaʊsiən/ *noun* *Statistics* = NORMAL DISTRIBUTION. [as GAUSS]

Gau·tama /ˈɡaʊtəmə/ the family name of the Buddha. [Sanskrit]

Gau·teng /xauˈteŋ/ a province of northeastern South Africa, formerly called Pretoria-Witwatersrand-Vereeniging; capital, Johannesburg.

Gau·tier /ɡoːˈtjei/ **Thé·o·phile** (1811–72), French poet, novelist, critic, and journalist, who played a prominent role in the romantic movement of the 1830s, and was closely associated with the doctrine of 'art for art's sake', expounded in the preface to his novel *Mademoiselle de Maupin* (1835).

gauze *noun* **1** a thin transparent fabric of silk, cotton, etc. **2** *Med.* thin loosely woven material used for dressings and swabs. **3** a fine mesh of wire etc. **4** a slight haze. [French *gaze* from *Gaza* in Palestine]

gauzy *adjective* (**gauz·i·er, gauz·i·est**) **1** like gauze; thin and translucent. **2** flimsy, delicate. □ **gauz·i·ly** *adverb* **gauz·i·ness** *noun*

gave past of GIVE.

gavel /ˈɡavəl/ ● *noun* a small hammer used by an auctioneer, or for calling a meeting to order. ● *verb* (**gav·elled, gavel·ling**; *US* **gav·eled, gavel·ing**) **1** *intransitive* use a gavel. **2** *transitive* call to order or end (a meeting) or dismiss (a speaker) by use of a gavel. [19th c.: origin unknown]

gavi·al *var.* of GHARIAL.

ga·votte /ɡəˈvɒt/ *noun* **1** a medium-paced French dance popular in the 18th c. **2 a** a piece of music for this, composed in common time beginning on the third beat of the bar. **b** a piece of music in this rhythm as a movement in a suite. [French from Provençal *gavoto* from *Gavot* native of a region in the Alps]

Gawd *interjection* *slang* God (see GOD 5). [alteration of GOD]

gawk ● *intransitive verb* *informal* stare stupidly. ● *noun* an awkward or bashful person. □ **gawk·er** *noun* **gawk·ish** *adjective* [related to obsolete *gaw* gaze, from Old Norse *gá* heed]

gawky *adjective* (**gawk·i·er, gawk·i·est**) awkward or ungainly. □ **gawk·i·ly** *adverb* **gawk·i·ness** *noun*

gaw·moge /ɡaˈmoːɡ/ *noun* *Cdn* (*Nfld*) **1** a clownish, mischievous person. **2** (usu. in *pl.*) clownish or mischievous behaviour (*look at the gawmoges of them*). [Irish *gamóg* a clown or simpleton]

gawp *intransitive verb* *informal* stare stupidly or obtrusively; gape. □ **gawp·er** *noun* [earlier *gaup, galp* from Middle English *galpen* yawn, related to YELP]

Gay, John (1685–1732), English poet and dramatist. He is now chiefly known for *The Beggar's Opera* (1728), a ballad opera combining burlesque and political satire.

gay ● *adjective* **1 a** homosexual. **b** of or pertaining to homosexuals (*a gay bar*). ¶ The use of *gay* to mean 'homosexual' is favoured by homosexuals, and is now well established and in widespread general use. In many instances it is restricted in application to male homosexuals and contrasted with *lesbian* when discussing homosexuals as a group. **2** *dated* **a** lighthearted and carefree; mirthful. **b** characterized by cheerfulness or pleasure (*a gay life*). **c** brightly coloured; showy, brilliant (*a gay scarf*). ● *noun* a homosexual, esp. male. □ **gay·ness** *noun* [Old French *gai*, of unknown origin]

Gaya /ˈɡɒjə/ a city in NE India, in the state of Bihar south of Patna; pop. (2001) 383,200. It is a place of Hindu pilgrimage.

ga·yal /ɡəˈjal/ *noun* a semi-domesticated ox, *Bos frontalis,* of India and SE Asia, which is black or brown with white legs, and possibly a variety of the gaur. [Hindi]

gay bashing *noun* esp. *N Amer. informal* **1** unprovoked verbal and esp. physical attacking of a homosexual or homosexuals. **2** an instance of this. □ **gay-bash** *transitive & intransitive verb* **gay-basher** *noun*

gay·dar *noun* *informal* an ability to discern that someone is gay by interpreting subtle signals conveyed by appearance, manner, interests, etc. [blend of GAY + RADAR]

gay·feather *noun* any of various plants of the genus *Liatris,* native to the prairies and eastern N America, with showy flowers in a long spike.

Gay-Lussac /ˈɡeɪluˈsak/ **Jo·seph Louis** (1778–1850), French chemist and physicist. Best known for his work on gases, he formulated the law usually known by his name (1808), that gases which combine chemically do so in volumes which are in a simple ratio to each other.

gay pride *noun* a sense of strong self-esteem associated with a person's public acknowledgement of their homosexuality.

gay·wings *noun* a low-growing evergreen plant of eastern N America, *Polygala paucifolia*, with two pink wing-like petals.

Gaza /ˈgazə, ˈgɒzə/ the acting administrative centre for the Gaza Strip; pop. (est. 1999) 388,031.

gaz·ania /gəˈzeɪnɪə/ *noun* any herbaceous plant of the genus *Gazania*, with showy yellow or orange daisy-shaped flowers. [18th c.: from Theodore of *Gaza*, Greek scholar d.1478]

Gaza Strip /ˈgazə/ a strip of territory in Palestine, on the SE Mediterranean coast, including the town of Gaza; pop. (2001) 1,178,119. Administered by Egypt from 1949, and occupied by Israel from 1967, it became a self-governing enclave under the PLO-Israeli accord of 1994 and elected its own legislative council in 1996. □ **Gazan** *noun*

gaze ● *intransitive verb* (foll. by *at, into, on, upon*, etc.) look fixedly. ● *noun* **1** a fixed or intent look. **2** *Cdn* (*Nfld*) a wall etc. for concealing a hunter; a blind. **3** *Cdn* (*Nfld*) a crest or point commanding a view of the sea or a harbour. □ **gaz·er** *noun* [Middle English: origin unknown; compare obsolete *gaw* GAWK]

gaz·ebo /gəˈziːbəʊ/ *noun* (*pl.* **-ebos** or **-eboes**) a small structure in a garden, park etc., usu. open or with screens on all sides to give a wide view. [perhaps jocular from GAZE, in imitation of Latin future tenses ending in *-ebo*: compare LAVABO]

gaz·elle /gəˈzel/ *noun* **1** any of various small graceful soft-eyed antelopes of Asia or Africa, esp. of the genus *Gazella*. **2** a small company which is expanding rapidly and consistently. [French prob. from Spanish *gacela* from Arabic *ġazāl*; sense 2 in reference to the company growing 'in leaps and bounds']

gaz·ette /gəˈzet/ ● *noun* **1** a newspaper (used esp. in names). **2** *hist.* a periodical publication giving current events. **3** (in Canada, the UK, and other Commonwealth countries) an official journal with a list of government appointments, bankruptcies, and other public notices. ● *transitive verb* (in Canada, the UK, and other Commonwealth countries) announce or publish in an official gazette. [earliest in sense 2: French from Italian *gazzetta*, originally Venetian *gazeta de la novita* 'a halfpennyworth of news' because sold for a *gazeta*, a Venetian small coin]

gaz·et·teer /ˌgazəˈtɪər/ *noun* a geographical index or dictionary. [earlier = journalist, for whom such an index was provided: from French *gazettier* from Italian *gazzettiere* (as GAZETTE)]

Gaz·ian·tep /ˌgazɪənˈtep/ a city in S Turkey, near the border with Syria; pop. (est. 2002) 795,300. Until 1921 it was called Aintab.

ga·zil·lion /gəˈzɪljən/ *noun N Amer. informal* **1** an exaggeratedly large number (*selling gazillions of dictionaries*). **2** (in *pl.*) an exaggeratedly large amount of money (*has made gazillions in real estate*). □ **ga·zil·lion·aire** *noun* [after BILLION, MILLION, etc.]

gaz·pa·cho /gəˈspatʃəʊ/ *noun* (*pl.* **-chos**) a Spanish soup made from tomatoes, peppers, cucumbers, garlic, etc., and served cold. [Spanish]

gaz·ump /gəˈzʌmp/ *transitive & intransitive verb Brit. informal* **1** (of a seller) raise the price of a property after having accepted an offer by (an intending buyer). **2** swindle. □ **gaz·ump·er** *noun* [20th c.: origin uncertain]

gaz·un·der /gəˈzʌndər/ *transitive & intransitive verb Brit. informal* (of a buyer) lower the amount of an offer made to (the seller) for a property, esp. just before exchange of contracts. [GAZUMP + UNDER]

GB *abbreviation* Great Britain.

GBE *abbreviation* (in the UK) Knight (or Dame) Grand Cross (of the Order) of the British Empire.

GBH *abbreviation Brit.* grievous bodily harm.

Gbyte *abbreviation* gigabyte.

GC *abbreviation* (in the UK) George Cross.

GCB *abbreviation* (in the UK) Knight (or Dame) Grand Cross (of the Order) of the Bath.

GCE *abbreviation* (in England, Wales, and Northern Ireland) GENERAL CERTIFICATE OF EDUCATION.

GCHQ *abbreviation* (in the UK) Government Communications Headquarters.

GCMG *abbreviation* (in the UK) Knight (or Dame) Grand Cross (of the Order) of St. Michael & St. George.

GCSE *abbreviation* (in England, Wales, and Northern Ireland) GENERAL CERTIFICATE OF SECONDARY EDUCATION.

Gd *symbol Chem.* the element gadolinium.

g.d. *abbreviation N Amer.* goddamn.

Gdańsk /gdansk/ (German **Danzig** /ˈdantsɪk/) an industrial port and shipbuilding centre in N Poland, on an inlet of the Baltic Sea; pop. (est. 2000) 456,574. It was a free city under a League of Nations mandate from 1910 until 1939, when it was annexed by Nazi Germany, precipitating hostilities with Poland and the outbreak of the Second World War. It passed to Poland in 1945. In the 1980s the Gdańsk shipyards were the site of the activities of the Solidarity movement, which eventually led to the collapse of the Communist regime in Poland in 1989.

Gdn *abbreviation* Garden.

Gdns *abbreviation* Gardens.

GDP *abbreviation* GROSS DOMESTIC PRODUCT.

GDR *abbreviation hist.* German Democratic Republic.

Gdynia /ˈgdɪnjə/ a port and naval base in N Poland, on the Baltic Sea northwest of Gdańsk; pop. (est. 2000) 255,549.

GE *abbreviation* **1** genetic engineering. **2** genetically engineered.

Ge¹ /geɪ/ *Gk Myth* = GAIA. [Greek, = earth]

Ge² *symbol Chem.* the element germanium.

gean /giːn/ *noun* **1** the wild sweet cherry, *Prunus avium*. **2** the fruit of this. [Old French *guine* (modern *guigne*)]

gear ● *noun* **1** (often in *pl.*) **a** a set of toothed wheels that work together to receive and transmit force and motion. **b** a mechanism using gears to transmit and control motion, esp. to the road wheels of a vehicle. **2** a particular state of adjustment of engaged gears (*low gear; second gear*). **3** a state of speed or activity (*the campaign moved into top gear*). **4** a mechanism of wheels, levers, etc., usu. for a special purpose (*winding gear*). **5** (in full **landing gear**) the undercarriage of an aircraft (*flew around with its gear down*). **6** equipment or tackle for a special purpose (*fishing gear*). **7** *informal* clothing, equipment, and accessories, especially for a specified purpose or of a specified type (*police in riot gear*). **8** an indeterminate quantity of belongings and objects, esp. if perceived as burdensome (*clear all of your old gear out of the attic*). **9** rigging. **10** a harness for a horse or draft animal. ● *verb* **1** *transitive* (usu. in *passive*; foll. by *to, towards*) adjust or adapt to suit a specified purpose, need, or recipient. **2** *transitive* (often foll. by *up*) equip with gears. **3** (usu. foll. by *up*) **a** *transitive* make ready or prepared. **b** *intransitive* prepare, get ready. **4** *transitive* put (machinery) in gear. **5** *intransitive* be in or come into gear. □ **be geared** (or **all geared**) **up** (often foll. by *for*, or *to* + infin.) *informal* be ready or enthusiastic. **gear down** engage a lower gear in a vehicle. **gear up 1** (of groups of people, cities, corporate bodies, etc.) prepare or equip, esp. over a period of time in anticipation of some intense activity. **2** speed up or intensify (*gear up production*). **3** engage a higher gear in a vehicle. **gear oneself up** provide oneself with progressively more supplies, courage, etc. in order to face a daunting prospect. **get one's ass** (or **butt**) **in gear** *slang* get moving. **give a person the gears** *Cdn* pester, hassle. **in gear 1** with a gear engaged. **2** operating properly or efficiently. **in high gear** *N Amer.* operating at maximum efficiency. **out of gear 1** with no gear engaged. **2** out of order. **shift** (or **change** etc.) **gears** change one's pace, direction, strategy, etc., esp. in progress. [Old Norse *gervi* from Germanic]

gear·box *noun* **1** the casing that encloses a set of gears. **2** a set of gears with its casing, esp. in a motor vehicle; transmission.

gear·head *noun* a person who is an expert in or enthusiastic about technical equipment.

gear·ing *noun* **1** a set or arrangement of gears in a machine. **2** *Brit. Business* the ratio of a company's loan capital (debt) to the value of its common shares (equity).

gear ratio *noun* (in a gearbox, transmission, etc.) the ratio between the rates at which the last and the first gears rotate.

gear·shift *noun* (also esp. *Brit.* **gear lever**) a lever used to engage or change gear, esp. in a motor vehicle.

gear·wheel *noun* a toothed wheel in a set of gears.

Geber /ˈdʒiːbər/ (Latinized name of Jabir ibn Hayyan, *c.*721–*c.*815), Arab chemist, attached to the court of Harūn ar-Rashīd. He was familiar with many chemicals and techniques, including distillation and sublimation, and many works are attributed to him.

gecko /ˈgekəʊ/ *noun* (*pl.* **geckos** or **geckoes**) any of various house lizards found in warm climates, with adhesive feet for climbing vertical surfaces. [Malay *chichak* etc., imitative of its cry]

GED *abbreviation N Amer.* General Educational Development, designating a certificate attesting that the holder has passed examinations considered by the Department of Education as equivalent to completion of high school.

gee¹ *interjection* N Amer. informal a mild expression of surprise, discovery, dismay, etc. [perhaps abbreviation of JESUS²]

gee² /dʒiː/ *interjection* **1** (often foll. by *up*) a command to a horse, dog team, etc., to go faster. **2** a similar command to turn to the right. [17th c.: origin unknown]

gee³ *noun* US slang (usu. in *pl.*) a thousand dollars. [the letter *G*, as initial of GRAND]

gee·gaw /'dʒiːɡɒ, 'ɡiː-/ *noun* var. of GEWGAW.

gee-gee /'dʒiːdʒiː/ *noun* esp. Brit. informal a horse. [originally a child's word, from GEE²]

geek *noun* esp. N Amer. informal **1** an uninteresting, ineffectual, socially inept person; a nerd. **2** a person thoroughly devoted to one usu. technical interest, study, etc., often at the expense of social interaction (*computer geek*). □ **geek·dom** *noun* **geek·i·ness** *noun* **geek·ish** *adjective* **geeky** *adjective* [from the English dialect *geck* fool]

geek chic *noun* informal a fashion style incorporating characteristics traditionally associated with computer geeks, e.g. heavy-rimmed glasses.

geek·speak *noun* computer jargon.

geese pl. of GOOSE.

gee whiz esp. N Amer. informal ● *interjection* = GEE¹. ● *attributive adjective* (usu. as **gee-whiz**) characterized by (often naive) astonishment or wonder, usu. at new technologies (*gee-whiz journalism*).

geez *interjection* N Amer. expressing annoyance, frustration, etc. [euphemism for JESUS²]

gee·zer *noun* slang a person, esp. an old man. [dial. pronunciation of *guiser* mummer]

ge·filte fish /ɡə'fɪltə/ *noun* a ball or small cake of chopped fish mixed with matzo meal, egg, and seasoning, and simmered in fish stock, usu. served cold. [Yiddish *gefilte* filled]

Ge·hen·na /ɡɪ'hɛnə/ *noun* (in Judaism and the New Testament) a name for hell as a place of fiery torment for the wicked. [ecclesiastical Latin from Greek from Hebrew *gēʾ hinnōm* hell, originally the valley of Hinnom near Jerusalem, where children were sacrificed]

Geh·rig /'ɡɛrɪɡ/ **Henry Louis ('Lou')** (1903–41), US baseball player. He was known as the 'Iron Horse', and his record for 2,130 consecutive major-league games for the New York Yankees (1925 to 1939) remained unbroken until 1995; he died from amyotrophic lateral sclerosis, now also known as Lou Gehrig's disease.

Gehry /'ɡɛri/ **Frank (Owen)** (b.1929), Canadian-born American architect. His buildings include the titanium-clad Guggenheim Museum in Bilbao (1997).

Geiger /'ɡaɪɡər/ **Hans (Jo·hann) Wil·helm** (1882–1945), German nuclear physicist. In 1908 he developed his prototype radiation counter for detecting alpha particles, later improving the sensitivity of his device with Walther Müller.

Geiger counter /'ɡaɪɡər/ *noun* a device for measuring radioactivity by detecting and counting ionizing particles. [GEIGER]

Geikie /'ɡiːki/ **Sir Archi·bald** (1835–1924), Scottish geologist. A leading figure in British geology, he specialized in Pleistocene geology, esp. the geomorphological effects of glaciations and the resulting deposits.

Geisel /'ɡaɪzəl/ **Theo·dor Seuss**, see SEUSS.

gei·sha /'ɡeɪʃə/ *noun* (*pl.* same or **geishas**) **1** a Japanese hostess trained in entertaining men with dance and song. **2** a Japanese prostitute. [Japanese]

Gejiu /ɡe'dʒuː/ (also **Geju**) a tin-mining city in S China, near the border with Vietnam; pop. (est. 2002) 163,600.

gel ● *noun* **1** a semi-solid colloidal suspension or jelly, of a solid dispersed in a liquid. **2** a jellylike substance used for setting hair. **3** a coloured transparent sheet of gelatin placed in front of a light source to change the colour of theatrical lighting. ● *verb* (**gelled, gel·ling**) **1** *intransitive* = JELL. **2** *transitive* apply gel to (hair etc.). [abbreviation of GELATIN]

gel·ada /dʒə'lɑːdə/ *noun* (*pl.* same or **gel·adas**) a brownish gregarious baboon, *Theropithecus gelada*, with a bare red patch on its chest, native to Ethiopia. [Amharic *čʾällada*]

gel·atin /'dʒɛlətɪn/ *noun* (also **gel·atine**) **1** a virtually colourless tasteless transparent water-soluble protein derived from collagen and obtained by prolonged boiling of animal skin, tendons, ligaments, etc., used in food preparation, photography, glue, etc. **2** any similar colloidal substance. □ **gel·atin·ize** /dʒɪ'lætɪˌnaɪz/ *transitive & intransitive*

verb (also esp. Brit. **-ise**). **gel·atin·iz·a·tion** /dʒɪˌlætɪnaɪ'zeɪʃən/ *noun* [French *gélatine* from Italian *gelatina* from *gelata* JELLY]

gel·atin·ous /dʒə'lætɪnəs/ *adjective* **1** of or like gelatin. **2** of a jellylike consistency. □ **gel·atin·ous·ly** *adverb*

gel·ation¹ /dʒə'leɪʃən/ *noun* solidification by freezing. [Latin *gelatio* from *gelare* freeze]

gel·ation² /dʒə'leɪʃən/ *noun* formation of or conversion into a gel. [GEL + -ATION]

gel·ato /dʒe'lɑːtoʊ, -'lɒtoʊ/ *noun* (*pl.* **gelati** /-ti/) an Italian sherbet-like ice cream made with milk or cream and relatively low in butterfat. [Italian, = frozen]

gel·cap *noun* a gelatin capsule containing a medication in liquid or gel form.

gel·coat *noun* a polyester resin coating applied to a mould on which fibreglass cloth is subsequently laid, setting to a hard surface over the fibreglass.

geld /ɡɛld/ *transitive verb* **1** deprive (a male animal) of the ability to reproduce; excise the testicles of; castrate. **2** deprive of some essential part; weaken. [Old Norse *gelda* from *geldr* barren, from Germanic]

Gel·der·land /'ɡɛldərˌlɑːnd/ a province of the Netherlands, on the border with Germany; capital, Arnhem.

geld·ing /'ɡɛldɪŋ/ *noun* a gelded animal, esp. a male horse. [Old Norse *geldingr*: see GELD]

gelid /'dʒɛlɪd/ *adjective* **1** icy, ice-cold. **2** chilly, cool. [Latin *gelidus* from *gelu* frost]

gel·ig·nite /'dʒɛlɪɡˌnaɪt/ *noun* a high explosive made from a gel of nitroglycerine and nitrocellulose in a base of wood pulp and sodium or potassium nitrate, much used in rock blasting. [GELATIN + Latin *ignis* fire + -ITE¹]

Gé·li·nas /ʒeɪliː'nɒ/ **Gra·tien** (1909–99), Canadian theatre actor, director, and producer. He created the popular character Fridolin for a series of revues (1938–46), and was known for his plays *Tit-Coq* (1948), *Bousille et les justes* (1959), and *Hier, les enfants dansaient* (1966).

Gell-Mann /'ɡɛlˌmæn/ **Mur·ray** (b.1929), US theoretical physicist. He coined the word *quark*, proposed the concept of strangeness in quarks, and made major contributions on the classification and interactions of subatomic particles; he was awarded the Nobel Prize for physics in 1969.

gelly /'dʒɛli/ *noun* Brit. slang gelignite. [abbreviation]

Gel·sen·kir·chen /'ɡɛlzənˌkɪrxən/ an industrial city in western Germany, in North Rhine-Westphalia northeast of Essen; pop. (est. 2002) 278,000.

gelt *noun* N Amer. slang money. [Yiddish, from German *geld*]

gem ● *noun* **1** a precious stone, esp. when cut and polished or engraved. **2** an object, person, event, etc. of great beauty, worth, or excellence. ● *transitive verb* (**gemmed, gem·ming**) adorn with or as with gems. □ **gem·like** *adjective* [Old French *gemme* from Latin *gemma* bud, jewel]

Ge·mara /ɡə'mɑːrə/ *noun* Judaism the later of the two parts of the Talmud, consisting of a rabbinical commentary on the first part (the Mishnah). [Aramaic *gᵊmārā* completion]

Gé·meaux /ʒeɪ'moʊ/ *noun* **1** Cdn any of several awards presented by the Academy of Canadian Cinema and Television for excellence in Canadian French-language television. **2** any of the statuettes symbolizing such an award. [French, = 'twins, Gemini']

Ge·mein·schaft /ɡə'maɪnˌʃɒft/ *noun* a form of social integration based on personal ties; community (compare GESELLSCHAFT). [German, from *gemein* common, general + *-schaft* -ship]

gem·in·ate ● *adjective* /'dʒɛmɪnət/ combined in pairs. ● *transitive verb* /'dʒɛmɪˌneɪt/ **1** double, repeat. **2** arrange in pairs. □ **gem·in·ation** /-'neɪʃən/ *noun* [Latin *geminatus* past participle of *geminare* from *geminus* twin]

Gem·ini /'dʒɛmɪˌnaɪ/ *noun* (*pl.* **-inis**) **1** a constellation between Taurus and Cancer, traditionally regarded as contained in the figures of twins. **2 a** the third sign of the zodiac. **b** a person born when the sun is in this sign, usu. between 21 May and 20 June. **3** Cdn **a** any of several awards presented by the Academy of Canadian Cinema and Television for excellence in Canadian English-language television. **b** any of the statuettes symbolizing such an award. □ **Gemi·nian** /ˌdʒɛmɪ'naɪən/ *noun & adjective* [Latin, = twins]

gem jar *noun* Cdn a Mason jar with a 78 mm diameter mouth.

gemma /'dʒɛmə/ *noun* (*pl.* **gem·mae** /-miː/) a small cellular body in cryptogams that separates from the mother plant and starts a new one; an asexual spore. [Latin: see GEM]

Consonants: b *but*   d *dog*   f *few*   g *get*   h *her*   j *yes*   k *cat*   l *leg*   m *man*   n *no*   p *pen*   r *red*   s *sit*

gem·ma·tion /dʒeˈmeiʃən/ *noun* reproduction by gemmae. [French from *gemmer* to bud, *gemme* bud]

gem·mule /ˈdʒemjuːl/ *noun* **1** a tough-coated dormant cluster of embryonic cells produced by a freshwater sponge, for development in more favourable conditions. **2** a small gemma. [French *gemmule* or Latin *gemmula* little bud (as GEM)]

gem·ol·ogy /dʒeˈmɒlədʒi/ *noun* the study of gems. □ **gem·ol·o·gist** *noun*

gems·bok /ˈgemzbɒk/ *noun* a large antelope, *Oryx gazella*, of SW and E Africa, having long straight horns and black markings on the face and flanks. [Afrikaans from Dutch, = chamois]

gem·stone /ˈdʒemstoːn/ *noun* a precious stone used as a gem.

gemüt·lich /ɡəˈmuːtlɪx/ *adjective* **1** pleasant and comfortable; cozy. **2** genial, agreeable. [German]

gemüt·lich·keit /ɡəˈmuːtlɪxkəit/ *adjective* the quality of being *gemütlich*. [German]

Gen. *abbreviation* **1** General. **2** *Bible* Genesis.

gen /dʒen/ *esp. Brit. slang* ● *noun* information. ● *transitive & intransitive verb* (**genned, gen·ning**) (foll. by *up*) provide with or obtain information. [perhaps from first syllable of *general information*]

-gen /dʒən/ *combining form* **1** *Chem.* that which produces (*hydrogen*; *antigen*; *carcinogen*). **2** *Bot.* growth (*endogen*; *exogen*). [French *-gène* from Greek *-genēs* -born, of a specified kind from *gen-* root of *gignomai* be born, become]

gen·darme /ˈʒɒndɑrm/ *noun* **1** a soldier employed in specific public police duties, esp. in some French-speaking countries. **2** a rock tower on a mountain, occupying and blocking an arête. [French from *gens d'armes* people of arms]

gen·darm·erie /ʒɒnˈdɑrməri/ *noun* **1** a force of gendarmes. **2** the headquarters of such a force.

gen·der /ˈdʒendər/ *noun* **1 a** the grammatical classification of nouns and related words, roughly corresponding to the two sexes and sexlessness. **b** each of the classes of nouns (see MASCULINE, FEMININE, NEUTER, COMMON *adjective* 6). **2** (of nouns and related words) the property of belonging to such a class. **3 a** a person's sex; either of the sexes. **b** one's characteristics or traits determined socially as a result of one's sex. □ **gender·less** *adjective* [Old French *gendre*, ultimately from Latin GENUS]

gender-bender *noun* a person who or thing which adopts or portrays non-traditional gender roles. □ **gender-bending** *noun* (often *attributive*)

gender bias *noun* the quality of concentrating more on males or of presenting them in a more favourable light than females in books, films, etc.

gen·dered /ˈdʒendərd/ *adjective* of, relating to, or determined by one's sex as expressed by social or cultural distinctions.

gen·der gap *noun* the discrepancy in opportunities, status, attitudes, etc. between men and women.

gender-neutral *adjective* **1** denoting a word which cannot be taken to refer to one sex only, e.g. *firefighter* as opposed to *fireman*. **2** (of language, a piece of writing, etc.) using gender-neutral words whenever appropriate.

gender role *noun* one's behaviour, lifestyle, etc. regarded in light of one's sex.

gender-specif·ic *adjective* characteristic of, pertaining to, or referring to one sex only.

gender tax *noun* a higher price charged to women than to men for similar goods and services.

gene /dʒiːn/ *noun* a unit of heredity composed of DNA or RNA and forming part of a chromosome etc., that determines a particular characteristic of an individual. [German *Gen*: see -GEN]

ge·nea·log·ic·al /ˌdʒiːniəˈlɒdʒɪkəl/ *adjective* **1** of or concerning genealogy. **2** tracing family descent. □ **ge·nea·log·ic·al·ly** *adverb*

ge·neal·ogy /ˌdʒiːniˈɒlədʒi/ *noun* (pl. **-gies**) **1 a** a line of descent traced continuously from an ancestor. **b** an account or exposition of this. **2** the study and investigation of lines of descent. **3** a plant's or animal's line of development from earlier forms. □ **ge·neal·o·gist** *noun* [Old French *genealogie* from Late Latin *genealogia* from Greek *genealogia* from *genea* race]

gene bank *noun* a collection of living organisms maintained as a repository of genetic material, esp. for developing new breeds etc. or safeguarding the survival of existing ones.

gene mapping *noun* the determination of a gene's location on a chromosome. □ **gene map** *noun*

gene pool *noun* the whole stock of different genes in an interbreeding population.

gen·era *pl. of* GENUS.

gen·er·al ● *adjective* **1 a** completely or almost universal. **b** including or affecting all or nearly all parts or cases of things. **2** prevalent, widespread, usual. **3** not partial, particular, local, or sectional. **4** not limited in application; relating to whole classes or all cases. **5** including points common to the individuals of a class and neglecting the differences (*a general term*). **6** not restricted or specialized (*general knowledge*). **7 a** roughly corresponding or adequate. **b** sufficient for practical purposes. **8** not detailed (*a general resemblance*; *a general idea*). **9** vague, indefinite (*spoke only in general terms*). **10** chief or principal; having overall authority (*Secretary-General*). **11** (in Alta., BC, Man., & Sask.) designating a film deemed suitable for all audiences. Abbr.: **G**. **12** *Med.* of the entire body (*general anaesthetic*; *general paralysis*). ● *noun* **1** (also **General**; abbr.: **Gen** *Cdn* or **Gen.**) **a** (in the Canadian Army or Air Force) an officer of the highest rank. **b** a similar officer in other military forces. **c** a lieutenant general, major general, or brigadier general. **d** (in the UK) an army officer ranking next below field marshal or above lieutenant general. **e** (in the US) an officer of the army or air force ranking above a lieutenant general and below a general of the army or a general of the air force. **f** (in the US) an army officer of any of the five highest ranks: brigadier general, major general, lieutenant general, general, or general of the army. **g** (in the US Marine Corps) an officer of the highest rank. **2** a commander of an army. **3** a tactician or strategist of specified merit (*a great general*). **4** the head of a religious order, e.g. of the Jesuits or Dominicans or the Salvation Army. □ **as a general rule** in most cases. **in general 1** as a normal rule; usually. **2** for the most part. □ **gen·er·al·ness** *noun* [Old French from Latin *generalis* (as GENUS)]

general admission *noun* **1** (often *attributive*) admission to unreserved seating at a concert, sports event, etc. (*general-admission tickets*; *we paid $5 for general admission*). **2** the section of a theatre, stadium, etc. with unreserved seats (*we sat in general admission*). **3** the admission fee to an event, museum, etc. charged to those who are not eligible for a discounted rate.

general alert *noun* *Cdn & Brit.* a generally-issued alert among police officers, esp. calling for the apprehension of a wanted person.

General American *noun* a form of English spoken in the US which is not markedly dialectal or regional.

general anaesthetic *noun* an anaesthetic that affects the whole body, usu. with loss of consciousness.

General Assembly *noun* **1** the main deliberative body of the United Nations, with a delegate from each member country. **2** (in Presbyterian churches) an annual national meeting of representative clergy and elders, constituting the highest court of the church. **3** (in the US) the legislature of some states.

general aviation *noun* aviation that is neither commercial nor military, including that using private, business, and agricultural aircraft.

General Certificate of Education *noun* (in England, Wales, and Northern Ireland) an examination for secondary-school students and required for entrance into university or college. Abbr.: **GCE**.

General Certificate of Secondary Education *noun* (in England, Wales, and Northern Ireland) an examination for 16-year-old students in specified subjects. Abbr.: **GCSE**.

general contractor *noun* a person or company that organizes and coordinates construction work performed by employees or subcontractors.

General Council *noun* (in the United Church of Canada) a national convention of representative clergy and elders, now held every three years, constituting the highest court of the church.

general delivery *noun* *N Amer.* the delivery of mail to a post office where addressees, e.g. those without a permanent address, can pick it up.

general election *noun* the election of representatives to a legislature from all constituencies of a country, province, etc.

general hospital *noun* a hospital which does not confine itself to patients suffering from one particular class of disease or to those of a particular sex or age group.

gen·er·al·is·simo /ˌdʒenərəˈliːsimoː/ *noun* (pl. **-simos**) **1** the supreme commander of a combined military force consisting of army, navy, and air force units. **2** *jocular* a pretentious leader. [Italian, superlative of *generale* GENERAL]

gen·er·al·ist *noun* a person competent or knowledgeable in several different fields or activities (*opp.* SPECIALIST).

gen·er·al·ity /ˌdʒenəˈralɪti/ *noun* (*pl.* **-ities**) **1** a statement or principle etc. having general validity or force. **2** applicability to a whole class of instances. **3** vagueness; lack of detail. **4** the state of being general. **5** (foll. by *of*) the main body or majority.

gen·er·al·iz·a·tion *noun* (also esp. *Brit.* **-isation**) **1** a general notion or proposition obtained by inference from (esp. limited or inadequate) particular cases. **2** the act or an instance of generalizing.

gen·er·al·ize *verb* (also esp. *Brit.* **-ise**) **1** *intransitive* **a** speak in general or indefinite terms. **b** form general principles or notions. **2** *transitive* reduce to a general statement, principle, or notion. **3** *transitive* **a** give a general character to. **b** call by a general name. **4** *transitive* infer (a law or conclusion) by induction. **5** *transitive Math. & Philos.* express in a general form; extend the application of. **6** *transitive* (in painting) render only the typical characteristics of. **7** *transitive* bring into general use. **8** *intransitive* (of a disease) spread to other parts of the body. □ **gen·er·al·iz·abil·ity** *noun* **gen·er·al·iz·able** *adjective* **gen·er·al·iz·er** *noun*

general ledger *noun* an accounting document recording all debits and all credits to all accounts for a business etc.

gen·er·al·ly *adverb* **1** usually; in most cases. **2** in a general sense; without regard to particulars or exceptions (*generally speaking*). **3** for the most part; extensively (*not generally known*). **4** in most respects (*they were generally well-behaved*).

general manager *noun* **1** the member of the administration of a sports team responsible for hiring, firing, trading etc. the players. **2** the person having overall responsibility for the operations of a company or other organization.

general meeting *noun* a meeting open to all the members of an association, shareholders of a corporation, etc.

general of the air force *noun* (in the US) the highest ranking officer in the Air Force.

general of the army *noun* (in the US) the highest ranking officer in the Army.

general practitioner *noun* a doctor working in the community and treating cases of all kinds in the first instance, as distinct from a consultant or specialist. Abbr.: **GP**. □ **general practice** *noun*

general public *noun* the people of a community collectively, esp. those not enjoying special privileges.

general-purpose *adjective* having a range of potential uses or functions; not specialized in design.

general relativity *noun see* RELATIVITY 2b.

general secretary *noun* a chief administrator of an organization.

gen·er·al·ship *noun* **1** the art or practice of exercising military command. **2** military skill; strategy. **3** skilful management; tact, diplomacy.

general staff *noun* the staff assisting a military commander in planning and administration.

general store *noun* esp. *N Amer.* a store selling a wide variety of goods for everyday needs.

general strike *noun* a strike of workers in all or most occupations.

General Synod *noun* the highest governing body in some national Anglican churches, including the Anglican Church of Canada.

gen·er·ate *transitive verb* **1** bring into existence; produce, evolve. **2** produce (electricity). **3** *Math.* (of a point, line, or surface) move and so notionally form or trace out (a line, surface, or solid). **4** *Math. & Linguistics* produce (a set or sequence of items) by performing specified operations on or applying specified rules to an initial set. □ **gen·er·able** *adjective* [Latin *generare* beget (as GENUS)]

generating station *noun* a power station for the generation of electricity.

gen·er·a·tion *noun* **1** all the people born at a particular time, regarded collectively (*my generation; the rising generation*). **2** a single step in descent or pedigree (*have known them for three generations; a second-generation Canadian*). **3** a stage in (esp. technological) development (*fourth-generation computers*). **4** members of a specific group or category who became prominent at the same time (*the new generation of rock guitarists*). **5** the individuals born at about the same time, with a specified common characteristic, attitude, etc. (*the Walkman generation*). **6** the average time in which children are ready to take the place of their parents (usu. reckoned at about 30 years). **7** production by natural or artificial process, esp. the production of electricity or heat. **8** procreation; the propagation of species. □ **gen·er·a·tion·al** *adjective*

generation gap *noun* differences of outlook or opinion between those of different generations.

Generation X *noun* the generation born after that of the baby boomers (roughly from the early 60s to mid-70s). □ **Generation Xer** *noun* [popularized, though not coined, by D. COUPLAND]

gen·er·a·tive /ˈdʒenərətɪv/ *adjective* **1** of or concerning procreation. **2** able to produce, productive.

generative grammar *noun* the theory that for each language a set of rules can be formulated capable of 'generating' the infinite number of possible sentences of that language and providing them with the correct structural description.

gen·er·a·tor *noun* **1** a machine for converting mechanical into electrical energy; a dynamo. **2** an apparatus for producing gas, steam, etc. **3** a person or thing that generates something.

gen·er·ic /dʒəˈnerɪk/ ● *adjective* **1** characteristic of or relating to an entire class; general, not specific or special. **2** *Biol.* characteristic of or belonging to a genus. **3** designating a word that can apply or refer to both men and women. **4** (of goods, esp. a drug) having no brand name; not protected by a registered trademark. ● *noun* a generic product, esp. a drug. □ **gen·er·ic·ally** *adverb* [French *générique* from Latin GENUS]

gen·er·ous *adjective* **1** (of a person or an institution) giving willingly more of something, esp. money, than is strictly necessary or expected. **2** (of help) given abundantly and willingly. **3** consisting of or representing a large amount of money, esp. when considered excessive or undeserved. **4** (of a person or an action) manifesting an inclination to recognize the positive aspects of someone or something, often disinterestedly. **5** (of something offered) favouring the recipient's interests rather than the giver's (*we offered them generous terms*). **6** liberal, broad, leaning towards the positive (*a generous estimate*). **7 a** ample, abundant, copious (*a generous portion*). **b** (of wine) rich and full. **8** (of rooms, houses, etc.) large, spacious; (of clothing) ample. □ **gen·er·os·ity** *noun* **gen·er·ous·ly** *adverb* **gen·er·ous·ness** *noun* [Old French *generus* from Latin *generosus* noble, magnanimous (as GENUS)]

Gen·esis /ˈdʒenəsɪs/ the first book of the Bible, containing an account of the creation of the universe and of the early history of humankind. [as GENESIS]

gen·esis /ˈdʒenəsɪs/ *noun* (*pl.* **gen·eses** /-siːz/) the origin, or mode of formation or generation, of a thing. [Latin from Greek from *gen-* be produced, root of *gignomai* become]

gene-splicing *noun* the process of removing a chosen gene or sequence of genes from one organism and causing it to be integrated into the genetic material of another, usu. a bacterium, in order that it may produce the protein for which the gene codes. □ **gene-spliced** *adjective*

Genet /ʒəˈneɪ/ **Jean** (1910–86), French novelist, poet, and dramatist. His early life in the criminal underworld provided the background for much of his work, including the autobiographical *Journal du Voleur* (1949) and *Notre-Dame des Fleurs* (1944); his plays include *Les Nègres* (1958).

genet /ˈdʒenɪt/ *noun* **1** any catlike mammal of the genus *Genetta*, native to Africa and S Europe, with spotted fur and a long ringed bushy tail. **2** the fur of the genet. [Old French *genete* from Arabic *jarnait*]

gene therapy *noun Med.* the introduction of normal genes into cells in place of missing or defective ones in order to correct genetic disorders.

gen·etic /dʒəˈnetɪk/ *adjective* **1** of genetics or genes; inherited. **2** of, in, or concerning origin; causal. □ **gen·etic·al·ly** *adverb* [GENESIS after *antithetic*]

genetically modified *adjective* (also **genetically altered**) **1** (of genetic material) artificially manipulated in order to produce a desired characteristic. **2** (of an organism or cell) containing such genetic material. **3** (of foodstuffs) containing or consisting of genetically altered plant or animal tissue.

genetic code *noun* the means by which genetic information is stored as sequences of nucleotide bases in the chromosomal DNA.

genetic counselling *noun* counselling given to prospective parents concerning their chances of passing on genetic disorders, or to someone who is undergoing genetic testing. □ **genetic counsellor** *noun*

genetic discrimination *noun* discrimination, esp. refusal to provide health benefits or denying employment to someone, based on the result of a genetic test that suggests that that person might have a genetic predisposition to a disease or disorder.

genetic drift *noun* variation in the relative frequency of different genotypes in a small population owing to the chance disappearance of particular genes as individuals die or do not reproduce.

genetic engineering noun the deliberate modification of the characteristics of an organism by the manipulation of the genetic material. □ **genetically engineered** adjective

genetic fingerprinting noun (also **genetic profiling**) the analysis of characteristic patterns in DNA as a means of identifying individuals. □ **genetic fingerprint** noun

genetic information noun the genetic potential of an organism carried in the base sequence of its DNA (or, in some viruses, RNA) according to the genetic code.

gen·eti·cist /dʒə'netɪsɪst/ noun a specialist in genetics.

genetic map noun a representation of a chromosome including the positions of its genes. □ **genetic mapping** noun

genetic marker noun an allele used to identify a chromosome or to locate other genes on a genetic map.

genetic modification noun deliberate alteration of genetic material by direct manipulation of the genome, esp. in agricultural crops.

genetic pollution noun the spread of altered genes from genetically engineered organisms to other, non-engineered organisms, esp. by cross-pollination.

gen·etics /dʒə'netɪks/ plural noun (treated as sing.) **1** the study of heredity and the variation of inherited characteristics. **2** (treated as sing. or pl.) the genetic properties or features of an organism, characteristic, etc. (the genetics of disease resistance).

genetic testing noun the analysis of DNA, RNA, or genetic markers to determine the presence of certain genes or mutations that cause or may be likely to cause a specific disease or condition.

Gen·eva /dʒə'niːvə/ a city in SW Switzerland, on Lake Geneva; pop. (est. 2002) 176,200. In the 16th c. it was a stronghold of John Calvin, who rewrote its laws and constitution. It was the site of the conclusion of the Geneva Conventions (1846–1949) and the headquarters of the League of Nations (1920–46). It is the headquarters of international bodies such as the Red Cross, various organizations of the UN, and the World Health Organization. □ **Gen·evan** noun & adjective

Geneva, Lake a lake in SW central Europe, between the Jura mountains and the Alps. Its southern shore forms part of the border between France and Switzerland.

gen·eva /dʒə'niːvə/ noun archaic Hollands gin. [Dutch genever from Old French genevre from Latin juniperus, assimilated to GENEVA]

Geneva bands plural noun two white cloth strips hanging from the collar of some Protestants' clerical dress. [GENEVA, where these were originally worn by Calvinists]

Geneva Convention noun an international agreement first made at Geneva in 1864 and later revised, governing the status and treatment of captured and wounded military personnel in wartime.

Geneva gown noun a loose full-length black gown with long wide sleeves worn by some Protestant clerics. [GENEVA, where this was originally worn by Calvinists]

Gen·ghis Khan /,ɡeŋgɪs 'kɒn, ,dʒeŋ-/ (born Temujin) (c.1162–1227), the founder of the Mongol Empire. He took the name Genghis Khan (= 'ruler of all') in 1206 after uniting the nomadic Mongol tribes under his command; at his death his empire extended from the shores of the Pacific to the northern shores of the Black Sea.

gen·ial /'dʒiːnɪəl/ adjective **1** jovial, sociable, kindly, cheerful. **2** (of the climate) mild and warm; conducive to growth. □ **geni·al·ity** /-'alɪti/ noun **geni·ial·ly** adverb [Latin genialis as GENIUS]

genic /'dʒiːnɪk/ adjective of or relating to genes.

-genic /'dʒenɪk/ combining form forming adjectives meaning: **1** producing (carcinogenic; pathogenic). **2** well suited to (photogenic; telegenic). **3** produced by (iatrogenic). □ **-genically** suffix. [-GEN + -IC]

genie /'dʒiːni/ noun **1 a** (pl. **genies** or **genii** /'dʒiːni,ai/) = JINNI. **b** a spirit of Arabian folklore, esp. one contained within a bottle, lamp, etc., and capable of granting wishes. **2** (**Genie**) Cdn **a** any of several awards presented by the Academy of Canadian Cinema and Television for excellence in filmmaking. **b** any of the statuettes symbolizing such an award. [French génie from Latin GENIUS: compare JINNI]

genii pl. of GENIE, GENIUS.

gen·is·ta /dʒɪ'nɪstə/ noun any almost leafless shrub of the genus Genista, with a profusion of yellow pea-shaped flowers, e.g. dyer's broom. [Latin]

genis·tein /dʒɪ'nɪsteiɪn/ noun a phytoestrogen found esp. in soybeans

and flaxseed which may have cancer-fighting properties. [GENISTA, because originally isolated in dyer's broom]

gen·ital /'dʒenɪtəl/ ● adjective of or relating to the reproductive organs. ● noun (in pl.) the external reproductive organs. [Old French génital or Latin genitalis from gignere genit- beget]

genital herpes noun a disease characterized by blisters in the genital area, caused by a variety of the herpes simplex virus.

gen·ital·ia /,dʒenɪ'teɪliə/ plural noun the genitals. [Latin, neuter pl. of genitalis: see GENITAL]

geni·tive /'dʒenɪtɪv/ Grammar ● noun the case of nouns and pronouns (and words in grammatical agreement with them) corresponding to of, from, and other prepositions and indicating possession or close association. ● adjective of or in the genitive. [Old French genetif, -ive or Latin genitivus from gignere genit- beget]

genito- /'dʒenɪto/ combining form genital.

gen·ito·urin·ary /,dʒenɪto'jʊrɪneri/ adjective of the genital and urinary organs.

genius /'dʒiːnjəs/ noun **1** (pl. **genius·es**) **a** an exceptional intellectual or creative power or other natural ability or tendency. **b** a person having this. **c** this ability as manifest in a work of art etc. (the genius of her painting). **2** (pl. **genii** /-ni,ai/) the tutelary spirit of a person, place, institution, etc. **3** a person or spirit regarded as powerfully influencing a person for good or evil. **4** the prevalent feeling or associations etc. of a nation, age, etc. [Latin (in sense 2) from the root of gignere beget]

genius loci /'loːsai, -kai, -si, -ki/ noun **1** the presiding god or guardian spirit of a place. **2** the body of associations connected with or inspirations derived from a place. [Latin, = genius of the place]

gen·lock /'dʒenlɒk/ noun **1** a device for maintaining synchronization between two different video signals, or between a video signal and a computer or audio signal, esp. enabling video images and computer graphics to be mixed. **2** this technique or process. □ **gen·lock·ing** noun [GENERATOR + LOCK¹]

Genoa /'dʒenoːə/ a seaport on the northwest coast of Italy, capital of Liguria region; pop. (2001) 603,560. It was the birthplace of Christopher Columbus. □ **Geno·ese** /,dʒenoː'iːz/ adjective & noun

genoa /'dʒenoːə/ noun (in full **genoa jib**) a large jib or foresail used esp. on racing yachts. [GENOA]

Genoa salami noun a salami of pork and veal or beef, usu. flavoured with garlic.

geno·cide /'dʒenə,said/ noun the mass extermination of human beings, esp. of a particular race or nation. □ **geno·cid·al** /-'saidəl/ adjective [Greek genos race + -CIDE]

gen·oise /'ʒenwɒz/ noun a sponge cake with melted butter incorporated into the batter. [French, = 'Genoese']

gen·ome /'dʒiːnoːm/ noun **1** the haploid set of chromosomes of an organism. **2** the genetic material of an organism. □ **genom·ic** /-'nɒmɪk/ adjective [GENE + CHROMOSOME]

genom·ics /dʒiː'nɒmɪks/ noun the branch of molecular biology concerned with the structure, function, evolution, and mapping of genomes.

geno·toxic /,dʒiːnoː'tɒksɪk/ adjective designating any substance, esp. a carcinogen, which has a direct and toxic effect upon the genetic material of an organism. □ **geno·tox·icity** noun

geno·type /'dʒiːno,taip/ noun Biol. the genetic constitution of an individual (compare PHENOTYPE). □ **geno·typ·ic** /-'tɪpɪk/ adjective [German Genotypus (as GENE, TYPE)]

-genous /'dʒenəs/ combining form **1** generated by or arising from (endogenous). **2** generating or producing (erogenous).

genre /'ʒɑ̃rə, 'ʒɒnrə/ ● noun **1** a kind or style, esp. of art or literature, e.g. novel, satire, science fiction. **2** (in full **genre painting**) the painting of scenes from ordinary life. ● attributive adjective denoting a film etc. following the conventions of a recognizable genre. [French, = a kind (as GENDER)]

gens /dʒenz/ noun (pl. **gen·tes** /-tiːz, -teiz/) **1** Rom. Hist. a group of families sharing a name and claiming a common origin. **2** Anthropology a number of people sharing descent through the male line. [Latin, from the root of gignere beget]

Gen·ser·ic /'ɡensərɪk, 'dʒen-/ (also **Gaiseric** /'ɡaizərɪk/) (d.477), king of the Vandals (428–77), who captured and plundered Rome in 455.

Gent see GHENT.

gent /dʒent/ noun informal (often jocular) **1** a gentleman. **2** (**the Gents**) Brit. informal a men's washroom. [abbreviation of GENTLEMAN]

gen·ta·micin /dʒentə'məisɪn/ noun a broad spectrum antibiotic used

u: mood ai my əi pipe au brown ʌu house ei day ɔi boy ā franglais ã Canadien ɔ̃ Brayon *(see over for consonants)*

esp. for severe systemic infections. [from *genta-*, of unknown origin + alteration of -MYCIN]

gen·teel /dʒen'tiːl/ *adjective* **1** affectedly or ostentatiously refined, stylish, or polite. **2** often *ironic* of or appropriate to the upper classes. □ **gen·teel·ly** *adverb* **gen·teel·ness** *noun* [earlier *gentile*, readoption of French *gentil* GENTLE]

gen·teel·ism /dʒen'tiːlɪzəm/ *noun* a word used because it is thought to be less vulgar than the commoner word, e.g. *perspire* for *sweat*.

gen·tes *pl. of* GENS.

gen·tian /'dʒenʃən, -ʃiən/ *noun* **1** any plant of the genus *Gentiana* or *Gentianella*, found esp. in mountainous regions, and usu. having violet or vivid blue trumpet-shaped flowers. **2** (in full **gentian bitter**) a tonic extracted from the root of the gentian. [Old English from Latin *gentiana* from *Gentius* king of Illyria]

gentian violet *noun* a violet dye formerly used as an antiseptic, esp. in the treatment of burns, now used as a treatment for thrush in breastfeeding.

gen·tile /'dʒentaɪl/ ● *adjective* **1** (**Gentile**) **a** not Jewish. **b** (of a person) not belonging to one's religious community, esp. *hist.* non-Mormon. **2** of or relating to a nation or tribe. ● *noun* (**Gentile**) a person who is not Jewish. [Latin *gentilis* from *gens gentis* family: see GENS]

gen·til·ity /dʒen'tɪlɪti/ *noun* **1** refined manners and habits, esp. as associated with wealthy and well-bred people. **2** affected or pretentious refinement or politeness. **3** people of noble birth. [Old French *gentilité* (as GENTLE)]

gen·tle ● *adjective* (**gent·ler**, **gent·lest**) **1** not rough; mild or kind. **2 a** moderate; not severe or drastic (*a gentle rebuke; a gentle breeze*). **b** gradual (*gentle progression; gentle slope*). **c** not harsh (*gentle hair-care products*). **3** (of birth, pursuits, etc.) honourable, of or fit for people of elevated social position. **4** (of an animal) quiet, tractable. **5** *archaic* generous, courteous. ● *transitive verb* **1** make gentle or docile. **2** handle (a horse etc.) firmly but gently. □ **gentle·ness** *noun* **gent·ly** *adverb* [Old French *gentil* from Latin *gentilis*: see GENTILE]

gentle·folk *plural noun literary* people of elevated social position.

gentle·man *noun* (*pl.* **-men**) **1** a man (in polite or formal use). **2** a chivalrous or well-bred man. **3** a man of good social position or of wealth and leisure (*country gentleman*). **4** a man of gentle birth attached to a royal household (*gentleman in waiting*). **5** (in *pl.* as a form of address) a male audience or the male part of an audience. [GENTLE + MAN after Old French *gentilz hom*]

gentleman farmer *noun* (*pl.* **gentlemen farmers**) a person who farms for pleasure, not to earn a living.

gentle·man·ly *adjective* like a gentleman in looks or behaviour; befitting a gentleman. □ **gentle·man·li·ness** *noun*

gentleman's agreement *noun* (also **gentlemen's agreement**) one which is binding in honour but not legally enforceable.

Gentleman Usher of the Black Rod *noun see* BLACK ROD.

gentle·woman *noun* (*pl.* **-women**) *archaic* a woman of good birth or breeding.

gen·too /'dʒentuː/ *noun* a penguin, *Pygoscelis papua*, esp. abundant in the Falkland Islands. [perhaps from Anglo-Indian *Gentoo* = Hindu, from Portuguese *gentio* GENTILE]

gen·tri·fy /'dʒentrɪfaɪ/ *transitive verb* (**-fies**, **-fied**) convert (a working-class or inner-city neighbourhood etc.) into an area of middle-class residence. □ **gen·tri·fi·ca·tion** *noun* **gen·tri·fied** *adjective* **gen·tri·fier** *noun*

gen·try /'dʒentri/ *plural noun* **1** people of high social standing. **2** (in the UK) the class of people next below the nobility in position and birth. **3** *derogatory* people (*these gentry*). [prob. from obsolete *gentrice* from Old French *genterise* var. of *gentelise* nobility, from *gentil* GENTLE]

genu·flect /'dʒenjuˌflekt/ *intransitive verb* **1** bend the knee to the ground, esp. in worship or as a sign of respect. **2** (foll. by *to, at*) display servile obedience or deference to. □ **genu·flec·tion** *noun* [ecclesiastical Latin *genuflectere genuflex-* from Latin *genu* the knee + *flectere* bend]

genu·ine /'dʒenjuɪn, -aɪn/ *adjective* **1** really coming from its stated, advertised, or reputed source. **2** properly so called; not sham. **3** (of an opinion etc.) sincere. **4** (of a person) free from affectation or hypocrisy. □ **genu·ine·ly** *adverb* **genu·ine·ness** *noun* [Latin *genuinus* from *genu* knee, with reference to a father's acknowledging a newborn child by placing it on his knee: later associated with GENUS]

genuine article *noun* (prec. by *the*) a person or thing that is exactly as described or promoted.

genus /'dʒiːnəs/ *noun* (*pl.* **gen·era** /'dʒenərə/) **1** *Biol.* a taxonomic grouping of organisms having common characteristics distinct from

those of other genera, usu. containing several or many species and being one of a series constituting a taxonomic family. **2** a kind or class having common characteristics. **3** *Logic* a class of things containing a number of subordinate classes with certain common attributes. [Latin *genus -eris* birth, race, stock]

Gen X *noun slang* = GENERATION X. □ **Gen-Xer** *noun*

-geny /dʒəni/ *combining form* forming nouns meaning 'mode of production or development of' (*anthropogeny; ontogeny; pathogeny*). [French *-génie* (as -GEN, -Y³)]

Geo. *abbreviation* George.

geo- *combining form* **1** earth (*geology*). **2** geographical (*geopolitics*). [Greek *geō-* from *gē* earth]

geo·cen·tric /ˌdʒiːoʊ'sentrɪk/ *adjective* **1** having or representing the earth as the centre; not heliocentric. **2** considered as viewed from the centre of the earth. □ **geo·cen·tric·ally** *adverb*

geo·chem·istry *noun* the chemistry of the earth and its rocks, minerals, etc. □ **geo·chem·ical** *adjective* **geo·chem·ist** *noun*

geo·chron·ol·ogy /ˌdʒiːoʊkrə'nɒlədʒi/ *noun* **1** the study and measurement of geological time by means of geological events. **2** the ordering of geological events. □ **geo·chrono·logic·al** /-ˌkrɒnə'lɒdʒɪkəl/ *adjective* **geo·chron·ol·o·gist** *noun*

geode /'dʒiːoʊd/ *noun* **1** a small cavity lined with crystals or other mineral matter. **2** a rock containing such a cavity. □ **geod·ic** /dʒiː'ɒdɪk/ *adjective* [Latin *geodes* from Greek *geōdēs* earthy, from *gē* earth]

geo·demo·graph·ic /ˌdʒiːoʊdemoʊ'grafɪk/ *adjective* of or pertaining to a combination of geographic and demographic information, obtained esp. by matching census data with neighbourhoods as defined by e.g. postal codes. □ **geo·demo·graph·ics** *noun*

geo·des·ic /ˌdʒiːoʊ'diːsɪk, -'desɪk/ ● *adjective* **1** of or relating to geodesy (*compare* GEODETIC). **2** of, involving, or consisting of a geodesic line. ● *noun* = GEODESIC LINE.

geodesic dome *noun* a dome constructed of short struts along geodesic lines, forming a light open framework of triangles or polygons, combining the structural advantages of the sphere and the tetrahedron.

geodesic line *noun* the shortest possible line on a surface between two points on that surface.

geod·esy /dʒiː'ɒdɪsi/ *noun* the branch of mathematics dealing with the figures and areas of the earth or large portions of it. □ **geod·esist** *noun* [modern Latin from Greek *geōdaisia* (as GEO-, *daiō* divide)]

geo·det·ic /dʒiːoʊ'detɪk/ *adjective* of or relating to geodesy, esp. as applied to land surveying. [Greek *geōdaitēs* 'land surveyor', from *geōdaisia* GEODESY]

geo·duck /'guːiːdʌk/ *noun* a giant mud-burrowing bivalve mollusc, *Panopea generosa*, occurring on the west coast of N America, where it is collected for food. [Chinook Jargon from Puget Salish *gwídeq*]

geo·econom·ics *plural noun* (treated as *sing.*) **1** the study of the relationship between geography and economics. **2** economics considered on the broadest global scale.

Geof·frey of Mon·mouth /'dʒefri/ (*c.*1100–*c.*1154), Welsh chronicler. His *Historia Regum Britanniae* (*c.*1139; first printed in 1508) was a major source for English literature, including Arthurian legend and the plots of some of Shakespeare's plays.

geo·graph·ic·al *adjective* (also **geo·graph·ic**) of or relating to geography. □ **geo·graph·ic·al·ly** *adverb*

geographic information system *noun* a computer system which allows the user to analyze, display and manipulate spatial data (e.g. data from remote sensing). Abbr.: **GIS**.

geog·raphy *noun* **1** the study of the earth's physical features, resources, and climate, and the physical aspects of its population. **2** the main physical features of an area. **3** the arrangement of features or layout of a region or thing. □ **geog·raph·er** *noun* [Greek *geōgraphia* from *gē* 'earth' + -*graphia* 'writing']

ge·oid /'dʒiːɔɪd/ *noun* the shape of the earth taken as mean sea level and its imagined extension under (or over) land areas. [Greek *geōeidēs* (as GEO-, -OID)]

geol. *abbreviation* **1** geology. **2** geological.

geo·logic·al /dʒiːə'lɒdʒɪkəl/ *adjective* (also **geo·logic**) of, pertaining to, or derived from geology. □ **geo·logic·al·ly** *adverb*

geological survey *noun* **1** a detailed investigation of the geological features and resources of a region. **2** (**Geological Survey**) an official body responsible for conducting such surveys.

geological time *noun* **1** the time which has elapsed since the earth's

Consonants: b *but* d *dog* f *few* g *get* h *her* j *yes* k *cat* l *leg* m *man* n *no* p *pen* r *red* s *sit*

formation (up to the beginning of the historical period). **2** time measured with reference to geological events.

geol·ogy /dʒɪˈɒlədʒi/ *noun* **1** the science of the earth, including the composition, structure, and origin of its rocks. **2** this science applied to any other planet or celestial body. **3** the geological features of a district. □ **geol·o·gist** *noun* [modern Latin *geologia* (as GEO-, -LOGY)]

geo·mag·net·ism *noun* the study of the magnetic properties of the earth. □ **geo·mag·net·ic** *adjective* **geo·mag·net·ical·ly** *adverb*

geo·mancy /ˈdʒɪːɔːˌmansi/ *noun* **1** the art of siting buildings etc. auspiciously. **2** divination from the configuration of a handful of earth or random dots. □ **geo·man·cer** *noun* **geo·man·tic** /-ˈmantɪk/ *adjective*

geo·mat·ics /ˌdʒiːɔːˈmatɪks/ *plural noun* (treated as *sing.*) computerization applied to geography. [GEOGRAPHY + INFORMATICS]

geom·eter /dʒiˈɒmɪtər/ *noun* **1** a person skilled in geometry. **2** any moth, esp. of the family Geometridae, having twig-like larvae which move by alternately hunching and stretching the body, as if measuring the ground.

geo·met·ric /ˌdʒiəˈmetrɪk/ ● *adjective* (also **geo·met·ric·al**) **1** of, according to, or like geometry. **2** (of a design, architectural feature, etc.) characterized by or decorated with regular lines and shapes. ● *noun* a print, pattern, fabric, etc. with a geometric design. □ **geo·met·ric·al·ly** *adverb*

geometric mean *noun* the central number in a geometric progression, also calculable as the nth root of a product of n numbers (as 9 from 3 and 27).

geometric progression *noun* a progression of numbers with a constant ratio between each number and the one before (as 1, 3, 9, 27).

geometric series *noun* a series in geometrical progression.

geom·etry /dʒiˈɒmətri/ *noun* **1 a** the branch of mathematics concerned with the properties and relations of points, lines, surfaces, and solids. **b** (*pl.* **-ries**) a particular system describing these properties etc. (*Euclidean geometry*). **2** the relative arrangement of objects or parts. □ **geo·met·ri·cian** /ˌdʒiːəmɪˈtrɪʃən/ *noun* [Old French *geometrie* from Latin *geometria* from Greek (as GEO-, -METRY)]

geo·morph·ol·ogy /ˌdʒiːɔːmɔrˈfɒlədʒi/ *noun* the study of the physical features of the surface of the earth and their relation to its underlying geological structures. □ **geo·morph·ic** *adjective* **geo·morpho·logic·al** *adjective* **geo·morph·ol·o·gist** *noun*

geo·phys·ics /ˌdʒiːɔːˈfɪzɪks/ *noun* the science concerned with all aspects of the physical properties and processes of the earth and planetary bodies, including seismology, gravity, magnetism, etc. □ **geo·physic·al** *adjective* **geo·physi·cist** *noun*

geo·pol·itics /ˌdʒiːɔːˈpɒlɪtɪks/ *noun* **1 a** the politics of a country as determined by its geographical features. **b** the study of this. **2** politics on a global scale. □ **geo·polit·ical** *adjective* **geo·polit·ical·ly** *adverb* **geo·polit·ician** *noun*

Geor·die /ˈdʒɔrdi/ *Brit. informal* ● *noun* **1** a native of the area around Newcastle in NE England. **2** the dialect spoken in this area. ● *adjective* of or relating to this area, its people, or its dialect. [the name *George* + -IE]

George ▶ **1 Dan** (1899–1981), Canadian actor. A longshoreman and logger, he was chief of the Squamish Band (1951–63), and was noted for his performances in the films *Smith* (1969) and *Little Big Man* (1970), and in plays such as George Ryga's *The Ecstasy of Rita Joe* (1970). **2 Henry** (1839–97), US economist, who is remembered for his *Progress and Poverty* (1879), in which he attributed poverty to rent, and proposed a tax on land as the remedy for social ills. **3 St.** (*fl.* 3rd c.), patron saint of England. He may have been martyred near Lydda in Palestine some time before the reign of Constantine (d.337), but his cult did not become popular until the 6th c., and the slaying of the dragon (possibly derived from the legend of Perseus) was not attributed to him until the 12th c. Feast day, 23 April.

George I (1660–1727), great-grandson of James I, king of Great Britain and Ireland 1714–27, and Elector of Hanover 1698–1727. Unpopular in England as a foreigner who never learned the English language, he left the administration of his new kingdom to his ministers and devoted himself to diplomacy and the interests of Hanover.

George II (1683–1760), son of George I, king of Great Britain and Ireland 1727–60, and Elector of Hanover 1727–60. Like his father, he depended heavily on his ministers, but took an active part in Britain's entry into the War of the Austrian Succession.

George III (1738–1820), grandson of George II, king of Great Britain and Ireland 1760–1820, Elector of Hanover 1760–1814 and king of Hanover 1815–20. He attempted to exercise royal control of

government to the fullest possible extent, and his determination to suppress the American Revolution dominated British war policy 1775–83; his political influence declined from 1788 after a number of bouts of mental illness, and in 1811 his son was made regent.

George IV (1762–1830), son of George III, king of Great Britain and Ireland 1820–30. Known as a patron of the arts and for his dissolute lifestyle, he was Prince Regent during his father's final period of insanity.

George V (1865–1936), son of Edward VII, king of Great Britain and Ireland 1910–36. He exercised restrained but none the less important influence over British politics, playing an esp. significant role in the formation of the national government in 1931.

George VI (1895–1952), son of George V, king of Great Britain and Ireland 1936–52. He was created Duke of York in 1920, and came to the throne on the abdication of his brother Edward VIII.

George Cross *noun* (also **George Medal**) (in the UK) decorations for bravery awarded esp. to civilians, instituted in 1940 by King George VI.

George·town 1 the capital of Guyana, a port at the mouth of the Demerara River; pop. (est. 2002) 225,800. **2** part of the town of Halton Hills in south central Ontario. [sense 2 after *George* Kennedy, founder and first settler d.1870]

George Town 1 the capital of the Cayman Islands, on the island of Grand Cayman; pop. (est. 2002) 27,800. **2** (also called **Penang**) the chief port of Malaysia and capital of the state of Penang, on Penang island; pop. (2000) 180,573.

geor·gette /dʒɔrˈdʒet/ *noun* a thin silk or crepe dress material. [*Georgette* de la Plante, French dressmaker fl. *ca.* 1900]

Geor·gia 1 a country of SE Europe, on the eastern shore of the Black Sea; pop. (est. 2002) 4,960,951; capital, Tbilisi. Since the breakup of the USSR in 1991, separatist movements among the Abkhazian and South Ossetian minorities have led to outbreaks of ethnic conflict. **2** a state of the southeastern US, on the Atlantic coast; pop. (2000) 8,186,453; capital, Atlanta. Founded as an English colony in 1732, it became one of the original thirteen states of the Union in 1788.

Georgia, Strait of a channel of the N Pacific, separating the southern half of Vancouver Island from mainland BC. [GEORGE III]

Geor·gian[1] *adjective* **1 a** of or characteristic of the time of Kings George I–IV of England (1714–1830). **b** designating or resembling the style of architecture of this period, typified in domestic architecture by red-brick houses with regularly spaced sash windows, white paintwork, and pedimented doorways. **2** of or characteristic of the time of Kings George V and VI of England (1910–52), esp. of the literature of 1910–20.

Geor·gian[2] ● *adjective* of or relating to the state of Georgia in the US. ● *noun* a native or resident of Georgia.

Geor·gian[3] ● *adjective* of or relating to the country Georgia. ● *noun* **1** a native of Georgia; a person of Georgian descent. **2** the language of Georgia.

Georgian Bay a large arm of Lake Huron, extending from the lake's northeastern end into south central Ontario. [GEORGE IV]

Georgian Bay Islands National Park a small park in south central Ontario, situated in the southeastern corner of Georgian Bay. Established in 1929, it encompasses close to sixty islands.

Georgian Triangle *noun* a roughly triangular area bordering on Nottawasaga Bay, extending from Meaford to Wasaga Beach and south to Creemore.

geor·gic /ˈdʒɔrdʒɪk/ ● *adjective literary* agricultural. ● *noun* a didactic poem giving instruction on farming, husbandry, etc., often involving praise of rural life. [Latin *georgicus* from Greek *geōrgikos*, from *geōrgos* farmer]

Geor·gina /dʒɔrˈdʒiːnə/ a town in south central Ontario, on Lake Simcoe; pop. (2001) 39,263. □ **Geor·gin·ian** *noun* [GEORGE III]

geo·science *noun* earth sciences, e.g. geology, geophysics. □ **geo·scien·tist** *noun*

geo·sphere *noun* **1** the solid surface of the earth. **2** any of the almost spherical concentric regions of the earth and its atmosphere.

geo·station·ary *adjective Electronics* (of an artificial satellite of the earth) moving in such an orbit as to remain above the same point on the earth's surface (*see also* GEOSYNCHRONOUS).

geo·stra·tegic *adjective* relating to the esp. military or economic global strategies of nations.

geo·stroph·ic /ˌdʒiːɔːˈstrɒfɪk/ *adjective* relating to or denoting the component of a wind or current that arises from a balance between pressure gradients and coriolis forces. [GEO- + Greek *strophē* a turning, from *strephō* to turn]

geo·syn·chron·ous /ˌdʒiːoʊˈsɪŋkrənəs/ *adjective* (of an artificial satellite of the earth) moving in an orbit equal to the earth's period of rotation (*see also* GEOSTATIONARY).

geo·tech·nic·al *adjective* of or pertaining to practical applications of geological science in engineering, building, etc.

geo·tex·tile *noun* a fabric used to cover or retain earth, as in construction work or gardening.

geo·ther·mal *adjective* relating to, originating from, or produced by the internal heat of the earth.

geo·trop·ism /dʒiˈɒtrəˌpɪzəm/ *noun* plant growth in relation to gravity. □ **geo·trop·ic** /ˌdʒiːoʊˈtrɒpɪk, -ˈtroʊpɪk/ *adjective* [GEO- + Greek *tropikos* from *tropē* a turning, from *trepō* to turn]

Gera /ˈɡiːrə/ an industrial city in east central Germany, in Thuringia; pop. (est. 2002) 109,800.

gera·nium /dʒəˈreɪniəm/ *noun* **1** any herb or shrub of the genus *Geranium* bearing fruit shaped like the bill of a crane, e.g. cranesbill. **2** (in general use) a cultivated pelargonium. **3** the colour of the scarlet geranium. [Latin from Greek *geranion* from *geranos* crane]

ger·bera /ˈdʒɜːrbərə/ *noun* any composite plant of the genus *Gerbera* of Africa or Asia, esp. the Transvaal daisy. [T. *Gerber*, German naturalist d.1743]

ger·bil /ˈdʒɜːrbɪl/ *noun* a mouselike desert rodent of the subfamily Gerbillinae, with long hind legs, esp. *Meriones unguiculatus* of Mongolia, commonly kept elsewhere as a pet. [French *gerbille* from modern Latin *gerbillus* diminutive of *gerbo* JERBOA]

ger·enuk /ˈdʒɛrəˌnʊk/ *noun* an antelope, *Litocranius walleri*, native to E Africa, with a very long neck and small head. [Somali]

geri·at·ric /ˌdʒɛriˈætrɪk/ ● *adjective* **1** of or relating to old age or old people. **2** *informal* old, outdated. ● *noun* **1** an old person, esp. one receiving special care. **2** *offensive* a person or thing considered as relatively old or outdated. [Greek *gēras* old age + *iatros* doctor]

geri·at·rics /ˌdʒɛriˈætrɪks/ *plural noun* (usu. treated as *sing.*) a branch of medicine or social science dealing with the health and care of old people. □ **geria·tri·cian** /-əˈtrɪʃən/ *noun*

Géri·cault /ˈʒɛriˌkoʊ/ **(Jean Louis André) Théo·dore** (1791–1824), French romantic painter. His most famous work, *The Raft of the Medusa* (1819), is notable for its realistic treatment of the macabre; he is also known for his paintings of horses.

Ger·itol /ˈdʒɛrɪtɒl/ *noun proprietary* a vitamin supplement used as a tonic for older people.

germ *noun* **1** a micro-organism, esp. one which causes disease. **2 a** a portion of an organism capable of developing into a new one; the rudiment of an animal or plant. **b** an embryo of a seed (*wheat germ*). **3** an original idea etc. from which something may develop; an elementary principle. □ **germy** *adjective* [French *germe* from Latin *germen germinis* sprout]

Ger·man ● *noun* **1** a native or national of Germany; a person of German descent. **2** the language of Germany, also used in Austria and Switzerland. ● *adjective* of or relating to Germany or its people or language. [Latin *Germanus* with reference to related peoples of Central and N Europe, a name perhaps given by Celts to their neighbours: compare Old Irish *gair* neighbour]

ger·man *adjective* (placed after *brother*, *sister*, or *cousin*) **1** having both parents the same (*brother german*). **2** having both grandparents the same on one side (*cousin german*). [Old French *germain* from Latin *germanus* genuine, of the same parents]

German Democratic Republic (abbr. **GDR**, **DDR**) *hist.* East Germany (see GERMANY).

ger·man·der /dʒɜːrˈmændɜːr/ *noun* any plant of the genus *Teucrium*, of the mint family, of which some are cultivated as ornamentals and some are used in herbal medicine. [medieval Latin *germandra*, ultimately from Greek *khamaidrus* from *khamai* on the ground + *drus* oak]

germander speedwell *noun* a creeping plant, *Veronica chamaedrys*, with germander-like leaves and blue flowers.

ger·mane /dʒɜːrˈmeɪn/ *adjective* (usu. foll. by *to*) relevant (to a subject under consideration). □ **ger·mane·ly** *adverb* **ger·mane·ness** *noun* [var. of GERMAN]

German East Africa a former German protectorate in East Africa (1891–1918), corresponding to present-day Tanzania, Rwanda, and Burundi.

German Empire (also called **Second Reich**) an empire in German-speaking central Europe, created in 1871 after the Franco-Prussian War when Bismarck united 25 German states under the King of Prussia. Allied with Austria-Hungary, the German Empire became the greatest industrial power in Europe. After World War I the empire collapsed and the Weimar Republic was created.

Ger·man·ic /dʒɜːrˈmænɪk/ ● *adjective* **1** of the languages or language group called Germanic. **2** of the Scandinavians, Anglo-Saxons, or Germans. **3** *hist.* of the Germans. **4** having characteristics considered typically German. ● *noun* **1** the branch of Indo-European languages including English, German, Dutch, and the Scandinavian languages. **2** the (unrecorded) early language from which other Germanic languages developed. [Latin *Germanicus* (as GERMAN)]

ger·man·ic /dʒɜːrˈmænɪk/ *adjective Chem.* of or containing germanium, esp. in its tetravalent state.

Ger·man·icus Caesar /dʒɜːrˈmænɪkəs/ (15 BC–AD 19), Roman general, the nephew and adopted son of Tiberius. He waged successful wars against the Germans (AD 14–16).

Ger·man·ist /ˈdʒɜːrmənɪst/ *noun* an expert in or student of the language, literature, and civilization of Germany, or Germanic languages.

ger·ma·nium /dʒɜːrˈmeɪniəm/ *noun Chem.* a lustrous brittle semi-metallic element occurring naturally in sulphide ores and used in semiconductors. Symbol: **Ge**; at. no.: 32. [modern Latin from *Germanus* GERMAN]

Ger·man·ize *transitive & intransitive verb* (also esp. *Brit.* **-ise**) make or become German; adopt or cause to adopt German customs etc. □ **Ger·man·iz·a·tion** *noun*

German measles *noun* a contagious disease, rubella, that resembles a mild form of measles but can cause fetal malformations if caught by a woman early in a pregnancy.

Germano- /dʒɜːrˈmanoʊ/ *combining form* German; German and.

German shepherd *noun* (also **German shepherd dog**) a large, strong, black and tan dog with erect ears and a shaggy tail, used as a guard dog and in police work.

German silver *noun* a white alloy of nickel, zinc, and copper.

German South West Africa a former German protectorate in SW Africa (1884–1918), corresponding to present-day Namibia.

Ger·many a country in central Europe; pop. (est. 2002) 83,251,851; capital, Berlin. After being defeated in the First World War, Germany was taken over in the 1930s by the Nazi dictatorship which led to a policy of expansionism and eventually to complete defeat in the Second World War. Germany was occupied for a time by the victorious Allies during which it was partitioned; some territory in the east, including East Prussia, was lost, mainly to Poland and the USSR. The western part (including West Berlin), which was occupied by the US, Britain, and France, became the Federal Republic of Germany (**West Germany**); the eastern part, occupied by the Soviet Union, became the German Democratic Republic (**East Germany**). The two parts reunited on 3 Oct. 1990.

germ cell *noun* **1** a cell containing half the number of chromosomes of a somatic cell and able to unite with one from the opposite sex to form a new individual; a gamete. **2** any embryonic cell with the potential of developing into a gamete.

germi·cide *noun* a substance destroying germs, esp. those causing disease. □ **germi·cid·al** *adjective*

ger·min·al /ˈdʒɜːrmɪnəl/ *adjective* **1** relating to or of the nature of a germ or germs (*see* GERM 1). **2** in the earliest stage of development. **3** productive of new ideas. [Latin *germen germin-* sprout: see GERM]

ger·min·ate /ˈdʒɜːrmɪˌneɪt/ *verb* **1 a** *intransitive* sprout, bud, or put forth shoots. **b** *transitive* cause to sprout or shoot. **2** *intransitive* come into existence. □ **ger·min·a·tion** *noun* **ger·min·a·tive** *adjective* **ger·min·ator** *noun* [Latin *germinare germinat-* (as GERM)]

Ger·mis·ton /ˈdʒɜːrmɪstən/ a city in South Africa, in the province of Gauteng, southeast of Johannesburg; pop. (1998) 166,142. It is the site of a large gold refinery, which serves the Witwatersrand gold-mining region.

germ layer *noun Biol.* each of the three layers of cells (ectoderm, mesoderm, and endoderm) that are formed in the early embryo.

germ line *noun Biol.* a series of germ cells each descended from earlier cells in the series, regarded as continuing through successive generations of an organism.

germ·plasm *noun* germ cells collectively; their genetic material.

germ warfare *noun* the systematic spreading of micro-organisms to cause disease in an enemy population.

Ger·on·imo[1] /dʒəˈrɒnɪˌmoʊ/ (*c.*1829–1909), Apache chief. He led his people in resistance to white encroachment on reservations in

Arizona, waging war against settlers and US troops in a series of raids, before surrendering in 1886.

Ger·on·imo² /dʒəˈrɒnɪˌmoː/ *interjection* expressing exhilaration or exultation. [after GERONIMO¹]

ger·on·toc·racy /dʒerɒnˈtɒkrəsi/ *noun* **1** government by old people. **2** a state or society so governed. □ **ger·on·to·crat** /dʒeˈrɒntəkrat/ *noun* **ger·on·to·crat·ic** /-ˈkratɪk/ *adjective* [Greek *gerōn -ontos* 'old man' + -CRACY]

ger·on·tol·ogy /ˌdʒerənˈtɒlədʒi/ *noun* the scientific study of old age, the process of aging, and the special problems of old people. □ **ger·on·to·logic·al** *adjective* **ger·on·tol·o·gist** *noun* [Greek *gerōn -ontos* old man + -LOGY]

-gerous /dʒərəs/ *combining form* forming adjectives meaning 'bearing' (*armigerous*).

gerry·man·der /ˈdʒeriˌmandər/ ● *transitive verb* **1** manipulate the boundaries of (a constituency etc.) so as to give undue influence to some party or class. **2** manipulate (a situation etc.) to gain advantage. ● *noun* this practice. □ **gerry·man·der·er** *noun* [the name of Governor *Gerry* of Massachusetts + (SALA)MANDER, from the shape of a district on a political map drawn when he was in office (1812)]

Gersh·win, **George** (born Jacob Gershvin) (1898–1937), US composer and pianist. He composed many popular songs, mainly with lyrics by his brother Ira (Israel, 1896–1983), the opera *Porgy and Bess* (1935), and works for piano and orchestra, including *Rhapsody in Blue* (1924) and *Concerto in F* (1925).

ger·und /ˈdʒerənd/ *noun* Grammar a noun formed from a verb, in English ending in *-ing*, and designating an action or state, e.g. *smoking is bad for you*. [Late Latin *gerundium* from *gerundum* var. of *gerendum*, the gerund of Latin *gerere* do]

ger·und·ive /dʒeˈrʌndɪv/ *noun* Grammar a form of a Latin verb and functioning as an adjective meaning 'that should or must be done' etc. [Late Latin *gerundivus* (*modus* mood) from *gerundium*: see GERUND]

Gesamt·kunst·werk /ɡəˈzamtkʊnstˌvɛrk/ *noun* a work of art in which drama, music, and other performing arts are integrated and each is subservient to the whole. [German, from *gesamt* total + *Kunstwerk* work of art]

Gesell·schaft /ɡəˈzelʃɒft/ *noun* a form of social integration based on impersonal ties, as duty to society or an organization (*compare* GEMEINSCHAFT). [German, from *Gesell*(e) companion + *-schaft* -ship]

Ges·ner /ˈɡesnər/ **Abra·ham** (1797–1864), Canadian geologist and inventor. He made a geological survey of New Brunswick (1838–43), and in 1852 patented a process for distilling kerosene.

ges·so /ˈdʒesoː/ *noun* (pl. **-soes**) plaster of Paris or gypsum as used in painting as a ground or in sculpture. □ **ges·soed** *adjective* [Italian from Latin *gypsum*: see GYPSUM]

ge·stalt /ɡəˈʃtɒlt/ *noun* Psych. an organized whole that is perceived as more than the sum of its parts. □ **ge·stalt·ism** *noun* **ge·stalt·ist** *noun* [German, = form, shape]

Ge·stalt psych·ol·ogy *noun* a system maintaining that perceptions, reactions, etc., are gestalts.

Ge·sta·po /ɡəˈstɒpoː/ *noun* **1** the German secret police under Nazi rule. Founded by Hermann Goering in 1933 and headed by Heinrich Himmler from 1936, the Gestapo ruthlessly suppressed opposition to the Nazis within Germany and in occupied Europe and was responsible for rounding up Jews and other groups to be sent to concentration camps. **2** (also **gestapo**) *derogatory* an organization compared to this. [German, from *Geheime Staatspolizei*, lit. 'Secret State Police']

ges·tate /ˈdʒesteit/ *transitive & intransitive verb* **1** carry (a fetus) in gestation. **2** develop (an idea etc.).

ges·ta·tion /dʒeˈsteiʃən/ *noun* **1 a** the process of carrying or being carried in the womb between conception and birth. **b** this period. **2** the development of a plan, idea, etc. □ **ges·ta·tion·al** *adjective* [Latin *gestatio* from *gestare* frequentative of *gerere* carry]

ges·ticu·late /dʒeˈstɪkjuˌleit/ *verb* **1** *intransitive* use esp. lively gestures instead of or in addition to speech. **2** *transitive* express with gestures. □ **ges·ticu·la·tion** *noun* **ges·ticu·la·tive** /-lətɪv/ *adjective* **ges·ticu·la·tor** *noun* **ges·ticu·la·tory** /-ˈtɔri/ *adjective* [Latin *gesticulari* from *gesticulus* diminutive of *gestus* GESTURE]

ges·ture /ˈdʒestʃər/ ● *noun* **1** a movement of a limb or the body as an expression of thought or feeling. **2** the use of such movements esp. to convey feeling or as a rhetorical device. **3** an action to evoke a response or convey intention, usu. friendly (*goodwill gesture*). ● *transitive & intransitive verb* gesticulate. □ **ges·tur·al** *adjective* **ges·tur·al·ly** *adverb* [medieval Latin *gestura* from Latin *gerere gest-* wield]

ge·sund·heit /ɡəˈzʊntaɪt, -haɪt/ *interjection* expressing a wish of good health to a person who has just sneezed. [German, = health]

get ● *verb* (**get·ting**; *past* **got**; *past participle* **got** or **got·ten**) **1** *transitive* come into the possession of; receive or earn (*get a job*; *got $200 a week*; *got first prize*). **2** *transitive* fetch, obtain, procure, purchase (*get my book for me*; *got a new car*). **3** *transitive* go to reach or catch (a bus, train, etc.). **4** *transitive* prepare (a meal etc.). **5** *intransitive & transitive* reach or cause to reach a certain state or condition; become or cause to become (*get rich*; *get one's feet wet*; *get to be famous*; *got them ready*; *got him into trouble*; *cannot get the key into the lock*). **6** *transitive* obtain as a result of calculation. **7** *transitive* contract (a disease etc.). **8** *transitive* establish or be in communication with via telephone or radio; receive (a radio signal, television channel, etc.). **9** *transitive* experience or suffer; have inflicted on one; receive as one's lot or penalty (*got four years in prison*). **10 a** *transitive* succeed in bringing, placing, etc. (*get it round the corner*; *get it on to the agenda*; *flattery will get you nowhere*). **b** *intransitive & transitive* succeed or cause to succeed in coming or going (*will get you there somehow*; *got absolutely nowhere*). **11** *transitive* (*prec. by* have) **a** possess (*have not got a penny*). **b** (*foll. by* to + infin.) be bound or obliged (*have got to see you*). **12** *transitive* (*foll. by* to + infin.) induce; prevail upon (*got them to help me*). **13** *transitive informal* understand (a person or an argument) (*have you got that?*; *I get your point*; *don't get me wrong*). **14** *transitive informal* inflict punishment or retribution on, esp. in retaliation (*I'll get you for that*). **15** *transitive informal* **a** annoy. **b** move; affect emotionally. **c** attract, obsess. **d** amuse. **16** *transitive* (*foll. by* to + infin.) develop an inclination as specified (*am getting to like it*). **17** *intransitive* (*foll. by* verbal noun) begin (*get going*). **18** *transitive* (esp. in *past* or *perfect*) catch in an argument; corner, puzzle. **19** *transitive* establish (an idea etc.) in one's mind. **20** *intransitive slang* be off; go away. **21** *transitive archaic* beget. **22** *transitive archaic* learn; acquire (knowledge) by study. **23** *transitive* answer (a telephone, doorbell, etc.). ● *noun dated* an offspring (of animals). □ **be getting on for** be approaching (a specified time, age, etc.). **get across 1** manage to communicate (an idea etc.). **2** (of an idea etc.) be communicated successfully. **3** Brit. informal annoy, irritate. **get ahead** be or become successful. **get along** (or **on**) **1** (foll. by *together*, *with*) live harmoniously. **2** (as *imperative*) nonsense! **get around 1** (also **get about**) **a** travel extensively or fast; go from place to place. **b** manage to walk, move about, etc. (esp. after illness). **c** (of news) be circulated, esp. orally. **2 a** evade (a law etc.). **b** successfully coax or cajole (a person) esp. to secure a favour. **get around to** deal with (a task etc.) in due course. **get at 1** reach; get hold of. **2** *informal* imply (*what are you getting at?*). **3** *informal* nag, criticize, bully. **get away 1** escape. **2** Brit. (as *imperative*) informal expressing disbelief or skepticism. **3** (foll. by *with*) escape blame or punishment for. **get back 1** move back or away. **2** return, arrive home. **3** recover (something lost). **4** (usu. foll. by *to*) contact later (*I'll get back to you*). **get back at** informal retaliate against. **get by** informal **1** just manage, even with difficulty. **2** be acceptable. **get down 1** alight, descend (from a vehicle, ladder, etc.). **2** record in writing. **3** manage to swallow. **4** lower oneself closer to the floor or ground. **5** N Amer. slang be uninhibited or unrestrained, esp. in dancing or socializing. **get a person down** depress or deject a person. **get down to** begin working on or discussing. **get even** (often foll. by *with*) **1** achieve revenge; act in retaliation. **2** equalize the score. **get his** (or **hers** etc.) slang **1** be killed. **2** suffer retribution. **get hold of 1** grasp (physically). **2** grasp (intellectually); understand. **3** make contact with (a person). **4** acquire. **get in 1** enter; gain entrance. **2** arrive. **3** be elected. **get into** become interested or involved in. **get it** slang be punished or in trouble. **get it into one's head** (foll. by *that* + clause) firmly believe or maintain; realize. **get nowhere** fail despite one's efforts. **get off 1** informal be acquitted; escape with little or no punishment. **2** start. **3** alight; alight from (a bus etc.). **4** slang reach orgasm. **5** go, or cause to go, to sleep. **6** (foll. by *with*, *together*) Brit. informal form an amorous or sexual relationship, esp. abruptly or quickly. **get (a crop** etc.) **off** harvest. **get a person off** informal cause a person to be acquitted. **get off on** slang be excited or aroused by; enjoy greatly. **get on 1** make progress; manage. **2** enter (a bus etc.). **3** = GET ALONG. **4** (usu. as **getting on**) informal grow old. **get on to** informal **1** make contact with. **2** understand; become aware of. **get out 1** leave or escape. **2** manage to go outdoors. **3** alight from a vehicle. **4** transpire; become known. **5** succeed in uttering, publishing, etc. **6** (as *interjection*) (also **get out of here!**, **get out of town!**) expressing disbelief. **get a person out** help a person to leave or escape. **get out of 1** avoid or escape (a duty etc.). **2** abandon (a habit) gradually. **get a thing out of** manage to obtain it from (a person) esp. with difficulty. **get over 1** recover from (an illness, upset, etc.). **2** overcome (a difficulty). **3** manage to communicate (an idea etc.). **4** overcome one's disbelief about. **get a thing over** (or **over with**) complete (a tedious task) promptly. **get one's own back** informal have one's revenge. **get rid of** *see* RID. **get somewhere** make progress; be initially successful. **get through 1** pass or assist in passing (an examination, an ordeal, etc.). **2** finish or use up (esp. resources). **3** make contact by telephone. **4** (foll. by *to*) succeed in making (a person) listen or understand. **get a thing through** cause it to overcome obstacles, difficulties, etc. **get to 1** reach. **2** annoy. **3** = GET DOWN TO. **get together 1** gather, assemble. **2** put (something) in order so as to perform effectively (*it's about time you got your act together*). **get up 1** rise or cause to rise from sitting etc., or from bed after sleeping or an illness. **2** ascend or mount, e.g. on a bicycle. **3** (of fire, wind, or the sea) begin to be strong or agitated. **4** prepare or organize. **5** enhance or refine one's knowledge of (a subject). **6** work up (a feeling, e.g. anger). **7** produce or stimulate (*get up steam; get up speed*). **8** (often *reflexive*) dress or arrange elaborately; make presentable; arrange the appearance of. **9** (foll. by *to*) *informal* indulge or be involved in (*always getting up to mischief*). **get it up** *slang* achieve an erection. **get the wind up** *see* WIND[1]. **get with child** *archaic* make pregnant. **have got it bad** (or **badly**) *slang* be obsessed or affected emotionally. □ **get·table** *adjective* [Old Norse *geta* obtain, beget, guess, corresponding to Old English *gietan* (recorded only in compounds), from Germanic]

get-at-able *adjective informal* accessible.

get·away *noun* **1** (often *attributive*) an escape, esp. after committing a crime (*made a clean getaway; police found the getaway car*). **2 a** a place far from work or home, visited for relaxation, e.g. a cottage, resort, etc. **b** a relaxing holiday, esp. far from one's work or home.

get-go *noun* esp. *N Amer. informal* the very beginning (of a project, enterprise, etc.) (*knew from the get-go that it was futile*).

Geth·sem·ane, Garden of /geθ'semənɪ/ a garden lying in the valley between Jerusalem and the Mount of Olives, where Christ went with his disciples after the Last Supper and which was the scene of his agony and betrayal (Matt. 26:36–46). [Hebrew *gath-shemen* oil press]

get-out *noun Brit.* a means of avoiding something. □ **as all get-out** *see* ALL.

get-rich-quick *attributive adjective* designed to make a lot of money fast (*a get-rich-quick scheme*).

get·ter ● *noun* **1** *in senses of* GET *verb.* **2** *Physics* a substance used to remove residual gas from an evacuated vessel. ● *transitive verb Physics* remove (gas) or evacuate (a vessel) with a getter.

get-togeth·er *noun informal* a social gathering.

get-tough *adjective* designating policies, programs, etc. that reflect a new more rigorous or aggressive and less compromising approach to a problem.

Getty ▸ 1 Don·ald Ross (b.1933), Canadian politician, Progressive Conservative premier of Alberta 1985–92. **2 Jean Paul** (1892–1976), US industrialist and art collector. He made an immense fortune in the oil industry, and founded the museum which bears his name in Malibu, California.

Gettys·burg, Battle of /'getɪz,bɜrg/ a decisive battle of the American Civil War fought near the town of Gettysburg, Pennsylvania in July 1863, in which the Union army under General Meade repulsed the Confederate army of General Lee, in a bloody three-day engagement, forcing him to abandon his invasion of the north.

Gettys·burg address a speech delivered on 18 Nov. 1863 by Abraham Lincoln at the dedication of the national cemetery on the site of the Battle of Gettysburg, reasserting the principles of freedom, equality, and democracy on which the United States was founded.

getup *noun informal* a style or arrangement of dress etc., esp. an elaborate one.

get-up-and-go *noun informal* energy, enthusiasm.

Getz /'gets/ **Stan** (born Stanley Gayetzby) (1927–91), US jazz saxophonist, who introduced the Brazilian bossa nova sound into jazz with works such as 'The Girl from Ipanema' (1964).

geum /'dʒiːəm/ *noun* any rosaceous plant of the genus *Geum*, with rosettes of leaves and yellow, red, or white flowers. [modern Latin, var. of Latin *gaeum*]

GeV *abbreviation* giga-electron volt (equivalent to 10^9 electron volts).

gew·gaw /'guːgɔ, 'gjuː-/ *noun* a gaudy ornament or trinket. [Middle English: origin unknown]

Ge·würz·tra·mi·ner /gə'vʊrtstrə,miːnər/ *noun* **1** a variety of grape most associated with Alsace but also grown in other cool climates. **2** the full-bodied and mildly spicy white wine made from this grape. [German, from *Gewürz* spice, perfume + *Traminer* a grape and white wine originally from *Tramin*, now *Termeno*, in N Italy]

gey·ser ● *noun* **1** /'gaizər/ **a** an intermittently gushing hot spring that throws up a tall column of water. **b** a jet of steam or liquid. **2** /'giːzər/ *Brit.* an apparatus for heating water rapidly for domestic use. ● *intransitive verb* (esp. of water or steam) gush or burst out with great force. [Icelandic *Geysir*, the name of a particular spring in Iceland, related to *geysa* to gush]

GFI *abbreviation* (also **GFCI**) *N Amer.* ground-fault (circuit) interrupter, a circuit breaker integrated into an outlet, esp. for use in bathrooms or outdoors.

G-force *noun* the force of acceleration due to gravity.

GG *abbreviation* **1** Governor General. **2** *Cdn* = GOVERNOR GENERAL'S AWARD.

Ghana /'gɒnə, 'ganə/ a country of West Africa, with its southern coastline bordering on the Atlantic Ocean; pop. (est. 2002) 20,244,154; capital, Accra. □ **Ghan·aian** /gə'neiən/ *adjective & noun*

ghar·ial /'geriəl, 'gariəl/ *noun* (also **gavial** /'geiviəl/) a large Indian crocodile, *Gavialis gangeticus*, having a long narrow snout widening at the nostrils. [Hindustani]

ghast·ly ● *adjective* (**ghast·li·er, ghastl·i·est**) **1** horrible, frightful. **2** *informal* objectionable, very unpleasant. **3** deathlike, pallid. ● *adverb* in a ghastly or sickly way (*ghastly pale*). □ **ghast·li·ness** *noun* [Middle English *gastlich* from obsolete *gast* terrify: *gh* after *ghost*]

ghat /gɒt/ *noun* (in India) **1** steps leading down to a river. **2** a defile or mountain pass. [Hindi *ghāt*]

Ghats, the /gɒts/ two mountain ranges in central and S India. Known as the **Eastern Ghats** and the **Western Ghats**, they run parallel to the coast on either side of the Deccan plateau, meeting at the southern tip of India.

ghaz·al /'gɒzɒl/ *noun* a usu. amatory Arabic, Turkish, Urdu, or esp. Persian lyric poem or song characterized by a limited number of stanzas and the recurrence of the same rhyme. [Persian from Arabic *ġazal*]

Ghazi /'gɒzi/ *noun* (pl. **Ghazis**) a Muslim fighter against non-Muslims. [Arabic *al-ġāzī* part. of *ġazā* raid]

Ghazi·abad /'gɒziə,bad/ a city in N India, in Uttar Pradesh east of Delhi; pop. (2001) 968,500.

Ghaz·na·vid /gaz'nɒvɪd/ *noun* a member of a Turkish Muslim dynasty founded in Ghazna, Afghanistan, in AD 977, whose power extended into Persia and the Punjab. Pressure from the Seljuk Turks in the 11th c. fragmented the dynasty, which was finally destroyed in 1186.

GHB *abbreviation* gamma hydroxy butyrate, a designer drug with anaesthetic properties, claimed also to be an aphrodisiac, and much used as a date-rape drug.

ghee /giː/ *noun* clarified butter as used in Indian cuisine, esp. from the milk of a buffalo or cow. [Hindi *ghī* from Sanskrit *ghrita-* sprinkled]

Ghent /gent/ a city in Belgium, capital of the province of East Flanders; pop. (est. 2002) 222,400. A port on the Scheldt River, it is connected by canal to the North Sea at Zeebrugge. It was formerly known in English as Gaunt (surviving in names, e.g. John of Gaunt).

ghe·rao /ge'rau/ *noun* (pl. **-raos**) (in India and Pakistan) coercion of employers, by which their workers prevent them from leaving the premises until certain demands are met. [Hindustani *gherna* besiege]

gher·kin /'gɜrkɪn/ *noun* **1** a small variety of cucumber, or a young green cucumber, used for pickling. **2 a** a trailing plant, *Cucumis sativus*, with cucumber-like fruits used for pickling. **b** this fruit. [Dutch *gurkkijn* (unrecorded), diminutive of *gurk*, from Slavic, ultimately from medieval Greek *aggourion*]

ghet·to *noun* (pl. **-tos** or **-toes**) **1** a part of a city, esp. a slum area, occupied by a minority group or groups. **2** *hist.* an area of a city in which Jews were required to live. **3** a situation in which a group is segregated because of discrimination or its own preference. [perhaps from Italian *getto* 'foundry' (applied to the site of the first ghetto in Venice in 1516)]

ghetto blaster *noun informal* a large powerful portable radio and cassette/CD player.

ghetto·ize *transitive verb* (also esp. *Brit.* **-ise**) restrict to a certain category by prejudice. □ **ghetto·iz·a·tion** *noun*

Ghi·bel·line /'gɪbə,liːn, -lain/ *noun* a member of one of the two great political factions in Italian medieval politics, traditionally supporting the Holy Roman emperor against the pope and his supporters (the Guelphs) during the long struggle between the papacy and the empire. [Italian *Ghibellino* perhaps from German *Waiblingen* estate belonging to Hohenstaufen emperors]

Ghi·ber·ti /gɪ'berti/ **Lor·enzo** (c.1378–1455), Italian sculptor and goldsmith, best known for his two pairs of bronze doors for the

Consonants: b *but*   d *dog*   f *few*   g *get*   h *her*   j *yes*   k *cat*   l *leg*   m *man*   n *no*   p *pen*   r *red*   s *sit*

Baptistery in Florence; the second, more famous, pair (1425–52) represents episodes from the Old Testament.

ghil·lie var. of GILLIE.

Ghir·lan·daio /ˌgɪːrlanˈdaɪoː/ (born Domenico Bigordi) (also **Ghir·lan·dajo**) (1449–94), Italian painter. His religious frescoes, painted in a naturalistic style and including detailed portraits of many leading citizens, include the cycle *Scenes from the Lives of the Virgin and St. John the Baptist* (1486–90) in Florence.

Ghiz /gɪz/ **Jo·seph At·al·lah** (1945–97), Canadian politician, premier of Prince Edward Island 1986–93. He enthusiastically supported the Meech Lake Accord and opposed the Free Trade Agreement.

ghost ● *noun* **1** the supposed apparition of a dead person or animal, often as a nebulous image; a disembodied spirit. **2** a shadow or mere semblance (*not a ghost of a chance*). **3** a secondary or duplicated image produced by defective television reception or by a telescope. **4** *archaic* a spirit or soul. ● *verb* **1 a** *intransitive* (often foll. by *for*) act as ghostwriter. **b** *transitive* act as ghostwriter of (a work). **2** *intransitive* move like a ghost. □ **give up the ghost** *informal* die. □ **ghost·like** *adjective* [Old English *gāst* from West Germanic: *gh*- occurs first in Caxton, prob. influenced by Flemish *gheest*]

ghost·bust·er *noun informal* a person who professes to banish ghosts, poltergeists, etc.

ghost car *noun Cdn informal* an unmarked police car.

Ghost Dance a Messianic movement which spread among N American Aboriginal peoples in the second half of the 19th c. Followers believed that the whites would be expelled, the traditional lands and way of life would be restored, and the dead would return; to these ends ritual dances were performed, sometimes for days on end, and a code was adopted that combined traditional with Christian elements. Advocated by the Sioux chief Sitting Bull, the movement led to the uprising that was crushed at the Battle of Wounded Knee.

ghost·ing *noun* **1** in senses of GHOST *verb*. **2** the appearance of a 'ghost' or secondary image in a television picture or on a computer screen.

ghost·ly *adjective* (**ghost·li·er**, **ghost·li·est**) like a ghost; spectral. □ **ghost·li·ness** *noun*

ghost town *noun* a deserted town with few or no remaining inhabitants.

ghost·writer *noun* a person who writes on behalf of the credited author of a work. □ **ghost·write** *transitive & intransitive verb*

ghoul /guːl/ *noun* **1** an evil spirit or phantom. **2** a person morbidly interested in death, disaster, etc. **3** a spirit in Arabic folklore preying on corpses. □ **ghoul·ish** *adjective* **ghoul·ish·ly** *adverb* **ghoul·ish·ness** *noun* [Arabic *ġūla* desert demon believed to rob graves and devour corpses]

GHQ *abbreviation* general headquarters.

Ghul·ghu·leh /gʊlˈgʊlə/ an ancient city, now ruined, near Bamian in central Afghanistan. The city was destroyed by Genghis Khan *c*.1221.

ghyll *Brit.* var. of GILL³.

GHz *abbreviation* gigahertz.

GI¹ /dʒiːˈaɪ/ ● *noun* a private soldier in the US Army. ● *adjective* of or for US servicemen. [abbreviation of *government* (or *general*) *issue*]

GI² *abbreviation* gastrointestinal.

gi /giː/ *noun* the loose white jacket worn in judo and karate. [Japanese]

Gia·co·met·ti /ˌdʒakəˈmeti/ **Al·berto** (1901–66), Swiss sculptor and painter. The characteristic style which he adopted after the Second World War, exemplified in such works as *Pointing Man* (1947), features emaciated and extremely elongated human figures.

giant ● *noun* **1** an imaginary or mythical being of human form but superhuman size. **2** (in Greek mythology) one of such beings who fought against the gods. **3** an abnormally tall or large person, animal, plant, or thing. **4** a person, company, etc. of exceptional ability, prominence, importance, etc. **5 a** a star of relatively great size and luminosity. **b** any of the enormous gaseous planets Jupiter, Saturn, Uranus, and Neptune. ● *attributive adjective* **1** of extraordinary size or force, gigantic. **2** of exceptional importance, ability, or prominence (*a giant leap in science*). **3** (of a plant or animal) of a very large kind. □ **giant·ism** **giant·like** *adjective* [Middle English *geant* (later influenced by Latin) from Old French, ultimately from Latin *gigas gigant-* from Greek]

giant·ess *noun* a female imaginary or mythical being of human form but superhuman size.

giant hyssop *noun see* HYSSOP 3.

giant-killer *noun* a person who defeats a seemingly much more powerful opponent.

Giant's Causeway a geological formation of basalt columns, dating from the Tertiary period, on the north coast of Northern Ireland. It was once believed to be the end of a road made by a legendary giant to Staffa in the Inner Hebrides, where there is a similar formation.

giant sequoia *noun see* SEQUOIA.

giant slalom *noun Skiing* a downhill event with a longer course and wider turns than standard slalom.

giant squid *noun* a deep-sea squid which is the largest known invertebrate, reaching a length of 18m (59 ft) or more.

giaour /ˈdʒaʊr/ *noun derogatory* a non-Muslim, esp. a Christian. [Turkish *gâvur* from Persian *gaur* var. of *gabr*, prob. from Arabic *kāfir* infidel, from *kafara* not believe]

gi·ar·dia /gɪˈɑrdiə/ *noun* a flagellate protozoan, *Giardia lamblia*, sometimes found in the mammalian intestines. [modern Latin genus name *Giardia* (from A. *Giard*, French biologist d.1908)]

gi·ar·dia·sis /dʒɪɑrˈdaɪəsɪs/ *noun Med.* infection of the intestines with giardia, often from drinking untreated lake water, causing diarrhea etc. *Also called* BEAVER FEVER.

Gib /dʒɪb/ *noun informal* Gibraltar. [abbreviation]

gib /dʒɪb, gɪb/ *noun* a wood or metal bolt, wedge, or pin for holding a machine part etc. in place. [18th c.: origin unknown]

gib·ber /ˈdʒɪbər/ ● *verb* **1** *intransitive* speak fast and inarticulately; chatter incoherently. **2** *transitive* utter in a gibber. ● *noun* such speech or sound. □ **gib·ber·ing** *noun* (usu. in *pl.*). [imitative]

gib·ber·el·lin /ˌdʒɪbəˈrelɪn/ *noun* one of a group of plant hormones that stimulate the growth of leaves and shoots. [*Gibberella* a genus of fungi, diminutive of genus name *Gibbera* from Latin *gibber* hump]

gib·ber·ish /ˈdʒɪbərɪʃ/ *noun* unintelligible or meaningless speech or writing; nonsense. [perhaps from GIBBER (but attested earlier) + -ISH¹ as used in *Spanish*, *Swedish*, etc.]

gib·bet /ˈdʒɪbət/ ● *noun hist.* **1 a** a gallows. **b** an upright post with an arm from which the bodies of executed criminals were hung for public viewing. **2** (prec. by *the*) death by hanging. ● *transitive verb* (**gib·bet·ed**, **gib·bet·ing**) **1** put to death by hanging. **2** expose on a gibbet. [Old French *gibet* gallows, diminutive of *gibe* club, prob. from Germanic]

Gib·bon /ˈgɪbən/ **Edward** (1737–94), English historian. His six-volume *The History of the Decline and Fall of the Roman Empire* (1776–88), aroused controversy for the critical account of the spread of Christianity in some chapters.

gib·bon /ˈgɪbən/ *noun* any small ape of the genus *Hylobates*, native to SE Asia, having a slender body and long arms. [French, of unknown origin]

Gib·bons /ˈgɪbənz/ **Or·lan·do** (1583–1625), English composer. He composed mainly sacred music, including anthems, motets, and several hymn tunes, and madrigals, notably *The Silver Swan* (1612).

gib·bous /ˈgɪbəs/ *adjective* **1** (of a moon or planet) having the bright part greater than a semicircle and less than a circle. **2** convex or protuberant; bulging. [Late Latin *gibbosus* from *gibbus* hump]

Gibbs /gɪbz/ **Jo·si·ah Wil·lard** (1839–1903), US physical chemist. He was the founder of the study of chemical thermodynamics and statistical mechanics, though the profound significance of his theoretical work was not generally appreciated until after his death.

gibe var. of JIBE¹.

gib·lets /ˈdʒɪbləts/ *plural noun* the liver, gizzard, heart, neck, etc., of a fowl, usu. removed and kept separate when the bird is prepared for cooking. [Old French *gibelet* game stew, perhaps from *gibier* game]

Gibral·tar /dʒɪˈbrɒltər/ a British dependency near the southern tip of the Iberian peninsula, at the eastern end of the Strait of Gibraltar; pop. (est. 2002) 27,714. Occupying a site of great strategic importance, Gibraltar consists of a fortified town and military base at the foot of a rocky headland (the **Rock of Gibraltar**) 426 m (1398 ft.) high. (*See also* PILLARS OF HERCULES.) □ **Gibral·tar·ian** /ˌdʒɪbrɒlˈteriən/ *adjective & noun* [Arabic *gebel-al-Tarik* hill of Tarik, 8th-c. Saracen commander]

Gibraltar, Strait of a channel between the southern tip of the Iberian peninsula and North Africa, forming the only outlet of the Mediterranean Sea to the Atlantic. Varying in width from 24km (15 miles) to 40 km (25 miles) at its western extremity, it stretches east-west for some 60 km (38 miles).

Gib·ran /dʒɪˈbran/ (also **Jub·ran**), **Kha·lil** (1883–1931), Lebanese-born US mystic poet, essayist, and painter, best known for *The Prophet* (1923).

Gib·son ▸ **1 Al·thea** (1927–2003), US tennis player. The first black player to compete successfully at the highest level of tennis, she won all the major world women's singles titles, including the British and American titles (1957 and 1958). **2 Mel (Colum·cille Ger·ard)**

(b.1956), American-born Australian actor and director. He acquired recognition with *Mad Max* (1979) and went on to star in the *Lethal Weapon* trilogy (1987, 1989, 1992) and *Braveheart*, which he also directed and which won five Oscars. **3 Wil·liam** (b.1948) US-born Canadian science-fiction writer, who first coined the term 'cyberspace' (*Neuromancer*, 1984).

Gibson Desert a desert region in Western Australia, to the southeast of the Great Sandy Desert.

Gibson girl *noun* a girl typifying the fashionable ideal of *c*.1900, wearing a long skirt, very tight waist, a high neckline, and full-length, usu. leg-of-mutton sleeves. [as represented in the work of C.D. *Gibson* US artist d.1944]

GIC *abbreviation Cdn* = GUARANTEED INVESTMENT CERTIFICATE.

giddy ● *adjective* (**gid·di·er**, **gid·di·est**) **1** having a sensation of whirling and a tendency to fall, stagger, or spin round; dizzy. **2 a** overexcited as a result of success, pleasurable emotion, etc.; mentally intoxicated. **b** excitable, frivolous. **3** tending to make one giddy. ● *transitive verb* (**-dies**, **-died**) (usu. as **giddy·ing** *adjective*) make giddy. □ **gid·di·ly** *adverb* **gid·di·ness** *noun* [Old English *gidig* insane, lit. 'possessed by a god']

giddy-up *interjection* (also **gid·dap**, **giddy·ap**) commanding a horse to go or go faster. [reproducing a pronunciation of *get up*]

Gide /ʒiːd/ **André (Paul Guil·laume)** (1869–1951), French novelist, essayist, and critic. His novels, which often deal with themes of self-fulfillment and renunciation, include *The Immoralist* (1902) and *The Counterfeiters* (1926); he received the Nobel Prize for literature in 1947.

Gid·eon /ˈɡɪdiən/ **1** *Bible* an Israelite leader, described in Judges 6:11 ff. **2** a member of the Gideons International.

Gideon Bible *noun* a Bible purchased by the Christian organization Gideons International and placed in a hotel room etc.

Gideons International an international Christian organization of business and professional people, founded in 1899 in the US with the aim of spreading the Christian faith by placing bibles in hotel rooms, hospital wards, etc.

gie /ɡiː/ *transitive & intransitive verb Scot.* = GIVE.

Giel·gud /ˈɡiːlɡʊd/ **Sir (Arthur) John** (1904–2000), English actor and director. One of the outstanding Shakespearean stage actors of the 20th c., he was also noted for his roles in films such as *Arthur* (1980), for which he won an Oscar, and *Prospero's Books* (1991).

GIF /ɡɪf/ *noun* **1** *computing* a format for image files, with built-in data compression. **2** a file in this format. [acronym from *graphic interchange format*]

GIFT /ɡɪft/ *noun* gamete intrafallopian transfer, a technique for assisting conception by introducing mixed ova and sperm into a Fallopian tube. [acronym]

gift ● *noun* **1 a** a thing given freely; a present. **b** (*attributive*) denoting a usu. decorated container or wrapping for gifts, given along with the presents (*gift bag*; *gift box*). **2** a natural ability or talent. **3** the power to give (*in his gift*). **4** the act or an instance of giving. ● *transitive verb* **1** endow with gifts. **2 a** (foll. by *with*) give to as a gift. **b** bestow as a gift. □ **look a gift horse in the mouth** (usu. *neg.*) find fault with what has been given. □ **gift·ing** *noun* [Old Norse *gipt* from Germanic, related to GIVE]

gift certificate *noun N Amer.* a certificate or voucher presented as a gift and exchangeable for a specified value of goods, usu. at a specific store.

gift·ed *adjective* **1** exceptionally talented or intelligent. **2** *N Amer.* designating programs of study for children of above average intelligence or artistic talent. □ **gifted·ness** *noun*

gift of tongues *noun see* TONGUE.

gift shop *noun* a small store, often within a museum, hospital, stadium, or other public venue, selling articles suitable as gifts.

gift·ware *noun* goods sold as being suitable as gifts.

gift-wrap ● *transitive verb* (**-wrapped**, **-wrap·ping**) wrap attractively as a gift. ● *noun* (**gift wrap**) decorative paper etc. for wrapping gifts.

Gifu /ˈɡiːfuː/ a city in central Japan, on the island of Honshu; pop. (est. 2002) 419,600.

gig¹ *informal* ● *noun* **1** an engagement of an entertainer, esp. of musicians to play jazz, rock, or dance music, usu. for a single appearance. **2** a performance of this kind. **3** a job or employment, esp. likely to be temporary. ● *intransitive verb* (**gigged**, **gig·ging**) perform in gigs or a gig. [20th c.: origin unknown]

gig² *noun* **1** a light two-wheeled one-horse carriage. **2** a light ship's boat for rowing or sailing. **3** a rowboat esp. for racing. [Middle English, perhaps originally = a flighty girl]

gig³ ● *noun* a kind of fishing spear, also used to catch frogs. ● *transitive & intransitive verb* spear (a fish or frog) with a gig. [short for *fizgig*, *fishgig*: compare Spanish *fisga* harpoon]

gig⁴ *noun* a gigabyte. [abbreviation]

giga- /ˈɡɪɡə/ *combining form* **1** denoting a factor of 10^9 (i.e. one billion) (*gigawatt*). **2** *Computing* (in the binary system) denoting a factor of 2^{30} (i.e. 1 073 741 824) (*gigabyte*; *gigabit*). [Greek *gigas* giant]

giga·byte /ˈɡɪɡəˌbaɪt/ *noun Computing* 1 073 741 824 (i.e. 2^{30}) bytes as a measure of data capacity, or loosely 1 000 000 000.

giga·flop /ˈɡɪɡəflɒp/ *noun Computing* a unit of computing speed equal to one billion floating-point operations per second.

giga·hertz *noun* a measure of frequency equivalent to one billion (10^9) cycles per second.

gi·gan·tic /dʒaɪˈɡantɪk/ *adjective* **1** very large; enormous. **2** like or suited to a giant. [Latin *gigas gigantis* GIANT]

gi·gan·tism /ˈdʒaɪɡanˌtɪzəm, dʒaɪˈɡantɪzəm/ *noun* **1** abnormal largeness. **2** *Med.* excessive growth due to hormonal imbalance. **3** *Bot.* excessive size due to polyploidy in plants.

gig·gle ● *intransitive verb* laugh in half-suppressed, high-pitched, spasms, esp. in a silly manner or out of nervousness. ● *noun* **1** such a laugh. **2** (**the giggles**) a fit of giggling. **3** *informal* an amusing person or thing; a joke. □ **gig·gler** *noun* **gig·gly** *adjective* (**gig·gli·er**, **gig·gli·est**). **gig·gli·ness** *noun* [imitative: compare Dutch *gichelen*, German *gickeln*]

GIGO /ˈɡaɪɡoʊ/ *abbreviation Computing* garbage in, garbage out.

gig·olo /ˈdʒɪɡəˌloʊ/ *noun* (*pl.* **-olos**) **1** a young man paid by an older woman to be her escort or lover. **2** a professional male dancing partner or escort. [French, formed as masc. of *gigole* dance hall woman]

gi·got /ʒiːˈɡoʊ/ *noun* a leg of mutton or lamb. [French, diminutive of dial. *gigue* leg]

gigue /ʒiːɡ/ *noun* a lively piece of music in duple or triple time, often with dotted rhythms and forming the last movement of a suite. [French, from JIG]

Gijón /ɡiˈhɒn/ a port and industrial city in N Spain, on the Bay of Biscay; pop. (est. 2001) 269,270.

Gila monster /ˈhiːlə/ *noun* a large carnivorous venomous lizard of Mexico and the southwestern US, *Heloderma suspectum*, black with orange or pink markings. [*Gila* river in New Mexico and Arizona]

Gil·bert ▶ **1 Sir Hum·phrey** (*c*.1539–83), English explorer. Following his unsuccessful attempt to colonize N America (1578–9), he claimed Newfoundland for Elizabeth I in 1583, establishing a colony at St. John's. **2 Wil·liam** (1544–1603), English physician and physicist. He worked on terrestrial magnetism, discovered how to make magnets, and coined the term *magnetic pole* in his work *De Magnete* (1600). **3 Sir Wil·liam Schwenck** (1836–1911), English humorist and librettist, whose collaboration with the composer Sir Arthur Sullivan produced 14 light operas between 1871 and 1896, including *HMS Pinafore* (1878), *The Pirates of Penzance* (1879), and *The Mikado* (1885).

Gil·bert and El·lice Islands a former British colony (1915–75) in the central Pacific, consisting of two groups of islands: the Gilbert Islands and the Ellice Islands.

Gilbert Islands a group of islands in the central Pacific, forming part of Kiribati. The islands straddle the equator and lie immediately west of the International Date Line.

gild¹ /ɡɪld/ *transitive verb* (*past participle* **gilded** or as adj. in sense 1 **gilt**) **1** cover thinly with gold or a substance resembling gold. **2** tinge with a golden colour or light. **3** give a specious or false brilliance to. □ **gild the lily** try to improve what is already beautiful or excellent. □ **gild·er** *noun* [Old English *gyldan* from Germanic]

gild² *archaic var. of* GUILD.

gilded age *noun* a period of great prosperity, esp. (**Gilded Age**) the period from *c*.1870-1898 in US history.

gilded cage *noun* luxurious but restrictive surroundings.

gilded youth *noun* young people of wealth, fashion, and privilege.

gild·ing *noun* **1** the act or art of applying gilt. **2** material used in applying gilt.

Gil·ga·mesh /ˈɡɪlɡəˌmeʃ/ a legendary Sumerian king who ruled some time during the first half of the 3rd millennium BC; the epic of Gilgamesh recounts his exploits in an ultimately unsuccessful quest for immortality.

Gil·git /ˈɡɪlɡɪt/ a town in a mountainous district of the same name, in the northern part of Pakistani Kashmir.

gill¹ /ɡɪl/ ● *noun* (usu. in *pl.*) **1** the respiratory organ in fishes and other aquatic animals. **2** the vertical radial plates on the underside of

Vowels: a cat ɑ arm e bed ɜr her ɜ: deux ə ago ɪ sit i cosy iː feed ɒ hot ɔ pore ɔː no ʌ run ʊ put

mushrooms and other fungi. **3** the flesh below a person's jaws and ears (*green at the gills*). ● *transitive verb* **1** gut or clean (a fish). **2** cut off the gills of (a mushroom). **3** catch in a gillnet. □ **to the gills** completely, thoroughly, fully (*fed to the gills*). □ **gilled** *adjective* (also in *combination*). [Old Norse *gil* (unrecorded) from Germanic]

gill² /dʒɪl/ *noun* a unit of liquid measure, equal to a quarter of a pint (142 ml in imperial measure, 118 ml in US measure). [Old French *gille*, medieval Latin *gillo* from Late Latin *gello, gillo* water pot]

gill³ /gɪl/ *noun* (also **ghyll**) *Brit.* **1** a deep usu. wooded ravine. **2** a narrow mountain torrent. [Old Norse *gil* glen]

gill⁴ /dʒɪl/ *noun* (also **Gill, jill, Jill**) *derogatory* a young woman. [Middle English, abbreviation of *Gillian*]

gill cover *noun* a bony case protecting a fish's gills; an operculum.

Giller Prize *noun Cdn* a prize awarded to the author of the best Canadian novel or short story collection published in English each year. [named in honour of the literary journalist Doris Giller (d.1993) by her husband Jack Rabinovitch, who established the prize in 1994]

Gil·les·pie /gɪˈlespi/ **John Birks ('Dizzy')** (1917–93), US jazz musician and bandleader. A virtuoso trumpet player, he was a leading exponent of the bebop style of jazz.

gil·lie /ˈgɪli/ *noun* (also **ghillie**) *Scot.* **1** a man or boy attending a person hunting or fishing. **2** *hist.* a Highland chief's attendant. [Gaelic *gille* lad, servant]

Gil·lis /ˈgɪlɪs/ **Mar·gie** (b.1953), Canadian modern dancer and choreographer. Known for her energetic dancing style, flowing hair and costumes, she has established an international reputation, and was created a Member of the Order of Canada in 1988.

gill·net /ˈgɪlnet/ *noun* a net suspended vertically to entangle fish by the gills. □ **gill·net·ting** *noun*

gill·net·ter /ˈgɪlnetər/ *noun* **1** a person who fishes using gillnets. **2** a ship or boat designed for fishing with gillnets.

gilly·flower /ˈdʒɪli,flaʊr/ *noun* **1** (in full **clove gillyflower**) a clove-scented pink (*see* CLOVE¹ 2). **2** any of various similarly scented flowers such as the wallflower or white stock. [Old French *gilofre, girofle*, from medieval Latin from Greek *karuophullon* clove tree, from *karuon* nut + *phullon* leaf, assimilated to FLOWER]

Gil·man /ˈgɪlmən/ **Char·lotte Anna Per·kins** (1860–1935), US feminist and writer, best known for the short story *The Yellow Wallpaper* (1892), the study *Women and Economics* (1898), and the utopian fantasy *Herland* (1915).

gilt¹ /gɪlt/ ● *adjective* **1** covered thinly with gold or a gold-like substance. **2** gold-coloured. ● *noun* **1** gold or a gold-like substance applied in a thin layer to a surface. **2** (often in *pl.*) *Brit.* a gilt-edged security. [past participle of GILD¹]

gilt² /gɪlt/ *noun* a young sow that has not been bred. [Old Norse *gyltr*]

gilt-edged *adjective* **1** (of a page, book, etc.) having a gilded edge. **2** of the highest quality; first-rate. **3** (of securities, stocks, etc.) having a high degree of reliability as an investment.

gim·bal /ˈdʒɪmbəl, ˈgɪmbəl/ *noun* (often in *pl.*) a contrivance, usu. of rings and pivots, for keeping objects, esp. instruments such as a compass and chronometer, horizontal aboard a ship or aircraft, etc. □ **gim·balled** *adjective* [var. of earlier *gimmal* from Old French *gemel* double finger ring, from Latin *gemellus* diminutive of *geminus* twin]

gim·crack /ˈgɪmkrak/ ● *adjective* showy but flimsy and worthless. ● *noun* a cheap showy ornament; a knick-knack. □ **gim·crack·ery** *noun* [Middle English *gibecrake* a kind of ornament, of unknown origin]

gim·let /ˈgɪmlət/ *noun* **1** a small tool with a screw tip for boring holes. **2** a cocktail usu. of gin or vodka and lime juice. [Old French *guimbelet*, diminutive of *guimble*, ultimately from Germanic]

gim·let eye *noun* an eye with a piercing glance. □ **gimlet-eyed** *adjective*

gimme /ˈgɪmi/ *informal* ● *contraction* give me. ● *interjection* give it to me. ● *noun N Amer.* **1** esp. *Sport* a task, e.g. kicking a short field goal or sinking a short putt, regarded as too easy to bungle; a sure thing. **2** *Golf* (in informal games) a short easy putt one is not required to attempt. ● *adjective N Amer.* designating an item given away, esp. for promotional purposes (*gimme cap*).

gim·mick /ˈgɪmɪk/ *noun informal* a trick or device, often underhanded, esp. for attracting attention, publicity, or trade. □ **gim·mickry** *noun* **gim·micky** *adjective* [20th c.: origin unknown]

gimp¹ /gɪmp/ *noun* **1** a twist of silk etc. with cord or wire running through it, used esp. as a trimming on upholstery. **2** a coarser thread outlining the design of lace. [Dutch: origin unknown]

gimp² /gɪmp/ *slang* ● *noun* **1** a lame person or leg. **2** a stupid or

contemptible person. ● *intransitive verb* limp, hobble. □ **gimpy** *adjective* [20th c. US: origin unknown]

gin¹ /dʒɪn/ *noun* **1** an alcoholic spirit distilled from grain or malt and flavoured esp. with juniper berries. **2** = GIN RUMMY. [abbreviation of GENEVA]

gin² /dʒɪn/ ● *noun* **1** a snare or trap. **2** a machine for separating cotton from its seeds. **3** a kind of crane and windlass. ● *transitive verb* (**ginned**, **gin·ning**) **1** treat (cotton) in a gin. **2** trap. □ **gin·ner** *noun* [Old French *engin* ENGINE]

gin-and-it *noun* a cocktail of gin and Italian vermouth. [abbreviation]

ginch *noun var. of* GOTCH. [alteration of GITCH]

gin clear *adjective* (of water) perfectly clear.

gin·ger ● *noun* **1 a** a hot spicy root used fresh or dried and powdered for use in cooking, or preserved in syrup, or candied. **b** the plant, *Zingiber officinale*, of SE Asia, having this root. **2** a light reddish-yellow colour. **3** spirit, mettle. **4** *N Amer.* ginger ale. ● *adjective* of a ginger colour. ● *transitive verb* **1** flavour with ginger. **2** (foll. by *up*) rouse or enliven. □ **gin·gery** *adjective* [Old English *gingifer* & Old French *gingi(m)bre*, both from medieval Latin *gingiber*, ultimately from Sanskrit *śṛngaveram* from *śṛngam* horn + *-vera* body, with reference to the antler shape of the root]

ginger ale *noun* a carbonated clear amber drink flavoured with ginger extract.

ginger beer *noun* **1** an effervescent, cloudy soft drink strongly flavoured with ginger. **2** an effervescent mildly alcoholic cloudy drink, made by fermenting a mixture of ginger and syrup.

ginger·bread *noun* **1** a cake or cookie made with molasses and flavoured with ginger (*gingerbread cookie; gingerbread man*). **2** (often *attributive*) elaborate carving or other trim on buildings, usu. along the eaves or on porches etc. **3** gaudy or tawdry decoration or ornament.

ginger group *noun Cdn & Brit.* a group within a party or movement that presses for stronger or more radical policy or action.

ginger jar *noun* a wide-mouthed ceramic jar that bulges outward at the top and tapers toward the base.

gin·ger·ly ● *adverb* in a careful or cautious manner. ● *adjective* showing great care or caution. □ **gin·ger·li·ness** *noun* [perhaps from Old French *gensor* delicate, comparative of *gent* graceful, from Latin *genitus* (well-)born]

ginger·snap *noun* a thin, brittle, ginger-flavoured cookie.

ginger wine *noun* a drink of fermented sugar, water, and bruised ginger.

ging·ham /ˈgɪŋəm/ *noun* a plain-woven cotton cloth of dyed yarn, esp. striped or checked. [Dutch *gingang* from Malay *ginggang* (originally adj. = striped)]

gin·giva /ˈdʒɪndʒɪvə, dʒɪnˈdʒaɪvə/ *noun* (*pl.* **gin·givae** /-,viː/) the gum. □ **gin·gi·val** /-ˈdʒaɪvəl/ *adjective* [Latin]

gin·gi·vitis /,dʒɪndʒɪˈvaɪtɪs/ *noun* inflammation of the gums.

gink /gɪŋk/ *noun slang* often *derogatory* a fellow; a man. [20th c.: origin unknown]

gink·go /ˈgɪŋkɡoː/ *noun* (also **ging·ko** /ˈgɪŋkoː/) (*pl.* **-gos** or **-goes**) **1** an originally Chinese and Japanese tree, *Ginkgo biloba*, with fan-shaped leaves and yellow flowers. *Also called* MAIDENHAIR TREE. **2** a herbal extract from its leaves, which improves circulation and brain function, esp. memory. [Japanese *ginkyo* from Chinese *yinxing* silver apricot]

gin mill *noun N Amer.* a bar, esp. a disreputable or seedy one.

gi·nor·mous /dʒaɪˈnɔrməs/ *adjective Cdn & Brit. slang* very large; enormous. [GIANT + ENORMOUS]

gin rummy *noun Cards* a form of rummy in which a player holding cards totalling ten or less may terminate play.

Gins·berg /ˈgɪnzbərg/ **Allen** (1926–97), US poet. A leading poet of the beat generation, he is best known for the poem *Howl* (1956), in which he attacked US society for its materialism and complacency.

gin·seng /ˈdʒɪnseŋ/ *noun* **1** any of several medicinal plants of the genus *Panax*, found in E Asia and N America. **2** the root of this. [Chinese *renshen* perhaps = man-image, with allusion to its forked root]

Gior·gione /dʒɔrˈdʒoːne/ (also called Giorgio Barbarelli or Giorgio da Castelfranco) (*c.*1478–1510), Italian painter. He was one of the earliest artists to specialize in small easel paintings intended for private collectors; his works, such as *The Tempest* (*c.*1505), typically feature enigmatic figures in pastoral settings.

Giotto /,dʒɒtoː/ (full name Giotto di Bondone) (*c.*1267–1337), Italian painter. His art marks a turning away from the flat patterns and symbols of the Byzantine tradition to the clear space and dignified human figures of Renaissance art; notable works include the frescoes in the Arena Chapel, Padua (1305–8) and those in the Church of Santa Croce, Florence (c.1320).

Gio·van·ni de' Med·ici see Leo X.

gippy tummy /ˈdʒɪpi/ noun (also **gyppy tummy**) esp. Cdn & Brit. informal an upset stomach, esp. accompanied by diarrhea and affecting visitors to hot countries. [abbreviation of EGYPTIAN]

gipsy var. of GYPSY.

gir·affe /dʒɪˈraf/ noun a ruminant mammal, Giraffa camelopardalis of Africa, the tallest living animal, with a long neck and forelegs and a skin of dark patches separated by lighter lines. [French girafe, Italian giraffa, ultimately from Arabic zarāfa]

gir·an·dole /ˈdʒɪrən,doːl/ noun **1** a revolving cluster of fireworks. **2** a branched support for candles or other lights, esp. projecting from a wall, and often incorporating a mirror. **3** an earring or pendant with a large central stone surrounded by small ones. [French from Italian girandola from girare GYRATE]

gira·sol /ˈdʒɪrə,sɒl/ noun (also **gira·sole** /-,soːl/) a kind of opal reflecting a reddish glow. [originally = sunflower, from French girasol or Italian girasole from girare (as GIRANDOLE) + sole sun]

Girau·doux /ʒɪroːˈduː/ **(Hip·po·lyte) Jean** (1882–1944), French dramatist, novelist, and diplomat, whose plays are frequently stylized and modernized versions of Biblical or classical legend, and include Amphitryon 38 (1929) and La Guerre de Troie n'aura pas lieu (1935).

gird verb (past and past participle **gird·ed**) literary **1** transitive encircle, attach, or secure with a belt or band. **2** transitive secure (clothes) on the body with a girdle or belt. **3** transitive enclose or encircle. **4** transitive **a** (foll. by with) equip with a sword in a belt. **b** fasten (a sword) with a belt. **5** intransitive (foll. by for) prepare for action, a conflict, etc. **6** transitive place (cord etc.) round. □ **gird** (or **gird up**) **one's loins** prepare for action. [Old English gyrdan from Germanic (as GIRTH)]

gird·er noun a large iron or steel beam or compound structure for bearing loads, esp. in bridge-building.

gir·dle¹ ● noun **1** a woman's corset extending from waist to thigh. **2** a belt or cord worn around the waist. **3** a thing that surrounds like a girdle. **4** the bony support for a limb (pelvic girdle). **5** the part of a cut gem dividing the crown from the base and embraced by the setting. **6** a ring around a tree made by the removal of bark. ● transitive verb **1** surround with or as with a girdle. **2 a** remove a ring of bark from (a branch or tree) to kill it. **b** remove a ring of bark from (a branch) to make the tree more fruitful. [Old English gyrdel: see GIRD]

gir·dle² noun Scot. & Northern England a circular iron plate placed over a fire or otherwise heated for baking, toasting, etc. [var. of GRIDDLE]

girl noun **1** a female child or youth. **2** informal a young (esp. unmarried) woman. **3** informal a daughter. **4** informal a girlfriend or sweetheart. **5** often offensive a female servant. **6** often offensive a grown woman. **7** a woman belonging to a specified group (a country girl). **8** (**the girls**) informal a group of women mixing socially. **9** (usu. as a form of address) a female animal (Steady, girl!). □ **girl·hood** noun [Middle English (denoting a child or young person of either sex) perhaps related to Low German gör child]

girl band noun (also **girl group**) a pop group composed of young attractive women, appealing esp. to a young audience.

girl Friday noun dated a woman who performs a variety of clerical and secretarial duties in a business office. [after MAN FRIDAY]

girl·friend noun **1** a regular female companion or lover. **2** a female friend.

Girl Guide noun Cdn, Brit., Austral., & NZ a member of a girls' organization promoting outdoor activity, leadership, and community service.

girl·ie (also **girly**) informal ● adjective **1** (of a magazine etc.) depicting nude or partially nude young women in erotic poses. **2** girlish. ● noun (pl. **-ies**) offensive a young woman.

girl·ish adjective of or like a young girl. □ **girl·ish·ly** adverb **girl·ish·ness** noun

girl power noun power exercised by girls, esp. a self-reliant attitude among girls and young women manifested in ambition, assertiveness, and individualism.

Girl Scout noun (in the US) a girl belonging to the Scout Association.

giro /ˈdʒaɪroː/ noun (pl. **giros**) Brit. **1** a system of credit transfer between banks, post offices, etc. **2** a cheque or payment by giro, esp. used for unemployment benefit or social security payments. [German from Italian, = circulation (of money)]

Gi·ronde /ʒɪˈrɒnd/ a river estuary in SW France, formed at the junction of the Garonne and Dordogne rivers, north of Bordeaux, and flowing northwest for 72 km (45 miles) into the Bay of Biscay.

Gi·ron·din /ʒɪːrɒˈdã/ noun (also **Gi·rond·ist** /ʒɪˈrɒndɪst/) a member of the French moderate republican party in power during the Revolution 1791–93, so called because the party leaders were the deputies from the department of the Gironde. [French]

girt¹ /gɜrt/ adjective literary **1** (in combination) surrounded (a sea-girt paradise). **2** (foll. by round) circumscribed.

girt² var. of GIRTH.

girth /gɜrθ/ noun **1 a** the distance around a thing. **b** size, esp. of an overweight person. **2** a band around the body of a horse to secure the saddle etc. [Old Norse gjörth, Gothic gairda from Germanic]

GIS abbreviation **1** Cdn GUARANTEED INCOME SUPPLEMENT. **2** geographic information system.

Gis·card d'Estaing /ʒɪskar destã/ **Va·léry** (b.1926), French conservative politician, secretary of state for finance 1959–62, finance minister 1962–6, and president 1974–81, regarded as the principal architect of France's economic growth in the 1960s and early 1970s.

Gish /gɪʃ/ **1 Dor·othy** (born Dorothy de Guiche) (1898–1968), US actress, who is noted for her roles in the silent films of D.W. Griffith, including Hearts of the World (1918) and Orphans of the Storm (1921). **2** her sister, **Lil·lian** (born Lillian de Guiche) (1896–1993), US actress, who starred alongside her sister in a number of silent films, and is remembered for her roles in The Birth of a Nation (1915) and Intolerance (1916).

gist /dʒɪst/ noun **1** the substance or essence of a matter (the gist of my argument). **2** Law the real ground of an action etc. [Old French, 3rd sing. pres. of gesir lie, from Latin jacēre]

git /gɪt/ ● interjection esp. N Amer. informal get going; get along. ● noun Brit. slang a silly or contemptible person. [var. of GET]

gitch /gɪtʃ/ noun Cdn slang underwear. [origin unknown, perhaps alteration of GOTCH]

Git·chi Mani·tou /,gɪtʃiː ˈmanɪ,tuː/ the 'Great Spirit' of the Ojibwa and neighbouring Algonquian peoples. [Ojibwa]

gîte /ʒiːt/ noun a furnished holiday house in a French-speaking area, usu. small and in a rural district. [originally = lodging: French from Old French giste, related to gésir lie]

Git·ksan /gɪtˈksɒn/ noun **1** an Aboriginal group living along the Skeena River in north central BC. **2** the Tsimshian language of this group. [Gitksan kitxsan, lit. 'people of the Skeena River']

git·tern /ˈgɪtɜrn/ noun a medieval stringed instrument, a forerunner of the guitar. [Old French guiterne: compare CITTERN, GUITAR]

give ● verb (past **gave**; past participle **given**) **1** transitive & intransitive (often foll. by to) transfer the possession of freely; hand over as a present (gave them her old curtains; gives to cancer research). **2** transitive **a** transfer the ownership of with or without actual delivery; bequeath (gave him $200 in her will). **b** transfer, esp. temporarily or for safekeeping; hand over; provide with (gave him the dog to hold; gave them a drink). **c** administer (medicine). **d** deliver (a message) (give her my best wishes). **3** transitive (usu. foll. by for) make over in exchange or payment; pay; sell (gave him $100 for the bicycle). **4** transitive **a** confer; grant (a benefit, an honour, etc.). **b** accord; bestow (one's affections, confidence, etc.). **c** award; administer (one's approval, blame, etc.); tell, offer (esp. something unpleasant) (gave him a talking-to; gave him my blessing; gave him the sack). **d** pledge, assign as a guarantee (gave her word). **5** transitive **a** effect or perform (an action etc.) (gave him a kiss). **b** utter (gave a shriek). **6** transitive allot; assign; grant (was given the contract). **7** transitive (in passive; foll. by to) be inclined to or fond of (is given to speculation). **8** transitive yield as a product or result (the lamp gives a bad light; the field gives fodder for twenty cows). **9** intransitive **a** yield to pressure; become relaxed; lose firmness (this elastic doesn't give properly). **b** collapse (the roof gave under the pressure). **c** slang concede defeat; surrender (I give! I give!). **10** intransitive (usu. foll. by of) grant; bestow (gave freely of his time). **11** transitive **a** commit, consign, or entrust (gave him into custody; gave her into your care). **b** sanction the marriage of (a daughter etc.). **12** transitive devote; dedicate (gave his life to table tennis; shall give it my attention). **13** intransitive informal tell what one knows (What happened? Come on, give!). **14** transitive present; offer; show; hold out (gives no sign of life; gave her his arm; gave him your ear). **15** transitive Theatre read, recite, perform, act, etc. (gave them Hamlet's soliloquy). **16** transitive impart; be a source of (gave him my sore throat; gave its name to the battle; gave me much pain; gives him a right to complain). **17** transitive allow (esp. a fixed amount of time) (can give you five minutes). **18** transitive (usu. foll. by for) value (something) (gives nothing for their opinions). **19** transitive concede; yield (I give you the victory; they did their part; I have to give them that). **20** transitive deliver (a judgment etc.) authoritatively (gave her verdict). **21** transitive introduce (a person, cause, etc.) (I give you our President). **22** transitive provide (a party, meal, etc.) as host (gave a banquet). ● noun **1** capacity to yield or bend under pressure;

elasticity (*there is no give in a stone floor*). **2** ability to adapt or comply (*no give in his attitudes*). □ **give and take** exchange (concessions, words, or blows). **give as good as one gets** retort adequately in words or blows. **give away 1** transfer as a gift. **2** hand over (a bride) ceremonially to a bridegroom. **3** betray or expose to ridicule or detection. **4** esp. *Sport* give inadvertently to the opposition (*gave away a penalty*). **5** *Austral.* abandon, desist from, give up, lose faith or interest in. **give back** return (something) to its previous owner or in exchange. **give birth** (**to**) see BIRTH. **give down** (of a cow) let (milk) flow. **give forth** emit; publish; report. **give the game** (or **show**) **away** reveal a secret or intention. **give a hand** see HAND. **give a person** (or **the devil**) **his or her due** acknowledge, esp. grudgingly, a person's rights, abilities, etc. **give in 1** cease fighting or arguing; yield. **2** hand in (a document etc.) to an official etc. **give in marriage** sanction the marriage of (one's daughter etc.). **give it to a person** informal scold or punish. **give me** I prefer or admire (*give me the Greek islands*). **give off** emit (vapour etc.). **give oneself** (of a woman) yield sexually. **give oneself airs** act pretentiously or snobbishly. **give oneself up** surrender to one's pursuers. **give oneself up to 1** abandon oneself to an emotion, esp. despair. **2** addict oneself to. **give on to** (or **into**) (of a window, corridor, etc.) overlook or lead into. **give or take** informal add or subtract (a specified amount or number) in estimating. **give out 1** announce; emit; distribute. **2** cease or break down from exhaustion etc. **3** run short. **give over 1** informal cease from doing; abandon (a habit etc.); desist (*give over sniffing*). **2** hand over. **3** devote. **give rise to** cause, induce, suggest. **give a person to understand** inform authoritatively. **give up 1** resign; surrender. **2** part with. **3** deliver (a wanted person etc.). **4** pronounce incurable or insoluble; renounce hope of. **5** renounce or cease (an activity). **give way** see WAY. **give a person what for** informal punish or scold severely. **give one's word** (or **word of honour**) promise solemnly. **what gives?** informal what is the news?; what's happening?; what's the problem? **would give the world** (or **one's right arm** etc.) for covet or wish for desperately. □ **giv·er** noun [Old English *g(i)efan* from Germanic]

give-and-go noun N Amer. Sport (in hockey, basketball, etc.) a play in which the player handling the puck or ball passes it to a teammate, rushes past an opponent, and immediately receives it again.

give-and-take noun an exchange of words, concessions, etc.; a compromise.

give·away noun informal **1** an inadvertent betrayal or revelation. **2** an act of giving away. **3** (often attributive) **a** something given away free. **b** something sold at a low price. **4** Sport the inadvertent turning over of the puck, ball, etc. to an opponent.

give·back noun N Amer. a union's agreement to reduce wages in exchange for benefits.

given ● adjective **1** as previously stated or assumed; granted; specified (*given that he is a liar, we cannot trust him; a given number of people*). **2** Law (of a document) signed and dated (*given this day the 30th June*). ● noun a known fact or situation. □ **given·ness** noun

given name noun N Amer. a name given to a child at or shortly after birth, as distinguished from the family name; a first name.

Giza /ˈɡiːzə/ (also **El Giza**) a city southwest of Cairo in N Egypt, on the west bank of the Nile, site of the pyramids of Cheops (including the Great Pyramid) and of the Sphinx; pop. (est. 2002) 2,541,000.

giz·mo /ˈɡɪzmoʊ/ noun (pl. **-mos**) informal a gadget. [20th c.: origin unknown]

giz·zard /ˈɡɪzərd/ noun **1** the second part of a bird's stomach, for grinding food usu. with grit. **2** a muscular stomach of some fish, insects, molluscs, and other invertebrates. **3** informal **a** the stomach, entrails. **b** the throat. □ **stick in one's gizzard** informal be distasteful. [Old French *giser*, ultimately from Latin *gigeria* cooked entrails of fowl]

GLA abbreviation GAMMA-LINOLENIC ACID.

gla·bella /ɡləˈbelə/ noun (pl. **gla·bel·lae** /-liː/) the smooth part of the forehead above and between the eyebrows. □ **gla·bel·lar** adjective [modern Latin from Latin *glabellus* (adj.) diminutive of *glaber* smooth]

gla·brous /ˈɡleɪbrəs/ adjective free from hair or down; smooth skinned. [Latin *glaber glabri* hairless]

glacé /ˈɡlaseɪ, ɡlaˈseɪ/ adjective **1** (of fruit, esp. cherries) preserved in sugar, usu. resulting in a glossy surface. **2** (of cloth, leather, etc.) smooth; polished. [French, past participle of *glacer* to ice, gloss from *glace* ice: see GLACIER]

Glace Bay /ɡleɪs ˈbeɪ/ a former coal-mining urban community on Cape Breton Island, part of the regional municipality of Cape Breton. It is situated on the Atlantic coast about 15 km east of Sydney; pop. (1996) 23,038. [from French *Baie de Glace* ice bay]

gla·cial /ˈɡleɪʃəl, -siəl/ adjective **1** of ice; icy. **2** of or pertaining to glaciers. **3** Geomorph. characterized or produced by the presence or agency of glaciers. **4** (of movement or progress) resembling that of a glacier; extremely slow. **5** Chem. forming ice-like crystals upon freezing (*glacial acetic acid*). □ **gla·cial·ly** adverb [French *glacial* or Latin *glacialis* icy, from *glacies* ice]

glacial lake noun a lake formed by glaciers, esp. a prehistoric lake formed by retreating ice sheets.

glacial period noun (also **glacial epoch**) a period when ice sheets were exceptionally extensive; an ice age.

glaci·ated /ˈɡleɪsiˌeɪtəd/ adjective **1** marked or polished by the action of ice. **2** covered or having been covered by glaciers or ice sheets. □ **glaci·ation** /-ˈeɪʃən/ noun [past participle of *glaciate* from Latin *glaciare* freeze, from *glacies* ice]

gla·cier /ˈɡleɪʃər, -ʃiər, -siər/ noun a slowly-moving mass or river of ice formed by the accumulation and compaction of snow on mountains or in areas of prolonged cold climate. [French from *glace* ice, ultimately from Latin *glacies*]

Glacier Bay National Park a national park in SE Alaska, on the Pacific coast. Extending over an area of 12 880 sq. km (4,975 sq. miles), it contains the terminus of the Grand Pacific Glacier.

glacier bear noun a rare smoky-blue phase of the black bear, found in Alaska and northern British Columbia.

glacier lily noun = AVALANCHE LILY.

Glacier National Park a park in the Selkirk Mountains of southeastern BC. Established in 1886, it has more than four hundred glaciers.

glaci·ol·ogy /ˌɡleɪsiˈɒlədʒi, ˌɡleɪʃi-/ noun the science of the internal dynamics and effects of glaciers. □ **glaci·o·logic·al** adjective **glaci·ol·o·gist** noun [Latin *glacies* ice + -LOGY]

gla·cis /ˈɡlasi, -sɪs, ˈɡleɪ-/ noun (pl. same /-siːz, -sɪz/) **1** a bank sloping down from a fort, on which attackers are exposed to the defenders' missiles etc. **2** a gently sloping bank. **3** Military (in full **glacis plate**) the front plate of armour on a tank. [French from Old French *glacier* to slip, from *glace* ice: see GLACIER]

glad¹ ● adjective (**glad·der**, **glad·dest**) **1** (predicative) **a** pleased; delighted. **b** relieved (*glad about the way it turned out*). **c** (usu. foll. by of) grateful (*would be glad of a chance to talk about it*). **d** (usu. foll. by to + infin.) willing and eager (*shall be glad to come*). **2** (attributive) **a** (of news, events, etc.) giving joy (*glad tidings*). **b** expressing joy (*a glad expression*). ● transitive verb (**glad·ded**, **glad·ding**) archaic make glad. □ **give a person the glad eye** informal cast an amorous glance at a person. □ **glad·ly** adverb **glad·ness** noun [Old English *glæd* from Germanic]

glad² noun informal a gladiolus. [abbreviation]

glad·den transitive verb make glad.

glade noun an open space in a wood or forest. [Middle English: origin unknown]

glad hand ● noun a warm, often superficial, greeting or welcome. ● transitive verb (**glad-hand**) (esp. of a politician, celebrity, etc.) greet or welcome warmly, often superficially. □ **glad-hander** noun **glad-hand·ing** noun & adjective

gladi·ator /ˈɡladiˌeɪtər/ noun **1** hist. a man trained to fight with a sword or other weapons at ancient Roman shows. **2** a person defending or opposing a cause. □ **gladi·a·tor·ial** /-əˈtɔriəl/ adjective [Latin from *gladius* sword]

gladi·ola /ˌɡladiˈoʊlə/ noun informal a gladiolus. [alteration of GLADIOLUS]

gladi·olus /ˌɡladiˈoʊləs/ noun (pl. **gladi·oli** /-laɪ/ or **gladi·olus·es**) any iridaceous plant of the genus *Gladiolus* with sword-shaped leaves and usu. brightly coloured flower spikes. [Latin, diminutive of *gladius* sword]

glad rags plural noun informal best clothes.

glad·some adjective archaic = GLAD¹.

Glad·stone /ˈɡladstoʊn, -stən/ **Wil·liam Ewart** (1809–98), English Liberal politician, prime minister 1868–74, 1880–5, 1886, and 1892–4. He introduced many social and political reforms, including the secret ballot and compulsory education, and campaigned for Home Rule for Ireland. □ **Glad·ston·ian** adjective

Gladstone bag noun a bag like a briefcase having two equal compartments joined by a hinge. [GLADSTONE]

Glago·lit·ic /ˌɡlaɡəˈlɪtɪk/ adjective of or relating to the alphabet ascribed to St. Cyril and formerly used in writing some Slavic

---

t top   v voice   w we   z zoo   ʃ she   ʒ vision   θ thin   ð this   ŋ ring   x loch   tʃ chip   dʒ jar   (see over for vowels)

languages. [modern Latin *glagoliticus* from Serbo-Croatian *glagolica* Glagolitic alphabet, from Old Slavic *glagol* word]

glair /gleɪr/ *noun* (also **glaire**) an adhesive preparation made from egg whites, used in bookbinding etc. [Old French *glaire*, ultimately from Latin *clara* fem. of *clarus* clear]

glaive /gleɪv/ *noun archaic* a sword. [Old French, apparently from Latin *gladius* sword]

glam *informal* ● *adjective* **1** glamorous. **2** (usu. *attributive*) designating a kind of pop music characterized by the extravagant dress, makeup, etc. of its performers, originally popular in the early 1970s (*glam rock*). ● *noun* glamour. ● *intransitive verb* (**glammed, glam·ming**) *informal* (foll. by *up*) make glamorous. □ **glammed-up** *adjective* **glammy** *adjective* [abbreviation]

Gla·mor·gan /ɡləˈmɔːrɡən/ a former county of South Wales, on the Bristol Channel. It was divided in 1974 into the counties of West Glamorgan, Mid Glamorgan, and South Glamorgan, and in 1996 was subdivided into smaller jurisdictions.

glam·or·ize *transitive verb* (also **glam·our·ize**, esp. *Brit.* **-ise**) make glamorous or attractive. □ **glam·or·iz·a·tion** *noun*

glam·our *noun* (also **glamor**) **1** physical attractiveness, esp. when achieved by makeup, elegant clothing, etc. **2** an attractive or exciting quality, esp. one which is inaccessible to the average person (*the glamour of New York*). □ **glam·our·less** *adjective* **glam·or·ous** *adjective* **glam·or·ous·ly** *adverb* [18th c.: var. of GRAMMAR, with reference to the occult practices associated with learning in the Middle Ages]

glamour girl *noun* (also **glamour boy**) an attractive young woman (or man), esp. a model etc.

glamour·puss *noun informal* a glamorous person, esp. deliberately or affectedly so.

glance[1] ● *verb* **1** *intransitive* (often foll. by *down, up*, etc.) cast a momentary look (*glanced up at the sky*). **2** *intransitive* (often foll. by *off*) (esp. of a bullet, ball, etc.) bounce (off an object) obliquely. **b** *transitive* (esp. of a weapon etc.) strike (an object) obliquely. **3** *intransitive* pass quickly over a subject or subjects (*the author glances over a number of difficult elements*). **4** *intransitive* (of a bright object or light) flash, dart, or gleam (*the sun glanced off the knife*). **5** *transitive Cricket* deflect (the ball) with an oblique stroke. ● *noun* **1** (usu. foll. by *at, into, over*, etc.) a brief look (*took a glance at the paper; threw a glance over her shoulder*). **2** a flash or gleam (*a glance of sunlight*). **3** *Cricket* a stroke with the bat's face turned slantwise to deflect the ball. □ **at a glance 1** immediately upon looking. **2** presented in a manageable format; condensed (*carpentry at a glance*). **at first glance** on the first impression; initially. **glance at 1** give a brief look at. **2** make a passing and usu. sarcastic allusion to. **glance over (or through)** read cursorily. □ **glan·cing·ly** *adverb* [Middle English *glence* etc., prob. a nasalized form of obsolete *glace* in the same sense, from Old French *glacier* to slip: see GLACIS]

glance[2] *noun* any lustrous sulphide ore (*copper glance; lead glance*). [German *Glanz* lustre]

gland[1] *noun* **1 a** an organ in an animal body secreting substances for use in the body or for ejection. **b** a structure resembling this, such as a lymph gland. **2** *Bot.* a secreting cell or group of cells on the surface of a plant structure. [French *glande* from Old French *glandre* from Latin *glandulae* throat glands]

gland[2] *noun* a sleeve used to produce a seal round a moving shaft. [19th c.: perhaps var. of *glam, glan* a vice, related to CLAMP[1]]

glan·ders *plural noun* (treated as *sing.*) **1** a contagious disease of horses, caused by a bacterium and characterized by swellings below the jaw and mucous discharge from the nostrils. **2** this disease in humans or other animals. [Old French *glandre*: see GLAND[1]]

gland·u·lar /ˈɡlandjʊlər/ *adjective* of or relating to a gland or glands. [French *glandulaire* (as GLAND[1])]

glandular fever *noun* an infectious viral disease characterized by swelling of the lymph glands and prolonged lassitude; infectious mononucleosis (see MONONUCLEOSIS).

glans /ɡlanz/ *noun* (pl. **glandes** /ˈɡlandiːz/) the rounded part forming the head of the penis or clitoris. [Latin, = acorn]

glare[1] ● *verb* **1** *intransitive* (usu. foll. by *at, upon*) look fiercely or fixedly. **2** *intransitive* shine or reflect light dazzlingly or disagreeably. **3** *transitive* express (hate, defiance, etc.) by a look. **4** *intransitive archaic* be over-conspicuous or obtrusive. ● *noun* **1** a strong fierce (often reflected) light, esp. sunshine. **b** oppressive public attention (*the glare of fame*). **2** a fierce or fixed look (*a glare of defiance*). □ **glare·less** *adjective* **glary** *adjective* [Middle English, prob. ultimately related to GLASS: compare Middle Dutch and Middle Low German *glaren* gleam, glare]

glare[2] *adjective N Amer.* (esp. of ice) smooth and glassy. [perhaps from *glare* frost (16th c., of uncertain origin)]

glar·ing *adjective* **1** obvious, conspicuous (*a glaring error*). **2** shining or reflecting light oppressively or harshly. **3** staring fiercely. □ **glar·ing·ly** *adverb*

Glaser /ˈɡleɪzər/ **Don·ald Ar·thur** (b.1926), US physicist, who invented the bubble chamber used to observe the paths of subatomic particles; he was awarded the Nobel Prize for physics in 1960.

Glas·gow /ˈɡlazɡoʊ/ a city in Scotland on the Clyde River; pop. (est. 2002) 609,400. It was formerly a major shipbuilding centre, is still an important commercial and cultural centre, and is the largest city in Scotland.

Glash·ow /ˈɡlaʃaʊ/ **Shel·don Lee** (b.1932), US theoretical physicist. Glashow independently developed a unified theory to explain electromagnetic interactions and the weak nuclear force, and extended the quark theory of Murray Gell-Mann. He received the Nobel Prize for physics (1979).

glas·nost /ˈɡlaznɒst, ˈɡlas-/ *noun hist.* (in the former Soviet Union) the policy or practice of more open consultative government and wider dissemination of information. [Russian *glasnost'*, lit. 'publicity', 'openness']

Glass, Phil·ip (b.1937), US composer. His minimalist works are influenced by Asian and North African music as well as jazz and rock, and include the opera *Einstein on the Beach* (1976), the ballet *Glass Pieces* (1982), and the orchestral symphony *Low Symphony* (1993).

glass ● *noun* **1 a** (often *attributive*) a hard, brittle, usu. transparent, translucent, or shiny substance, made by fusing sand with soda and lime and sometimes other ingredients, and used most commonly in windows and bottles (compare FLINT GLASS, PLATE GLASS). **b** any similar substance which has solidified from a molten state without crystallizing (*volcanic glass*). **c** = PLEXIGLAS. **2** (often *collective*) an object or objects made from, or partly from, glass, esp.: **a** a drinking vessel. **b** a mirror. **c** an hourglass. **d** a window. **e** a greenhouse (*rows of lettuce under glass*). **f** glass ornaments. **g** a barometer. **h** *Brit.* a glass disc covering a watch face. **i** a magnifying lens. **j** a monocle. **3** (in *pl.*) **a** eyeglasses. **b** binoculars; opera glasses. **4** the amount of liquid contained in a glass; a drink (*has had four glasses*). ● *transitive verb* **1** (usu. as **glassed** *adjective*) fit with glass; glaze. **2** *poet.* reflect as in a mirror. **3** look at or for with binoculars. ● *adjective* of or made from glass. □ **glass·ful** *noun* (pl. **-fuls**). **glass·less** *adjective* **glass·like** *adjective* [Old English *glæs* from Germanic: compare GLAZE]

glass-blowing *noun* the blowing of semi-molten glass to make glassware. □ **glass-blower** *noun*

glass ceiling *noun* an unacknowledged barrier to personal advancement.

glass cloth *noun* **1** a linen cloth for drying glasses. **2** *Brit.* a cloth covered with powdered glass or abrasive, like glasspaper. **3** a woven fabric of fine-spun glass.

glass cutter *noun* **1** a worker who cuts glass. **2** a tool used for cutting glass.

glassed-in *adjective* surrounded by or enclosed in glass (*glassed-in sundeck*).

glass eye *noun* a false eye made from glass.

glass fibre *noun* esp. *Brit.* **1** a filament or filaments of glass made into fabric. **2** such filaments embedded in plastic as reinforcement.

glass harmonica *noun* a musical instrument consisting of a set of chromatic glass bowls kept moist and played by finger pressure or by means of a keyboard.

glass·house *noun* **1** *Brit.* & *Cdn* a greenhouse. **2** *Brit. slang* a military prison. **3** a building where glass is made.

glass·ie *var.* of GLASSY *noun*.

glass·ine /ˈɡlaˈsiːn/ *noun* a glossy transparent paper. [GLASS]

glass lizard *noun* (also **glass snake**) any of various snakelike lizards of the genus *Ophiosaurus*, of the southern US, with a very brittle tail.

glass-making *noun* the manufacture of glass. □ **glass-maker** *noun*

glass noodle *noun* = CELLOPHANE NOODLE.

glass·paper *noun* paper covered with powdered glass and used for smoothing and polishing.

glass·ware *noun* articles made from glass, esp. drinking glasses, tableware, etc.

glass wool *noun* glass in the form of fine fibres used for packing and insulation.

Vowels: a cat ɑ arm e bed ɜr her ɜː *deux* ə ago ɪ sit i cosy iː feed ɒ hot ɔ pore ɔː no ʌ run ʊ put

glass·works *plural noun* (treated as *sing.*) a factory where glass is manufactured or worked.

glass·wort /ˈɡlaswɜrt, -wɔrt/ *noun* any plant of the genus *Salicornia* or *Salsola* formerly used for use in glass-making.

glassy ● *adjective* (**glass·i·er**, **glass·i·est**) **1** of or resembling glass, esp. in smoothness. **2** (of the eye, the expression, etc.) abstracted; dull; fixed (*fixed her with a glassy stare*). ● *noun* (also **glassie**) (*pl.* **-ies**) *Cdn & Austral.* a glass marble. □ **glass·i·ly** *adverb* **glass·i·ness** *noun*

Glas·ton·bury /ˈɡlastənbəri/ a town in Somerset, England; pop. (1998) 8,200. It is the legendary burial place of King Arthur and Queen Guinevere and the site of a ruined abbey held by legend to have been founded by Joseph of Arimathea. It was identified in medieval times with the mythical Avalon.

Glas·we·gian /ɡlazˈwiːdʒən, glas-/ ● *adjective* of or relating to Glasgow. ● *noun* **1** a native of Glasgow. **2** the dialect or accent of people from Glasgow. [*Glasgow* on the pattern of *Norwegian*]

glatt kosher /ɡlat/ *adjective* strictly kosher. [Yiddish *glat*, = only, from Middle High German *glat*, + KOSHER]

Glau·ber's salt /ˈɡlaubɜrz, ˈɡlɔ-/ *noun* (also **Glauber's salts**) a crystalline hydrated form of sodium sulphate used in detergents and in the textile, glass and paper industries. [J. R. *Glauber*, German chemist d.1668]

glau·coma /ɡlɔˈkoːmə/ *noun* a condition of the eye with increased pressure within the eyeball, causing gradual loss of sight. [Latin from Greek *glaukōma -atos*, ultimately from *glaukos*: see GLAUCOUS]

glau·cous /ˈɡlɔkəs/ *adjective* **1** of a dull greyish green or blue. **2** covered with a powdery bloom as of grapes. [Latin *glaucus* from Greek *glaukos* bluish-green or bluish-grey]

glaucous gull *noun* a large grey and white gull, *Larus hyperboreus*, of Arctic coasts.

glaucous-winged gull *noun* a large pink-legged gull of the west coast of N America, *Larus glaucescens*, having grey wing tips.

glaze ● *verb* **1** *transitive* **a** fit (a window, picture, etc.) with glass. **b** provide (a building) with glass windows. **2** *transitive* **a** cover (pottery etc.) with a glaze. **b** fix (paint) on pottery with a glaze. **3** *transitive* cover (pastry, meat, etc.) with a glaze. **4** *intransitive* (often foll. by *over*) (of the eyes) become fixed or glassy (*his eyes glazed over*). **5** *transitive* cover (cloth, paper, leather, a painted surface, etc.) with a glaze. **6** *transitive* give a glassy surface to, e.g. by rubbing. **7** *transitive* coat with a thin layer of ice. ● *noun* **1** a vitreous substance, usu. a special glass, used to glaze pottery. **2 a** a smooth shiny coating of milk, sugar, jam, gelatin, etc., on food. **b** a semi-liquid icing, often with a glossy sheen. **3** a thin topcoat of transparent paint used to modify the tone of the underlying colour. **4** a smooth surface formed by glazing. **5** *N Amer.* a thin coating of ice. □ **glaz·er** *noun* [Middle English from an oblique form of GLASS]

glaz·ier /ˈɡleiziɜr, -ʒɜr/ *noun* a person whose trade is glazing windows etc. □ **glaz·iery** *noun*

glaz·ing *noun* **1** the act or an instance of glazing. **2** windows (*see also* DOUBLE GLAZING). **3** material used to produce a glaze.

Glaz·unov /ˈɡlazuˌnɒf/ **Alek·sandr (Kon·stan·tin·ovich)** (1865–1936), Russian composer. A student of Rimsky-Korsakov (1880–1), he was influenced by Liszt and Wagner, and his work includes orchestral and chamber music, songs, and the ballet *The Seasons* (1901).

GLBT *abbreviation* gay, lesbian, bisexual, and transgendered.

GLC *abbreviation* **1** *Chem.* gas–liquid chromatography. **2** *hist.* (in the UK) Greater London Council.

gleam ● *noun* **1** a reflected, brief, or faint light (*a gleam of sunlight*). **2** a faint, sudden, intermittent, or temporary show or expression (*not a gleam of hope*; *a gleam in her eye*). ● *intransitive verb* **1** emit gleams. **2** shine with a reflected, intermittent, or faint brightness. **3** (of a quality) be indicated (*fear gleamed in his eyes*). □ **a gleam in someone's eye** something that is as yet no more than an idea or dream. □ **gleam·ing·ly** *adverb* **gleamy** *adjective* [Old English *glǣm*: compare GLIMMER]

glean *verb* **1** *transitive* collect or scrape together (news, facts, gossip, etc.) in small quantities. **2 a** *transitive & intransitive* gather (ears of grain etc.) after the harvest. **b** *transitive* strip (a field etc.) after a harvest. □ **glean·er** *noun* [Old French *glener* from Late Latin *glennare*, prob. of Celtic origin]

glean·ings *plural noun* things gleaned, esp. facts.

glebe *noun* **1** a piece of land serving as part of a clergyman's benefice and providing income. **2** *archaic* earth; land; a field. [Latin *gl(a)eba* clod, soil]

glee *noun* **1** mirth; delight, esp. triumphant (*watched the enemy's defeat with glee*). **2** a song for three or more, esp. adult male, voices, singing different parts simultaneously, usu. unaccompanied. [Old English *glío*, *glēo* minstrelsy, jest, from Germanic]

glee club *noun* esp. *N Amer.* a choir, esp. at a school or university.

glee·ful *adjective* full of glee; joyful. □ **glee·ful·ly** *adverb* **glee·ful·ness** *noun*

gleet *noun* *Med.* a watery discharge from the urethra caused by gonorrheal infection. [Old French *glette* 'slime, secretion']

Gleich·schal·tung /ˈɡlaixˌʃaltʊŋ/ *noun* the standardization of political, economic, and social institutions in authoritarian states. [German]

glen *noun* a narrow valley. [Gaelic & Irish *gleann*]

glen check *noun* (also **glen plaid**) **1** (often *attributive*) a plaid pattern consisting of light and dark stripes alternating both vertically and horizontally. **2** a garment or fabric in this pattern.

Glen·coe, Massacre of a massacre in 1692 of about thirty members of the Jacobite MacDonald clan, including their chief, by soldiers of the Campbell clan, which took place near Glencoe in the Scottish Highlands after the MacDonald clan had failed to swear allegiance to William III. Though the chief of the Campbell clan was held responsible, the massacre was almost certainly instigated by the government.

Glen·dower /ɡlenˈdauɜr/ **Owen** (also **Glyn·dwr**) (*c*.1355–*c*.1416), Welsh chieftain. A legendary symbol of Welsh nationalism, he proclaimed himself Prince of Wales and led an unsuccessful national uprising against Henry IV (1400–15).

Glen·eagles /ɡlenˈiːɡəlz/ a valley in E Scotland, southwest of Perth, site of a noted hotel and golfing centre.

glen·garry /ɡlenˈɡeri/ *noun* (*pl.* **-ries**) a brimless Scottish hat with a cleft down the centre and usu. two ribbons hanging at the back, chiefly worn as part of Highland dress. [*Glengarry* in Scotland]

Glen More an alternative name for the GREAT GLEN.

Glenn, John Her·schel, Jr. (b.1921), US astronaut and politician. He was the first US astronaut to orbit the earth (1962), and later served as a senator (1974–98).

glen·oid /ˈɡliːnɔid/ *adjective* designating a shallow depression on a bone, esp. the scapula and temporal bone, receiving the projection of another bone to form a joint. [French *glénoïde* from Greek *glēnoeidēs* from *glēnē* socket]

gley /ɡlei/ *noun* a tacky waterlogged soil grey to blue in colour. [Ukrainian, = sticky blue clay, related to CLAY]

glia /ˈɡlaiə, ˈɡliːə/ *noun* the connective tissue supporting the central nervous system. □ **glial** *adjective* [Greek, = glue]

glib *adjective* (**glib·ber**, **glib·best**) **1** (of a speaker, speech, etc.) fluent and voluble but insincere and shallow. **2** *Cdn* (esp. *PEI*) (usu. *attributive*) slippery, smooth (*glib ice*). □ **glib·ly** *adverb* **glib·ness** *noun* [related to obsolete *glibbery* slippery, from Germanic: perhaps imitative]

Glick, Srul Irv·ing (1934–2002), Canadian composer. His prolific musical output, much of it vocal or choral for synagogue liturgies, combined contemporary, classical, and Hebraic influences.

glide ● *verb* **1** *intransitive* (of a bird, boat, skater, stream, snake, etc.) move with a smooth continuous motion. **2 a** *intransitive* (of an aircraft, esp. a glider) fly without engine power. **b** (of a pilot) fly a glider. **3** *intransitive* of time etc.: **a** pass gently and imperceptibly. **b** (often foll. by *into*) pass and change gradually and imperceptibly (*night glided into day*). **4** *intransitive* move quietly or stealthily. **5** *transitive* cause to glide (*breezes glided the ship on its course*). ● *noun* **1 a** the act of gliding. **b** an instance of this. **2** *Phonetics* a gradually changing sound made in passing from one position of the speech organs to another. **3** a gliding dance or dance step. **4** a flight in a glider. **5** a device affixed to the bottom of chair or table legs so that they can be slid across a floor more easily. [Old English *glīdan* from West Germanic]

glide path *noun* (also **glide·slope**) an aircraft's line of descent to land, esp. as indicated by ground radar.

glider *noun* **1 a** an aircraft that flies without an engine. **b** a glider pilot. **2** a person or thing that glides.

glim *noun* *archaic* **1** a faint light. **2** a candle; a lantern. [17th c.: perhaps abbreviation of GLIMMER or GLIMPSE]

glim·mer ● *intransitive verb* shine faintly or intermittently. ● *noun* **1** a feeble or wavering light. **2** (usu. foll. by *of*) a faint gleam (of hope, understanding, etc.). **3** a glimpse. [Middle English prob. from Scandinavian from West Germanic: see GLEAM]

glim·mer·ing ● *noun* **1** in senses of GLIMMER *verb*. **2** = GLIMMER *noun*. **3** an act of glimmering. ● *adjective* that glimmers. □ **glim·mer·ing·ly** *adverb*

glimpse ● *noun* (often foll. by *of*) **1** a momentary or partial view (*caught a glimpse of her*). **2** a faint and transient appearance (*glimpses of the truth*). ● *verb* **1** *transitive* see faintly or partly (*glimpsed his face in the crowd*). **2** *intransitive* (often foll. by *at*) cast a passing glance. **3** *intransitive archaic* **a** shine faintly or intermittently. **b** appear faintly; dawn. [Middle English *glimse* corresponding to Middle High German *glimsen* from West Germanic (as GLIMMER)]

Glin·ka, Mik·hail (Ivan·ovich) (1804–57), Russian composer. Regarded as the father of the Russian national school of music, he is best known for his operas *A Life for the Tsar* (1836) and *Russlan and Ludmilla* (1842).

glint ● *transitive & intransitive verb* flash or cause to flash; glitter; sparkle; reflect (*eyes glinted with amusement; the sword glinted fire*). ● *noun* a brief flash of light; a sparkle. [alteration of Middle English *glent*, prob. of Scandinavian origin]

gli·oma /glaiˈoːmə/ *noun* (*pl.* **-omas, -mata** /-mətə/) any malignant tumour of non-nervous cells in the nervous system. [from GLIA + -OMA]

gli·osis /glaiˈoːsɪs/ *noun* reparative or pathological proliferation of glial cells. [from GLIA + -OSIS]

glis·sade ● *noun* **1** /glɪˈsɒd, -ˈseɪd/ an act of sliding down a steep slope of snow or ice, usu. on the feet with the support of an ice axe etc. **2** /gliˈsɒd/ *Dance* a movement in which one leg is brushed outwards from the body and then the second leg is brushed inward to meet it. ● *intransitive verb* /glɪˈsɒd, -ˈseɪd/ perform a glissade. [French from *glisser* slip, slide]

glis·sando /glɪˈsandoː, -ˈsɒndoː/ *noun* (*pl.* **glis·sandi** /-sandi/ or **-dos**) *Music* a continuous rapid slide of adjacent notes upwards or downwards. [Italian from French *glissant* sliding (as GLISSADE)]

glis·sé /ˈglisei/ *noun Dance* a step in which one foot is slid briskly outward from the body, extended slightly off the ground, and returned to a closed position. [French, past participle of *glisser*: see GLISSADE]

glis·ten /ˈglɪsən/ ● *intransitive verb* shine, esp. like a wet object, snow, etc.; glitter. ● *noun* a glitter; a sparkle. □ **glis·ten·ing·ly** *adverb* [Old English *glisnian* from *glisian* shine]

glis·ter /ˈglɪstər/ *archaic* ● *intransitive verb* sparkle; glitter. ● *noun* a sparkle; a gleam. [Middle Low German *glistern*, Middle Dutch *glisteren*, related to GLISTEN]

glitch *noun* a sudden irregularity or malfunction (of equipment, a plan, etc.). □ **glitch·less** *adjective* **glitchy** *adjective* [20th c.: origin unknown]

glit·ter ● *intransitive verb* **1** shine, esp. with a bright reflected light; sparkle. **2** (usu. foll. by *with*) **a** be showy or splendid (*glittered with diamonds*). **b** be ostentatious or flashily brilliant (*glittering rhetoric*). ● *noun* **1** a gleam; a sparkle. **2** showiness; splendour. **3** tiny pieces of sparkling material. **4** *Cdn* (*Nfld*) **a** (often *attributive*) freezing rain (*glitter storm*). **b** the coating of ice deposited by a glitter storm. □ **glit·ter·ing·ly** *adverb* **glit·tery** *adjective* [Old Norse *glitra* from Germanic]

glit·ter·ati /ˌglɪtəˈrɒti, -ˈrati/ *plural noun informal jocular* the fashionable, wealthy set of literary or show-business people. [GLITTER + LITERATI]

Glit·ter·tind /ˈglɪtərˌtɪn/ a mountain in Norway, in the Jotunheim range. Rising to 2 470 m (8,104 ft.), it is the highest mountain in the country.

glitz *noun informal* extravagant but superficial display; show-business glamour. [back-formation from GLITZY]

glitzy *adjective* (**glitz·i·er, glitz·i·est**) *informal* extravagant, ostentatious; tawdry, gaudy. □ **glitz·i·ly** *adverb* **glitz·i·ness** *noun* [GLITTER, after RITZY: compare German *glitzerig* glittering]

Gli·wice /glɪˈviːtsə/ a mining and industrial city in S Poland, near the border with the Czech Republic; pop. (est. 2000) 209,356.

gloam·ing *noun* twilight; dusk. [Old English *glōmung* from *glōm* twilight, related to GLOW]

gloat ● *intransitive verb* (often foll. by *on, upon, over*) consider or contemplate with malice, triumph, etc. (*gloated over their victory*). ● *noun* **1** the act of gloating. **2** a look or expression of triumphant satisfaction. □ **gloat·er** *noun* **gloat·ing·ly** *adverb* [16th c.: origin unknown, but perhaps related to Old Norse *glotta* grin, Middle High German *glotzen* stare]

glob *noun* a mass or lump of semi-liquid substance, e.g. mud. [20th c.: perhaps from BLOB and GOB[2]]

global *adjective* **1** worldwide (*global marketplace*). **2 a** relating to or embracing a group of items etc.; total. **b** *Computing* operating or applying through the whole of a file, program, etc. □ **global·ly** *adverb*

global·ism *noun* the operation or planning of economic and foreign policy on a global basis.

global·iz·a·tion *noun* **1** the act or fact of globalizing. **2** an increase in free trade and open markets throughout the world, usu. accompanied by an increase in the international dominance of multinational corporations; the trend toward an integrated global economy.

global·ize *transitive & intransitive verb* (also esp. *Brit.* **-ise**) develop or be developed so as to make possible international influence or operation.

Global Positioning System *noun* a system of satellites and portable receivers able to pinpoint each receiver's location anywhere on the earth's surface, used in navigating, surveying, etc. Abbr.: **GPS**.

global village *noun* the world considered as a single interdependent community linked by telecommunications.

global warming *noun* the increase in temperature of the earth's atmosphere supposedly caused by the greenhouse effect.

globe ● *noun* **1 a** (prec. by *the*) the planet earth. **b** a planet, star, or sun. **c** any spherical body; a ball. **2** a spherical representation of the earth or of the constellations with a map on the surface. **3** a golden sphere as an emblem of sovereignty; an orb. **4** any spherical glass vessel, esp. a fishbowl, a lamp, etc. ● *transitive & intransitive verb* make (usu. in *passive*) or become globular. □ **globe·like** *adjective* **glob·oid** *adjective & noun* **glob·ose** *adjective* [French *globe* or Latin *globus* 'spherical object']

globe artichoke *noun* the partly edible head of the artichoke plant.

globe·fish *noun* any of various chiefly tropical fishes with more or less rounded bodies.

globe·flower *noun* any ranunculaceous plant of the genus *Trollius* with globular usu. yellow flowers.

globe-trotting ● *noun* frequent and extensive travelling. ● *attributive adjective* engaging in this (*a globe-trotting executive*). □ **globe·trot·ter** *noun*

glo·bi·ger·ina /gloːˌbɪdʒəˈrainə, -ˈriːnə/ *noun* any planktonic protozoan of the genus *Globigerina*, living near the surface of the sea. The shells collect as a deposit (**globigerina ooze**) over much of the ocean floor. [modern Latin from Latin *globus* globe + *-ger* carrying + -INA]

glo·bin /ˈgloːbɪn/ *noun* any of various polypeptides forming the protein component of hemoglobin and related compound proteins. [abbreviation of HEMOGLOBIN]

globu·lar /ˈglɒbjʊlər/ *adjective* **1** globe-shaped, spherical. **2** composed of globules.

globular cluster *noun Astronomy* a large compact spherical star cluster usu. of old stars in the outer regions of a galaxy.

glob·ule /ˈglɒbjuːl/ *noun* a small globe or round particle; a drop. [French *globule* or Latin *globulus* (as GLOBE)]

globu·lin /ˈglɒbjʊlɪn/ *noun* any of a group of simple proteins characterized by solubility only in salt solutions and esp. forming a large fraction of blood serum protein. [archaic sense GLOBULE = blood corpuscle + -IN]

Glock *noun proprietary* a semi-automatic handgun. [name of the Austrian manufacturer]

glock·en·spiel /ˈglɒkənˌspiːl, -ˌʃpiːl/ *noun* a musical instrument consisting of a series of bells or metal bars or tubes suspended or mounted in a frame and struck by hammers. [German, = bell-play]

glom *verb* (**glommed, glom·ming**) *N Amer. slang* **1** *transitive & intransitive* steal. **2** *intransitive* (usu. foll. by *on to, into*) **a** grab, clutch. **b** latch on to, get hooked on (an idea, trend, etc.). [var. of Scots *glaum* (18th c., of unknown origin)]

glom·eru·lo·neph·ritis /gləˌmerjʊloːnəˈfraɪtəs/ *noun* a disease of the kidneys, usu. allergic in origin, resulting in acute inflammation.

glom·eru·lus /gləˈmerələs, -jələs/ *noun* (*pl.* **glom·eruli** /-ˌlaɪ/) a cluster of small organisms, tissues, or blood vessels, esp. of the capillaries of the kidney. □ **glom·eru·lar** *adjective* [modern Latin, diminutive of Latin *glomus -eris* ball]

gloom ● *noun* **1** darkness; obscurity. **2** melancholy; despondency. **3** *poet.* a dark place. ● *verb* **1** *intransitive* be gloomy or melancholy; frown. **2** *intransitive* (of the sky etc.) be dull or threatening. **3** *intransitive* appear darkly or obscurely. **4** *transitive* cover with gloom; make dark or dismal. [Middle English *gloum(b)e*, of unknown origin: compare GLUM]

gloom and doom *noun* = DOOM AND GLOOM.

gloom·ster *noun* a person who habitually predicts dire consequences.

gloomy *adjective* (**gloom·i·er, gloom·i·est**) **1** dark; unlighted. **2** depressed; sullen. **3** dismal; depressing. □ **gloom·i·ly** *adverb* **gloom·i·ness** *noun*

gloomy Gus *noun N Amer.* a habitually gloomy or pessimistic person.

Consonants:　b *but*　　d *dog*　　f *few*　　g *get*　　h *her*　　j *yes*　　k *cat*　　l *leg*　　m *man*　　n *no*　　p *pen*　　r *red*　　s *sit*

gloop *noun informal* semi-liquid or sticky material. ☐ **gloopy** *adjective* [imitative: compare GLOP]

Gloos·cap /ˈgluːskap/ (also **Glus·kap**) a trickster and hero in the mythology of the Maliseet, Mi'kmaq, and Passamaquoddy.

glop *N Amer. slang* ● *noun* a liquid or sticky mess. ● *verb* (**glopped**, **glop·ping**) **1** *transitive* scoop, drop, or toss (a semi-liquid substance). **2** *intransitive* (of a semi-liquid substance) drop, collect, ooze, or splat. ☐ **gloppy** *adjective* [imitative: compare obsolete *glop* swallow greedily]

Glor·ia *noun* **1** any of various Christian prayers or hymns beginning with the word *Gloria*, esp. the *Gloria in excelsis Deo* (Glory to God in the highest), as part of the Mass, or the *Gloria Patri* (Glory be to the Father). **2** a musical setting of this. [Latin, = glory]

glori·fy *transitive verb* (**-fies, -fied**) **1** reveal or make clearer the glory of (God) by one's actions (*God can be glorified through a life of scholarship*). **2** give praise to (God). **3** (often as **glori·fied** *adjective*) describe or represent as admirable, esp. unjustifiably or undeservedly (*just a glorified office boy; a movie glorifying violence*). ☐ **glori·fi·ca·tion** *noun*

glori·osa daisy /glɔriˈoːsə/ *noun* a plant of the genus *Rudbeckia*, with daisy-like flowers. [Latin, = glorious]

glori·ous *adjective* **1** possessing glory; illustrious. **2** conferring glory; honourable (*a glorious sacrifice*). **3** *informal* splendid; magnificent; delightful (*a glorious day; glorious fun*). **4** *ironic* intense; unmitigated (*a glorious muddle*). ☐ **glori·ous·ly** *adverb*

Glorious Revolution the events that led to the removal of James II from the English throne and his replacement by his daughter Mary II and her husband William of Orange (1688), with their acceptance of the conditions laid down in the Bill of Rights.

Glorious Twelfth *noun* (prec. by *the*) the anniversary of the Battle of the Boyne in Ireland on 12 July 1690, at which the Protestant army of William III of England defeated the Catholic army of the recently deposed James II, celebrated esp. by Protestants of Irish descent.

glory ● *noun* (*pl.* **-ies**) **1** high renown or fame; honour. **2** adoring praise and thanksgiving (*Glory to the Lord*). **3** resplendent majesty or magnificence; great beauty (*the glory of Versailles; the glory of the rose*). **4** a thing that brings renown or praise; a distinction. **5** the bliss and splendour of heaven. **6** *informal* a state of exaltation, prosperity, happiness, etc. (*is in his glory playing with his trains*). **7** a luminous ring or halo. ● *intransitive verb* (often foll. by *in*) take great pride or pleasure (*glory in their skill*). ☐ **go to glory** *slang* die; be destroyed. [Old French *glorie* from Latin *gloria*]

Glory Be ● *noun* a Christian prayer of praise to the Holy Trinity beginning with the words 'Glory be to the Father'. ● *interjection* (**glory be**) **1** a devout exclamation. **2** *informal* an exclamation of surprise or delight.

glory days *plural noun* (also **glory years** etc.) the period of one's highest achievement, greatest fame, etc.

glory hole *noun* **1** *informal* an untidy storage place, esp. a room or cupboard. **2** *slang* a hole in a wall through which fellatio or masturbation is conducted incognito between male homosexuals.

glory lily *noun* a climbing lily of the genus *Gloriosa*, with bright red and yellow flowers. *Also called* CLIMBING LILY.

glory-of-the-snow *noun* = CHIONODOXA.

gloss[1] ● *noun* **1 a** a surface shine or lustre. **b** an instance of this; a smooth finish. **2 a** a deceptively attractive appearance. **b** an instance of this. **3** (in full **gloss paint**) paint formulated to give a hard glossy finish (*compare* MATTE[1]). **4** a cosmetic applied to add lustre to skin (*lip gloss*). ● *transitive verb* make glossy. ☐ **gloss over 1** seek to conceal beneath a false appearance. **2** conceal or evade by mentioning briefly or misleadingly. [16th c.: origin unknown]

gloss[2] ● *noun* **1 a** an explanatory word or phrase inserted between the lines or in the margin of a text. **b** a comment, explanation, interpretation, or paraphrase. **2 a** a glossary. **b** an interlinear translation or annotation. ● *verb* **1** *transitive* **a** add a gloss or glosses to (a text, word, etc.). **b** read a different sense into; explain away. **2** *intransitive* write or introduce glosses. [Old French *glose* suggested by medieval Latin *glossa* 'explanation of a difficult word' from Greek *glōssa* tongue]

glos·sary /ˈglɒsəri/ *noun* (*pl.* **-ies**) **1** (also **gloss**) an alphabetical list of terms or words found in or relating to a specific subject or text, with explanations; a brief dictionary. **2** a collection of glosses. ☐ **glos·sar·ial** /glɒˈseriəl/ *adjective* [Latin *glossarium* from *glossa* GLOSS[2]]

glos·so·lalia /ˌglɒsəˈleɪliə/ *noun* = GIFT OF TONGUES (see TONGUE). [modern Latin from Greek *glōssa* tongue + *-lalia* speaking]

gloss·o·pharyn·geal /ˌglɒsəfəˈrɪndʒiəl, -fərənˈdʒiːəl/ ● *adjective* of or relating to the tongue and pharynx. ● *noun* (in full **glossopharyngeal nerve**) either of the ninth pair of cranial nerves, supplying the tongue and pharynx. [Greek *glōssa* 'tongue' + *pharyngeal*: see PHARYNX]

glossy ● *adjective* (**gloss·i·er, gloss·i·est**) **1** having a shine; smooth. **2** (of paper etc.) smooth and shiny. **3** (of a magazine etc.) printed on such paper. **4** having a deceptively smooth and attractive external appearance. ● *noun* (*pl.* **-ies**) *informal* **1** a glossy magazine. **2** a photograph with a glossy surface. ☐ **gloss·i·ly** *adverb* **gloss·i·ness** *noun*

glot·tal /ˈglɒtəl/ *adjective* of or produced by the glottis.

glottal stop *noun* a plosive sound produced by the sudden opening or shutting of the glottis before or after an emission of breath or voice.

glot·tis /ˈglɒtɪs/ *noun* the space at the upper end of the windpipe and between the vocal cords, affecting voice modulation through expansion or contraction. [modern Latin from Greek *glōttis* from *glōtta* var. of *glōssa* tongue]

Glouces·ter /ˈglɒstər/ **1** a city in SW England, the county town of Gloucestershire; pop. (est. 2002) 117,900. **2** a former city in E Ontario, now part of the city of Ottawa; pop. (2001) 110,264. [sense 2 after Prince William Frederick, Duke of *Gloucester*, nephew of George III d.1834]

Glouces·ter·shire /ˈglɒstərˌʃɪr/ a county of SW England; county town, Gloucester.

glove ● *noun* **1** a covering for the hand, of wool, leather, cotton, etc., worn esp. for protection against cold or dirt, and usu. having separate fingers. **2** a padded protective glove, esp.: **a** used for catching, as by a goaltender or a baseball player. **b** a hockey player's glove. **c** a boxing glove. ● *transitive verb* **1** (usu. as **gloved** *adjective*) cover or provide with a glove or gloves. **2** *N Amer.* catch (a ball, puck, etc.) in a glove. ☐ **drop the** (or **one's**) **gloves 1** *N Amer.* (in hockey) remove one's gloves to indicate willingness to fight. **2** *Cdn* engage in or indicate willingness to engage in a debate, confrontation, etc. (*halfway through the interview, he dropped the gloves*). **fit like a glove** fit exactly. **take off the gloves** *Cdn* ready oneself or indicate readiness for a confrontation. **with the gloves off** mercilessly; unfairly; with no compunction. ☐ **glove·less** *adjective* **glove·like** *adjective* [Old English *glōf*, corresponding to Old Norse *glófi*, perhaps from Germanic]

glove·box *noun* **1** = GLOVE COMPARTMENT. **2** a closed chamber with sealed-in gloves for handling infants, radioactive material, etc.

glove compartment *noun* a recess for small articles in the dashboard of a motor vehicle.

glove hand *noun* *Hockey* the hand on which the goalie wears a catching glove.

glove puppet *noun* a small cloth puppet fitted on the hand and worked by the fingers.

glov·er *noun* a person who makes or sells gloves.

glove side *noun* *Hockey* the area of the net to that side of a goalie on which the catching glove is worn.

glow ● *intransitive verb* **1 a** throw out light and heat; be incandescent. **b** shine with a steady light like something heated in this way. **2** (of the cheeks) redden, esp. from cold or exercise. **3** (often foll. by *with*) **a** (of the body) be heated, esp. from exertion; sweat. **b** express or experience strong emotion, esp. joy (*glowed with pride; glowing with indignation*). **4** show a warm colour (*the painting glows with warmth*). ● *noun* **1** a glowing state. **2** a bright warm colour, esp. the red of cheeks. **3** a feeling induced by good health, exercise, etc.; well-being. [Old English *glōwan* from Germanic]

glow·er /ˈglaʊər/ ● *intransitive verb* (often foll. by *at*) stare or scowl angrily. ● *noun* a glowering look. ☐ **glower·ing·ly** *adverb* [origin uncertain: perhaps Scots var. of Middle English *glore* from Low German or Scandinavian, or from obsolete (Middle English) *glow* stare + -ER[4]]

glow·ing *adjective* expressing pride or praise (*a glowing report*). ☐ **glow·ing·ly** *adverb*

Glow Stick *noun* *proprietary* = LIGHT STICK.

glow-worm *noun* any beetle of the genus *Lampyris* whose wingless female emits light from the end of the abdomen.

glox·inia /glɒkˈsɪniə/ *noun* a tropical plant, *Sinningia speciosa*, native to S America, with large bell-shaped flowers of various colours, cultivated as a houseplant. [modern Latin from B. P. *Gloxin*, 18th-c. German botanist]

gluca·gon /ˈgluːkəgɒn/ *noun* a polypeptide hormone formed in the pancreas, which aids the breakdown of glycogen to glucose. [Greek *glukus* sweet + *agōn* leading]

Gluck /glʊk/ **Chris·toph Willi·bald von** (1714–87), German operatic composer, whose later 'reform' operas reduced the emphasis on the star singer and attempted a continuous musical unfolding of the narrative; they include *Orfeo ed Eurydice* (1762) and *Alceste* (1767).

gluco·cor·ti·coid /ˌgluːkoːˈkɔrtɪˌkɔɪd/ *noun* any of a group of corticosteroids which are involved in the metabolism of carbohydrates, proteins, and fats.

glu·cos·a·mine /gluːˈkoːsəmiːn/ *noun* a crystalline amino sugar that is derived from glucose and is the principal constituent of chitin.

glucosamine sulphate *noun* a nutritional supplement that is a sulphate of glucosamine and which relieves the symptoms and delays the progress of osteoarthritis.

glu·cose /ˈgluːkoːs, -oːz/ *noun* **1** a simple sugar containing six carbon atoms, found mainly in its dextrorotatory form (*see* DEXTROSE), which is an important energy source in living organisms and obtainable from some carbohydrates by hydrolysis. Chem. formula: $C_6H_{12}O_6$. **2** a syrup containing glucose sugars from the incomplete hydrolysis of starch, used in the food industry. [French from Greek *gleukos* sweet wine, related to *glukus* sweet]

gluco·side /ˈgluːkəˌsaɪd/ *noun* a compound yielding glucose and other products upon hydrolysis.

glue ● *noun* an adhesive substance used for sticking objects or materials together. ● *transitive verb* (**glues, glued, glu·ing** or **glue·ing**) **1** fasten or join with glue. **2** keep or put very close. **3** set fixedly (*eyes glued to the TV*). □ **glue-like** *adjective* **gluer** *noun* **gluey** /ˈgluːi/ *adjective* (**glu·i·er, glu·i·est**) **gluey·ness** *noun* [Old French *glu* (n.), *gluer* (v.), from Late Latin *glus glutis* from Latin *gluten*]

glue gun *noun* an electric tool resembling a handgun, used for melting and applying glue stored as hard sticks.

glue sniffing *noun* the inhalation of intoxicating fumes from the solvents in adhesives etc. □ **glue sniffer** *noun*

glue stick *noun* a type of solid glue in a retractable tube.

glug ● *verb* (**glugged, glug·ging**) **1** *intransitive* make a hollow, usu. repetitive gurgling sound, as of liquid being poured from a bottle. **2** *transitive* pour or drink (a liquid) with such a sound. ● *noun* such a sound. [imitative]

glum *adjective* (**glum·mer, glum·mest**) looking or feeling dejected; sullen, morose. □ **glum·ly** *adverb* **glum·ness** *noun* [related to dial. *glum* (v.) frown, var. of *gloume* GLOOM *verb*]

glume /gluːm/ *noun* **1** a membranous bract surrounding the spikelet of grasses or the florets of sedges. **2** the husk of grain. [Latin *gluma* husk]

gluon /ˈgluːɒn/ *noun Physics* any of a group of elementary particles that are thought to bind quarks together. [GLUE + -ON]

Glus·kap var. of GLOOSCAP.

glut ● *noun* **1** *Econ.* supply exceeding demand; a surfeit (*a glut in the market*). **2** an excessive quantity (*the information glut*). **3** *archaic* full indulgence; one's fill. ● *transitive verb* (**glut·ted, glut·ting**) **1** *Econ.* overstock (a market) with goods. **2** supply or fill to excess; choke up. [prob. Old French *gloutir* swallow, from Latin *gluttire*: compare GLUTTON]

gluta·mate /ˈgluːtəˌmeɪt/ *noun* any salt or ester of glutamic acid, esp. a sodium salt used to enhance the flavour of food.

glu·tam·ic acid /gluːˈtamɪk/ *noun* a naturally occurring amino acid, a constituent of many proteins. [GLUTEN + AMINE + -IC]

gluta·mine /ˈgluːtəmiːn/ *noun Biochem.* a hydrophilic amino acid present in many proteins. [GLUTAMIC ACID + AMINE]

gluta·thi·one /ˌgluːtəˈθaɪoːn/ *noun* a compound present in the body and involved as a coenzyme in oxidation-reduction reactions in cells. It is derived from glutamic acid, cysteine, and glycine.

glutch *Cdn (Nfld)* ● *transitive & intransitive verb* gulp, swallow. ● *noun* a gulp or swallow. [origin unknown]

glute /gluːt/ *noun slang* (usu. in *pl.*) a gluteus muscle. [abbreviation]

glu·ten /ˈgluːtən/ *noun* a mixture of proteins present in cereal grains, responsible for the elastic cohesion of dough. [French from Latin *gluten glutinis* glue]

glu·teus /ˈgluːtiəs/ *noun* (pl. **glutei** /-tiˌaɪ/) any of the three muscles in each buttock. □ **glu·teal** *adjective* [modern Latin from Greek *gloutos* buttock]

glu·teus max·imus /ˈgluːtiəs ˈmaksɪməs/ *noun* (pl. **glu·tei max·imi** /ˈgluːtiˌaɪ ˈmaksɪmaɪ/) **1** the largest and outermost muscle of each buttock. **2** *slang* the buttocks.

glu·tin·ous /ˈgluːtɪnəs/ *adjective* sticky; like glue. □ **glu·tin·ous·ly** *adverb* [French *glutineux* or Latin *glutinosus* (as GLUTEN)]

glut·ton *noun* **1** an excessively greedy eater. **2** (often foll. by *for*) *informal* a person insatiably eager (*a glutton for work*). □ **a glutton for punishment** a person eager to take on hard or unpleasant tasks.

□ **glut·ton·ous** *adjective* **glut·ton·ous·ly** *adverb* [Old French *gluton, gloton* from Latin *glutto -onis* from *gluttire* swallow, *gluttus* greedy]

glut·tony *noun* habitual greed or excess in eating.

gly·cemic index /glaɪˈsiːmɪk/ *noun* (also *Brit.* **gly·caemic index**) the ability of a food to increase blood sugar, calculated as the increase in blood glucose over 2 hours after consuming 50 g of carbohydrate, expressed as a percentage of that after 50 g of glucose.

gly·cer·ide /ˈglɪsəˌraɪd/ *noun* any fatty-acid ester of glycerol.

gly·cer·ine /ˈglɪsəˌriːn/ *noun* (esp. *US* **gly·cer·in** /-rɪn/) = GLYCEROL. [French *glycerin* from Greek *glukeros* sweet]

gly·cer·ol /ˈglɪsəˌrɒl/ *noun* a colourless sweet viscous liquid formed as a by-product in the manufacture of soap, used as an emollient and laxative, and for making explosives and antifreeze. Chem. formula: $C_3H_8O_3$. Also called GLYCERINE. [GLYCERINE + -OL[1]]

gly·cine /ˈglaɪsiːn/ *noun* the simplest naturally occurring amino acid, a general constituent of proteins. [German *Glycin* from Greek *glukus* sweet]

glyco- /ˈglaɪkoː/ *combining form* sugar. [Greek *glukus* sweet]

glyco·gen /ˈglaɪkədʒən/ *noun* a polysaccharide serving as a store of carbohydrates, esp. in animal tissues, and yielding glucose on hydrolysis. □ **glyco·gen·ic** *adjective*

gly·col /ˈglaɪkɒl/ *noun* a diol, esp. ethylene glycol. □ **gly·col·ic** /-ˈkɒlɪk/ *adjective* [GLYCERINE + -OL[1], originally as being intermediate between glycerine and alcohol]

glycolic acid *noun* a crystalline acid which occurs in sugar-cane syrup which is used as an exfoliant and has numerous industrial uses.

glyco·lipid /ˌglaɪkoːˈlɪpɪd/ *noun* any compound in which a sugar or other carbohydrate is combined with a lipid.

gly·coly·sis /glaɪˈkɒlɪsɪs/ *noun Biochem.* the breakdown of glucose by enzymes in most living organisms to release energy and pyruvic acid or lactic acid. □ **glyco·lytic** /-ˈlɪtɪk/ *adjective*

glyco·pro·tein /ˌglaɪkoːˈproːtiːn/ *noun* any of a group of compounds consisting of a protein combined with a carbohydrate.

glyco·side /ˈglaɪkəˌsaɪd/ *noun* a compound formed from a simple sugar and another compound by replacement of a hydroxyl group in the sugar molecule. Many drugs and poisons derived from plants are glycosides. □ **glyco·sid·ic** /-ˈsɪdɪk/ *adjective* [GLYCO-, after GLUCOSIDE]

gly·cos·uria /ˌglaɪkəˈsjʊriə/ *noun* a condition characterized by an excess of sugar in the urine, associated with diabetes, kidney disease, etc. [French *glycose* glucose + -URIA]

Glynde·bourne /ˈglaɪndbɔrn/ an estate near Lewes in SE England, where an annual opera festival is held.

Glyn·dwr *see* GLENDOWER.

glyph /glɪf/ *noun* **1** a sculptured character or symbol. **2** a vertical groove, esp. that on a Greek frieze. **3** a symbol or pictorial representation, as in computing or on a public sign. □ **glyph·ic** *adjective* [French *glyphe* from Greek *gluphē* carving, from *gluphō* carve]

gly·phos·ate /ˈglaɪfəˌseɪt/ *noun* a non-selective systemic herbicide that is especially effective against perennial weeds. [GLYCINE + PHOSPHO- + -ATE[1]]

glyp·tic /ˈglɪptɪk/ *adjective* of or concerning carving, esp. on precious stones. [French *glyptique* or Greek *gluptikos* from *gluptēs* carver, from *gluphō* carve]

glyp·to·dont /ˈglɪptəˌdɒnt/ *noun* an extinct mammal of Cenozoic times whose few teeth were grooved, related to the armadillos but much larger and with a bony shield round the body and tail. [modern Latin from Greek *gluptos* carved + *odous odontos* tooth]

GM *abbreviation* **1** General Motors. **2** general manager. **3** genetically modified.

gm *abbreviation* gram(s).

G-man *noun* (pl. **G-men**) *US informal* a federal criminal-investigation officer; an FBI agent. [Government + MAN]

GMO *abbreviation* genetically modified organism.

GMT *abbreviation* GREENWICH MEAN TIME.

GN *abbreviation Cdn* Government of Nunavut.

gnarled /nɑrld/ *adjective* (of a tree, hands, etc.) knobbly, twisted, rugged. [var. of *knarled*, related to KNURL]

gnarly /ˈnɑrli/ *adjective* **1** = GNARLED. **2** *N Amer. slang* excitingly rough or dangerous. [in sense 2 orig. surfers' slang, perhaps from the appearance of rough seas]

gnash /naʃ/ *verb* **1** *transitive* grind (the teeth), esp. in anger or exasperation. **2** *intransitive* (of the teeth) strike together; grind. [var. of obsolete *gnacche* or *gnast*, related to Old Norse *gnastan* a gnashing (imitative)]

gnat /nat/ *noun* any small two-winged biting fly, e.g. a midge or blackfly. [Old English *gnætt*]

gnat·catch·er /ˈnatkatʃər/ *noun* any of various tiny birds, related to the kinglets, of the genus *Polioptila*.

gnaw /nɒ/ *verb* **1** *a transitive* (usu. foll. by *away*, *off*, *in two*, etc.) bite persistently; wear away by biting. **b** *intransitive* (often foll. by *at*, *into*) bite, nibble. **2 a** *intransitive* (often foll. by *at*, *into*) (of a destructive agent, pain, fear, etc.) corrode; waste away; consume; torture. **b** *transitive* corrode, consume, torture, etc. with pain, fear, etc. (*was gnawed by doubt*). [Old English *gnagen*, ultimately imitative]

gnaw·ing /ˈnɒɪŋ/ *adjective* persistent; worrying. □ **gnaw·ing·ly** *adverb*

gneiss /nəɪs/ *noun* a usu. coarse-grained metamorphic rock foliated by mineral layers, principally of feldspar, quartz, and ferromagnesian minerals. □ **gneiss·ic** *adjective* [German]

gnoc·chi /ˈnjɒki/ *plural noun* an Italian dish of small dumplings usu. made from potato, semolina flour, etc. [Italian, pl. of *gnocco* from *nocchio* knot in wood]

gnome¹ /nəʊm/ *noun* **1 a** a dwarfish legendary creature supposed to guard the earth's treasures underground; a goblin. **b** a figure of a gnome, esp. as a garden ornament. **2** (esp. in *pl.*) *informal* a person with sinister influence, esp. financial (*gnomes of Zurich*). □ **gnom·ish** *adjective* [French from modern Latin *gnomus*, a word used by Paracelsus as a synonym of *Pygmaeus* denoting a mythical race of very small people said to inhabit parts of Ethiopia and India]

gnome² /nəʊm, ˈnəʊmi/ *noun* a maxim; an aphorism. [Greek *gnōmē* opinion from *gignōskō* know]

gnom·ic /ˈnəʊmɪk/ *adjective* **1** expressed in or of the nature of short, pithy maxims or aphorisms. **2** enigmatic, ambiguous. [Greek *gnōmikos* (as GNOME²)]

gno·mon /ˈnəʊmɒn/ *noun* **1** the rod or pin etc. on a sundial that shows the time by the position of its shadow. **2** *Math.* the part of a parallelogram left when a similar parallelogram has been taken from its corner. □ **gno·mon·ic** /-ˈmɒnɪk/ *adjective* [French or Latin *gnomon* from Greek *gnōmōn* indicator etc. from *gignōskō* know]

gno·sis /ˈnəʊsɪs/ *noun* esoteric knowledge of spiritual mysteries. [Greek *gnōsis* knowledge (as GNOMON)]

gnos·tic /ˈnɒstɪk/ ● *adjective* **1** relating to knowledge, esp. esoteric mystical knowledge. **2** (**Gnostic**) of or concerning Gnosticism or the Gnostics; occult; mystic. ● *noun* (**Gnostic**) (usu. in *pl.*) an adherent of Gnosticism. [ecclesiastical Latin *gnosticus* from Greek *gnōstikos* (as GNOSIS)]

Gnos·ti·cism /ˈnɒstɪˌsɪzəm/ *noun* a heretical movement prominent in the Christian Church in the 2nd c., emphasizing the power of gnosis, the supposed revealed knowledge of God, to redeem the spiritual element in humankind; they contrasted the supreme remote divine being with the demiurge or creator god, who controlled the world and was antagonistic to all that was purely spiritual.

GNP *abbreviation* gross national product.

gns. *abbreviation* Brit. hist. guineas.

gnu /nuː, njuː/ *noun* any antelope of the genus *Connochaetes*, native to S Africa, with a large erect head and brown stripes on the neck and shoulders. *Also called* WILDEBEEST. [Bushman *nqu*, prob. through Dutch *gnoe*]

GNWT *abbreviation* Cdn Government of the Northwest Territories.

go¹ ● *verb* (3rd sing. present **goes**; past **went**; past participle **gone**) **1** *intransitive* **a** start moving or be moving from one place or point in time to another; travel, proceed. **b** (foll. by *to* + infin., or *and* + verb) proceed in order to (*went to find him*; *go and buy some bread*). **c** (foll. by *and* + verb) *informal* expressing annoyance (*you went and told him*; *they've gone and broken it*; *she went and won*). **2** *intransitive* (foll. by verbal noun) make a special trip for; participate in; proceed to do (*went skiing*; *then went shopping*; *often goes running*). **3** *intransitive* lie or extend in a certain direction (*the road goes to Antigonish*). **4** *intransitive* leave; depart (*they had to go*). **5** *intransitive* move, act, work, etc. (*the clock doesn't go*; *her brain is going all the time*). **6** *intransitive* **a** make a specified movement (*go like this with your foot*). **b** make a sound (often of a specified kind) (*the gun went bang*; *the doorbell went*). **c** *informal* say (*so he goes to me, 'Why didn't he like it?'*). **d** (of an animal) make (its characteristic cry) (*the cow went 'moo'*). **7** *intransitive* be in a specified state (*go hungry*; *went in fear of his life*). **8** *intransitive* **a** pass into a specified condition (*gone bad*; *went mad*; *went to sleep*). **b** *informal* die. **c** proceed or escape in a specified condition (*the poet went unrecognized*; *the crime went unnoticed*). **9** *intransitive* (of time or distance) pass, elapse; be traversed (*ten days to go before Christmas*; *the last*

mile went quickly). **10** *intransitive* **a** (of a document, verse, song, etc.) have a specified content or wording (*the tune goes like this*). **b** be current or accepted (*so the story goes*). **c** be suitable; fit; match (*the shoes don't go with the hat*). **d** be regularly kept or put (*the forks go here*). **e** find room; fit (*this won't go into the cupboard*). **11** *intransitive* **a** turn out, proceed; take a course or view (*things went well*; *Montreal went Liberal*). **b** be successful (*make the party go*). **c** progress (*we've still a long way to go*). **12** *intransitive* **a** be sold (*went for $50*; *went cheap*). **b** (of money) be spent (*$200 went on a new jacket*). **13** *intransitive* **a** be relinquished, dismissed, or abolished (*the car will have to go*). **b** fail, decline; give way, collapse (*his sight is going*; *the bulb has gone*). **14** *intransitive* be acceptable or permitted; be accepted without question (*anything goes*; *what Susan says goes*). **15** *intransitive* (often foll. by *by*, *with*, *on*, *upon*) be guided by; judge or act on or in harmony with (*have nothing to go on*; *a good rule to go by*). **16** *intransitive* attend or visit or travel to regularly (*goes to church*; *goes to school*; *this train goes to Edmonton*). **17** *intransitive* (foll. by pres. part.) *informal* proceed (often foolishly) to do (*went running to the police*; *don't go making him angry*). **18** *intransitive* act or proceed to a certain point (*will go so far and no further*; *went as high as $100*). **19** *intransitive* (of a number) be capable of being contained in another (*6 goes twice into 12*; *6 doesn't go into 5*). **20** *transitive* Cards bid; declare (*has gone two spades*). **21** *intransitive* (usu. foll. by *to*) be allotted or awarded; pass (*first prize went to the girl*; *the job went to his rival*). **22** *intransitive* (foll. by *to*, *towards*) amount to; contribute to (*this will go towards your holiday*). **23** *intransitive* (in *imperative*) begin motion (a starter's order in a race) (*ready, set, go!*). **24** *intransitive* (usu. foll. by *to*) refer or appeal (*go to him for help*). **25** *intransitive* (often foll. by *on*) take up a specified profession (*went on the stage*; *gone soldiering*; *went to sea*). **26** *intransitive* (usu. foll. by *by*, *under*) be known or called (*goes by the name of Droopy*). **27** *transitive* (in *imperative*) *informal* proceed to (*go jump in the lake*). **28** *intransitive* (foll. by *for*) apply to; have relevance for (*that goes for me too*). **29** *intransitive* urinate or defecate (*I have to go*; *the dog went on the carpet*). ● *noun* (*pl.* **goes**) **1** the act or an instance of going. **2** mettle; spirit; dash; animation (*she has a lot of go in her*). **3** vigorous activity (*it's all go*). **4** *informal* a success (*made a go of it*). **5** *informal* a turn; an attempt (*I'll have a go*; *it's my go*; *all in one go*). **6** esp. *Brit. informal* a state of affairs (*a rum go*). **7** esp. *Brit. informal* an attack of illness (*a bad go of flu*). **8** esp. *Brit. informal* a quantity of liquor, food, etc. served at one time. **9** *N Amer.* a project, undertaking, etc. which has been given the go-ahead (*the new subway line is a go*). **10** an experience (*had a rough go of it*). ● *adjective informal* functioning properly (*all systems are go*). □ **as** (or **so**) **far as it goes** an expression of caution against taking a statement too positively (*the work is good as far as it goes*). **as** (**a person or thing**) **goes** as the average is (*a good actor as actors go*). **don't go there** *informal* don't proceed any further along the line of thought you are following. **from the word go** *informal* from the very beginning. **give it a go** *informal* make an effort to succeed. **go about 1** busy oneself with; set to work at. **2** be socially active. **3** = GO AROUND 2. **4** *Naut.* change to an opposite tack. **go against 1** be contrary to (*goes against my principles*). **2** have an unfavourable result for (*decision went against them*). **go ahead** proceed without hesitation. **go along with** agree to; take the same view as. **go around 1** (foll. by *with*) be regularly in the company of. **2** (foll. by pres. part.) make a habit of doing (*goes around telling lies*). **go at** take in hand energetically; attack. **go away** depart, esp. from home for a holiday etc. **go back 1** return (to). **2 a** extend backwards in space or time (*goes back to the 18th century*). **b** (also **go way back**) (of two or more people or things) have known one another for a very long time (*Marty and I go way back*). **3** (of the hour, a clock, etc.) be set to an earlier standard time (*the clocks go back in the autumn*). **go back on** fail to keep (one's word, promise, etc.). **go begging** see BEG. **go by 1** pass. **2** be dependent on; be guided by. **go down 1 a** (of an amount) become less (*the coffee has gone down a lot*). **b** subside (*the flood went down*). **c** decrease in price; lose value. **2 a** (of a ship) sink. **b** (of an aircraft) crash. **c** (of the sun) set. **3** (usu. foll. by *to*) be continued to a specified point. **4** deteriorate; fail (*a computer network etc.*) cease to function. **5 a** be recorded in writing. **b** be remembered (*this will go down as their greatest triumph*). **6** (of a baby) have a nap. **7** be swallowed. **8** (often foll. by *with*) find acceptance. **9** *Brit. informal* leave university. **10** *Brit. informal* be sent to prison (*went down for ten years*). **11** (often foll. by *before*) fall (before a conqueror). **12** *N Amer. slang* happen. **go down on** *slang* perform fellatio or cunnilingus on. **go down with** *Brit.* begin to suffer from (a disease). **go far** be very successful. **go for 1** be accounted as or achieve (*went for nothing*). **2** prefer; choose (*that's the one I go for*). **3** *informal* strive to attain (*go for it!*). **4** *informal* attack (*the dog went for him*). **go forward 1** proceed, progress (*go forward into the next round*). **2** (of the hour, a clock, etc.) be set to a later time, esp. daylight time. **go great guns** see GUN. **go halves** (or **shares**) (often foll. by *with*) share equally. **go in 1** enter a room, house, etc. **2** Cricket take or begin an innings. **3** (of the sun etc.)

become obscured by cloud. **go in for** take as one's object, style, pursuit, principle, etc. **going!, gone!** an auctioneer's announcement that bidding is closing or closed. **go into 1** enter (a profession, Parliament, etc.). **2** take part in; be a part of. **3** investigate. **4** allow oneself to pass into (hysterics etc.). **5** dress oneself in (mourning etc.). **6** elaborate on (*went into the family's history*). **go it alone** see ALONE. **go a long way 1** (often foll. by *towards*) have a great effect. **2** (of food, money, etc.) last a long time, buy much. **3** = GO FAR. **go off 1** explode. **2** leave the stage. **3** gradually cease to be felt. **4** (esp. of foodstuffs) deteriorate; decompose. **5** go to sleep; become unconscious. **6** begin. **7** (of an alarm) begin to sound. **8** *informal* lose one's taste or enthusiasm for (*I've gone off sweet things*). **go off at** *Austral. & NZ slang* reprimand, scold. **go off well** (or **badly** etc.) (of an enterprise etc.) be received or accomplished well (or badly etc.). **go on 1** (often foll. by pres. part.) continue, persevere (*decided to go on with it; went on trying; unable to go on*). **2** *informal* **a** talk at great length. **b** (foll. by *at*) admonish (*went on and on at him*). **3** (foll. by *to* + infin.) proceed (*went on to become a star*). **4** happen (*what's going on?*). **5** conduct oneself (*shameful, the way they went on*). **6** *Theatre* appear on stage. **7** *Cricket* begin bowling. **8** (of a garment) be large enough for its wearer. **9** take one's turn to do something. **10** *informal* use as evidence (*police don't have anything to go on*). **go on!** *informal* an expression of encouragement or disbelief. **go out 1** leave a room, house, etc. **2 a** be broadcast. **b** be distributed. **3** be extinguished. **4** (often foll. by *with*) be dating. **5** leave one's home for recreation, esp. to visit a restaurant, friends, etc. **6** (of a government) leave office. **7** cease to be fashionable. **8** *informal* lose consciousness. **9** (of workers) strike. **10** (usu. foll. by *to*) (of the heart etc.) expand with sympathy etc. towards (*my heart goes out to them*). **11** *Golf* play the first nine holes in a round. **12** *Cards* be the first to dispose of one's hand. **13** (of a tide) turn to low tide. **14** *Cdn* (of winter ice on a lake, river, etc.) break up in the spring. **go over 1** inspect the details of; rehearse; retouch. **2** (often foll. by *to*) change one's allegiance or religion. **3** (of a play, joke, etc.) be successful (*went over well in Vancouver*). **go round 1** spin, revolve. **2** be long enough to encompass. **3** (of food etc.) suffice for everybody. **4** (usu. foll. by *to*) visit informally. **5** = GO AROUND. **go through 1** be dealt with or completed. **2** discuss in detail; scrutinize in sequence. **3** perform (a ceremony, a recitation, etc.). **4** undergo. **5** *informal* use up; spend (money etc.). **6** make holes in. **7** (of a book) be successively published (in so many editions). **go through with** not leave unfinished; complete. **go to!** *archaic* an exclamation of disbelief, impatience, admonition, etc. **go to hell** (or **blazes** etc.) *slang* an exclamation of dismissal, contempt, etc. **go to the country** see COUNTRY. **go together 1** match; fit. **2** be dating. **go to it!** *informal* begin work! **go to show** (or **prove**) serve to demonstrate (or prove). **go under** sink; fail; succumb. **go up 1** increase in price. **2** be consumed (in flames etc.); explode. **3** (of a building) be under construction. **4** *Brit. informal* enter university. **go well** (or **ill** etc.) (often foll. by *with*) turn out well, (or ill etc.). **go with 1** be harmonious with; match. **2** agree to; take the same view as. **3 a** be a pair with. **b** be dating. **4** follow the drift of. **go without** manage without; forgo (*we shall just have to go without*). **have a go at 1** attempt, try. **2** esp. *Brit.* attack, criticize. **on the go** *informal* **1** in constant motion. **2** constantly working. **3** in progress; happening. **to go 1** still to be dealt with. **2** *N Amer.* (of fast food etc.) to be consumed off the premises. **who goes there?** a sentry's challenge. **you go, girl** *N Amer. informal* expressing encouragement to a girl or woman. [Old English *gān* from Germanic: *went* originally past of WEND]

go² *noun* a Japanese board game of territorial possession and capture. [Japanese]

Goa /ˈɡəʊə/ a state on the west coast of India; capital, Panaji. Formerly a Portuguese territory, it was seized by India in 1961. □ **Goan** *adjective & noun* **Goan·ese** /ˌɡəʊəˈniːz/ *adjective & noun*

goad ● *noun* **1** an implement, such as a pointed or electrified rod, used for herding cattle etc. **2** anything that torments, incites, or stimulates. ● *transitive verb* **1** urge on with a goad. **2** (usu. foll. by *on, into*) irritate; stimulate (*goaded him into retaliating; goaded me on to win*). [Old English *gād*, related to Lombard *gaida* arrowhead, from Germanic]

go-ahead ● *noun* permission to proceed. ● *adjective* **1** enterprising (*a go-ahead business*). **2** *N Amer. Sport* designating a goal, run, touchdown, etc. which puts the scoring team ahead of its opponent (*scored the go-ahead goal*).

goal *noun* **1** the object of an ambition or effort; a destination; an aim (*fame is his goal; Fredericton was our goal*). **2 a** (in hockey, soccer, etc.) a pair of posts with a crossbar between which the puck or ball has to be sent to score. **b** a cage or basket used similarly in other sports. **c** a successful attempt to score (*it's a goal!*). **d** a point won (*scored 3 goals*). **3** a point marking the end of a race. **4** the position of goalkeeper (*has

played goal since childhood*). □ **in goal** in the position of goalkeeper. □ **goal·less** *adjective* [16th c.: origin unknown: perhaps identical with Middle English *gol* boundary]

goal·ball *noun* a team game for visually handicapped players, in which a ball emitting a sound is thrown at a goal to score points.

goal·ie *noun* = GOALKEEPER.

goalie pads *plural noun* *Hockey* (also **goal pads**) a pair of very thick rectangular pads worn on the legs by a goaltender.

goal·keep·er *noun* a player stationed to protect the goal in various sports. □ **goal·keep·ing** *noun*

goal kick *noun* **1** *Soccer* a kick by the defending side after attackers send the ball over the goal line without scoring. **2** *Rugby* an attempt to kick a goal. □ **goal-kicker** *noun* (in sense 2). **goal-kicking** *noun* (in sense 2).

goal line *noun* *Sport* a line across which a ball or puck must cross for points to be scored, esp.: **1** (in hockey) a red line between each pair of goalposts. **2** (in soccer) a line between each pair of goalposts, also extending beyond the posts to form the end boundary of the field of play (compare TOUCHLINE). **3** (in football) the line separating each end zone from the rest of the field.

goal·mouth *noun* (in hockey, soccer, etc.) the space between or directly in front of the goalposts.

goal-oriented *noun* consciously or unconsciously directing one's behaviour and actions towards a given result.

goal pads *plural noun* = GOALIE PADS.

goal·post *noun* either of the two upright posts of a goal. □ **move the goalposts** *Brit.* alter the basis or scope of a procedure during its course.

goals-against average *noun* *Hockey* the average number of goals scored per game against a specified goaltender. Abbr.: **GAA**.

goal scorer *noun* **1** a player who scores a goal. **2** a player proficient in scoring goals. □ **goal-scoring** *adjective & noun*

goal suck *noun* *Hockey slang* a player who lets teammates do the hard work bringing the puck down the ice, then lingers by the goal so as to score easily.

goal·tend·er *noun* *N Amer.* (esp. in hockey) a goalkeeper.

goal·tend·ing *noun* **1** *N Amer.* (esp. in hockey) the action of defending a goal (*the team got good goaltending in the playoffs*). **2** (in basketball) the illegal blocking or deflecting of an attempted basket while the ball is descending or on the rim.

go·an·na /ɡəʊˈanə/ *noun* any of various lizards, esp. large monitors of the genus *Varanus*. [corruption of IGUANA]

goat *noun* **1 a** a hardy lively frisky short-haired domesticated mammal, *Capra aegagrus*, having horns and (in the male) a beard, and kept for its milk and meat. **b** = MOUNTAIN GOAT. **2** any other mammal of the genus *Capra*, including the ibex. **3** *informal* a foolish person. **4** a lecherous man. **5** (**the Goat**) the zodiacal sign or constellation Capricorn. **6** *Sports slang* a player who is responsible for a team's misfortune (*his terrible goaltending made him the biggest goat of the playoffs*). □ **get a person's goat** *informal* irritate a person. □ **goat·ish** *adjective* **goat·like** *adjective* **goaty** *adjective* [Old English *gāt* she-goat]

goat-antelope *noun* any antelope-like member of the goat family, including the chamois, goral, and Rocky Mountain goat.

goat cheese *noun* *N Amer.* (also esp. *Brit.* **goat's cheese**) cheese made from goat's milk.

goa·tee /ɡəʊˈtiː/ *noun* a small beard on the point of the chin, like that of a goat. □ **goa·teed** *adjective*

goat·herd *noun* a person who tends goats.

goat's beard *noun* **1** a meadow plant, *Tragopogon pratensis*, with plumed seeds forming a large ball. **2** a herbaceous plant, *Aruncus dioicus*, with long plumes of white flowers.

goat·skin *noun* **1** the skin of a goat. **2** a garment or bottle made out of goatskin.

goat·suck·er *noun* any nocturnal bird of the family Caprimulgidae, having a characteristic harsh cry, including nighthawks and whippoorwills.

gob¹ *noun* esp. *Brit. slang* the mouth. [perhaps from Gaelic & Irish, = beak, mouth]

gob² *slang* ● *noun* **1** a clot or lump of esp. slimy or soft matter. **2** *slang* **a** *Cdn & Brit.* spittle. **b** a globule of spittle. **3** (in *pl.*; foll. by *of*) lots of. ● *intransitive verb* (**gobbed**, **gob·bing**) *Cdn & Brit.* spit. [Old French *go(u)be* mouthful]

gob³ *noun* *slang* a US sailor. [20th c.: origin unknown, perhaps from GOB²]

Consonants: b *but*   d *dog*   f *few*   g *get*   h *her*   j *yes*   k *cat*   l *leg*   m *man*   n *no*   p *pen*   r *red*   s *sit*

Göb·bels see GOEBBELS.

gob·bet *noun* a piece or lump, esp. of raw meat, flesh, food, etc. [Old French *gobet* (as GOB[2])]

gob·ble[1] *verb* **1** *transitive & intransitive* eat hurriedly and noisily; devour. **2** *transitive* (often foll. by *up*) **a** seize avidly, grab, snatch. **b** consume, use up. □ **gob·bler** *noun* [prob. dial. from GOB[2]]

gob·ble[2] ● *intransitive verb* **1** (of a male turkey) make a characteristic swallowing sound in the throat. **2** make such a sound when speaking, esp. when excited, angry, etc. ● *noun* such a sound. [imitative: perhaps based on GOBBLE[1]]

gobble·dy·gook /ˈgɒbəldɪˌgʊk, -ˌguːk/ *noun* (also **gobble·de·gook**) *informal* unintelligible jargon. [prob. imitative of a male turkey]

gob·bler *noun informal* a turkeycock.

Go·be·lin /ˈgəʊbəlɪn, gɔˈblæ̃/ *noun* (in full **Gobelin tapestry**) **1** a tapestry made at the Gobelins factory. **2** a tapestry imitating this. [name of a state factory in Paris, called *Gobelins* after its original owners]

go-between *noun* an intermediary; a negotiator.

Gobi Desert /ˈgəʊbi/ a barren plateau of S Mongolia and N China.

gob·let *noun* **1** a drinking vessel with a foot and a stem, usu. of glass. **2** *archaic* a metal or glass bowl-shaped drinking cup without handles, sometimes with a foot and a cover. [Old French *gobelet* diminutive of *gobel* cup, of unknown origin]

gob·lin *noun* a mischievous ugly dwarf-like creature of folklore. [prob. from Anglo-French *gobelin*, medieval Latin *gobelinus*, prob. from name diminutive of *Gobel*, related to German *Kobold*: see COBALT]

gobo /ˈgəʊbəʊ/ *noun* (*pl.* **gobos**, **goboes**) **1** a portable screen used to shield a camera lens from light or a microphone from noise. **2** a partial screen used in front of a spotlight to project a shape. [origin unknown, perhaps from *go between*]

gob·shite *noun* esp. *Irish coarse slang* a stupid, foolish, or incompetent person. [prob. from GOB[2] + *shite*, Irish variant of SHIT]

gob·smacked *adjective Brit. slang* astounded; utterly astonished. □ **gob·smack·ing** *adjective* **gob·smack·ing·ly** *adverb* [GOB[1] + SMACK[1]: with reference to clapping a hand to one's mouth in astonishment]

gob·stop·per *noun* a very large hard usu. spherical candy, esp. one revealing different concentric layers of colour as it dissolves slowly. [GOB[1] + STOP *verb* 7]

goby /ˈgəʊbi/ *noun* (*pl.* **-bies**) any small marine fish of the family Gabiidae, having ventral fins joined to form a sucker or disc. [Latin *gobius*, *cobius* from Greek *kōbios* GUDGEON[1]]

go-by *noun informal* a snub; a slight (*gave us the go-by*).

GOC *abbreviation* General Officer Commanding.

go-cart *noun* **1** = GO-KART. **2** an unpowered small esp. homemade riding cart, either sent down a slope or pushed.

god *noun* **1 a** (in many religions) a superhuman being or spirit worshipped as having power over nature, human fortunes, etc.; a deity. **b** an image, idol, animal, or other object worshipped as divine or symbolizing a god. **2** (**God**) (in monotheistic religions) the creator and ruler of the universe; the supreme being. **3 a** an adored, admired, or influential person. **b** something worshipped like a god (*makes a god of success*). **4** (in *pl.*) *Brit.* **a** the uppermost balcony in a theatre. **b** the people sitting in it. **5** (**God!**) an exclamation of surprise, anger, etc. □ **by God!** an exclamation of surprise etc. **for God's sake!** see SAKE[1]. **God bless** an expression of good wishes on parting. **God bless me** (or **my soul**) see BLESS. **God damn** (**you, him**, etc.) may (you etc.) be damned. **God the Father, Son, and Holy Ghost** (in the Christian tradition) the Persons of the Trinity. **God grant** (foll. by *that* + clause) may it happen. **God help** (**you, him**, etc.) an expression of concern for or sympathy with a person. **God knows 1** it is beyond all knowledge (*God knows what will become of him*). **2** I call God to witness that (*God knows we tried hard enough*). **God willing** if Providence allows. **in God's name** an appeal for help. **my** (or **oh**) **God!** an exclamation of surprise, anger, etc. **play God** attempt to control people or events, esp. in matters traditionally outside the realm of human influence. **with God** dead and in Heaven. □ **god·hood** *noun* **god·ship** *noun* [Old English from Germanic]

Go·dard /gɒˈdɑr/ **Jean-Luc** (b.1930), French film director. His films, frequently dealing with existentialist themes, use improvised dialogue, disjointed narratives, and unconventional shooting and cutting techniques; they include *Breathless* (1960), *Alphaville* (1965), and *Hail Mary* (1985).

Go·dav·ari River /gəʊˈdɒvəri/ a river in central India which rises in the state of Maharashtra and flows about 1 440 km (900 miles) southeast across the Deccan plateau to the Bay of Bengal.

god·awful *adjective slang* extremely unpleasant, inferior, etc.

God·bout /gɒdˈbuː/ **Jacques** (b.1933), Canadian novelist, poet, and filmmaker. His works include the novels *L'aquarium* (1962), *Salut Galarneau* (1967), *Les têtes à Papineau* (1981), and *Une Histoire américaine* (1986).

god·child *noun* (*pl.* **-chil·dren**) a person in relation to a godparent.

god·damm·it *interjection* (also **god·damn·it**) *informal* expressing annoyance, anger, etc.

god·damn *adjective* (also **god·dam** or **god·damned**) *slang* accursed, damnable.

God·dard /ˈgɒdərd/ **Rob·ert Hutch·ings** (1882–1945), US physicist. He carried out pioneering work in rocketry, and designed and built the first successful liquid-fuelled rocket.

god·daugh·ter *noun* a female godchild.

god·dess *noun* **1** a female deity. **2** a woman who is adored, esp. for her beauty.

Gode·froy de Bouil·lon /ˈgɒdfrwɒ də buːˈjɔ̃/ (*c.*1060–1100), duke of Lower Lorraine 1089–1100. He led the First Crusade (1096–99) and was proclaimed 'Protector of the Holy Sepulchre' in Jerusalem (1099).

Gödel /ˈgɜːdəl/ **Kurt** (1906–78), Austrian-born US mathematician. He made several contributions to mathematical logic, esp. the *incompleteness theorem* (Gödel's proof): that in any sufficiently powerful, logically consistent formulation of logic or mathematics there must be true formulas which are neither provable nor disprovable.

God·erich /ˈgɒdrɪtʃ/ a town in SW Ontario, situated on Lake Huron, about 65 km northwest of Stratford; pop. (2001) 7,604. □ **God·erich·ite** *noun* [F. J. Robinson, Viscount *Goderich* and Earl of Ripon d.1859]

go·det /gəʊˈdet, ˈgəʊdeɪ/ *noun* a triangular piece of material inserted in a dress, glove, etc. [Old French]

go·detia /gəʊˈdiːʃə/ *noun* a North American plant of the genus *Clarkia* with showy lilac to red flowers. [C. *Godet* Swiss botanist d.1879]

go-devil *noun N Amer.* **1** *hist.* a crude sled used for dragging logs etc. **2** an instrument used to clean the inside of pipes etc.

god·father *noun* **1** a male godparent. **2** a person directing an illegal organization, esp. the Mafia. **3** the most experienced or influential member of an organization, group, etc., treated with deference and respect.

God-fearing *adjective* **1** having a deep respect for God and leading a virtuous life. **2** earnestly religious.

god·for·saken *adjective* (also **God-forsaken**) **1** (of a place) dismal; dreary; lacking in comfort. **2** remote; isolated.

God game *noun* a computer game which places the player in a simulated situation where he or she can manage all the resources of a community or company etc.

God-given *adjective* received as from God; possessed from birth or by divine authority.

god·head *noun* (also **Godhead**) **1 a** the state of being God or a god. **b** divine nature. **2** a deity. **3** (**the Godhead**) God.

Go·diva /gəˈdaɪvə/ **Lady** (d.1080), English noblewoman, wife of Leofric, Earl of Mercia (d.1057). According to a 13th-c. legend, she agreed to her husband's proposition that he would reduce some unpopular taxes if she rode naked on horseback through the marketplace of Coventry.

god·less *adjective* **1** impious; wicked. **2** without a god. **3** not recognizing God. □ **god·less·ness** *noun*

god·like *adjective* **1** resembling God or a god in some quality, esp. in omnipotence. **2** befitting or appropriate to God or a god.

godly *adjective* religious, pious, devout. □ **god·li·ness** *noun*

god·mother *noun* **1** a female godparent. **2** a woman who is the most experienced or influential member of an organization, group, etc., treated with deference and respect.

go·down /gəʊˈdaʊn/ *noun* a warehouse in parts of E Asia, esp. in India. [Portuguese *gudão* from Malay *godong* perhaps from Telugu *gidangi* place where goods lie, from *kidu* lie]

god·parent *noun* a person who presents a child at baptism and responds on the child's behalf.

God's acre *noun* a graveyard, esp. one near a church.

God's country *noun N Amer.* a natural earthly paradise.

god·send *noun* an unexpected but welcome event, thing, or person.

God's gift *noun* often *ironic* a person or thing that is of supreme benefit to someone or something specified (*God's gift to dance; thinks he's God's gift to women*).

Gods Lake a lake in east central Manitoba, about 250 km northeast of Lake Winnipeg. [translation of Cree MANITOU, in the 'Great Spirit' sense, i.e. the supreme deity (identified by some as God)]

god·son *noun* a male godchild.

God·speed *noun* (as an expression of good wishes to a person starting a journey, new undertaking, etc.) good fortune.

God's truth *noun* the absolute truth.

Godt·håb /ˈɡɒdhɒb/ the former name (until 1979) for NUUK.

Godu·nov /ˈɡʊdʊˌnɒf/ **Boris (Fyodor·ovich)** (*c*.1550–1605), czar of Russia 1598–1605. His reign was overshadowed by famine, doubts over his involvement in the earlier death of Ivan the Terrible's eldest son, and the appearance of a pretender, the so-called False Dimitry.

God·win, Wil·liam (1756–1836), English philosopher and novelist. His best-known and most influential work, *An Enquiry Concerning Political Justice* (1793), advocated anarchism and the perfectibility of human beings; his novels include *Caleb Williams* (1794). He was married to Mary Wollstonecraft and was the father of Mary Shelley.

Godwin-Austen, Mount an alternative name for K2.

god·wit *noun* any wading bird of the genus *Limosa*, with long legs and a long straight or slightly upcurved bill. [16th c.: of unknown origin]

Goeb·bels /ˈɡɜːbəlz/ **(Paul) Jo·seph** (also **Göb·bels**) (1897–1945), German Nazi leader and politician. In 1933 he became Hitler's Minister of Propaganda, with control of the press, radio, and all aspects of culture, and manipulated these in order to further Nazi aims; he committed suicide shortly after Hitler.

goer *noun* **1** (often in *combination*) a person who attends, esp. regularly (*a churchgoer; balletgoer*). **2** a person or thing that goes (*a slow goer*). **3** *Brit. informal* **a** a lively or persevering person. **b** a sexually promiscuous person. **4** *Brit. & Austral. informal* a project likely to be accepted or to succeed.

Goer·ing *var. of* GÖRING.

goes *3rd sing. present of* GO¹.

goest *archaic 2nd sing. present of* GO¹.

goeth *archaic 3rd sing. present of* GO¹.

Goethe /ˈɡɜːtə/ **Jo·hann Wolf·gang von** (1749–1832), German poet, dramatist, and scholar. His poetry, plays, and novels contributed greatly to the development of German literature, and his best-known works include the epic drama *Götz von Berlichingen* (1773), the epistolary novel *The Sorrows of Young Werther* (1774), and the two-part poetic drama *Faust* (1808–32).

Goeth·ean /ˈɡɜːtɪən/ (also **Goeth·ian**) ● *adjective* of, relating to, or characteristic of J. W. von Goethe. ● *noun* an admirer or follower of Goethe.

go·fer /ˈɡoːfər/ *noun esp. N Amer. informal* a person who runs errands, esp. in an office. [*go for* (see GO¹)]

gof·fer /ˈɡoːfər, ˈɡɒf-/ ● *transitive verb* make wavy, flute, or crimp (a lace edge, a trimming, etc.) with heated irons. ● *noun* **1** an iron used for goffering. **2** ornamental braiding used for frills etc. [French *gaufrer* stamp with a patterned tool, from *gaufre* honeycomb, related to WAFER, WAFFLE²]

Gog and Magog /ɡɒɡ, ˈmeiɡɒɡ/ **1** in the Bible, the names of enemies of God's people. In Ezek. 38–9, Gog appears to be a ruler from the land of Magog. In Rev. 20:8, Gog and Magog are nations under the dominion of Satan. **2** (in medieval legend) opponents of Alexander the Great, living north of the Caucasus.

go-getter *noun informal* an aggressively enterprising person, esp. in business. □ **go-getting** *adjective*

gog·gle ● *noun* **1** (in *pl.*) **a** eyeglasses for protecting the eyes from glare, dust, water, etc. **b** *informal* eyeglasses. **2** an expression with wide-open or protuberant eyes. ● *intransitive verb* **1** (often foll. by *at*) stare with wide, round eyes, esp. in surprise or wonder. **2** (of the eyes) be rolled about; protrude. ● *adjective* (usu. *attributive*) (of the eyes) protuberant or rolling. □ **gog·gly** *adjective* [Middle English, prob. from a base *gog* (unrecorded) expressive of oscillating movement]

goggle·box *noun Brit. informal* a television set.

goggle-eyed *adjective* having staring or protuberant eyes.

Gogh see VAN GOGH.

go-go *adjective* **1 a** (of a dancer) performing at a nightclub or disco, esp. in scanty clothing. **b** (of a disco or nightclub) featuring go-go dancers. **2** *informal* unrestrained; energetic. **3** *informal* (of investment) speculative.

Gogol /ˈɡoːɡɒl/ **Niko·lai (Vasili·evich)** (1809–52), Ukrainian-born Russian novelist, dramatist, and short-story writer, who is best known

for his satirical play *The Inspector General* (1836), and his comic epic novel *Dead Souls* (1842), widely regarded as the foundation of the modern Russian novel. □ **Gogol·ian** *adjective*

Goi·ânia /ɡɔːˈjɒnjə/ a city in south central Brazil; pop. (est. 2002) 1,132,600.

Goi·del /ˈɡɔɪdəl/ *noun* a Celt who speaks Irish Gaelic, Scottish Gaelic, or Manx. [Old Irish *Góidel*]

Goi·del·ic /ɡɔɪˈdɛlɪk/ ● *noun* the northern group of the Celtic languages, comprising Irish Gaelic, Scottish Gaelic, and Manx. ● *adjective* of or relating to the Goidelic or the Goidels.

go·ing ● *noun* **1 a** the act or process of going. **b** an instance of this; a departure. **2 a** the condition of the ground for walking, riding, etc. **b** progress affected by this (*found the going through the tall grass very laborious*). **c** progress affected by all circumstances (*it'll be tough going for the party this election*). ● *adjective* **1** in or into action (*set the clock going*). **2** existing, available; to be had (*one of the best defencemen going*). **3** current, prevalent (*the going rate*). □ **get going** start steadily talking, working, etc. (*can't stop them when they get going*). **going away** with victory foreseen before the end of a competition or contest (*with another three-run homer in the eighth, Montreal won going away*). **going for one** *informal* acting in one's favour (*he's got a lot going for him*). **going on fifteen** etc. esp. *N Amer.* approaching one's fifteenth etc. birthday. **going on for** approaching (a time, an age, etc.) (*must be going on for 6 years*). **going to** intending or intended to; about to; likely to (*it's going to sink!*). **to be going on with** to start with; for the time being. **while the going is good** while conditions are favourable.

going away *noun* a departure, as to another city, job, etc. (often, with hyphen, *attributive*: *going-away party*).

going concern *noun* a thriving business.

going-over *noun* (*pl.* **goings-over**) **1** *informal* an inspection or overhaul. **2** *slang* a thrashing. **3** *N Amer. informal* a scolding.

goings-on *plural noun* unusual, surprising, or morally undesirable happenings or events.

goitre /ˈɡɔɪtər/ *noun* (esp. *US* **goiter**) *Med.* a swelling of the neck resulting from enlargement of the thyroid gland. □ **goitred** *adjective* **goi·trous** *adjective* [French, back-formation from *goitreux* or from Provençal *goitron*, ultimately from Latin *guttur* throat]

go-kart *noun* a miniature racing car with a skeleton body.

Golan Heights /ˈɡoːlan/ a range of hills on the border between Syria and Israel, northeast of the Sea of Galilee. Formerly under Syrian control, the area was occupied by Israel in 1967 and annexed in 1981. Negotiations for the withdrawal of Israeli troops from the region began in 1992.

Gol·con·da /ɡɒlˈkɒndə/ *noun* a mine or source of wealth, advantages, etc. [city near Hyderabad, India]

gold ● *noun* **1** a yellow malleable ductile high density metallic element resistant to chemical reaction, occurring naturally in quartz veins and gravel, and precious as a monetary medium, in jewellery, etc. Symbol: **Au**; at. no.: 79. **2** the colour of gold. **3 a** coins or articles made of gold. **b** money in large sums, wealth. **4** something precious, beautiful, or brilliant (*all that glitters is not gold*). **5** = GOLD MEDAL. **6** *Cdn* (usu. in *pl.*) a gold seat in a hockey arena etc., usu. among those closest to the playing surface. **7** the bull's eye of an archery target (usu. gilt). ● *adjective* **1** made wholly or chiefly of gold. **2** coloured like gold. **3** (of an album, CD, etc.) having sold a specified high number of copies. [Old English from Germanic]

gol·darn /ɡɒlˈdɑːn/ *transitive verb N Amer. informal* euphemism for *god damn*. □ **gol·darned** *adjective*

gold·brick esp. *US slang* ● *noun* **1** a thing with only a surface appearance of value, a sham or fraud. **2** *US* a lazy person or malingerer. ● *intransitive verb* **1** be lazy. **2** malinger.

gold card *noun* a credit card issued only to people with a high credit rating and giving benefits not available to holders of the standard card.

Gold Coast 1 the former name (until 1957) for GHANA. **2** a resort region on the east coast of Australia, to the south of Brisbane.

gold·crest *noun* a tiny olive-green Eurasian kinglet, *Regulus regulus*, with a golden crest.

gold digger *noun* **1** *slang* a woman who uses her sexual attraction to acquire wealth and material possessions, esp. through marriage. **2** a person who digs for gold.

gold disc *noun Brit.* = GOLD RECORD.

gold dust *noun* **1** gold in fine particles as often found naturally. **2** a plant, *Alyssum saxatile*, with many small yellow flowers.

gold·en *adjective* **1 a** made or consisting of gold. **b** yielding gold.

2 coloured or shining like gold (*golden hair; bake till golden brown*). **3** precious; valuable; excellent; important (*a golden memory; a golden opportunity*). **4** (esp. in nicknames for places) wealthy (*Golden Horseshoe*). □ **gold·en·ly** *adverb*

golden age *noun* **1** a supposed past age when people were happy and innocent. **2** the period of greatest esp. artistic achievement (*the golden age of comics*). **3** (usu. *attributive*) old age, esp. after retirement.

golden ager *noun N Amer.* an old person, esp. a retired person over 65.

golden arches *plural noun* a McDonald's fast-food restaurant, identifiable by the large yellow letter M which resembles two arches.

golden bean *noun* = BUFFALO BEAN.

golden boy *noun informal* a popular or successful man or boy.

Golden Calf *noun* **1** (in the Bible) an image of gold in the shape of a calf, made by Aaron in response to the Israelites' pleas for a god as they awaited Moses' return from Mount Sinai, where he was receiving the Ten Commandments (Exod. 32). **2** (**golden calf**) wealth as an object of worship.

golden chain *noun* the laburnum.

Golden Delicious *noun see* DELICIOUS *noun*.

golden eagle *noun* a large eagle, *Aquila chrysaetos*, with yellow-tipped head feathers.

golden·eye *noun* a diving duck of the genus *Bucephala*, esp. the common goldeneye *B. clangula*, a migratory Holarctic duck with a large dark head and bright yellow eyes.

Golden Fleece *noun* (in Greek mythology) a fleece of gold sought and won by Jason.

Golden Gate a deep channel connecting San Francisco Bay with the Pacific Ocean, spanned by a suspension bridge (completed 1937).

golden girl *noun informal* a popular or successful woman or girl.

Golden Globe *noun* an award given and voted upon by the Hollywood Foreign Press Association to recognize merit in filmmaking, television, and theatre.

golden goal *noun* (in some soccer competitions) a goal scored in sudden-death overtime.

golden goose *noun* a continuing source of wealth or profit.

golden hamster *noun* a usu. tawny hamster, *Mesocricetus auratus*, kept as a pet or laboratory animal.

golden handcuffs *plural noun informal* benefits to discourage an employee from taking employment elsewhere.

golden handshake *noun informal* a payment given as compensation for dismissal or compulsory retirement.

golden hello *noun Brit. informal* a payment made by an employer to a keenly sought recruit.

Golden Hinde /ˈhaɪnd/ a mountain of central Vancouver Island, west of Courtenay. Rising to a height of 2 200 m, it is the highest peak on the island. [the name of Sir Francis Drake's ship]

Golden Horde a Mongol and Tartar host under the leadership of the descendants of Genghis Khan that overran Asia and part of E Europe in the 13th c., and maintained an empire of varying size until the end of the 15th c. [so called because of the magnificence of its leader's camp]

Golden Horn a curved inlet of the Bosporus, forming the harbour of Istanbul.

Golden Horseshoe a region of S Ontario, characterized as an industrial heartland, stretching around the western end of Lake Ontario from St. Catharines to Oshawa. [so called with reference to the area's wealth and horseshoe-like shape]

golden jubilee *noun* **1** the fiftieth anniversary of a sovereign's accession. **2** any other fiftieth anniversary.

golden mean *noun* **1** the principle of moderation, as opposed to excess. **2** = GOLDEN SECTION.

golden number *noun* the number of a year in the Metonic lunar cycle, used to fix the date of Easter.

golden oldie *noun informal* **1** an old hit record or film etc. that is still well known and popular. **2** any person or thing still popular or successful after a long period.

golden oriole *noun* a European oriole, *Oriolus oriolus*, of which the male has yellow and black plumage and the female has mainly green plumage.

golden parachute *noun informal* financial compensation guaranteed to company executives dismissed as a result of a merger or takeover.

golden plover *noun* either of two plovers, the N American *Pluvialis dominica* (also **lesser golden plover**) or the Eurasian *P. apricaria*

(also **greater golden plover**), having golden brown plumage on the head, back, and wings.

golden po·thos /ˈpoːθɒs/ *noun* = DEVIL'S IVY. [modern Latin from Sinhalese *pōtha*]

golden raisin *noun N Amer.* a yellowish raisin made by mechanically dehydrating a Thompson grape and treating it with sulphur dioxide.

golden retriever *noun* a retriever with a thick coat ranging in colour from pale yellow to golden-orange, and feathering on the neck, legs, and tail.

golden·rod *noun* any plant of the genus *Solidago* with a rod-like stem and a spike of small bright yellow flowers.

golden rule *noun* a basic principle of action, esp. 'do unto others as you would have them do unto you'.

golden russet *noun see* RUSSET 3.

golden·seal *noun* a N American woodland plant of the buttercup family, *Hydrastis canadensis*, with a bright yellow root that is used in herbal medicine as a remedy for indigestion or postpartum bleeding.

golden section *noun* the division of a line so that the whole is to the greater part as that part is to the smaller part, a proportion that is considered to be particularly pleasing to the eye.

golden shower *noun slang* the action of urinating on a sexual partner for sexual gratification.

Golden State *noun* a nickname for California.

golden syrup *noun Cdn & Brit.* a bright golden-yellow syrup drained off in the process of obtaining refined crystallized sugar.

golden triangle *noun* **1** any roughly triangular area with a high concentration of wealth. **2** an area at the meeting point of Burma (Myanmar), Laos, and Thailand, where much opium is grown.

golden wedding *noun* the fiftieth anniversary of a wedding.

gold·eye *noun* (also **Winnipeg goldeye**) a silvery freshwater fish, *Hiodon alosoides*, with a golden iris, of central N America, much favoured as a delicacy in Manitoba, esp. when smoked, when it becomes a reddish-gold colour.

gold fever *noun informal* a sudden lust for wealth.

gold·field *noun* a district in which gold is found as a mineral.

gold-filled *adjective* (esp. of jewellery) consisting of a base metal covered in a thin layer of gold.

gold·finch *noun* any of various bright-coloured songbirds of the genus *Carduelis* with predominantly yellow plumage, esp. the N American *C. tristis* or the Eurasian *C. carduelis*.

gold·fish *noun* a small reddish-golden Chinese carp kept for ornament or as a pet, *Carassius auratus*.

goldfish bowl *noun* **1** a globular glass container for goldfish. **2** a situation lacking privacy.

gold foil *noun* gold beaten into a thin sheet.

Gold Glove *noun N Amer.* Baseball an award presented annually in both major leagues to the best defensive player at each position. □ **Gold Glov·er** *noun*

Gold·ing, Sir Wil·liam (Ger·ald) (1911–93), English novelist. In his best-known novel, *Lord of the Flies* (1954), he explores the human capacity for evil and guilt, a predominant theme throughout his work; he was awarded the Nobel Prize for literature in 1983.

gold leaf *noun* gold beaten into a very thin sheet (often, with hyphen, *attributive*: *gold-leaf decor*).

Gold·man, Emma (1869–1940), Lithuanian-born US political activist. She founded the New York anarchist monthly *Mother Earth* (1906–17), was jailed for opposing US conscription (1917), and deported to Russia (1919); *My Disillusionment in Russia* (1923) relates her disenchantment with and opposition to the Soviet system.

Gold·mark, Peter Carl (1906–77), Hungarian-born US inventor and engineer. He made the first colour television broadcast in 1940, invented the long-playing record in 1948, and pioneered videocassette recording.

gold medal *noun* **1** a medal of gold, usu. awarded as first prize (often, with hyphen, *attributive*: *gold-medal performance*). **2** a gold or gold-coloured medal awarded to a graduating university student who has the highest academic standing in the university or a department of it. □ **gold medallist** *noun*

gold mine *noun* **1** a place where gold is mined. **2** *informal* a source of wealth. □ **gold miner** *noun* **gold mining** *noun*

Gol·doni /ɡɒlˈdoːni/ **Carlo** (1707–93), Italian dramatist, whose comedy is based on the society of his native Venice; his more than 150 comedies include *La locandiera* (1753) and *I rusteghi* (1760).

---

uː mood   aɪ my   əɪ pipe   au brown   ʌu house   ei day   ɔi boy   ā franglais   ã Canadien   ɔ̃ Brayon   (see over for consonants)

gold pan·ner *noun* a person who pans for gold. □ **gold pan·ning** *noun*

gold plate ● *noun* **1** vessels made of gold. **2** material plated with gold. ● *transitive verb* (**gold-plate**) plate with gold.

gold-plated *adjective* **1** plated with gold. **2** wealthy or opulent, esp. excessively so.

gold record *noun* N Amer. an award given to a recording artist or group for sales of a record etc. exceeding a specified high figure (which varies from country to country).

gold reserve *noun* a reserve of gold coins or bullion held by a central bank etc.

gold rush *noun* a rush to a newly discovered goldfield. The first major gold rush, across the US to California after the discovery of gold there in 1848, was followed by similar rushes in Australia (1851–3), South Africa (1884), and the Klondike (1897–8).

Gold·schmidt /'gɒldʃmɪt/ **Vic·tor Mor·itz** (1888–1947), Swiss-born Norwegian chemist, the founder of modern geochemistry. He suggested a law relating crystal structure to chemical composition, and used X-ray crystallography to determine the structure of many compounds.

gold seeker *noun* esp. Cdn a person who searches for gold. □ **gold seeking** *noun*

Gold·smith, **Oli·ver** (1730–74), Irish novelist, poet, essayist, and dramatist. He is now best known for his novel *The Vicar of Wakefield* (1766), the poem *The Deserted Village* (1770), a nostalgic lament for village life as it declines under economic pressures, and the comic play *She Stoops to Conquer* (1773).

gold·smith *noun* a worker in gold, a manufacturer of gold articles.

gold standard *noun* **1** a system in which the value of a currency is defined in terms of gold, for which the currency may be exchanged. **2** the best or most prestigious thing of its type.

gold thread *noun* **1** a thread of silk etc. with gold wire wound around it. **2** (**gold·thread**) any of several plants of the genus *Coptis* with bright yellow, bitter, threadlike rhizomes.

gold-tone *adjective* (of buttons, jewellery, etc.) coloured or coated to resemble gold.

Gold·wyn /'gɒldwɪn/ **Sam·uel** (born Samuel Gelbfisz; changed to Goldfish then Goldwyn) (1882–1974), Polish-born US film producer. He founded the Metro-Goldwyn-Mayer (MGM) film company with Louis B. Mayer (1924), and produced many successful films. His illogical use of English, as in the phrase 'Include me out', was notorious.

go·lem /'gɒːləm/ *noun* **1** (in Jewish legend) a clay figure supernaturally brought to life. **2** an automaton; a robot. [Yiddish *goylem* from Hebrew *gōlem* shapeless mass]

golf ● *noun* a game played on a park-like course, in which a small hard ball is driven with clubs into a series of 18 or 9 holes with the fewest possible strokes. ● *intransitive verb* play golf. □ **golf·er** *noun* [Middle English: perhaps related to Dutch *kolf* club]

golf bag *noun* a bag used for carrying golf clubs and balls.

golf ball *noun* a small, hard dimpled ball used in golf.

golf cart *noun* **1** a trolley used for carrying clubs in golf. **2** a motorized cart for golfers and equipment.

golf club *noun* **1** a long thin club with a metal or wooden head used in golf. **2 a** an association for playing golf. **b** the premises used by a golf club.

golf course *noun* (also **golf links**) the course on which golf is played.

golf shirt *noun* N Amer. a light short-sleeved collared shirt, usu. of a knit fabric, with buttons at the neck only.

golf umbrella *noun* an umbrella with a very large diameter.

Golgi /'gɒldʒi/ **Cam·illo** (1844–1926), Italian histologist and anatomist. He devised a method of staining nerve tissue to reveal details of the cells and nerve fibres, and described what is now known as the *Golgi body*; he shared a Nobel Prize in 1906.

Golgi body /'gɒldʒi, -gi/ *noun* (also **Golgi apparatus**) Biol. an organelle of vesicles and folded membranes within the cytoplasm of most eukaryotic cells, involved esp. in the secretion of substances. [GOLGI]

Gol·go·tha /'gɒlgəθə/ the site of the crucifixion of Jesus; Calvary (Mark 15:22). [Late Latin from Greek from Aramaic from Hebrew *gulgoleth* skull]

Gol·iath /gə'laɪəθ/ Bible a Philistine giant, according to legend slain by David (1 Sam. 17) with a slingshot, but according to another tradition slain by Elhanan (2 Sam. 21:19).

Goliath beetle *noun* any large beetle of the genus *Goliathus*, esp. *G. giganteus* native to Africa.

Goliath frog *noun* a giant frog, *Rana goliath*, of central Africa.

gol·li·wog *noun* a black-faced brightly dressed soft doll with fuzzy hair. [from *Golliwogg*, the name of a doll character in books by B. Upton, US writer d.1912; perhaps suggested by GOLLY + POLLIWOG]

golly *interjection* expressing mild surprise. [euphemism for GOD]

gom·been /gɒm'biːn/ *noun* Irish usury. □ **gom·been·ism** *noun* [Irish *gaimbín* perhaps from the same Old Celtic source as medieval Latin *cambire* CHANGE]

gombeen man *noun* Irish a moneylender.

Gom·or·rah /gə'mɒrə/ a town of ancient Palestine, probably south of the Dead Sea. According to Gen. 19:24, it was destroyed by fire from heaven, along with Sodom, for the wickedness of its inhabitants.

Gom·pers /'gɒmpərz/ **Sam·uel** (1850–1924), English-born US labour leader, who was one of the founders of the American Federation of Labour (1886), and served as its president (1886–94 and 1896–1924).

-gon *combining form* forming nouns denoting plane figures with a specified number of angles (*hexagon*). [Greek *-gōnos* -angled]

go·nad /'gɒnad/ *noun* an animal organ producing gametes, e.g. the testis or ovary. □ **go·nad·al** /gɒ'neɪdəl/ *adjective* [modern Latin *gonas gonad-* from Greek *gonē, gonos* generation, seed]

go·nad·o·trop·ic hormone /ˌgɒnədəˈtrɒpɪk, -ˈtrɒpɪk, gɒˌnadə-/ *noun* (also **go·nad·o·troph·ic** /-ˈtrɒfɪk, -ˈtrɒfɪk/) = GONADOTROPIN.

gonad·o·trop·in /ˌgɒnədəˈtrɒpɪn, gɒˌnadə-/ *noun* (also **go·nad·o·troph·in** /-ˈtrɒfɪn/) Biochem. any of various hormones stimulating the activity of the gonads.

gonch *noun var. of* GAUNCH.

Gon·cha·rov /'gɒntʃəˌrɒf/ **Ivan** (1812–91), Russian novelist. He is best known for his novel *Oblomov* (1857), which is regarded as one of the greatest and most representative works of Russian realism.

Gon·court /gɔ̃'kuːr/ **Ed·mond de** (1822–96) and **Jules de** (1830–70), French novelists and critics. They collaborated closely in their writing, producing art criticism, realist novels such as *Germinie Lacerteux* (1864), and the *Journal des Goncourt* (1851–96); in his will Edmond provided for the establishment of the Académie Goncourt, which awards the annual Prix Goncourt for French fiction.

gon·do·la /'gɒndələ/ *noun* **1** a light flat-bottomed boat used on Venetian canals, with a central cabin and a high point at each end, worked by one oar at the stern. **2** an enclosed compartment suspended from an airship or balloon. **3** an enclosed cabin suspended from a cable, as in a ski lift. **4** (also **gondola car**) N Amer. a railway car with an open top. [Venetian Italian, perhaps from Byzantine Greek *kondoura* small boat]

gon·do·lier /ˌgɒndə'liːr/ *noun* the oarsman on a gondola. [French from Italian *gondoliere* (as GONDOLA)]

Gond·wana /gɒn'dwɒnə/ (also **Gond·wana·land** /gɒn'dwɒnə,land/) a vast continental area believed to have existed in the southern hemisphere and to have resulted from the breakup of Pangaea in Mesozoic times. It comprised the present Arabia, Africa, South America, Antarctica, Australia, and the peninsula of India. [*Gondwana* land of the Gonds, a Dravidian people of central India]

gone ● *verb* past participle of GO[1]. ● *adjective* **1 a** lost; hopeless. **b** dead. **2** used up, consumed. **3** informal pregnant for a specified time (*already three months gone*). **4** slang completely enthralled or entranced, esp. by rhythmic music, drugs, etc. **5** Brit. (of time) past (*not until gone nine*). □ **gone on** slang infatuated with.

gon·er *noun* slang a person or thing that is doomed, ended, irrevocably lost, etc.; a person beyond hope or help.

gon·fa·lon /'gɒnfələn/ *noun* **1** a banner, often with streamers, hung from a crossbar; a pennant. **2** hist. such a banner as the standard of some Italian republics. □ **gon·fa·lon·ier** /ˌgɒnfələ'niːr/ *noun* [Italian *gonfalone* from Germanic (compare VANE)]

gong ● *noun* **1** a metal disc with a turned rim, giving a resonant note when struck. **2** a saucer-shaped bell. **3** the resonant sound of a struck gong. ● *intransitive verb* make a reverberating sound like that of a gong. [Malay *gong, gung* of imitative origin]

gon·iff *noun* (also **gonif**) N Amer. informal a disreputable or dishonest person (often used as a general term of abuse). [Yiddish *ganev* from Hebrew *gannāb* 'thief']

goni·om·eter /ˌgɒni'ɒmɪtər/ *noun* any of various instruments for measuring angles, as in crystallography, medicine (e.g. in the study of joints), etc. □ **goni·om·etry** *noun* **gonio·met·ric** /-ə'metrɪk/ *adjective* [French *goniomètre* from Greek *gōnia* angle]

Consonants: b *but*   d *dog*   f *few*   g *get*   h *her*   j *yes*   k *cat*   l *leg*   m *man*   n *no*   p *pen*   r *red*   s *sit*

gonna *contraction informal* going to (*we're gonna win; it's gonna be tough*). ¶ *Gonna* is non-standard and should generally be avoided in writing. [*corruption*]

gono·coc·cus /ˌɡɒnəˈkɒkəs/ *noun* (*pl.* **gono·cocci** /-kai, -ksai, -ki, -ksi/) a bacterium causing gonorrhea. □ **gono·coc·cal** *adjective* [Greek *gonos* generation, semen + COCCUS]

gon·or·rhea /ˌɡɒnəˈriːə/ *noun* (also esp. *Brit.* **gon·or·rhoea**) a sexually transmitted disease with inflammatory discharge from the urethra or vagina. □ **gon·or·rhe·al** *adjective* [Late Latin from Greek *gonorrhoia* from *gonos* semen + *rhoia* flux]

gonzo *adjective* esp. *N Amer.* **1** *informal* bizarre; crazy. **2** of or associated with journalistic writing of an exaggerated, subjective, and fictionalized style. [perhaps from Italian *gonzo* 'foolish' or Spanish *ganso* 'goose, fool']

goo *noun informal* **1** a sticky or slimy substance. **2** sickly sentiment. [20th c.: perhaps from *burgoo* (Naut. slang) = porridge]

goo·ber *noun N Amer. informal* **1** (in full **goober pea**) a peanut or peanut plant. **2** a stupid or inept person. [Kikongo (and other West central African languages) *nguba* peanut]

good ● *adjective* (**better**, **best**) **1** having the right or desired qualities; satisfactory, adequate. **2 a** (of a person) efficient, competent (*good at French; a good driver*). **b** (of a thing) reliable, efficient (*good brakes*). **c** (of health etc.) strong (*good eyesight*). **3 a** kind, benevolent (*good of you to come*). **b** morally excellent; virtuous (*a good deed*). **c** charitable (*good works*). **d** well-behaved (*a good child*). **4** enjoyable, agreeable (*a good party; good news*). **5** thorough, considerable (*gave it a good wash*). **6 a** not less than (*waited a good hour*). **b** considerable in number, quality, etc. (*a good many people*). **7** healthy, beneficial (*milk is good for you*). **8 a** valid, sound (*a good reason*). **b** financially sound (*her credit is good*). **c** (usu. foll. by *for*) *N Amer.* (of a ticket) valid. **9** in exclamations of surprise (*good heavens!*). **10** right, proper, expedient (*thought it good to have a try*). **11** fresh, eatable, untainted (*is the meat still good?*). **12** (sometimes patronizing) commendable, worthy (*good old Joan; your good self; good men and true; my good man*). **13** well shaped, attractive (*has a good body; good looks*). **14** in courteous greetings and farewells (*good afternoon*). ● *noun* **1** (only in *sing.*) that which is good; what is beneficial or morally right (*only good can come of it; did it for your own good; what good will it do?*). **2** (only in *sing.*) a desirable end or object; a thing worth attaining (*sacrificing the present for a future good*). **3** (in *pl.*) **a** movable property or merchandise. **b** *Brit.* things to be transported, as distinct from passengers; freight. **c** (prec. by *the*) *informal* what one has undertaken to supply (esp. *deliver the goods*). **d** (prec. by *the*) *slang* the real thing; the genuine article. **4** (as *pl.*; prec. by *the*) virtuous people. ● *adverb N Amer. informal disputed* well (*doing pretty good*). □ **as good as** practically (*he as good as told me*). **as good as gold** extremely well-behaved. **be so good as** (or **be good enough**) **to** (often in a request) be kind and do (a favour) (*be so good as to open the window*). **be (a certain amount) to the good** have as net profit or advantage. **do good** show kindness, act philanthropically. **do a person good** be beneficial to. **for good (and all)** finally, permanently. **good and** *informal* used as an intensifier before an adj. or adv. (*raining good and hard; was good and angry*). **good for 1** beneficial to; having a good effect on. **2** able to perform; inclined for (*good for a ten-mile walk*). **3** able to be trusted to pay (*is good for $100*). **good for you!** (or **him!**, **her!**, etc.) exclamation of approval towards a person. **good God!** (or **good Lord!**) an exclamation of surprise, anger, etc. **good on you!** (or **him!** etc.) = GOOD FOR YOU! **goods and chattels** see CHATTEL. **have a good mind** see MIND. **have** (or **get**) **the goods on a person** *slang* have (or acquire) advantageous information about a person. **have a good time** enjoy oneself. **in a person's good books** see BOOK. **in good faith** with honest or sincere intentions. **in good form** see FORM. **in good time 1** with no risk of being late. **2** (also **all in good time**) in due course but without haste. **make good 1** make up for, compensate for, pay (an expense). **2** fulfill (a promise); effect (a purpose or an intended action). **3** demonstrate the truth of (a statement); substantiate (a charge). **4** gain and hold (a position). **5** replace or restore (a thing lost or damaged). **6** accomplish what one intended. **no good** useless (*it is no good arguing; said my idea was no good*). **take in good part** not be offended by. **to the good** having as profit or benefit. **up to no good** making mischief. □ **good·ish** *adjective* [Old English *gōd* from Germanic]

good afternoon ● *interjection* expressing greeting or farewell in the afternoon. ● *noun* an instance of saying 'good afternoon'.

Good Book *noun* (prec. by *the*) the Bible.

good breeding *noun* correct or courteous manners.

good·bye (*US* also **good·by**) ● *interjection* expressing good wishes on parting, ending a telephone conversation, etc., or said with reference to a thing got rid of or irrevocably lost. ● *noun* (*pl.* **good·byes** or also *US* **good·bys**) the saying of 'goodbye'; a parting; a farewell. [contraction of *God be with you!* with *good* substituted after *good night* etc.]

good cholesterol *noun N Amer.* high-density lipoprotein.

good cop/bad cop *adjective N Amer. informal* designating a procedure or routine used in interrogating, negotiating, or in public relations, in which one of two partners assumes a harsh, uncompromising attitude and the other a more lenient or mild one.

good day ● *interjection* expressing greeting or farewell during the day. ● *noun* an instance of saying 'good day'.

good egg *noun* a reliable or pleasant person.

good evening ● *interjection* expressing greeting or farewell in the evening. ● *noun* an instance of saying 'good evening'.

good faith *noun* honesty or sincerity of intention.

good·fella *noun N Amer. informal* a gangster, esp. a member of a Mafia family.

good form *noun* what complies with current social conventions. □ **in good form** in a state of good health or training.

good-for-nothing ● *adjective* worthless. ● *noun* a worthless person.

Good Friday *noun* the Friday before Easter Sunday, commemorating the Crucifixion of Christ.

good guy *noun* esp. *N Amer. informal* a person viewed favourably in a conflict.

good-hearted *adjective* kindly, well-meaning.

Good Hope, Cape of see CAPE OF GOOD HOPE.

good humour *noun* a genial mood.

good-humoured *adjective* cheerful, amiable. □ **good-humoured·ly** *adverb*

good·ie *var. of* GOODY[1] *noun*.

goodie bag *noun* a bag of treats, goodies, or promotional items, given as a gift or prize.

good job *noun* a fortunate state of affairs (*it's a good job you came early*).

good life *noun* (prec. by *the*) esp. *N Amer.* a life of luxury, pleasure, and material comfort.

good-looker *noun* a handsome or attractive person.

good-looking *adjective* handsome; attractive.

good luck ● *noun* **1** good fortune. **2** an omen of this. ● *interjection* exclamation of well-wishing.

good·ly *adjective* (**goodli·er**, **good·li·est**) **1** good-looking, handsome. **2** of imposing size etc. □ **good·li·ness** *noun*

Good·man, **Ben·ja·min David** (**'Benny'**) (1909–86), US jazz clarinetist and bandleader. Nicknamed 'the King of Swing' because of his new style of jazz playing, he also gave performances of classical works, including pieces written for him by Bartók and others.

good money *noun* **1** genuine money; money that might usefully have been spent elsewhere. **2** *informal* high wages.

good morning ● *interjection* expressing good wishes on seeing someone in the morning. ● *noun* an instance of saying 'good morning'.

good nature *noun* a friendly disposition.

good-natured *adjective* kind, patient; easygoing. □ **good-natured·ly** *adverb*

good·ness ● *noun* **1** virtue; excellence, esp. moral. **2** kindness, generosity (*had the goodness to wait*). **3** what is good or beneficial in a thing (*vegetables with all the goodness boiled out*). ● *interjection* (as a substitution for 'God') expressing surprise, anger, etc. (*goodness me!; goodness knows; for goodness' sake!*).

good night ● *interjection* **1** expressing good wishes on parting in the evening or at bedtime. **2** expressing surprise. ● *noun* an instance of saying 'good night'.

good offices *plural noun* influence, esp. as used to others' benefit; connections.

good old boy *noun* usu. *derogatory* an unsophisticated man esp. of the rural areas of the southern US; a redneck.

good riddance *interjection* expressing welcome relief from an unwanted person or thing.

goods and services tax *noun Cdn & NZ* a value-added tax levied on a broad range of consumer goods and services. Abbr.: **GST**.

Good Shepherd (prec. by *the*) Christ.

good-tempered *adjective* not easily annoyed. □ **good-tempered·ly** *adverb*

good-time *attributive adjective* recklessly pursuing pleasure. □ **good-timer** *noun*

good times *plural noun* a period of prosperity.

good·wife *noun* (*pl.* **-wives**) *Scot. archaic* the mistress of a household.

good·will *noun* **1** kindly feeling. **2** the established reputation of a business etc. as enhancing its value. **3** cheerful consent or acquiescence; readiness, zeal.

goodwill ambassador *noun* a person who serves to increase goodwill between countries or organizations (*Canada's goodwill ambassadors: the Snowbirds aerobatic team*).

good word *noun* (often in phr. **put in a good word for**) words in recommendation or defence of a person.

good works *plural noun* charitable acts.

goody[1] ● *noun* (also **goodie**) (*pl.* **-ies**) **1** (usu. in *pl.*) something good or attractive, esp. to eat, often given as a treat or reward. **2** = GOODY-GOODY *noun*. **3** *informal* a good or favoured person, esp. a hero in a story, film, etc. ● *interjection* expressing childish delight.

goody[2] *noun* (*pl.* **good·ies**) *archaic* (often as a title prefixed to a surname) an elderly woman of humble station (*Goody Blake*). [for GOODWIFE: compare HUSSY]

Good·year, **Charles** (1800–60), US inventor, who developed vulcanized rubber in 1839.

goody-goody *informal* ● *noun* (*pl.* **goody-goodies**) a smug or obtrusively virtuous person. ● *adjective* obtrusively or smugly virtuous.

goody two-shoes *noun* = GOODY-GOODY. [the nickname of the heroine of the *History of Little Goody Two-shoes* (1766)]

gooey *adjective* (**goo·i·er**, **goo·i·est**) *slang* **1** viscous, sticky. **2** sickly, sentimental. □ **gooey·ness** *noun*

goof *informal* ● *noun* **1** a foolish or stupid person. **2** a mistake, a blunder. ● *verb* **1** *transitive* (foll. by *up*) bungle, mess up. **2** *intransitive* (often foll. by *up*) blunder, make a mistake. **3** *intransitive* (often foll. by *off*) idle. **4** *intransitive* (foll. by *around*, *about*) fool around, mess about. [early 20th c: origin uncertain]

goof·ball esp. *N Amer. informal* ● *noun* **1** a blundering or eccentric person. **2** a pill containing a narcotic drug, esp. a barbiturate. ● *adjective* eccentric or silly; foolish.

goofed *adjective informal* stupefied with drugs.

goof-proof *N Amer.* ● *adjective* (of a product, procedure, etc.) designed to be simple enough for anyone to use or implement. ● *transitive verb* design or adapt (a product etc.) so that it becomes simple enough for anyone to use.

goof-up *noun informal* a mistake, a blunder.

goofy *adjective* (**goof·i·er**, **goof·i·est**) silly, ridiculous, odd. □ **goof·i·ly** *adverb* **goof·i·ness** *noun*

google *transitive verb* search (a term) on the Internet using the search engine Google.

googlie-eyed *adjective* (also **googly-eyed**) = GOGGLE-EYED.

goo·gol /ˈguːgəl/ *noun* ten raised to the hundredth power (10[100]). ¶ *Googol* is a fanciful word, not found in technical use. [arbitrary formation]

goo·gol·plex /ˈguːgəlˌplɛks/ *noun* ten raised to the power of a googol. ¶ Not found in technical use. [GOOGOL + *-plex* as in MULTIPLEX]

goo-goo *adjective N Amer.* **1** designating the behaviour etc. of a baby; infantile (*taunted them with goo-goo sounds*). **2** indicating excessive or foolish infatuation (*making goo-goo eyes*). [imitative]

gook /guːk, gʊk/ *noun N Amer. slang* **1** *offensive* a foreigner, esp. a person of E Asian descent. **2** a slimy or sticky substance. [20th c.: origin unknown]

goo·lie *noun* (also **gooly**) (*pl.* **-lies**) **1** (usu. in *pl.*) esp. *Brit. slang* a testicle. **2** *Austral. slang* a stone or pebble. [apparently of Indian origin; compare Hindustani *golī* bullet, ball, pill]

goom·bah /ˈguːmˌbɒ/ *noun N Amer. slang* **1** a member of a criminal gang; a Mafioso. **2** a boss or mentor; a crony. [Italian dialect *compare* 'godfather, friend, accomplice']

goon *noun slang* **1** esp. *N Amer.* a person employed to terrorize esp. political or industrial opponents; a thug. **2** *N Amer. informal* a hockey player who intimidates opponents by rough play and fighting. **3** a stupid person; a dolt. □ **goon·ery** *noun* **goony** *adjective* [perhaps from dial. *gooney* booby: influenced by the subhuman cartoon character 'Alice the *Goon*']

goon·da *noun* (in the Indian subcontinent) a hired thug or bully. [Hindi *guṇḍā* 'rascal']

goon hockey *noun informal* an excessively rough or violent style of hockey playing.

goon squad *noun* a group of hired thugs or aggressive people.

goop *noun* esp. *N Amer.* = GLOOP. □ **goopy** *adjective* (**goop·i·er**, **goop·i·est**). **goop·i·ness** *noun* [imitative: compare GOO, GLOOP]

goose ● *noun* (*pl.* **geese**) **1 a** any of various large water birds of the family Anatidae, with short legs, webbed feet, and a broad bill. **b** the female of this (*opp.* GANDER). **c** the flesh of a goose as food. **2** *informal* a silly person. **3** (*pl.* **gooses**) a tailor's flatiron, having a handle like a goose's neck. ● *transitive verb* **1** *slang* poke (a person) in the buttocks. **2** esp. *US informal* (often foll. by *up*) energize, strengthen, invigorate, or increase. □ **what's good** (or **sauce**) **for the goose is good** (or **sauce**) **for the gander** what is appropriate in one case is appropriate in others. [Old English *gōs* from Germanic]

goose·berry /ˈguːzˌbɛri, -bəri, ˈguːz-/ *noun* (*pl.* **-berries**) **1** a round edible yellowish-green berry with a thin usu. translucent skin enclosing seeds in a juicy flesh. **2** any of various thorny shrubs, esp. *Ribes grossularia*, bearing this fruit. **3** *Brit. informal* an unwanted extra (usu. third) person (esp. in phr. **play gooseberry**). [the first element perhaps from GOOSE, or perhaps based on Old French *groseille* 'currant', altered because of an unexplained association with the bird]

goose·bumps *plural noun* (also **goose pimples**, **goose·flesh** *noun*) *N Amer.* the small pimple-like bumps appearing on the skin because of cold, fright, etc.

goose egg *noun N Amer. informal* **1** a zero score in a game or examination. **2** a lump appearing after hitting one's head etc. or being hit.

goose·foot *noun* (*pl.* **-foots**) any plant of the genus *Chenopodium*, having leaves shaped like the foot of a goose.

goose grass *noun* **1** cleavers. **2** any of various grasses, e.g. *Puccinellia* of salty or alkaline places of N America, providing an important food source for geese.

goose·neck *noun N Amer.* (often *attributive*) a long thin flexible metal tube resembling the neck of a goose (*gooseneck lamp*).

goose pimples *plural noun* = GOOSEBUMPS.

goose step ● *noun* a marching step in which the knees are kept locked and the legs are lifted high, usu. associated with militaristic regimes. ● *intransitive verb* (**goose-step**) march in this way.

goose·tongue *noun* a coastal plant, *Plantago juncoide*, eaten cooked as greens.

GOP *abbreviation US* Grand Old Party (the Republican Party).

go·pher /ˈgoʊfər/ *noun* **1** a buff-coloured ground squirrel of the prairies of western N America; a Richardson's ground squirrel. **2** (in full **pocket gopher**) any burrowing rodent of the family Geomyidae, native to North and Central America, having external cheek pouches and sharp front teeth. **3** a turtle, *Gopherus polyphemus*, native to the southern US, that excavates tunnels as shelter from the sun. **4** *Computing* a computer program designed to help users reach and search other sites on the Internet. **5** *N Amer.* = GOFER. [18th c.: origin uncertain]

gopher ball *noun Baseball informal* a pitch hit for a home run.

gopher snake *noun* = BULL SNAKE.

gopik /ˈgoʊpɪk/ *noun* (*pl.* same or **gopiks**) a monetary unit of Azerbaijan, equal to one-hundredth of a manat. [Azerbaijani, = KOPECK]

Gor·ak·pur /ˈgɔːrəkˌpʊr/ an industrial city in NE India, in Uttar Pradesh near the border with Nepal; pop. (2001) 624,600.

gor·al /ˈgɔːrəl/ *noun* a goat-antelope, *Nemorhaedus goral*, native to mountainous regions from N India to Siberia, having short horns curving to the rear. [local (Himalayan) name]

Gor·ba·chev /ˈgɔːrbəˌtʃɒf/ **Mik·hail (Serge·evich)** (b.1931), Soviet leader, general secretary of the Communist Party of the USSR 1985–91 and president 1988–91. He signed arms control treaties with the US in 1987 and 1990, introduced major political, economic, and cultural reforms in the USSR, and resigned in 1991 after losing his political battle to retain a centrally controlled union of Soviet states against his opponent, Boris Yeltsin; he was awarded the Nobel Peace Prize in 1990.

gor·blimey /ɡɔːrˈblaɪmi/ *interjection Brit. informal* an expression of surprise, indignation, etc. [corruption of *God blind me*]

Gor·dian knot /ˈɡɔːrdiən/ *noun* **1** an intricate knot. **2** a difficult problem or task. □ **cut the Gordian knot** solve a problem by force or by evasion. [*Gordius*, king of Phrygia, who tied an intricate knot that remained tied until cut by Alexander the Great]

Gor·di·mer /ˈɡɔːrdɪmər/ **Na·dine** (b.1923), South African novelist and short-story writer. Her works examine issues of race, class, and gender in apartheid and post-apartheid South Africa, and include *The*

Vowels: a *cat* ɑ *arm* e *bed* ɜr *her* ɜː *deux* ə *ago* ɪ *sit* i *cosy* iː *feed* ɒ *hot* ɔ *pore* oː *no* ʌ *run* ʊ *put*

Conservationist (1974), *Burger's Daughter* (1979), and *None to Accompany Me* (1994); she was awarded the Nobel Prize for literature in 1991.

Gor·dium /ˈgɔːdiəm/ an ancient city of Asia Minor, the capital of Phrygia in the 8th and 9th c. BC. According to legend the city was founded by Gordius, who tied the knot cut by Alexander the Great during his expedition of 334 BC (see GORDIAN KNOT).

Gor·don ▸ **1 Charles George** (1833–85), English general and colonial administrator. He was known as 'Chinese Gordon' after defeating rebels in China; sent to help Egyptian troops fighting the Mahdi, he was trapped in the garrison at Khartoum and killed there after a ten-month siege. **2 Charles Wil·liam** (pseudonym Ralph Connor) (1860–1937), Canadian novelist. A Presbyterian minister, he helped to found the United Church of Canada (1925), and his novels are characterized by action-packed plots in which Christian virtues are upheld; they include *The Sky Pilot* (1899), *The Man from Glengarry* (1901), and *Glengarry School Days* (1902). **3 Wal·ter Lock·hart** (1906–87), Canadian politician. He was chairman of the Royal Commission on Canada's Economic Prospects, known as the Gordon Commission (1955–7), and minister of finance (1963–5) under Pearson.

Gordon riots a series of anti-Catholic riots in London on 2–9 June 1780, in which about 300 people were killed. The riots were provoked by a petition presented to Parliament by Lord George Gordon against the relaxation of restrictions on the holding of landed property by Roman Catholics.

Gordon setter *noun* a black and tan breed of setter, used as a gun dog. [4th Duke of *Gordon*, d.1827, promoter of the breed]

Gordy, Berry Jr. (b.1929), US record producer. He founded the Motown record company in 1959.

gore¹ *noun* **1** blood that has been shed, esp. as a result of violence. **2** bloodshed, carnage. [Old English *gor* dung, dirt]

gore² *transitive verb* pierce with a horn, tusk, etc. [Middle English: origin unknown]

gore³ ● *noun* **1** a wedge-shaped piece in a garment. **2** a triangular or tapering piece in an umbrella etc. **3** esp. *N Amer.* a small strip or tract of land lying between larger divisions such as townships etc. ● *transitive verb* shape with a gore. □ **gored** *adjective* [Old English *gāra* triangular piece of land, related to Old English *gār* spear, a spearhead being triangular]

Gó·recki /gɔˈretski/ **Hen·ryk** (b.1933), Polish composer whose work blends modern musical techniques with traditional Polish themes and music. He gained international recognition for his *Symphony of Sorrowful Songs* for soprano and orchestra (1976).

gore·fest *noun* *informal* a movie involving much bloodshed.

Gör·eme /ˈgɜːriːmi/ a valley in Cappadocia in central Turkey, noted for its cave dwellings, hollowed out of the rock. In the Byzantine era these contained hermits' cells, monasteries, and more than 400 churches.

Gore-Tex *noun* *proprietary* a breathable laminated waterproof fabric.

Gorey, Ed·ward (St. John) (1925–2000), American illustrator and writer. His Gothic, often macabre, illustrations and stories have appeared on television and on the stage, though he is perhaps best known for his books, including *The Gashlycrumb Tinies* (1962) and the anthology *Amphigorey* (1972).

gorge ● *noun* **1** a narrow opening between hills or a rocky ravine, often with a stream running through it. **2** an act of gorging; a feast. **3** the contents of the stomach; what has been swallowed. **4** the neck of a bastion or other outwork; the rear entrance to a fortification. **5** a mass of ice etc. blocking a narrow passage. ● *verb intransitive* or *reflexive* (usu. foll. by *on*) feed greedily. □ **one's gorge rises** one is sickened or disgusted. □ **gor·ger** *noun* [Old French *gorge* throat, ultimately from Latin *gurges* whirlpool]

gor·geous *adjective* **1** strikingly beautiful. **2** very pleasant, splendid (*gorgeous weather*). **3** richly coloured, sumptuous, magnificent. □ **gor·geous·ly** *adverb* **gor·geous·ness** *noun* [earlier *gorgayse*, *-yas* from Old French *gorgias* fine, elegant, of unknown origin]

gor·get /ˈgɔːdʒət/ *noun* **1** a patch of colour on the throat of a bird, insect, etc. **2** *hist.* **a** a piece of armour for the throat. **b** an ornament for the neck; a necklace, decorative collar, etc. [Old French *gorgete* (as GORGE)]

Gor·gon /ˈgɔːgən/ *noun* **1** (in Greek mythology) each of three snake-haired sisters (esp. Medusa) with the power to turn anyone who looked at them to stone. **2** (often **gorgon**) a frightening or repulsive person, esp. a woman. □ **Gor·gon·ian** /gɔːˈgoːniən/ *adjective* [Latin *Gorgo -onis* from Greek *Gorgō* from *gorgos* terrible]

gor·gon·ian /gɔːˈgoːniən/ ● *noun* a usu. brightly coloured horny coral of the order Gorgonacea, having a treelike skeleton bearing polyps, e.g.

a sea fan. ● *adjective* of or relating to the Gorgonacea. [modern Latin (as GORGON), with reference to its petrifaction]

Gor·gon·zola /ˌgɔːgənˈzoːlə/ *noun* a type of rich cheese with bluish-green veins. [*Gorgonzola*, a village in Northern Italy]

gor·illa /gəˈrɪlə/ *noun* **1** the largest anthropoid ape, *Gorilla gorilla*, native to Central Africa, having a large head, short neck, and prominent mouth. **2** *informal* a heavily built man of aggressive demeanour. [adopted as the specific name in 1847 from Greek *Gorillai* an African tribe noted for hairiness]

Gör·ing /ˈgɜːrɪŋ/ **Her·mann Wil·helm** (also **Goer·ing**) (1893–1946), German Nazi leader and politician. He commanded the Luftwaffe, founded and headed the Gestapo, and directed the German economy (1936–43), but was dismissed (1945) after unauthorized attempts to make peace with the Allies; sentenced to death at the Nuremberg trials, he committed suicide in his cell.

Gorky¹ ▸ the name from 1932 to 1991 of NIZHNI NOVGOROD.

Gorky² **1 Ar·shile** (born Vosdanik Adoian) (1904–48), Turkish-born US painter. His abstract expressionist work of the early 1940s uses ambiguous biomorphic forms, bright colours, and black sinuous outlines. **2 Maxim** (pseudonym of Aleksei Maksimovich Peshkov) (1868–1936), Russian novelist, dramatist, and short-story writer. He is known for his short stories of the 1890s, the play *The Lower Depths* (1901), and his autobiographical trilogy (1915–23); imprisoned for his involvement in the Russian Revolution of 1905 and exiled, he was honoured in 1931 as the founder of the new socialist realism.

Gor·lov·ka /ˈgɔːrləfkə/ the Russian name for HORLIVKA.

gorm·less *adjective* esp. *Brit. informal* foolish, lacking sense. □ **gorm·less·ly** *adverb* **gorm·less·ness** *noun* [originally *gaumless* from dial. *gaum* understanding]

Gorno-Altai /ˌgɔːrnɔːˈaltai/ an autonomous republic in south central Russia, on the border with Mongolia; pop. (est. 2002) 294,800; capital, Gorno-Altaisk.

Gorno-Altaisk /ˌgɔːrnɔːˈaltaisk/ a city in south central Russia, capital of the republic of Gorno-Altai; pop. (est. 2002) 53,500. It was known as Ulala until 1932 and as Oirot-Tura from 1932 until 1948.

go-round *noun* esp. *N Amer.* **1** each of several recurring turns, opportunities, or chances (*we'll do better on the next go-round*). **2** a fight; a beating; an argument.

gorp *noun* *N Amer.* = TRAIL MIX. [origin obscure, influenced by slang *gorp* 'eat greedily'; the theory that the word is an acronym of 'good old raisins and peanuts' is unsubstantiated]

gorse /gɔːrs/ *noun* any spiny yellow-flowered shrub of the genus *Ulex*, esp. growing on European wastelands. *Also called* FURZE. [Old English *gors(t)* related to Old High German *gersta*, Latin *hordeum*, barley]

Gor·sedd /ˈgɔːrseð/ *noun* a meeting of Welsh etc. bards and druids (esp. as a daily preliminary to the eisteddfod). [Welsh, lit. 'throne']

gory *adjective* (**gor·i·er**, **gor·i·est**) **1** involving or depicting bloodshed; bloodthirsty (*a gory film*). **2** covered in gore. **3** resembling gore (*a gory red*). □ **gory details** *jocular* explicit details. □ **gor·i·ly** *adverb* **gor·i·ness** *noun*

gosh *interjection* expressing mild surprise. [euphemism for GOD]

gos·hawk /ˈgɒshɔːk/ *noun* a large short-winged hawk, *Accipiter gentilis*. [Old English *gōs-hafoc* (as GOOSE, HAWK¹)]

gos·ling /ˈgɒzlɪŋ/ *noun* a young goose. [Middle English, originally *gesling* from Old Norse *gǽslingr*]

go-slow *noun* (usu. *attributive*) **1** an instance of proceeding slowly, esp. intentionally out of caution (*go-slow approach to privatization*). **2** esp. *Brit.* a form of job action in which employees deliberately work slowly.

gos·pel /ˈgɒspəl/ *noun* **1** the teaching or revelation of Christ. **2** (**Gospel**) **a** the record of Christ's life and teaching in the first four books of the New Testament. **b** each of these books. **c** a portion from one of them read at a service. **3** (also **gospel truth**) a thing regarded as absolutely true (*take my word as gospel*). **4** a principle one acts on or advocates. **5** (in full **gospel music**) a fervent, spirited style of evangelical religious music, esp. as originally sung by US Blacks. [Old English *gōdspel* (as GOOD, *spel* news, SPELL²), rendering ecclesiastical Latin *bona annuntiatio*, *bonus nuntius* = *evangelium* EVANGEL: assoc. with GOD]

gos·pel·ler /ˈgɒspələr/ *noun* (*US* **gos·pel·er**) a person who preaches or promotes the Gospel or a gospel.

gos·pel·ly *adjective* resembling gospel music.

Gospel side *noun* the side of a church to the left of the altar (as viewed by the congregation).

gos·sa·mer /ˈgɒsəmər/ ● *noun* **1** a filmy substance of small spiders' webs. **2** delicate filmy material. **3** a thread of gossamer. ● *adjective* **1** light and flimsy. **2** frivolous, volatile. [Middle English *gos(e)somer(e)*, apparently from GOOSE + SUMMER[1] (*goose summer* = St. Martin's summer, i.e. early November when geese were eaten, gossamer being common then)]

gos·sip ● *noun* **1 a** easy or unconstrained talk or writing esp. about persons or social incidents. **b** idle talk; groundless rumour. **c** (usu. *attributive*) denoting a tabloid or section of a newspaper etc. devoted to news or rumours about celebrities (*gossip columnist*; *gossip rag*). **2** a person who indulges in gossip. ● *intransitive verb* (**gos·siped**, **gos·sip·ing**) talk or write gossip. □ **gos·sip·er** *noun* **gos·sipy** *adjective* [earlier sense 'godparent': from Old English *godsibb* person related to one in GOD: see SIB]

gossip·monger /'gɒsɪp,mʌ̩ŋgɜr, -,mʌŋgɜr/ *noun* a perpetrator of gossip.

gos·soon /gɒ'suːn/ *noun Irish* a lad. [earlier *garsoon* from French *garçon* boy]

got *past and past participle of* GET.

gotch *noun Cdn slang* underpants. [prob. of Eastern European origin: compare Hungarian *gatya*, Serbo-Croat *gaće*]

gotcha *informal* ● *interjection* esp. *N Amer.* expressing satisfaction at having exploited another's gullibility or weakness, uncovered another's faults, etc. ● *noun* **1** (often *attributive*) an instance of catching someone out, esp. by surprise. **2** a sudden unforeseen problem or difficulty, esp. in something one has already purchased, committed oneself to, etc. [corruption of (*I have*) *got you*]

gotch·ies *plural noun Cdn slang* underpants. [diminutive of GOTCH]

Goth *noun* **1** a member of a Germanic tribe that invaded the Roman Empire in the 3rd–5th c. **2** an uncivilized or ignorant person. **3** (**goth**) **a** a style of rock music derived from punk, often with apocalyptic or mystical lyrics. **b** a member of a subculture favouring black clothing, white and black makeup, metal jewellery, and goth music. [Late Latin *Gothi* (pl.) from Greek *Go(t)thoi* from Gothic]

Gotha /'gɒːtə, 'gɒːθə/ a city in central Germany, in Thuringia; pop. (1998) 49,753. From 1640 until 1918 it was the residence of the dukes of Saxe-Gotha and Saxe-Coburg-Gotha.

Goth·am 1 /'gɒːtəm/ a village in Nottinghamshire. It is associated with the English folk tale *The Wise Men of Gotham*, in which the inhabitants of the village demonstrated cunning by feigning stupidity. **2** /'gɒθəm/ a nickname for New York City, applied originally by Washington Irving in *Salmagundi* (1807–8) and associated with the popular science fiction story *Batman*. □ **Goth·am·ite** *noun*

Goth·en·burg /'gɒθən,bɜrg/ a seaport in SW Sweden, on the Kattegat strait; pop. (2000) 466,990. It is the second largest city in Sweden.

Goth·ic /'gɒθɪk/ ● *adjective* **1** of the Goths or their language. **2** in the style of architecture prevalent in W Europe in the 12th–16th c., characterized by pointed arches, flying buttresses, and ribbed vaults. **3** (of a novel etc.) in a style popular in the 18th–19th c., with supernatural or horrifying events. **4** barbarous, uncouth. **5** *Typography* (of type) old-fashioned German, black letter, or sans serif. ● *noun* **1** the Gothic language. **2** Gothic architecture. **3** *Typography* Gothic type. □ **Goth·ic·ally** *adverb* **Gothi·cism** /-,sɪzəm/ *noun* **Gothi·cize** /-,saɪz/ *transitive & intransitive verb* (also esp. *Brit.* **-cise**). [French *gothique* or Late Latin *gothicus* from *Gothi*: see GOTH]

Gothic revival *noun* the reintroduction of a Gothic style of architecture towards the middle of the 19th c.

Got·land /'gɒtlənd/ an island and province of Sweden, in the Baltic Sea; pop. (2000) 57,313; capital, Visby.

go-to guy *noun* (also **go-to person** etc.) *N Amer. slang* (esp. in sports) the person on a team most often relied on to accomplish a task.

go-to-meeting *attributive adjective informal* (of clothes etc.) suitable for wearing to church.

gotta *informal* have got to (*we gotta go*). [corruption]

got·ten *N Amer. past participle of* GET.

Göt·ter·däm·mer·ung /,gɒtɜr'damə,rʊŋ/ *noun* **1** the twilight (i.e. downfall) of the gods. **2** the complete downfall of a regime etc. [German, esp. as the title of an opera by Wagner]

Göt·ting·en /'gɜtɪŋən/ a town in north central Germany, on the Leine River; pop. (est. 2002) 129,800. It is noted for its university, which was founded in 1734 by George II of England.

gou·ache /guː'ɒʃ, gwɒʃ/ *noun* **1** a method of painting in opaque pigments ground in water and thickened with a glue-like substance. **2** these pigments. **3** a picture painted in this way. [French from Italian *guazzo*]

Gouda[1] /'guːdə/ a market town in the Netherlands, just northeast of Rotterdam; pop. (est. 2002) 73,200.

Gouda[2] /'guːdə/ *noun* a flat round usu. Dutch cheese with a yellow rind. [GOUDA[1], where originally made]

gouge /gaudʒ/ ● *noun* **1** a chisel with a concave blade, used in carpentry, sculpture, and surgery. **2** a groove or mark made by gouging. **3** an act of gouging. ● *verb* **1** *transitive* cut with or as with a gouge. **2** *transitive* **a** (foll. by *out*) force out (esp. an eye with the thumb) with or as with a gouge. **b** force out the eye of (a person). **3** *transitive & intransitive N Amer. informal* take an unjustly large sum of money from (someone); swindle (*price gouging*; *they're gouging us!*). □ **goug·er** *noun* [French from Late Latin *gubia*, perhaps of Celtic origin]

Gouin /gwã/ **Sir Jean-Lomer** (1861–1929), Canadian politician, Liberal premier of Quebec 1905–20. He oversaw a period of great economic growth in Quebec, later serving as federal minister of justice (1921–4) and Lieutenant-Governor of Quebec (1929).

Gouin, Ré·ser·voir /gwã/ a reservoir in central Quebec, situated at the head of the Rivière Saint-Maurice, west of Lac Saint-Jean. [GOUIN]

gou·lash /'guːlaʃ/ *noun* a highly-seasoned Hungarian soup or stew of meat and vegetables, usu. flavoured with paprika. [Magyar *gulyás-hús* from *gulyás* herdsman + *hús* meat]

Gould /'guːld/ **1 Glenn (Her·bert)** (1932–82), Canadian pianist. Internationally acclaimed as a concert pianist and known for his unorthodox playing style, he retired from live performance in 1964 to concentrate on recording and broadcasting; he is best known for his interpretations of Bach's *Goldberg Variations*, and works by Beethoven, Hindemith, and Schoenberg. **2 Ste·phen Jay** (1941–2002) US paleontologist. He proposed that evolution does not occur at a steady rate but can go through accelerated phases (the concept of punctuated equilibrium), and was esp. interested in the social context of scientific theory; his books include *Ever Since Darwin* (1977), *Hen's Teeth and Horses' Toes* (1983), and *Bully for Brontosaurus* (1992).

Gou·nod /'guːnoː/ **Charles (Fran·çois)** (1818–93), French composer, conductor, and organist. He is best known for the operas *Faust* (1859) and *Roméo et Juliette* (1867).

gou·rami /'gʊrəmi, -'rɒmi/ *noun* **1 a** a large freshwater fish, *Osphronemus goramy*, native to SE Asia, used as food. **b** any small fish of the family Osphronemidae, usu. kept in aquariums. **2** any small brightly coloured freshwater fish of the family Belontiidae, usu. kept in aquariums. [Malay *gurāmi*]

gourd /gʊrd/ *noun* **1 a** any of various fleshy usu. large fruits with a hard skin, often used as containers, ornaments, etc. **b** any of various climbing or trailing plants of the family Cucurbitaceae bearing this fruit. *Also called* CUCURBIT. **2** the hollow hard skin of the gourd fruit, dried and used as a drinking vessel, water container, etc. □ **out of one's gourd** *N Amer. slang* crazy. □ **gourd·ful** *noun* (*pl.* **-fuls**). [Old French *gourde*, ultimately from Latin *cucurbita*]

gourde /gʊrd/ *noun* the basic monetary unit of Haiti, equal to 100 centimes. [French, feminine of *gourd*, heavy, dull]

gour·mand /gʊr'mɒnd/ *noun* **1** a glutton. **2** a gourmet. [Old French, of unknown origin]

gour·mand·ise /'gʊrmã,diːz/ *noun* the habits of a gourmand; gluttony. [French (as GOURMAND)]

gour·mand·ize /'gʊrmən,daiz/ *verb* (also esp. *Brit.* **-ise**) **1** *intransitive & transitive* eat or devour voraciously. **2** *intransitive* indulge in good eating.

gour·met /gɔr'mei, 'gʊr-, 'gɔr-/ ● *noun* a connoisseur of good food, having a discerning palate. ● *attributive adjective* **1** (of food) of very high quality, suitable to refined tastes. **2** of, relating to, or suitable for a gourmet. [French, = wine taster: sense influenced by GOURMAND]

gout *noun* **1** a disease with inflammation of the smaller joints, esp. the toe, as a result of excess uric acid salts in the blood. **2 a** a drop, esp. of blood. **b** a splash or spot. □ **gouty** *adjective* [Old French *goute* from Latin *gutta* drop, with reference to the medieval theory of the flowing down of humours]

gout·weed *noun* a widely-distributed plant originally from Eurasia, *Aegopodium podagraria*, formerly used medicinally for gout, now both a garden weed and cultivated in a variegated form.

Gou·zen·ko /guː'zenko/ **Igor (Sergei·evich)** (1919–82), Russian-born Canadian intelligence officer. A cipher clerk with the Soviet Embassy in Ottawa from 1943, he defected in 1945 with documents confirming the existence of a Soviet spy ring in N America.

Gov. *abbreviation* **1** Governor. **2** Government.

gov·ern *verb* **1 a** *transitive* rule or control (a state, subject, etc.) with authority; conduct the policy and affairs of (an organization etc.). **b** *intransitive* be in government. **2 a** *transitive* control or influence (a

---

Consonants:　b *but*　　d *dog*　　f *few*　　g *get*　　h *her*　　j *yes*　　k *cat*　　l *leg*　　m *man*　　n *no*　　p *pen*　　r *red*　　s *sit*

person, a function, the course of events, etc.). **b** *intransitive* be the predominating influence. **3** *transitive* be a standard or principle for; constitute a law for; serve to decide (a case). **4** *transitive* check or control (esp. passions). **5** *transitive Grammar* (esp. of a verb or preposition) have (a noun or pronoun or its case) depending on it. **6** *transitive* be in military command of (a fort, town). □ **gov·ern·able** *adjective*

gov·ern·abil·ity *noun* [Old French *governer* from Latin *gubernare* steer, rule, from Greek *kubernaō*]

gov·ern·ance *noun* **1** the act or manner of governing. **2** the office or function of governing. **3** sway, control.

gov·ern·ess *noun* a woman employed to teach children in a private household. [earlier *governeress* from Old French *governeresse* (as GOVERNOR)]

gov·ern·essy *adjective* considered characteristic of a governess; prim and reproving.

governing body *noun* **1** the board of directors of a university or other institution. **2** an organization that establishes and enforces rules for a sport or other activity.

gov·ern·ment /ˈɡʌvənmənt, ˈɡʌvərmənt/ *noun* **1** the act or manner of governing. **2** the system by which a state or community is governed. **3 a** a body of persons governing a state or community. **b** (usu. **Government**) a particular administration in office. **4** the state as an agent. **5** (*attributive*) denoting something produced, issued, or funded by a government or state. **6** *Grammar* the relation between a governed and a governing word. □ **gov·ern·ment·al** /-ˈmentəl/ *adjective* **gov·ern·ment·al·ly** /-ˈmentəli/ *adverb*

Government House *noun* the official residence of the representative of the Crown, e.g. a Lieutenant-Governor.

gov·ernment-in-exile *noun* a temporary government established in a foreign country by exiles hoping to form a government in their native country once they can return there.

government issue *adjective US* (of equipment) provided by the government.

Government Leader *noun* (in Canada) the leader of any of the Territorial governments.

government securities *plural noun* bonds etc. issued by the government.

government surplus *noun* unused equipment sold by the government.

government wharf *noun Cdn* a wharf built by the government.

gov·ern·or /ˈɡʌvənər, ˈɡʌvərnər/ *noun* **1** a person who governs; a ruler. **2 a** (also **gov·ernor-in-chief**) an official governing a province, town, etc. **b** a representative of the Crown in a colony. **3** the executive head of each state or territory of the US. **4** an officer commanding a fortress or garrison. **5** the head or a member of a governing body of an institution. **6** *Cdn hist.* **a** the officer in charge of a fort or factory of the Hudson's Bay Company. **b** (in full **gov·ernor-in-chief**) the Hudson's Bay Company's chief officer in Canada. **7** *Brit.* the official in charge of a prison. **8** *Brit.* **a** *slang* one's employer. **b** *slang* one's father. **c** *informal* (as a form of address) sir. **9** *Mech.* an automatic regulator controlling the speed of an engine etc. □ **gov·ern·or·ate** /-rət/ *noun* **gov·ern·or·ship** *noun*

Governor General *noun* (*pl.* **Governors General**) the representative of the Crown in a Commonwealth country that regards the Queen as head of state.

Governor General's Award *noun* (in full **Governor General's Literary Award**) *Cdn* an award presented annually by the Governor General in each of several categories of Canadian literature.

Gov·ernor-in-Council *noun* (also **Governor-General-in-Council**) the Governor General acting formally as an instrument for legalizing decisions of the cabinet.

Gov. Gen. *abbreviation* Governor General.

Govt. *abbreviation* (also **govt., gov't.**) government.

gowan /ˈɡauən/ *noun Scot.* **1** a daisy. **2** any white or yellow field flower. [prob. var. of dial. *gollan* ranunculus etc., and related to *gold* in *marigold*]

gowk /ɡauk/ *noun esp. Brit. dialect* an awkward or halfwitted person; a fool. [Old Norse *gaukr* from Germanic]

gown ● *noun* **1** a loose flowing garment, esp. a long dress worn by a woman. **2** the official robe of a judge, cleric, member of a university, etc. **3** a protective garment worn in a hospital etc. by a staff member during surgery or by a patient. **4** the members of a university as distinct from the permanent residents of the university town (*compare* TOWN 3). ● *transitive verb* (usu. as **gowned** *adjective*) attire in a gown. [Old

French *goune*, *gon(n)e* from Late Latin *gunna* fur garment: compare medieval Greek *gouna* fur]

goy *noun* (*pl.* **goyim** /ˈɡɔiim/ or **goys**) *slang* a non-Jew. □ **goy·ish** *adjective* (also **goy·ishe** /ˈɡɔiʃə/). [Hebrew *gōy* people, nation]

GP *abbreviation* **1** general practitioner. **2** Grand Prix.

GPA *abbreviation N Amer.* GRADE POINT AVERAGE.

GPO *abbreviation* **1** General Post Office. **2** *US* Government Printing Office.

GPRS *abbreviation* general packet radio services, a technology for radio transmission of small packets of data, especially between mobile phones and the Internet.

GPS *abbreviation* GLOBAL POSITIONING SYSTEM.

GR *abbreviation* King George. [Latin *Georgius Rex*]

gr *abbreviation* (also **gr.**) **1** gram(s). **2** grains. **3** gross. **4** grey.

Graaf·ian follicle /ˈɡrɒfiən/ *noun* a follicle in the mammalian ovary in which an ovum develops prior to ovulation. [R. de *Graaf*, Dutch anatomist d.1673]

grab ● *verb* (**grabbed**, **grab·bing**) **1** *transitive* **a** seize suddenly, roughly, or firmly. **b** capture, arrest. **2** *transitive* take greedily or unfairly. **3** *transitive slang* attract the attention of, impress. **4** *intransitive* (foll. by *at*) make a sudden snatch at. **5** *transitive* purchase, obtain, or consume (esp. food) hastily (*grabbed a pizza*). **6** *intransitive* (of the brakes of a motor vehicle) act harshly or jerkily. ● *noun* **1** a sudden clutch or attempt to seize. **2** a mechanical device for clutching. **3** the practice of grabbing; rapacious proceedings esp. in politics and commerce. □ **up for grabs** *slang* easily obtainable; inviting capture; available. □ **grab·ber** *noun* [Middle Low German, Middle Dutch *grabben*: compare GRIP, GRIPE, GROPE]

grab bag *noun esp. N Amer.* **1** a bag concealing various prizes, treats, etc., from which one draws blindly. **2** an assortment of small items in a sealed bag which one buys or is given without knowing what the contents are. **3** a miscellaneous assortment, hodgepodge.

grab bar *noun esp. N Amer.* a bar or rail fixed to a wall as an aid in entering or leaving a bathtub etc.

grab·ble *intransitive verb* **1** grope about, feel for something. **2** (often foll. by *for*) sprawl on all fours, scramble (for something). [Dutch & Low German *grabbeln* scramble for a thing (as GRAB)]

grabby *adjective informal* **1** tending to grab; greedy, grasping. **2** attention-getting (*a grabby headline*).

gra·ben /ˈɡrɒbən/ *noun* (*pl.* same or **-bens**) *Geol.* a depression of the earth's surface between faults. [German, originally = ditch]

grab rail *noun* (also **grab handle** etc.) a handle or rail etc. by grabbing which one may maintain one's balance, steady oneself, etc.

Grac·chus /ˈɡrakəs/ **Ti·ber·ius Sem·pro·nius** (*c.*164–133 BC), and his brother, **Gaius Sem·pro·nius** (*c.*153–121 BC) (known as 'the Gracchi'), Roman tribunes. They pushed through radical social and economic legislation to redistribute land and relieve poverty; Tiberius was killed by his opponents, and Gaius later committed suicide.

grace ● *noun* **1** attractiveness, esp. in elegance of proportion or manner or movement; gracefulness. **2** courteous good will (*had the grace to apologize*). **3** an attractive feature; an accomplishment (*social graces*). **4 a** (in Christian belief) the unmerited favour of God; a divine saving and strengthening influence. **b** the state of receiving this. **c** a divinely given talent. **5** goodwill, favour (*fall from grace*). **6** delay granted as a favour (*a year's grace*; *a five-day grace period*). **7** a short thanksgiving before or after a meal. **8** (**Grace**) (in Greek mythology) each of three beautiful sister goddesses, bestowers of beauty and charm. **9** (**Grace**) (prec. by *His*, *Her*, *Your*) forms of description or address for a duke, duchess, or archbishop. ● *transitive verb* (often foll. by *with*) add grace to, enhance; confer honour or dignity on (*graced us with his presence*). □ **days of grace** the time allowed by law for payment of a sum due. **in a person's good** (or **bad**) **graces** regarded by a person with favour (or disfavour). **with good** (or **bad**) **grace** as if willingly (or reluctantly). [Old French from Latin *gratia* from *gratus* pleasing: compare GRATEFUL]

grace·ful *adjective* having or showing grace or elegance. □ **grace·ful·ly** *adverb* **grace·ful·ness** *noun*

grace·less *adjective* lacking grace or elegance or charm. □ **grace·less·ly** *adverb* **grace·less·ness** *noun*

grace note *noun Music* an extra note as an embellishment not essential to the harmony or melody.

Gra·cias a Dios, Cape /ˈɡrɒsiˌɒs ɒ ˈdiːɒs/ a cape forming the easternmost extremity of the Mosquito Coast in Central America, on the border between Nicaragua and Honduras. The cape was named by Columbus, who, in 1502, had been becalmed off the coast but was able to continue his voyage with the arrival of a following wind. [Spanish, = thanks (be) to God]

gra·cile /'grasail, -sɪl/ *adjective* slender; gracefully slender.
□ **gra·cil·ity** /grə'sɪlɪti/ *noun* [Latin *gracilis* slender]

gra·cious /'greiʃəs/ ● *adjective* **1** kindly, courteous. **2** (of God) merciful, benign. **3** condescendingly indulgent and beneficent. **4** characterized by elegance and usu. wealth (*gracious grandeur; gracious rooms*). ● *interjection* expressing surprise. □ **gra·cious·ly** *adverb* **gra·cious·ness** *noun*

grackle *noun* **1** any of various New World birds of the genus *Quiscalus* and related genera, the males of which are shiny black with a blue-green sheen. *Also called* BLACKBIRD. **2** any of various mynas, esp. of the genus *Gracula*, native to Asia. [modern Latin *Gracula* from Latin *graculus* jackdaw]

grad *noun informal* **1** = GRADUATE *noun* 1. **2** *Cdn* a graduation ceremony; commencement. **3** *Cdn* a dinner dance to celebrate graduation; a prom. [abbreviation]

grad·ate /'greideit/ *verb* **1** *intransitive & transitive* pass or cause to pass by gradations from one shade to another. **2** *transitive* arrange in steps or grades of size etc. [back-formation from GRADATION]

grada·tion /grei'deiʃən, grə-/ *noun* (usu. in *pl.*) **1** a stage of transition or advance. **2 a** a certain degree in rank, intensity, merit, divergence, etc. **b** an arrangement in such degrees. **3** (of paint etc.) the gradual passing from one shade, tone, etc., to another. □ **grada·tion·al** *adjective* **grada·tion·al·ly** *adverb* [Latin *gradatio* from *gradus* step]

grade ● *noun* **1 a** a certain degree in rank, merit, proficiency, quality, etc. **b** a class of persons or things of the same grade. **2** a step or stage in a process. **3** a mark indicating the quality of a student's work. **4 a** *N Amer.* a class in school, concerned with a particular year's work and usu. numbered from one upwards. **b** (in *combination*) *Cdn* a pupil of a specified grade in a school (*the grade threes are visiting the museum on Thursday*). **5 a** a gradient or slope. **b** the rate of ascent or descent. **c** *N Amer.* the level at which the ground meets the foundation of a building (*hardwood floors are not recommended below grade*). **6 a** a variety of cattle produced by crossing native stock with a superior breed. **b** a group of animals at a similar level of development. ● *verb* **1** *transitive* arrange in or allocate to grades; class, sort. **2** *intransitive* (foll. by *up, down, off, into*, etc.) pass gradually between grades, or into a grade. **3** *transitive* give a grade to (a student or academic work). **4** *intransitive* be of good or specified quality; reach a required or expected standard. **5** *transitive* blend so as to affect the grade of colour with tints passing into each other. **6** *transitive* reduce (a road etc.) to easy gradients or to a level. **7** *transitive* (often foll. by *up*) cross (livestock) with a better breed. □ **at grade** *N Amer.* on the same level. **make the grade** *informal* succeed; reach the desired standard. [French *grade* or Latin *gradus* step]

grade A *noun* **1** the highest quality of certain food products etc., e.g. eggs and meat. **2** (*attributive*) designating something that is of the highest order (*I got a grade A case of the creeps*).

grade crossing *noun N Amer.* = LEVEL CROSSING.

grade inflation *noun* the awarding of higher academic grades than students' work deserves.

grade point *noun N Amer.* (esp. in post-secondary education) a numerical value assigned to a grade received in a course, multiplied by the number of credits awarded for the course.

grade point average *noun N Amer.* (esp. in post-secondary education) an indication of a student's academic achievement, being the total number of grade points received divided by the number of credits awarded.

grad·er *noun* **1** a person or thing that grades. **2** (in *combination*) *N Amer.* a pupil of a specified grade in a school. **3** = ROAD GRADER.

grade school *noun N Amer.* elementary school. □ **grade schooler** *noun*

Grad·grind /'gradgraind/ *noun* a person who is hard and cold and solely interested in facts, esp. one who advocates the rote acquisition of factual knowledge as the basis for education. □ **Grad·grind·ian** *adjective* [name of a character in Charles Dickens's *Hard Times*]

gra·di·ent /'greidiənt/ *noun* **1 a** a stretch of road, railway, etc., that slopes from the horizontal. **b** the amount of such a slope. **2** the rate of rise or fall of temperature, pressure, etc., in passing from one region to another. [prob. formed on GRADE after *salient*]

grad·ual /'gradʒʊəl/ ● *adjective* **1** taking place or progressing slowly or by degrees. **2** not rapid or steep or abrupt. ● *noun Christianity* **1** an antiphon sung or recited between the Epistle and Gospel in the Mass. **2** a book of music for the sung parts of the Mass. □ **grad·ual·ly** *adverb* **grad·ual·ness** *noun* [medieval Latin *gradualis, -ale* from Latin *gradus*

step, the noun referring to the altar steps on which the response was sung]

grad·ual·ism /'gradʒʊə,lizəm/ *noun* **1** a policy of gradual reform rather than sudden change or revolution. **2** the theory of or belief in gradual evolutionary change. □ **grad·ual·ist** *noun* **grad·ual·is·tic** *adjective*

gradu·and /'gradjʊ,and/ *noun Cdn & Brit.* a person about to receive a degree or other academic qualification. [medieval Latin *graduandus* gerundive of *graduare* GRADUATE]

gradu·ate ● *noun* /'gradʒʊət/ **1 a** a person who has been awarded an academic degree. **b** (*attributive*) designating or involved in education undertaken beyond the first or bachelor's degree (*graduate student*). **2** *N Amer.* a person who has completed a course of study. ● *verb* /'gradʒʊeit/ **1** *intransitive* **a** receive an academic degree or (*N Amer.*) a high school diploma. **b** (foll. by *from*) be a graduate of a specified university. **c** (foll. by *from*) complete a course of study at a specified place or level. **d** (foll. by *in*) be a graduate in a specified subject. **2** *transitive N Amer.* confer a degree, diploma, etc. upon; send out as a graduate from a university etc. **3** *intransitive* **a** (foll. by *to*) move up to (a higher grade of activity etc.). **b** (foll. by *as, in*) gain specified qualifications. **4** *transitive* mark out in degrees or parts. **5** *transitive* arrange in gradations; apportion (e.g. tax) according to a scale. **6** *intransitive* (foll. by *into, away*) pass by degrees. [medieval Latin *graduari* take a degree, from Latin *gradus* step]

gradu·at·ed /'gradʒʊ,eitɪd/ *adjective* **1** arranged in grades or gradations; advancing or proceeding by degrees. **2** marked with lines to indicate degrees, grades, or quantities.

graduated licensing *noun* a gradual process of awarding driving privileges to new drivers, in which novice drivers are allowed to drive only under certain conditions for a specified period and must pass a road test before privileges are increased.

graduate school *noun N Amer.* **1** a department of a university for advanced work by graduates. **2** study undertaken at a university by graduates.

gradu·a·tion /gradʒʊ'eiʃən/ *noun* **1** the act or an instance of graduating or being graduated. **2** a ceremony at which degrees are conferred. **3** each or all of the marks on a vessel or instrument indicating degrees of quantity etc.

Grae·cism /'griːsizəm/ *noun* (also **Gre·cism**) **1** a Greek idiom, esp. as imitated in another language. **2 a** the Greek spirit, style, mode of expression, etc. **b** the imitation of these. [French *grécisme* or medieval Latin *Graecismus* from *Graecus* GREEK]

Grae·cize /'griːsaiz/ *transitive verb* (also **Gre·cize**, esp. *Brit.* **-cise**) give a Greek character or form to. [Latin *Graecizare* (as GRAECISM)]

Graeco- *var. of* GRECO-.

Graf /'graf/ **Steffi** (b.1969), German tennis player. In 1988 she won the Australian, French, and US Open championships, as well as the Wimbledon trophy and an Olympic gold medal; she won her seventh Wimbledon singles title in 1996. She retired in 1999.

graf·fiti /grə'fiːti/ ● *plural noun* (often treated as *sing.*) (*sing.* **graf·fito** /-toː/) inscriptions or drawings scribbled, scratched, or sprayed on a surface. ● *transitive verb* (**graf·fi·tied**) **1** cover (a surface) with graffiti. **2** write as graffiti (*graffitied initials*). □ **graf·fi·tist** *noun* [Italian, from *graffio* 'a scratch']

graft[1] ● *noun* **1** *Bot.* **a** a shoot or scion inserted into a slit of stock, from which it receives sap. **b** the place where a graft is inserted. **c** an instance or the process of inserting a shoot or scion. **2** *Surgery* **a** a piece of living tissue, organ, etc., transplanted surgically. **b** an instance or the process of doing this. **3** *Brit. slang* hard work. ● *verb* **1** *transitive* **a** (often foll. by *into, on, together*, etc.) insert (a scion) as a graft. **b** insert a graft on (a stock). **2** *intransitive* insert a graft. **3** *transitive Surgery* transplant (living tissue). **4** *transitive* (foll. by *in, on*) insert or fix (a thing) permanently to another. **5** *intransitive Brit. slang* work hard. □ **graft·er** *noun* [Old French *grafe, grefe* from Latin *graphium* from Greek *graphion* stylus, from *graphō* write]

graft[2] *informal* ● *noun* **1** practices, esp. bribery, used to secure illicit gains in politics or business. **2** such gains. ● *intransitive verb* seek or make such gains. □ **graft·er** *noun* [19th c.: origin unknown]

Gra·ham /'greiəm/ **1 Martha** (1894–1991), US dancer, teacher, and choreographer. An influential teacher of modern dance, she evolved a new dance language using more flexible movements intended to express psychological complexities and emotional power; her works include *Appalachian Spring* (1944) and *Care of the Heart* (1946). **2 Thom·as** (1805–69), Scottish physical chemist. He suggested a law which relates a gas's rate of diffusion to its density; he also investigated the passage of dissolved substances through porous

Vowels: a cat ɑ arm e bed ɜr her ɜː deux ə ago ɪ sit i cosy iː feed ɒ hot ɔ pore oː no ʌ run ʊ put

membranes, and coined the words *osmosis* and *colloid*. **3 Wil·liam Frank·lin ('Billy')** (b.1918), US evangelical preacher. A minister of the Southern Baptist Church, he is internationally famous as a mass evangelist, conducting large, theatrically staged religious meetings throughout the world.

gra·ham /'greɪəm, gram/ *adjective* esp. *N Amer.* designating unbolted whole wheat flour, or crackers etc. made from this. [Sylvester *Graham* (d.1851), US advocate of dietary reform]

Gra·hame /'greɪəm/ **Ken·neth** (1859-1932), Scottish writer, whose classic children's book *The Wind in the Willows* (1908) is a collection of stories about the riverbank animals Toad, Mole, Rat, and Badger.

Graham Island /'greɪəm/ an island off the central coast of BC, the largest of the Queen Charlotte Islands. [Sir J. R. *Graham*, English statesman d.1861]

Graham Land the northern part of the Antarctic Peninsula. It is the only part of Antarctica lying outside the Antarctic Circle. Discovered in 1831-2 by the English navigator John Biscoe (1794-1843), it now forms part of British Antarctic Territory, but is claimed also by Chile and Argentina.

Grail *noun* (in full **Holy Grail**) (also **grail**) **1** (in medieval legend) the cup or platter used by Christ at the Last Supper, and in which Joseph of Arimathea received Christ's blood at the Cross. Quests for it undertaken by medieval knights are described in versions of the Arthurian legends written from the early 13th century onwards. **2** a thing which is being earnestly pursued or sought after (*profit has become the holy grail*). [Old French *graal* etc. from medieval Latin *gradalis* dish, of unknown origin]

grain ● *noun* **1 a** wheat or any other cereal plant used as food. **b** their fruit. **c** any particular species of cereal plant. **2** a fruit or seed of a cereal. **3 a** a small hard particle of salt, sand, etc. **b** a discrete particle or crystal, usu. small, in a rock or metal. **c** a piece of solid propellant for use in a rocket engine. **4** the smallest unit of weight in the troy and avoirdupois systems (approx. 0.0648 grams), equivalent to $^1/_{5760}$ of a pound troy and $^1/_{7000}$ of a pound avoirdupois. **5** the smallest possible quantity (*not a grain of truth in it*). **6 a** a roughness of surface. **b** *Photog.* each of the tiny light-sensitive particles in a photograph or negative. **7** the texture of skin, wood, stone, etc.; the arrangement and size of constituent particles. **8 a** a pattern of lines of fibre in meat, wood, fabric, or paper. **b** lamination or planes of cleavage in stone, coal, etc. **9 a** (in full **grain side**) the side of a piece of leather on which the hair originally grew. **b** the rough or wrinkled pattern on the grain side of leather or any similar artificially-produced material. ● *verb* **1** *transitive* paint in imitation of the grain of wood or marble. **2** *transitive* give a granular surface to. **3** *transitive & intransitive* form into grains. **4** *transitive* remove hair from (hides). □ **against the grain** contrary to one's natural inclination or feeling. □ **grained** *adjective* (also in *combination*). **grain·less** *adjective* [Old French from Latin *granum*]

grain alcohol *noun* ethanol fermented from grain.

grain elevator *noun N Amer.* = ELEVATOR 2.

Grain·ger /'greɪndʒər/ **(George) Percy Ald·ridge** (1882-1961), Australian-born US composer and pianist, who is best known for his light music incorporating traditional melodies, such as *Shepherd's Hey*, *Country Gardens*, and *Handel in the Strand*, and for his arrangements of English folk songs.

grains of paradise *plural noun* capsules of a W African plant (*Aframomum melegueta*), used as a spice and a drug.

grainy *adjective* (**grain·i·er, grain·i·est**) **1** granular. **2** resembling the grain of wood. **3** *Photog.* having a granular appearance. □ **grain·i·ness** *noun*

gram¹ *noun* (*Brit.* also **gramme**) a metric unit of mass equal to one-thousandth of a kilogram. [French *gramme* from Greek *gramma* small weight]

gram² *noun* any of various pulses used as food. [Portuguese *grão* from Latin *granum* grain]

gram³ *noun* var. of GRAMMA.

-gram *combining form* forming nouns denoting a thing written or recorded or expressed (often in a certain way) (*anagram*; *epigram*; *monogram*; *telegram*; *kissogram*). □ **-grammatic** *combining form*. [from or after Greek *gramma -atos* thing written, letter of the alphabet, from *graphō* write]

grama /'grɑmə/ *noun* (also **grama grass**) any of various chiefly N American pasture and ornamental grasses of the genus *Bouteloua*. [Spanish, = 'grass']

gram-atom *noun Chem.* the quantity of a chemical element equal to its relative atomic mass in grams (see MOLE⁴).

gram-equiva·lent *noun Chem.* the quantity of a substance equal to its relative atomic or molecular weight in grams.

gram·in·aceous /ˌgramɪ'neɪʃəs/ *adjective* of or like grass; grassy. [Latin *gramen -inis* grass]

gram·ma /'gramə, 'gramɒ/ *noun N Amer. informal* = GRANDMA. [corruption]

gram·mar *noun* **1 a** the branch of language study or linguistics which deals with the means of showing the relationship between words in use, traditionally including morphology and syntax, and often phonology. **b** a body of forms and usages in a specified language (*French grammar*). **2** a person's manner of using grammatical forms; speech or writing judged as good or bad according to its conformity to rules of grammar. **3** a book on grammar. **4** the elements or rudiments of an art or science. **5** *Brit. informal* = GRAMMAR SCHOOL 2. □ **gram·mar·less** *adjective* [Old French *gramaire* from Latin *grammatica* from Greek *grammatikē* (*tekhnē*) (art) of letters, from *gramma -atos* letter of the alphabet]

grammar checker *noun* a software program that works with a word processor to alert the user to possible grammar, syntax, punctuation, and style errors.

gram·mar·ian /grə'meriən/ *noun* an expert in grammar.

grammar school *noun* **1** *US* an elementary school. **2** *Brit. esp. hist.* a selective state secondary school with a mainly academic curriculum. **3** *Brit. hist.* a school founded in or before the 16th c. for teaching Latin, later becoming a secondary school teaching academic subjects.

gram·mat·ic·al /grə'matɪkəl/ *adjective* **1** of or relating to grammar. **2** conforming to the rules of grammar. □ **gram·mat·ic·al·ity** /grəˌmatɪ'kalɪti/ *noun* **gram·mat·ic·al·ly** *adverb* [French *grammatical* or Late Latin *grammaticalis* from Latin *grammaticus* from Greek *grammatikos* (as GRAMMAR)]

grammatical gender *noun Linguistics* gender determined by the form of a word, not by the real or attributed sex.

gramme *Brit.* var. of GRAM¹.

gram-molecule *noun Chem.* the quantity of a substance equal to its relative molecular mass in grams.

Gram·my *noun* (*pl.* **Gram·mys**) *proprietary* (in the US) any of several annual awards given by the American National Academy of Recording Arts and Sciences for outstanding achievements in the record industry. [from GRAMOPHONE after EMMY]

Gram-negative *adjective Biol.* (of bacteria) not retaining the first (violet) dye of Gram stain. [see GRAM STAIN]

gram·o·phone *noun dated* a record player. [formed by inversion of PHONOGRAM]

gram·pa /'grampə, 'grampɒ/ *noun* (also **gramps**, **grampy**) *N Amer. informal* = GRANDPA. [corruption]

Gram·pian /'grampiən/ a former local government region in NE Scotland, divided in 1996 into Moray and Aberdeenshire.

Grampian Mountains (also **Grampians**) **1** a mountain range in north central Scotland. Its southern edge forms a natural boundary between the Highlands and the Lowlands. **2** a mountain range in SE Australia, in Victoria. It forms a spur of the Great Dividing Range at its western extremity.

Gram-positive *adjective Biol.* (of bacteria) retaining the first (violet) dye of Gram stain. [see GRAM STAIN]

gram·pus *noun* (*pl.* **gram·pus·es**) **1** a dolphin, *Grampus griseus*, with a blunt snout and long pointed black flippers. **2** the killer whale. [earlier *graundepose*, *grapeys* from Old French *grapois* etc. from medieval Latin *craspiscis* from Latin *crassus piscis* fat fish]

Gram stain *noun* (also **Gram's stain**) *Biol.* a technique for identifying bacteria of different cell wall types by successive application of a violet dye, a decolorizing agent, and a red dye. [H.C.J. *Gram*, Danish physician d.1938]

gran *noun informal* grandmother (*compare* GRANNY). [abbreviation]

Gran·ada /grə'nadə, -nɒdə/ **1** a city in Andalusia in S Spain; pop. (est. 2001) 243,341. Founded in the 8th c., it became the capital of the Moorish kingdom of Granada in 1238. It is the site of the Alhambra palace. **2** a city in Nicaragua, on the northwest shore of Lake Nicaragua; pop. (est. 2002) 91,900. Founded by the Spanish in 1523, it is the oldest city in the country.

grana·dilla /ˌgranə'dɪlə/ var. of GRENADILLA.

Gran·ados /grə'nadoːs/ **En·ri·que** (1867-1916), Spanish composer and pianist, who is best known for his piano works, the *Goyescas* (1911-13), which were adapted into an opera of the same name (1916).

gran·ary /'greɪnəri, 'gran-/ *noun* (*pl.* **-aries**) **1** a storehouse for threshed grain. **2** a region producing, and esp. exporting, much grain. [Latin *granarium* from *granum* grain]

Gran·by an industrial city in south central Quebec, west of Sherbrooke; pop. (2001) 44,121. [J. Manners, 4th Duke of Rutland and Marquess of *Granby* d.1770]

Gran Can·aria /ˌgran kəˈnɑriə/ a volcanic island in the Atlantic Ocean off the northwest coast of Africa, one of the Canary Islands, of which its chief town, Las Palmas, a port on the north coast, is the capital.

Gran Chaco /gran ˈtʃɒkɔː/ (also **Chaco**) a lowland plain in central S America, extending from S Bolivia through Paraguay to N Argentina. [Spanish, = great hunting ground or riches]

grand ● *adjective* **1 a** splendid, magnificent, imposing, dignified. **b** solemn or lofty in conception, execution, or expression; noble. **c** showy, ostentatious. **2** main; of chief importance (*grand staircase*; *grand entrance*). **3** of the highest rank; surpassing all others (*grand chief*; *grand champion*). **4** *informal* excellent, enjoyable (*had a grand time*; *in grand condition*). **5** belonging to high society; wealthy (*a grand affair*). **6** (*in combination*) in names of family relationships, denoting the second degree of ascent or descent (*granddaughter*). **7** great (*grand army*; *Grand Monarch*; *Grand Hotel*). **8** comprehensive, final (*grand total*). **9** *Law* serious, important (*grand larceny*) (*compare* COMMON 8, PETTY 4). ● *noun* **1** = GRAND PIANO. **2** (*pl.* same) (usu. in *pl.*) esp. *N Amer. slang* a thousand dollars or pounds. □ **grand·ly** *adverb* **grand·ness** *noun* [Old French *grant* from Latin *grandis* full-grown]

gran·dam *noun* **1** (also **gran·dame**) *archaic* grandmother. **2** an old woman. [Anglo-French *graund dame* (as GRAND, DAME)]

grand-aunt *noun* = GREAT-AUNT.

Grand Banks a submarine plateau of the continental shelf, situated off the southern coast of Newfoundland and consisting of several banks (the most prominent being Grand, Green and St. Pierre). It is a meeting place of the warm Gulf Stream and the cold Labrador Current, a phenomenon which promotes the growth of plankton, making the waters an important feeding area for fish.

Grand Canal 1 a series of waterways in E China, extending from Beijing southward to Hangzhou, a distance of 1 700 km (1,060 miles). First constructed in 486 BC as a link between the Yangtze and the Yellow River to transport rice from the river valleys to the cities, it reached its present length in AD 1327. **2** the main waterway of Venice in Italy. It is lined on each side by fine palaces and spanned by the Rialto Bridge.

Grand Canyon a deep gorge in Arizona, formed by the Colorado River. It is about 440 km (277 miles) long, 8 to 24 km (5 to 15 miles) wide, and, in places, 1 800 m (6,000 ft.) deep. The area was designated a national park in 1919.

grand chief *noun* the chief of a grand council or national or regional Aboriginal organization.

grand·child *noun* (*pl.* **-chil·dren**) a child of one's son or daughter.

grand council *noun* a group of chiefs representing several different First Nations, organized as a council for political discussions etc.

grand·dad *noun* (also **gran·dad**) *informal* **1** grandfather. **2** an elderly man.

grand·daddy *noun* (also **gran·daddy**) esp. *N Amer. informal* **1** = GRANDDAD. **2** the greatest or most notable example or instance of something (*the granddaddy of all winter storms*).

grand·daugh·ter *noun* a female grandchild.

grand duchess *noun* **1** a princess or noble woman ruling over a territory. **2** the wife or widow of a grand duke.

grand duchy *noun* a state ruled by a grand duke or duchess.

grand duke *noun* **1** a prince or noble person ruling over a territory. **2** *hist.* the son or grandson of a Russian czar.

Grande Com·ore /ˌgrand kəˈmɔrei/ the largest of the islands of the Comoros, off the northwest coast of Madagascar; pop. (est. 2002) 340,000; chief town (and capital of the Comoros), Moroni.

grande dame /grãd ˈdɒm/ *noun* (*pl.* **grandes dames** *pronunc.* same) **1** a dignified woman of high rank or eminence. **2** a venerable institution, esp. an old and impressive hotel, theatre, etc. [French, lit. = 'great lady']

gran·dee /granˈdiː/ *noun* **1** a Spanish or Portuguese nobleman of the highest rank. **2** a person of high rank or eminence. [Spanish & Portuguese *grande*, assimilated to -EE]

grand entry *noun* a procession of dancers and drummers as part of an Aboriginal powwow or festival.

Grande Prairie /ˌgrand ˈpreri/ a city in west central Alberta, about

425 km northwest of Edmonton; pop. (2001) 36,983. □ **Grande Prairi·an** *noun* [French, lit. 'great prairie']

grand·eur /ˈgrandʒər, -dʒɔər/ *noun* **1** majesty, splendour; dignity of appearance or bearing. **2** nobility of character. [French from *grand* great, GRAND]

Grand Falls a town in NW New Brunswick, situated on the Saint John River, about 55 km southeast of Edmundston; pop. (2001) 5,858. [the name of the falls, a translation and shortening from its early French name, *Grand Sault Saint Jean-Baptiste*]

Grand Falls-Windsor a pulp and paper town in central Newfoundland, situated on the Exploits River, about 90 km west of Gander; pop. (2001) 13,340. [from the amalgamation of two towns: *Grand Falls* (after the name of the river's falls) + WINDSOR² 1)]

grand·father ● *noun* **1** a male grandparent. **2** (*attributive*) *Cdn & Brit.* designating a long-sleeved collarless esp. flannel shirt with a short buttoned placket at the neck. ● *transitive verb* esp. *N Amer.* exempt a pre-existing class of people or things from the requirements of a new regulation. □ **grand·father·ly** *adjective*

grandfather clause *noun* a legal provision exempting certain pre-existing classes of people or things from the requirements of a new regulation.

grandfather clock *noun* a clock in a tall wooden case, driven by weights and a pendulum.

grand finale *noun* **1** the usu. elaborate final scene of a theatrical performance, often involving the whole cast. **2** an elaborate or impressive conclusion to anything (*the grand finale to the meal was a chocolate torte*).

Grand Gui·gnol /ˌgrã giːˈnjɒl/ *noun* a dramatic entertainment of a sensational or horrific nature. [the name (= Great Punch) of a theatre in Paris]

gran·di·flora /ˌgrandɪˈflɔrə/ *adjective* bearing large flowers. [modern Latin (often used in specific names of large-flowered plants) from Latin *grandis* great + FLORA]

grand·il·o·quent /granˈdɪləkwənt/ *adjective* **1** pompous or inflated in language. **2** given to boastful talk. □ **grand·il·o·quence** *noun* **grand·il·o·quent·ly** *adverb* [Latin *grandiloquus* (as GRAND, -*loquus* -speaking from *loqui* speak), after *eloquent* etc.]

Grand Inquisitor *noun* the director of the court of Inquisition in some countries.

gran·di·ose /ˌgrandiˈɔːs, ˈgran-/ *adjective* **1** producing or meant to produce an imposing effect. **2** planned on an ambitious or magnificent scale. **3** (of speech, manner, etc.) characterized by esp. affected grandeur or stateliness; pompous, arrogant. □ **gran·di·ose·ly** *adverb* **gran·di·os·ity** /-ˈɒsɪti/ *noun* [French from Italian *grandioso* (as GRAND, -OSE¹)]

grand jeté /grã ʒəˈtei/ *noun* (*pl.* **grands jetés** *pronunc.* same) *Dance* a jump in which the dancer extends one leg forward and the other backwards. [French]

grand jury *noun Law* (in the US and formerly in Nova Scotia) a jury selected to examine the validity of an accusation prior to trial.

grand·kid *noun N Amer. informal* = GRANDCHILD.

Grand Lake 1 the largest lake in New Brunswick, situated in the south central part of the province, east of Fredericton. **2** the largest lake in Newfoundland, 91 km in length, situated in the west central part of the island, east of Corner Brook.

grand·ma /ˈgranmə, ˈgrand-, -mɒ/ *noun* (also *archaic* **grand·mama** /ˈgranmə,mɒ, ˈgrand-/) *informal* grandmother.

grand mal /grã ˈmal/ *noun* a serious form of epilepsy with loss of consciousness (*compare* PETIT MAL). [French, = great sickness]

Grandma Moses see MOSES 2.

Grand Manan Island /ˌgrand məˈnan/ (also **Grand Manan**) an island of SW New Brunswick, situated at the entrance to the Bay of Fundy. □ **Grand Manan·er** *noun* [French *grand* great + *manan* (alteration of Passamaquoddy, Maliseet & Penobscot *munanook* island)]

Grand Mar·nier /grã marˈnjei, ˈmarnjei/ *noun proprietary* an orange-flavoured cognac-based liqueur. [*Marnier*-Lapostolle, the manufacturer's name.]

grand·master *noun* **1** a chess player of the highest class. **2** (**Grand Master**) the head of a military order of knighthood, of Freemasons, etc.

Grand-Mère /grãˈmer/ (also **Grand'Mère**) a former town in south central Quebec, about 45 km north of Trois-Rivières, now part of Shawinigan; pop. (2001) 13,179. [French translation of Algonquin *kokomis* grandmother, with reference to a rock resembling the profile of an old woman]

Consonants: b *but*   d *dog*   f *few*   g *get*   h *her*   j *yes*   k *cat*   l *leg*   m *man*   n *no*   p *pen*   r *red*   s *sit*

grand·mother *noun* a female grandparent. □ **teach one's grandmother to suck eggs** presume to advise a more experienced person. □ **grand·mother·ly** *adjective*

grandmother clock *noun* a clock like a grandfather clock but in a smaller case.

grand·nephew *noun* = GREAT-NEPHEW.

grand·niece *noun* = GREAT-NIECE.

grand old man *noun* a venerated person esp. in a specified field or position.

grand opening *noun N Amer.* the usu. festive first opening of a new store etc. to the public.

grand opera *noun* opera on a serious theme, or in which the entire libretto (including dialogue) is sung.

grand·pa /ˈɡranpə, ˈɡrand-, -pɒ/ *noun* (also archaic **grand·papa** /-pə,pɒ/, *N Amer.* **grand·pappy**) *informal* grandfather.

grand·par·ent *noun* a parent of one's father or mother.

grand piano *noun* a large full-toned piano standing on three legs, with the body, strings, and soundboard arranged horizontally and in line with the keys.

Grand Pré /ɡrãˈpreɪ/ a historic site in central Nova Scotia, located on the shores of Minas Basin, about 80 km northwest of Halifax. Originally settled by Acadians *c.*1680, the site today commemorates their expulsion in 1755. [French, = big meadow]

Grand Prix /ɡrã ˈpriː/ *noun* (*pl.* **Grands Prix** *pronunc.* same) any of several important international sporting events, esp. in auto racing. [French, = great or chief prize]

grand prize *noun* the most valuable prize in a raffle etc. for which many prizes are given.

Grand River a river in SW central Ontario, rising south of Collingwood and winding southward through Fergus, Kitchener, Cambridge, Paris and Brantford to empty into Lake Erie just southeast of Dunnville. [from its early French name *Grande Rivière*]

grand sei·gneur /ɡrã seˈnjɜr/ *noun* (*pl.* **grands sei·gneurs** *pronunc.* same) a person of high rank or noble presence.

grand·sire /ˈɡran,saɪr, ˈɡrand-/ *noun archaic* grandfather, old man, ancestor.

grand slam *noun* **1** *Bridge* the winning of 13 tricks. **2 a** the winning of all of the most important championships or matches in a sport, esp. tennis. **b** (*attributive*) designating each of these championships (*won three of four grand slam events this year*). **3** *Baseball* a home run hit when all three bases are occupied by a runner, thus scoring four runs.

grand·son *noun* a male grandchild.

grand·stand ● *noun* the main stand, usu. roofed, for spectators at a racetrack etc. ● *intransitive verb* seek to impress others, esp. by acting showily or ostentatiously. □ **grand·stand·er** *noun*

grand tour *noun hist.* a long tour of major cities and places of interest, formerly undertaken esp. in Europe as part of an Englishman's education.

grand-uncle *noun* = GREAT-UNCLE.

grand unified theory *noun Physics* a theory attempting to give a single explanation of the strong, weak, and electromagnetic interactions between subatomic particles.

grange /ɡreɪndʒ/ *noun* **1** *Brit.* a country house with farm buildings. **2** *archaic* a barn. [Old French from medieval Latin *granica* (*villa*), ultimately from Latin *granum* GRAIN]

gran·ita /ɡrəˈniːtə/ *noun* (*pl.* **-itas**) **1** a coarse sherbet. **2** a drink made with crushed ice. [Italian (see GRANITE)]

gran·ite /ˈɡranɪt/ *noun* **1** a granular crystalline igneous rock of quartz, mica, feldspar, etc., used for building. **2** a hard, determined or resolute thing, quality, attitude, etc. **3** *Curling* curling rocks. □ **gran·it·ic** /ɡrəˈnɪtɪk/ *adjective* **gran·it·oid** *adjective & noun* [Italian *granito*, lit. 'grained' from *grano* from Latin *granum* GRAIN]

granite·ware /ˈɡranɪt,wer/ *noun* **1** a speckled form of earthenware imitating the appearance of granite. **2** a kind of enamelled ironware.

gran·iv·or·ous /ɡrəˈnɪvərəs/ *adjective* feeding on grain. □ **grani·vore** /ˈɡranɪ,vɔr/ *noun* [Latin *granum* GRAIN]

granny *noun* (also **gran·nie**) (*pl.* **-nies**) *informal* grandmother. [obsolete *grannam* for GRANDAM + -Y²]

granny flat *noun* part of a house made into self-contained accommodation, as for an elderly relative.

granny glasses *plural noun* round wire-rimmed eyeglasses.

granny knot *noun* a reef knot crossed the wrong way and therefore insecure.

Granny Smith *noun* an originally Australian variety of bright green apple. [Maria Ann ('Granny') *Smith*, d.1870]

granny square *noun N Amer.* a knitted or crocheted square of yarn, stitched to others like it to form an afghan.

grano·dior·ite /ɡranoˈdaɪərəɪt/ *noun Geol.* a coarse-grained plutonic rock containing quartz and plagioclase, between granite and diorite in composition. [GRANITE + -O- + DIORITE]

gran·ola /ɡrəˈnoːlə/ *N Amer.* ● *noun* a mixture of rolled oats, nuts, raisins, brown sugar, etc. eaten as a breakfast cereal or pressed into bars. ● *adjective jocular* designating persons having liberal political views, esp. concerned with the protection of the environment, and typified as leading an unconventional or hippy lifestyle including the eating of health foods. [from *gran-* representing GRAIN + -OLA]

Grant ▸ 1 Cary (born Alexander Archibald Leach) (1904–86), English-born US actor. Noted for his image of sophisticated and amiable assurance, he acted in more than 70 films, including *Holiday* (1938), *The Philadelphia Story* (1940), and *North by Northwest* (1959). **2 Cuth·bert** (*c.*1793–1854), Canadian Metis fur trader. A clerk in the North West Company, he was the captain of the group of Metis sent by the company to destroy the Red River Settlement (1815), an event which resulted in the massacre at Seven Oaks (1816); he later founded the Metis settlement of Grantown (1824), and was made warden of the plains by the Hudson's Bay Company (1828). **3 George Par·kin** (1918–88), Canadian social philosopher. His works analyze contemporary social and political behaviour, and include *Philosophy in the Mass Age* (1959), the influential *Lament for a Nation: The Defeat of Canadian Nationalism* (1965), in which he proclaims the death of Canada as a victim of continentalism and technology, and *Technology and Justice* (1986). **4 Ulys·ses Simp·son** (born Hiram Ulysses Grant) (1822–85), US general and 18th president of the US 1869–77. He won a series of victories on the Union side in the American Civil War (most notably the capture of Vicksburg in 1863), and was made supreme commander of the Unionist armies; his policy of attrition against the Confederate army proved successful in ending the war.

grant ● *transitive verb* **1 a** consent to fulfill (a request, wish, etc.) (*granted all they asked*). **b** allow (a person) to have (a thing) (*granted me my freedom*). **c** (as **grant·ed**) *informal* apology accepted; pardon given. **2** give (rights, property, etc.) formally; transfer legally. **3** (often foll. by *that* + clause) admit as true; concede, esp. as a basis for argument. ● *noun* **1** the process of granting or a thing granted. **2 a** a sum of money given by the state for any of various purposes, e.g. to finance education. **b** a tract of land given by the state to private interests. **3** *Law* **a** a legal conveyance by written instrument. **b** formal conferment. □ **take for granted 1** assume something to be true or valid. **2** cease to appreciate through familiarity. □ **grant·able** *adjective* **gran·tee** *noun* (esp. in sense 2 of *verb*). **grant·er** *noun* **grant·or** *noun* (esp. in sense 2 of *verb*). [Old French *gr(e)anter* var. of *creanter*, ultimately from part. of Latin *credere* entrust]

Granth /ɡrʌnt/ *noun* (in full **Granth Sahib**) = ADI GRANTH.

grant-in-aid *noun* (*pl.* **grants-in-aid**) a grant by a central government to a local government or an institution.

grants·man·ship *noun* skill in obtaining research grants from funding agencies.

granu·lar /ˈɡranjʊlər/ *adjective* **1** of or like grains or granules. **2** having a granulated surface or structure. □ **granu·lar·ity** /-ˈlerɪti/ *noun* [Late Latin *granulum* GRANULE]

granu·late /ˈɡranjʊ,leɪt/ *verb* **1** *transitive & intransitive* form into grains (*granulated sugar*). **2** *transitive* roughen the surface of. **3** *intransitive* (of a wound etc.) form small prominences as the beginning of healing or joining. □ **granu·la·tor** *noun*

granu·la·tion /ɡranjʊˈleɪʃən/ *noun* **1** the action or process of forming into granules or grains. **2** the formation of multiple small prominences on the surface of injured tissue, as part of the growth of new connective tissue.

gran·ule /ˈɡranjuːl/ *noun* a small grain. [Late Latin *granulum*, diminutive of Latin *granum* grain]

granu·lo·cyte /ˈɡranjʊlə,saɪt/ *noun* any of various white blood cells having granules in their cytoplasm. □ **granu·lo·cyt·ic** /-ˈsɪtɪk/ *adjective*

granu·loma /ɡranjʊˈloːmə/ *noun* a mass of granulation tissue produced in any of various disease states, usu. in response to infection, inflammation, or the presence of a foreign substance. □ **granu·lo·ma·tous** /,ɡranjʊˈloːmətəs/ *adjective* [GRANULE + -OMA]

Gran·ville a former name (1870–1886) for Vancouver. [G. Leveson-Gower, 2nd Earl of *Granville*, British statesman d.1891]

Granville-Barker, Harley (1877–1946), English dramatist, critic, theatre director, and actor. One of the leading figures in progressive theatre at the beginning of the 20th c., he presented plays incorporating social comment and greater realism.

grape *noun* **1** a berry (usu. purple, black, or green) growing in clusters on a vine, eaten fresh or dried and used in making wine. **2** (prec. by *the*) *informal* wine. **3** = GRAPESHOT. **4** (in *pl.*) a diseased growth like a bunch of grapes on the pastern of a horse etc., or on a pleura in cattle. □ **grapey** *adjective* (also **grapy**). [Old French *grape* bunch of grapes, prob. from *graper* gather (grapes) from *grap(p)e* hook, ultimately from Germanic]

grape fern *noun* any of various ferns of the genus *Botrychium*, with grape-like spore clusters.

grape·fruit *noun* (*pl.* same or **-fruits**) **1** a large round yellow citrus fruit with an acid juicy pulp. **2** the tree, *Citrus paradisi*, bearing this fruit.

grape hyacinth *noun* any liliaceous plant of the genus *Muscari*, with clusters of usu. blue flowers.

grape·shot *noun hist.* small balls used as charge in a cannon and scattering when fired.

grape·vine *noun* **1** any of various vines of the genus *Vitis*, esp. *Vitis vinifera*. **2** *informal* the means of transmission of unofficial information or rumour (*heard it through the grapevine*).

graph¹ ● *noun* **1** a diagram showing the relation between variable quantities, usu. of two variables, each measured along one of a pair of axes at right angles. **2** *Math.* a collection of points whose coordinates satisfy a given relation. ● *transitive verb* plot or trace on a graph. [abbreviation of *graphic formula*]

graph² *noun Linguistics* a visual symbol, esp. a letter or letters, representing a unit of sound or other feature of speech. [Greek *graphē* writing]

-graph *combining form* forming nouns and verbs meaning: **1** a thing written or drawn etc. in a specified way (*autograph*; *photograph*). **2** an instrument that records (*heliograph*; *seismograph*; *telegraph*).

graph·eme /'grafiːm/ *noun Linguistics* **1** a class of letters etc. representing a unit of sound. **2** a feature of a written expression that cannot be analyzed into smaller meaningful units. □ **graph·em·ic** /grə'fiːmɪk/ *adjective* **graph·em·ic·ally** /grə'fiːmɪkli/ *adverb* [GRAPH² + -EME]

-grapher *combining form* forming nouns denoting a person concerned with a subject (*geographer*; *photographer*). [from or after Greek *-graphos* writer + -ER¹]

graph·ic ● *adjective* **1** of or relating to the visual or descriptive arts, esp. writing and drawing. **2** vividly descriptive; conveying all (esp. unwelcome or unpleasant) details. **3** (of minerals) showing marks like writing on the surface or in a fracture. **4** = GRAPHICAL. ● *noun* a visual image (*compare* GRAPHICS). □ **graph·ic·al·ly** *adverb* **graphic·ness** *noun* [Latin *graphicus* from Greek *graphikos* from *graphē* writing]

-graphic *combining form* (also **-graphical**) forming adjectives corresponding to nouns in *-graphy* (*see* -GRAPHY). □ **-graphically** *combining form.* [from or after Greek *-graphikos* (as GRAPHIC)]

graph·ic·al *adjective* **1** of or in the form of graphs (*see* GRAPH¹). **2** graphic. □ **graph·ic·al·ly** *adverb*

graphical user interface *noun* (also **graphical interface**) software which provides a computer user with icons or other simple graphic representations of a program's available commands or options, which can be manipulated directly, e.g. with a mouse. Abbr.: **GUI**.

graphic arts *plural noun* the visual and technical arts involving design, writing, drawing, printing, etc. □ **graphic artist** *noun*

graphic equalizer *noun* a device enabling the quality of an audio signal to be varied by adjusting its strength in each of a series of frequency bands independently, usu. by means of slides.

graphic novel *noun* a full-length story in the form of a comic strip, published as a book.

graph·ics *plural noun* (usu. treated as *sing.*) **1** the products of the graphic arts, esp. commercial design or illustration. **2** the use of diagrams in calculation and design. **3** (in full **computer graphics**) *Computing* **a** the use of computers linked to monitors to generate and manipulate visual images. **b** visual images produced by computer processing.

graphics card *noun* (also **graphics board**) a circuit board which when connected to a computer increases the computer's ability to produce, display, or manipulate graphics.

graph·ite *noun* a crystalline allotropic form of carbon used as a solid lubricant, in pencils, and as a moderator in nuclear reactors etc. □ **graph·itic** /grə'fɪtɪk/ *adjective* **graph·it·ize** /-fɪˌtaɪz/ *transitive &*

intransitive verb (also esp. *Brit.* **-ise**). [German *Graphit* from Greek *graphō* write]

graph·ol·ogy /grə'fɒlədʒi/ *noun* **1** the study of handwriting esp. as a supposed guide to character. **2** *Linguistics* the study of systems of writing. □ **graph·o·logic·al** /-fə'lɒdʒɪkəl/ *adjective* **graph·ol·o·gist** *noun* [Greek *graphē* writing]

graph paper *noun* paper with intersecting lines forming small squares of equal size, used for drawing graphs.

-graphy *combining form* forming nouns denoting: **1** a descriptive science (*bibliography*; *geography*). **2** a technique of producing images (*photography*; *radiography*). **3** a style or method of writing, drawing, etc. (*calligraphy*). [from or after French or German *-graphie* from Latin *-graphia* from Greek *-graphia* writing]

gra·ple /'greipəl/ *noun Cdn* (*Nfld*) a small anchor used to moor fishing equipment or small boats. [as GRAPPLE]

grap·nel /'grapnəl/ *noun* **1** a device with iron claws, attached to a rope and used for dragging or grasping. **2** a small anchor with several flukes. [Old French *grapon* from Germanic: compare GRAPE]

grap·pa /'grapə/ *noun* a brandy distilled from the fermented residue of grapes after they have been pressed in winemaking. [Italian, lit. = 'grape stalk']

Grap·pelli /grə'peli/ **Ste·phane** (1908–97), French jazz violinist. With the guitarist Django Reinhardt he formed the Quintette du Hot Club de France (1934–39), becoming famous for his improvisational style of swing; he went on to lead a successful international career.

grap·ple ● *verb* **1** *intransitive* (often foll. by *with*) fight at close quarters or in close combat. **2** *intransitive* (foll. by *with*) try to manage or overcome a difficult problem etc. **3** *transitive* **a** grip with the hands; come to close quarters with. **b** seize with or as with a grapnel; grasp. ● *noun* **1 a** a hold or grip in or as in wrestling. **b** a contest at close quarters. **2** a grapnel. □ **grap·pler** *noun* [Old French *grapil* (n.) from Provençal, diminutive of *grapa* hook (as GRAPNEL)]

grapple yarder *noun* (also **grapple skidder**) a powerful tractor-like vehicle with a large set of claws, used to haul logs to a landing.

grap·pling hook *noun* (also **grap·pling iron**) = GRAPNEL 1.

grap·to·lite /'graptəˌlaɪt/ *noun* an extinct marine invertebrate animal found as a fossil in lower Paleozoic rocks. [Greek *graptos* marked with letters + -LITE]

Gras·mere /'grasmɪːr/ a village in Cumbria, beside a small lake of the same name; pop. (est. 1998) 1,500. It is associated with William and Dorothy Wordsworth, who settled there in 1799.

grasp ● *verb* **1** *transitive* **a** clutch at; seize greedily. **b** hold firmly; grip. **2** *intransitive* (foll. by *at*) try to seize; accept avidly. **3** *transitive* understand or realize (a fact or meaning). ● *noun* **1** a firm hold; a grip. **2** (foll. by *of*) **a** mastery or control (*a grasp of the situation*). **b** a mental hold or understanding (*a grasp of the facts*). □ **grasp at straws** *see* STRAW. **within one's grasp** capable of being grasped, achieved, or comprehended by one. □ **grasp·able** *adjective* **grasp·er** *noun* [Middle English *graspe*, *grapse* perhaps from Old English *græpsan* (unrecorded) from Germanic, related to GROPE: compare Low German *grapsen*]

grasp·ing *adjective* avaricious, greedy. □ **grasp·ing·ly** *adverb*

Grass, Gün·ter Wil·helm (b.1927), German novelist, poet, and dramatist. An outspoken socialist, he drew on his experiences as a youth in Nazi Germany for his picaresque novel *The Tin Drum* (1959). He was awarded the Nobel Prize for literature in 1999.

grass ● *noun* **1 a** vegetation belonging to a group of small plants with green blades that are eaten by cattle, horses, sheep, etc. **b** any species of this. **c** any plant of the family Gramineae (or Poaceae), which includes cereals, reeds, and bamboos. **2** pasture land. **3** grass-covered ground; lawn (*keep off the grass*). **4** *slang* marijuana. **5** *Brit. slang* an informer, esp. a police informer. **6** *Brit.* the earth's surface above a mine; the pithead. ● *verb* **1** *transitive* cover with turf. **2** *Brit. slang* **a** *transitive* betray, esp. to the police. **b** *intransitive* inform the police. □ **not let the grass grow under one's feet** be quick to act or to seize an opportunity. **out to grass 1** out to pasture. **2** in retirement. □ **grass·less** *adjective* **grass·like** *adjective* [Old English *græs* from Germanic, related to GREEN, GROW]

grass carp *noun* a large Chinese freshwater fish, farmed for food in SE Asia and introduced elsewhere to control the growth of vegetation in waterways.

grass·cloth *noun* a linen-like cloth woven from ramie or other strong plant fibres.

grass court *noun* a grass-covered tennis court.

grass·cyc·ling *noun* the practice of leaving grass clippings on a lawn after mowing, so that they fall between the growing blades and act as fertilizer. □ **grass·cycle** *intransitive verb* [blend of GRASS + RECYCLE]

grass dance *noun* a competitive N American Aboriginal men's dance, originating on the Plains, noted for its fluid movements and sliding steps. [originally as young men tramping down the grass to get ready for dancing]

grass hockey *noun Brit. & Cdn* (esp. *BC*) = FIELD HOCKEY.

grass·hop·per *noun* **1** a plant-eating insect of the order Orthoptera, characterized by having legs adapted for jumping, flat-sided heads with large compound eyes, and antennae of various sizes, and the ability of the males to make chirping sounds. **2** a cocktail usu. consisting of cream, crème de cacao, and crème de menthe in equal portions.

grasshopper pie *noun* a frozen dessert consisting of a base of chocolate cookie crumbs and a mint cream or ice cream topping.

grass·land *noun* a large open area covered with grass, e.g. a prairie.

Grass·lands National Park a park in SW Saskatchewan, located on the border with Montana. Established in 1981, the park preserves various species of prairie flora and fauna.

grass of Par·nas·sus *noun* any of several herbaceous plants of the genus *Parnassia*, with white petals striped with green veins.

grass·roots *plural noun* **1** a fundamental level or source. **2** (often *attributive*) ordinary people, esp. as voters; the rank and file of an organization, esp. a political party (*a grassroots movement*).

grass ski *noun* each of a pair of short skis with small wheels or rollers for skiing down grass-covered slopes. □ **grass skiing** *noun*

grass skirt *noun* a skirt made of long grass and leaves fastened to a waistband.

grass snake *noun* **1** *N Amer.* the common green snake, *Opheodrys vernalis*. **2** *Brit.* the common ringed snake, *Natrix natrix*.

grass tree *noun* any tree of the genus *Xanthorrhea*, native to Australia, with a thick dark trunk and a head of grasslike leaves.

grass widow *noun* a person whose spouse is away for a prolonged period. □ **grass widower** *noun* [orig. denoting an unmarried woman with a child, perhaps from the idea of the couple having lain in the grass instead of in bed]

grassy *adjective* (**grass·i·er**, **grass·i·est**) **1** covered with or abounding in grass. **2** resembling grass. □ **grass·i·ness** *noun*

grate[1] *verb* **1** *transitive* reduce to small shreds by rubbing on a serrated surface. **2** *intransitive* (often foll. by *against, on*) rub with a harsh scraping sound. **3** *transitive* utter in a harsh tone. **4** *intransitive* (often foll. by *on*) **a** sound harshly or discordantly. **b** have an irritating effect. **5** *transitive* grind (one's teeth). **6** *intransitive* (of a hinge etc.) creak. [Old French *grater*, ultimately from West Germanic]

grate[2] *noun* **1** = GRATING[2] 1. **2** a frame of metal bars for holding the fuel in the recess of a fireplace etc. **3** the recess of a fireplace or furnace. [Middle English, = grating, from Old French, ultimately from Latin *cratis* hurdle]

grate·ful *adjective* **1** thankful; feeling or showing gratitude (*am grateful to you for helping*). **2** pleasant, acceptable. □ **grate·ful·ly** *adverb* **grate·ful·ness** *noun* [obsolete *grate* (adj.) from Latin *gratus* + -FUL]

grat·er *noun* a device for reducing cheese or other food to small shreds.

Gra·tian /ˈgreiʃən, -ʃiən/ (full name Flavius Gratianus Augustus) (359–83), Roman emperor 367–83. Most of his reign was spent in defence of Gaul; in 379 he appointed Theodosius I as emperor of the Eastern Empire.

grat·i·fy /ˈgratɪˌfaɪ/ *transitive verb* (-**fies**, -**fied**) **1 a** please, delight. **b** please by compliance; assent to the wish of; satisfy. **2** indulge in or yield to (a feeling or desire). □ **grati·fi·ca·tion** *noun* **grati·fi·er** *noun* **grati·fy·ing** *adjective* **grati·fy·ing·ly** *adverb* [French *gratifier* or Latin *gratificari* do a favour to, make a present of, from *gratus* pleasing]

gra·tin /ˈgratɑ̃/ *noun Cooking* **1** a crisp brown crust usu. of bread crumbs or melted cheese. **2** a dish cooked with this (*compare* AU GRATIN).

gra·ti·née /ˈgratiˈneɪ/ *adjective* = AU GRATIN. □ **gra·ti·néed** *adjective*

grat·ing[1] /ˈgreɪtɪŋ/ *adjective* **1** sounding harsh or discordant (*a grating laugh*). **2** having an irritating effect. □ **grat·ing·ly** *adverb*

grat·ing[2] /ˈgreɪtɪŋ/ *noun* **1** a framework of parallel or crossed metal bars. **2** *Optics* a set of parallel wires, lines ruled on glass, etc., for producing spectra by diffraction.

grat·is /ˈgratɪs/ *adverb & adjective* free; without charge. [Latin, contracted ablative pl. of *gratia* favour]

grati·tude /ˈgratɪˌtjuːd, -ˌtʃuːd/ *noun* the feeling of being grateful or the desire to express one's thanks. [French *gratitude* or medieval Latin *gratitudo* from *gratus* thankful]

gra·tuit·ous /grəˈtuːɪtəs, -ˈtjuːɪtəs/ *adjective* **1** uncalled for; unwarranted; lacking good reason (*a gratuitous insult; gratuitous depictions of violence*). **2** given or done free of charge. □ **gra·tuit·ous·ly** *adverb* **gra·tuit·ous·ness** *noun* [Latin *gratuitus* spontaneous: compare *fortuitous*]

gra·tu·ity /grəˈtuːɪti, -ˈtjuːɪti/ *noun* (pl. -**ies**) money given in recognition of services; a tip. [Old French *gratuité* or medieval Latin *gratuitas* gift, from Latin *gratus* grateful]

gra·va·men /grəˈveɪmen/ *noun* (pl. **gra·va·mina** /-mɪnə/) **1** *Law* the essential or most serious part of an accusation; the part that bears most heavily on the accused. **2** a grievance. [Late Latin, = inconvenience, from Latin *gravare* to load from *gravis* heavy]

grave[1] *noun* **1 a** a hole or trench dug in the ground to receive a dead body. **b** the place where someone is buried, often marked by a mound or stone. **2** (prec. by *the*) death. **3** something compared to or regarded as a grave. □ **have one foot in the grave** *see* FOOT. **turn** (or **roll**) **over in one's grave** (of a dead person) react with imagined disgust or repugnance at the actions of those still living (*Dad must be turning over in his grave because of all of this*). [Old English *græf* from West Germanic]

grave[2] ● *adjective* **1 a** serious, weighty, important (*a grave matter*). **b** dignified, solemn, sombre (*a grave look*). **2** extremely serious or threatening (*grave danger*). ● *noun* /grɒv/ = GRAVE ACCENT. □ **grave·ly** *adverb* **grave·ness** *noun* [French *grave* or Latin *gravis* heavy, serious]

grave[3] /greɪv/ *transitive verb* (*past participle* **graven** or **graved**) **1** (foll. by *in, on*) fix indelibly (on one's memory). **2** *archaic* engrave, carve. [Old English *grafan* dig, engrave, from Germanic: compare GROOVE]

grave[4] /greɪv/ *transitive verb* clean (a ship's bottom) by burning off accretions and by tarring. [perhaps French dial. *grave* = Old French *greve* shore (because originally the ship would have been run aground)]

grave[5] /ˈgrɑːveɪ/ *adverb & adjective Music* with slow and solemn movement. [French or Italian, = GRAVE[2]]

grave accent /grɒv/ *noun* a mark (`) placed over a vowel in some languages to denote pronunciation, length, etc., originally indicating low or falling pitch.

grave·dig·ger *noun* a person who digs graves.

grav·el ● *noun* **1 a** a mixture of coarse sand and small water-worn or pounded stones, used for paths and roads and as an aggregate. **b** *Geol.* a stratum of this. **2** *Med.* aggregations of crystals formed in the urinary tract. ● *transitive verb* (**grav·elled**, **grav·el·ling**; *US* **grav·eled**, **grav·el·ing**) lay or strew with gravel. [Old French *gravel(e)* diminutive of *grave* (as GRAVE[4])]

gravel bar *noun* a long narrow accumulation of gravel in a river, the top of which is just above or below the water surface.

grav·el·ly *adjective* **1** of or like gravel. **2** having or containing gravel. **3** (of a voice) deep and rough-sounding.

gravel pit *noun* an excavation from which gravel is obtained.

grave marker *noun* a usu. inscribed stone, plaque, etc. marking a grave.

grav·en *past participle of* GRAVE[3].

Grav·en·hurst /ˈgreɪvənˌhɜrst/ a town in south central Ontario, about 35 km north of Orillia; pop. (2001) 10,899. [the name of a literary place in W. Irving's novel *Bracebridge Hall*]

graven image *noun* an idol.

Grav·en·stein /ˈgravənˌstiːn/ *noun* a medium-sized, red, cooking and eating apple streaked with yellow. [German name for *Graasten*, a village in Denmark (formerly in Schleswig-Holstein, Germany)]

grav·er *noun* an engraving tool; a burin.

Graves[1], **Rob·ert Ranke** (1895–1985), English poet, novelist, and critic. His writing reflects his interest in classics and mythology, and includes autobiography (*Good-bye to All That*, 1929, recounting his experiences in the First World War), historical fiction (*I, Claudius*, 1934; *Claudius the God*, 1934), and non-fiction (*The White Goddess*, 1948).

Graves[2] /grɒv/ *noun* a light usu. white wine from Graves in France.

Graves' disease /greɪvz/ *noun* exophthalmic goitre with characteristic swelling of the neck and protrusion of the eyes, resulting from an overactive thyroid gland. [R. J. *Graves*, Irish physician d.1853]

grave·side *noun* the ground at the edge of a grave.

grave·site *noun N Amer.* the location of a grave.

grave·stone *noun* = TOMBSTONE.

grave·yard *noun* **1** a cemetery, esp. one located near a church. **2** *informal* = GRAVEYARD SHIFT. **3** a place in which obsolete or derelict objects are stored (*an appliance graveyard*).

uː mood   ai my   əi pipe   au brown   ʌu house   ei day   ɔi boy   ã franglais   ã Canadien   ɔ̃ Brayon   (*see over for consonants*)

graveyard shift *noun* esp. *N Amer.* **1** a work shift beginning around midnight and lasting until morning. **2** the workers on duty during this period.

grav·id /ˈɡravɪd/ *adjective literary* or *Zool.* pregnant. [Latin *gravidus* from *gravis* heavy]

grav·im·eter /ɡrəˈvɪmɪtər/ *noun* an instrument for measuring the difference in the force of gravity from one place to another. [French *gravimètre* from Latin *gravis* heavy]

grav·i·met·ric /ˌɡravɪˈmetrɪk/ *adjective* **1** of or relating to the measurement of weight. **2** denoting chemical analysis based on weighing reagents and products.

grav·im·etry /ɡrəˈvɪmɪtri/ *noun* the measurement of weight.

grav·ing dock *noun* = DRY DOCK.

grav·itas /ˈɡravɪˌtas/ *noun* solemn demeanour; seriousness. [Latin from *gravis* serious]

grav·i·tate *verb* **1** *intransitive* (foll. by *to*, *towards*) move or be attracted to some source of influence. **2** *transitive & intransitive* **a** move or tend by force of gravity towards. **b** sink by or as if by gravity. [modern Latin *gravitare* GRAVITAS]

gravi·ta·tion *noun Physics* **1** a force of attraction between any particle of matter in the universe and any other. **2** the effect of this, esp. the falling of bodies to the earth. **3** a natural tendency or movement towards a person or thing. □ **gravi·ta·tion·al** *adjective* **gravi·ta·tion·al·ly** *adverb*

gravitational constant *noun* the constant in Newton's law of gravitation relating gravity to the masses and separation of particles. Symbol: **G**.

gravitational field *noun* the region of space surrounding a body in which another body experiences a force of attraction.

gravitational lens *noun Astronomy* a region of space containing a massive body whose gravitational field acts like a lens in refracting electromagnetic radiation. □ **gravitational lensing** *noun*

gravitational wave *noun* (also called **gravity wave**) a wave propagated though a gravitational field caused by an accelerating mass.

gravi·ton /ˈɡravɪtɒn/ *noun Physics* a hypothetical quantum of gravitational energy. [GRAVITY + -ON]

grav·ity *noun* **1 a** the force that attracts a body towards the centre of the earth or towards any other physical body having mass. **b** the degree of intensity of this measured by acceleration. **c** gravitational force. **d** (usu. *attributive*) operating or functioning by the effect of gravity (*gravity bin*). **2** the property of having weight. **3 a** importance, seriousness; the quality of being grave. **b** solemnity, sobriety; serious demeanour. [French *gravité* or Latin *gravitas* from *gravis* heavy]

gravity box *noun* (also **gravity wagon**) a farm wagon for hauling grain etc., having a bottom that is sloped towards an opening on one side so that the contents may be unloaded by gravity.

gravity feed *noun* the supply of material by its fall under gravity. □ **gravity-fed** *adjective*

grav·lax /ˈɡravlaks/ *noun* (also **grav·ad·lax** /ˈɡravədlaks/) a Scandinavian dish of dry-cured salmon marinated in salt, sugar, and dill etc. [Swedish *gravlax*, from *grav* 'trench' + *lax* 'salmon', from the former practice of marinating the salmon in a hole in the ground]

Grav·ol /ˈɡravɒl/ *noun Cdn proprietary* = DIMENHYDRINATE.

grav·ure /ɡrəˈvjʊr/ *noun* = PHOTOGRAVURE. [abbreviation]

gravy *noun* (pl. **-vies**) **1 a** the juices and fat from cooked meat. **b** a dressing or sauce for food, made from these or from other materials, e.g. stock. **2** *slang* **a** money easily acquired. **b** an unexpected bonus. [Middle English, perhaps from a misreading as *gravé* of Old French *grané*, prob. from *grain* spice: see GRAIN]

gravy boat *noun* a long, low jug used for serving gravy.

gravy browning *noun* = BROWNING.

gravy train *noun slang* a source of easy financial benefit.

Gray ▸ **1 Asa** (1810–88), US botanist, whose many works helped to popularize the study of botany, and to expound, as well as criticize, Darwin's evolutionary theory. **2 James Henry** (1906–1998), Canadian popular historian. His works include *The Winter Years* (1966), an autobiographical account of the Depression on the Prairies, *A Brand of its Own* (1985), and *Talk to My Lawyer* (1987). **3 John Ham·il·ton** (1811–87), Canadian politician, premier of PEI 1863–4, Father of Confederation. He attended the Charlottetown and Quebec conferences on Confederation, which was rejected by the province until 1873. **4 John Ham·il·ton** (1814–89), Bermudan-born Canadian politician, premier of New Brunswick 1856–7, Father of Confederation.

He attended the Charlottetown and Quebec conferences as an advocate of Confederation. **5 Thom·as** (1716–71), English poet. He is best known for the 'Elegy Written in a Country Church-Yard' (1751) and the two Pindaric odes, 'The Bard' (1757) and 'The Progress of Poesy' (1757), often considered precursors of Romanticism.

gray¹ *var.* of GREY.

gray² *noun Physics* the SI unit of the absorbed dose of ionizing radiation, corresponding to one joule per kilogram. Abbr.: **Gy**. [L. H. Gray, English radiobiologist d.1965]

gray·beard *var.* of GREYBEARD.

gray·ling *noun* any silver-grey freshwater fish of the genus *Thymallus*, with a long high dorsal fin. [gray var. of GREY + -LING²]

gray·wacke *var.* of GREYWACKE.

Graz /ɡrɑːts/ a city in S Austria, on the Mur River, capital of the state of Styria; pop. (2001) 226,400.

graze¹ *verb* **1** *intransitive* (of cattle, sheep, etc.) eat growing grass. **2** *transitive* **a** feed (cattle etc.) on growing grass. **b** feed on (grass). **3** *intransitive informal* **a** eat snacks or small meals throughout the day. **b** casually sample something, esp. food on a store shelf. **c** flick rapidly between television channels. □ **graz·er** *noun* [Old English *grasian* from *græs* GRASS]

graze² ● *verb* **1** *transitive* rub or scrape (a part of the body, esp. the skin) so as to break the surface without causing bleeding. **2 a** *transitive* touch lightly in passing. **b** *intransitive* (foll. by *against*, *along*, etc.) move with a light passing contact. ● *noun* a superficial wound; a scrape. [perhaps a specific use of GRAZE¹, as if 'take off the grass close to the ground' (of a shot etc.)]

gra·zier /ˈɡreɪʒər/ *noun* esp. *Brit.* a person who feeds cattle for market.

graz·ing *noun* **1** in senses of GRAZE¹, ². **2** grassland suitable for pasturage.

GRE *abbreviation* Graduate Record Examination.

grease ● *noun* **1** oily or fatty matter esp. in a semi-solid state and as a lubricant in engines etc. **2** the melted fat of a dead animal. **3** oily matter in unprocessed wool. ● *transitive verb* **1** smear or lubricate with grease. **2** smear (a cookie sheet, baking pan, etc.) with butter, margarine, shortening, etc. before using. □ **grease the palm of** *informal* bribe. **like greased lightning** *informal* very fast. □ **grease·less** *adjective* [Old French *graisse*, ultimately from Latin *crassus* (adj.) fat]

grease·ball *noun N Amer. slang* a greasy or slimy person.

grease gun *noun* a device for forcing grease into the parts of a machine.

grease monkey *noun slang* a mechanic.

grease·paint *noun* a waxy composition used as makeup for theatrical performers.

grease pencil *noun* a pencil made of grease coloured with a pigment, used esp. for marking glossy surfaces.

grease·proof *adjective* (esp. of paper) impervious to the penetration of grease.

greas·er *noun* **1** a person or thing that greases an engine etc., esp. on a ship. **2** *slang* a tough youth, esp. male, with the greased hair characteristic of members of motorcycle gangs of the 1950s. **3** *US slang offensive* a Mexican or Spanish-American. **4** *Cdn & Brit. slang* a gentle landing of an aircraft.

grease trail *noun Cdn* any of the forest paths connecting the Pacific coast with the interior, used for centuries as trade routes. [named by European settlers after eulachon oil, one of the most important commodities traded]

grease·wood *noun* any of various resinous shrubs of the goosefoot family, esp. *Sarcobatus vermiculatus*, which grow in dry alkaline valleys in western N America.

greasy *adjective* (**greas·i·er**, **greas·i·est**) **1 a** of or like grease. **b** smeared or covered with grease. **c** containing or having too much grease. **2 a** slippery. **b** (of a person or manner) unpleasantly unctuous, smarmy. □ **greas·i·ly** *adverb* **greas·i·ness** *noun*

greasy pole *noun informal* **1** a pole smeared with grease and difficult to climb. **2** a difficult pathway to success.

greasy spoon *noun* esp. *N Amer. informal* a cheap diner serving greasy food.

great ● *adjective* **1 a** of a size, amount, extent, or intensity considerably above the normal or average; big (*a great boulder*; *take great care*; *lived to a great age*). **b** also with implied surprise, admiration, contempt, etc., esp. in exclamations (*great stuff!*; *look at that great wasp!*). **c** reinforcing other words denoting size, quantity, etc. (*a great big hole*;

Consonants: **b** *but* **d** *dog* **f** *few* **g** *get* **h** *her* **j** *yes* **k** *cat* **l** *leg* **m** *man* **n** *no* **p** *pen* **r** *red* **s** *sit*

a great many). **2** important, pre-eminent; worthy or most worthy of consideration (*the great thing is not to get caught*). **3** grand, imposing (*a great occasion; the great hall*). **4 a** (esp. of a public or historic figure) distinguished; prominent. **b** (**the Great**) as a title denoting the most important of the name (*Alfred the Great*). **5 a** (of a person) remarkable in ability, character, achievement, etc. (*a great thinker*). **b** (of a thing) outstanding of its kind (*the Great Lakes*). **6** (foll. by *at, on*) competent, skilled, well-informed. **7** fully deserving the name of; doing a thing habitually or extensively (*a great believer in tolerance; not a great one for travelling*). **8** (also **greater**) the larger of the name, species, etc. (*great auk; greater celandine*). **9** (**Greater**) (of a city etc.) including adjacent urban areas (*Greater Toronto*). **10** *informal* very enjoyable or satisfactory; attractive, fine (*had a great time; it would be great if we won*). **11** (in *combination*) (in names of family relationships) denoting one degree further removed upwards or downwards (*great-uncle; great-great-grandmother*). ● *noun* **1** a great or outstanding person or thing. **2** (in *pl.*) (**Greats**) *Brit. informal* (at Oxford University) an honours course or final examinations in classics and philosophy. ● *adverb informal* excellently, well, successfully. ● *interjection* **1** used to express admiration, approval, appreciation, etc. (*Great! Thanks for doing them for me!*). **2** *ironic* used to express dismay, disappointment, etc. (*Great! The tire's flat again!*). □ **great and small** all classes or types. (**the**) **great and** (**the**) **good** often *ironic* distinguished and worthy people. **to a great extent** largely. □ **great·ness** *noun* [Old English *grēat* from West Germanic]

great ape *noun* any of the large apes of the family Pongidae, closely related to humans, including the gorilla, orangutan, and chimpanzee.

great auk *noun* an extinct flightless auk, *Pinguinus impennis*, of the N Atlantic.

great-aunt *noun* a parent's aunt.

Great Australian Bight a wide bay on the south coast of Australia, part of the S Indian Ocean.

Great Barrier Reef a coral reef in the W Pacific, off the coast of Queensland, Australia. It extends for about 2 000 km (1,250 miles), roughly parallel to the coast, and is the largest coral reef in the world.

Great Basin an arid region of the western US between the Sierra Nevada and the Rocky Mountains, including most of Nevada and parts of the adjacent states.

Great Bear *noun* = BIG DIPPER.

Great Bear Lake a large lake in the northeastern NWT, situated between the Mackenzie and Coppermine rivers, its northern arm lying over the Arctic Circle. With an area of 31 328 sq. km, it is the largest lake lying wholly within Canadian boundaries and the fourth largest in N America. [the name of the river, so called with reference to the bears in the area]

great blue heron *noun* a heron, *Ardea herodias*, widespread throughout N America, predominantly greyish blue but having a white head with a broad black stripe on either side.

Great Britain England, Wales, and Scotland considered as a unit (*see also* BRITAIN); the name is also often used loosely to refer to the United Kingdom (*see also* UNITED KINGDOM).

great circle *noun* a circle on the surface of a sphere whose plane passes through the sphere's centre.

Great Coalition *noun Cdn hist.* the coalition government formed in the Province of Canada in 1864 to pursue the federation of British North America, prominent members of which included John A. Macdonald, George Brown, and George-Étienne Cartier.

great·coat *noun* a long heavy overcoat.

Great Dane *noun* a breed of very large, powerful short-haired dog.

great deal *noun see* DEAL[1] *noun* 1.

Great Depression *noun* = DEPRESSION 2b.

Great Dismal Swamp (also **Dismal Swamp**) an area of swampland in SE Virginia and NE North Carolina.

Great Divide[1] **1** see CONTINENTAL DIVIDE. **2** see GREAT DIVIDING RANGE.

Great Divide[2] *noun* (prec. by *the*) **1** the boundary between life and death. **2** (usu. **great divide**) *jocular* or *literary* the boundary between two contrasting conditions, cultures, etc.

Great Dividing Range (also **Great Divide**) a mountain system in E Australia. Curving roughly parallel to the coast, it extends from E Victoria to N Queensland.

Greater Antilles see ANTILLES.

Greater Bairam *noun see* BAIRAM.

Greater London a metropolitan area comprising central London and the surrounding regions. It is divided administratively into the City of London, thirteen inner London boroughs, and twenty outer London boroughs.

Greater Manchester a former metropolitan county of NW England including the city of Manchester and adjacent areas.

Greater Napanee a town in E Ontario, about 35 km west of Kingston, incorporating the former town of Napanee and surrounding townships; pop. (2001) 15,132.

greater shearwater *noun* an Atlantic white-bellied shearwater, *Puffinus gravis*, common in summer in the Strait of Belle Isle and along the Atlantic coast.

Greater Sudbury a city in N central Ontario, incorporating the former cities of Sudbury and Valley City and the former towns of Nickel Centre, Capreol, Onaping Falls, Rayside-Balfour, and Walden; pop. (2001) 155,219.

Greater Sunda Islands see SUNDA ISLANDS.

Greater Toronto Area the heavily-populated urban area surrounding and including the city of Toronto, extending from Burlington in the west to Oshawa in the east, and as far north as Lake Simcoe.

greatest hits *plural noun* a compilation of the most popular pieces in the repertoire of a composer, singer, band, or genre (*Arnold Schoenberg's greatest hits*).

Great Exhibition the first international exhibition of the products of industry, held in the Crystal Palace in London in 1851.

Great Famine *noun* the potato famine in Ireland 1845–49.

Great Fire see FIRE OF LONDON.

Great Glen (also called **Glen More**) a valley in Scotland, extending from the Moray Firth southwest to Loch Linnhe, and containing Loch Ness.

great-grand·child *noun* a grandchild's son or daughter.

great-grand·daugh·ter *noun* a grandchild's daughter.

great-grand·fath·er *noun* a grandparent's father.

great-grand·moth·er *noun* a grandparent's mother.

great-grand·par·ent *noun* a grandparent's parent.

great-grand·son *noun* a grandchild's son.

great grey owl *noun* a very large grey hornless owl, *Strix nebulosa*, of northern coniferous forests of N America and Eurasia, having a large facial disc, yellow eyes, and long tail.

Great Grims·by see GRIMSBY.

great-hearted *adjective* magnanimous; having a noble or generous mind. □ **great-hearted·ness** *noun*

great horned owl *noun* a large powerful N American owl, *Bubo virginianus*, with prominent ear tufts.

Great Indian Desert an alternative name for the THAR DESERT.

Great Lakes a group of five large interconnected lakes in central N America, consisting of Lakes Superior, Michigan, Huron, Erie, and Ontario. With the exception of Lake Michigan, which is wholly within the US, they lie on the Canada–US border. They constitute the largest area of freshwater in the world. Connected to the Atlantic Ocean by the St. Lawrence Seaway, the Great Lakes form an important commercial waterway.

Great Lakes-St. Law·rence Low·lands a physiographic region of SE Canada, consisting of south central and SE Ontario and Quebec, including Manitoulin and Anticosti islands, as well as the west coast of the island of Newfoundland.

Great Leap Forward an unsuccessful attempt made under Mao Zedong in China 1958–60 to hasten the process of industrialization and improve agricultural production by reorganizing the population into large rural collectives and adopting labour-intensive industrial methods.

great·ly *adverb* by a considerable amount; much (*greatly admired; greatly superior*).

Great Mother see MOTHER GODDESS.

great-nephew *noun* a nephew's or niece's son.

great-niece *noun* a nephew's or niece's daughter.

great northern diver *noun* a diving seabird, *Gavia immer*, of the northern hemisphere; the common loon.

Great Northern Peninsula see NORTHERN PENINSULA.

Great Northern War a conflict 1700–21 in which Russia, Denmark, and Poland-Saxony opposed Sweden. As a result of the war, Sweden lost imperial possessions in central Europe, and Russia under Peter the Great became a major power in the Baltic.

Great Ouse River see OUSE RIVER 1.

---

t top   v voice   w we   z zoo   ʃ she   ʒ vision   θ thin   ð this   ŋ ring   x loch   tʃ chip   dʒ jar   (*see over for vowels*)

great outdoors *noun* (prec. by *the*) the open air.

Great Plague a serious outbreak of bubonic plague in England, 1665-6, in which about one fifth of the population of London died before the Fire of London destroyed much of the poor housing in which the disease had flourished (*see also* PLAGUE 1).

Great Plains a vast area of plains to the east of the Rocky Mountains in N America, extending from the valleys of the Mackenzie River in Canada to S Texas.

Great Rebellion the Royalist name for the English Civil War.

Great Rift Valley a large system of rift valleys running for some 5 000 km (3,000 miles) from the Jordan valley in Syria, along the Red Sea into Ethiopia, and through Kenya, Tanzania, and Malawi into Mozambique; it is marked by a chain of lakes and a series of volcanoes, including Mount Kilimanjaro.

great room *noun* N Amer. a spacious multi-purpose open concept living area in a house.

Great Russian ● *noun* **1** a Russian. **2** the Russian language. ● *adjective* Russian.

Great Salt Lake a salt lake in N Utah, near Salt Lake City. With an area of approximately 4 400 sq. km (1,700 miles), it is the largest salt lake in N America.

Great Sand Sea an area of desert in NE Africa, on the border between Libya and Egypt.

Great Sandy Desert 1 a large tract of desert in north central Western Australia. **2** an alternative name for the RUBʻ AL KHALI.

Great Schism 1 the breach between the Eastern and the Western Churches, traditionally dated to 1054, when, in an attempt to assert the primacy of the papacy, Cardinal Humbert excommunicated the patriarch of Constantinople and the latter excommunicated the Western legates. **2** the period 1378–1417, when the Western Church was divided by the creation of antipopes. The Council of Constance ended the schism by the election of Martin V in 1417.

Great Seal *noun* the seal used for the authentication of state documents of the highest importance.

Great Slave Lake a large lake in the southern NWT, about 100 km north of the border with Alberta. At a depth of 615 m (2,015 ft.), it is the deepest lake in N America. [SLAVEY]

Great Society *noun* a reform program instigated in the United States in the 1960s by President Lyndon B. Johnson, involving federal legislation aiming to improve education, urban life, and health care, eliminate poverty and racial discrimination, and address environmental issues.

Great Spirit the Creator in N American Aboriginal spirituality.

Great Terror *noun see* TERROR 4.

great toe *noun* = BIG TOE.

Great Trek the northward migration 1835–7 of large numbers of Boers, discontented with British rule in the Cape, to the areas where they eventually founded the Transvaal Republic and the Orange Free State.

great-uncle *noun* a parent's uncle.

great unwashed *plural noun informal* (prec. by *the*) the mass or multitude of ordinary people.

Great Victoria Desert a desert region of Australia, which straddles the boundary between Western Australia and South Australia.

Great Vowel Shift *noun* a series of changes between medieval and modern English affecting the long vowels of the standard language.

Great Wall of China a defensive wall in northern China, extending some 2400 km (1,500 miles) from Kansu province to the Yellow Sea north of Peking. Dating from *c.*210 BC, it was rebuilt in medieval times largely against the Mongols; the present wall dates from the Ming dynasty. The wall also served as a means of communication: for most of its length it was wide enough to allow five horses to travel abreast.

Great War (prec. by *the*) = FIRST WORLD WAR.

Great Whale River a river in NW Quebec, rising from Lac Bienville in the north central part of the province and flowing westward 724 km to Hudson Bay at Kuujjuarapik, a village on the bay's southeastern shore.

great white combine *noun* Cdn (Sask.) slang hail.

great white hope *noun* = WHITE HOPE.

Great White North *noun* Cdn jocular (prec. by *the*) Canada.

great white shark *noun* a large and dangerous greyish shark, *Carcharadon carcharias*, found in the temperate and tropical regions of all oceans.

Great White Way a nickname for BROADWAY.

Great Zimbabwe a complex of stone ruins in a fertile valley in Zimbabwe, about 270 km (175 miles) south of Harare, discovered by Europeans in 1868. [Shona *dzimbabwe* walled grave]

greave /griːv/ *noun* (usu. in *pl.*) a piece of armour for the shin. [Old French *greve* shin, greave, of unknown origin]

grebe /griːb/ *noun* any diving bird of the family Podicipedidae, with a long neck, lobed toes, and almost no tail. [French *grèbe*, of unknown origin]

Gre·cian /ˈɡriːʃən/ *adjective* (of architecture or beauty) following Greek models or ideals. [Old French *grecien* or medieval Latin *graecianus* (unrecorded) from Latin *Graecia* Greece]

Gre·cism *var. of* GRAECISM.

Gre·cize *var. of* GRAECIZE.

Greco- /ˈɡriːkoː/ *combining form* (also **Graeco-**) Greek; Greek and. [Latin *Graecus* GREEK]

Greco, El see EL GRECO.

Greco-Roman *adjective* (also **Graeco-Roman**) **1** of or relating to the Greeks and Romans. **2** *Wrestling* denoting a style attacking only the upper part of the body.

Greece a country in SE Europe; pop. (est. 2002) 10,645,343; capital, Athens. Greece consists of a mountainous peninsula bounded by the Ionian, Mediterranean, and Aegean Seas, and many outlying islands, of which the largest are Crete, Euboea, Lesbos, Chios and Rhodes.

greed *noun* an excessive desire, esp. for wealth or food. [back-formation from GREEDY]

greed·head *noun* slang an avaricious person.

greedy *adjective* (**greed·i·er**, **greed·i·est**) **1** wanting wealth to excess. **2** having or showing an excessive appetite for food or drink. **3** (foll. by *for*, or *to* + infin.) very keen or eager; needing intensely (*greedy for affection*; *greedy to learn*). □ **greed·i·ly** *adverb* **greed·i·ness** *noun* [Old English *grǣdig* from Germanic]

Greek ● *noun* **1 a** a native or national of modern Greece; a person of Greek descent. **b** a native or citizen of any of the ancient states of Greece; a member of the Greek people. **2** the Indo-European language of Greece. ● *adjective* of Greece or its people or language; Hellenic. □ **Greek to me** *informal* incomprehensible to me. □ **Greek·ness** *noun* [Old English *Grēcas* (pl.) from Germanic from Latin *Graecus* from Greek *Graikoi*, the prehistoric name of the Hellenes (in Aristotle)]

Greek cross *noun* a cross with four equal arms.

Greek fire *noun* hist. a combustible composition for igniting enemy ships etc.

Greek key *noun* a pattern of interlocking right-angled spirals.

Greek Orthodox Church *noun* (also **Greek Church**) the national Church of Greece (see also ORTHODOX CHURCH).

Greek salad *noun* a salad consisting of lettuce, tomatoes, cucumbers, olives, feta cheese, and olive oil and vinegar dressing.

Gree·ley, Hor·ace (1811–72), US journalist and editor. He founded and edited the *New York Tribune* (1841–72), which was notable for its anti-slavery editorials.

green ● *adjective* **1** of the colour between blue and yellow in the spectrum; coloured like grass, emeralds, etc. **2 a** covered with leaves or grass. **b** mild and without snow (*a green Christmas*). **3** (of fruit etc. or wood) unripe or unseasoned. **4 a** not dried, smoked, or tanned. **b** Cdn (Nfld) (of cod) split and salted, but not dried. **5** inexperienced, naive, gullible. **6 a** (of the complexion) pale, sickly-hued. **b** jealous, envious. **7** young, flourishing. **8** not withered or worn out (*a green old age*). **9** vegetable (*green salad*). **10 a** (also **Green**) concerned with or supporting protection of the environment as a political principle. **b** (of a consumer product) not harmful to the environment in its manufacture or use. **11** *archaic* fresh; not healed (*a green wound*). ● *noun* **1** a green colour or pigment. **2** green clothes or material (*dressed in green*). **3 a** a piece of public or common grassy land (*village green*). **b** a grassy area used for a special purpose (*putting green*; *bowling green*). **c** Golf a putting green. **4** (in *pl.*) green vegetables. **5** vigour, youth, virility (*in the green*). **6** a green light. **7 a** a green ball, piece, etc., in a game or sport. **b** Cdn (usu. in *pl.*) a green seat in a hockey arena etc. **8** (also **Green**) a member or supporter of an environmentalist group or party. **9** *slang* low-grade marijuana. **10** *slang* money. **11** green foliage or growing plants. ● *transitive & intransitive verb* make or become green. □ **green up** (of vegetation or a landscape etc.) become green, as in the spring. **too green to burn** Cdn (Nfld) extremely gullible. □ **green·ish** *adjective* **green·ly** *adverb* **green·ness** *noun* [Old English *grēne* (adj. & n.), *grēnian* (v.), from Germanic, related to GROW]

green alder *noun* a large shrub, *Alnus viridis crispa*, of northern Canada and the Maritime provinces.

green alga *noun* an alga with esp. two types of chlorophyll, cellulose cell walls, and starch grains.

green ash *noun* a variety of the ash *Fraxinus pennsylvanica*, common in the Prairie provinces.

Green·away ▸ 1 Cath·er·ine ('Kate') (1846–1901), English artist, who is known esp. for her illustrations of children's books such as *Under the Windows* (1879) and *Mother Goose* (1881). **2 Peter** (b.1942), English film director, whose films include *A Zed and Two Noughts* (1985), *The Draughtsman's Contract* (1982), and *The Cook, the Thief, his Wife, and her Lover* (1990).

green·back *noun* **1 a** a US legal tender note. **b** the US dollar. **2** any of various green-backed animals.

green bean *noun* **1** any bean plant, esp. the French bean *Phaseolus vulgaris*, grown for its edible young pods rather than for its seeds. **2** the pod of such a plant.

green·belt *noun* an area of open land around a city, the development of which is restricted.

Green Beret *noun informal* an American or British commando.

green bin *noun* a green plastic bin used for curbside collection of recyclable or compostable materials, esp. (in Canada) one for organic waste.

green·brier *noun* (also **green·briar**) a climbing vine of the genus *Smilax* of the lily family, with dark blue berries. *Also called* CATBRIER.

green card *noun* US a permit allowing a foreign national to live and work permanently in the US.

green·chain *noun* Forestry an endless conveyor taking trimmed lumber from the saws to a sorting area. [see GREEN *adjective* 3]

green chamber *noun* Cdn the House of Commons or a provincial legislature.

green Christmas *noun* Christmas day without snow (in places where snow might be expected).

green dragon *noun* a plant of the arum family, *Arisaema dracontium*, of eastern N America, with a long, slender spadix.

Greene ▸ 1 (Henry) Gra·ham (1904–91), English novelist. He converted to Roman Catholicism in 1926, and the moral paradoxes of his faith underlie much of his work, which includes *Brighton Rock* (1938), *The Power and the Glory* (1940), and *Travels with My Aunt* (1969). **2 Lorne (Hyman)** (1915–87), Canadian actor. He was the chief news announcer for CBC Radio (1939–42), and is best known for his portrayal of Ben Cartwright in the popular television program 'Bonanza' (1959–72), and for his television series 'Lorne Greene's New Wilderness'. **3 Nancy** (b.1943), Canadian alpine skier. An outstanding skier, she won the World Cup in 1967, and at the Winter Olympics in 1968 she won a gold and a silver medal.

green earth *noun* a hydrous silicate of potassium, iron, and other metals.

green·ery *noun* green foliage or growing plants.

green-eyed *adjective* **1** having green eyes. **2** jealous.

green-eyed monster *noun* (prec. by *the*) *informal* jealousy.

green fee *noun* Golf a charge for playing one round on a course.

green feed *noun* Cdn, Austral., & NZ forage grown to be fed fresh to livestock.

green·field *noun* (attributive) esp. Brit. (of a site, in terms of its potential development) having no previous building development on it.

Green·field Park a former city in south central Quebec, located on the St. Lawrence, opposite Montreal, now part of Longueuil; pop. (2001) 16,978. [origin uncertain: perhaps a reference to the area's grassy park-like landscape]

green·finch *noun* a finch, *Carduelis chloris*, with green and yellow plumage, native to Europe but a popular cage bird.

green fingers *plural noun* esp. Brit. = GREEN THUMB. □ **green-fingered** *adjective*

green·fly *noun* (pl. **-flies**) esp. Brit. a green aphid.

green·gage *noun* a roundish green fine-flavoured variety of plum. [Sir W. *Gage* d.1727]

green·grocer /ˈɡriːnˌɡroʊsər, -ʃər/ *noun* a retailer of fruit and vegetables.

green·grocery /ˈɡriːnˌɡroʊsəri, -ʃri, -sri/ *noun* (pl. **-ies**) **1** the business of a greengrocer. **2** goods sold by a greengrocer.

green·heart *noun* **1** any of several tropical American trees, esp. *Ocotea rodiaei*. **2** the hard greenish wood of one of these.

green·horn *noun* an inexperienced or foolish person; a new recruit.

green hornet *noun* Cdn slang (in Ottawa and Toronto) a city employee who issues parking tickets. [in reference to their green uniforms and their 'stinging' of parking offenders]

green·house *noun* a transparent glass or plastic building for rearing or hastening the growth of plants.

greenhouse effect *noun* the heating of the earth's surface and lower atmosphere attributed to an increase in carbon dioxide and other gases, which are more transparent to incoming solar radiation than to reflected radiation from the earth.

greenhouse gas *noun* any of various gases, esp. carbon dioxide, that contribute to the greenhouse effect.

green·ie *noun informal* a person concerned about environmental issues.

green·ing¹ *noun* **1** the process or result of making something green, or becoming green. **2** the planting of trees etc. in urban or desert areas. **3** the process of becoming or making aware of or sensitive to ecological issues.

green·ing² *noun* **1** a variety of apple that is green when ripe. **2** (**Greening**) = RHODE ISLAND GREENING. [prob. from Middle Dutch *groeninc* (as GREEN)]

green·keep·er *noun* = GREENSKEEPER.

Green·land a large island lying to the northeast of N America and mostly within the Arctic Circle; pop. (est. 2002) 56,376; capital, Nuuk (Godthåb). Only five per cent of Greenland is habitable; the population is largely Inupiat. □ **Green·land·er** *noun*

Greenland halibut *noun* an edible halibut, *Reinhardtius hippoglossoides*, with a black or dark brown upper side, which is found in cold deep waters off Greenland, Baffin Island, Labrador, and Newfoundland. *Also called* TURBOT.

Green·land·ic *noun* a dialect of Inuit which is one of the official languages of Denmark.

green light *noun* **1** a signal to proceed on a road, railway, etc. **2** *informal* permission to go ahead with a project. □ **green-light** *transitive verb*

green·ling *noun* any of several fish of the family Hexagrammidae of the N Pacific and adjacent Arctic oceans, related to the sculpins. [GREEN + LING¹]

green·mail *noun* Stock Exch. the practice of buying enough shares in a company to threaten a takeover, thereby forcing the owners to buy them back at a higher price in order to retain control of the business. □ **green·mail·er** *noun* [GREEN + BLACKMAIL]

green manure *noun* growing plants plowed into the soil as fertilizer.

green monkey *noun* a common African guenon, *Cercopithecus aethiops*, with greenish-brown upper parts and a black face.

green olive *noun* a cured unripe olive.

green onion *noun* N Amer. an onion taken from the ground before the bulb has formed, with slender green hollow leaves.

Green Paper *noun* Cdn & Brit. a preliminary report of Government proposals, for discussion.

Green·peace an international organization that campaigns actively but non-violently for conservation of the environment and the preservation of endangered species. It was first active in BC in 1971.

green pepper *noun* the unripe fruit of *Capsicum annuum*.

green revolution *noun* **1** an increase in crop production, esp. in developing countries, achieved by using artificial fertilizers, pesticides, and high-yield crop varieties. **2** a rise of environmental concern in industrialized countries.

green roof *noun* a roof (usu. a flat roof of an office building or apartment block) specially designed to include a thin layer of soil for growing plants, to increase insulation and decrease heat absorption.

green room *noun* a room in a theatre, studio, etc. in which performers may relax when they are not on stage, on the air, etc.

green·sand *noun* **1** a greenish kind of sandstone, often imperfectly cemented. **2** a stratum largely formed of this sandstone.

greens fee *noun* N Amer. var. of GREEN FEE.

greens·keep·er *noun* esp. N Amer. the keeper of a golf course.

green snake *noun* a harmless snake of eastern and central North America with a green back and white or yellowish underparts.

green space *noun* **1** an area of grass, trees, or other vegetation set apart for recreational or aesthetic purposes in an otherwise urban environment. **2** these collectively.

green-stick fracture *noun* a bone fracture, esp. in children, in which one side of the bone is broken and one only bent.

Green·stone a town in NW Ontario, extending eastward from the eastern shore of Lake Nipigon, incorporating the former towns of Geraldton and Longlac; pop. (2001) 5,662.

green·stone *noun* **1** any dark green igneous rock, esp. containing chlorite, epidote, hornblende, etc. **2** a variety of jade found in New Zealand.

green·sward /ˈɡriːnswɔːd/ *noun* **1** grassy turf. **2** an expanse of this.

green tea *noun* tea made from steam-dried, not fermented, leaves.

green thumb *noun informal esp. N Amer.* a talent for gardening. □ **green-thumbed** *adjective* **green-thumber** *noun*

green turtle *noun* a green-shelled sea turtle, *Chelonia mydas*, highly regarded as food.

green·wash ● *transitive & intransitive verb* attempt to diminish the perceived extent of environmental damage caused by (an accident etc. or those responsible for it). ● *noun* an act or instance of greenwashing (*applied a greenwash to their account of the spill*). [from GREEN after WHITEWASH]

green·way *noun esp. N Amer.* an undeveloped strip of land in an urban area, usu. including a trail and following a natural feature such as a river or ridge.

green·weed *noun see* DYER'S GREENWEED.

Green·wich Mean Time /ˈɡrenɪtʃ/ *noun* the local time on the 0° meridian, used as an international basis of time reckoning. Abbr.: **GMT**. [*Greenwich* in London, former site of the Royal Observatory]

Green·wich meridian *noun* the prime meridian, which passes through the former Royal Observatory at Greenwich, a London borough on the south bank of the Thames. It was adopted internationally as the zero of longitude in 1884.

Green·wich Village /ˈɡrenɪtʃ/ a residential area of New York City on the lower west side of Manhattan, traditionally associated with writers, artists, and musicians.

green-winged teal *noun see* TEAL *noun* 1.

green·wood *noun* a woodland or forest in leaf, esp. as the typical setting of medieval outlaw life.

green woodpecker *noun* a large green and yellow European woodpecker, *Picus viridis*, with a red crown.

greeny *adjective* greenish (*greeny yellow*).

Greer, Ger·maine (b.1939), Australian feminist and writer. She first achieved recognition with her influential book *The Female Eunuch* (1970), an analysis of women's subordination in a male-dominated society; her other books include *The Change* (1991), about social attitudes to female aging.

greet¹ *transitive verb* **1** address politely or welcomingly on meeting or arrival. **2** receive or acknowledge in a specified way (*was greeted with derision*). **3** (of a sight, sound, etc.) become apparent to or noticed by. □ **greet·er** *noun* [Old English *grētan* handle, attack, salute, from West Germanic]

greet² *intransitive verb Scot.* weep. [Old English *grētan, grēotan*, of uncertain origin]

greet·ing *noun* **1** the act or an instance of welcoming or addressing politely. **2** words, gestures, etc., used to greet a person. **3** (often in *pl.*) an expression of goodwill.

greeting card *noun* (*Brit.* **greetings card**) a decorative card sent to convey greetings.

gre·gar·i·ous /ɡrɪˈɡeərɪəs/ *adjective* **1** fond of company. **2** living in flocks or communities. **3** growing in clusters. □ **gre·gar·i·ous·ly** *adverb* **gre·gar·i·ous·ness** *noun* [Latin *gregarius* from *grex gregis* flock]

Greg·or·ian calendar /ɡrəˈɡɔːrɪən/ *noun* the general calendar in use today, introduced in 1582 by Pope Gregory XIII as a correction of the Julian calendar, with 365 days in standard years and 366 days in all years exactly divisible by 4 except century years, which must be exactly divisible by 400 to have 366 days.

Greg·or·ian chant /ɡrəˈɡɔːrɪən/ *noun* church music sung as a single vocal line in free rhythm and a restricted scale (plainsong), in a style developed for the medieval Latin liturgy. [after GREGORY I]

Greg·ory /ˈɡreɡəri/ **Lady Isa·bel·la Au·gus·ta** (1852–1932), Irish dramatist. A leading figure in the Irish literary revival, she was one of the founders of the Abbey Theatre (Dublin) and wrote translations of Irish legends and plays, including *The Workhouse Ward* and *The Gaol Gate*.

Gregory I /ˈɡreɡəri/ **St.** (known as 'Gregory the Great') (540–604), pope 590–604. He established the temporal power of the papacy by appointing governors to the Italian cities, sent St. Augustine to England to lead the country's conversion to Christianity, and is credited with the invention of Gregorian chant. Feast day, 12 March.

Gregory XIII /ˈɡreɡəri/ (born Ugo Buoncompagni) (1502–85), pope 1572–85. He established numerous seminaries, mainly under the direction of the Jesuits, fostered missions in the Far East, and instituted the Gregorian calendar (1582).

Gregory of Nazi·an·zus, St. /ˈɡreɡəri, naziˈanzəs/ (329–89), Doctor of the Church, bishop of Constantinople. With St. Basil and St. Gregory of Nyssa he was an upholder of Orthodoxy against the heresies of the time, and influential in restoring adherence to the Nicene creed. Feast day, (in the Eastern Church) 25 and 30 January; (in the Western Church) 2 January (formerly 9 May).

Gregory of Nyssa, St. /ˈɡreɡəri, ˈnɪsə/ (*c*.330–*c*.395), Doctor of the Eastern Church, bishop of Nyssa in Cappadocia. With his brother St. Basil and St. Gregory of Nazianzus, he opposed Arianism. Feast day, 9 March.

Gregory of Tours, St. /ˈɡreɡəri, tʊr/ (*c*.540–94), Frankish bishop and historian. He was elected bishop of Tours in 573; his writings provide the chief authority for the early Merovingian period of French history. Feast day, 17 November.

Gregory the Great see GREGORY I.

grem·lin *noun informal* **1** an imaginary mischievous sprite regarded as responsible for mechanical faults. **2** any similar cause of trouble. [20th c.: origin unknown, but prob. after *goblin*]

gremo·lata /ˌɡreməˈlɒtə/ *noun* a mixture of parsley, grated lemon rind, and garlic, used to add zest to a dish. [Italian]

Gre·nache /ɡrəˈnaʃ/ *noun* **1** a variety of esp. black grape that is widely planted in southern France, Spain, California, and elsewhere. **2** a wine made from this grape. [French]

Gren·ada /ɡrəˈneɪdə/ a country in the W Indies, consisting of the island of Grenada (the southernmost of the Windward Islands) and the S Grenadines; pop. (est. 2002) 89,211; capital, St. George's. □ **Gren·adi·an** *adjective & noun*

gren·ade /ɡrəˈneɪd/ *noun* **1** a small bomb thrown by hand (**hand grenade**) or launched mechanically. **2** a similar missile containing chemicals which disperse on impact, used for extinguishing fires etc. [French from Old French *grenate* and Spanish *granada* POMEGRANATE]

grena·dier /ˌɡrenəˈdɪːr/ *noun* **1 a** *Brit.* (**Grenadiers** or **Grenadier Guards**) the first regiment of the royal household infantry. **b** *hist.* a soldier armed with grenades. **c** *hist.* a soldier selected for height and strength to be part of an elite unit. **2** any deep-sea fish of the family Macrouridae, with a long tapering body and pointed tail, and secreting luminous bacteria when disturbed. [French (as GRENADE)]

grena·dilla /ɡrenəˈdɪlə/ *noun* (also **grana·dilla** /ɡran-/) a passion fruit. [Spanish *granadilla*, diminutive of *granada* POMEGRANATE]

grena·dine /ˈɡrenəˌdiːn/ *noun* a sweet red syrup flavoured with pomegranates. [French from *grenade*: see GRENADE]

Grena·dine Islands (also **Grena·dines**) a chain of small islands in the W Indies, part of the Windward Islands. They are divided administratively between St. Vincent and Grenada.

Gren·del /ˈɡrendəl/ (in Old English legend) the monster slain by Beowulf.

Gren·fell /ˈɡrenfəl/ **Sir Wil·fred Thoma·son** (1865–1940), English missionary and medical doctor. As superintendent of the Royal National Mission to Deep Sea Fisherman (1889–1912), he began to establish hospitals, nursing stations and orphanages in Newfoundland and Labrador in 1892, as well as setting up co-operatives to sell handwoven cloth and Inuit handicrafts.

Gre·noble /ɡrəˈnoːbl/ a city in SE France; pop. (1999) 153,317. It is an important industrial city and a winter-sports centre.

Gren·ville ▶ **1 George** (1712–70), English Whig politician, prime minister 1763–5. His American Stamp Act (1765), intended to raise revenue from the colonies through taxation, was one of the causes of the American Revolution. **2 Sir Rich·ard** (*c*.1542–91), English naval officer, who led an unsuccessful expedition to colonize Virginia (1585) and supplied some of the ships organized against the Spanish Armada (1588).

Gresh·am /ˈɡreʃəm/ **Sir Thom·as** (*c*.1519–79), English financier. He founded the Royal Exchange in 1566 and exerted considerable influence over Elizabethan economic policy.

Gresh·am's law /ˈɡreʃəmz/ *noun* the tendency for money of lower intrinsic value to circulate more freely than money of higher intrinsic and equal nominal value. [GRESHAM]

Gret·na Green a village in Scotland just north of the Scottish–English border near Carlisle, from 1753 to the mid 19th c. a popular place for runaway couples from England to be married according to

Consonants: b *but*   d *dog*   f *few*   ɡ *get*   h *her*   j *yes*   k *cat*   l *leg*   m *man*   n *no*   p *pen*   r *red*   s *sit*

Scots law without the parental consent required in England for people under a certain age.

Gretz·ky, Wayne (b.1961), Canadian hockey player. With the Edmonton Oilers (1978-88) he broke records for goals, assists, and total points in a season, leading the team to four Stanley Cups before being traded to Los Angeles; after a brief stint in St. Louis and three seasons with the New York Rangers, he retired in 1999 as the NHL's all-time leading point-scorer. During his illustrious career Gretzky received numerous awards and distinctions, including ten scoring titles and nine Hart Trophies as the league's most valuable player.

Greuze /grɜːz/ **Jean-Baptiste** (1725–1805), French painter. His early paintings were sentimental and melodramatic genre scenes, while his later works consisted of pictures of young women containing thinly-veiled sexual allusions, as in *The Broken Pitcher* (c.1773).

grew past of GROW.

Grey ▶ 1 Al·bert Henry George, 4th Earl (1851–1917), Governor General of Canada 1904–11. A staunch imperialist, Grey tried to encourage both the Canadian public and Prime Minister Wilfrid Laurier to adopt close ties to the rest of the Empire, esp. in matters of defence. He attempted to bring Newfoundland into Confederation, and donated the Grey Cup in 1909. **2 Charles, 2nd Earl** (1764–1845), English politician, prime minister 1830–4. He was an advocate of electoral reform and his government passed the first Reform Act (1832) as well as important factory legislation and the Act abolishing slavery throughout the British Empire. **3 Lady Jane** (1537–54), queen of England 9–19 July 1553, granddaughter of the sister of Henry VIII. The Duke of Northumberland forced her to marry his son and persuaded the Protestant king Edward VI to declare that she should succeed to the throne rather than his Catholic half-sister Mary Tudor. Jane was queen for nine days before being deposed by forces loyal to Mary, and later executed to avoid possible rebellions by Protestants. **4 Zane** (1872–1939), US writer of western novels, who is best known for *Riders of the Purple Sage* (1912).

Grey, Point a peninsula at the west end of Vancouver, jutting into the Strait of Georgia. [G. *Grey*, English naval commander d.1828]

grey (also **gray**) ● *adjective* **1** of a colour intermediate between black and white, as of ashes or lead. **2** (of the weather etc.) dull, dismal; heavily overcast. **b** bleak, depressing; (of a person) depressed. **3 a** (of hair) turning white with age etc. **b** (of a person) having grey hair. **4** anonymous, nondescript, unidentifiable. ● *noun* **1 a** a grey colour or pigment. **b** grey clothes or material (*dressed in grey*). **2** a cold sunless light. **3** *Cdn* (usu. in *pl.*) a grey seat in a hockey arena etc., often the farthest from the playing surface. **4** a grey or white horse. ● *verb* **1** *transitive & intransitive* make or become grey. **2** *intransitive informal* become older; age. □ **grey·ish** *adjective* **grey·ly** *adverb* **grey·ness** *noun* [Old English *græg* from Germanic]

grey area *noun* **1** an ill-defined situation, field, etc., not readily categorized or conforming to an existing set of rules. **2** *Brit.* an area in economic decline.

grey·beard *noun* often *derogatory* an old man.

Grey Cup *noun Cdn* **1** the trophy presented each year to the team winning the Canadian Football League championship (often *attributive*: *Grey Cup game*). **2** the game deciding this championship. [4th Earl GREY, who donated the trophy]

greyed-out *adjective* (of an icon etc. on a computer screen) displayed in grey or faint tones, to indicate that it is not available.

grey eminence *noun* = ÉMINENCE GRISE.

Grey Friar *noun* a Franciscan friar.

grey goose *noun* = GREYLAG.

grey·hound *noun* a breed of tall slender dog having keen sight and capable of high speed, used in racing. [Old English *grighund* from *grieg* bitch (unrecorded: compare Old Norse *grey*) + *hund* dog, related to HOUND]

grey jay *noun* a common N American jay, *Perisoreus canadensis*, having grey, black, and white plumage, notorious for its boldness in scavenging from backwoods camps and picnic grounds. *Also called* CANADA JAY, WHISKY JACK.

grey·lag *noun* (in full **greylag goose**) a large grey, brown, and white Eurasian wild goose, *Anser anser*. [GREY + LAG¹ (because of its late migration)]

grey market *noun* the unofficial but not illegal buying and selling of goods, esp. that bypassing standard channels of distribution. □ **grey marketer** *noun*

grey matter *noun* **1** the darker tissues of the brain and spinal cord

consisting of nerve cell bodies and branching dendrites. **2** *informal* intelligence.

grey mullet *noun* any mullet of the family Mugilidae, usu. found near coasts and having a thick body and blunt head, often used as food.

Grey Nun *noun* a member of any of five Roman Catholic women's communities, each with a history traceable to the community founded by Marguerite d'Youville, the Sisters of Charity of the Hôpital Général, in Montreal.

Grey Owl a name taken by **Archi·bald Stans·feld Bel·aney** (1888–1938), English-born Canadian conservationist and writer. Shortly after his arrival in Canada he adopted the name Grey Owl, describing himself as the son of a Scot and an Apache; his works, which have a theme of conservation, include *The Men of the Last Frontier* (1931) and *Tales of an Empty Cabin* (1936).

grey partridge *noun see* PARTRIDGE 1.

grey power *noun informal* political or other pressure applied or held by senior citizens.

grey-scale *Computing* ● *attributive adjective* designating the production of black and white images by the assigning of one of several shades of grey to each pixel (*compare* DITHERING 2). ● *noun* a grey-scale image.

grey seal *noun* a large seal, *Halichoerus grypus*, of the N Atlantic and Baltic.

grey squirrel *noun* a common grey or black squirrel of eastern N America, *Sciurus carolinensis*, introduced into Europe.

grey·stone *noun Cdn* **1** grey stones used in building walls, houses, etc. (also *attributive*: *a greystone mansion*). **2** a house etc. made of greystone.

grey·wacke /ˈɡreɪˌwakə, -ˌwak/ *noun* (also **gray·wacke**) *Geol.* a dark and coarse-grained sandstone, usu. with an admixture of clay. [anglicized from German *Grauwacke* from *grau* grey: see WACKE]

grey water *noun* mildly contaminated household waste water from sinks, washing machines, etc.

grey whale *noun* a large mottled grey baleen whale of N Pacific waters, *Eschrichtius robustus*.

grey wolf *noun* = WOLF *noun* 1.

grid *noun* **1 a** a framework of spaced parallel bars; a grating. **b** a network of lines, esp. of two series of regularly spaced lines crossing one another at right angles. **c** a set of points arranged so that lines passing through them would form a grid. **2** a system of numbered squares printed on a map and forming the basis of map references. **3 a** a network of water mains, gas lines, etc. **b** = POWER GRID. **4** a pattern of lines marking the starting places on a motor racing track. **5** the wire network between the filament and the anode of a thermionic valve etc. **6** an arrangement of town or city streets in a rectangular pattern. **7** *Cdn* (*Sask.*) = GRID ROAD. □ **grid·ded** *adjective* [back-formation from GRIDIRON]

grid computing *noun Computing* the linking of numerous computer systems so that they may share processing power.

grid·dle *noun* a flat pan with little or no rim, used esp. for frying. [Old French *gridil* gridiron, ultimately from Latin *craticula* diminutive of *cratis* hurdle; compare GRATE², GRILL¹]

grid·dle cake *noun* = PANCAKE 1.

grid·iron *noun* **1** a cooking utensil of metal bars for broiling or grilling. **2** *N Amer.* **a** a football field (with parallel lines marking out the area of play). **b** *informal* the game of football (*the gridiron season is drawing to a close*). **3** *Theatre* an open framework over a stage supporting the mechanism for drop scenes etc. **4** = GRID 6. [Middle English *gredire*, var. of *gredil* GRIDDLE, later assoc. with IRON]

grid·lock *noun* **1** a traffic jam affecting a whole network of intersecting streets. **2** = DEADLOCK *noun* 1. □ **grid·locked** *adjective*

grid road *noun Cdn* **1** a road following the surveyed divisions of a township, municipality, etc. **2** (*Sask.*) a road forming part of a provincial grid system constructed in the 1950s, with north-south roads one mile apart, and east-west roads two miles apart.

grief *noun* **1** deep or intense sorrow or mourning. **2** the cause of this. **3** *informal* trouble; annoyance. □ **come to grief** meet with disaster; fail. **good grief!** an exclamation of surprise, alarm, etc. [Anglo-French *gref*, Old French *grief* from *grever* GRIEVE]

Grieg /ɡriːɡ/ **Ed·vard Hage·rup** (1843–1907), Norwegian composer. Much of his music, like the popular Piano Concerto in A Minor (1869) and the suite for Ibsen's *Peer Gynt* (1876), was inspired by his country's folk music, though he rarely used its tunes directly.

Grier·son /ˈɡriːrsən/ **John** (1898–1972), Scottish film director and producer, creator of the National Film Board of Canada (1939). After ten years of pioneering work in British documentary filmmaking, he was invited to Canada to study the government's use of film, and

t *top*   v *voice*   w *we*   z *zoo*   ʃ *she*   ʒ *vision*   θ *thin*   ð *this*   ŋ *ring*   x *loch*   tʃ *chip*   dʒ *jar*   (see over for vowels)

established the National Film Board as one of the most creative and productive film centres in the world. He headed it until 1945, giving a strong impetus to the fledgling film industry in Canada. Among his films, *Night Mail* (1936), with a verse commentary by W. H. Auden, is considered a classic of documentary filmmaking.

griev·ance *noun* **1** a real or fancied cause for complaint. **2** an official allegation that something is unjust, inequitable, or illegal (*the union has filed a grievance*). [Middle English, = injury, from Old French *grevance* (as GRIEF)]

grieve *verb* **1** *intransitive* suffer grief, esp. at another's death. **2** *transitive* cause grief or great distress to. **3** *transitive* file a grievance against (a person or thing). □ **griev·er** *noun* [Old French *grever*, ultimately from Latin *gravare* from *gravis* heavy]

griev·ous /ˈɡriːvəs/ *adjective* very severe or serious. □ **griev·ous·ly** *adverb* **griev·ous·ness** *noun*

grievous bodily harm *noun* esp. *Brit. Law* serious physical injury inflicted on a person by the deliberate action of another.

grif·fin *noun* (also **gryphon**) a mythical creature with an eagle's head and wings and a lion's body. [Old French *grifoun*, ultimately from Late Latin *gryphus* from Latin *gryps* from Greek *grups*]

Grif·fith ▸ **1 Ar·thur** (1872–1922), Irish nationalist leader, president of the Irish Free State 1922. He founded and became president of Sinn Fein (1905) and led the Irish delegation during negotiations for the Anglo-Irish treaty (1921); he died in office several months after being elected president. **2 David Wark** (1875–1948), US film director. One of the most influential figures in the early history of film, he is best known for his silent films, which include *The Birth of a Nation* (1915), on the American Civil War, *Intolerance* (1916), and *Broken Blossoms* (1919).

grif·fon *noun* **1** a small terrier-like breed of dog with coarse or smooth hair. **2** (in full **griffon vulture**) a large vulture, *Gyps fulvus*. [French (in sense 1) or var. of GRIFFIN]

grift esp. *US slang* ● *noun* = GRAFT² *noun*. ● *intransitive verb* = GRAFT² *verb*. □ **grift·er** *noun* [perhaps alteration of GRAFT²]

grig *noun* a small eel. □ **merry** (or **lively**) **as a grig** full of fun; extravagantly lively. [Middle English, originally = dwarf: origin unknown]

grill¹ ● *noun* **1 a** a cooking apparatus consisting of a series of metal bars over a heat source. **b** this series of metal bars, on which food is directly placed for cooking. **c** *Brit.* = BROILER 1. **2** a dish of food cooked on a grill. **3** (in full **grill room**) a restaurant serving grilled food. ● *verb* **1** *transitive & intransitive* cook or be cooked on a grill or griddle. **2** *transitive & intransitive* subject or be subjected to extreme heat, esp. from the sun. **3** *transitive* subject to severe questioning or interrogation. □ **grill·er** *noun* **grill·ing** *noun* (in sense 3 of *verb*). [French *gril* (n.), *griller* (v.), from Old French forms of GRILLE]

grill² var. of GRILLE.

grille /ɡrɪl/ *noun* (also **grill**) **1** a grating or latticed screen, used as a partition or to allow discreet vision. **2** a metal grid protecting the radiator of a motor vehicle. [French from Old French *graille* from medieval Latin *graticula, craticula*: see GRIDDLE]

grilled cheese *noun* (in full **grilled cheese sandwich**) *N Amer.* a cheese sandwich that has been fried on both sides.

grill room *noun see* GRILL¹ *noun* 3.

grilse /ɡrɪls/ *noun* (*pl.* same) a young salmon that has returned to fresh water from the sea for the first time. [Middle English: origin unknown]

grim *adjective* (**grim·mer**, **grim·mest**) **1** having a stern or forbidding appearance. **2** harsh, merciless, severe. **3** ghastly, joyless, sinister (*has a grim truth in it*). **4** unpleasant, unattractive. **5** ominous, dreadful. □ **like grim death** with great determination. □ **grim·ly** *adverb* **grim·ness** *noun* [Old English from Germanic]

grim·ace /ˈɡrɪməs/ ● *noun* a distortion of the face made in disgust etc. or to amuse. ● *intransitive verb* make a grimace. [French from Spanish *grimazo* from *grima* fright]

Gri·mal·di /ɡrɪˈmaldi/ **1** the name of the royal family of Monaco since 1297. **2 Fran·ces·co Ma·ria** (1618–63), Italian Jesuit physicist and astronomer. He discovered the diffraction of light, verified Galileo's law of the uniform acceleration of falling bodies, and began the practice of naming lunar features after astronomers and physicists.

gri·mal·kin /ɡrɪˈmalkɪn, -ˈmɒlkɪn/ *noun archaic* **1** an old female cat. **2** a spiteful old woman. [GREY + *Malkin* diminutive of the name *Matilda*]

grime ● *noun* dirt or soot, esp. ingrained in a surface. ● *transitive verb* blacken with grime; befoul. [originally as verb: from Middle Low German & Middle Dutch]

Grimm, Jacob Lud·wig Carl (1785–1863) and **Wil·helm Carl** (1786–1859), German philologists and folklorists. They are remembered for the anthology of German fairy tales which they compiled (1812–22), and the dictionary of German on historical principles which they jointly inaugurated (1852–60).

Grim Reaper *noun* a personification of death, esp. as a skeletal or faceless hooded figure with a scythe.

Grims·by 1 (official name **Great Grimsby**) a port in E England, on the south shore of the Humber estuary; pop. (est. 2002) 90,600. **2** a town in S Ontario, situated on Lake Ontario, about halfway between Hamilton and St. Catharines; pop. (2001) 21,297.

grimy *adjective* (**grim·i·er**, **grim·i·est**) covered with grime; dirty. □ **grim·i·ly** *adverb* **grim·i·ness** *noun*

grin ● *verb* (**grinned**, **grin·ning**) **1** *intransitive* **a** smile broadly, showing the teeth. **b** make a forced, unrestrained, or stupid smile. **2** *transitive* express by grinning (*grinned his satisfaction*). **3** *intransitive* draw back the lips and reveal the teeth, esp. in pain. ● *noun* the act or action of grinning. □ **grin and bear it** take pain or misfortune stoically. □ **grin·ner** *noun* **grin·ning·ly** *adverb* [Old English *grennian* from Germanic]

grinch *noun* a person that seeks to deprive others of joy or happiness. [from the name of a character in Dr. Seuss's *How the Grinch Stole Christmas* (1957)]

grind ● *verb* (*past and past participle* **ground**) **1 a** *transitive* reduce to small particles or powder by crushing esp. by passing through a mill. **b** *intransitive* (of a mill, machine, etc.) move with a crushing action. **2 a** *transitive* reduce, sharpen, or smooth by friction. **b** *transitive & intransitive* rub or rub together gratingly (*grind one's teeth*). **3** *transitive* (often foll. by *down*) oppress; harass with exactions (*grinding poverty*). **4** *intransitive* **a** (often foll. by *away*) work or study hard. **b** (foll. by *out*) produce with effort (*grinding out verses*). **c** (foll. by *on*) (of a sound) continue gratingly or monotonously. **5** *transitive* turn the handle of a barrel organ etc. **6** *intransitive slang* rotate the hips or pelvis in a suggestive manner, esp. in a dance. **7** *intransitive Brit. coarse slang* have sexual intercourse. ● *noun* **1** the act or an instance of grinding. **2** *informal* hard dull work; a laborious task (*the daily grind*). **3** the fineness of something that has been ground (*a very coarse grind*). **4** *slang* the action of rotating the hips or pelvis in a dance etc. **5** *Brit. coarse slang* an act of sexual intercourse. □ **grind to a halt** stop laboriously. □ **grind·ing·ly** *adverb* [Old English *grindan*]

grind·er *noun* **1** a person or thing that grinds, esp. a machine (often in combination: *coffee grinder; organ grinder*). **2** *N Amer. slang* an athlete known more for consistently working hard than for remarkable skill. **3** a molar tooth.

grind·stone *noun* a thick revolving disc used for grinding, sharpening, and polishing. □ **keep one's nose to the grindstone** work hard and continuously.

gringo *noun* (*pl.* **-gos**) often *derogatory* a foreigner, esp. a N American or British person, in a Latin American country. [Spanish, = gibberish, foreigner]

Grin·nell Peninsula /ɡrɪˈnel/ a peninsula of the northwestern coast of Devon Island, Nunavut. [H. G. Grinnell, US philanthropist d.1874]

griot /ˈɡriːɒt, ɡriˈoʊ/ *noun* (in W Africa) a member of a hereditary caste whose main function is to maintain an oral history of their tribe or village. [French]

grip ● *verb* (**gripped**, **grip·ping**) **1 a** *transitive* grasp tightly; take a firm hold of. **b** *intransitive* take a firm hold, esp. by friction. **2** *transitive* (of a feeling or emotion) deeply affect (a person) (*was gripped by fear*). **3** *transitive* compel the attention or interest of. ● *noun* **1 a** a firm hold; a tight grasp or clasp. **b** a manner of grasping or holding. **2** the power of holding attention. **3 a** mental or intellectual understanding or mastery. **b** effective control of a situation or one's behaviour etc. (*lose one's grip*). **4 a** a part of a machine that grips or holds something. **b** a part or attachment by which a tool, implement, weapon, etc., is held in the hand. **5 a** a member of a camera crew responsible for moving and setting up equipment. **b** a stagehand. **6** a travelling bag. **7** (in full **hairgrip**) *Brit.* = BOBBY PIN. □ **come** (or *Brit.* **get**) **to grips with** approach purposefully; begin to deal with. **get a grip** gain or regain composure or control. **in the grip of** dominated or affected by (esp. an adverse circumstance or unpleasant sensation). □ **grip·per** *noun* **grip·ping·ly** *adverb* **grip·py** *adjective* (**grip·pi·er**, **grip·pi·est**) [Old English *gripe, gripa* handful (as GRIPE)]

gripe ● *verb* **1** *intransitive informal* complain, esp. peevishly. **2** *transitive* affect with gastric or intestinal pain. **3** *transitive archaic* clutch, grip. **4** *Naut.* **a** *transitive* secure with gripes. **b** *intransitive* turn to face the wind in spite of the helm. ● *noun* **1** *informal* **a** a complaint. **b** the act of griping. **2** (usu. in *pl.*) gastric or intestinal pain; colic. **3** a grip or clutch.

4 (in *pl.*) *Naut.* lashings securing a boat in its place. □ **grip·er** *noun*

grip·ing·ly *adverb* [Old English *grīpan* from Germanic: compare GROPE]

gripe water *noun* a solution containing sodium bicarbonate and oils of fennel, dill, and anise, to relieve colic and stomach ailments in infants.

grippe /grip/ *noun archaic* or *informal* influenza. [French from *gripper* seize]

Gris /griːs/ **Juan** (born José Victoriano González) (1887–1927), Spanish cubist painter. His work, such as *The Sunblind* (1914), uses collage and paint in simple fragmented shapes which are arranged to create interplays and contrasts of textures, colours, and forms.

gris·aille /gri'zaɪ/ *noun* **1** a method of painting in grey monochrome, often to imitate sculpture. **2** a painting or stained glass window of this kind. [French from *gris* grey]

Grise Fiord /griːz/ **1** a fjord of the southern coast of Ellesmere Island. **2** a hamlet situated at its entrance, on Jones Sound; pop. (2001) 166. It is the most northerly permanent community in Canada. [Norwegian *grise* pig]

griseo·ful·vin /ˌgrɪziəʊˈfʊlvɪn/ *noun* an antibiotic used against fungal infections of the hair and skin. [modern Latin *griseofulvum* from medieval Latin *griseus* grey + Latin *fulvus* reddish yellow]

gris·ly *adjective* (**gris·li·er**, **gris·li·est**) causing horror, disgust, or fear. □ **gris·li·ness** *noun* [Old English *grislic* terrifying]

grist *noun* **1 a** grain to be ground. **b** grain that has been ground. **c** the measure of grain ground at one time. **2** malt crushed for brewing. **3** = GRIST FOR THE MILL. □ **grist for the mill** (also **grist for one's mill**) a subject to be used, discussed, processed, etc., esp. for profit or advantage. [Old English from Germanic, related to GRIND]

gris·tle /ˈɡrɪsəl/ *noun* tough cartilaginous tissue, esp. as occurring in meat. □ **grist·ly** *adjective* [Old English *gristle*]

grist·mill *noun* a mill for grinding grain. □ **grist·mill·er** *noun*

grit ● *noun* **1** small particles of stone or sand. **2** coarse sandstone. **3** the texture or coarseness of sandpaper, stone, etc. **4** (**Grit**) *Cdn* **a** a supporter or member of the Liberal Party. **b** *hist.* = CLEAR GRIT. **5** *informal* pluck, endurance; strength of character. ● *verb* (**grit·ted**, **grit·ting**) **1** *transitive* clench (the teeth). **2** *transitive Brit.* spread grit on (icy roads etc.). **3** *intransitive* make or move with a grating sound. [Old English *grēot* from Germanic: compare GRITS, GROATS]

grits *plural noun* **1** (treated as *sing.* or *pl.*) esp. *US* **a** a coarsely ground grain, esp. corn. **b** = HOMINY. **2** oats that have been husked but not ground. [Old English *grytt(e)*: compare GRIT, GROATS]

grit·ty *adjective* (**grit·ti·er**, **grit·ti·est**) **1** containing or covered with grit. **2** showing courage and resolve (*a typically gritty performance by the Habs*). **3** tough and uncompromising, esp. in depicting sordid or ugly details (*a gritty look at urban life*). □ **grit·ti·ly** *adverb* **grit·ti·ness** *noun*

griz *noun* (*pl.* same) *N Amer. slang* a grizzly bear.

griz·zle[1] *intransitive verb Brit. informal* **1** (esp. of a child) cry fretfully. **2** complain whiningly. [19th c.: origin unknown]

griz·zle[2] ● *adjective* (esp. of hair or fur) having dark and white hairs mixed. ● *noun* a mixture of dark and white hairs. [Old French *grisel* from *gris* grey]

griz·zled *adjective* having, or streaked with, grey hair.

griz·zly ● *adjective* (**griz·zli·er**, **griz·zli·est**) grizzled. ● *noun* (*pl.* **-zlies**) (in full **grizzly bear**) a large variety of brown bear, *Ursus arctos*, found in N America and N Russia.

groan ● *verb* **1 a** *intransitive* make a deep sound expressing pain, grief, disapproval, or pleasure. **b** *transitive* utter with groans. **2** *intransitive* complain; grumble. **3** *intransitive* (usu. foll. by *under, beneath, with*) be loaded or oppressed. **4** (of a thing) make a low creaking or moaning sound when weight or pressure is applied. ● *noun* the sound made in groaning. □ **groan·ing·ly** *adverb* [Old English *grānian* from Germanic, related to GRIN]

groan·er *noun* **1** a person who groans or complains. **2** a bad joke or pun.

groan·ing board *noun* a table abundantly laden with food.

groat *noun hist.* **1** an English silver coin worth four old pence. **2** *archaic* a small sum (*don't care a groat*). [Middle Dutch *groot*, originally = great, i.e. thick (penny)]

groats *plural noun* hulled or crushed grain, esp. oats. [Old English *grotan* (*pl.*): compare *grot* fragment, *grēot* GRIT, *grytt* bran]

gro·cer /ˈɡrəʊsər, -ʃər/ *noun* a person who owns or operates a grocery store. [Anglo-French *grosser*, originally one who sells in the gross, from Old French *grossier* from medieval Latin *grossarius* (as GROSS)]

gro·cery /ˈɡrəʊsəri, -ʃəri, -ʃri/ *noun* (*pl.* **-ies**) **1** (in *pl.*) food and other general household supplies. **2** (in full **grocery store**) a store where groceries are sold.

grocery cart *noun N Amer.* = SHOPPING CART 1.

gro·ceter·ia /ˌgrəʊsəˈtɪːriə/ *noun N Amer.* (used esp. in names) a usu. small grocery store. [GROCERY, after CAFETERIA]

Grod·no Russian name for HRODNA.

grog *noun* **1** a drink of spirits (originally rum) and water. **2** *informal* any alcoholic drink. [said to be from 'Old Grog', the reputed nickname (from his GROGRAM cloak) of Admiral Vernon, who in 1740 first had rum served to sailors diluted rather than straight]

grog·gy *adjective* (**grog·gi·er**, **grog·gi·est**) dazed or unsteady, as from a hangover, blows, lack of sleep, etc. □ **grog·gi·ly** *adverb* **grog·gi·ness** *noun*

grog·ram /ˈɡrɒɡrəm/ *noun* a coarse fabric of silk, or of mohair and wool, or of a mixture of all these, often stiffened with gum. [French *gros grain* coarse grain (as GROSS, GRAIN)]

groin[1] ● *noun* **1** the part of the body where the thighs meet the abdomen. **2 a** the lower abdomen. **b** the esp. male genitals. **3** *Archit.* **a** an edge formed by intersecting vaults. **b** an arch supporting a vault. ● *transitive verb Archit.* build with groins. [Middle English *grynde*, perhaps from Old English *grynde* depression]

groin[2] esp. *US var.* of GROYNE.

grom·met *noun* a metal, plastic, or rubber eyelet, esp. placed in a hole to protect or insulate a rope or cable etc. passed through it. [obsolete French *grommette* from *gourmer* to curb, of unknown origin]

Gro·myko /grəˈmiːkəʊ/ **An·drei Andre·evich** (1909–89), Soviet leader, foreign minister 1957–85, and president 1985–8. As foreign minister he represented the Soviet Union abroad throughout most of the Cold War; his appointment as president, then largely a formal position, was widely interpreted as a manoeuvre by Gorbachev to reduce Gromyko's influence on Soviet affairs.

Gron·ing·en /ˈɡrəʊnɪŋən/ a city in the N Netherlands, capital of a province of the same name; pop. (est. 2002) 168,500.

groom ● *noun* **1** = BRIDEGROOM. **2** a person employed to take care of horses. **3** *Brit. Military* any of certain officers of the Royal Household. ● *transitive verb* **1 a** tend to, esp. brush the coat of (a horse, dog, etc). **b** (of an animal) clean the fur of (another) (also *reflexive*). **2 a** give a neat or tidy appearance to (a person etc.). **b** carefully attend to (a lawn). **c** keep (snowmobile or cross-country ski trails) open. **3** prepare or train (a person) for a particular purpose or activity (*was groomed for the top job*). □ **groom·er** *noun* [Middle English, originally = boy: origin unknown]

grooms·man *noun* (*pl.* **-men**) a male friend attending the bridegroom at a wedding; an usher or best man.

groove ● *noun* **1 a** a channel or hollow, esp. one made to guide motion or receive a corresponding ridge. **b** a spiral track cut in a phonograph record. **2** an established routine or habit. **3** *slang* an established rhythmic pattern (*got a groove going*). ● *verb* **1** *transitive* make a groove or grooves in. **2** *intransitive slang* **a** play music (esp. jazz or dance music) rhythmically. **b** dance or move rhythmically to music. **c** enjoy oneself. □ **in the groove** *slang* **1** doing or performing well. **2** fashionable. [Middle English, = mine shaft, from obsolete Dutch *groeve* furrow, from Germanic]

groover *noun informal* **1** a person who plays or dances to esp. jazz music. **2** a tune with a groove.

groovy *adjective* (**groov·i·er**, **groov·i·est**) **1** *slang* (esp. dated or *jocular*) fashionable and exciting; enjoyable, excellent. **2** of or like a groove. □ **groov·i·ly** *adverb* **groov·i·ness** *noun*

grope ● *verb* **1** *intransitive* (usu. foll. by *for*) feel about or search blindly or uncertainly with the hands. **2** *intransitive* (foll. by *for, after*) search mentally (*was groping for the answer*). **3** *transitive* feel (one's way) towards something. **4** *transitive slang* fondle clumsily for sexual pleasure. ● *noun* the process or an instance of groping. □ **grop·er** *noun* **grop·ing·ly** *adverb* [Old English *grāpian* from Germanic]

Gro·pius /ˈɡrəʊpɪəs/ **Wal·ter Adolph** (1883–1969), German-born US architect. He was the first director of the Bauhaus School of Design (1919–28) and a pioneer of the International Style; his intention was to relate architecture more closely to social needs and to the industrial techniques and modern construction materials on which it was increasingly coming to rely.

gros·beak /ˈɡrəʊsbiːk/ *noun* any of various finch-like birds with heavy bills and usu. brightly coloured plumage. [French *grosbec* (as GROSS)]

Gro·seil·liers *see* DES GROSEILLIERS.

gros·grain /ˈɡrəʊɡreɪn/ *noun* any of various heavily ribbed fabrics, esp. of silk or rayon. [French, = coarse grain (as GROSS, GRAIN)]

Gros Morne National Park /ˈɡrəʊs ˌmɔrn/ a park located on the west central coast of the island of Newfoundland. Known for its ice-carved fjords and hiking trails, it is a designated World Heritage Site. [French, lit. 'great height']

gros point /ˈɡrəʊ pɔɪnt/ *noun* any of various embroidery stitches worked over two or more horizontal and vertical threads of the canvas. [French (as GROSS, POINT)]

Gross /ɡrəʊs/ **Paul** (b.1959), Canadian actor and writer. He earned a Gemini award in 1986 for writing the TV drama *In This Corner*, before become internationally known for his acting role in the comedy *Due South*.

gross ● *adjective* **1** overfed, bloated; repulsively fat. **2** (of a person, manners, or morals) noticeably coarse, unrefined, or indecent. **3** *slang* very unpleasant, repulsive, disgusting. **4** flagrant; conspicuously wrong (*gross negligence*). **5** total; without deductions; not net (*gross tonnage; gross income*). **6 a** luxuriant, rank. **b** thick, solid, dense. **7** (of the senses etc.) dull; lacking sensitivity. ● *transitive verb* produce or earn as gross profit or income. ● *noun* (*pl.* same) **1** gross income, receipts, etc. (*deduct ten per cent of the gross*). **2** an amount equal to twelve dozen. □ **gross out** *N Amer. slang* disgust, esp. by repulsive or obscene behaviour. **gross up** increase (a net amount) to its value before deductions. □ **gross·ly** *adverb* **gross·ness** *noun* [Old French *gros grosse* large, from Late Latin *grossus*: (n.2) from French *grosse douzaine* large dozen]

gross domestic product *noun* the annual total value of goods produced and services provided in a country excluding transactions with other countries. Abbr.: **GDP**.

Grosse-Île /ɡrəʊsˈiːl/ a historic site in SE central Quebec, situated in the St. Lawrence River, just northeast of Île d'Orléans. From 1832 to 1937 the island served as a quarantine station for immigrants, esp. the Irish; the site commemorates those who died there or en route to Canada. [alteration of its original name *Île de Grâce*]

Gross·glock·ner /ˈɡrəʊsˌɡlɒknər/ the highest mountain in Austria, in the E Tyrolean Alps, rising to a height of 3 797 m (12,457 ft.).

gross indecency *noun* **1** *Cdn hist.* any of various sexual offences considered an outrage to public morals, e.g. sex in public places, homosexual sex, sex with minors. **2** *Brit.* sexual activity between two adult males in public or with a third person present.

gross margin *noun Business* the difference between the dealer's cost and the selling price; the profit margin.

gross national product *noun* the annual total value of goods produced and services provided in a country. Abbr.: **GNP**.

gross-out *noun* esp. *N Amer. slang* (often *attributive*) something that is repulsive or disgusting (*a gross-out horror flick; one gross-out after another.*)

gross ton *noun see* TON 5a.

Gros Ventre /ˈɡrəʊ vɒnt/ *noun* (*pl.* same or **Gros Ventres**) **1** a member of an Aboriginal people living in Montana and (formerly) in S Saskatchewan. **2** the Algonquian language of these people. [French, = 'big bellies']

Grosz /ɡrəʊs/ **George** (1893–1959), German-born US painter. His satirical drawings and paintings characteristically depict a decaying society in which gluttony and depraved sensuality are juxtaposed with poverty and disease; major works include the paintings *Metropolis* (1917) and *Suicide* (1916).

grosz /ɡrɒʃ/ *noun* (*pl.* **groszy** or **grosze** /ˈɡrɒʃi/) a monetary unit of Poland, equal to one-hundredth of a zloty. [Polish]

gro·tesque /ɡrəʊˈtesk/ ● *adjective* **1** comically or repulsively distorted; monstrous, unnatural. **2** incongruous, ludicrous, absurd. ● *noun* **1** a decorative form interweaving human and animal features. **2** a comically distorted figure or design. □ **gro·tesque·ly** *adverb* **gro·tesque·ness** *noun* **gro·tes·quer·ie** /-ˈteskəri/ *noun* (also **gro·tes·query**). [Italian *grottesca* grotto-like (painting etc.) fem. of *grottesco* (as GROTTO, -ESQUE)]

Gro·tius /ˈɡrəʊʃəs, ˈɡrəʊtɪəs/ **Hugo** (Latinized name of Huig de Groot) (1583–1645), Dutch jurist and diplomat. His legal treatise *De Jure Belli et Pacis* (1625) established the basis of modern international law.

grot·to *noun* (*pl.* **-toes** or **-tos**) **1** a small picturesque cave. **2** an artificial ornamental cave, e.g. in a park or large garden. [Italian *grotta*, ultimately from Latin *crypta* (as CRYPT)]

grotty *adjective* (**grot·ti·er**, **grot·ti·est**) *slang* unpleasant, dirty, shabby, unattractive. □ **grot·ti·ness** *noun* [shortening of GROTESQUE + -Y¹]

grouch *informal* ● *noun* **1** a discontented person. **2** a fit of grumbling or bad temper. **3** a cause of discontent. ● *intransitive verb* grumble. [var. of *grutch*: see GRUDGE]

grouchy *adjective* (**grouch·i·er**, **grouch·i·est**) *informal* discontented, grumpy. □ **grouch·i·ly** *adverb* **grouch·i·ness** *noun*

Groulx /ɡruː/ **Lionel-Adolphe** (1878–1967), Canadian historian, Catholic priest and Quebec nationalist. As professor of Canadian history at the Université de Montréal 1915–49, he took the then novel view that the Conquest was a disaster for French Canada. Encouraging French Canadians to look to their past, their culture, and the Catholic church for inspiration, he challenged them to create for themselves an equal place within Confederation.

ground¹ ● *noun* **1 a** the surface of the earth, esp. as contrasted with the air around it. **b** a part of this specified in some way (*low ground*). **2** the substance of the earth's surface; soil, earth (*stony ground; dug deep into the ground*). **3 a** a position, area, or distance on the earth's surface. **b** the extent of activity etc. achieved or of a subject dealt with (*the book covers a lot of ground*). **4** (often in *pl.*) a foundation, motive, or reason (*excused on the grounds of poor health; there is ground for concern; boycotted classes on the grounds that content was inadequate*). **5** an area of a special kind or designated for special use (often in *combination: fishing grounds*). **6** (in *pl.*) an area of usu. enclosed land attached to a building. **7** an area or basis for consideration, agreement, etc. (*common ground; on firm ground*). **8 a** (in painting) the prepared surface giving the predominant colour or tone. **b** (in embroidery, ceramics, etc.) the undecorated surface. **9** (in full **ground bass**) *Music* a short theme in the bass constantly repeated with the upper parts of the music varied. **10** (in *pl.*) solid particles, esp. of coffee, forming a residue. **11** esp. *N Amer. Electricity* a connection between an electrical circuit and the ground, conducting electricity harmlessly to the ground in case of a fault. **12** the bottom of the sea or a large body of water (*the ship touched ground*). **13** esp. *Brit.* the floor of a room etc. **14** a piece of wood fixed to a wall as a base for boards, plaster, or joinery. **15** (*attributive*) **a** (of animals) living on or in the ground. **b** (of fish) living at the bottom of water. **c** (of plants) dwarfish or trailing. **d** relating to or concerned with the ground (*ground staff*). **e** *Mil.* designating units etc. operating on land, as opposed to naval or air units (*ground support; ground troops*). ● *verb* **1** *transitive* **a** prevent (a pilot, airline passenger, or an aircraft) from flying. **b** *informal* temporarily restrict the esp. social activities of (esp. a child or teenager), usu. as a punishment. **2 a** *transitive* run (a ship) aground; strand. **b** *intransitive* (of a ship) run aground. **3** *transitive* (foll. by *in*) instruct thoroughly (in a subject). **4** *transitive* (often as **ground·ed** *adjective*) (foll. by *on*) base (a principle, conclusion, etc.) on. **5** *transitive* (often as **ground·ed** *adjective*) esp. *N Amer.* connect (an electrical circuit) to the ground, directly or indirectly, so that the electricity is conducted harmlessly to the earth in case of a fault. **6** *intransitive* alight on the ground. **7** *intransitive Baseball* hit the ball along the ground, esp. for an easy out (*grounded to second*). **8** *transitive* place or lay (esp. weapons) on the ground. □ **break ground 1** begin the excavation for a new construction project. **2** (also **break new ground**) introduce or discover a new method, system, etc.; innovate. **cut the ground from under a person's feet** anticipate and pre-empt a person's arguments, plans, etc. **down to the ground** esp. *Brit. informal* thoroughly; in every respect. **fall to the ground** (of a plan etc.) fail. **from the ground up 1** completely, thoroughly. **2** from the most basic stage to the most complex (*completely redesigned from the ground up*). **gain** (or **make**) **ground 1** advance steadily; make progress. **2** (foll. by *on*) get closer to (a person or thing pursued). **get off the ground** *informal* make a successful start. **go to ground 1** (of a fox etc.) enter its earth or burrow etc. **2** (of a person) become inaccessible for a prolonged period. **ground out** *Baseball* hit the ball along the ground to an infielder and be put out at first base. **hold** (or **stand**) **one's ground** not retreat or give way. **lose ground 1** retreat, decline. **2** lose the advantage or one's position in an argument, contest, etc. **on the ground** at the point of production or operation; in practical conditions. **on one's own ground** on one's own territory or subject; on one's own terms. **thin on the ground** not numerous. **work** (or **run** etc.) **oneself into the ground** *informal* work etc. to the point of exhaustion. [Old English *grund* from Germanic]

ground² past and past participle of GRIND.

ground·bait *noun Brit., Austral. & NZ* bait thrown to the bottom of a fishing ground.

ground ball *noun* = GROUNDER.

ground bass *noun see* GROUND¹ *noun* 9.

ground·break·ing ● *adjective* **1** innovative, pioneering. **2** of or relating to a groundbreaking. ● *noun* the act or ceremony of breaking ground for a new construction project.

ground cherry *noun* *esp. N Amer.* any of several plants of the genus *Physalis* of the tomato family, bearing fruit in a papery calyx. *See also* CHINESE LANTERN 2.

ground control *noun* the personnel and equipment that monitor and direct the landing etc. of aircraft or spacecraft from the ground. □ **ground controller** *noun*

ground cover *noun* **1** a plant covering the surface of the earth, esp. a low-growing spreading plant that inhibits the growth of weeds. **2** such plants collectively.

ground crew *noun* the people at an airfield whose job is to repair and refuel aircraft.

ground·ed *adjective* **1** (of an airplane, pilot, etc.) unable, or not allowed, to fly. **2** (of a child) confined to his or her home outside of school hours as a punishment. **3** (of a person) having his or her feet on the ground; realistic, sensible, well-balanced. **4** electrically connected with the ground, either directly or through another conductor. □ **ground·ed·ness** *noun* (in sense 3).

ground·er *noun* (esp. in baseball) a ball that is hit or passed along the ground.

ground-fault interrupter *noun* (also **ground-fault circuit interrupter**) *see* GFI.

ground fire *noun* **1** *Military* fire directed from the ground against aircraft. **2** *N Amer.* a forest fire spreading among the smaller growth, having yet to reach the branches and crowns of the taller trees.

ground·fish *noun* any fish living on or near the bottom of the sea, including halibut, sole, cod, etc.

ground floor *noun* the floor of a building at ground level. □ **get in on the ground floor** become part of an enterprise in its early stages.

ground glass *noun* **1** glass made non-transparent by grinding etc. **2** glass ground to a powder.

ground hemlock *noun* a N American yew, *Taxus canadensis*, growing as a straggling shrub.

ground·hog *noun* *N Amer.* a woodchuck.

Ground·hog Day *noun* *N Amer.* 2 February, when the groundhog is said to come out of hibernation; according to folklore, if it sees its shadow on that day, six more weeks of winter may be expected.

ground·ing *noun* basic training or instruction in a subject.

ground ivy *noun* = CREEPING CHARLIE.

ground·less *adjective* without motive or foundation. □ **ground·less·ly** *adverb* **ground·less·ness** *noun*

ground level *noun* **1** the level of the ground. **2** the ground floor.

ground·ling *noun* **1 a** a creeping or dwarf plant. **b** an animal that lives near the ground, at the bottom of a lake, etc., esp. a groundfish. **2** a person on the ground as opposed to one in an aircraft. **3** a spectator or reader of inferior taste (with reference to Shakespeare's *Hamlet* III. ii. 11).

ground·nut *noun* **1 a** a N American wild bean. **b** its edible tuber. **2** *Brit.* = PEANUT 1, 2.

ground·out *noun* *Baseball* a play in which the batter hits a ball along the ground to an infielder and is put out at first base.

ground pine *noun* any of several clubmosses resembling miniature conifers, esp. *Lycopodium obscurum* and *L. tristachyum*.

ground plan *noun* **1** the plan of a building at ground level. **2** the general outline of a scheme.

ground rent *noun* rent for land leased for building.

ground rule *noun* a basic principle.

ground rule double *noun* *Baseball* a double awarded automatically, according to the rules of a particular stadium, on a base hit that leaves the playing field, e.g. by bouncing into the stands or over the outfield fence.

ground school *noun* the part of a pilot's training conducted on the ground, including instruction in subjects such as navigation, meteorology, and theory of aerodynamics as they apply to flying.

ground·sel /ˈgraʊnsəl/ *noun* any composite plant of the genus *Senecio*, esp. *S vulgaris*, used as a food for caged birds. [Old English *grundeswylige*, *gundæswelgiæ* (perhaps = pus-absorber from *gund* pus, with reference to use for poultices)]

ground·sheet *noun* a waterproof sheet spread on the ground to give protection from moisture, esp. in a tent.

grounds·keep·er *noun* (also *Brit.* **grounds·man**) *N Amer.* a person who maintains a playing field or court etc.

ground·speed *noun* an aircraft's speed relative to the ground (*compare* AIRSPEED).

ground squirrel *noun* **1** a squirrel-like rodent, e.g. a chipmunk, gopher, etc. **2** any squirrel of the genus *Spermophilus* living in burrows.

ground staff *noun* the non-flying personnel of an airport or air base.

ground state *noun* *Physics* the lowest energy state of an atom etc.

ground·stroke *noun* *Tennis* a stroke played after the ball has bounced.

ground·swell *noun* **1** a large or extensive swell of the sea caused by a distant or past storm or an earthquake. **2** an increasingly forceful presence (esp. of public opinion).

ground·water *noun* water held in soil or rock, esp. that below the water table.

ground·wood *noun* (*attributive*) designating low-grade newsprint, pulp, etc. that has not been treated or coated.

ground·work *noun* **1** preliminary or basic work. **2** a foundation or basis.

ground zero *noun* **1** the point on the ground or on the surface of the water directly under or above an exploding (usu. nuclear) bomb. **2** *N Amer. informal* the very beginning or starting point.

group ● *noun* **1** a number of persons or things located close together, or considered or classed together. **2** (*attributive*) concerning or done by a group (*a group photograph*; *a group hug*). **3** a number of people working together or sharing beliefs, e.g. part of a political party. **4** a number of commercial companies under common ownership. **5** a small band, esp. one that plays popular music. **6** a division of an air force. **7** *Math.* a set of elements, together with an associative binary operation, which contains an inverse for each element and an identity element. **8** *Chem.* **a** a set of ions or radicals giving a characteristic qualitative reaction. **b** a set of elements occupying a column in the periodic table and having broadly similar properties. **c** a combination of atoms having a recognizable identity in a number of compounds. **9** a stratigraphic unit consisting of two or more formations. ● *verb* **1** *transitive & intransitive* form or be formed into a group. **2** *transitive* (often foll. by *with*) place in a group or groups. **3** *transitive* form (colours, figures, etc.) into a well-arranged and harmonious whole. **4** *transitive* classify. □ **group·age** *noun* [French *groupe* from Italian *gruppo* from Germanic, related to CROP]

group captain *noun* (also **Group Captain**) (currently in the RAF and *hist.* in the RCAF) an officer ranking next below air commodore and above wing commander. Abbr.: **Gp. Capt.**

group dynamics *plural noun* *Psych.* (also treated as *sing.*) the field of social psychology concerned with the nature, development, and interactions of human groups.

group·er *noun* any marine fish of the family Serranidae, with a heavy body, big head, and wide mouth. [Portuguese *garupa*, prob. from an Aboriginal name in S America]

group home *noun* a home where several unrelated people live together under supervision or care.

group·ie *noun* *slang* **1** an ardent follower of touring pop groups, esp. a young woman seeking sexual relations with them. **2** a fan, enthusiast, or follower (*literary groupie*).

group·ing *noun* **1** a process or system of allocation to groups. **2** a formation or arrangement in a group or groups.

group insurance *noun* *esp. N Amer.* a life, health, or accident insurance policy covering a group of people (esp. the employees of a company) at a reduced rate under a single contract.

Group of Eight the eight leading industrial nations i.e. the US, Canada, Japan, Germany, France, the UK, Italy, and Russia. Abbr.: **G8**.

Group of Five the five countries of France, Japan, the UK, the US, and (West) Germany, whose financial representatives, at a meeting in New York in September 1985, agreed to take measures to establish greater stability of international currency.

Group of Seven 1 a group of Canadian landscape painters, officially established in 1920, who formed the first major national movement in Canadian art. The founding members were Franklin Carmichael, Lawren Harris, A.Y. Jackson, Franz Johnston, Arthur Lismer, J.E.H. MacDonald, and F.H. Varley. A.J. Casson, Edwin Holgate, and L.L. Fitzgerald joined subsequently. Their work exhibited a bold and colourful expressionistic style, depicting especially, but not exclusively, Canadian landscapes. **2** *hist.* the seven leading industrial nations outside the former Communist bloc, i.e. the US, Canada, Japan, (West) Germany, France, the UK, and Italy. Abbr.: **G7**.

Group of Seventy-Seven a coalition of (orig. 77) developing countries aiming to promote their collective economic interests and economic and technical co-operation in the developing world.

Group of Ten the ten relatively prosperous industrial countries (Belgium, Canada, France, Italy, Japan, the Netherlands, Sweden, (West)

---

t *top*   v *voice*   w *we*   z *zoo*   ʃ *she*   ʒ *vision*   θ *thin*   ð *this*   ŋ *ring*   x *loch*   tʃ *chip*   dʒ *jar*   (*see over for vowels*)

Germany, the UK, and the US) who agreed in 1962 to lend money to the IMF to be used to give financial assistance to other members of the fund.

Group of Three the three largest industrialized economies (the US, Germany, and Japan).

group practice *noun* a medical practice in which several doctors are associated.

group therapy *noun* therapy in which patients with a similar condition are brought together to assist one another psychologically.

group·think *noun* esp. *N Amer.* the practice of thinking or making decisions as a group, often resulting in poor quality decision-making. [modelled on DOUBLETHINK]

group·ware *noun* *Computing* software designed to facilitate collective working by a number of different users.

group work *noun* work done by a group of people working in close association.

grouse[1] /grʌus/ *noun* (*pl.* same) **1** any of various game birds of the family Tetraonidae, with a plump body and feathered legs. **2** the flesh of a grouse used as food. [16th c.: origin uncertain]

grouse[2] /grʌus/ *informal* ● *intransitive verb* grumble or complain pettily. ● *noun* a complaint. □ **grous·er** *noun* [19th c.: origin unknown]

grout ● *noun* a thin mortar for filling gaps in tiling etc. ● *transitive verb* provide or fill with grout. □ **grout·er** *noun* [perhaps from obsolete *grout* 'sediment, dregs', but compare French dial. *grouter* grout a wall]

Grove, Fred·er·ick Phil·ip (1879–1948) (born Felix Paul Berthold Friedrich Greve), German-born Canadian author, teacher, and translator who emigrated to Canada in 1909. His works, largely neglected during his lifetime, include the novels *Over Prairie Trails* (1922) and *Fruits of the Earth* (1933), as well as a fictionalized autobiography, *In Search of Myself* (1946), which won a Governor General's Award.

grove *noun* **1** a small wood or group of trees, esp. one with little or no undergrowth. **2** an orchard planted for the cultivation of citrus fruit, olives, etc. [Old English *grāf*, related to *grǣfa* brushwood]

grov·el /ˈgrɒvəl/ *intransitive verb* (**grov·elled, grov·el·ling**; also **grov·eled, grov·el·ing**) **1** behave obsequiously in seeking favour or forgiveness. **2** lie or move abjectly on the ground with one's face downwards. □ **grov·el·ler** *noun* **grov·el·ling** *adjective* **grov·el·ling·ly** *adverb* [back-formation from obsolete *grovelling* (adv.) from *gruf* face down, from *on grufe* from Old Norse *á grúfu*, later taken as pres. part.]

grow *verb* (*past* **grew**; *past participle* **grown**) **1** *intransitive* increase in size, height, quantity, degree, or in any way regarded as measurable, e.g. authority or reputation (often foll. by *in*: *grew in stature*). **2** *intransitive* **a** develop or exist as a living plant or natural product. **b** develop in a specific way or direction (*began to grow sideways*). **c** germinate, sprout; spring up. **3** *intransitive* be produced; come naturally into existence; arise. **4** *intransitive* **a** become gradually (*grow rich; grow less*). **b** (foll. by *to* + infin.) come by degrees (*grew to like it*). **5** *intransitive* (foll. by *into*) **a** become, having grown or developed (*the acorn has grown into a tall oak; will grow into a fine athlete*). **b** become large enough for or suited to (*will grow into the coat; grew into her new job*). **6** *intransitive* (foll. by *on*) become gradually more favoured by. **7** *transitive* **a** produce (plants, fruit, wood, etc.) by cultivation. **b** bring forth. **c** allow (a beard etc.) to develop or increase in length. **8** *transitive* (in *passive*; foll. by *over, up*) be covered with a growth. **9** *transitive* cause (the economy, a corporation, etc.) to grow or increase in size, value, etc. (*a plan designed to grow the company's market share*). □ **grow out of 1** become too large to wear (a garment). **2** become too mature to retain (a childish habit etc.). **3** be the result or development of. **grow together** coalesce. **grow up 1 a** advance to maturity. **b** (esp. in *imperative*) begin to behave sensibly. **2** (of a custom) arise, become common. □ **grow·able** *adjective* [Old English *grōwan* from Germanic, related to GRASS, GREEN]

grow·er *noun* **1** (often in *combination*) a person growing produce (*fruit grower*). **2** a plant that grows in a specified way (*a fast grower*).

growing pains *plural noun* **1** early difficulties in the development of an enterprise etc. **2** neuralgic pain in children's legs due to fatigue etc.

growl ● *verb* **1** *intransitive* **a** (often foll. by *at*) (esp. of a dog) make a low guttural sound, usu. of anger. **b** murmur angrily. **2** *intransitive* rumble. **3** *transitive* (often foll. by *out*) utter with a growl. ● *noun* **1** a growling sound, esp. made by a dog. **2** an angry murmur; a complaint. **3** a rumble. □ **growl·ing·ly** *adverb* **growly** *adjective* (**growl·i·er, growl·i·est**). [prob. imitative]

growl·er *noun* **1** a person or thing that growls. **2** a small iceberg.

grow light *noun* an artificial light designed to stimulate the growth of plants.

grown ● *verb* past participle of GROW ● *adjective* fully matured; adult.

grown-up ● *adjective* **1** adult. **2** suitable for or characteristic of an adult. ● *noun* an adult person.

grow op *noun* *Cdn informal* an illegal marijuana-growing operation, usu. in someone's home.

growth *noun* **1** the act or process of growing. **2** an increase in size or value. **3** something that has grown or is growing. **4** *Med.* an abnormal formation, esp. a tumour. **5** the cultivation of produce. **6** a crop or yield of grapes.

growth factor *noun* any substance required by an organism in minute amounts to maintain growth.

growth hormone *noun* a substance which stimulates the growth of a plant or animal.

growth industry *noun* an industry that is developing rapidly.

growth ring *noun* a concentric layer of wood, shell, etc., developed during an annual or other regular period of growth.

growth stock *noun* stock that tends to increase in capital value rather than yield high income.

groyne /grɔin/ *noun* (also esp. *US* **groin**) a timber framework or low broad wall built out from a shore to check erosion of a beach. [dial. *groin* snout, from Old French *groign* from Late Latin *grunium* pig's snout]

Groz·ny /ˈgrɒznji/ a city in SW Russia, near the border with Georgia, capital of the Chechen Republic; pop. (est. 2002) 123,300. It is a major centre of the oil industry.

grr *interjection* representing the sound of growling, esp. to express anger or annoyance. [imitative]

grrrl *noun* a young woman perceived as strong or aggressive, esp. in her attitude to men or in her expression of feminine independence and sexuality. [blend of GRR + GIRL]

grub ● *noun* **1** the larva of an insect, esp. of a beetle. **2** *informal* food. ● *verb* (**grubbed, grub·bing**) **1** *transitive & intransitive* dig superficially. **2** *transitive* **a** clear (the ground) of roots and stumps. **b** clear away (roots etc.). **3** *transitive* (foll. by *up, out*) **a** get by digging (*grubbing up weeds*). **b** extract (information etc.) by searching in books etc. **4** *intransitive* search in an undignified or grovelling manner; rummage. **5** *intransitive* (foll. by *on, along, away*) toil, plod. [Middle English, (v.) perhaps corresponding to Old English *grybban* (unrecorded) from Germanic]

grub·ber *noun* **1** (usu. in *combination*) *derogatory* a person devoted to amassing something (*vote-grubber*) (compare MONEY-GRUBBER). **2** an implement for digging up weeds etc. **3** a person who or animal which grubs.

grub box *noun* *Cdn & US* (*Alaska*) a box or other container for carrying and storing food on an expedition etc.

grubby *adjective* (**grub·bi·er, grub·bi·est**) **1** dirty, grimy, slovenly. **2** of or infested with grubs. □ **grub·bi·ly** *adverb* **grub·bi·ness** *noun*

grub·stake *N Amer. informal* ● *noun* material or provisions supplied to an enterprise in return for a share in the resulting profits (originally in prospecting for ore). ● *transitive verb* provide with a grubstake. □ **grub·sta·ker** *noun*

Grub Street *noun* (often *attributive*) the world or class of literary hacks and impoverished authors. [name of a street (later Milton St.) in Moorgate, London, inhabited by these in the 17th c.]

grudge ● *noun* a persistent feeling of ill will or resentment, esp. one due to an insult or injury (*bears a grudge against me*). ● *transitive verb* **1** be resentfully reluctant to give, grant, or allow (a thing). **2** (foll. by verbal noun or *to* + infin.) be reluctant to do (a thing) (*grudged paying so much*). [Middle English *grutch* from Old French *grouchier* murmur, of unknown origin]

grudge match *noun* esp. *N Amer.* a contest or competition involving personal antipathy between competitors.

grudg·ing *adjective* reluctant; not willing. □ **grudg·ing·ly** *adverb* **grudg·ing·ness** *noun*

gruel *noun* a liquid food of oatmeal etc. boiled in milk or water. [Old French, ultimately from Germanic, related to GROUT]

gruel·ling (also **gruel·ing**) ● *adjective* extremely demanding, severe, or tiring. ● *noun* a harsh or exhausting experience. □ **gruel·ling·ly** *adverb* [GRUEL as verb, = exhaust, punish]

grue·some *adjective* horrible, grisly, disgusting. □ **grue·some·ly** *adverb* **grue·some·ness** *noun* [Scots *grue* to shudder, from Scandinavian +-SOME[1]]

gruff *adjective* **1 a** (of a voice) low and harsh. **b** (of a person) having a gruff voice. **2** surly, terse, rough-mannered. □ **gruff·ly** *adverb*

Vowels: a cat ɑ arm e bed ɜr her ɜː deux ə ago ɪ sit i cosy iː feed ɒ hot ɔ pore ɔː no ʌ run ʊ put

gruff·ness *noun* [Dutch, Middle Low German *grof* coarse, from West Germanic (related to ROUGH)]

grum·ble ● *verb* **1** *intransitive* **a** (often foll. by *at, about, over*) complain peevishly. **b** be discontented. **2** *intransitive* **a** utter a dull inarticulate sound; murmur, growl faintly. **b** rumble. **3** *transitive* (often foll. by *out*) utter complainingly. ● *noun* **1** a complaint. **2 a** a dull inarticulate sound; a murmur. **b** a rumble. □ **grum·bler** *noun* **grum·bling** *adjective & noun* **grum·blingly** *adverb* **grum·bly** *adjective* [obsolete *grumme*: compare Middle Dutch *grommen*, Middle Low German *grommelen*, from Germanic]

grump *informal* ● *noun* **1** a grumpy person. **2** (in *pl.*) a fit of sulks. ● *verb* **1** *intransitive* sulk, be grumpy. **2** *transitive* utter grumpily. [imitative]

grumpy *adjective* (**grump·i·er**, **grump·i·est**) morosely irritable; surly. □ **grump·i·ly** *adverb* **grump·i·ness** *noun*

Grundy *noun* (*pl.* **-dies**) (in full **Mrs. Grundy**) a person embodying narrow-minded propriety and prudery. □ **Grundy·ism** *noun* [a person repeatedly mentioned in T. Morton's comedy *Speed the Plough* (1798)]

Grüne·wald /ˈɡruːnəˌvalt/ **Mathias** (born Mathis Nithardt; also called Mathis Gothardt) (*c.*1470–1528), German painter. The nine-panel *Isenheim Altar* (completed 1516), exemplifies his style: figures with twisted limbs, contorted postures, and expressive faces, painted in glowing colour against a dark background.

grunge *noun* **1** *esp. N Amer.* grime, dirt. **2** (in full **grunge rock**) an aggressive style of rock music characterized by a raucous guitar sound and lazy delivery (also *attributive*: *grunge band*). **3** a style of dress associated with this music, characterized by loose-fitting, often second-hand clothes. □ **grun·gi·ness** *noun* **grungy** *adjective* (**-gi·er**, **-gi·est**). [perhaps suggested by GRUBBY, DINGY, etc.]

grun·ion /ˈɡrʌnjən/ *noun* a slender Californian marine fish, *Leuresthes tenuis*, that comes ashore to spawn. [prob. from Spanish *gruñón* grunter]

grunt ● *noun* **1** a low guttural sound made by a pig. **2** a sound resembling this. **3** *slang* a low-ranking labourer (also *attributive*: *grunt work*). **4** *N Amer. slang* an infantry soldier. **5** any of numerous tropical marine fishes of the family Haemulidae, which produce a grunting sound by grinding together the pharyngeal teeth. **6** *N Amer.* a dessert of berries (esp. blueberries) baked with a doughy topping. ● *verb* **1** *intransitive* (of a pig) make a grunt or grunts. **2** *intransitive* (of a person) make a low inarticulate sound resembling this, esp. to express discontent, dissent, fatigue, etc. **3** *transitive* utter with a grunt. [Old English *grunnettan*, prob. originally imitative]

grunt·er *noun* **1** a person or animal that grunts, esp. a pig. **2** a grunting fish, esp. = GRUNT *noun* 5.

Gru·yère /ˈɡruːjɛr/ *noun* a firm pale yellow cheese made from cow's milk. [*Gruyère*, a district in Switzerland where it was first made]

gryph·on *var. of* GRIFFIN.

GSC *abbreviation* Geological Survey of Canada.

GSM *abbreviation* Global System (or Standard) for Mobile Communication, a standardized international system for digital mobile communication.

G spot *noun* a sensitive area of the anterior wall of the vagina believed by some to be highly erogenous and capable of ejaculation. [*G* from Ernst *Gräfenberg*, German-born US gynecologist d.1957, who first described it]

GST *abbreviation* GOODS AND SERVICES TAX.

G-string *noun* **1** a narrow strip of cloth etc. covering only the genitals and attached to a string around the waist, as worn esp. by strippers. **2** (usu. **G string**) *Music* a string sounding the note G.

G-suit *noun* a garment with inflatable pressurized pouches, worn by pilots and astronauts to enable them to withstand high acceleration. [*g* = gravity + SUIT]

GT *noun* a fast high-performance luxury touring sedan. [abbreviation from Italian *gran turismo* great touring]

Gt. *abbreviation* Great.

GTA *abbreviation* Greater Toronto Area.

GTi *adjective* designating a high-performance car with a fuel-injected engine. [GT + injection]

gua·ca·mole /ˌɡwɑːkəˈmoʊli/ *noun* a dip or spread made from mashed avocados mixed with chopped onion, tomatoes, chili peppers, and seasoning. [Latin American Spanish from Nahuatl *ahuacamolli* from *ahuacatl* avocado + *molli* sauce]

Gua·da·la·jara /ˌɡwɒdələˈhɑːrə/ **1** a city in west central Mexico, capital of the state of Jalisco; pop. (2000) 3,847,000. **2** a city in central Spain, to the northeast of Madrid; pop. (2001) 67,640.

Gua·dal·canal /ˌɡwɒdəlkəˈnal/ an island in the S Pacific, one of the Solomon Islands; pop. (2000) 115,400. During the Second World War it was the scene of the first major US offensive against the Japanese (August 1942), bitter fighting on land and at sea continuing for several months before victory was secured.

Guadal·qui·vir River /ˌɡwɒdəlkwiˈviːr/ a river of Andalusia in S Spain. It flows for 657 km (410 miles) through Cordoba and Seville to reach the Atlantic northwest of Cadiz.

Gua·de·loupe /ˌɡwɒdəˈluːp/ a group of islands in the Lesser Antilles, forming an overseas department of France; pop. (est. 2002) 435,739; capital, Basse-Terre. □ **Gua·de·loup·ian** *adjective & noun*

Guadi·ana River /ˌɡwɒdiˈɒnə/ a river of Spain and Portugal. Rising southeast of Madrid, it flows southwestward for some 580 km (360 miles), and forms the border between Spain and Portugal before entering the Atlantic at the Gulf of Cadiz.

guai·ac·ol /ˈɡwaɪəkɒl/ *noun* a liquid with a penetrating aromatic odour obtained by the fractional distillation of wood tar and the dry distillation of guaiacum resin. [GUAIACUM + -OL¹]

guai·ac·um /ˈɡwaɪəkəm/ *noun* **1** any tree of the genus *Guaiacum*, native to tropical America. **2** (also **guaiac** /ˈɡwaɪak/) **a** the hard dense oily timber of some of these, esp. *G. officinale*. Also called LIGNUM VITAE. **b** the resin from this used medicinally. [modern Latin from Spanish *guayaco* of Haitian origin]

guai·fen·esin /ɡwaɪˈfenəsɪn/ *noun* a substance derived from guaiacol, having expectorant properties and commonly used in cough medicines. [GUAIACOL + respelling of PHENOL + arbitrary suffix -*esin*]

Guam /ɡwɒm/ the largest and southernmost of the Mariana Islands, an unincorporated territory of the US; pop. (est. 2002) 160,796; capital, Agaña.

guan /ɡwɒn/ *noun* any of various game birds of the family Cracidae, of tropical America. [from Latin American Spanish from Miskito *kwamu*]

gua·naco /ɡwəˈnɒkoː/ *noun* (*pl.* **-nacos**) an Andean mammal, *Lama guanicoe*, related to the llama and camel, with a coat of soft pale brown hair used for wool. [Spanish, from Quechua *huanacu*]

Gua·na·juato /ˌɡwɒnəˈhwɒtoː/ **1** a state of central Mexico. **2** its capital city; pop. (2000) 74,900. The city developed as a silver-mining centre after a rich vein of silver was discovered there in 1558.

Guang·dong /ɡwaŋˈdʊŋ/ (also **Kwangtung** /kwaŋˈtʊŋ/) a province of S China, on the South China Sea; capital, Guangzhou (Canton).

Guang·xi Zhuang /ɡwaŋ ʃiː ˈʒwaŋ/ (also **Kwangsi Chuang** /ˌkwaŋsiː ˈtʃwaŋ/) an autonomous region of S China, on the Gulf of Tonkin; capital, Nanning.

Guang·zhou /ɡwaŋˈdʒoː/ (also **Canton** /kanˈtɒn/, **Kwangchow** /kwaŋˈtʃaʊ/) a city in S China, the capital of Guangdong province; pop. (est. 2002) 5,230,700. It is a leading industrial and commercial centre of S China.

guan·ine /ˈɡwɒniːn/ *noun* *Biochem.* a purine found in all living organisms as a component base of DNA and RNA. Symbol: **G**. [GUANO + -INE⁴]

guano /ˈɡwɒnoː/ *noun* (*pl.* **-os**) **1** the excrement of seabirds, esp. that found in the islands off Peru and used as manure. **2** an artificial manure, esp. that made from fish. [Spanish from Quechua *huanu* dung]

Guan·tán·amo Bay /ɡwɒnˈtɒnəmoː/ a bay on the southeast coast of Cuba. It is the site of a US naval base established in 1903.

guar /ɡwɑr/ *noun* a drought-resistant leguminous plant, *Cyamopsis tetragonoloba*, grown esp. in the Indian subcontinent as a vegetable and fodder crop and as a source of guar gum. [Hindi *guār*]

guar·ana /ɡwəˈrɑːnə/ *noun* **1** a Brazilian shrub, *Paullinia cupana*. **2** a substance prepared from the seeds of this shrub, used as a tonic or stimulant. [Tupi]

Guar·ani /ɡwɒrəˈniː/ ● *noun* (*pl.* same or **Guar·anis**) **1 a** a member of a S American Aboriginal people of Paraguay and adjacent regions. **b** the language of this people. **2** the chief monetary unit of Paraguay, equal to 100 centimos. ● *adjective* of or relating to the Guarani or their language. [Spanish]

guar·an·tee /ˌɡerənˈtiː/ ● *noun* **1 a** a formal promise or assurance, esp. that an obligation will be fulfilled or that something is of a specified quality and durability. **b** a document giving such an undertaking. **2** = GUARANTY. **3** a person making a guaranty or giving a security. **4** a thing that makes something certain to happen or be the case (*there's no guarantee that she will show up*). ● *transitive verb* (**guar·an·tees**, **guar·an·teed**) **1 a** give or serve as a guarantee for; answer for the due fulfillment of (a contract etc.) or the genuineness of (an article). **b** assure the permanence etc. of. **c** provide with a guarantee. **2** (foll. by *that* + clause, or *to* + infin.) give a promise or assurance. **3 a** (foll. by *to*) secure the possession of (a thing) for a person. **b** make (a person) secure against a risk or in possession of a thing. [earlier *garante*, perhaps from Spanish *garante* = French *garant* WARRANT: later influenced by French *garantie* guaranty]

Guaranteed Income Supplement *noun Cdn* a federally-supported supplement to the monthly pension payments of those with little income other than that derived from Old Age Security. Abbr.: **GIS**.

guaranteed investment certificate *noun Cdn* a certificate guaranteeing a fixed interest rate on a sum of money deposited with a financial institution for a fixed term, usu. between one and seven years, which may not be withdrawn before term. Abbr.: **GIC**.

guar·an·tor /ˈɡerənˌtɔr, ˌɡerənˈtɜr/ *noun* a person who gives a guarantee or guaranty.

guar·anty /ˈɡerənti/ *noun* (*pl.* **-ties**) **1** a written or other undertaking to answer for the payment of a debt or for the performance of an obligation by another person liable in the first instance. **2** a thing serving as security for a guaranty. [Anglo-French *guarantie*, var. of *warantie* WARRANTY]

guard ● *verb* **1** *transitive* (often foll. by *from*, *against*) watch over and defend or protect from harm. **2** *transitive* keep watch by (a door etc.) so as to control entry or exit. **3** *transitive* supervise (prisoners etc.) and prevent from escaping. **4** *transitive* provide (machinery) with a protective device. **5** *transitive* keep (thoughts or speech) in check. **6** *transitive* provide with safeguards. **7** *intransitive* (foll. by *against*) take precautions. **8** *transitive* (in various games) protect (a piece, card, etc.) with set moves. ● *noun* **1** a state of vigilance or watchfulness. **2** a person who keeps watch at a prison etc., or who protects. **3** a body of soldiers etc. serving to protect a place or person; an escort. **4** a part of an army detached for some purpose (*advance guard*). **5** (in *pl.*) (usu. **Guards**) any of various bodies of troops nominally employed to guard a ruler. **6 a** a thing that protects or defends. **b** a piece of protective equipment designed to prevent injury to a usu. specified part of the body (*mouth guard*; *shin guard*). **7** (often in *combination*) a device fitted to a machine, vehicle, weapon, etc., to prevent injury or accident to the user (*fireguard*). **8** a protective or defensive player, esp.: **a** (in football) the player on either side of the centre on the offensive line. **b** (in basketball) either of the two players positioned in the backcourt. **9** (in curling) a rock positioned in front of the house to protect those behind it. **10** a defensive posture or motion. **11** = FIREBREAK. **12** *Brit.* an official who rides with and is in general charge of a train. □ **be on** (or **keep** or **stand**) **guard** (of a sentry etc.) keep watch. **lower one's guard** (also **let one's guard down**) reduce vigilance against attack. **off** (or **off one's**) **guard** unprepared for some surprise or difficulty. **on** (or **on one's**) **guard** prepared for all contingencies; vigilant. **raise one's guard** become vigilant against attack. [Old French *garde*, *garder*, ultimately from West Germanic: related to WARD *noun*]

guard cell *noun Bot.* either of a pair of cells surrounding the stomata in plants.

guard dog *noun* = WATCHDOG 1.

guard·ed *adjective* **1** (of a remark etc.) cautious, avoiding commitment. **2** defended, protected; kept under guard. □ **guard·ed·ly** *adverb* **guard·ed·ness** *noun*

guard hair *noun* each of the long coarse hairs forming an animal's outer fur.

guard·house *noun* a building used to accommodate a military guard or to detain prisoners.

guard·ian *noun* **1** a defender, protector, or keeper. **2** a person having legal custody of another person and his or her property when that person is incapable of managing his or her own affairs. □ **guard·ian·ship** *noun* [Anglo-French *gardein*, Old French *garden* from Frankish, related to WARD, WARDEN]

guardian angel *noun* a spirit conceived as watching over a specific person or place.

guard·rail *noun* a rail fitted as a support or to prevent an accident, e.g. along the edge of a highway or balcony.

guard·room *noun* a room used to accommodate a military guard or to detain prisoners.

guards·man *noun* (*pl.* **-men**) a soldier belonging to a body of guards.

guar gum *noun* a fine powder obtained by grinding the endosperm of seeds of guar, used in food as an emulsifier and filler, and also in the paper and textile industries.

Guar·neri /ɡwɑrˈneri/ **Giu·seppe ('del Gesù')** (1687–1744), Italian violin maker. The most famous of a family of three generations of

violin makers based in Cremona, he gave particular attention to the tone quality of his instruments, which do not conform to any standard shape or dimensions.

Gua·te·mala /ˌɡwɒtəˈmɒlə/ a country in Central America, bordering on the Pacific Ocean and with a short coastline on the Caribbean Sea; pop. (est. 2002) 13,314,079; capital, Guatemala City. □ **Gua·te·mal·an** *adjective & noun*

Gua·te·mala City the capital of Guatemala; pop. (est. 2002) 2,564,900.

gua·va /ˈɡwɒvə/ *noun* **1** a small tropical American tree, *Psidium guajava*, bearing an edible pale yellow fruit with pink juicy flesh. **2** this fruit. [Spanish *guayaba* prob. from a S American name]

guaya·bera /ɡaiəˈbeirə/ *noun* a lightweight open-necked Cuban or Mexican shirt with two breast pockets and two pockets over the hips, typically having short sleeves and worn untucked. [Cuban Spanish: apparently orig. from the name of the *Yayabo* river, influenced by Spanish *guayaba* guava.]

Guaya·quil /ˌɡwɒjəˈkiːl/ a seaport in Ecuador, the country's principal port and second largest city; pop. (est. 2002) 2,196,800.

gub·bins *noun Brit.* **1** *informal* paraphernalia. **2** a gadget. **3** something of little value; rubbish. [originally = fragments, from obsolete *gobbon*: perhaps related to GOBBET]

gu·ber·na·tor·ial /ˌɡuːbɜrnəˈtɔriəl/ *adjective* esp. *US* of or relating to a governor. [Latin *gubernator* governor]

guck *noun* esp. *N Amer. slang* a sticky or slimy substance. [origin unknown]

gudg·eon¹ /ˈɡʌdʒən/ *noun* a small European freshwater fish, *Gobio gobio*, often used as bait. [Old French *goujon* from Latin *gobio -onis* GOBY]

gudg·eon² /ˈɡʌdʒən/ *noun* **1** any of various kinds of pivot working a wheel, bell, etc. **2** the tubular part of a hinge into which the pin fits to effect the joint. **3** a socket at the stern of a boat, into which a rudder is fitted. **4** a pin holding two blocks of stone etc. together. [Old French *goujon* diminutive of *gouge* GOUGE]

Gud·run /ˈɡʊdruːn/ (also **Guth·run** /ˈɡʊθruːn/) *Scand. Myth* the wife of Sigurd, and following his death, of Atli. She killed Atli to avenge his murder of her brother Gunnar; she corresponds to Kriemhild in the *Nibelungenlied*.

guel·der rose /ˈɡeldɜr/ *noun* a deciduous shrub, *Viburnum opulus*, with round bunches of creamy-white flowers. Also called CRAMP BARK, SNOWBALL TREE. [Dutch *geldersch* from *Gelderland* a province in the Netherlands]

Guelph¹ /ɡwelf/ a city in south central Ontario, about 20 km northeast of Kitchener; pop. (2001) 106,170. □ **Guelph·ite** *noun* [GUELPH² 2]

Guelph² /ɡwelf/ *noun* **1** a member of one of the two great factions in Italian medieval politics, traditionally supporting the pope against the Holy Roman emperor (see GHIBELLINE). **2** a member of a princely family of Swabian origin from which the British royal house is descended through George I. [Italian *Guelfo* from Middle High German *Welf* name of German noble family]

gue·non /ɡəˈnɒn/ *noun* any African monkey of the genus *Cercopithecus*, having a characteristic long tail, e.g. the vervet. [French: origin unknown]

guer·don /ˈɡɜrdən/ *literary* ● *noun* a reward or recompense. ● *transitive verb* give a reward to. [Old French from medieval Latin *widerdonum* from West Germanic *widarlōn* (as WITH, LOAN), assimilated to Latin *donum* gift]

Gue·ricke /ˈɡerikə/ **Otto von** (1602–86), German engineer and physicist. He invented the air pump, using it to produce a partial vacuum, and investigated the properties of a vacuum using the Magdeburg hemispheres; he also built the first known electrostatic machine.

guer·il·la *var.* of GUERRILLA.

Guer·nica /ɡwerˈniːkə, ɡer-/ (also **Guernica y Luno** /ɡerˌnika i ˈluno/) a town in the Basque Provinces of N Spain, to the east of Bilbao; pop. (2001) 15,264. Formerly the seat of a Basque parliament, it was bombed in 1937, during the Spanish Civil War, by German planes in support of Franco, an event depicted in a famous painting by Picasso.

Guern·sey¹ /ˈɡɜrnzi/ an island in the English Channel, to the northwest of Jersey; pop. (2001) 62,650; capital, St. Peter Port. It is the second largest of the Channel Islands.

Guern·sey² /ˈɡɜrnzi/ *noun* (*pl.* **-seys**) a light brown and white dairy cow of a breed originally from Guernsey.

guernsey lily *noun* an amaryllis of the genus *Nerine* originally from southern Africa, with large pink lily-like flowers.

Consonants: b *but* d *dog* f *few* g *get* h *her* j *yes* k *cat* l *leg* m *man* n *no* p *pen* r *red* s *sit*

Guer·rero /geˈreroː/ a state of SW central Mexico, on the Pacific coast; capital, Chilpancingo.

guer·ril·la /gəˈrɪlə/ noun (also **guer·illa**) **1** a person taking part in an irregular war waged by small bands operating independently, often against a stronger, more organized force, with surprise attacks etc. (also attributive: guerrilla warfare). **2** informal an activist using controversial or sensational means to support a cause. [Spanish guerrilla, diminutive of guerra war]

guess ● verb **1** transitive & intransitive estimate or suppose without calculation or measurement, or on the basis of inadequate data. **2** transitive conjecture or estimate correctly by guessing (you have to guess the weight). **3** intransitive (foll. by at) make a conjecture about. **4** transitive informal suppose (I guess you're right). ● noun **1** an estimate or conjecture reached by guessing. **2** an act or instance of guessing. □ **anybody's** (or **anyone's**) **guess** something very vague or difficult to determine. **by guess and by golly** (or **gosh** or **God**) informal by instinct rather than logic or knowledge; by the seat of one's pants. **I guess** informal I think it likely; I suppose. **keep a person guessing** informal withhold information. □ **guess·able** adjective **guess·er** noun [Middle English gesse, of uncertain origin: compare Old Swedish gissa, Middle Low German, Middle Dutch gissen: from the root of GET verb]

guess·ing game noun informal a situation in which desired information is withheld.

guess·ti·mate (also **gues·ti·mate**) informal ● noun an estimate based more on guesswork than calculation. ● transitive & intransitive verb form a guesstimate of. [GUESS + ESTIMATE]

guess·work noun the process of or results obtained by guessing.

guest- combining form as a guest (he now guest-conducts the Chicago Symphony; a guest-curated exhibition).

guest ● noun **1** a person (usu. invited) visiting another's house or invited to have a meal etc. at the expense of the inviter. **2** a person lodging at a hotel, boarding house, etc. **3 a** a visiting performer invited to take part with a regular body of performers (also attributive: guest artist). **b** a person who takes part by invitation in a radio or television program (often attributive: guest star). **4** a person attending a social gathering at the request of or accompanying someone invited specifically. **5** (attributive) **a** serving or set aside for guests (guest room). **b** acting as a guest (guest speaker). **6** an organism living in close association with another. ● intransitive verb be a guest on a radio or television show or in a theatrical performance etc. □ **be my guest** informal make what use you wish of the available facilities. [Old Norse gestr from Germanic]

guest book noun a book in a restaurant, hotel, or other public place, in which guests write their names or record comments on their stay.

guest house noun a private house offering paid accommodation.

gues·ti·mate var. of GUESSTIMATE.

guest of honour noun the most important guest at an occasion.

guest ranch noun N Amer. a ranch where guests pay to lodge and participate in daily activities.

guest worker noun = GASTARBEITER. [translation of German]

Gue·vara /gəˈvarə/ **'Che'** (born Ernesto Guevara de la Serna) (1928–67), Argentinian revolutionary and guerrilla leader. He played a significant part in the Cuban revolution (1956–9) and served as a government minister under Castro; in 1967 he was captured and executed while training guerrillas for a planned uprising against the Bolivian government.

Guèvre·mont /ˈɡevrəmɔ̃/ **Ger·maine** (1893–1968) (born Marianne-Germaine Grignon), French-Canadian journalist and novelist. She is best known for her novels Le Survenant (1945) and Marie-Didace (1947) (translated together into English in 1950 as The Outlander).

guff noun slang **1** nonsense; foolish talk. **2** insolent talk. □ **no guff** Cdn **1** a declaration of truthfulness. **2** an expression of mock surprise at a statement. [19th c., originally = 'puff': imitative]

guf·faw /ɡʌˈfɒ/ ● noun a coarse or boisterous laugh. ● verb **1** intransitive utter a guffaw. **2** transitive say with a guffaw. [originally Scots: imitative]

Gug·gen·heim /ˈɡʊɡənˌhaɪm/ **Meyer** (1828–1905), Swiss-born US industrialist. The fortune he amassed in large mining and metal-processing companies was used to fund the Guggenheim Foundation, established in 1925 to provide funding for scholars, artists, and writers.

GUI /ˈɡuːi/ noun Computing a graphical user interface. [acronym]

Gui·ana /ɡaɪˈanə/ a region in northern S America, bounded by the Orinoco, Negro, and Amazon rivers and the Atlantic Ocean. It now comprises Guyana, Suriname, French Guiana, and the Guiana Highlands of SE Venezuela and N Brazil.

Guiana Highlands a mountainous plateau region of northern S America, lying between the Orinoco and Amazon river basins, largely in SE Venezuela and N Brazil. Its highest peak is Roraima (2 774 m; 9,094 ft.).

Gui·bord /ɡiːˈbɔr/ **Jo·seph** (d.1869), Canadian, member of the Institut canadien. Guibord died a few months after the Institut was placed under interdict by Bishop Bourget of Montreal for possession of banned books, and was thus denied burial in consecrated ground. In 1874 the Judicial Committee of the Privy Council reversed Bourget's decision, and Guibord's body was interred in a Catholic cemetery in 1875 in the presence of a military guard. The cemetery itself was immediately deconsecrated by Bourget.

guid·ance noun **1** advice or information aimed at resolving a problem, difficulty, etc. **2** the process of guiding or being guided. **3** the control of a missile or spacecraft in its course.

guidance counsellor noun N Amer. a person, esp. at a school, who counsels others regarding career decisions etc. □ **guidance counselling** noun

guide ● noun **1** a person who leads or shows the way, or directs the movements of a person or group. **2 a** a person who conducts travellers on tours etc. **b** a professional mountain climber in charge of a group. **c** someone hired to lead a hunting or fishing expedition. **3** an adviser. **4** a directing principle or standard (let your conscience be your guide). **5** a book with essential information on a subject, esp. = GUIDEBOOK 1. **6** a thing marking a position or guiding the eye. **7** a soldier, vehicle, or ship whose position determines the movements of others. **8** Mech. **a** a bar, rod, etc., directing the motion of something. **b** a gauge etc. controlling a tool. **9** (**Guide**) Cdn, Brit., Austral., & NZ = GIRL GUIDE. ● transitive verb **1 a** act as guide to; lead or direct. **b** arrange the course of (events). **2** be the principle, motive, or ground of (an action, judgment, etc.). **3** direct the affairs of (a nation etc.). □ **guid·er** noun [Old French guide (n.), guider (v.), earlier guier, ultimately from Germanic, related to WIT²]

guide·book noun **1** a book of information about a place for visitors, tourists, etc. **2** a manual or handbook.

guided missile noun a missile directed to its target by remote control or by internal equipment.

guide dog noun a dog trained to guide a blind person.

guide·line noun (often in pl.) a principle or criterion guiding or directing action.

guide·post noun = SIGNPOST.

Guid·er noun an adult leader of a group of Girl Guides.

guide·way noun a groove or track that guides movement, e.g. of a monorail.

Guid·ing noun the Girl Guide movement.

Guido d'Arezzo /ˈɡwiːdoː dəˈretsoː/ (c.990–1050), Italian Benedictine monk and music theorist, the inventor of solmization.

gui·don /ˈɡaɪdən/ noun a pennant narrowing to a point or fork at the free end, esp. one used as the standard of a light cavalry regiment. [French from Italian guidone from guida GUIDE]

Gui·enne see GUYENNE.

guild /ɡɪld/ noun **1** an association of people for mutual aid or the pursuit of a common goal. **2** a medieval association of craftsmen or merchants. [prob. from Middle Low German, Middle Dutch gilde from Germanic: related to Old English gild payment, sacrifice]

guil·der /ˈɡɪldər/ noun **1** the former chief monetary unit of the Netherlands, now replaced by the euro. **2** the chief monetary unit of Suriname and Netherlands Antilles, equal to 100 cents. **3** hist. a gold coin of the Netherlands and Germany. [Middle English, alteration of Dutch gulden: see GULDEN]

Guild·ford /ˈɡɪlfərd/ a city in Surrey, S England; pop. (est. 2002) 68,300.

guild·hall /ɡɪldˈhɒl, ˈɡɪld-/ noun **1 a** the meeting place of a guild or corporation. **b** Brit. a town hall. **2** (**Guildhall**) (in the UK) the hall of the Corporation of the City of London, used for ceremonial occasions.

guilds·man /ˈɡɪldzmən/ noun (pl. **-men**) a member of a guild. □ **guilds·woman** /ˈɡɪldzwʊmən/ noun (pl. **-women**).

guile /ɡaɪl/ noun clever and esp. deceitful behaviour. □ **guile·ful** adjective **guile·less** adjective **guile·less·ly** adverb **guile·less·ness** noun [Old French, from Germanic]

Guilin /ɡweɪˈlɪn/ a city in S China, on the Li River, in the autonomous region of Guangxi Zhuang; pop. (est. 2002) 749,300.

Guillaume-Delisle, Lac /ɡiːˈjoːm dəˈliːl/ a saltwater lake in NW

Quebec, situated near the east central shore of Hudson Bay. [*Guillaume Delisle*, French map-maker d.1726]

guil·le·mot /ˈgɪlɪˌmɒt/ *noun* any of several diving seabirds of northern latitudes constituting the genera *Uria* and *Cepphus*, of the auk family, with black (or brown) and white plumage and pointed bills. [French from *Guillaume* William]

guil·loche /gɪˈlɒʃ/ *noun* an ornament imitating braided ribbons. [French *guillochis* (or *guilloche* the tool used)]

guil·lo·tine /ˈgɪləˌtiːn, ˌgiːə-/ ● *noun* **1** *hist.* a machine with a heavy knife blade sliding vertically in grooves, used for beheading. **2** a device for cutting paper, metal, etc. **3** a surgical instrument for excising the tonsils etc. **4** *Parl.* a method of preventing delay in the discussion of a legislative bill by fixing times at which various parts of it must be voted on. ● *transitive verb* **1** use a guillotine on. **2** *Parl.* end discussion of (a bill) by applying a guillotine. □ **guil·lo·tin·er** *noun* [French from J.-I. *Guillotin*, French physician d.1814, who recommended its use for executions in 1789]

guilt ● *noun* **1** the fact of having committed a specified or implied offence. **2 a** culpability. **b** the feeling of this. ● *transitive verb informal* cause (someone) to feel guilty. □ **guilt by association** guilt ascribed to a person not because of any evidence but because of his or her association with an offender. [Old English *gylt*, of unknown origin]

guilt complex *noun* a mental obsession with the idea of having done wrong.

guilt·less *adjective* **1** (often foll. by *of* an offence) innocent; not blameworthy. **2** (foll. by *of*) not having knowledge or possession of. □ **guilt·less·ly** *adverb* **guilt·less·ness** *noun*

guilt-ridden *adjective* consumed by guilt.

guilt trip ● *noun* **1** an intense feeling of guilt, esp. induced by others pointing out offences. **2** an attempt to make another feel guilty by pointing out (supposed) offences. ● *transitive verb* (**guilt-trip**) (**-tripped**, **-tripping**) attempt to induce a feeling of guilt in (someone), esp. by pointing out (supposed) offences.

guilty *adjective* (**guilt·i·er**, **guilt·i·est**) **1** culpable of or responsible for a wrong. **2** conscious of or affected by guilt (*a guilty conscience; a guilty look*). **3** concerning guilt (*a guilty secret*). **4 a** (often foll. by *of*) having committed a (specified) offence. **b** *Law* adjudged to have committed a specified offence, esp. by a verdict in a trial. □ **guilt·i·ly** *adverb* **guilt·i·ness** *noun*

Guinea /ˈgɪni/ a country on the west coast of Africa; pop. (est. 2002) 7,775,065; capital, Conakry. The country is estimated to contain one-third of the world's reserves of bauxite. □ **Guin·ean** *adjective & noun*

Guinea, Gulf of a large inlet of the Atlantic Ocean bordering the southern coast of West Africa.

guin·ea /ˈgɪni/ *noun* **1** *Brit.* the sum of 21 old shillings (£1.05), used esp. in determining professional fees. **2** *hist.* a former British gold coin worth 21 shillings, first coined for the African trade. [GUINEA]

Guinea-Bissau /ˌgɪnɪbɪˈsaʊ/ a country on the west coast of Africa, between Senegal and Guinea; pop. (est. 2002) 1,345,479; capital, Bissau. It was formerly known as Portuguese Guinea.

guinea fowl *noun* any originally African fowl of the family Numididae, esp. *Numida meleagris*, with slate-coloured white-spotted plumage, raised for food.

guinea hen *noun* a female guinea fowl, esp. as food.

guinea pig *noun* **1** a domesticated S American cavy, *Cavia porcellus*, kept as a pet or for research in biology etc. **2** a person or thing used as a subject for experiment.

guinea worm *noun* a very long parasitic nematode worm, *Dracunculus medinensis*, which lives under the skin of infected people in rural tropical Africa and Asia.

Guin·evere /ˈgwɪnɪvɪr/ (in Arthurian legend) the wife of King Arthur and lover of Lancelot.

Guin·ness /ˈgɪnəs/ **Sir Alec** (1914–2000), English actor. His stage career ranged from Shakespeare to contemporary drama, and his films included *Great Expectations* (1946), *The Bridge on the River Kwai* (1957), for which he won an Oscar, and *Star Wars* (1977).

guiro /ˈgiːrəʊ, ˈgwiː-/ *noun* (*pl.* **guiros**) a Latin American musical instrument consisting of a gourd with an artificially serrated surface which gives a rasping sound when scraped with a stick. [Spanish, = gourd]

Guis·card /giːˈskɑr/ **Rob·ert** (*c.*1015–85), Norman military leader, who extended Norman rule over much of S Italy.

guise /gaiz/ *noun* **1** an assumed appearance; a pretense (*under the guise of friendship*). **2** external appearance. **3** *archaic* style of attire, garb. [Old French, ultimately from Germanic]

gui·tar *noun* a usu. six-stringed musical instrument with a fretted fingerboard, played by plucking or strumming with the fingers or a plectrum. □ **guitar·ist** *noun* [Spanish *guitarra* (partly through French *guitare*) from Greek *kithara*: see CITTERN, GITTERN]

Gui·yang /gweiˈjaŋ/ (also **Kweiyang** /kwei-/) an industrial city in S China, capital of Guizhou province; pop. (est. 2002) 1,898,600.

Gui·zhou /gweiˈdʒəʊ/ (also **Kweichow** /kweiˈtʃaʊ/) a province of S China; capital, Guiyang.

Gui·zot /giːˈzəʊ/ **Fran·çois Pierre Guil·laume** (1787–1874), French historian, premier 1847–8. He introduced educational reforms and advocated a constitutional monarchy.

Gu·ja·rat /ˌguːdʒəˈrɒt/ a state in W India, with an extensive coastline on the Arabian Sea; capital, Gandhinagar.

Gu·ja·rati /ˌguːdʒəˈrɒti/ ● *noun* (*pl.* **Gu·ja·ratis**) **1** the language of Gujarat. **2** a native of Gujarat. ● *adjective* of or relating to Gujarat or its language.

Guj·ran·wala /ˌguːdʒrənˈwɒlə/ a city of Pakistan, in Punjab province, northwest of Lahore; pop. (1998) 1,217,600. It was the birthplace of the Sikh ruler Ranjit Singh, and was an important centre of Sikh influence in the early 19th c.

Guj·rat /ˈguːdʒrɒt/ a city of Pakistan, in Punjab province, north of Lahore; pop. (1998) 250,100.

gu·lag /ˈguːlag/ *noun* **1** (also **Gulag**) *hist.* **a** the system of forced-labour camps in the Soviet Union, specifically in the period 1930–55, in which hundreds of thousands, perhaps millions, died. Besides ordinary criminals, inmates included dissident intellectuals, members of the ethnic groups suspected of disloyalty, and members of political factions who had lost power. **b** a camp or prison within this system. **2** any extremely oppressive environment. [Russian acronym, from *Glavnoe upravlenie ispravitel'no-trudovykh lagerei*, lit. 'Chief Administration for Corrective Labour Camps']

Gul·barga /gʊlˈbɑːgə/ a city in south central India, in the state of Karnataka; pop. (2001) 427,900.

gulch *noun* *N Amer.* **1** a ravine, esp. one in which a stream flows. **2** a steep, narrow ravine or cove cutting inland from a shoreline cliff. **3** *Cdn* (*Nfld*) a narrow depression in the bottom of the sea. [perhaps dial. *gulch* to swallow]

gul·den /ˈgʊldən/ *noun* = GUILDER. [Dutch & German, = GOLDEN]

gules /gjuːlz/ *noun & adjective* (usu. placed after noun) *Heraldry* red. [Old French *goules* red-dyed fur neck ornaments, from *gole* throat]

gulf *noun* **1** a stretch of sea consisting of a deep inlet with a narrow mouth. **2** (**the Gulf**) **a** the Gulf of Mexico. **b** the Persian Gulf. **c** the Gulf of St. Lawrence. **3** a deep hollow; a chasm or abyss. **4** a wide difference of feelings, opinion, etc. [Old French *golfe* from Italian *golfo*, ultimately from Greek *kolpos* 'bosom, gulf']

Gulf Islands a group of over 200 islands and islets in the Strait of Georgia, situated off the southeastern coast of Vancouver Island. [after the *Gulf of Georgia*, the original name for the strait]

Gulf Islands National Park Reserve a park reserve consisting of lands (including an intertidal zone) on 16 islands and numerous small islets and reef areas in the southern Gulf Islands.

Gulf States 1 the states of the US bordering on the Gulf of Mexico (Florida, Alabama, Mississippi, Louisiana, and Texas). **2** the states bordering on the Persian Gulf (Iran, Iraq, Kuwait, Saudi Arabia, Bahrain, Qatar, the United Arab Emirates, and Oman).

Gulf Stream a warm ocean current which flows from the Gulf of Mexico parallel with the coast of N America towards Newfoundland, continuing across the Atlantic Ocean towards NW Europe as the North Atlantic Drift.

Gulf War the war of January and February 1991 between Iraq and an international coalition of forces led by the US, in which Iraq was compelled to withdraw with very heavy casualties from Kuwait, which it had invaded and occupied in August 1990.

Gulf War syndrome *noun* a disorder of the nervous system alleged to have been contracted by soldiers serving in the Gulf War of 1991.

gulf·weed *noun* = SARGASSO.

gull[1] *noun* any of various long-winged web-footed seabirds of the family Laridae, usu. having white plumage with a mantle varying from pearly-grey to black, and a bright bill. □ **gul·lery** *noun* (*pl.* **-ies**). [Middle English, ultimately from Old Celtic]

gull[2] *transitive verb* (usu. in *passive*; foll. by *into*) dupe, fool. [perhaps from obsolete *gull* yellow, from Old Norse *gulr*]

Gul·lah /ˈgʌlə/ ● *noun* **1** a member of a people living on the coast of S Carolina or the nearby sea islands. **2** the Creole language spoken by them. ● *adjective* of or relating to the Gullahs or their language. [perhaps a shortening of *Angola*, or from a tribal name *Golas*]

gul·let *noun* **1** the food passage extending from the mouth to the stomach; the esophagus. **2** the throat. **3** the space between the teeth of a saw. [Old French diminutive of *go(u)le* throat, from Latin *gula*]

gul·lible *adjective* easily persuaded or deceived; credulous. □ **gul·li·bil·ity** *noun*

gull-wing *adjective* **1** (of a car door) hinged along the top and opening outwards and upwards. **2** (of a car) having gull-wing doors.

gully ● *noun (pl.* **-lies**) (also **gulley** *pl.* **-leys**) **1** a small ravine, esp. formed by water after heavy rain. **2** a deep artificial channel; a gutter or drain. **3** *Cdn (Nfld)* a pond in a marsh, esp. one linked to others. **4** *Austral. & NZ* a river valley. ● *transitive verb* (**-lies**, **-lied**) **1** form (channels) by water action. **2** make gullies in. [French *goulet* bottleneck (as GULLET)]

gulp ● *verb* **1** *transitive* (often foll. by *down*) swallow hastily, greedily, or with effort. **2** *intransitive* swallow gaspingly or with difficulty; choke. **3** *transitive* (foll. by *down, back*) stifle, suppress (esp. tears). ● *noun* **1** an act of gulping (*drained it in one gulp*). **2** an effort to swallow. **3** a large mouthful of a drink. □ **gulp·er** *noun* **gulpy** *adjective* [prob. from Middle Dutch *gulpen* (imitative)]

gum¹ ● *noun* **1 a** a viscous secretion of some trees and shrubs that hardens on drying but is soluble in water (*compare* RESIN 1). **b** an adhesive substance made from this. **2** *N Amer.* **a** = CHEWING GUM. **b** = BUBBLE GUM. **3** *Brit.* = GUMDROP. **4** = GUM ARABIC. **5** = GUM TREE. ● *verb* (**gummed, gum·ming**) **1** *transitive* smear or cover with gum. **2** *transitive* (usu. foll. by *down, together*, etc.) fasten with gum. **3** *transitive* make (a birchbark canoe) watertight by sealing its seams with melted pine gum. **4** *intransitive* exude gum. □ **gum up 1** (of a mechanism etc.) become clogged or obstructed with stickiness. **2** *informal* interfere with the smooth running of (*gum up the works*). [Old French *gomme*, ultimately from Latin *gummi, cummi* from Greek *kommi* from Egyptian *kemai*]

gum² ● *noun* (usu. in *pl.*) the firm flesh around the roots of the teeth. ● *transitive verb* (of someone without teeth) chew with the gums as though with teeth. [Old English *gōma* related to Old High German *guomo*, Old Norse *gómr* roof or floor of the mouth)

gum³ *noun informal* (in oaths) God (*by gum!*). [corruption of *God*]

gum arabic *noun* a gum exuded by some kinds of acacia, esp. *Acacia senegal*, and used as glue and as an emulsifier.

gum benjamin *noun* benzoin.

gum·bo *noun (pl.* **-bos**) *N Amer.* **1 a** okra. **b** a spicy chicken or seafood soup thickened with okra, rice, etc. **2** a heavy clayey soil that is sticky and non-porous when wet; thick clinging mud. **3** (**Gumbo**) a French-based creole spoken in some Black communities in Louisiana. [of African origin: compare Bantu (Angolan) *kingombo* okra]

gum·boil *noun* a small abscess on the gums.

gum·boot *noun* a rubber boot usu. reaching the knee.

gum·drop *noun* a soft coloured candy made with gelatin or gum arabic.

gum line *noun* the point where the tooth protrudes from the gum.

gumma *noun (pl.* **gum·mas** or **gum·mata** /-mətə/) *Med.* a small soft swelling occurring in the connective tissue of the liver, brain, testes, and heart, and characteristic of the late stages of syphilis. □ **gum·ma·tous** *adjective* [modern Latin from Latin *gummi* GUM¹]

gummi *noun* a rubbery, coloured and flavoured candy, often in the shape of animals, insects, etc. (also *attributive*: *gummi spiders*). [German]

gummy¹ *adjective* (**gum·mi·er, gum·mi·est**) **1** viscous, sticky. **2** abounding in or exuding gum. □ **gum·mi·ness** *noun*

gummy² *adjective* (**gum·mi·er, gum·mi·est**) toothless. □ **gum·mi·ly** *adverb*

gump·tion *noun informal* **1 a** resourcefulness, initiative; enterprising spirit. **b** courage. **2** common sense. [18th-c. Scots: origin unknown]

gum resin *noun* a vegetable secretion of resin mixed with gum, e.g. gamboge.

gum·shield *noun* a pad protecting a boxer's teeth and gums.

gum·shoe ● *noun* **1** a galosh. **2** *N Amer. informal* a detective. ● *intransitive verb* (**-shoed, -shoe·ing**) *N Amer. informal* **1** move or act stealthily. **2** act as a detective.

gum tree *noun* a tree exuding gum, esp. a eucalyptus. □ **up a gum tree** *informal* in great difficulties.

gum·weed *noun* a plant, *Grindelia squarrosa*, with dark green gummy leaves and showy yellow flowers with sticky bracts, widespread in W Canada.

gum·wood *noun* the wood of a gum tree.

gun ● *noun* **1** a kind of weapon (of any size from a hand-held pistol to a mounted piece of artillery), consisting of a metal tube from which bullets or other missiles are propelled with great force, esp. by a contained explosion. **2** any device imitative of this, e.g. a starting pistol. **3** a device for discharging something under pressure (often in *combination*: *grease gun; staple gun*). **4** *N Amer.* a gunman. **5** the firing of a gun. **6** *N Amer. Sport informal* (esp. in hockey) a prolific scorer. ● *verb* (**gunned, gun·ning**) **1** *transitive* **a** (often foll. by *down*) shoot (a person) with a gun. **b** shoot at with a gun. **2** *transitive informal* accelerate (an engine or vehicle). **3** *intransitive* go hunting with a gun. **4** *intransitive* (foll. by *for*) **a** seek out determinedly to attack or rebuke. **b** go determinedly or energetically after. □ **go great guns** *informal* proceed forcefully or vigorously or successfully. **jump the gun** *informal* start before a signal is given, or before an agreed time. **put** (or **hold**) **a gun to someone's head** subject someone to extreme coercive pressure. **stick to one's guns** *informal* maintain one's position under attack. **under the gun** *informal* under pressure (*we're under the gun to get this thing finished*). □ **gun·less** *adjective* **gunned** *adjective* [Middle English *gunne, gonne*, perhaps from the Scandinavian name *Gunnhildr*, from *gunnr + hildr*, both meaning 'war']

gun·boat *noun* a small vessel of shallow draft and having relatively heavy guns.

gunboat diplomacy *noun* political negotiation supported by the use or threat of military force.

gun carriage *noun* a wheeled support for a gun.

gun control *noun N Amer.* the legislated regulation or restriction of private firearm ownership.

gun cotton *noun* an explosive used for blasting, made by steeping cotton in nitric and sulphuric acids.

gun crew *noun* a team operating a gun.

gun deck *noun* **1** a deck on a ship on which guns are placed. **2** *hist.* the lowest such deck on a battleship.

gun dog *noun* a dog bred or trained to assist hunters, e.g. by pointing, retrieving, flushing, etc.

gun·fight *noun* a fight with firearms. □ **gun·fight·er** *noun*

gun·fire *noun* **1** the firing of a gun or guns, esp. repeatedly. **2** the noise from this.

gunge *informal* ● *noun* = GUNK *noun*. ● *transitive verb* (usu. foll. by *up*) clog or obstruct with gunge. □ **gungy** *adjective* [20th c.: origin uncertain: compare GOO, GUNK]

gung-ho *adjective* **1** enthusiastic, eager. **2** uninhibited; quick to take action. [Chinese *gonghe* 'work together', slogan adopted by US Marines in 1942]

gunk *esp. N Amer. slang* ● *noun* sticky or viscous matter, esp. when messy or indeterminate. ● *transitive verb* (often foll. by *up*) soil or clog with gunk. □ **gunky** *adjective* (**-ier, -iest**). [20th c.: originally the proprietary name of a degreasing substance]

gunk·hole ● *noun* a shallow inlet that is difficult or dangerous to navigate. ● *intransitive verb* cruise in and out of such inlets or coves. [20th c.: orig. unknown]

gun·lock *noun* a mechanism by which the charge of a gun is exploded.

gun·man *noun (pl.* **-men**) a person armed with a gun, esp. in committing a crime.

gun·metal ● *noun* **1** (in full **gunmetal grey, gunmetal blue**) a dull bluish-grey colour. **2** an alloy of copper and tin or zinc (formerly used for guns). ● *adjective* dull bluish grey.

Gun·nar /ˈɡʊnɑr/ *Scand. Myth* the brother of Gudrun and husband of Brynhild; he corresponds to Gunther in the *Nibelungenlied*.

gun·nel¹ /ˈɡʌnəl/ *noun* any small eel-shaped marine fish of the family Pholidae. [17th c.: origin unknown]

gun·nel² *var. of* GUNWALE.

gun·ner *noun* **1 a** (also **Gunner**) a private in the artillery. Abbr.: **Gnr**. **b** any member of the artillery. **2** a person who operates a gun, esp. on an aircraft or ship. **3** a person who hunts game with a gun.

gun·nera /ˈɡʌnərə/ *noun* any plant of the genus *Gunnera* from S America and New Zealand, having large leaves and often grown for ornament. [J. E. *Gunnerus*, Norwegian botanist d.1773]

gun·nery *noun* **1** the design and operation of esp. large guns. **2** the firing of guns.

gunny *noun (pl.* **-nies**) *N Amer.* **1** coarse sacking, usu. of jute fibre; burlap. **2** (in full **gunny sack**) a sack made of this. [Hindi & Marathi *gōni* from Sanskrit *gōni* sack]

gun·play *noun* the use of guns.

gun·point *noun* the point of a gun. □ **at gunpoint** threatened with a gun or an ultimatum etc.

gun·powder *noun* **1** an explosive powder made of potassium nitrate, sulphur, and charcoal, used for fuses, fireworks, and blasting. **2** a fine green tea of granular appearance.

Gunpowder Plot a conspiracy by a small group of extremist Catholics to blow up James I and his Parliament on 5 Nov. 1605. The day before the scheduled attack, one of the conspirators, Guy Fawkes, was found in the cellars of the Houses of Parliament, the plot having been uncovered. Under torture he betrayed his colleagues, some of whom were killed resisting arrest; he and others were arrested and executed. The plot is commemorated in Britain on 5 Nov. with bonfires, fireworks, and with the burning of an effigy of Guy Fawkes.

gun·room *noun* a room in a house for storing guns.

gun·run·ner *noun* a person engaged in the illegal sale or importing of firearms or other weapons. □ **gun-running** *noun*

gun·ship *noun* a heavily-armed helicopter or other aircraft.

gun·shot *noun* **1** a shot fired from a gun. **2** the sound of this. **3** the range of a gun (*within gunshot*).

gun·shy *adjective* **1** (esp. of a hunting dog) afraid of a gun or the sound that it makes. **2** hesitant or nervous, esp. because of a previous unpleasant experience.

gun·sight *noun* a sight on a gun (see SIGHT *noun* 7).

gun·sling·er *noun* esp. *US slang* a gunfighter. □ **gun·sling·ing** *noun & adjective*

gun·smith *noun* a person who makes, sells, and repairs firearms. □ **gun·smith·ing** *noun*

gun·stock *noun* the esp. wooden mounting for the barrel and firing mechanism of a rifle etc.

Gun·ter /ˈɡʌntər/ **Ed·mund** (1581–1626), English mathematician, who invented a number of measuring instruments and introduced the terms *cosine* and *tangent*.

Gun·ther /ˈɡʊntər/ (in the *Nibelungenlied*) a king of Burgundy, who was allied with Siegfried; he corresponds to Gunnar in Scandinavian mythology.

Gun·tur /ɡʊnˈtʊr/ a city in E India, in Andhra Pradesh; pop. (2001) 514,700.

gun·wale /ˈɡʌnəl/ *noun* (also **gun·nel**) the upper edge of the side of a boat or ship. [GUN + WALE (because formerly used to support guns)]

Guo·min·dang *var. of* KUOMINTANG.

guppy *noun* (pl. **-pies**) a small freshwater fish, *Poecilia reticulata*, of the W Indies and S America, frequently kept in aquariums, and giving birth to live young. [R. J. L. *Guppy*, 19th-c. Trinidad clergyman who sent the first specimen to the British Museum]

Gupta /ˈɡʊptə/ the name of a Hindu dynasty established in AD 320 by Chandra Gupta I in Bihar, eventually controlling most of northern India before disintegrating until only northern Bengal was left by the middle of the 6th c. □ **Gup·tan** *adjective*

gurd·wara /ɡɜrdˈwʊrə/ *noun* a Sikh temple. [Punjabi *gurduārā* from Sanskrit *guru* teacher + *dvāra* door]

gurdy *noun* (pl. **-dies**) *N Amer.* a winch on a fishing boat used to haul in a line, net, etc. [prob. from earlier HURDY-GURDY in this sense]

gur·gle ● *verb* **1** *intransitive* make a bubbling sound as of water from a bottle or flowing over stones. **2** *intransitive* (of liquid) flow with such a sound. **3** *transitive* utter with such a sound. ● *noun* a gurgling sound. □ **gurg·ly** *adjective* [imitative, or from Dutch *gorgelen*, German *gurgeln*, or medieval Latin *gurgulare*, from Latin *gurgulio* 'gullet']

Gur·kha /ˈɡɜrkə/ *noun* **1** a member of the principal Hindu race in Nepal. **2** a Nepalese soldier serving in the British army. [name of locality from Sanskrit *goraksa* cowherd (from *go* cow + *raks-* protect) as epithet of patron deity]

gur·nard /ˈɡɜrnərd/ *noun* = SEA ROBIN. [Old French *gornart* from *grondir* to grunt, from Latin *grunnire*]

gur·ney *noun N Amer.* a wheeled stretcher used to transport patients in a hospital etc. [apparently named after J. T. *Gurney*, US designer of a two-wheeled horse-drawn cab in 1883]

gurry *noun N Amer.* fish entrails or offal as refuse from cleaning fish. [origin unknown]

guru /ˈɡuːruː, ˈɡʊruː/ *noun* **1** a Hindu spiritual teacher or head of a religious sect. **2** often *derogatory* **a** an influential teacher. **b** a revered mentor. [Sanskrit *guru* elder, teacher]

gush ● *verb* **1** *transitive & intransitive* emit or flow in a sudden and copious stream. **2** *intransitive* speak or behave with effusiveness or sentimental affectation. ● *noun* **1** a sudden or copious stream. **2** an effusive or

sentimental outburst or manner. □ **gush·ing** *adjective* **gush·ing·ly** *adverb* [Middle English *gosshe*, *gusche*, prob. imitative]

gush·er *noun* **1** an oil well from which oil flows without being pumped. **2** an effusive person.

gushy *adjective* (**gush·i·er**, **gush·i·est**) excessively effusive or sentimental. □ **gush·i·ly** *adverb* **gush·i·ness** *noun*

gus·set *noun* **1** a piece of material let into a garment etc. to strengthen or enlarge a part. **2** a bracket strengthening an angle of a structure. □ **gus·set·ed** *adjective* [Old French *gousset* flexible piece filling up a joint in armour, from *gousse* pod, shell]

gussy *transitive verb* (**-sies, -sied**) (esp. in *passive*; foll. by *up*) esp. *N Amer. informal* dress up, esp. for a special occasion. [perhaps from *Gussie* pet form of the name *Augustus*]

gust ● *noun* **1** a sudden strong rush of wind. **2** a burst of rain, fire, smoke, or sound. **3** a passionate or emotional outburst. ● *intransitive verb* blow in gusts. [Old Norse *gustr*, related to *gjósa* to gush]

gus·ta·tory /ˈɡʌstətˌɔri/ *adjective* concerned with tasting or the sense of taste. [Latin *gustat-* past participle stem of *gustare* to taste + -ORY²]

Gus·ta·vus I /ɡʊˈstɒvəs/ (born Gustavus Vasa) (*c.*1496–1560), king of Sweden 1523–60. He fought against the Danes (1517–23), modernized the Swedish economy, and established Lutheranism as the state religion (1527).

Gustavus II see GUSTAVUS ADOLPHUS.

Gustavus VI /ɡʊˈstɒvəs/ (born Oscar Fredrik Wilhelm Olaf Gustaf Adolf) (1882–1973), king of Sweden 1950–73, who was the last Swedish monarch to hold real political power before the constitutional reforms of 1971.

Gus·ta·vus Adol·phus /ɡʊˌstɒvəs əˈdɒlfəs/ (also **Gustavus II**) (1594–1632), king of Sweden 1611–32. He raised Sweden to the status of a European power by his victories against Denmark, Poland, and Russia in the first part of his reign, and in 1630 intervened on the Protestant side in the Thirty Years War.

gusto /ˈɡʌstoː/ *noun* zest; enthusiasm or vigour in doing something. [Italian from Latin *gustus* taste]

gusty *adjective* (**gust·i·er**, **gust·i·est**) **1** characterized by or blowing in strong winds. **2** marked by sudden bursts of feeling or action. **3** characterized by gusto. □ **gust·i·ly** *adverb* **gust·i·ness** *noun*

gut ● *noun* **1 a** the lower alimentary canal or a part of this; the intestine. **b** *informal* the abdomen or belly (*punched in the gut*). **2** (in *pl.*) the bowel or entrails, esp. of animals. **3** (in *pl.*) *informal* personal courage and determination; vigorous application and perseverance. **4** (in *pl.*) *informal* the belly as the source of appetite. **5** (in *pl.*) **a** the contents of anything, esp. representing substantiality. **b** the essence of a thing, e.g. of an issue or problem. **6 a** material for violin or racquet strings or surgical use made from the intestines of animals. **b** material for fishing lines made from the silk glands of silkworms. **7 a** a narrow water passage; a sound or strait. **b** a defile or narrow passage. **8** (*attributive*) **a** instinctive (*a gut reaction; a gut feeling*). **b** fundamental (*a gut issue*). ● *transitive verb* (**gut·ted, gut·ting**) **1** (often in *passive*) remove or destroy (esp. by fire) the internal fittings of (a house etc.). **2** take out the guts of (a fish). **3** remove the essential components of. **4** extract the essence of (a book etc.). □ **hate a person's guts** *informal* dislike a person intensely. **have someone's guts for garters** *Cdn & Brit.* be extremely angry at someone. **spill one's guts** see SPILL¹. **split a gut** see SPLIT. **sweat** (or **work** etc.) **one's guts out** *informal* work etc. extremely hard or energetically. [Old English *guttas* (pl.), prob. related to *gēotan* pour]

gut·bucket *adjective* designating a very spirited, robust, or raw style of music, esp. jazz. [GUT + BUCKET, a bucket used to collect drippings from liquor barrels in bars where such jazz was originally played]

gut-busting *adjective* **1** hilariously funny. **2** (of food) very dense or rich and filling. □ **gut-buster** *noun*

gut check *noun N Amer. slang* **1** (esp. in sport) a re-examination of one's level of effort, followed by renewed determination, effort, etc. **2** an occasion on which one examines one's gut instinct in relation to a risky undertaking etc.

Guten·berg /ˈɡuːtənˌbɜrɡ/ **Jo·hannes** (born Johannes Gensfleisch) *c.*1400–68), German printer. He invented printing using movable type, and by *c.*1455 he had produced an edition of the Vulgate which later became known as the Gutenberg Bible.

gut·ful *noun* = BELLYFUL.

Guth·rie /ˈɡʌθri/ **Woody** (born Woodrow Wilson Guthrie) (1912–1967), US folksinger and songwriter, who is known for his radical political stance, and for his protest songs about the US rural poor during the Depression, which include 'This Land is Your Land' (1944).

Consonants: b *but* d *dog* f *few* g *get* h *her* j *yes* k *cat* l *leg* m *man* n *no* p *pen* r *red* s *sit*

Guth·run *var. of* GUDRUN.

gut·less *adjective informal* lacking courage or determination; feeble. □ **gut·less·ly** *adverb* **gut·less·ness** *noun*

gut-level *attributive adjective* instinctive; heartfelt.

gut-shot *adjective N Amer.* (esp. of game) shot in the abdomen, esp. fatally. □ **gut-shoot** *verb* **gut-shooter** *noun* **gut-shooting** *noun*

gutsy *adjective* (**guts·i·er**, **guts·i·est**) *informal* courageous; tough. □ **guts·i·ly** *adverb* **guts·i·ness** *noun*

gutta per·cha /ˌɡʌtəˈpɜrtʃə/ *noun* a tough plastic substance obtained from the latex of various Malaysian trees. [Malay *getah* gum + *percha* name of a tree]

gut·tate /ˈɡʌteɪt/ *adjective Biol.* having drop-like markings. [Latin *guttatus* speckled from *gutta* drop]

gut·ted *adjective* **1** *in senses of* GUT *verb.* **2** *Brit. slang* bitterly disappointed; deeply upset.

gut·ter ● *noun* **1 a** a channel at the side of a street to carry away runoff. **b** *esp. US & Brit.* = EAVESTROUGH. **2** (prec. by *the*) **a** a poor or degraded background or environment (*worked their way out of the gutter*). **b** a sordid or vulgar situation (*get your mind out of the gutter*). **3** an open conduit or channel along which liquid etc. flows out. **4** a groove. **5** a track made by the flow of water. **6** the channel running along each side of a bowling lane. **7** the space between open pages of a book, magazine, etc. ● *intransitive verb* **1** (of a candle) melt away as the wax forms channels down the side. **2** (of a candle flame) flicker before being extinguished, esp. as the last wax melts away. [Anglo-French *gotere* ultimately from Latin *gutta* drop]

gut·ter·ing *noun* **1 a** the gutters of a building etc. **b** a section or length of a gutter. **2** material for gutters.

gutter press *noun* sensational journalism concerned esp. with the private lives of public figures.

gutter·snipe *noun* **1** a street urchin. **2** an ill-mannered street person or vagrant.

gut·tur·al /ˈɡʌtərəl/ *adjective* **1** (of a sound) produced at the back of the throat. **2** (of speech) characterized by guttural sounds. □ **gut·tur·al·ly** *adverb* [French *guttural* or medieval Latin *gutturalis* from Latin *guttur* throat]

gutty *adjective* = GUTSY.

gut-wrenching *adjective* emotionally devastating.

guv *noun slang* = GOVERNOR 8c. [abbreviation]

Guy, John (d.1629), merchant and colonizer, governor (1610–15) of the first English colony in Newfoundland. After his return to England, he continued to support permanent colonies in Newfoundland against the interests of English migratory fishermen.

guy[1] ● *noun* **1** *informal* a man; a fellow. **2** (in *pl.*) *N Amer. informal* a person of either sex. **3** *Brit.* an effigy of Guy Fawkes in ragged clothing, burned on a bonfire on 5 Nov. **4** *Brit.* a grotesquely dressed person. ● *transitive verb* **1** ridicule. **2** exhibit in effigy. [*Guy* FAWKES]

guy[2] ● *noun* a rope , wire, cable, etc. used to secure a tent or keep something upright. ● *transitive verb* secure with a guy or guys. [prob. of Low German origin]

Guy·ana /ɡaiˈanə/ a country on the northeast coast of S America; pop. (est. 2002) 698,209; capital, Georgetown. □ **Guyan·ese** /ˌɡaiəˈniːz/ *adjective & noun*

Guy·enne /ɡiːˈen/ (also **Guienne**) a region and former province of S France, stretching from the Bay of Biscay to the southwestern edge of the Massif Central.

Guy Fawkes' Night *noun Brit.* 5 Nov., on which fireworks are displayed and an effigy of Guy Fawkes burned.

guy wire *noun* a wire or cable used to secure a tent or keep something upright.

guz·zle *transitive & intransitive verb* eat, drink, or consume excessively or greedily. □ **guz·zler** *noun* [perhaps from Old French *gosiller* chatter, vomit, from *gosier* throat]

GVRD *abbreviation* Greater Vancouver Regional District.

Gwaii Haa·nas National Park Reserve and Haida Heritage Site /ɡwai ˈhɒnɒs/ *noun* a park reserve on the southern part of the Queen Charlotte Islands, which includes the World Heritage Site SGaang Gwaii. [Haida, = 'beautiful land' from *gwaii* 'land' + *haana* 'beautiful']

Gwa·lior /ˈɡwɒliˌɔr/ a city in a district of the same name in Madhya Pradesh, central India; pop. (2001) 826,900.

Gwent /ɡwent/ a former county of SE Wales on the Bristol Channel bordering Gloucestershire, formed in 1974 and dissolved in 1996.

Gwich'in /ˈɡwitʃin/ ● *noun* **1** a member of an Aboriginal people living in Alaska, the Yukon, and the NWT. **2** the Athapaskan language of the Gwich'in. ● *adjective* of or relating to this people or their language or culture. [Gwich'in, = 'people, dwellers']

Gwyn, Elea·nor ('Nell') (1650–87), English actress. Originally an orange seller, she became famous as a comedic actress and as the mistress of Charles II.

Gwyn·edd /ˈɡwɪneð/ **1** a county in the NW corner of Wales, formed in 1974 from Anglesey, Caernarvonshire, part of Denbighshire, and most of Merionethshire, and re-formed in 1996 with a smaller area; administrative centre, Caernarvon. **2** a former principality of N Wales. Powerful in the mid-13th c. under Llewelyn, it was finally subjugated by the English forces of Edward I in 1282, following Llewelyn's death.

Gy *abbreviation* = GRAY[2].

gybe /dʒaib/ (also **jibe**) ● *verb* **1** *intransitive* (of a fore-and-aft sail or boom) swing across in wearing or running before the wind. **2** *transitive* cause (a sail) to do this. **3** *intransitive* (of a ship or its crew) change course so that this happens. ● *noun* a change of course causing gybing. [obsolete Dutch *gijben*]

gym *noun informal* **1** a gymnasium. **2** physical education. **3** gymnastics. [abbreviation]

gym·khana /dʒɪmˈkɒnə/ *noun* an equestrian day event comprising races and other competitions on horseback, esp. for children. [Hindustani *gendkhāna* ball house, racquet court, assimilated to GYMNASIUM]

gym·na·sium /dʒɪmˈneiziəm/ *noun* (*pl.* **gym·na·siums** or *rare* **gym·na·sia** /-ziə/) **1** a room or building equipped for gymnastics, indoor sports, physical training, etc. **2** a school, esp. in Germany or Scandinavia, that prepares pupils for university entrance. [Latin from Greek *gumnasion* from *gumnazō* exercise, from *gumnos* naked]

gym·nast /ˈdʒɪmnast, -nəst/ *noun* an expert in gymnastics. [French *gymnaste* or Greek *gumnastēs* athlete trainer, from *gumnazō*: see GYMNASIUM]

gym·nas·tic /dʒɪmˈnastɪk/ *adjective* of or involving gymnastics. □ **gym·nas·tic·ally** *adverb*

gym·nas·tics /dʒɪmˈnastɪks/ *plural noun* (also treated as *sing.*) **1** exercises developing or displaying physical agility and coordination, usu. in competition. **2** other forms of physical or mental agility (*verbal gymnastics*).

gym·na·tor·ium *noun N Amer.* a large room in a school, church hall, etc. that serves as both a gymnasium and an auditorium.

gymno- /ˈdʒɪmnoː/ *combining form Biol.* bare, naked. [Greek *gumnos* naked]

gym·noso·phist /dʒɪmˈnɒsəfɪst/ *noun* a member of an ancient contemplative Hindu sect wearing little clothing. □ **gym·noso·phy** *noun* [ultimately from Greek *gumnosophistai*: see GYMNO-, SOPHIST]

gymno·sperm /ˈdʒɪmnoːˌspɜrm/ *noun* any of various plants having seeds unprotected by an ovary, including conifers, cycads, and ginkgos (*opp.* ANGIOSPERM). □ **gymno·sperm·ous** /-ˈspɜrməs/ *adjective*

gym rat *noun slang* a person who enjoys spending a great deal of time in gyms, e.g. to play basketball or to weight train.

gym shoe *noun* = RUNNING SHOE.

gym·slip *noun Brit.* a sleeveless tunic, usu. belted, formerly worn by schoolgirls.

gy·nae·ceum *var. of* GYNOECIUM.

gynaeco- *combining form var. of* GYNECO-.

gyneco- /ˈɡainəkoː, ˌɡainəˈkɒ-/ *combining form* (also **gynaeco-**) woman, women; female. [Greek *gunē gunaikos* woman]

gyne·col·ogy /ˌɡainəˈkɒlədʒi/ *noun* (also **gynae·col·ogy**) the science of the physiological functions and diseases of women and girls, esp. those affecting the reproductive system. □ **gyne·co·logic·al** *adjective* **gyne·co·logic·al·ly** *adverb* **gyne·col·o·gist** *noun*

gyne·co·mas·tia /ˌɡainəkoːˈmastiə/ *noun* (also **gynae·co·mas·tia**) *Med.* enlargement of a man's breasts, usu. due to hormone imbalance or hormone therapy.

gynie *noun informal* **1** a gynecologist. **2** gynecology.

gyno- /ˈɡainoː, ˈdʒɪ-/ *combining form* **1** woman, women. **2** *Bot.* female. [Greek *gunē* woman]

gyno /ˈɡainoː/ *noun N Amer. informal* a gynecologist.

gyno·cen·tric /ˌɡainoːˈsentrɪk/ *adjective* (of an attitude, viewpoint, society, etc.) based on women's perspectives.

gy·noe·cium /ɡaiˈniːsiəm, dʒɪ-/ *noun* (also **gynae·ceum**) (*pl.* **-cia** /-siə/) *Bot.* the carpels of a flower taken collectively. [modern Latin from Greek *gunaikeion* women's apartments (as GYNECO-, Greek *oikos* house)]

-gynous /ˈɡinəs, ˈdʒɪnəs/ *combining form* **1** of or pertaining to women (*androgynous*). **2** *Bot.* forming adjectives meaning 'having specified female organs or pistils' (*monogynous*). [as GYNO-]

gyp¹ /dʒɪp/ *noun* Brit. informal **1** pain or severe discomfort. **2** a scolding (*gave them gyp*). [19th c.: perhaps from *gee-up* (see GEE²)]

gyp² /dʒɪp/ *slang* ● *transitive verb* (**gypped**, **gyp·ping**) cheat, swindle. ● *noun* an act of cheating; a swindle. [19th c.: origin unknown]

gyp·po /ˈdʒɪpoː/ *noun* (also **gypo**) (usu. *attributive*) N Amer. a minor or small-time logging operator or contractor (*gyppo outfit*; *gyppo show*). [GYP²]

gyppy tummy *var. of* GIPPY TUMMY.

Gyp·roc /ˈdʒɪprɒk/ *noun* proprietary Cdn & Austral. = DRYWALL *noun*. [GYPSUM + ROCK¹]

gyp·so·phila /dʒɪpˈsɒfɪlə/ *noun* any plant of the genus *Gypsophila*, with a profusion of small usu. white composite flowers, esp. baby's breath. [modern Latin from Greek *gupsos* chalk + *philos* loving]

gyp·sum /ˈdʒɪpsəm/ *noun* a hydrated form of calcium sulphate occurring naturally and used in the building industry and to make plaster of Paris. [Latin from Greek *gupsos*]

gypsum·board /ˈdʒɪpsəmˌbɔːd/ *noun* N Amer. = DRYWALL.

gypsy /ˈdʒɪpsi/ *noun* (also **gipsy**) (pl. **-sies**) **1** (also **Gypsy**) a member of a nomadic people of Europe and N America, of Hindu origin, speaking a language (Romany) related to Hindi. **2** a person resembling or living like a Gypsy. □ **gypsy·ish** *adjective* [earlier *gipcyan*, *gipsen* from EGYPTIAN, from the supposed origin of gypsies when they appeared in England in the early 16th c.]

gypsy moth *noun* a kind of tussock moth, *Lymantria dispar*, of which the larvae are very destructive to foliage.

gyr·ate /ˈdʒaɪreɪt/ ● *intransitive verb* (also /dʒaɪˈreɪt/) **1** revolve around a fixed point or axis; go in a circle or spiral. **2** move one's hips rhythmically in a circular pattern, esp. in a sexually suggestive way. ● *adjective* Bot. arranged in rings or convolutions. □ **gyr·a·tion** /-ˈreɪʃən/ *noun* **gyra·tory** /-rəˌtɔri/ *adjective* [Latin *gyrare gyrat-* revolve, from *gyrus* ring, from Greek *guros*]

gyre /ˈdʒaɪr/ esp. literary ● *intransitive verb* whirl, gyrate. ● *noun* **1** a whirling, a vortex; a gyration. **2** a circulatory ocean current. [Latin *gyrus* 'ring' from Greek *guros*]

gyr·falcon /ˈdʒɜːrˌfɒlkən/ *noun* a large falcon, *Falco rusticolus*, of the northern hemisphere. [Old French *gerfaucon* from Frankish *gērfalco* from Old Norse *geirfálki*: see FALCON]

gyri pl. of GYRUS.

gyro¹ /ˈdʒaɪroː/ *noun* (pl. **gyros**) informal **1** = GYROSCOPE. **2** = GYROCOMPASS. [abbreviation]

gyro² /ˈjiːroː/ *noun* (pl. **gyros**) N Amer. a sandwich of pita bread filled with slices of spiced meat cooked on a spit, tomatoes, onions, etc. [modern Greek *guros* turning]

gyro- /ˈdʒaɪroː/ *combining form* **1** rotation. **2** gyroscopic. [Greek *guros* 'ring']

gyro·com·pass /ˈdʒaɪroːˌkʌmpəs/ *noun* a non-magnetic compass giving true north and bearings from it by means of a gyroscope.

gyro·mag·net·ic /ˌdʒaɪroːmagˈnetɪk/ *adjective* Physics of the magnetic and mechanical properties of a rotating charged particle.

gyro·scope /ˈdʒaɪrəˌskoːp/ *noun* a wheel or disc mounted so as to spin rapidly about an axis whose orientation is not fixed but is unperturbed by tilting of the mount, esp. used in stabilizers, gyrocompasses, navigation systems, etc. □ **gyro·scop·ic** /-ˈskɒpɪk/ *adjective* **gyro·scop·ic·ally** /-ˈskɒpɪkli/ *adverb* [French (as GYRO-, SCOPE²)]

gyro·stabil·iz·er /ˈdʒaɪroːˌsteɪbɪˌlaɪzər/ *noun* a gyroscopic device for maintaining the equilibrium of a ship, aircraft, platform, etc.

gyrus /ˈdʒaɪrəs/ *noun* (pl. **gyri** /-riˌ/) a fold or convolution, esp. of the brain. [Latin from Greek *guros* ring]

Gzow·ski /ˈzɒski/ **Peter** (1934–2002), Canadian broadcaster and writer. He hosted the highly popular CBC Radio programs 'This Country in the Morning' (1971–74) and 'Morningside' (1982–97), and also wrote several non-fiction books, including *The Game of Our Lives* (1981) and *The New Morningside Papers* (1987).

Vowels: a cat ɑ arm e bed ɜr her ɜː deux ə ago ɪ sit i cosy iː feed ɒ hot ɔ pore ɔː no ʌ run ʊ put

Hh

H¹ /eitʃ/ *noun* (also **h**) (*pl.* **Hs** or **H's**) **1** the eighth letter of the alphabet (*see* AITCH). **2** anything having the form of an H (esp. in *combination*: *H-girder*).

H² *abbreviation* (also **H.**) **1** hardness. **2** (of a pencil lead) hard. **3** (water) hydrant. **4** *slang* heroin.

H³ *symbol* **1** the element hydrogen. **2** henry(s). **3** magnetic field strength.

h¹ *abbreviation* (also **h.**) **1** height. **2** horse. **3** hot. **4** hour(s). **5** husband. **6** *Baseball* hit. **7** harbour. **8** *Music* horn. **9** hundred.

h² *symbol* **1** hecto-. **2** Planck's constant.

Ha *symbol Chem.* the element hahnium.

ha¹ *interjection* (also **hah**) expressing surprise, suspicion, triumph, etc. (*compare* HA HA). [Middle English]

ha² *abbreviation* hectare(s).

Haakon VII /ˈhɒkʊn/ (1872–1957), King of Norway 1905–57. During the German occupation of Norway (1940–45), he coordinated Norwegian resistance from England.

haar /hɑr/ *noun dialect* a cold sea fog on the east coast of England or Scotland. [perhaps from Old Norse *hárr* hoar, hoary]

Haar·lem /ˈhɑrləm/ a city in the Netherlands, near Amsterdam; pop. (est. 2002) 148,000. It is the capital of the province of North Holland and commercial centre of the Dutch bulb industry.

Hab·ak·kuk /ˈhæbəkək, həˈbak-/ **1** a Hebrew minor prophet probably of the 7th c. BC. **2** a book of the Bible bearing his name.

haba·nera /ˌhæbəˈnerə, -ˈnjerə/ *noun* **1** a Cuban dance in slow duple time. **2** the music for this. [Spanish, short for *danza habanera* dance of Havana, fem. of *habanero* 'of HAVANA¹']

haba·nero /ˌhæbəˈneroː/ *noun* a small, green, fiery hot chili pepper. [Spanish *habanero* 'of HAVANA¹']

hab·eas cor·pus /ˌheibiəs ˈkɔrpəs/ *noun* **1** a writ requiring a person to be brought before a judge or into court, esp. to investigate the lawfulness of his or her detention. **2** the right to such a writ as protection against unlawful detention. [Latin, = you must have the body]

haber·dash·er /ˈhæbərˌdæʃər/ *noun* **1** *N Amer.* a dealer in men's clothing and accessories. **2** *Brit.* a dealer in small articles related to dress or sewing, such as thread, tape, ribbons, etc. [Middle English, prob. ultimately from Anglo-French *hapertas* perhaps the name of a fabric]

haber·dash·ery /ˈhæbərˌdæʃəri/ *noun* (*pl.* **-eries**) **1** the goods and wares sold by a haberdasher. **2** the shop or establishment of a haberdasher, esp. as a department in a store.

Haber·mas, Jür·gen /ˈhæbərmæs; ˈjʊrgən/ (b.1929), German social philosopher. A leading figure of the Frankfurt School, he developed its cultural reappraisal of Marxism and is especially noted for his work on communication theory. □ **Haber·mas·ian** *adjective*

ha·bili·ment /həˈbɪləmənt/ *noun* (usu. in *pl.*) **1** clothes suited to a particular purpose. **2** *jocular* ordinary clothes. [Old French *habillement* from *habiller* fit out, from *habile* ABLE]

hab·it *noun* **1** (often foll. by *of* + verbal noun) a customary practice or way of acting (*has a habit of ignoring me*). **2** a practice that a person does often and almost without thinking, esp. one that is hard to give up. **3** a person's mental or moral constitution, disposition, qualities, or character. **4** *Psych.* an automatic reaction to a specific situation, acquired by learning or repetition. **5** *informal* **a** a craving for or

dependency on an addictive drug or drugs. **b** the practice of taking such a drug or drugs. **6 a** the dress of a particular religious order. **b** (in full **riding habit**) an outfit designed to be worn by a rider on horseback. **7** *Biol. & Mineralogy* the characteristic mode of growth and general external form of a plant or mineral. □ **make a habit of** do regularly. [Old French *abit* from Latin *habitus* from *habēre habit-* have, be constituted]

habit·able /ˈhæbɪtəbəl/ *adjective* fit or suitable for habitation; that can be inhabited. □ **habit·abil·ity** /-ˈbɪlɪti/ *noun* [Old French from Latin *habitabilis* (as HABITANT)]

habi·tant /ˌæbiˈtɑ̃/ *noun hist.* (in Canada) a French settler in rural Quebec up until the early 20th c., esp. a farmer. [French from Old French *habiter* from Latin *habitare* inhabit (as HABIT)]

habi·tat /ˈhæbɪˌtat/ *noun* **1 a** the natural environment characteristically occupied by an organism. **b** an area distinguished by the set of organisms which occupy it. **c** such areas collectively. **2** a person's usual or preferred surroundings. [Latin, = it dwells: see HABITANT]

habi·ta·tion /ˌhæbɪˈteiʃən/ *noun* **1** the action of dwelling in or inhabiting; occupancy by inhabitants (*not fit for human habitation*). **2** a house or home. [Old French from Latin *habitatio -onis* (as HABITANT)]

habitat loss *noun* the destruction or restriction of a species' habitat, esp. by human intervention.

habit-forming *adjective* causing addiction.

ha·bitu·al /həˈbɪtʃuəl/ *adjective* **1** done constantly or as a habit. **2** regular, continual, usual. **3** given to a specified habit (*a habitual smoker*). □ **ha·bitu·al·ly** *adverb* [medieval Latin *habitualis* (as HABIT)]

ha·bitu·ate /həˈbɪtʃuˌeit/ *transitive & intransitive verb* (often foll. by *to*) esp. *Zool.* make or become accustomed or used to something, esp. to living in close contact with humans. □ **ha·bitu·a·tion** *noun* [Late Latin *habituare* (as HABIT)]

habi·tué /həˈbɪtʃuˌei/ *noun* a habitual visitor to a place. [French, past participle of *habituer* (as HABITUATE)]

Habs·burg *var. of* HAPSBURG.

há·ček /ˈhatʃek/ *noun* a diacritical mark (ˇ) placed over letters to modify the sound in some Slavic and Baltic languages. [Czech, diminutive of *hák* hook]

Hachi·oji /ˌhatʃiˈoːdʒi/ a city in south central Japan, west of Tokyo; pop. (est. 1995) 503,363.

ha·cien·da /ˌhasiˈendə/ *noun* (in Spanish-speaking countries) **1** an estate or plantation, esp. one used for farming or ranching. **2** the house on such an estate. [Spanish from Latin *facienda* things to be done]

hack¹ ● *verb* **1** *transitive* cut or chop with heavy blows, esp. in a rough or random fashion. **2** *intransitive* (often foll. by *at*) deliver cutting blows. **3** *transitive* cut (a trail, one's way, etc.) through thick foliage etc. **4** *transitive* (of an editor etc.) shorten (a piece of writing, film footage, etc.), esp. detrimentally. **5** *informal* **a** *intransitive* (usu. foll. by *into*) use a computer to gain unauthorized access to data in a system. **b** *transitive* gain unauthorized access to (data in a computer etc.). **6** *transitive slang* cope with, manage, tolerate, or accept. **7** *intransitive* cough repeatedly with a short, dry cough. ● *noun* **1** an act of hacking or chopping, esp. a hacking blow. **2** a gash or wound, esp. from a kick. **3** an implement used in agriculture, mining, etc. for breaking or chopping up, esp. a two-pronged tool resembling a mattock. **4** a short, dry, hard cough. **5** *Curling* a rubber, metal, or wooden insert in the ice, used as a starting block to steady the foot when delivering a stone. **6** *informal* an attempt to break into a computer system. □ **hack around** *informal* **1** idly pass the time or wander aimlessly. **2** pass the time by computer hacking. **hacked off** *informal* annoyed, embarrassed, disconcerted, confused. [Old English *haccian* cut in pieces, from West Germanic]

hack² ● *noun* **1 a** a writer of mediocre literary or journalistic work. **b** *informal* usu. *derogatory* a journalist. **2** a person hired to do dull routine work. **3** *N Amer.* **a** a taxi. **b** a taxi driver. **4 a** a horse for ordinary riding. **b** a horse that may be hired. **c** = JADE² 1. ● *attributive adjective* **1** typical of a hack; commonplace (*hack journalism*). **2** used as a hack. ● *verb* **1** *intransitive* write like or work as a hack. **2 a** *intransitive* ride on horseback on a road at an ordinary pace. **b** *transitive* ride (a horse) in this way. [abbreviation of HACKNEY]

hack³ *noun* **1** a rack holding fodder for cattle. **2** a board on which a hawk's meat is laid. [var. of HATCH¹]

hacka·more *noun* *N Amer.* a bridle without a bit, having a hard, oval noseband which allows pressure to be exerted on the nose of a horse, used esp. in breaking colts. [perhaps from Spanish *jaquima*, formerly *xaquima* halter]

hack·berry *noun* (*pl.* **-berries**) *N Amer.* **1** any tree of the genus *Celtis*, native to N America, bearing purple edible berries. **2** the berry of this tree. [var. of *hagberry*, of Norse origin]

hack·er *noun* **1** a person or thing that hacks or cuts roughly. **2** *informal* **a** a computer user who attempts to gain unauthorized access to computer systems. **b** a computer user who is expert in programming. **3** *N Amer.* a person who engages in esp. a sporting activity in an unskilful fashion. □ **hack·ery** *noun*

hack·ing *adjective* (of a cough) short, dry, and frequently repeated.

hackle ● *noun* **1** a long feather or series of feathers on the neck or saddle of certain birds, e.g. the domestic rooster. **2** (in *pl.*) the erectile hairs along the back of a dog, which rise when it is angry or alarmed. **3** a feather in a Highland soldier's bonnet. **4** *Fishing* an artificial fly dressed wholly or chiefly with a hackle. **5** a steel comb for dressing flax. ● *transitive verb* dress or comb with a hackle. □ **make a person's hackles rise** or **raise some** (or **a person's**) **hackles** anger or annoy a person. [Middle English *hechele, hakele*, prob. from Old English from West Germanic]

hack·ma·tack /ˈhakmətak/ *noun* = TAMARACK. [perhaps from Western Abenaki]

hack·ney *noun* (*pl.* **-neys**) **1 a** a light harness horse with a compact body and a characteristic high-stepping trot. **b** a horse of average size and quality for ordinary riding. **2** (*attributive*) designating any of various vehicles kept for hire (*hackney carriage*). [Middle English, perhaps from *Hackney* (formerly *Hakenei*) in London, where horses were pastured]

hack·neyed *adjective* (of a phrase etc.) made commonplace or trite by overuse.

hack·saw *noun* a saw with a narrow blade set in a frame, for cutting metal.

hack·tiv·ism *noun* the commission of computer crimes, e.g. hacking into military or financial etc. computer systems, to further social or political ends. □ **hack·tiv·ist** *noun* [blend of HACK¹ + ACTIVISM]

hack·work *noun* mediocre esp. literary work done primarily or solely to make money.

had *past and past participle of* HAVE.

Hadar /ˈhadar, hɒˈdar/ a giant star, the second brightest in the constellation Centaurus. [Arabic *Ḥadār* ground, perhaps for the star's low position]

Ha·das·sah /həˈdasə/ *noun* a N American Jewish women's organization, founded in 1912 to support social and medical services in Israel. [Hebrew *hădassāh* myrtle, the name of the Biblical character Esther (Esther 2:7)]

had·dock /ˈhadək/ *noun* (*pl.* same) a marine fish, *Melanogrammus aeglefinus*, of the N Atlantic, related to the cod, but smaller, and popular as a food fish. [Middle English, prob. from Anglo-French *hadoc*, Old French *(h)adot*, of unknown origin]

hade /heɪd/ *Geol.* ● *noun* an incline from the vertical. ● *intransitive verb* incline from the vertical. [17th c., perhaps dial. form of *head*]

Hades /ˈheɪdiːz/ **1** *Gk Myth* **a** one of the sons of Cronus, lord of the lower world, the abode of the spirits of the dead. Also called PLUTO. **b** the kingdom of the dead. **2** *Bible* (esp. in the New Testament) the state or abode of spirits of the dead, esp. as a place of waiting before judgment. **3** *informal* (in imprecations) hell. □ **Hade·an** /heɪˈdiːən, ˈheɪdiən/ *adjective* [Greek *haidēs*, originally a name of Pluto]

Hadhra·maut /ˌhadrəˈmɔːt/ a narrow region on the southern coast of Yemen, separating the Gulf of Aden from the desert land of the S Arabian peninsula.

Had·ith /ˈhadɪθ, haˈdiːθ/ *noun* a collection of traditions containing sayings of the Prophet Muhammad, which, with accounts of his daily practice (see SUNNA), constitute the major source of guidance for Muslims after the Quran. [Arabic *ḥadīt* tradition]

hadj *var. of* HAJJ.

had·ji *var. of* HAJJI.

hadn't *contraction* had not.

Had·rian /ˈheɪdriən/ (full name Publius Aelius Hadrianus) (AD 76–138), Roman emperor 117–38. He spent much of his reign touring the provinces of the Empire and securing the frontiers; the building of Hadrian's Wall was begun after his visit to England in 122.

Hadrian's Wall a stone wall built by the Romans across northern England to defend the province of Britain against invasions by tribes from the north, stretching from the Solway Firth in the west to the mouth of the Tyne in the east (about 120 km, 74 miles).

had·ron /ˈhadrɒn/ *noun* *Physics* any of a class of subatomic particles including baryons and mesons, which can take part in the strong interaction. □ **had·ron·ic** /-ˈdrɒnɪk/ *adjective* [Greek *hadros* bulky]

hadro·saur /ˈhadrəsɔːr/ *noun* a large herbivorous usu. bipedal dinosaur of the family Hadrosauridae, of the late Cretaceous period, with jaws flattened like the bill of a duck. [modern Latin genus name *Hadrosaurus*, from Greek *hadros* 'thick, stout' + *sauros* 'lizard']

hadst *archaic* 2nd sing. past of HAVE.

Haeck·el /ˈhekəl/ **Ernst Hein·rich** (1834–1919), German biologist and philosopher. He popularized Darwin's theories and saw evolution as providing a framework for describing the world, with the German Empire representing the highest evolved form of a civilized nation.

haem esp. *Brit. var. of* HEME.

haem·al esp. *Brit. var. of* HEMAL.

haemato- etc. esp. *Brit. var. of* HEMATO- etc.

-haemia esp. *Brit. var. of* -EMIA.

haemo- etc. esp. *Brit. var. of* HEMO- etc.

hafiz /ˈhafɪz/ *noun* a Muslim who knows the Quran by heart. [Persian from Arabic *ḥāfiz* guardian]

haf·ni·um /ˈhafniəm/ *noun* *Chem.* a silvery lustrous metallic element occurring naturally with zirconium, used in tungsten alloys for filaments and electrodes. Symbol: **Hf**; at. no.: 72. [modern Latin from *Hafnia* Copenhagen]

haft ● *noun* the handle of a dagger or knife etc. ● *transitive verb* provide with a haft. [Old English *hæft* from Germanic]

Haf·tar·ah /hafˈtɔːrə, ˈhaftəˌrɑ/ *noun* (*pl.* **-tar·ot** /-ˈtɒrɒt/) the selection from the Prophets read following the Torah passage in synagogues on Sabbaths and festivals.

Hag. *abbreviation* Haggai (Old Testament).

hag¹ *noun* **1** an ugly old woman. **2** a witch. **3** = HAGFISH. [Middle English *hegge, hagge*, perhaps from Old English *hægtesse*, Old High German *hagazissa*, of unknown origin]

hag² *noun* *Scot. & Northern England* **1** a soft place on a moor. **2** a firm place in a bog. [Old Norse *hǫgg* gap, originally 'cutting blow', related to HEW]

Hagar /ˈheɪgɑr/ (in the Bible) the Egyptian maid of Abraham's wife Sarah, who bore Ishmael to Abraham (Gen. 16, 21). She and Ishmael were driven away after the birth of Isaac.

Hagen /ˈhɒgən/ an industrial city in NW Germany, in North Rhine-Westphalia; pop. (est. 2002) 205,500.

hag·fish *noun* any of various scavenging or predatory cyclostome fishes of the family Myxinidae, having an eel-like body without paired fins, slime glands, and a jawless mouth with movable toothed plates, found chiefly in oxygen-poor mud in deep cold seas and estuaries. [HAG¹]

Hag·gad·ah /həˈgadə, hagaˈdɑ/ *noun* (*pl.* **-gad·ahs, -gad·oth**) **1** the non-legal element of the Talmud, consisting esp. of illustrative legends or parables (*compare* HALACHA). **2** a book containing the text recited at the Seder, on the first two nights of Passover. □ **Hag·gad·ic** /-ˈgadɪk/ *adjective* [Hebrew, = tale, from *higgîd* tell]

Hag·gai /ˈhagɪˌaɪ, ˈhagaɪ/ **1** a Hebrew minor prophet of the 6th c. BC. **2** a book of the Bible containing his prophecies of a glorious future in the Messianic age.

Hag·gard /ˈhagɑrd/ **Sir Henry Rider** (1856–1925), English novelist. He is famous for his adventure novels, many of them set in Africa, such as *King Solomon's Mines* (1885) and *She* (1889).

hag·gard /ˈhagɑrd/ *adjective* looking exhausted and distraught, esp. from fatigue, worry, privation, etc. □ **hag·gard·ly** *adverb* **hag·gard·ness** *noun* [French *hagard*, of uncertain origin: later influenced by HAG¹]

hag·gis /ˈhagɪs/ *noun* a Scottish dish consisting of a sheep's or calf's offal mixed with suet, oatmeal, etc., and boiled in a bag made from the animal's stomach or in an artificial bag. [Middle English: origin unknown]

hag·gle ● *intransitive verb* (often foll. by *about, over*) dispute or wrangle over a price, deal, etc. ● *noun* a dispute or wrangle, esp. about a price etc. □ **hag·gler** *noun* **hag·gling** *noun* [earlier sense 'hack' from Old Norse *höggva* HEW]

Hagia So·phia /ˌhagiə səˈfiːə/ = ST. SOPHIA. [Greek, = holy wisdom]

hagio- /ˈhagiɔː/ *combining form* of or pertaining to saints or holiness. [Greek *hagios* holy]

Hagi·og·rapha /ˌhagiˈɒɡrəfə/ *noun* the last of the three canonical divisions of the Hebrew Scriptures, additional to the Law and the Prophets and comprising Psalms, Proverbs, Job, Canticles, Ruth, Lamentations, Ecclesiastes, Esther, Daniel, Ezra, Nehemiah, and Chronicles. *Also called* THE WRITINGS (*see* WRITING 5).

hagi·og·raph·er /ˌhagiˈɒɡrəfər/ *noun* **1** a writer of the lives of saints. **2** a writer of any of the Hagiographa.

hagi·og·raphy /ˌhagiˈɒɡrəfi/ *noun* (*pl.* **-ies**) **1** the writing of the lives of saints. **2** an idealized biography of any person. □ **hagio·graph·ic** *adjective* **hagio·graph·ic·al** *adjective*

hagi·ol·ogy /ˌhagiˈɒlədʒi/ *noun* (*pl.* **-gies**) **1 a** literature dealing with the lives and legends of saints. **b** a catalogue of saints. **2** the history of sacred writings. □ **hagio·logic·al** /-giəˈlɒdʒɪkəl/ *adjective* **hagi·ol·o·gist** *noun*

hag-ridden *adjective* very worried, harassed, or troubled by anxiety.

Hague, The /heig/ the seat of government and administrative centre of the Netherlands, on the North Sea coast, capital of the province of South Holland; pop. (est. 2002) 444,400. The International Court of Justice is based at The Hague.

hah *var. of* HA[1].

ha ha *interjection* representing laughter. [Old English: compare HA[1]]

ha-ha *noun* **1** a ditch with a wall on its inner side below ground level, forming a boundary to a park or garden without interrupting the view. **2** a structure, geographic feature, etc. which unexpectedly proves to be other than it initially appears. [French, perhaps from the cry of surprise on encountering it]

Hahn /hɒn/ **Otto** (1879–1968), German chemist. His partnership with Lise Meitner began with the discovery of the new element protactinium in 1917 and culminated in 1938 when, with Fritz Strassmann (1902–80), they discovered nuclear fission. He was awarded the Nobel Prize for chemistry in 1944.

Hah·ne·mann /ˈhɒnəmən/ **(Chris·tian Frie·drich) Sam·uel** (1755–1843), German physician and founder of homeopathy.

hahn·ium /ˈhɒniəm/ *noun* Chem. the name formerly proposed by the American Chemical Society for the chemical element of atomic number 105 (now called DUBNIUM) and by IUPAC for element 108 (now called HASSIUM). [O. HAHN + -IUM]

Haida /ˈhaidə/ ● *noun* **1** (*pl.* same or **Haidas**) a member of an Aboriginal people living on the west coast of Canada. **2** the language of this people. ● *adjective* of or relating to this people or their language or culture. [Haida, = people]

Haida Gwaii /ˈhaidə gwai/ the Haida name for the QUEEN CHARLOTTE ISLANDS.

Haifa /ˈhaifə/ the chief port of Israel, in the northwest of the country on the Mediterranean coast; pop. (2000) 270,500. It is the site of the Baha'i shrine.

Haig /heig/ **Doug·las, 1st Earl Haig of Bemer·syde** (1861–1928), British Field Marshal. During the First World War he served as commander-in-chief of British forces in France (1915–18). His policy of defeating Germany by a war of attrition on the Western Front resulted in massive loss of life.

Haig-Brown /heigˈbraun/ **Rod·er·ick** (1908–1976), British-born Canadian writer and conservationist, noted for his nature writing and for his condemnation of the exploitation of nature that characterized the development of the Canadian West. His children's book *Saltwater Summer* (1948) received a Governor General's Award.

haik /həik, heik/ *noun* (also **haick**) a large outer wrap, usu. white, covering the head and body and worn by Arabs of both sexes. [Moroccan Arabic *ḥā'ik*]

Hai·kou /hai'koː/ the capital of Hainan autonomous region, a port on the northeast coast of Hainan island; pop. (est. 1999) 438,262.

haiku /ˈhaikuː/ *noun* (*pl.* same) **1** a type of very short Japanese poem, having three parts, usu. 17 syllables, and often about a subject in nature. **2** an imitation of this in another language. [Japanese]

hail[1] ● *noun* **1** pellets of frozen rain falling in showers from cumulonimbus clouds. **2** (foll. by *of*) a barrage or onslaught (of bullets, curses, questions, etc.). ● *verb* **1** *intransitive* (prec. by *it* as subject) hail falls (*it is hailing; if it hails*). **2** *transitive* pour down (blows, words, etc.). [Old English *hagol, hægl, hagalian* from Germanic]

hail[2] ● *verb* **1** *transitive* (often foll. by *as*) acclaim, commend, or endorse vigorously (*hailed him king; hailed as a success*). **2** *transitive* signal to or attract the attention of (*hailed a taxi*). **3** *intransitive* (foll. by *from*) (of a person) have one's home or origins in (a place) (*hails from Thunder Bay*). **4** *transitive* greet enthusiastically. ● *interjection* expressing greeting. ● *noun* **1** distance as affecting the possibility of hailing (*was within hail*). **2** a greeting or act of hailing. **3** N Amer. a periodic count of a fishing vessel's catch, usu. made by the captain. □ **hail·er** *noun* [elliptical use of obsolete *hail* (adj.) from Old Norse *heill* sound, WHOLE]

Haile Sel·as·sie /ˌhaili səˈlasi/ (born Tafari Makonnen) (1892–1975), emperor of Ethiopia 1930–74. He lived in exile in Britain during the Italian occupation of Ethiopia (1936–41), but was restored to the throne by the Allies and ruled until deposed in a Communist military coup in 1974.

Hail·ey /ˈheili/ **Ar·thur** (b.1920), Canadian novelist. Some of his bestselling books, including *Airport* (1968), became the basis for popular movies.

Hailey·bury /ˈheiləbəri/ a town in NE Ontario, situated north of North Bay, close to the border with Quebec; pop. (2001) 4,543. □ **Hailey·bur·ian** *noun* [after *Haileybury* Public School in Hertfordshire, England]

hail-fellow-well-met ● *adjective* showing much or excessive familiarity or affability. ● *noun* an exceedingly affable, genial person.

Hail Holy Queen *noun* = SALVE REGINA.

Hail Mary *noun* **1** the prayer to the Virgin Mary beginning with the words used by Gabriel in Luke 1:28 and incorporating Elizabeth's words from Luke 1:42. **2** N Amer. Football (*attributive*) a very long forward pass made in the final seconds of a half or game, esp. as a desperate effort to score when completion is unlikely.

hail·stone *noun* a pellet of hail.

hail·storm *noun* a period of heavy hail.

Hai·nan /hai'nan/ an island in the South China Sea, forming an autonomous region of China; pop. (est. 2002) 8,035,000; capital, Haikou.

Hai·naut /ei'noː/ a province of S Belgium; capital, Mons.

Hai·phong /hai'fɒŋ/ a port in northern Vietnam, on the delta of the Red River in the Gulf of Tonkin; pop. (est. 2002) 572,100.

hair *noun* **1 a** any of the fine threadlike strands growing from the skin of mammals, esp. from the human head. **b** these collectively (*has red hair*). **2** anything resembling a hair. **3** a fine, elongated plant structure, esp. an outgrowth from the epidermis of a plant, e.g. a root hair. **4** a very small degree, quantity, or extent. □ **get in a person's hair** *informal* persistently irritate or annoy a person. **hair of the dog (that bit you)** an alcoholic drink taken to cure a hangover, so called because it is a cure consisting of a small amount of the cause. **let one's hair down** *informal* abandon restraint, behave freely or wildly. **make one's hair stand on end** alarm or horrify one. **not turn a hair** remain apparently unmoved or unaffected. □ **haired** *adjective* (also in *combination*). **hair·less** *adjective* **hair·like** *adjective* [Old English *hær* from Germanic]

hair·ball *noun* a ball of hair which collects in the stomach of a cat etc. as a result of the animal licking its coat.

hair·breadth *noun* = HAIR'S BREADTH (esp. *attributive*: *a hairbreadth escape*).

hair·brush *noun* a brush for arranging or smoothing the hair.

hair clip *noun* = BARRETTE.

hair·cloth *noun* stiff cloth woven from hair, used in upholstery etc.

hair colour *noun* a dye, tint, etc. used on the hair. □ **hair colouring** *noun* **hair colourist** *noun*

hair·cut *noun* **1** an act of cutting the hair. **2** the style in which the hair is cut. □ **hair·cut·ter** *noun* **hair·cut·ting** *noun*

hair·do *noun* (*pl.* **-dos**) the particular way in which esp. a woman's hair is styled.

hair·dress·er *noun* **1** a person who cuts and styles hair, esp. professionally. **2** the business or establishment of a hairdresser. □ **hair·dress·ing** *noun*

hair dryer *noun* (also **hair drier**) an electrical device for drying the hair by blowing warm air over it.

hair grass *noun* any of various grasses, esp. of the genera *Deschampsia*, *Corynephorus*, *Aira*, etc., with slender stems.

hair·grip *noun Brit.* = BOBBY PIN.

hair·line *noun* **1** the natural line on the head at which a person's hair stops growing, esp. on the forehead. **2** (also *attributive*) a very thin line or crack etc. (*a hairline fracture*).

hair·net *noun* a fine, light net worn on the head to keep the hair in place.

hair·piece *noun* a piece of false hair, such as a fall or toupée, augmenting a person's natural hair or covering a bald spot.

hair·pin *noun* **1** a U-shaped pin for fastening the hair. **2** (usu. *attributive*) (of a bend in a road etc.) curving sharply.

hair-raising *adjective* extremely alarming; terrifying.

hair's breadth *noun* a very small amount or margin.

hair shirt *noun* **1** a shirt of haircloth, worn by penitents and ascetics. **2** (**hair-shirt**) (*attributive*) austere, harsh, self-sacrificing.

hair·split·ting *adjective & noun* making overfine distinctions; quibbling. □ **hair·split·ter** *noun*

hair·spray *noun* a fixative solution sprayed onto the hair to keep it in place.

hair·spring *noun* a fine spring regulating the balance wheel in a watch.

hair·streak *noun* any of various butterflies belonging to the genus *Thecla*, and related genera, having fringed wings often with pale markings like streaks.

hair·style *noun* a particular way of arranging or dressing the hair. □ **hair·styl·ing** *noun* **hair·styl·ist** *noun*

hair-trigger *noun* **1** a trigger of a firearm set for release at the slightest pressure. **2** (usu. *attributive*) (of a reaction, mood, etc.) quickly and easily provoked.

hair·wing *noun* a highly buoyant type of fishing lure made or tied with hair from a deer etc.

hairy *adjective* (**hair·i·er**, **hair·i·est**) **1** made of or covered with hair. **2** having the feel or appearance of hair. **3** *slang* difficult, frightening, or problematic. □ **give someone the hairy eyeball** *N Amer. slang* look malevolently or threateningly at someone, esp. through narrowed eyes so that one is looking through the eyelashes. □ **hair·i·ness** *noun*

hairy woodpecker *noun* a large black and white N American woodpecker, *Picoides villosus*.

Hais·la /ˈhəɪslə/ ● *noun* (*pl.* same or **Hais·las**) **1** a member of a major language group of northern Wakashan, living in the watershed of the Douglas Channel in NW BC. **2** the language of the Haisla. ● *adjective* of or relating to this people or their culture or language. [those living at the river mouth and downriver]

Haiti /ˈheiti/ a country in the Caribbean, occupying the western part of the island of Hispaniola; pop. (est. 2002) 7,063,722; capital, Port-au-Prince.

Hai·tian /ˈheiʃən/ ● *noun* **1** a native or inhabitant of Haiti. **2** (also **Haitian Creole**) the French-based Creole language spoken in Haiti. ● *adjective* of or relating to the Haitians or their language.

Hai·tink /ˈhaitɪŋk/ **Ber·nard (Jo·hann Her·man)** (b.1929), Dutch conductor. As principal conductor of the Amsterdam Concertgebouw (1964–87) he made notable recordings of all of Mahler's and Bruckner's symphonies. He was also principal conductor of the London Philharmonic Orchestra (1967–79) and musical director of Glyndebourne (1977–87) and Covent Garden (1987–2002).

hajj /hadʒ/ *noun* (also **hadj**) the pilgrimage to Mecca undertaken in the twelfth month of the Muslim year, constituting one of the religious duties of Islam. [Arabic *ḥājj* pilgrimage]

haj·ji /ˈhadʒi/ *noun* (also **hadji**) (*pl.* **-jis**) a Muslim who has been to Mecca as a pilgrim: also (**Hajji**) used as a title. [Persian *ḥājī* (partly through Turkish *hacı*) from Arabic *ḥājj*: see HAJJ]

hake *noun* **1** any of various blue-grey and silver fishes related to the cod, of shallow temperate seas, of the genus *Merluccius*, or the family Merlucciidae, having a rather elongate body with two dorsal fins, most species being commercially fished. **2** either of two reddish-brown food fishes related to the cod, *Urophycis chuss* and *U. tenuis*, of the northwestern Atlantic. [Middle English, perhaps ultimately from dial. *hake* hook + FISH[1]]

ha·ken·kreuz /ˈhɒkənˌkrɔits/ *noun* a swastika, esp. as a Nazi symbol. [German from *Haken* hook + *Kreuz* CROSS]

ha·kim[1] /həˈkiːm/ *noun* (in India and Muslim countries) a physician. [Arabic *ḥakīm* wise man, physician]

ha·kim[2] /ˈhɒkɪm/ *noun* (in India and Muslim countries) a judge, ruler, or governor. [Arabic *ḥākim* governor]

Hak·luyt /ˈhakluːt/ **Rich·ard** (c.1552–1616), English geographer and historian. He compiled *Principal Navigations, Voyages, and Discoveries of the English Nation* (1589), a collection of accounts of famous voyages of discovery.

Hako·date /ˌhakəˈdati/ a port in N Japan, on the southern tip of the island of Hokkaido; pop. (est. 2002) 302,700.

Ha·la·cha /həˈlɒxə/ *noun* (also **Ha·la·kah**) (*pl.* **-chahs**, **-choth**) **1** Jewish law and jurisprudence, based on the Talmud, esp. the Mishnah, and subsequent rabbinical rulings (*compare* HAGGADAH 1). **2** a law, tradition, or legal ruling included as a binding part of this law. □ **Ha·la·chic** *adjective* [Aramaic *hᵃlākāh* law]

halal /haˈlal/ (also **hallal**) ● *transitive verb* (**ha·lalled**, **halal·ling**) kill (an animal) as prescribed by Muslim law. ● *noun* (often *attributive*) meat prepared in this way; lawful food. [Arabic *ḥalāl* lawful]

ha·la·lah /həˈlalə/ *noun* a monetary unit of Saudi Arabia, equal to one-hundredth of a riyal.

hal·berd /ˈhalbərd/ *noun* (also **hal·bert**) *hist.* a weapon consisting of a long handle ending in a combined spearhead and battle-axe, used esp. in the 15th and 16th c. [French *hallebarde* from Italian *alabarda* from Middle High German *helmbarde* from *helm* handle + *barde* hatchet]

hal·berd·ier /ˌhalbərˈdiːr/ *noun hist.* a soldier armed with a halberd or a guard carrying a halberd as a badge of office.

Hal·cion /ˈhalsiːɒn/ *noun N Amer.* proprietary a tranquilizer of the benzodiazepine group. [altered form of HALCYON]

hal·cyon /ˈhalsiən/ ● *adjective* **1** calm, peaceful (*halcyon days*). **2** (of a period) happy, prosperous. ● *noun* **1** any kingfisher of the genus *Halcyon*, native to Europe, Africa, and Australasia, with brightly coloured plumage. **2** *Myth* a bird thought in antiquity to breed in a nest floating at sea at the winter solstice, charming the wind and waves into calm. [Latin *(h)alcyon* from Greek *(h)alkuōn* kingfisher]

Hal·di·mand County /ˈhɒldəmənd/ a city in SW central Ontario, between Hamilton and Lake Erie; pop. (2001) 43,728. [Sir F. *Haldimand*, British army officer and former Governor of Quebec d.1791]

Hale, George Ellery (1868–1938), US astronomer. He discovered that sunspots are associated with strong magnetic fields, invented the spectroheliograph, and initiated the construction of several large telescopes.

hale[1] *adjective* (esp. of an old person) strong and healthy (esp. in **hale and hearty**). [Old English *hāl* WHOLE]

hale[2] *transitive verb* drag or draw forcibly. [Old French *haler* from Old Norse *hala*]

haler /ˈhalər/ *noun* (*pl.* same or **haleru** /ˈhaləru/) a monetary unit of the Czech Republic and Slovakia, equal to one-hundredth of a koruna. [Czech *haléř* from Middle High German *haller*]

Haley /ˈheili/ **Wil·liam John Clif·ton** ('Bill') (1925–81), US rock 'n' roll singer. He was the first to popularize rock 'n' roll with the release of his song 'Rock Around the Clock' (1954), recorded with his group the Comets.

half ● *noun* (*pl.* **halves**) **1** either of two equal or corresponding parts, groups, etc. into which a thing is or might be divided. **2** either of two equal periods of play in sports, usu. separated by an interval or intermission. **3** esp. *Soccer & Rugby informal* = HALFBACK. **4** *informal* half a pint, esp. of beer etc. **5** *Golf* a score on a hole or in a round that is the same as one's opponent's. ● *adjective* **1** of an amount or quantity equal to a half, or loosely, to a part thought of as roughly a half (*take half the men; spent half the time reading; half a pint; a half-pint; half-price*). **2** forming a half (*a half share*). **3** partial, incomplete, imperfect, or falling short of a full or perfect amount, degree, type, etc. (*half measures*). ● *adverb* **1** (often in *combination*) partly, nearly, or to the extent of half (*only half cooked; half-frozen; half-laughing*). **2** to a certain extent, somewhat, esp. in idiomatic phrases (*half dead; am half inclined to agree*). **3** (in reckoning time) by an amount of half (an hour etc.) (*half past two*). □ **at half cock** see COCK[1]. **by half** (prec. by *too* + adj.) excessively (*too clever by half*). **by halves** imperfectly or incompletely (*never does things by halves*). **go halves** (or **half and half**) share equally in something with another person. **half the battle** see BATTLE. **half a chance** *informal* the slightest opportunity (esp. *given half a chance*). **half an eye** *Brit.* the slightest degree of perceptiveness. **half a mind** see MIND. **the half of it** *informal* the rest or more important part of something (usu. after *neg.: you don't know the half of it*). **half past** (of time) thirty minutes past the hour. **half the time** see TIME. **not half 1** not nearly (*not half long enough*). **2** *informal* not at all (*not half bad*). [Old English *half, healf* from Germanic, originally = 'side']

half a crown var. of HALF-CROWN.

half a dozen var. of HALF-DOZEN.

half-and-half ● *adverb* in equal parts. ● *adjective* that is half one thing and half another. ● *noun* **1** something that is half one thing and half another. **2** *N Amer.* a mixture of milk and cream having 10% milk fat, used esp. in coffee.

half-assed *slang* ● *adjective* incompetent, inadequate. ● *adverb* in an inadequate, inept fashion.

half·back *noun* **1** *Football* a back lined up on one or the other side of the fullback. **2** *Soccer* a player positioned behind the forwards and in front of the fullbacks. **3** *Rugby* a forward playing primarily in an offensive capacity, e.g. the scrum half or the stand-off half.

half-baked *adjective* **1** incompletely considered or planned. **2** stupid or foolish.

half bath *noun N Amer.* a washroom in a residence containing only a toilet and sink (*compare* FULL BATH).

half·beak *noun* any fish of the family Hemirhamphidae with the lower jaw projecting beyond the upper.

half binding *noun* a type of bookbinding in which the spine and corners are bound in one material (usu. leather) and the sides in another.

half-blood *noun* **1** a person having one parent in common with another. **2** this relationship. **3** = HALF-BREED.

half-blooded *adjective* born from parents of different races.

half board *noun* provision of bed, breakfast, and one main meal at a hotel etc.

half-bottle *noun* **1** a bottle that is half the standard size, esp. a 375 ml bottle of wine. **2** its contents or the amount that will fill it.

half-breed *noun offensive* a person of mixed race.

half-brother *noun* a male related to one or more other persons, male or female, by having one biological parent in common.

half-caste *offensive* ● *noun* a person whose parents are of different races, esp. the offspring of a European father and an East Indian mother. ● *adjective* of or relating to such a person.

half-circle *noun* a semicircle.

half-cock *noun* the position of the hammer of a gun when pulled halfway back.

half-cocked *adjective* **1** incompletely prepared or realized. **2** (of a gun) at half-cock.

half course *noun N Amer.* a university course extending over half the academic year or one equivalent to it in credits acquired.

half court *noun* **1** either side's section of a court in basketball, tennis, etc. **2** (**half-court**) (*attributive*) esp. *Basketball* designating an offensive or defensive game plan devised to be used within one half of the court.

half-crown *noun* (also **half a crown**) (in the UK) a former coin and monetary unit equal to two shillings and sixpence.

half-cut *adjective Cdn & Brit. slang* fairly drunk.

half day *noun* **1** half a working day, esp. taken as a holiday. **2** a period equal either to twelve hours or one half of a work day (also *attributive: a half-day strike*).

half-dead *adjective* **1** in a state in which death seems as likely as recovery. **2** in a state of extreme exhaustion or weakness.

half-decent *adjective* moderately decent.

half dollar *noun* **1** (in Canada, the US, etc.) a coin worth fifty cents. **2** the amount represented by this.

half-dozen *noun* (also **half a dozen**) six or about six.

half-drunk *adjective* **1** partially intoxicated. **2** (of a drink etc.) partially consumed.

half-duplex *adjective* (of a communications circuit etc.) allowing the transmission of signals in both directions but not simultaneously.

half-hardy *adjective* (of a plant) able to grow in the open air at all times except in severe frost.

half-hear *transitive verb* (*past and past participle* **half-heard**) hear (a thing) incompletely (*only half-heard the shout above the sound of the television*).

half-hearted *adjective* lacking in courage, enthusiasm, or determination. □ **half-hearted·ly** *adverb* **half-hearted·ness** *noun*

half hitch *noun* a noose or knot formed by passing the end of a rope around its standing part and then through the loop.

half-hour *noun* **1** (also **half an hour**) a period of 30 minutes. **2** a point of time 30 minutes after any hour o'clock. □ **half-hourly** *adjective & adverb*

half-integer *noun* a number obtained by dividing an odd integer by two. □ **half-integral** *adjective*

half-life *noun* **1** the time taken for half of a sample of a particular radioactive isotope to decay into other materials. **2** the time taken for half of a dose of a drug etc. to disappear in the body after administration. **3** an unsatisfactory way of life.

half-light *noun* a dim, imperfect light, esp. that at dusk or dawn.

half-litre *noun* (also esp. *US* **half-liter**) a unit of capacity half as large as a litre.

half-marathon *noun* a long-distance running race, usu. of 13 miles 352 yards (21.243 km).

half-mast *noun* **1** the position of a flag halfway down the mast, as a mark of respect for a person who has died. **2** *informal* the position of a garment halfway to that normal (*trousers at half-mast*).

half measures *plural noun* an unsatisfactory or inadequate compromise, policy, etc.

half moon *noun* **1** the moon when only half its illuminated surface is visible from earth. **2** the time when this occurs. **3** a semicircular object.

half-naked *adjective* nearly naked; partially unclothed.

half nelson *noun Wrestling see* NELSON.

half note *noun esp. N Amer. Music* a note having the time value of two quarter notes or half a whole note and represented by a hollow ring with a stem.

half pay *noun* reduced income, esp. on retirement.

half·penny /ˈheipəni, ˈheipni/ *noun* (also **ha'penny**) (*pl.* **-pen·nies** or **-pence** /ˈheipəns/) (in the UK) a former bronze coin worth half a penny, withdrawn in 1984 (*compare* FARTHING).

half·penny·worth /ˈheipɜrθ/ *noun* (also **ha'p'orth**) *Brit.* **1** as much as could be bought for a halfpenny. **2** *informal* (esp. after *neg.*) a negligible amount (*doesn't make a halfpennyworth of difference*).

half-pint *noun* **1** an amount of liquid equal to half a pint. **2** *slang* a short person.

half-pipe *noun* a snow tunnel or U-shaped cut in the snow, similar to the stunt ramps used by skateboarders, but used by snowboarders.

half rest *noun N Amer. Music* a rest having the time value of a half note.

half seas over *adjective esp. Brit. slang* fairly drunk.

half section *noun N Amer.* (*West*) a half of a square mile of esp. agricultural land, 320 acres (approx. 130 hectares).

half shell *noun* half of the shell of an oyster etc., esp. as used for serving food (*oysters on the half shell*).

half-sister *noun* a female related to one or more other persons, male or female, by having one biological parent in common.

half size *noun* a size of clothing designed for full-figured, short-waisted women, having extra room in the bust, waist, and hip and shorter length proportions.

half-slip *noun* an article of lingerie resembling a skirt, worn underneath dresses and skirts.

half-sole *noun* the sole of a boot or shoe from the shank to the toe.

half-sovereign *noun hist.* (in the UK) a former gold coin and monetary unit equal to ten shillings (50p).

half-staff *noun N Amer.* = HALF-MAST.

half-starved *adjective* poorly fed; suffering from malnourishment; having insufficient food.

half-step *noun* **1** *Music* a semitone. **2** a small or partial step in a specific direction.

half-term *noun Brit.* a period about halfway through a school term, when a short holiday is usually taken.

half-timbered *adjective* (also **half timber**) *Archit.* having walls with a timber frame and a brick or plaster filling. □ **half-timber·ing** *noun*

half·time *noun* **1** the time at which half of a game or contest is completed. **2** a short interval occurring at this time.

half-title *noun* **1** the title or short title of a book, printed on the recto of the leaf preceding the title page or at the head of the first page. **2** the title of a section of a book printed on the recto of the leaf preceding it.

half-ton *noun esp. Cdn* a pickup truck with a carrying capacity of approximately half a ton.

half·tone *noun* **1 a** an image, produced by photographic or electronic means, in which an effect of continuous tone is simulated by dots of various sizes or lines of various thicknesses. **b** the process which produces such an image. **2** *N Amer. Music* a semitone. **3** an intermediate tone between the extreme lights and extreme shades.

half-track *noun* **1** a propulsion system for land vehicles with wheels at the front and an endless driven belt at the back. **2** a vehicle equipped with this.

half-truth *noun* a statement that conveys only part of the truth, esp. deliberately.

half·way ● *adverb* **1** at or to a point equidistant between two others (*we were halfway to Regina*). **2** to some extent, more or less (*is halfway decent*). ● *adjective* midway or equidistant between two points (*reached a halfway point*).

halfway house *noun* **1** a residence where ex-prisoners, psychiatric patients, etc. live and receive treatment to help prepare them for their return to society. **2** *hist.* an inn midway between two towns. **3** esp. *Brit.* a compromise. **4** the halfway point in a progression.

half·wit *noun informal* an extremely foolish or stupid person. □ **half·wit·ted** *adjective* **half·wit·ted·ly** *adverb* **half·wit·ted·ness** *noun*

half-yearly *adjective & adverb* esp. *Brit.* at intervals of six months.

Hali·bur·ton /ˈhalɪˌbɜːrtən/ **Thom·as Chand·ler** (1796–1865), Nova Scotian author, lawyer, judge, and politician. He wrote numerous works on the history and politics of the British colonies in North America but is best known for his works of fiction. Haliburton's social satire *The Clockmaker; or the Sayings and Doings of Sam Slick of Slickville*, which was first published in book form in 1836, won international attention throughout the 19th c.

hali·but /ˈhalɪbət/ *noun* (*pl.* same) any of several very large flatfishes fished intensively for food, esp. (also **Atlantic halibut**), *Hippoglossus hippoglossus*, (also **Pacific halibut**) *Hippoglossus stenolepis*, and (also **Greenland halibut**) *Reinhardtius hippoglossoides*. [Middle English from *haly* HOLY + obsolete sense of BUTT[3] flatfish, perhaps because eaten on holy days]

Hali·car·nas·sus /ˌhaləkɑːrˈnasəs/ an ancient Greek city on the southwest coast of Asia Minor, at what is now the Turkish city of Bodrum. It is the site of the Mausoleum of Halicarnassus, one of the Seven Wonders of the World.

Halicarnassus, Dionysius of *see* DIONYSIUS OF HALICARNASSUS.

hal·ide /ˈhalaɪd, ˈheɪl-/ *noun Chem.* a binary compound of a halogen with another group or element.

Hali·fax[1] the capital city of Nova Scotia and Canada's principal ice-free port on the Atlantic coast, now including the former city of Dartmouth and former town of Bedford; pop. (2001) 359,111. [G. M. Dunk, 2nd Earl of HALIFAX]

Hali·fax[2], George Mon·tagu Dunk, 2nd Earl of (1716–71), British statesman. As president of the Board of Trade from 1748, he was active in colonial development and founded Halifax, Nova Scotia. His other positions of state include Lord Lieutenant of Ireland (1761–3), Lord Privy Seal (1770), and Secretary of State for the Northern Department (1762–3, 1771).

Halifax explosion a massive explosion in Halifax Harbour on the morning of December 6, 1917, caused when a ship collided with a munitions carrier. The blast and subsequent fire destroyed 2.5 km[2] of the city, killed 1600 people and injured another 9000, and was the world's biggest man-made explosion before Hiroshima.

Hali·gon·ian /halɪˈɡoːniən/ ● *noun* a native or resident of Halifax. ● *adjective* of or pertaining to Halifax or Haligonians. [from medieval Latin *Haligonia* Halifax + -AN]

hali·otis /ˌhalɪˈoːtɪs/ *noun* any edible gastropod mollusc of the genus *Haliotis* with an ear-shaped shell lined with mother-of-pearl. [Greek *hals* hali- sea + *ous ōt-* ear]

hal·ite /ˈhalaɪt/ *noun* rock salt. [modern Latin *halites* from Greek *hals* salt]

hali·to·sis /ˌhalɪˈtoːsɪs/ *noun* = BAD BREATH. [modern Latin from Latin *halitus* breath]

Halko·mel·em /ˌhɒlkəˈmeɪləm/ *noun* the Salishan language of the Halqʼemeylem.

Hall ▶ **1 Charles Mar·tin** (1863–1914), US industrial chemist. He determined that electrolysis was the most effective process for producing aluminum from bauxite. A similar method was developed independently in France by P. T. Héroult (1863–1914), so the technique is known as the *Hall–Héroult process*. **2 (Mar·guer·ite) Rad·clyffe** (1883–1943), English novelist and poet. Her novels attracted both acclaim and outrage; while *Adam's Breed* (1926) was awarded the James Tait Black Memorial Prize, *The Well of Loneliness* (1928), with its explicit depiction of lesbianism, was banned for obscenity in Britain.

hall *noun* **1 a** *N Amer.* a corridor or passage in a building. **b** a space or passage into which the front entrance of a house etc. opens. **2** a large room or building for meetings, meals, concerts, etc. **3** a building

containing lecture rooms etc. that is part of a university (*Tabaret Hall*). **4** (*Brit.* in full **hall of residence**) a university residence for students. **5 a** (in a college etc.) a common dining room, esp. for members of the institution. **b** *Brit.* dinner in this. **6** the building of a union, fraternity, guild, etc. (*Elks' Hall*). **7 a** a large public room in a palace etc. **b** the principal living room of a medieval house. **8** *Brit.* a large country house, esp. with a landed estate. [Old English = *hall* from Germanic, related to HELL]

hal·lal *var. of* HALAL.

Halle /ˈhalə/ a city in east central Germany, on the Saale River, in Saxony-Anhalt; pop. (est. 2002) 245,300.

Hal·lel /haˈleɪl, ˈhalel/ *noun* a portion of the service for certain Jewish festivals, consisting of Psalms 113 to 118 inclusive. [Hebrew *hallēl* praise]

hal·le·lu·jah *var. of* ALLELUIA.

Hal·ler /ˈhalər/ **Al·brecht von** (1708–77), Swiss anatomist and physiologist. He pioneered the study of neurology and experimental physiology.

Hal·ley /ˈhali/ **Ed·mond** or **Ed·mund** (1656–1742), English astronomer and mathematician. He realized that nebulae were clouds of luminous gas among the stars, and that the aurora was related to the earth's magnetism. He is best known for recognizing that a bright comet (later named after him) had appeared several times, and for successfully predicting its return.

Halley's comet /ˈhaliːz, ˈheɪliːz/ *noun* a bright comet, first recorded in 240 BC, which reappears about every 76 years.

hall·mark ● *noun* **1** a mark used by British assay offices for indicating the standard of gold, silver, and platinum. **2** any distinctive feature esp. of excellence. ● *transitive verb* **1** stamp with a hallmark. **2** designate as excellent. [Goldsmith's *Hall* in London, England, where articles are tested and stamped]

hallo esp. *Brit.* **1** *var. of* HELLO. **2** *var. of* HALLOO.

Hall of Fame *noun* **1** esp. *N Amer.* a building with memorials of people who have excelled in a specific activity, esp. in a particular sport. **2** (usu. **hall of fame**) a group of people famous in a particular sphere. □ **Hall of Famer** *noun*

hall of residence *noun see* HALL 4.

hal·loo /həˈluː/ (also **hallo**) ● *interjection* **1** (in fox hunting) a cry inciting dogs to the chase. **2** calling attention. **3** expressing surprise. ● *noun* the cry 'halloo'. ● *verb* (**hal·loos, hal·looed**) **1** *intransitive* cry 'halloo', esp. to dogs. **2** *intransitive* shout to attract attention. **3** *transitive* urge on (dogs etc.) with shouts. [perhaps from *hallow* pursue with shouts, from Old French *halloer* (imitative)]

hal·low /ˈhaloː/ *noun archaic* a saint or holy person. [Old English *hālgian*, *hālga* from Germanic]

hal·lowed *adjective* **1** respected and important (*the hallowed halls of Parliament*). **2** that has been consecrated (*buried in hallowed ground*).

Hal·low·een /ˌhaləˈwiːn, ˌhɒl-/ *noun* (also **Hallowe'en**) the eve of All Saints' Day, 31 October. [HALLOW + EVEN[2]]

Halloween apples *interjection Cdn* (*Prairies*) uttered by children going door to door on Halloween to collect candies etc.

Hall Peninsula a broad peninsula at the southeastern end of Baffin Island. [C. *Hall*, English explorer *c.*1576]

hall·stand *noun* esp. *Brit.* a stand in the hall of a house, with pegs for hanging coats, a mirror, etc.

Hall·statt /ˈhɒlʃtat/ *adjective* of or relating to the early Iron Age in Europe, as attested by archaeological finds at Hallstatt in Upper Austria.

hal·lu·ces *pl. of* HALLUX.

hal·lu·cin·ate /həˈluːsəˌneɪt/ *verb* **1** *intransitive* experience hallucinations. **2** *transitive* produce illusions in the mind of (a person). [Latin (h)*allucinari* 'wander in mind' from Greek *alussō* 'be uneasy']

hal·lu·cin·a·tion /həˌluːsəˈneɪʃən/ *noun* the apparent or alleged perception of an object not actually present. □ **hal·lu·cina·tory** /həˈluːsɪnəˌtɔri/ *adjective* [Latin *hallucinatio* (as HALLUCINATE)]

hal·lu·cino·gen /həˈluːsənədʒən/ *noun* a drug causing hallucinations. □ **hal·lu·cino·gen·ic** /-ˈdʒenɪk/ *adjective*

hal·lux /ˈhalʌks/ *noun* (*pl.* **halluces** /-juːˌsiːz/) **1** the big toe. **2** the innermost digit of the hind foot of vertebrates. [modern Latin from Latin *allex*]

hall·way *noun* an entrance hall or corridor.

hallway medicine *noun N Amer.* the practice of treating hospital patients on beds in hallways because of a shortage of hospital rooms.

halm *var. of* HAULM.

Consonants: b *but* d *dog* f *few* g *get* h *her* j *yes* k *cat* l *leg* m *man* n *no* p *pen* r *red* s *sit*

Hal·ma·hera /ˌhalməˈhiːrə/ the largest of the Molucca Islands.

halo /ˈheɪləʊ/ ● *noun* (*pl.* **halos** or **ha·loes**) **1** a disc or circle of light shown surrounding the head of a sacred person. **2** the glory associated with an idealized person etc. **3** a circle of white or coloured light around a luminous body, esp. the sun or moon. **4** a circle or ring. ● *transitive verb* (**-loes, -loed**) surround with a halo. [medieval Latin from Latin from Greek *halōs* threshing floor, disc of the sun or moon]

halo effect *noun* the tendency of a favourable (or unfavourable) impression created by an individual in one area to influence one's judgment of him or her in another area.

halo·gen /ˈhalədʒən/ *noun Chem.* **1** any of the group of non-metallic elements (fluorine, chlorine, bromine, iodine, and astatine) which form halides (e.g. sodium chloride) by simple union with a metal. **2** (*attributive*) (of lamps and radiant heat sources) using a filament surrounded by a halogen, usu. iodine vapour. □ **halo·gen·ic** /-ˈdʒenɪk/ *adjective* [Greek *hals halos* salt]

halo·gen·a·tion /ˌhalədʒəˈneɪʃən/ *noun* the introduction of a halogen atom into a molecule. □ **halo·gen·at·ed** /həˈlɒdʒɪneɪtəd/ *adjective*

ha·lon /ˈheɪlɒn/ *noun Chem.* any of a class of compounds in which the hydrogen atoms of a hydrocarbon (usually methane or ethane) are replaced by bromine and other halogens, many of which are gases noted for their lack of reactivity and useful in firefighting. [as HALOGEN + -ON]

halo·peri·dol /haləˈperɪdɒl, heɪlə-/ *noun Pharm.* a drug used to treat psychotic disorders, esp. mania. [HALOGEN + PIPERIDINE + -OL¹]

halo·phyte /ˈhaləfʌɪt, ˈheɪlə-/ *noun* a plant adapted to saline conditions. □ **halo·phyt·ic** *adjective* [Greek *hals halos* 'salt' + -PHYTE]

halo·thane /ˈhaləθeɪn/ *noun Med.* a volatile liquid used as a general anaesthetic, a halogenated derivative of ethane. [HALOGEN + ETHANE]

Halqʼemeyʼlem /ˈhɒlkəˈmeɪləm/ ● *noun* (*pl.* same) **1** a member of an Aboriginal people living in southwestern BC. **2** the Salishan language of the Halqʼemeylem, particularly the upriver dialect spoken by the Sto:lo. ● *adjective* of or relating to this people or their culture or language.

Hals /hals/ **Frans** (*c.*1580–1666), Dutch portrait and genre painter. His bold brushwork, capturing the character, mood, and facial expressions of his subjects, gave vitality to his portraits and represented a departure from conventional portraiture.

halt¹ ● *noun* **1** a usu. temporary stop; an interruption of progress (*come to a halt*). **2** a temporary stoppage on a march or journey. **3** *Brit.* a minor stopping place on a local railway line, usu. without permanent buildings. ● *transitive & intransitive verb* stop; come or bring to a halt. □ **call a halt (to)** decide to stop. [originally in phr. *make halt* from German *Halt machen* from *halten* hold, stop]

halt² ● *intransitive verb* **1** (esp. as **halt·ing** *adjective*) lack smooth progress. **2** hesitate. **3** walk hesitatingly. **4** *archaic* be lame. ● *adjective archaic* lame or crippled. □ **halt·ing** *adjective* **halt·ing·ly** *adverb* [Old English *halt, healt, healtian* from Germanic]

hal·ter ● *noun* **1** a rope or strap with a noose or headstall for horses or cattle. **2** (also **halter top**) a style of woman's top fastened behind the neck and across the back, leaving the arms, shoulders, upper back, and often the midriff bare. **3 a** a rope with a noose for hanging a person. **b** death by hanging. ● *transitive verb* **1** put a halter on (a horse etc.). **2** hang (a person) with a halter. [Old English *hælftre*: compare HELVE]

halter-break *transitive verb* accustom (a horse) to a halter.

hal·ter·es /halˈtiːriːz/ *plural noun* the balancing organs of dipterous insects. [Greek, = weights used to aid leaping, from *hallomai* to leap]

Hal·ton Hills a town in south central Ontario, northwest of Oakville; pop. (2001) 48,184. [Major W. *Halton*, secretary to Lt.-Gov. Sir F. Gore d.1821]

hal·vah /ˈhalvə/ *noun* (also **halva**) a sweet confection of sesame flour and honey. [Yiddish from Turkish *helva* from Arabic *ḥalwā*]

halve *transitive verb* **1** divide into two halves or parts. **2** reduce by half. **3** share equally (with another person etc.). **4** *Golf* use the same number of strokes as one's opponent in (a hole or match). [Middle English *halfen* from HALF]

halves *pl.* of HALF.

halwa /ˈhalwɒ/ *noun* a sweet Indian dish consisting of carrots and semolina boiled with milk, almonds, sugar, butter, and cardamom. [Arabic, lit. = 'sweetmeat']

hal·yard /ˈhaljərd/ *noun Naut.* a rope or tackle for raising or lowering a sail or yard etc. [Middle English *halier* from HALE² + -IER, assoc. with YARD¹]

Ham (in the Bible) a son of Noah (Gen. 10:1), traditional ancestor of the Hamites.

ham ● *noun* **1 a** the upper part of a pig's leg salted and dried or smoked for food. **b** the meat from this. **2** the back of the thigh; the thigh and buttock. **3** *slang* (often *attributive*) an inexpert or unsubtle actor or piece of acting. **4** *informal* the operator of an amateur radio station (also *attributive*: **ham radio**). ● *transitive & intransitive verb* (**hammed, ham·ming**) *slang* overact; act or treat emotionally or sentimentally. □ **ham it up** ham; overact. [Old English *ham, hom* from a Germanic root meaning 'be crooked']

hama·dryad /ˌhaməˈdrʌɪad/ *noun* **1** (in Greek and Roman mythology) a nymph who lives in a tree and dies when it dies. **2** the king cobra. [Latin *hamadryas* from Greek *hamadruas* from *hama* with + *drus* tree]

hama·dryas /ˌhaməˈdrʌɪəs/ *noun* (also **hamadryas baboon**) a large Arabian baboon, *Papio hamadryas*, with a silvery-grey cape of hair over the shoulders, held sacred in ancient Egypt.

Hamal /həˈmɒl/ a giant star, the brightest in the constellation Aries. [Arabic, = sheep]

Hama·matsu /ˌhaməˈmatsuː/ an industrial city on the southern coast of the island of Honshu, Japan; pop. (est. 2002) 589,500.

hama·melis /ˌhaməˈmiːlɪs/ *noun* any shrub of the genus *Hamamelis*, e.g. witch hazel. [modern Latin from Greek *hamamēlis* medlar]

ham·an·tasch·en /ˈhamənˌtaʃən/ *noun* (in Jewish cuisine) a triangular pastry with a prune or poppyseed filling, served traditionally at Purim. [Yiddish, = 'Haman's hat' (Haman being a Persian official who plotted to kill all Jews but was defeated by Esther)]

ha·mar·tia /həˈmɑːtɪə/ *noun* (in Greek tragedy) the fatal flaw leading to the destruction of the tragic hero or heroine. [Greek, = fault, failure]

Hamas /haˈmas/ a Palestinian Islamic fundamentalist movement which has become a focus for Arab resistance in the Israeli-occupied territories; it opposes peace with Israel and has come into conflict with the more moderate Palestine Liberation Organization.

ha·mat·sa /həˈmatsə/ *noun* **1** a dance among the Kwagiulth in which the main dancer is inspired by the spirit of a man-eating monster hungering for human flesh. **2** a dancer embodying the man-eating monster. [Kwagiulth]

Ham·burg /ˈhambɜːg/ a city in N Germany, on the Elbe River; pop. (est. 2002) 1,688,300. It is the largest port in Germany, with extensive shipyards.

ham·burg *noun N Amer.* = HAMBURGER. [abbreviation]

ham·burg·er *noun* **1** a patty of ground beef, seasonings, etc. **2** this fried or grilled and eaten in a soft bread roll. **3** *N Amer.* ground beef. [German, = of Hamburg]

hamburger disease *noun N Amer.* a disease, characterized by diarrhea and kidney failure, caused by toxins produced by *Escherichia coli* bacteria. [so called because it is often caused by improperly cooked hamburgers]

Ham·eln /ˈhɒməln/ (also **Ham·elin** /ˈhamlɪn/) a town in NW Germany, in Lower Saxony, on the Weser River; pop. (est. 2002) 59,400. It was a medieval market town, the setting of the legend of the Pied Piper of Hamelin, which may be based on events which occurred in 1284.

hames /heɪmz/ *plural noun* two curved pieces of iron or wood forming the collar or part of the collar of a draft horse, to which the traces are attached. [Middle Dutch *hame*]

ham-fisted *adjective informal* = HAM-HANDED. □ **ham-fisted·ly** *adverb* **ham-fisted·ness** *noun*

ham-handed *adjective informal* clumsy, heavy-handed, bungling. □ **ham-handed·ly** *adverb* **ham-handed·ness** *noun*

Ham·hung /ham·hʌŋ/ an industrial city in eastern N Korea; pop. (est. 2002) 821,200 (with Hungnam). It was the centre of government of NE Korea during the Yi dynasty of 1392–1910.

Ham·il·car /haˈmɪlkɑː, ˈhamɪlkɑː/ (*c.*270–229 BC), Carthaginian general and father of Hannibal. He fought Rome in the First Punic War and negotiated terms of peace after the Carthaginian defeat of 241, which led to the loss of Sicily to the Romans. From 237 he and Hannibal were engaged in the conquest of Spain.

Ham·il·ton¹ 1 a port and steel-manufacturing city in S Ontario, situated at the western end of Lake Ontario, about 75 km southwest of Toronto; pop. (2001) 490,268. **2** the capital of Bermuda; pop. (est. 2002) 980. □ **Ham·il·ton·ian** /ˌhaməlˈtoːnɪən/ *noun & adjective* [sense 1 after G. *Hamilton*, local landowner and founder of the city *c.*1815]

Ham·il·ton² ▸ 1 Alex·an·der (*c.*1757–1804), US Federalist politician. As First Secretary of the Treasury (1789–95) under Washington, he established the US central banking system. **2 Lady Emma** (born Amy Lyon) (*c.*1765–1815), Englishwoman best known as the mistress of Lord Nelson. **3 Sir Wil·liam Rowan** (1806–65), Irish mathematician and theoretical physicist. Hamilton made influential contributions to optics and the foundations of algebra, and invented quaternions while investigating the subject of complex numbers. □ **Ham·il·ton·ian** /ˌhaməlˈtoːnɪən/ adjective

Hamilton Inlet an inlet of the N Atlantic, extending some 250 km (to the head of Lake Melville) into the southeastern coast of Labrador. [Sir C. *Hamilton*, English admiral and governor of Newfoundland d.1849]

Ham·ite /ˈhamaɪt/ noun a member of a group of North African peoples, including the ancient Egyptians and Berbers. [HAM, son of Noah, from whom they are supposedly descended]

Ham·it·ic /həˈmɪtɪk/ ● noun a group of African languages including ancient Egyptian and Berber. ● adjective **1** of or relating to this group of languages. **2** of or relating to the Hamites.

Hamito-Semitic noun & adjective = AFRO-ASIATIC.

ham·let noun a small village, esp. one that is unincorporated. [Anglo-French *hamelet(t)e*, Old French *hamelet* diminutive of *hamel* diminutive of *ham* from Middle Low German *hamm*]

Hamm an industrial city in NW Germany, in North Rhine-Westphalia, on the Lippe River; pop. (est. 2002) 178,000.

Ham·mar·skjöld /ˈhamərˌʃoːld/ **Dag Hjal·mar Agné Carl** (1905–61), Swedish statesman; Secretary-General of the United Nations (1953–61). He was awarded the Nobel Peace Prize posthumously in 1961.

ham·mer ● noun **1 a** a tool with a heavy metal head at right angles to the handle, used for breaking, driving nails, etc. **b** a machine with a metal block serving the same purpose. **c** a similar contrivance, as for exploding the charge in a gun, striking the strings of a piano, etc. **2** an auctioneer's mallet, indicating by a rap that an article is sold. **3 a** a metal ball of about 7 kg, attached to a wire for throwing in an athletic contest. **b** the sport of throwing the hammer. **4** a bone of the middle ear; the malleus. **5** *Curling* the last rock of an end. ● verb **1 a** transitive & intransitive hit or beat with or as with a hammer. **b** intransitive strike loudly; knock violently (esp. on a door). **2** transitive **a** drive in (nails) with a hammer. **b** fasten or secure by hammering (*hammered the lid down*). **3** transitive (often foll. by *in*) inculcate (ideas, knowledge, etc.) forcefully or repeatedly. **4** transitive informal utterly defeat; inflict heavy damage on. **5** intransitive (foll. by *at, away at*) work hard or persistently at. □ **under the hammer** to be sold at an auction. **hammer out 1** make flat or smooth by hammering. **2** work out the details of (a plan, agreement, etc.) laboriously. **3** play (a tune, esp. on the piano) loudly or clumsily. □ **hammer·er** noun **hammer·ing** noun (esp. in sense 4 of *verb*). **hammer·less** adjective [Old English *hamor, hamer*]

hammer and sickle noun the symbols of the industrial worker and the peasant used as the emblem of the former USSR and of international communism.

hammer and tongs adverb informal with great vigour and commotion.

hammer·beam noun a wooden beam (often carved) projecting from a wall to support the principal rafter or the end of an arch.

hammer drill noun a drill with a bit that moves backwards and forwards while rotating.

ham·mered adjective **1** (of metal, etc.) shaped or formed with a hammer (*hammered brass*). **2** N Amer. informal drunk.

hammer·head noun **1** any of a number of sharks of the genus *Sphyrna*, with a flattened, laterally elongated head bearing the eyes and nostrils at the extremities. **2** a long-legged African marsh bird, *Scopus umbretta*, with a thick bill and an occipital crest.

hammer·lock noun **1** a hold in which an opponent's arm is twisted and bent behind the back. **2** a strong hold.

hammer price noun the price realized by an item sold at auction.

Ham·mer·stein /ˈhamərˌstaɪn/ **Oscar** (full name Oscar Hammerstein II) (1895–1960), US librettist. He collaborated with the composers Jerome Kern (*Showboat*, 1927), Sigmund Romberg, and most notably with Richard Rodgers (*South Pacific*, 1949; *The Sound of Music*, 1959).

hammer·toe noun a deformity in which the toe is bent permanently downwards.

Ham·mett, (Sam·uel) Dash·iell (1894–1961), US novelist. His detective fiction, based in part on his own experiences as a detective, is characterized by a hard-boiled style. Many of his stories, including *The Maltese Falcon* (1930) and *The Thin Man* (1932), were made into successful films.

ham·mock¹ noun a bed of canvas or rope network, suspended by cords at the ends. [earlier *hamaca* from Spanish, from Taino *hamaka*]

ham·mock² var. of HUMMOCK 2.

Ham·mu·rabi /ˌhamʊˈrɒbi/ (d.1750 BC), the sixth king of the first dynasty of Babylonia (1792–1750 BC). He made Babylon the capital of Babylonia, extended the Babylonian Empire, and instituted one of the earliest known legal codes, which took the form of 282 case laws dealing with the economy and with family, criminal, and civil law.

hammy adjective (**ham·mi·er, ham·mi·est**) **1** of or like ham. **2** informal (of an actor or acting) over-theatrical. □ **ham·mi·ly** adverb **ham·mi·ness** noun

ham·per¹ noun **1** a large basket usu. with a hinged lid and containing food (*picnic hamper*). **2** a package of food or other essentials for a needy person (*distributing Christmas hampers*). **3** N Amer. a usu. covered basket or other receptacle for dirty laundry. **4** Brit. a selection of food, drink, etc., for an occasion. [Middle English from obsolete *hanaper*, Anglo-French from Old French *hanapier* case for a goblet, from *hanap* goblet]

ham·per² ● transitive verb **1** prevent the free movement or activity of. **2** impede, hinder. ● noun Naut. necessary but cumbersome equipment on a ship. [Middle English: origin unknown]

Hamp·shire /ˈhampʃɪr/ a county on the coast of S England; county town, Winchester. The cities of Southampton and Portsmouth, now independent jurisdictions, were part of the county until 1996. [after SOUTHAMPTON¹]

Hamp·stead 1 /ˈhampstəd/ a residential suburb of NW London. It contains Hampstead Heath, a large tract of open common land within the city, popular for recreation. **2** /ˈhamsted/ a former town in south central Quebec, on the southern part of the Island of Montreal, now part of the city of Montreal; pop. (2001) 6,974.

Hamp·ton¹ a city in SE Virginia, on the harbour of Hampton Roads, on Chesapeake Bay; pop. (2000) 146,400.

Hamp·ton², Lionel (1913–2002), US musician. He was the first jazz musician to use the vibraphone.

Hampton Roads a deepwater estuary 6 km (4 miles) long, formed by the James River where it joins Chesapeake Bay, on the Atlantic coast in SE Virginia. The ports of Newport News and Hampton are situated on it.

ham·ster noun any of various rodents of the subfamily Cricetinae, esp. *Cricetus cricetus*, having a short tail and large cheek pouches for storing food, kept as a pet or laboratory animal. [German from Old High German *hamustro* corn weevil]

ham·string ● noun **1** each of five tendons at the back of the knee in humans. **2** the great tendon at the back of the hock in quadrupeds. ● transitive verb (*past* and *past participle* **ham·strung**) **1** cripple by cutting the hamstrings of (a person or animal). **2** prevent the activity or efficiency of (a person or enterprise).

Ham·sun /ˈhamsʊn/ **Knut** (pseudonym of Knut Pedersen) (1859–1952), Norwegian novelist. His novels, including *Hunger* (1890) and *Growth of the Soil* (1917), explore the human psyche and are written in a fragmentary, vivid style. He was awarded the Nobel Prize for literature in 1920.

ham·ulus /ˈhamjʊləs/ noun (pl. **ham·uli** /-ˌlaɪ/) Anat., Zool., & Bot. a hooklike projection. [Latin, diminutive of *hamus* hook]

Han¹ /hɒn/ ● noun **1** a member of a small Aboriginal group living along the Yukon River. **2** the Athapaskan language of this people. ● adjective of or relating to this people or their culture or language. [Gwich'in *han-gwich'in* 'river dwellers']

Han² /han/ the Chinese dynasty that ruled, with only a brief interruption, from 206 BC until AD 220, during which time Chinese rule was extended over Mongolia. The dynasty was marked by the flourishing of the arts, the recognition of Confucianism as the state philosophy, and by technical advances including the invention of paper. The term is now also used to describe the dominant ethnic group in China (as distinct from the many minority groups).

Han·cock, John (1737–93), US politician. He was the first person to sign the Declaration of Independence.

hand ● noun **1 a** the end part of the human arm beyond the wrist, including the fingers and thumb. **b** in other primates, the end part of a forelimb, also used as a foot. **2 a** (often in *pl.*) control, management, custody, disposal (*is in good hands*). **b** agency or influence (*suffered at their hands*). **c** a share in an action; active support. **3** help or assistance (*Katie gave me a hand with this*). **4** a thing compared with a hand or its functions, esp. the pointer of a clock or watch. **5** the right or left side or direction relative to a person or thing. **6 a** a skill, esp. in something practical (*a hand for making pastry*). **b** a person skilful in some respect. **7** a person who does or makes something, esp. distinctively (*a picture by the same hand*). **8** an individual's writing or the style of this; a signature (*a legible hand; in one's own hand; witness the hand of …*). **9** a person etc. as the source of information etc. (*at first hand*). **10** a pledge of marriage. **11** a person as a source of manual labour esp. in a factory, on a farm, or on board ship. **12 a** the playing cards dealt to a player. **b** the player holding these. **c** a round of play. **13** *informal* applause (*got a big hand*). **14** the unit of measure of a horse's height, equal to 4 inches (10.16 cm). **15** a bunch of bananas. **16** (*attributive*) **a** operated or held in the hand (*hand drill; hand baggage*). **b** done by hand and not by machine (*hand-knitted*). ● *transitive verb* **1** (foll. by *in, to, over,* etc.) deliver; transfer by hand or otherwise. **2** convey verbally (*handed me a lot of abuse*). **3** *informal* give away too readily (*handed them the advantage*). □ **all hands 1** the entire crew of a ship. **2** the entire workforce. **all hands on deck 1** a cry or signal used on board ship, typically in an emergency, to indicate that all crew members are to go on deck. **2** used to indicate that the involvement of all members of a team is required. **at hand 1** close by. **2** about to happen. **by hand 1** by a person and not a machine. **2** delivered privately, rather than by the post office. **from hand to mouth** satisfying only one's immediate needs (also *attributive: a hand-to-mouth existence*). **get** (or **have** or **keep**) **one's hand in** become (or be or remain) practised in something. **give** (or **lend**) **a hand** assist in an action or enterprise. **hand and foot** completely; satisfying all demands (*waited on them hand and foot*). **hand down 1 a** pass the ownership or use of to another. **b** transmit (a custom etc.) from one generation to the next. **2 a** transmit (a decision) from a higher court etc. **b** *N Amer.* express (an opinion or verdict). **hand in glove** in collusion or association. **hand in hand 1** holding hands. **2** in close association. **hand it to** *informal* acknowledge the merit of (a person). **hand off 1** *Football* hand (the ball) to another player, rather than passing or throwing it. **2** give or hand (a thing) to another person. **3** *Rugby* push off (a tackling opponent) with the hand. **hand on** pass (a thing) to the next in a series or succession. **hand out 1** serve, distribute. **2** award, allocate (*the judges handed out stiff sentences*). **hand over** deliver; surrender possession of. **hand over fist** *informal* with rapid progress. **hand round** distribute. **hands down** (esp. of winning) with no difficulty. **hands off 1** a warning not to touch or interfere with something. **2** *Computing etc.* not requiring manual use of controls. **hands on** *Computing* **1** of or requiring personal operation at a keyboard. **2** involving or offering active participation rather than theory; direct, practical. **a hand's turn** *informal* a stroke of work. **hands up!** an instruction to raise one's hands in surrender or to signify assent or participation. **hand-to-hand** (of fighting) at close quarters. **have** (or **take**) **a hand in** share or take part in. **have one's hand in the till** steal from one's employer; embezzle; take bribes. **have one's hands full** be fully occupied. **have one's hands tied** *informal* be unable to act. **hold one's hand** = STAY ONE'S HAND. **in hand 1** receiving attention. **2** in reserve; at one's disposal. **3** under one's control. **lay** (or **put**) **one's hands on** see LAY[1]. **off one's hands** no longer one's responsibility. **on every hand** (or **all hands**) to or from all directions. **on hand 1** available. **2** present, in attendance. **on one's hands** resting on one as a responsibility. **on (one's) hands and knees** crouching down with the palms and the knees touching the ground. **on the one** (or **the other**) **hand** from one (or another) point of view. **out of hand 1** out of control. **2** peremptorily (*refused out of hand*). **put** (or **set**) **one's hand to** start work on; engage in. **stay one's hand** *archaic* or *literary* refrain from action. **to hand 1** within easy reach. **2** (of a letter) received. **turn one's hand to** undertake (as a new activity). □ **hand·ed** *adjective* **hand·less** *adjective* [Old English *hand, hond*]

Han·dan /han'dan/ a city in Hebei province, E China; pop. (est. 1999) 1,005,834.

hand axe *noun* a prehistoric stone implement, normally oval or pear-shaped and worked on both sides, used for chopping, cutting, and scraping things.

hand·bag *noun* a woman's purse.

hand·ball *noun* **1 a** a game in which a ball is hit with the hand in a walled court. **b** the small, hard ball used in this game. **2** *Brit.* a game similar to soccer in which the ball is thrown rather than kicked. **3** *Soccer* intentional touching of the ball with the hand or arm by a player other than the goalkeeper in the goal area, constituting a foul.

hand barrow *noun Cdn (Nfld)* = BARROW[1] 2.

hand·basket *noun* esp. *N Amer.* a small basket. □ **go to hell in a handbasket** degenerate, esp. rapidly (*the company's going to hell in a handbasket*).

hand·bell *noun* a small bell, usu. tuned to a particular note and rung by hand, esp. one of a set giving a range of notes.

hand·bill *noun* a printed notice distributed by hand.

hand blender *noun* a hand-held electrical kitchen appliance with rotating blades at one end, plunged into soup etc. to purée it.

hand·book *noun* a short manual or guidebook.

hand·brake *noun* a brake operated by hand.

hand·car *noun* a small, four-wheeled railway car propelled by hand, used for inspecting tracks etc.

hand·cart *noun* a small cart pushed or drawn by hand. □ **go to hell in a handcart** = GO TO HELL IN A HANDBASKET (see HANDBASKET).

hand-carve *transitive verb* carve (a thing) by hand. □ **hand-carved** *adjective*

hand·clap *noun* a clapping of the hands.

hand·craft ● *noun* = HANDICRAFT. ● *transitive verb* make by handicraft. □ **hand·craft·ed** *adjective*

hand cream *noun* a cream for softening and moisturizing the skin of the hands.

hand·cuff ● *noun* (in *pl.*) a pair of lockable linked metal rings for securing a person's wrists. ● *transitive verb* **1** put handcuffs on. **2** prevent (a person) from acting freely or effectively.

-handed *adjective* (in combination) **1** for or involving a specified number of hands (in various senses) (*two-handed*). **2** using chiefly the hand specified (*left-handed*). □ **-handedly** *adverb* **-handedness** *noun* (both in sense 2).

hand·ed·ness *noun* the tendency to use or the preference for the use of either the right or the left hand.

Han·del /'handǝl/ **George Fred·erick** (1685–1759), German-born composer, resident in England from 1712. A major baroque composer whose prolific output included choral works, chamber music, operas, concerti grossi, and orchestral pieces, he is now chiefly remembered for his oratorios, the most famous of which is the *Messiah* (1742). □ **Han·del·ian** /han'diːliǝn/ *adjective*

hand·ful *noun* (*pl.* **-fuls**) **1** a quantity that fills the hand. **2** a small number or amount. **3** *informal* a troublesome person or task.

hand game *noun* a usu. gambling game involving sleight of hand, esp. requiring players to guess in which hand an object is concealed.

hand·glass *noun* **1** a magnifying glass held in the hand. **2** a small mirror with a handle.

hand grenade *noun* see GRENADE 1.

hand·grip *noun* **1** a grasp with the hand. **2** a handle designed for easy holding.

hand·gun *noun* a small firearm held in and fired with one hand.

hand-held ● *adjective* designed to be held in the hand. ● *noun* a small hand-held computer.

hand·hold *noun* something for the hands to grip on (in climbing, sailing, etc.).

handi·cap ● *noun* **1 a** a disadvantage imposed on a superior competitor in order to make the chances more equal. **b** a race or contest in which this is imposed. **2** the number of strokes by which a golfer normally exceeds par for the course. **3** a thing that makes progress or success difficult. **4** a physical or mental disability. ● *transitive verb* (**handi·capped, handi·cap·ping**) **1** impose a handicap on. **2** place (a person) at a disadvantage. **3** act as an impediment to. □ **handi·cap·per** *noun* [originally a game in which participants deposited forfeit money in a cap: the name prob. from the phrase *hand in cap*]

handi·capped *adjective* suffering from a physical or mental disability.

handi·craft *noun* **1** an art, skill, or trade that requires both manual and artistic ability. **2** work produced by such a skill or art (*local handicrafts are on sale*). **3** manual skill or dexterity. [Middle English, alteration of earlier HANDCRAFT after HANDIWORK]

hand·i·ly *adverb* **1** in a handy manner. **2** *N Amer.* easily (*she won the contest handily*). **3** conveniently.

handi·work *noun* work done or a thing made by hand, or by a particular person. [Old English *handgeweorc*]

hand job *noun coarse slang* an act of masturbation, esp. as performed on a man by someone else.

hand·ker·chief /'haŋkǝrtʃif, -,tʃiːf/ *noun* (*pl.* **hand·ker·chiefs** or **-chieves** /-,tʃiːvz/) a square of cotton, linen, silk, etc., usu. carried in the pocket for wiping one's nose, etc.

han·dle ● *noun* **1** the part by which a thing is held, carried, or controlled. **2** a fact that may be taken advantage of (*gave a handle to his critics*). **3** *informal* a personal name or title. **4** the feel of goods, esp. textiles, when handled. **5** the total amount of money bet at an event or time. ● *verb* **1** *transitive* touch, feel, operate, or move with the hands. **2** *transitive* manage or deal with; treat in a particular or correct way (*knows how to handle people; unable to handle the situation*). **3** *transitive* deal in (goods). **4** *transitive* discuss or write about (a subject). **5** *intransitive* (of a vehicle, machine, tool, etc.) react or behave in a specified way in response to use, operation, or direction. **6** *reflexive* behave, esp. under pressure. □ **get a handle on** *informal* understand the basis of or reason for a situation, circumstance, etc. **fly off the handle** *see* FLY[1]. □ **handle·able** *adjective* **handle·abil·ity** *noun* **han·dled** *adjective* (also in *combination*). **handle·less** *adjective* [Old English *handle, handlian* (as HAND)]

handle·bar *noun* (often in *pl.*) the steering bar of a bicycle etc., with a handgrip at each end.

handlebar moustache *noun* a thick moustache with ends curving upwards.

hand·ler *noun* **1** a person or thing that handles something. **2** a person who handles or deals in certain commodities. **3** a person who trains and looks after an animal (esp. a police dog). **4** a person who looks after or represents a public figure, esp. a politician.

hand·line *noun* a fishing line worked or drawn by hand. □ **hand·liner** *noun* **hand·lining** *noun*

hand·ling *noun* **1** the act or an instance of handling. **2** treatment or manner of dealing with something. **3** the process of packing, transporting, and delivering goods etc. (also *attributive*: *handling charges*). **4** the way in which a vehicle handles.

hand·log·ger *noun* N Amer. a person who logs by hand, using tools such as an axe or saw rather than a feller-buncher or other more mechanized methods. □ **hand·log·ging** *noun*

hand·made *adjective* made by hand and not by machine, esp. as designating superior quality.

hand·maid *noun* (also **hand·maiden**) **1** *archaic* a female servant or helper. **2** something that supports and helps something else.

hand-me-down *noun* an article of clothing etc. passed on from another person.

hand-off *noun* the act or an instance of handing off.

hand·out *noun* **1** something given free to a needy person. **2** a statement given to the press etc. **3** a fact sheet, graph, summary of a speech, etc. distributed to a class or audience. **4** anything given away free, e.g. a sample of a product. **5** a payment made by esp. a government to a person, agency, etc. perceived as providing nothing in return.

hand·over *noun* the act or an instance of handing over.

hand-pick *transitive verb* **1** pick (fruit etc.) by hand. **2** choose carefully or personally. □ **hand-picked** *adjective*

hand·print *noun* the print or mark of a hand (*left handprints all over the window*).

hand pump *noun* a pump operated by hand.

hand·rail *noun* a narrow rail for holding as a support on stairs etc.

hand·saw *noun* a saw worked by one hand.

hands-down *adjective* unrivalled, without competition (*the hands-down favourite*).

hand·set *noun* a telephone mouthpiece and earpiece forming one unit.

hands-free *adjective* (of a telephone etc.) designed to be operated without the use of the hands.

hand·shake *noun* the shaking of a person's hand with one's own as a greeting etc.

hand signal *noun* a manual indication by a cyclist or driver of a motor vehicle of his or her intention to stop, turn, etc.

hands-off *adjective* **1** (of a policy, attitude, etc.) characterized by the lack of intervention (*a hands-off approach to the problem*). **2** (of flying, driving, etc.) without the use of the hands (*hands-off piloting*).

hand·some /ˈhansəm/ *adjective* (**hand·som·er, hand·som·est**) **1** (of a person) good-looking. **2** (of a building etc.) imposing, attractive. **3 a** generous, liberal (*a handsome present; handsome treatment*). **b** (of a price, fortune, etc., as assets gained) considerable. □ **hand·some·ness** *noun* [Middle English, = easily handled, from HAND + -SOME[1]]

hand·some·ly /ˈhansəmli/ *adverb* **1** generously, liberally. **2** finely, beautifully. **3** *Naut.* carefully.

hands-on *adjective* characterized by active participation or involvement (*hands-on computer experience*).

hand·spring *noun* a somersault in which one lands first on the hands and then on the feet.

hand·stand *noun* the act or an instance of balancing on one's hands with the feet in the air or against a wall.

hand tool *noun* a tool operated by hand, without electricity.

hand·wash·ing *noun* **1** washing of the hands. **2** washing by hand. **3** the act of renouncing responsibility.

hand·work *noun* work done with the hands, esp. as opposed to machinery. □ **hand·worked** *adjective*

hand·woven *adjective* (of cloth) woven by hand, as opposed to by a machine.

hand-wringing ● *noun* exaggerated lamentation or anguish. ● *adjective* characterized by hand-wringing.

hand·writing *noun* **1** writing with a pen, pencil, etc. **2** a person's particular style of writing. □ **the handwriting is on the wall** N Amer. there are clear signs of approaching failure or disaster. □ **hand·writ·ten** *adjective*

Handy, Wil·liam Chris·to·pher (1873-1958), US blues musician and songwriter. His works include 'St. Louis Blues' (1911).

handy *adjective* (**hand·i·er, hand·i·est**) **1** convenient to handle or use; useful. **2** ready to hand; placed or occurring conveniently. **3** clever with the hands. □ **hand·i·ness** *noun*

handy-dandy *adjective informal* extremely handy.

handy·man *noun* (*pl.* **-men**) a person able or employed to do occasional domestic repairs and minor renovations.

handyman's special *noun* N Amer. something, esp. a house, that is for sale at a reduced price because of the many repairs or renovations needed.

hang ● *verb* (*past and past participle* **hung** except in sense 7) **1** *transitive* **a** secure or cause to be supported from above, esp. with the lower part free. **b** (foll. by *up, on, on to,* etc.) attach loosely by suspending from the top. **2** *transitive* set up (a door, gate, etc.) on its hinges so that it moves freely. **3** *transitive* place (a picture) on a wall or in an exhibition. **4** *transitive* attach (wallpaper) in vertical strips to a wall. **5** *transitive* (foll. by *on*) *informal* attach the blame for (a thing) to (a person) (*you can't hang that on me*). **6** *transitive* (foll. by *with*) decorate by hanging pictures or decorations etc. (*a hall hung with tapestries*). **7** *transitive & intransitive* (*past and past participle* **hanged**) **a** suspend or be suspended by the neck with a noosed rope until dead, esp. as a form of capital punishment. **b** as a mild oath (*hang the expense; let everything go hang; hanged if I know*). **8** *transitive* let droop (*hung her head*). **9** *transitive* suspend (meat or game) from a hook and leave it until dry or tender or high. **10** *intransitive* be or remain hung (in various senses). **11** *intransitive* remain static in the air. **12** *intransitive* (often foll. by *over*) be present or imminent, esp. oppressively or threateningly (*a hush hung over the room*). **13** *intransitive* (foll. by *on*) **a** be contingent or dependent on (*everything hangs on the discussions*). **b** listen closely to (*hangs on their every word*). **14** *transitive* prevent (a jury) from reaching a verdict. **15** *intransitive* (of a computer or computer system) cease to respond to input from the keyboard or mouse. **16** *intransitive* N Amer. *slang* (usu. foll. by *with*) associate with (a person). ● *noun* **1** the way a thing hangs or falls. **2** a downward droop or bend. □ **get the hang of** *informal* understand the technique or meaning of. **hang a left** (or **right**) N Amer. *informal* make a left (or right) turn. **hang around** (also Brit. **about**) **1 a** loiter or dally; not move away. **b** linger near (a person or place). **c** wait. **2** (often foll. by *with*) associate with (a person etc.). **hang back 1** show reluctance to act or move. **2** remain behind. **hang fire** be slow in taking action or in progressing. **hang heavily** (or **heavy**) (of time) pass slowly. **hang in** esp. N Amer. *informal* **1** persist, persevere. **2** linger. **hang in there** expressing encouragement to persevere. **hang loose** *informal* be casual or unconcerned. **hang on** *informal* **1** continue or persevere, esp. with difficulty. **2** (often foll. by *to*) continue to hold or grasp. **3** (foll. by *to*) retain; fail to give back. **4 a** wait for a short time. **b** (in telephoning) continue to listen during a pause in the conversation. **hang one's hat** N Amer. be resident. **hang out 1** hang from a window, clothesline, etc. **2** protrude or cause to protrude downwards. **3** (foll. by *of*) lean out of (a window etc.). **4** *slang* reside or be often present. **5** = HANG AROUND 2. **hang a person out to dry** abandon a person to a usu. unpleasant fate. **hang ten** *slang* (of a surfer) ride (a surfboard) with all ten toes curled over the board's front edge. **hang together 1** make sense. **2** remain associated. **hang tough** N Amer. *informal* be or remain inflexible. **hang up 1** hang from a hook, peg, hanger, etc. **2** (often foll. by *on*) end a telephone conversation, esp. abruptly (*then he hung up on me*). **3** cause delay or difficulty to. **4** (usu. in *passive*, foll. by *on*) *slang* be a psychological or emotional obsession or problem to (*is really hung up on her father*). **5** = HANG verb 15. **hang up one's skates** Cdn give up; quit or retire (*the premier has announced he will hang up his skates next spring*). **let it all hang out** *slang* be uninhibited or relaxed. **might as well be hanged for a sheep as a lamb** if the penalty for a more serious crime, offence, act of foolishness, etc. is no greater than for a less serious one, then one might as well continue in one's criminal, foolish, etc. behaviour. **not care** (or **give**) **a hang** *informal* not care at all. [Old Norse *hanga* (tr.) = Old English *hōn*, & from Old English *hangian* (intr.), from Germanic]

hang·ar *noun* a building with extensive floor area, for housing aircraft etc. □ **hangar·age** *noun* [French, of unknown origin]

hang·ashore *Cdn* (*Nfld & Maritimes*) (also **angishore**, **angashore** /ˈaŋəʃɔr/) **1** a weak or sickly person. **2** an idle person, esp. one regarded as too lazy to fish. [Irish Gaelic *aindeiseoir* 'weak, sickly person']

Hang·chow see HANGZHOU.

hang·dog *adjective* having a dejected or guilty appearance; shamefaced.

hang·er *noun* **1** a person or thing that hangs. **2** (also **coat hanger**) a shaped piece of wood or plastic etc. from which clothes may be hung.

hanger-on *noun* (*pl.* **hangers-on**) a follower or dependant, esp. an unwelcome one.

hang-glider *noun* **1** a frame with a fabric airfoil stretched over it, from which the operator is suspended and controls flight by body movement. **2** a person who practises hang-gliding. □ **hang-glide** *intransitive verb* **hang-gliding** *noun*

hang·ing ● *noun* **1** the act or practice of executing a person by hanging. **2** a tapestry hung on a wall etc. ● *adjective* **1** that hangs or is hung; suspended. **2** (of a crime) punishable by hanging (*a hanging offence*). **3** (of a judge, jury, etc.) inclined towards giving a death sentence (*a hanging judge*).

hanging basket *noun* a basket or similar container which can be suspended from a building and in which decorative esp. flowering plants are grown.

hanging gardens *plural noun* gardens laid out on a steep slope.

Hanging Gardens of Babylon *plural noun* terraced gardens at Babylon, watered by pumps from the Euphrates, whose construction was ascribed to Nebuchadnezzar (*c.* 600 BC). They were one of the Seven Wonders of the World.

hanging valley *noun* a valley, usu. tributary, above the level of the valleys or plains it joins.

hang·man *noun* (*pl.* **-men**) **1** an executioner who hangs condemned persons. **2** a word game for two players, in which the tally of failed guesses is kept by drawing a representation of a body on a gallows.

hang·nail *noun* a piece of torn skin at the root of a fingernail or toenail. [alteration of *agnail* (from Old English *angnægl* from *nægl* NAIL *noun* 1), influenced by HANG]

hang·out *noun* *informal* a place one frequently visits, esp. to relax or socialize etc.

hang·over *noun* **1** a severe headache and other after-effects caused by drinking an excess of alcohol. **2** a survival from the past.

Hang Seng index *noun* a figure indicating the relative price of representative shares on the Hong Kong Stock Exchange. [*Hang Seng*, name of a Hong Kong bank]

hang tag *noun* a tag attached to an item of clothing etc. giving information about its use, care, etc.

hang-up *noun* *slang* an emotional problem or inhibition.

Hang·zhou /haŋˈʒoː/ (also **Hang·chow** /-ˈtʃau/) the capital of Zhejiang province in E China, situated on Hangzhou Bay, an inlet of the Yellow Sea, at the southern end of the Grand Canal; pop. (est. 2002) 3,010,000.

hank *noun* **1** a usu. thick clump of hair. **2** a coil or skein of wool or thread etc. **3** any of several measures of length of cloth or yarn, e.g. 840 yds. (767 m) for cotton yarn and 560 yds. (512 m) for worsted. **4** *Naut.* a ring of rope, iron, etc., for securing the staysails to the stays. [Old Norse *hönk*: compare Swedish *hank* string, Danish *hank* handle]

han·ker *intransitive verb* (foll. by *for*, *after*, or *to* + infin.) long for; crave. □ **han·ker·er** *noun* **han·ker·ing** *noun* [obsolete *hank*, prob. related to HANG]

Hanks, Thom·as J. ('Tom') (b.1956), US actor. Lighthearted films such as *Splash!* (1984) and *Big* (1988) brought him international success. He went on to win Oscars for his roles in *Philadelphia* (1993) and *Forrest Gump* (1994), and was nominated for his performances in *Saving Private Ryan* (1998) and *Cast Away* (2000).

hanky *noun* (also **hankie**) (*pl.* **-kies**) *informal* a handkerchief. [abbreviation]

hanky-panky *noun* *slang* **1** naughtiness, esp. sexual misbehaviour. **2** dishonest dealing; trickery. [19th c.: perhaps based on *hocus-pocus*]

Han·lan /ˈhanlən/ **Ed·ward** ('Ned') (1855–1908), Canadian athlete, the first to become a world champion. He took the Canadian sculling championship in 1877 and the US championship in 1878. In 1879

Hanlan defeated the English champion by 11 lengths, and went on to hold the world championship 1880–1884.

Han·ni·bal /ˈhanɪbəl/ (247–182 BC), Carthaginian general. In 218 he led an army of about 30,000 over the Alps into Italy, and inflicted a series of defeats on the Romans, campaigning for sixteen years undefeated but failing to take Rome itself.

Hanoi /haˈnɔi/ the capital of Vietnam, situated on the Red River in the north of the country; pop. (est. 2002) 1,372,800. It was the capital of French Indochina from 1887 to 1946 and of North Vietnam before the reunification of North and South Vietnam.

Han·over[1] /ˈhanoːvər/ **1** an industrial city in NW Germany, on the Mittelland Canal; pop. (est. 2002) 516,800. It is the capital of Lower Saxony. **2** a former state and province in N Germany. **3** a town in SW central Ontario, about 60 km south of Owen Sound; pop. (2001) 6,869. □ **Han·over·ian** /ˌhanəˈviːrɪən/ *adjective & noun*

Han·over[2] /ˈhanoːvər/ the British royal house from 1714 to the death of Queen Victoria in 1901. □ **Han·over·ian** /ˌhanəˈviːrɪən/ *adjective & noun*

Hansa /ˈhansə/ *noun* (also **Hanse**) **1 a** a medieval guild of merchants. **b** the entrance fee to a guild. **2** = HANSEATIC LEAGUE. □ **Han·se·atic** /-siˈatɪk/ *adjective* [Middle High German *hanse*, Old High German, Gothic *hansa* company]

Han·sard /ˈhansərd/ *noun* the official verbatim record of debates in parliaments in Canada, the UK, and many other parliaments throughout the Commonwealth. [T. C. *Hansard*, English printer d.1832, who first printed it]

Han·se·atic League /ˌhansiˈatɪk/ a commercial alliance of north German cities, formed in 1241. With about 100 member towns in the later Middle Ages, the League functioned as an independent political power, with its own army and navy. It began to collapse in the early 17th c. and was finally broken up in the 19th. [HANSA]

Han·sen /ˈhansən/ **Rick** (b.1957), Canadian athlete. Between 1985 and 1987, he travelled around the world in his wheelchair to raise money for spinal cord research, propelling himself by hand through 34 countries including Australia, China, and Canada. He is the subject of the film *Man in Motion* (1987).

Hansen's disease *noun* leprosy. [G. H. A. *Hansen*, Norwegian physician d.1912]

Hans Island /hanz/ a small uninhabited island in the Arctic, situated in Nares Strait roughly midway between Ellesmere Island and Greenland. Currently under territorial dispute, the island is claimed both by Canada and Denmark.

han·som /ˈhansəm/ *noun* (in full **hansom cab**) *hist.* a two-wheeled horse-drawn cab accommodating two inside, with the driver seated behind. [J. A. *Hansom*, English architect d.1882, who designed it]

hanta·virus /ˈhantəˌvaɪrəs/ *noun* any of various viruses of the family Bunyaviridae, spread mainly by rodents and causing acute respiratory disease, kidney failure, etc. [Modern Latin from *Hantaan* River in Korea (where the virus was first isolated in 1976) + VIRUS]

Ha·nuk·kah /ˈhɒnəkə/ *noun* (also **Chanukah**) the eight-day Jewish festival of lights, usu. in December, commemorating the purification of the Temple in 165 BC. [Hebrew *ḥānukkāh* consecration]

hanu·man /ˌhanuˈmʊn/ *noun* **1** a common grey monkey of India, *Presbytis entellus*, venerated by Hindus. **2** (**Hanuman**) (in Hindu mythology) a semi-divine being represented as resembling a monkey with extraordinary powers. [Hindi]

Haora see HOWRAH.

hap *archaic* ● *noun* **1** chance, luck. **2** a chance occurrence. ● *intransitive verb* (**happed**, **hap·ping**) **1** come about by chance. **2** (foll. by *to* + infin.) happen to. [Old Norse *happ*]

hapax leg·om·en·on /ˌhapaks ləˈgɒməˌnɒn/ *noun* (*pl.* **hapax leg·om·ena** /-mənə/) a word of which only one instance of use is recorded. [Greek, = a thing said once]

ha'penny *var.* of HALFPENNY.

hap·haz·ard /hapˈhazərd/ ● *adjective* done etc. by chance; random. ● *adverb* at random. □ **hap·haz·ard·ly** *adverb* **hap·haz·ard·ness** *noun* [HAP + HAZARD]

hap·less *adjective* unlucky. □ **hap·less·ly** *adverb* **hap·less·ness** *noun* [HAP + -LESS]

hap·loid /ˈhaplɔɪd/ ● *adjective* *Biol.* (of an organism or cell) with a single set of chromosomes. ● *noun* a haploid organism or cell. [German from Greek *haplous* single + *eidos* form]

hap·lol·ogy /hapˈlɒlədʒi/ *noun* the omission of a sound when this is repeated within a word (e.g. *mirror* pronounced /ˈmiːr/). [Greek *haplous* 'single' + -LOGY]

hap·lo·type noun Genetics a set of genetic determinants located on a single chromosome.

ha'p'orth Brit. var. of HALFPENNYWORTH.

hap·pen ● intransitive verb 1 occur (by chance or otherwise). 2 (foll. by to + infin.) have the (good or bad) fortune to (I happened to meet her). 3 (foll. by to) be the (esp. unwelcome) fate or experience of (what happened to you?). 4 (foll. by on) encounter or discover by chance. 5 esp. N Amer. (foll. by along, by, etc.) come or turn up in a place casually or as if by chance. ● adverb Northern England dialect perhaps, maybe (happen it'll rain). □ **as it happens** in fact; in reality (as it happens, it turned out well). [Middle English from HAP + -EN¹]

hap·pen·ing ● noun 1 an event or occurrence. 2 an improvised or spontaneous theatrical etc. performance. ● adjective slang exciting, fashionable, trendy.

happen·stance noun esp. N Amer. a thing that happens by chance. [HAPPEN + CIRCUMSTANCE]

hap·pi noun (pl. **hap·pis**) (also **happi coat**) a loose informal Japanese coat. [Japanese]

happy adjective (**hap·pi·er**, **hap·pi·est**) 1 feeling or showing pleasure or contentment. 2 a fortunate; characterized by happiness. b (of words, behaviour, etc.) apt, pleasing. 3 informal slightly drunk. 4 (in combination) informal inclined to use excessively or at random (trigger-happy). □ **hap·pi·ly** adverb **hap·pi·ness** noun [Middle English from HAP + -Y¹]

happy camper noun N Amer. informal a happy or contented person.

happy event noun informal the birth of a child.

happy face noun = SMILEY FACE.

happy-go-lucky adjective cheerfully casual.

happy hour noun a period of the day when drinks are sold at reduced prices in bars, hotels, etc.

happy hunting ground noun a place where success or enjoyment is obtained.

happy medium noun a compromise; the avoidance of extremes.

happy pill noun slang a drug which makes people artificially happy; an antidepressant.

Happy Valley-Goose Bay a town in south central Labrador, at the mouth of the Churchill River where it empties into Goose Bay; pop. (2001) 7,969.

Haps·burg one of the principal dynasties of central Europe from medieval to modern times. The family established a hereditary monarchy in Austria in 1282 and by 1452 had secured the title of Holy Roman emperor. Austrian and Spanish branches were created when Emperor Charles V divided the territories between his son Philip II and his brother Ferdinand; the branch in Spain ruled 1504–1700, while the Austrian branch finally collapsed in 1918.

hap·tic adjective relating to the sense of touch. [Greek haptikos able to touch, from haptō fasten]

hara-kiri /ˌherəˈkɪri/ noun 1 ritual suicide by disembowelment with a sword, formerly practised by Samurai to avoid dishonour. 2 a self-destructive action or course (political hara-kiri). [informal Japanese from hara belly + kiri cutting]

har·angue /həˈraŋ/ ● noun 1 a lengthy and earnest speech. 2 a passionate verbal attack or reprimand. ● transitive & intransitive verb lecture or make a harangue (to). □ **har·anguer** noun [Old French arenge from medieval Latin harenga, perhaps from Germanic]

Har·ap·pa /həˈrapə/ an ancient city of the Indus valley civilization (c.2600–1700 BC), in N Pakistan. The site of the ruins was discovered in 1920.

Har·are /həˈrɑri/ the capital of Zimbabwe; pop. (1992) 1,864,400. It was known as Salisbury until 1982.

ha·rass /həˈras, ˈherəs/ transitive verb 1 trouble and annoy continually or repeatedly. 2 make repeated attacks on (an enemy or opponent). ¶ The pronunciation with the stress on the second syllable is the most common pronunciation, but is considered incorrect by some people. □ **ha·rass·er** noun **ha·rass·ing** noun & adjective **ha·rass·ing·ly** adverb **ha·rass·ment** noun [French harasser from Old French harer set a dog on]

Har·bin /ˈhɑrbɪn, -ˈbiːn/ the capital of Heilongjiang province in NE China, on the Songhua River; pop. (est. 2002) 4,438,200.

har·bin·ger /ˈhɑrbɪndʒər/ noun 1 a person or thing that announces or signals the approach of another. 2 a forerunner. [earlier = 'one who provides lodging': Middle English herbergere from Old French from herberge lodging, from Germanic]

har·bour (also **har·bor**) ● noun 1 a place of shelter for ships. 2 a shelter; a place of refuge or protection. ● verb 1 transitive give shelter to (esp. a criminal or wanted person). 2 transitive keep in one's mind, esp. resentfully (harbour a grudge). 3 intransitive come to anchor in a harbour. [Old English hereborg perhaps from Old Norse, related to HARBINGER]

har·bour·front N Amer. ● noun (usu. **harbour front**) land adjacent to a harbour. ● adjective situated or occurring beside a harbour.

Harbour Grace a town on the Avalon Peninsula in SE Newfoundland, situated on the west side of Conception Bay; pop. (2001) 3,380. □ **Harbour Gra·cian** noun [prob. after French Havre de Grâce, the original name for port Le Havre, France]

harbour·master noun an official in charge of a harbour.

harbour porpoise noun the common porpoise, Phocoena phocoena.

harbour seal noun N Amer. a small seal, Phoca vitulina, of coastal marine waters and estuaries.

hard ● adjective 1 (of a substance, material, etc.) firm and solid; unyielding to pressure; not easily cut. 2 a difficult to understand or explain (a hard problem). b difficult to accomplish (a hard decision). c (foll. by to + infin.) not easy to (hard to believe; hard to please). 3 difficult to bear; entailing suffering (a hard life; hard luck). 4 (of a person) unfeeling; severely critical. 5 (of a season or the weather) severe, harsh (a hard winter; a hard frost). 6 harsh or unpleasant to the senses (a hard voice; hard colours). 7 a strenuous, enthusiastic, intense (a hard worker; a hard fight). b severe, uncompromising (a hard blow; a hard bargain; hard words). c (of a turn) sharp, extreme (make a hard left at the corner). d Politics extreme; most radical (the hard right). 8 a (of liquor) strongly alcoholic; designating spirits rather than wine or beer. b N Amer. (of a beverage) containing alcohol; fermented (hard cider). 9 (of drugs) potent and addictive. 10 (of pornography) highly suggestive and explicit. 11 (of water) containing mineral salts that make lathering difficult. 12 slang (of the penis) erect. 13 (of a person) disreputable. 14 established; not disputable; reliable (hard facts; hard data). 15 (of a shape, boundary, etc.) clearly defined, unambiguous. 16 (of wheat) containing a hard kernel rich in gluten, used to make bread flour (compare SOFT adjective 20). 17 (of money) a in coins as opposed to paper currency. b in currency as opposed to cheques etc. 18 Phonetics (of a consonant) guttural (as c in cat, g in go). 19 (of radiation) highly penetrating. ● adverb 1 strenuously, intensely, copiously; with one's full effort (try hard; look hard at; is raining hard; hard-working). 2 with difficulty or effort (hard-earned). 3 so as to be hard or firm (frozen hard). 4 in close proximity (following hard on their heels). 5 with great force or genuine sorrow (she took his death very hard). ● noun Brit. 1 a sloping roadway across a foreshore. 2 slang = HARD LABOUR (got two years hard). □ **be hard on 1** be difficult for. 2 be severe in one's treatment or criticism of. 3 be unpleasant to (the senses). **be hard put** (also esp. Brit. **be hard put to it**) (usu. foll. by to + infin.) find it difficult. **give someone a hard time** make things difficult for someone, esp. by criticizing, berating, or teasing them. **go hard with** turn out to (a person's) disadvantage. **hard at it** informal busily working or occupied. **hard by** near; close by. **a hard** (or **tough**) **nut to crack** informal 1 a difficult problem. 2 a person or thing not easily understood or influenced. **hard on** (or **upon**) close to in pursuit etc. □ **hard·ish** adjective **hard·ness** noun [Old English hard, heard from Germanic]

hard and fast adjective (of a rule or a distinction made) definite, unalterable, strict.

hard-ass noun slang a tough, demanding, inflexible person. □ **hard-assed** adjective

hard·back = HARDCOVER.

hard·ball N Amer. ● noun 1 = BASEBALL. 2 slang uncompromising methods or dealings, esp. in politics (play hardball; political hardball). ● adjective tough; uncompromising (hardball tactics).

hard·bit·ten adjective informal tough and cynical.

hard·board noun stiff board made of compressed and treated wood pulp.

hard·body noun (pl. **-ies**) informal a sexually attractive person with a very thin muscular body.

hard-boiled adjective 1 (also **hard-cooked**) (of an egg) cooked in water in the shell until the white and the yolk are solid. 2 (of a person) tough, shrewd.

hard bread noun Cdn (Nfld) a thick, oval biscuit baked without salt and dried in a kiln.

hard candy noun N Amer. a candy made of corn syrup and boiled sugar, usu. coloured and flavoured.

hard·case noun a tough or intractable person.

hard copy noun printed material produced by computer, usu. on paper. □ **hard-copy** adjective

hard core ● *noun* **1** an irreducible nucleus. **2** *informal* **a** the most active or committed members of a society etc. **b** a conservative or reactionary minority. **3** (usu. **hard·core**) a type of punk rock music characterized by a fast tempo and more emphasis on rhythm than melody. **4** (usu. **hard·core**) *Brit.* solid material, esp. rubble, forming the foundation of a road etc. ● *adjective* (usu. **hard-core**) **1** forming a nucleus or centre. **2** active, committed, uncompromising (*the show's hard-core fans*). **3** (of pornography) explicit, obscene. **4** (of drug addiction) relating to 'hard' drugs, esp. heroin.

hard·cover *adjective & noun* esp. *N Amer.* ● *adjective* (of a book) bound in stiff covers. ● *noun* a hardcover book.

hard disk *noun* (also **hard drive**) *Computing* a large-capacity rigid usu. magnetic storage disk.

hard done by *adjective Cdn & Brit.* harshly or unfairly treated.

hard-earned *adjective* that has taken a great deal of effort to earn or acquire.

Har·de·ca·nute /ˌhardəkəˈnuːt/ (also **Har·di·ca·nute**) (*c.*1019–42), king of Denmark (1035–42) and of England (1040–42). The son of Canute, he claimed the English throne after the death of Harold I.

hard-edged *adjective* aggressive, uncompromising; not gentle or emotional etc.

hard·en *verb* **1** *transitive & intransitive* make or become hard or harder. **2** *intransitive & transitive* become, or make (one's attitude etc.), uncompromising or less sympathetic. **3** *intransitive* (of prices etc.) cease to fall or fluctuate. □ **harden off** inure (a plant) to cold by gradual increase of its exposure. □ **hard·en·abil·ity** *noun* **hard·en·able** *adjective* **hard·en·er** *noun*

hard·en·ing *noun* **1** the process or an instance of becoming hard. **2** (in full **hardening of the arteries**) *Med.* = ARTERIOSCLEROSIS.

hard feelings *plural noun* feelings of resentment.

hard·hack *noun* a shrub, *Spiraea tomentosa*, with woolly leaves and pink or white flowers clustered in a spike.

hard hat *noun* **1** protective headgear worn on construction sites, logging sites, etc. **2** *informal* a construction worker. **3** *informal* a conservative member of the working class.

hard-headed *adjective* **1** practical, realistic; not sentimental. **2** esp. *N Amer.* stubborn. □ **hard-headed·ly** *adverb* **hard-headed·ness** *noun*

hard-hearted *adjective* unfeeling, unsympathetic. □ **hard-hearted·ly** *adverb* **hard-hearted·ness** *noun*

hard hit *adjective* badly affected.

hard-hitting *adjective* forceful, tough; not sparing the feelings (*a hard-hitting report*).

Har·di·ca·nute *see* HARDECANUTE.

har·di·hood *noun* boldness, daring.

Har·ding, War·ren Gama·liel (1865–1923), US Republican politician, 29th president of the US (1921–3). His administration was beset by scandal and mismanagement, and he died in office.

hard knocks *noun* painful or difficult experiences.

hard labour *noun* heavy manual work as a punishment, esp. in a prison.

hard landing *noun* **1** a clumsy or rough landing of an aircraft. **2** an uncontrolled landing in which a spacecraft is destroyed.

hard line ● *noun* unyielding adherence to a firm policy. ● *attributive adjective* (**hard·line**) unyielding, strict, firm. □ **hard-liner** *noun*

hard luck *noun* worse fortune than one deserves.

hard·ly *adverb* **1** scarcely; only just (*we hardly knew them*). **2** only with difficulty (*could hardly speak*). **3** probably not or almost certainly not (*she will hardly come now*). ¶ *Hardly* should not be used with negative constructions. Expressions such as *I couldn't hardly see* are non-standard; the correct form is *I could hardly see*. □ **hardly any** almost no; almost none. **hardly ever** very rarely.

hard maple *noun* = SUGAR MAPLE.

hard news *noun* news that is of immediate interest to a very broad audience, usu. dealing with serious issues such as politics, wars, disasters, etc. (*compare* SOFT NEWS).

hard-nosed *adjective informal* realistic, uncompromising.

hard nut *noun slang* (also **tough nut**) a tough, aggressive person. □ **hard nut to crack** *see* NUT.

hard of hearing *adjective* somewhat deaf.

hard-on *noun coarse slang* an erection of the penis.

hard·pack *noun N Amer.* snow with a very dense, tightly packed surface.

hard palate *noun* the front part of the palate.

hard·pan *noun Geol.* a hardened layer of clay occurring in or below the soil profile.

hard-pressed *adjective* **1** closely pursued. **2** burdened or oppressed (with work, etc.). **3** in (esp. financial) difficulty (*hard-pressed taxpayers*). **4** (usu. **hard pressed**) (foll. by *to* + infin.) unable or barely able (*you'd be hard pressed to find a better player anywhere*).

hard return *noun* a carriage return inserted by the operator of a word processor, e.g. at the end of a paragraph (*compare* SOFT RETURN).

hard rock *noun* rock music characterized by a heavy beat, distorted amplified guitar playing, and loud vocals.

hard·rock mining *noun* mining performed underground in large formations of esp. igneous or metamorphic rock, e.g. the Canadian Shield. □ **hard·rock miner** *noun*

hard roe *noun see* ROE[1] 1.

hard sauce *noun* a sauce of butter and sugar, often with brandy etc. added.

hard·scrab·ble *adjective N Amer.* providing or yielding a meagre output and requiring much effort (*earned a hardscrabble living*).

hard sell *noun* aggressive salesmanship or advertising.

hard-shell *adjective* (also **hard-shelled**) **1** having a hard shell. **2** esp. *N Amer.* rigid, orthodox, uncompromising.

hard·ship *noun* **1** severe suffering or privation. **2** the circumstance causing this.

hard stuff *noun slang* hard drugs or strong liquor.

hard·tack *noun* = SHIP'S BISCUIT. [origin obscure]

hard·top *noun* **1** *N Amer.* **a** a road paved with a hard surface, esp. tar and gravel. **b** the material used for such a road. **2** a car with a rigid (sometimes detachable) roof.

hard up *adjective* **1** short of money. **2** (foll. by *for*) at a loss for; lacking.

Har·dwar /harˈdwar/ a city in Uttar Pradesh, N India, on the Ganges River; pop. (1991) 175,000. It is a place of Hindu pilgrimage.

hard·ware *noun* **1** tools, building materials, and household articles. **2** heavy machinery or armaments. **3** the mechanical and electronic components of a computer etc. (*compare* SOFTWARE 1).

hardware cloth *noun N Amer.* heavy-duty galvanized wire screening.

hard-wearing *adjective* able to stand much wear.

hard-wired *adjective* **1** involving or achieved by permanently connected circuits designed to perform a specific function. **2** furnished or equipped with a natural ability to do something, as if programmed. **3** (of an ability) innate and difficult to modify (*fear is hard-wired into our brains*).

hard·wood ● *noun* **1** the wood from a deciduous broadleaf tree, as distinguished from that of conifers. **2** a tree producing such wood. ● *adjective* **1** made of hardwood (*hardwood floor*). **2** containing hardwoods (*hardwood forest*).

hard-working *adjective* diligent.

Hardy ▸ **1 Oli·ver**, *see* LAUREL AND HARDY. **2 Thom·as** (1840–1928), English novelist and poet. In novels such as *The Mayor of Casterbridge* (1886), *Tess of the D'Urbervilles* (1891), and *Jude the Obscure* (1896), and eight volumes of poems, he depicts the struggle of human beings against the indifferent force that inflicts the sufferings and ironies of life.

hardy *adjective* (**har·di·er, har·di·est**) **1** robust; capable of enduring difficult conditions. **2** (of a plant) able to withstand winter in the open air. □ **har·di·ly** *adverb* **har·di·ness** *noun* [Old French *hardi* past participle of *hardir* become bold, from Germanic, related to HARD]

hardy annual *noun* an annual plant that may be sown in the open.

hardy har har *var. of* HAR HAR.

Hare /her/ *noun* **1** a member of a North Slavey group living along the north Mackenzie River. **2** the Athapaskan language of this people. [name given by Europeans to reflect the dependence of the people on the snowshoe hare for food and clothing]

hare ● *noun* any of various mammals of the family Leporidae, esp. of the genus *Lepus*, like a large rabbit, with tawny fur, long ears, short tail, and hind legs longer than forelegs, inhabiting fields, hills, etc. ● *intransitive verb* run with great speed. □ **hare off** depart, esp. rapidly or impulsively. **run with the hare and hunt with the hounds** try to remain on good terms with both sides. [Old English *hara* from Germanic]

hare and hounds *noun* a paper chase.

hare·bell *noun* a plant, *Campanula rotundifolia*, with slender stems and pale-blue bell-shaped flowers. Also called BLUEBELL.

hare-brained *adjective* (also **hair-brained**) rash, wild.

Ha·redi /haˈredi/ *noun* (*pl.* **Ha·red·im**) a member of any of various Orthodox Jewish sects characterized by strict adherence to the traditional form of Jewish law and rejection of modern secular culture, many of whom do not recognize the modern state of Israel as a spiritual authority. [Hebrew, lit. 'one who trembles (in awe at the word of God)']

Hare·foot *see* HAROLD I.

Hare Krish·na /ˌhɑri ˈkrɪʃnə, ˌheri/ *noun* **1** a sect devoted to the worship of the Hindu deity Krishna (an incarnation of Vishnu). **2** (*pl.* **Hare Krish·nas**) a member of this sect. [the title of a mantra based on the name *Krishna*, from Sanskrit *O Hari!* an epithet of Krishna]

hare·lip *noun* often *offensive* = CLEFT LIP. □ **hare·lipped** *adjective*

har·em /ˈherəm/ *noun* **1** (*hist.* or in conservative Muslim communities) **a** the women of a Muslim household, esp. the wives and concubines, living in a separate part of the house. **b** separate women's quarters designed for privacy and seclusion in a Muslim household. **2** a group of female animals sharing a mate. [Arabic *ḥarām*, *ḥarīm*, originally = prohibited, prohibited place, from *ḥarama* prohibit]

harem pants *plural noun* women's pants of a full, billowy cut gathered at the ankle, supposedly resembling the costume traditionally worn by an inhabitant of a harem.

hare's-foot *noun* (in full **hare's-foot clover**) a clover, *Trifolium arvense*, with soft hair around the flowers.

hare·wood *noun* stained sycamore wood used for making furniture. [German dial. *Ehre* from Latin *acer* maple + WOOD]

Har·geisa /hɑrˈgeisə/ (also **Har·geysa**) a city in NW Somalia; pop. (est. 2002) 231,000. It was the capital of British Somaliland between 1941 and 1960.

Har·greaves /ˈhɑrgriːvz/ **James** (1720–78), English inventor. A pioneer of the Lancashire cotton industry, he patented his most famous invention, the spinning jenny, in 1770.

har har *interjection* (also **hardy har har**) expressing (esp. mirthless or disparaging) laughter. [variant of HA HA]

hari·cot /ˈheriˌkoː/ *noun* **1** (in full **haricot bean**) a variety of French bean with small white seeds. **2** the dried seed of this used as a vegetable. [French]

Hari·jan /ˈhɑrɪdʒən/ *noun* a member of the class of untouchables in the Indian subcontinent. [Sanskrit, = a person dedicated to Vishnu, from *Hari* Vishnu, *jana* person]

har·is·sa /ˈherɪsə/ *noun* a spicy, North African chili paste used as an accompaniment to couscous dishes. [Arabic *harisa* a dish of meat and bulgur, from *harasa* crush, pound, tenderize by beating]

hark *intransitive verb* (usu. in *imperative*) listen attentively. □ **hark back** mention again or remember an earlier subject, event, etc. [Middle English *herkien* from Old English *heorcian* (unrecorded): compare HEARKEN: *hark back* was originally a hunting call to retrace steps]

hark·en *var. of* HEARKEN.

Har·lem a district of New York City, situated to the north of 96th Street in NE Manhattan. It has a mainly black population and in the 1920s and 30s was noted for its nightclubs and jazz bands.

har·le·quin /ˈhɑrləkwɪn/ ● *noun* **1** (**Harlequin**) **a** a mute character in pantomime, usu. masked and dressed in a diamond-patterned costume. **b** *hist.* a stock comic character in Italian *commedia dell'arte*. **2** (in full **harlequin duck**) a duck of northern coasts and rivers, *Histrionicus histrionicus*, the breeding males having deep grey-blue plumage with chestnut and white markings. ● *adjective* **1** gaily coloured. **2** (esp. of an animal) in varied colours; variegated. [French from earlier *Herlequin* leader of a legendary troupe of demon horsemen]

har·le·quin·ade /ˌhɑrləkwɪˈneid/ *noun* **1** the part of a pantomime featuring Harlequin. **2** buffoonery. [French *arlequinade* (as HARLEQUIN)]

Har·ley Street a street in London long associated with the premises of eminent physicians and surgeons. The name is also used allusively to refer to medical specialists.

har·lot *noun* a prostitute or promiscuous woman. □ **har·lotry** *noun* [Old French *harlot*, *herlot* lad, knave, vagabond]

Har·low /ˈhɑrloː/ **Jean** (born Harlean Carpenter) (1911–37), US actress. Her films, which made her a sex symbol of the 1930s, include *Hell's Angels* (1930) and *Red Dust* (1932).

harm ● *noun* **1** hurt, damage. **2** moral evil; wrong. ● *transitive verb* cause harm to. □ **do more harm than good** make matters worse (despite good intentions). **out of harm's way** in safety. [Old English *hearm*, *hearmian* from Germanic]

har·mat·tan /hɑrˈmatən/ *noun* a parching dusty land-wind of the West African coast occurring from December to February. [Fanti or Twi *haramata*]

harm·ful *adjective* causing or likely to cause harm. □ **harm·ful·ly** *adverb* **harm·ful·ness** *noun*

harm·less *adjective* **1** not able or likely to cause harm. **2** inoffensive. □ **harm·less·ly** *adverb* **harm·less·ness** *noun*

har·mo·lod·ics *noun* a form of free jazz in which musicians improvise simultaneously on a melodic line at various pitches. □ **har·mo·lod·ic** *adjective* [coined by the American saxophonist Ornette Coleman (b.1930) and said to be a blend of *harmony*, *movement*, and *melodic*]

har·mon·ic /hɑrˈmɒnɪk/ ● *adjective* **1** of or characterized by harmony; harmonious. **2** *Music* **a** of or relating to harmony. **b** (of a tone) produced by vibration of a string etc. in an exact fraction of its length. **3** *Math.* **a** of or relating to quantities whose reciprocals are in arithmetical progression (*harmonic progression*). **b** expressible in the form of sine and cosine functions. ● *noun* **1** *Music* an overtone accompanying at a fixed interval (and forming a note with) a fundamental. **2** *Physics* a component frequency of wave motion. □ **har·mon·ic·ally** *adverb*

har·mon·ica /hɑrˈmɒnɪkə/ *noun* a small rectangular wind instrument with a row of metal reeds along its length, held against the lips and moved from side to side to produce different notes by blowing or sucking. [Latin, fem. sing. or neuter pl. of *harmonicus*: see HARMONIC]

harmonic motion *noun* (in full **simple harmonic motion**) oscillatory motion under a retarding force proportional to the amount of displacement from an equilibrium position.

harmonic progression *noun* (also **harmonic series**) *Math.* a series of quantities whose reciprocals are in arithmetical progression.

har·moni·ous /hɑrˈmoːniəs/ *adjective* **1** sweet-sounding, tuneful. **2** forming a pleasing or consistent whole; concordant. **3** free from disagreement or dissent. □ **har·moni·ous·ly** *adverb* **har·moni·ous·ness** *noun*

har·mon·ist /ˈhɑrmənɪst/ *noun* a person skilled in musical harmony, a harmonizer.

har·mon·ium /hɑrˈmoːniəm/ *noun* a keyboard instrument in which the notes are produced by air driven through metal reeds by bellows operated by the feet. [French from Latin (as HARMONY)]

har·mon·ize /ˈhɑrməˌnaiz/ *verb* (also esp. *Brit.* **-ise**) **1** *transitive* add notes to (a melody) to produce harmony. **2** *transitive & intransitive* (often foll. by *with*) bring into or be in harmony. **3** *intransitive* sing or play in harmony. **4** *intransitive* make or form a pleasing or consistent whole. **5** *transitive* coordinate or make consistent. □ **har·mon·iz·a·tion** *noun* **har·mon·iz·er** *noun*

harmonized sales tax *noun* *Cdn* a value-added tax on goods and services combining the GST and the provincial sales tax in Nova Scotia, New Brunswick, and Newfoundland and Labrador. Abbr.: **HST**.

har·mony /ˈhɑrməni/ *noun* (*pl.* **-ies**) **1 a** a combination of simultaneously sounded musical notes to produce chords and chord progressions, esp. as having a pleasing effect. **b** the study of this. **c** the parts of a harmonized piece of music other than the melody. **2 a** an apt or aesthetic arrangement of parts. **b** the pleasing effect of this. **3** agreement, concord. **4** a collation of parallel narratives, esp. of the Gospels. □ **in harmony 1** (of singing etc.) producing chords; not discordant. **2** (often foll. by *with*) in agreement. **harmony of the spheres** *see* SPHERE. [Old French *harmonie* from Latin *harmonia* from Greek *harmonia* joining, concord, from *harmos* joint]

harm reduction *noun* a philosophy of dealing with drug addiction that focuses on reducing the risks associated with drug use, e.g. by providing needle exchanges and methadone programs to prevent HIV infection from shared needles among heroin addicts.

Harms·worth, Al·fred Charles Wil·liam, *see* NORTHCLIFFE.

har·ness ● *noun* **1** the equipment of straps and fittings by which a horse or other draft animal is fastened to a cart etc. and controlled. **2** a similar arrangement for fastening a thing to a person's body, for restraining a young child, etc. ● *transitive verb* **1 a** put a harness on (esp. a horse). **b** (foll. by *to*) attach by a harness. **2** make use of (natural resources) esp. to produce energy. ● *adjective* of or relating to harness racing (*harness horse*; *harness driver*). □ **in harness** in the routine of daily work. □ **har·ness·er** *noun* [Old French *harneis* military equipment, from Old Norse *hernest* (unrecorded) from *herr* army + *nest* provisions]

harness racing *noun* *N Amer.* a form of horse racing in which a horse

---

Consonants: b *but*   d *dog*   f *few*   g *get*   h *her*   j *yes*   k *cat*   l *leg*   m *man*   n *no*   p *pen*   r *red*   s *sit*

pulls a two-wheeled vehicle and its driver with a trotting or pacing gait. □ **harness race** *noun*

Har·non·court /ˈhɑrnənkuːr/ **Niko·laus** (b.1929), Austrian conductor, cellist and musicologist who began his career as a cellist with the Vienna Symphony Orchestra (1952–69). He is perhaps best known for reviving interest in the performance of early music on original period instruments when he co-founded the instrumental ensemble *Concentus Musicus Wien* in 1953, which is still among the best known early music ensembles in the world.

Har·noy /ˈhɑrnɔɪ/ **Ofra** (b.1965), Canadian cellist. She is known for her classical recordings of pieces by Offenbach and Vivaldi, and also for recording contemporary arrangements of popular songs.

Har·old I (known as 'Harold Harefoot') (d.1040), king of England 1035–40. An illegitimate son of Canute, he came to the throne when his half-brother Hardecanute (Canute's legitimate heir) was king of Denmark and thus absent at the time of his father's death.

Harold II (c.1019–66), reigned 1066, the last Anglo-Saxon king of England. He succeeded Edward the Confessor, having dominated the latter's court in the last years of his reign, but was faced with two invasions within months of his accession. He was killed and his army defeated at the Battle of Hastings; the victor, William, Duke of Normandy, took the throne as William I.

Haro Strait /ˈhɛroː/ a passage of the N Pacific, lying off the west coast of N America. It connects the Strait of Georgia and the Juan de Fuca Strait, thereby separating the San Juan Islands of Washington state from Vancouver Island, BC. [G. López de *Haro*, first mate on the British vessel *Princess Royal c.*1790]

Haroun-al-Raschid see HARŪN AR-RASHĪD.

harp ● *noun* **1** a usu. large upright roughly triangular musical instrument consisting of a frame housing a graduated series of vertical strings, played by plucking with the fingers. **2** (in full **mouth harp**) *informal* a mouth organ; harmonica. ● *intransitive verb* **1** (foll. by *on, on about*) talk repeatedly and tediously about. **2** play on a harp. □ **harp·er** *noun* **harp·ist** *noun* [Old English *hearpe* from Germanic]

Har·pers Ferry a small town in Jefferson County, West Virginia, at the junction of the Potomac and Shenandoah rivers. In Oct. 1859, John Brown and a group of abolitionists captured a Federal arsenal there in a raid aimed at establishing a state for freed slaves; by antagonizing slave-owners in the South, this helped precipitate the Civil War.

Har·poc·ra·tes /hɑrˈpɒkrəˌtiːz/ see HORUS.

har·poon ● *noun* a barbed spear-like missile with a rope attached, for hunting seals, whales, etc. ● *transitive verb* spear with or as with a harpoon. □ **har·poon·er** *noun* [French *harpon* from *harpe* clamp, from Latin *harpa* from Greek *harpē* sickle]

harp seal *noun* a seal, *Phoca groenlandica*, with a harp-shaped dark mark on its back, of the NW Atlantic and the Barents and White Seas.

harp·si·chord /ˈhɑrpsɪˌkɔrd/ *noun* a keyboard instrument with horizontal strings which are plucked mechanically. □ **harp·si·chord·ist** *noun* [obsolete French *harpechorde* from Late Latin *harpa* harp, + *chorda* string, the *-s-* being unexplained]

harpy *noun* (*pl.* **-pies**) **1** (in Greek and Roman mythology) a monster with a woman's head and body and bird's wings and claws. **2** a nagging unpleasant woman. **3** a greedy, cruel or grasping person. [French *harpie* or Latin *harpyia* from Greek *harpuiai* snatchers (compare *harpazō* snatch)]

harpy eagle *noun* a S American crested bird of prey, *Harpia harpyja*, one of the largest of eagles.

har·que·bus /ˈhɑrkwəbəs/ *noun* (also **arquebus** /ˈɑrk-/) *hist.* an early type of portable gun supported on a tripod or on a forked rest. [French (h)*arquebuse*, ultimately from Middle Low German *hakebusse* or Middle High German *hakenbühse*, from *haken* hook + *busse* gun]

Harri·cana, Ri·vière /ari'kanə/ a river in NW central Quebec, 480 km long, which rises west of Val-d'Or and flows northwestward to James Bay, crossing the Ontario border near its mouth. [Algonquin, = river of biscuits, with reference to the fact that early explorers carried hardtack]

har·ri·dan /ˈhɛrɪdən/ *noun* a bad-tempered woman. [17th-c. cant, perhaps from French *haridelle* old horse]

har·ri·er[1] *noun* a person who harries or lays waste.

har·ri·er[2] *noun* **1** a hound used for hunting hares. **2** a cross-country runner. [HARE + -IER, assimilated to HARRIER[1]]

har·ri·er[3] *noun* any bird of prey of the genus *Circus*, with long wings for swooping over the ground. [*harrower* from *harrow* harry, rob, assimilated to HARRIER[1]]

Har·ring·ton, Rex (b.1962), Canadian dancer. Known for his

performances of classical prince roles, and his skill as a partner, he became a principal dancer with the National Ballet of Canada in 1988 and retired from principal roles in 2004.

Har·ris[1] the southern part of the island of Lewis with Harris, in the Outer Hebrides.

Har·ris[2] ▶ **1 Frank** (1856–1931), Irish-born writer. Among his best-known works is the autobiographical *My Life and Loves* (1923-27). **2 Joel Chand·ler** (1848–1908), US writer. He wrote *Uncle Remus: His Songs and His Sayings* (1880). **3 Law·ren Stew·art** (1885–1970), Canadian painter, leader of the Group of Seven. A member of the successful Harris farm machinery family, he studied art in Berlin, and soon became friends with J.E.H. MacDonald and Tom Thomson. His landscapes reduce mountains, trees, clouds, and lakes to their essential elements, creating an austere yet forceful effect. **4 Mi·chael Deane** ('Mike') (b.1945), Canadian Conservative politician, premier of Ontario 1995–2002. He cut income tax and public spending, and also reformed the health, education, and welfare systems, and repealed various labour laws. **5 Roy Ells·worth** (1898–1979), US composer. He is noted for his orchestral and choral music which frequently incorporates American folk tunes.

Harris·burg the state capital of Pennsylvania, on the Susquehanna River; pop. (2000) 49,000. The nearby nuclear power station at Three Mile Island suffered a serious accident in 1979 (see THREE MILE ISLAND).

Har·ri·son ▶ **1 Ben·ja·min** (1833–1901), US Republican politician, 23rd president of the US 1889–93. He was the grandson of William Henry Harrison. **2 George** (1943–2001), British singer and songwriter; member of the Beatles 1962–70. **3 Sir Rex** (born Reginald Carey Harrison) (1908–90), English actor. His most famous role was as Professor Higgins in the stage and film musical *My Fair Lady* (1956, 1964). **4 Wil·liam Henry** (1773–1841), US Whig politician, 9th president of the US, 1841. He died of pneumonia one month after his inauguration. He was the grandfather of Benjamin Harrison.

Harrison Lake a lake in southwestern BC, situated just northeast of Chilliwack. [B. *Harrison*, director of the Hudson's Bay Co. *c.*1828]

Harris tweed *noun* *proprietary* a kind of tweed woven by hand in the Outer Hebrides, esp. on the island of Lewis with Harris.

har·row ● *noun* a heavy frame with iron teeth dragged over plowed land to break up clods, remove weeds, cover seed, etc. ● *transitive verb* **1** draw a harrow over (land). **2** (usu. as **har·row·ing** *adjective*) distress greatly. □ **har·row·ing·ly** *adverb* [Old Norse *hervi*]

Har·row·ing of Hell *noun* (in medieval Christian theology) the defeat of the powers of evil and the release of its victims, by the descent of Christ into hell after his death.

har·rumph (also **ha·rumph**) ● *verb* **1** *intransitive* clear the throat or make a similar sound, esp. ostentatiously. **2** *transitive* say gutturally, esp. expressing disapproval. ● *interjection* expressing disapproval. ● *noun* a guttural sound made by clearing the throat, expressing disapproval. [imitative]

harry *transitive verb* (**-ries**, **-ried**) **1** ravage or despoil. **2** harass; annoy with repeated requests, questions, etc. [Old English *herian*, *hergian* from Germanic, related to Old English *here* army]

harsh *adjective* **1** unpleasantly rough, sharp, or irritating, esp. to the senses. **2** severe, cruel. **3** physically disagreeable; bleak, stark (*harsh terrain*). □ **harsh·ly** *adverb* **harsh·ness** *noun* [Middle Low German *harsch* rough, lit. 'hairy', from *haer* HAIR]

Hart ▶ **1 Eve·lyn Anne** (b.1956), Canadian ballet dancer. After joining the Royal Winnipeg Ballet in 1976, she became a principal dancer in 1979. She is noted for her highly fluid and lyrical style. **2 John** (1879–1957), Irish-born Canadian businessman and politician. First elected to the BC legislature in 1916, he sat as a Liberal MLA for over twenty-five years, serving as finance minister and later as premier (1941–1947). Under his premiership BC saw rural electrification and highway expansion. **3 Lor·enz Mil·ton** (1895–1943), US lyricist. He collaborated with Richard Rodgers, and is known for songs such as 'With a Song in My Heart' (1929), 'Blue Moon' (1934), and 'The Lady is a Tramp' (1937). **4 Moss** (1904–61), US playwright and director. He collaborated with George Kaufmann on musicals such as *The Man Who Came to Dinner* (1939).

hart *noun* the male of the European red deer, usu. over five years old. [Old English *heor(o)t* from Germanic]

har·tal /ˈhɑrtəl/ *noun* the closing of shops and offices in the Indian subcontinent as a mark of protest or sorrow. [Hindustani *hartāl*, *haṭṭāl* from Sanskrit *haṭṭa* shop + *tālaka* lock]

Harte, (Fran·cis) Bret (1836–1902), US short-story writer and poet.

His short stories about life in a gold-mining settlement are collected in works such as *The Luck of Roaring Camp* (1870).

harte·beest /ˈhɑːtəˌbiːst/ *noun* any large African antelope of the genus *Alcelaphus*, with ringed horns bent back at the tips. [Afrikaans from Dutch *hert* HART + *beest* BEAST]

Hart·ford the state capital of Connecticut, situated in the centre of the state on the Connecticut River; pop. (2000) 121,600.

harts·horn /ˈhɑːtshɔːn/ *noun archaic* (in full **spirit of hartshorn**) an aqueous solution of ammonia used as smelling salts, formerly prepared from the horns of a deer.

hart's tongue *noun* a fern, *Phyllitis scolopendrium*, with narrow undivided fronds.

ha·rumph *var. of* HARRUMPH.

harum-scarum *informal* ● *adjective* wild and reckless. ● *noun* such a person. ● *adverb* in a wild and reckless manner. [rhyming formation on HARE, SCARE]

Harūn ar-Rashīd /hɑˌruːn ɑrɑˈʃiːd/ (also **Haroun-al-Raschid** /-alrɑˈʃiːd/) (763–809), fifth Abbasid caliph of Baghdad 786–809. He was the most powerful and vigorous of the Abbasid caliphs; he and his court were made famous by their portrayal in the *Arabian Nights*.

ha·rus·pex /həˈrʌspɛks/ *noun* (*pl.* **ha·rus·pi·ces** /-spɪˌsiːz/) a Roman religious official who interpreted omens from the inspection of animals' entrails. □ **ha·rus·picy** /-spɪsi/ *noun* [Latin]

Har·vard, John (1607-38), US cleric. On his death, he donated his library and half of his estate to the college in Cambridge, Massachusetts that bears his name.

Harvard classification *noun Astronomy* a system of classification of stars based on their spectral types, the chief classes (O, B, A, F, G, K, M) forming a series from very hot bluish-white stars to cool dull red stars. [named after the observatory at Harvard, Massachusetts, where it was devised]

har·vest ● *noun* **1 a** the process of gathering in crops etc. **b** the season when this takes place. **2** the season's yield or crop. **3** the product or result of any action. ● *transitive verb* **1** gather (crops, timber, etc.) as a harvest; reap. **2** kill or remove (wild animals) for food, sport, or population control (*harvest lobsters*). **3** remove (cells, tissues, organs) from a person or animal for experimental purposes or for transplants. **4** experience (consequences). □ **har·vest·able** *adjective* [Old English *hærfest* from Germanic]

har·vest·er *noun* **1** a person who harvests crops, fish, etc., esp. one hired temporarily to do so. **2** a machine for reaping and esp. also for binding up sheaves.

harvest excursion *noun Cdn hist.* a low-priced train trip for workers travelling to the West to harvest crops.

harvest festival *noun* a thanksgiving festival for the harvest.

harvest gold *noun N Amer.* a rich yellow-gold shade, offered as a colour choice for kitchen appliances.

harvest home *noun* **1** the fact, time, or occasion of bringing in the last of the harvest. **2** *Brit.* the festival to mark this.

har·vest·man *noun* (*pl.* **-men**) = DADDY-LONG-LEGS 1.

harvest mite *noun* = CHIGGER 1.

harvest moon *noun* the full moon nearest to the autumnal equinox.

harvest table *noun N Amer.* a large rectangular wooden dining table.

Har·vey ▸ 1 Doug·las ('**Doug**') (1924–89), Canadian hockey player. The greatest defenceman of his time, he played for the Montreal Canadiens from 1947 to 1961, winning the James Norris trophy as outstanding defenceman 7 times. **2 Wil·liam** (1578–1657), English physician, who discovered the circulation of the blood.

Har·vey Wall·bang·er *noun* a cocktail of vodka and orange juice often with Galliano. [20th c.: origin unknown]

Har·y·ana /ˌhʌriˈɒnə/ a state of N India; capital, Chandigarh. It was formed in 1966, mostly from Hindi-speaking parts of the former state of Punjab.

Harz Mountains a range of mountains in central Germany, the highest of which is the Brocken. The region is the source of many legends about witchcraft and sorcery.

has *3rd sing. present of* HAVE.

has-been *noun informal* a person or thing that has lost a former importance or usefulness.

Has·dru·bal /ˈhazdrʊbəl/ (d.207 BC), Carthaginian general, the son of Hamilcar and younger brother of Hannibal. In 218 he was left in command of Carthaginian forces in Spain after Hannibal's departure for Italy. Hasdrubal campaigned with only moderate success before setting out across the Alps to join Hannibal, but was intercepted and killed in battle.

hash¹ ● *noun* **1** a dish of cooked meat cut into small pieces and re-cooked, usu. with vegetables. **2 a** a mixture; a jumble. **b** a mess. **3** reused or recycled material. ● *transitive verb* (often foll. by *up*) **1** cut (meat etc.) into a small pieces; make into a hash. **2** (often foll. by *out, over*) *informal* talk over, discuss exhaustively. □ **make a hash of** *informal* make a mess of; bungle. **settle a person's hash** *informal* deal with and subdue a person. **sling hash** *see* SLING¹. [French *hacher* from *hache* HATCHET]

hash² *noun informal* hashish. [abbreviation]

hash brownies *noun informal* chocolate brownies containing hashish.

hash browns *plural noun* esp. *N Amer.* chopped boiled potatoes, sometimes mixed with chopped onions, fried until brown.

Hash·em·ite /ˈhaʃəˌmaɪt/ *of*, relating to, or denoting an Arab princely family claiming descent from Hashim, great-grandfather of Muhammad. (See also JORDAN¹).

ha·shish /haˈʃiːʃ, ˈha-/ *noun* a resinous product of the top leaves and tender parts of hemp, smoked or chewed for its narcotic effects. [Arabic *ḥašīš* dry herb; powdered hemp leaves]

hash mark *noun* **1** the symbol #. **2** *Football* a short cross stripe on each five-yard line, 24 yards in from and parallel to each sideline, enclosing a central zone within which all plays must start. **3** *Hockey* one of four short lines on the edges of each faceoff circle. **4** *N Amer. informal* a military service stripe.

Hasid /ˈhasɪd, haˈsiːd/ *noun* (*pl.* **Hasid·im**) (also **Chas·sid, Chasid, Has·sid**) a member of any of several mystical Jewish sects, esp. one founded in the 18th c. □ **Hasid·ic** /-ˈsɪdɪk/ *adjective* **Hasid·ism** /ˈhasɪˌdɪzəm, -ˈsɪdɪzəm/ *noun* [Hebrew *ḥasīd* pious]

Has·kal·ah /həˈskala, ˌhaskəˈlɒ/ *noun* a Jewish movement in central and E Europe in the 18th and 19th c. that advocated the adoption of secular European culture and customs in order to modernize Judaism. [Hebrew, 'enlightenment']

Has·mo·nean /ˌhazməˈniən/ *of*, relating to, or denoting the Jewish dynasty established by the Maccabees. [Greek *Asmōnaios* from Hebrew *ḥašmônây* Hasmon, name of reputed ancestor]

hasn't *contraction* has not.

hasp ● *noun* a hinged metal clasp that fits over a staple and can be secured by a padlock. ● *transitive verb* fasten with a hasp. [Old English *hæpse, hæsp*]

Has·san II /haˈsan/ (born Mawley Hassan Muhammad Ibn Yusuf) (b.1929), Moroccan king (1961–1999). Though criticized for human rights abuses against political prisoners in the early 1990s, he is credited for instituting many political reforms in Morocco, and playing an instrumental role in the Middle East peace process.

has·sium *noun* a very unstable chemical element made by high-energy atomic collisions. Symbol: **Hs**; at. no. 108. [modern Latin, from Latin *Hassias* 'Hesse' (the German state); it was discovered in Darmstadt in 1984]

has·sle *informal* ● *noun* **1** a prolonged trouble or inconvenience. **2** an argument or involved struggle. ● *verb* **1** *transitive* harass, annoy; cause trouble to. **2** *intransitive* argue, quarrel. [20th c.: originally dial.]

has·sock *noun* **1** a thick firm cushion used to rest the feet on or, esp. in church, to kneel on. **2** = OTTOMAN 1a. **3** a tuft of matted grass etc. [Old English *hassuc*]

hast *archaic 2nd sing. present of* HAVE.

hast·ate /ˈhasteɪt/ *adjective Bot.* triangular like the head of a spear. [Latin *hastatus* from *hasta* spear]

haste ● *noun* **1** quickness or speed of motion or action, esp. as prompted by urgency or pressure. **2** quickness of action without due consideration; rashness, precipitancy (*in my haste, I forgot to lock the door*). ● *intransitive verb archaic* = HASTEN. □ **in haste** quickly, hurriedly. **make haste** hurry; be quick. [Old French *haste, haster* from West Germanic]

hast·en /ˈheɪsən/ *verb* **1** *intransitive* (often foll. by *to* + infin.) make haste; hurry. **2** *transitive* cause to occur or be ready or be done sooner.

Hast·ings¹ one of several former communities (est. *c.*1860s), around which the city of Vancouver eventually grew. It now forms an urban area of Vancouver.

Hast·ings², War·ren (1732–1818), British colonial administrator. In 1774 he became India's first Governor General. Impeached for corruption in 1785 on his return to England, he was acquitted in 1795 after a seven-year trial before the House of Lords.

Hastings, Battle of a decisive battle which took place in 1066 just north of the town of Hastings, East Sussex, in which William the Conqueror defeated the Anglo-Saxon king Harold II and launched the

Vowels: a *cat* ɑ *arm* e *bed* ɜr *her* ɜː *deux* ə *ago* ɪ *sit* i *cosy* iː *feed* ɒ *hot* ɔ *pore* oː *no* ʌ *run* ʊ *put*

Norman Conquest of England. Harold died in the battle, leaving the way open for William to seize London and the vacant throne.

hasty *adjective* (**hasti·er**, **hasti·est**) **1** hurried; acting quickly or hurriedly. **2** said, made, or done too quickly or too soon; rash, unconsidered. **3** quick-tempered. □ **hasti·ly** *adverb* **hasti·ness** *noun*

hasty note *noun Cdn* (also **hasti-note**) (usu. in *pl.*) a small folded card or sheet of paper with a decoration on the front and the rest left blank for writing short letters etc.

hat ● *noun* **1** a covering for the head, often with a brim and worn out of doors. **2** *informal* a person's occupation or capacity, esp. one of several (*wearing his managerial hat*). **●** *transitive verb* (**hat·ted**, **hat·ting**) cover or provide with a hat. □ **hang one's hat** *see* HANG. **hat in hand** in a supplicatory manner; obsequiously. **hats off** (as *interjection*; foll. by *to*) expressing admiration or appreciation. **keep it under one's hat** *informal* keep it secret. **out of a hat** by random selection. **pass the hat** collect contributions of money. **take off one's hat to** *informal* acknowledge admiration for. **throw (or toss) one's hat in the ring** take up a challenge. □ **hat·ful** *noun* (*pl.* **-fuls**). **hat·less** *adjective* **hat·ted** *adjective* (also in *combination*). [Old English *hætt* from Germanic]

hat·band *noun* a band of ribbon etc. around a hat above the brim.

hat box *noun* a box to hold a hat, esp. for travelling.

hatch¹ *noun* **1 a** an opening in a door, floor, or ceiling of a building. **b** an opening in a wall between two rooms, esp. a kitchen and a dining area, through which dishes etc. are passed. **2** an opening or door in an aircraft, spacecraft, etc. **3** *Naut.* **a** an opening in a ship's deck for lowering cargo into the hold. **b** a trap door or cover for this (often in *pl.*: *batten the hatches*). **4** the rear hinged door of a hatchback. □ **down the hatch** *slang* (as a drinking toast) drink up, cheers! [Old English *hæcc* from Germanic]

hatch² **●** *verb* **1** *intransitive* **a** (of a young bird or fish etc.) emerge from the egg. **b** (of an egg) produce a young animal. **2** *transitive* incubate (an egg). **3** *transitive* devise (a plot etc.). **●** *noun* **1** the act or an instance of hatching. **2** a brood hatched. □ **hatch·abil·ity** *noun* **hatch·er** *noun* [Middle English *hacche*, of unknown origin]

hatch³ *transitive verb* mark (a surface, e.g. a map or drawing) with close parallel lines. [French *hacher* from *hache* HATCHET]

hatch·back *noun* **1** a car with a sloping back hinged at the top to form a door. **2** the rear hinged door of such a car.

hatch·ery *noun* (*pl.* **-eries**) a place for hatching eggs, esp. of fish or poultry.

hatch·et *noun* **1** a light short-handled axe. **2** *N Amer.* a tomahawk. [Old French *hachette* diminutive of *hache* axe, from medieval Latin *hapia* from Germanic]

hatchet-faced *adjective informal* sharp-featured or grim-looking.

hatchet job *noun informal* a fierce verbal attack on a person, esp. in print.

hatchet·man *noun* (*pl.* **-men**) *informal* **1** a hired killer. **2** a harsh or vindictive critic. **3** a person employed to carry out unpleasant tasks, e.g. reducing staff and expenditure in a firm, etc.

hatch·ing *noun Art & Archit.* close parallel lines forming shading esp. on a map or an architectural drawing.

hatch·ling *noun* a bird or fish that has just hatched.

hatch·ment *noun* a large usu. diamond-shaped tablet with a deceased person's armorial bearings, affixed to that person's house, tomb, etc. [prob. from French *hachement* from Old French *acesmement* adornment]

hatch·way *noun* = HATCH¹ 3a.

hate ● *transitive verb* **1** feel hatred or intense dislike towards. **2** *informal* **a** dislike. **b** (foll. by verbal noun or *to* + infin.) be reluctant (to do something) (*I hate to disturb you*). **●** *noun* **1** hatred; intense dislike. **2** *informal* a hated person or thing. **3** (*attributive*) motivated by sexual, racial, or other forms of intolerance (*hate crime; hate literature*). □ **hate someone's guts** *informal* dislike (someone) intensely. □ **hate·able** *adjective* **hater** *noun* [Old English *hatian* from Germanic]

hate crime *noun* a crime, usu. violent, motivated by hatred or intolerance of another social group, esp. on the basis of race or sexual orientation.

hate·ful *adjective* **1** arousing hatred; odious. **2** full of hatred (*a hateful diatribe*). □ **hate·ful·ly** *adverb* **hate·ful·ness** *noun*

hate mail *noun* letters sent (usu. anonymously) in which the sender expresses hostility towards the recipient.

hate-monger *noun* a person who promotes hatred and intolerance against an identifiable group. □ **hate-monger·ing** *noun*

hate speech *noun* speech expressing hatred or intolerance of other social groups, esp. on the basis of race or sexual orientation.

Hat·field, **Rich·ard Ben·nett** (1931–1991), Canadian politician, premier of New Brunswick (1970–1987). First elected as an MLA in 1961, he became leader of the New Brunswick Conservatives in 1969. As premier, he supported national unity, linguistic equality, and the patriation of the constitution. His government was re-elected repeatedly up until the election of 1987, when the Conservatives lost in every riding; he resigned as leader immediately.

hath *archaic* 3rd *sing. present of* HAVE.

Hatha·way, **Anne** (*c.*1557–1623), the wife of Shakespeare, whom she married in 1582.

hatha yoga /ˈhaθə/ *noun* a system of physical exercises and breathing control used in yoga. [Sanskrit *haṭha* force: see YOGA]

Hath·or /ˈhaθɔr/ *Egyptian Myth* a sky goddess, the patron of love and joy, represented variously as a cow, with a cow's head or ears, or with a solar disc between a cow's horns. Her name means 'House of Horus'.

hat·pin *noun* a long pin, often decorative, for securing a hat to the head.

hatred *noun* intense dislike or ill will. [Middle English from HATE + *-red* from Old English *rǣden* condition]

Hat·shep·sut /hatˈʃepsuːt/ (d.1482 BC), Egyptian queen of the 18th dynasty, reigned *c.*1503–1482 BC. She was the wife of her half-brother Tuthmosis II; on his death she became regent for her nephew Tuthmosis III, proclaiming herself co-ruler and dominating the partnership until her death. Her reign was predominantly peaceful and she promoted Egypt's cultural life.

hat stand *noun* a stand with hooks on which to hang hats.

Hat·ter *noun* a native or resident of Medicine Hat.

hat·ter *noun* a maker or seller of hats. □ **mad as a hatter** wildly eccentric.

hat trick *noun* **1** *Hockey etc.* the scoring of three goals, points etc. by one person during a game. **2** *Cricket* the taking of three wickets by the same bowler with three successive balls. **3** three successes.

Hat·tu·sa /ˈhatuːˌsa/ the capital of the ancient Hittite Empire, situated in central Turkey about 35 km (22 miles) east of Ankara. It is the site of the modern Turkish village of Bogazköy.

hau·berk /ˈhɒbɜrk/ *noun hist.* a coat of mail. [Old French *hau(s)berc* from Frankish, = neck protection, from *hals* neck + *berg-* from *beorg* protection]

Hau·deno·saunee /hɒdənəˈsɒni/ *noun & adjective* = IROQUOIS. [Mohawk, lit. 'people of the longhouse']

haughty *adjective* (**haught·i·er**, **haught·i·est**) arrogantly self-admiring and disdainful. □ **haught·i·ly** *adverb* **haught·i·ness** *noun* [extension of *haught* (adj.), earlier *haut* from Old French *haut* from Latin *altus* high]

haul ● *verb* **1** *transitive* pull or drag forcibly. **2** *transitive* transport by truck, cart, etc. **3** *transitive* **a** draw (a net) through water to catch fish. **b** lift (fish) in a net or on a line to the surface. **4** *intransitive* turn a ship's course. **5** *transitive* (usu. foll. by *into*, *up*) *informal* bring for reprimand or trial. **●** *noun* **1** the act or an instance of hauling. **2 a** an amount gained or acquired. **b** the quantity of fish caught in one draft of the net. **3** a distance to be traversed (*a short haul*). □ **haul ass** *N Amer.* move fast; hurry, leave. **haul off** *N Amer. informal* **1** withdraw a little in preparation (*he hauled off and hit me*). **2** leave, depart. **haul out 1** take or drag out. **2** (of seals and walruses) come out of the water to rest on the rocky slopes of the shore. **haul over the coals** *see* COAL. [var. of HALE²]

haul·age *noun* **1** the commercial transport of goods. **2** a charge for this.

haul·back *noun Forestry* a lighter line for drawing a cable back to its original position after it has been used to move a log away.

haul·er *noun* (also *Brit.* **haul·ier**) **1** a person or thing that hauls. **2** a person or firm engaged in the transport of goods.

haul·ing *noun Forestry* the process of transporting logs from the cutting area to the mill or shipping point.

haulm /hɒm/ *noun* (also **halm**) **1** a stalk or stem. **2** the stalks or stems collectively of peas, beans, potatoes, etc., without the pods etc. [Old English *h(e)alm* from Germanic]

haul·out *noun* **1** the action of hauling a boat out of water. **2** a place along the shore where marine mammals haul out.

haul road *noun* a dirt or gravel road through the bush etc. used for transporting equipment, supplies, ore, logs, etc. to and from a mining or lumber camp.

haunch *noun* **1** (often in *pl.*) the fleshy part of the buttock with the thigh. **2** the leg and loin of a deer etc. as food. **3** the side of an arch between the crown and the pier. [Old French *hanche*, of Germanic origin: compare Low German *hanke* hind leg of a horse]

haunt ● *transitive verb* **1** (of a ghost) visit (a place) regularly, usu. reputedly giving signs of its presence. **2** (of a person or animal) frequent or be persistently in (a place). **3** (of a memory etc.) return repeatedly to the mind of, esp. in a distressing manner. **4** (of an action, a phenomenon, etc.) cause difficulty or problems to (a person, organization, etc.), usu. long after the fact (*that letter will come back to haunt you*). ● *noun* **1** (often in *pl.*) a place frequented by a person. **2** a place frequented by animals, esp. for food and drink. □ **haunt·er** *noun* [Old French *hanter* from Germanic]

haunt·ed *adjective* **1** frequented by a ghost (*a haunted house*). **2** troubled, world-weary (*a haunted face*).

haunt·ing ● *adjective* (of a memory, melody, etc.) poignant, wistful, evocative. ● *noun* a visitation by a ghost. □ **haunt·ing·ly** *adverb*

Haupt·mann /ˈhauptman/ **Ger·hart** (1862–1946), German dramatist. He was an early pioneer of naturalism in the German theatre; his plays, such as *Before Sunrise* (1889) and *The Weavers* (1892), treat social and moral issues with directness and realism. He was awarded the Nobel Prize for literature in 1912.

Hausa /ˈhausə, -zə/ ● *noun* (*pl.* same or **Hau·sas**) **1 a** a people of West Africa and the Sudan. **b** a member of this people. **2** the Hamitic language of this people, widely used in West Africa. ● *adjective* of or relating to this people or language. [Hausa]

haus·frau /ˈhʌusfrau/ *noun* a housewife. [German from *Haus* house + *Frau* woman]

Hauss·mann /ˈhausman/ **Baron Georges-Eugène** (1809-91), French civil servant, noted for his rebuilding of Paris during the reign of Napoleon III.

haut·boy /ˈhoːbɔɪ/ *archaic var. of* OBOE.

haute /oːt, hoːt/ *adjective* upper-class, elegant, prestigious (*a haute university*). [French, lit. = high]

haute couture /ˌhoːt kuːˈtʃur, -tur, -tjur, oːt/ *noun* high fashion; the leading fashion houses or their products. [French, lit. = high dressmaking]

haute cuisine /ˌoːt kwiˈziːn/ *noun* cooking of a high standard, esp. of the French traditional school. [French, lit. = high cookery]

Haute-Norman·die /oːt ˌnɔrmaˈdiː/ a region of N France, on the coast of the English Channel, including the city of Rouen. It was formed from part of the former province of Normandy.

hau·teur /oʊˈtɜr/ *noun* haughtiness of manner. [French from *haut* high]

haut monde /oː ˈmɒnd/ *noun* fashionable society. [French, lit. = high world]

haut relief /oʊriˈliːf/ *noun Sculpture* **1** = HIGH RELIEF (see RELIEF 6a). **2** a sculpture, carving, etc. in high relief. [French, = high relief; compare BAS-RELIEF]

Ha·vana[1] /həˈvanə/ the capital of Cuba, situated on the north coast; pop. (est. 2002) 2,328,000.

Ha·vana[2] /həˈvanə/ *noun* (in full **Havana cigar**) a cigar made at Havana or elsewhere in Cuba.

ha·varti /həˈvarti/ *noun* a mild, semi-soft Danish cheese with small irregular holes. [name of the farm of Hanne Nielsen, 19th c. Danish cheese maker]

have ● *verb* (*3rd sing. present* **has**; *past and past participle* **had**) ● *transitive verb* **1** hold in possession as one's property or at one's disposal; be provided with (*has a car; had no time to read; has nothing to wear*). **2** hold in a certain relationship (*has a sister; had no equals*). **3** contain as a part or quality (*house has two floors; has green eyes*). **4 a** undergo, experience, enjoy, suffer (*had a good time; had a shock; has a headache*). **b** be subjected to a specified state (*had my car stolen; the book has a page missing*). **c** cause, instruct, or invite (a person or thing) to be in a particular state or take a particular action (*had him dismissed; had us worried; had my hair cut; had a copy made; had them over for dinner*). **5 a** engage in (an activity) (*had an argument; had sex*). **b** hold (a meeting, party, etc.). **6** eat or drink (*had a beer*). **7** (usu. in *neg.*) accept or tolerate; permit to (*I won't have it; will not have you say such things*). **8 a** let (a feeling etc.) be present (*have no doubt; has a lot of sympathy for me; have nothing against them*). **b** show or feel (mercy, pity, etc.) towards another person (*have pity on him; have mercy!*). **c** (foll. by *to* + infin.) show by action that one is influenced by (a feeling, quality, etc.) (*have the goodness to leave now*). **9 a** give birth to (offspring). **b** conceive mentally (an idea etc.). **10** receive, obtain (*had a letter from him; not a ticket to be had*). **11** be burdened with or committed to (*has a job to do; have my garden to attend to*). **12 a** have obtained (a qualification) (*has a Ph.D.*). **b** know (a language) (*has no Latin*). **13** *slang* **a** get the better of (*I had him there*). **b** (usu. in *passive*) cheat, deceive (*you*

were had). **14** have sexual intercourse with. ● *auxiliary verb* (with *past participle* or *elliptical*, to form the perfect, pluperfect, and future perfect tenses, and the conditional mood) (*have worked; had seen; will have been; had I known, I would have gone; have you met her? yes, I have*). ● *noun* (usu. in *pl.*) *informal* a person who has wealth or resources. □ **had best** *see* BEST. **had better** would find it prudent to. **had rather** *see* RATHER. **have a care** *see* CARE. **have done, have done with** *see* DONE. **have an eye for, have eyes for, have an eye to** *see* EYE. **have a good mind to** *see* MIND. **have got to** *informal* = HAVE TO. **have had it** *informal* **1** have missed one's chance. **2** be no longer useful or appropriate (*these old boots have had it*). **3** have been killed, defeated, etc. **4** be tired or fed up with (*I've had it with your excuses!*). **have it 1** (foll. by *that* + clause) express the view that. **2** win a decision in a vote etc. **3** *informal* have found the answer etc. **have it away** (or **off**) *Brit. coarse slang* have sexual intercourse. **have it both ways** *see* BOTH. **have it coming** can expect unpleasant consequences to follow. **have it in for** *informal* be hostile or ill-disposed towards. **have it out** (often foll. by *with*) *informal* attempt to settle a dispute by discussion or argument. **have it one's own way** *see* WAY. **have nothing to do with** *see* DO[1]. **have on 1** be wearing (clothes). **2** be committed to (an engagement). **3** *informal* tease, play a trick on. **have out** get (a tooth etc.) extracted (*had her tonsils out*). **have something** (or **nothing**) **on a person 1** know something (or nothing) discreditable or incriminating about a person. **2** have an (or no) advantage or superiority over a person. **have to** be obliged to, must. **have up** *informal* bring (a person) before a court of justice, interviewer, etc. [Old English *habban* from Germanic, prob. related to HEAVE]

Havel /ˈhɒvel/ **Vác·lav** (b.1936), Czech dramatist and politician, president of Czechoslovakia 1989–92 and of the Czech Republic 1993–2003. His early plays, such as *The Garden Party* (1963), were critical of totalitarianism; in the 1970s he became a leading spokesman for human rights groups and was twice imprisoned as a dissident.

ha·ven *noun* **1** a harbour or port. **2** a place of refuge. [Old English *hæfen* from Old Norse *höfn*]

have-not *noun* (usu. in *pl.*) *informal* a person etc. lacking wealth or resources.

have-not province *noun Cdn* a province whose per capita tax revenue falls below a certain average level and which is therefore entitled to receive equalization payments from the federal government.

haven't *contraction* have not.

have province *noun Cdn* a province whose per capita tax revenue exceeds a certain average level and which does not therefore receive equalization payments from the federal government.

ha·ver /ˈheivər/ ● *intransitive verb Brit.* **1** talk foolishly; babble. **2** vacillate, hesitate. ● *noun* (usu. in *pl.*) *Scot.* foolish talk; nonsense. [18th c.: origin unknown]

haver·sack /ˈhavər.sak/ *noun* a stout bag for provisions etc., carried on the back or over the shoulder. [French *havresac* from German *Habersack* from *Haber* oats + *Sack* SACK[1]]

haver·sine /ˈhavər.sain/ *noun Math.* half of a versed sine. [contraction]

havoc *noun* widespread destruction; great confusion or disorder. □ **play havoc with** *informal* cause great confusion or difficulty to. **wreak havoc** devastate, cause damage to. [Anglo-French *havok* from Old French *havo(t)*, of unknown origin]

haw[1] *noun* the hawthorn or its fruit. [Old English *haga* from Germanic, related to HEDGE]

haw[2] *noun* the nictitating membrane of a horse, dog, etc., esp. when inflamed. [16th c.: origin unknown]

haw[3] ● *interjection* expressing hesitation. ● *intransitive verb* (in **hum and haw** or **hem and haw**; *see* HUM[1]) [imitative: compare HA[1]]

haw[4] *N Amer.* ● *interjection* a command to a horse, dog team, etc. to turn to the left. ● *transitive & intransitive verb* turn to the left or command (a horse, dog team, etc.) to turn to the left.

Ha·waii /həˈwaiiː/ **1** a state of the US comprising a group of over 20 islands in the N Pacific; capital, Honolulu (on Oahu); pop. (2000) 1,211,537. Originally called the Sandwich Islands, the group came to be known as Hawaii, after the largest of the islands, in the 19th c. **2** the largest island in the state of Hawaii.

Ha·wai·ian /həˈwaiən/ ● *noun* **1 a** a native of Hawaii. **b** a person of Hawaiian descent. **2** the Malayo-Polynesian language of Hawaii. ● *adjective* **1** of or relating to Hawaii or its people or language. **2** *N Amer.* (of pizza) garnished with ham and pineapple.

Hawaiian guitar *noun* a steel-stringed musical instrument, usu. held horizontally, in which a characteristic glissando effect is produced by sliding a metal bar along the strings as they are plucked.

Hawaiian shirt *noun* a brightly coloured and gaily patterned shirt.

haw·eater *noun Cdn* a long-time resident of Manitoulin Island.

haw haw *interjection* used to represent the sound of a loud or boisterous laugh. [imitative]

hawk[1] ● *noun* **1** any of various diurnal birds of prey of the family Accipitridae, having a characteristic curved beak, rounded short wings, and a long tail. **2** *Politics* a person who advocates an aggressive or warlike policy, esp. in foreign affairs. **3** a rapacious person. ● *verb* **1** *intransitive* hunt game with a hawk. **2** *intransitive & transitive* attack, as a hawk does. **3** *intransitive* (of a bird) hunt on the wing for food. □ **watch like a hawk** watch intently and unceasingly. □ **hawk·ish** *adjective* **hawk·ish·ly** *adverb* **hawk·ish·ness** *noun* **hawk-like** *adjective* [Old English *h(e)afoc, hæbuc* from Germanic]

hawk[2] *transitive verb* **1** carry about or offer around (goods) for sale. **2** (often foll. by *about*) relate (news, gossip, etc.) freely. [back-formation from HAWKER[1]]

hawk[3] *verb* **1** *intransitive* clear the throat noisily. **2** *transitive* (foll. by *up*) bring (phlegm etc.) up from the throat. [prob. imitative]

hawk[4] *noun* a plasterer's square board with a handle underneath for carrying plaster or mortar. [17th c.: origin unknown]

Hawke, Rob·ert James Lee (b.1929), Australian Labor politician, who as prime minister 1983–91 pursued an economic program based on free-market policies and tax reform.

Hawke Bay a bay on the east coast of North Island, New Zealand. The port of Napier lies on its southern shore. [E. *Hawke*, British admiral d.1781]

hawk·er[1] *noun* a person who travels about selling goods. [16th c.: prob. from Low German or Dutch; compare HUCKSTER]

hawk·er[2] *noun* a falconer.

Hawke's Bay an administrative region on the eastern coast of North Island, New Zealand.

Hawkes·bury a town in E Ontario, situated on the Ottawa River, about 85 km east of Ottawa; pop. (2001) 10,314. □ **Hawkes·bur·ian** *noun* [either after C. Jenkinson, Baron *Hawkesbury* and Lord Liverpool d.1808, or his son, R. Banks Jenkinson, prime minister of Great Britain d.1828]

hawk-eyed *adjective* keen-sighted.

Haw·king, Ste·phen Wil·liam (b.1942), English theoretical physicist. Despite being afflicted with a degenerative nervous disease, he has made major contributions to the theory of space-time, quantum mechanics, and black holes, and his book *A Brief History of Time* (1988) has proved a popular bestseller.

Haw·kins ▶ 1 Cole·man Ran·dolph (1904–69), US jazz saxophonist. During the 1920s and 1930s he was influential in making the tenor saxophone popular as a jazz instrument. **2 Sir John** (also **Haw·kyns**) (1532–95), English sailor. As treasurer of the Elizabethan navy in 1573, he played an important part in building up the fleet which defeated the Spanish Armada in 1588, during which time he was third in command of the English forces.

hawk moth *noun* any darting and hovering moth of the family Sphingidae, having narrow forewings and a stout body.

hawk-nosed *adjective* having an aquiline nose.

hawk owl *noun* a somewhat long-tailed, partly diurnal owl, *Surnia ulula*, of northern coniferous woodlands.

hawks·bill *noun* (in full **hawksbill turtle**) a small turtle of tropical seas with hooked jaws, *Eretmochelys imbricata*, yielding tortoiseshell.

Hawks·moor, Nicho·las (1661–1736), English architect. From 1690 onward he worked with Vanbrugh at Castle Howard in Yorkshire and Blenheim Palace in Oxfordshire. In 1711 he was commissioned to design six London churches.

hawk·weed *noun* any composite plant of the genus *Hieracium*, with yellow or orange flowers. *Also called* PAINTBRUSH.

Haw·kyns see Sir J. HAWKINS.

Haw·ley, San·ford Des·mond ('Sandy') (b.1949), Canadian jockey, the first jockey to win 500 races in a single year (1973).

Ha·worth /ˈhauwɜrθ/ **Sir Wal·ter Nor·man** (1883–1950), English organic chemist. He made major contributions to the understanding of the structure and classification of sugars and polysaccharides, determined the structure of vitamin C, and later synthesized it, the first vitamin to be made artificially. He shared the Nobel Prize for chemistry in 1937.

hawse /hɒz/ *noun* **1** the part of a ship's bows in which hawse holes or hawse pipes are placed. **2** the space between the head of an anchored vessel and the anchors. **3** the arrangement of cables when a ship is moored with port and starboard forward anchors. [prob. from Old Norse *háls* neck, ship's bow]

hawse hole *noun* a hole in the side of a ship through which a cable or anchor rope passes.

hawse pipe *noun* a metal pipe lining a hawse hole.

haws·er /ˈhɒzər/ *noun Naut.* a thick rope or cable for mooring or towing a ship. [Old French *haucier* hoist, ultimately from Latin *altus* high]

haw·thorn *noun* any thorny shrub or tree of the genus *Crataegus*, with white, red, or pink blossoms and small red or black apple-like fruit.

Haw·thorne, Na·than·iel (1804–64), US novelist and short-story writer. Much of his fiction deals with the effects of Puritanism in New England; his works include *The Scarlet Letter* (1850) and *The House of the Seven Gables* (1851).

hay ● *noun* grass, clover, alfalfa, etc., cut and dried for animal fodder. ● *verb* **1** *intransitive* make hay. **2** *transitive* make (grass etc.) into hay. □ **hit the hay** *informal* go to bed. **make hay of** throw into confusion. **make hay (while the sun shines)** seize opportunities for profit or enjoyment. **make hay out of** turn to one's advantage. **a roll in the hay** see ROLL *noun* 6c. □ **hay·ing** *noun* [Old English *hēg, hieg, hīg* from Germanic]

hay·cock *noun* a conical heap of hay in a field. [HAY + COCK[2]]

Haydn /ˈhaidn/ **Franz Jo·seph** (1732–1809), Austrian composer. He was a major exponent of the classical style, a teacher of Mozart and Beethoven, and musical director in the household of the Hungarian Prince Esterházy from 1761 to 1790. He wrote more than 100 symphonies and many string quartets and keyboard sonatas, twelve masses, and the oratorios *The Creation* (1796–8) and *The Seasons* (1799–1801).

Hayek /ˈhaijek/ **Frie·drich Aug·ust von** (1899–1992), Austrian-born economist known as a leading advocate of the free market and a critic of Keynesian economics. He shared the Nobel Prize for economics with Gummar Myrdal (1898–1987) in 1974.

Hayes, 1 Helen (1900–1993) US actress. In a career spanning over 80 years, she was acclaimed for both her stage and film work, winning Academy Awards for *The Sin of Madelon Claudet* (1931, best actress) and *Airport* (1970, best supporting actress). **2 Ruther·ford Bir·chard** (1822–93), US Republican politician, 19th president of the US 1877–81. His administration marked an end to the Reconstruction era.

Hayes River a river in NE Manitoba, flowing 420 km northeastward from Molson Lake (situated northeast of Lake Winnipeg) into Hudson Bay. [Sir J. *Hayes*, secretary to Prince Rupert and charter member of the Hudson's Bay Co. *c.*1684]

hay fever *noun* an allergic reaction to the airborne pollen of grasses or other plants, manifested in summer and causing sneezing, nasal congestion, conjunctival irritation, and in some cases asthmatic symptoms.

hay·field *noun* a field where hay is being or is to be made.

hay fork *noun* **1** a long-handled fork for moving hay; pitchfork. **2** esp. *hist.* a device for lifting hay into a loft etc.

hay·lage /ˈheilɪdʒ/ *noun* silage made from grass etc. which has been partially dried. [HAY *noun* + (SI)LAGE]

hay·loft *noun* = LOFT *noun* 2.

hay·maker *noun* **1** a person who tosses and spreads hay to dry after mowing. **2** an apparatus for shaking and drying hay. **3** *slang* a forceful blow or punch. □ **hay·making** *noun*

hay·mow /ˈheimau, -mɒ/ *noun* **1** hay stored in a stack or barn. **2** the part of a barn for the storage of hay.

hay privilege *noun Cdn* (*Man.*) *hist.* **1** the right of Red River settlers to cut hay on the uncultivated land lying behind each river lot. **2** the land to which this right pertained.

hay·rack *noun* **1** a rack for holding hay for feeding animals. **2** a light framework projecting from the sides of a wagon to increase its carrying capacity for hay or other bulky material. **3** a wagon together with such a rack.

hay rake *noun* **1** a hand rake used in haymaking. **2** an implement drawn by a tractor, horse, etc. for raking hay into windrows.

hay rick *noun* = HAYSTACK.

hay·ride *noun* esp. *N Amer.* a pleasure ride in an open wagon etc. filled with hay or straw.

Hay River 1 a river in NW Alberta and the southern NWT, 702 km long, rising in Alberta west of the Peace River and flowing first westward into BC, then curving back into Alberta to flow generally northeastward into the NWT to Great Slave Lake. **2** a town in the southern NWT, situated at the mouth of the Hay River, on the south shore of Great Slave Lake; pop. (2001) 3,510. □ **Hay River·ite** *noun* [after the grass along the riverbanks]

hay·seed *noun* **1** grass seed obtained from hay. **2** *N Amer. informal* a rustic or yokel.

hay·stack *noun* a packed pile of hay with a pointed or ridged top.

hay wagon *noun N Amer.* a wagon for carrying bales of hay etc.

hay·wire ● *noun* wire for binding bales of hay, straw, etc. ● *adjective informal* **1** badly disorganized, out of control. **2** (of a person) badly disturbed; erratic. □ **go haywire** go wrong; become confused or crazy. [HAY + WIRE, from the use of hay-baling wire in makeshift repairs]

Haz·ara /haˈzɑːrə/ *noun* **1** a member of a people of Mongolian descent inhabiting the mountainous region of central Afghanistan and parts of northern Iran and Pakistan. **2** the Iranian language of this people. [Persian *hazār* 'thousand']

haz·ard ● *noun* **1** a danger or risk. **2** a source of this. **3** chance. **4** a dice game with a complicated arrangement of chances. **5** *Golf* an obstruction in playing a shot, e.g. a bunker, water, etc. **6** (in *pl.*) = HAZARD LIGHTS. ● *transitive verb* **1** venture on; suggest tentatively (*hazard a guess*). **2** run the risk of. **3** expose to danger; risk. [Old French *hasard* from Spanish *azar* from Arabic *az-zahr* chance, luck]

hazard lights *plural noun* (also *Brit.* **hazard warning lights**) flashing lights on a vehicle (usu. the turn signals operating simultaneously) warning that the vehicle is stationary or slowing or reversing unexpectedly.

haz·ard·ous *adjective* **1** risky, dangerous. **2** dependent on chance. □ **haz·ard·ous·ly** *adverb* **haz·ard·ous·ness** *noun*

haze[1] ● *noun* **1** obscuration of the atmosphere near the earth by fine particles of water, smoke, or dust. **2** mental obscurity or confusion. ● *transitive & intransitive verb* make or become hazy. [prob. back-formation from HAZY]

haze[2] *transitive verb* **1** *Naut.* harass with overwork. **2** esp. *N Amer.* subject (new students, recruits, etc.) to abuse and ridicule. **3** drive (cattle etc.) while on horseback. [origin uncertain: compare obsolete French *haser* tease, insult]

ha·zel ● *noun* **1** any shrub or small tree of the genus *Corylus*, bearing round brown edible nuts. **2** wood from the hazel. **3** a golden-brown or greenish-brown colour (esp. of the eyes). ● *adjective* (esp. of the eyes) of a golden-brown or greenish-brown colour. [Old English *hæsel* from Germanic]

hazel grouse *noun* a brown speckled grouse of European woodlands, *Tetrastes bonasia*.

hazel·nut *noun* the fruit of the hazel.

Haz·litt, Wil·liam (1778–1830), English essayist and critic. From about 1812 he wrote many articles on diverse subjects for several periodicals. His style, marked by clarity and conviction, brought a new vigour to English prose writing.

haz·mat *noun* hazardous material.

hazy *adjective* (**hazi·er**, **hazi·est**) **1** misty. **2** vague, indistinct. **3** confused, uncertain. □ **hazi·ly** *adverb* **hazi·ness** *noun* [17th c. in nautical use: origin unknown]

HB *abbreviation* hard black (pencil lead).

Hb *symbol* hemoglobin.

HBC *abbreviation Cdn* Hudson's Bay Company.

HBM *abbreviation* Her or His Britannic Majesty (or Majesty's).

H-bomb *noun* = HYDROGEN BOMB.

HC *abbreviation* House of Commons.

HCF *abbreviation* highest common factor.

HCFC *abbreviation* hydrochlorofluorocarbon (similar to CFC but thought to be less harmful to the ozone layer).

hCG *abbreviation* HUMAN CHORIONIC GONADOTROPIN.

HCV *abbreviation* hepatitis C virus.

H.D. *see* DOOLITTLE, HILDA.

HDL *abbreviation* HIGH-DENSITY LIPOPROTEIN.

HDPE *abbreviation* high-density polyethylene.

HDTV *abbreviation* high-definition television.

HE *abbreviation* **1** His or Her Excellency. **2** His Eminence. **3** high explosive.

He *symbol Chem.* the element helium.

he ● *pronoun* **1** the man or boy or male animal previously named or in question. **2** a person etc. of unspecified sex, esp. referring to one

already named or identified (*if anyone comes he will have to wait*). ¶ Many people perceive this usage as sexist, and prefer to use *they*; however, this alternative is condemned by others. If possible, recasting the sentence to avoid using a pronoun (e.g. *Anyone who comes will have to wait*) is the best way to avoid censure. ● *noun* **1** a male; a man. **2** (in combination) male (*he-goat*). [Old English from Germanic]

Head, Sir Fran·cis Bond (1793–1875), British soldier and colonial administrator, Lieutenant-Governor of Upper Canada 1835–38. Initially welcomed by the Reform interests in the colony, he ignored both the Executive Council and the Assembly, and his indifference to the need for political reform helped push Reform extremists towards rebellion in 1837. He was recalled in 1838.

head ● *noun* **1** the upper part of the human body, or the foremost or upper part of an animal's body, containing the brain, mouth, and sense organs. **2 a** the head regarded as the seat of intellect or repository of comprehended information. **b** intelligence; imagination (*use your head*). **c** mental aptitude or tolerance (usu. foll. by *for*: *a good head for business; no head for heights*). **3** *informal* a headache, esp. resulting from a blow or from intoxication. **4** a thing like a head in form or position, esp.: **a** the part of a tool, weapon, golf club, etc. used to strike with. **b** the flattened top of a nail. **c** the ornamented top of a pillar. **d** a mass of leaves or flowers at the top of a stem. **e** the flat end of a drum. **f** the foam on top of a glass of beer etc. **g** the upper horizontal part of a window frame, door frame, etc. **h** = SHOWER HEAD. **5** life when regarded as vulnerable (*it cost him his head*). **6 a** a person in charge; a director or leader (esp. *Brit.* the principal teacher at a school or college). **b** a position of leadership or command. **7** the front or forward part of something, e.g. a procession. **8** the upper end of something, e.g. a table or bed. **9** the top or highest part of something, e.g. a page, stairs, etc. **10** a person or individual regarded as a numerical unit (*$10 per head*). **11** (*pl.* same) **a** an individual animal as a unit. **b** (as *pl.*) a number of cattle or game as specified (*20 head*). **12 a** the side of a coin bearing the image of a head. **b** (usu. in *pl.*) this side as a choice when tossing a coin. **13 a** the source of a river, stream etc. **b** the end of a lake, bay, etc. at which a river enters it. **c** *Cdn (Nfld)* the innermost area of a bay, harbour, etc. **14** the height or length of a head as a measure (*his horse won by a head*). **15** the component of a machine that is in contact with or very close to what is being processed or worked on, esp.: **a** the component on a tape recorder that touches the moving tape in play and converts the signals. **b** the part of a record player that holds the playing cartridge and stylus. **c** = PRINTHEAD. **16 a** a confined body of water or steam in an engine etc. **b** the pressure exerted by this. **17** a promontory (esp. in place names). **18** *Naut.* **a** the bows of a ship or boat. **b** (often in *pl.*) a latrine on a ship or boat. **c** *Cdn (Nfld)* the seaward end of a wharf. **19** a main topic or category for consideration or discussion. **20** *Journalism* = HEADLINE *noun*. **21** a culmination, climax, or crisis. **22** the fully developed top of a boil etc. **23** *slang* a habitual taker of drugs; a drug addict. ● *attributive adjective* chief or principal (*head gardener; head office*). ● *verb* **1** *transitive* be at the head or front of. **2** *transitive* (often foll. by *up*) be in charge of (*headed a small team*). **3** *transitive* **a** provide with a head or heading. **b** (of an inscription, title, etc.) be at the top of, serve as a heading for. **4 a** *intransitive* face or move in a specified direction or towards a specified result (often foll. by *for*: *is heading for trouble*). **b** *transitive* direct in a specified direction. **5** *transitive Soccer* strike (the ball) with the head. **6 a** *transitive* (often foll. by *down*) cut the head off (a plant etc.). **b** *intransitive* (of a plant etc.) form a head. **7 a** *transitive* go around the head of (a stream or lake). **b** *intransitive* (of a river or stream) have its source; rise. □ **above** (or **over**) **one's head** beyond one's ability to understand. **bang** (or **beat**) **one's head against** (a **brick**) **wall** *informal* be frustrated in an attempt to do something. **come to a head** (of a boil etc.) suppurate. **2** reach a crisis or climax. **enter** (or **come into**) **one's head** *informal* occur to one. **from head to toe** (or **foot**) all over a person's body. **get it into one's head** (foll. by *that* + clause or *to* + infin.) form a definite idea or plan, esp. mistakenly or impetuously. **get one's head around** *slang* understand or concentrate on. **get one's head down** *Cdn & Brit. slang* **1** go to bed. **2** concentrate on the task in hand. **give a person his** or **her head** allow a person to act freely. **give head** *coarse slang* perform oral sex. **go to one's head 1** (of liquor) make one dizzy or slightly drunk. **2** (of success) make one conceited. **have one's head** (**screwed**) **on straight** be sensible. **head and shoulders** *informal* by a considerable amount. **head back** return home etc. **head in the sand** refusal to acknowledge an obvious danger or difficulty. **head off 1** get ahead of so as to intercept and turn aside. **2** forestall. **a head of steam** momentum. **head over heels 1** turning over completely in forward motion as in a somersault etc. **2** topsy-turvy. **3** utterly, completely (*head over heels in love*). **heads will roll** *informal* people will be disgraced or dismissed. **head to head** in direct competition or conflict. **hold up one's head** be confident or unashamed. **in one's head 1** in one's thoughts or imagination. **2** by mental process without use of physical aids. **keep one's head** remain calm. **keep one's head above water** *informal* **1** keep out of debt. **2** avoid succumbing to difficulties. **keep one's head down** *informal* remain inconspicuous in difficult or dangerous times. **lose one's head** lose self-control; panic. **make head(s) or tail(s) of** (usu. with *neg.* or *interrogative*) understand at all. **off one's head** *slang* crazy. **off the top of one's head** *informal* impromptu; without careful thought or investigation. **one's head off** noisily or excessively (*laughed his head off*). **on one's** (or **one's own**) **head** as one's sole responsibility. **out of one's head 1** *slang* crazy or delirious. **2** from one's imagination or memory. **over one's head 1** beyond one's ability to understand. **2** without one's knowledge or involvement, esp. when one has a right to this. **3** with disregard for one's own (stronger) claim (*was promoted over their heads*). **put heads together** consult together. **put into a person's head** suggest to a person. **turn a person's head** make a person conceited. **turn heads** cause people to notice. **with one's head in the clouds** see CLOUD. □ **head·ed** *adjective* (also in *combination*). **head·less** *adjective* [Old English *hēafod* from Germanic]

-head *suffix* = -HOOD (*godhead*; *maidenhead*). [Middle English *-hed*, *-hede* = -HOOD]

head·ache *noun* **1** a continuous pain in the head. **2** *informal* **a** a worrying problem. **b** a troublesome person. □ **head·achy** *adjective*

head·band *noun* **1** a band worn around the head as decoration or to keep the hair off the face. **2** an ornamental band of silk etc. fastened to the inner back of a bound book at the head and tail.

head·bang·er *noun* *slang* **1** a fan of heavy metal music. **2** *Brit.* a crazy or eccentric person.

head·bang·ing *noun* (often *attributive*) **1** vigorous head-shaking in time to heavy metal music. **2** the brisk forceful disciplining of uncooperative persons.

head·board *noun* an upright panel forming or placed behind the head of a bed etc.

head-butt ● *noun* a forceful thrust with the top of the head into the chin or body of another person. ● *transitive verb* attack (another person) with a head-butt.

head case *noun* *informal* a mentally ill or unstable person.

head·cheese *noun* *N Amer.* a jellied preparation of the chopped meat from a boiled pig's head.

head·cloth *noun* a cloth or covering for the head.

head cold *noun* *N Amer.* a cold characterized esp. by sneezing and a stuffy or runny nose.

head count *noun* **1** a counting of individual people or animals. **2** a total number of people, esp. the number of people employed in a particular organization.

head·dress *noun* an ornamental covering or band for the head.

head·end *noun* a control centre in a cable television system, at which the various signals are introduced into the cable network.

head·er *noun* **1** *Soccer* a shot or pass made with the head. **2** *informal* a headlong fall or dive. **3** a line or block of text appearing at the top of each page of a document etc. (*compare* FOOTER 2). **4** a brick or stone laid at right angles to the face of a wall (*compare* STRETCHER 2). **5** a beam crossing and supporting the ends of joists, studs, or rafters. **6** a tank of water etc. maintaining pressure in a plumbing system. **7** a person or thing which removes the head, esp. a reaping machine which cuts off the heads of grain. **8** *N Amer.* the top part of an automobile's windshield.

head fake ● *noun* *Sport* a feint of the head intended to deceive an opponent. ● *intransitive verb* attempt to deceive with a head fake.

head·first ● *adverb* **1** with the head foremost. **2** precipitately. ● *adjective* with the head foremost.

head·frame *noun* a structure at the head of a shaft in a mine to support the hoisting equipment.

head game *noun* *N Amer. informal* **1** (often in *pl.*) psychological manipulation. **2** a mental exercise to improve memory etc.

head·gear *noun* **1 a** something worn on the head, as a hat, cap, or headdress. **b** a protective covering for the head, as a helmet. **2** machinery etc. at the top of a mine shaft. **3** the parts of a harness around a horse's head. **4** orthodontic equipment worn on the head and attached to braces on the teeth.

head·hunt·er *noun* **1** a person who collects the heads of dead enemies as trophies. **2** an employment agency or agent specializing in the recruitment for an organization etc. of skilled personnel.

□ **head·hunt** *transitive & intransitive verb* **head·hunt·ing** *noun*

head·ing *noun* **1 a** a title at the head of a page or section of a book etc. **b** a division or section of a subject of discourse etc. **2 a** a horizontal passage made in preparation for building a tunnel. **b** *Mining* = DRIFT *noun* 6. **3** the extension of the top of a curtain above the tape that carries the hooks or the pocket for a wire. **4** the course of an aircraft, ship, etc. **5** the angle between the direction of the longitudinal axis of an aircraft and a specified meridian, as magnetic north.

head·lamp *noun* **1** = HEADLIGHT. **2** a small lamp attached to a hat or worn strapped to the forehead.

head·land *noun* **1** a promontory. **2** a strip left unplowed at the end of a field, for machinery to pass along.

head lettuce *noun* lettuce having tightly clustered, usu. pale leaves forming a round compact head (*compare* LEAF LETTUCE).

head·light *noun* **1** a strong light at the front of a motor vehicle or railway engine. **2** the beam from this. **3** (usu. in *pl.*) *N Amer. slang* a woman's breast.

head·line ● *noun* **1** a heading at the top of an article or page, esp. in a newspaper. **2** (in *pl.*) the most important items of news in a newspaper or broadcast news bulletin. ● *verb* **1** *transitive* give a headline to. **2** *intransitive* headlines appear as the chief performer (at). □ **hit** (or **make**) **the headlines** *informal* be given prominent attention as news.

head·liner *noun* a headlining performer; a star.

head·lock *noun* a hold with an arm around the opponent's head.

head·long *adverb & adjective* **1** with the head foremost. **2** in a rush. [Middle English *headling* (as HEAD, -LING²), assimilated to -LONG]

head·man *noun* (*pl.* **-men**) the chief man of a village, tribe etc.

head·man *transitive verb* *Hockey* pass (the puck) to a team member who is closer to the opposing team's net than the passer.

head·master *noun* a man who is the principal of a school.

head·mis·tress *noun* a woman principal in charge of a school.

head·most *adjective* (esp. of a ship) foremost.

head·note *noun* **1** a note or comment at the head of a document, page, etc. **2** *Law* a summary giving the principle of a decision and an outline of the facts, prefixed to the report of a decided case.

head of hair *noun* the hair on a person's head, esp. as a distinctive feature.

head of state *noun* (*pl.* **heads of state**) the title of the head of a state, usu. the leader of the ruling party or a monarch.

head-on *adjective & adverb* **1** with the front foremost (*a head-on crash*; *hit us head-on*). **2** in direct confrontation.

head·phone *noun* (usu. in *pl.*) a pair of earphones joined by a band placed over the head or around the neck, for listening to audio equipment etc.

head·piece *noun* **1** any covering for the head, esp. a decorative one worn by a bride. **2** a helmet. **3** an ornamental engraving at the head of a chapter etc.

head·pond *noun* *Cdn* (*Maritimes*) a pond created behind a dam.

head·quar·ter *verb* esp. *N Amer.* **1** *transitive* (usu. in *passive*) provide with headquarters (at a specific location). **2** *intransitive* set up headquarters.

head·quar·ters *noun* (as *sing.* or *pl.*) **1** the administrative centre of an organization. **2** the premises occupied by a military commander and the commander's staff. Abbr.: **HQ**.

head·rail *noun* a horizontal rail at the top of something, esp. a window.

head·rest *noun* a support for the head attached to a dentist's chair, the seat of a motor vehicle, etc.

head·room *noun* **1** the space above a driver's or passenger's head in a vehicle, between a person's head and a doorway, ceiling, etc. **2** the space or clearance between the top of a vehicle and the underside of a bridge etc. which it passes under.

head·sail *noun* a sail on a ship's foremast or bowsprit.

head scarf *noun* a scarf worn around the head and tied under the chin.

head-scratch·ing *noun* puzzlement.

head·set *noun* a set of headphones, often with a microphone attached, used esp. in telephone and radio communication.

head·ship *noun* the position of chief or leader, esp. *Brit.* of a headmaster or headmistress.

head shop *noun* *slang* a store selling drug paraphernalia.

head·shot *noun* a photograph of a person from the shoulders or neck up.

head-shrink·er *noun slang* a psychiatrist.

heads·man *noun* (*pl.* **-men**) *hist.* an executioner who beheads.

Head-Smashed-In Buffalo Jump a UNESCO World Heritage site west of Lethbridge in S Alberta, an exceptionally large and well-preserved buffalo jump in existence since 5500 BCE.

head·space *noun* **1** space left in the top of a jar, bottle, etc. to allow room for expansion of contents. **2** mindset, attitude. **3** a gap between the bolt face and breech of a gun using rimless ammunition.

head·spring *noun* **1** the main source of a stream. **2** a principal source of ideas etc.

head·stall *noun esp. N Amer.* the part of a halter or bridle that fits around a horse's head.

head·stand *noun* an act or instance of balancing on one's head.

head start *noun* an advantage granted or gained at an early stage.

head·stock *noun* a set of bearings in a machine, supporting a revolving part, e.g. the part of a lathe that holds the rotating spindle.

head·stone *noun* a (usu. inscribed) stone set up at the head of a grave.

head·stream *noun* a stream that forms the source of a larger stream or river.

head·strong *adjective* self-willed and obstinate.

heads-up *N Amer. informal* ● *noun* a warning (*gave the department a heads-up*). ● *adjective* alert, perceptive (*a heads-up baseball player*). ● *interjection* (**heads up**) look out!

head table *noun N Amer.* a table at a wedding, conference, etc. where the guests of honour sit.

head tax *noun* a tax levied esp. on new immigrants to a country.

head·teach·er *noun esp. Brit.* the teacher in charge of a school.

head-to-head ● *attributive adjective* involving two parties confronting each other. ● *adverb* confronting another party. ● *noun Brit.* a conversation, confrontation, or contest between two parties. [translation of French *tête-à-tête*]

head-turner *noun* an extremely attractive person. □ **head-turning** *adjective*

head-up *adjective* (of instrument readings in an aircraft, vehicle, etc.) shown so as to be visible without lowering the eyes.

head voice *noun* the high register of the voice in speaking or singing.

head waiter *noun* a waiter who supervises other waiters, busboys, etc.

head·water *noun* (in *sing.* or *pl.*) streams flowing from the sources of a river.

head·way *noun* **1** progress. **2** the rate of progress of a ship. **3** = HEADROOM.

head·wind *noun* a wind blowing from directly in front.

head·word *noun* a word forming a heading, e.g. of an entry in a dictionary or encyclopedia.

head·work *noun* mental work or effort.

heady *adjective* (**head·i·er**, **head·i·est**) **1** (of liquor) potent, intoxicating. **2** light-headed, giddy. **3** affecting the senses strongly (*a heady aroma*). **4** exhilarating; very exciting (*the heady days of youth*). **5** (of a person, thing, or action) impetuous, foolhardy. □ **head·i·ly** *adverb* **head·i·ness** *noun*

heal *verb* **1** *intransitive* (often foll. by *up*) (of a wound or injury) become sound or healthy again. **2** *transitive* cause (a wound, disease, or person) to heal or be cured, or be made sound again. **3** *transitive* repair, correct (an undesirable condition, esp. a breach of relations); put right (differences etc.). **4** *transitive* alleviate (sorrow etc.). **5** *intransitive* (of a person) recover from mental trauma. □ **heal·able** *adjective* **heal·ing** *noun & adjective* [Old English *hælan* from Germanic, related to WHOLE]

heal-all *noun* a popular name of various medicinal plants.

heal·er *noun* **1** a person who heals others, esp. a faith healer. **2** a thing which heals or assists in healing.

Healey /ˈhiːli/ **Jeff** (b.1966), Canadian blues musician. His records include *See the Light* (1988) and *Hell to Pay* (1990), recorded with his trio, The Jeff Healey Band.

healing circle *noun* **1** a traditional Aboriginal ceremony that promotes emotional healing, in which participants are arranged in a circle and each in turn is invited to speak by passing a talking stick or other token around the circle. **2** any gathering or forum that uses shared prayer, chanting, song, meditation, etc. to promote emotional or physical healing.

health *noun* **1** the state of being well in body or mind. **2** a person's mental or physical condition (*in poor health*) (often *attributive*: *health insurance*). **3** the delivery of medical services (*the government will increase health spending this year*). **4** soundness, esp. financial or moral (*the health of the nation*). **5** a toast drunk in someone's honour. [Old English *hælth* from Germanic]

health card *noun Cdn* a card identifying a person as eligible to receive medical treatment paid for by a public insurance plan.

health care *noun* the maintenance and improvement of health, esp. as administered by organized medical services and facilities.

health centre *noun* the headquarters of a group of local medical services.

health certificate *noun* a certificate attesting fitness or good health.

health club *noun* an establishment providing facilities for exercise, massage, etc.

health farm *noun* a residential establishment where people seek improved health by a regime of dieting, exercise, etc.

health food *noun* natural food eaten for its health-giving qualities (often *attributive*: *health food store*).

health·ful *adjective* conducive to good health; beneficial. □ **health·ful·ly** *adverb* **health·ful·ness** *noun*

health maintenance organization *noun US* an organization which delivers prepaid health care services to enrolled members and their families within a certain geographic area. Abbr.: **HMO**.

health plan *noun* a medical insurance plan, either one provided by a government or one offered as an employment benefit.

health service *noun Brit.* a public service providing medical care.

health visitor *noun Brit.* = VISITING NURSE.

healthy *adjective* (**health·i·er**, **health·i·est**) **1** having, showing, or promoting good health. **2** beneficial, helpful (*a healthy respect for experience*). **3** ample, considerable (*a healthy portion*). **4** (of a business etc.) sound, functioning well. □ **health·i·ly** *adverb* **health·i·ness** *noun*

Hea·ney /ˈhiːni/ **Sea·mus Jus·tin** (b.1939), Irish poet. His early poetry, such as *Death of a Naturalist* (1966), reflects the rural life of his youth, while his later poetry deals with wider social and cultural themes. He received the Nobel Prize for Literature in 1995.

heap ● *noun* **1 a** a collection of things lying haphazardly one on another. **b** a mass of something in an untidy pile (*she collapsed in a heap on the floor*). **2** (esp. in *pl.*) *informal* a large number or amount (*there's heaps of time*). **3** *slang* an old or dilapidated thing, esp. a motor vehicle or building. ● *verb* **1** *transitive & intransitive* (foll. by *up*, *together*, etc.) collect or be collected in a heap. **2** *transitive* (foll. by *with*) load copiously or to excess. **3** *transitive* (foll. by *on*, *upon*) accord or offer copiously to (*heaped insults on them*). [Old English *hēap*, *hēapian* from Germanic]

heaped *adjective Brit.* = HEAPING.

heap·ing *adjective N Amer.* (of a spoonful etc.) with the contents piled above the brim.

hear *verb* (*past* and *past participle* **heard**) **1** *transitive & intransitive* perceive (sound etc.) with the ear. **2** *transitive* **a** listen to (*heard them on the radio*). **b** listen to (a recital, religious service, etc.) as a member of an audience or congregation. **3** *transitive* listen judicially to and judge (a case, plaintiff, etc.). **4** *intransitive* (foll. by *about*, *of*, or *that* + clause) be told or informed. **5** *intransitive* (foll. by *from*) be contacted by, esp. by letter or telephone. **6** *transitive* be ready to obey (an order) (*you're not going out – do you hear me?*). **7** *transitive* grant (a prayer). **8** listen or pay attention to, or acknowledge what another is saying (*I hear you, brother*; *I hear what you're saying*). □ **be unable to hear oneself think** be unable to think clearly because of the noise. **have heard of** be aware of; know of the existence of. **hear a pin drop** hear the slightest noise. **hear! hear!** *interjection* expressing agreement (esp. with something said in a speech). **hear a person out** listen to all that a person says. **hear tell** (usu. foll. by *of*, or *that* + clause) be informed. **will not hear of** will not allow or agree to. □ **hear·able** *adjective* **hear·er** *noun* [Old English *hīeran* from Germanic]

Heard and Mc·Don·ald Islands a group of uninhabited islands in the S Indian Ocean, administered by Australia since 1947 as an external territory.

hear·ing *noun* **1** the faculty of perceiving sounds. **2** the range within which sounds may be heard; earshot (*within hearing*; *in my hearing*). **3** the action or an act of listening. **4** an opportunity to state one's case (*give them a fair hearing*). **5** the listening to evidence and pleadings in a law court or other officially constituted body.

hearing aid *noun* a small device to amplify sound, worn by a partially deaf person in or behind the ear.

hearing ear dog *noun* (also **hearing dog**) a guide dog trained to guide a deaf person.

hearing impaired ● *plural noun* people who have some hearing loss. **●** *adjective* (**hearing-impaired**) having some hearing loss.

hark·en /ˈhɑrkən/ *intransitive verb* (also **hark·en**) (often foll. by *to*) *archaic* or *literary* listen. □ **hearken back** mention again or remember an earlier subject, event, etc. [Old English *heorcnian* (as HARK)]

Hearne /hɜrn/ **Sam·uel** (1745–92), Canadian explorer and fur trader. He joined the Hudson's Bay Company in 1766, and was chosen to look for a trade route across the Barrens. After two unsuccessful attempts, he succeeded (1770–1772) in reaching the Coppermine River and following it to the Arctic Ocean, though he could not find a feasible trade route. Following his return, he attempted to solve the problem of competition for furs by establishing Cumberland House, the HBC's first inland trading post, on the Saskatchewan River.

hear·say *noun* rumour, gossip.

hearsay evidence *noun* evidence given by a witness based on information received from others rather than personal knowledge.

hearse /hɜrs/ *noun* a vehicle for conveying the coffin at a funeral. [Old French *herse* harrow, from medieval Latin *herpica*, ultimately from Latin *hirpex -icis* large rake]

Hearst[1] /hɜrst/ a mining town in NE Ontario, about 250 km northwest of Timmins; pop. (2001) 5,825. [Sir W. H. HEARST]

Hearst[2] /hɜrst/ **1 Sir Wil·liam How·ard** (1864–1941), Canadian lawyer and politician, Conservative premier of Ontario 1914–1919. During his premiership he enfranchised women, legislated prohibition, and authorized construction of a hydroelectric plant at Queenston, which was the largest in the world when it opened in 1921. **2 Wil·liam Ran·dolph** (1863–1951), US newspaper publisher and tycoon, noted for his introduction of large headlines, sensational crime reporting, and other features designed to increase circulation; these innovations revolutionized American journalism.

heart *noun* **1** a hollow muscular organ maintaining the circulation of blood by rhythmic contraction and dilation. **2** the region of the heart; the breast. **3 a** the heart regarded as the centre of thought, feeling, and emotion (esp. love). **b** a person's capacity for feeling emotion (*has no heart*). **4 a** courage or enthusiasm (*take heart; lose heart*). **b** one's mood or feeling (*change of heart*). **5 a** the central or innermost part of something. **b** the vital part or essence (*the heart of the matter*). **6** the close compact head of a cabbage, lettuce, etc. **7 a** a heart-shaped thing. **b** a conventional representation of a heart with two equal curves meeting at a point at the bottom and a cusp at the top. **8 a** a playing card of a suit denoted by a red figure of a heart. **b** (in *pl.*) this suit. **c** (in *pl.*) a card game in which players avoid taking tricks containing a card of this suit. **9** condition of land as regards fertility (*in good heart*). **10** a beloved person (*dear heart*). □ **after one's own heart** such as one likes or desires. **at heart 1** in one's innermost feelings. **2** basically, essentially. **break a person's heart** overwhelm a person with sorrow, esp. by ending a romantic relationship. **by heart** in or from memory. **close** (or **near**) **to one's heart 1** dear to one. **2** affecting one deeply. **from the heart** (or **the bottom of one's heart**) sincerely, profoundly. **give** (or **lose**) **one's heart** (often foll. by *to*) fall in love (with). **have a heart** be merciful. **have the heart** (usu. with *neg.*; foll. by *to* + infin.) be insensitive or hard-hearted enough (*didn't have the heart to ask him*). **have** (or **put**) **one's heart in** be keenly involved in or committed to (an enterprise etc.). **have one's heart in one's mouth** be greatly alarmed or apprehensive. **have one's heart in the right place** be sincere or well-intentioned. **heart and soul** (with) all one's energies and affections. **heart of gold** a generous nature. **heart of stone** a stern or cruel nature. **hearts and minds** emotional and intellectual support. **heart to heart** candidly, intimately. **in one's heart of hearts** in one's innermost feelings. **sing** (or **play** etc.) **one's heart out** sing or play etc. to the fullest extent of one's ability. **take to heart** be much affected or distressed by. **to one's heart's content** *see* CONTENT[1]. **wear one's heart on one's sleeve** make one's feelings apparent. **with all one's heart** sincerely; with all goodwill. **with one's whole heart** with enthusiasm; without doubts or reservations. □ **-hearted** *adjective* [Old English *heorte* from Germanic]

heart·ache *noun* mental anguish or grief.

heart attack *noun* a sudden occurrence of coronary thrombosis usu. resulting in the death of part of a heart muscle.

heart·beat *noun* **1** a pulsation of the heart. **2** the central or most important part or place (*the heartbeat of the nation*). □ **in a heartbeat** in a very brief space of time.

heart·break *noun* overwhelming sorrow or distress. □ **heart·break·er** *noun* **heart·break·ing** *adjective* **heart·break·ing·ly** *adverb* **heart·broken** *adjective*

heart·burn *noun* a burning sensation in the chest resulting from indigestion; pyrosis.

heart·en *transitive & intransitive verb* make or become more cheerful. □ **heart·en·ing** *adjective* **heart·en·ing·ly** *adverb*

heart failure *noun* a severe failure of the heart to function properly, esp. as a cause of death.

heart·felt *adjective* sincere; deeply felt.

hearth /hɑrθ/ *noun* **1 a** the floor of a fireplace. **b** the area in front of a fireplace. **2** this symbolizing the home. **3** the bottom of a blast furnace where molten metal collects. □ **hearth and home** the home and its comforts. [Old English *heorth* from West Germanic]

heart-healthy *adjective* = HEART-SMART.

hearth rug *noun* a rug laid before a fireplace.

hearth·stone /ˈhɑrθstoːn/ *noun* a flat stone forming a hearth.

heart·i·ly *adverb* **1** in a hearty manner; with goodwill, appetite, or courage. **2** very; to a great degree (esp. with reference to personal feelings) (*am heartily sick of it; disliked him heartily*).

heart·land *noun* the central or most important part of an area.

heart·less *adjective* unfeeling, pitiless. □ **heart·less·ly** *adverb* **heart·less·ness** *noun*

heart-lung machine *noun* a machine that temporarily takes over the functions of the heart and lungs, esp. in surgery.

heart murmur *noun* = MURMUR 3.

heart of darkness *noun* **1** the depths of human evil. **2** a dark, frightening place, esp. a jungle, associated with evil. [after Joseph Conrad's novella *Heart of Darkness* (1902), telling of an encounter in the farthest reaches of the Congo with a corrupt European colonist who has abandoned all moral and ethical considerations]

heart rate *noun* the pulse, calculated by counting the number of beats of the heart per unit of time.

heart-rending *adjective* causing great sorrow or distress. □ **heart-rending·ly** *adverb*

heart-search·ing *noun* the thorough examination of one's own feelings and motives.

hearts·ease /ˈhɑrtsiːz/ *noun* (also **heart's-ease**) a pansy.

heart·sick *adjective* very despondent. □ **heart·sick·ness** *noun*

heart-smart *adjective informal* (of food, meals, etc.) low in fat and high in fibre, thus helping to prevent heart disease.

heart·sore *adjective archaic* or *literary* grieving, heartsick.

heart-stopping *adjective* very suspenseful or thrilling (*a heart-stopping hockey game*). □ **heart-stopper** *noun*

heart·strings *plural noun* one's deepest feelings or emotions.

heart·throb *noun* **1** *informal* an extremely attractive (usu. male) person, esp. an actor or other celebrity. **2** beating of the heart.

heart-to-heart ● *adjective* (of a conversation etc.) candid, intimate. **●** *noun* a candid or personal conversation.

heart·warm·ing *adjective* emotionally rewarding or uplifting. □ **heart·warm·ing·ly** *adverb*

heart·wood *noun* the dense inner part of a tree trunk yielding the hardest timber.

heart·worm *noun* **1** a parasitic nematode worm which infests the hearts of dogs and other canids. **2** the disease due to infestation by heartworm.

heart-wrenching *adjective* emotionally devastating.

hearty ● *adjective* (**heart·i·er, heart·i·est**) **1** strong, vigorous (*hale and hearty*). **2** spirited. **3** (of a meal or appetite) large. **4** warm, friendly (*a hearty welcome*). **5** heartfelt, genuine, sincere. **●** *noun* (*pl.* **-ies**) **1** *Brit.* a hearty person, esp. one ostentatiously so. **2** (usu. in *pl.*) (as a form of address) fellows, esp. fellow sailors. □ **heart·i·ness** *noun*

heat ● *noun* **1 a** the condition of being hot. **b** the sensation or perception of this. **c** high temperature of the body. **2** *Physics* **a** a form of energy arising from the random motion of the molecules of bodies, which may be transferred by conduction, convection, or radiation. **b** the amount of this needed to cause a specific process, or evolved in a process (*heat of formation; heat of solution*). **3** hot weather (*succumbed to the heat*). **4 a** warmth of feeling. **b** anger or excitement (*the heat of the argument*). **5** (foll. by *of*) the most intense part or period of an activity (*in the heat of the battle*). **6** a (usu. preliminary or trial) round in a race or contest. **7** the receptive period of the sexual cycle, esp. in female mammals. **8** redness of the skin with a sensation of heat (*prickly heat*). **9** pungency of flavour. **10** *slang* intensive pursuit, e.g. by the police. **11** *N Amer. slang* adverse criticism; blame. **●** *verb* (often foll. by *up*) **1** *transitive & intransitive* make or become hot or warm. **2** *transitive* inflame;

excite or intensify. □ **in the heat of the moment** during or resulting from intense activity, without pause for thought. **in heat** (of mammals, esp. females) sexually receptive. **turn the heat on** *informal* concentrate an attack or criticism on (a person). □ **heat·less** *adjective* [Old English *hætu* from Germanic]

heat capacity *noun* the number of units of heat needed to raise the temperature of a body by one degree.

heat death *noun Physics* a state of uniform distribution of energy, esp. viewed as a possible fate of the universe.

heat·ed *adjective* **1** (of a person, discussions, etc.) angry; inflamed with passion or excitement. **2** made hot. □ **heat·ed·ly** *adverb*

heat·er *noun* **1** a device for warming the air in a room, car, etc. **2** a container with an element etc. for heating the contents (*water heater*). **3** *N Amer. slang* a gun. **4** *Baseball slang* = FASTBALL 1.

heat exchanger *noun* a device for the transfer of heat from one medium to another.

heat gun *noun* an electrical device like a blow-dryer but generating much greater heat for use in stripping paint etc.

Heath, Sir Ed·ward Rich·ard George (b.1916), British Conservative politician, prime minister 1970–74. His term of office was marked by problems of inflation and balance of payments; attempts to restrain wage increases led to widespread strikes.

heath *noun* **1** an area of flattish uncultivated land with low shrubs. **2** a plant growing on a heath, esp. of the genus *Erica* or *Calluna* (e.g. heather). □ **heathy** *adjective* [Old English *hæth* from Germanic]

hea·then /ˈhiːðən/ ● *noun* **1** *derogatory* a person who does not belong to a widely held religion (esp. who is not Christian, Jewish, or Muslim) as regarded by those that do. **2** an unenlightened person; a person regarded as lacking culture or moral principles. **3** (**the heathen**) heathen people collectively. **4** *Bible* a Gentile. ● *adjective* **1** of or relating to heathens; pagan. **2** having no religion. □ **hea·then·dom** *noun* **hea·then·ism** *noun* [Old English *hæthen* from Germanic]

hea·ther /ˈheðər/ *noun* **1** an evergreen shrub, *Calluna vulgaris*, with purple bell-shaped flowers. **2** any of various shrubs, e.g. of the genus *Erica* or *Phyllodoce*, growing esp. on moors or in mountainous regions. □ **hea·thery** *adjective* [Middle English, Scots, & Northern English *hathir* etc., of unknown origin: assimilated to *heath*]

heather mixture *noun Brit.* **1** a fabric of mixed hues supposed to resemble heather. **2** the colour of this.

heath·land *noun* an extensive area of heath.

Heath Rob·in·son *adjective Brit.* absurdly ingenious and impracticable in design or construction. [W. *Heath Robinson*, English cartoonist d.1944 who drew such contrivances]

Heath·row an international airport situated 25 km (15 miles) west of the centre of London, England.

heat·ing *noun* **1** the imparting or generation of heat. **2** equipment or devices used to provide heat, esp. to a building.

heating pad *noun* a fabric-covered pad containing an electric heating element, placed on the body to relieve aches and pains.

heat island *noun* (also **urban heat island**) an area, usu. a city, which has a higher temperature than its surroundings, esp. due to higher energy output from vehicles etc. and to the retention by roads, rooftops, etc. of heat from insolation.

heat lamp *noun* a lamp used for its heat as well as its light.

heat lightning *noun* lightning that is too far away for the associated thunder to be heard.

heat·proof *adjective* able to resist great heat.

heat pump *noun* a device for the transfer of heat from a colder area to a hotter area by using mechanical energy.

heat rash *noun* = PRICKLY HEAT.

heat-resist·ant *adjective* = HEATPROOF.

heat-seeking *adjective* (of a missile etc.) able to detect infrared radiation to guide it to its target. □ **heat seeker** *noun*

heat shield *noun* a device for protection from excessive heat, esp. fitted to a spacecraft.

heat sink *noun* a device or substance for absorbing excessive or unwanted heat.

heat·stroke *noun* a feverish condition caused by excessive exposure to high temperature.

heat treatment *noun* the use of heat to modify the properties of a metal etc. □ **heat-treat** *transitive verb*

heat wave *noun* a prolonged period of abnormally hot weather.

heave ● *verb* (*past* and *past participle* **heaved** or esp. *Naut.* **hove**) **1** *transitive* lift or haul (a heavy thing) with great effort. **2** *transitive* utter

with effort or resignation (*heaved a sigh*). **3** *transitive* throw. **4** *intransitive* rise and fall rhythmically or spasmodically. **5** *transitive Naut.* haul by rope. **6** *intransitive* retch or vomit. **7** *intransitive* rise up above the general surface; expand, shift (*the floor heaved during the winter*). ● *noun* **1 a** an instance of heaving. **b** an uneven area of road etc. caused by heaving due to frost. **2** *Geol.* a sideways displacement in a fault. **3** (in *pl.*) a disease of horses, characterized by laboured breathing due to ruptured air cells in the lungs. **4** (in *pl.*; prec. by *the*) *slang* a bout of retching or vomiting. □ **heave in sight** (or **into view**) come into view. **heave to** esp. *Naut.* bring or be brought to a standstill. □ **heav·er** *noun* [Old English *hebban* from Germanic, related to Latin *capere* take]

heave-ho ● *noun* (usu. prec. by *the* or *the old*) *slang* rejection or dismissal (*the bank gave him the heave-ho*). ● *interjection* a sailors' cry, esp. on raising the anchor.

heav·en *noun* **1** (also **Heaven**) a place regarded in some religions as the abode of God and the angels, and of the good after death, often characterized as above the sky. **2** a place or state of supreme bliss. **3** *informal* something delightful. **4** God, Providence (often in *sing.* or *pl.* as an exclamation or mild oath: *for heaven's sake*). **5** (**the heavens**) the sky as the abode of the sun, moon, and stars and regarded from earth. □ **the heavens opened** rain started to pour down. **in seventh heaven** in a state of ecstasy. **move heaven and earth** (foll. by *to* + infin.) make extraordinary efforts. □ **heaven·ward** *adjective & adverb* **heaven·wards** *adverb* [Old English *heofon*]

heav·en·ly *adjective* **1** of heaven; divine. **2** of the heavens or sky. **3** *informal* very pleasing; wonderful. □ **heav·en·li·ness** *noun*

heavenly body *noun* a natural object in outer space, e.g. the sun, a star, a planet, etc.; a celestial object.

heavenly hash *noun N Amer.* a flavour of ice cream combining chocolate ice cream, marshmallow, chocolate chunks, and chocolate-coated almonds.

heavenly host *noun see* HOST[1] 3.

heaven-sent *adjective* providential; wonderfully opportune.

heavier-than-air *adjective* (of an aircraft) weighing more than the air it displaces.

Heavi·side /ˈhevɪˌsaɪd/ **Oli·ver** (1850–1925), English physicist and electrical engineer. He contributed to long-distance telephone communication and cable and wireless telegraphy, and suggested the existence of what is now called the Heaviside layer in 1902.

Heaviside layer *noun* (in full **Heaviside–Kennelly layer**) = E-LAYER. [O. HEAVISIDE and A.E. KENNELLY]

heavy ● *adjective* (**heav·i·er**, **heav·i·est**) **1 a** of great or exceptionally high weight; difficult to lift. **b** (of a person) fat, overweight. **2 a** of great density. **b** *Physics* having a greater than the usual mass (esp. of isotopes and compounds containing them). **3** abundant, considerable (*a heavy crop*). **4** severe, intense, extensive, excessive (*heavy fighting; a heavy sleep*). **5** doing something to excess (*a heavy drinker*). **6 a** striking or falling with force (*heavy blows; heavy rain*). **b** (of a body of water) having large powerful waves. **7** (of rock music etc.) highly amplified with a strong beat. **8** (of machinery, artillery, etc.) very large of its kind; large in calibre etc. **9** causing a strong impact (*heavy drugs*). **10** needing much physical effort (*heavy work*). **11** (foll. by *with*) laden. **12** carrying heavy weapons (*the heavy brigade*). **13 a** (of a speech, writing, etc.) serious or sombre in tone or attitude; dull, tedious. **b** (of temperament) dignified, stern. **c** (of an issue etc.) grave; important, weighty. **14 a** (of food) hard to digest. **b** (of a literary work etc.) hard to read or understand. **15** (of bread etc.) too dense from not having risen. **16** (of ground) difficult to traverse or work. **17 a** oppressive; hard to endure (*a heavy fate; heavy demands*). **b** (of the atmosphere, weather, etc.) overcast; oppressive, sultry. **18 a** coarse, ungraceful (*heavy features*). **b** unwieldy. **19** sad, dejected (*a heavy heart*). **20** loud and deep in sound (*a heavy thud*). **21** *slang* **a** dangerous, threatening (*a heavy scene*). **b** excellent, cool. **c** important, profound. **22** strong, sturdy (*heavy canvas*). ● *noun* (*pl.* **-ies**) **1** *informal* a large violent person; a thug. **2** a villainous or tragic role or actor in a play etc. (usu. in *pl.*). **3** anything large or heavy of its kind, e.g. a piece of artillery. ● *adverb* heavily (esp. in *combination*: *heavy-laden*). □ **heavy on** using a lot of (*heavy on gas*). **make heavy weather of** *see* WEATHER. □ **heav·i·ly** *adverb* **heav·i·ness** *noun* [Old English *hefig* from Germanic, related to HEAVE]

heavy breathing *noun* breathing that is audible through being deep or laboured, esp. in sleep, as a result of exertion, or due to sexual excitement, esp. of an obscene phone caller. □ **heavy breather** *noun*

heavy chemicals *plural noun* bulk chemicals used in industry and agriculture.

heavy cream *noun N Amer.* = WHIPPING CREAM.

heavy-duty *adjective* **1** intended to withstand hard use. **2** *N Amer. informal* significant in size, amount, etc.

heavy-footed *adjective* awkward, ponderous.

heavy going *noun* slow or difficult to progress with (*found Proust heavy going*).

heavy-handed *adjective* **1** clumsy. **2** overbearing, oppressive. □ **heavy-handed·ly** *adverb* **heavy-handed·ness** *noun*

heavy-hearted *adjective* sad, doleful.

heavy hitter *noun N Amer. informal* an important or powerful person.

heavy hydrogen *noun* = DEUTERIUM.

heavy industry *noun* industry producing metal, machinery, etc.

heavy lifting *noun* **1** lifting of heavy objects. **2** *US informal* hard work.

heavy metal *noun* **1** (often *attributive*) a type of highly amplified, loud, vigorous rock music with a strong, usu. fast beat and often theatrical performance. **2** metal of high density. **3** heavy guns.

heavy oil *noun* **1** any oil of a high relative density. **2** such an oil obtained from coal tar by distillation.

heavy petting *noun* erotic fondling between two people involving stimulation of the genitals but stopping short of intercourse.

heavy-set *adjective* (of a person) stocky, burly.

heavy sleeper *noun* a person who sleeps deeply.

heavy water *noun* a form of water consisting of deuterium oxide, used as a moderator in nuclear reactors.

heavy weather *noun* **1** weather with high winds and waves, rain, etc. **2** difficult circumstances. □ **make heavy weather** encounter difficulties.

heavy·weight *noun* **1 a** a weight in certain sports, in the amateur boxing scale over 81 kg but differing for professional boxers and wrestlers (*attributive: heavyweight championship*). **b** a sportsman of this weight. **2** a person, animal, or thing of above average weight (also *attributive: heavyweight cotton*). **3** *informal* a person of influence or importance.

Heb. *abbreviation* Hebrews (New Testament).

heb·dom·adal /hɛbˈdɒmədəl/ *adjective formal* weekly, esp. meeting weekly. [Late Latin *hebdomadalis* from Greek *hebdomas, -ados* from *hepta* seven]

Hebe /ˈhiːbi/ **1** *Gk Myth* daughter of Hera and Zeus, and cupbearer of the gods. **2** *Astronomy* asteroid 6, discovered in 1847 (diameter 192 km). [Greek *hēbē* youthful beauty]

Hebei /həˈbeɪ/ (also **Hopeh** /hoːˈpeɪ/) a province of NE central China; capital, Shijiazhuang.

Hé·bert /eɪˈbɛːr/ **1 Anne** (1916–2000), Canadian poet, novelist and playwright. Her numerous plays, poems and novels, many of which have also been translated into English, feature characters who revolt in one way or another against the life which they are asked to lead. **2 Jacques** (b.1923), Canadian writer, publisher, and senator. After a career that included writing for *Le Devoir*, *Cité Libre*, and Radio-Canada as well as producing novels and non-fiction books, he was appointed to the Senate in 1983. **3 Louis** (*c.*1575–1627), French-Canadian colonist and apothecary. After visiting New France three times between 1604 and 1613, he settled in Quebec City with his family in 1617. His wife, Marie Rollet, was the first Frenchwoman to cultivate the soil of New France.

hebe·tude /ˈhɛbə̩tjuːd/ *noun literary* dullness, lethargy. [Late Latin *hebetudo* from *hebes, -etis* blunt]

Heb·raic /hɪˈbreɪɪk/ *adjective* of Hebrew or the Hebrews. [Late Latin from Greek *Hebraikos* (as HEBREW)]

Heb·ra·ism /ˈhiːbreɪˌɪzəm/ *noun* **1** a Hebrew idiom or expression, esp. in the Greek of the Bible. **2** an attribute of the Hebrews. **3** the Hebrew system of thought or religion. □ **Heb·raize** *transitive & intransitive verb* (also esp. *Brit.* **-raise**). [French *hébraïsme* or modern Latin *Hebraismus* from late Greek *Hebraïsmos* (as HEBREW)]

Heb·ra·ist /ˈhiːbreɪɪst/ *noun* a Hebrew scholar; an expert in Hebrew.

Heb·rew /ˈhiːbruː/ ● *noun* **1** a member of a Semitic people originally centred in ancient Palestine and having a descent traditionally traced from Abraham, Isaac, and Jacob. **2 a** the language of this people. **b** a modern form of this used esp. in Israel. ● *adjective* **1** of or in Hebrew. **2** of the Hebrews or the Jews. [Old French *Ebreu* from medieval Latin *Ebreus* from Latin *hebraeus* from Greek *Hebraios* from Aramaic *'ibray* from Hebrew *'ibrī* one from the other side (of the river)]

Hebrew Bible *noun* the sacred writings of Judaism, called by Christians the Old Testament, consisting of the Torah (the Law or Pentateuch), the Prophets, and the Hagiographa or Writings.

Hebrews /ˈhiːbruːz/ a book of the New Testament, traditionally included among the letters of St. Paul but now generally held to be non-Pauline.

Heb·ri·des, the /ˈhɛbrɪˌdiːz/ (also called **Western Isles**) a group of about 500 islands off the northwest coast of Scotland. The **Inner Hebrides** include the islands of Skye, Mull, Jura, Islay, Iona, Coll, Eigg, Rhum, Staffa and Tiree. The Little Minch separates this group from the **Outer Hebrides**, which include the islands of Lewis with Harris, Barra, Benbecula, North and South Uist, and the island group of St. Kilda. □ **Heb·ri·dean** /ˌhɛbrɪˈdiːən/ *adjective & noun*

Heb·ron /ˈhɛbrɒn/ a Palestinian city on the West Bank of the Jordan; pop. (est. 2002) 133,900. It is one of the most ancient cities in the Middle East, probably founded in the 18th c. BC. As the home of Abraham it is a holy city of both Judaism and Islam.

Heb·ros River /ˈhiːbrɒs/ (also **Heb·rus River**) the ancient Greek name for the MARITSA RIVER.

Hec·ate /ˈhɛkəti/ (also **Hekate**) *Gk Myth* a goddess of dark places, often associated with ghosts and sorcery. She is frequently identified with Artemis and Selene. [Greek, = the distant one]

Hecate Strait /ˈhɛkət/ a channel of the Canadian N Pacific, separating the Queen Charlotte Islands from mainland BC. [*Hecate*, survey ship of the Royal Navy *c.*1862]

heca·tomb /ˈhɛkə̩tuːm/ *noun* **1** *hist.* (in ancient Greece or Rome) a great public sacrifice, originally of 100 oxen. **2** any extensive sacrifice. [Latin *hecatombe* from Greek *hekatombē* from *hekaton* hundred + *bous* ox]

heck ● *interjection* a mild exclamation of surprise or dismay. ● *adverb* as an intensifier (*a heck of a job; what the heck are you doing?; beats the heck out of watching a movie*). □ **what the heck** expressing indifference, dismissal of a difficulty, etc. [alteration of HELL]

heckle ● *transitive verb* **1** interrupt and harass (a public speaker). **2** dress (flax or hemp). ● *noun* an act of heckling. □ **heck·ler** *noun* [Middle English, northern and eastern form of HACKLE]

heckuva *adjective & adverb informal* = HELLUVA. [alteration of 'heck of a']

hec·tare /ˈhɛktɛː/ *noun* a metric unit of land measure, equal to 100 ares (2.471 acres or 10,000 square metres). Abbr.: **ha**. [French (as HECTO-, ARE²)]

hec·tic ● *adjective* **1** busy and confused; characterized by feverish excitement or haste. **2** *Med. hist.* having a hectic fever; abnormally flushed. ● *noun Med. hist.* **1** a hectic fever or flush. **2** a patient suffering from this. □ **hec·tic·ally** *adverb* [Old French *etique* from Late Latin *hecticus* from Greek *hektikos* habitual, from *hexis* habit, assimilated to French *hectique* or Late Latin]

hectic fever *noun* (also **hectic flush**) *hist.* a fever which accompanies consumption and similar diseases, with flushed cheeks and hot dry skin.

hecto- *combining form* a hundred, esp. of a unit in the metric system. Abbr.: **h**. [French, irreg. from Greek *hekaton* hundred]

hecto·gram *noun* a metric unit of mass, equal to one hundred grams.

hecto·litre *noun* (also esp. *US* **hecto·liter**) a metric unit of capacity, equal to one hundred litres.

hecto·metre *noun* (also esp. *US* **hecto·meter**) a metric unit of length, equal to one hundred metres.

Hec·tor *Gk Myth* a Trojan warrior, son of Priam and Hecuba and husband of Andromache. He was killed by Achilles, who dragged his body three times round the walls of Troy.

hec·tor *verb* **1** *transitive* bully, intimidate. **2** *intransitive* brag, bluster, domineer. □ **hec·tor·ing** *adjective* **hec·tor·ing·ly** *adverb* [HECTOR, from its earlier use to mean 'swaggering fellow']

Hec·uba /ˈhɛkjʊbə/ *Gk Myth* the wife of King Priam of Troy, and mother of numerous sons, including Hector, Paris, and Troilus.

he'd *contraction* **1** he had. **2** he would.

hed·dle *noun* one of the sets of small cords or wires between which the warp is passed in a loom before going through the reed. [apparently from Old English *hefeld*]

he·der *var. of* CHEDER.

hedge ● *noun* **1** a fence or boundary formed by closely growing bushes or shrubs. **2** a protection against possible loss or diminution. **3** an equivocal or evasive statement. ● *verb* **1** *transitive* surround or bound with or as with a hedge. **2** *transitive* (foll. by *in*) enclose. **3 a** *transitive* reduce one's risk of loss on (a bet or speculation) by compensating transactions on the other side. **b** *intransitive* avoid a definite decision or commitment. **4** *intransitive* make or trim hedges. □ **hedge one's bets** protect oneself against loss or error by supporting more than one side in a contest, an argument, etc. □ **hedg·er** *noun* [Old English *hegg* from Germanic]

hedge fund *noun* an esp. offshore investment fund usu. formed as a private limited partnership that engages in speculation using credit or borrowed capital.

hedge·hog *noun* **1** any small nocturnal insect-eating mammal of the Old World genus *Erinaceus*, esp. *E. europaeus*, having a piglike snout and a coat of spines, and rolling itself up into a ball for defence. **2** a porcupine or other animal similarly covered with spines. [Middle English from HEDGE (from its habitat) + HOG (from its snout)]

hedge-hop *intransitive verb* fly at a very low altitude. □ **hedge-hopper** *noun* **hedge-hopping** *adjective & noun*

hedge·row *noun* a row of bushes etc. forming a hedge.

hedge trimmer *noun* an electric device for trimming hedges.

he·don·ic /hiːˈdɒnɪk, he-/ *adjective* **1** of or characterized by pleasure. **2** *Psych.* of pleasant or unpleasant sensations. [Greek *hēdonikos* from *hēdonē* pleasure]

hedon·ism /ˈhiːdəˌnɪzəm/ *noun* **1** belief in pleasure as the highest good and mankind's proper aim. **2** behaviour based on this; devotion to or pursuit of pleasure. □ **hedon·ist** *noun* **hedon·is·tic** /-ˈnɪstɪk/ *adjective* [Greek *hēdonē* pleasure]

-hedron /ˈhiːdrən, ˈhedrən/ *combining form* (*pl.* **-hedrons** or **-hedra** /-drə/) forming nouns denoting geometrical solids with various numbers or shapes of faces (*dodecahedron*; *rhombohedron*). □ **-hedral** *combining form*. [Greek *hedra* seat]

he·dys·arum /heˈdɪsərəm/ *noun* a leguminous plant of the genus *Hedysarum* including both poisonous species and those with edible roots, e.g. licorice root. [Greek name for some plant, *hedysaron*, used by Linnaeus]

heebie-jeebies *plural noun* (prec. by *the*) *slang* a state of nervous depression or anxiety. [20th c.: origin unknown]

heed ● *transitive verb* attend to; take notice of. ● *noun* careful attention. [Old English *hēdan* from West Germanic]

heed·ful *adjective* (often foll. by *of*) mindful, attentive; careful, cautious.

heed·less *adjective* (often foll. by *of*) inattentive, regardless; careless (*went out, heedless of the rain*). □ **heed·less·ly** *adverb* **heed·less·ness** *noun*

hee-haw ● *noun* the bray of a donkey. ● *intransitive verb* emit a braying sound. [imitative]

hee hee *interjection* representing laughter, esp. in amusement, derision, triumph, etc. [imitative]

heel¹ ● *noun* **1** the back part of the foot below the ankle. **2** the corresponding part in vertebrate animals. **3 a** the part of a sock etc. covering the heel. **b** the part of a shoe or boot supporting the heel. **c** (in *pl.*) high-heeled shoes. **4** a thing like a heel in form or position, e.g. the part of the palm next to the wrist, the end of a violin bow at which it is held, or the part of a golf club near where the head joins the shaft. **5** the crust end of a loaf of bread. **6** *informal* a person regarded with contempt or disapproval. **7** (as *interjection*) a command to a dog to walk close to a person's heels. **8** *Naut.* **a** the after end of a ship's keel and the lower end of the sternpost to which it is connected. **b** the lower end of a mast, boom, or bowsprit. ● *verb* **1** *transitive* fit or renew a heel on (a shoe or boot). **2** *intransitive* touch the ground with the heel as in dancing. **3** *intransitive* (of a dog) follow obediently at a person's heels. **4** *intransitive* (foll. by *out*) Rugby pass the ball with the heel. **5** *transitive* Golf strike (the ball) with the heel of the club. □ **at** (or **on**) **the heels of** following closely after (a person or event). **cool** (or *Brit.* **kick**) **one's heels** be kept waiting. **down at heel** *see* DOWN-AT-THE-HEELS. **take to one's heels** run away. **to heel 1** (of a dog) close behind. **2** (of a person etc.) under control. **turn on one's heel** turn sharply round. □ **heel·less** *adjective* [Old English *hēla*, *hæla* from Germanic]

heel² ● *verb* **1** *intransitive* (of a ship etc.) lean over owing to the pressure of wind or an uneven load (*compare* LIST²). **2** *transitive* cause (a ship etc.) to do this. ● *noun* the act or amount of heeling. [prob. from obsolete *heeld*, *hield* incline, from Old English *hieldan*, Old Saxon *-heldian* from Germanic]

Hefei /heˈfeɪ/ (also **Hofei** /hoːˈfeɪ/) an industrial city in E China, capital of Anhui province; pop. (est. 2002) 1,334,300.

heft ● *transitive verb* lift (something heavy), esp. to judge its weight. ● *noun* N Amer. *informal* weight, heaviness. [prob. from HEAVE after *cleft*, *weft*]

hefty *adjective* (**heft·i·er**, **heft·i·est**) **1** (of a person) big and strong. **2** (of a thing) large, heavy, powerful. **3** substantial, considerable (*a hefty fee increase*). □ **heft·i·ly** *adverb* **heft·i·ness** *noun*

Hegel /ˈheɪɡəl/ **Georg Wil·helm Frie·drich** (1770–1831), German philosopher. He is esp. known for his three-stage process of dialectical reasoning (set out in his *Science of Logic*, 1812–16), which underlies his idealist concepts of historical development and the evolution of ideas; Marx based his theory of dialectical materialism on this aspect of Hegel's work. □ **He·gel·ian** /həˈɡeɪlɪən/ **He·gel·ian·ism** *noun*

hegem·on *noun* a paramount leader.

hegem·onic /ˌhedʒəˈmɒnɪk/ *adjective* ruling or dominant in a political or social context.

he·gem·ony /həˈdʒeməni, ˈhedʒəˌmoːni/ *noun* (*pl.* **-onies**) leadership or dominance, esp. by one state or social group over others. [Greek *hēgemonia* from *hēgemōn* leader, from *hēgeomai* lead]

hegi·ra /ˈhedʒɪrə, hɪˈɡiːrə/ *noun* (also **hejira**, **hijra** /ˈhɪdʒrə/) **1** (**Hegira**) **a** Muhammad's departure from Mecca to Medina in AD 622. **b** the Muslim era reckoned from this date. **2** a general exodus or departure. [medieval Latin *hegira* from Arabic *hijra* departure from one's country, from *hajara* separate]

heh heh *interjection* expressing chuckling. [imitative]

Hei·deg·ger /ˈhaɪdeɡər/ **Mar·tin** (1889–1976), German philosopher whose works, such as *Being and Time* (1927), significantly influenced existentialist philosophers such as Sartre. □ **Hei·deg·ger·ian** *adjective & noun*

Hei·del·berg /ˈhaɪdəlˌbɜrɡ/ a city in SW Germany, on the Neckar River, in Baden-Württemberg; pop. (est. 2002) 138,100. It is noted for its university, which received its charter in 1386 and is the oldest in Germany, and for its medieval castle.

heif·er /ˈhefɜr/ *noun* **1** a female domestic bovine animal that has not borne a calf, or has borne only one calf. **2** *slang offensive* a woman. [Old English *heahfore*]

Hei·fetz /ˈhaɪfəts/ **Ja·scha** (1901–87), US violinist. Born in Russia, he was considered among the best in the world from the age of 13.

heigh-ho /heɪˈhoː/ *interjection* expressing boredom, resignation, etc. [imitative]

height *noun* **1** the measurement from base to top or (of a standing person) from head to foot. **2** the elevation above ground or a recognized level (usu. sea level). **3** any considerable elevation (*situated at a height*). **4** (often in *pl.*) **a** a high place or area. **b** rising ground. **c** the state of being high above the ground (*afraid of heights*). **5** the top of something. **6** *Typography* the distance from the foot to the face of type. **7 a** the most intense part or period of anything (*at its height*). **b** an extreme instance or example (*the height of fashion*). [Old English *hēhthu* from Germanic]

height·en *transitive & intransitive verb* make or become higher or more intense. □ **height·ened** *adjective*

height of land *noun* esp. *Cdn* a watershed.

Hei·long·jiang /ˌheɪlʊŋdʒˈjaŋ/ (also **Hei·lung·kiang** /-lʊŋˈjaŋ/) a province of NE China, on the Russian frontier; capital, Harbin.

Heil·tsuk /ˈhaɪltsʊk/ ● *noun* **1** (*pl.* same) a member of an Aboriginal group living on the islands and waterways of Milbanke Sound in BC. **2** the Wakashan language of this people. ● *adjective* of or relating to the Heiltsuk or their culture or language. [Heiltsuk, = 'people']

Heim·lich manoeuvre /ˈhaɪmlɪk/ *noun* a first aid procedure to dislodge a foreign object from the windpipe of a choking person by administering a sudden upward thrust of the fist to the victim's upper abdomen. [H.J. *Heimlich*, US surgeon b.1920]

Heine /ˈhaɪnə/ (**Chris·tian Jo·hann**) **Hein·rich** (born Harry Heine) (1797–1856), German poet, known esp. for his lyric poetry, particularly that in *Das Buch der Lieder* (1827), much of which was set to music by Schumann and Schubert.

heinie *noun* N Amer. *slang* the buttocks. [alteration of HINDER²]

hein·ous /ˈheɪnəs/ *adjective* (of a crime or criminal) utterly odious or wicked. □ **hein·ous·ly** *adverb* **hein·ous·ness** *noun* [Old French *haïneus*, ultimately from *hair* to hate, from Frankish]

Heinz 57 /haɪnz/ *noun slang* a mongrel, esp. a dog. [with reference to 'Heinz 57 Varieties', the slogan of H. J. Heinz Company condiment manufacturer]

heir /er/ *noun* **1** a person entitled to property or rank as the legal successor of its former owner (often foll. by *to*: *heir to the throne*). **2** a person deriving or morally entitled to some thing, quality, etc., from a predecessor. □ **heir·less** *adjective* **heir·ship** *noun* [Old French *eir* from Late Latin *herem* from Latin *heres -edis*]

heir apparent *noun* (*pl.* **heirs apparent**) **1** an heir whose claim cannot be set aside by the birth of another heir. **2** a person considered likely to succeed to another, e.g. as head of political party or corporation. ¶ This sense derives from a misunderstanding of the original meaning of *heir apparent* as 'seeming heir', but it is well established.

heir-at-law *noun* (*pl.* **heirs-at-law**) an heir by right of blood, esp. to the real property of an intestate.

heir·ess /ˈerəs/ *noun* **1** a woman entitled to property or rank as the legal successor of its former owner (often foll. by *to*: *heiress to a huge fortune*). **2** a woman deriving or morally entitled to some thing, quality, etc., from a predecessor.

heir·loom /ˈerluːm/ ● *noun* **1** a piece of personal property that has been in a family for several generations. **2** a piece of property received as part of an inheritance. ● *adjective* **1** of or designating seeds that have been passed down from one generation to another. **2** of or designating fruits or vegetables grown with these seeds. [HEIR + LOOM[1] in the sense 'tool']

heir presumptive *noun* (*pl.* **heirs presumptive**) an heir whose claim may be set aside by the birth of another heir.

Hei·sen·berg /ˈhaizənˌbɜrg/ **Wer·ner Karl** (1901–76), German mathematical physicist and philosopher, who developed a system of quantum mechanics based on matrix algebra. He was awarded the 1932 Nobel Prize for physics.

Heisenberg uncertainty principle *noun* see UNCERTAINTY PRINCIPLE.

heist /həist/ *N Amer. slang* ● *noun* a robbery. ● *transitive verb* rob. [representing a local pronunciation of HOIST]

Hejaz /hɪˈdʒaz/ (also **Hijaz**) a coastal region of W Saudi Arabia, extending along the Red Sea.

heji·ra *var. of* HEGIRA.

Hek·ate *see* HECATE.

Hekla /ˈheklə/ an active volcano in SW Iceland, rising to a height of 1 491 m (4,840 ft.).

Hel /hel/ (also **Hela** /ˈhelə/) *Scand. Myth* **1** the goddess of the underworld. **2** the underworld of the dead not killed in battle.

HeLa cell /ˈhelə/ *noun* (usu. in *pl.*) a human epithelial cell of a strain maintained in tissue culture since 1951 and used in research, esp. in virology. [Henrietta Lacks, whose cervical carcinoma provided the original cells]

held *past and past participle of* HOLD[1].

hel·den·tenor /ˈheldənteˌnɔr/ *noun* **1** a powerful tenor voice suitable for heroic roles in opera. **2** a singer with this voice. [German from *Held* a hero]

Helen *Gk Myth* the daughter of Zeus and Leda. In the Homeric poems, she is the wife of Menelaus, and her abduction by Paris (to whom she had been promised, as a bribe, by Aphrodite) leads to the Trojan War.

Hel·ena[1] /ˈhelənə/ the state capital of Montana; pop. (2000) 25,780.

Hel·ena[2] /ˈhelənə/ **St.** (*c.*255–*c.*330), Roman empress and mother of Constantine the Great. After converting to Christianity, she visited the Holy Land in 326, where, according to tradition, she found the cross on which Christ was crucified. Feast day (in the Eastern Church) 21 May; (in the Western Church) 18 Aug.

he·len·ium /heˈliːniəm/ *noun* any composite plant of the genus *Helenium*, with daisy-like flowers having prominent central discs. [modern Latin from Greek *helenion*, possibly commemorating Helen of Troy]

heli- *combining form* helicopter (*heliport*; *heli-fishing*).

he·li·acal /hɪˈlaiəkəl/ *adjective Astronomy* relating to or near the sun. [Late Latin *heliacus* from Greek *hēliakos* from *hēlios* sun]

heliacal rising *noun* (also **heliacal setting**) the first rising (or setting) of a star after (or before) a period of invisibility due to conjunction with the sun.

heli·an·the·mum /ˌhiːliˈanθəməm/ *noun* any evergreen shrub of the genus *Helianthemum*, with saucer-shaped flowers. *Also called* ROCK ROSE. [modern Latin from Greek *hēlios* sun + *anthemon* flower]

heli·an·thus /ˌhiːliˈanθəs/ *noun* any plant of the genus *Helianthus*, including the sunflower and Jerusalem artichoke. [modern Latin from Greek *hēlios* sun + *anthos* flower]

hel·ical /ˈhelikəl/ *adjective* having the form of a helix. □ **hel·ical·ly** *adverb* **heli·coid** *adjective & noun*

heli·ces *pl. of* HELIX.

heli·chry·sum /ˌheliˈkraizəm/ *noun* any composite plant of the genus *Helichrysum*, with flowers retaining their appearance when dried. [Latin from Greek *helikhrusos*, from *helix* spiral + *khrusos* gold]

he·li·city /həˈlisiti/ *noun* (*pl.* **-ties**) **1** esp. *Biochem.* helical character. **2** *Physics* a combination of the spin and the linear motion of a subatomic particle. [HELICAL + -ITY]

heli·con /ˈhelikɒn/ *noun* a large spiral bass tuba played encircling the player's head and resting on the shoulder. [Latin from Greek *Helikōn* Mount Helicon: later associated with HELIX]

Helicon, Mount /ˈhelikɒn/ a mountain in Boeotia, central Greece, to the north of the Gulf of Corinth, rising to 1 750 m (5741 ft.). It was believed by the ancient Greeks to be the home of the Muses.

heli·cop·ter ● *noun* a type of aircraft without wings, obtaining lift and propulsion from horizontally revolving overhead blades or rotors, and capable of moving vertically and horizontally. ● *transitive & intransitive verb* transport or fly by helicopter. [French *hélicoptère* from Greek *helix* (see HELIX) + *pteron* wing]

Heli·go·land /ˈheligoˌland/ a small island in the North Sea, one of the North Frisian Islands, off the coast of Germany.

heli-hiking *noun* hiking in remote locations accessible only by helicopter. □ **heli-hiker** *noun*

heli-logging *noun N Amer.* the removal of felled timber by helicopter. □ **heli-log** *transitive verb* **heli-logger** *noun*

helio- /ˈhiːlio/ *combining form* the sun. [Greek *hēlios* sun]

helio·cen·tric /ˌhiːlioˈsentrik/ *adjective* **1** having, representing, or regarding the sun as centre. **2** considered as viewed from the sun's centre. □ **helio·cen·trism** *noun*

He·lio·gaba·lus /ˌhiːlioˈɡabələs/ (also **Elagabalus** /ˌelə-/) (real name Varius Avitus Bassianus) (AD 204–22), Roman emperor 218–22. He was notorious for his dissipated lifestyle and neglect of state affairs, and was eventually murdered.

helio·graph /ˈhiːlioˌɡraf/ ● *noun* **1** a signalling apparatus reflecting sunlight in flashes from a movable mirror. **2** an apparatus for photographing the sun. ● *transitive verb* send (a message) by heliograph. □ **helio·graph·ic** *adjective*

heli·om·eter /ˌhiːliˈɒmɪtər/ *noun* a refracting telescope with a split objective lens, used to measure angular distances between stars etc. (originally used for measuring the diameter of the sun).

Heli·op·olis /ˌhiːliˈɒpəlis/ **1** an ancient Egyptian city situated near the apex of the Nile delta at what is now Cairo. It was an important religious centre and the centre of sun worship, and was the original site of the obelisks known as Cleopatra's Needles. **2** the ancient Greek name for BAALBEK. [Greek, = city of the sun]

He·li·os /ˈhiːliɒs/ *Gk Myth* the sun, personified as a god, father of Phaethon, often represented as a charioteer driving daily across the sky. In Rhodes he was the chief national god. [Greek *hēlios* sun]

helio·trope /ˈhiːlioˌtroːp/ *noun* **1 a** any plant of the genus *Heliotropium*, with fragrant purple flowers. **b** the scent of these. **2** a light purple colour. **3** bloodstone. [Latin *heliotropium* from Greek *hēliotropion* plant turning its flowers to the sun, from *hēlios* sun + *-tropos* from *trepō* turn]

helio·trop·ism /ˌhiːliˈɒtrəˌpizəm/ *noun* the directional growth of a plant in response to sunlight (*compare* PHOTOTROPISM). □ **helio·trop·ic** /ˌhiːlioˈtrɒpik/ *adjective*

heli·pad *noun* a landing pad for helicopters.

heli·port *noun* an airport or landing place for helicopters.

heli-skiing *noun* skiing in remote mountain locations accessible only by helicopter. □ **heli-skier** *noun*

heli·tack *noun* the use of helicopters to fight forest fires, e.g. to deploy ground crews or to transport and release extinguishing substances. [blend of HELICOPTER + ATTACK]

he·li·um /ˈhiːliəm/ *noun Chem.* a colourless, light, inert, gaseous element occurring in deposits of natural gas, used in airships and as a refrigerant. Symbol: **He**; at. no.: 2. [Greek *hēlios* sun (having been first identified in the sun's atmosphere)]

helix /ˈhiːliks/ *noun* (*pl.* **heli·ces** /ˈhiːliˌsiːz/) **1** an object of coiled form, either a spiral curve round an axis like a corkscrew or a coiled curve in one plane like a watchspring. **2** *Math.* a three-dimensional curve on a conical or cylindrical surface which becomes a straight line when the surface is unrolled into a plane. **3** *Archit.* a volute or spiral ornament. **4** *Anat.* the curved fold which forms the rim of the external ear. [Latin *helix -icis* from Greek *helix -ikos*]

hell ● *noun* **1 a** the abode of the dead; in Christian, Jewish, and Islamic belief, the place of punishment or torment where the souls of the damned are confined after death. **b** the kingdom, power, inhabitants, or forces of hell collectively. **2 a** a place or state of suffering, misery, or wickedness. **b** extreme chaos, turmoil, discord, etc. (*all hell broke loose*). ● *interjection informal* used as an exclamation of surprise, annoyance, etc. □ **as hell** *informal* as an intensifier (*sure as hell*). **beat** (or **knock, scare,** etc.) **the hell out of** *informal* beat, scare, etc. excessively, severely, or beyond all measure. **be hell on** *slang* be unpleasant or harmful to, tough on, etc. (**come**) **hell or high water** (through) great difficulties, (despite) any obstacles or problems. **for the hell of**

---

it *informal* for fun; on impulse. **from hell** *slang* indicating the worst possible example, instance, etc. (*the date from hell*). **get** (or **catch**) **hell** *informal* be severely scolded or punished. **give** (**a person**) **hell** *informal* **1** scold or punish (a person). **2** make things extremely difficult, challenging, or unpleasant for (a person, another team, etc.). **go to hell** be damned, get lost, go away. **the hell** (usu. prec. by *what, where, who, etc.*) expressing anger, disbelief, etc. or merely emphatic (*who the hell are you?; a hell of a mess*). **hell** (or **hell-bent**) **for leather** at full speed. **hell of a** (or **helluva**) exceedingly bad, good, remarkable, etc. (*one hell of an athlete*). **hell on wheels** a wild or terrible person or thing, esp. one of great speed or ferocity. **hell's bells** expressing anger or annoyance. **hell's half acre** a great distance. **hell to pay** great trouble, discord, pandemonium, etc., esp. as a result of previous action. **in hell** as an intensifier (*what in hell have you done?*). **like hell** *informal* **1** recklessly, desperately, exceedingly. **2** *ironic* not at all, on the contrary. **not a hope in hell** *informal* no chance at all. **play hell** (or **merry hell**) **with** *informal* **1** be upsetting or disruptive to. **2** damage. **raise hell** cause trouble, create chaos. **till** (or **until** or **when**) **hell freezes over** never or to (or at) some date in the impossibly distant future. **to hell** as an intensifier (*shot to hell*). **to hell and gone 1** a great distance. **2** endlessly, forever. **to hell with 1** expressing exasperated dismissal of (a person, thing, etc.). **2** endlessly, forever. **what the hell** *informal* expressing dismissal of a difficulty etc., i.e. it is of no importance. □ **hell-like** *adjective* **hell-ward** *adverb & adjective* [Old English *hel, hell* from Germanic]

he'll *contraction* he will; he shall.

hell·acious /he'leɪʃəs/ *adjective N Amer. slang* **1** hellish, extremely awful. **2** tremendous, spectacularly awesome. □ **hell·acious·ly** *adverb* [HELL + -*acious*, perhaps suggested by BODACIOUS]

Hel·lad·ic /he'ladɪk/ *adjective* of or belonging to the Bronze Age culture of mainland Greece, lasting from *c.*2800–*c.*1200 BC. [Greek *Helladikos* from *Hellas* -*ados* Greece]

hell-bent *adjective* (foll. by *on*) recklessly determined.

hell·cat *noun* a spiteful violent woman.

hell·diver *noun N Amer.* a small grebe.

hel·le·bore /'hɛlɪˌbɔr/ *noun* **1** any evergreen plant of the genus *Helleborus*, having large white, green, or purplish flowers, e.g. the Christmas rose. **2** a liliaceous plant, *Veratrum album*. **3** *hist.* any of various plants supposed to cure madness. **4** (in full **false hellebore**) *see* INDIAN POKE. [Old French *elebore* from Latin *elleborus* from Greek (*h*)*elleboros*]

hel·le·bor·ine /'hɛlɪbəˌriːn/ *noun* any orchid of the genus *Epipactis* or *Cephalanthera*. [French or Latin *helleborine* or Latin from Greek *helleborinē* plant like hellebore (as HELLEBORE)]

Hel·len *Gk Myth* the son or brother of Deucalion and ancestor of all the Hellenes or Greeks.

Hel·lene /'hɛliːn/ *noun* **1** a native or citizen of modern Greece. **2** an ancient Greek. □ **Hel·len·ic** /he'lɛnɪk/ *adjective* [Greek *Hellēn* a Greek]

Hel·len·ism /'hɛləˌnɪzəm/ *noun* **1** Greek character or culture (esp. of ancient Greece). **2** the study or imitation of Greek culture. □ **Hel·len·ize** *transitive & intransitive verb* (also esp. *Brit.* -**ise**). **Hel·len·iz·a·tion** *noun* [(as HELLENE)]

Hel·len·ist /'hɛlɪnɪst/ *noun* **1** an expert on Greek language or culture. **2** (in ancient times) a non-Greek, esp. a Jew, who adopted the Greek language, ideals, modes of dress, etc.

Hel·len·is·tic /ˌhɛləˈnɪstɪk/ *adjective* of or relating to the period of Greek history, language, and culture from the death of Alexander the Great in 323 BC to the defeat of Cleopatra and Mark Antony by Octavian in 31 BC, during which Greek culture spread through the Mediterranean and into the Near East and Asia.

Hel·ler, Jo·seph (1923–99), US novelist. His best-known novel is *Catch-22* (1961), an absurdist black comedy satirizing war.

Heller·work *noun* a form of alternative therapy which combines massage, body movements, and exploration of emotional issues. [J. *Heller*, US engineer b.1940 who developed the method]

Hel·les·pont /'hɛləsˌpɒnt/ the ancient name for the Dardanelles.

hell·fire *noun* **1** the fire or fires of hell. **2 a** the punishments and torments of hell. **b** (*attributive*) (esp. of preaching) emphasizing the damnation of unsaved souls and the eternal punishments of hell.

hell·gram·mite /'hɛlɡrəˌmaɪt/ *noun N Amer.* an aquatic larva of an insect, esp. the fly *Corydalus cornutus*, often used as fishing bait. [19th c.: origin unknown]

hell·hole *noun* an extremely oppressive or unbearable place.

hell-hound *noun* a fiend.

hel·lion *noun N Amer. informal* **1** a rowdy, troublemaking, disreputable person. **2** a rowdy, mischievous, or difficult child. [perhaps from dial. *hallion* a worthless fellow, assimilated to HELL]

hell·ish ● *adjective* **1** of or like hell. **2** *informal* extremely difficult or unpleasant. ● *adverb Brit. informal* (as an intensifier) extremely (*hellish expensive*). □ **hell·ish·ly** *adverb* **hell·ish·ness** *noun*

Hell·man, Lil·lian Flor·ence (1907–84), US dramatist. Her plays, such as *The Children's Hour* (1934), *The Little Foxes* (1939), and *Watch on the Rhine* (1941), frequently reflect her socialist and feminist political concerns.

hel·lo (also esp. *Brit.* **hallo, hullo**) ● *interjection* **1 a** an expression of informal greeting, or of surprise. **b** used to begin a telephone conversation. **2** used to call attention. **3** *N Amer.* used to reproach ignorance or inattention. ● *noun* (*pl.* -**los**) an instance of saying 'hello'. [var. of earlier *hollo*]

hell-rais·er *noun* a person who causes trouble or creates chaos, esp. habitually. □ **hell-rais·ing** *adjective & noun*

Hells Angel *noun* a member of a gang of motorcyclists notorious for violent behaviour and disturbances of the civil order.

Hells Canyon a chasm in Idaho, cut by the Snake River and forming the deepest gorge in the US. Flanked by the Seven Devils Mountains, the canyon drops to a depth of 2 433 m (7,900 ft.).

Hell's Gate *noun* a narrow gorge of the Fraser River Canyon, about 50 km north of Hope, BC, with dramatic rapids.

helluva *informal* = HELL OF A (*see* HELL).

helm¹ ● *noun* **1** a tiller or wheel by which a ship's rudder is controlled. **2** the amount by which this is turned (*more helm needed*). **3** a position of leadership or government. ● *transitive verb* **1** steer or guide with a helm. **2** lead; control. □ **at the helm** in control; at the head (of an organization etc.). [Old English *helma*, prob. related to HELVE]

helm² *noun archaic* a helmet. [Old English from Germanic]

Hel·mand /'hɛlmənd/ the longest river in Afghanistan. Rising in the Hindu Kush, it flows 1 125 km (700 miles), generally southwest, before emptying into marshland near the Iran–Afghanistan frontier.

Helm·cken Falls /'hɛlmkən/ a waterfall in east central BC, situated on the Murtle River, north of Kamloops. With a vertical drop of 137 m, it is the fifth highest waterfall in Canada. [J. S. *Helmcken*, Canadian physician and politician d.1920]

hel·met *noun* **1 a** any of various protective head coverings worn by soldiers, miners, athletes, motorcyclists, etc. **b** a device fitting over the head and including a screen on which virtual reality images are displayed. **2** *Bot.* the arched upper part of the corolla in some flowers. **3** the shell of a gastropod mollusc of the genus *Cassis*, used in jewellery. □ **hel·met·ed** *adjective* **helmet·less** *adjective* [Old French, diminutive of *helme* from West Germanic (as HELM²)]

Helm·holtz /'hɛlmhɒlts/ **Her·mann Lud·wig Fer·di·nand von** (1821–94), German physiologist and physicist. He formulated the principle of the conservation of energy in 1847, and contributed to the study of sense perception, nerve impulses, hydrodynamics and electric currents.

hel·minth /'hɛlmɪnθ/ *noun* any of various parasitic worms including flukes, tapeworms, and nematodes. □ **hel·minth·ic** /-ˈmɪnθɪk/ *adjective* **hel·minth·oid** /-ˈmɪnθɔɪd/ *adjective* **hel·minth·ol·ogy** /-mɪnˈθɒlədʒi/ *noun* [Greek *helmins* -*inthos* intestinal worm]

hel·minth·ia·sis /ˌhɛlmɪnˈθaɪəsɪs/ *noun* a disease characterized by the presence of any of several parasitic worms in the body.

Hel·mont /'hɛlmɒnt/ **Jo·an·nes Bap·tis·ta van** (1597–1644), Belgian chemist and physician. He made early studies on the conservation of matter, was the first to distinguish gases, and coined the word *gas*.

helms·man *noun* (*pl.* -**men**) a person who steers a ship. □ **helms·man·ship** *noun*

helo /'hiːloʊ/ *noun N Amer. slang* a helicopter.

Hé·lo·ïse /ˌeloˈiːz/ (1098–1164), French abbess. She is chiefly remembered for her passionate but tragic love affair with Abelard, which began after she became his pupil *c.*1118. After giving birth to a son, she was forced by relatives to enter a convent.

hel·ot /'hɛlət/ *noun* **1** a slave or serf. **2** (esp. **Helot**) a member of a class of serfs in ancient Sparta, intermediate in status between slaves and citizens. □ **helot·ism** *noun* **hel·otry** *noun* [Latin *helotes* pl. from Greek *heilōtes*, -*ōtai*, erroneously taken as = inhabitants of *Helos*, a Laconian town]

help ● *verb* **1** *transitive* aid, assist, or provide (a person etc.) with what is needed or sought (*helped me with my work; helped me (to) pay my debts*). **2** *transitive* (foll. by *up, down, on with*, etc.) assist or give support to (a person) in moving etc. as specified (*helped her into the chair; helped him on *with his coat).* **3 a** *transitive & intransitive* benefit, do good to, or be of use or service to (a person) (*does that help?*). **b** *transitive* assist in achieving, promote, further, or make (an action, process, etc.) more effective. **4** *transitive* contribute to alleviating (a pain, difficulty, misfortune, etc.). **5** *transitive* prevent, remedy, or cause to be otherwise (*it can't be helped*). **6** (usu. with *neg.*) **a** *transitive* refrain from (*could not help laughing*). **b** *reflexive* refrain from acting (*couldn't help himself*). **7** *transitive* (often foll. by *to*) serve (food etc.) (*help yourself to the butter tarts*). ● *noun* **1** aid, assistance, or the act of helping or being helped (*we need your help*). **2** a source or means of assistance, esp. a person or thing that helps. **3** an employee or domestic servant, or several collectively. **4** a remedy or escape (*there is no help for it*). □ **can't** (or **cannot**) **help but** be obliged to or unable to do other (*can't help but share his worry*). **help oneself** (often foll. by *to*) **1** serve oneself (with food). **2** take without seeking help or permission. **help a person out** give a person help, esp. in difficulty. **not if I can help it** not if I can prevent it. **so help me** (or **help me God**) (as an invocation or oath) as I keep my word, as I speak the truth, etc. □ **help·er** *noun* [Old English *helpan* from Germanic]

help·desk *noun* a service which assists customers or users who have problems with esp. computer equipment or software.

help·ful *adjective* (of a person or thing) giving or productive of help; useful. □ **help·ful·ly** *adverb* **help·ful·ness** *noun*

help·ing *noun* **1** a portion of food esp. at a meal. **2** a portion of something offered (*generous helpings of propaganda*).

helping hand *noun* an act of assistance.

helping profession *noun* one of the professions whose function is to provide help to people, e.g. medicine, social work, teaching, ministry, etc. □ **helping professional** *noun*

help·less *adjective* **1** unable to function independently or act without help. **2** lacking help or protection; defenceless. **3** unable to help. □ **help·less·ly** *adverb* **help·less·ness** *noun*

help·line *noun* a telephone service providing help and advice, either for personal problems or for an item one has bought.

help·mate *noun* (also **help·meet**) a helpful companion or partner, usu. a spouse. [*helpmeet* from an erroneous reading of Gen. 2:18, 20, where Adam's future wife is described as 'an help meet for him', i.e. a suitable helper for him)]

help-wanted index *noun* Cdn a rough, seasonally adjusted measure of the job market calculated from help-wanted advertisements in newspapers.

Hel·sin·ki /hel'sɪŋki/ the capital of Finland, a port in the south on the Gulf of Finland; pop. (2001) 559,128.

helter-skelter ● *adverb & adjective* in disorderly haste, random order, or confusion. ● *noun* **1** disorder or confusion. **2** *Brit.* a tall spiral slide round a tower, at a fairground etc. [imitative, originally in a rhyming jingle, perhaps from Middle English *skelte* hasten]

helve /helv/ *noun* the handle or shaft of a weapon or a tool. [Old English *helfe* from West Germanic]

Hel·ve·tian /hel'viːʃən/ ● *adjective* Swiss. ● *noun* a native of Switzerland. [Latin *Helvetia* Switzerland]

Hel·vet·ica /hel'vetɪkə/ *noun* proprietary a sans serif typeface.

Hel·vé·tius /hel'viːʃəs/ **Claude Ad·rien** (1715–71), French philosopher. In his best-known work, *De l'Esprit* (1758), he argues that human action arises out of self-interest, and that differences in intellect are strictly due to differences in education.

hem¹ ● *noun* **1** the border of a piece of cloth, esp. a cut edge turned under and sewn down. **2** HEMLINE. ● *transitive verb* (**hemmed**, **hem·ming**) turn under and sew in the edge of (a piece of cloth etc.). □ **hem in** confine; restrict the movement of. □ **hem·mer** *noun* [Old English, perhaps related to dial. *ham* enclosure]

hem² ● *interjection* calling attention or expressing hesitation by a slight cough or clearing of the throat. ● *noun* an utterance of this. ● *intransitive verb* (**hemmed**, **hem·ming**) say *hem*; hesitate in speech. □ **hem and haw** hesitate in speaking, esp. through indecision, disagreement, etc. [imitative]

hem·ag·glu·tin·ate /hiːmə'gluːtɪneit/ *transitive verb* (also esp. *Brit.* **haem·ag·glu·tin·ate**) cause (red blood cells) to coagulate. □ **hem·ag·glu·tin·a·tion** /hiːmə,gluːtɪ'neiʃən/ *noun* (also esp. *Brit.* **haem·ag·glu·tin·a·tion**). [HEMO- + AGGLUTINATE]

hem·ag·glu·tin·in /hiːmə'gluːtɪnɪn/ *noun* (also esp. *Brit.* **haem·ag·glu·tin·in**) a substance, such as a viral protein, which causes hemagglutination.

hemal /'hiːməl/ *adjective* (also esp. *Brit.* **haem·al**) *Anat.* **1** of or concerning the blood or circulatory system. **2 a** belonging to, situated on, or

towards the same side of the body as the heart and major blood vessels. **b** (esp. with reference to animals) ventral. [Greek *haima* blood]

he-man *noun* (*pl.* **-men**) *informal* often *ironic* a particularly strong, masterful, or virile man.

he·mat·ic /hi'matɪk/ *adjective* (also esp. *Brit.* **hae·mat·ic**) *Med.* **1** of or containing blood. **2** acting on the blood. [Greek *haimatikos* (as HEMATIN)]

hema·tin /'hiːmətɪn/ *noun* (also esp. *Brit.* **haema·tin**) *Anat.* a bluish-black derivative of hemoglobin, formed by removal of the protein part and oxidation of the iron atom. [Greek *haima -matos* blood]

hema·tite /'hiːmə,tait/ *noun* (also esp. *Brit.* **haema·tite**) ferric oxide occurring as a dark red mineral which constitutes an important ore of iron. [Latin *haematites* from Greek *haimatitēs* (*lithos*) blood-like (stone) (as HEMATIN)]

hemato- /'hiːməto/ *combining form* (also esp. *Brit.* **haemato-**) = HEMO-. [Greek *haima haimat-* blood]

hema·to·cele /'hiːməto,siːl/ *noun* (also esp. *Brit.* **haema·to·cele**) *Med.* a swelling caused by blood collecting in a body cavity.

hema·to·crit /'hiːməto,krɪt/ *noun* (also esp. *Brit.* **haema·to·crit**) *Physiol.* **1** the ratio of the volume of red blood cells to the total volume of blood. **2** an instrument for measuring this. [HEMATO- + Greek *kritēs* judge]

hema·tol·ogy /,hiːmə'tɒlədʒi/ *noun* (also esp. *Brit.* **haema·tol·ogy**) the branch of medicine that deals with the blood, esp. in disorders. □ **hema·to·logic** /-tə'lɒdʒɪk/ *adjective* **hema·to·logic·al** /-tə'lɒdʒɪkəl/ *adjective* **hema·tol·o·gist** *noun*

hema·toma /,hiːmə'toːmə/ *noun* (also esp. *Brit.* **haema·toma**) *Med.* a solid swelling of clotted blood within the tissues.

hema·toxy·lin /,hiːmə'tɒksəlɪn/ *noun* (also esp. *Brit.* **haema·toxy·lin**) *Chem.* a colourless crystalline polycyclic phenol present in logwood that can be easily converted into red, blue, or purple dyes and used as a biological stain. [modern Latin *Haematoxylum* genus name for logwood, as HEMATO- + Greek *xulon* wood]

hema·turia /,hiːmə'tjuriə/ *noun* (also esp. *Brit.* **haema·turia**) *Med.* the presence of blood in urine.

heme /hiːm/ *noun* (also esp. *Brit.* **haem**) a non-protein compound containing iron, and responsible for the red colour of hemoglobin. [Greek *haima* blood, or from HEMOGLOBIN]

hem·ero·cal·lis /,hemərə'kalɪs/ *noun* = DAY LILY. [Latin *hemerocalles* from Greek *hēmerokalles*, a kind of lily, from *hēmera* 'day' + *kallos* 'beauty']

hemi- /'hemi/ *combining form* half. [Greek *hēmi-* = Latin *semi-*: see SEMI-]

-hemia var. of -EMIA.

hemi·cellu·lose /hemi'selju,loːz, -s/ *noun* any of various polysaccharides forming the matrix of plant cell walls in which cellulose is embedded.

hemi·chord·ate /hemi'kɔːdeit/ ● *noun* a wormlike marine invertebrate of the phylum *Hemichordata*, comprising the acorn worms, possessing a notochord in the larval stage. ● *adjective* of or relating to this phylum.

hemi·demi·semi·quaver /'hemidemi,semikweivɜr/ *noun* Brit. Music = SIXTY-FOURTH NOTE.

hemi·hed·ral /hemi'hiːdrəl/ *adjective* (of a crystal) having half the number of planes required for symmetry of the holohedral form.

Hem·ing·way, Er·nest (Mil·ler) (1899–1961), US novelist. His early novels (such as *The Sun also Rises*, 1926, and *A Farewell to Arms*, 1929) reflect the disillusionment of the postwar 'lost generation', while in his later works (such as *For Whom the Bell Tolls*, 1940, and *The Old Man and the Sea*, 1952) there is a developing theme of strength and dignity of the human spirit. He was awarded the Nobel Prize for literature in 1954. □ **Hem·ing·way·esque** *adjective*

hemi·ola /,hiːmi'oːlə, hem-/ *noun* Music a rhythmic device consisting of superimposing two notes in the time of three, or three in the time of two, e.g. two dotted quarter notes in a 3/4 bar. [medieval Latin *hemiolia* from Greek *hēmiolia*, *-lios*, in the ratio of one and a half to one, from as HEMI- + *holos* whole]

hemi·plegia /hemi'pliːdʒiə/ *noun* Med. paralysis of one side of the body. □ **hemi·plegic** *noun & adjective* [modern Latin from Greek *hēmiplēgia* 'paralysis' (as HEMI-, *plēgē* 'stroke')]

hem·ip·ter·ous /he'mɪptərəs/ *adjective* of the insect order *Hemiptera* including aphids, bugs, and cicadas, with piercing or sucking mouthparts. [HEMI- + Greek *pteron* 'wing']

hemi·sphere /'hemisfiːr/ *noun* **1** a half of the earth, esp. as divided by the equator (into *northern* and *southern hemisphere*) or by an imaginary line passing through the poles (into *eastern* and *western hemisphere*). **2** *Anat.* (in full **cerebral hemisphere**) each of the halves of the cerebrum. **3** half of a sphere. □ **hemi·spher·al** *adjective* **hemi·spher·ic** *adjective* **hemi·spher·ic·al** *adjective* **hemi·spher·ic·al·ly** *adverb*

hemi·stich /ˈhemɪstɪk/ *noun* a half of a line of verse or a line of less than the usual length. [Late Latin *hemistichium* from Greek *hēmistikhion* (as HEMI-, *stikhos* 'line')]

Hem·kund, Lake /hemˈkund/ a lake in N India, in the Himalayan foothills of Uttar Pradesh. It is regarded as holy by Sikhs.

hem·line *noun* the line or level of the lower edge of a skirt, dress, or coat.

hem·lock *noun* **1 a** a poisonous umbelliferous plant, *Conium maculatum*, with fern-like leaves and small white flowers. **b** a poisonous potion obtained from this. **2** (in full **hemlock fir** or **hemlock spruce**) **a** any coniferous tree of the genus *Tsuga*, having foliage that smells like hemlock when crushed. **b** the timber or pitch of these trees. [Old English *hymlic(e)*]

hemo- /ˈhiːmoʊ/ *combining form* (also esp. *Brit.* **haemo-**) blood. [abbreviation of HEMATO-]

hemo·coel /ˈhiːməsiːl/ *noun* (also esp. *Brit.* **haemo·coel** /ˈhiːm-, ˈhem-/) *Zool.* the primary body cavity of most invertebrates, containing circulatory fluid. [HEMO- + Greek *koilos* 'hollow, cavity']

hemo·cya·nin /ˌhiːməˈsaɪənɪn/ *noun* (also esp. *Brit.* **haemo·cya·nin** /ˌhiː-, -hem-/) an oxygen-carrying substance containing copper, present in the blood plasma of arthropods and molluscs, that is blue when oxygenated and colourless otherwise. [HEMO- + *cyanin* blue pigment (as CYAN)]

hemo·di·aly·sis /ˌhiːmoʊdaɪˈælɪsɪs/ *noun* (also esp. *Brit.* **haemo·di·aly·sis**) = DIALYSIS 2.

hemo·glo·bin /ˈhiːməˌɡloʊbɪn/ *noun* (also esp. *Brit.* **haemo·glo·bin** /ˌhiː-, -he-/) a red, oxygen-carrying substance containing iron, present in the red blood cells of vertebrates. [shortened from *hematoglobin*, compound of HEMATIN + GLOBULIN]

hemo·lymph /ˈhiːməlɪmf/ *noun* (also esp. *Brit.* **haemo·lymph** /ˈhiː-', ˈhe-/) a fluid equivalent to blood in invertebrate animals.

he·moly·sis /hiːˈmɒlɪsɪs/ *noun* (also esp. *Brit.* **hae·moly·sis** /hiː-, he-/) the loss of hemoglobin from red blood cells. □ **hemo·lytic** /-məˈlɪtɪk/ *adjective*

Hémon /eiˈmɔ̃/ **Louis** (1880–1913), French-born Canadian novelist who immigrated to Canada in 1911. His novel *Maria Chapdelaine: récit du Canada français* (published posthumously in 1914) depicted Québécois peasant life in the Lac Saint-Jean region and earned him worldwide fame.

hemo·philia /ˌhiːməˈfiːliə/ *noun* (also esp. *Brit.* **haemo·philia**) a usu. hereditary disorder with a tendency to bleed severely from even a slight injury, through the failure of the blood to clot normally. □ **hemo·phil·ic** *adjective* [modern Latin (as HEMO-, -PHILIA)]

hemo·phil·iac /ˌhiːməˈfiːliˌak/ *noun* (also esp. *Brit.* **haemo·phil·iac** /ˌhiː-, -he-/) a person with hemophilia.

hem·or·rhage /ˈheməridʒ/ (also esp. *Brit.* **haem·or·rhage**) ● *noun* **1** an escape of blood from a ruptured blood vessel, esp. when profuse. **2** a damaging or uncontrolled outflow of something, esp. of people or assets from a country, organization, etc. ● *verb* **1** *intransitive* undergo a hemorrhage; bleed heavily. **2** *intransitive* be extensively lost or dissipated. **3** *transitive* expend (money etc.) in large amounts; lose or dissipate, esp. wastefully (*Bay Street has been hemorrhaging jobs since the recession*). □ **hem·or·rhag·ic** /ˌheməˈradʒɪk/ *adjective* [ultimately from Greek *haimorrhagia* from *haima* blood + stem of *rhēgnumi* burst]

hem·or·rhoid /ˈheməˌrɔɪd/ *noun* (also esp. *Brit.* **haem·or·rhoid**) (usu. in *pl.*) swollen veins at or near the anus; piles. □ **hem·or·rhoid·al** /-ˈrɔɪdəl/ *adjective* [Greek *haimorrhoides* (*phlebes*) bleeding (veins) from *haima* blood, *-rhoos* -flowing]

hemo·stat /ˈhiːmoʊˌstat/ *noun* (also esp. *Brit.* **haemo·stat**) an instrument for stopping the flow of blood by compression of a blood vessel. □ **hemo·stat·ic** *adjective*

hemp *noun* **1** (in full **Indian hemp**) a herbaceous plant, *Cannabis sativa*, native to Asia. **2** its fibre extracted from the stem and used to make rope and stout fabrics. **3** any of several narcotic drugs made from the hemp plant (*compare* CANNABIS, MARIJUANA). **4** any of several other plants yielding fibre, including manila hemp. [Old English *henep*, *hænep* from Germanic, related to Greek *kannabis*]

hemp agrimony *noun* a composite plant, *Eupatorium cannabinum*, with pale-purple flowers and hairy leaves.

hemp·en *adjective* made from or resembling hemp.

hemp nettle *noun* any of various nettle-like plants of the genus *Galeopsis*.

hem·stitch ● *noun* a decorative stitch used in sewing hems. ● *transitive verb* hem with this stitch. □ **hem·stitch·ing** *noun*

hen *noun* **1 a** a female bird, esp. of a domestic fowl. **b** (in *pl.*) domestic fowls of either sex. **2** a female lobster or crab or salmon. □ **rare as hen's teeth** exceedingly rare. [Old English *henn* from West Germanic]

Henan /həˈnan/ (also **Honan** /hoːˈnan/) a province of NE central China; capital, Zhengzhou.

hen and chickens *noun* any of several plants, esp. the houseleek.

hen·bane *noun* **1** a poisonous herbaceous plant, *Hyoscyamus niger*, with sticky hairy leaves and an unpleasant smell. **2** a narcotic drug obtained from this.

hence *adverb* **1** from this time (*two years hence*). **2 a** for this reason; as a result of inference (*hence we seem to be wrong*). **b** from this source, fact, or circumstance. **3** *archaic* from here; from this place. [Middle English *hens*, *hennes*, *henne* from Old English *heonan* from the root of HE]

hence·forth *adverb* (also **hence·for·ward**) from this time onward.

hench·man *noun* (*pl.* **-men**) **1** usu. *derogatory* **a** a trusted supporter or faithful follower who always obeys the orders of his or her leader. **b** an often unscrupulous, self-serving, and ambitious subordinate or lackey. **2** *hist.* a squire; a page of honour. [Middle English *henxman*; *hengestman* from Old English *hengst* male horse]

Hen·day /ˈhendei/ **An·thony** (*fl.*1750–62), Canadian explorer. An employee of the Hudson's Bay Company at York Factory, he volunteered to lead a party into the interior in 1754–55 to encourage greater trade in furs. In this journey he travelled further west than any European explorer had done previously, reaching a camp of Gros Ventre near the present site of Red Deer, Alberta.

hendeca- /henˈdekə/ *combining form* eleven. [Greek *hendeka* eleven]

Hen·der·son, Ar·thur (1863–1935), British Labour politician, foreign secretary (1929–31). Henderson supported the League of Nations and international disarmament, and was awarded the Nobel Peace Prize in 1934.

hen·dia·dys /henˈdaɪədɪs/ *noun* the expression of an idea by two words connected with 'and', instead of one modifying the other, e.g. *nice and warm* for *nicely warm*. [medieval Latin from Greek *hen dia duoin* one thing by two]

Hen·drix, Jimi (born James Marshall Hendrix) (1942–70), US rock guitarist and singer, one of the first to develop the potential of the electric guitar. His best-known singles include 'Purple Haze' (1967) and 'All Along the Watchtower' (1968).

hene·quen /ˈhenɪˌken/ *noun* **1** a Mexican agave, *Agave fourcroydes*. **2** the sisal-like fibre obtained from this. [Spanish *jeniquen*]

henge /hendʒ/ *noun* any large circular monument, usu. of later neolithic date, comprising a bank and internal ditch which may enclose massive stone or wooden structures. [back-formation from STONEHENGE]

Hen·gist and Horsa /ˈheŋɡɪst, ˈhɔrsə/ (d.488 & d.455), semi-mythological Jutish leaders. According to Bede, the brothers were invited to Britain by the British king Vortigern in 449 to assist in defeating the Picts, and later established an independent Anglo-Saxon kingdom in Kent.

hen·house *noun* a building in which poultry roost.

Henie /ˈheni/ **Sonja** (1912–69), Norwegian figure skater, winner of ten world championships (1927–36).

Hen·ley *noun* N Amer. (usu. *attributive*) a long-sleeved pullover with a round neckline and a short buttoned placket. [possibly alluding to Henley in England, where prestigious rowing races are held]

hen·na ● *noun* **1** a tropical shrub, *Lawsonia inermis*, having small pink, red, or white flowers. **2** the reddish dye from its shoots and leaves esp. used to colour hair. ● *transitive verb* dye (hair) with henna. □ **hen·naed** *adjective* [Arabic *ḥinnā*]

hen party *noun* informal derogatory a social gathering of women.

hen·peck *transitive verb* (of a woman) constantly harass, nag, or domineer over (a man, esp. her husband). □ **hen·pecked** *adjective*

Henry ▸ **1** (**'the Navigator'**) (1394–1460), Portuguese prince. The third son of John I of Portugal, he was a leading patron of voyages of exploration. **2** **Jo·seph** (1791–1878), US physicist. He conducted extensive research into electromagnetism, and constructed the first electromagnetic motor (1829). **3** **Mar·tha** (b.1938), American-born Canadian actress. In her association with the Stratford Festival from

1962, Henry has performed most of Shakespeare's major roles as well as a wide range of other parts. She has also starred in several films, including the film adaptation of Timothy Findley's *The Wars* (1984), and has won three Genie awards. **4 O.** (pseudonym of William Sidney Porter) (1862–1910), US short-story writer, whose works are characterized by irony and plots frequently dependent on coincidence and the surprise ending; they are collected in volumes such as *Cabbages and Kings* (1904) and *The Four Million* (1906). **5 Pat·rick** (1736–99), US statesman, a leading opponent of British rule during the American Revolution. **6 Wil·liam Alex·an·der** (1816–1888), Canadian lawyer, politician, and judge. After service as an MLA and cabinet minister in Nova Scotia under both the Liberals and Conservatives, Henry was a delegate to all three Confederation conferences and may have helped draft the BNA Act. He was appointed to the Supreme Court in 1875.

Henry I (1068–1135), king of England 1100–35. Youngest son of William I, he established a bureaucracy to support the English monarchy and set up a system of travelling judges.

Henry II ▶ 1 (1133–89), king of England 1154–89. The first Plantagenet king, he restored order after the civil war of 1139–53, but his reign was overshadowed by his dispute with Thomas Becket over the rights of the church. **2** (1519–59), king of France 1547–59. He recovered Calais from England, and suppressed the Huguenots.

Henry III ▶ 1 (1207–72), king of England 1216–72. Unpopular because of his financial mismanagement and his reliance on foreign advisers, he was deposed in 1264. He was restored the next year, but most of the real power in the kingdom passed to his son, who eventually succeeded him as Edward I. **2** (1551–1589), king of France 1574–1589. The last of the Valois kings, he continued the wars of religion and nearly bankrupted France.

Henry IV ▶ 1 (1050–1106), king of Germany (1056–1105) and Holy Roman Emperor (1084–1105). He was excommunicated twice by Pope Gregory VII, whom he eventually deposed. **2** (known as 'Henry Bolingbroke') (1367–1413), son of John of Gaunt, king of England 1399–1413. He returned from exile in 1399 to overthrow Richard II and establish the Lancastrian dynasty. His reign was scarred by rebellion, both in Wales and in the north. **3** (known as 'Henri of Navarre') (1553–1610), king of France 1589–1610. He founded the Bourbon dynasty, established religious freedom with the Edict of Nantes (1598), and restored order after prolonged civil war.

Henry V (1387–1422), son of Henry IV, king of England 1413–22. He renewed the Hundred Years War soon after coming to the throne and defeated the French at Agincourt in 1415.

Henry VI (1421–71), king of England 1422–61 and 1470–71. He proved too unfit to rule effectively on his own. During his reign the Hundred Years War was lost, and after intermittent civil war, he was deposed in 1461 by Edward IV. In 1470 Henry briefly regained his throne, but was deposed again and murdered soon after.

Henry VII (known as 'Henry Tudor') (1457–1509), the first Tudor king of England (1485–1509). In 1485 he returned from exile in France to defeat and kill Richard III at Bosworth Field. As king he modernized and strengthened the system of royal government.

Henry VIII (1491–1547), son of Henry VII, king of England 1509–47. He divorced his first wife, Catherine of Aragon, breaking with the Roman Church to do so, and dissolved the monasteries in England. He had six wives, two of whom he had executed and two of whom he divorced.

henry *noun* (*pl.* **-ries** or **henrys**) *Electricity* the SI unit of inductance which gives an electromotive force of one volt in a closed circuit with a uniform rate of change of current of one ampere per second. Abbr.: **H.** [J. HENRY]

Hen·son, Jim (1936–90), US puppeteer. He created the Muppets, including Kermit the Frog, Miss Piggy, and Big Bird.

Henze /'hentsə/ **Hans Wer·ner** (b.1926), German composer and conductor. His abundant and diverse works, influenced by serialism, classical composers, and Italian opera, sometimes reflect his left-wing ideals, such as in *The Raft of the Medusa* (1968) (a requiem for Che Guevara) and the opera *We Come to the River* (1974–6).

hep¹ *var. of* HIP³.

hep² *Brit. var. of* HIP².

hep³ *noun informal* hepatitis. [abbreviation]

HEPA /'hepə/ *abbreviation* high efficiency particulate air (HEPA *filter*).

hep·ar·in /'hepərɪn/ *noun Biochem.* a sulphur-containing polysaccharide with anticoagulant properties, present in the blood and various bodily organs and tissues. □ **hep·ar·in·iz·a·tion** *noun* **hep·ar·in·ized** *adjective* [Latin from Greek *hēpar* liver]

hep·atic /hɪ'patɪk/ *adjective* **1** of or relating to the liver. **2** dark brownish red; liver-coloured. [Latin *hepaticus* from Greek *hēpatikos* from *hēpar -atos* liver]

hep·at·ica /hɪ'patɪkə/ *noun* any plant of the genus *Hepatica*, with reddish-brown lobed leaves resembling the liver. [medieval Latin fem. of *hepaticus*: see HEPATIC]

hepa·titis /ˌhepə'təitɪs/ *noun* inflammation of the liver. [modern Latin: see HEPATIC]

hepatitis A *noun* a form of viral hepatitis transmitted in food, causing fever and jaundice. *Also called* INFECTIOUS HEPATITIS.

hepatitis B *noun* a severe form of viral hepatitis transmitted in infected blood and other body fluids, causing fever, debility, and jaundice. *Also called* SERUM HEPATITIS.

hepatitis C *noun* a very serious form of hepatitis, transmitted through untreated blood and blood products and often resulting in chronic disease. *Also called* NON-A, NON-B HEPATITIS.

hepato- /'hepatoː/ *combining form* liver. [Greek *hēpar, hēpat-* liver]

Hep·burn ▶ 1 Aud·rey (1929–93), US actress, born in Belgium. After a career as a stage and film actress in England, she moved to Hollywood, where she starred in such films as *Roman Holiday* (1953), for which she won an Oscar, and the film musical *My Fair Lady* (1964). **2 Kath·ar·ine** (1909–2003), US actress. Her films include *The Philadelphia Story* (1940), *Woman of the Year* (1942), *The African Queen* (1952), and *On Golden Pond* (1981), for which she won her fourth Oscar. **3 Mitch·ell Fred·erick** (1896–1953), Canadian Liberal politician. As premier of Ontario (1934–42) he broke with Prime Minister King over the 1937 strike at General Motors in Oshawa; the dispute with King ruined both Hepburn's health and the provincial Liberals.

hep·cat *noun slang* **1** a jazz musician. **2** a hip person. [HEP¹, var. of HIP³]

Heph·aes·tus /hə'faistəs/ *Gk Myth* the god of fire (esp. the smithy fire) and of craftsmen. The son of Zeus and Hera, he was identified with Vulcan by the Romans.

Hepple·white¹, George (d.1786), English cabinetmaker and furniture designer. The posthumously published book of his designs, *The Cabinet-Maker and Upholsterer's Guide* (1788), contains almost 300 designs, characterized by light and elegant lines, which sum up neoclassical taste.

Hepple·white² *noun* a late 18th-c. style of furniture, originally as made by the English cabinetmaker George Hepplewhite, characterized by lightness, delicacy, and graceful curves.

Hepp·ner, Ben (b.1956), Canadian opera singer. Known worldwide for his powerful tenor voice, he has performed diverse roles at most of the world's major opera houses, including the Metropolitan Opera House, Covent Garden, and La Scala, and made numerous award-winning recordings.

hepta- *combining form* seven. [Greek *hepta* seven]

hept·ad *noun* a group of seven. [Greek *heptas -ados* set of seven (*hepta*)]

hepta·gon *noun* a plane figure with seven sides and angles. □ **hept·ag·on·al** /-'tagənəl/ *adjective*

hepta·hed·ron /ˌheptə'hiːdrən/ *noun* (*pl.* **-hed·rons** or **-hedra** /-drə/) a solid figure with seven faces. □ **hepta·hed·ral** *adjective* [HEPTA- + -HEDRON after POLYHEDRON]

hept·am·eter /hep'tamətər/ *noun* a line or verse of seven metrical feet. [Latin *heptametrum* from Greek (as HEPTA-, -METER)]

hept·ane *noun Chem.* a liquid hydrocarbon of the alkane series, obtained from petroleum. Chem. formula: C_7H_{16}. [HEPTA- + -ANE²]

hept·archy /'heptɑrki/ *noun* (*pl.* **-ies**) **1 a** a government by seven rulers. **b** an instance of this. **2** *hist.* the supposed seven kingdoms of the Angles and the Saxons in Britain in the 7th–8th c. □ **hept·arch·ic** /-'tɑrkɪk/ *adjective* **hept·arch·ic·al** /-'tɑrkɪkəl/ *adjective* [HEPTA- after *tetrarchy*]

Hepta·teuch /'heptəˌtjuːk/ *noun* the first seven books of the Bible. [Latin from Greek from *hepta* seven + *teukhos* book, volume]

hept·ath·lon /hep'taθlɒn/ *noun* an athletic contest, usu. for women, in which each competitor takes part in seven events. □ **hept·ath·lete** /-liːt/ *noun* [HEPTA-, on the pattern of DECATHLON]

hepta·valent /ˌheptə'veilənt/ *adjective Chem.* having a valence of seven.

Hep·worth, Dame (Joce·lyn) Bar·bara (1903–75), English sculptor. A pioneer of abstraction in British sculpture, her works include the nine-piece group *The Family of Man* (1972).

her ● *pronoun* **1** objective case of SHE (*I like her*). **2** *informal* she (*it's her all right; am older than her*). ● *possessive adjective* (attributive) **1** of or belonging to her or herself (*her house; her own business*). **2** (**Her**) (in titles) that she is (*Her Majesty*). [Old English *hi(e)re* dative & genitive of *hio, hēo* fem. of

HE] ¶ The use of *her* instead of *she* after the verb 'to be' (as in *It's her all right; I am older than her*) is considered by some to be incorrect but is normal in ordinary usage. The notion that the subjective rather than the objective case should be used after 'to be' is based partly on logic — the references of the grammatical subject and the complement are the same — and partly on the grammar of languages such as Latin, which are more highly inflected than English, but not on actual English usage. *Him, me, them,* and *us* are used similarly, e.g. *It's them on the phone again; It's us who will have to pay for it*. See also Usage Note at THAN.

Hera /'hɛrə, 'hɪːrə/ *Gk Myth* the wife and sister of Zeus and the daughter of Cronus and Rhea. Worshipped as the queen of heaven and as a marriage goddess, and probably of pre-Hellenic origin, she was identified by the Romans with Juno. [Greek *Hēra* (perhaps as a title, = lady, fem. of *hērōs* hero)]

Her·a·cles /'hɛrəˌkliːz/ the Greek form of HERCULES.

Hera·cli·tus /ˌhɛrə'klaɪtəs/ (c.500 BC), Greek philosopher. He regarded the universe as a ceaselessly changing conflict of opposites, all things being in a harmonious process of constant change.

Her·ac·lius /he'rakliəs/ (c.575–641), Byzantine emperor (610–641). In the first of the crusades, he recaptured the Cross and much of the Holy Land from the Persians.

Her·ak·lion /hɪ'rakliən/ a port in and the capital of Crete, on the north coast of the island; pop. (est. 2002) 135,300.

her·ald ● *noun* **1** an official messenger bringing news. **2** a forerunner (*spring is the herald of summer*). **3** *hist.* an officer responsible for state ceremonial and etiquette. ● *transitive verb* **1** proclaim the approach of; usher in (*her arrival heralds a new era*). **2** acclaim; praise (*heralded as the year's biggest success*). [Old French *herau(l)t, herauder* from Germanic]

her·ald·ic /he'raldɪk/ *adjective* of or concerning heraldry.
□ **her·ald·ic·al·ly** *adverb*

her·aldry *noun* **1** the science or art of a herald, esp. that of blazoning armorial bearings and deciding the rights of people to bear arms. **2** heraldic pomp, or the ceremony characteristic of a herald. **3 a** the heraldic charge or device which is pictured on a coat of arms. **b** heraldic devices collectively.

Herat /hə'rat/ a city in W Afghanistan; pop. (est. 2002) 116,600.

herb /hɜrb, ɜrb/ *noun* **1** any non-woody seed-bearing plant which dies down to the ground after flowering. **2** any plant with leaves, seeds, or flowers used for flavouring, food, medicine, scent, etc. □ **herb·like** *adjective* [Old French *erbe* from Latin *herba* grass, green crops, herb]

herb·aceous /hɜr'beɪʃəs/ *adjective* **1** of or like herbs (*see* HERB 1). **2 a** (of a plant) not woody or not having a woody stem. **b** resembling a leaf in colour or texture. □ **herb·aceous·ness** *noun* [Latin *herbaceus* grassy (as HERB)]

herbaceous border *noun* esp. *Brit.* a garden border containing esp. perennial flowering plants.

herbaceous perennial *noun* a plant whose growth dies down annually but whose roots etc. survive.

herb·age /'hɜrbɪdʒ, 'ɜrb-/ *noun* **1** herbs collectively. **2** the succulent part of herbs, esp. as pasture. [Old French *erbage* from medieval Latin *herbaticum, herbagium* right of pasture, from Latin *herba* herb]

herb·al /'hɜrbəl, 'ɜrbəl/ ● *adjective* pertaining to or containing herbs, esp. in therapeutic and culinary use. ● *noun* a book with descriptions and accounts of the properties of these.

herb·al·ist /'hɜrbəlɪst, 'ɜrb-/ *noun* **1 a** a person who practises or advocates the use of herbs to treat disease. **b** a dealer in medicinal herbs. **2** a person skilled in herbs, esp. an early botanical writer.
□ **herb·al·ism** *noun*

herbal tea *noun* (also **herb tea**) an infusion of dried herbs, usu. non-caffeinated.

herb·arium /hɜr'bɛriəm, ɜrb-/ *noun* (*pl.* **herb·aria** /-riə/) **1** a systematically arranged collection of dried plants. **2** a book, room, or building for these.

herbed /hɜrbd, ɜrbd/ *adjective* flavoured with herbs.

Her·bert, George (1593–1633), English metaphysical poet. His devout religious verse, marked by metrical versatility and homely imagery, is pervaded by simple piety and reflects his spiritual conflicts.

herbi·cide /'hɜrbɪˌsaɪd, 'ɜrb-/ *noun* a substance toxic to plants and used to destroy unwanted vegetation. □ **herbi·cid·al** *adjective*

herbi·vore /'hɜrbɪˌvɔr, 'ɜrb-/ *noun* an animal that feeds on plants.
□ **herb·iv·or·ous** /-'bɪvɜrəs/ *adjective* [Latin *herba* herb + -VORE (see -VOROUS)]

herb·ol·ogy *noun* the use of herbs to treat disease. □ **herb·ol·o·gist** *noun*

herb Rob·ert *noun* a common cranesbill, *Geranium robertianum*, with red-stemmed leaves and pink flowers.

herby /'hɜrbi, 'ɜrbi/ *adjective* (**herb·i·er, herb·i·est**) **1** abounding in herbs. **2** of the nature of a culinary or medicinal herb.

Her·ce·go·vina see HERZEGOVINA.

Her·cu·la·neum /ˌhɜrkjʊ'leɪniəm/ an ancient Roman town, near Naples, on the lower slopes of Vesuvius. The volcano's eruption in AD 79 buried it deeply under volcanic ash, along with Pompeii, and thus largely preserved it.

Her·cu·lean /ˌhɜrkjʊ'liːən, ˌhɜr'kjuːliən/ *adjective* **1** having or requiring great strength or effort. **2** of, like, or pertaining to Hercules.

Her·cu·les /'hɜrkjuˌliːz/ **1** (also **Heracles**) *Gk & Rom. Myth* a hero of superhuman strength and courage who performed twelve immense tasks or 'labours' imposed on him by Eurystheus, king of Argos, and who after death was ranked among the gods. **2** a man of exceptional strength or size. **3** *Astronomy* a large northern constellation, said to represent the figure of Hercules kneeling on his right knee. It contains the brightest globular cluster in the northern hemisphere, but no bright stars.

Her·cyn·ian /hɜr'sɪniən/ *adjective Geol.* designating a time during which mountains were formed in the eastern hemisphere during the late Paleozoic era. [Latin *Hercynia silva* forested mountains of central Germany]

herd ● *noun* **1** a large number of animals, esp. cattle, feeding, travelling, or kept together. **2** *derogatory* **a** a large number of people; a mob. **b** (prec. by *the*) the majority viewed as mindless followers (*prefers not to follow the herd*). **3** (esp. in *combination*) a keeper of herds; a herdsman (*cowherd*). ● *verb* **1** *intransitive & transitive* go, drive, or cause to go together in or as in a herd (*herded together for warmth*). **2** *transitive* tend (sheep, cattle, etc.) (*they herd the goats*). **3** *transitive* drive (an animal, a person) in a particular direction (*stopped to herd a cow off the road*).
□ **herding cats** *N Amer.* engaging in an impossible undertaking.
ride herd on *N Amer.* keep watch on or control over, esp. by close supervision. □ **herd·er** *noun* **herd·ing** *noun* [Old English *heord, hirdi,* from Germanic]

Her·der /'hɜrdər/ **Jo·hann Gott·fried von** (1744–1803), German philosopher, critic, and poet, the primary figure in the *Sturm und Drang* school of German literature.

herd instinct *noun* (usu. prec. by *the*) the tendency of associating or conforming with one's own kind for support etc.

herds·man *noun* (*pl.* **-men**) **1** the owner or keeper of herds (of domestic animals). **2** (usu. **Herdsman**) the constellation Boötes.

here ● *adverb* **1** in or at or to this place or position (*put it here; has lived here for many years; comes here every day*). **2** indicating a person's presence or a thing offered (*here is your coat; my son here will show you*). **3** at this point in the argument, situation, etc. (*here I have a question*). ● *noun* this place (*get out of here; lives near here; fill it up to here*). ● *interjection* **1** calling attention: short for *come here, look here,* etc. (*here, where are you going with that?*). **2** indicating one's presence in a roll call: short for *I am here*.
□ **here and now 1** at this very moment; immediately. **2** (prec. by *the*) the present reality. **here and there** in various places. **here goes!** *informal* an expression indicating the start of a bold act. **here's to** I drink to the health, success, etc. of. **here we are** *informal* **1** said as acknowledgement of a given state (*here we are, broke again*). **2** said on arrival at one's destination. **here we go again** *informal* the same, usu. undesirable, events are recurring. **here you are 1** (also **here you go**) said on handing something to somebody. **2** said in acknowledgement of an individual's presence, condition, or achievement (*and here you are, a doctor*). **neither here nor there** of no importance or relevance. [Old English *hēr* from Germanic: compare HE]

here·abouts *adverb* (also **here·about**) about or near this place.

here·after ● *adverb* **1 a** from now on; in the future. **b** *formal* HEREINAFTER. **2** in the world to come (after death). ● *noun* **1** the future. **2** life after death.

here·at *adverb archaic* as a result of this.

here·by *adverb* by this means; as a result of this.

her·ed·it·able /hɪ'rɛdɪtəbəl/ *adjective* that can be inherited. [obsolete French *héréditable* or medieval Latin *hereditabilis* from ecclesiastical Latin *hereditare* from Latin *heres -edis* heir]

her·ed·ita·ment /ˌhɛrɪ'dɪtəmənt, hɪ'rɛdɪ-/ *noun Law* anything, esp. property, that can be inherited. [medieval Latin *hereditamentum* (as HEREDITABLE)]

her·edi·tary /hə'rɛdɪtɜri/ *adjective* **1** (of a characteristic, disease, etc.) able to be passed down from one generation to another.

2 a descending by inheritance. **b** holding a position by inheritance. **3** the same as or resembling what one's parents had (*a hereditary hatred*). **4** of or relating to inheritance. □ **her·edi·tar·ily** *adverb* [Latin *hereditarius* (as HEREDITY)]

hereditary chief *noun* a chief of an Indian band through hereditary right, as opposed to one who has been elected.

her·ed·ity /həˈredɪti/ *noun* **1 a** the passing on of physical or mental characteristics genetically from one generation to another. **b** these characteristics in a particular individual. **2** the genetic constitution of an individual. [French *hérédité* or Latin *hereditas* heirship (as HEIR)]

Here·ford[1] /ˈherəfərd/ a city in west central England, on the Wye River in the county of Herefordshire; pop. (est. 2002) 57,200.

Here·ford[2] /ˈhɜrfərd, ˈherəfərd/ *noun* **1** an animal of a breed of red and white beef cattle. **2** this breed. [HEREFORD[1], where it originated]

Hereford and Worcester a former county of west central England, on the border with Wales. It was formed in 1974 from the counties of Herefordshire and Worcestershire, which were reinstated in 1998.

Here·ford·shire /ˈherəfərdˌʃɪr/ a county of west central England, on the border with Wales. Between 1974 and 1998 it was part of the county of Hereford and Worcester.

here·in *adverb formal* **1** in this document, book, etc. **2** in this matter, particular, case, etc.

here·in·after *adverb esp. Law formal* **1** from this point on. **2** in a later part of this document etc.

here·of *adverb formal* of or concerning this.

Her·ero /həˈrerɔ, -ˈriːrɔ/ *noun (pl.* same or **Her·eros**) **1** a member of any of several peoples, speaking a Bantu language, of Namibia, Angola, and Botswana. **2** the language of these peoples.

her·esi·arch /heˈriːziˌɑrk/ *noun* the leader or founder of a heresy. [ecclesiastical Latin *haeresiarcha* from Greek *hairesiarkhēs* (as HERESY + *arkhēs* ruler)]

her·esy /ˈherəsi/ *noun (pl.* **-esies**) **1 a** belief or practice contrary to the orthodox doctrine of a given religion. **b** an instance of this. **2 a** opinion contrary to what is normally accepted or maintained in any subject, field, etc. (*it's heresy to suggest that instant coffee is as good as the real thing*). **b** an instance of this. [Old French (*h*)*eresie*, from ecclesiastical Latin *haeresis*, in Latin = school of thought, from Greek *hairesis* choice, sect, from *haireomai* choose]

her·et·ic /ˈherətɪk/ *noun* **1** the holder of an unorthodox opinion in a subject, field, etc. **2** esp. *hist.* a person believing in or practising religious heresy. □ **her·et·ic·al** /hɪˈretɪkəl/ *adjective* **her·et·ic·al·ly** *adverb* [Old French *heretique* from ecclesiastical Latin *haereticus* from Greek *hairetikos* able to choose (as HERESY)]

here·to *adverb formal* with regard to this point or to this matter, subject, etc.

here·to·fore *adverb formal* formerly, before this time.

here·under *adverb formal* below (in a book, legal document, etc.).

here·upon *adverb* after this; in consequence of this.

here·with *adverb* **1** with this (esp. of an enclosure in a letter etc.). **2** hereby.

herit·able /ˈherɪtəbəl/ *adjective* **1** *Law* **a** (of property) capable of being inherited by heirs-at-law (*compare* MOVABLE 2). **b** capable of inheriting. **2** *Biol.* (of a characteristic) transmissible from parent to offspring. □ **herit·abil·ity** *noun* [Old French from *heriter* from ecclesiastical Latin *hereditare*: see HEREDITABLE]

herit·age /ˈherɪtɪdʒ/ *noun* **1 a** things such as works of art, cultural achievements and folklore that have been passed on from earlier generations. **b** a nation's buildings, monuments, countryside, etc., esp. when regarded as worthy of preservation. **c** (*attributive*) esp. *Cdn* designating a building, site, river, etc. significant for its historic, architectural, or environmental value and which is protected from alteration, development, etc. by the government. **2** that which is or may be inherited. **3** inherited circumstances, benefits, etc. (*a heritage of violence*). **4** *Bible* **a** the ancient Israelites. **b** the Church. [Old French (as HERITABLE)]

Heritage Day *noun Cdn* **1** the third Monday in February, marked unofficially as a celebration of Canada's history and culture. **2** (in the Yukon) the fourth Friday in February, observed as a holiday in the public service and some other workplaces. **3** a day designated by a particular region, ethnic group, etc. as a time to celebrate a shared history and culture.

heritage fund *noun esp. Cdn* (often **Heritage Fund**) a fund established by a province, region, city, etc. from supplementary

revenue either as a hedge against difficult economic times or as a resource for future social and cultural development.

heritage language *noun Cdn* a language, other than English or French, which is a person's mother tongue or that of his or her ethnocultural group.

herky-jerky *adjective N Amer. slang* (of a movement) spasmodic or occurring at an irregular rate. [reduplication of JERKY[1]]

herm *noun Gk Hist.* a squared stone pillar with a head (esp. of Hermes) on top, used as a boundary marker, signpost, etc. (*compare* TERMINUS 5). [Latin *Herma* from Greek HERMES]

Her·man, Wood·row Charles ('Woody') (1913–87), US jazz musician and bandleader. Primarily known as a clarinetist and saxophonist, he enjoyed great success from the 1930s to the 1980s.

herm·aphro·dite /hərˈmafrəˌdaɪt/ ● *noun* **1 a** *Zool.* an animal normally having both male and female sexual organs, e.g. many snails and earthworms. **b** *Bot.* a plant having stamens and pistils in the same flower. **2** a human being in whom both male and female sex organs are present, or in which the sex organs contain both ovarian and testicular tissue. **3** a person or thing combining opposite qualities or characteristics. ● *adjective* **1** combining the characteristics of or consisting of both sexes. **2** combining opposite qualities or characteristics. □ **herm·aphro·dit·ic** /-ˈdɪtɪk/ *adjective* **herm·aphro·dit·ism** *noun* [HERMAPHRODITUS]

hermaphrodite brig *noun hist.* a two-masted sailing ship rigged on the foremast as a brig and on the mainmast as a schooner.

Herm·aphro·ditus /hər mafrəˈdaitəs/ *Gk Myth* a son of Hermes and Aphrodite, with whom the nymph Salmacis fell in love and prayed to be forever united. As a result the two became joined in a single body which retained characteristics of either sex.

her·men·eut·ic /ˌhɜrmɪˈnuːtɪk, -ˈnjuː-/ *adjective* of or concerning interpretation or theories of interpretation, esp. of Scripture or literary texts. □ **her·men·eut·ic·al** *adjective* **her·men·eut·ic·al·ly** *adverb* [Greek *hermēneutikos* from *hermēneuō* interpret]

her·men·eut·ics /ˌhɜrmɪˈnuːtɪks, -ˈnjuː-/ *plural noun* (also treated as *sing.*) the branch of knowledge that deals with interpretation and the theories of interpretation, esp. of Scripture or literary texts.

Her·mes /ˈhɜrmiːz/ *Gk Myth* the son of Zeus and Maia, the messenger of the gods and god of merchants, thieves, and oratory. Identified by the Romans with Mercury, he was represented in human form as a herald with broad-brimmed hat, winged shoes, and a winged rod. [prob. from Greek *herma* 'heap of stones']

Her·mes Tris·me·gis·tus /ˌtrɪsməˈdʒɪstəs/ a legendary figure regarded by Neoplatonists and others as the author of certain works on astrology, magic, and alchemy. [Latin, = thrice-greatest Hermes, irreg. translation of 'Thoth the very great' (see THOTH)]

her·met·ic /hərˈmetɪk/ *adjective* (also **her·met·ic·al**) **1** completely airtight. **2** protected from outside influences or agencies. **3 a** esoteric. **b** of alchemy or other occult sciences (*hermetic art*). □ **her·met·ic·al·ly** *adverb* **her·meti·cism** /hərˈmetɪsɪzəm/ *noun* [modern Latin *hermeticus* irreg. from HERMES TRISMEGISTUS]

her·mit *noun* **1** a person who, from religious motives, has retired into the solitary life, esp. an early Christian recluse. **2** any person living in solitude or shunning human society. **3** *N Amer.* a soft spicy cookie, usu. containing raisins and nuts. □ **her·mit·ic** /-ˈmɪtɪk/ *adjective* [Old French (*h*)*ermite* or from Late Latin *eremita* from Greek *erēmitēs* from *erēmia* desert, from *erēmos* solitary]

her·mit·age /ˈhɜrmɪtɪdʒ/ *noun* **1** a hermit's dwelling. **2** a solitary or secluded dwelling. **3** a French wine produced near Valence.

hermit crab *noun* any crab of the family Paguridae that lives in a cast-off mollusc shell for protection.

hermit thrush *noun* a N American thrush, *Catharus guttatus*, predominantly olive brown with a reddish-brown tail, noted for its beautiful bell-like song.

Her·mo·sillo /ˌerməˈsiːjo/ a city in NW Mexico, capital of the state of Sonora; pop. (2000) 545,900.

Herne /ˈhernə/ an industrial city in North Rhine-Westphalia, Germany; pop. (est. 1999) 176,200.

her·nia *noun (pl.* **her·nias**) a rupture or the abnormal displacement and protrusion of part of an organ through the wall of the cavity containing it, esp. of the abdomen. □ **herni·at·ed** *adjective* **herni·ation** *noun* [Latin]

herniated disc *noun* a disc between vertebrae that has become displaced, causing pain because of pressure on the nerves of the spine.

Hero /ˈhiːrɔ/ **1** *Gk Myth* a beautiful priestess of Aphrodite at Sestos on the European shore of the Hellespont, whose lover Leander, a youth of

Abydos on the opposite shore, swam the strait nightly to visit her until one stormy night he was drowned, and Hero in grief threw herself into the sea. **2 of Alexandria** (1st c.) (also **Heron**), Greek mathematician and inventor. He described a number of hydraulic, pneumatic, and other mechanical devices, including elementary applications of the power of steam.

hero noun (pl. **heroes**) **1** a person distinguished by courage, noble deeds, outstanding achievements, etc. (*Terry Fox became a national hero*). **2** the chief, esp. male, character in a poem, play, story, etc. **3** *Gk Hist.* a man of superhuman strength, courage, or qualities, favoured by the gods; a demigod. **4** (in full **hero sandwich**) *US* = SUB 2. □ **hero's welcome** a rapturous welcome, like that given to a successful warrior. [Latin *heros* from Greek *hērōs*]

Herod /'herəd/ 'the Great' (c.74–4 BC), king of Judea 37–4 BC. He built the palace of Masada and rebuilt the temple in Jerusalem. Jesus was born during his reign; according to the New Testament (Matt. 2:16), Herod ordered the Massacre of the Innocents.

Herod Agrippa I /ə'grɪpə/ (called 'Herod' in Acts) (10 BC–AD 44), grandson of Herod the Great, king of Judea AD 41–44. According to the New Testament, he imprisoned St. Peter and put St. James the Great to death.

Herod Agrippa II /ə'grɪpə/ (AD 27–c.93), son of Herod Agrippa I, king of various territories in northern Palestine 50–c.93. He presided over the trial of St. Paul (Acts 25:13 ff.).

Herod Antipas /'antɪpas/ (22 BC–AD c.40), son of Herod the Great, tetrarch of Galilee and Peraea 4 BC–AD 40. He married Herodias and was responsible for the beheading of John the Baptist. According to the New Testament (Luke 23:7), Pilate sent Jesus to be questioned by him before his crucifixion.

Herodias /he'rɔːdiəs/ (c.14 BC–c.40 AD), niece and second wife of Herod Antipas, and mother of Salome.

Herodotus /hə'rɒdətəs/ (5th c. BC), Greek historian (known as 'the Father of History'), the first to collect his materials systematically, test their accuracy as far as possible, and arrange them in a well-constructed and vivid narrative.

heroic /hɪ'rɔːɪk/ ● adjective **1 a** (of an act or a quality) bold, daring, or characteristic of or fit for a hero. **b** (of an effort etc.) great or courageous, but also desperate. **c** (of a person) like a hero. **2 a** (of language) grand, high-flown, dramatic. **b** (of a work of art) extravagant or unusually large, esp. between life-size and colossal. **3** (of poetry etc.) dealing with heroes and their deeds, esp. those of ancient Greece. ● noun (in pl.) heroic behaviour, esp. if unduly, extravagantly, or recklessly bold. □ **heroically** adverb

heroic age noun **1** = GOLDEN AGE 2. **2** (usu. prec. by *the*) **a** the period in ancient culture when heroes of legends lived and ruled. **b** the period in Greek history before the return from Troy.

heroic couplet noun two lines of rhyming iambic pentameters.

heroic verse noun a type of verse used for heroic poetry, esp. the hexameter, the iambic pentameter, or the alexandrine.

heroin noun a highly addictive white crystalline analgesic drug derived from morphine, often used as a narcotic. [German (as HERO, from its effects on the user's self-esteem)]

heroin chic noun a glamorization esp. in the mid to late 1990s of the culture and appearance of heroin users, characterized esp. by the use of very thin, wan fashion models.

heroine noun **1** a woman noted or admired for nobility, courage, outstanding achievements, etc. **2** the chief female character in a poem, play, story, etc. [Greek *hērōinē*, fem. of *hērōs* HERO]

heroism /'herəʊˌɪzəm/ noun heroic conduct or qualities.

Heron /'hiːrɒn/ see HERO 2.

heron noun any of various large wading birds of the family Ardeidae, esp. *Ardea herodias*, with long legs and a long S-shaped neck. [Old French *hairon* from Germanic]

heronry noun (pl. **-ries**) a place where herons breed; a colony of herons.

Herophilus /hiː'rɒfɪləs/ (4th–3rd c. BC), Greek anatomist, regarded as the father of human anatomy. He contributed to knowledge of the brain, eyes, reproductive organs, nerves, and veins and arteries. None of his works survive.

hero sandwich noun *US* = SUB 2.

hero-worship ● noun **1** idealization of an admired person. **2** *Gk Hist.* worship of the ancient heroes. ● transitive verb (-**worshipped**, -**worshipping**; *US* -**worshiped**, -**worshiping**) idolize or be excessively devoted to (a person). □ **hero-worshipper** noun

herpes /'hɜːpiːz/ noun any of several infectious diseases caused by a

herpesvirus and characterized by outbreaks of blisters on the skin etc. □ **herpetic** /-'petɪk/ adjective [Greek *herpēs -ētos* shingles, from *herpō* creep]

herpes simplex noun a viral infection producing usu. localized inflammation, as blisters, cold sores, conjunctivitis, oral and vaginal inflammation, etc.

herpesvirus /'hɜːpiːzˌvaɪrəs/ noun any of a group of related viruses that includes those causing shingles and chicken pox, esp. *Herpesvirus hominis*, the cause of herpes simplex.

herpes zoster /'hɜːpiːz 'zɒstər/ noun = SHINGLES. [Greek *zōstēr* belt, girdle]

herpetology /ˌhɜːpɪ'tɒlədʒi/ noun the branch of zoology concerned with the study of reptiles and amphibians. □ **herpetological** /-tə'lɒdʒɪkəl/ adjective **herpetologist** noun [Greek *herpeton* reptile, from *herpō* creep]

Herr /her/ noun (pl. **Herren** /'herən/) **1** the title of a German man; Mr. **2** a German man. [German from Old High German *hērro* comparative of *hēr* exalted]

Herrenvolk /'herənˌfɒlk, -ˌfoːk/ noun **1** the German nation characterized by the Nazis as born to mastery. **2** a group regarding itself as naturally superior. [German, = master-race (as HERR, FOLK)]

Herrick, Robert (1591–1674), English poet, writer of both secular and religious verse. His secular poems, such as 'Gather ye Rosebuds While ye may', treat such subjects as country rituals, folklore, and love.

herring noun any of various chiefly marine fishes of the family Clupeidae, which form shoals in coastal waters at spawning time, including several important food fishes esp. *Clupea harengus* of the N Atlantic or *C. pallasi* of the N Pacific. [Old English *hæring*, *hēring* from West Germanic]

herringbone ● noun **1** any zigzag pattern or arrangement resembling the pattern of a herring's bones, as of stones, bricks, tiles, etc. **2** a stitch with a similar zigzag pattern. **3** this pattern, or cloth woven in it. **4** *Skiing* a method of ascending a slope with the skis pointing outwards. **5** (attributive) **a** (of cloth) having a zigzag weave. **b** (of brickwork etc.) having a zigzag pattern. **c** resembling the bones of a herring. ● verb **1** transitive **a** mark with a herringbone pattern. **b** work with a herringbone stitch. **2** intransitive *Skiing* ascend a slope using the herringbone technique.

herring choker noun *Cdn* esp. (*Maritimes*) informal a Maritimer, esp. a New Brunswicker.

herring gull noun a large, widely distributed gull, *Larus argentatus*, with dark wing tips, scavenging from fishing boats, garbage dumps, canneries, etc.

herring roe noun the yellowish eggs of pregnant herring on their way to spawn, eaten as a food and considered a delicacy.

herring scull noun (also **herring school**) *Cdn* (*Nfld*) a school of herring appearing in inshore waters.

herring skiff noun (also **herring punt**) *N Amer.* (*BC*, *Alaska*, *& Pacific Northwest*) a broad, flat-bottomed, open, usu. aluminum boat with a low freeboard, used for herring fishing.

Herriot, James (pseudonym of James Alfred Wight) (1916–95), English short-story writer and veterinarian. His experiences as a vet are collected in *All Creatures Great and Small* (1972) and other books.

hers possessive pronoun the one or ones belonging to or associated with her (*it is hers; hers are over there*). □ **of hers** of or belonging to her (*a friend of hers*).

Herschel /'hɜːʃəl/ **1 Caroline Lucretia** (1750–1848), German-born British astronomer. The sister and colleague of Sir William Herschel, she published a star catalogue. **2 Sir (Frederick) William** (1738–1822), German-born British astronomer, the father of stellar astronomy. His painstaking cataloguing of the skies resulted in the discovery of the planet Uranus. **3 Sir John (Frederick William)** (1792–1871), British astronomer and physicist, son of William Herschel. He extended the sky survey to the southern hemisphere and carried out pioneering work in photography.

Herschel Island /'hɜːʃəl/ a small island in the Beaufort Sea, situated just off the northern coast of Yukon Territory. [Sir W. HERSCHEL]

herself pronoun **1 a** emphatic form of SHE or HER (*she herself will do it*). **b** reflexive form of HER (*she has hurt herself*). **2** in her normal state of body or mind (*does not feel quite herself today*). □ **be herself** act in her normal unconstrained manner. **by herself** see BY ONESELF (see BY).

Hertford /'hɑːtfərd/ the county town of Hertfordshire; pop. (est. 2002) 21,800.

Consonants: b *but*   d *dog*   f *few*   g *get*   h *her*   j *yes*   k *cat*   l *leg*   m *man*   n *no*   p *pen*   r *red*   s *sit*

Hert·ford·shire /ˈhɑːtfəd.ʃɪr/ a county of SE England, one of the Home Counties; county town, Hertford.

Hertz /hɜːts/ **1 Gus·tav Lud·wig** (1887–1975), German atomic physicist. He shared the 1925 Nobel Prize for physics with James Franck, for confirming the theory that energy can be absorbed by an atom only in definite amounts. **2 Hein·rich Ru·dolf** (1857–94), German physicist and pioneer of radio communication, the first to broadcast and receive radio waves.

hertz /hɜːts/ noun (pl. same) the SI unit of frequency, equal to one cycle per second. Abbr.: **Hz**. [H.R. HERTZ]

Hertz·ian wave /ˈhɜːtsiən/ noun an electromagnetic wave of a length suitable for use in radio. [H.R. HERTZ]

Herz·berg, Ger·hard (1904–99), German-born Canadian chemist, winner of the 1971 Nobel Prize for chemistry, known as the father of molecular spectroscopy.

Her·ze·go·vina /ˌhɜːtsəgəˈviːnə/ (also **Hercegovina**) a region in the Balkans forming the southern part of Bosnia and Herzegovina and separated from the Adriatic by part of Croatia. Its chief town is Mostar. □ **Her·ze·go·vin·ian** /-ˈviːniən/ adjective & noun

Herzl /ˈhɜːtsəl/ **Theo·dor** (1860–1904), Hungarian-born journalist, dramatist, and Zionist leader. As a writer and journalist in Vienna he advocated the establishment of a Jewish state in Palestine; in 1897 he founded the Zionist movement.

Her·zog /ˈhɜːtsɒg/ **Wer·ner** (born Werner Stipetic) (b.1942), German film director. Themes of remoteness in time and space dominate his films, which include *The Enigma of Kaspar Hauser* (1974) and *Fitzcarraldo* (1982).

he's contraction **1** he is. **2** he has.

he-said-she-said adjective designating a situation in which two people give conflicting accounts of an event, with little or no evidence to support either.

he/she pronoun a written representation of 'he or she' used to indicate both sexes.

Hes·iod /ˈhiːsiəd/ (c.700 BC), one of the earliest known Greek poets. His hexametric poem the *Theogony* deals with the origin and genealogies of the gods; his *Works and Days* contains moral and practical advice for agricultural work.

hes·i·tant /ˈhezɪtənt/ adjective tending to be slow in speaking or acting because of uncertainty or unwillingness. □ **hesi·tance** noun **hesi·tancy** noun **hesi·tant·ly** adverb

hes·i·tate /ˈhezɪˌteɪt/ intransitive verb **1** (often foll. by *about*, *over*) show or feel indecision or uncertainty; pause in doubt (*hesitated over her choice*). **2** (often foll. by *to* + infin.) be deterred by scruples; be reluctant (*I hesitate to inform against him*). **3** stammer, falter, or pause momentarily in speech. □ **hesi·tat·ing·ly** adverb **hesi·ta·tion** noun [Latin *haesitare* frequentative of *haerēre haes-* stick fast]

Hes·peler /ˈhesplər/ part of the city of Cambridge, Ontario; it was amalgamated with the city of Galt and the town of Preston in 1973. [J. *Hespeler*, miller and first postmaster c.1851]

Hes·per·ian /heˈspɪəriən/ adjective poet. **1** western. **2** (in Greek mythology) of or concerning the Hesperides. [Latin *Hesperius* from Greek *Hesperios* (as HESPERUS)]

Hes·peri·des /heˈsperəˌdiːz/ Gk Myth nymphs, the daughters of Hesperus, who kept watch with a dragon over a tree of golden apples in the Islands of the Blessed.

Hes·per·us /ˈhespərəs/ the evening star, Venus. [Greek *hesperos* (adj. & n.) western, evening (star)]

Hes·qui·aht /ˈheʃkwɪt/ ● noun **1** a member of a Nuu-chah-nulth Aboriginal group living on the west coast of Vancouver Island. **2** the Wakashan language of the Hesquiaht. ● adjective of or relating to this people or their culture or language. [Hesquiaht, 'people who eat herring eggs off eel grass']

Hess ▸ 1 Vic·tor Fran·cis (1883–1964), Austrian-born US physicist who pioneered the study of cosmic rays. He shared the Nobel Prize for physics in 1936 with C. D. Anderson. **2 Wal·ther Rich·ard Ru·dolf** (1894–1987), German politician, deputy leader of the Nazi Party (1934–41) and close friend of Hitler. In 1941, secretly and independently, he parachuted into Scotland to negotiate peace with Britain. Imprisoned for the duration of the war, he was sentenced to life imprisonment during the Nuremberg trials.

Hesse[1] /hes/ a state of western Germany; capital, Wiesbaden.

Hesse[2] /hes, ˈhesə/ **Her·mann** (1877–1962), German-born Swiss novelist and poet. His work, including *Siddhartha* (1922) and *Steppenwolf* (1927), emphasizes spiritual values as expressed in Eastern religion; he was awarded the Nobel Prize for literature in 1946.

Hes·sian /ˈhesən/ ● noun **1** (**hessian**) esp. *Brit.* = BURLAP. **2** a native of Hesse. ● adjective of or concerning Hesse. [HESSE[1]]

Hessian boot noun a tasselled high boot fashionable in England in the early 19th c. [first worn by Hessian troops]

Hessian fly noun a midge, *Mayetiola destructor*, whose larva destroys growing wheat. [thought to have been brought to N America by Hessian troops]

hest noun archaic behest. [Old English *hæs* (see HIGHT), assimilated to Middle English nouns in *-t*]

Hes·tia /ˈhestiə/ Gk Myth the goddess of the hearth, called Vesta by the Romans.

het slang = HETEROSEXUAL. [abbreviation]

he·taera /hɪˈtiːrə/ noun (also **he·taira** /-ˈtaɪrə/) (pl. **-ras**, **he·tae·rae** /-ˈtiːriː/, or **he·tai·rai** /-ˈtaɪraɪ/) a courtesan or mistress, esp. in ancient Greece. [Greek *hetaira*, fem. of *hetairos* companion]

het·ero /ˈhetərəʊ/ informal ● noun (pl. **-eros**) a heterosexual. ● adjective heterosexual. [abbreviation]

hetero- /ˈhetərəʊ/ combining form other, different (often opp. HOMO-). [Greek *heteros* other]

hetero·clite /ˈhetərəˌklaɪt/ ● adjective **1** abnormal. **2** Grammar (esp. of a noun) irregularly declined. ● noun **1** an abnormal thing or person. **2** Grammar an irregularly declined word, esp. a noun. □ **hetero·clit·ic** adjective [Late Latin *heteroclitus* from Greek (as HETERO-, *klitos* from *klinō* bend, inflect)]

hetero·cyclic /ˌhetərəʊˈsaɪklɪk, -ˈsɪklɪk/ adjective Chem. (of a compound) with a bonded ring of atoms of more than one kind.

hetero·dox /ˈhetərəˌdɒks/ adjective (of a person, opinion, etc.) not orthodox. □ **hetero·doxy** noun [Late Latin *heterodoxus* from Greek (as HETERO-, *doxos* from *doxa* opinion)]

hetero·dyne /ˈhetərəˌdaɪn/ ● adjective relating to the production of a lower radio frequency from the combination of two almost equal high radio frequencies. ● intransitive verb produce a lower radio frequency in this way.

hetero·gen·eous /ˌhetərəʊˈdʒiːniəs/ adjective **1** diverse in character. **2** varied in content. **3** Math. incommensurable through being of different kinds or degrees. □ **hetero·gen·eity** /-dʒɪˈneɪɪti/ noun **hetero·gen·eous·ly** adverb **hetero·gen·eous·ness** noun [medieval Latin *heterogeneus* from Greek *heterogenēs* (as HETERO-, *genos* kind)]

heter·ol·o·gous /ˌhetəˈrɒləgəs/ adjective not homologous. □ **heter·ol·ogy** noun

hetero·morph·ic /ˌhetərəʊˈmɔːfɪk/ adjective (also **hetero·morph·ous** /-ˈmɔːfəs/) Biol. **1** of dissimilar forms. **2** (of insects) existing in different forms at different stages in their life cycle.

hetero·morph·ism /ˌhetərəʊˈmɔːfɪzəm/ noun the quality or condition of existing in various forms.

heter·on·om·ous /ˌhetəˈrɒnəməs/ adjective **1** subject to an external law (compare AUTONOMOUS). **2** Biol. subject to different laws (of growth etc.).

heter·on·omy /ˌhetəˈrɒnəmi/ noun **1** the presence of a different law. **2** subjection to an external law.

hetero·polar /ˌhetərəʊˈpəʊlər/ adjective having dissimilar poles, esp. Electricity with an armature passing north and south magnetic poles alternately.

heter·op·ter·an /ˌhetəˈrɒptərən/ noun any insect of the suborder Heteroptera with non-uniform forewings having a thickened base and membranous tip (compare HOMOPTERAN). □ **heter·op·ter·ous** adjective [HETERO- + Greek *pteron* wing]

hetero·sex·ism /hetərəʊˈseksɪzəm/ noun discrimination or prejudice by heterosexuals against or towards homosexuals. □ **hetero·sex·ist** adjective & noun

hetero·sex·ual /ˌhetərəʊˈsekʃʊəl/ ● adjective **1** feeling or involving sexual attraction to persons of the opposite sex. **2** concerning heterosexual relations or people. **3** relating to the opposite sex. ● noun a heterosexual person. □ **hetero·sex·u·al·ity** /-ˈalɪti/ noun **hetero·sex·ual·ly** adverb

hetero·troph·ic /ˌhetərəʊˈtrɒfɪk/ adjective Biol. deriving its nourishment and carbon requirements from organic substances; not autotrophic. [HETERO- + Greek *trophos* feeder]

hetero·zygote /ˌhetərəʊˈzaɪgəʊt/ noun Biol. an individual having two different alleles of a particular gene or genes, and so giving rise to varying offspring (compare HOMOZYGOTE). □ **hetero·zygous** adjective

het·man /ˈhetmən/ noun (pl. **-mans**) a Polish or Cossack military commander. [Polish, prob. from German *Hauptmann* captain]

---

t top   v voice   w we   z zoo   ʃ she   ʒ vision   θ thin   ð this   ŋ ring   x loch   tʃ chip   dʒ jar   (see over for vowels)

het up *adjective informal* excited, overwrought. [*het* dial. past participle of HEAT]

heu·chera /ˈhjuːkərə, ˈhɔɪk-/ *noun* any N American herbaceous plant of the genus *Heuchera*, with dark green round or heart-shaped leaves and tiny flowers. [modern Latin from J. H. von *Heucher*, German botanist d.1747]

heur·is·tic /hjuˈrɪstɪk/ ● *adjective* **1** allowing or assisting to discover. **2** *Computing* proceeding to a solution by trial and error. ● *noun* **1** the science of heuristic procedure. **2** a heuristic process or method. **3** (in *pl.*, usu. treated as *sing.*) *Computing* the study and use of heuristic techniques in data processing. □ **heur·is·tic·al·ly** *adverb* [irreg. from Greek *heuriskō* find]

heuristic method *noun* a system of education under which pupils are trained to find out things for themselves.

he·vea /ˈhiːvɪə/ *noun* any S American tree of the genus *Hevea*, yielding a milky sap used for making rubber. [modern Latin from Quechua *hyeve*]

Hev·esy /ˈhevəʃi/ **George Charles de** (1885–1966), Hungarian-born radiochemist. He made fundamental contributions to the study of radioisotopes and co-discovered the element hafnium (1923). He was awarded the Nobel Prize for chemistry in 1943.

HEW *abbreviation* (in the US) Department of Health, Education, and Welfare.

hew *verb* (past participle **hewn** or **hewed**) **1** *transitive* **a** (often foll. by *down, away, off*) chop or cut (a thing) with an axe, a sword, etc. **b** cut (a block of wood etc.) into shape. **2** *intransitive* (often foll. by *at, among*, etc.) strike cutting blows. **3** *intransitive N Amer.* (usu. foll. by *to*) conform. □ **hew one's way** make a way for oneself by hewing. [Old English *hēawan* from Germanic]

hew·er *noun* **1** a person who hews. **2** a person who cuts coal from a seam. □ **hewers of wood and drawers of water** menial drudges; labourers (Josh. 9:21).

Hew·itt, Fos·ter Wil·liam (1902–1985), Canadian hockey broadcaster. For many years his voice brought hockey games into homes across Canada via both radio and television, and he gave sports broadcasting much of its vocabulary, including the line 'He shoots! He scores!'.

hex ● *verb* **1** *intransitive* practise witchcraft. **2** *transitive* bewitch. ● *noun* **1** a magic spell. **2** a witch. [Pennsylvania Dutch *hexe* (v.), *Hex* (n.), from German *hexen*, *Hexe*]

hex² *adjective & noun* esp. *Computing* = HEXADECIMAL. [abbreviation]

hex³ *adjective* hexagonal (*hex nut*). [abbreviation]

hexa- *combining form* (also **hex-** esp. before a vowel) six. [Greek *hex* six]

hexa·chord /ˈheksəkɔːd/ *noun* a diatonic series of six notes with a semitone between the third and fourth, used at three different pitches in medieval music. [HEXA- + CHORD¹]

hex·ad /ˈheksad/ *noun* a group of six. [Greek *hexas -ados* from *hex* six]

hexa·deci·mal /ˌheksəˈdesɪməl/ esp. *Computing* ● *adjective* relating to or using a system of numerical notation that has 16 rather than 10 as a base. ● *noun* the hexadecimal system; hexadecimal notation.

hexa·gon /ˈheksəgɒn/ *noun* a plane figure with six sides and angles. □ **hex·ag·on·al** /-ˈsagənəl/ *adjective* **hex·ag·on·al·ly** *adverb*

hexa·gram /ˈheksəˌgram/ *noun* **1** a figure formed by two intersecting equilateral triangles. **2** a figure of six lines.

hexa·hed·ron /ˌheksəˈhiːdrən/ *noun* (*pl.* **-hed·rons** or **-hedra** /-drə/) a solid figure with six faces. □ **hexa·hed·ral** *adjective*

hex·am·eter /hekˈsamɪtər/ *noun* a line or verse of six metrical feet. □ **hexa·met·ric** /-səˈmetrɪk/ *adjective*

hex·ane /ˈheksein/ *noun Chem.* a liquid hydrocarbon of the alkane series. Chem. formula: C_6H_{14}.

hexa·pod /ˈheksəˌpɒd/ ● *noun* any arthropod with six legs; an insect. ● *adjective* having six legs. [Greek *hexapous*, *hexapod-* (as HEXA-, *pous* pod-foot)]

Hexa·teuch /ˈheksəˌtuːk, -ˌtjuːk/ *noun* the first six books of the Old Testament. [Greek *hex* six + *teukhos* book]

hexa·valent /ˌheksəˈveilənt/ *adjective* having a valence of six.

hex·ose /ˈheksoːs, -soːz/ *noun Biochem.* a monosaccharide with six carbon atoms in each molecule, e.g. glucose or fructose. [HEXA- + -OSE²]

hey *interjection* **1** calling attention or expressing joy, surprise, inquiry, enthusiasm, etc. **2** expressing greeting (*Hey, Katherine, how are you?*). **3** indicating feigned or real unconcern about something one has just stated (*I'm not beautiful, but hey, beauty is only skin deep*). □ **what the hey** *N Amer.* = WHAT THE HELL (see HELL). [Middle English: compare Old French *hay*, Dutch, German *hei*]

hey·day *noun* the flush or full bloom of youth, vigour, prosperity, etc.

[archaic *heyday* expression of joy, surprise, etc.: compare Low German *heidi*, *heida*, exclamation denoting gaiety]

Heyer·dahl /ˈheɪər,dɒl/ **Thor** (1914–2000), Norwegian anthropologist, noted for his ocean voyages in the primitive craft the *Kon-Tiki* (1947) and the *Ra* (1969) to demonstrate his theories of cultural diffusion.

hey presto! *interjection Cdn & Brit.* a phrase announcing the successful completion of a magical trick or other surprising achievement.

Hez·bol·lah /ˌhezbəˈlɒ, ˈhezbʊlə/ an extremist Shiite Muslim group which has close links with Iran, created after the Iranian revolution of 1979 and active esp. in Lebanon. [Arabic *ḥizbullah* Party of God, from *ḥezb* party + *allāh* ALLAH]

Hez·ekiah /ˌhezəˈkaɪə/ (late 8th–early 7th c. BC) king of Judah (*c.*715–*c.*686 BC), noted for his religious reforms.

HF *abbreviation* HIGH FREQUENCY.

Hf *symbol* the element hafnium.

HG *abbreviation* Her or His Grace.

Hg *symbol* the element mercury. [modern Latin *hydrargyrum*]

hg *abbreviation* hectogram(s).

HGH *abbreviation* HUMAN GROWTH HORMONE.

HH *abbreviation* **1** Her or His Highness. **2** His Holiness. **3** double-hard (pencil lead).

hh. *abbreviation* hands (see HAND *noun* 14).

H-hour *noun* the hour at which an operation is scheduled to begin. [*H* for *hour* + HOUR]

HI *abbreviation* **1** Hawaii (also in official postal use). **2** the Hawaiian Islands.

hi *interjection* as a greeting or calling attention. [parallel form to HEY]

hia·tus /haɪˈeɪtəs/ *noun* (*pl.* **hia·tus·es**) **1** a break or gap, esp. in a series, account, or chain of proof. **2** *Prosody & Grammar* a break between two vowels coming together but not in the same syllable, as in *the ear*. [Latin, = gaping from *hiare* gape]

hiatus hernia *noun Med.* the protrusion of an organ, esp. the stomach, through the esophageal opening in the diaphragm.

Hia·watha /ˌhaɪəˈwɒθə/ (*c.*1450), Onondaga chief who is credited with the formation of the Iroquois Confederacy.

Hib /hɪb/ *noun Med.* a bacterium, *Haemophilus influenzae* type B, causing infant meningitis (often *attributive*: *Hib vaccine*). [acronym]

hib·achi /hɪˈbɒtʃi, hɪˈbatʃi/ *noun* (*pl.* **-achis**) a small, portable charcoal brazier with a grill. [Japanese, from *hi* fire + *hachi* bowl, pot]

hiber·nacu·lum /haɪbərˈnakjuːləm/ *noun* **1** a structure which protects a plant or animal during hibernation. **2** the place or nest in which an animal hibernates. [as HIBERNATE + -CULE]

hiber·nate /ˈhaɪbərˌneɪt/ *intransitive verb* **1** (of some animals) spend the winter in a dormant state. **2** remain inactive. **3** (of human beings) escape or withdraw from a harsh winter. □ **hiber·na·tion** *noun* **hiber·na·tor** *noun* [Latin *hibernare* from *hibernus* wintry]

Hi·bern·ian /haɪˈbɜːniən/ ● *adjective* of or concerning Ireland. ● *noun* a native of Ireland. [Latin *Hibernia*, *Iverna* from Greek *Iernē* from Old Celtic]

Hiberno- /haɪˈbɜːnoː/ *combining form* Irish (*Hiberno-British*). [medieval Latin *hibernus* Irish (as HIBERNIAN)]

hi·bis·cus /hɪˈbɪskəs, haɪ-/ *noun* any plant of the genus *Hibiscus*, often cultivated for its large bright-coloured flowers. *Also called* ROSE MALLOW. [Latin from Greek *hibiskos* marsh mallow]

hic *interjection* expressing the sound of a hiccup, esp. a drunken hiccup. [imitative]

hic·cough dated var. of HICCUP.

hic·cup ● *noun* **1 a** an involuntary spasm of the diaphragm and respiratory organs, with sudden closure of the glottis and characteristic cough-like sound. **b** (in *pl.*) an attack of such spasms. **2** a temporary or minor stoppage or difficulty. ● *verb* (**hic·cuped**, **hic·cup·ing** or **hic·cupped**, **hic·cup·ping**) **1** *intransitive* make a hiccup or series of hiccups. **2** *transitive* utter with a hiccup. □ **hic·cupy** *adjective* [imitative]

hick *informal derogatory* ● *noun* a country dweller; a provincial. ● *adjective* rural or unsophisticated. [pet form of the name *Richard*: compare DICK¹]

hick·ey *noun* (*pl.* **-eys**) *N Amer. informal* **1** a red mark on the skin, caused by biting or sucking during sexual play. **2** a gadget (compare DOOHICKEY). [20th c.: origin unknown]

Hick·ok /ˈhɪkɒk/ **James But·ler** ('Wild Bill') (1837–76), US frontier scout and marshal, noted for his pursuit of outlaws.

hick·ory *noun* (*pl.* **-ies**) **1** any N American tree of the genus *Carya*, yielding tough heavy wood, and bearing sometimes edible nuts (see PECAN). **2 a** the wood of these trees. **b** a stick made of this. [earlier *pohickery*, from Virginia Algonquian *pocohiquara* milky drink prepared from hickory nuts]

hicks·ville *noun* *N Amer.* *derogatory* a non-urban area.

hid *past of* HIDE[1].

Hi·dal·go /hɪˈdalɡoː/ a state of S Mexico; capital, Pachuca de Soto.

hi·dal·go /hɪˈdalɡoː/ *noun* (*pl.* **-gos**) a Spanish gentleman. [Spanish from *hijo dalgo* 'son of something' (i.e. of an important person)]

hid·den *past participle of* HIDE[1]. □ **hid·den·ly** *adverb* **hid·den·ness** *noun*

hidden agenda *noun* a secret or ulterior motive behind an action, statement, etc.

hidden reserves *noun* extra profits, resources, etc. kept concealed in reserve.

hidden tax *noun* a tax paid by a manufacturer, distributor, or retailer, that is included in the price charged to the consumer.

hide[1] ● *verb* (*past* **hid**; *past participle* **hid·den** or *archaic* **hid**) **1** *transitive* put or keep out of sight (*hid it under the cushion*; *hid her in the cupboard*). **2** *intransitive* conceal oneself. **3** *transitive* (usu. foll. by *from*) keep (a fact) secret (*hid his real motive from her*). **4** *transitive* conceal (a thing) from sight intentionally or not (*trees hide the house*). ● *noun* *Brit.* = BLIND *noun* 3. □ **hide one's light under a bushel** conceal one's merits (Matthew 5:15). **hide out** (or **up**) remain in concealment. □ **hider** *noun* [Old English *hȳdan* from West Germanic]

hide[2] ● *noun* **1** the skin of an animal, esp. when tanned or dressed. **2** *informal* the human skin (*saved her own hide*; *I'll tan your hide*). ● *transitive verb* *informal* flog. □ **neither hide nor hair** not the slightest trace (*I've seen neither hide nor hair of them since last week*). □ **hided** *adjective* (also in combination). [Old English *hȳd* from Germanic]

hide[3] *noun* (in England) a former measure of land large enough to support a family and its dependants, usu. between 60 and 120 acres (24 to 48 hectares). [Old English *hī(gi)d* from *hīw-*, *hīg-* household]

Hide-A-Bed *noun* *N Amer.* *proprietary* a couch that folds out into a bed.

hide-and-seek *noun* **1** (also **hide-and-go-seek**) a children's game in which one or more players hide and the other or others look for them. **2** a process of attempting to find an evasive person or thing.

hide·away ● *noun* a hiding place or place of retreat. ● *adjective* hidden or concealed, esp. when not in use (*hideaway bed*).

hide·bound *adjective* **1 a** narrow-minded; bigoted. **b** conservative; constricted by tradition. **2** *archaic* (of cattle) with the skin clinging close as a result of bad feeding. [HIDE[2] + BOUND[4]]

hid·eous /ˈhɪdɪəs/ *adjective* **1** frightful, repulsive, or revolting, to the senses or the mind. **2** *informal* unpleasant. □ **hid·eos·ity** *noun* (*pl.* **-ities**). **hid·eous·ly** *adverb* **hid·eous·ness** *noun* [Old French *hideus*, from Old French *hide* fear, of unknown origin]

hide·out *noun* *informal* a hiding place.

hidey-hole *noun* (also **hidy-hole**) *informal* a hiding place.

hid·ing[1] *noun* **1** the act or an instance of hiding. **2** the state of remaining hidden (*go into hiding*).

hid·ing[2] *noun* *informal* a thrashing.

hie *intransitive verb & reflexive* (**hies**, **hied**, **hie·ing** or **hying**) *archaic* or *literary* go quickly (*hie to your chamber*; *hied him to the chase*). [Old English *hīgian* strive, pant, of unknown origin]

hier·arch /ˈhaɪɑrˌɑrk/ *noun* **1** a chief priest. **2** *Catholicism* a bishop or archbishop. □ **hier·arch·al** /-ˈɑrkəl/ *adjective* [medieval Latin from Greek *hierarkhēs* from *hieros* sacred + *-arkhēs* ruler]

hier·archy /ˈhaɪɑrˌɑrki/ *noun* (*pl.* **-ies**) **1 a** a system in which grades or classes of status or authority are ranked one above the other (*ranks third in the hierarchy*). **b** the hierarchical system (of government, management, etc.). **c** (foll. by *of*) a range in order of importance (*hierarchy of values*). **2 a** priestly government. **b** a priesthood organized in grades. **3 a** each of the three divisions of angels. **b** the angels. □ **hier·arch·ic** /-ˈɑrkɪk/ *adjective* **hier·arch·ic·al** *adjective* **hier·arch·ize** *transitive verb* (also esp. *Brit.* **-ise**).

hier·atic /ˌhaɪəˈratɪk/ *adjective* **1** of or concerning priests. **2** of the ancient Egyptian writing of abridged hieroglyphics as used by priests (*compare* DEMOTIC *noun* 2). **3** of or concerning Egyptian or Greek traditional styles of art. **4** priestly. [Latin from Greek *hieratikos* from *hieraomai* be a priest, from *hiereus* priest]

hiero- /ˈhaɪroː/ *combining form* sacred, holy. [Greek *hieros* sacred + *-o-*]

hiero·glyph /ˈhaɪrəɡlɪf/ *noun* **1 a** a picture of an object representing a word, syllable, or sound, as used in ancient Egyptian and other

writing. **b** a writing consisting of characters of this kind. **2** a secret or enigmatic symbol. [back-formation from HIEROGLYPHIC]

hiero·glyph·ic /ˌhaɪrəˈɡlɪfɪk/ ● *adjective* **1** of or written in hieroglyphs. **2** symbolical. ● *noun* (in *pl.*) **1** hieroglyphs. **2** handwriting that is difficult to read. [Greek *hieroglyphikos* (as HIERO-, *gluphikos* from *gluphē* carving)]

hiero·phant /ˈhaɪrəˌfant/ *noun* **1** *Gk Hist.* an initiating or presiding priest; an official interpreter of sacred mysteries. **2** an interpreter of sacred mysteries or any esoteric principle. □ **hiero·phant·ic** /-ˈfantɪk/ *adjective* [Late Latin *hierophantes* from Greek *hierophantēs* (as HIERO-, *phantēs* from *phainō* show)]

hi-fi *informal* ● *adjective* of or relating to high fidelity. ● *noun* (*pl.* **hi-fis**) a set of equipment for high-fidelity sound reproduction. [abbreviation]

higgledy-piggledy ● *adverb & adjective* in confusion or disorder. ● *noun* a state of disordered confusion. [rhyming jingle, prob. with reference to the irregular herding together of pigs]

Higgs *noun* (also **Higgs boson** or **Higgs particle**) a subatomic particle whose existence is predicted by the theory which unified the weak and electromagnetic interactions. [P.W. *Higgs*, English physicist b.1929]

high ● *adjective* **1 a** of great vertical extent (*a high building*). **b** (*predicative*; often in *combination*) of a specified height (*one inch high*; *water was waist-high*). **2 a** far above ground or sea level etc. (*a high altitude*; *the high country*). **b** inland, esp. when raised (*High Sierra*). **3** extending above the normal or average level (*high boots*; *a sweater with a high neck*). **4** of exalted, esp. spiritual, quality (*high minds*; *high principles*; *high art*). **5 a** of exalted social station (*in high society*). **b** (usu. foll. by *up*) placed near the top of a hierarchy (*is high up in the government*). **6 a** great; intense; extreme; powerful (*high praise*; *high temperature*). **b** greater than normal (*high prices*). **7** *Brit.* extreme in political opinion (*high Tory*). **8** *Christianity* tending towards or involving an elaborate or formal style of worship (*high Anglican*; *high Lutheran*). **9** (of physical action, esp. athletics) performed at, to, or from a considerable height (*high diving*; *high flying*). **10** *informal* **a** (often foll. by *on*) intoxicated by alcohol or esp. drugs. **b** exhilarated; ecstatic. **11** (of a sound or note) of high frequency; at the top end of the scale or of a singer's register etc. **12** (of a period, an age, a time, etc.) at its peak (*high noon*; *high summer*; *High Renaissance*). **13 a** (of meat) beginning to go bad; off. **b** (of game) well-aged and slightly decomposed. **14** *Geog.* (of latitude) near the North or South Pole. **15** *Phonetics* (of a vowel) close (see CLOSE[1] *adjective* 14). **16** (of a gear) having an output speed relatively close to that of the input speed. **17** (foll. by *in*) having an elevated proportion of (*high in fibre*). ● *noun* **1** a high, or the highest, level or figure. **2** an area of high barometric pressure. **3** *informal* **a** a euphoric drug-induced state. **b** a state of excitement. **4** top gear in a motor vehicle. **5** the setting of a cooking element, microwave oven, etc. giving the most heat or power. **6** the highest temperature reached during a specified period (*daytime highs of 37°*). **7** *N Amer.* *informal* (esp. in names) high school. ● *adverb* **1** far up; aloft (*flew the flag high*). **2** in or to a high degree. **3** at a high price. **4** (of a sound) at or to a high pitch (*sang high*). □ **ace** (or **King** or **Queen** etc.) **high** (in card games) having the ace etc. as the highest-ranking card. **from on high** from heaven or a high place. **high old** *informal* most enjoyable (*had a high old time*). **high on the agenda** (or **list**) considered a priority for discussion or action. **high opinion of** a favourable opinion of. **high, wide, and handsome** *informal* in a carefree or stylish manner. **on high** in or to heaven or a high place. **on one's high horse** *informal* behaving superciliously or arrogantly. **play high 1** play for high stakes. **2** play a card of high value. **run high 1** (of the sea) have a strong current with high tide. **2** (of feelings) be strong. **to high heaven** to a high degree (*stank to high heaven*). [Old English *hēah* from Germanic]

high achiever *noun* a person who excels at something, esp. one who excels at many different activities, e.g. academics, sports, work, etc. □ **high-achiev·ing** *adjective*

high altar *noun* the chief altar of a church.

high and dry *adverb* (usu. in phr. **leave high and dry**) **1** stranded without resources. **2** (of a ship) out of the water, esp. stranded.

high and low *adverb* (esp. in phr. **search high and low**) everywhere.

high and mighty *adjective* **1** *informal* arrogant. **2** *archaic* of exalted rank.

High Arctic *noun* the part of the Canadian Arctic that lies within the Arctic Circle.

high·ball *N Amer.* ● *noun* **1** a drink of liquor diluted with a soft drink etc., served with ice in a tall glass. **2** a railway signal to proceed. ● *verb* *informal* **1** *intransitive* move at full speed. **2** *transitive* drive (a train, car, etc.) at full speed.

highball glass *noun N Amer.* a tall glass with straight sides.

high beam *noun N Amer.* (usu. in *pl.*) a bright headlight beam, used for long-range illumination.

high-born *adjective* of noble birth.

high·boy *noun N Amer.* a tall chest of drawers on legs.

high·brow *informal* ● *adjective* intellectual; cultural. ● *noun* an intellectual or cultured person.

high·bush *noun* **1** (in full **highbush blueberry**) a shrub of the genus *Vaccinium* of eastern N America, with sweet, juicy, dark blue fruit. **2** (in full **highbush cranberry**) a shrub, *Viburnum triloba*, with lobed leaves and red, juicy berries, found across Canada and the northern US.

high card *noun* a card that outranks others, esp. an ace or a face card.

high chair *noun* an infant's chair with long legs and a tray, for use at meals.

high cheek·boned *adjective* having prominent cheekbones located near the eye socket.

High Church ● *noun* a tradition within the Anglican Church emphasizing ritual, priestly authority, sacraments, and historical continuity with Catholic Christianity. ● *adjective* of or relating to this tradition.

High Church·man *noun* (*pl.* **-men**) an advocate of High Church principles.

high-class *adjective* of high quality.

high colour *noun* a flushed complexion.

high command *noun* **1** the leaders of a military force and associated staff. **2** the chief headquarters of a military force.

High Commission 1 an embassy from one Commonwealth country to another. **2** an international commission, such as one under the auspices of the United Nations. □ **High Commissioner** *noun*

high-concept *noun* (*attributive*) designating films etc. based on an uncomplicated and easily promoted central theme.

High Court *noun* (also in England **High Court of Justice**) a supreme court of justice for civil cases.

high-cut *adjective* (of shorts, underpants, bodysuits, etc.) having the leg holes cut high up on the side.

high day *noun* a festal day.

high-defini·tion *adjective* designating or providing a relatively clear or distinct image (*high-definition TV*).

high-density *adjective* **1** (of a substance) very dense. **2** accommodating a large number of people in a relatively small area (*high-density housing*).

high-density lipoprotein *noun* the form of lipoprotein involved in the transport of cholesterol and associated with decreased risk of arteriosclerosis and heart attack.

high-end *adjective* of, relating to or associated with the most expensive section of the market (*a high-end stereo*).

high·er *adjective* **1** comparative of HIGH. **2** *Computing* designating software releases that are more recent than one specified (*use Adobe Acrobat 4.0 or higher*).

higher animal *noun* an animal showing relatively advanced characteristics, e.g. a placental mammal.

higher court *noun* a court that can overrule the decision of another.

higher criticism *noun* the critical study of the literary methods and sources used by the authors of esp. Biblical writings (*compare* TEXTUAL CRITICISM 2).

higher education *noun* post-secondary education at university, college, etc.

higher mathematics *plural noun* (usu. treated as *sing.*) advanced mathematics as taught at university etc.

higher plant *noun* a plant showing relatively advanced characteristics, e.g. a flowering plant.

higher power *noun* a spiritual or other determining force that is more powerful than human beings, e.g. a divinity.

higher-up *noun* (*pl.* **higher-ups**) *informal* a person of higher rank; a superior.

highest bidder *noun* **1** the person who makes the highest bid for an item sold at auction. **2** a person, corporation, etc. that pays a higher price for something than any other contender.

highest common factor *noun* the highest number that can be divided exactly into each of two or more numbers.

high explosive *noun* an extremely explosive substance used in shells, bombs, etc.

high·falu·tin *adjective* (also **high·falu·ting**) *informal* absurdly pretentious. [HIGH + *fluting* pres. part. of FLUTE *verb*]

high fashion *noun* = HAUTE COUTURE.

high fidelity *noun* the reproduction of sound with little distortion, giving a result very similar to the original (also *attributive*: *high-fidelity sound*).

high finance *noun* financial transactions involving large sums.

high-five *N Amer. slang* ● *noun* a gesture of celebration or greeting in which two people slap each other's palms with their arms outstretched over their heads. ● *verb* **1** *transitive* greet with a high-five. **2** *intransitive* make a high-five. □ **high-fiving** *noun*

high-flown *adjective* (of language etc.) extravagant, bombastic.

high flyer *noun* (also **high flier**) **1** an ambitious person. **2** a person or thing with great potential for achievement.

high-flying *adjective* **1** (of a person) ambitious. **2** (of stocks, securities, etc.) having great value or perceived value. **3** (of an airplane, ball, etc.) flying high in the air.

high frequency *noun* a frequency, esp. in radio, of 3 to 30 megahertz. Abbr.: **HF**. □ **high-frequen·cy** *adjective*

high gear *noun* **1** a gear such that the driven end of a transmission revolves faster than the driving end. **2** a state of intensified activity (*the project has moved into high gear*).

High German *noun* standard written and spoken German.

high-grade ● *adjective* **1** of high quality. **2** (of ore) rich in metal value and commercially profitable. ● *transitive & intransitive verb* **1** steal (high-grade ore) from a mine. **2** *N Amer.* cut down (the best trees) from a forest. □ **high-grading** *noun*

high ground *noun* **1** ground that is naturally elevated and therefore strategically advantageous. **2** the position of esp. moral superiority in a debate etc.

high-handed *adjective* disregarding others' feelings; overbearing. □ **high-handed·ly** *adverb* **high-handed·ness** *noun*

high hat ● *noun* **1** a top hat. **2** = HI-HAT. **3** a snobbish or overbearing person. ● *adjective* (**high-hat**) supercilious; snobbish. ● *transitive verb* (**high-hat**) (**-hatted, -hatting**) *N Amer.* treat superciliously.

high heels *plural noun* women's shoes with high heels. □ **high-heeled** *adjective*

High Holidays *plural noun* the Jewish festivals of Rosh Hashanah and Yom Kippur.

high-impact *adjective* **1** (of plastics, etc.) able to withstand great impact without breaking. **2** designating esp. aerobic exercises that place a great deal of potentially harmful stress on the body. **3** having a great effect or lasting impression (*it was a high-impact movie*).

high·jinks *var.* of HIJINKS.

high jump *noun* **1** an athletic event consisting of jumping as high as possible over a bar of adjustable height. **2** *Brit. informal* a drastic punishment. □ **high jumper** *noun* **high jumping** *noun*

high kick *noun* **1** a kick high in the air, esp. in dancing. **2** a traditional Inuit game in which participants attempt to kick an object suspended above them and land on the foot used to kick with. □ **high-kicking** *attributive adjective*

high·land ● *noun* (usu. in *pl.*) **1** an area of high land. **2** (**the Highlands**) **a** the mountainous part of Scotland. **b** any similar area of hilly plateau (*Cape Breton Highlands*; *Haliburton Highlands*; *Okanagan Highlands*). ● *adjective* of or in a highland or the Highlands. □ **high·land·er** *noun* (also **Highlander**). [Old English *hēahlond* promontory (as HIGH, LAND)]

Highland cattle *noun* a breed of shaggy-haired cattle with long, curved, widely spaced horns.

Highland clearances the forced removal of crofters from their land in the Scottish Highlands in the late 18th and early 19th c., carried out by absentee landlords wanting to make way for sheep on their estates. The clearances led to widespread emigration to N America and elsewhere.

Highland dancing *noun* a style of dancing based on traditional dances of Scottish highland folk, e.g. the Highland fling and the sword dance etc.

Highland dress *noun* the clothing traditionally worn by Highlanders, including the kilt, sporran, etc.

Highland fling *noun see* FLING *noun* 3.

Highland games *plural noun* a Scottish sports meeting and cultural festival, typically consisting of athletic events such as tossing the caber

---

Consonants: b *but* d *dog* f *few* g *get* h *her* j *yes* k *cat* l *leg* m *man* n *no* p *pen* r *red* s *sit*

and putting the shot as well as other activities such as dancing and bagpipe playing.

Highland Region a local government region of N Scotland; administrative centre, Inverness.

high lead /liːd/ *noun Cdn Forestry* the cable or line used to haul logs when using a system of spar trees etc. for yarding (also *attributive*: *high-lead operation*).

high-level *adjective* **1** (of negotiations etc.) conducted by high-ranking people. **2** *Computing* (of a programming language) that is not machine-dependent and is usu. at a level of abstraction close to natural language.

high life *noun* **1** (also **high living**) a luxurious existence. **2** (usu. **high·life**) a West African style of dance music characterized by traditional drumming and syncopated melodies.

high·light ● *noun* **1** (in a painting etc.) a light area, or one seeming to reflect light. **2** a moment or detail of vivid interest; an outstanding feature. **3** (usu. in *pl.*) a bright tint in the hair produced by bleaching. **●** *transitive verb* **1** bring into prominence; draw attention to. **2** mark with a highlighter. **3** create highlights in (the hair).

high·light·er *noun* a marker pen which overlays colour on a printed word etc., leaving it legible and emphasized.

high·ly *adverb* **1** in a high degree (*highly amusing*; *highly probable*; *commend it highly*). **2** favourably (*think highly of her*).

highly-strung *adjective* = HIGH-STRUNG.

high maintenance *adjective* requiring much or frequent maintenance, attention, etc. (*a high maintenance machine*).

high marks *plural noun N Amer.* **1** the maximum award in an examination, competition, etc. **2** full credit (*I give them high marks for resourcefulness*).

High Mass *noun* a Mass in which the prayers are sung rather than spoken.

high-minded *adjective* having high moral principles. □ **high-minded·ly** *adverb* **high-minded·ness** *noun*

high muckamuck *noun N Amer.* = MUCKY-MUCK. [perhaps from Chinook *hiu* plenty + *muckamuck* (as MUCKY-MUCK)]

high·ness *noun* **1** the state of being high (*highness of taxation*) (compare HEIGHT). **2** (**Highness**) a title used in addressing and referring to a prince or princess (*Her Highness*; *Your Royal Highness*).

high-occupancy vehicle lane *noun* a traffic lane reserved for buses, taxis, and cars with at least two or three occupants.

high-octane *adjective* **1** (of fuel used in internal combustion engines) having good anti-knock properties, not detonating readily during the power stroke. **2** high-powered; potent (*a high-octane dessert*; *a high-octane performance*).

high performance *adjective* **1** designating items that will perform well even under extreme conditions. **2** (of a car, boat, etc.) capable of achieving high speed. **3** (in reference to sporting competition) designating a very high level of skill and achievement (*steroid use amongst high-performance athletes*).

high-pitched *adjective* **1** (of a sound) high. **2** (of a roof) steep. **3** (of style etc.) lofty.

high places *plural noun* the upper ranks of an organization etc. (*has friends in high places*).

high point *noun* the maximum or best state reached (*the high point of her career*).

high polymer *noun* a polymer having a high molecular weight.

high-powered *adjective* (also **high-power**) **1** having great power or energy. **2** important or influential.

high pressure ● *noun* **1** a high degree of activity or exertion. **2** a condition of the atmosphere with the pressure above 101.3 kilopascals. **●** *adjective* (usu. **high-pressure**) **1** having or involving a pressure that is above the ordinary (*high-pressure propane*). **2** (of a job, etc.) demanding; having a high level of stress. **3** (of a sales technique, etc.) forceful, persistent.

high-pressure system *noun Meteorol.* a large expanse of air at high atmospheric pressure.

high priest *noun* **1** a chief priest in some non-Christian religions. **2** a chief exponent of a political or cultural movement, esp. one who promotes the cause with dogmatism and fervour. □ **high priesthood** *noun*

high priestess *noun* **1** a chief priestess in some non-Christian religions. **2** a chief exponent of a political or cultural movement, esp. one who promotes the cause with dogmatism and fervour.

high profile *noun* exposure to attention or publicity. □ **high-profile** *adjective*

high-quality *adjective* of high quality.

high-ranking *adjective* of high rank, senior.

high relief *noun see* RELIEF 6a.

high-resolution *adjective* (also **high-res**, **hi-res**) (of a display or a photographic or video image) showing a large amount of detail.

high rigger *noun* the logger responsible for climbing, topping, and rigging the spar tree.

high-rise ● *attributive adjective* (of a building) having many storeys. **●** *noun* such a building.

high-risk *attributive adjective* involving or exposed to danger (*high-risk sports*; *high-risk pregnancy*).

High River a town in SW Alberta, about 50 km south of Calgary; pop. (2001) 9,345. □ **High River·ite** *noun* [the name of the river, originally called *High Woods River*, a translation of Blackfoot *ispitsi* tall timbers, with reference to the unusually tall trees lining its banks]

high road *noun* **1** *Brit.* a main road. **2** (usu. foll. by *to*) a direct route (*on the high road to success*).

high roller *noun N Amer. slang* a person who gambles large sums or spends freely. □ **high-rolling** *adjective*

high school *noun* **1** *N Amer., Scot., Austral.,* & *NZ* a secondary school. **2** *Brit.* a grammar school. □ **high-schooler** *noun*

high sea *noun* (also **high seas**) open seas not within any country's jurisdiction.

high season *noun* the period during which the most people travel, book accommodation, etc.

high-security *attributive adjective* **1** (of a prison, lock, etc.) extremely secure. **2** (of a prisoner) kept in a high-security prison.

High Sheriff *noun Brit. see* SHERIFF 3a.

high sign *noun N Amer.* a surreptitious gesture indicating that all is well or that the coast is clear.

High·smith, Pa·tri·cia (born Patricia Plangman) (1921–95), US writer of detective fiction. Many of her novels have been made into films, including *Strangers on a Train* (1949), filmed by Alfred Hitchcock in 1951. Novels featuring her psychotic hero Tom Ripley include *The Talented Mr Ripley* (1956) and *Ripley Under Water* (1991).

high-sounding *adjective* pretentious, bombastic.

high-speed *attributive adjective* **1** moving, operating, or happening very quickly. **2** (of steel) suitable for tools, cutting so rapidly as to become red-hot. **3** (of photographic film) needing little light or only short exposure.

high-spirit·ed *adjective* vivacious; cheerful.

high spirits *plural noun* vivacity; energy; cheerfulness.

high spot *noun informal* an important place or feature.

high-stakes *adjective* **1** designating a gambling game where the stakes are high. **2** (of an activity) highly risky; dangerous.

high steel *noun N Amer.* steel used as the framework for high-rise buildings, esp. steel girders high above the ground (also *attributive*: *high steel workers*).

high-step *intransitive verb* walk or move lifting one's feet high off the ground. □ **high-stepper** *noun* **high-stepping** *adjective*

high-sticking *noun* (in ice and field hockey) an illegal raising of the blade of the stick above shoulder level. □ **high stick** *noun* **high-stick** *transitive verb*

high street *noun Brit.* **1** a main road, esp. the principal shopping street of a town (usu. hyphenated when *attributive*: *high-street bank*). **2** designating stores, particularly belonging to chains, typically found in high streets, or the goods sold in them.

high-strung *adjective* very sensitive or nervous.

hight /haɪt/ *adjective archaic* called; named. [past participle (from 14th c.) of Old English *hātan* command, call]

high table *noun* (in some colleges in Britain and those elsewhere established on a British model) a table on a platform at a public dinner or for the fellows of a college.

high·tail *transitive verb N Amer. informal* □ **hightail it** hurry (*hightailed it to the grocery store*).

high tea *noun Brit.* a main evening meal usu. consisting of a cooked dish, bread and butter, tea, etc.

high-tech ● *adjective* **1** (of interior design etc.) imitating styles more usual in industry etc., esp. using steel, glass, or plastic in a functional way. **2** employing, requiring, or involved in high technology. **●** *noun* (**high tech**) = HIGH TECHNOLOGY.

high technology *noun* advanced technological development, esp. in electronics.

high-tensile *adjective* (of metal) having great tensile strength.

high tension *noun* = HIGH VOLTAGE.

high tide *noun* **1** the tide at its fullest. **2** the time of this.

high time *noun* a time that is late or overdue (*it is high time they arrived*).

high-toned *adjective* stylish; dignified; superior.

high-top *N Amer.* ● *adjective* designating shoes, esp. athletic shoes, whose uppers come above the ankle bone. ● *noun* (in *pl.*) high-top shoes.

high treason *noun see* TREASON 1.

high voltage ● *noun* electrical potential large enough to cause injury or damage if diverted. ● *adjective* (also **high-voltage**) **1** involving high electrical voltage. **2** displaying a great deal of energy (*a high-voltage performance*).

high water *noun* = HIGH TIDE.

high-water mark *noun* **1** the level reached at high water. **2** the maximum recorded value or highest point of excellence.

High·way, Tom·son (b.1951), Canadian Cree writer. He has won two Dora Mavor Moore Awards for his plays *The Rez Sisters* (1986) and *Dry Lips Oughta Move to Kapuskasing* (1989), and wrote the novel *Kiss of the Fur Queen* (1998), about two Cree brothers at a residential school.

high·way *noun* **1 a** a main road, esp. one between towns or cities. **b** a public road. **c** a much-travelled route leading directly to a place (*the Mackenzie River: history's highway to the Arctic Ocean*). **2** a direct course of action (*on the highway to success*).

highway·man *noun* (*pl.* **-men**) *hist.* a man, usu. mounted and armed with a gun, who robbed travellers on public roads.

highway robbery *noun informal* a price or charge that is unreasonably or exorbitantly high.

high wire ● *noun* a high tightrope. ● *adjective* (**high-wire**) requiring great skill or judgment (*a high-wire act of diplomacy*).

high yellow *noun US slang offensive* a light-skinned person of mixed black and white parentage.

HIH *abbreviation* Her or His Imperial Highness.

hi-hat *noun* a pair of cymbals mounted one above the other on an upright rod, with a sprung pedal at the base to move the upper cymbal down onto the other.

hi·jab /hɪˈʒɒb, -ˈdʒɒb/ *noun* a veil worn by some Muslim women to cover the hair, forehead, etc. [Arabic]

hi·jack ● *transitive verb* **1** seize control of (an aircraft in flight, a loaded truck, etc.), esp. to force it to a different destination. **2** seize (goods) in transit. **3** take over (an organization etc.) by force or subterfuge in order to redirect it. ● *noun* an instance of hijacking. □ **hi·jack·er** *noun* [20th c.: origin unknown]

Hijaz *see* HEJAZ.

hi·jinks *plural noun* (also **highjinks**) boisterous joking or merrymaking.

hijra *var. of* HEGIRA.

hike ● *noun* **1** a long walk, esp. in the country, taken for pleasure or exercise. **2** an increase (of prices etc.). ● *verb* **1** *intransitive* go for a long walk, esp. across country. **2** (usu. foll. by *up*) **a** *transitive* hitch up (clothing etc.); hoist; shove. **b** *intransitive* work upwards out of place, become hitched up. **3** *transitive* increase (prices etc.). □ **take a hike** esp. *N Amer.* go away (*she told him to take a hike*). □ **hik·er** *noun* [19th-c. dial.: origin unknown]

hiking boot *noun* a moderately low-cut leather boot with a heavy tread, worn esp. when hiking.

Hila /ˈhiːlə/ an Inuit deity, the spirit of the wind and the supreme force underlying all natural phenomena.

hila *pl. of* HILUM.

hil·ari·ous /hɪˈlɛriəs/ *adjective* **1** exceedingly funny. **2** boisterously merry. □ **hil·ari·ous·ly** *adverb* **hil·ari·ous·ness** *noun* **hil·ar·ity** *noun* [Latin *hilaris* from Greek *hilaros* cheerful]

Hil·ary term /ˈhɪləri/ *noun Brit.* the university term beginning in January, esp. at Oxford. [*Hilarius* bishop of Poitiers d.367, with a festival on 13 January]

Hil·bert, David (1862–1943), German mathematician. He contributed to the knowledge of algebraic numbers, and reorganized the axiomatic foundations of geometry.

Hilda, St. (614–80), English abbess. Related to the Saxon kings of Northumbria, around 658 she founded a monastery for both men and women at Whitby. She was one of the leaders of the Celtic Church delegation at the Synod of Whitby. Feast day, 17 November.

Hilde·gard of Bing·en, St. (1098–1179), German abbess, scholar, composer, and mystic. A Benedictine nun, she described and illustrated her mystical experiences in *Scivias*, wrote poetry, and composed sacred music.

hill ● *noun* **1** a naturally raised area of land, not as high as a mountain. **2** (often in *combination*) a heap; a mound (*anthill; dunghill*). **3** a sloping piece of road. **4** (**the Hill**) **a** (in Canada) = PARLIAMENT HILL. **b** (in the US) = CAPITOL HILL. **5 a** a heap formed around a plant by banking up soil. **b** a cluster of plants in such a hill or on level ground. ● *transitive verb* **1** form into a hill. **2** (usu. foll. by *up*) bank up (plants) with soil. □ **old as the hills** very ancient. **over the hill** *informal* **1** past the prime of life; declining. **2** past the crisis. **up hill and down dale** *see* UP. [Old English *hyll*]

Hil·lary, Sir Ed·mund Per·ci·val (b.1919), New Zealand mountaineer and explorer. In 1953, he and Tenzing Norgay were the first to reach the summit of Mount Everest.

hill·billy esp. *US* ● *noun* (*pl.* **-lies**) **1** *informal*, often *derogatory* a person from a remote or mountainous area, esp. in the Appalachians. **2** country music of or like that of the southern US. ● *adjective* of, like, or relating to hillbillies. [HILL + *Billy*, pet form of the name *William*]

hill climb *noun* a race for vehicles up a steep hill.

Hil·lel /ˈhɪləl/ (1st c. BC–1st c. AD), rabbi, president of the Sanhedrin. He was the first to formulate principles of Biblical interpretation.

hill fort *noun* a fort built on a hill.

Hil·liard /ˈhɪliɑrd/ **Nicho·las** (1547–1619), English painter, known for his miniatures of Queen Elizabeth I and her court.

hill·ock /ˈhɪlək/ *noun* a small hill or mound. □ **hill·ocky** *adjective*

hill·side ● *noun* the sloping side of a hill. ● *adjective* located on the side of a hill.

hill station *noun Anglo-Indian* a government settlement, esp. for holidays etc. during the hot season, in the low mountains of the northern Indian subcontinent.

hill·top *noun* the summit of a hill.

hilly *adjective* (**hill·i·er, hill·i·est**) having many hills. □ **hill·i·ness** *noun*

hilt ● *noun* **1** the handle of a sword, dagger, etc. **2** the handle of a tool. ● *transitive verb* provide with a hilt. □ **to the hilt** completely. [Old English *hilt(e)* from Germanic]

hilum /ˈhaɪləm/ *noun* (*pl.* **hila** /-lə/) **1** *Bot.* the point of attachment of a seed to its seed vessel. **2** *Anat.* a notch or indentation where a vessel enters an organ. [Latin, = little thing, trifle]

him *pronoun* **1** *objective case of* HE (*I saw him*). **2** *informal* he (*it's him again; is taller than him*). ¶ See Usage Note at HER. [Old English, masc. and neuter dative sing. of HE, IT]

Hi·ma·chal Pra·desh /hɪˌmʌtʃəl prəˈdeʃ/ a mountainous state in N India; capital, Simla.

Hima·lay·as, the /ˌhɪməˈleɪəz/ a vast mountain system in S Asia, extending 2 400 km (1500 miles) from Kashmir eastward to Assam. The Himalayas consist of a series of parallel ranges rising up from the Ganges basin to the Tibetan plateau, at over 3 000 m above sea level, and include the Karakoram, Zaskar, and Ladakh ranges. The backbone is the Great Himalayan Range, the highest mountain range in the world, with several peaks rising to over 7 700 m (25,000 ft.), the highest peak being Mount Everest. □ **Hima·lay·an** *adjective* [Sanskrit from *hima* snow + *ālaya* abode]

hi·mat·ion /hɪˈmatɪən/ *noun hist.* the outer garment worn by the ancient Greeks over the left shoulder and under the right. [Greek]

Himm·ler, Hein·rich (1900–45), German Nazi leader, chief of the SS (1929–45) and of the Gestapo (1936–45). He established and oversaw the program of systematic genocide of over 6 million Jews and other disfavoured groups between 1941 and 1945.

Hims *see* HOMS.

him·self *pronoun* **1 a** *emphatic form of* HE or HIM (*he himself will do it*). **b** *reflexive form of* HIM (*he has hurt himself*). **2** in his normal state of body or mind (*does not feel quite himself today*). **3** esp. *Irish* a third party of some importance; the master of the house. □ **be himself** act in his normal unconstrained manner. **by himself** *see* BY ONESELF (*see* BY).

Hi·na·yana /ˌhiːnəˈjɒnə/ *noun* a name given by the followers of Mahayana Buddhism to the more orthodox and, as they thought, less central, schools of early Buddhism. The Hinayana tradition died out in India by the 7th c. AD but survived in Ceylon (Sri Lanka) as the Theravada school and was taken from there to Burma, Thailand, and other regions of SE Asia. [Sanskrit from *hīna* lesser + *yāna* vehicle]

hind¹ *adjective* (esp. of parts of the body) situated behind or at the back, posterior (*hind leg*) (*opp.* FORE). [Middle English, perhaps shortened from Old English *bihindan* BEHIND]

hind² *noun* a female deer (usu. a red deer or sika), esp. in and after the third year. [Old English from Germanic]

hind³ *noun hist.* a servant, esp. an agricultural worker. [Old English *hīne* (pl.) apparently from *hī(g)na* genitive pl. of *hīgan*, *hīwan* 'members of a family' (compare HIDE³): for -d compare SOUND³]

hind·brain *noun Anat.* the lower part of the brain stem, comprising the cerebellum, pons, and medulla oblongata.

Hin·de·mith /ˈhɪndəˌmɪt/ **Paul** (1895–1963), German composer and theorist. His music, which includes operas (such as *Mathis der Maler*, 1938), concertos, and orchestral and chamber music, is basically contrapuntal and forms part of the neoclassical trend which began in the 1920s.

Hin·den·burg¹ /ˈhɪndənˌbɜrk/ the former German name (1915–45) for ZABRZE.

Hin·den·burg² /ˈhɪndənˌbɜrg/ **Paul Lud·vig von Ben·eck·en·dorff und von** (1847–1934), German Field Marshal and president of the Weimar Republic 1925–34. Commander-in-chief of German forces from 1916, he directed the war effort in partnership with Ludendorff. He appointed Hitler as Chancellor in 1933.

Hin·den·burg Line (also called the **Siegfried Line**) in the First World War, the fortified line of defence on the German Western Front, to which Hindenburg directed retreat and which was not breached until near the end of the war.

hin·der¹ /ˈhɪndər/ *transitive & intransitive verb* impede, delay, prevent, or obstruct (*you will hinder him*; *hindered me from working*). [Old English *hindrian* from Germanic]

hin·der² /ˈhaɪndər/ *adjective* rear, hind (*the hinder part*). [Middle English, perhaps from Old English *hinderweard* backward: compare HIND¹]

hind·gut *noun* the end part of an animal's intestine.

Hindi /ˈhɪndi/ ● *noun* **1** a group of spoken dialects of N India. **2** a literary form of Hindustani with a Sanskrit-based vocabulary and the Devanagari script, an official language of India. ● *adjective* of or concerning Hindi. [Urdu *hindī* from *Hind* India]

hind·milk *noun* breast milk exuded after the first part of a feeding, containing more fat and nutrients than the milk at the beginning of the feeding.

hind·most *adjective* furthest behind; most remote.

hind·quar·ters *plural noun* the hind legs and adjoining parts of a quadruped.

hin·drance /ˈhɪndrəns/ *noun* **1 a** the act or an instance of hindering. **b** the state of being hindered. **2** a person or thing that hinders; an obstacle.

hind·sight *noun* wisdom after the event (*realized with hindsight that they were wrong*) (*opp.* FORESIGHT 1).

hind tit *noun slang* a position of inferiority. □ **suck the hind tit** be in a position of inferiority, esp. in receiving less money than others.

Hin·du /ˈhɪnduː/ (also *archaic* **Hin·doo**) ● *noun* (*pl.* **Hin·dus**) **1** a follower of Hinduism. **2** *archaic* an Indian. ● *adjective* **1** of or concerning Hindus or Hinduism. **2** *archaic* Indian. [Urdu from Persian from *Hind* India]

Hindu·ism /ˈhɪnduːˌɪzəm/ *noun* the main religious and social system of India, including a belief in reincarnation, the worship of several gods, and an ordained caste system as the basis of society. □ **Hindu·ize** *transitive verb* (also esp. *Brit.* **-ise**).

Hindu Kush /ˌhɪnduː ˈkuːʃ, ˈkuʃ/ a range of high mountains in N Pakistan and Afghanistan, forming a westward continuation of the Himalayas. Several peaks exceed 6 150 m (20,000 ft.), the highest being Tirich Mir.

Hindu·stan /ˌhɪnduˈstɑn/ *hist.* the Indian subcontinent in general, more specifically that part of India north of the Deccan, esp. the plains of the Ganges and Jumna rivers.

Hindu·stani /ˌhɪnduˈstɑni/ ● *noun hist.* **1** a group of mutually intelligible languages and dialects spoken in NW India, principally Hindi and Urdu. **2** the Delhi dialect of Hindi, widely used throughout India as a lingua franca. ¶ *Hindustani* was the usual term in the 18th and 19th c. for the native language of NW India. The usual modern term is *Hindi*, although *Hindustani* is still sometimes used to refer to the lingua franca. ● *adjective* of or relating to Hindustan or its people, or Hindustani. [Urdu from Persian *hindūstānī* (as HINDU + -*stān* 'country')]

hind·wing *noun* either of the posterior wings of an insect.

Hines, Earl 'Fatha Hines' (1905–83), US jazz pianist, bandleader, and songwriter.

hinge ● *noun* **1 a** a movable, usu. metal, joint or mechanism on which a lid, door, gate, etc. turns or swings as it opens and closes. **b** *Biol.* a natural joint performing a similar function, e.g. that of a bivalve shell. **2** a central point or principle on which everything depends. **3** a small piece of gummed, transparent paper used for fixing a postage stamp in an album etc. ● *verb* **1** *intransitive* (foll. by *on*) depend (on a principle, an event, etc.) (*everything hinges on his acceptance*). **b** (of a door etc.) hang and turn (on a post etc.). **2** *transitive* attach with or as if with a hinge. □ **hinged** *adjective* **hinge·less** *adjective* [Middle English *heng* etc., related to HANG]

hinky *adjective* esp. *N Amer. informal* **1** (of a person) dishonest or suspect. **2** (of an object) unreliable. [20th c.: origin uncertain]

hinny¹ *noun* (*pl.* **-nies**) the offspring of a female donkey and a male horse. [Latin *hinnus* from Greek *hinnos*]

hinny² *noun* (also **hin·nie**) (*pl.* **-nies**) *Scot. & Northern England* (esp. as a form of address) darling, sweetheart. [var. of HONEY]

Hin·shel·wood, Sir Cyril Nor·man (1897–1967), English physical chemist. He made contributions to reaction kinetics in gases and liquids, suggested the role of nucleic acids in protein synthesis, and shared the Nobel Prize for chemistry in 1956.

hint ● *noun* **1** a slight or indirect indication or suggestion (*took the hint and left*). **2** a small piece of practical information; a tip (*handy hints on cooking*). **3** a very small trace, a slight indication (*a hint of perfume*; *a hint of sadness in his voice*). ● *transitive verb* (often foll. by *that* + clause) suggest slightly or indirectly (*hinted the contrary*; *hinted that they were wrong*). □ **hint at** give a hint of or refer indirectly to. **take a** (or **the**) **hint** understand what is meant or stated indirectly and act accordingly. [apparently from obsolete *hent* grasp, lay hold of, from Old English *hentan*, from Germanic, related to HUNT]

hin·ter·land *noun* **1** a remote or fringe area; backcountry. **2** the often deserted or uncharted areas beyond a coastal district or a river's banks. **3** an area served by a port or other centre. [German from *hinter* behind + *Land* LAND]

Hin·ton a town in west central Alberta, about 275 km west of Edmonton; pop. (2001) 9,405. □ **Hinton·ite** *noun* [after the *Hinton Trail*, a route leading from Jasper to Yukon, after W. P. *Hinton*, president and general manager of the Grand Trunk Pacific Railway *c.*1917]

hip¹ *noun* **1** a projection of the pelvis and upper thigh bone on each side of the body in human beings and quadrupeds. **2** (often in *pl.*) the part on each side of the human body between the top of the legs and the waist. **3** *Archit.* the sharp edge of a roof from ridge to eaves where two sides meet. □ **hip·less** *adjective* [Old English *hype* from Germanic, related to HOP¹]

hip² *noun* (*Brit.* also **hep**) the fruit of a rose, esp. a wild kind. [Old English *hēope*, *hīope* from West Germanic]

hip³ *slang* ● *adjective* (also **hep**) (**hip·per**, **hip·pest** or **hep·per**, **hep·pest**) **1** following the latest fashion in esp. music, clothes, etc.; stylish. **2** (often foll. by *to*) understanding, aware. ● *transitive verb* (**hipped**, **hip·ping**) (often foll. by *to*) make (a person) hip; inform, tell. □ **hiply** *adverb* **hip·ness** *noun* [20th c.: origin unknown]

hip⁴ *interjection* introducing a united cheer (*hip, hip, hooray*). [19th c.: origin unknown]

hip bone *noun* a bone forming the hip, esp. the ilium.

hip boot *noun* a tall boot reaching to the hip, usu. made of rubber, worn by firefighters, fly fishermen, etc.

hip cat *noun* = HEPCAT.

hip check *Hockey* ● *noun* a type of bodycheck in which a player suddenly thrusts his or her hips to the side to obstruct or hit an opponent who is attempting to skate past. ● *transitive verb* (**hip-check**) hit or obstruct in this way.

hip dysplasia *noun* an abnormal development of the hip joint in some mid- to large-sized dogs caused by a combination of hereditary and environmental factors and resulting in pain, an impaired gait, lameness, etc.

hip flask *noun* a small metal bottle for liquor etc., carried in a hip pocket.

hip hop *noun* **1** a style of popular music of US black origin, featuring frequently politically inspired raps delivered above spare, electronic backing. **2** the subculture associated with this, including graffiti art, urban fashion, breakdancing, etc. □ **hip-hopper** *noun* [20th c.: perhaps from HIP¹, reduplicated with alteration of vowel as a jingling refrain]

hip-huggers *plural noun* snugly fitting pants or shorts hanging from the hips rather than the waist. □ **hip-hugger** *adjective* **hip-hugging** *adjective*

hip joint *noun* the articulation of the head of the thigh bone with the ilium.

hip-length *adjective* (of a garment) reaching down to the hips.

Hip·par·chus /hɪˈpɑːkəs/ (*c*.190–after 126 BC) Greek astronomer and geographer. He discovered the precession of the equinoxes, suggested improved methods of determining latitude and longitude, and developed trigonometry.

hip·pe·as·trum /ˌhɪpɪˈastrəm/ *noun* any S American bulbous plant of the genus *Hippeastrum* with showy white or red flowers. [modern Latin from Greek *hippeus* horseman (the leaves appearing to ride on one another) + *astron* star (from the shape of the flower)]

hipped *adjective* (usu. foll. by *on*) esp. *US slang* enthusiastic about, obsessed with. [past participle of *hip* (v.) = make hip (HIP³)]

hipped roof *var. of* HIP ROOF.

hip·pie *noun* (also **hippy**) (*pl.* **-pies**) *informal* **1** (esp. in the 1960s) a young person who rejected traditional societal values, advocated free love, peace, etc., and adopted an unconventional appearance, typically with long hair, jeans, beads, etc. **2** a person resembling a hippie in dress, beliefs, etc. □ **hippie·dom** *noun* [HIP³]

hip·po *noun* (*pl.* **-pos**) *informal* a hippopotamus. [abbreviation]

hippo·cam·pus /ˌhɪpəˈkampəs/ *noun* (*pl.* **hippo·campi** /-pi/) **1** a sea horse. **2** *Anat.* the elongated ridges on the floor of each lateral ventricle of the brain, thought to be the centre of emotion and the autonomic nervous system. □ **hippo·cam·pal** *adjective* [Latin from Greek *hippokampos* from *hippos* horse + *kampos* sea monster]

hip pocket *noun* a pocket just behind the hip on pants etc. □ **in one's hip pocket** *N Amer. informal* completely under control.

hip·po·cras /ˈhɪpəˌkras/ *noun hist.* wine flavoured with spices. [Old French *ipocras* Hippocrates (see HIPPOCRATIC OATH), prob. because strained through a filter called 'Hippocrates' sleeve']

Hip·poc·ra·tes /hɪˈpɒkrəˌtiːz/ (*c*.460–377 BC), Greek physician, commonly regarded as the father of modern medicine. He regarded the body as a single organism, and formulated a theory of disease.

Hip·po·crat·ic oath /ˌhɪpəˈkratɪk/ *noun* (*hist.* except in revised form in certain medical schools) an oath, taken by doctors prior to beginning medical practice, affirming their obligations and proper conduct. [medieval Latin *Hippocraticus* from HIPPOCRATES]

Hip·po·crene /ˈhɪpəˌkriːn/ *noun literary* poetic or literary inspiration. [name of a fountain on Mount Helicon sacred to the Muses: Latin from Greek from *hippos* horse + *krēnē* fountain, as having been produced by a stroke of Pegasus' hoof]

hippo·drome /ˈhɪpəˌdroʊm/ *noun* **1** *hist.* a dance hall. **2** (in ancient Greece or Rome) a course for chariot races etc. [French *hippodrome* or Latin *hippodromus* from Greek *hippodromos* from *hippos* horse + *dromos* race, course]

hippo·griff /ˈhɪpəˌgrɪf/ *noun* (also **hippo·gryph**) a mythical creature with the body and hindquarters of a horse and the wings and head of a griffon. [French *hippogriffe* from Italian *ippogrifo* from Greek *hippos* horse + Italian *grifo* GRIFFIN]

Hip·poly·ta /hɪˈpɒlɪtə/ *Gk Myth* the queen of the Amazons, killed by Hercules in battle for her belt as one of his labours.

Hip·poly·tus /hɪˈpɒlɪtəs/ *Gk Myth* the son of Theseus, killed after being falsely accused of rape by his stepmother Phaedra.

Hip·pom·enes /hɪˈpɒmɪˌniːz/ *Gk Myth* the husband of Atalanta (*see* ATALANTA).

hippo·pota·mus /ˌhɪpəˈpɒtəməs/ *noun* (*pl.* **hippo·pota·mus·es** or **hip·po·pota·mi** /-ˌmaɪ/) **1** a large thick-skinned four-legged mammal, *Hippopotamus amphibius*, native to Africa, inhabiting rivers, lakes, etc. **2** (in full **pygmy hippopotamus**) a smaller related mammal, *Choeropsis liberiensis*, native to Africa, inhabiting forests and swamps. [Latin from Greek *hippopotamos* from *hippos* horse + *potamos* river]

hippy¹ *var. of* HIPPIE. □ **hippy·ish** *adjective*

hippy² *adjective* having large hips.

hippy-dippy *adjective informal* rejecting conventional practices or behaviour in a way perceived to be vague and unconsidered or foolishly idealistic.

hip roof *noun* (also **hipped roof**) a roof with both the sides and the ends inclined.

hip·ster¹ ● *noun* **1** hip-hugger underpants. **2** *Brit.* (in *pl.*) = HIP-HUGGERS. ● *adjective Brit.* (of a garment) hanging from the hips rather than the waist.

hip·ster² *noun slang* a person who is hip; a hepcat. □ **hip·ster·ism** *noun*

hip waders *plural noun* waders that come up to the hips.

hira·gana /ˌhɪrəˈɡanə/ *noun* the cursive form of Japanese syllabic writing or kana (*compare* KATAKANA). [Japanese, lit. 'plain kana']

hire ● *transitive verb* **1** esp. *N Amer.* employ (a person) for wages or a fee. **2** (often foll. by *from*) procure the temporary use of (a thing) for an agreed payment. ● *noun* **1** an act or instance of hiring or being hired. **2** payment for this. **3** *N Amer.* a recently hired employee. □ **for** (or **on**) **hire** ready to be hired. **hire on** *N Amer.* take a job or obtain employment, esp. at a specific task, company, etc. **hire out 1** grant the temporary use of (a thing) for an agreed payment. **2** *reflexive* make oneself available for employment. □ **hir·er** *noun* [Old English *hȳrian*, *hȳr* from West Germanic]

hire car *noun Brit.* a rental car.

hired girl *noun* (also **hired man**) *N Amer.* a domestic servant, esp. on a farm.

hired gun *noun* esp. *N Amer. informal* **1 a** an expert brought in to resolve complex esp. legal or financial problems, disputes, etc. **b** a person, e.g. a lobbyist, able to attain power or influence for others quickly and efficiently. **2 a** a bodyguard, mercenary, or other person hired to protect or fight for another. **b** a person contracted to kill another, e.g. a hit man or gunfighter.

hired hand *noun N Amer.* a person employed to do usu. manual work on a farm, ranch, etc.

hire·ling *noun* usu. *derogatory* a person who works primarily for monetary gain, esp. without other motives such as job satisfaction etc. [Old English *hȳrling* (as HIRE, -LING¹)]

hire purchase *noun Brit.* = INSTALMENT PLAN.

hi-res *adjective* high resolution.

Hiro·hito /ˌhɪrəˈhiːtoʊ/ (born Michinomiya Hirohito) (1901–89), emperor of Japan 1926–89. He was obliged to renounce his divinity and become a constitutional monarch by the terms of the constitution established in 1946.

Hiro·shige /ˌhɪrəˈʃiːɡeɪ/ **Ando** (1797–1858), Japanese artist known esp. for his colour woodblock prints.

Hiro·shi·ma /ˌhɪrəˈʃiːmə, hɪˈroʊʃɪmə/ a city on the south coast of the island of Honshu, W Japan, capital of Chugoku region; pop. (est. 2002) 1,132,900. It was the target of the first atomic bomb, which was dropped by the US on 6 Aug. 1945 and resulted in the deaths of about one-third of the city's population of 300,000. Together with a second attack, on Nagasaki three days later, this led to Japan's surrender and the end of the Second World War.

Hirsch /hɜːʃ/ **John Ste·phen** (1930–1989), Hungarian-born Canadian theatre, film and television director. He was chief of television drama for the CBC (1974–78) and artistic director of the Stratford Festival (1981–85).

hir·sute /ˈhɜːsuːt, ˈhɜːsuːt, -sjuːt/ *adjective* **1** hairy, shaggy. **2** *Bot. & Zool.* covered with long soft or moderately stiff hairs. □ **hir·sute·ness** *noun* [Latin *hirsutus*]

hir·sut·ism /ˈhɜːsjuːˌtɪzəm/ *noun* the excessive growth of hair on the face and body.

his *possessive adjective* **1** (*attributive*) of or belonging to him or himself (*his house; his own business*). **2** the one or ones belonging to or associated with him (*it is his; his are over there*). **3** (**His**) (*attributive*) (in titles) that he is (*His Majesty*). □ **his and hers** *jocular* (of matching items) for husband and wife, or men and women. **of his** of or belonging to him (*a friend of his*). [Old English, genitive of HE, IT]

His·pan·ic /hɪˈspanɪk/ ● *adjective* **1** of or relating to Spain or to Spanish-speaking countries. **2** of or relating to Hispanics. ● *noun* a Spanish-speaking person living in the US or Canada, esp. one of Latin American descent. □ **His·pani·cize** /-ˌsaɪz/ *transitive verb* (also esp. *Brit.* **-cise**). [Latin *Hispanicus* from *Hispania* Spain]

His·pani·ola /ˌhɪspaniˈoʊlə/ an island of the Greater Antilles in the W Indies, divided into the states of Haiti and the Dominican Republic. [from Spanish *La Isla Española* the Spanish island, so named by Columbus]

His·pan·ist /ˈhɪspənɪst/ *noun* an expert in or student of the language, literature, and civilization of Spain or Spanish-speaking countries.

Hispano- /hɪˈspanoʊ/ *combining form* Spanish. [Latin *Hispanus* Spanish]

his·pid /ˈhɪspɪd/ *adjective Bot. & Zool.* bristly; covered with short stiff hairs. [Latin *hispidus*]

hiss ● *verb* **1** *intransitive* **a** make a sharp sibilant sound (*the goose hissed at me angrily; the water hissed on the hot plate*). **b** make this sound to show disapproval or derision (*the audience booed and hissed*). **2** *transitive* express disapproval of (a person etc.) by hisses. **3** *transitive* whisper (a threat etc.) urgently or angrily (*'Get back!' he hissed*). ● *noun* **1** a sharp sibilant sound as of the letter *s*. **2** *Electronics* unwanted interference at audio frequencies. □ **hiss off** hiss (actors etc.) so that they leave the stage. □ **hiss·er** noun **hissy** adjective [Middle English: imitative]

hissy fit noun N Amer. informal a temper tantrum; an angry outburst.

hist interjection archaic used to call attention, enjoin silence, incite a dog, etc. [16th c.]

hist. abbreviation **1** history. **2** historical.

his·ta·mine /ˈhɪstəmɪn, ˈhɪstəˌmiːn/ noun Biochem. an amine causing contraction of smooth muscle and dilation of capillaries, released by most cells in response to injury and in allergic and inflammatory reactions. [HISTO- + AMINE]

his·ti·dine /ˈhɪstɪˌdiːn/ noun Biochem. an amino acid present in proteins and from which histamine is derived. [Greek histos web, tissue]

histo- combining form (also **hist-** before a vowel) Biol. tissue. [Greek histos web]

histo·chem·istry noun the study of the identification and distribution of the chemical constituents of tissues by means of stains, indicators, and microscopy. □ **histo·chem·ical** adjective

histo·com·pat·ibil·ity noun compatibility between the tissue of different individuals, so that one accepts a graft from the other without giving an immune reaction.

histo·gen·esis /ˌhɪstəˈdʒɛnəsɪs/ noun the production and differentiation of organic tissues. □ **histo·gen·etic** /-dʒəˈnɛtɪk/ adjective

histo·gram noun Statistics a chart consisting of rectangles (usu. drawn vertically from a base line) whose areas and positions are proportional to the value or range of a number of variables. [Greek histos mast + -GRAM]

his·tol·ogy /hɪˈstɒlədʒi/ noun **1** the study of the microscopic structure of tissues. **2** the microscopic structure of tissues. □ **histo·logic** adjective **histo·logic·al** adjective **histo·logic·al·ly** adjective **his·tol·o·gist** noun

his·tone /ˈhɪstoːn/ noun Biochem. any of a group of proteins found in chromatin. [German Histon perhaps from Greek histamai arrest, or as HISTO-]

histo·path·ol·ogy /ˌhɪstoːpəˈθɒlədʒi/ noun **1** changes in tissues caused by disease. **2** the study of these. □ **histo·patho·logic** /ˌhɪstoːpaθəˈlɒgɪk/ adjective **histo·patho·logic·al** adjective **histo·path·ol·o·gist** noun

histo·plas·mo·sis /ˌhɪstoːplazˈmoːsɪs/ noun infection with Histoplasma capulatum, a fungus found in the droppings of birds and bats in humid areas, which may be a transient benign infection of the lungs or a disseminated usu. fatal disease of the reticuloendothelial system.

his·tor·ian noun **1** a writer of history, esp. a critical analyst, rather than a compiler. **2** a person learned in history, esp. one professionally engaged in teaching and researching history (Canadian historian; ancient historian).

his·tori·ated /hɪˈstɔriˌeɪtɪd/ adjective decorated with historical, legendary, or emblematic designs.

his·tor·ic adjective **1** famous or important in history or potentially so (a historic moment). **2** archaic or disputed = HISTORICAL. **3** Grammar (of a tense) normally used in the narration of past events, esp. Latin & Greek imperfect and pluperfect (compare PRIMARY adjective 8).

his·tor·ic·al adjective **1** of or concerning history (historical evidence). **2** belonging to history, not to prehistory or legend. **3** (of the study of a subject) based on an analysis of its development over a period. **4** belonging to the past, not the present. **5** (of a novel, a film, etc.) dealing or professing to deal with historical events. **6** in connection with history, from the historian's point of view (of purely historical interest).

his·tor·ic·al·ly adverb **1** with reference to past events (a historically accurate reconstruction). **2** in the past (historically, government policy has favoured urban dwellers).

his·tori·cism noun **1** a the theory that social and cultural phenomena are determined by history. **b** the belief that historical events are governed by laws. **2** the tendency to regard historical development as the most basic aspect of human existence. **3** an excessive regard for past styles etc. □ **his·tori·cist** noun

his·tori·city /ˌhɪstəˈrɪsɪti/ noun the historical genuineness of an event etc.

his·tori·cize /hɪˈstɒrəsaɪz, -stɒrə-/ transitive verb make or represent as historical. □ **his·tori·ciz·a·tion** noun **his·tori·cized** adjective **his·tori·ciz·ing** noun & adjective

his·tori·ograph·er /hɪˌstɔriˈɒgrəfər, -stɒri-/ noun **1** an expert in or student of historiography. **2** a writer of history, esp. an official historian.

his·tori·og·raphy /hɪˌstɔriˈɒgrəfi, -stɒri-/ noun **1** the writing of history. **2** the study of history-writing. **3** written history. □ **his·torio·graph·ic** /-ˈgrafɪk/ adjective **his·torio·graph·ic·al** adjective **his·torio·graph·ic·al·ly** adverb

his·tory noun (pl. **-ies**) **1** a continuous, usu. chronological, record of important or public events. **2 a** the study of past events, esp. human affairs. **b** the total accumulation of past events, esp. relating to human affairs or to the accumulation of developments connected with a particular nation, person, thing, etc. (the history of Canada; the history of astronomy; has a history of illness). **3** an eventful past (this house has a history). **4 a** a systematic or critical account of or research into a past event, development, movement, etc. (the history of broadcasting). **b** a similar record or account of natural phenomena. **5** a historical play. □ **be history** informal be no longer existing, relevant, or important (one more mistake and I'll be history). **go down in history** be remembered or recorded in history. **make history 1** do or take part in something important enough to be recorded in the world's or one's country's history. **2** do something unusual or important, esp. something never before done in an art, science, profession, sport, etc. **the rest is history** a concluding statement suggesting that the events succeeding those already related are so familiar as to need no repetition. [Latin historia from Greek historia finding out, narrative, history, from histōr learned, wise man, related to WIT²]

history-making adjective important enough to be recorded in the world's or one's country's history.

his·tri·on·ic /ˌhɪstriˈɒnɪk/ ● adjective **1** (of behaviour) theatrical; dramatically exaggerated. **2** of or concerning actors or acting. ● noun **1** (in pl.) insincere and dramatic behaviour designed to impress. **2** theatricals; theatrical art. □ **his·tri·on·ic·ally** adverb [Late Latin histrionicus from Latin histrio -onis actor]

hit ● verb (**hit·ting**; past and past participle **hit**) **1** transitive **a** strike with a blow or a flying object. **b** (of a moving object) strike against, crash into, or collide with (the plane hit the ground). **c** reach (a target, a person, etc.) with a directed flying object (hit the window with the ball). **2** transitive affect the feelings, conscience, etc. of a person, esp. deeply or painfully (the loss hit him hard). **3** intransitive (often foll. by at, against, upon) direct a blow. **4** transitive (often foll. by against, on) knock (a part of the body) (hit his head on the door frame). **5** transitive light upon; get at (a thing aimed at) (he's hit the truth at last; tried to hit the right tone in his apology) (see HIT ON 1). **6** transitive informal **a** encounter (hit a snag). **b** arrive at (hit an all-time low; hit the town). **c** indulge in, esp. liquor etc. (hit the bottle). **7** transitive esp. N Amer. slang kill, attack, or rob. **8** transitive **a** occur forcefully to (the seriousness of the situation only hit him later). **b** come suddenly to mind; occur to (a person) (couldn't remember where I'd seen him before, and then it suddenly hit me). **9** transitive Sport **a** propel (a ball etc.) with a bat, club, etc. to score runs or points. **b** score (runs or points) in this way. **c** Baseball make (a base hit). **10** transitive & intransitive slang give (a person) a playing card, alcoholic drink, etc. **11** transitive esp. N Amer. (also foll. by up) request, ask, or beg (a person), esp. for money. **12** transitive represent or imitate exactly (hit the exact colour). ● noun **1 a** a blow; a stroke. **b** a collision. **2** a shot etc. that hits its target. **3** informal **a** a popular success, esp. in entertainment. **b** a successful pop record. **4** a stroke of sarcasm, wit, etc. **5** esp. N Amer. slang **a** a violent crime, esp. a contract killing. **b** a dose of something, esp. an illegal drug. **6** Baseball = BASE HIT. **7** esp. Brit. a stroke of good luck. **8** a successful attempt, esp. an instance of identifying an item of data which matches the requirements of a search etc. □ **hit back** retaliate. **hit below the belt 1** esp. Boxing hit an opponent below the waist, esp. in the genitals. **2** treat or behave unfairly. **hit the books** N Amer. study, esp. intensely or diligently. **hit the bottle** (or **booze** etc.) informal drink too much habitually or over a period of time. **hit the bricks** N Amer. slang go on strike. **hit for the cycle** Baseball (of a player) hit a single, double, triple, and home run in a single game. **hit the deck** informal fall to the floor, ground, etc. **hit the ground running** esp. N Amer. informal **1** begin a task, endeavour, etc. with the basic preparation already completed. **2** proceed with enthusiasm and dynamism. **hit the headlines** see HEADLINE. **hit home 1** become fully and often painfully clear. **2** (of remarks etc.) have the intended, often painful, effect. **hit it** Music begin playing. **hit it off** (often foll. by with, together) informal get on well or have a good and harmonious relationship (with a person). **hit the nail on the head** guess correctly or express the truth precisely. **hit on 1** (also **hit upon**) find (what is sought), esp. by chance. **2** slang make sexual overtures toward (a person). **hit out** deal vigorous physical or verbal blows (hit out at her enemies). **hit the road** (also N Amer. **trail**) slang depart. **hit the roof** see ROOF. **hit the sack** (also **hit the hay**) informal go to bed. **make** (or **be**) **a hit** (usu. foll. by with) be successful or popular. □ **hit·less** adjective **hit·table** adjective **hit·ter** noun [Old English hittan from Old Norse hitta meet with, of unknown origin]

t top   v voice   w we   z zoo   ʃ she   ʒ vision   θ thin   ð this   ŋ ring   x loch   tʃ chip   dʒ jar   (see over for vowels)

hit-and-miss *adjective* (also **hit-or-miss**) aimed or done carelessly, at random, or haphazardly.

hit and roll *Curling* ● *noun* a play in which a curled rock strikes and glances off a stationary rock, sliding into a better position and usu. knocking the other rock into a less advantageous position. ● *intransitive verb* make such a play.

hit and run ● *noun* **1 a** a motor vehicle accident in which the driver who caused the accident flees the scene. **b** a military etc. attack using swift actions followed by immediate withdrawals. **2** *Baseball* the departure of a runner from his or her base as soon as the pitcher begins to throw to the batter. ● *adjective* (**hit-and-run**) relating to or (of a person) committing a hit and run (*hit-and-run fatalities*).

hit and stay (also **hit and stick**) *Curling* ● *noun* a play in which a curled rock strikes an opponent's rock directly, knocking it into a less advantageous position and, at the same time, assumes the position of the previously stationary rock. ● *intransitive verb* make such a shot.

hitch ● *verb* **1 a** *transitive* fasten with a loop, hook, etc., tether (*hitched the horse to the cart*). **b** *intransitive* (often foll. by *in, on to*, etc.) become fastened in this way (*the rod hitched in to the bracket*). **2 a** *transitive* move (a thing) with a jerk; shift slightly (*hitched the pillow to a comfortable position*). **b** *intransitive* move jerkily or unsteadily (*the snowmobile began to hitch*). **3** *informal* **a** *intransitive* = HITCHHIKE. **b** *transitive* obtain (a lift) by hitchhiking. **4** *intransitive* catch, snag, or become caught on something. ● *noun* **1** an impediment; a temporary obstacle (*the unit ran without a hitch*). **2 a** an abrupt pull or push; a jerk. **b** *Baseball* a flaw in batting style in which the batter brings the bat forward and then draws it back slightly before swinging. **3** any of various kinds of noose or knot used to fasten one thing temporarily to another (*diamond hitch; clove hitch*). **4** a contrivance for fastening one thing to another (*trailer hitch*). **5** *N Amer. slang* a period of service in the military etc. **6** *informal* a free ride in a vehicle. □ **get hitched** *informal* marry. **hitch up 1** lift (esp. clothing) with a jerk. **2** meet, join, or become associated with. **hitch one's wagon to a star** associate oneself with a person more prominent than oneself; make use of powers or opportunities greater than one's own. □ **hitch·er** *noun* [Middle English: origin uncertain]

Hitch·cock, Sir Al·fred (Jo·seph) (1899–1980), English film director. His films, such as *The Thirty-Nine Steps* (1935), *Rebecca* (1940), *Psycho* (1960) and *The Birds* (1963), are notable for their technical ingenuity and ability to create suspense. □ **Hitch·cock·i·an** *adjective*

hitch·hike *intransitive verb* travel by seeking free lifts in passing vehicles. □ **hitch·hik·er** *noun* **hitch·hik·ing** *noun*

hitching post *noun* (also **hitching rail**) a fixed post or rail for tethering a horse.

hi-tech *adjective* = HIGH-TECH. [respelling]

hither usu. *formal* or *literary* ● *adverb* to or towards this place. ● *adjective* *archaic* situated on this side; the nearer (of two). [Old English *hider*: compare THITHER]

hither and thither *adverb* (also **hither and yon**) here and there, in various directions, to and fro.

hither·to *adverb* until this time, up to now.

Hit·ler[1], **Adolf** (1889–1945), Austrian-born German Chancellor and Nazi Leader 1933–45, co-founder of the National Socialist Workers' Party (1919). Imprisoned in 1923, he wrote *Mein Kampf*, an exposition of his political ideas. Following his release, his powers as an orator enabled him to overthrow the Weimar Republic and establish the totalitarian Third Reich, proclaiming himself *Führer*. His expansionist foreign policy precipitated the Second World War, and his fanatical anti-Semitism led to the deaths of millions of Jews in an attempt to create an Aryan German state. □ **Hit·ler·ian** /hɪtˈlɛrɪən/ *adjective* **Hit·ler·ite** *noun & adjective*

Hit·ler[2] *noun* a tyrannical, dictatorial person, esp. a ruler (*a little Hitler*). [HITLER[1]]

Hit·ler·ism *noun* the political principles or policy of the Nazi Party in Germany. [HITLER[1]]

hit list *noun slang* **1** a list of prospective victims esp. of assassination. **2** a list of people, programs, etc. against whom some action is being planned (*which industries are on the government's privatization hit list?*).

hit·maker *noun informal* an entertainer, esp. a musician, who consistently produces bestselling records etc.

hit man *noun slang* a hired assassin.

hit-or-miss *adjective* = HIT-AND-MISS.

hit parade *noun informal* **1** a list of the current bestselling records of popular music. **2** any listing of popular people, things, etc. in a specified field.

Hit·tite /ˈhɪtaɪt/ ● *noun* **1** a member of an ancient, non-Semitic people of Asia Minor and Syria. **2** the Indo-European language of the Hittites, written in cuneiform and deciphered in the early 20th c. ● *adjective* of or relating to the Hittites or their language. [Hebrew *Ḥittīm*]

hit woman *noun slang* a female hired assassin.

HIV *abbreviation* human immunodeficiency virus, a retrovirus which causes AIDS.

hive ● *noun* **1 a** a beehive. **b** the bees in a hive. **2** a busy, swarming place. **3** a swarming multitude. **4** a thing shaped like a hive in being domed. ● *verb* **1** *transitive* place (bees) in a hive. **2** *intransitive* (of bees) enter a hive. **3** *transitive* gather, hoard, store up, as bees with honey. □ **hive off 1** separate from a larger group. **2 a** form into or assign (work) to a subsidiary department or company. **b** denationalize or privatize (an industry etc.). [Old English *hȳf* from Germanic]

hives *plural noun* any of various skin conditions characterized by itchy red weals caused by allergic reaction, emotional stress, etc. [16th c. (originally Scots): origin unknown]

hiya *interjection informal* a word used in greeting. [corruption of *how are you?*]

HK *abbreviation* **1** Hong Kong. **2** *N Amer.* housekeeping (*HK cottages*).

HL *abbreviation* (in the UK) House of Lords.

hl *abbreviation* hectolitre(s).

HLA *abbreviation* human leukocyte antigen, any of a number of genetically determined antigens that occur on the surface of all nucleated cells and play a major role in crossmatching procedures to determine whether a transplanted organ etc. will be rejected.

HM *abbreviation* *Brit.* **1** Her (or His) Majesty('s). **2 a** headmaster. **b** headmistress. **3** *Mus.* heavy metal.

hm *abbreviation* hectometre(s).

HMCS *abbreviation* Her (or His) Majesty's Canadian Ship (as a designation for a Canadian naval vessel).

HMD *abbreviation* head-mounted display, a viewing system that is worn on and moves with the head, allowing the person wearing it to participate interactively in a virtual reality environment.

HMG *abbreviation* (in the UK) Her (or His) Majesty's Government.

HMI *abbreviation* (in the UK) Her (or His) Majesty's Inspector (of Schools).

hmm *interjection* (also **hmmm**) indicating hesitation, contemplation, etc.

HMO *abbreviation US* = HEALTH MAINTENANCE ORGANIZATION.

Hmong /hmɒŋ/ ● *noun* (*pl.* same) **1** a member of a people living in isolated mountain villages throughout SE Asia. **2** the language of this people, occurring in a large number of highly distinct dialects. ● *adjective* relating to or denoting this people or their language. [Chinese, self-designation]

HMS *abbreviation* Her (or His) Majesty's Ship (as a designation for a British naval vessel).

Hna·tyshyn /nəˈtɪʃən/ **Ramon John** 'Ray' (1934–2002), Canadian lawyer and politician. First elected to the House of Commons as a Conservative MP in 1974, he served as minister of energy (1979–80), government leader (1984–86), and minister of justice (1986–88). He was Governor General 1990–95 and inaugurated the Governor General's Performing Arts Awards.

Ho *symbol Chem.* the element holmium.

ho[1] *interjection* **1 a** an expression of admiration or (often repeated as **ho! ho!**), derision, surprise, or triumph. **b** (in *combination*) (*heigh-ho*). **2** a call for attention. **3** (in *combination*) an addition to the name of a destination etc. (*westward ho*). [Middle English, imitative: compare Old Norse *hó*]

ho[2] *noun* (*pl.* **hos**) esp. *N Amer. slang* **1** a prostitute. **2** *derogatory* a woman. [representing a pronunciation of WHORE *noun*]

hoag·ie *noun* (also **hoagy**) *US* = SUB *noun* 2.

hoar *literary* ● *adjective* **1** grey-haired with age. **2** greyish-white. **3** (of a thing) grey with age. ● *noun* **1** = HOARFROST. **2** hoariness. [Old English *hār* from Germanic]

hoard ● *noun* **1** a stock or store (esp. of money) put away. **2** an amassed store of facts etc. **3** *Archaeology* an ancient store of treasure etc. ● *verb* **1** *transitive & intransitive* (often foll. by *up*) amass (money etc.) and put away; store. **2** *intransitive* accumulate more than one's current requirements of food etc. in a time of scarcity. □ **hoard·er** *noun* [Old English *hord* from Germanic]

hoard·ing *noun* **1** a temporary board fence erected around a construction site etc. **2** *Brit.* = BILLBOARD. [obsolete *hoard* from Anglo-French *h(o)urdis* from Old French *hourd, hort*, related to HURDLE]

hoar·frost *noun* frozen water vapour deposited in clear still weather on vegetation etc.

hoarse *adjective* **1** (of the voice) rough and deep; husky; croaking.

Vowels: a *cat*   ɑ *arm*   e *bed*   ɜr *her*   ɜː *deux*   ə *ago*   ɪ *sit*   i *cosy*   iː *feed*   ɒ *hot*   ɔ *pore*   ɔː *no*   ʌ *run*   ʊ *put*

2 having such a voice, due to illness, shouting, etc. □ **hoarse·ly** *adverb* **hoarse·ness** *noun* [Old Norse *hārs* (unrecorded) from Germanic]

hoary *adjective* (**hoar·i·er, hoar·i·est**) **1 a** (of hair) grey or white with age. **b** (of a person) having such hair; aged, venerable. **2** old and trite (*a hoary joke*). **3** *Bot. & Zool.* covered with short white hairs. □ **hoar·i·ly** *adverb* **hoar·i·ness** *noun*

hoary marmot *noun* a large marmot, *Marmota caligata*, of mountains of NW America, which has greyish-brown fur with a mantle of white on the shoulders and back, and a piercing whistling call. *Also called* WHISTLER.

ho·at·zin /hoʊˈatsɪn/ *noun* a tropical American bird, *Opisthocomus hoatzin*, whose young climb by means of hooked claws on their wings. [Latin American Spanish from Nahuatl *uatzin*, prob. imitative]

hoax ● *noun* a humorous or malicious deception; a practical joke. ● *transitive verb* deceive (a person) with a hoax. □ **hoax·er** *noun* [18th c.: prob. contraction from HOCUS]

hob[1] *noun* **1 a** *Brit.* a cooking appliance or the flat top part of a stove, with hot plates or burners. **b** a flat metal shelf at the side of a fireplace, having its surface level with the top of the grate, used esp. for heating a pan etc. **2** a tool used for cutting gears etc. [perhaps var. of HUB, originally = lump]

hob[2] *noun* **1** a male ferret. **2** a hobgoblin. □ **play** (or **raise**) **hob** *N Amer.* cause mischief or act disruptively. [Middle English, familiar form of *Rob*, short for *Robin* or *Robert*]

Ho·bart /ˈhoʊbɑrt/ the capital and chief port of Tasmania; pop. (2001) 197,800.

Hob·bema /ˈhɒbəmə/ **Mein·dert** (1638–1709), Dutch landscape painter. His work often includes a water mill and trees around a pool.

Hobbes /hɒbz/ **Thom·as** (1588–1679), English philosopher. A materialist and cynic, his view of society was expressed in his most famous work, *Leviathan* (1651), in which he argued that simple rationality made social institutions and even absolute monarchy inevitable and stated that human life was 'solitary, poor, nasty, brutish, and short'. □ **Hobbes·ian** *adjective & noun*

hob·bit *noun* a member of an imaginary race similar to humans, of small size and with hairy feet, in stories by J.R.R. Tolkien. [invented by J.R.R. TOLKIEN, and said by him to mean 'hole-dweller']

hob·ble ● *verb* **1** *intransitive* **a** walk lamely; limp. **b** proceed haltingly in action or speech (*hobbled lamely to his conclusion*). **2** *transitive* **a** tie together the legs of (a horse etc.) to prevent it from straying etc. **b** tie or fasten (a horse's etc. legs). **3** *transitive* **a** cause (a person etc.) to limp. **b** hinder, interfere with, foil, or perplex (a person, plan, etc.). ● *noun* **1** an uneven or infirm gait. **2** a rope, clog, etc. used for hobbling a horse etc. [prob. from Low German: compare Dutch *hobbelen* rock from side to side]

hobble·bush *noun* = MOOSEWOOD 2.

hobble·de·hoy *noun* *informal* a clumsy or awkward youth. [16th c.: origin unknown]

hobble skirt *noun* a skirt so narrow at the hem as to impede walking.

hobby[1] *noun* (pl. **-bies**) **1** a favourite leisure-time activity or occupation. **2** *archaic* a small horse. □ **hobby·ist** *noun* [Middle English *hobyn, hoby*, from pet forms of *Robin*: compare DOBBIN]

hobby[2] *noun* (pl. **-bies**) any of several small long-winged Eurasian falcons, esp. *Falco subbuteo*, catching prey on the wing. [Old French *hobé, hobet* diminutive of *hobe* small bird of prey]

hobby farm *noun* *N Amer. & Austral.* a very small farm operated primarily for pleasure rather than profit. □ **hobby farmer** *noun*

hobby horse *noun* **1** a child's toy consisting of a long stick with a figure of a horse's head on one end. **2** a preoccupation; a favourite topic of conversation. **3** a model of a horse, esp. of wicker, used in pantomime, morris dancing, etc. **4** a rocking horse. **5** a horse on a merry-go-round.

hob·gob·lin *noun* **1** a mischievous imp or sprite. **2** something to be feared superstitiously; a bogey, a bugbear. [HOB[2] + GOBLIN]

hob·nail *noun* **1** a heavy-headed nail used for boot soles. **2** a pattern in glass etc. consisting of closely spaced studs or bosses, often in the shape of diamonds. □ **hob·nailed** *adjective* [HOB[1] + NAIL]

hob·nob *intransitive verb* (**hob·nobbed, hob·nob·bing**) (usu. foll. by *with*) mix socially or informally. □ **hob·nob·ber** *noun* [*hob* or *nob* = give or take, of alternate drinking; earlier *hab nab*, = have or not have]

hobo *noun* (pl. **hoboes** or **hobos**) esp. *N Amer.* **1** a tramp or vagrant. **2** an unskilled worker who moves from place to place. [19th c.: origin unknown]

Hobson's choice *noun* a choice of taking the thing offered or

nothing. [T. *Hobson*, Cambridge carrier d.1631, who let out horses on the basis that customers must take the one nearest the door]

Ho·che·laga /ˌhɒʃəˈlɒgə/ a former Iroquoian village, an agricultural community located at the present-day site of Montreal. Jacques Cartier arrived there in the fall of 1535.

Ho Chi Minh /ˌhoʊ tʃiː ˈmɪn/ (born Nguyen That Thanh) (1890–1969), Vietnamese Communist leader, president of North Vietnam 1954–69. A committed nationalist, he was instrumental in gaining his country's independence from France.

Ho Chi Minh City the official name (since 1975) for SAIGON.

hock[1] *noun* **1** the joint of a quadruped's hind leg between the knee and the fetlock. **2** a knuckle of pork; the lower joint of a ham. [obsolete *hockshin* from Old English *hōhsinu* hamstring]

hock[2] *noun* esp. *Brit.* a German white wine from the Rhineland (properly that of Hochheim on the Main River). [abbreviation of obsolete *hockamore* from German *Hochheimer*]

hock[3] *transitive verb* esp. *N Amer. informal* pawn. □ **in hock 1** in debt. **2** in pawn. [Dutch *hok* hutch, prison, debt]

hock·ey *noun* **1** (often *attributive*) *N Amer.* **a** a game played on ice between two teams of six players each, in which players try to shoot a puck into the opposing team's net with sticks. **b** any of a number of variations of this game, such as street hockey or shinny. **2** *Brit.* = FIELD HOCKEY. [16th c.: origin unknown]

hockey bag *noun* a large esp. nylon bag for carrying hockey equipment, usu. with pockets for skates.

hockey club *noun* a hockey team.

hockey cushion *noun* *Cdn* a skating rink with hockey boards, esp. an outdoor rink of natural ice.

hockey glove *noun* a padded glove worn by hockey players for protection against slashing etc.

hockey hair *noun* *slang* = MULLET[2].

hockey jacket *noun* *Cdn* an outer jacket, usu. of nylon with a quilted lining, with a hockey team's crest on the chest and the owner's name, position, number, etc. embroidered on the arm.

hockey mom *noun* (also **hockey mother**) *N Amer.* a mother deeply committed to a child's hockey practice, career, etc., who spends much time, effort, and money to ensure the child receives the best training, advantages, etc.

hockey pants *plural noun* knee-length, high-waisted padded pants worn by hockey players to protect their thighs, hips, and kidneys.

hockey puck *noun* **1** = PUCK 1. **2** an object the size or shape of a hockey puck.

hockey socks *plural noun* long woollen leggings extending from thigh to ankle, held up by a garter belt and with stirrups for the feet, worn by hockey players.

hockey stick *noun* a stick with a flat, slightly curved blade at the lower end, used to control, pass, and shoot the puck in hockey.

hockey tape *noun* an adhesive tape used esp. on the blade of a hockey stick to strengthen it or on the handle to improve the grip.

Hock·ney, David (b.1937), English artist, best known for paintings, such as *A Bigger Splash* (1967), which depict flat, almost shadowless architecture, lawns, and swimming pools.

Hoc·quart /ɒˈkɑr/ **Gilles** (1694–1783), intendant of New France 1731–1748. He encouraged agriculture, shipbuilding, and ironworking, and built roads to connect Quebec City to Montreal and Montreal to Lake Champlain. These policies were offset by the lack of government funding, crop failures, and by war with the British.

hocus *transitive verb* (**ho·cussed, hocus·sing**; *US* ho·cused, hocus·ing) **1** take in; hoax. **2** stupefy (a person) with drugs. **3** add a drug to (liquor). [obsolete *noun hocus* = HOCUS-POCUS]

hocus-pocus *noun* **1** a deception; trickery. **b** magic, dazzle. **2 a** a typical verbal formula used in conjuring. **b** esoteric or in-group jargon. [17th-c. sham Latin]

hod *noun* **1** a V-shaped open trough on a pole used for carrying bricks, mortar, etc. **2** a portable receptacle for coal. [prob. = dial. *hot* from Old French *hotte* pannier, from Germanic]

Ho·dei·da /hoʊˈdeɪdə/ the chief port of Yemen, on the Red Sea; pop. (est. 2002) 382,400.

hodge·podge *noun* esp. *N Amer.* **1** a mixture of heterogeneous things, a jumble. **2** *Cdn* (*Maritimes*) a dish of potatoes and other vegetables cooked in milk and butter. [variant of HOTCHPOTCH assimilated to *Hodge*, nickname for *Roger*]

Hodg·kin ▸ 1 Alan Lloyd (1914–98), English physiologist. Working with A.F. Huxley, he explained the chemical and physical aspects of nervous impulses; they shared a Nobel Prize in 1963. **2 Dor·othy Crow·foot** (1910–94), Egyptian-born British chemist who studied the chemical structure of insulin; she won the Nobel Prize for chemistry in 1964.

Hodgkin's disease *noun* a malignant but often curable disease of the lymphatic system usu. characterized by enlargement of the lymph nodes, liver, and spleen. [T. *Hodgkin*, English physician d.1866]

hodo·graph /ˈhɒdəˌɡrɑːf/ *noun* a curve in which the radius vector represents the velocity of a moving particle. [Greek *hodos* way + -GRAPH]

hoe ● *noun* a long-handled tool with a thin metal blade, used for weeding etc. ● *verb* (**hoes, hoed, hoe·ing**) **1** *transitive* weed (crops); loosen (earth); dig up or cut down with a hoe. **2** *intransitive* use a hoe. [Old French *houe* from Germanic]

hoe·cake *noun US* a coarse cake of cornmeal originally baked on the blade of a hoe.

hoe·down *noun N Amer.* **1** a lively party with square dancing, country music, etc. **2** the music played at such a party.

Hofei see HEFEI.

Hoffa, James Rid·dle 'Jimmy' (1913–75), US labour leader, President of the International Brotherhood of Teamsters 1957–71. Known to have ties with organized crime, he disappeared in 1975.

Hoff·man, Dus·tin Lee (b.1937), US actor. He has appeared in a wide variety of films including *The Graduate* (1967), *Midnight Cowboy* (1969), *Rain Man* (1989), for which he received his second Oscar, and *Wag the Dog* (1997).

Hof·mann, Hans (1880–1966), German-born US artist, a pioneer of abstract expressionism in painting.

Hof·manns·thal /ˈhɒfmənsˌtɑːl/ **Hugo von** (1874–1929), Austrian poet and dramatist. He wrote the libretti for Richard Strauss's operas *Elektra* (1909), *Der Rosenkavalier* (1911), *Ariadne auf Naxos* (1912), and *Arabella* (1933), and helped found the Salzburg Festival.

hog ● *noun* **1 a** a domesticated pig, esp. a castrated male reared for slaughter. **b** any of several other pigs of the family Suidae, e.g. a warthog. **2** *informal* **a** a greedy person. **b** a person who hoards selfishly or monopolizes something (*a puck hog*). **3** *N Amer. slang* a large, heavy motorcycle. ● *verb* (**hogged, hog·ging**) **1** *transitive informal* take greedily; hoard selfishly; monopolize. **2** *transitive & intransitive* raise (the back), or rise in an arch in the centre. □ **go (the) whole hog** *informal* do something completely or thoroughly. **live high on** (or **off**) **the hog** *N Amer. informal* live luxuriously.

Hogan /ˈhoʊɡən/ **(Wil·liam) Ben·ja·min** (1912–97), US golfer. He won the PGA championship in 1948, and the US Open championship in 1948, 1950, 1951, and 1953.

Ho·garth /ˈhoʊɡɑːrθ/ **Wil·liam** (1697–1764), English painter and engraver. His satirical paintings include his series of engravings on 'modern moral subjects', such as *A Rake's Progress* (1735).
□ **Ho·garth·ian** *adjective*

hog·back *noun* (also **hog's back**) a ridge of land sloping steeply on each side.

hog fuel *noun* sawdust, wood chips, bark waste, etc. produced by sawmills or pulp and paper mills and used as fuel, landfill, animal feed, etc. [earlier sense of HOG, 'a traction engine, esp. a machine that grinds waste wood into small pieces']

Hogg, James (1770–1835), Scottish poet. After spending his youth and early adulthood as a shepherd, he earned a literary reputation as a writer of Romantic ballads.

Hog·gar Mountains /ˈhɒɡɑːr/ (also **Ahaggar Mountains** /ɒˈhɒɡɑːr/) a mountain range in the Saharan desert of S Algeria, rising to a height of 2 918 m (9,573 ft.) at Tahat.

hog heaven *noun informal* a place or condition of foolish or idle bliss.

hog line *noun Curling* a line drawn across each end of a rink at one-sixth of the rink's length from the tee, over which a rock must cross to count in the game.

Hog·ma·nay /ˌhɒɡməˈneɪ/ *noun Scot.* **1** New Year's Eve. **2** a celebration on this day. **3** a gift of cake etc. demanded by children at Hogmanay. [17th c.: perhaps from Norman French *hoguinané* from Old French *aguillanneuf* (also = new year's gift)]

hog·nose snake *noun* any of several harmless colubrid snakes constituting the N American genus *Heterodon*, which have an upturned snout and defensive behaviour including hissing, flattening the head, inflating the body, and feigning death.

hog's back *var. of* HOGBACK.

hogs·head *noun* **1** a large cask. **2** a liquid or dry measure, varying according to the commodity, but usu. about 220 to 245 litres (roughly 50 imperial gallons). [Middle English from HOG, HEAD: reason for the name unknown]

hog-tie *transitive verb* (**-tying**) *N Amer.* **1** secure by fastening the hands and feet or all four feet together. **2** restrain, impede.

Hog·town a nickname for Toronto. □ **Hog·town·er** *noun* [origin uncertain: perhaps with reference to the city's expanding farmers' markets and livestock trading during the early 19th c.]

hog·wash *noun* **1** *informal* nonsense, rubbish. **2** kitchen swill etc. for pigs.

hog·weed *noun* any of various coarse weeds of the genus *Heracleum*, esp. *H. sphondylium*.

hog-wild *adjective N Amer. informal* exceedingly excited or enthusiastic.

Hohen·stau·fen /ˈhoʊənˌʃtaʊfən/ the name of a German dynastic family, some of whom ruled as Holy Roman emperors between 1138 and 1254, among them Frederick I (Barbarossa).

Hohen·zol·lern /ˈhoʊənˌzɒlərn/ the name of a German dynastic family from which came the kings of Prussia from 1701 to 1918 and German emperors from 1871 to 1918.

Hoh·hot /hoʊˈhɒt/ (also **Huhe·hot** /ˌhuːheɪˈhɒt/) the capital of Inner Mongolia autonomous region, NE China; pop. (est. 2002) 1,036,700.

ho ho *interjection* **1** representing deep jolly laughter. **2** expressing surprise, triumph, or derision. [reduplication of HO[1]]

Ho·ho·kam /hoʊˈhoʊkəm/ ● *noun* **1** an extinct N American Aboriginal people. **2** the culture of this people, flourishing in Arizona after *c.*450, characterized by irrigated agriculture and houses built in pits. ● *adjective* of or pertaining to this people or culture. [Uto-Aztecan *hùhukam*, old one]

ho-hum ● *adjective* dull, routine, boring. ● *interjection* expressing boredom. [imitative of yawn]

hoick *verb informal* (often foll. by *out*) lift or pull, esp. with a jerk. [perhaps var. of HIKE]

hoi pol·loi /ˌhɔɪ pəˈlɔɪ/ *noun* (often prec. by *the*) the masses; the common people. ¶ Some object vehemently to the use with *the*, since *hoi* = 'the', but this construction is well established in English and it is neither necessary nor idiomatic to omit *the*. [Greek, = the many]

hoi·sin sauce /ˈhɔɪzɪn/ *noun* a sweet, spicy, dark red sauce made from soybeans, vinegar, sugar, garlic, and various spices, widely used in southern Chinese cooking. [Cantonese *hoisin*, seafood, from *hoi* sea + *sin* fresh]

hoist ● *transitive verb* **1** raise or haul up. **2** raise by means of ropes and pulleys etc. ● *noun* **1** an apparatus for hoisting. **2** an act of hoisting, a lift. **3 a** the perpendicular height of a flag or sail (*compare* FLY[1] *noun* 8a). **b** the part of a flag nearest the staff (*compare* FLY[1] *noun* 8b). **c** a group of flags raised as a signal. □ **hoist with one's own petard** *see* PETARD. □ **hoist·er** *noun* [16th c.: alteration of *hoise* from (15th-c.) *hysse*, prob. of Low German origin: compare Low German *hissen*]

hoity-toity ● *adjective* haughty, snobbish, pretentious. ● *interjection* expressing surprised protest at presumption etc. [obsolete *hoit* indulge in riotous mirth, of unknown origin]

Hokan /ˈhoʊkən/ ● *noun* a group of languages spoken by certain Aboriginal peoples of California, the US southwest, and Mexico. ● *adjective* designating or pertaining to such languages. [Hokan *hok* approximate form of 'two' + -AN]

hoke *transitive verb N Amer. slang* (foll. by *up*) make hokey. □ **hoked-up** *adjective*

hokey *adjective* (**hoki·er, hoki·est**) *N Amer. slang* sentimental, artificial. □ **hokey·ness** *noun* [HOKUM + -Y[2]]

hokey-cokey *noun Brit.* = HOKEY-POKEY 1. [perhaps from HOCUS-POCUS]

hokey-pokey *noun informal* **1** *N Amer.* a communal dance performed in a circle with synchronized shaking of the limbs in turn. **2** = HOCUS-POCUS. [HOCUS-POCUS]

Hok·kai·do /hɒˈkaɪdoʊ/ the most northerly of the four main islands of Japan, constituting an administrative region; pop. (est. 1999) 5,720,000; capital, Sapporo.

hokku /ˈhɒkuː/ *noun* (*pl.* same) = HAIKU. [Japanese]

hokum *noun* esp. *N Amer. slang* **1** sentimental, popular, sensational, or unreal situations, dialogue, etc., in a film or play etc. **2** bunkum; rubbish. [20th c.: origin unknown]

Ho·ku·sai /ˈhɒkuˌsaɪ, ˌhɒkʊˈsaɪ/ **Kat·su·shika** (1760–1849), Japanese painter and engraver. His woodcuts vividly depict Japanese everyday life, and his prints had a significant influence on Impressionist and Post-Impressionist artists such as Van Gogh.

Hol·arc·tic /hɒˈlɑːrktɪk/ ● *adjective* of, relating to, or found throughout the Nearctic and Palearctic regions considered together as a single zoogeographical region. ● *noun* the Holarctic region. [HOLO- + ARCTIC]

Hol·bein /ˈhɒlbaɪn/ **1 Hans** ('the Elder') (1465–1524), German painter, best known for his many magnificent altarpieces. **2** his son **Hans** ('the Younger') (1497–1543), German painter and engraver. He produced the series of woodcuts the *Dance of Death* (*c*.1523–6), and served as court painter to Henry VIII from 1536, painting many well known portraits, e.g. Henry VIII, Jane Seymour, Anne of Cleves, and Thomas More.

hold¹ ● *verb* (*past* and *past participle* **held**) **1** *transitive* **a** keep fast; grasp (esp. in the hands or arms). **b** (also *reflexive*) keep or sustain (a thing, oneself, one's head, etc.) in a particular position (*hold it to the light; held himself up*). **c** grasp so as to control (*hold the reins*). **2** *transitive* (of a vessel etc.) contain or be capable of containing (*the jug holds two litres; the hall holds 900*). **3** *transitive* possess, gain, or have, esp.: **a** be the owner or tenant of (land, property, stocks, etc.) (*holds the farm in trust*). **b** gain or have gained as an honour, achievement, or qualification (a degree, record, etc.) (*holds the long jump record*). **c** have the position of (a job or office). **d** have (a specified playing card) in one's hand. **e** keep possession of (a place, a person's thoughts, etc.) esp. against attack (*held the fort against the enemy; held her place in our estimation*). **4** *intransitive* remain unbroken; not give way (*the roof held under the storm*). **5** *transitive* observe; celebrate, conduct (a meeting, festival, conversation, etc.). **6** *transitive* **a** keep (a person etc.) in a specified condition, place, etc. (*held him prisoner; held him at arm's length*). **b** detain, esp. in custody (*hold him until I arrive*). **7** *transitive* **a** engross (a person or a person's attention) (*the book held him for hours*). **b** dominate (*held the stage*). **8** *transitive* (foll. by *to*) make (a person etc.) adhere to (terms, a promise, etc.). **9** *intransitive* (of weather) remain free of rain, snow etc.; continue sunny and clear. **10** *transitive* (often foll. by *to* + infin., or *that* + clause) think; believe (*held it to be self-evident; held that the earth was flat*). **11** *transitive* regard with a specified feeling (*held him in contempt*). **12** *transitive* **a** cease; restrain (*hold your fire*). **b** *N Amer. informal* withhold; not use (*a burger please, and hold the onions!*). **13** *transitive* keep or reserve (*will you hold our seats please?*). **14** *transitive* be able to drink (liquor) without obvious effect. **15** *transitive* (usu. foll. by *that* + clause) (of a judge, a court, etc.) decide; state as an authoritative opinion; lay down as a point of law. **16** *transitive Music* sustain (a note). **17** *intransitive archaic* restrain oneself. **18** *intransitive* remain connected by telephone without speaking to someone. **19** *transitive* (of a computer, answering machine, etc.) retain or temporarily store information, data, messages, etc. **20** *transitive N Amer. informal* be in possession of illegal drugs, esp. for sale. ● *noun* **1** a grasp (*get hold of him; keep a hold on him*). **2** (often in *combination*) a thing to hold by (*seized the handhold*). **3** (foll. by *on*, *over*) a controlling influence over (*has a strange hold over them*). **4** a manner of holding in wrestling etc. **5** a facility offered by some telephone systems whereby an incoming connection is held open until a specified recipient can take the call. **6** a pause, delay, or postponement. **7** a request ordering or reserving (a book, video, etc.). □ **get (a) hold of 1** acquire, obtain, etc. **2** contact or communicate with, esp. by telephone. **hold (a thing) against (a person)** resent or regard (a thing) as discreditable to (a person). **hold aloof** avoid communication with people etc. **hold back 1** impede the progress of; restrain. **2** keep (a thing) to or for oneself. **3** (often foll. by *from*) hesitate; refrain. **hold one's breath** see BREATH. **hold by** (or **to**) adhere to (a choice, purpose, etc.). **hold dear** regard with affection. **hold down 1** repress. **2** *informal* be competent enough to keep (one's job etc.). **3** secure, restrain, or limit. **hold everything!** cease action or movement. **hold the fort 1** act as a temporary substitute. **2** cope in an emergency. **hold forth 1** offer (an inducement etc.). **2** usu. *derogatory* speak at length or tediously. **hold one's ground** see GROUND¹. **hold one's hand** = STAY ONE'S HAND (see HAND). **hold a person's hand** give a person guidance or moral support. **hold hands** grasp one another by the hand as a sign of affection or for support or guidance. **hold harmless** *Law* indemnify. **hold one's head high** behave proudly and confidently. **hold one's horses** *informal* stop; slow down. **hold in** keep in check, confine. **hold it!** stop; cease and desist. **hold the line 1** not yield. **2** maintain a telephone connection. **hold one's nose 1** compress the nostrils to avoid a bad smell. **2** repress one's repugnance about doing something (*hold your nose and vote Conservative*). **hold off 1** delay; not begin. **2** keep one's distance. **hold on 1** keep one's grasp on something. **2** wait a moment. **3** (when telephoning) not hang up. **hold out 1** stretch forth (a hand etc.). **2** offer (an inducement etc.). **3** maintain resistance. **4** persist or last. **hold out for** continue to demand. **hold out on** *informal* refuse something to (a person). **hold over 1** postpone, keep for future consideration. **2** retain for an additional period (*the movie was held over for another week*). **hold something over** threaten (a person) constantly with something. **hold one's own** see OWN. **hold together 1** cohere. **2** cause to cohere. **3** retain its composure, esp.

in difficult circumstances. **hold one's tongue** *informal* be silent. **hold to ransom 1** keep (a person) prisoner until a ransom is paid. **2** demand concessions from by threats of damaging action. **hold that thought** an instruction to someone not to say anything further on a subject for the moment. **hold true** (or **good**) be valid; apply. **hold up 1 a** support; sustain. **b** maintain (the head etc.) erect. **2** exhibit; display. **3** arrest the progress of; obstruct. **4** stop and rob by violence or threats. **hold water** (of reasoning) be sound; bear examination. **hold with** (usu. with *neg*.) *informal* approve of (*don't hold with motorbikes*). **on hold 1** (when telephoning) holding the line. **2** reserved (*the book is on hold*). **3** (esp. in phr. **put on hold**) temporarily inactive or receiving little attention. **take hold** (of a custom or habit) become established. **there is no holding him** (or **her** etc.) he (or she etc.) is restive, high-spirited, determined, etc. **with no holds barred** with no restrictions, all methods being permitted. □ **hold·able** *adjective* [Old English *h(e)aldan*, *heald*]

hold² *noun* a cavity in the lower part of a ship or aircraft in which the cargo is stowed. [obsolete *holl* from Old English *hol* (originally adj. = hollow), related to HOLE, assimilated to HOLD¹]

hold·all *noun* esp. *Brit.* a portable case or bag for miscellaneous articles.

hold·back *noun* **1** something that restrains or holds back. **2** *N Amer.* a thing held back, e.g. a fee, tax, etc.

hold'em *noun* a type of poker in which players are dealt a two-card hand, which they combine with three of five cards dealt to the centre of the table.

hold·er *noun* **1** (often in *combination*) a device or implement for holding something (*cigarette holder*). **2 a** the possessor of a title, record, etc. **b** the occupant of an office etc. **c** a person who holds a bank account, credit card, company share, etc. **3** *Brit.* = SMALLHOLDER.

hold·fast *noun* **1** a firm grasp. **2** the attachment organ of an alga etc. **3** a staple or clamp securing an object to a wall etc.

hold·ing *noun* **1 a** a land held by lease. **b** the tenure of land. **2** (usu. in *pl.*) stocks, property, etc. held. **3** *Sport* the action of illegally restraining or obstructing one's opponent. **4** the collection of books, journals, artworks, etc. in a library or museum.

holding cell *noun* a small cell in a courthouse in which prisoners are kept awaiting court appearances or during recesses.

holding company *noun* a company created to hold the shares of other companies, which it then controls.

holding pattern *noun* **1** the (usu. circular) flight path maintained by an aircraft awaiting permission to land. **2** a state or period of no progress or change.

holding pen *noun* **1** a paddock where sheep or cattle are kept until required (for driving, shearing, etc.). **2** any actual or notional place in which people are kept together to wait for something (*the green room was the holding pen for the show's guests; the fashion section was the traditional holding pen for female journalists*).

holding tank *noun* **1** a tank for short-term storage of a substance. **2** *slang* a holding cell for prisoners. **3** any actual or notional place in which people stay while waiting for something (*have the universities become holding tanks for those who cannot find jobs?*).

hold·out *noun* **1** an act of holding out against some trend, or of staying out of some activity. **2** a person who does this, esp. *N Amer.* a baseball player who refuses to play until paid more.

hold·over *noun* **1** *N Amer.* a person or thing left over from the past; a relic. **2** a person who remains in office, on a team, etc. beyond the regular term etc.

hold·up *noun* **1** a stoppage or delay by traffic, inclement weather, etc. **2** a robbery, esp. by the use of threats or violence.

hole ● *noun* **1 a** an empty space in a solid body. **b** an aperture in or through something. **2** an animal's burrow. **3** a cavity or receptacle into which the ball must be propelled in various sports or games, e.g. golf. **4** *informal* a small, mean, or dingy abode. **5** a dungeon or prison cell, esp. a cell used for solitary confinement. **6** *informal* an awkward or embarrassing situation. **7** a deep place in a river, stream, etc. (*swimming hole*). **8** *Golf* **a** a point scored by a player who gets the ball from tee to hole with the fewest strokes. **b** the terrain or distance from tee to hole. **9** an opening or vacancy (*the hiring filled a hole in our department*). **10** a position from which an electron is absent, esp. acting as a mobile positive particle in a semiconductor. ● *verb* **1** *transitive* make a hole or holes in. **2** *transitive* pierce the side of (a ship etc.). **3** *transitive* put into a hole. **4** *transitive & intransitive* (often foll. by *out*) send (a golf ball) into a hole. □ **dig a hole for oneself** create a difficult situation for oneself, from which escape is difficult. **hole up** *N Amer. informal* **1** hide oneself. **2** take shelter (for the night, the winter, etc.). **in the hole** *N Amer. informal* in debt. **make a hole in** use a large amount of. **a**

round (or **square**) **peg in a square** (or **round**) **hole** *see* PEG.
□ **holey** *adjective* [Old English *hol, holian* (as HOLD²)]

hole-and-corner *adjective* secret; underhand.

hole card *noun* **1** (in stud poker) a card which has been dealt face down. **2** *informal* something held in reserve until it can be used to one's advantage.

hole-in-one *noun* (*pl.* **holes-in-one**) *Golf* a shot that enters the hole from the tee.

hole in the heart *noun* a congenital defect in the heart septum.

hole in the wall *noun* **1** a small dingy place (esp. of business). **2** *Brit.* a bank machine in the wall of a building.

-holer *combining form* *informal* **1** designating a privy etc. with a specified number of toilet seats (*one-holer*). **2** designating a golf course with a specified number of holes (*nine-holer*).

Holi /ˈhoːliː/ *noun* the Hindu spring festival in honour of Krishna the amorous cowherd. [Hindustani *holī*]

Hol·i·day, Bil·lie (born Eleanora Fagan) (1915–59), US jazz singer who began her career in 1933 with Benny Goodman's band. Her style was characterized by dramatic intensity and vocal agility.

holi·day ● *noun* **1 a** a day on which most work, school, and business ceases, esp. in honour of a person or event (*compare* STATUTORY HOLIDAY). **b** a religious festival. **2** esp. *Cdn, Brit., Austral. & NZ* (often in *pl.*) a period of rest from work, school, etc., usu. for a certain number of weeks per year. **3** (in *pl.*) (also **holiday season**) the festive period surrounding Christmas, Hanukkah, and New Year's. **4** (*attributive*) (of clothes etc.) festive. ● *intransitive verb* spend a holiday. □ **take a holiday** have a break from work. □ **holi·day·er** *noun* [Old English *hāligdæg* (HOLY, DAY)]

holiday·maker *noun* esp. *Brit.* a person on holiday.

holiday weekend *noun* a long weekend on which the Friday or Monday is a holiday.

holier-than-thou *adjective* *informal* self-righteous.

hol·i·ly *adverb* in a holy manner.

hol·i·ness *noun* **1** sanctity; the state of being holy. **2** (**Holiness**) a title used when referring to or addressing the Pope.

Hol·in·shed /ˈhɒlɪnˌʃed/ **Raph·ael** (died *c.*1580), English chronicler. He compiled *The Chronicles of England, Scotland and Ireland* (1577), which was widely used by Shakespeare and other dramatists.

hol·ism /ˈhoːlɪzəm/ *noun* (also **wholism**) **1** *Philos.* the theory that certain wholes are to be regarded as greater than the sum of their parts (*compare* REDUCTIONISM 2). **2** *Med.* the treating of the whole person including mental and social factors rather than just the symptoms of a disease. □ **hol·ist** *noun* **hol·is·tic** *adjective* **hol·is·tic·ally** *adverb* [as HOLO- + -ISM]

Hol·land **1** the Netherlands. **2** a former province of the Netherlands, comprising the coastal parts of the country. It is now divided into **North Holland** and **South Holland**.

hol·land *noun* a smooth, hard-wearing, linen fabric. [HOLLAND, where it was originally made]

hol·land·aise sauce /ˈhɒlənˌdeɪz/ *noun* a creamy sauce of melted butter, egg yolks, lemon juice, etc., served esp. with fish or in eggs benedict. [French, fem. of *hollandais* Dutch, from *Hollande* Holland]

Hol·land·er *noun* a native of Holland (the Netherlands).

Hol·lands *noun* gin made in Holland. [Dutch *hollandsch genever* Dutch gin]

hol·ler esp. *N Amer. informal* ● *verb* **1** *intransitive* make a loud cry or noise. **2** *transitive* express with a loud cry or shout. ● *noun* a loud cry, noise, or shout. [var. of earlier *hollo*]

Hol·ler·ith /ˈhɒlərɪθ/ **Her·man** (1860–1929), US computer scientist. He invented a tabulating machine using punched cards for computation, and founded a company in 1896 that later expanded to become the IBM Corporation.

hol·low ● *adjective* **1 a** having a hole or cavity inside; not solid throughout. **b** having a depression; sunken (*hollow cheeks*). **2** (of a sound) echoing, as though made in or on a hollow container. **3** empty; hungry. **4** without significance; meaningless (*a hollow triumph*). **5** insincere; cynical; false (*a hollow laugh; hollow promises*). ● *noun* **1** a hollow place; a hole. **2** a valley; a basin. **3** (also **hollow of the hand**) the enclosed space formed by the palm of the hand with the fingers curled inwards. ● *transitive verb* (often foll. by *out*) make hollow; excavate. ● *adverb* *informal* completely (*beaten hollow*). □ **hol·low·ly** *adverb* **hol·low·ness** *noun* [Middle English *holg, holu, hol(e)we* from Old English *holh* cave, related to HOLE]

hollow-cheeked *adjective* with sunken cheeks.

hollow-eyed *adjective* with eyes deeply sunk, or appearing to be deeply sunk, esp. due to lack of sleep.

hollow leg *noun* *informal* a seemingly limitless capacity for food, alcohol, etc.

hollow-point ● *adjective* (of ammunition) made with a hollow point, so as to shatter on impact. ● *noun* a hollow-point bullet.

hollow·ware *noun* hollow articles of metal, china, etc., such as pots, kettles, jugs, etc. (opp. FLATWARE 2).

Holly, Buddy (born Charles Harden Holley) (1936–59), US rock 'n' roll singer, guitarist, and songwriter. His hit songs, all from the late 1950s, include 'That'll be the Day' and 'Peggy Sue'.

holly *noun* (*pl.* **-lies**) **1** any of various shrubs or small trees of the genus *Ilex*, esp. the evergreen *Ilex aquifolium*, with prickly usu. dark green leaves, small white flowers, and red berries. **2** its branches and foliage used as decorations at Christmas. [Old English *hole(g)n*]

holly fern *noun* any of various ferns with dark glossy leaves, esp. woodland ferns of the genus *Polystichum*, and *Cyrtomium falcatum*, grown as a houseplant.

holly·hock *noun* a tall plant, *Alcea rosea*, with large showy flowers of various colours. [Middle English (originally = marsh mallow) from HOLY + obsolete *hock* mallow, Old English *hoc*, of unknown origin]

Holly·wood *noun* the American motion picture industry or its products, with its principal centre at Hollywood in California.

holm /hoːm/ *noun* (in full **holm oak**) an evergreen oak, *Quercus ilex*, with holly-like young leaves. [Middle English alteration of obsolete *holin* (as HOLLY)]

Holmes /hoːmz/ **1 Ar·thur** (1890–1965), English geologist and geophysicist. He pioneered the dating of rocks using isotopic decay, and was one of the first supporters of the theory of continental drift. **2 Oli·ver Wen·dell** (1809–94), US physician, poet, and essayist. His best-known works are the essays known as 'table talks', which began with *The Autocrat of the Breakfast Table* (1857–8). **3** his son **Oli·ver Wen·dell** (1841–1935), US jurist, who served on the US Supreme Court (1902–32) and is noted for his liberal judgments.

Holmes·ian /ˈhoːmziən/ *adjective* of, pertaining to, or characteristic of Sherlock Holmes, the brilliant amateur detective in the stories of A. Conan Doyle.

hol·mium /ˈhoːlmiəm/ *noun* *Chem.* a soft silvery metallic element of the lanthanide series occurring naturally in apatite. Symbol: **Ho**; at. no.: 67. [modern Latin from *Holmia* Stockholm]

holo- /ˈhɒloː/ *combining form* whole (*Holocene; holocaust*). [Greek *holos* whole]

holo·caust /ˈhɒləˌkɒst/ *noun* **1** a case of large-scale destruction, esp. by fire or nuclear war. **2** (**the Holocaust**) the mass murder esp. of Jews under the Nazi regime. After the Nazis came to power in 1933, Jews were systematically deprived of civil rights, confined to ghettoes, and persecuted; in 1941 Eichmann's 'final solution' introduced the program of extermination at concentration camps. More than 6 million European Jews (about two-thirds of the total number) were murdered in the period 1941–5. **3** a sacrifice wholly consumed by fire. □ **holo·caust·al** *adjective* [Old French *holocauste* from Late Latin *holocaustum* from Greek *holokauston* (as HOLO-, *kaustos* burned, from *kaiō* burn)]

Holocaust denier *noun* a person who engages in a persistent campaign of denying that the Holocaust occurred, or insists that it has been greatly exaggerated, usu. as part of a general espousal of extreme right-wing or neo-Nazi ideology. □ **Holocaust denial** *noun*

Holo·cene /ˈhɒləˌsiːn/ *Geol.* ● *adjective* of or relating to the second epoch of the Quaternary period, following the Pleistocene and lasting from about 10,000 years ago to the present, coinciding with the development of human agricultural settlement and civilization. ● *noun* this geological period or system. *Also called* RECENT. [HOLO- + Greek *kainos* new]

holo·enzyme /ˌhɒloːˈenzaɪm/ *noun* *Biochem.* the active complex of an enzyme with a coenzyme.

Holo·fer·nes /ˌhɒloːˈfɜːrniːz, həˈlɒfɜrˌniːz/ *Bible* the Assyrian general of Nebuchadnezzar's forces who was killed by Judith (Judith 4:1 ff.).

holo·gram /ˈhɒləˌgram/ *noun* *Physics* **1** a three-dimensional image formed by the interference of light beams from a coherent light source. **2** a photograph of the interference pattern, which when suitably illuminated produces a three-dimensional image.

holo·graph /ˈhɒləˌgraf/ ● *adjective* wholly written by hand by the person named as the author. ● *noun* a holograph document.

hol·og·raphy /həˈlɒgrəfi/ *noun* *Physics* the study or production of holograms. □ **holo·graph·ic** *adjective* **holo·graph·ic·ally** *adverb*

holo·hed·ral /ˌhɒləˈhiːdrəl/ *adjective Crystallog.* having the full number of planes required by the symmetry of a crystal system.

holo·phyte /ˈhɒləˌfaɪt/ *noun* an organism that synthesizes complex organic compounds by photosynthesis. □ **holo·phyt·ic** /-ˈfɪtɪk/ *adjective*

holo·thur·ian /ˌhɒləˈθʊəriən/ ● *noun* any echinoderm of the class Holothurioidea, with a wormlike body, e.g. a sea cucumber. ● *adjective* of or relating to this class. [modern Latin *Holothuria* (n.pl.) from Greek *holothourion*, a zoophyte]

holo·type /ˈhɒləˌtaɪp/ *noun* the specimen used for naming and describing a species.

hols *plural noun Brit. informal* holidays. [abbreviation]

Holst /hoːlst/ **Gus·tav (Theo·dore)** (1874–1934), English composer, of Swedish and Russian descent. His music, which was strongly influenced by folk music, is marked by a visionary quality. His best-known work is the orchestral suite *The Planets* (1914–16).

Hol·stein /ˈhoːlstiːn/ *noun N Amer.* (in full **Holstein-Friesian**) a large black and white breed of dairy cattle, noted for high milk production. [*Holstein* in NW Germany]

hol·ster /ˈhoːlstər/ *noun* a leather case for a pistol or revolver, worn on a belt or under an arm or fixed to a saddle. [17th c., synonymous with Dutch *holster*: origin unknown]

holt[1] /hoːlt/ *noun Brit.* **1** an animal's (esp. an otter's) lair. **2** *informal* or *dialect* grip, hold. [var. of HOLD[1]]

holt[2] /hoːlt/ *noun archaic* or *dialect* **1** a wood or copse. **2** a wooded hill. [Old English from Germanic]

hol·ub·tsi /ˈhɒlʌpˌtʃi/ *plural noun Cdn* esp. (*West*) cabbage rolls. [Ukrainian]

holus-bolus /ˌhoːləsˈboːləs/ *adverb* all in a lump, altogether. [apparently sham Latin, perhaps = 'whole lump': compare BOLUS]

holy (**hol·i·er**, **hol·i·est**) ● *adjective* **1** morally and spiritually excellent or perfect, and to be revered. **2** belonging to, devoted to, or empowered by, God. **3** consecrated, sacred. **4** used in exclamations (*holy cow!*; *holy mackerel!*; *holy Moses!*; *holy smokes!*). ● *interjection* expressing amazement etc. [Old English *hālig* from Germanic, related to WHOLE]

Holy Alliance a loose and largely uninfluential alliance of conservative and autocratic European powers proclaimed at the Congress of Vienna (1815) by the emperors of Austria and Russia and the king of Prussia, who pledged to uphold the principles of the Christian religion. It was joined by most other European monarchs.

Holy Ark *noun* a chest or cabinet containing the Torah scrolls in a synagogue.

Holy Bible *noun* = BIBLE 1a.

Holy City *noun* **1** a city held sacred by the adherents of a religion, esp. Jerusalem. **2** Heaven.

Holy Communion *noun see* COMMUNION 3a.

holy day *noun* a religious festival.

holy day of obligation *noun* a day on which Roman Catholics are obliged to attend Mass.

Holy Family *noun* **1** the young Jesus with his mother and St. Joseph. **2** (also **Feast of the Holy Family**) *Catholicism* a feast day falling on the first Sunday after Christmas, commemorating the life together of the Holy Family and emphasizing religious family life.

Holy Father *noun* the Pope.

Holy Ghost *noun see* HOLY SPIRIT.

Holy Grail *noun see* GRAIL.

Holy·head /ˈhɒliˌhed/ a port on Holy Island, off Anglesey, in NW Wales; pop. (est. 2002) 11,500.

Holy Innocents *plural noun* **1** the children massacred by King Herod in his attempt to kill the child Jesus. **2** (also **Feast of the Holy Innocents**) a feast day commemorating this, celebrated in some Western Christian churches on Dec. 28 and in Eastern churches on Dec. 29.

Holy Island 1 an alternative name for LINDISFARNE. **2** a small island off the western coast of Anglesey in N Wales. It contains the ferry port of Holyhead.

Holy Joe *noun informal* **1** a clergyman. **2** a pious person.

holy jumpin' *interjection Cdn slang* expressing surprise, disbelief, etc. [possibly a corruption of or euphemism for JESUS[2]]

Holy Land a region on the eastern shores of the Mediterranean, in what is now Israel. It has religious significance for Judaism, Christianity, and Islam.

Holy League any of various European alliances sponsored by the papacy during the 15th, 16th, and 17th c. They include the League of 1511–13, formed to expel Louis XII of France from Italy; the French Holy League (also called the **Catholic League**) of 1576 and 1584, a Catholic extremist league formed during the French Wars of Religion; and the Holy (or Catholic) League of 1609, a military alliance of the German Catholic princes.

holy moly *interjection* (also **holy moley**) expressing great surprise, admiration, etc. [reduplication, possibly corruption of 'holy Moses']

Holy Mother *noun* **1** Mary, the mother of Jesus. **2** (also **Holy Mother Church**) the Roman Catholic Church.

Holy Name *noun Catholicism* the name of Jesus as an object of formal devotion.

Holy Office *noun* an ecclesiastical court established in 1542 as the final court of appeal in trials of heresy. Renamed the Sacred Congregation for the Doctrine of the Faith in 1965, its function is to promote as well as to safeguard sound doctrine in the Roman Catholic Church.

holy of hol·ies *noun* **1** the inner chamber of the sanctuary in the Jewish temple, separated by a veil from the outer chamber. **2** an innermost shrine. **3** a thing regarded as most sacred.

holy orders *plural noun* the status of a member of the clergy, esp. the grades of bishop, priest, and deacon.

holy place *noun* **1** a place to which religious pilgrimage is made. **2** the outer chamber of the sanctuary in the Jewish temple.

holy roller *noun slang derogatory* **1** a member of a Pentecostal or other charismatic group characterized by religious excitement. **2** a highly vocal devout person.

Holy Roman Empire the empire set up in Western Europe following Charlemagne's coronation as emperor in the year 800 and lasting until 1806. Created by the medieval papacy as a secular deputy to rule Christendom, the office of the emperor proved to be more often a rival than an ally. From Otto I's coronation (962) the title was largely the preserve of German dynasties ruling Germany, Austria, Switzerland, and parts of Italy and the Netherlands.

Holy Sacrament *noun see* SACRAMENT 3.

Holy Saturday *noun* Saturday in Holy Week.

Holy Scripture *noun* the Bible.

Holy See *noun* the papacy or the papal court.

Holy Sepulchre *noun* the tomb in which Christ was laid.

Holy Spirit (also called **Holy Ghost**) (in Christian theology) the third person of the Trinity. Regarded as God spiritually active in the world, the Holy Spirit was received by the Apostles at Pentecost (Acts 2), and is usu. symbolized by a white dove.

holy·stone *Naut.* ● *noun* a piece of soft sandstone used for scouring decks. ● *transitive verb* scour with this. [19th c.: prob. from HOLY + STONE: the stones were called *bibles* etc., perhaps because used while kneeling]

holy terror *noun see* TERROR 2b.

Holy Thursday *noun* the Thursday before Easter.

Holy Trinity *noun* **1** *see* TRINITY 1. **2** (**holy trinity**) a group of three persons or things considered exemplary in their field.

holy war *noun* a war waged in support of a religious cause. □ **holy warrior** *noun*

holy water *noun* water dedicated to holy uses, or blessed by a priest.

Holy Week *noun* the week before Easter.

Holy Writ *noun* holy writings collectively, esp. the Bible.

Holy Year *noun Catholicism* a period of remission from the penal consequences of sin, granted under certain conditions for a year usu. at intervals of 25 years.

hom /hoːm/ *noun* (also **homa** /ˈhoːmə/) **1** the soma plant. **2** the juice of this plant as a sacred drink of the Parsis. [Persian *hōm*, *hūm*, Avestan *haoma*]

hom·age /ˈhɒmɪdʒ, ˈɒm-/ *noun* **1** acknowledgement of superiority, dutiful reverence (*pay homage to*; *do homage to*). **2** *hist.* formal public acknowledgement of feudal allegiance. **3** an act of homage. [Old French (*h*)*omage* from medieval Latin *hominaticum* from Latin *homo -minis* man]

hom·bre /ˈɒmbreɪ, ˈhɒm-/ *noun N Amer. slang* a man. [Spanish]

hom·burg /ˈhɒmbɜrg/ *noun* a man's felt hat with a narrow curled brim and a lengthwise dent in the crown. [*Homburg* in Germany, where first worn]

home ● *noun* **1 a** the place where one lives; the fixed residence of a family or household. **b** a house or dwelling place. **c** the residence of a person's parents (*are you going home for the holidays?*). **d** a building etc. providing a locale for a company's activities (*the ballet company has a new home*). **2** the members of a family collectively; one's family background (*comes from a good home*). **3** the native land of a person or of a person's ancestors. **4** an institution for persons needing care, rest, or refuge (*nursing home*). **5** the place where a thing originates or is native or most common. **6 a** *Baseball* = HOME PLATE. **b** the finishing point in a race. **c** (in games) the place where one is free from attack. **d** (in some sports) the goal. **e** *Lacrosse* a player in an attacking position near the opponents' goal. **7** *Sport* a home game or win. • *attributive adjective* **1 a** of or connected with one's home. **b** carried on, done, or made at home (*home movies*). **c** proceeding from home. **2 a** carried on or produced in one's own country (*home industries; the home market*). **b** esp. *Brit.* dealing with the domestic affairs of a country. **3** *Sport* played on one's own ground etc. (*home game; home win*). **4** in the neighbourhood of home. **5** main; principal. • *adverb* **1 a** to one's home or country (*go home*). **b** arrived at home (*is he home yet?*). **c** *N Amer.* at home (*stay home*). **2 a** to the point aimed at (*the thrust went home*). **b** as far as possible (*drove the nail home; pressed her advantage home*). • *verb* **1** *intransitive* (esp. of a trained pigeon) return home (*compare* HOMING 1). **2** *intransitive* (often foll. by *on, in on*) (of a vessel, missile, etc.) be guided towards a destination or target by a landmark, radio beam, etc. **3** *transitive* send or guide homewards. **4** *transitive* provide with a home. □ **at home 1** in one's own house or native land. **2** at ease as if in one's own home (*make yourself at home*). **3** (usu. foll. by *in, on, with*) familiar or well informed. **4** available to callers. **come home to** become fully realized by. **come home to roost** *see* ROOST. **heading home** *Curling* in or during the final end of a game (*we'll have the hammer heading home; was leading by two points heading home*). **home and dry** *Brit.* having achieved one's purpose. **home free** *N Amer.* assured of success or safety (*if we make it to the border we're home free*). **home, James!** *jocular* drive home quickly! **near home** affecting one closely. □ **home·like** *adjective* [Old English *hām* from Germanic]

home-and-home *adjective* *N Amer.* designating a pair of usu. back-to-back matches between two teams, the first at one team's venue and the second at the other's.

home and school *noun* (in full **home and school association**) esp. *Cdn* a local organization of parents and teachers to promote better communication and improve educational facilities.

home away from home *noun* a place other than one's home where one feels at home; a place providing homelike amenities.

home-baked *adjective* (of food) baked at home or at the restaurant etc. where it is served. □ **home baking** *noun*

home base *noun* **1** headquarters (*our home base is in Brampton*). **2** *Baseball* = HOME PLATE.

home-based *adjective* (of a person, business, etc.) operating out of a private home.

home·body *noun* (pl. **-ies**) a person who likes to stay at home.

home·bound *adjective* **1** confined to one's home, esp. by illness or disability. **2** = HOMEWARD-BOUND.

home·boy *noun* esp. *US slang* **1** a person from one's own town or neighbourhood. **2** a close friend, esp. a member of one's gang.

home·brew *noun* **1** beer or other alcoholic drink brewed at home. **2** *Cdn* a person, esp. a sports competitor, who is a native of the country or locality where the competition is held. □ **home-brewed** *adjective* **home brewer** *noun* **home brewing** *noun*

home builder *noun* **1** a person who builds houses. **2** a person who builds something in their home.

home·built *adjective* (of a thing) built in an individual's home.

home·buy·er *noun* a person who buys a house, condominium, etc.

home care *noun* care, esp. medical care, given or received at home (also *attributive*: *home care nurse*). □ **home carer** *noun*

home child *noun* *Cdn* (usu. in *pl.*) one of a number of orphaned or destitute children sent from Britain to Canada from the mid-19th to the early 20th c. to serve as farm or domestic help.

home·com·ing *noun* **1** arrival at home. **2** *N Amer.* a reunion, esp. of former students of a university, college, or high school.

Home Counties (in the UK) the counties surrounding London, into which London has extended, comprising chiefly Essex, Kent, Surrey, and Hertfordshire.

home ec *noun* *N Amer.* home economics. [abbreviation]

home economics *plural noun* (often treated as *sing.*) the study of household management, usu. including cooking, nutrition, sewing, child-raising, budgeting, etc. □ **home economist** *noun*

home entertainment *noun* entertainment provided in the home by electronic equipment such as televisions, VCRs, stereos, etc. (also *attributive*: *home entertainment centre*).

home fires *plural noun* the fire etc. used to warm a family home.

□ **keep the home fires burning** maintain a family home, esp. while one of its members is away for a prolonged period.

home from home *noun* *Brit.* = HOME AWAY FROM HOME.

home fry *noun* *N Amer.* (pl. **fries**) (usu. in *pl.*) a slice of usu. boiled potato that has been fried in a frying pan, as opposed to being deep-fried.

home·girl *noun* esp. *US slang* **1** a girl from one's own town or neighbourhood. **2** a close friend, esp. a member of one's gang.

home ground *noun* a subject or area with which one is familiar.

home·grown *adjective* **1** raised or cultivated on one's own land. **2** native to or produced in one's own country, locality, etc.

Home Guard *noun* *hist.* a local reserve force to defend a country from invasion.

home help *noun* *Brit.* a person employed to help in another's home, esp. one provided by a local social agency.

home ice *noun* the rink where a hockey team or curling rink normally plays its home games.

home invasion *noun* *N Amer.* a robbery usu. perpetrated by a group while the occupants are present.

Homel /ˈhɒmɪl/ an industrial city in SE Belarus; pop. (est. 2002) 502,600.

home·land *noun* **1 a** one's native land. **b** the country where one lives. **2** *hist.* a partially self-governing area in South Africa set aside for a particular indigenous African people or peoples under the former policy of separate development; the homelands were abolished in 1994. **3** any similar semi-autonomous area.

home·less *adjective* **1** without a home, esp. living on the streets. **2** pertaining to people who have no home and live on the streets (*homeless advocates; homeless shelters*). □ **home·less·ness** *noun*

home loan *noun* a loan advanced to a person to assist in buying a house, condominium, etc.

home·ly *adjective* (**home·li·er**, **home·li·est**) **1** *N Amer.* (esp. of people or their features) unattractive. **2 a** simple, plain. **b** unpretentious. **c** primitive. **3** comfortable in the manner of a home, cozy. □ **home·li·ness** *noun*

home·made *adjective* made at home.

home·maker *noun* *N Amer.* **1** a person who runs a household for their family, esp. as a primary occupation. **2** a person who cooks meals, cleans house, etc. for an elderly, sick, or disabled person. □ **home·making** *adjective & noun*

home movie *noun* (or **home video**) a film (or video) made at home or of one's own activities.

home office *noun* **1** *N Amer.* an office in a private home. **2** (**Home Office**) (in the UK) **a** the government department dealing with law and order, immigration, etc., in England and Wales. **b** the building used for this. **3** the head office of a corporation.

Home of the Hir·sel of Cold·stream /ˈhɜrsəl, ˈkoːldstriːm/ **Baron**, *see* DOUGLAS-HOME.

homeo·path /ˈhoːmɪoˌpaθ/ *noun* (also *Brit.* **homoeo·path**) a person who practises homeopathy.

hom·eop·athy /ˌhoːmɪˈɒpəθi/ *noun* (also *Brit.* **hom·oeop·athy**) the treatment of disease by minute doses of drugs that in a healthy person would produce symptoms of the disease (*compare* ALLOPATHY). □ **homeo·path·ic** /-ˈpaθɪk/ *adjective* **homeo·path·ic·ally** /-ˈpaθɪkli/ *adverb* **hom·eop·ath·ist** *noun* [German *Homöopathie* from Greek *homoios* like + *patheia* -PATHY]

home opener *noun* *N Amer.* a sports team's first home game of a new season.

homeo·sta·sis /ˌhoːmɪoˈsteɪsɪs/ *noun* (also **homoeo·sta·sis**) (pl. **-sta·ses** /-siːz/) the tendency towards a relatively stable equilibrium between interdependent elements, esp. as maintained by physiological processes. □ **homeo·stat·ic** *adjective* [modern Latin, from Greek *homoios* 'like' + -STASIS]

homeo·therm /ˈhoːmɪoˌθɜrm/ *noun* an organism that maintains its body temperature at a constant level, usu. above that of the environment, by its metabolic activity; a warm-blooded organism (*compare* POIKILOTHERM). □ **homeo·therm·ic** *adjective* **homeo·thermy** *noun* [modern Latin from Greek *homoios* like + *thermē* heat]

home·owner *noun* a person who owns his or her own home. □ **home ownership** *noun*

home page *noun* *Computing* a computer screen that serves as an introduction to a network site, from which a number of options may be selected.

home perm *noun* (in full **home permanent**) a hair permanent made using a kit sold for home use.

home plate *noun Baseball* a base beside which the batter stands and which a runner must reach safely to score a run.

home port *noun* the port from which a ship originates.

Homer ▸ **1** (*c*.700 BC), Greek epic poet, traditionally held to be the author of the *Iliad* and the *Odyssey*. In later antiquity Homer was regarded as the greatest and unsurpassable poet, and his poems were constantly used as a model and source by others. **2 Wins·low** (1836–1910), US painter. He is known for his seascapes and realistic scenes of American working life.

homer ● *noun* **1** *Baseball* a home run. **2** a homing pigeon. ● *intransitive verb Baseball* hit a homer.

Ho·mer·ic /hoʊˈmɛrɪk, hə'm-/ *adjective* **1** of, or in the style of, Homer or the epic poems ascribed to him. **2** of Bronze Age Greece as described in these poems. **3** epic, large-scale, titanic (*Homeric conflict*).

home·room *noun N Amer.* **1** a classroom in which a group of students assembles daily with the same teacher for announcements, opening exercises, etc. before dispersing to other classes. **2** the period during which students assemble in a homeroom. **3** the group of students who assemble for a given homeroom.

home rule *noun* (also **Home Rule**) a movement for the government of a colony, dependent country, etc. by its own citizens, esp. the movement advocating devolved government for Ireland, 1870–1914.

home run *noun Baseball* a hit that allows the batter to make a complete circuit of the bases.

home-school·ing *noun N Amer.* the practice of teaching one's own children in one's own home instead of sending them to a school. □ **home-school** *transitive verb* **home-school·er** *noun*

Home Secretary *noun* (in the UK) the Secretary of State in charge of the Home Office.

home shopping *noun* shopping carried out from home using catalogues, TV channels, etc.

home show *noun* a fair or exposition at which home construction and renovation products are displayed.

home·sick *adjective* depressed by longing for one's home during absence from it. □ **home·sick·ness** *noun*

home·site *noun* esp. *N Amer., Austral. & NZ* a lot or piece of land suitable for building a house on.

home·spun ● *adjective* **1 a** (of cloth) made of yarn spun at home. **b** (of yarn) spun at home. **2** plain, simple, unsophisticated, homely. ● *noun* **1** homespun cloth. **2** anything plain or homely.

home·stand *noun* a series of games played at a team's own venue.

home·stay *noun* a period during which a foreign visitor stays with a local family.

home·stead ● *noun* **1** *N Amer.* an area of public land (usu. a quarter section) granted to a settler in exchange for a small fee, and on certain conditions, usu. that the settler establish a dwelling and cultivate a certain area of land within a specified time. **2** a house, esp. a farmhouse, and outbuildings. **3** *Austral. & NZ* the owner's residence on a sheep or cattle station. ● *verb N Amer.* **1** *transitive* settle on (land) as a homestead. **2** *intransitive* settle on a homestead. □ **home·stead·er** *noun* [Old English *hāmstede* (as HOME, STEAD)]

home stretch *noun* (*Brit.* also **home straight**) **1** the straight section of a racetrack leading to the finish line. **2** the final stage or phase of anything.

home·style *adjective N Amer.* (esp. of food) of a kind made or done at home.

home theatre *noun* a home audio-video system designed to simulate as closely as possible the viewing conditions in a movie theatre, e.g. with a very large flat screen and high quality sound.

home·town *noun* the town of one's birth or early life or present fixed residence.

home truth *noun* basic but unwelcome information concerning oneself.

home turf *noun* one's own territory (*defeated them on their home turf*).

home video *noun* **1** = HOME MOVIE. **2** a theatrical movie released on video for home viewing rather than broadcast.

home·ward ● *adverb* (also **home·wards**) towards home. ● *adjective* going or leading towards home.

homeward bound ● *adverb* preparing to go, or on the way, home. ● *adjective* (**homeward-bound**) preparing to go, or on the way, home.

home·work *noun* **1** work to be done at home, esp. by a school pupil. **2** preparatory work or study.

home·work·er *noun* a person who works from home, esp. doing low-paid piecework.

home wrecker *noun N Amer. slang* a person, esp. a woman, who causes the breakup of a family by seducing one of the spouses.

homey *adjective* (also **homy**) (**hom·i·er**, **hom·i·est**) suggesting home; cozy. □ **homey·ness** *noun* (also **hom·i·ness**)

homi·cide /ˈhɒmɪˌsaɪd/ *noun* **1** the killing of a human being by another. **2** a person who kills a human being. □ **homi·cid·al** *adjective* [Old French from Latin *homicidium* (sense 1), *homicida* (sense 2) (HOMO man)]

homie *noun* esp. *US slang* a homeboy or homegirl.

homi·let·ic /ˌhɒmɪˈlɛtɪk/ ● *adjective* (also **homi·let·ic·al**) of homilies. ● *noun* (usu. in *pl.*) the art of preaching.

hom·ily /ˈhɒmɪli/ *noun* (*pl.* **-ilies**) **1** a sermon. **2** a tedious moralizing discourse. □ **hom·il·ist** *noun* [Greek *homilia* from *homilos* crowd]

hom·ing *attributive adjective* **1** (of a pigeon) trained to fly home, bred for long-distance racing, carrying messages, etc. **2** (of a device) for guiding (something) to a target etc. **3** that goes home.

homing instinct *noun* the instinct of certain animals to return to the territory from which they have been moved.

hom·in·id /ˈhɒmɪnɪd/ ● *noun* a primate of the family Hominidae, which includes human beings (*Homo sapiens*), and several fossil forms. ● *adjective* of or relating to this family. [modern Latin *Hominidae* from Latin *homo hominis* man]

hom·in·oid /ˈhɒmɪˌnɔɪd/ ● *adjective* **1** like a human. **2** hominid or pongid. ● *noun* an animal resembling a human.

hom·iny /ˈhɒmɪni/ *noun* esp. *US* coarsely ground kernels of corn esp. boiled with water or milk. [contraction of Virginia Algonquian *uskatahomen*]

homme du nord /ɒm duː 'nɔr/ *noun* (*pl.* **hommes du nord**) *Cdn hist.* a voyageur who spent winters in the interior. [Canadian French]

hom·mos *var. of* HUMMUS.

Homo /ˈhoʊmoʊ/ *noun* **1** any primate of the genus *Homo*, including modern humans and various extinct species. **2** (with Latin or mock-Latin adjectives in imitation of zoological nomenclature) in names intended to personify some aspects of human life or behaviour (*Homo economicus*). [Latin, = man]

homo¹ /ˈhoʊmoʊ/ *noun* (*pl.* **homos**) *informal offensive* a homosexual. [abbreviation]

homo² /ˈhoʊmoʊ/ *noun Cdn* homogenized milk typically having a butterfat content of 3.25 per cent. [abbreviation]

homo- /ˈhoʊmoʊ, ˈhɒmoʊ/ *combining form* same (often opp. HETERO-). [Greek *homos* same]

homo·cen·tric /ˌhoʊmoʊˈsɛntrɪk, ˌhɒmoʊ-/ *adjective* having the same centre.

homo·cyst·eine /ˌhoʊmoʊˈsɪstiːiːn/ *noun* an amino acid which occurs in the body as an intermediate in the metabolism of methionine and cysteine.

homoeo·path etc. *Brit. var. of* HOMEOPATH etc.

homoeo·sta·sis *var. of* HOMEOSTASIS.

homo·erot·ic /ˌhoʊmoʊɪˈrɒtɪk/ *adjective* **1** homosexual. **2** arousing sexual desire in a person of the same sex. □ **homo·erotic·ally** *adverb* **homo·eroti·cism** *noun* (also **homo·erot·ism**).

hom·og·amy /həˈmɒɡəmi/ *noun Bot.* **1** a state in which the flowers of a plant are hermaphrodite or of the same sex. **2** the simultaneous ripening of the stamens and pistils of a flower. □ **hom·og·am·ous** *adjective* [Greek *homogamos* (as HOMO-, *gamos* marriage)]

hom·ogen·ate /həˈmɒdʒɪˌneɪt/ *noun* a suspension produced by homogenizing.

homo·gene·ous /ˌhoʊməˈdʒiːniəs, ˌhoʊmə-/ *adjective* (also *disputed* **hom·ogen·ous** /həˈmɒdʒənəs/) **1** of the same kind. **2** consisting of parts all of the same kind; uniform. **3** *Math.* containing terms all of the same degree. ¶ The variant *homogenous* is considered incorrect by many people and is best avoided. It is found especially in spoken English and arose perhaps under the influence of the verb *homogenize*. The technical term *homogenous* (see HOMOGENOUS¹) is quite different in meaning and has now been largely replaced by HOMOGENETIC. □ **homo·gen·eity** /-dʒɪˈneɪəti/ *noun* **homo·gen·eous·ly** *adverb* **homo·gene·ous·ness** *noun* [medieval Latin *homogeneus* from Greek *homogenēs* (as HOMO-, *genēs* from *genos* kind)]

homo·gen·etic /ˌhoʊmoʊdʒɪˈnɛtɪk, ˌhɒmoʊ-/ *adjective Biol.* having a common descent or origin.

hom·ogen·ize /həˈmɒdʒəˌnaɪz/ *verb* (also esp. *Brit.* **-ise**) **1** *transitive & intransitive* make or become homogeneous. **2** *transitive* treat (milk) so that the fat droplets are emulsified and the cream does not separate. □ **hom·ogen·iz·a·tion** *noun* **hom·ogen·iz·er** *noun*

hom·ogen·ized *adjective* **1** homogeneous. **2** (of milk) having the fat droplets emulsified, esp. (in Canada) designating homogenized milk with a butterfat content of 3.25 per cent.

hom·ogen·ous[1] /həˈmɒdʒɪnəs/ *adjective Biol. archaic* = HOMOGENETIC. [HOMOGENY + -OUS]

hom·ogen·ous[2] *adjective see* HOMOGENEOUS. [alteration of HOMOGENEOUS, perhaps influenced by HOMOGENIZE]

hom·ogeny /həˈmɒdʒəni/ *noun Biol.* similarity due to common descent. □ **hom·ogen·ous** *adjective*

homo·graft /ˈhɒməˌɡrɑft/ *noun* a graft of living tissue from one to another of the same species but different genotype.

homo·graph /ˈhɒməˌɡrɑf/ *noun* a word spelled like another but of different meaning or origin (e.g. POLE[1], POLE[2]). □ **homo·graph·ic** *adjective*

homoio·therm *var. of* HOMEOTHERM.

homo·log *var. of* HOMOLOGUE.

hom·olo·gate /həˈmɒləˌɡeɪt/ *transitive verb* **1** acknowledge, admit. **2** confirm, accept. **3** approve (a car, boat, engine, etc.) for use in a particular class of racing. □ **hom·olo·ga·tion** *noun* [medieval Latin *homologare* agree, from Greek *homologeō* (as HOMO-, *logos* word)]

hom·olo·gize /həˈmɒləˌdʒaɪz/ *verb* (also esp. *Brit.* **-gise**) **1** *intransitive* be homologous; correspond. **2** *transitive* make homologous.

hom·olo·gous /həˈmɒləɡəs/ *adjective* **1 a** having the same relation, relative position, etc. **b** corresponding. **2** *Biol.* (of organs etc.) similar in position and structure but not necessarily in function. **3** *Biol.* (of chromosomes) pairing at meiosis and having the same structural features and pattern of genes. **4** *Chem.* (of a series of chemical compounds) having the same functional group but differing in composition by a fixed group of atoms. [medieval Latin *homologus* from Greek (as HOMO-, *logos* ratio, proportion)]

homo·logue /ˈhɒməˌlɒɡ/ *noun* (also **homo·log**) a homologous thing. [French from Greek *homologon* (neuter adj.) (as HOMOLOGOUS)]

hom·ol·ogy /həˈmɒlədʒi/ *noun* a homologous state or relation; correspondence. □ **homo·logic·al** /ˌhɒməˈlɒdʒɪkəl/ *adjective*

homo·nym /ˈhɒmənɪm/ *noun* **1** a word of the same spelling or sound as another but of different meaning; a homograph or homophone. **2** a namesake. □ **homo·nym·ic** /-ˈnɪmɪk/ *adjective* **hom·onym·ous** /həˈmɒnɪməs/ *adjective* [Latin *homonymum* from Greek *homōnumon* (neuter adj.) (as HOMO-, *onoma* name)]

homo·phob·ia /ˌhɒməˈfəʊbiə/ *noun* a hatred or fear of or prejudice against homosexuals or homosexuality. □ **homo·phobe** *noun* **homo·phob·ic** *adjective*

homo·phone /ˈhɒməˌfəʊn/ *noun* **1** a word having the same sound as another but of different meaning or origin (e.g. *pair, pear*). **2** a symbol denoting the same sound as another.

homo·phon·ic /ˌhɒməˈfɒnɪk/ *adjective Music* in unison; characterized by movement of all parts to the same melody. □ **homo·phon·ic·ally** *adverb* **hom·oph·ony** *noun*

hom·op·ter·an /həˈmɒptərən/ *noun* any insect of the suborder Homoptera, including aphids and cicadas, with wings of uniform texture (*compare* HETEROPTERAN). □ **hom·op·ter·ous** *adjective* [HOMO- + Greek *pteron* wing]

Homo sa·pi·ens /ˌhɒmoː ˈseɪpiɛnz/ *noun* modern humans regarded as a species. [Latin, = wise man]

homo·sex·ual /ˌhɒmoːˈsekʃʊəl/ ● *adjective* **1** feeling or involving sexual attraction to persons of the same sex. **2** concerning homosexual relations or people. ● *noun* a homosexual person. □ **homo·sex·u·al·ity** *noun* **homo·sex·ual·ly** *adverb*

homo·social *adjective* of or relating to social interaction between members of the same sex, typically men.

homo·zygote /ˌhɒmoːˈzaɪɡoːt, ˌhɒmɒ-/ *noun Biol.* an individual having two identical alleles of a particular gene or genes and so breeding true for the corresponding characteristic. □ **homo·zygos·ity** *noun* **homo·zygous** *adjective*

Homs /hɒms, hɒmz/ (also **Hims** /hɪms, hɪmz/) an industrial city in W Syria, on the Orontes River; pop. (est. 2002) 724,700. It occupies the site of ancient Emesa, lying at the junction of north–south and east–west trade routes.

hom·un·cu·lus /həˈmʌŋkjʊləs/ *noun* (pl. **hom·un·culi** /-ˌlaɪ/) a small person. [Latin *homunculus* from *homo -minis* man]

homy *var. of* HOMEY.

Hon. *abbreviation* **1** Honourable. **2** Honorary.

hon *noun informal* = HONEY 5. [abbreviation]

Honan 1 see HENAN. **2** a former name for LUOYANG.

hon·cho *N Amer. slang* ● *noun* (pl. **-chos**) a leader or manager, the person in charge. ● *transitive verb* (**-choes, -choed**) be in charge of, oversee. [Japanese *han'chō* group leader]

Honda *noun proprietary Cdn (North)* an all-terrain vehicle.

Hon·dur·as /hɒnˈdjʊərəs, -ˈdʊr-/ a country of Central America, bordering on the Caribbean Sea and with a short coastline on the Pacific Ocean; pop. (est. 2002) 6,560,608; capital, Tegucigalpa. (*See also* BRITISH HONDURAS.) □ **Hon·dur·an** *adjective & noun*

hone ● *transitive verb* **1** sharpen on a whetstone. **2** make more effective or focused (*honing her skills as a performer*). ● *noun* **1** a whetstone, esp. for straight razors. **2** any of various stones used as material for this. [Old English *hān* stone, from Germanic]

Hon·eck·er /ˈhɒnəkər/ **Erich** (1912–1994), East German Communist leader, head of state 1976–89. His repressive regime was marked by a close allegiance to the Soviet Union, and he was ousted in 1989 after a series of pro-democracy demonstrations.

Hon·eg·ger /ˈɒnəɡər/ **Ar·thur** (1892–1955), French composer, of Swiss descent, a member of the anti-romantic group Les Six. His works include *Pacific 231* (1924), a musical representation of a steam locomotive.

hon·est /ˈɒnɪst/ ● *adjective* **1** fair and just in character or behaviour, not cheating or stealing. **2** free of deceit and untruthfulness, sincere. **3** fairly earned (*an honest living*). **4** (of an act or feeling) showing fairness. **5** (of a thing) unadulterated, unsophisticated. ● *adverb informal* genuinely, really (*I didn't take it, honest!*). □ **do one's honest best** do the best that one can. **make an honest woman of** *informal* marry (esp. a pregnant woman). [Old French (*h)oneste* from Latin *honestus* from *honos* HONOUR]

honest broker *noun* a mediator in international, industrial, etc., disputes.

honest Injun *interjection slang offensive* genuinely, really.

hon·est·ly ● *adverb* **1** in an honest way. **2** really (*I don't honestly know*). ● *interjection* expressing exasperation, dismay, etc. (*Honestly! You're always complaining!*).

honest-to-God (also **honest-to-goodness**) *informal* ● *adjective* genuine, real. ● *adverb* genuinely, really.

hon·esty *noun* **1** the quality of being honest. **2** truthfulness. **3** a plant of the genus *Lunaria* with purple or white flowers, so called from its flat round semi-transparent seed pods. *Also called* SILVER DOLLAR.

hon·ey *noun* (pl. **-eys**) **1** a sweet sticky yellowish fluid made by bees and other insects from nectar collected from flowers. **2** the colour of this. **3 a** a sweetness. **b** a sweet thing. **4** a person or thing excellent of its kind (*a honey of a movie*). **5** esp. *N Amer.* (usu. as a form of address) darling, sweetheart. **6** (*attributive*) designating something that is used to hold or carry sewage, manure, etc. (*honey bucket; honey cart*). □ **honey-like** *adjective* [Old English *hunig* from Germanic]

honey bag *noun Cdn (North) informal* a plastic bag used as a receptacle for human waste.

honey·bee *noun* the common hive bee, *Apis mellifera*.

honey bucket *noun N Amer. informal* a receptacle for excrement, e.g. in an outdoor toilet.

honey·bun *noun* **1** (also **honey·bunch**) (esp. as a form of address) darling. **2** *N Amer.* a sweet bread roll in the shape of a spiral, coated with a honey glaze.

honey cake *noun* a dark, dense, chewy cake sweetened with honey.

honey·comb ● *noun* **1** a structure of hexagonal cells of wax, made by bees to store honey and eggs. **2 a** a pattern arranged hexagonally. **b** fabric made with a pattern of raised hexagons etc. **3** tripe from the second stomach of a ruminant. **4** a cavernous flaw in metalwork, esp. in guns. ● *transitive verb* **1** fill with cavities or tunnels, undermine. **2** mark with a honeycomb pattern. □ **honey·combed** *adjective*

honey·dew *noun* **1** a sweet sticky substance found on leaves and stems, excreted by aphids. **2** a variety of melon with smooth pale skin and sweet green flesh.

honey·eater *noun* any Australasian bird of the family Meliphagidae with a long tongue that can take nectar from flowers.

honeyed *adjective* (also **honied**) **1** of or containing honey. **2** sweet, pleasant. **3** flattering.

honey·guide *noun* any small bird of the family Indicatoridae of the Old World tropics which feeds on beeswax and insects.

honey locust *noun* a spiny N American leguminous tree, *Gleditsia triacanthos*, with pinnate leaves.

honey·moon ● *noun* **1** a holiday spent together by a newly married couple. **2** an initial period of enthusiasm or goodwill. **●** *intransitive verb* (usu. foll. by *in*, *at*) spend a honeymoon. □ **honey·moon·er** *noun* [HONEY + MOON, originally with reference to waning affection, not to a period of a month]

honey mushroom *noun* (also **honey fungus**) a parasitic fungus, *Armillaria mellea*, with honey-coloured edible toadstools.

honey sac *noun* an enlarged part of a bee's gullet where honey is formed.

honey·suckle *noun* any shrub of the genus *Lonicera* with fragrant yellow, orange, white or pink flowers. [as HONEY, SUCK]

honey-sweet *adjective* sweet as honey.

honey·trap *noun* a stratagem in which an attractive person entices another person into revealing information.

honey wagon *noun* *informal* **1** a vehicle which carries away human waste. **2** *N Amer.* a manure spreader.

Hong Kong a Special Administrative Region of China (a British dependency from 1898 to 1997) on the southeast coast, comprising Hong Kong Island, the Kowloon peninsula, and the New Territories, additional areas of the mainland; pop. (2001) 6,708,389; capital, Victoria. One of the world's major financial and manufacturing centres, Hong Kong is guaranteed, for a period of fifty years following China's resumption of sovereignty in 1997, the preservation of the systems and lifestyles established under British rule. □ **Hong Kong·er** *noun*

Hon·gue·do Strait /ɔ̃gweiˈdoː/ a channel linking the St. Lawrence River and the Gulf of St. Lawrence to E Quebec. It separates Anticosti Island from the Gaspé Peninsula. [origin uncertain: possibly from Mi'kmaq, = gathering place, or from Algonquian *hehonguesto* his own nose]

Ho·ni·ara /ˌhoːniˈɑrə/ a port and the capital of the Solomon Islands, situated on the northwest coast of the island of Guadalcanal; pop. (est. 2002) 52,900.

hon·ied *var. of* HONEYED.

honk ● *noun* **1** the cry of a goose. **2** the harsh sound of a car horn. **3** a sound similar to either of these, e.g. of a person blowing their nose. **●** *verb* **1** *intransitive* emit or give a honk. **2** *transitive* cause to do this. [imitative]

honk·er *noun* **1** *N Amer. informal* a goose, esp. a wild goose. **2** a person or thing that honks.

honk·ing *adjective* (also **honkin'**) *N Amer. slang* very large.

honky *noun* (pl. **-kies**) *N Amer. slang offensive* a white person. [20th c.: origin unknown]

honky-tonk *noun informal* **1** ragtime piano music. **2** a cheap or disreputable nightclub, dance hall, etc. [20th c.: origin unknown]

Hono·lulu /ˌhɒnəˈluːluː/ the capital and principal port of Hawaii, situated on the southeast coast of the island of Oahu; pop. (2000) 371,657.

hon·or *var. of* HONOUR.

honor·able *var. of* HONOURABLE.

honor·and /ˈɒnəˌrand/ *noun* a person to be honoured, esp. with an honorary degree. [Latin *honorandus* (as HONOUR)]

honor·ari·um /ˌɒnəˈreriəm/ *noun* (pl. **honor·ari·ums** or **honor·aria** /-riə/) a fee, esp. a voluntary payment for professional services rendered without the normal fee. [Latin, neuter of *honorarius*: see HONORARY]

honor·ary /ˈɒnəreri/ *adjective* (also **honourary**) **1 a** conferred as an honour, without the usual requirements, functions, etc. (*honorary degree*). **b** holding such a title or position (*honorary colonel*). **2** (of an office or its holder) unpaid (*honorary secretaryship*; *honorary treasurer*). **3** (of an obligation) depending on honour, not legally enforceable. [Latin *honorarius* (as HONOUR)]

honorary pallbearer *noun* a person who is given an honorary role in a funeral as a sign of respect for their closeness to the deceased, but does not carry the coffin.

honor·ific /ˌɒnəˈrɪfɪk/ **●** *adjective* **1** conferring honour. **2** (esp. of oriental forms of speech) implying respect. **●** *noun* an honorific form of words. □ **honor·ific·ally** *adverb* [Latin *honorificus* (as HONOUR)]

hon·or·is causa /ɒˌnɔrɪs ˈkauzə/ *adverb* (esp. of a degree awarded without examination) as a mark of esteem. [Latin, = for the sake of honour]

hon·our /ˈɒnər/ (also **honor**) **●** *noun* **1** high respect; glory; credit; reputation, good name. **2** adherence to what is right or to a conventional standard of conduct. **3** nobleness of mind, magnanimity (*honour among thieves*). **4** a thing conferred as a distinction, esp. an official award for bravery or achievement. **5** (foll. by *of* + verbal noun, or *to* + infin.) privilege, special right (*had the honour of being invited*). **6 a** exalted position. **b** (**Honour**) (prec. by *your*, *his*, *her*, etc.) a title of respect given to a lower court judge, (in the US) a mayor, etc. **7** (foll. by *to*) a person or thing that brings honour (*she is an honour to her profession*). **8** *archaic* **a** chastity (esp. of a woman). **b** the reputation for this. **9** (in *pl.*) **a** special distinction for proficiency in an examination. **b** a course of degree studies more specialized than for a general degree. **10 a** *Bridge* the ace, king, queen, jack, and ten, esp. of trumps, or the four aces at no trumps. **b** (in whist) the ace, king, queen, and jack, esp. of trumps. **11** *Golf* the right of driving off first as having won the last hole (*it is my honour*). **●** *transitive verb* **1** respect highly. **2** confer honour on. **3** accept or pay (a bill or cheque) when due. **4** acknowledge. □ **do the honours** perform the duties of a host to guests etc. **in honour bound** *see* ON ONE'S HONOUR. **in honour of** as a celebration of. **on one's honour** (usu. foll. by *to* + infin.) under a moral obligation. **on** (or **upon**) **my honour** an expression of sincerity. [Old French (*h*)*onor* (n.), *onorer* (v.) from Latin *honor*, *honorare*]

hon·our·able /ˈɒnərəbəl/ *adjective* (also **honor·able**) **1 a** worthy of honour. **b** bringing honour to its possessor. **c** showing honour, not base. **d** consistent with honour. **e** *informal* (of the intentions of a man courting a woman) directed towards marriage. **2** (**Honourable**) a title indicating eminence or distinction, given esp. to an MP, an upper court judge, a Lieutenant-Governor, etc. □ **hon·our·able·ness** *noun* **hon·our·ably** *adverb*

honourable mention *noun* a citation given to a contestant, entry, etc. which has considerable merit but has not been awarded a prize.

hon·our·ary *var. of* HONORARY.

hon·our·ee /ˈɒnɔrˌiː/ *noun* (also **honor·ee**) a person who is honoured, esp. by receiving an award or special presentation.

honour point *noun* *Heraldry* the point halfway between the top of a shield and the fess point.

honour roll *noun* *N Amer.* **1** a list of students who have achieved grades above a certain average during a term or school year. **2** a list of the local citizens, members of a church, etc., who died or served in the armed forces.

honours list *noun* *Brit.* a list of persons awarded honours.

honours of war *plural noun* privileges granted to a capitulating force, e.g. that of marching out with colours flying.

honours student *noun* *N Amer.* **1** (also **honour student**) a student who has high grades. **2** a student in an honours program at university.

honour system *noun* a system of conduct which relies on the honour of those concerned to adhere to certain standards of behaviour, unenforced by supervision etc.

Hons. *abbreviation* honours (in reference to a bachelor's degree).

Hon. Sec. *abbreviation* Honorary Secretary.

Hon·shu /ˈhɒnʃuː/ the largest of the four main islands of Japan; pop. (2000) 102,318,000.

hoo *interjection* expressing surprise or apprehension, or requesting attention (*hoo boy!*).

Hooch *see* DE HOOCH.

hooch¹ *noun* (also **hootch**) *N Amer. informal* alcoholic liquor, esp. inferior or illicit whisky. [abbreviation of earlier *hoochinoo*, originally the name of a Tlingit village in Alaska, from *xutsnuːwú*, lit. 'brown bear's fort']

hooch² *noun* (also **hootch**) *US Military slang* living quarters, esp. a dugout or temporary shelter. [originally applied to thatched huts in SE Asia during the Korean and Vietnam Wars: perhaps from Japanese *uchi* 'dwelling']

Hood, Thom·as (1799–1845), English poet and humorist, known for his serious poems, including 'I remember, I remember' (1824), and protest ballads such as 'The Bridge of Sighs' (1844).

hood¹ ● *noun* **1 a** a covering for the head and neck, whether part of a coat etc. or separate. **b** a separate hoodlike garment worn over a university gown or a surplice to indicate the wearer's degree. **2** *N Amer.* a hinged cover over the engine of a motor vehicle. **3** *Brit.* a folding waterproof top of a car, baby carriage, etc. **4** a canopy to protect users of machinery or incorporating a fan to remove fumes, cooking odours, etc. **5** the hoodlike structure or marking on the head or neck of a cobra, seal, etc. **6** a leather covering for a hawk's head. **●** *transitive verb* cover with a hood. □ **hood·less** *adjective* **hood·like** *adjective* [Old English *hōd* from West Germanic, related to HAT]

hood² *noun* esp. *N Amer. slang* a gangster or gunman. [abbreviation of HOODLUM]

'hood *noun* esp. *US slang* a neighbourhood, esp. one in the inner city. [abbreviation]

-hood *suffix* forming nouns: **1** of condition or state (*childhood*; *falsehood*). **2** indicating a collection or group (*sisterhood*; *neighbourhood*). [Old English *-hād*, originally an independent noun, = person, condition, quality]

hood·ed *adjective* **1** having a hood; covered with or as with a hood. **2** wearing a hood. **3** (of eyes) having large, partly closed eyelids.

hooded crow *noun* a piebald grey and black crow, *Corvus cornix*, found in N and E Europe and parts of Asia.

hooded seal *noun* a seal, *Cystophora cristata*, of the Arctic and N Atlantic Oceans, grey with black blotches, the male of which has inflatable nasal sacs used in display.

hooded sweatshirt *noun* a sweatshirt with a hood, often with a front pouch.

hood·ie *noun* *informal* a hooded sweatshirt.

Hood·less, Adel·aide (born Adelaide Hunter) (1857–1910), Canadian educator. After losing an infant son due to impure milk, she campaigned for the teaching of home economics in secondary schools, and founded the first Women's Institute (in Stoney Creek, Ontario) in 1897. She helped found the Victorian Order of Nurses, the National Council of Women, and the national YWCA.

hood·lum /ˈhudləm,ˈhuːd-/ *noun* **1** a street hooligan, a young thug. **2** a gangster. [19th c.: origin unknown]

hoo·doo ● *noun* **1** *N Amer.* a fantastic rock pinnacle or column of rock formed by erosion etc. **2** *esp. US* voodoo. **3** *esp. US* **a** bad luck. **b** a thing or person that brings or causes this. ● *transitive verb* (**hoo·doos, hoo·dooed**) *esp. US* **1** make unlucky. **2** bewitch. [alteration of VOODOO]

hood ornament *noun* a usu. metallic emblem on the front of the hood of a car, usu. distinctive to the manufacturer.

hood·wink *transitive verb* deceive, delude. [originally 'blindfold', from HOOD[1] *noun* + WINK]

hooey *noun & interjection* *slang* nonsense, humbug. [20th c.: origin unknown]

hoof /huf, huːf/ ● *noun* (pl. **hoofs** or **hooves** /huːvz, huvz/) **1** the horny part of the foot of a horse, antelope, and other ungulates. **2** *jocular* the human foot. ● *transitive verb* *slang* kick or shove. □ **hoof it** *slang* **1** go on foot. **2** dance. **on the hoof 1** (of cattle) not yet slaughtered. **2** (of an action etc.) extempore. □ **hoofed** *adjective* (also in *combination*). [Old English *hōf* from Germanic]

hoof-and-mouth disease *noun* = FOOT-AND-MOUTH DISEASE.

hoof·beat *noun* the sound made by a horse's hoof striking the ground.

hoof·er /ˈhufər, ˈhuːf-/ *noun* *informal* a professional dancer, esp. a tap or jazz dancer.

hoof·print *noun* the impression in the ground made by an animal's hoof.

Hoogh·ly River /ˈhuːgli/ (also **Hugli River**) the most westerly of the rivers of the Ganges delta, in West Bengal, India. It flows for 192 km (120 miles) into the Bay of Bengal and is navigable to Calcutta.

hoo-ha (also **hoo-hah, hoo-haw**) *slang* ● *noun* a commotion, a row; uproar, trouble. ● *interjection* expressing feigned surprise or excitement. [20th c.: origin unknown]

hook ● *noun* **1 a** a piece of metal or other material bent back at an angle or with a round bend, for catching hold or for hanging things on. **b** in full **fish hook**) a bent piece of wire, usu. barbed and baited, for catching fish. **2** a curved cutting instrument (*pruning hook*). **3 a** a sharp bend, e.g. in a river. **b** a projecting point of land (*Hook of Holland*). **c** a sand spit with a curved end. **4** *Hockey* an instance of hooking (*see* sense 7 of *verb*). **5** *Golf, Baseball, etc.* **a** a ball or bowl's deviation from a straight line. **b** the action or an act of hooking a ball (*see* sense 8 of *verb*). **c** = HOOK SHOT. **6** *Boxing* a short swinging blow with the elbow bent and rigid. **7** *esp. N Amer.* **a** something that captures attention or entices (*a marketing hook*). **b** an item or theme around which a news story, radio segment, etc. can be developed. **8** a memorable musical phrase in a pop or rock song etc. **9** a trap, a snare. **10 a** a curved stroke in handwriting, esp. as made in learning to write. **b** *Music* an added stroke transverse to the stem in the symbol for an eighth note etc. **11** (in *pl.*) *slang* hands or fingers. ● *verb* **1** *transitive* **a** grasp with a hook. **b** secure with a hook or hooks. **2** (often foll. by *on, up*) **a** *transitive* attach with or as with a hook. **b** *intransitive* be or become attached with a hook. **3** *transitive* catch with or as with a hook (*he hooked a fish; she hooked a husband*). **4** (foll. by *up*) **a** *transitive* connect or set up (stereo components, a VCR, etc.). **b** *transitive* attach (a house, vehicle, etc.) to a central source of electricity, water, etc. **c** *intransitive* *informal* meet or become involved with (*got hooked up with a guy from Amsterdam*). **5** *transitive* *slang* steal. **6** *intransitive* work as a prostitute. **7** *transitive* *Hockey* illegally hinder the advancement of the person with the puck by tugging at his or her body from the side or rear with the blade of one's stick. **8** *transitive & intransitive* *Golf* strike (the ball) so that it deviates towards the opposite side of the striker from that where it lay. **9** *transitive* *Rugby* secure (the ball) and pass it backward with the foot in the scrum. **10** *transitive* *Boxing* strike (one's opponent) with the elbow bent and rigid. **11** *transitive* make (a rug) using a hook to pull yarn, rag, etc. through canvas, burlap, etc. □ **by hook or by crook** by one means or another, by fair means or foul. **get one's hooks on** (or **into**) get hold of. **get the hook** *N Amer. slang* be fired. **give someone the hook** *N Amer. slang* fire or demote (a person). **hook, line, and sinker** entirely. **off the hook 1** *informal* no longer in difficulty or trouble. **2** (of a telephone receiver) not on its rest, and so preventing incoming calls. **on one's own hook** *esp. US slang* on one's own account. **on the hook** *informal* responsible for (*on the hook for a bad loan*). **ring off the hook** *see* RING[2]. **sling one's hook** *Brit. slang* make off, run away. □ **hook·less** *adjective* **hook·like** *adjective* [Old English *hōc*: sense 3 of *noun* prob. influenced by Dutch *hoek* corner]

hook·ah /ˈhukə/ *noun* an oriental tobacco pipe with a long tube passing through water for cooling the smoke as it is drawn through. [Urdu from Arabic *ḥuḳḳah* casket]

hook and eye *noun* **1** a small metal hook and loop as a fastener on a garment. **2** a similar device consisting of a hook and screw eye used to fasten or secure esp. a door.

hook-and-ladder *noun* (also **hook-and-ladder truck**) a large fire truck equipped with long ladders.

hook-and-loop *adjective* designating a fastener for clothes, shoes, etc. consisting of two strips of nylon fabric, one with tiny hooks and the other with thick pile, which adhere when pressed together.

Hooke /huk/ **Rob·ert** (1635–1703), English scientist. He formulated Hooke's law, introduced the term *cell* to biology, and studied light, gravity, and the earth's orbit. He also designed several of London's prominent buildings.

hooked *adjective* **1** hook-shaped (*hooked nose*). **2** furnished with a hook or hooks. **3** *in senses of* HOOK *verb*. **4** (of a rug or mat) made by pulling woollen yarn through canvas with a hook. **5** *informal* (often foll. by *on*) addicted to or captivated by.

Hook·er ▸ 1 Sir Jo·seph Dal·ton (1817–1911), English botanist and pioneer in plant geography. Following a voyage to the Antarctic he proposed that Australia and S America had once been joined, and he introduced rhododendrons to England. **2 Rich·ard** (1554–1600), English theologian. In *The Laws of Ecclesiastical Polity*, which was incomplete at his death, he established Anglican theology as distinct from Roman Catholicism, puritanism, and Geneva Protestantism.

hook·er[1] *noun* **1** *esp. N Amer. slang* a prostitute. **2** a person or thing that hooks. **3** *N Amer.* = HOOKTENDER. **4** *N Amer. slang* a drink of liquor. **5** *Rugby* the player in the middle of the front row of the scrum who tries to hook the ball.

hook·er[2] *noun* **1** a small Dutch or Irish fishing vessel. **2** *slang* an old or fondly-regarded boat. [Dutch *hoeker* from *hoek* HOOK]

Hooke's law /huks/ *noun* the law that the strain in a solid is proportional to the applied stress within the elastic limit of that solid. [HOOKE]

hook·ing *noun* *Hockey* an illegal check in which a player attempts to hinder or pull down an opponent by tugging with the blade of the stick, usu. from behind.

hook nose *noun* an aquiline nose. □ **hook-nosed** *adjective*

Hook of Holland a cape and port of the Netherlands, near The Hague.

hook shot *noun* *Basketball* a one-handed shot in which the player lobs the ball over the head with a sweeping movement of the arm.

hook·tend·er *noun* *N Amer.* a person in charge of the chokermen on a logging crew.

hook·up *noun* **1** a connection, esp. an interconnection of broadcasting equipment for special transmissions. **2** a link to a source of electricity, water, etc. in a campground etc. **3** an act or instance of hooking up (also *attributive: expensive hookup fees*).

hook·worm *noun* **1** any of various nematode worms, with hooklike mouthparts for attachment and feeding, infesting humans and animals. **2** a disease caused by one of these, often resulting in severe anemia.

hooky[1] *noun* (also **hook·ey**) *N Amer.* □ **play hooky** *slang* play truant. [19th c.: origin unknown]

hooky[2] *adjective* **1** (of a song) having a memorable hook; catchy. **2** shaped like a hook.

Consonants: **b** *but* **d** *dog* **f** *few* **g** *get* **h** *her* **j** *yes* **k** *cat* **l** *leg* **m** *man* **n** *no* **p** *pen* **r** *red* **s** *sit*

hoo·li·gan *noun* a noisy and violent person. □ **hoo·li·gan·ism** *noun* [19th c.: perhaps from *Hooligan*, surname of a fictional rowdy Irish family]

hoop ● *noun* **1** a circular band of metal, wood, etc., esp. for binding the staves of casks etc. or for forming part of a framework. **2 a** a ring of wood, plastic, or metal rolled along as a toy or used in various exercises, esp. by children. **b** a large ring usu. with paper stretched over it for circus performers to jump through. **3** *Basketball* **a** the round metal frame of the basket. **b** (also **hoops**) the game of basketball. **4** a circle of flexible material for expanding a woman's petticoat or skirt. **5 a** a circular earring. **b** the circular band of a finger ring. **6** an arch of iron etc. through which the balls are hit in croquet. ● *transitive verb* **1** bind with a hoop or hoops. **2** encircle with or as with a hoop. □ **jump** (or **be put**) **through the hoop** (or **hoops**) make (or force to make) an extraordinary effort. [Old English *hōp* from West Germanic]

hoop dance *noun* a form of dance among certain N American Aboriginal peoples in which the dancer suspends many, often multicoloured hoops with the arms, legs, and body, to create patterns. □ **hoop dancer** *noun*

hoop·la *noun* **1** *informal* extravagant publicity; hype. **2** *informal* commotion; excitement; lively activity. **3** *Brit.* a game in which rings are thrown in an attempt to encircle one of various prizes.

hoo·poe /'huːpuː/ *noun* a salmon-pink Eurasian bird, *Upupa epops*, with black and white wings and tail, a large erectile crest, and a long downward-curving bill. [alteration of Middle English *hoop* from Old French *huppe* from Latin *upupa*, imitative of its cry]

hoop·ster *noun* N Amer. slang a basketball player.

hoo·ray *interjection* = HURRAH. [var. of HURRAH]

Hooray Henry *noun* Brit. slang a rich ineffectual young man, esp. one who is fashionable, extroverted, and conventional.

hoose·gow /'huːsgau/ *noun* N Amer. slang a prison. [Latin American Spanish *juzgao*, Spanish *juzgado* tribunal, from Latin *judicatum* neuter past participle of *judicare* JUDGE]

Hoo·sier /'huːʒɪr/ *noun* a native or inhabitant of the state of Indiana (used as a nickname). [origin unknown]

hoot ● *noun* **1** an owl's cry. **2** the sound made by a train whistle etc. **3** a shout expressing scorn or disapproval; an inarticulate shout. **4** *informal* **a** a shout of laughter. **b** a cause of laughter or merriment (*the party was a hoot*). **5** (also **two hoots**) slang anything at all (*don't give a hoot; doesn't matter two hoots*). ● *verb* **1** *intransitive* **a** (of an owl) utter its cry. **b** (of a train whistle etc.) make a hoot. **c** (often foll. by *at*) make loud sounds, esp. of scorn or merriment (*hooted with laughter*). **2** *transitive* **a** assail with scornful shouts. **b** (often foll. by *out, away*) drive away by hooting. [Middle English *hūten* (v.), perhaps imitative]

hootch var. of HOOCH[1],[2].

hootchy-kootchy *noun* a kind of erotic dance similar to a belly dance. [origin unknown]

hoot·en·anny /'huːtənani/ *noun* (pl. **-nies**) esp. US informal an informal gathering with folk music. [originally dial., = 'gadget']

hoot·er *noun* **1** esp. Brit. a siren or steam whistle, esp. as a signal for work to begin or cease. **2** esp. Brit. the horn of a motor vehicle. **3** slang a nose. **4** a person or animal that hoots. **5** (usu. in pl.) N Amer. slang a woman's breast.

hoots *interjection* Scot. & Northern England expressing dissatisfaction or impatience. [compare Swedish *hut* begone, Welsh *hwt* away, Irish *ut* out, all in similar sense]

Hoo·ver[1] ▶ **1 Her·bert Clark** (1874–1964), US Republican politician, 31st president of the US 1929–33. He is also known for his work in organizing food production and distribution in the US and Europe after both World Wars. **2 John Edgar** (1895–1972), US lawyer and director of the FBI 1924–72. Although he came under criticism for the FBI's anti-Communist stance in the 1960s, he was instrumental in reorganizing it into an efficient law enforcement agency. **3 Wil·liam Henry** (1849–1932), US industrialist. In 1908 he bought the patent of a lightweight electric cleaning machine from James Murray Spangler, a janitor, and formed a company to manufacture it. The machine proved an international success and in 1910 the company was renamed Hoover.

Hoo·ver[2] ● *noun* proprietary Brit. a vacuum cleaner. ● *verb* (**hoover**) **1** *transitive* Brit. clean (a carpet etc.) with a vacuum cleaner. **2** (foll. by *up*) Brit. **a** *transitive* suck up with a vacuum cleaner (*hoovered up the crumbs*). **b** *intransitive* clean a room etc. with a vacuum cleaner (*decided to hoover before they arrived*). **3** *informal* suck up or remove with great force (*hoovered up two slices of cake*). [W. H. HOOVER]

Hoo·ver·ville *noun* (in the US) any of the shantytowns built by unemployed and destitute people during the Great Depression of the early 1930s. [H. C. HOOVER, the president of the day]

hooves pl. of HOOF.

hop[1] ● *verb* (**hopped, hop·ping**) **1** *intransitive* (of a bird, frog, etc.) spring with two or all feet at once. **2** *intransitive* (of a person) **a** jump on one foot. **b** make small jumps up and down on both feet. **3** *transitive* move or go quickly (*hopped out of his chair*). **4** *transitive* cross (a ditch etc.) by hopping. **5** *intransitive* *informal* **a** make a quick trip. **b** make a quick change of position or location (*bar-hop*). **6** *transitive* *informal* jump into or board (a vehicle, plane, etc.). **7** *transitive* (usu. as **hop·ping** *noun*) (esp. of aircraft) pass quickly from one (place of a specified type) to another (*hedge-hopping*). ● *noun* **1** a hopping movement. **2** *informal* an informal gathering for dancing. **3** a short trip, esp. in an aircraft; the distance travelled by air without landing; a stage of a flight or journey. **4** N Amer. a bounce of a ball etc. □ **hop in** (or **out**) *informal* get into (or out of) a car etc. **hop it** Brit. slang go away. **a hop, skip, and a jump** slang a short distance. **hop the twig** (or **stick**) slang **1** depart suddenly. **2** die. **on the hop** Brit. *informal* **1** unprepared (*caught on the hop*). **2** bustling about. [Old English *hoppian*]

hop[2] ● *noun* **1** a climbing plant, *Humulus lupulus*, cultivated for the cones borne by the female. **2** (in pl.) **a** the ripe cones of this, used to give a bitter flavour to beer. **b** *informal* beer. **3** US dated slang opium or any other narcotic. ● *verb* (**hopped, hop·ping**) *transitive* flavour with hops. [Middle Low German, Middle Dutch *hoppe*]

hopak /'hoːpak/ *noun* a lively Ukrainian dance in 2/4 time. [Ukrainian, from *hop*, interjection uttered during the dance]

Hope ▶ **1 An·thony** (1863–1933), English author known for his cloak-and-dagger romances, including *The Prisoner of Zenda* (1894). **2 Bob** (born Leslie Townes Hope) (1903–2003), British-born US comedian, known for his dry allusive style in his films and variety shows.

hope ● *noun* **1** (in sing. or pl.; often foll. by *of*, *that*) expectation and desire combined, e.g. for a certain thing to occur (*has high hopes of getting the job*). **2 a** a person, thing, or circumstance that gives cause for hope. **b** grounds for hope; promise. **3** what is hoped for. ● *verb* **1** *intransitive* (often foll. by *for*) feel hope. **2** *transitive* expect and desire (*I hope you can leave early*). **3** *transitive* feel fairly confident; trust. □ **hope against hope** continue to hope for something even though it is very unlikely. **not a hope** (**in hell**) *informal* no chance at all. □ **hoper** *noun* [Old English *hopa*]

hope chest *noun* N Amer. a chest containing linen, clothing, china, etc. stored by a woman in preparation for her marriage.

hope·ful ● *adjective* **1** feeling hope. **2** causing or inspiring hope. **3** likely to succeed; promising. ● *noun* **1** a person likely to succeed. **2** *ironic* a person likely to be disappointed. □ **hope·ful·ness** *noun*

hope·ful·ly *adverb* **1** in a hopeful manner. **2** (qualifying a whole sentence) disputed it is to be hoped (*hopefully, the car will be ready by then*). ¶ The use of *hopefully* in sense 2 is extremely common, but it is still considered incorrect by some people. However, there are no grounds for condemning this use; many other adverbs, such as *thankfully* and *mercifully*, function in the same way.

Hopeh see HEBEI.

hope·less *adjective* **1** having or feeling no hope; despairing. **2** feeling or causing despair (*a hopeless case*). **3** inadequate, incompetent (*am hopeless at tennis*). **4** without hope of success; futile. □ **hope·less·ly** *adverb* **hope·less·ness** *noun*

hop·head *noun* esp. US slang a drug addict.

hop hornbeam *noun* a deciduous tree of eastern N America, *Ostrya virginiana*, with very hard wood. Also called IRONWOOD. [so-called because of the resemblance of the ripe catkins to hops]

Hopi /'hoːpi/ ● *noun* (pl. same or **Hopis**) **1** a member of a N American Aboriginal people living chiefly in NE Arizona. **2** the Uto-Aztecan language of these people. ● *adjective* of or pertaining to the Hopi or their language. [Hopi]

Hop·kins ▶ **1 Sir An·thony (Phil·ip)** (b.1937), Welsh actor. His films include *The Elephant Man* (1980), *The Bounty* (1984), and *The Remains of the Day* (1993). He won an Oscar for his performance in *The Silence of the Lambs* (1991). **2 Sir Fred·erick Gow·land** (1861–1947), English biochemist, considered the father of British biochemistry. He carried out pioneering work on 'accessory food factors' (later called vitamins), and shared a Nobel Prize in 1929. **3 Ger·ard Man·ley** (1844–89), English poet. In poems such as 'Windhover' and 'Pied Beauty' (both 1877), he explored religious themes through original style and

t *top*   v *voice*   w *we*   z *zoo*   ʃ *she*   ʒ *vision*   θ *thin*   ð *this*   ŋ *ring*   x *loch*   tʃ *chip*   dʒ *jar*   (*see over for vowels*)

wordplay. **4 Johns** (1795–1873), US financier. He provided endowments for the creation of the hospital and university in Baltimore that bear his name.

hop·lite /ˈhɒplaɪt/ *noun* a heavily-armed foot soldier of ancient Greece. [Greek *hoplitēs* from *hoplon* weapon]

hopped up *adjective* N Amer. slang **1** intoxicated; stimulated with or as with a drug. **2** excited, enthusiastic. **3** (of a motor vehicle) having its engine altered to give improved performance; souped-up.

Hop·per, Ed·ward (1882–1967), US realist painter, best known for his mature works, such as *Early Sunday Morning* (1930) and *Nighthawks* (1942), depicting scenes from everyday American urban life.

hop·per *noun* **1** a person who hops. **2** a grasshopper or other hopping insect. **3 a** a container tapering downward (originally having a hopping motion) through which grain passes into a mill. **b** a similar contrivance in various machines. **4 a** a barge carrying away mud etc. from a dredging machine and discharging it. **b** (in full **hopper car**) a railway car able to discharge grain etc. through openings in its floor. **5** *Baseball slang* a ball which having been struck rebounds from the ground.

hop·ping *adjective* **1** *in senses of* HOP[1]. **2** esp. N Amer. informal very active, lively (*a hopping party*).

hop·ping mad *adjective* informal very angry.

hoppy *adjective* (**hop·pi·er**, **hop·pi·est**) tasting strongly of hops. □ **hop·pi·ness** *noun*

hop·sack *noun* (also **hop·sack·ing**) **1 a** a coarse material made from hemp etc. **b** sacking for hops made from this. **2** a coarse clothing fabric of a loose plain weave.

hop·scotch ● *noun* a children's game of hopping on one foot into and over squares or oblongs marked on the ground in order to retrieve a stone etc. thrown into one of these compartments. ● *intransitive verb* N Amer. **1** play hopscotch. **2** jump, as if playing hopscotch (*hopscotched out of the way*). **3** travel from place to place (*hopscotched from Calgary to Winnipeg and then home*). [HOP[1] + SCOTCH[1]]

hora *noun* a Jewish and Romanian traditional dance in which the dancers form a circle. [Hebrew *hōrāh*, Romanian *horă*]

Hor·ace /ˈhɒrəs/ (full name Quintus Horatius Flaccus) (65–8 BC), Roman poet of the Augustan period. His works include the *Odes*, the *Satires*, and the *Ars Poetica*, which influenced Dryden and the 18th-c. Augustans in their critical writing. □ **Hor·atian** /həˈreɪʃən/ *adjective*

horde *noun* **1 a** usu. *derogatory* a large group, a gang. **b** a moving swarm or pack (of insects, wolves, etc.). **2** a troop of Tartar or other nomads. [Polish *horda* from Turkic *ordī, ordŭ* camp: compare URDU]

hore·hound *noun* **1 a** a herbaceous plant, *Marrubium vulgare*, with a white cottony covering on its stem and leaves. **b** its bitter aromatic juice used against coughs etc. **2** a herbaceous plant, *Ballota nigra*, with an unpleasant aroma. [Old English *hāre hūne* from *hār* HOAR + *hūne* a plant]

hor·izon *noun* **1 a** the line at which the earth and sky appear to meet. **b** (in full **apparent horizon, sensible horizon,** or **visible horizon**) the line at which the earth and sky would appear to meet but for irregularities and obstructions; a circle where the earth's surface touches a cone whose vertex is at the observer's eye. **c** (in full **celestial horizon** or **true horizon**) a great circle of the celestial sphere, the plane of which passes through the centre of the earth and is parallel to that of the apparent horizon of a place. **2** range or limit of mental perception, experience, interest, etc. **3** a geological stratum or set of strata, a layer of soil, with particular characteristics. **4** *Archaeology* the level at which a particular set of remains is found. □ **on the horizon** (of an event) just imminent or becoming apparent. □ **hor·izon·less** *adjective* [Old French *orizon(te)* from Late Latin *horizon -ontis* from Greek *horizōn (kuklos)* limiting (circle)]

hori·zon·tal ● *adjective* **1 a** parallel to the plane of the horizon, at right angles to the vertical (*horizontal plane*). **b** (of machinery etc.) having its parts working in a horizontal direction. **2 a** combining firms engaged in the same stage of production (*horizontal integration*). **b** of or concerned with the same work, status, etc. (*a horizontal move rather than a promotion*). **3** of or at the horizon. ● *noun* a horizontal line, plane, etc. □ **hori·zon·tal·ity** *noun* **hori·zon·tal·ly** *adverb* [French *horizontal* or modern Latin *horizontalis* (as HORIZON)]

horizontal mambo *noun* slang sexual intercourse.

hork N Amer. slang ● *transitive & intransitive verb* spit. ● *noun* the act of spitting. [alteration of HAWK[3]]

Hor·liv·ka /ˈhɔːrljuːkə/ (Russian **Gorlovka**) an industrial city in SE Ukraine, in the Donets Basin; pop. (est. 2001) 292,000.

hor·mone *noun* **1** a regulatory substance produced in an organism

and transported in tissue fluids such as blood or sap to stimulate cells or tissues into action. **2** a synthetic substance with a similar effect. **3** (in *pl.*) *informal* the hormones regulating the sex drive. □ **hor·mon·al** *adjective* **hor·mon·al·ly** *adverb* [Greek *hormōn* part. of *hormaō* impel]

hormone replacement therapy *noun* treatment with estrogens to alleviate menopausal symptoms. Abbr.: **HRT**.

Hor·muz /ˈhɔːrmuz/ (also **Ormuz** /ˈɔːrmuz/) an Iranian island at the mouth of the Persian Gulf, in the Strait of Hormuz. It is the site of an ancient city, which was an important centre of commerce in the Middle Ages.

Hormuz, Strait of a strait linking the Persian Gulf with the Gulf of Oman, which leads to the Arabian Sea, and separating Iran from the Arabian peninsula. It is of strategic and economic importance as a waterway through which sea traffic to and from the oil-rich states of the Gulf must pass.

horn ● *noun* **1 a** a hard permanent outgrowth, often curved and pointed, on the head of cattle, rhinoceroses, giraffes, and other esp. hoofed mammals, found singly, in pairs, or one in front of another. **b** the structure of a horn, consisting of a core of bone encased in keratinized skin. **2** each of two deciduous branched appendages on the head of (esp. male) deer. **3** a hornlike projection on the head of other animals, e.g. a snail's tentacle, the crest of a horned owl, etc. **4** the substance of which horns are composed. **5** anything resembling or compared to a horn in shape. **6** *Music* **a** = FRENCH HORN. **b** a wind instrument played by lip vibration, originally made of horn, now usu. of brass. **c** a horn player. **7** an instrument sounding a warning or other signal (*car horn; foghorn*). **8** a receptacle or instrument made of horn, e.g. a drinking vessel. **9** a horn-shaped projection, e.g. on a saddle. **10** N Amer. informal a telephone. **11** the extremity of the moon or other crescent. **12** an arm or branch of a river, bay, etc. **13** a pyramidal peak formed by glacial action. **14** coarse slang an erect penis. **15** the hornlike emblem of a cuckold. **16** a representation of an animal's horn as appearing on the head of a supernatural (esp. evil) being. **17** a cone-shaped apparatus (esp. part of an early gramophone etc.) for the collection or amplification of sound. ● *transitive verb* gore with the horns. □ **horn in** slang **1** (usu. foll. by *on*) intrude. **2** interfere. **horn of plenty** a cornucopia. **on the horns of a dilemma** faced with a decision involving equally unfavourable alternatives. **pull** (or **draw**) **in one's horns** become less assertive or ambitious; draw back. □ **horn·ist** *noun* (in sense 6 of *noun*). **horn·less** *adjective* **horn·like** *adjective* [Old English from Germanic, related to Latin *cornu*]

Horn, Cape (also **the Horn**) the southernmost point of S America, on a Chilean island south of Tierra del Fuego. The region is notorious for its storms, and until the opening of the Panama Canal in 1914 constituted the only sea route between the Atlantic and Pacific Oceans. [*Hoorn*, birthplace of W. C. Schouten, Dutch navigator who discovered the cape in 1616]

horn·beam *noun* any tree of the genus *Carpinus*, with a smooth bark and a hard tough wood. Also called IRONWOOD.

horn·bill *noun* any bird of the family Bucerotidae, with a hornlike excrescence on its large red or yellow curved bill.

horn·blende *noun* a dark brown, black, or green mineral occurring in many igneous and metamorphic rocks, and composed of calcium, magnesium, and iron silicates. [German (as HORN, BLENDE)]

horn·book *noun* **1** hist. a teaching aid consisting of a leaf of paper containing the alphabet, the Lord's Prayer, etc., mounted on a wooden tablet with a handle, and protected by a thin plate of horn. **2** a treatise on the rudiments of a subject.

Horn·by Island one of the Gulf Islands in the Strait of Georgia, BC, situated west of Texada Island. [Sir P. *Hornby*, English admiral d.1867]

horned *adjective* **1** having a horn or horns. **2** crescent-shaped (*horned moon*).

horned grebe *noun* a small grebe, *Podiceps auritus*, with a short straight bill, a chestnut neck, and buff ear tufts against a black head.

horned lark *noun* a brown and white lark, *Eremophila alpestris*, which has two black tufts on the head, and is of worldwide distribution.

horned owl *noun* = GREAT HORNED OWL.

horned toad *noun* **1** (also **horned lizard**) a small spiny American lizard of the genus *Phrynosoma*, esp. *P. cornutum*, sometimes kept as a pet. **2** any SE Asian toad of the family Pelobatidae, with horn-shaped extensions over the eyes.

horned viper *noun* = ASP 2b.

hor·net *noun* any of various large social wasps of the family Vespidae, with a severe sting. [prob. from Middle Low German, Middle Dutch *horn(e)te*, corresponding to Old English *hyrnet*, perhaps related to HORN]

Vowels: a cat ɑ arm e bed ɜr her ɜ: deux ə ago ɪ sit i cosy iː feed ɒ hot ɔ pore ɔː no ʌ run ʊ put

hornet's nest *noun* a state of trouble, outrage, opposition, etc. (*stir up a hornet's nest*).

horn·fels /ˈhɔrnfelz/ *noun* a dark fine-grained metamorphic rock composed mainly of quartz, mica, and feldspars. [German, lit. = 'horned rock']

Horn of Africa, the (also called **Somali Peninsula**) a peninsula of NE Africa, comprising Somalia and parts of Ethiopia. It lies between the Gulf of Aden and the Indian Ocean.

horn·pipe *noun* **1** a lively dance, usu. for one person, originally to the accompaniment of a wind instrument, and esp. associated with the merrymaking of sailors. **2** the music for this. [name of an obsolete wind instrument partly of horn: Middle English, from HORN + PIPE]

horn-rimmed *adjective* (esp. of eyeglasses) having rims made of horn or a substance resembling it. □ **horn-rims** *plural noun*

horn·swog·gle *transitive verb slang* cheat, hoax. □ **horn·swog·gler** *noun* [19th c.: origin unknown]

horn·worm *noun N Amer.* any of several hawk moth larvae having a hornlike spike on the tail, esp. the vegetable pests *Manduca sexta* and *M. quinquemaculata*.

horn·wort /ˈhɔrnwɜrt, -wɔrt/ *noun* any aquatic rootless plant of the genus *Ceratophyllum*, with forked leaves.

horny *adjective* (**horn·i·er**, **horn·i·est**) **1** of or like horn. **2** hard like horn, callous (*horny-handed*). **3** wearing or having a horn or horns. **4** *slang* **a** sexually excited. **b** lecherous. □ **horn·i·ness** *noun*

hor·ol·ogy /həˈrɒlədʒi/ *noun* the art of measuring time or making clocks, watches, etc.; the study of this. □ **horo·logic·al** *adjective* **hor·ol·o·gist** *noun* [Greek *hōra* time + -LOGY]

horo·scope /ˈhɔrəˌskoʊp/ *noun Astrology* **1** a forecast of a person's future based on a diagram showing the relative positions of the stars and planets at a particular time, e.g. the time of that person's birth. **2** such a diagram (*cast a horoscope*). □ **horo·scop·ic** /-ˈskɒpɪk/ *adjective* **hor·os·copy** /həˈrɒskəpi/ *noun* [French from Latin *horoscopus* from Greek *hōroskopos* from *hōra* time + *skopos* observer]

Horo·witz /ˈhɒrəvɪts/ **Vlad·i·mir** (1904–89), Russian-born pianist. He toured the US in 1928, and settled there soon afterwards. A leading international virtuoso, he was best known for his performances of Scarlatti, Liszt, Scriabin, and Prokofiev.

hor·ren·dous /həˈrendəs/ *adjective* horrifying; awful. □ **hor·ren·dous·ly** *adverb* [Latin *horrendus* gerundive of *horrēre*: see HORRID]

hor·rible *adjective* **1** causing or likely to cause horror; hideous, shocking. **2** unpleasant, excessive (*horrible weather; horrible noise*). □ **hor·rible·ness** *noun* **hor·ribly** *adverb* [Old French (h)*orrible* from Latin *horribilis* from *horrēre*: see HORRID]

hor·rid *adjective* **1** horrible, revolting. **2** unpleasant, disagreeable (*horrid weather; horrid children*). □ **hor·rid·ly** *adverb* **hor·rid·ness** *noun* [Latin *horridus* from *horrēre* bristle, shudder]

hor·rif·ic *adjective* horrifying. □ **hor·rif·ic·ally** *adverb* [French *horrifique* or Latin *horrificus* from *horrēre*: see HORRID]

hor·rify *transitive verb* (**-fies**, **-fied**) arouse horror in; shock, scandalize. □ **hor·ri·fy·ing** *adjective* **hor·ri·fy·ing·ly** *adverb* [Latin *horrificare* (as HORRIFIC)]

hor·ri·pi·la·tion /ˌhɒrɪpəˈleɪʃən/ *noun literary* = GOOSEBUMPS. [Late Latin *horripilatio* from *horrēre* to bristle + *pilus* hair]

hor·ror *noun* **1** an intense feeling of loathing and fear. **2 a** (often foll. by *of*) intense dislike. **b** (often foll. by *at*) *informal* intense dismay. **3 a** a person or thing causing horror (*the horrors of war*). **b** *informal* a bad or mischievous person etc. **c** *informal* something considered ugly or tacky (*this chesterfield is a horror!*). **4** (in *pl.*; prec. by *the*) *informal* a fit of horror, depression, or nervousness, esp. as in delirium tremens. **5** a genre of literature, film, etc. designed to excite pleasurable feelings of horror by depiction of the supernatural, violence, etc. (often attributive: *horror movie*). □ **horror of horrors** used to emphasize how bad a situation is (*I stood up to speak and–horror of horrors–realized I had left my notes behind*). [Old French (h)*orrour* from Latin *horror -oris* (as HORRID)]

hor·rors *interjection* an exclamation of (esp. mock) dismay.

horror story *noun* **1** a story about frightening, esp. supernatural things that is designed to entertain people. **2** a report that describes an experience of a situation as very unpleasant (*horror stories about visits to the dentist*).

horror-strick·en *adjective* (also **horror-struck**) horrified, shocked.

hors de combat /ˌɔr də kɔ̃ˈbɑ/ *adjective* out of the fight or the running. [French]

hors d'oeuvre /ɔrˈdɜrv/ *noun* (*pl.* same or **hors d'oeuvres** *pronunc.* same or /ˈdɜrvz/) a small item of food served as an appetizer or at a

cocktail reception etc. [French, lit. 'outside the work', as being outside the main course of the meal]

horse ● *noun* **1 a** a solid-hoofed plant-eating quadruped, *Equus caballus*, with flowing mane and tail, used for riding and to carry and pull loads. **b** an adult male horse; a stallion or gelding. **c** any other four-legged mammal of the genus *Equus*, including asses and zebras. **d** (*collective*; as *sing.*) cavalry. **e** a representation of a horse. **2** = VAULTING HORSE. **3 a** a frame or structure on which something is mounted or supported. **b** = SAWHORSE. **c** = CLOTHES HORSE 1. **4** *slang* heroin. **5** *informal* a unit of horsepower. **6** *Naut.* any of various ropes and bars. **7** *Mining* an obstruction in a vein. **8** *Chess informal* a knight. ● *verb* **1** *intransitive informal* (foll. by *around*) fool around. **2** *transitive* provide (a person or vehicle) with a horse or horses. **3** *intransitive* mount or go on horseback. □ **change horses in midstream** change one's ideas, plans, etc. in the middle of a project or process. **flog a dead horse** see DEAD HORSE. **from the horse's mouth** (of information etc.) from the person directly concerned or another authoritative source. **hold one's horses** see HOLD¹. **horse of a different** (or **another**) **colour** a thing significantly different. **horses for courses** *Brit.* the matching of tasks and talents. **if wishes were horses** see WISH. **on one's high horse** see HIGH. **to horse!** (as a command) mount your horses. □ **horse·less** *adjective* **horse·like** *adjective* [Old English *hors* from Germanic]

horse-and-buggy *attributive adjective N Amer.* old-fashioned, bygone.

horse·back ● *noun* the back of a horse, esp. as sat on in riding. ● *adverb & adjective* on horseback (*rode horseback; horseback riding*). □ **on horseback** mounted on a horse.

horse blanket *noun* a blanket placed over a horse's body esp. after exercise.

horse·box *noun Brit.* a closed vehicle for transporting a horse or horses.

horse brass *noun* see BRASS *noun* 5.

horse bun *noun Cdn slang* a piece of horse manure.

horse car *noun N Amer. hist.* a horse-drawn streetcar or railway car.

horse chestnut *noun* **1** any large ornamental tree of the genus *Aesculus*, with upright conical clusters of white or pink or red flowers. **2** the dark brown fruit of this (like an edible chestnut, but with a coarse bitter taste).

horse doctor *noun* a veterinary surgeon attending horses.

horse-drawn *adjective* (of a vehicle) pulled by a horse or horses.

horse feathers *noun* = HORSESHIT 2.

horse·flesh *noun* **1** (also **horse·meat**) the flesh of a horse, esp. as food. **2** horses collectively.

horse·fly *noun* (*pl.* **-flies**) any of various flies of the family Tabanidae (esp. of the genus *Tabanus*), the females of which inflict a painful bite to suck blood from their victims.

Horse Guards *plural noun* **1** (in the UK) the cavalry brigade of the household troops. **2** the headquarters of such cavalry, esp. a building in Whitehall.

horse·hair *noun* hair from the mane or tail of a horse, used for padding etc. (often *attributive*: *a horsehair sofa*).

horse·head *noun* a pump used for extracting crude oil, consisting of a raised horizontal beam that functions like a see-saw, with a counterweight at one end that is shaped somewhat like a horse's head.

horse·hide *noun* **1** the hide of a horse. **2** leather made from the hide of a horse. **3** *informal* a baseball.

horse latitudes *plural noun* a belt of calms in each hemisphere, at the latitudes 30–35° north and south of the equator, between the trade winds and the westerlies. [18th c.: origin uncertain]

horse laugh *noun* a loud coarse laugh.

horse·leech *noun* a large freshwater leech of the genus *Haemopis*, feeding by swallowing not sucking.

horse mackerel *noun* any large fish of the mackerel type, e.g. the tuna.

horse·man *noun* (*pl.* **-men**) **1** a rider on horseback. **2** a skilled rider. **3** *Cdn slang* a member of the Royal Canadian Mounted Police.

horse·man·ship *noun* the art of riding on horseback; skill in doing this.

horse·meat *noun* = HORSEFLESH 1.

horse mushroom *noun* a large edible mushroom, *Agaricus arvensis*.

horse opera *noun slang* a western film.

horse pill *noun slang* a very large pill.

horse·play *noun* boisterous play.

horse·play·er *noun* a person who gambles on horse races.

horse pond *noun* a pond for watering and washing horses, proverbial as a place for ducking obnoxious persons.

horse·power *noun* (*pl.* same) **1** an imperial unit of power equal to 550 foot-pounds per second (about 750 watts). Abbr.: **hp**. **2** the power of an engine etc. measured in terms of this.

horse race *noun* **1** a race between horses with riders. **2** any close competition, e.g. an election etc. □ **horse racing** *noun*

horse·radish *noun* **1** a cruciferous plant, *Armoracia rusticana*, with long lobed leaves. **2** the pungent root of this scraped or grated as a condiment, often made into a sauce.

horse sense *noun informal* plain common sense.

horse·shit *noun coarse slang* **1** excrement from a horse. **2** (often as *interjection*) nonsensical, foolish, or deceptive talk or writing.

horse·shoe *noun* **1** an iron shoe for a horse shaped like the outline of the hard part of the hoof. **2** a representation of this as a good luck charm. **3** an object shaped like C or U (e.g. a magnet, a table, a Spanish or Islamic arch). **4** (in *pl.*) esp. *N Amer.* a game in which horseshoes are tossed at an iron stake.

horseshoe bat *noun* a bat of the Old World family Rhinolophidae, usu. with a horseshoe-shaped ridge on the nose.

horseshoe crab *noun* a large marine arthropod, *Limulus polyphemus*, with a horseshoe-shaped shell and a long tail spine. *Also called* KING CRAB.

Horseshoe Falls see NIAGARA FALLS 1.

horseshoe pit *noun N Amer.* a sandy area for playing horseshoes.

horse·tail *noun* **1** the tail of a horse (formerly used in Turkey as a standard, or as an ensign denoting the rank of a pasha). **2** any cryptogamous plant of the genus *Equisetum*, like a horse's tail, with a hollow jointed stem and scale-like leaves.

horse-trading *noun* **1** *N Amer.* dealing in horses. **2** shrewd bargaining. □ **horse-trade** *intransitive verb* **horse trader** *noun*

horse·whip ● *noun* a whip for driving horses. ● *transitive verb* (**-whipped, -whip·ping**) beat with a horsewhip.

horse whisperer *noun* a person who tames or trains horses using whispering and other non-aggressive methods. □ **horse whispering** *noun*

horse·woman *noun* (*pl.* **-women**) **1** a woman who rides on horseback. **2** a skilled woman rider.

horsey *adjective* (also **horsy**) (**hors·i·er, hors·i·est**) **1** of, pertaining to, or resembling a horse or horses. **2** concerned with or devoted to horses or horse racing (*the horsey set*).

hors·ie *noun* a child's name for a horse.

horst *noun Geol.* a raised elongated block of land bounded by faults on both sides. [German, = heap]

hor·ta·tory /ˈhɔːtətɔri/ *adjective* (also **hor·ta·tive** /ˈhɔːtətɪv/) tending or serving to exhort. [Latin *hortativus* from *hortari* exhort]

hor·ten·sia /hɔːˈtensiə/ *noun* a kind of hydrangea, *Hydrangea macrophylla*, with large rounded infertile flower heads. [modern Latin from *Hortense* Lepaute, 18th-c. Frenchwoman]

horti·cul·ture /ˈhɔːtɪˌkʌltʃər/ *noun* the art or science of garden cultivation. □ **horti·cul·tur·al** *adjective* **horti·cul·tur·al·ist** *noun* **horti·cul·tur·al·ly** *adverb* **horti·cul·tur·ist** *noun* [Latin *hortus* garden, after AGRICULTURE]

Hor·ton River a river in the northwestern NWT, rising north of Great Bear Lake and flowing 618 km northwestward into Franklin Bay, an inlet of the Beaufort Sea. [Sir R. W. *Horton*, Undersecretary of State for the colonies d.1841]

Horus *Egyptian Myth* a sky god, regarded as the protector of the monarchy, usu. depicted as a falcon-headed man. In the myth of Isis and Osiris he was the posthumous son of Osiris, whose murder he avenged.

Hos. *abbreviation* Hosea (Old Testament).

ho·san·na /həʊˈzanə/ *noun & interjection* (in Biblical, Judaic, and Christian use) a shout of adoration. [Greek *hōsanna* from Hebrew *hôšaʿnâ* for *hôšîʿa-nnâ* save now!]

hose ● *noun* **1** a flexible tube conveying water for watering plants, putting out fires, etc. **2 a** (as *pl.*) stockings and socks. **b** *hist.* breeches (*doublet and hose*). ● *transitive verb* **1** (often foll. by *down*) water or spray or drench with a hose. **2** provide with hose. **3** *slang* deceive, swindle. [Old English from Germanic]

Hosea /həʊˈzeiə/ **1** a Hebrew minor prophet of the 8th c. BC. **2** a book of the Bible containing his prophecies.

hose·pipe *noun Brit.* = HOSE *noun* 1.

hos·er *noun Cdn slang* **1** an idiot; a goof. **2** an uncultivated person, esp. an unintelligent, inarticulate, beer-drinking lout.

hos·iery /ˈhəʊzəri, ˈhəʊʒəri/ *noun* stockings and socks collectively.

hos·pice /ˈhɒspɪs/ *noun* **1** a home for people who are ill (esp. terminally). **2** *archaic* a lodging for travellers, esp. one kept by a religious order. [French from Latin *hospitium* (as HOST²)]

hos·pit·able /hɒˈspɪtəbəl, ˈhɒsp-/ *adjective* **1** giving or disposed to give welcome and entertainment to strangers or guests. **2** (of an environment) pleasant and favourable for living in. □ **hos·pit·ably** *adverb* [French from *hospiter* from medieval Latin *hospitare* entertain (as HOST²)]

hos·pi·tal *noun* **1 a** an institution providing medical and surgical treatment and nursing care for ill or injured people. **b** an establishment for the treatment of sick or injured animals. **c** an establishment that repairs something specified (*doll hospital*). **2** *hist.* **a** a hospice. **b** an establishment of the Knights Hospitallers. [Old French from medieval Latin *hospitale* neuter of Latin *hospitalis* (adj.) (as HOST²)]

hospital corners *plural noun* a way of tucking in sheets by creating a mitred corner.

hos·pi·tal·er *US var. of* HOSPITALLER.

Hos·pita·let /ɒsˌpɪtəˈlet/ (in full **Hos·pita·let de Llobre·gat** /-de ˌjʊvrəˈɡat/) a city in NE Spain, part of the conurbation of Barcelona; pop. (est. 1998) 248,521.

hospital gown *noun* a garment of a thin fabric, covering the shoulders to the knees, and fastening at the back with ties at the neck and waist, worn by patients in hospital and for medical examinations.

hos·pi·tal·ity *noun* the friendly and generous reception and entertainment of guests or strangers. [Old French *hospitalité* from Latin *hospitalitas -tatis* (as HOSPITAL)]

hospitality home *noun N Amer.* **1** a guest home, sometimes providing breakfast with accommodation. **2** (also **hospitality house**) a house providing temporary lodging for friends or relatives attending on hospital patients, prison inmates, etc.

hospitality industry *noun* the business of providing lodging and usu. meals for travellers.

hospitality suite *noun* (also **hospitality room**) a suite or room in a hotel etc. set aside for the entertainment of guests.

hos·pi·tal·ize *transitive verb* (also esp. *Brit.* **-ise**) send or admit (a patient) to hospital. □ **hos·pi·tal·iz·a·tion** *noun*

hos·pi·tal·ler /ˈhɒspɪtələr/ *noun* (*US* **hospitaler**) (also **Hospitaller**) a member of a charitable religious order.

hospital ship *noun* a ship to receive sick and wounded sailors, or to take sick and wounded military personnel home.

Host *noun* the bread consecrated in the Eucharist. [Old French (h)oiste from Latin *hostia* victim]

host¹ *noun* **1** (usu. foll. by *of*) a large number of people or things. **2** *archaic* an army. **3** (in full **heavenly host, host of heaven**) *Bible* **a** the sun, moon, and stars. **b** the angels. [Old French from Latin *hostis* stranger, enemy, in medieval Latin 'army']

host² ● *noun* **1** a person who receives or entertains another as a guest. **2** an emcee or interviewer, esp. on a television or radio program. **3** *Biol.* an animal or plant having a parasite or commensal. **4** an animal or person that has received a transplanted organ etc. **5** the landlord or landlady of an inn. ● *transitive verb* act as host to (a person) or at (an event). [Old French *oste* from Latin *hospes -pitis* host, guest]

hos·ta /ˈhɒstə/ *noun* any perennial garden plant of the genus *Hosta* (formerly *Funkia*) with green or variegated ornamental leaves and loose clusters of tubular mauve or white flowers. [modern Latin, from N. T. *Host*, Austrian physician d.1834]

hos·tage /ˈhɒstɪdʒ/ *noun* **1** a person seized or held as security for the fulfilment of a condition. **2** the state of being held as a hostage. □ **hos·tage·ship** *noun* [Old French (h)ostage ultimately from Late Latin *obsidatus* 'the state of being a hostage' from Latin *obses obsidis* hostage]

hostage to fortune *noun* an acquisition, commitment, etc., regarded as endangered by unforeseen circumstances.

host computer *noun* a computer attached to a network, which controls or executes certain functions for other linked computers.

hos·tel /ˈhɒstəl/ *noun* **1** a place providing temporary accommodation for the homeless etc. **2** = YOUTH HOSTEL. **3** *Brit. & Cdn* a house of residence or lodging for students, nurses, etc. **4** *archaic* an inn. [Old French (h)ostel from medieval Latin (as HOSPITAL)]

hos·tel·ling /ˈhɒstəlɪŋ/ *noun* (also esp. *US* **hostel·ing**) the practice of staying in youth hostels, esp. while travelling. □ **hos·tel·ler** *noun*

---

hos·tel·ry /'hɒstəlri/ *noun* (*pl.* **-ries**) *archaic* or *literary* an inn.

host·ess *noun* **1** a woman who receives or entertains a guest. **2 a** a woman employed to welcome and seat customers of a restaurant etc. **b** a woman employed to greet and entertain esp. male customers of a nightclub etc. **3** a woman employed as an emcee or interviewer, esp. on a television or radio program. **4** a woman employed to tend to passengers on an aircraft, train, etc. (*air hostess*).

hostess gift *noun* a small gift given by a party guest or house guest to the hostess.

hos·tile /'hɒstail, 'hɒstəl/ *adjective* **1** of an enemy. **2 a** (often foll. by *to*) aggressively opposed; showing strong rejection. **b** showing strong dislike; aggressive. **3** (of a takeover bid) liable to be opposed by the management of the target company. □ **hos·tile·ly** *adverb* [French *hostile* or Latin *hostilis* (as HOST¹)]

hostile witness *noun Law* a witness who appears hostile to the party calling him or her and therefore untrustworthy.

hos·til·i·ty /hɒ'stɪlɪti/ *noun* (*pl.* **-ities**) **1** being hostile, enmity. **2** a state of warfare. **3** (in *pl.*) acts of warfare. **4** opposition (in thought etc.). **5** a hostile act. [French *hostilité* or Late Latin *hostilitas* (as HOSTILE)]

host·ler /'hɒslər, 'ɒslər/ *noun hist.* **1** a stableman at an inn. **2** *US* a person in charge of vehicles or machines, esp. railway engines, when they are not in use. [Middle English from *hosteler* (as OSTLER)]

hot ● *adjective* (**hot·ter**, **hot·test**) **1 a** having a relatively or noticeably high temperature. **b** (of food or drink) prepared by heating and served without cooling. **2** producing the sensation of heat (*hot fever*; *hot flash*). **3** (of pepper, spices, etc.) pungent. **4** (of a person) feeling heat. **5 a** ardent, passionate, excited. **b** (often foll. by *for*, *on*) eager, keen (*in hot pursuit*). **c** angry or upset. **d** lustful. **e** exciting. **f** performing exceptionally well. **6** (of news etc.) fresh, recent. **7** *Hunting* (of the scent) fresh and strong, indicating that the quarry has passed recently. **8 a** (of a player) very skilful. **b** (of a competitor in a race or other sporting event) strongly favoured to win. **c** (of a hit, return, etc., in ball games) difficult for an opponent to deal with. **9** (of music, esp. jazz) strongly rhythmical and emotional. **10** *slang* (of goods) stolen, esp. easily identifiable and hence difficult to dispose of. **b** (of a person) wanted by the police. **11** *slang* radioactive. **12** *informal* (of information) unusually reliable (*hot tip*). **13** (of a colour, shade, etc.) suggestive of heat; intense, bright. **14** *informal* currently popular or in demand (*spring's hottest fashions*). **15** *slang* good-looking; sexy. **16** (of a participant in a children's seeking or guessing game) very close to finding or guessing what is sought. **17** *informal* (of a motor vehicle or aircraft) fast or powerful, esp. in relation to its size. **18** at a high voltage; live (*a hot wire*). **19** (of metal, esp. iron) sufficiently high above melting point to flow readily. **20** as an intensifier (*hot damn!*). **21** *N Amer.* (of a sandwich) served hot and covered in gravy (*hot chicken sandwich*). **22** (of an oven temperature) above 400° F. ● *verb* (**hot·ted**, **hot·ting**) (usu. foll. by *up*) *informal* **1** *transitive & intransitive* make or become hot. **2** *transitive & intransitive* make or become active, lively, exciting, or dangerous. ● *adverb* **1** hotly; in a hot manner. **2** with or to great heat. □ **blow** (or **run**) **hot and cold** *informal* vacillate; be alternately enthusiastic and indifferent. **have the hots for** *slang* be sexually attracted to. **hot and bothered** in a state of exasperated agitation. **hot and heavy** *N Amer.* intense. **hot off the press** very recently published. **hot on the heels of** in close pursuit of. **hot under the collar** feeling anger, resentment, or embarrassment. **in one's hot little hand** firmly in one's grasp or possession. **make it** (or **things**) **hot for a person** persecute a person. **not so hot** *informal* only mediocre. □ **hot·ness** *noun* **hot·tish** *adjective* [Old English *hāt* from Germanic: compare HEAT]

hot air *noun informal* empty, boastful, or excited talk.

hot-air balloon *noun* a balloon (*see* BALLOON *noun* 2) consisting of a bag in which air is heated by burners located below it, causing it to rise. □ **hot-air ballooning** *noun*

hot and sour soup *noun* an Oriental soup having a spicy and slightly acidic broth.

hot·bed *noun* **1** a bed of earth heated by fermenting manure, for raising or forcing plants. **2** (foll. by *of*) an environment promoting the growth of something, esp. something unwelcome (*hotbed of vice*).

hot-blooded *adjective* ardent, passionate.

hot button *noun* esp. *N Amer. informal* **1** (often *attributive*) an emotionally or politically sensitive topic or issue. **2** a commercially attractive feature of a new product.

hot·cake *noun US* = PANCAKE 1b. □ **sell like hotcakes** sell rapidly and in great numbers.

hot chocolate *noun* a drink of hot water or milk flavoured with chocolate.

hotch·potch *noun* esp. *Brit.* **1** = HODGEPODGE. **2** a dish of many mixed ingredients, esp. a mutton broth or stew with vegetables. [Old French *hochepot* from Old French *hocher* shake + POT¹: *-potch* by assimilation]

hot corner *noun Baseball* **1** third base. **2** the position of third baseman.

hot cross bun *noun* a sweet bun, usu. containing raisins and dried fruit peel, marked with a cross, traditionally eaten on Good Friday.

hot damn *interjection* expressing admiration.

hot dark matter *noun see* DARK MATTER.

hot dog ● *noun* **1 a** a hot sausage, usu. a wiener, sandwiched in an elongated soft roll. **b** a wiener. **2** *N Amer. slang* a person who performs stunts, esp. when skiing or surfing. ● *interjection N Amer. slang* expressing approval. ● *intransitive verb* (**hot-dog**) (**hot-dogged**, **hot-dogging**) *N Amer. slang* perform stunts. □ **hot-dogger** *noun*

ho·tel *noun* **1** an establishment providing accommodation and meals for payment. **2** *Austral., NZ,* & *Cdn* a tavern. [French *hôtel*, later form of HOSTEL]

Hotel-Dieu /'ho:teldjɜ/ *noun* a name given to a hospital in French-speaking areas or to one established by a French-speaking order of nuns. [French *hôtel-Dieu*, *hôtel* being a medieval doublet of *hospital* + *Dieu* = God]

ho·tel·ier /ho:'teliɜr/ *noun* a person who owns or manages a hotel. [French *hôtelier* from Old French *hostelier*: see HOSTELRY]

hot flash *noun* esp. *N Amer.* (also esp. *Brit.* **hot flush**) a sudden feeling of heat during menopause.

hot·foot ● *adverb* in eager haste. ● *transitive verb* hurry eagerly (esp. *hotfoot it*). ● *noun* a practical joke in which a lighted match is inserted between the soles and uppers of a person's shoe.

hot·head *noun* an impetuous, fiery, quick-tempered person. □ **hot·head·ed** *adjective* **hot·head·ed·ly** *adverb* **hot·head·ed·ness** *noun*

hot·house ● *noun* **1** a heated building, usu. largely of glass, for rearing plants out of season or in a climate colder than is natural for them (often attributive: *hothouse flowers*). **2** an environment that encourages the rapid growth or development of something. ● *adjective* characteristic of something reared in a hothouse; sheltered, sensitive.

hot key *Computing* ● *noun* a key or combination of keys that has been programmed to cause an immediate change in the operating environment, such as the execution of a program. ● *intransitive verb* use such a key or keys.

hot·line *noun* **1** a direct exclusive communication link between heads of government etc., esp. for emergencies. **2** a telephone link that is specially arranged and kept for a particular purpose (*a hotline for reporting stolen travellers' cheques*). **3** *Cdn* a radio phone-in show.

hot·liner *noun Cdn* **1** an on-air personality who runs a radio phone-in show. **2** a person who calls a radio phone-in show.

hot·link *noun* = HYPERLINK.

hotly *adverb* **1** eagerly (*hotly anticipated*). **2** passionately (*hotly debated*). **3** angrily.

hot metal *noun Typography* type made from molten metal (also attributive: *hot-metal printing*).

hot money *noun* capital transferred at frequent intervals.

hot pants *plural noun* very brief, tight shorts worn by women.

hot pepper *noun* any of various very spicy fruits of plants of the genus *Capsicum*.

hot pink ● *noun* a bright, deep pink colour. ● *adjective* of this colour.

hot plate *noun* an electrical appliance with a flat heated metal surface, used for cooking food or keeping it hot.

hot·pot *noun* esp. *Brit.* a casserole of meat and vegetables, usu. with a layer of potato on top.

hot potato *noun informal* **1** a controversial or awkward matter or situation. **2** a children's game in which an object is passed rapidly between participants while music plays, the one left holding it when the music stops being eliminated.

hot-press ● *noun* a press of glazed boards and hot metal plates for smoothing paper or cloth or making plywood. ● *transitive verb* press (paper etc.) in this.

hot rod ● *noun* a motor vehicle modified to have extra power and speed. ● *verb* (**hot-rod**) (**-rodded**, **-rodding**) **1** *transitive* soup up (a vehicle, amplifier, etc.). **2** *intransitive* drive a hot rod. □ **hot rod·der** *noun*

hot sauce *noun* a very spicy sauce, usu. made with chilies, used as a condiment.

t *top*   ʋ *voice*   w *we*   z *zoo*   ʃ *she*   ʒ *vision*   θ *thin*   ð *this*   ŋ *ring*   x *loch*   tʃ *chip*   dʒ *jar*   (*see over for vowels*)

hot seat *noun slang* **1** a position of difficult responsibility. **2** the electric chair.

hot shoe *noun Photog.* a socket on a camera with electrical contacts for a flash gun etc.

hot·shot *informal* ● *noun* **1** an important or exceptionally able person. **2** *Sport* a skilful player of football, basketball, etc., esp. one who is showy. **3** *N Amer.* an express freight train. ● *adjective (attributive)* **1** important, able, expert, suddenly prominent (*a hotshot lawyer*). **2** displaying skills in a flamboyant manner (*a hotshot ballplayer*).

hot spot *noun* **1** a small region that is relatively hot. **2** a place of significant activity or danger.

hot spring *noun* (usu. in *pl.*) a spring of naturally hot water.

Hot·spur *see* PERCY 1.

hot·spur *noun* a rash person. [late Middle English: literally 'a person whose spur is hot from rash or constant riding']

hot stove league *noun N Amer.* a group of fans who gather to discuss their favourite sport, esp. in the off-season.

hot stuff *noun informal* **1** an important, impressive, or popular person or thing. **2** a sexually attractive person.

hot-swap *transitive verb informal* fit or replace (a computer part) with the power still connected. □ **hot-swappable** *adjective*

hot-tempered *adjective* impulsively angry.

Hot·ten·tot /ˈhɒtənˌtɒt/ *often offensive* ● *noun* = NAMA *noun* 1, 2. ● *adjective* = NAMA *adjective*. ¶ Nama is now the preferred name for this people and their language. [Dutch, prob. originally a repetitive formula in a Nama dancing song, transferred by Dutch sailors to the people themselves]

hot ticket *noun informal* a person or thing that is much in demand (*Dance Theatre is one of the hottest tickets anywhere*).

hot·tie *noun N Amer. slang* a sexually attractive person.

hot-to-trot *adjective* **1** eager, enthusiastic. **2** sexually active or excited.

hot tub *noun* a large tub filled with hot aerated water and used by one or several people for recreation or physical therapy. □ **hot tub·ber** *noun* **hot tub·bing** *noun*

hot walker *noun N Amer.* a worker at a racetrack, stable, etc. who walks a horse to cool it down after its training.

hot war *noun* an open war, with active hostilities.

hot water *noun informal* difficulty, trouble, or disgrace (*be in hot water*; *get into hot water*).

hot water bottle *noun* a container, usu. made of rubber, filled with hot water, esp. to warm a bed.

hot well *noun* a reservoir in a condensing steam engine.

hot-wire ● *transitive verb esp. N Amer. slang* start the engine of (a car etc.) by bypassing the ignition system. ● *adjective* operated by the expansion of heated wire.

Houde /uːd/ **Camil·lien** (1889–1958), Canadian politician, the mayor of Montreal, with only a few brief interruptions, from 1928–1954. His administrations were marked by widespread patronage and corruption.

Hou·dini[1] /huːˈdiːni/ **Harry** (born Erik Weisz) (1874–1926), Hungarian-born US magician and escape artist. In the early 1900s he became famous for his ability to escape from all kinds of bonds and containers.

Hou·dini[2] /huːˈdiːni/ *noun* **1** an ingenious escape. **2** a person skilled at escaping.

hound ● *noun* **1 a** a dog used for hunting, esp. one able to track by scent. **b** (also **hound dog**) *informal* any dog. **c** (**the hounds**) *Brit.* a pack of foxhounds. **2** *informal* a despicable man. **3** a runner who follows a trail in hare and hounds. **4** (usu. in *combination*) a person keen in pursuit of something (*publicity hound*; *newshound*). ● *transitive verb* **1** harass or pursue relentlessly. **2** urge on or nag (a person). **3** chase or pursue with a hound. □ **ride to hounds** go fox hunting on horseback. [Old English *hund* from Germanic]

hound's tongue *noun* a tall plant, *Cynoglossum officinale*, with tongue-shaped leaves.

hounds·tooth *noun* a check pattern with notched corners suggestive of a canine tooth.

houn·gan /ˈhuːŋɡən/ *noun* a voodoo priest. [Fon *hun* voodoo deity + *ga* chief]

hour *noun* **1** a twenty-fourth part of a day and night, 60 minutes. **2** a definite time of day, a specific point in time (*a late hour; what is the hour?*). **3** (in *pl.*, with preceding numerals in form 18:00, 20:30, etc.) this number of hours and minutes past midnight on the 24-hour clock (*will assemble at 20:00 hours*). **4 a** a period set aside for some purpose (*lunch hour*). **b** (in *pl.*) a fixed period of time for work, use of a building, etc. (*office hours; opening hours*). **c** (in *pl.*) one's habitual time of getting up or esp. going to bed (*keeps late hours*). **5** a short indefinite period of time (*an idle hour*). **6** the present time (*question of the hour*). **7 a** a time for action etc. (*the hour has come*). **b** the moment of one's death (*your hour has come*). **8** the distance travelled in one hour (*we are an hour from Fredericton*). **9** *Catholicism* **a** prayers to be said at one of seven fixed times of day (*book of hours*). **b** any of these times. **10** (prec. by *the*) the point of time at which each of the twelve or twenty-four hours measured by a timepiece ends and the next begins (*buses leave on the hour; at quarter past the hour*). **11** *Astronomy & Geog.* 15° of longitude or right ascension. □ **after hours** after the normally permitted business hours. **at all hours** at any hour of the day, no matter how early or late. **till** (or **until**) **all hours** till very late. **the wee** (**small**) **hours** the hours after midnight, usu. 1 to 4 o'clock. [Old French *ore*, *eure* from Latin *hora* from Greek *hōra* season, hour]

hour·glass *noun* **1** a reversible device with two connected glass bulbs containing sand that takes an hour to pass from the upper to the lower bulb. **2** (*attributive*) shaped like an hourglass, i.e. narrow in the middle and curving strongly outward above and below (*hourglass figure*).

hour hand *noun* the short hand on a clock or watch which indicates the hours.

houri /ˈhuːri/ *noun* (*pl.* **houris**) a beautiful young woman, esp. in the Muslim Paradise. [French via Persian ḥūrī from Arabic ḥūr pl. of ḥawra‘ gazelle-like (of the eyes)]

hour-long ● *adjective* lasting for one hour. ● *adverb* for one hour.

hour·ly ● *adjective* **1** done or occurring every hour. **2** frequent, continual. **3 a** reckoned hour by hour (*hourly wage*). **b** (of a worker etc.) hired or paid by the hour. ● *adverb* **1** every hour. **2** frequently, continually.

House, Chris·to·pher Max·well (b.1955), Canadian modern dancer, choreographer, and company director. Resident choreographer of the Toronto Dance Theatre since 1981 and artistic director since 1994, he has helped broaden the company's audience and establish an international reputation for it. His choreography is noted for its speed and fluidity and his eclectic choice of music.

house ● *noun* **1 a** a building for human habitation. **b** a family, household, or occupants of a house collectively (*the head of the house*). **c** (*attributive*) (of an animal) kept in, frequenting, or infesting houses (*house cat; housefly*). **2** a building for a special purpose (*opera house*). **3** (in *combination*) a building for keeping animals etc. or for the storage or protection of something (*henhouse; boathouse*). **4 a** a religious community. **b** the buildings occupied by it. **5** *Brit.* **a** a body of pupils living in the same building at a boarding school. **b** such a building. **c** a division of a day school for games, competitions, etc. **6** *Brit.* a college of a university. **7** a family, esp. a royal family; a dynasty (*House of Windsor*). **8 a** a firm or institution, esp. a printing or publishing firm, or a couture establishment. **b** its place of business. **c** (*attributive*) of or pertaining to a specific commercial house or business establishment (*house rules*). **9** (**the House**) *Brit. informal* the Stock Exchange. **10** (*attributive*) belonging to, working for, or associated with a hotel or other establishment (*house phone; house detective*). **11 a** a legislative or deliberative assembly. **b** the building where it meets. **12** (**the House**) **a** (in Canada) the House of Commons. **b** (in the UK) the House of Commons or Lords. **c** (in the US) the House of Representatives. **13 a** an audience in a theatre etc. **b** a theatre. **14** *Astrology* **a** a twelfth part of the heavens. **b** any of the signs of the zodiac considered as the seat of the greatest influence of a particular planet. **15** (*attributive*) (of wine etc.) selected by the management of a restaurant, hotel, etc. to be offered at a special price. **16** *Curling* the space within the outermost circle drawn round either tee. **17** = HOUSE MUSIC. **18 a** a casino or other establishment for gambling. **b** the management of such an establishment against which bets are placed. **19** the natural habitat of an animal, e.g. a den, burrow, nest, or the shell of a snail or tortoise, etc. **20** *Cdn hist.* a trading post, esp. inland, for the fur trade. **21** (**the House**) *Brit. hist.* euphemism the workhouse. ● *transitive verb* **1** provide (a person, a population, etc.) with a house or houses or other accommodation. **2 a** store (goods etc.). **b** *Naut.* place in a secure or sheltered position. **3** enclose or encase (a part or fitting). **4** fix (a piece of wood etc.) in a socket, joint, mortise, etc. □ **as safe as houses** thoroughly or completely safe. **bring the house down** make the audience laugh or applaud loudly. **clean house** *N Amer.* **1** do housework. **2** wipe out corruption, inefficiency, etc. **a house divided** a home, organization, party, etc. with dissension in its ranks. **keep house** provide for, maintain, or manage a household. **like a house on fire 1** vigorously, fast. **2** successfully, excellently. **on the house** at the management's expense; free. **play house** (esp. of children) play by pretending to be a family in its home. **put** (or **get, set,** etc.) **one's house in order** organize one's own affairs efficiently, esp. before telling others how to organize their affairs. **set up house** begin to live in a separate dwelling. □ **house·ful** noun (pl. **-fuls**). **house·less** adjective [Old English hūs, hūsian, from Germanic]

house and home noun (as an emphatic) home (eating us out of house and home).

house arrest noun detention in one's own house etc., not in prison.

house band noun a band that regularly performs at a certain club.

house·boat noun a boat equipped for living in, usu. on inland waters. □ **house·boat·ing** noun

house·bound adjective unable to leave one's house through illness etc.

house·boy noun = HOUSEMAN 1.

house brand noun N Amer. a food item or household product that bears the name of the store which sells it and usu. costs less than its brand name equivalent.

house·break transitive verb N Amer. train (a pet) not to urinate and defecate inside the house. □ **house·broken** adjective

house·break·er noun a person who breaks into a house or building with the intent to steal. □ **house·break·ing** noun

house call noun a visit made to a patient in his or her own home by a doctor etc.

house·carl noun (also **house·carle**) hist. a member of the bodyguard of a Danish or English king or noble. [Old English húscarl from Old Norse húskarl from hús HOUSE + karl man: compare CARL]

house church noun **1** a charismatic church independent of traditional denominations. **2** a group meeting in a house as part of the activities of a church.

house·clean·ing noun **1** the cleaning of the interior of a house or apartment. **2** N Amer. the revamping of a company, department etc. by eliminating personnel, reorganizing systems, etc. □ **house·clean** transitive & intransitive verb

house·coat noun a woman's long garment for informal wear in the house, usu. worn over a nightgown or pyjamas; a dressing gown.

house·dress noun N Amer. a plain dress usu. of light cotton, for wearing around the house while doing housework, etc.

house father noun a man who supervises young people living in a dormitory, hostel, etc.

house finch noun a red-breasted N American finch, Carpodacus mexicanus.

house flag noun a flag indicating to what firm a ship belongs.

house·fly noun any fly of the family Muscidae, esp. Musca domestica, breeding in decaying organic matter and often entering houses.

house front noun the front or face of a house.

house guest noun a guest staying for some days in a private house.

house·hold noun **1** the occupants of a house regarded as a unit. **2** a house and its affairs. **3** (attributive) of, pertaining to, or for use in a house (vinegar as a household cleaner; household appliances).

household effects plural noun the movable contents of a house, e.g. furniture, appliances, etc.

house·hold·er noun **1** a person who owns or rents a house. **2** the head of a household.

household gods plural noun **1** gods presiding over a household, esp. Rom.Hist. the lares and penates. **2** Brit. informal the essentials of home life.

household name noun (also **household word**) a person or thing that is well known to the general public.

house hunting noun the process of seeking a house to live in. □ **house hunter** noun

house·husband noun a husband who works full-time in the home, taking care of the children, managing the household, etc., while his wife goes out to work.

house·keep·er noun **1** a person employed to manage a household. **2** a person employed to manage the cleaning staff in a hotel, hospital, etc.

house·keep·ing noun **1 a** the maintenance of a household, including esp. the domestic chores of cleaning etc. **b** operations of maintenance, record-keeping, etc. in an organization. **c** the cleaning staff in a hotel etc. **2** N Amer. (usu. attributive) (of rental cabins, cottages, etc.) having a stove, refrigerator, and other basic facilities. **3** Computing the general maintenance operations enhancing, but not directly affecting, a computer system's performance, e.g. elimination of obsolete files etc. **4** money allowed or set aside for the management of household affairs etc.

house leader noun **1** (also **House Leader**) (in Canada) a Member of Parliament chosen by his or her party to coordinate the party's strategy in the House of Commons, supervise the party whip, schedule speakers during question period, etc. **2** (in the US) a politician holding a position of prominence in the House of Representatives.

house league noun Cdn **1** a sports league in which the players on all teams are members of the same school, organization, etc. **2** a league in children's sports in which any child may play without having to pass a tryout.

house·leek noun a plant, Sempervivum tectorum, with pink flowers and fleshy leaves, cultivated in gardens and as a houseplant.

house lights plural noun the lights in the auditorium of a theatre etc.

house magazine noun = HOUSE ORGAN.

house·maid noun a female servant in a house, esp. one who cleans rooms etc.

housemaid's knee noun inflammation of the kneecap, often due to excessive kneeling.

house·man noun (pl. **-men**) **1** a male employee responsible for general duties in a house, hotel, etc. **2** Brit.= INTERN noun 1a.

house martin noun a black and white Eurasian swallow-like bird, Delichon urbica, which builds a mud nest on house walls etc.

house·master noun the male teacher in charge of a house at a boarding school.

house·mate noun a fellow occupant of a house, apartment, etc.

house·mis·tress noun the female teacher in charge of a house at a boarding school.

house mother noun a woman who supervises young people living in a dormitory, hostel, etc.

house mouse noun a usu. grey mouse, Mus musculus, very common as a scavenger around human dwellings, and bred as a pet and experimental animal.

house music noun (also **house**) a form of popular dance music characterized by the extensive use of drum machines and sampling, and having a fast beat and heavy synthesized bass lines. [prob. from The Warehouse, a Chicago nightclub]

House of Assembly noun **1** Cdn (in Nova Scotia and Newfoundland and Labrador) the provincial legislature. **2** Cdn hist. the legislature in a province of British North America, usu. the lower, elected house. **3** the legislature in certain Commonwealth nations.

house of cards noun **1** an insecure scheme etc. **2** a tower-like structure built by balancing playing cards against and on top of each other.

House of Commons noun (in Canada and the UK) **1** the lower house of Parliament, composed of elected members. **2** the building in which this assembly meets.

house officer noun Brit. a hospital doctor of one of the more junior grades.

house of God noun a place of worship, e.g. a church, chapel, temple, etc.

house of ill repute noun (also **house of ill fame**) euphemism a brothel.

House of Lords noun (in the UK) the chamber of Parliament composed of peers and bishops.

House of Representatives noun the lower house of the US Congress and other legislatures.

house of worship noun = HOUSE OF GOD.

house organ noun a publication produced by a company or society and dealing mainly with its own activities.

house parent noun a house mother or house father.

house party noun **1** esp. N Amer. a social gathering in a private home, usu. with music, food, dancing, etc. **2** Brit. a party, usu. at a country house, at which the guests stay for several days.

house phone noun a phone for internal calls only, esp. in a hotel or apartment building.

house·plant noun a plant that is suitable for growing indoors.

house-proud adjective attentive to, or unduly preoccupied with, the care and appearance of the home.

house·room noun space or accommodation in one's house. □ **not give houseroom to** not have in any circumstances.

house rules plural noun rules that are in effect at a particular locality, e.g. a gambling club, legislature, club, etc.

house-sit intransitive verb live in and look after a house while its owner is away. □ **house-sitter** noun **house-sitting** noun

Houses of Parliament *plural noun* (in Canada and the UK) the legislative body, composed of a lower elected chamber and an upper appointed chamber.

house sparrow *noun* a common brown and grey sparrow, *Passer domesticus*, which nests in the eaves and roofs of houses.

house style *noun* a particular printer's or publisher's etc. preferred way of presenting text, including rules for spelling, punctuation, etc.

house-to-house *adjective & adverb* calling at each house in turn (*made house-to-house inquiries; travelled house-to-house*).

house·top *noun* the roof of a house.

house trailer *noun* N Amer. **1** a trailer, such as that used in camping, that can be pulled by a car or truck and is equipped with beds, sinks, etc. **2** = MOBILE HOME.

house-train *transitive verb* esp. Brit. = HOUSEBREAK. □ **house-trained** *adjective*

house·wares *plural noun* N Amer. utilitarian household items, esp. kitchen utensils.

house·warm·ing *noun* a party celebrating a move to a new home.

house·wife *noun* (*pl.* **-wives**) **1** a woman (usu. married) managing a household, esp. as her primary occupation. **2** /ˈhʌzɪf/ esp. Brit. a case for needles, thread, etc. □ **house·wife·ly** *adjective*

house·wifery /ˈhaʊs.wɪfəri, -.wɪfri/ *noun* **1** housekeeping. **2** skill in this.

house·work *noun* regular work done in housekeeping, esp. cleaning, laundry, etc.

house·wrap *noun* N Amer. a large sheet of thin plastic that is applied over insulation and sheathing before siding is applied to a house, to prevent drafts penetrating through hard-to-insulate areas.

housey *adjective informal* in the style of house music.

hous·ing[1] *noun* **1 a** houses, apartments, etc. collectively. **b** the provision of these. **2** shelter, lodging, accommodation. **3** a rigid casing, esp. for moving or sensitive parts of a machine. **4** the hole or niche cut in one piece of wood to receive some part of another in order to join them.

hous·ing[2] *noun* a cloth covering put on a horse for protection or ornament. [Middle English = covering, from obsolete *house* from Old French *houce* from medieval Latin *hultia* from Germanic]

housing association *noun* esp. Brit. a society formed with the aim of providing housing at relatively low cost and without making a profit.

housing development *noun* **1** = DEVELOPMENT 5. **2** the act or process of planning and building a large group of homes.

housing estate *noun* Brit. a residential area planned as a unit and often having its own shops and other facilities.

housing project *noun* N Amer. a government-subsidized housing development with relatively low rents.

housing start *noun* an instance of beginning construction on a house, the number of these occurring over a certain period being used as an indicator of the strength of the economy.

Hous·man /ˈhaʊsmən/ **Al·fred Ed·ward** (1859–1936), English poet and classical scholar, remembered for the poems in *A Shropshire Lad* (1896), a series of nostalgic verses largely based on ballad forms.

Hous·ton /ˈhjuːstən/ an inland port of Texas, linked to the Gulf of Mexico by the Houston Ship Canal; pop. (2000) 1,953,631. Since 1961 it has been a centre for space research and manned space flight; it is the site of the NASA Space Center. □ **Hous·ton·ian** /hjuːˈstoʊniən/ *noun & adjective*

HOV *abbreviation* N Amer. high-occupancy vehicle (*HOV lane*).

hove *past of* HEAVE.

hovel /ˈhɒvəl, ˈhʌv-/ *noun* **1** a small miserable dwelling. **2** an open shed or other construction used for sheltering cattle, storing grain, etc. [Middle English: origin unknown]

hover /ˈhɒvər/ ● *intransitive verb* **1 a** (of a bird, insect, etc.) hang suspended in the air, esp. with a fluttering or wavering movement, by rapidly beating the wings. **b** (of a helicopter etc.) maintain a stationary position in the air. **2** (often foll. by *about, around*) wait close at hand, linger. **3** be in an indeterminate or irresolute state, waver (*the Canadian dollar hovered around 62 cents US*). ● *noun* **1** an act or state of hovering. **2** a shelter used in the brooding of chickens. □ **hover·er** *noun* [Middle English from obsolete *hove* hover, linger]

hover·craft /ˈhɒvərˌkrɑːft/ *noun* (*pl.* same) a vehicle that travels over land or water supported on a cushion of air produced by jet engines.

hover·fly /ˈhɒvərˌflaɪ/ *noun* (*pl.* **-flies**) any fly of the dipteran family

Syrphidae, the members of which resemble wasps but are stingless and often hover in the air.

hover·port /ˈhʌvərˌpɔːrt/ *noun* a terminal for hovercraft.

how[1] ● *interrog. adverb* **1** by what means, in what way or manner (*how do you do it?; tell me how you do it; how could you behave so badly?; but how to bridge the gap?*). **2 a** by what name (*how does one address the prime minister?*). **b** *informal* to what effect, with what meaning (*how did he mean that?*). **3** in what condition, esp. of health (*how is the patient?; how do things stand?*). **4 a** to what extent (*how far is it?; how would you like to take my place?; how we laughed!*). **b** to what extent good or well, what ... like (*how was the movie?; how did they play?*). ● *relative adverb* in whatever way, as (*do it how you can*). ● *conjunction informal* that (*told us how he'd been in Thailand*). ● *noun* the way a thing is done (*the how and why of it*). □ **and how!** *slang* very much so (chiefly used ironically or intensively). **how about 1** would you like (*how about a game of chess?*). **2** what is to be done about. **3** what is the news about. **how come?** *see* COME. **how many** what number. **how much 1** what amount (*how much do I owe you?; did not know how much to take*). **2** what price (*how much is it?*). **how now?** *archaic* what is the meaning of this? **how so?** how can you show that that is so? **how's that?** what is your opinion or explanation of that? **how's that for . . ?** isn't that a remarkable instance of . . ? (*how's that for irony?*). [Old English *hū* from West Germanic]

how[2] *interjection* a greeting attributed to N American Indians. [perhaps from Sioux *háo*, Omaha *hau*]

How·ard ▸ **1 Cath·er·ine** (c.1521–1542), fifth wife of Henry VIII. She married Henry soon after his divorce from Anne of Cleves in 1540; accused of infidelity, she confessed and was beheaded in 1542. **2 John** (1726–90), English philanthropist and prison reformer. His tour of British prisons (1773) led to acts of Parliament setting down sanitary standards. **3 John Win·ston** (b.1939), Australian Liberal politician, Prime Minister from 1996. **4 Les·lie** (born Leslie Howard Stainer) (1893–1943), English actor. After making his film debut in *Outward Bound* (1930) he played the archetypal English gentleman in films such as *The Scarlet Pimpernel* (1935) and *Pygmalion* (1938). He also starred in *Gone with the Wind* (1939). **5 Trev·or (Wal·lace)** (1916–88), English actor. He starred in *Brief Encounter* (1945) and *The Third Man* (1949) and had a distinguished career in film and television. He later played character roles, often eccentric ones, in films such as *Gandhi* (1985) and *White Mischief* (1987).

how·beit /haʊˈbiːɪt/ *adverb archaic* nevertheless.

how·dah /ˈhaʊdə/ *noun* a seat for two or more, usu. with a canopy, for riding on the back of an elephant. [Urdu *hawda* from Arabic *hawdaj* litter]

how do you do (also *informal* **how-de-do**) (*pl.* **-dos**) ● *interjection* a greeting on first being introduced. ● *noun* **1** an inquiry of 'how do you do?'. **2** (**how-do-you-do**) an awkward or embarrassing situation (*what a fine how-do-you-do that would be*).

howdy *interjection* N Amer. *informal* hello. [corruption of HOW DO YOU DO?]

Howe ▸ **1 Cla·rence Deca·tur** ('C.D.') (1886–1960), American-born Canadian engineer and Liberal politician. As minister of munitions and supply (from 1940) and minister of reconstruction (from 1944) he transformed Canada into an efficient producer of military supplies and then prepared for the postwar era of free enterprise. As minister of trade and commerce he played a key role in the pipeline debate which led to the Liberals' defeat in 1957. **2 Elias** (1819–67), US inventor. In 1846 he patented a sewing machine with an eyed needle to carry the upper thread and a holder resembling a shuttle for the lower thread. **3 Gor·don** ('Gordie') (b.1928), Canadian hockey player. Over a long professional career that began in 1946 with the Detroit Red Wings and ended in 1980 with the Hartford Whalers, he established NHL records for the most seasons, most games, most goals and most assists; he won the leading scorer award 6 times, the most valuable player award 6 times, and played in 21 all star games. In 1997 he appeared in one game in the International Hockey League to become the first player to play professional hockey in 6 decades. He is known for the strength, speed and stamina of his playing. **4 Jo·seph** (1804–73), Canadian journalist and politician, premier of Nova Scotia 1861–63. First elected to the Nova Scotia House of Assembly in 1836, he was both committed to responsible government and loyal to Britain. The leader of the anti-Confederation movement between 1866 and 1868, Howe became a federal cabinet minister once it became evident that further opposition would be fruitless, and played a key role in bringing Manitoba into Confederation. **5 Rich·ard, 4th Viscount Howe** (1726–99), British admiral who served in wars against the US and France. **6** his brother **Wil·liam, 5th Viscount Howe** (1729–1814),

British general who served as commander-in-chief of British forces during the American Revolution.

howe'er *adverb literary* = HOWEVER.

Howe Sound an inlet of the Strait of Georgia, situated on the southwestern coast of BC, immediately northwest of North Vancouver. [R. HOWE]

Howe Street *noun Cdn* **1** a street in Vancouver where the offices of many financial institutions are located. **2** the moneyed interests of Vancouver, esp. as opposed to other regions of Canada.

how·ever *adverb* **1** nevertheless; yet. **2 a** in whatever way (*do it however you want*). **b** to whatever extent, no matter how (*must go however inconvenient*). **3** *informal* (as an emphatic) in what way, by what means (*however did that happen?*).

how·itz·er /ˈhaʊɪtsər/ *noun* a short, relatively light gun for high-angle firing of shells at low velocities. [Dutch *houwitser* from German *Haubitze* from Czech *houfnice* catapult]

howl ● *noun* **1** a long loud doleful cry uttered by a dog, wolf, etc. **2** a prolonged wailing noise, e.g. as made by a strong wind. **3** a loud cry of pain, rage, anguish, etc. **4** a yell of derision or merriment. **5** *informal* a cause of laughter or merriment. **6** *Electronics* a howling noise in a loudspeaker due to electrical or acoustic feedback. ● *verb* **1** *intransitive* **a** (of a dog, wolf, etc.) emit a long, loud, doleful cry. **b** (of a person) utter a long, loud, cry of pain, derision, laughter, etc. **2** *intransitive* (esp. of a child) weep loudly. **3** *transitive* utter (words) with a howl. **4** *intransitive* (of an inanimate object, esp. the wind, a storm, etc.) make a prolonged wailing noise. □ **howl down 1** prevent (a speaker) from being heard by howls of derision. **2** *N Amer.* move very quickly with or as with a howling noise (*the police cruiser howled down the street*). [Middle English *houle* (v.), prob. imitative]

How·land ▸ Sir Wil·liam P. (1811–1907), US-born Canadian businessman and politician, Father of Confederation. First elected to the legislative assembly in 1857, he was a minister in the Great Coalition and attended the London Conference. He was Lieutenant-Governor of Ontario 1868–73.

howl·er *noun* **1** (in full **howler monkey**) any of several S American monkeys constituting the genus *Alouatta*, which have long prehensile tails and make loud howling noises. **2** *informal* a glaring and usu. amusing mistake, esp. in the use of words. **3** a person or animal that howls.

howl·ing *adjective* **1** that howls. **2** *slang* extreme (*a howling shame*).

Howlin' Wolf (real name Chester Burnett) (1910–76), US blues singer and songwriter.

How·rah /ˈhaʊrə/ (also **Haora**) a city in E India, on the Hooghly River opposite Calcutta; pop. (2001) 1,008,700.

how·so·ever *adverb* (also *literary* **howsoe'er**) **1** in whatsoever way. **2** to whatsoever extent.

how-to ● *adjective* instructive; of the nature of a manual (*a how-to book*). ● *noun* the instructions for doing something (*the how-tos of plumbing*).

Hoxha /ˈhɒdʒə/ **Enver** (1908–85), Albanian leader, prime minister 1944–54 and First Secretary of the Albanian Communist Party 1954–85. In 1941 he founded the Albanian Communist Party and led the fight for national independence. As head of state, he isolated Albania from Western influences and implemented a program of nationalization and collectivization.

hoy[1] *interjection* used to call attention, drive animals, or *Naut.* hail or call aloft. [Middle English]

hoy[2] *noun hist.* a small vessel, usu. rigged as a sloop, carrying passengers and goods esp. for short distances. [Middle Dutch *hoei*, *hoede*, from unknown origin]

hoya *noun* any climbing shrub of the genus *Hoya*, with pink, white, or yellow waxy flowers. [modern Latin from T. *Hoy*, English gardener d.1821]

hoy·den *noun* a boisterous girl; a tomboy. □ **hoy·den·ish** *adjective* [originally = rude fellow, prob. from Middle Dutch *heiden* (= HEATHEN)]

Hoyle[1]**, Sir Fred** (1915–1995), English astrophysicist, one of the proponents of the steady-state theory of cosmology. His publications include works of popular science and science fiction.

Hoyle[2] *noun* □ **according to Hoyle** correctly, exactly; according to plan or the rules. [E. *Hoyle*, English writer on card games d.1769]

h.p. *abbreviation* (also **HP**) **1** horsepower. **2** high pressure. **3** *Brit.* hire purchase.

HPLC *abbreviation* high performance liquid chromatography.

HPV *abbreviation* = HUMAN PAPILLOMA VIRUS.

HQ *abbreviation* headquarters.

HR *abbreviation* **1** *Baseball* home run. **2** (in the US) House of Representatives. **3** HUMAN RESOURCES.

hr. *abbreviation* hour.

HRDC *abbreviation Cdn* Human Resources Development Canada, the federal government department responsible for employment and income support programs.

HRH *abbreviation* Her or His Royal Highness.

HRM *abbreviation* Halifax Regional Municipality.

Hrod·na /ˈhrɒdnə/ (Russian **Grodno** /ˈɡrɒdnɔ/) a city in W Belarus, on the Neman River near the borders with Poland and Lithuania; pop. (est. 2002) 312,900.

hrs. *abbreviation* hours.

HRT *abbreviation* = HORMONE REPLACEMENT THERAPY.

hryv·nya /ˈhrɪvnjə/ *noun* (also **hryv·nia**) the monetary unit of Ukraine. [Ukrainian]

HSH *abbreviation* Her or His Serene Highness.

Hsian see XIAN.

Hsi·ning see XINING.

HSS *abbreviation* high speed steel.

HST *abbreviation Cdn* HARMONIZED SALES TAX.

HT *abbreviation Physics* high tension.

HTLV *abbreviation* human T-cell lymphotrophic virus, a small family of retroviruses causing diseases of the immune system, such as certain leukemias.

HTML *abbreviation* HYPERTEXT MARKUP LANGUAGE.

http *abbreviation Computing* hypertext transfer protocol, a protocol that supports the retrieval of data on the Internet, esp. of hypertext on the World Wide Web.

Huai·nan /hwaiˈnan/ a city in the province of Anhui, in east central China; pop. (est. 2002) 1,427,500.

Hual·laga River /hwɒˈjɒɡə/ a river in central Peru, one of the headwaters of the Amazon. Rising in the central Andes, it flows generally northeastward for 1 100 km (700 miles) and emerges into the Amazon Basin at Lagunas. The remote upper river valley is one of the world's chief coca-growing regions.

Huam·bo /ˈwambɔ/ a city in the mountains in W Angola; pop. (est. 2002) 168,300. It was known by its Portuguese name of Nova Lisboa until 1978.

Huás·car /ˈwɒskɑr/ (d.1533), Inca chieftain. After succeeding his father in 1525, he faced both Spanish invasion and opposition from his younger brother, who eventually had him assassinated.

Huas·ca·rán /ˌwɑskəˈrɒn/ an extinct volcano in the Peruvian Andes, west central Peru, rising to 6 768 m (22,205 ft.). It is the highest peak in Peru.

hub *noun* **1** the central part of a wheel, rotating on or with the axle, and from which the spokes radiate. **2** a central point of interest, importance, activity, etc. **3** a large regional airport serving as a transfer point between flights. **4** *Computing* a common connection point for devices in a network. □ **hotter** (or **harder**) **than the hubs of hell** *N Amer. informal* exceedingly hot (or hard). □ **hub·less** *adjective* [16th c.: perhaps = HOB[1]]

hub and spoke *adjective* of or designating an air transportation system in which local flights take passengers to a large regional airport, where they are put on other flights to their final destinations.

hubba hubba *interjection N Amer. slang* expressing approval, excitement, or enthusiasm, esp. for another person's physical appearance. [origin unknown]

Hub·bard, Mount a peak (4 577 m) in the St. Elias Mountains, situated on the Yukon–Alaska border. [G. G. *Hubbard*, founder of the National Geographic Society d.1897]

Hub·bard squash *noun* a variety of winter squash, usu. oval with pointed ends, with green skin and orange flesh.

Hub·ble, Ed·win Pow·ell (1889–1953), US astronomer. In 1929 he demonstrated that the distance of a galaxy is directly proportional to its observed velocity of recession from us.

hubble-bubble *noun* **1** a rudimentary form of hookah. **2** a bubbling sound. **3** confused talk. [reduplication of BUBBLE]

Hubble constant *noun Astronomy* **1** the ratio of the speed of recession of a galaxy to its distance from the observer. **2** the reciprocal of this, interpretable as the age of the universe. [HUBBLE]

hub·bub *noun* **1** a confused din, esp. from a crowd of people. **2** a disturbance or uproar. [perhaps of Irish origin: compare Gaelic *ubub* interjection of contempt, Irish *abú*, used in battle cries]

t *top*　v *voice*　w *we*　z *zoo*　ʃ *she*　ʒ *vision*　θ *thin*　ð *this*　ŋ *ring*　x *loch*　tʃ *chip*　dʒ *jar*　(*see over for vowels*)

hubby *noun* (*pl.* **-bies**) *informal* a husband. [abbreviation]

hub·cap *noun* a cover for the hub of a vehicle's wheel.

Hubei /huːˈbei/ (also **Hupeh** /-ˈpei/) a province of E China; capital, Wuhan.

Hubli /ˈhuːbliː/ (also **Hubli-Dharwad** /ˌhuːblidɑːrˈwɒd/, **Hubli-Dharwar** /-ˈwɑːr/) a city in SW India; pop. (2001) 786,000.

hu·bris /ˈhjuːbrɪs/ *noun* **1** arrogant pride or presumption. **2** (in Greek tragedy) excessive pride towards or defiance of the gods, leading to nemesis. □ **hu·bris·tic** *adjective* **hu·bris·tic·ally** *adverb* [Greek]

huck *transitive verb Cdn* (*West*) *informal* throw (*hucked some rocks at the truck*). [var. of dialect *hike* throw; compare HOICK]

huckle·berry *noun* (*pl.* **-berries**) **1** any of various low-growing N American shrubs, esp. of the genus *Gaylussacia*. **2** the blue or black soft fruit of this plant. [prob. alteration of *hurtleberry*, WHORTLEBERRY]

huck·ster ● *noun* **1** a mercenary person ready to make a profit out of anything. **2** *N Amer.* a person who uses aggressive methods to sell things, esp. one working in advertising. **3** a peddler or hawker. ● *verb* **1** *transitive* promote or sell (an often questionable product) aggressively. **2** *intransitive* bargain, haggle. □ **huck·ster·ing** *noun* **huck·ster·ish** *adjective* **huck·ster·ism** *noun* [prob. from Low German: compare dial. *huck* to bargain, HAWKER¹]

HUD *abbreviation* head-up display.

Hud·ders·field a town in N England, in West Yorkshire; pop. (est. 2002) 143,500.

hud·dle ● *verb* **1** *transitive & intransitive* (often foll. by *up*) crowd together; nestle closely. **2** *intransitive & reflexive* (often foll. by *up*) coil one's body into a small space. **3** *intransitive* confer, discuss. ● *noun* **1** (in team sports, esp. football) a brief gathering of players during a game to receive instructions on the next play. **2** *informal* a close or secret conference, esp. in *go into a huddle*. **3** a confused or crowded mass of people or things. [16th c.: perhaps from Low German and ultimately related to HIDE³]

Hud·son¹, a town in south central Quebec, situated on the south shore of Lac des Deux Montagnes, southwest of Montreal; pop. (2001) 4,796. □ **Hud·son·ite** *noun* [E. *Hudson*, who established a glassworks there *c.*1845]

Hud·son² Henry (*fl.*1607–11), English explorer. He made two voyages (in 1607 and 1608) in search of a sea route to Asia via Norway and Russia, and then turned his attention to N America, travelling up the Hudson River in 1609. In 1610, he attempted to find the Northwest Passage to the Spice Islands. He succeeded in travelling down the east shore of Hudson Bay into James Bay, where he and his crew spent the winter; his crew mutinied, and Hudson, his son, and 7 others were set adrift in an open shallop.

Hudson Bay¹ a large inland sea in NE Canada, with shoreline in Quebec, Ontario, Manitoba and Nunavut. The largest inland sea in the world, it is connected to the Arctic via Foxe Channel and Fury and Hecla Strait and to the Labrador Sea via the Hudson Strait. [HUDSON²]

Hudson Bay² *noun Cdn* **1 a** = HUDSON'S BAY COMPANY. **b** (*attributive*) of, associated with, or pertaining to the Hudson's Bay Company. **2** = HUDSON'S BAY BLANKET.

Hudson Bay Lowlands (also called **Hudson Platform**) a sub-region of the Canadian Shield, a lowland extending around the southwestern shoreline of Hudson Bay and James Bay. It is part of a sedimentary basin, most of which lies beneath the two bays.

Hudson River a river of eastern N America, which rises in the Adirondack Mountains and flows southward for 560 km (350 miles) into the Atlantic at New York. [HUDSON²]

Hudson's Bay blanket *noun Cdn* a durable woollen blanket woven in a variety of patterns, including cream with wide stripes of green, red, yellow, and indigo, and scarlet or green with black stripes.

Hudson's Bay blanket coat *noun* (also **Hudson's Bay coat**) a warm, heavy, woollen winter coat or parka, made of Hudson's Bay blanket cloth.

Hudson's Bay Company originally a British colonial trading company set up by Royal Charter in 1670 and granted all lands draining into Hudson Bay for purposes of commercial exploitation, principally trade in fur. The company amalgamated with the rival North-West Company in 1821 and continued to operate in the area until finally handing over control of its territory to the new Canadian government in 1870. It is now a retail and wholesale operation.

Hudson's Bay point blanket *noun Cdn* = HUDSON'S BAY BLANKET.

Hudson's Bay tea *noun Cdn* (*North*) & *Alaska* = LABRADOR TEA.

Hudson Strait a channel connecting the Labrador Sea and Hudson Bay. It separates the Ungava Peninsula from Baffin Island. [HUDSON²]

Hué /hwei/ a city in central Vietnam; pop. (est. 2002) 266,800.

hue *noun* **1 a** a colour or tint. **b** a variety or shade of colour caused by the admixture of another. **2** the attribute of a colour by virtue of which it is discernible as red, green, etc. □ **-hued** *adjective* [Old English *hīew*, *hēw* form, beauty, from Germanic: compare Old Norse *hȳ* down on plants]

hue and cry *noun* **1** a loud clamour or outcry. **2** *hist.* **a** a loud cry raised for the pursuit of a wrongdoer. **b** a proclamation for the capture of a criminal. [Anglo-French *hu e cri* from Old French *hu* outcry (from *huer* shout) + *e* and + *cri* cry]

huevos ran·cheros /ˌweivɒs ranˈtʃeroːs/ *plural noun* eggs, fried or poached with onions and peppers, topped with salsa, guacamole, etc., and often served on a tortilla. [Latin American Spanish, = eggs cooked in a country or ranch style]

huff ● *verb* **1** *intransitive* give out loud puffs of air, steam, etc. **2** *intransitive & transitive* take or cause to take offence. **3** *intransitive* bluster loudly or threateningly. **4** *transitive N Amer. slang* inhale (gasoline fumes etc.) in a quick gasp of air to get high. ● *noun* a fit of petty annoyance. □ **in a huff** annoyed and offended. □ **huff·ish** *adjective* [imitative of the sound of blowing]

huffy *adjective* (**huff·i·er**, **huff·i·est**) **1** apt to take offence. **2** offended. □ **huff·i·ly** *adverb* **huff·i·ness** *noun*

hug ● *transitive verb* (**hugged**, **hug·ging**) **1** squeeze tightly in one's arms, esp. with affection. **2 a** keep close to (the shore, curb, etc.). **b** fit tightly around. **3** cherish or cling to (beliefs, prejudices etc.). ● *noun* a strong esp. affectionate clasp with the arms (*I gave Rebecca a hug*). □ **hug·gable** *adjective* **hug·ger** *noun* (also in *combination*). **huggy** *adjective* [16th c.: prob. from Scandinavian: compare Old Norse *hugga* console]

hug drug *noun slang* the drug ecstasy. [with reference to the drug's tendency to make people feel affectionate toward others]

huge /hjuːdʒ, juːdʒ/ *adjective* **1** extremely large; enormous. **2** (of immaterial things) very great (*a huge success; a huge fan of yours*). **3** *informal* very popular, fashionable, or important. □ **huge·ness** *noun* [Old French *ahuge*, *ahoge*, of unknown origin]

huge·ly /ˈhjuːdʒliː, ˈjuːdʒliː/ *adverb* **1** enormously (*hugely successful*). **2** very much (*enjoyed it hugely*).

hugger-mugger ● *noun* **1** secrecy. **2** confusion. ● *adjective & adverb* **1** in secret. **2** confused; in confusion. [prob. related to Middle English *hoder* huddle, *mokere* conceal: compare 15th-c. *hoder moder*, 16th-c. *hucker mucker* in the same sense]

Hug·gins, Sir Wil·liam (1824–1910), British astronomer. He pioneered spectroscopic analysis in astronomy and discovered the red shift in stellar spectra.

Hugh Capet *see* CAPET.

Hughes ▶ **1 Ed·ward James** ('Ted') (1930–98), English poet, Poet Laureate from 1984. His work, including *The Hawk in the Rain* (1957), is pervaded by his vision of the natural world as a place of violence, terror, and beauty. **2 (James Mer·cer) Lang·ston** (1902–67), US writer, known for his interpretations of black American life published in collections such as *The Poetry of the Negro* (1949). **3 How·ard (Rob·ard)** (1905–76), US industrialist, film producer, and aviator. Extremely wealthy, for the last twenty-five years of his life he lived as a total recluse.

Hugli River *see* HOOGHLY RIVER.

Hugo, Vic·tor (Marie) (1802–85), French poet, novelist, and dramatist. A leading figure of French Romanticism, he brought a new freedom of diction, subject, and versification to French poetry. *Hernani* (1830), *Notre Dame de Paris* (1831) and *Les Misérables* (1862) are among his best-known novels.

Hu·gue·not /ˈhjuːgənɒt, -ˌnoː/ *noun hist.* a French Protestant in the 16th or 17th c., esp. one persecuted for his or her beliefs or involved in civil war with the Catholic majority. [French, assimilation of *eiguenot* (from Dutch *eedgenot* from Swiss German *Eidgenoss* confederate) to the name of a Geneva burgomaster *Hugues*]

huh *interjection* **1** expressing disgust, surprise, inquiry, etc. **2** inviting assent (*busy, huh?*). [imitative]

Huhe·hot *see* HOHHOT.

Hui·chol /wiːˈtʃoːl/ ● *noun* (*pl.* same or **-chols**) **1** a member of a Mexican Indian people. **2** the language of this people. ● *adjective* of or pertaining to the Huichol or their language. [Spanish, from Huichol]

hula *noun* (also **hula-hula**) a Hawaiian dance with six basic steps and flowing arm movements symbolizing or imitating natural phenomena, historical events, etc. [Hawaiian]

hula hoop *noun* a large, usu. plastic hoop for spinning around the body by hula-like movements of the waist and hips.

hula skirt *noun* a long grass skirt as worn by a hula dancer.

hulk ● *noun* **1 a** the body of a dismantled ship (*rotting hulks on the beach*). **b** (in *pl.*) *hist.* this used as a prison. **2** an unwieldy vessel. **3** *informal* a large unwieldy person or thing. **4** the shell of something abandoned or destroyed (*the empty hulk of the burned out mill*). ● *intransitive verb* **1** move or behave in a clumsy or idle way. **2** be bulky or massive; rise like a hulk. [Old English *hulc* & Middle Low German, Middle Dutch *hulk*: compare Greek *holkas* cargo ship]

hulk·ing *adjective informal* bulky; large and clumsy.

Hull¹ 1 (official name **Kingston-upon-Hull**) a city and port in NE England, situated where the Hull River meets the Humber; pop. (est. 2002) 309,100. **2** a former city in SW Quebec, located on the Ottawa River, opposite Ottawa, now merged with Gatineau.

Hull² ▶ 1 Cor·dell (1871–1955), US secretary of state (1933–44) who helped to found the UN. **2 Robert Mar·vin** ('Bobby') (b.1939), Canadian hockey player. He joined the Chicago Black Hawks in 1957, and soon developed a reputation for his speed and power. He led Chicago to its first Stanley Cup in 23 years (1961), and went on to score 610 goals in 15 NHL seasons.

hull¹ ● *noun* the body or frame of a ship, airship, flying boat, etc. ● *transitive verb* pierce the hull of (a ship) with gunshot etc. [Middle English, perhaps related to HOLD²]

hull² ● *noun* **1** the outer covering of a fruit, esp. the pod of peas and beans, the husk of grain, or the green calyx of a strawberry. **2** a covering. ● *transitive verb* remove the hulls from (fruit etc.). [Old English *hulu*, ultimately from *helan* cover]

hul·la·ba·loo *noun* (*pl.* **hul·la·ba·loos**) an uproar or clamour. [18th c.: reduplication of *hallo, hullo,* etc.]

hullo esp. *Brit. var.* OF HELLO.

hum¹ ● *verb* (**hummed, hum·ming**) **1** *intransitive* make a low steady continuous sound like that of a bee. **2** *transitive & intransitive* sing (a wordless tune) with closed lips. **3** *intransitive* utter a slight inarticulate sound. **4** *intransitive informal* be in an active state (*really made things hum*). **5** *intransitive Brit. & Cdn informal* smell unpleasantly. ● *noun* **1** a humming sound. **2** an unwanted low-frequency noise in an amplifier etc., caused by variation of electric current. **3** esp. *Brit. informal* a bad smell. □ **hum and haw** hesitate, esp. in speaking. [Middle English, imitative]

hum² *interjection* expressing hesitation or dissent. [imitative]

hu·man /ˈhjuːmən, ˈjuː-/ ● *adjective* **1** of, belonging to, or characteristic of people or humankind; of or belonging to the genus *Homo*. **2** consisting of human beings (*the human race*). **3** of or characteristic of humankind as opposed to God, animals, or machines, esp. susceptible to the weaknesses of humankind (*is only human*). **4** showing (esp. the better) qualities of humankind, e.g. kindness, compassion, etc. (*proved to be very human*). ● *noun* a human being, esp. as distinguished from an animal or (in science fiction and fantasy) a Martian, an elf, etc. □ **human·ness** *noun* [Old French *humain(e)* from Latin *humanus* from *homo* human being]

human being *noun* any man or woman or child of the species *Homo sapiens*.

human capital *noun* the training, skills, education, etc. of an individual or group of individuals collectively, viewed as a resource contributing to economic growth.

human chain *noun* a line of people formed for passing things along, e.g. buckets of water to the site of a fire.

human chorionic gonadotropin *noun* gonadotropin secreted by the placenta that stimulates the production of estrogen and progestin; estimation of its presence in the urine is the basis of most pregnancy tests. Abbr.: **hCG**.

human condition *noun* the common experience shared by all human beings.

hu·mane /hjuːˈmein, juː-/ *adjective* **1** benevolent, compassionate. **2** inflicting the minimum of pain (*humane trap*). **3** (of a branch of learning) tending to civilize or confer refinement. □ **hu·mane·ly** *adverb* **hu·mane·ness** *noun* [var. of HUMAN, differentiated in sense in the 18th c.]

human ecology *noun see* ECOLOGY 2.

human engineering *noun* **1** the scientific study of the interaction of human beings and their working environment and the exploitation of this interaction in the interests of efficiency. **2** the application of the human sciences to the design of machines.

human error *noun* an error caused by human judgement or

weakness, rather than mechanical or computer failure, esp. as the cause of a plane crash etc.

humane society *noun* an organization concerned with the protection and humane treatment of animals, which usu. operates shelters for stray, sick, or abused animals.

human factors *plural noun* = HUMAN ENGINEERING.

human geography *noun* the branch of geography dealing with how human activity affects or is influenced by the earth's surface.

human growth hormone *noun* a hormone secreted by the pituitary gland which stimulates the growth of bone and body tissue and affects the metabolism of proteins, carbohydrates, and lipids. Abbr.: **HGH**.

human immunodeficiency virus *noun* = HIV.

human interest *noun* (often *attributive*) (in a newspaper story etc.) reference to personal experience and emotions etc.

human·ism /ˈhjuːməˌnɪzəm, ˈjuː-/ *noun* **1** an outlook or system of thought concerned with human rather than divine or supernatural matters. **2** a belief or outlook emphasizing common human needs, seeking solely rational ways of solving human problems, and being concerned with humanity as responsible and progressive intellectual beings. **3** (often **Humanism**) literary culture, esp. that of the Renaissance humanists.

human·ist /ˈhjuːmənɪst, ˈjuː-/ *noun* **1** an adherent of humanism. **2** a humanitarian, a person concerned with or interested in human affairs. **3** *hist.* a student (esp. in the 14th–16th c.) of Roman and Greek literature and antiquities. □ **human·is·tic** *adjective* **human·is·tic·al·ly** *adverb*

hu·mani·tar·ian /hjuːˌmanɪˈteriən, juː-/ ● *noun* **1** a person who seeks to promote human welfare. **2** a person who advocates or practises humane action; a philanthropist. ● *adjective* **1** concerned with improving the lives of humanity and reducing suffering, esp. by social reform, aid, etc. **2** relating to or holding the views of humanitarians. □ **hu·mani·tar·ian·ism** *noun*

hu·man·ity /hjuːˈmanɪti, juː-/ *noun* (*pl.* **-ities**) **1 a** the human race. **b** human beings collectively. **c** the fact, quality, or condition of being human. **2** humaneness, kindness, benevolence. **3** (in *pl.*) **a** learning concerned with human culture, esp. the study of literature, art, philosophy, etc. **b** the study of Latin and Greek literature and philosophy.

human·ize *transitive verb* (also esp. *Brit.* **-ise**) **1** make human; give a human character to. **2** make humane; soften, refine, civilize. □ **human·iz·a·tion** *noun*

human·kind *noun* human beings collectively.

human·ly *adverb* **1** by human means (*I will do it if it is humanly possible*). **2** in a human manner. **3** from a human point of view. **4** with human kindness or feelings.

human nature *noun* the general characteristics and feelings shared by humankind.

human·oid ● *adjective* having human form or character. ● *noun* a humanoid animal or thing.

human papilloma virus *noun* the virus that causes genital warts. Abbr.: **HPV**.

human race *noun* the division of living creatures to which people belong; humankind.

human relations *plural noun* the study of relations with or between people or individuals usu. to enhance performance, esp. in a work environment.

human resources *plural noun* **1** people, esp. personnel or workers, as a significant asset of a business, organization, etc. **2** the department in a business, organization, etc. which deals with the hiring, training, management, etc. of employees.

human rights *plural noun* basic rights held to belong to every living person, e.g. the right to freedom, justice, etc.

human shield *noun* a person or group of persons held hostage and placed in a potential line of fire in order to deter attack.

Hum·ber an estuary in NE England. It flows 60 km (38 miles) eastward to enter the North Sea. The major port of Hull is situated on its north bank. The estuary is spanned by the world's largest suspension bridge, opened in 1981, having a span of 1 410 m (4,626 ft.).

Humber River 1 a river in W Newfoundland, rising in the Long Range Mountains and flowing 153 km generally southwestward through Deer Lake and emptying into the Humber Arm, an inlet of the Bay of Islands, at Corner Brook. **2** a river in south central Ontario, which rises just east of Orangeville and flows southeastward to Lake Ontario. [HUMBER]

---

uː mood   ai my   əi pipe   au brown   ʌu house   ei day   ɔi boy   ɑ̃ franglais   ã Canadien   ɔ̃ Brayon   (*see over for consonants*)

Hum·ber·side a former county of NE England. It was formed in 1974 from parts of the East and West Ridings of Yorkshire and the northern part of Lincolnshire, and dissolved in 1996.

hum·ble ● adjective **1 a** (of a person) not proud; having or showing a low or modest estimate of one's own importance. **b** offered with or affected by such an estimate (*if you want my humble opinion*). **2** of low social or political rank (*humble origins*). **3** (of a thing) of modest pretensions, dimensions, etc. ● transitive verb **1** make humble; bring low; abase. **2** lower the rank or status of. □ **eat humble pie** make a humble apology; accept humiliation. □ **humble·ness** noun **hum·bly** adverb [Old French *umble* from Latin *humilis* lowly, from *humus* ground: *humble pie* from UMBLES]

humble·bee noun = BUMBLEBEE. [prob. from Middle Low German *hummelbē*, Middle Dutch *hommel*, Old High German *humbal*]

Hum·boldt[1] /'hʌmbəʊlt/ a city in central Saskatchewan, 113 km east of Saskatoon; pop. (2001) 5,161. □ **Hum·boldt·onian** noun [F. H. Alexander, Baron von HUMBOLDT]

Hum·boldt[2] /'hʌmbəʊlt/ **1 Frie·drich Hein·rich Alex·an·der, Baron von** (1769–1859), German explorer and scientist. He travelled in Central and S America (1799–1804), proved that the Amazon and Orinoco river systems are connected, and wrote extensively. **2 Baron (Karl) Wil·helm von** (1767–1835), German philologist, philosopher and educational reformer. He suggested that language expresses the culture and individuality of the speaker and that humans understand the world through language.

hum·bug ● noun **1** deceptive or false talk or behaviour. **2** an imposter. **3** Brit. & Cdn a hard candy usu. flavoured with peppermint. **4** nonsense, rubbish. ● verb (**hum·bugged, hum·bug·ging**) **1** intransitive be or behave like an imposter. **2** transitive deceive, hoax. □ **humbug·gery** noun [18th c.: origin unknown]

hum·ding·er /'hʌmˌdɪŋər/ noun slang an excellent or remarkable person or thing. [20th c.: origin unknown]

hum·drum ● adjective **1** commonplace, dull. **2** monotonous. ● noun **1** commonplaceness, dullness. **2** a monotonous routine etc. □ **hum·drum·ness** noun [16th c.: prob. from HUM[1] by reduplication]

Hume /hjuːm/ **1 David** (1711–76), Scottish philosopher, economist, and historian. His philosophy rejected the possibility of certainty in knowledge, and he agreed with Locke that there are no innate ideas and that all the data of reason stem from experience. **2 John** (b.1937), Northern Irish Catholic Nationalist leader. He shared the 1998 Nobel Peace Prize with Protestant Unionist David Trimble for their efforts in securing the accord known as the 'Good Friday Agreement'. □ **Hum·ean** /'hjuːmiən/ noun & adjective

hu·mec·tant /hjuˈmɛktənt/ ● adjective retaining or preserving moisture. ● noun a substance, esp. a food additive, used to reduce loss of moisture. [Latin (*h*)*umectant*- part. stem of (*h*)*umectare* moisten, from *umēre* be moist]

hu·mer·al /'hjuːmərəl/ adjective **1** of the humerus or shoulder. **2** worn on the shoulder.

hu·mer·us /'hjuːmərəs/ noun (*pl.* **hu·meri** /-ˌraɪ/) **1** the bone of the upper arm in humans. **2** the corresponding bone in other vertebrates. [Latin, = shoulder]

humic /'hjuːmɪk/ adjective of or consisting of humus.

humid adjective (of the air or climate) warm and damp. □ **humid·ly** adverb [French *humide* or Latin *humidus* from *umēre* be moist]

humi·dex noun Cdn a scale indicating the personal discomfort level resulting from combined heat and humidity, calculated by adding a given value based on the dew point level to the temperature of the atmosphere. [HUMIDITY + INDEX, first used by the Toronto Weather Office in 1965]

hu·midi·fi·er noun a device for keeping the atmosphere moist in a room etc.

hu·mid·ify transitive verb (**-fies, -fied**) make (air etc.) humid or damp. □ **hu·midi·fi·ca·tion** noun

hu·midi·stat noun a machine or device which automatically regulates the humidity of the air in a room or building. [HUMIDITY + -STAT]

hu·mid·ity noun (*pl.* **-ities**) **1 a** = RELATIVE HUMIDITY. **b** the degree of moisture esp. in the atmosphere. **2** the state or quality of being humid. **3** moisture or dampness.

humi·dor /'hjuːmɪˌdɔːr/ noun a room or container for keeping cigars or tobacco moist. [HUMID after *cuspidor*]

hu·mili·ate /hjuˈmɪliˌeɪt/ transitive verb make humble; injure the dignity or self-respect of. □ **hu·mili·at·ing** adjective **hu·mili·at·ing·ly** adverb **hu·mili·a·tion** noun **hu·mili·ator** noun [Late Latin *humiliare* (as HUMBLE)]

hu·mil·ity /hjuˈmɪlɪti/ noun **1** humbleness, meekness. **2** a humble condition. [Old French *humilité* from Latin *humilitas -tatis* (as HUMBLE)]

hum·int /'hjuːmɪnt/ noun covert intelligence-gathering by agents or others. [from *human intelligence*]

hum·mable adjective (of a tune) catchy enough to be easily hummed.

hum·mer noun **1** a person or thing that hums. **2** a hummingbird.

hum·ming·bird noun any of numerous very small birds of the New World family Trochilidae having usu. long, thin bills and iridescent plumage, which feed from flowers while hovering and make a characteristic humming sound when in flight.

hum·mock noun **1** a hillock or knoll. **2** (also **hammock**) N Amer. a piece of forested ground rising above a marsh. **3** a hump or ridge in an icefield. □ **hum·mocky** adjective [16th c.: origin unknown]

hum·mus noun (also **hom·mos**) a thick sauce or spread made from ground chickpeas and sesame oil flavoured with lemon and garlic. [Turkish *humus* mashed chickpeas]

hu·mon·gous /hjuˈmʌŋgəs/ adjective (also **hu·mun·gous**) slang huge, enormous. [20th c.: origin unknown; compare HUGE, MONSTROUS, STUPENDOUS, etc.]

hu·mor var. of HUMOUR.

humor·al /'hjuːmərəl/ adjective **1** Med. relating to body fluids, esp. as distinct from cells. **2** hist. of the four bodily humours. [French *humoral* or medieval Latin *humoralis* (as HUMOUR)]

humor·esque noun a short lively piece of music. [German *Humoreske* from *Humor* HUMOUR]

humor·ist noun a person who is known for his or her humorous writing or talking. □ **humor·is·tic** adjective

humor·ous adjective **1** showing humour or a sense of humour (*a humorous person*). **2** comic, funny (*a humorous remark*). □ **humor·ous·ly** adverb **humor·ous·ness** noun

hu·mour /'hjuːmər, 'juːmər/ (also **hu·mor**) ● noun **1 a** the condition of being amusing or comic. **b** the expression of humour in literature, speech, etc. **2** (in full **sense of humour**) the ability to perceive or express humour or take a joke. **3** a mood or state of mind (*bad humour*). **4** an inclination or whim. **5** (in full **cardinal humour**) hist. each of the four chief fluids of the body (blood, phlegm, yellow bile, black bile), thought to determine a person's physical and mental qualities. ● transitive verb **1** gratify or indulge (a person or taste etc.). **2** adapt oneself to; make concessions to. □ **out of humour** displeased. □ **-humoured** adjective **-humouredly** adverb **humour·less** adjective **humour·less·ly** adverb **humour·less·ness** noun [Anglo-French *umour, humour*, Old French *umor, humor* from Latin *humor* moisture (as HUMID)]

hump ● noun **1** a rounded protuberance on the back of a camel etc., or as an abnormality on a person's back. **2 a** a rounded, raised mound of earth etc. **b** N Amer. a mountain or mountain range. **3** a critical point in an undertaking, ordeal, etc. **4** Cdn (BC) = HUMPBACK SALMON. **5** coarse slang an act or instance of sexual intercourse. **6** (prec. by the) Brit. slang a fit of depression or vexation (*it gives me the hump*). **7** a mound over which railway vehicles are pushed so as to run by gravity to the required place in a marshalling yard. ● verb **1** transitive informal lift or carry (heavy objects etc.) with difficulty. **2 a** transitive make humped or hump-shaped. **b** intransitive rise in a hump-like shape. **3** transitive annoy, depress. **4** transitive & intransitive coarse slang have sexual intercourse (with). **5** reflexive & intransitive slang hurry, move, or act, esp. with effort. □ **over the hump** over the worst; well begun. □ **humped** adjective **hump·less** [17th c.: perhaps related to Low German *humpel* hump, Low German *humpe*, Dutch *homp* lump, hunk (of bread)]

hump·back noun **1** (in full **humpback whale**) a large black baleen whale with white markings on the flippers, *Megaptera novaeangliae*, with a dorsal fin forming a hump. **2** = HUMPBACK SALMON. **3** = HUNCHBACK.

hump·backed adjective **1** = HUNCHBACKED. **2** (esp. of a bridge) having a hump in the middle.

humpback salmon noun = PINK SALMON.

Hum·per·dinck, En·gel·bert (1854–1921), German composer. Influenced by Wagner, he is chiefly remembered as the composer of the opera *Hänsel und Gretel* (1893).

humph ● interjection an inarticulate sound expressing doubt or dissatisfaction. ● intransitive verb utter 'humph'. ● noun an utterance of 'humph'. [imitative]

hump·ty dump·ty noun (*pl.* **-ties**) **1** a person or thing that, once damaged or overthrown, cannot be restored. **2** esp. Brit. a short dumpy person. [the nursery rhyme *Humpty Dumpty*, perhaps ultimately from HUMPY[1], DUMPY]

humpy[1] *adjective* (**hump·i·er**, **hump·i·est**) **1** having a hump or humps. **2** hump-like. **3** *Brit. informal* annoyed, depressed, out of humour.

humpy[2] *noun* (*pl.* **-ies**) esp. *Austral.* a primitive hut. [Yagara *ngumbi*]

hu·mun·gous *var. of* HUMONGOUS.

humus /ˈhjuːməs/ *noun* the organic constituent of soil, usu. formed by the decomposition of plants and leaves by soil bacteria. □ **humusy** *adjective* [Latin, = soil]

Hun *noun* **1** a member of a warlike Asiatic nomadic people who invaded and ravaged Europe in the 4th–5th c. **2** *dated informal offensive* a German (esp. in military contexts). **3** an uncivilized devastator; a vandal. □ **Hun·nish** *adjective* [Old English *Hūne* pl. from Late Latin *Hunni* from Greek *Hounnoi* from Turkic *Hun-yü*]

Hunan /huˈnan/ a province of east central China; capital, Changsha.

hunch ● *verb* **1** *transitive* (usu. in *passive*) bend or arch into a hump. **2** *transitive* thrust out or up to form a hump. **3** *intransitive* (often foll. by *up*) esp. *N Amer.* sit with the body hunched. ● *noun* **1** an intuitive feeling or conjecture. **2** a hump. **3** a thick piece. [16th c.; origin unknown]

hunch·back *noun* **1** a person having a deformed, hunched or protruding back. **2** such a back. □ **hunch·backed** *adjective*

hun·dred ● *noun* (*pl.* **hun·dreds** or (in sense 1) **hun·dred**) (in *sing.*, prec. by *a* or *one*) **1** the number equal to ten times ten. **2** a symbol for this (100, c, C). **3** a set of a hundred things, people, etc. **4** (in *sing.* or *pl.*) *informal* a large number. **5** a hundred-dollar bill, hundred-pound note, etc. **6** (in *pl.*) the years of a specified century (*the seventeen hundreds*). **7** (in *pl.*) the numbers from 100 to 109 (or 199) inclusive, esp. as denoting years of a decade or century or units of a scale of temperature. **8** (in *pl.*) the digit third from the right of a whole number in decimal notation, representing a multiple of one hundred less than a thousand (*numbered in the hundreds rather than the thousands*). **9** *Brit. hist.* a subdivision of a county or shire, having its own court. ● *adjective* **1** that amount to or approximate a hundred. **2** used to express whole hours in the 24-hour system (*thirteen hundred hours*). □ **a** (or **one**) **hundred per cent** *adverb* entirely, completely. ● *adjective* **1** entire, complete. **2** (usu. with *neg.*) fully recovered. □ **hundred·fold** *adjective & adverb* **hun·dredth** *adjective & noun* [Old English from Germanic]

Hundred Flowers a period of debate in China 1956–7, when, under the slogan 'Let a hundred flowers bloom and a hundred schools of thought contend', citizens were invited by Mao Zedong and others to voice their opinions of the Communist regime. The period was forcibly concluded after social unrest and fierce criticism of the government, ending in the prosecution of those who had exercised their right to voice their opinions.

hundreds and thousands *noun* esp. *Brit.* tiny multicoloured bits of candy used chiefly for decorating cakes etc.; coloured sprinkles.

hundred·weight *noun* (*pl.* same or **-weights**) **1** (in full **metric hundredweight**) a unit of weight equal to 50 kg. **2** (in full **long hundredweight**) *Brit.* a unit of weight equal to 112 lb. avoirdupois (about 50.8 kg). **3** (in full **short hundredweight**) *US* a unit of weight equal to 100 lb. (about 45.4 kg). Abbr.: **cwt**.

Hundred Years War a war between France and England, conventionally dated 1337–1453, in which successive English kings attempted to dominate France. Edward III claimed the French throne following the death of the last Capetian king, but despite early English military successes at Crécy and Poitiers, the House of Valois retained its position. Henry V's victory at Agincourt in 1415 resulted in the English occupation of much of northern France, but under the regency of Henry VI the English gradually lost control of the conquered territory to French forces, revitalized in the first instance by Joan of Arc. With the exception of Calais, all English conquests had been lost by 1453.

hung ● *verb* past and past participle of HANG. ● *adjective* **1** *N Amer.* (of a jury) unable to agree on a verdict. **2** (of an elected body) in which no political party has a clear majority. **3** *slang* (of a male) having large sexual organs.

Hun·gar·ian /hʌŋˈɡeriən/ ● *noun* **1 a** a native or national of Hungary. **b** a person of Hungarian descent. **2** the Finno-Ugric language of Hungary. ● *adjective* of or relating to Hungary or its people or language. [medieval Latin *Hungaria* from *Hungari* Magyar nation]

Hungarian partridge *noun* the grey partridge, *Perdix perdix*.

Hun·gary /ˈhʌŋɡəri/ a country in central Europe; pop. (est. 2002) 10,075,034; capital, Budapest.

hun·ger ● *noun* **1 a** a feeling of pain, weakness, or discomfort, or (in extremes) an exhausted condition, caused by lack of food. **b** lack of food; famine (*alleviate world hunger*). **2** (often foll. by *for*, *after*) a strong desire. ● *intransitive verb* **1** (often foll. by *for*, *after*) have a craving or strong desire. **2** feel hunger. [Old English *hungor*, *hyngran* from Germanic]

hunger strike *noun* the refusal of food as a form of protest, esp. by prisoners. □ **hunger striker** *noun*

hung·over *adjective informal* suffering from a hangover.

hun·gry *adjective* (**hun·gri·er**, **hun·gri·est**) **1** feeling or showing hunger; needing food. **2** (also in *combination*) eager, greedy, craving, esp. for money, power, etc. **3** (of a period, place, etc.) marked by famine or a scarcity of food. **4** (of soil) poor, barren. □ **hun·gri·ly** *adverb* **hun·gri·ness** *noun* [Old English *hungrig* (as HUNGER)]

hunk *noun* **1 a** a large piece cut off (*a hunk of bread*). **b** a thick or clumsy piece. **2** *informal* a sexually attractive, well built, and ruggedly handsome man. [19th c.: prob. from Flemish *hunke*]

hun·ker *intransitive verb* (often foll. by *down*) esp. *N Amer. & Scot.* **1** squat or crouch with the haunches nearly touching the heels, esp. for shelter or concealment. **2** hide or take shelter (*hunkered down for the winter*). □ **hunker down** apply oneself, knuckle down. [related to Middle Dutch *hucken*, Middle Low German *hūken*, Old Norse *húka*; compare German *hocken* 'squat']

hun·kers *plural noun* the haunches. [originally Scots, from HUNKER]

hunky[1] *adjective* (**hunk·i·er**, **hunk·i·est**) **1** shaped like a hunk. **2** (of a man) well built and sexually attractive.

hunky[2] *noun* (also **hun·kie**) (*pl.* **-ies**) *N Amer. slang offensive* a person of Slavic, esp. Ukrainian, or Hungarian origin or descent. [earlier *hunk*, prob. alteration of HUNGARIAN (compare BOHUNK)]

hunky-dory *adjective informal* excellent. [19th c.: origin unknown]

Hun·len Falls /ˈhʌnlən/ a waterfall in west central BC, situated on the Atnarko River in Tweedsmuir Provincial Park, west of Williams Lake. With a drop of over 250 m, it is the third highest waterfall in Canada.

Hunt ► **1 (James Henry) Leigh** (1784–1859), English poet, essayist and editor who was a friend and supporter of Keats, Shelley, and other Romantic poets. **2 (William) Holman** (1827–1910), English painter of the Pre-Raphaelite school who specialized in landscapes, Biblical scenes and paintings with a moral message. His best-known work is *The Light of the World* (1854).

hunt ● *verb* **1** *transitive & intransitive* **a** pursue and kill (wild animals or game) for sport or food. **b** *Brit.* pursue on horseback and usu. kill (a fox) using hounds. **c** *Brit.* use (hounds or a horse) for hunting. **d** (of an animal) chase (its prey). **2** *intransitive* (foll. by *after, for*) seek, search (*hunting for a job*). **3** *transitive* pursue with hostility. **4** *transitive* scour (a district) in pursuit of game. ● *noun* **1** an act of looking for something; a search (*scavenger hunt; the hunt is on for a suitable candidate*). **2** an act of hunting wild animals (*the seal hunt*). **3** *Brit.* **a** an association of people engaged in hunting with hounds. **b** an area where hunting takes place. □ **hunt down** pursue and capture. **hunt out** find by searching; track down. □ **hunt·able** *adjective* [Old English *huntian*, weak grade of *hentan* seize]

hunt-and-peck *adjective N Amer.* designating a method of typing in which the typist looks for each key before striking it, usu. using only the index fingers.

hunt camp *noun N Amer.* a camp or cabin, esp. in a remote area, used by hunters.

hunt·ed *adjective* (of a look etc.) expressing alarm or terror as of one being hunted.

Hun·ter, John (1728–93), Scottish anatomist. Regarded as a founder of scientific surgery, he made valuable investigations in pathology, physiology, dentistry, and biology.

hunt·er *noun* **1 a** a person or animal that hunts. **b** a horse used in hunting. **2** a person who seeks something.

hunter-gather·er *noun* a member of a people whose mode of subsistence is based on hunting animals and gathering plants etc.

hunter green ● *noun* a dark, slightly yellowish green. ● *adjective* of this colour.

hunter orange *adjective & noun N Amer.* = BLAZE ORANGE.

hunter's moon *noun* the next full moon after the harvest moon.

hunt farm *noun Cdn* a farm on which wild animals are kept in enclosures for hunting.

hunt·ing *noun* the practice of pursuing and killing wild animals (also *attributive*: *hunting camp*).

hunting camp *noun* **1** a location where tents are set up (esp. by nomadic peoples) as a base from which to hunt. **2** = HUNT CAMP.

hunting dog *noun* = GUN DOG.

Hun·ting·don·shire a former county of SE England. It became part of Cambridgeshire in 1974.

hunting ground *noun* **1** a place suitable for hunting. **2** a source of information or object of exploitation likely to be fruitful.

hunting horn *noun* a horn blown to give signals during fox hunting etc.

hunting knife *noun* a large, sharp knife used for cutting up, skinning, and sometimes killing game.

hunting pink *noun see* PINK¹ *noun* 6.

hunting territory *noun esp. Cdn hist.* the area in which a particular person, family, Aboriginal band, etc. was allowed to hunt, esp. for furs.

Hun·ting·ton Beach a city on the Pacific coast, to the south of Long Beach, in S California; pop. (2000) 189,600. It is noted as a surfing locality.

Hun·ting·ton's disease *noun* (also **Huntington's chorea**) a hereditary disease marked by degeneration of the brain cells and causing chorea and progressive dementia. [G. *Huntington* US neurologist d.1916]

hunt·ress *noun literary* a woman or female animal that hunts.

hunts·man *noun* (*pl.* **-men**) **1** a hunter. **2** a hunt official in charge of hounds.

Hunts·ville 1 a city in N Alabama; pop. (2000) 342,376. It is a centre for space exploration and solar energy research. **2** a town in south central Ontario, about 70 km east of Parry Sound; pop. (2001) 17,338. □ **Hunts·vil·lian** *noun* (in sense 2) [sense 2 after G. *Hunt*, British military officer and first postmaster d.1882]

Hupeh *see* HUBEI.

hur·dle ● *noun* **1** *Athletics* **a** each of a series of light frames to be cleared by athletes in a race. **b** (in *pl.*) a hurdle race. **2** an obstacle or difficulty. **3** *Brit.* a portable rectangular frame strengthened with withes or wooden bars, used as a temporary fence etc. **4** *Brit. hist.* a frame on which traitors were dragged to execution. ● *verb* **1** *Athletics* **a** *intransitive* run in a hurdle race. **b** *transitive* clear (a hurdle). **2** *transitive Brit.* fence off etc. with hurdles. **3** *transitive* overcome (a difficulty). □ **hurd·ler** *noun* [Old English *hyrdel* from Germanic]

hurdy-gurdy *noun* (*pl.* **-gurdies**) **1** a musical instrument with a droning sound, played by turning a handle, esp. one with a rosined wheel turned by the right hand to sound the drone strings, and keys played by the left hand. **2** *informal* a barrel organ. [prob. imitative]

hurl ● *verb* **1** *transitive* throw with great force. **2** *transitive* utter (abuse etc.) vehemently. **3** *intransitive N Amer. slang* vomit. **4** *transitive & intransitive Baseball slang* pitch. **5** *intransitive* play hurley. ● *noun* **1** a forceful throw. **2** the act of hurling. [Middle English, prob. imitative, but corresponding in form and partly in sense with Low German *hurreln*]

hurl·er *noun* **1** a person or thing that hurls. **2** *Baseball* a pitcher.

hur·ley *noun* **1** (also **hurl·ing**) an Irish game somewhat resembling field hockey, played with broad sticks. **2** a stick used in this.

hurly-burly *noun* boisterous activity; commotion. [reduplication from HURL]

Huron /ˈhjʊərˌən, -ɒn/ ● *noun* **1** a member of an Aboriginal group formerly living around Lake Simcoe, with present-day populations living north of Quebec City and in Oklahoma. **2** the Iroquoian language of this people. ● *adjective* of or relating to the Huron or their language or culture. [French]

Huron, Lake /ˈhjʊərˌən, -ɒn/ the second largest of the Great Lakes (63 096 sq. km), situated between Lakes Erie and Superior, on the border between Ontario and Michigan. [HURON]

Huron East a town in SW Ontario, about 40 km east of Goderich; pop. (2001) 9,680.

Hur·onia /hjʊərˈoːniə/ **1** a popular tourist region situated around the lower end of Georgian Bay in south central Ontario, north of Barrie. It includes the towns of Collingwood, Midland, Penetanguishene and Wasaga Beach. **2** *hist.* the territory occupied by the Huron from 1615 to 1650. [French *Huronie*]

hur·rah (also **hur·ray**) ● *interjection & noun* an exclamation of joy or approval. ● *intransitive verb* cry or shout 'hurrah' or 'hurray'. [alteration of earlier *huzza* (see HUZZAH)]

hur·ri·cane /ˈhɜrɪˌkeɪn/ *noun* **1** a tropical cyclone with winds greater than 65 knots (75 mph) accompanied by heavy rain, esp. one originating in the western North Atlantic. **2** *Meteorol.* a wind of 65 knots (75 mph) or more, force 12 on the Beaufort scale. [Spanish *huracan* & Portuguese *furacão* of Carib origin]

hurricane deck *noun* a light upper deck on a ship etc.

hurricane lamp *noun* an oil lamp having a curved glass chimney to protect the flame from wind or drafts.

hur·ried *adjective* **1** hasty; done rapidly owing to lack of time (*had a hurried supper*). **2** pressed for time (*hurried waiters*). □ **hur·ried·ly** *adverb*

hurry ● *noun* (*pl.* **-ries**) **1 a** great haste. **b** (with *neg.* or *interrogative*) a need for haste (*there is no hurry*; *what's the hurry?*). **2** (often foll. by *for*, or *to* + *infin.*) eagerness to get a thing done quickly. ● *verb* (**-ries**, **-ried**) **1** move or act with great or undue haste. **2** *transitive* (often foll. by *away*, *along*) cause to move or proceed in this way. **3** *Curling* sweep. □ **hurry up** (or **along**) make or cause to make haste. **in a hurry 1** hurrying, rushed; in a rushed manner. **2** *informal* easily or readily (*you won't beat that in a hurry*; *won't ask again in a hurry*). [16th c.: imitative]

hurry-up *adjective N Amer. informal* showing, involving, or requiring haste or urgency (*a hurry-up reform package*).

hurst *noun archaic* **1** a hillock. **2** a sandbank in the sea or a river. **3** a wood or wooded eminence. [Old English *hyrst*, related to Old Saxon, Old High German *hurst*, *horst*]

hurt ● *verb* (*past and past participle* **hurt**) **1** *transitive & intransitive* cause pain or injury to. **2** *transitive* cause mental pain or distress to (a person, feelings, etc.). **3** *intransitive* suffer physical pain or mental anguish (*my arm hurts*; *her boyfriend dumped her and she's really hurting*). **4** *intransitive N Amer.* (foll. by *for*) have a pressing need for. **5** *intransitive informal* experience harm or misfortune (*sales have been hurting since the funding cuts*). **6** *transitive* influence adversely (*the recession has hurt ticket sales*). ● *noun* **1** bodily or material injury. **2** harm, wrong. ● *adjective* **1** physically injured (*a hurt knee*). **2** emotionally wounded (*hurt pride*). **3** (of a facial expression, etc.) suggesting that one has been emotionally injured or offended (*a hurt look*). [Old French *hurter*, *hurt*, ultimately perhaps from Germanic]

hurt·ful *adjective* causing (esp. mental) hurt. □ **hurt·ful·ly** *adverb* **hurt·ful·ness** *noun*

hurt·ing *adjective* **1** suffering, esp. mentally. **2** (of music, esp. country and western songs) lamenting one's misfortunes. **3** *N Amer. slang* pitiful, contemptible.

hur·tle *transitive & intransitive verb* move or hurl rapidly or with a clattering sound. [HURT in obsolete sense 'strike forcibly']

Hus *see* HUSS.

Hus·ain *var. of* HUSSEIN 2, 3.

hus·band ● *noun* a married man esp. in relation to his wife. ● *transitive verb* manage thriftily; use (resources) economically. □ **hus·band·less** *adjective* **hus·band·ly** *adjective* [Old English *hūsbonda* house dweller, from Old Norse *húsbóndi* (as HOUSE, *bóndi* one who has a household)]

hus·band·ry *noun* **1** the cultivation of plants and animals; farming. **2** the application of science to farming, esp. to raising livestock. **3** careful or thrifty management of resources etc.

hush ● *transitive & intransitive verb* make or become silent or quiet. ● *interjection* calling for silence. ● *noun* an expectant stillness or silence. □ **hush up 1** *N Amer.* be quiet. **2** suppress public mention of (an affair). [back-formation from obsolete *husht* interj., = quiet!, taken as a past participle]

hush·a·by *interjection* (also **hush·a·bye**) used to lull a child.

hush-hush *adjective informal* (esp. of an official plan or enterprise etc.) highly secret or confidential.

hush money *noun* money paid to prevent the disclosure of a discreditable matter.

hush puppy *noun* (*pl.* **-pies**) *US* (*South*) a deep-fried ball of cornmeal batter.

husk ● *noun* **1** the dry outer covering of some fruits or seeds, esp. of a nut or grain. **2** *N Amer.* the coarse leaves enclosing an ear of corn. **3** the worthless outside part of a thing. ● *transitive verb* remove a husk or husks from. [Middle English, prob. from Low German *hūske* sheath, diminutive of *hūs* HOUSE]

husky¹ *adjective* (**husk·i·er**, **husk·i·est**) **1** (of a person or voice) sounding rough as if dry in the throat, often because of emotion; hoarse. **2** (of or full of husks). **3** dry as a husk. **4** big and strong. □ **husk·i·ly** *adverb* **husk·i·ness** *noun*

husky² *noun* (*pl.* **-ies**) a breed of dog used in the Arctic for pulling sleds. [abbreviation of *husky dog*, *husky breed*; compare Nfld. and Labrador dial. *Husky* 'a Labrador Inuit' from earlier *Huskemaw*, *Uskemaw*, ultimately from the same Algonquian root as ESKIMO]

Huss /hʌs/ **John** (Czech name Jan Hus) (*c.*1372–1415), Bohemian religious reformer. His Wycliffite views and attacks on ecclesiastical abuses aroused the hostility of the Church, and he was excommunicated (1411), tried (1414), and burned at the stake (*see also* HUSSITE).

hus·sar /hʊˈzɑr/ *noun* **1** a soldier of a light cavalry regiment. **2** a

Vowels: a *cat* ɑ *arm* e *bed* ɜr *her* ɜː *deux* ə *ago* ɪ *sit* i *cosy* iː *feed* ɒ *hot* ɔ *pore* ɔː *no* ʌ *run* ʊ *put*

Hungarian light horseman of the 15th c. [Magyar *huszár* from Old Serbian *husar* from Italian *corsaro* CORSAIR]

Hus·sein /hʊ'sein/ **1** see ABDULLAH IBN HUSSEIN. **2** (also **Hus·ain**) (1935–99), king of Jordan 1953–99. He gained the West Bank for Jordan in the Arab–Israeli War (1948–9), but lost it to Israel during the Six Day War of 1967. **3 Sad·dam** (also **Hus·ain**) (b.1937), Iraqi president, prime minister, and head of the armed forces 1979–2003. As president he suppressed opposing parties, built up the army and its weaponry, and made himself the object of an extensive personality cult. During his presidency Iraq fought a war with Iran (1980–8) and invaded Kuwait (1990), from which Iraqi forces were expelled in the Gulf War (1991). He was captured after the US-led invasion of Iraq in 2003.

Hus·serl /'hʊsərl/ **Ed·mund (Gus·tav Al·brecht)** (1859–1938), German philosopher. His work forms the basis of the school of phenomenology.

Hus·site /'hʌsʌit/ *noun* a member or follower of a religious and nationalist movement begun by John Huss. After Huss's execution the Hussites took up arms against the Holy Roman Empire and demanded a set of ecclesiastical reforms. The movement was split by a schism in which the more extreme faction was defeated, but most of the demands of the moderate Hussites were then granted (1436), and a Church established that retained a measure of independence from the Roman Catholic Church until 1620. □ **Hus·sit·ism** *noun*

hussy *noun* (*pl.* **-sies**) *derogatory* a wanton or impudent girl or woman. [phonetic reduction of HOUSEWIFE (the original sense)]

hus·tings *noun* **1** the political campaigning leading up to an election, e.g. canvassing votes and making speeches. **2** *Brit. hist.* a platform from which (before 1872) candidates for Parliament were nominated and addressed electors. [late Old English *husting* from Old Norse *hústhing* house of assembly]

hus·tle ● *verb* **1** *transitive* push or move (someone) in a specified direction in a hurried, esp. rough and aggressive way (*hustled the protesters off the premises; was hustled into a waiting car*). **2** *intransitive* move quickly (*if we want to catch the train, we'll have to hustle*). **3 a** *intransitive* work hard (*if you want it, you'll have to hustle for it*). **b** *transitive* obtain by hard work and persistence. **4** *transitive & intransitive N Amer.* sell or obtain (illegal or stolen goods) using aggressive tactics (*they survive by hustling on the streets*). **5** *transitive & intransitive N Amer.* market or sell aggressively. **6 a** *intransitive slang* engage in prostitution. **b** *transitive* (esp. of a prostitute) solicit (a sexual partner). ● *noun* **1** (also **hustle and bustle**) busy movement or activity, esp. of many people (*get away from the hustle of the big city*). **2** the quality or an instance of working hard or aggressively. **3** an act or instance of hustling. **4** *informal* a fraud or swindle. **5** a fast, vigorous dance popular particularly during the disco craze of the 1970s, set to a strong beat and incorporating Latin American, swing, and rock elements. □ **hustle one's buns** (or **butt**) *N Amer. slang* get a move on; move or act quickly. [Middle Dutch *husselen* shake, toss, frequentative of *hutsen*, originally imitative]

hust·ler *noun slang* **1** an active, enterprising, or unscrupulous individual. **2** a prostitute.

Hus·ton /'hjuːstən/ **John** (1906–87), US-born Irish film director. He made his debut as a film director in 1941 with *The Maltese Falcon*. A number of successful adventure films followed, including *The Asphalt Jungle* (1950), *The African Queen* (1951), and *Prizzi's Honour* (1985).

hut *noun* **1** a small simple or crude house or shelter. **2** *Military* a temporary wooden etc. house for troops. [French *hutte* from Middle High German *hütte*]

hutch *noun* **1** a box or cage, usu. with a wire mesh front, for keeping small animals, esp. rabbits. **2** *N Amer.* **a** a usu. open shelving unit placed on top of a sideboard, desk, etc. **b** a piece of furniture incorporating this. [Middle English, = coffer, from Old French *huche* from medieval Latin *hutica*, of unknown origin]

Hutch·i·son, (Wil·liam) Bruce (1901–1992), Canadian journalist and writer. He was an editor for the *Winnipeg Free Press*, Victoria *Times*, and *Vancouver Sun*. His books, most of which share a nationalistic theme, include *The Incredible Canadian* (1953) (a biography of Mackenzie King) and three more general books on Canada: *The Unknown Country* (1942), *Canada: Tomorrow's Giant* (1957), and *The Unfinished Country* (1985).

hut·ment *noun Military* an encampment of huts.

Hutt, Wil·liam Ian de·Witt (b.1920), Canadian actor and director. He has performed at the Stratford Festival since its inaugural season in 1953; he has also acted and directed throughout Canada, the US, and Britain. He was named a Companion of the Order of Canada in 1969 and won several awards for his portrayal of Sir John A. Macdonald in the CBC's production of *The National Dream*.

Hut·ter·ite ● *noun* a member of an Anabaptist sect living esp. in rural

communal settlements and holding all property in common. ● *adjective* of or relating to the Hutterites or their beliefs. [Jacob *Hutter*, Moravian Anabaptist d.1536, + -ITE¹]

Hut·ton, James (1726–97), Scottish geologist. His theories on the age and creation of the earth, controversial at the time, became accepted tenets of modern geology.

Hutu /'huːtu/ ● *noun* (*pl.* same or **Hutus**) a member of a Bantu-speaking people forming the majority population in Rwanda and Burundi. ● *adjective* of or relating to the Hutu people. [Bantu]

Hux·ley ▶ **1 Al·dous Leon·ard** (1894–1963), English novelist and essayist, best known for the futuristic novel *Brave New World* (1932), which portrays a highly mechanized totalitarian universe where science and technology are exploited to control mankind. **2 Sir An·drew Field·ing** (b.1917), British physiologist, noted for his research into nerves and nerve impulses. He shared a Nobel Prize in 1963. **3 Sir Jul·ian** (1887–1975), English biologist, grandson of T. H. Huxley. He contributed to the development of the study of animal behaviour, made science accessible to the public through writing and broadcasting, and became the first director general of UNESCO (1946–8). **4 Thom·as Henry** (1825–95), English biologist. He studied marine biology and fossils, esp. of fishes and reptiles, became a supporter of Darwinism, and coined the word *agnostic* to describe his own beliefs.

Huy·gens /'haiɡənz/ **Chris·tiaan** (1629–95), Dutch physicist, mathematician, and astronomer, best known for his pendulum-regulated clock. He improved the telescope, discovered a satellite and the rings of Saturn, and formulated a wave theory of light.

Huys·mans /'wiːsmãs/ **Joris Karl** (1848–1907), French novelist. His early work was influenced by naturalists such as Zola but his later work, such as *À rebours* (1884), often highly autobiographical, focused on aesthetic and spiritual concerns.

huz·zah /'hʌzə/ *noun* a shout or cheer; a hurrah. [earlier *huzza*, perhaps originally a sailor's cry when hauling: compare German *Hussa* a cry of pursuit and exaltation]

HVAC *abbreviation* heating, ventilating, and air conditioning.

HWM *abbreviation* HIGH-WATER MARK.

hwy. *abbreviation N Amer.* highway.

hwyl /'huːil/ *noun* an emotional quality inspiring impassioned eloquence. [Welsh]

hya·cinth /'haiəsinθ/ *noun* **1** any bulbous plant of the genus *Hyacinthus* with racemes of usu. purplish-blue, pink, or white bell-shaped fragrant flowers. **2** (also **wild hyacinth**) any of various plants of the lily family resembling this. **3** = GRAPE HYACINTH. **4** the purplish-blue colour of the hyacinth flower. **5** an orange variety of zircon used as a precious stone. □ **hya·cinth·ine** /-'sinθiːn/ *adjective* [French *hyacinthe* from Latin *hyacinthus* from Greek *huakinthos*, HYACINTHUS]

Hya·cin·thus /ˌhaiə'sinθəs/ *Gk Myth* a pre-Hellenic god, said to have been a beautiful boy whom the god Apollo loved but killed accidentally with a discus. From his blood Apollo caused the flower that bears his name to spring up.

Hya·des /'haiəˌdiːz/ **1** *Gk Myth* daughters of Atlas and sisters of the Pleiades, placed by Zeus among the stars. **2** a group of stars in Taurus near the Pleiades, whose heliacal rising was once thought to foretell rain. [Greek *Huades* (by popular etymology from *huō* rain, but perhaps from *hus* pig)]

hyal·in /'haiəlin/ *noun* a clear substance esp. produced as a result of the degeneration of certain body tissues. *Compare* HYALINE. [Greek *hualos* glass + -IN]

hyal·ine /'haiəlin, -ˌlain, -ˌliːn/ ● *adjective* **1** *Anatomy & Zoology* having a glassy or translucent appearance. **2** *Anat. & Zool.* characterized by the formation of hyaline material. ● *noun Anat. & Zool.* = HYALIN. [Latin *hyalinus* from Greek *hualinos* from *hualos* glass]

hyaline cartilage *noun* a translucent bluish-white type of cartilage present in the joints and respiratory tract, and in the immature skeleton.

hyal·oid membrane *noun* a thin transparent membrane enveloping the vitreous humour of the eye. [French *hyaloïde* from Late Latin *hyaloides* from Greek *hualoeidēs* 'like glass' from *hualos* glass]

hyal·uron·ic acid /ˌhaiəljʊ'rɒnik/ *noun Biochem.* a viscous fluid carbohydrate found in synovial fluid, the vitreous humour of the eye, etc. [HYALOID + -uronic chemical suffix]

hy·brid ● *noun* **1** *Biol.* the offspring of two plants or animals of different species or varieties. **2** *offensive* a person of mixed racial or cultural origin. **3** a thing composed of mixed or incongruous elements. **4** *Linguistics* a word with parts taken from different languages. ● *adjective* **1** bred as a hybrid from different species or varieties. **2** formed from mixed, esp. incongruous elements; heterogeneous. □ **hy·brid·ist** *noun* **hy·brid·ity** *noun* [Latin *hybrida*, (*h*)*ibrida* offspring of a tame sow and wild boar, child of a freeman and slave, etc.]

hy·brid·ize *verb* (also esp. *Brit.* **-ise**) **1** *transitive* subject (a species etc.) to crossbreeding. **2** *intransitive* **a** produce hybrids. **b** (of an animal or plant) interbreed. □ **hy·brid·iz·able** *adjective* **hy·brid·iz·a·tion** *noun* **hy·brid·iz·er** *noun*

hybrid offence *noun Cdn* a crime which may be treated as either a summary conviction offence or an indictable offence, at the discretion of the Crown.

hy·brid·oma /ˌhaɪbrɪˈdoʊmə/ *noun* (*pl.* **-omas** or **-omata**) a culture of cells produced by hybridization, esp. one in which myeloma cells are hybridized with antibody-producing lymphocytes, used to produce monoclonal antibodies.

hybrid tea *noun* any rose of a group of hybrids now much grown, evolved from crosses between various hybrids, including the tea rose.

hybrid vigour *noun* heterosis.

hyda·tid /ˈhaɪdətɪd/ *noun Med.* **1** a cyst containing watery fluid (esp. one formed by, and containing, a tapeworm larva). **2** a tapeworm larva. □ **hyda·tidi·form** /-ˈtɪdɪˌfɔrm/ *adjective* [modern Latin *hydatis* from Greek *hudatis -idos* watery vesicle, from *hudōr hudatos* water]

Hyde ▸ **1 Doug·las** (1860–1949), Irish scholar and writer; first president of the Republic of Eire (1938–45). **2 Ed·ward**, *see* CLARENDON.

Hy·dera·bad /ˈhaɪdərəˌbad/ **1** a city in central India, capital of the state of Andhra Pradesh; pop. (2001) 3,449,900. **2** *hist.* a former large princely state of south central India, divided in 1956 between Maharashtra, Mysore, and Andhra Pradesh. **3** a city in SE Pakistan, in the province of Sind, on the Indus River; pop. (1998) 1,151,300.

Hydra /ˈhaɪdrə/ **1** *Gk Myth* a many-headed snake of the marshes of Lerna in the Peloponnese, whose heads grew again as they were cut off, killed by Hercules. **2** *Astronomy* the largest constellation (the Water Snake or Sea Monster), said to represent the beast slain by Hercules.

hy·dra /ˈhaɪdrə/ *noun* **1** a freshwater polyp of the genus *Hydra* with a tubular body and tentacles around the mouth. **2** something which is hard to destroy. [Latin from Greek *hudra* water snake]

hy·dran·gea /haɪˈdreɪndʒə, -dʒiə/ *noun* any shrub of the genus *Hydrangea* with large white, pink, or blue flowers. [modern Latin from Greek *hudōr* water + *aggos* vessel (from the cup shape of its seed capsule)]

hy·drant /ˈhaɪdrənt/ *noun* = FIRE HYDRANT. [irreg. from HYDRO- + -ANT]

hy·drate /ˈhaɪdreɪt/ ● *noun Chem.* a compound of water combined with another compound or with an element. ● *transitive verb* **1** combine chemically with water. **2** cause to absorb water. □ **hy·dra·tion** /-ˈdreɪʃən/ *noun* **hy·dra·tor** *noun* [French from Greek *hudōr* water]

hy·drat·ed /ˈhaɪdreɪtəd/ *adjective* chemically bonded to water.

hy·draul·ic /haɪˈdrɒlɪk/ *adjective* **1** (of water, oil, etc.) conveyed through pipes or channels usu. by pressure. **2** (of a mechanism etc.) operated by liquid moving in this manner (*hydraulic brakes*; *hydraulic lift*). **3** of or concerned with hydraulics (*hydraulic engineer*). **4** hardening under water (*hydraulic cement*). □ **hy·draul·ic·ally** *adverb* [Latin *hydraulicus* from Greek *hudraulikos* from *hudōr* water + *aulos* pipe]

hydraulic brake *noun* **1** a brake that uses a piston or rotor in a liquid-filled chamber to produce the slowing down. **2** a brake on a vehicle that is activated hydraulically but operates through friction.

hydraulic press *noun* a device in which the force applied to a fluid creates a pressure which when transmitted to a larger volume of fluid gives rise to a greater force.

hy·draul·ics /haɪˈdrɒlɪks/ *plural noun* **1** (usu. treated as *sing.*) the science of the conveyance of liquids through pipes etc. esp. as motive power. **2** hydraulically operated devices.

hy·dra·zine /ˈhaɪdrəˌziːn/ *noun Chem.* a colourless alkaline liquid which is a powerful reducing agent and is used as a rocket propellant. Chem. formula: N_2H_4. [HYDROGEN + AZO- + -INE⁴]

hy·dride /ˈhaɪdraɪd/ *noun Chem.* a binary compound of hydrogen with an element, esp. with a metal.

hy·dro ● *noun* (*pl.* **-dros**) **1** *Cdn* electricity. **2** hydroelectricity. **3** a hydroelectric power plant. **4** (**Hydro**) *Cdn* an electric utility. **5** *Brit. informal* a hotel or clinic etc. originally providing hydropathic treatment. ● *adjective* **1** *Cdn* of or relating to electricity (*hydro bill*). **2** of or relating to hydroelectricity (*hydro dam*). [abbreviation]

hydro- *combining form* (also **hydr-** before a vowel) **1** having to do with water (*hydroelectric*). **2** *Med.* affected with an accumulation of serous fluid (*hydrocele*). **3** *Chem.* combined with hydrogen (*hydrochloric*). [Greek *hudro-* from *hudōr* water]

hydro·bro·mic acid /ˌhaɪdrəˈbroʊmɪk/ *noun Chem.* a solution of the colourless gas hydrogen bromide in water. Chem. formula: HBr.

hydro·bro·mide *noun* a compound formed by the combination of hydrobromic acid with an organic radical.

hydro·car·bon /ˌhaɪdrəˈkɑrbən/ *noun Chem.* a compound of hydrogen and carbon.

hydro·cele /ˈhaɪdrəˌsiːl/ *noun Med.* the accumulation of serous fluid in a body sac.

hydro·ceph·al·us /ˌhaɪdrəˈsefələs/ *noun Med.* an accumulation of fluid in the brain, esp. in young children, which makes the head enlarge and can cause mental handicap. □ **hydro·ceph·alic** /-sɪˈfalɪk/ *adjective & noun*

hydro·chlor·ic acid /ˌhaɪdrəˈklɔrɪk/ *noun Chem.* a solution of the colourless gas hydrogen chloride in water. Chem. formula: HCl.

hydro·chlor·ide /ˌhaɪdrəˈklɔraɪd/ *noun Chem.* a compound of an organic base with hydrochloric acid.

hydro corridor *noun Cdn* a right-of-way for a hydro line.

hydro·corti·sone /ˌhaɪdrəˈkɔrtɪˌzoʊn/ *noun Biochem.* a steroid hormone produced by the adrenal cortex, used medicinally to treat inflammation and rheumatism. Chem. formula: $C_{21}H_{30}O_5$.

hydro·cyan·ic acid /ˌhaɪdrəsaɪˈanɪk/ *noun Chem.* a highly poisonous volatile liquid with a characteristic odour of bitter almonds. Chem. formula: HCN. *Also called* PRUSSIC ACID.

hydro·dynam·ics /ˌhaɪdroʊdaɪˈnamɪks/ *noun* the science of forces acting on or exerted by fluids (esp. liquids). □ **hydro·dynam·ic** *adjective* **hydro·dynam·i·cist** /-sɪst/ *noun*

hydro·elec·tric *adjective* **1** generating electricity by utilization of water power. **2** (of electricity) generated in this way. □ **hydro·elec·tri·city** *noun*

hydro·fluor·ic acid /ˌhaɪdrəˈflʊrɪk/ *noun Chem.* a solution of the colourless liquid hydrogen fluoride in water. Chem. formula: HF.

hydro·foil *noun* **1** a boat equipped with a device consisting of planes for lifting its hull out of the water to increase its speed. **2** this device. [HYDRO-, after AIRFOIL]

hydro·gel *noun* a gel in which the liquid component is water.

hy·dro·gen *noun Chem.* a colourless gaseous element, without taste or odour, the lightest of the elements and occurring in water and all organic compounds. Symbol: **H**; at. no.: 1. □ **hy·dro·gen·ous** /haɪˈdrɒdʒɪnəs/ *adjective* [French *hydrogène* (as HYDRO-, -GEN)]

hy·dro·gen·ase /haɪˈdrɒdʒɪˌneɪz, -ˌneɪs/ *noun Biochem.* any enzyme that catalyzes the reduction of a substrate by hydrogen, as in some micro-organisms.

hy·dro·gen·ate /haɪˈdrɒdʒɪˌneɪt, ˈhaɪdrədʒəˌneɪt/ *transitive verb* **1** charge with or cause to combine with hydrogen. **2** (often as **hy·dro·gen·at·ed** *adjective*) add hydrogen to (an edible oil) to convert it into a saturated fat, usu. solid at room temperature. □ **hy·dro·gen·a·tion** *noun*

hydrogen bomb *noun* an immensely powerful bomb utilizing the explosive fusion of hydrogen nuclei. *Also called* H-BOMB.

hydrogen bond *noun* a weak electrostatic interaction between an electronegative atom and a hydrogen atom bonded to a different electronegative atom.

hydrogen peroxide *noun* **1** a colourless viscous unstable liquid with strong oxidizing properties. Chem. formula: H_2O_2. **2** an aqueous solution of this used esp. as a disinfectant or bleach.

hydrogen sulphide *noun* (also **hydrogen sulfide**) a colourless poisonous gas with a disagreeable smell, formed by rotting animal matter. Chem. formula: H_2S.

hydro·geol·ogy *noun* the branch of geology dealing with underground and surface water. □ **hydro·geo·logic·al** *adjective* **hydro·geol·o·gist** *noun*

hy·drog·raphy /haɪˈdrɒɡrəfɪ/ *noun* the science of surveying and charting seas, lakes, rivers, etc. □ **hy·drog·raph·er** *noun* **hydro·graph·ic** /ˌhaɪdrəˈɡrafɪk/ *adjective* **hydro·graph·ic·al·ly** /ˌhaɪdrəˈɡrafɪkli/ *adverb*

hy·droid /ˈhaɪdrɔɪd/ *noun* any usu. polypoid hydrozoan of the order Hydroida, including hydra.

hydro·lase /ˈhaɪdrəˌleɪz, -ˌleɪs/ *noun Biochem.* any enzyme which catalyzes the hydrolysis of a substrate.

hydro line *noun Cdn* an elevated or buried wire for the transmission of electricity.

hydro·logic·al cycle *noun* the circulation of water between the atmosphere and the earth's surface through precipitation and evaporation.

hy·drol·ogy /haɪˈdrɒlədʒi/ *noun* the science of the properties of the earth's water, esp. of its movement in relation to land. □ **hydro·logic** /ˌhaɪdrəˈlɒdʒɪk/ *adjective* **hydro·logic·al** /ˌhaɪdrəˈlɒdʒɪkəl/ *adjective* **hy·drol·o·gist** *noun*

hy·droly·sis /haɪˈdrɒlɪsɪs/ *noun* the chemical reaction of a substance with water, usu. resulting in decomposition. □ **hydro·lytic** /ˌhaɪdrəˈlɪtɪk/ *adjective*

hydro·lyze /ˈhaɪdrəˌlaɪz/ *transitive & intransitive verb* (also **hydro·lyse**) subject to or undergo the chemical action of water.

hydro·lyzed vegetable protein *noun* (also **hydrolyzed plant protein**) a flavour-enhancing food additive made from plant protein that has been broken down into amino acids.

hy·drom·eter /haɪˈdrɒmɪtər/ *noun* an instrument for measuring the density of liquids. □ **hydro·met·ric** /ˌhaɪdrəˈmetrɪk/ *adjective* **hy·drom·etry** *noun*

hy·drop·athy /haɪˈdrɒpəθi/ *noun* the treatment of disorders by external and internal application of water. □ **hydro·path·ic** /ˌhaɪdrəˈpaθɪk/ *adjective* [HYDRO-, after HOMEOPATHY etc.]

hydro·phil·ic /ˌhaɪdrəˈfɪlɪk/ *adjective* **1** having an affinity for water. **2** readily mixable with or wettable by water. [HYDRO- + Greek *philos* loving]

hydro·phobia /ˌhaɪdrəˈfoːbiə/ *noun* **1** a morbid aversion to water, esp. as a symptom of rabies in humans. **2** rabies, esp. in humans.

hydro·phob·ic /ˌhaɪdrəˈfoːbɪk/ *adjective* **1** of or suffering from hydrophobia. **2 a** lacking an affinity for water. **b** not readily wettable. □ **hydro·phob·icity** /-foːˈbɪsɪti/ *noun*

hydro·phone /ˈhaɪdrəˌfoːn/ *noun* an instrument for the detection of sound waves in water.

hydro·plane /ˈhaɪdrəˌpleɪn/ ● *noun* **1** a light fast motorboat designed to skim over the surface of water. **2** a fin-like attachment which enables a submarine to rise and fall in water. ● *intransitive verb* **1** (of a vehicle) glide uncontrollably on the wet surface of a road. **2** (of a boat) skim over the surface of water with its hull lifted.

hydro pole *noun Cdn* an esp. wooden vertical pole supporting a hydro line.

hydro·pon·ics /ˌhaɪdrəˈpɒnɪks/ *noun* the process of growing plants in sand, gravel, or liquid, without soil and with added nutrients. □ **hydro·ponic** *adjective* **hydro·pon·ic·ally** *adverb* [HYDRO- + Greek *ponos* labour]

hydro power *noun* hydroelectricity.

hydro·quin·one /ˌhaɪdrəˈkwɪnoːn/ *noun* a substance formed by the reduction of benzoquinone, used as a photographic developer and in skin-bleaching creams.

hydro·sphere *noun* the waters of the earth's surface.

hydro·stat·ic *adjective* of the equilibrium of liquids and the pressure exerted by liquid at rest. □ **hydro·stat·ic·al·ly** *adverb* [prob. from Greek *hudrostatēs* hydrostatic balance (as HYDRO-, STATIC)]

hydro·stat·ics *plural noun* (usu. treated as *sing.*) the branch of mechanics concerned with the hydrostatic properties of fluids.

hydro station *noun Cdn* **1** a hydroelectric generating station. **2** a station reducing the high voltage of electric power transmission to that suitable for supply to customers; a substation.

hydro·ther·apy *noun* the use of water in the treatment of disorders, usu. exercises in swimming pools for arthritic or partially paralyzed patients. □ **hydro·ther·apist** *noun*

hydro·ther·mal *adjective* of or relating to the action of heated water in the earth's crust. □ **hydro·ther·mal·ly** *adverb*

hydro tower *noun Cdn* a tall metal structure erected as a support for high-voltage electrical transmission lines.

hy·drous /ˈhaɪdrəs/ *adjective Chem. & Mineralogy* containing water. [Greek *hudōr hudro-* water]

hy·drox·ide /haɪˈdrɒksaɪd/ *noun Chem.* a metallic compound containing oxygen and hydrogen either in the form of the hydroxide ion (OH-) or the hydroxyl group (-OH).

hydroxy- /haɪˈdrɒksi/ *combining form Chem.* having a hydroxide ion (or ions) or a hydroxyl group (or groups) (*hydroxybenzoic acid*). [HYDROGEN + OXYGEN]

hy·droxyl /haɪˈdrɒksɪl/ *noun Chem.* the monovalent group containing hydrogen and oxygen, as -OH. [HYDROGEN + OXYGEN + -YL]

hydro·zoan /ˌhaɪdrəˈzoːən/ ● *noun* any aquatic coelenterate of the class Hydrozoa of mainly marine polyp or medusoid forms, including hydra

and Portuguese man-of-war. ● *adjective* of or relating to this class. [modern Latin *Hydrozoa* (as HYDRA, Greek *zōion* animal)]

hyena /haɪˈiːnə/ *noun* any of several carnivorous scavenging animals somewhat resembling a dog, but with the hind limbs shorter than the forelimbs, belonging to the genera *Hyaena* and *Crocuta* (family Hyaenidae). [Old French *hyene* & Latin *hyaena* from Greek *huaina* fem. of *hus* pig]

Hy·geia /haɪˈdʒiːə/ *Gk Myth* the goddess of health.

hy·giene /ˈhaɪdʒiːn/ *noun* **1** the branch of knowledge that deals with the maintenance of health, esp. the conditions and practices conducive to it. **2** conditions or practices conducive to maintaining health. **3** cleanliness. [French *hygiène* from modern Latin *hygieina* from Greek *hugieinē (tekhnē)* (art) of health, from *hugiēs* healthy]

hy·gien·ic /haɪˈdʒenɪk, haɪˈdʒiːnɪk/ *adjective* conducive to health; clean and sanitary. □ **hy·gien·ic·ally** *adverb*

hy·gien·ist /haɪˈdʒenɪst, haɪˈdʒiːnɪst/ *noun* **1** a specialist in the promotion and practice of cleanliness for the preservation of health. **2** = DENTAL HYGIENIST.

hygro- /ˈhaɪgroː/ *combining form* moisture. [Greek *hugro-* from *hugros* wet, moist]

hy·grom·eter /haɪˈgrɒmɪtər/ *noun* an instrument for measuring the humidity of the air or a gas. □ **hygro·met·ric** /ˌhaɪgrəˈmetrɪk/ *adjective* **hy·grom·etry** *noun*

hygro·scope /ˈhaɪgrəˌskoːp/ *noun* an instrument which indicates approximately the humidity of the air.

hygro·scop·ic /ˌhaɪgrəˈskɒpɪk/ *adjective* (of a substance) tending to absorb moisture from the air. □ **hygro·scop·icity** /-skɒpˈɪsɪti/ *noun*

hying *pres. part. of* HIE.

hylo- /ˈhaɪloː/ *combining form* matter. [Greek *hulo-* from *hulē* matter]

Hymen /ˈhaɪmen/ *Gk Myth* the god of marriage, the son of Apollo and a muse of Dionysus and Aphrodite. In other sources, he was a handsome young man whose happy marriage was legendary.

hy·men /ˈhaɪmen/ *noun* a membrane which partially closes the opening of the vagina and is usu. broken at the first occurrence of sexual intercourse. □ **hy·men·al** *adjective* [Late Latin from Greek *humēn* membrane]

hy·men·eal /ˌhaɪmɪˈniːəl/ *adjective literary* of or concerning marriage. [HYMEN]

hy·men·ium /haɪˈmiːniəm/ *noun* (*pl.* **hy·menia** /-niə/) the spore-bearing surface of certain fungi. [modern Latin from Greek *humenion* diminutive of *humēn* membrane]

hy·men·op·ter·an /ˌhaɪməˈnɒptərən/ *noun* any insect of the order Hymenoptera having four transparent wings, including bees, wasps, and ants. □ **hy·men·op·ter·ous** *adjective* [modern Latin *hymenoptera* from Greek *humenopteros* membrane-winged (as HYMENIUM, *pteron* wing)]

hymn /hɪm/ ● *noun* **1** a song of praise, esp. to God in Christian worship, usu. a metrical composition sung in a religious service. **2** a song of praise in honour of a god or other exalted being or thing. ● *verb* **1** *transitive* praise or celebrate in hymns. **2** *intransitive* sing hymns. □ **hym·nic** /ˈhɪmnɪk/ *adjective* [Old French *ymne* from Latin *hymnus* from Greek *humnos* song in praise of a god or hero]

hym·nal /ˈhɪmnəl/ ● *noun* a hymn book. ● *adjective* of hymns.

hym·nary /ˈhɪmnɹi/ *noun* (*pl.* **-ies**) a hymn book.

hymn book *noun* a book of hymns. □ **sing from the same hymn book** be in agreement; express the same ideas.

hym·nody /ˈhɪmnədi/ *noun* (*pl.* **-ies**) the singing or composition of hymns. [medieval Latin *hymnodia* from Greek *humnōidia* from *humnos* hymn: compare PSALMODY]

hym·nol·ogy /hɪmˈnɒlədʒi/ *noun* (*pl.* **-gies**) the composition or study of hymns. □ **hym·nol·o·gist** *noun*

hy·oid /ˈhaɪɔɪd/ ● *noun* (in full **hyoid bone**) a U-shaped bone in the neck which supports the tongue. ● *adjective* of or relating to this. [French *hyoïde* from modern Latin *hyoïdes* from Greek *huoeidēs* shaped like the letter upsilon (hu)]

hyos·cine /ˈhaɪəˌsiːn/ *noun* = SCOPOLAMINE. [from HYOSCYAMINE]

hyos·cya·mine /ˌhaɪəˈsaɪəˌmiːn/ *noun* a poisonous alkaloid obtained from henbane, having similar properties to scopolamine. [modern Latin *hyoscyamus* from Greek *huoskuamos* henbane, from *hus huos* pig + *kuamos* bean]

hype¹ *slang* ● *noun* **1** extravagant or intensive publicity or promotion. **2** a dubious or questionable statement, method, etc., used to promote a product or service. **3** cheating; a trick. ● *transitive verb* **1** promote (a product) with extravagant publicity. **2** cheat, trick. [20th c.: origin unknown]

hype² *noun slang* **1** a drug addict. **2** a hypodermic needle or injection. □ **hyped up** stimulated by or as if by a hypodermic injection. [abbreviation of HYPODERMIC]

hyper *adjective slang* hyperactive, highly strung; extraordinarily energetic.

hyper- *prefix* **1** over, beyond, above (*hyperthermia*). **2** exceeding (*hypersonic*). **3** excessively; above normal (*hyperinflation; hypersensitive*). **4** *informal* extremely, to the utmost degree (*hypercool*). [Greek *huper* over, beyond]

hyper·active *adjective* **1** (of a person, esp. a child) abnormally active. **2** (of a child) showing constantly active and sometimes disruptive behaviour. □ **hyper·active·ly** *adverb* **hyper·activ·ity** *noun*

hyper·aemia *var. of* HYPEREMIA.

hyper·baric /ˌhaɪpərˈberɪk/ *adjective* (of a gas) at a pressure greater than normal. [HYPER- + Greek *barus* heavy]

hyperbaric chamber *noun* = DECOMPRESSION CHAMBER.

hyper·bola /haɪˈpɜrbələ/ *noun* (pl. **hy·per·bolas** or **hy·per·bolae** /-ˌliː/) *Geom.* the plane curve of two equal branches, produced when a cone is cut by a plane that makes a larger angle with the base than the side of the cone (*compare* ELLIPSE). [modern Latin from Greek *huperbolē* excess (as HYPER-, *ballō* to throw)]

hyper·bole /haɪˈpɜrbəli/ *noun* **1** an exaggerated statement not meant to be taken literally. **2** extravagant exaggeration. [Latin (as HYPERBOLA)]

hyper·bolic /ˌhaɪpərˈbɒlɪk/ *adjective* **1** *Geom.* of or relating to a hyperbola. **2** of the nature of or using hyperbole; exaggerated. □ **hyper·bolic·al·ly** *adverb*

hyperbolic function *noun* a function related to a rectangular hyperbola, e.g. a hyperbolic cosine.

hy·per·bol·ize /haɪˈpɜrbəlaɪz/ *intransitive verb* exaggerate; use hyperbole.

hy·per·bol·oid /haɪˈpɜrbəˌlɔɪd/ *noun Geom.* a solid or surface having plane sections that are hyperbolas, ellipses, or circles. □ **hy·per·bol·oid·al** *adjective*

hyper·choles·terol·emia /ˌhaɪpərkəˌlestɜrəˈliːmiə/ *noun* (also **hyper·choles·terol·aemia**) an excess of cholesterol in the bloodstream.

hyper·con·scious *adjective* acutely or excessively aware.

hyper·critic·al *adjective* excessively critical, esp. of small faults. □ **hyper·critic·al·ly** *adverb*

hyper·cube *noun* a geometrical figure in four or more dimensions, analogous to a cube in three dimensions.

hyper·drive *noun* (in science fiction) a supposed propulsion system for travel in hyperspace.

hyper·emia /ˌhaɪpəˈriːmiə/ *noun* (also **hyper·aemia**) an excessive quantity of blood in the vessels supplying an organ or other part of the body. □ **hyper·emic** *adjective* [modern Latin (as HYPER-, -EMIA)]

hyper·extend *transitive verb* bend (a limb, digit, etc.) so that it makes an abnormally great angle. □ **hyper·exten·si·bil·ity** *noun* **hyper·exten·sible** *adjective* **hyper·exten·sion** *noun*

hyper·focal distance *noun* the distance on which a camera lens can be focused to bring the maximum range of object-distances into focus.

hyper·gly·cemia /ˌhaɪpərɡlaɪˈsiːmiə/ *noun* (also **hyper·gly·caemia**) an excess of glucose in the bloodstream, often associated with diabetes mellitus. □ **hyper·gly·cemic** *adjective* [HYPER- + GLYCO- + -EMIA]

hy·peri·cin /haɪˈperɪsɪn/ *noun* a substance found in St John's Wort, credited with chemical and pharmacological properties similar to those of antidepressants. [from HYPERICUM]

hy·peri·cum /haɪˈperɪkəm/ *noun* any shrub of the genus *Hypericum* with five-petalled yellow flowers. *Also called* ST. JOHN'S WORT. [Latin from Greek *hupereikon* (as HYPER-, *ereikē* heath)]

hyper·infla·tion *noun* monetary inflation at a very high rate.

Hy·peri·on /haɪˈpiːriən/ **1** *Gk Myth* a Titan, son of Uranus (Heaven) and Gaia (Earth). **2** *Astronomy* satellite VII of Saturn, the sixteenth closest to the planet, discovered in 1848. Its irregular shape suggests that it is a remnant of a larger body.

hyper·kinet·ic /ˌhaɪpərkɪˈnetɪk/ *adjective* **1** characterized by excessive or spasmodic movement. **2** hyperactive.

hyper·link ● *noun* a link from a hypertext file or document to another location or file, typically activated by clicking on a highlighted word or image at a particular location on the screen. ● *transitive verb* connect by means of a hyperlink.

hyper·market *noun* (in Europe) a very large supermarket with extensive parking facilities.

hyper·media *noun* = MULTIMEDIA *noun*.

hy·per·on /ˈhaɪpəˌrɒn/ *noun Physics* an unstable subatomic particle classified as a baryon, heavier than the neutron and proton. [HYPER- + -ON]

hyper·pla·sia /ˌhaɪpərˈpleɪziə/ *noun* the enlargement of an organ or tissue from the increased production of cells. [HYPER- + Greek *plasis* formation]

hyper·real *adjective* (esp. of an artificial environment or an artistic creation) created or represented with such meticulous attention to detail as to appear more real than reality. □ **hyper·real·ism** *noun* **hyper·real·ist** *adjective* **hyper·real·is·tic** *adjective* **hyper·real·ity** *noun*

hyper·sensi·tive *adjective* **1** abnormally or excessively sensitive. **2** (of an individual) having an adverse bodily reaction to a particular substance in doses that do not affect most individuals. □ **hyper·sensi·tiv·ity** *noun*

hyper·sonic *adjective* relating to speeds of more than five times the speed of sound (Mach 5). □ **hyper·sonic·ally** *adverb* [HYPER-, after SUPERSONIC, ULTRASONIC]

hyper·space *noun* space of more than three dimensions, esp. (in science fiction) a notional space-time continuum in which motion and communication at speeds greater than that of light are supposedly possible. □ **hyper·spa·tial** *adjective*

hyper·ten·sion *noun* **1** abnormally high blood pressure. **2** a state of great emotional tension. □ **hyper·ten·sive** *adjective & noun*

hyper·text *noun Computing* a software system allowing extensive cross-referencing between related sections of text and associated graphic material. □ **hyper·text·ual** *adjective* **hyper·text·ual·ly** *adverb*

Hypertext Markup Language *noun* the system of tagging used in hypertext to indicate how any downloaded text should be formatted.

hyper·ther·mia *noun Med.* the condition of having a body temperature greatly above normal. □ **hyper·ther·mic** *adjective* [HYPER- + Greek *thermē* heat]

hyper·thyroid·ism *noun Med.* overactivity of the thyroid gland, resulting in rapid heartbeat and an increased rate of metabolism. □ **hyper·thyroid** *noun & adjective*

hyper·tonic *adjective* **1** (of muscles) having high tension. **2** (of a solution) having a greater osmotic pressure than another solution.

hy·per·trophy /haɪˈpɜrtrəfi/ *noun* **1** the enlargement of an organ or tissue from the increase in size of its cells. **2** excessive growth or development. □ **hyper·troph·ic** /ˌhaɪpərˈtrɒfɪk/ *adjective* **hy·per·troph·ied** *adjective* [modern Latin *hypertrophia* (as HYPER-, Greek *-trophia* nourishment)]

hyper·venti·la·tion *noun* breathing at an abnormally rapid rate, resulting in an increased loss of carbon dioxide, and often accompanied by dizziness. □ **hyper·venti·late** *intransitive verb*

hypha /ˈhaɪfə/ *noun* (pl. **hyphae** /-fiː/) a filament in the mycelium of a fungus. □ **hy·phal** *adjective* [modern Latin from Greek *huphē* web]

hy·phen ● *noun* the sign (-) used to join words semantically or syntactically (as in *pick-me-up, rock-forming*), to indicate the division of a word at the end of a line, or to indicate a missing or implied element (as in *man- and womankind*). ● *transitive verb* = HYPHENATE *verb*. [Late Latin from Greek *huphen* together, from *hupo* under + *hen* one]

hy·phen·ate ● *transitive verb* **1** write (a compound word) with a hyphen. **2** join (words) with a hyphen. ● *noun N Amer.* a person who works in more than one (related) occupation, e.g both directing a film and acting in it. □ **hy·phen·a·tion** *noun*

hy·phen·at·ed *adjective* **1** (of a word) spelled with a hyphen. **2** (of a person) having dual nationality or mixed background or ancestry, e.g. *Scottish-Canadian*.

hyp·na·gogic *adjective Psych.* of or pertaining to the state immediately before falling asleep. [French *hypnagogique* from Greek *hypnos* 'sleep' and *agōgos* 'leading']

hypno- /ˈhɪpnəʊ/ *combining form* sleep, hypnosis. [Greek *hupnos* sleep]

Hyp·nos /ˈhɪpnɒs/ *Gk Myth* the god of sleep, son of Nyx (Night). [Greek *hupnos* sleep]

hyp·no·sis /hɪpˈnəʊsɪs/ *noun* a state like sleep in which the subject acts only on external suggestion. [modern Latin from Greek *hupnos* sleep + -OSIS]

hypno·ther·apy /ˌhɪpnəʊˈθerəpi/ *noun* psychotherapy involving the use of hypnotism. □ **hypno·ther·apist** *noun*

Vowels: a *cat* ɑ *arm* e *bed* ɜr *her* ɜː *deux* ə *ago* ɪ *sit* i *cosy* iː *feed* ɒ *hot* ɔ *pore* oː *no* ʌ *run* ʊ *put*

hyp·not·ic /hɪpˈnɒtɪk/ ● *adjective* **1** of or producing hypnotism. **2** (of a drug) soporific. **3** (of a person's gaze, musical rhythms, etc.) producing a trancelike state or fascination. ● *noun* **1** a thing, esp. a drug, that produces sleep. **2** a person under or open to the influence of hypnotism. □ **hyp·not·ic·al·ly** *adverb* [French *hypnotique* from Late Latin *hypnoticus* from Greek *hupnōtikos* from *hupnoō* put to sleep]

hypno·tism /ˈhɪpnəˌtɪzəm/ *noun* the study or practice of hypnosis. □ **hypno·tist** *noun*

hypno·tize /ˈhɪpnəˌtaiz/ *transitive verb* (also esp. *Brit.* **-tise**) **1** produce hypnosis in. **2** fascinate; capture the mind of (a person). □ **hypno·tiz·able** *adjective*

hypo¹ *noun Photog.* the chemical sodium thiosulphate (incorrectly called hyposulphite) used as a photographic fixer. [abbreviation]

hypo² *noun* (*pl.* **hypos**) *informal* = HYPODERMIC *noun*. [abbreviation]

hypo- *prefix* (before a vowel or h usu. **hyp-**) **1** under (*hypodermic*). **2** below normal (*hypoxia*). **3** slightly (*hypomania*). **4** *Chem.* containing an element combined in low valence (*hypochlorous*). [Greek from *hupo* under]

hypo·aller·gen·ic /ˌhaipoːˈalərˈdʒenɪk/ *adjective* having little tendency, or a specially reduced tendency, to cause an allergic reaction.

hypo·blast *noun Biol.* = ENDODERM.

hypo·caust *noun* a hollow space under the floor in ancient Roman houses, into which hot air was sent for heating a room or bath. [Latin *hypocaustum* from Greek *hupokauston* place heated from below (as HYPO-, *kaiō, kau-* burn)]

hypo·chlor·ite /ˌhaipoːˈklɔːrait/ *noun Chem.* a salt of hypochlorous acid.

hypo·chlor·ous acid /ˌhaipoːˈklɔːrəs/ *noun Chem.* an unstable acid existing only in dilute solution and used in bleaching and water treatment. Chem. formula: HOCl. [HYPO- + CHLORINE + -OUS]

hypo·chon·dria /ˌhaipəˈkɒndriə/ *noun* abnormal and unnecessary anxiety about one's health. [Late Latin from Greek *hupokhondria* soft parts of the body below the ribs, where melancholy was thought to arise (as HYPO-, *khondros* 'sternal cartilage')]

hypo·chon·dri·ac /ˌhaipəˈkɒndriˌak/ ● *noun* a person suffering from hypochondria. ● *adjective* (also **hypo·chon·dri·ac·al** /-ˈdraiəkəl/) of or affected by hypochondria. [French *hypocondriaque* from Greek *hupokhondriakos* (as HYPOCHONDRIA)]

hypo·cotyl /ˌhaipəˈkɒtɪl/ *noun Bot.* the part of the stem of an embryo plant beneath the stalks of the seed leaves or cotyledons and directly above the root.

hyp·ocrisy /hɪˈpɒkrəsi/ *noun* (*pl.* **-sies**) **1** the assumption or postulation of moral standards, principles, etc. to which one's own behaviour does not conform; dissimulation, pretense. **2** an instance of this. [Old French *ypocrisie* from ecclesiastical Latin *hypocrisis* from Greek *hupokrisis* acting of a part, pretense (as HYPO-, *krinō* decide, judge)]

hypo·crite /ˈhɪpəkrɪt/ *noun* a person given to hypocrisy. □ **hypo·crit·ical** /-ˈkrɪtɪkəl/ *adjective* **hypo·crit·ic·al·ly** /-ˈkrɪtɪkli/ *adverb*

hypo·cyc·loid /ˌhaipəˈsaikloid/ *noun Math.* the curve traced by a point on the circumference of a circle rolling on the interior of another circle. □ **hypo·cyc·loid·al** /-ˈklɔidəl/ *adjective*

hypo·der·mic /ˌhaipəˈdərmɪk/ ● *adjective Med.* **1** of or relating to the area beneath the skin. **2 a** (of a drug etc. or its application) injected beneath the skin. **b** (of a needle, syringe, etc.) used to do this. ● *noun* a hypodermic injection or syringe. □ **hypo·der·mic·al·ly** *adverb* [HYPO- + Greek *derma* skin]

hypo·gas·trium /ˌhaipəˈɡastriəm/ *noun* (*pl.* **hypo·gas·tria** /-striə/) the part of the central abdomen which is situated below the region of the stomach. □ **hypo·gas·tric** *adjective* [modern Latin from Greek *hupogastrion* (as HYPO-, *gastēr* belly)]

hypo·geal /ˌhaipəˈdʒiːəl/ *adjective* **1** (existing or growing) underground. **2** (of seed germination) with the seed leaves remaining below the ground. [Late Latin *hypogeus* from Greek *hupogeios* (as HYPO-, *gē* earth)]

hypo·gly·cemia /ˌhaipoːɡlaiˈsiːmiə/ *noun* (also **hypo·gly·caemia**) a deficiency of glucose in the bloodstream. □ **hypo·gly·cemic** *adjective* [HYPO- + GLYCO- + -EMIA]

hy·poid gear /ˈhaipoid/ *noun* a gear with the pinion offset from the centre-line of the wheel, to connect non-intersecting shafts. [perhaps from HYPERBOLOID]

hypo·mania /ˌhaipəˈmeiniə/ *noun* a minor form of mania. □ **hypo·manic** /-ˈmanɪk/ *adjective & noun* [modern Latin from German *Hypomanie* (as HYPO-, MANIA)]

hypo·nasty /ˈhaipəˌnasti/ *noun Bot.* the tendency in plant organs for growth to be more rapid on the underside. □ **hypo·nas·tic** /-ˈnastɪk/ *adjective* [HYPO- + Greek *nastos* pressed]

hy·pophy·sis /haiˈpɒfɪsɪs/ *noun* (*pl.* **hy·pophy·ses** /-ˌsiːz/) *Anat.* the pituitary gland. □ **hypo·phys·eal** /ˌhaipəˈfɪziəl/ *adjective* (also **-physial**). [modern Latin from Greek *hupophusis* offshoot (as HYPO-, *phusis* growth)]

hy·pos·ta·sis /haiˈpɒstəsɪs/ *noun* (*pl.* **hy·pos·ta·ses** /-ˌsiːz/) **1** *Med.* an accumulation of fluid or blood in the lower parts of the body or organs under the influence of gravity, in cases of poor circulation. **2** *Metaphysics* an underlying substance, as opposed to attributes or to that which is unsubstantial. **3** (in Christian theology) **a** the person of Christ, combining human and divine natures. **b** each of the three persons of the Trinity. [ecclesiastical Latin from Greek *hupostasis* (as HYPO-, STASIS standing, state)]

hy·pos·ta·size /haiˈpɒstəsaiz/ *transitive verb* (also **-sise**) *Brit.* = HYPOSTATIZE.

hypo·stat·ic /ˌhaipəˈstatɪk/ *adjective* (also **hypo·stat·ic·al**) (in Christian theology) relating to the three persons of the Trinity.

hypostatic union *noun* the divine and human natures in Christ.

hy·pos·ta·tize /haiˈpɒstətaiz/ *transitive verb N Amer.* make into or represent as a substance or concrete reality; embody, personify. □ **hy·pos·ta·tiz·a·tion** *noun*

hypo·style /ˈhaipəˌstail/ *adjective Archit.* having a roof supported by pillars. [Greek *hupostulos* (as HYPO-, STYLE)]

hypo·taxis /ˌhaipəˈtaksɪs/ *noun Grammar* the subordination of one clause to another. □ **hypo·tac·tic** /-ˈtaktɪk/ *adjective* [Greek *hupotaxis* (as HYPO-, *taxis* arrangement)]

hypo·ten·sion /ˌhaipəˈtenʃən/ *noun* abnormally low blood pressure. □ **hypo·ten·sive** *adjective*

hy·pot·en·use /haiˈpɒtəˌnuːs, -ˌnjuːz, -ˌnuːz/ *noun* the side opposite the right angle of a right-angled triangle. [Latin *hypotenusa* from Greek *hupoteinousa* (*grammē*) subtending (line) fem. part. of *hupoteinō* (as HYPO-, *teinō* stretch)]

hypo·thal·amus /ˌhaipəˈθaləməs/ *noun* (*pl.* **-ami** /-ˌmai/) *Anat.* the region of the brain which controls body temperature, thirst, hunger, etc. □ **hypo·thal·amic** *adjective* [modern Latin formed as HYPO-, THALAMUS]

hypo·ther·mia /ˌhaipəˈθərmiə/ *noun Med.* the condition of having an abnormally low body temperature. □ **hypo·ther·mic** *adjective* [HYPO- + Greek *thermē* heat]

hy·poth·esis /haiˈpɒθɪsɪs/ *noun* (*pl.* **hy·poth·eses** /-ˌsiːz/) **1** a proposition made as a basis for reasoning, without the assumption of its truth. **2** a supposition made as a starting point for further investigation from known facts (*compare* THEORY 1). [Late Latin from Greek *hupothesis* foundation (as HYPO-, THESIS)]

hy·poth·esize /haiˈpɒθɪˌsaiz/ *verb* (also esp. *Brit.* **-esise**) **1** *intransitive* frame a hypothesis. **2** *transitive* assume as a hypothesis. □ **hy·poth·esist** /-sɪst/ *noun* **hy·poth·esiz·er** *noun*

hypo·thet·ical /ˌhaipəˈθetɪkəl/ ● *adjective* **1** of or based on or serving as a hypothesis. **2** supposed but not necessarily real or true. ● *noun* a hypothetical proposition, phrase, statement, etc. □ **hypo·thet·ical·ly** *adverb*

hypo·thyroid·ism /ˌhaipoːˈθairɔiˌdizəm/ *noun Med.* subnormal activity of the thyroid gland, resulting in cretinism in children, and mental and physical slowing in adults. □ **hypo·thyroid** *noun & adjective*

hypo·venti·la·tion /ˌhaipoːˌventiˈleiʃən/ *noun* breathing at an abnormally slow rate, resulting in an increased amount of carbon dioxide in the blood.

hypox·emia /ˌhaipɒkˈsiːmiə/ *noun* (also **hypox·aemia**) *Med.* an abnormally low concentration of oxygen in the blood. □ **hypox·emic** *adjective* [modern Latin (as HYPO-, OXYGEN, -EMIA)]

hy·poxia /haiˈpɒksiə/ *noun Med.* a deficiency of oxygen reaching the tissues. □ **hy·pox·ic** *adjective* [HYPO- + OX- + -IA¹]

hyrax /ˈhaiˌraks/ *noun* a mammal of the order Hyracoidea, comprising small stumpy animals of Africa and the Middle East which resemble rodents but are actually related to ungulates and sirenians, having feet with nails like hoofs. [modern Latin from Greek *hurax* shrew mouse]

hys·sop /ˈhisəp/ *noun* **1** any small bushy aromatic herb of the genus *Hyssopus*, esp. *H. officinalis*, formerly used medicinally. **2** *Bible* **a** a plant whose twigs were used for sprinkling in Jewish rites. **b** a bunch of this used in purification. **3** (in full **giant hyssop**) any of various tall labiate plants of the genus *Agastache*. [Old English (h)ysope from Latin *hyssopus* from Greek *hyssōpos* from Semitic origin]

hyster·ec·tomy /ˌhistəˈrektəmi/ *noun* (*pl.* **-mies**) the surgical removal of the uterus. □ **hyster·ec·to·mize** *transitive verb* (also esp. *Brit.* **-mise**). [Greek *hustera* womb + -ECTOMY]

hys·ter·esis /ˌhɪstəˈriːsɪs/ *noun Physics* the lagging behind of an effect when its cause varies in amount etc., esp. of magnetic induction behind the magnetizing force. [Greek *husterēsis* from *hustereō* be behind, from *husteros* coming after]

hys·teria /hɪˈsteriə, -ˈstiːriə/ *noun* **1** an emotional state, caused by grief or fear etc., accompanied by uncontrollable laughter, weeping, etc. **2** a functional disturbance of the nervous system, of psychoneurotic origin. **3** an excited and exaggerated reaction to an event (*public hysteria about AIDS*). [modern Latin (as HYSTERIC)]

hys·ter·ic /hɪˈsterɪk/ ● *noun* **1** (in *pl.*) **a** a fit of hysteria. **b** *informal* overwhelming mirth or laughter (*we were in hysterics*). **2** a hysterical person. ● *adjective* = HYSTERICAL. [Latin from Greek *husterikos* of the womb (*hustera*), hysteria previously being thought to occur more frequently in women than in men and to be associated with the womb]

hys·ter·ic·al /hɪˈsterɪkəl/ *adjective* **1** of or affected with hysteria. **2** morbidly or uncontrollably emotional. **3** *informal* extremely funny or amusing. □ **hys·ter·ic·al·ly** *adverb*

hystero- *combining form* of the uterus. [Greek *hustera* uterus]

hys·ter·on pro·ter·on /ˌhɪstərɒn ˈprɒtəˌrɒn/ *noun Rhetoric* a figure of speech in which what should come last is put first; an inversion of the natural order (e.g. *I die! I faint! I fall!*). [Late Latin from Greek *husteron proteron* the latter (put in place of) the former]

Hz *abbreviation* hertz.

Ii

I¹ *noun* (also **i**) (*pl.* **Is** or **I's**) **1** the ninth letter of the alphabet. **2** (as a Roman numeral) 1.

I² ● *pronoun* used by a speaker or writer to refer to himself or herself. ● *noun* (**the I**) *Metaphysics* the ego; the subject or object of self-consciousness. [Old English from Germanic]

I³ *symbol Chem.* **1** the element iodine. **2** electric current.

I⁴ *abbreviation* (also **I.**) **1** Island(s). **2** Isle(s). **3** (in the US) (used in designating highways) interstate (*I-95*). **4** institute.

i *symbol Math.* the imaginary square root of minus one.

-i¹ /i, ai/ *suffix* forming the plural of nouns from Latin in *-us* or from Italian in *-e* or *-o* (*foci*; *dilettanti*; *timpani*). ¶ Plurals in *-s* or *-es* are often also possible esp. when the word is well established in English, e.g. *cactus*, plural *cacti* or *cactuses*.

-i² *suffix* forming adjectives from names of countries or regions in the Near or Middle East (*Israeli*; *Pakistani*). [adj. suffix in Semitic and Indo-Iranian languages]

-i- a connecting vowel esp. forming words in *-ana*, *-ferous*, *-fic*, *-form*, *-fy*, *-gerous*, *-vorous* (compare **-o-**). [from or after French from Latin]

IA *abbreviation* Iowa (in official postal use).

Ia. *abbreviation* Iowa.

-ia¹ *suffix* **1** forming abstract nouns (*mania*; *utopia*), often in *Med.* (*anemia*; *pneumonia*). **2** *Bot.* forming names of classes and genera (*dahlia*). **3** forming names of countries (*Australia*; *India*). [from or after Latin & Greek]

-ia² *suffix* forming plural nouns or the plural of nouns: **1** from Greek in *-ion* or Latin in *-ium* (*paraphernalia*; *regalia*; *amnia*; *labia*). **2** *Zool.* the names of groups (*Mammalia*).

IAEA *abbreviation* International Atomic Energy Agency.

-ial *suffix* forming adjectives (*celestial*; *dictatorial*; *trivial*). [from or after French *-iel* or Latin *-ialis*: compare **-AL**]

iamb /ˈaiamb/ *noun Prosody* a foot consisting of one short (or unstressed) followed by one long (or stressed) syllable. [anglicized from IAMBUS]

iam·bic /aiˈambɪk/ *Prosody* ● *adjective* of or using iambs. ● *noun* (usu. in *pl.*) iambic verse.

iam·bus /aiˈambəs/ *noun* (*pl.* **iam·bus·es** or **iambi** /-bai/) = IAMB. [Latin from Greek *iambos* iambus, lampoon, from *iaptō* assail in words, from its use by Greek satirists]

-ian *var. of* -AN. [from or after French *-ien* or Latin *-ianus*]

-iana *var. of* -ANA.

Iap·etus /aiˈapɪtəs/ **1** *Gk Myth* a Titan, son of Uranus (Heaven) and Gaia (Earth). **2** *Astronomy* satellite VIII of Saturn, the seventeenth closest to the planet, discovered by Cassini in 1671 (diameter 1,440 km). It is unusual in having one side bright, icy, and cratered, and the other side covered with very dark material.

Iaşi /ˈjaʃi/ (German **Jassy** /ˈjasi/) a city in E Romania; pop. (est. 2002) 354,800. Between 1565 and 1859 it was the capital of the principality of Moldavia.

-iasis /ˈaiəsɪs/ *suffix* the usual form of -ASIS.

IATA /aiˈatə, iː-/ *abbreviation* International Air Transport Association.

iatro·genic /ai,atrəˈdʒɛnɪk/ *adjective* (of a disease etc.) caused by medical examination or treatment. □ **iatro·gen·esis** *noun* [Greek *iatros* physician + -GENIC]

IB *abbreviation* INTERNATIONAL BACCALAUREATE.

ib. *var. of* IBID.

Iba·dan /iˈbadən/ the second largest city of Nigeria, situated 160 km (100 miles) northeast of Lagos; pop. (est. 2002) 3,078,400.

Iban /ˈiːban/ *noun* (*pl.* same) **1** a member of a group of non-Muslim indigenous peoples of Sarawak. **2** the language of the Iban, belonging to the Indonesian branch of the Malayo-Polynesian group of languages. [Iban]

Ibar·ruri Gomez /iː,barʊri ˈɡoːmez/ **Dol·ores** (known as 'La Pasionaria') (1895–1989), Spanish Communist politician. A founder of the Spanish Communist Party (1920), she became famous as an inspirational leader of the Republicans during the Spanish Civil War.

IBC *abbreviation* Inuit Broadcasting Corporation.

IBD *abbreviation* INFLAMMATORY BOWEL DISEASE.

I-beam *noun* a girder with a cross-section shaped like an I.

Iberia /aiˈbiːriə/ the ancient name for what is now Spain and Portugal; the Iberian peninsula. □ **Iber·ian** *adjective & noun* [Latin from Greek *Ibēr* Spaniard]

Iberian peninsula /aiˈbiːriən/ the extreme southwestern peninsula of Europe, containing present-day Spain and Portugal. In ancient times it was a centre of Carthaginian colonization until the third Punic War, after which it came increasingly under Roman influence.

Ibero- /ɪˈbero:/ *combining form* Iberian; Iberian and (*Ibero-American*).

Iber·ville¹ /iːbɛrˈviːl/ a former town in south central Quebec, situated on the Richelieu, now part of the city of Saint-Jean-sur-Richelieu; pop. (2001) 9,424. [D'IBERVILLE]

Iber·ville² /ˈiːbɛrviːl/ **Pierre Le Moyne d'**, see D'IBERVILLE.

ibex /ˈaibɛks/ *noun* (*pl.* **ibex·es**) a wild goat-antelope, *Capra ibex*, esp. of mountainous areas of Europe, N Africa, and Asia, with a chin beard and thick curved ridged horns. [Latin]

ibid. *abbreviation* (also **ib.**) in the same book or passage etc. [Latin *ibidem* in the same place]

-ibility *suffix* forming nouns from, or corresponding to, adjectives in *-ible* (*possibility*; *credibility*). [French *-ibilité* or Latin *-ibilitas*]

ibis /ˈaibɪs/ *noun* (*pl.* **ibis·es**) any wading bird of the family Threskiornithidae with a curved bill, long neck, and long legs, and nesting in colonies. [Latin from Greek]

Ibiza /ɪˈbiːθə/ **1** the westernmost of the Balearic Islands. **2** its capital city and port; pop. (2001) 34,826.

-ible *suffix* forming adjectives meaning 'able to be, suitable for being' (*terrible*; *forcible*; *possible*). See also -ABLE. [French *-ible* or Latin *-ibilis*]

-ibly *suffix* forming adverbs corresponding to adjectives in *-ible*.

ibn Hus·sein *see* ABDULLAH IBN HUSSEIN.

ibn-Saud /,ɪbən ˈsaud/ **Abdul-Aziz** (c.1880–1953), the first king of Saudi Arabia 1932–53, who was largely responsible for his country's fabulous wealth as an oil producer.

Ibo /ˈiːboː/ ● *noun* (also **Igbo**) (*pl.* same or **Ibos**) **1** a member of a people of SE Nigeria. **2** the Kwa language of this people. ● *adjective* of or relating to this people or their language. [African name]

ibo·gaine /ɪˈboːɡein/ *noun* a hallucinogenic compound derived from the roots of a West African shrub, sometimes used as a treatment for heroin or cocaine addiction. [from a blend of *iboga* (local name for the compound) and COCAINE]

IBRD *abbreviation* International Bank for Reconstruction and Development (*see* WORLD BANK).

IBS *abbreviation* IRRITABLE BOWEL SYNDROME.

Ibsen, Hen·rik (Johan) (1828–1906), Norwegian dramatist. After the

---

t top v voice w we z zoo ʃ she ʒ vision θ thin ð this ŋ ring x loch tʃ chip dʒ jar (*see over for vowels*)

success of his verse drama *Peer Gynt* (1867), he turned to writing prose plays on social issues, including *A Doll's House* (1879) and *Ghosts* (1881); his later works deal with the forces of the unconscious, and include *Hedda Gabler* (1890) and *The Master Builder* (1892).

ibu·pro·fen /aɪbjuːˈprəʊfən/ *noun* an analgesic and anti-inflammatory drug used esp. as a stronger alternative to acetylsalicylic acid. [ISO- + BUTYL + PROPIONIC ACID + *-fen* representing PHENYL, elements of the chemical name]

IC *abbreviation* integrated circuit.

i/c *abbreviation* in charge.

-ic *suffix* **1** forming adjectives (*Arabic*; *classic*; *public*) and nouns (*critic*; *epic*; *mechanic*; *music*). **2** *Chem.* in higher valence or degree of oxidation (*ferric*; *sulphuric*) (*see also* -OUS). **3** denoting a particular form or instance of a noun in *-ics* (*aesthetic*; *tactic*). [from or after French *-ique* or Latin *-icus* or Greek *-ikos*: compare -ATIC, -ETIC, -FIC, -OTIC]

-ical *suffix* **1** forming adjectives corresponding to nouns or adjectives, usu. in *-ic* (*classical*; *comical*; *farcical*; *musical*). **2** forming adjectives corresponding to nouns in *-y* (*pathological*).

-ically *suffix* forming adverbs corresponding to adjectives in *-ic* or *-ical* (*comically*; *musically*; *tragically*).

ICAO /ɪˈkeɪoʊ/ *abbreviation* International Civil Aviation Organization.

Ica·rus /ˈɪkərəs/ *Gk Myth* the son of Daedalus, who escaped from Crete on wings made by his father but was killed when he flew too near the sun and the wax attaching his wings melted.

ICBM *abbreviation* INTERCONTINENTAL BALLISTIC MISSILE.

ICC *noun* International Criminal Court.

ice ● *noun* **1 a** frozen water, a brittle transparent crystalline solid. **b** a sheet of this on the surface of water (*fell through the ice*). **c** a sheet of ice used as a playing surface for hockey, curling, broomball, etc. **2** a frozen mixture of fruit juice or flavoured water and sugar. **3** *Brit.* a portion of ice cream or water ice (*would you like an ice?*). **4** *slang* diamonds. **5** *slang* a crystalline form of the drug methamphetamine, inhaled or smoked (illegally) as a stimulant. **●** *verb* **1** *transitive* mix with or cool in ice (*iced drinks*). **2** *transitive & intransitive* (often foll. by *over*, *up*) **a** cover or become covered with ice. **b** freeze. **3** *transitive* spread or cover (a cake etc.) with icing. **4** *transitive Hockey* shoot (the puck) from one's own half of the rink to the far end of the other half. **5** *transitive Cdn* select (a team or individual) to play in a hockey game. **6** *transitive N Amer. slang* murder (a person). **7** *transitive N Amer. informal* clinch (a victory, deal, etc.). □ **break the ice** *see* BREAK[1]. **on ice 1** (of an entertainment, sport, etc.) performed by skaters. **2** *informal* held in reserve; awaiting further attention. **on thin ice** in a risky situation. [Old English *īs* from Germanic]

-ice *suffix* forming (esp. abstract) nouns (*avarice*; *justice*; *service*) (*compare* -ISE[2]).

ice age *noun* a period when ice sheets were particularly extensive, esp. in the Pleistocene epoch.

ice axe *noun* a tool used by mountain climbers and ice climbers for cutting footholds.

ice bag *noun* = ICE PACK 2.

ice bear *noun* = POLAR BEAR.

Ice Beer *noun proprietary* beer brewed using a process in which the temperature is lowered until ice crystals form in the beer, which are then removed.

ice·berg *noun* **1** a large floating mass of ice detached from a glacier or ice sheet and carried out to sea. **2** an unemotional or cold-blooded person. □ **the tip of the iceberg** a small perceptible part of something (esp. a difficulty) the greater part of which is hidden. [prob. from Dutch *ijsberg* from *ijs* ice + *berg* hill]

iceberg lettuce *noun* any of various crisp lettuces with pale, compact leaves.

ice·blink *noun* a luminous appearance on the horizon, caused by a reflection from ice.

ice-blue ● *noun* a clear, piercing blue, like that seen in a block of ice. **●** *adjective* of this colour.

ice·boat *noun* **1** a lightly built boat with runners and a sail for travelling at speed over ice, esp. as a sport. **2** *N Amer.* a fishing vessel with facilities for the refrigeration of fish. □ **ice·boat** *intransitive verb* **ice·boat·er** *noun* **ice·boat·ing** *noun*

ice·bound *adjective* **1** (of a ship) confined by ice. **2** (of a harbour, coast, etc.) obstructed or sealed off by ice.

ice·box *noun* **1** an insulated chest, cabinet, etc. for storing food, cooled by means of a block of ice. **2** *US* a refrigerator.

ice·break·er *noun* **1** a ship specially built or adapted for breaking a

channel through ice. **2** something that serves to relieve inhibitions, start a conversation, etc. □ **ice·break·ing** *noun & adjective*

ice bridge *noun Cdn* a formation of ice across a river solid enough to support traffic.

ice bucket *noun* a usu. insulated bucket-like container in which ice cubes are kept temporarily, for adding to drinks or to keep a bottle of wine chilled.

ice cake *noun* = ICE PAN.

ice candle *noun Cdn* (*Nfld*) an icicle.

ice canoe *noun Cdn* a small, sturdy boat used to cross a partially frozen river.

ice cap *noun* a permanent covering of ice e.g. in polar regions. □ **ice-capped** *adjective*

ice chest *noun* an insulated, chest-shaped cooler.

ice climbing *noun* the action or activity of climbing glaciers etc., esp. as a recreational sport. □ **ice climber** *noun*

ice-cold *adjective* as cold as ice.

ice cream *noun* a frozen dessert made of cream or milk, sugar, flavourings or fruit, etc.

ice cream cake *noun* a slab of ice cream, usu. on a cookie-crumb base, formed and iced to look like a cake.

ice cream cone *noun* **1** a crisp, thin, usu. conical wafer for holding ice cream. **2** such a cone containing ice cream.

ice cream headache *noun* a severe pain in the front of the head caused by exposure to cold.

ice cube *noun* a small block of ice made in a refrigerator.

ice dam *noun* an accumulation of ice at the edge of a roof that prevents melting snow from draining off the roof.

ice dancing *noun* (also **ice dance**) a form of esp. competitive figure skating based on ballroom dancing and performed by couples. □ **ice dancer** *noun*

iced tea *noun* (also **ice tea**) a cold drink of sweetened tea, often flavoured with lemon etc.

ice·fall *noun* a steep part of a glacier like a frozen waterfall.

ice·field *noun* **1** an expanse of ice, esp. in polar regions. **2** a large flat area of floating ice.

ice fishing *noun N Amer.* the act or an instance of fishing through holes cut in the ice on the surface of a lake etc. □ **ice-fish** *intransitive verb* **ice fisherman** *noun*

ice-fishing hut *noun Cdn* = FISH HUT.

ice floe *noun* = FLOE.

ice fog *noun* fog made up of minute ice crystals suspended in the air.

ice-free *adjective* (of a harbour, river, etc.) free from ice.

ice hockey *noun* = HOCKEY 1.

ice hole *noun Cdn* a hole cut through the ice on the surface of a lake etc., used for ice fishing.

ice house *noun* a building often partly or wholly underground for storing ice.

ice hunter *noun Cdn* (*Nfld*) a person engaged in the seal hunt. □ **ice hunting** *noun*

ice hut *noun Cdn* = FISH HUT.

ice island *noun* a very large floating mass of Arctic ice.

ice jam *noun N Amer.* an obstruction in a river etc. caused by broken ice.

Ice·land an island country in the N Atlantic; pop. (est. 2002) 279,384; capital, Reykjavik. Iceland lies just south of the Arctic Circle, and only about 21 per cent of the land area is habitable. Situated at the north end of the Mid-Atlantic Ridge, it is volcanically active. □ **Ice·land·er** *noun*

Ice·land·ic ● *adjective* of or relating to Iceland. **●** *noun* the language of Iceland, a Scandinavian language which is the purest descendant of Old Norse.

Iceland lichen *noun* (also **Iceland moss**) a mountain and moorland lichen, *Cetraria islandica*, with edible branching fronds.

Iceland poppy *noun* an Arctic poppy, *Papaver nudicaule*, with red or yellow flowers.

Iceland spar *noun* a transparent variety of calcite with the optical property of strong double refraction.

ice lolly *noun* (also **iced lolly**) *Brit.* a piece of flavoured ice, often with chocolate or ice cream, on a stick.

ice·maker *noun* **1** an electric appliance for making ice cubes etc. **2** the person who maintains the ice at a curling or skating rink.

ice·man *noun* (pl. **-men**) esp. *N Amer.* a person who sells or delivers ice.

Vowels: a cat   ɑ arm   e bed   ɜː her   ɜ: deux   ə ago   ɪ sit   i cosy   iː feed   ɒ hot   ɔ pore   ɔː no   ʌ run   ʊ put

ice margin *noun* **1** the edge of a glacier. **2** the edge of an ice floe.

ice milk *noun N Amer.* a sweet frozen food similar to ice cream but containing less butterfat.

Iceni /aiˈsiːnai/ *noun* a tribe of ancient Britons inhabiting an area of SE England, whose queen, Boudicca, led an unsuccessful rebellion against the Romans in AD 60. [Latin]

ice-out *noun N Amer.* the time of year at which a body of water becomes free of ice.

ice pack *noun* **1** = PACK ICE. **2** a waterproof package containing ice or another frozen substance, used to cool an injured or inflamed part of the body or to keep food cold.

ice pad *noun Cdn* = RINK 1.

ice palace *noun* **1** *Cdn informal* a hockey arena. **2** *N Amer.* a large building made or carved from ice.

ice pan *noun* a slab of floating ice.

ice pellets *plural noun Cdn* a form of precipitation consisting of raindrops that freeze into small grains of ice before reaching the ground.

ice pick *noun* a pointed implement for breaking up pieces of ice.

ice pilot *noun Cdn* a pilot who guides ships through sea ice etc.

ice plant *noun* **1** a plant, *Mesembryanthemum crystallinum*, with leaves covered with crystals or vesicles looking like ice specks. **2** a machine or factory for making ice, e.g. at a skating rink.

ice queen *noun* **1** (also **ice princess**, **ice maiden**) an aloof, unemotional woman. **2** a female figure skater.

ice rink *noun* = RINK *noun* 1.

ice road *noun Cdn* a winter road built across frozen lakes, rivers, muskeg, etc.

ice·scape *noun* a landscape covered with ice. [after LANDSCAPE]

ice sculpture *noun* **1** the art of carving representational forms in blocks of ice. **2** a sculpture carved in ice.

ice sheet *noun* a permanent layer of ice covering an extensive tract of land.

ice shelf *noun* a floating sheet of ice permanently attached to a land mass.

ice show *noun* a show performed by figure skaters.

ice skate ● *noun* = SKATE *noun* 1. ● *intransitive verb* (**ice-skate**) skate on ice. □ **ice-skater** *noun* **ice-skating** *noun*

ice station *noun* a meteorological research centre in polar regions.

ice storm *noun esp. N Amer.* a storm of freezing rain, that leaves a deposit of ice.

ice tea *var. of* ICED TEA.

ice time *noun esp. Hockey* **1** time spent by a hockey etc. player engaged in play (*got a lot of ice time in the playoffs*). **2** the time during which a team, league, etc. may use an ice rink (*our league could only get ice time at midnight*).

ice water *noun* water from, or cooled by the addition of, ice.

ice·wine *noun* **1** *esp. Cdn* a very sweet wine made from ripe grapes left to freeze on the vine before being picked, and still frozen when they go into the press. **2** a similar wine made in California from artificially frozen grapes. [German *Eiswein*]

ice·worm *noun* **1** a small oligochaete worm, *Mesenchytraeus solifugus*, found in N American glaciers and icefields. **2** a mythical worm said to inhabit the Northern ice.

I Ching /ˈiː ˈtʃɪŋ/ *noun* an ancient Chinese manual of divination based on symbolic trigrams and hexagrams. [Chinese *yijing* book of changes]

ich·neu·mon /ɪkˈnjuːmən/ *noun* **1** (in full **ichneumon wasp**) any small hymenopterous insect of the family Ichneumonidae, depositing eggs in or on the larva of another insect as food for its own larva. **2** a mongoose of N Africa, *Herpestes ichneumon*, noted for destroying crocodile eggs. [Latin from Greek *ikhneumōn* spider-hunting wasp, from *ikhneuō* trace, from *ikhnos* footstep]

ichor /ˈaikɔr/ *noun* **1** (in Greek mythology) fluid flowing like blood in the veins of the gods. **2** *literary* blood-like fluid. **3** *hist.* a watery fetid discharge from a wound etc. □ **ichor·ous** /ˈaikərəs/ *adjective* [Greek *ikhōr*]

ichthyo- /ˈɪkθiɔ:/ *combining form* fish. [Greek *ikhthus* fish]

ich·thy·ol·ogy /ˌɪkθiˈɒlədʒi/ *noun* the study of fishes. □ **ich·thy·o·logic·al** /-əˈlɒdʒɪkəl/ *adjective* **ich·thy·ol·o·gist** *noun*

ich·thyo·saur /ˈɪkθiə.sɔr/ *noun* (also **ich·thyo·saur·us** /ˌɪkθiəˈsɔrəs/) any extinct marine reptile of the order Ichthyosauria, with long head, tapering body, four flippers, and usu. a large tail. [ICHTHYO- + Greek *sauros* lizard]

-ician *suffix* forming nouns denoting persons skilled in or concerned with subjects having nouns (usu.) in *-ic* or *-ics* (*magician*; *politician*). [from or after French *-icien* (as *-IC*, *-IAN*)]

icicle *noun* **1** a hanging tapering piece of ice, formed by the freezing of dripping water. **2** a long thin strip of foil or silver-coloured Mylar plastic used as a Christmas tree decoration. [Middle English from ICE + *ickle* (now dial.) icicle]

icicle lights *plural noun* a string of tiny usu. uncoloured Christmas lights hung esp. from eavestroughs to resemble icicles.

Icicle Pansy *noun proprietary* a pansy that is planted in the fall, survives the winter in relatively cold climates, and blooms again in the spring.

icing *noun* **1** a sweet mixture of sugar with butter or egg whites and flavouring etc., used as a coating or filling for cakes etc. **2** the formation of ice on a ship or aircraft. **3** *Hockey* **a** the act of icing the puck (see ICE *verb* 4). **b** the penalty for this. □ **icing on the cake** an attractive though inessential addition or enhancement.

icing sugar *noun Cdn, Brit., Austral. & NZ* finely powdered sugar, usu. combined with a small amount of cornstarch, for making icing for cakes etc.

-icist *suffix* = -ICIAN (*classicist*). [-IC + -IST]

-icity *suffix* forming abstract nouns esp. from adjectives in *-ic* (*authenticity*; *publicity*). [-IC + -ITY]

ICJ *abbreviation* INTERNATIONAL COURT OF JUSTICE.

ick *esp. N Amer. informal* ● *interjection* an expression of distaste or revulsion. ● *noun* something sticky, congealed, or disgusting.

-ick *archaic var. of* -IC.

icky *adjective* (**-ier**, **-iest**) *informal* **1** sweet, sticky, sickly. **2** (as a general term of disapproval) nasty, repulsive. □ **ick·i·ness** *noun* [20th c.: origin unknown]

-icle *suffix* forming (originally diminutive) nouns (*article*; *particle*). [formed as -CULE]

icon /ˈaikɒn/ *noun* **1** (also **ikon**) a devotional painting or carving, usu. on wood, of Christ or another holy figure, esp. in the Eastern Church. **2** (also **ikon**) an image or statue. **3** *Computing* a symbol or small graphic representation on a computer screen of a program, option, or window, esp. one of several for selection. **4** an object of particular admiration, esp. as a representative symbol of something (*a cultural icon of the 1960s*). **5** *Linguistics* a sign which has a characteristic in common with the thing it signifies. [Latin from Greek *eikōn* image]

icon·ic /aiˈkɒnɪk/ *adjective* **1** of or having the nature of an image or portrait. **2** of or pertaining to a computer icon. **3** constituting a cultural icon. **4** (of a statue) following a conventional type. **5** *Linguistics* that is an icon. □ **icon·ic·ally** *adverb* **icon·icity** /aikəˈnɪsiti/ *noun* (esp. in sense 3). [Latin *iconicus* from Greek *eikonikos* (as ICON)]

icono·clasm /aiˈkɒnə.klazəm/ *noun* **1** the breaking of images. **2** the assailing of cherished beliefs or conventions. [ICONOCLAST after *enthusiasm* etc.]

icono·clast /aiˈkɒnə.klast/ *noun* **1** a person who attacks cherished beliefs or conventions. **2** a person who destroys images used in religious worship, esp. *hist.* during the 8th–9th c. in the Churches of the East, or as a Puritan of the 16th–17th c. □ **icono·clas·tic** /-ˈklastɪk/ *adjective* **icono·clas·tic·ally** /-ˈklastɪkli/ *adverb* [medieval Latin *iconoclastes* from ecclesiastical Greek *eikonoklastēs* (as ICON, *klaō* break)]

icon·og·raphy /ˌaikəˈnɒɡrəfi/ *noun* (pl. **-ies**) **1 a** the visual images and symbols typical of an art form, an artistic movement, an artist, a culture, etc. **b** the interpretation of the significance of these. **2** the illustration of a subject by drawings or figures. **3** the study of portraits, esp. of an individual. □ **icon·og·raph·er** *noun* **icono·graph·ic** /aikɒnəˈɡrafɪk/ *adjective* **icono·graph·ic·al** *adjective* **icono·graph·ic·al·ly** *adverb* [Greek *eikonographia* sketch (as ICON + -GRAPHY)]

icon·os·ta·sis /ˌaikəˈnɒstəsɪs, ai.kɒnəˈstasɪs/ *noun* (pl. **icon·os·ta·ses** /-.siːz/) (in the Eastern Church) a screen bearing icons and separating the sanctuary from the nave. [modern Greek *eikonostasis* (from Greek *eikōn* likeness + STASIS)]

icosa·hed·ron /ˌaikəsəˈhiːdrən/ *noun* (pl. **-hed·rons** or **-hedra** /-drə/) a solid figure with twenty faces. □ **icosa·hed·ral** *adjective* [Late Latin *icosahedrum* from Greek *eikosaedron* from *eikosi* twenty + -HEDRON]

-ics *suffix* (treated as *sing.* or *pl.*) forming nouns denoting arts or sciences or branches of study or action (*athletics*; *politics*) (*compare* -IC 3). ¶ A word ending in *-ics* meaning 'a subject of study or branch of knowledge' will generally be treated as singular, e.g. *Aerodynamics is a mathematical science*, but the same word may be used in the plural to mean 'particular aspects of something considered collectively', e.g. *The aerodynamics of this car are rather primitive*. [from or after French pl. *-iques* or Latin pl. *-ica* or Greek pl. *-ika*]

ic·ter·us /ˈɪktɜrəs/ *noun Med.* = JAUNDICE. □ **ic·ter·ic** /ɪkˈtɛrɪk/ *adjective* [Latin from Greek *ikteros*]

Ic·ti·nus /ɪkˈtaɪnəs/ (*fl.* 5th c. BC), Greek architect. He is said to have designed the Parthenon in Athens (448–437 BC) with the architect Callicrates and the sculptor Phidias.

ictus *noun* (*pl.* same or **ictus·es**) **1** *Prosody* rhythmical or metrical stress. **2** *Med.* a stroke or seizure; a fit. [Latin, = blow, from *icere* strike]

ICU *abbreviation* intensive care unit.

icy *adjective* (**icier, iciest**) **1** very cold. **2** covered with or abounding in ice. **3** (of a tone or manner) unfriendly, hostile (*an icy stare*). **4** like ice (*icy blue eyes*). □ **icily** *adverb* **ici·ness** *noun*

ID *abbreviation* **1** identification, identity (*ID card*). **2** Idaho (in official postal use). ● *transitive verb* (**ID's, ID'd, ID'ing**) identify.

I.D. *abbreviation Cdn* (*Alta.*) IMPROVEMENT DISTRICT.

Id /iːd/ *noun* (also **Eid**) **1** (in full **Id al-Fitr** /iːdblˈfɪtrə/) a Muslim festival celebrating the end of the fast of Ramadan. **2** (in full **Id al-Adha** /iːdblˈədɑ/) a Muslim festival marking the culmination of the annual pilgrimage to Mecca. [Arabic *'id* feast]

I'd *contraction* **1** I had. **2** I would.

id *noun Psych.* the inherited instinctive impulses of the individual as part of the unconscious. [Latin, = that, translation of German *es*]

id. *abbreviation* = IDEM.

i.d. *abbreviation* inner diameter.

-id¹ *suffix* forming adjectives (*arid; rapid*). [French *-ide* from Latin *-idus*]

-id² *suffix* forming nouns: **1** general (*pyramid*). **2** *Biol.* of structural constituents (*plastid*). **3** *Bot.* of a plant belonging to a family with a name in *-aceae* (*orchid*). [from or after French *-ide* from Latin *-is -idis* from Greek *-is -ida* or *-idos*]

-id³ *suffix* forming nouns denoting: **1** *Zool.* an animal belonging to a family with a name in *-idae* or a class with a name in *-ida* (*canid; arachnid*). **2** a member of a person's family (*Seleucid* from Seleucus). **3** *Astronomy* **a** a meteor in a group radiating from a specified constellation (*Leonid* from Leo). **b** a star of a class like one in a specified constellation (*Cepheid*). [from or after Latin *-ides*, pl. *-idae* or *-ida*]

Ida /ˈaɪdə/ **1** a mountain in central Crete, associated in classical times with the god Zeus. Rising to 2 456 m (8,058 ft.), it is the highest peak on the island. **2** *Astronomy* asteroid 243. It is irregular in shape, 52 km long, and has many craters, some of which are large and degraded. It also has a tiny moon, about 1.5 km across.

Idaho /ˈaɪdəˌhoʊ/ a state of the northwestern US, bordering on BC to the north and containing part of the Rocky Mountains; pop. (2000) 1,293,953; capital, Boise. □ **Ida·ho·an** *noun & adjective*

Ida·red /ˌaɪdə ˈrɛd/ *noun* (also **Ida Red**) *N Amer.* a large, tart, red cooking and eating apple with greenish-yellow patches. [abbreviation of *Idaho*, having first been developed at the Idaho Agricultural Experiment Station, + RED]

-ide *suffix* (also **-id**) *Chem.* forming nouns denoting: **1** binary compounds of an element (the suffix *-ide* being added to the abbreviated name of the more electronegative element etc.) (*sodium chloride; lead sulphide; calcium carbide*). **2** various other compounds (*amide; anhydride; peptide; saccharide*). **3** elements of a series in the periodic table (*actinide; lanthanide*). [originally in OXIDE]

idea *noun* **1** a conception or plan formed by mental effort (*have you any ideas?; had the idea of writing a book*). **2 a** a mental impression or notion; a concept. **b** a vague belief or fancy (*had an idea you were married; had no idea where you were*). **3** an intention, purpose, or essential feature (*the idea is to make money*). **4** an archetype or pattern as distinguished from its realization in individual cases. **5** *Philos.* **a** (in Platonism) an eternally existing pattern of which individual things in any class are imperfect copies. **b** a concept of pure reason which transcends experience. □ **get** (or **have**) **ideas** *informal* be ambitious, rebellious, etc. **give a person ideas** give a person expectations or hopes that may not be realized. **have no idea** *informal* **1** not know at all. **2** be completely incompetent. **not one's idea of** *informal* not what one regards as (*not my idea of a pleasant evening*). **put ideas into a person's head** suggest ambitions etc. he or she would not otherwise have had. **that's an idea** *informal* that proposal etc. is worth considering. **that's the idea!** that's the correct way to proceed etc. **the** (**very**) **idea!** *informal* an exclamation of disapproval or disagreement. **what's the big idea?** expressing disapproval of effrontery, stupidity, etc. □ **idea·less** *adjective* [Greek *idea* form, pattern from stem *id-* see]

ideal ● *adjective* **1** satisfying one's conception of what is perfect; most suitable. **2** existing only in the imagination; desirable or perfect but not likely to become a reality. **3** representing an abstract or hypothetical optimum. ● *noun* **1** a person or thing regarded as perfect. **2** a standard of perfection; a principle to be aimed at. □ **ideal·ly** *adverb*

ideal gas *noun* a hypothetical gas consisting of molecules occupying negligible space and without attraction for each other, thereby obeying simple laws.

ideal·ism *noun* **1** the practice of forming or following after ideals, esp. unrealistically (*compare* REALISM). **2** the representation of things in ideal or idealized form. **3** imaginative treatment. **4** *Philos.* any of various systems of thought in which the objects of knowledge are held to be in some way dependent on the activity of mind (*compare* REALISM). □ **ideal·ist** *noun* **ideal·is·tic** *adjective* **ideal·is·tic·ally** *adverb*

ideal·ity /ˌaɪdiˈalɪti/ *noun* (*pl.* **-ities**) the quality of being ideal.

ideal·ize *transitive & intransitive verb* (also esp. *Brit.* **-ise**) consider or represent (a person or thing) as perfect or ideal. □ **ideal·iz·a·tion** *noun*

idea man *noun* (also **idea person, ideas man, ideas person**) a person who is adept at thinking of innovative ideas, esp. one who does not become involved in the practicalities of their implementation.

ideate /ˈaɪdiˌeɪt/ *verb Psych.* **1** *transitive* imagine, conceive. **2** *intransitive* form ideas. □ **idea·tion** /-ˈeɪʃən/ *noun* **idea·tion·al** /-ˈeɪʃənəl/ *adjective* **idea·tion·al·ly** /-ˈeɪʃənəli/ *adverb* [medieval Latin *ideare* form an idea (as IDEA)]

idée fixe /ˌiːdeɪ ˈfiːks/ *noun* (*pl.* **idées fixes** *pronunc.* same) an idea that dominates the mind; an obsession. [French, lit. 'fixed idea']

idée reçue /iːˌdeɪ rəˈsuː/ *noun* (*pl.* **idées reçues** *pronunc.* same) a generally accepted notion or opinion. [French]

idem /ˈɪdɛm/ ● *adverb* in the same author, work, etc. ● *noun* the same work or author etc. [Latin]

ident *noun* short for IDENTIFICATION, esp. in informal or technical use.

iden·ti·cal /aɪˈdɛntɪkəl/ *adjective* **1** (often foll. by *with*) (of different things) exactly the same in every detail. **2** (of one thing viewed at different times) one and the same. **3** (of twins) developed from a single fertilized ovum, therefore of the same sex and usu. very similar in appearance. **4** *Logic & Math.* expressing an identity. □ **iden·ti·cal·ly** *adverb* [medieval Latin *identicus* (as IDENTITY)]

iden·ti·fi·ca·tion /aɪˌdɛntɪfɪˈkeɪʃən/ *noun* **1** the act or an instance of identifying. **2** a means of identifying a person. **3** (*attributive*) serving to identify (esp. the bearer) (*identification card*).

identification parade *noun Brit.* an assembly of persons from whom a suspect is to be identified.

iden·ti·fi·er /aɪˈdɛntɪˌfaɪr/ *noun* **1** a person or thing that identifies. **2** *Computing* a sequence of characters used to identify or refer to a set of data.

iden·tify /aɪˈdɛntɪˌfaɪ/ *verb* (**-fies, -fied**) **1** *transitive* establish the identity of; recognize. **2** *transitive* establish or select by consideration or analysis of the circumstances (*identify the best method of solving the problem*). **3** *transitive* (foll. by *with*; also *reflexive*) associate (a person or oneself) inseparably or very closely (with a party, policy, etc.). **4** *transitive* (often foll. by *with*) treat (a thing) as identical. **5** *intransitive* (foll. by *with*) **a** regard oneself as sharing characteristics of (another person). **b** associate oneself. □ **identify oneself** state or show who one is. □ **iden·ti·fi·able** *adjective* **iden·ti·fi·ably** *adverb* [medieval Latin *identificare* (as IDENTITY)]

Identi·kit /aɪˈdɛntɪkɪt/ *noun* (often *attributive*) a reconstructed picture of a person (esp. one sought by the police) assembled from transparent strips showing typical facial features according to witnesses' descriptions. [IDENTITY + KIT¹]

iden·tity /aɪˈdɛntɪti/ *noun* (*pl.* **-ties**) **1 a** the quality or condition of being a specified person or thing. **b** individuality, personality (*felt she had lost her identity*). **2** identification or the result of it (*a case of mistaken identity; identity card*). **3** the state of being the same in substance, nature, qualities, etc.; absolute sameness (*no identity of interests between them*). **4** *Algebra* **a** the equality of two expressions for all values of the quantities expressed by letters. **b** an equation expressing this, e.g. $(x + 1)^2 = x^2 + 2x + 1$. **5** *Math.* **a** (in full **identity element**) an element in a set, left unchanged by any operation to it. **b** a transformation that leaves an object unchanged. [Late Latin *identitas* from Latin *idem* same]

identity crisis *noun* a period of emotional disturbance in which a person has difficulty in determining his or her identity and role in relation to society.

identity parade *noun Brit.* = IDENTIFICATION PARADE.

Consonants: b *but*   d *dog*   f *few*   g *get*   h *her*   j *yes*   k *cat*   l *leg*   m *man*   n *no*   p *pen*   r *red*   s *sit*

identity politics *noun* political activity predicated on one's belonging to a group considered to be socially marginalized.

identity theft *noun* the obtaining of someone's personal information such as social insurance numbers, credit card numbers, bank account numbers, etc. in order to defraud the victim of money or impersonate them. □ **identity thief** *noun*

ideo·gram /ˈɪdɪəˌgram/ *noun* a character symbolizing the idea of a thing without indicating the sequence of sounds in its name (e.g. a numeral, and many Chinese characters). [Greek *idea* form + -GRAM]

ideo·graph /ˈɪdɪəˌgraf/ *noun* = IDEOGRAM. □ **ideo·graph·ic** /-ˈgrafɪk/ *adjective* [Greek *idea* form + -GRAPH]

ideo·logue /ˈaɪdɪəˌlɒg, -ˈdiː-/ *noun* **1** an adherent of an ideology. **2** a theorist; a visionary. [French *idéologue* from Greek *idea* (see IDEA) + -LOGUE]

ideol·ogy /ˌaɪdɪˈɒlədʒi, ˌɪd-/ *noun* (*pl.* **-gies**) a system of ideas or way of thinking, usu. relating to politics or society, or to the conduct of a class or group, and regarded as justifying actions, esp. one that is held implicitly or adopted as a whole and maintained regardless of the course of events. □ **ideo·logic·al** /-əˈlɒdʒɪkəl/ *adjective* **ideo·logic·al·ly** /-əˈlɒdʒɪkli/ *adverb* **ideol·o·gist** *noun* [French *idéologie* (as IDEOLOGUE)]

ides /aɪdz/ *plural noun* the eighth day after the nones in the ancient Roman calendar (the 15th day of March, May, July, October, the 13th of other months). [Old French from Latin *idus* (pl.), perhaps from Etruscan]

-idine /ɪdiːn/ *suffix* *Chem.* forming names of usu. cyclic organic compounds containing nitrogen. [-IDE + -INE⁴]

idiocy /ˈɪdiəsi/ *noun* (*pl.* **-cies**) utter foolishness; idiotic behaviour or an idiotic action.

idio·lect /ˈɪdiəˌlekt/ *noun* the linguistic system of an individual person, differing in some details from that of all other speakers of the same dialect or language. □ **idio·lect·al** *adjective* [Greek *idios* own + -*lect* in DIALECT]

idiom /ˈɪdiəm/ *noun* **1** a group of words established by usage and having a meaning not deducible from those of the individual words, e.g. *down in the dumps*. **2** a form of expression peculiar to a language, person, or group of people. **3 a** the language of a people or country. **b** the specific character of this. **4** a characteristic mode of expression in music, art, etc. [French *idiome* or Late Latin *idioma* from Greek *idiōma -matos* private property, from *idios* own, private]

idio·mat·ic /ˌɪdiəˈmatɪk/ *adjective* **1** relating to or conforming to idiom. **2** characteristic of a particular language. □ **idio·mat·ic·al·ly** *adverb* **idio·mati·city** *noun*

idio·path·ic /ˌɪdiəˈpaθɪk/ *adjective* *Med.* (of a disease or condition) of unknown cause or arising spontaneously. [modern Latin *idiopathia* from Greek *idiopatheia* from *idios* own + -PATHY]

idio·syn·crasy /ˌɪdioʊˈsɪŋkrəsi/ *noun* (*pl.* **-sies**) **1** a person's particular way of thinking, behaving, etc. that is clearly different from that of others. **2** anything highly individualized or eccentric. **3** a mode of expression peculiar to an author. **4** *Med.* a physical constitution peculiar to a person. □ **idio·syn·crat·ic** /-ˈkratɪk/ *adjective* **idio·syn·crat·ic·al·ly** /-ˈkratɪkli/ *adverb* [orig. in the sense 'physical constitution particular to an individual', from Greek *idiosugkrasia* from *idios* own + *sun* with + *krasis* mixture]

idiot *noun* **1** a stupid person; an utter fool. **2** (in a former system of classification of mental retardation) a person deficient in mind and permanently incapable of rational conduct. □ **idi·ot·ic** *adjective* **idi·ot·ic·al·ly** *adverb* [Old French from Latin *idiota* ignorant person, from Greek *idiōtēs* private person, layman, ignorant person, from *idios* own, private]

idiot board *noun* (also **idiot card**) *informal* a board displaying a television script to a speaker as an aid to memory.

idiot box *noun* *informal* **1** television. **2** a television set.

idiot light *noun* a warning light that goes on when a fault occurs in a device or machine, esp. a motor vehicle.

idiot-proof *adjective* = FOOLPROOF.

idiot savant /ˈidiət səˈvɑ̃/ *noun* (*pl.* **idiot savants** or **idiots savants** *pronunc.* same) a person considered mentally retarded but who displays brilliance in a specific area esp. related to memory skills. [French, = learned idiot]

idiot string *noun* (also **idiot strings**) *Cdn* a string attached to each of two mittens or gloves and strung through the sleeves and across the inside back of a child's coat, to prevent the mittens etc. from being lost.

idle ● *adjective* (**idler**, **idlest**) **1 a** (of a person) not working, doing nothing. **b** lazy, indolent, having a dislike for work or activity. **2** (of a thing) inactive, not in use, not moving or in operation. **3** (of time etc.) unoccupied. **4 a** (of a thought, speculation, etc.) baseless, groundless, meaningless (*idle rumour*; *idle curiosity*). **b** (of an action, word, etc.) vain, trifling, ineffective, or worthless. **5** useless. **6** (of money) out of circulation; not earning interest, investment income, etc. ● *verb* **1 a** *intransitive* (of an engine) run slowly without doing any work. **b** *transitive* cause (an engine) to idle. **2 a** *intransitive* be idle, pass the time in idleness. **b** *transitive* take out of use or employment (*the store closure idled 750 workers*). **3** *transitive* (foll. by *away*) pass (time etc.) in idleness. ● *noun* **1** an act of idling. **2** idling or idling speed of an engine. **3** an idle person. □ **idle·ness** *noun* **idly** *adverb* [Old English *īdel* empty, useless]

idler *noun* **1** a person who idles or is idle. **2** a habitually lazy person.

Ido /ˈiːdoʊ/ *noun* an artificial universal language based on Esperanto. [Ido, = offspring]

idol *noun* **1** an image of a deity etc. used as an object of worship. **2** *Bible* a false god. **3** a person or thing that is the object of excessive or supreme adulation (*teen idol*). [Old French *idole* from Latin *idolum* from Greek *eidōlon* phantom, from *eidos* form]

idol·ater /aɪˈdɒlətər/ *noun* **1** a worshipper of idols. **2** (often foll. by *of*) a devoted admirer. □ **idol·atrous** *adjective*

idol·atry /aɪˈdɒlətri/ *noun* (*pl.* **-atries**) **1** the worship of idols. **2** excessive devotion to or veneration for a person or thing.

idol·ize *verb* (also esp. *Brit.* **-ise**) *transitive* admire, revere, or love greatly or excessively. □ **idol·iz·a·tion** *noun* **idol·iz·er** *noun*

Idom·en·eus /aɪˈdɒmɪˌnjuːs/ *Gk Myth* a king of Crete. He was forced to sacrifice his son in consequence of a vow, made on his return from the Trojan War, to sacrifice the first living thing that met him on his return.

idyll /ˈɪdɪl/ *noun* (also **idyl**) **1** an extremely happy, peaceful, or picturesque episode or scene, typically an idealized or unsustainable one. **2** a short description in verse or prose of a picturesque scene or incident, esp. in rustic life. [Latin *idyllium* from Greek *eidullion*, diminutive of *eidos* form]

idyl·lic /aɪˈdɪlɪk, ɪd-/ *adjective* **1** blissfully peaceful and happy. **2** of or like an idyll. □ **idyl·lic·ally** *adverb*

i.e. *abbreviation* that is to say. [Latin *id est*]

-ie /i/ *suffix* **1** var. of -Y² (*dearie*; *nightie*). **2** archaic var. of -Y¹, -Y³ (*litanie*; *prettie*). [earlier form of -Y]

IEEE *abbreviation* Institute of Electrical and Electronic Engineers, a US organization responsible for setting industry standards in the fields of electric and electronic engineering.

-ier *suffix* forming personal nouns denoting an occupation or interest: **1** with stress on the preceding element (*courier*). **2** with stress on the suffix (*cashier*; *brigadier*). [sense 1 Middle English of various origins; sense 2 French *-ier* from Latin *-arius*]

IF *abbreviation* intermediate frequency.

if ● *conjunction* **1** introducing a conditional clause: **a** on the condition or supposition that; in the event that (*if he comes I will tell him*; *if you are tired we will rest*). **b** (with past tense) implying that the condition is not fulfilled (*if I were you*; *if I knew I would say*). **2** even though (*I'll finish it, if it takes me all day*). **3** whenever (*if I am not sure I ask*). **4** whether (*see if you can find it*). **5 a** expressing wish or surprise (*if I could just try!*; *if it isn't my old hat!*). **b** expressing a request (*if you wouldn't mind opening the door?*). **6** with implied reservation, = perhaps not (*very rarely if at all*). **7** (with reduction of the protasis to its significant word) if there is or it is etc. (*took little if any*). **8** despite being (*a useful if cumbersome device*). ● *noun* **1** a condition or supposition (*too many ifs about it*). **2** an uncertainty (*if he wins—and it's a big if—he'll be the first Canadian to do so*). □ **if and only if** introducing a condition which is necessary as well as sufficient. **if and when** used to express uncertainty about a possible event in the future (*if and when we ever meet again*). **if anything** if any degree, perhaps even (*if anything, it's too large*; *if anything, she finds math easier*). **if not 1** otherwise. **2** used after a *yes/no* question to give a promise, warning, etc. (*Are you ready? If not, I'm going without you*). **3** perhaps even (*cost thousands if not millions of dollars*). **4** although not; but not (*it was a good if not very imaginative performance*). **if only 1** even if for no other reason than (*I'll come if only to see her*). **2** (often *elliptical*) an expression of regret (*if only I had thought of it*; *if only I could swim!*). **3** an expression of a wish with reference to present or future time. **ifs, ands, or buts** (usu. in *neg.*) reservations, arguments against. **if so** if that is the case. **only if** only on the condition that. [Old English *gif*]

Ife /ˈiːfeɪ/ an industrial city in SW Nigeria; pop. (est. 2002) 313,400. It was a major centre of the Yoruba kingdom from the 14th to the 17th c., noted for its bronze artwork, which dates back to the 12th c.

iff *conjunction* Logic & Math. = if and only if (see IF). [arbitrary extension of *if*]

iffy *adjective* (**if·fi·er**, **if·fi·est**) *informal* **1** uncertain, doubtful. **2** of questionable quality. □ **if·fi·ly** *adverb* **if·fi·ness** *noun*

-ific *suffix see* -FIC.

-ification *suffix see* -FICATION.

Ifni /ˈɪfni/ a former overseas province of Spain, on the southwest coast of Morocco.

-iform *suffix see* -FORM.

IFR *abbreviation Aviation* = INSTRUMENT FLIGHT RULES.

Ig *abbreviation* immunoglobulin.

Igbo *var. of* IBO.

ig·loo *noun* (also **iglu**) **1** a dome-shaped Inuit dwelling built of snow. **2** any other dome-shaped Inuit dwelling. [Inuktitut, = house]

Ig·lu·lik /ɪgˈluːlɪk/ *noun* (also **Ig·loo·lik**) **1** a member of an Inuit people inhabiting the eastern Arctic, esp. living on Baffin Island and the Melville Peninsula. **2** the language of the Iglulik. [Inuktitut, = 'there is an igloo here']

Ig·nati·eff /ɪgˈnɒtiːef/ **George** (1913–1989), Russian-born Canadian diplomat. His long career with the Department of External Affairs included terms as ambassador to Yugoslavia 1956–58, permanent representative to NATO 1963–66, ambassador to the UN 1966–69, and president of the UN Security Council 1968–69.

Ig·na·tius /ɪgˈneɪʃəs/ **St.** (died c.107), bishop of Antioch. On his journey from Antioch to Rome, where he was martyred for his Christianity, he wrote seven letters which were influential in the early Christian Church. Feast day (in the Western Church) 17 Oct. or 17 Dec.; (in the Eastern Church) 20 Dec.

Ignatius Loyola, St. /ɪgˌneɪʃəs lɔɪˈoːlə/ (1491–1556), Spanish theologian. He founded the Society of Jesus (1534) and became its first general; his *Spiritual Exercises* (1548), an ordered scheme of meditations on the life of Christ and Christian faith, is still used in the training of Jesuits. Feast day, 31 July.

ig·ne·ous /ˈɪgniəs/ *adjective Geol.* (of rock) having solidified from lava or magma. [Latin *igneus* from *ignis* fire]

ignis fatu·us /ˌɪgnɪs ˈfatʃʊəs/ *noun* (*pl.* **ignes fatui** /ˌɪgniːz ˈfatʃuai/) **1** a phosphorescent light seen hovering or floating over marshy ground, perhaps due to the combustion of methane; a will-o'-the-wisp. **2** a delusive guiding principle, hope, aim, etc. [modern Latin, = foolish fire, because of its erratic movement]

ig·nite *verb* **1** *transitive* set fire to; cause to burn. **2** *intransitive* catch fire. **3** *transitive Chem.* heat to the point of combustion or chemical change. **4** *transitive* provoke or excite (feelings etc.). □ **ignit·able** *adjective* [Latin *ignire ignit-* from *ignis* fire]

ignit·er *noun* a person who or device which ignites something, esp. a device to set fire to an explosive or combustible.

ig·ni·tion *noun* **1 a** the action of igniting the fuel in the cylinder of an internal combustion engine. **b** the mechanism for starting this process. **2** the act or an instance of igniting or being ignited.

ig·noble *adjective* (**ig·nob·ler**, **ig·nob·lest**) **1** dishonourable. **2** of low birth, position, or reputation. □ **ig·no·bil·ity** *noun* **ig·nobly** *adverb* [French *ignoble* or Latin *ignobilis* (as IN-¹, *nobilis* noble)]

ig·no·mini·ous /ˌɪgnəˈmɪniəs/ *adjective* **1** causing or deserving ignominy. **2** humiliating (*an ignominious defeat*). □ **ig·no·mini·ous·ly** *adverb* **ig·no·mini·ous·ness** *noun*

ig·no·miny /ˈɪgnəməni, ˈɪgnəmɪni/ *noun* (*pl.* **-ies**) dishonour, disgrace. [French *ignominie* or Latin *ignominia* (as IN-¹, *nomen* name)]

ig·nor·amus /ˌɪgnəˈreɪməs, -ˈrɑːməs/ *noun* (*pl.* **ig·nor·amus·es**) an extremely ignorant person. [Latin, = we do not know: in legal use (formerly of a grand jury rejecting a bill) we take no notice of it; modern sense perhaps from a character in George Ruggle's *Ignoramus* (1615) exposing lawyers' ignorance]

ig·nor·ance /ˈɪgnərəns/ *noun* (often foll. by *of*) lack of knowledge (about a thing).

ig·nor·ant /ˈɪgnərənt/ *adjective* **1 a** lacking knowledge or experience. **b** (foll. by *of*, *in*) uninformed (about a fact or subject). **2** *informal* ill-mannered, uncouth. □ **ig·nor·ant·ly** *adverb*

ig·nore /ɪgˈnɔr/ *transitive verb* refuse to take notice of or accept; intentionally disregard. □ **ig·nor·able** *adjective* **ig·nor·er** *noun* [French *ignorer* or Latin *ignorare* not know, ignore (as IN-¹, *gno-* know)]

Igua·çu River /ˌiːgwəˈsuː/ a river of S Brazil, rising in the Serra do Mar in SE Brazil and flowing westward for 1 300 km (800 miles) to the Paraná River, which it joins at the point where the frontiers between

Brazil, Paraguay, and Argentina meet, shortly below the Iguaçu Falls, a spectacular series of waterfalls.

igua·na /ɪgˈwɒnə/ *noun* any of various large lizards of the family Iguanidae native to America, the W Indies, and the Pacific islands, having a dorsal crest and throat appendages. [Spanish from Carib *iwana*]

iguan·o·don /ɪˈgwɒnəˌdɒn/ *noun* a large extinct plant-eating dinosaur of the genus *Iguanodon*, of late Jurassic and early Cretaceous times, with forelimbs smaller than hind limbs. [IGUANA (from its resemblance to this), after *mastodon* etc.]

i.h.p. *abbreviation* indicated horsepower.

IHS *abbreviation* Jesus. [Late Latin, representing Greek IHΣ = *Iēs(ous)* Jesus: often taken as an abbreviation of various Latin words]

IJC *abbreviation* INTERNATIONAL JOINT COMMISSION.

IJssel·meer /ˌəisəlˈmer/ a shallow lake in the NW Netherlands, created in 1932 by the building of a dam across the entrance to the old Zuider Zee. The salt water of the Zuider Zee was gradually replaced by fresh water flowing in from the IJssel River and large areas of land that had been under water were reclaimed as polders.

IJssel River /ˈəisəl/ a river in the Netherlands. In part it is a distributary of the Rhine, which it leaves at Arnhem, joining the Oude IJssel a few kilometres downstream, and flows 115 km (72 miles) northward through the E Netherlands to the IJsselmeer.

ikat /ˈiːkat/ *noun* **1** a fabric made using an Indonesian technique of textile decoration in which warp or weft threads, or both, are tied at intervals and dyed before weaving. **2** this technique. [Malay, = tie, fasten]

ike·bana /ˌɪkəˈbanə/ *noun* the art of Japanese flower arrangement, with formal display according to strict rules. [Japanese, = living flowers]

Ikh·na·ton see AKHENATEN.

ikon *var. of* ICON 1, 2.

IL¹ *abbreviation* Illinois (in official postal use).

IL² *abbreviation* = INTERLEUKIN.

il- *prefix* assimilated form of IN-¹, IN-² before l.

-il *suffix* (also **-ile**) forming adjectives or nouns denoting relation (*civil*; *utensil*) or capability (*agile*). [Old French from Latin *-ilis*]

ilang-ilang *var. of* YLANG-YLANG.

ilea *pl. of* ILEUM.

Île-de-France /iːldəˈfrɑ̃s/ a region of north central France, incorporating the city of Paris.

ile·itis /ˌɪliˈaɪtɪs/ *noun Med.* **1** inflammation of the ileum. **2** = CROHN'S DISEASE.

ileos·tomy /ˌɪliˈɒstəmi/ *noun* (*pl.* **-mies**) **1** a surgical operation in which a damaged part is removed from the ileum and the cut end directed to an artificial opening in the abdominal wall. **2** the opening so created. [ILEUM + Greek *stoma* mouth]

Il·esha /ɪˈleɪʃə/ a city in SW Nigeria; pop. (est. 2002) 561,200.

ileum /ˈɪliəm/ *noun* (*pl.* **ilea** /ˈɪliə/) *Anat.* the third and last portion of the small intestine. □ **ileac** *adjective* **ileal** *adjective* (var. of ILIUM)

ileus /ˈɪliəs/ *noun Med.* any painful obstruction of the intestine, esp. of the ileum. [Latin from Greek (*e)ileos* colic]

ilex /ˈaɪleks/ *noun* **1** any tree or shrub of the genus *Ilex*, esp. the common holly. **2** the holm oak. [Latin]

ilia *pl. of* ILIUM.

iliac /ˈɪliˌak/ *adjective* of the lower body or ilium (*iliac artery*). [Late Latin *iliacus* (as ILIUM)]

Ilium /ˈɪliəm/ the alternative name for TROY, denoting esp. the Greek city built there in the 7th c. BC.

ilium /ˈɪliəm/ *noun* (*pl.* **ilia** /ˈɪliə/) **1** the bone forming the upper part of each half of the human pelvis. **2** the corresponding bone in animals. [Latin]

ilk *noun* **1** *informal* usu. *derogatory* a family, class, or set (*for John and his ilk, there is only one kind of music*). **2** (in **of that ilk**) *Scot.* of the same (name) (*Guthrie of that ilk* = of Guthrie). [Old English *ilca* same]

ILL *abbreviation* interlibrary loan.

Ill. *abbreviation* Illinois.

I'll *contraction* I will; I shall.

ill ● *adjective* **1** (usu. *predicative*; often foll. by *with*) out of health; sick (*is ill*; *was taken ill with pneumonia*; *mentally ill*). **2** (of health) unsound, disordered. **3** (of an omen, condition, etc.) unlucky, unfavourable, disastrous (*ill fortune*; *ill luck*). **4** harmful, disagreeable, objectionable (*ill effects*). **5** hostile, unkind (*ill feeling*). **6** immoral, wicked (*house of ill repute*). ● *adverb* **1** badly, wrongly, unskilfully, or inefficiently

---

Vowels: a cat ɑ arm e bed ɜr her ɜː deux ə ago ɪ sit i cosy iː feed ɒ hot ɔ pore oː no ʌ run ʊ put

(ill-matched). **2 a** imperfectly (ill-provided). **b** scarcely (can ill afford to do it). **3** unfavourably or unhappily (it would have gone ill with them). ● noun **1** injury, harm. **2** evil; the opposite of good. **3** something unfriendly, unfavourable, or injurious. □ **ill at ease** embarrassed, uneasy. **speak ill of** say something unfavourable about. [Old Norse illr, of unknown origin]

ill. abbreviation **1** illustrated. **2** illustration. **3** illustrator.

ill-advised adjective **1** acting foolishly or imprudently. **2** (of a plan etc.) not well formed or considered. □ **ill-advised·ly** adverb

ill-assort·ed adjective not well matched.

il·la·tion /ɪˈleɪʃən/ noun **1** a deduction or conclusion. **2** a thing deduced. [Latin illatio from illatus past participle of inferre INFER]

il·la·tive /ɪˈleɪtɪv, ˈɪlətɪv/ adjective **1 a** (of a word) stating or introducing an inference. **b** inferential. **2** Grammar (of a case) denoting motion into. □ **il·la·tive·ly** adverb [Latin illativus (as ILLATION)]

ill-behaved adjective having bad manners or conduct.

ill-bred adjective badly brought up, badly behaved, rude. □ **ill breeding** noun

ill-conceived adjective badly planned or conceived.

ill-consid·ered adjective = ILL-ADVISED 2.

ill-defined adjective not accurately analyzed or described (an ill-defined role).

ill-disposed adjective **1** (often foll. by towards) not friendly or pleasant; unfavourably disposed. **2** disposed to evil; malevolent.

ill effect noun (usu. in pl.) a harmful or unpleasant consequence, result, effect, etc.

il·legal ● adjective **1** not legal. **2** contrary to law. **3** Sport against or prohibited by the rules or regulations. ● noun an illegal immigrant. □ **il·legal·ity** noun (pl. **-ities**). **il·legal·ly** adverb

il·legi·ble /ɪˈledʒɪbəl/ adjective difficult or impossible to read; not legible. □ **il·legi·bil·ity** noun **il·legi·bly** adverb

il·legit·im·ate /ˌɪləˈdʒɪtəmət/ ● adjective **1** (of a child) born of parents not married to each other. **2** not authorized by law or custom; unlawful. **b** not in accordance with a rule; abnormal. **3** improper. **4** wrongly inferred. ● noun a person whose position is illegitimate, esp. by birth. □ **il·legit·im·acy** noun **il·legit·im·ate·ly** adverb

ill-equipped adjective (often foll. by to + infin.) not adequately or appropriately equipped, qualified, or prepared.

ill fame noun disrepute.

ill-fated adjective unlucky, doomed; bringing or having bad fortune (an ill-fated voyage).

ill-favoured adjective (also **ill-favored**) unattractive, displeasing, objectionable.

ill feeling noun bad feeling; animosity.

ill-fitting adjective fitting badly (an ill-fitting suit).

ill-founded adjective (of an idea etc.) not based on fact or truth; groundless.

ill-gotten adjective gained by dishonest or unlawful means.

ill health noun poor physical or mental condition.

il·lib·er·al adjective **1** intolerant, narrow-minded. **2** not generous; stingy. □ **il·lib·er·al·ity** noun (pl. **-ities**). **il·lib·er·al·ly** adverb

il·licit /ɪˈlɪsɪt/ adjective **1** unlawful, forbidden (illicit dealings). **2** secret, furtive (an illicit affair). □ **il·licit·ly** adverb **il·licit·ness** noun

il·limit·able adjective limitless, boundless. □ **il·limit·ably** adverb

ill-informed adjective inadequately or wrongly informed.

Il·li·nois /ˌɪləˈnɔɪ/ a state in the Midwest of the US; pop. (2000) 12,419,293; capital, Springfield.

il·liquid /ɪˈlɪkwɪd/ adjective (of assets) not easily converted into cash. □ **il·liquid·ity** noun

il·lit·er·ate /ɪˈlɪtərət/ ● adjective **1** unable to read or write. **2 a** having or showing little or no education. **b** ignorant in a particular field (culturally illiterate). ● noun an illiterate person. □ **il·lit·er·acy** noun

ill-judged adjective unwise; badly considered.

ill luck noun bad luck, misfortune.

ill-mannered adjective having bad manners; rude.

ill-matched adjective badly matched; unsuited.

ill-natured adjective churlish, unkind. □ **ill-natured·ly** adverb

ill·ness noun **1** a disease, ailment, or malady. **2** the state of being ill.

il·logic·al adjective devoid of or contrary to logic. □ **il·logic** noun **il·logic·al·ity** noun (pl. **-ities**). **il·logic·al·ly** adverb

ill-omened adjective inauspicious; attended by bad omens.

ill-prepared adjective badly or inadequately prepared.

ill-starred adjective unlucky; destined to failure.

ill-suited adjective **1** not suited to doing something; unsuitable. **2** inappropriate.

ill temper noun irritability, sullenness. □ **ill-tempered** adjective

ill-timed adjective done or occurring at an inappropriate or unsuitable time.

ill-treat transitive verb treat badly or cruelly; abuse. □ **ill-treatment** noun

il·lume /ɪˈluːm/ transitive verb literary light up; make bright. [shortening of ILLUMINE]

il·lumin·ance /ɪˈluːmɪnəns/ noun Physics the amount of luminous flux per unit area.

il·lumin·ant /ɪˈluːmɪnənt/ ● noun a means of illumination. ● adjective serving to illuminate.

il·lumin·ate /ɪˈluːmɪˌneɪt/ transitive verb **1** light up; make bright. **2** help to explain (a subject etc.). **3** decorate (an initial letter, a manuscript, etc.) with elaborate designs in gold, silver, or brilliant colours. **4** enlighten spiritually or intellectually. **5** decorate (buildings etc.) with lights as a sign of festivity. □ **il·lumin·at·ing** adjective **il·lumin·at·ing·ly** adverb **il·lumin·ator** noun [Latin illuminare (as IN-², lumen luminis light)]

il·lumin·ati /ɪˌluːmɪˈnɑːti, -ˈnɒti/ plural noun **1** persons claiming to possess special knowledge or enlightenment. **2** (**Illuminati**) hist. any of various intellectual movements or societies of illuminati. □ **il·lumin·ism** /ɪˈluːmɪˌnɪzəm/ noun **il·lumin·ist** /ɪˈluːmɪnɪst/ noun [pl. of Latin illuminatus or Italian illuminato past participle (as ILLUMINATE)]

il·lumin·a·tion /ɪˌluːmɪˈneɪʃən/ noun **1** the act or an instance of shedding light on something or lighting something up. **2** spiritual or intellectual enlightenment. **3 a** the decoration of a medieval manuscript with elaborate tracery or designs in gold, silver, bright colours, etc. **b** a design or illustration used in such decoration. **c** a page so decorated. **4** esp. Brit. (in pl.) coloured lights arranged in designs to decorate a street, building, etc. **5** = ILLUMINANCE.

il·lumine /ɪˈluːmɪn/ transitive verb literary **1** light up; make bright. **2** enlighten spiritually. [Old French illuminer from Latin (as ILLUMINATE)]

illus. abbreviation **1** illustration. **2** illustrated.

ill-use ● transitive verb treat unkindly or badly. ● noun (also **ill-usage**) ill-treatment. □ **ill-used** adjective

il·lu·sion /ɪˈluːʒən/ noun **1** deception, delusion. **2** a misapprehension of the true state of affairs. **3** Psych. **a** the faulty perception of an external object. **b** an instance of this. **4** a figment of the imagination. **5** = OPTICAL ILLUSION. **6** a thin and transparent kind of tulle. □ **be under no illusions** have no esp. positive expectations. **be under the illusion** (foll. by that + clause) believe mistakenly. □ **il·lu·sion·al** adjective [French from Latin illusio -onis from illudere mock (as IN-², ludere lus- play)]

il·lu·sion·ist /ɪˈluːʒənɪst/ noun a person who produces illusions, esp. a conjuror. □ **il·lu·sion·ism** noun **il·lu·sion·is·tic** /-ˈnɪstɪk/ adjective

il·lu·sive /ɪˈluːsɪv/ adjective = ILLUSORY. [medieval Latin illusivus (as ILLUSION)]

il·lu·sory /ɪˈluːzəri, -səri/ adjective **1** deceptive (esp. as regards value or content). **2** having the character of an illusion. [ecclesiastical Latin illusorius (as ILLUSION)]

illus·trate /ˈɪləˌstreɪt/ transitive verb **1 a** provide (a book, newspaper, etc.) with pictures. **b** elucidate (a description etc.) by drawings or pictures. **2** serve as an example of. **3** explain or make clear, esp. by examples. [Latin illustrare (as IN-², lustrare light up]

illus·tra·tion /ˌɪləˈstreɪʃən/ noun **1** a drawing or picture illustrating a book, magazine article, etc. **2** an example serving to elucidate. **3** the act or an instance of illustrating. □ **illus·tra·tion·al** adjective

illus·tra·tive /ˈɪləˌstreɪtɪv, ɪˈlʌstrətɪv/ adjective (often foll. by of) serving as an explanation or example.

illus·tra·tor /ˈɪləˌstreɪtər/ noun a person who makes illustrations, esp. for magazines, books, advertising copy, etc.

il·lus·tri·ous /ɪˈlʌstriəs/ adjective distinguished, renowned. □ **il·lus·tri·ous·ly** adverb **il·lus·tri·ous·ness** noun [Latin illustris (as ILLUSTRATE)]

ill will noun bad feeling; animosity.

ill wind noun an unfavourable or untoward circumstance. [with reference to the proverb it's an ill wind that blows nobody good]

ill-wisher noun a person who harbours ill will towards another.

Il·lyria /ɪˈlɪriə/ an ancient region along the east coast of the Adriatic Sea, including Dalmatia and what is now Montenegro and N Albania.

Il·lyr·ian /ɪˈlɪrɪən/ ● *adjective* **1** of or relating to ancient Illyria. **2** of the language group represented by modern Albanian. ● *noun* **1 a** a native of Illyria, esp. a member of an Indo-European people inhabiting ancient Illyria. **b** a person of Illyrian descent. **2 a** the ancient language of Illyria. **b** the language group represented by modern Albanian.

il·men·ite /ˈɪlmə,naɪt/ *noun* a black ore of titanium. [*Ilmen* mountains in the Urals]

ILO *abbreviation* International Labour Organization.

Ilo·ilo /ˌiːloˈiːloː/ a port on the south coast of the island of Panay in the Philippines; pop. (est. 2002) 378,200.

Il·orin /ɪˈlɔrɪn/ a city in W Nigeria; pop. (est. 2002) 756,400.

ILS *abbreviation Aviation* = INSTRUMENT LANDING SYSTEM.

-ily /ɪli/ *suffix* forming adverbs corresponding to adjectives in -*y* (*see* -Y[1], -LY[2]).

IM *abbreviation* intramuscular.

I'm *contraction* I am.

im- *prefix assimilated form of* IN-[1], IN-[2] before *b*, *m*, *p*.

image /ˈɪmɪdʒ/ ● *noun* **1** a representation of a person or thing in sculpture, painting, photography, etc. **2** the character or reputation of a person, organization, product, etc. as generally perceived by the public, esp. a cultivated favourable reputation. **3** an optical appearance or counterpart produced by light or other radiation from an object reflected in a mirror, refracted through a lens, etc. **4** semblance, likeness (*God created man in His own image*). **5** a person or thing that closely resembles another (*is the image of his father*). **6 a** a typical example. **b** a symbol or emblem. **7 a** a simile, metaphor, or figure of speech. **b** a spoken or written description, esp. a vivid or graphic one. **8** an idea, conception, or mental representation. **9** *Math.* a set formed by mapping from another set. ● *transitive verb* **1 a** make an image of; portray. **b** imagine or form a mental picture of. **2** reflect, mirror. **3** describe or depict vividly. **4** obtain a representation of by radar, X-rays, etc. □ **image·able** *adjective* **image·less** *adjective* **im·ager** *noun* [Old French from Latin *imago -ginis*, related to IMITATE]

image consultant *noun* a person or company that advises on the improvement of the public image of a person, company, organization, etc.

image intensifier *noun* a device used to make a brighter version of an image on a photoelectric screen.

image-maker *noun* **1** a person employed to create a public image for a politician, product, etc. **2** a carver, sculptor, etc. of images. □ **image-making** *noun*

image processing *noun* (also **image manipulation**) the analysis and manipulation of a usu. digitized image, esp. to improve its quality. □ **image processor** *noun*

im·agery /ˈɪmɪdʒri/ *noun* (*pl.* -ries) **1** figurative illustration, esp. as used by an author for particular effects. **2** pictures, photographs (*satellite imagery*). **3** mental images collectively. **4** statuary, carving.

im·agin·able /ɪˈmadʒɪnəbəl/ *adjective* that can be conceived or imagined (*the greatest difficulty imaginable*).

im·agin·al /ɪˈmadʒɪnəl/ *adjective* **1** of or an image or images. **2** *Zool.* of or pertaining to an insect imago. [Latin *imago imagin-*: see IMAGE]

im·agin·ary /ɪˈmadʒɪneri/ *adjective* **1** existing only in the imagination. **2** *Math.* being the square root of a negative quantity, and plotted graphically in a direction usu. perpendicular to the axis of real quantities (*see* REAL[1] *adjective* 9). [Latin *imaginarius* (as IMAGE)]

im·agin·a·tion /ɪˌmadʒɪˈneɪʃən/ *noun* **1 a** a mental faculty forming images or concepts of external objects not present to the senses. **b** the action or process of imagining or forming such images. **2** the ability of the mind to be creative or resourceful.

im·agin·a·tive /ɪˈmadʒɪnətɪv/ *adjective* **1** having or showing imagination. **2** given to using the imagination. **3** of or pertaining to the imagination or its use. □ **im·agin·a·tive·ly** *adverb*

im·agine /ɪˈmadʒɪn/ *transitive verb* **1 a** form a mental image or concept of. **b** picture to oneself (something non-existent or not present to the senses). **2** (often foll. by *to* + infin.) think or conceive (*imagined them to be soldiers*). **3** guess (*cannot imagine what they are doing*). **4** (often foll. by *that* + clause) suppose, be of the opinion (*I imagine you will need help*). **5** (in imperative) as an exclamation of surprise (*just imagine!*). □ **im·agin·er** *noun* [Old French *imaginer* from Latin *imaginari* (as IMAGE)]

im·agin·eer ● *noun* a person who devises and implements a new or highly imaginative concept or technology, in particular one who devises the attractions in Walt Disney theme parks. ● *transitive verb* devise and implement (such a concept). [blend of IMAGINE + ENGINEER]

im·agi·nes *pl.* of IMAGO.

im·aging *noun* **1** *Med.* the creation of images of internal organs etc. through tomography etc., used as a diagnostic tool. **2** *Psych.* the practice of formulating and using mental pictures to control pain, disease, distress, etc.

im·agin·ings *plural noun* things imagined; fancies, fantasies.

im·agism /ˈɪmə,dʒɪzəm/ *noun* a movement in early 20th-c. poetry which, in revolt against Romanticism, sought clarity of expression through the use of precise images and free verse. □ **im·agist** *noun & adjective* **im·agis·tic** /-ˈdʒɪstɪk/ *adjective* **im·agis·tic·ally** *adverb*

im·ago /ɪˈmeɪgoː/ *noun* (*pl.* **imagos** or **im·agi·nes** /ɪˈmadʒɪ,niːz/) **1** the final and fully developed stage of an insect after all metamorphoses, e.g. a butterfly or beetle. **2** *Psych.* an idealized, unconscious image of oneself or someone, esp. a parent, which influences a person's behaviour etc. [modern Latin sense of *imago* IMAGE]

imam /ɪˈmam, -mɒm/ *noun* **1** a leader of prayers in a mosque. **2** a title of various Muslim leaders, esp. of one succeeding Muhammad as leader of Shiite Islam. □ **imam·ate** /-meit/ *noun* [Arabic *'imām* leader from *'amma* precede]

Imari /ɪˈmɑri/ *noun* (*attributive*) designating a high-quality Japanese porcelain with rich decoration and delicate colouring. [a town in NW Kyushu, Japan]

IMAX /ˈaɪmaks/ *noun proprietary* a technique of widescreen cinematography in which 70mm film is shot and projected in such a way as to produce a celluloid image approximately ten times larger than that normally obtained from standard 35 mm film. [from image + *maximum*]

im·bal·ance *noun* **1** lack of balance. **2** a lack of proportion or relation between corresponding things. □ **im·bal·anced** *adjective*

im·be·cile /ˈɪmbəsɪl/ ● *noun informal* a stupid person. ● *adjective* mentally weak; stupid, idiotic. □ **im·becil·ic** /-ˈsɪlɪk/ *adjective* **im·becil·ity** /-ˈsɪlɪti/ *noun* (*pl.* -**ities**). [French *imbécil(l)e* from Latin *imbecillus* (as IN-[1], *baculum* stick) originally in sense 'without supporting staff']

imbed *var.* of EMBED.

im·bibe *verb* **1** *transitive & intransitive* drink (esp. alcoholic liquor). **2** *transitive* **a** absorb or assimilate (ideas etc.). **b** absorb (moisture, heat, etc.). □ **im·bib·er** *noun* **im·bib·ition** /ˌɪmbɪˈbɪʃən/ *noun* [Latin *imbibere* (as IN-[2], *bibere* drink)]

im·bri·cate ● *transitive & intransitive verb* /ˈɪmbrɪ,keit/ arrange (leaves, the scales of a fish, etc.), or be arranged, so as to overlap like roof tiles. ● *adjective* /ˈɪmbrɪkət/ having leaves, scales, etc. arranged in this way. □ **im·bri·ca·tion** *noun* [Latin *imbricare imbricat-* cover with roof tiles from *imbrex -icis* roof tile from *imber* shower of rain]

im·bro·glio /ɪmˈbroːlioː/ *noun* (*pl.* -**glios**) a complicated, confused, or embarrassing situation, esp. a political or interpersonal one. [Italian *imbrogliare* confuse (as EMBROIL)]

Im·bros /ˈɪmbrɒs/ a Turkish island in the NE Aegean Sea, near the entrance to the Dardanelles.

imbue /ɪmˈbjuː/ *transitive verb* (**imbues**, **imbued**, **imbu·ing**) (often foll. by *with*) **1** inspire or permeate (with feelings, opinions, or qualities). **2** saturate, soak through. **3** dye, tinge. [originally as past participle, from French *imbu* or Latin *imbutus* from *imbuere* moisten]

IMF *abbreviation* International Monetary Fund, an organization established in 1945 to promote international trade and monetary co-operation and the stabilization of exchange rates.

IMHO *abbreviation* in my humble opinion.

Im·ho·tep /ɪmˈhoːtep/ (*fl.* 27th c. BC), Egyptian architect and scholar. He is usually credited with designing the step pyramid built at Saqqara for the 3rd-dynasty pharaoh Djoser (*c.*2686–*c.*2613 BC); he was later deified in Egypt and identified with the god Asclepius in Greece.

im·ide /ˈɪmaɪd/ *noun Chem.* an organic compound containing the group (-CO.NH.CO-) formed by replacing two of the hydrogen atoms in ammonia by carbonyl groups. [originally French: arbitrary alteration of AMIDE]

im·ine /ˈɪmiːn/ *noun Chem.* a compound containing the group (-NH-) formed by replacing two of the hydrogen atoms in ammonia by other groups. [German *Imin* arbitrary alteration of *Amin* AMINE]

im·ip·ra·mine /ɪˈmɪprə,miːn/ *noun Pharm.* a tricyclic tertiary amine used to treat depression. Chem. formula $C_{19}H_{24}N_2$. [IMINE + PROPYL + AMINE]

imi·tate *transitive verb* **1** follow the example of; copy the action(s) of. **2** mimic. **3** make a copy of; reproduce. **4** be, become, or make oneself like, intentionally or unintentionally. □ **imit·able** *adjective* **imi·ta·tor** *noun* [Latin *imitari imitat-*, related to *imago* IMAGE]

imi·ta·tion ● *noun* **1** the act or an instance of imitating or being imitated (*does a good imitation of Elvis*). **2** a copy. **3** a counterfeit; something made to look like something else. **4** *Music* the repetition of a phrase etc., usu. at a different pitch, in another part or voice. ● *adjective* made in imitation of a real or genuine article or substance (*imitation leather*).

imi·ta·tive *adjective* **1** imitating; following a model or example. **2** following a model or example without any attempt at originality. **3** of a word: **a** that reproduces a natural sound, e.g. *fizz*. **b** whose sound is thought to correspond to the appearance etc. of the object or action described, e.g. *blob*. □ **imi·ta·tiv·ely** *adverb*

im·mac·u·late /ɪˈmakjʊlət/ *adjective* **1** pure, spotless; perfectly clean and tidy. **2** perfectly or extremely well executed (*an immaculate performance*). **3** free from moral stain or fault; innocent. **4** *Biol.* not spotted. □ **im·mac·u·lacy** *noun* **im·mac·u·late·ly** *adverb* **im·mac·u·late·ness** *noun* [Latin *immaculatus* (as IN-¹, *maculatus* from *macula* spot)]

Immaculate Conception *noun Catholicism* **1** the doctrine that God preserved the Virgin Mary from the taint of original sin from the moment she was conceived. **2** 8 Dec., the feast of the Immaculate Conception.

im·ma·nent /ˈɪmənənt/ *adjective* **1** (often foll. by *in*) naturally present; indwelling, inherent. **2** (of the supreme being) permanently pervading the universe (*opp.* TRANSCENDENT 4). **3** *Philos.* (of an action) performed entirely within the mind of the subject, and producing no external effect. □ **im·ma·nence** *noun* **im·ma·nent·ism** *noun* **im·ma·nent·ist** *noun* [Late Latin *immanēre* (as IN-², *manēre* remain)]

Im·man·uel *var. of* EMMANUEL.

im·ma·te·ri·al *adjective* **1** of no essential consequence; unimportant, irrelevant. **2** not material; incorporeal, without physical form or substance. □ **im·ma·te·ri·al·ity** *noun*

im·ma·te·ri·al·ism *noun* the doctrine that all things exist only as ideas or perceptions of a mind, that matter has no objective existence. □ **im·ma·te·ri·al·ist** *noun*

im·ma·ture *adjective* **1 a** (of cells, animals, etc.) not mature or fully developed. **b** (of plants, fruit, etc.) unripe. **2** lacking emotional or intellectual development. □ **im·ma·ture·ly** *adverb* **im·ma·tur·ity** *noun*

im·meas·ur·able *adjective* not measurable; immense. □ **im·meas·ur·abil·ity** *noun* **im·meas·ur·ably** *adverb*

im·me·di·ate *adjective* **1** occurring or done at once or without delay (*an immediate reply*). **2 a** nearest in time or space (*the immediate future; the immediate vicinity*). **b** (of family) designating those of closest relation, usu. parents, children, spouses, and siblings. **3** most pressing or urgent; of current concern (*our immediate concern was to get him to the hospital*). **4** (of a thing or action in relation to another) having direct effect; not separated by an intervening medium or agency (*the immediate cause of death*). **5** (of knowledge, reactions, etc.) intuitive, gained or exhibited without reasoning. □ **im·me·di·acy** *noun* (*pl.* -acies). **im·me·di·ate·ness** *noun* [French *immédiat* or Late Latin *immediatus* (as IN-¹, MEDIATE)]

im·me·di·ate·ly ● *adverb* **1** instantly, without pause or delay (*answered the phone immediately*). **2** without intermediary; in direct connection or relation (*who is immediately responsible?*). **3** with no object, distance, time, etc. intervening (*the door immediately in front of you; the years immediately following the war*). ● *conjunction esp. Brit.* as soon as.

im·me·mo·ri·al /ˌɪməˈmɔːriəl/ *adjective* **1** ancient beyond memory or record. **2** very old or long established. □ **im·me·mo·ri·al·ly** *adverb*

im·mense *adjective* immeasurably large or great; huge. □ **im·mens·ity** *noun* (*pl.* -ities) [French from Latin *immensus* immeasurable (as IN-¹, *mensus* past participle of *metiri* measure)]

im·mense·ly *adverb* **1** very much (*enjoyed myself immensely*). **2** to an immense degree.

im·merse *transitive verb* **1 a** (often foll. by *in*) dip, plunge, or submerge in a liquid. **b** cause (a person) to be completely under water. **2** (often *reflexive* or in *passive*; often foll. by *in*) absorb or involve deeply in a particular activity or condition. [Latin *immergere* (as IN-², *mergere* mers-dip)]

im·mer·sion *noun* **1** *esp. N Amer.* **a** (often *attributive*) a method of teaching a foreign language by the exclusive use of that language, usu. at a special school, in a special class, etc. **b** a class, course, or system of study based on the immersion method. **2 a** the act or an instance of immersing. **b** the process of being immersed. **3** baptism by immersing the whole person in water. **4** mental absorption in an activity etc. **5** *Astronomy* the disappearance of a celestial body behind another or in its shadow, as in an eclipse or occultation.

immersion heater *noun esp. Brit.* an electric heater designed for direct immersion in a liquid to be heated, esp. as a fixture in a hot water heater.

immersion suit *noun* a waterproof suit designed to give the wearer buoyancy and insulation when in the water.

im·mi·grant ● *noun* **1** a person who immigrates. **2 a** an animal or plant that has migrated into a given area, esp. one now living there. **b** an animal (esp. a bird) that regularly or occasionally migrates into a given area. ● *adjective* of, pertaining to, or concerning immigrants or immigration.

im·mi·grate *intransitive verb* **1** come as a permanent resident to a country other than one's native land. **2** (of an animal or plant) migrate to a different geographical region, esp. when this leads to continuous occupation of the area by the species. [Latin *immigrare* (as IN-², MIGRATE)]

im·mi·gra·tion /ˌɪmɪˈɡreɪʃən/ *noun* **1 a** the process of coming to live in another country permanently. **b** an instance of this. **2** (often *attributive*) the process of authorizing or monitoring immigration (*immigration officer*). **3** (**Immigration**) the government ministry in charge of regulating immigration. **4** a control point at an airport, border, etc. where the documentation of people wanting to enter a country is checked.

immigration building *noun* (also **immigration hall**, **immigration shed**) *Cdn hist.* a building used to shelter new immigrants to the country until they found their own homes.

im·mi·nent /ˈɪmɪnənt/ *adjective* **1** (of an event, esp. danger) impending; about to happen. **2** *archaic* overhanging. □ **im·mi·nence** *noun* **im·mi·nent·ly** *adverb* [Latin *imminēre* imminent- overhang, project]

im·mis·ci·ble /ɪˈmɪsɪbəl/ *adjective* (often foll. by *with*) unable to be mixed (*oil and water are immiscible*). □ **im·mis·ci·bil·ity** /-ˈbɪlɪti/ *noun* [Late Latin *immiscibilis* (as IN-¹, MISCIBLE)]

im·mis·er·a·tion *noun* economic impoverishment. [translation of German *Verelendung*]

im·mo·bile /ɪˈmoʊbaɪl, -bəl/ *adjective* **1** not moving. **2** not able to move or be moved. □ **im·mo·bil·ity** *noun*

im·mo·bil·ize *transitive verb* (also esp. *Brit.* -ise) **1** make or keep immobile. **2** restrict the free movement of. **3** make (esp. a vehicle or troops) incapable of being moved. **4** keep (a limb or patient) restricted in movement for healing purposes. □ **im·mo·bil·iz·a·tion** *noun* **im·mo·bil·iz·er** *noun*

im·mod·er·ate *adjective* excessive; lacking moderation. □ **im·mod·er·ate·ly** *adverb* **im·mod·er·ate·ness** *noun* **im·mod·er·a·tion** *noun*

im·modest *adjective* **1** lacking modesty. **2** lacking due decency (*immodest dress*). □ **im·modest·ly** *adverb* **im·modesty** *noun*

im·mo·late /ˈɪməˌleɪt/ *transitive verb* kill or offer as a sacrifice, esp. by burning. □ **im·mo·la·tion** *noun* **im·mo·la·tor** *noun* [Latin *immolare* sprinkle with sacrificial meal (as IN-², *mola* MEAL²)]

im·moral *adjective* **1** not conforming to accepted standards of morality (*compare* AMORAL). **2** morally wrong, esp. in sexual matters. **3** depraved, dissolute. □ **im·moral·ist** *noun* **im·moral·ity** *noun* (*pl.* -ities). **im·moral·ly** *adverb*

im·mor·tal ● *adjective* **1 a** living forever; not mortal. **b** divine. **2** unfading, incorruptible. **3** likely or worthy to be famous for all time. ● *noun* **1 a** an immortal being. **b** (in *pl.*) the gods of antiquity. **2** a person (esp. an author) of enduring fame. □ **im·mor·tal·ity** *noun* **im·mor·tal·ize** *transitive verb* (also esp. *Brit.* -ise). **im·mor·tal·iz·a·tion** *noun* **im·mor·tal·ly** *adverb*

im·mor·telle /ˌɪmɔːrˈtel/ *noun* a flower of the daisy family with papery texture, retaining its shape and colour after being dried, esp. a helichrysum. [French, fem. of *immortel* IMMORTAL]

im·mov·able /ɪˈmuːvəbəl/ ● *adjective* **1** unable to be moved. **2** steadfast, unyielding. **3** emotionless, impassive. **4** fixed, not subject to change (*immovable law*). **5** motionless, stationary. **6** *Law* (of property) permanent, not liable to be removed, e.g. land, houses, etc. ● *noun* (in *pl.*) *Law* immovable property. □ **im·mov·ably** *adverb*

immovable feast *noun* a religious feast day that occurs on the same date each year.

im·mune /ɪˈmjuːn/ *adjective* **1 a** (often foll. by *against, from, to*) *Biol.* resistant to a particular infection, toxin, etc., owing to the presence of specific antibodies or sensitized white blood cells. **b** of, pertaining to, or producing immunity (*immune mechanism*). **2** (foll. by *from, to*) free or exempt from or not subject to (some undesirable factor or circumstance) (*immune from prosecution; immune to criticism*). [Latin *immunis* exempt from public service or charge (as IN-¹, *munis* ready for service): sense 1 from French *immun*]

immune response *noun* the reaction of the body to the introduction into it of an antigen.

immune system *noun* those structures and functions of an organism responsible for maintaining immunity.

im·mun·ity /ɪˈmjuːnɪti/ *noun* (pl. **-ities**) **1** *Biol.* the ability of an organism to resist a specific infection, toxin, etc. **2** freedom or exemption from an obligation, penalty, or unfavourable circumstance. **3** ability to be unaffected by something (*immunity to virulent ideas*).

im·mun·ize /ˈɪmjʊˌnaɪz/ *transitive verb* (also esp. *Brit.* **-ise**) make immune, esp. to infection, usu. by inoculation. □ **im·mun·iz·a·tion** /-ˈzeɪʃən/ *noun* (also esp. *Brit.* **-isation**) **im·mun·iz·er** *noun*

immuno- /ˈɪmjuːnoː, ɪˈmjuːnoː/ *combining form* immune, immunity.

immuno·assay /ˌɪmjʊnoːˈasei, ɪˌmjuːnoː-/ *noun Biochem.* the determination of the presence or quantity of a substance, esp. a protein, through its properties as an antigen or antibody.

immuno·chem·istry /ˌɪmjʊnoːˈkemɪstri, ɪˌmjuːnoː-/ *noun* **1** the chemical study of immune systems. **2** the use of specific immune reactions in the study of biological molecules.

immuno·com·pro·mised /ˌɪmjʊnoːˈkɒmprəmaɪzd, ɪˌmjuːnoː-/ *adjective Med.* having an impaired immune system.

immuno·defi·ciency /ˌɪmjʊːnoːdəˈfɪʃənsi, ɪˌmjuːnoː-/ *noun* (pl. **-cies**) a reduction in a person's normal immune defences. □ **immuno·defi·cient** *adjective*

immuno·fluor·es·cence /ˌɪmjʊnoːfləˈresəns, ɪˌmjuːnoː-/ *noun* a technique for determining the location of an antigen or antibody in tissues by reaction with an antibody or antigen labelled with a fluorescent dye. □ **immuno·fluor·es·cent** *adjective*

immuno·genic /ˌɪmjʊnoːˈdʒenɪk, ɪˌmjuːnoː-/ *adjective Biochem.* of, relating to, or possessing the ability to elicit an immune response. □ **immuno·gen·icity** /-dʒəˈnɪsɪti/ *noun*

immuno·globu·lin /ˌɪmjʊnoːˈglɒbjʊlɪn, ɪˌmjuːnoː-/ *noun Biochem.* any of a group of structurally related proteins which function as antibodies. Abbr.: **Ig**.

immun·ol·ogy /ˌɪmjʊˈnɒlədʒi/ *noun* (pl. **-gies**) the scientific study of resistance to infection in humans and animals. □ **immuno·logic** /-nəˈlɒdʒɪk/ *adjective* **immuno·logic·al** /-nəˈlɒdʒɪkəl/ *adjective* **immuno·logic·al·ly** /-nəˈlɒdʒɪkli/ *adverb* **immun·ol·o·gist** *noun*

immuno·sup·pressed /ˌɪmjʊnoːsəˈprest, ɪˌmjuːnoː-/ *adjective* (of an individual) rendered partially or completely unable to react immunologically.

immuno·sup·pres·sion /ˌɪmjʊnoːsəˈpreʃən, ɪˌmjuːnoː-/ *noun Biochem.* the partial or complete suppression of the immune response of an individual, esp. to maintain the survival of an organ after a transplant operation. □ **immuno·sup·pres·sant** *noun*

immuno·sup·pres·sive /ˌɪmjʊnoːsəˈpresɪv, ɪˌmjuːnoː-/ ● *adjective* partially or completely suppressing the immune response of an individual. ● *noun* an immunosuppressive drug.

immuno·ther·apy /ˌɪmjʊnoːˈθerəpi, ɪˌmjuːnoː-/ *noun* (pl. **-apies**) *Med.* the prevention or treatment of disease with substances that stimulate the immune response. □ **immuno·thera·peut·ic** /-ˈpjuːtɪk/ *adjective*

im·mure /ɪˈmjʊr/ *transitive verb* **1 a** enclose within walls; imprison. **b** enclose, surround, confine. **2** *reflexive* shut oneself away. □ **im·mure·ment** *noun* [French *emmurer* or medieval Latin *immurare* (as IN-², *murus* wall)]

im·mut·able /ɪˈmjuːtəbəl/ *adjective* **1** unchangeable. **2** not subject to variation in different cases. □ **im·mut·abil·ity** *noun* **im·mut·ably** *adverb*

i-mode *noun* a technology that allows data to be transferred to and from Internet sites via mobile phones. [from I² (referring to the user's ability to interact directly with the Internet) + MODE]

imp *noun* **1** a mischievous child. **2** a small mischievous devil or sprite. [Old English *impa, impe* young shoot, scion, *impian* graft: ultimately from Greek *emphutos* implanted, past participle of *emphuō*]

im·pact ● *noun* **1** (often foll. by *on, against*) the action of one body coming forcibly into contact with another. **2** an effect or influence, esp. when strong. ● *transitive verb* **1** *intransitive* (often foll. by *on, against,* etc.) come forcibly into contact with a usu. larger body or surface. **2 a** *intransitive* (often foll. by *on*) have an impact. **b** *transitive* have an impact on (*how are the cuts to welfare impacting low-income families?*) ¶ Some people object to these uses of *impact*, but they are well established in both spoken and written English and are acceptable. However, the use of 'impact' may sound jargony and lead to imprecise sentences such as 'The marathon will impact the reliability of our services' when what is meant is 'The marathon will cause delays'. **3** (often foll. by *in, into*) press closely or fix firmly. □ **im·pact·ful** *adjective* **im·pac·tion** *noun* **im·pact·or** *noun* [Latin *impact-* part. stem of *impingere* IMPINGE]

impact crater *noun* a crater or hollow supposedly produced by the impact of a meteorite.

im·pact·ed *adjective* **1 a** (of a tooth) wedged between another tooth and the jaw. **b** (of a fractured bone) with the parts crushed together. **c** (of feces) lodged in the intestine. **2 a** (of an area) overcrowded, esp. so as to put severe pressures on public services, etc. **b** pressed closely in, firmly fixed.

impact statement *noun* a formal written account of how a person, place, etc. has been or will be affected by a specific incident, process etc. (*victim impact statement; environmental impact statement*).

im·pair *transitive verb* damage or weaken. □ **im·pair·ment** *noun* [Old French *empeirier* (as IN-², Late Latin *pejorare* from Latin *pejor* worse)]

im·paired *adjective* **1** *Cdn* (of driving or the driver of a car, boat, snowmobile, etc.) adversely affected by alcohol or narcotics, specifically for legal purposes, having a blood alcohol level greater than .08. **2** (usu. in *combination*) disabled, handicapped (*hearing impaired*). **3** that has been impaired.

im·pala /ɪmˈpalə, -pɒl-/ *noun* (pl. same) a medium-sized reddish-brown grazing antelope, *Aepyceros melampus*, of southern and eastern African savannah, the male of which has lyre-shaped horns. [Zulu]

im·pale *transitive verb* **1** (foll. by *on, upon, with*) transfix or pierce with a sharp instrument. **2** *Heraldry* combine (two coats of arms) by placing them side by side on one shield separated by a vertical line down the middle. □ **im·pale·ment** *noun* **im·paler** *noun* [French *empaler* or medieval Latin *impalare* (as IN-², *palus* stake)]

im·palp·able /ɪmˈpalpəbəl/ *adjective* **1** not easily grasped by the mind; intangible. **2** imperceptible to the touch. □ **im·palp·abil·ity** /-ˈbɪlɪti/ *noun* **im·palp·ably** *adverb*

im·panel *var. of* EMPANEL.

im·part *transitive verb* (often foll. by *to*) **1** communicate (news etc.). **2** bestow (a quality). [Old French *impartir* from Latin *impartire* (as IN-², *pars* part)]

im·par·tial *adjective* treating all sides in a dispute etc. equally; unprejudiced, fair. □ **im·par·tial·ity** *noun* **im·par·tial·ly** *adverb*

im·pass·able *adjective* that cannot be traversed. □ **im·pass·abil·ity** *noun* **im·pass·ably** *adverb*

im·passe /ˈɪmpɑs/ *noun* a position from which progress is impossible; deadlock. [French (as IN-¹, *passer* PASS¹)]

im·pas·sible *adjective* (in Christian theology) not subject to suffering. □ **im·pas·si·bil·ity** *noun* ¶ Do not confuse with *impassable*.

im·pas·sioned *adjective* deeply felt; ardent (*an impassioned plea*).

im·pas·sive *adjective* not feeling or showing emotion. □ **im·pas·sive·ly** *adverb* **im·pas·siv·ity** *noun*

im·pasto /ɪmˈpɑstoː/ *noun Art* **1 a** the process of laying on paint thickly. **b** the paint so applied. **2** this technique of painting. □ **im·pastoed** *adjective* [Italian *impastare* (as IN-², *pastare* paste)]

im·patiens /ɪmˈpeɪʃəns, -ɒnz/ *noun* any plant of the genus *Impatiens*, including busy Lizzie and touch-me-not. [modern Latin from IMPATIENT]

im·patient *adjective* **1 a** (often foll. by *at, with*) lacking patience or tolerance. **b** (of an action) showing a lack of patience. **2** (often foll. by *for,* or *to* + infin.) restlessly eager. **3** (foll. by *of*) intolerant. □ **im·pa·tience** *noun* **im·patient·ly** *adverb*

im·peach *transitive verb* **1** esp. *US* charge (the holder of a public office) with misconduct. **2** *Brit.* charge with a crime against the state, esp. treason. **3** call in question, disparage (a person's integrity etc.). □ **im·peach·able** *adjective* **im·peach·ment** *noun* [Old French *empecher* impede, from Late Latin *impedicare* entangle (as IN-², *pedica* fetter from *pes pedis* foot)]

im·pec·cable *adjective* **1** (of behaviour, performance, etc.) faultless, exemplary. **2** (of clothing, grooming, accommodations, etc.) flawlessly clean and tidy. □ **im·pec·ca·bil·ity** *noun* **im·pec·cably** *adverb* [Latin *impeccabilis* (as IN-¹, *peccare* sin)]

im·pecu·ni·ous /ˌɪmpɪˈkjuːniəs/ *adjective* having little or no money. □ **im·pecu·ni·os·ity** /-ˈɒsɪti/ *noun* **im·pecu·ni·ous·ly** *adverb* **im·pecu·ni·ous·ness** *noun* [IN-¹ + obsolete *pecunious* having money, from Latin *pecuniosus* from *pecunia* money from *pecu* cattle]

im·ped·ance /ɪmˈpiːdəns/ *noun* **1** *Electricity* the total effective resistance of an electric circuit etc. to alternating current, arising from ohmic resistance and reactance. **2** an analogous mechanical property. [IMPEDE + -ANCE]

im·pede /ɪmˈpiːd/ *transitive verb* retard by obstructing; hinder. [Latin *impedire* shackle the feet of (as IN-², *pes* foot)]

im·pedi·ment /ɪmˈpedəmənt/ *noun* **1** a hindrance or obstruction. **2** a defect in speech, e.g. a lisp or stammer. **3** *Law* an obstruction, usu. closeness of blood or affinity, to the making of a marriage contract. □ **im·pedi·ment·al** /-'mentəl/ *adjective* [Latin *impedimentum* (as IMPEDE)]

im·pedi·menta /ɪm,pedə'mentə/ *plural noun* equipment for an expedition, esp. when considered as bulky or an encumbrance. [Latin, pl. of *impedimentum*: see IMPEDIMENT]

impel *transitive verb* (**im·pelled**, **im·pel·ling**) **1** drive, force, or urge into action. **2** drive forward; propel. [Latin *impellere* (as IN-², *pellere* puls-drive)]

im·pel·ler *noun* **1** a person who or thing which impels. **2** the rotating part of a machine designed to move a fluid by rotation, as a centrifugal pump or a compressor.

im·pend *intransitive verb* be about to happen. □ **im·pend·ing** *adjective* [Latin *impendēre* (as IN-², *pendēre* hang)]

im·pene·trable /ɪm'penətrəbəl/ *adjective* **1 a** that cannot be penetrated, pierced or entered. **b** that cannot be seen through (*impenetrable fog*). **2** inscrutable, unfathomable; impossible to understand. **3** inaccessible to ideas, influences, etc. **4** *Physics* (of matter) having the property such that a body is incapable of occupying the same place as another body at the same time. □ **im·pene·tra·bil·ity** /-'bɪlɪti/ *noun* **im·pene·trably** *adverb*

im·peni·tent /ɪm'penɪtənt/ *adjective* not repentant or penitent. □ **im·peni·tence** *noun* **im·peni·tent·ly** *adverb* [ecclesiastical Latin *impaenitens* (as IN-¹, PENITENT)]

im·pera·tive /ɪm'perətɪv/ ● *adjective* **1** urgent. **2** obligatory. **3** commanding, peremptory (*an imperative tone of voice*). **4** *Grammar* (of a mood) expressing a command (e.g. *wait!*). ● *noun* **1** *Grammar* **a** the imperative mood. **b** a word, form, etc. in the imperative mood. **2** a command. **3** an essential or urgent thing (*a moral imperative*). □ **im·pera·tive·ly** *adverb* **im·pera·tive·ness** *noun* [Late Latin *imperativus* from *imperare* command (as IN-², *parare* make ready)]

im·pera·tor /,ɪmpə'rɑːtɔr, -'reɪ-, -tər/ *noun Rom. Hist.* commander (a title conferred under the Republic on a victorious general and under the Empire on the emperor). □ **im·pera·tor·ial** /ɪm,perə'tɔriəl/ *adjective* [Latin (as IMPERATIVE)]

im·per·cep·tible /,ɪmpər'septəbəl/ *adjective* **1** that cannot be perceived. **2** very slight, gradual, or subtle. □ **im·per·cep·ti·bil·ity** /-'bɪlɪti/ *noun* **im·per·cep·tibly** *adverb*

im·per·cipi·ent /,ɪmpər'sɪpiənt/ *adjective* lacking in perception. □ **im·per·cipi·ence** *noun*

im·per·fect ● *adjective* **1** not fully formed or done; faulty, incomplete. **2** *Grammar* (of a tense) denoting a (usu. past) action in progress but not completed at the time in question (e.g. *they were singing*). **3** *Music* (of a cadence) ending on the dominant chord. **4** *Bot.* (of a flower) lacking some normal part, esp. functional stamens or pistils. **5** *Law* not binding. ● *noun* **1** the imperfect tense. **2** a word, form, etc. in the imperfect. □ **im·per·fect·ly** *adverb*

im·per·fec·tion *noun* **1** incompleteness. **2 a** faultiness. **b** a fault or blemish.

im·per·fec·tive *Grammar* ● *adjective* (of a verb aspect etc.) expressing an action without reference to its completion (*opp.* PERFECTIVE). ● *noun* an imperfective aspect or form of a verb.

imperfect rhyme *noun* a rhyme in which the final consonants of stressed syllables agree but the vowel sounds do not match (e.g. *love* and *move*).

im·per·for·ate /ɪm'pɜrfərət/ *adjective* **1** not perforated. **2** *Anat.* lacking the normal opening. **3** (of a postage stamp) lacking perforations.

im·per·ial /ɪm'pɪriəl/ ● *adjective* **1** of or characteristic of an empire or comparable sovereign state. **2 a** of or characteristic of an emperor or empress. **b** supreme in authority. **c** majestic, august. **3** (of non-metric weights and measures) used or formerly used by statute in the UK and other Commonwealth jurisdictions (*imperial gallon*). **4** designating any of various products or commodities of a certain (esp. great) size or quality. ● *noun* **1** a former size of paper, 762 × 559 mm (30 × 22 inches). **2** a small pointed beard growing below the lower lip (associated with Napoleon III of France). □ **im·per·ial·ly** *adverb* [Old French from Latin *imperialis* from *imperium* command, authority]

imperial gallon *noun* = GALLON 1a.

im·per·ial·ism *noun* **1** an imperial rule or system. **2** usu. *derogatory* a policy of acquiring dependent territories or extending a country's influence over less developed countries through trade, diplomacy, etc. **3** the domination or attempted domination of another country's economic, political, or cultural institutions, without actually seizing

governmental control. **4** advocacy or support for imperial interests. □ **im·per·ial·ize** *transitive verb* (also esp. *Brit.* **-ise**).

im·per·ial·ist ● *noun* usu. *derogatory* an advocate or agent of imperial rule or of imperialism. ● *adjective* of or relating to imperialism or imperialists. □ **im·per·ial·is·tic** *adjective* **im·per·ial·is·tic·ally** *adverb*

Imperial Order Daughters of the Empire *noun* a Canadian women's organization founded in 1900 to promote British institutions in Canada, but more recently focusing on community affairs and supporting educational, cultural, and social causes in Canada.

imperial preference *noun* a system of tariff concessions granted by members of the Commonwealth (or formerly British Empire) to one another.

imperial roll *noun* (in Vietnamese cuisine) a large deep-fried spring roll with a stuffing of meat, fish, vegetables etc. in a rice paper wrapper.

im·peril *transitive verb* (**im·perilled**, **im·peril·ling**; esp. *US* **im·periled**, **im·peril·ing**) bring or put into danger.

im·peri·ous /ɪm'pɪriəs/ *adjective* **1** overbearing, domineering, expecting obedience. **2** urgent, imperative. □ **im·peri·ous·ly** *adverb* **im·peri·ous·ness** *noun* [Latin *imperiosus* from *imperium* command, authority]

im·perish·able *adjective* that cannot perish. □ **im·perish·ably** *adverb*

im·per·ium /ɪm'pɪriəm/ *noun* **1** absolute power or authority. **2** empire; sphere of control. [Latin, = command, authority]

im·perma·nent *adjective* not permanent; transient. □ **im·perma·nence** *noun* **im·perma·nent·ly** *adverb*

im·perme·able /ɪm'pɜrmiəbəl/ *adjective* **1** that cannot be penetrated. **2** *Physics* that does not permit the passage of fluids. □ **im·perme·abil·ity** *noun* [French *imperméable* or Late Latin *impermeabilis* (as IN-¹, PERMEABLE)]

im·permis·sible *adjective* not allowable. □ **im·permis·si·bil·ity** *noun*

im·person·al *adjective* **1** not influenced by, showing or involving human emotions (*a vast impersonal organization*). **2** having no personal reference; objective (*an impersonal assessment*). **3** having no personality; not existing as a person (*an impersonal deity*). **4** *Grammar* **a** (of a verb) used only with a formal subject (usu. *it*) and expressing an action not attributable to a definite subject (e.g. *it is snowing*). **b** (of a pronoun) = INDEFINITE 3. □ **im·person·al·ity** *noun* **im·person·al·ly** *adverb* [Late Latin *impersonalis* (as IN-¹, PERSONAL)]

im·person·ate *transitive verb* **1** pretend to be (another person) in order to deceive others (*impersonated a police officer*). **2** mimic the speech, behaviour, etc. of (another person) in order to entertain others. □ **im·person·a·tion** *noun* **im·person·ator** *noun* [IN-² + Latin *persona* PERSON]

im·pertin·ent /ɪm'pɜrtɪnənt/ *adjective* **1** rude or insolent; lacking proper respect. **2** esp. *Law* irrelevant, intrusive. □ **im·pertin·ence** *noun* **im·pertin·ent·ly** *adverb*

im·per·turb·able /,ɪmpər'tɜrbəbəl/ *adjective* not excitable; calm. □ **im·per·turb·abil·ity** /-'bɪlɪti/ *noun* **im·per·turb·ably** *adverb*

im·pervi·ous /ɪm'pɜrviəs/ *adjective* (usu. foll. by *to*) **1** not responsive (to an argument, outside influence, etc.). **2** not allowing water, gas, etc. to pass through. **3** able to withstand wear and tear; resistant. □ **im·pervi·ous·ness** *noun* [Latin *impervius* (as IN-¹, PERVIOUS)]

im·pe·tigo /,ɪmpə'taɪgo/ *noun* a contagious bacterial skin infection forming pustules and yellow crusty sores. [Latin *impetigo -ginis* from *impetere* assail]

im·petu·ous /ɪm'petʃuəs/ *adjective* **1** acting or done rashly or with sudden energy. **2** moving forcefully or rapidly. □ **im·petu·os·ity** /-'ɒsɪti/ *noun* **im·petu·ous·ly** *adverb* **im·petu·ous·ness** *noun* [Old French *impetueux* from Late Latin *impetuosus* (as IMPETUS)]

im·petus /'ɪmpɪtəs/ *noun* **1** the force or energy with which a body moves. **2** a driving force or impulse. [Latin, = assault, force, from *impetere* assail (as IN-², *petere* seek)]

Im·phal /'ɪmfəl, ɪm'fɒl/ the capital of the state of Manipur in the far northeast of India, lying close to the border with Burma (Myanmar); pop. (2001) 217,300. It was the scene of an important victory in 1944 by Anglo-Indian forces over the Japanese.

impi /'ɪmpi/ *noun* (pl. **impis**) esp. *hist.* a body of Zulu warriors or armed tribesmen. [Zulu, = regiment, armed band]

im·piety /ɪm'paɪəti/ *noun* (pl. **-pieties**) **1** a lack of piety or reverence. **2** an act etc. showing this.

im·pinge /ɪm'pɪndʒ/ *transitive verb* (usu. foll. by *on, upon*) **1** make an impact; have an effect. **2** encroach. **3** strike, come into forcible contact;

uː m**oo**d   ai m**y**   əi p**i**pe   au br**ow**n   ʌu h**ou**se   ei d**ay**   ɔi b**oy**   ã fr**an**glais   ā C**a**nadien   ɔ̃ Br**ay**on   (*see over for consonants*)

collide. □ **im·pinge·ment** *noun* [Latin *impingere* drive (a thing) at (as IN-², *pangere* fix, drive)]

im·pious /ˈɪmpɪəs/ *adjective* **1** not pious; lacking reverence for God or a god. **2** wicked, profane. □ **im·pious·ly** *adverb* **im·pious·ness** *noun*

imp·ish *adjective* of or like an imp; mischievous. □ **imp·ish·ly** *adverb* **imp·ish·ness** *noun*

im·plac·able /ɪmˈplakəbəl/ *adjective* **1** that cannot be appeased or placated. **2** unstoppable, inexorable. □ **im·plac·abil·ity** /-ˈbɪlɪti/ *noun* **im·plac·ably** *adverb* [ultimately from Latin *placare* appease]

im·plant ● *verb* **1** *transitive* (often foll. by *in*) insert or fix. **2** *transitive* (often foll. by *in*) instill (a principle, idea, etc.) in a person's mind. **3** *transitive* plant, set in the ground. **4** *Med.* **a** *transitive* insert (tissue, a substance, or an artificial object) in a living body. **b** *intransitive* (of a fertilized ovum) become attached to the wall of the uterus. ● *noun* **1** a thing implanted. **2** a thing implanted or grafted into the body, e.g. a piece of tissue, hair, or a capsule containing material for radium therapy. □ **im·plant·a·tion** *noun*

im·plaus·ible /ɪmˈplɔzəbəl/ *adjective* not plausible. □ **im·plaus·ibil·ity** *noun* **im·plaus·ibly** *adverb*

im·ple·ment ● *noun* /ˈɪmpləmənt/ **1** a tool, instrument, or utensil. **2** a piece of farm machinery, e.g. a plow, manure spreader, combine, etc. (also *attributive*: *implement shed*). **3** (in *pl.*) equipment; articles of furniture, dress, etc. **4** an agent, channel (*an implement for change*). ● *transitive verb* /ˈɪmpləˌment/ **1** put (a decision, plan, etc.) into effect. **2** fulfill (an undertaking). □ **im·ple·ment·able** *adjective* **im·ple·men·ta·tion** *noun* **im·ple·ment·er** *noun* [medieval Latin *implementa* (pl.) from *implēre* employ (as IN-², Latin *plēre plet-* fill)]

im·pli·cate /ˈɪmplɪˌkeɪt/ *transitive verb* **1** (often foll. by *in*) show (a person or thing) to be concerned or involved (in a charge, crime, etc.). **2** (in *passive*; often foll. by *in*) be affected or involved. [Latin *implicatus* past participle of *implicare* (as IN-², *plicare*, *plicat-* or *plicit-* fold)]

im·pli·ca·tion /ˌɪmplɪˈkeɪʃən/ *noun* **1** what is involved in or implied by something else. **2** the act of implicating or implying. □ **by implication** by what is implied or suggested rather than by formal expression.

im·plicit /ɪmˈplɪsɪt/ *adjective* **1** implied though not plainly expressed. **2** (often foll. by *in*) essentially or very closely connected with; always to be found in. **3** absolute, unquestioning, unreserved (*implicit obedience*). **4** *Math.* (of a function) not expressed directly in terms of independent variables. □ **im·plicit·ly** *adverb* **im·plicit·ness** *noun* [French *implicite* or Latin *implicitus* (as IMPLICATE)]

im·plode *verb* **1** *intransitive & transitive* burst or cause to burst inwards. **2** *intransitive* collapse or disintegrate internally (*factors which caused the Soviet Union to implode*). □ **im·plo·sion** *noun* **im·plo·sive** *adjective* [IN-² + Latin *-plodere*, after EXPLODE]

im·plore *verb* **1** *transitive* (often foll. by *to* + infin.) entreat (a person). **2** *transitive* beg earnestly for (help, forgiveness, etc.). **3** *intransitive* utter entreaties; supplicate. □ **im·plor·ing·ly** *adverb* [French *implorer* or Latin *implorare* invoke with tears (as IN-², *plorare* weep)]

im·ply *transitive verb* (**-plies**, **-plied**) **1** (often foll. by *that* + clause) strongly suggest the truth or existence of (a thing not expressly asserted). ¶ See Usage Note at INFER. **2** involve as a necessary consequence. **3** insinuate, hint (*what are you implying?*). **4** (of a word etc.) signify. □ **im·plied** *adjective* **im·plied·ly** *adverb* [Old French *emplier* from Latin *implicare* (as IMPLICATE)]

im·polite *adjective* ill-mannered, uncivil, rude. □ **im·polite·ly** *adverb* **im·polite·ness** *noun*

im·politic /ɪmˈpɒlɪtɪk/ *adjective* failing to possess or display prudence; unwise.

im·ponder·able /ɪmˈpɒndərəbəl/ ● *adjective* **1** that cannot be estimated or assessed in any definite way. **2** *Physics* having no weight. ● *noun* (often in *pl.*) something difficult or impossible to assess. □ **im·ponder·abil·ity** /-ˈbɪlɪti/ *noun* **im·ponder·ably** *adverb*

im·port ● *transitive verb* **1** bring in (esp. foreign goods or services) to a country. **2** bring or introduce from an external source or from one use etc. to another (*theories imported from the business world.*) **3** (often foll. by *that* + clause) imply, indicate, signify. **4** *Computing* bring (files etc.) from one application program into another. ● *noun* **1** the process of importing. **2 a** an imported article or service. **b** (in *pl.*) an amount imported (*imports exceeded $50 million*). **3** what is implied; meaning. **4** importance. **5** *Cdn Sport* **a** a player who is enlisted from elsewhere to play for a team representing a city, school, etc. **b** any player who is not from the area his or her team represents. **c** *Football* a professional player who learned to play football outside of Canada (usu. in the US) before the age of seventeen, or who started to learn football after the

age of seventeen outside Canada. **6** esp. *Cdn* a person recently arrived in one country from another. □ **im·port·able** *adjective*

im·port·a·tion *noun* **im·port·ed** *adjective* **im·port·er** *noun* (all in sense 1 of *verb*). [Latin *importare* bring in, in medieval Latin = imply, be of consequence (as IN-², *portare* carry)]

im·port·ance *noun* **1** the state of being important. **2** weight, significance. **3** personal consequence; dignity (*a woman of great importance*).

im·port·ant *adjective* **1** of great effect or consequence; significant. **2** (of a person) having high rank or status, or great authority. **3** pretentious, pompous. **4** of great concern to; highly prized (*my family is very important to me*). **5** (in parenthetic construction) what is a more, or most, significant point or matter (*they are willing and, more important, able*). ¶ Some usage commentators have objected to the use of the adverbial *more importantly* rather than *more important* in sentences such as this, but *more importantly* is overwhelmingly more common and totally unobjectionable. □ **im·port·ant·ly** *adverb* (see note above). [French from medieval Latin (as IMPORT)]

im·por·tun·ate /ɪmˈpɔrtʃənət/ *adjective* making persistent or pressing requests, demands for attention, etc. □ **im·por·tun·ate·ly** *adverb* **im·por·tun·ity** /ˌɪmpɔrˈtuːnɪti, -ˈtjuː-/ *noun* [Latin *importunus* inconvenient (as IN-¹, *portunus* from *portus* harbour)]

im·por·tune /ˈɪmpɔrtuːn, -ˈtjuːn/ *transitive verb* solicit (a person) pressingly; beg or demand insistently. [French *importuner* or medieval Latin *importunari* (as IMPORTUNATE)]

im·pose *verb* **1** *transitive* (often foll. by *on*, *upon*) require (a tax, duty, charge, or obligation) to be paid or undertaken (by a person etc.). **2** *transitive* enforce compliance with (*imposed his will*). **3** *intransitive & reflexive* (foll. by *on*, *upon*) demand the attention or commitment of (a person); take advantage of (*I do not want to impose on you any longer; I did not want to impose*). **4** *transitive* (often foll. by *on*, *upon*) palm (a thing) off on (a person). **5** *transitive* lay (pages of type) in the proper order ready for printing. **6** *intransitive* (foll. by *on*, *upon*) exert influence by an impressive character or appearance. [French *imposer* from Latin *imponere imposit-* inflict, deceive (as IN-², *ponere* put)]

im·pos·ing *adjective* impressive, formidable, esp. in appearance. □ **im·pos·ing·ly** *adverb*

im·pos·ition /ˌɪmpəˈzɪʃən/ *noun* **1** the act or an instance of imposing; the process of being imposed. **2** an unfair or resented demand or burden. **3** *Christianity* **a** the laying on of hands in blessing, ordination, etc. **b** the placing of ashes upon a person's forehead on Ash Wednesday. **4** the imposing of pages.

im·pos·si·bil·ity *noun* (*pl.* **-ities**) **1** the fact or condition of being impossible. **2** an impossible thing or circumstance.

im·pos·sible *adjective* **1** not possible; that cannot occur, exist, or be done (*such a thing is impossible; it is impossible to alter them*). **2** (loosely) extremely difficult, inconvenient, or implausible. **3** *informal* (of a person or thing) outrageous, intolerable. □ **im·pos·sibly** *adverb*

im·post¹ /ˈɪmpoʊst/ *noun* **1** a tax, duty, or tribute. **2** a weight carried by a horse in a handicap race. [French from medieval Latin *impost-* part. stem of Latin *imponere*: see IMPOSE]

im·post² /ˈɪmpoʊst/ *noun* the upper course of a pillar, often in the form of a projecting ornamental moulding, on which the foot of an arch rests. [French *imposte* or Italian *imposta* fem. past participle of *imporre* from Latin *imponere*: see IMPOSE]

im·pos·ter /ɪmˈpɒstər/ *noun* (also **im·pos·tor**) a person who assumes a false character or pretends to be someone else. [French *imposteur* from Late Latin *impostor* (as IMPOST¹)]

im·pos·ture /ɪmˈpɒstʃər/ *noun* the act or an instance of fraudulent deception. [French from Late Latin *impostura* (as IMPOST¹)]

im·po·tent /ˈɪmpətənt/ *adjective* **1 a** powerless; lacking all strength. **b** helpless. **c** ineffective. **2** (of a male) unable, esp. for a prolonged period, to achieve an erection or orgasm. **3** *informal* unable to procreate; sterile. □ **im·po·tence** *noun* **im·po·tency** *noun* **im·po·tent·ly** *adverb*

im·pound *transitive verb* **1** confiscate; take legal possession of. **2** shut up (animals) in a pound. **3** shut up (a person or thing) as in a pound. **4** (of a dam etc.) collect or confine (water). □ **im·pound·ment** *noun*

im·pover·ish /ɪmˈpɒvərɪʃ/ *transitive verb* (often as **im·pover·ished** *adjective*) **1** make poor. **2** exhaust the natural fertility of. **3** weaken or reduce the quality of; deprive of some quality; affect adversely (*a culturally impoverished society*). □ **im·pover·ish·ment** *noun* [Old French *empoverir* (as EN-¹, *povre* POOR)]

im·prac·tic·able /ɪmˈpraktɪkəbəl/ *adjective* **1** impossible in practice. **2** (of a road etc.) impassable. □ **im·prac·tic·abil·ity** *noun* **im·prac·tic·ably** *adverb*

im·prac·tical /ɪmˈpraktɪkəl/ *adjective* **1** not practical. **2** esp. *N Amer.* not practicable. □ **im·prac·ti·cal·ity** /-'kalɪti/ *noun* **im·prac·tical·ly** *adverb*

im·pre·ca·tion /ˌɪmprə'keiʃən/ *noun* **1** a spoken curse; a malediction. **2** the act of uttering an imprecation.

im·pre·ca·tory /'ɪmprɪˌkeitəri, -kəˌtɔri/ *adjective* expressing or involving imprecation.

im·precise *adjective* not precise. □ **im·precise·ly** *adverb* **im·precise·ness** *noun* **im·pre·ci·sion** /-'sɪʒən/ *noun*

im·preg·nable¹ /ɪm'pregnəbəl/ *adjective* **1** (of a fortress etc.) that cannot be taken by force. **2** resistant to attack or criticism. **3** unable to be broken down or overcome (*impregnable shyness*). □ **im·preg·nabil·ity** *noun* **im·preg·nably** *adverb* [Old French *imprenable* (as IN-¹, *prendre* take)]

im·preg·nable² /ɪm'pregnəbəl/ *adjective* that can be impregnated.

im·preg·nate /ɪm'preg,neit/ *transitive verb* **1 a** make (a female) pregnant. **b** *Biol.* fertilize (a female reproductive cell or ovum). **2** (often foll. by *with*) fill or saturate. **3** (often foll. by *with*) imbue, fill (with feelings, moral qualities, etc.). □ **im·preg·na·tion** *noun* [Late Latin *impregnare impregnat-* (as IN-², *pregnare* be pregnant)]

im·pres·ario /ˌɪmprə'sɑrio, -'serio/ *noun* (*pl.* **-arios**) an organizer of public entertainments, esp. a manager or promoter of performing arts companies or productions. [Italian from *impresa* undertaking]

im·pre·scrip·tible /ˌɪmprɪ'skrɪptɪbəl/ *adjective Law* (of rights) that cannot be taken away by prescription or lapse of time. [medieval Latin *imprescriptibilis* (as IN-¹, PRESCRIBE)]

im·press¹ ● *verb* /ɪm'pres/ **1** (often foll. by *with*) **a** *transitive* affect or influence deeply. **b** *transitive & intransitive* evoke a favourable opinion or reaction from (a person) (*was most impressed with your efforts*). **2** *transitive* (often foll. by *on, upon*) emphasize (an idea etc.) (*must impress on you the need to be prompt*). **3** *transitive* (often foll. by *on*) **a** imprint or stamp. **b** apply (a mark etc.) with pressure. **4** *transitive* make a mark or design on (a thing) with a stamp, seal, etc. **5** *transitive Electricity* apply (voltage etc.) from outside. ● *noun* /'ɪmpres/ **1** the act or an instance of impressing. **2** a mark made by a seal, stamp, etc. **3** a characteristic mark or quality. **4** = IMPRESSION 1. □ **im·press·ible** /ɪm'presɪbəl/ *adjective* [Old French *empresser* (as EN-¹, PRESS¹)]

im·press² /ɪm'pres/ *transitive verb hist.* **1** force (men) to serve in the army or navy. **2** seize (goods etc.) for public service. □ **im·press·ment** *noun* [IN-² + PRESS²]

im·pres·sion *noun* **1 a** an effect produced (esp. on the mind, conscience, or feelings). **b** a striking or positive effect (*made an impression on the talent scout*). **2** a notion or belief (esp. a vague or mistaken one) (*my impression is they are afraid*). **3** an imitation of a person or sound, esp. done to entertain. **4 a** the impressing of a mark. **b** a mark impressed. **5** a reprint without editorial corrections (esp. as distinct from *edition*). **6 a** the number of copies of a book, newspaper, etc., issued at one time. **b** the printing of these. **7** a print taken from a wood engraving. **8** *Dentistry* a mould (from which a positive cast is usu. made) of the teeth or mouth made by pressing them into a soft substance.

im·pres·sion·able *adjective* easily influenced; susceptible to impressions. □ **im·pres·sion·abil·ity** *noun* **im·pres·sion·ably** *adverb*

Im·pres·sion·ism *noun* (also **impressionism**) **1** an artistic style or movement originating in France in the late 19th c., characterized by a concern with depicting the visual impression of the moment, esp. in terms of the shifting effect of light and colour. **2** a style of music or writing that seeks to describe a feeling or experience rather than achieve accurate depiction or systematic structure. [French *impressionnisme* (after *Impression: Soleil levant*, title of a painting by Monet, 1872)]

im·pres·sion·ist ● *noun* **1** an entertainer who impersonates famous people etc. **2** (**Impressionist**) an adherent or practitioner of Impressionism. ● *adjective* (**Impressionist**) of or relating to Impressionism or Impressionists.

im·pres·sion·is·tic *adjective* **1** (**Impressionistic**) in the style of Impressionism. **2** subjective, unsystematic; based on impressions. □ **im·pres·sion·is·tic·ally** *adverb*

im·pres·sive *adjective* **1** impressing the mind or senses, esp. so as to cause approval or admiration. **2** (of language, a scene, etc.) tending to excite deep feeling. □ **im·pres·sive·ly** *adverb* **im·pres·sive·ness** *noun*

im·prest /'ɪmprest/ *noun* an advance; a loan. [originally *in prest* from Old French *prest* loan, advance pay: see PRESS²]

im·pri·ma·tur /ˌɪmprɪ'mɑtɜr, -'meitɜr, -tʊr/ *noun* **1** *Catholicism* an official

licence to print (an ecclesiastical or religious book etc.). **2** official approval. [Latin, = let it be printed]

im·print ● *transitive verb* **1** (often foll. by *on*) impress or establish firmly, esp. on the mind. **2 a** (often foll. by *on*) make a stamp or impression of (a figure etc.) on a thing. **b** make an impression on (a thing) with a stamp etc. **3** (usu. in *passive*; often foll. by *on* or *to*) *Biol.* cause (a young animal etc.) to recognize another as a parent or object of habitual trust. ● *noun* **1** a mark produced by pressure on a surface; an impression or stamp. **2** a lasting impression or sign of some emotion, experience, action, etc.; an influence, an effect. **3 a** the printer's or publisher's name and other details printed in a book, usu. on the title page or at the foot of a single sheet. **b** a line of specific titles issued by a publishing company. [Old French *empreinter empreint* from Latin *imprimere*: see IMPRESSION]

im·pris·on *transitive verb* **1** put into prison. **2** confine; shut up. □ **im·pris·on·ment** *noun*

im·pro *noun* (*pl.* **impros**) *Brit. informal* = IMPROV. [abbreviation]

im·prob·able *adjective* **1** not likely to be true or to happen. **2** difficult to believe. □ **im·prob·abil·ity** *noun* **im·prob·ably** *adverb*

im·promp·tu ● *adjective & adverb* without preparation; on the spur of the moment; unrehearsed. ● *noun* **1** an improvised performance or speech. **2** a short piece of usu. solo instrumental music, often song-like. [French from Latin *in promptu* in readiness: see PROMPT]

im·proper *adjective* **1 a** unseemly; indecent. **b** not in accordance with accepted rules of behaviour. **2** wrong or incorrect (*improper use of a tool*). **3** dishonest, irregular (*improper business practices*). □ **im·proper·ly** *adverb*

improper fraction *noun* a fraction in which the numerator is greater than or equal to the denominator.

im·pro·pri·ety /ˌɪmprə'praiəti/ *noun* (*pl.* **-eties**) **1** lack of propriety; indecency. **2** an instance of improper conduct, language etc. **3** incorrectness, inaccuracy. **4** unfitness, inappropriateness.

im·prov *noun* (often *attributive*) *informal* **1** improvisation, esp. as a theatrical technique. **2** an instance of this. [abbreviation]

im·prove *verb* **1 a** *transitive & intransitive* make or become better. **b** *intransitive* (foll. by *on, upon*) produce something better than. **2** *transitive* make (land) more productive or valuable by cultivation, clearing, etc. □ **im·prov·able** *adjective* **im·prov·abil·ity** *noun* **im·proved** *adjective* **im·prov·er** *noun* [originally *emprowe, improwe* from Anglo-French *emprower* from Old French *emprou* from *prou* profit, influenced by PROVE]

im·prove·ment *noun* **1** the act or an instance of improving or being improved. **2** something that improves, esp. an addition or alteration that adds to value (*home improvements*). **3** something that has been improved.

improvement district *noun Cdn* (*Alta., Ont., & BC*) a sparsely populated region which does not have a municipal government and is therefore administered by provincial officials. Abbr.: **I.D.**

im·provi·dent /ɪm'provɪdənt/ *adjective* **1** lacking foresight or care for the future. **2** not frugal. **3** heedless, incautious. □ **im·provi·dence** *noun* **im·provi·dent·ly** *adverb*

im·pro·vise /'ɪmprəˌvaiz/ *transitive & intransitive verb* **1 a** compose or perform (music, dialogue, etc.) on the spur of the moment, not working from a text or score, etc. **b** say or do (something) without preparation (*I didn't know the answer, so I had to improvise*). **2** provide or construct (a thing) from whatever is available, without preparation. □ **im·provi·sa·tion** *noun* **im·pro·vis·a·tion·al** *adjective* **im·pro·visa·tory** /-'provəzəˌtɔri/ *adjective* **im·pro·vis·er** *noun* [French *improviser* or Italian *improvvisare* from *improvviso* extempore, from Latin *improvisus* past participle (as IN-¹, PROVIDE)]

im·pru·dent *adjective* rash, indiscreet. □ **im·pru·dence** *noun* **im·pru·dent·ly** *adverb*

im·pu·dent /'ɪmpjʊdənt/ *adjective* **1** insolently disrespectful; impertinent. **2** shamelessly presumptuous. □ **im·pu·dence** *noun* **im·pu·dent·ly** *adverb* [Latin *impudens* (as IN-¹, *pudēre* be ashamed)]

im·pugn /ɪm'pjuːn/ *transitive verb* challenge or call in question (a statement, action, someone's character, etc.). □ **im·pugn·ment** *noun* [Latin *impugnare* assail (as IN-¹, *pugnare* fight)]

im·pulse *noun* **1** the act or an instance of impelling; a push. **2** impetus (*gave an impulse to industrial expansion*). **3** incitement or stimulus to action arising from a state of mind or feeling (*a selfish impulse*). **4** a sudden desire or tendency to act without reflection (*did it on impulse*). **5** *Physics* **a** an indefinitely large force acting for a very short time but producing a finite change of momentum (e.g. the blow of a hammer). **b** the change of momentum produced by this or any force. **6 a**

stimulating force in a nerve or an electric circuit that causes a reaction. [Latin *impulsus* (as IMPEL)]

impulse buying *noun* the unpremeditated buying of goods as a result of a whim or impulse. □ **impulse buy** *noun & intransitive verb* **impulse buyer** *noun*

impulse purchase *noun* a purchase made on impulse, without premeditation.

im·pul·sion *noun* **1** the act or an instance of impelling. **2** a mental impulse. **3** impetus. [Old French from Latin *impulsio -onis* (as IMPEL)]

im·pul·sive *adjective* **1** (of a person or conduct etc.) apt to be affected or determined by sudden impulse. **2** *Physics* acting as an impulse. □ **im·pul·sive·ly** *adverb* **im·pul·sive·ness** *noun* **im·pul·siv·ity** *noun*

im·pun·ity /ɪmˈpjuːnɪti/ *noun* exemption from punishment or from the injurious consequences of an action. □ **with impunity** without having to suffer the normal injurious consequences (of an action). [Latin *impunitas* from *impunis* (as IN-[1], *poena* penalty)]

im·pure *adjective* **1** mixed with foreign matter; adulterated (*impure metals*). **2 a** dirty or contaminated. **b** ceremonially unclean. **3** unchaste; not morally pure (*impure thoughts*). **4** (of a colour) mixed with another colour. **5** (of architecture, design, etc.) mixed in style. □ **im·pure·ly** *adverb*

im·pur·ity *noun* (*pl.* **-ities**) **1** the quality or condition of being impure. **2 a** an impure thing or constituent. **b** *Electronics* a trace element deliberately added to a semiconductor; a dopant. [French *impurité* or Latin *impuritas* (as IMPURE)]

im·pute *transitive verb* (foll. by *to*) **1** regard (esp. something undesirable) as being done or caused or possessed by. **2** (in Christian theology) ascribe (righteousness, guilt, etc.) to (a person) by virtue of a similar quality in another. **3** *Econ.* attribute or assign (value) to a product or process by inference from the value of the products or processes to which it contributes. □ **im·put·able** *adjective* **im·pu·ta·tion** *noun* [Old French *imputer* from Latin *imputare* enter in the account (as IN-[2], *putare* reckon)]

IN *abbreviation* Indiana (in official postal use).

In *symbol Chem.* the element indium.

in ● *preposition* **1** expressing inclusion or position within limits of space, time, circumstance, etc. (*in Canada; in bed; in the rain*). **2** during the time of (*in the night; in 1989*). **3** within the time of (*will be back in two hours*). **4 a** with respect to (*blind in one eye; good in parts*). **b** as a kind of (*the latest thing in luxury*). **5** as a proportionate part of (*one in three failed*). **6** with the form or arrangement of (*packed in tens; falling in folds*). **7** as a member of (*in the army*). **8** concerned with (*is in politics*). **9** as or regarding the content of (*there is something in what you say*). **10** within the ability of (*does he have it in him?*). **11** having the condition of; affected by (*in bad health; in danger*). **12** having as a purpose (*in search of; in reply to*). **13** by means of or using as material (*drawn in pencil; modelled in bronze*). **14 a** using as the language of expression (*written in French*). **b** (of music) having as its key (*symphony in C*). **15** wearing as dress (*in blue; in a suit*). **16** with the identity of (*found a friend in Mary*). **17** (of an animal) pregnant with (*in calf*). **18** into (with a verb of motion or change: *put it in the box; cut it in two*). **19** introducing an indirect object after a verb (*believe in; engage in; share in*). **20** forming adverbial phrases (*in any case; in reality; in short*). **21** in the process of; in the act of (*in climbing the wall he skinned his knee*). ● *adverb* expressing position within limits, or motion to such a position: **1** into a room, house, etc. (*come in*). **2** at home, in one's office, etc. (*is not in*). **3** so as to be enclosed or confined (*locked in*). **4** in a publication (*is the advertisement in?*). **5** in or to the inward side (*rub it in*). **6 a** in fashion, season, or office (*long skirts are in; strawberries are not yet in*). **b** elected (*the Liberal got in*). **7** exerting favourable action or influence (*their luck was in*). **8** *Sport* **a** (of a shot, serve, etc.) within the boundary of the playing area. **b** (of a player or side) having the turn to play. **c** (of a hockey puck, soccer ball, etc.) between and behind the goalposts. **d** (of a baseball infielder or outfielder) playing closer to home plate than usual. **9** (of transport) at the platform etc. (*the train is in*). **10** (of a season, harvest, order, etc.) having arrived or been received. **11** *Brit.* (of a fire) continuing to burn. **12** denoting effective action (*join in*). **13** (of the tide) at the highest point. **14** (in *combination*) *informal* denoting prolonged or concerted action, esp. by large numbers (*sit-in; teach-in*). ● *adjective* **1** internal; living in; inside (*in-patient*). **2** fashionable, esoteric (*the in thing to do*). **3** confined to or shared by a group of people (*in-joke*). ● *noun* (foll. by *with*) *informal* an introduction to, or influence with, a person of power or authority. □ **in all** *see* ALL. **in at** present at; contributing to (*in at the kill*). **in between** *see* BETWEEN *adverb* **in for 1** about to undergo (esp. something unpleasant). **2** competing in or for. **3** involved in; committed to. **in on** sharing in; privy to (a secret etc.). **ins and outs**

(often foll. by *of*) all the details (of a procedure etc.). **in so far as** *see* FAR. **in that** because; in so far as. **in with** on good terms with. [Old English *in, inn*, originally as adv. with verbs of motion]

in. *abbreviation* inch(es).

in-[1] *prefix* (also **il-** before *l*, **im-** before *b, m, p*, **ir-** before *r*) added to: **1** adjectives, meaning 'not' (*inedible; insane*). **2** nouns, meaning 'without, lacking' (*inaction*). [Latin]

in-[2] *prefix* (also **il-** before *l*, **im-** before *b, m, p*, **ir-** before *r*) in, on, into, towards, within (*induce; influx; insight; intrude*). [IN, or from or after Latin *in* IN *preposition*]

-in *suffix Chem.* forming names of organic compounds, pharmaceutical products, proteins, etc. (*dioxin; fibrin; gelatin; penicillin*). [-INE[4]]

-ina *suffix* denoting: **1** feminine names and titles (*Georgina; czarina*). **2** names of musical instruments (*concertina*). **3** names of zoological classification categories (*globigerina*). [Italian or Spanish or Latin]

in·abil·ity *noun* **1** the state of being unable. **2** a lack of power or means.

in ab·sen·tia /ˌɪn abˈsenʃə, -ˌʃɪə, -tɪə/ *adverb* in (his, her, or their) absence. [Latin]

in·access·ible *adjective* **1** not accessible; that cannot be reached. **2** (of a person) not open to advances or influence; unapproachable. □ **in·access·ibil·ity** *noun* **in·access·ibly** *adverb*

in·accur·ate *adjective* not accurate; inexact, imprecise, incorrect. □ **in·accur·acy** *noun* (*pl.* **-acies**). **in·accur·ate·ly** *adverb*

in·action *noun* **1** lack of action. **2** sluggishness, inertness.

in·acti·vate *transitive verb* make inactive or inoperative. □ **in·acti·va·tion** *noun*

in·active *adjective* **1** not active or inclined to act. **2** passive. **3** sedentary, indolent (*an inactive lifestyle*). **4** not participating fully in a club, team, etc. (*inactive members of the music society*). **5** *Chem.* not rotating the plane of polarization of polarized light. □ **in·active·ly** *adverb* **in·activ·ity** *noun*

in·ad·equate /ɪnˈadəkwət/ *adjective* **1** not adequate; insufficient. **2** (of a person) incompetent; unable to deal with a situation. □ **in·ad·equa·cy** *noun* (*pl.* **-cies**). **in·ad·equate·ly** *adverb*

in·admis·sible /ˌɪnədˈmɪsəbəl/ *adjective* that cannot be admitted or allowed (*inadmissible evidence*). □ **in·admis·si·bil·ity** *noun*

in·adver·tent /ˌɪnədˈvɜːtənt/ *adjective* **1** (of an action) unintentional. **2** (of a mistake) made through lack of care. □ **in·adver·tence** *noun* **in·adver·tent·ly** *adverb* [IN-[1] + obsolete *advertent* 'attentive' (as ADVERT[2])]

in·advis·able /ˌɪnədˈvaizəbəl/ *adjective* not advisable. □ **in·advis·abil·ity** *noun*

in·alien·able /ɪnˈeɪlɪənəbəl/ *adjective* that cannot be transferred to another; not alienable (*inalienable rights*). □ **in·alien·ably** *adverb*

in·alter·able *adjective* not alterable; that cannot be changed. □ **in·alter·ably** *adverb*

in·amor·ata /ɪnˌaməˈrɑːtə/ *noun* (*pl.* **-atas**) a female lover. [feminine of INAMORATO]

in·amor·ato /ɪnˌaməˈrɑːtoʊ/ *noun* (*pl.* **-atos**) a lover. [Italian, past participle of *inamorare* 'enamour' (as IN-[2], *amore* from Latin *amor* 'love')]

inane /ɪˈneɪn/ *adjective* silly, senseless (*inane remarks*). □ **inane·ly** *adverb* **in·an·ity** /-ˈanɪti/ *noun* (*pl.* **-ities**). [Latin *inanis* 'empty, vain']

in·ani·mate /ɪnˈanəmət/ *adjective* **1** not animate; not endowed with (esp. animal) life. **2** lifeless; showing no sign of life. □ **in·ani·ma·tion** *noun*

in·ani·tion /ˌɪnəˈnɪʃən/ *noun* **1** exhaustion resulting from lack of nourishment. **2** lack of mental or spiritual vigour and enthusiasm. [Late Latin *inanitio* from Latin *inanire* make empty (as INANE)]

in·appar·ent /ˌɪnəˈperənt/ *adjective Med.* causing no noticeable signs or symptoms.

in·applic·able /ˌɪnəˈplɪkəbəl, ɪnˈaplɪk-/ *adjective* (often foll. by *to*) not relevant or appropriate. □ **in·applic·abil·ity** *noun* **in·applic·ably** *adverb*

in·appos·ite /ɪnˈapəzɪt/ *adjective* not apposite; unsuitable, not pertinent.

in·appro·pri·ate /ˌɪnəˈproʊprɪət/ *adjective* not appropriate; unsuitable. □ **in·appro·pri·ate·ly** *adverb* **in·appro·pri·ate·ness** *noun*

inapt *adjective* unsuitable or inappropriate in the circumstances. □ **inapt·ly** *adverb* ¶ See Usage Note at INEPT.

in·arch /ɪnˈɑːtʃ/ *transitive verb* graft (a plant) by connecting a growing branch without separation from the parent stock. [IN-[2] + ARCH[1] *verb*]

Vowels: a *cat*   ɑ *arm*   e *bed*   ɜr *her*   ɜ: *deux*   ə *ago*   ɪ *sit*   i *cosy*   iː *feed*   ɒ *hot*   ɔ *pore*   oː *no*   ʌ *run*   ʊ *put*

in·argu·able *adjective* that cannot be argued about or disputed. □ **in·argu·ably** *adverb*

in·articu·late /ˌɪnɑrˈtɪkjʊlət/ *adjective* 1 unable to speak distinctly or express oneself clearly or fluently. 2 (of speech, a sound, etc.) **a** not articulate; indistinctly pronounced. **b** having no distinct meaning; unintelligible (*inarticulate gibberish*). 3 not clearly or well expressed (*an inarticulate speech*). 4 unable to speak (*inarticulate with anger*). 5 not expressed; unspoken. 6 *Zool. & Bot.* not jointed or hinged. □ **in·articu·lacy** *noun* **in·articu·late·ly** *adverb* **in·articu·late·ness** *noun*

in·artis·tic *adjective* having or showing a lack of skill or talent in art.

in·as·much *adverb* (foll. by *as*) 1 since, because, seeing or considering that. 2 in so far as, to the extent that.

in·atten·tive *adjective* 1 not paying due attention; heedless. 2 neglecting to show courtesy. □ **in·atten·tion** *noun* **in·atten·tive·ly** *adverb* **in·atten·tive·ness** *noun*

in·aud·ible *adjective* not audible; not able to be heard. □ **in·audi·bil·ity** *noun* **in·aud·ibly** *adverb*

in·augur·al /ɪˈnɒɡjʊrəl, -ɡɜr-/ ● *adjective* 1 of, pertaining to, or forming part of an inauguration or inauguration ceremony. 2 (of a lecture, series, etc.) first in a series or course. ● *noun* an inaugural speech, lecture, ceremony, etc.

in·augur·ate /ɪˈnɒɡjʊˌreit, -ɡɜr-/ *transitive verb* 1 admit (a person) formally to office (*inaugurated the president*). 2 open or dedicate (a building etc.) to public use by a ceremony. 3 **a** begin, introduce, initiate (*the moon landing inaugurated a new era in space exploration*). **b** enter into (an undertaking, course of action, etc.) formally or ceremoniously. □ **in·augur·a·tion** *noun* **in·augur·ator** *noun* [Latin *inaugurare* (as IN-², *augurare* take omens: see AUGUR)]

Inauguration Day *noun* (in the US) the day on which the president is inaugurated, being the January 20th following the presidential election.

in·auspi·cious /ˌɪnɔˈspɪʃəs/ *adjective* not conducive to success; unpromising. □ **in·auspi·cious·ly** *adverb* **in·auspi·cious·ness** *noun*

in·authen·tic /ˌɪnɔˈθentɪk/ *adjective* 1 not in fact what it is said to be. 2 not genuinely belonging to a time or period. 3 lacking full reality or sincerity. □ **in·authen·ti·city** /-ˈtɪsɪti/ *noun*

in-basket *noun* N Amer. a tray on an office desk etc. for incoming documents, letters, etc.

in-between ● *attributive adjective* informal intermediate (*at an in-between stage*). ● *noun* informal a person or thing that fills, occupies, or takes up an intermediate space, position, or attitude.

in·between·er *noun* 1 an assistant animator who produces the drawings that fill in the action between the key drawings done by the major animator. 2 a person who occupies or takes up an intermediate position or attitude.

in·board ● *adjective* situated within or towards the centre of a boat, aircraft, vehicle, etc.; interior. ● *adverb* within the sides of or towards the centre of a boat, aircraft, or vehicle. ● *noun* esp. N Amer. 1 a boat equipped with a motor mounted within the hull. 2 a motor so mounted.

in·born *adjective* 1 (of a quality etc.) innate, existing from birth. 2 (of a metabolic disorder etc.) congenital and hereditary.

in·bound ● *adjective* coming in, headed inward, or homeward bound. ● *transitive verb* Basketball throw (the ball) in bounds from the sidelines.

in·bounds *attributive adjective* Basketball (of a pass) thrown in bounds from the sidelines.

in·box *noun* 1 the window in which an individual user's received email messages (and other communications such as voice mail messages, faxes, etc.) are displayed. 2 the file space in which such communications are received and stored.

in·bred *adjective* 1 inborn, innate, inherent. 2 characterized or produced by inbreeding.

in·breed·ing *noun* breeding from closely related animals or persons. □ **in·breed** *transitive & intransitive verb & noun* (past and past participle **inbred**).

in·built *adjective* 1 incorporated as part of a structure. 2 already part of or present in something, esp. naturally.

Inc. *abbreviation* 1 N Amer. Incorporated. 2 (**inc.**) including, included.

Inca *noun* a member of a S American Aboriginal people who established an empire in the central Andes before the Spanish conquest in the early 16th c. □ **Inca·ic** /ɪŋˈkeiɪk/ *adjective* **Incan** *adjective* [Quechua, = lord, royal person]

in·calcul·able /ɪnˈkalkjʊləbəl/ *adjective* 1 too great for calculation.

2 that cannot be estimated, forecast, or reckoned beforehand. 3 (of a person, character, etc.) uncertain, unpredictable. □ **in·calcul·abil·ity** *noun* **in·calcul·ably** *adverb*

in camera *see* CAMERA.

in·can·desce /ˌɪnkanˈdes/ *intransitive verb* glow with heat. [back-formation from INCANDESCENT]

in·can·des·cent /ˌɪnkanˈdesənt/ ● *adjective* 1 (of an electric or other light) produced by a glowing white-hot filament. 2 glowing with heat. 3 intense in feeling, expression, etc. ● *noun* an incandescent light bulb. □ **in·can·des·cence** *noun* **in·can·des·cent·ly** *adverb* [French from Latin *incandescere* (as IN-², *candescere* inceptive of *candēre* be white)]

in·can·ta·tion /ˌɪnkanˈteiʃən/ *noun* 1 **a** a magical formula chanted or spoken. **b** the use of this. 2 a spell or charm. □ **in·cant** *transitive & intransitive verb* **in·can·ta·tion·al** *adjective* **in·can·ta·tory** *adjective* [Old French from Late Latin *incantatio -onis* from *incantare* chant, bewitch (as IN-², *cantare* sing)]

in·cap·able /ɪnˈkeipəbəl/ *adjective* 1 (often foll. by *of*) **a** incompetent, not capable. **b** lacking the required quality or characteristic (favourable or adverse) for a specified purpose, action, etc. (*incapable of hurting anyone*). 2 not, esp. legally, capable of rational conduct or of managing one's own affairs. □ **in·cap·abil·ity** *noun* **in·cap·ably** *adverb*

in·capa·ci·tate /ˌɪnkəˈpasɪˌteit/ *transitive verb* 1 render incapable or unfit. 2 disqualify, esp. legally. □ **in·capa·ci·tant** *noun* **in·capa·ci·ta·tion** /-ˈteiʃən/ *noun*

in·capa·city /ˌɪnkəˈpasɪti/ *noun* (pl. **-ties**) 1 inability; lack of the necessary power or resources. 2 legal disqualification. 3 an instance of incapacity.

in·car·cer·ate /ɪnˈkɑrsəˌreit/ *transitive verb* imprison or confine. □ **in·car·cer·a·tion** *noun* **in·car·cer·ator** *noun* [medieval Latin *incarcerare* (as IN-², Latin *carcer* prison)]

in·car·na·dine /ɪnˈkɑrnəˌdain/ *literary* ● *adjective* crimson or flesh-coloured. ● *noun* crimson or flesh colour. ● *transitive verb* dye incarnadine. [French *incarnadin -ine* from Italian *incarnadino* (for *-tino*) from *incarnato* INCARNATE *adjective*]

in·car·nate *adjective* /ɪnˈkɑrnət/ 1 (of a person, spirit, quality, etc.) embodied in flesh, esp. in human form (*is the devil incarnate*). 2 represented in a recognizable or typical form (*folly incarnate*). ● *transitive verb* /ɪnˈkɑrneit/ 1 embody in flesh or esp. a human form. 2 put (an idea etc.) into concrete form; realize. 3 (of a person etc.) be the living embodiment or type of (a quality etc.). [ecclesiastical Latin *incarnare incarnat-* make flesh (as IN-², Latin *caro carnis* flesh)]

in·car·na·tion /ˌɪnkɑrˈneiʃən/ *noun* 1 **a** the form, appearance, or mode of presentation assumed by a person or thing at a particular time (*the party's present political incarnation*). **b** the period of time spent in such an incarnation. 2 **a** the embodiment of a deity etc. in esp. human flesh. **b** (**the Incarnation**) (in Christian theology) the embodiment of God the Son in human flesh as Jesus Christ. 3 (often foll. by *of*) a living type or embodiment (of a quality etc.) (*she's the incarnation of femininity*).

in·cau·tious *adjective* heedless, rash. □ **in·cau·tion** *noun* **in·cau·tious·ly** *adverb*

in·cen·di·ary /ɪnˈsendieri/ ● *adjective* 1 (of a substance or device, esp. a bomb) designed to cause fires. 2 tending to stir up strife. 3 *informal* exciting, powerful, impressive (*an incendiary guitar solo*). ● *noun* (pl. **-aries**) 1 an incendiary bomb or device. 2 **a** an arsonist. **b** a person who stirs up strife. □ **in·cen·di·ar·ism** *noun* [Latin *incendiarius* from *incendium* conflagration from *incendere incens-* set fire to]

in·cense¹ /ˈɪnsens/ *noun* 1 a gum or spice producing a sweet smell when burned. 2 the smoke or perfume of this, used esp. in religious ceremonies. [Old French *encens, encenser* from ecclesiastical Latin *incensum* a thing burned, incense: see INCENDIARY]

in·cense² /ɪnˈsens/ *transitive verb* (often foll. by *at, with, against*) enrage; make angry. [Old French *incenser* (as INCENDIARY)]

in·cen·tive /ɪnˈsentiv/ ● *noun* 1 (often foll. by *to*) a motive or incitement, esp. to action. 2 a payment or concession to stimulate greater output by workers. ● *adjective* serving to motivate or incite. □ **in·cent** *transitive verb* **in·cen·tiv·ize** *transitive verb* (also esp. *Brit.* **-ise**). [Latin *incentivus* setting the tune, from *incinere incent-* sing to (as IN-², *canere* sing)]

in·cep·tion *noun* a beginning. [Old French *inception* or Latin *inceptio incipere incept-* begin (as IN-², *capere* take)]

in·cep·tive ● *adjective* 1 **a** beginning. **b** initial. 2 *Grammar* (of a verb) that denotes the beginning of an action. ● *noun* an inceptive verb.

in·certi·tude *noun* uncertainty, doubt.

in·ces·sant /ɪnˈsesənt/ *adjective* unceasing, continual, repeated.

□ **in·ces·sant·ly** adverb [French incessant or Late Latin incessans (as IN-[1], cessans pres. part. of Latin cessare CEASE)]

in·cest noun sexual intercourse between parent and child or grandchild, or between siblings or half-siblings. [Latin incestus (as IN-[1], castus CHASTE)]

in·ces·tu·ous /ɪnˈsestʃʊəs/ adjective 1 involving or guilty of incest. 2 unwholesomely close; interconnected (the incestuous literary world). □ **in·ces·tu·ous·ly** adverb **in·ces·tu·ous·ness** noun

inch[1] ● noun 1 a unit of linear measure equal to one-twelfth of a foot (2.54 cm). 2 a (as a unit of rainfall) a quantity that would cover a horizontal surface to a depth of 1 inch. b (of atmospheric or other pressure) an amount of pressure that balances the weight of a column of mercury 1 inch high. 3 (as a unit of scale on a map) so many inches representing 1 mile on the ground. 4 a small amount (usu. with neg.: would not budge an inch). ● transitive & intransitive verb move gradually in a specified way (inched forward). □ **by inches** 1 only just (missed me by inches). 2 gradually (dying by inches). **every inch** 1 (often foll. by a, the) entirely (looked every inch a lady). 2 (usu. foll by of) the whole distance or area (combed every inch of the garden). **give a person an inch and he** (or **she**) **will take a mile** a person once conceded to will demand much. **inch by inch** gradually; bit by bit. **within an inch of** almost to the point of. **within an inch of one's life** 1 extremely severely. 2 almost to death. [Old English ynce from Latin uncia twelfth part: compare OUNCE[1]]

inch[2] noun esp. Scot. a small island (esp. in place names). [Middle English from Gaelic innis]

inch·er noun (with a numeral prefixed) a thing having a length, diameter, etc. of the number of inches specified.

in·cho·ate /ɪnˈkoːət, -eit, ˈɪn-/ adjective 1 incipient, just begun. 2 undeveloped, rudimentary, unformed. ¶ Inchoate, meaning 'just begun' or 'undeveloped', should not be confused with incoherent or chaotic, although all these words can often be found in similar contexts. Inchoate scribbles thus means 'undeveloped' rather than 'incoherent' pieces of writing. □ **in·cho·ate·ly** adverb **in·cho·ative** /-ˈkoːətɪv/ adjective [Latin inchoatus past participle of inchoare (as IN-[2], choare begin)]

In·chon /ɪnˈtʃɒn/ a port on the west coast of S Korea, on the Yellow Sea near Seoul; pop. (est. 2002) 2,433,000.

inch·worm noun the caterpillar of the geometer moth.

in·ci·dence /ˈɪnsɪdəns/ noun 1 (often foll. by of) the fact, manner, or rate of occurrence or action of a phenomenon among a group of people (high incidence of suicide attempts). 2 the range, scope, or extent of a thing or a thing's influence. 3 Physics a the way in which esp. a ray of light strikes a surface. b = ANGLE OF INCIDENCE. 4 the act or an instance of falling upon, affecting, or coming into contact with a thing.

in·ci·dent /ˈɪnsɪdənt/ ● noun 1 a an event or occurrence. b a minor or detached event attracting general attention or noteworthy in some way. 2 a a hostile clash, esp. of troops of countries at war (a border incident). b an accident, public disturbance, or other trouble (the night passed without incident). 3 a distinct piece of action in a play or a poem. ● adjective 1 a (often foll. by to) apt or liable to happen. b (foll. by to) naturally connected with or forming an expected part of something. 2 (often foll. by on, upon) (of light etc.) falling upon or striking against a surface. [French incident or Latin incidere (as IN-[2], cadere fall)]

in·ci·dent·al /ˌɪnsɪˈdentəl/ ● adjective 1 (often foll. by to) a having a minor role in relation to a more important thing, event, etc. b not essential. 2 (foll. by to) liable to happen. 3 (foll. by on, upon) following as a subordinate event. 4 (of an expense or charge) incurred apart from the main sum disbursed. ● noun (usu. in pl.) a minor detail, expense, event, etc.

in·ci·dent·al·ly /ˌɪnsɪˈdentəli/ adverb 1 by the way; as a further thought or unconnected remark. 2 in an incidental way.

incidental music noun music used as a background to the action of a film, broadcast, play, etc.

in·cin·er·ate /ɪnˈsɪnəˌreit/ transitive verb destroy completely by burning; reduce to ashes. □ **in·cin·er·a·tion** noun [medieval Latin incinerare (as IN-[2], cinis -eris ashes)]

in·cin·er·ator /ɪnˈsɪnəˌreitər/ noun a furnace or apparatus for burning esp. waste to ashes.

in·cipi·ent /ɪnˈsɪpiənt/ adjective 1 beginning. 2 in an initial or early stage. □ **in·cipi·ence** noun [Latin incipere incipient- (as INCEPTION)]

in·cise /ɪnˈsaiz/ transitive verb 1 cut into or make a cut in. 2 engrave (letters, an inscription, etc.). □ **in·cised** adjective [French inciser from Latin incidere incis- (as IN-[2], caedere cut)]

in·ci·sion /ɪnˈsɪʒən/ noun 1 a a cut; a division produced by cutting. b the esp. initial cut through the surface of the body made during surgery. 2 the act of cutting into a thing.

in·ci·sive /ɪnˈsaisɪv/ adjective 1 mentally sharp; acute. 2 clear and effective. 3 (of a comment etc.) cutting, penetrating. □ **in·ci·sive·ly** adverb **in·ci·sive·ness** noun

in·cis·or /ɪnˈsaizər/ noun a sharp cutting tooth, esp. in humans, any of the eight teeth at the front of the mouth.

in·cite /ɪnˈsait/ transitive verb (often foll. by to) urge or stir up. □ **in·cite·ment** noun **in·cit·er** noun [French inciter from Latin incitare (as IN-[2], citare rouse)]

in·civil·ity /ˌɪnsɪˈvɪliti/ noun (pl. -ities) 1 rudeness, discourtesy. 2 a rude or discourteous act.

incl. abbreviation 1 including. 2 inclusive.

in·clem·ent /ɪnˈklemənt/ adjective (of the weather or climate) severe, esp. cold, rainy, or stormy. □ **in·clem·en·cy** noun (pl. -cies).

in·clin·a·tion /ˌɪnklɪˈneiʃən/ noun 1 (often foll. by to) a disposition, tendency, or propensity. 2 (often foll. by for) a liking or affection. 3 a a leaning, slope, or slant. b the amount of the deviation (of a surface etc.) from the normal horizontal or vertical position. 4 the act or action of bending towards something, esp. a bending of the body or head in a bow. 5 Math. the difference of direction of two lines or planes, esp. as measured by the angle between them. 6 the dip of a magnetic needle. 7 Astronomy the angle between the orbital plane of a planet, comet, etc. and the plane of the ecliptic.

in·cline ● verb 1 transitive (usu. in passive; often foll. by to, for, or to + infin.) a make (a person, feelings, etc.) willing or favourably disposed (am inclined to think so). b give a specified tendency to (a thing) (the door is inclined to bang). 2 intransitive a be disposed (I incline to think so). b (often foll. by to, towards) tend. 3 intransitive & transitive lean or turn away from a given direction (the land inclines towards the shore; the bench is inclined at a 30° angle). 4 transitive bend (the head, body, or oneself) forward, downward, or toward a thing. ● noun 1 a slope, esp. on a road or railway. 2 an inclined plane or surface. □ **incline one's ear** (often foll. by to) listen favourably. □ **in·clin·er** noun [Old French encliner from Latin inclinare (as IN-[2], clinare bend)]

in·clined adjective 1 sloping, slanted. 2 having a natural ability in a specified subject (musically inclined).

inclined plane noun a sloping plane, esp. as a means of reducing the force needed to raise a load.

in·clin·om·eter /ˌɪnklɪˈnɒmətər/ noun 1 an instrument for measuring the angle between the direction of the earth's magnetic field and the horizontal. 2 an instrument for measuring the inclination of an aircraft or ship to the horizontal. 3 an instrument for measuring the inclination of a slope.

in·clude transitive verb 1 involve, comprise, or reckon in as part of a whole. 2 treat or regard as part of the whole. □ **include out** informal or jocular specifically exclude. [Latin includere inclus- (as IN-[2], claudere shut)]

in·clud·ed adjective 1 that is included. 2 (of a stamen or style) not protruding beyond the corolla.

in·clud·ing preposition if one takes into account, inclusive of (six members, including the chairman).

in·clu·sion noun 1 the act of including someone or something. 2 a the fact or condition of being included. b an instance of this. 3 a thing which is included. 4 a body or particle distinct from the substance in which it is embedded, esp. a solid fragment or globule of liquid or gas enclosed within a rock or mineral.

in·clu·sive adjective 1 (often foll. by of) including, comprising. 2 with the inclusion of the extreme limits stated (pages 7 to 26 inclusive). 3 including all the normal services etc. (a hotel offering inclusive terms). 4 a not excluding any section of society. b (of language) deliberately non-sexist, esp. avoiding the use of masculine pronouns to cover both men and women. □ **in·clu·sive·ly** adverb **in·clu·sive·ness** noun **in·clu·siv·ity** noun [medieval Latin inclusivus (as INCLUDE)]

in·cog·nito /ˌɪnkɒgˈniːtoː/ ● adjective & adverb with one's name or identity kept secret (was travelling incognito). ● noun (pl. -nitos) 1 a person who is incognito. 2 the pretended identity or anonymous character of such a person. [Italian, = unknown, from Latin incognitus (as IN-[1], cognitus past participle of cognoscere know)]

in·cog·ni·zant /ɪnˈkɒgnɪzənt/ adjective (foll. by of) unaware; not knowing.

in·coher·ent /ˌɪnkoˈhiːrənt/ adjective 1 (of a person) unable to speak intelligibly. 2 (of speech, thought, etc.) disjointed, lacking logic or consistency. 3 Physics (of waves) having no definite or stable phase relationship. □ **in·co·her·ence** *noun* **in·co·her·ency** *noun* (*pl.* **-cies**). **in·co·her·ent·ly** *adverb*

in·com·bust·ible /ˌɪnkəmˈbʌstɪbəl/ *adjective* that cannot be burned or consumed by fire. □ **in·com·bust·ibil·ity** *noun*

in·come *noun* the money or other assets received, esp. periodically or in a year, from one's business, work, investments, etc. [Middle English (originally = arrival), prob. from Old Norse *innkoma*: in later use from *come in*]

income group *noun* a section of the population determined by income.

in·com·er *noun* **1** a person who comes in. **2** esp. *Brit.* a person who arrives to settle in a place; an immigrant.

-incomer *combining form* earning a specified kind or level of income (*middle-incomer*).

income support *noun* esp. *Brit.* a government benefit for those with low incomes, esp. those who are unemployed, elderly, bringing up children alone, or unable to work through disability or through caring for relatives.

income tax *noun* a tax levied on income.

in·com·ing *adjective* **1 a** coming in (*the incoming tide; incoming telephone calls*). **b** starting, beginning (*incoming students*). **2** succeeding another person or persons (*the incoming tenant*).

in·com·men·sur·able /ˌɪnkəˈmenʃərəbəl/ ● *adjective* **1** not worthy of being compared with; utterly disproportionate to. **2** *Math.* **a** (often foll. by *with*) (of a magnitude or magnitudes) having no common factor, integral or fractional. **b** irrational. ● *noun* (usu. in *pl.*) an incommensurable quantity. □ **in·com·men·sur·abil·ity** *noun*

in·com·men·sur·ate /ˌɪnkəˈmenʃərət/ *adjective* **1** (often foll. by *with*, *to*) out of proportion; inadequate (*his abilities are incommensurate with the demands of the job*). **2** = INCOMMENSURABLE *adjective* 1.

in·com·mode /ˌɪnkəˈmoːd/ *transitive verb* **1** hinder, inconvenience. **2** trouble, annoy. [French *incommoder* or Latin *incommodare* (as IN-¹, *commodus* convenient)]

in·com·mun·ic·able /ˌɪnkəˈmjuːnɪkəbəl/ *adjective* that cannot be communicated or shared.

in·com·muni·cado /ˌɪnkəˌmjuːnɪˈkɒdoː, -adoː/ *adjective & adverb* **1** without or deprived of the means of communication with others. **2** in solitary confinement (*the prisoner was held incommunicado*). [Spanish *incomunicado* past participle of *incomunicar* deprive of communication]

in·com·par·able /ɪnˈkɒmpərəbəl, -prəbəl/ *adjective* **1** without an equal; matchless (*incomparable beauty*). **2** (often foll. by *with*, *to*) not to be compared. □ **in·com·par·abil·ity** *noun* **in·com·par·ably** *adverb*

in·com·pat·ible /ˌɪnkəmˈpatɪbəl/ *adjective* **1** opposed in character; discordant. **2** (often foll. by *with*) not consistent or in logical agreement (*behaviour incompatible with the aims of the society*). **3** (of persons) unable to live, work, etc., together in harmony. **4** (of drugs) not suitable for taking at the same time. **5** (of equipment, machinery, etc.) not capable of being used in combination with some other item. □ **in·com·pat·ibil·ity** *noun* (*pl.* **-ities**).

in·com·pe·tent /ɪnˈkɒmpətənt/ ● *adjective* **1 a** not qualified or able to perform a particular task or function (*an incompetent buyer*). **b** (of a witness, evidence, etc.) not legally qualified or qualifying. **2** showing a lack of skill (*an incompetent performance*). **3** *Med.* (esp. of a valve or sphincter) not able to perform its function. ● *noun* an incompetent person. □ **in·com·pe·tence** *noun* **in·com·pe·tency** *noun* (*pl.* **-cies**). **in·com·pe·tent·ly** *adverb*

in·com·plete *adjective* **1** not complete, finished, or fully formed. **2** imperfect, not whole, lacking something. **3** *Football* (of a forward pass) not completed. □ **in·com·plete·ly** *adverb* **in·com·plete·ness** *noun* **in·com·ple·tion** *noun*

in·com·pre·hen·sible /ɪnˌkɒmprəˈhensɪbəl/ *adjective* (often foll. by *to*) that cannot be understood. □ **in·com·pre·hen·si·bil·ity** *noun* **in·com·pre·hen·sibly** *adverb*

in·com·pre·hen·sion /ɪnˌkɒmprəˈhenʃən/ *noun* failure to understand.

in·com·press·ible /ˌɪnkəmˈpresɪbəl/ *adjective* that cannot be compressed into a smaller volume. □ **in·com·press·ibil·ity** *noun*

in·con·ceiv·able /ˌɪnkənˈsiːvəbəl/ *adjective* **1** unthinkable, unimaginable. **2** unbelievable. □ **in·con·ceiv·abil·ity** /-ˈbɪlɪti/ *noun* **in·con·ceiv·ably** *adverb*

in·con·clu·sive /ˌɪnkənˈkluːsɪv/ *adjective* (of an argument, evidence, or action) not leading to a definite decision, conclusion, or result. □ **in·con·clu·sive·ly** *adverb* **in·con·clu·sive·ness** *noun*

in·con·gru·ous /ɪnˈkɒŋgruəs/ *adjective* **1** not appropriate; out of place. **2** (often foll. by *with*) discordant, inconsistent; disagreeing in character

or qualities. **3** having disparate or inharmonious parts or elements. □ **in·con·gru·ity** /-ˈgruːɪti/ *noun* (*pl.* **-ities**). **in·con·gru·ous·ly** *adverb* **in·con·gru·ous·ness** *noun*

in·connu /ˈɪnkənuː/ *noun* (*pl.* same) a predatory freshwater salmonid game fish *Stenodus leucichthys*, of the Eurasian and N American Arctic. [French = 'unknown']

in·con·secu·tive /ˌɪnkənˈsekjʊtɪv/ *adjective* not in order or following continuously.

in·con·se·quent /ɪnˈkɒnsəkwənt/ *adjective* **1** irrelevant. **2** lacking logical sequence. **3** (of ideas or subjects) disconnected, haphazard. □ **in·con·se·quence** *noun*

in·con·se·quen·tial /ɪnˌkɒnsəˈkwenʃəl/ *adjective* trivial, unimportant, of no consequence. □ **in·con·se·quen·tial·ity** *noun* (*pl.* **-ities**). **in·con·se·quen·tial·ly** *adverb*

in·con·sider·able /ˌɪnkənˈsɪdərəbəl/ *adjective* **1** of small size, value, etc. **2** not worth considering.

in·con·sider·ate /ˌɪnkənˈsɪdərət/ *adjective* thoughtlessly causing hurt or inconvenience to others. □ **in·con·sider·ate·ly** *adverb* **in·con·sider·ate·ness** *noun*

in·con·sis·tent /ˌɪnkənˈsɪstənt/ *adjective* **1** acting at variance with one's own principles or former conduct. **2** (often foll. by *with*) not in keeping; discordant, at variance. **3** not staying the same throughout; having self-contradictory elements. □ **in·con·sis·tency** *noun* (*pl.* **-cies**). **in·con·sis·tent·ly** *adverb*

in·consol·able /ˌɪnkənˈsoːləbəl/ *adjective* (of a person, grief, etc.) that cannot be consoled or comforted. □ **in·consol·ably** *adverb*

in·con·spicu·ous /ˌɪnkənˈspɪkjʊəs/ *adjective* **1** not conspicuous; not easily noticed. **2** *Bot.* (of flowers) small, pale, or green. □ **in·con·spicu·ous·ly** *adverb* **in·con·spicu·ous·ness** *noun*

in·con·stant *adjective* **1** (of a person) fickle, changeable. **2** frequently changing; variable, irregular. □ **in·con·stancy** *noun* (*pl.* **-cies**). **in·con·stant·ly** *adverb*

in·contest·able *adjective* unquestionable, indisputable, not open to argument. □ **in·contest·abil·ity** *noun* **in·contest·ably** *adverb*

in·contin·ent /ɪnˈkɒntɪnənt/ *adjective* **1** unable to control movements of the bowels or bladder or both. **2** lacking self-restraint, esp. in regard to sexual desire; promiscuous. **3** unrestrained, unchecked (*incontinent bombing*). □ **in·contin·ence** *noun* **in·contin·ent·ly** *adverb*

in·contro·vert·ible /ˌɪnkɒntrəˈvɜːtɪbəl/ *adjective* indisputable, indubitable. □ **in·contro·vert·ibil·ity** *noun* **in·contro·vert·ibly** *adverb*

in·conven·ience ● *noun* **1** lack of suitability to personal requirements or ease. **2** a cause or instance of this. ● *transitive verb* cause inconvenience to.

in·conven·ient *adjective* causing trouble, difficulty, or discomfort; not convenient. □ **in·conven·ient·ly** *adverb*

in·con·vert·ible *adjective* (esp. of currency) not convertible into another form on demand.

in·coordin·a·tion *noun* lack of coordination, esp. of muscular action.

in·cor·por·ate ● *verb* **1** *transitive* (often foll. by *in*, *with*) unite; form into one body or whole. **2** *intransitive* become incorporated. **3** *transitive* combine (ingredients) into one substance. **4** *transitive* admit as a member of a company etc. **5** *transitive* combine or form into an organization, esp. constitute as a legal corporation. ● *adjective* (of a company etc.) formed into a legal corporation. □ **in·cor·por·a·tion** *noun* **in·cor·por·ator** *noun* [Late Latin *incorporare* (as IN-², Latin *corpus -oris* body)]

in·cor·por·ated *adjective* forming a legal corporation (*an incorporated town*).

in·cor·por·eal /ˌɪnkɔːrˈpɔːriəl/ *adjective* **1** without a body or material form. **2** of, pertaining to, or characteristic of immaterial beings. **3** *Law* having no material existence in itself, but connected as a right to some actual thing. [Latin *incorporeus* (as INCORPORATE)]

in·correct *adjective* **1** not in accordance with fact; wrong. **2** not in accordance with accepted standards; improper (*incorrect behaviour*). □ **in·correct·ly** *adverb* **in·correct·ness** *noun*

in·corri·gible /ɪnˈkɒrɪdʒɪbəl/ ● *adjective* **1** (of a person or habit) incurably bad or depraved. **2** not readily improved. ● *noun* an incorrigible person. □ **in·corri·gi·bil·ity** *noun* **in·corri·gibly** *adverb*

in·corrupt·ible /ˌɪnkəˈrʌptɪbəl/ *adjective* **1** unable to be corrupted, esp. unable to be bribed. **2** not susceptible to decay; everlasting. □ **in·corrupt·ibil·ity** *noun* **in·corrupt·ibly** *adverb*

in·crease ● *verb* **1** *transitive & intransitive* make or become greater in size, amount, etc., or more numerous. **2** *intransitive* advance (in quality, attainment, etc.). **3** *transitive* intensify (a quality). ● *noun* **1** the act or process of becoming greater or more numerous; growth, enlargement. **2** (of people, animals, or plants) growth in numbers; multiplication. **3** the amount or extent of an increase. □ **on the increase** increasing, esp. in frequency. □ **in·creased** *adjective* **in·creas·ing·ly** *adverb* [Old French *encreiss-* stem of *encreistre* from Latin *increscere* (as IN-², *crescere* grow)]

in·cred·ible *adjective* **1** that cannot be believed. **2** *informal* amazing, extraordinary (*we had an incredible time in San Francisco*). □ **in·cred·ibil·ity** *noun* **in·cred·ibly** *adverb*

in·credu·lous /ɪnˈkredjʊləs/ *adjective* **1** unwilling to believe, skeptical. **2** showing disbelief (*an incredulous look*). □ **in·credu·lity** /ˌɪnkrəˈdjuːlɪti/ *noun* **in·credu·lous·ly** *adverb* **in·credu·lous·ness** *noun*

in·cre·ment /ˈɪnkrəmənt/ *noun* **1 a** the action or process of increasing or becoming greater, esp. gradually. **b** an increase or addition, esp. one of a series on a fixed scale. **c** the amount of this. **2** *Math.* a small amount by which a variable quantity increases. □ **in·cre·men·tal** /-ˈmentəl/ *adjective* **in·cre·men·tal·ism** *noun* **in·cre·men·tal·ly** *adverb* [Latin *incrementum* from *increscere* INCREASE]

in·crim·in·ate /ɪnˈkrɪmɪˌneɪt/ *transitive verb* (esp. as **in·crim·in·at·ing** *adjective*) tend to prove the guilt of (*incriminating evidence*). □ **in·crim·in·a·tion** *noun* **in·crim·in·a·tory** *adjective* [Late Latin *incriminare* (as IN-², Latin *crimen* offence)]

in·crust·a·tion *var. of* ENCRUSTATION.

in·cu·bate /ˈɪŋkjʊbeɪt/ *verb* **1** *transitive* sit on or artificially heat (eggs) in order to bring forth young birds etc. **2** *transitive* maintain (cells, micro-organisms, etc.) in a controlled environment suitable for growth and development. **3** *intransitive* **a** sit on eggs; brood. **b** undergo incubation. **4** *transitive & intransitive* develop or grow slowly (*incubate a plan*). [Latin *incubare* (as IN-², *cubare* *cubit-* or *cubat-* lie)]

in·cu·ba·tion /ˌɪŋkjʊˈbeɪʃən/ *noun* **1** the act of incubating. **2** *Med.* **a** (in full **incubation period**) the period between exposure to an infection and the appearance of the first symptoms. **b** the processes occurring during this.

in·cu·ba·tor /ˈɪŋkjʊˌbeɪtər/ *noun* **1** an apparatus used to provide a suitable temperature and environment for a premature baby or one of low birth weight. **2** an apparatus used to hatch eggs or grow micro-organisms under artificially controlled conditions. **3** a place, organization, etc. providing a supportive and nurturing environment for the growth of an idea, business, etc.

in·cu·bus /ˈɪŋkjʊbəs/ *noun* (*pl.* **in·cu·bus·es** or **in·cubi** /-ˌbaɪ/) **1** a male demon believed to have sexual intercourse with sleeping women. **2** a nightmare. **3** a person or thing that oppresses or troubles like a nightmare. [Late Latin, = Latin *incubo* nightmare (as INCUBATE)]

in·cu·des *pl. of* INCUS.

in·cul·cate /ˈɪnkʌlˌkeɪt/ *transitive verb* (often foll. by *in*) urge or impress (a fact, habit, idea, etc.) persistently (*inculcate in young people a respect for the law*). □ **in·cul·ca·tion** *noun* **in·cul·ca·tor** *noun* [Latin *inculcare* (as IN-², *calcare* tread from *calx calcis* heel)]

in·cul·pate /ˈɪnkʌlpeɪt/ *transitive verb* **1** involve in a charge; incriminate. **2** accuse, blame. □ **in·cul·pa·tion** /-ˈpeɪʃən/ *noun* **in·cul·pa·tory** /ɪnˈkʌlpətəri/ *adjective* [Late Latin *inculpare* (as IN-², *culpare* blame, from *culpa* fault)]

in·cum·bent /ɪnˈkʌmbənt/ ● *adjective* **1** currently holding office (*the incumbent prime minister*). **2** (foll. by *on, upon*) resting or falling upon a person as a duty or obligation (*it is incumbent on you to warn them*). ● *noun* the holder of an office or post. □ **in·cum·ben·cy** *noun* (*pl.* **-cies**). [Anglo-Latin *incumbens* pres. part. of Latin *incumbere* lie upon (as IN-², *cubare* lie)]

in·cun·able /ɪnˈkjuːnəbəl/ *noun* = INCUNABULUM. [French, formed as INCUNABULUM]

in·cu·nabu·lum /ˌɪnkjuːˈnabjʊləm/ *noun* (*pl.* **in·cu·nab·ula** /-lə/) a book printed at an early date, esp. before 1501. [Latin *incunabula* swaddling clothes, cradle (as IN-², *cunae* cradle)]

incur *transitive verb* (**in·curred**, **in·cur·ring**) suffer, experience, or become subject to (something unpleasant) as a result of one's own behaviour etc. (*incurred huge debts*). □ **in·cur·rable** *adjective* [Latin *incurrere incurs-* (as IN-², *currere* run)]

in·cur·able *adjective* **1** unable to be cured. **2** inveterate; not likely to change (*an incurable romantic*). □ **in·cur·ably** *adverb*

in·curi·ous *adjective* lacking curiosity. □ **in·curi·os·ity** *noun* **in·curi·ous·ly** *adverb*

in·cur·sion *noun* **1** an invasion or attack, esp. when sudden or brief.

2 an interruption or disturbance. [Middle English from Latin *incursio* (as INCUR)]

in·curve *transitive verb* bend into a curve. □ **in·curv·a·tion** *noun*

in·curved *adjective* curved inwards.

incus /ˈɪŋkəs/ *noun* (*pl.* **in·cu·des** /-ˈkjuːdiːz/) the small anvil-shaped bone in the middle ear, in contact with the malleus and stapes. [Latin, = anvil]

in·cuse /ɪŋˈkjuːz/ ● *noun* an impression hammered or stamped on a coin. ● *transitive verb* **1** mark (a coin) with a figure by stamping. **2** impress (a figure) on a coin by stamping. ● *adjective* hammered or stamped on a coin. [Latin *incusus* past participle of *incudere* (as IN-², *cudere* forge)]

Ind. *abbreviation* **1** Independent. **2 a** India. **b** Indian. **3** Indiana.

in·debt·ed *adjective* (usu. foll. by *to*) **1** owing gratitude or obligation. **2** owing money. □ **in·debt·ed·ness** *noun*

in·decent *adjective* **1** offending against recognized standards of decency. **2** unbecoming; highly unsuitable (*with indecent haste*). □ **in·decen·cy** *noun* (*pl.* **-cies**). **in·decent·ly** *adverb*

indecent assault *noun* *Cdn hist. & Brit.* an offence of a sexual nature, not involving rape. ¶ In Canada, the legal offence of *indecent assault* was repealed in 1982. It was replaced with the offences of *sexual assault*, of which there are three categories.

indecent exposure *noun* the intentional act of publicly and indecently exposing one's body, esp. the genitals.

in·de·cipher·able /ˌɪndəˈsaɪfərəbəl/ *adjective* that cannot be deciphered; incoherent or illegible.

in·deci·sion /ˌɪndɪˈsɪʒən/ *noun* lack of decision; hesitation.

in·deci·sive /ˌɪndɪˈsaɪsɪv/ *adjective* **1** not decisive or conclusive (*an indecisive battle*). **2** (of a person) undecided, hesitating. **3** characteristically unable to make decisions. □ **in·deci·sive·ly** *adverb* **in·deci·sive·ness** *noun*

in·declin·able /ˌɪndɪˈklaɪnəbəl/ *adjective* *Grammar* **1** that cannot be declined. **2** having no inflections.

in·decor·ous /ɪnˈdekərəs/ *adjective* **1** improper. **2** in bad taste. □ **in·decor·ous·ly** *adverb* **in·decor·ous·ness** *noun*

in·deed ● *adverb* **1** in truth; really (*they are, indeed, a remarkable family*). **2** expressing emphasis or intensification (*I shall be very glad indeed; indeed it is; very, indeed inordinately, proud of it*). **3** admittedly (*there are indeed exceptions*). **4** in point of fact (*if indeed such a thing is possible*). **5** expressing an approving or ironic echo (*who is this Mr. Smith? — who is he indeed?*). ● *interjection* expressing irony, contempt, incredulity, etc.

in·deedy *interjection* *informal* indeed (adding emphasis to an affirmative).

in·defatig·able /ˌɪndɪˈfatɪɡəbəl/ *adjective* (of a person, quality, etc.) that cannot be tired out; unwearying, unremitting. □ **in·defatig·abil·ity** *noun* **in·defatig·ably** *adverb* [obsolete French *indéfatigable* or Latin *indefatigabilis* (as IN-¹, *defatigare* wear out)]

in·defeas·ible /ˌɪndɪˈfiːzəbəl/ *adjective* *literary* (esp. of a claim, rights, etc.) that cannot be lost. □ **in·defeas·ibil·ity** *noun* **in·defeas·ibly** *adverb*

in·defect·ible /ˌɪndɪˈfektəbəl/ *adjective* **1** unfailing; not liable to defect or decay. **2** faultless. [IN-¹ + *defectible* from Late Latin *defectibilis* (as DEFECT)]

in·defens·ible /ˌɪndɪˈfensəbəl/ *adjective* that cannot be defended, justified, or maintained in argument. □ **in·defens·ibil·ity** *noun* **in·defens·ibly** *adverb*

in·defin·able /ˌɪndɪˈfaɪnəbəl/ *adjective* that cannot be defined or exactly described. □ **in·defin·ably** *adverb*

in·defin·ite /ɪnˈdefənɪt/ *adjective* **1** not clearly defined or stated; vague (*an indefinite answer*). **2** of undetermined extent, amount or number; unlimited. **3** *Grammar* not determining the person, thing, time, etc., referred to. □ **in·defin·ite·ness** *noun*

indefinite article *noun* *Grammar* a word (*a* and *an* in English) preceding a noun and implying lack of specificity (as in *bought me a book; government is an art*).

indefinite integral *noun* *Math.* an integral expressed without limits, and so having the same derivative if an arbitrary constant is added.

in·defin·ite·ly /ɪnˈdefənɪtli/ *adverb* **1** for an unlimited time (*was postponed indefinitely*). **2** in an indefinite manner; vaguely.

indefinite pronoun *noun* a pronoun indicating a person, amount, etc., without being definite or particular, e.g. *any, some, anyone*.

in·dehis·cent /ˌɪndɪˈhɪsənt/ *adjective* *Bot.* (of fruit) not splitting open when ripe. □ **in·dehis·cence** *noun*

in·del·ible /ɪnˈdeləbəl/ *adjective* **1** that cannot be rubbed out or (in abstract senses) removed; permanent. **2** (of ink etc.) that makes indelible marks. □ **in·del·ibil·ity** /-ˈbɪlɪti/ noun **in·del·ibly** adverb [French indélébile or Latin indelebilis (as IN-¹, delebilis from delēre efface)]

in·deli·cate adjective **1** coarse, unrefined. **2** tactless. **3** tending to indecency. □ **in·deli·cacy** noun (pl. **-cies**). **in·deli·cate·ly** adverb

in·dem·nify /ɪnˈdemnə,faɪ/ transitive verb (**-fies, -fied**) **1** (often foll. by from, against) protect or secure (a person) against harm, loss, etc. **2** (often foll. by for) secure (a person) against legal responsibility for actions. **3** (often foll. by for) compensate (a person) for a loss, expenses, etc. □ **in·dem·ni·fi·ca·tion** noun [Latin indemnis unhurt (as IN-¹, damnum loss, damage)]

in·dem·nity /ɪnˈdemnɪti/ noun (pl. **-ties**) **1 a** compensation for loss incurred. **b** a sum paid for this, esp. a sum exacted by a victor in war etc. as one condition of peace. **2** security against loss. **3** legal exemption from penalties etc. incurred. **4** Cdn the salary paid to a Member of Parliament or of a Legislative Assembly. [French indemnité or Late Latin indemnitas -tatis (as INDEMNIFY)]

ind·ene /ˈɪndiːn/ noun Chem. a colourless flammable liquid hydrocarbon obtained from coal tar and used in making synthetic resins. [INDOLE + -ENE]

in·dent¹ ● transitive verb /ɪnˈdent/ **1** start (a line of print or writing) further from the margin than other lines, e.g. to mark a new paragraph. **2** divide (a document drawn up in duplicate) into its two copies with a zigzag line dividing them and ensuring identification. **3** make toothlike notches in. **4** form deep recesses in (a coastline etc.). ● noun /ˈɪndent/ **1** an indentation in printing or writing; an indented line. **2** an incision in the edge of a thing; a deep angular recess. **3** an indenture. □ **in·dent·er** noun **in·dent·or** noun [Anglo-French endenter from Anglo-Latin indentare (as IN-², Latin dens dentis tooth)]

in·dent² ● transitive verb /ɪnˈdent/ **1** make a dent in the surface of (a thing). **2** impress (a mark etc.). ● noun /ˈɪndent/ a dent or depression in a surface. [Middle English from IN-² + DENT]

in·den·ta·tion noun **1** the act or an instance of indenting; the process of being indented. **2** a cut or notch. **3** a zigzag. **4** a deep recess in a coastline etc.

in·den·ture /ɪnˈdentʃər/ ● noun **1** an indented document (see INDENT¹ verb 2). **2** (usu. in pl.) **a** a sealed agreement or contract. **b** a contract binding a person to service. **3** a formal list, certificate, voucher, etc. ● transitive verb bind (a person) by indentures, esp. as an apprentice or servant. □ **in·den·tured** adjective **in·den·ture·ship** noun [Anglo-French endenture (as INDENT¹)]

in·dépen·dan·tiste /ãdepãdãˈtiːst/ Cdn ● noun a person who supports the idea of Quebec independence; a sovereignist. ● adjective of or relating to the sovereignist movement in Quebec. [French]

in·depend·ence /ˌɪndɪˈpendəns/ noun **1** (often foll. by of, from) the state of being independent. **2** the fact or process of becoming independent (a new constitution was introduced after independence).

Independence Day noun a day celebrating the anniversary of national independence, esp. 4 July in the US.

in·depend·ent /ˌɪndɪˈpendənt/ ● adjective **1 a** (often foll. by of) not depending on authority or control. **b** (of a state) self-governing. **2 a** not depending on another person for one's opinion or livelihood. **b** (of income or resources) making it unnecessary to earn one's living (a woman of independent means). **3** unwilling to be under an obligation to others. **4** Politics not belonging to or supported by a party. **5** not depending on something else for its validity, efficiency, value, etc. (independent proof). **6** impartial; conducted or originating outside a given institution, group, etc. (an independent inquiry). **7** (of broadcasting, a school, etc.) not supported by public funds. **8 a** (of a film, recording, etc.) produced without the support of a major studio, record label, etc. **b** (of a store, business, business person, etc.) not part of a chain or larger corporate structure (an independent bookstore; an independent contractor). **9** Grammar (of a clause) able to stand alone as a complete sentence. ● noun **1** a person or thing which is independent, esp. a retailer whose store is not part of a chain. **2** a person who is politically independent. □ **in·depend·ent·ly** adverb

independent variable noun Math. a variable whose variation does not depend on that of another.

in-depth attributive adjective thorough; done in depth.

in·describ·able /ˌɪndɪˈskraɪbəbəl/ adjective **1** too unusual or extreme to be described. **2** vague, indefinite. □ **in·describ·ably** adverb

in·de·struct·ible /ˌɪndɪˈstrʌktəbəl/ adjective that cannot be destroyed. □ **in·de·struct·ibil·ity** /-ˈbɪlɪti/ noun **in·de·struct·ibly** adverb

in·deter·min·able /ˌɪndɪˈtɜːmɪnəbəl/ adjective **1** that cannot be ascertained. **2** (of a dispute etc.) that cannot be settled.

in·deter·min·ate /ˌɪndɪˈtɜːmɪnət/ adjective **1** not fixed in extent,

character, etc. **2** left doubtful; vague. **3** Math. (of a quantity) not limited to a fixed value by the value of another quantity. **4** (of a judicial sentence) such that the convicted person's conduct determines the date of release. **5** Bot. (of a plant shoot) not having all the axes terminating in a flower bud and so producing a shoot of indefinite length. **6** Med. (of a condition) from which a diagnosis of the underlying cause cannot be made (indeterminate colitis). □ **in·deter·min·acy** noun **in·deter·min·ate·ly** adverb

indeterminate vowel noun the obscure vowel /ə/ heard in 'a moment ago'; a schwa.

in·deter·min·ism /ˌɪndɪˈtɜːmɪˌnɪzəm/ noun the belief that human action is not wholly determined by motives. □ **in·deter·min·is·tic** adjective

index ● noun (pl. **in·dex·es** or esp. in technical use **in·di·ces** /ˈɪndɪˌsiːz/) **1** an alphabetical list of names, subjects, etc., with references, usu. at the end of a book. **2** = CARD INDEX. **3** a scale relating the level of prices, wages, etc. at a particular time to those at a date taken as a base (consumer price index; Dow Jones index). **4** Math. **a** the exponent of a number. **b** the power to which it is raised. **5 a** a pointer, esp. on an instrument, showing a quantity, a position on a scale, etc. **b** (usu. foll. by of) a sign, token, or indication of something. **6** Physics a number expressing a physical property etc. in terms of a standard (refractive index). **7** Computing a set of items each of which specifies one of the records of a file and contains information about its address. **8** (**Index**) Catholicism hist. a list of books forbidden to Roman Catholics to read. **9** Printing a symbol shaped like a pointing hand, used to draw attention to a note etc. ● transitive verb **1** provide (a book etc.) with an index. **2** enter in an index. **3** relate (wages etc.) to the value of a price index. **4** serve as an index to; indicate. □ **in·dex·er** noun [Latin index indicis forefinger, informer, sign: sense 8 from Latin Index librorum prohibitorum list of prohibited books]

in·dex·a·tion noun the adjustment in rates of payment etc. to reflect variations in the cost-of-living index or other economic indicator.

index card noun a small rectangular card made of heavy paper, used in writing or recording notes, information, etc.

index case noun Med. the first identified case in a group of related cases of a particular communicable or hereditable disease.

index finger noun the forefinger.

index futures plural noun contracts to buy a range of shares at an agreed price but delivered and paid for later.

index-linked adjective Brit. related to the value of a retail price index. □ **index-linking** noun

India a country in S Asia occupying the greater part of the Indian subcontinent; pop. (est. 2002) 1,045,845,226; capital, New Delhi. India is the second most populous country in the world.

India ink noun esp. N Amer. **1** a black pigment made originally in China and Japan. **2** a dark ink made from this, used esp. in drawing and technical graphics.

In·di·an ● noun **1 a** a native or national of India. **b** a person of Indian descent. **2 a** a member of the Aboriginal peoples of North and South America, or their descendants. **b** any of the languages of the Aboriginal peoples of North and South America. **c** Cdn a status Indian. ¶ Although the use of Indian in sense 2 has declined because it is thought to reflect Columbus's mistaken idea that he had landed in India in 1492, it is common in the usage of many Aboriginal people and embedded in legislation that is still in effect. It is also the only clear way to distinguish among the three general categories of Aboriginal people (Indians, Inuit, and Metis). ● adjective **1** of or relating to India, or to the subcontinent comprising India, Pakistan, and Bangladesh. **2** of or relating to the Aboriginal peoples of North and South America. □ **In·dian·iz·a·tion** noun **In·dian·ize** transitive verb **In·dian·ness** noun

In·di·ana a state in the Midwest of the US; pop. (2000) 6,080,485; capital, Indianapolis. □ **In·di·an·an** noun & adjective

Indian agent noun Cdn hist. a person appointed by the Department of Indian Affairs to supervise government programs on a reserve or in a specific region.

In·dian·ap·olis /ˌɪndiəˈnapəlɪs/ the state capital of Indiana; pop. (2000) 791,926. The city hosts an annual 500-mile (804.5-km) motor race, known as the Indy 500.

Indian bean tree noun = CATALPA.

Indian club noun each of a pair of bottle-shaped clubs swung to exercise the arms in gymnastics.

Indian corn noun **1** = CORN¹ 1. **2** multicoloured corn on the cob, used esp. as a decoration.

Indian cucumber-root *noun see* CUCUMBER-ROOT.

Indian elephant *noun* the elephant, *Elephas maximus*, of India, which is smaller than the African elephant.

Indian file *noun* = SINGLE FILE.

Indian hemp *noun* **1** = HEMP 1. **2** = DOGBANE.

Indian ice cream *noun Cdn* (*BC*) a dessert or drink made from whipped soapberries, sugar, and water.

Indian ink *noun* esp. *Brit.* = INDIA INK.

Indian Mutiny a revolt of Indians against British rule, 1857–8. After a series of sieges (most notably that of Lucknow) and battles, the revolt was put down; it was followed by the institution of direct rule by the British Crown in place of the East India Company administration.

Indian Ocean the ocean to the south of India, extending from the east coast of Africa to the East Indies and Australia.

Indian paintbrush *noun N Amer.* any of various plants of the genus *Castilleja*, chiefly of western N America, with flowers hidden by brightly coloured bracts.

Indian pear *noun* **1** any of several N American shrubs of the genus *Amelanchier*, of the rose family, with showy white flowers. **2** the fruit of this shrub.

Indian pipe *noun* a usu. white, low, saprophytic plant, *Monotropa uniflora*, with a solitary drooping flower.

Indian poke *noun* a liliaceous plant of the genus *Veratrum* with clusters of yellowish green flowers. *Also called* FALSE HELLEBORE.

Indian red ● *noun* **1** a yellowish red earth containing ferric oxide. **2** the colour of various red pigments prepared by oxidation of ferrous salts. ● *adjective* of this colour.

Indian rice *noun* = CHOCOLATE LILY.

Indian subcontinent the part of Asia south of the Himalayas which forms a peninsula extending into the Indian Ocean, between the Arabian Sea and the Bay of Bengal. Historically forming the whole territory of greater India, the region is now divided between India, Pakistan, and Bangladesh.

Indian summer *noun* **1** a period of dry warm weather occurring in the fall after colder weather has already set in. **2** a late period (of life, of an epoch etc.) characterized by comparative calm.

Indian title *noun Cdn* the claim by Indians to rights of ownership of land by virtue of its being occupied by Indians before the arrival of Europeans.

Indian tobacco *noun* **1** a N American medicinal plant, *Lobelia inflata*, which tastes like tobacco when chewed. **2** any of various plants used as a tobacco substitute.

Indian turnip *noun* **1** the jack-in-the-pulpit plant. **2** the edible corm of this.

India paper *noun* **1** a soft absorbent paper originally imported from China, used for proofs of engravings. **2** a very thin tough opaque printing paper.

India rubber *noun* = RUBBER¹ 1.

Indic ● *adjective* of or relating to a group of Indo-European languages comprising Sanskrit and the modern Indian languages which are its descendants. ● *noun* this language group. [Latin *Indicus* from Greek *Indikos* INDIAN]

indi·cate *transitive verb* (often foll. by *that* + clause) **1** point out; make known; show. **2** be a sign or symptom of; express the presence of. **3** (often in *passive*) suggest; call for; require or show to be necessary (*stronger measures are indicated*). **4** admit to or state briefly (*indicated his disapproval*; *she indicated that she was 'investigating the matter'*). **5** (of a gauge etc.) give as a reading. [Latin *indicare* (as IN-², *dicare* make known)]

indi·ca·tion *noun* **1 a** the act or an instance of indicating. **b** something that suggests or indicates; a sign or symptom. **2** something indicated or suggested. **3** a reading given by a gauge or instrument.

in·dic·a·tive /ɪnˈdɪkətɪv/ ● *adjective* **1** (foll. by *of*) suggestive; serving as an indication. **2** *Grammar* (of a mood) denoting simple statement of a fact. ● *noun Grammar* **1** the indicative mood. **2** a verb in this mood. □ **in·dic·a·tive·ly** *adverb*

indi·ca·tor *noun* **1** a person or thing that indicates, esp. performance, change, etc. (*economic indicators*). **2 a** a device indicating the condition of a machine etc. **b** a pointer, light, etc., which draws attention or gives warning. **3** a recording instrument attached to an apparatus. **4** *Brit.* a board in a railway station etc. giving current information. **5** (in full **turning indicator**) *Brit.* = TURN SIGNAL. **6** a substance which changes to a characteristic colour in the presence of a particular concentration

of an ion, so indicating e.g. acidity. **7** *Biol.* a species or group which acts as a sign of particular environmental conditions.

indicator species *noun* a species of plant or animal found in a particular environment whose condition reflects conditions in that environment.

in·di·ces *pl. of* INDEX.

in·di·cia /ɪnˈdɪʃɪə/ *plural noun* **1** distinguishing or identifying marks. **2** signs, indications. [pl. of Latin *indicium* (as INDEX)]

in·dict /ɪnˈdaɪt/ *transitive verb* **1** charge (a person) with a crime, esp. formally by legal process. **2** bring accusations against (a person or thing). □ **in·dict·ee** /-ˈtiː/ *noun* **in·dict·er** *noun* [Anglo-French *enditer* from Old French *enditier* declare, from Romanic *indictare* (unrecorded: as IN-², DICTATE)]

indictable offence *noun Cdn & Brit.* a more serious criminal offence, such as murder, which is triable by way of indictment (*compare* SUMMARY CONVICTION OFFENCE).

in·dict·ment /ɪnˈdaɪtmənt/ *noun* **1** the act of indicting or the state of being indicted. **2 a** a formal accusation. **b** a legal process in which this is made. **c** a document containing a charge. **3** something that serves to condemn or censure (*his book is an indictment of the previous government*).

in·die *informal* ● *noun* **1** an independent record or film company. **2 a** a musician or band whose music is recorded by an independent company. **b** a film produced by an independent company. **3** a bookstore that is not part of a chain. ● *adjective* **1** (of a pop group, record label, film, etc.) independent, not belonging to one of the major record companies or film studios. **2** characteristic of the deliberately unpolished or uncommercial style of indie bands.

In·dies *plural noun* (prec. by *the*) *archaic* India and adjacent regions (*see also* EAST INDIES, WEST INDIES). [pl. of obsolete *Indy* India]

in·dif·fer·ence *noun* **1** lack of interest or attention. **2** unimportance (*a matter of indifference*).

in·dif·fer·ent *adjective* **1** (foll. by *to*) having no partiality for or against; having no interest in or sympathy for. **2** neither good nor bad; average, mediocre. **3 a** not especially good. **b** fairly bad. **4** (often prec. by *very*) decidedly inferior. **5** chemically, magnetically, etc., neutral. □ **in·dif·fer·ent·ly** *adverb*

in·dif·fer·ent·ism *noun* an attitude of indifference, esp. in religious matters.

indi·gene /ˈɪndɪdʒiːn/ *noun* a native or aboriginal inhabitant of a region etc. [French *indigène* from Latin *indigena*]

in·digen·ize /ɪnˈdɪdʒə,naɪz/ *transitive verb* (also esp. *Brit.* **-ise**) make indigenous; subject to native influence. □ **in·digen·iz·a·tion** /-ˈzeɪʃən/ *noun*

in·digen·ous /ɪnˈdɪdʒənəs/ *adjective* **1 a** (esp. of flora or fauna) originating naturally in a region. **b** (of people) born in a region. **c** (of a musical style, sport, etc.) characteristic of or originating in a region. **2** (foll. by *to*) belonging naturally to a place. **3** of, pertaining to, or concerned with the aboriginal inhabitants of a region. □ **in·digen·ous·ly** *adverb* [Latin *indigena* from *indi-* = IN-² + *gen-* be born]

indi·gent /ˈɪndɪdʒənt/ ● *adjective* needy, poor. ● *noun* an indigent person. □ **indi·gence** *noun* [Old French from Late Latin *indigēre* from *indi-* = IN-² + *egēre* need]

in·digest·ible /ˌɪndɪˈdʒɛstəbəl/ *adjective* **1** difficult or impossible to digest. **2** too complex or awkward to read or comprehend easily. □ **in·digest·ibil·ity** /-ˈbɪlɪti/ *noun* **in·digest·ibly** *adverb*

in·diges·tion /ˌɪndɪˈdʒɛstʃən/ *noun* **1** difficulty in digesting food. **2** pain or discomfort caused by this.

Indi·gir·ka River /ˌɪndɪˈɡiːrkə/ a river of far E Siberia, which flows northward for 1 779 km (1,112 miles) to the Arctic Ocean, where it forms a wide delta.

in·dig·nant /ɪnˈdɪɡnənt/ *adjective* feeling or showing scornful anger. □ **in·dig·nant·ly** *adverb* [Latin *indignari indignant-* regard as unworthy (as IN-¹, *dignus* worthy)]

in·dig·na·tion /ˌɪndɪɡˈneɪʃən/ *noun* scornful anger at supposed unjust or unfair conduct or treatment. [Old French *indignation* or Latin *indignatio* (as INDIGNANT)]

in·dig·nity /ɪnˈdɪɡnɪti/ *noun* (pl. **-ties**) **1** unworthy treatment. **2** a slight or insult. **3** the humiliating quality of something (*the indignity of my position*).

in·digo /ˈɪndɪˌɡoʊ/ ● *noun* (pl. **-digos**) **1 a** a natural blue dye obtained from the indigo plant. **b** a synthetic form of this dye. **2** any plant of the genus *Indigofera*. **3** (in full **indigo blue**) a colour between blue and violet in the spectrum. ● *adjective* of this colour. [16th-c. *indico* (from

Spanish), *indigo* (from Portuguese) from Latin *indicum* from Greek *indikon* INDIAN (dye)]

indigo bunting *noun* a N American bunting, *Passerina cyanea*, the male of which has bright blue plumage.

In·dira Gan·dhi Canal /ɪnˌdiːrə ˈgandi, ˌɪndɜrə/ (formerly called **Rajasthan Canal**) a massive canal in NW India, bringing water to the Thar Desert of Rajasthan from the Harike Barrage on the Sutlej River. The canal, which is 650 km (406 miles) long, was completed in 1986.

in·direct *adjective* **1 a** allusive; not going straight to the point (*an indirect answer*). **b** not acting or exercised with direct force; roundabout. **2** (of a route etc.) not straight; circuitous. **3** not directly sought or aimed at (*an indirect result*). **4** (of lighting) from a concealed source and diffusely reflected. □ **in·direc·tion** *noun* **in·direct·ly** *adverb* **in·direct·ness** *noun*

indirect object *noun Grammar* a person or thing affected by a verbal action but not primarily acted on, e.g. *him* in *give him the book*.

indirect question *noun Grammar* a question in reported speech, e.g. *they asked who I was*.

indirect speech *noun* (esp. *N Amer.* also **indirect discourse**) = REPORTED SPEECH.

indirect tax *noun* a tax that is paid to the government by the taxpayer through an intermediary rather than directly, e.g. sales tax.

in·discern·ible /ˌɪndɪˈsɜrnəbəl/ *adjective* that cannot be discerned or distinguished from another. □ **in·discern·ibly** *adverb*

in·disci·pline /ɪnˈdɪsɪplɪn/ *noun* lack of discipline. □ **in·disci·plined** *adjective*

in·discreet *adjective* **1** not discreet; revealing secrets. **2** injudicious, unwary. □ **in·discreet·ly** *adverb*

in·dis·crete *adjective* not divided into distinct parts.

in·dis·cre·tion /ˌɪndɪˈskreʃən/ *noun* **1** lack of discretion; indiscreet conduct. **2** an indiscreet action, remark, etc.

in·dis·crim·in·ate /ˌɪndɪˈskrɪmɪnət/ *adjective* **1** (of an action etc.) not distinguished by discernment or discrimination; haphazard, not selective (*indiscriminate bombing of enemy targets*). **2** (of a person) acting without careful judgment; not using or exercising discrimination. □ **in·dis·crim·in·ate·ly** *adverb* **in·dis·crim·in·ate·ness** *noun* **in·dis·crim·in·a·tion** /-ˈneiʃən/ *noun*

in·dis·pens·able /ˌɪndɪˈspensəbəl/ ● *adjective* **1** (often foll. by *to, for*) that cannot be dispensed with; necessary. **2** (of a law, duty, etc.) that is not to be set aside. ● *noun* an indispensable person or thing. □ **in·dis·pens·abil·ity** *noun* **in·dis·pens·ably** *adverb*

in·dis·pose *transitive verb* (often foll. by *towards, from*, or *to* + infin.) make averse.

in·dis·posed *adjective* **1** slightly unwell. **2** averse or unwilling. □ **in·dis·pos·ition** *noun*

in·disput·able *adjective* **1** that cannot be disputed. **2** unquestionable. □ **in·disput·abil·ity** *noun* **in·disput·ably** *adverb*

in·dis·sol·uble /ˌɪndɪˈsɒljʊbəl/ *adjective* **1** that cannot be dissolved or decomposed. **2** lasting, stable (*an indissoluble bond*). □ **in·dis·solu·bil·ity** *noun* **in·dis·sol·ubly** *adverb*

in·dis·tinct *adjective* **1** not distinct. **2** confused, obscure. □ **in·dis·tinct·ly** *adverb* **in·dis·tinct·ness** *noun*

in·dis·tin·guish·able *adjective* (often foll. by *from*) not distinguishable. □ **in·dis·tin·guish·abil·ity** *noun* **in·dis·tin·guish·ably** *adverb*

in·dium /ˈɪndiəm/ *noun Chem.* a soft silvery-white metallic element occurring naturally in zinc blende etc., used for electroplating and in semiconductors. Symbol: **In**; at. no.: 49. [Latin *indicum* indigo, with reference to its characteristic spectral lines]

in·di·vid·ual ● *adjective* **1** single, separate. **2** particular, special; not general. **3** having a distinct character. **4** characteristic of a particular person. **5** designed for use by one person (*individual portions*). ● *noun* **1** a single human being as distinct from a family or group. **2** a person (*a most unpleasant individual*). **3** a person who does not conform to the majority. **4** a single member of a class or group. **5** *Biol.* a single member of a species, or of a colonial or compound organism. [Middle English, = indivisible, from medieval Latin *individualis* (as IN-¹, *dividuus* from *dividere* DIVIDE)]

in·di·vid·ual·ism *noun* **1** the habit or principle of being independent and self-reliant. **2** a social theory favouring the free action of individuals. **3** self-centred feeling or conduct; egoism. **4** = INDIVIDUALITY 1. □ **in·di·vid·ual·ist** *noun* **in·di·vid·ual·is·tic** *adjective* **in·di·vid·ual·is·tic·ally** *adverb*

in·di·vid·u·al·ity *noun* (pl. **-ities**) **1** the sum of the attributes which distinguish one person or thing from others of the same kind; strongly marked individual character. **2** the fact or condition of separate existence.

in·di·vid·ual·ize *transitive verb* (also esp. *Brit.* **-ise**) **1** give an individual character to. **2** (esp. as **in·di·vid·ual·ized** *adjective*) personalize or tailor to suit the individual (*individualized notepaper; individualized training course*). □ **in·di·vid·ual·iz·a·tion** *noun*

in·di·vid·ual·ly *adverb* **1** personally; in an individual capacity. **2** in a distinctive manner. **3** one by one; not collectively.

in·di·vidu·ate *transitive verb* distinguish from others of the same kind; single out. □ **in·di·vidu·a·tion** *noun*

in·divis·ible /ˌɪndɪˈvɪzɪbəl/ *adjective* **1** not divisible. **2** (of a number) unable to be divided by another number exactly without leaving a remainder. □ **in·divis·ibil·ity** *noun* **in·divis·ibly** *adverb*

Indo- *combining form* Indian; Indian and. [Latin *Indus* from Greek *Indos*]

Indo-Aryan /ˌɪndoːˈeriən/ ● *noun* **1** a member of any of the Aryan peoples of India. **2** the Indic group of languages. ● *adjective* of or relating to the Indo-Aryans or Indo-Aryan.

Indo-Canadian ● *noun* a Canadian born in the Indian subcontinent, esp. India, or one of Indian descent. ● *adjective* of or relating to Indo-Canadians.

Indo·china the peninsula of SE Asia containing Burma (Myanmar), Thailand, Malaya, Laos, Cambodia, and Vietnam; esp. the part of this area consisting of Laos, Cambodia, and Vietnam, which was a French dependency (**French Indochina**) from 1862 to 1954. □ **Indo·chinese** *adjective & noun*

in·doc·trin·ate /ɪnˈdɒktrɪˌneɪt/ *transitive verb* teach (a person or group) systematically or for a long period to accept (esp. partisan or tendentious) ideas uncritically. □ **in·doc·trin·a·tion** *noun* **in·doc·trin·ator** *noun*

Indo-European /ˌɪndoːjʊərəˈpiːən/ ● *adjective* **1** of or relating to the family of languages spoken over the greater part of Europe and Asia as far as N India. **2** of or relating to the hypothetical parent language of this family. ● *noun* **1** the Indo-European family of languages. **2** the hypothetical parent language of all languages belonging to this family. **3** (usu. in *pl.*) a speaker of an Indo-European language.

Indo-Iranian /ˌɪndoːɪˈreɪniən/ ● *adjective* of or relating to the subfamily of Indo-European languages spoken chiefly in northern India and Iran. ● *noun* this subfamily.

ind·ole /ˈɪndoːl/ *noun Chem.* an organic compound with a characteristic odour formed on the reduction of indigo. [INDIGO + Latin *oleum* oil]

indole·acet·ic acid /ˌɪndoːləˈsiːtɪk/ *noun Biochem.* any of the several isomeric acetic acid derivatives of indole, esp. one found as a natural growth hormone in plants. Abbr.: **IAA**. [INDOLE + ACETIC]

in·dol·ent /ˈɪndələnt/ *adjective* **1** lazy; wishing to avoid activity or exertion. **2** *Med.* causing no pain (*an indolent tumour*). □ **in·dol·ence** *noun* **in·dol·ent·ly** *adverb* [Late Latin *indolens* (as IN-¹, *dolere* suffer pain)]

Ind·ol·ogy /ɪnˈdɒlədʒi/ *noun* the study of the history, literature, etc. of India. □ **Ind·ol·o·gist** *noun*

in·domit·able /ɪnˈdɒmɪtəbəl/ *adjective* impossible to subdue or defeat. □ **in·domit·abil·ity** *noun* **in·domit·ably** *adverb* [Late Latin *indomitabilis* (as IN-¹, Latin *domitare* tame)]

Indo·nesia /ˌɪndəˈniːʒə/ a SE Asian country consisting of many islands in the Malay Archipelago; pop. (est. 2002) 231,328,092; capital, Jakarta (on Java). Indonesia consists of the territories of the former Dutch East Indies, of which the largest are Java, Sumatra, S Borneo, W New Guinea, the Moluccas, and Sulawesi. The majority of Indonesia's population is Javanese, with Java the most densely populated of the country's islands.

Indo·nes·ian /ˌɪndəˈniːʒən/ ● *noun* **1 a** a native or national of Indonesia. **b** a person of Indonesian descent. **2** a member of the chief pre-Malay population of the E Indies. **3 a** the western branch of the Austronesian language family. **b** = BAHASA. ● *adjective* of or relating to Indonesia or its people or language. [*Indonesia* from INDIES after *Polynesia*]

in·door *adjective* situated, carried on, or used within a building or under cover (*indoor antenna; indoor games*).

indoor-outdoor *adjective N Amer.* designating a sturdy carpet that can be used both inside and outside a house etc.

in·doors *adverb* into or within a building.

In·dore /ɪnˈdɔr/ a manufacturing city of Madhya Pradesh in central India; pop. (2001) 1,597,400.

Indra *Hinduism* the warrior king of the heavens, god of war and storm, to whom many of the prayers in the Rig-Veda are addressed. [Sanskrit, = lord]

---

t *top* v *voice* w *we* z *zoo* ʃ *she* ʒ *vision* θ *thin* ð *this* ŋ *ring* x *loch* tʃ *chip* dʒ *jar* (*see over for vowels*)

in·draft *noun* (esp. *Brit.* **in·draught**) an inward flow or current.

in·drawn *adjective* **1** (of breath etc.) drawn in. **2** aloof.

in·dri /ˈɪndri/ *noun* (*pl.* **in·dris**) a large woolly black and white lemur of Madagascar, *Indri indri*, having long hind legs and a short tail and progressing by long leaps between trees. [Malagasy *indry* behold, mistaken for its name]

in·dubit·able /ɪnˈduːbɪtəbəl, -ˈdjuː-/ *adjective* that cannot be doubted. □ **in·dubit·ably** *adverb* [French *indubitable* or Latin *indubitabilis* (as IN-¹, *dubitare* to doubt)]

in·duce *verb* **1** *transitive* (often foll. by *to* + infin.) prevail on; persuade. **2** *transitive* bring about; give rise to. **3** *transitive & intransitive Med.* bring on (labour) artificially, esp. by use of drugs. **4** *transitive Electricity* produce (a current) by induction. **5** *transitive Physics* cause (radioactivity) by bombardment. **6** *transitive* infer; derive as a deduction. **7** *transitive Biol.* cause (a bacterium) to begin the lytic cycle. □ **in·du·cer** *noun* **in·du·cible** *adjective* [Latin *inducere induct-* (as IN-², *ducere* lead)]

in·duce·ment *noun* **1** (often foll. by *to*) an attraction that leads one on. **2** a thing that induces (*a financial inducement*).

in·duct *transitive verb* (often foll. by *to, into*) **1 a** introduce formally into an office, position, etc. **b** introduce (a member of the clergy) formally into possession of a benefice. **2** introduce, initiate (*inducted into a secret brotherhood*). **3 a** *US* enlist (a person) for military service. **b** admit as a new member (*inducted him into the band*). □ **in·duc·tee** *noun* [Middle English (as INDUCE)]

in·duct·ance *noun Electricity* **1** the property of an electric circuit that causes an electromotive force to be generated by a change in the current flowing. **2** INDUCTOR 1.

in·duc·tion *noun* **1** the act or an instance of inducting or inducing. **2** *Med.* the process of bringing on (esp. labour) by artificial means. **3** *Logic* **a** the inference of a general law from particular instances (*compare* DEDUCTION 2a). **b** *Math.* a means of proving a theorem by showing that if it is true of any particular case it is true of the next case in a series, and then showing that it is indeed true in one particular case. **c** (foll. by *of*) the production of (facts) to prove a general statement. **4** (often *attributive*) *Brit.* a formal introduction to a new job, position, etc. (*attended an induction course*). **5** *Electricity* **a** the production of an electric or magnetic state by the proximity (without contact) of an electrified or magnetized body. **b** the production of an electric current in a conductor by a change of magnetic field. **6** the drawing of a fuel mixture into the cylinders of an internal combustion engine. **7** *US* enlistment for military service. **8** *Biochem.* initiation or acceleration of synthesis of an enzyme as a result of the introduction of a specific substance (the inducer).

induction coil *noun* a coil for generating intermittent high voltage from a direct current.

induction heating *noun* heating by an induced electric current.

in·duct·ive *adjective* **1** (of reasoning etc.) of or based on induction. **2** of electric or magnetic induction. □ **in·duct·ive·ly** *adverb*

in·duct·or *noun* **1** *Electricity* a component (in a circuit) which possesses inductance. **2** a person who inducts or initiates.

in·dulge *verb* **1** *intransitive* (often foll. by *in*) allow oneself to enjoy the pleasure of something. **2** *transitive* yield freely to (a desire etc.). **3** *transitive* gratify the wishes of; favour (*indulged them with money*). **4** *reflexive* give free rein to one's inclination or liking. **5** *intransitive informal* take alcoholic liquor. **6** *transitive* grant (a debtor) an extension of time for payment of (a debt, etc.). □ **in·dul·ger** *noun* [Latin *indulgēre indult-* give free rein to]

in·dul·gence *noun* **1 a** the act of indulging. **b** the state of being indulgent. **c** lenient or liberal treatment. **2** something indulged in. **3** *Catholicism* the remission of punishment in purgatory, still due for sins even after sacramental absolution. **4** a privilege granted.

in·dul·gent *adjective* **1** ready or too ready to overlook faults etc. **2** indulging or tending to indulge. □ **in·dul·gent·ly** *adverb*

in·duna /ɪnˈduːnə/ *noun South Africa* **1** a tribal councillor or headman. **2 a** an African foreman. **b** a person in authority. [Nguni *inDuna* captain, councillor]

in·dur·ate /ˈɪndjʊˌreɪt/ *transitive & intransitive verb* make or become hard. [Latin *indurare* (as IN-², *durus* hard)]

in·du·sium /ɪnˈduːzɪəm, -ˈdjuː-/ *noun* (*pl.* **in·dusia** /-zɪə/) **1** a membranous shield covering the fruit cluster of a fern. **2** a collection of hairs enclosing the stigma of some flowers. **3** the case of a larva. [Latin, = tunic, from *induere* put on (a garment)]

Indus River /ˈɪndəs/ a river of S Asia, about 2 900 km (1,800 miles) in length, flowing from Tibet through Kashmir and Pakistan to the Arabian Sea. Along its valley an early civilization flourished from *c.*2600 to 1760 BC.

in·dus·trial ● *adjective* **1 a** of or relating to industry or industries. **b** employed in industry (*industrial workers*). **2** designed or suitable for industrial use (*industrial alcohol*). **3** characterized by highly developed industries (*the industrial nations*). **4** of or relating to a form of popular dance music characterized by a heavy mechanical beat and a dissonant sound. ● *noun* **1** (in *pl.*) shares in industrial companies. **2** a promotional film profiling an industry, company, etc. □ **in·dus·trial·ly** *adverb*

industrial action *noun* esp. *Brit.* any action, esp. a strike or work to rule, taken by employees as a protest.

industrial archaeology *noun* the study of machines, factories, bridges, etc., formerly used in industry.

industrial arts *plural noun N Amer.* woodworking, metalwork, etc., esp. as taught in schools and colleges.

industrial base *noun* an established industry or industries forming the basis of a region's economy.

industrial design *noun* the act or art of designing objects for manufacture. □ **industrial designer** *noun*

industrial diamond *noun* a small diamond, not of gem quality, used in abrasives and in cutting and drilling tools.

industrial dispute *noun* a dispute between employers and employees.

industrial engineering *noun* the branch of engineering that deals with the development, design, and construction of industrial operations. □ **industrial engineer** *noun*

industrial espionage *noun* spying directed towards discovering the secrets of a rival manufacturer or other industrial company.

industrial estate *noun Brit.* = INDUSTRIAL PARK.

in·dus·trial·ism *noun* a social or economic system in which manufacturing industries are prevalent.

in·dus·trial·ist *noun* a person engaged in the management of an industrial enterprise.

in·dus·trial·ize *verb* (also esp. *Brit.* **-ise**) **1** *transitive* introduce industries to (a country or region etc.). **2** *intransitive* become industrialized. □ **in·dus·trial·iz·a·tion** *noun*

industrial league *noun Cdn informal* a sports league, esp. in hockey, of teams sponsored by corporations.

industrial mall *noun N Amer.* a strip mall or plaza housing a number of individual industrial enterprises, usu. located in a suburban area.

industrial park *noun N Amer.* an area of land developed for the siting of industrial enterprises.

industrial quantities *plural noun* very large quantities, as of something mass-produced.

industrial relations *plural noun* **1** the relations between management and workers in industries. **2** the study or management of such relations.

Industrial Revolution the dramatic transformation of society resulting from the bulk of the working population turning from agriculture to industry, esp. that which occurred in Britain in the second half of the 18th c. and the first half of the 19th c.

in·dustrial-strength *adjective* (often *attributive*) esp. *N Amer.* often *jocular* strong, powerful (*industrial-strength coffee*).

Industrial Workers of the World a radical US labour movement, popularly known as the **Wobblies**, founded in 1905 and dedicated to the overthrow of capitalism. By 1925 its membership was insignificant. Abbr.: **IWW**.

in·dus·tri·ous *adjective* diligent, hard-working. □ **in·dus·tri·ous·ly** *adverb* **in·dus·tri·ous·ness** *noun*

in·dus·try *noun* (*pl.* **-tries**) **1 a** a branch of trade or manufacture. **b** trade and manufacture collectively (*incentives to industry*). **c** any commercial undertaking that provides services (*hospitality industry*). **2** concerted or copious activity (*the building was a hive of industry*). **3 a** diligence. **b** *informal* the diligent study of a particular topic (*the Shakespeare industry*). [French *industrie* or Latin *industria* diligence]

in·dwell *verb* (*past* and *past participle* **in·dwelt**) *literary* **1** *intransitive* (often foll. by *in*) be permanently present as a spirit, principle, etc. **2** *transitive* inhabit spiritually.

in·dwell·ing *adjective Med.* (of a catheter, needle, etc.) fixed in a person's body for a long period of time.

Indy¹ see D'INDY.

Indy² *noun* **1** (in full **Indy 500**) the annual Indianapolis 500-mile motor race. **2** (usu. *attributive*) any of a series of similar competitive circuit races. [abbreviation of INDIANAPOLIS]

Vowels: a *cat* ɑ *arm* e *bed* ɜr *her* ɜ: *deux* ə *ago* ɪ *sit* i *cosy* iː *feed* ɒ *hot* ɔ *pore* ɔː *no* ʌ *run* ʊ *put*

Indy·car *noun* **1** a rear-engine, turbocharged race car designed to compete in Indy racing. **2** (*attributive*) = INDY² 2 (*Indycar champion*). [abbreviation of INDIANAPOLIS]

-ine¹ *suffix* forming adjectives, meaning 'belonging to, of the nature of' (*Alpine; asinine*). [from or after French *-in -ine*, or from Latin *-inus*]

-ine² *suffix* forming adjectives esp. from names of minerals, plants, etc. (*crystalline*). [Latin *-inus* from or after Greek *-inos*]

-ine³ *suffix* forming feminine nouns (*heroine; margravine*). [French from Latin *-ina* from Greek *-inē*, or from German *-in*]

-ine⁴ *suffix* **1** forming (esp. abstract) nouns (*discipline; medicine*). **2** *Chem.* forming nouns denoting derived substances, esp. alkaloids, halogens, amines, and amino acids. [French from Latin *-ina* (fem.) = -INE¹]

in·ebri·ate ● *transitive verb* /ɪˈniːbriˌeit/ make drunk; intoxicate. ● *adjective* /ɪˈniːbriət/ excited. ● *noun* /ɪˈniːbriət/ a drunken person, esp. a habitual drunkard. □ **in·ebri·at·ed** *adjective* **in·ebri·a·tion** *noun* **in·ebri·ety** /-ˈbraiəti/ *noun* [Latin *inebriatus* past participle of *inebriare* (as IN-², *ebrius* drunk)]

in·edible *adjective* not edible, esp. not suitable for eating (*compare* UNEATABLE). □ **in·edi·bil·ity** *noun*

in·educ·able /ɪnˈedʒʊkəbəl, -djʊ-/ *adjective* incapable of being educated. □ **in·educ·abil·ity** *noun*

in·effable /ɪnˈefəbəl/ *adjective* **1** unutterable; too great for description in words; indefinable. **2** that must not be uttered. □ **in·effa·bil·ity** *noun* **in·effably** *adverb* [Old French *ineffable* or Latin *ineffabilis* (as IN-¹, *effari* speak out, utter)]

in·efface·able /ˌɪnɪˈfeisəbəl/ *adjective* that cannot be effaced.

in·effect·ive *adjective* **1** not producing any effect or the desired effect. **2** (of a person) inefficient; not achieving results. □ **in·effect·ive·ly** *adverb* **in·effect·ive·ness** *noun*

in·effec·tual *adjective* **1 a** without effect. **b** not producing the desired or expected effect. **2** (of a person) lacking the ability to achieve results (*an ineffectual leader*). □ **in·effec·tual·ity** *noun* **in·effec·tual·ly** *adverb* **in·effec·tual·ness** *noun*

in·effi·ca·cious /ˌɪnefɪˈkeiʃəs/ *adjective* (of a remedy etc.) not producing the desired effect. □ **in·effi·ca·cious·ly** *adverb* **in·effi·cacy** /ɪnˈefɪkəsi/ *noun*

in·effi·cient *adjective* **1** (of a machine, process, etc.) wasting time or resources (*an inefficient heating system*). **2** (of a person or organization) failing to make the best use of the available time and resources. □ **in·effi·ciency** *noun* **in·effi·cient·ly** *adverb*

in·egali·tar·ian /ˌɪnɪɡælɪˈteriən/ *adjective* of or pertaining to inequality; favouring or marked by inequality. □ **in·egali·tar·ian·ism** *noun*

in·elas·tic *adjective* **1** not elastic. **2** unadaptable, inflexible, unyielding. **3** *Physics* (of a collision etc.) involving an overall loss of translational kinetic energy. **4** *Econ.* (of demand or supply) unresponsive to, or varying less than in proportion to, changes in price. □ **in·elas·tic·ally** *adverb* **in·elas·ti·city** *noun*

in·elegant *adjective* **1** not elegant. **2 a** unrefined. **b** (of a style) unpolished. □ **in·ele·gance** *noun* **in·elegant·ly** *adverb*

in·eli·gible /ɪnˈelɪdʒəbəl/ *adjective* not eligible; not having the appropriate or necessary qualifications (for an office, position, etc). □ **in·eligi·bil·ity** *noun*

in·eluct·able /ˌɪnɪˈlʌktəbəl/ *adjective* unable to be resisted or avoided; inescapable (*ineluctable fate*). □ **in·eluct·abil·ity** *noun* **in·eluct·ably** *adverb* [Latin *ineluctabilis* (as IN-¹, *eluctari* struggle out)]

inept *adjective* **1** unskilful, incompetent. **2** absurd, silly. □ **in·epti·tude** *noun* **in·ept·ly** *adverb* **in·ept·ness** *noun* [Latin *ineptus* (as IN-¹, APT)]

in·equal·ity *noun* (*pl.* **-ities**) **1 a** lack of equality between persons or things; disparity in size, number, quality, etc. **b** an instance of this. **2 a** difference of rank or circumstance; social or economic disparity (*inequality between the rich and the poor*). **b** unfairness, inequity. **3** *Math.* a formula affirming that two expressions are not equal. **4** *Astronomy* a deviation from uniformity in the motion of a planet or satellite.

in·equit·able /ɪnˈekwɪtəbəl/ *adjective* unfair, unjust. □ **in·equit·ably** *adverb*

in·equity /ɪnˈekwɪti/ *noun* (*pl.* **-ties**) **1** unfairness, bias. **2** an instance of this.

in·eradic·able /ˌɪnɪˈradɪkəbəl/ *adjective* unable to be eradicated or rooted out. □ **in·eradic·ably** *adverb*

in·err·ant /ɪnˈerənt/ *adjective* (esp. in reference to the Bible) incapable of being wrong. □ **in·err·ancy** *noun* **in·errant·ist** *noun* [Latin *inerrans* (as IN-¹, ERR)]

inert /ɪˈnɜrt/ *adjective* **1** without inherent power of action, motion, or resistance. **2** without active chemical or other properties. **3** inactive, slow. **4** lacking vigour or interest. □ **inert·ly** *adverb* **inert·ness** *noun* [Latin *iners inert-* (as IN-¹, *ars* ART¹)]

inert gas *noun* = NOBLE GAS.

in·er·tia /ɪˈnɜrʃə/ *noun* **1** *Physics* a property of matter by which it continues in its existing state of rest or uniform motion in a straight line, unless that state is changed by an external force. **2 a** inertness; lack of vigour or will to move. **b** a tendency to remain unchanged. □ **in·er·tial** *adjective* [Latin (as INERT)]

inertial guidance *noun* (also **inertial navigation**) guidance of a missile by internal instruments which measure its acceleration and compare the calculated position with stored data.

in·escap·able *adjective* that cannot be escaped or avoided. □ **in·escap·abil·ity** *noun* **in·escap·ably** *adverb*

-iness *suffix* forming nouns corresponding to adjectives in *-y* (see -Y¹, -LY²).

in·essen·tial ● *adjective* not necessary; dispensable. ● *noun* an inessential thing.

in·estim·able /ɪnˈestɪməbəl/ *adjective* too great, intense, precious, etc., to be estimated. □ **in·estim·ably** *adverb*

in·evit·able /ɪnˈevɪtəbəl/ ● *adjective* **1 a** unavoidable; sure to happen. **b** that is bound to occur or appear. **2** *informal* that is tiresomely familiar. ● *noun* (prec. by *the*) that which is inevitable. □ **in·evit·abil·ity** *noun* **in·evit·ably** *adverb* [Latin *inevitabilis* (as IN-¹, *evitare* avoid)]

in·exact *adjective* not exact. □ **in·exact·i·tude** *noun* **in·exact·ly** *adverb* **in·exact·ness** *noun*

in·excus·able *adjective* (of a person, action, etc.) that cannot be excused or justified. □ **in·excus·ably** *adverb*

in·exhaust·ible *adjective* that cannot be used up (*an inexhaustible resource*). □ **in·exhaust·ibil·ity** *noun* **in·exhaust·ibly** *adverb*

in·exor·able /ɪnˈeksərəbəl/ *adjective* **1** relentless. **2** (of a person or attribute) that cannot be persuaded by request or entreaty. □ **in·exor·abil·ity** *noun* **in·exor·ably** *adverb* [French *inexorable* or Latin *inexorabilis* (as IN-¹, *exorare* entreat)]

in·expedi·ent /ˌɪnɪkˈspiːdiənt/ *adjective* not expedient. □ **in·expedi·ency** *noun*

in·expen·sive *adjective* not expensive, cheap. □ **in·expen·sive·ly** *adverb*

in·experi·ence *noun* lack of experience, or of the resulting knowledge or skill. □ **in·experi·enced** *adjective*

in·expert *adjective* unskilful; lacking expertise. □ **in·expert·ly** *adverb* **in·expert·ness** *noun*

in·explic·able /ˌɪnɪkˈsplɪkəbəl, ɪnˈeks-/ *adjective* that cannot be explained or accounted for. □ **in·explic·abil·ity** /-ˈbɪlɪti/ *noun* **in·explic·ably** *adverb*

in·express·ible *adjective* that cannot be expressed in words. □ **in·express·ibly** *adverb*

in·expres·sive *adjective* not expressive. □ **in·expres·sive·ly** *adverb* **in·expres·sive·ness** *noun*

in ex·ten·so /ˌɪn ekˈstensoː/ *adverb* in full; at length. [Latin]

in·extin·guish·able *adjective* **1** unquenchable; indestructible. **2** (of laughter etc.) irrepressible.

in ex·tre·mis /ˌɪn ekˈstremɪs, -triːmɪs/ *adjective* **1** at the point of death. **2** in great difficulties. [Latin]

in·extric·able /ɪnɪkˈstrɪkəbəl/ *adjective* **1** (of a circumstance) that cannot be escaped from. **2** (of a knot, problem, etc.) that cannot be unravelled or solved. **3** intricately confused. □ **in·extric·ably** *adverb*

INF *abbreviation* intermediate-range nuclear force(s).

in·falli·ble /ɪnˈfalɪbəl/ *adjective* **1** incapable of error. **2** (of a method, test, proof, etc.) unfailing; sure to succeed. **3** *Catholicism* (of the Pope) unable to err in pronouncing dogma as doctrinally defined. □ **in·falli·bil·ity** *noun* **in·falli·bly** *adverb*

in·fam·ous /ˈɪnfəməs/ *adjective* **1** well-known for being bad, wicked, etc.; notorious. **2** abominable. □ **in·fam·ous·ly** *adverb* **in·famy** /ˈɪnfəmi/ *noun* (*pl.* **-ies**)

in·fancy /ˈɪnfənsi/ *noun* (*pl.* **-cies**) **1** early childhood; babyhood. **2** an early state in the development of an idea, undertaking, etc. **3** *Law* the state of being a minor.

in·fant *noun* **1** a child during the earliest period of its life. **b** *Brit.* a schoolchild below the age of seven years. **2** (*attributive*) **a** of or relating to infants or infancy. **b** made or intended for young children (*infant car seat*). **3** (esp. *attributive*) a person or thing in an early stage of its development. **4** *Law* a minor; a person under 18. [Old French *enfant* from Latin *infans* unable to speak (as IN-[1], *fans fantis* pres. part. of *fari* speak)]

in·fan·ta /ɪnˈfantə/ *noun hist.* a daughter of the ruling monarch of Spain or Portugal (usu. the eldest daughter who is not heir to the throne). [Spanish & Portuguese, fem. of INFANTE]

in·fan·te /ɪnˈfantɪ/ *noun hist.* a son of the ruling monarch of Spain or Portugal other than the heir to the throne, esp. the second son. [Spanish & Portuguese from Latin (as INFANT)]

in·fan·ti·cide /ɪnˈfantɪˌsaɪd/ *noun* **1** the killing of an infant soon after birth. **2** the practice of killing newborn infants. **3** a person who kills an infant. □ **in·fan·ti·cid·al** *adjective*

in·fan·tile /ˈɪnfənˌtaɪl/ *adjective* **1** like or characteristic of a child. **2** childish, immature (*infantile humour*). □ **in·fan·til·i·ty** /-ˈtɪlɪti/ *noun*

infantile paralysis *noun* poliomyelitis.

in·fan·til·ism /ɪnˈfantɪˌlɪzəm/ *noun* **1** childish behaviour. **2** *Psych.* the persistence of infantile characteristics or behaviour in adult life; abnormal physical, sexual, or psychological immaturity.

in·fan·til·ize /ɪnˈfantɪlaɪz/ *transitive verb* (also esp. *Brit.* **-ise**) treat (a person) as a child or in a way that denies their maturity or experience. □ **in·fan·til·i·za·tion** *noun*

infant mortality *noun* death before the age of one.

in·fan·try /ˈɪnfəntri/ *noun* (pl. **-tries**) a body of soldiers who march and fight on foot; foot soldiers collectively. [French *infanterie* from Italian *infanteria* from *infante* youth, infantryman (as INFANT)]

in·fan·try·man /ˈɪnfəntrɪmən/ *noun* (pl. **-men**) a soldier of an infantry regiment.

in·farct /ˈɪnfɑrkt/ *noun Med.* a small localized area of dead tissue caused by an inadequate blood supply. □ **in·farct·ed** *adjective* **in·farc·tion** /ɪnˈfɑrkʃən/ *noun* [modern Latin *infarctus* (as IN-[2], Latin *farcire farct-* stuff)]

in·fatu·at·ed /ɪnˈfatʃuːˌeitɪd, -tjuː-/ *adjective* (often foll. by *with*) affected by an intense fondness or admiration. □ **in·fatu·a·tion** *noun* [Latin *infatuare* (as IN-[2], *fatuus* foolish)]

in·fauna /ˈɪnˌfɒnə/ *noun* any animals which live just below the surface of the seabed. □ **in·faun·al** *adjective* [Danish *ifauna* (as IN-[2], FAUNA)]

in·feas·ible /ɪnˈfiːzɪbəl/ *adjective* not feasible; that cannot easily be done. □ **in·feas·ibil·ity** *noun*

in·fect *transitive verb* **1** contaminate (air, water, etc.) with harmful organisms or noxious matter. **2 a** affect (a person) with disease etc; introduce a disease-causing micro-organism into. **b** affect (a computer system) with a virus. **3** instill bad feeling or opinion into (a person). [Latin *inficere infect-* taint (as IN-[2], *facere* make)]

in·fec·tion *noun* **1** the process of infecting or state of being infected. **2** an instance of this; an infectious disease. **3** the presence of a virus in, or its entry into, a computer system.

in·fec·tious *adjective* **1** infecting with disease. **2** (of a disease) liable to be transmitted by air, water, etc. **3** (of emotions etc.) apt to spread; quickly affecting others. □ **in·fec·tious·ly** *adverb* **in·fec·tious·ness** *noun*

infectious hepatitis *noun* = HEPATITIS A.

in·fect·ive *adjective* capable of infecting with disease.

in·feed *noun* **1** the action or process of supplying material to a machine. **2** a mechanism which does this.

in·felici·tous /ˌɪnfəˈlɪsɪtəs/ *adjective* unfortunate or inappropriate. □ **in·felici·tous·ly** *adverb*

in·felici·ty /ˌɪnfɪˈlɪsɪti/ *noun* (pl. **-ties**) a thing that is inappropriate, esp. a remark or expression.

infer *transitive verb* (**in·ferred**, **in·fer·ring**) (often foll. by *that* + clause) **1** deduce or conclude from facts and reasoning. **2** *disputed* imply, suggest. ¶ The use of *infer* in sense 2 is considered incorrect by many people since it is the reverse of the primary sense of the verb. It should be avoided by using *imply* or *suggest*. □ **in·fer·able** *adjective* (also **in·fer·rable**). [Latin *inferre* (as IN-[2], *ferre* bring)]

in·fer·ence /ˈɪnfərəns/ *noun* **1** the act or an instance of inferring. **2** *Logic* **a** the forming of a conclusion from premises. **b** a thing inferred. □ **in·fer·en·tial** /-ˈrenʃəl/ *adjective* **in·fer·en·tial·ly** *adverb*

in·fer·ior /ɪnˈfiːriər/ ● *adjective* **1** of lower rank, quality, etc. **2** lower; in a lower position. **3** poor in quality. **4** (of a planet) having an orbit within the earth's. **5** *Bot.* situated below an ovary or calyx. **6** (of figures or letters) written or printed below the line, e.g. the 2 in CO₂. ● *noun* **1** a person inferior to another, esp. in rank. **2** an inferior letter or figure. □ **in·fer·ior·ly** *adverb* [Latin, comparative of *inferus* that is below]

in·fer·ior·ity /ɪnˌfiːriˈɒrɪti, -DrI-/ *noun* the state of being inferior.

inferiority complex *noun* an unrealistic feeling of general

inadequacy caused by actual or supposed inferiority in one sphere, sometimes marked by aggressive behaviour in compensation.

in·fer·nal *adjective* **1 a** of hell or the underworld. **b** hellish, fiendish. **2** *informal* detestable, tiresome. □ **in·fer·nal·ly** *adverb* [Old French from Late Latin *infernalis* from Latin *infernus* situated below]

in·fer·no *noun* (pl. **-nos**) **1** a raging fire. **2** a scene of horror or distress. **3** hell. [Italian from Late Latin *infernus* (as INFERNAL)]

in·fertile *adjective* not fertile. □ **in·fertil·ity** *noun*

in·fest *transitive verb* (of harmful persons or things, esp. vermin or disease) overrun (a place) in large numbers. □ **in·fest·a·tion** *noun* [French *infester* or Latin *infestare* assail, from *infestus* hostile]

in·fibu·late /ɪnˈfɪbjʊleit/ *transitive verb* (usu. as **in·fibu·lat·ed** *adjective*) subject to infibulation. [Latin *infibulat-*, past participle stem of *infibulare* (as IN-[2] + FIBULA)]

in·fibu·la·tion /ɪnˌfɪbjʊˈleiʃən/ *noun* the practice in some cultures of partially stitching together the labia, often after excision of the clitoris, to prevent sexual intercourse.

in·fidel /ˈɪnfɪdəl, -ˌdel/ ● *noun* **1** usu. *derogatory* a person who does not believe in religion or in a particular religion; an unbeliever. **2** *hist.* an adherent of a religion other than one's own, esp.: **a** (from a Christian point of view) a Muslim. **b** (from a Muslim point of view) a Christian. **c** (from a Jewish point of view) a Gentile. ● *adjective* **1** that is an infidel. **2** of unbelievers. [French *infidèle* or Latin *infidelis* (as IN-[1], *fidelis* faithful)]

in·fidel·ity /ˌɪnfɪˈdelɪti/ *noun* (pl. **-ities**) **1 a** disloyalty, or esp. unfaithfulness to a sexual partner. **b** an instance of this. **2** lack of faith; disbelief in religious matters or a particular religion, esp. Christianity.

in·field *noun* **1** *Baseball* **a** the area bounded by the baselines. **b** the fielders positioned along the baseline from first base to third base. **c** a team's defensive ability in the infield. **2** *N Amer.* the area enclosed by a racetrack. **3** the usu. arable farmland lying near a farmstead.

in·field·er *noun Baseball* any of the fielders, i.e. the first baseman, second baseman, third baseman, and shortstop, stationed in the infield.

in·fight·ing *noun* **1** hidden conflict or competitiveness within an organization. **2** boxing at closer quarters than arm's length. □ **in·fight·er** *noun*

in·fill ● *noun* (also **in·fill·ing**) **1** material used to fill a hole, gap, etc. **2** the placing of buildings to occupy the space between existing ones. **3 a** the building of a house on a lot cleared by demolishing an existing, usu. smaller house. **b** a house built where the previous one has been demolished. ● *transitive verb* fill in (a cavity etc.).

in·fil·trate *verb* **1 a** *transitive & intransitive* gain entrance or access to surreptitiously and by degrees (as spies etc.). **b** *transitive* cause to do this. **2** *transitive & intransitive* permeate by filtration. **3** *transitive & intransitive* (often foll. by *into*, *through*) introduce (fluid) by filtration. □ **in·fil·tra·tion** *noun* **in·fil·tra·tor** *noun*

infin. *abbreviation* infinitive.

in·fin·ite /ˈɪnfɪnɪt/ ● *adjective* **1** boundless, endless. **2** very great. **3** (usu. with *pl.*) innumerable; very many (*infinite resources*). **4** *Math.* **a** greater than any assignable quantity or countable number. **b** (of a series) that may be continued indefinitely. **5** *Grammar* (of a verb part) not limited by person or number, e.g. infinitive, gerund, and participle. ● *noun* (**the Infinite**) God. **2** (**the infinite**) infinite space. □ **in·fin·ite·ly** *adverb* **in·fin·ite·ness** *noun* [Latin *infinitus* (as IN-[1], FINITE)]

in·fini·tes·imal /ˌɪnfɪnɪˈtesɪməl/ ● *adjective* infinitely or very small. ● *noun* an infinitesimal amount. □ **in·fini·tes·imal·ly** *adverb* [modern Latin *infinitesimus* from INFINITE: compare CENTESIMAL]

infinitesimal calculus *noun* the differential and integral calculi regarded as one subject.

in·fini·tive /ɪnˈfɪnɪtɪv/ ● *noun* a form of a verb expressing the verbal notion without reference to a particular subject, tense, etc. (e.g. *see* in *we came to see*, or *let her see*). ● *adjective* having this form. □ **in·fini·tival** /-ˈtaɪvəl/ *adjective* **in·fini·tival·ly** /-ˈtaɪvəli/ *adverb* [Latin *infinitivus* (as IN-[1], *finitivus* definite, from *finire finit-* define)]

in·fini·tude /ɪnˈfɪnɪˌtjuːd, -tjuːd/ *noun* **1** the state of being infinite; boundlessness. **2** (often foll. by *of*) a boundless number or extent.

in·fin·ity /ɪnˈfɪnɪti/ *noun* (pl. **-ities**) **1** the state of being infinite. **2** an infinite number or extent. **3** infinite distance. **4** *Math.* infinite quantity. Symbol: ∞.

in·firm *adjective* **1** physically weak, esp. through age. **2** (of a person, mind, judgment, etc.) weak, irresolute. □ **in·firm·ity** *noun* (pl. **-ities**).

in·firm·ary /ɪnˈfɜrməri/ *noun* (pl. **-aries**) **1** a place for those who are ill in a boarding school, prison, camp, monastery, etc. **2** a hospital.

infix ● *transitive verb* **1** implant or insert (a thing) firmly in another. **2** *Linguistics* insert (a formative element) into the body of a word. ● *noun* *Linguistics* a formative element inserted in a word. □ **in·fix·a·tion** *noun*

in fla·grante de·licto /ˌɪn fləˌgrantɪ dɪˈlɪktəʊ/ *adjective* in the very act of committing an offence. [Latin, = in blazing crime]

in·flame *verb* **1** *transitive & intransitive* provoke or become provoked to strong feeling, esp. anger. **2** *transitive* *Med.* cause inflammation or fever in (a body etc.). **3** *transitive* aggravate. [Old French *enflammer* from Latin *inflammare* (as IN-², *flamma* flame)]

in·flamed *adjective* **1** (of a part of the body) red, painful, and often swollen, esp. as a reaction to injury or infection. **2** full of anger or violent feelings.

in·flam·mable ● *adjective* **1** easily set on fire; flammable. **2** easily excited. ¶ See Usage Note at FLAMMABLE. ● *noun* (usu. in *pl.*) an inflammable substance. □ **in·flam·mabil·ity** *noun* [INFLAME after French *inflammable*]

in·flam·ma·tion *noun* **1** the act or an instance of inflaming. **2** *Med.* a localized physical condition with heat, swelling, redness, and usu. pain, esp. as a reaction to injury or infection. [Latin *inflammatio* (as INFLAME)]

in·flam·ma·tory /ɪnˈflamətəri, -tri/ *adjective* **1** (esp. of speeches, leaflets, etc.) tending to cause anger etc. **2** of or tending to inflammation of the body.

inflammatory bowel disease *noun* either of two diseases, Crohn's disease and ulcerative colitis, which cause an inflammation of the bowel. Abbr.: **IBD**.

in·flat·able ● *adjective* that can be inflated. ● *noun* an inflatable plastic or rubber object, esp. an inflatable boat.

in·flate *verb* **1** *transitive* distend (a balloon etc.) with air. **2** *transitive* (usu. foll. by *with*; usu. in *passive*) puff up (a person with pride etc.). **3 a** *transitive & intransitive* bring about inflation (of the currency). **b** *transitive* raise (prices) artificially. **4** *transitive* exaggerate or embellish. **5** *intransitive* become inflated. □ **in·fla·tor** *noun* [Latin *inflare inflat-* (as IN-², *flare* blow)]

in·flat·ed *adjective* **1** swollen or distended. **2** (esp. of language, sentiments, etc.) bombastic. **3** (of prices, costs, etc.) unreasonably increased in amount, level, etc. **4** (of a person) puffed up (with pride etc.). **5** *Bot.* & *Zool.* having a bulging form and hollow interior, as if filled with air.

in·fla·tion *noun* **1** *Econ.* **a** a general increase in prices and fall in the purchasing value of money. **b** an increase in available currency regarded as causing this. **2 a** the act or condition of inflating or being inflated. **b** an instance of this. □ **in·fla·tion·ary** *adjective* **in·fla·tion·ist** *noun & adjective*

in·flation-adjusted *adjective* *N Amer.* (of income, a return on an investment, etc.) adjusted to take inflation into account.

in·flect *verb* **1** *transitive* change the pitch of (the voice, a musical note, etc.). **2** *Grammar* **a** *transitive* change the form of (a word) to express tense, gender, number, mood, etc. **b** *intransitive* (of a word, language, etc.) undergo such change. **3** *transitive* bend inwards; curve. **4** *transitive* (usu. as **in·flect·ed** *adjective*, in *combination*) influence or modify, esp. by the addition of characteristics of another culture, musical style, etc. (*jazz-inflected style of singing*). □ **in·flect·ive** *adjective* [Latin *inflectere inflex-* (as IN-², *flectere* bend)]

in·flec·tion *noun* (*Brit.* also **in·flex·ion**) **1 a** the act or condition of inflecting or being inflected. **b** an instance of this. **2** *Grammar* **a** the process or practice of inflecting words. **b** an inflected form of a word. **c** a suffix etc. used to inflect, e.g. *-ed*. **3** a modulation of the voice. **4** *Geom.* a change of curvature from convex to concave at a particular point on a curve. □ **in·flec·tion·al** *adjective* **in·flec·tion·al·ly** *adverb* **in·flec·tion·less** *adjective*

in·flex·ible *adjective* **1** that cannot be changed or adapted to particular circumstances (*an inflexible system*). **2** (of a person) unwilling to change or adapt (*inflexible in their attitudes*). **3** unbendable. □ **in·flex·ibil·ity** *noun* **in·flex·ibly** *adverb*

in·flict *transitive verb* (usu. foll. by *on, upon*) **1** cause (injury, defeat, damage, punishment etc.). **2** (also *reflexive*) often *jocular* impose (something objectionable or unwelcome) on (*shall not inflict myself on you any longer*). [Latin *infligere inflict-* (as IN-², *fligere* strike)]

in·flic·tion *noun* **1** the act or an instance of inflicting. **2** something inflicted.

in·flight *attributive adjective* occurring or provided during an aircraft flight.

in·flor·es·cence /ˌɪnfləˈresəns/ *noun* **1** *Bot.* **a** the complete flower head of a plant including stems, stalks, bracts, and flowers. **b** the

arrangement of this. **2** the process of flowering. [modern Latin *inflorescentia* from Late Latin *inflorescere* (as IN-², FLORESCENCE)]

in·flow *noun* **1** a flowing in. **2** something, e.g. a liquid, money, etc., that flows in. □ **in·flow·ing** *noun & adjective*

in·flu·ence ● *noun* **1 a** (usu. foll. by *on, upon*) the effect a person or thing has on another. **b** (usu. foll. by *over, with*) moral ascendancy or power. **c** a thing or person exercising such power (*is a good influence on them*). **2** the ability to obtain favourable treatment by means of acquaintance, wealth, status, etc. **3** *Astrology* an ethereal fluid supposedly flowing from the stars and affecting character and destiny. ● *transitive verb* **1** exert influence on; have an effect on. **2** persuade or induce (a person) to do or think something. □ **under the influence** *informal* affected by alcoholic drink. □ **in·flu·ence·able** *adjective* **in·flu·en·cer** *noun* [Old French *influence* or medieval Latin *influentia* inflow, from Latin *influere* flow in (as IN-², *fluere* flow)]

influence peddler *noun* *N Amer.* a person who uses his or her position or political influence in exchange for money or favours. □ **influence peddling** *noun*

in·flu·ent /ˈɪnfluːənt/ ● *adjective* flowing in. ● *noun* a tributary stream. [Middle English from Latin (as INFLUENCE)]

in·flu·en·tial /ˌɪnfluˈenʃəl/ ● *adjective* having a great influence or power (*influential in the financial world*). ● *noun* an influential person. □ **in·flu·en·tial·ly** *adverb*

in·flu·enza /ˌɪnfluˈenzə/ *noun* a highly contagious virus infection causing fever, severe aching, weakness, and coughing. □ **in·flu·en·zal** *adjective* [Italian from medieval Latin *influentia* INFLUENCE]

in·flux *noun* **1** a continual entry of people (esp. visitors or immigrants) into a place, esp. in large numbers. **2** (usu. foll. by *into*) a flowing in of a substance, esp. in large quantities (*the influx of heroin into the market*). **3** the point at which a stream or river flows into another body of water. [French *influx* or Late Latin *influxus* (as IN-², FLUX)]

info *noun & combining form* *informal* information. [abbreviation]

Info·bahn /ˈɪnfəʊˌbɒn/ *noun* *informal* = INFORMATION SUPERHIGHWAY. [blend of INFORMATION + AUTOBAHN]

info centre *noun* a booth or office etc. providing information to the public on a particular subject or region.

in·fold ● *transitive & intransitive verb* fold inwards. ● *noun* a convolution; a fold. □ **in·fold·ing** *noun*

info·medi·ary *noun* an Internet company that gathers and links information on particular subjects on behalf of commercial organizations and their potential customers.

info·mer·cial *noun* esp. *N Amer.* a usu. lengthy television commercial which promotes a particular product using a documentary, testimonial, talk show, or demonstration format etc. to convey information. [blend of INFORMATION + COMMERCIAL]

in·form *verb* **1** *transitive* (usu. foll. by *of, about*, or *that, how* + clause) tell (*informed them of their rights; informed us that the train was late*). **2** *intransitive* (usu. foll. by *against, on*) make an accusation. **3** *transitive* (usu. foll. by *with*) *literary* inspire or imbue (a person, heart, or thing) with a feeling, principle, quality, etc. **4** *transitive* impart its quality to; permeate. **5** *intransitive* give or supply information or knowledge (*the magazine's task is to inform*). [Old French *enfo(u)rmer* from Latin *informare* give shape to, fashion, describe (as IN-², *forma* form)]

in·formal *adjective* **1** without ceremony or formality (*just an informal chat*). **2** (of clothing, etc.) everyday; casual. **3** (of language, writing, etc.) relaxed or conversational in style; not formal. □ **in·for·mal·ity** *noun* (*pl.* **-ities**). **in·formal·ly** *adverb*

in·form·ant *noun* **1** a person who gives information. **2** a person who informs against another, esp. in criminal matters; an informer. **3** a person from whom a linguist, anthropologist, etc., obtains information about language, dialect, or culture.

in·form·at·ics *plural noun* (usu. treated as *sing.*) the science of processing data for storage and retrieval; information science. [translation of Russian *informatika* (as INFORMATION, -ICS)]

in·for·ma·tion *noun* **1 a** something told; knowledge. **b** (usu. foll. by *on, about*) items of knowledge; news (*the latest information on the crisis*). **2** a booth, office or agency providing information, esp. on a specific subject or location (*go and ask at information*). **3** *Law* (usu. foll. by *against*) a charge or complaint lodged with a court or magistrate. **4 a** the act of informing or telling. **b** an instance of this. **5** data as processed or stored etc. by a computer system. **6** (in information theory) a mathematical quantity expressing the probability of occurrence of a particular sequence of symbols etc. □ **in·for·ma·tion·al** *adjective* **in·for·ma·tion·al·ly** *adverb*

information age *noun* the current historical period, characterized by the capacity to store, retrieve, and transmit large volumes of information using computer technology.

information architect *noun* a specialist in the organization and presentation of information, e.g. on a website. □ **information architecture** *noun*

information broker *noun* a person or organization which retrieves pertinent information for a client, esp. using electronic means.

Information Commissioner *noun* an official responsible for investigating complaints from those who feel they have been denied rights under access to information legislation.

information overload *noun* **1** the provision or receipt of an excessive quantity of information, such that it cannot be processed fully or efficiently by the recipient. **2** a situation resulting from this.

information retrieval *noun* the tracing of information stored esp. in a computer system.

information science *noun* the study of the processes for storing and retrieving information.

information superhighway *noun* (also **information highway**) a means of rapid transfer of information in different digital forms (e.g. video, sound, and graphics) via an extensive electronic network.

information technology *noun* the study or use of systems (esp. computers, telecommunications, etc.) for storing, retrieving, and sending information.

information theory *noun* *Math.* the quantitative study of the transmission of information by signals etc.

information warfare *noun* **1** the strategic use of information or information technology for competitive, aggressive, or military purposes. **2** the deliberate disruption of information and communications systems for similar purposes.

in·forma·tive *adjective* giving information; instructive. □ **in·forma·tive·ly** *adverb*

in·formed *adjective* **1** with knowledge of the facts (*their answers show that they are badly informed*). **2** educated; knowledgeable (*informed readers*).

informed consent *noun* a patient's agreement to a certain course of treatment etc. given after being advised of the relevant medical facts, risks, etc.

in·form·er *noun* **1** a person who informs against another. **2** a person who informs or advises.

info·sphere *noun* the sphere of human activity concerned with the collection and processing of information, esp. by computer.

info·tain·ment *noun* broadcast material intended both to entertain and to inform. [INFORMATION + ENTERTAINMENT]

infra *adverb* below, further on (in a book or writing). [Latin, = below]

infra- *combining form* **1** below (opp. SUPRA-). **2** *Anat.* below or under a part of the body. [from or after Latin *infra* below, beneath]

infra·class *noun* a taxonomic category below a subclass.

in·frac·tion *noun* esp. *Law* a violation or infringement. [Latin *infractio* (as INFRINGE)]

infra dig *predicative adjective* *informal* beneath one's dignity; unbecoming. [abbreviation of Latin *infra dignitatem*]

in·fran·gible /ɪnˈfrandʒɪbəl/ *adjective* **1** unbreakable. **2** inviolable. [as IN-¹, FRANGIBLE]

infra·red ● *adjective* **1** having a wavelength just greater than the red end of the visible light spectrum but less than that of radio waves. **2** of or using such radiation. **●** *noun* the infrared part of the spectrum.

infra·sonic *adjective* of or relating to sound waves with a frequency below the lower limit of human audibility. □ **infra·sonic·ally** *adverb*

infra·sound *noun* sound waves with frequencies below the lower limit of human audibility.

infra·struc·ture *noun* **1 a** the basic structural foundations of a society or enterprise; a substructure or foundation. **b** roads, bridges, sewers, etc., regarded as a country's economic foundation. **2** permanent installations as a basis for military etc. operations. □ **infra·struc·tur·al** *adjective*

in·fre·quent *adjective* not frequent. □ **in·fre·quen·cy** *noun* **in·fre·quent·ly** *adverb*

in·fringe *verb* **1** *transitive* **a** act contrary to; violate (a law, an oath, etc.). **b** act in defiance of (another's rights etc.). **2** *intransitive* (usu. foll. by *on*, *upon*) affect something so as to limit or restrict it (*this infringes on our rights*; *they are infringing on our privacy*). □ **in·fringe·ment** *noun* **in·frin·ger** *noun* [Latin *infringere infract-* (as IN-², *frangere* break)]

in·fula /ˈɪnfjʊlə/ *noun* (pl. **in·fulae** /-ˌliː/) Christianity either of the two ribbons on a bishop's mitre. [Latin, = woollen fillet worn by priest etc.]

in·fun·dibu·lar /ˌɪnfʌnˈdɪbjʊlər/ *adjective* funnel-shaped. [Latin *infundibulum* funnel, from *infundere* pour in (as IN-², *fundere* pour)]

in·furi·ate *transitive verb* fill with fury; enrage. □ **in·furi·at·ing** *adjective* **in·furi·at·ing·ly** *adverb*

in·fuse *verb* **1** *transitive* (usu. foll. by *with*) imbue; pervade (*anger infused with resentment*). **2** *transitive* steep (herbs, tea, etc.) in liquid to extract the content. **3** *transitive* (usu. foll. by *into*) instill (grace, spirit, life, etc.). **4** *intransitive* undergo infusion (*let it infuse for five minutes*). □ **in·fus·er** *noun* [Latin *infundere infus-* (as IN-², *fundere* pour)]

in·fus·ible *adjective* not able to be fused or melted. □ **in·fus·ibil·ity** *noun*

in·fusion *noun* **1** a liquid obtained by infusing. **2** the introduction of someone or something new that will have a positive influence (*an infusion of cash*). **3** *Med.* a slow injection of a substance into a vein or tissue. **4 a** the act of infusing. **b** an instance of this.

-ing¹ *suffix* forming gerunds and nouns from verbs (or occas. from nouns) denoting: **1 a** the verbal action or its result (*asking*; *carving*; *fighting*; *learning*). **b** the verbal action as described or classified in some way (*tough going*). **2** material used for or associated with a process etc. (*piping*; *washing*). **3** an occupation or event (*banking*; *wedding*). **4** a set or arrangement of (*colouring*; *feathering*). [Old English *-ung*, *-ing* from Germanic]

-ing² *suffix* **1** forming the present participle of verbs (*asking*; *fighting*), often as adjectives (*charming*; *strapping*). **2** forming adjectives from nouns (*hulking*) and verbs (*balding*). [Middle English alteration of Old English *-ende*, later *-inde*]

-ing³ *suffix* forming derivative nouns with the sense 'one belonging to or of the kind of', hence as patronymics or diminutives (*farthing*; *gelding*). [Old English from Germanic]

in·gather·ing *noun* a gathering together, esp. of dispersed peoples.

In·gen·housz /ˈɪŋən.huːs/ **Jan** (1730–99), Dutch scientist, best known for discovering that sunlit green plants take in carbon dioxide, fix the carbon, and 'restore' the air (oxygen) required for respiration.

in·gen·ious /ɪnˈdʒiːnɪəs/ *adjective* **1** clever at inventing, constructing, organizing, etc.; skilful; resourceful. **2** (of a machine, theory, etc.) cleverly contrived. ¶ See Usage Note at INGENUOUS. □ **in·gen·ious·ly** *adverb* **in·gen·ious·ness** *noun* [Middle English, = talented, from French *ingénieux* or Latin *ingeniosus* from *ingenium* cleverness: compare ENGINE]

in·genue /ˌãʒəˈnjuː, -nuː/ *noun* **1** an innocent or unsophisticated young woman. **2 a** such a part in a play. **b** the actress who plays this part. [French, fem. of *ingénu* INGENUOUS]

in·genu·ity /ˌɪndʒɪˈnjuːɪtɪ/ *noun* skill in devising or contriving; ingeniousness. [Latin *ingenuitas* ingenuousness (as INGENUOUS): English meaning by confusion of INGENIOUS with INGENUOUS]

in·genu·ous /ɪnˈdʒenjʊəs/ *adjective* **1** innocent; artless. **2** open; frank. ¶ *Ingenuous*, meaning 'open, frank, innocent', should not be confused with *ingenious*, which means 'clever at inventing, resourceful'. □ **in·genu·ous·ly** *adverb* **in·genu·ous·ness** *noun* [Latin *ingenuus* freeborn, frank (as IN-², root of *gignere* beget)]

Inger·soll /ˈɪŋɡərsɒl/ a town in SW central Ontario, situated on the Thames River, about 35 km east of London; pop. (2001) 10,977. [T. Ingersoll, early settler d.1812]

in·gest /ɪnˈdʒest/ *transitive verb* take in (food etc.); eat. □ **in·ges·tion** /ɪnˈdʒestʃən/ *noun* **in·gest·ive** *adjective* [Latin *ingerere ingest-* (as IN-², *gerere* carry)]

ingle·nook *noun* a space within the opening on either side of a large fireplace. [dial. (originally Scots) *ingle* fire burning on a hearth, perhaps from Gaelic *aingeal* fire, light, + NOOK]

in·glori·ous *adjective* **1** shameful; ignominious. **2** not famous. □ **in·glori·ous·ly** *adverb* **in·glori·ous·ness** *noun*

-ingly *suffix* forming adverbs esp. denoting manner of action or nature or condition (*dotingly*; *charmingly*; *slantingly*).

in·going *adjective* going in; entering.

in·got /ˈɪŋɡət/ *noun* a usu. oblong piece of cast metal, esp. of gold, silver, or steel. [Middle English: perhaps from IN¹ + *goten* past participle of Old English *geotan* cast]

in·grain ● *adjective* (of textiles) dyed in the fibre, before being woven. **●** *transitive verb* implant (a habit, belief, or attitude) ineradicably in a person. [Old French *engrainer* dye in grain (*en graine*): see GRAIN]

in·grained *adjective* **1** deeply rooted; inveterate. **2** thorough. **3** (of dirt etc.) deeply embedded.

in·grate /ˈɪŋɡreɪt/ **●** *noun* an ungrateful person. **●** *adjective* ungrateful. [Latin *ingratus* (as IN-¹, *gratus* grateful)]

in·grati·ate /ɪnˈgreiʃi,eit/ *reflexive verb* (usu. foll. by *with*) bring oneself into favour. □ **in·grati·at·ing** *adjective* **in·grati·at·ing·ly** *adverb* **in·grati·a·tion** *noun* [Latin *in gratiam* into favour]

in·grati·tude *noun* a lack of due gratitude.

in·gredi·ent *noun* **1** any of the foods that are combined to make a particular dish (*mix all the ingredients in a bowl*). **2** any of the things or qualities of which something is made (*the basic ingredients of a good mystery story*). [Latin *ingredi ingress-* enter (as IN-², *gradi* step)]

Ingres /ãgr/ **Jean Au·guste Domi·nique** (1780–1867), French painter. A vigorous opponent of Delacroix's romanticism, he upheld neoclassicism in paintings such as *Ambassadors of Agamemnon* (1801), and his many nudes, including the *Bather* (1808), reflect his skills as a draftsman.

in·gress /ˈɪngres/ *noun* **1** the act or right of going in or entering. **2** *Astronomy* the start of an eclipse or transit. □ **in·gres·sion** *noun* [Latin *ingressus* (as INGREDIENT)]

in-ground *attributive adjective N Amer.* (of a swimming pool, etc.) sunk into the earth.

in-group *noun* a small exclusive group of people with a common interest.

in·grow·ing *adjective* growing inwards, esp. (of a toenail) growing into the flesh. □ **in·growth** *noun*

in·grown *adjective* (of a toenail, hair, etc.) grown into the flesh.

in·guin·al /ˈɪŋgwɪnəl/ *adjective* of the groin. [Latin *inguinalis* from *inguen -inis* groin]

in·habit *transitive verb* (**in·habit·ed**, **in·habit·ing**) (of a person or animal) dwell in; occupy (a region, town, house, etc.). □ **in·habit·able** *adjective* **in·habit·ant** *noun* **in·habit·a·tion** *noun* [Old French *enhabiter* or Latin *inhabitare* (as IN-², *habitare* dwell): see HABIT]

in·habit·ed /ɪnˈhabɪtəd/ *adjective* having inhabitants; lived-in (*an inhabited planet*).

in·hal·ant /ɪnˈheilənt/ ● *noun* **1** a medicinal preparation for inhaling. **2** a substance inhaled by drug abusers. ● *adjective* of or relating to inhalation or inhalants.

in·hale *verb* **1** *transitive & intransitive* breathe in. **2** *transitive & intransitive* take (esp. tobacco smoke) into the lungs. **3** *transitive N Amer. informal* devour (food etc.) rapidly (*inhaled the meal*). □ **in·hal·ation** /,ɪnhəˈleɪʃən/ *noun* [Latin *inhalare* breathe in (as IN-², *halare* breathe)]

in·hal·er *noun* a portable device for administering a medicinal or anaesthetic gas or vapour, esp. to relieve nasal or bronchial congestion, e.g. in asthmatics.

in·har·moni·ous *adjective* esp. *Music* not harmonious.

in·here *intransitive verb* (often foll. by *in*) **1** exist essentially or permanently in (*goodness inheres in my child*). **2** (of rights etc.) be vested in (a person etc.). [Latin *inhaerere inhaes-* (as IN-², *haerēre* to stick)]

in·her·ent /ɪnˈherənt/ *adjective* (often foll. by *in*) **1** existing in something, esp. as a permanent or characteristic attribute. **2** vested in (a person etc.) as a right or privilege. □ **in·her·ent·ly** *adverb*

in·her·it *verb* (**in·herit·ed**, **in·herit·ing**) **1** *transitive & intransitive* receive (property, rank, title, etc.) by legal descent or succession. **2** *intransitive* succeed as an heir (*a younger son rarely inherits*). **3** *transitive* receive or have from a predecessor or predecessors in office etc. (*inherited a lot of problems from the previous government*). **4** *transitive* come into possession of (clothing, etc.) from someone else (*inherits all her clothes from her older sisters*). **5** *transitive* derive (a characteristic, disorder, etc.) genetically from one's ancestors. [Old French *enheriter* from Late Latin *inhereditare* (as IN-², Latin *heres heredis* heir)]

in·herit·able *adjective* capable of being inherited. □ **in·herit·abil·ity** *noun*

in·herit·ance *noun* **1** something that is inherited. **2 a** the act of inheriting. **b** an instance of this.

inheritance tax *noun* a tax levied on property etc. acquired by inheritance.

in·herit·or *noun* an heir; a person who inherits.

in·heri·trix *noun* (also **in·heri·tress**) an heiress; a woman who inherits.

in·hib·it *transitive verb* (**in·hib·it·ed**, **in·hib·it·ing**) **1** hinder, restrain, or prevent (an action or progress). **2** prevent (a person) from acting freely. **3** (of a drug or other substance) slow down or prevent (a process, reaction, or function) or reduce the activity of (an enzyme or other agent). □ **in·hib·it·ive** *adjective* **in·hib·it·or** *noun* **in·hib·it·ory** *adjective* [Latin *inhibēre* (as IN-², *habēre* hold)]

in·hib·it·ed *adjective* subject to inhibition; unable to express feelings or impulses.

in·hib·ition /,ɪnhɪˈbɪʃən/ *noun* **1** *Psych.* a restraint on the direct expression of an instinct. **2** a feeling of nervousness or embarrassment which prevents one from relaxing or behaving naturally (*has inhibitions about singing in public*). **3 a** the act of inhibiting. **b** the process of being inhibited.

in·homo·gen·eous /ɪn,homəˈdʒiːniəs, ɪn,hɒm-/ *adjective* not homogeneous. □ **in·homo·gen·eity** /-dʒəˈneiːɪti/ *noun*

in·hos·pit·able /,ɪnhɒˈspɪtəbəl, ɪnˈhɒsp-/ *adjective* **1** not hospitable. **2** (of a region, coast, etc.) not affording shelter etc. □ **in·hos·pit·able·ness** *noun* **in·hos·pit·ably** *adverb*

in·hospi·tal·ity *noun* the act or process of being inhospitable.

in-house ● *adjective* done or existing within an institution, company, etc. (*an in-house project*). ● *adverb* internally, without outside assistance.

in·human *adjective* **1** (of a person, conduct, etc.) brutal; unfeeling; barbarous. **2** not of a human type. **3** (of living conditions, etc.) not suitable for humans. □ **in·human·ly** *adverb* **in·human·ness** *noun*

in·humane *adjective* not humane. □ **in·humane·ly** *adverb*

in·human·ity *noun* (*pl.* **-ities**) **1** brutality; barbarousness; callousness. **2** an inhumane act.

in·imical /ɪˈnɪmɪkəl/ *adjective* (usu. foll. by *to*) **1** hostile. **2** harmful. □ **in·imical·ly** *adverb* [Late Latin *inimicalis* from Latin *inimicus* (as IN-¹, *amicus* friend)]

in·imit·able /ɪˈnɪmɪtəbəl/ *adjective* impossible to imitate. □ **in·imit·abil·ity** /-ˈbɪlɪti/ *noun* **in·imit·ably** *adverb*

in·iquity /ɪˈnɪkwɪti/ *noun* (*pl.* **-ties**) **1** wickedness. **2** a gross injustice. □ **in·iqui·tous** *adjective* **in·iqui·tous·ly** *adverb* **in·iqui·tous·ness** *noun* [Old French *iniquité* from Latin *iniquitas -tatis* from *iniquus* (as IN-¹, *aequus* just)]

in·itial ● *adjective* of, existing at, or occurring at the beginning; first (*initial stage*; *initial expenses*). ● *noun* **1** (usu. in *pl.*) the first letters of two or more names of a person, or of words forming any name or phrase. **2** = INITIAL LETTER. ● *transitive verb* (**in·itialled**, **in·itial·ling**; also **in·itialed**, **in·itial·ing**) mark or sign with one's initials. □ **in·itial·ly** *adverb* [Latin *initialis* from *initium* beginning, from *inire init-* go in]

in·itial·ism *noun* a group of initial letters used as an abbreviation for a name or expression, each letter being pronounced separately, e.g. *CBC* (compare ACRONYM).

in·itial·ize *transitive verb* (also esp. *Brit.* **-ise**) *Computing* **1** set to the value or put in the condition appropriate to the start of an operation. **2** format (a disk). □ **in·itial·iz·a·tion** *noun*

initial letter *noun* a letter at the beginning of a word.

initial public offering *noun* the first offering by a private company of stock for public purchase, usu. to raise start-up or expansion capital.

in·iti·ate ● *transitive verb* /ɪˈnɪʃi,eit/ **1** cause (a process or action) to begin. **2 a** (usu. foll. by *into*) admit (a person) into a society, an office, a secret, etc., esp. with a ritual. **b** (usu. foll. by *in*, *into*) instruct (a person) in science, art, etc. ● *noun* /ɪˈnɪʃiət/ a person who has been newly initiated; a beginner, a novice. ● *adjective* /ɪˈnɪʃiət/ (of a person) newly initiated (*an initiate member*). □ **in·iti·a·tion** *noun* **in·iti·ator** *noun* **in·itia·tory** /ɪˈnɪʃiətɔri/ *adjective* [Latin *initiare* from *initium*: see INITIAL]

in·itia·tive /ɪˈnɪʃətɪv, ɪˈnɪʃjətɪv/ *noun* **1** the ability to initiate things; enterprise, self-motivation (*I'm afraid he lacks initiative*). **2 a** an act or strategy intended to resolve a difficulty or improve a situation; a fresh approach to something (*a new recycling initiative*). **b** a proposal made by one group, nation, etc. to another, with a view to improving relations between them (*a peace initiative*). **3** the power or right to begin something. **4** *Politics* (esp. in Switzerland and some US states) the right of citizens outside the legislature to originate legislation. □ **on one's own initiative** without being prompted by others. **take the initiative** (often foll. by *in* + verbal noun) be the first to take action. [French (as INITIATE)]

in·ject *transitive verb* **1 a** (usu. foll. by *into*) drive or force (a fluid, medicine, etc.) under pressure into a passage, cavity, or solid material. **b** (usu. foll. by *with*) introduce by injection. **c** administer medicine etc. to (a person) by injection. **2** introduce suddenly, with force, or by way of interruption; interject (*may I inject a note of realism?*). **3** introduce (a new quality, element, etc.) into something (*inject some fresh ideas into the project*; *inject $200,000 of new capital*). □ **in·ject·able** *adjective & noun* **in·ject·or** *noun* [Latin *injicere* (as IN-², *jacere* throw)]

in·jec·tion *noun* **1 a** the act of injecting. **b** an instance of this. **2** a liquid or solution (to be) injected (*prepare a morphine injection*). **3** = FUEL INJECTION.

injection moulding *noun* the shaping of rubber or plastic articles by injecting heated material into a mould. □ **in·jection-moulded** *adjective*

in·jera /ɪnˈdʒɪːrə/ *noun* a soft, white, spongy Ethiopian bread made from teff flour. [Amharic]

in-joke *noun* a joke which can be appreciated by only a limited group of people because of shared experiences etc.

in·judi·cious /ˌɪndʒuːˈdɪʃəs/ *adjective* unwise, showing lack of judgment or discretion. □ **in·judi·cious·ly** *adverb* **in·judi·cious·ness** *noun*

in·junc·tion *noun* **1** an authoritative warning or order. **2** *Law* a judicial order restraining a person or a corporation from an act or compelling redress to an injured party (compare RESTRAINING ORDER). □ **in·junc·tive** *adjective* [Late Latin *injunctio* from Latin *injungere* ENJOIN]

in·jure *transitive verb* **1** do esp. physical harm or damage to; hurt (*was injured in a car accident*). **2** harm or impair (*gossip has injured her reputation*). **3** do injustice or wrong to. [back-formation from INJURY]

in·jured harmed and hurt (*the injured passengers*). **2** offended; wronged (*in an injured tone*).

in·juri·ous /ɪnˈdʒʊriəs/ *adjective* **1** causing or likely to cause damage or harm. **2** (of language) insulting; libellous. □ **in·juri·ous·ly** *adverb*

in·jury *noun* (*pl.* **-ies**) **1 a** physical harm or damage. **b** an instance of this (*suffered head injuries*). **2** esp. *Law* a wrongful action or treatment, esp. the violation of another's rights. **b** an instance of this. **3** damage to one's feelings, reputation, etc. [Anglo-French *injurie* from Latin *injuria* a wrong (as IN-¹, *jus juris* right)]

injury time *noun* Soccer & Rugby extra playing time allowed by a referee to compensate for time lost in dealing with injuries.

in·jus·tice *noun* **1** a lack of fairness or justice. **2** an unjust act. □ **do a person an injustice** judge a person unfairly.

ink ● *noun* **1** a coloured fluid or paste used for writing, drawing, printing, etc. **2** *Zool.* a black liquid ejected by a cuttlefish, octopus, etc. to confuse a predator. **3** *informal* press coverage; publicity. ● *transitive verb* **1** (usu. foll. by *in*, *over*, etc.) **a** mark with ink. **b** go over or trace around with ink. **2** cover (type etc.) with ink before printing. **3** apply ink to. **4** esp. *N Amer. informal* sign, put one's signature to (a contract etc.). □ **ink out** obliterate with ink. □ **ink·er** *noun* [Old French *enque* from Late Latin *encau(s)tum* from Greek *egkauston* purple ink used by Roman emperors for signature (as EN-², CAUSTIC)]

In·ka·tha /ɪnˈkatə/ *noun* (in full **Inkatha Freedom Party**) a mainly Zulu political party and organization in South Africa, founded in 1928 by the Zulu king Solomon as a cultural and social movement and revived by Mangosuthu Buthelezi in 1975. [Zulu *inKhata* crown of woven grass, a tribal emblem symbolizing the force unifying the Zulu nation]

ink blot test *noun* = RORSCHACH TEST.

ink cap *noun* any fungus of the genus *Coprinus*.

ink·horn *noun hist.* **1** a small portable horn container for ink. **2** (*attributive*) (of a term, word, language, etc.) obscure; literary.

in-kind *adjective* (of a donation etc.) in goods or labour rather than money.

ink-jet printer *noun Computing* a printer that creates characters and graphics by firing a stream of minute ink drops at a surface from one or more banks of tiny nozzles. □ **ink-jet printing** *noun*

ink·ling *noun* (often foll. by *of*) a slight knowledge or suspicion; a hint. [Middle English *inkle* utter in an undertone, of unknown origin]

ink pad *noun* = STAMP PAD.

ink·stand *noun* a stand for one or more ink bottles, often incorporating a pen tray etc.

ink·well *noun* a pot for ink usu. housed in a hole in a desk.

inky *adjective* of, as black as, or stained with ink.

in·laid ● *transitive verb past and past participle of* INLAY. ● *adjective* (of a piece of furniture etc.) ornamented by inlaying.

in·land ● *adjective* **1** pertaining to or situated in the interior of a country (*inland waterway*). **2** inhabiting the interior of a country (*inland Algonquians*). **3** esp. *Cdn & Brit.* carried on within the limits of a country; domestic (*inland trade*). **4** conducted or occurring away from the coast or borders (*inland fishing*). ● *noun* **1** the parts of a country remote from the coast or borders; the interior. **2** *Cdn hist.* (*attributive*) denoting persons, places, or things involved with the inland fur trade (*an inland post*). ● *adverb* in or towards the interior of a country. □ **in·land·er** *noun*

inland navigation *noun* transportation by rivers and canals.

inland revenue *noun* **1** *Brit.* revenue consisting of taxes and inland duties. **2** (**Inland Revenue**) (in the UK) the government department responsible for assessing and collecting such taxes.

Inland Sea an almost landlocked arm of the Pacific Ocean, surrounded by the Japanese islands of Honshu, Shikoku, and Kyushu. Its chief port is Hiroshima.

inland sea *noun* an entirely landlocked large body of salt or fresh water.

Inland Tlingit *noun* **1** a member of an Aboriginal group living in northern BC and the southern Yukon Territory. **2** the Tlingit language of this people.

in-law ● *noun* (usu. in *pl.*) a relative by marriage. ● *combining form* denoting a relation by marriage (*father-in-law*; *sister-in-law*).

in-law suite *noun* (also **in-law apartment**) *N Amer.* an extension added or a room, suite, etc. renovated to form a small apartment within an existing house.

inlay ● *transitive verb* (*past* and *past participle* **inlaid**) **1 a** (usu. foll. by *in*) embed (a thing in another) so that the surfaces are even. **b** (usu. foll. by *with*) ornament (a thing) by inserting another material in its surface in a decorative design. **2** insert (a page, an illustration, etc.) in a space cut in a larger thicker page. ● *noun* **1** inlaid work. **2** a piece of material inlaid or prepared for inlaying. **3** a filling shaped to fit a tooth cavity.

in·let *noun* **1** a small arm of the ocean, a lake, or a river. **2** a valve, device, etc. that controls incoming air, water, etc. **3** a way of entry. **4** a piece inserted, esp. in dressmaking etc. [Middle English from IN + LET¹ *verb*]

in·lier /ˈɪnlaɪr/ *noun Geol.* a structure or area of older rocks completely surrounded by newer rocks. [IN, after *outlier*]

in-line *adjective* **1 a** having parts arranged in a line. **b** (of an internal combustion engine) having usu. vertical cylinders arranged in one or more rows. **2** involving, employing, or forming part of a continuous, usu. linear, sequence of operations or machines, as in an assembly line. **3** *Computing* designating data processing which does not require input data to be sorted into batches.

in-line skate *noun* a skate resembling an ice skate, but having a line of usu. four rubber wheels instead of a blade, for use on paved surfaces etc. □ **in-line skater** *noun* **in-line skating** *noun*

in loco pa·ren·tis /ɪn ˌloːkoː pəˈrentɪs/ *adverb* in the place or position of a parent (used by a teacher etc. responsible for children). [Latin]

inly /ˈɪnli/ *adverb literary* inwardly; in the heart.

In·mar·sat *noun* an international organization that operates a system of satellites providing telecommunication services, as well as distress and safety communication services, to the world's shipping, aviation, and offshore industries. [*International Maritime Satellite Organization*]

in·mate *noun* a person confined in a prison, hospital, etc. [prob. originally INN + MATE¹, assoc. with IN]

in med·ias res /ɪn ˌmiːdias ˈreɪz/ *adverb* **1** into the midst of things. **2** into the middle of a story, without preamble. [Latin]

in me·mor·iam /ɪn məˈmɔriəm/ ● *preposition* in memory of (a dead person). ● *noun* a written article or notice etc. in memory of a dead person; an obituary. [Latin]

in·most *adjective* **1** most inward. **2** most intimate; deepest (*inmost secrets*).

inn *noun* **1** a small hotel, esp. in the country. **2** a tavern. [Old English *inn* (as IN)]

in·nards *plural noun informal* **1** entrails. **2** the inner workings (of an engine etc.). [dial. etc. pronunciation of *inwards*: see INWARD]

in·nate *adjective* **1** inborn; natural (*an innate sense of style*). **2** *Philos.* originating in the mind. □ **in·nate·ly** *adverb* **in·nate·ness** *noun* [Latin *innatus* (as IN-², *natus* past participle of *nasci* be born)]

in·ner ● *adjective* (usu. *attributive*) **1 a** further in; inside; interior (*the inner compartment*). **b** further inshore, nearer the land (*inner islands*). **2** (of thoughts, feelings, etc.) deeper, more secret. **3** designating the mind or soul; mental; spiritual. ● *noun* **1** the inner part of something. **2** *Archery* **a** a division of the target next to the bull's eye. **b** a shot that strikes this. □ **inner·most** *adjective* **inner·ness** *noun* [Old English *innera* (adj.), comparative of IN]

inner cabinet *noun* a small group of powerful decision-makers within a ministerial cabinet.

inner child *noun Psych.* **1** a person's supposed original or authentic self, esp. regarded as damaged or concealed by negative childhood experiences. **2** that part of an individual's personality which manifests itself in or enjoys childish activities.

inner circle *noun* an exclusive group of close friends or associates within a larger group.

inner city *noun* the central area of a city, esp. if dilapidated, or characterized by overcrowding, poverty, etc. (also *attributive: inner-city housing*).

inner-direct·ed *adjective Psych.* governed by one's own standards, not by external pressures.

inner ear *noun* the semicircular canals and cochlea, which form the organs of balance and hearing and are embedded in the temporal bone.

Inner Hebrides see HEBRIDES, THE.

inner man *noun* the soul or mind.

Inner Mongolia an autonomous region of N China, on the border with Mongolia; capital, Hohhot.

inner planet *noun* one of the four planets closest to the sun, i.e. Mercury, Venus, Earth, or Mars.

inner sanctum *noun* **1** the most sacred place in a temple or church. **2** a private or secret place to which few other people are admitted.

inner space *noun* **1 a** the region between the earth and outer space. **b** the region below the surface of the sea. **2** the part of the mind not normally accessible to consciousness.

inner·spring *adjective N Amer.* (of a mattress etc.) with coiled springs inside.

Inner Temple *noun* one of the two Inns of Court on the site of the Temple in London (*compare* MIDDLE TEMPLE).

inner tube *noun* an inflatable rubber tube inside a tire.

in·nerv·ate /'ɪnɜr,veɪt, ɪ'nɜr-/ *transitive verb* supply (an organ etc.) with nerves or nervous stimulation. ☐ **in·nerv·a·tion** /-'veɪʃən/ *noun* [IN-² + Latin *nervus* nerve + -ATE³]

in·ning *noun N Amer.* each of the divisions of a baseball game during which both sides have a turn at bat. [*in* (v.) go in (from IN)]

in·nings *noun* (*pl.* same or *informal* **in·nings·es**) **1** esp. *Cricket* **a** the part of a game during which a side is in or batting. **b** the play of or score achieved by a player during a turn at batting. **2** esp. *Brit.* **a** a period during which a person can achieve something. **b** *informal* a person's life span (*had a good innings and died at 94*).

Innis, Har·old Adams (1894–1952), Canadian political economist. His two major works, *The Fur Trade in Canada* (1930) and *The Cod Fisheries* (1940) introduced the staple thesis of economic development and suggested that Canada's political development as distinct from the United States was a natural outcome of its economic development.

Innis·fail /'ɪnəsfeɪl/ a town in south central Alberta, about 110 km north of Calgary; pop. (2001) 6,928. [*Innis Fail* isle of destiny, a poetic name for Ireland]

Innis·fil /'ɪnəsfɪl/ a town in south central Ontario, south of Barrie; pop. (2001) 28,666. [var. of INNISFAIL]

inn·keep·er *noun* a person who manages or owns an inn.

In·no·cent III (born Giovanni Lotario di Segni) (*c.*1160–1216), pope 1198–1216. An active reformer, he oversaw the Fourth Crusade (1202–4), ordered a crusade against the Albigenses (1208), and summoned the fourth Lateran Council (1215).

in·no·cent ● *adjective* **1** free from moral wrong; sinless. **2** (usu. foll. by *of*) not guilty (of a crime etc.). **3** free from responsibility for an event yet suffering its consequences (*innocent bystanders*). **4** simple; guileless; naive. **5** harmless; not intending to hurt or offend (*an innocent question*). **6** (foll. by *of*) *informal* without, lacking (*innocent of hypocrisy*). **●** *noun* **1** an innocent person, esp. a young child. **2** a person involved by chance in a situation, esp. a victim of crime or war. **3** (in *pl.*) the young children killed by Herod after the birth of Jesus (Matt. 2:16). ☐ **in·no·cence** *noun* **in·no·cent·ly** *adverb* [Old French *innocent* or Latin *innocens* *innocent-* (as IN-¹, *nocēre* hurt)]

in·nocu·ous /ɪ'nɒkjuəs/ *adjective* **1** not injurious; harmless. **2** inoffensive. ☐ **in·nocu·ous·ly** *adverb* **in·nocu·ous·ness** *noun* [Latin *innocuus* (as IN-¹, *nocuus* formed as INNOCENT)]

Inn of Court *noun Brit. Law* **1** each of the four legal societies having the exclusive right of admitting people to the English bar. **2** any of the sets of buildings in London belonging to these societies.

in·nomin·ate /ɪ'nɒmɪnət/ *adjective* not having a name; unnamed. [Late Latin *innominatus* (as IN-¹, NOMINATE)]

innominate bone *noun Anat.* the bone formed from the fusion of the ilium, ischium, and pubis; the hip bone.

in·nov·ate *verb* **1** *intransitive* bring in new methods, ideas, etc. (*the company collapsed because of its failure to innovate*). **2** *intransitive* (often foll. by *in*) make changes. **3** *transitive* introduce (a product) for the first time,

esp. to the market. ☐ **in·nov·a·tion** *noun* **in·nov·a·tive** *adjective* **in·nov·a·tive·ly** *adverb* **in·nov·a·tive·ness** *noun* **in·nov·a·tor** *noun* **in·nov·a·tory** /'ɪnəvə,tɔri/ *adjective* [Latin *innovare* make new, alter (as IN-², *novus* new)]

Inns·bruck /'ɪnzbrʊk/ a city in W Austria, capital of Tyrol; pop. (2001) 113,800.

inn-to-inn *adjective* designating a network of trails for cross-country skiing, snowmobiling, etc. on which inns are strategically located as rest stops.

Innu /'ɪnuː/ **●** *noun* **1** a member of an Aboriginal people living in Labrador and northern Quebec (*see also* MONTAGNAIS, NASKAPI). **2** the Cree language of this people. **●** *adjective* of or relating to this people or their culture or language. [Innu *innu*, human being]

in·nu·en·do /,ɪnju'endoʊ/ *noun* (*pl.* **-does** or **-dos**) **1** an allusive or oblique remark or hint, usu. disparaging. **2** a remark with a double meaning, usu. suggestive. [Latin, = by nodding at, by pointing to: ablative gerund of *innuere* nod at (as IN-², *nuere* nod)]

In·nu·itian Region /,ɪnjuː'ɪʃən, ,ɪnʊ-/ a largely mountainous and upland region of the Canadian High Arctic, including most of the islands north of Parry Channel. [from Innuit (a former spelling of INUIT) + -IAN]

in·numer·able /ɪ'nuːmərəbəl, -'njuː-/ *adjective* too many to be counted.

in·numer·ate /ɪ'nuːmərət, -'njuː-/ *adjective* without a basic knowledge of mathematics and arithmetic. ☐ **in·numer·acy** /-əsi/ *noun*

in·ocu·late /ɪ'nɒkjʊ,leɪt/ *transitive verb* **1** treat (a person or animal) with a vaccine containing a dead or modified disease-causing agent, usu. by injection, to promote immunity against the disease. **2** introduce (an infective agent) into an organism. **3** introduce (cells or organisms) into a culture medium. ☐ **in·ocu·la·tion** *noun* **in·ocu·la·tor** *noun* [originally in sense 'insert (a bud) into a plant': Latin *inoculare inoculat-* implant (as IN-², *oculus* eye, bud)]

in·ocu·lum /ɪ'nɒkjʊləm/ *noun* (*pl.* **in·ocula** /-lə/) (also **in·ocu·lant** /ɪ'nɒkjʊlənt/) any substance used for inoculation. [modern Latin (as INOCULATE)]

in·offen·sive *adjective* **1** not objectionable or offensive; not causing offence. **2** innocuous, unoffending; doing or causing no harm. ☐ **in·offen·sive·ly** *adverb* **in·offen·sive·ness** *noun*

İnönü /'iːnə,nuː/ **Ismet** (1884–1973), Turkish prime minister 1923–37 and 1961–5 and president 1938–50. Although considered a dictator from 1939 to 1946, he emerged as a defender of democracy and introduced several social and political reforms to westernize Turkey.

in·oper·able *adjective* **1** *Surgery* that cannot be operated on successfully (*inoperable cancer*). **2** that cannot be operated; inoperative. **3** impractical, unworkable.

in·opera·tive *adjective* **1** not working or taking effect. **2** *Law* without practical force, invalid. ☐ **in·opera·tive·ness** *noun*

in·oppor·tune *adjective* not appropriate, esp. as regards time; inconvenient. ☐ **in·oppor·tune·ly** *adverb* **in·oppor·tune·ness** *noun*

in·ordin·ate /ɪn'ɔrdɪnət/ *adjective* unusually or disproportionately large; excessive (*inordinate delays*). ☐ **in·ordin·ate·ly** *adverb* [Latin *inordinatus* (as IN-¹, *ordinatus* past participle of *ordinare* ORDAIN)]

in·organ·ic ● *adjective* **1** *Chem.* (of a compound) not organic, usu. of mineral origin; not derived from or found in living organisms (*opp.* ORGANIC). **2** without organized physical structure or systematic arrangement. **3** not arising or growing naturally from an organization or structure; artificial, extraneous. **4** *Linguistics* not explainable by normal etymology. **●** *noun* an inorganic chemical. ☐ **in·organ·ic·ally** *adverb*

inorganic chemistry *noun* the branch of chemistry that deals with the properties and reactions of inorganic compounds.

in·osi·tol /ɪ'nɒsɪtɒl/ *noun* each of the nine stereoisomers in $C_6H_{12}O_6$, a substance acting as a growth factor in plants, animals, etc. [Greek *in-* + *is* sinew + -ITE¹ + -OL¹]

in-patient *noun* a patient who stays in hospital for a period of days while receiving treatment.

in pro·pria per·sona /ɪn ,prɒprɪə pɜr'soʊnə/ *adverb* in his or her own person. [Latin]

input ● *noun* **1 a** what is put in or taken in, or operated on by any process or system. **b** the total resources including raw materials, manpower, etc. necessary to production, which are deducted from output in calculating profits. **2** *Electronics* **a** a place where, or a device through which, energy, information, etc. enters a system (*a tape recorder with inputs for microphone and radio*). **b** energy supplied to a device or system; an electrical signal. **3** the information fed into a computer. **4** the action or process of putting in or feeding in. **5** a contribution of information etc. ● *transitive verb* (**in·put·ting**; *past* and *past participle* **input** or **in·put·ted**) (often foll. by *into*) **1** put in. **2** *Computing* supply (data, programs, etc., to a computer, program, etc.).

input device *noun* *Computing* a piece of equipment by which data, programs, or signals are transferred to a computer.

input/output *attributive adjective* (also **input-output**) *Computing etc.* of, relating to, or for input and output. Abbr.: **I/O**.

in·quest *noun* **1** *Law* **a** an inquiry by a coroner's court into the cause of a sudden, unexplained, or suspicious death. **b** a coroner's jury. **2** *informal* a discussion analyzing the outcome of a game, an election, etc. [Old French *enqueste* (as INQUIRE)]

in·quire *verb* (also **enquire**) **1 a** *intransitive* (often foll. by *of*) seek information; ask a question (of a person). **b** *transitive* ask for information as to (*inquired my name*; *inquired whether we were coming*). **2** *intransitive* seek information formally; make a formal investigation. **3** *intransitive* (foll. by *after, for*) ask about a person, a person's health, etc. **4** *intransitive* (foll. by *for*) ask about the availability of. □ **in·quir·er** *noun* **in·quir·ing** *adjective* **in·quir·ing·ly** *adverb* [Old French *enquerre*, ultimately from Latin *inquirere* (as IN-², *quaerere quaesit-* seek)]

in·quiry /ɪnˈkwaɪri/ *noun* (*pl.* **-ies**) (also **enquiry**) **1** the act or an instance of asking or seeking information. **2** a question, a query. **3** (also /ˈɪnkwəri/) a formal or judicial investigation into a matter of public concern (*a public inquiry into the accident*).

in·qui·si·tion /ˌɪnkwəˈzɪʃən/ *noun* **1** usu. *derogatory* **a** an intensive search or investigation. **b** a relentless, sustained, or unwelcome questioning of a person. **2** a judicial or official inquiry. **3** (**the Inquisition**) *Catholicism hist.* **a** an ecclesiastical court established by Pope Gregory IX *c.*1232 for the detection of heretics, at a time when certain heretical groups were regarded as enemies of society; condemned heretics who refused to recant were handed over to the civil authorities for punishment. **b** (in full **Spanish Inquisition**) a similar but separate body, established by the Spanish crown in 1478 and directed originally against converts from Judaism and Islam; it operated with great severity, especially under its first inquisitor, Torquemada. [Old French from Latin *inquisitio -onis* examination (as INQUIRE)]

in·quis·i·tive /ɪnˈkwɪzɪtɪv/ *adjective* **1** seeking knowledge; inquiring. **2** unduly curious; prying. □ **in·quis·i·tive·ly** *adverb* **in·quis·i·tive·ness** *noun* [Old French *inquisitif -ive* from Late Latin *inquisitivus* (as INQUISITION)]

in·quis·i·tor /ɪnˈkwɪzɪtər/ *noun* **1** an official investigator, esp. one who proceeds ruthlessly, unrelentingly, etc. **2** *hist.* an officer of the Inquisition. [French *inquisiteur* from Latin *inquisitor -oris* (as INQUIRE)]

Inquisitor-General *noun* *hist.* the head of the Spanish Inquisition.

in·quis·i·tor·i·al /ɪnˌkwɪzɪˈtɔriəl/ *adjective* **1** of or like an inquisitor. **2** offensively prying. **3** *Law* (of a trial etc.) in which the judge, rather than a prosecutor, has the prosecuting role (*opp.* ACCUSATORIAL). □ **in·quis·i·tor·i·al·ly** *adverb*

in re /ɪn ˈriː, ˈreɪ/ *preposition* = RE¹. [Latin, = in the matter of]

INRI *abbreviation* Jesus of Nazareth, King of the Jews. [Latin *Iesus Nazarenus Rex Iudaeorum*]

in·road *noun* **1** (usu. in *pl.*) **a** (usu. foll. by *on, into*) an encroachment; a using up of resources etc. (*makes inroads on my time*). **b** (usu. foll. by *in, into*) progress; an advance (*making inroads into a difficult market*). **2** a hostile attack; a raid. [IN + ROAD in sense 'riding']

in·rush *noun* a rushing in; an influx. □ **in·rush·ing** *adjective & noun*

ins. *abbreviation* **1** inches. **2** insurance.

in·sa·lu·bri·ous /ˌɪnsəˈluːbriəs/ *adjective* (of a place) seedy and rundown; unwholesome.

in·sane *adjective* **1 a** mentally deranged; not of sound mind. **b** characteristic of an insane person (*an insane laugh*). **2** (of an action) extremely foolish; irrational. □ **in·sane·ly** *adverb* **in·san·i·ty** *noun* (*pl.* **-ies**). [Latin *insanus* (as IN-¹, *sanus* healthy)]

in·san·i·tary *adjective* not sanitary; dirty or germ-carrying.

in·sa·ti·a·ble /ɪnˈseɪʃəbəl/ *adjective* **1** unable to be satisfied. **2** (usu. foll. by *of*) extremely greedy. □ **in·sa·ti·a·bil·i·ty** *noun* **in·sa·ti·a·bly** *adverb* [Old French *insaciable* or Latin *insatiabilis* (as IN-¹, SATIATE)]

in·sa·ti·ate /ɪnˈseɪʃiət/ *adjective* never satisfied.

in·scape *noun* *literary* the unique inner quality or essence of an object etc. as shown in a work of art, esp. a poem.

in·scribe *transitive verb* **1 a** (usu. foll. by *in, on*) write or carve (words etc.) on stone, metal, paper, a book, etc. **b** (usu. foll. by *with*) mark (a sheet, tablet, etc.) with characters. **2** (usu. foll. by *to*) write an informal dedication (to a person) in or on (a book etc.). **3** enter the name of (a person) on an official document or list; enrol. **4** *Math.* draw (a figure)

within another so that some or all of their boundaries touch but do not intersect (*compare* CIRCUMSCRIBE). □ **in·scrib·a·ble** *adjective* **in·scrib·er** *noun* [Latin *inscribere inscript-* (as IN-², *scribere* write)]

in·scrip·tion *noun* **1** words inscribed, esp. on a monument, coin, stone, or in a book etc. **2 a** the act of inscribing, esp. the informal dedication of a book etc. **b** an instance of this. □ **in·scrip·tion·al** *adjective* **in·scrip·tive** *adjective* [Latin *inscriptio* (as INSCRIBE)]

in·scrut·a·ble /ɪnˈskruːtəbəl/ *adjective* wholly mysterious, impenetrable. □ **in·scrut·a·bil·i·ty** *noun* **in·scrut·a·ble·ness** *noun* **in·scrut·a·bly** *adverb* [ecclesiastical Latin *inscrutabilis* (as IN-¹, *scrutari* search: see SCRUTINY)]

in·seam *noun* *N Amer.* the inner seam on the leg of a pair of pants, extending from crotch to cuff.

in·sect *noun* **1 a** any arthropod of the class Insecta, having a head, thorax, abdomen, two antennae, three pairs of thoracic legs, and usu. one or two pairs of thoracic wings. **b** (loosely) any other small invertebrate animal esp. with several pairs of legs. **2** an insignificant or contemptible person or creature. □ **in·sect·ile** *adjective* [Latin *insectum (animal)* notched (animal) from *insecare insect-* (as IN-², *secare* cut)]

in·sect·ar·i·um *noun* (*pl.* **in·sect·ar·i·ums**) a place for keeping insects, esp. an institution where insects are on public display for educational purposes.

in·sec·ti·cide *noun* a substance used for killing insects. □ **in·sec·ti·cid·al** *adjective*

in·sec·ti·vore *noun* **1** any animal that feeds on insects, esp. a mammal of the order Insectivora, including shrews, hedgehogs, and moles. **2** any plant which captures and absorbs insects. □ **in·sect·iv·or·ous** *adjective*

in·se·cure *adjective* **1** (of a person or state of mind) uncertain; lacking confidence. **2 a** unsafe, not firm or fixed. **b** (of ice, ground, etc.) not providing good support, liable to give way. □ **in·se·cure·ly** *adverb* **in·se·cur·i·ty** *noun* (*pl.* **-ities**)

in·sem·in·ate /ɪnˈseməˌneɪt/ *transitive verb* introduce semen into (a female) by natural or artificial means. □ **in·sem·in·a·tion** *noun* [Latin *inseminare* (as IN-², SEMEN)]

in·sen·sate *adjective* **1** without physical sensation or feeling; inanimate. **2** without sensibility; unfeeling. **3** stupid, foolish. □ **in·sen·sate·ly** *adverb* [ecclesiastical Latin *insensatus* (as IN-¹, *sensatus* from *sensus* SENSE)]

in·sen·si·bil·i·ty *noun* (*pl.* **-ities**) **1** unconsciousness. **2** a lack of mental feeling or emotion; hardness. **3** (often foll. by *to*) indifference.

in·sen·si·ble *adjective* **1 a** without one's mental faculties; unconscious. **b** (of the extremities etc.) numb; without feeling. **2** (usu. foll. by *of, to*) unaware; indifferent (*insensible to her needs*). **3** without emotion; callous. **4** too small or gradual to be perceived; inappreciable. □ **in·sen·si·bly** *adverb*

in·sen·si·tive *adjective* (often foll. by *to*) **1** showing or feeling no sympathetic or emotional response; indifferent, callous. **2** not sensitive to physical stimuli. **3** (of a substance, device, etc.) not susceptible or responsive to some physical influence, e.g. light, radiation, etc. □ **in·sen·si·tive·ly** *adverb* **in·sen·si·tiv·i·ty** *noun* (*pl.* **-ities**)

in·sen·tient /ɪnˈsenʃənt/ *adjective* not sentient; inanimate. □ **in·sen·tience** *noun*

in·sep·ar·a·ble *adjective* **1** unable or unwilling to be separated (*inseparable concepts*; *inseparable friends*). **2** *Grammar* (of a prefix, or a verb with respect to it) unable to be used as a separate word, e.g.: *dis-, mis-, un-*. □ **in·sep·ar·a·bil·i·ty** *noun* **in·sep·ar·a·ble·ness** *noun* **in·sep·ar·a·bly** *adverb*

in·sert ● *transitive verb* **1** (usu. foll. by *in, into, between*, etc.) place, fit, or thrust (a thing) into another (*insert a key in a lock*). **2** (usu. foll. by *in, into*) introduce (a letter, word, etc.) into a piece of text etc. (*inserted a new paragraph*). ● *noun* something inserted, e.g. an additional section in a magazine, a piece of cloth in a garment, a shot in a film, etc. □ **in·sert·a·ble** *adjective* **in·sert·er** *noun* [Latin *inserere* (as IN-², *serere sert-* join)]

in·sert·ed *adjective* **1** (of a thing) placed, put, or included in another. **2** *Anat. etc.* (of a muscle etc.) attached (at a specific point).

in·ser·tion *noun* **1** the act or an instance of inserting. **2** an amendment etc. inserted in writing or printing. **3** each appearance of an advertisement in a newspaper etc. **4** an ornamental section of needlework inserted into plain material (*lace insertions*). **5** the manner or place of attachment of a muscle, an organ, etc. **6** the placing of a spacecraft in an orbit.

in-service ● *attributive adjective* (of training) intended for those actively engaged in the profession or activity concerned. ● *noun* an in-service training session, e.g. a professional development day for teachers.

inset ● *noun* **1** (often *attributive*) something set in or inserted (*an inset photo; an inset of burl walnut*). **2 a** a small map, photograph, etc., inserted within the border of a larger one. **b** an extra page or pages inserted in a folded sheet or in a book; an insert. **3** a piece set into a garment as decoration etc. ● *transitive verb* (**in·set·ting**) *past* and *past participle* **inset** or **in·set·ted**) **1** set or put in as an inset; insert. **2** decorate with an inset.

in·shal·lah /ɪnˈʃalə/ *interjection* if Allah wills it. [Arabic *in šā' Allah*]

in·shore ● *adjective* **1** situated at sea close to the shore. **2** of or pertaining to fishing conducted from small boats in coastal waters. ● *adverb* **1** at sea but close to the shore. **2** towards the shore.

in·side ● *noun* **1 a** the inner side or surface of a thing. **b** the inner part; the interior. **2 a** the side of a path or sidewalk furthest away from the road. **b** the part of a track or curving road nearest to the inner or shorter side of the curve. **3** (usu. in *pl.*) *informal* **a** the stomach and bowels (*something wrong with my insides*). **b** the operative part of a machine etc. **4** *informal* a position affording inside information (*knows someone on the inside*). ● *adjective* **1** situated on or in, or derived from, the inside. **2** (of information etc.) available only to those on the inside. **3** *Baseball* **a** (of a pitched ball) missing the plate on the batter's side. **b** (of the strike zone) nearest the batter. **4** (in some team sports) denoting positions nearer to the centre of the field (*inside linebacker*). ● *adverb* **1 a** on, in, or to the inside. **b** indoors. **2** *slang* in prison. **3** *Cdn* (*North*) within the Yukon, Northwest Territories, or Nunavut (*compare* OUTSIDE *adverb* 4). ● *preposition* **1** on the inner side of; within (*inside the house*). **2** in less than (*inside an hour*). □ **inside of** *informal* in less than (a week etc.)

inside information *noun* information not accessible to outsiders.

inside job *noun informal* a crime committed by or involving the help of a person living or working on the premises burgled etc.

inside joke *noun* = IN-JOKE.

inside out ● *adverb* with the inner surface turned outwards. ● *attributive adjective* (**inside-out**) in this condition. □ **know a thing inside out** know a thing thoroughly. **turn inside out 1** turn the inner surface outwards. **2** *informal* cause confusion or a mess in.

Inside Passage (also called **Inland Passage**) a sheltered, natural sea route extending some 1 600 km northwestward along the Pacific coast of N America, from Seattle, Washington to Skagway, Alaska. The cities of Victoria, Vancouver and Prince Rupert, BC and Juneau, Alaska are situated along its route.

in·sid·er *noun* **1** a person who is within a society, organization, etc. **2** a person privy to a secret, esp. when using it to gain advantage.

insider trading *noun* (esp. *Brit.* **insider dealing**) *Stock Exch.* the illegal use of confidential information as a basis for share trading. □ **insider trader** *noun*

inside track *noun* **1** a position of advantage. **2** the track of a racecourse etc. which is shorter, because of the curve.

in·sid·i·ous /ɪnˈsɪdiəs/ *adjective* **1** proceeding or progressing inconspicuously but harmfully (*an insidious disease*). **2** treacherous; crafty. □ **in·sid·i·ous·ly** *adverb* **in·sid·i·ous·ness** *noun* [Latin *insidiosus* cunning, from *insidiae* ambush (as IN-², *sedēre* sit)]

in·sight *noun* **1 a** the capacity of understanding hidden truths etc., esp. of character or situations. **b** an instance of this. **2** a sudden perception of the solution to a problem or difficulty. □ **in·sight·ful** *adjective* **in·sight·ful·ly** *adverb* [Middle English, = 'discernment', prob. of Scandinavian & Low German origin (as IN-², SIGHT)]

in·sig·ni·a /ɪnˈsɪɡniə/ *noun* (pl. same or **-nias**) a badge or distinguishing mark of military rank, office, or membership of an organization or other symbols of rank or authority (*wore his insignia of office*). [Latin, pl. of *insigne* neuter of *insignis* distinguished (as IN-², *signis* from *signum* SIGN)]

in·sig·nif·i·cant *adjective* **1** unimportant; trifling. **2** (of a person) undistinguished. **3** meaningless. □ **in·sig·nif·i·cance** *noun* **in·sig·nif·i·cant·ly** *adverb*

in·sin·cere *adjective* not sincere; not candid. □ **in·sin·cere·ly** *adverb* **in·sin·cer·i·ty** *noun* (pl. **-ities**).

in·sin·u·ate /ɪnˈsɪnjuˌeɪt/ *transitive verb* **1** (often foll. by *that* + clause) convey indirectly or obliquely; hint (*insinuated that she was lying*). **2** (often *reflexive*; usu. foll. by *into*) **a** introduce (oneself, a person, etc.) into favour, office, etc., by subtle manipulation. **b** introduce (a thing, oneself, etc.) subtly or deviously into a place (*insinuated himself back into my life*). □ **in·sin·u·at·ing** *adjective* **in·sin·u·at·ing·ly** *adverb*

in·sinu·a·tion /-ˈeɪʃən/ *noun* [Latin *insinuare insinuat-* (as IN-², *sinuare* to curve)]

in·sip·id /ɪnˈsɪpɪd/ *adjective* **1** lacking vigour or interest; dull, boring. **2** lacking flavour; tasteless. □ **in·sip·id·ity** /-ˈpɪdɪti/ *noun* **in·sip·id·ly** *adverb* **in·sip·id·ness** *noun* [French *insipide* or Late Latin *insipidus* (as IN-¹, *sapidus* SAPID]

in·sist *transitive & intransitive verb* (usu. foll. by *that* + clause) maintain or demand positively and assertively (*insisted that he was innocent; let me pay! I insist!*). □ **insist on** insistently maintain or make a persistent demand for (something) (*I insist on being present; insists on his suitability*). [Latin *insistere* stand on, persist (as IN-², *sistere* stand)]

in·sist·ent *adjective* **1** insisting; demanding positively or continually. **2** regular and repeated; demanding attention (*the insistent rattle of the window*). □ **in·sist·ence** *noun* **in·sist·ent·ly** *adverb*

in situ /ɪn ˈsɪtjuː, sɪtuː, ˈsiː-/ *adverb* in its original or proper place. [Latin]

in·sobri·ety /ˌɪnsəˈbraɪəti/ *noun* lack of sobriety; intemperance, esp. in drinking.

in·so·far *adverb* (usu. foll. by *as*) to the extent that.

in·so·la·tion /ˌɪnsəʊˈleɪʃən/ *noun* **1** exposure to the sun's rays, esp. for drying or bleaching or as a medical treatment. **2** the amount of solar radiation reaching a given area. [Latin *insolatio* from *insolare* (as IN-², *solare* from *sol* sun)]

in·sole *noun* **1** a removable sole worn in a boot or shoe for comfort, warmth etc. **2** the fixed inner sole of a boot or shoe.

in·sol·ent /ˈɪnsələnt/ *adjective* rude, disrespectful; offensively contemptuous or arrogant. □ **in·sol·ence** *noun* **in·sol·ent·ly** *adverb* [Middle English, = 'arrogant', from Latin *insolens* (as IN-¹, *solens* pres. part. of *solēre* be accustomed)]

in·sol·uble /ɪnˈsɒljʊbəl/ *adjective* **1** (of a difficulty, problem, etc.) incapable of being solved. **2** incapable of being dissolved in a liquid.

in·sol·vent ● *adjective* **1** unable to pay one's debts. **2** relating to insolvency (*insolvent laws*). ● *noun* a debtor. □ **in·sol·vency** *noun* (pl. **-cies**)

in·som·nia *noun* habitual sleeplessness; inability to sleep. □ **in·som·niac** *noun & adjective* [Latin from *insomnis* sleepless (as IN-¹, *somnus* sleep)]

in·so·much *adverb* **1** (foll. by *that* + clause) to such an extent. **2** (foll. by *as*) inasmuch.

in·souci·ant /ɪnˈsuːsiənt/ *adjective* carefree; unconcerned. □ **in·souci·ance** *noun* **in·souci·ant·ly** *adverb* [French (as IN-¹, *souciant* pres. part. of *soucier* care)]

Insp. *abbreviation* Inspector.

in·spect *transitive verb* **1** look closely at or into, esp. to assess quality or check for shortcomings. **2** examine (a document etc.) officially. □ **in·spec·tion** *noun* [Latin *inspicere inspect-* (as IN-², *specere* look at), or its frequentative *inspectare*]

in·spect·or *noun* **1** a person who inspects. **2** an official employed to supervise a service, system, machine, etc., and make reports (*school inspector; building inspector*). **3** (in some municipal police forces in Canada) an officer ranking above staff sergeant and below staff inspector or superintendent. **4** (in the Sûreté du Québec) an officer ranking above captain and below chief inspector. **5** (in Quebec municipal police forces) an officer ranking above captain and below deputy director. **6** (in the Ontario Provincial Police) an officer ranking above sergeant major and below superintendent. **7** (in the Royal Newfoundland Constabulary) an officer ranking above lieutenant and below superintendent. **8** (in the RCMP) an officer ranking above corps sergeant major and below superintendent. **9** (in the UK) a police officer below a superintendent and above a sergeant in rank. □ **in·spect·or·ate** *noun* **in·spec·tor·ial** *adjective* **in·spec·tor·ship** *noun*

inspector general *noun* a chief inspector.

in·spir·a·tion *noun* **1 a** a supposed force or influence on poets, artists, musicians, etc., stimulating creativity, ideas, etc. **b** a person, principle, faith, etc. as a source of esp. artistic creativity or moral fervour. **c** a similar divine influence supposed to have led to the writing of Scripture etc. **2** a sudden brilliant, creative, or timely idea etc. **3** a drawing in of breath; inhalation. □ **in·spir·a·tion·al** *adjective* **in·spir·a·tion·al·ly** *adverb*

in·spira·tory *adjective* of or relating to inhalation.

in·spire *verb* **1** *transitive* (often foll. by *to*) stimulate or arouse (a person) to esp. creative activity or moral fervour (*inspired her to write; inspired by God*). **2** *transitive* **a** (usu. foll. by *with*) animate (a person) with a feeling. **b** (usu. foll. by *into*) instill (a feeling) into a person etc. **c** (usu. foll. by *in*) create (a feeling) in a person. **3** *transitive* prompt; give rise to (*the poem* *was inspired by the autumn*). **4** *transitive & intransitive* esp. *literary* breathe in (air etc.); inhale. □ **in·spir·er** *noun* **in·spir·ing** *adjective* **in·spir·ing·ly** *adverb* [Old French *inspirer* from Latin *inspirare* breathe in (as IN-², *spirare* breathe)]

in·spired *adjective* **1** (of a work of art etc.) as if prompted by or emanating from a supernatural source; characterized by inspiration (*an inspired speech*). **2** (of a guess) intuitive but accurate. □ **in·spired·ly** *adverb*

in·spirit *transitive verb* (**in·spirit·ed**, **in·spirit·ing**) **1** put life into; animate. **2** (usu. foll. by *to*, or *to* + infin.) encourage (a person). □ **in·spirit·ing** *adjective* **in·spirit·ing·ly** *adverb*

in·spis·sat·ed /ɪnˈspɪseɪtəd/ *adjective* thickened; condensed. [Late Latin *inspissare inspissat-* (as IN-², Latin *spissus* thick)]

inst. *abbreviation* **1** (**Inst.**) institute. **2** (**Inst.**) institution. **3** = INSTANT *adjective* **4** (*the 6th inst.*).

in·stabil·ity *noun* (*pl.* **-ities**) **1 a** a lack of stability. **b** an instance of instability. **2** *Psych.* a tendency to unpredictable behaviour or erratic changes of mood. **3** a meteorological tendency towards precipitation, high winds, etc.

in·stall *transitive verb* (also **instal**) (**in·stalled**, **in·stall·ing**) **1** place (equipment, machinery, etc.) in position ready for use. **2** *Computing* take (software), e.g. from a floppy disk, CD-ROM, tape, or remote networked computer, and place it in its permanent location from where it will be executed. **3** place (a person) in an office or rank with ceremony (*installed in the office of chancellor*). **4** establish (oneself, a person, etc.) in a place, condition, etc. (*installed herself at the head of the table*). □ **in·stall·er** *noun* [medieval Latin *installare* (as IN-², *stallare* from *stallum* STALL¹)]

in·stal·la·tion *noun* **1 a** the act or an instance of installing. **b** the process or an instance of being installed. **2** a piece of apparatus, a machine, etc. installed. **3 a** a large work of art, esp. a sculpture or mixed media piece, specially created or constructed for display in a gallery, museum, or other site. **b** an exhibition of such works. **4** a subsidiary military or industrial establishment.

in·stal·ment *noun* (also **in·stall·ment**) **1** a sum of money due as one of several usu. equal payments for something, spread over an agreed period of time. **2** any of several parts, esp. of a television or radio series or a magazine story, broadcast or published in sequence at intervals. [alteration of obsolete *estallment* from Anglo-French *estalement* from *estaler* fix: prob. assoc. with INSTALLATION]

instalment plan *noun* a method of buying something by paying for it in instalments.

in·stance ● *noun* **1** an example or illustration of (*just another instance of his lack of determination*). **2** a particular case (*that's not true in this instance*). **3** *Law* a legal suit. ● *transitive verb* cite (a fact, case, etc.) as an instance. □ **at the instance of** at the request or suggestion of. **for instance** as an example. **in the first** (or **second** etc.) **instance** in the first (or second etc.) place; at the first (or second etc.) stage of a proceeding. [Old French from Latin *instantia* (as INSTANT)]

in·stant ● *adjective* **1 a** occurring immediately (*gives an instant result*). **b** designed to produce quick or immediate results (*instant lottery; instant camera*). **2 a** (of food etc.) processed to allow quick preparation. **b** prepared hastily and with little effort (*I have no instant solution*). **3** urgent; pressing. **4** *Business archaic* of the current month (*the 6th instant*). **5** of the present moment. ● *noun* **1** a precise moment of time, esp. the present (*come here this instant; went that instant; told you the instant I heard*). **2** a short space of time (*was there in an instant*). **3** an instant food or beverage, esp. instant coffee. [French from Latin *instare instant-* be present, press upon (as IN-², *stare* stand)]

instant book *noun* a book which is written and published in an extremely short time to take advantage of a topical subject.

instant coffee *noun* **1** dried coffee granules. **2** the beverage made by adding boiling water to these granules.

in·stan·ter /ɪnˈstantər/ *adverb archaic* immediately. [Latin from *instans* (as INSTANT)]

in·stan·tiate /ɪnˈstanʃiˌeɪt/ *transitive verb* represent by an instance. □ **in·stan·ti·a·tion** *noun* [Latin *instantia*: see INSTANCE]

in·stant·ly *adverb* immediately; at once.

instant messaging *noun Computing* real-time communication through the Internet or another network, esp. using software that informs people when friends are online. □ **instant message** *noun*

instant replay *noun* esp. *N Amer.* **1** the recording and immediate rebroadcasting of part of a televised sports event, often in slow motion. **2** the part recorded and rebroadcast. **3** any immediate recollection, re-enactment, or review of an event, conversation, etc.

Instant Teller *noun Cdn proprietary* an automated banking machine.

instant-win *adjective* designating a lottery ticket which one scratches, rips open, etc. to reveal a winning number etc.

in·star /ˈɪnstɑr/ *noun* a stage in the life of an insect etc. between two periods of moulting. [Latin, = form]

in·state *transitive verb* (often foll. by *in*) install; establish. [IN-² + STATE]

in statu pu·pil·lari /ɪn ˌstatjuː ˌpjuːpɪˈlɑːri/ *adjective* **1** under guardianship, esp. as a pupil. **2** in a junior position at university; not having a master's degree. [Latin]

in·staur·a·tion /ˌɪnstɔːˈreɪʃn/ *noun formal* restoration; renewal. [Latin *instauratio* from *instaurare* (as IN-²: compare RESTORE)]

in·stead *adverb* **1** (foll. by *of*) as a substitute or alternative to; in place of (*instead of this one; stayed instead of going*). **2** as an alternative (*took me instead*) (compare STEAD). [Middle English, from IN + STEAD]

in·step *noun* **1** the inner arch of the foot between the toes and the ankle. **2** the part of a shoe etc. fitting over or under this.

in·sti·gate /ˈɪnstɪˌɡeɪt/ *transitive verb* **1** bring about by incitement or persuasion; provoke (*who instigated the inquiry?*). **2** (usu. foll. by *to*) urge on, incite (a person etc.) to esp. a foolhardy or drastic act. □ **in·sti·ga·tion** *noun* **in·sti·ga·tor** *noun* [Latin *instigare instigat-*]

in·still *transitive verb* (also **instil**) (**in·stilled**, **in·still·ing**) (often foll. by *into*) **1** introduce (a feeling, idea, etc.) into a person's mind etc. gradually. **2** put (a liquid) into something in drops. □ **in·stil·la·tion** *noun* [Latin *instillare* (as IN-², *stillare* drop): compare DISTILL]

in·stinct ● *noun* **1 a** an innate, usu. fixed, pattern of behaviour in most animals in response to certain stimuli. **b** a similar propensity in human beings to act without conscious intention; innate impulsion. **2** (usu. foll. by *for*) unconscious skill; intuition. ● *predicative adjective* (foll. by *with*) imbued, filled (with life, beauty, force, etc.). □ **in·stinc·tual** *adjective* **in·stinc·tual·ly** *adverb* [Middle English, = 'impulse', from Latin *instinctus* from *instinguere stinct-* prick)]

in·stinct·ive *adjective* **1** relating to or prompted by instinct. **2** apparently unconscious or automatic (*an instinctive reaction*). □ **in·stinct·ive·ly** *adverb*

in·sti·tute ● *noun* **1 a** a society or organization for the promotion of science, education, etc. **b** a building used by an institute. **2** *Law* (usu. in *pl.*) a digest of the elements of a legal subject (*Institutes of Justinian*). **3** a principle of instruction. **4** *N Amer.* a brief course of instruction for teachers etc. **5** a unit within a university, college, etc. devoted to advanced teaching and research in a specialized field. **6** *Cdn see* COLLEGIATE INSTITUTE. ● *transitive verb* **1** establish; found. **2 a** initiate (an inquiry etc.). **b** begin (proceedings) in a court. **3** (usu. foll. by *to*, *into*) place (a person, esp. a cleric) officially in a new post with a formal ceremony. [Latin *institutum* design, precept, neuter past participle of *instituere* establish, arrange, teach (as IN-², *statuere* set up)]

in·sti·tu·tion *noun* **1** the act or an instance of instituting. **2 a** a society or organization founded esp. for charitable, religious, educational, or social purposes. **b** a business or governmental establishment providing a service to the public, e.g. a bank, prison, etc. (*financial institution; minimum-security institution*). **c** a building used by an institution. **3** a residential centre for the care of psychiatric or disabled patients etc. **4** an established law, practice, or custom (*the institution of marriage*). **5** *informal* (of a person, a custom, etc.) a familiar object. **6 a** the establishment of a sacrament by Christ, esp. the Eucharist. **b** a passage, e.g. *this is my body, this is my blood*, of the prayer used in consecrating the Eucharist. **c** the establishment of a cleric etc. in a church.

in·sti·tu·tion·al *adjective* **1** of or like an institution. **2** typical of institutions, esp. in being regimented or unimaginative (*the food was dreadfully institutional*). **3** (of religion) expressed or organized through institutions (*churches etc.*). □ **in·sti·tu·tion·al·ism** *noun* **in·sti·tu·tion·al·ly** *adverb*

institutional investor *noun* a large institution, e.g. an insurance company, bank, etc. that invests substantial amounts of money in the stock market.

in·sti·tu·tion·al·ize *transitive verb* (also esp. *Brit.* **-ise**) **1** (esp. as **in·sti·tu·tion·al·ized**) establish in practice or custom (*institutionalized racism*). **2** place or keep (a person) in an institution. **3** convert into an institution; make institutional. □ **in·sti·tu·tion·al·iz·a·tion** *noun*

Consonants: b *but*   d *dog*   f *few*   g *get*   h *her*   j *yes*   k *cat*   l *leg*   m *man*   n *no*   p *pen*   r *red*   s *sit*

in·sti·tu·tion·al·ized *adjective* (of a prisoner, a long-term patient, etc.) made apathetic and dependent after a long period in an institution.

in-store ● *adjective* available or occurring inside a store (*an in-store promotion*). ● *adverb* inside a store.

in·struct *transitive verb* **1** (often foll. by *in*) teach (a person) a subject etc. (*instructed her in French*). **2** (usu. foll. by *to* + infin.) direct; command (*instructed him to fill in the hole*). **3** (often foll. by *of*, or *that* etc. + clause) inform (a person) of a fact etc. **4** *N Amer.* (of a judge) advise (a jury), prior to its deliberations, of the legal principles applicable to the case under consideration. **5** *Brit.* **a** (of a client or solicitor) give information to (a solicitor or counsel). **b** authorize (a solicitor or counsel) to act for one. [Latin *instruere instruct-* build, teach (as IN-², *struere* pile up)]

in·struc·tion *noun* **1** (often in *pl.*) a direction; an order (*read the instructions; gave him his instructions*). **2** teaching; education (*individualized instruction in the classroom*). **3** *Law* (in *pl.*) **a** *N Amer.* a judge's directions to a jury, prior to its deliberations, on the legal principles applicable to the case under consideration. **b** *Brit.* directions to a solicitor or counsel. **4** the act or an instance of teaching or directing. **5** *Computing* a direction in a computer program defining and effecting an operation. □ **in·struc·tion·al** *adjective*

in·struc·tive *adjective* tending to instruct; conveying a lesson; enlightening (*found the experience instructive*). □ **in·struc·tive·ly** *adverb*

in·struc·tor *noun* **1** a person who instructs; a teacher. **2** *N Amer.* a university teacher ranking below assistant professor. □ **in·struc·tor·ship** *noun*

in·struc·tress *noun* a woman who instructs; a teacher.

in·stru·ment ● *noun* **1** a tool or implement, esp. for delicate or scientific work. **2** (in full **musical instrument**) a device for producing musical sounds by vibration, wind, percussion, etc. **3 a** a thing used in performing an action; a means (*the meeting was an instrument in her success*). **b** a person made use of (*is merely their instrument*). **4** a measuring device, esp. in a car or aircraft, serving to gauge position, speed, etc. **5** a formal, esp. legal, document. **6** an investment option such as derivatives, stocks, bonds, etc. ● *transitive verb* equip with instruments (for measuring, recording, controlling, etc.). □ **in·stru·ment·ed** *adjective* [Old French *instrument* or Latin *instrumentum* (as INSTRUCT)]

in·stru·men·tal ● *adjective* **1** (usu. foll. by *to*, *in*, or *in* + verbal noun) serving as an instrument or means (*was instrumental in finding the money*). **2** (of music) performed on instruments, without singing (*compare* VOCAL *adjective* 3). **3** of, or arising from, an instrument (*instrumental error*). **4** *Grammar* of or in the instrumental. ● *noun* **1** a piece of music performed by instruments, not by the voice. **2** *Grammar* the case of nouns and pronouns (and words in grammatical agreement with them) indicating a means or instrument. □ **in·stru·men·tal·ly** *adverb*

in·stru·men·tal·ism *noun* **1** a pragmatic philosophical approach which regards an activity (such as science, law, or education) chiefly as an instrument or tool for some practical purpose, rather than in more absolute or ideal terms. **2** (esp. in Marxist theory) the view that the state and social organizations are tools which are exploited by the ruling class or by individuals in their own interests.

in·stru·men·tal·ist *noun* **1** a player of a musical instrument. **2** an adherent of instrumentalism.

in·stru·men·tal·ity *noun* (*pl.* **-ities**) **1** the fact or quality of serving as an instrument or means to an end. **2** a thing which serves as an instrument or means to an end.

in·stru·men·ta·tion *noun* **1 a** the arrangement or composition of music for a particular group of musical instruments. **b** the instruments used in any one piece of music. **2 a** the design, provision, or use of instruments in industry, science, etc. **b** such instruments collectively.

instrument flight rules *plural noun* rules for controlling and navigating an aircraft by using instruments only. Abbr.: **IFR**.

instrument landing system *noun* a system for landing an aircraft in which the pilot uses only instruments and ground-based electronics rather than visual cues as a guide. Abbr.: **ILS**.

instrument panel *noun* a surface, esp. in a car or aircraft, containing the dials etc. of measuring devices.

instrument rating *noun* a certification that a pilot is able to fly using only instruments and ground-based electronics rather than visual cues as a guide. □ **instrument-rated** *adjective*

in·sub·ord·in·ate /ˌɪnsəˈbɔːrdɪnət/ *adjective* refusing to obey instructions or show respect. □ **in·sub·ord·in·ate·ly** *adverb* **in·sub·ord·in·a·tion** /-ˈneɪʃən/ *noun*

in·sub·stan·tial *adjective* **1** lacking solidity or substance; weak, flimsy. **2** not real; imaginary (*an insubstantial vision*). **3** not large in size or amount (*an insubstantial raise*). □ **in·sub·stan·tial·ity** *noun* **in·sub·stan·tial·ly** *adverb*

in·suf·fer·able *adjective* **1** intolerable. **2** unbearably arrogant or conceited etc. □ **in·suf·fer·able·ness** *noun* **in·suf·fer·ably** *adverb*

in·suf·fi·cien·cy *noun* (*pl.* **-cies**) **1 a** the condition of being insufficient; inadequacy. **b** an instance of this. **2** *Med.* the inability of an organ to perform its normal function (*renal insufficiency*).

in·suf·fi·cient *adjective* not sufficient; inadequate. □ **in·suf·fi·cient·ly** *adverb*

in·suf·flate /ˈɪnsəˌfleɪt/ *transitive verb* **1** *Med.* **a** blow or breathe (air, gas, powder, etc.) into a cavity of the body etc. **b** treat (the nose etc.) in this way. **2** (in Christian theology) blow or breathe on (a person) to symbolize spiritual influence. □ **in·suf·fla·tion** /-ˈfleɪʃən/ *noun* [Late Latin *insufflare insufflat-* (as IN-², *sufflare* blow upon)]

in·su·lar /ˈɪnsʊlər, ˈɪnsjʊ-/ *adjective* **1 a** of or like an island. **b** separated or remote, like an island. **c** inhabiting or situated on an island. **2** ignorant of or indifferent to cultures, peoples, etc., outside one's own experience; narrow-minded. □ **in·su·lar·ity** /-ˈlerɪti/ *noun* [Late Latin *insularis* (as INSULATE)]

in·su·late /ˈɪnsəˌleɪt, ˈɪnsjə-/ *transitive verb* **1** prevent the passage of electricity, heat, or sound from (a thing, room, etc.) by interposing non-conductors. **2** detach (a person or thing) from its surroundings; isolate. □ **in·su·la·tive** *adjective* [Latin *insula* island + -ATE³]

in·su·la·tion *noun* **1** the action of insulating or the condition of being insulated against the passage of electricity, heat, or sound. **2** materials used for this, such as foam, fibreglass, or rockwool.

in·su·la·tor *noun* **1** a thing or substance used for insulation against electricity, heat, or sound. **2** an insulating device to support telephone wires etc. **3** a device preventing contact between electrical conductors.

insul·brick /ˈɪnsʊlbrɪk/ *noun Cdn* simulated-brick asphalt siding used on houses etc. [INSULATION + BRICK]

in·su·lin /ˈɪnsʊlɪn, ˈɪnsjə-/ *noun Biochem.* **1** a polypeptide hormone produced in the pancreas by the islets of Langerhans, which regulates the amount of glucose in the blood, and the lack of which causes diabetes. **2** a commercial preparation of this substance, used in the treatment of diabetes. [Latin *insula* island + -IN]

in·sult ● *transitive verb* speak to or treat with scornful abuse or disrespect. ● *noun* **1** an insulting remark or action. **2** something so worthless or contemptible as to be offensive (*an insult to his intelligence*). **3** *Med.* **a** an event or occurrence causing damage to the body. **b** such damage. □ **add insult to injury** behave offensively as well as harmfully. □ **in·sult·er** *noun* **in·sult·ing** *adjective* **in·sult·ing·ly** *adverb* [French *insulte* or Latin *insultare* (as IN-², *saltare* frequentative of *salire salt-* leap)]

in·super·able /ɪnˈsuːpərəbəl, ɪnˈsjuː-, -ˈprəbəl/ *adjective* **1** (of a barrier) impossible to surmount. **2** (of a difficulty etc.) impossible to overcome. □ **in·super·ably** *adverb* [IN- + Latin *superabilis* from *superare* overcome]

in·sup·port·able *adjective* **1** unable to be endured; insufferable. **2** unjustifiable. □ **in·sup·port·ably** *adverb*

insurable earnings *plural noun Cdn* income on which employment insurance premiums are paid.

in·sur·ance *noun* **1** the act or an instance of insuring property, life, etc. **2 a** a sum paid for this; a premium. **b** a sum paid out as compensation for theft, damage, loss, etc. **3** the business of providing insurance policies. **4** = INSURANCE POLICY. **5** a measure taken to provide for a possible contingency (*take an umbrella as insurance; insurance goal*). **6** a system of contributions from workers and employers, or one funded entirely by tax revenue, to provide government assistance in sickness, unemployment, retirement, etc. (*health insurance; employment insurance*).

insurance agent *noun* a person employed by an insurance company to sell insurance policies.

insurance broker *noun* a self-employed person who buys and sells insurance policies on behalf of clients.

insurance company *noun* a company engaged in the business of insurance.

insurance policy *noun* **1** a contract of insurance. **2** a document detailing such a policy and constituting a contract.

in·sure *verb* **1** *transitive & intransitive* (often foll. by *against*) secure the payment of a sum of money in the event of loss or damage to (property, life, a person, etc.) by regular payments or premiums (*insured the house for $250,000; we have insured against flood damage*) (*compare* ASSURE 3). **2** *transitive* (of the owner of a property, an insurance company, etc.)

t *top*   v *voice*   w *we*   z *zoo*   ʃ *she*   ʒ *vision*   θ *thin*   ð *this*   ŋ *ring*   x *loch*   tʃ *chip*   dʒ *jar*   (see over for vowels)

secure the payment of (a sum of money) in this way. **3** *transitive* (usu. foll. by *against*) provide for (a possible contingency) (*insured themselves against the rain by taking umbrellas*). **4** *transitive N Amer.* = ENSURE 1-3. □ **in·sur·able** *adjective* **in·sur·abil·ity** *noun* [Middle English, var. of ENSURE]

in·sured ● *adjective* covered by insurance. ● *noun* (usu. prec. by *the*) a person etc. covered by insurance.

in·sur·er *noun* a person or company offering insurance policies for premiums; an underwriter.

in·sur·gent /ɪnˈsɜrdʒənt/ ● *adjective* rising in active revolt; rebellious. ● *noun* a rebel; a revolutionary. □ **in·sur·gence** *noun* **in·sur·gen·cy** *noun* (*pl.* **-cies**). [French from Latin *insurgere insurrect-* (as IN-², *surgere* rise)]

in·sur·mount·able *adjective* unable to be surmounted or overcome. □ **in·sur·mount·ably** *adverb*

in·sur·rec·tion *noun* a rising in open resistance to established authority; a rebellion. □ **in·sur·rec·tion·ary** *adjective* **in·sur·rec·tion·ist** *noun & adjective* [Old French from Late Latin *insurrectio -onis* (as INSURGENT)]

int. *abbreviation* **1** interior. **2** internal. **3** international.

in·tact *adjective* entire; undamaged. □ **in·tact·ness** *noun* [Latin *intactus* (as IN-¹, *tactus* past participle of *tangere* touch)]

in·tagli·at·ed /ɪnˈtɑli,eɪtɪd/ *adjective* decorated with surface carving. [Italian *intagliato* past participle of *intagliare* cut into]

in·taglio /ɪnˈtɑlioʊ/ ● *noun* (*pl.* **-taglios**) **1** a gem with an incised design (*compare* CAMEO 1). **2** an engraved design. **3** a carving, esp. incised, in hard material. **4** a printing process in which the image is engraved or etched into a metal plate or cylinder so that it lies below the non-printing areas. ● *transitive verb* (**-glioes, -glioed**) **1** engrave (material) with a sunken pattern or design. **2** engrave (such a design). [Italian (as INTAGLIATED)]

in·take *noun* **1 a** the action of taking in. **b** an instance of this. **2 a** a number (of people etc.) or the amount taken in or received (*this year's intake of students*). **b** such people etc. **3** a place where water is taken into a channel or pipe from a river, or fuel or air enters an engine etc.

in·tan·gible /ɪnˈtandʒəbəl/ ● *adjective* **1** unable to be touched; not solid. **2** unable to be grasped mentally. **3** (of a business asset, e.g. a patent, trademark, or copyright) saleable, but having no value in itself. ● *noun* something that cannot be precisely measured or assessed. □ **in·tan·gibil·ity** /-ˈbɪlɪti/ *noun* **in·tan·gibly** *adverb*

in·tar·sia /ɪnˈtɑrsiə/ *noun* **1 a** the craft of using wood inlays, esp. as practised in 15th-c. Italy. **b** similar inlaid work in stone, metal, or glass. **2** a method of knitting with a number of colours in which a separate length or ball of yarn is used for each area of colour (as opposed to different yarns being carried at the back of the work). [Italian *intarsio*]

in·teger /ˈɪntɪdʒər/ *noun* **1** a whole number. **2** a thing complete in itself. [Latin (adj.) = untouched, whole: see ENTIRE]

in·te·gral ● *adjective* /ˈɪntɪɡrəl, ɪnˈtɛɡrəl/ **1 a** of a whole or necessary to the completeness of a whole. **b** forming a whole (*integral design*). **c** whole, complete. **d** included as part of the whole, rather than supplied from outside (*a machine with an integral power source*). **2** *Math.* **a** of or denoted by an integer. **b** involving only integers, esp. as coefficients of a function. ● *noun* /ˈɪntɪɡrəl/ *Math.* **1** a quantity of which a given function is the derivative, i.e. which yields that function when undifferentiated, and which may express the area under the curve of a graph of the function (see DEFINITE INTEGRAL, INDEFINITE INTEGRAL). **2** a function satisfying a given differential equation. □ **in·te·gral·ity** /-ˈɡralɪti/ *noun* **in·te·gral·ly** *adverb* [Late Latin *integralis* (as INTEGER)]

integral calculus *noun* mathematics concerned with finding integrals, their properties and application, etc. (*compare* DIFFERENTIAL CALCULUS).

in·te·grand /ˈɪntəˌɡrand/ *noun Math.* a function that is to be integrated. [Latin *integrandus* gerundive of *integrare*: see INTEGRATE]

in·te·grate /ˈɪntəˌɡreɪt/ *verb* **1** *transitive* **a** combine (parts) into a whole. **b** complete (an imperfect thing) by the addition of parts. **2** *transitive & intransitive* bring or come into equal participation in or membership of society, a school, etc. **3** *transitive* desegregate, esp. racially (a school etc.). **4** *transitive Math.* find the integral of. □ **in·te·grable** /ˈɪntəɡrəbəl/ *adjective* **in·te·gra·tive** /ˈɪntəˌɡreɪtɪv/ *adjective* [Latin *integrare integrat-* make whole (as INTEGER)]

in·te·grat·ed /ˈɪntəˌɡreɪtɪd/ *adjective* **1** combined into a whole; united; undivided. **2** designating or characterized by a personality in which the component elements combine harmoniously. **3** uniting several components previously regarded as separate. **4** (of an institution, group, etc.) not divided by considerations of race, culture, ability, etc.;

not segregated. **5** *Math.* indicating the mean value or total sum of (temperature, an area, etc.).

integrated circuit *noun* a small chip etc. of material replacing several separate components in a conventional electrical circuit.

integrated school *noun Cdn* (*Nfld*) *hist.* a public school established, maintained, and operated jointly by members of the Anglican, United, and Presbyterian Churches and the Salvation Army.

integrated services digital network *noun* a telecommunications network through which sound, images, and data can be transmitted as digitized signals. Abbr.: **ISDN**.

in·te·gra·tion /ˌɪntəˈɡreɪʃən/ *noun* **1** the act or an instance of integrating. **2** the intermixing of persons previously segregated. **3** *Psych.* the combination of the diverse elements of perception etc. in a personality. **4** *Math.* the process or an instance of obtaining the integral of a function. □ **in·te·gra·tion·ist** *noun & adjective* [Latin *integratio* (as INTEGRATE)]

in·te·gra·tor /ˈɪntəˌɡreɪtər/ *noun* **1** an instrument for indicating or registering the total amount or mean value of some physical quality, as area, temperature, etc. **2** a person or thing that integrates.

in·teg·rin /ˈɪntəˌɡrɪn/ *noun* any of a class of animal transmembrane proteins which are involved in the adhesion of cells to each other and to their substrate.

in·teg·rity /ɪnˈtɛɡrɪti/ *noun* **1** moral uprightness; honesty. **2** wholeness; completeness. **3** soundness; unimpaired or uncorrupted condition. [French *intégrité* or Latin *integritas* (as INTEGER)]

in·tegu·ment /ɪnˈtɛɡjumənt/ *noun* **1** a natural outer covering, as a skin, husk, rind, etc. **2** something with which an object is covered, enclosed, or clothed; a covering or coating. □ **in·teg·ment·ary** /-ˈmɛntəri/ *adjective* [Latin *integumentum* from *integere* (as IN-², *tegere* cover)]

in·tel·lect *noun* **1 a** the faculty of reasoning, knowing, and thinking, as distinct from feeling. **b** the understanding or mental powers (of a particular person etc.) (*his intellect is not great*). **2 a** a clever or knowledgeable person. **b** the intelligentsia regarded collectively (*the combined intellect of four universities*). [Old French or Latin *intellectus* understanding (as INTELLIGENT)]

in·tel·lec·tion *noun* **1** the action or process of understanding (*opp.* IMAGINATION). **2** a notion; an idea. □ **in·tel·lect·ive** *adjective*

in·tel·lec·tual ● *adjective* **1** of or relating to the intellect. **2 a** possessing a high level of understanding or intelligence. **b** valuing or interested in matters appealing to the intellect. **3** requiring, appealing to, or engaging the intellect. ● *noun* **1** a person of superior intelligence. **2** a person who is interested in intellectual matters. **3** a person professionally engaged in intellectual activity. □ **in·tel·lec·tual·ity** *noun* **in·tel·lec·tual·ly** *adverb*

intellectual capital *noun* the knowledge possessed by people, esp. as seen as an asset to a business.

in·tel·lec·tual·ism *noun* **1** devotion to intellectual pursuits. **2** the exercise, esp. when excessive, of the intellect at the expense of the emotions. **3** *Philos.* the theory that knowledge is wholly or mainly derived from pure reason. □ **in·tel·lec·tual·ist** *noun*

in·tel·lec·tual·ize *verb* (also esp. *Brit.* **-ise**) **1** *transitive* make intellectual; give an intellectual character to. **2** *intransitive* exercise the intellect; talk or write intellectually. □ **in·tel·lec·tual·iz·a·tion** *noun*

intellectual property *noun Law* non-tangible property that is the result of creativity, such as patents, copyrights, etc.

in·tel·li·gence *noun* **1 a** the intellect; the understanding. **b** (of a person or an animal) quickness of understanding and reasoning; wisdom. **2 a** the collection of information, esp. of military or political value (also *attributive*: *intelligence operation*). **b** a group or agency that collects such information. **c** information so collected. **d** information in general; news. **3** an intelligent or rational being.

intelligence quotient *noun* a number denoting the ratio of a person's intelligence to the statistical norm, 100 being average. Abbr.: **IQ**.

intelligence service *noun* (also **intelligence agency**) a usu. government body engaged in collecting esp. secret information.

intelligence test *noun* a test designed to measure intelligence rather than acquired knowledge.

in·tel·li·gent *adjective* **1** having the faculty of understanding; possessing or showing intelligence, esp. of a high level (*intelligent life on other planets*; *an intelligent remark*). **2** quick of mind; clever. **3 a** (of a device or machine) able to vary its behaviour in response to varying situations and requirements and past experience. **b** (esp. of a computer terminal) having its own data-processing capability; incorporating a microprocessor (opp. DUMB adjective 7). **c** (of a building, office, etc) equipped with sophisticated telecommunications and computer technology. □ **in·tel·li·gent·ly** adverb [Latin intelligere intellect- understand (as INTER-, legere gather, pick out, read)]

intelligent agent noun a computer program which can seek or sort information with minimal supervision by the user.

in·tel·li·gent·sia noun **1** the class of intellectuals regarded as possessing culture and political initiative. **2** people doing intellectual work; intellectuals. [Russian from Polish inteligencja from Latin intelligentia (as INTELLIGENT)]

in·tel·li·gible /ɪnˈtelɪdʒəbəl/ adjective **1** (often foll. by to) able to be understood; comprehensible. **2** Philos. able to be understood only by the intellect, not by the senses. □ **in·tel·li·gi·bil·ity** noun **in·tel·li·gibly** adverb [Latin intelligibilis (as INTELLIGENT)]

In·tel·sat /ˈɪntelˌsat/ noun an international organization of countries operating a system of commercial communication satellites. [International Telecommunications Satellite Consortium]

in·temper·ate /ɪnˈtempərət, -prət/ adjective **1** (of a person, conduct, or speech) immoderate; unbridled; violent (used intemperate language). **2 a** given to excessive indulgence in alcohol. **b** excessively indulgent in one's appetites. **c** characterized by overindulgence or profligacy (an intemperate lifestyle). □ **in·temper·ance** noun **in·temper·ate·ly** adverb

in·tend transitive verb **1** have as one's purpose; propose (we intend to go; we intend that it shall be done). **2** (usu. foll. by to + infin.) design or destine (a person or a thing) (I intend him to go). **3** (often foll. by as) mean (what does he intend by that?; intended it as a warning). **4** (in passive; foll. by for) **a** be meant for a person to have or use etc. (they are intended for the children). **b** be designed for (intended for a small child's hand). [Old French entendre, intendre from Latin intendere intent- or intens- strain, direct, purpose (as IN-², tendere stretch, tend)]

in·tend·ant /ɪnˈtendənt/ noun (often **Intendant**) hist. a high-ranking administrative official in French, Portuguese, and Spanish provinces and colonies, responsible for economic development, settlement, and the administration of justice. **2** a superintendent or manager of a department of public business etc. □ **in·tend·an·cy** noun [French from Latin intendere (as INTEND)]

in·tend·ed ● adjective **1** done on purpose; intentional. **2** designed, meant (the intended audience). **3** future; prospective (my intended spouse). ● noun informal the person one intends to marry; one's fiancé or fiancée (is this your intended?).

in·tend·ing adjective who intends to be (an intending visitor).

in·tense adjective (**in·tens·er**, **in·tens·est**) **1** (of a quality, feeling etc.) existing in a high degree; extremely strong, esp. so severe as to be difficult to withstand or endure (intense cold; subjected to intense scrutiny). **2 a** (of an emotion) deeply or strongly felt. **b** (of a person) extremely earnest and serious (very intense about my music). **c** (of an activity) characterized by emotional tension. **d** expressing strong emotion (a deeply intense poem). **3** (of a colour) very strong or deep. **4** (of an action etc.) requiring a great deal of emotional, intellectual, or physical effort concentrated in a short time (intense thought). □ **in·tense·ly** adverb **in·tense·ness** noun [Old French intens or Latin intensus (as INTEND)]

in·ten·si·fi·er noun **1** a person or thing that intensifies. **2** Grammar a word or prefix used to give force or emphasis.

in·ten·si·fy verb (**-fies**, **-fied**) **1** transitive (often in passive) **a** (of a person) make (esp. something that causes stress) more intense. **b** increase the quantity or strength of (something). **2** intransitive (of any activity, esp. a conflict; also of emotions, colours, physical sensations) become much stronger, esp. rapidly. **3** transitive Photog. increase the opacity of (a negative). □ **in·ten·si·fi·ca·tion** noun

in·ten·sion noun Logic the internal content of a concept. □ **in·ten·sion·al** adjective **in·ten·sion·al·ly** adverb [Latin intensio (as INTEND)]

in·ten·sity noun (pl. **-ties**) **1** the quality of being intense. **2** concentration of feeling, emotional depth, earnestness or passion. **3** esp. Physics the measurable amount of some quality, e.g. force, brightness, a magnetic field, etc.

in·ten·sive ● adjective **1** characterized by a great deal of concentrated effort, usu. over a short period of time (intensive study; intensive bombardment). **2** of or relating to intensity as opposed to extent; producing intensity. **3** serving to increase production in relation to costs (intensive farming methods) (compare EXTENSIVE adjective 3). **4** (usu. in combination) Econ. making much use of (a labour-intensive industry). **5** Grammar (of an adjective, adverb, etc.) expressing intensity; giving force, as really in my feet are really cold. ● noun Grammar an intensive

adjective, adverb, etc.; an intensifier. □ **in·ten·sive·ly** adverb [French intensif -ive or medieval Latin intensivus (as INTEND)]

intensive care noun **1** medical treatment with constant monitoring etc. of a dangerously ill patient (also attributive: intensive care unit). **2** a part of a hospital devoted to this.

in·ten·siv·ist noun a physician in charge of an intensive care unit.

in·tent ● noun (usu. without article) **1** intention; a purpose (my intent to reach the top; with evil intent). **2** Law a person's state of mind that directs him or her to perform an action (with intent to defraud). ● adjective **1** (usu. foll. by on) **a** resolved; bent; determined (was intent on succeeding). **b** attentively occupied (intent on her books). **2** (esp. of a look) earnest; eager; meaningful. □ **to** (or **for**) **all intents and purposes** practically; virtually. □ **in·tent·ly** adverb **in·tent·ness** noun [Old French from Latin intentus (as INTEND)]

in·ten·tion noun **1** (often foll. by to + infin., or of + verbal noun) a thing intended; an aim or purpose (it was not his intention to interfere; have no intention of staying). **2** the action or fact of intending (done without intention). **3** informal (usu. in pl.) a person's, esp. a man's, designs in respect to marriage (are his intentions honourable?). **4** Logic a conception. **5** Catholicism = SPECIAL INTENTION. □ **in·ten·tioned** adjective (usu. in combination). [Old French from Latin intentio stretching, purpose (as INTEND)]

in·ten·tion·al adjective **1** done with an aim or purpose; deliberate. **2** of or pertaining to intention; existing only in intention. **3** Philos. of or pertaining to the operation of the mind; existing in or for the mind. □ **in·ten·tion·al·ity** noun **in·ten·tion·al·ly** adverb

intentional walk noun Baseball a tactical play in which a pitcher deliberately walks a batter.

inter /ɪnˈtɜr/ transitive verb (**in·terred**, **inter·ring**) deposit (a corpse etc.) in the earth, a tomb, etc.; bury. [Old French enterrer from Romanic (as IN-², Latin terra earth)]

inter. abbreviation intermediate.

inter- combining form **1** between, among (intercontinental). **2** mutually, reciprocally (interbreed). [Old French entre- or Latin inter between, among]

In·ter·ac noun Cdn proprietary a system of payment by means of a debit card, in which funds are transferred electronically from the cardholder's bank account to the account of a merchant etc.

inter·act intransitive verb **1** act reciprocally; act on each other. **2** (of people) work together or communicate. □ **inter·act·ant** adjective & noun

inter·action noun **1** reciprocal action or influence. **2** Physics the action of atomic and subatomic particles on each other. □ **inter·action·al** adjective

inter·action·ism noun Philos. the theory that there are two entities, mind and body, each of which can have an effect on the other. □ **inter·action·ist** noun & adjective

inter·active adjective **1** reciprocally active; acting upon or influencing each other. **2** (of a computer, television, or other electronic device) allowing a two-way flow of information between it and a user; responding to the user's input. □ **inter·active·ly** adverb **inter·activ·ity** noun

inter alia /ˌɪntər ˈeiliə, ˈaliə/ adverb among other things. [Latin]

inter·atomic adjective between atoms.

inter·bank adjective agreed, arranged, or operating between banks (interbank loan).

inter·bed transitive verb (**-bed·ded**, **-bed·ding**) embed (esp. a stratum) among others.

inter·breed transitive & intransitive verb (past and past participle **-bred**) breed or cause to breed with members of a different stock, race, or species to produce a hybrid.

in·ter·cal·ary /ɪnˈtɜrkələri, -ˈkaləri/ adjective **1 a** (of a day or a month) inserted in the calendar to harmonize it with the solar year, e.g. 29 Feb. in leap years. **b** (of a year) having such an addition. **2** interpolated; intervening. [Latin intercalari(u)s (as INTERCALATE)]

in·ter·cal·ate /ɪnˈtɜrkəˌleit/ transitive verb **1** insert (an intercalary day etc.). **2** interpose (anything out of the ordinary course). □ **in·ter·cal·a·tion** noun [Latin intercalare intercalat- (as INTER-, calare proclaim)]

in·ter·cal·at·ed /ɪnˈtɜrkəˌleitid/ adjective (of strata etc.) interposed.

inter·cede intransitive verb **1** (usu. foll. by with) interpose or intervene on behalf of another; plead (they interceded with the authorities for her release). **2** mediate between two people, groups, etc. [French intercéder or Latin intercedere intercess- intervene (as INTER-, cedere go)]

inter·cellu·lar *adjective Biol.* located or occurring between cells.

inter·cept ● *transitive verb* **1** seize, catch, or stop (a person, message, vehicle, ball, puck, etc.) going from one place to another. **2** check or stop (motion etc.). **3** overtake and destroy (an aircraft, missile, etc.). **4** *Math.* mark off (a space) between two points etc. ● *noun* **1** *Math.* the part of a line between two points of intersection with usu. the coordinate axes or other lines. **2** a message, signal, etc. intended for someone else and obtained by covert means, esp. in espionage or warfare. □ **inter·cep·tion** *noun* **inter·cep·tive** *adjective* [Latin *intercipere intercept-* (as INTER-, *capere* take)]

inter·cept·or *noun* **1** an aircraft used to intercept enemy aircraft. **2** a person or thing that intercepts.

inter·ces·sion *noun* **1** the act of interceding, esp. by prayer. **2** an instance of this, esp. a prayer on behalf of another. □ **inter·ces·sor** *noun* **inter·ces·sory** *adjective* [French *intercession* or Latin *intercessio* (as INTERCEDE)]

inter·change ● *transitive verb* **1** (of two people) exchange (things) with each other. **2** put each of (two things) in the other's place; alternate. ● *noun* **1** (often foll. by *of*) a reciprocal exchange between two people etc. **2** alternation (*the interchange of woods and fields*). **3** an intersection of two or more highways designed on several levels to allow vehicles to go from one road to another without crossing a flow of traffic. □ **inter·change·able** *adjective* **inter·change·abil·ity** *noun* **inter·change·ably** *adverb*

inter-church *adjective* concerning or composed of several Christian denominations (*an inter-church coalition*).

inter·city *adjective* existing or travelling between cities (*an intercity bus*).

inter-class *adjective* existing or conducted between different social classes.

inter·collegi·ate *adjective* existing or conducted between colleges or universities.

inter·coloni·al ● *adjective* existing or conducted between colonies. ● *noun* usu. (**Intercolonial**) (in full **Intercolonial Railway**) *Cdn hist.* a railway connecting the Maritimes with Quebec and Ontario, incorporated into the Canadian National Railways in 1919.

inter·com *noun* **1** a system of intercommunication by radio or telephone between or within offices, aircraft, etc. **2** an instrument used in this. [abbreviation]

inter·com·muni·cate *intransitive verb* **1** communicate reciprocally. **2** (of rooms etc.) have free passage into each other; have a connecting door. □ **inter·com·muni·ca·tion** *noun*

inter·com·mun·ion *noun* **1** mutual fellowship, esp. mutual sharing of the Eucharist by Christian denominations. **2** mutual action or relationship, esp. between Christian denominations.

inter·com·mun·ity ● *noun* **1** the quality of being common to various groups etc. **2** having things in common. ● *adjective* of or between communities.

inter·con·nect *transitive & intransitive verb* connect with each other. □ **inter·connect·ed** *adjective* **inter·connect·ed·ness** *noun* **inter·connect·ing** *adjective* **inter·connec·tion** *noun* **inter·connec·tiv·ity** *noun*

inter·contin·ent·al *adjective* connecting or travelling between continents.

intercontinental ballistic missile *noun* a ballistic missile able to be sent from one continent to another. Abbr.: **ICBM**.

inter·con·vert *transitive & intransitive verb* convert into each other. □ **inter·con·ver·sion** *noun* **inter·convert·ible** *adjective*

inter·cool·er *noun* an apparatus for cooling gas between successive compressions, esp. in a car or truck engine. □ **inter·cool** *transitive verb*

inter·costal /ˌɪntər'kɒstəl/ ● *adjective* between the ribs (of the body or a ship). ● *noun* (in *pl.*) intercostal muscles, nerves, arteries, etc.

inter·course *noun* **1** = SEXUAL INTERCOURSE. **2** communication or dealings between individuals, nations, etc. [Old French *entrecours* exchange, commerce, from Latin *intercursus* (as INTER-, *currere curs-* run)]

inter·crop (**-cropped**, **-crop·ping**) ● *transitive & intransitive verb* raise (a crop) among plants of a different kind, usu. in the space between rows. ● *noun* a crop raised by intercropping. □ **inter·crop·ping** *noun*

inter·cross *verb* **1** *transitive & intransitive* lay or lie across each other. **2 a** *intransitive* (of animals) breed with each other. **b** *transitive* cause to do this.

inter·cultur·al *adjective* taking place between cultures; belonging to or derived from different cultures. □ **inter·cultur·al·ism** *noun*

inter·cut (**-cut·ting**; *past* and *past participle* **-cut**) *Film* ● *verb* **1** *transitive* alternate (scenes or shots) with contrasting scenes or shots to make

one composite scene. **2** *intransitive* switch from one shot or scene to another (*intercut from the actor standing to sitting*). ● *noun* a sequence or scene in a film, video, etc. formed by intercutting.

inter·denomin·a·tion·al *adjective* concerning more than one (religious) denomination.

inter·den·tal *adjective* **1** situated or placed between the teeth. **2** pronounced by placing the tip of the tongue between the teeth.

inter·depart·ment·al *adjective* concerning more than one department. □ **inter·depart·ment·al·ly** *adverb*

inter·depend·ent *adjective* dependent on each other. □ **inter·depend** *intransitive verb* **inter·depend·ence** *noun* **inter·depend·ency** *noun* **inter·depend·ent·ly** *adverb*

inter·dict ● *noun* **1** an authoritative prohibition. **2** *Catholicism* a sentence debarring a person, or esp. a place, from ecclesiastical functions and privileges. ● *transitive verb* **1** prohibit (an action). **2** forbid the use of. **3** (usu. foll. by *from* + verbal noun) restrain (a person). **4 a** *Military* impede (an enemy force), esp. by bombing lines of communication or supply. **b** intercept (a prohibited commodity); prevent (its movement). □ **inter·dic·tion** *noun* **inter·dict·ory** *adjective* [Latin *interdictum* past participle of *interdicere* interpose, forbid by decree (as INTER-, *dicere* say)]

inter·digi·tate *intransitive verb* interlock like clasped fingers. [INTER- + Latin *digitus* finger + -ATE³]

inter·disci·plin·ary *adjective* of or between more than one branch of learning. □ **inter·disci·plin·ar·ity** *noun*

in·ter·est ● *noun* **1 a** concern; curiosity (*have no interest in fishing*). **b** a quality exciting curiosity or holding the attention (*this magazine lacks interest*). **c** the power of an issue, action, etc. to hold the attention; noteworthiness, importance (*findings of no particular interest*). **2** a subject, hobby, etc., in which one is concerned (*her interests are gardening and sports*). **3** advantage or profit, esp. when financial (*it is in your interest to go; look after your own interests*). **4 a** money paid for the use of money lent, or for not requiring the repayment of a debt. **b** = INTEREST RATE. **5** (usu. foll. by *in*) **a** a financial stake (in an undertaking etc.). **b** a legal concern, title, or right (in property). **6 a** a party or group having a common interest (*the brewing interest*). **b** a principle in which a party or group is concerned. **7** the selfish pursuit of one's own welfare, self-interest. ● *transitive verb* **1** excite the curiosity or attention of (*your story interests me greatly*). **2** (usu. foll. by *in*) cause (a person) to take a personal interest or share (*can I interest you in a holiday abroad?*). □ **declare an** (or **one's**) **interest** make known one's financial etc. interests in an undertaking before it is discussed. **in the best interests of** to the greatest advantage or benefit of. **in the interest** (or **interests**) **of** as something that is advantageous to. **lose interest** become bored or boring. **with interest 1** with interest charged or paid. **2** with increased force etc. (*returned the blow with interest*). [Latin *interest*, 3rd sing. pres. of *interesse* matter, make a difference (as INTER-, *esse* be)]

in·ter·est·ed *adjective* **1** showing or having curiosity or concern (*an interested audience*). **2** having a private interest; not impartial or disinterested (*an interested party*). □ **in·ter·est·ed·ly** *adverb* **in·ter·est·ed·ness** *noun*

interest group *noun* a group of people sharing a common identifying interest, concern, or purpose.

in·ter·est·ing *adjective* causing curiosity; holding the attention. □ **in·ter·est·ing·ly** *adverb* **in·ter·est·ing·ness** *noun*

interest rate *noun* a charge made for borrowing a sum of money, expressed as a percentage of the total sum loaned, for a stated period of time.

inter-ethnic *adjective* occurring or existing between ethnic groups.

inter·face ● *noun* **1** esp. *Physics* a surface forming a common boundary between two regions. **2** a point where interaction occurs between two systems, processes, subjects, etc. (*the interface between psychology and education*). **3** *Computing* **a** an apparatus for connecting two pieces of equipment or systems so that they can be operated jointly or communicate with each other. **b** the way in which a program accepts information from or presents information to the user, e.g. the layout of the screen, command structure, etc. ● *verb* **1** *transitive & intransitive* (often foll. by *with*) connect with (another piece of equipment etc.) by an interface. **2** *intransitive* interact with (another person etc.).

inter·facial *adjective* **1** included between two faces of a crystal or other solid. **2** of or forming an interface.

inter·facing *noun* **1** a stiffish material, esp. buckram, between two layers of fabric in collars etc. **2** *in senses of* INTERFACE *verb*.

Consonants: b *but*   d *dog*   f *few*   g *get*   h *her*   j *yes*   k *cat*   l *leg*   m *man*   n *no*   p *pen*   r *red*   s *sit*

inter·faith *adjective* of, relating to, or between different religions or members of different religions.

inter·fere *intransitive verb* **1** (usu. foll. by *with*) **a** (of a person) meddle; obstruct a process etc. **b** (of a thing) be a hindrance; get in the way. **2** (usu. foll. by *in*) take part or intervene, esp. without invitation or necessity. **3** *Sport* (foll. by *with*) unlawfully obstruct an opposing player. **4** (foll. by *with*) *Cdn & Brit.* molest or assault sexually. **5** *Physics* (of light or other waves) combine so as to cause interference. **6** (of a horse) knock one leg against another. □ **inter·fer·er** *noun* **inter·fer·ing** *adjective* **inter·fer·ing·ly** *adverb* [Old French *s'entreferir* strike each other (as INTER-, *ferir* from Latin *ferire* strike)]

inter·fer·ence *noun* **1** (usu. foll. by *with*) **a** the act of interfering. **b** an instance of this. **2 a** the fading or disturbance of received radio signals by the interference of waves from different sources, or esp. by atmospherics or unwanted signals. **b** the distorted reception caused by this. **3** *Physics* the combination of two or more wave motions to form a resultant wave in which the displacement is reinforced or cancelled. **4 a** *Football* the legal blocking of an opposing player to clear a way for the ball carrier. **b** *Sport* the illegal blocking or hindering of an opponent. **5** *Linguistics* the use of the vocabulary, syntax, etc. of one language when speaking or writing another. **6** *Law* sexual abuse of a minor. □ **run interference** *N Amer.* intervene on someone's behalf, esp. to protect them from distraction, annoyance, etc. □ **inter·fer·en·tial** /ˌɪntɜrfəˈrenʃəl/ *adjective*

inter·fer·om·eter /ˌɪntɜrfəˈrɒmɪtər/ *noun* an instrument for measuring wavelengths etc. by means of interference phenomena. □ **inter·fero·met·ric** /-ˌferəˈmetrɪk/ *adjective* **inter·fero·met·ric·ally** /-ˌferəˈmetrɪkli/ *adverb* **inter·fer·om·etry** *noun*

inter·feron /ˌɪntɜrˈfiːrɒn/ *noun Biochem.* any of various proteins released by cells, usu. in response to a virus, and able to inhibit viral replication. [INTERFERE + -ON]

inter·file *transitive verb* **1** file (two sequences) together. **2** file (one or more items) into an existing sequence.

inter·galac·tic /ˌɪntɜrgəˈlaktɪk/ *adjective* of or situated between two or more galaxies. □ **inter·galac·tic·ally** *adverb*

inter·gener·a·tion·al *adjective* **1** existing or occurring between different generations of people. **2** involving more than one generation.

inter·glacial ● *adjective* of or relating to a period of milder climate between glacial periods. ● *noun* such a period.

inter·govern·ment·al *adjective* concerning or conducted between two or more governments. □ **inter·govern·ment·al·ly** *adverb*

inter·grade ● *intransitive verb* merge gradually one into another by passing through a series of intermediate stages. ● *noun* such an intermediate stage. □ **inter·grada·tion** *noun*

inter·group *adjective* existing or occurring between different groups or members of different groups, esp. different social or political groups.

inter·growth *noun* the growing of things into each other.

in·ter·im ● *noun* the intervening time (*in the interim she had died*). ● *adjective* in or for the intervening period; provisional, temporary. [Latin, as INTER- + adv. suffix *-im*]

interim moderator *noun* (in Presbyterian churches) a minister who takes temporary responsibility for a pastoral charge while it is without a permanent minister.

In·ter·ior, the an inland region of mainland BC, extending the length of the southern half of the province, between the Coast and Rocky mountain ranges.

in·ter·ior ● *adjective* **1** inner (*opp.* EXTERIOR). **2** remote from the coast or frontier; inland. **3** internal; domestic (*opp.* FOREIGN). **4** (usu. foll. by *to*) situated further in or within. **5** existing in the mind or soul; inward. **6** drawn, photographed, etc. within a building. **7** coming from inside. ● *noun* **1** the interior part; the inside. **2** the interior part of a country or region. **3 a** the home affairs of a country. **b** a department dealing with these (*Minister of the Interior*). **4 a** the inside of a building, room, etc. **b** a representation of this in art or photography (*Dutch interior*). **5** the inner nature; the soul. □ **in·ter·ior·ity** *noun* **in·ter·ior·ize** *transitive verb* (also esp. *Brit.* **-ise**). **in·ter·ior·iza·tion** *noun* [Latin, comparative from *inter* among]

interior angle *noun* the angle between adjacent sides of a rectilinear figure.

interior design *noun* (also **interior decoration**) the decoration or design of the interior of a building, a room, etc. □ **interior designer** *noun* (also **interior decorator**).

interior monologue *noun* a form of writing expressing a character's inner thoughts.

Interior Plains (also called **Interior Platform**) a lowland region of W Canada, extending from the NWT through Alberta and Saskatchewan and into SW Manitoba.

interj. *abbreviation* interjection.

inter·ject *transitive verb* introduce abruptly, esp. into a conversation; remark parenthetically or as an interruption. [Latin *interjicere* (as INTER-, *jacere* throw)]

inter·jec·tion *noun* an exclamation, esp. as a part of speech (e.g. *hey!, dear me!*).

inter·lace *verb* **1** *transitive* bind intricately together; interweave. **2** *transitive* mingle, intersperse. **3** *intransitive* cross each other intricately. □ **inter·lace·ment** *noun*

inter·lacrosse *noun* a coeducational, non-contact version of lacrosse played indoors or outdoors with a moulded plastic stick and a soft, air-filled ball, and involving continuous running. [*inter-* designating at once French *intérieur* 'indoor', *international*, and 'between', inter-lacrosse providing an opportunity to play lacrosse in the winter, between box lacrosse seasons]

Inter·lake a region in south central Manitoba, between Lakes Winnipeg and Manitoba.

Inter·laken /ˈɪntɜrˌlɒkən/ the chief town of the Bernese Alps in central Switzerland, situated on the Aare River between Lake Brienz and Lake Thun; pop. (est. 1998) 5,052.

inter·lan·guage *noun* a language or use of language having features of two others, often a pidgin or dialect form.

inter·lard *transitive verb* (usu. foll. by *with*) mix (writing or speech) with particular, esp. contrasting, words or phrases. [French *entrelarder* (as INTER-, LARD *verb*)]

inter·layer *noun* a layer sandwiched between two others.

inter·leave *transitive verb* **1** insert (usu. blank) leaves between the leaves of (a book etc.). **2** insert something at regular intervals between (the parts of).

inter·leukin /ˌɪntɜrˈluːkɪn/ *noun Biochem.* any of several glycoproteins produced by leukocytes for regulating immune responses. Abbr.: **IL**. [INTER- + LEUKOCYTE]

inter·library *adjective* between libraries (*interlibrary loan*).

inter·line[1] ● *verb* **1** *transitive* insert words between the lines of (a document etc.). **2** *transitive* insert (words) in this way. **3** *intransitive* **a** make use of transportation by more than one route, service, etc. **b** provide interconnections with another route, service, etc. ● *adjective* of or relating to the transfer of passengers or freight from one route or service to another during travel or shipment (*interline service*). □ **inter·linea·tion** /-ˌlɪniˈeɪʃən/ *noun*

inter·line[2] *transitive verb* put an extra lining between the ordinary lining and the fabric of (a garment) esp. for added stiffness or warmth.

inter·linear /ˌɪntɜrˈlɪniːər/ *adjective* written or printed between the lines of a text.

inter·lining *noun* material used to interline a garment.

inter·link *transitive & intransitive verb* link or be linked together. □ **inter·link·age** *noun* **inter·linked** *adjective*

inter·lock ● *verb* **1** *intransitive* engage with each other by overlapping or by the fitting together of projections and recesses. **2** *transitive* (usu. in *passive*) lock or clasp within each other. **3** *intransitive* be intimately connected (*interlocking responsibilities*). ● *adjective* (of a fabric) knitted with closely interlocking stitches. ● *noun* **1** a device or mechanism for connecting or coordinating the function of different components. **2** a knitted fabric with closely interlocking stitches. **3** *N Amer.* = INTERLOCKING BRICK. □ **inter·lock·ing** *adjective*

interlocking brick *noun* (also **interlocking stone**) a paving material formed into shapes that interlock.

inter·locu·tor /ˌɪntɜrˈlɒkjʊtər/ *noun* a person who takes part in a dialogue or conversation. □ **inter·locu·tion** /-ləˈkjuːʃən/ *noun* [modern Latin from Latin *interloqui interlocut-* interrupt in speaking (as INTER-, *loqui* speak)]

inter·locu·tory /ˌɪntɜrˈlɒkjʊtəri/ *adjective* **1** of dialogue or conversation. **2** *Law* (of a decree etc.) given provisionally in a legal action.

inter·lop·er /ˈɪntɜrˌloʊpər/ *noun* an intruder. □ **inter·lope** *intransitive verb* [INTER- + *loper* as in *landloper* vagabond from Middle Dutch *landlooper*]

inter·lude *noun* **1 a** an intervening time, space, or event that contrasts with what goes before or after. **b** a temporary amusement or entertaining episode. **2** a piece of music, esp. an instrumental passage, played between other pieces etc. [Middle English, = a light dramatic item between the acts of a morality play, from medieval Latin *interludium* (as INTER-, *ludus* play)]

inter·mar·riage *noun* **1** marriage between people of different races, tribes, religions, etc. **2** marriage between near relations.

inter·marry *intransitive verb* (**-marries, -married**) (foll. by *with*) (of people belonging to different races, tribes, religions, etc.) become connected by marriage.

inter·medi·ary /ˌɪntɜrˈmiːdiˌeri/ ● *noun* (*pl.* **-aries**) **1** a person who acts as a link or helps to negotiate between two or more others; a mediator. **2** something acting between persons or things. ● *adjective* intermediate; serving as a means of mediation or interaction. [French *intermédiaire* from Italian *intermediario* from Latin *intermedius* (as INTERMEDIATE)]

inter·medi·ate /ˌɪntɜrˈmiːdiət/ ● *adjective* coming between two things in time, place, order, character, etc. ● *noun* **1** an intermediate thing. **2** a chemical compound formed by one reaction and then used in another, esp. during synthesis. ● *intransitive verb* /-diˌeit/ (foll. by *between*) act as intermediary; mediate. □ **inter·medi·acy** /-si/ *noun* **inter·medi·ate·ly** *adverb* **inter·medi·a·tion** *noun* [medieval Latin *intermediatus* (as INTER-, *medius* middle)]

intermediate frequency *noun* the frequency to which a radio signal is converted during heterodyne reception.

intermediate host *noun Zool.* an organism infected by a juvenile or asexual stage of a parasitic animal.

inter·ment *noun* the act or an action of interring; burial. ¶ See Usage Note at INTERNMENT.

inter·mesh *transitive & intransitive verb* make or become meshed together.

inter·metal·lic ● *adjective* designating compounds made from two or more metals. ● *noun* such a compound.

inter·mezzo /ˌɪntɜrˈmetsoː/ *noun* (*pl.* **inter·mezzi** /-tsi/ or **-mezzos**) **1 a** a short connecting instrumental movement in an opera or other musical work. **b** a similar piece performed independently. **c** a short piece for a solo instrument. **2** a short light dramatic or other performance inserted between the acts of a play. [Italian from Latin *intermedium* interval (as INTERMEDIATE)]

in·termin·able /ɪnˈtɜrmɪnəbəl/ *adjective* **1** endless; having no prospect of an end. **2** tediously long or habitual. □ **in·termin·ably** *adverb*

inter·min·gle *transitive & intransitive verb* (often foll. by *with*) mix together; mingle.

inter·minister·ial *adjective Cdn & Brit.* occurring between or involving several government ministries (*an inter-ministerial committee*).

inter·mis·sion *noun* **1** a pause or break between parts of a play, film, concert, etc. **2** a pause or cessation. **3** a period of inactivity. [French *intermission* or Latin *intermissio* (as INTERMIT)]

inter·mit *verb* (**inter·mit·ted**, **inter·mit·ting**) **1** *intransitive* esp. *Med.* stop or cease activity briefly (e.g. of a fever, or a pulse). **2** *transitive* suspend; discontinue for a time. [Latin *intermittere intermiss-* (as INTER-, *mittere* let go)]

inter·mit·tent *adjective* occurring at intervals; not continuous or steady. □ **inter·mit·tence** *noun* **inter·mit·tency** *noun* **inter·mit·tent·ly** *adverb*

intermittent claudication *noun* a cramping pain, esp. in the leg, caused by arterial obstruction.

inter·mix *transitive & intransitive verb* mix together. □ **inter·mix·able** *adjective* **inter·mix·ture** *noun* [back-formation from *intermixed*, *intermixt* from Latin *intermixtus* past participle of *intermiscēre* mix together (as INTER-, *miscēre* mix)]

inter·modal *adjective* involving two or more different modes, esp. modes of transport in conveying goods.

inter·molecu·lar *adjective* between molecules.

inter·mon·tane /ˌɪntɜrˈmontein/ *adjective* situated between mountains (*intermontane plateau*).

in·tern ● *noun* esp. *N Amer.* **1** a recent medical graduate, resident and working under supervision in a hospital as part of his or her training. **2** a person in any profession gaining practical experience under supervision. ● *verb* **1** *intransitive* esp. *N Amer.* serve as an intern. **2** *transitive* confine; oblige (a prisoner, alien, etc.) to reside within prescribed limits. □ **intern·ship** *noun* [French *interne* from Latin *internus* internal]

in·ter·nal ● *adjective* **1** of or situated in the inside or invisible part. **2** relating or applied to the inside of the body (*internal injuries*). **3** of or relating to political, economic, etc. activity happening entirely within a country rather than with other countries; domestic (*internal flight*).

4 used or applying within an organization. **5 a** of the inner nature of a thing; intrinsic. **b** of the mind or soul. **6** *Brit.* (of a student) attending a university etc. as well as taking its examinations. ● *noun* (in *pl.*) inner parts, features, etc. □ **in·ter·nal·ity** *noun* **in·ter·nal·ly** *adverb* [modern Latin *internalis* (as INTERN)]

internal combustion engine *noun* an engine in which motive power is generated by the expansion of exhaust gases from the burning of fuel (e.g. gasoline, diesel, etc.) with air inside the engine.

internal evidence *noun* evidence derived from the contents of the thing discussed.

internal exile *noun* penal banishment from a part of one's own country.

in·ter·nal·ize *transitive verb* (also esp. *Brit.* **-ise**) **1** *Psych.* make (attitudes, behaviour, etc.) part of one's nature by learning or unconscious assimilation. **2** *Econ.* incorporate (costs) as part of the internal structure, esp. social costs resulting from the manufacture and use of a product. □ **in·ter·nal·iz·a·tion** *noun*

internal medicine *noun* the branch of medicine that deals with the diagnosis and treatment, by non-surgical means, of diseases of internal organs.

Internal Revenue Service *noun* (in the US) the government department responsible for collecting domestic taxes. Abbr.: **IRS**.

internal rhyme *noun* a poetic device in which two or more words rhyme within the same line of verse.

internat. *abbreviation* international.

inter·nation·al ● *adjective* **1** existing, involving, or carried on between two or more nations. **2** agreed on or used by all or many nations (*international money order*). **3** of or pertaining to relations between nations (*international law*). **4** available for the use of all nations (*international waters*). ● *noun* **1 a** (**International**) any of four associations founded (1864–1936) to promote socialist or communist action. **b** a member of any of these. **2** *Brit.* **a** a contest, esp. in sport, between teams representing different countries. **b** a member of such a team. □ **inter·nation·al·ly** *adverb*

international airport *noun* an airport providing customs and immigration clearance facilities for passengers arriving from other countries.

International Atomic Energy Agency *noun* an international organization set up in 1957 to promote research into and development of atomic energy for peaceful purposes. Its headquarters are in Vienna.

International Baccalaureate *noun* **1** a set of examinations intended to qualify successful candidates for higher education in any of several countries. Abbr.: **IB**. **2** a qualification awarded for satisfactory performance in these examinations.

International Brigade an international group of volunteers (mainly from Europe and N America) raised by Communist parties to fight on the Republican side in the Spanish Civil War.

International Civil Aviation Organization *noun* a United Nations agency founded in 1947 to study problems of international civil aviation and establish standards and regulation etc. Its headquarters are in Montreal.

International Court of Justice *noun* an international judicial court of the United Nations, which meets at The Hague and adjudicates disputes between nations in accordance with international law. Abbr.: **ICJ**.

International Date Line *noun see* DATE LINE *noun* 1.

Inter·na·tio·nale /ˌɪntɜrˌnaʃəˈnɑl/ *noun* (prec. by *the*) an (originally French) revolutionary song adopted by socialists. [French, fem. of *international* (adj.) from INTERNATIONAL]

inter·nation·al·ism *noun* **1** the advocacy of a community of interests among nations. **2** the quality or state of being international. **3** (**Internationalism**) the principles of any of the Internationals. □ **inter·nation·al·ist** *noun & adjective*

inter·nation·al·ize *transitive verb* (also esp. *Brit.* **-ise**) **1** make international. **2** bring under the protection or control of two or more nations. □ **inter·nation·al·iz·a·tion** *noun*

International Joint Commission *noun* a commission comprising three Canadian and three US members dealing with questions concerning water resources along the Canada-US boundary. Abbr.: **IJC**.

international law *noun* a body of rules established by custom or treaty and agreed as binding by nations in their relations with one another.

International Monetary Fund *noun see* IMF.

International Phonetic Alphabet *noun* an internationally recognized set of phonetic symbols used to transcribe the pronunciation of words etc. Abbr.: **IPA**.

International Reply Coupon *noun* a voucher sold by a post office, exchangeable for stamps in a foreign post office.

International Style *noun* a 20th c. style of architecture characterized by simple geometric forms and the use of unornamented glass, steel, and reinforced concrete.

international system of units *noun* a system of physical units based on the metre, kilogram, second, ampere, kelvin, candela, and mole, with prefixes to indicate multiplication or division by a power of ten. Abbr.: **SI**.

international unit *noun* a standard quantity of a vitamin etc. Abbr.: **IU**.

inter·necine /ˌɪntər'nesiːn/ *adjective* **1** mutually destructive. **2** of or relating to conflict within a group or organization etc. [originally = deadly, from Latin *internecinus* from *internecio* massacre, from *internecare* slaughter (as INTER-, *necare* kill)]

in·tern·ee *noun* a person interned.

In·ter·net *noun* a global computer network providing a variety of information and communication facilities, consisting of interconnected networks using standardized communication protocols. [abbreviation of INTERNETWORK]

Internet café *noun* a café, bar, etc. where customers can sit at computer terminals to surf the Internet, use email, etc.

Internet Protocol *noun* a standard that specifies the format and addressing scheme of packets of data sent over the Internet or other network.

Internet service provider *noun* an organization that provides access to the Internet, usu. on a commercial basis, either via a modem or through a permanent line, and usu. also offers services relating to websites etc.

Internet time *noun* time seen as passing at an accelerating rate because of ever more efficient technology and/or its ever quicker obsolescence.

inter·net·work *noun* several computer networks connected together to form a single, higher-level network. □ **inter·net·work·ing** *noun* [INTER- + NETWORK]

in·tern·ist *noun* esp. *N Amer.* a specialist in internal medicine.

in·tern·ment *noun* **1** the act of interning someone. **2** confinement; the state of being interned. ¶ *Internment* should not be confused with either *interment* 'burial' or *internship* 'position of, or period of serving as, an intern'.

inter·node *noun* **1** *Bot.* a part of a stem between two of the knobs from which leaves arise. **2** *Anat.* a slender part between two joints or nodes.

intern·ship *noun* esp. *N Amer.* **1** the position of an intern. **2** the period of such a position. ¶ See Usage Note at INTERNMENT.

inter·nuclear *adjective* between nuclei.

inter-office *adjective* serving to communicate or occurring between the offices of a corporation etc. (*an inter-office memo*).

inter·oper·able *adjective* able to operate in conjunction. □ **inter·oper·abil·ity** *noun*

inter·parlia·ment·ary *adjective* between parliaments.

inter·pel·late /ɪn'tɜrpəˌleɪt/ *transitive verb* (in European parliaments) interrupt the order of the day by demanding an explanation from (the minister concerned). □ **in·ter·pel·la·tion** *noun* **in·ter·pel·la·tor** *noun* [Latin *interpellare interpellat-* (as INTER-, *pellere* drive)]

inter·pene·trate *verb* **1** *intransitive* (of two things) penetrate each other. **2** *transitive* pervade; penetrate thoroughly. □ **inter·pene·tra·tion** *noun* **inter·pene·tra·tive** *adjective*

inter·person·al *adjective* **1** (of relations) occurring between persons, esp. reciprocally. **2** of or relating to relationships between people (*interpersonal skills*). □ **inter·person·al·ly** *adverb*

inter·phase *noun* *Biol.* the resting phase between successive divisions of a cell.

inter·planet·ary *adjective* **1** between planets. **2** relating to travel between planets.

inter·plant *transitive verb* plant (a specified crop or plant) together with another crop or plant.

inter·play *noun* the way in which two or more things influence or affect each other.

In·ter·pol *noun* the International Criminal Police Organization, an organization that coordinates investigations with an international dimension made by the police forces of member countries. [abbreviation]

in·ter·pol·ate /ɪn'tɜrpəˌleɪt/ *transitive verb* **1** interject (a remark) in a conversation. **2** insert as something additional or different. **3** estimate (values) from known ones in the same range (*compare* EXTRAPOLATE 2). **4 a** insert (words) in a book etc., esp. to give false impressions as to its date etc. **b** make such insertions in (a book etc.). □ **in·ter·pol·a·tion** *noun* **in·ter·pol·ator** *noun* [Latin *interpolare* furbish up (as INTER-, *polire* POLISH)]

inter·pose *verb* **1** *transitive* (often foll. by *between*) place or insert (a thing) between others. **2** *transitive* say (words) as an interruption. **3** *transitive* exercise or advance (a veto or objection) so as to interfere. **4** *intransitive* (foll. by *between*) intervene (between parties). □ **inter·pos·ition** *noun* [French *interposer* from Latin *interponere* put (as INTER-, POSE¹)]

in·ter·pret *verb* (**in·ter·pret·ed**, **in·ter·pret·ing**) **1** *transitive* explain the meaning of. **2** *transitive* perform a piece of music, a dramatic role, etc. **3** *transitive & intransitive* translate orally or in sign language from one language into another. **4** *transitive* explain or understand (behaviour etc.) in a specified manner (*interpreted her gesture as mocking*). □ **in·ter·pret·able** *adjective* **in·ter·pret·abil·ity** *noun* **in·ter·pret·a·tion** *noun* **in·ter·pret·a·tion·al** *adjective* **in·ter·pret·a·tive** *adjective* **in·ter·pret·ive** *adjective* **in·ter·pret·ive·ly** *adverb* [Old French *interpreter* or Latin *interpretari* explain, translate, from *interpres -pretis* explainer]

in·ter·pret·er *noun* **1** a person who translates from one language to another either orally or using sign language. **2** a person who interprets. **3** *Computing* a program that can analyze and execute a program line by line. **4** an employee of a park, museum, etc. who gives tours, answers visitors' questions, etc.

interpretive centre *noun* a building or complex at a historic site, national park, etc., which contains displays and exhibits related to the site.

inter·prov·in·cial *adjective* situated or carried on between provinces. □ **inter·pro·vin·cial·ly** *adverb*

inter·racial *adjective* existing between or affecting different races. □ **inter·racial·ly** *adverb*

inter·regional *adjective* between regions.

inter·reg·num *noun* (*pl.* **inter·reg·nums** or **inter·regna**) **1** an interval when the normal government is suspended, esp. between successive reigns or regimes. **2** an interval or pause. [Latin (as INTER-, *regnum* reign)]

inter·relate *verb* **1** *transitive* relate (two or more things) to each other. **2** *intransitive* (of two or more things) relate to each other. □ **inter·related·ness** *noun* **inter·rela·tion** *noun* **inter·rela·tion·ship** *noun*

interrog. *abbreviation* interrogative.

in·terro·gate *transitive verb* **1** ask questions of (a person) esp. closely, thoroughly, or formally. **2** examine closely (data, social systems, etc.) so as to find answers. □ **in·terro·ga·tor** *noun* [Latin *interrogare interrogat-* ask (as INTER-, *rogare* ask)]

in·terro·ga·tion *noun* **1** the act or an instance of interrogating; the process of being interrogated. **2** a question or inquiry. □ **in·terro·ga·tion·al** *adjective*

in·ter·roga·tive /ˌɪntə'rɒɡətɪv/ ● *adjective* **1 a** of or like a question; used in questions. **b** *Grammar* (of an adjective or pronoun) asking a question (e.g. *who?, which?*). **2** having the form or force of a question. **3** suggesting inquiry (*an interrogative tone*). ● *noun* an interrogative word (e.g. *what?, why?*). □ **in·ter·roga·tive·ly** *adverb*

in·ter·roga·tory /ˌɪntə'rɒɡətəri/ ● *adjective* questioning; of or suggesting inquiry (*an interrogatory eyebrow*). ● *noun* (*pl.* **-ies**) a formal set of questions, esp. *Law* one formally put to an accused person etc.

in·ter·rupt ● *verb* **1 a** *transitive* act so as to break the continuous progress of (something) temporarily. **b** *transitive & intransitive* stop (someone) speaking, by speaking oneself or causing some other disturbance. **2** *transitive* obstruct (a person's view etc.). **3** *transitive* break an even or continuous line, surface, etc. ● *noun* *Computing* a signal causing an interruption of a program, e.g. to allow immediate execution of another program. □ **in·ter·rupt·ible** *adjective*

in·ter·rup·tion *noun* **in·ter·rupt·ive** *adjective* [Latin *interrumpere interrupt-* (as INTER-, *rumpere* break)]

in·ter·rupt·er *noun* (also **in·ter·rupt·or**) **1** a person or thing that interrupts. **2** a device for interrupting, esp. an electric circuit.

inter·schol·as·tic /ˌɪntərskə'læstɪk/ *adjective* occurring between schools.

inter·sect *verb* **1** *transitive* divide (a thing) by passing or lying across it. **2** *intransitive* (of lines, roads, etc.) cross or cut each other. **3** *intransitive*

Geom. have one or more points in common. [Latin *intersecare intersect-* (as INTER-, *secare* cut)]

inter·sec·tion *noun* **1 a** esp. *N Amer.* a place where two or more roads intersect. **b** the place where two things intersect or cross (*at the intersection of the nave and the transept*). **2** a point or line common to lines or planes that intersect. **3** *Math. & Logic* the set which comprises all the elements common to two or more given sets, and no others. **4** the act of intersecting. □ **inter·sec·tion·al** *adjective* [Latin *intersectio* (as INTERSECT)]

inter·ses·sion *noun* **1** *Cdn* a short university term, usu. in May and June, in which the course material usually covered in thirteen weeks is condensed into five or six weeks of intensive study. **2** *US* a short period between university terms, esp. in January, sometimes used by students to engage in special projects not usually offered as part of the academic program.

inter·sex *noun* **1** the abnormal condition of being intermediate between male and female. **2** an individual in this condition.

inter·sex·ual *adjective* **1** existing between the sexes. **2** of intersex. □ **inter·sex·u·al·ity** *noun*

inter·space ● *noun* an interval of space or time. ● *transitive verb* put interspaces between.

inter·specif·ic *adjective* (also **inter·species**) **1** relating to or occurring between one or more species. **2** formed from different species.

inter·sperse *transitive verb* **1** (often foll. by *between, among*) scatter; place here and there. **2** (foll. by *with*) diversify (a thing or things with others so scattered). □ **inter·sper·sion** *noun* [Latin *interspergere interspers-* (as INTER-, *spargere* scatter)]

inter·squad *adjective* designating a competition between members of the same team.

inter·stadi·al /ˌɪntərˈsteidiəl/ ● *adjective* of or relating to a minor period of ice retreat during a glacial period. ● *noun* such a period. [INTER- + Latin *stadium* 'stage' + -AL]

inter·state ● *adjective* existing or carried on between states, esp. of the US or Australia. ● *noun US* each of a system of highways between states.

inter·stel·lar *adjective* occurring or situated between stars.

in·ter·stice /ɪnˈtərstɪs/ *noun* **1** an intervening space. **2** a chink or crevice. [Latin *interstitium* (as INTER-, *sistere stit-* stand)]

inter·stitial /ˌɪntərˈstɪʃəl/ ● *adjective* **1** of, forming, or occupying interstices. **2** designating an advertisement that appears between pages being loaded from a website. ● *noun* an interstitial advertisement. □ **inter·stitial·ly** *adverb*

inter·subject·ive /ˌɪntərsʌbˈdʒɛktɪv/ *adjective Philos.* existing between or shared by more than one conscious mind. □ **inter·subject·ive·ly** *adverb* **inter·subjec·tiv·ity** *noun*

inter·text·u·al·ity /ˌɪntərˌtɛkstʃʊˈalɪti/ *noun* the relationship between esp. literary texts; the fact of relating or alluding to other texts. □ **inter·text·ual** *adjective*

inter·tidal *adjective* of or relating to the area which is under water at high tide and exposed at low tide.

inter·track *adjective* (of betting, esp. on horse races) involving bets placed at racetracks other than the one at which the race betted on is being run.

inter·tribal *adjective* existing or occurring between different tribes.

inter·twine *verb* **1** *transitive* (often foll. by *with*) entwine (together). **2** *intransitive* become entwined.

inter·univer·sity *adjective* existing or carried on between universities.

inter·urban *adjective* (of a transit system) linking different urban areas.

inter·val *noun* **1** an intervening time or space. **2** an open space between two things or two parts of the same thing; a gap or opening. **3** the difference in pitch between two sounds. **4** *Brit.* = INTERMISSION 1. □ **at intervals** here and there; now and then. □ **inter·val·lic** /-ˈvalɪk/ *adjective* (also **inter·val·ic**). [Middle English, ultimately from Latin *intervallum* space between ramparts, interval (as INTER-, *vallum* rampart)]

inter·vale *noun N Amer.* (*Maritimes, Nfld & New England*) a low, level tract of land, esp. along a river. [var. of INTERVAL, influenced by VALE through folk etymology]

interval house *noun Cdn* = WOMEN'S SHELTER.

inter·vene *intransitive verb* (often foll. by *between, in*) **1** occur in time between events. **2** come between so as to prevent or modify the result or course of events. **3** occur in time between events. **4** be situated between things. **5** *Law* interpose in a lawsuit as a third party. □ **inter·ven·or** *noun* (also **inter·ven·er**) [Latin *intervenire* (as INTER-, *venire* come)]

inter·ven·tion *noun* **1** the act or an instance of intervening. **2** interference, esp. by one country in another's affairs. **3** mediation. **4** action or an action taken to improve a situation, esp. a medical disorder. □ **inter·ven·tion·al** *adjective* [Latin *interventio* (as INTERVENE)]

inter·ven·tion·ist ● *adjective* **1** favouring intervention, esp. by a government in its domestic economy or by one state in the affairs of another. ● *noun* a person who favours intervention of this kind. □ **inter·ven·tion·ism** *noun*

inter·ver·te·bral /ˌɪntərˈvərtəbrəl/ *adjective* between vertebrae.

inter·view ● *noun* **1** a meeting at which a job applicant, student, etc. is questioned to determine their suitability. **2 a** a conversation between a reporter etc. and a person of public interest, used as a basis of a broadcast or publication. **b** the published or broadcast result of this. **3** a meeting of persons face to face, esp. for consultation. **4** a session of formal questioning by the police. ● *verb* **1** *transitive* hold an interview with. **2** *transitive* question to discover the opinions or experience of (a person). **3** *intransitive* participate in an interview; perform (well etc.) at an interview. □ **inter·view·ee** *noun* **inter·view·er** *noun* [French *entrevue* from *s'entrevoir* see each other (as INTER-, *voir* from Latin *vidēre* see: see VIEW)]

inter·vocal·ic /ɪntərvoˈkalɪk/ *adjective Linguistics* occurring between vowels.

inter·war *attributive adjective* existing in the period between two wars, esp. the two world wars.

inter·weave *verb* (*past* **-wove**; *past participle* **-woven**) **1** *transitive* (often foll. by *with*) weave together. **2** *transitive* blend intimately. **3** *intransitive* be or become interwoven.

inter·work *verb* **1** *intransitive* work together or interactively. **2** *transitive* interweave.

inter·woven *adjective* **1** woven together; interlaced. **2** intimately linked.

in·tes·tate /ɪnˈtesteit/ ● *adjective* not having made a will before death. ● *noun* a person who has died intestate. □ **in·tes·tacy** /-təsi/ *noun* [Latin *intestatus* (as IN-¹, *testari testat-* make a will from *testis* witness)]

intestinal flora *plural noun* = FLORA 3.

intestinal fortitude *noun* courage; guts.

in·tes·tine /ɪnˈtestain, -ɪn/ *noun* (in *sing.* or *pl.*) **1** the lower part of the alimentary canal from the end of the stomach to the anus. **2** *Zool.* (esp. in invertebrates) the whole alimentary canal. □ **in·tes·tin·al** (/ɪnˈtestɪnəl, ˌɪnteˈstainəl/) *adjective* [Latin *intestinum* from *intestinus* 'internal']

inti /ˈɪnti/ *noun* (*pl.* same or **intis**) a former monetary unit of Peru, equal to 100 centimos. [Spanish from Quechua *ynti*, sun, the Inca sun god]

in·ti·fada /ˌɪntəˈfʊdə/ *noun* a movement of Palestinian uprising in the Israeli-occupied West Bank and Gaza Strip, beginning in 1987. [Arabic, = uprising]

in·tim·acy /ˈɪntɪməsi/ *noun* (*pl.* **-acies**) **1** close familiarity or friendship; closeness. **2** an intimate act, esp. sexual intercourse. **3** a private cozy atmosphere. **4** an intimate remark; an endearment.

in·tim·ate¹ /ˈɪntɪmət/ ● *adjective* **1** closely acquainted; familiar, close (*an intimate friend; an intimate relationship*). **2** private and personal, often in a sexual way (*intimate details about his family life; the most intimate parts of her body*). **3** (usu. foll. by *with*) having sexual relations. **4** (of knowledge) detailed, thorough. **5** (of a relationship between things) close. **6** (of mixing etc.) thorough. **7** essential, intrinsic. **8** (of a place etc.) cozy; suggesting intimacy (*an intimate restaurant; an intimate dinner*). ● *noun* **1** a very close friend. **2** (in *pl.*) undergarments or lingerie. □ **in·tim·ate·ly** *adverb* [Latin *intimus* inmost]

in·tim·ate² /ˈɪntɪˌmeit/ *transitive verb* **1** (often foll. by *that* + clause) state or make known. **2** imply, hint. □ **in·tim·a·tion** *noun* [Late Latin *intimare* announce, from Latin *intimus* inmost]

in·timi·date /ɪnˈtɪmɪˌdeit/ *transitive verb* frighten or overawe, esp. to subdue or influence. □ **in·timi·dat·ing** *adjective* **in·timi·dat·ing·ly** *adverb* **in·timi·da·tion** *noun* **in·timi·da·tor** *noun* [medieval Latin *intimidare* (as IN-², *timidare* from *timidus* TIMID)]

in·tinc·tion *noun Christianity* the dipping of the Eucharistic bread in the wine so that the communicant receives both together. [Late Latin *intinctio* from Latin *intingere intinct-* (as IN-², TINGE)]

into *preposition* **1** expressing motion or direction to a point on or within (*walked into a tree; ran into the house*). **2** expressing direction of attention or concern (*will look into it*). **3** expressing a change of state (*turned into a*

Consonants: b *but*   d *dog*   f *few*   g *get*   h *her*   j *yes*   k *cat*   l *leg*   m *man*   n *no*   p *pen*   r *red*   s *sit*

dragon; *separated into groups*; *forced into it*). **4** *informal* interested in; knowledgeable about (*is really into ballet*). **5** after the beginning of (*five minutes into the game*). **6** *Math.* expressing the relationship of a divisor to a dividend (*8 into 24 is 3*). [Old English *intō* (as IN, TO)]

in·tol·er·able /ɪnˈtɒlərəbəl/ *adjective* that cannot be endured. □ **in·tol·er·ably** *adverb*

in·tol·er·ance /ɪnˈtɒlərəns/ *noun* **1** lack of tolerance for difference of opinion or practice, esp. in political or religious matters. **2** severe sensitivity or allergy to a substance, esp. a food or drug (*lactose intolerance*).

in·tol·er·ant /ɪnˈtɒlərənt/ *adjective* **1** not tolerant, esp. of views, beliefs, or behaviour differing from one's own. **2** (usu. foll. by *of*) not having the capacity to tolerate or endure a specified thing. □ **in·tol·er·ant·ly** *adverb*

in·ton·a·tion /ˌɪntəˈneɪʃən/ *noun* **1** modulation of the voice; accent. **2** the act of intoning. **3** accuracy of pitch in playing or singing (*watch your intonation, altos!*). **4** the opening phrase of a plainsong melody. □ **in·ton·a·tion·al** *adjective*

in·tone *transitive verb* **1** recite (prayers etc.) with prolonged sounds, esp. in a monotone. **2** chant (psalms, parts of a liturgical service, etc.). **3** utter in a solemn or pompous tone. [medieval Latin *intonare* (as IN-², Latin *tonus* TONE)]

in toto *adverb* completely. [Latin]

in·tox·i·cant /ɪnˈtɒksɪkənt/ *noun* an intoxicating substance.

in·tox·i·cate /ɪnˈtɒksɪˌkeɪt/ *transitive verb* **1** make drunk. **2** excite or elate beyond self-control. □ **in·tox·i·cat·ing** *adjective* **in·tox·i·cat·ing·ly** *adverb* **in·tox·i·ca·tion** *noun* [medieval Latin *intoxicare* (as IN-², *toxicare* poison, from Latin *toxicum*): see TOXIC]

intr. *abbreviation* intransitive.

intra- *prefix* forming adjectives usu. from adjectives, meaning 'on the inside, within' (*intramural*). [Latin *intra* inside]

intra·cel·lu·lar *adjective* *Biol.* located or occurring within a cell or cells. □ **intra·cel·lu·lar·ly** *adverb*

intra·crani·al /ˌɪntrəˈkreɪniəl/ *adjective* within the skull.

in·tract·able /ɪnˈtraktəbəl/ *adjective* **1** hard to control or deal with. **2** (of a disease) not easily treated. **3** (of a person or animal) not manageable or docile; stubborn. □ **in·tract·abil·ity** *noun* **in·tract·ably** *adverb*

intra·day *adjective* *Stock Exch.* occurring within one day (*intraday low*).

in·tra·dos /ɪnˈtreɪdɒs/ *noun* the lower or inner curve of an arch. [French (as INTRA-, *dos* back, from Latin *dorsum*)]

intra·molecu·lar /ˌɪntrəməˈlekjʊlər/ *adjective* within a molecule.

intra·mural /ˌɪntrəˈmjʊrəl/ ● *adjective* **1 a** esp. *N Amer.* taking place within a single (esp. educational) institution (*intramural floor hockey league*). **b** forming part of normal university or college studies. **2** situated or done within walls. ● *noun* (in *pl.*) *N Amer.* intramural sports. □ **intra·mural·ly** *adverb*

intra·muscu·lar *adjective* in or into a muscle or muscles. □ **intra·muscu·lar·ly** *adverb*

intra·net *noun* *Computing* a communications network within an organization, employing the same technology as the Internet.

in·transi·gent /ɪnˈtranzɪdʒənt, -sɪdʒənt/ ● *adjective* uncompromising, stubborn. ● *noun* an intransigent person. □ **in·transi·gence** *noun* **in·transi·gency** *noun* **in·transi·gent·ly** *adverb* [French *intransigeant* from Spanish *los intransigentes*, a name adopted by the extreme republicans in the Cortes, ultimately formed as IN-¹ + Latin *transigere transigent-* 'come to an understanding' (as TRANS-, *agere* 'act')]

in·transi·tive /ɪnˈtranzɪtɪv, -sɪtɪv/ *adjective* (of a verb or sense of a verb) that does not take or require a direct object (whether expressed or implied), e.g. *look* in *look at the sky* (opp. TRANSITIVE). Abbr.: **intr**. □ **in·transi·tive·ly** *adverb* **in·transi·tiv·ity** /-ˈtɪvɪti/ *noun*

intra·psych·ic /ˌɪntrəˈsaɪkɪk/ *adjective* *Psych.* occurring or existing within the psyche or self.

intra·specif·ic /ˌɪntrəspəˈsɪfɪk/ *adjective* produced, occurring, or existing within a single taxonomic species or between individuals of a single species.

intra·uter·ine /ˌɪntrəˈjuːtəˌrɪn, -ˌraɪn/ *adjective* within the uterus.

intrauterine device *noun* a contraceptive device fitted inside the uterus and physically preventing the implantation of fertilized ova. Abbr.: **IUD**.

intra·vascu·lar /ˌɪntrəˈvaskjʊlər/ *adjective* situated or occurring within a vessel of an animal or plant, esp. within a blood vessel.

intra·venous /ˌɪntrəˈviːnəs/ ● *adjective* in or into a vein or veins. ● *noun*

an intravenous injection or feeding. □ **intra·venous·ly** *adverb* [INTRA- + Latin *vena* vein]

intra vires /ˌɪntrə ˈvaɪriːz/ *adverb* *Law* within the powers or legal authority of (a legislative body, etc.). [Latin, = 'within the powers']

in-tray /ˈɪntreɪ/ *noun* = IN-BASKET.

in·trep·id /ɪnˈtrepɪd/ *adjective* fearless; very brave. □ **in·trep·id·ity** /-trɪˈpɪdɪti/ *noun* **in·trep·id·ly** *adverb* [French *intrépide* or Latin *intrepidus* (as IN-¹, *trepidus* alarmed)]

in·tri·cate /ˈɪntrɪkət/ *adjective* very complicated; perplexingly detailed. □ **in·tri·cacy** *noun* (*pl.* **-cies**). **in·tri·cate·ly** *adverb* [Latin *intricare intricat-* (as IN-², *tricare* from *tricae* tricks)]

in·trigue ● *verb* /ɪnˈtriːg/ (**in·trigues**, **in·trigued**, **in·triguing**) **1** *transitive* provoke (a person's) interest or curiosity (*what you say intrigues me*). **2** *intransitive* (foll. by *with*) make and carry out secret plans, often with other people, with the aim of causing someone harm, doing something illegal, etc.; plot (*she was intriguing with the leader of a rival gang*). ● *noun* /ˈɪntriːg, ɪnˈtriːg/ **1** the making of secret plans to cause somebody harm, do something illegal, etc. (*a novel of mystery and intrigue*). **2 a** a secret plan to cause someone harm, etc. (*political intrigues*). **b** a secret arrangement (*amorous intrigues*). □ **in·triguer** *noun* **in·triguing** *adjective* (esp. in sense 1 of *verb*). **in·triguing·ly** *adverb* [French *intrigue* (n.), *intriguer* (v.) from Italian *intrigo*, *intrigare* from Latin (as INTRICATE)]

in·trin·sic /ɪnˈtrɪnzɪk/ *adjective* inherent, essential; belonging naturally (*intrinsic value*). □ **in·trin·sic·ally** *adverb* [Middle English, = interior, from French *intrinsèque* from Late Latin *intrinsecus* from Latin *intrinsecus* (adv.) inwardly]

in·tro /ˈɪntroʊ/ *informal* ● *noun* (*pl.* **-tros**) an introduction. ● *adjective* introductory. [abbreviation]

intro- /ˈɪntroʊ/ *combining form* into (*introgression*). [Latin *intro* to the inside]

intro·duce *transitive verb* **1** (foll. by *to*) make (a person or oneself) known by name to another, esp. formally. **2** announce or present to an audience. **3** bring (a custom, idea, etc.) into use. **4** bring (a piece of legislation) before a legislative assembly. **5** (foll. by *to*) draw the attention or extend the understanding of (a person) to a subject, activity, etc. (*introduced me to curling*). **6** insert; place in. **7** bring in; usher in; bring forward. **8** begin; occur just before the start of. **9** bring (a plant, animal, disease, etc.) to a place where it does not normally occur. □ **intro·du·cer** *noun* [Latin *introducere introduct-* (as INTRO-, *ducere* lead)]

intro·duc·tion *noun* **1** the act or an instance of introducing; the process of being introduced. **2** a formal presentation of one person to another. **3** an explanatory section at the beginning of a book etc. **4** a preliminary section in a piece of music, often thematically different from the main section. **5** an introductory treatise on a subject. **6** a thing introduced. [Latin *introductio* (as INTRODUCE)]

intro·duc·tory *adjective* serving as an introduction; preliminary.

in·troit /ˈɪntrɔɪt/ *noun* **1** a psalm or antiphon sung or said while the priest approaches the altar for the Eucharist. **2** a choral response used at the start of a worship service. [Old French from Latin *introitus* from *introire introit-* enter (as INTRO-, *ire* go)]

intro·jec·tion /ˌɪntrəˈdʒekʃən/ *noun* the unconscious incorporation of external ideas into one's mind. □ **intro·ject** *transitive verb* [INTRO- after projection]

intro·mis·sion /ˌɪntrəˈmɪʃən/ *noun* the action or process of inserting the penis into the vagina in sexual intercourse.

in·tron *noun* **1** a segment of an RNA molecule which does not code for proteins, is excised during or soon after transcription, and takes no part in forming the eventual gene product. **2** a section of DNA that codes for this (*compare* EXON). [INTRA- + -ON]

intro·spec·tion *noun* the examination or observation of one's own mental and emotional processes etc. □ **intro·spec·tive** *adjective* **intro·spec·tive·ly** *adverb* [Latin *introspicere introspect-* look inwards (as INTRO-, *specere* look)]

intro·vert ● *noun* /ˈɪntrəˌvɜrt/ **1** *Psych.* a person predominantly concerned with his or her own thoughts and feelings rather than with external things. **2** a shy, inwardly thoughtful person (*compare* EXTROVERT). ● *adjective* /ˈɪntrəˌvɜrt/ (also **intro·vert·ed**) typical or characteristic of an introvert. ● *transitive verb* /ˌɪntrəˈvɜrt/ **1** *Psych.* direct (one's thoughts or mind) inwards. **2** *Zool.* withdraw (an organ etc.) within its own tube or base, like the finger of a glove. □ **intro·ver·sion** /-ˈvɜrʒən/ *noun* **intro·vert·ed** *adjective* [INTRO- + *vert* as in INVERT]

in·trude *verb* (foll. by *on*, *upon*, *into*) **1** *intransitive* come uninvited or unwanted; force oneself abruptly on others. **2** *transitive* thrust or force (something unwelcome) on a person. **3** *Geol.* **a** *transitive* thrust or force (esp. molten rock material) into. **b** *intransitive* (of rock material) be forced or thrust into as an intrusion. [Latin *intrudere intrus-* (as IN-², *trudere* thrust)]

in·trud·er *noun* a person who intrudes, esp. into a building with criminal intent.

in·tru·sion *noun* **1** the act or an instance of intruding. **2** an unwanted interruption etc. **3** *Geol.* an influx of molten rock between or through strata etc. but not reaching the surface.

in·tru·sive *adjective* **1** that intrudes or tends to intrude. **2** characterized by intrusion. **3** *Phonetics* (of a sound) pronounced between words or syllables to facilitate pronunciation, as in the pronunciation /ˈaθəˌliːt/ for *athlete*. □ **in·tru·sive·ly** *adverb* **in·tru·sive·ness** *noun*

in·tub·ate /ˈɪntʊˌbeɪt, -tjʊ-/ *transitive verb Med.* insert a tube into the trachea for ventilation, usu. during anaesthesia. □ **in·tub·a·tion** *noun* [IN-² + Latin *tuba* tube]

in·tuit /ɪnˈtuːɪt, -tjuː-/ *verb* **1** *transitive* know by intuition. **2** *intransitive* receive knowledge by direct perception. [Latin *intueri intuit-* consider (as IN-², *tueri* look)]

in·tu·ition /ˌɪntuˈɪʃən, -tjuː-/ *noun* **1** the power of understanding situations or people's feelings immediately, without the need for conscious reasoning or study (*use your intuition*). **2** an idea or piece of knowledge gained by this power (*had an intuition you were here*).

in·tu·ition·ism /ˌɪntuˈɪʃəˌnɪzəm, -tjuː-/ *noun* (also **in·tu·ition·al·ism**) *Philos.* the belief that primary truths and principles (esp. of ethics and metaphysics) are known directly by intuition. □ **in·tu·ition·ist** *noun*

in·tu·itive /ɪnˈtuːɪtɪv, -tjuː-/ *adjective* **1** of, characterized by, or possessing intuition. **2** perceived by intuition. **3** capable of being easily understood or grasped by intuition (*some computer programs are more intuitive than others*). □ **in·tu·itive·ly** *adverb* **in·tu·itive·ness** *noun*

in-turn *noun* Curling **1** an inward turn of the elbow and an outward turn of the hand made in delivering a stone, thus giving it a clockwise rotation. **2** a stone delivered with such a motion.

intus·sus·cep·tion /ˌɪntəssəˈsepʃən/ *noun* **1** *Med.* the inversion of one portion of the intestine within another. **2** *Bot.* the deposition of new cellulose particles in a cell wall, to increase the surface area of the cell. [modern Latin *intussusceptio* from Latin *intus* within + *susceptio* from *suscipere* take up]

Inuin·naq·tun /iːˌnuːiːnˈʌktuːn/ *noun* an Inuit language spoken in the Coronation Gulf area of the Central Arctic.

Inuit /ˈɪnjuːɪt, ˈɪnʊɪt/ ● *noun* (*pl.* same) **1** any of several Aboriginal peoples inhabiting the Arctic coasts of Canada, Greenland, and Alaska. **2** the language of the Inuit; Inuktitut. ● *adjective* of or relating to the Inuit or their culture or language. [Inuktitut *inuit* 'the people']

Inuit Ta·piri·it Kana·tami a national organization, founded in 1971, representing the Inuit of Nunavut, the NWT, northern Quebec and Labrador. [Inuktitut, = 'Inuit are united with Canada']

Inuit Ta·piri·sat of Canada *noun* the former name of INUIT TAPIRIIT KANATAMI.

Inuk /ɪnˈuːk/ *noun* (*pl.* **Inuit**) a member of any of the Inuit peoples. [Inuktitut *inuk* person]

inuk·shuk /ˈɪnʊkˌʃʊk/ *noun* (also **inuk·suk**) (*pl.* **inuk·shuks** or **inuk·suit**) a figure of a human made of stones, originally used among the Inuit to scare caribou into an ambush, and as a marker to guide travellers, now also found as decorative sculptures in southern Canada. [Inuktitut]

Inuk·ti·tut /ɪnˈʊktɪtʊt/ *noun* the language of the Inuit. [Inuktitut]

inu·lin /ˈɪnjəlɪn/ *noun Biochemistry* a complex of sugar present in the root of various plants and used medically to test kidney function. It is a polysaccharide based on fructose. [Latin *inula* (identified by medieval herbalists with elecampane) + -IN]

in·un·date /ˈɪnənˌdeɪt/ *transitive verb* (often foll. by *with*) **1** flood. **2** overwhelm (*inundated with inquiries*). □ **in·un·da·tion** *noun* [Latin *inundare* flow, from *unda* wave]

Inupi·aq /ɪˈnuːpiak/ *noun* an Inuit language spoken in Canada, Alaska, and Greenland. [Inuktitut, from *inuk* 'person' + *piaq* 'genuine']

In·upi·at /ɪˈnuːpiat/ (*pl.* same) ● *noun* **1** a member of an Inuit people inhabiting areas of northern Alaska. **2** the Inuit language spoken by the Inupiat. ● *adjective* of or relating to the Inupiat or their culture or language. [INUPIAQ]

inure /ɪˈnjʊr/ *verb* **1** *transitive* (often in *passive*; foll. by *to*) accustom (a person) to something esp. unpleasant. **2** *intransitive Law* come into operation; take effect. □ **inure·ment** *noun* [Anglo-French *eneurer* from

phr. en eure (both unrecorded) in use or practice, from *en* in + Old French *e(u)vre* work, from Latin *opera*]

in utero /ɪn ˈjuːtərəʊ/ *adverb* in the womb; before birth. [Latin]

Inu·vi·alu·it /ɪˌnuːviːˈaluːɪt/ ● *noun* an Inuit people of the W Canadian Arctic, speaking Inuvialuktun. ● *adjective* of or relating to this people. [Inuvialuktun]

Inu·via·luk /ɪˌnuːviˈaluk/ ● *noun* a member of the Inuvialuit people. ● *adjective* designating a member of the Inuvialuit people.

Inu·via·luk·tun /ɪˌnuːviəˈluktuːn/ *noun* an Inuit language of the western Arctic. [Inuvialuktun]

Inu·vik /ɪˈnuːvɪk/ a town in the northwestern region of the NWT, situated on the East Channel of the Mackenzie River, about 1 125 km (by air) northwest of Yellowknife; pop. (2001) 2,894. [Inuvialuktun, = place of man]

in vacuo /ɪn ˈvakjʊoʊ/ *adverb* in a vacuum. [Latin]

in·vade *transitive & intransitive verb* **1** enter (a country etc.) under arms, with intent to control or subdue it. **2** enter in large numbers; swarm into (*every summer tourists invade the city*). **3** (of a disease) attack (a body etc.). **4** encroach upon (a person's rights, esp. privacy). □ **in·vad·er** *noun* [Latin *invadere invas-* (as IN-², *vadere* go)]

in·vagin·ate /ɪnˈvadʒɪˌneɪt/ *verb* **1** *transitive* turn or double (a tubular anatomical structure) inside out or back within itself. **2** *intransitive* become invaginated. □ **in·vagin·a·tion** *noun* [IN-² + Latin *vagina* sheath]

in·valid¹ /ˈɪnvəˌlɪd/ ● *noun* **1** a person weakened or disabled by illness or injury, esp. chronically or permanently. **2** (*attributive*) **a** being an invalid (*caring for her invalid mother*). **b** of or for invalids. ● *transitive verb* (**in·valid·ed, in·valid·ing**) **1** esp. *Brit.* (often foll. by *out* etc.) remove from active service (one who has become an invalid). **2** (usu. in *passive*) disable (a person) by illness. □ **in·valid·ism** *noun* [Latin *invalidus* weak, infirm (as IN-¹, VALID)]

in·valid² /ɪnˈvalɪd/ *adjective* **1** not officially acceptable or usable, esp. having no legal force. **2** not true or logical; not supported by reasoning (*an invalid argument*). □ **in·valid·ly** *adverb* [Latin *invalidus* (as INVALID¹)]

in·vali·date /ɪnˈvaliˌdeɪt/ *transitive verb* **1** make (esp. an argument etc.) invalid. **2** remove the validity or force of (a treaty, contract, etc.). □ **in·vali·da·tion** *noun*

in·valid·ity /ˌɪnvəˈlɪdɪti/ *noun* (*pl.* **-ities**) **1** lack of validity. **2** the condition of being an invalid; bodily infirmity.

in·valu·able *adjective* above valuation; inestimable. □ **in·valu·ably** *adverb*

in·vari·able *adjective* **1** unchangeable; always the same. **2** *Math.* constant, fixed. □ **in·vari·abil·ity** *noun* **in·vari·ably** *adverb*

in·vari·ant ● *adjective* unvarying, invariable. ● *noun Math.* a function which remains unchanged when a specified transformation is applied. □ **in·vari·ance** *noun*

in·va·sion *noun* **1** the act of invading or process of being invaded. **2** an entry of a hostile army into a country or territory. **3** the entry or arrival of a large number of people in a place (*an invasion of tourists*). **4** a harmful incursion of any kind, e.g. of disease, moral evil, etc. **5** the spreading to new sites of pathogenic micro-organisms or malignant cells already in the body. **6** intrusion; encroachment upon a person's property, rights, privacy, etc.

in·va·sive *adjective* **1** (of weeds, cancer cells, etc.) tending to spread. **2** (of medical procedures etc.) involving the introduction of instruments into the body. **3** tending to encroach on the privacy, rights, etc., of others. □ **in·va·sive·ness** *noun*

in·vec·tive *noun* insulting, abusive, or highly critical language. [Old French from Late Latin *invectivus* attacking (as INVEIGH)]

in·veigh /ɪnˈveɪ/ *intransitive verb* (foll. by *against*) speak or write with strong hostility, esp. to denounce, reproach, or censure. [Latin *invehi* go into, assail (as IN-², *vehere vect-* carry)]

in·veigle /ɪnˈveɪɡəl/ *transitive verb* (foll. by *into*, or *to* + infin.) entice; persuade by guile. □ **in·veigle·ment** *noun* [earlier *enve(u)gle* from Anglo-French *envegler*, Old French *aveugler* to blind, from *aveugle* blind, prob. from Romanic *ab oculis* (unrecorded) without eyes]

in·vent *transitive verb* **1** create by thought; devise; originate (a new method, an instrument, etc.). **2** concoct (a false story etc.). [Middle English, = discover, from Latin *invenire invent-* find, contrive (as IN-², *venire vent-* come)]

in·ven·tion *noun* **1** the process of inventing. **2** a thing invented; a contrivance, esp. one for which a patent is granted. **3** a fictitious statement or story; a fabrication. **4** creativity, inventiveness. **5** *Music* a short piece for keyboard, developing a simple idea.

in·vent·ive *adjective* **1** able or inclined to invent; original in devising.

2 showing ingenuity of devising. **3** of or pertaining to invention. □ **in·vent·ive·ly** *adverb* **in·vent·ive·ness** *noun*

in·vent·or *noun* a person who invents things, esp. as an occupation.

in·ven·tory /'ɪnvənˌtɔri/ ● *noun* (*pl.* **-ies**) **1 a** a complete list of goods in stock, house contents, etc. **b** the goods listed in this. **c** the action of compiling such a list. **2** any list, catalogue, or detailed account (*an inventory of jobs to do*). **3** *N Amer.* the total of a firm's commercial assets. **4** *N Amer.* a means of taking stock of the quality, characteristics, and growth of various forest areas through aerial mapping and sampling on the ground. ● *transitive verb* (**-ies, -ied**) **1** make an inventory of. **2** enter (goods) in an inventory. [medieval Latin *inventorium* from Late Latin *inventarium* (as INVENT)]

Inver·car·gill /ˌɪnvərˈkɑrɡɪl/ a city in New Zealand, capital of Southland region, South Island; pop. (2001) 50,118.

Inver·ness /ˌɪnvərˈnes/ a city in Scotland at the mouth of the Ness River; pop. (est. 2002) 43,100.

in·verse /'ɪnvɜrs, -'vɜrs/ ● *adjective* inverted in position, order, or relation. ● *noun* **1** the state or condition of being inverted. **2** (often foll. by *of*) a thing that is the opposite or reverse of another. **3** *Math.* an element which, when combined with a given element in an operation, produces the identity element for that operation. □ **in·verse·ly** *adverb* [Latin *inversus* past participle of *invertere*: see INVERT]

inverse proportion *noun* (also **inverse ratio**) a relation between two quantities such that one increases in proportion as the other decreases.

inverse square law *noun* a law by which the intensity of an effect, such as gravitational force, illumination, etc., changes in inverse proportion to the square of the distance from the source.

in·ver·sion *noun* **1 a** the act of turning upside down, inside out, or inwards. **b** the state of being so turned. **2** the reversal of a normal order, position, sequence, or relation. **3** the reversal of the order of words, for rhetorical effect. **4 a** the reversal of the normal variation of air temperature with altitude, i.e. an increase of temperature with height instead of the normal decrease. **b** (also **inversion layer**) a layer of air having such a reversed gradient. **5** *Music* the process or result of inverting an interval, chord, phrase, or subject. **6 a** the decomposition of an optically active carbohydrate, esp. sucrose, by which the direction of the optical rotatory power is reversed. **b** the reversal of direction of rotation of a plane of polarized light. **7** *Psych.* dated homosexuality. **8** the conversion of direct current into alternating current. **9** *Geol.* the folding back of stratified rocks upon each other, so that older strata overlie newer. □ **in·ver·sive** *adjective* [Latin *inversio* (as INVERT)]

in·vert ● *transitive verb* /ɪnˈvɜrt/ **1** turn upside down, inside out, or inwards. **2** reverse the position, order, or relation of. **3** *Music* change the relative position of the notes of (a chord or interval) by placing the lowest note higher, usu. by an octave. **4** subject to inversion. ● *noun* /'ɪnvɜrt/ **1** *Psych. dated* a homosexual. **2** an inverted arch, as at the bottom of a sewer. □ **in·vert·er** /ɪnˈvɜrtər/ *noun* **in·vert·ibil·ity** /-ˈbɪlɪti/ *noun* **in·vert·ible** /ɪnˈvɜrtɪbəl/ *adjective* [Latin *invertere invers-* (as IN-², *vertere* turn)]

in·vert·ase /ɪnˈvɜrteɪz/ *noun* *Biochem.* an enzyme from yeast which catalyzes the inversion of sucrose to produce invert sugar. [INVERT + -ASE]

in·ver·te·brate /ɪnˈvɜrtəˌbreɪt, -brət/ ● *adjective* (of an animal) not having a backbone or spinal column. ● *noun* an invertebrate animal. [modern Latin *invertebrata* (pl.) (as IN-¹, VERTEBRA)]

inverted comma *noun* esp. *Brit.* = QUOTATION MARK.

inverted snobbery *noun* pride in what a snob might be expected to disapprove of; a liking asserted for unfashionable things.

invert sugar *noun* a mixture of glucose and fructose obtained by the hydrolysis of sucrose.

in·vest *verb* **1** *transitive* (often foll. by *in*) **a** apply or use (money), esp. for profit. **b** devote (time, effort etc.) to an enterprise. **2** *intransitive* (foll. by *in*) **a** put money for profit (into stocks etc.). **b** *informal* buy (something useful) (*invested in a new car*). **3** *transitive* **a** (foll. by *with*) provide or credit (a person or thing with qualities, insignia, or rank). **b** (foll. by *in*) attribute or entrust (qualities or feelings to a person). **4** *transitive* lay siege to. □ **in·vest·able** *adjective* **in·vest·or** *noun* [French *investir* or Latin *investire investit-* (as IN-², *vestire* clothe, from *vestis* clothing): sense 1 from Italian *investire*]

in·ves·ti·gate *verb* **1** *transitive* **a** inquire into; examine; study carefully. **b** make an official inquiry into. **2** *intransitive* make a systematic inquiry or search. □ **in·ves·ti·ga·tor** *noun* **in·ves·ti·ga·tory** *adjective* [Latin *investigare investigat-* (as IN-², *vestigare* track)]

in·ves·ti·ga·tion *noun* **1** the process or an instance of investigating. **2** a formal examination or study. □ **in·ves·ti·ga·tion·al** *adjective*

in·ves·ti·ga·tive *adjective* **1 a** (of journalism or broadcasting) investigating and seeking to expose malpractice, miscarriage of justice, etc. **b** (of a journalist etc.) engaged in this. **2** characterized by or inclined to investigation.

in·ves·ti·ture /ɪnˈvestɪˌtʃər/ *noun* the formal investing of a person with honours or rank. [medieval Latin *investitura* (as INVEST)]

in·vest·ment *noun* **1 a** the act or process of investing money, time, effort, etc. **b** an instance of this. **2** money etc. invested. **3** property etc. in which money is or may be invested.

investment bank *noun* a financial institution that specializes in financing commercial loans, mergers and acquisitions, foreign trade, etc. □ **investment banker** *noun* **investment banking** *noun*

investment company *noun* (also esp. *Brit.* **investment trust**) a company that invests the funds provided by shareholders in a variety of selected securities, its profits being made from the income and capital gains provided by these securities.

investment dealer *noun* *Cdn* **1** = INVESTMENT COMPANY. **2** a person working as a broker for an investment company.

investment income *noun* **1** a person's income derived from investments. **2** the income of a business derived from its outside investments rather than from its trading activities.

in·veter·ate /ɪnˈvetərət/ *adjective* **1** (of a person) confirmed in an esp. undesirable habit etc. (*an inveterate gambler*). **2 a** (of a habit etc.) long established, ingrained. **b** (of an activity, esp. an undesirable one) habitual. □ **in·veter·ate·ly** *adverb* [Latin *inveterare inveterat-* make old (as IN-², *vetus veteris* old)]

in·vidi·ous /ɪnˈvɪdiəs/ *adjective* (of an action, conduct, attitude, etc.) likely to excite resentment or indignation against the person responsible, esp. by real or seeming injustice (*an invidious position; an invidious task*). □ **in·vidi·ous·ly** *adverb* **in·vidi·ous·ness** *noun* [Latin *invidiosus* from *invidia* ENVY]

in·vigi·late /ɪnˈvɪdʒɪˌleɪt/ *intransitive verb* *Cdn & Brit.* supervise candidates at an examination. □ **in·vigi·la·tion** *noun* **in·vigi·la·tor** *noun* [originally = keep watch, from Latin *invigilare invigilat-* (as IN-², *vigilare* watch, from *vigil* watchful)]

in·vigor·ate *transitive verb* give vigour or strength to. □ **in·vigor·at·ing** *adjective* **in·vigor·at·ing·ly** *adverb* **in·vigor·a·tion** *noun* [IN-² + medieval Latin *vigorare vigorat-* make strong]

in·vin·cible *adjective* **1** unconquerable; that cannot be defeated. **2** insurmountable. □ **in·vinci·bil·ity** /-ˈbɪlɪti/ *noun* **in·vin·cible·ness** *noun* **in·vin·cibly** *adverb* [Latin *invincibilis* (as IN-¹ + *vincibilis* from *vincere* overcome)]

in·viol·able /ɪnˈvaɪələbəl/ *adjective* not to be violated, dishonoured, or profaned (*inviolable rights*). □ **in·viol·abil·ity** *noun* **in·viol·ably** *adverb* [French *inviolable* or Latin *inviolabilis* (as IN-¹, VIOLATE)]

in·viol·ate /ɪnˈvaɪələt/ *adjective* **1** not violated or profaned. **2** safe from violation or harm. [Latin *inviolatus* (as IN-¹, *violare, violat-* treat violently)]

in·vis·ible *adjective* **1 a** unable to be seen; that by its nature is not perceivable by the eye. **b** not in sight; hidden, obscured, secret. **2** too small or inconspicuous to be seen or noticed; imperceptible. **3** artfully concealed (*invisible mending*). □ **in·visi·bil·ity** *noun* **in·vis·ible·ness** *noun* **in·vis·ibly** *adverb*

invisible ink *noun* ink which becomes invisible when on paper so that writing cannot be seen until the paper is heated or otherwise treated.

in·vi·ta·tion *noun* **1** the process of inviting or fact of being invited, esp. to a social occasion. **2** the spoken or written form in which a person is invited (*birthday party invitations*). **3** the action or an act of enticing; attraction, allurement.

in·vi·ta·tion·al esp. *N Amer.* ● *adjective* (of a tournament, contest etc.) open only to those invited. ● *noun* an invitational contest etc.

in·vite ● *verb* **1** *transitive* (often foll. by *to*, or *to* + infin.) ask (a person) courteously to come, or to do something (*were invited to lunch; invited them to reply*). **2** *transitive* make a formal courteous request for (*invited comments*). **3** *transitive* tend to call forth unintentionally (something unwanted) (*inviting trouble*). **4 a** *transitive* attract. **b** *intransitive* be attractive. ● *noun* /'ɪnvaɪt/ *informal* an invitation. □ **in·vit·ee** *noun* **in·vit·er** *noun* [French *inviter* or Latin *invitare*]

in·vit·ing *adjective* **1** attractive. **2** enticing, tempting. □ **in·vit·ing·ly** *adverb*

in vitro /ɪn ˈviːtroʊ/ *adverb* *Biol.* (of processes or reactions) performed, obtained, or occurring in a test tube, culture dish, or elsewhere outside a living organism (*opp.* IN VIVO). [Latin, = in glass]

uː m*oo*d aɪ m*y* əɪ p*i*pe aʊ br*ow*n ʌʊ h*ou*se eɪ d*ay* ɔɪ b*oy* ã fr*anglais* ā *Canadien* ɔ̃ Br*ayon*   (*see over for consonants*)

in vitro fertilization *noun* a method of fertilizing an ovum in a test tube, culture dish, etc. and then implanting it in a uterus for gestation. Abbr.: **IVF**.

in vivo /ɪn ˈviːvoʊ/ *adverb Biol.* (of processes) taking place in a living organism (*opp.* IN VITRO). [Latin, = in a living thing]

in·vo·ca·tion /ˌɪnvəˈkeɪʃən/ *noun* **1 a** the act or an instance of invoking an authority, a precedent, etc. **b** the act or an instance of calling upon God, a deity, etc. in prayer. **2** an appeal to a supernatural being or beings, e.g. the Muses, for psychological or spiritual inspiration. **3** *Christianity* the words 'In the name of the Father' etc. used at the beginning of a religious service, as the preface to a sermon, etc. □ **in·voc·a·tory** /ɪnˈvɒkətəri/ *adjective*

in·voice ● *noun* a list of goods shipped or sent, or services rendered, with prices and charges; a bill. ● *transitive verb* **1** make an invoice of (goods and services). **2** send an invoice to (a person). [earlier *invoyes* pl. of *invoy* = ENVOI]

in·voke *transitive verb* **1 a** appeal to (the law, a person's authority, etc.), esp. for support, confirmation, etc. **b** put or call (a law, model, etc.) into operation or effect. **2** call on (a deity etc.) in prayer or as a witness. **3** ask earnestly for (vengeance, help, etc.). **4** summon (a spirit) by charms. **5** *Computing* cause (a procedure etc.) to be carried out. □ **in·vok·er** *noun* [French *invoquer* from Latin *invocare* (as IN-², *vocare* call)]

in·vo·lu·cre /ˈɪnvəˌluːkər/ *noun* **1** *Anat.* a membranous envelope. **2** *Bot.* a whorl of bracts surrounding an inflorescence. [French *involucre* or Latin *involucrum* (as INVOLVE)]

in·vol·un·tary /ɪnˈvɒləntəri/ *adjective* **1** not done willingly or by choice; unintentional. **2** (of a nerve, muscle, or movement) not under the control of the will. □ **in·vol·un·tar·i·ly** *adverb*

in·vo·lute /ˈɪnvəˌluːt/ ● *adjective* **1** involved, intricate. **2** rolled up in a spiral. **3** (of a shell) having the whorls wound closely around the axis. **4** *Bot.* (of a leaf etc.) rolled inwards at the edges. ● *noun Geom.* the locus of a point fixed on a straight line that rolls without sliding on a curve and is in the plane of that curve (*compare* EVOLUTE). [Latin *involutus* past participle of *involvere*: see INVOLVE]

in·vo·lut·ed /ˈɪnvəˌluːtəd/ *adjective* **1** complicated, abstruse. **2** = INVOLUTE *adjective* 2.

in·vo·lu·tion /ˌɪnvəˈluːʃən/ *noun* **1** the action of involving or the fact of being involved. **2** an entanglement. **3** intricacy. **4** a folding, curling, or turning inwards. **5** *Physiol.* the reduction in size of an organ in old age, or when its purpose has been fulfilled, esp. the uterus after childbirth. □ **in·vo·lu·tion·al** *adjective* [Latin *involutio* (as INVOLVE)]

in·volve *transitive verb* **1** (often foll. by *in*) cause (a person or thing) to participate, or share the experience or effect (of a situation, activity, etc.). **2** imply, entail, make necessary. **3** (foll. by *in*) implicate (a person in a charge, crime, etc.). **4** include or affect in its operations. [Middle English from Latin *involvere involut-* (as IN-², *volvere* roll)]

in·volved *adjective* **1** (often foll. by *in*) **a** connected or associated with (*involved in biotechnology*). **b** implicated (*involved in drug dealing*). **2** complicated in thought or form (*an involved process*). **3** (often foll. by *with*) engaged in a romantic relationship (*involved with a married man*).

in·volve·ment *noun* **1** (often foll. by *in*, *with*) **a** the action or process of involving something or someone. **b** the fact or condition of being involved. **2** a complicated affair, relationship, or concern.

in·vul·ner·a·ble *adjective* **1** that cannot be wounded or hurt, physically or mentally. **2** unassailable; not liable to damage or harm, esp. from attack. □ **in·vul·ner·a·bil·ity** *noun* **in·vul·ner·a·bly** *adverb*

-in-waiting *combining form* **1** attending another person (*lady-in-waiting*). **2** future (*leader-in-waiting*).

in·ward ● *adjective* **1** directed toward the inside; going in. **2** situated within; that is the inner or innermost part. **3** mental, spiritual. ● *adverb* (also **in·wards**) **1** (of motion or position) towards the inside. **2** in the mind or soul.

inward-looking *adjective* introverted, self-absorbed, insular.

in·ward·ly *adverb* **1** on the inside. **2 a** in the mind or soul. **b** at heart, in reality, secretly. **3** (of speaking) not aloud; inaudibly.

in·ward·ness *noun* **1** inner nature; essence. **2** the condition of being inward. **3 a** introspection. **b** spirituality.

in·wards *var. of* INWARD *adverb*.

in-your-face *adjective* (also **in your face** *predicative*) *slang* aggressively blatant or provocative (*an in-your-face attitude*). [from *in your face* used as a derisive insult]

I/O *abbreviation Computing* = INPUT/OUTPUT.

Io /ˈaɪoʊ/ **1** *Gk Myth* a priestess of Hera who was loved by Zeus. Trying to protect her from the jealousy of Hera, he turned her into a heifer,

which wandered far and wide being constantly stung by a gadfly. **2** *Astronomy* satellite I of Jupiter, the fifth closest to the planet, and one of the Galilean moons (diameter 3 630 km).

IOC *abbreviation* International Olympic Committee.

IODE *abbreviation Cdn* IMPERIAL ORDER DAUGHTERS OF THE EMPIRE.

iodic /aɪˈɒdɪk/ *adjective Chem.* containing iodine in chemical combination (*iodic acid*). □ **iod·ate** /ˈaɪəˌdeɪt/ *noun*

iod·ide /ˈaɪəˌdaɪd/ *noun Chem.* any compound of iodine with another element or group.

iodin·ate /ˈaɪədɪneɪt, aɪˈɒdɪneɪt/ *transitive verb* treat or combine with iodine. □ **iodin·a·tion** /-ˈneɪʃən/ *noun*

iod·ine /ˈaɪəˌdaɪn/ *noun* **1** *Chem.* a non-metallic element of the halogen group, forming black crystals and a violet vapour, used in medicine and photography, and important as an essential element for living organisms. Symbol: **I**; at. no.: 53. **2** a solution of this in alcohol used as a mild antiseptic. [French *iode* from Greek *iōdēs* violet-like, from *ion* violet + -INE⁴]

iod·ize /ˈaɪəˌdaɪz/ *transitive verb* (also esp. *Brit.* **-ise**) treat or impregnate with iodine. □ **iod·iz·a·tion** *noun*

iodo- /aɪˈoːdoʊ/ *combining form* (usu. **iod-** before a vowel) *Chem.* iodine.

IOF *abbreviation* Independent Order of Foresters.

ion /ˈaɪən, ˈaɪɒn/ *noun* an atom, molecule, or group that has lost one or more electrons (= CATION), or gained one or more electrons (= ANION). [Greek, neuter pres. part. of *eimi* go]

-ion *suffix* (usu. as **-sion**, **-tion**, **-xion**; *see* -ATION, -ITION, -UTION) forming nouns denoting: **1** verbal action (*excision*). **2** an instance of this (*a suggestion*). **3** a resulting state or product (*vexation*; *concoction*). [from or after French *-ion* or Latin *-io -ionis*]

Iona /aɪˈoʊnə/ a small island in the Inner Hebrides, off the west coast of Mull. It is the site of a monastery founded by St. Columba in about 563, which became the centre for Christian missions in Scotland.

Ion·esco /ˌiːəˈnɛskoʊ/ **Eu·gène** (1912–94), Romanian-born French dramatist. A leading exponent of the theatre of the absurd, he achieved fame with his first play *The Bald Prima Donna* (1950), which blended a dialogue of empty platitudes with absurd logic and surrealist effects.

ion exchange *noun* the exchange of ions of the same charge between a usu. aqueous solution and a solid, used in water-softening, separation of chemical compounds, etc. □ **ion exchanger** *noun*

Ionia /aɪˈoːnɪə/ in classical times, the central part of the west coast of Asia Minor. In the 11th c. BC peoples speaking the Ionic dialect of Greek (the Ionians) settled in the Aegean Islands and in the western part of Asia Minor, part of which was named Ionia after them. This area was also colonized by Greeks from the mainland from about the 8th c. BC. □ **Ion·ian** *noun & adjective*

Ionian Islands a chain of about 40 Greek islands off the western coast of mainland Greece, in the Ionian Sea, including Corfu, Cephalonia, and Ithaca.

Ionian mode *noun Music* the mode represented by the natural diatonic scale C–C.

Ionian Sea the part of the Mediterranean Sea between W Greece and S Italy, at the mouth of the Adriatic. [according to legend, after Io]

Ionic /aɪˈɒnɪk/ ● *adjective* **1** of the order of Greek architecture characterized by a column with scroll shapes on either side of the capital. **2** of the ancient Greek dialect used in Ionia. ● *noun* the Ionic dialect. [Latin *Ionicus* from Greek *Iōnikos*]

ionic /aɪˈɒnɪk/ *adjective* of, relating to, or using ions. □ **ion·ic·ally** *adverb*

ion·iz·a·tion /ˌaɪənaɪˈzeɪʃən/ *noun* (also esp. *Brit.* **-isation**) the process of producing ions as a result of solvation, heat, radiation, etc.

ionization chamber *noun* an instrument for gauging radiation intensity by measuring the charge on the ions produced by the radiation in a volume of gas.

ion·ize /ˈaɪəˌnaɪz/ *transitive & intransitive verb* (also esp. *Brit.* **-ise**) convert or be converted into an ion or ions. □ **ion·iz·able** *adjective*

ion·iz·er /ˈaɪəˌnaɪzər/ *noun* any thing which produces ionization, esp. a device used to improve the quality of the air in a room etc.

ionizing radiation *noun* a radiation of sufficient energy to cause ionization in the medium through which it passes.

iono·phore /aɪˈɒnəfər/ *noun Biol.* an agent which is able to transport ions across a lipid membrane in a cell. [ION + -O- + -PHORE]

iono·sphere /aɪˈɒnəˌsfɪːr/ *noun* an ionized region of the atmosphere above the stratosphere, extending to about 1 000 km above the earth's surface and able to reflect radio waves for long-distance transmission around the earth (*compare* TROPOSPHERE). □ **iono·spher·ic** /-'sferɪk/ *adjective*

IOOF *abbreviation* Independent Order of Oddfellows.

-ior¹ *suffix* forming adjectives of comparison (*senior*; *ulterior*). [Latin]

-ior² *var. of* -IOUR.

iota /aɪ'əʊtə/ *noun* **1** the ninth letter of the Greek alphabet (Ι, ι). **2** (usu. with *neg.*) the smallest possible amount. [Greek *iōta*]

IOU /ˌaɪəʊ'juː/ *noun* a signed document acknowledging a debt. [abbreviation of *I owe you*]

-iour *suffix* (also **-ior**) forming nouns (*saviour*; *warrior*). [-I- (as a stem element) + -OUR², -OR¹]

-ious *suffix* forming adjectives meaning 'characterized by, full of', often corresponding to nouns in *-ion* (*cautious*; *curious*; *spacious*). [from or after French *-ieux* from Latin *-iosus*]

Iowa /'aɪəwə/ a state in the Midwest of the US; pop. (2000) 2,926,324; capital, Des Moines. □ **Iowan** *adjective & noun*

Iowa City a city in E Iowa; pop. (2000) 62,200. It was the state capital until replaced by Des Moines in 1858.

IPA *abbreviation* **1** INTERNATIONAL PHONETIC ALPHABET. **2** International Phonetic Association.

IP address /aɪ 'piː/ *noun* *Computing* a unique string of numbers separated by periods that identifies each computer attached to the Internet. [abbreviation of *Internet protocol*]

Ipati·eff /ɪ'patief/ **Vlad·i·mir Niko·lai·evich** (1867–1952), Russian-born US chemist. He worked mainly on the catalysis of hydrocarbons, esp. the use of high-pressure catalysis and of metallic oxides as catalysts; these techniques became vitally important to the petrochemical industry.

IPCC *noun* Intergovernmental Panel on Climate Change.

ipe·cac /'ɪpɪˌkak/ *noun* ipecacuanha. [abbreviation]

ipe·cacu·anha /ˌɪpɪˌkakjuˈanə/ *noun* **1** the root of a S American shrub, *Cephaelis ipecacuanha*, used as an emetic and expectorant. **2** (in full **American ipecacuanha**) a plant of the rose family of the genus *Gillenia* of the eastern US. [Portuguese from Tupi-Guarani *ipekaaguéne* emetic creeper]

Iphi·genia /ˌɪfɪdʒəˈnaɪə/ *Gk Myth* the daughter of Agamemnon, who was obliged to offer her as a sacrifice to Artemis when the Greek fleet was becalmed on its way to the Trojan War; Artemis took her to Tauris in the Crimea, where she became a priestess until rescued by her brother Orestes.

IPO *abbreviation* INITIAL PUBLIC OFFERING.

Ipoh /'iːpəʊ/ the capital of the state of Perak in W Malaysia; pop. (2000) 574,401. It replaced Taiping as state capital in 1937.

ipo·moea /ˌɪpəˈmiːə/ *noun* any twining plant of the genus *Ipomoea*, having trumpet-shaped flowers, e.g. the sweet potato and morning glory. [modern Latin from Greek *ips ipos* worm + *homoios* like]

ips *abbreviation* (also **i.p.s.**) inches per second.

ipse dixit /ˌɪpsi 'dɪksɪt/ *noun* an unproven assertion resting only on the speaker's authority. [Latin, he himself said it (originally of Pythagoras)]

ipsi·lat·eral /ˌɪpsəˈlatərəl/ *adjective* belonging to or occurring on the same side of the body. [irreg. from Latin *ipse* self + LATERAL]

ip·sis·sima verba /ɪpˌsɪsəmə 'vɜːbə/ *plural noun* the precise words. [Latin]

ipso facto /ˌɪpsəʊ 'faktəʊ/ *adverb* **1** by that very fact or act. **2** thereby. [Latin]

Ips·wich /'ɪpswɪtʃ/ the county town of Suffolk, a port and industrial town on the estuary of the Orwell River in E England; pop. (2001) 117,074.

IQ *abbreviation* = INTELLIGENCE QUOTIENT.

Iqal·uit /ɪ'kaluːɪt/ (formerly **Frobisher Bay**) a town at the southern end of Baffin Island situated at the head of Frobisher Bay, the capital of Nunavut; pop. (2001) 5,236. □ **Iqal·ung·miut** /ɪkaˈluŋmiːʊt/ *plural noun & adjective* [Inuktitut, = place of fish]

Iqui·tos /iˈkiːtɒs/ a city in NE Peru, a river port on the west bank of the Amazon; pop. (est. 2002) 349,300. Situated in tropical rainforest, it is a centre for oil exploration.

IR *abbreviation* infrared.

I.R. *abbreviation* *Cdn* Indian Reserve.

Ir *symbol* *Chem.* the element iridium.

ir- /ɪr/ *prefix* assimilated form of IN-¹, IN-² before *r*.

IRA *abbreviation* = IRISH REPUBLICAN ARMY.

Iran /ɪ'ran, -'rɒn/ a country in the Middle East, between the Caspian Sea and the Persian Gulf; pop. (est. 2002) 66,622,704; capital, Tehran.

Previously known as Persia, the country adopted the name Iran in 1935. Iran was a monarchy until 1979, when a popular uprising led to the establishment of an Islamic republic. (*See also* PERSIA.)

Iran-Contra affair (also called **Iran–Contra scandal** or **Iran·gate**) a US political scandal of 1987, involving the covert selling of arms by the US to Iran (at a time when official relations between the countries were suspended), the subsequent release of American hostages held in the Middle East, and the use of the proceeds from the sales to supply arms to the anti-Communist Contras in Nicaragua (despite Congressional prohibition).

Iran·ian /ɪ'reɪnɪən/ ● *adjective* **1** of or relating to Iranians or Iran. **2** of the Indo-European group of languages including Persian, Pashto, Avestan, and Kurdish. ● *noun* **1 a** a native or national of Iran. **b** a person of Iranian descent. **2** the Iranian languages.

Iran-Iraq War the war of 1980–8 between Iran and Iraq in the general area of the Persian Gulf, which ended inconclusively after great hardship and loss of life on both sides.

Iraq /ɪ'rak, -'rɒk/ a country in the Middle East, on the Persian Gulf; pop. (est. 2002) 24,001,816; capital, Baghdad. Iraq is traversed by the Tigris and Euphrates rivers, whose valley was the site of the ancient civilizations of Mesopotamia. The country was at war with Iran in 1980–8, and in the Gulf War of 1991 it was expelled from Kuwait (which it had invaded the previous year) by an international coalition of forces. In 2003, after its failure to comply fully with a UN resolution that it should disarm, it was invaded by US-led forces and the regime of Saddam Hussein was overthrown.

Iraqi /ɪ'raki, -'rɒki/ ● *adjective* of or relating to Iraqis. ● *noun* (*pl.* **Iraqis**) **1 a** a native or national of Iraq. **b** a person of Iraqi descent. **2** the form of Arabic spoken in Iraq.

iras·cible /ɪ'rasɪbəl/ *adjective* **1** irritable, hot-tempered, easily provoked to anger or resentment. **2** (of an emotion, action, etc.) characterized by, arising from, or exhibiting anger. □ **iras·ci·bil·ity** *noun* **iras·cibly** *adverb* [French from Late Latin *irascibilis* from Latin *irasci* grow angry, from *ira* anger]

irate /aɪ'reɪt/ *adjective* **1** angry, enraged. **2** (of an action etc.) characterized by, arising from, or exhibiting anger (*an irate letter*). □ **irate·ly** *adverb* **irate·ness** *noun* [Latin *iratus* from *ira* anger]

IRB *abbreviation* *Cdn* Immigration and Refugee Board.

IRC *abbreviation* **1** International Reply Coupon. **2** *Computing* Internet Relay Chat.

ire *noun* anger, wrath. □ **ire·ful** *adjective* [Old French from Latin *ira*]

Ire·land an island of the British Isles, lying west of Great Britain. Approximately four-fifths of the area of Ireland forms the Republic of Ireland, with the remaining one-fifth forming the UK province of Northern Ireland (*see* IRELAND, REPUBLIC OF and NORTHERN IRELAND).

Ireland, Republic of (also **Irish Republic**) a country forming approximately four-fifths of Ireland; pop. (est. 2002) 3,883,159; capital, Dublin (*see* IRISH FREE STATE and EIRE).

iren·ic /aɪ'riːnɪk/ *adjective* (also **eirenic**) *literary* aiming or aimed at peace. [Greek *eirēnikos* from *eirēnikos* peace]

Irgun /ɪːr'ɡʊn/ a violent Zionist organization (founded in 1931) which from 1937 to 1948 carried out attacks on Arabs in its campaign to establish a Jewish state. [modern Hebrew *'irgūn ṣēḇā'ī lĕ'ummī* = national military organization]

Irian Jaya /ˌiːrɪən 'dʒaɪə/ (also **West Irian**) a province of E Indonesia comprising the western half of the island of New Guinea together with the adjacent small islands; capital, Jayapura. Until its incorporation into Indonesia in 1963 it was known as Dutch New Guinea.

iri·da·ceous /ˌɪrɪ'deɪʃəs/ *adjective* *Bot.* of or relating to the family Iridaceae of plants growing from bulbs, corms, or rhizomes, e.g. iris, crocus, and gladiolus. [modern Latin *iridaceus* (as IRIS)]

iri·des·cent /ˌɪrɪ'desənt/ *adjective* **1** showing rainbow-like luminous or gleaming colours. **2** changing colour with position. □ **iri·des·cence** *noun* **iri·des·cent·ly** *adverb* [Latin IRIS + -ESCENT]

irid·ium /ɪ'rɪdɪəm/ *noun* *Chem.* a hard white metallic element of the platinum group, used esp. in alloys. Symbol: **Ir**; at. no.: 77. [modern Latin from Latin IRIS + -IUM]

iri·dol·ogy /ɪrɪ'dɒlədʒi/ *noun* (in alternative medicine) diagnosis by examination of the iris of the eye. □ **iri·dol·o·gist** *noun* [Greek *iris iridos* 'iris' + -LOGY]

Iris /'aɪrɪs/ *Gk Myth* the goddess of the rainbow, who acted as a messenger of the gods.

iris *noun* **1** the flat circular coloured membrane behind the cornea of the eye, with a circular opening (pupil) in the centre. **2** any herbaceous plant of the genus *Iris*, usu. with tuberous roots, sword-shaped leaves,

t *top*   v *voice*   w *we*   z *zoo*   ʃ *she*   ʒ *vision*   θ *thin*   ð *this*   ŋ *ring*   x *loch*   tʃ *chip*   dʒ *jar*   (see over for vowels)

and showy flowers. **3** (in full **iris diaphragm**) an adjustable diaphragm of thin overlapping plates for regulating the size of a central hole esp. for the admission of light to a lens. **4** *literary* a rainbow. [Latin *iris iridis* from Greek *iris iridos* rainbow, iris]

Irish ● *adjective* of or relating to Ireland, its people, or the Celtic language of Ireland. ● *noun* **1** (prec. by *the*; treated as *pl.*) the people of Ireland, or their immediate descendants in other countries, esp. those of Celtic origin. **2** the Celtic language of Ireland. **3** *informal* temper, passion (*don't get your Irish up*). □ **Irish·ness** *noun* [Middle English from Old English *Iras* the Irish]

Irish bull *noun* = BULL³.

Irish coffee *noun* hot coffee mixed with Irish whiskey and served with whipped cream on top.

Irish Free State the name for southern Ireland from 1921, when it gained dominion status on the partition of Ireland, until 1937, when it became the sovereign state of Eire (*see* IRELAND, REPUBLIC OF).

Irish·man *noun* (*pl.* **-men**) a man who is Irish by birth or descent.

Irish moss *noun* = CARRAGEEN.

Irish Republic *see* IRELAND, REPUBLIC OF.

Irish Republican Army *noun* the military arm of Sinn Fein, formed during the struggle for independence from Britain in 1916-21, and aiming for union between the Republic of Ireland and Northern Ireland. Its Provisional branch often engages in terrorist acts. Abbr.: **IRA**.

Irish Sea the sea separating Ireland from England and Wales.

Irish setter *noun* a breed of setter with a long silky dark red coat and a long feathered tail.

Irish stew *noun* a stew of lamb, potato, and onion.

Irish terrier *noun* a rough-haired, light reddish-brown breed of terrier.

Irish whiskey *noun* a whisky made in Ireland from malted barley and seldom blended.

Irish wolfhound *noun* a breed of large, rough-coated hound, often grey in colour.

Irish·woman *noun* (*pl.* **-women**) a woman who is Irish by birth or descent.

irk *transitive verb* (often prec. by *it* as subject) irritate, bore, annoy. [Middle English: origin unknown]

irk·some *adjective* tedious, annoying, tiresome. □ **irk·some·ly** *adverb* **irk·some·ness** *noun* [Middle English, = tired etc., from IRK + -SOME¹]

Ir·kutsk /ir'kutsk/ the chief city of Siberia, situated on the western shore of Lake Baikal in E Russia; pop. (est. 2002) 594,200.

IRO *abbreviation* International Refugee Organization.

iron ● *noun* **1** *Chem.* a silver-white ductile metallic element occurring naturally as hematite, magnetite, etc., much used for tools and implements, and an essential element in all living organisms. Symbol: Fe; at. no.: 26. **2** this as a type of unyieldingness or a symbol of firmness (*man of iron; will of iron*). **3** a tool or implement made of iron (*branding iron*). **4** a household appliance with a flat base which uses dry heat or steam to remove wrinkles from fabric when passed over it. **5** a golf club with an iron or steel sloping head which is angled in order to loft the ball (often in *combination* with a number indicating the degree of angle: *seven-iron*). **6** a preparation of iron as a tonic or dietary supplement, used to treat anemia etc. (*iron pills*). **7** (usu. in *pl.*) a fetter (*clapped in irons*). **8** (usu. in *pl.*) a stirrup. **9** a harpoon. ● *adjective* **1 a** consisting or made of iron. **b** resembling iron, esp. in appearance or hardness. **2** very robust, tough, enduring. **3 a** firm, inflexible, stubborn, unyielding (*iron determination*). **b** cruel, merciless, implacable, severe. ● *verb* **1 a** *transitive* smooth (clothes etc.) with an iron. **b** *intransitive* (of a garment, material, etc.) become smooth by being pressed with an iron. **2** *transitive* shackle with irons. □ **in irons 1** handcuffed, chained, etc. **2** (of a sailing vessel) head to wind and unable to come about or tack either way. **iron in the fire** an undertaking, opportunity, or commitment (usu. in *pl.*: *too many irons in the fire*). **iron out** remove or smooth over (difficulties etc.). □ **iron·er** *noun* **iron·less** *adjective* **iron-like** *adjective* [Old English *iren*, *isern* from Germanic, prob. from Celtic]

Iron Age *noun* the period following the Bronze Age when iron replaced bronze in the making of implements and weapons, lasting in Europe until the Roman period.

iron·bark *noun* any of various eucalyptus trees with a thick solid bark and hard dense timber.

iron-bound *adjective* **1** bound with iron. **2** rigorous; hard and fast.

Iron Chancellor the nickname of Otto von Bismarck after he used

the phrase 'blood and iron' in a speech in 1862, referring to war as an instrument of foreign policy.

iron·clad ● *adjective* **1** strict, rigorous, hard and fast. **2** clad or protected with iron. ● *noun* *hist.* an early name for a 19th-c. warship built of iron or protected by iron plates.

Iron Cross *noun* a German military decoration for bravery, originally awarded in Prussia (instituted 1813), revived by Hitler on the invasion of Poland by German forces in Sept. 1939.

Iron Curtain *noun* the notional barrier to the passage of people and information which existed between the West and the countries of the former Soviet bloc until the decline of Communism.

Iron Duke the nickname of the Duke of Wellington.

iron fist *noun* firmness or ruthlessness.

Iron Gate a gorge through which a section of the Danube River flows, forming part of the boundary between Romania and Serbia.

iron hand *noun* = IRON FIST (*compare* VELVET GLOVE). □ **iron·hand·ed** *adjective*

iron horse *noun* N Amer. informal a locomotive or train.

iron·ic /ai'ronik/ *adjective* (also **iron·ic·al**) **1** using or displaying irony. **2** in the nature of irony. ¶ It is not recommended to use *ironic* to describe any mildly surprising, unexpected, coincidental, or paradoxical state of affairs. □ **iron·ic·al·ly** *adverb*

iron·ing *noun* **1** the pressing and smoothing of clothes etc. with a heated iron. **2** clothes etc. which are to be or have just been ironed.

ironing board *noun* a long narrow flat surface usu. on legs and of adjustable height, on which clothes etc. are ironed.

iron·ist /'airnist/ *noun* a person who uses irony. □ **iron·ize** *intransitive verb* (also esp. *Brit.* **-ise**).

iron lung *noun* a rigid airtight metal case fitted over a patient's body, used for administering prolonged artificial respiration by means of mechanical pumps.

iron maiden *noun* *hist.* a medieval instrument of torture consisting of a coffin-shaped box lined with iron spikes, into which the victim is shut.

iron man *noun* **1** a brave or robust man, esp. a powerful athlete. **2** (**Iron·man**) *proprietary* a multi-event sporting contest demanding stamina, esp. a consecutive triathlon of swimming, cycling, and running.

iron·master *noun* a manufacturer of iron.

iron·monger /'airn,mʌŋgər/ *noun* Brit. a hardware dealer. □ **iron·mongery** *noun* (*pl.* **-ies**).

iron-on *adjective* able to be fixed to the surface of a fabric etc. by ironing.

iron ore *noun* any rock or mineral from which iron is or may be extracted.

iron pyrites *noun* see PYRITE.

iron rations *plural noun* a small emergency supply of food, esp. for military personnel.

Iron Ring *noun* Cdn a ring made of iron worn on the little finger by engineers who have undergone a special ritual involving a statement of their commitment to the highest professional standards.

Iron·sides *noun* **1** a man of great bravery. **2** a nickname for Oliver Cromwell.

iron·stone *noun* **1** any rock containing a substantial proportion of an iron compound. **2** a kind of hard white opaque stoneware.

iron·ware *noun* small articles made of iron, esp. domestic implements.

iron·weed *noun* any of several herbaceous plants of the genus *Vernonia*, with clusters of purple flowers.

iron·wood *noun* any of various trees with strong wood, esp. the hornbeam and hop hornbeam of the birch family, growing in eastern N America.

iron·work *noun* **1** things made of iron. **2** work in iron. □ **iron·work·er** *noun* **iron·work·ing** *noun*

iron·works *noun* (as *sing.* or *pl.*) a place where iron is smelted or iron goods are made.

irony¹ /'airəni, 'airni/ *noun* (*pl.* **-ies**) **1 a** the expression of meaning using language that normally expresses the opposite. **b** an instance of this; an ironic utterance or expression. **2** a discrepancy between the expected and actual state of affairs. **3** a literary technique in which the audience can perceive hidden meanings unknown to the characters. [Latin *ironia* from Greek *eirōneia* simulated ignorance, from *eirōn* dissembler]

irony² /'airni/ *adjective* of or like iron.

Iro·quoi·an /ˌɪrəˈkwɔɪən/ ● *noun* **1** a major Aboriginal linguistic group, including Cayuga, Mohawk, Oneida, Onondaga, Seneca, and Tuscarora. **2** a member of the Iroquois. ● *adjective* of or relating to the Iroquois or the Iroquoian linguistic group or one of its members.

Iro·quois /ˈɪrəˌkwɒɪ/ ● *noun* (*pl.* same) **1 a** an Aboriginal confederacy of Iroquoian peoples (originally including the Cayuga, Mohawk, Oneida, Onondaga, and Seneca, and later also the Tuscarora) living in Ontario, Quebec, and New York. **b** a member of any of the peoples of this confederacy. **2** any of the languages of these peoples. ● *adjective* of or relating to the Iroquois or their languages. [French from Algonquin]

Iroquois Falls a town in NE central Ontario, situated on the Abitibi River, about 60 km northeast of Timmins; pop. (2001) 5,217. [perhaps from a legend about Huron women who, as an act of vengeance for the mass slaughter of their men, sent the Iroquois over the falls to their deaths]

ir·radi·ance /ɪˈreidiːənʃ/ *noun* the flux of radiant energy per unit area, normal to the direction of flow of radiant energy through a medium.

ir·radi·ate /ɪˈreidiˌeit/ *transitive verb* **1** subject to any form of radiation. **2** make brighter, light up (*faces irradiated with joy*). **3** throw light on (a subject). [Latin *irradiare irradiat-*, *radiare* from *radius* RAY¹)]

ir·radi·a·tion /ɪˌreidiˈeiʃən/ *noun* **1 a** the action or process of irradiating. **b** an instance of this. **2 a** the use of radiation for diagnostic or therapeutic purposes. **b** the process of exposing food to gamma rays to kill micro-organisms. **3** the apparent extension of the edges of an illuminated object seen against a dark background.

ir·ration·al *adjective* **1** illogical; unreasonable. **2** not capable of reasoning. **3** *Math.* (of a root etc.) not rational; not commensurate with the natural numbers, e.g. a non-terminating decimal. ☐ **ir·ration·al·ism** *noun* **ir·ration·al·ist** *noun* **ir·ration·al·ity** *noun* **ir·ration·al·ly** *adverb*

Irra·waddy /ˌɪrəˈwɒdi/ the principal river of Burma (Myanmar), 2 090 km (1,300 miles) long. It flows in a large delta into the eastern part of the Bay of Bengal.

ir·recon·cil·able /ɪˈrekənˌsailəbəl/ ● *adjective* **1** implacably hostile. **2** (of ideas, actions, etc.) incompatible, unable to be made consistent or brought into harmony (*irreconcilable differences*). ● *noun* **1** an uncompromising opponent of a political measure etc. **2** (usu. in *pl.*) any of two or more items, ideas, etc., that cannot be made to agree. ☐ **ir·recon·cil·abil·ity** /-ˈbɪlɪti/ *noun* **ir·recon·cil·ably** *adverb*

ir·recov·er·able *adjective* **1** that cannot be recovered or retrieved. **2** that cannot be remedied or rectified. ☐ **ir·recov·er·ably** *adverb*

ir·redeem·able *adjective* **1** that cannot be redeemed or bought back. **2 a** hopeless, absolute, fixed. **b** beyond redemption, thoroughly depraved. **3** (of paper currency) that cannot be exchanged for money in coins. ☐ **ir·redeem·ably** *adverb*

ir·reden·tist /ˌɪrɪˈdentɪst/ ● *noun* a person, originally in 19th-c. Italy, advocating the restoration to his or her country of any territory formerly belonging to it. ● *adjective* of, pertaining to, or advocating irredentism. ☐ **ir·reden·tism** *noun* [Italian *irredentista* from (*Italia*) *irredenta* unredeemed (Italy)]

ir·redu·cible *adjective* **1 a** that cannot be reduced or made smaller. **b** that cannot be simplified. **2** (often foll. by *to*) that cannot be brought to a desired condition. ☐ **ir·reduci·bil·ity** *noun* **ir·redu·cibly** *adverb*

ir·ref·rag·able /ɪˈrefrəgəbəl/ *adjective* **1** (of a statement, argument, or person) unanswerable, indisputable. **2** (of rules etc.) inviolable. [Late Latin *irrefragabilis* (as IN-¹, *refragari* oppose)]

ir·refut·able /ˌɪrɪˈfjuːtəbəl, ɪˈrefjutəbəl/ *adjective* that cannot be refuted or disproved. ☐ **ir·refut·ably** *adverb*

ir·regu·lar ● *adjective* **1** not regular; unsymmetrical, uneven; varying in form. **2** (of a surface) uneven. **3** contrary to a rule, moral principle, or custom. **4** uneven in duration, order, etc.; not occurring at regular intervals. **5** (of troops) not belonging to the regular or established army. **6** *Grammar* (of a verb, noun, etc.) not inflected according to the usual rules. **7** *N Amer.* (of clothing, cloth, etc.) flawed or damaged, and thus often offered for sale at a reduced price. **8** (of a flower) having unequal petals etc. **9** (of a galaxy) having an irregular shape, esp. lacking any apparent axis of symmetry or central nucleus. **10** not having regular bowel movements or menstrual periods. ● *noun* **1 a** (in *pl.*) irregular troops. **b** a member of an irregular military force. **2** *N Amer.* (usu. in *pl.*) an imperfect piece of merchandise, esp. cloth or clothing, often sold at a reduced price. ☐ **ir·regu·lar·ity** *noun* (*pl.* **-ities**). **ir·regu·lar·ly** *adverb*

ir·rel·evant *adjective* (often foll. by *to*) not relevant; not applicable (to a matter in hand). ☐ **ir·rel·evance** *noun* **ir·rel·evancy** *noun* (*pl.* **-cies**). **ir·rel·evant·ly** *adverb*

ir·reli·gion *noun* **1** disregard of or hostility to religion. **2** lack of religion.

ir·reli·gious *adjective* **1** indifferent or hostile to religion. **2** lacking a religion.

ir·remedi·able /ˌɪrɪˈmiːdiəbəl/ *adjective* that cannot be remedied. ☐ **ir·remedi·ably** *adverb* [Latin *irremediabilis* (as IN-¹, REMEDY)]

ir·remov·able *adjective* that cannot be removed, esp. from office. ☐ **ir·remov·ably** *adverb*

ir·repar·able /ɪˈrepərəbəl/ *adjective* (of an injury, loss, etc.) that cannot be rectified or made good. ☐ **ir·repar·ably** *adverb*

ir·replace·able *adjective* that cannot be replaced if lost or damaged (*an irreplaceable antique vase*). ☐ **ir·replace·abil·ity** *noun* **ir·replace·ably** *adverb*

ir·repress·ible *adjective* that cannot be repressed or restrained. ☐ **ir·repress·ibil·ity** *noun* **ir·repress·ibly** *adverb*

ir·re·proach·able *adjective* faultless, blameless. ☐ **ir·re·proach·abil·ity** *noun* **ir·re·proach·ably** *adverb*

ir·resist·ible *adjective* **1** too strong or convincing to be resisted. **2** delightful; alluring. ☐ **ir·resist·ibil·ity** *noun* **ir·resist·ibly** *adverb*

ir·reso·lute /ɪˈrezəˌluːt/ *adjective* **1** hesitant, undecided. **2** lacking in resoluteness. ☐ **ir·reso·lute·ly** *adverb* **ir·reso·lute·ness** *noun* **ir·reso·lu·tion** *noun*

ir·resolv·able *adjective* **1** that cannot be resolved into its components. **2** (of a problem) that cannot be solved. ☐ **ir·resolv·abil·ity** *noun*

ir·respec·tive *adjective* (foll. by *of*) not taking into account; regardless of. ☐ **ir·respec·tive·ly** *adverb*

ir·respon·sible *adjective* **1** acting or done without due sense of responsibility. **2** not responsible for one's conduct. ☐ **ir·respon·sibil·ity** *noun* **ir·respon·sibly** *adverb*

ir·retriev·able *adjective* that cannot be retrieved or restored. ☐ **ir·retriev·ably** *adverb*

ir·rever·ent /ɪˈrevərənt, -ˈrevrənt/ *adjective* lacking reverence; disrespectful. ☐ **ir·rever·ence** *noun* **ir·rever·ent·ly** *adverb*

ir·revers·ible *adjective* not reversible or alterable, irrevocable. ☐ **ir·revers·ibil·ity** *noun* **ir·revers·ibly** *adverb*

ir·revoc·able /ɪˈrevəkəbəl, ɪrəˈvoːk-/ *adjective* **1** unalterable. **2** gone beyond recall. ☐ **ir·revoc·abil·ity** *noun* **ir·revoc·ably** *adverb* [Latin *irrevocabilis* (as IN-¹, REVOKE)]

ir·rig·ate *transitive verb* **1** supply (land or a crop) with water, esp. by means of specially constructed channels or pipes. **2** *Med.* supply (a wound etc.) with a constant flow of liquid. ☐ **ir·rig·able** *adjective* **ir·riga·tion** *noun* **ir·rig·ator** *noun* [Latin *irrigare* (as IN-², *rigare* moisten)]

irrit·able *adjective* **1** easily annoyed or angered. **2** (of an organ etc.) very sensitive to contact. **3** *Biol.* responding actively to physical stimulus. ☐ **irrit·abil·ity** *noun* **irrit·ably** *adverb*

irritable bowel syndrome *noun* a condition involving abdominal pain and diarrhea or constipation and associated with stress, depression, etc. Abbr.: **IBS**.

irri·tant ● *adjective* causing irritation. ● *noun* an irritant substance. ☐ **irri·tancy** *noun*

irri·tate *transitive verb* **1** excite to anger; annoy. **2** stimulate discomfort or pain in (a part of the body). **3** *Biol.* stimulate (an organ) to action. ☐ **irri·tat·ed·ly** *adverb* **irri·tat·ing** *adjective* **irri·tat·ing·ly** *adverb* **irri·ta·tion** *noun* **irri·ta·tive** *adjective* [Latin *irritare irritat-*]

ir·rupt /ɪˈrʌpt/ *intransitive verb* (foll. by *into*) enter forcibly or violently. [Latin *irrumpere irrupt-* (as IN-², *rumpere* break)]

ir·rup·tion /ɪˈrʌpʃən/ *noun* **1** the action of irrupting; a sudden incursion. **2** a sudden temporary increase in the local population of a migrant bird or animal species. ☐ **ir·rupt·ive** *adjective*

IRS *abbreviation* (in the US) INTERNAL REVENUE SERVICE.

Ir·tysh River /ɪrˈtɪʃ/ a river of central Asia, which rises on the slopes of the Altai Mountains in N China and flows westward into NE Kazakhstan, where it turns northwest into Russia, joining the Ob River near its mouth at the head of the Gulf of Ob; length, 4 248 km (2,655 miles).

Irv·ing ▸ **1 Sir Henry** (born John Henry Brodribb) (1838–1905), English actor and theatre manager. He managed the Lyceum Theatre, London (1878–1902), and entered into a celebrated acting partnership with Ellen Terry; they were noted esp. for their performances in Irving's productions of Shakespeare. **2 John (Wins·low)** (b.1942), US novelist, whose works include *The World According to Garp* (1978), *A Prayer for Owen Meany* (1989), and *A Son of the Circus* (1994). **3 Ken·neth Colin** (1899–1992), Canadian industrialist. Irving's business interests

uː mood   aɪ my   əi pipe   au brown   ʌu house   ei day   ɔi boy   ã franglais   ã Canadien   ɔ̃ Brayon   (*see over for consonants*)

grew from a single car dealership and gas station to a commercial empire that included oil refining, pulp and paper, newspapers, and broadcasting, dominating the Maritimes petroleum industry and the New Brunswick forestry sector. **4 Wash·ing·ton** (1783–1859), US writer, who is remembered for *The Sketch Book of Geoffrey Crayon, Gent* (1819–20), which contains such tales as 'Rip Van Winkle' and 'The Legend of Sleepy Hollow'.

Is. *abbreviation* **1 a** Island(s). **b** Isle(s). **2** (also **Isa.**) *Bible* Isaiah.

is *3rd sing. present of* BE.

Isaac a Hebrew patriarch, son of Abraham and Sarah and father of Jacob and Esau. He was nearly sacrificed by Abraham at God's command (Gen. 21:3 etc.).

Isa·bel·la I (known as 'Isabella of Castile' or 'Isabella the Catholic') (1451–1504), queen of Castile 1474–1504 and of Aragon 1479–1504. Her marriage to Ferdinand of Aragon (1469) joined together the Christian kingdoms of Castile and Aragon, and marked the beginning of the unification of Spain; as joint monarchs they instituted the Spanish Inquisition (1478) and supported Columbus's expedition to the New World (1492).

Isaiah /aɪˈzeɪə, aɪˈzaɪə/ **1** a Hebrew major prophet of Judea in the 8th c. BC, who taught the supremacy of the God of Israel and emphasized the moral demands on worshippers. He foretold the coming to the people of Israel of a saviour and ruler (interpreted by Christians as a reference to Christ). **2** the book of the Bible containing his prophecies.

ISBN *abbreviation* international standard book number, a ten-digit number assigned to every book before publication, recording such details as language, country of publication, and publisher.

is·chemia /ɪˈskiːmɪə/ *noun* (also esp. *Brit.* **is·chaemia**) *Med.* a reduction of the blood supply to part of the body. □ **is·chemic** *adjective* [modern Latin from Greek *iskhaimos* from *iskhō* keep back]

is·chi·um /ˈɪskɪəm/ *noun* (*pl.* **ischia** /-kɪə/) the curved bone forming the base of each half of the pelvis. □ **is·chi·al** *adjective* [Latin from Greek *iskhion* hip joint: compare SCIATIC]

ISDN *abbreviation* INTEGRATED SERVICES DIGITAL NETWORK.

Ise /ˈiːseɪ/ a city in central Honshu island, Japan, on Ise Bay; pop. (est. 2002) 106,200. It has several noted Shinto shrines, including one dedicated to the sun goddess, from whom the Japanese royal family were once claimed to be descended. The city was known as Ujiyamada until 1956.

-ise¹ esp. *Brit.* var. of -IZE.

-ise² *suffix* forming nouns of quality, state, or function (*exercise*; *expertise*; *franchise*). [from or after French or Old French *-ise* from Latin *-itia* etc.]

-ise³ var. of -ISH².

Ise·ler, Elmer Wal·ter (1927–98), Canadian choral conductor. From 1954 to 1978 he conducted the Festival Singers of Canada, which in 1968 became the first professional choir in Canada. From 1964 to 1997 he conducted the Toronto Mendelssohn Choir, and in 1978 he founded the Elmer Iseler Singers.

isen·trop·ic /ˌaɪsɛnˈtrɒpɪk/ *adjective* having constant or equal entropy. [ISO- + ENTROPY]

Is·eult /ɪˈsuːlt/ (also **Isolde** /ɪˈzɒldə/) (in medieval legend) the sister or daughter of the king of Ireland, and wife of King Mark of Cornwall, loved by Tristan; in another account she was the daughter of the king of Brittany, and the wife of Tristan.

Isfa·han /ˌɪsfəˈhɒn/ (also **Esfahan** /ˌɛsfə-/, **Ispahan** /ˌɪspə-/) an industrial city in central Iran, the country's third largest city; pop. (1996) 1,266,072. It was the capital from 1598 until destroyed by the Afghans in 1722.

-ish¹ *suffix* forming adjectives: **1** from nouns, meaning: **a** having the qualities or characteristics of (*boyish*). **b** of the nationality of (*Danish*). **2** from adjectives, meaning 'somewhat' (*thickish*). **3** *informal* denoting an approximate age or time of day (*fortyish*; *six-thirtyish*). [Old English *-isc*]

-ish² *suffix* (also **-ise**) forming verbs (*vanish*; *advertise*). [from or after French *-iss-* (in extended stems of verbs in *-ir*) from Latin *-isc-* inceptive suffix]

Isher·wood, Chris·to·pher (Wil·liam Brad·shaw) (1904–86), English-born US novelist. The musical *Cabaret* was based on his novel *Goodbye to Berlin* (1939), which vividly portrays Germany on the eve of Hitler's rise to power.

Ishi·guro /ˌɪʃɪˈɡʊrəʊ/ **Kazuo** (b.1954), Japanese-born English novelist, whose works include *The Remains of the Day* (1989), which won the Booker Prize, and *The Unconsoled* (1995).

Ish·mael /ˈɪʃmeɪəl/ (in the Bible) a son of Abraham and his wife Sarah's maid Hagar, driven away with his mother after the birth of

Isaac (Gen. 16:12); he is the traditional ancestor of Muhammad and of the Arab peoples. □ **Ish·mael·ite** /ˈɪʃmeɪəˌlaɪt/ *noun*

Ish·tar /ˈɪʃtɑr/ *Myth* a Babylonian and Assyrian goddess whose name and functions correspond to those of Astarte.

Isi·dore of Seville, St. /ˈɪzɪˌdɔr/ (Latin name Isidorus Hispalensis) (AD *c.*560–636), Spanish archbishop and Doctor of the Church. He is noted for his *Etymologies*, an encyclopedic work used by many medieval authors. Feast day, 4 Apr.

isin·glass /ˈaɪzɪŋˌɡlas/ *noun* a kind of gelatin obtained from fish, esp. sturgeon, and used in making jellies, glue, etc. [corruption of obsolete Dutch *huisenblas* sturgeon's bladder, assimilated to GLASS]

Isis /ˈaɪsɪs/ *Egyptian Myth* a nature goddess, wife of Osiris and mother of Horus. Her worship spread to western Asia, Greece, and Rome, where she was identified with many and varied local goddesses.

Is·ken·de·run /ɪsˈkɛndəˌruːn/ a port and naval base in S Turkey, on the Mediterranean coast; pop. (est. 2002) 180,400. Formerly named Alexandretta, it lies on or near the site of Alexandria ad Issum, founded by Alexander the Great in 333 BC.

Islam /ˈɪzlam, -lɒm, -ˈlam/ *noun* **1** the religion of the Muslims, a monotheistic faith regarded as revealed through Muhammad as the Prophet of Allah. **2** the Muslim world. □ **Is·lam·ic** *adverb* **Is·lam·ic·ally** *adjective* **Islam·ize** *transitive verb* (also **Islam·i·cize**) (also esp. *Brit.* **-cise**). **Islam·iz·a·tion** *noun* (also **Islam·i·ciz·a·tion**) [Arabic *islām* submission (to God), from *aslama* resign oneself]

Is·lama·bad /ɪzˈlɑːməˌbad/ the capital of Pakistan, a modern planned city in the north of the country, which replaced Rawalpindi as capital in 1967; pop. (1998) 529,200.

Islam·i·cist *noun* **1** a person who is an expert in Islamic culture, history, etc. **2** ISLAMIST. See ISLAMISM.

Islamic state *noun* a state governed under Islamic rather than secular law.

Islam·ism *noun* a political and cultural movement favouring the establishment of Islamic states. □ **Islam·ist** *noun & adjective*

Islam·o·phobia *noun* hatred or fear of Islam or of Muslims, esp. as a political force.

island ● *noun* **1** a piece of land surrounded by water. **2** anything compared to an island, esp. in being isolated or surrounded in some way. **3** a free-standing cupboard unit with a countertop, esp. in a kitchen, allowing access from all sides. **4** = TRAFFIC ISLAND. **5** a clump of woodland surrounded by prairie. **6 a** a detached or isolated thing. **b** *Physiol.* a detached portion of tissue or group of cells (compare ISLET 2). **7** *Naut.* a ship's superstructure, bridge, etc. ● *transitive verb* **1** make into an island. **2** isolate. [Old English *igland* from *ig* island + LAND: first syllable influenced by ISLE]

island arc *noun* a curved chain of esp. volcanic islands typically located at a tectonic plate margin and having a deep trench on the convex side.

island·er *noun* **1** a native or inhabitant of an island. **2** (**Islander**) (in Canada) a native or resident of Prince Edward Island, Vancouver Island, etc.

island-hop *transitive verb* move from one island to another, esp. as a tourist in an area of small islands. □ **island-hopping** *noun*

Island of Montreal see MONTRÉAL, ÎLE DE.

Islands of the Blessed a mythical abode, often located near where the sun sets in the west, to which people in classical times believed the souls of the good were conveyed to a life of bliss.

isle *noun* an island, esp. a small one (esp. in place names). [Middle English *ile* (later *isle*) via Old French *île*, *isle* from Latin *insula*]

Isle of Man an island in the Irish Sea which is a British Crown possession with its own legislature and judicial system; pop. (2001) 76,315; capital, Douglas. Its ancient language, Manx, is still occasionally used for ceremonial purposes.

Isle of Wight /waɪt/ an island off the south coast of England, a county since 1974; pop. (2001) 132,719; administrative centre, Newport.

islet /ˈaɪlət/ *noun* **1** a small island. **2** *Anat.* a portion of tissue structurally distinct from surrounding tissues. [Old French, diminutive of *isle* ISLE]

islets of Lan·ger·hans /ˈlaŋərhanz/ *plural noun* groups of pancreatic cells secreting insulin and glucagon. [P. *Langerhans* (d.1888), German physician]

ism *noun informal* usu. *derogatory* any distinctive but unspecified doctrine or practice of a kind with a name ending in *-ism*.

-ism *suffix* forming nouns, esp. denoting: **1** an action or its result (*baptism*; *organism*). **2** a system, principle, or ideological movement (*Conservatism*; *jingoism*; *feminism*). **3** a state or quality (*heroism*; *barbarism*).

Consonants: b *but*   d *dog*   f *few*   g *get*   h *her*   j *yes*   k *cat*   l *leg*   m *man*   n *no*   p *pen*   r *red*   s *sit*

4 a basis of prejudice or discrimination (*racism*; *sexism*). **5** a peculiarity or characteristic of a nation, individual, etc., esp. in language (*Canadianism*). **6** a pathological condition (*alcoholism*; *Parkinsonism*). [from or after French *-isme* from Latin *-ismus* from Greek *-ismos* or *-isma* from *-izō* -IZE]

Is·maili /ɪzˈmaɪli/ *noun* (*pl.* **Is·mailis**) a member of a Shiite Muslim branch that seceded from the main group in the 8th c. over the question of succession to the position of imam. [*Ismail* a son of the patriarch Ibrāhīm (= Abraham)]

Ismail Sam·ani Peak /ˈɪzmail səˈmɒni/ one of the principal peaks in the Pamir Mountains of Tajikistan, rising to 7 495 m (24,590 ft.). It was known as Mount Garmo until 1933, Stalin Peak until 1962, and Communism Peak until 1998.

isn't *contraction* is not.

ISO *abbreviation* **1** International Organization for Standardization. **2** the numerical exposure index assigned to a photographic film to indicate its sensitivity to light.

iso- /ˈaɪsəʊ/ *combining form* **1** equal (*isometric*). **2** *Chem.* isomeric, esp. of a hydrocarbon with a branched chain of carbon atoms (*isobutane*). [Greek *isos* equal]

iso·bar /ˈaɪsəʊˌbɑr/ *noun* **1** a line on a map connecting positions having the same atmospheric pressure at a given time or on average over a given period. **2** each of two or more isotopes of different elements, with the same atomic weight. □ **iso·bar·ic** /-ˈbɛrɪk/ *adjective* [Greek *isobarēs* of equal weight (as ISO-, *baros* weight)]

iso·chron·ous /aɪˈsɒkrənəs/ *adjective* **1** occurring at the same time. **2** occupying equal time. □ **iso·chron·ous·ly** *adverb* [ISO- + Greek *khronos* time]

iso·clinal /ˌaɪsəʊˈklaɪnəl/ *adjective* **1** *Geol.* (of a fold) in which the two limbs are parallel. **2** corresponding to equal values of magnetic dip. [ISO- + CLINE]

iso·cyan·ate /ˌaɪsəʊˈsaɪəneɪt/ *noun* the radical ·N=C=O, or any of the class of compounds containing this radical, some of which are used in making polyurethane. [ISO- + *cyanate* (as CYANIC ACID + -ATE²)]

iso·elec·tric /ˌaɪsəʊɪˈlɛktrɪk/ *adjective* having or involving no net electric charge or difference in electrical potential.

isoelectric focusing *noun* (also **isoelectric focussing**) *Biochem.* a form of high-resolution electrophoresis.

iso·enzyme /ˈaɪsəʊˌɛnzaɪm/ *noun Biochem.* one of two or more enzymes with identical function but different structure.

iso·fla·vone /ˈaɪsəʊˌfleɪvəʊn/ *noun* a phytoestrogen found in leguminous plants such as chickpeas and soybeans. □ **iso·flavon·oid** *noun*

iso·gloss /ˈaɪsəʊˌɡlɒs/ *noun* a line on a map marking an area having a distinct linguistic feature.

iso·hyet /ˌaɪsəʊˈhaɪɪt/ *noun* a line on a map connecting places having the same amount of precipitation in a given period. [ISO- + Greek *huetos* rain]

iso·kin·etic /ˌaɪsəʊkɪˈnɛtɪk/ *adjective* **1** characterized by or producing a constant speed. **2** *Physiol.* of or relating to muscular action with a constant rate of movement.

iso·late ● *transitive verb* **1 a** place apart or alone, cut off from society. **b** place (a patient thought to be contagious or infectious) in quarantine. **2 a** identify and separate for attention (*isolated the problem*). **b** *Chem.* separate (a substance) from a mixture. **3** insulate (electrical apparatus). ● *adjective* = ISOLATED. ● *noun* **1** an isolated person or thing. **2** a language that is not related historically or structurally to any other known language. □ **isol·able** *adjective* **iso·lat·able** *adjective*

iso·la·tor *noun* [originally in past participle, from French *isolé* from Italian *isolato* from Late Latin *insulatus* from Latin *insula* island]

iso·lat·ed *adjective* **1** lonely; cut off from society or contact; remote (*feeling isolated*; *an isolated farmhouse*). **2** untypical, unique (*an isolated incident*).

iso·lat·ing *adjective* (of a language) having each element as an independent word without inflections.

iso·la·tion *noun* **1** the act or an instance of isolating. **2** the state of being isolated or separated. **3** (*attributive*) designating a hospital ward etc. for patients with contagious or infectious diseases. □ **in isolation** considered singly and not relatively.

iso·la·tion·ism *noun* the policy of holding aloof from the affairs of other countries or groups esp. in politics. □ **iso·la·tion·ist** *noun & adjective*

isolation pay *noun Cdn* a financial supplement to the salary of an employee who works in an isolated area, usu. in the Far North.

Is·olde see ISEULT.

iso·leu·cine /ˌaɪsəʊˈluːsiːn/ *noun Biochem.* an amino acid that is a constituent of proteins and an essential nutrient. [German *Isoleucin* (see ISO-, LEUCINE)]

iso·mer /ˈaɪsəmɛr/ *noun* **1** *Chem.* one of two or more compounds with the same molecular formula but a different arrangement of atoms and different properties. **2** *Physics* one of two or more atomic nuclei that have the same atomic number and the same mass number but different energy states. □ **iso·mer·ic** /-ˈmɛrɪk/ *adjective* **isom·er·ism** /aɪˈsɒməˌrɪzəm/ *noun* **isom·er·ize** /aɪˈsɒməˌraɪz/ *transitive verb* (also esp. *Brit.* **-ise**). **isom·er·iz·a·tion** *noun* [German from Greek *isomerēs* sharing equally (as ISO-, *meros* share)]

iso·met·ric /ˌaɪsəʊˈmɛtrɪk/ *adjective* **1** of equal measure. **2** *Physiol.* (of muscle action) developing tension while the muscle is prevented from contracting. **3** (of a drawing etc.) with the plane of projection at equal angles to the three principal axes of the object shown. **4** *Math.* (of a transformation) without change of shape or size. □ **iso·met·ric·ally** *adverb* **isom·etry** /aɪˈsɒmɪtri/ *noun* (in sense 4). [Greek *isometria* equality of measure (as ISO-, -METRY)]

iso·met·rics /ˌaɪsəʊˈmɛtrɪks/ *plural noun* a system of physical exercises in which muscles are caused to act against each other or against a fixed object.

iso·morph /ˈaɪsəʊˌmɔrf/ *noun* an isomorphic substance or organism. [ISO- + Greek *morphē* form]

iso·morph·ic /ˌaɪsəʊˈmɔrfɪk/ *adjective* (also **iso·morph·ous** /-fəs/) **1** exactly corresponding in form and relations. **2** *Mineralogy* having the same form. □ **iso·morph·ism** *noun*

-ison /ɪsən/ *suffix* forming nouns, = -ATION (*comparison*; *garrison*; *jettison*; *venison*). [Old French *-aison* etc. from Latin *-atio* etc.: see -ATION]

iso·ni·azid /ˌaɪsəʊˈnaɪəzɪd/ *noun* a soluble colourless crystalline compound used as a bacteriostatic drug, esp. in the treatment of tuberculosis. [ISO- + NICOTINE + *hydrazide* (as HYDRAZINE)]

iso·pleth /ˈaɪsəʊˌplɛθ/ *noun* a line on a map connecting places having equal incidence of a geographical or meteorological feature. [ISO- + Greek *plēthos* fullness]

iso·pod /ˈaɪsəʊˌpɒd/ *noun* any crustacean of the order Isopoda, including sowbugs, often parasitic and having a flattened body with seven pairs of legs. [French *isopode* from modern Latin *Isopoda* (as ISO-, Greek *pous podos* foot)]

iso·propyl alcohol /ˌaɪsəˈprəʊpəl/ *noun* a colourless secondary alcohol used in antifreeze and as a solvent. Chem. formula: C_3H_8O.

isos·celes /aɪˈsɒsɪˌliːz/ *adjective* (of a triangle) having two sides equal. [Late Latin from Greek *isoskelēs* (as ISO-, *skelos* leg)]

isos·tasy /aɪˈsɒstəsi/ *noun Geol.* the general state of equilibrium thought to exist within the earth's crust. □ **iso·stat·ic** /ˌaɪsəʊˈstatɪk/ *adjective* **iso·stat·ic·ally** *adverb* [ISO- + Greek *stasis* station]

iso·therm /ˈaɪsəʊˌθɜrm/ *noun* **1** a line on a map connecting places having the same temperature at a given time or on average over a given period. **2** a curve for changes in a physical system at a constant temperature. □ **iso·therm·al** *adjective* **iso·therm·al·ly** *adverb* [French *isotherme* (as ISO-, Greek *thermē* heat)]

iso·ton·ic /ˌaɪsəʊˈtɒnɪk/ *adjective* **1** designating or relating to a solution having the same osmotic pressure as some particular solution (esp. that in a cell, or a body fluid). **2** of or relating to a solution having the same salt concentration as blood, used esp. by athletes to restore lost salt. **3** *Physiol.* (of muscle action) taking place with normal contraction. □ **iso·ton·ic·ally** *adverb* [Greek *isotonos* (as ISO-, TONE)]

iso·tope /ˈaɪsəˌtəʊp/ *noun Chem.* each of two or more forms of an element differing from each other in relative atomic mass, and in nuclear but not chemical properties. □ **iso·top·ic** /-ˈtɒpɪk/ *adjective* **iso·top·ic·ally** *adverb* [ISO- + Greek *topos* place (i.e. in the periodic table of elements)]

iso·tre·tino·in /ˌaɪsəʊtrɛˈtɪnəʊɪn/ *noun* an isomer of retinoic acid, given orally in the treatment of severe acne and other skin disorders. [ISO- + TRETINOIN]

iso·trop·ic /ˌaɪsəʊˈtrɒpɪk/ *adjective* having the same physical properties in all directions (opp. ANISOTROPIC). □ **iso·trop·ic·ally** *adverb* **isot·ropy** /aɪˈsɒtrəpi/ *noun* [ISO- + Greek *tropos* turn]

ISP *noun* Internet service provider.

Ispa·han see ISFAHAN.

I spy *noun* a children's game in which players try to identify something observed by one of them and identified by its colour or initial letter.

Is·rael 1 /ˈɪzriəl, -reɪəl/ a country in the Middle East, on the Mediterranean Sea; pop. (est. 2002) 6,029,529; capital (not recognized as such by the UN), Jerusalem. The modern state of Israel was established as a Jewish homeland in 1948, on land that was at that time part of the British mandated territory of Palestine. **2** /ˈɪzreiel, -rai-/ (also **children of Israel**) the Hebrew nation or people. According to tradition they are descended from the patriarch Jacob (his alternative name was Israel), whose twelve sons became founders of the twelve tribes. **3** /ˈɪzreiel, -rai-/ the northern kingdom of the Hebrews (*c.*930–721 BC), formed after the reign of Solomon, whose inhabitants were carried away to captivity in Assyria (*see* JUDAH). [Hebrew *yisrā'ēl* he that strives with God; see Gen. 32:28]

Is·rae·li /ɪzˈreili/ ● *adjective* of or relating to the modern state of Israel. ● *noun* **1** a native or national of Israel. **2** a person of Israeli descent.

Is·rael·ite /ˈɪzriə‚ləit, -rə‚ləit/ ● *noun* a member of the ancient Hebrew nation or people, esp. an inhabitant of the northern kingdom of the Hebrews (*c.*930–721 BC). ● *adjective* of or relating to the Israelites.

Is·ra·fel /ˈɪzrə‚fel/ (in Muslim tradition) the angel of music, who will sound the trumpet on the Day of Judgment.

Issei /ˈiːsei/ *noun* (*pl.* same) *N Amer.* a member of the first generation of Japanese immigrants to N America, who immigrated in the late 19th and early 20th c. [Japanese, = generation]

ISSN *abbreviation* international standard serial number, a number assigned to periodicals before publication.

issu·ant /ˈɪʃuːənt/ *adjective Heraldry* (esp. of a beast with only the upper part shown) rising from the bottom or top of a bearing.

issue ● *noun* **1 a** a giving out or circulation of shares, notes, stamps, etc. **b** a quantity of coins, supplies, copies of a newspaper or book etc., circulated or put on sale at one time. **c** an item or amount given out or distributed, esp. by a military force. **d** each of a regular series of a magazine etc. (*the May issue*). **2 a** an outgoing, an outflow. **b** a way out, an outlet, esp. the place of the emergence of a stream etc. **3** a point in question; an important subject of debate or litigation. **4** *informal* a problem (*he has commitment issues; airlines with bankruptcy issues*). **5** a result; an outcome; a decision. **6** *Law* children, progeny (*died without issue*). **7** *archaic* a discharge of blood etc. ● *verb* (**issues, issued, issu·ing**) **1** *intransitive* (often foll. by *out, forth*) *literary* go or come out. **2** *transitive* a send forth; publish; put into circulation. **b** (foll. by *to, with*) supply, esp. officially or authoritatively (*issued them with passports; issued orders to the staff*). **3** *intransitive* **a** (often foll. by *from*) be derived or result. **b** (foll. by *in*) end, result. **4** *intransitive* (foll. by *from*) emerge from a condition. □ **at issue 1** under discussion; in dispute. **2** at variance. **make an issue of** make a fuss about; turn into a subject of contention. **take issue** (foll. by *with*) disagree. □ **issu·able** *adjective* **issu·ance** *noun* **issue·less** *adjective* **issu·er** *noun* [Old French ultimately from Latin *exitus* past participle of *exire* EXIT]

-ist *suffix* forming personal nouns (and in some senses related adjectives) denoting: **1** an adherent of a system etc. in *-ism*: *see* -ISM 2 (*Marxist; fatalist*). **2 a** a member of a profession (*pathologist*). **b** a person concerned with something (*tobacconist*). **3** a person who uses a thing (*violinist; balloonist; motorist*). **4** a person who does something expressed by a verb in *-ize* (*plagiarist*). **5** a person who subscribes to a prejudice or practises discrimination (*racist; sexist*). [Old French *-iste*, Latin *-ista* from Greek *-istēs*]

Is·tan·bul /‚ɪstanˈbul/ a port in Turkey on the Bosporus, lying partly in Europe, partly in Asia; pop. (est. 2002) 9,216,400. It was the capital of Turkey from 1453 until 1923, when it was replaced by Ankara. Formerly the Roman city of Constantinople (330–1453), it was built on the site of the ancient Greek city of Byzantium, founded in the 7th c. BC.

isth·mian /ˈɪsmiən, ˈɪsθ-/ *adjective* of or relating to an isthmus, esp. (**Isthmian**) to the Isthmus of Panama or the Isthmus of Corinth.

Isthmian games *plural noun* games held by the ancient Greeks every other year near the Isthmus of Corinth.

isth·mus /ˈɪsməs, ˈɪsθ-/ *noun* **1** a narrow piece of land connecting two larger bodies of land. **2** *Anat.* a narrow part connecting two larger parts. [Latin from Greek *isthmos*]

IT *abbreviation* information technology.

It. *abbreviation* Italian.

it *pronoun* (*possessive* **its**; *pl.* **they**) **1** the thing (or occas. the animal or child) previously named or in question (*took a stone and threw it*). **2** the person in question (*Who is it? It is I; is it a boy or a girl?*). **3** as the subject of an impersonal verb (*it is raining; it is winter; it is Tuesday; it is two kilometres to Whitehorse*). **4** as a substitute for a deferred subject or object (*it is intolerable, this delay; it is silly to talk like that; I take it that you agree*). **5** as a substitute for a vague object (*brazen it out; run for it!*). **6** as the antecedent to a relative word (*it was an owl I heard*). **7** exactly what is needed (*absolutely it*). **8** the extreme limit of achievement. **9** *informal* **a** sexual intercourse. **b** sex appeal. **10** (in children's games) a player who has to perform a required feat, esp. to catch the others. □ **that's**

it *informal* that is: **1** what is required. **2** the difficulty. **3** the end, enough. **this is it** *informal* **1** the expected event is at hand. **2** this is the difficulty. [Old English *hit* neuter of HE]

ital. *abbreviation* italic (type).

Ital·ian ● *noun* **1 a** a native or national of Italy. **b** a person of Italian descent. **2** the Romance language used in Italy and parts of Switzerland. ● *adjective* of or relating to Italy or its people or language. □ **Ital·ian·ize** *transitive verb*

Ital·ian·ate /ɪˈtaljə‚neit/ *adjective* of Italian style or appearance.

Italian bread *noun* a crusty white bread usually baked in large oval loaves.

Italian dressing *noun* a salad dressing of oil and vinegar seasoned with garlic, oregano, basil, dill, fennel, and sometimes minced red pepper.

Italian parsley *noun* a flat-leaved parsley with a stronger flavour than curly-leaved parsley.

Italian sausage *noun* a pork sausage flavoured with anise or fennel seeds and sometimes hot red pepper flakes.

Italian vermouth *noun* a sweet kind of vermouth.

ital·ic /aiˈtalɪk, ɪ-/ ● *adjective* **1 a** *Typography* of the sloping kind of letters now used esp. for emphasis or distinction and in foreign words. **b** (of handwriting) compact and pointed like early Italian handwriting. **2** (**Italic**) of ancient Italy. ● *noun* **1** a letter in italic type. **2** this type. [Latin *italicus* from Greek *italikos* Italian (because introduced by Aldo Manuzio of Venice)]

ital·i·cize /ɪˈtalɪ‚saiz/ *transitive verb* (also esp. *Brit.* **-cise**) print in italics. □ **ital·i·ci·za·tion** *noun*

Ital·iot /ɪˈtaliət/ ● *noun* an inhabitant of the Greek colonies in ancient Italy. ● *adjective* of or relating to the Italiots. [Greek *Italiōtēs* from *Italia* Italy]

Italo- *combining form* Italian; Italian and.

Italy a country in S Europe; pop. (est. 2002) 57,715,625; capital, Rome. Most of mainland Italy forms a peninsula extending south from the Alps into the Mediterranean Sea. There are also several offshore islands, of which the largest are Sicily and Sardinia.

Ita·nagar /‚iːtəˈnʌgər/ a city in the far northeast of India, north of the Brahmaputra River, capital of the state of Arunachal Pradesh; pop. (2001) 35,000.

Itar-Tass /ˈaitɑr/ *noun* the official news agency of Russia. [the initials of Russian *Informatsionnoe telegrafnoe agentstvo Rossii* 'Information Telegraph Agency of Russia' + TASS]

itch ● *noun* **1** an irritation in the skin. **2** an impatient desire; a hankering. **3** (prec. by *the*) (in general use) scabies. ● *intransitive verb* **1** feel an irritation in the skin, causing a desire to scratch it. **2** (usu. foll. by *to* + infin.) (of a person) feel a desire to do something (*am itching to tell you the news*). [Old English *gycce, gyccan* from West Germanic]

itchy *adjective* (**itch·i·er, itch·i·est**) having or causing an itch. □ **have itchy feet** *informal* **1** be restless. **2** have a strong urge to travel. □ **itch·i·ness** *noun*

it'd *contraction* **1** it had. **2** it would.

-ite¹ *suffix* forming nouns meaning 'a person or thing connected with': **1** in names of persons: **a** as natives or residents of a country, city, etc. (*Israelite; Vancouverite*). **b** often *derogatory* as followers of a movement etc. (*pre-Raphaelite; Trotskyite*). **2** in names of things: **a** fossil organisms (*ammonite*). **b** minerals (*graphite*). **c** constituent parts of a body or organ (*somite*). **d** explosives (*dynamite*). **e** commercial products (*ebonite; vulcanite*). **f** salts of acids having names in *-ous* (*nitrite; sulphite*). [from or after French *-ite* from Latin *-ita* from Greek *-itēs*]

-ite² *suffix* **1** forming adjectives (*erudite; favourite*). **2** forming nouns (*appetite*). **3** forming verbs (*expedite; unite*). [from or after Latin *-itus* past participle of verbs in *-ēre, -ere,* and *-ire*]

item ● *noun* **1 a** any of a number of enumerated or listed things. **b** an entry in an account. **2** an article, esp. one for sale (*household items*). **3** a separate or distinct piece of news, information, etc. **4** *informal* a couple in a romantic or sexual relationship. ● *adverb archaic* (introducing the mention of each item) likewise, also. [originally as adv.: Latin, = in like manner, also]

item·ize *transitive verb* (also esp. *Brit.* **-ise**) state or list item by item. □ **item·iza·tion** *noun*

item veto *noun US* = LINE-ITEM VETO.

it·er·ate /ˈɪtə‚reit/ *transitive verb* **1** perform or utter repeatedly. **2** make repeated use of a mathematical or computational procedure, applying it each time to the result of the previous application, typically as a means of obtaining successively closer approximations to the solution of a problem. □ **it·er·a·tion** *noun* [Latin *iterare iterat-* from *iterum* again]

it·era·tive /ˈɪtɜrətɪv/ *adjective Grammar* **1** = FREQUENTATIVE *adjective.* **2** characterized by repeating or being repeated. □ **it·era·tive·ly** *adverb*

Ith·aca /ˈɪθəkə/ an island off the western coast of Greece in the Ionian Sea, the legendary home of Odysseus.

ithy·phal·lic /ˌɪθɪˈfalɪk/ *adjective Gk Hist.* (esp. of a statue of a Greek deity, painting of a satyr, etc.) having an erect penis. [Late Latin *ithyphallicus* from Greek *ithuphallikos* from *ithus* straight, *phallos* PHALLUS]

-itic *suffix* forming adjectives and nouns corresponding to nouns in *-ite*, *-itis*, etc. (*parasitic*; *arthritic*; *syphilitic*). [from or after French *-itique* from Latin *-iticus* from Greek *-itikos*; see -IC]

itin·er·ant /aiˈtɪnɜrənt, ɪ-/ ● *adjective* **1** travelling from place to place. **2** (of a judge, minister, etc.) travelling within a circuit. **3** (of a teacher) working at more than one school. ● *noun* a person who travels from place to place, esp. as a minister etc. □ **itin·er·ancy** *noun* [Late Latin *itinerari* travel, from Latin *iter itiner-* journey]

itin·er·ary /aiˈtɪnɜreri, ɪ-/ *noun* (*pl.* **-aries**) **1** a detailed route. **2 a** a record of a journey. **b** a listing of the departure and arrival times etc. of aircraft, trains, or other means of transport taken on a journey, usu. accompanying the ticket. [Late Latin *itinerarius* (adj.), *-um* (n.) from Latin *iter*: see ITINERANT]

-ition *suffix* forming nouns, = -ATION (*admonition*; *perdition*; *position*). [from or after French *-ition* or Latin *-itio -itionis*]

-itious[1] *suffix* forming adjectives corresponding to nouns in *-ition* (*ambitious*). [Latin *-itio* etc. + -OUS]

-itious[2] *suffix* forming adjectives meaning 'related to, having the nature of' (*adventitious*). [Latin *-icius* + -OUS, commonly written with *t* in medieval Latin manuscripts]

-itis *combining form* forming nouns, esp.: **1** names of inflammatory diseases (*appendicitis*; *bronchitis*). **2** *informal* in extended uses with reference to conditions compared to diseases (*electionitis*). [Greek *-itis*, forming fem. of adjectives in *-itēs* (with *nosos* 'disease' implied)]

-itive *suffix* forming adjectives, = -ATIVE (*positive*; *transitive*). [from or after French *-itif -itive* or Latin *-itivus* from participial stems in *-it-*: see -IVE]

it'll *contraction* it will; it shall.

ITO *abbreviation* International Trade Organization.

Ito /ˈiːtoː/ **Prince Hiro·bumi** (1841–1909), Japanese statesman, premier four times between 1884 and 1901. He was prominent in drafting the Japanese constitution (1889), and helped to establish a bicameral national Diet (1890); he was assassinated by a member of the Korean independence movement.

-itor *suffix* forming agent nouns, usu. from Latin words (sometimes via French) (*creditor*). See also -OR[1].

-itory *suffix* forming adjectives meaning 'relating to or involving (a verbal action)' (*inhibitory*). See also -ORY[2]. [Latin *-itorius*]

-itous *suffix* forming adjectives corresponding to nouns in *-ity* (*calamitous*; *felicitous*). [from or after French *-iteux* from Latin *-itosus*]

its *possessive adjective* of it; of itself (*can see its advantages*). ¶ Care should be taken not to confuse *its* with *it's*. *Its*, meaning 'of or belonging to it', does not have an apostrophe, e.g. *Its handle had fallen off*. The apostrophe is used only in the short form of *it is* or *it has*, e.g. *It's raining*; *It's been a long time since we met*.

it's *contraction* **1** it is. **2** it has. ¶ See Usage Note at ITS.

it·self *pronoun* emphatic and reflexive form of IT. □ **by itself** apart from its surroundings, automatically, spontaneously. **in itself** viewed in its essential qualities (*not in itself a bad thing*).

itsy-bitsy *adjective* (also **itty-bitty**) *informal* usu. *derogatory* tiny, insubstantial, slight. [reduplication of LITTLE, influenced by BIT[1]]

ITU *abbreviation* International Telecommunication Union.

-ity *suffix* forming nouns denoting: **1** quality or condition (*authority*; *humility*; *purity*). **2** an instance or degree of this (a *monstrosity*; *humidity*). [from or after French *-ité* from Latin *-itas -itatis*]

IU *abbreviation* INTERNATIONAL UNIT.

IUD *abbreviation* INTRAUTERINE DEVICE.

-ium *suffix* forming nouns denoting esp.: **1** (also **-um**) names of metallic elements (*uranium*; *tantalum*). **2** a region of the body (*pericardium*; *hypogastrium*). **3** a biological structure (*mycelium*; *prothallium*). [from or after Latin *-ium* from Greek *-ion*]

IV *abbreviation* intravenous.

Ivan I (*c.*1304–40), grand duke of Muscovy 1328–40. He strengthened

and enlarged the duchy, making Moscow the ecclesiastical capital in 1326.

Ivan III (known as 'Ivan the Great') (1440–1505), grand duke of Muscovy 1462–1505. He consolidated and enlarged his territory, defending it against a Tartar invasion in 1480, and adopting the title of 'Ruler of all Russia' in 1472.

Ivan IV (known as 'Ivan the Terrible') (1530–84), grand duke of Muscovy 1533–47 and first czar of Russia 1547–84. His expansionist foreign policy resulted in the capture of Kazan (1552), Astrakhan (1556), and Siberia (1581); the Tartar siege of Moscow (1572) and Ivan's defeat by the Poles in the Livonian War (1558–82) left Russia weak and divided.

Ivan the Great see IVAN III.

Ivan the Terrible see IVAN IV.

I've *contraction* I have.

-ive *suffix* forming adjectives meaning 'tending to, having the nature of', and corresponding nouns (*suggestive*; *corrosive*; *palliative*; *coercive*; *talkative*). □ **-ively** *suffix* **-iveness** *suffix*. [from or after French *-if -ive* from Latin *-ivus*]

iver·mec·tin /ˌaivɜrˈmektɪn/ *noun* a medication used for treating heartworm in dogs. [*i* + *avermectin*, an anthelmintic isolated from the bacterium *Streptomyces avermitilis*]

Ives, Charles (Edward) (1874–1954), US composer. Influenced by popular music and the sounds of everyday life, he developed the use of polytonality, quarter-tones, note-clusters, and aleatoric techniques; he is noted for his second piano sonata *Concord* (1915), and his chamber work *The Unanswered Question* (1906).

IVF *abbreviation* in vitro fertilization.

ivied *adjective* overgrown with ivy.

Ivor·ian /aiˈvɔːrɪən/ ● *noun* a person from Ivory Coast. ● *adjective* relating to Ivory Coast.

Ivory, James (b.1928), US film director. He has made a number of films in partnership with Ismail Merchant, including *Heat and Dust* (1983), *A Room with a View* (1986), and *Howards End* (1992).

ivory (*pl.* **-ies**) ● *noun* **1** a hard creamy-white substance composing the main part of the tusks of an elephant, hippopotamus, walrus, or narwhal. **2** the colour of this. **3** a substance resembling ivory, or made in imitation of it. **4** (usu. in *pl.*) **a** an article made of ivory. **b** *slang* a piano key or a tooth. ● *adjective* of the colour of ivory; creamy white. □ **tickle** (or **tinkle**) **the ivories** *informal* play the piano. [Old French *yvoire* ultimately from Latin *ebur eboris*]

ivory black *noun* black pigment from calcined ivory or bone.

Ivory Coast a country in West Africa, on the Gulf of Guinea; pop. (est. 2002) 16,804,784; capital, Yamoussoukro.

ivory nut *noun* the seed of a corozo palm, *Phytelephas macrocarpa*, used as a source of vegetable ivory for carving: also called COROZO-NUT.

ivory tower *noun* a state or place of seclusion or separation from the ordinary world and the harsh realities of life (*universities are often described as ivory towers*).

Iv·va·vik National Park /ˈɪvəvɪk/ a park in NW Yukon, bordering on the Beaufort Sea and Alaska, established in 1984 to preserve the migratory route of the barren ground caribou. [Inuvialuktun, = place where the young [caribou] are raised]

ivy *noun* (*pl.* **ivies**) **1** a climbing evergreen shrub, *Hedera helix*, with usu. dark green shining five-angled leaves. **2** any of various other climbing plants including ground ivy and poison ivy. [Old English *ifig*]

Ivy League ● *noun* a group of universities in the eastern US, with a reputation for scholastic and social prestige, including Harvard, Princeton, Yale, Columbia, Dartmouth, Cornell, the University of Pennsylvania, and Brown. ● *adjective* of or relating to the schools of the Ivy League or their students. □ **Ivy Leaguer** *noun* [with reference to the ivy traditionally growing over the walls of these institutions]

IWC *abbreviation* International Whaling Commission.

Iwo Jima /ˌiːwoː ˈdʒiːmə/ a small volcanic island, the largest of the Volcano Islands in the W Pacific, 1 222 km (760 miles) south of Tokyo. During the Second World War it was the heavily fortified site of a Japanese air base, and its attack and capture in 1944–5 was one of the severest US campaigns. It was returned to Japan in 1968.

IWW *abbreviation* see INDUSTRIAL WORKERS OF THE WORLD.

ixia /ˈɪksɪə/ *noun* any iridaceous plant of the genus *Ixia* of S Africa, with large showy flowers. [Latin from Greek, a kind of thistle]

Ixion /ɪkˈsaiən/ *Gk Myth* a king who tried to seduce Hera, for which he was punished by being pinned to a fiery wheel that revolved unceasingly through the underworld.

---

uː mood ai my əi pipe au brown ʌu house ei day ɔi boy ã franglais ā Canadien ɔ̃ Brayon   (see over for consonants)

ixnay *interjection slang* no. [pig Latin for NIX]

Iyen·gar /aɪˈjɛnɡɑr/ *noun* a type of hatha yoga focusing on the correct alignment of the body, making use of straps, wooden blocks, and other objects as aids to achieving the correct postures. [B.K.S. *Iyengar* Indian yoga teacher b.1918, who devised it]

-ize *suffix* (also esp. *Brit.* **-ise**) forming verbs, meaning: **1** make or become such (*Canadianize; pulverize; realize*). **2** treat in such a way (*monopolize; pasteurize*). **3 a** follow a special practice (*economize*). **b** have a specified feeling (*sympathize*). **4** affect with, provide with, or subject to (*oxidize; hospitalize*). □ **-ization** *suffix*. **-izer** *suffix*. ¶ Some Canadians mistakenly believe that the *-ise* spelling for this suffix is the "Canadian" spelling because they are aware that Americans use only the *-ize* variant and that the British now prefer the *-ise* variant. However, this British preference is only recent, and *-ize* has always been the preference of Oxford University Press and until recently *The Times* of London, with the justification being that this suffix is ultimately derived from a Greek and Latin spelling in which *z* rather than *s* is used. The vast majority of Canadians who do use the *-ize* spellings are therefore following, not American practice, but former British practice and long-standing Canadian practice. [from or after French *-iser* from Late Latin *-izare* from Greek *-izō*]

Izhevsk /iˈʒɛfsk/ an industrial city in central Russia, capital of the republic of Udmurtia; pop. (est. 2002) 652,400. It was known as Ustinov from 1984 to 1987.

Izmir /ˈɪzmiːr/ a seaport and naval base in W Turkey, on an inlet of the Aegean Sea; pop. (est. 2002) 2,322,500. Formerly known as Smyrna, it is the third largest city in Turkey.

Izmit /ˈɪzmɪt/ a city in NW Turkey, situated on the Gulf of Izmit, an inlet of the Sea of Marmara; pop. (est. 1994) 221,100.

Iznik /ˈɪznɪk/ a town in NW Turkey, situated to the southeast of the Sea of Marmara; pop. (1990) 17,230. Built on the site of ancient Nicaea, it has been a noted centre for the production of coloured tiles since the 16th c.

Consonants: b *but* d *dog* f *few* g *get* h *her* j *yes* k *cat* l *leg* m *man* n *no* p *pen* r *red* s *sit*

Jj

J¹ *noun* (also **j**) (*pl.* **Js** or **J's**) **1** the tenth letter of the alphabet. **2** (as a Roman numeral) = *i* in a final position (*ij*; *vj*).

J² *abbreviation* (also **J.**) **1** Judge. **2** Justice. **3** (in cards) jack. **4** Journal.

J³ *symbol* joule(s).

jab ● *verb* (**jabbed**, **jab·bing**) **1** *transitive* pierce or poke with the end or point of something; stab. **2** *transitive* punch (a person etc.), esp. with a short, sharp blow. **3** *transitive* (foll. by *into*) thrust (a thing) hard or abruptly. **4** *intransitive* punch or poke with short, sharp blows (*jabbed at it with a stick*). ● *noun* **1** an abrupt blow with one's fist or a pointed implement. **2** *N Amer. informal* a satirical or cutting remark or comment. **3** esp. *Brit. informal* a hypodermic injection, esp. a vaccination. [originally Scots var. of *job*, prod]

Jab·al·pur /ˌdʒʌbəlˈpʊr/ an industrial city and military post in Madhya Pradesh, central India; pop. (2001) 951,500.

jab·ber ● *verb* **1** *intransitive* chatter volubly and incoherently. **2** *transitive* utter (words) fast and indistinctly. ● *noun* meaningless jabbering. [imitative]

jab·ber·wocky /ˈdʒæbərˌwɒki/ *noun* (*pl.* **-ies**) a piece of nonsensical writing or speech, esp. for comic effect. [title of a poem in Lewis Carroll's *Through the Looking-Glass* (1871)]

Jabir ibn Hay·yan /ˈdʒɒbiːr ɪbən hɒˈjɒn/ see GEBER.

jab·iru /ˈdʒæbɪˌruː/ *noun* a large stork, *Jabiru mycteria*, of Central and S America. [Tupi-Guarani *jabirú*]

jabo·ran·di /ˌdʒæbəˈrandi/ *noun* (*pl.* **jabo·ran·dis**) **1** any shrub of the genus *Pilocarpus*, of S America. **2** the dried leaflets of this, having diuretic and diaphoretic properties. [Tupi-Guarani *jaburandi*]

ja·bot /ˈʒaboː/ *noun* an ornamental frill or ruffle of lace etc. on the front of a shirt or blouse. [French, originally = crop of a bird]

jaca·mar /ˈdʒækəmɑr/ *noun* a small insect-eating bird with partly iridescent plumage, of the tropical S American family Galbulidae. [French, apparently from Tupi]

jaca·na /ˈdʒækənə, -sənə/ *noun* any of various small tropical wading birds of the family Jacanidae, with elongated toes and hind claws which enable them to walk on floating leaves etc. [Portuguese *jaçanã* from Tupi-Guarani *jasaná*]

jaca·ran·da /ˌdʒækəˈrandə/ *noun* **1** any tropical American tree of the genus *Jacaranda*, with trumpet-shaped blue flowers. **2** any tropical American tree of the genus *Dalbergia*, with hard scented wood. [Tupi-Guarani *jacarandá*]

jack¹ ● *noun* **1** a device for lifting heavy objects, esp. the axle of a vehicle off the ground while changing a wheel etc. **2** a playing card with a picture of a soldier, servant, etc. **3** a ship's flag, esp. one flown from the bow and showing nationality. **4** a female connecting device in an electrical circuit (*telephone jack*). **5** a small white ball in lawn bowling, at which the players aim. **6 a** = JACKSTONE. **b** (in *pl.*) a game of jackstones. **7** (**Jack**) the familiar form of *John* esp. typifying the common man (*I'm all right, Jack*). **8** *US slang* money. **9** *N Amer. informal* = LUMBERJACK. **10** = STEEPLEJACK. **11** a device for turning a spit. **12 a** any of various marine perch-like fish of the family Carangidae, including the amberjack. **b** a pike or pickerel. **13** the male of various animals (*jackass*). **14** a species or variety of animal smaller than other similar kinds. **15** a device for plucking the string of a harpsichord etc., one being operated by each key. **16** *Cdn (Nfld) hist.* = JACK BOAT. **17** *N Amer. slang* = JACK SHIT (*doesn't know jack about it*). **18** esp. *US* a mild cheddar cheese. ● *verb* **1** *transitive* (usu. foll. by *up*) **a** raise (a car, etc.) with or as with a jack (in sense 1). **b** *informal* increase (prices, volume, etc.) (*jacked up the rent; jack up the volume on the TV*). **2** *transitive & intransitive N Amer.* hunt or fish using a jacklight. □ **every man jack** each and every person. **jack around** *N Amer. slang* deal deceitfully or dishonestly with. **jack into** *slang* access (the Internet, a home page, etc.). **jack off** *coarse slang* masturbate. [Middle English *Iakke*, a pet name for *John*, erroneously associated with French *Jacques* James]

jack² *noun* **1** *hist.* = BLACKJACK². **2** *hist.* a sleeveless padded tunic worn by foot soldiers. [Old French *jaque*, of uncertain origin]

jack³ *transitive verb slang* **1** steal. **2** mug. [from HIJACK]

jack·al /ˈdʒækəl/ *noun* any of various wild doglike mammals of the genus *Canis*, esp. *C. aureus*, found in Africa and S Asia, usu. hunting or scavenging for food in packs. [Turkish *çakal* from Persian *šagāl*]

jack·a·napes /ˈdʒækəˌneips/ *noun archaic* **1** an impertinent person. **2** a mischievous child. **3** a tame monkey. [earliest as *Jack Napes* (1450): supposed to refer to the Duke of Suffolk, whose badge was an ape's clog and chain]

Jack and Jill *N Amer.* ● *adjective* **1** (of a competition, etc.) open to both women and men. **2** designating a party held for a couple soon to be married, in which both men and women are invited. ● *noun* a Jack and Jill party. [from the personal names *Jack* and *Jill*, influenced by the nursery rhyme 'Jack and Jill went up the hill']

jack·ass *noun* **1** a male donkey or ass. **2** a stupid person.

jack boat *noun Cdn (Nfld) hist.* a small fishing schooner with two masts.

jack·boot *noun* **1** a large boot reaching above the knee worn chiefly by soldiers, e.g. those under the Nazi regime. **2** this as a symbol of fascism or military oppression. □ **jack·boot·ed** *adjective*

jack cheese *noun N Amer.* = MONTEREY JACK.

jack·daw *noun* a small grey-headed Eurasian bird of the crow family, *Corvus monedula*, often frequenting rooftops and nesting in tall buildings, and noted for its inquisitiveness. [JACK¹ + DAW]

jacked *adjective* (also **jacked up**) *slang* **1** excited. **2** intoxicated.

jack·et ● *noun* **1 a** a sleeved short outer garment. **b** a thing worn esp. round the torso for protection or support (*life jacket*). **2** a casing or covering, e.g. as insulation around a boiler. **3** = DUST JACKET. **4** the skin of a potato, esp. when baked whole. **5** an animal's coat. ● *transitive verb* (**jack·et·ed**, **jack·et·ing**) cover with a jacket. □ **jack·et·ed** *adjective* **jacket·less** *adjective* [Old French *ja(c)quet* diminutive of *jaque* JACK²]

jacket potato *noun Brit.* a baked potato served with the skin on.

jack·fish *noun* (*pl.* same) = PIKE¹.

Jack Frost *noun* frost personified.

jack·fruit *noun* **1** an East Indian tree, *Artocarpus heterophyllus*, bearing fruit resembling breadfruit. **2** this fruit. [Portuguese *jaca* from Malayalam *chakka* + FRUIT]

jack·ham·mer esp. *N Amer.* ● *noun* a portable pneumatic hammer or drill. ● *transitive verb* drill or break up using a jackhammer.

jack-in-the-box *noun* a toy in the form of a box with a figure inside on a spring that jumps up when the lid is opened.

jack-in-the-pulpit *noun* any of several small woodland plants of the arum family, in N America esp. of the genus *Arisaema*. [from the erect spadix overarched by the spathe, resembling a person in a pulpit]

jack·knife ● *noun* (*pl.* **-knives**) **1** a large pocket knife. **2** a dive in which the body is first bent at the waist and then straightened. ● *verb* (**-knifed**, **-knif·ing**) **1** *intransitive* (of an articulated vehicle) fold against itself in an accidental skidding movement. **2** *intransitive & transitive* fold like a jackknife. **3** *intransitive* perform a jackknife dive.

jack·light *N Amer.* ● *noun* a light used illegally as a lure when hunting or fishing at night. ● *intransitive verb* hunt or fish using a jacklight. □ **jack·light·er** *noun* **jack·light·ing** *noun*

jack of all trades *noun* a person who can do many different kinds of work.

jack-off *noun coarse slang* **1** an act of masturbation. **2** a stupid or contemptible person.

jack-o'-lantern *noun* **1** a lantern made esp. from a hollowed-out pumpkin carved to resemble a face. **2** a will-o'-the wisp.

Jack pine *noun* a pine of northern N America, *Pinus banksiana*, with short needles.

jack plane *noun* a long heavy carpenter's plane used for rough work.

jack·pot *noun* a large prize or amount of winnings, esp. accumulated in a game or lottery etc. □ **hit the jackpot** *informal* **1** win a large prize. **2** have remarkable luck or success. [JACK¹ *noun* 2 + POT¹: originally in a form of poker with two jacks as minimum to open the pool]

jack·rabbit *noun* any of various large N American prairie hares of the genus *Lepus* with very long ears and hind legs.

Jack Rus·sell *noun* (in full **Jack Russell terrier**) a breed of terrier with short legs. [Rev. John (*Jack*) *Russell*, English clergyman and dog breeder d.1883]

jack shit *noun* esp. *US coarse slang* nothing at all; anything at all.

jack·snipe *noun* a small Eurasian snipe, *Lymnocryptes minimus*.

Jack·son¹ the state capital of Mississippi; pop. (2000) 184,256.

Jack·son² ▸ **1 Alex·an·der Young** (1882–1974), Canadian painter and writer, a leading member of the Group of Seven. His landscapes of various remote areas of Canada depict a country that is rolling and unpopulated. **2 An·drew** (known as 'Old Hickory') (1767–1845), US general and Democratic politician, 7th president of the US 1829–37. He defeated the British army at New Orleans (1815) and successfully invaded Florida (1818); he strengthened presidential powers and made many patronage appointments. **3 Don·ald** (b.1940), Canadian figure skater. The winner of the Canadian senior men's figure skating championship from 1959 to 1962, he won the bronze medal in the Olympics and placed second in the world championships in 1960. After winning the world title in 1962, he turned professional, and won the world professional championship in 1970. **4 Ma·ha·lia** (1911–72), US gospel singer. A prominent civil rights activist in the 1950s and 1960s, she is known for her renditions of songs such as 'Move on up a Little Higher' (1945) and 'We Shall Overcome' (1968). **5 Mi·chael (Joe)** (b.1958), US singer and songwriter. He first came to prominence in the 1970s with his four older brothers in the pop group the Jackson Five; his successful solo career began with the album *Off the Wall* (1979), and subsequent albums, including *Bad* (1987), confirmed his status as the most commercially successful US star of the decade. **6 Thom·as Jona·than** (known as 'Stonewall Jackson') (1824–63), US Confederate general in the American Civil War, who got his nickname from the firmness of his resistance to the Northern army at the battle of Bull Run in 1861. He was shot and killed accidentally by one of his own soldiers at the battle of Chancellorsville. **7 Wil·liam Henry** (also known as Honoré Joseph Jaxon) (1861–1952), Canadian-born labour leader, secretary to Louis Riel 1884–87. As the secretary of the farmers' union in Prince Albert, he met Riel and became sympathetic to the Metis cause. Moving to Batoche, he converted first to Catholicism and then to Riel's new religion. He was found insane and committed to an asylum following the Riel rebellion, but escaped to the US where he spent most of his life as a union organizer in Chicago. □ **Jack·son·ian** /ˌdʒakˈsɔːniən/ *noun*

Jack·son·ville an industrial city and port in NE Florida; pop. (2000) 735,617.

jack·staff *noun Naut.* **1** a staff at the bow of a ship for a jack. **2** a staff carrying the flag that is to show above the masthead.

jack·stone *noun* **1** a small piece of metal etc. used with others in tossing games. *Also called* JACK¹ *noun* 6a. **2** (in *pl.*) **a** a game with a ball and jackstones. **b** the game of jacks.

jack·straw *noun* **1** a thin strip of wood etc., esp. as used in the game of jackstraws. **2** (in *pl.*) a game in which a heap of jackstraws is to be removed one at a time without moving the others.

Jack tar *noun* a sailor.

Jack the Ripper (19th c.), an unidentified English murderer, who brutally killed at least six prostitutes in the East End of London between August and November 1888.

Jacob a Hebrew patriarch, the younger of the twin sons of Isaac and Rebecca, who persuaded his brother Esau to sell him his birthright and tricked him out of his father's blessing (Gen. 25, 27); his twelve sons became the founders of the twelve tribes of ancient Israel.

Jaco·bean /ˌdʒakəˈbiːən/ ● *adjective* **1** of or relating to the reign of James I of England. **2** (of furniture) in the style prevalent then, esp. of the colour of dark oak. ● *noun* a person of the time of James I. [modern Latin *Jacobaeus* from ecclesiastical Latin *Jacobus* 'James', from Greek *Iakōbos* Jacob]

Jac·obi ▸ **1** /ˈdʒakəbi/ **Derek (George)** (b.1938), English actor, who is noted for his performances in Shakespearean roles, the title role in the television series *I, Claudius* (1976) and *Cadfael* (1994), and films, including *Dead Again* (1991). **2** /dʒəˈkoːbi/ **Karl Gus·tav Jacob** (1804–51), German mathematician. He worked on the theory of elliptic functions independently of Niels Abel, and investigated number theory and differential equations; his work on determinants is important in dynamics and quantum mechanics.

Jaco·bin /ˈdʒakəbɪn/ *noun* **1** *hist.* a member of a democratic club established in Paris in 1789. The Jacobins were among the most radical and ruthless of the political groups formed in the wake of the French Revolution, championing the poor and the people of Paris. In association with Robespierre they instituted the Terror of 1793-4. **2** any extreme radical. □ **Jaco·bin·ic** /-ˈbɪnɪk/ *adjective* **Jaco·bin·ic·al** /-ˈbɪnɪkəl/ *adjective* **Jaco·bin·ism** *noun* [Old French from medieval Latin *Jacobinus* from ecclesiastical Latin *Jacobus* 'James'. The term was applied to the Dominican friars in Old French in reference to their church in Paris, St-Jacques, near which they built their first convent; the building eventually became the headquarters of the French revolutionary group]

Jaco·bite /ˈdʒakəˌbɔɪt/ *noun* a supporter of the deposed James II and his descendants in their claim to the British throne after the Revolution of 1688. The Jacobites, who drew most of their support from Catholic clans of the Scottish Highlands, launched three serious attempts to regain the throne in 1689–90, 1715, and 1745-6, but support finally collapsed when the clans were suppressed after the Battle of Culloden. □ **Jaco·bit·ism** *noun*

Ja·cobs, Jane (b.1916), US-born Canadian urban theorist, who is known for her influential books on urban planning and design; these include *The Death and Life of Great American Cities* (1961).

Jacob's ladder *noun* **1** a plant, *Polemonium caeruleum*, with corymbs of blue or white flowers, and leaves suggesting a ladder. **2** *Naut.* a rope or chain ladder. [from Jacob's dream of a ladder reaching to heaven, as described in Gen. 28:12]

jaco·net /ˈdʒakənət/ *noun* a lightweight cotton cloth with a smooth and slightly stiff finish. [Urdu *jagannāthī* from *Jagannath* (now Puri) in India, its place of origin: see JUGGERNAUT]

Jac·quard /ˈdʒakɑːrd/ **Jo·seph Marie** (1752–1834), French inventor, who designed the innovative weaving device named after him (1805).

jac·quard /ˈdʒakɑːrd/ *noun* **1** an apparatus with perforated cards, fitted to a loom to facilitate the weaving of figured fabrics. **2** (in full **jacquard loom**) a loom fitted with this. **3** a fabric or article made with this, with an intricate variegated pattern. [JACQUARD]

Jacques-Cartier, Mont /ˌʒakkɑːrtˈjei/ the highest mountain (1 268 m) in the Chic-Chocs mountain range of E Quebec, situated southeast of Sainte-Anne-des-Monts. [J. CARTIER]

Jacques Cartier Strait /ˌʒak kɑːrtˈjei/ a northern channel linking the St. Lawrence River and the Gulf of St. Lawrence. It separates Anticosti Island from the north shore of E Quebec. [J. CARTIER]

jacti·ta·tion /ˌdʒaktɪˈteiʃən/ *noun Med.* **1** the restless tossing of the body in illness. **2** the twitching of a limb or muscle. [earlier *jactation*, from Latin *jactare* throw]

Ja·cuzzi /dʒəˈkuːzi/ *noun* (*pl.* **Ja·cuz·zis**) proprietary **1** = WHIRLPOOL BATH (see WHIRLPOOL 2). **2** = HOT TUB. [C. *Jacuzzi*, American inventor, d.1986]

jade¹ ● *noun* **1 a** a hard usu. green stone composed of silicates of calcium and magnesium, or of sodium and aluminum, used for ornaments and implements. **b** an ornament etc. made of jade. **2** the green colour of jade. ● *adjective* of this colour. [French *le jade* for *l'ejade*, from Spanish *piedra de ijada* 'stone of the flank', i.e. stone for colic (which it was believed to cure)]

jade² *noun* **1** an inferior or worn-out horse. **2** *derogatory* a disreputable woman. [Middle English: origin unknown]

jaded *adjective* tired, bored or lacking enthusiasm, typically after having had too much of something. □ **jaded·ly** *adverb* **jaded·ness** *noun*

jade·ite *noun* a green, blue, or white sodium aluminum silicate form of jade.

Vowels: a *cat* ɑ *arm* e *bed* ɜr *her* ɜː *deux* ə *ago* ɪ *sit* i *cosy* iː *feed* ɒ *hot* ɔ *pore* ɔː *no* ʌ *run* ʊ *put*

jade plant *noun* a succulent plant, *Crassula argentea*, with thick shiny dark green leaves, frequently grown as a houseplant.

j'adoube /ʒaˈduːb/ *interjection* Chess a declaration by a player intending to adjust the placing of a piece without making a move with it. [French, = I adjust]

jae·ger /ˈjeigər/ *noun* N Amer. a seabird of the skua family, esp. one of the smaller kinds, of the genus *Stercorarius*. [German *Jäger* hunter, from *jagen* to hunt]

Jaffa[1] a city and port on the Mediterranean coast of Israel, forming a southern suburb of the Tel Aviv conurbation, and since 1949 united with Tel Aviv.

Jaffa[2] *noun* Brit. a large oval thick-skinned variety of orange. [JAFFA[1], near where it was first grown]

Jaff·na a city and port on the Jaffna peninsula at the northern tip of Sri Lanka; pop. (est. 2002) 162,000. It has a predominantly Tamil population and until the 17th c. was the capital of a Tamil monarchy.

JAG /dʒag/ *abbreviation* = JUDGE ADVOCATE GENERAL.

jag[1] ● *noun* a sharp projection of rock etc. ● *transitive verb* (**jag·ged**, **jag·ging**) **1** cut or tear unevenly. **2** make indentations in. [Middle English, prob. imitative]

jag[2] *noun* esp. N Amer. informal **1** a drinking bout; a spree. **2** a period of indulgence in an activity, emotion, etc. (*a crying jag*). **3** a load of (hay, logs, etc.). [originally = load for one horse: 16th c., origin unknown]

jagd·wurst /ˈjɒgdwərst/ *noun* a cured German sausage with chunks of ham in a pâté base, often with whole mustard seeds, pistachios, and pimentos. [German, = 'hunter's sausage']

jag·ged /ˈdʒagɪd/ *adjective* **1** with an unevenly cut or torn edge. **2** deeply indented; with sharp points. **3** having a harsh or irregular quality; not smooth. □ **jag·ged·ly** *adverb* **jag·ged·ness** *noun*

Jag·ger, Sir Mick (full name Michael Philip Jagger) (b.1943), English rock singer and songwriter. As the lead singer of the Rolling Stones he has become an international celebrity; his songs with the group include 'Satisfaction' (1965) and 'Start Me Up' (1981).

jaggy *adjective* (**jag·gi·er**, **jag·gi·est**) **1** = JAGGED. **2** Scot. prickly.

jag·uar /ˈdʒagwər, -juər/ *noun* a large carnivorous feline, *Panthera onca*, of Central and S America, mainly yellowish-brown with dark spots grouped in rosettes. [Tupi-Guarani *jaguara*]

jag·uar·undi /ˌdʒagwəˈrʌndi/ *noun* (pl. **jag·uar·un·dis**) a wild cat, *Felis yagouaroundi*, larger than the domestic cat, with a long body and tail and inhabiting forest and scrub from Arizona to Argentina. [Tupi-Guarani]

Jah /dʒɑː, jɑː/ *noun* the Rastafarian name of God. [representing Hebrew *Yāh*, abbreviation of YAHWEH]

jai alai /ˌhaiəˈlai/ *noun* a game like pelota played with large curved wicker baskets. [Spanish from Basque *jai* festival + *alai* merry]

jail (also esp. Brit. **gaol**) ● *noun* **1** a public prison for the detention of persons committed by process of law. **2** confinement in a jail. ● *transitive verb* put in jail. [Old French *jaiole* from Romanic diminutive of Latin *cavea* CAGE]

jail·bait *noun* slang a young woman, or young women collectively, considered in sexual terms but under the age of consent.

jail·bird *noun* a prisoner or habitual criminal.

jail·break *noun* an escape from jail.

jail·er *noun* (also **jail·or**, esp. Brit. **gaoler**) **1** a person in charge of a jail or of the prisoners in it. **2** a person who keeps another person forcibly confined.

jail·house *noun* esp. N Amer. a prison.

jail yard *noun* a yard enclosed within a prison's walls.

Jain /dʒain/ ● *noun* an adherent of a non-Brahmanical Indian religion characterized by its stress on non-violence and strict asceticism as means to liberation. ● *adjective* of or relating to this religion. □ **Jain·ism** *noun* **Jain·ist** *noun* [Hindi from Sanskrit *jainas* saint, victor, from *jina* victorious]

Jai·pur /dʒaiˈpʊr/ a city in W India, the capital of Rajasthan; pop. (2001) 2,324,300.

Ja·kar·ta /dʒəˈkɑrtə/ (also **Djakarta**) the capital of Indonesia, situated in NW Java; pop. (est. 2002) 10,810,400.

jake *adjective* slang all right; satisfactory. [20th c.: origin uncertain]

Jal·an·dhar see JULLUNDUR.

Ja·lapa /hɑˈlɒpɑ/ (in full **Ja·lapa En·rí·quez** /enˈriːkez/) a city in east central Mexico, capital of the state of Veracruz; pop. (est. 2002) 387,700.

jala·peno /halɑˈpiːnɔː, -ˈpiːnjɔː, -ˈpeinjɔː/ *noun* (pl. **-penos**) (also

jalapeno pepper) a very hot green chili pepper, used esp. in Mexican-style cooking. [Latin American Spanish (*chile*) *jalapeño*]

Jal·isco /həˈliːskɔː/ a state of west central Mexico, on the Pacific coast; capital, Guadalajara.

jal·opy /dʒəˈlɒpi/ *noun* (pl. **-ies**) informal a dilapidated old car, truck, etc. [20th c.: origin unknown]

jal·ou·sie /ˈʒaləˌziː/ *noun* a blind or shutter made of a row of angled slats to keep out rain etc. and control the influx of light. [French (as JEALOUSY)]

Jam. *abbreviation* **1** Jamaica. **2** James (New Testament).

jam[1] ● *transitive & intransitive verb* (**jammed**, **jam·ming**) **1 a** *transitive* (usu. foll. by *into*) squeeze or wedge into a space. **b** *transitive* (usu. foll. by *in*) bruise or crush by pressure (*jammed my finger in the drawer*). **c** *intransitive* become wedged. **2 a** *transitive* cause (machinery or a component) to become wedged or immovable so that it cannot work. **b** *intransitive* become jammed in this way. **3** *transitive* push or cram together in a compact mass. **4** *intransitive* (foll. by *in*, *on to*) push or crowd (*they jammed on to the bus*). **5 a** *transitive* block (a passage, road, etc.) by crowding or obstructing. **b** *transitive* (foll. by *in*) obstruct the exit of (*we were jammed in*). **c** *intransitive* (of ice, logs, etc.) form an obstruction in a river, stream, etc. **6** *transitive* (usu. foll. by *on*) **a** apply (brakes etc.) forcefully or abruptly. **b** put on (an item of clothing etc.) in a determined or angry manner (*jammed his hat on his head and walked out the door*). **7** *transitive* make (a radio transmission) unintelligible by causing interference. **8** *intransitive* informal (in jazz etc.) extemporize with other musicians. ● *noun* **1** a squeeze or crush. **2** a crowded mass (*traffic jam*). **3** informal an awkward situation or predicament. **4** a stoppage (of a machine etc.) due to jamming. **5** (in full **jam session**) informal improvised playing by a group of jazz etc. musicians. □ **jam·mer** *noun* [imitative]

jam[2] *noun* a conserve of fruit and sugar boiled to a thick consistency. [perhaps = JAM[1]]

Ja·maica an island country in the Caribbean Sea, southeast of Cuba; pop. (est. 2002) 2,680,029; capital, Kingston. □ **Ja·mai·can** *adjective* & *noun*

Jamaican patty *noun* a half-moon shaped turnover with yellow pastry with a spicy filling of ground meat.

Jamaican satinwood *noun* see SATINWOOD 1b.

jamb /dʒam/ *noun* Archit. a side post or surface of a doorway, window, or fireplace. [Old French *jambe* ultimately from Late Latin *gamba* hoof]

jam·ba·laya /ˌdʒambəˈlaiə/ *noun* **1** a Cajun dish of rice with shrimps, chicken, etc. **2** a mixture; jumble. [Louisiana French from modern Provençal *jambalaia*]

jam·bo·ree /ˌdʒambəˈriː/ *noun* **1** a celebration or merrymaking. **2** a large rally of Scouts. [19th c.: origin unknown]

jam·bust·er *noun* Cdn (Man. & NW Ont.) a jelly-filled doughnut.

James ▸ 1 Henry (1843–1916), US-born English novelist, short-story writer, and critic. He settled in England in 1876, and his novels often explore the relationship between European civilization and American life, and include *The Portrait of a Lady* (1881), *The Bostonians* (1886), and *The Ambassadors* (1903); he was the brother of William James. **2 Jesse (Wood·son)** (1847–82), US outlaw, who joined with his brother Frank (1843–1915) and others to form a notorious band of outlaws, specializing in bank and train robberies. **3 Dame Phyl·lis Dor·othy** (b.1920), English writer of detective fiction. She is noted for her novels featuring the poet-detective Adam Dalgleish, including *Death of an Expert Witness* (1977) and *A Taste for Death* (1986). **4 St.** (known as 'James the Great') (died AD 44), an Apostle, son of Zebedee, and brother of John. He was put to death by Herod Agrippa I; afterwards, according to a Spanish tradition, his body was taken to Santiago de Compostela. Feast day, 25 July. **5 St.** (known as 'James the Less') (died AD 62), an Apostle. Feast day (in the Eastern Church) 9 October; (in the Western Church) 1 May. **6 a St.** (died AD 61), leader of the Church at Jerusalem, who was put to death by the Sanhedrin. Feast day, 1 May. **b** the epistle of the New Testament traditionally ascribed to him. **7 Thom·as** (1593–1635), English explorer of northern Canada. In 1631 he sailed from Bristol to Hudson Bay, and explored the west coast of James Bay, which he named after himself. He was the first European to deliberately winter in the north, spending a miserable winter on Charlton Island, and returned to England in 1632 without finding the northwest passage. **8 Wil·liam** (1842–1910), US philosopher and psychologist. A leading exponent of pragmatism, he sought a functional definition of truth rather than a depiction of a structural relation between ideas and reality, and his works include *The Will to Believe* (1907) and *The Meaning of Truth* (1909); he was the brother of Henry James.

James I ▸ 1 (1394–1437), son of Robert III, king of Scotland 1406–37.

Captured by the English while a child, James remained a captive until 1424; he returned to a country divided by baronial feuds, but managed to restore some measure of royal authority. **2** (1566–1625), son of Mary, Queen of Scots, king of Scotland (as James VI) 1567–1625, and of England and Ireland 1603–25. He inherited the English throne on the death of Elizabeth I, and his declaration of the divine right of kings, favouritism towards the Duke of Buckingham, and intended alliance with Spain made him unpopular with Parliament.

James II ▸ 1 (1430–60), son of James I, king of Scotland 1437–60. After ascending the throne as a minor, he eventually overthrew his regents and considerably strengthened the position of the Crown by crushing the powerful Douglas family (1452–5). **2** (1633–1701), son of Charles I, king of England, Ireland, and (as James VII) Scotland 1685–8. His Catholic beliefs led to the rebellion of the Duke of Monmouth (1685) and to his deposition in favour of William of Orange and Mary II (1688); attempts to regain the throne resulted in James's defeat at the Battle of the Boyne (1690), and he died in exile in France.

James III ▸ (1452–88), son of James II, king of Scotland 1460–88. He proved increasingly unable to control his nobles who eventually raised an army against him in 1488, using his son, the future James IV, as a figurehead.

James IV (1473–1513), son of James III, king of Scotland 1488–1513. He re-established royal power throughout the realm and forged a dynastic link with England by marrying Margaret Tudor, the daughter of Henry VII; in 1513 he invaded England and was killed when his army was defeated at Flodden.

James V (1512–42), son of James IV, king of Scotland 1513–42. During his reign Scotland was dominated by French interests; relations with England deteriorated in the later years of his reign, culminating in an invasion by Henry VIII's army and the defeat of James's troops near the border at Solway Moss in 1542.

James VI the Scottish title of James I of England.

James VII the Scottish title of James II of England.

James Bay a shallow southern arm of Hudson Bay. Though it straddles the border between Ontario and Quebec its islands are administered by Nunavut. [T. JAMES]

Jame·son Raid /ˈdʒeɪmsən/ an abortive raid into Boer territory made in 1895 by pro-British extremists led by Dr L. S. Jameson, which seriously heightened tension in South Africa and contributed to the eventual outbreak of the Second Boer War.

James·town 1 a British settlement established in Virginia in 1607, during the reign of King James I. Built on a marshy and unhealthy site, it was abandoned when the state capital of Virginia was moved to Williamsburg at the end of the 17th c. **2** the capital and chief port of the island of St. Helena; pop. (est. 2002) 1,500.

jam·mies plural noun N Amer. slang = PYJAMAS 1. [abbreviation]

Jammu /ˈdʒʌmuː/ a town in NW India; pop. (2001) 378,400. It is the winter capital of the state of Jammu and Kashmir.

Jammu and Kashmir a mountainous state of NW India, at the western end of the Himalayas; capitals, Srinagar (in summer) and Jammu (in winter). See also KASHMIR.

jammy adjective (**jam·mi·er, jam·mi·est**) **1** of or like jam in taste, consistency, etc. **2** Brit. informal lucky.

Jam·nagar /dʒʌmˈnʌgər/ a port and walled city in the state of Gujarat, W India; pop. (2001) 446,700. It was famous in the past for its pearl fishing and for its tie-dyed fabrics.

jam-packed adjective informal full to capacity.

jam-pail curling noun Cdn (Prairies) a form of curling in which the rocks are replaced by ice-filled four-pound jam tins, with a bent steel rod serving as a handle.

jam session noun see JAM¹ noun 5.

Jam·shed·pur /ˌdʒʌmˈʃedˈpʊr/ an industrial city in the state of Bihar, NE India; pop. (2001) 570,300.

Jam·shid /dʒʌmˈʃiːd/ a legendary early king of Persia, reputed inventor of the arts of medicine, navigation, and ironworking. According to legend, he was king of the peris (or fairies), condemned to assume human form for boasting of his immortality, and ruled Persia for 700 years.

Jan. abbreviation January.

Janá·ček /ˈjanəˌtʃek/ **Leoš** (1854–1928), Czech composer. He was greatly influenced by Czech folk music and the rhythms of Czech speech, and is best known for his nine operas, notably Jenůfa (1904) and The Cunning Little Vixen (1924), the Sinfonietta (1926), and the Glagolitic Mass (1927).

Jane Doe noun a woman whose name is unknown.

jan·gle ● verb **1** intransitive & transitive make, or cause (a bell etc.) to make, a harsh metallic sound. **2** transitive irritate (the nerves etc.) by discordant sound or speech etc. ● noun a harsh metallic sound. □ **jan·gly** adjective [Old French jangler, of uncertain origin]

janis·sary /ˈdʒanəseri/ noun (also **jani·zary** /-zeri/) (pl. **-ies**) **1** (often **Janissary**) hist. a member of the Turkish infantry forming the Sultan's guard and the main fighting force of the Turkish army from the late 14th to early 19th c. **2** a devoted follower or supporter. [ultimately from Turkish yeniçeri from yeni new + çeri troops]

jani·tor /ˈdʒanɪtər/ noun a caretaker of a school, office building, etc., responsible for its cleaning, heating, etc. □ **jani·tor·ial** adjective [Latin from janua door]

janny (pl. **-nies**) (also **janney**) Cdn (Nfld) ● noun a costumed person who participates in group festivities and pranks at Christmas; a mummer. ● intransitive verb (often foll. by up) participate in mumming activities. □ **janny·ing** noun [prob. var. of JOHNNY]

Jan·sen /ˈdʒansən/ **Cor·nel·ius Otto** (1585–1638), Flemish Roman Catholic theologian. He was made bishop of Ypres in 1636, and his major work, the four-volume Augustinus (1640), emphasized St. Augustine's teachings on grace, predestination, and free will, and formed the basis of the anti-Jesuit movement known as Jansenism.

Jan·sen·ism /ˈdʒansəˌnɪzəm/ noun a Christian movement of the 17th and 18th c., based on the writings of Jansen and characterized by asceticism and moral rigour. Its most famous exponent was Pascal. □ **Jan·sen·ist** noun

Janu·ary noun (pl. **-aries**) the first month of the year. [Latin Januarius (mensis) (month) of Janus]

Janus /ˈdʒeɪnəs/ Rom. Myth an ancient Italian deity, guardian of doorways, gates, and beginnings, and protector of the state in time of war; he is usually represented with two faces, so that he looks both forwards and backwards.

Jap noun & adjective informal offensive = JAPANESE. [abbreviation]

Japan a country in E Asia, occupying an archipelago in the Pacific roughly parallel with the east coast of the Asiatic mainland; pop. (est. 2002) 126,974,628; capital, Tokyo. [a rendering of Chinese Riben, a form of Nippon, the Japanese name of the country, lit. 'rising sun']

Japan, Sea of the sea between Japan and the mainland of Asia.

japan ● noun **1** a hard usu. black varnish, esp. of a kind brought originally from Japan. **2** work in a Japanese style. ● transitive verb (**ja·panned, japan·ning**) **1** varnish with japan. **2** make black and glossy as with japan. [JAPAN]

Jap·an·ese ● noun (pl. same) **1 a** a native or national of Japan. **b** a person of Japanese descent. **2** the language of Japan. ● adjective of or relating to Japan, its people, or its language. □ **Japan·ese·ness** noun

Japanese beetle noun a chafer, Popillia japonica, which is a plant pest in eastern N America.

Japanese cedar noun = CRYPTOMERIA.

Japanese knotweed noun a tall Japanese plant, Polygonum japonica, with clusters of small white flowers, grown for ornament and now widely naturalized.

Japanese lantern noun = CHINESE LANTERN.

Japanese maple noun any of several maples native to Japan cultivated for their decorative foliage.

Japanese print noun a colour print from woodblocks.

Japanese quince noun = JAPONICA.

Japan·ima·tion noun = ANIME. [blend of JAPAN + ANIMATION]

jape ● noun a jest or joke. ● intransitive verb say or do something in jest or mockery; joke. □ **japer** noun **japery** noun [Middle English: origin uncertain]

japon·ica /dʒəˈpɒnɪkə/ noun any flowering shrub of the genus Chaenomeles, esp. C. speciosa, with round white, green, or yellow edible fruits and bright red flowers. Also called JAPANESE QUINCE. [modern Latin, fem. of japonicus Japanese]

Jaques-Dalcroze /ˈʒɒk ˌdalˈkroːz/ **Émile** (1865–1950), Austrian-born Swiss music teacher and composer. While professor of harmony at the Geneva Conservatory, he evolved the eurhythmics method of music teaching; he established a school for eurhythmics instruction in 1910.

jar¹ noun **1 a** a container of glass, earthenware, plastic, etc., usu. cylindrical. **b** the contents of this. **2** Brit. & Cdn informal a glass of beer etc. □ **jar·ful** noun (pl. **-fuls**). [French jarre from Arabic jarra]

jar² ● verb (**jarred, jar·ring**) **1** intransitive (often foll. by on) (of sound, words, manner, etc.) sound discordant or grating (on the nerves etc.). **2 a** transitive (foll. by against, on) strike or cause to strike with vibration or a grating sound. **b** intransitive (of a body affected) vibrate gratingly.

Consonants: b but d dog f few g get h her j yes k cat l leg m man n no p pen r red s sit

3 *transitive* send a shock through (a part of the body) (*the fall jarred his neck*). **4** *intransitive* (often foll. by *with*) (of an opinion, fact, etc.) be at variance; be in conflict or in dispute. ● *noun* **1** a jarring sound or sensation. **2** a physical shock or jolt. **3** lack of harmony; disagreement. □ **jar·ring** *adjective* **jar·ring·ly** *adverb* [16th c.: prob. imitative]

jar·di·nière /ˌʒɑrdɪˈnjɛr/ *noun* **1** an ornamental pot or stand for the display of growing plants. **2** a dish of mixed vegetables. [French]

jar·gon¹ *noun* **1** words or expressions used by a particular group or profession (*medical jargon*). **2** language marked by affected or convoluted syntax, vocabulary, or meaning. **3** unintelligible or meaningless talk or writing; gibberish. **4** a pidgin (*Chinook Jargon*). □ **jar·gon·is·tic** *adjective* **jar·gon·ize** *transitive & intransitive verb* (also esp. *Brit.* **-ise**). **jar·gony** *adjective* [Old French: origin unknown]

jar·gon² /ˈdʒɑrgən/ *noun* (also **jar·goon** /dʒɑrˈguːn/) a translucent, colourless, or smoky variety of zircon. [French from Italian *giargone*, prob. ultimately formed as ZIRCON]

jargon buster *noun* a glossary, esp. online, that explains in plain language the jargon associated with a particular field.

jarl /jɑrl/ *noun hist.* a Norse or Danish chief. [Old Norse, originally = man of noble birth, related to EARL]

Jarls·berg /ˈjɑrlzbɜrg/ *noun proprietary* a yellow hard cheese with holes, similar in taste to Swiss. [*Jarlsberg* in Norway, where it originated]

Jar·man /ˈdʒɑrmən/ **Derek** (1942–94), English film director and painter. Jarman worked in costume and set design for the Royal Ballet and was a production designer for Ken Russell's *The Devils* (1970). His controversial films, which often explore gay sensibilities, include *Sebastiane* (1976), *Caravaggio* (1985), and *The Last of England* (1987).

jar·rah /ˈdʒɑrə/ *noun* **1** the Australian mahogany gum tree, *Eucalyptus marginata*. **2** the durable timber of this. [Aboriginal *djarryl*]

jarred *adjective* preserved in a jar (*jarred baby food*).

Jar·row a town in NE England, on the Tyne estuary; pop. (est. 2002) 28,200. From the 7th c. until the Viking invasions its monastery was a centre of Northumbrian Christian culture; the Venerable Bede lived and worked there.

Ja·ru·zel·ski /ˌjɑruˈzelski/ **Woj·ciech (Wit·old)** (b.1923), Polish general and Communist leader, prime minister 1981–5, head of state 1985–9, and president 1989–90. He responded to Poland's economic crisis and the rise of Solidarity by imposing martial law and banning trade union operation; following the victory of Solidarity in 1989, he supervised Poland's transition to a novel 'socialist pluralist' democracy.

Jas. *abbreviation* James (also in New Testament).

Jas·min /ʒazˈmɑ̃/ **Claude** (b.1930), Canadian novelist, playwright, essayist and scenographer. He won numerous awards for his fiction and plays, and his fictionalized autobiography *La Petite Patrie* (1972) became a popular TV series in Quebec from 1974–76.

jas·mine /ˈdʒazmɪn/ *noun* (also **jas·min, jessa·mine** /ˈdʒɛsəmɪn/) any of various ornamental shrubs of the genus *Jasminum* usu. with white or yellow flowers. [French *jasmin, jessemin* from Arabic *yās(a)mīn* from Persian *yāsamīn*]

jasmine rice *noun* a fragrant long-grain rice grown in Thailand.

jasmine tea *noun* a tea perfumed with dried jasmine blossom.

Jason *Gk Myth* the son of the king of Iolcos in Thessaly, and leader of the Argonauts in the quest for the Golden Fleece.

Jas·per an improvement district and resort centre in the Rocky Mountains of W Alberta, situated on the Athabasca River, southwest of Hinton; pop. (2001) 4,180. □ **Jas·per·ite** *noun* [from *Jasper House*, a North West Co. trading post, after *Jasper* Hawes, who oversaw its workings *c.*1817]

jas·per *noun* **1** an opaque variety of quartz, usu. red, yellow, or brown in colour. **2** (in full **jas·per·ware**) a kind of fine white stoneware invented by Josiah Wedgwood, usu. stained powder blue and with white cameo decoration. [Old French *jaspre* from Latin *iaspis* from Greek, of oriental origin]

Jasper National Park a park in the Rocky Mountains of W Alberta, northwest of Banff National Park. It was established in 1907. [as JASPER]

Jas·pers /ˈjaspɜrz/ **Karl (Theo·dor)** (1883–1969), German philosopher, who was one of the founders of existentialism; his works include *Philosophy* (1932) and *The Future of Mankind* (1958).

Jassy see IAȘI.

Jat /dʒat/ *noun* a member of an Indic people widely distributed in NW India. [Hindi *jāt*]

Jat·aka /ˈdʒʌtəkə/ *noun* any of the various stories of the former lives of the Buddha found in Buddhist literature. [Sanskrit, from *jata* born]

jaun·dice /ˈdʒɔːndɪs/ ● *noun* **1** *Med.* a condition with yellowing of the skin or whites of the eyes, often caused by obstruction of the bile duct or by liver disease. **2** envy, resentment, jealousy. ● *transitive verb* **1** affect with jaundice. **2** (esp. as **jaun·diced** *adjective*) affect (a person) with envy, resentment, disillusionment, or jealousy. [Old French *jaunice* yellowness, from *jaune* yellow]

jaunt ● *noun* a short excursion for enjoyment. ● *intransitive verb* take a jaunt. [16th c.: origin unknown]

jaunting car *noun hist.* a light two-wheeled horse-drawn vehicle formerly used in Ireland.

jaunty *adjective* (**jaunt·i·er, jaunt·i·est**) **1** cheerful and self-confident; carefree. **2** dashing, pert (*a jaunty hat*). □ **jaunt·i·ly** *adverb* **jaunt·i·ness** *noun* [earlier *jentee* from French *gentil* GENTLE]

Jau·rès /ʒɔˈrɛs/ **Jean Léon** (1859–1914), French journalist and politician, who co-founded the socialist newspaper *l'Humanité* (1904) and helped to create a unified French socialist party (1905); he was assassinated.

Java¹ /ˈdʒɑːvə/ a large island in the Malay Archipelago, forming part of Indonesia; pop. (2000) 122,759,800 (with Madura).

Java² /ˈdʒɑːvə, dʒɒvə/ *noun proprietary* a general-purpose programming language designed to produce programs that will run on any computer system and used esp. for creating applications for the Internet and other networks.

java /ˈdʒɑːvə, dʒɒvə/ *noun N Amer. slang* coffee. [JAVA]

Java Man *noun* a fossil human of the species *Homo erectus* (formerly *Pithecanthropus*) whose remains were found in Java, Indonesia in 1891.

Javan *noun & adjective* = JAVANESE.

Java·nese ● *noun* (*pl.* same) **1 a** a native or inhabitant of Java. **b** a person of Javanese descent. **2** the Austronesian language of central Java. ● *adjective* of or relating to Java, its people, or its language.

Java Sea a sea in the Malay Archipelago of SE Asia, surrounded by the islands of Borneo, Java, and Sumatra.

jav·elin /ˈdʒavəlɪn, -vlɪn/ *noun* **1** a light spear thrown in a competitive sport or as a weapon. **2** the athletic event or sport of throwing the javelin. [French *javeline, javelot* from Gallo-Roman *gabalottus*]

jave·lina /havəˈliːnə/ *noun N Amer.* = PECCARY. [Spanish *jabalina*, from the feminine form of *jabalí* 'wild boar', from Arabic *jabali* 'mountaineer']

Javex /ˈdʒaveks/ *noun Cdn proprietary* chlorine bleach. [from *Javel* water from French *eau de javel* from *Javelle*, a village, now a suburb of Paris, where sodium hypochlorite solution was first used as bleach]

Jaw, the a nickname for Moose Jaw. [abbreviation]

jaw ● *noun* **1 a** each of the upper and lower bony structures in vertebrates forming the framework of the mouth and containing the teeth. **b** the parts of certain invertebrates used for the ingestion of food. **2 a** (in *pl.*) the mouth with its bones and teeth. **b** the narrow mouth of a valley, channel, etc. **c** the gripping parts of a tool or machine. **d** gripping power (*jaws of death*). **3** *informal* **a** talkativeness; tedious talk (*hold your jaw*). **b** a conversation. ● *verb informal* **1** *intransitive* speak esp. at tedious length; gossip. **2** *transitive* admonish or lecture. □ **jawed** *adjective* (also in *combination*). **jaw·less** *adjective* [Old French *joe* cheek, jaw, of uncertain origin]

jaw·bone ● *noun* **1** a bone of the jaw, esp. that of the lower jaw (the mandible), or either half of this. **2** *Cdn slang* deferred payment; credit. ● *transitive & intransitive verb* seek to restrain (a union or other body in a dispute) by persuasion. □ **jaw·bon·ing** *noun*

jaw·break·er *noun informal* **1** a word that is very long or hard to pronounce. **2** a large, round, hard candy. □ **jaw·break·ing** *adjective*

jaw-dropping *adjective* amazing. □ **jaw-dropper** *noun* **jaw-droppingly** *adverb*

jaw·line *noun* the outline of the jaw.

jaws of life *noun* a powerful hydraulic tool that can pry apart twisted metal, used esp. to rescue people trapped in wrecked vehicles.

Jay, John (1745–1829), US jurist and diplomat, who served as the first chief justice of the US Supreme Court (1789–95) and negotiated the Jay Treaty (1794) with Great Britain, which settled outstanding disputes resulting from the American Revolution.

jay *noun* **1** any of various medium-sized birds of the crow family, with varied, often colourful, plumage, e.g. a blue jay, grey jay, Steller's jay, etc. **2** a noisy chattering European bird, *Garrulus glandarius*, with vivid pinkish-brown, blue, black, and white plumage. [Old French from Late Latin *gaius, gaia*, perhaps from Latin praenomen *Gaius*: compare *jackdaw, robin*]

---

t **top**   v **voice**   w **we**   z **zoo**   ʃ **she**   ʒ **vision**   θ **thin**   ð **this**   ŋ **ring**   x **loch**   tʃ **chip**   dʒ **jar**   (*see over for vowels*)

Jay·cee noun N Amer., Austral., & NZ a member of a Junior Chamber of Commerce. [Junior Chamber]

jay·walk intransitive verb (of a pedestrian) cross a street at a place other than an intersection, crosswalk, etc. or against a red light, esp. with disregard for traffic. □ **jay·walk·er** noun **jay·walk·ing** noun

jazz ● noun **1 a** a type of music of African-American origin, characterized by improvisation, syncopated phrasing, and a regular or forceful rhythm. **b** (attributive) designating a style of music containing elements of jazz (jazz-rock). **2** (also **jazz ballet, jazz dance**) a style of theatrical dance performed to jazz or popular music, and incorporating elements of popular dance. **3** slang pretentious talk or behaviour, nonsensical stuff. **4** slang energy, excitement, excitability. ● verb **1** intransitive play or dance to jazz. **2** transitive excite, energize. □ **all that jazz** all that sort of thing. **jazz up** brighten or enliven. □ **jazz·er** noun [20th c.: origin uncertain]

Jazz Age noun the 1920s in the US characterized as a period of carefree hedonism, wealth, freedom, and youthful exuberance.

jazz·bo noun slang a jazz musician or fan. [origin unknown]

Jazz·er·cise noun proprietary physical exercise in the form of dancing to the accompaniment of jazz music. [JAZZ + EXERCISE]

jazz-funk noun a style of popular dance music incorporating elements of jazz and funk.

jazz·man noun (pl. **-men**) a male jazz musician.

jazzy adjective (**jazz·i·er, jazz·i·est**) **1** of or like jazz. **2** slang spirited, lively, exciting. **3** slang flashy, showy (a jazzy car). □ **jazz·i·ly** adverb **jazz·i·ness** noun

JB abbreviation JERUSALEM BIBLE.

J-Cloth noun Cdn & Brit. proprietary a type of light, absorbent, reusable cloth used for household cleaning.

Jct. abbreviation JUNCTION 2.

jeal·ous adjective **1** (often foll. by of) envious or resentful (of a person or a person's advantages etc.). **2** afraid, suspicious, or resentful of rivalry in love or affection. **3** (often foll. by of) fiercely protective (of rights etc.). **4** (of God) intolerant of disloyalty. □ **jeal·ous·ly** adverb [Old French gelos from medieval Latin zelosus ZEALOUS]

jeal·ousy noun (pl. **-ies**) **1** a jealous state or feeling. **2** an instance of this.

jean noun **1** a heavy twilled cotton fabric, now usu. denim (usu. attributive: jean jacket). **2** (usu. in pl.) hard-wearing pants made of this fabric. [from jean 'twilled cotton cloth' from Middle English, attributive use of Jene from Old French Janne, from medieval Latin Janua 'Genoa']

Jeans, Sir James (Hop·wood) (1877–1946), English physicist and astronomer. He proposed a theory for the formation of the solar system, according to which the planets formed from natural material pulled out of the sun by the gravity of a passing star, and was the first to propose that matter is continuously created throughout the universe, one of the tenets of the steady-state theory.

jeans·wear noun clothing made from denim.

Jed·dah see JIDDAH.

Jed·dore Lake /dʒeˈdɔr/ a lake in south central Newfoundland, situated north of Bay d'Espoir. [possibly after N. Jeddore, Mi'kmaq chief d.1944]

Jeep noun proprietary a sturdy, four-wheel drive motor vehicle, suitable for off-road travel. [from GP = general purposes, influenced by 'Eugene the Jeep', an animal in a comic strip]

jeep·ers interjection (also **jeepers creepers**) N Amer. slang expressing surprise etc. [corruption of JESUS²]

jeep·ney noun (in the Philippines) a jitney bus converted from a Jeep. [blend of JEEP + JITNEY]

jeer ● verb **1** intransitive (usu. foll. by at) speak or call out in derision or mockery; scoff derisively. **2** transitive scoff at; deride. **3** (usu. foll. by down, from, out, etc.) drive or force away by jeering. ● noun a scoff or taunt. □ **jeer·ing·ly** adverb [16th c.: origin unknown]

jeez interjection (also **jeeze**) slang a mild expression of surprise, discovery, etc. (compare GEE¹). [abbreviation of JESUS²]

jeez·ly adjective (also **jeeze·ly, jees·ly**) Cdn slang used as an intensifier (you're a jeezly fool!). [corruption of JESUS²]

Jef·fer·son, Thom·as (1743–1826), US Democratic Republican leader, 3rd president of the US 1801–9. He was the principal drafter of the Declaration of Independence (1776), was a key leader during the American Revolution, advocated decentralization, and as president, secured the Louisiana Purchase (1803).

Jefferson City the state capital of Missouri; pop. (2000) 39,636.

Jef·fer·son·ian /ˌdʒefərˈsoːniən/ ● adjective of or pertaining to Thomas Jefferson or his political principles, esp. minimal intervention by the state, individual rights, and democracy. ● noun a supporter of Thomas Jefferson or Jeffersonianism. □ **Jef·fer·son·ian·ism** noun

Je·hosha·phat /dʒəˈhɒsəˌfat, -ˈhɔːʃ-/ Bible the fourth king of Judah (c.874–50 BC), who entered into alliances with the kings of Israel (I Kings 22:41–50).

Je·ho·vah /dʒəˈhoːvə/ noun a form of the Hebrew name of God used in some translations of the Old Testament. [medieval Latin Iehoua(h) from Hebrew YHVH (with the vowels of adonai 'my lord' included): see ADONAI, YAHWEH]

Jehovah's Witness noun a member of a fundamentalist millenarian Christian sect rejecting the supremacy of the state and religious institutions over personal conscience, faith, etc.

Je·hov·ist /dʒəˈhoːvɪst/ noun = YAHWIST.

je·june /dʒɪˈdʒuːn/ adjective **1** intellectually unsatisfying; shallow. **2** puerile, childish; naive. **3** (of ideas, writings, etc.) meagre, scanty; dry and uninteresting. □ **je·june·ly** adverb [originally = fasting, from Latin jejunus]

je·junum /dʒɪˈdʒuːnəm/ noun Anat. the part of the small intestine between the duodenum and ileum. □ **je·jun·al** adjective [Latin, neuter of jejunus fasting]

Jek·yll and Hyde /ˌdʒekəl ənd ˈhaɪd/ noun a person alternately displaying opposing good and evil personalities (also attributive: a Jekyll-and-Hyde existence). [R. L. Stevenson's story The Strange Case of Dr. Jekyll and Mr. Hyde]

jell intransitive verb informal **1 a** set as a jelly. **b** (of ideas etc.) take a definite form. **2** (of people) readily co-operate or reach an understanding. [back-formation from JELLY]

jel·la·ba var. of DJELLABA.

jel·lied adjective set into a jelly (jellied chicken stock).

jellied salad noun Cdn a sweet or savoury dish made of fruit or chopped vegetables in fruit-flavoured gelatin.

Jell-O noun N Amer. proprietary **1** a fruit-flavoured gelatin dessert. **2** the powder used to make this.

jelly ● noun (pl. **-lies**) **1 a** a type of jam made of fruit juice boiled with sugar and cooled to a semi-solid consistency (crabapple jelly). **b** a dessert made of juice, fruit-flavoured water, etc., sugar and gelatin, set to a soft semi-solid consistency, often in a mould. **c** a similar preparation derived from meat, bones, etc., and gelatin. **2** any substance of a similar consistency (petroleum jelly). **3** (usu. in pl.) a plastic shoe, usu. a sandal, worn by girls and women. ● verb (**-lies, -lied**) **1** intransitive & transitive set or cause to set as a jelly, congeal. **2** transitive set (food) in a jelly. □ **jelly·like** adjective [Old French gelee frost, jelly, from Romanic gelata from Latin gelare freeze, from gelu frost]

jelly baby noun Cdn & Brit. a soft fruit-flavoured candy in the shape of a baby, made from gelatin.

jelly bag noun a bag, usu. of cheesecloth, for straining juice for jelly.

jelly bean noun a bean-shaped candy with a gelatinous centre and a hard sugar coating.

jelly doughnut noun N Amer. a round jam-filled doughnut, usu. coated in icing sugar.

jelly·fish noun (pl. usu. same) **1** a marine coelenterate of the class Scyphozoa having an umbrella-shaped jellylike body and stinging tentacles. **2** informal a feeble person.

jelly roll noun N Amer. a thin, flat, rectangular sponge cake spread with jam or other filling and rolled up to form a cylindrical cake with a spiral cross-section.

jemmy esp. Brit. var. of JIMMY.

Jena /ˈjeɪnə/ a university town in central Germany, in Thuringia; pop. (est. 2002) 97,800. It was the scene of a battle (1806) in which Napoleon defeated the Prussians.

je ne sais quoi /ʒə nə seɪ ˈkwʌ/ noun an indefinable something. [French, = I do not know what]

Jen·ghis Kahn /ˈdʒeŋɡɪs ˈkɒn/ see GENGHIS KAHN.

Jen·kins's Ear, War of /ˈdʒeŋkɪnzɪz/ a naval war between England and Spain (1739), precipitated by the appearance before Parliament in 1738 of Robert Jenkins, a British sea captain, who produced what he claimed was his ear, cut off by the Spanish while they were carrying out a search of his ship. His story was probably at least partially fabricated, but it caused great popular indignation.

Jen·ner, Ed·ward (1749–1823), English physician. The pioneer of vaccination, he demonstrated that people deliberately infected with cowpox were protected from smallpox; the practice eventually led to the eradication of smallpox in the late 20th c.

Jen·ness /ˈdʒɛnɪs/ **Dia·mond** (1886–1969), New Zealand-born Canadian anthropologist. A member of the Canadian Arctic Expedition (1913–18), he joined the staff of the National Museum of Canada after World War I and served as its chief anthropologist from 1926. His bibliography of some 100 titles includes *The People of the Twilight* (1928) and *The Indians of Canada* (1932).

jenny *noun* (pl. **-nies**) **1** *hist.* = SPINNING JENNY. **2** a female donkey or female bird. [pet form of the name *Janet*]

Jen·sen /ˈjɛnsən/ **Jo·han·nes Vil·helm** (1873–1950), Danish novelist, poet, and essayist, whose best-known work is his series of six novels on human history entitled *The Long Journey* (1908–22); he was awarded the Nobel Prize for literature in 1944.

jeop·ard·ize /ˈdʒɛpərˌdaɪz/ *transitive verb* (also esp. *Brit.* **-ise**) endanger; put into jeopardy.

jeop·ardy /ˈdʒɛpərdi/ *noun* **1** danger, esp. of severe harm or loss. **2** *Law* the risk of being convicted and punished for a criminal offence. [Middle English *iuparti* from Old French *ieu parti* divided (i.e. even) game, from Latin *jocus* game + *partitus* past participle of *partire* divide from *pars partis* part]

Jeph·thah /ˈdʒɛfθə/ (in the Bible) a judge of Israel who sacrificed his daughter in consequence of a vow that if victorious in battle he would sacrifice the first living thing that met him on his return (Judges 11, 12).

Jer. *abbreviation* Jeremiah (Old Testament).

jer·boa /dʒɜrˈboʊə/ *noun* any small desert rodent of the family Dipodidae with long hind legs and the ability to make large jumps. [modern Latin from Arabic *yarbū'* flesh of loins, jerboa]

jere·miad /ˌdʒɛrəˈmaɪəd, -ad/ *noun* a doleful complaint or lamentation; a list of woes. [French *jérémiade* from *Jérémie* Jeremiah, with reference to the Lamentations of Jeremiah in the Old Testament]

Jere·miah /ˌdʒɛrəˈmaɪə/ **1** *Bible* a Hebrew major prophet (c.650–c.585 BC), who saw the fall of Assyria, the conquest of his country by Egypt and then by Babylon, and the destruction of Jerusalem. **2** a book of the Bible containing his prophecies. **3** *noun* a prophet of doom; a denouncer of the times.

Jerez /heˈreθ/ (in full **Jerez de la Fron·tera** /dei la frɒnˈterə/) a town in Andalusia, Spain; pop. (est. 2002) 186,000. It is the centre of the sherry-making industry.

Jeri·cho /ˈdʒɛrɪˌkoʊ/ a town in Palestine, in the West Bank north of the Dead Sea. It has been occupied from at least 9000 BC. According to the Bible, Jericho was a Canaanite city destroyed by the Israelites after they crossed the Jordan into the Promised Land; its walls were flattened by the shout of the army and the blast of the trumpets. Occupied by the Israelis since the Six Day War of 1967, in 1994 Jericho was the first area given partial autonomy under the PLO-Israeli peace accord.

jerk[1] ● *noun* **1** a sharp sudden pull, twist, twitch, start, etc. **2** a spasmodic muscular twitch. **3** *slang* an obnoxious or inconsiderate person. **4** (prec. by *the*) *Weightlifting* the raising of a barbell to above the head by a rapid extension of the arms, following an initial lift to shoulder level. ● *verb* **1** *intransitive* move with a jerk. **2** *transitive* pull, thrust, twist, etc., with a jerk. **3** *transitive* throw with a suddenly arrested motion. **4** *transitive Sport* (in weightlifting) raise (a weight) from shoulder level to above the head. **5** *transitive N Amer. informal* serve (sodas, milkshakes, etc.) at a soda fountain. □ **jerk around** *N Amer. slang* deal with unfairly; deceive or mislead. **jerk off** *coarse slang* (of a male) masturbate. □ **jerk·er** *noun* [16th c.: perhaps imitative]

jerk[2] ● *transitive verb* cure (meat) by cutting it in slices and drying it in the sun. ● *noun* (*attributive*) designating an originally Jamaican method of preparing meat, esp. pork or chicken, by cutting it into strips, seasoning highly with pepper and spices, esp. allspice, and barbecuing (*jerk chicken*; *jerk spices*). [Latin American Spanish *charquear* from *charqui* from Quechua *echarqui* dried flesh]

jer·kin *noun* **1** a sleeveless jacket. **2** *hist.* a man's close-fitting jacket, often of leather. [16th c.: origin unknown]

jerk-off *coarse slang* ● *noun* a contemptible person. ● *adjective* contemptible.

jerk·water *adjective N Amer. informal* (of a town etc.) small and remote; insignificant. [JERK[1] + WATER, from the need of early railway engines in remote locations to be supplied with water from streams using a bucket on a rope]

jerky[1] *adjective* (**jerk·i·er**, **jerk·i·est**) having sudden abrupt movements; spasmodic. □ **jerk·i·ly** *adverb* **jerk·i·ness** *noun*

jerky[2] *noun* meat that has been cured by being cut into long, thin strips and dried.

jero·boam /ˌdʒɛrəˈboʊəm/ *noun* a wine bottle of 4 times the ordinary size. [*Jeroboam* King of Israel (1 Kings 11:28, 14:16)]

Jer·ome ▸ **1 St.** (c.342–420), Doctor of the Church. Born in Dalmatia, he ruled a newly founded monastery in Bethlehem and devoted his life to study. He is well known for his compilation of the Vulgate. Feast day, 30 September. **2 Harry Win·ston** (1940–1982), Canadian track and field athlete. After tying the world record for 100 metre and 100 yard races in 1960 and 1962, he represented Canada at the 1960, 1964 and 1968 Olympics, winning a bronze medal in the 100 metres in 1964 and a gold in the 100 metres at the 1967 Pan-American Games.

Jerry *noun* (pl. **-ries**) esp. *Brit. dated slang* **1** a German (esp. in military contexts). **2** the Germans collectively. [prob. alteration of *German*]

jerry-built *adjective* (also **jerry-rigged**) **1** built insubstantially from inferior materials. **2** developed or produced in a slapdash manner. □ **jerry-build** *transitive verb* (also **jerry-rig**). **jerry-building** *noun* [19th c.: origin unknown]

jerry can *noun* (also **jerri·can**) a kind of (originally German) gasoline or water can. [JERRY + CAN[2]]

Jer·sey the largest of the Channel Islands; pop. (2001) 87,200; capital, St. Helier.

jer·sey *noun* (pl. **-seys**) **1** a soft, fine, usu. stretchy knitted fabric. **2** a knitted usu. woollen pullover or similar garment. **3** a distinguishing sweater or shirt worn by members of a hockey, soccer, etc. team. **4** (**Jersey**) a light brown dairy cow of a breed originally from Jersey. [JERSEY]

Jer·sey·an *noun* a native or inhabitant of New Jersey.

Jersey City an industrial city in NE New Jersey, on the Hudson River opposite New York City; pop. (2000) 240,055.

Jersey Mac *noun* a variety of round red eating apple. [*Jersey* from NEW JERSEY, where originally developed, + MAC[2]]

Jeru·sa·lem /dʒəˈruːsələm, -ˈruːz-/ a city lying in the Judean hills about 30 km (20 miles) west of the Jordan River; pop. (2000) 617,000. As the site of the Temple, built by Solomon (957 BC), it became the centre of the Jewish religion; by Christians it is revered as the site of Christ's death and resurrection, and by Muslims as the site of the Dome of the Rock. The city was divided between the states of Israel and Jordan from 1947 until 1967, when the Israelis occupied the whole city and proclaimed it the capital of Israel. *See also* NEW JERUSALEM. □ **Jeru·sa·lem·ite** *noun*

Jerusalem artichoke *noun* **1** a species of sunflower, *Helianthus tuberosus*, with edible underground tubers. **2** this tuber used as a vegetable. [corruption of Italian *girasole* sunflower]

Jerusalem Bible *noun* an English version of the Hebrew Bible, published in 1966, which transliterates the Hebrew names for God into the English text. Abbr.: **JB**.

Jes·per·sen /ˈjɛspərsən/ **(Jens) Otto (Harry)** (1860–1943), Danish philologist, grammarian, and educator. He promoted the use of the 'direct method' in language teaching with the publication of his theoretical work *How to Teach a Foreign Language* (1904); other books include his seven-volume *Modern English Grammar* (1909–49).

jess *noun* a short strap of leather, silk, etc., put round the leg of a hawk in falconry. [Old French *ges, get* ultimately from Latin *jactus* a throw, from *jacere jact-* to throw]

jessa·mine *var. of* JASMINE.

Jesse /ˈdʒɛsi/ *Bible* the father of David (1 Sam. 16), hence represented as the first in the genealogy of Jesus Christ.

jest ● *noun* **1 a** a joke. **b** fun. **2 a** a raillery, banter. **b** an object of derision (*a standing jest*). ● *intransitive verb* **1** joke; make jests. **2** fool about; play or act triflingly. □ **in jest** in fun. □ **jest·ing·ly** *adverb* [originally = exploit: Old French *geste* from Latin *gesta*, neuter pl. past participle of *gerere* 'do']

jest·er *noun hist.* a professional joker or fool at a medieval court etc., traditionally wearing a cap and bells and carrying a mock sceptre.

Jesu /ˈdʒiːzjuː, ˈdʒeɪ-/ Jesus (as an archaic form of address).

Jes·uit /ˈdʒɛzjʊɪt, ˈdʒɛzə- ˈdʒɛzjʊɪt/ *noun* a member of the Society of Jesus, a Roman Catholic order founded by St. Ignatius Loyola and others in 1534. [French *jésuite* or modern Latin *Jesuita* from *Jesus*: see JESUS[1]]

Jesu·it·ical /ˌdʒɛzjʊˈɪtɪkəl, ˈdʒɛz- -jʊɪt/ *adjective* **1** of or concerning the Jesuits. **2** *offensive* dissembling or equivocating, in the manner once associated with Jesuits. □ **Jesu·it·ical·ly** *adverb*

Jesus[1] (also **Jesus Christ** or **Jesus of Nazareth**) the central figure of the Christian religion. He was a Jew, the son of Mary, living in

Palestine at the beginning of the 1st c. AD who in about AD 28–30 conducted a mission of preaching and healing (with reported miracles), which is described in the New Testament. He was arrested and put to death by crucifixion. His followers believed him to be the Christ or Messiah, and the Son of the living God, and belief in his resurrection from the dead, as recorded in the Gospels, became a central tenet of Christianity.

Jesus² *interjection* (also **Jesus Christ**, **Jesus H. Christ**) *taboo slang* an exclamation of surprise, dismay, anger, etc.

Jésus, Île /ʒeiˈzuː/ an island in south central Quebec, situated between Île de Montréal and mainland Quebec. The city of Laval is situated on it. [after the Jesuits, who were granted the land *c*.1636: see Jesuit]

Jesus freak *noun slang* a (usu. young) person combining a hippie lifestyle with fervent evangelical Christianity.

Jesus, Mary, and Joseph *interjection* esp. *Cdn* (Maritimes) & *Irish informal* an exclamation of surprise, dismay, etc.

Jesus wept *interjection* expressing pain, exasperation, surprise, etc.

jet¹ ● *noun* **1** a stream of liquid, gas, or (more rarely) solid particles shot out, esp. from a small opening. **2** a spout or nozzle for emitting water etc. in this way. **3 a** a jet engine (also *attributive: jet fighter*). **b** an aircraft powered by one or more jet engines. ● *verb* (**jet·ted**, **jet·ting**) **1** *intransitive & transitive* spurt out or cause to spurt out in jets. **2** *transitive & intransitive* send or travel by jet plane. □ **cool one's jets** *N Amer. informal* be calm or patient. [earlier as verb (in sense 1): French *jeter* throw, ultimately from Latin *jactare* frequentative of *jacere* *jact-* throw]

jet² ● *noun* **1 a** a hard black variety of lignite capable of being carved and highly polished. **b** (*attributive*) made of this. **2** the colour of jet; a deep glossy black. ● *adjective* of this colour. [Middle English via Anglo-French *geet*, Old French *jaiet*, and Latin *gagates* from Greek (*lithos*) *gagatēs* '(stone) from *Gagai*', a town in Asia Minor]

jet black ● *noun* a black colour like jet; a glossy black. ● *adjective* (**jet-black**) of this colour.

jet boat *noun* a small boat without a propeller, the engine of which expels a jet of water to provide thrust. □ **jet boater** *noun* **jet boating** *noun*

jeté /ʒeˈtei/ *noun Dance* a jump or leap with one leg thrown forwards or outwards; a grand jeté or petit jeté. [French, past participle of *jeter* throw: see JET¹]

jet engine *noun* an engine using jet propulsion for forward thrust, esp. of an aircraft.

jet lag *noun* extreme tiredness and disrupted biological rhythms felt after a long flight in which different time zones are crossed in a relatively short time. □ **jet-lagged** *adjective*

jet·lin·er *noun* a commercial airplane equipped with jet engines.

jet·pack *noun* (esp. in science fiction) a backpack-like device containing jets used to transport the person wearing it.

jet-propelled *adjective* **1** having jet propulsion. **2** (of a person etc.) very fast.

jet propulsion *noun* propulsion by the backward ejection of a high-speed jet of gas etc.

jet·sam *noun* discarded material washed ashore, esp. that thrown overboard to lighten a ship etc. (*compare* FLOTSAM). [contraction of JETTISON]

jet set *noun informal* wealthy people frequently travelling by air, esp. for pleasure (also *attributive: a jet-set lifestyle*). □ **jet-setter** *noun* **jet-setting** *adjective*

Jet Ski ● *noun proprietary* a jet-propelled watercraft ridden like a motorbike. ● *intransitive verb* (**jet ski**) ride on a jet ski. □ **jet skier** *noun* **jet skiing** *noun*

jet stream *noun* **1** a narrow current of very strong winds encircling the globe several miles above the earth. **2** the stream from a jet engine.

jet·ted *adjective* (esp. of a bathtub) equipped with nozzles emitting a strong jet of water.

jet·ti·son /ˈdʒetisən, -zən/ ● *transitive verb* **1** throw (esp. heavy material) overboard to lighten an aircraft, ship, hot-air balloon, etc. **2** release or drop from a spacecraft in flight. **3** abandon; get rid of (something no longer wanted). ● *noun* the act of jettisoning. [Anglo-French *getteson*, Old French *getaison* from Latin *jactatio -onis* from *jactare* throw: see JET¹]

jetty *noun* (pl. **-ties**) **1** a landing pier. **2** a pier or breakwater constructed to protect or defend a harbour, coast, etc. [Old French *jetee*, fem. past participle of *jeter* throw: see JET¹]

Jet·way *noun proprietary* a portable bridge or walkway connecting the

door of an airliner with a departure gate at an airport to allow passengers to board and disembark.

jeu d'esprit /ˌʒɜ deˈspriː/ *noun* (*pl.* **jeux d'esprit** *pronunc.* same) a witty or humorous (usu. literary) trifle. [French, = game of the spirit]

jeun·esse dorée /ˌʒɜnes ˈdɔrei/ *noun* = GILDED YOUTH. [French]

Jew *noun* a person of Hebrew descent or whose religion is Judaism. [Middle English via Old French *giu* and Latin *judaeus* from Greek *ioudaios*, ultimately via Hebrew *yᵉhûdî* from *yᵉhûdâh* Judah]

jewel ● *noun* **1 a** a precious stone; a gem. **b** this as used for its hardness as a bearing in watchmaking. **2** a personal ornament containing a jewel or jewels. **3** a precious person or thing; something of great beauty or worth. **4** (*attributive*) cut or shaped like a jewel (*a jewel neckline*). **5** (*attributive*) having the intense colour of a jewel (*jewel tones such as emerald, ruby, and sapphire*). ● *transitive verb* (**jew·elled**, **jew·el·ling**; esp. *US* **jew·eled**, **jew·el·ing**) (esp. as **jew·elled** *adjective*) adorn or set with jewels. □ **jewel in the crown** the best in a particular class of assets. □ **jewel-like** *adjective* [Anglo-French *juel*, *jeuel*, Old French *joel*, of uncertain origin]

jewel box *noun* (also **jewel case**) **1** a small, usu. ornamental box for storing jewellery or other valuables. **2** the hinged plastic case in which a compact disc is packaged.

jewel fish *noun* a scarlet and green tropical cichlid fish, *Hemichromis bimaculatus*.

jewel·ler *noun* (esp. *US* **jewel·er**) a person who makes or sells jewels or jewellery.

jeweller's rouge *noun* finely ground ferric oxide for polishing metal.

jewel·lery /ˈdʒuːləri, ˈdʒuːəlri, dʒuːlri/ *noun* (also **jewel·ry**) ornamental objects for personal adornment, e.g. rings and necklaces, esp. made of precious metal and set with jewels.

jewellery box *noun* = JEWEL BOX 1.

jewel·weed *noun* either of two N American balsams, the orange-flowered *Impatiens capensis* and the yellow-flowered *I. pallida*.

Jew·ess /ˈdʒuːɪs/ *noun offensive* a female Jew.

Jew·ish *adjective* **1** of or relating to Jews. **2** of Judaism. □ **Jew·ish·ly** *adverb* **Jew·ish·ness** *noun*

Jewi·son /ˈdʒuːəsən/ **Nor·man Fred·erick** (b.1926), Canadian film director and producer. His films, which often combine popular appeal with social commentary, include *In the Heat of the Night* (1967; Academy Award for best picture), *Fiddler on the Roof* (1971), *Jesus Christ Superstar* (1973) and *Moonstruck* (1987).

Jewry /ˈdʒʊri/ *noun* (*pl.* **-ries**) **1** the Jewish people, nation, or community; Jews collectively. **2** *hist.* the district inhabited by Jews in a town or city.

Jew's ear *noun* a rubbery cup-shaped fungus, *Auricularia auricula-judae*, growing on trees. [mistranslation of medieval Latin *auricula Judae* 'Judas's ear', from its shape and its occurrence on the elder, said to be the tree from which Judas Iscariot hanged himself]

Jew's harp *noun* a small lyre-shaped musical instrument held between the teeth and struck with the finger.

Jez·ebel /ˈdʒezəˌbel/ **1** a 9th-c. BC Phoenician princess, traditionally the great-aunt of the legendary Dido and in the Bible the wife of Ahab king of Israel. She was denounced by Elijah for introducing the worship of Baal into Israel (1 Kings 16:31, 21:5–15, 2 Kings 9:30–7). **2** *noun* a shameless or immoral woman.

Jhan·si /ˈdʒɒnsi/ a city in the state of Uttar Pradesh, N India; pop. (2001) 383,200.

Jhe·lum River /ˈdʒiːləm/ a river which rises in the Himalayas and flows for about 720 km (450 miles) through the Vale of Kashmir into the province of Punjab in Pakistan, where it meets the Chenab River. It is one of the five rivers that gave Punjab its name.

J.H.S. *abbreviation N Amer.* JUNIOR HIGH SCHOOL.

Jiang Jie Shi see CHIANG KAI-SHEK.

Jiang·su /dʒaŋˈsuː/ (also **Kiangsu** /kjaŋ-/) a province of E China; capital, Nanjing. It includes much of the Yangtze delta.

Jiang·xi /dʒaŋˈʃiː/ (also **Kiangsi** /kjaŋˈsiː/) a province of SE China; capital, Nanchang.

jib¹ ● *noun* **1** a triangular staysail from the outer end of the jib-boom to the top of the foremast or from the bowsprit to the masthead. **2** the projecting arm of a crane. ● *transitive & intransitive verb* (**jibbed**, **jib·bing**) (of a sail etc.) pull or swing round from one side of the ship to the other; gybe. □ **the cut of someone's jib** someone's appearance. [17th c.: origin unknown]

jib² *intransitive verb* (**jibbed**, **jib·bing**) **1 a** (of an animal, esp. a horse) stop and refuse to go on; move backwards or sideways instead of going on. **b** (of a person) refuse to continue. **2** (foll. by *at*) show aversion to (a person or course of action). □ **jib·ber** *noun* [19th c.: origin unknown]

jib·ba *noun* (also **jib·bah, djibba, djibbah**) a long coat worn by Muslim men. [Egyptian var. of Arabic *jubba*]

jib-boom *noun* a spar run out from the end of the bowsprit.

jibe¹ (also **gibe**) ● *noun* an instance of mocking or taunting. ● *verb* **1** *intransitive* (often foll. by *at*) jeer, mock. **2** *transitive* sneer at, taunt, mock. [perhaps from Old French *giber* handle roughly]

jibe² *var. of* GYBE.

jibe³ *intransitive verb* N Amer. (also **jive**) (usu. foll. by *with*) *informal* agree; be in accord. [19th c.: origin unknown]

Jib·uti see DJIBOUTI.

jica·ma /ˈhiːkəmə/ *noun* the crisp white-fleshed edible tuber of the yam bean, used esp. in Mexican cuisine. [Mexican Spanish *jícama* from Nahuatl *xicama*]

Jid·dah /ˈdʒɪdə/ (also **Jeddah** /ˈdʒedə/) a seaport on the Red Sea coast of Saudi Arabia, near Mecca; pop. (est. 2002) 2,674,000.

jiffy *noun* (*pl.* **-fies**) (also **jiff**) *informal* a short time; a moment (*in a jiffy*). [18th c.: origin unknown]

jig ● *noun* **1 a** a lively dance with springs and hops. **b** the music for this, usu. in triple time. **2** a device that holds a piece of work and guides the tools operating on it. **3** a device for catching fish that is jerked up and down through the water. ● *verb* (**jigged, jig·ging**) **1** *intransitive* dance a jig. **2** *transitive & intransitive* move quickly and jerkily up and down. **3** *transitive* work on or equip with a jig or jigs. **4** *transitive & intransitive* fish (for) or catch with a jig or jigger. □ **in jig time** *N Amer. informal* extremely quickly; in a short time. **the jig is up** *N Amer. informal* the scheme is revealed or foiled. [16th c.: origin unknown]

jig·ger¹ ● *noun* **1** *Naut.* **a** a small tackle consisting of a double and single block with a rope. **b** a small sail at the stern. **c** a small fishing boat having this. **2** *Golf* an iron club with a narrow face. **3 a** a small glass or metal cup marked for measuring liquor. **b** the quantity of liquor contained in this. **4** *Cdn* **a** a device upon which a gillnet is hung underneath ice. **b** a piece of lead shaped like a fish, with two hooks in the mouth, fastened on the end of a heavy fishing line. **5** *Cdn & NZ* a small manually or power operated railway car used by railway workers. **6** a person or thing that jigs. ● *transitive verb* **1** (usu. in phr. **I'll be jiggered**) *slang* confound, damn. **2** *Brit.* exhaust; damage, break. [JIG *verb*]

jig·ger² *noun* **1** = CHIGOE. **2** *US* = CHIGGER 1. [corruption]

jiggery-pokery *noun* esp. *Brit. informal* deceitful or dishonest dealing, trickery. [compare Scots *joukery-pawkery* from *jouk* dodge, skulk]

jig·gle ● *verb* **1** *transitive & intransitive* shake lightly; rock jerkily. **2** *intransitive* fidget. ● *noun* a light shake. □ **jig·gly** *adjective* [JIG or JOGGLE¹]

Jiggs' dinner *noun Cdn (Nfld)* a boiled dinner of corned beef, potatoes, and other vegetables, esp. cabbage. [possibly from the American cartoon character *Jiggs*]

jiggy *adjective* **1** jittery, fidgety; trembling, esp. as the result of drug withdrawal. **2** mentally agitated or disturbed. **3** excitedly energetic; uninhibited, often in a sexual manner.

jig·saw *noun* **1 a** (in full **jigsaw puzzle**) a puzzle consisting of a picture on board or wood etc. cut into irregular interlocking pieces to be reassembled. **b** a mental puzzle resolvable by assembling various pieces of information. **2** (**jig saw**) a machine saw with a fine blade enabling it to cut curved lines in a sheet of wood, metal, etc.

jihad /dʒɪˈhad/ *noun* **1** a holy war undertaken by Muslims for the propagation or defence of Islam. **2** a campaign or crusade in some cause. [Arabic *jihād*]

ji·hadi /dʒɪˈhadi/ *noun* (also **jihad·ist**) a person taking part in a jihad.

Jilin /dʒiːˈlɪn/ (also **Kirin** /kiːˈrɪn/) **1** a province of NE China; capital, Changchun. **2** an industrial city in Jilin province; pop. (est. 2002) 1,517,000.

jill *var. of* GILL⁴.

jil·lion *noun N Amer. informal* a great many, an extremely large quantity. □ **jil·lionth** *adjective* [fanciful formation after BILLION, MILLION]

jilt ● *transitive verb* abruptly reject or abandon (a lover etc.). ● *noun* a person (esp. a woman) who jilts a lover. [17th c.: origin unknown]

Jim Crow *noun US* the practice of segregating or discriminating against blacks (also *attributive*: *Jim Crow laws*). □ **Jim Crow·ism** *noun* [from the name of a black character in a 19th c. song]

jim-dandy ● *adjective* excellent; outstanding. ● *noun* an excellent person or thing. [from *Jim*, pet form of the name *James* + DANDY]

Ji·mé·nez /hiˈmenes/ **Juan Ramón** (1881–1958), Spanish poet, who

is known for poetry collections such as *Sonetos espirituales 1914–5* (1916) and the prose work *Platero y yo* (1917); he was awarded the Nobel Prize for literature in 1956.

Ji·mé·nez de Cis·ner·os /hiˌmenez də sɪsˈnerɒs/ (also **Ximenes de Cisneros**), **Fran·cis·co** (1436–1517), Spanish statesman, regent of Spain 1506–7 and 1516–17. He was made Cardinal (1507), and served as Grand Inquisitor for Castile and Léon (1507–17), during which time he undertook a massive campaign against heresy, having some 2,500 alleged heretics put to death.

jim-jams *plural noun slang* **1** a fit of depression or nervousness. **2** *Brit.* pyjamas. [fanciful reduplication]

Jimmu /ˈdʒɪmuː/ the legendary first emperor of Japan (660 BC), descendant of the sun goddess and founder of the imperial dynasty.

jimmy *N Amer.* (esp. *Brit.* **jemmy**) ● *noun* (*pl.* **-mies**) a burglar's short crowbar, usu. made in sections. ● *transitive verb* (**-mies, -mied**) force open with a jimmy. [pet form of the name *James*]

jim·son *noun* (in full **jimson weed**) *US* a highly poisonous tall weed, *Datura stramonium*, with large trumpet-shaped flowers. *See also* THORNAPPLE. [corruption of *Jamestown* in Virginia]

Jin (also **Chin**) **1** a dynasty that ruled China AD 265–420, commonly divided into *Western Jin* (265–317) and *Eastern Jin* (317–420). **2** a dynasty that ruled Manchuria and northern China AD 1115–1234.

Jinan /dʒiːˈnan/ (also **Tsinan** /tsiː-/) a city in E China, the capital of Shandong province; pop. (est. 2002) 2,433,600.

jin·gle ● *noun* **1 a** a mixed noise as of bells or light metal objects being shaken together. **b** a thing that jingles, esp. a bell. **2 a** a repetition of the same sound in words, esp. as an aid to memory or to attract attention. **b** a short verse of this kind used in advertising etc. ● *verb* **1** *intransitive & transitive* make or cause to make a jingling sound. **2** *intransitive* proceed or move with such a sound. **3** *intransitive* (of writing) be full of alliterations, rhymes, etc. □ **give a person a jingle** *N Amer. informal* telephone a person. □ **jin·gly** *adjective* (**jin·gli·er, jin·gli·est**). [Middle English: imitative]

jingle dress *noun* a usu. cotton or taffeta dress covered with jingling metal ornaments, worn by Aboriginal women in performing certain traditional dances.

jingo *noun* (*pl.* **-goes**) a supporter of policy favouring war; a blustering patriot. □ **by jingo!** a mild oath. [17th c.: originally a conjuror's word: political sense from use of *by jingo* in a popular song, then applied to patriots]

jingo·ism *noun* extreme patriotism, esp. in the form of aggressive or warlike foreign policy. □ **jingo·ist** *noun* **jingo·is·tic** *adjective*

jink ● *intransitive verb* move elusively; dodge. ● *noun* an act of dodging or eluding. [originally Scots: prob. imitative of nimble motion]

jink·er *noun Cdn (Nfld)* a person who brings bad luck or who puts a jinx on someone or something. [alteration of JINX v. + -ER¹]

Jin·nah /ˈdʒɪnə/ **Muham·mad Ali** (1876–1948), Indian nationalist and founder of Pakistan. He headed the Muslim League in its struggle with the Hindu-oriented Indian National Congress, and, from 1928 onward, championed the rights of the Muslim minority at conferences on Indian independence; with the establishment of Pakistan in 1947, he became its first Governor General.

jinni /dʒɪˈniː/ *noun* (also **jin·nee, jinn, djinn** /dʒɪn/) (*pl.* **jinn** or **djinn**) (in Muslim mythology) an intelligent being lower than the angels, able to appear in human and animal forms, and having power over people. [Arabic *jinnī*, pl. *jinn*: compare GENIE]

jinx *informal* ● *noun* **1** a person or thing that seems to cause bad luck. **2** bad luck; a curse. ● *transitive verb* (often in *passive*) subject (a person) to an unlucky force. [perhaps var. of *jynx* wryneck, charm]

jism *noun coarse slang* (also **jizz**) semen. [19th c.: origin unknown]

JIT *abbreviation* Business just-in-time.

jit·ney *noun N Amer.* a bus or other vehicle carrying passengers for a low fare, originally five cents. [origin unknown]

jit·ter *informal* ● *noun* **1** (**the jit·ters**) extreme nervousness. **2** *Electronics* **a** slight random or irregular variation, esp. in the shape or timing of a regular pulse. **b** unsteadiness of an image etc. due to this. ● *intransitive verb* be nervous; act nervously. □ **jit·tery** *adjective* **jitter·i·ness** *noun* [20th c.: origin unknown]

jitter·bug ● *noun* **1** *hist.* a fast dance popular in the 1940s, performed chiefly to swing music. **2** a person fond of dancing this. ● *intransitive verb* (**-bugged, -bug·ging**) dance the jitterbug. □ **jitter·bug·ger** *noun*

jiu-jitsu /dʒuːˈdʒɪtsuː/ *noun* (also **ju-jitsu, ju-jutsu**) a Japanese system of unarmed combat using an opponent's strength and weight to his or her disadvantage, now also practised as physical training. [Japanese *jūjutsu* from *jū* gentle + *jutsu* skill]

jive ● noun **1** a jerky lively style of dance esp. popular in the 1950s, performed to jazz or rock'n'roll music. **2** music for this dance. **3** a variety of American black English associated esp. with jazz musicians and enthusiasts. **4** slang talk, conversation, esp. when misleading or pretentious. ● verb **1** intransitive play jive music. **2** intransitive dance the jive. **3** slang **a** transitive mislead, fool (are you jiving me?). **b** intransitive fool around; talk nonsense. **4** N Amer. informal var. of JIBE³. □ **jiv·er** noun **jivey** adjective [20th c.: origin uncertain]

jizz noun **1** the combination of characteristics by which a given plant, bird, etc. can be quickly recognized in the field. **2** = JISM. [20th c.: origin unknown]

JK abbreviation Cdn (Ont.) JUNIOR KINDERGARTEN.

Jnr. abbreviation Junior.

Joa·chim, St. /ˈdʒoːəˌkɪm/ (in Christian tradition) the husband of St. Anne and father of the Virgin Mary. He is first mentioned in an apocryphal work of the 2nd c., and then rarely referred to until much later times.

Joan of Arc, St. (known as 'the Maid of Orleans') (c.1412–31), French national heroine. Guided by divine 'voices' she led the French armies against the English in the Hundred Years War, relieving besieged Orleans, and ensured that the dauphin was crowned Charles VII in Reims; captured by the Burgundians (1430), she was handed over to the English and burned at the stake as a heretic. She was canonized in 1920. Feast day, 30 May.

João Pes·soa /ˌʒwau peˈsoːə/ a city in NE Brazil, on the Atlantic coast; pop. (est. 2002) 614,900.

Job /dʒoːb/ **1** Bible a prosperous man whose patience and exemplary piety are tried by dire and undeserved misfortunes, and who, in spite of his bitter lamentations, remains finally confident in the goodness and justice of God. **2** a book of the Bible telling of Job.

job ● noun **1** a piece of work, esp. one done for hire or profit. **2** a paid position of employment. **3 a** anything one has to do. **b** responsibility (it's your job to do the dishes). **c** a specified operation or other matter, esp. an operation involving plastic surgery (a nose job; a paint job). **4 a** informal a difficult task (had a job to find them). **b** performance; carrying out of a task (did a poor job on the exam). **5** slang an example of its type (that car's a neat little job). **6** Computing an item of work regarded separately. **7** slang a crime, esp. a robbery. **8** a transaction in which private advantage prevails over duty or public interest. **9** informal a state of affairs or set of circumstances (is a bad job). ● verb (**jobbed**, **job·bing**) **1 a** intransitive do jobs; do piecework. **b** transitive (usu. foll by out) let or deal with for profit; subcontract. **2 a** intransitive deal in stocks. **b** transitive buy and sell (stocks or goods) as a middleman. **3 a** intransitive turn a position of trust to private advantage. **b** transitive deal corruptly with (a matter). **4** transitive N Amer. slang swindle. □ **do the job** succeed in doing what is required or desired. **get on with the job** proceed with one's work; continue with one's affairs. **jobs for the boys** Brit. informal preferment for one's supporters or favourites. **just the job** Brit. informal exactly what is wanted. **make a job** (or **good job**) **of** Brit. do thoroughly or successfully. **on the job 1** at work; in the course of doing a piece of work. **2** Brit. informal engaged in sexual intercourse. **out of a job** unemployed. [16th c.: origin unknown]

job action noun N Amer. an organized protest by employees, such as a work slowdown.

job·ber noun **1** a wholesaler. **2** a pieceworker. **3** a person who uses a public office or position of trust for private or party advantage.

job·bery noun corrupt dealing.

job·bie noun slang an example of its type (one of those fancy new jobbies).

job·bing adjective working on separate or occasional jobs.

job creation noun the provision of new opportunities for paid employment, esp. as part of a policy to provide work for the unemployed.

job description noun a written description of the exact responsibilities of a job.

job fair noun an event at which a number of employers set up booths to recruit employees.

job-hopping noun moving frequently from one job to another. □ **job-hop** intransitive verb **job-hopper** noun

job-hunt intransitive verb seek employment. □ **job hunt·er** noun **job-hunting** noun

job killer noun a piece of legislation, a technology, etc. the introduction of which will cause a drop in employment.

job·less adjective without a job; unemployed. □ **job·less·ness** noun

job lot noun a miscellaneous group of articles, esp. bought together.

job one noun the most important task; the priority.

job satisfaction noun fulfillment gained from doing one's job.

Job's comforter /dʒoːbz/ noun a person who under the guise of comforting aggravates distress. [JOB]

job shadowing noun accompanying a person at work to acquire training, work experience, or knowledge of their work.

job-sharing noun an arrangement by which a full-time job is done jointly by two or more part-time employees who share the remuneration etc. □ **job-share** noun & intransitive verb **job-sharer** noun

Job's tears /dʒoːbz/ plural noun the seeds of a grass, Coix lacryma-jobi, used as beads. [the patriarch JOB]

jobs·worth noun Brit. informal an official who upholds petty rules. [contraction of 'it's more than my job's worth (not) to']

Jo·burg /ˈdʒoːbɜrg/ an informal name for JOHANNESBURG.

Jo·casta /dʒəˈkastə/ Gk Myth a Theban woman, the wife of Laius and mother of Oedipus, whom she later unwittingly married.

Jock noun slang a Scotsman. [Scots form of the name Jack (see JACK¹)]

jock¹ noun N Amer. informal **1** = JOCKSTRAP. **2** an esp. male athlete or sports fan, esp. one not interested in intellectual or artistic pursuits. □ **jock·dom** noun **jock·ish** adjective **jocky** adjective [abbreviation]

jock² noun informal **1** a disc or video jockey (shock jock). **2** an enthusiast or devotee of some activity (computer jock). **3** a jockey. [abbreviation]

jock·ette noun a female athlete or sports fan, esp. one not interested in intellectual or artistic pursuits.

jockey ● noun (pl. **-eys**) **1** a rider in horse races, esp. a professional one. **2** esp. N Amer. informal (usu. in combination) a person having control, guidance, or direction of something (desk jockey; gas jockey). ● verb (**-eys**, **-eyed**) **1** intransitive (usu. foll. by for) try to gain an advantageous position esp. by skilful manoeuvring or unfair action (jockey for position). **2** transitive ride (a horse) as a jockey. **3** transitive trick, cheat, or outwit (a person). [diminutive of JOCK]

Jockey Club noun (also **jockey club**) a club or association for the promotion and regulation of horse racing.

Jockey shorts plural noun N Amer. proprietary men's or boys' close-fitting underpants with elasticized waist and leg openings and a triangular flap opening at the front.

jock itch noun a fungal infection of the groin area.

jock·strap noun a close-fitting undergarment functioning as a support or protection for the male genitals, usu. worn by athletes. [slang jock genitals + STRAP]

joc·ose /dʒəˈkoːs/ adjective playful or humorous. □ **joc·ose·ly** adverb **joc·os·ity** /-ˈkɒsɪti/ noun (pl. **-ities**). [Latin jocosus from jocus jest]

jocu·lar /ˈdʒɒkjʊlər/ adjective **1** (of speech, action, etc.) of the nature of a joke; said, done, etc. jokingly. **2** (of a person, disposition, etc.) fond of joking; speaking or acting in jest or merriment. □ **jocu·lar·ity** /-ˈlerɪti/ noun (pl. **-ities**). **jocu·lar·ly** adverb [Latin jocularis from joculus jest]

joc·und /ˈdʒɒkənd/ adjective literary merry, cheerful. □ **joc·und·ity** /dʒəˈkʌndɪti/ noun [Old French from Latin jocundus, jucundus from juvare delight]

Jodh·pur /ˈdʒɒdpʊr/ **1** a city of W India, in Rajasthan; pop. (1991) 846,400. **2** a former princely state of India, now part of Rajasthan.

jodh·purs /ˈdʒɒdpɜrz/ plural noun long breeches for riding etc., wide around the hips and thighs but close-fitting from the knee to the ankle. [JODHPUR]

joe¹ noun slang (also attributive) a fellow or average man (the average joe; joe citizen).

joe² noun N Amer. coffee. [20th c.: origin unknown]

Joe Average noun informal = JOE BLOW.

Joe Bloggs noun Brit. informal = JOE BLOW.

Joe Blow noun N Amer. informal a hypothetical average man.

joe-boy noun N Amer. informal a person required to perform menial tasks for another.

joe job noun Cdn a menial or monotonous task.

Joel ▶ 1 a Hebrew minor prophet of the 5th or possibly 9th c. BC. **2** a book of the Bible containing his prophecies.

Joe Public noun informal (a member of) the general public.

Joe-pye weed noun (also **Joe-pie weed**) any of various tall perennial plants of the genus Eupatorium of the composite family, bearing large clusters of small tubular flowers. [origin unknown]

Joe Schmo noun N Amer. slang (pl. **Schmoes**) an ordinary, unremarkable person.

Joe Sixpack noun esp. US slang a usu. working-class, esp. redneck, member of the general public.

joey *noun* (*pl.* **joeys**) *Austral.* **1** a young kangaroo. **2** a young animal. [19th c.: origin unknown]

Jof·fre /ˈʒɔfrə/ **Jo·seph Jacques Cé·saire** (1852–1931), French Marshal. Commander-in-chief of the French army on the Western Front (1914–16), he was chiefly responsible for the Allied victory in the first battle of the Marne (1914), but resigned after the French defeat at Verdun (1916).

jog¹ ● *verb* (**jogged, jog·ging**) **1** *intransitive* run at a slow pace, esp. as physical exercise. **2** *intransitive* (of a horse) move at a jogtrot. **3** *intransitive* (often foll. by *on, along*) proceed, go on one's way, get through the time, esp. laboriously (*the industry is jogging along at a respectable growth rate*). **4** *transitive* nudge (a person), esp. to arouse attention. **5** *transitive* shake or bump with a push or jerk. **6** *transitive* give a gentle reminder to (a person's or one's own memory). ● *noun* **1 a** a slow walk or trot. **b** a gentle run taken as a form of exercise. **2** a shake, push, or nudge. [Middle English: apparently imitative]

jog² *N Amer.* ● *noun* **1** a short bend, turn, or change of direction in a road etc., after which the road continues in its original direction. **2** a notch, step, or jag in an otherwise level surface or straight line. ● *intransitive verb* bend, turn, or suddenly change course or direction. [prob. var. of JAG¹]

jog·ger *noun* a person who jogs, esp. regularly for exercise.

jog·ging *noun* running at a gentle, regular pace as a form of exercise (also *attributive*: *jogging suit*).

jog·gle¹ ● *transitive & intransitive verb* shake or move by or as if by repeated jerks. ● *noun* **1** a slight shake. **2** the act or action of joggling. [frequentative of JOG¹]

jog·gle² ● *noun* **1** a joint of two pieces of stone or timber, contrived to prevent their sliding on one another. **2** a notch in one of the two pieces, a projection in the other, or a small piece let in between the two, for this purpose. ● *transitive verb* join with a joggle. [perhaps from *jog* = JAG¹]

Jog·ja·kar·ta see YOGYAKARTA.

jog·trot ● *noun* **1** a slow regular trot or pace. **2** a steady, monotonous way of doing something. ● *intransitive verb* go or move at a jogtrot.

Jogues /ʒɒg/ **Isaac, St.** (1607–46), French Jesuit missionary and martyr. Sent to Canada in 1636, he was captured and tortured by the Iroquois in 1642, and, aided by Dutch traders, escaped back to France in 1643. He returned to Canada in 1644 and volunteered for a peace mission to the Iroquois in 1646. He was murdered that year, and was canonized in 1930.

Jo·han·nes·burg /dʒəʊˈhanɪsˌbɜrg/ a city in South Africa, the capital of the province of Gauteng; pop. (est. 2002) 1,646,400. The largest city in South Africa and the centre of its gold-mining industry, it was founded in 1886. [prob. after *Johannes* Meyer, its first mining commissioner]

John ▸ **1** (known as 'John Lackland') (1167–1216), son of Henry II, king of England 1199–1216. He lost Normandy and most of his French possessions to Philip II of France by 1205, and in 1215 he was forced to sign Magna Carta by his barons; when he ignored its provisions, civil war broke out and he died on campaign. **2 Au·gus·tus (Edwin)** (1878–1961), Welsh painter. He is best known for *The Smiling Woman* (1908), a portrait of his second wife Dorelia; he was subsequently noted for his portraits of the wealthy and famous, particularly prominent writers, including Hardy, Shaw, Yeats, Joyce, and Dylan Thomas. He was the brother of Gwen John. **3 Sir Elton (Her·cu·les)** (born Reginald Kenneth Dwight) (b.1947), English pop and rock singer, pianist, and songwriter. With lyricist Bernie Taupin (b.1950), he has written many hit songs blending pop and rock, including 'Your Song' (1970), 'Goodbye Yellow Brick Road' (1973), and 'Candle in the Wind' (1987, reissued in 1997 as a tribute to the Princess of Wales). **4 Gwen** (1876–1939), Welsh painter. Her paintings, mainly watercolours, often depict nuns or girls in interior settings and are noted for their grey tonality; she was the sister of Augustus John. **5 a St.** (known as 'St. John the Evangelist' or 'St. John the Divine') an Apostle, son of Zebedee and brother of James, credited with the authorship of the fourth Gospel, Revelation, and three epistles of the New Testament. Feast day, 27 Dec. **b** the fourth Gospel. **c** any of the three epistles of the New Testament attributed to him.

John I (known as 'John the Great') (1357–1433), king of Portugal 1385–1433. Reinforced by an English army, he won independence for Portugal with his victory over the Castilians at Aljubarrota (1385); he patronized many voyages of discovery.

John III (known as 'John Sobieski') (1629–96), king of Poland 1674–96. He was elected king of Poland after a distinguished early career as a

soldier; in 1683 he relieved Vienna when it was besieged by the Turks, thereby becoming the hero of the Christian world.

John IV (known as 'John the Fortunate') (1604–56), king of Portugal 1640–56. The founder of the Braganza dynasty, he expelled a Spanish usurper and proclaimed himself king; he defeated the Spanish at Montijo (1644) and drove the Dutch out of Brazil (1654).

John XXIII (born Angelo Giuseppe Roncalli) (1881–1963), pope 1958–63. He convened the Second Vatican Council (1962–5), and was respected internationally for his efforts to bring about peace between East and West.

john *noun* *N Amer.* *informal* **1** a toilet. **2** a washroom. **3** a prostitute's customer. [the name *John*]

John Birch·er *noun* = BIRCHER.

john·boat *noun* *N Amer.* a small, square-ended, flat-bottomed boat chiefly for use on inland waterways.

John Bull *noun* a personification of England or the typical Englishman. [the name of a character representing the English nation in J. Arbuthnot's satire *Law is a Bottomless Pit* (1712)]

John Chrysostom, St. see CHRYSOSTOM, ST. JOHN.

John Doe *noun* *N Amer.* **1 a** a person whose real name is unknown. **b** *Law* an anonymous party, usu. the plaintiff, in a legal action. **2** *informal* = JOE BLOW.

John Dory *noun* (*pl.* **-ies**) a dory, *Zeus faber*, found in inshore waters of the eastern Atlantic and the Mediterranean, with a laterally flattened body and a black spot on each side.

John Hancock *noun* *slang* a signature. [HANCOCK]

John·ny *noun* = LITTLE JOHNNY.

john·ny *noun* (*pl.* **-nies**) esp. *Brit.* *informal* a fellow; a man. [familiar form of the name *John*]

johnny·cake *noun* *N Amer.* a cornmeal bread usu. baked or fried on a griddle. [unknown first element + CAKE]

John·ny Can·uck *noun* *Cdn informal* **1** a native, inhabitant, or citizen of Canada. **2** a Canadian soldier, esp. during the world wars. **3** Canada personified.

johnny collar *noun* a small, pointed, close-fitting collar, usu. associated with casual or sports clothing.

johnny-come-lately *noun* (*pl.* **-lately**) *informal* a person who has recently arrived or come to prominence, esp. one who quickly makes use of advantages earned by those who were there before; an upstart.

Johnny-jump-up *noun* *N Amer.* any of several kinds of wild or cultivated pansy or violet.

johnny-one-note *noun* *N Amer.* *informal* a person who is obsessed with or competent in only one limited subject.

Johnny-on-the-spot *noun* a person who is immediately available in a place when a service is required or an opportunity presents itself.

John of Austria (known as 'Don John') (1547–78), Spanish general and admiral. The illegitimate son of the Holy Roman emperor Charles V, he commanded the fleet that defeated the Turks at Lepanto (1571) and went on to conquer Tunis (1573).

John of Damascus, St. (c.675–749), Syrian theologian and Doctor of the Church. He championed image veneration against the iconoclasts, and wrote an encyclopedic work on Christian theology, *The Fount of Wisdom* (c.743), which was influential for centuries in both Eastern and Western Churches. Feast day, 4 Dec.

John of Gaunt (1340–99), son of Edward III. He was effective ruler of England during the final years of his father's reign and the minority of Richard II.

John o'Groats a village at the extreme northeastern point of the Scottish mainland.

John Paul I (born Albino Luciani) (1912–78), pope 1978, who served for only 34 days.

John Paul II (born Karol Jozef Wojtyla) (b.1920), Polish cleric, pope since 1978. The first non-Italian pope since 1522, he has travelled abroad extensively during his papacy, and has upheld traditional Catholic teaching. His papacy provided crucial moral and political support for the popular uprising against Communism in Poland and other E European countries.

John Q. Public *noun* *N Amer.* *informal* the general public or a member thereof.

Johns, Jasper (b.1930), US painter, sculptor, and printmaker. A key figure in the development of pop art, he rebelled against abstract expressionism and depicted commonplace and universally recognized images such as the US flag; he is best known for his *Flags, Targets*, and *Numbers* series produced in the mid-1950s.

John·son ▸ 1 Al·bert (the 'Mad Trapper') (d.1932), Canadian trapper and sharpshooter. On 31 December 1931 he killed an RCMP officer sent to investigate poaching claims. Johnson then led police, assisted by pilot Wop May, on a 48-day chase, covering a total of over 240 km in temperatures averaging -40°C. He was killed by the RCMP in a shootout that also left one officer dead and another badly injured. **2 An·drew** (1808–75), US Democratic politician, 17th president of the US 1865–9. His lenient policy towards the southern states after the American Civil War brought him into bitter conflict with the Republican majority in Congress who attempted to impeach him (1868); he was acquitted by a single vote. **3 Ben** (b.1961), Jamaican-born Canadian sprinter. He set a number of national and international records in the 100m, posting record times of 9.93 seconds at the World Championships in Rome (1987) and 9.79 seconds at the Olympics in Seoul (1988). Upon testing positive for steroids at the latter competition, he was stripped of these titles and suspended from competition for two years. After returning to competition in 1991, Johnson again tested positive in 1993 and was banned for life. **4 Byron Inge·mar** (1890–1964), Canadian businessman and politician, premier of BC 1947–52. His government introduced the retail sales tax and compulsory hospital insurance. **5 Dan·iel** (1915–1968), Canadian lawyer and politician, premier of Quebec 1966–68. First elected as a Union Nationale MNA in 1946, he entered the Duplessis cabinet ten years later, and was elected party leader in 1961. He continued the reforms of the Quiet Revolution, establishing the Université du Québec and Radio-Québec as well as the foundations for a provincial health insurance program. **6 Earvin ('Magic')** (b.1959), US basketball player. He played for the Los Angeles Lakers from 1979 to 1991, winning the NBA's Most Valuable Player of the Year award three times. He won an Olympic gold medal in 1992. **7 Jack** (1878–1946), US boxer. In 1908 he became the first black holder of the world heavyweight title, retaining it until 1915. **8 John Mer·cer** (1818–68), British-born Canadian lawyer and politician, Father of Confederation. After attending both the Quebec and London conferences on Confederation, he was elected to the House of Commons in 1867. **9 Lyn·don Baines** (known as 'L.B.J.') (1908–73), US Democratic politician, 36th president of the US 1963–9. His administration continued the program of social and economic reform initiated by John F. Kennedy, notably passing the 1964 and 1965 Civil Rights Acts; increasing involvement of the US in the Vietnam War eventually undermined his popularity. **10 Rob·ert** (*c.*1911–38), US blues guitarist, singer, and songwriter. Considered one of the most influential blues musicians of the early 20th c., he is best known for songs such as 'Crossroad Blues' (1936), 'Hellbound on My Trail' (1937), and 'Love in Vain' (1937). **11 Sam·uel** (known as 'Dr. Johnson') (1709–84), English lexicographer, writer, critic, and conversationalist. A leading figure in the literary London of his day, he is known for his *Dictionary of the English Language* (1755), one of the first to use illustrative quotations, an edition of Shakespeare (1765), and *The Lives of the English Poets* (1777).

John·son·grass *noun* a tall, coarse, highly invasive perennial grass, *Sorghum halepense*, with stout rhizomes, orig. Mediterranean but now a common weed in North America. [W. Johnson, 19th c. American agriculturalist]

John·son·ian /dʒɒnˈsoːniən/ *adjective* **1** of or relating to Samuel Johnson. **2** typical of his style of writing, e.g. having many words derived or formed from Latin.

John·ston /ˈdʒɒnsən/ **1 Fran·cis Hans** (later **Franz**) (1888–1949), Canadian painter. Although he was one of the artists who founded the Group of Seven in 1920, he participated only in the Group's first show. A landscape painter, his works have an atmospheric and decorative quality that sets them apart from most of the Group's paintings. **2 Lynn** (b.1947), Canadian cartoonist. Her comic strip 'For Better or For Worse', chronicling the daily activities of a family, which she started in 1979, is syndicated to over 450 newspapers in 19 countries.

John·stone Strait /ˈdʒɒnstoːn/ a narrow passage of the N Pacific, situated between the northeastern coast of Vancouver Island and mainland BC; it connects the Strait of Georgia and the Queen Charlotte Strait. [J. Johnstone, master of the tender ship *Chatham c.*1792]

John the Baptist, St. a preacher and prophet, son of Elizabeth and Zacharias and contemporary of Jesus, whom he baptized. In AD *c.*27 he preached on the banks of the Jordan, demanding repentance and baptism from his hearers in view of the approach of God's judgment; he was imprisoned and beheaded by Herod Antipas (Matt. 14:1–12). Feast day, 24 June.

John Thomas *noun slang* the penis.

Johor Ba·haru /dʒoːˈhɔr bəˌharuː/ a city in Malaysia, situated at the southern tip of the Malay Peninsula, opposite the island of Singapore; pop. (2000) 630,603.

joie de vivre /ˌʒwɒ də ˈviːvrə/ *noun* a feeling of healthy and exuberant enjoyment of life. [French, = joy of living]

join ● *verb* **1** *transitive* (often foll. by *to*, *together*) put together; fasten, unite (one thing or person to another or several together). **2** *transitive* connect (points) by a line etc. **3** *transitive* become a member of (an association, society, organization, etc.). **4** *transitive* take one's place with or in (a company, group, procession, etc.). **5** *transitive* **a** come into the company of (a person). **b** (foll. by *in*) take part with (others) in an activity etc. (*joined me in condemnation of the outrage*). **c** (foll. by *for*) share the company of (a person) for a specified occasion (*may I join you for lunch?*). **6** *intransitive* (often foll. by *with*, *to*) come together, be united, esp. in action or purpose. **7** *intransitive* (often foll. by *in*) take part with others in an activity etc. **8** *transitive* be or become connected or continuous with (*the Liard joins the Mackenzie at Fort Simpson*). **9** *transitive* link or unite (people etc. together) in marriage, friendship, or other alliance. ● *noun* a point, line, or surface at which two or more things are joined. □ **join battle** begin fighting. **joined at the hip** inseparable. **join forces** combine efforts. **join hands 1 a** clasp each other's hands. **b** clasp one's hands together. **2** combine in an action or enterprise. **join up 1** enlist for military service. **2** (often foll. by *with*) unite, connect. [Old French *joindre* (stem *joign-*) from Latin *jungere junct-* join]

join·der *noun Law* the act of bringing together. [Anglo-French from Old French *joindre* to join]

joined-up *adjective* (of handwriting) written with the characters joined; cursive.

join·er *noun* **1** *informal* a person who readily joins groups, associations, etc. **2** esp. *Brit.* a person who makes furniture and light woodwork. **3** a device used for making carpentry joints.

join·ery *noun* **1** the construction of wooden furniture etc. **2** carpentry joints collectively.

joint ● *noun* **1 a** a place at which things or parts are joined together. **b** a point at which, or a contrivance by which, two parts of an artificial structure are joined either rigidly or so as to allow movement. **2 a** a structure in an animal body by which two bones are fitted and held together, usu. so that relative movement is possible. **b** the place of connection of two movable parts in an invertebrate, esp. an arthropod. **3 a** any of the parts into which an animal carcass is divided for food. **b** a part of a plant, animal, etc. connected by a joint to an adjacent part, esp. such a part of a digit or limb. **4** *slang* **a** often *derogatory* a place where people go for eating, drinking, entertainment, etc. (*a strip joint; a burger joint*). **b** a residence or establishment (*let's case the joint*). **c** N *Amer.* prison. **5** *slang* a marijuana cigarette. **6** the part of a stem from which a leaf or branch grows. **7** *Geol.* a crack or fissure intersecting a mass of rock. ● *adjective* **1** (of a single thing) held or done by, or belonging to, two or more persons etc. in conjunction (*a joint venture*). **2** (of a person or persons) sharing with another in some action, state, etc. (*joint author*). **3** of, concerning, or involving both houses of a bicameral parliament. ● *transitive verb* **1** connect or fasten by joints. **2** divide (a body or member) at a joint or into joints. **3** prepare (a board etc.) for being joined to another by planing its edge. **4** file, sharpen, and even up the teeth of a saw blade. □ **joint and several** (of a bond etc.) signed by more than one person, of whom each is liable for the whole sum. **out of joint 1** (of a bone) dislocated. **2** disordered, out of order. □ **joint·less** *adjective* **joint·ly** *adverb* [Old French, past participle of *joindre* JOIN]

joint account *noun* a bank account held by more than one person, each of whom has the right to deposit and withdraw funds.

joint address *noun Cdn* a vote taken before both the House of Commons and the Senate.

Joint Chiefs of Staff *plural noun* (in the US) the chief military advisory body to the President, consisting of a chairperson, the Chiefs of Staff of the Army and Air Force, the Chief of Naval Operations, and the Commandant of the Marine Corps.

joint committee *noun* a committee composed of members nominated by two or more distinct bodies.

joint custody *noun* legal custody of a child or children shared by both parents after separation or divorce.

joint·ed *adjective* **1** provided with, constructed with, or having joints. **2** having joints of a specified kind. **3** *Bot.* **a** having or appearing to have joints. **b** separating readily at the joints.

joint·er *noun* **1** (in full **jointer plane**) a long plane used in jointing. **2** a worker employed in jointing wires, pipes, etc.

joint stock *noun* capital held jointly; a common fund.

joint-stock company *noun* a company, usu. unincorporated, that has its members' capital pooled in a common fund.

joint venture *noun* a commercial enterprise undertaken jointly by two or more parties otherwise retaining their separate identities.

Join·ville /ʒwãˈviːl/ **Jean de** (c.1224–1317), French historian and courtier, who is known for his *Histoire de St. Louis*, an account of the Seventh Crusade (1248–54).

joist *noun* each of a series of parallel supporting beams of timber, steel, etc., used in floors, ceilings, etc. [Old French *giste*, ultimately from Latin *jacēre* lie]

jo·joba /hoːˈhoːbə/ *noun* a plant, *Simmondsia chinensis*, with seeds yielding an oily extract used in cosmetics etc. [Latin American Spanish]

joke ● *noun* **1 a** a thing said or done to excite laughter. **b** a witticism, jest, or short humorous anecdote. **2** a ridiculous thing, person, or circumstance. **3 a** something trifling; a matter that is not serious, true, or worthy of concern (*that theory is a joke*). **b** *N Amer. informal* something very easy (*that exam was a joke*). ● *verb* **1** *intransitive* make a joke or jokes. **2** *transitive* utter as a joke. □ **(all) joking aside** speaking seriously. **no joke** *informal* a serious matter. □ **jok·ing·ly** *adverb* **jokey** *adjective* **jok·i·ness** *noun* [17th c. (*joque*), originally slang: perhaps from Latin *jocus* jest]

jok·er *noun* **1** a person who jokes. **2** a person who is considered foolish or inept and so not treated seriously. **3** a playing card usu. with a figure of a jester, used in some games esp. as a wild card. **4** *US* a clause unobtrusively inserted in a bill or document and affecting its operation in a way not immediately apparent. **5** an unexpected factor or resource. □ **the joker in the pack** an unpredictable factor or participant.

joke·ster *noun* a person who makes esp. petty jokes.

jolie laide /ˌʒɒliˈled/ *noun* (pl. **jolies laides** *pronunc.* same) a woman whose face is attractive despite having features conventionally considered to be plain. [French from *jolie* pretty + *laide* ugly]

Jo·liet *var.* of JOLLIET.

Jo·li·ette /ʒɒˈljet/ a city in south central Quebec, about 50 km northeast of Laval; pop. (1996) 17,837. [B. *Joliette*, founder of the city d.1850]

Joliot-Curie /ʒɔljoːkjʊˈri/ **Jean-Frédéric** (1900–58) and **Irène** (1897–1956) (daughter of Marie and Pierre Curie), French nuclear physicists. Their joint discovery of artificial radioactivity earned them the 1935 Nobel Prize for chemistry.

Jol·liet /dzɒliˈet/ **Louis** (1645–1700), Canadian explorer. Born in Quebec, he was sent in 1672 to find and explore the Mississippi River, which was then known to Europeans only through second-hand accounts. He entered the river in 1673, and followed it to the mouth of the Arkansas before turning back.

jol·lify *transitive & intransitive verb* (**-fies, -fied**) make or be jolly. □ **jol·li·fi·ca·tion** *noun*

jol·lity *noun* (pl. **-ties**) **1** the quality or condition of being jolly, cheerful, or festive. **2** merrymaking; festiveness.

jolly¹ ● *adjective* (**jol·li·er, jol·li·est**) **1** cheerful and good-humoured. **2** lively and very pleasant; delightful or enjoyable. ● *adverb* *Brit. informal* very (*they were jolly unlucky*). ● *transitive verb* (**-lies, -lied**) **1** (usu. foll. by *up, along*) *informal* keep or make (a person) jolly or cheerful by friendly behaviour etc. **2** poke fun at, tease. ● *noun* (pl. **-lies**) **1** *N Amer. informal* (usu. in *pl.*) a thrill or cause of excitement or pleasure. **2** esp. *Brit.* a trip or excursion, esp. one made at public expense by a politician etc. **3** *Brit. informal* a party or celebration. □ **jolly well** *Brit.* (used as an intensifier, esp. in annoyance) certainly (*if you don't come now, you can jolly well walk home*). □ **jol·li·ness** *noun* [Old French *jolif* gay, pretty, perhaps from Old Norse *jól* YULE]

jolly² *noun* (pl. **-lies**) (in full **jolly boat**) a clinker-built ship's boat smaller than a cutter, with a bluff bow and very wide transom. [18th c.: origin unknown: perhaps related to YAWL]

Jolly Jumper *noun* *Cdn proprietary* an infant swing which suspends a baby in a harness in a standing position just above the floor, allowing the child to jump, exercise its legs, etc.

Jolly Roger *noun* a pirate's black flag, usu. with the skull and crossbones.

Jol·son /ˈdzoːlsən/ **Al** (born Asa Yoelson) (1886–1950), Russian-born US singer, film actor, and comedian. He made the Gershwin song 'Swanee' his trademark, and appeared in the first full-length talking film *The Jazz Singer* (1927).

jolt ● *verb* **1** *transitive* disturb or shake from the normal position with a jerk. **2** *transitive* give a mental shock to; perturb. **3** *transitive* invigorate suddenly or abruptly (*jolt the failing economy back to life*). **4** *intransitive* **a** move with a jolt. **b** (of a vehicle) move along with jerks, as on a rough road. ● *noun* **1** an abrupt movement or jerk. **2** a surprise or mental shock. **3** a sudden invigorating sensation (*caffeine provides a jolt*). □ **jolty** *adjective* (**jolt·i·er, jolt·i·est**). [16th c.: origin unknown]

Jon. *abbreviation* Jonah.

Jona·gold *noun* an apple that is a cross of Jonathan and Golden Delicious apples, with a yellowish-green skin with red stripes.

Jo·nah¹ ▸ **1** a Hebrew minor prophet. Called by God to preach in Nineveh, he disobeyed and attempted to escape by sea; in a storm he was thrown overboard as a bringer of bad luck and swallowed by a great fish, only to be saved and finally succeed in his mission. **2** a book of the Bible telling of Jonah.

Jo·nah² *noun* a person who seems to bring bad luck.

Jona·mac *noun* an apple that is a cross of Jonathan and McIntosh.

Jona·than¹ (in the Bible) the son of Saul and friend of David, killed at the battle of Mount Gilboa (1 Sam. 13 ff.).

Jona·than² *noun* a red-skinned cooking apple with a yellowish flesh. [Jonathan Hasbrouck, US lawyer d.1846]

Jones ▸ **1 Chuck** (born Charles Martin Jones) (1912–2002), American animator who created popular cartoon characters Bugs Bunny, Daffy Duck and Elmer Fudd, among others. He won an Academy Award for lifetime achievement in 1996. **2 Inigo** (1573–1652), English architect and stage designer. He introduced the Palladian style to England; he also pioneered the use of the proscenium arch and movable stage scenery in England, and was involved with costume design for court masques. **3 John Paul** (born John Paul) (1747–92), Scottish-born US admiral. He became famous for his raids off the northern coasts of Britain during the American Revolution. **4 John Wal·ter** (1878–1954), premier of PEI 1943–53. An outspoken and successful farmer, Jones was first elected to the PEI legislature as a Liberal in 1935. As premier, he championed rural interests, for example by seizing a strikebound Canada Packers plant in 1947, hiring scab labour, and outlawing all unions affiliated with national or international labour organizations. He was appointed to the Senate in 1953. **5 (Ev·er·ett) LeRoi** (Muslim name Imamu Amiri Baraka) (b.1934), US playwright, poet, novelist, and essayist. A committed black political activist, he is known for plays such as the one-act *Four Black Revolutionary Plays* (1969), the novel *The System of Dante's Hell* (1965), and essay collections such as *Home* (1966).

jones esp. *US slang* ● *noun* **1** a fixation on or compulsive desire for someone or something, esp. a drug; an addiction. **2** a craving. ● *intransitive verb* (often foll. by *for*) **1** have a fixation on; be addicted to. **2** have a craving for. [said to come from *Jones* Alley in Manhattan, associated with drug addicts]

Jones·es *plural noun* a person's neighbours or social equals. □ **keep up with the Joneses** try to emulate or not be outdone by one's neighbours. [*Jones*, a common British surname]

jon·gleur /dʒɔ̃ˈglɔːr/ *noun* *hist.* an itinerant minstrel in the Middle Ages. [French, var. of *jougleur* JUGGLER]

Jon·quière /ʒɔ̃ˈkjer/ a former city in NE central Quebec, just west of Chicoutimi, now merged with Chicoutimi, La Baie, Laterrière and other communities into the city of Saguenay; pop. (2001) 54,842. [J.-P. de Taffanel, Marquis de *Jonquière*, Governor General of New France d.1752]

jon·quil /ˈdʒɒnkwɪl/ *noun* a bulbous plant, *Narcissus jonquilla*, with clusters of small fragrant yellow flowers. [modern Latin *jonquilla* and French *jonquille* from Spanish *junquillo* diminutive of *junco*: see JUNCO]

Jon·son, Ben·ja·min ('Ben') (1572–1637), English dramatist and poet. With his play *Every Man in his Humour* (1598), he established his 'comedy of humours' whereby each character is dominated by a particular obsession; his vigorous and often savage wit is evident in his comedies *Volpone* (1606) and *Bartholomew Fair* (1614).

Jop·lin ▸ **1 Janis (Lyn)** (1943–70), US rock singer, who was known for her hoarse, bluesy voice and rebellious, uninhibited personality; her albums include *Cheap Thrills* (1968), *Kosmic Blues* (1969), and the posthumously-released *Pearl* (1971). **2 Scott** (1868–1917), US pianist and composer. One of the creators of ragtime, he was the first to write down his compositions, and is known for rags such as 'Maple Leaf Rag' (1899), and 'The Entertainer' (1902).

Jor·dan¹ (in full **Hashemite Kingdom of Jordan**) a country in the Middle East, east of the Jordan River; pop. (est. 2002) 5,307,470; capital, Amman. During the war of 1948–9 following the establishment of the state of Israel the Jordanians took over a large area on the west bank of the river, but were driven out by Israel in the Six Day War of 1967 (see WEST BANK); many Palestinian refugees then

---

t *top*   v *voice*   w *we*   z *zoo*   ʃ *she*   ʒ *vision*   θ *thin*   ð *this*   ŋ *ring*   x *loch*   tʃ *chip*   dʒ *jar*   (*see over for vowels*)

entered the country, and the PLO maintained its headquarters there until it was expelled following the short civil war of 1970. A peace treaty with Israel in 1994 ended an official state of war between the two countries. □ **Jor·dan·ian** /dʒɔrˈdeiniən/ *adjective & noun*

Jor·dan², **Mi·chael (Jef·frey)** (b.1963), US basketball player. He won six NBA championships with the Chicago Bulls (1991–93 and 1996–98), and won the league scoring title a record ten times.

Jordan River a river flowing southward for 320 km (200 miles) from the Anti-Lebanon mountains through the Sea of Galilee into the Dead Sea. John the Baptist baptized Christ in the Jordan River. It is regarded as sacred not only by Christians but also by Jews and Muslims.

jor·um /ˈdʒɔrəm/ *noun* **1** a large drinking bowl. **2** its contents, esp. punch. [perhaps from *Joram* (2 Sam. 8:10)]

Jos /dʒɔːs/ a city in central Nigeria; pop. (est. 1991) 510,300.

Jo·seph ▶ **1** a Hebrew patriarch, son of Jacob. He was given a coat of many colours by his father, but was then sold by his jealous brothers into captivity in Egypt, where he attained high office (Gen. 30–50). **2 St.** (*fl.* 1st c. AD), a carpenter of Nazareth, husband of the Virgin Mary; at the time of the Annunciation, he was betrothed to Mary. Feast day, 19 Mar.

Joseph II (1741–90), Holy Roman emperor 1765–90. He was co-regent of Austria with his mother Maria Theresa from 1765 and sole ruler 1780–90; he abolished serfdom, curtailed the privileges of the nobles, and issued edicts in 1781 granting toleration to Jews and Protestants.

Joseph, Lake a lake in south central Ontario, situated off the eastern shore of Georgian Bay, southeast of Parry Sound. [*Joseph* Dennis, father of surveyor J. S. Dennis *c.*1860]

Jo·seph·ine (born Marie Joséphine Rose Tascher de la Pagerie) (1763–1814), empress of France 1796–1809. Born in the West Indies, she was married to the Viscount de Beauharnais before marrying Napoleon in 1796; their marriage proved childless and Napoleon divorced her in 1809.

Jo·seph of Ari·ma·thea /ˌɛriməˈθiːə/ a member of the council at Jerusalem who, after the Crucifixion, asked Pilate for Christ's body, which he buried. He is also known from the medieval story that he came to England with the Holy Grail and built the first church at Glastonbury.

Jo·seph·us /dʒɔˈsiːfəs/ **Flav·ius** (born Joseph ben Matthias) (*c.*37–*c.*100), Jewish historian and general. A leader of the Jewish revolt against the Romans from 66, he was captured in 67 but was spared when he prophesied that Vespasian would become emperor; his works include the *History of the Jewish War* (75–9), and *Antiquities of the Jews* (93), a history until 66.

Josh. *abbreviation* Joshua, a book of the Bible.

josh *slang* ● *verb* **1** *transitive* tease or joke with. **2** *intransitive* indulge in banter. ● *noun* a good-natured or teasing joke. □ **josh·er** *noun* **josh·ing** *noun* **josh·ing·ly** *adverb* [19th c.: origin unknown]

Joshua ▶ **1** the Israelite leader (probably 13th c. BC) who succeeded Moses and led his people into the Promised Land. **2** the sixth book of the Bible, telling of the conquest of Canaan and its division among the twelve tribes of Israel.

Joshua tree *noun* a yucca, *Yucca brevifolia*, of arid parts of western N America. [apparently from JOSHUA, the plant being likened to a man brandishing a spear (Joshua 8:18)]

Jo·siah /dʒɔˈsaiə/ (also **Jo·sias** /dʒɔːˈsaiəs/) (died *c.*609 BC), king of Judah *c.*640–*c.*609, who undertook a major reform of religion in and around Jerusalem.

Jos·quin des Prez /ʒɒskä dei ˈprei/ (also **des Prés**, **Deprez**) (*c.*1440–1521), Flemish composer. One of the leading composers of the Renaissance, he wrote masses, motets, and songs.

joss *noun* **1** a Chinese figure of a god. **2** = JOSS STICK. [perhaps ultimately from Portuguese *deos* from Latin *deus* god]

joss house *noun* a Chinese temple.

joss stick *noun* a stick of fragrant tinder mixed with clay, burned as incense.

jos·tle ● *verb* **1** *transitive* knock or come into rough collision with. **2** *transitive* (often foll. by *away*, *from*, etc.) push (a person) roughly or unceremoniously. **3** *intransitive* push, shove, or come into collision with, esp. in a crowd. **4** *intransitive* (often foll. by *for*, *with*) vie, struggle, or compete forcefully in order to gain something. ● *noun* **1** the act or an instance of jostling. **2** a collision, rough push, or thrust. □ **jos·tler** *noun* [Middle English: earlier *justle* from JOUST + -LE⁴]

jot ● *transitive verb* (**jot·ted**, **jot·ting**) (usu. foll. by *down*) write briefly or hastily. ● *noun* (often with *neg.* expressed or implied) a very small

amount (*not one jot or tittle*). [earlier as noun: Latin from Greek *iōta*: see IOTA]

jot·ter *noun* *Brit.* a small pad or notebook for making notes etc.

jot·ting *noun* **1** (usu. in *pl.*) a note; something jotted down. **2** the act or an instance of hastily writing something down.

joual /ʒuːˈɒl/ *noun* a variety of Canadian French considered to be uneducated, characterized by non-standard grammar and syntax and, esp. in cities, numerous English borrowings. [dial. Canadian French from French *cheval*, lit. 'horse']

jouis·sance /ʒwiˈsɒns/ *noun* pleasure or delight, esp. from the possession and use of something advantageous or pleasing. [French *jouir*, lit. 'enjoy']

Joule /ˈdʒuːl/ **James Pres·cott** (1818–89), English physicist. He established that all forms of energy were basically the same and interchangeable; he also established the law governing the thermal effects of an electric current due to the resistance of the wire, and with Thomson, later Lord Kelvin, discovered the fall in temperature when gases expand (the Joule–Thomson effect, 1852), which led to the development of the refrigerator and to the science of cryogenics.

joule /dʒuːl/ *noun* the SI unit of work or energy equal to the work done by a force of one newton when its point of application moves one metre in the direction of action of the force, equivalent to a watt-second. Symbol: **J**. [JOULE]

jounce ● *transitive & intransitive verb* bump, bounce, jolt. ● *noun* a bump, jolt, or a jolting pace. □ **joun·cing** *noun & adjective* **jouncy** *adjective* [Middle English: origin unknown]

jour·nal *noun* **1** a daily record of events; a diary. **2 a** a periodical, esp. an academic one dealing with a specialized subject. **b** an esp. daily newspaper. **3** *Naut.* a logbook. **4** a book in which business transactions are entered, with a statement of the accounts to which each is to be debited and credited. **5** the part of a shaft or axle that rests on bearings. **6** (**the Journals**) a record of daily proceedings in a legislative assembly. [Old French *jurnal* from Late Latin *diurnalis* DIURNAL]

jour·nal·ese *noun* a hackneyed style of language characteristic of some newspaper writing.

jour·nal·ism *noun* **1** the work of collecting, writing, and reporting news items in the press or on television or radio. **2** the news media collectively. **3** material published or broadcast by the news media. □ **jour·nal·ist** *noun* **jour·nal·is·tic** *adjective* **jour·nal·is·tic·ally** *adverb*

jour·ney ● *noun* (*pl.* **-neys**) **1** an act of going from one place to another, esp. at a long distance. **2** the distance travelled in a specified time (*a day's journey*). **3** the travelling of a vehicle along a route at a stated time. **4** one's passage or progress through life. ● *intransitive verb* (**-neys**, **-neyed**) make a journey. □ **jour·ney·er** *noun* [Old French *jornee* day, day's work or travel, ultimately from Latin *diurnus* daily]

journey·man *noun* (*pl.* **-men**) **1** a person who, having served an apprenticeship, is qualified to work in a craft or trade under the direction of another more qualified person. **2** a reliable but not outstanding worker. [JOURNEY in obsolete sense 'day's work' + MAN]

Journey Prize *noun* (in full **The Writers' Trust of Canada/McClelland & Stewart Journey Prize**) an annual prize awarded to a new writer for a short story published in a Canadian literary publication. [funded by James A. Michener's donation of the Canadian royalties from his novel *Journey*]

jour·no *noun* (*pl.* **-nos**) esp. *Brit. slang* a journalist.

joust ● *noun* **1** *hist.* a combat between two knights on horseback with lances. **2** a verbal, political, etc. encounter or contest, esp. between two individuals. ● *intransitive verb* engage in a joust. □ **joust·er** *noun* [Old French *juster* bring together, ultimately from Latin *juxta* near]

Jove *noun* (in Roman mythology) Jupiter. □ **by Jove!** an exclamation of surprise or approval. [Latin *Jovis* used as genitive of JUPITER]

jov·ial /ˈdʒoːviəl/ *adjective* merry, convivial, hearty and good-humoured. □ **jovi·al·ity** /-ˈaliti/ *noun* **jov·ial·ly** *adverb* [French from Late Latin *jovialis* of Jupiter (as JOVE), with reference to the supposed influence of the planet Jupiter on those born under it]

Jov·ian /ˈdʒoːviən/ *adjective* **1** (in Roman mythology) of or like Jupiter. **2** of the planet Jupiter. **3** designating the class of planets that resemble Jupiter in mass and density, esp. Jupiter, Saturn, Uranus, and Neptune in the Earth's solar system.

jowar /dʒauˈwɑr/ *noun* = DURRA. [Hindi *jawār*]

jowl¹ *noun* **1** the jaw or jawbone. **2** the cheek (*cheek by jowl*). □ **-jowled** *adjective* (in *combination*). [Middle English *chavel* jaw, from Old English *ceafl*]

jowl² noun **1** the external loose skin on the throat or neck when prominent. **2** the dewlap of oxen, wattle of a bird, etc. **3 a** *Cdn* (*Nfld*) the meat of the cheek of cod eaten as food. **b** *N Amer.* the meat of the cheek of a pig eaten as food. □ **jowly** *adjective* [Middle English *cholle* neck, from Old English *ceole*]

joy noun **1** (often foll. by *at*, *in*) a vivid emotion of pleasure; extreme gladness. **2** a thing that causes joy. **3** *informal* satisfaction, success (*got no joy*). □ **wish a person joy of** *ironic* be gladly rid of (what that person has to deal with). □ **joy·less** *adjective* **joy·less·ly** *adverb* [Old French *joie*, ultimately from Latin *gaudium* from *gaudēre* rejoice]

joy buzzer noun *N Amer.* a device concealed in the palm of the hand with which, as a practical joke, one surprises another with a buzzing noise and unpleasant vibrating sensation while shaking hands.

Joyce, James (Au·gus·tine Aloy·sius) (1882–1941), Irish novelist and short-story writer. His two greatest works, *Ulysses* (1922) and *Finnegans Wake* (1939) revolutionized the techniques of fiction-writing, introducing the 'stream of consciousness', inventing words, and experimenting with syntax; his earlier books include *Dubliners* (1914) and the autobiographical *A Portrait of the Artist as a Young Man* (1914–15).

Joy·cean /ˈdʒɔisiən/ ● *adjective* of or characteristic of James Joyce or his work. ● *noun* a specialist in or admirer of Joyce's works.

joy·ful *adjective* full of, showing, or causing joy. □ **joy·ful·ly** *adverb* **joy·ful·ness** *noun*

joy·ous *adjective* (of an occasion, circumstance, etc.) characterized by pleasure or joy; joyful. □ **joy·ous·ly** *adverb* **joy·ous·ness** *noun*

joy·ride *informal* ● *noun* **1** a car ride taken for fun and excitement, usu. without the owner's permission. **2** a pleasurable, often exciting, and usu. brief experience. ● *intransitive verb* (*past* **-rode**; *past participle* **-rid·den**) go for a joyride. □ **joy·rid·er** *noun* **joy·rid·ing** *noun*

joy·stick noun **1** *informal* the control column of an aircraft. **2** a lever that can be moved in several directions to control the movement of an image on a video or computer screen.

JP *abbreviation* JUSTICE OF THE PEACE.

JPEG /ˈdʒeipeg/ noun **1** a technique and standard for the compression of continuous-tone digital images. **2** an image encoded as a file in this format. [acronym from Joint Photographic Experts Group, the name of the committee who devised the standard]

Jr. *abbreviation* Junior.

J-school noun *N Amer. slang* journalism school.

J-stroke noun *Canoeing* a paddle stroke made in the shape of a letter J, used to bring the canoe back on course after drifting sideways.

Juan Car·los /hwɒn ˈkɑrlos/ (b.1938), grandson of Alfonso XIII, king of Spain since 1975. He was nominated by Franco as his successor and became king when Franco died; his reign has seen Spain's increasing liberalization and its entry into NATO and the European Community.

Juan de Fuca Strait /ˌwɒn də ˈfjuːkə, ˈfuːkə/ a passage of the N Pacific, lying between the south coast of Vancouver Island and Washington state. It connects the Pacific Ocean and the Strait of Georgia. [*Juan de Fuca* (or *Iwannis Phokas*), Greek sea captain in the service of Spain d.1602]

Juan Fer·nan·dez Islands /ˌhwɒn fərˈnandez/ a group of three almost uninhabited islands in the Pacific Ocean 640 km (400 miles) west of Chile.

Juá·rez /ˈhwɑrez/ **Benito (Pablo)** (1806–72), Mexican leader, president 1861–4 and 1867–72. His refusal to repay Mexico's foreign debts led to the occupation of Mexico by Napoleon III and the establishment of Maximilian as emperor of Mexico (1864); with the withdrawal of the occupying French forces (1867) Maximilian was executed and Juárez returned to power.

Juba /ˈdʒuːbə/ the capital of the southern region of Sudan, on the White Nile; pop. (est. 2002) 151,000. Since 1983 it has been virtually isolated by the civil war in Sudan.

Jubal /ˈdʒuːbəl/ *Bible* a descendant of Cain, and the alleged inventor of musical instruments (Gen. 4:21).

Jubba River /ˈdʒʊbə, ˈdʒuːbə/ (also **Juba River**) a river in East Africa, rising in the highlands of central Ethiopia and flowing southward for about 1 600 km (1,000 miles) through Somalia to the Indian Ocean.

ju·bi·lant /ˈdʒuːbɪlənt/ *adjective* exultant, rejoicing, joyful. □ **ju·bi·lance** *noun* **ju·bi·lant·ly** *adverb* [Latin *jubilare jubilant-* shout for joy]

Ju·bi·late /juːbɪˈlatei, ˈdʒuː-/ *noun* **1** Psalm 100, beginning *Jubilate deo* 'Be joyful in God', used as a canticle. **2** a musical setting of this. [Latin]

ju·bi·late /ˈdʒuːbɪˌleit/ *intransitive verb* exult; be joyful. □ **ju·bi·la·tion** /-ˈleiʃən/ *noun* [Latin *jubilare* (as JUBILANT)]

ju·bi·lee /ˈdʒuːbɪˈliː, ˈdʒuː-/ *noun* **1** an anniversary, esp. the 25th, 50th, or 60th. **2** a time or season of rejoicing. **3 a** *Jewish Hist.* a year of emancipation and restoration, kept every 50 years. **b** a time of restitution, remission, or release. **4** *Catholicism* a period, usu. every 25 years, during which indulgences are granted under certain conditions. [Old French *jubilé* from Late Latin *jubilaeus* (*annus*) (year) of jubilee, ultimately from Hebrew *yōḇēl*, originally = ram, ram's-horn trumpet]

Jub·ran *see* GIBRAN.

Jud. *abbreviation* **1** (also **Judg.**) Judges, a book of the Bible. **2** Judith, a book of the Apocrypha.

Ju·daea *var. of* JUDEA.

Judaeo- *combining form var. of* JUDEO-.

Judah /ˈdʒuːdə/ **1** the most powerful of the twelve tribes of Israel. After the reign of Solomon it formed a separate kingdom (Judea), which outlasted that of the northern tribes. **2** = JUDEA.

Ju·da·ic /dʒuːˈdeiɪk/ *adjective* of or characteristic of the Jews or Judaism. [Latin *Judaicus* from Greek *Ioudaïkos* from *Ioudaios* JEW]

Ju·da·ica /dʒuːˈdeiɪkə/ *plural noun* (treated as *sing.*) **1** the literature, customs, ritual objects, artifacts, etc. which are of particular relevance to Jews or Judaism. **2** such items or aspects of Jewish life individually.

Ju·da·ism /ˈdʒuːˌdeiˌɪzəm/ *noun* **1** the religion of the Jews, with a belief in one God and a basis in Mosaic and rabbinical teachings. **2** the cultural practices, social identity, etc. based on this religion. **3** *hist.* the Jews collectively. [Late Latin *Judaismus* from Greek *Ioudaismos* (as JUDAIC)]

Ju·da·ize /ˈdʒuːˌdeiˌaiz/ *verb* (also esp. *Brit.* **-ise**) **1** *intransitive* follow Jewish customs or rites. **2** *transitive* **a** make Jewish. **b** convert to Judaism. **3** *transitive* imbue with Jewish doctrines or principles. □ **Ju·da·iz·a·tion** *noun* **Ju·da·ized** *adjective* **Ju·da·iz·er** *noun* [Late Latin *judaizare* from Greek *ioudaizō* (as JUDAIC)]

Judas¹ *see* JUDE, ST.

Judas² /ˈdʒuːdəs/ ● *noun* **1** a person who betrays a friend. **2** (**judas**) (also **judas hole**, **judas window**) a peephole in a door. ● *adjective* an animal used to lead others of its kind to destruction (*judas goat*). [JUDAS ISCARIOT]

Judas Is·car·iot /ɪˈskeriət/ (died *c.* AD 30), an Apostle. He betrayed Jesus to the Jewish authorities in return for 30 pieces of silver; he later committed suicide.

Judas Mac·ca·baeus /ˌmakəˈbiːəs/ (died *c.*161 BC), Jewish leader. He led the Jewish revolt in Judea against the Seleucid king, Antiochus IV Epiphanes, from around 167, so recovering Jerusalem, dedicating the Temple anew, and protecting Judaism from Hellenization.

Judas tree noun a Mediterranean tree, *Cercis siliquastrum*, with purple flowers usu. appearing before the leaves.

jud·der ● *intransitive verb* (esp. of a mechanism) shake or vibrate noisily or violently. ● *noun* **1** an instance of juddering. **2** the condition of juddering. □ **jud·dery** *adjective* [imitative: compare SHUDDER]

Jude, St. 1 (known as 'Judas') an Apostle, supposed brother of James. According to tradition, he was martyred in Persia with St. Simon. Feast day (with St. Simon), 28 October. **2** the last epistle of the New Testament, ascribed to St. Jude.

Judea /dʒuːˈdiːə/ the southern part of ancient Palestine, corresponding to the former kingdom of Judah. The Jews returned to the region in 537 BC after the Babylonian Captivity, and in 165 the Maccabees again established it as an independent kingdom. It became a province of the Roman Empire in 63 BC, and was subsequently amalgamated with Palestine (*see also* JUDAH 2). □ **Ju·dean** *adjective*

Judeo- /dʒuːˈdeiːoː/ *combining form* (also **Judaeo-**) **1** pertaining to the Jews, Judaism, or things Jewish. **2** Jewish and (*Judeo-Christian*). [Latin *judaeus* Jewish]

Judg. *abbreviation* Judges, a book of the Old Testament.

judge ● *noun* **1** a public officer appointed to hear and try causes in a court of justice. **2** a person appointed to decide a competition, contest, dispute, etc. **3 a** a person who decides anything in question. **b** a person regarded in terms of capacity to decide on the merits of a thing or question (*am no judge of that; a good judge of art*). **4** *Jewish Hist.* a leader having temporary authority in Israel in the period between Joshua and the Kings. ● *verb* **1** *transitive* **a** try (a cause) in a court of justice. **b** pronounce sentence on (a person). **2** *transitive* form an opinion about; estimate, appraise. **3** *transitive* act as a judge of (a dispute or contest). **4** *transitive* (often foll. by *to* + infin. or *that* + clause) conclude, consider, or suppose. **5** *intransitive* **a** form a judgment. **b** act as judge. □ **judge·like** *adjective* **judge·ship** *noun* [Old French *juge* (n.), *juger* (v.) from Latin *judex judicis* from *jus* law + *-dicus* speaking]

judge advocate *noun* a lawyer who advises a court martial on points of law and sums up the case.

Judge Advocate General *noun* an officer in supreme control of the courts martial in the armed forces.

judge-made *adjective* (of law) constituted by judicial decisions (*compare* CASE LAW, COMMON LAW).

Judg·es the seventh book of the Bible, describing the gradual conquest of Canaan under various leaders (known as judges) in an account that is parallel to that of the Book of Joshua and is probably more accurate historically.

judg·ment *noun* (also **judge·ment**) **1** the critical faculty; discernment (*an error of judgment*). **2** good sense. **3** an opinion or estimate (*in my judgment*). **4 a** the sentence of a court of justice. **b** judicial decision or order in court. **5** criticism. **6 a** a divine decree, decision, or sentence. **b** often *jocular* a misfortune viewed as a deserved recompense (*it is a judgment on you for getting up late*). **7** = LAST JUDGMENT. □ **against one's better judgment** contrary to what one really feels to be advisable.

judg·ment·al *adjective* (also **judge·ment·al**) **1** of, concerning, or by way of judgment. **2** condemning, critical, esp. in moral matters. □ **judg·ment·al·ly** *adverb*

judgment call *noun* a decision made on personal observation, by subjective determination, etc., esp. when the facts of a situation are indeterminate.

judgment creditor *noun* a creditor in whose favour a judgment has been given ordering the payment of the debt due.

Judgment Day *noun* the day on which the Last Judgment is believed to take place; doomsday.

judgment debtor *noun* a debtor against whom a judgment ordering payment has been given.

judi·care /ˈdʒuːdɪkɛr/ *noun Cdn* a form of legal aid in which lawyers bill the province for services to poor clients rather than receiving a salary. [blend of JUDICIAL + CARE, after MEDICARE]

judi·ca·ture /ˈdʒuːdɪkətʃər, -ˈdɪkətʃər/ *noun* **1** the administration of justice. **2** the office, function, or authority of a judge. **3** judges collectively. **4** a court of justice. [medieval Latin *judicatura* from Latin *judicare* to judge]

ju·di·cial /dʒuːˈdɪʃəl/ *adjective* **1** of, done by, or proper to a court of law. **2** having the function of judgment; invested with the authority to judge causes (*a judicial assembly*). **3** of or proper to a judge. **4** giving or being disposed to pass judgment on a matter; critical. **5** judicious, impartial, having or showing sound judgment. **6** regarded as a divine judgment. □ **ju·di·cial·ly** *adverb* [Latin *judicialis* from *judicium* judgment, from *judex* JUDGE]

Judicial Committee *noun Law Cdn* a committee made up of chief judges, either nationally or from a specific province or territory, which considers proposed appointments to the bench, reports to the Attorney General, vets complaints about judges, etc.

Judicial Committee of the Privy Council *noun esp. hist.* the final court for the disposal of appeals made to the King or Queen in Council from colonial countries. Established in 1832, it was the final court of appeal for Canadians until 1949 and continues as such for certain Commonwealth countries.

judicial district *noun Cdn Law* (in certain provinces) a territory, county, or district subdivided for purposes of holding district or county courts, with a judge having jurisdiction over each subdivision.

judicial review *noun Law* a procedure by which a superior judicial body may pronounce on (in Canada) the conduct of an inferior court, committee, etc. to ensure the conduct was proper, (in the US) the validity of an act of legislature, (in the UK) a decision of an inferior court or public authority.

ju·di·ciary /dʒuːˈdɪʃəri, -ieri/ *noun* (*pl.* **-ies**) the judges of a nation collectively. ● *adjective* = JUDICIAL 1, 2, 3. [Latin *judiciarius* (as JUDICIAL)]

ju·di·cious /dʒuːˈdɪʃəs/ *adjective* **1** sensible, prudent, proceeding from or showing sound judgment esp. in practical matters. **2** (of a person, the faculties, etc.) sound in discernment and judgment. □ **ju·di·cious·ly** *adverb* **ju·di·cious·ness** *noun* [French *judicieux* from Latin *judicium* (as JUDICIAL)]

Ju·dith ▸ **1** (in the Apocrypha) a rich Israelite widow who saved the town of Bethulia from Nebuchadnezzar's army by captivating the besieging general Holofernes and cutting off his head while he slept. **2** a book of the Apocrypha recounting the story of Judith.

judo *noun* a refined form of jiu-jitsu using principles of movement and balance, practised as a sport or form of physical exercise. □ **judo·ist** *noun* [Japanese from *jū* gentle + *dō* way]

judo·ka /ˈdʒuːdoːkə/ *noun* a person who practises or is an expert in judo. [Japanese, from JUDO + -*ka* 'person, profession']

Judy *noun* (*pl.* **-dies**) **1** the wife of Punch (*see* PUNCH 1). **2** (also **judy**) esp. *Brit. slang* a woman. [pet form of the name *Judith*]

jug ● *noun* **1 a** *N Amer.* a large, deep vessel, usu. of glass or earthenware, with a narrow neck and usu. a handle. **b** *Cdn & Brit.* a deep vessel for holding liquids, with a handle and often with a spout or lip shaped for pouring. **2** the contents of a jug; a jugful. **3** *slang* prison. **4** (in *pl.*) *N Amer. slang* a woman's breasts. ● *transitive verb* (**jugged**, **jug·ging**) **1** (in rock or ice climbing etc.) climb a rope like a ladder. **2** *slang* imprison. □ **jug·ful** *noun* (*pl.* **-fuls**). [perhaps from *Jug*, pet form of the name *Joan* etc.]

jug band *noun* a folk or blues band in which jugs are played by blowing across the opening to produce bass notes, usu. accompanied by other makeshift or simple instruments such as washboards, kazoos, etc.

jug-eared *adjective* having large, protruding ears.

jug·ger·naut *noun* **1** a huge or overwhelming force or object. **2** esp. *Brit.* a large heavy motor vehicle, esp. an articulated truck. [Hindi *Jagannath* from Sanskrit *Jagannātha* = lord of the world: name of an idol of Krishna in Hindu belief, carried in procession on a huge cart under which devotees are said to have formerly thrown themselves]

jug·gle ● *verb* **1 a** *intransitive* (often foll. by *with*) perform feats of dexterity, esp. by tossing objects in the air and catching them, keeping several in the air at the same time. **b** *transitive* perform such feats with. **2** *transitive* continue to deal with (several activities) at once, esp. with ingenuity. **3** *intransitive & transitive* **a** change the arrangement of something adroitly to achieve a more viable or satisfactory result (*juggle bookings*). **b** manipulate or misrepresent (facts etc.), esp. to deceive or cheat. ● *noun* an act or instance of juggling. [Middle English, back-formation from JUGGLER or from Old French *jogler*, *jugler* from Latin *joculari* jest, from *joculus* diminutive of *jocus* jest]

jug·gler *noun* **1** a person who juggles. **2** a trickster or imposter. □ **jug·glery** *noun*

jug·head *noun* a stupid person.

jug milk *noun* (also **jug milk store**, **jug milk outlet**, etc.) *Cdn (Ont.)* a convenience store at which milk may be bought in returnable plastic jugs.

Jugo·slav *var. of* YUGOSLAV.

jugu·lar /ˈdʒʌɡjʊlər/ ● *adjective* **1 a** of the neck or throat. **b** designating or pertaining to any of several large veins of the neck. **2** (of fish) having ventral fins in front of the pectoral fins, in the throat region. ● *noun* **1** = JUGULAR VEIN. **2** the weakest point in an opponent's argument etc., esp. when subject to fierce attack (*a go-for-the-jugular campaign*). [Late Latin *jugularis* from Latin *jugulum* collarbone, throat, diminutive of *jugum* YOKE]

jugular vein *noun* any of several large veins of the neck which carry blood from the face, head, brain, etc.

juice ● *noun* **1** the extractable liquid part of a vegetable or fruit, commonly containing its characteristic flavour etc. **2 a** the fluid part of an animal body or substance, esp. a secretion (*gastric juice*). **b** the fluid naturally contained in or coming from anything. **3 a** the essence or spirit of anything. **b** (in *pl.*) a person's vitality or creative, expressive, etc. faculties. **c** strength or vigour. **4** *informal* gasoline or electricity as a source of power. **5** *N Amer. slang* **a** influence or money, esp. that obtained by or used in corrupt or criminal activities. **b** money lent at a usurious rate of interest or the interest extorted usuriously. **6** *N Amer. slang* gossip, rumour, scandal. **7** *N Amer. slang* alcoholic drink; liquor. ● *transitive verb* extract the juice from (a fruit etc.). □ **juice up** **1** increase the power, potential, or performance of. **2** heighten the enthusiasm, energy, or style of. □ **juice·less** *adjective* [Old French *jus* from Latin *jus* broth, juice]

juice bar *noun N Amer.* **1** a café-style establishment serving esp. freshly squeezed fruit juices. **2** a nightclub for teenagers, where only non-alcoholic beverages are served.

juice box *noun N Amer.* a small box comprising layers of foil, plastic, waxed cardboard, etc., with a short straw attached, containing an individual serving of fruit juice.

juiced *adjective* **1** *N Amer. slang* intoxicated. **2** *N Amer. slang* (of a baseball, card deck, etc.) being inexplicably and perhaps illicitly altered and enhanced for superior results. **3** (of fruit etc.) having had its juice extracted.

juicer *noun* **1** an appliance or device used to extract juice from fruit or vegetables. **2** *N Amer.* an alcoholic.

juicy *adjective* (**juici·er**, **juici·est**) **1** full of juice; succulent. **2** *informal*

Consonants: b *but* d *dog* f *few* g *get* h *her* j *yes* k *cat* l *leg* m *man* n *no* p *pen* r *red* s *sit*

a substantial or interesting (*always gets the juicy roles*). **b** racy, scandalous (*juicy gossip*). **3** *informal* profitable. □ **juici·ly** *adverb*

juici·ness *noun*

ju-jitsu /dʒuːˈdʒɪtsuː/ *var. of* JIU-JITSU.

juju /ˈdʒuːdʒuː/ *noun* **1** a charm or fetish of some W African peoples. **2** a supernatural power attributed to this. **3** *Music* a flowing, sonorous, and complex musical style of Yoruba origin, usu. combining numerous interrelating drums, guitars, and call-and-response singing. [perhaps from French *joujou* toy]

ju·jube *noun* **1 a** any plant of the genus *Zizyphus* bearing edible acidic berry-like fruits. **b** this fruit. **2** a small, flavoured, jellylike candy. [French *jujube* or medieval Latin *jujuba*, ultimately from Greek *zizuphon*]

ju-jutsu *var. of* JIU-JITSU.

juke ● *noun* **1** *US* **a** = JUKE JOINT. **b** = JUKEBOX. **2** a feigned move or gesture, esp. intended to confuse or deceive. ● *verb* **1** *transitive & intransitive* feign or make a sham move to confuse or mislead (one's opponent). **2** *intransitive* move in a zigzag fashion. **3** *intransitive* dance, esp. at a juke joint or to the music of a jukebox. [prob. from Gullah *juke*, *joog*, 'disorderly, wicked' of W African origin]

juke·box *noun* **1** a machine that automatically plays a selected musical recording when a coin is inserted. **2** *Computing* a device for holding a number of CD-ROMs in such a way that any of them can be played or accessed.

juke joint *noun N Amer.* a roadhouse, nightclub, etc., esp. one providing food, drinks, and music for dancing.

juku /ˈdʒuːkuː/ *noun* (in Japan) a place of study, complementing one's normal schooling, where students cram, are tutored, etc. in preparation for university entrance examinations.

Jul. *abbreviation* July.

ju·lep /ˈdʒuːlep/ *noun* **1** *N Amer.* = MINT JULEP. **2 a** a sweet drink, esp. as a vehicle for medicine. **b** a medicated drink as a mild stimulant etc. [Old French from Arabic *julāb* from Persian *gulāb* from *gul* rose + *āb* water]

Jul·ian¹ (full name Flavius Claudius Julianus) (AD *c.*331–63), Roman emperor 361–3, nephew of Constantine. Known as 'the Apostate', he restored paganism as the state cult in place of Christianity, but this move was reversed after his death while on campaign against the Persians.

Jul·ian² *adjective* **1** of or associated with Julius Caesar. **2** of or pertaining to the calendar reform instituted by him in 46 BC. [Latin *Julianus* from *Julius*]

Juli·ana (full name Juliana Louise Emma Marie Wilhelmina) (1909–2004), queen of the Netherlands 1948–80. She resided in Ottawa during the Second World War, and later abdicated in favour of her eldest daughter Beatrix.

Julian Alps an Alpine range in W Slovenia and NE Italy, rising to a height of 2 863 m (9,395 ft.) at Triglav.

Julian calendar *noun* a calendar introduced by Julius Caesar, in which the year consisted of 365 days, every fourth year having 366 (*compare* GREGORIAN CALENDAR).

Ju·lien /ʒuːlˈjã/ **Paul·ine** (1928–98), Canadian singer, songwriter and actor. After making her debut in Paris around 1957, she returned to Quebec where she introduced the songs of Kurt Weill and Bertolt Brecht. She recorded her first album in 1962, and began writing some of her own material in 1968. She also appeared in several films.

juli·enne /ˌdʒuːliˈen/ ● *noun* **1** food, esp. vegetables, cut into short thin strips. **2** a dish of assorted vegetables cut into thin strips. ● *adjective* **1** (of a vegetable etc.) cut into thin strips. **2** (of a dish or garnish) consisting of or containing such strips. ● *transitive verb* slice (esp. vegetables) into short, thin strips. □ **juli·enned** *adjective* [French from the name *Jules* or *Julien*]

Juliet cap /ˈdʒuːliet/ *noun* a small ornamental skullcap, often decorated with pearls, worn by brides etc. [the heroine of Shakespeare's *Romeo & Juliet*]

Jul·ius Caesar see CAESAR¹.

Jul·lun·dur /ˈdʒʌləndər/ (also **Jalandhar**) a city in Punjab, NW India; pop. (2001) 701,200. It has long been an important communications centre and was capital of Punjab from 1947 to 1954.

July *noun* (*pl.* **Julys**) the seventh month of the year in the Gregorian calendar. Abbr.: **Jul.** [Anglo-French *julie* from Latin *Julius* (*mensis* month), named after Julius Caesar]

jumar /ˈdʒuːmər/ ● *noun* a clamp that is attached to a fixed rope and automatically tightens when weight is applied and relaxes when it is removed. ● *intransitive verb* climb with the aid of such a clamp. [orig. in Swiss use; of unknown origin]

jum·bie *noun* esp. *West Indies* a ghost; an evil spirit. [Kikongo *zumbi* fetish: compare ZOMBIE]

jum·ble ● *noun* **1** a confused state or heap; a muddle. **2** *Brit.* articles collected for a rummage sale. ● *verb* **1** *transitive* (often foll. by *up*) **a** mix or mingle (objects etc.) in a confused and disordered way. **b** confuse or mix up (memories etc.) mentally. **2** *intransitive* move about in disorder. □ **jum·bled** *adjective* [prob. imitative]

jumble sale *noun* esp. *Brit.* a rummage sale.

jum·bo *informal* ● *noun* (*pl.* **-bos**) **1** a large animal (esp. an elephant), person, or thing. **2** (in full **jumbo jet**) a large airliner with capacity for several hundred passengers. ¶ Usu. applied specifically to the Boeing 747. ● *adjective* **1** very large of its kind. **2** extra large. [19th c. (originally of a person): origin unknown: popularized as the name of a zoo elephant sold in 1882]

Jumbo Pass a pass (2 270 m) through the central part of the Purcell Mountains in southeastern BC. [as JUMBO]

Jumbo·tron *noun proprietary* a gigantic television screen used esp. for relaying pictures of an event in stadiums etc.

Jumna River /ˈdʒʌmnə/ a river of N India, which rises in the Himalayas and flows about 1 370 km (850 miles) in a large arc southward and southeastward, through Delhi, joining the Ganges below Allahabad. Its source (Yamunotri) and its confluence with the Ganges are both Hindu holy places.

jump ● *verb* **1** *intransitive* move off the ground or other surface (usu. upward, at least initially) by sudden muscular effort in the legs. **2** *intransitive* (often foll. by *up*, *from*, *in*, *out*, etc.) move suddenly or hastily in a specified way (*we jumped into the car*). **3** *intransitive* give a sudden bodily movement from shock or excitement etc. **4** *intransitive* undergo a rapid change, esp. an advance in status. **5** *intransitive* (often foll. by *around*, *about*) change or move rapidly from one idea or subject to another, omitting intermediate stages. **6 a** *intransitive* rise or increase suddenly (*prices jumped*). **b** *transitive* cause to do this. **7** *transitive* **a** pass over (an obstacle, barrier, etc.) by jumping. **b** move or pass over (an intervening thing) to a point beyond. **8** *transitive* skip, ignore, or pass over (a passage in a book etc.). **9** *transitive* cause (a thing, or an animal, esp. a horse) to jump. **10** *intransitive* (foll. by *to*, *at*) reach a conclusion hastily, esp. without examining the premises. **11** *transitive* (of a train) leave (the rails) owing to a fault. **12** *transitive* **a** anticipate and respond prematurely to (permission or a signal to act). **b** ignore and pass (a red traffic light etc.). **13** *transitive* get on or off (a train etc.) quickly, esp. illegally or dangerously. **14** *transitive* pounce on or attack (a person) unexpectedly. **15** *transitive* take summary possession of (a claim allegedly abandoned or forfeit by the former occupant). **16** *transitive slang* have sexual intercourse with. **17** *transitive* start (a car) using jumper cables. **18** *intransitive* (often foll. by *in*, *into*) join in eagerly and enthusiastically. **19** *intransitive* parachute from a flying plane. **20 a** *transitive & intransitive Bridge* raise (a bid) higher than necessary in the suit concerned. **b** *transitive* (in checkers) jump over and so take (an opposing piece). **21** *intransitive* **a** (of a nightclub etc.) be full of excitement, pulsate with activity. **b** (of jazz or similar music) have a strong or exciting rhythm. **22** *intransitive* obey, respond, or react to another's word, instantly and eagerly. ● *noun* **1** the act or an instance of jumping. **2** *Sport* **a** an act or type of jumping, as an athletic performance. **b** a distance jumped. **c** a place to be jumped from, as in ski jumping etc. **3** an obstacle to be jumped, esp. by a horse. **4** a sudden bodily movement caused by shock or excitement. **5** an abrupt rise in amount, price, value, status, etc. **6 a** a sudden transition from one thing, idea etc. to another, omitting intermediate stages. **b** an interval or gap in argument, technological development, etc. **7** the motion of a firearm, after discharge, which throws the muzzle away from the mounting. □ **get** (or **have**) **the jump on** *informal* get (or have) an advantage over (a person) by prompt action. **jump at** accept eagerly. **jump bail** *see* BAIL¹. **jump down a person's throat** *informal* berate, reprimand, or contradict a person fiercely. **jump the gun** *see* GUN. **jump for joy** be joyfully excited; show one's delight by excited movements. (**go**) **jump in the lake** *informal* (usu. in *imperative*) go away and stop being a nuisance. **jump on** *informal* attack or criticize severely and without warning. **jump out at** **1** grab the attention; be blatantly apparent. **2** suddenly spring out at and surprise (a person). **jump out of one's skin** *informal* be extremely startled. **jump the queue** **1** *Brit.* go to the front of a line of people without waiting one's turn. **2** take unfair precedence over others. **jump rope** *N Amer.* skip with a skipping rope. **jump ship** **1** abandon an organization, effort, etc. before one's commitment is up, an undertaking is finished, etc. **2** (of a seaman) desert. **jump to it** *informal* act promptly and energetically. □ **jump·able** *adjective* **jump·ing** *noun & adjective* [16th c.: prob. imitative]

jump ball *noun Basketball* a ball thrown vertically between two opposing players by the referee to start or resume play.

jump-cut *Film* ● *noun* **1** the excision of part of a shot in order to break its continuity of action and time. **2** the abrupt transition from one scene to another which is discontinuous in time. ● *transitive verb* join (a scene) to others via a jump-cut.

jumped-up *adjective informal* newly or suddenly risen in status or importance, esp. when presumptuously arrogant.

jump·er[1] *noun* **1** *N Amer.* a collarless, sleeveless dress worn over a blouse or sweater. **2** *Brit.* a knitted pullover. [prob. from (17th-c., now dial.) *jump* short coat, perhaps from French *jupe* from Arabic *jubba*]

jump·er[2] *noun* **1** a person or animal that jumps, esp.: **a** a horse trained for show jumping. **b** an athlete in a sport such as ski jumping, high jump, etc. **c** *informal* a person who commits suicide by leaping from a bridge, tall building, etc. **d** *slang* a person who frequently or dramatically changes jobs, religions, etc. **2** *Electricity* **a** a short wire used to make or break a circuit. **b** (usu. in *pl.*) = JUMPER CABLE. **3** *Basketball slang* **a** = JUMPSHOT. **b** = JUMP BALL. **4** *Cdn* = JOLLY JUMPER. **5** a heavy, chisel-ended bore or iron bar worked by hand or a hammer, for drilling blastholes in rock etc.

jumper cable *noun* esp. *N Amer.* either of a pair of heavy electric cables ending in alligator clips, used for conveying current from the battery of one motor vehicle to boost (or recharge) another.

jumping bean *noun* the seed of a Mexican plant, esp. *Sebastiana pavoniana*, that jumps with the movement of the larva inside.

jumping castle *noun N Amer.* an inflatable structure, sometimes in a castle-like shape but also in shapes of animals etc., on which children jump and bounce.

jumping gene *noun* = TRANSPOSON.

jumping jack *noun* **1** *N Amer.* an exercise performed by standing with legs together and arms at one's side, jumping to a position with legs spread and arms fully extended above the head, then returning to the initial stance. **2** a toy figure with movable limbs esp. attached to strings. **3** *Brit.* a small firework producing repeated explosions.

jumping mouse *noun* any of several mouselike rodents of the palearctic family Zapodidae, having long hind feet and a long tail, and able to jump distances as great as 3 m.

jumping-off point *noun* (also **jumping-off place** etc.) **1** the place or point from where a journey, plan, campaign, etc. is begun or launched. **2** *N Amer.* a place regarded as being the furthest limit of civilization or settlement. **3** a place from which a person moves into another, esp. remote region beyond.

jump jet *noun* a jet aircraft that can take off and land vertically.

jump lead *noun Brit.* = JUMPER CABLE.

jump·off *noun* **1** a deciding round in a show jumping competition. **2** = JUMPING-OFF POINT.

jump rope *noun N Amer.* **1** a skipping rope. **2** an exercise or child's game done or played with a skipping rope.

jump seat *noun N Amer.* a folding extra seat in a motor vehicle, aircraft, etc.

jump·shot *noun Basketball* a shot at the net made at the apex of a vertical leap.

jump·sies *noun Cdn (Ont.)* a form of skipping in which a circle of elastic is looped around the ankles of two participants then moved progressively higher while the other participants attempt various jumping manoeuvres.

jump-start ● *transitive verb* **1** start (a motor vehicle) with jumper cables. **2** revitalize, energize, or stimulate (a team, effort, etc.). ● *noun* the action of jump-starting.

jump·suit *noun* a one-piece garment for the whole body, of a kind originally worn by paratroopers.

jumpy *adjective* (**jump·i·er**, **jump·i·est**) **1** nervous; easily startled. **2** making sudden movements, esp. of nervous excitement.
□ **jump·i·ly** *adverb* **jump·i·ness** *noun*

Jun. *abbreviation* **1** June. **2** (also **jun.**) Junior.

jun·co /ˈdʒʌŋkoʊ/ *noun* (*pl.* **-cos**) any of several small birds of Central and N America of the genus *Junco*. [Spanish from Latin *juncus* rush plant]

junc·tion *noun* **1** a point at which two or more things are joined. **2** a place where two or more railway lines or roads meet, unite, or cross. **3** the act or an instance of joining. **4** *Electronics* a region of transition in a semiconductor between regions where conduction is mainly by electrons and regions where it is mainly by holes. □ **junc·tion·al** *adjective* [Latin *junctio* (as JOIN)]

junction box *noun* a rigid box or casing used to enclose and protect junctions of electrical wires, cables, etc.

junc·ture *noun* **1** a critical convergence of events; a critical point of time (*at this juncture*). **2** a place where things join. **3** an act of joining. [Latin *junctura* (as JOIN)]

June *noun* the sixth month of the year in the Gregorian calendar. [Old French *juin* from Latin *Junius* var. of *Junonius* sacred to Juno]

Ju·neau /ˈdʒuːnoʊ/ the state capital of Alaska, a seaport on an inlet of the Pacific Ocean in the south of the state; pop. (2000) 30,700.

June·berry *noun* (*pl.* **-berries**) **1** any of several N American shrubs of the genus *Amelanchier*, of the rose family, with showy white flowers. **2** the fruit of this shrub.

June bug *noun* (also **June beetle**) any of various large beetles of the genus *Phyllophaga*, esp. N American chafers, appearing in early summer.

June grass *noun* any of various grasses, esp. bluegrass.

June·teenth *noun US* the 19th of June, celebrated as a holiday by African-Americans to commemorate the emancipation of slaves in Texas on that date in 1865.

June War *see* SIX DAY WAR.

Jung /jʊŋ/ **Carl (Gus·tav)** (1875–1961), Swiss psychologist. After first collaborating with Sigmund Freud, he eventually opposed Freud's theory of a sexual basis for neurosis. He established the concept of introvert and extrovert personality, and of the four psychological functions of sensation, intuition, thinking, and feeling; in his major work, *The Psychology of the Unconscious* (1912), he proposed the existence of a collective unconscious, which he combined with a theory of archetypes for studying the history and psychology of religion.

Jung·frau /ˈjʊŋfraʊ/ a mountain in the Swiss Alps, 4 158 m (13,642 ft.) high. [German, = virgin]

Jung·ian /ˈjʊŋiən/ ● *adjective* of Carl Jung or his system of analytical psychology. ● *noun* a supporter of Jung or of his system.

jun·gle *noun* **1 a** land overgrown with underwood or tangled vegetation, esp. in the tropics. **b** the luxuriant and often almost impenetrable vegetation covering such land. **2** a wild tangled mass. **3 a** a scene or place of ruthless competition, struggle, or exploitation (*urban jungle*). **b** a place of bewildering complexity or confusion. **4** (in full **jungle music**) a type of fast dance music with an exaggerated bass line, influenced by reggae and soul. **5** *N Amer. slang* an often illicit camp for and established by the homeless, unemployed, etc. □ **law of the jungle** a state of ruthless competition. □ **jungly** *adjective* [Hindi *jangal* from Sanskrit *jangala* desert, forest]

jungle fever *noun* a severe form of malaria.

jungle gym *noun* monkey bars for a children's playground, usu. having various bars, tubes, slides, etc.

jungl·ist *noun* a performer of or enthusiast for jungle music.

jun·ior ● *adjective* **1 a** (foll. by *to*) inferior in age, standing, or position. **b** of less or least standing; of the lower or lowest position (*junior partner*). **2 a** less advanced in age. **b** intended for children or young people (*junior dictionary*). **3** the younger (esp. appended to a name for distinction from an older person of the same name). **4** smaller than usual. **5** *Sport* of, for, or pertaining to (usu. amateur) athletes under 20 years of age. **6** esp. *US* of the year before the final year at university, high school, etc. **7** *Brit.* (of a school) having pupils in a younger age range, usu. 7 - 11. ● *noun* **1** a person who holds a low rank in a profession, is inferior in length of service, etc. **2** a person who is a specified number of years younger than another (*10 years his junior*). **3** *Sport* **a** a junior athlete. **b** the level of competition for junior athletes (*spent three years playing junior*). **4** esp. *US* a student in the third year of a four-year program at high school, college, or university. **5** *Brit.* a pupil in the younger age range, roughly between 7 and 11. **6** *N Amer. informal* a young male child, esp. in relation to his family. **7** (in *pl.*) *N Amer.* a range of garment sizes, odd-numbered from 5 to 15, for well-proportioned, short-waisted women of slightly less than average height. **8 a** *Cdn* a junior partner in a law firm. **b** (in England) a barrister who is not a QC. ● *intransitive verb* (of a lawyer) assist the lead lawyer on a case. □ **jun·ior·ity** *noun* [Latin, comparative of *juvenis* young]

Junior A *noun* **1** *Hockey* the highest level of amateur competition below major junior, for players under 20 years of age. **2** *hist.* = MAJOR JUNIOR.

Junior B *noun Hockey* the level of amateur competition below Junior A.

Junior C *noun Hockey* the level of amateur competition below Junior B.

junior college *noun* **1** *Cdn (Que.) informal* a CEGEP. **2** *US* a college offering the first two years of a university education.

junior common room *noun* **1** *Cdn & Brit.* (in certain universities) a room for social use by undergraduates, esp. for reading, watching TV, etc. **2** *Brit.* the undergraduates collectively.

Junior Forest Wardens *plural noun Cdn (West)* an organization for young people interested in conservation, hunter education, etc.

junior high school *noun N Amer.* (also *informal* **junior high**) a school intermediate between elementary school and high school, usu. from Grade 7 to Grade 9.

junior kindergarten *noun Cdn (Ont.)* a class for young children, usu. ages 3 to 4, which prepares them for kindergarten through games, singing, socialization, etc. Abbr.: **JK**.

Junior League *noun* a women's organization involved in charitable works.

junior lightweight *noun* **1** a weight in professional boxing of 57.1–59 kg. **2** a professional boxer of this weight.

junior management *noun* **1** the lowest level of management in an organization. **2** the managers at this level usu. with supervisory rather than full management responsibility (compare MIDDLE MANAGEMENT, SENIOR MANAGEMENT).

junior matriculation *noun* (also *informal* **junior matric**) *Cdn hist.* (in certain provinces) completion of secondary education to a level one year short of the requirements for admission to university (compare SENIOR MATRICULATION).

junior middleweight *noun* **1** a weight in professional boxing of 66.7–69.8 kg. **2** a professional boxer of this weight.

junior minister *noun Cdn & Brit.* a cabinet minister with responsibility for certain matters within a larger portfolio, assisting and reporting to the minister in charge.

junior welterweight *noun* **1** a weight in professional boxing of 61.2–63.5 kg. **2** a professional boxer of this weight.

juni·per /ˈdʒuːnɪpər/ *noun* any evergreen shrub or tree of the genus *Juniperus*, esp. *J. communis*, with prickly leaves and dark blue berry-like cones. [Latin *juniperus*]

junk¹ ● *noun* **1** anything regarded as useless or of little value. **2** old or unwanted articles that are discarded or sold cheaply. **3** *slang* a narcotic drug, esp. heroin. **4** *Baseball* a pitch effective because of unpredictable movement rather than speed, e.g. a knuckleball. **5** old cables or ropes cut up for oakum etc. **6** esp. *Brit.* a lump or chunk. **7** *Naut.* hard salt meat. **8** *Cdn* (esp. *Maritimes & Nfld*) a short log, esp. cut to fit a stove, fireplace, etc. **9** = JUNK FOOD. **10** = JUNK BOND. **11** a lump of fibrous tissue in the sperm whale's head, containing spermaceti. **12** (*attributive*) unsolicited advertising material etc. sent to large numbers of people by mail, email, fax, etc. ● *transitive verb* discard as junk. [Middle English: origin unknown]

junk² *noun* a flat-bottomed sailing vessel used in the China seas, with a prominent stem and lugsails. [obsolete French *juncque*, Portuguese *junco*, or Dutch *jonk*, from Javanese *djong*]

junk bond *noun* a high-yielding high-risk security, esp. one issued to finance a takeover.

Jun·ker /ˈjuŋkər/ *noun hist.* **1** a member of an exclusive (Prussian) aristocratic party concerned with maintaining the exclusive privileges of their class. **2** a German noble, esp. a younger, narrow-minded, overbearing one. □ **junker·dom** *noun* [German, earlier *Junkher* from Old High German (as YOUNG, HERR)]

junk·er /ˈdʒʌŋkər/ *noun N Amer. informal* **1** an old, dilapidated automotive vehicle, aircraft, boat, etc. **2** a junk dealer.

Jun·kers /ˈjuŋkərz/ **Hugo** (1859–1935), German aircraft designer, who developed the first successful all-metal plane (1915), and designed a number of aircraft used by Germany during the Second World War.

jun·ket ● *noun* **1 a** esp. *N Amer.* an extensive tour taken esp. for promotional purposes, usu. with the traveller's expenses paid. **b** a pleasure outing, esp. with eating, drinking, etc. **2** a dish of sweetened and flavoured curds, often served with fruit or cream. ● *intransitive verb* (**jun·ket·ed, jun·ket·ing**) esp. *N Amer.* go on a pleasure excursion. □ **jun·ket·eer** *noun* **jun·ket·eer·ing** *noun & adjective* **jun·ket·ing** *noun* [Middle English *jonket* from Old French *jonquette* rush basket (used to carry junket) from *jonc* rush, from Latin *juncus*]

junk food *noun* food with low nutritional value.

junk heap *noun* **1** an accumulation of junk. **2** a notional place to which discarded ideas, trends, etc. are consigned.

junk·ie *noun informal* (also **junky**) **1** a drug addict. **2** *informal* an aficionado of some specified activity (*a baseball junkie*).

junk shop *noun* a shop selling cheap second-hand goods or antiques.

junk science *noun* faulty or misleading scientific data or analysis, esp. when used to promote a specific agenda.

junk shop *noun* a shop selling cheap second-hand goods or antiques.

junky *adjective* (**junk·i·er, junk·i·est**) of or like junk. ● *noun* (pl. **-ies**) var. of JUNKIE.

junk·yard *noun* a place where junk is collected for storage or resale.

Juno¹ ▶ **1** *Rom. Myth* the most important goddess of the Roman state, wife of Jupiter, identified with the Greek goddess Hera. **2** *Astronomy* asteroid 3, discovered in 1804 (diameter 244 km).

Juno² *noun Cdn* (pl. **Junos**) **1** any of several awards presented by the Canadian Academy of Recording Arts and Sciences for excellence in Canadian music recording. **2** any of the statuettes symbolizing such an award. [after JUNO¹ and P. *Juneau* b.1922, chairman of the CRTC who introduced Canadian content rules for broadcasting]

Juno·esque *adjective* (of a woman) imposingly tall and shapely.

jun·ta /ˈhʊntə, ˈhʌn-, ˈdʒʌn-/ *noun* **1 a** a political or military clique or faction taking power after a revolution or coup. **b** a secretive group; a cabal. **2** a deliberative or administrative council in Spain, Portugal, or Latin America. [Spanish & Portuguese from Latin *juncta*, fem. past participle (as JOIN)]

Ju·pi·ter /ˈdʒuːpɪtər/ *noun* **1** *Rom. Myth* the chief god of the Roman state, giver of victory, identified with Zeus. He was originally a sky god, associated with lightning and the thunderbolt; his wife was Juno. **2** *Astronomy* the fifth planet from the sun and the largest planet in the solar system, orbiting between Mars and Saturn; equatorial diameter 142 800 km. [Latin *Jovis pater* father of the bright heaven]

Jura¹ /ˈjʊərə/ a system of mountain ranges on the border of France and Switzerland. It has given its name to the Jurassic period, when most of its rocks were laid down.

Jura² /ˈdʒʊərə/ an island of the Inner Hebrides, separated from the west coast of Scotland by the Sound of Jura.

Jur·as·sic /dʒʊˈrasɪk/ *Geol.* ● *adjective* of or relating to the second period of the Mesozoic era, between 213 and 144 million years ago, between the Triassic and Cretaceous periods, with evidence of many large dinosaurs, the first birds (including Archaeopteryx), and mammals. ● *noun* the Jurassic period or geological system. [French *jurassique* from JURA¹ + -*assic* from TRIASSIC]

jur·at /ˈdʒʊərat/ *noun* a statement of the circumstances in which an affidavit was made. [Latin *juratum* neuter past participle of *jurare* swear]

jur·id·ical /dʒʊˈrɪdɪkəl/ *noun* **1** of judicial proceedings. **2** relating to the law. □ **jur·id·ical·ly** *adverb* [Latin *juridicus* from *jus juris* law + -*dicus* saying, from *dicere* say]

jur·ied *adjective* judged or selected by a jury or panel.

juris·con·sult /ˌdʒʊərɪskənˈsʌlt/ *noun* a person learned in law; a jurist. [Latin *jurisconsultus* from *jus juris* law + *consultus* skilled: see CONSULT]

juris·dic·tion /ˌdʒʊərɪsˈdɪkʃən/ *noun* **1** (often foll. by *over*) the administration of justice. **2 a** legal or other authority. **b** the extent of this; the territory it extends over. □ **juris·dic·tion·al** *adjective* [Latin *jurisdictio* from *jus juris* law + *dictio* DICTION]

juris·pru·dence /ˌdʒʊərɪsˈpruːdəns/ *noun* **1** the science or philosophy of law. **2** a system or body of law. **3** a branch of law (*constitutional jurisprudence*). **4** legal decisions collectively. □ **juris·pru·den·tial** /-ˈdenʃəl/ *adjective* [Late Latin *jurisprudentia* from Latin *jus juris* law + *prudentia* knowledge: see PRUDENT]

jur·ist *noun* a person who is knowledgeable in legal matters, e.g. a judge, legal writer, etc. [French *juriste* or medieval Latin *jurista* from *jus juris* law]

jur·or /ˈdʒʊərər/ *noun* **1** a member of a jury. **2** a person who takes an oath. [Old French *jureor* from Latin *jurator -oris* from *jurare jurat-* swear]

jury ● *noun* (pl. **-ies**) **1** a body of usu. twelve persons sworn to render a verdict on the basis of evidence submitted to them in a court of justice. **2** a body of persons selected to award prizes in a competition. ● *transitive verb* select or judge (entries etc.) by or as if by a jury. □ **the jury is** (or **is still**) **out** (often foll. by *on*) a decision has not yet been reached. [Old French *juree* oath, inquiry, from *jurata* fem. past participle of Latin *jurare* swear]

jury box *noun* the enclosure for the jury in a law court.

jury·man *noun* (pl. **-men**) a member of a jury.

jury-rig *transitive verb* (often as **jury-rigged** *adjective*) assemble (something) hastily, using whatever materials are at hand. [originally Naut., with reference to temporary makeshift rigging: perhaps ultimately from Old French *ajurie* aid + RIG]

jury·woman *noun* (pl. **-women**) a woman member of a jury.

jus /ʒuː/ *noun* (esp. in French cuisine) an unthickened sauce.

Jus·sieu /ʒʊsˈjɜː/ **An·toine Lau·rent de** (1748–1836), French botanist, who grouped plants into families on the basis of common essential properties and, in *Genera Plantarum* (1789), developed the system on which modern plant classification is based.

just ● *adjective* **1** acting or done in accordance with what is morally right or fair. **2** (of treatment etc.) deserved (*a just reward*). **3** (of feelings, opinions, etc.) well-grounded (*just resentment*). **4** right in amount etc.; proper. ● *adverb* **1** exactly (*just what I need*). **2** exactly or nearly at this or that moment; a little time ago (*I have just seen them*). **3** *informal* simply, merely (*we were just good friends; it just doesn't make sense*). **4** barely; no more than (*I just managed it; just a minute*). **5** *informal* positively (*it is just splendid*). **6** quite (*not just yet*). **7** *informal* as an intensifier (*just you wait!*). **8** in questions, seeking precise information (*just how did you manage?*). □ **just about** *informal* almost exactly; almost completely. **just as well** convenient; fortunate (*it is just as well that I checked*). **just in case** as a precaution. **jut like that** without difficulty, hindrance, or hesitation. **just now 1** at this moment. **2** a little time ago. **just so 1** exactly arranged (*they like everything just so*). **2** it is exactly as you say. □ **just·ly** *adverb* **just·ness** *noun* [Old French *juste* from Latin *justus* from *jus* right]

jus·tice *noun* **1** just conduct; fairness. **2** the law and its administration (*the criminal justice system*). **3** judgment by legal process (*was brought to justice*). **4 a** a judge, esp. of a court of appeal. **b** (**Justice**) (usu. prec. by (*Cdn & Brit.*) *Mr.*, (*Cdn*) *Madame*, or (*Brit.*) *Mrs.*) a title given to an appeal court judge. □ **do justice to** treat fairly or appropriately; show due appreciation of. **do oneself justice** perform in a manner worthy of one's abilities. **in justice to** out of fairness to. **with (some) justice** reasonably. □ **justice·ship** *noun* (in sense 4).

Justice of the Peace *noun* a local public official appointed to hear minor cases, take oaths, solemnize marriages, etc. Abbr.: **JP**.

Justice of the Peace Court *noun Cdn* (in the NWT and Nunavut) a court presided over by a Justice of the Peace, with jurisdiction to hear all summary conviction matters, offences against municipal bylaws, etc.

jus·ti·ciable /dʒʌˈstɪʃəbəl/ *adjective* liable to be tried in a court of justice; subject to jurisdiction. [Old French from *justicier* bring to trial, from medieval Latin *justitiare* (as JUSTICE)]

justi·fi·able /ˈdʒʌstɪˌfaɪəbəl/ *adjective* that can be justified or defended. □ **justi·fi·abil·ity** *noun* **justi·fi·ably** *adverb*

justifiable homicide *noun* killing regarded as lawful and without criminal guilt, esp. the execution of a death sentence.

jus·tify *transitive verb* (**-fies**, **-fied**) **1** show the justice or rightness of (a person, act, etc.). **2** demonstrate the correctness of (an assertion etc.). **3** provide adequate grounds for (conduct, a claim, etc.). **4** (esp. in *passive*) (of circumstances) be a good reason or excuse for (*tiredness cannot justify such behaviour; a rise in prices cannot be justified*). **5** (as **jus·ti·fied** *adjective*) just, right (*am justified in assuming*). **6** *Theol.* (of God) free (a person) from the consequences of sin. **7** *Printing* adjust (a line of type) to fill a space evenly. □ **justi·fi·ca·tion** *noun* **justi·fi·ca·tory** /-fɪˌkeɪtəri, -ˈtɪfɪkəˌtɔri/ *adjective* **jus·ti·fi·er** *noun* [French *justifier* from Late Latin *justificare* do justice to, from Latin *justus* JUST]

Jus·tin, St. 'the Martyr' (*c.*100–165), Christian philosopher. He is remembered for his *Apologia* (*c.*150) defending Christianity; tradition holds that he was martyred in Rome together with some of his followers. Feast day, 1 June.

Jus·tin·ian /dʒʌˈstɪniən/ (Latin name Flavius Petrus Sabbatius Justinianus) (483–565), Byzantine emperor 527–65. Under his general Belisarius (*c.*505–65), he succeeded in reclaiming North Africa from the Vandals, Italy from the Ostrogoths, and Spain from the Visigoths; he codified Roman law in the *Codex Justinianus* (534).

just-in-time *noun* (often *attributive*) **1** a manufacturing system in which production is operated in very small batches. **2** a factory system in which materials are delivered immediately before they are required in order to minimize storage costs.

jut ● *intransitive verb* (**jut·ted**, **jut·ting**) (often foll. by *out*, *into*) protrude, project. ● *noun* a projection; a protruding point. [var. of JET[1]]

Jute *noun* a member of a Germanic tribe that settled in Britain in the 5th–6th c. □ **Jut·ish** *adjective* [representing medieval Latin *Jutae*, *Juti*, in Old English *Eotas*, *Iotas* = Icelandic *Iótar* people of JUTLAND]

jute *noun* **1** a rough fibre made from the bark of a jute plant, used for making twine and rope, and woven into sacking, mats, etc. **2** an Asian plant of the genus *Corchorus* yielding this fibre. [Bengali *jhōto* from Sanskrit *jūṭa* = *jaṭā* braid of hair]

jut-jawed *adjective* having a protruding lower jaw.

Jut·land a peninsula of NW Europe, forming the mainland of Denmark together with the N German state of Schleswig-Holstein.

Jutland, Battle of a major naval battle in the First World War, fought between British and German fleets in the North Sea west of Jutland on 31 May 1916. Although the battle itself was indecisive, the German fleet never again sought a full-scale engagement, and British control of the North Sea remained unshaken.

Jutra /ˈʒuːtrɒ/ **Claude** (1930–1986), Canadian filmmaker. He joined the National Film Board in 1956, and his film *Mon oncle Antoine* (1971) launched a new movement in Quebec film. After 1977 he worked in English for the CBC, then returned to the cinema for several films including an adaptation of Margaret Atwood's *Surfacing* (1981).

Ju·ven·al /ˈdʒuːvənəl/ (Latin name Decimus Junius Juvenalis) (*c.*60–*c.*140), Roman satirist. His sixteen verse satires present a savage attack on the vice and folly of Roman society.

ju·ven·al /ˈdʒuːvənəl/ *noun* esp. *N Amer.* = JUVENILE *noun* 3. [Latin *juvenalis*, = *juvenilis* (as JUVENILE)]

ju·ven·ile /ˈdʒuːvəˌnaɪl/ ● *adjective* **1 a** young, youthful. **b** of or for young persons. **2** suited to or characteristic of youth. **3** often *derogatory* immature (*behaving in a very juvenile way*). **4** *Cdn* (of a sports team, league, player, etc.) involving teenagers, esp. between the ages of 15 and 19 (*played hockey in a juvenile league*). **5** of or relating to a juvenile bird, animal, etc. (*juvenile feathers*). ● *noun* **1** a young person, esp. one below the age at which ordinary criminal prosecution is possible. **2** a book intended for young people. **3** a young bird, animal, etc., esp.: **a** a bird in its first full plumage, but not yet having adult plumage. **b** a two-year-old racehorse. □ **juven·il·ity** /-ˈnɪlɪti/ *noun* [Latin *juvenilis* from *juvenis* young]

juvenile court *noun* = YOUTH COURT.

juvenile delinquency *noun* offences committed by a person or persons below the age of legal responsibility. □ **juvenile delinquent** *noun*

juvenile diabetes *noun* (also **juvenile-onset diabetes**) a type of diabetes mellitus in which insulin is not produced by the body in sufficient quantities and must therefore be injected.

juven·ilia /ˌdʒuːvəˈnɪliə, -ˈnaɪljə/ *plural noun* works produced by an author or artist in youth.

juvie /ˈdʒuːviː/ *noun slang* **1** a juvenile delinquent. **2** a detention centre for juvenile delinquents. [abbreviation]

juxta·pose *transitive verb* **1** place (things) side by side. **2** (foll. by *to*, *with*) place (a thing) beside another. **3** set (something) in close association with another, esp. to highlight a contrast (*consumerist ideals juxtaposed with a non-materialistic lifestyle*). □ **juxta·pos·ition** *noun* **juxta·pos·ition·al** *adjective* [French *juxtaposer* from Latin *juxta* next: see POSE[1]]

Kk

K¹ *noun* (also **k**) (*pl.* **Ks** or **K's**) the eleventh letter of the alphabet.

K² *abbreviation* (also **K.**) **1** kelvin(s). **2** King, King's. **3** Köchel (catalogue of Mozart's works). **4** (also **k**) (prec. by a numeral) **a** *Computing* a unit of 1,024 (i.e. 2¹⁰) bytes or bits, or loosely 1,000. **b** 1,000. **5** *informal* one thousand dollars (*earns 50 K*). **6** *N Amer.* kindergarten. **7** kilometre (*ran 30 K*). **8** (in *pl.*) kilometres per hour. [sense 4 as abbreviation of KILO-]

K³ *symbol Chem.* the element potassium.

K⁴ *noun N Amer.* a strikeout.

K⁵ *noun slang* = KETAMINE.

k¹ *abbreviation* knot(s).

k² *symbol* **1** kilo-. **2** *Math.* a constant.

K2 (also called **Dapsang**) the highest mountain in the Karakoram range, on the border between Pakistan and China. It is the second highest peak in the world, rising to 8 611 m (28,250 ft.). [so called because it was the second peak to be surveyed in the Karakoram range]

K-9 *abbreviation* designating police canine units.

ka *noun* (in ancient Egypt) the spiritual part of an individual human being or god, which survived (with the soul) after death and could reside in a statue of the dead person. [Ancient Egyptian]

ka- *prefix* forming nouns and interjections imitative of a loud sound (*kaboom; ka-pow*). [imitative]

Kaaba /ˈkɑːbə/ *noun* (also **Caaba**) a building in the centre of the Great Mosque at Mecca, the Muslim Holy of Holies, containing a sacred black stone, in the direction of which Muslims must face when praying. [Arabic *Kaʿba*]

kab·ad·di /kəˈbɒdi/ *noun* a game popular in northern India and Pakistan played between two teams of nine who rush and tackle one another. [Tamil]

Kaba·lega Falls /ˌkabəˈleigə/ a waterfall on the lower Victoria Nile near Lake Albert, in NW Uganda. It is a central feature of the Kabalega National Park and is formed at a point where the river narrows to 6 m (20 ft.) and drops 120 m (400 ft.). It was formerly known as Murchison Falls.

Kabardino-Balkaria /ˌkabarˈdiːnoː balˈkariə/ (also called **Kabarda-Balkar Republic** /ˌkabərdə balˈkar/) an autonomous republic of SW Russia, on the border with Georgia; pop. (est. 2002) 749,400; capital, Nalchik.

Kab·balah /kəˈbɒlə, ˈkabələ/ *noun* (also **Kab·bala**, **Cabala**, **cabbala**) a Jewish mystical tradition. □ **kab·bal·ism** *noun* **kab·bal·ist** *noun* **kab·bal·is·tic** /-ˈlɪstɪk/ *adjective* [medieval Latin from Rabbinical Hebrew *ḳabbālā* tradition]

Kabi·nett /ˌkabɪˈnet/ *noun* a wine of exceptional quality, esp. one made in Germany from grapes that can ferment without added sugar. [German *Kabinettwein*, lit. 'cabinet or chamber wine', from its originally being kept in a special cellar]

kab·loo·na /kəˈbluːnə/ *noun* (*pl.* same or **kab·loo·nas** or **kab·loo·nat**) a person who is not Inuit, esp. a white person. [Inuktitut *kabluna* 'bushy eyebrow']

ka·bob *var. of* KEBAB.

ka·bocha /kəˈbɒtʃə/ *noun* any of various Japanese pumpkins or squashes with a rough dark-green skin and a flattened turban shape. [Japanese]

ka·boodle esp. *N Amer. var. of* CABOODLE.

ka·boom *noun* a sudden loud sound, as of an explosion. [imitative]

ka·bu·ki /kəˈbuːki/ *noun* a form of popular traditional Japanese drama with highly stylized song, acted by males only. [Japanese from *ka* song + *bu* dance + *ki* art]

Kabul /ˈkɒbul/ the capital of Afghanistan; pop. (est. 2002) 2,142,300. It is situated in the northeast of the country, with a strategic position commanding the mountain passes through the Hindu Kush, esp. the Khyber Pass. It has existed for more than 3,000 years and has been destroyed and rebuilt several times in its history. □ **Kab·uli** *noun*

Kabwe /ˈkabwei/ a town in central Zambia, situated to the north of Lusaka; pop. (est. 2002) 213,800. One of the oldest mining towns in Zambia, it is the site of a cave which has yielded human fossils associated with the Upper Pleistocene period. It was known as Broken Hill from 1904 to 1965.

ka·chi·na /kəˈtʃiːnə/ *noun* **1** a Pueblo Indian ancestral spirit. **2** (in full **kachina dancer**) a person who represents a kachina in ceremonial dances. [Hopi *kacina* 'supernatural']

kachina doll *noun* a wooden doll representing a kachina.

ka-ching *interjection N Amer.* imitating the sound made by a cash register.

Kádár /ˈkodɑr/ **János** (1912–89), Hungarian leader, first secretary of the Hungarian Socialist Workers' Party 1956–88 and prime minister 1956–8 and 1961–5. He consistently supported the Soviet Union, involving Hungarian troops in the 1968 invasion of Czechoslovakia; his policy of 'consumer socialism' made Hungary the most affluent state in E Europe.

Kad·dish /ˈkadɪʃ/ *noun* **1** a Jewish mourner's prayer. **2** a doxology in the synagogue service. [Aramaic *ḳaddīš* holy]

kadi *var. of* QADI.

kaffee·klatsch /ˈkafei,klatʃ/ *noun* = COFFEE KLATCH.

Kaf·fir /ˈkafər/ *noun* **1 a** *hist.* a member of the Xhosa-speaking peoples of South Africa. **b** the language of these peoples. **2** *South Africa offensive* any black African (now an actionable insult). [originally = a non-Muslim: Arabic *kāfir* 'infidel' from *kafara* 'not believe']

kaf·fir lime *noun* a citrus fruit, *Citrus hystrix*, with a knobbly bitter fruit whose juice and the plant's leaves are much used in SE Asian cooking.

kaf·fi·yeh /keˈfiːjei/ *noun* (also **keffiyeh**) a headdress worn by Arab men, consisting of a square of material fastened by a cord around the crown of the head. [Arabic *keffiya*, *kūfiyya*, perhaps from Late Latin *cofea* COIF¹]

Kafir /ˈkafɜr/ *noun* a native of the Hindu Kush mountains of NE Afghanistan. [formed as KAFFIR]

Kafka /ˈkafkə/ **Franz** (1883–1924), Czech novelist, who wrote in German. His work, haunted by a sense of guilt, portrays an enigmatic and nightmarish reality where the individual is perceived as lonely, perplexed, and threatened; his novels include *The Metamorphosis* (1917), *The Trial* (1925), and *The Castle* (1926).

Kafka·esque /ˌkafkəˈesk/ *adjective* (of a situation, atmosphere, etc.) impenetrably oppressive, nightmarish, in a manner characteristic of the fictional world of Franz Kafka.

kaf·tan *var. of* CAFTAN.

ka·fuf·fle *var. of* KERFUFFLE.

Kago·shima /ˌkagəˈʃiːmə/ a city and port in Japan; pop. (est. 2002) 553,600. It is situated on the southern coast of Kyushu island, on the Satsuma Peninsula and is noted for its porcelain, Satsuma ware.

Kahna·wake /ɡɒˈnɒwəɡei/ a Mohawk reserve south of Montreal. [Mohawk, = 'at the rapids', in reference to the Lachine rapids nearby]

Kahra·man·ma·raş /ˌkʊrəˌmanməˈraʃ/ (also **Maras**) a city in south central Turkey; pop. (1997) 303,594.

ka·hu·na noun see BIG KAHUNA.

Kai·feng /kaiˈfeŋ/ a city in Henan province, E China, on the Yellow River; pop. (est. 2002) 851,900. Established in the 4th c. BC, it is one of the oldest cities in China.

Kai·gani /kaiˈɡani/ noun a member of a division of the Haida, who left the Queen Charlotte Islands in the early 18th c. and settled on the southern shores of Prince of Wales Island (Alaska).

Kain, Karen (b.1951), Canadian ballet dancer. One of Canada's finest ballerinas, she was a principal dancer in the National Ballet of Canada from 1969 until her retirement in 1997, and established herself as a dancer of international stature much in demand by companies throughout the world.

Kai·nai /ˈkainai/ plural noun = BLOOD. [Blood, = 'many chiefs']

Kai·rouan /ˌkairʊˈɒn/ a city in NE Tunisia; pop. (2000) 113,100. It is a Muslim holy city and a place of pilgrimage.

kai·ser /ˈkaizər/ noun **1** hist. an emperor, esp. the German Emperor, the Emperor of Austria, or the head of the Holy Roman Empire. **2** N Amer. (in full **kaiser roll**) a large crusty bread roll made by folding the corners of a square of bread dough into the centre, resulting in a pinwheel pattern when baked. **3** Cdn (Sask.) a whist-based card game played esp. in Saskatchewan. [in modern English from German Kaiser and Dutch keizer; in Middle English from Old English cāsere from Germanic adoption (through Greek kaisar) of Latin Caesar: see CAESAR[1]]

kaizen /kaiˈzen/ noun a Japanese business philosophy of continuous improvement of working practices, personal efficiency, etc. [Japanese, = improvement]

kaka[1] /ˈkɒkɒ/ noun (pl. **kakas**) a large New Zealand parrot, Nestor meridionalis, with olive-brown plumage. [Maori]

kaka[2] /ˈkɒkɒ/ noun informal **1** excrement. **2** rubbish. [French]

Kaka·beka Falls /ˌkakəˈbekə/ a waterfall in NW Ontario, 47 m high, situated on the Kaministiquia River, west of Thunder Bay. [Ojibwa kakabika steep rock with a waterfall]

kaka·po /ˈkɒkəˌpoː/ noun (pl. **-pos**) an owl-like flightless New Zealand parrot, Strigops habroptilus. [Maori, = night kaka]

kaki·vak /ˈkakiˌvak/ noun a three-pronged fish spear used by the Inuit. [Inuktitut]

kala azar /ˌkɒlə əˈzɑr/ noun a tropical disease caused by the parasitic protozoan Leishmania donovani, which is transmitted to humans by sandflies. [Assamese from kālā black + āzār disease]

Kala·hari /ˌkaləˈhari/ (in full **Kalahari Desert**) a high, vast, arid plateau in southern Africa north of the Orange River. It comprises most of Botswana with parts in Namibia and South Africa.

kala·mata /kaləˈmatə/ noun (also **calamata**) a medium-sized, firm, flavourful, Greek variety of purplish-black olive. [Kalamáta, a port in the S Peloponnese, where they are grown]

kalan·choe /kalənˈkoːi/ noun a succulent plant of the mainly African genus Kalanchoe, which includes several houseplants, some producing miniature plants from the edges of the leaves. [modern Latin from French, ultimately from Chinese gāláncài]

Ka·lash·nikov /kəˈlaʃnɪkɒf/ noun a type of rifle or submachine gun made in Russia (also attributive: Kalashnikov rifle). [M.T. Kalashnikov (b.1919), its Russian developer]

kale noun **1** a variety of cabbage which forms no compact head. Also called CURLY KALE. **2** US slang money. [Middle English, northern form of COLE]

ka·leido·scope /kəˈlaidəˌskoːp/ noun **1** a tube containing mirrors and pieces of coloured glass or paper, whose reflections produce changing patterns when the tube is rotated. **2** a constantly and quickly changing pattern. □ **ka·leido·scop·ic** adjective **ka·leido·scop·ic·ally** adverb [Greek kalos beautiful + eidos form + -SCOPE]

kal·ends var. of CALENDS.

Kal·goor·lie /kalˈɡʊrli/ a gold-mining town in Western Australia; pop. (2001) 29,735. Gold was discovered there in 1887, leading to a gold rush in the 1890s.

Kali /ˈkɒli/ Hinduism the most terrifying goddess, wife of Shiva, often identified with Durga. She is usually depicted as black, naked, old, and hideous, with a necklace of skulls, a belt of severed hands, and a protruding bloodstained tongue.

Kali·man·tan /ˌkaliˈmantan/ a region of Indonesia, comprising the southern part of the island of Borneo.

ka·limba /kəˈlɪmbə/ noun a type of African thumb piano. [Bantu]

Ka·li·nin[1] /kəˈliːnɪn/ the former name (1931–91) for TVER.

Ka·li·nin[2] /kəˈliːnɪn/ **Mik·hail Ivan·ovich** (1875–1946), Soviet leader, head of state of the USSR 1919–46. He was a founder of Pravda ('Truth'), then an underground Bolshevik newspaper, in 1912.

Ka·li·nin·grad /kəˈliːnɪnˌɡrad/ **1** a port on the Baltic coast of E Europe, capital of the Russian region of Kaliningrad; pop. (est. 2002) 425,200. It was known by its German name of Königsberg until 1946, when it was ceded to the Soviet Union under the Potsdam Agreement. Its port is a significant naval base for the Russian fleet. **2** a region of Russia, an enclave situated on the Baltic coast of E Europe; capital, Kaliningrad. It shares its borders with Lithuania and Poland and is separated from Russia by the intervening countries of Lithuania, Latvia, and Belarus. [KALININ[2]]

Kal·mar, Union of the treaty which joined together the crowns of Denmark, Sweden, and Norway in 1397, dissolved in 1523.

kal·mia /ˈkalmiə/ noun a N American evergreen shrub of the genus Kalmia, esp. sheep laurel, K. angustifolia, with showy pink flowers. [modern Latin from P. Kalm, Swedish botanist d.1779]

Kal·muck /ˈkalmʌk/ (also **Kal·myk** /ˈkalmɪk/ or **Kal·myks**) ● noun (pl. same or **Kal·mucks** or **Kal·myks**) **1** a member of a Buddhist Mongolian people living in the west of the former USSR. **2** the Ural-Altaic language of this people. ● adjective of or relating to this people or their language. [Russian kalmyk]

Kal·mykia /kalˈmɪkiə/ (official name **Republic of Kalmykia-Khalmg Tangch**) an autonomous republic in SW Russia, on the Caspian Sea; pop. (est. 2002) 310,500; capital, Elista.

kal·ong /ˈkɒlɒŋ/ noun any of several fruit bats of SE Asia and Indonesia, esp. the large common flying fox, Pteropus vampyrus. [Malay]

Kaloo·kan /kəˈluːkan/ a city in the Philippines, part of the conurbation of Manila; pop. (est. 2000) 1,177,604.

kalpa /ˈkalpə/ noun Hinduism & Buddhism the period between the beginning and the end of the world considered as the day of Brahma (4,320 million human years). [Sanskrit]

Ka·luga /kəˈluːɡə/ an industrial city and river port in European Russia, on the Oka River southwest of Moscow; pop. (est. 2002) 366,800.

Kal·yan /kʌlˈjɒn/ a city on the west coast of India, in the state of Maharashtra, northeast of Bombay (Mumbai); pop. (2001) 1,193,300.

Kama /ˈkɒmə/ Hinduism the god of sexual love, usually represented as a beautiful youth with a bow of sugar cane, a bowstring of bees, and arrows of flowers.

Kama Sutra /ˈsuːtrə/ noun an ancient Sanskrit treatise on the art of erotic love. [Sanskrit, = love treatise]

Kam·chat·ka /kamˈtʃatkə/ a vast mountainous peninsula of the northeast coast of Siberian Russia, separating the Sea of Okhotsk from the Bering Sea; chief port, Petropavlovsk. It is a volcanically active zone containing twenty-two active volcanoes and many hot springs.

kame noun a short ridge of sand and gravel deposited from the water of a melted glacier. [Scots form of COMB]

kam·eez /kaˈmiːz/ noun a long tunic worn by many people from the Indian subcontinent, typically with a shalwar or churidars. [Arabic ḳamīs, perhaps from late Latin camisia (see CHEMISE)]

Ka·men·skoe /kaˈmjenskɔijə/ a former name (until 1936) of DNIPRODZERZHINSK.

Kamensk-Uralsky /ˌkɒmənskuˈralski/ an industrial city in central Russia, in the eastern foothills of the Urals; pop. (est. 2002) 188,800.

Kamer·lingh Onnes /ˌkamərlɪŋ ˈɒnəs/ **Heike** (1853–1926), Dutch physicist, who studied cryogenic phenomena. He succeeded in liquefying helium in 1908, and achieved a temperature of less than one degree above absolute zero; he discovered the phenomenon of superconductivity in 1911, and was awarded the Nobel Prize for his work on low temperature physics in 1913.

kami /ˈkɒmiː/ noun a divine being in the Shinto religion. [Japanese]

kamik /ˈkɒmɪk, ˈkam-/ noun a traditional Inuit boot made from seal or caribou skin. [Inuktitut]

kami·kaze /ˌkɒmɪˈkɒzi, ˌkamɪˈkazi/ ● noun hist. (during the Second World War) **1** a Japanese aircraft loaded with explosives and deliberately crashed by its pilot on its target. **2** the pilot of such an aircraft. ● adjective **1** of or relating to a kamikaze. **2** reckless, dangerous, potentially self-destructive. [Japanese from kami divinity + kaze wind]

Ka·mila·roi /kəˈmɪlərɔi/ noun an Aboriginal language formerly spoken in New South Wales and S Queensland. [Kamilaroi]

Kam·loops a city in south central BC, located at the confluence of the North and South Thompson rivers, 355 km northeast of Vancouver; pop. (2001) 77,281. □ **Kam·loops·ian** *noun* [Shuswap *kahmoloops* meeting of the waters]

Kamloops trout *noun Cdn* a bright silvery rainbow trout found in lakes.

kamo·tik *noun* (also **kamo·tiq**) *var. of* KOMATIK.

Kam·pala /kamˈpɒlə/ the capital of Uganda; pop. (est. 2002) 953,400. It is situated on the northern shores of Lake Victoria and replaced Entebbe as capital when the country became independent in 1963.

kam·pong /ˈkampɒŋ/ *noun* a Malayan enclosure or village. [Malay: compare COMPOUND²]

Kam·pu·chea /ˌkampʊˈtʃiːə/ the former name (1976–89) for CAMBODIA.

Kam·pu·chean /ˌkampʊˈtʃiən/ *noun & adjective* = CAMBODIAN.

Kamut /kɒˈmuːt/ *noun proprietary* a variety of high-protein unhybridized wheat.

Kan. *abbreviation* Kansas.

kana /ˈkɒnə/ *noun* **1** Japanese syllabic writing. **2** a character or syllabary in this. [Japanese]

ka·naka /kəˈnakə, -ˈnɒkə/ *noun* a South Sea Islander, esp. (formerly) one employed as a labourer in either Canada or Australia. [Hawaiian, = person, human being]

Kana·rese /ˌkanəˈriːz/ *noun* (also **Canarese**) (*pl.* same) **1** a member of a Dravidian people living in western India. **2** the language of this people. [*Kanara* in India]

Ka·nata /kəˈnatə/ a former city in E Ontario, now part of Ottawa; pop. (2001) 58,636. [Iroquoian *kanata* cluster of dwellings, so called because the city's neighbourhoods were arranged in clusters: compare CANADA¹]

Kan·chen·junga /ˌkantʃenˈdʒʌŋgə/ (also **Kang·chen·junga**, **Kin·chin·junga** /ˌkɪntʃɪn-/) a mountain in the Himalayas, on the border between Nepal and Sikkim. Rising to a height of 8 598 m (28,209 ft.), it is the world's third-highest mountain. [Tibetan, = the five treasures of the snows, with reference to its summit which is split into five separate peaks]

Kan·da·har /ˈkandəˌhɑr/ a city in S Afghanistan; pop. (est. 2002) 339,200. It was the first capital of Afghanistan after the country became independent, from 1748 until replaced by Kabul in 1773.

Kan·din·sky /kanˈdɪnski/ **Was·sily** (1866–1944), Russian painter and theorist. A pioneer of abstract art, he co-founded the Munich-based *Blaue Reiter* group of artists (1911) and later taught at the Bauhaus (1922–33); his paintings from this time are notable for conveying energy and movement purely by colour, line, and shape.

Kandy /ˈkandi/ a city in the highlands of central Sri Lanka; pop. (2001) 110,000. It was the capital (1480–1815) of the former independent kingdom of Kandy and contains one of the most sacred Buddhist shrines, the Dalada Maligava (Temple of the Tooth).

Kane, Paul (1810–71), Irish-born Canadian painter. In 1845 he travelled around the Great Lakes sketching, and in 1846 travelled to the Lakehead, where he joined the trading brigades and journeyed to the west coast via Fort Garry and Fort Edmonton. He spent 8 months on the coast, and then returned to Toronto, having made some 700 sketches of Aboriginal life and western scenery.

Kane Basin /kein/ a body of water lying between Ellesmere Island and Greenland, north of Baffin Bay. [E. K. *Kane*, US physician and Arctic explorer d.1857]

Kane·sa·take /ˌkɒŋeisɒtɒˈkei/ a Mohawk reserve near Oka, Quebec, site of a confrontation between Mohawks and non-Indians in 1990. [Mohawk, = 'at the bottom of the hill']

kan·ga·roo *noun* (*pl.* **-roos**) **1** a plant-eating marsupial of the genus *Macropus*, native to Australia and New Guinea, with a long tail and strongly developed hind quarters enabling it to travel by jumping. **2** *Cdn* (*attributive*) designating a hooded garment, usu. of fleece material, with a front pouch (*kangaroo jacket*). [*ganurru*, the name of a specific kind of kangaroo in Guugu Yimidhirr (an extinct Aboriginal language of N Queensland)]

kangaroo care *noun* a method of nurturing premature babies by holding them upright skin-to-skin against a parent's chest for increasing lengths of time.

kangaroo court *noun* **1** an illegal court formed by a group of prisoners, strikers, etc. to settle disputes among themselves. **2** any trial, court, public hearing, or disciplinary proceeding operating unfairly and rendering an unjust verdict. **3** a mock trial, usu. for comic effect and often to raise funds for a charity, where participants are tried for trivial offences and given comic punishments.

kangaroo mouse *noun* any small rodent of the genus *Microdipodops*, native to N America, with long hind legs for hopping.

kan·ga·roo paw *noun* any plant of the genus *Angiozanthos*, with green and red woolly flowers.

kangaroo rat *noun* any burrowing rodent of the genus *Dipodomys*, having elongated hind feet.

kangaroo vine *noun* an evergreen climbing plant, *Cissus antarctica*, with toothed leaves.

Kanien·ke·haka /kanˌjenkeiˈhɒkɒ/ *noun* (*pl.* same) **1** the Mohawk people. **2** their Iroquoian language. [Mohawk, = 'people of the flint']

kanji /ˈkandʒi/ *noun* Japanese writing using Chinese characters. [Japanese from *kan* Chinese + *ji* character]

Kan·nada /ˈkanədə/ *noun* the Kanarese language. [Kanarese]

Kano /ˈkɒnɒː/ a city in N Nigeria; pop. (1998) 746,538.

Kan·pur /kɒnˈpʊr/ (also **Cawnpore** /kɒnˈpɔr/) a city in Uttar Pradesh, N India, on the Ganges River; pop. (2001) 2,532,100. It was the site of a massacre of British soldiers and European families in July 1857, during the Indian Mutiny.

Kans. *abbreviation* Kansas.

Kan·sas /ˈkanzəs/ a state in the central US; pop. (2000) 2,688,418; capital, Topeka. □ **Kan·san** *adjective & noun*

Kansas City each of two adjacent cities in the US, situated at the junction of the Missouri and Kansas rivers, one in NE Kansas (2000 pop. 146,866) and the other in NW Missouri (2000 pop. 441,545).

Kansu see GANSU.

Kant /kant/ **Im·man·uel** (1724–1804), German philosopher. In the *Critique of Pure Reason* (1781), he countered Hume's empiricism by arguing that the human mind can neither confirm, deny, nor scientifically demonstrate the ultimate nature of reality, but claimed that it can know the objects of experience, which it interprets with notions of space and time; his *Critique of Practical Reason* (1788) affirms the existence of an absolute moral law, the categorical imperative, whose motivation is reason. □ **Kant·ian** *adjective & noun* **Kant·ian·ism** *noun*

Kanto /kanˈtoː/ a region of Japan, on the island of Honshu; capital, Tokyo.

Kao·hsiung /kauˈʃjʊŋ/ the chief port of Taiwan, on the southwest coast; pop. (est. 2002) 1,506,300.

kao·lin /ˈkeiəlɪn/ *noun* a fine soft white clay produced by the decomposition of other clays or feldspar, used esp. for making porcelain and in medicines. *Also called* CHINA CLAY. □ **kao·lin·ic** /-ˈlɪnɪk/ *adjective* [French from Chinese *gaoling* the name of a mountain, from *gao* high + *ling* hill]

kaon /ˈkeiɒn/ *noun Physics* a meson having a mass several times that of a pion. [*ka* representing the letter *K* (as symbol for the particle) + -ON]

Kapa·chira Falls /ˌkapəˈtʃiːrə/ a waterfall on the Shire River in S Malawi.

kapell·meis·ter /kəˈpelˌmaistər/ *noun* (*pl.* same) *hist.* the conductor of an orchestra, opera, choir, etc., attached to a German court. [German from *Kapelle* 'court orchestra', from Italian *cappella* CHAPEL + *Meister* master]

Ka·pitza /kəˈpɪtsə/ **Pyotr Leonid·ovich** (1894–1984), Russian physicist, who was noted for his work in the field of low temperature physics; he shared the Nobel Prize for physics in 1978.

kapok /ˈkeipɒk/ *noun* **1** a fine fibrous cotton-like substance found surrounding the seeds of a tropical tree, *Ceiba pentandra*, used for stuffing cushions, soft toys, etc. **2** the tree itself. [ultimately from Malay *kāpoq*]

Kaposi's sarcoma /kəˈpoːsiːz/ *noun* a form of cancer involving multiple tumours of the lymph nodes or skin, occurring esp. in people with depressed immune systems, e.g. as a result of AIDS. Abbr.: **KS**. [M.K. *Kaposi*, Hungarian dermatologist d.1902]

kapow *noun N Amer. informal* a sudden sharp sound, like a gunshot or explosion. [imitative]

kappa *noun* the tenth letter of the Greek alphabet (K, κ). [Greek]

Kap·us·ka·sing /ˌkapəsˈkeisɪŋ/ a town in NE central Ontario, situated on the Kapuskasing River, about 150 km northwest of Timmins; pop. (2001) 9,238. [see KAPUSKASING RIVER]

Kapuskasing River a river in NE central Ontario, which rises northeast of Sault Ste. Marie and flows northward to join the Mattagami River. [Cree *kepuskaskikwa* 'it branches from a river']

kaput /kaˈpʊt/ *predicative adjective slang* broken, ruined; done for. [German *kaputt*]

kara·biner *var. of* CARABINER.

---

uː m**oo**d   ai m**y**   əi p**i**pe   au br**ow**n   ʌu h**ou**se   ei d**ay**   ɔi b**oy**   ɑ̃ fr**an**glais   ã Canadi**en**   ɔ̃ Bray**on**   (*see over for consonants*)

Karachai-Cherkes·sia /ˌkarəˌtʃai tʃerˈkesiə/ (official name **Karachai-Cherkess Republic**) an autonomous republic in the N Caucasus, SW Russia; pop. (est. 2002) 430,800; capital, Cherkessk.

Ka·rachi /kəˈratʃi/ a major city and port in Pakistan, capital of Sind province; pop. (1998) 9,269,300. Situated on the Arabian Sea, it was the capital of Pakistan 1947–59, before being replaced by Rawalpindi.
  □ **Ka·rachi·ite** *noun*

Kara·futo /ˌkarəˈfuːtoː/ the Japanese name for the southern part of the island of Sakhalin.

karahi /kʌˈrai/*noun* a small, bowl-shaped frying pan with two handles used in Indian cooking, esp. for preparing balti dishes. [Hindi]

Karaj /kaˈrɒdʒ/ a city in N Iran, to the west of Tehran; pop. (est. 2002) 1,075,200.

Kara·jan /ˈkarəˌjan/ **Her·bert von** (1908–89), Austrian conductor. He is chiefly remembered as the principal conductor of the Berlin Philharmonic Orchestra (1955–89), although he was also associated with the Vienna State Opera (1957–64).

Kara·kor·am /ˌkarəˈkɔrəm/ a great mountain system of central Asia, extending over 480 km (300 miles) southeastward from NE Afghanistan to Kashmir and forming part of the borders of India and Pakistan with China. One of the highest mountain systems in the world, it consists of a group of parallel ranges, forming a westward continuation of the Himalayas, with many peaks over 7 900 m (26,000 ft.), the highest being K2. Virtually inaccessible, it also contains the highest passes in the world, at elevations over 4 900 m (16,000 ft.), including Karakoram Pass and Khardungla Pass.

Kara·kor·um /ˌkarəˈkɔrəm/ an ancient city in central Mongolia, now ruined, which was the capital of the Mongol Empire, established by Genghis Khan in 1220. The capital was later moved by Kublai Khan to Khanbaliq (modern Beijing) in 1267, and Karakorum was destroyed by Chinese forces in 1388.

kara·kul /ˈkarəˌkʊl/ *noun* (also **caracul**) **1** a variety of Asian sheep with a dark curled fleece when young. **2** fur made from or resembling this. *Also called* PERSIAN LAMB. [Russian]

Kara Kum /ˌkarə ˈkuːm/ a desert in central Asia, to the east of the Caspian Sea, covering much of Turkmenistan.

Kara·man·lis /ˌkarəmanˈliːs/ **Kon·stan·tinos** (1907–98), Greek politician, prime minister 1955–63 and 1974–80, and president 1980–5 and 1990–95. As prime minister he was responsible for the referendum abolishing the monarchy and establishing a republic (1974) with a new constitution (passed in 1975).

kara·oke /ˌkeriːˈoːkiː/ *noun* a form of entertainment in which people sing popular songs as soloists against a pre-recorded backing (often *attributive*: *karaoke bar*). [Japanese, = empty orchestra]

Kara Sea /ˈkarə/ an arm of the Arctic Ocean off the northern coast of Russia, bounded to the east by the islands of Severnaya Zemlya and to the west by Novaya Zemlya.

kar·at /ˈkerət/ *noun* (also **carat**) a measure of purity of gold, pure gold being 24 karats. Abbr.: **kt**. [as CARAT]

karate /kəˈrɒti/ *noun* a Japanese system of unarmed combat using the hands and feet as weapons. [Japanese from *kara* empty + *te* hand]

karate chop ● *noun* a forceful, usu. downward motion with the side of the hand. ● *transitive verb* (**karate-chop**) (**-chopped, -chopping**) strike with a karate chop.

Kar·bala /ˈkarbələ/ a city in S Iraq; pop. (est. 2002) 549,700. A holy city for Shiite Muslims, it is the site of the tomb of Husayn, grandson of Muhammad, who was killed here in AD 680.

Ka·relia /kəˈriːliə, -ˈreiliə/ a region of NE Europe on the border between Russia and Finland. After the Russo-Finnish war of 1939–40 the greater part of Finnish Karelia was ceded to the Soviet Union and the area now constitutes the Republic of Karelia; pop. (est. 2001) 766,000; capital, Petrozavodsk. The remaining part of Karelia constitutes a province of E Finland. □ **Ka·rel·ian** *adjective & noun*

Karen /kəˈren/ ● *noun* **1** a member of a non-Burmese Mongoloid people, most of whom live in eastern Burma (Myanmar). **2** the language spoken by this people, which is probably of the Sino-Tibetan family. ● *adjective* of or relating to the Karens or their language. [Burmese *ka-reng* 'wild unclean man']

Karen State (also called **Kawthoolay, Kawthulei**) a state in SE Burma (Myanmar), on the border with Thailand; capital, Pa-an. Its people are engaged in armed conflict with the Burmese government in an attempt to gain independence.

Ka·riba, Lake /kəˈriːbə/ a large artificial lake on the Zambia–Zimbabwe border in central Africa. It was created by the damming of the Zambezi River. On its northern shore is Kariba, a resort town.

Kariba Dam /kəˈriːbə/ a concrete arch dam on the Zambezi River, 385 km (240 miles) downstream from Victoria Falls. It was built in 1955–59, creating Lake Kariba and providing a bridge over the Zambezi between Zambia and Zimbabwe. It is the chief source of hydroelectric power for both Zimbabwe and Zambia.

Karl XII see CHARLES XII.

Karl-Marx-Stadt /karl'marksʃtat/ the former name (1953–1990) of CHEMNITZ.

Kar·loff, Boris (born William Henry Pratt) (1887–1969), English-born US actor, whose name is chiefly linked with horror films, such as *Frankenstein* (1931) and *The Mummy* (1932).

Kar·lovy Vary /ˌkarləvi ˈvari/ a spa town in the W Czech Republic; pop. (2001) 53,570. Founded in the 14th c. by the Holy Roman emperor Charles IV, it is famous for its alkaline thermal springs.

Karls·bad /ˈkarlsbɒt/ the German name for KARLOVY VARY.

Karls·ruhe /ˈkarlzˌruː/ an industrial town and port on the Rhine in western Germany; pop. (est. 2002) 277,500.

karma *noun* **1 a** *Buddhism & Hinduism* the sum of a person's actions in previous states of existence, viewed as deciding his or her fate in future existences. **b** *Jainism* subtle physical matter which binds the soul as a result of bad actions. **2** destiny. **3** the positive or negative feelings or energy felt to be produced by a person or thing. □ **kar·mic** *adjective* **kar·mic·ally** *adverb* [Sanskrit, = action, fate]

Kar·nak /ˈkarnak/ a village in Egypt, on the Nile near Luxor. It is the site of the northern complex of monuments of ancient Thebes, including the great temple of Amun.

Kar·nat·aka /karˈnɒtəkə/ a state in SW India; capital, Bangalore. It was known as Mysore until 1973.

Karoo /kəˈruː/ *noun* (also **Kar·roo**) an elevated semi-desert plateau in South Africa.

Kar·pov /ˈkarpɒf/ **Ana·toli (Yev·geny·evich)** (b.1951), Russian chess player. He was world champion from 1975 until defeated by Kasparov in 1985. He regained the title from Kasparov in 1993.

Kars /kars/ a city and province in NE Turkey; pop. (est. 2002) 103,800. In the 9th and 10th c. it was the capital of an independent Armenian principality.

Karsh, You·suf (1908–2002), Armenian-born Canadian photographer renowned for his portraits of influential people. His 1941 photograph of Winston Churchill was used on the cover of *Life* magazine and remains one of the most reproduced pictures in the history of photography. His work has been collected in several books and hangs in galleries worldwide.

karst /karst/ *noun* a limestone region with underground drainage and many cavities and passages caused by the dissolution of the rock.
  □ **karst·ic** *adjective* [the *Karst*, a limestone region in Slovenia]

kart *noun* = GO-KART. [var. of CART]

karyo- /ˈkeriːo/ *combining form Biol.* denoting the nucleus of a cell. [Greek *karuon* kernel]

karyo·kin·esis /ˌkeriːokɪˈniːsɪs/ *noun Biol.* the division of a cell nucleus during mitosis. [KARYO- + Greek *kinēsis* movement from *kineō* move]

karyo·type /ˈkeriːoˌtaip/ *noun* the number and structure of the chromosomes in the nucleus of a cell. □ **karyo·typic** /-əˈtɪpɪk/ *adjective* **karyo·typ·ing** *noun*

kas·bah *var. of* CASBAH.

kasha /ˈkaʃə/ *noun* a soft food made of boiled or baked grain, esp. buckwheat. [Russian]

Kash·mir /kaʃˈmiːr/ a region on the northern border of India and NE Pakistan. Formerly a state of India, it has been disputed between India and Pakistan since partition in 1947. The northwestern part is controlled by Pakistan, most of it forming the state of Azad Kashmir, while the remainder is incorporated into the Indian state of Jammu and Kashmir.

Kashmir goat *noun* a goat of a Himalayan breed yielding fine soft wool (used to make cashmere).

Kash·miri /kaʃˈmiːri/ ● *adjective* of or relating to Kashmir or its people or language. ● *noun* **1** a native or inhabitant of Kashmir. **2** the Indic language of Kashmir. [KASHMIR + -I²]

Kash·ruth /ˈkaʃruːθ/ *noun* (also **Kash·rut** /ˈkaʃruːt/) *Judaism* **1** the body of religious laws relating to the suitability of food, ritual objects, etc. **2** the condition of being fit for ritual use. [Hebrew, = 'legitimacy (in religion)': as KOSHER]

Kaska /ˈkaskə/ ● *noun* **1** a member of a Dene Aboriginal group living in northwestern BC. **2** the Athapaskan language of this people.

● *adjective* of or relating to this people or their culture or language. [from the native name of a creek in the area]

Kas·pa·rov /ˈkæspəˌrɒf/ **Gary** (born Gary Weinstein) (b.1963), Azerbaijani chess player of Armenian-Jewish descent. At the age of 22, he became the youngest-ever world champion, defeating Karpov in 1985; he defended the title until 2000 when he lost to Vladimir Kramnik. In recent years, he has gained attention for his matches against computers.

Kas·sel /ˈkæsəl/ a city in central Germany, in Hesse; pop. (est. 2002) 194,600. It was formerly the capital of the kingdom of Westphalia (1807–13) and of the Prussian province of Hesse-Nassau (1866–1944).

Kasur /kəˈsʊr/ a city in Punjab province, NE Pakistan; pop. (1998) 241,600.

kata /ˈkɒtɒ/ *noun* a system of basic exercises or postures used to teach and improve the execution of techniques in judo and other martial arts. [Japanese]

kata·batic /ˌkætəˈbætɪk/ *adjective Meteorol.* (of wind) caused by air flowing downwards (*compare* ANABATIC). [Greek *katabatikos* from *katabainō* go down]

kata·kana /ˌkætəˈkɒnə/ *noun* an angular form of Japanese kana or writing (*compare* HIRAGANA). [Japanese, = side kana]

Ka·tan·ga /kəˈtæŋgə/ the former name (until 1972) of SHABA.

Kath·ak /ˈkʌtʌk/ *noun* a type of northern Indian classical dance alternating passages of mime with passages of dance. [Sanskrit *kathaka* 'professional storyteller', from *kathā* 'story']

Katha·kali /ˌkɒtəˈkɒli/ *noun* a form of dramatic dance of southern India, based on Hindu literature and characterized by masks, stylized costume and makeup, and frequent use of mime. [Malayalam, from Sanskrit *kathā* 'story' + Malayalam *kali* 'play']

Kathia·war /ˌkætiəˈwɑr/ a peninsula on the western coast of India, in the state of Gujarat, separating the Gulf of Kutch from the Gulf of Cambay.

Kath·man·du /ˌkætmænˈduː/ the capital of Nepal; pop. (2001) 696,852. It is situated in the Himalayas at an altitude of 1 370 m (4,450 ft.).

ka·thump *noun* a loud thudding sound, e.g. of a heart beating rapidly.

Kato·wice /ˌkætəˈviːtsə/ a city in SW Poland; pop. (est. 2000) 340,539. It is the industrial centre of the Silesian coal-mining region.

kat·sura tree /katˈsʊrə/ *noun* a tree native to eastern Asia, *Cercidiphyllum japonicum*, with leaves resembling redbud, grown as an ornamental. [Japanese]

Katte·gat /ˈkatˌgat/ a strait, 225 km (140 miles) in length, between Sweden and Denmark. It is linked to the North Sea by the Skagerrak and to the Baltic Sea by the Øresund.

katy·did /ˈkeitidɪd/ *noun* any of various N American green grasshoppers of the family Tettigoniidae. [imitative of the sound it makes]

Kauai /kəˈwɒi/ an island in the state of Hawaii, separated from Oahu by the Kauai Channel; chief town, Lihue.

Kauff·mann /ˈkaufmən/ **(Maria Anna Cath·a·rina) An·geli·ca** (also **Kauff·man**) (1741–1807), Swiss painter. In London from 1766, she became well known for her neoclassical and allegorical paintings (e.g. *Self-Portrait Hesitating Between the Arts of Music and Painting*, 1791), and for her decorative wall paintings in houses designed by Robert Adam.

Kau·nas /ˈkaunəs/ an industrial city and river port in S Lithuania, at the confluence of the Vilnya and Neman rivers; pop. (1999) 414,174.

Ka·un·da /kɒˈʊndə/ **Ken·neth (David)** (b.1924), Zambian leader, president 1964–91. In 1964 he became prime minister and was appointed the first president of independent Zambia; as chairman of the Organization of African Unity (1970–1; 1987–8), he played a key role in the negotiations leading to Namibian independence (1990).

kauri /ˈkauri/ *noun* (*pl.* **kauris**) a coniferous New Zealand tree, *Agathis australis*, which produces valuable timber and a resin. [Maori]

Kaus Aus·tral·is /ˌkaus ɒsˈtrælɪs/ the brightest star in the constellation Sagittarius located in the southern part of the archer's bow. [Arabic *kaus* 'bow' + Latin *australis* 'southern']

kava /ˈkɒvə/ *noun* 1 a Polynesian shrub, *Piper methysticum*. 2 an intoxicating drink made from the crushed roots of this. 3 (also **kava kava**) an extract of this used to treat anxiety and as a sedative, now banned in Canada and Europe as implicated in liver damage. [Polynesian]

Kav·eri River see CAUVERY RIVER.

Ka·war·tha Lakes /kəˈwɔrθə/ 1 a series of small interconnected lakes in south central Ontario, situated near Peterborough and forming part of the Trent-Severn Waterway. 2 a city roughly contiguous with this region, including the former town of Lindsay and

surrounding areas; pop. (2001) 69,179. [corruption of Huron *kawatha* land of reflections]

Kawa·saki /ˌkɒwəˈsɒki/ an industrial city on the southeast coast of the island of Honshu, Japan; pop. (est. 2002) 1,271,600.

Kawasaki disease *noun* a disease in young children with an unknown cause, giving rise to a rash, glandular swelling and sometimes damage to the heart. [T. *Kawasaki*, Japanese physician]

Kaw·thoo·lay /kɒθuːˈlei/ (also **Kaw·thu·lei**) a former name (1964–74) for KAREN STATE.

kay·ak /ˈkaiak/ ● *noun* 1 an Inuit one-man canoe consisting of a light wooden frame covered with sealskins. 2 a small covered canoe modelled on this, used for touring or sport. ● *verb* (**ka·yaked**, **kayak·ing**) 1 *intransitive* travel by kayak. 2 *transitive* paddle a kayak on or along (a river, the ocean, etc.). □ **kay·ak·er** *noun* **kay·ak·ing** *noun* [Inuktitut]

Kaye, Danny (born David Daniel Kominski) (1913–87), US actor and comedian. After a successful Broadway career he went on to star in a number of films and became known for his mimicry, comic songs, and slapstick humour; his films include *The Secret Life of Walter Mitty* (1947) and *Hans Christian Andersen* (1952).

kayo /keiˈoː/ *informal* ● *transitive verb* (**kayoes**, **kayoed**) knock out; stun by a blow. ● *noun* (*pl.* **kayos**) a knockout. [representing pronunciation of KO]

Kay·seri /ˈkaisəri/ a city in central Turkey, capital of a province of the same name; pop. (est. 2002) 555,900.

Kaz·akh /kəˈzɒk/ ● *noun* 1 (*pl.* **Kaz·akhs**) a member of a Turkic people of central Asia, esp. of Kazakhstan. 2 the language of this people. ● *adjective* of or relating to the Kazakhs or their language.

Kaz·akh·stan /ˌkazəkˈstɑn/ a republic in central Asia; population (est. 1996) 16,677,000; capital, Astana. Situated on the southern border of Russia, it extends from the Caspian Sea eastward to the Altai Mountains and China.

Kazan¹ /kəˈzan, -ˈzɒn/ a port situated on the Volga River to the east of Nizhni Novgorod in Russia, capital of the autonomous republic of Tatarstan; pop. (est. 2002) 1,109,500.

Kazan² /kəˈzan/ **Elia** (born Elia Kazanjoglous) (1909–2003), Turkish-born US film and theatre director. He co-founded the Actors' Studio (1947), one of the leading centres of method acting, and is best known for the stage production of *A Streetcar Named Desire* (1947), which he made into a film (1951), and the films *On the Waterfront* (1954) and *East of Eden* (1955).

Kazan River /kəˈzan/ a river in the southwestern Nunavut, 732 km long, rising north of the Saskatchewan border and flowing generally northeastward into Baker Lake. [Chipewyan, = white partridge]

Kaz·an·tza·kis /ˌkazandˈzakɪs/ **Nikos** (1885–1957), Greek novelist, poet, and playwright, whose writings show a deep concern with metaphysical and religious issues; they include the epic poem *The Odyssey: A Modern Sequel* (1938), and the novels *Zorba the Greek* (1946) and *The Last Temptation of Christ* (1955).

ka·zil·lion /kəˈzɪljən/ *noun N Amer.* = GAZILLION.

kazoo /kəˈzuː/ *noun* a toy or jazz musical instrument consisting of a tube with a membrane at each end or over a hole in the side, which produces a buzzing noise when hummed into. [19th c., apparently with reference to the sound produced]

KB *abbreviation* 1 kilobyte(s). 2 KING'S BENCH.

Kb *abbreviation* kilobit(s).

kb *abbreviation* kilobar(s).

KBE *abbreviation* (in the UK) Knight Commander of the Order of the British Empire.

KBps *abbreviation* kilobytes per second.

Kbps *abbreviation* kilobits per second.

kbyte *abbreviation* kilobyte(s).

KC *abbreviation* 1 KING'S COUNSEL. 2 Kansas City. 3 Kennel Club.

kc *abbreviation* kilocycle(s).

kcal *abbreviation* kilocalorie(s).

KCB *abbreviation* (in the UK) Knight Commander of the Order of the Bath.

KCMG *abbreviation* (in the UK) Knight Commander of the Order of St. Michael and St. George.

KE *abbreviation* kinetic energy.

kea /ˈkiːə, ˈkeiə/ *noun* a parrot, *Nestor notabilis*, of New Zealand, with brownish-green and red plumage. [Maori, imitative]

Kean, Ed·mund (1787–1833), English actor, who became particularly renowned for his interpretations of Shakespearean villains, notably Macbeth and Iago.

Keat·ing, **Paul (John)** (b.1944), Australian Labor politician, prime minister 1991–96.

Kea·ton, **Bus·ter** (born Joseph Francis Keaton) (1895–1966), US actor and director. His straight face and acrobatic skills contributed to his popularity as a silent-film mime artist; major films include *Our Hospitality* (1923), *The Navigator* (1924), and *The General* (1926).

Keats, **John** (1795–1821), English poet. A principal figure of the romantic movement, he was noted for his spiritual and intellectual contemplation of beauty, and wrote his most famous poems in 1818, including 'The Eve of St. Agnes', 'La Belle Dame sans Merci', 'Ode to a Nightingale', 'Ode on a Grecian Urn', and 'Ode to Autumn'. □ **Keats·ian** *adjective*

ke·bab /kə'bɒb, -bab/ *noun* (also **kabob** /-'bɒb/) a dish of pieces of marinated meat and vegetables cooked and served on a skewer. [Urdu from Arabic *kabāb*]

Keble /'kiːbəl/ **John** (1792–1866), English churchman. His sermon on national apostasy (1833) is generally held to mark the beginning of the Oxford Movement; the work of Keble's followers did much to revive traditional Catholic teaching within the Church of England.

Keb·ne·kaise /ˌkebnə'kəisə/ the highest peak in Sweden, in the north of the country, rising to a height of 2 117 m (6,962 ft.).

Kedah /'kedə/ a state of NW Malaysia, on the west coast of the Malay Peninsula; capital, Alor Setar.

kedge ● *verb* **1** *transitive* move (a ship) by hauling in a hawser attached to a small anchor dropped at some distance. **2** *intransitive* (of a ship) move in this way. ● *noun* (in full **kedge anchor**) a small anchor for this purpose. [perhaps a specific use of obsolete *cagge*, dial. *cadge* bind, tie]

kedg·eree /'kedʒəri, -'riː/ *noun* **1** an Indian dish of rice, split pulse, onions, eggs, etc. **2** a European dish of fish, rice, hard-boiled eggs, etc. [Hindi *khichṛī*, Sanskrit *k'rsara* dish of rice and sesame]

keek *Scot.* ● *intransitive verb* peep; peek. ● *noun* a peep or glance. [Middle English *kike*: compare Middle Dutch, Middle Low German *kiken*]

keel ● *noun* **1** the lengthwise timber or steel structure along the base of a ship, airship, or some aircraft, on which the framework of the whole is built up. **2** *literary* a ship. **3** a ridge along the breastbone of many birds; a carina. **4** *Bot.* a prow-shaped pair of petals in a corolla etc. ● *transitive & intransitive verb* turn keel upwards. □ **keel over 1** fall down; faint. **2** fall over sideways. **3** die. **4** capsize. **on an even keel 1** (of a ship or aircraft) not listing. **2** (of a plan or person) untroubled. □ **keel·less** *adjective* [Middle English *kele* from Old Norse *kjǫlr* from Germanic]

keel·boat *noun* **1** a yacht built with a permanent keel instead of a centreboard. **2** a large flat boat used to transport freight on rivers.

keel·haul *transitive verb* **1** drag (a person) through the water under the keel of a ship as a punishment. **2** scold or rebuke severely.

Kee·ling Islands an alternative name for the COCOS ISLANDS.

keel·son *noun* (also **kelson**) a line of timber fastening a ship's floor timbers to its keel. [Middle English *kelswayn*, perhaps from Low German *kielswîn* from *kiel* KEEL + (prob.) *swîn* SWINE used as the name of a timber]

keen¹ *adjective* **1** (of a person, desire, or interest) eager, ardent (*a keen curler*). **2** (foll. by *on*) much attracted by; fond of or enthusiastic about. **3 a** (of the senses) sharp; highly sensitive. **b** (of feelings) intense, strong, deep. **4** intellectually acute. **5 a** having a sharp edge or point. **b** (of an edge etc.) sharp. **6** (of a sound, light, etc.) penetrating, vivid, strong. **7** (of a wind, frost, etc.) piercingly cold. **8** (of a pain etc.) acute, bitter. **9** *informal* excellent. **10** *Curling* (of ice) allowing fast movement of the rock, esp. with a little curl. □ **keen·ly** *adverb* **keen·ness** *noun* [Old English *cēne* from Germanic]

keen² ● *noun* an Irish funeral song accompanied with wailing. ● *verb* **1** *intransitive* make a high-pitched sound like wailing (*wind keened through the walls*). **2** *intransitive* utter the keen. **3** *transitive* bewail (a person) in this way. **4** *transitive* utter in a wailing tone. [Irish *caoine* from *caoinim* wail]

keen·er *noun* *Cdn informal* a person, esp. a student, who is extremely eager, zealous, or enthusiastic. [KEEN¹ + -ER¹]

keep ● *verb* (*past* and *past participle* **kept**) **1** *transitive* have continuous charge of; retain possession of. **2** *transitive* (foll. by *for*) retain or reserve for a future occasion or time (*will keep it for tomorrow*). **3** *transitive & intransitive* retain or remain in a specified condition, position, course, etc. (*keep cool*; *keep off the grass*; *keep them happy*). **4** *transitive* put or store in a regular place (*knives are kept in this drawer*). **5** *transitive* (foll. by *from*) cause to avoid or abstain from something (*will keep you from going too*

fast). **6** *transitive* detain; cause to be late (*what kept you?*). **7** *transitive* **a** observe or pay due regard to (a law, custom, etc.). **b** honour or fulfill (a commitment, undertaking, etc.) (*keep one's word*). **c** respect the commitment implied by (a secret etc.). **d** act fittingly on the occasion of (*keep the Sabbath*). **8** *transitive* own and look after (animals) for amusement or profit (*keeps bees*). **9** *transitive* **a** provide for the sustenance of (a person, family, etc.). **b** (foll. by *in*) maintain (a person) with a supply of. **10** *transitive* carry on; manage (a shop, business, etc.). **11 a** *transitive* maintain (accounts, a diary, etc.) by making the requisite entries. **b** *transitive* maintain (a house) in proper order. **12** *transitive* have (a commodity) regularly on sale (*we don't keep that book in stock*). **13** *transitive* guard or protect (a person or place, a goal in hockey, etc.). **14** *transitive* preserve in being; continue to have (*keep order*). **15** *intransitive* (foll. by verbal noun) continue or do repeatedly or habitually (*why do you keep saying that?*). **16** *transitive* continue to follow (a way or course). **17** *intransitive* **a** (esp. of perishable commodities) remain in good condition. **b** (of news or information etc.) admit of being withheld for a time. **18** *transitive* remain in (one's bed, room, house, etc.). **19** *transitive* retain (one's seat, ground, etc.) against opposition or difficulty. **20** *transitive* maintain (a person) in return for sexual favours (*a kept woman*). ● *noun* **1** food, clothes, and other things needed for living (*it's time you got a job to earn your keep*; *is in your keep*). **2** charge or control (*is in your keep*). **3** *hist.* a tower or stronghold. □ **for keeps** *informal* (esp. of something received or won) permanently, indefinitely. **how are you keeping?** how are you? **keep at** persist or cause to persist with. **keep away** (often foll. by *from*) **1** avoid being near. **2** prevent from being near. **keep back 1** remain or keep at a distance. **2** retard the progress of. **3** conceal; decline to disclose. **4** retain, withhold (*kept back $50*). **keep one's balance** remain stable; avoid falling. **keep down 1** hold in subjection. **2** keep low in amount. **3** lie low; stay hidden. **4** manage not to vomit (food eaten). **keep one's feet** manage not to fall. **keep one's hand in** *see* HAND. **keep in 1** confine or restrain (one's feelings etc.). **2** remain or confine indoors. **keep off 1** stay or cause to stay away from. **2** ward off; avert. **3** abstain from. **4** avoid (a subject) (*let's keep off religion*). **keep on 1** continue to do something; do continually (*kept on laughing*). **2** continue to use or employ. **3** (foll. by *at*) pester or harass. **keep on keeping on** endure, esp. in spite of hardship. **keep oneself to oneself** not mingle or associate with others. **keep out 1** keep or remain outside. **2** exclude. **keep one's temper** control one's anger. **keep to 1** adhere to (a course, schedule, etc.). **2** observe (a promise). **3** confine oneself to. **keep to oneself 1** avoid contact with others. **2** refuse to disclose or share. **keep together** remain or keep in harmony. **keep track of** *see* TRACK¹. **keep under** hold in subjection. **keep up 1** maintain (progress etc.). **2** prevent (prices, one's spirits, etc.) from sinking. **3** keep in repair, in an efficient or proper state, etc. **4** carry on (a correspondence etc.). **5** prevent (a person) from going to bed, esp. when late. **6** (often foll. by *with*) manage not to fall behind. **keep up with the Joneses** strive to compete socially with one's neighbours. □ **keep·able** *adjective* [Old English *cēpan*, of unknown origin]

keep·er *noun* **1** a person who keeps or looks after something or someone (also in *combination*: *zookeeper*; *lighthouse keeper*). **2** a device for keeping something in place, esp. a loop securing the end of a buckled strap. **3** a fruit or other product that keeps in a specified way. **4** *Football* an offensive play in which the quarterback runs with the ball. **5** *informal* something that one wishes to keep as valuable (*that cookie recipe is definitely a keeper*). **6** *N Amer.* a fish that is large enough that it need not be released if caught. **7 a** a plain stud or ring worn to preserve a hole in a pierced earlobe. **b** a ring worn to guard against the loss of a more valuable one. **8** a bar of soft iron across the poles of a horseshoe magnet to maintain its strength.

keep-fit *noun* esp. *Brit.* (often *attributive*) regular exercises to promote personal fitness and health.

keep·ing *noun* **1** custody, charge (*into your keeping*). **2** conformity, harmony (*in keeping with his wishes*; *out of keeping*).

keep·sake *noun* a thing kept for the sake of or in remembrance of the giver.

kees·hond /'keishɒnd/ *noun* (pl. **-honds** or **-hond·en**) a breed of dog with long thick grey hair; a variety of the spitz. [Dutch, from *Kees* pet form of male name Cornelius + *hond* dog]

kees·ter *N Amer.* var. of KEISTER.

Kee·wa·tin /kiː'weitən/ an administrative region of Nunavut, including Southampton and Coats Islands and the southern part of the mainland. [Ojibwa, = north wind]

Keewatin, District of /kiː'weitən/ a former district (est. 1876) of the NWT, occupying the eastern mainland region, but originally encompassing much of N Manitoba and NW Ontario as well.

kef *noun* (also **kif**) **1** a drowsy state induced by marijuana etc. **2** the enjoyment of idleness. **3** a substance smoked to produce kef. [Arabic *kayf* enjoyment, well-being]

kefa·lo·tiri /ˌkefəloˈtiːriː/ *noun* (also **kefalotyri**) a hard, salty, yellow, Greek ewe's or goat's cheese similar to Parmesan. [Greek, = 'hat cheese', its shape being similar to that of a brimless hat]

kef·fi·yeh *var.* of KAFFIYEH.

Kef·la·vik /ˈkeflaˌvɪk/ a fishing port in SW Iceland; pop. (1999) 7,671. Iceland's international airport is located nearby.

keg *noun* **1** a small barrel. **2** *Cdn* (*Nfld*) a small barrel used as a buoy or float for a fishnet etc. (also *attributive*: keg buoy). [Middle English *cag* from Old Norse *kaggi*, of unknown origin]

keg beer *noun* beer supplied from a sealed metal container.

Kegel exercise /ˈkeɡəl/ *noun* (also **Kegel**) an exercise consisting of contraction and release of the muscles of the genitourinary tract so as to strengthen them in preparation for childbirth and improve bladder control. [A. H. Kegel, US physician d.1972, who invented the exercise]

keg party *noun* (*pl.* **-ties**) *N Amer.* a usu. large, informal party at which the primary refreshment is a keg of beer.

kei·retsu /keiˈretsuː/ *noun* (*pl.* same) (in Japan) a conglomeration of businesses linked together by cross-shareholdings to form a robust corporate structure. [Japanese, from *kei* 'systems' + *retsu* 'tier']

keis·ter /ˈkiːstər/ *noun* (also **keester**) *N Amer. slang* the buttocks. [origin unknown: original sense 'suitcase, satchel, handbag']

Kei·tel /ˈkaɪtəl/ **Wil·helm (Bode·win Jo·hann Gus·tav)** (1882–1946), German field marshal, who served as supreme commander of Hitler's forces throughout the Second World War.

Kejim·kujik National Park /ˌkedʒɪmˈkuːdʒɪk/ a park in SW central Nova Scotia, southeast of Annapolis Royal. [the name of a local lake, from Mi'kmaq, possibly = swollen private parts, with reference to the exertion required when paddling across the lake]

Kek·ulé von Strad·onitz /ˈkekjuˌlei fɒn ˈʃtraːdɒnɪts/ **(Frie·drich) Aug·ust** (1829–96), German chemist. One of the founders of structural organic chemistry, he suggested in 1858 that carbon was tetravalent, and that carbon atoms could combine with others to form complex chains; he discovered the ring structure of benzene, the key to understanding many organic compounds.

Ke·lan·tan /kəˈlantən/ a state of N Malaysia, on the east coast of the Malay Peninsula; capital, Kota Baharu.

Kel·ler, Helen (Adams) (1880–1968), US writer, social reformer, and academic. Blind and deaf from the age of 19 months, she learned how to read, type, and speak, and is particularly remembered for her campaigning in aid of the American Foundation for the Blind.

Kel·logg, Will Keith (1860–1951), US food manufacturer. The breakfast cereal consisting of crisp flakes of rolled and toasted wheat and corn which he developed for sanatorium patients was the foundation of a vast food company.

Kel·logg Pact (also called **Kellogg-Briand Pact**) a treaty renouncing war as an instrument of national policy, signed in Paris in 1928 by representatives of 15 nations. It grew out of a proposal made by the French Premier Aristide Briand (1862–1932) to Frank B. Kellogg (1856–1937), US Secretary of State.

Kelly ▶ 1 Gene (born Eugene Curran Kelly) (1912–1996), US dancer and choreographer. He began his career on Broadway in 1938 and went on to perform in and choreograph many film musicals, including *Anchors Aweigh* (1945), *An American in Paris* (1951) and *Singin' in the Rain* (1952). **2 Grace (Pa·tri·cia)** (known as 'Princess Grace of Monaco' from 1956) (1928–82), US film actress. She starred in successful films such as *High Noon* (1952), *The Country Girl* (1954), for which she won an Oscar, and *Rear Window* (1954), before retiring from films in 1956 on her marriage to Prince Rainier III of Monaco. **3 Petra (Karin)** (1947–92), German political leader. Formerly a member of the German Social Democratic Party, she became disillusioned with their policies and in 1979 co-founded the Green Party, a broad alliance of environmentalists, feminists, and anti-nuclear activists; she was found dead, allegedly after committing suicide, in 1992.

kelly green *N Amer.* ● *noun* a bright yellowish-green colour. ● *adjective* of this colour. [prob. from the Irish surname *Kelly*]

ke·loid /ˈkiːlɔɪd/ *noun* fibrous tissue formed at the site of a scar or injury. □ **ke·loid·al** *adjective* [Greek *khēlē* claw + -OID]

Ke·low·na /kəˈloʊnə/ a city in south central BC, situated on Okanagan Lake, 163 km southeast of Kamloops; pop. (2001) 96,288. [Okanagan, = female grizzly bear]

kelp *noun* **1** any of several large broad-bladed brown seaweeds esp. of the genus *Laminaria*, suitable for use as fertilizer. **2** the calcined ashes of seaweed used for the salts of sodium, potassium, and iodine which they contain. [Middle English *cülp(e)*, of unknown origin]

kel·pie¹ *noun* (in Scottish folklore) a water spirit, usu. in the form of a horse, reputed to delight in the drowning of travellers etc. [perhaps from Gaelic *cailpeach, colpach* bullock, colt]

kel·pie² *noun* a smooth-coated, prick-eared, Australian breed of sheepdog derived from imported Scottish collies. [apparently from the name of a particular bitch, *King's Kelpie* (c.1870)]

kel·son *var.* of KEELSON.

Kelt *var.* of CELT.

kelt *noun* a salmon or sea trout after spawning. [Middle English: origin unknown]

Kel·vin, Wil·liam Thom·son, 1st Baron (1824–1907), Scottish physicist. He formulated the second law of thermodynamics in 1850, and introduced the absolute scale of temperature; his concept of an electromagnetic field influenced Maxwell's electromagnetic theory of light, which Kelvin never accepted, and he was involved in the laying of the first Atlantic cable, for which he invented several instruments.

kel·vin *noun* the SI unit of thermodynamic temperature, equal in magnitude to the degree celsius. Abbr.: **K**. [KELVIN]

Kelvin scale *noun* a scale of temperature with absolute zero as zero.

Kemal /keˈmɒl/ see ATATÜRK.

Keme·rovo /ˈkeməˌrəvə/ an industrial city in south central Russia, to the east of Novosibirsk; pop. (est. 2000) 489,300.

Kempe /ˈkemp/ **Mar·gery** (c.1373–c.1440), English mystic, who gave up married life to devote herself to religion and travelled widely on pilgrimage; her autobiographical *Book of Margery Kempe* recounts her visions and general experiences.

Kem·pis see THOMAS À KEMPIS.

kempt *adjective* combed; neatly kept. [past participle of (now dial.) *kemb* COMB *verb* from Old English *cemban* from Germanic]

ken ● *noun* range of sight or knowledge (*it's beyond my ken*). ● *transitive verb* (**ken·ning**; *past* and *past participle* **kenned** or **kent**) *Scot. & Northern England* **1** recognize at sight. **2** know. [Old English *cennan* from Germanic]

Ken·dall, Ed·ward Cal·vin (1886–1972), US biochemist. He was the first to isolate crystalline thyroxine from the thyroid gland, and he obtained a number of steroid hormones from the adrenal cortex, several of which are now valuable in the treatment of rheumatic, allergic, and inflammatory diseases; he shared a Nobel Prize in 1950.

kendo *noun* a Japanese form of fencing with two-handed bamboo swords. [Japanese, = sword way]

Ken doll *noun* *N Amer.* a good-looking and well built but vacuous young man. [name of a male doll]

Ken·drew, Sir John Cowd·ery (1917–97), English molecular biologist, who determined the structure of the muscle protein myoglobin; he shared the Nobel Prize for chemistry in 1962.

Ken·nebe·casis River /ˈkenəbəˌkeɪsɪs/ a river in S New Brunswick, rising southeast of Moncton and flowing generally southwestward to Kennebecasis Bay, an arm of the Saint John River. [Mi'kmaq, = little bay place]

Ken·nedy ▶ 1 a Ed·ward Moore ('Teddy') (b.1932), US Democratic politician. The brother of John F. Kennedy and Robert F. Kennedy, he was elected to the Senate in 1962; his subsequent political career was overshadowed by his involvement in a mysterious fatal car accident at Chappaquiddick Island (1969). **b Jacque·line Bou·vier,** see ONASSIS 2. **c John Fitz·ger·ald** (known as 'J.F.K.') (1917–63), US Democratic politician, 35th president of the US 1961–3. A national war hero during the Second World War, he became, at 43, the youngest man and first Roman Catholic ever to be elected president; he gained a popular reputation as an advocate of civil rights, and in 1962 successfully demanded the withdrawal of Soviet missiles from Cuba, and negotiated the Nuclear Test-Ban Treaty of 1963 with the USSR and the UK. He was assassinated while riding in a motorcade through Dallas, Texas, in Nov. 1963. **d** his brother, **Rob·ert Fran·cis** (1925–68), US Democratic politician. He closely assisted his brother John in domestic policy, serving as his Attorney General (1961–4), and was a champion of the civil-rights movement; he stood as a prospective presidential candidate in 1968, but was assassinated during his campaign. **2 Nigel** (b.1956), British violinist. He achieved mainstream popularity with recordings of classical music such as Vivaldi's *Four Seasons* (1990) and performances of improvisational concerts with Stephane Grappelli. □ **Kennedy·esque** *adjective*

Kennedy, Mount a peak (4 238 m) in the St. Elias Mountains of SW Yukon Territory, east of Mount Alverstone. [J. F. KENNEDY]

uː mood ai my əi pipe au brown ʌu house ei day ɔi boy ā franglais ã Canadien ɔ̃ Brayon   (*see over for consonants*)

ken·nel ● *noun* **1** a small shelter for a dog. **2** (in *pl.*) a breeding or boarding establishment for dogs. ● *verb* (**ken·nelled, ken·nel·ling**; also esp. *US* **ken·neled, ken·nel·ing**) **1** *transitive* put into or keep in a kennel. **2** *intransitive* live in or go to a kennel. [Old French *chenil* from medieval Latin *canile* (unrecorded) from Latin *canis* dog]

kennel club *noun* an organization which establishes dog breeds, records pedigrees, issues the rules for dog shows and trials, etc.

kennel cough *noun* a highly contagious condition, characterized by a hacking cough, that commonly spreads among dogs at boarding kennels, animal shelters, dog shows, etc.

Ken·nel·ly, Ar·thur Edwin (1861–1939), English-born US electrical engineer. His principal work was on the theory of alternating currents, and he also worked on the practical problems of electrical transmission; he proposed the existence of the ionosphere (1902).

Ken·neth I (known as 'Kenneth MacAlpin') (d.858), king of Scotland *c*.844–58. He is traditionally viewed as the founder of the kingdom of Scotland, following his defeat of the Picts in about 844.

ken·ning *noun* a compound expression in Old English and Old Norse poetry, e.g. *oar-steed* = ship. [Middle English, = 'teaching' etc. from KEN]

keno /ˈkiːno/ *noun* a game of chance resembling bingo, based on the drawing of numbers and covering of corresponding numbers on cards. [19th c.: origin unknown]

Ke·no·ju·ak /ˈkenˈoːdʒuːak/ **Ashe·vak** (b.1927), Canadian artist. The first Inuk woman to become involved with the Cape Dorset printmaking shop, she is best known for her prints but has also sculpted. Her work, mostly depicting birds, is characterized by colour and strong composition.

Ken·ora /kəˈnɔrə/ a city in NW Ontario, situated on the northern shore of Lake of the Woods, close to the border with Manitoba; pop. (2001) 15,838. □ **Ken·or·an** *noun* **Ken·ora·ite** *noun* [combination of the first two letters of each of the following: *Keewatin* + *Norman* (two communities to the west of Kenora) + *Rat Portage* (the former name for Kenora)]

ken·osis /kɪˈnoːsɪs/ *noun Theol.* the renunciation of the divine nature, at least in part, by Christ in the Incarnation. □ **ken·otic** /-ˈnɒtɪk/ *adjective* [Greek *kenōsis* from *kenoō* to empty, from *kenos* empty]

ken·speckle /ˈkenˌspekəl/ *adjective Scot.* conspicuous. [*kenspeck* of Scandinavian origin; related to KEN]

Kent¹, a county on the southeast coast of England; county town, Maidstone. □ **Kent·ish** *adjective*

Kent², Wil·liam (*c*.1685–1748), English architect and landscape gardener. He promoted the Palladian style of architecture in England.

kent *past and past participle of* KEN.

kente /ˈkentei/ *noun* (in full **kente cloth**) a brightly coloured banded woven fabric of Ghanaian origin. [Twi, = cloth]

kent·ledge /ˈkentlədʒ/ *noun Naut.* pig iron etc. used as permanent ballast. [French *quintelage* ballast, assimilated to *kentle* obsolete var. of QUINTAL]

Ken·ton, Stan (born Stanley Newcomb) (1912–79), US bandleader, composer, and arranger. Kenton formed his own orchestra in 1940 and is particularly associated with the big-band jazz style of the 1950s.

Kent Peninsula a peninsula of the north central coast of mainland Nunavut, south of Victoria Island, separating Coronation and Queen Maud gulfs. [*Duchess of Kent*, Victoria Mary Louisa, mother of Queen Victoria d.1861]

Ken·tucky a state in the southeastern US; pop. (2000) 4,041,769; capital, Frankfort. It is also known as the Bluegrass state. □ **Ken·tuck·ian** *noun & adjective*

Kentucky bluegrass *noun* the grass *Poa pratensis*, used for fodder and in lawns.

Kentucky coffee tree *noun* a leguminous tree of eastern N America, *Gymnocladus dioicus*, with large doubly-pinnate leaves and brown seed pods.

Kentucky Derby *noun* an annual horse race for three-year-olds held at Louisville, Kentucky.

Kent·ville a town in central Nova Scotia, about 25 km inland from the Bay of Fundy, northwest of Halifax; pop. (2001) 5,610. □ **Kent·vill·ite** *noun* [Prince Edward, Duke of *Kent* and Strathearn d.1820]

Kenya /ˈkenjə, ˈkiːn-/ an equatorial country in East Africa, on the Indian Ocean; pop. (est. 2002) 31,138,735; capital, Nairobi. □ **Ken·yan** *adjective & noun*

Kenya, Mount a mountain in central Kenya, the second-highest in Africa, just south of the equator, rising to a height of 5 200 m (17,058 ft.).

Ken·yat·ta /kenˈjatə/ **Jomo** (*c*.1891–1978), Kenyan leader, who led his country's fight for independence and was its president from 1964 until his death.

kepi /ˈkepi, ˈkeipi/ *noun* (*pl.* **kepis**) a French military cap with a flat circular top and a horizontal peak. [French *képi* from Swiss German *käppi* diminutive of *kappe* cap]

Kep·ler, Jo·han·nes (1571–1630), German astronomer. One of the founders of modern astronomy, he discovered the three laws governing planetary motion that are named after him; he also made discoveries in optics, general physics, and geometry. □ **Kep·ler·ian** /kepˈliːriən/ *adjective*

Kepler's laws *plural noun* three theorems describing orbital motion: that the planets move in ellipses having the sun at one focus; that the radius vector of a planet sweeps out equal areas in equal times; and that the square of a planet's orbital period is directly proportional to the cube of its mean distance from the sun.

kept *past and past participle of* KEEP.

ker- *prefix* forming nouns and interjections imitative of a loud sound (*kerplunk*; *ker-thud*). [imitative]

Ker·ala /ˈkerələ/ a state on the coast of SW India; capital, Trivandrum. It was created in 1956 from the former state of Travancore-Cochin and part of Madras. □ **Keral·ite** *adjective & noun*

kera·tin /ˈkeratɪn/ *noun* a fibrous protein which occurs in hair, feathers, hooves, claws, horns, etc. [Greek *keras keratos* horn + -IN]

kera·tin·ize /ˈkeratɪˌnaɪz/ *transitive & intransitive verb* (also esp. *Brit.* **-ise**) cover or become covered with a deposit of keratin. □ **kera·tin·iz·a·tion** *noun*

kera·titis /kerəˈtaɪtɪs/ *noun Med.* inflammation of the cornea of the eye. [*kerat-* denoting the cornea (from Greek *keras keratos* 'horn') + -ITIS]

kera·to·sis /ˌkerəˈtoːsɪs/ *noun* (*pl.* **-to·ses**) **1** a skin condition marked by horny growths. **2** such a growth. □ **kera·tot·ic** *adjective* [Greek *keras keratos* horn + -OSIS]

kera·tot·omy /kerəˈtɒtəmi/ *noun Med.* a surgical operation involving cutting into the cornea of the eye, esp. (in full **radial keratotomy**) to correct myopia. [*kerat-* denoting the cornea (compare KERATITIS) + -TOMY]

kerb *Brit. var. of* CURB *noun* 1.

kerb-crawler *noun Brit.* a (usu. male) person who drives slowly near the edge of the road in an attempt to engage a prostitute or harass esp. female passersby. □ **kerb-crawling** *noun*

kerb·side *Brit. var. of* CURBSIDE.

kerb·stone *Brit. var. of* CURBSTONE.

Kerch /kɜrtʃ/ a city in S Ukraine, the chief port and industrial centre of the Crimea, at the eastern end of the Kerch peninsula; pop. (est. 2001) 157,000.

ker·chief /ˈkɜrtʃɪf, -tʃiːf/ *noun* a cloth used to cover the head. □ **ker·chiefed** *adjective* [Anglo-French *courchef*, Old French *couvrechief* from *couvrir* COVER + CHIEF head]

Ke·ren·sky /kəˈrenski/ **Alek·sandr Fyodor·ovich** (1881–1970). Russian leader. He was prime minister of the Russian provisional government (1917) but lost power to the Bolsheviks after the October Revolution (1917).

kerf ● *noun* a slit made by cutting, esp. with a saw. ● *transitive verb* make a kerf in (a piece of wood etc.). [Old English *cyrf* from Germanic (as CARVE)]

ker·fuf·fle *noun* (also **kafuffle**) *Cdn, Brit., & Austral. informal* a fuss or commotion. [Scots *curfuffle* from *fuffle* to disorder: imitative]

Ker·gue·len Islands /ˈkɜrgələn, kɜrˈgeilən/ a group of islands in the S Indian Ocean, comprising the island of Kerguelen and some 300 small islets, forming part of French Southern and Antarctic Territories. The only settlement is a scientific base. [Y.-J. de *Kerguélen*-Trémarec, Breton navigator who discovered them in 1772]

Ker·man·shah /ˌkɜrmənˈʃɒ/ (also **Bakhtaran** /ˌbɒxtəˈrɒn/) a city in W Iran; pop. (est. 1996) 692,986.

ker·mes /ˈkɜrmiːz/ *noun* **1** (in full **kermes oak**) a small evergreen oak, *Quercus coccifera*, of the Mediterranean region. **2 a** the female of a scale insect, *Kermes ilicis*, which forms berry-like galls on the kermes oak. **b** a red dye made from the dried bodies of these insects. [French *kermès* from Arabic & Persian *kirmiz*: related to CRIMSON]

ker·mis /ˈkɜrmɪs/ *noun* a periodical country fair, esp. in the Netherlands. [Dutch, originally = mass on the anniversary of the dedication of a church, when a yearly fair was held: from *kerk* formed as CHURCH + *mis, misse* MASS²]

ker·mode /kɜr'moːdi/ *noun* (also **kermode bear**) a subspecies of the black bear, *Ursus americanus kermodei*, which can have either black or white fur, found in the coastal mainland and some coastal islands of British Columbia. [F. *Kermode*, Canadian museum administrator d.1946]

Kern, Jer·ome (David) (1885–1945), US composer and songwriter. He wrote several influential musicals including *Showboat* (1927), which featured the song 'Ol' Man River'.

kern¹ *Printing* ● *noun* the part of a metal type projecting beyond its body or shank. ● *transitive verb* **1** provide (type) with kerns; make (letters) overlap. **2** adjust the spacing between (characters). □ **kerned** *adjective* [perhaps from French *carne* corner, from Old French *charne* from Latin *cardo cardinis* hinge]

kern² (also **kerne**) **1** *hist.* a light-armed Irish foot soldier. **2** a peasant; a boor. [Middle English from Irish *ceithern*]

ker·nel *noun* **1** a central, softer, usu. edible part within a hard shell of a nut, fruit stone, seed, etc. **2** the whole seed of a cereal. **3** the nucleus or essential part of anything. **4** *Computing* the lowest layer into which a large operating system is subdivided, responsible for allocating hardware resources to processes and programs. [Old English *cyrnel*, diminutive of CORN¹]

kero·sene /'kerəˌsiːn/ *noun* esp. *N Amer.* a petroleum distillate widely used as a fuel and solvent. [Greek *kēros* wax + -ENE]

Ker·ou·ac /'keruˌak/ **Jack** (born Jean-Louis Lebris de Kérouac) (1922–69), US novelist and poet, of French-Canadian descent. A leading figure of the beat generation, he is best known for his semi-autobiographical novel *On the Road* (1957).

ker·plunk *noun* *N Amer. informal* a loud sound of something falling. [imitative]

Kerry a county of the Republic of Ireland, on the southwest coast in the province of Munster; county town, Tralee.

Kerry blue *noun* a breed of terrier with a silky blue-grey coat. [KERRY]

ker·sey /'kɜrzi/ *noun* (pl. **-seys**) **1** a kind of coarse narrow cloth woven from short-stapled wool, usu. ribbed. **2** a variety of this. [Middle English, prob. from *Kersey* in Suffolk]

ker·sey·mere /'kɜrzimiːr/ *noun* a twilled fine woollen cloth. [alteration of *cassimere*, var. of CASHMERE, assimilated to KERSEY]

Ker·tész /'kɜrteis/ **Imre** (b.1929). Hungarian writer whose best-known works, including *Sorstalanság* (*Fateless*), draw on his experiences as a holocaust survivor. Many of his works were not published until after the fall of communism in Hungary in 1989, and he was awarded the Nobel Prize for literature in 2002.

Kes·sel·ring /'kesəlrɪŋ/ **Al·bert** (1885–1960), German air force chief and field marshal, who directed German air attacks on Poland, France, and Britain (1939–40) and was noted for his tactical defensive campaign in Italy (1943–5).

kes·trel /'kestrəl/ *noun* any of several falcons distinguished by the habit of hunting by sustained hovering, esp. the American kestrel *Falco sparverius* or the Eurasian kestrel *F. tinnunculus*, widely distributed in the Old World. [Middle English *castrell*, perhaps from French dial. *casserelle*, French *créc(er)elle*, perhaps imitative of its cry]

keta /kiːtə/ *noun* = CHUM³. [Russian]

ké·taine /kei'ten/ *adjective* *Cdn* (*Que.*) in poor taste; tacky or kitschy. [Canadian French]

keta·mine /'kiːtəmiːn/ *noun* an anaesthetic and painkilling drug, also used (illicitly) as a hallucinogen. [KETONE + AMINE]

ketch *noun* a two-masted fore-and-aft rigged sailing boat with a mizzen-mast located forward of the rudder and smaller than its foremast. [Middle English *catche*, prob. from CATCH]

ketch·up *noun* (also esp. *US* **catsup**) a thick sauce made from tomatoes, vinegar, sugar, etc., used as a condiment. □ **ketch·upy** *adjective* [perhaps from Cantonese *k'ê chap* 'tomato juice']

ke·tone /'kiːtoːn/ *noun* any of a class of organic compounds in which two hydrocarbon groups are linked by a carbonyl group, e.g. propanone (acetone). □ **ke·tonic** /kɪ'tɒnɪk/ *adjective* [German *Keton* alteration of *Aketon* ACETONE]

ketone body *noun* *Biochem.* any of several ketones produced in the body during the metabolism of fats.

keton·uria /ˌkiːtoːˈnjʊriə/ *noun* the excretion of abnormally large amounts of ketone bodies in the urine, characteristic of diabetes mellitus, starvation, etc.

ke·to·sis /kɪ'toːsɪs/ *noun* a condition characterized by raised levels of ketone bodies in the body, associated with fat metabolism and diabetes. □ **ke·tot·ic** /-'tɒtɪk/ *adjective*

Ket·ter·ing, Charles Frank·lin (1876–1958), US inventor and automobile engineer. He developed the first electric cash register (1905) and made a number of advances in automotive technology, including the development of electric ignition (1912).

ket·tle *noun* **1** a vessel with a spout and handle, for boiling water in. **2** a large usu. open pot for cooking foods, boiling liquids, etc. **3** = KETTLE HOLE. □ **a different kettle of fish** a different matter altogether. **a pretty** (or **fine**) **kettle of fish** an awkward state of affairs. □ **kettle·ful** *noun* (pl. **-fuls**). [Old Norse *ketill* ultimately from Latin *catillus* diminutive of *catinus* deep food-vessel]

kettle·drum *noun* a large drum shaped like a bowl with a membrane adjustable for tension (and so pitch) stretched across. □ **kettle·drum·mer** *noun*

ket·tle hole *noun* a depression in the ground resulting from the melting of an ice block trapped in glacial deposits.

keV *abbreviation* kilo-electron volt.

Kev·lar *noun* *proprietary* a synthetic fibre of high tensile strength used esp. as a reinforcing agent in the manufacture of rubber products, e.g. tires.

Kew Gardens the Royal Botanic Gardens at Kew, in Richmond, London. Developed by the mother of George III with the aid of Sir Joseph Banks, the gardens were presented to the nation in 1841 and are now an important botanical institution.

kewpie doll *noun* (also **kewpie**) a small chubby doll with a curl or topknot. [CUPID + -IE]

key¹ ● *noun* (pl. **keys**) **1** an instrument, usu. of metal, for moving the bolt of a lock forwards or backwards to lock or unlock. **2** a similar implement for operating a switch in the form of a lock. **3** an instrument for grasping screws, pegs, nuts, etc., e.g. one for winding a clock etc. **4** a lever depressed by the finger in playing the organ, piano, flute, concertina, etc. **5** (often in *pl.*) each of several buttons for operating a word processor, computer terminal, typewriter, etc. **6** what gives or precludes the opportunity for or access to something. **7** a place that by its position gives control of a sea, territory, etc. **8 a** a solution or explanation. **b** a word or system for solving a cipher or code. **c** an explanatory list of symbols used in a map, table, etc. **d** a book of solutions to mathematical problems etc. **e** a literal translation of a book written in a foreign language. **f** the first move in a chess problem solution. **9** *Music* a system of notes definitely related to each other, based on a particular note, and predominating in a piece of music (*a study in the key of C major*). **10** a tone or style of thought or expression. **11** a piece of wood or metal inserted between others to secure them. **12** the samara of a maple etc. **13** a mechanical device for making or breaking an electric circuit, e.g. in telecommunications. **14** the dominant tonality of a photograph or painting. **15** (in basketball) the area beneath each basket, extending from the end line to a circle surrounding the free throw line. ● *adjective* essential; of vital importance (*the key element in the problem; productivity is key*). ● *transitive verb* (**keys, keyed**) **1** (foll. by *in, on*, etc.) fasten with a pin, wedge, bolt, etc. **2** (often foll. by *in*) enter (data) by means of a keyboard. **3** (foll. by *to*) align or link (one thing to another). **4** regulate the pitch of the strings of (a violin etc.). □ **key** (**in**) **on** focus on; zero in on. **key up** (often foll. by *to*, or *to* + infin.) make (a person) nervous or tense; excite. □ **key·er** *noun* **key·less** *adjective* [Old English *cæg*, of unknown origin]

key² *noun* a low-lying island or reef, esp. off the coast of Florida or in the W Indies (*compare* CAY). [Spanish *cayo* shoal, reef, influenced by QUAY]

key·board ● *noun* **1** a set of keys on a computer, piano, typewriter, etc. **2** an electronic musical instrument with keys arranged as on a piano. ● *verb* **1** *transitive* enter (data) by means of a keyboard. **2** *intransitive* work at a keyboard. □ **key·board·er** *noun* (in sense 1 of noun). **key·board·ist** *noun* (in sense 2 of noun).

key card *noun* a small plastic card, sometimes used instead of a door key in hotels, bearing magnetically encoded data that can be read and processed by an electronic device.

key chain *noun* a short, often decorated chain for carrying keys.

key escrow *noun* a system involving the holding by an independent agency of decryption keys to encrypted data, for controlled access by authorized persons or bodies.

key·frame *noun* the frozen image at the beginning or end of a sequence of animation.

key grip *noun* the chief grip on a film set etc.

key·hole *noun* **1** a hole by which a key is put into a lock. **2** a means to very private or intimate information. **3** something shaped like a keyhole, with a circle above a vertical oblong, often flared at the bottom (*a keyhole neckline*).

keyhole surgery *noun Brit.* minimally invasive surgery carried out through a very small incision; laparoscopic surgery.

Key Largo a resort island off the south coast of Florida, the northernmost and the longest of the Florida Keys.

key lime *noun* a small yellowish tart lime. [the Florida *Keys*]

key lime pie *noun* a pie with a filling made of key lime juice, sweetened condensed milk, and eggs, baked in a graham cracker crust and topped with meringue.

Keynes /'keinz/ **John May·nard, 1st Baron** (1883–1946), English economist. He laid the foundations of modern macroeconomics with *The General Theory of Employment, Interest and Money* (1936), arguing that full employment is not a natural condition but is determined by effective demand, and advocating stimulating this by government spending on public works.

Keynes·ian /'keinziən/ ● *adjective* of or relating to the economic theories of J. M. Keynes, esp. regarding state control of the economy through money and taxation. ● *noun* an adherent of these theories. □ **Keynes·ian·ism** *noun*

key·note *noun* **1** a prevailing tone or idea (*the keynote of the whole occasion*). **2** (*attributive*) intended to set the prevailing tone at a meeting or conference (*keynote address*). **3** *Music* the note on which a key is based.

key·pad *noun* a miniature keyboard or set of buttons for operating a portable electronic device, telephone, etc.

key·press *noun* = KEYSTROKE.

key·punch ● *noun* a keyboard device for transferring data by punching holes or notches in a series of cards or paper tape. ● *transitive verb* transfer (data) by means of a keypunch. □ **key·punch·er** *noun*

key ring *noun* a ring for keeping keys on.

key signature *noun Music* any of several combinations of sharps or flats after the clef at the beginning of each staff indicating the key of a piece of music.

key·stone *noun* **1** the central principle of a system, policy, etc., on which all the rest depends. **2** a central stone at the summit of an arch locking the whole together.

keystone species *noun* any species exerting a major influence upon an ecosystem, esp. one upon whose activities the survival of the other species depends.

key·stroke *noun* a single depression of a key on a keyboard.

key·way *noun* a slot for receiving a machined key.

Key West a city in S Florida, at the southern tip of the Florida Keys; pop. (2000) 25,478. It is the southernmost city in the continental US.

key·word *noun* **1** the key to a cipher etc. **2 a** a word of great significance. **b** a significant word used in indexing.

KG *abbreviation* (in the UK) Knight of the Order of the Garter.

kg *abbreviation* kilogram(s).

KGB the Soviet secret police organization (1953–91) created on Stalin's death to take over state security, with responsibility for external espionage, internal counter-intelligence, and internal 'crimes against the state'. [Russian, abbreviation of *Komitet gosudarstvennoĭ bezopasnosti* committee of state security]

Kgs. *abbreviation Bible* Kings.

Kha·bar·ovsk /kə'bɑrɒfsk/ **1** a krai on the east coast of Siberian Russia; pop. (est. 2000) 1,518,000. **2** its capital, a city on the Amur River, on the Chinese border; pop. (est. 1999) 614,000.

Kha·cha·tur·ian /ˌkɒtʃə'tʊəriən/ **Aram Ilich** (1903–78), Russian composer, whose work was deeply influenced by Armenian folk music, and includes a piano concerto (1936) and the ballets *Gayaneh* (1942), which includes the 'Sabre Dance', and *Spartacus* (1954).

khadi /'kɒdi/ *noun* (also **khad·dar** /'kɒdɜr/) Indian homespun cloth. [Hindi]

Kha·kas·sia /kɒ'kasiə/ an autonomous republic in south central Russia; pop. (est. 2002) 573,000; capital, Abakan.

khaki /'kaki, 'kɒki, 'kɑrki/ ● *adjective* dust-coloured; dull brownish yellow. ● *noun* (*pl.* **khakis**) **1** khaki fabric of twilled cotton or wool, used esp. in military dress. **2** the dull brownish-yellow colour of this. **3** (*in pl.*) esp. military clothing made from this. [Urdu *kākī* dust-coloured, from *kāk* dust]

Kha·lid /kɒ'liːd/ (full name Khalid ibn Abdul Aziz), king of Saudi Arabia 1975–82.

Khal·sa /'kɒlsə/ *noun* the fraternity of warriors into which Sikh males

are initiated at puberty. [Punjabi from Urdu from Persian *kāl(i)ṣa* from fem. of Arabic *kāl(i)ṣ*, 'pure, free, belonging to']

Kham·bat, Gulf of see CAMBAY, GULF OF.

kham·sin /'kamsɪn/ *noun* an oppressive hot south or southeast wind occurring in Egypt for about 50 days in March, April, and May. [Arabic *kamsīn* from *kamsūn* fifty]

khan[1] /kɒn, kan/ *noun* **1** a title given to rulers and officials in Central Asia, Afghanistan, etc. **2** *hist.* **a** the supreme ruler of the Turkish, Tartar, and Mongol tribes. **b** the emperor of China in the Middle Ages. □ **khan·ate** *noun* [Turkic *kān* lord]

khan[2] /kɒn, kan/ *noun* a caravanserai. [Arabic *kān* inn]

Kharg Island /kɑrg/ a small island at the head of the Persian Gulf, site of Iran's principal deepwater oil terminal.

Khar·kiv /'kɑrkɪf/ an industrial city in NE Ukraine, in the Donets basin; pop. (est. 2001) 1,470,000. It was the first capital of the Ukrainian Soviet Socialist Republic from 1919 until replaced by Kiev in 1934.

Khar·toum /kɑr'tuːm/ the capital of Sudan, situated at the junction of the Blue Nile and the White Nile; pop. (est. 2002) 1,244,500.

khat /kɒt/ *noun* **1** a shrub, *Catha edulis*, grown in Arabia. **2** the leaves of this shrub, chewed or infused as a stimulant. [Arabic *kāt*]

Khay·litsa /kai'lɪtsə/ a township 40 km (25 miles) southeast of Cape Town, South Africa. Designed to accommodate 250,000 people, it was built in 1983 for black Africans from the squatter camps of Crossroads, Langa, and KTC.

Khay·yám see OMAR KHAYYÁM.

Khe·dive /kɪ'diːv/ *noun hist.* the title of the viceroy of Egypt under Turkish rule 1867–1914. □ **Khe·dival** *adjective* **Khe·div·ial** *adjective* [French *khédive*, ultimately from Persian *kadīv* prince]

Kher·son /ker'sɒn/ a port on the south coast of Ukraine, on the Dnieper estuary; pop. (est. 2001) 328,000.

Khmer /kmer/ ● *noun* **1** a native of the ancient Khmer kingdom in SE Asia, or of modern Cambodia. **2** the language of this people. ● *adjective* of the Khmers or their language. [Khmer]

Khmer Republic the former official name (1970–5) for CAMBODIA.

Khoi·khoi /'kɔikɔi/ *noun* see NAMA. [Nama, lit. 'men of men']

Khoi·san /'kɔisɒn/ *noun* **1** a collective term for the Nama (Khoikhoi) and the San (Bushmen) of southern Africa. **2** a southern African language family, the smallest in Africa, spoken mainly by the Nama and the San. Khoisan languages are distinguished by clicks (made by suction with the tongue), which function as consonants. [KHOIKHOI + SAN]

Kho·meini /koː'meini, xɒ-/ **Ru·hol·lah** (known as 'Ayatollah Khomeini') (1900–89), Iranian Shiite Muslim leader. After sixteen years in exile, he returned to Iran in 1979 to lead the Islamic revolution; with the overthrow of the Shah he established a fundamentalist Islamic republic, supported the seizure of the US embassy (1979), and pursued the war with Iraq (1980–8).

Khon·su /'kɒnsuː/ *Egyptian Myth* a moon god, whose principal cult centre was at Thebes, a member of the Theban triad as the divine son of Amun and Mut. [Ancient Egyptian, = 'he who crosses']

Khor·ram·shahr /ˌxɒrəm'ʃɑr/ an oil port on the Shatt al-Arab waterway in W Iran. It was almost totally destroyed during the Iran–Iraq war of 1980–8.

khoum /kuːm/ *noun* a monetary unit of Mauritania, equal to one-fifth of an ouguiya. [Arabic *kums* one-fifth]

Khrush·chev /'krʊʃtʃɒf/ **Ni·kita (Sergey·evich)** (1894–1971), Soviet leader, premier of the USSR 1958–64. In the power struggle that followed Stalin's death, Khrushchev became first secretary of the Communist Party of the USSR (1953–64) and played a prominent part in the 'de-Stalinization' program after 1956; he came close to war with the US over the Cuban Missile Crisis (1962) and was ousted two years later largely as a result of his antagonism to China.

Khufu /'kuːfuː/ see CHEOPS.

Khul·na /'kʊlnɒ/ an industrial city in S Bangladesh, on the Ganges delta; pop. (est. 2002) 1,190,000.

Khun·je·rab Pass /'kʌnjəˌrɒb/ a high-altitude pass through the Himalayas, on the Karakoram highway at a height of 4 700 m (15,519 ft.), linking China and Pakistan.

Khyber Pass /'kaibər/ a mountain pass in the Hindu Kush, on the border between Pakistan and Afghanistan at a height of 1 067 m (3,520 ft.). The pass was for long of great commercial and strategic importance, the route by which successive invaders entered India, and was garrisoned by the British intermittently between 1839 and 1947.

kHz *abbreviation* kilohertz.

KIA *abbreviation* killed in action.

kiack /ˈkaiak/ *noun Cdn (Nova Scotia)* = GASPEREAU. [prob. from Mi'kmaq]

kiang /kiˈaŋ/ *noun* a wild Tibetan ass, *Equus hemionus kiang*, with a thick furry coat. [Tibetan *kyang*]

Kiang·si see JIANGXI.

Kiang·su see JIANGSU.

kib·beh /kɪˈbeɪ/ *noun* an originally Middle Eastern dish of meatballs with bulgur wheat, onions, seasoning, etc. [Arabic]

kib·ble¹ ● *noun N Amer.* ground meal shaped into pellets esp. for pet food. ● *transitive verb* grind or chop (dried grain, beans, etc.) coarsely. [18th c.: origin unknown]

kib·ble² *noun Brit.* an iron hoisting bucket used in mines. [German *Kübel* (compare Old English *cyfel*) from medieval Latin *cupellus*, corn-measure, diminutive of *cuppa* cup]

kib·butz /kɪˈbuts/ *noun* (*pl.* **kib·butz·im** /-ˈtsiːm/) a collective esp. farming settlement in Israel. [modern Hebrew *ḳibbūṣ* gathering]

kib·butz·nik /kɪˈbutsnɪk/ *noun* a member of a kibbutz. [Yiddish (as KIBBUTZ)]

kibe *noun* an ulcerated chilblain, esp. on the heel. [Middle English, prob. from Welsh *cibi*]

ki·bit·ka /kɪˈbɪtkə/ *noun* **1** a type of Russian hooded sled or wagon. **2 a** a Tartar's circular tent, covered with felt. **b** a Tartar household. [Russian from Tartar *kibitz*]

kib·itz /ˈkɪbɪts/ *intransitive verb N Amer. informal* **1** chat or joke lightheartedly. **2** offer unwanted advice to card players. **3** meddle; give unsolicited advice. □ **kib·itz·er** *noun* [Yiddish from German *kiebitzen* lapwing, busybody]

ki·bosh /ˈkaibɒʃ/ *esp. N Amer. slang* ● *noun* nonsense. ● *transitive verb* put an end to; dispose of. □ **put the kibosh on** put an end to; finally dispose of. [19th c.: origin unknown]

kick ● *verb* **1** *transitive* strike or propel forcibly with the foot or hoof etc. **2** *intransitive* (usu. foll. by *at*, *against*) **a** strike out with the foot. **b** extend the leg and foot forcefully out from the body. **c** express annoyance at or dislike of (treatment, a proposal, etc.); rebel against. **3** *transitive informal* give up (a habit). **4** *transitive* (often foll. by *out* etc.) expel or dismiss forcibly. **5** *reflexive* be annoyed with oneself (*I'll kick myself if I'm wrong*). **6** *transitive* (in soccer, football, etc.) score (a goal or field goal) by a kick. ● *noun* **1 a** a blow with the foot or hoof etc. **b** the delivery of such a blow. **c** an instance of extending the leg and foot forcefully out from the body. **2** *informal* **a** a sharp stimulant effect, esp. of alcohol (*has some kick in it; a cocktail with a kick in it*). **b** (often in *pl.*) a pleasurable thrill (*did it just for kicks; got a kick out of flying*). **3** strength, resilience (*have no kick left*). **4** *informal* a specified temporary interest or enthusiasm (*on a jogging kick*). **5** the recoil of a gun when discharged. □ **kick around** (or **about**) *informal* **1 a** drift idly from place to place. **b** be unused or unwanted. **2 a** treat roughly or scornfully. **b** discuss (an idea) unsystematically. **kick against the pricks** see PRICK. **kick (some) ass** (or **butt**) *N Amer. slang* act forcefully or in a domineering manner; dominate (*compare* KICK-ASS). **kick at the can** (or **cat**) *Cdn informal* an opportunity to achieve something. **kick back 1** recoil. **2** *informal* relax. **kick the bucket** *slang* die. **kick one's heels** see HEEL¹. **kick in 1** knock down (a door etc.) by kicking. **2** esp. *N Amer. slang* contribute (esp. money); pay one's share. **3** become activated, start. **kicking and screaming** reluctantly; with much resistance. **kick in the pants** *informal* **1** a reprimand or setback seen as an incentive. **2** (also **kick in the teeth, ass** etc.) a humiliating punishment or setback. **kick off 1 a** (in football or soccer) begin or resume a match. **b** *informal* begin. **2** remove (shoes etc.) by kicking. **kick over the traces** see TRACE². **kick up** stir up; cause to move upward. **kick up a fuss** *informal* create a disturbance; object or register strong disapproval. **kick up one's heels** esp. *N Amer.* have a lively, enjoyable time. **kick a person upstairs** *informal* shelve a person by giving him or her an ostensible promotion or title. □ **kick·able** *adjective* [Middle English *kike*, of unknown origin]

kick-ass *attributive adjective* (also **kick-butt**) *N Amer. slang* **1** forceful, aggressive, domineering. **2** impressive, powerful.

kick·back *noun informal* **1** the force of a recoil. **2** payment for collaboration, esp. collaboration for illicit profit.

kick·ball *noun N Amer.* **1** an informal children's game involving kicking a ball, more or less as in soccer. **2** a game combining elements of baseball and soccer, in which a soccer ball is 'pitched' to a 'batter' who kicks it and proceeds to run the bases.

kick-boxing *noun* a form of boxing characterized by the use of blows with the feet as well as with gloved fists. □ **kick-boxer** *noun*

kick drum *noun* a bass drum played using a pedal.

kick·er *noun* **1** a person or thing that kicks, esp. a football player. **2** *N Amer.* a surprising fact, circumstance, etc. which comes as a conclusion, often as a disappointment. **3** a small, electrically powered outboard motor.

kick·ing *adjective slang* lively, exciting; excellent.

Kicking Horse Pass a rail and road pass (1 627 m) through the Rocky Mountains, situated on the BC–Alberta border, just west of Lake Louise. [with reference to an incident involving a member of a geological expedition and a pack horse *c.*1858]

kick·off *noun* **1** (in football or soccer) the start or resumption of a match. **2** the kick marking this. **3** an event marking the beginning of a campaign etc.

kick·plate *noun* a protective covering for the lowest portion of a door.

kick-pleat *noun* a pleat in a narrow skirt to allow freedom of movement (often *attributive*: *kick-pleat skirt*).

kick·shaw *noun* **1** something elegant but insubstantial; a toy or trinket. **2** *archaic*, usu. *derogatory* a fancy dish in cooking. [French *quelque chose* something]

kick·stand *noun* a rod attached to a bicycle or motorcycle and kicked into a vertical position to support the vehicle when stationary.

kick-start ● *noun* **1** (also **kick-starter**) a device to start the engine of a motorcycle etc. by the downward thrust of a pedal. **2** an act of starting a motorcycle etc. in this way. **3** an impetus given to get a thing started or restarted. ● *transitive verb* **1** start (a motorcycle etc.) in this way. **2** start or restart (a process etc.) by providing some initial impetus.

kick the can *noun N Amer.* a children's game involving chasing and capturing, in which a can must be kicked to set free those captured.

kicky *adjective* (**kick·i·er, kick·i·est**) *N Amer. informal* exciting, amusing, pleasurable.

Kid see KYD.

kid¹ ● *noun* **1** a young goat. **2** the leather made from its skin. **3** *informal* **a** a child or young person. **b** (*attributive*) designating something pertaining to or characteristic of children. **4** (as a form of address) any person (*here's lookin' at you, kid!*). ● *intransitive verb* (**kid·ded, kid·ding**) (of a goat) give birth. □ **kids'** (or **kid** or **kid's**) **stuff** *informal* something very simple. **new kid on the block** *N Amer.* a person, company, etc., newly arrived within a group. [Middle English *kide* from Old Norse *kith* from Germanic]

kid² *verb* (**kidded, kidding**) *informal* **1** *transitive* (also *reflexive*) deceive, trick (*don't kid yourself*). **2** *transitive & intransitive* tease, joke with (*only kidding*). □ **no kidding** (also **I kid you not**) *informal* that is the truth. □ **kid·der** *noun* **kid·ding·ly** *adverb* [perhaps from KID¹]

kid brother *noun* (or **sister**) *informal* a younger brother or sister.

Kidd, Wil·liam (known as 'Captain Kidd') (1645–1701), Scottish privateer and pirate. He was commissioned to put down piracy in the Indian Ocean (1695) but joined with other pirates and plundered the Malabar coast of India (1697–9); he was arrested and hanged in London.

kid·die *noun* (also **kiddy**) (*pl.* **-dies**) *informal* = KID¹ *noun* 3.

kiddo *noun* (*pl.* **-dos**) *informal* (esp. as a form of address) = KID¹ *noun* 3, 4.

kid·dush /kɪˈduːʃ, ˈkɪdəʃ/ *noun* a ceremony of prayer and blessing over wine, performed by the head of a Jewish household at the meal ushering in the Sabbath or a holy day. [Hebrew *qiddûš* sanctification]

kiddy *var. of* KIDDIE.

kid glove *noun* **1** a glove made from kid leather. **2** (*attributive*) dainty or delicate. □ **handle with kid gloves** handle in a gentle, delicate, or gingerly manner.

kid·lit *noun* literature intended for children. [KID¹ 3 + LIT²]

kid·nap (**kid·napped, kid·nap·ping**; *US* also **kid·naped, kid·nap·ing**) ● *transitive verb* carry off (a person etc.) by illegal force or deception, esp. to obtain a ransom. ● *noun* (usu. *attributive*) an instance of kidnapping (*kidnap victims*). □ **kid·nap·per** *noun* **kid·nap·ping** *noun* [back-formation from *kidnapper*, from KID¹ + *nap* = NAB¹]

kid·ney *noun* (*pl.* **-neys**) **1** either of a pair of organs in the abdominal cavity of mammals, birds, and reptiles, which remove nitrogenous wastes from the blood and excrete urine. **2** the kidney of a pig etc. as food. **3** temperament, nature, kind (*a man of that kidney; of the right kidney*). [Middle English *kidnei*, pl. *kidneiren*, apparently partly from *ei* EGG¹]

kidney bean *noun* an edible esp. dark red kidney-shaped bean.

kidney dish *noun* a kidney-shaped dish, esp. one used in surgery.

kidney-shaped *adjective* shaped like a kidney, with one side concave and the other convex.

kid·skin *noun* = KID¹ *noun* 2.

---

uː mo**o**d ai m**y** əi p**i**pe au br**ow**n ʌu h**ou**se ei d**ay** ɔi b**oy** ā fr**an**glais ã C**an**adien ɔ̃ Br**ay**on   (*see over for consonants*)

kid·vid *noun informal* **1** children's television or video entertainment. **2** a children's television program or videotape. [KID[1] 3 + VIDEO]

Kiel /kiːl/ a naval port in N Germany, capital of Schleswig-Holstein, on the Baltic Sea coast at the eastern end of the Kiel Canal; pop. (est. 2002) 231,700.

kiel·basa /kiːlˈbɒsə/ *noun* a type of highly seasoned sausage of Eastern European origin, usu. containing garlic. [Polish *kiełbasa* sausage]

Kiel Canal an artificial waterway, 98 km (61 miles) in length, in NW Germany, running westward from Kiel to Brunsbüttel at the mouth of the Elbe. It connects the North Sea with the Baltic.

Kielce /ˈkjeltsə/ an industrial city in S Poland; pop. (est. 2002) 210,956.

Kier·ke·gaard /ˈkiːrkə‚ɡard/ **Søren (Aabye)** (1813–55), Danish religious philosopher. Viewed as one of the founders of existentialism, he opposed the prevailing Hegelian philosophy of the time by affirming the importance of individual experience and choice; his works include *Either/Or* (1843), *Fear and Trembling* (1843), *The Concept of Dread* (1844), and *The Sickness unto Death* (1849). □ **Kier·ke·gaard·ian** /ˈkiːr‚kəˈɡardiən/ *adjective*

kie·sel·guhr /ˈkiːzəl‚ɡʊr/ *noun* = DIATOMACEOUS EARTH. [German from *Kiesel* gravel + dial. *Guhr* earthy deposit]

Kies·low·ski /kɪˈslɒfski/ **Krzysz·tof** (1941–96), Polish film director. Noted for their mannered style and their artistic, philosophical nature, his films include the series *Dekalog* (1988), each film being a visual interpretation of one of the Ten Commandments, *The Double Life of Veronique* (1991), and the trilogy *Three Colors* (1993–4).

Kiev /ˈkiːef/ (Ukrainian **Kyiv** /ˈkiːɪf/) the capital of Ukraine, an industrial city and port on the Dnieper River; pop. (est. 2001) 2,602,000.

kif *var. of* KEF.

Ki·gali /kɪˈɡɒli/ the capital of Rwanda; pop. (est. 2002) 290,600.

kike *noun esp. N Amer. slang offensive* a Jew. [20th c.: origin uncertain]

Ki·kongo /kɪˈkɒŋɡoː/ ● *noun* the Bantu language of the Kongo people, used in the Republic of the Congo, Congo (formerly Zaire), and adjacent areas. ● *adjective* of or pertaining to this language. [Kikongo, from *ki-* prefix + KONGO]

Ki·kuyu /kɪˈkuːjuː/ ● *noun* (*pl.* same or **Ki·ku·yus**) **1** a member of a Bantu-speaking people constituting the largest ethno-linguistic group in Kenya. **2** the language of this people. **3** (**kikuyu**) (also **kikuyu grass**) a creeping perennial grass, *Pennisetum clandestinum*, which is native to Kenya and cultivated elsewhere as a lawn and fodder grass. ● *adjective* of or relating to the Kikuyu or their language. [Bantu]

Kil·dare /kɪlˈder/ a county of the Republic of Ireland, in the east, in the province of Leinster; county town, Naas.

kil·der·kin /ˈkɪldərkɪn/ *noun* **1** a cask for liquids etc., usu. holding 18 imperial gallons (about 82 litres). **2** this measure. [Middle English, alteration of *kinderkin* from Middle Dutch *kinderkin, kinneken*, diminutive of *kintal* QUINTAL]

kilim /kɪˈliːm, ˈkiːlɪm/ ● *noun* a pileless woven carpet, rug, etc., made in Turkey, Kurdistan, and neighbouring areas. ● *attributive adjective* designating such a carpet, rug, etc. [Turkish from Persian *gelim*]

Kili·man·jaro /‚kɪləmənˈdʒɑroː/ an extinct volcano in N Tanzania. It has twin peaks, the higher of which, Kibo (5 895 m, 19,340 ft.), is the highest mountain in Africa.

Kil·ken·ny /kɪlˈkeni/ **1** a county of the Republic of Ireland, in the southeast, in the province of Leinster. **2** its county town; pop. (est. 2002) 19,500. It was the capital of the ancient kingdom of Ossory.
□ **fight like Kilkenny cats** fight persistently (like the two cats from Kilkenny who according to legend fought until only their tails remained).

kill ● *verb* **1 a** *transitive* deprive of life or vitality; put to death; cause the death of. **b** *intransitive* cause or bring about death (*must kill to survive*). **2** *transitive* destroy; put an end to (feelings etc.) (*overwork killed my enthusiasm*). **3** *reflexive* (often foll. by pres. part.) **a** overexert oneself (*don't kill yourself lifting them all at once*). **b** laugh heartily. **4** *transitive informal* overwhelm (a person) with amusement, disbelief, etc. (*the things he says really kill me*). **5** *transitive* switch off (a spotlight, engine, etc.). **6** *transitive Computing* **a** delete (a line, paragraph, etc.) from a computer file. **b** cause (a process) to stop running. **7** *transitive informal* cause pain or discomfort to (*my feet are killing me*). **8** *transitive* pass (time, or a specified amount of it) usu. while waiting for a specific event (*had an hour to kill before the interview*). **9** *transitive* defeat (a bill in a legislative assembly). **10** *transitive informal* consume the entire contents of (a bottle of wine etc.). **11** *transitive Hockey* **a** (often foll. by *off*) (of a team) endure (a penalty) without being scored on. **b** (of a player) play during (a penalty) while the team is short-handed. **12** *transitive* **a** *Tennis etc.* hit (the ball) so skilfully that it cannot be returned. **b** stop (the ball) dead. **13** *transitive* neutralize or render ineffective (taste, sound, colour, etc.) (*thick carpet killed the sound of footsteps*). **14** *transitive* cancel publication or broadcast of (a news story or other item). ● *noun* **1** an act of killing (esp. an animal). **2** an animal or animals killed, esp. by a hunter. **3** *informal* the destruction or disablement of an enemy aircraft, submarine, etc.
□ **dressed to kill** dressed showily, alluringly, or impressively. **go** (or **move in** or **close in**) **for the kill** take decisive action to turn a situation to one's advantage. **in at the kill** present at or benefiting from the successful conclusion of an enterprise. **kill off 1** get rid of or destroy completely (esp. a number of persons or things). **2** (of an author) bring about the death of (a fictional character). **kill or cure** (usu. *attributive*) (of a remedy etc.) drastic, extreme. **kill two birds with one stone** achieve two aims at once. **kill with kindness** spoil (a person) with overindulgence. [Middle English *cülle, kille*, perhaps, ultimately related to QUELL]

Kil·lam, Izaak Wal·ton (1885–1955), Canadian financier. Beginning as a bank clerk in 1901, he built up an extensive investment empire in Canada and Latin America, including holdings in publishing, pulp and paper, utilities, construction and filmmaking. Described as the richest Canadian of his day, he was a patron of the arts and education; the initial funding for the Canada Council came mostly from the $50 million inheritance tax levied on his estate.

Kil·lar·ney /kɪˈlɑrni/ a town in the southwest of the Republic of Ireland, in County Kerry, famous for the beauty of the nearby lakes and mountains; pop. (est. 2002) 12,500.

kill·deer *noun* a large N American plover, *Charadrius vociferus*, with a plaintive song. [imitative]

kill·er *noun* **1 a** a person, animal, or thing that kills. **b** a murderer. **2** *informal* **a** an impressive or formidable thing (*this one is quite difficult, but the next one is a real killer*). **b** a decisive blow (*his brilliant short-handed goal proved to be the killer*). **c** an excellent thing (also *attributive*: *killer abs*).

killer app *noun* (also **killer application**) *Computing* **1** an application which is particularly significant or useful. **2** a feature, function or application of a new technology or product which is presented as virtually indispensable or much superior to rival products.

killer bee *noun informal* a very aggressive hybrid honeybee.

killer cell *noun Physiol.* a white blood cell which destroys infected or cancerous cells.

killer instinct *noun* **1** an innate tendency to kill. **2** a ruthless streak.

killer whale *noun* a predatory toothed whale, *Orcinus orca*, with black and white markings and a high narrow dorsal fin. *Also called* ORCA.

kill fee *noun* compensation paid to an author by a magazine etc. for cancelling the publication of a piece it had previously agreed to publish.

kil·lick /ˈkɪlɪk/ *noun* **1** a heavy stone used by small craft as an anchor. **2** a small anchor. [17th c.: origin unknown]

killi·fish /ˈkɪlɪfɪʃ/ *noun* **1** any of several small, often brightly coloured fish of the families Cyprinodontidae and Poeciliidae, esp. any of the genus *Fundulus*, found esp. in sheltered rivers and estuaries of eastern N America. **2** a brightly coloured tropical aquarium fish, *Pterolebias peruensis*. [perhaps from *kill* stream, from Dutch *kil* + FISH[1]]

kill·ing ● *noun* **1** in senses of KILL *verb*. **2** a great (esp. financial) success (*make a killing*). ● *adjective* **1** that kills (*a killing frost*). **2** *informal* overwhelmingly funny. **3** *informal* exhausting; very strenuous.
□ **kill·ing·ly** *adverb*

killing field *noun* (usu. in *pl.*) (also **killing ground**) an area where mass killing is carried out.

Kil·li·niq Island /ˈkɪlɪnɪk/ an island just off the northern tip of Labrador, shared by Newfoundland and Nunavut. Cape Chidley is located there.

kill·joy *noun* a person who throws gloom over or prevents other people's enjoyment.

kiln *noun* a furnace or oven for burning, baking, or drying, esp. for firing pottery, calcining lime, drying lumber, etc. [Old English *cylene* from Latin *culina* kitchen]

kilo /ˈkiːloː/ *noun* (*pl.* **kilos**) **1** a kilogram. **2** a kilometre. [French: abbreviation]

kilo- /ˈkɪloː/ *combining form* denoting a factor of 1,000 (esp. in metric units). Abbr.: **k**, or **K** in *Computing*. [French from Greek *khilioi* thousand]

kilo·bit *noun Computing* a unit of memory size equal to 1,024 (i.e. 2^{10}) bits.

kilo·byte *noun Computing* 1,024 (i.e. 2^{10}) bytes as a measure of memory size. Abbr.: **KB** or **kbyte**.

kilo·cal·orie *noun* = CALORIE 1.

Consonants: b *but* d *dog* f *few* g *get* h *her* j *yes* k *cat* l *leg* m *man* n *no* p *pen* r *red* s *sit*

kilo·cycle *noun* a former measure of frequency, equivalent to 1 kilohertz. Abbr.: **kc**.

kilo·gram *noun* the SI unit of mass, equivalent to the international standard kept at Sèvres near Paris (approx. 2.205 lb.). Abbr.: **kg**. [French *kilogramme* (as KILO-, GRAM[1])]

kilo·hertz *noun* a measure of frequency equivalent to 1,000 cycles per second. Abbr.: **kHz**.

kilo·joule *noun* 1,000 joules, esp. as a measure of the energy value of foods. Abbr.: **kJ**.

kilo·litre *noun* (also **-liter**) 1,000 litres (equivalent to 220 imperial gallons). Abbr.: **kl**.

kilo·met·rage /ˈkɪləmiːtərɪdʒ/ *noun* **1** a number of kilometres travelled, used, etc., esp. by motor vehicle. **2** the number of kilometres travelled by a vehicle per unit (usu. per litre) of fuel. **3** expenses (as depreciation, fuel, etc.) reimbursed per kilometre travelled.

kilo·metre /kɪˈlɒmɪtər, ˈkɪləˌmiːtər/ *noun* (also **kilo·meter**) a metric unit of measurement equal to 1 000 metres (approx. 0.62 miles). Abbr.: **km**. □ **kilo·met·ric** /ˌkɪləˈmetrɪk/ *adjective* [French *kilomètre* (as KILO-, METRE[1])]

kilo·pas·cal /ˈkɪloˌpaskəl, ˌkɪloːˈpasˈkal/ *noun* a metric unit of pressure equal to 1,000 pascals. Abbr.: **kPa**.

kilo·ton *noun* a unit of explosive power equivalent to 1,000 tons of TNT. Abbr.: **kt**.

kilo·volt *noun* 1,000 volts. Abbr.: **kV**.

kilo·watt *noun* 1,000 watts. Abbr.: **kW**.

kilowatt hour *noun* a measure of electrical energy equivalent to a power consumption of 1,000 watts for one hour. Abbr.: **kWh**.

kilt ● *noun* **1** a skirt-like garment, usu. of pleated tartan cloth and reaching to the knees, as worn by Highland men traditionally or by some soldiers when in dress uniform. **2** a similar garment worn by women and children. ● *transitive verb* tuck up (skirts) around the body. [originally as verb: Middle English, of Scandinavian origin]

kilt·ed *adjective* **1** provided with or wearing a kilt. **2** gathered in vertical pleats.

kil·ter *noun* good working order (esp. *out of kilter*; *off-kilter*). [17th c.: origin unknown]

kilt·ie *noun* **1** a wearer of a kilt, esp. a soldier with a kilted dress uniform. **2 a** a dress shoe with a folded fringed tongue and tassels covering the laces. **b** this tongue.

Kim·ber·ley **1** a city in South Africa, in the province of Northern Cape; pop. (est. 2002) 192,800. It has been a diamond-mining centre since the early 1870s and gave its name to kimberlite. **2** a city in southeastern BC, just northwest of Cranbrook; pop. (2001) 6,484. **3** (also **the Kimberleys**) a plateau region in the far north of Western Australia. A mining and cattle-ranching region, it was the scene of a gold rush in 1885. [sense 1 after J. Wodehouse, 1st Earl of *Kimberley*, British Colonial Secretary d.1902; sense 2 after the South African diamond-mining centre, so called in the hope that the local mines would yield comparable wealth]

kim·ber·lite *noun* a rare igneous blue-tinged rock sometimes containing diamonds, found in northern Canada, South Africa, and Siberia. [KIMBERLEY in South Africa]

kim·chee /ˈkɪmtʃi/ *noun* (also **kim·chi**) a dish of raw, highly spiced, pickled or fermented cabbage, the Korean national dish. [Korean]

Kim Dae-jung /ˌkɪm deiˈʒʊŋ/ (b.1925), South Korean politician, president since 1997. He was awarded the Nobel Peace Prize in 2000 for his contributions to democracy and human rights in Asia, and for his efforts to promote reconciliation with North Korea.

Kim Il Sung /ˌkɪm ɪl ˈsʊŋ/ (born Kim Song Ju) (1912–94), Korean Communist leader, first premier of North Korea 1948–72 and president 1972–94. He ordered his forces to invade South Korea in 1950, precipitating the Korean War (1950–3); he later pressed for the peaceful reunification of the country and created a personality cult around himself and his family.

ki·mo·no /kɪˈmoːnoː, -nə/ *noun* (pl. **-nos**) **1** a long loose Japanese robe worn with a sash. **2** a wraparound dressing gown modelled on this. □ **ki·mo·noed** *adjective* [Japanese]

kin ● *noun* **1** one's relatives or family. **2** a group of similar or related things. ● *predicative adjective* (of a person) related (*we are kin; he is kin to me*). □ **kith and kin** *see* KITH. [Old English *cynn* from Germanic]

-kin *suffix* forming diminutive nouns (*catkin; manikin*). [from or after Middle Dutch *-kijn, -ken*, Old High German *-chin*]

kina /ˈkiːnə/ *noun* the chief monetary unit of Papua New Guinea, equal to 100 toea. [Papuan]

Kina·balu, Mount /ˌkɪnəbəˈluː/ a mountain in the state of Sabah in E Malaysia, on the north coast of Borneo. Rising to 4 094 m (13,431 ft.), it is the highest peak of Borneo and of SE Asia.

kin·aes·the·sia *var. of* KINESTHESIA.

kin·ase /ˈkaineiz, ˈkɪneɪz, -eis/ *noun* Biochem any of various enzymes that catalyze the transfer of a phosphate group from ATP to another molecule. [from Greek *kinein* move + -ASE]

Kin·bas·ket Lake /ˈkɪnˌbaskət/ a long, narrow reservoir in southeastern BC, impounded by the Mica Dam on the Columbia River route. It was created in 1973, the smaller original lake being submerged in the process. [P. I. *Kinbaskit*, Shuswap chief *c*.1866]

Kin·car·dine /kɪnˈkardən/ a township in SW Ontario, situated on the eastern shore of Lake Huron, about 50 km north of Goderich; pop. (2001) 11,029. □ **Kin·car·din·ite** *noun* [J. Bruce, 12th Earl of *Kincardine* and Governor General of Canada d.1863]

Kin·car·dine·shire /kɪnˈkardənˌʃɪːr/ a former county of E Scotland. In 1975 it became part of Grampian region and in 1996 part of Aberdeenshire.

Kin·chin·junga *see* KANCHENJUNGA.

kind[1] *noun* **1 a** a race or species (*human kind*). **b** a natural group of animals, plants, etc. (*the wolf kind*). **2** class, type, sort, variety (*what kind of job are you looking for?*). ¶ In sense 2, *these* (or *those*) *kind* is often encountered when followed by a plural, as in *I don't like these kind of things*, but *this kind* and *these kinds* are usually preferred. **3** each of the elements of the Eucharist (*communion in both kinds*). **4** the manner or fashion natural to a person etc. (*act after their kind; true to kind*). **5** character, quality (*differ in degree but not in kind*). □ **all kinds of** very many, esp. of different varieties. **in kind 1** in the same form, likewise (*was insulted and replied in kind*). **2** (of payment) in goods or labour as opposed to money (*received their wages in kind*). **kind of** *informal* to some extent (*felt kind of sorry; I kind of expected it*). **a** (or **some**) **kind of** used to imply looseness, vagueness, exaggeration, etc., in the term used (*a kind of Jane Austen of our times; I suppose he's some kind of doctor*). **nothing of the kind 1** not at all like the thing in question. **2** (expressing denial) not at all. **of a kind 1** similar in some important respect (*they're two of a kind*). **2** *derogatory* scarcely deserving the name (*a choir of a kind*). **something of the kind** something like the thing in question. **it takes all kinds** (or *Brit.* **sorts**) (**to make a world**) people vary greatly in character, tastes, and abilities (often used as a comment on what the speaker feels to be strange behaviour). [Old English *cynd(e), gecynd(e)* from Germanic]

kind[2] *adjective* **1** of a friendly, generous, benevolent, or gentle nature. **2** (usu. foll. by *to*) showing friendliness, affection, or consideration. **3** showing kindness (*kind words*). [Old English *gecynde* (as KIND[1]): originally = 'natural, native']

kinda *adverb* *informal* = KIND OF (*see* KIND[1]). [corruption]

kin·der·gart·en /ˈkɪndərˌgartən/ *noun* a class or school for young children, usu. five-year-olds, in preparation for grade one. Abbr.: **K**. □ **kin·der·gart·ner** /ˈkɪndərˌgartnər/ *noun* [German, = children's garden]

Kin·ders·ley /ˈkɪndərzli/ a town in west central Saskatchewan, 198 km southwest of Saskatoon; pop. (2001) 4,548. [Sir R. *Kindersley*, prominent stockholder in the Canadian Northern Railway *c*.1909]

kind-hearted *adjective* of a kind disposition. □ **kind-hearted·ly** *adverb* **kind-hearted·ness** *noun*

kin·dle /ˈkɪndəl/ *verb* **1** *transitive* light or set on fire (a flame, fire, substance, etc.), esp. gradually. **2** *intransitive* catch fire, burst into flame. **3** *transitive* arouse or inspire (*kindle enthusiasm for the project; kindle jealousy in a rival*). **4** *intransitive* become animated, glow with passion etc. (*her imagination kindled*). **5** *transitive & intransitive* make or become bright (*kindle the embers to a glow*). [Old Norse *kynda*, kindle: compare Old Norse *kindill* candle, torch]

kin·dling /ˈkɪndlɪŋ/ *noun* small sticks etc. for lighting fires.

kind·ly[1] *adverb* **1** in a kind manner (*spoke to the child kindly*). **2** often *ironic* used in a polite request or demand (*kindly acknowledge this letter; kindly leave me alone*). □ **look kindly upon** regard sympathetically. **take a thing kindly** like or be pleased by it. **take kindly to** be pleased by or endeared to (a person or thing). **thank kindly** thank very much. [Old English *gecyndelīce* (as KIND[2])]

kind·ly[2] *adjective* (**kind·li·er**, **kind·li·est**) **1** kind, kind-hearted. **2** (of climate etc.) pleasant, genial. □ **kind·li·ness** *noun* [Old English *gecyndelic* (as KIND[1])]

kind·ness *noun* **1** the state or quality of being kind. **2** a kind act.

kin·dred /ˈkɪndrəd/ ● *noun* **1** one's relatives, referred to collectively. **2** a relationship by blood. ● *adjective* **1** related by blood or marriage.

t top v voice w we z zoo ʃ she ʒ vision θ thin ð this ŋ ring x loch tʃ chip dʒ jar (*see over for vowels*)

2 allied or similar in character (*other kindred symptoms*). [Middle English from KIN + -*red* from Old English *ræden* condition]

kindred spirit *noun* a person whose character and outlook have much in common with one's own.

kine *archaic pl. of* COW[1].

kin·emat·ics /ˌkɪnəˈmatɪks/ *plural noun* (usu. treated as *sing.*) the branch of mechanics concerned with the motion of objects without reference to the forces which cause the motion. □ **kin·emat·ic** *adjective* **kin·emat·ic·ally** *adverb* [Greek *kinēma -matos* motion, from *kineō* move + -ICS]

kin·esics /kɪˈniːsɪks/ *plural noun* (usu. treated as *sing.*) **1** the study of body movements and gestures which contribute to communication. **2** these movements; body language. [Greek *kinēsis* motion (as KINETIC)]

kin·esi·ol·ogy /kɪˌniːsɪˈɒlədʒi, -zi-/ *noun* the study of the mechanics of esp. human body movements. □ **kin·esi·ol·o·gist** *noun*

kin·esis /kɪˈniːsɪs/ *noun* **1** movement, motion. **2** *Biol.* undirected movement of an organism in response to a stimulus (*compare* TAXIS 2). [Greek *kinēsis* 'movement']

kin·es·the·sia /ˌkɪnəsˈθiːziə, -ʒə/ *noun* (also **kin·aes·the·sia**) a sense of awareness of the position and movement of the voluntary muscles of the body. □ **kin·es·thet·ic** /-ˈθetɪk/ *adjective* (also **kin·aes·thet·ic**). [Greek *kineō* move + *aisthēsis* sensation]

kin·etic /kɪˈnetɪk/ *adjective* of or due to motion. □ **kin·etic·ally** *adverb* [Greek *kinētikos* from *kineō* move]

kinetic art *noun* a form of art that depends on movement for its effect.

kinetic energy *noun* energy which a body possesses by virtue of being in motion.

kin·et·ics /kɪˈnetɪks/ *plural noun* (usu. treated as *sing.*) **1** = DYNAMICS 1a. **2** the branch of physical chemistry or biochemistry concerned with measuring and studying the rates of chemical or biochemical reactions.

kinetic theory *noun* a theory which explains the physical properties of matter in terms of the motions of its constituent particles.

Kin·ette /kɪˈnet/ *noun* Cdn a member of a women's organization associated with the Kinsmen. [KINSMAN + -ETTE]

kin·folk *plural noun* (also **kins·folk**) people to whom one is related by blood.

King ▸ 1 B. B. (born Riley B. King) (b.1925), US blues singer and guitarist. An immensely influential blues musician, he is known for his clear falsetto vocal style and trademark 'bent' vibrato note, a feature developed in his single-string guitar solos; his songs include 'Three O'Clock Blues' (1950), 'Sweet Little Angel' (1956) and 'The Thrill is Gone' (1970). **2 Billie Jean** (b.1943), US tennis player. She won a record twenty Wimbledon titles, including six singles titles (1966–8; 1972–3; 1975), ten doubles titles, and four mixed doubles titles; she retired in 1983. **3 George Edwin** (1839–1901), Canadian lawyer, politician, and judge, premier of New Brunswick 1872–78. He was appointed to the New Brunswick Supreme Court in 1880 and to the Supreme Court of Canada in 1893. **4 Mar·tin Lu·ther** (1929–68), US Baptist minister and civil-rights leader. He opposed discrimination against blacks by organizing non-violent resistance and peaceful mass demonstrations, including the March on Washington (1963) at which he delivered his celebrated speech beginning 'I have a dream'; he was awarded the Nobel Peace Prize in 1964 and was later assassinated in Memphis. **5 Ste·phen (Edwin)** (b.1947), American writer. He is best known for his horror novels, including *The Shining* (1977) and *Misery* (1987), many of which have been made into films. **6 Thom·as** (b.1943), Canadian writer of Cherokee origin, whose works often include aboriginal themes. His novels include *Green Grass, Running Water* (1993) and *Truth and Bright Water* (1999). He also wrote and performed in the radio comedy *Dead Dog Café* (1997-2000). **7 Wil·liam Lyon Mac·ken·zie** (1874–1950), Canadian Liberal politician, prime minister 1921–6, 1926–30, and 1935–48. The grandson of William Lyon Mackenzie, he became leader of the Liberal Party on the death of Laurier (1919). At the imperial conferences in London (1923; 1926; 1927), he established the status of the self-governing nations of the Commonwealth; he went on to strengthen ties with the UK and the US and introduced a number of social reforms, including unemployment insurance (1940).

king ● noun 1 (as a title usu. **King**) a male sovereign, esp. the hereditary ruler of an independent state. **2** a person or thing pre-eminent in a specified field or class (*railway king*). **3** a large (or the largest) kind of plant, animal, etc. (*king penguin*). **4** *Chess* **a** a piece on each side which can move only one square in any direction, and which the opposing side has to checkmate to win. **b** (**king's**) designating pieces that start on the king's side of the board. **5** a piece in checkers with extra capacity of moving, made by crowning an ordinary piece that has reached the far end of the board. **6** a playing card bearing a representation of a king and usu. ranking next below an ace. **7** (**the King**) (in Canada and the UK) the anthem 'God Save the King'. ● *transitive verb* make (a person) king. ● *adjective* denoting a king-size bed, mattress, sheets, etc. (*see* KING-SIZE 2). □ **king·hood** *noun* **king·less** *adjective* **king·like** *adjective* **king·ly** *adjective* **king·li·ness** *noun* [Old English *cyning*, *cyng* from Germanic]

king·bird *noun* any of several N American tyrant flycatchers of the genus *Tyrannus*.

King Charles spaniel *noun* a small black and tan breed of spaniel.

king cobra *noun* a large and venomous hooded Indian snake, *Ophiophagus hannah*.

king crab *noun* **1** = HORSESHOE CRAB. **2** any of various very large crabs of the family Lithodidae, which resemble the spider crabs and are found in cold waters of the N Pacific.

king·craft *noun* *archaic* the skilful exercise of kingship.

king·cup *noun* *Brit.* a marsh marigold.

king devil *noun* a hawkweed, *Hieracium pratense*, naturalized in N America, with yellow composite flowers.

king·dom *noun* **1** an organized community headed by a king or queen. **2** the territory subject to a king or queen. **3** *Christianity* **a** the spiritual reign attributed to God (*Thy kingdom come*). **b** the sphere of this (*kingdom of heaven*). **4** a domain belonging to a person, animal, etc. **5** a province of nature (*the vegetable kingdom*). **6** a specified mental or emotional province (*kingdom of the heart*; *kingdom of fantasy*). **7** *Biol.* the highest category in taxonomic classification.

kingdom come *noun* *informal* eternity; the next world. □ **till kingdom come** forever; for an indefinitely long period.

king eider *noun* an arctic eider, *Somateria spectabilis*, distinguished by the orange bill and frontal shield of the male.

king·fish *noun* any of various large fish, esp. the opah or croaker.

king·fish·er *noun* any bird of the family Alcedinidae, often stocky with crested heads, which dive for fish in rivers etc., esp. the N American belted kingfisher or the European *Alcedo atthis*, with a long beak and brilliant blue and orange plumage.

King George's War the North American phase of the War of the Austrian Succession, 1740–48 (*see* AUSTRIAN SUCCESSION, WAR OF THE). In the most decisive engagement of the war, Louisbourg was captured by forces from Massachusetts in 1745, but the fortress was returned to France by the terms of the Treaty of Aix-la-Chapelle (1748).

King James Version *noun* (also **King James Bible**) a 1611 English translation of the Bible made under James I and still widely used. Abbr.: **KJV**. *Also called* AUTHORIZED VERSION.

king·let *noun* **1** any of several tiny N American birds of the genus *Regulus*, e.g. the golden-crowned kinglet, *R. satrapa*, and the ruby-crowned kinglet, *R. calendula*. **2** a petty king.

king·maker *noun* a person who makes kings, leaders, etc., through the exercise of political influence, originally with reference to the Earl of Warwick in the reign of Henry VI of England.

king of beasts *noun* the lion.

King of Kings *noun* **1** God. **2** *hist.* a title assumed by certain kings of the ancient world who ruled over other kings.

King of the Castle *noun* Cdn & Brit. a children's game consisting of trying to displace a rival from an elevated position.

King Peak (also **Mount King**) a peak in the St. Elias Mountains of SW Yukon Territory, west of Mount Logan. Rising to a height of 5 173 m, it is the fourth highest mountain in Canada. [W. F. *King*, Canadian astronomer d.1916]

king·pin *noun* **1** an essential person or thing, esp. in a complex system. **2 a** a main or large bolt in a central position. **b** a vertical bolt used as a pivot.

king post *noun* an upright post from the tie beam of a roof to the apex of a truss.

Kings either of two books of the Bible recording the history of Israel and Judea from the accession of Solomon to the destruction of the Temple in 586 BC.

king salmon *noun* = CHINOOK 2.

King's Bench *noun* see QUEEN'S BENCH.

King's Canyon a national park in the Sierra Nevada, California, to the north of Sequoia National Park. Established in 1940, it preserves groves of ancient sequoia trees, including some of the largest in the world.

King's Counsel *noun* = QUEEN'S COUNSEL.

King's English *noun* = QUEEN'S ENGLISH.

king's evil *noun hist.* scrofula, formerly held to be curable by the royal touch.

King's highway *noun* = QUEEN'S HIGHWAY.

king·ship *noun* the office of king; the fact of ruling as a king.

king-size *adjective* (also **king-sized**) **1** larger than normal; very large. **2** designating the largest standard size of mattress, usu. 193 by 203 cm (76 by 80 in.), or the bed frame, sheets, etc. designed for such a mattress.

king's ransom *noun* a fortune.

King's speech *noun Brit. hist.* = QUEEN'S SPEECH.

Kings·ton 1 the capital and chief port of Jamaica; pop. (est. 2002) 539,900. **2** a city in SE Ontario, situated at the eastern end of Lake Ontario where it joins the St. Lawrence, about 250 km east of Toronto; pop. (2001) 114,195. □ **Kings·ton·ian** /kɪŋˈstoːniən/ *noun & adjective* [sense 2 from a shortening of *King's Town*, in honour of George III]

Kingston-upon-Hull the official name for HULL[1] 1.

Kings·town the capital and chief port of St. Vincent in the W Indies; pop. (est. 2002) 17,400.

Kings·ville a town in SW Ontario, situated on Lake Erie, southeast of Windsor; pop. (2001) 19,619. [Colonel J. *King*, first resident *c.*1843]

King William Island a large island off the northeastern shore of mainland Nunavut, between Victoria Island and the Boothia Peninsula. [WILLIAM IV]

kinin /ˈkaɪnɪn/ *noun* any of a group of polypeptides of low molecular weight which are formed in tissue (from inactive precursors in the blood) in response to injury and have local effects that typically include pain and the dilatation of the blood vessels. [Greek *kinein* 'set in motion' + -IN[1]]

kink ● *noun* 1 a a short twist or bend in wire or tubing etc. such as may cause an obstruction. **b** a tight wave in human or animal hair. **2** a flaw or glitch in a mechanism, plan, etc. **3** a crick or stiffness in the neck or back. **4** an esp. mental twist or quirk. **5** kinky sex. **●** *transitive & intransitive verb* form or cause to form a kink. [Middle Low German *kinke* (v.) prob. from Dutch *kinken*]

kin·ka·jou /ˈkɪŋkəˌdʒuː/ *noun* a Central and S American nocturnal fruit-eating mammal, *Potos flavus*, related to the raccoon, with a prehensile tail and living in trees. [French *quincajou*, alteration of CARCAJOU influenced by Ojibwa *kwi:nkwa'a:ke:* wolverine]

Kinki /ˈkiːŋkiː/ a region of Japan, on the island of Honshu; capital, Osaka.

kinky *adjective* (**kink·i·er, kink·i·est**) **1** *informal* **a** given to or involving bizarre or unusual sexual behaviour. **b** (of clothing etc.) bizarre in a sexually provocative way. **2** strange, eccentric. **3** having kinks or twists. □ **kink·i·ly** *adverb* **kink·i·ness** *noun* [KINK + -Y[1]]

kin·ni·kin·nick /ˌkɪnɪkɪˈnɪk/ *noun* **1** a mixture formerly used by some Aboriginal peoples of N America as a substitute for tobacco or for mixing with it, usu. consisting of dried bearberry or sumac leaves and the inner bark of dogwood or willow. **2** any of the various plants used for this, esp. bearberry. [Delaware, = admixture]

Kinross-shire /kɪnˈrɒsʃɪr/ a former county of east central Scotland. In 1975 it became part of Tayside region, and since 1996 has been part of Perth and Kinross.

-kins *suffix* = -KIN, often with suggestions of endearment (*babykins*).

Kin·sel·la /kɪnˈselə/ **Wil·liam Pat·rick** (b.1935), Canadian writer. His short stories and novels have two major settings: Native reserves in central Alberta and the realm of baseball. His works include the novel *Shoeless Joe* (1985) and the short story collection *The Fencepost Chronicles* (1986), which won a Stephen Leacock Medal in 1987.

Kin·sey /ˈkɪnzi/ **Alfred Charles** (1894–1956), US zoologist and sex researcher. His *Sexual Behaviour in the Human Male* (1948) (often referred to as the *Kinsey Report*), was controversial but highly influential; it was followed five years later by a companion volume on female sexual behaviour.

kins·folk *var. of* KINFOLK.

Kin·shasa /kɪnˈʃɒsə, -ˈʃɒzə/ the capital of Congo (formerly Zaire), a port on the Congo River, in the southwest; pop. (est. 2002) 6,301,100. It was known until 1966 as Léopoldville. It became capital of the Republic of Zaire (now Congo) in 1960.

kin·ship *noun* **1** blood relationship. **2** the sharing of characteristics or origins.

kins·man *noun* (*pl.* **-men**) **1** a blood relative or *disputed* a relative by marriage. **2** a member of one's own tribe or people. **3** (**Kinsman**) *Cdn*

a member of a fraternal organization for esp. businessmen and professionals, founded in 1920. □ **kins·woman** *noun* (*pl.* **-women**).

Kin·tyre /kɪnˈtair/ a peninsula on the west coast of Scotland, to the west of Arran, extending southward for 64 km (40 miles) into the North Channel and separating the Firth of Clyde from the Atlantic Ocean. Its southern tip is the Mull of Kintyre.

kiosk /ˈkiːɒsk/ *noun* **1** a light open-fronted booth or cubicle from which refreshments, newspapers, tickets, etc. are sold or information for tourists is provided. **2** esp. *Brit.* a telephone booth. **3** a light open pavilion in Turkey and Iran. [French *kiosque* from Turkish *kiūshk* pavilion, from Persian *guš*]

Kiowa /ˈkaɪəwə/ **●** *noun* **1** a member of an Aboriginal people from the southern US plains. **2** the language of these people. **●** *adjective* of or pertaining to the Kiowa or their language. [Latin American Spanish *Caygua* from Kiowa *kóygú* (pl.)]

kip[1] *Brit. slang* **●** *noun* **1** a sleep or nap. **2** a bed or cheap lodging house. **●** *intransitive verb* (**kipped, kip·ping**) sleep, take a nap. [18th c., origin uncertain: compare Danish *kippe* hovel, tavern]

kip[2] *noun* the hide of a young or small animal as used for leather. [Middle English: origin unknown]

kip[3] *noun* (*pl.* same or **kips**) the basic monetary unit of Laos, equal to 100 at. [Thai]

Kip·ling, (Jo·seph) Rud·yard (1865–1936), Indian-born English novelist, short-story writer, and poet. Poems such as 'The White Man's Burden', 'If', and 'Gunga Din', and his tales for children, notably *The Jungle Book* (1894), *Kim* (1901), and the *Just So Stories* (1902) reflect themes of British imperialism and life in India under British rule; in 1907 he was the first English writer to be awarded the Nobel Prize for literature. □ **Kip·ling·esque** *adjective*

kip·per ● *noun* **1** a fish, esp. herring that has been cured by splitting, salting, and drying in the open air or smoke. **2** a male salmon in the spawning season. **●** *transitive verb* cure (a herring etc.) by splitting open, salting, and drying in the open air or smoke. [Middle English: origin uncertain]

kir /kiːr/ *noun* a drink made from dry white wine and crème de cassis. [Canon Felix *Kir* d.1968, said to have invented the recipe]

Kirch·hoff /ˈkiːrkɒf/ **Gus·tav Rob·ert** (1824–87), German physicist, a pioneer in spectroscopy. Working with Bunsen, he developed a spectroscope, discovered that solar absorption lines are specific to certain elements, developed the concept of black body radiation, and discovered the elements cesium and rubidium.

Kirch·ner /ˈkiːrʃnər, ˈkiːrk-/ **Ernst Lud·wig** (1880–1938), German expressionist painter, whose works, such as *Five Women in the Street* (1913), are characterized by bright contrasting colours and angular outlines, and often depict claustrophobic street scenes; he committed suicide after condemnation of his work by the Nazis.

Kir·ghiz *var. of* KYRGYZ.

Kir·ghi·zia /kiːrˈɡiːziə/ an alternative name for KYRGYZSTAN.

Kiri·bati /ˈkiːrəbəs, ˌkiːriˈbɒti/ a country in the SW Pacific including the Gilbert Islands, the Line Islands, the Phoenix Islands, and Banaba (Ocean Island); pop. (est. 2002) 96,335; capital, Bairiki (on Tarawa).

Kirin see JILIN.

Kiriti·mati /kəˈrɪsɪməs/ an island in the Pacific Ocean, one of the Line Islands of Kiribati; pop. (est. 2002) 5,300. It is the largest atoll in the world. Known as Christmas Island until 1981, it was discovered by Captain James Cook on Christmas Eve 1777. In the 1950s it was used as an operational base for US and British nuclear weapons testing.

kirk *noun* **1** esp. *Scot.* a church. **2** (**the Kirk** or **the Kirk of Scotland**) the Church of Scotland (Presbyterian). [Old Norse *kirkja* from Old English *cir(i)ce* CHURCH]

Kirk·cud·bright·shire /kərˈkuːbriˌʃɪr/ a former county of SW Scotland. It became part of the region of Dumfries and Galloway in 1975.

Kirke, Sir David (*c.*1597–1654), English adventurer. In 1628 he and his three brothers captured Tadoussac and demanded that Champlain surrender Quebec to them; when this demand was refused they withdrew, but returned the next year and succeeded in taking Quebec. Forced to return the colony to the French in 1632, Kirke became the first Governor of Newfoundland in 1637. He was recalled in 1651 on charges of withholding tax money.

Kirk·land a former city in south central Quebec, towards the southwest end of the Island of Montreal, now part of the city of Montreal; pop. (2001) 20,434. [Dr. C.-A. *Kirkland*, Canadian politician d.1961]

Kirkland Lake a gold-mining town in NE Ontario, about 225 km north of North Bay, close to the border with Quebec; pop. (2001) 8,616. [W. *Kirkland*, secretary in the Ontario Department of Mines *c.*1907]

kirk session *noun* (in Presbyterian churches) = SESSION 6.

Kir·kuk /kɜrˈkʊk/ an industrial city in N Iraq, centre of the oil industry in that region; pop. (est. 2002) 728,800.

Kirov /ˈkiːrɒf/ the former name (1934–92) for VYATKA.

Kirov·a·bad /ˌkiːrəvəˈbad/ a former name (1935–89) for GÄNCÄ.

Kirov·o·hrad /kɪˈrɒvəˌhrad/ a city in central Ukraine; pop. (est. 1998) 270,200.

kir·pan /kɜrˈpan, -ˈpɒn/ *noun* the dagger or sword worn by Sikhs as a religious symbol. [Punjabi and Hindi *kirpān* from Sanskrit *kṛpāṇa* sword]

kir royale /kiːr rɔɪˈjal/ *noun* a drink made from sparkling white wine and crème de cassis.

kirsch /kiːrʃ/ *noun* a brandy distilled from the fermented juice of cherries. [German *Kirsche* cherry]

kir·tle *noun archaic* **1** a woman's gown or outer petticoat. **2** a man's tunic or coat. [Old English *cyrtel* from Germanic, ultimately perhaps from Latin *curtus* short]

Ki·san·gani /ˌkisaŋˈɡɒni/ a city in N Congo (formerly Zaire), on the Congo River; pop. (est. 2002) 510,300. Founded in 1882 by the explorer Sir Henry Morton Stanley, it was known as Stanleyville until 1966.

kis·met /ˈkɪzmɛt, ˈkɪs-/ *noun* destiny, fate. [Turkish from Arabic *ḳisma(t)* from *ḳasama* divide]

kiss ● *verb* **1** *transitive* touch with the lips, esp. as a sign of love, affection, greeting, or reverence. **2** *transitive* express (greeting or farewell) in this way. **3** *intransitive* (of two persons) touch each other's lips in this way. **4** *transitive* touch very lightly or briefly. **5** *transitive & intransitive* (of a snooker ball etc. in motion) lightly touch (another ball). ● *noun* **1** a touch with the lips in kissing. **2** a very light or brief touch. **3** the slight impact when one snooker ball etc. lightly touches another. **4** a bite-sized baked meringue or esp. chocolate candy. □ **kiss and tell** recount one's romantic encounters or sexual exploits. **kiss ass** (or **kiss a person's ass**) *coarse slang* act obsequiously (towards a person) (*compare* KISS-ASS). **kiss away** remove (tears etc.) by kissing. **kiss goodbye to** *informal* accept the loss of. **kiss the ground** prostrate oneself as a token of homage. **kiss off** esp. *N Amer. slang* dismiss, get rid of, esp. roughly or abruptly. **kiss up to** *N Amer. informal* act sycophantically or obsequiously towards in order to obtain something. □ **kiss·able** *adjective* [Old English *cyssan* from Germanic]

kiss-and-cry *noun* (usu. *attributive*) the area beside the ice in which figure skaters and their coaches etc. await the posting of the judges' marks at a competition.

kiss and ride *noun N Amer. & Austral.* an area at a public transit station where passengers may be picked up or dropped off by the driver of a car.

kiss-and-tell *adjective* revealing confidential material.

kiss-ass *noun* esp. *N Amer. coarse slang* an obsequious, bootlicking toady; a sycophant.

kiss-curl *noun* a small curl of hair on the forehead, at the nape, or in front of the ear.

kiss·er *noun* **1** a person who kisses. **2** *slang* the mouth; the face.

kissing cousin *noun* **1** a relative or friend with whom one is on close enough terms to greet with a kiss. **2** something related or similar.

kissing disease *noun* a disease transmitted by contact with saliva infected with a virus, esp. mononucleosis.

Kis·sin·ger /ˈkɪsɪndʒər/ **Henry (Al·fred)** (b.1923), German-born US politician and diplomat, secretary of state under Nixon and Ford 1973–77. He helped to improve relations with both China and the Soviet Union, ordered the bombing and invasion of Cambodia during the Vietnam War, negotiated the withdrawal of US troops from South Vietnam (1973), and restored US diplomatic relations with Egypt in the wake of the Yom Kippur War (1973); he shared the Nobel Peace Prize in 1973.

kissing gate *noun Brit.* a gate hung at the narrow end of a V- or U-shaped enclosure, to let one person through at a time.

kiss of death *noun* an act or situation (often apparently friendly) which causes ruin.

kiss-off *noun* esp. *N Amer. slang* an abrupt or rude dismissal.

kiss of life *noun* **1** mouth-to-mouth resuscitation. **2** an act or thing which revitalizes.

kiss of peace *noun Christianity* a ceremonial kiss or other greeting, esp. during the Eucharist, as a sign of unity.

kiss·o·gram *noun* a novelty telegram or greeting delivered with a kiss.

kissy *adjective informal* pertaining to or given to kissing (*not the kissy type*).

kissy-face *noun N Amer.* a puckering of the lips as if to kiss someone.

Ki·swa·hili /ˌkɪswəˈhiːli/ *noun* a major language of the Bantu family, spoken widely in Kenya, Tanzania, and elsewhere in E Africa, where it serves as a lingua franca. [Swahili *ki-* prefix for an abstract or inanimate object]

kit¹ ● *noun* **1** a set of articles, equipment, documents, or clothing needed for a specific purpose (*first aid kit; bicycle-repair kit; press kit*). **2** a container for such a set. **3** the clothing, gear, etc. needed for any activity (*battle kit*). **4** a set of all the parts needed to assemble an item, e.g. a piece of furniture, a model, etc. (also *attributive*: *kit car*). **5** = DRUM KIT. ● *transitive verb* (**kit·ted, kit·ting**) esp. *Brit.* (often foll. by *out, up*) equip with the appropriate clothing or tools. □ **the whole kit and caboodle** *see* CABOODLE. [Middle Dutch *kitte* wooden vessel, of unknown origin]

kit² *noun* **1** a kitten. **2** a young fox, beaver, etc. [abbreviation]

kit³ *noun hist.* a small fiddle esp. as used by a dancing master. [perhaps from Latin *cithara*; see CITTERN]

Kita·kyu·shu /ˌkiːtəˈkjuːʃu/ a port in S Japan, on the north coast of Kyushu island; pop. (est. 2002) 1,102,500.

kit bag *noun* a large, often cylindrical bag or sack used for carrying the equipment of a soldier, traveller, etc.

kitch·en *noun* **1 a** a room or area where food is prepared and cooked. **b** kitchen appliances, fixtures, etc., esp. as sold together. **2** (*attributive*) of or belonging to the kitchen (*kitchen knife; kitchen table*). **3** the staff working in the kitchen of a restaurant etc. □ **everything but the kitchen sink** everything imaginable. [Old English *cycene* from Latin *coquere* 'cook']

kitchen cabinet *noun* a group of unofficial advisers thought to be unduly influential.

Kitch·en·er¹ a city in SW central Ontario, situated about 50 km northwest of Hamilton, forming a conurbation with Waterloo; pop. (2001) 190,399. Settled by German Mennonites in 1806 as Sand Hills, it was renamed Berlin in 1830 and Kitchener in 1916. [KITCHENER²]

Kitch·en·er², (Hor·atio) Her·bert, 1st Earl Kitch·en·er of Khar·toum (1850–1916), Irish-born English field marshal. He led British and Egyptian forces to victory in the Battle of Omdurman (1898), served as commander-in-chief during the Boer War (1902–9), and was war minister during the First World War; he died when the ship taking him to Russia was sunk by a mine.

kitchen·ette *noun* a small kitchen or part of a room, boat, etc. fitted as a kitchen.

kitchen garden *noun* a garden where vegetables and sometimes fruit or herbs are grown for personal use.

kitchen midden *noun* a prehistoric refuse heap which marks an ancient settlement, chiefly containing bones, seashells, etc.

kitchen party *noun Cdn* (*Maritimes*) **1** an informal entertainment held in a person's home, at which participants play music, sing, dance, etc. **2** a party where the partygoers congregate in the kitchen.

kitchen racket *noun Cdn* (*Nfld & Cape Breton*) = KITCHEN PARTY.

kitchen-sink *adjective* (in art forms) depicting extreme realism, esp. drabness or sordidness (*kitchen-sink school of painting; kitchen-sink drama*).

kitchen·ware *noun* the utensils used in the kitchen.

kite ● *noun* **1** a toy consisting of a light frame with thin material stretched over it, flown in the wind at the end of a long string. **2** any of various medium-sized birds of prey of the family Accipitridae, with long wings and usu. a forked tail and soaring flight. **3** *Brit. slang* an airplane. **4** *slang* a fraudulent cheque, bill, or receipt. **5** *slang* a letter or note, esp. one that is illicit or surreptitious. **6** (in *pl.*) the highest sail of a ship, set only in a light wind. ● *verb* **1** *intransitive* soar like a kite. **2** *transitive & intransitive N Amer.* originate or pass (fraudulent cheques, bills, or receipts). **3** *transitive & intransitive* raise (money) by dishonest means (*kite a loan*). □ **go fly a kite** *informal* get lost; go away. **high as a kite** *informal* **1** intoxicated by alcohol or drugs. **2** excited; happy. □ **kit·ing** *noun* [Old English *cȳta*, of unknown origin]

Kite·mark *noun Brit.* an official kite-shaped mark on goods approved by the British Standards Institution.

kite·surf·ing *noun* (also **kite·board·ing**) a sport in which one rides a surfboard pulled by a kite.

kith *noun* friends, acquaintances, or neighbours. □ **kith and kin** friends and relations. [Old English *cȳthth* from Germanic]

Ki·tik·meot /kɪˈtɪkˌmiɒt/ an administrative region of Nunavut including the Central Arctic. [Inuinnaqtun, = 'from the centre']

Kiti·mat /ˈkɪtiˌmat/ a district municipality in western BC, about 60 km

Consonants: b *but* d *dog* f *few* g *get* h *her* j *yes* k *cat* l *leg* m *man* n *no* p *pen* r *red* s *sit*

south of Terrace; pop. (2001) 10,285. □ **Kiti·ma·tian** /kɪtɪˈmeiʃən/ *noun* [Tsimshian *Kitamaat* = people of the falling snow]

kitsch *noun* (often *attributive*) garish, tasteless, or sentimental art (*kitsch plastic models of the royal family*). □ **kitsch·i·fi·ca·tion** *noun* **kitsch·i·ness** *noun* **kitschy** *adjective* (**kitsch·i·er**, **kitsch·i·est**). [German]

Kit·se·las /ˈkɪtsələs/ *noun* **1** a member of an Aboriginal people living along the Skeena River in northwestern BC. **2** the Tsimshian language of this people. [Kitselas *git'selasu* = 'people of the canyon']

kit·ten ● *noun* **1** a young cat. **2** the young of certain other animals, as the fox, ferret, etc. ● *transitive & intransitive verb* (of a cat etc.) give birth or give birth to. □ **have kittens** *informal* be extremely upset, anxious, or nervous. [Middle English *kito(u)n, ketoun* from Old French *chitoun, chetoun* diminutive of *chat* CAT]

kit·ten·ish *adjective* **1** like a young cat; playful and lively. **2** flirtatious, coy. □ **kit·ten·ish·ly** *adverb*

kit·ti·wake /ˈkɪtɪˌweik/ *noun* either of two small gulls, *Rissa tridactyla* and *R. brevirostris*, nesting on sea cliffs. [imitative of its cry]

kit·ty¹ *noun* (*pl.* **-ties**) **1** a fund of money for communal use. **2** a pool of money in some card games made up of contributions from each player and used as winnings or for refreshments etc. **3** the jack in bowls. [19th c.: origin unknown]

kit·ty² *noun* (*pl.* **-ties**) a pet name or a child's name for a kitten or cat.

kitty-corner *N Amer.* ● *adjective* placed or situated diagonally. ● *adverb* diagonally. [from *cater-cornered*, alteration of dial. *cater* diagonally (compare *cater* the four on dice, from French *quatre* from Latin *quattor* four)]

Kitty Hawk a town on a narrow sand peninsula on the Atlantic coast of N Carolina. The Wright brothers made the first powered airplane flight there in 1903.

Kitty Litter *noun proprietary* = CAT LITTER.

Kit·wan·ga Fort /ˈkɪtwɒŋɡə/ a historic site in west central BC, located at the confluence of the Skeena and Kitwanga rivers, northeast of Terrace. A legendary Aboriginal stronghold, it was a site of inter-tribal trade and warfare. [ultimately from Gitksan, lit. 'people of the place of rabbits']

Kitwe /ˈkɪtwei/ a city in the Copperbelt mining region of N Zambia; pop. (est. 2002) 305,000.

Kitz·bühel /ˈkɪtsbjuːl/ a town in the Tyrol, W Austria; pop. (2000) 8,625, a popular resort and competition centre for winter sports.

kiva /ˈkiːvə/ *noun* a chamber, built wholly or partly underground, used by male Pueblo Indians for religious rites etc. [Hopi]

Kivu, Lake /ˈkiːvuː/ a lake in central Africa, on the border between Congo (formerly Zaire) and Rwanda.

Ki·wan·is /kɪˈwɒnɪs/ *noun N Amer.* a society of business and professional people founded in 1915 for the maintenance of commercial ethics and as a social and charitable organization. □ **Ki·wan·ian** *noun* [origin unknown]

kiwi /ˈkiːwiː/ *noun* (*pl.* **kiwis**) **1** a flightless New Zealand bird of the genus *Apteryx* with hairlike feathers and a long bill. *Also called* APTERYX. **2 a** a climbing plant, *Actinidia chinensis*, bearing fruits with a thin hairy skin, green flesh, and black seeds. **b** (also **kiwi fruit**) this fruit. *Also called* CHINESE GOOSEBERRY. **3** (**Kiwi**) *informal* a New Zealander, esp. a soldier or member of a national sports team. [Maori]

kJ *abbreviation* kilojoule(s).

KJV *abbreviation* KING JAMES VERSION.

KKK *abbreviation* KU KLUX KLAN.

KL *abbreviation informal* Kuala Lumpur.

kl *abbreviation* kilolitre(s).

Klag·en·furt /ˈklɒɡənˌfʊrt/ a city in S Austria, capital of Carinthia; pop. (2000) 90,300.

Klai·peda /ˈklaipədə/ a city and port in Lithuania, on the Baltic Sea; pop. (1999) 202,528. It was known as Memel when under German control (1918-23 and 1941-4).

Klan *noun* (usu. prec. by *the*) KU KLUX KLAN.

Klans·man *noun* (*pl.* **-men**) a member of the Ku Klux Klan.

Klans·woman *noun* (*pl.* **-women**) a female member of the Ku Klux Klan.

Klap·roth /ˈklaproːt/ **Mar·tin Hein·rich** (1743–1817), German chemist, one of the founders of analytical chemistry. He discovered zirconium, uranium, and titanium and helped to introduce Lavoisier's new system of chemistry into Germany.

klap skate *noun var.* OF CLAP SKATE.

klax·on /ˈklaksən/ *noun* a horn, originally on a motor vehicle. [name of the manufacturing company]

Klee /ˈklei/ **Paul** (1879–1940), Swiss painter, resident in Germany from 1906. One of the most imaginative, prolific and influential of 20th-c. masters, he worked in many styles, both representational and abstract, and his paintings often have a childlike quality, as in *A Tiny Tale of a Tiny Dwarf* (1925).

Klee·nex *noun* (*pl.* same or **Klee·nex·es**) *proprietary* an absorbent disposable paper tissue, used esp. as a handkerchief.

Klein /ˈklain/ **1 Abra·ham Moses** (1909–72), Ukrainian-born Canadian lawyer, poet and writer. Much of Klein's work was Jewish in character, and he contributed a great deal to the development of Jewish-Canadian culture. His poetry includes *Hath Not a Jew* (1940) and *The Hitleriad* (1944); he also served as editor of the weekly *Canadian Jewish Chronicle* from 1938 to 1955. **2 Cal·vin (Rich·ard)** (b.1942), US fashion designer of understated and sophisticated fashions for both men and women. **3 Mel·anie** (1882–1960), Austrian-born English psychoanalyst. The first psychologist to specialize in the psychoanalysis of small children, she discovered surprising levels of aggression and sadism in young infants, and made an important contribution to the understanding of the more severe mental disorders found in children. **4 Ralph** (b.1942), Canadian Conservative politician, premier of Alberta since 1992. He eliminated his province's deficit by cutting government expenditure and encouraging growth in the gambling industry, and then moved to bring private hospitals into the health care system and introduce a single-rate tax system.

Klein bottle /ˈklain/ *noun Math.* a closed surface with only one side, formed by passing the neck of a tube through the side of the tube to join the hole in the base. [F. *Klein*, German mathematician d.1925]

Klem·perer /ˈklempərər/ **Otto** (1885–1973), German-born conductor and composer. His readings of symphonies by Beethoven, Brahms, and Mahler, and particularly his recordings of the Beethoven cycle in the 1950s, were highly acclaimed; he adopted Israeli citizenship in 1970.

klep·toc·racy /klepˈtɒkrəsi/ *noun* (*pl.* **-cies**) **1** government by a group who enrich themselves on the country's resources. **2** a nation ruled in this way. □ **klepto·crat** *noun* [Greek *klepto-* (see KLEPTOMANIA) + -CRACY]

klepto·mania /ˌkleptoˈmeiniə/ *noun* a recurrent urge to steal, usu. without regard for need or profit. □ **klepto·maniac** *noun & adjective* [Greek *kleptēs* thief + -MANIA]

Klerk *see* DE KLERK.

Klerks·dorp /ˈklɜrksdɔrp/ a city in South Africa, in North-West Province, southwest of Johannesburg; pop. (est. 2002) 152,700.

klez·mer /ˈklezmɜr/ *noun* **1** a member of a group of musicians playing traditional eastern European Jewish music. **2** (in full **klezmer music**) this type of music. [Yiddish, contraction of Hebrew *kĕlēy zemer* musical instrument]

klick *noun N Amer. slang* a kilometre. [origin unknown; used by US servicemen during the Vietnam War]

klieg light /kliːɡ/ *noun* a powerful lamp in a film studio etc. [A. T. & J. H. *Kliegl*, US inventors d.1927, 1959]

Klimt /ˈklɪmt/ **Gus·tav** (1862–1918), Austrian painter and designer. His work combines stylized human forms with decorative and ornate clothing or backgrounds in elaborate mosaic patterns, often using gold leaf; he painted allegorical and mythological subjects, as well as portraits, and is known for *Judith I* (1901) and *The Kiss* (1908).

Kline, Franz (1910–62), US abstract expressionist painter. His works, such as *Chief* (1950) and *Two Horizontals* (1954), are reminiscent of oriental calligraphy in their use of thick bold black lines against a white background.

Kling·on *noun* **1** a member of a warlike humanoid alien species in the TV series *Star Trek* and its spinoffs. **2** the language of the Klingons, artificially created, and used by *Star Trek* fans. [invented name]

klip·spring·er *noun* a S African dwarf antelope, *Oreotragus oreotragus*, which can bound up and down rocky slopes. [Afrikaans from *klip* rock + *springer* jumper]

klis·ter *noun Skiing* a soft wax for applying to the running surface of skis to facilitate movement, used esp. when the temperature is above freezing. [Norwegian, = paste]

Klon·dike *noun* a source of valuable material. [The KLONDIKE]

Klon·dike, the the region of west central Yukon Territory surrounding the Klondike River. In 1897-8, following the discovery of gold in nearby Bonanza Creek in 1896, a gold rush brought thousands to the area, and the town of Dawson was established. Within ten years the area was exhausted and the population dramatically decreased. Today, the

t *top*   v *voice*   w *we*   z *zoo*   ʃ *she*   ʒ *vision*   θ *thin*   ð *this*   ŋ *ring*   x *loch*   tʃ *chip*   dʒ *jar*   (*see over for vowels*)

Klondike Gold Fields and the city of Dawson are designated historic sites. [see KLONDIKE RIVER]

Klon·dik·er *noun hist.* a prospector who took part in the Klondike gold rush of 1897–8.

Klondike River a river in west central Yukon Territory, which rises in the Ogilvie Mountains and flows 160 km (100 miles) westward to join the Yukon River at Dawson. [Gwich'in *thronduik* hammer water, with reference to the salmon-trapping practice of driving stakes into the river bottom]

kloof *noun South Africa* a steep-sided ravine or valley. [Dutch, = cleft]

Klos·ters /'klɔːstɜrz/ an Alpine winter-sports resort in E Switzerland, near the Austrian border.

Klu·ane Lake /kluːˈoni/ a small lake in SW Yukon Territory, situated almost 200 km northwest of Whitehorse. [Tlingit, = whitefish place]

Klu·ane National Park a park in the southwestern corner of Yukon Territory. Designated a World Heritage Site, it surrounds the St. Elias mountain range, preserving Canada's highest peak, Mount Logan. [as KLUANE LAKE]

kludge *noun slang* **1** an ill-assorted collection of poorly matching parts. **2** *Computing* a machine, system, or program that has been badly put together. ☐ **kludgy** *adjective* [invented word, perhaps influenced by FUDGE]

klutz *noun esp. N Amer. informal* **1** a clumsy, awkward person. **2** a fool. ☐ **klutzy** *adjective* [Yiddish, from German *Klotz* 'wooden block']

klys·tron /'klɔistrɒn/ *noun* an electron tube that generates or amplifies microwaves by velocity modulation. [Greek *kluzō klus-* wash over]

km *abbreviation* kilometre(s).

K-meson /keiˈmezɒn, -'miːzɒn/ *noun* = KAON. [K (see KAON) + MESON]

km/h *abbreviation* kilometres per hour.

kn. *abbreviation Naut.* knot(s).

knack *noun* **1** an acquired or intuitive faculty of doing a thing adroitly. **2** a trick or habit of action or speech etc. (*has a knack of offending people*). **3** *archaic* an ingenious device; a trinket (see KNICK-KNACK). [Middle English, prob. identical with *knack* sharp blow or sound, from Low German, ultimately imitative]

knack·er *Brit.* ● *noun* **1** a buyer of useless horses for slaughter. **2** a buyer of old houses, ships, etc. for the materials. ● *transitive verb slang* (esp. as **knack·ered** *adjective*) exhaust, wear out. [19th c.: origin unknown]

knack·wurst /'nakwɜrst/ *noun* a type of short fat highly seasoned German sausage. [German from *knacken* make a cracking noise + *Wurst* sausage]

knap[1] *noun esp. dialect* the crest of a hill or of rising ground. [Old English *cnæp(p)*, perhaps related to Old Norse *knappr* knob]

knap[2] *transitive verb* (**knapped**, **knap·ping**) break (esp. a stone) with a sharp blow from a hammer etc. ☐ **knap·per** *noun* [Middle English, imitative]

knap·sack *noun* a bag of canvas, nylon, or other weatherproof material, carried strapped on the back by hikers, students, soldiers, etc. [Middle Low German, prob. from *knappen* bite + SACK[1]]

knap·weed *noun* any of various plants of the genus *Centaurea*, having thistle-like purple flowers. [Middle English, originally *knopweed* from *knop* knob + WEED]

knar *noun* a knot or protuberance in a tree trunk, root, etc. [Middle English *knarre*, related to Middle Low German, Middle Dutch, Middle High German *knorre* knobbed protuberance]

knave *noun* **1** a rogue, a scoundrel. **2** = JACK[1] *noun* 2. ☐ **knav·ery** *noun* (*pl.* **-eries**). **knav·ish** *adjective* [Old English *cnafa* boy, servant, from West Germanic]

knawel /'nɒəl/ *noun* any low-growing plant of the genus *Scleranthus*. [German *Knauel*]

knead *transitive verb* **1 a** work (dough, clay, etc.) into a smooth mass by pressing and folding. **b** make (bread, pottery, etc.) in this way. **2** blend or weld together (*kneaded them into a unified group*). **3** massage or pummel (muscles etc.) as if kneading. ☐ **knead·er** *noun* [Old English *cnedan* from Germanic]

knee ● *noun* **1 a** (often *attributive*) the joint between the thigh and the lower leg in humans. **b** the corresponding joint in other animals. **c** the area around this. **d** the upper surface of the thigh of a sitting person; the lap (*held her on his knee*). **2** the part of a garment covering the knee. **3** anything resembling a knee in shape or position, esp. a piece of wood or iron bent at an angle, a sharp turn in a graph, etc. **4** a conical protuberance on the roots of the bald cypress and tupelo, rising above the water in which the tree grows. ● *transitive verb* (**knees**,

kneed, **knee·ing**) touch or strike with the knee (*kneed the ball past him; kneed him in the groin*). ☐ **bend the knee 1** kneel in submission, worship, or supplication. **2** submit. **bring to its** (or **his** or **her**) **knees** reduce (a thing or person) to a state of weakness or submission. **learn** (**something**) **at one's mother's knee** learn something at an early age. **on bended knee** (also **on one's bended knees**) kneeling, esp. in supplication, submission, or worship. **on one's knees 1** kneeling. **2** (of a country, business, etc.) seriously weakened, just short of total collapse. [Old English *cnēo(w)*]

knee bend *noun* the action of bending the knee, esp. as a physical exercise in which the body is raised and lowered without the use of the hands.

knee·board ● *noun* a short surfboard ridden in a kneeling position. ● *intransitive verb* ride a kneeboard. ☐ **knee·board·er** *noun* **knee·board·ing** *noun*

knee breeches *plural noun* close-fitting trousers reaching to or just below the knee.

knee·cap ● *noun* **1** the convex bone in front of the knee joint; the patella. **2** a protective covering for the knee. ● *transitive verb* (**-capped**, **-cap·ping**) shoot (a person) in the knee or leg as a punishment, esp. for betraying a terrorist group. ☐ **knee·cap·per** *noun* **knee·cap·ping** *noun*

knee-deep *adjective* **1** (usu. foll. by *in*) **a** immersed up to the knees. **b** deeply involved. **c** having more than one needs or wants of a specified thing. **2** (of water, snow, mud, etc.) so deep as to reach the knees.

knee-high ● *adjective* **1** reaching as high as the knees. **2** (of a person) very small or very young. ● *noun* (usu. in *pl.*) *N Amer.* a sock reaching just below the knee. ☐ **knee-high to a grasshopper** very small or very young.

knee·hole *noun* (often *attributive*) a space for the knees, esp. under a desk.

knee-jerk ● *noun* a sudden involuntary kick caused by a blow on the tendon just below the knee. ● *attributive adjective* predictable, automatic, stereotyped (*a knee-jerk reaction*).

knee joint *noun* **1** = KNEE *noun* 1a, b. **2** a joint made of two pieces hinged together.

kneel *intransitive verb* (*past* and *past participle* **knelt** or esp. *N Amer.* **kneeled**) **1** fall or rest on the knees or a knee. **2** (of a bus) lower its platform to street level to facilitate entry and exit. [Old English *cnēowlian* (as KNEE)]

knee-length *adjective* reaching the knees.

kneel·er *noun* **1** a low padded bench or cushion used for kneeling, esp. in church. **2** a person who kneels.

knee pad *noun* a pad of foam, plastic, etc. worn to protect the knee, esp. in sports activities.

knee pants *plural noun* trousers reaching to or near the knee, esp. as formerly worn by young boys.

knee-slapper *noun N Amer. informal* an uproariously funny joke. ☐ **knee-slapping** *adjective*

knee sock *noun* (usu. in *pl.*) a sock covering the lower leg to just below the knee.

knees-up *noun Brit. informal* a lively party or gathering.

knee-trembler *noun slang* an act of sexual intercourse between people in a standing position.

knee wall *noun* a short side wall, as of an attic room under a sloped roof.

knell ● *noun* **1** the sound of a bell, esp. when rung solemnly for a death or funeral. **2** an announcement, event, etc., regarded as a solemn warning of disaster. ● *verb* **1** *intransitive* **a** (of a bell) ring solemnly, esp. for a death or funeral. **b** make a doleful or ominous sound. **2** *transitive* proclaim by or as by a knell (*knelled the death of all their hopes*). ☐ **ring the knell of** announce or herald the end of. [Old English *cnyll*, *cnyllan*: perhaps influenced by *bell*]

knelt *past* and *past participle of* KNEEL.

Knes·set /'knesit/ *noun* the parliament of modern Israel, established in 1949. [Hebrew, lit. 'gathering']

knew *past of* KNOW.

knicker·bock·er *noun* **1** (in *pl.*) loose-fitting breeches gathered at the knee or calf. **2** (**Knickerbocker**) **a** a New Yorker. **b** a descendant of the original Dutch settlers in New York. [Diedrich *Knickerbocker*, pretended author of W. Irving's *History of New York* (1809)]

knick·ers *plural noun* **1** *N Amer.* **a** knickerbockers. **b** a boy's short trousers. **2** *Brit.* a woman's or girl's underpants. ☐ **get one's**

knickers (or **shirt**) **in a knot** (or **twist**) become agitated or upset. [abbreviation of KNICKERBOCKER]

knick-knack noun **1** a useless and usu. worthless ornament; a trinket. **2** a small, dainty article of furniture, dress, etc. □ **knick-knackery** noun [reduplication of knack in obsolete sense 'trinket']

knife ● noun (pl. **knives**) **1 a** a metal blade used as a cutting tool with usu. one long sharp edge fixed rigidly in a handle or hinged. **b** a similar tool used as a weapon. **2** a cutting blade forming part of a machine. ● verb **1** transitive cut or stab with or as with a knife. **2** transitive slang bring about the defeat of (a person) by underhand means. **3** intransitive (usu. foll. by through) cut or move through like a knife. □ **go under the knife** informal have surgery. **like a** (**hot**) **knife through butter** easily; without meeting any resistance or difficulty. **that one could cut with a knife** informal (of an accent, atmosphere, etc.) very obvious, oppressive, etc. □ **knife·like** adjective **knif·er** noun [Old English cnif from Old Norse knifr, from Germanic]

knife block noun a usu. wooden block used for storing knives, with long narrow slots for the blades.

knife-edge noun **1** the edge of a knife. **2** a position of extreme danger or uncertainty. **3** a steel wedge on which a pendulum etc. oscillates. **4** = ARÊTE.

knife-pleat noun a narrow flat pleat on a skirt etc., usu. overlapping another. □ **knife-pleated** adjective

knife·point noun the pointed end of a knife, esp. as directed at a person as a threat. □ **at knifepoint** under threat of being stabbed.

knife-throwing noun a circus etc. act in which knives are thrown at targets. □ **knife-thrower** noun

knif·ing noun an instance of stabbing with a knife.

knight ● noun **1** a man awarded a non-hereditary title (Sir) by a sovereign in recognition of merit or service. **2** hist. **a** a man, usu. noble, raised esp. by a sovereign to honourable military rank after service as a page and squire. **b** a military follower or attendant, esp. of a lady as her champion in a war or tournament. **3** a man devoted to the service of a woman, cause, etc. **4** Chess a piece usu. shaped like a horse's head. **5 a** Rom. Hist. a member of the class of equites, originally the cavalry of the Roman army. **b** Gk Hist. a citizen of the second class in Athens. **6** (in full **knight of the shire**) Brit. hist. a gentleman representing a shire or county in parliament. ● transitive verb confer a knighthood on. □ **knight·hood** noun **knight·ly** adjective **knight·li·ness** noun [Old English cniht boy, youth, hero, from West Germanic]

knight bachelor noun (pl. **knights bachelor**) a knight not belonging to a special order.

knight commander noun see COMMANDER 2.

knight errant noun **1** hist. a medieval knight wandering in search of chivalrous adventures. **2** a man of a chivalrous or quixotic nature. □ **knight-errantry** noun

Knight Hospitaller a member of a military religious order founded as the Knights of the Hospital of St. John at Jerusalem in the 11th c. Originally protectors of pilgrims, they also undertook the care of the sick. The order was responsible for the foundation of the St. John Ambulance Association in 1878 and the St. John Ambulance Brigade in 1888 (see ST. JOHN AMBULANCE).

Knight Inlet a fjord of Queen Charlotte Strait, extending some 95 km into the western coast of mainland BC. [Sir J. Knight, English admiral d.1831]

knight in shining armour noun a chivalrous rescuer or helper, esp. of a woman.

knight of the road noun Brit. informal **1** hist. a highwayman. **2** a travelling sales representative. **3** a tramp. **4** a truck or taxi driver.

knight of the shire noun see KNIGHT noun 6.

Knights of Columbus plural noun an esp. N American society of Roman Catholic men founded at New Haven, Connecticut, in 1882.

Knight Templar noun (pl. **Knights Templar**) **1** hist. a member of a religious and military order for the protection of pilgrims to the Holy Land, suppressed in 1312. **2** US a member of an American Masonic order.

knish /knɪʃ/ noun a dumpling of flaky dough filled with cheese etc. and baked or fried. [Yiddish from Russian]

knit ● verb (**knit·ting**; past and past participle **knit·ted** or (esp. in senses 2–4) **knit**) **1** transitive & intransitive **a** make (a garment, blanket, etc.) by interlocking loops of yarn with knitting needles or by machine. **b** make (a plain stitch) in knitting (knit one, purl one). **2 a** transitive contract (the forehead) in vertical wrinkles. **b** intransitive (of the forehead) contract; frown. **3** transitive & intransitive (often foll. by together) make or become close or compact esp. by common interests etc. (a

close-knit group). **4** intransitive (often foll. by together) (of parts of a broken bone) become joined; heal. ● noun knitted material or a knitted garment (also attributive: a knit sleeper). □ **knit up 1 a** make or repair by knitting. **b** (Nfld & PEI) knot twine into meshes to make a fishnet or the heads on a lobster trap. **2** conclude, finish, or end. □ **knit·ter** noun [Old English cnyttan from West Germanic: compare KNOT¹]

knit·ting noun **1** a garment etc. in the process of being knitted. **2 a** the act of knitting. **b** an instance of this.

knitting machine noun a machine used for mechanically knitting garments etc.

knitting needle noun a thin pointed rod of steel, wood, plastic, etc., used esp. in pairs for knitting.

knit·wear noun knitted garments.

knives pl. of KNIFE.

knob ● noun **1 a** a rounded protuberance, esp. at the end or on the surface of a thing. **b** a handle of a door, drawer, etc., shaped like a knob. **c** a knob-shaped attachment for pulling, turning, etc. (press the knob under the desk). **2 a** a small, usu. round, piece (of butter, coal, etc.). **b** Cdn (Nfld) a hard candy. **3** esp. N Amer. a prominent round hill. **4** coarse slang the penis. **5** slang a stupid or contemptible person. ● transitive verb (**knobbed, knob·bing**) provide with knobs. □ **with knobs on** Brit. slang that and more (used as a retort to an insult, in emphatic agreement, etc.) (and the same to you with knobs on). □ **knob·by** adjective **knob-like** adjective [Middle Low German knobbe 'knot, knob, bud': compare NOB², NUB]

knob·bly adjective having many small knobs.

knob·kerrie /ˈnɒbˌkeri/ noun a short stick with a knobbed head used as a weapon esp. in S Africa. [after Afrikaans knopkierie]

knock ● verb **1 a** transitive strike (a hard surface) with an audible sharp blow (knocked the table three times). **b** intransitive strike, esp. a door to gain admittance (can you hear someone knocking?; knocked at the door). **2** transitive make (a hole, a dent, etc.) by knocking (knock a hole in the fence). **3** transitive (usu. foll. by in, out, off, etc.) drive (a thing, a person, etc.) by striking (knocked the ball into the hole; knocked those ideas out of his head; knocked her hand away). **4** transitive informal criticize. **5** intransitive come into collision with something (he knocked into the desk). **6** transitive cause (a person) to be in a certain state or position by striking (the fall knocked me senseless). **7** intransitive (of a motor or other engine) make a thumping or rattling noise, esp. due to faulty combustion. **8** transitive Brit. coarse slang offensive have sexual intercourse with. ● noun **1** an act of knocking. **2** a sharp rap, esp. at a door. **3** an audible sharp blow. **4** the sound of knocking in an engine, esp. in a motor engine. **5 a** a misfortune, a setback. **b** adverse criticism. □ **knock around** (or **about**) **1** strike repeatedly; treat roughly (knocked him around). **2** lead a wandering adventurous life; wander aimlessly. **3** be present without design or volition (there's a cup knocking about somewhere). **4** discuss casually (knocked a couple of ideas around). **knock against** collide with. **knock back 1** informal eat or drink, esp. quickly. **2** Brit. & Cdn informal disconcert. **3** reverse the progress of. **4** Brit., Austral., & NZ informal refuse, rebuff. **knock down 1** strike (esp. a person) to the ground with a blow. **2** demolish. **3** (usu. foll. by to) (at an auction) dispose of (an article) to a bidder by a knock with a hammer (knocked the Picasso down to him for a million). **4** informal lower the price of (an article). **5** take (machinery, furniture, etc.) apart for transportation. **6** US slang earn as a wage. **knock one's head against** come into collision with (unfavourable facts or conditions). **knock into a cocked hat** see COCKED HAT. **knock into the middle of next week** informal send (a person) flying, esp. with a blow. **knock it off!** stop it! **knock off 1** strike off with a blow. **2** informal **a** finish work (knocked off at 5:30). **b** finish (work) (knocked off work early). **3** informal rapidly produce (a work of art, verses, etc.). **4** (often foll. by from) deduct (a sum) from a price, bill, etc. **5** slang **a** steal or burglarize (knocked off a convenience store). **b** copy, plagiarize. **6** coarse slang offensive have sexual intercourse with (a woman). **7** slang kill. **8** N Amer. slang defeat (knocked off the top team in the league). **9** remove or reduce by (knocked a second off the previous world record). **knock on** Rugby drive (a ball) with the hand or arm towards the opponents' goal line. **knock on the head 1** stun or kill (a person) by a blow on the head. **2** Brit. informal put an end to (a scheme etc.). **knock (on) wood** N Amer. = TOUCH WOOD (SEE TOUCH). **knock out 1** make (a person) unconscious by a blow on the head. **2** knock down (a boxer) for a count of 10, thereby winning the contest. **3 a** defeat, esp. in a knockout competition. **b** get rid of; destroy (a computer program to knock out viruses). **4** informal astonish, esp. by unexpected excellence, generosity, etc. **5** (reflexive) informal exhaust (knocked themselves out swimming). **6** informal make or write (a plan etc.) hastily. **7** empty (a tobacco pipe) by tapping. **knock over 1** cause to fall, spill, or overturn. **2** slang rob, burglarize. **knock sideways** Brit.

uː mood   aɪ my   əɪ pipe   aʊ brown   ʌʊ house   eɪ day   ɔɪ boy   ã franglais   ã Canadien   ɔ̃ Brayon   (see over for consonants)

informal disconcert; astonish. **knock one's socks off** astound, amaze. **knock spots off** *Brit.* defeat easily. **knock together** put together or assemble hastily or roughly. **knock up 1** esp. *N Amer. slang* make pregnant. **2 a** become exhausted or ill. **b** exhaust or make ill. **3** *Brit.* arouse (a person) by a knock at the door. **4** *Brit.* make or arrange hastily. **take a knock** be hard hit financially or emotionally. [Middle English from Old English *cnocian*: prob. imitative]

knock·about ● *attributive adjective* **1** (of comedy) boisterous; slapstick. **2** (of clothes) suitable for rough use. **3** rough, unruly. ● *noun* **1** *Austral.* a farm or station handyman. **2** a sloop-rigged sailboat or a sailboat without a bowsprit. **3** a knockabout performer or performance.

knock-back *noun Brit., Austral., & NZ informal* a refusal, a rebuff.

knock-down ● *attributive adjective* **1** (of a blow, misfortune, argument, etc.) overwhelming. **2** *informal* (of a price) very low. **3** (of a price at auction) reserve. **4** (of furniture etc.) easily dismantled and reassembled. **5** (of an insecticide) rapidly immobilizing. ● *noun* an act or instance of knocking down.

knock-down, drag-out *adjective* esp. *N Amer.* (also **knock-down, drag-'em-out**) (of a brawl, argument, etc.) violent, vicious.

knock·er *noun* **1** a metal or wooden instrument hinged to a door for knocking to call attention. **2** a person or thing that knocks. **3** (in *pl.*) *coarse slang* a woman's breasts. **4** *informal* a person who continually finds fault. □ **on the knocker 1** (buying or selling) from door to door. **2** *Austral. & NZ informal* promptly.

knocking-shop *noun Brit. slang* a brothel.

knock knees *plural noun* an abnormal condition with the legs curved inwards at the knee. □ **knock-kneed** *adjective*

knock-knock joke *noun* a variety of joke beginning with the line 'knock knock' and usu. ending with a pun.

knock-off *noun* (often *attributive*) *informal* a copy or imitation made esp. for commercial gain.

knock-on *noun Rugby* an act of knocking on.

knock-on effect *noun* esp. *Brit.* a secondary, indirect, or cumulative effect.

knock·out *noun* **1** the act of making unconscious by a blow. **2** *Boxing etc.* a blow that knocks an opponent out. **3** a competition in which the loser in each round is eliminated (also *attributive*: *a knockout round*). **4** *informal* an outstanding or irresistible person or thing.

knockout drops *plural noun* a drug added to a drink to cause unconsciousness.

knockout mouse *noun* a laboratory mouse that has had a certain gene disabled so that geneticists can study the function of the disabled gene.

knoll¹ /nəʊl/ *noun* a small hill or mound. [Old English *cnoll* hilltop, related to Middle Dutch, Middle High German *knolle* clod, Old Norse *knollr* hilltop]

knoll² /nəʊl/ *archaic* ● *verb* **1** *transitive & intransitive* = KNELL *verb.* **2** *transitive* summon by the sound of a bell. ● *noun* = KNELL *noun.* [Middle English, var. of KNELL: perhaps imitative]

Knos·sos /ˈknɒsəs, ˈnɒs-/ the principal city of Minoan Crete, the remains of which are situated on the north coast of Crete. Excavations have revealed the remains of a luxurious and spectacularly decorated complex of buildings, named the Palace of Minos, with frescoes of landscapes, animal life, and the sport of bull-leaping. The city site was occupied from neolithic times until *c*.1200 BC; in *c*.1450 BC Crete was overrun by the Mycenaeans, but the palace was not destroyed until the 14th or early 13th c. BC.

knot¹ ● *noun* **1 a** an intertwining of a rope, string, tress of hair, etc., with another, itself, or something else to join or fasten together. **b** a set method of tying a knot (*a reef knot*). **c** a ribbon etc. tied as an ornament and worn on a dress etc. **d** a tangle in hair, knitting, etc. **2 a** a unit of a ship's or aircraft's speed equivalent to one nautical mile per hour (*see* NAUTICAL MILE). **b** a division marked by knots on a line or rope attached to a ship's log, used as a measure of speed. **c** *informal* a nautical mile. **3** (usu. foll. by *of*) a group or cluster (*a small knot of journalists at the gate*). **4** something forming or maintaining a union; a bond or tie, esp. of wedlock. **5** a hard lump of tissue in an animal or human body. **6 a** a knob or protuberance in a stem, branch, or root. **b** a hard mass formed in a tree trunk at the intersection with a branch. **c** a round cross-grained piece in timber where a branch has been cut through. **d** a node on the stem of a plant. **7** a difficulty; a problem. **8** a central point in a problem or the plot of a story etc. **9** a sensation of contortion felt in the stomach or throat, caused by stress or nervousness. ● *verb* (**knot·ted, knot·ting**) **1** *transitive* **a** tie (a string etc.) in a knot. **b** secure (something) with a knot. **2 a** *transitive* entangle.

b *intransitive* become entangled. **3** *transitive* form lumps, knobs, or knots on or in; make knotty. **4** *transitive* N *Amer. slang* tie (a score, game, etc.). **5 a** *intransitive* make knots for fringing. **b** *transitive* make (a fringe) with knots. □ **at a rate of knots** *informal* very fast. **get knotted!** *Brit. slang* an expression of disbelief, annoyance, etc. **tie in knots** *informal* baffle or confuse completely. **tie the knot** *informal* get married. □ **knot·less** *adjective* **knot·ter** *noun* **knot·ting** *noun* (esp. in sense 5 of *verb*). [Old English *cnotta* from West Germanic]

knot² *noun* (in full **red knot**) a small sandpiper, *Calidris canutus*, with a bright red throat and breast. [Middle English: origin unknown]

knot garden *noun* an intricately designed formal garden.

knot·grass *noun see* KNOTWEED.

knot·head *noun N Amer. informal* a stupid person or animal. □ **knot·head·ed** *adjective*

knot·hole *noun* **1** a hole in a piece of timber where a knot has fallen out. **2** a hollow formed in a tree trunk by the decay of a branch.

knot·ty *adjective* (**knot·ti·er, knot·ti·est**) **1** full of knots. **2** hard to explain; puzzling (*a knotty problem*). □ **knot·ti·ly** *adverb* **knot·ti·ness** *noun*

knot·weed *noun* **1** (also **knotgrass**) any of various plants of the genus *Polygonum*, with stems with thickened joints. **2** (in full **Japanese knotweed**) a fast-growing plant, *Polygonum cuspidatum* (*Reynoutria japonica*), with stems like bamboo, cultivated as an ornamental but often becoming a weed.

knout /naʊt/ ● *noun hist.* a scourge used in imperial Russia, often causing death. ● *transitive verb* flog with a knout. [French from Russian *knut* from Icelandic *knútr*, related to KNOT¹]

know ● *verb* (*past* **knew**; *past participle* **known**) **1** (often foll. by *that, how, what,* etc.) **a** *transitive* have in the mind; have learned; be able to recall (*knows a lot about cars; knows what to do*). **b** *transitive & intransitive* be aware of (a fact) (*she knows I am waiting; I think he knows*). **c** *transitive* have a good command of (a subject or language) (*knew German; knows her times tables*). **2** *transitive* be acquainted or friendly with (a person or thing). **3** *transitive* **a** recognize; identify (*I knew him at once*). **b** (foll. by *to* + infin.) be aware of (a person or thing) as being or doing what is specified (*knew them to be thugs*). **c** (foll. by *from*) be able to distinguish (one from another) (*did not know him from Adam*). **4** *transitive* be subject to (*her joy knew no bounds*). **5** *transitive* have personal experience of (fear etc.). **6** *intransitive* have understanding or knowledge. **7** *transitive archaic* have sexual intercourse with. ● *noun* (in phr. **in the know**) *informal* well informed; having special knowledge. □ **before one knows it** with baffling speed. **be not to know 1** have no way of learning (*wasn't to know they'd arrive late*). **2** be not to be told (*she's not to know about the party*). **don't I know it!** *informal* an expression of rueful assent. **don't you know** *informal* or *jocular* an expression used for emphasis (*such a bore, don't you know*). **for all I know** so far as my knowledge extends. **have been known to** have occasionally in the past (*they have been known to turn up late*). **I knew it!** I was sure that this would happen. **I know what** I have a new idea, suggestion, etc. **know about** have information about. **know best** be or claim to be better informed etc. than others. **know better than** (foll. by *that,* or *to* + infin.) be wise, well informed, or well-mannered enough to avoid (specified behaviour etc.). **know by name 1** have heard the name of. **2** be able to give the name of. **know by sight** recognize the appearance (only) of. **know how** know the way to do something. **know of** be aware of; have heard of (*not that I know of*). **know one's own mind** be decisive, not vacillate. **know the ropes** (or **one's stuff**) be fully knowledgeable or experienced. **know a thing or two** be experienced or shrewd. **know what's what** have adequate knowledge of the world, life, etc. **know who's who** be aware of who or what each person is. **not know from** *N Amer.* not know anything about. **not know that . . .** *informal* be fairly sure that . . . not (*I don't know that I want to go*). **not know the meaning of the word** behave as if one does not know such an idea exists. **not know what hit one** be suddenly disconcerted, injured, killed, etc. **not want to know** refuse to take any notice of. **what do you know** (or **know about that?**) *informal* an expression of surprise. **you know** *informal* **1** an expression implying something generally known or known to the hearer (*you know, the restaurant on the corner*). **2** an expression used as a gap-filler in conversation. **you know something** (or **what?**) I am going to tell you something. **you never know** nothing in the future is certain. □ **know·able** *adjective* **know·er** *noun* [Old English (*ge*)*cnāwan*, related to CAN¹, KEN]

know-all *noun* esp. *Brit.* = KNOW-IT-ALL.

know-how *noun* **1** practical knowledge; technique, expertise. **2** natural skill or invention.

Consonants: b *but*   d *dog*   f *few*   g *get*   h *her*   j *yes*   k *cat*   l *leg*   m *man*   n *no*   p *pen*   r *red*   s *sit*

know·ing ● *noun* the state of being aware or informed of any thing. ● *adjective* **1** usu. *derogatory* cunning; sly. **2** showing knowledge or awareness; shrewd. □ **there is no knowing** no one can tell. □ **know·ing·ness** *noun*

know·ing·ly *adverb* **1** consciously; intentionally (*had never knowingly injured him*). **2** in a knowing manner (*smiled knowingly*).

know-it-all *noun* esp. *N Amer. informal* (often *attributive*) a person who seems or pretends to know everything.

know·ledge *noun* **1 a** (usu. foll. by *of*) awareness or familiarity gained by experience (of a person, fact, or thing) (*have no knowledge of that*). **b** a person's range of information (*is not within his knowledge*). **2 a** (usu. foll. by *of*) a theoretical or practical understanding of a subject, language, etc. (*has a good knowledge of Greek*). **b** the sum of what is known (*every branch of knowledge*). **3** *Philos.* true, justified belief; certain understanding, as opposed to opinion. **4** *archaic* sexual intercourse. □ **come to one's knowledge** become known to one. **to (the best of) my knowledge 1** so far as I know. **2** as I know for certain. [Middle English *knaulege*, with earlier *knawlechen* (v.) formed as KNOW + Old English ·*lǣcan* from *lāc* as in WEDLOCK]

know·ledge·able *adjective* (also **know·ledg·able**) well-informed; intelligent. □ **know·ledge·abil·ity** /-ˈbɪlti/ *noun* **know·ledge·ably** *adverb*

knowledge base *noun* **1** the underlying set of facts, assumptions, and inference rules which a computer system has available to solve a problem. **2** a store of information (in a database, from one's personal experience, etc.) available to draw upon.

knowledge-based *adjective* **1** (of an economy, industry, etc.) producing information rather than manufactured goods, natural resources, etc. **2** (of a computer system) incorporating a set of facts, assumptions, or inference rules derived from human knowledge.

knowledge engineering *noun* *Computing* the subdiscipline of artificial intelligence concerned with building expert systems. □ **knowledge engineer** *noun*

knowledge worker *noun* a person employed in a knowledge-based industry such as computer programming, research and development, etc.

known ● *verb* past participle of KNOW. ● *adjective* **1** publicly acknowledged (*a known thief*; *a known fact*). **2** *Math.* (of a quantity etc.) having a value that can be stated.

know-nothing *noun* **1** an ignorant person. **2** (also **Know-Nothing**) *US hist.* a member of a political party of the 1850s known as the Know-Nothing Party because its members denied its own existence and hence its policies, which were primarily opposition to immigrants, esp. Catholics. □ **know-nothing·ism** *noun* (in sense 2 of *noun*).

Knox, John (*c.*1514–72), Scottish Protestant reformer. Influenced by Calvin during a stay in Geneva, he returned to Scotland in 1559 and helped to overthrow the French regency and establish the Presbyterian Church of Scotland within a Scottish Protestant state.

Knox·ville a port on the Tennessee River, in E Tennessee; pop. (2000) 173,890. It was twice the state capital (1796–1812 and 1817–19).

Knt. *abbreviation* Knight.

knuckle ● *noun* **1** the bone at a finger joint, esp. that adjoining the hand. **2 a** a projection of the carpal or tarsal joint of a quadruped. **b** a cut of meat consisting of this with the adjoining parts, esp. of bacon or pork. **3** something shaped, angled, or protruding like a knuckle. ● *transitive verb* strike, press, or rub with the knuckles. □ **knuckle down** (often foll. by *to*) **1** apply oneself seriously (to a task etc.). **2** (also **knuckle under**) give in; submit. **rap a person's knuckles** see RAP[1]. □ **-knuckled** *adjective* (in combination). **knuck·ly** *adjective* [Middle English *knokel* from Middle Low German, Middle Dutch *knökel*, diminutive of *knoke* bone]

knuckle·ball *noun* (also **knuckler**) *Baseball* a slow pitch which moves erratically, made by gripping the ball with the knuckles or fingernails and throwing it with little spin. □ **knuckle·ball·er** *noun*

knuckle·bone *noun* **1** bone forming a knuckle. **2** the bone of a sheep or other animal corresponding to or resembling a knuckle. **3** a knuckle of meat. **4** (in *pl.*) **a** animal knucklebones used in the game of jacks. **b** the game of jacks.

knuckle-dragger *noun* *informal* an old-fashioned or reactionary person; a Neanderthal. □ **knuckle-dragging** *adjective*

knuckle-duster *noun* a metal guard worn over the knuckles in fighting, esp. to increase the effect of the blows.

knuckle·head *noun* *informal* a stupid or dull-witted person. □ **knuckle·headed** *adjective*

knuck·ler *noun* *N Amer. slang* a knuckleball.

knuckle sandwich *noun* *slang* a punch in the mouth.

knur /nɜr/ *noun* (also **knurr**) a hard excrescence on the trunk of a tree. [Middle English *knorre*, var. of KNAR]

knurl /nɜrl/ ● *noun* a small projecting knob, ridge, etc. ● *transitive verb* make knurls on the edge of (a coin etc.). □ **knurled** /nɜrld/ *adjective* [KNUR]

Knut see CANUTE.

KO /ˈkeɪoʊ/ ● *noun* a knockout in boxing etc. ● *transitive verb* (**KO's, KO'd KO'ing**) **1** knock out (an opponent) in boxing etc. **2** *informal* destroy, defeat. ● *abbreviation* knockout.

koa /ˈkoʊə/ *noun* **1** a Hawaiian tree, *Acacia koa*, which produces dark red wood. **2** this wood. [Hawaiian]

ko·ala /koʊˈɑːlə/ *noun* (in full **koala bear**) an Australian bearlike marsupial, *Phascolarctos cinereus*, having thick grey fur and feeding on eucalyptus leaves. [Aboriginal *kūl(l)a*]

koan /ˈkoʊɑːn/ *noun* a paradoxical anecdote or riddle without a solution, used in Zen Buddhism to demonstrate the inadequacy of logical reasoning and provoke enlightenment. [Japanese, = public matter (for thought)]

kob *noun* (*pl.* same) (in full **kob antelope**) a grazing antelope, *Kobus kob*, native to African savannah. [Wolof *kooba*]

Kobe /ˈkoʊbeɪ/ a port in central Japan, on the island of Honshu; pop. (est. 2002) 1,517,700. The city was severely damaged by an earthquake in Jan. 1995.

kobo /ˈkoʊboʊ/ *noun* (*pl.* same) a monetary unit of Nigeria, equal to one-hundredth of a naira.

ko·bold /ˈkoʊbəld/ *noun* (in Germanic mythology) a spirit who haunts houses or lives underground in mines or caves. [German]

Koch /kɒx/ **(Hein·rich Her·mann) Rob·ert** (1843–1910), German bacteriologist. He successfully identified and cultured the bacillus causing anthrax in cattle, identified the organisms causing tuberculosis and cholera, and studied typhoid fever, malaria, and other tropical diseases; he was awarded a Nobel Prize in 1905.

Köchel number /ˈkɜːʃəl/ *noun* *Music* a number given to each of Mozart's compositions in the complete catalogue of his works compiled by Köchel and his successors. [L. von *Köchel*, Austrian scientist d.1877]

Kodak moment *noun* *N Amer.* an event or picturesque scene worthy of a photograph. [*Kodak*, proprietary name of a brand of photographic film]

Ko·dály /koʊˈdaɪ/ **Zol·tán** (1882–1967), Hungarian composer and educator. Noted for his study of Hungarian folk music, he is best known for the choral work *Psalmus Hungaricus* (1923), the opera *Háry János* (1925–7), and the *Marosszék Dances* (1930); he also originated methods for teaching young children music.

Ko·di·ak /ˈkoʊdiˌak/ *noun* (in full **Kodiak bear**) a large variety of grizzly found in Alaska. [*Kodiak* Island, Alaska]

Koest·ler /ˈkɜːstlər/ **Ar·thur** (1905–83), Hungarian-born English novelist and essayist. His best-known novel, *Darkness at Noon* (1940), exposed the Stalinist purges of the 1930s; his later works include *The Sleepwalkers* (1959) and *The Ghost in the Machine* (1967).

K of C *abbreviation* KNIGHTS OF COLUMBUS.

Koff·man, Mor·ris ('Moe') (1928–2001), Canadian flutist and saxophonist. Koffman rose to the top of the Toronto jazz and studio worlds with a 1957 recording of his flute tune 'Swinging Shepherd Blues'. He made more than 20 recordings.

kofta *noun* (in Indian cooking) a spiced meatball (or fish or vegetable ball). [Urdu and Persian *koftah* pounded meat]

Ko·gawa /koʊˈɡɒwə/ **Joy Nozo·mi** (b.1935), Canadian poet and novelist, known for works inspired by her Japanese ancestry, including *The Splintered Moon* (1967), *Jericho Road* (1977), and the novel *Obasan* (1981), which deals with internment of Japanese Canadians during World War II. She has also written a children's book, *Naomi's Road* (1986).

Ko·hima /koʊˈhiːmə/ a city in the far northeast of India, capital of the state of Nagaland; pop. (2001) 78,600.

Kohl /ˈkoʊl/ **Hel·mut** (b.1930), German politician, chancellor of the Federal Republic of Germany 1982–98. As Chancellor he showed a strong commitment to NATO and to closer European union within the European Community; in 1990 he presided over the reunification of East and West Germany and was elected chancellor of the united country later the same year.

kohl /koʊl/ *noun* a black powder, usu. antimony sulphide or lead sulphide, used as eye makeup esp. in Eastern countries. [Arabic *kuhl*]

---

t top   v voice   w we   z zoo   ʃ she   ʒ vision   θ thin   ð this   ŋ ring   x loch   tʃ chip   dʒ jar   (*see over for vowels*)

kohl·rabi /koːlˈrabi, -robi/ *noun* (*pl.* **kohl·rab·ies**) a variety of cabbage with an edible turnip-like swollen stem. [German from Italian *cavoli rape* (pl.) from medieval Latin *caulorapa* (as COLE, RAPE²)]

koi /kɔi/ *noun* (also **koi carp**) (*pl.* same) a carp of a large ornamental variety bred in Japan. [Japanese]

koine /ˈkɔini/ *noun* **1** the common language of the Greeks from the close of the classical period to the Byzantine era. **2** a common language shared by various peoples; a lingua franca. [Greek *koinē* (*dialektos*) common (language)]

ko·kanee /ˈkoːkəˌni/ *noun* (*pl.* same) a non-migratory form of sockeye salmon found in lakes in western N America. [Shuswap]

Ko·kosch·ka /kəˈkɒʃkə/ **Oskar** (1886–1980), Austrian expressionist painter and writer, who is known for his portraits, such as *Portrait of Auguste Forel* (1910).

Kok·so·ak River /ˈkɒksəwak/ a river in N Quebec, 874 km long (together with its main branch, the Caniapiscau River), which rises over 600 km north of Tadoussac and flows generally northward through Kuujjuaq to empty into Ungava Bay. [Inuktitut, = big river]

kokum¹ /ˈkoːkəm/ *noun* (also **kookum**) /ˈkuːkəm/ (among Cree, Ojibwa, and some Metis peoples) a grandmother. [Algonquian]

kokum² /ˈkoːkəm/ *noun* (also **kokam**) an East Indian tree, *Garcinia indica*, related to the mangosteen, with round purple fruits used to impart an acidic flavour to foods, and the seeds of which yield an oil or butter used in soaps and skin preparations. [Hindi]

kola *var. of* COLA 1.

Kola Peninsula /ˈkoːlə/ a peninsula on the northwest coast of Russia, separating the White Sea from the Barents Sea. The port of Murmansk lies on its northern coast.

kol·bas·sa /koˈbɒˈsɒ, ˈkuˌbəˌsɒ, koːˈbasə/ *noun* a type of highly seasoned sausage, usu. containing garlic. [Russian *kolbasa* or Ukrainian *kovbasa* 'sausage']

Kol·ha·pur /ˌkoːlhəˈpʊr/ an industrial city in the state of Maharashtra, W India; pop. (2001) 485,200.

ko·lin·sky /kəˈlɪnski/ *noun* (*pl.* **-skies**) **1** the Siberian mink, *Mustela sibirica*, having a brown coat in winter. **2** the fur of this. [Russian *kolinskiĭ* from *Kola* in NW Russia]

kol·khoz /ˈkɒlkɒz, ˌkʌlkˈhɒz/ *noun* a collective farm in the former USSR. [Russian from *kollektivnoe khozyaĭstvo* collective farm]

Koll·witz /ˈkoːlwɪtz, ˈkɒlvɪtz/ **Käthe** (1867–1945), German graphic artist and sculptor. Much of her work was intended as a social protest against the working conditions of the urban poor, and she is known for her series of etchings *Weavers' Revolt* (1897–8) and *Peasants' War* (1902–8).

Koly·ma River /ˌkɒliˈmɒ/ a river of far eastern Siberia, which flows approximately 2 400 km (1,500 miles) northward to the Arctic Ocean.

koma·tik /ˈkɒmətɪk/ *noun* an Inuit sled consisting of two parallel wooden runners connected by wooden slats, usu. pulled by a dog team or snowmobile. [Inuktitut *qamutiq*]

kombu /ˈkɒmbuː/ *noun* a brown seaweed of the genus *Laminaria*, used in Japanese cooking, esp. as a base for stock. [Japanese]

Komi /ˈkoːmi/ an autonomous republic of NW Russia; pop. (est. 2002) 1,085,400; capital, Syktyvkar.

Ko·mo·do /kəˈmoːdoː/ a small island in Indonesia, in the Lesser Sunda Islands, situated between the islands of Sumbawa and Flores.

Komodo dragon /kəˈmoːdoː/ *noun* (also **Komodo monitor**) a large monitor lizard, *Varanus komodoensis*, native to the E Indies. [KOMODO]

Kom·so·mol /ˈkɒmsəˌmɒl/ *noun hist.* **1** an organization for Communist youth in the former Soviet Union. **2** a member of this. [Russian from *Kommunisticheskiĭ soyuz molodezhi* Communist League of Youth]

Kom·so·molsk /ˌkɒmsəˈmɒlsk/ (also **Komsomolsk-on-Amur** /-ˌɒnəˈmʊr/) an industrial city in the far east of Russia, on the Amur River; pop. (est. 2002) 286,600.

Kongo (*pl.* same or **Kongos**) ● *noun* **1** a member of a Bantu-speaking people inhabiting the region of the Congo River in west central Africa. **2** the language of this people. ● *adjective* of or relating to this people or their language. [Kikongo]

Kö·nigs·berg /ˈkɜːnɪɡzˌbɜːɡ/ the German name for KALININGRAD.

Konya /ˈkɒnjə/ a city in SW central Turkey; pop. (est. 2002) 695,500.

koo·doo *var. of* KUDU.

kook *noun* N Amer. slang a strange or eccentric person. [20th c.: prob. from CUCKOO]

kooka·burra /ˈkʊkəˌbʌrə/ *noun* any Australian kingfisher of the genus *Dacelo*, esp. *D. novaeguineae*, which makes a strange laughing cry. *Also called* LAUGHING JACKASS. [Wiradhuri *gugubarra*]

koo·kum *noun var. of* KOKUM¹.

kooky *adjective* (**kook·i·er**, **kook·i·est**) *slang* strange, eccentric. □ **kook·i·ly** *adverb* **kook·i·ness** *noun*

Kool-Aid *noun* N Amer. proprietary **1** a fruit-flavoured powder mixed with water and sugar to make a drink. **2** such a drink.

Koo·ning *see* DE KOONING.

Koo·te·nay (also **Koo·te·nai**) *var. of* KUTENAI.

Kootenay Lake /ˈkuːtəˌnaɪ/ a long, narrow lake in southeastern BC, situated east of Nelson, close to the border with Idaho. [as KOOTENAY RIVER]

Kootenay National Park a park reserve in the Rocky Mountains of southeastern BC, bordering Banff and Yoho national parks. It was established in 1920. [as KOOTENAY RIVER]

Kootenay River a river in southeastern BC, 780 km long, flowing first from the Rocky Mountains west of Banff to Montana, then turning northwestward to flow through Idaho and into BC again to Kootenay Lake, and finally flowing southwestward to join the Columbia River at Castlegar. [Blackfoot pronunciation of *Ktunaxa* (*see* KTUNAXA KINBASKET)]

Koo·ten·ays, the *noun* the region in the SE corner of BC including the two valleys of the Kootenay river.

ko·peck /ˈkoːpek/ *noun* (also **kopek**) a monetary unit of Russia and some other countries of the former USSR, equal to one-hundredth of a ruble. [Russian *kopeĭka* diminutive of *kop'ë* lance (from the figure of Ivan IV bearing a lance instead of a sword in 1535)]

kopje /ˈkɒpi/ *noun* (also **kop·pie**) South Africa a small hill. [Afrikaans *koppie*, Dutch *kopje*, diminutive of *kop* head]

kora /ˈkɔrə/ *noun* a stringed W African instrument resembling a harp. [from a W African language]

Koran *var. of* QURAN.

Korch·noi /ˈkɔrtʃnɔi/ **Vik·tor (Lvo·vich)** (b.1931), Russian chess player. He ranked third (*c.*1967–75) and then second (*c.*1975–80) in the world. In 1976 he left the USSR feeling that his career was in jeopardy, and played for Switzerland in the 1978 Olympics.

Kor·do·fan /ˌkɔrdəˈfɒn/ a region of central Sudan.

Korea /kəˈriə/ a region of E Asia forming a peninsula between the Sea of Japan and the Yellow Sea, now divided into the countries of North Korea and South Korea. After the Japanese surrender at the end of the Second World War, Korea was partitioned along the 38th parallel, the north being occupied by the Soviets and the south by the US (*see also* KOREAN WAR, NORTH KOREA, SOUTH KOREA).

Korea, Democratic People's Republic of see NORTH KOREA.

Korea, Republic of see SOUTH KOREA.

Ko·rean /kəˈriːən/ ● *noun* **1** a native or national of N or S Korea in SE Asia. **2** the language of Korea. ● *adjective* of or relating to Korea or its people or language.

Korean War the war of 1950–3 between North and South Korea, which began with the invasion of the South by North Korean forces. The United Nations voted to oppose the invasion, and UN troops, dominated by US forces, invaded and advanced to North Korea's border with China. China intervened on the side of the North, and for a time there appeared to be a danger of global conflict; peace negotiations began in 1951, and the war ended two years later with the restoration of previous boundaries.

korma *noun* a mildly-spiced Indian curry dish of meat or fish marinated in yogourt or curds. [Urdu *ḳormā* from Turkish *kavurma*]

Koror /kɒˈrɔr/ the capital of Palau; pop. (est. 2000) 13,303.

kor·una /ˈkɒrunə, kəˈruːnə/ *noun* the chief monetary unit of the Czech Republic and Slovakia, equal to 100 haleru. [Czech, = crown]

Korup /ˈkɒrəp/ a national park in W Cameroon, on the border with Nigeria, established in 1961 to protect a large area of rainforest.

Kor·zyb·ski /kɔrˈzɪbski/ **Al·fred (Hab·dank Skar·bek)** (1879–1950), Polish-born US philosopher and semanticist, who originated the system of linguistic philosophy known as general semantics; his works include *Science and Sanity: An Introduction to Non-Aristotelian Systems and General Semantics* (1933).

Kos /kɒs/ (also **Cos**) a Greek island in the SE Aegean, one of the Dodecanese group.

Kosci·usko /ˌkɒsiˈʌskoʊ/ **Thad·deus** (Polish name Tadeusz Kościuszko) (1746–1817), Polish soldier and patriot, who fought for the American colonists during the American Revolution (1775–83); he returned to Poland (1784) and led an unsuccessful nationalist uprising against Russian forces (1794).

Kosci·usko, Mount a mountain in SE Australia, in the Great

Vowels: a *cat* ɑ *arm* e *bed* ɜr *her* ɜː *deux* ə *ago* ɪ *sit* i *cosy* iː *feed* ɒ *hot* ɔ *pore* ɔː *no* ʌ *run* ʊ *put*

Dividing Range in SE New South Wales. Rising to a height of 2 228 m (7,234 ft.), it is the highest mountain in Australia. [Kosciusko]

ko·sher /ˈkoːʃər/ ● *adjective* **1** (of food or premises in which food is sold, cooked, or eaten) fulfilling the requirements of Jewish law. **2** *informal* correct; genuine; legitimate. ● *noun* **1** kosher food. **2** the Jewish law regarding food (*keep kosher*). ● *transitive verb* prepare (food) according to the Jewish law. [Hebrew *kāšēr* proper]

Koš·ice /ˈkɒʃɪtsə/ an industrial city in S Slovakia; pop. (2001) 236,093.

Kos·ovar /ˈkɒsəˌvɑr/ ● *noun* an esp. Albanian-speaking native or inhabitant of Kosovo. ● *adjective* of or relating to Kosovo or its inhabitants.

Kos·ovo /ˈkɒsəvoː/ an autonomous province of Serbia; pop. (est. 1997) 2,228,000; capital, Priština. It borders on Albania, and the majority of the people are of Albanian descent.

Kos·suth /ˈkɒsuːθ, ˈkɒʃuːt/ **Lajos** (1802–94), Hungarian leader and patriot. Long an opponent of Hapsburg domination of Hungary, he led the 1848 insurrection and was appointed governor of the country during the brief period of independence which followed (1849).

Kos·tro·ma /ˌkɒstrəˈmɒ/ an industrial city in European Russia, situated on the Volga River to the northwest of Nizhni Novgorod; pop. (est. 2002) 288,900.

Ko·sy·gin /kəˈsiːgɪn/ **Alek·sei Niko·lay·evich** (1904–80), Soviet leader, premier of the USSR 1964–80. He succeeded Khrushchev as premier (1964), but devoted most of his attention to internal economic affairs, being gradually eased out of the leadership by Brezhnev; he resigned owing to ill health in 1980.

Kota /ˈkoːtə/ an industrial city in Rajasthan state, in NW India, on the Chambal River; pop. (2001) 695,900.

Kota Ba·haru /ˌkoːtə bəˈhɑru/ a city in Malaysia, on the east coast of the Malay Peninsula, the capital of the state of Kelantan; pop. (2000) 252,714.

Kota Kina·balu /ˌkoːtə ˌkɪnəbəˈluː/ a port in Malaysia, on the north coast of Borneo, capital of the state of Sabah; pop. (2000) 305,382.

Kotch·eff /ˈkɒtʃəf/ **Wil·liam** ('Ted') (b.1931), Canadian film and television director. He directed two films based on the novels of Mordecai Richler, *The Apprenticeship of Duddy Kravitz* (1974) and *Joshua Then and Now* (1985), as well as many other films and television shows.

koto /ˈkoːtoː/ *noun* (pl. **kotos**) a Japanese musical instrument with 13 long esp. silk strings. [Japanese]

Kou·chi·bou·guac National Park /ˈkuːʃɪbuːˌgwak/ a park reserve on the eastern coast of New Brunswick, bordering the Northumberland Strait. [Mi'kmaq *pijeboogwek* river of the long tideway]

kou·miss /ˈkuːmɪs/ *noun* (also **kumiss, kumis**) a fermented liquor prepared from esp. mare's milk, used by Asian nomads and medicinally. [Tartar *kumiz*]

kou·prey /ˈkuːpreɪ/ *noun* a rare grey ox, *Bos sauveli*, native to forests in Indochina. [Cambodian]

Kou·rou /kuːˈruː/ a town on the north coast of French Guiana; pop. (1999) 19,200. Nearby is a satellite-launching station of the European Space Agency, established in 1967.

Kow·loon /kauˈluːn/ a densely populated peninsula on the southeast coast of China, forming part of Hong Kong. It is separated from Hong Kong Island by Victoria Harbour.

kow·tow ● *noun hist.* the Chinese custom of kneeling and touching the ground with the forehead in worship or submission. ● *intransitive verb* **1** (usu. foll. by *to*) act obsequiously. **2** *hist.* perform the kowtow. [Chinese *ketou* from *ke* knock + *tou* head]

KP *noun* esp. *US Military informal* **1** enlisted men detailed to help the cooks. **2** kitchen duty. [abbreviation of *kitchen police*]

kPa *abbreviation* kilopascal(s).

k.p.h. *abbreviation* kilometres per hour.

Kr *symbol Chem.* the element krypton.

Kra, Isthmus of the narrowest part of the Malay Peninsula, forming part of S Thailand.

kraal *South Africa* ● *noun* **1** a village of huts enclosed by a fence. **2** an enclosure for cattle or sheep. ● *transitive verb* enclose (animals) in a kraal or stockade. [Afrikaans from Portuguese *corral*]

Kraatz, Victor, *see* BOURNE AND KRAATZ.

Krafft-Ebing /kraftˈebɪŋ/ **Rich·ard, Baron von** (1840–1902), German physician and psychologist. He is best known for establishing the relationship between syphilis and general paralysis, and for his *Psychopathia Sexualis* (1886), which pioneered the systematic study of aberrant sexual behaviour.

kraft *noun* (in full **kraft paper**) a kind of strong smooth brown wrapping paper. [German from Swedish, = strength]

Kragu·jevac /ˈkraɡujəˌvats/ a city in central Serbia; pop. (est. 2002) 177,500. It was the capital of Serbia from 1818 to 1839.

krai /kraɪ/ *noun* (also **kray**) an administrative territory of Russia. [Russian, = edge, border]

krait /kraɪt/ *noun* any venomous snake of the genus *Bungarus* of E Asia. [Hindi *karait*]

Kraka·toa /ˌkrakəˈtoːə/ a small volcanic island in Indonesia, lying between Java and Sumatra, scene of a great eruption in 1883 which destroyed most of the island.

krak·en /ˈkrakən/ *noun* a large mythical sea monster said to appear off the coast of Norway. [Norwegian]

Krall /krɒl/ **Diana** (b.1964), Canadian jazz singer and pianist. Her many recordings include *When I Look in Your Eyes* (1999), which won Grammy and Juno awards.

Kra·ma·torsk /krаməˈtɔrsk/ a city in E Ukraine, north of Donetsk; pop. (est. 1998) 190,800.

Kras·no·dar /ˌkrasnəˈdɑr/ **1** a krai in the N Caucasus, on the Black Sea in S Russia; pop. (est. 2000) 5,067,000. **2** its capital, a port on the lower Kuban River; pop. (est. 2002) 643,000. It was known until 1922 as Yekaterinodar (Ekaterinodar).

Kras·no·yarsk /ˌkrasnəˈjɑrsk/ **1** a krai in central Siberian Russia; pop. (est. 2000) 2,978,000. **2** its capital, a port on the Yenisei River; pop. (est. 2002) 870,000.

Kraut *noun slang offensive* a German. [shortening of SAUERKRAUT]

Kraut·rock *noun* an experimental style of rock music associated with German groups of the 1970s, characterized by improvisation and strong, hypnotic rhythms. □ **Kraut·rock·er** *noun*

Krav Maga /ˌkrɒv məˈɡɒ/ *noun* a form of self-defence and physical training, first developed by the Israeli army in the 1940s, based on the use of reflexive responses to threatening situations. [Hebrew, = 'contact combat']

Krebs, Sir Hans Adolf (1900–81), German-born English biochemist. He discovered the cyclical series of biochemical reactions by which organisms break down food using oxygen; he shared a Nobel Prize for this in 1953.

Kre·feld /ˈkreifelt/ an industrial town and port on the Rhine in western Germany, in North Rhine-Westphalia; pop. (est. 2002) 238,200.

Kreis·ler /ˈkraɪslər/ **Fritz** (1875–1962), Austrian-born US violinist and composer. He was a noted interpreter of the standard classics, and in 1910 gave the first performance of Elgar's violin concerto, which was dedicated to him.

Krem·en·chuk /ˌkremənˈtʃuk/ an industrial city in east central Ukraine, on the Dnieper River; pop. (est. 2001) 234,000.

krem·lin *noun* **1** a citadel within a Russian town. **2** (**the Kremlin**) **a** the citadel in Moscow. **b** the Russian or (formerly) USSR government housed within it. [French, from Russian *Kreml'*, of Tartar origin]

Krem·lin·ol·ogy *noun* the study and analysis of Soviet or Russian policies. □ **Krem·lin·ol·o·gist** *noun*

krep·lach /ˈkreplax/ *plural noun* triangular dumplings of noodle dough filled with chopped meat or cheese and served with soup. [Yiddish *kreplech* pl. of *krepel* from dial. German *Kräppel* 'fritter']

Krieg·hoff /ˈkriːɡhɒf/ **Cor·nel·ius David** (1815–1872), Dutch-born Canadian painter. He painted more than 2,000 canvases, mostly depicting habitant and Aboriginal life in 19th c. Quebec, many of which contain visible narratives. One of his most famous works is *Merrymaking* (1860), which portrays a winter gathering at a country inn.

krieg·spiel /ˈkriːɡspiːl/ *noun* **1** a war game in which blocks representing armies etc. are moved about on maps. **2** a form of chess with an umpire, in which each player has only limited information about the opponent's moves. [German from *Krieg* war + *Spiel* game]

Kriem·hild /ˈkriːmhɪlt/ (also **Kriem·hilde** /ˈkriːmˌhɪldə/) (in the *Nibelungenlied*) the wife of Siegfried; she corresponds to Gudrun in Scandinavian mythology.

krill *noun* **1** a small shrimp-like planktonic crustacean of the order Euphausiacea, important as food for fish, and for some whales and seals. **2** these collectively. [Norwegian *kril* tiny fish]

krim·mer *noun* a grey or black fur obtained from the wool of young Crimean lambs. [German from *Krim* Crimea]

kris /kriːs/ *noun* a Malay or Indonesian dagger with a wavy blade. [ultimately from Malay *k(i)rīs*]

Krish·na /ˈkrɪʃnə/ *Hinduism* one of the most popular gods, the eighth

---

uː m**oo**d aɪ m**y** əi p**i**pe au br**ow**n ʌu h**ou**se ei d**ay** ɔi b**oy** ã fr**an**glais ã C**an**adien ɔ̃ Br**ay**on *(see over for consonants)*

and most important avatar or incarnation of Vishnu. He is worshipped in several forms: as the child god whose miracles and pranks are extolled in the Puranas; as the divine cowherd whose erotic exploits, esp. with his favourite, Radha, have produced both romantic and religious literature; and as the divine charioteer who preaches to Arjuna on the battlefield in the Bhagavad-Gita. [Sanskrit, = black]

Krish·na·ism /ˈkrɪʃnəˌɪzəm/ *noun Hinduism* the worship of Krishna as an incarnation of Vishnu.

Krishna River a river which rises in the Western Ghats of S India and flows generally eastward for 1 288 km (805 miles) to the Bay of Bengal.

Kris Krin·gle /krɪs ˈkrɪŋɡəl/ *N Amer.* **1** = SANTA CLAUS. **2** a Christmas party at which each person brings a gift (usu. not exceeding a specified value) and receives another, sometimes anonymously, and sometimes involving each person drawing the name of another as the gift recipient. [prob. alteration of German *Christkindl* 'Christmas present', 'Christ child']

Kris·tall·nacht /ˈkrɪstəlˌnɒxt/ the occasion of concerted violence by Nazis throughout Germany and Austria against Jews and their property on the night of 9–10 Nov. 1938, marking an escalation of the persecution of Jews in the Third Reich. [German, lit. 'night of crystal' or 'of (broken) glass', in reference to the broken glass produced by the smashing of store windows]

Kris·ti·ania see CHRISTIANIA.

Kroetsch /krɔːtʃ/ **Rob·ert** (b.1927), Canadian writer, editor and teacher. His novels, including *The Studhorse Man* (1969), which won a Governor General's Award, and *Badlands* (1975), are mostly set in Alberta. He has also published several volumes of poetry, and writes extensively on contemporary literary theory.

krona /ˈkrɔːnə/ *noun* **1** (*pl.* **kro·nor** /ˈkrɔːnɔːr/) the chief monetary unit of Sweden. **2** (*pl.* **kro·nur** /ˈkrɔːnɜːr/) the chief monetary unit of Iceland. [Swedish & Icelandic, = CROWN]

krone /ˈkrɔːnə/ *noun* (*pl.* **kro·ner** /ˈkrɔːnɜːr/) the chief monetary unit of Denmark and of Norway, equal to one hundred ore. [Danish & Norwegian, = CROWN]

Kro·nos = CRONUS.

Kron·stadt /ˈkrɔːnʃtat/ the German name for BRAŞOV.

kroon /kruːn/ *noun* the basic monetary unit of Estonia, equal to 100 sents. [Estonian, = 'crown']

Kro·pot·kin /krəˈpɒtkɪn/ **Prince Peter** (Russian name Pyotr Alexeyevich) (1842–1921), Russian anarchist. He became an influential exponent of anarchism through works such as *Modern Science and Anarchism* (1903).

Kru (also **Kroo**) ● *noun* (*pl.* same) **1** a member of a seafaring people on the coast of Liberia. **2** their language. ● *adjective* of or concerning the Kru, their language, or the group of languages including it. [W African]

Kru Coast a section of the coast of Liberia to the northwest of Cape Palmas, inhabited by the Kru people.

Kru·ger /ˈkruːɡər/ **Ste·phan·us Jo·han·nes Paul·us** (known as 'Oom Paul') (1825–1904), South African soldier. He led the Afrikaners to victory in the First Boer War (1881) and served as president of the Transvaal (1883–99); his refusal to allow equal rights to non-Boer immigrants was one of the causes of the Second Boer War, during which Kruger was forced to flee the country.

Kruger National Park a national park in South Africa, in Eastern Transvaal on the Mozambique border. Designated a national park in 1926, it was originally a game reserve. [KRUGER]

kru·ger·rand /ˈkruːɡəˌrand, -ˌrɑnt/ *noun* (also **Krugerrand**) a South African gold coin depicting President Kruger. [KRUGER + RAND¹]

krumm·holz /ˈkrʌmhɒlts/ *noun Bot.* a region of dwarfed, crooked trees found in alpine regions, esp. just below the timberline. [German, 'crooked wood']

Krupp /krʊp/ **Al·fred** (1812–87), German arms manufacturer. The Krupp works in Essen, originally an iron foundry, grew to become the largest arms manufacturer in Europe and played a pre-eminent part in German arms production through to the end of the Second World War.

kryp·ton /ˈkrɪptɒn/ *noun Chem.* an inert gaseous element of the noble gas group, forming a small portion of the earth's atmosphere and used in fluorescent lamps etc. Symbol: **Kr**; at. no.: 36. [Greek *krupton* hidden, neuter adj. from *kruptō* hide]

kryp·ton·ite *noun* a mythical mineral capable of defeating even the strongest man. [a substance in the *Superman* comic book series capable of incapacitating the otherwise invincible superhero]

Kryvy Rih /krɪˌviː ˈrɪx/ an industrial city in S Ukraine, at the centre of an iron-ore mining region; pop. (est. 2001) 667,000.

KS *abbreviation* **1** Kansas (in official postal use). **2** KAPOSI'S SARCOMA.

Kshat·riya /ˈkʃatriə, ˈkʃɒ-/ *noun* a member of the second of the four great Hindu castes, the military caste. [Sanskrit from *kshatra* rule]

KT *abbreviation* **1** Knight Templar. **2** (in the UK) Knight of the Order of the Thistle.

Kt. *abbreviation* Knight.

kt. *abbreviation* **1** knot. **2** karat. **3** kiloton.

Ktu·naxa Kin·bas·ket /ktuːˈnɒxɒ ˈkɪnˌbasket/ ● *noun* **1** a member of an Aboriginal people living in southeastern BC and northeastern Washington. **2** the language of this people, a language isolate. ● *adjective* of or relating to this people or their culture or language. *Also called* KUTENAI. [Ktunaxa, *ktunaxa* (self-designation) + name of Chief *Kinbaskit* of the Secwepemc Nation, whose clan joined with the Ktunaxa in the 19th c.]

Kuala Lum·pur /ˌkwɒlə ˈlʊmpʊr/ the capital of Malaysia, in the southwest of the Malay Peninsula; pop. (2000) 1,297,526. It is a major commercial centre in the middle of a rubber-growing and tin-mining region.

Kuala Treng·ganu /ˌkwɒlə trəŋˈɡanuː/ (also **Kuala Terengganu**) the capital of the state of Trengganu in Malaysia, on the east coast of the Malay Peninsula at the mouth of the Trengganu River; pop. (2000) 255,109.

Kuan·tan /kwɒnˈtɒn/ the capital of the state of Pahang in Malaysia, on the east coast of the Malay Peninsula; pop. (2000) 298,395.

Kuan Yin /kwɒn ˈjɪn/ (in Chinese Buddhism) the goddess of compassion.

ku·basa /kuːˈbɒsɒ, ˈkuːbəsɒ/ *noun Cdn* a garlic sausage of Ukrainian origin. [corruption of Ukrainian *kovbasa*, 'sausage']

kubie /ˈkuːbiː/ *noun Cdn* (*Alta.*) kubasa, esp. when eaten on a hot dog bun. [abbreviation of KUBASA]

kubie burger *noun Cdn* (*Alta.*) kubasa pressed into a patty and eaten on a bun, like a hamburger.

Kub·lai Khan /ˌkuːblai ˈkɒn/ (1216–94), Mongol emperor of China, grandson of Genghis Khan. Between 1252 and 1259 he conquered S China with his brother Mangu (then Mongol Khan); on Mangu's death (1259) he was elected Khan himself, completing the conquest of China and founding the Yuan dynasty.

Kub·rick /ˈkuːbrɪk/ **Stan·ley** (1928–99), US film director, producer, and writer, whose films include the black comedy *Dr. Strangelove* (1964), the science fiction film *2001: A Space Odyssey* (1968), the violent and futuristic *A Clockwork Orange* (1971), the horror film *The Shining* (1980), and *Full Metal Jacket* (1987), about the Vietnam War. □ **Kub·rick·ian** *adjective*

ku·chen /ˈkuːxən/ *noun* a cake topped with sliced fruit and sprinkled with sugar before baking. [German 'cake']

Ku·ching /ˈkuːtʃɪŋ/ a port in Malaysia, on the Sarawak River near the northwest coast of Borneo, capital of the state of Sarawak; pop. (2000) 423,873.

Ku·del·ka /kəˈdelkə/ **James** (b.1955), Canadian choreographer and artistic director. He choreographed throughout his career as a dancer, first with the National Ballet of Canada (1972–81) and then with Les Grands Ballets Canadiens (1981–84). He has been artistic director of the National Ballet of Canada since 1996. His ballets, which combine classical and contemporary idioms, include a full-length *Nutcracker* (1995), *Swan Lake* (1999), and *The Four Seasons* (1997).

kud·lik /ˈkuːdlɪk/ *noun* an Inuit soapstone seal oil lamp, providing both light and heat. [Inuktitut *qulliq*]

kudos /ˈkuːdɒz, -dɒs/ *noun informal* **1** *N Amer.* (often treated as *pl.*) expressions of praise. **2** glory; renown. [Greek] ¶ The plural use of *kudos* has been criticized on the grounds that the Greek word is singular, but it is well established in North American English.

kudu /ˈkuːduː/ *noun* (also **koodoo**) either of two African antelopes, *Tragelaphus strepsiceros* or *T. imberbis*, with white stripes and corkscrew-shaped ridged horns. [Xhosa-Kaffir *iqudu*]

kudzu /ˈkʌdzuː/ *noun* (in full **kudzu vine**) a quick-growing climbing plant, *Pueraria thunbergiana*, with reddish-purple flowers. [Japanese *kuzu*]

Kuer·ti /ˈkwertiː/ **Anton Emil** (b.1938), Austrian-born Canadian pianist, composer, and teacher. He has toured 39 countries and made many recordings. He has a vast repertoire, but is perhaps best known for his performances of Beethoven.

Kufic /ˈkuːfɪk/ (also **Cufic**) ● *noun* an early angular form of the Arabic alphabet found chiefly in decorative inscriptions. ● *adjective* of or in this type of script. [*Cufa*, a city south of Baghdad in Iraq]

Ku·gaar·uk /ˈkuːˈɡɑrʌk/ a hamlet, formerly called Pelly Bay, on the southeast corner of Pelly Bay, NU; pop. (2001) 605. [Inuktitut]

kugel /ˈkuːɡəl/ *noun* a baked sweet or savoury dish of potatoes or noodles mixed with eggs, cottage cheese, etc. and served as a separate course or as a side dish. [Yiddish 'ball' from Middle High German *kugel(e)* 'ball, globe']

Ku·gluk·tuk /kuːˈɡluːktʌk/ a hamlet on the northern coast of mainland Nunavut, situated at the mouth of the Coppermine River at the Coronation Gulf, about 600 km (by air) north of Yellowknife; formerly known as Coppermine; pop. (2001) 1,212. [Inuktitut, = place of rapids, prob. with reference to nearby Bloody Falls]

Kui·by·shev /ˈkwiːbəˌʃef/ the former name (1935–1991) for SAMARA.

Kuiper belt /ˈkaipər/ *noun Astronomy* a zone stretching outward from the orbit of Neptune containing many asteroids. [G. *Kuiper*, Dutch-born US astronomer d.1973, who postulated its existence]

Ku Klux Klan *noun* a secret society of white people in the United States, originally formed in the southern states after the Civil War and revived in 1915 to harass and intimidate Blacks and other ethnic or religious minorities through violence, terrorism, and murder. □ **Ku Klux·er** *noun* **Ku Klux Klans·man** *noun* (*pl.* **-men**). [perhaps from Greek *kuklos* circle + CLAN]

kukri /ˈkʊkri/ *noun* (*pl.* **kuk·ris**) a curved knife broadening towards the point, used by Gurkhas. [Hindi *kukrī*]

kulak /ˈkuːlak/ *noun hist.* a peasant in Russia wealthy enough to own a farm, hire labour, and engage in moneylending. When kulaks resisted Stalin's forced collectivization of agriculture from 1929, they were destroyed as a class, with millions being arrested, sent to Siberia, or killed. [Russian, = fist, tight-fisted person]

kulfi /ˈkʊlfi/ *noun* an East Indian ice-cream-like dessert flavoured with nuts, esp. pistachios or almonds, and mangoes, etc. [Hindi/Urdu]

Kul·tur /kʊlˈtʊr/ *noun* esp. *derogatory* German civilization and culture seen as racist, authoritarian, and militaristic. [German from Latin *cultura* CULTURE]

Kultur·kampf /kʊlˈtʊrkampf/ *noun* the conflict between the German government (headed by Bismarck) and the papacy for the control of schools and Church appointments (1872–87). Bismarck passed legislation in an attempt to break the authority and influence of the Catholic Church in Germany, but he was later forced to repeal most of it. [German (as KULTUR, *Kampf* struggle)]

Kum see QOM.

Kuma·moto /ˌkuːməˈmoːtoː/ a city in S Japan, on the west coast of Kyushu island; pop. (est. 2002) 666,000.

Ku·masi /kuːˈmasi/ a city in S Ghana; pop. (est. 2002) 627,600. It is the capital of the Ashanti region.

kumis (also **ku·miss**) *var. of* KOUMISS.

küm·mel /ˈkʊməl/ *noun* (also **kum·mel**) a sweet liqueur flavoured with caraway and cumin seeds. [German (as CUMIN)]

kum·quat /ˈkʌmkwɒt/ *noun* **1** an orange-like fruit with a sweet rind and acid pulp, used in preserves. **2** any shrub or small tree of the genus *Fortunella* yielding this. [Cantonese var. of Mandarin *kin kü* golden orange]

Kun /ˈkuːn/ **Béla** (1886–*c*.1939), Hungarian Communist leader, president of the Hungarian Soviet Republic 1919. With the collapse of the republic (1919) he fled abroad, eventually settled in Russia, and died in one of Stalin's purges.

Kuna /ˈkuːnə/ (*pl.* same or **Kunas**) ● *noun* **1** a member of an Indian people of the isthmus of Panama. **2** the language of this people. ● *adjective* of or pertaining to the Kuna or their language. [Kuna]

kuna /ˈkuːnə/ *noun* (*pl.* **kune** /ˈkuːnei/) the basic monetary unit of Croatia, equal to 100 lipa. [Serbo-Croat, literally 'marten' (the fur of the marten was formerly a medium of exchange)]

kun·da·lini /ˈkuːndəˌlini/ *noun* **1** (in yoga) latent female energy believed to lie coiled at the base of the spine. **2** (in full **kundalini yoga**) a type of meditation which aims to direct and release this energy. [Sanskrit, *kuṇḍalinī*, lit. 'snake']

Kun·dera /ˈkʊndərə/ **Milan** (b.1929), Czech novelist. His books were proscribed in Czechoslovakia following the Soviet military invasion (1968) and he emigrated to France (1975); his novels include *The Book of Laughter and Forgetting* (1979), *The Unbearable Lightness of Being* (1984), and *Immortality* (1991).

Kung /kʊŋ/ ● *noun* (*pl.* same) **1** a member of a San (Bushman) people of the Kalahari Desert in southern Africa, maintaining to some extent a nomadic way of life dependent on hunting and gathering. **2** the Khoisan language of the Kung. ● *adjective* of or relating to the Kung or their language.

Küng /ˈkʊŋ/ **Hans** (b.1928), Swiss Roman Catholic theologian, who was banned from teaching as a Catholic theologian (1979) for his questioning of traditional Church doctrines such as papal infallibility.

kung fu /kʌŋ ˈfuː/ *noun* the Chinese form of unarmed combat similar to karate. [Chinese *gongfu* from *gong* merit + *fu* master]

K'ung Fu-tzu /kʊŋ fuː dzuː/ see CONFUCIUS.

Kun·lun Shan /ˌkʊnlʊn ˈʃɒn/ a range of mountains in W China, on the northern edge of the Tibetan plateau, extending eastward for over 1 600 km (1,000 miles) from the Pamir Mountains. Its highest peak is Muztag, which rises to 7 723 m (25,338 ft.).

Kun·ming /kʊnˈmɪŋ/ a city in SW China, capital of Yunnan province; pop. (est. 2002) 1,938,900.

Kuo·min·tang /ˌkwoːmɪnˈtaŋ/ (also **Guomindang**) a nationalist party founded in China under Sun Yat-sen in 1912, which held power from 1928 until the Communist Party took power in Oct. 1949. The Kuomintang subsequently formed the central administration of Taiwan. [Chinese, = national people's party]

Kuo·pio /kʊˈoːpiˌoː/ a city in S Finland, capital of a province of the same name; pop. (2001) 87,347.

kur·cha·tov·ium /ˌkɜrtʃəˈtoːviəm/ *noun Chem. hist.* a name proposed in the former USSR for the artificial radioactive element of atomic number 104, now called RUTHERFORDIUM. [I. V. *Kurchatov*, Russian physicist d.1960]

Kurd *noun* a member of a mainly pastoral Muslim people living chiefly in eastern Turkey, northern Iraq, western Iran, and eastern Syria. [Kurdish]

Kurd·ish ● *adjective* of or relating to the Kurds or their language. ● *noun* the Iranian language of the Kurds.

Kurdi·stan an extensive plateau and mountainous region in the Middle East, south of the Caucasus, including large parts of E Turkey, N Iraq, W Iran, E Syria, Armenia, and Azerbaijan. For centuries it has been the traditional home of the Kurdish people, but the creation of a separate state of Kurdistan is opposed by Iraq, Iran, Syria, and Turkey.

Kure /kuːˈrei/ a city in S Japan, on the south coast of the island of Honshu, near Hiroshima; pop. (est. 2002) 213,700.

Kur·elek /ˈkɜrələk/ **Wil·liam** (1927–1977), Canadian painter, writer and evangelist. His paintings, influenced by Bosch and Brueghel, combine images from his prairie childhood, his Ukrainian heritage, and his Catholic faith. His religious works include a series of 160 paintings depicting the Passion according to St. Matthew. He also collected several of his paintings, together with simple texts, into children's books such as *A Prairie Boy's Winter* (1973), *A Prairie Boy's Summer* (1975), and *A Northern Nativity* (1976).

Kur·gan /kʊrˈɡan/ a city in central Russia, commercial centre for an agricultural region; pop. (est. 2002) 364,400.

Kurile Islands /kʊˈriːl/ (also **Kuril Islands** or **Kurils**) a chain of 56 islands, belonging to Russia, between the Sea of Okhotsk and the N Pacific, stretching from the southern tip of the Kamchatka peninsula to the northeast corner of the Japanese island of Hokkaido. They are a continuing source of dispute between Japan and Russia.

Kuro·sawa /ˌkʊrəˈsɒwə/ **Akira** (1910–98), Japanese film director, who gained international acclaim for blending the traditional with the modern in his films; these include *Rashomon* (1950), *Kagemusha* (1980), *Ran* (1985), a Japanese version of Shakespeare's *King Lear*, and *Rhapsody in August* (1991).

Kursk /kʊrsk/ an industrial city in SW Russia; pop. (est. 2002) 443,200. It was the scene of an important Soviet victory in the Second World War.

kur·ta /ˈkɜrtə/ *noun* a loose shirt or tunic worn by esp. Hindu men and women. [Hindustani]

kurt·o·sis /kɜrˈtoːsɪs/ *noun Statistics* the sharpness of the peak of a frequency-distribution curve. [modern Latin from Greek *kurtōsis* bulging, from *kurtos* convex]

kur·ush /kəˈruːʃ/ *noun* (*pl.* same) a monetary unit of Turkey, equal to one-hundredth of a lira. [Turkish *kuruş*]

Kush *var. of* CUSH.

Kuta·isi /ˌkʊtəˈiːsi/ an industrial city in the central Republic of Georgia; pop. (est. 2002) 267,300. One of the oldest cities in Transcaucasia, it has been the capital of various kingdoms, including Colchis and Abkhazia.

Kutch, Gulf of /kʌtʃ, kʊtʃ/ an inlet of the Arabian Sea on the west coast of India.

Kutch, Rann of /kʌtʃ, kʊtʃ, ran/ a vast salt marsh on the eastern shores of the Arabian Sea, on the frontier between India and Pakistan. Most of it lies in the state of Gujarat in NW India, the remainder in the province of Sind in SE Pakistan.

Kutch·in /kuːˈtʃɪn/ noun = GWICH'IN.

Ku·te·nai /ˈkuːtənˌei/ noun & adjective (also **Kootenay, Kootenai**) = KTUNAXA KINBASKET. [corruption of KTUNAXA]

Kuuj·ju·aq /ˈkuːjuːaq/ a village in N Quebec, situated on the Koksoak River, about 50 km upriver from its mouth where it joins Ungava Bay; pop. (2001) 1,932. [contemporary spelling of Koksoak: see KOKSOAK RIVER]

Ku·wait /kʊˈweit/ a country on the northwest coast of the Persian Gulf; pop. (est. 2002) 2,111,561; capital, Kuwait City. One of the world's leading oil-producing countries, Kuwait was invaded by Iraq in Aug. 1990, the occupying forces being expelled in the Gulf War of Jan.–Feb. 1991. □ **Ku·waiti** adjective & noun

Ku·wait City a port on the Persian Gulf, the capital city of Kuwait; pop. (est. 2002) 32,100.

Kuz·nets /ˈkuznɪtz/ **Simon (Smith)** (1901–85), Russian-born US economist and statistician, who was awarded the 1971 Nobel Prize for economics for his research on social change and economic growth.

Kuz·nets Basin /kuzˈnjets/ (also **Kuz·netsk** /-ˈnjetsk/ or **Kuzbas** /-ˈbas/) an industrial region of S Russia, situated in the valley of the Tom River, between Tomsk and Novokuznetsk. The region is rich in iron and coal deposits.

kV abbreviation kilovolt(s).

kvass /kvas/ noun (esp. in Russia) a fermented beverage, low in alcohol, made from rye flour or bread with malt. [Russian kvas]

kvell /kvel/ intransitive verb informal be extremely pleased or bursting with pride. [Yiddish kveln, 'be delighted']

kvetch /kvetʃ/ esp. N Amer. slang ● transitive verb complain and whine, esp. continually. ● noun (also **kvetch·er** /kvetʃər/) a person who complains a great deal. □ **kvetch·ing** noun **kvetchy** adjective [Yiddish kvetsh from Yiddish verb kvetshn from German Quetsche 'crusher, presser', quetschen 'crush, press']

K-W abbreviation Kitchener-Waterloo.

kW abbreviation kilowatt(s).

Kwa /kwɒ/ ● noun **1** the group of related languages, spoken from Ivory Coast to Nigeria, which includes Ibo and Yoruba. **2** (pl. same) a member of a Kwa-speaking people. ● adjective of or relating to this group of languages. [Kwa]

kwa·cha /ˈkwɒtʃə/ noun the chief monetary unit of Zambia and Malawi, equal to 100 ngwee in Zambia and 100 tambala in Malawi. [Bantu = dawn]

Kwa·giulth /kwɒˈgiːʊlθ/ ● noun (pl. same) **1** a member of an Aboriginal people living in parts of coastal BC and northern Vancouver Island. Also called KWAKIUTL. **2** the Kwakwala language of this people. ● adjective of or relating to this people or their culture or language. [Kwagiulth Kʷágułɬ]

Kwa·ki·utl /ˌkwɒkiːˈuːtəl/ noun & adjective (pl. same) = KWAGIULTH. [corruption of KWAGIULTH]

Kwa·kwaka'wakw /kwɒˈkwɒkiˌwɒk/ ● noun (pl. same) a member of an Aboriginal people living in southwestern BC. ● adjective of or relating to this people. [Kwakwala, = 'those who speak Kwakwala']

Kwa·kwala /kwɒˈkwɒlə/ noun the Wakashan language of the Kwakwaka'wakw and Kwagiulth. [Kwakwala]

Kwa·Nde·bele /ˌkwɒəndəˈbiːli/ a former homeland established in South Africa for the Ndebele people, now part of the province of Mpumalanga (see also HOMELAND 2).

Kwang·chow see GUANGZHOU.

Kwang·ju /kwaŋˈdʒuː/ a city in southwestern S Korea; pop. (est. 2002) 1,371,000.

Kwang·si Chuang see GUANGXI ZHUANG.

Kwang·tung see GUANGDONG.

Kwan·za /ˈkwɒnzə/ noun (also **Kwan·zaa**) N Amer. a festival observed from 26 Dec. to 1 Jan. in celebration of black cultural heritage. [Swahili matunda ya kwanza 'first fruits']

kwan·za /ˈkwɒnzə/ noun (pl. same or **kwan·zas**) the chief monetary unit of Angola. [prob. from the name of the Kwanza (now Cuanza) River, in Angola]

kwa·shi·or·kor /ˌkwɒʃiˈɔrkɔr/ noun a form of malnutrition caused by a severe dietary protein deficiency, esp. in young children in the tropics. [local name in Ghana]

Kwa·Zulu /kwɒˈzuːluː/ a former homeland established in South Africa for the Zulu people, now part of the province of KwaZulu-Natal. The general area was formerly known as Zululand.

KwaZulu-Natal /kwɒˈzuːluː nəˈtal/ a province of eastern South Africa, on the Indian Ocean, formerly called Natal; capital, Pietermaritzburg.

Kwei·chow see GUIZHOU.

Kwei·lin see GUILIN.

Kwei·yang see GUIYANG.

Kwe·sui /kweiˈswei/ a former name for HOHHOT.

kWh abbreviation kilowatt hour(s).

KWIC /kwɪk/ noun Computing etc. keyword in context. [abbreviation]

KY abbreviation Kentucky (in official postal use).

Ky. abbreviation Kentucky.

kyan·ite /ˈkaiəˌnait/ noun a crystalline mineral of aluminum silicate, usu. blue, greenish, or colourless. [Greek kuanos dark blue]

kyat /kiˈat/ noun (pl. same or **kyats**) the chief monetary unit of Burma (Myanmar). [Burmese]

Kyd /kɪd/ **Thom·as** (also **Kid**) (1558–94), English dramatist, who is best known for The Spanish Tragedy (1592), an early example of revenge tragedy; other works attributed to Kyd include a lost pre-Shakespearean play on Hamlet.

Kyiv see KIEV.

kylin /ˈkiːlɪn/ noun a mythical composite animal figured on Chinese and Japanese ceramics. [Chinese qilin from qi male + lin female]

kym·o·graph /ˈkaiməˌgraf/ noun an instrument for recording variations in pressure, e.g. in sound waves or in blood within blood vessels, by the trace of a stylus on a rotating cylinder. □ **kym·o·graph·ic** /-ˈgrafɪk/ adjective [Greek kuma wave + -GRAPH]

Kyoto /kiˈoːtoː/ an industrial city in central Japan, on the island of Honshu; pop. (est. 2002) 1,472,000. Founded in the 8th c., it was the imperial capital from 794 until 1868.

ky·pho·sis /kaiˈfoːsɪs/ noun excessive outward curvature of the spine, causing hunching of the back (opp. LORDOSIS). □ **ky·phot·ic** /-ˈfɒtɪk/ adjective [modern Latin from Greek kuphōsis from kuphos bent]

Kyr·gyz /kiːrˈgɪz, ˈkɜrgɪz/ noun (also **Kirghiz**) (pl. same) **1** a member of a traditionally nomadic Sunni Muslim Mongol people living between the Volga and the Irtysh rivers, chiefly in Kyrgyzstan but also in Tajikistan, Uzbekistan, and parts of China and Afghanistan. **2** the Turkic language of the Kyrgyz. [Kyrgyz]

Kyr·gyz·stan /ˌkɜrgɪˈstan/ (also called **Kirghizia; Kyrgyz Republic**) a mountainous country in central Asia, on the northwestern border of China; population (est. 1996) 4,512,000; capital, Bishkek.

Kyrie /ˈkiːriˌei/ noun (in full **Kyrie eleison** /ei'leiiˌsɒn, e'lei-, i'lei-, -ˌzɒn/) **1** a short repeated invocation (in Greek or translated) beginning with the words 'Lord, have mercy' used in many Christian liturgies, esp. at the beginning of the Eucharist or as a response in a litany. **2** a musical setting of the Kyrie. [Greek, 'Lord, have mercy']

Kyu·shu /kiˈuːʃuː/ the most southerly of the four main islands of Japan, constituting an administrative region; pop. (2000) 13,446,000; capital, Fukuoka.

Kyzyl /kəˈzɪl/ a city in south central Russia, on the Yenisei River, capital of the republic of Tuva; pop. (est. 2002) 103,300.

Kyzyl Kum /kuːm/ an arid desert region in central Asia, extending eastward from the Aral Sea to the Pamir Mountains and covering part of Uzbekistan and S Kazakhstan.

Vowels: a cat ɑ arm e bed ɜr her ɜː deux ə ago ɪ sit i cosy iː feed ɒ hot ɔ pore ɔː no ʌ run ʊ put

Ll

L¹ *noun* (also **l**) (*pl.* **Ls** or **L's**) **1** the twelfth letter of the alphabet. **2** (as a Roman numeral) 50. **3** a thing shaped like an L, esp. a joint connecting two pipes at right angles.

L² *abbreviation* (also **L.**) **1** Lake. **2** (esp. on clothing etc.) large. **3** Liberal. **4** (in academic degrees) Licentiate. **5** *Biol.* Linnaeus. **6** litre. **7** *Brit.* learner driver.

L³ *symbol* **1** levorotatory. **2** Avogadro's constant.

l *abbreviation* (also **l.**) **1** left. **2** line. **3** litre(s). **4** length. **5** (esp. *pl.* **ll.**) (of poetry) line. **6** liquid.

£ *abbreviation* (preceding a numeral) pound or pounds (of money). [Latin *libra*]

LA *abbreviation* **1** Los Angeles. **2** Louisiana (in official postal use).

La *symbol Chem.* the element lanthanum.

La. *abbreviation* Louisiana.

la *noun* (also **lah**) *Music* **1** (in tonic sol-fa) the sixth note of a major scale. **2** the note A in the fixed-do system. [Latin *labii*: see GAMUT]

laa·ger /ˈlɒɡɑr/ *noun* **1 a** esp. *South Africa* a camp or encampment, originally formed by a circle of wagons. **b** a defensive position, esp. one protected by armoured vehicles. **2** an entrenched policy, viewpoint, etc. under attack from opponents (also *attributive*: *a laager mentality*). [Afrikaans from Dutch *leger*: see LEAGUER²]

laari /ˈlɑri/ *noun* (*pl.* same or **laaris**) a monetary unit of the Maldives, equal to one-hundredth of a rufiyaa. [Persian]

Laa·youne see LA·YOUN.

Lab *noun* esp. *N Amer.* a Labrador retriever. [abbreviation]

Lab. *abbreviation* **1** Labrador. **2** (in the UK) the Labour Party.

lab *noun informal* a laboratory. [abbreviation]

La Baie /la ˈbeɪ/ a city in NE central Quebec, located at the head of Baie des Ha! Ha! on the Saguenay River, southeast of Chicoutimi, now merged with Chicoutimi, Jonquière, Laterrière and other communities into the city of Saguenay; pop. (2001) 19,940. [French, = the bay]

Laba·no·ta·tion /ˈlɑbənoːteiʃən/ *noun* a system of dance notation devised by the Hungarian-born dancer and choreographer Rudolf von Laban, born Rudolf Laban von Varlja (1879-1958).

la Barca see CALDERÓN DE LA BARCA.

La Barre /laˈbɑr/ **Joseph-Antoine Le Febvre de** (1622-88), French colonial administrator, Governor of New France 1682-85. During his short term as Governor, La Barre attempted to gain personal wealth through the fur trade, esp. by seizing the trading posts belonging to La Salle. In 1684, he launched a disastrous campaign against the Iroquois; the French troops, weakened by disease, were forced to conclude a humiliating peace agreement and La Barre was recalled.

lab·a·rum /ˈlɑbərəm/ *noun* **1** a symbolic banner. **2** Constantine the Great's imperial standard, with Christian symbols added to Roman military symbols. [Late Latin: origin unknown]

La·batt ▸ 1 John (1838-1915), Canadian brewer and entrepreneur. He expanded his family's brewing company using railway transport, bottling agencies, and advertising, and specialized in an English-type India pale ale. In 1911 he incorporated the firm as John Labatt Corporation. **2** his father, **John Kin·der** (1803-66), Irish-born Canadian farmer and brewer. In 1846 he sold his farm near London, Ontario, and bought a partnership in a small London brewery, becoming sole owner in 1855. **3 John Sack·ville** (1880-1952), Canadian brewer, eldest son of John Labatt. As president of the family firm 1915-1950, he survived prohibition in Ontario (1916-27) and the US (1920-33). In August 1934 he became the first Canadian businessman to be kidnapped and held for a large ransom; the ransom was never paid and he was released unharmed.

lab coat *noun* a coat of a light, usu. white fabric, worn over clothing to protect it from stains etc., esp. in a laboratory or by doctors etc.

lab·da·num /ˈlabdənəm/ *noun* (also **ladanum** /ˈladənəm/) a gum resin from plants of the genus *Cistus*, used in perfumery etc. [Latin from Greek *ladanon* from *lēdon* mastic]

label ● *noun* **1** a usu. small piece of paper, card, cloth, metal, etc. attached to or beside an object, item of food, etc., giving its name, information about it, instructions for use, etc. **2** esp. *derogatory* a short classifying phrase or name applied to a person, a work of art, etc. **3 a** a small fabric label sewn into a garment bearing the maker's name. **b** the logo, title, or trademark of esp. a fashion or recording company (*brought it out under his own label*). **c** the clothing or recordings produced under such a trademark. **d** the identifying material affixed to or imprinted upon a CD, cassette, etc. describing its contents etc. **e** a recording company or part of one producing CDs, cassettes, etc. under a distinctive name. **4** a paper sticker used for addressing envelopes, magazines etc. for mailing. **5** a word placed before, after, or in the course of a dictionary definition etc. to specify its subject, register, nationality, etc. **6** *Archit.* a moulding over a door, window or other opening. **7** *Biol. & Chem.* a radioactive isotope, fluorescent dye, etc. used to label another substance. **8** *Computing* **a** an arbitrary name for a statement in a program which facilitates reference to it elsewhere in the program. **b** a set of data recorded on a reel of magnetic tape describing its contents and serving for identification by a computer. **●** *transitive verb* (**labelled, label·ling**; esp. *US* **labeled, label·ing**) **1** attach a label to, mark with a label. **2** (usu. foll. by *as*) assign to a category, describe or designate as with a label (*labelled them as irresponsible*). **3** make (a substance, molecule, etc.) experimentally recognizable but essentially unaltered in behaviour, so that its path may be followed or its distribution ascertained, esp. by replacing a constituent atom by one of a different isotope or by attaching a usu. fluorescent dye to the molecule. □ **label·ler** *noun* [Old French, = ribbon, prob. from Germanic (as LAP¹)]

La Belle Province /la bel prɒˈvæs/ the province of Quebec.

la·bel·lum /ləˈbeləm/ *noun* (*pl.* **la·bel·la** /-lə/) **1** *Zool.* each of a pair of lobes at the tip of the proboscis in some insects. **2** *Bot.* a central petal at the base of an orchid flower, usu. large and unlike the others. [Latin, diminutive of *labrum* 'lip']

label·mate *noun* a performer in relation to one or more others whose recordings are produced by the same record company.

La·berge /laˈberʒ/ **1 Al·bert** (1871-1960), Canadian journalist and author. From 1896 to 1932 he worked as a sportswriter and arts critic at *La Presse*. His novel *La Scouine* (1918), one of the first naturalistic novels written by a Canadian, portrays the misery of the Beauharnois peasantry. He also published several volumes of stories and criticism. **2 Louis** (1924-2002), Canadian labour leader. He was president of the Conseil des métiers et du travail de Montréal 1956-63 and of the Fédération des travailleurs du Québec 1964-1991. Under his leadership the FTQ became a major supporter of Quebec nationalism.

La·berge, Lake /ləˈbɑrdʒ/ a small lake in S Yukon Territory, a widening of the Yukon River, situated immediately north of Whitehorse. It was immortalized in Robert Service's poem *The Cremation of Sam McGee* (1907).

u: m**oo**d ai m**y** əi p**i**pe au br**ow**n ʌu h**ou**se ei d**ay** ɔi b**oy** ū fr**an**glais ã C**an**adien ɔ̃ Br**ay**on   (*see over for consonants*)

labia pl. of LABIUM.

labi·al /ˈleibiəl/ ● adjective **1 a** of the lips. **b** Zool. pertaining to, of the nature of, associated with, or situated on a lip or labium. **2** Dentistry designating the surface of a tooth adjacent to the lips. **3** Phonetics (of a sound) requiring partial or complete closure of the lips, e.g. the consonants p, b, f, v, and m and vowels and semi-vowels in which lips are rounded, e.g. w and oo in moon. ● noun Phonetics a labial sound. □ **labi·al·ize** transitive verb (also esp. Brit. **-ise**). **labi·al·ly** adverb [medieval Latin labialis from Latin labia lips]

labial pipe noun Music an organ pipe having lips; a flue pipe.

labia ma·jora /məˈdʒɔrə/ plural noun (usu. treated as sing.) the larger, outer pair of labia of the vulva.

labia mi·nora /mɪˈnɔrə/ plural noun (usu. treated as sing.) the smaller, inner pair of labia of the vulva.

labi·ate /ˈleibiət/ ● noun any plant of the family Labiatae, including mint and rosemary, having square stems and a corolla or calyx divided into two parts suggesting lips. ● adjective **1** Bot. of or relating to the Labiatae. **2** Bot. & Zool. like a lip, lips, or labium. [modern Latin labiatus (as LABIUM)]

labile /ˈleibail, -bɪl/ adjective Chem. **1** (of a compound) liable to displacement or change esp. if an atom or group is easily replaced by other atoms or groups. **2** unstable, liable to undergo change in nature, form, etc. □ **la·bil·ity** /ləˈbɪlɪti/ noun [Late Latin labilis from labi to fall]

labio- /ˈleibiɔ/ combining form of the lips. [as LABIUM]

labio·den·tal /ˌleibiɔˈdentəl/ ● adjective (of a sound) made with the lips and teeth, e.g. f and v. ● noun a sound formed with the lips and teeth.

labio·velar /ˌleibiɔˈviːlər/ ● adjective (of a sound) made with the lips and soft palate, e.g. w. ● noun a sound formed with the lips and soft palate.

labi·um /ˈleibiəm/ noun (pl. **labia** /-biə/) **1** (usu. in pl.) Anat. each of the two pairs of skin folds that enclose the vulva. **2** the lower lip in the mouthparts of an insect or crustacean. **3** a lip, esp. the lower one of a labiate plant's corolla. [Latin, = lip]

labor etc. var. of LABOUR etc.

lab·ora·tory /ˈlabrə,tɔri, ləˈbɔrə-, ləˈbɔrətri-/ noun (pl. **-ies**) **1** a room or building fitted out for scientific experiments, research, teaching, or the manufacture of drugs and chemicals. **2** a class in which students engage in learning activities by practice such as language drill, mapping, conducting experiments, etc. [medieval Latin laboratorium from Latin laborare LABOUR]

laboratory animal noun any animal, such as a rat, monkey, mouse, etc. commonly used for experiments in a laboratory.

laboratory technician noun a person trained to perform practical tasks in a laboratory, e.g. conducting tests, maintaining equipment, compiling data, etc.

la·bor·i·ous /ləˈbɔriəs/ adjective **1** needing hard work or toil (a laborious task). **2** (esp. of literary style) showing signs of toil; not fluent. □ **la·bor·i·ous·ly** adverb **la·bor·i·ous·ness** noun

labour (also **labor**) ● noun **1 a** physical or mental work; exertion; toil. **b** such work considered as supplying the needs of a community. **2** workers, esp. manual, considered as a class or political force (a dispute between capital and labour). **3** the process of childbirth, esp. the period from the start of uterine contractions to delivery (has been in labour for three hours). **4** a particular task, esp. of a difficult nature. **5** (**Labour**) = LABOUR PARTY. ● verb **1** intransitive **a** work hard or exert oneself physically or mentally. **b** do esp. manual work to earn one's living. **2** intransitive (usu. foll. by for, or to + infin.) strive for a purpose (laboured to fulfill his promise). **3** transitive treat or insist upon at excessive length; elaborate needlessly (I will not labour the point). **4** intransitive (often foll. by under) suffer under (a disadvantage or delusion) (laboured under universal disapproval). **5** intransitive proceed with trouble or difficulty (laboured slowly up the hill). **6** intransitive **a** (of a ship) roll or pitch heavily. **b** (of an engine) work noisily and with difficulty, esp. when under load. **7** intransitive (of a woman) be in labour, give birth. □ **labour in vain** make a fruitless effort. **labour of love** a task done for pleasure, not reward. □ **labour·ing·ly** adverb [Old French labo(u)r, labourer from Latin labor, -oris, laborare]

labour board noun (in full **Labour Relations Board**) a tribunal, either provincial or federal, empowered to mediate and resolve labour disputes.

labour camp noun **1** a prison camp enforcing a regime of hard labour. **2** a camp providing shelter for migratory workers, esp. farm labourers.

labour coach noun N Amer. a person who provides emotional and physical help to a woman in labour, e.g. by helping with breathing exercises, giving massages, etc.

labour code noun a law or body of laws regulating working practices, conditions, etc.

Labour Day noun (US **Labor Day**) a holiday in celebration of working people, observed in Canada and the US on the first Monday in September and elsewhere on 1 May.

la·boured adjective **1** not natural or spontaneous; showing signs of too much effort. **2** (esp. of breathing) slow and difficult.

labour·er noun (also **labor·er**) **1** a person doing unskilled, usu. manual, work for wages. **2** a person who labours.

labour exchange noun = EMPLOYMENT AGENCY.

labour force noun **1** the number of people in the population employed or seeking work. **2** the body of workers employed, esp. at a single plant, company, etc.

labour-intensive adjective (of a process or industry) having labour as the largest factor or cost.

labour·ite noun **1** (also **labor·ite**) a supporter of organized labour. **2** (**Labourite**) a member or follower of a Labour Party.

labour law noun **1** the area of law pertaining to and governing the relationship between employers and employees, management and unions, etc. **2** a law affecting or controlling working conditions etc.

labour market noun the supply of labour considered with reference to the demand on it.

labour movement noun **1** the effort by organized labour to improve conditions for workers. **2** the organizations and individuals involved in this.

Labour Party noun **1** a British political party formed to represent the interests of ordinary working people. **2** any similar political party in other countries.

labour relations noun (often treated as sing.) the relations between management and employees.

labour-saving adjective (of an appliance etc.) designed to reduce or eliminate the work needed to do something.

labour temple noun N Amer. a building providing facilities for various union-related activities, e.g. for meetings, social activities, benevolent societies, printing, etc.

labour theory of value noun the Marxist theory that the value of a commodity should be determined by the amount of human labour used in its production.

labour union noun N Amer. an organized association of workers formed to protect and further their rights and interests and to bargain collectively with employers.

labra pl. of LABRUM.

Lab·ra·dor¹ /ˈlabrəˌdɔr, ˈlabrəˌdɔr/ a coastal region of E Canada, which forms the mainland part of the province of Newfoundland and Labrador. Formerly disputed between Newfoundland and Quebec, the area was awarded to Newfoundland in 1927. □ **Lab·ra·dor·ian** noun & adjective [Portuguese lavrador small landholder]

Lab·ra·dor² /ˈlabrəˌdɔr/ noun **1** (in full **Labrador dog**, **Labrador retriever**) a breed of retriever with a black or golden coat often used as a gun dog or as a guide for a blind person. **2** Cdn (Nfld) a type of heavily salted, semi-cured cod from the Labrador fishery. [from LABRADOR¹]

Labrador City an iron-ore mining town in W Labrador, near the border with Quebec; pop. (2001) 7,744.

Labrador Current a cold ocean current which flows southward from the Arctic Ocean along the northeast coast of N America. It meets the warm Gulf Stream in an area off the coast of Newfoundland which is noted for its dense fogs.

Labrador Highlands a mountainous region in Labrador, extending roughly from Cape Chidley to Nain. It includes the Torngat Mountains.

Labrador Inuit noun **1** the Inuit people living in N Labrador. **2** the language of this people.

lab·ra·dor·ite /ˈlabrəˈdɔrəit/ noun a kind of plagioclase feldspar, often showing iridescence from internal reflective planes. [LABRADOR¹]

Labrador Peninsula (also **Labrador-Ungava**) a broad peninsula of E Canada, between Hudson Bay, the N Atlantic and the Gulf of St. Lawrence. Consisting of the Ungava Peninsula and Labrador, it contains most of Quebec and the mainland part of the province of Newfoundland and Labrador. It is very sparsely inhabited.

Labrador Sea the part of the N Atlantic between the coast of Labrador and Greenland. It is linked to Hudson Bay via Hudson Strait and to Baffin Bay via Davis Strait.

Labrador tea noun **1** a shrub of the genus *Ledum* of the heath family, which has leathery evergreen leaves used to make an infusion. **2** an infusion made from these leaves.

lab rat noun **1** a rat used for experiments in a laboratory. **2** a researcher who spends excessive amounts of time in a laboratory.

lab·ret /ˈlabrɪt/ noun a piece of shell, bone, etc., inserted in the lip as an ornament. [LABRUM]

la·brum /ˈleibrəm/ noun (pl. **labra** /-brə/) the upper lip in the mouthparts of an insect. [Latin, = lip: related to LABIUM]

la·brus·ca /ləˈbruskə/ noun **1** a wild vine, *Vitis labrusca*, of eastern N America, from which many cultivated varieties have been derived. **2** the grape of this vine. **3** a wine made from this grape. [Latin *labrusca*, a wild vine]

La Bru·yère /ˌlabruːˈjɛr/ **Jean de** (1645–96), French moralist. He is known for his *Caractères* (1688), consisting of short character studies exposing the vanity and corruption of human behaviour by satirizing Parisian society.

lab technician noun (also *N Amer. informal* **lab tech**) = LABORATORY TECHNICIAN.

La·bu·an /ləˈbuːən/ a small Malaysian island off the north coast of Borneo; pop. (est. 2002) 74,300; capital Victoria.

la·bur·num /ləˈbɜrnəm/ noun any small tree of the genus *Laburnum* with racemes of golden flowers yielding poisonous seeds. *Also called* GOLDEN CHAIN. [Latin]

lab·y·rinth /ˈlabərɪnθ/ noun **1** a complicated irregular network of passages or paths etc.; a maze. **2 a** an intricate or tangled arrangement, esp. of streets or buildings. **b** a complex or confusing situation. **3** *Anat.* the complex arrangement of bony and membranous canals and chambers of the inner ear which constitute the organs of hearing and balance. **4** any of various devices containing or consisting of winding passages, esp. a series of chambers designed to absorb unwanted vibrations in a loudspeaker. □ **lab·y·rinth·ian** /-ˈrɪnθiən/ adjective **lab·y·rinth·ine** /-ˈrɪnθaɪn/ adjective [ultimately from Greek *laburinthos*]

LAC abbreviation LEADING AIRCRAFTMAN.

lac[1] noun a resinous substance secreted as a protective covering by the lac insect, and used to make varnish and shellac. [ultimately from Hindustani *lākh* from Prakrit *lakkha* from Sanskrit *lākṣā*]

lac[2] var. of LAKH.

LACAC /ˈlakak/ abbreviation Cdn (Ont.) Local Architectural Conservation Advisory Committee.

L'Acadie /lakaˈdiː/ a former municipality in S Quebec, now part of Saint-Jean-sur-Richelieu; pop. (2001) 5,526. [French, lit. = 'Acadia', because settled by Acadians after the Expulsion]

Lacan /laˈkɑ̃/ **Jacques (Marie Émile)** (1901–81), French psychoanalyst. He reinterpreted Freudian psychoanalysis in the light of structural linguistics and anthropology; he saw the unconscious as developing simultaneously with language. □ **La·can·ian** /ləˈkaniən/ noun & adjective **La·can·ian·ism** noun

Lac-Brome /lakˈbroːm/ a town in S Quebec, situated at the southern end of Lac Brome, about 40 km southwest of Sherbrooke; pop. (2001) 5,444. [ultimately after *Brome Hall*, residence of Charles, 1st Marquess Cornwallis and Viscount *Brome*: see CORNWALLIS 1]

Lac·ca·dive Islands /ˈlakədiːv/ one of the groups of islands forming the Indian territory of Lakshadweep in the Indian Ocean.

lac·co·lith /ˈlakəlɪθ/ noun *Geol.* a lens-shaped intrusion of igneous rock which thrusts the overlying strata into a dome. [Greek *lakkos* reservoir + -LITH]

Lac des Deux Mon·tagnes /lakdeidøˈtainjə/ a widening of the Ottawa River as it joins the St. Lawrence at the southwestern end of the Island of Montreal. [with reference to two hills, Mont-Rigaud on the south side and Mont Oka on the north side]

lace ● noun **1** a fine open fabric, esp. of cotton or silk, made by weaving thread in patterns and used esp. as a trim or to make tablecloths. **2** a cord or leather strip passed through eyelets or hooks on opposite sides of a shoe, skate, garment, etc., pulled tight and fastened. **3** braid used for trimming esp. dress uniforms (*gold lace*). ● attributive adjective made of lace. ● verb **1** transitive (usu. foll. by *up*) **a** fasten or tighten (a shoe, garment, etc.) with a lace or laces usu. passed alternately through two rows of eyelet holes or around two rows of hooks, studs, etc. **b** fasten (a person) into a garment etc. by means of a lace or laces. **2** transitive **a** (usu. foll. by *with*) add an ingredient to (a drink, dish, substance, etc.) to enhance or adulterate flavour, strength, effect, etc. **b** intermingle (*ribaldry laced with philosophy*). **3** transitive (usu. foll. by *with*) **a** streak (a sky etc.) with colour

(*cheek laced with blood*). **b** interlace or embroider (fabric) with thread etc. **4** transitive & intransitive informal thrash, beat, or abuse, physically or verbally. **5** transitive (often foll. by *through*) pass (a shoelace etc.) through. **6** transitive pass (film, tape, etc.) between the guides and other parts of a projector, tape recorder, etc. so it runs from one spool to the other. **7** transitive trim with lace. [Old French *laz, las, lacier*, ultimately from Latin *laqueus* noose]

lace curtain ● noun a window curtain made of lace which lets in light but makes seeing into the room difficult. ● adjective (also **lace-curtain**) **1** having social pretensions. **2** genteel.

laced adjective **1 a** (of shoes etc.) made to be fastened or tightened with a lace or laces. **b** (of a shoe etc.) so fastened. **2 a** (of a drink etc.) mixed with a small measure of some other substance such as liquor, a drug, etc. **b** marked with streaks of colour. **3** ornamented or trimmed with lace or laces.

lace·maker noun a person who makes lace, esp. professionally. □ **lace·making** noun

la·cer·ate /ˈlasəˌreit/ transitive verb **1** tear or cut (esp. flesh or tissue). **2** distress or cause pain to (the feelings etc.). □ **la·cer·at·ed** adjective **la·cer·a·tion** noun [Latin *lacerare* from *lacer* torn]

la·cer·tian /ləˈsɜrtiən/ (also **lacer·til·ian** /ˌlasɜrˈtiliən/, **lacer·tine** /ˈlasɜrˌtain/) ● noun any reptile of the suborder Lacertilia, including lizards. ● adjective of or relating to the Lacertilia. [Latin *lacerta* lizard]

lace-up ● noun a shoe, boot, etc. fastened with a lace. ● attributive adjective (of a shoe etc.) fastened by a lace or laces.

lace·wing noun any of various predatory insects with delicate lace-like wings.

lace·work noun **1** work done in lace. **2** woodwork, ironwork etc. made to resemble lace.

Lac Guillaume-Delisle see GUILLAUME-DELISLE, LAC.

La·che·naie /laʃənˈei/ a former town in south central Quebec, located on the Rivière des Mille-Îles, northeast of Montreal, now part of Terrebonne; pop. (2001) 21,709. [alteration of C. Aubert de *La Chesnaye*, fur trader d.1702]

lach·es /ˈlatʃɪz, ˈlei-/ noun Law unjustifiable, inexcusable, or unreasonable delay in performing a legal duty, asserting a right, claiming a privilege, etc. [Anglo-French *laches(se)*, Old French *laschesse* from *lasche*, ultimately from Latin *laxus* loose]

Lach·es·is /ˈlakɪsɪs/ Gk Myth one of the three Fates, the measurer of the thread of human destiny. [Greek, = getting by lot]

La·chine /laˈʃiːn/ a former city in south central Quebec, on the south shore of the Island of Montreal, now part of the city of Montreal; pop. (2001) 40,222. [French *la Chine*, lit. 'China', a derisive name for the land grant belonging to La Salle, who was unsuccessful in his attempt to reach China c.1669]

Lachine Canal a historic canal in south central Quebec, extending through the southeastern corner of Île de Montréal. Operating from 1825 to 1970, the canal was integral to the industrialization of Canada, providing a vital link from the lower St. Lawrence to the Great Lakes. In 1959, it was superseded by the St. Lawrence Seaway.

Lachine Rapids a set of rapids in south central Quebec, situated at the southeastern end of the Island of Montreal, where Lac Saint-Louis narrows and becomes the St. Lawrence.

Lachlan River /ˈlaklən/ a river of New South Wales, Australia, which rises in the Great Dividing Range and flows some 1 472 km (920 miles) northwest then southwest to join the Murrumbidgee River near the border with Victoria. [*Lachlan* Macquarie, Scottish-born Australian colonial administrator d.1824]

lach·rym·al var. of LACRIMAL.

lach·rym·ose /ˈlakrɪˌmoːs/ adjective formal **1** given to weeping; tearful. **2** melancholy; inducing tears. □ **lach·rym·ose·ly** adverb **lach·rym·os·ity** noun [Latin *lacrimosus* from *lacrima* tear]

La·chute /laˈʃuːt/ a town in south central Quebec, located west of Montreal on the Rivière du Nord; pop. (2001) 11,628. [French *la chute*, lit. 'the fall', with reference to the waterfalls located there]

lacing noun **1** the act or an instance of lacing something. **2** something that laces or fastens, esp. a laced fastening on a shoe etc. **3** ornamental lace trimming or braiding. **4** informal a beating.

la·cini·ate /ləˈsɪniət/ adjective (also **la·cini·at·ed** /-ˌeitəd/) Bot. & Zool. divided into deep narrow irregular segments; fringed. □ **la·cini·a·tion** noun [Latin *lacinia* flap of a garment]

lac insect noun an Asian scale insect, *Laccifer lacca*, living in trees.

lack ● noun (usu. foll. by *of*) an absence, want, or deficiency (*a lack of talent; felt the lack of warmth*). ● transitive verb be without or deficient in (*lacks courage*). □ **for lack of** owing to the absence of (*went hungry for* lack of money). **lack for** lack (never lacks for odd jobs). [Middle English *lac*, *lacen*, corresponding to Middle Dutch, Middle Low German *lak* deficiency, Middle Dutch *laken* to lack]

lack·a·dais·ic·al /ˌlakəˈdeɪzɪkəl/ adjective unenthusiastic, lacking vigour and determination. □ **lack·a·dais·ic·al·ly** adverb **lack·a·dais·ic·al·ness** noun [archaic lackaday, -daisy (interj.): see ALACK]

lack·ey noun (pl. **-eys**) **1** derogatory **a** a servile political follower. **b** an obsequious parasitical person. **2 a** a usu. liveried footman or manservant. **b** a servant. [French laquais, obsolete alaquais from Catalan alacay = Spanish ALCALDE]

lack·ing predicative adjective **1** (of a thing) not available, missing (money was lacking). **2** inadequate or deficient (is lacking in determination).

lack·lustre adjective (also esp. US **lack·luster**) **1** lacking in vitality, force, or conviction. **2** (of the eye, hair, etc.) dull.

Lac la Ronge /lak la ˈrɒ̃ʒ/ a lake in central Saskatchewan, over 200 km north of Prince Albert. [from French ronger to gnaw, with reference either to the gnawed appearance of the jagged shoreline or to the activity of beavers in the area]

La·clos /laˈklo/ **Pierre (Am·broise Fran·çois) Cho·der·los de** (1741–1803), French novelist. His epistolary novel Les Liaisons dangereuses (1782), depicting the corrupt, erotic schemes of an aristocratic couple, caused a scandal.

Lac-Mégantic /lakmeɪgãˈtiːk/ a town in S Quebec, situated at the northern end of Lac Mégantic, northeast of Sherbrooke; pop. (2001) 5,897. [ultimately from Abenaki namagôtegw at the camp of the salmon trout]

Lac Mem·phré·ma·gog see MEMPHRÉMAGOG, LAC.

Lac Mis·tas·sini see MISTASSINI, LAC.

La·combe[1] /laˈkoːmb/ a town in central Alberta, north of Red Deer; pop. (2001) 9,384. □ **La·comb·ian** noun [LACOMBE[2]]

La·combe[2] /laˈkõb/ **Al·bert** (1827–1916), Canadian Oblate priest and missionary. Starting in 1852, except for a period as a parish priest in Winnipeg (1872–82), he worked among the Metis and Indians in what would later become Alberta. In 1883 he served as a mediator between the CPR and the Blackfoot, whom he convinced to allow the railway across their reserve. He also wrote a Cree grammar and a Cree dictionary.

La·co·nia /ləˈkoːniə/ (also **Lakonia**) a modern department and ancient region of Greece, in the SE Peloponnese. Throughout the classical period the region was dominated by its capital, Sparta, which remains the administrative centre of the modern department. □ **La·co·nian** adjective & noun

la·con·ic /ləˈkɒnɪk/ adjective **1** (of a style of speech or writing) brief; concise; terse. **2** (of a person) laconic in speech etc. □ **la·con·ic·ally** adverb **la·coni·cism** noun [Latin from Greek Lakōnikos from Lakōn Spartan, the Spartans being known for their terse speech]

La Cor·uña see CORUNNA.

lac·quer /ˈlakər/ ● noun **1** a sometimes coloured varnish made of shellac dissolved in alcohol, or of synthetic substances, that dries to form a hard protective coating for wood, brass, etc. **2** any of the various resinous wood varnishes capable of taking a hard polish, esp. the sap of the lacquer tree. **3** esp. Brit. hairspray. **4** Art decorative ware made of wood coated with lacquer. ● transitive verb coat with lacquer. □ **lac·quered** adjective [obsolete French lacre sealing wax, from unexplained var. of Portuguese laca LAC[1]]

lacquer tree noun an E Asian tree, Rhus verniciflua, the sap of which is used as a hard-wearing varnish for wood.

lac·quer·ware noun decorative articles made of wood coated with lacquer, often inlaid with ivory, mother-of-pearl, etc.

lac·rim·al /ˈlakrɪməl/ adjective (also **lachrymal**) **1** (usu. as **lacrimal**) Anat. concerned with the secretion of tears (lacrimal canal; lacrimal duct). **2** literary of or for tears. [medieval Latin lachrymalis from Latin lacrima tear]

lac·rim·a·tion /ˌlakrɪˈmeɪʃən/ noun formal the flow of tears. [Latin lacrimatio from lacrimare weep (as LACRIMAL)]

la·crosse /ləˈkrɒs/ noun a game, originally played by N American Indians, in which a ball is thrown, carried and caught with a lacrosse stick. [French from la the + CROSSE]

lacrosse stick noun the long-handled stick used in lacrosse, having a curved L-shaped or triangular frame at one end with a piece of shallow netting in the angle.

Lac-Saint-Charles /lak sã ʃarl/ a former city in SE central Quebec, now part of the city of Québec; pop. (2001) 8,912. [named after the lake

on which it is located, which was named by Récollet missionaries in honour of Charles Desboues, vicar of Pontoise, France.]

Lac Saint-Jean see SAINT-JEAN, LAC.

Lac Saint-Louis see SAINT-LOUIS, LAC.

Lac Saint-Pierre see SAINT-PIERRE, LAC.

Lac Seul /lak ˈsœl/ a lake in NW Ontario, situated about 50 km north of Dryden, northwest of Thunder Bay. [French, lit. 'alone lake']

lac·tase /ˈlakteɪz, -teɪs/ noun Biochem. any of a group of enzymes which catalyze the hydrolysis of lactose to glucose and galactose. [French from lactose LACTOSE]

lac·tate[1] /ˈlakteɪt/ intransitive verb (of mammals) secrete milk. □ **lac·tat·ing** adjective [as LACTATION]

lac·tate[2] /ˈlakteɪt/ noun Chem. any salt or ester of lactic acid.

lac·ta·tion /lakˈteɪʃən/ noun **1** the secretion of milk by the mammary glands. **2 a** the period of milk secretion normally following childbirth. **b** the suckling of young. [Latin lactare suckle, from lac lactis milk]

lac·teal /ˈlaktɪəl/ ● adjective **1** of, pertaining to, consisting of, or resembling milk. **2** Anat. (of a vessel etc.) conveying chyle or other milky fluid. ● noun (in pl.) the lymphatic vessels of the small intestine which absorb digested fats. [Latin lacteus from lac lactis milk]

Lac Té·mis·ca·mingue see TIMISKAMING, LAKE.

Lac Témis·coua·ta see TÉMISCOUATA, LAC.

lac·tic adjective Chem. of, relating to, or obtained from milk. [Latin lac lactis milk]

lactic acid noun a clear odourless syrupy carboxylic acid formed in sour milk, and produced in the muscle tissues during strenuous exercise.

lac·tif·er·ous /lakˈtɪfərəs/ adjective yielding milk or milky fluid. [Late Latin lactifer (as LACTIC)]

lacti·tol noun an artificial sweetener derived from lactulose. [lacto- + -ITE[1] + -OL[1]]

lacto- combining form milk. [Latin lac lactis milk]

lacto·ba·cil·lus /ˌlaktoːbəˈsɪləs/ noun (pl. **-bacil·li** /-laɪ/) Biol. any Gram-positive rod-shaped bacterium of the genus Lactobacillus, producing lactic acid from the fermentation of carbohydrates.

lac·tom·eter /lakˈtɒmɪtər/ noun an instrument for testing the relative density of milk.

lac·tone noun Chem. any of a class of cyclic esters formed by the elimination of water from a hydroxy-carboxylic acid. [German Lacton]

lacto-ovo-vegetar·ian ● adjective (of a diet) consisting only of dairy products, eggs, and vegetables. ● noun a person who subsists on such a diet.

lacto·pro·tein noun a protein which occurs normally in milk.

lac·tose /ˈlaktoːs, -toːz/ noun Chem. a sugar that occurs in milk, and is less sweet than sucrose. [as LACTO-]

lactose intolerance noun an inability to digest lactose due to a deficiency of lactase, usu. resulting in abdominal cramps and gas after the consumption of dairy products. □ **lactose intolerant** adjective

lactu·lose /ˈlaktjuːloːs, -loːz/ noun a disaccharide of galactose and fructose which is formed in heated milk by the isomerization of lactose.

la·cu·na /ləˈkjuːnə/ noun (pl. **la·cu·nae** /-niː/ or **la·cu·nas**) **1** a hiatus, blank, or gap. **2 a** a missing portion or empty page, esp. in an ancient manuscript, book, etc. **b** something missing or left out, esp. by oversight, incompetence, etc. **3** Anat. a space, cavity, or depression within or between the tissues of an organism, esp. in bone. □ **la·cu·nar** adjective [Latin = pool, from lacus LAKE[1]]

la·cus·trine /ləˈkʌstraɪn/ adjective formal **1** of or relating to lakes. **2** (of plants and animals) living or growing in or beside a lake. **3** Geol. originating by deposition at the bottom of a lake. [Latin lacus LAKE[1], after palustris marshy]

LACW abbreviation (in the RAF and hist. in the RCAF) Leading Aircraftwoman.

lacy adjective (**lacier**, **laci·est**) of, trimmed with, or resembling lace. □ **laci·ly** adverb **laci·ness** noun

lad noun **1 a** a boy or youth. **b** a young son. **2** (esp. in pl.) informal a man; a fellow, esp. a workmate, drinking companion, etc. (he's one of the lads). **3** Brit. informal a high-spirited or roguish man, esp. one who is very interested in sexual conquest (he's a bit of a lad). **4** Brit. a stable hand of any age and of either gender. □ **laddy** adjective [Middle English ladde, of unknown origin]

La·dakh /ləˈdɒk/ a high-altitude region of NW India, Pakistan, and China, containing the Ladakh and Karakoram mountain ranges and

Vowels: a cat ɑ arm e bed ɜr her ɜ: deux ə ago ɪ sit i cosy iː feed ɒ hot ɔ pore ɔː no ʌ run ʊ put the upper Indus valley; chief town, Leh (in India). It is one of the highest regions of the world.

lada·num *var. of* LABDANUM.

lad·der ● *noun* **1 a** a fixed or portable device usu. made of wood, metal, or rope, consisting of a series of bars, rungs, or steps fixed between two supports and used as a means of climbing up or down. **b** anything resembling a ladder in appearance or function (*fish ladder*). **2 a** a hierarchical structure perceived as resembling a ladder. **b** such a structure as a means of advancement, promotion, etc. **3** *Brit.* a run in a stocking. ● *verb Brit.* **1** *intransitive* (of a stocking etc.) develop a run. **2** *transitive* cause a run in (a stocking etc.). [Old English *hlǣd(d)er*, ultimately from Germanic]

lad·der·back *noun* an upright chair with a back formed of horizontal pieces of wood, resembling a ladder.

ladder truck *noun* an emergency vehicle carrying ladders, hooks, etc. for firefighters.

lad·die *noun informal* a young boy or lad.

lad·dish *adjective esp. Brit.* characteristic of a young man who behaves in a boisterously macho manner. □ **lad·dish·ly** *adverb* **lad·dish·ness** *noun* **lad·dism** *noun*

lade *verb* (*past participle* **laden**) **1** *transitive* **a** put cargo on board (a ship). **b** ship (goods) as cargo. **2** *intransitive* (of a ship) take on cargo. [Old English *hladan*]

laden *adjective* **1** (in *combination*) having a high proportion of the specified quality, substance, etc. (*debt-laden; sugar-laden*). **2** (usu. foll. by *with*) heavily loaded, abundantly filled. **3** (of the conscience, spirit, etc.) painfully burdened with guilt etc.

la-di-da *adjective informal* (also **la-de-da**, **lah-di-dah**) affectedly genteel or refined. [imitative of an affected manner of speech]

ladies *pl. of* LADY.

Ladies' Aid *noun* (in full **Ladies' Aid Society**) *N Amer.* an organization of women who support the work of a church by fundraising, arranging social activities, etc.

ladies' man *noun* (also **lady's man**) a man fond of and very successful with women.

ladies' night *noun* **1** a designated night at a bar, club, etc. on which admission for women is free or at a reduced price. **2** a function at a men's club etc. to which women are invited.

ladies' room *noun* a women's washroom.

ladies who lunch *plural noun* affluent women of leisure, pursuing a life of cultural diversions and social events, esp. lunches in expensive restaurants and charity fundraisers.

Ladin /ləˈdiːn/ *noun* the Rhaeto-Romance dialect of the Engadine area of SE Switzerland and the adjoining areas of N Italy. [Romansh, from Latin *latinus* LATIN]

lading *noun* **1** a cargo. **2** the act or process of lading.

La·di·no /ləˈdiːno/ *noun* (*pl.* **-nos**) **1** a language based on Old Spanish and written in modified Hebrew characters, used by some Sephardic Jews, esp. in Mediterranean countries. **2** a mestizo or Spanish-speaking white person in Central America. [Spanish, originally = 'Latin', from Latin (as LADIN)]

la·di·no /ləˈdiːno/ *noun* (*pl.* **-nos**) a large variety of white clover (*Trifolium repens*) native to Italy and cultivated for fodder. [Italian]

ladle ● *noun* **1** a long-handled spoon with a cup-shaped bowl for serving or transferring liquids. **2** a vessel for transporting molten metal in a foundry. ● *transitive verb* (often foll. by *out*) transfer (liquid) from one receptacle to another. □ **ladle out** distribute, esp. lavishly. □ **ladle·ful** *noun* (*pl.* **-fuls**). [Old English *hlǣdel* from *hladan* LADE]

Lado·ga, Lake /ˈlɒdəgə/ a large lake in NW Russia, northeast of St. Petersburg, near the border with Finland. It is the largest lake in Europe, with an area of 17 700 sq. km (6,837 sq. miles).

lady *noun* (*pl.* **ladies**) **1 a** a woman regarded as being of superior social status or as having the refined manners associated with this (*compare* GENTLEMAN). **b** (**Lady**) a title used by peeresses, female relatives of peers, the wives and widows of knights, etc. **2 a** any woman (*ask that lady over there*). **b** often *offensive* as a form of address (*hey lady, move your car*). **3** *informal* **a** a wife or consort. **b** a man's girlfriend or mistress. **4** the female head of a household (*lady of the house; lady of the manor*). **5** (in *pl.* as a form of address) a female audience or the female part of an audience. **6** *hist.* a woman who is the object of chivalrous devotion, esp. one loved and courted by a knight. **7** a queen in a pack of playing cards. **8** an honorific title, used preceding the names of goddesses, allegorical figures, personifications, etc. (*Lady Philosophy*). □ **the Ladies** (or **Ladies'**) a women's public washroom. □ **lady·hood** *noun*

lady·ness *noun* [Old English *hlǣfdige* from *hlāf* LOAF[1] + (unrecorded) *dig-* knead, related to DOUGH)]

Lady altar *noun* the altar in a Lady chapel.

lady beetle *noun* = LADYBUG.

lady·bird *noun* esp. *Brit.* = LADYBUG.

Lady Bountiful *noun* a charitable but patronizing lady. [after a character in George Farquhar's *The Beaux' Stratagem*, 1707]

lady·bug *noun* *N Amer.* a coleopterous insect of the family Coccinellidae, with wing covers usu. of a reddish-brown colour with black spots.

Lady chapel *noun* a chapel dedicated to the Virgin Mary, situated within a larger church.

Lady Day *noun* the Feast of the Annunciation, 25 Mar.

lady fern *noun* a slender woodland fern, *Athyrium filix-femina*.

lady·finger *noun* *N Amer.* a finger-shaped sponge cake.

lady friend *noun* a regular female companion or lover.

lady-in-waiting *noun* a lady attending a queen or princess.

lady-killer *noun* **1** a practised and habitual seducer. **2** a dangerously attractive man.

lady·like *adjective* with the modesty, comportment, etc., thought characteristic of a well brought-up lady.

lady love *noun* a female sweetheart or lover.

Lady Luck *noun informal* a female personification of luck.

Lady Mayoress *noun* the wife of a Lord Mayor.

Lady Muck *noun* esp. *Brit. slang derogatory* a socially pretentious woman.

lady of the bedchamber *noun* = LADY-IN-WAITING.

lady of the house *noun* the female head of a household.

lady of the night *noun* a prostitute.

lady's bedstraw *noun* = OUR LADY'S BEDSTRAW.

lady·ship *noun archaic* being a lady. □ **her** (or **your** or **their**) **ladyship** (or **ladyships**) **1** a respectful form of reference or address to a Lady or Ladies. **2** *ironic* a form of reference or address to a woman thought to be giving herself airs.

lady's maid *noun* a lady's personal maidservant.

lady's mantle *noun* any rosaceous plant of the genus *Alchemilla* with yellowish-green clustered flowers.

Lady·smith 1 a town on the eastern coast of Vancouver Island, about 20 km southeast of Nanaimo; pop. (2001) 6,587. **2** a town in E South Africa, in KwaZulu-Natal. It was subjected to a four-month siege by Boer forces during the Second Boer War and was finally relieved on 28 Feb. 1900. [sense 2 after the wife of the governor of Natal, Sir H. *Smith*; sense 1 from sense 2]

lady-smock *noun* (also **lady's smock**) = CUCKOO FLOWER.

lady's slipper *noun* any orchid of the genus *Cypripedium*, with a slipper-shaped lip on its flowers, the floral emblem of PEI. (Also called **moccasin flower**.)

lady's tresses *plural noun* (also **ladies' tresses**) any white-flowered orchid of the genus *Spiranthes*.

laevo- /ˈliːvo/ *var. of* LEVO-. [Latin *laevus* left]

laevo·ro·ta·tory *var. of* LEVOROTATORY.

laevul·ose *var. of* LEVULOSE.

La·fay·ette /ˌlafaiˈet/ (also **La Fay·ette**), **Marie Jo·seph Paul Yves Roch Gil·bert du Mo·tier, Mar·quis de** (1757–1834), French soldier and liberal statesman. He fought alongside the American colonists in the American Revolution, and, commanding the National Guard (1789–91), played a crucial part in the early phase of the French Revolution.

laff riot *noun* *N Amer. informal* often *ironic* an instance or occasion of great mirth. [respelling of LAUGH]

La·fleur /laˈflɜr/ **Guy Da·mien** (b.1951), Canadian hockey player. After an outstanding junior year in 1971 during which he scored 131 goals, he joined the Montreal Canadiens as a right winger. His accurate shot and instinct for the game helped him to six consecutive 50-goal seasons. In 1983 he became the tenth NHL player to reach the 500 career goal plateau; he retired during the 1984–85 season.

La·Fon·taine /lafɔ̃ˈten/ **Sir Louis-Hippolyte** (1807–64), Canadian lawyer and politician. First elected to the Lower Canadian Assembly in 1830, he was a follower of Papineau, but opposed taking up arms in 1837. After the Union of the two Canadas in 1841 he worked with Robert Baldwin and Francis Hincks in the formation of a party of Upper and Lower Canadian reformers; he and Baldwin formed a government in 1842 but resigned in 1843. In 1848 he was asked to form the first administration under the new policy of responsible government; over his three-year ministry he created the University of Toronto out of King's College and passed an amnesty act for the rebels of 1837–38.

La·fon·taine /lafɔ̃'tɛn/ a former town in south central Quebec, now part of Saint-Jérôme; pop. (2001) 9,477. [LAFONTAINE]

La Fon·taine /lafɔ̃'tɛn/ **Jean de** (1621–95), French poet. His *Fables* (1668–94), drawn from oriental, classical, and contemporary sources, include such tales as 'The Grasshopper and the Ant' and 'The Crow and the Fox'.

lag[1] ● *intransitive verb* (**lagged**, **lag·ging**) **1** (often foll. by *behind*) fall behind; not keep pace. **2** *Billiards* make the preliminary strokes that decide which player shall begin. ● *noun* **1 a** = LAG TIME. **b** a delay. **2** *Physics* **a** a retardation in a current or movement. **b** the amount of this. **3** *Geol.* (in full **lag fault**) a type of overthrust formed when the uppermost of a series of rocks moves more slowly than the lower ones. □ **lag·ger** *noun* [originally = hindmost person, hang back: perhaps from a fanciful distortion of LAST[1] in a children's game (*fog, seg, lag*, = 1st, 2nd, last, in dial.)]

lag[2] ● *transitive verb* (**lagged**, **lag·ging**) enclose or cover in lagging. ● *noun* **1** the non-heat-conducting cover of a boiler etc.; lagging. **2** a piece of this. [prob. from Scandinavian: compare Old Norse *lögg* barrel rim, related to LAY[1]]

lag[3] *slang* ● *noun* esp. *Brit.* (esp. as **old lag**) a convict, esp. a habitual criminal. ● *transitive verb* (**lagged**, **lag·ging**) **1** send to prison. **2** apprehend; arrest. [19th c.: origin unknown]

lagan /'lagən/ *noun* goods or wreckage lying on the bed of the sea, sometimes with a marking buoy etc. for later retrieval. [Old French, perhaps of Scandinavian origin, from root of LIE[1], LAY[1]]

lager *noun* (in full **lager beer**) **1** a kind of beer, effervescent and light in colour and body. **2** a serving of this. [German *Lagerbier* beer brewed for keeping from *Lager* store]

Lager·kvist /'lɒɡərkvɪst/ **Pär (Fabian)** (1891–1974), Swedish novelist, poet, and playwright. His novels explore good and evil, life's ambiguities, and the fear of death, and include *The Dwarf* (1944) and *Barabbas* (1950); he won the Nobel Prize for literature in 1951.

Lager·löf /'lɒɡər,lɜːf/ **Selma (Ottil·iana Lovi·sa)** (1858–1940), Swedish novelist. She made her name with *Gösta Berlings Saga* (1891), a book inspired by local legends and traditions; she won the Nobel Prize for literature in 1909, the first woman Nobel laureate.

lager lout *noun Brit. informal* a youth who behaves badly as a result of excessive drinking.

lag·gard /'laɡərd/ ● *noun* a dawdler; a person who lags behind. ● *adjective* dawdling; slow; lagging behind. □ **lag·gard·ly** *adjective & adverb* **lag·gard·ness** *noun* [LAG[1]]

lag·ging *noun* material providing heat insulation for a boiler, pipes, etc. [LAG[2]]

Lagi·mo·dière /laʒɪmoːdi'er/ **1 Jean-Baptiste** (1778–1855), Canadian fur trader. He lived as a trapper and hunter in the Red River and Fort Edmonton areas from about 1800 on. During the 1815 troubles in the Red River settlement he travelled 3000 km to Montreal in five months, much of it by snowshoe, to take a message to Lord Selkirk. On his return to the west he was given a grant of land across from Fort Garry. **2** his wife, **Marie-Anne** (1780–1875), Canadian western settler. She moved west with her husband following her marriage in 1806, becoming one of the first white women on the prairies. She was the mother of the first legitimate white child born in the west, and the grandmother of Louis Riel.

lagni·appe /la'njap/ *noun US* something given as a bonus or gratuity. [Louisiana French, from Spanish *la ñapa*]

lago·morph /'laɡə,mɔrf/ *noun* any mammal of the order Lagomorpha, including hares and rabbits. [Greek *lagōs* hare + *morphē* form]

la·goon *noun* **1** a bay separated from the sea, a large lake, etc. by a low sandbank or similar barrier. **2** the enclosed water of an atoll or inside a barrier reef. **3** an artificial pool for the treatment of effluent or to accommodate an overspill from surface drains during heavy rain. □ **la·goon·al** *adjective* [French *lagune* or Italian & Spanish *laguna* from Latin *lacuna*: see LACUNA]

Lagos /'leɪɡɒs/ the chief city of Nigeria, a port on the Gulf of Guinea; pop. (est. 1995) 1,484,000. It became capital of the newly independent Nigeria in 1960. It was replaced as capital by Abuja in 1982.

La Grande Ri·vière /la ˌɡrɑ̃d riv'jer/ a river in N Quebec, 893 km long, rising in the central part of the province and flowing first southwestward and then westward to empty into James Bay at Chisasibi, a Cree village on the bay's northeastern shore. [French, lit. 'the great river']

La·grange /lə'ɡrɑ̃ʒ/ **Jo·seph Louis, Comte de** (1736–1813), Italian-born French mathematician. His *Traité de mécanique analytique* (1788), was the culmination of his extensive work on mechanics and its application to the description of planetary and lunar motion. □ **La·gran·gian** /lə'ɡrɑ̃ʒiən/ *adjective*

La·gran·gian point /lə'ɡrɑ̃ʒiən/ *noun* each of five points in the plane of orbit of one body around another, e.g. the moon around the earth, at which a small third body can remain stationary with respect to both. [LAGRANGE]

lag screw *noun N Amer.* a large wood screw with a square or hexagonal head, driven with a wrench rather than a screwdriver.

lag time *noun* (also **lag**) a period of time separating two events, esp. an action and its effect.

La Guar·dia /lə 'ɡwardiə/ **Fio·rel·lo Henry** (1882–1947), US politician and mayor of New York 1933–45, who was responsible for wide-ranging civic improvements.

lah *var. of* LA.

lahal /'ləhɒl, 'ləhəl/ *noun* (also **slahal**) a game common amongst Pacific Northwest Aboriginal peoples in which teams attempt to win carved sticks by guessing in which hands of their opponents four bones are concealed. Singing, drumming, and often gambling accompany the game. [Pacific Northwest languages]

lahar /'lɒhar/ *noun* a mudflow composed mainly of volcanic debris. [Javanese]

La·Have River /lə'heɪv/ a river in W Nova Scotia, rising in the west central part of the province and flowing 75 km southeastward through Bridgewater to empty into the Atlantic Ocean. [LE HAVRE]

La·hore /lə'hɔr/ the capital of Punjab province and second largest city of Pakistan, situated near the border with India; pop. (1998) 5,063,500. It was the capital of the former province of West Pakistan between 1955 and 1970.

laic /'leɪɪk/ *rare* ● *adjective* non-clerical. ● *noun formal* a lay person; a non-cleric. □ **laicism** *noun* [Late Latin from Greek *laïkos* from *laos* people]

laicize /'leɪɪ,saɪz/ *transitive verb* (also esp. *Brit.* **laicise**) **1** make (an office etc.) tenable by lay people. **2** subject (a school or institution) to the control of lay people. **3** secularize. □ **laiciz·a·tion** *noun*

laid *past and past participle of* LAY[1].

laid-back *adjective informal* relaxed, unbothered, easygoing.

laid paper *noun* paper having a ribbed appearance made by parallel wires in the mould or on the dandy roller.

laid up *predicative adjective* **1** (of a person) confined to bed or the house, esp. because of illness or injury. **2** (of a ship, vehicle, etc.) taken out of service. **3 a** (of goods, provisions, etc.) saved, stored up, or put away for safety. **b** *informal* (of a person etc.) hidden.

lain *past participle of* LIE[1].

Laing /laŋ/ **Ron·ald David** (1927–89), Scottish psychiatrist. He had controversial views on schizophrenia, proposing that what society calls insanity is in fact a defensive facade in response to the tensions of the close-knit nuclear family; his books include *The Divided Self* (1960), *Sanity, Madness, and the Family* (1965), and *The Politics of the Family* (1971).

lair *noun* **1 a** a wild animal's den or resting place. **b** a person's hiding place, retreat, or secret base (*tracked him to his lair*). **2** *Brit.* a shed or enclosure for cattle on the way to market. □ **lair·age** *noun Brit.* [Old English *leger* from Germanic]

laird *noun Scot.* a landed proprietor. □ **laird·ship** *noun* [Scots form of LORD]

laissez-faire /ˌleseɪ'fer/ *noun* (also **laisser-faire**) **1** the theory or practice of governmental abstention from interference in the workings of the market etc. **2** non-interference or non-involvement in, or indifference to, the affairs of others generally. [French, = let act]

laissez-passer /ˌleseɪpa'seɪ/ *noun* (also **laisser-passer**) a document allowing the holder to pass; a permit. [French, = let pass]

laity /'leɪɪti/ *noun* (usu. prec. by *the*; usu. treated as *pl.*) **1** lay people, as distinct from the clergy. **2** ordinary people, as distinct from experts or professionals.

Laius /'laɪəs/ *Gk Myth* a king of Thebes, the father of Oedipus and husband of Jocasta.

La Jon·quière /laʒɔ̃ki'er/ **Jacques-Pierre de Taf·fa·nel de** (1685–1752), French naval officer, Governor of New France 1749–52. Serving in an official period of peace, he was chiefly occupied with preparing the forts in Acadia and on the Great Lakes for the next conflict.

lake[1] *noun* **1** a large body of water surrounded by land. **2** an expanse or surplus of liquid. **3** *Cdn* (*Nfld*) (often in **lake of water**) an expanse of open sea water in an icefield. □ **(go) jump in the lake** see JUMP. [Old French *lac* from Latin *lacus* basin, pool, lake]

lake² *noun* **1** a reddish colouring originally made from lac (*crimson lake*). **2** an insoluble pigment made by combining a soluble dye and an insoluble mordant. [var. of LAC¹]

Lake Abitibi see ABITIBI, LAKE.

Lake Agassiz see AGASSIZ, LAKE.

Lake Albert see ALBERT, LAKE.

Lake Athabasca see ATHABASCA, LAKE.

Lake Baikal (also **Lake Baykal**) see BAIKAL, LAKE.

Lake Balaton see BALATON, LAKE.

Lake Balqash see BALQASH, LAKE.

lake boat *noun Cdn* a boat or ship designed for sailing on the Great Lakes.

Lake Chad see CHAD, LAKE.

Lake Champlain see CHAMPLAIN, LAKE.

Lake Claire see CLAIRE, LAKE.

Lake Como see COMO, LAKE.

Lake Constance see CONSTANCE, LAKE.

Lake Couchiching see COUCHICHING, LAKE.

Lake Diefenbaker see DIEFENBAKER, LAKE.

Lake District (also **the Lakes**, **Lakeland**) a region of lakes in Cumbria, NW England.

Lake Edward see EDWARD, LAKE.

lake effect *noun* the influence of a large lake on weather patterns, esp. increasing snowfall downwind and moderating the temperature of surrounding areas (also *attributive*: *lake effect snow*).

Lake Erie see ERIE, LAKE.

Lake Eyre see EYRE, LAKE.

lake·fill *noun* an artificial shoreline or land area built by filling a lake etc.

lake·front *noun N Amer.* the shore of a lake (also *attributive*: *lakefront cottages*).

Lake Garda see GARDA, LAKE.

Lake Geneva see GENEVA, LAKE.

Lake·head, the an informal name for Thunder Bay.
□ **Lake·head·er** *noun*

lake·head *noun Cdn* the area along a lakeshore farthest from the lake's outlet.

Lake Hemkund see HEMKUND, LAKE.

lake herring *noun* a cisco or whitefish found in lakes.

Lake Huron see HURON, LAKE.

Lake Joseph see JOSEPH, LAKE.

Lake Kariba see KARIBA, LAKE.

Lake Kivu see KIVU, LAKE.

Lake Laberge see LABERGE, LAKE.

Lake Ladoga see LADOGA, LAKE.

lake·land *noun* **1** an area with many lakes. **2** (**Lakeland**) = LAKE DISTRICT.

Lakeland terrier *noun* a rough-coated, red or black and tan terrier with a stocky body and a broad muzzle, belonging to a breed developed in the Lake District of NW England.

Lake Lou·ise 1 a lake in SW Alberta, situated in Banff National Park. **2** a resort community nearby; pop. (2001) 1,497. [Princess *Louise*, 4th daughter of Queen Victoria and wife of the Marquess of Lorne, d.1939]

Lake Lucerne see LUCERNE, LAKE.

Lake Mac·qua·rie /məˈkwɒri/ a city on the coast of New South Wales, Australia, northeast of Sydney; pop. (est. 1998) 180,826.

Lake Magadi see MAGADI, LAKE.

Lake Maggiore see MAGGIORE, LAKE.

Lake Malawi see MALAWI, LAKE.

Lake Manitoba see MANITOBA, LAKE.

Lake Maracaibo see MARACAIBO, LAKE.

Lake Melville see MELVILLE, LAKE.

Lake Michigan see MICHIGAN, LAKE.

Lake Muskoka see MUSKOKA, LAKE.

Lake Nasser see NASSER, LAKE.

Lake Natron see NATRON, LAKE.

Lake Neuchâtel see NEUCHÂTEL, LAKE.

Lake Nicaragua see NICARAGUA, LAKE.

Lake Nipigon see NIPIGON, LAKE.

Lake Nipissing see NIPISSING, LAKE.

Lake Nyasa see NYASA, LAKE.

Lake of the Four Cantons see FOUR CANTONS, LAKE OF THE.

Lake of the Woods a lake situated in NW Ontario, straddling the borders with Manitoba and Minnesota. It has an area of 4 472 sq. km. [translation of French *Lac des Bois*]

Lake Ohrid see OHRID, LAKE.

Lake Okeechobee see OKEECHOBEE, LAKE.

Lake Onega see ONEGA, LAKE.

Lake Ontario see ONTARIO, LAKE.

Lake Poets the English poets Coleridge, Southey, and Wordsworth, who lived in and were inspired by the Lake District.

lak·er *noun informal* **1** *N Amer.* = LAKE TROUT. **2** a ship designed for sailing on lakes, esp. the Great Lakes.

Lake Rosseau see ROSSEAU, LAKE.

Lake Rossignol see ROSSIGNOL, LAKE.

Lake Rudolf see RUDOLF, LAKE.

Lake St. Clair see ST. CLAIR, LAKE.

Lake St. Francis see ST. FRANCIS, LAKE.

Lake·shore a town in SW Ontario, along the southern shore of Lake St. Clair; pop. (2001) 28,746.

lake·shore *noun N Amer.* the shore of a lake.

lake·side ● *attributive adjective* beside a lake. ● *noun* the area beside a lake.

Lake Simcoe see SIMCOE, LAKE.

Lake Superior see SUPERIOR, LAKE.

Lake Tana see TANA, LAKE.

Lake Tanganyika see TANGANYIKA, LAKE.

Lake Taupo see TAUPO, LAKE.

Lake Temagami see TEMAGAMI, LAKE.

Lake Tiberias see TIBERIAS, LAKE.

Lake Timiskaming see TIMISKAMING, LAKE.

Lake Titicaca see TITICACA, LAKE.

lake trout *noun* **1** the salmonid *Salvelinus namaycush*, occurring in N American lakes, an important sport fish. **2** a large, pale, partly migrating form of the trout, *Salmo trutta*, occurring in N European lakes.

Lake Turkana see TURKANA, LAKE.

Lake Van see VAN, LAKE.

Lake Vänern see VÄNERN, LAKE.

Lake Victoria see VICTORIA, LAKE.

lake·view *attributive adjective N Amer.* overlooking a lake (*lakeview suite*).

lake·ward /ˈleikwɜrd/ *N Amer.* ● *adjective* (of something on a lakeshore) facing the lake, as opposed to the land. ● *adverb* (also **lake·wards** /ˈleikwɜrdz/) towards a lake.

Lake Winnipeg see WINNIPEG, LAKE.

Lake Winnipegosis see WINNIPEGOSIS, LAKE.

lakh /lak, lɒk/ *noun* (also **lac**) *Ind.* (usu. foll. by *of*) a hundred thousand (rupees etc.). [Hindustani *lākh* from Sanskrit *lakṣa*]

La·ko·ta /ləˈkoːtə/ ● *noun* **1** (*pl.* same or **-tas**) a member of an Aboriginal people of western South Dakota. **2** the Sioux language of the Lakota. ● *adjective* of or relating to the Lakota or their language. [Lakota *lakhóta* 'allies']

Lak·shad·weep Islands /lakˈʃadwiːp/ a group of islands off the Malabar Coast of SW India, constituting a Union Territory in India; pop. (2000) 60,600; capital, Kavaratti. The group consists of the Laccadive, Minicoy, and Amindivi Islands.

Lak·shmi /ˈlʌkʃmi/ *Hinduism* the goddess of prosperity, consort of Vishnu. She assumes different forms, e.g. Radha, Sita, in order to accompany her husband in his various incarnations. [Sanskrit, = prosperity]

la-la land *noun N Amer. informal* **1** a fanciful state or dream world. **2** (**La-La Land**) California, esp. the world of movies and television based there. **3** *Cdn* (**La-La Land**) British Columbia. [20th c.: origin unknown]

lala·pa·loo·za *var. of* LOLLAPALOOZA.

Lale·mant /laləˈmɑ̃/ **1 Charles** (1587–1674), French Jesuit missionary. He organized the first Jesuit mission to Canada in 1625, and returned to France in 1627. He was in Canada again 1634–38, ministering to the

French immigrants, then returned to Paris to serve until 1650 as procurator of the missions to New France; in this position he helped to create the Société de Notre-Dame de Montréal. **2** his brother **Jé·rôme** (1593–1673), French Jesuit missionary. Arriving in Canada in 1638, he was made superior of the Huron missions. He made the first census of an Aboriginal nation and in 1639 centralized mission operations in a model community at Sainte-Marie-Among-the-Hurons. He also served as superior at Quebec 1645–50 and 1659–65.

La·lique /laˈliːk/ **René** (1860–1945), French jeweller. He achieved fame with his display of art nouveau brooches and combs at the International Exhibition in Paris in 1900. He developed a personal style of moulded glass with iced surfaces and patterns in relief.

Lal·lan /ˈlalən/ Scot. ● noun (now usu. **Lal·lans**) a Lowland Scots dialect, esp. as a literary language. ● adjective of or concerning the Lowlands of Scotland. [var. of LOWLAND]

lally·gag var. of LOLLYGAG.

Lam. abbreviation Bible Lamentations.

lam[1] verb (**lammed, lam·ming**) slang **1** transitive thrash; hit. **2** intransitive (foll. by into) hit (a person etc.) hard with a stick etc. [perhaps from Scandinavian: compare Old Norse lemja beat so as to LAME]

lam[2] noun □ **on the lam** N Amer. slang in flight, esp. from the police. [20th c.: origin unknown]

lama /ˈlɒmə, lɑmə/ noun a Tibetan or Mongolian Buddhist monk. [Tibetan blama (with silent b)]

Lama·ism /ˈlɒmə,ɪzəm/ noun the system of doctrine and observances inculcated and maintained by lamas; Tibetan Buddhism. (See DALAI LAMA, TIBETAN BUDDHISM.) □ **Lama·ist** noun

La Mal·baie /lamalˈbei/ a town in E Quebec, on the north shore of the St. Lawrence at the mouth of the Rivière Malbaie, about 150 km downstream from Quebec City; pop. (2001) 9,143. [French, lit. 'bad bay', because the bay is completely drained at low tide]

La·marck /laˈmɑrk/ **Jean Bap·tiste (Pierre An·toine) de Monet, Cheva·lier de** (1744–1829), French naturalist, an early proponent of organic evolution. He suggested that species could have evolved from each other by small changes in their structure, and that the mechanism of such change was that characteristics acquired in order to survive could be passed on to offspring. □ **La·marck·ian** noun & adjective **La·marck·ism** noun

La·Marsh /laˈmɑrʃ/ **Julia Ver·lyn** 'Judy' (1924–1980), Canadian lawyer, politician, broadcaster and writer. As a Liberal MP for Niagara Falls 1960–68, she served in the Pearson cabinet first as minister of national health and welfare (1963–65) and then as secretary of state (1965–68). She implemented the Canada Pension Plan and helped design the medicare system.

Lamar·tine /ˌlamɑrˈtiːn/ **Al·phonse Marie Louis de** (1790–1869), French poet, statesman, and historian. His first volume of poems, _Méditations poétiques_ (1820), established him as a leading figure of French Romanticism; his other works include _Histoire des Girondins_ (1847).

lama·sery /ˈlɒməseri/ noun (pl. **-ies**) a monastery of lamas. [French lamaserie irreg. from lama LAMA]

La Ma·tan·za /lamaˈtanzə/ (formerly **San Justo**) a city in central Argentina, pop. (est. 1999) 1,241,264.

La Mau·ri·cie National Park /lamɔriˈsiː/ a park in south central Quebec, situated on the Rivière Saint-Maurice, northwest of Trois-Rivières. [ultimately from the name of the river: see SAINT-MAURICE, RIVIÈRE]

La·maze /laˈmɒz/ noun (attributive) N Amer. designating a method of childbirth which emphasizes the use of psychological and physical preparation and breathing routines to control pain and minimize the need for drugs. [F. Lamaze, French physician d.1957, who advocated it]

Lamb ▶ **1 Charles** (1775–1834), English essayist and critic. He and his sister **Mary** (1764–1847) wrote _Tales from Shakespeare_ (1807), which, with his anthology _Specimens of English Dramatic Poets_ (1808), revived interest in Elizabethan drama. His semi-autobiographical essays were collected as _Essays of Elia_ (1823). **2 Wil·liam**, see MELBOURNE[2]. **3 Wil·lis Eu·gene, Jr.** (b.1913), US physicist. He discovered the Lamb shift, the small variation in energy between two states of the hydrogen atom, which led to a fundamental revision of quantum theory; he shared the Nobel Prize for physics in 1955.

lamb ● noun **1** a young sheep. **2** the flesh of a lamb as food. **3** a mild or gentle person, esp. a young child. **4** = LAMB OF GOD. ● verb **1 a** transitive (in passive) (of a lamb) be born. **b** intransitive (of a ewe) give birth to lambs. **2** transitive tend (lambing ewes). □ **like a lamb** meekly, obediently.

lamb·kin noun **lamb·like** adjective [Old English lamb from Germanic]

lam·bada /ləmˈbɒdə/ noun a fast erotic Brazilian dance which became internationally popular for a brief period in the late 1980s. [Portuguese, = a beating]

lam·baste /lamˈbeist/ transitive verb **1** thrash; beat. **2** criticize severely. [LAM[1] + BASTE[3]]

lamb·da /ˈlamdə/ noun **1** the eleventh letter of the Greek alphabet (Λ, λ). **2** (as λ) the symbol for wavelength. [Greek la(m)bda]

lam·bent /ˈlambənt/ adjective **1** (of a flame or a light) playing on a surface with a soft radiance but without burning. **2** (of the eyes, sky, etc.) softly radiant. **3** (of wit etc.) lightly brilliant. □ **lam·ben·cy** noun **lam·bent·ly** adverb [Latin lambere lambent- lick]

lam·bert /ˈlambɜrt/ noun a former unit of luminance, equal to the emission or reflection of one lumen per square centimetre. [J. H. _Lambert_, German physicist d.1777]

Lam·beth /ˈlambəθ/ a borough of inner London, on the south bank of the Thames; pop. (1991) 220,100. It is the site of Lambeth Palace, the London residence of the Archbishop of Canterbury.

Lambeth Conference noun a consultative gathering of all Anglican bishops, usu. held every ten years. [_Lambeth_ Palace, where the Conference is usually held]

lambie noun a term of endearment for a lamb.

lamb·kill noun = SHEEP LAUREL.

Lamb of God noun **1** a name for Christ (see John 1:29). **2** = AGNUS DEI 2.

Lam·bor·ghi·ni /lamborˈgiːni/ **Fer·ruc·cio** (1916–1993), Italian industrialist. In 1963 he set up a company to produce expensive, high-performance sports cars to rival those produced by Ferrari, and by the end of the 60s Lamborghini cars were much in demand.

lam·bre·quin /ˈlambrɪkɪn, ˈlambɜr-/ noun a short piece of drapery hung over the top of a door or a window or draped on a mantelpiece. [French from Dutch (unrecorded) lamperkin, diminutive of lamper veil]

lamb's ears noun a garden plant, _Stachys byzantina_, with whitish woolly leaves.

lamb·skin noun prepared skin from a lamb, with the wool on or as leather.

lamb's lettuce noun a plant, _Valerianella locusta_, used in salad. Also called CORN SALAD, MÂCHE.

lamb's quarters noun a herbaceous European plant of the goosefoot family, _Chenopodium album_, naturalized in N America.

lambs·wool ● noun soft fine wool from a young sheep used in knitted garments etc. ● adjective made of lambswool.

Lamb·ton Shores a town in SW Ontario, on the southern shore of Lake Huron northeast of Sarnia; pop. (2001) 10,571. [in honour of Sir John _Lambton_, Lord DURHAM[2]]

lame ● adjective **1 a** unable to walk without difficulty as the result of an injury or illness affecting the foot or leg. **b** (of a leg or foot) affected in this way. **2** (of an argument, story, excuse, etc.) unconvincingly feeble. **3** N Amer. pathetic or contemptible, esp. because unfashionable. **4** (of something intended to be entertaining) uninspiring and dull. ● transitive verb make lame. □ **lame·ly** adverb **lame·ness** noun [Old English lama from Germanic]

lamé /laˈmei, ˈlamei/ ● noun a fabric with gold or silver threads interwoven. ● adjective (of fabric, a dress, etc.) having such threads. [French]

lame·brain noun N Amer. informal a stupid person. □ **lame·brained** adjective

lame duck noun (often, with hyphen, attributive) **1** a disabled or powerless person or thing. **2** (in the US) the President in the final period of office, after the election of a successor. **3** any person or thing soon to be replaced.

la·mel·la /ləˈmelə/ noun (pl. **la·mel·lae** /-liː/) (usu. in pl.) **1** a thin layer, membrane, scale, or plate-like tissue or part, esp. in bone tissue. **2** Bot. a membranous fold in a chloroplast. □ **la·mel·lar** adjective

lam·el·late /ˈlaməleit/ adjective **lam·el·lat·ed** /ˈlaməleitəd/ adjective [Latin, diminutive of lamina: see LAMINA]

la·mel·li·branch /ləˈmelɪ,braŋk/ noun = BIVALVE. [LAMELLA + Greek bragkhia gills]

la·mel·li·corn /ləˈmelɪ,kɔrn/ noun the former name for SCARABAEOID. [modern Latin lamellicornis from Latin lamella (see LAMELLA) + cornu horn]

la·ment /ləˈment/ ● noun **1** a passionate expression of grief. **2** a song or poem of mourning or sorrow. ● verb **1** transitive & intransitive express or feel grief (for or about). **2** *transitive* regret (*lamented the lack of information*). **3** *transitive* utter with a lament. □ **lament for** (or **over**) mourn or regret. □ **la·ment·er** *noun* [Latin *lamentum*]

la·ment·able /ləˈmentəbəl, ˈlaməntəbəl/ *adjective* **1** (of circumstances or conditions.) deplorably bad. **2** (of an event, action, or attitude) unfortunate; regrettable. □ **la·ment·ably** *adverb*

lam·en·ta·tion /ˌlamənˈteɪʃən/ *noun* **1** the act or an instance of lamenting. **2** a lament.

Lam·en·ta·tions (in full **The Lamentations of Jeremiah**) a book of the Bible traditionally ascribed to Jeremiah but probably of a later period, telling of the desolation of Judah after the destruction of Jerusalem in 586 BC.

la·ment·ed *adjective* a conventional expression referring to a recently dead person (*your late lamented father*).

La·mèque, Île /ləˈmek/ an island off the northeastern corner of New Brunswick, situated at the entrance to Chaleur Bay. [Mi'kmaq]

lam·ina /ˈlaminə/ *noun* (*pl.* **lam·inae** /-ˌniː/) a thin plate or scale, e.g. of bone, stratified rock, or vegetable tissue. □ **lamin·ose** *adjective* [Latin, = 'layer']

lamin·ar /ˈlaminər/ *adjective* **1** consisting of laminae. **2** *Physics* (of a flow) taking place along constant streamlines, not turbulent.

lamin·ate ● *verb* /ˈlamiˌneit/ **1** *transitive* overlay with a thin plastic layer, metal plates, etc. **2** *transitive* beat or roll (metal) into thin plates. **3** *transitive* manufacture by placing layer on layer. **4** *transitive & intransitive* split or be split into layers or leaves. ● *noun* /ˈlaminət/ a laminated structure or material, esp. of layers fixed together to form rigid or flexible material. ● *adjective* /ˈlaminət/ in the form of lamina or laminae. □ **lamin·a·tion** *noun* **lamin·ator** *noun*

lamin·itis /ˌlamiˈnaitis/ *noun* inflammation of the laminae of the hoof in horses and other animals.

Lam·mas /ˈlaməs/ *noun* (in full **Lammas Day**) the first day of August, formerly observed in England as harvest festival. [Old English *hlāfmæsse* (as LOAF[1], MASS[2])]

lam·mer·geier /ˈlamərˌgaiər/ *noun* (also **lam·mer·geyer**) a large Eurasian vulture, *Gypaetus barbatus*, with a very large wingspan (often of 3 m) and dark beard-like feathers on either side of its beak. [German *Lämmergeier*, from *Lämmer* lambs + *Geier* vulture]

Lamon /ləˈmɒn/ **Jeanne** (b.1949), Canadian violinist and conductor. She became musical director of the chamber orchestra Tafelmusik in 1981, and has made several acclaimed recordings, including Bach's *Brandenburg Concertos* (1993), for which she won a Juno award.

lamp *noun* **1** a device for producing a steady light, esp.: **a** an electric bulb, and usu. its holder and shade or cover (*bedside lamp*). **b** an oil lamp. **c** a usu. glass holder for a candle. **d** a gas jet and mantle. **2** a source of spiritual or intellectual inspiration. **3** *literary* the sun, the moon, or a star. **4** a device producing ultraviolet, infrared, or other radiation, for tanning skin, keeping food warm, or as a treatment for various complaints. □ **lamp·less** *adjective* [Old French *lampe* and Late Latin *lampada* from the accusative of Latin *lampas* 'torch', from Greek]

lamp·black *noun* a black pigment made from soot.

Lam·pe·dusa /ˌlampiˈduːzə/ **Giu·seppe Tomasi de** (1896–1957), Italian novelist. His only novel *Il Gattopardo* (*The Leopard*) was originally rejected by publishers but won worldwide acclaim on its posthumous publication in 1958.

lamp·light *noun* light given by a lamp or lamps. □ **lamp·lit** *adjective*

lamp·light·er *noun* *hist.* a person who lights street lamps.

Lamp·man, Archi·bald (1861–1899), Canadian poet. Employed as a postal clerk in Ottawa from 1883 until his death, Lampman had to publish his first collection, *Among the Millet* (1888), himself. His strikingly simple impressions of the Cdn landscape, esp. in *Lyrics of the Earth* (1895), made him the finest of the Confederation Poets.

lam·poon ● *noun* a satirical attack on a person etc. ● *transitive verb* satirize. □ **lam·poon·er** *noun* **lam·poon·ery** *noun* **lam·poon·ist** *noun* [French *lampon*, conjectured to be from *lampons* 'let us drink' from *lamper* 'gulp down' from *laper* LAP[3]]

lamp·post *noun* a tall post supporting a street light.

lam·prey /ˈlampri/ *noun* (*pl.* **-preys**) any eel-like aquatic vertebrate of the family Petromyzonidae, without scales, paired fins, or jaws, but having a sucker mouth with horny teeth and a rough tongue. [Old French *lampreie* from medieval Latin *lampreda*: compare Late Latin *lampetra* perhaps from Latin *lambere* lick + *petra* stone]

lamp·shade *noun* a cover for a lamp, used to soften or direct its light.

lamp·stand *noun* a pole or stand for supporting a lamp, light bulb, etc.

lamp standard *noun* = LAMPPOST.

LAN /lan/ *noun* Computing local area network. [abbreviation]

la·nai /ləˈnai/ *noun* a porch or veranda, originally in Hawaii. [Hawaiian]

Lan·ark·shire /ˈlanərkˌʃir/ a former county of SW central Scotland, now divided into North Lanarkshire and South Lanarkshire. It was part of Strathclyde region from 1975 to 1996.

Lan·ca·shire /ˈlaŋkəˌʃir/ a county of NW England, on the Irish Sea; administrative centre, Preston. The county was noted for the production of textiles, esp. cotton goods, between the 16th and 19th c.

Lan·cas·ter[1] /ˈlaŋˌkastər/ a city in Lancashire, on the estuary of the Lune River; pop. (est. 2002) 48,800. It was the county town and administrative centre of Lancashire until 1974.

Lan·cas·ter[2] /ˈlaŋˌkastər/ **1 Bur·ton Ste·phen 'Burt'** (1913–94), US film actor. He made his film debut in *The Killers* (1946) and was often cast in 'tough guy' roles. He took more dramatic parts in films such as *From Here to Eternity* (1953), *Elmer Gantry* (1960), for which he won an Oscar, and *Field of Dreams* (1989). **2 Ron·ald 'Ron'** (b.1938), American-born Canadian football player and coach. During his career as a CFL quarterback, in Ottawa from 1960–63 and in Saskatchewan from 1963–78, he took his team to the playoffs 17 times, winning the Grey Cup twice, and set 30 CFL records. He also served as head coach of the Saskatchewan Roughriders, Edmonton Eskimos, and Hamilton Tiger-Cats.

Lancaster Sound /ˈlankastər/ a passage in the Canadian Arctic, separating Devon Island from Baffin Island. It is connected to the Labrador Sea through Baffin Bay. [Sir J. *Lancaster*, English merchant and promoter of Arctic exploration d.1618]

Lan·cas·trian /lanˈkastriən/ ● *noun* **1** a native of Lancashire or Lancaster. **2** *hist.* a follower of the House of Lancaster or of the Red Rose party supporting it in the Wars of the Roses (compare YORKIST). ● *adjective* of or concerning Lancashire or Lancaster, or the House of Lancaster.

lance ● *noun* **1 a** a long weapon with a wooden shaft and a pointed steel head, used by a horseman in charging. **b** a similar weapon used for spearing a fish, killing a harpooned whale, etc. **2** a metal pipe supplying oxygen to burn metal. **3** = LANCER 1. ● *verb* **1** *transitive* Surgery prick or cut open with a lancet. **2** *transitive* pierce with or as with a lance. **3** *intransitive* (of a ray of light etc.) pierce through a narrow opening. □ **lance the boil** relieve simmering tension or an unpleasant situation, esp. by taking drastic or painful measures. [Old French *lancier* from Latin *lancea*]

lance bombardier *noun* (also **Lance Bombardier**) (in the UK and formerly in Canada) a non-commissioned officer of the lowest rank in the artillery. Abbr.: **LBdr**.

lance corporal *noun* the lowest rank of NCO in some armies. [on analogy of obsolete *lancepesade* lowest grade of NCO, ultimately from Italian *lancia spezzata* broken lance]

lance·let *noun* any small non-vertebrate fishlike chordate of the family Branchiostomidae, that burrows in sand. [LANCE *noun* + -LET, with reference to its thin form]

Lan·ce·lot (in Arthurian legend) a knight of the Round Table, and the lover of Guinevere.

lan·ceo·late /ˈlansiələt/ *adjective* shaped like the head of a lance, narrow and tapering at each end. [Late Latin *lanceolatus* from *lanceola* diminutive of *lancea* lance]

lan·cer *noun* **1** *hist.* a soldier of a cavalry regiment armed with lances. **2** (in *pl.*) **a** a quadrille for 8 or 16 pairs. **b** the music for this.

lan·cet /ˈlansət/ *noun* **1** a small broad two-edged surgical knife with a sharp point. **2** (in full **lancet arch**, **lancet window**) a narrow arch or window with a pointed head. □ **lan·cet·ed** *adjective* [Old French *lancette* (as LANCE)]

lanch /lanʃ/ *transitive verb* Cdn (Nfld) **1** push or haul (a boat etc.) over ice. **2** move (a house or other building) over land, water, or ice. [obsolete form of LAUNCH[1]]

Lan·chow see LANZHOU.

L'Ancienne-Lorette /ˌlɑ̃sjenlɔrˈet/ a former city in SE central Quebec, now part of the city of Québec; pop. (2001) 15,929. [French, lit. 'Old Lorette', in contrast to *Nouvelle-Lorette* (now Loretteville), both ultimately after LORETO]

Lancs. *abbreviation* Lancashire.

Land[1], **Edwin Her·bert** (1909–91), US inventor and physicist, who designed a polarizing filter, and developed the instant camera manufactured as the Polaroid Land Camera (1947).

Land[2] /lɒnt/ *noun* (*pl.* **Länder** /ˈlendər/) a state of Germany or Austria. [German (as LAND]]

u: m**oo**d ai m**y** əi p**i**pe au br**ow**n ʌu h**ou**se ei d**ay** ɔi b**oy** ã fr**an**glais ã Ca**na**dien ɔ̃ Br**ay**on   (*see over for consonants*)

land ● *noun* **1 a** the solid part of the earth's surface, as opposed to large bodies of water or air. **b** (*attributive*) designating armies rather than navies or air forces (*land forces*). **2 a** an expanse of country; ground; soil. **b** such land in relation to its use, quality, etc., or (often prec. by *the*) as a basis for agriculture or hunting, fishing, and gathering (*building land; this is good land; works on the land; a dogsled trip out on the land*). **3** a country, nation, or state (*our home and native land*). **4 a** landed property. **b** (in *pl.*) estates. **5** the space between the rifling grooves in a gun. **6** a figurative domain or sphere (*TV land*). ● *verb* **1 a** *transitive & intransitive* set or go ashore. **b** *intransitive* (often foll. by *at*) disembark (*landed at the harbour*). **2** *transitive* bring (an aircraft, its passengers, etc.) to the ground or the surface of water. **3** *intransitive* (of an aircraft, bird, parachutist, etc.) alight on the ground or water. **4** *transitive* bring (a fish) to land, esp. with a hook or net. **5** *transitive & intransitive* (also *reflexive*; often foll. by *up*) *informal* bring to, reach, or find oneself in a certain situation, place, or state (*landed himself in jail; landed up in France; landed her in trouble; landed up penniless*). **6** *transitive informal* **a** deal (a person etc. a blow etc.) (*landed him one in the eye*). **b** (foll. by *with*) esp. *Brit.* present (a person) with (a problem, job, etc.). **7** *transitive* set down (a person, cargo, etc.) from a vehicle, ship, etc. **8** *transitive informal* win or obtain (a prize, job, etc.) esp. against strong competition. □ **how the land lies** what the state of affairs is. **in the land of the living** *jocular* still alive. **land of Nod** sleep (with pun on the phr. in Gen. 4:16). **land on one's feet** emerge unharmed from a difficult situation. □ **land·less** *adjective* [Old English from Germanic]

Land Acts a series of British parliamentary acts concerning land tenure in Ireland, passed in 1870, 1881, 1903, and 1909, intended to give tenants greater security and further rights.

land agent *noun* **1** *Cdn hist.* an agent who helped settlers find homesteads, esp. on the Prairies. **2** *Brit.* the steward of an estate. **3** *Brit.* an agent for the sale of estates. □ **land agency** *noun*

land assembly *noun* the acquisition of adjacent pieces of land for one large development.

Lan·dau /ˈlandau/ **Lev David·ovitch** (1908–68), Soviet theoretical physicist. He was awarded the 1962 Nobel Prize for physics for his work on the superfluidity and thermal conductivity of liquid helium.

lan·dau /ˈlandau/ *noun* **1** a four-wheeled horse-drawn carriage, with folding front and rear hoods enabling it to travel open, half-open, or closed. **2** a car with a folding leather hood over the rear seats. [*Landau* near Karlsruhe in Germany, where it was first made]

land bank *noun* **1** a bank issuing banknotes on the securities of landed property. **2** land held in trust, esp. for future development.

land base *noun* esp. *Cdn* a territory under the control of a specified group, e.g. a logging company or Aboriginal group.

land bridge *noun* a neck of land joining two large land masses.

land claim *noun* esp. *Cdn* a legal claim by an Aboriginal group concerning the use of an area of land.

land crab *noun* a crab, *Cardisoma guanhumi*, that lives in burrows inland and migrates in large numbers to the sea to breed.

land·ed *adjective* **1** *Cdn* denoting official recognition of immigration to Canada (*landed immigrant; seeking landed status*). **2** owning land (*landed gentry*). **3** consisting of, including, or relating to land (*landed property*).

Länd·er *pl.* of LAND².

land·er *noun* a spacecraft designed to land on the surface of a planet or moon.

Lan·ders /ˈlandərz/ **Ann** (born Esther Pauline Friedman Lederer) (b.1918–2002), US advice columnist, syndicated in more than 1,200 newspapers. Soon after she took over the 'Ask Ann Landers' column in the *Chicago Sun-Times*, her twin sister Pauline Esther started a successful rival column called 'Dear Abby'.

land·fall *noun* the first sight of or approach to land after a journey by sea or by air over open water.

land·fast *attributive adjective* *N Amer.* (also **shorefast**) (of ice covering a frozen body of water) firmly attached to the shore; not floating freely.

land·fill ● *noun* **1** the disposal of refuse by burying it under layers of earth. **2** refuse disposed of in this way. **3** an area filled in by this process. ● *verb* **1** *transitive & intransitive* dispose of (refuse) in this way. **2** *transitive* fill (a piece of land) with refuse in this way.

landfill gas *noun* gas, esp. methane, given off by decomposing refuse in landfills.

Land Forces Command *noun* *Cdn* the official name for the Canadian army.

land·form *noun* a natural feature of the earth's surface.

land grant ● *noun* *N Amer.* **1** the donation of land by a government to an individual, institution, etc. **2** the land so granted. **3** the agreement, treaty, etc. authorizing the grant. ● *attributive adjective* (**land-grant**) *US* designating a college etc. established with government grants.

land·hold·er *noun* the owner or the tenant of land.

land·hold·ing *noun* **1** a piece of land owned or rented. **2** the owning or renting of land.

land·ing *noun* **1 a** the act or process of coming to land or the ground, floor etc. **b** an instance of this. **c** a place in a harbour for disembarking, loading, unloading, etc. **2** a level place between two flights of stairs, or at the top or bottom of a flight. **3** *Cdn Forestry* an area where logs are piled before being loaded for transportation. **4** a quantity of fish landed at one time.

landing card *noun* a card issued to a passenger on an international flight or voyage, which they fill out with details of their citizenship, travel itinerary, and sometimes goods being imported, which is surrendered to customs and immigration authorities upon landing.

landing craft *noun* any of several types of craft esp. designed for putting troops and equipment ashore.

landing gear *noun* the undercarriage of an aircraft.

landing light *noun* **1** a light on a runway to guide an aircraft in a night landing. **2** (usu. in *pl.*) a powerful light attached to an aircraft to illuminate the landing path ahead.

landing net *noun* a net for landing a large fish which has been hooked.

landing pad *noun* a small area designed for helicopters to land on and take off from.

landing stage *noun* a platform, often floating, on which goods and passengers are disembarked.

landing strip *noun* an airstrip.

land·lady *noun* (pl. **-ladies**) **1** a woman who rents land, a building, part of a building, etc., to a tenant. **2** a woman who keeps a boarding house or rooming house. **3** *Brit.* a woman responsible for a pub.

Land League an Irish organization formed in 1879 to campaign for tenants' rights, in particular fair rents and security of tenure. Among its techniques was the use of the boycott against anyone taking on a farm from which the tenant had been evicted.

länd·ler /ˈlendlər/ *noun* **1** an Austrian dance in triple time, a precursor of the waltz. **2** the music for a ländler. [German from *Landl* Upper Austria]

land line *noun* a conventional telecommunications connection made at least partly by cable laid across land, esp. in reference to a telephone service attached to a given address in contrast to a cellular phone connection.

land·locked *adjective* **1** almost or entirely enclosed by land. **2** (of fish, esp. salmon) living in fresh water cut off from the sea.

land·lord *noun* **1** a person who rents land, a building, part of a building, etc., to a tenant. **2** a person who keeps a boarding house or rooming house. **3** *Brit.* a man responsible for a pub.

land·lord·ism *noun* the system whereby property is owned by landlords and leased or rented to tenants.

land·lub·ber *noun* a person unfamiliar with the sea or sailing. [LAND + LUBBER]

land·mark *noun* **1 a** an object or feature of a landscape or town that is easily seen and recognized from a distance, esp. one that enables someone to establish their location. **b** an important building, monument, etc. **2** an event, change, etc. marking a stage or turning point in history etc. (also *attributive*: *a landmark decision*).

land mass *noun* a large area of land.

land mine *noun* an explosive mine laid in or on the ground.

land office *noun* *N Amer.* an office recording dealings in public land.

land-office business *noun* *N Amer.* an enormously successful business.

Lan·dor, Wal·ter Sav·age (1775–1864), English poet and essayist. In verse and prose his style shows a clear debt to classical forms and themes; his best-known prose work, *Imaginary Conversations of Literary Men and Statesmen* (1824–8), was composed during his long residence in Italy (1815–35).

land·owner *noun* an owner of land. □ **land·owner·ship** *noun* **land·own·ing** *adjective & noun*

Lan·dow·ska /lanˈdɒfskə/ **Wanda** (1877–1959), Polish-born US pianist and harpsichordist, who was a leading figure in the 20th-c. revival of baroque harpsichord music.

Land·race *noun* a pig of a large white breed, originally developed in Denmark. [Danish, = national breed]

land registry office *noun* *Cdn* (in the Atlantic provinces, Quebec, and parts of Ontario and Manitoba) a government office where documents concerning property are kept but where the government does not guarantee their validity (compare LAND TITLES OFFICE).

Land·sat Island an island off the northeastern coast of Labrador. [Landsat-1, the US remote-sensing satellite that detected the island (blend of land(sensing) + satellite)]

land·scape ● noun **1** natural or imaginary scenery, as seen in a broad view. **2** (often attributive) a picture representing this; the genre of landscape painting. **3** (of a page, book, etc., or the manner in which it is set or printed) having or in a rectangular shape with the width greater than the height (compare PORTRAIT). **4** the general characteristics of an activity, field, sphere, etc. (the political landscape). ● transitive & intransitive verb alter (a piece of land) by landscape gardening. □ **land·scap·er** noun **land·scap·ing** noun **land·scap·ist** noun [Middle Dutch landscap (as LAND, -SHIP)]

landscape architecture noun the art or practice of planning and designing the environment, esp. with reference to built areas. □ **landscape architect** noun

landscape fabric noun a woven water-permeable material placed over the earth in a flower bed etc. to deter the growth of weeds.

landscape gardening noun the art or practice of laying out ornamental grounds or grounds imitating natural scenery. □ **landscape gardener** noun

Land·seer /ˈlandsiːr/ **Sir Edwin (Henry)** (1802–73), English painter, esp. of domestic and wild animals, and sculptor of the bronze lions at the base of Nelson's Column in Trafalgar Square, London (1867).

Land's End a rocky promontory in SW Cornwall, which forms the westernmost point of England.

land·slide noun **1 a** (Brit. also **land·slip**) the sliding down of a mass of land from a mountain, cliff, etc. **b** the mass of land which has so fallen. **2** an overwhelming majority for one side in an election.

lands·man[1] noun (pl. **-men**) **1** a non-sailor. **2** Cdn (Nfld) a sealer based on land rather than on a ship.

lands·man[2] noun (pl. **-men**) (esp. among Jews) a compatriot. [Yiddish, from Middle High German lantsman, lantman a native]

Land·stein·er /ˈland.staɪnər/ **Karl** (1868–1943), Austrian-born US immunologist. He devised the system of classifying blood into four main immunological groups (A, B, AB, and O), which made successful blood transfusions possible, and was the first to describe the rhesus factor in blood (1940); he was awarded a Nobel Prize in 1930.

land titles office noun Cdn & Austral. a government agency which keeps track of ownership of property by maintaining documents pertaining to the property once it has determined their validity (compare LAND REGISTRY OFFICE).

land·ward ● adjective facing the land, as opposed to the sea. ● adverb (also **land·wards**) towards the land.

land·wash noun Cdn (Nfld) the area along a shore between the high-water mark and the sea.

land wind noun a wind blowing seaward from the land.

lane noun **1** a narrow road, street, or path. **2** a division of a road for a stream of traffic (four-lane highway; bicycle lane). **3** a strip of track or water for a runner, rower, or swimmer, usu. marked out and separated from parallel ones by lines or ropes. **4** a path or course prescribed for or regularly followed by a ship, aircraft, etc. (ocean lane). **5** the long alley down which a bowling ball is thrown. **6** a gangway between crowds of people, objects, etc. **7** Basketball **a** = KEY[1] noun 15. **b** any open area on the court through which a player can move towards the hoop (drive the lane). [Old English: origin unknown]

lane·way noun **1** = LANE 1. **2** Cdn a narrow urban street, esp. behind houses or stores; a back alley.

Lang, **Fritz** (1890–1976), Austrian-born US film director. A pioneer of German cinema, during the 1920s he directed such notable silent films as the dystopian Metropolis (1927); in the US from 1935 he made a range of films, including westerns (such as Rancho Notorious, 1952) and films noirs (such as The Big Heat, 1953).

lang, k.d. (Kathy Dawn Lang) (b.1961), Canadian singer and songwriter. She gained a wide audience in the mid-1980s with a musical style blending country, pop, and blues, moving into a more mainstream pop style in the 90s. She won Grammys for Absolute Torch and Twang (1989) and Ingenue (1992).

Lan·ge·vin /lãʒəˈvã/ **1 André** (b.1927), Canadian writer. His early work, including Poussière sur la ville (1953), was inspired by existentialism and humanism and brought a new outlook to Quebec writing. All of his novels deal with humanity's attempts to escape fate. **2 Sir Hector-Louis** (1826–1906), Canadian lawyer, politician and

journalist, Father of Confederation. His varied career included terms as mayor of Quebec City (1857–61), member of the legislative assembly (1857–67), Solicitor General for Canada East (1864–66) and postmaster general (1866–67). He attended all three Confederation conferences, and served as secretary of state and superintendent of Indian affairs (1867–69), minister of public works (1869–73 and 1879–91), and leader of the Quebec wing of the Conservative Party (1873–91).

Lang·land /ˈlaŋlənd/ **Wil·liam** (c.1330–c.1400), English poet. He is credited with writing Piers Plowman (c.1367–70), an allegorical poem in alliterative verse in which the narrator is guided on a spiritual pilgrimage by the Plowman and experiences a series of visions on his journey in search of Truth.

lang·lauf /ˈlaŋlʌuf/ noun cross-country skiing; a cross-country skiing race. [German, = long run]

Lang·ley[1] a city in southwestern BC, about 45 km east of Vancouver; pop. (2001) 23,643. [see FORT LANGLEY]

Lang·ley[2], **Sam·uel Pier·point** (1834–1906), US astronomer and aviation pioneer. He invented the bolometer and used it to study the radiant energy of the sun; his work on aerodynamics contributed to the design of early airplanes.

Lang·muir /ˈlaŋmjʊr/ **Irv·ing** (1881–1957), US chemist and physicist. He studied adsorption and its application to catalysis; while studying atomic structure he introduced the terms covalence and electrovalence. He won the Nobel Prize for chemistry in 1932.

lan·gouste /lãˈguːst, ˈlɒŋguːst/ noun a spiny lobster. [French]

lan·gous·tine /ˌlãguːˈstiːn, ˈlɒŋguˌstiːn/ noun = NORWAY LOBSTER. [French]

lang syne /laŋ ˈzaɪn/ Scot. ● adverb in the distant past. ● noun the old days (compare AULD LANG SYNE). [= long since]

Lang·ton, Ste·phen (c.1150–1228), English clergyman. As Archbishop of Canterbury (1213–28) he defended the Church's interests against King John, was intermediary during the negotiations leading to the signing of Magna Carta (1215), and protected the young Henry III against baronial domination.

Lang·try, Lillie (born Emilie Charlotte le Breton) (known as 'the Jersey Lily') (1853–1929), English actress. She was noted for her beauty, and made her stage debut in 1881; she became the mistress of the Prince of Wales, later Edward VII.

lan·guage noun **1** the method of human communication, either spoken or written, consisting of the use of words in an agreed way. **2** the language of a particular community or country etc. (speaks several languages). **3** any method of expression (body language; sign language). **4 a** the faculty of speech. **b** a style or the faculty of expression; the use of words, etc. (his language was poetic; hasn't the language to express it). **c** (also **bad language**) coarse, crude, or abusive speech (didn't like his language). **5** a system of symbols and rules for writing computer programs or algorithms. **6** a professional or specialized vocabulary. **7** literary style. □ **speak the same language** understand; have a similar outlook, manner of expression, etc. [Old French langage, ultimately from Latin lingua tongue]

language arts plural noun those subjects (as reading, writing, spelling, etc.) taught in schools to develop oral and written communication skills.

language laboratory noun (also **language lab**) **1** a room equipped with tape recorders etc. where foreign languages are learned by means of repeated oral practice. **2** a class which takes place in a language laboratory.

language police noun derogatory **1** Cdn (Que.) the officials of the Commission de Protection de la Langue Française responsible for ensuring that the province of Quebec's language laws are enforced. **2** a group, often self-appointed, which criticizes what it considers to be unacceptable language.

langue de chat /ˌlãg də ˈʃp/ noun (pl. **langues de chat** pronunc. same) a very thin finger-shaped crisp cookie or piece of chocolate. [French, = cat's tongue]

Langue·doc /lãgəˈdɒk/ a former province of S France, which extended from the Rhone valley to the northern foothills of the E Pyrenees.

langue d'oc /lãg ˈdɒk/ noun the form of medieval French spoken south of the Loire, the basis of modern Occitan (compare LANGUE D'OÏL). [Old French langue language, from Latin lingua tongue + de of + oc (from Latin hoc) the form for yes]

Languedoc-Roussil·lon /lãgəˌdɒk ruːsiːˈjɔ̃/ a region of S France, on the Mediterranean coast, extending from the Rhone delta to the border with Spain.

---

t top   v voice   w we   z zoo   ʃ she   ʒ vision   θ thin   ð this   ŋ ring   x loch   tʃ chip   dʒ jar   (see over for vowels)

langue d'oïl /lãg 'dɔil/ *noun* medieval French as spoken north of the Loire, the basis of modern French (compare LANGUE D'OC). [as LANGUE D'OC + *oïl* (from Latin *hoc ille*) the form for *yes*]

lan·guid /'laŋgwɪd/ *adjective* **1** moving slowly and involving little physical effort or emotion. **2** (of ideas etc.) lacking force; uninteresting. **3** faint; weak. □ **lan·guid·ly** *adverb* **lan·guid·ness** *noun* [French *languide* or Latin *languidus* (as LANGUISH)]

lan·guish /'laŋgwɪʃ/ *intransitive verb* **1** be or grow feeble; lose or lack vitality. **2** live under conditions which lower the vitality or depress the spirits (*languished in graduate school*). **3** (foll. by *for*) pine or long for. **4** suffer neglect. [Old French *languir*, ultimately from Latin *languêre*, related to LAX]

lan·guor /'laŋgɜr/ *noun* **1** the state or feeling, often pleasant, of being lazy and lacking energy. **2** an oppressive stillness (of the air etc.). □ **lan·guor·ous** *adjective* **lan·guor·ous·ly** *adverb* [Old French from Latin *languor -oris* (as LANGUISH)]

lan·gur /lʌn'guːr/ *noun* any of various Asian long-tailed monkeys esp. of the genus *Presbytis*. [Hindi]

La Niña /la 'niːnjə/ *noun* a cooling of the water in the equatorial Pacific, which occurs at irregular intervals, and is associated with widespread changes in weather patterns complementary to those of El Niño, but less extensive and damaging in their effect. [Spanish = 'the girl', after EL NIÑO]

lank *adjective* **1** (of hair, grass, etc.) long, limp, and straight. **2** thin and tall. □ **lank·ly** *adverb* **lank·ness** *noun* [Old English *hlanc* from Germanic]

lanky *adjective* (**lank·i·er**, **lank·i·est**) (of limbs, a person, etc.) ungracefully thin and long or tall. □ **lank·i·ly** *adverb* **lank·i·ness** *noun*

lan·ner *noun* a S European falcon, *Falco biarmicus*, esp. the female. [Old French *lanier* perhaps from Old French *lanier* cowardly, originally = weaver, from Latin *lanarius* wool merchant, from *lana* wool]

lan·ner·et *noun* a male lanner, smaller than the female.

Lan·ois /lan'wɒ/ **Dan·iel** (b.1951), Canadian musician and producer. He has worked with British composer Brian Eno to produce several albums by the rock band U2, and has also worked with Peter Gabriel, Bob Dylan, and others, while pursuing his own critically acclaimed solo music career.

lan·o·lin /'lanəlɪn/ *noun* a fat found naturally on sheep's wool and used purified for cosmetics etc. [German from Latin *lana* wool + *oleum* oil]

Lans·downe, Henry Charles Keith Petty-Fitzmaurice, 5th Marquess of (1845–1927), British politician, Governor General of Canada 1883–88. As Governor General he presided over the period of the Northwest Rebellion; following his term in Canada he was viceroy of India 1888–93.

L'Anse aux Meadows /ˌlãsoːme'doːz/ a historic site in N Newfoundland, at the northernmost tip of the island. It is the location of a Norse settlement established *c.*1000 AD, and was designated a World Heritage Site in 1978. [alteration of French *anse aux méduses* jellyfish cove]

Lan·sing the state capital of Michigan; pop. (2000) 119,128.

lans·quenet /'lanskənət/ *noun* **1** a card game of German origin. **2** a German mercenary soldier in the 16th–17th c. [French from German *Landsknecht* (as LAND, *Knecht* soldier, from Old High German *kneht*: see KNIGHT)]

lan·tana /lan'teinə, -'tanə, -'tɒnə/ *noun* any evergreen shrub of the genus *Lantana*, with usu. yellow or orange flowers. [modern Latin]

Lan·tau /lan'tau/ an island of Hong Kong, situated to the west of Hong Kong Island and separated from it by the Lamma Channel.

lan·tern *noun* **1 a** a portable lamp with a transparent or translucent case, e.g. of glass or paper, protecting a flame. **b** a similar electric etc. lamp. **c** its case. **2 a** a raised structure on a dome, room, etc., glazed to admit light. **b** a similar structure for ventilation etc. **3** the light chamber of a lighthouse. **4** = MAGIC LANTERN. [Old French *lanterne* from Latin *lanterna* from Greek *lamptêr* torch, lamp]

lantern fish *noun* any marine fish of the family Myctophidae, having small light organs on the head and body.

lantern jaw *noun* a long thin chin and jaw, giving a hollow look to the face. □ **lantern-jawed** *adjective*

lantern slide *noun hist.* a slide for projection by a magic lantern etc. (see SLIDE *noun* 4).

lan·tha·nide /'lanθə,naid/ *noun Chem.* an element of the lanthanide series. [German *Lanthanid* (as LANTHANUM)]

lanthanide series *noun* a series of 15 metallic elements from lanthanum (at. no.: 57) to lutetium (at. no.: 71), inclusive, in the periodic table, having similar chemical properties. *Also called* RARE EARTHS.

lan·tha·num /'lanθənəm/ *noun Chem.* a silvery metallic element of the lanthanide series which is used in the manufacture of alloys and catalysts. Symbol: **La**; at. no.: 57. [Greek *lanthanō* 'escape notice', from having remained undetected in cerium oxide]

la·nu·go /lə'nuːgoː, -'njuː-/ *noun* fine soft hair, esp. that which covers the body and limbs of a human fetus. [Latin, = 'down' from *lana* wool]

lan·yard /'lanjərd, -jɑrd/ *noun* **1** a cord hanging around the neck or looped around the shoulder, to which a knife, a whistle, etc., may be attached. **2** *Naut.* a short rope or line used for securing, tightening, etc. **3** a cord attached to a breech mechanism for firing a gun. [Old French *laniere, lasniere*: assimilated to YARD[1]]

Lan·za·rote /ˌlanzə'rɒti/ one of the Canary Islands, the most easterly island of the group; chief town, Arrecife. It is noted for the black sand of its beaches and for the 'Mountains of Fire' in the southwest, an area of many volcanic cones.

Lan·zhou /lan'dʒoː/ (also **Lanchow** /-'tʃau/) a city of N China, on the upper Yellow River, capital of Gansu province; pop. (est. 2002) 1,880,400.

Laoc·o·on /lei'ɒkɒ,ɒn/ *Gk Myth* a Trojan priest who, with his two sons, was crushed to death by two sea serpents as a penalty for warning the Trojans against drawing the wooden horse of the Greeks into Troy.

Lao·di·cean /ˌleiɒdɪ'siːən/ ● *adjective* lukewarm or half-hearted, esp. in religion or politics. ● *noun* such a person. [Latin *Laodicea* in Asia Minor (with reference to the early Christians there: see Rev. 3:16)]

Laois /liːʃ/ (also **Laoighis, Leix**) a county of the Republic of Ireland, in the province of Leinster; county town, Portlaoise. It was formerly called Queen's County.

Laos /laus, 'lɑɒs/ a landlocked country in SE Asia; pop. (est. 2002) 5,777,180; capital, Vientiane.

Lao·tian /'lauʃən, lə'ɒʃən/ ● *noun* **1 a** a native or national of Laos in SE Asia. **b** a person of Laotian descent. **2** the language of Laos. ● *adjective* of or relating to Laos or its people or language.

Lao-tzu /lau'tsuː/ (also **Laoze** /-'tsei/) **1** the legendary founder of Taoism (fl. 6th c. BC) and traditional author of the *Tao-te Ching*, its most sacred scripture. **2** the *Tao-te Ching*. [Chinese, = Lao the Master]

lap[1] *noun* **1 a** the front of the body from the waist to the knees of a sitting person (*sat on her lap*; *caught it in his lap*). **b** the clothing, esp. a skirt, covering the lap. **c** the front of a skirt held up to catch or contain something. **2** care, charge, etc. (*thrown into the laps of the teachers*). **3** a condition or position of extreme comfort, ease, etc. (*in the lap of luxury*). **4** a hollow among hills. **5** a hanging flap on a garment, a saddle, etc. □ **in the lap of the gods** (of an event etc.) open to chance; beyond human control. □ **lap·ful** *noun* (*pl.* **-fuls**). [Old English *læppa* fold, flap]

lap[2] ● *noun* **1 a** one circuit of a racetrack etc. **b** a swim from one end of a pool to the other and back again; two lengths. **c** a swim from one end of a pool to the other; a length. **d** a section of a journey etc. (*finally we were on the last lap*). **2 a** an amount of overlapping. **b** an overlapping or projecting part. **3 a** a layer or sheet (of cotton etc. being made) wound on a roller. **b** a single turn of rope, silk, thread, etc., around a drum or reel. **4** a rotating disc for polishing a gem or metal. ● *verb* (**lapped, lap·ping**) **1** *transitive* lead or overtake (a competitor in a race) by one or more laps. **2** *transitive* (often foll. by *about, round*) coil, fold, or wrap (a garment etc.) around esp. a person. **3** *transitive* (usu. foll. by *in*) enfold or swathe (a person) in wraps etc. **4** *transitive* surround (a person) with an influence etc. **5** *intransitive* (usu. foll. by *over*) project; overlap. **6** *transitive* cause to overlap. **7** *transitive* polish (a gem etc.) with a lap. [Middle English, prob. from LAP[1]]

lap[3] ● *verb* (**lapped, lap·ping**) **1 a** *transitive & intransitive* (usu. of an animal) drink (liquid) with the tongue. **b** *transitive* (usu. foll. by *up, down*) consume (liquid) greedily. **c** *transitive* (usu. foll. by *up*) consume (gossip, praise, etc.) greedily. **2 a** *transitive* (of water) move or beat upon (a shore) with a rippling sound as of lapping. **b** *intransitive* (of waves etc.) move in ripples; make a lapping sound. ● *noun* **1 a** the process or an act of lapping. **b** the amount of liquid taken up. **2** the sound of wavelets on a beach. [Old English *lapian* from Germanic]

La Palma /la 'palmə, 'pɒmə/ one of the Canary Islands, the most northwesterly in the group, the site of an astronomical observatory with several major telescopes.

laparo·scope /'lapərə,skoːp/ *noun* a fibre optic instrument inserted through the abdominal wall to give a view of the organs in the abdomen. □ **laparo·scop·ic** /-'skɒpɪk/ *adjective* **lapa·ros·copy** /-'rɒskəpi/ *noun* (*pl.* **-ies**). [Greek *lapara* flank + -SCOPE]

lapa·rot·omy /ˌlapə'rɒtəmi/ *noun* (*pl.* **-omies**) a surgical incision into the abdominal cavity for exploration or diagnosis. [Greek *lapara* flank + -TOMY]

La Paz /la ˈpaz/ **1** the capital of Bolivia, in the northwest of the country near the border with Peru; pop. (2001) 789,585. The judicial capital is Sucre. Situated in the Andes at an altitude of 3 660 m (12,000 ft.), La Paz is the highest capital city in the world. **2** a city in Mexico, near the southern tip of the Baja California peninsula, capital of the state of Baja California Sur; pop. (2000) 163,000.

lap belt *noun* a seat belt worn across the lap.

lap dance *noun* a dance performed by a stripper sitting on a paying customer's lap. □ **lap dancer** *noun* **lap dancing** *noun*

lap·dog *noun* **1** a small pet dog. **2** a person or organization which is influenced or controlled by another (*the government and its media lapdogs*).

lapel /ləˈpel/ *noun* the part of the front of a coat, jacket, etc., which is folded over towards either shoulder. □ **la·pelled** *adjective* [LAP¹ + -EL]

lapi·dary /ˈlapɪˌderi/ ● *adjective* **1** concerned with stone or stones. **2** engraved upon stone. **3** (of writing style) dignified and concise, suitable for inscriptions. ● *noun* (*pl.* -**ies**) a cutter, polisher, or engraver of gems. [Latin *lapidarius* from *lapis -idis* stone]

lap·il·li /ləˈpɪlaɪ/ *plural noun* stone fragments ejected from volcanoes. [Italian from Latin, pl. diminutive of *lapis* stone]

lapis laz·uli /ˌlapɪs ˈlazuli/ (also **lapis**) ● *noun* **1** a blue mineral containing sodium aluminum silicate and sulphur, used as a gemstone. **2** a bright blue pigment formerly made from this. **3** its colour. ● *adjective* of this mineral, pigment, or colour. [Latin *lapis* 'stone' + medieval Latin *lazuli*, genitive of *lazulum*, from Persian (as AZURE)]

La·pita /laˈpiːtə/ an ancient Oceanic culture centred on Melanesia around *c*.1500 BC, characterized by pottery distinctively stamped with a toothed instrument.

Lap·ith /ˈlapɪθ/ *noun Gk Myth* a member of a Thessalian people who fought and defeated the centaurs.

lap joint *noun* the joining of rails, shafts, etc., by halving the thickness of each at the joint and fitting them together.

La·place /laˈplas/ **Pierre Simon, Marquis de** (1749–1827), French applied mathematician and theoretical physicist. His *Mécanique céleste* (1799–1825) is an extensive mathematical analysis of geophysical matters and of planetary and lunar motion; he also did innovative work on partial differential equations and contributed to probability theory. □ **La·pla·cian** *adjective*

La Plaine /laˈplen/ a former town in south central Quebec, northeast of Montreal, now part of Terrebonne; pop. (2001) 15,673. [with reference to the surrounding flat land]

Lap·land a region of N Europe which extends from the Norwegian Sea to the White Sea and lies mainly within the Arctic Circle. It consists of the northern parts of Norway, Sweden, and Finland, and the Kola Peninsula of Russia. □ **Lap·land·er** *noun*

Lapland rosebay *noun* a dwarf rhododendron found across northern Canada, with purple flowers.

La Plata /la ˈplɒtə/ a port in Argentina, on the Plate River southeast of Buenos Aires; pop. (est. 1999) 556,308.

La Poca·tière /laˌpɒkaˈtjer/ a town in SE central Quebec, situated on the south shore of the St. Lawrence, about 60 km southwest of Rivière-du-Loup; pop. (2001) 4,518. [F. Pollet de La Combe-*Pocatière*, first seigneur *c*.1672]

La·pointe /laˈpɔɪnt/ **Er·nest** (1876–1941), Canadian lawyer and politician. He served as a Liberal MP from 1904 until his death, and was minister of marine and fisheries (1921–24) and minister of justice (1924–30 and 1935–41). He was King's Quebec lieutenant, and helped to ensure Québécois support for Canada's role in the Second World War by promising there would be no conscription for overseas duty. His legacy, in the form of Quebec support for the federal Liberal Party, lasted long after his death.

La·porte /laˈpɔrt/ **Pierre** (1921–1970), Canadian journalist and politician. He was minister of immigration and of labour and manpower in Robert Bourassa's government, and was kidnapped by a cell of the FLQ on October 10, 1970. He was murdered on October 17, one day after the federal government invoked the War Measures Act, and his death intensified the October Crisis.

Lapp ● *noun* **1** a member of the indigenous population of the extreme north of Scandinavia. **2** the language of this people. ● *adjective* of or relating to the Lapps or their language. ¶ The Lapps' own name for themselves, *Sami*, is now often preferred with reference to the people. [Swedish *Lapp*, perhaps originally a term of contempt: compare Middle High German *lappe* simpleton]

lap·pet *noun* **1** a small flap or fold of a garment etc. **2** a hanging or loose piece of flesh, such as a lobe or wattle. □ **lap·pet·ed** *adjective* [LAP¹ + -ET¹]

Lap·pish ● *adjective* = LAPP. ● *noun* the Lapp language.

lap pool *noun N Amer.* a narrow pool suitable for swimming laps.

La Prai·rie /la preˈriː/ a town in south central Quebec, situated on the St. Lawrence, opposite Montreal; pop. (2001) 18,896. [French, lit. 'the prairie', with reference to the surrounding area]

lap robe *noun N Amer.* a thick blanket draped over the lap and legs for warmth.

Lap·sang /ˈlapsaŋ/ *noun* (usu. *attributive*) a variety of souchong tea with a smoky flavour. [invented term]

lapse ● *noun* **1** a slight error; a slip of memory etc. **2** a weak or careless decline into an inferior state. **3** (foll. by *of*) an interval or passage of time (*after a lapse of three years*). **4** *Law* the termination of a right or privilege through disuse or failure to follow appropriate procedures. ● *intransitive verb* **1** fail to maintain a position or standard. **2** (foll. by *into*) fall back into an inferior or previous state. **3** (of a right or privilege etc.) become invalid because it is not used or claimed or renewed. [Latin *lapsus* from *labi laps-* glide, slip, fall]

lapsed *adjective* designating a person who has abandoned a formerly adhered-to religion, philosophy, etc.

lapse rate *noun Meteorol.* the rate at which the temperature falls with increasing altitude.

lap steel *noun* = HAWAIIAN GUITAR.

lap·strake ● *noun* a clinker-built boat. ● *adjective* clinker-built.

lap·sus lin·guae /ˌlapsəs ˈlɪŋgwaɪ/ *noun* (*pl.* same) a slip of the tongue. [Latin: see LAPSE]

Lap·tev Sea /ˈlaptef/ a part of the Arctic Ocean, lying to the north of Russia between the Taimyr Peninsula and the New Siberian Islands.

lap·top *noun* (often *attributive*) a microcomputer that is portable and suitable for use while travelling.

lap·wing *noun* a plover, *Vanellus vanellus*, with black and white plumage, crested head, and a shrill cry. [Old English *hlēapewince* from *hlēapan* LEAP + the base of WINK, meaning 'move from side to side': assimilated to LAP¹, WING (named from its manner of flying)]

lar·board /ˈlɑrbərd/ *noun & adjective Naut. archaic* = PORT³. [Middle English *lade-, ladde-, lathe-* (perhaps = LADE + BOARD): later assimilated to *starboard*]

lar·ceny /ˈlɑrsəni/ *noun* (*pl.* -**ies**) the theft of personal property. □ **lar·cen·ist** *noun* **lar·cen·ous** *adjective* **lar·cen·ous·ly** *adverb* [Old French *larcin* from Latin *latrocinium* from *latro* robber, mercenary, from Greek *latreus*]

larch *noun* **1** a deciduous coniferous tree of the genus *Larix*, with soft needles and producing tough timber. **2** (also **larch·wood**) its wood. [Middle High German *larche*, ultimately from Latin *larix -icis*]

lard ● *noun* the internal fat of the abdomen of pigs, esp. when rendered and clarified for use in cooking and pharmacy. ● *transitive verb* **1** insert strips of fat or bacon in (meat etc.) before cooking. **2** (foll. by *with*) embellish or enrich (esp. talk or writing) with foreign material, esp. to excess. [Old French *lard* bacon, from Latin *lardum, laridum*, related to Greek *larinos* fat]

lard-ass *noun* (often *attributive*) *N Amer. derogatory* a person with fat buttocks.

larder *noun* **1** a room or cupboard for storing food. **2** a store of food. [Old French *lardier* from medieval Latin *lardarium* (as LARD)]

lar·don /ˈlɑrdən/ *noun* (also **lar·doon** /-ˈduːn/) a strip of fat bacon used to lard meat. [French *lardon* (as LARD)]

lardy *adjective* (-**ier, -iest**) like or with lard.

lardy cake *noun Brit.* a cake made of a leavened dough sprinkled with lard, sugar, and currants before baking.

lares /ˈlerɪz/ *plural noun Rom. Hist.* gods worshipped, together with the penates, by households in ancient Rome. They are probably originally deities of the farmland. □ **lares and penates** the home. [Latin]

large ● *adjective* **1** of considerable or relatively great size or extent. **2** of the larger kind (*the large intestine*). **3** of wide range; comprehensive. **4** pursuing an activity on a large scale (*large landowner; large manufacturer*). ● *noun* **1** a garment of a size suited for people moderately larger than average. **2** a large serving of a beverage or food that is sold in more than one size. □ **at large 1** at liberty; not confined. **2** as a body or whole (*popular with the people at large*). **3** (of a narration etc.) at full length and with all details. **4** without a specific target (*scatters insults at large*). **5** *US* representing a whole area and not merely a part of it (*congressman at large*). **in large measure** (or **part**) to a significant extent. **large as life** see LIFE. **larger than life** see LIFE. **live large** be very wealthy; have an extravagant lifestyle. □ **large·ness** noun **larg·ish** adjective [Old French from fem. of Latin largus copious]

large calorie noun see CALORIE 1.

large cap noun a company with a relatively large market capitalization (usu. with hyphen, attributive: large-cap stocks).

large intestine noun the cecum, colon, and rectum collectively.

large·ly adverb to a great extent; principally (is largely due to laziness).

large-minded adjective liberal; not narrow-minded.

large·mouth noun (pl. same or **large·mouths**) (in full **largemouth bass**) a N American freshwater bass, Micropterus salmoides of the sunfish family, an important sport fish.

large-print adjective designating a book etc. printed in large type.

large-scale adjective made or occurring on a large scale or in large amounts.

lar·gesse /larˈdʒes, -ˈʒes/ noun (also **lar·gess**) **1** generosity in bestowing money or gifts upon others. **2** money or gifts given generously. [Old French largesse, ultimately from Latin largus copious]

large·tooth aspen noun (also **bigtooth aspen**) a poplar of eastern N America, Populus gradidentata, similar to trembling aspen, with leaves with large teeth.

lar·ghet·to /larˈgetoː/ Music ● adverb & adjective in a fairly slow tempo. ● noun (pl. **-tos**) a larghetto passage or movement. [Italian, diminutive of LARGO]

largo Music ● adverb & adjective in a slow tempo and dignified in style. ● noun (pl. **largos**) a largo passage or movement. [Italian, = broad]

lari /ˈluri/ noun (pl. same) a monetary unit of Georgia, equal to one hundred tetri. [Georgian]

lar·iat /ˈleriət/ noun **1** a lasso. **2** a tethering rope, esp. used by cowboys. [Spanish la reata from reatar tie again (as RE-, Latin aptare adjust from aptus APT, fit)]

lar·i·gan /ˈlarɪɡən, ˈler-/ noun (also **lar·ri·gan**) N Amer. a tanned leather moccasin boot almost reaching the knee. [origin unknown]

La Rioja /ˌla riˈɒhə/ an autonomous region of N Spain, in the wine-producing valley of the Ebro River; capital, Logroño.

La·ris·sa /ləˈrɪsə/ a city in Greece, the chief town of Thessaly; pop. (est. 2002) 132,900.

lark[1] noun **1** any small singing bird of the family Alaudidae with brown plumage and an elongated hind claw, esp. the Eurasian skylark or the horned lark. **2** any of various birds resembling but not related to the true larks, e.g. the meadowlark. [Old English lāferce, lǣwerce, of unknown origin]

lark[2] informal ● noun **1** a carefree frolic or spree; an amusing incident; a practical joke. **2** Brit. a type of activity, affair, etc. (fed up with this digging lark). ● intransitive verb (usu. foll. by about) play tricks; frolic. □ **larky** adjective **lark·i·ness** noun **lark·ish** adjective **lark·ish·ness** noun [19th c.: origin uncertain]

Lar·kin, Philip (Ar·thur) (1922–85), English poet and novelist. He adapted everyday speech rhythms and vocabulary to poetic metre, and many of his poems are set in urban and suburban landscapes pervaded by an air of melancholy, bitterness, and stoic wit; his volumes of poetry include The Less Deceived (1955), The Whitsun Weddings (1964), and High Windows (1974).

lark·spur noun **1** a plant of the genus Consolida (buttercup family), with spurred flowers. **2** a delphinium.

larn verb informal or jocular **1** intransitive = LEARN. **2** transitive teach (that'll larn you). [dial. form of LEARN]

La Roche·fou·cauld /la rɒʃfuːˈkoː/ **Fran·çois de Mar·sillac, Duc de** (1613–80), French moralist. His chief work, Réflexions, ou sentences et maximes morales (1665), consists of 504 epigrammatic reflections on human conduct, finding self-interest to be its driving force.

La Ro·chelle /ˌla rɒˈʃel/ a port on the Atlantic coast of W France; pop. (1999) 76,584.

La Rocque /laˈrɒk/ **Mar·guer·ite de**, French-born Canadian heroine. In 1542 she set out from France to accompany a close relative, the Sieur de Roberval, on a voyage to Canada. Shocked by her behaviour in taking a lover, Roberval put Marguerite, her lover and a female servant ashore on the Île des Démons in the St. Lawrence River. The lover, servant, and a child Marguerite bore all died; she herself was picked up by fishermen a few years later.

la Ronge, Lac see LAC LA RONGE.

La·rousse /laˈruːs/ **Pierre (Atha·nase)** (1817–75), French lexicographer, encyclopedist, and founder (1852) of the publishing house Larousse. His 15-volume Grand dictionnaire universel du XIXᵉ siècle (1866–76) aimed to treat every area of human knowledge.

lar·ri·kin /ˈlarɪkɪn/ noun Austral. a hooligan. [also English dial.: perhaps from the name Larry (pet form of Lawrence) + -KIN]

lar·rup /ˈlerəp/ transitive verb (**lar·ruped, lar·rup·ing**) informal thrash. [dial.: perhaps from LATHER]

larva noun (pl. **lar·vae** /ˈlarviː/) **1** the stage of development of an insect between egg and pupa, e.g. a caterpillar. **2** an immature form of other animals that undergo some metamorphosis, e.g. a tadpole. □ **lar·val** adjective [Latin, = ghost, mask]

lar·vi·cide /ˈlarvɪˌsaɪd/ ● noun a preparation adapted to kill larvae. ● transitive & intransitive verb use larvicide (in). □ **lar·vi·cid·al** adjective

laryn·geal /ləˈrɪndʒiəl/ adjective **1** of or relating to the larynx. **2** Phonetics (of a sound) designating a speech sound made in the larynx with the vocal cords partly closed and partly vibrating.

laryn·gec·tomy /ˌlerɪnˈdʒektəmi/ noun **1** surgical removal of the larynx. **2** an instance of this.

laryn·gitis /ˌlerɪnˈdʒaɪtəs/ noun inflammation of the larynx.

laryn·gol·ogy /ˌlerɪnˈɡɒlədʒi/ noun the branch of medicine that deals with the larynx. □ **laryn·gol·o·gist** noun

laryn·go·scope /ləˈrɪŋɡəˌskoːp/ noun an instrument for examining the larynx, or for inserting a tube through it.

laryn·got·omy /ˌlerɪnˈɡɒtəmi/ noun (pl. **-omies**) a surgical incision of the larynx, esp. to provide an air passage when breathing is obstructed.

larynx /ˈlerɪŋks/ noun (pl. **larynx·es** or **la·ryn·ges** /ləˈrɪndʒiːz/) the hollow muscular organ forming an air passage to the lungs and holding the vocal cords in humans and other mammals; the voice box. [modern Latin from Greek larugx -ggos]

la·sa·gna /ləˈzɒnjə/ noun (also **lasagne**) **1** pasta in the form of wide ribbons, usu. with ruffled edges. **2** a baked dish made from layers of lasagna, usu. filled with tomato sauce, cheese, and ground meat. [Italian, from Latin lasanum cooking pot]

La·Salle /laˈsal, ləˈsal/ **1** a city in south central Quebec, on the south shore of the Island of Montreal, now part of the city of Montreal; pop. (2001) 73,983. **2** a town in SW Ontario, directly south of Windsor on the Detroit River; pop. (2001) 25,285. [LA SALLE]

La Salle /la ˈsal/ **René-Robert Cavel·ier, Sieur de** (1643–87), French explorer. A settler in French Canada, he sailed down the Ohio and Mississippi rivers in 1682, naming the Mississippi basin Louisiana in honour of Louis XIV; in 1684 he led an expedition to establish a French colony on the Gulf of Mexico, and after an unsuccessful search for the Mississippi delta his followers mutinied and he was murdered.

La Sarre /laˈsɑr/ a town in NW central Quebec, situated north of Rouyn-Noranda, near the border with Ontario; pop. (2001) 7,728. [after the La Sarre Regiment, which was sent to New France c.1756]

las·car /ˈlaskər/ noun a sailor from India or SE Asia. [ultimately from Urdu & Persian laškar army]

las·civ·i·ous /ləˈsɪviəs/ adjective **1** lustful. **2** inciting to or evoking lust. □ **las·civ·i·ous·ly** adverb **las·civ·i·ous·ness** noun [Late Latin lasciviosus from Latin lascivia lustfulness, from lascivus sportive, wanton]

lase /leiz/ intransitive verb **1** function as or in a laser. **2** (of a substance) undergo the physical processes employed in a laser. [back-formation from LASER]

laser /ˈleizər/ ● noun a device that generates an intense beam of coherent monochromatic light (or other electromagnetic radiation) by stimulated emission from excited atoms or molecules. Lasers are used in drilling and cutting, alignment and guidance, surgery, recording and playing compact discs, etc. (compare MASER). ● verb **1** transitive remove or treat (cells, tissue, etc.) with a laser. **2** transitive inscribe or engrave (words, a design, etc.) onto a surface using a laser. **3** intransitive travel with great speed and precision (the ball lasered towards his head). [light amplification by stimulated emission of radiation]

laser disc noun a disc on which signals and data are recorded digitally as a series of pits and bumps under a protective coating, and which is read optically by a laser beam reflected from the surface.

laser printer noun a high-speed computer printer in which a laser is used to form a pattern of dots on a photosensitive drum corresponding to the pattern of print required on the page.

laser show noun a display of laser lights at a rock concert, sports event, etc.

laser tag noun a game in which individuals or teams use laser beams to 'tag' opponents wearing vests with sensors in a large indoor maze.

lash ● verb **1** transitive & intransitive make a sudden whip-like movement (lashed his tail; lashing backwards and forwards). **2** transitive beat with a

Consonants: b *but* d *dog* f *few* g *get* h *her* j *yes* k *cat* l *leg* m *man* n *no* p *pen* r *red* s *sit*

whip, rope, etc. **3** *intransitive* pour or rush with great force. **4** *intransitive* (foll. by *at*, *against*) strike violently. **5** *transitive* castigate in words. **6** *transitive* urge on as with a lash. **7** *transitive* (foll. by *down*, *together*, etc.) fasten with a cord, rope, etc. **8** *transitive* (of rain, wind, etc.) beat forcefully upon. ● *noun* **1 a** a sharp blow made by a whip, rope, etc. **b** (prec. by *the*) punishment by beating with a whip etc. **c** something that goads or hurts like a blow from a whip (*the lash of her tongue*). **d** a powerful impact (*the lash of the storm*). **2** the flexible end of a whip. **3** (usu. in *pl.*) an eyelash. □ **lash out 1** (often foll. by *at*) speak or hit out angrily. **2** *Brit.* spend money extravagantly, be lavish. □ **lash·er** *noun* **lash·less** *adjective* [Middle English: prob. imitative]

lash·ing *noun* **1 a** a beating. **b** a scolding; reprimand. **2** cord used for lashing.

lash·ings *plural noun* esp. *Brit. informal* (foll. by *of*) plenty; an abundance.

lash-up *noun* a makeshift or improvised structure or arrangement.

LASIK /ˈleɪzɪk/ *noun* laser in situ keratomileusis, a form of eye surgery which uses a laser to carve the interior of the cornea, e.g. to correct myopia (*compare* PRK).

Las·kin /ˈlaskɪn/ **Bora** (1912–1984), Canadian lawyer and judge, chief justice of Canada 1973–84.

Las Pal·mas /las ˈpalmas/ (in full **Las Pal·mas de Gran Ca·na·ria** /də ˌgran kəˈnɑriə/) a port and resort on the north coast of the island of Gran Canaria, capital of the Canary Islands; pop. (est. 2002) 366,000.

La Spe·zia /la ˈspetsiə/ an industrial port in NW Italy; pop. (2001) 91,027. It is Italy's chief naval station.

Las·queti Island /ləˈskiːtiː/ an island in the Strait of Georgia, situated off the east central coast of Vancouver Island, southwest of Texada Island. [J. M. *Lasqueti*, Spanish naval officer *c.*1791]

lass *noun* *Scot. & Northern England* or *literary* a girl or young woman. [Middle English *lasce* from Old Norse *laskwa* unmarried (fem.)]

Lassa fever /ˈlasə/ *noun* an acute and often fatal febrile viral disease of tropical Africa. [*Lassa* in Nigeria, where first reported]

lassi /ˈlasi/ *noun* a drink, originally from the Indian subcontinent, made from a buttermilk or yogourt base with water. [Hindi]

las·sie¹ *noun informal* = LASS.

las·sie² *noun* (also **lassy**) *Cdn* (*Nfld*) *informal* = MOLASSES.

las·si·tude /ˈlasɪˌtuːd, -ˌtjuːd/ *noun* **1** languor, weariness. **2** disinclination to exert or interest oneself. [French *lassitude* or Latin *lassitudo* from *lassus* tired]

las·so /ləˈsuː, ˈlasoː/ ● *noun* (*pl.* **-sos** or **-soes**) a rope with a noose at one end, used esp. in N America for catching cattle etc. ● *transitive verb* (**-soes**, **-soed**) catch with or as with a lasso. □ **las·so·er** *noun* [Spanish *lazo* LACE]

L'Assomp·tion /lasɔ̃ˈpsjɔ̃/ a town in south central Quebec, situated on the St. Lawrence, northeast of Montreal; pop. (2001) 15,615. [see ASSUMPTION 4]

lassy bread *noun* *Cdn* (*Nfld*) a sweet yeast bread with molasses, raisins, and spices.

last¹ ● *adjective* **1** after all others; coming at or belonging to the end. **2 a** most recent; next before a specified time (*last Christmas; last week*). **b** preceding; previous in a sequence (*got on at the last station*). **3** only remaining; final (*the last cookie; our last chance*). **4** (prec. by *the*) least likely or suitable (*the last person I'd want; the last thing I'd have expected*). **5** the lowest in rank (*the last place*). **6** individual, single (*every last one of them*). ● *adverb* **1** after all others (esp. in *combination*: *last-mentioned*). **2** on the last occasion before the present (*when did you last see him?*). **3** (esp. in enumerating) lastly. ● *noun* **1** a person or thing that is last, last-mentioned, most recent, etc. **2** (prec. by *the*) the last mention or sight etc. (*shall never hear the last of it*). **3** the last performance of certain acts (*breathed his last*). **4** (prec. by *the*) **a** the end or last moment. **b** death. □ **at last** (or **long last**) in the end; after much delay. **last but not least** last in order of mention or occurrence but not of importance. **on one's last legs** *see* LEG. **pay one's last respects** *see* PAY¹. **to** (or **till**) **the last** till the end; esp. till death. [Old English *latost* superlative: see LATE]

last² *intransitive verb* **1** remain unexhausted or adequate or alive for a specified or considerable time; suffice (*enough food to last us a week; the battery lasts and lasts*). **2** continue for a specified time (*the journey lasts an hour*). □ **last out** remain adequate or in existence for the whole of a period previously stated or implied. [Old English *læstan* from Germanic]

last³ *noun* a shoemaker's model for shaping or repairing a shoe or boot. [Old English *læste* last, *læst* boot, *låst* footprint, from Germanic]

last best West *noun* *Cdn* a nickname for the Canadian prairies in promotional literature attracting homesteaders in the early 1900s.

last call *noun* *N Amer.* the final opportunity to order alcoholic drinks from a bar before it must legally stop serving alcohol for the evening.

last-ditch *adjective* (of an effort etc.) made at the last minute in an attempt to avert disaster.

last gasp ● *noun* **1** the final attempt to draw breath before dying. **2** the final hours, days etc. of an event, season, etc. (*the last gasp of winter*). ● *adjective* (**last-gasp**) last-minute (*last-gasp negotiations*).

last hurrah *noun* **1** any final performance, effort, or success. **2** the final act in a politician's career.

last·ing *adjective* **1** continuing, permanent. **2** durable. □ **last·ing·ly** *adverb* **last·ing·ness** *noun*

Last Judgment *noun* (in some beliefs) the judgment of humankind expected to take place at the end of the world, when each person is rewarded or punished according to his or her merits.

last·ly *adverb* finally; in the last place.

last minute ● *noun* (also **last moment**) the time just before an important event. ● *adjective* (**last-minute**) done at the last minute (*last-minute Christmas shopping*).

Last Mountain Lake a long, narrow lake in south central Saskatchewan, about 50 km northwest of Regina.

last name *noun* surname.

last post *noun* *Brit. & Cdn* **1** the last of several bugle calls giving notice of the hour of retiring at night. **2** this call blown at military funerals etc.

last rites *noun* sacred rites for a person about to die.

Last Supper *noun* the supper eaten by Christ and his disciples on the eve of the Crucifixion, as recorded in the New Testament.

last thing *adverb* very late, esp. as a final act before going to bed.

last trump *noun* (prec. by *the*) the trumpet blast to wake the dead on Judgment Day.

last word *noun* (prec. by *the*) **1** a final or definitive statement (*always has the last word; is the last word on this subject*). **2** (often foll. by *in*) the latest fashion.

Las Vegas /lɒs ˈveɪgəs/ a city in S Nevada; pop. (2000) 478,434. It is noted for its casinos and nightclubs.

lat¹ *noun* (usu. in *pl.*) *slang* = LATISSIMUS DORSI.

lat² *noun* (also **lats**) (*pl.* **lati** or **lats**) a monetary unit of Latvia, equal to 100 santimi. [Latvian *lats*]

lat. *abbreviation* latitude.

Lata·kia /ˌlatəˈkiːə/ a seaport on the coast of W Syria, opposite the northeastern tip of Cyprus; pop. (est. 2002) 404,000. It is famous for its tobacco.

latch ● *noun* **1** a bar with a catch and lever used as a fastening for a gate etc. **2** a spring lock preventing a door from being opened from the outside without a key after being shut. ● *transitive & intransitive verb* fasten or be fastened with a latch. □ *informal* **latch on** (often foll. by *to*) **1** attach oneself (to). **2** *N Amer.* obtain, get. **3** associate oneself strongly with. **4** become very interested in. [prob. from (now dial.) *latch* (v.) seize, from Old English *læccan* from Germanic]

latch·key *noun* (*pl.* **-keys**) a key of an outer door.

latchkey child *noun* (also *informal* **latchkey kid**) a child who is alone at home after school until a parent returns from work.

late ● *adjective* **1 a** after the due or usual time; occurring or done after the proper time (*late for dinner; a late delivery*). **b** *informal* (of a woman) whose menstrual period has failed to occur at the expected time. **2 a** far on in the day or night or in a specified time or period (*the late 1500s*). **b** belonging to an advanced stage in the development of a person or thing, the history of a science, language, etc. **3** flowering or ripening towards the end of the season (*late strawberries*). **4** (prec. by *the* or *my*, *his*, etc.) no longer alive or having the specified status (*my late husband; the late president*). **5** (esp. in *superlative*) of recent date (*the late storms; the latest songs*). ● *adverb* **1** after the due or usual time (*arrived late; married late*). **2** far on in time (*this happened later on*). **3** at or till a late hour. **4** at a late stage of development. **5** formerly but not now (*late of Halifax*). **6** (in *comparative*) subsequently (*this issue will be examined later in this chapter; three months later*). □ **at the latest** as the latest time envisaged (*will have done it by six at the latest*). **late in the day** (or **game**) *informal* at a late stage in the proceedings, esp. too late to be useful. **of late** lately, recently (*have you heard the latest?*). □ **late·ness** *noun* [Old English *læt* (adj.), *late* (adv.) from Germanic]

late bloomer *noun* *N Amer.* **1** a flower that blooms towards the end of the season. **2** a person who develops a skill, interest, etc. later in life. □ **late-blooming** *adjective*

late-breaking *adjective* (of a news story) becoming public close to or after the print or broadcast deadline for a newspaper or newscast etc.

late·comer *noun* **1** a person who arrives late. **2** a recent arrival; a newcomer.

la·teen /ləˈtiːn/ *adjective* (of a ship) rigged with a lateen sail.

lateen sail *noun* a triangular sail on a long yard at an angle of 45° to the mast. [French (*voile*) *latine* Latin (sail), because common in the Mediterranean]

late immersion *noun* Cdn a French immersion program started in grade 6 or later.

Late Latin *noun* Latin of about AD 200–600.

late Loyalist *noun* (also **later Loyalist**) *Cdn hist.* an American settler who came to Canada between 1790 and 1800 after the influx of the first United Empire Loyalists.

late·ly *adverb* not long ago; recently; in recent times.

late-model *adjective* (of a car, electronic component, etc.) of a recent make.

La Tène /la ˈten/ *adjective* of or relating to the second cultural phase of the Iron Age in central and W Europe, lasting from the 5th to the 1st c. BC. [*La Tène* in Switzerland, where remains of it were first identified]

latent /ˈleɪtənt/ *adjective* **1** concealed, dormant. **2** existing but not developed or manifest. □ **laten·cy** *noun* **latent·ly** *adverb* [Latin *latēre* *latent-* be hidden]

latent heat *noun* Physics the heat required to convert a solid into a liquid or vapour, or a liquid into a vapour, without change of temperature.

latent image *noun* Photog. an image not yet made visible by developing.

-later /lətər/ *combining form* denoting a person who worships a particular thing or person (*idolater*). [obsolete *latria* from Greek *latreia* worship, from *latreuō* serve]

later *interjection* see you later.

lat·eral /ˈlatərəl/ ● *adjective* **1** of, at, towards, or from the side or sides. **2** of or pertaining to a new job which is neither a promotion nor a demotion (*a lateral move*). ● *noun* **1** a side part etc., esp. a lateral shoot or branch. **2** (in full **lateral pass**) Football a sideways pass. ● *verb* (**lat·eralled**, **lat·eral·ling**; esp. *US* **lat·eraled**, **lat·eral·ing**) Football **1** *intransitive* make a sideways pass. **2** *transitive* throw (the ball) in a lateral pass. □ **lat·eral·ly** *adverb* [Latin *lateralis* from *latus lateris* side]

lateral line *noun* Zool. a visible line along the side of a fish consisting of a series of sense organs acting as vibration receptors.

lateral thinking *noun* a method of solving problems indirectly or by apparently illogical methods (*opp.* VERTICAL THINKING).

Lat·eran /ˈlatərən/ the site in Rome containing the basilica of St. John the Baptist (St. John Lateran), which is the cathedral church of Rome, and the Lateran Palace where the popes resided until the 14th c.

Lateran Council any of five general councils of the Western Church held in the Lateran Palace, Rome, in 1123, 1139, 1179, 1215, and 1512–17. The fourth council (1215) was the most important and involved the condemnation of the Albigenses as heretical.

Lateran Treaty a treaty signed in 1929 in the Lateran Palace in Rome, a concordat between the kingdom of Italy (represented by Mussolini) and the Holy See (represented by Pope Pius XI), which recognized as fully sovereign and independent the papal state under the name Vatican City.

lat·erite /ˈlatəˌraɪt/ *noun* a red or yellow ferruginous clay, friable and hardening in air, used for making roads in the tropics. □ **lat·erit·ic** /-ˈrɪtɪk/ *adjective* [Latin *later* brick + -ITE¹]

La·ter·rière /laterˈjer/ a town in NE central Quebec, south of Chicoutimi, now merged with Chicoutimi, Jonquière, La Baie and other communities into the city of Saguenay; pop. (2001) 4,969. [M.-P. de Sales *Laterrière*, member of the Legislative Assembly of United Canada d.1872]

latex /ˈleɪteks/ *noun* (pl. **latex·es**) **1** a milky fluid of mixed composition found in various plants and trees, esp. the rubber tree, and used for commercial purposes. **2** a synthetic product resembling this, used in paints, adhesives, etc. **3** (in full **latex paint**) paint having latex as its binding medium. [Latin, = liquid]

lath /laθ/ ● *noun* (pl. **laths** /laθs, laðz/) **1** a thin flat strip of wood, esp. each of a series forming a framework or support for plaster etc. **2** (esp. in phr. **lath and plaster**) laths collectively as a building material,

esp. as a foundation for supporting plaster. ● *transitive verb* attach laths to (a wall or ceiling). [Old English lætt]

lathe /leɪð/ *noun* a machine for shaping wood, metal, etc., by means of a rotating drive which turns the piece being worked on against changeable cutting tools. [prob. related to Old Danish *lad* structure, frame, from Old Norse *hlath*, related to *hlatha* LADE]

lath·er /ˈlaðər/ ● *noun* **1** a froth produced by agitating soap etc. and water. **2** frothy sweat, esp. of a horse. **3** a state of agitation. ● *verb* **1** *intransitive* (of soap etc.) form a lather. **2** *transitive* cover with lather. **3** *intransitive* (of a horse etc.) develop or become covered with lather. **4** *transitive informal* thrash. [Old English *lēathor* (n.), *lēthran* (v.)]

lathi /ˈlati/ *noun* (pl. **lathis**) (in India) a long heavy iron-bound bamboo stick used as a weapon, esp. by police. [Hindi *lāthī*]

Lati·mer /ˈlatɪmər/ **Hugh** (c.1485–1555), English Protestant clergyman and martyr. He became one of Henry VIII's chief advisers when the king formally broke with the papacy in 1534, and was made bishop of Worcester in 1535; under Mary I he was imprisoned for heresy and burned at the stake with Ridley at Oxford.

Lat·in ● *noun* **1** the Italic language of ancient Rome and its empire, originating in Latium. **2** *Rom. Hist.* an inhabitant of ancient Latium in Central Italy. **3** a native or inhabitant of any of the various countries in Europe (France, Italy, Spain, etc.) and Latin America whose language is developed from Latin. ● *adjective* **1** of or in Latin. **2 a** of the countries or peoples using languages developed from Latin. **b** Latin-American. **3** *Rom. Hist.* of or relating to ancient Latium or its inhabitants. **4** of the Roman Catholic Church. **5** of or relating to the Latin alphabet. □ **Lat·in·ism** *noun* **Lat·in·ist** *noun* [Old French *Latin* or Latin *Latinus* from *Latium*]

Lat·ina /laˈtiːnə/ ● *noun* a female Latin American inhabitant of N America. ● *adjective* of or relating to these inhabitants. [Latin American Spanish]

Latin America the parts of the Americas where Spanish or Portuguese is the main language. □ **Latin American** *adjective & noun*

Lat·in·ate /ˈlatɪˌneɪt/ *adjective* having the character of Latin.

Latin Church *noun* the Roman Catholic Church.

Latin cross *noun* a cross in which the transverse bar is shorter than the vertical post and the lowest of the four segments is the longest.

Lat·in·ize *verb* (also esp. *Brit.* **-ise**) **1** *transitive* give a Latin or Latinate form to. **2** *transitive* translate into Latin. **3** *transitive* make conformable to the ideas, customs, etc., of the ancient Romans, Latin peoples, or Latin Church. **4** *intransitive* use Latin forms, idioms, etc. □ **Lat·in·iz·a·tion** *noun*

Lat·ino /laˈtiːnoː/ ● *noun* (pl. **-inos**) a Latin American inhabitant of N America. ● *adjective* of or relating to these inhabitants. [Latin American Spanish]

Latin Quarter *noun* the district of Paris on the left or south bank of the Seine, where Latin was spoken in the Middle Ages, and where students and artists live and the principal university buildings are situated.

Latin rite *noun* a religious ceremony using Latin, esp. in the Roman Catholic Church.

latish /ˈleɪtɪʃ/ *adjective & adverb* fairly late.

la·tis·si·mus dorsi /ləˈtɪsəməs ˈdɔrsaɪ, ˈdɔrsi/ *noun* (pl. **la·tis·si·mi dorsi** /ləˈtɪsəmaɪ/) either of a pair of large, roughly triangular muscles covering the lower part of the back, from the sacral, lumbar, and lower thoracic vertebrae to the armpits. [modern Latin, ellipt. for *musculus latissimus dorsi* lit. 'the broadest muscle of the back']

lati·tude /ˈlatɪˌtud, -ˌtjuːd/ *noun* **1** Geog. **a** the angular distance on its meridian of any place on the earth's surface from the equator, expressed in degrees and minutes north or south of the equator. **b** (usu. in *pl.*) regions or climes, esp. with reference to temperature (*warm latitudes*). **2** freedom from narrowness; liberality of interpretation. **3** tolerated variety of action or opinion (*was allowed much latitude*). **4** *Astronomy* the angular distance of a celestial body or point from the ecliptic. **5** *Photog.* the range of exposures for which an emulsion, printing paper, etc. will give acceptable contrast. □ **lati·tud·in·al** *adjective* **lati·tud·in·ally** *adverb* [Middle English, = breadth, from Latin *latitudo -dinis* from *latus* broad]

lati·tudi·nar·ian /ˌlatɪˌtuːdɪˈnerɪən, -ˌtjuːd-/ ● *adjective* allowing latitude esp. in religion; showing no preference among varying creeds and forms of worship. ● *noun* a person with a latitudinarian attitude. □ **lati·tudi·nar·ian·ism** *noun* [Latin *latitudo -dinis* breadth + -ARIAN]

La·tium /ˈleɪʃiəm/ an ancient region of west central Italy, west of the Apennines and south of the Tiber River. It was settled during the early part of the first millennium BC by a branch of the Indo-European people known as the Latini. By the end of the 4th c. BC, Rome dominated the region. It is part of the modern region of Lazio.

lat·ke /ˈlatkə/ *noun* (in Jewish cooking) a pancake made with grated potato. [Yiddish from Russian *latka* earthenware cooking vessel, (dial.) dish cooked in such a vessel]

La·to·na /ləˈtoːnə/ *Rom. Myth* the Roman name of Leto.

La Tour /la ˈtuːr/ **1 Charles de Saint-Étienne de** (1593–1663), French-born colonizer and trader in Acadia. La Tour first visited Acadia as early as 1606, and lived there from 1610. In 1623 he assumed leadership of the colony and was made Lieutenant-Governor 8 years later, but he soon fell out with the governor, Charles de Menou d'Aulnay, who in 1645 attacked his base and killed its defenders. La Tour returned to Acadia in 1650, and later used his title of knight-baronet of Scotland to give legitimacy to the English takeover of the colony. **2** his wife, **Françoise-Marie de Saint-Étienne de** (1602–1645), Acadian heroine. Married in 1640, she travelled to France, England and Boston to secure support for her husband's fight against d'Aulnay. When d'Aulnay attacked Fort La Tour in her husband's absence, she took command, and succeeded in holding off the much larger force for three days. She died three weeks after watching d'Aulnay massacre her soldiers. **3 Georges de** (1593–1652), French painter, best known for his nocturnal religious scenes in which a candle is the source of illumination, such as *St. Joseph the Carpenter* (*c.*1645).

la·trine /ləˈtriːn/ *noun* a communal lavatory, esp. in a camp, barracks, etc. [French from Latin *latrina*, shortening of *lavatrina* from *lavare* wash]

-latry /lətri/ *combining form* denoting worship (*idolatry*). [Greek *latreia* worship, from *latreuō* serve]

latte /ˈlatei, ˈlɒtei/ *noun* a drink made by adding a shot of espresso coffee to a cup of frothy hot milk. [Italian, abbreviation of CAFFE LATTE].

lat·ten /ˈlatən/ *noun* an alloy of copper and zinc, often rolled into sheets, and formerly used for monumental brasses and church articles. [Old French *laton*, *leiton* 'brass']

lat·ter ● *noun* (prec. by *the*) the second-mentioned or *disputed* last-mentioned person or thing (*opp.* FORMER[1] *noun*). ¶ The use of *latter* to mean 'last-mentioned of three or more' is considered incorrect by some people. ● *adjective* **1** nearer to the end (*the latter part of the year*). **2** recent. **3** belonging to the end of a period, of the world, etc. [Old English *lætra*, comparative of *læt* LATE]

latter-day *attributive adjective* modern, contemporary.

Latter-day Saint *noun* a member of the Mormon Church (officially called the Church of Jesus Christ of Latter-day Saints).

lat·ter·ly *adverb* **1** in the latter part of life or of a period. **2** recently.

lat·tice /ˈlatɪs/ *noun* **1 a** a structure of crossed laths or bars with spaces between, used as a screen, fence, etc. **b** = LATTICEWORK. **2** something with an open interlaced structure like that of a lattice. **3** a regular periodic arrangement of atoms, ions, or molecules in a crystalline solid. □ **lat·ticed** *adjective* [Old French *lattis* from *latte* lath, from West Germanic]

lattice window *noun* a window with small panes set in diagonally crossing strips of lead.

lat·tice·work *noun* laths arranged in lattice formation.

La Tuque /la ˈtuːk/ a town in SE central Quebec, situated on the Rivière Saint-Maurice, northwest of Quebec; pop. (2001) 13,151. [after a mountain nearby, which resembles a toque]

Lat·via a country on the eastern shore of the Baltic Sea, between Estonia and Lithuania; pop. (est. 2002) 2,366,515; capital, Riga.

Lat·vian ● *noun* **1 a** a native of Latvia. **b** a person of Latvian descent. **2** the language of Latvia. ● *adjective* of or relating to Latvia or its people or language.

Laud, Wil·liam (1573–1645), English clergyman, Archbishop of Canterbury 1633–45. His persecution of Puritans and moves to impose liturgical uniformity by restoring pre-Reformation practices aroused great hostility, and were a contributory cause of the English Civil War; in 1640 he was impeached and imprisoned, and later executed for treason.

laud ● *transitive verb* praise or extol. ● *noun* **1** *archaic* praise; a hymn of praise. **2** (in *pl.*) the office of the first canonical hour of prayer, originally said at daybreak. [Middle English: (n.) from Old French *laude*, (v.) from Latin *laudare*, from Latin *laus laudis* praise]

laud·able *adjective* commendable, praiseworthy. ¶ *Laudable* 'praiseworthy' is sometimes confused with *laudatory* 'expressing praise'. The difference is illustrated by the sentence *Her laudable efforts*

were recognized in the mayor's laudatory speech. □ **laud·abil·ity** *noun* **laud·ably** *adverb*

laud·a·num /ˈlɒdənəm/ *noun* a solution containing morphine and prepared from opium, formerly used as a narcotic painkiller. [modern Latin, the name given by Paracelsus to a costly medicament, later applied to preparations containing opium: perhaps var. of LADANUM]

laud·a·tory *adjective* expressing praise. ¶ See Usage Note at LAUDABLE.

laugh ● *verb* **1** *intransitive* **a** make the spontaneous sounds and movements usual in expressing lively amusement, scorn, derision, etc. **b** have the emotion expressed by laughing (*laughed inwardly at his foolishness*). **2** *transitive* express by laughing. **3** *transitive* bring (a person) into a certain state by laughing (*laughed them into agreeing*). **4** *intransitive* (foll. by *at*) ridicule, make fun of (*laughed at us for going*). **5** *intransitive* (in phr. **be laughing**) *informal* be in a fortunate or successful position. **6** *intransitive* esp. *literary* make sounds reminiscent of laughing (*the wind laughed in the trees*). ● *noun* **1** the sound or act or manner of laughing. **2** *informal* a comical, entertaining or ridiculous person or thing (*the party was a laugh*). □ **for laughs** for amusement or enjoyment. **have the last laugh** be ultimately the winner. **laugh all the way to the bank** be in an enviable financial position. **a laugh a minute** very funny or amusing. **laugh in a person's face** show open scorn for a person. **laugh off** get rid of (embarrassment or humiliation) by joking. **laugh out of the other side of one's face** (or **mouth**) change from enjoyment or amusement to displeasure, shame, apprehension, etc. **laugh out of court** deprive of a hearing by ridicule. **laugh over** discuss with laughter or amusement. **laugh up one's sleeve** be secretly or inwardly amused. [Old English *hlæhhan*, *hliehhan*, from Germanic]

laugh·able *adjective* ludicrous; highly amusing. □ **laugh·ably** *adverb*

laugh·er *noun* **1** a person who laughs. **2** *N Amer. Sport slang* an easily won game; a walkover.

laugh·ing ● *noun* laughter. ● *adjective* in senses of LAUGH *verb*. □ **no laughing matter** something serious. □ **laugh·ing·ly** *adverb*

laughing gas *noun* nitrous oxide as an anaesthetic, formerly used without oxygen and causing an exhilarating effect when inhaled.

laughing hyena *noun* the spotted hyena, *Crocuta crocuta*, whose howl is compared to a fiendish laugh.

laughing jackass *noun* = KOOKABURRA.

laugh·ing·stock *noun* a person or thing open to general ridicule.

laugh line *noun* **1** (also esp. *Brit.* **laughter line**) (usu. in *pl.*) a wrinkle around the eye or mouth formed over the years by smiling or laughing. **2** a line in a play, movie, etc. designed to make the audience laugh.

laugh·ter *noun* the act or sound of laughing. [Old English *hleahtor* from Germanic]

Laugh·ton /ˈlɒtən/ **Charles** (1899–1962), English-born US actor, whose films include *The Private Life of Henry VIII* (1933), for which he won an Oscar, *Mutiny on the Bounty* (1935), *The Hunchback of Notre Dame* (1939), and *Witness for the Prosecution* (1957).

laugh track *noun* *N Amer.* pre-recorded laughter added to a radio or television show to simulate or encourage audience response.

Lau·mann /ˈlaumən/ **Sil·ken** (b.1965), Canadian rower. She won several world rowing titles, including the World Cup championship and the World Championship in 1991, and won the Lou Marsh award as Canada's outstanding athlete, but suffered a broken ankle when her boat was rammed before the 1992 Olympics. She achieved a bronze medal despite the injury, and then won an Olympic silver medal in 1996.

launce /lans/ *noun* = SAND LANCE. [perhaps from LANCE: compare *garfish*]

launch[1] ● *verb* **1 a** *transitive* set (a vessel) afloat. **b** *transitive* set afloat (a newly built vessel) for the first time, often with ceremonies. **c** *intransitive* (often foll. by *out*) (of a vessel) put out to sea etc. **2** *transitive* hurl or send forth (a weapon, rocket, etc.). **3** *transitive* start or set in motion (an enterprise, a person on a course of action, etc.). **4** *transitive* formally introduce (a new product) with publicity etc. **5** *intransitive* **a** (foll. by *out*, *into*) make a start, esp. on an ambitious enterprise. **b** (foll. by *into*) begin suddenly (a tirade, speech, song, etc.). ● *noun* the act or an instance of launching. [Anglo-French *launcher*, Old Norman French *lancher*, Old French *lancier* LANCE *verb*]

launch[2] *noun* **1** a large motorboat, used esp. for pleasure. **2** *hist.* a man-of-war's largest boat. [Spanish *lancha* pinnace, perhaps from Malay *lancharan* from *lanchār* swift]

launch·er *noun* a structure or device to hold a rocket, missile, etc. during launching.

launching pad *noun* (also **launch pad**) **1** a platform with a supporting structure, from which rockets are launched. **2** a starting point for a career, enterprise, etc.

launch vehicle *noun* a rocket-powered vehicle used to send artificial satellites or spacecraft into space.

laun·der ● *verb* **1 a** *transitive & intransitive* wash and dry (clothes, bed or table linen, etc.). **b** *intransitive* (of a fabric, garment, etc.) bear laundering without damage to the texture, colour, etc. **2** *transitive informal* transfer (funds) to conceal a dubious or illegal origin. **3** *transitive* treat or process (something) to make it appear acceptable. ● *noun* a channel for conveying liquids, esp. molten metal. □ **laun·der·er** *noun* [Middle English *launder* (n.) washer of linen, contraction of *lavander* from Old French *lavandier*, ultimately from Latin *lavanda* things to be washed, neuter pl. gerundive of *lavare* wash]

laun·der·ette *noun* (also **laun·drette**) a laundromat.

laun·dress *noun* a woman whose job is to launder clothes, linen, etc.

laun·dro·mat *noun* esp. *N Amer.* an establishment with coin-operated washing machines and dryers for public use. [from LAUNDRY + -*mat*, suffix designating establishments using automatic machines]

laun·dry *noun* (pl. **-dries**) **1** clothes or linen for laundering or newly laundered. **2 a** a room or building for washing clothes etc. **b** a business washing clothes etc. commercially. **3** the action of laundering clothes etc. [contraction of *lavendry* (from Old French *lavanderie*), influenced by LAUNDER]

laundry list *noun* esp. *N Amer.* a long list of assorted items (*a laundry list of complaints*).

laundry·man *noun* (pl. **-men**) a person who launders clothes etc. or who collects and delivers laundry.

laundry·woman *noun* (pl. **-women**) a woman who launders clothes etc. or who collects and delivers laundry.

Laur·asia /lɔːˈreɪʒə/ a vast continental area believed to have existed in the northern hemisphere and to have resulted from the breakup of Pangaea in Mesozoic times. It comprised the present North America, Greenland, Europe, and most of Asia north of the Himalayas. [*Laurentia*, name given to the ancient forerunner of North America + Eurasia]

Laure /lɔr/ **Ca·role** (b.1949) (born Carole Chambers, later Carole Lord), Canadian actor and singer. After studying to be a concert pianist, she moved into theatre and then film. She has acted in several films directed by Gilles Carles, including *La Mort d'un bûcheron* (1973) and *Maria Chapdelaine* (1983). She has also released two solo albums.

laure·ate /ˈlɔrɪət/ ● *noun* **1** a person who is honoured for outstanding creative or intellectual achievement (*Nobel laureate*). **2** = POET LAUREATE. ● *adjective* wreathed with laurel as a mark of honour. □ **laureate·ship** *noun* [Latin *laureatus* from *laurea* laurel wreath, from *laurus* laurel]

laur·el /ˈlɔrəl/ ● *noun* **1** = BAY² 1. **2 a** (in *sing.* or *pl.*) the foliage of the bay tree used as an emblem of victory or distinction in poetry, usu. formed into a wreath or crown. **b** (in *pl.*) honour or distinction. **3** any plant with dark green glossy leaves like a bay tree, e.g. cherry laurel, mountain laurel, spurge laurel. ● *transitive verb* (**laur·elled**, **laur·el·ling**; esp. *US* **laur·eled**, **laur·el·ing**) **1** wreathe with laurel. **2** confer honourable distinction upon. □ **look to one's laurels** beware of losing one's pre-eminence. **rest on one's laurels** be satisfied with what one has done and not seek further success. [Old French *lorier* from Provençal *laurier* from Latin *laurus*]

Laurel and Hardy /ˈlɔrəl, ˈhardi/ **Stan Laurel** (born Arthur Stanley Jefferson) (1890–1965) and **Oli·ver Hardy** (born Oliver Norvell Hardy, Jr.) (1892–1957), US comedy duo. English-born Stan Laurel played the bullied, ever-tearful child while Oliver Hardy ('Ollie') played the pompous bullying father figure; they brought their distinctive slapstick comedy to many films from 1927 onward.

Lau·ren /lɔrˈen/ **Ralph** (b.1939) (born Ralph Lipschitz), US fashion designer known for his classic men's, women's, and children's wear and home furnishings.

Laur·ence, **Mar·garet** (1926–87) (born Jean Margaret Wemyss), Canadian novelist. She published her first major work, *The Tomorrow-Tamer*, a collection of stories set in Africa, in 1963. She is probably best known for her novels set in the fictional Manawaka, inspired by her hometown of Neepawa, Manitoba, including *The Stone Angel* (1964) and *The Diviners* (1974).

Lau·ren·deau /ˌlɔrənˈdoː/ **(Joseph-Edmond-)André** (1912–1968), Canadian journalist, politician, and playwright. As the editor of *l'Action Nationale* (1937–42) and Quebec leader of the Bloc populaire (1944–7) he campaigned against the Union Nationale government. He was editor of *Le Devoir* 1958–68, and co-chaired the Royal Commission on Bilingualism and Biculturalism.

Lau·ren·tian /ləˈrenʃən/ *adjective* **1** designating or pertaining to a geological region in eastern Canada of Precambrian age or the period in which it was formed, esp. designating a group of granites found northwest of the St. Lawrence River. **2** of or pertaining to the Laurentian Mountains. [Latin *Laurentius* Laurence, from the St. Lawrence River + -AN]

Laurentian Mountains (also **Laurentians**) a mountain range (maximum elevation: 1 200 m) in south central Quebec, forming a portion of the Canadian Shield and comprising, in particular, the area bounded by the Ottawa, St. Lawrence and Saguenay rivers.

Laurentian Shield *noun* see CANADIAN SHIELD.

Laurentide Ice Sheet *noun* the ice sheet that covered the eastern part of North America during the most recent glaciation. [French *Laurentides* = LAURENTIAN MOUNTAINS]

Lau·rier /ˈlɔriːeɪ/ **Sir Wil·frid** (1841–1919), Canadian lawyer, journalist, and politician, seventh prime minister of Canada 1896–1911. A staunch opponent of Confederation, he was a liberal MNA from 1871 to 1874, then reconciled himself to federalism and became a Liberal MP, a position he held for the next 45 years. He was leader of the Liberal party 1887–1919. A skilled and charismatic politician, he led Canada through a period of dramatic change, including massive immigration and the establishment of two new provinces, Alberta and Saskatchewan. An ardent nationalist, he sought compromise whenever possible.

laurus·ti·nus /ˌlɔrəˈstaɪnəs/ *noun* an evergreen winter-flowering shrub, *Viburnum tinus*, with dense glossy green leaves and white or pink flowers. [modern Latin from Latin *laurus* laurel + *tinus* wild laurel]

Lau·sanne /loːˈzan/ a town in SW Switzerland, on the north shore of Lake Geneva; pop. (est. 2002) 115,500.

Lau·son /loːˈsɔ̃/ **Jean de** (c.1584–1666) French governor of New France (1651–56). Even before he arrived in the colony, he accumulated vast estates on the St. Lawrence. As governor, he concentrated mainly on enriching himself and his family through the fur trade.

lav *noun informal* a lavatory. [abbreviation]

lava /ˈlɑːvə, ˈlɑːvə/ *noun* **1** the molten matter which flows from a volcano. **2** the solid substance which it forms on cooling. □ **lava·like** *adjective* [Italian from *lavare* wash, from Latin]

lav·abo /ləˈveɪboː, -ˈvɑːboː/ *noun* (pl. **-abos**) **1** *Catholicism* **a** the ritual washing of the celebrant's hands at the offertory of the Mass. **b** a towel or basin used for this. **2** a monastery washing trough. [Latin, = I will wash, first word of Psalm 26:6]

lava flow *noun* a mass of flowing or solidified lava.

lav·age /ləˈvɒʒ, ˈlavɪdʒ/ *noun Med.* the washing out of a body cavity, such as the colon or stomach, with water or a medicated solution. [French from *laver* wash: see LAVE]

Laval¹ /laˈval, lə-/ a city in south central Quebec, located on Île Jésus, just northwest of Montreal; pop. (2001) 343,005. [F. de LAVAL²]

Laval² /laˈval/ **1 Fran·çois de** (1623–1708), French clergyman, first Roman Catholic bishop of Quebec. **2 Pierre** (1883–1945), French politician and prime minister 1931–2, 1935–6, and 1942–4, whose collaboration with the Germans during the Second World War led to his execution for treason in 1945.

lava lamp *noun* a lamp designed as an upright tube containing coloured liquid which swirls and separates like lava when the lamp is plugged in.

lava·liere /ˌlavəˈliːr/ *noun* (also **lava·lier**, **laval·liere**) **1** (in full **lavaliere microphone**) a small microphone worn hanging around the neck. **2** a pendant necklace. **3** a loosely tied cravat. [Louise de *la Vallière*, French courtesan d.1710]

La·val·lée /lavaˈlei/ **Ca·lixa** (1842–1891), Canadian composer and pianist. His most famous composition is the music for 'O Canada', but he also wrote a comic opera, two symphonies, and many overtures and marches.

La·val·trie /lavalˈtriː/ a town in south central Quebec on the north side of the St. Lawrence downstream from Montreal; pop. (2001) 5,967. [in honour of the Sieur de Lavaltrie d.1699]

lava·tera /lavəˈterə/ *noun* a plant of the genus *Lavatera*, of the mallow family, bearing pink, white, or purple flowers. [Modern Latin, after the brothers *Lavater*, 17th- and 18th-c. Swiss naturalists]

lav·a·tor·ial /lavəˈtɔriəl/ *adjective* **1** of or relating to lavatories, esp. resembling the architecture or decoration of public lavatories. **2** (of humour etc.) scatological.

lav·a·tory /ˈlavətɔri/ *noun* (pl. **-ies**) **1** = TOILET 1. **2** a room or compartment containing one or more toilets. [Middle English, = washing vessel, from Late Latin *lavatorium* from Latin *lavare lavat-* wash]

lava tube *noun* a tubular cave occurring naturally in some solidified lava flows.

lave /leɪv/ *transitive verb literary* **1** wash, bathe. **2** (of water) wash against; flow along. [Old French *laver* from Latin *lavare* wash, perhaps coalescing with Old English *lafian*]

lav·en·der /ˈlavəndər/ ● *noun* **1 a** any small evergreen shrub of the genus *Lavandula*, with narrow leaves and blue, purple, or pink aromatic flowers. **b** its flowers and stalks dried and used to scent linen, clothes, etc. **2** (in full **oil of lavender** or **lavender oil**) the oil obtained by distillation of the blossoms of cultivated lavender, used in medicine and perfume. **3** a pale blue colour with a trace of mauve. ● *adjective* **1** of the colour or fragrance of lavender flowers. **2 a** refined, sentimental, genteel. **b** *informal* of or relating to homosexuality. [Anglo-French *lavendre*, ultimately from medieval Latin *lavandula*]

lavender water *noun* a perfume made from distilled lavender, alcohol, and ambergris.

Laver /ˈleɪvər/ **Rod·ney George ('Rod')** (b.1938), Australian tennis player. In 1962 he became the second player (after Don Budge in 1938) to win the four major singles championships (Australia, Britain, France, and the US) in one year; in 1969 he was the first to repeat this.

laver[1] /ˈleɪvər, ˈlɑːvər/ *noun* any of various edible seaweeds, esp. *Porphyra umbilicalis*, having sheet-like fronds. [Latin]

laver[2] /ˈleɪvər/ *noun* **1** *Bible* a large brass vessel for Jewish priests' ritual ablutions. **2** *archaic* a washing or fountain basin; a font. [Old French *laveo(i)r* from Late Latin (as LAVATORY)]

La Véren·drye /ˌlavəˈrɑ̃dri/ **Pierre Gaul·tier de Va·rennes et de** (1685–1749), Canadian military officer, fur trader and explorer. In 1728 he was appointed commandant of the French posts on the north shore of Lake Superior. Between 1731 and 1737 he built several trading posts between Lake Superior and Lake Winnipeg; in 1738 he travelled southwest to the area of the Missouri River. He was responsible for opening a large area of the west to French traders.

lav·ish ● *adjective* **1** giving or producing in large quantities; profuse. **2** generous, unstinting. **3** excessive, overabundant. **4** great in extent, rich in quality, and usu. expensive (*a lavish new production* of Swan Lake). ● *transitive verb* (often foll. by *on*) bestow or spend (money, effort, praise, etc.) abundantly. □ **lav·ish·ly** *adverb* **lav·ish·ness** *noun* [Middle English from obsolete *lavish, lavas* (n.) profusion, from Old French *lavasse* deluge of rain, from *laver* wash]

La·voi·sier /laˈvwʊzi,eɪ/ **An·toine Lau·rent** (1743–94), French scientist, regarded as the father of modern chemistry. He realized that it was Priestley's 'dephlogisticated air' that combined with substances during burning, and (believing it to be a constituent of acids) he renamed the gas *oxygen* (1779).

Law ▸ **1 (An·drew) Bonar** (1858–1923), Canadian-born English Conservative politician, prime minister 1922–3. He was leader of the British Conservative Party (1911–21; 1922–3) and held several ministerial posts from 1915 until retiring in 1921; in Oct. 1922 he returned from retirement to become prime minister following Lloyd George's resignation, but himself resigned six months later because of ill health. **2 John** (1671–1729), Scottish financier. He set up the first French state bank (1716) and a trading company to develop French territories in Louisiana; this 'Mississippi scheme' collapsed in 1720.

law *noun* **1 a** a rule enacted or customary in a community and recognized as enjoining or prohibiting certain actions and enforced by the imposition of penalties. **b** a body of such rules (*the law of the land*; *forbidden under Canadian law*). **2** the controlling influence of laws; a state of respect for laws (*law and order*). **3** laws collectively as a social system or subject of study. **4** (with defining word) any of the specific branches or applications of law (*commercial law*; *law of contract*). **5** binding force or effect (*their word is law*). **6** (prec. by *the*) **a** the legal profession. **b** *informal* the police. **7** the statute and common law (*opp.* EQUITY 2). **8** jurisprudence. **9 a** the judicial remedy; litigation. **b** the law courts as providing this (*go to law*). **10** a rule of action or procedure, e.g. in a game, social context, form of art, etc. **11** a regularity in natural occurrences, esp. as formulated or propounded in particular instances (*the laws of nature*; *the law of gravity*; *Parkinson's law*). **12 a** the body of divine commandments as expressed in the Bible or other sources. **b** (**Law of Moses**) the precepts of the Pentateuch. **c** (**the Law**) the Pentateuch as distinguished from the other parts of the Hebrew Bible (the Prophets and the Writings) (*compare* TORAH). □ **be a law unto oneself** do what one feels is right; disregard custom. **go to law** take legal action; make use of the law courts. **in** (or **at**) **law** according to the laws. **lay down the law** be dogmatic or

authoritarian. **take the law into one's own hands** redress a grievance by one's own means, esp. by force. [Old English *lagu* from Old Norse *lag*, something 'laid down' or fixed, related to LAY[1]]

law-abiding *adjective* obedient to the laws. □ **law-abiding·ness** *noun*

law·break·er *noun* a person who breaks the law. □ **law-breaking** *noun & adjective*

law clerk *noun* **1** = CLERK 4b. **2** = ARTICLED CLERK.

law court *noun* a court of law.

law·ful *adjective* conforming with, permitted by, or recognized by law; not illegal or (of a child) illegitimate. □ **law·ful·ly** *adverb* **law·ful·ness** *noun*

law·giver *noun* a person who lays down laws.

law·less *adjective* **1** having no laws or enforcement of them. **2** disregarding laws. **3** unbridled, uncontrolled. □ **law·less·ly** *adverb* **law·less·ness** *noun*

Law Lord *noun* (in the UK) a member of the House of Lords qualified to perform its legal work.

law·maker *noun* a legislator. □ **law-making** *adjective & noun*

law·man *noun* (*pl.* **-men**) esp. *US* a law enforcement officer, esp. a sheriff or police officer.

lawn[1] ● *noun* a piece of grass kept mown and smooth in a garden, park, etc. ● *transitive verb* turn into lawn, lay with lawn. [Middle English *laund* 'glade' via Old French *launde* from Celtic: related to LAND]

lawn[2] *noun* a fine linen or cotton fabric used for clothes. [Middle English, prob. from *Laon* in France]

lawn bowling *noun N Amer.* any of several bowling games played on grass or dirt surfaces in which players attempt to roll a ball as close as possible to a smaller ball. □ **lawn bowler** *noun*

lawn chair *noun N Amer.* a usu. folding chair for use out of doors.

lawn dart *noun* **1** (in *pl.*; usu. treated as *sing.*) an outdoor game in which large darts are thrown at an area of grass enclosed by a hoop. **2** a dart used in this game.

lawn mower *noun* a machine for cutting the grass on a lawn.

lawn party *noun N Amer.* a social event held on a lawn; a garden party.

lawn sale *noun N Amer.* a sale of used household goods, clothes, books, etc. held on the lawn of a private house.

lawn tennis *noun* the usual form of tennis, played with a soft ball on outdoor grass or a hard court (*compare* COURT TENNIS).

law of nations *noun* international law.

law of nature *noun* = NATURAL LAW.

law of the jungle *noun* a state of ruthless competition.

Law·rence ▸ **1 Charles** (*c*.1709–1760), British military officer. He was posted to Nova Scotia in 1747; in 1753 he was placed in charge of settling German Protestants at Lunenburg. He was named Lieutenant-Governor of Nova Scotia in 1754, and served as governor 1756–60; he was the force behind the expulsion of the Acadians in 1755. **2 David Her·bert** (1885–1930), English novelist, poet, and essayist. He is chiefly remembered for his views on the destructive nature of industrial society and his controversial exploration of sexual relationships; his novels include *Sons and Lovers* (1913), *The Rainbow* (1915), *Women in Love* (1921), and *Lady Chatterley's Lover* (1928). **3 Er·nest Or·lan·do** (1901–58), US physicist. He developed the first circular particle accelerator, later called a cyclotron, capable of achieving very high electron voltages; he also worked on providing fissionable material for the atomic bomb, and received the Nobel Prize for physics in 1939. **4 St.** (Latin name Laurentius) (d.258), Roman martyr and deacon of Rome. According to tradition, he was ordered by the prefect of Rome to deliver up the treasure of the Church; when in response to this order he presented the poor people of Rome to the prefect, he was roasted to death on a gridiron. Feast day, 10 August. **5 Sir Thom·as** (1769–1830), English painter. He first achieved success with his full-length portrait of Queen Charlotte (1789); by 1810 he was recognized as the leading portrait painter of his time. **6 Thom·as Ed·ward** (known as 'Lawrence of Arabia') (1888–1935), Welsh-born English soldier and writer. From 1916 onward he helped to organize and lead the Arab revolt against the Turks in the Middle East, and his campaign of guerrilla raids contributed to Allenby's eventual victory in Palestine in 1918; Lawrence described this period in *The Seven Pillars of Wisdom* (1926).

law·ren·cium /lɒˈrensiəm/ *noun Chem.* an artificially made transuranic radioactive metallic element. Symbol **Lr**, formerly **Lw**; at. no.: 103. [E. O. LAWRENCE]

t top   v voice   w we   z zoo   ʃ she   ʒ vision   θ thin   ð this   ŋ ring   x loch   tʃ chip   dʒ jar   (*see over for vowels*)

law reports *plural noun* a publication of accounts of judicial proceedings and judgments.

law school *noun* an institution of higher education, usu. part of a university, at which lawyers are trained.

Law Society *noun Cdn & Brit.* a professional body representing lawyers.

law·suit *noun* the process of bringing a dispute, claim, etc. before a law court for settlement.

law·yer ● *noun* a member of the legal profession. ● *intransitive verb* follow the profession of lawyer; act as a lawyer. □ **law·yer·ly** *adjective* [Middle English *law(i)er* from LAW]

lax *adjective* **1** not strict or severe enough. **2** *Phonetics* pronounced with the vocal muscles relaxed. □ **lax·ity** *noun* **lax·ly** *adverb* **lax·ness** *noun* [Middle English, = loose, from Latin *laxus*: related to SLACK[1]]

lax·a·tive ● *adjective* tending to stimulate or facilitate evacuation of the bowels. ● *noun* a laxative medicine. [Old French *laxatif -ive* or Late Latin *laxativus* from Latin *laxare* loosen (as LAX)]

Lax·ness, Hall·dór (pseudonym of Halldór Kiljan Gudjónsson) (1902–98), Icelandic novelist. His novels of the 1930s and 1940s reflect his socialist interests, and include *Independent People* (1934–5) and the four-volume *World Light* (1937–40); he was awarded the Nobel Prize for literature in 1955.

lay¹ ● *verb (past* and *past participle* **laid**) **1** *transitive* place on a surface, esp. horizontally in a position of rest (*laid the book on the table*). **2** *transitive* **a** put or bring into a certain or the required position or state (*lay a carpet; laid a cable*). **b** deposit (a corpse) in a grave; bury. **3** *intransitive disputed* lie. ¶ Although the intransitive use of the verb *lay* in this sense is very common, especially in spoken English, it is considered erroneous in standard English. Its use arises probably as a result of confusion with *lay* as the past of *lie*, as in *The dog lay on the floor* which is correct. *The dog is laying on the floor* is not considered standard by many people, and in this sentence *laying* should be *lying*. **4** *transitive* make by laying (*lay the foundations*). **5** *transitive & intransitive* (of a hen bird) produce (an egg). **6** *transitive* **a** cause to subside or lie flat. **b** deal with to remove (a ghost, fear, etc.). **7** *transitive* place or present for consideration (a case, proposal, etc.). **8** *transitive* set down as a basis or starting point. **9** *transitive* (usu. foll. by *on*) attribute or impute (blame etc.). **10** *transitive* locate (a scene etc.) in a certain place. **11** *transitive* prepare or make ready (a plan or a trap). **12** *transitive* prepare (a table) for a meal. **13** *transitive* place or arrange the material for (a fire). **14** *transitive* put down as a wager; stake. **15** *transitive* (foll. by *with*) coat or strew (a surface). **16** *transitive slang offensive* have sexual intercourse with. ● *noun* **1** the way, position, or direction in which something lies. **2** *slang offensive* **a** a partner in sexual intercourse. **b** an act of sexual intercourse. **3** the direction or amount of twist in rope strands. □ **lay about one 1** hit out on all sides. **2** criticize indiscriminately. **lay aside 1** put to one side. **2** cease to practise or consider. **3** save (money etc.) for future needs. **lay something at a person's door** see DOOR. **lay back** cause to slope back from the vertical. **lay bare** expose, reveal. **lay a charge** make an accusation. **lay claim to** claim as one's own. **lay down 1** put on the ground or other surface. **2** relinquish; give up (an office). **3** formulate or insist on (a rule or principle). **4** pay or wager (money). **5** begin to construct (a ship or railway). **6** store (wine) in a cellar. **7** set down on paper. **8** sacrifice (one's life). **9** convert (land) into pasture. **10** record (esp. popular music). **lay down the law** see LAW. **lay an egg** see EGG[1]. **lay hands on 1** seize or attack. **2** place one's hands on or over, esp. in confirmation, ordination, or spiritual healing. **3** (also **lay one's hands on**) obtain, acquire, locate. **lay hold of** seize or grasp. **lay in** provide oneself with a stock of. **lay into** *informal* attack violently with words or blows. **lay it on** (**thick** or **with a shovel** or *Brit.* **with a trowel**) *informal* flatter or exaggerate grossly. **lay low 1** overthrow, kill, or humble. **2** incapacitate by illness. **3** *disputed* lie low. **lay off 1** discharge (workers) temporarily or permanently because of a shortage of work; make redundant. **2** *informal* (often in *imperative*) stop bothering (a person). **3** *informal* stop working (*laid off around 4:00*). **4** abstain from or stop using (something) (*lay off beer*). **5** (of a bookmaker) insure against a substantial loss resulting from (a large bet) by placing a similar bet with another bookmaker. **lay on 1** provide (a facility, amenity, etc.). **2** impose (a penalty, obligation, etc.). **3** inflict (blows, damage, etc.). **4** spread on (paint etc.). **lay on the table** see TABLE. **lay open 1** break the skin of. **2** (foll. by *to*) expose (to criticism etc.). **lay out 1** spread out. **2** expose to view. **3** prepare (a corpse) for burial. **4** *informal* knock unconscious. **5** dispose (grounds etc.) according to a plan. **6** expend (money). **7** reveal or explain in detail (*she laid out the rules for us*). **8** *reflexive* (foll. by *to* + infin.) *Brit.* take pains (to do something) (*laid themselves out to help*). **lay store by** see STORE. **lay to rest** see REST[1]. **lay up 1** store, save. **2** put (a ship

etc.) out of service. **3** (usu. in *passive*) confine to bed through illness, injury, etc.; be taken ill (*was laid up with a cold*). **lay waste** see WASTE. [Old English *lecgan*, from Germanic]

lay² *adjective* **1 a** non-clerical. **b** designating a person who has taken the vows of a religious order but is not ordained and is employed in ancillary or manual work (*lay brother; lay sister*). **2 a** not professionally qualified, esp. in law or medicine. **b** of or done by such persons. [Old French *lai* from ecclesiastical Latin *laicus* from Greek *laïkos* LAIC]

lay³ *noun* **1** a short lyric or narrative poem meant to be sung. **2** a song. [Old French *lai*, Provençal *lais*, of unknown origin]

lay⁴ *past of* LIE[1].

lay·about *noun* a habitual loafer or idler.

Laya·mon /ˈlaɪəmɒn/ (late 12th c.), English poet and priest. He wrote the verse chronicle known as the *Brut*, a history of England which introduces for the first time in English the story of King Arthur.

lay·away *noun N Amer.* a system of purchasing an article by making usu. monthly payments until the entire cost has been paid, at which point the article is released to the customer.

lay·back spin *noun Figure Skating* a spin on one foot with the other leg extended backwards and turned out, with the upper body arched backwards.

lay-by *noun (pl.* **lay-bys**) **1** *Brit.* an area at the side of an open road where vehicles may stop. **2** a similar arrangement on a canal or railway.

lay·er ● *noun* **1** a thickness of matter, esp. one of several, laid over a surface or forming a horizontal division (*wore layers of clothing; a layer of clay; ozone layer*). **2** a person or thing that lays. **3** a hen that lays eggs, esp. with reference to its productivity (*a good layer*). **4** a shoot fastened down to take root while attached to the parent plant. ● *verb* **1** *transitive* **a** arrange (something) in layers. **b** cut (hair) in layers. **2** *transitive* propagate (a plant) as a layer. **3** *intransitive* form layers. **4** *intransitive* wear several layers of clothing so that layers can be removed or put back on to adjust to temperature variations. □ **lay·ered** *adjective* **layer·ing** *noun*

layer cake *noun esp. N Amer.* a cake of two or more layers with icing, filling, etc. between.

lay·ette *noun* a set of clothing, toilet articles, and bedclothes for a newborn child. [French, diminutive of Old French *laie* drawer, from Middle Dutch *laege*]

lay figure *noun* a dummy or jointed figure of a human body used by artists for arranging drapery on etc. [*lay* from obsolete *layman* from Dutch *leeman* from obsolete *led* joint]

laying on of hands *noun* **1** a religious rite in which a person being ordained, confirmed, etc. is touched by a cleric. **2** the act of placing the hands, esp. by a faith healer, evangelist, etc., on a person seeking healing, faith, etc.

lay·man *noun (pl.* **-men**) **1** any non-ordained member of a church. **2** a person without professional or specialized knowledge in a particular subject.

lay·off *noun* **1** a temporary or permanent dismissal of workers. **2** a period when this is in force. **3** a rest, a respite (*came back from a six-month layoff to win the race*).

lay of the land *noun N Amer.* **1** the disposition of natural features in a landscape. **2** the current state of affairs.

La'youn /lɒˈjuːn/ (also **Laayoune**) the capital of Western Sahara; pop. (est. 2002) 190,500.

lay·out *noun* **1** the disposing or arrangement of a site, ground, etc. **2** the way in which plans, printed matter, etc., are arranged or set out. **3** something arranged or set out in a particular way. **4** the makeup of a book, newspaper, etc.

lay·over *noun* a period of rest or waiting before a further stage in a journey etc.; a stopover.

lay·person *noun (pl.* **lay people** or **lay·persons**) a layman or laywoman.

lay reader *noun* (in the Anglican Church) a lay person licensed to conduct some religious services.

Lay·ton, Irv·ing Peter (b.1912) (born Israel Lazarovitch), Romanian-born Canadian poet, writer, and essayist. His early poems were published in the journal *First Statement* (1942–5). His first collection, *Here and Now*, was published in 1945; since then he has released approximately 50 volumes of poetry and fiction.

lay·up *noun* **1** *Basketball* a shot made close to the basket, in which the shooter often lays the ball against the backboard so it will rebound into the basket. **2** plies or layers assembled for the manufacture of plywood or other laminated material.

Vowels: a *cat* ɑ *arm* e *bed* ɜr *her* ɜ: *deux* ə *ago* ɪ *sit* i *cosy* iː *feed* ɒ *hot* ɔ *pore* oː *no* ʌ *run* ʊ *put*

lay·woman *noun* (*pl.* **-women**) **1** any non-ordained female member of a church. **2** a woman without professional or specialized knowledge in a particular subject.

laz·ar /ˈlazər/ *noun archaic* a poor and diseased person, esp. a leper. [medieval Latin *lazarus* from LAZARUS 2]

laz·ar·et /ˌlazəˈret/ *noun* (also **laz·ar·ette, laz·ar·etto** /-ˈretoː/) (*pl.* **laz·ar·ets, laz·ar·ettes,** or **laz·ar·et·tos**) **1** a hospital for diseased people, esp. lepers. **2** a building or ship for quarantine. **3** the after part of a ship's hold, used for stores. [(French *lazaret*) from Italian *lazzaretto* from *lazzaro* LAZAR]

Laz·ar·ist /ˈlazərɪst/ *noun* a member of a religious body, the Congregation of the Mission, established at the priory of St. Lazare in Paris in 1625 by St. Vincent de Paul. Set up to preach to the rural poor and train candidates for the priesthood, the Lazarists now have foundations worldwide. *Also called* VINCENTIAN. [French, from LAZARUS 2]

Laz·a·rus /ˈlazərəs/ *New Testament* **1** the brother of Martha and Mary, whom Jesus raised from the dead (John 11–12). **2** (in a parable in Luke 16:19–31) a diseased beggar who lay by the gate of a rich man, hoping for scraps from his table, and who, upon his death, was taken into heaven while the rich man was sent to eternal torment.

laze *verb* **1** *intransitive* spend time lazily or idly. **2** *transitive* (often foll. by *away*) pass (time) in this way. [back-formation from LAZY]

Lazio /ˈlatsiˌoː/ an administrative region of west central Italy, on the Tyrrhenian Sea, including the ancient region of Latium; capital, Rome.

lazy *adjective* (**laz·i·er, laz·i·est**) **1** disinclined to work, doing little work. **2** of or inducing idleness. **3** (of a river etc.) slow-moving. **4** (of a brand letter or mark on cattle etc.) placed on its side rather than upright (*a lazy E*). □ **laz·i·ly** *adverb* **laz·i·ness** *noun* [earlier *laysie, lasie, laesy,* perhaps from Low German: compare Low German *lasich* idle]

lazy·bones *noun* (*pl.* same) *informal* a lazy person.

lazy eye *noun* an amblyopic eye in which underuse has contributed to its poor vision.

Lazy Su·san *noun* (also **lazy Susan**) **1** a revolving stand on a table to hold condiments etc. **2** *N Amer.* an esp. kitchen cupboard or shelf designed to revolve in order to provide easy access to its contents.

lb. *abbreviation* a pound or pounds (weight). [Latin *libra*]

LBdr *abbreviation* LANCE BOMBARDIER.

LBO *abbreviation* LEVERAGED BUYOUT.

LC *abbreviation* **1** LIBRARY OF CONGRESS CLASSIFICATION. **2** *Cdn* LIQUOR COMMISSION.

l.c. *abbreviation* **1** in the passage etc. cited. **2** lower case. **3** letter of credit. [sense 1 from Latin *loco citato*]

LCBO *abbreviation Cdn* (*Ont.*) Liquor Control Board of Ontario.

LCD *abbreviation* **1** LIQUID CRYSTAL DISPLAY. **2** lowest (or least) common denominator.

LCdr *abbreviation Cdn* LIEUTENANT COMMANDER.

l'chaim /ləˈxaɪɪm/ *interjection* a drinking toast. [Hebrew, = 'to life!']

LCM *abbreviation* lowest (or least) common multiple.

LCol *abbreviation Cdn* LIEUTENANT COLONEL.

LD *abbreviation* **1** lethal dose, usu. with a following numeral indicating the percentage of a group of animals killed by such a dose (LD_{50}). **2** learning disability.

Ld. *abbreviation* Lord.

LDC *abbreviation* less developed country.

LDL *abbreviation* LOW-DENSITY LIPOPROTEIN.

L-dopa *noun Biochem.* the levorotatory form of dopa, used to treat Parkinson's disease. *Also called* LEVODOPA.

LDP *abbreviation* (in Japan) Liberal Democratic Party.

LDS *abbreviation* Latter-day Saints.

-le¹ *suffix* forming nouns, esp.: **1** names of appliances or instruments (*handle; thimble*). **2** names of animals and plants (*beetle; thistle*). ¶ The suffix has ceased to be syllabic in *snail, stile.* [ultimately from or representing Old English *-el* etc. from Germanic, with many Indo-European cognates]

-le² *suffix* (also **-el**) forming nouns with (or originally with) diminutive sense (*angle; castle; mantle; syllable; novel; tunnel*). [Middle English *-el, -elle* from Old French, ultimately from Latin forms *-ellus, -ella,* etc.]

-le³ *suffix* forming adjectives, often with (or originally with) the sense 'apt or liable to' (*brittle; fickle; little; nimble*). [Middle English from Old English *-el* etc. from Germanic, corresponding to Latin *-ulus*]

-le⁴ *suffix* forming verbs, esp. expressing repeated action or movement

or having diminutive sense (*bubble; crumple; wriggle*). [Old English *-lian* from Germanic]

lea /liː/ *noun literary* a piece of meadowland, or pasture land, or arable land. [Old English *lēa(h)* from Germanic]

leach *verb* **1** *transitive* make (a liquid) percolate through some material. **2** *transitive* subject (bark, ore, ash, or soil) to the action of percolating fluid. **3** *transitive & intransitive* (foll. by *away, out*) remove (soluble matter) or be removed in this way. **4** *transitive* slowly deprive of. □ **leach·able** *adjective* **leach·abil·ity** *noun* [prob. representing Old English *leccan* 'to water', from West Germanic]

leach·ate /ˈliːtʃeɪt/ *noun* a quantity of liquid that has percolated through a solid and leached out some of the constituents.

Leach's storm petrel *noun* (also **Leach's petrel**) a storm petrel of the N Atlantic and N Pacific, *Oceanodroma leucorhoa,* with a forked tail, which flies in a distinctive darting manner close to the sea. [W. *Leach* English naturalist d.1836]

Lea·cock, Ste·phen (1869–1944), English-born Canadian humorist, essayist, political economist and historian. He taught in the department of economics and political science at McGill University from 1903 until he retired in 1936. His first book, *Elements of Political Science* (1906) became a bestselling textbook, but he is best remembered for *Sunshine Sketches of a Little Town* (1912), a humorous examination of the social, political, business and religious life of the fictional small Canadian town of Mariposa.

lead¹ /liːd/ ● *verb* (*past* and *past participle* **led**) **1** *transitive* cause to go with one, esp. by guiding or showing the way or by going in front and taking a person's hand or an animal's halter etc. **2** *transitive* **a** direct the actions or opinions of. **b** (often foll. by *to,* or *to* + infin.) guide by persuasion or example or argument (*what led you to that conclusion?; was led to think you may be right*). **c** (of a lawyer) put a question to (a witness) in such a way as to suggest the answer required. **3** *transitive & intransitive* provide access to; bring to a certain position or destination (*this door leads you into a small room; the road leads to Moncton; the path leads uphill*). **4** *transitive* pass or go through (a life etc. of a specified kind) (*led a miserable existence*). **5 a** *transitive* have the first place in (*the mayor led the parade; leads the world in sugar production*). **b** *intransitive* go first; be ahead in a race or game. **c** *intransitive* be pre-eminent in some field. **d** *intransitive* guide one's partner through the steps of a dance. **6** *transitive* be in charge of (*leads a team of researchers*). **7** *transitive* **a** direct by example. **b** set (a fashion). **c** be the principal player of (a group of musicians). **8** *transitive & intransitive Cards* begin a round of play by playing (a card) or a card of (a particular suit). **9** *intransitive* (foll. by *to*) have as an end or outcome; result in (*what does all this lead to?*). **10** *intransitive* (foll. by *with*) *Boxing* make an attack (with a particular blow). **11 a** *intransitive* (foll. by *with*) (of a newspaper, newscast, etc.) use a particular item as the main story (*led with the Stock Market crash*). **b** *transitive* (of a story) be the main feature of (a newspaper or part of it or a newscast) (*the election will lead the front page*). **12** *transitive* (foll. by *through*) make (a liquid, strip of material, etc.) pass through a pulley, channel, etc. ● *noun* **1** guidance given by going in front; example (*I'll follow her lead*). **2 a** a leading place; the leadership (*is in the lead; take the lead*). **b** the amount by which a competitor is ahead of the others (*a lead of ten points*). **3** a clue, esp. an early indication of the resolution of a problem (*is the first real lead in the case*). **4** = LEASH *noun.* **5** a conductor (usu. a wire) conveying electric current from a source to an appliance. **6 a** the chief part in a play etc. **b** the person playing this. **c** the chief performer or instrument of a specified type (also *attributive: lead guitar*). **7** (in full **lead story**) the item of news given the greatest prominence in a newspaper, magazine, or newscast. **8** the member of a curling rink who delivers the first two rocks for their rink in each end. **9 a** the act or right of playing first in a game or round of cards. **b** the card led. **10** the distance advanced by a screw in one turn. **11 a** an artificial watercourse, esp. one leading to a mill. **b** a channel of water in an icefield. **12** an alluvial deposit of gold along the bed of an ancient river. **13** *Cdn* (*Nfld*) a stretch of low, open land passing through an area covered with lakes, trees, or hills. □ **lead astray** *see* ASTRAY 1. **lead by the nose** cajole (a person) into compliance. **lead a person a dance** *see* DANCE. **lead off 1** begin; make a start. **2** *Baseball* be the first batter for a team in (an inning or game). **lead on 1** entice into going further than was intended. **2** mislead or deceive. **lead the way** *see* WAY. □ **lead·able** *adjective* [Old English *lǣdan* from Germanic]

lead² /led/ ● *noun* **1** *Chem.* a heavy bluish-grey soft ductile metallic element occurring naturally in galena and other minerals. Symbol: **Pb**; at. no.: 82. **2 a** graphite. **b** a thin length of this for use in a pencil. **3** a lump of lead used in sounding water. **4** (in *pl.*) *Brit.* **a** strips of lead covering a roof. **b** a piece of lead-covered roof. **5** (in *pl.*) lead frames holding the glass of a lattice or stained glass window. **6** *Printing* a blank space between lines of print (originally with reference to the metal strip used to give this space). **7** (*attributive*) made of lead. **8** bullets collectively. ● *transitive verb* **1** cover, weight, or frame (a roof or windowpanes) with lead. **2** *Printing* separate lines of (printed matter) with leads. **3** add a lead compound in response to (gasoline etc.). □ **get the lead out** *N Amer. slang* hurry up; move or work more quickly. **go over like a lead balloon** *N Amer. slang* (of an idea etc.) fail to generate enthusiasm or interest. □ **lead·less** *adjective* [Old English *léad* from West Germanic]

Lead·bel·ly /'led,beli/ (born Huddie William Ledbetter) (c.1885–1949), US guitarist, blues and folk singer, and songwriter, known for songs such as 'Midnight Special', 'Rock Island Line', and 'Goodnight, Irene'.

lead crystal /led/ *noun* crystal containing a substantial proportion of lead oxide, making it more refractive.

lead dog /liːd/ *noun N Amer.* the primary dog in a team, responsible for leading the rest of the team in response to the driver's commands.

leaded /'ledəd/ *adjective* **1** (of gasoline) containing tetraethyl lead as an additive. **2** (of glass or crystal) containing a high proportion of lead oxide, making it more refractive. **3** (of a window) containing panes of glass set in lead strips.

leaden /'ledən/ *adjective* **1** of or like lead. **2** heavy, slow, burdensome (*leaden limbs*). **3** inert, depressing (*leaden rule*). **4** lead-coloured (*leaden skies*). □ **leaden·ly** *adverb*

lead·er /'liːdər/ *noun* **1 a** a person or thing that leads. **b** a person followed by others. **2 a** the principal player in a music group. **b** *Brit.* = CONCERTMASTER. **c** a conductor, esp. of a small musical group. **3 a** short strip of non-functioning material at each end of a reel of film or recording tape for connection to the spool. **4** a shoot of a plant at the apex of a stem or of the main branch. **5** (in *pl.*) *Printing* a series of dots or dashes across the page to guide the eye, esp. in tabulated material. **6** the horse or dog placed at the front of a team. **7** a length of line or wire connecting the end of a fishing line to a hook or fly. **8** a net placed to intercept fish and lead them into a trap, weir, etc. **9** (in full **Leader of the House**) *Brit.* a member of the government officially responsible for initiating business in Parliament. **10** *Brit.* = LEADING ARTICLE. □ **leader·less** *adjective* **leader·ship** *noun*

leader·board *noun* a scoreboard, esp. at a golf course, showing the names etc. of the leading competitors.

leadership convention *noun Cdn* a convention held by a political party for the purpose of electing a new leader.

leadership race *noun Cdn, Brit., Austral., & NZ* a campaign of several candidates for the leadership of a political party.

lead foot /led/ *noun N Amer. informal* the practice of driving too quickly, esp. habitually (*drives with a lead foot*).

lead-footed /led/ *adjective N Amer.* **1** slow or sluggish (*a lead-footed skater*). **2** tending to drive too quickly (*a lead-footed driver*).

lead-free *adjective* (of gasoline) without added tetraethyl lead.

lead head /led/ *noun* (in full **lead head jig**) a simple fishing lure consisting of a single hook extending horizontally from a blob of lead.

lead-in *noun* **1** an introduction, opening, etc. **2** a wire leading in from outside, esp. from an antenna to a receiver or transmitter.

lead·ing¹ /'liːdɪŋ/ ● *adjective* **1** chief; most important (*the leading scholar in her field; a leading cause of death*). **2** first in position (*the leading runner rounded the corner*). **3** bestselling; most popular (*uses the leading brand*). **4** most likely to succeed, win, etc. (*the leading candidate for the job*). ● *noun* guidance, leadership.

lead·ing² /'ledɪŋ/ *noun Printing* = LEAD² *noun* 6.

leading aircraftman /'liːdɪŋ/ *noun* (also **Leading Aircraftman**) (currently in the RAF or *hist.* in the RCAF) a serviceman of the rank above aircraftman (*see* AIRCRAFTMAN). Abbr.: **LAC**.

leading article /'liːdɪŋ/ *noun Brit.* a newspaper article giving the editorial opinion.

leading edge /'liːdɪŋ/ *noun* **1** the foremost edge of an airfoil, esp. a wing or propeller blade. **2** the forefront of development, esp. in technology (also *attributive*: *leading-edge company*). **3** *Electronics* the part of a pulse in which the amplitude increases (*opp.* TRAILING EDGE).

leading lady /'liːdɪŋ/ *noun* the actress or film star who plays the principal female part in a play or film.

leading light /'liːdɪŋ/ *noun* a prominent and influential person.

leading man /'liːdɪŋ/ *noun* the actor or film star who plays the principal male part in a play or film.

leading note /'liːdɪŋ/ *noun Music* = SUBTONIC.

leading question /'liːdɪŋ/ *noun* **1** *Law* a question that prompts the

answer wanted. **2** a craftily worded question intended to lead the questioned person to say something incriminating.

leading seaman /'liːdɪŋ/ *noun* **1** (also **Leading Seaman**) a member of the Canadian Navy of the rank above able seaman and below master seaman. Abbr.: **LS**. **2** a person of similar rank in other navies.

leading tone /'liːdɪŋ/ *noun N Amer. Music* = SUBTONIC.

lead·off /'liːdɒf/ *noun* an action beginning a process. ● *adjective* **1** *Baseball* of or relating to the player who bats first in either the batting order or an inning (*leadoff hitter; leadoff triple*). **2** of or relating to something that serves as a beginning or introduction (*a leadoff news story*).

lead pencil /led/ *noun* a pencil of graphite enclosed in wood.

lead poisoning /led/ *noun* acute or chronic poisoning by absorption of lead into the body.

lead shot /led/ *noun* = SHOT¹ 3b.

lead time /liːd/ *noun* the time between the initiation and completion of a process.

leaf ● *noun* (*pl.* **leaves**) **1 a** each of several flattened usu. green structures of a plant, growing on the side of a stem or branch and the main organ of photosynthesis. **b** other similar plant structures, e.g. bracts, sepals, and petals (*floral leaf*). **2 a** foliage regarded collectively. **b** the state of having leaves out (*a tree in leaf*). **3** a single thickness of paper, esp. in a book with each side forming a page. **4** a very thin sheet of metal, esp. gold or silver. **5 a** the hinged part or flap of a door, shutter, table, etc. **b** an extra section inserted to extend a table. ● *intransitive verb* put forth leaves. □ **leaf through** turn over the pages of (a book etc.). **take a leaf out of a person's book** imitate a person. **turn over a new leaf** improve one's conduct or performance. □ **leaf·age** *noun* **leaf·less** *adjective* **leaf·like** *adjective* [Old English *léaf* from Germanic]

leaf blower *noun* a device for blowing leaves off a lawn or into piles etc., used as an alternative to raking.

leaf·cut·ter *noun* **1** (in full **leafcutter ant**, **leaf-cutting ant**) an ant of the mainly tropical American genus *Atta*, which cuts pieces from leaves to cultivate fungus. **2** (in full **leafcutter bee**) a solitary bee of the family Megachilidae which lines its nest with leaf fragments.

leafed *adjective var. of* LEAVED.

leaf-green ● *noun* the colour of green leaves. ● *adjective* of this colour.

leaf·hop·per *noun* any homopterous insect of the family Cicadellidae, which sucks the sap of plants and often causes damage and spreads disease.

leaf insect *noun* any insect of the family Phylliidae, having a flattened body resembling a leaf.

leaf·let ● *noun* **1** a printed sheet of paper, usu. folded and free of charge, containing information. **2** a young leaf. **3** *Bot.* any division of a compound leaf. ● *transitive verb* (**leaf·let·ed**, **leaf·let·ing** or **leaf·let·ted**, **leaf·let·ting**) distribute leaflets to.

leaf lettuce *noun* lettuce with loose leaves (*compare* HEAD LETTUCE).

leaf miner *noun* any of various larvae burrowing in leaves.

leaf mould *noun* soil consisting chiefly of decayed leaves.

leaf·roll *noun* a virus disease of potatoes characterized by upward curling of the leaves.

leaf·roll·er *noun* an insect, esp. a small moth, whose larvae roll up the leaves of plants which they feed upon.

leaf spot *noun* any of numerous fungal and bacterial plant diseases which cause leaves to develop discoloured spots.

leaf spring *noun* a spring consisting of a number of strips of metal curved slightly upwards and clamped together one above the other.

leaf stalk *noun* a petiole.

leafy *adjective* (**leaf·i·er**, **leaf·i·est**) **1 a** having many leaves. **b** (of a place) rich in foliage; verdant. **2** producing broad-bladed leaves, as distinct from other types of foliage (*green leafy vegetables*). **3** resembling a leaf. □ **leaf·i·ness** *noun*

league¹ ● *noun* **1** a collection of people, countries, groups, etc., combining for a particular purpose, esp. mutual protection or co-operation. **2** an agreement to combine in this way. **3** a group of sports teams of a similar level organized to compete among themselves. **4** a class or category (*as a musician, I'm not in your league*). ● *intransitive verb* (**leagues**, **leagued**, **leaguing**) (often foll. by *together*) join in a league. □ **in league** allied, conspiring. [French *ligue* or Italian *liga*, var. of *lega* from *legare* bind, from Latin *ligare*]

league² *noun archaic* a variable measure of distance, usu. about three miles (4.8 km). [Middle English, ultimately from Late Latin *leuga*, *leuca*, of Gaulish origin]

league-leading *adjective* **1** (of a team or player) occupying first place in any classification of all teams or players in a league. **2** designating a statistic which surpasses that of every other player or team in a league (*a league-leading 43 goals*).

League of Arab States *noun* an organization of Arab nations, founded in 1945 with headquarters in Cairo, whose purpose is to ensure co-operation among its member states and protect their independence and sovereignty. *Also called* ARAB LEAGUE.

League of Nations *noun* an association of countries established in 1919 to promote international co-operation and achieve international peace and security; it was replaced after World War II by the United Nations.

leaguer[1] *noun* esp. *N Amer.* a member of a league (esp. in *combination*: *minor-leaguer*).

leaguer[2] *noun & verb* = LAAGER. [Dutch *leger* camp, related to LAIR]

league table *noun Brit.* **1** a listing of competitors as a league, showing their ranking according to performance. **2** any list of ranking order.

Leah /ˈliːə/ *Bible* the first wife of Jacob and elder sister of Rachel (Genesis 29).

leak ● *noun* **1 a** a hole in a pipe, container, etc. caused by wear or damage, through which matter, esp. liquid or gas, passes accidentally in or out. **b** the matter passing in or out through this. **c** the act or an instance of leaking. **2 a** a similar escape of electrical charge. **b** the charge that escapes. **3** the intentional disclosure of secret information. ● *verb* **1 a** *intransitive* (of liquid, gas, etc.) pass in or out through a leak. **b** *transitive* lose or admit (liquid, gas, etc.) through a leak. **2** *transitive* intentionally disclose (secret information). **3** *intransitive* (often foll. by *out*) (of a secret, secret information) become known. □ **take a leak** *slang* urinate. □ **leak·er** *noun* [Middle English prob. from Low German]

leak·age *noun* **1** the action or result of leaking. **2** what leaks in or out. **3** an intentional disclosure of secret information.

Lea·key ▸ **1 Louis (Sey·mour Bazett)** (1903–72), Kenyan archaeologist and anthropologist, whose discoveries of fossil hominids in E Africa established that region as the likely origin of *Homo sapiens*; his books include *Adam's Ancestors* (1934), *Olduvai Gorge* (1952), and *Unveiling Man's Origins* (1968). **2** his wife, **Mary Doug·las** (1913–96), English archaeologist and anthropologist, who discovered *Australopithecus* (or *Zinjanthropus*) *boisei* at Olduvai in 1959; her books include *Olduvai Gorge: My Search for Early Man* (1979) and *Disclosing the Past* (1984). **3** their son, **Rich·ard (Ers·kine Frere)** (b.1944), English anthropologist and paleontologist, who has continued his parents' work on early hominids, and was appointed director of the Kenya Wildlife Service in 1989; his books include *Origins* (1977) and *The Making of Mankind* (1981).

leak-proof *adjective* designed in such a way as to prevent leakage (*a leak-proof diaper*).

leaky *adjective* (**leak·i·er**, **leak·i·est**) having a leak or leaks. □ **leak·i·ness** *noun*

Leam·ing·ton /ˈliːmɪŋtən/ a town in SW Ontario, situated on Lake Erie, southeast of Windsor; pop. (2001) 27,138. □ **Leam·ing·ton·ian** *noun* [Leamington Spa, a town in Warwickshire]

Lean, Sir David (1908–91), English film director. He made many notable films, including *Great Expectations* (1946), *The Bridge on the River Kwai* (1957), *Lawrence of Arabia* (1962), *Doctor Zhivago* (1965), and *A Passage to India* (1984).

lean[1] ● *verb* (*past* and *past participle* **leaned** or (esp. *Brit.*) **leant** /lent/) **1** *intransitive & transitive* (often foll. by *across, back, over*, etc.) be or place in a sloping position; incline from the perpendicular. **2** *intransitive & transitive* (foll. by *against, on, upon*) rest or cause to rest for support against etc. **3** *intransitive* (foll. by *on, upon*) rely on; derive support from. **4** *intransitive* (foll. by *to, towards*) be inclined or partial to; have a tendency towards. ● *noun* a deviation from the perpendicular; an inclination (*has a decided lean to the right*). □ **lean on** *informal* put pressure on (a person) to act in a certain way. [Old English *hleonian, hlinian* from Germanic]

lean[2] ● *adjective* **1** (of a person or animal) thin; having no superfluous fat. **2** (of meat) containing little fat. **3** meagre; of poor quality (*lean crop*). **4** (also **lean, mean**, or **leaner and meaner**) (of a business, sector of the economy, etc.) rendered more efficient or competitive through the reduction of unnecessary costs or expenditure. **5** (of a period of time) not prosperous; marked by austerity and restraint (*went through some lean times together*). **6** (of a vaporized fuel mixture) having a high proportion of air (*compare* RICH 7). ● *noun* the lean part of meat. □ **lean·ly** *adverb* **lean·ness** *noun* [Old English *hlæne* from Germanic]

lean-burn *adjective* of or relating to an internal combustion engine designed to run on a lean mixture to reduce pollution.

Le·ander /liˈandər/ *Gk Myth* a young man, the lover of the priestess Hero. He was drowned swimming across the Hellespont to visit her.

lean·ing *noun* a tendency or partiality.

lean-to *noun* (*pl.* **-tos**) **1** *N Amer.* a usu. temporary shelter consisting of an inclined roof supported at one side by trees or posts and covered with canvas, branches, etc. **2** a roof that has a single slope and is supported at its upper end by a wall or building etc. **3** a room or building with such a roof.

leap ● *verb* (*past* and *past participle* **leaped** or **leapt** /lept/) **1** *intransitive* jump or spring forcefully. **2** *transitive* jump across. **3** *intransitive* (of prices etc.) increase dramatically. **4** *intransitive* move quickly or suddenly; rush (*leaped into the car*). **5** *intransitive* spring or arise quickly, as if by a leap (*the idea just leapt into my mind*). **6** *intransitive* (foll. by *up*) spring suddenly to one's feet; rise with a bound from a sitting or reclining position. **7** *intransitive* (often foll. by *at*) accept something eagerly (*leaped at the chance to go to Yellowknife*). ● *noun* **1** a forceful jump. **2** a large, sudden increase (*a leap in prices*). **3** an abrupt or sudden transition. **4** the distance covered by a leap or jump. **5** a thing to be leaped over or from. □ **by leaps and bounds** with startlingly rapid progress. **leap in the dark** a daring step or enterprise whose consequences are unpredictable. **leap to the eye** be immediately apparent. □ **leap·er** *noun* [Old English *hlýp, hléapan* from Germanic]

leap·frog ● *noun* a game in which players in turn vault with parted legs over another who is bending down. ● *verb* (**-frogged, -frog·ging**) **1** *intransitive* (foll. by *over*) perform such a vault. **2** *transitive* vault over in this way. **3** *transitive & intransitive* (of two or more people, vehicles, etc.) overtake alternately. **4** *transitive & intransitive* (of a person, corporation, etc.) overtake or surpass a competitor or competitors.

leap of faith *noun* the act or an instance of accepting or believing something that cannot be proven.

leap year *noun* a year, occurring one in four, with 366 days (including 29th February as an intercalary day). [prob. from the fact that feast days after February in such a year fell two days later (as opposed to one day in other years) than in the previous year]

Lear ▸ **1 Ed·ward** (1812–88), English humorist and illustrator, who is best known for his nonsense verse and limericks. **2 Wil·liam Pow·ell** (1902–78), US inventor and industrialist. After an early career producing radio and navigational aids for aircraft, he founded Lear Jet, Inc. which produced very popular private jet aircraft.

learn *verb* (*past* and *past participle* **learned** or **learnt**) **1** *transitive* gain knowledge of or skill in by study, experience, or being taught. **2** *transitive* (foll. by *to* + infin.) acquire or develop a particular ability (*learn to swim*). **3** *transitive* commit to memory (*will try to learn your names*). **4** *intransitive* (foll. by *of*) be informed about. **5** *transitive* (foll. by *that, how*, etc. + clause) become aware of by information or from observation. **6** *intransitive* receive instruction; acquire knowledge or skill. **7** *transitive* *slang* or *archaic* teach. ¶ Usually regarded as an uneducated use, and unacceptable in spoken and written English except jocularly or in fixed informal phrases, e.g. *that'll learn you!* □ **learn one's lesson** see LESSON. □ **learn·abil·ity** *noun* **learn·able** *adjective* [Old English *leornian* from Germanic: related to LORE[1]]

learn·ed /ˈlɜːrnəd/ *adjective* **1** (of a person) having much knowledge acquired by study. **2** showing or requiring learning (*a learned work*). **3** studied or pursued by learned persons. **4** concerned with the interests of learned persons; scholarly (*a learned journal*). **5** /lɜːrnd/ acquired by learning or experience; not innate (*learned behaviour*). **6** *Cdn & Brit.* as a courteous description of a lawyer in certain formal contexts (*my learned friend*). □ **learn·ed·ly** *adverb* **learn·ed·ness** *noun*

learned helplessness *noun* *Psych.* a condition of apathy and lack of motivation in which a person suffers from a sense of powerlessness, arising from a traumatic event or persistent failure to succeed.

learn·er *noun* **1** a person who is learning a subject, language, or skill. **2** a person who is learning to drive a motor vehicle and has not yet passed a driving test.

learn·ing *noun* **1** knowledge acquired by study. **2** the act or process of learning (also *attributive: learning experience*).

learning curve *noun* **1** the rate of progress in learning or gaining experience. **2** a graph of this.

learning disability *noun* a difficulty in learning caused by a physical or psychological dysfunction. □ **learning disabled** *adjective*

Leary, Tim·othy (Fran·cis) (1920–96), US psychologist and drug pioneer. After he began experimenting with mind-altering drugs including LSD, he was dismissed from his teaching post at Harvard

University in 1963 and became a figurehead for the hippy drug culture. He was imprisoned for possession of marijuana (1970–6).

lease ● noun **1** an agreement by which the owner of a building, apartment, vehicle, piece of land, etc. allows another to use it for a specified time in return for payment. **2** the period of time for which such an agreement is made. ● transitive verb grant or take on lease. □ **a new lease on** (Brit. **of**) **life** a substantially improved prospect of living, or of use after repair. □ **leas·able** adjective **leas·er** noun [Old French lais, leis from lesser, laissier leave, from Latin laxare make loose (laxus)]

lease·back noun the leasing of a property back to the vendor.

lease·hold ● noun **1** the holding of property by lease. **2** property held by lease. ● adjective held by lease. □ **lease·hold·er** noun

leash ● noun a strip of rope etc. for leading or controlling a dog. ● transitive verb **1** put a leash on. **2** restrain. □ **keep a person on a long** (or **short**) **leash** give a person considerable (or little) freedom of action. **straining at the leash** eager to begin. [Old French lesse, laisse from specific use of laisser let run on a slack lead: see LEASE]

least ● adjective **1** smallest, slightest, most insignificant. **2** (prec. by the; esp. with neg.) any at all (it does not make the least difference). **3** (of a species or variety) very small (least bittern). ● noun the least amount. ● adverb in the least degree. □ **at least 1** at all events; anyway; even if there is doubt about a more extended statement. **2** (also **at the least**) not less than. **in the least** (or **the least**) (usu. with neg.) in the smallest degree; at all (not in the least offended). **least said, soonest mended** a difficult situation will be resolved more quickly if there is no more discussion of it. **to say the least** (or **the least of it**) used to imply the moderation of a statement (that is doubtful to say the least). [Old English lǣst, lǣsest from Germanic]

least bittern noun a small bittern, Ixobrychus exilis, found from southern Canada to S America.

least common denominator noun = LOWEST COMMON DENOMINATOR.

least common multiple noun = LOWEST COMMON MULTIPLE.

least squares noun (in full **method** or **principle of least squares**) a method of estimating a quantity or fitting a graph to data so as to minimize the sum of the squares of the differences between the observed values and the estimated values.

least·ways adverb (also **least·wise**) informal at least, rather.

leath·er ● noun **1** material made from the skin of an animal by tanning or a similar process. **2** a thing made wholly or partly of leather. **3 a** (usu. in pl.) leather clothes, esp. for wearing on a motorcycle. **b** leather clothing, esp. as intended to express extreme masculinity, aggression, or sado-masochistic tendencies, or to arouse sexual desire. **4** a thong (stirrup leather). **5** dried puréed fruit cut into sheets (fruit leather). ● adjective **1** made of or resembling leather. **2** of or relating to leather clothing or persons wearing such clothing (leather bar). ● transitive verb **1** cover with leather. **2** polish or wipe with a leather. **3** beat, thrash (originally with a leather thong). [Old English lether from Germanic]

leather·back noun a large marine turtle, Dermochelys coriacea, having a thick leathery carapace.

leather-bound adjective (esp. of a book) bound in leather.

leather·ette noun imitation leather.

leather·leaf noun an ericaceous shrub, Chamaedaphne calyculata, found across Canada, with leathery leaves and small white flowers.

leather·man noun (pl. **-men**) a gay man who is involved in sado-masochistic practices.

leathern noun archaic made of leather.

leather·neck noun slang a US marine. [with reference to the leather-lined collar formerly worn by them]

leather·wear noun articles of clothing made of leather.

leather·wood noun a shrub or small tree, Dirca palustris, of eastern N America, with soft bark formerly used by Aboriginal peoples to make thongs. Also called MOOSEWOOD.

leath·ery adjective **1** like leather. **2** (esp. of meat etc.) tough. □ **leather·i·ness** noun

leave[1] verb (past and past participle **left**) **1 a** transitive go away from; cease to remain in or on (left him quite well an hour ago; leave the track; leave here). **b** intransitive (often foll. by for) depart (we leave tomorrow; has just left for St. John's). **2** transitive cause to or let remain; depart without taking (has left his gloves; left a slimy trail; left a bad impression). **3** transitive & intransitive cease to reside at or attend or belong to or work for (has left the school; I am leaving for another job). **4** transitive abandon, forsake, desert. **5** transitive have remaining after one's death (leaves a husband and

two children). **6** transitive bequeath. **7** transitive (foll. by to + infin.) allow (a person or thing) to do something without interference or assistance (leave the future to take care of itself). **8** transitive (foll. by to) commit or refer to another person (leave that to me; nothing was left to chance). **9** transitive **a** abstain from consuming or dealing with. **b** (in passive; often foll. by over) remain over. **10** transitive **a** deposit or entrust (a thing) to be attended to, collected, delivered, etc., in one's absence (left a message with her secretary). **b** depute (a person) to perform a function in one's absence. **11** transitive allow to remain or cause to be in a specified state or position (left the door open; the performance left them unmoved; left nothing that was necessary undone). **12** to have a particular amount remaining after subtraction (six from seven leaves one). □ **be left with 1** retain (a feeling etc.). **2** be burdened with (a responsibility etc.). **have left** have remaining (has no friends left). **leave alone 1** refrain from disturbing, not interfere with. **2** not have dealings with. **3** = LET ALONE (see LET[1]). **leave be** informal refrain from disturbing, not interfere with. **leave behind 1** go away without. **2** leave as a consequence or a visible sign of passage. **3** pass. **leave a person cold** (or **cool**) not impress or excite a person. **leave go** informal relax one's hold. **leave hold of** cease holding. **leave it at that** informal abstain from comment or further action. **leave much** (or **a lot** etc.) **to be desired** be highly unsatisfactory. **leave off 1** come to or make an end. **2** discontinue (leave off work; leave off talking). **3** omit from (was left off the list). **4** cease to wear. **leave out** omit, not include. **leave over** Brit. leave to be considered, settled, or used later. **leave a person to himself** or **herself 1** not attempt to control a person. **2** leave a person solitary. **left at the post** beaten from the start of a race. **leave for dead** abandon as being beyond rescue. □ **leav·er** noun [Old English lǣfan from Germanic]

leave[2] noun **1** (often foll. by to + infin.) permission. **2 a** (in full **leave of absence**) permission to be absent from duty, work, etc. **b** the period for which this lasts. □ **on leave** legitimately absent from duty, work, etc. **take one's leave** bid farewell. **take one's leave of** bid farewell to. **take leave of one's senses** see SENSE. [Old English lēaf from West Germanic: related to LIEF, LOVE]

leaved adjective (also **leafed**) **1** having leaves. **2** (in combination) having a leaf or leaves of a specified kind or number (broad-leaved weeds).

leave-in adjective designating or relating to a hair-care product (esp. a conditioner) which does not need to be washed out after application.

leaven /ˈlevən/ ● noun **1** archaic a substance added to dough to make it ferment and rise, esp. yeast, or fermenting dough reserved for the purpose. **2 a** a pervasive transforming influence. **b** (foll. by of) a tinge or admixture of a specified quality. ● transitive verb **1** cause (dough, batter) to rise. **2 a** permeate and transform. **b** (foll. by with) modify with a tempering element. □ **leaven·er** noun [Old French levain from Gallo-Roman spec. use of Latin levamen relief, from levare lift]

leaven·ing /ˈlevənɪŋ/ noun **1** a substance, e.g. yeast or baking powder, that causes dough or batter to rise. **2** the act or an instance of causing fermentation by using leaven. **3** = LEAVEN noun 2.

leaves pl. of LEAF.

leave-taking noun the act of taking one's leave.

leav·ings plural noun things left over, esp. as worthless.

Lea·vis, Frank Ray·mond (1895–1978), English literary critic. He taught English at Cambridge from the 1920s, founded and edited the quarterly Scrutiny (1932–53), and had considerable influence on 20th-c. literary criticism; his books include The Great Tradition (1948) and The Common Pursuit (1952). □ **Lea·vis·ite** adjective & noun

Leb·a·non a country in the Middle East with a coastline on the Mediterranean Sea; pop. (est. 2002) 3,677,780; capital, Beirut. □ **Leb·a·nese** adjective & noun

Lebanon Mountains a range of mountains in Lebanon. Running parallel to the Mediterranean coast, it rises to a height of 3 087 m (10,022 ft.) at Qornet es Saouda. It is separated from the Anti-Lebanon range, on the border with Syria, by the Bekaa valley.

Lebens·raum /ˈleibənzˌraum/ noun the territory which a nation etc. believes is needed for its natural development. [German, = living space (originally with reference to Germany, esp. in the 1930s)]

Le·Blanc /ləˈblɑ̃/ **Roméo A.** (b.1927), Canadian journalist and politician, Governor General 1995–99, the first Acadian to hold that post.

Le·blanc /ləˈblɑ̃/ **Nico·las** (c.1742–1806), French surgeon and chemist. He developed a process for making soda ash (sodium carbonate) from common salt, making possible the large-scale manufacture of glass, soap, paper, and other chemicals.

Le·brun /ləbrɑ̃/ **1 Al·bert** (1871–1950), French politician and president 1932–40. He acquiesced in the French armistice (1940) that led to the Vichy government of Marshal Pétain, and was interned in Austria (1943–4). **2 Charles** (also **Le Brun**) (1619–90), French painter, designer, and decorator. He was a founder (1648) and director (from 1663) of the Royal Academy of Painting and Sculpture, and his work for Louis XIV at Versailles (1661–83), which included painting, furniture, and tapestry design, established him as a leading exponent of 17th-c. French classicism.

Le Carré /lə ˈkareɪ/ **John** (pseudonym of David John Moore Cornwell) (b.1931), English novelist. His spy novels present an unromanticized view of espionage and frequently explore the moral dilemmas inherent in such work; they include *The Spy Who Came in from the Cold* (1963), *Tinker, Tailor, Soldier, Spy* (1974), and *A Perfect Spy* (1986).

lech /letʃ/ *informal* ● *intransitive verb* feel lecherous; behave lustfully. ● *noun* **1** a strong, esp. sexual, desire. **2** a lecher. [back-formation from LECHER: (n.) perhaps from *letch* longing]

lech·er /ˈletʃər/ *noun* a lecherous man. [Old French *lecheor* etc. from *lechier* live in debauchery or gluttony, from Frankish, related to LICK]

lech·er·ous /ˈletʃərəs/ *adjective* having or showing excessive or offensive sexual desire. □ **lech·er·ous·ly** *adverb* **lech·er·ous·ness** *noun*

lech·ery /ˈletʃəri/ *noun* unrestrained indulgence of sexual desire.

leci·thin /ˈlesɪθɪn/ *noun* **1** any of a group of phospholipids found naturally in animals, egg yolk, and some higher plants. **2** a preparation of this used to emulsify foods etc. [Greek *lekithos* egg yolk + -IN]

Le·clerc /ləˈkler/ **Félix** (1914–88), Canadian singer, songwriter, poet, novelist, playwright and actor. A radio announcer with the CBC from 1934 to 1942, reading and (after 1939) singing his own material, he founded the VLM Troupe in 1948 to produce his own plays. He was well known both in Canada and in Europe, especially in France; he was made a Member of the Order of Canada in 1985.

Le Cor·bu·sier /lə kɔrbuːziˈeɪ/ (born Charles Édouard Jeanneret) (1887–1965), Swiss-born French architect and town planner. A pioneer of the International Style, he developed his theories on functionalism, the use of new materials and industrial techniques in architecture, and the Modulor, a modular system of standard-sized units, in books such as *Towards a New Architecture* (1923) and *Le Modulor I* (1948); his works include the *unité d'habitation* ('living unit', 1945–50) in Marseilles, and the city of Chandigarh in India (1954).

lec·tern *noun* **1** a stand for holding a book in a church, esp. for a bible from which readings are made. **2** a similar stand for a lecturer etc. [Old French *let(t)run*, medieval Latin *lectrum* from *legere lect-* read]

lec·tin *noun Biochem.* any of a class of proteins, usu. of plant origin, causing the agglutination of particular cell types. [Latin *legere, lect-* 'choose, select' + -IN]

lec·tion *noun* a reading of a text found in a particular copy or edition. [Latin *lectio* reading (as LECTERN)]

lec·tion·ary *noun* (*pl.* **-aries**) **1** a list of portions of Scripture for reading at a religious service. **2** a book containing such portions of Scripture.

lec·tor *noun* **1** *Catholicism* a person designated to read aloud certain readings, prayers, psalms, etc. at Mass. **2** a lecturer or reader, esp. at a European university. [Latin from *legere lect-* read]

lec·ture ● *noun* **1** a discourse giving information about a subject to a class or other audience. **2** a long serious speech esp. as a scolding or reprimand. ● *verb* **1** *intransitive* (often foll. by *on*) deliver a lecture or lectures. **2** *transitive* talk seriously or reprovingly to (a person). **3** *transitive* instruct or entertain (a class or other audience) by a lecture. [Old French *lecture* or medieval Latin *lectura* from Latin (as LECTOR)]

lec·tur·er *noun* a person who lectures, esp. as a teacher in post-secondary education. **2** *N Amer.* a university professor ranking below assistant professor.

lec·ture·ship *noun* a position as a lecturer.

LED *abbreviation* light-emitting diode, a semiconductor diode which glows when a voltage is applied (often *attributive*: *LED display*).

led *past and past participle of* LEAD[1].

Leda /ˈliːdə/ *Gk Myth* the wife of Tyndareus king of Sparta. She was loved by Zeus, who visited her in the form of a swan; among her children were the Dioscuri, Helen, and Clytemnestra.

Led·better see LEADBELLY.

Leder·berg /ˈledərˌbɜrg/ **Joshua** (b.1925), US geneticist, who discovered genetic recombination in bacteria, for which he received the Nobel Prize for physiology or medicine in 1958.

leder·hosen /ˈleɪdərˌhoʊzən/ *plural noun* leather shorts with braces worn by men in Bavarian traditional dress. [German, = leather trousers]

ledge *noun* **1** a narrow horizontal surface projecting from a wall etc. **2** a shelf-like projection on the side of a rock or mountain. **3** a ridge of rocks, esp. below water. **4** *Mining* a stratum of metal-bearing rock. □ **ledged** *adjective* **ledgy** *adjective* [perhaps from Middle English *legge* LAY[1]]

ledg·er *noun* **1** a book or computer document in which a business, bank, etc. records its financial accounts. **2** a flat tombstone. [Middle English from senses of Dutch *ligger* and *legger* (from *liggen* LIE[1], *leggen* LAY[1]) & pronunciation of Middle English *ligge*, *legge*]

ledger line *noun Music* a short line added for notes above or below the range of a staff.

ledger-tackle *noun* a kind of fishing tackle in which a lead weight keeps the bait on the bottom.

Leduc[1] /ləˈduːk/ a city in central Alberta, about 30 km south of Edmonton, site of the first oil well in Western Canada, which launched the boom in oil production in Alberta; pop. (2001) 15,032. □ **Ledu·cian** /leˈduːʃiən/ *noun* **Leduc·ite** /leˈduːsaɪt/ *noun* [Fr. H. *Leduc*, Oblate missionary d.1918]

Leduc[2] /ləˈduːk/ **Ozias** (1864–1955), Canadian painter. He is known both for his landscapes (esp. of the Saint-Hilaire region, where he was born and lived) and still lifes, and for the many churches he decorated throughout Quebec, Nova Scotia and the eastern US. Remaining largely outside of contemporary Canadian art movements, he became quite popular towards the end of his life.

Lee ▶ **1 Ang** (b.1954), Taiwanese-born film director. His movies include *Eat Drink Man Woman* (1994), *Sense and Sensibility* (1995), and *The Ice Storm* (1997). **2 Bruce** (born Lee Yuen Kam) (1941–73), US actor, an expert in kung fu who starred in martial arts films featuring elaborately staged fight scenes; these include *Fists of Fury* (1972) and *Enter the Dragon* (1973). **3 Den·nis Bey·non** (b.1939), Canadian teacher, editor, writer and poet. He has written a variety of books ranging from *Savage Fields: An Essay in Literature and Cosmology* (1977) to the popular children's book *Alligator Pie* (1974). **4 James Mat·thew** (b.1937), Canadian businessman and politician, Progressive Conservative premier of PEI 1982–86. **5 (Nelle) Har·per** (b.1926), US novelist. She won a Pulitzer Prize with her only novel, *To Kill a Mockingbird* (1960), about the sensational trial of a black man falsely charged with raping a white woman, as seen through the eyes of the daughter of the white defence lawyer. **6 Rich·ard Henry** (1732–94), US revolutionary leader, who introduced the motion that led to the Declaration of Independence (1776). **7 Rob·ert Ed·ward** (1807–70), US general. He was the commander of the Confederate army of N Virginia, leading it for most of the American Civil War; his invasion of the North was repulsed by General Meade at the Battle of Gettysburg (1863) and he eventually surrendered to General Grant in 1865. **8 Spike (Shel·ton Jack·son)** (b.1957), US film director, screenwriter, and actor. His films address the racial, economic, and social experiences of urban black Americans, and include *She's Gotta Have It* (1986), *Jungle Fever* (1991), and the biographical *Malcolm X* (1992). **9 Tsung-Dao** (b.1926), Chinese-born US physicist. He was awarded the 1957 Nobel Prize for physics with Yang for their discovery that the conservation of parity principle does not apply to the weak interaction.

lee *noun* **1** shelter given by a neighbouring object (*under the lee of*). **2** (in full **lee side**) the sheltered side, the side away from the wind (*opp.* WEATHER SIDE). [Old English *hlēo* from Germanic]

lee·board *noun* a plank frame fixed to the side of a flat-bottomed vessel and let down into the water to diminish leeway.

leech[1] ● **1** *noun* any freshwater or terrestrial annelid worm of the class Hirudinea with suckers at both ends, esp. *Hirudo medicinalis*, a bloodsucking parasite of vertebrates formerly much used medically. **2** a person who extorts profit from or sponges on others. ● *intransitive verb* habitually exploit or rely on (*he's leeching off the abilities of others*). □ **like a leech** persistently or clingingly present. [Old English *lǣce*, assimilated to LEECH[2]]

leech[2] *noun archaic* or *jocular* a physician; a healer. [Old English *lǣce* from Germanic]

leech[3] *noun* **1** a perpendicular or sloping side of a square sail. **2** the side of a fore-and-aft sail away from the mast or stay. [Middle English, perhaps related to Old Norse *lik*, a nautical term of uncertain meaning]

leech·craft *noun archaic* the art of healing. [Old English *lǣcecræft* (as LEECH[2], CRAFT)]

Leeds an industrial city in West Yorkshire; pop. (est. 1998) 727,400. It became a centre of the clothing trade in the Industrial Revolution.

leek *noun* an alliaceous plant, *Allium porrum*, with flat overlapping leaves forming an elongated cylindrical bulb, used as food and as a Welsh national emblem. [Old English *lēac* from Germanic]

Lee Kuan Yew /liː ˈkwɒn ˈjuː/ (b.1923), first prime minister of the Republic of Singapore 1965–90. He was criticized for repressing political opposition and praised for Singapore's economic progress.

leer ● *intransitive verb* look slyly or lasciviously or maliciously. ● *noun* a leering look. □ **leer·ing·ly** *adverb* [perhaps from obsolete *leer* cheek, from Old English *hlēor*, as though 'to glance over one's cheek']

leery *adjective* (**leer·i·er, leer·i·est**) *slang* 1 (usu. foll. by *of*) wary. 2 *archaic* knowing, sly. □ **leer·i·ness** *noun* [perhaps from obsolete *leer* looking askance, from LEER + -Y¹]

lees *plural noun* 1 the sediment of wine etc. (*drink to the lees*). 2 dregs, refuse. [pl. of Middle English *lie* from Old French *lie* from medieval Latin *lia* from Gaulish]

lee shore *noun* the shore to leeward of a ship.

Leeu·wen·hoek /ˈleivən,huːk/ **Anton van** (1632–1723), Dutch naturalist and microscopist. He developed a lens and was the first to observe bacteria, protozoa, and yeast, and accurately described red blood corpuscles, capillaries, striated muscle fibres, spermatozoa, and the crystalline lens of the eye.

lee·ward /ˈliːwərd, *Naut.* ˈluːərd/ ● *adjective & adverb* on or towards the side sheltered from the wind (*opp.* WINDWARD). ● *noun* the leeward region, side, or direction (*to leeward*; *on the leeward of*).

Leeward Islands /ˈliːwərd/ a group of islands in the W Indies, constituting the northern part of the Lesser Antilles. The group includes Guadeloupe, Antigua, St. Kitts, and Montserrat. [so called with reference to their position further downwind, in terms of the prevailing southeasterly winds, than the Windward Islands]

lee·way *noun* 1 a allowable deviation or freedom of action (*give her some leeway*). b additional or extra time, materials, etc. (*have plenty of leeway*). 2 the sideways drift of a ship to leeward of the desired course.

Le·febvre /ləˈfevrə/ **Jean-Pierre** (b.1941), Canadian filmmaker. After producing three films independently and spending a brief period with the NFB (1967), Lefebvre formed his own company, Cinak. Since that time he has produced such films as *Les Maudits sauvages* (1971); the majority of these low-budget films advance his humanitarian view of the world.

left¹ ● *adjective* 1 a on or towards the side of the human body which corresponds to the position of west if one regards oneself as facing north. b on or towards the part of an object which is analogous to a person's left side or (with opposite sense) which is nearer to an observer's left hand (*opp.* RIGHT 5). 2 (also **Left**) *Politics* of the Left. ● *adverb* on or to the left side. ● *noun* 1 the left side or area (*on my left*). 2 a the road etc. on the left (*take the next left*). b a left turn. 3 *Boxing* a the left hand. b a blow with this. 4 (often **Left**) *Politics* a group or section favouring socialism; socialists collectively. 5 = STAGE LEFT. □ **have two left feet** *informal* be clumsy. **left and right** (also **left, right, and centre**) = RIGHT AND LEFT (see RIGHT). □ **left·ish** *adjective* [Middle English *lüft, lift, left,* from Old English, original sense 'weak, worthless'; political sense originally with reference to the more radical section of a European legislature, seated on the president's left]

left² *past and past participle of* LEAVE¹.

left bank *noun* the bank of a river on the left facing downstream.

left bower *noun Cards see* BOWER³.

left brain *noun* the left cerebral hemisphere, which controls the right side of the body; in humans, it normally controls language skills and numerical calculations.

left-centre *noun* (in full **left-centre field**) *Baseball* the part of the outfield between centre field and left field (*a fly to deep left-centre*).

left field *noun* 1 *Baseball* a the part of the outfield to the left of the batter as he or she faces the pitcher. b the position of the fielder who covers this area (*playing left field for this game*). 2 *N Amer. informal* a position, state, experience, etc., that is removed from the mainstream or ordinary (*the proposal came from left field*). □ **out in left field** *N Amer. slang* completely wrong or mistaken. □ **left fielder** *noun*

left-footed *adjective* 1 using the left foot by preference as more serviceable than the right. 2 (of a kick etc.) done or made with the left foot.

left-hand *adjective* 1 on or towards the left side of a person or thing (*left-hand drawer*). 2 to the left (*a left-hand turn*). 3 done with the left hand (*left-hand blow*). 4 a (of rope) twisted counter-clockwise. b (of a screw) = LEFT-HANDED 4b.

left-handed ● *adjective* 1 a using the left hand by preference as more serviceable than the right. b using a tool etc. by preference on one's left side (*left-handed batter*). 2 (of a tool etc.) designed for use by left-handed people. 3 (of a blow) struck with the left hand. 4 a turning to the left; towards the left. b (of a screw) advanced by turning to the left (counter-clockwise). 5 awkward, clumsy. 6 a (of a compliment) ambiguous. b of doubtful sincerity or validity. ● *adverb* with the left hand or to the left side (*shoots left-handed*; *she writes left-handed*). □ **left-hand·ed·ly** *adverb* **left-hand·ed·ness** *noun*

left-hander *noun* 1 a left-handed person. 2 a left-handed blow.

left·ie *var. of* LEFTY.

left·ism *noun Politics* the principles or policy of the left. □ **left·ist** *noun & adjective*

left-leaning *adjective* (of a person, group, etc.) favouring or tending towards the political left.

left·most *adjective* furthest to the left.

left-of-centre *adjective* (of political parties, voters, etc.) having somewhat leftist views, policies, etc.

left·over ● *noun* (usu. in *pl.*) an item (esp. of food) remaining after the rest has been used. ● *adjective* remaining over, surplus.

left·ward ● *adverb* (also **left·wards**) towards the left. ● *adjective* going towards or facing the left.

left wing ● *noun* 1 the radical or socialist section of a political party. 2 *Hockey* a the forward position to the left of centre (facing the opponent's goal). b the player at this position. 3 the left side of an army. ● *adjective* (usu. **left-wing**) socialist or radical. □ **left-winger** *noun*

lefty ● *noun* (also **leftie**) (pl. **-ies**) *informal* 1 a left-handed person. 2 *Politics* a left-winger. ● *adjective* (of a person) 1 left-handed. 2 leftist. ● *adverb* esp. *Baseball* with the left hand or to the left side (*batting lefty*).

leg. /ledʒ/ *noun Cdn informal* a legislature.

leg *noun* 1 a each of the limbs on which a person or animal walks and stands. b the part of this from the hip to the ankle. 2 a leg of an animal or bird as food. 3 a part of a garment covering a leg or part of a leg. 4 a support of a chair, table, bed, etc. 5 a a section of a journey. b a section of a relay race. c a stage in a competition. d one of two or more games constituting a round. 6 one branch of a forked object (*the leg of a compass*). 7 one of the sides of a triangle other than the base or hypotenuse. 8 *Naut.* a run made on a single tack. 9 *N Amer.* a device for lifting grain in a grain elevator, consisting of a series of buckets attached to a vertical conveyor belt. □ **as fast as one's legs can** (or **would**) **carry one** as fast as one is able to. **find one's legs** 1 gain momentum. 2 acquire or regain mastery of a skill. **give a person a leg up** help a person to mount a horse etc. or get over an obstacle or difficulty. **have legs** *informal* (of a book, movie, etc.) have the potential to be highly successful and run a long time. **have no legs** *informal* (of a golf ball etc.) have not enough momentum to reach the desired point. **leg it** *informal* walk or run hard. **not have a leg to stand on** be unable to support one's argument by facts or sound reasons. **on one's last legs** near death or the end of one's usefulness etc. [Old Norse *leggr* from Germanic]

leg·acy /ˈlegəsi/ ● *noun* (pl. **-acies**) 1 a gift left in a will. 2 something handed down by a predecessor (*legacy of corruption*). ● *adjective* denoting software or hardware that has been superseded but is difficult to replace because of its wide use. [Old French *legacie* legateship, from medieval Latin *legatia* from Latin *legare* bequeath]

legal *adjective* 1 of or based on law; concerned with law; falling within the province of law. 2 appointed or required by law. 3 permitted by law, lawful. 4 *Sport* permitted by the rules (*a legal tackle*). 5 *N Amer.* a designating a size of paper 22 by 35.5 cm (8¹⁄₂ by 14 inches). b designating office supplies, e.g. file folders etc., designed to be used with this size of paper. 6 recognized by law, as distinct from equity. □ **legal·ly** *adverb* [French *légal* or Latin *legalis* from *lex legis* law: compare LOYAL]

legal aid *noun* payment from public funds allowed, in cases of need, to help pay for legal advice or proceedings.

legal clinic *noun N Amer.* a clinic offering legal advice and assistance, paid for by legal aid.

legal eagle *noun* (also **legal beagle**) *informal* a lawyer, esp. one who is keen or astute.

legal·ese *noun informal* the technical language of legal documents.

legal fiction *noun* an assertion accepted as true (though probably fictitious) to achieve a useful purpose, esp. in legal matters.

legal holiday *noun N Amer.* = STATUTORY HOLIDAY.

legal·ism *noun* excessive adherence to law or formula. □ **legal·ist** *noun* **legal·is·tic** *adjective* **legal·is·tic·ally** *adverb*

legal·ity *noun* (pl. **-ities**) 1 lawfulness. 2 legalism. 3 (in *pl.*) obligations imposed by law.

Consonants: b *but* d *dog* f *few* g *get* h *her* j *yes* k *cat* l *leg* m *man* n *no* p *pen* r *red* s *sit*

legal·ize *transitive verb* (also esp. *Brit.* **-ise**) **1** make lawful. **2** bring into harmony with the law. □ **legal·iz·a·tion** *noun*

legal proceedings *plural noun see* PROCEEDING 2.

legal separation *noun see* SEPARATION 3.

legal tender *noun* currency that cannot legally be refused in payment of a debt.

Lega·nés /ˌleganˈes/ a city in central Spain, part of the conurbation of Madrid; pop. (est. 1998) 173,163.

Le Gar·deur /ləgɑrˈdər/ a former town in south central Quebec, northeast of Montreal, now part of Repentigny; pop. (2001) 17,688. [either P. *Legardeur* de Repentigny, who was granted the seigneuries of L'Assomption and La Chesnaye in 1647, or his son, J.-B. *Legardeur* de Repentigny]

Lé·ga·ré /leigaˈrei/ **Jo·seph** (1795–1855), Canadian painter and art collector. The first Canadian-born painter to concentrate on landscapes, he opened Canada's first art gallery (1833–35). In total he painted some 250 oils.

leg·ate /ˈlegət/ *noun* **1** a member of the clergy representing the Pope. **2** *Rom. Hist.* **a** a deputy of a general. **b** a governor or deputy governor of a province. **3** *archaic* an ambassador or delegate. □ **legate·ship** *noun* [Old English from Old French *legat* from Latin *legatus* past participle of *legare* depute, delegate]

lega·tee /ˌlegəˈtiː/ *noun* the recipient of a legacy. [as LEGATOR + -EE]

lega·tion /lɪˈgeiʃən/ *noun* **1** a body of deputies. **2 a** the office and staff of a diplomatic minister (esp. when not having ambassadorial rank). **b** the official residence of a diplomatic minister. **3** the sending of a legate or deputy.

le·gato /ləˈgɑːtoː/ *Music* ● *adverb & adjective* in a smooth flowing manner, without breaks between notes (*compare* STACCATO, TENUTO). ● *noun* (*pl.* **-gatos**) **1** a legato passage. **2** legato playing. [Italian, = bound, past participle of *legare* from Latin *ligare* bind]

leg·ator /lɪˈgeitər/ *noun* the giver of a legacy. [archaic *legate* bequeath, from Latin *legare* (as LEGACY)]

leg curl *noun* an exercise for strengthening the leg muscles in which the heels, with or without added weights, are drawn up to the buttocks.

legend /ˈledʒənd/ *noun* **1 a** a traditional story sometimes popularly regarded as historical but unauthenticated; a myth. **b** such stories collectively. **c** a popular but unfounded belief. **d** *informal* a subject of such beliefs (*became a legend in her own lifetime*). **2 a** an inscription, esp. on a coin or medal. **b** *Printing* a caption. **c** a key to the symbols used on a map etc. **3** *hist.* **a** the story of a saint's life. **b** a collection of lives of saints or similar stories. [Old French *legende* from medieval Latin *legenda* what is to be read, neuter pl. gerundive of Latin *legere* read]

legend·ary /ˈledʒəndˌeri/ *adjective* **1** of or connected with legends. **2** described in a legend. **3** remarkable enough to be a subject of legend. **4** based on a legend. □ **legend·ar·i·ly** *adverb*

Le·gendre /ləˈʒɑ̃drə/ **Ad·rien Marie** (1752–1833), French mathematician, who classified elliptic integrals into their standard forms, and did significant work on number theory.

Léger /leiˈʒei/ **1 Fer·nand** (1881–1955), French cubist painter, who was influenced by industrial technology; his static and precise paintings often include representations of mechanical parts. **2 Jules** (1913–80), Canadian diplomat and Governor General. He was Canada's ambassador to Mexico (1953), Italy (1962), France (1964), and Belgium and Luxembourg (1973), winning particular admiration for his handling of de Gaulle's attitudes towards Quebec separatism. He served as Governor General 1974–79, overcoming the difficulties caused by a stoke suffered early in his term. **3** his brother **Paul-Émile** (1904–91), Canadian priest and cardinal. Ordained in 1929, he served in France, Japan and Rome before being named archbishop of Montreal in 1950. He was made a cardinal in 1953, and worked on a preparatory commission leading to the Second Vatican Council (1962–65). In 1967 he resigned as archbishop to work as a missionary among lepers and handicapped children in Cameroon.

leger·de·main /ˌledʒərdəˈmein/ *noun* **1** sleight of hand; conjuring or juggling. **2** trickery, sophistry. [French *léger de main* light of hand, dexterous]

Legge /leg/ **Fran·cis** (*c.*1719–83), British soldier, governor of Nova Scotia 1773–76. He alienated the local oligarchy by attempting to improve the colony's economic situation and administration and by trying to audit the provincial accounts and recover missing funds in the courts. With his own Council and Assembly strongly opposed to him, he was recalled just as the American Revolution broke out.

legged *adjective* having legs, esp. of a specified kind or number (*long-legged*).

leg·ging *noun* (usu. in *pl.*) **1** close-fitting stretch trousers for women or children. **2** an outer garment for keeping the legs warm.

leg·gy ● *adjective* (**leg·gi·er**, **leg·gi·est**) **1 a** long-legged. **b** (of a woman) having attractively long legs. **2** long-stemmed. ● *noun* *Cdn* (*Nfld*) (*pl.* **-gies**) a small cod that has been cleaned, salted, and dried but not split, usu. intended for home consumption. □ **leg·gi·ness** *noun*

leg·hold trap *noun* (also **leg·hold**) a type of trap with a mechanism which catches and holds an animal by one of its legs.

Leg·horn *see* LIVORNO.

leg·horn *noun* **1** (**Leghorn**) **a** a bird of a small hardy breed of domestic fowl. **b** this breed. **2 a** fine braided straw. **b** a hat of this. [LEGHORN]

legi·ble /ˈledʒɪbəl/ *adjective* (of handwriting, print, etc.) clear enough to read; readable. □ **legi·bil·ity** *noun* **legi·bly** *adverb* [Late Latin *legibilis* from *legere* read]

le·gion /ˈliːdʒən/ ● *noun* **1** a vast host, multitude, or number. **2** (**Legion**) any of various national associations of ex-servicemen and ex-servicewomen (*Royal Canadian Legion*). **3** *N Amer.* = LEGION HALL. **4** *Rom. Hist.* a division of 3,000–6,000 soldiers, including a complement of cavalry. **5** a large military force. ● *predicative adjective* great in number (*her good works have been legion*). [Old French from Latin *legio -onis* from *legere* choose]

le·gion·ary /ˈliːdʒəneri/ ● *adjective* of a legion or legions. ● *noun* (*pl.* **-aries**) a soldier of a legion.

le·gion·ella /ˌliːdʒəˈnelə/ *noun* the bacterium *Legionella pneumophila*, which causes legionnaires' disease.

legion hall *noun* *N Amer.* a building serving as the headquarters for a local Legion branch, usu. incorporating facilities for entertainment, e.g. an auditorium, banquet hall, bar, etc.

le·gion·naire /ˌliːdʒəˈner/ *noun* **1** a member of a foreign legion. **2** a member of a Legion. [French *légionnaire* (as LEGION)]

legionnaires' disease *noun* a form of bacterial pneumonia first identified after an outbreak at an American Legion meeting in 1976 and spread esp. by water droplets through air conditioning systems etc. (*compare* LEGIONELLA).

Legion of Honour *noun* a French order of distinction founded in 1802. [French *Légion d'honneur*]

leg iron *noun* a shackle or fetter for the leg.

legis·late /ˈledʒɪsˌleit/ *verb* **1** *intransitive* make laws. **2** *transitive* create or control by means of legislation (*the government is legislating pay equity*). [back-formation from LEGISLATION]

legis·la·tion /ˌledʒɪsˈleiʃən/ *noun* **1** the process of making laws. **2** a law or series of laws. [Late Latin *legis latio* from *lex legis* law + *latio* proposing, from *lat-* past participle stem of *ferre* bring]

legis·la·tive /ˈledʒɪsˌleitɪv/ *adjective* **1** of or empowered to make legislation. **2** of or pertaining to a legislature (*the legislative library*). □ **legis·la·tive·ly** *adverb*

legislative assembly *noun* **1** the legislative body of a nation, province, etc. **2** (in Canada) an elected provincial or (*hist.*) colonial legislature.

legislative building *noun* *Cdn* the building in which a provincial legislature meets.

legislative council *noun* *Cdn hist.* **1** the upper house of a provincial legislature, consisting of members appointed by the government. **2** (in colonial governments) a body of advisers appointed by the governor, serving either as a unicameral legislature or as the upper house of a bicameral legislature.

legis·la·tor /ˈledʒɪsˌleitər/ *noun* **1** a member of a legislative body. **2** a lawgiver.

legis·la·ture /ˈledʒɪsˌleitʃər/ *noun* **1** the legislative body of a nation, province, etc. **2** *Cdn* = LEGISLATIVE BUILDING.

legit /lɪˈdʒɪt/ *adjective informal* legitimate. [abbreviation]

legit·im·ate ● *adjective* /lɪˈdʒɪtɪmət/ **1 a** (of a child) born of parents lawfully married to each other, entitled in law to full filial rights. **b** (of a parent, birth, descent, etc.) with, of, through, etc., a legitimate child. **2 a** conformable to, sanctioned or authorized by, law or principle; lawful. **b** conforming to a recognized standard. **3** sanctioned by the laws of reasoning; logically admissible or inferable. **4** (of a monarch, sovereignty, etc.) justified or validated by the strict principle of hereditary right. **5** designating or pertaining to art considered to have aesthetic merit or serious intent, esp.: **a** conventional theatre or drama as distinct from musical comedy, farce, etc. **b** classical music as

distinct from jazz or other popular music. ● *transitive verb* /lɪˈdʒɪtɪˌmeɪt/ **1** make legitimate by decree, enactment, or proof. **2** authorize or justify by word or example; serve as a justification for.
□ **legit·im·acy** /-məsi/ *noun* **legit·im·ate·ly** /-mətli/ *adverb*
legit·im·at·ing *adjective* **legit·im·a·tion** *noun* [medieval Latin *legitimare* from Latin *legitimus* lawful, from *lex legis* law]

legit·im·ism /lɪˈdʒɪtɪˌmɪzəm/ *noun* adherence to a sovereign or pretender whose claim is based on direct descent (esp. in French and Spanish history). □ **legit·im·ist** *noun & adjective*

legit·im·ize /lɪˈdʒɪtɪˌmaɪz/ *transitive verb* (also esp. *Brit.* **-ise**) **1** make legitimate. **2** serve as a justification for. □ **legit·im·iz·a·tion** /-ˈzeɪʃən/ *noun* **legit·im·iz·ing** *noun & adjective*

leg·less *adjective* **1** having no legs. **2** *Brit. slang* drunk, esp. too drunk to stand.

leg·man *noun* (*pl.* **-men**) a person employed to go about gathering news or running errands etc.

Lego /ˈleɡoʊ/ *noun* proprietary a construction toy consisting of interlocking plastic building blocks. [Danish *legetøj* toys, from *lege* to play]

leg-of-mutton *adjective* **1** designating a style of sleeve which is full and loose on the upper arm but close-fitting on the forearm. **2** designating a triangular mainsail.

leg-over *noun Brit. slang* an act of sexual intercourse.

leg rest *noun* a support for a seated person's leg or legs.

leg·room *noun* the space available for the legs of a seated person in a car, theatre, etc.

leg trap *noun* = LEGHOLD TRAP.

leg·ume /ˈleɡjuːm/ *noun* **1** any seed, pod, or other edible part of a leguminous plant used as food. **2** a leguminous plant. **3** the seed pod of a leguminous plant. [French *légume* from Latin *legumen -minis* from *legere* pick, because they can be picked by hand]

le·gum·in·ous /lɪˈɡjuːmɪnəs/ *adjective* of or like the family Leguminosae, including peas and beans, having seeds in pods and usu. root nodules able to fix nitrogen.

leg-up *noun* **1** an act of helping someone or something to improve their situation (*he gave hip hop a much-needed leg-up*). **2** *N Amer.* an advantage (*he'd certainly have a leg-up on the competition*).

leg warmer *noun* either of a pair of tubular, usu. knitted garments covering the leg from ankle to thigh, but often worn gathered below the knee to the ankle.

leg·work *noun* work which involves a lot of walking, travelling, or physical activity to collect information, deliver messages, etc.

Leh /leɪ/ a town in Jammu and Kashmir, N India, to the east of Srinagar near the Indus River; pop. (2001) 27,500. It is the chief town of the Himalayan region of Ladakh, and the administrative centre of Ladakh district in Jammu and Kashmir.

Lehár /ˈleɪhɑːr/ **Franz (Fer·encz)** (1870–1948), Hungarian composer. He is chiefly known for his operettas, of which the most famous is *The Merry Widow* (1905).

Le Havre /lə ˈɒvrə/ a port in N France, on the English Channel at the mouth of the Seine; pop. (1999) 190,905.

lehr /lɪːr/ *noun* a slow-cooling, tunnel-like furnace used for the annealing of glass. [17th c.: origin unknown]

lei¹ /ˈleɪiː, leɪ/ *noun* a garland of flowers, feathers, shells, etc. often given as a symbol of affection. [Hawaiian]

lei² *pl.* of LEU.

Leib·niz /ˈlaɪbnɪts/ **Gott·fried Wil·helm** (also **Leib·nitz**) (1646–1716), German rationalist philosopher and mathematician. An exponent of optimism, he believed that the world is fundamentally harmonious and good, being composed of single units (monads), each of which is self-contained, but acts in harmony with every other to form an ascending hierarchy culminating in God; he also devised a method of calculus independently of Newton. □ **Leib·niz·ian** /laɪbˈnɪtsiən/ *noun & adjective*

Leibo·vitz /ˈliːbəˌvɪts/ **Annie** (b.1950), US photographer. She was chief photographer of *Rolling Stone* magazine (1973–83) before moving to *Vanity Fair*. She has produced many celebrity portraits and had numerous exhibitions, including those at the Smithsonian National Portrait Gallery, Washington, DC (1991).

Leices·ter¹ /ˈlestər/ a city in central England, east of Birmingham; pop. (est. 2002) 319,100.

Leices·ter² /ˈlestər/ see DUDLEY.

Leices·ter³ /ˈlestər/ *noun* a kind of mild firm cheese, usu. orange-coloured and originally made in Leicestershire.

Leices·ter·shire /ˈlestərˌʃɪr/ a county of central England.

Lei·den /ˈlaɪdən/ (also **Leyden**) a city in the W Netherlands, 15 km (9 miles) northeast of The Hague; pop. (1991) 119,500. It is the site of the country's oldest university, founded in 1575.

Leif Erics·son see ERICSSON 2.

Leigh /liː/ **Vivien** (born Vivien Mary Hartley) (1913–67), English stage and film actress, who won Oscars for her portrayal of Scarlett O'Hara in *Gone with the Wind* (1939) and Blanche du Bois in *A Streetcar Named Desire* (1951).

Lein·ster /ˈlenstər/ a province of the Republic of Ireland, in the southeast of the country, centred on Dublin.

Leip·zig /ˈlaɪpsɪɡ/ an industrial city in east central Germany; pop. (est. 2002) 409,800. It is a centre of publishing and music. An annual trade fair has been held there since the 12th c.

leish·man·ia·sis /ˌliːʃməˈnaɪəsɪs/ *noun* any of several diseases caused by parasitic protozoans of the genus *Leishmania* transmitted by the bite of sandflies. [W. B. *Leishman*, British physician d.1926]

leis·ter /ˈliːstər/ ● *noun* a pronged spear for catching salmon. ● *transitive verb* pierce with a leister. [Old Norse *ljóstr* from *ljósta* to strike]

lei·sure /ˈliːʒər, ˈle-/ *noun* **1** free time; time at one's own disposal. **2** enjoyment of free time. **3** (usu. foll. by *for*, or *to* + infin.) opportunity afforded by free time. □ **at leisure 1** not occupied. **2** in an unhurried manner. **at one's leisure** when one has time. [Anglo-French *leisour*, Old French *leisir*, ultimately from Latin *licēre* be allowed]

leisure centre *noun* (also **leisure complex**) *Cdn & Brit.* a large public building with sports facilities, bars, etc.

leisure class *noun* a usu. moneyed social class, with little need to work, or to work long hours, and so having ample time for leisure activities etc.

lei·sured *adjective* **1** having ample leisure (*the leisured classes*). **2** leisurely.

lei·sure·ly ● *adjective* **1** relaxed, having leisure, able to proceed without haste. **2** (of an action or agent) performed or operating at leisure or without haste; unhurried. ● *adverb* without haste or hurry. □ **lei·sure·li·ness** *noun*

leisure suit *noun* a man's casual outfit having matching trousers and top usu. of a knitted polyester fabric, with the jacket functioning as both shirt and jacket.

leisure wear *noun* informal clothes, esp. track suits and other sportswear.

leit·mo·tif /ˈlaɪtmoʊˌtiːf/ *noun* (also **leit·mo·tiv**) **1** a recurrent theme associated throughout a musical, literary, etc. composition with a particular person, idea, or situation. **2** any recurring theme, symbol, image, etc. [German *Leitmotiv* (as LEAD¹, MOTIVE)]

Lei·trim /ˈliːtrɪm/ a county of the Republic of Ireland, in the province of Connacht; county town, Carrick-on-Shannon.

Leix see LAOIS.

Le Jeune /lə ˈʒʌn/ **Paul** (1591–1664), French Jesuit missionary and author. After converting to Catholicism at age 16, he was superior of the Jesuits at Quebec from 1632 to 1639. From 1639 to 1649 he served as a missionary priest throughout New France.

lek¹ *noun* the chief monetary unit of Albania. [Albanian]

lek² *noun* **1** a patch of ground used by groups of certain birds during the breeding season as a setting for the males' display and their meeting with the females. **2** such a gathering or display. [perhaps from Swedish *leka* to play]

Lek·wil·tok /ˈlekwɪltɒk/ *noun* **1** a member of large group of the Kwakwaka'wakw living between Knight and Bute Inlets, on the west coast of BC. **2** the Kwakwala language of the Lekwiltok, of the Wakashan linguistic group.

Le Lou·tre /lə ˈluːtrə/ **Jean-Louis** (1709–72), French priest and missionary. He travelled to Louisbourg in 1737, and was appointed to serve the parish of Annapolis Royal, which was in British territory. He spent the next 18 years working in various capacities to help the Acadian settlers and the French army in their fight against the British. Imprisoned by the British 1755–63, he worked after his release to help deported Acadians who wished to settle in France.

Lely /ˈliːli/ **Sir Peter** (Dutch name Pieter van der Faes) (1618–80), Dutch portrait painter, resident in England from 1641. As principal court painter to Charles II he consolidated the tradition of society portrait painting.

LEM *abbreviation* lunar excursion module (*compare* LUNAR MODULE).

Vowels: a *cat* ɑ *arm* e *bed* ɜr *her* ɜː *deux* ə *ago* ɪ *sit* i *cosy* iː *feed* ɒ *hot* ɔ *pore* ɔː *no* ʌ *run* ʊ *put*

Le·maî·tre /ləˈmetrə/ **Georges (Édouard)** (1894–1966), Belgian astronomer and cosmologist, who proposed the big bang theory of the universe in 1927.

lem·an /ˈlemən/ *noun* (*pl.* **lem·ans**) *archaic* **1** a lover or sweetheart. **2** an illicit lover, esp. a mistress. [Middle English *leofman* (as LIEF, MAN)]

Le Mans /lə ˈmɑ̃/ an industrial town in NW France; pop. (1999) 146,105. It is the site of a motor-racing circuit, on which a 24-hour endurance race is held each summer.

LeMay Doan /ləˈmeidɔːn/ **Catriona** (b.1970), Canadian speed skater, winner of Olympic gold medals in 1998 and 2002.

Le·mieux /ləˈmjɜ, ləˈmjuː/ **Mario** (b.1965), Canadian hockey player. One of the greatest scorers of all time, he has won the NHL scoring title six times despite having had his career interrupted by Hodgkin's disease and serious back trouble. He led the Pittsburgh Penguins to back-to-back Stanley Cups (1991, 1992), and returned from retirement in 2000 as both player and franchise owner. He also played a key role in the Canadian national team's victories in the 1987 Canada Cup and the 2002 Olympics.

lem·ma *noun* **1** an assumed or demonstrated proposition used in an argument or proof. **2 a** a word or phrase defined in a dictionary, glossed in a glossary, entered in a word list, etc. **b** the form of a word or phrase chosen to represent all inflectional and spelling variants in a dictionary entry etc. **3 a** (*pl.* **lemmata** /ˈlemətə/) a heading indicating the subject or argument of a literary composition, annotation, etc. **b** a motto appended to a picture etc. [Latin from Greek *lēmma -matos* thing assumed, from the root of *lambanō* take]

lemme *informal* let me. [corruption]

lem·ming *noun* **1** any of several short-tailed esp. Arctic rodents of the genus *Lemmus* and related genera of the family Muridae, noted for their fluctuating populations and periodic mass migrations. **2** a person who unthinkingly joins a mass movement, esp. a headlong rush to destruction. □ **lemming-like** *adjective* [Norwegian]

Lem·mon, Jack (born John Uhler Lemmon III) (1925–2001), US actor. He made his name in comedy films such as *Some Like It Hot* (1959), and later played serious dramatic parts in such films as *Save the Tiger* (1973), for which he won an Oscar, *The China Syndrome* (1979), and *Missing* (1981).

Lem·nos /ˈlemnɒs/ a Greek island in the N Aegean Sea; chief town, Kástron.

lem·on ● *noun* **1 a** a pale-yellow thick-skinned oval citrus fruit with acidic juice. **b** a tree of the species *Citrus limon* which produces this fruit. **2** = LEMON YELLOW. **3** *informal* **a** a thing which is bad, unsatisfactory, or disappointing, esp. a substandard or defective car. **b** a loser, simpleton, or person who is easily deluded or taken advantage of. ● *adjective* of or resembling the colour, flavour, or fragrance of a lemon; pale yellow. □ **lem·ony** *adjective* [Old French *limon* from Arabic *līma*: compare LIME²]

lem·on·ade *noun* **1** a drink made of lemon juice and water, usu. sweetened with sugar. **2** *Brit.* a colourless, carbonated, lemon-flavoured drink.

lemon balm *noun* a bushy plant, *Melissa officinalis*, with leaves smelling and tasting of lemon.

lemon butter *noun* **1** (also **lemon curd**) a thick filling made from lemons, butter, eggs, and sugar. **2** a mixture of butter, lemon juice, and seasonings, used as a garnish for fish, vegetables, etc.

lemon drop *noun* a hard candy flavoured with lemon.

lemon geranium *noun* a lemon-scented pelargonium, *Pelargonium crispum*.

lemon grass *noun* any fragrant tropical grass of the genus *Cymbopogon*, yielding an oil smelling of lemon.

lemon law *noun* N Amer. *informal* a law requiring the manufacturer or seller to replace a defective car.

lemon meringue *noun* (in full **lemon meringue pie**) an open pie consisting of a pastry crust with a lemon filling and a topping of meringue.

lemon oil *noun* **1** an essential oil obtained from the rind of lemons, used in cooking, perfumes, etc. **2** a lemon-scented petroleum distillate used as a furniture polish.

lemon-scented *adjective* having a smell suggestive of lemons.

lemon sole *noun* **1** a flatfish, *Microstomus kitt*, of the flounder family, an important food fish. **2** the flesh of any of various other flounders as food. [French *limande*]

lemon thyme *noun* a herb, *Thymus citriodorus*, with lemon-scented leaves used for flavouring.

lemon verbena *noun* (also **lemon plant**) a shrub, *Aloysia triphylla* (*Lippia citriodora*), with lemon-scented leaves.

lemon yellow ● *noun* a pale yellow colour. ● *adjective* (hyphenated when *attributive*) of this colour.

Le·Moyne /ləˈmwɒn/ a former town in south central Quebec, located on the St. Lawrence, opposite Montreal, now part of Longueuil; pop. (2001) 4,855. [C. LE MOYNE]

Le Moyne /leˈmwɒn/ **Charles Le Moyne de Lon·gueuil et de Châ·teau·guay** (1626–85), French soldier. Coming to New France at the age of fifteen, he worked among the Hurons with the Jesuits. He settled at Ville-Marie in 1646, and was granted the seigneuries of Longueuil and Châteauguay for his actions against the Iroquois. He was named governor of Montreal in 1683.

lem·pira /lemˈpiːrə/ *noun* the chief monetary unit of Honduras, equal to 100 centavos. [named after *Lempira*, 16th-c. chieftain who opposed the Spanish conquest of Honduras]

le·mur /ˈliːmər/ *noun* any arboreal primate of the family Lemuridae native to Madagascar, with a pointed snout and long tail. [modern Latin from Latin *lemures* (pl.) spirits of the dead, from its spectre-like face]

Lena River /ˈleinə/ a river in Siberia, which rises in the mountains on the western shore of Lake Baikal and flows generally northeast and north for 4 400 km (2,750 miles) into the Laptev Sea. It is famous for the goldfields in its basin.

lend *transitive verb* (*past* and *past participle* **lent**) **1** (usu. foll. by *to*) grant (to a person) the use of (a thing) on the understanding that it or its equivalent shall be returned. **2** allow the use of (money) at interest. **3** bestow or contribute (something temporary) (*lend assistance*; *lends a certain charm*). □ **lend an ear** (or **one's ears**) listen. **lend a hand** see HAND. **lend itself to** (of a thing) allow, be suitable for. **lend oneself to** accommodate oneself to (a policy or purpose). **lend one's name to** allow one's self, name, or reputation to be associated with some cause etc. □ **lend·er** *noun* **lend·ing** *noun & adjective* [Middle English, earlier *lēne(n)* from Old English *lǣnan* from *lǣn* LOAN]

lending library *noun* a library from which books may be temporarily taken away with or without direct payment.

Lendl, Ivan (b.1960), Czech-born US tennis player. He won many singles titles in the 1980s and early 1990s, including the US, Australian, and the French Open championships. He retired from the sport in 1994.

Lend-Lease *noun* *hist.* an arrangement made in 1941 whereby the US supplied equipment etc. to the UK and its allies, originally as a loan in return for the use of British-owned military bases.

length /leŋθ, leŋθ/ *noun* **1 a** the linear extent of a thing from end to end. **b** the greater of two or the greatest of three dimensions of a body or figure. **c** the quality or fact of being long. **2 a** extent from beginning to end, esp. of a period of time, etc. (*the length of a speech*). **b** a period or duration of time, esp. a long period (*a stay of some length*). **3** the distance a thing extends (*at arm's length*; *ships a cable's length apart*). **4 a** the length of a swimming pool as a measure of the distance swum. **b** the length of a horse, boat, etc., as a measure of the lead in a race. **c** the length of a car, usu. as a measure of separation from the vehicle in front. **5** a long stretch, piece, or extent of land, hair, tubing, etc. **6** a degree of thoroughness in action (*went to great lengths*; *prepared to go to any length*). **7** a piece of material of a certain or distinct length (*a length of cloth*). **8** the quantity, esp. long quantity, of a vowel or syllable. **9** the extent of a garment, curtains, etc. in a vertical direction when worn or hung (*a floor-length veil*). **10** the full extent of one's body. □ **at length 1** (also **at full** or **great** etc. **length**) in detail, without curtailment. **2** after a long time, at last. **length and breadth** the whole area; all places or directions. [Old English *lengthu* from Germanic (as LONG¹)]

length·en *verb* **1** *transitive & intransitive* make or become longer. **2** *transitive* make (a vowel) long. □ **length·en·ing** *noun & adjective*

length·wise ● *adverb* (also esp. *Brit.* **length·ways**) in a direction parallel with a thing's length. ● *adjective* lying or moving lengthwise.

lengthy *adjective* (**length·i·er**, **length·i·est**) **1** (of a period of time) long, extended, of unusual length. **2** (of speech, writing, style, a speaker, etc.) tedious, excessively detailed. □ **length·i·ly** *adverb* **length·i·ness** *noun*

leni·ent /ˈliːnɪənt/ *adjective* **1** merciful, tolerant, not disposed to severity. **2** (of punishment etc.) mild. □ **leni·en·cy** *noun* **leni·ent·ly** *adverb* [Latin *lenire lenit-* soothe, from *lenis* gentle]

Lenin /ˈlenɪn/ **Vlad·i·mir Ilich** (born Vladimir Ilich Ulyanov) (1870–1924), the principal figure in the Russian Revolution and first premier of the Soviet Union 1918–24. The originator of Marxism-Leninism, he led the Bolsheviks to power in the October Revolution (1917), and as the first head of the communist Soviet state he founded the Third International or Comintern (1919), defeated counter-revolutionary forces in the Russian Civil War (1918–21), and instituted the New Economic Policy (1921) emphasizing economic reconstruction and education.

Len·in·grad a former name (1924–91) for St. Petersburg 1.

Len·in·ism *noun* Marxism as interpreted and applied by Lenin. □ **Len·in·ist** *noun & adjective*

le·ni·tion /lɪˈnɪʃən/ *noun* the process or result of a consonant being weakly articulated or lost. [Latin *lenis* soft, after German *Lenierung*]

Len·non, John (1940–80), English pop and rock singer, guitarist, and songwriter. A founding member of the Beatles, he wrote most of their songs in collaboration with Paul McCartney, and his subsequent recording career, in which he often collaborated with his second wife Yoko Ono, included the albums *Imagine* (1971) and *Double Fantasy* (1980); he was murdered in 1980.

Len·nox, Charles, (4th Duke of Rich·mond and Len·nox) (1764–1819), British soldier and colonial administrator. Lord Lieutenant of Ireland 1807–13, he was appointed governor-in-chief of British North America in 1818. He died shortly after his arrival in Canada, having developed rabies after being bitten by his pet fox.

Len·nox·ville a former town in S Quebec, situated on the Rivière Saint-François, now part of Sherbrooke; pop. (2001) 4,963. Bishop's University is located there. [C. Lennox]

Le Nôtre /lə ˈnoːtr/ **André** (1613–1700), French landscape gardener. He designed many formal gardens, including the parks of Vaux-le-Vicomte and Versailles, begun in 1655 and 1662 respectively, which incorporate his ideas on architecturally conceived garden schemes.

lens ● *noun* **1** a piece of a transparent substance with one or usu. both sides curved for concentrating or dispersing light rays esp. in optical instruments. **2** (also **compound lens**) such a lens or combination of lenses used in photography. **3** *Anat.* = CRYSTALLINE LENS. **4** *Physics* a device for focusing or otherwise modifying the direction of movement of light, sound, electrons, etc. **5 a** a piece of glass or plastic enclosed in a frame for wearing in front of the eyes to correct the vision. **b** = CONTACT LENS. **6** a biconvex body of any material, as rock, ice, water, etc. **7** a viewpoint, perspective (*see life through a new lens*). ● *verb* **1 a** *transitive* film (a movie etc.). **b** *intransitive* (of a movie etc.) be filmed. **2** *intransitive Astronomy & Physics* (often in *passive*) see or transmit through or as through a lens, esp. by the bending of radiation by a strong gravitational field. **3** *intransitive Geol.* (of a body of rock) become gradually thinner along a particular direction to the point of extinction. □ **lensed** *adjective* **lens·ing** *noun* **lens·less** *adjective* [Latin *lens lentis* lentil (from the similarity of shape)]

lens cap *noun* (also **lens cover**) a protective cover that fits over the end of a camera lens tube.

lens·man *noun* (*pl.* **-men**) = CAMERAMAN.

Lent *noun Christianity* the period of fasting and penitence preceding Easter, now beginning in most of the Western Church on the 7th Wednesday before Easter (Ash Wednesday). [Middle English from LENTEN]

lent *past and past participle of* LEND.

-lent *suffix* forming adjectives (*pestilent; violent*) (*compare* -ULENT). [Latin *-lentus* -ful]

Lent·en *adjective* of, in, or appropriate to Lent. [originally as noun, = spring, from Old English *lencten* from Germanic, related to LONG[1], perhaps with reference to lengthening of the day in spring: now regarded as adj. from LENT + -EN[2]]

len·ti·cel /ˈlentɪˌsel/ *noun Bot.* any of the raised pores in the stems of woody plants that allow gas exchange between the atmosphere and the internal tissues. [modern Latin *lenticella* diminutive of Latin *lens*: see LENS]

len·tic·u·lar /lenˈtɪkjʊlər/ *adjective* **1** having a flattened shape with a dense centre and thin edges, like a lentil or biconvex lens (*lenticular galaxy*). **2** of, pertaining to, or using a lens or lenses. **3 a** (of a film, screen, etc.) embossed with minute, usu. cylindrical, lenses so that two or more images can be interspersed. **b** designating a method of colour photography using such a film together with filters. [Latin *lenticularis* (as LENTIL)]

len·til *noun* **1** a leguminous plant, *Lens culinaris*, yielding edible biconvex seeds. **2** this seed, esp. used as food with the husk removed. [Old French *lentille* from Latin *lenticula* (as LENS)]

lento *Music* ● *adjective* slow. ● *adverb* slowly. [Italian]

Leo *noun* (*pl.* **Leos**) **1** a constellation between Virgo and Cancer, traditionally regarded as contained in the figure of a lion. **2 a** the fifth sign of the zodiac. **b** a person born when the sun is in this sign, usu. between 23 July and 22 August. [Old English from Latin, = LION]

Leo I (known as 'the Great'; canonized as St. Leo I) (d.461), pope from 440 and Doctor of the Church. His statement of the doctrine of the Incarnation was accepted at the Council of Chalcedon (451); and he extended and consolidated the power of the Roman see, claiming jurisdiction in Africa, Spain, and Gaul.

Leo X (born Giovanni de' Medici) (1475–1521), pope from 1513. He excommunicated Luther, bestowed on Henry VIII of England the title of Defender of the Faith, and was a noted patron of learning and the arts.

León /leiˈɒn/ **1** a city in N Spain; pop. (est. 2001) 137,384. It is the capital of the province and former kingdom of León, now part of Castilla-León region. **2** an industrial city in central Mexico; pop. (est. 2002) 1,397,300. **3** a city in W Nicaragua, the second largest city in the country; pop. (est. 2002) 158,600.

Leon·ard /ˈlenərd/ **Sugar Ray** (born Ray Charles Leonard) (b.1954), US boxer, who was world welterweight champion five times between 1976 and 1988.

Leo·nar·do da Vinci /ˌliːəˌnɑːrdoː də ˈvɪntʃi/ (1452–1519), Italian painter, scientist, and engineer. His nature studies and use of *sfumato* are reflected in paintings such as *The Virgin of the Rocks* (1483–5), *The Last Supper* (1498), and *Mona Lisa* (1504–5). His 19 notebooks contain studies and drawings on a wide range of subjects, from anatomy and biology to mechanics and hydraulics.

Leon·ca·vallo /leiɔːnkəˈvɒloː/ **Rug·giero** (1858–1919), Italian composer, who is known for the opera *Pagliacci* (1890).

leone /liˈoːn, -oːni/ *noun* the basic monetary unit of Sierra Leone, equal to 100 cents. [Sierra Leone]

Leo·nid /ˈliːənɪd/ *noun* any of the meteors that seem to radiate from the direction of the constellation Leo in November. [Latin *leo* (see LEO) *leonis* + -ID[3]]

Leoni·das /liˈɒnɪdæs/ (d.480 BC), king of Sparta, who was commander of the Greeks at the battle of Thermopylae in 480.

Leo·nine /ˈliːəˌnain/ *adjective* **1** of, pertaining to, made or invented by any of the popes named Leo. **2** (of poetry) having an internal rhyme. [the name *Leo* (as LEONINE); sense 2 may be from the name of an unknown medieval poet]

leo·nine /ˈliːəˌnain/ *adjective* **1** like a lion. **2** of or relating to lions. [Old French *leonin -ine* or Latin *leoninus* from *leo leonis* lion]

Leonine City the part of Rome in which the Vatican stands, walled and fortified by Pope Leo IV (d.855).

leop·ard /ˈlepərd/ *noun* **1** any large African or Asian flesh-eating cat, *Panthera pardus*, with either a black-spotted yellowish-fawn or all black coat. *Also called* PANTHER. **2** *Heraldry* a lion passant guardant as in the arms of England. **3** (*attributive*) spotted like a leopard (*leopard moth*). [Old French from Late Latin from late Greek *leopardos* (as LION, PARD)]

leop·ard·ess /ˈlepərdes/ *noun* a female leopard.

leopard frog *noun* **1** a N American frog, *Rana pipiens*, that is green with black pale-ringed blotches. **2** any of various similar N American frogs.

leopard's bane *noun* any plant of the genus *Doronicum*, with large yellow daisy-like flowers.

leopard skin *noun* **1** the skin of a leopard. **2** (also **leopard print**) fabric printed in imitation of a leopard skin, with tawny colours and brown blotches.

Leopold I ▶ 1 (1640–1705), Holy Roman emperor 1658–1705, whose long reign saw a major revival of Hapsburg power. **2** (1790–1865), first king of Belgium 1831–65. In 1830 he refused the throne of Greece, but a year later accepted that of the newly independent Belgium, reigning peacefully thereafter.

Leopold II (1835–1909), king of Belgium 1865–1909, who became the first sovereign of the Congo Free State in 1885.

Léo·pold·ville the former name (until 1966) for KINSHASA.

leo·tard *noun* **1** a close-fitting one-piece garment worn by dancers, gymnasts, etc. **2** *N Amer.* (usu. in *pl.*) heavy tights. [J. *Léotard*, French trapeze artist d.1870]

Le·page /ləˈpɒʒ/ **Rob·ert** (b.1957), Canadian theatre, opera and film director, actor, and writer. He has achieved international acclaim with his innovative, often startling productions including the film *Le Confessionnal* (1995), which swept the Genie awards.

Le·pan·to, Battle of /ləˈpantoː/ a naval battle fought in 1571 at the entrance to the Gulf of Lepanto, in which the forces of Rome, Venice,

---

Consonants: **b** *but* **d** *dog* **f** *few* **g** *get* **h** *her* **j** *yes* **k** *cat* **l** *leg* **m** *man* **n** *no* **p** *pen* **r** *red* **s** *sit*

and Spain, under the command of Don John of Austria, defeated a large Turkish fleet, ending for the time being Turkish naval domination in the eastern Mediterranean.

Le·pan·to, Gulf of /ləˈpantəʊ/ an alternative name for the Gulf of Corinth (see CORINTH, GULF OF).

lep·er /ˈlepər/ *noun* **1** a person suffering from leprosy. ¶ Now usu. avoided in medical usage. **2** a person who is shunned, esp. on moral grounds; an outcast. [Old French *lepre* from Latin *lepra* from Greek, fem. of *lepros* scaly, from *lepos* scale]

lepi·dop·ter·ist /lepɪˈdɒptərɪst/ *noun* a person who studies or collects butterflies.

lepi·dop·ter·ous /ˌlepɪˈdɒptərəs/ *adjective* of the order Lepidoptera of insects, with four scale-covered wings often brightly coloured, including butterflies and moths. □ **lepi·dop·ter·an** *adjective & noun* [Greek *lepis -idos* scale + *pteron* wing]

Lepi·dus /ˈlepɪdəs/ **Mar·cus Aemil·ius** (died *c.*13 BC), Roman statesman, who formed the triumvirate with Antony and Octavian (later Augustus) in 43.

lep·re·chaun /ˈleprəˌkɒn/ *noun* a small, usu. mischievous being of human form in Irish folklore, often associated with shoemaking or buried treasure. [Old Irish *luchorpán* from *lu* small + *corp* body]

lep·ro·sarium /leprəˈsɑːriəm/ *noun* (*pl.* **-saria**) a hospital for people with leprosy.

lep·ro·sy /ˈleprəsi/ *noun* **1** a contagious bacterial disease that affects the skin, mucous membranes, and nerves, causing disfigurement. *Also called* HANSEN'S DISEASE. **2** corruption or contagion, esp. social, moral, etc.

lep·rous /ˈleprəs/ *adjective* **1** suffering from leprosy. **2** like or relating to leprosy. [Old French from Late Latin *leprosus* from *lepra*: see LEPER]

lepta *pl. of* LEPTON[1].

lep·tin *noun* a protein produced by fatty tissue which is believed to regulate fat storage in the body. [Greek *leptos* 'thin, fine' + -IN]

Lep·tis Magna /ˌleptɪs ˈmaɡnə/ an ancient seaport and trading centre on the Mediterranean coast of North Africa, near present-day Al Khums in Libya. Most of its impressive remains date from the reign of Septimius Severus (AD 193–211), a native of the city.

lepto- *combining form* small, narrow. [Greek *leptos* fine, small, thin, delicate]

lep·ton[1] /ˈleptən/ *noun* (*pl.* **lepta** /-tə/) a Greek monetary unit worth one-hundredth of a drachma. [Greek *lepton* (*nomisma* coin) neuter of *leptos* small]

lep·ton[2] /ˈleptɒn/ *noun* (*pl.* **lep·tons**) Physics any of a class of elementary particles which do not undergo strong interaction, e.g. an electron, muon, or neutrino. [LEPTO- + -ON]

lep·to·spir·o·sis /ˌleptəspɪˈrəʊsɪs/ *noun* an infectious disease caused by bacteria of the genus *Leptospira*, that occurs in rodents, dogs, and other mammals, and can be transmitted to humans.

lep·to·tene /ˈleptəˌtiːn/ *noun* Biol. the first stage of the prophase of meiosis in which each chromosome is apparent as two fine chromatids. [LEPTO- + Greek *tainia* band]

Ler·mon·tov /ˈlermən,tɒf/ **Mik·hail (Yuri·evich)** (1814–41), Russian romantic poet and novelist, who wrote lyric and narrative poetry on the themes of disillusionment, rebellion, and personal freedom, and is known for the influential novel *A Hero of Our Time* (1840).

Ler·ner, Alan Jay (1918–86), US lyricist, who is best known for his collaboration with the songwriter Frederick Loewe in musicals such as *Brigadoon* (1947), *My Fair Lady* (1956), and *Camelot* (1960).

Ler·wick /ˈlɜrwɪk/ the capital of the Shetland Islands, on the island of Mainland; pop. (est. 1999) 7,500. The most northerly town in the British Isles, it is a fishing centre and a service port for the oil industry.

Le·sage /ləˈsɒʒ/ **1 Alain-René** (also **Le Sage**) (1668–1747), French novelist and dramatist, who is known for the picaresque novel *Gil Blas* (1715–35). **2 Jean** (1912–80), Canadian lawyer and politician, premier of Quebec 1960–66. A Liberal MP (1945–57) and federal cabinet minister (1953–57), he left federal politics following the fall of the St. Laurent government and became the leader of the Quebec provincial liberals in 1958, a position which he held until 1970. As premier, he led the Quebec government through the Quiet Revolution.

les·bian /ˈlezbiən/ ● *noun* a woman who is sexually attracted to other women. ● *adjective* **1** of or pertaining to lesbians. **2** (**Lesbian**) of Lesbos. □ **les·bian·ism** *noun* [via Latin from Greek *Lesbios* from LESBOS, home of Sappho, who expressed affection for women in her poetry]

lesbi·gay /ˈlezbaɪɡeɪ/ ● *adjective* being or relating to lesbians, bisexuals,

or male homosexuals. ● *noun* a member of one of these groups. [blend of *lesbian*, *bisexual*, and *gay*]

lesbo /ˈlezbəʊ/ *noun informal* a lesbian.

Les·bos /ˈlezbɒs/ a Greek island in the E Aegean, off the coast of NW Turkey; chief town, Mytilene. Its artistic golden age of the late 7th and early 6th c. BC produced the poets Alcaeus and Sappho.

lèse-majesté /ˌlez maʒəˈsteɪ, ˈmaʒ-/ *noun* (also **lese-majesty** /liːz ˈmadʒɪsti/) **1** treason. **2** an insult to a sovereign or ruler. **3** presumptuous conduct or disrespect from a junior person. [French from Latin *laesa majestas* injured sovereignty, from *laedere laes-* injure + *majestas* MAJESTY]

Les Îles de la Madeleine /leiziːldəlamadˈlen/ a municipality encompassing the towns and villages of the Magdalen Islands; pop. (2001) 12,824. [*Madeleine* Fontaine, wife of F. Doublet, early seigneur *c.*1663]

le·sion /ˈliːʒən/ *noun* **1** Med. a pathological change in the functioning or structure of an organ, organism, etc. **2** injury, harm, damage; a wound or blemish. □ **le·sioned** *adjective* [Old French from Latin *laesio -onis* from *laedere laes-* injure]

Le·so·tho /ləˈsuːtu, -səʊtəʊ/ a landlocked mountainous country forming an enclave in South Africa; pop. (est. 2002) 2,207,954; capital, Maseru.

less ● *adjective* **1** smaller in extent, degree, duration, number, etc. (*of less importance*). **2** of smaller quantity, not so much (opp. MORE) (*find less difficulty; eat less meat*). **3** *disputed* fewer (*eat less cookies*). ¶ The use of *less* with countable nouns is considered incorrect in formal English, although it is frequent in informal usage. Strictly, *less* should be used only with uncountable nouns as the comparative of *little*, e.g. *I have little time; she has even less*, but *I have few books; she has even fewer*. **4** of lower rank, status, etc. (*no less a person than; St. James the Less*). ● *adverb* to a smaller extent, in a lower degree. ● *pronoun* a smaller amount, quantity, or number (*cannot take less; for less than $10; is little less than disgraceful*). ● *preposition* minus (*made $1,000 less GST*). □ **in less than no time** *informal* very quickly or soon. **less and less** to an extent that is becoming continuously smaller. **less of** to a smaller extent. **much** (or **still**) **less** with even greater force of denial (*do not suspect him of negligence, much less of dishonesty*). **no less** (as an intensifier) what's more. [Old English *lǣssa* (adj.), *lǣs* (adv.), from Germanic]

-less *suffix* forming adjectives and adverbs: **1** from nouns, meaning 'not having, without, free from' (*doubtless; powerless*). **2** from verbs, meaning 'not affected by or doing the action of the verb' (*fathomless; tireless*). □ **-lessly** *suffix*. **-lessness** *suffix*. [Old English *-lēas* from *lēas* devoid of]

les·see *noun* a person to whom a lease is granted or who holds a property by lease, esp. a tenant. □ **les·see·ship** *noun* [Anglo-French past participle, Old French *lessé* (as LEASE)]

less·en *transitive & intransitive verb* make or become less, diminish.

Les·seps /ˈlesəps/ **Fer·di·nand (Marie), Vi·comte de** (1805–94), French diplomat. He oversaw the building of the Suez Canal (1859–69), and embarked on the first attempt to build the Panama Canal (1881–9).

less·er *adjective* (usu. *attributive*) **1 a** not so great or much as the other or the rest (*the lesser evil*). **b** (*attributive*) smaller, inferior, or of lower status or worth. **2** designating the smaller of two similar or related plants, animals, anatomical parts, or places (*the lesser celandine*).

Lesser Antilles see ANTILLES.

lesser-known *adjective* known less well than others of the same kind.

Lesser Slave Lake a lake in central Alberta, over 200 km northwest of Edmonton. [see GREAT SLAVE LAKE]

Lesser Sunda Islands see SUNDA ISLANDS.

Les·sing ▸ 1 Doris (May) (b.1919), English novelist and short-story writer, brought up in Rhodesia. Her fiction is concerned with left-wing politics, sexual conflict, and the position of women, and includes *The Golden Notebook* (1962), *Briefing for a Descent into Hell* (1971), and a quintet of science fiction novels collectively entitled *Canopus in Argus: Archives* (1979–83). **2 Gott·hold Eph·raim** (1729–81), German dramatist and critic, who wrote tragedies such as *Miss Sara Sampson* (1755), the comedy *Minna von Barnhelm* (1767), and the dramatic poem *Nathan der Weise* (1779), a plea for religious toleration; in his critical work *Laokoon* (1766) he criticized the reliance of German literature on the conventions of the French classical school.

less is more ● *noun* an aesthetic etc. favouring minimalism. ● *adjective* (**less-is-more**) of, pertaining to, or representing this aesthetic.

les·son *noun* **1 a** a continuous portion of teaching given to a student or class at one time. **b** the time assigned to this. **c** any of the portions into which a course of instruction is divided. **2** (in *pl.*; foll. by *in*) systematic instruction (*gives lessons in dancing*; *took lessons in French*). **3** a thing learned or to be learned by a student, esp. a section of a book etc. to be studied. **4 a** an occurrence, example, rebuke, or punishment, that serves or should serve to warn or encourage (*let that be a lesson to you*). **b** a thing inculcated by experience or study. **5** a passage from the Bible read aloud during a church service. □ **learn one's lesson** be wiser as a result of an unpleasant, painful, etc. experience. **teach a person a lesson** punish a person, esp. as a deterrent. [Old French *leçon* from Latin *lectio -onis*: see LECTION]

les·sor *noun* a person who lets a property by lease. [Anglo-French from *lesser*: see LEASE]

lest *conjunction* **1** in order that not, for fear that (*lest we forget*). **2** that (*afraid lest we should be late*). [Old English *thȳ lǽs the* whereby less that, later the *lǽste*, Middle English *lest(e)*] ¶ The verb in the clause introduced by *lest* is usually in the subjunctive; less frequently, it is preceded by *should*.

let¹ ● *verb* (**let·ting**; *past* and *past participle* **let**) **1** *transitive* **a** allow to, not prevent or forbid (*we let them go*). **b** cause to (*let me know*; *let it be known*). **2** *transitive* (foll. by *into*) **a** allow to enter. **b** make acquainted with (a secret etc.). **3** *transitive Brit.* grant the use of (rooms, land, etc.) for rent or hire (*was let to the new tenant for a year*). **4** *transitive* allow or cause (liquid or air) to escape (*let blood*). **5** *transitive* award (a contract for work). **6** *aux.* supplying the first and third persons of the imperative in exhortations (*let's eat!*), commands (*let it be done at once*; *let there be light*), assumptions (*let AB be equal to CD*), and permission or challenge (*let him do his worst*). ● *noun Brit.* the act or an instance of letting a house, room, etc. (*a long let*). □ **let alone** (also **leave alone**) **1** not to mention, far less or more (*hasn't got a television, let alone a DVD player*). **2** = LET BE. **let be** not interfere with, attend to, or do. **let down 1** lower. **2** fail to support or satisfy, disappoint. **3** lengthen (a garment). **4** loosen, untie, or allow to hang freely. **let down gently** avoid disappointing or humiliating abruptly. **let fly 1** (often foll. by *at*) attack physically or verbally. **2** (often foll. by *with*) throw, hurl, or hit vigorously. **let go 1** release, set at liberty. **2 a** (often foll. by *of*) relax or relinquish one's hold. **b** lose hold of. **3 a** cease to think or talk about; dismiss from one's thoughts. **b** cease to attend to or control; take no further action concerning. **c** dismiss (an employee). **let oneself go 1** give way to enthusiasm, impulse, etc. **2** cease to take trouble, neglect one's appearance or habits. **let in 1** allow to enter (*let the dog in*; *let in a flood of light*; *this would let in all sorts of evils*). **2** (usu. foll. by *for*) involve (a person, often oneself) in loss or difficulty. **3** (foll. by *on*) allow (a person) to share privileges, information, etc. **4** inlay (a thing) in another. **let oneself in** enter someone else's residence etc. by means of a key. **let it drop** (usu. in *imperative*) let the matter end there, not continue with the matter. **let know** inform (a person). **let loose 1** release or unleash. **2** loosen. **3** (also foll. by *with*) emit abruptly (a scream, tirade, etc.). **4** (often foll. by *on*) allow (a person) free access to (*once they're trained, we'll let them loose on the new computers*). **let off 1 a** fire (a gun). **b** explode (a bomb or firework). **2** allow or cause (steam, liquid, etc.) to escape. **3** allow to alight from a vehicle etc. **4 a** not punish or compel. **b** (foll. by *with*) punish lightly. **c** excuse, free (*was let off work early*). **let off steam** see STEAM. **let on** *informal* **1** reveal a secret. **2** pretend (*let on that he had succeeded*). **let out 1** allow to go out, esp. through a doorway. **2** release from restraint. **3** (often foll. by *that* + clause) reveal (a secret etc.). **4** make (a garment) looser esp. by adjustment at a seam. **5** esp. *Brit.* put out to rent esp. to several tenants, or to contract. **6** *N Amer.* (of a class, meeting, etc.) finish, come to an end. **let (a person) have it 1** direct a blow or shot at a person. **2** assail with blows or words. **let rip** see RIP¹. **let slip** see SLIP¹. **let through** allow to pass. **let up** *informal* **1** become less intense or severe. **2** relax one's efforts. **to let** esp. *Brit.* available for rent. [Old English *lǽtan* from Germanic, related to LATE]

let² *noun* **1** (in tennis, squash, etc.) an obstruction of a ball or a player in certain ways, requiring the ball to be served again. **2** *archaic* **without let or hindrance** obstruction, hindrance. [Old English *lettan* from Germanic, related to LATE]

-let *suffix* forming nouns, usu. diminutives (*piglet*; *leaflet*) or denoting articles of ornament or dress (*anklet*). [originally corresponding (in *bracelet*, *crosslet*, etc.) to French *-ette* added to nouns in *-el*]

let·down *noun* **1** a disappointment, drawback, or disadvantage. **2** the release of milk in a nursing mother or lactating animal as a reflex response to suckling or massage.

leth·al *adjective* **1** causing or sufficient to cause death. **2** harmful, injurious, destructive. □ **leth·al·ity** *noun* **leth·al·ly** *adverb* [Latin *let(h)alis* from *letum* death]

lethal dose *noun* the amount of a toxic compound or drug that causes death in humans or animals.

lethal injection *noun* an injection of various deadly chemicals used for capital punishment in certain judicial systems.

leth·argy /ˈleθərdʒi/ *noun* **1** lack of energy or vitality; a torpid, inert, or apathetic state. **2** *Med.* a pathological state of sleepiness or deep unresponsiveness and inactivity. □ **leth·ar·gic** /lɪˈθɑrdʒɪk/ *adjective* **leth·ar·gic·al·ly** *adverb* [Old French *litargie* from Late Latin *lethargia* from Greek *lēthargia* from *lēthargos* forgetful, from *lēth-*, *lanthanomai* forget]

Leth·bridge a city in S Alberta, located on the Oldman River, about 200 km southeast of Calgary; pop. (2001) 67,374. [W. *Lethbridge*, first president of the North Western Coal and Navigation Company d.1901]

Lethe /ˈliːθiː/ *noun* **1** (in Greek mythology) a river in Hades producing forgetfulness of the past. □ **Lethe·an** /liːˈθiːən/ *adjective* [Latin, use of Greek *lēthē* forgetfulness (as LETHARGY)]

Le·ticia /ləˈtiːsiə/ a town and river port at the southern tip of Colombia, on the upper reaches of the Amazon on the border with Brazil and Peru; pop. (est. 2002) 27,100.

Leto /ˈliːtoː/ *Gk Myth* the daughter of a Titan, mother (by Zeus) of Artemis and Apollo; the Roman Latona was identified with her.

let-off *noun* the action of pulling a trigger of a rifle, releasing the tension on a bow to fire an arrow, etc.

le tout /lə ˈtuː/ *adjective* designating everyone who is anyone in a specified city etc. (*le tout Saskatoon turned out for the gala*). [French, lit. 'all']

let-out *noun informal Brit.* (in full **let-out clause**) a clause specifying a circumstance in which the terms of an agreement, contract, etc. shall not apply; an opportunity to escape.

LETS *abbreviation Cdn & Brit.* Local Exchange Trading System, a barter system within and among participating communities which allows payments to be made in currency or goods or a combination of the two.

let's *contraction* let us (*let's go now*).

Lett *noun archaic* = LATVIAN *noun*. [German *Lette* from Lettish *Latvi*]

let·ter ● *noun* **1 a** a character representing one or more of the simple or compound sounds used in speech; any of the alphabetic symbols. **b** (in *pl.*) *informal* the initials of a degree etc. after the holder's name. **c** *US* a school or college initial as a mark of proficiency in athletics etc. **2 a** a written, typed, or printed communication, usu. sent by mail or messenger. **b** (in *pl.*) an addressed legal or formal document for any of various purposes. **3** the precise terms or strict verbal interpretation of a statement or document (*opp.* SPIRIT *noun* 6) (*according to the letter of the law*). **4** (in *pl.*) **a** literature in general. **b** acquaintance with books, erudition (*Canadian man of letters George Woodcock*). **c** authorship (*the profession of letters*). **5 a** types collectively. **b** a font of type. **6** *N Amer.* (*attributive*) **a** designating a size of paper 22 by 28 cm (8¹⁄₂ by 11 inches). **b** designating office supplies, e.g. files etc., designed to hold this size paper. **7** the smallest meaningful unit of a code, esp. the genetic code. ● *verb* **1** *transitive* **a** write, paint, inscribe, etc. letters on. **b** write, paint, inscribe, etc. (a word or words) on. **2** *intransitive US* earn a school letter in sports etc. □ **to the letter 1** with adherence to every detail. **2** in accordance with a strict literal interpretation. [Old French *lettre* from Latin *litera*, *littera* letter of alphabet, (in pl.) epistle, literature]

letter bomb *noun* a terrorist explosive device disguised as a letter and sent through the mail.

letter box ● *noun* **1** esp. *Brit.* a public mailbox into which letters are deposited for delivery by the postal service. **2** esp. *Brit.* **a** a private mailbox to which letters etc. are delivered. **b** = MAIL SLOT. **3** (**letter·box**) (usu. *attributive*) designating an adaptation of a motion picture for showing on television, maintaining the aspect ratio of a movie screen and thus producing an image with black borders above and below (*compare* PAN AND SCAN). ● *transitive verb* (**letter·box**) adapt a film for television broadcast in letterbox format. □ **letter·boxed** *adjective* **letter·box·ing** *noun*

letter carrier *noun N. Amer.* a person who delivers mail for the postal service.

let·tered *adjective* **1 a** printed, marked, inscribed, etc. with or as with letters. **b** (of a book) having the title etc. on the back or spine in gilt or coloured letters. **2** well read or educated; literate, learned.

letter·form *noun* the graphic form of a letter of an alphabet.

letter grade *noun N Amer.* a grade given for school work expressed as a letter (A, B, C, etc.).

letter·head *noun* **1** a printed heading on stationery, containing the address etc. of an organization or individual. **2** stationery with this.

Vowels: a cat ɑ arm e bed ɜr her ɜː deux ə ago ɪ sit i cosy iː feed ɒ hot ɔ pore oː no ʌ run ʊ put

letter·ing noun **1** the process of writing, inscribing, etc. letters. **2** letters written, painted, inscribed, etc. on something.

letter·man noun (pl. **-men**) US a person who has earned a school letter in sports.

letter of comfort noun an assurance about a debt, short of a legal guarantee, given to a bank by a third party.

letter of credit noun a letter from a banker authorizing a person to draw money up to a specified amount, usu. from another bank.

letter of intent noun a document containing a declaration of the intentions of the writer.

letter of introduction noun a letter written by one person and given to another introducing him or her to the addressee.

letter opener noun a knife with a long, narrow, blunt blade for slitting open envelopes etc.

letter-perfect adjective **1 a** literally correct, verbally exact. **b** flawless. **2** knowing one's part perfectly.

letter·press noun **1 a** the contents of an illustrated book other than the illustrations. **b** printed matter relating to illustrations. **2 a** a method of printing from raised type, not from lithography etc. **b** matter so printed.

letter-quality adjective **1** (esp. of a printer attached to a computer) producing print of a quality suitable for a business letter. **2** (of a letter etc.) printed to this quality.

letters of administration noun authority to administer the estate of an intestate.

letters of marque plural noun (also **letters of marque and reprisal**) hist. a licence to fit out an armed vessel and employ it in the capture of an enemy's merchant shipping and to commit acts which would otherwise have constituted piracy. [French from Provençal *marca* from *marcar* seize as a pledge]

letters patent plural noun an open document issued by a sovereign or government in order to record a contract, authorize or command an action, or confer a right, privilege, title, etc.

Let·tish adjective & noun archaic = LATVIAN.

let·tuce noun **1** a composite plant, *Lactuca sativa*, with crisp edible leaves used in salads. **2** any of various plants resembling this. [Middle English *letus(e)*, related to Old French *laitue* from Latin *lactuca* from *lac lactis* milk, with reference to its milky juice]

let-up noun informal **1** a reduction in intensity or severity. **2** a relaxation of effort.

leu /ˈleiuː/ noun (pl. **lei** /lei/) the basic monetary unit of Romania and Moldova, equal to 100 bani. [Romanian, = lion]

leu·cine /ˈluːsiːn/ noun Biochem. an amino acid which is a constituent of most proteins and is essential in the diet of vertebrates. [French from Greek *leukos* white + -IN]

leuco- var. of LEUKO-.

leuc·o·cyte var. of LEUKOCYTE.

leuc·o·cyt·o·sis var. of LEUKOCYTOSIS.

leuc·oma var. of LEUKOMA.

leuc·o·penia var. of LEUKOPENIA.

leuc·or·rhea /ˌluːkəˈriːə/ noun (also **leuc·or·rhoea**) a whitish or yellowish discharge of mucus from the vagina.

leuc·o·sis var. of LEUKOSIS.

leuc·ot·omy /luːˈkɒtəmi/ noun (pl. **-omies**) the surgical cutting of white nerve fibres of the frontal lobes of the brain, formerly used to treat intractable psychiatric disorders.

leuk·emia /luːˈkiːmiə/ noun (also esp. Brit. **leuk·aemia**) any of a group of malignant diseases in which the bone marrow and other blood-forming organs produce increased numbers of leukocytes. □ **leuk·emic** adjective [modern Latin from German *Leukämie* from Greek *leukos* white + *haima* blood]

leuko- /ˈluːkɔː/ combining form (also **leuco-**) white. [Greek *leukos* white]

leuk·o·cyte /ˈluːkəˌsɔit/ noun (also **leuc·o·cyte**) **1** a white blood cell. **2** any blood cell that contains a nucleus. □ **leuk·o·cyt·ic** /-ˈsɪtɪk/ adjective

leuk·o·cyt·o·sis /ˌluːkɔːsaiˈtɔːsɪs/ noun (also **leuc·o·cyt·o·sis**) (pl. **-ses**) an increase in the number of leukocytes in the blood.

leuk·oma /luːˈkɔːmə/ noun (also **leuc·oma**) a white opacity in the cornea of the eye.

leuk·o·penia /ˌluːkɔːˈpiːniːə/ noun (also **leuc·o·penia**) a reduction in the number of white cells in the blood.

leuk·o·sis /luːˈkɔːsɪs/ noun (also **leuc·o·sis**) esp. Vet. a leukemic

disease of animals, esp. any of a group of malignant viral diseases of poultry (*avian* or *fowl leukosis*) or of cattle (*bovine leukosis*).

leuk·o·tri·ene /ˌluːkəˈtraiiːn/ noun any of a group of biologically active metabolites related to prostaglandins, originally isolated from leukocytes, and contributing to asthma, other bronchial reactions, etc.

Leu·ven /ˈlɜːvən/ (French **Louvain** /luːˈvã/) a town in Belgium, east of Brussels; pop. (est. 2002) 88,300. From the 11th to the 15th c. it was the capital of the former duchy (now province) of Brabant.

Lev. abbreviation Leviticus (Bible).

lev noun (also **leva**) (pl. **leva**, **levas**, or **levs**) the chief monetary unit of Bulgaria. [Bulgarian, 'lion']

Le·vant /lɪˈvant/ noun (prec. by the) hist. or literary the eastern part of the Mediterranean with its islands and neighbouring countries. [French, pres. part. of *lever* rise, used as noun = point of sunrise, east]

le·vant·er /lɪˈvantər/ noun **1** a strong easterly Mediterranean wind. **2** (**Levanter**) a native or inhabitant of the Levant.

Le·vant·ine /lɪˈvantain, ˈlevən-/ ● adjective of or trading to the Levant. ● noun a native or inhabitant of the Levant.

le·va·tor /lɪˈveitɜːr/ noun a muscle whose contraction causes the raising of a part of the body. [Latin, = one who lifts from *levare* raise]

levee¹ /ˈlevi/ noun **1** Cdn a New Year's Day reception held by the Governor General or by a Lieutenant-Governor, or by a mayor, bishop, etc. **2** N Amer. an assembly of visitors or guests, esp. at a formal reception. **3** hist. an assembly held by the sovereign or sovereign's representative at which men only were received. **4** hist. a reception of visitors on rising, from bed. [French *levé* var. of *lever* rising from *lever* to rise: see LEVY]

levee² /ˈlevi, lɪˈviː/ noun N Amer. **1 a** an embankment against river floods. **b** any of a series of continuous embankments surrounding irrigated fields. **2** a natural embankment built up by a river. **3** a landing place, a pier, or a quay. [French *levée* fem. past participle of *lever* raise: see LEVY]

level ● noun **1 a** a horizontal line or plane. **b** a horizontal position or the condition of being horizontal. **2 a** a position marked by a horizontal line (*eye level*). **b** a position on a real or imaginary scale with respect to amount, intensity, extent, etc. (*danger level*). **c** a relative height, amount, or value (*sugar level in the blood*). **3** a standard or plane in social, moral, or intellectual matters. **4** a plane of rank or authority, esp. in a hierarchy (*discussions at Cabinet level*). **5 a** an instrument giving a line parallel to the plane of the horizon for testing whether things are horizontal. **b** Surveying an instrument for giving a horizontal line of sight. **c** a real or imaginary horizontal line in relation to which elevation is measured. **6 a** a more or less level or flat surface. **b** a floor or storey in a building. **c** a stratum in the earth. **7** a flat tract of land; a stretch of land without hills. **8 a** a facet or layer of significance or meaning, esp. in a literary or artistic work. **b** the aspect or aspects of a subject, situation, etc. being considered at a particular time. **9** a nearly horizontal passage or gallery in a mine, esp. one used for drainage. ● adjective **1** having a flat and even surface; not bumpy. **2 a** horizontal; perpendicular to the plumb line. **b** lying, moving, or directed in an approximately horizontal plane. **3** (often foll. by *with*) **a** (of two or more things) situated in the same horizontal plane. **b** having equality with something else. **c** (of a spoonful etc.) with the contents even with the brim; not rounded or heaped. **4 a** (of a person, judgment, etc.) well-balanced, sensible, not agitated or confused. **b** of even, uniform, or equable quality, tone, style, etc. **5** (of a race etc.) having the leading competitors close together. ● verb (**lev·elled**, **level·ling**; esp. US **lev·eled**, **level·ing**) **1** transitive make (a surface) level, even, or uniform, esp. by removing or reducing irregularities. **2** transitive **a** raze or demolish. **b** beat or knock (a person) down. **3** transitive & intransitive aim (a missile or gun). **4** transitive & intransitive (foll. by *at*, *against*) direct (an accusation, criticism, or satire). **5** transitive standardize, reduce or remove (distinctions) to produce evenness or equality. **6** intransitive (usu. foll. by *with*) informal be frank or honest. **7** transitive place (two or more things, people, etc.) on the same level. **8** transitive & intransitive Surveying **a** ascertain differences in the height of (land). **b** determine the height of a point or points relative to a given horizontal plane. **9** transitive & intransitive (foll. by *off*, *out*) **a** bring (an aircraft) into horizontal flight. **b** (of an aircraft) assume or resume horizontal flight. □ **do one's level best** informal do one's utmost; make all possible efforts. **find its level** (or **its own level**) **1** (of a liquid) reach the same height in containers etc. which communicate with each other. **2** reach a stable level, value, position, etc. with respect to something else (*the dollar found its level against the yen*). **find one's level** reach the right social, intellectual, etc. place in relation to others. **level down** bring down to a standard. **level off 1** make or become level or smooth. **2** cease or cause to cease ascending or descending, increasing or decreasing. **level out** make or become level, remove differences, irregularities, etc. from. **level up** bring up to a standard. **on the level** *informal adverb* **1** honestly, without deception. **2** on a given plane, horizontal, etc. ● *adjective* **1** honest, truthful. **2** on a given plane, horizontal, etc. **on a level with 1** equal with. **2** in the same horizontal plane as. □ **level·ly** *adverb* **level·ness** *noun* [Old French *livel*, ultimately from Latin *libella* diminutive of *libra* scales, balance]

level crossing *noun Cdn & Brit.* a place at which a road and a railway, or two railways, cross each other at the same level.

level-headed *adjective* mentally well-balanced, cool, sensible. □ **level-headed·ly** *adverb* **level-headed·ness** *noun*

level·ler *noun* (also esp. *US* **level·er**) **1 a** a person who advocates the abolition of social distinctions. **b** a thing which brings all people to a common level (*death the great leveller*). **2** (**Leveller**) *hist.* an extreme radical dissenter in 17th-c. England, professing egalitarian principles. **3** a person or thing that levels.

level playing field *noun* a state of equitable conditions for trading or competing.

lever /ˈliːvər, levər/ ● *noun* **1** a projecting handle moved to operate a mechanism. **2** a bar resting on a pivot, used to help lift or dislodge a heavy or firmly fixed object. **3** *Mech.* a simple machine consisting of a rigid bar pivoted about a fulcrum (fixed point) which can be acted upon by a force (effort) in order to move a load. **4** a means of exerting moral pressure. ● *verb* **1** *intransitive* use a lever. **2** *transitive* (often foll. by *away, out, up,* etc.) lift, move, or act on with or as with a lever. [Old French *levier, leveor* from *lever* raise: see LEVY]

lever-action *adjective* (of a rifle) having the shell case ejected and the weapon re-cocked by a manually operated lever arm situated in front of the trigger housing.

lever·age /ˈlevrɪdʒ, ˈliːvr-/ ● **1** the action of a lever; a way of applying a lever. **2** the power of a lever; the mechanical advantage gained by use of a lever. **3** advantage for accomplishing a purpose; increased power or influence of action. **4** *N Amer. Business* **a** the earning potential created by the ratio of capital to shares. **b** the use of borrowed capital to enhance this. **5** *N Amer. Business* **a** the ratio of a company's loan capital (debt) to the value of its common shares (equity). **b** the effect of this on share prices. ● *verb* **1** *transitive & intransitive verb* speculate or cause to speculate financially on borrowed capital expecting profits made to be greater than interest payable. **2** *transitive verb* bring into a specified, usu. advantageous, position by or as by applying a lever.

leveraged buyout *noun* esp. *N Amer.* the buyout of a company by its management using outside capital. Abbr.: **LBO**.

lev·er·et /ˈlevərət/ *noun* a young hare, esp. one in its first year. [Anglo-French, diminutive of *levre*, Old French *lievre* from Latin *lepus leporis* hare]

Lever·ku·sen /ˈleivər,kuːzən/ an industrial city in western Germany, in North Rhine-Westphalia, on the Rhine River north of Cologne; pop. (est. 2002) 162,500.

Le Ver·rier /lə ˈveriei/ **Ur·bain (Jean Jo·seph)** (1811–77), French mathematician and astronomer, whose study of irregularities in the orbit of Uranus led to the discovery of the planet Neptune (1846).

Lé·vesque /lei'vek/ **René** (1922–87), Canadian journalist and politician, premier of Quebec 1976–85. After an influential career in journalism, he was elected as a Liberal MNA in 1960, and became a minister in the Lesage government, but, holding increasingly separatist views, resigned from the party in 1967 to found what eventually became the Parti Québécois. As premier, he held the initial referendum on sovereignty-association in 1980.

Levi /ˈliːvai/ **1** a Hebrew patriarch, son of Jacob and Leah (Gen. 29:34). **2** the tribe of Israel traditionally descended from him.

levi·able *see* LEVY.

le·via·than /ləˈvaiəθən/ *noun* **1** *Bible* a sea monster. **2** an imaginary or real aquatic animal of enormous size. **3** anything monstrously large. **4** an autocratic monarch or nation (in allusion to a book by Hobbes, 1651). [Late Latin from Hebrew *liwyātān*]

levir·ate /ˈliːvɪrət, ˈlev-/ *noun* a custom of the ancient Jews and some other peoples by which a man is obliged to marry his brother's widow. [Latin *levir* brother-in-law + -ATE[1]]

Lévis[1] /leiˈviː/ a city in SE central Quebec, located on the south shore of the St. Lawrence, opposite Quebec City; pop. (2001) 121,999. [F.-G. de LÉVIS]

Lévis[2] /leiˈviː/ **François-Gaston de, Duc de Lévis** (1719–87), French military officer. Sent to Canada during the Seven Years War, he was made second-in-command of the regular French army in Canada

in 1756. On Montcalm's death, he took over command, but although he experienced some initial success in his attempt to retake Quebec he was ultimately defeated in 1760.

Lévi-Strauss /ˌleviˈstraus/ **Claude** (b.1908), Belgian-born French social anthropologist. An influential pioneer of structuralism, he regarded language as an essential common denominator underlying cultural phenomena, and is known for his theories concerning the relationships of such societal elements as religion, myth, and kinship; his books include the two-volume *Structural Anthropology* (1958; 1973).

levi·tate /ˈlevɪˌteit/ *verb* **1** *intransitive* rise and float in the air (esp. with reference to spiritualism). **2** *transitive* cause to do this. **3** *transitive* cause (something heavier than the surrounding medium) to rise or remain suspended without visible means, e.g. using magnetic forces. □ **levi·ta·tion** *noun* **levi·ta·tor** *noun* [Latin *levis* light, after GRAVITATE]

Le·vite /ˈliːvəit/ *noun* a member of the tribe of Levi, esp. of that part of it which provided assistants to the priests in the worship in the Jewish temple. [Late Latin *levita* from Greek *leuitēs* from *Leui* from Hebrew *lēwī* Levi]

Le·vit·ical /ləˈvɪtɪkəl/ *adjective* **1** of the Levites or the tribe of Levi. **2** of or pertaining to the ancient Jewish system of ritual administered by the Levites. **3** of or pertaining to the Biblical book of Leviticus.

Le·vit·icus /ləˈvɪtɪkəs/ the third book of the Bible, containing details of laws and ritual. [Latin, = (book) of the Levites]

lev·ity /ˈlevɪti/ *noun* the treatment of a serious matter with humour or in a manner lacking due respect. [Latin *levitas* from *levis* light]

levo- /ˈliːvoː/ *combining form* (also esp. *Brit.* **laevo-**) on or to the left. [Latin *laevus* left]

levo·do·pa /ˌliːvəˈdoːpə/ *noun* = L-DOPA.

levo·nor·ges·trel /ˌliːvoːnɔrˈdʒestrəl/ *noun* a synthetic steroid hormone which has a similar effect to progesterone and is used in some contraceptive pills. [LEVO- (it being a levorotatory isomer) + *norgestrel* a synthetic steroid hormone]

levo·rota·tory /ˌliːvoːroːˈteitəri/ *adjective* (also esp. *Brit.* **laevorotatory**) *Chem.* having the property of rotating the plane of a polarized light ray to the left (counter-clockwise facing the oncoming radiation).

levu·lose /ˈliːvjuˌloːs, -ˌloːz/ *noun* (also esp. *Brit.* **laevulose**) = FRUCTOSE. [LEVO- + -ULE + -OSE[2]]

levy /ˈlevi/ ● *verb* (**-ies, -ied**) **1 a** *transitive* raise (contributions, taxes) or impose (a rate, toll, fee, etc.) as a levy. **b** *transitive & intransitive* raise (a sum of money) by legal execution or process (*the debt was levied on the debtor's goods*). **c** *transitive* seize (goods) in this way. **2** *transitive* enlist or enrol (troops etc.). **3** *transitive* (usu. foll. by *upon, against*) wage, proceed to make (war). ● *noun* (*pl.* **-ies**) **1 a** the collecting of a contribution, tax, etc., or of property to satisfy a legal judgment. **b** a contribution, tax, etc., levied. **2 a** the act or an instance of enrolling troops etc. **b** (in *pl.*) troops enrolled. **c** a body of troops enrolled. □ **levi·able** *adjective* [Old French *levee* fem. past participle of *lever* from Latin *levare* raise, from *levis* light]

lewd *adjective* **1** lustful, lecherous, wanton. **2** indecent, obscene. □ **lewd·ly** *adverb* **lewd·ness** *noun* [Old English *lǣwede* LAY[2], of unknown origin]

Lewis[1] the northern part of the island of Lewis with Harris, in the Outer Hebrides of Scotland.

Lewis[2] ▶ **1 Cecil Day**, see DAY-LEWIS 1. **2 Clive Staples** (1898–1963), British novelist, theologian, and scholar. His works frequently deal with religious and moral themes and reflect his Christian faith; they include the theological study *The Screwtape Letters* (1942) and a series of children's stories about the imaginary country of 'Narnia', beginning with *The Lion, The Witch, and The Wardrobe* (1950). **3 David** (1909–81), Russian-born Canadian lawyer and politician. National secretary of the CCF 1936–50, he was one of the key architects of the NDP in 1961. He was elected as an MP 1962–63 and 1965–74, and served as leader of the NDP 1971–75, during which time the party held the balance of power in the Liberal minority government of 1972–74. **4 Fred·erick Carle·ton ('Carl')** (b.1961), US athlete. In 1984 he won four Olympic gold medals (in the 100 and 200 metres, long jump, and 4×100 metre relay) and he repeated his victories in the 100 metres and long jump in the 1988 Olympics. He won gold again in the long jump in the 1992 and 1996 Olympics, and retired from competition in 1997. **5 (Harry) Sin·clair** (1885–1951), US novelist. His novels often use satire and caricature to attack small-town life in the American Midwest, and include *Main Street* (1920), *Babbitt* (1922), *Elmer Gantry* (1927), and *Dodsworth* (1929); in 1930 he was the first American to win the Nobel Prize for literature. **6 Jerry Lee** (b.1935), US rock and roll singer and pianist. In 1957 he joined Sun Records in Memphis, and in

Consonants: b *but*   d *dog*   f *few*   ɡ *get*   h *her*   j *yes*   k *cat*   l *leg*   m *man*   n *no*   p *pen*   r *red*   s *sit*

the same year had hits with 'Whole Lotta Shakin' Going On' and 'Great Balls of Fire'. His career was interrupted when his marriage to his 14-year-old cousin caused a public outcry. **7 Len·nox** (b.1965), English boxer. After a successful amateur career in Canada, culminating in a gold medal at the 1988 Olympics, he returned to England to pursue a professional career, and became world heavyweight champion in 1999. He retired in 2004 with a record of 41 wins, two losses, and one draw. **8 Mat·thew Greg·ory** (known as 'Monk Lewis') (1775–1818), English novelist and dramatist, known for the Gothic novel *The Monk* (1796). **9 Meri·wether** (1774–1809), US explorer. He was the joint leader, with William Clark, of an expedition to explore the newly acquired Louisiana Purchase; the Lewis and Clark expedition crossed the US from St. Louis to the Pacific coast (1804–6). **10 (Percy) Wynd·ham** (1882–1957), English novelist, critic, and painter. A leader of the vorticist movement, he is also known for his portraits; his satirical novels and polemical works include *The Apes of God* (1930), the trilogy *The Human Age* (1928–55), and *Time and Western Man* (1927).

lewis *noun* an iron contrivance for gripping heavy blocks of stone or concrete for lifting. [18th c.: origin unknown]

Lewis gun *noun* a light magazine-fed, gas-operated, air-cooled machine gun. [I. N. *Lewis*, US soldier d.1931, its inventor]

lewis·ite *noun* a dark oily liquid or gas that causes respiratory irritation and produces blisters, developed for use in chemical warfare. [W. L. *Lewis*, US chemist d.1943 + -ITE[1]]

Lewis with Harris (also **Lewis and Harris**) the largest and northernmost island of the Outer Hebrides in Scotland; chief town, Stornoway. The island, which is separated from the mainland by the Minch, consists of a northern part, Lewis, and a smaller, more mountainous southern part, Harris.

Lexan *noun* proprietary a transparent plastic (polycarbonate) of high impact strength, used for cockpit canopies, bulletproof screens, etc. [invented name]

lex·eme /'leksiːm/ *noun* Linguistics a basic lexical unit of a language comprising one or several words, the elements of which do not separately convey the meaning of the whole. [LEXICON + -EME]

lex·ical *adjective* **1** of the words of a language. **2** of or as of a lexicon. □ **lex·ical·ly** *adverb*

lexical item *noun* (also **lexical unit**) a word or string of words (e.g. an idiomatic phrase, a compound word, etc.) having a distinct meaning.

lexi·cog·raphy /ˌleksɪˈkɒɡrəfi/ *noun* the compiling, writing, or editing of dictionaries. □ **lexi·cog·raph·er** *noun* **lex·ico·graph·ic** *adjective* **lex·ico·graph·ical** *adjective* **lex·ico·graph·ical·ly** *adverb*

lexi·col·ogy *noun* the study of the form, history, and meaning of words. □ **lex·ico·logic·al** *adjective* **lex·ico·logic·ally** *adverb* **lexi·col·o·gist** *noun*

lexi·con /'leksɪkɒn/ *noun* **1** a dictionary, esp. of Greek, Hebrew, Syriac, or Arabic. **2 a** the vocabulary of a person, language, branch of knowledge, etc. **b** a book listing this vocabulary. [modern Latin from Greek *lexikon* (*biblion* book), neuter of *lexikos* from *lexis* word, from *legō* speak]

Lex·ing·ton 1 a city in north central Kentucky; pop. (2000) 260,512 (with Fayette). It is a noted horse-breeding centre. **2** a residential town northwest of Boston, Massachusetts; pop. (2000) 30,355. It was the scene in 1775 of the first battle in the American Revolution.

lexis /'leksɪs/ *noun* **1** words, vocabulary. **2** the total stock of words in a language. [Greek: see LEXICON]

lex loci /leks 'loːsaɪ/ *noun* Law the law of the country in which a transaction is performed, a tort is committed, or a property is situated. [Latin]

lex tali·onis /ˌleks taliˈoːnɪs/ *noun* the law of retaliation, whereby a punishment resembles the offence committed, in kind and degree. [Latin]

ley[1] /leɪ/ *noun* esp. *Brit.* a field temporarily under grass. [Middle English (originally adj.), perhaps from Old English, related to LAY[1], LIE[1]]

ley[2] /leɪ, liː/ *noun* (in full **ley line**) (in the UK) one of a network of hypothetical lines or ancient tracks connecting prehistoric sites etc. [variant of LEA]

Ley·den see LEIDEN.

Ley·den jar /'laɪdən/ *noun* an early form of capacitor consisting of a glass jar with layers of metal foil on the outside and inside. [LEYDEN var. of LEIDEN where it was invented (1745)]

Ley·rac /leɪˈrak/ **Mo·nique** (born Monique Tremblay) (b.1928), Canadian singer and actress, known as an interpreter of Québécois popular music.

Leyte /'leɪti/ an island in the central Philippines; pop. (2000) 1,952,496; chief town, Tacloban.

lez·zie *noun offensive* a lesbian. [abbreviation]

LF *abbreviation* low frequency.

LGen *abbreviation Cdn* LIEUTENANT GENERAL.

LH *abbreviation Biochem.* LUTEINIZING HORMONE.

l.h. *abbreviation* left hand.

Lhasa[1] /'lasə/ the capital of Tibet; pop. (1999) 121,568. It is situated in the N Himalayas at an altitude of 3600 m (*c.*11,800 ft.), on a tributary of the Brahmaputra. Its inaccessibility and the hostility of the Tibetan Buddhist priests to foreign visitors—to whom Lhasa was closed until the 20th c.—earned it the title of the Forbidden City. The spiritual centre of Tibetan Buddhism, it was the seat of the Dalai Lama until 1959, when direct Chinese administration was imposed on the city.

Lhasa[2] /'lasə/ *noun* (in full **Lhasa Apso** /apsoː/ *pl.* **Apsos**) a breed of small long-coated dog, often gold or grey and white. [LHASA[1], second term from Tibetan]

LI *abbreviation* **1** Light Infantry. **2** (in the US) Long Island.

Li *symbol Chem.* the element lithium.

lia·bil·ity *noun* (*pl.* **-ities**) **1** the state of being liable. **2** a person or thing that causes one problems or puts something at risk. **3** what a person or company is liable for, esp. (in *pl.*) debts or pecuniary obligations.

liability insurance *noun* insurance that covers compensation payments and court costs for which a policyholder is legally liable because of claims for injury to other people or damage to their property resulting from the policyholder's negligence.

li·able /'laɪəbəl/ *predicative adjective* **1** legally bound. **2** (foll. by *to*) subject to (a tax or penalty). **3** (foll. by *to* + infin.) under an obligation. **4** (foll. by *to*) exposed or open to (something undesirable). **5** (foll. by *to* + infin.) apt, likely (*these sorts of people are liable to suffer from depression*). **6** (foll. by *for*) answerable. [Middle English perhaps from Anglo-French from Old French *lier* from Latin *ligare* bind]

li·aise /liˈeɪz/ *intransitive verb* (foll. by *with*, *between*) establish co-operation, act as a link. [back-formation from LIAISON]

li·aison /liˈeɪzɒn/ *noun* **1 a** communication or co-operation, esp. between groups within an organization. **b** a person or association coordinating the co-operation of different groups. **2** an illicit sexual relationship. **3** the binding or thickening agent of a sauce. **4** the sounding of an ordinarily silent final consonant before a word beginning with a vowel (or a mute *h* in French). [French from *lier* bind, from Latin *ligare*]

liaison officer *noun* **1** an officer acting as a link between allied forces or units of the same force. **2** a person whose job is to promote communication between different groups within an organization or between organizations and the public etc.

li·ana /liˈanə/ *noun* (also **liane** /-ˈan/) any of several climbing and twining plants of tropical forests. [French *liane*, *lierne* clematis, of uncertain origin]

Liao /ljaʊ/ a dynasty which ruled much of Manchuria and part of NE China AD 947–1125.

Liao·dong Peninsula /ljaʊˈdʊŋ/ a peninsula in NE China, which extends southward into the Yellow Sea between Bo Hai and Korea Bay. It contains the major port and industrial centre of Luda, and forms part of Liaoning province.

Liao·ning /ljaʊˈnɪŋ/ a province of NE China, bordered on the east by N Korea; capital, Shenyang.

Liao River /ljaʊ/ a river of NE China, which rises in Inner Mongolia and flows about 1 450 km (900 miles) east and south to the Gulf of Liaodong at the head of the gulf of Bo Hai.

liar *noun* a person who tells a lie or lies, esp. habitually.

Liard River /'liːɑrd, liːˈɑrd/ a river, 1 115 km long, which rises in the Pelly Mountains in south central Yukon and flows southeastward through Watson Lake and into the Rocky Mountains of BC, where it turns northeastward and flows into the NWT to join the Mackenzie River at Fort Simpson. [French, = cottonwood (poplar) tree, so called because these trees were abundant along the riverbank]

lias /'laɪəs/ *noun* **1** (**Lias**) *Geol.* the lower strata of the Jurassic system of rocks, consisting of shales and limestones rich in fossils. **2** a blue limestone rock found in SW England. □ **Lias·sic** /laɪˈasɪk/ *adjective* (in sense 1). [Old French *liois* hard limestone, prob. from Germanic]

li·at·ris /laɪˈatrɪs/ *noun* any of various N American plants of the genus *Liatris*, of the composite family, cultivated for their long spikes of purple or white flower heads. *Also called* BLAZING STAR. [19th c.: origin unknown]

Lib. *abbreviation* Liberal.

lib *noun informal* **1** liberation (*women's lib*). **2** a liberal. **3** (**Lib**) a Liberal. [abbreviation]

li·ba·tion /laɪˈbeɪʃən/ *noun* **1 a** the pouring out of a drink offering to a god. **b** such an offering. **2** *jocular* a drink. [Latin *libatio* from *libare* pour as offering]

lib·ber *noun informal* **1** an advocate of women's liberation. **2** an advocate of the liberation of a specified group (*animal libbers*).

Libby, Wil·lard Frank (1908–80), US chemist, who was awarded the 1960 Nobel Prize for chemistry for his discovery of radiocarbon dating.

Lib Dem *noun Brit. informal* a Liberal Democrat. [abbreviation]

libel /ˈlaɪbəl/ ● *noun* **1** *Law* **a** a published false statement damaging to a person's reputation (*compare* SLANDER 3). **b** the act or crime of publishing this. **2 a** a false and defamatory written statement. **b** (foll. by *on*) a thing that brings discredit by misrepresentation etc. (*the portrait is a libel on him; the book is a libel on human nature*). ● *transitive verb* (**libelled, libel·ling**; esp. *US* **libeled, libel·ing**) **1** defame by libellous statements. **2** accuse falsely and maliciously. **3** *Law* publish a libel against. □ **libel·ler** *noun* [Old French from Latin *libellus* diminutive of *liber* book]

libel·lous /ˈlaɪbələs/ *adjective* (also **libel·ous**) containing or constituting a libel. □ **libel·lous·ly** *adverb* (also **libel·ous·ly**).

Lib·erace /ˌlɪbəˈrɑːtʃi/ (full name Wladziu Valentino Liberace) (1919–87), US pianist and entertainer, who was known for his romantic arrangements of popular piano classics and for his flamboyant costumes.

lib·er·al ● *adjective* **1 a** given freely. **b** ample, abundant. **2** (often foll. by *with*) giving freely, generous, not sparing. **3** open-minded, not prejudiced. **4** not strict or rigorous; (of interpretation) not literal. **5** for general broadening of the mind, not professional or technical (*liberal education*). **6 a** favouring a relaxing of social traditions and a significant role for the state in matters of economics and social justice. **b** favouring individual liberty and limited government involvement in economic affairs. **7** (**Liberal**) of or characteristic of Liberals or a Liberal Party. **8** *Theol.* regarding many traditional beliefs as dispensable, invalidated by modern thought, or liable to change (*liberal Protestant; liberal Judaism*). ● *noun* **1** a person of liberal views. **2** (**Liberal**) a supporter or member of a Liberal Party. □ **lib·er·al·ly** *adverb*

lib·er·al·ness *noun* [Middle English, originally = befitting a free man, from Old French from Latin *liberalis* from *liber* free (man)]

liberal arts *plural noun* **1** *N Amer.* the humanities, esp. as studied at university, leading to a broad general education. **2** *hist.* the medieval trivium and quadrivium.

Liberal-Conserva·tive Party *noun Cdn hist.* the dominant political party of the Province of Canada, formed in the mid-19th c. as a coalition of moderate Reformers and Tories and holding power for most of the period leading to Confederation, which it strongly promoted.

Liberal Democrats *plural noun* (in the UK) a party formed from the Liberal Party and the Social Democratic Party. Founded in 1988 as the Social and Liberal Democrats, it changed its name in 1989.

lib·er·al·ism *noun* **1** a political and social philosophy emphasizing the freedom of the individual, democratic government characterized by progress and reform, and the protection of civil liberties. **2** the quality of being liberal; open-mindedness. **3** (**Liberalism**) the principles and practices of a Liberal party.

lib·er·al·ity *noun* **1** generosity. **2** respect for political, moral, or religious views which one does not agree with.

lib·er·al·ize *transitive & intransitive verb* (also esp. *Brit.* **-ise**) make or become more liberal or less strict. □ **lib·er·al·iz·a·tion** *noun* **lib·er·al·iz·er** *noun*

Liberal Party 1 (in Canada) one of the two historically most important political parties, generally advocating a centrist position. **2** (in the UK) a political party advocating liberal policies. ¶ In the UK the name was discontinued in official use in 1988, when the party regrouped with others to form the Social and Liberal Democrats (*see* LIBERAL DEMOCRATS).

Liberal Unionist *noun* (in the UK) a member of a group of Liberal MPs who left the party in 1886 because of Gladstone's support for Irish Home Rule, first forming an alliance with the Conservative Party, then merging officially with them in 1909 as the Conservative and Unionist Party.

lib·er·ate *transitive verb* **1** (often foll. by *from*) set at liberty, set free.

2 free (a country etc.) from an oppressor or an enemy occupation. **3** (often as **lib·er·at·ed** *adjective*) free (a person or group) from rigid social conventions or stigmas. **4** *slang jocular* steal. **5** *Chem.* release (esp. a gas) from a state of combination. □ **lib·er·ator** *noun* **lib·er·atory** *adjective* [Latin *liberare liberat-* from *liber* free]

lib·er·ation *noun* **1** the act or an instance of liberating; the state of being liberated. **2** the freeing of a person or group from restrictive social conventions. □ **lib·er·ation·ist** *noun & adjective*

liberation theology *noun Christianity* a theory which interprets liberation from social, political, and economic oppression as an anticipation of ultimate salvation.

Li·beria /laɪˈbɪəriə/ a country on the Atlantic coast of West Africa; pop. (est. 2002) 3,288,198; capital, Monrovia. Liberia was founded in 1822 as a settlement for freed slaves from the US, although indigenous peoples form the majority of the population. □ **Li·ber·ian** *adjective & noun* [Latin *liber* free]

lib·er·tar·ian /ˌlɪbərˈteriən/ ● *noun* **1** an advocate of liberty, esp. of an almost absolute freedom of expression and action. **2** a believer in free will (*opp.* NECESSITARIAN). ● *adjective* believing in free will. □ **lib·er·tar·ian·ism** *noun*

lib·er·tine /ˈlɪbərˌtiːn, -ˌtaɪn/ ● *noun* **1** a man who behaves without moral principles or a sense of responsibility, esp. in sexual matters. **2** a free thinker on religion. **3** a person who follows his or her own inclinations in spite of social conventions. ● *adjective* **1** licentious, dissolute. **2** freethinking. **3** following one's own inclinations. □ **lib·er·tin·age** *noun* **lib·er·tin·ism** *noun* [Latin *libertinus* freedman, from *libertus* made free, from *liber* free]

lib·er·ty *noun* (*pl.* **-ties**) **1 a** freedom from captivity, imprisonment, slavery, or despotic control. **b** a personification of this. **2 a** the right or power to do as one pleases. **b** (foll. by *to* + infin.) right, power, opportunity, permission. **c** *Philos.* freedom from control by fate or necessity. **3** (usu. in *pl.*) a right, privilege, or immunity, enjoyed by prescription or grant. **4** setting aside of rules or convention, esp. concerning intimacy (*permitted no liberties*). **5** *Naut.* leave of absence. □ **at liberty 1** free, not imprisoned (*set at liberty*). **2** (foll. by *to* + infin.) entitled, permitted. **3** available, disengaged. **take liberties 1** (often foll. by *with*) behave in an unduly familiar manner. **2** (foll. by *with*) deal freely or superficially with rules or facts. **take the liberty** (foll. by *to* + infin., or *of* + verbal noun) presume, venture. [Old French *liberté* from Latin *libertas -tatis*, from *liber* 'free']

liberty hall *noun* a place where one may do as one likes.

liberty of the subject *noun* the rights of a subject under constitutional rule.

Liberty ship *noun hist.* a prefabricated US-built freighter of the Second World War.

li·bid·in·ous /lɪˈbɪdɪnəs/ *adjective* lustful. □ **li·bid·in·ous·ly** *adverb* **li·bid·in·ous·ness** *noun* [Latin *libidinosus* from *libido -dinis* lust]

li·bi·do /lɪˈbiːˌdoʊ/ *noun* (*pl.* **-dos**) **1** the sexual drive or instinct. **2** *Psych.* psychic drive or energy inherent in instinctive mental desires and drives. □ **li·bid·in·al** /lɪˈbɪdɪnəl/ *adjective* **li·bid·in·al·ly** *adverb* [Latin: see LIBIDINOUS]

Li Bo see LI PO.

Lib·ra /ˈliːbrə/ *noun* **1** a constellation near Virgo, traditionally regarded as contained in the figure of scales. **2 a** the seventh sign of the zodiac. **b** a person born when the sun is in this sign, usu. between 23 September and 22 October. □ **Lib·ran** *noun & adjective* [Latin, originally = pound weight]

li·brar·ian /laɪˈbreriən/ *noun* **1** a person professionally trained in library science. **2** a person in charge of, or an assistant in, a library. □ **li·brar·ian·ship** *noun*

li·brary /ˈlaɪˌbreri/ *noun* (*pl.* **-ies**) **1 a** a collection of books, periodicals, recordings, electronic reference materials, etc. for use by the public or by members of a group. **b** a person's collection of books. **2** a room or building containing a collection of books (for reading or reference rather than for sale). **3 a** a similar collection of films, records, computer routines, genetic material, etc. **b** the place where these are kept. **4** a series of books issued by a publisher in similar bindings etc., usu. as a set. **5** a public institution charged with the care of a collection of books, films, etc. [Old French *librairie* from Latin *libraria* (*taberna* shop), fem. of *librarius* bookseller's, of books, from *liber libri* book]

library card *noun* a card entitling the bearer to borrow books from a library.

Library of Congress Classification *noun N Amer.* a classification system for library holdings based on that of the Library of Congress in Washington and used in most N American academic libraries. Abbr.: **LC**.

library school *noun* a college or a department in a university etc. teaching library science.

library science *noun* the study of the collection, organization, use, and dissemination of information resources within libraries and other information institutions.

li·bra·tion /laɪˈbreɪʃən/ *noun* an apparent oscillation of a heavenly body, esp. the moon, by which the parts near the edge of the disc are alternately in view and out of view. [Latin *libratio* from *librare* from *libra* balance]

li·bret·to /lɪˈbretoː/ *noun* (*pl.* **-tos** or **li·bret·ti** /-tiː/) **1** the text of an opera or other long musical vocal work. **2** a synopsis of the action of a ballet. □ **li·bret·tist** *noun* [Italian, diminutive of *libro* book, from Latin *liber libri*]

Libre·ville /ˈliːbrəˌvɪl/ the capital of Gabon, a port on the Atlantic coast at the mouth of the Gabon River; pop. (est. 2002) 541,000.

Lib·rium /ˈlɪbriəm/ *noun* proprietary a benzodiazepine drug used as a tranquilizer.

Libya /ˈlɪbiə/ a country in North Africa; pop. (est. 2002) 5,368,585; capital, Tripoli.

Liby·an /ˈlɪbiən, ˈlɪbjən/ ● *adjective* **1** of or relating to modern Libya. **2** of ancient N Africa west of Egypt. **3** of or relating to the Berber group of languages. ● *noun* **1 a** a native or national of modern Libya. **b** a person of Libyan descent. **2** an ancient language of the Berber group.

Lic. *abbreviation* licensed.

lice *pl.* of LOUSE 1.

li·cence *noun* (also esp. *US* **li·cense**) **1** a permit from an authority to own or use something (esp. a dog, gun, or vehicle), do something (esp. construct a building, drive a motor vehicle, or marry), or carry on a trade (esp. in liquor). **2 a** liberty of action, esp. when excessive; disregard of law or propriety, abuse of freedom. **b** licentiousness. **3** a writer's or artist's irregularity in grammar, metre, perspective, etc., or deviation from fact, esp. for effect (*poetic licence*). **4** *literary* permission (*granted them licence to do as they saw fit*). [Old French from Latin *licentia* from *licēre* be lawful: *-se* by confusion with LICENSE]

licence number *noun* N Amer. a unique sequence of numbers or letters identifying a motor vehicle.

licence plate *noun* N Amer. a plate fixed prominently to all licensed motor vehicles, bearing the licence number.

li·cense *transitive verb* (also **licence**) **1** grant a licence to (a person). **2** authorize the use of (premises) for a certain purpose, esp. the sale and consumption of alcoholic liquor. **3** authorize the publication of (a book etc.) or the performance of (a play). **4** authorize the use of a logo or proprietary name on (merchandise). □ **li·cens·able** *adjective* **li·cen·sor** *noun*

li·censed *adjective* (also **li·cenced**) **1** having a specified or appropriate licence (*licensed mechanic*). **2** (of a restaurant etc.) having a licence to sell alcoholic drinks. **3** (of a consumer product) bearing a logo, trademark, etc. which the manufacturer was licensed to use. **4** (of a Baptist preacher) authorized by the Church to preach but not ordained.

licensed practical nurse *noun* a person who has a licence to perform basic nursing tasks under the direction of a physician or registered nurse. Abbr.: **LPN**.

li·cen·see *noun* the holder of a licence.

li·cen·sure *noun* esp. *N Amer.* the granting of a licence, esp. to carry on a profession.

li·cen·tiate /laɪˈsenʃiət, -ʃət/ *noun* **1** a holder of a certificate of competence to practise a certain profession. **2 a** a degree between that of bachelor and doctor, esp. in European universities. **b** a holder of such a degree.

li·cen·tious /laɪˈsenʃəs/ *adjective* sexually promiscuous or unrestrained. □ **li·cen·tious·ly** *adverb* **li·cen·tious·ness** *noun* [Latin *licentiosus* from *licentia*: see LICENCE]

li·chee *var.* of LYCHEE.

li·chen /ˈlaɪkən/ *noun* **1** any plant organism of the group Lichenes, composed of a fungus and an alga in symbiotic association, usu. of green, grey, or yellow tint and growing on and colouring rocks, tree trunks, roofs, walls, etc. **2** any of several types of skin disease in which small round hard lesions occur close together. □ **li·chened** *adjective* (in sense 1). **li·chen·ol·ogy** *noun* (in sense 1). **li·chen·ous** *adjective* (in sense 2). [Latin from Greek *leikhēn*]

Lich·ten·stein /ˈlɪktənˌstaɪn/ **Roy** (1923–97), US painter and sculptor.

A leading exponent of pop art, he became known in the 1960s for paintings inspired by comic strips, such as *Whaam!* (1963).

licit /ˈlɪsɪt/ *adjective* not forbidden; lawful. □ **licit·ly** *adverb* [Latin *licitus* past participle of *licēre* be lawful]

lick ● *transitive & intransitive verb* **1** *transitive* pass the tongue over, esp. to taste, eat, moisten, or (of animals) clean. **2** *transitive* bring into a specified condition or position by licking (*licked it all up*; *licked it clean*). **3 a** *transitive* (of a flame, waves, etc.) touch; play lightly over. **b** *intransitive* move gently or caressingly. **4** *informal* **a** defeat, excel. **b** surpass the comprehension of (*has got me licked*). **5** *informal* thrash. **6** *N Amer.* solve (a problem); overcome (a difficulty). ● *noun* **1** an act of licking with the tongue. **2** = SALT LICK. **3** *informal* a fast pace (*at a lick*; *at full lick*). **4** *informal* **a** a small amount (foll. by *of*: *doesn't make a lick of sense*). **b** a hastily-done activity, esp. a wash. **5** a smart blow with a stick etc. **6** *slang Music* a short ornamental solo passage. □ **a lick and a promise** *informal* a hasty performance of a task, esp. of housecleaning etc. **lick a person's boots** (or **shoes**) toady; be servile. **lick into shape** see SHAPE. **lick one's lips** (or **chops**) **1** look forward with relish. **2** show one's satisfaction. **lick one's wounds** try to recover one's strength or confidence after defeat or disappointment. □ **lick·er** *noun* (also in combination). [Old English *liccian* from West Germanic]

licker·ish *adjective archaic* **1** lecherous. **2 a** fond of fine food. **b** greedy, longing. [Middle English *lickerous* from Old French *lecheros*: see LECHER]

lickety-split *informal* ● *adverb* at full speed; headlong. ● *attributive adjective* quick. [prob. from LICK (compare *at full lick*) + SPLIT]

lick·ing *noun informal* **1** a thrashing. **2** a defeat.

lick·spit·tle *noun* a toady.

lic·o·rice /ˈlɪkərɪʃ, ˈlɪkrɪʃ/ *noun* (also **liquorice**) **1** the leguminous plant *Glycyrrhiza glabra*. **2** a black substance extracted from its root, used as a sweet and in medicine. **3** candy flavoured with this, usu. in long black rubbery strips. **4** a rubbery candy similar to this, in any of several flavours and colours. [Anglo-French *lycorys*, Old French *licoresse* from Late Latin *liquiritia* from Greek *glukurrhiza* from *glukus* sweet + *rhiza* root]

licorice root *noun* N Amer. **1** a leguminous plant, *Glycyrrhiza lepidota* of western and central N America. Also called WILD LICORICE. **2** a leguminous plant, the circumboreal *Hedysarum alpinum*. Also called BEAR ROOT, HEDYSARUM.

licorice whip *noun* N Amer. a long thin strand of licorice candy.

lic·tor /ˈlɪktər/ *noun* (usu. in *pl.*) *Rom. Hist.* an officer attending the consul or other magistrate, bearing the fasces, and executing sentence on offenders. [Latin, perhaps related to *ligare* bind]

lid *noun* **1** a hinged or removable cover, esp. for the top of a container. **2** = EYELID. **3** *informal* a restraint, check, or brake (*keep a lid on the information*). **4** the operculum of a shell or a plant. **5** *slang* a hat or helmet. □ **blow the lid off** *informal* expose (a scandal etc.). **put a lid on it** *informal* stop talking. □ **lid·ded** *adjective* (also in combination). **lid·less** *adjective* [Old English *hlid* from Germanic]

lidar /ˈlaɪdɑr/ *noun* a detection system which works on the principle of radar, but uses light from a laser. [blend of LIGHT¹ + RADAR]

Lido /ˈliːdoː/ **1** (in full **Lido di Mala·moc·co** /di ˌmaləˈmɒkoː/) an island reef off the coast of NE Italy, in the N Adriatic. It separates the Lagoon of Venice from the Gulf of Venice. **2** (also **the Lido**) a town and beach resort in NE Italy, on the Lido reef opposite Venice; pop. (est. 2000) 18,800. [from Latin *litus* shore]

lido /ˈliːdoː, ˈlaɪ-/ *noun* (*pl.* **lidos**) *Brit.* a public open-air swimming pool or beach. [Italian from LIDO 2]

lido·caine /ˈlaɪdəˌkeɪn/ *noun Pharm.* a local anaesthetic for the gums, mucous membranes, or skin, usu. given by injection. [from ACETANILIDE + -O- + -CAINE]

Lie /ˈliː/ **Tryg·ve (Halv·dan)** (1896–1968), Norwegian Labour politician and first Secretary-General of the United Nations 1946–52.

lie¹ ● *intransitive verb* (**lying**; *past* **lay**; *past participle* **lain**) **1** be in or assume a horizontal position on a supporting surface; be at rest on something. **2** (of a thing) rest flat on a surface (*snow lay on the ground*). **3** (of abstract things) remain undisturbed or undiscussed etc. (*let matters lie*). **4 a** be kept or remain or be in a specified, esp. concealed, state or place (*lie hidden*; *lie in wait*; *malice lay behind those words*; *they lay dying*; *the books lay unread*; *the money is lying in the bank*). **b** (of abstract things) exist, reside; be in a certain position or relation (foll. by *in*, *with*, etc.: *the answer lies in education*; *my sympathies lie with the family*). **5 a** be situated or stationed (*the village lay to the east*; *the ships are lying off the coast*). **b** (of a road, route, etc.) lead (*the road lies over mountains*). **c** be spread out to view (*the desert lay before us*). **6** (of the dead) be buried in a grave. **7** (foll. by *with*) *archaic* have sexual intercourse. **8** *Law* be admissible or sustainable (*the objection will not lie*). **9** (of a game bird) not rise. ● *noun* **1 a** the way or direction or position in which a thing lies. **b** *Golf* the position of a golf ball when about to be struck. **2** the place of cover of an animal or a bird. □ **as far as in me lies** to the best of my power. **let lie** not raise (a controversial matter etc.) for discussion etc. **lie ahead** be going to happen; be in store. **lie around** (or **about**) be left carelessly out of place. **lie back** recline so as to rest. **lie down** assume a lying position; have a short rest. **lie heavy** cause discomfort or anxiety. **lie in 1** *Brit.* remain in bed in the morning. **2** *archaic* be brought to bed in childbirth. **lie in state** (of a deceased great personage) be laid in a public place of honour before burial. **lie low 1** keep quiet or unseen. **2** be discreet about one's intentions. **lie off** *Naut.* stand some distance from shore or from another ship. **lie over** be deferred. **lie to** *Naut.* come almost to a stop facing the wind. **lie up** (of a ship) go into dock or be out of commission. **lie with** (often foll. by *to* + infin.) be the responsibility of (a person) (*it lies with you to answer*). **take lying down** (usu. with *neg.*) accept (defeat, rebuke, etc.) without resistance or protest etc. [Old English *licgan* from Germanic]

lie² ● *noun* **1** an intentionally false statement (*tell a lie*; *pack of lies*). **2** imposture; false belief (*live a lie*). ● *transitive & intransitive verb* (**lies**, **lied**, **lying**) **1** *intransitive* **a** tell a lie or lies (*they lied to me*). **b** (of a thing) be deceptive (*the camera cannot lie*). **2** *transitive* (usu. *reflexive*; foll. by *into*, *out of*) get (oneself) into or out of a situation by lying (*lied my way out of danger*). □ **give the lie to** serve to show the falsity of (a supposition etc.). **lie through one's teeth** lie brazenly. [Old English *lyge lēogan* from Germanic]

Lieb·frau·milch /ˈliːbfraʊmɪlk/ *noun* a light white wine from the Rhine region. [German from *Liebfrau* the Virgin Mary, the patroness of the convent where it was first made + *Milch* milk]

Liebig /ˈliːbɪx/ **Jus·tus von, Baron** (1803–73), German chemist and educator. He applied chemistry to physiology and agriculture, stressed the importance of artificial fertilizers, and developed techniques for quantitative organic analysis.

Lieb·knecht /ˈliːp‚knɛkt/ **Karl** (1871–1919), German socialist and revolutionary leader. With Rosa Luxemburg he founded the Spartacus League (1916) and the German Communist Party (1918); he and Luxemburg were assassinated during an unsuccessful Communist uprising.

Liech·ten·stein /ˈliːxtən‚staɪn/ a small independent principality in the Alps, between Switzerland and Austria; pop. (est. 2002) 32,842; capital, Vaduz. Liechtenstein is economically integrated with Switzerland. □ **Liech·ten·stein·er** *noun*

lied /liːd, liːt/ *noun* (pl. **lieder** /ˈliːdər/) a type of German song, esp. of the Romantic period, usu. for solo voice with piano accompaniment. [German]

lie detector *noun* an instrument for determining whether a person is telling the truth by testing for physiological changes considered to be symptomatic of lying.

lie-down *noun* a short rest.

lief /liːf/ *adverb archaic* gladly, willingly. (usu. **had lief, would lief**) [originally as adj. from Old English *lēof* dear, pleasant, from Germanic, related to LEAVE², LOVE]

Liège /liˈɛʒ/ **1** a province of E Belgium. **2** its capital city; pop. (est. 2002) 184,300. Situated at the junction of the Meuse and Ourthe rivers, it is a major river port and industrial centre.

liege /liːdʒ, liːʒ/ usu. *hist.* ● *adjective* (of a superior) entitled to receive or (of a vassal) bound to give feudal service or allegiance. ● *noun* **1** (in full **liege lord**) a feudal superior or sovereign. **2** (usu. in *pl.*) a vassal or subject. [Old French *lige, liege* from medieval Latin *laeticus*, prob. from Germanic]

lie-in *noun Brit.* a prolonged stay in bed in the morning.

lien /liːn, ˈliːən/ *noun Law* a right over another's property to protect a debt charged on that property. [French from Old French *loien* from Latin *ligamen* bond, from *ligare* bind]

lie of the land *noun esp. Brit.* = LAY OF THE LAND.

lieu /luː, ljuː/ *noun Cdn* (*attributive*: *lieu time*) designating time taken off work in compensation for overtime worked. □ **in lieu 1** instead. **2** (foll. by *of*) in the place of. [French from Latin *locus* place]

Lieut. *abbreviation* Lieutenant.

lieu·ten·ant /lɛfˈtɛnənt, luː-/ *noun* **1** a deputy or substitute acting for a superior (*the prime minister's Quebec lieutenant*). **2** (also **Lieutenant**; abbr.: **Lt** *Cdn*, **Lt.**, or **Lieut.**) **a** (in the Canadian Army and Air Force and the British Army) an officer next in rank below captain. **b** (in the Canadian Navy and other navies) an officer next in rank below

lieutenant commander, equivalent to a captain in the other commands. Abbr.: **Lt(N)**. **3** (in Quebec and the US) a police officer next in rank below captain. **4** (in the Royal Newfoundland Constabulary) an officer of a rank between staff sergeant and inspector. □ **lieu·ten·ancy** *noun* (*pl.* **-cies**). [Old French (as LIEU, TENANT)] ¶ The pronunciation /lɛfˈtɛnənt/ is used in the Canadian Forces. Many Canadians object to /luːˈtɛnənt/ as being American, but outside of the Armed Forces, it is probably somewhat more common amongst Canadians than /lɛfˈtɛnənt/, except for the word *Lieutenant-Governor*, where usage is more equally divided.

lieutenant colonel *noun* (also **Lieutenant Colonel**) an officer ranking next below colonel and above major. Abbr.: **LCol** *Cdn* or **Lt. Col.**

lieutenant commander *noun* (also **Lieutenant Commander**) a naval officer ranking below a commander and above a lieutenant. Abbr.: **LCdr** *Cdn* or **Lt. Cmdr.**

lieutenant general *noun* (also **Lieutenant General**) (in the Canadian or US Army or Air Force and other armies) an officer ranking above a major general. Abbr.: **LGen** *Cdn* or **Lt. Gen.**

lieu·tenant-govern·or *noun* (*pl.* **lieu·tenant-govern·ors**) **1** (**Lieutenant-Governor**) *Cdn* the representative of the Crown in a province. Abbr.: **Lt.-Gov. 2** the acting or deputy governor of a state, province, etc., under a governor or Governor General.

LIF /lɪf/ *abbreviation Cdn* LIFE INCOME FUND.

life *noun* (*pl.* **lives**) **1** the condition which distinguishes active animals and plants from inorganic matter, including the capacity for growth, functional activity, and continual change preceding death. **2 a** living things and their activity (*insect life*; *is there life on Mars?*). **b** human presence or activity (*no sign of life*). **c** the human condition; existence (*such is life*). **3 a** the period during which life lasts, or the period from birth to the present time or from the present time to death (*have done it all my life*; *will regret it all my life*; *life membership*). **b** the duration of a thing's existence or of its ability to function; validity, efficacy, etc. (*the battery has a life of two years*). **4 a** a person's state of existence as a living individual (*sacrificed their lives*; *took many lives*). **b** a living person (*many lives were lost*). **c** life seen as a right to which the unborn are entitled (*pro-life*). **5 a** an individual's occupation, actions, or fortunes; the manner of one's existence (*that would make life easy*; *start a new life*). **b** a particular aspect of this (*how's your love life?*; *private life*). **c** one's romantic life (*is there someone in your life?*). **6** the active part of existence; the business and pleasures of the world (*travel is the best way to see life*). **7** earthly or supposed future existence (*this life and the next*). **8 a** energy, liveliness, animation (*full of life*; *put some life into it*). **b** an animating influence (*was the life of the party*). **9** the living, esp. nude, form or model (*life drawing classes*). **10** a written account of a person's life; a biography. **11** *informal* a sentence of imprisonment for life (*they were all serving life*). **12** a chance; a fresh start (*cats have nine lives*). □ **come to life 1** emerge from unconsciousness or inactivity; begin operating. **2** (of an inanimate object) assume an imaginary animation. **for dear** (or **one's**) **life** as if or in order to escape death; as a matter of extreme urgency (*hanging on for dear life*; *run for your life*). **for life** for the rest of one's life. **for the life of** (foll. by personal pronoun) even if (one's) life depended on it (*cannot for the life of me remember*). **get a life** begin to live a meaningful or useful life. **give one's life 1** (foll. by *for*) die; sacrifice oneself. **2** (foll. by *to*) dedicate oneself. **large as life** *informal* in person, esp. prominently (*stood there large as life*). **larger than life 1** exaggerated. **2** (of a person) having an exuberant personality. **life and limb** life and personal health and safety (*she would risk life and limb to save him*). **lose one's life** be killed. **not on your life** *informal* most certainly not. **save a person's life 1** prevent a person's death. **2** save a person from serious difficulty. **take one's life in one's hands** take a crucial personal risk. **to the life** true to the original. [Old English *līf* from Germanic]

life-and-death *adjective* **1** determining life or death (*a life-and-death struggle*). **2** vitally important.

life assurance *noun esp. Brit.* = LIFE INSURANCE. ¶ In Canada used only in proper names of some life insurance companies.

life·belt *noun* a belt of buoyant or inflatable material for keeping a person afloat in water.

life·blood *noun* **1** the blood, as being necessary to life. **2** the vital factor or influence.

life·boat *noun* a small rescue or safety boat for use during emergencies at sea.

life·buoy /ˈlaɪfbɔɪ/ *noun* a buoyant support (usu. a ring) for keeping a person afloat in water, esp. in an emergency.

life coach *noun* a person who gives professional guidance on how to attain one's social, work-related, or personal goals. □ **life coaching** *noun*

life cycle *noun* **1** the series of developmental stages through which an organism passes, from one state to the same state in the next generation. **2** the series of developmental stages of any thing, from beginning to end.

life event *noun* an event that causes a major change in a person's life, e.g. the death of a spouse, marriage, etc.

life expectancy *noun* the average period that a person or other organism may expect to live.

life force *noun* the vital force which gives energy, inspiration, etc. to a living being.

life form *noun* an organism.

life-giving *adjective* that sustains life or uplifts and revitalizes.

life·guard *noun* an expert swimmer employed to rescue swimmers from drowning. □ **life·guard·ing** *noun*

Life Guards *plural noun* (in the UK) a regiment of the royal household cavalry.

life history *noun* the story of the development of a person or thing, from beginning to end.

life income fund *noun Cdn* a tax-sheltered fund providing annual income to its holder, not falling below an established minimum percentage of the fund, but also not exceeding a maximum payment. Abbr.: **LIF**.

life insurance *noun* insurance for a sum to be paid to named beneficiaries on the death of the insured person.

life jacket *noun* a buoyant or inflatable jacket for keeping a person afloat in water, esp. in an emergency.

life·less *adjective* **1** lacking life; no longer living; dead. **2** unconscious. **3** lacking movement or vitality. □ **life·less·ly** *adverb* **life·less·ness** *noun*

life·like *adjective* closely resembling the person or thing represented. □ **life·like·ness** *noun*

life·line *noun* **1 a** a rope etc. used for life-saving, e.g. that attached to a lifebuoy. **b** a diver's signalling line. **2 a** a sole means of communication or transport. **b** a vital source of aid or sustenance. **3** a fold in the palm of the hand, regarded as significant in palmistry. **4** an emergency telephone counselling service.

life list *noun* a record of all species sightings made by a birdwatcher etc. in a lifetime.

life·long *adjective* lasting a lifetime.

life member *noun* a person who has lifelong membership of a society etc.

life of Riley *noun* a carefree or comfortable existence. [20th c.: origin unknown]

life-or-death *adjective* = LIFE-AND-DEATH.

life partner *noun* a person engaged in a permanent sexual and romantic relationship with another.

life peer *noun Brit.* a peer whose title lapses on death.

life preserver *noun* **1** a life jacket etc. **2** *Brit.* a short stick with a heavily loaded end.

lif·er *noun slang* **1** a person serving a life sentence. **2** a person seemingly destined to remain in the same job, position, etc. for life.

life raft *noun* an inflatable or timber etc. raft for use in an emergency instead of a boat.

life·saver *noun* **1** a buoyant ring for keeping a person afloat in an emergency. **2** *informal* a thing that saves one from serious difficulty (*your letter was a lifesaver!*). □ **life-saving** *noun & adjective*

life sciences *plural noun* biology and related subjects.

life sentence *noun* **1** a sentence of imprisonment for life. **2** (in Canada) a jail sentence of 25 years. **3** an illness or commitment etc. perceived as a continuing threat to one's freedom.

life-sized *adjective* (also **life-size**) of the same size as the person or thing represented.

life skills *plural noun* the basic skills needed to function normally in society.

life·span *noun* the length of time for which a person or creature lives, or for which a thing exists or is functional.

life story *noun* the story of a person's life, esp. told at tedious length.

life·style *noun* **1** the particular way of life of a person or group; a way or style of living. **2** (*attributive*) of or relating to a particular way of living, esp. designating advertising, products, etc. designed to appeal to a consumer by association with a particular, desirable lifestyle.

lifestyle drug *noun* a drug used to treat a condition that is not (necessarily) life-threatening but that has a significant impact on the quality of life.

life-support ● *attributive adjective* (of equipment or a system of machines) allowing vital functions, such as breathing, to continue in an adverse environment or during severe disability. ● *noun* a life-support system (*has been on life-support for a week*).

life's work *noun* (also **life work**) the work of a lifetime; a task, project, etc. pursued throughout one's life.

life-threaten·ing *adjective* (of an illness etc.) that endangers life.

life·time *noun* **1** the duration of a person's life. **2** the duration of a thing or its usefulness. **3** *informal* an exceptionally long time. □ **of a lifetime** such as does not occur more than once in a person's life (*the chance of a lifetime; the journey of a lifetime*).

life·way *noun esp. Anthropology* a way of life or lifestyle, esp. of a specific group or community.

Lif·fey River a river of E Ireland, which flows for 80 km (50 miles) from the Wicklow Mountains to Dublin Bay. The city of Dublin is situated at its mouth.

Lif·ford /ˈlɪfɜrd/ the county town of Donegal, in the Republic of Ireland; pop. (est. 2002) 1,700.

lift ● *verb* **1** *transitive* (often foll. by *up, off, out*, etc.) raise or remove to a higher position. **2** *intransitive* go up; be raised; yield to an upward force (*the window will not lift*). **3** *transitive* give an upward direction to (the eyes or face). **4** *transitive* **a** elevate to a higher plane of thought or feeling (*the news lifted their spirits*). **b** make less heavy or dull; add interest to (something esp. artistic). **c** enhance, improve (*lifted their game in the third period*). **5** *intransitive* (of a cloud, fog, rain, etc.) rise, disperse. **6** *transitive* remove (a barrier or restriction). **7** *transitive* transport supplies, troops, etc. by air. **8** *transitive informal* **a** steal. **b** plagiarize (a passage of writing etc.). **9** *Phonetics* **a** transitive make louder; raise the pitch of. **b** *intransitive* (of the voice) rise. **10** *transitive* dig up (esp. potatoes etc.). **11** *intransitive* (of a floor) swell upwards, bulge. **12** *transitive* hold or have on high (*the church lifts its spire*). **13** *transitive* hit (a baseball, puck, etc.) into the air (*lifted one over second base*). **14** *transitive* (usu. in *passive*) perform cosmetic surgery on (esp. the face or breasts) to reduce sagging. ● *noun* **1** the act of lifting or process of being lifted. **2** a free ride in another person's vehicle (*gave them a lift*). **3 a** *Brit.* = ELEVATOR 1. **b** an apparatus for carrying persons up or down a mountain etc. (see SKI LIFT). **c** a device for lifting things. **4 a** transport by air (see AIRLIFT *noun*). **b** a quantity of goods transported by air. **5** the upward pressure which air exerts on an airfoil to counteract the force of gravity. **6** a supporting or elevating influence; a feeling of elation (*that really gave me a lift*). **7** a layer of leather in the heel of a boot or shoe, esp. to correct shortening of a leg or increase height. **8** a rise in the level of the ground. **9** a movement in which a dancer or figure skater lifts another in the air. **10** cosmetic surgery to reduce sagging. **11** an exercise consisting of lifting a limb or other part of the body repeatedly to develop strength. □ **lift down** pick up and bring to a lower position. **lift a finger** (or **hand** etc.) (in *neg.*) make the slightest effort (*didn't lift a finger to help*). **lift off 1** (of a spacecraft or rocket) rise from the launching pad. **2** (of an aircraft) rise from the runway during takeoff. **lift his leg** (of a male dog) urinate. **lift up one's head** hold one's head high with pride. **lift up one's voice** sing out. □ **lift·able** *adjective* **lift·er** *noun* [Old Norse *lypta* from Germanic]

lift·gate *noun N Amer.* (in a motor vehicle) a hinged back panel that opens upwards.

lift·off *noun* **1** the vertical takeoff of a spacecraft or rocket. **2** an aircraft's rising from the runway during takeoff.

lift ticket *noun N Amer.* (*Brit.* **lift pass**) a ticket or tag entitling the bearer to use a ski lift.

liga·ment /ˈlɪgəmənt/ *noun* **1** a short band of tough flexible fibrous connective tissue linking bones together. **2** any membranous fold keeping an organ in position. □ **liga·ment·ary** *adjective* **liga·ment·ous** *adjective* [Latin *ligamentum* bond from *ligare* bind]

lig·and /ˈlɪgənd/ *noun* **1** *Chem.* an ion or molecule attached to a metal atom by covalent bonding in which both electrons are supplied by one atom. **2** *Biochem.* a molecule that binds to another (usu. larger) molecule. [Latin *ligandus*, gerundive of *ligare* bind]

lig·ase /ˈlɪgeɪz/ *noun* an enzyme which catalyzes the linking together of two molecules, esp. with a simultaneous conversion of ATP to ADP. [Latin *ligare*, bind + -ASE]

li·gate /lɪˈgeɪt/ *transitive verb Surgery* tie up (a bleeding artery etc.). □ **li·ga·tion** *noun* [Latin *ligare ligat-*]

liga·ture /ˈlɪgətʃər/ ● *noun* **1** a tie or bandage, esp. in surgery for a bleeding artery etc. **2** *Music* a slur; a tie. **3** *Printing* two or more letters joined, e.g. æ. **4** a bond; a thing that unites. **5** the act of tying or binding. ● *transitive verb* bind or connect with a ligature. [Late Latin *ligatura* from Latin *ligare ligat-* tie, bind]

li·ger /'laɪɡər/ *noun* the offspring of a male lion and a female tiger (*compare* TIGON). [blend of LION + TIGER]

light¹ ● *noun* **1** the natural agent (electromagnetic radiation of wavelength between about 390 and 740 nm) that stimulates sight and makes things visible. **2** the medium or condition of the space in which this is present. **3** an appearance of brightness (*saw a distant light*). **4 a** a source of light, e.g. the sun, or a lamp, fire, etc. **b** an illuminated, usu. coloured electrical device used as a signal (*the red light went on to indicate a goal*). **5** (often in *pl.*) a traffic light (*went through a red light; stop at the lights*). **6 a** the amount or quality of illumination in a place (*bad light stopped play*). **b** one's fair or usual share of this (*you are standing in my light*). **7 a** a flame or spark serving to ignite (*struck a light*). **b** a device producing this (*have you got a light?*). **8** the aspect in which a thing is regarded or considered (*appeared in a new light*). **9 a** mental illumination; elucidation, enlightenment. **b** hope, happiness; a happy outcome. **c** spiritual illumination by divine truth. **10** vivacity, enthusiasm, or inspiration visible in a person's face, esp. in the eyes. **11** (in *pl.*) a person's mental powers or ability (*by Mom's lights, he'd been a success*). **12** an eminent person (*a leading light*). **13 a** the bright part of a thing; a highlight. **b** the bright parts of a picture etc. esp. suggesting illumination (*light and shade*). **14 a** a window or opening in a wall to let light in. **b** the perpendicular division of a mullioned window. **c** a pane of glass, esp. in a door. ● *verb* (*past* **lit**; *past participle* **lit** or (*attributive*) **light·ed**) **1** *transitive & intransitive* set burning or begin to burn; ignite. **2** *transitive* provide with light or lighting. **3** *transitive* show (a person) the way or surroundings with a light. ● *adjective* **1** well provided with light; not dark. **2** (of a colour) pale (*light blue; a light blue ribbon*). ● *combining form* forming compounds designating the distance travelled by light in a specified time (*light year; light-minute*). □ **bring** (or **come**) **to light** reveal or be revealed. **in a good** (or **bad**) **light** giving a favourable (or unfavourable) impression. **in** (**the**) **light of** considering; in view of; drawing information from. **light at the end of the tunnel** a long-awaited sign that a period of hardship or adversity is coming to an end. **light of one's life** usu. *jocular* a much-loved person. **the lights are on, but nobody's home** *informal* there is an absence of intelligence and sense (referring to a dull, stupid, or mentally incompetent person). **light up 1** *informal* begin to smoke a cigarette etc. **2** switch on lights or lighting; illuminate a scene. **3** (of a light or a panel etc. covered with lights) become illuminated. **4** (of the face or eyes) brighten with animation. **out like a light** deeply asleep or unconscious. **throw** (or **shed**) **light on** help to explain. □ **light·ish** *adjective* **light·less** *adjective* **light·ness** *noun* [Old English *lēoht, līht, līhtan* from Germanic]

light² ● *adjective* **1** of little weight; not heavy; easy to lift. **2 a** relatively low in weight, amount, density, intensity, etc. (*light arms; light traffic; light metal; light rain; a light breeze*). **b** deficient in weight (*light coin*). **c** (of an isotope etc.) having not more than the usual mass. **3 a** carrying or suitable for small loads (*light aircraft; light railway*). **b** (of a ship) unladen. **c** carrying only light arms, armaments, etc. (*light brigade; light infantry*). **d** (of a locomotive) with no train attached. **4 a** (of food, a meal, etc.) small in amount; easy to digest (*had a light lunch*). **b** (of a foodstuff) low in fat, cholesterol, or sugar, etc. **c** (of a foodstuff) lower in calories, fat, etc. than a comparable product. **d** (of drink) not heavy on the stomach or not strongly alcoholic. **5 a** (of entertainment, music, etc.) intended for amusement, rather than edification; not profound. **b** frivolous, thoughtless, trivial (*a light remark*). **6** (of sleep or a sleeper) easily disturbed. **7** easily borne or done (*light housekeeping*). **8** nimble; quick-moving (*a light step; light of foot; a light rhythm*). **9** (of a building etc.) graceful, elegant, delicate. **10** (of type) not heavy or bold. **11 a** free from sorrow; cheerful (*a light heart*). **b** giddy (*light in the head*). **12** (of soil) not dense; porous. **13** (of a dessert) fluffy and well-aerated. **14** *archaic* unchaste or wanton; fickle. **15** *Phonetics* (of a syllable) unstressed. ● *adverb* **1** in a light manner (*tread light; sleep light*). **2** with a minimum load or minimum luggage (*travel light*). ● *intransitive verb* (*past* and *past participle* **lit** or **light·ed**) **1** (foll. by *on, upon*) come upon or find by chance. **2** *archaic* **a** alight, descend. **b** (foll. by *on*) land on (shore etc.). □ **light into** *informal* attack. **light out** *informal* depart. **make light of** treat as unimportant. **make light work** of do a thing quickly and easily. **trip the light fantastic** *see* TRIP. □ **light·ish** *adjective* **light·ness** *noun* [Old English *lēoht, līht, līhtan*, from Germanic, the verbal sense from the idea of relieving a horse etc. of weight]

light air *noun Meteorol.* a very light wind, 1–6 km/h.

light box *noun* any apparatus with a translucent surface lit from behind, used to view slides, film, transparencies, etc.

light breeze *noun Meteorol.* **1** a light wind, 7–12 km/h. **2** any light wind.

Light Brigade, Charge of the *see* CHARGE OF THE LIGHT BRIGADE.

light bulb *noun* a glass bulb containing an inert gas and a metal filament, providing light when an electric current is passed through.

light cream *noun* **1** esp. *US* a table cream generally with 18% milk fat. **2** *Cdn* a table cream having 7% milk fat.

light-emitting diode *noun* = LED.

light·en¹ *verb* **1 a** *transitive & intransitive* make or become lighter in weight. **b** *transitive* reduce the weight or load of. **2** *transitive* bring relief to (the heart, mind, etc.). **3** *transitive* mitigate (a penalty). □ **lighten up** *informal* become less earnest or intense; relax. □ **light·en·er** *noun*

light·en² *verb* **1 a** *transitive* shed light on. **b** *transitive & intransitive* make or grow bright. **c** make less dark. **2** *intransitive* **a** shine brightly; flash. **b** emit lightning (*it is lightening*). □ **light·en·er** *noun*

light·er¹ *noun* a device for lighting cigarettes, barbecues, etc.

light·er² *noun* a boat, usu. flat-bottomed, for transferring goods from a ship to a wharf or another ship. [Middle Dutch *lichter* (as LIGHT² in the sense 'unload')]

light·er·age *noun* **1** the transference of cargo by means of a lighter. **2** a charge made for this.

lighter fluid *noun* a petrochemical fuel, esp. naphtha, used to work a cigarette lighter.

lighter-than-air *attributive adjective* (of an aircraft) weighing less than the air it displaces, e.g. a blimp.

light·fast *adjective* (of a dye, pigment, etc.) resistant to alteration on exposure to light. □ **light·fast·ness** *noun*

light-fingered *adjective* given to stealing.

light flyweight *noun* **1** a weight in amateur boxing up to 48 kg. **2** an amateur boxer of this weight.

Light·foot, Gor·don Mer·e·dith (b.1939), Canadian singer and songwriter. He became widely known in 1965 as the writer of the hit 'Early Morning Rain'. Other hit songs include 'Sundown', 'Did She Mention My Name', and 'The Wreck of the *Edmund Fitzgerald*'. He has received numerous Juno awards and was promoted from Officer to Companion of the Order of Canada in 2003.

light-footed *adjective* nimble.

light-handed *adjective* having a light, delicate, or deft touch.

light-headed *adjective* giddy, faint. □ **light-headed·ly** *adverb* **light-headed·ness** *noun*

light-heart·ed *adjective* **1** cheerful. **2** (unduly) casual, thoughtless. □ **light-heart·ed·ly** *adverb* **light-heart·ed·ness** *noun*

light heavyweight *noun* **1** the weight in some sports between middleweight and heavyweight, in the amateur boxing scale 75-81 kg: *also called* CRUISERWEIGHT. **2** an athlete of this weight.

light·house *noun* a tower or other structure containing a beacon light to warn or guide ships.

light industry *noun* the manufacture of small or light articles, esp. consumer goods.

light·ing *noun* **1** equipment on a street or in a room etc. for producing light. **2** the arrangement or effect of lights.

light·keep·er *noun* a person in charge of a lighthouse.

light·ly *adverb in senses of* LIGHT² *adjective*. □ **get off lightly** escape with little or no punishment. **take lightly** not be serious about (a thing).

light meter *noun* an instrument for measuring the intensity of the light, esp. to show the correct photographic exposure.

light middleweight *noun* **1** a weight in amateur boxing of 67-71 kg. **2** an amateur boxer of this weight.

light·ning ● *noun* a flash of bright light produced by an electric discharge between clouds or between clouds and the ground. ● *attributive adjective* very quick (*with lightning speed*). [Middle English, differentiated from *lightening*, verbal noun from LIGHTEN²]

lightning bug *noun N Amer.* a firefly.

lightning rod *noun* (also **lightning conductor**) **1** a metal rod or wire fixed to an exposed part of a building or to a mast to divert lightning into the earth or sea. **2** a person or thing that attracts criticism.

light of day *noun* **1** daylight, sunlight. **2** general notice; public attention. □ **in the cold** (**hard**) **light of day** when confronted with reality after one's initial enthusiasm has worn off. **see the light of day** (usu. with *neg.*) come into existence (*that book will never see the light of day*).

light opera *noun* = OPERETTA.

light pen *noun* **1** a pen-like photosensitive device held to the screen of a computer terminal for passing information on to it. **2** a light-emitting device used for reading bar codes.

light pollution *noun* excessive brightening of the night sky by street lights etc., esp. as obscuring the stars etc.

light·proof *adjective* (of a container, barrier, etc.) not permitting the passage of light.

lights *plural noun* the lungs of sheep, pigs, steers, etc., used as a food esp. for pets. □ **punch a person's lights out** beat a person soundly. [Middle English, noun use of LIGHT²: compare LUNG; the idiom may also be derived from LIGHT¹; it is certainly often understood in that sense]

light·ship *noun* a moored or anchored ship with a beacon light.

light show *noun* a display of changing coloured lights for entertainment.

light·some *adjective* gracefully light; nimble; merry.

lights out *noun* the time all lights are to be shut off in a dormitory etc.

light·speed *informal* ● *noun* the speed of light. ● *attributive adjective* **1** at the speed of light. **2** very fast.

light station *noun* = LIGHTHOUSE.

light stick *noun* a plastic tube containing two chemicals which when combined (by bending the tube) glow by chemical luminescence.

light table *noun* a table with a translucent top lit from below, used to view film, slides, etc.

light touch *noun* delicate or tactful treatment.

light·weight ● *adjective* **1** (of a person, animal, garment, etc.) of below average weight. **2** of little importance or influence. ● *noun* **1** a lightweight person, animal, or thing. **2 a** a weight in certain sports intermediate between featherweight and welterweight, in the amateur boxing scale 57–60 kg but differing for professionals and wrestlers. **b** an athlete of this weight. **3** a person of little influence or significance.

light welterweight *noun* **1** a weight in amateur boxing of 60-63.5 kg. **2** an amateur boxer of this weight.

light year *noun* **1** *Astronomy* the distance light travels in one mean solar year, approximately 9.46×10^{12} km (5.88×10^{12} miles). **2** (in *pl.*) a long distance or great amount.

lig·neous /ˈlɪgnɪəs/ *adjective* **1** (of a plant) woody (*opp.* HERBACEOUS 2a). **2** of the nature of wood. [Latin *ligneus* (as LIGNI-)]

ligni- /ˈlɪgnɪ/ *combining form* wood. [Latin *lignum* wood]

lig·ni·fy *transitive & intransitive verb* (**-fies**, **-fied**) *Bot.* make or become woody by the deposition of lignin. □ **lig·ni·fi·ca·tion** *noun*

lig·nin *noun Bot.* a complex organic polymer deposited in the cell walls of many plants making them rigid and woody.

lig·nite *noun* a soft brown coal showing traces of plant structure, intermediate between bituminous coal and peat. *Also called* BROWN COAL.

lig·num vitae /ˌlɪgnəm ˈvaiti, ˈviːtai/ *noun* = GUAIACUM 2a. [Latin, = wood of life]

lig·ul·ate /ˈlɪgjʊlət/ *adjective Bot.* having strap-shaped florets.

lig·ule /ˈlɪgjuːl/ *noun Bot.* a narrow projection from the top of the sheath which encloses a leaf of a grass. [Latin *ligula* strap, spoon, from *lingere* lick]

Li·gu·ria /lɪˈgjʊriə/ a coastal region of NW Italy, which extends along the Mediterranean coast from Tuscany to the border with France; capital, Genoa. In ancient times, prior to its occupation by the Celts and then the Romans, Liguria was much more extensive (see LIGURIAN *adjective* 2). [Latin, from *Ligur* Ligurian, from Greek *Ligus*]

Li·gu·rian /lɪˈgjʊriən/ ● *adjective* **1** of or relating to Liguria, its people, or their language or dialect. **2** of or relating to an ancient people inhabiting NW Italy, Switzerland, and SE Gaul and speaking a pre-Italic Indo-European language. ● *noun* **1** a native or inhabitant of ancient or modern Liguria. **2** the language of the ancient Ligurians. **3** the dialect of modern Liguria.

Li·gu·rian Sea a part of the N Mediterranean, between Corsica and the northwest coast of Italy.

li·gus·trum /lɪˈgʌstrəm/ *noun* = PRIVET. [Latin]

lik·able *var. of* LIKEABLE.

like¹ ● *adjective* (often governing a noun as if a transitive participle such as *resembling*) (**more like**, **most like**) having some or all of the qualities of another or each other or an original; alike (*in like manner; is very like her brother*). ● *preposition* **1** resembling in some way, such as; in the same class as (*good writers like Dickens*). **2** (usu. in pairs correlatively) as one is so will the other be (*like mother, like daughter*). **3** characteristic of (*it is not like them to be late*). **4** in a suitable state or mood for (doing or having something) (*felt like working; felt like a cup of tea*). **5** in the manner of; to the same degree as (*drink like a fish; sell like hotcakes; acted like an idiot*). ● *adverb* **1** *slang* so to speak (*did a quick getaway, like; as I said, like, I'm no Shakespeare*). **2** *informal* likely, probably (*as like as not*). **3** *archaic* likely (*they will come, like enough*). **4** *archaic* in the same manner (foll. by *as*: *like as the hart desireth the water brooks*). ● *conjunction informal disputed* **1** as (*cannot do it like you do*). **2** as if (*ate like they were starving*). ● *noun* **1** a counterpart; an equal; a similar person or thing (*shall not see its like again; compare like with like*). **2** (prec. by *the*) a thing or things of the same kind (*will never do the like again*). □ **and the like** and similar things; et cetera (*music, painting, and the like*). **be nothing like** be in no way similar or comparable or adequate. **like anything** *see* ANYTHING. **like** (or **as like**) **as not** *informal* probably. **like so** *informal* like this; in this manner. **the likes of** *informal* a person such as. **more like it** *informal* nearer what is required. **of like** (or **of a like**) **mind** = LIKE-MINDED. **what is he** (or **she** or **it** etc.) **like?** what sort of characteristics does he (or she, or it, etc.) have? [Middle English *lic, lik*, shortened form of Old English *gelic* ALIKE] ¶ When *like* means 'such as' (see sense 1 of the preposition), some people prefer *such as* to be used in formal contexts when more than one example is mentioned, e.g. *good writers such as Dickens, Shakespeare, and Hardy*. The use of *like* as a conjunction, e.g. *He did it like he'd never done it before*, is very common, especially in spoken English. However, there is a long tradition of opposition to this usage, and it is therefore best avoided in formal contexts by using instead *as* or *as if*.

like² ● *verb* **1** *transitive* **a** find agreeable or enjoyable or satisfactory (*like reading; like to dance*). **b** be fond of (a person). **2** *transitive* **a** choose to have; prefer (*like my coffee black; do not like such things discussed*). **b** wish for or be inclined to (*would like a cup of tea; would like to come*). **3** *transitive* (usu. in *interrogative*; prec. by *how*) feel about; regard (*how would you like it if it happened to you?*). **4** *intransitive* feel inclined; choose (*we could go out if you like*). ● *noun* (in *pl.*) the things one likes or prefers. □ **like it or not** *informal* whether it is acceptable or not. [Old English *lician* from Germanic]

-like *combining form* forming adjectives from nouns, meaning 'similar to, characteristic of' (*doglike; shell-like; tortoise-like*). ¶ In formations intended as nonce words, or not generally current, the hyphen should be used. It may be omitted when the first element is of one syllable, but nouns in *-l* always require it.

like·able *adjective* (also **likable**) pleasant; easy to like. □ **like·abil·ity** *noun* **like·able·ness** *noun* **like·ably** *adverb*

like·li·hood *noun* probability; the quality or fact of being likely. □ **in all likelihood** very probably.

like·ly ● *adjective* **1** probable; such as well might happen or be true (*it is not likely that they will come; the most likely place is Saskatoon; a likely story*). **2** (foll. by *to* + infin.) to be reasonably expected (*he is not likely to come now*). **3** promising; apparently suitable (*this is a likely spot; three likely lads*). ● *adverb* probably (*is very likely true*). ¶ Although some people consider it incorrect, use of the adverb *likely* without a qualifying adverb such as *more*, *most*, or *very* is common among educated speakers. □ **as likely as not** probably. **not likely** *informal* certainly not. □ **like·li·ness** *noun*

like-minded *adjective* having the same tastes, opinions, etc. □ **like-minded·ly** *adverb* **like-minded·ness** *noun*

lik·en *transitive verb* (foll. by *to*) represent as similar; point out the resemblance of (a person or thing to another).

like·ness *noun* **1** (foll. by *between, to*) resemblance. **2** (foll. by *of*) a semblance or guise (*in the likeness of a ghost*). **3** a portrait or representation (*is a good likeness*).

like·wise *adverb* **1** also, moreover, too. **2** similarly (*do likewise*). [for *in like wise*]

lik·ing *noun* **1** what one likes; one's taste (*is it to your liking?*). **2** (foll. by *for*) regard or fondness; taste or fancy (*had a liking for toffee*).

Likud /lɪˈkuːd/ *noun* a coalition of right-wing Israeli political parties, formed in 1973, that won power in the Israeli elections of 1977 and governed under Menachem Begin until 1984, Benjamin Netanyahu (1996–99) and Ariel Sharon since 2000. [Hebrew, = consolidation, unity]

---

uː m**oo**d   ai m**y**   əi p**i**pe   au br**ow**n   ʌu h**ou**se   ei d**ay**   ɔi b**oy**   ɑ̃ fr**an**glais   ã Canadi**en**   ɔ̃ Bray**on**   (*see over for consonants*)

li·kuta /lɪˈkuːtə/ *noun* (*pl.* **makuta**) a monetary unit of Congo (formerly Zaire), equal to one-hundredth of a zaire. [Kikongo]

li'l *adjective informal jocular* little.

lilac /ˈlaɪlək, -lɒk, -lak/ ● *noun* **1** any shrub or small tree of the genus *Syringa*, esp. *S. vulgaris* with fragrant purple, mauve, pink, or white blossoms. **2** a pale pinkish-violet colour. **3** the scent of lilac. ● *adjective* of this colour. [obsolete French from Spanish from Arabic *līlāk* from Persian *līlak*, var. of *nīlak* bluish, from *nīl* blue]

lilan·geni /ˌliːlanˈɡeini/ *noun* (*pl.* **emalangeni** /iˈmɒlan-/) the basic monetary unit of Swaziland, equal to 100 cents. [Bantu, from *li-*, singular prefix (*ema-*, plural prefix) + *-langeni* member of royal family]

L'Île-Bizard a former city in south central Quebec, on Île Bizard, now part of the city of Montreal; pop. (2001) 13,861.

L'Île-Perrot /liːlperˈoː/ a town in south central Quebec, located on Île Perrot, at the point where Lac des Deux Montagnes drains into Lac Saint-Louis; pop. (2001) 9,375. [F.-M. *Perrot*, local seigneur and governor of Montreal d.1691]

lili·aceous /ˌlɪliˈeiʃəs/ *adjective* **1** of or relating to the family Liliaceae of plants with elongated leaves growing from a corm, bulb, or rhizome, e.g. tulip, lily, or onion. **2** lily-like.

Lili·en·thal /ˈliːliənˌtɒl/ **Otto** (1848–96), German engineer and pioneering designer of gliders. He constructed a variety of flying machines, and with his brother Gustavus made over 2,000 flights in various gliders before being killed in a crash.

Lil·ith /ˈlɪlɪθ/ a female demon of Jewish folklore, who tries to kill newborn children; in the Talmud she is the first wife of Adam, dispossessed by Eve. [Hebrew, = night monster]

Liliu·oka·lani /lɪˌliːuːoːkɒˈlɒni/ **Lydia Kame·ke·ha** (1838–1917), queen of the Hawaiian Islands 1891–5, who unsuccessfully attempted to eliminate US influence and restore autocracy.

Lille /liːl/ an industrial city in N France, near the border with Belgium; pop. (1999) 184,493. With the neighbouring cities of Tourcoing and Roubaix, Lille forms one of the largest conurbations in France and is the traditional textile centre of the country.

Lil·li·pu·tian /ˌlɪlɪˈpjuːʃən/ ● *noun* a diminutive person or thing. ● *adjective* **1** tiny, diminutive. **2** of petty mind or character. [the imaginary country of *Lilliput* in Swift's *Gulliver's Travels*, inhabited by people 15 cm (6 inches) high]

Lil·loo·et /ˈlɪloːet/ *noun* (also **Lil'wat**) = STL'ATL'IMX. [the native name for Mount Currie]

Lillooet River /ˈlɪloːet/ a river in southwestern BC, 165 km long, which rises in the Coast Mountains northwest of Whistler and flows southeastward to Harrison Lake. [LILLOOET]

Li·lon·gwe /lɪˈlɒŋwei/ the capital of Malawi; pop. (est. 2002) 486,000.

lilt ● *noun* a characteristic rising and falling cadence or inflection (of a voice, accent, music, etc.). ● *intransitive verb* (esp. as **lilt·ing** *adjective*) speak or sound etc. with a lilt (*a lilting melody*). [Middle English *lilte*, *lülte*, of unknown origin]

lily *noun* (*pl.* **-ies**) **1** any bulbous plant of the genus *Lilium* with large trumpet-shaped often spotted flowers on a tall slender stem, e.g. the madonna lily and tiger lily. **2** any of several other plants of the lily family with similar flowers, e.g. the day lily. **3** the water lily. □ **lily-like** *adjective* [Old English *lilie* from Latin *lilium* prob. from Greek *leirion*]

lily-livered *adjective* cowardly.

lily of the valley *noun* (*pl.* **lilies of the valley**) any liliaceous plant of the genus *Convallaria*, with oval leaves in pairs and racemes of white bell-shaped fragrant flowers.

lily pad *noun* a floating leaf of a water lily.

lily-white *adjective* **1** as white as a lily. **2** faultless. **3** in favour of, committed to, or pertaining to a policy excluding non-whites.

Lima /ˈliːmə/ the capital of Peru; pop. (est. 2002) 1,603,500. Founded in 1535 by Francisco Pizarro, it was the capital of the Spanish colonies in S America until the 19th c.

lima bean /ˈlaɪmə/ *noun* **1** a tropical American bean plant, *Phaseolus limensis*, having large flat white edible seeds. **2** the seed of this plant. [LIMA]

limb¹ ● *noun* **1** a projecting part of a person's or animal's body such as an arm, leg, or wing. **2** a large branch of a tree. **3** a projecting part of a thing, e.g. the branch of a cross. **4** either half of an archery bow. **5** a section, element, or component part of something. ● *transitive verb* remove branches from (a tree). □ **out on a limb** alone; without supporters. **tear limb from limb** violently dismember. □ **limbed** *adjective* (also *in combination*). **limb·less** *adjective* [Old English *lim* from Germanic]

limb² *noun* **1** *Astronomy* **a** a specified edge of the sun, moon, etc. (*eastern limb*; *lower limb*). **b** the graduated edge of a quadrant etc. **2** *Bot.* the broad part of a petal, sepal, or leaf. [French *limbe* or Latin *limbus* hem, border]

lim·ber¹ ● *adjective* **1** lithe, agile, nimble. **2** flexible. ● *verb* (usu. foll. by up) **1** *transitive* make (oneself or a part of the body etc.) supple. **2** *intransitive* warm up in preparation for athletic etc. activity. □ **lim·ber·ness** *noun* [16th c.: origin uncertain]

lim·ber² ● *noun* the detachable front part of a gun carriage, consisting of two wheels, axle, pole, and ammunition box. ● *transitive verb* attach a limber to (a gun etc.). [Middle English *limo(u)r*, apparently related to medieval Latin *limonarius* from *limo -onis* shaft]

limber pine *noun* a small pine tree, *Pinus flexilis*, with tough pliant branches, which is native to the Rockies.

lim·bic /ˈlɪmbɪk/ *adjective* of or relating to a part of the brain concerned with basic emotions and instinctive actions. [French *limbique*, from Latin *limbus* 'edge']

lim·bo¹ *noun* (*pl.* **-bos**) **1** (in some Christian beliefs) the supposed abode of the souls of unbaptized infants, and of the just who died before Christ. **2** an intermediate state or condition of awaiting a decision etc. **3** a state of neglect or oblivion. [medieval Latin phr. *in limbo*, from *limbus*: see LIMB²]

lim·bo² ● *noun* (*pl.* **-bos**) a W Indian dance in which the dancer bends backwards to pass under a horizontal bar which is progressively lowered to a position just above the ground. ● *intransitive verb* dance in such a way. [a Caribbean word, perhaps = LIMBER¹]

Lim·burg a former duchy of Lorraine, divided in 1839 between Belgium and the Netherlands. It now forms a province of NE Belgium (capital, Hasselt) and a province of the SE Netherlands (capital, Maastricht).

Lim·burg·er *noun* a soft white cheese with a characteristic strong smell, originally made in Limburg. [Dutch from LIMBURG]

lime¹ ● *noun* **1** (in full **quicklime**) a white caustic alkaline substance (calcium oxide) obtained by heating limestone and used for making mortar or as a fertilizer or bleach etc. **2** (in full **slaked lime**) a white substance (calcium hydroxide) made by adding water to quicklime, used esp. in cement. **3** calcium or calcium salts, esp. calcium carbonate in soil etc. **4** *archaic* = BIRDLIME. ● *transitive verb* **1** treat (wood, skins, land, etc.) with lime. **2** *archaic* catch (a bird etc.) with birdlime. □ **limy** *adjective* (**limi·er**, **limi·est**). [Old English *līm* from Germanic: related to LOAM]

lime² ● *noun* **1 a** a rounded citrus fruit like a lemon but greener, smaller, and more acid. **b** (in full **lime tree**) the tree, *Citrus aurantifolia*, bearing this. **2** (in full **lime juice**) the juice of limes, used in drinks and cooking. **3** = LIME GREEN. ● *adjective* of this colour. [French via modern Provençal *limo*, Spanish *lima* from Arabic *līma*: compare LEMON]

lime³ *noun* **1** (in full **lime tree**) any ornamental tree of the genus *Tilia*, esp. *T. europaea* with heart-shaped leaves and fragrant yellow blossom. *Also called* LINDEN. **2** the wood of this. [alteration of *line* = Old English *lind* = LINDEN]

lime grass *var. of* LYME GRASS.

lime green ● *noun* a bright pale green colour like that of a lime (see LIME² 1a). ● *adjective* (**lime-green**) of this colour.

lime kiln *noun* a kiln for heating limestone to produce quicklime.

lime·light *noun* (prec. by *the*) the full glare of publicity; the focus of attention.

Lim·erick /ˈlɪmərɪk/ **1** a county of the Republic of Ireland, in the west in the province of Munster. **2** its county town, on the Shannon River; pop. (2002) 54,058.

lim·erick /ˈlɪmərɪk/ *noun* a humorous or comic form of five-line poem with a rhyme scheme *aabba*. [said to be from the chorus 'will you come up to Limerick?' sung between improvised verses at a gathering: from LIMERICK]

lime rickey *noun* N Amer. a carbonated lime-flavoured drink, sometimes served as a cocktail with gin. [origin uncertain: possibly after a Colonel *Rickey*]

lime·stone *noun* a sedimentary rock composed mainly of calcium carbonate, used as building material and in the making of cement.

lime·wash *noun Brit.* a mixture of lime and water for coating walls.

lime water *noun* an aqueous solution of calcium hydroxide used esp. to detect the presence of carbon dioxide.

Limey (*pl.* **Limeys**) N Amer. slang offensive ● *noun* a British person (originally a sailor) or ship. ● *adjective* British. [LIME², because of the former enforced consumption of lime juice in the Royal Navy to prevent scurvy on long sea voyages]

lim·inal /ˈlɪmɪnəl/ *adjective* **1 a** of or relating to a transitional or initial stage. **b** marginal, insignificant. **2** occupying a position on, or on both sides of, a boundary or threshold. □ **limi·nal·ity** /-ˈnalɪti/ *noun* [Latin *limin-, limen* 'threshold' + -AL]

lim·it ● *noun* **1** a point, line, or level beyond which something does not or may not extend or pass. **2** (often in *pl.*) the boundary of an area. **3** *Cdn Forestry* an area of forested land in which an individual or company has the right to fell and remove timber. **4** the greatest or smallest amount permissible or possible (*upper limit; lower limit*). **5** *Math.* a quantity which a function or sum of a series can be made to approach as closely as desired. ● *transitive verb* (**lim·it·ed, lim·it·ing**) **1** set or serve as a limit to. **2** (foll. by *to*) restrict. □ **be the limit** *informal* be intolerable or extremely irritating. **go (to) the limit 1** behave in an extreme way. **2** allow sexual intercourse. **off limits** out of bounds; forbidden. **within limits** to a moderate extent. **without limit** with no restriction. □ **lim·it·able** *adjective* **lim·it·ing** *adjective* [Latin *limes limitis* boundary, frontier]

lim·it·a·tion *noun* **1** the act or an instance of limiting; the process of being limited. **2** (often in *pl.*) a condition of limited ability (*know one's limitations*). **3** (often in *pl.*) a limiting rule or circumstance (*has its limitations*). **4** a legally specified period beyond which an action cannot be brought, or a property right is not to continue.

lim·it·ed *adjective* **1** confined within limits. **2** not great in scope or talents (*has limited experience*). **3 a** few, scanty, restricted (*a limited budget*). **b** restricted to a few examples (*limited printing*). **4** (**Limited**) *Cdn & Brit.* (after a company name) being a limited company. Abbr.: **Ltd.** **5** (of a monarchy, government, etc.) exercised under limitations of power prescribed by a constitution. **6** *N Amer.* (of a train, bus, etc.) making few stops; express. □ **lim·it·ed·ness** *noun*

limited company *noun* (also **limited liability company**) *Cdn & Brit.* a company whose owners are legally responsible only to a limited amount for its debts.

limited edition *noun* an edition of a book, or reproduction of an object, limited to some specific number of copies.

limited liability *noun Cdn & Brit.* the status of being legally responsible only to a limited amount for debts of a company.

limited partnership *noun* a partnership in which the liability of some partners is legally limited to the extent of their investment. □ **limited partner** *noun*

lim·it·er *noun* **1** a person or thing that limits something. **2** *Electronics* a device whose output is restricted to a certain range of values irrespective of the size of the input.

lim·it·less *adjective* **1** extending or going on indefinitely (*a limitless expanse*). **2** unlimited (*limitless generosity*). □ **lim·it·less·ly** *adverb* **lim·it·less·ness** *noun*

limn /lɪm/ *transitive verb* **1** paint or draw (a picture or portrait); portray (a subject). **2** *archaic* illuminate (manuscripts). **3** portray or represent (esp. a person) in words. **4** suffuse or highlight (something) with a bright colour or light. □ **lim·ner** /ˈlɪmnər/ *noun* [obsolete *lumine* illuminate, from Old French *luminer* from Latin *luminare*: see LUMEN]

lim·nol·o·gy /lɪmˈnɒlədʒi/ *noun* the study of the physical phenomena of lakes and other fresh waters. □ **lim·no·logic·al** *adjective* **lim·nol·o·gist** *noun* [Greek *limnē* lake + -LOGY]

limo *noun* (*pl.* **limos**) *informal* a limousine. [abbreviation]

Li·moges /lɪˈmoːʒ/ **1** a city in west central France, the principal city of Limousin; pop. (1999) 133,968. It has been noted since the 18th c. for the production of porcelain. **2** the porcelain and painted enamels produced there.

limon·ene /ˈlɪməniːn/ *noun* a colourless liquid hydrocarbon with a lemon-like scent, present in the oils of citrus fruits and other essential oils. [modern Latin *limonum* 'lemon' + -ENE]

limon·ite /ˈlaɪmənaɪt/ *noun* an amorphous secondary material now recognized as a mixture of hydrous ferric oxides and important as an iron ore. [German *Limonit*, prob. from Greek *leimōn* meadow, after the earlier German name *Wiesenerz* lit. 'meadow ore']

limon·ium /lɪˈmoːniəm/ *noun* = SEA LAVENDER. [Greek *leimōnion* from *leimōn* meadow]

Li·mou·sin¹ /liːmuːˈzã/ a region and former province of central France, centred on Limoges.

Li·mou·sin² /liːmuːˈzã/ *noun* a breed of white beef cattle originating in Limousin.

lim·ou·sine /ˌlɪməˈziːn, ˈlɪməˌziːn/ *noun* **1** a large luxurious automobile, often with a partition behind the driver. **2** *N Amer.* a large sedan or

minibus for carrying people over a fixed route to and from an airport etc. [French, originally a caped cloak worn in LIMOUSIN¹]

limousine liberal *noun* esp. *US derogatory* a wealthy person with liberal political views.

limp¹ ● *intransitive verb* **1** walk lamely. **2** (of a damaged ship, aircraft, etc.) proceed with difficulty. **3** (of a business, event, etc.) progress slowly or weakly (*his company limped along for years before going under last month*). **4** (of verse) be metrically defective. ● *noun* a lame walk. [related to obsolete *limphalt* 'lame', Old English *lemp-healt*]

limp² *adjective* **1** not stiff or firm; easily bent. **2** without energy or will. **3** (of a book) having a soft cover. □ **limp·ly** *adverb* **limp·ness** *noun* [18th c.: origin unknown: perhaps related to LIMP¹ in the sense 'hanging loose']

lim·pet *noun* **1** any of various marine gastropod molluscs, esp. the common limpet *Patella vulgata*, with a shallow conical shell and a broad muscular foot that sticks tightly to rocks. **2** a clinging person. [Old English *lempedu* from medieval Latin *lampreda* limpet, LAMPREY]

limpet mine *noun* a mine designed to be attached to a ship's hull and set to explode after a certain time.

lim·pid *adjective* **1** (of water, eyes, etc.) clear, transparent. **2** (of writing) clear and easily comprehended. **3** calm, tranquil. □ **lim·pid·ity** *noun* **lim·pid·ly** *adverb* **lim·pid·ness** *noun* [French *limpide* or Latin *limpidus*, perhaps related to LYMPH]

limp·kin *noun* a wading marsh bird, *Aramus guarauna*, of tropical America. [LIMP¹, with reference to the bird's limping gait]

Lim·po·po /lɪmˈpoːpoː/ a province of northern South Africa, known as Northern Province until 2002; capital Polokwane.

Lim·po·po River /lɪmˈpoːpoː/ a river of SE Africa. Rising as the Crocodile River near Johannesburg, it flows 1 770 km (1,100 miles) in a sweeping curve to the north and east to meet the Indian Ocean in Mozambique, north of Maputo.

limp-wristed *adjective informal offensive* **1** effeminate. **2** ineffectual, feeble.

linage /ˈlaɪnɪdʒ/ *noun* **1** the number of lines in printed or written matter. **2** payment by the line.

Lin Biao /lɪn ˈbjau/ (also **Lin Piao**) (1908–71), Chinese Communist leader and general. He was appointed minister of defence (1959) and vice-chairman under Mao (1966), and nominated to become Mao's successor (1969); after staging an unsuccessful coup (1971) he was reportedly killed in an airplane crash while fleeing to the Soviet Union.

LINC /lɪŋk/ *abbreviation Cdn* Language Instruction for Newcomers to Canada.

linch·pin *noun* (also **lynchpin**) **1** a pin passed through the end of an axle to keep a wheel in position. **2** a person or thing vital to an enterprise, organization, etc. [Middle English *linch* from Old English *lynis* + PIN]

Lin·coln¹ /ˈlɪŋkən/ **1** the state capital of Nebraska; pop. (2000) 225,581. **2** a city in E England, the county town of Lincolnshire; pop. (1998) 82,800. Its 11th-c. cathedral houses one of the four original copies of Magna Carta. **3** a town in S Ontario, situated between Hamilton and St. Catharines; pop. (2001) 20,612. □ **Lin·coln·ite** *noun* (in sense 3) [sense 1 after LINCOLN²; sense 3 after sense 2]

Lin·coln² /ˈlɪŋkən/ **Abra·ham** (1809–65), US Republican politician, 16th president of the US 1861–5. His election as president on an anti-slavery platform helped precipitate the American Civil War; emancipation was formally proclaimed on New Year's Day, 1864, and Lincoln was assassinated by John Wilkes Booth shortly after the surrender of the main Confederate army had ended the war.

Lincoln green *noun* a bright green cloth of a kind originally made at Lincoln in England.

Lin·coln·shire /ˈlɪŋkənˌʃɪr/ a county on the east coast of England, county town Lincoln.

linc·tus *noun Brit.* a syrupy medicine, esp. a soothing cough mixture. [Latin from *lingere* lick]

Lind ▸ 1 James (1716–94), Scottish physician, who demonstrated that sailors could be cured of scurvy by supplementing their diet with citrus fruit; this practice was adopted by the Royal Navy in 1796. **2 Jenny** (born Johanna Maria Lind Goldschmidt) (1820–87), Swedish soprano. Known as 'the Swedish nightingale' for the purity and agility of her voice, she achieved international success with her performances in opera, oratorios, and concerts.

lin·dane /ˈlɪndeɪn/ *noun Chem.* a synthetic organochlorine insecticide, now generally restricted in use owing to its toxicity and persistence in the environment. [T. van der *Linden*, Dutch chemist b.1884]

Lind·bergh /ˈlɪndbɜrg/ **Charles Au·gus·tus** (1902–74), US aviator. In 1927 he made the first solo transatlantic flight, in a single-engined monoplane, *Spirit of St. Louis*; he moved to Europe with his wife to escape the publicity surrounding the kidnapping and murder of their two-year-old son in 1932.

Lin·de·mann /ˈlɪndəmən/ see CHERWELL.

lin·den noun a basswood tree. [originally as adj. from Old English *lind* lime tree: compare LIME[3]]

Lin·dis·farne /ˈlɪndəsˌfɑrn/ (also called **Holy Island**) a small island off the coast of Northumberland, north of the Farne Islands. It is linked to the mainland by a causeway exposed only at low tide. It is the site of a church and monastery founded by St. Aidan in 635, which was a missionary centre of the Celtic Church.

Lind·say[1] a former town in south central Ontario, located on the Scugog River, west of Peterborough, now part of Kawartha Lakes; pop. (2001) 16,930. [after a man called *Lindsay*, who was accidentally shot and killed during the survey of the townsite in 1834]

Lind·say[2], **(Nicho·las) Va·chel** (1879–1931), US poet, whose work combines idealism, mysticism, and fundamentalism, and includes the ballads 'General William Booth' (1913) and 'The Congo' (1914).

lindy (in full **lindy hop**) ● noun a dance originating as a form of the jitterbug among blacks in Harlem, New York. ● intransitive verb dance the lindy. [nickname of Charles A. *Lindbergh*]

line[1] ● noun **1** a continuous mark or band made on a surface (*drew a line*). **2** use of lines in art, esp. draftsmanship or engraving (*boldness of line*). **3** a thing resembling such a mark, esp. a furrow or wrinkle. **4** *Music* **a** each of (usu. five) horizontal marks forming a staff in musical notation. **b** a sequence of notes or tones forming an instrumental or vocal melody. **5 a** a straight or curved continuous extent of length without breadth. **b** the track of a moving point. **6 a** a contour or outline, esp. as a feature of design (*admired the sculpture's clean lines; the pure line of a tailored jacket; the ship's lines*). **b** a facial feature (*the cruel line of his mouth*). **c** *Dance* the alignment of the head, torso and extended limbs in a pose etc., esp. when pleasing (*a beautiful arabesque line*). **7 a** (on a map or graph) a curve connecting all points having a specified common property. **b** the Equator. **8 a** (**the Line**) the Equator. **8 a** a real or notional limit or boundary (*town line; below the poverty line*). **b** a border, esp. the border between Canada and the US. **c** a mark limiting or dividing the area of play, the starting or finishing point in a race, etc. **d** the boundary between a credit and a debit in an account. **9 a** a row of persons or things. **b** a direction as indicated by them (*line of march*). **c** *N Amer.* a row or sequence of people, vehicles, etc. awaiting their turn to be attended to or to proceed. **10 a** a row of printed or written words. **b** a portion of verse written in one line. **11** (in *pl.*) **a** a piece of poetry. **b** the words of an actor's part. **c** a specified amount of text etc. to be written out as a school punishment. **12** a short letter or note (*drop me a line*). **13** a length of cord, rope, wire, etc., usu. serving a specified purpose, esp. a fishing line or clothesline. **14** a pipe, conduit, etc. through which a substance is conveyed (*the fuel lines were cut*). **15 a** a wire or cable for a telephone or telegraph. **b** a connection by means of this (*am trying to get a line*). **c** an individual telephone number or extension (*she's on the other line; installed a toll-free line*). **d** a wire or cable serving as a conductor of electric current (*the storm brought down hydro lines*). **16 a** a single track of a railway. **b** one branch or route of a railway system, or the whole system under one management. **c** a bus route. **17 a** a regular succession of buses, ships, aircraft, etc., plying between certain places. **b** a company conducting this (*shipping line*). **18** a connected series of persons following one another in time (esp. several generations of a family); stock, succession (*a long line of craftsmen; next in line to the throne*). **19 a** a course or manner of procedure, conduct, thought, etc. (*did it along these lines; don't take that line with me*). **b** policy (*the party line*). **c** conformity (*bring them into line*). **20** a direction, course, or channel (*lines of communication*). **21** a department of activity; a branch of business (*not in my line*). **22** a class of commercial goods (*a new line in hats*). **23** *informal* **a** a false or exaggerated account or story; a dishonest approach (*gave me a line about missing the bus*). **b** a piece of information; tip (*I've got a line on a job*). **c** an utterance, esp. when rehearsed (*fifty best opening lines*). **24** a sequence of events in a story etc. (*plot line*). **25 a** a connected series of military fieldworks, defences, etc. (*behind enemy lines*). **b** an arrangement of soldiers or ships side by side; a line of battle (*ship of the line*). **c** the fighting forces of an army or navy (excluding auxiliary forces). **26** each of the very narrow horizontal sections forming a television picture. **27** a narrow range of the spectrum that is noticeably brighter or darker than the adjacent parts. **28** the level of the base of most letters in printing and writing. **29** (as a measure) one twelfth of an inch. **30** an assembly line. **31** a dose of cocaine laid out in a line for snorting. **32** *Football* **a** = LINE OF SCRIMMAGE. **b** either of the two front rows of opposing players facing each other on the line of scrimmage. **33** *Hockey & Lacrosse* a shift of players, esp. the three forwards. **34** *Cdn* (esp. *Ont*) = CONCESSION 4b. **35** *Cdn* (*Nfld*) a road cut through rough country to link coastal settlements. **36** a series of traps for catching game strung out across a territory. ● verb **1** *transitive* mark with lines. **2** *transitive* cover with lines (*a face lined with pain*). **3** *transitive & intransitive* position or stand at intervals along (*crowds lined the route*). **4** *transitive* delineate, sketch. **5** *transitive & intransitive* *Baseball* hit (a ball) straight and low above the ground; play (a shot) as a line drive. **6** *transitive & intransitive* *N Amer.* guide or control (a boat or canoe) from the bank or shore of a stretch of inland water by means of a rope or ropes. **7** *transitive* read out (a metrical psalm, a hymn, etc.) line by line for a congregation to sing. □ **all along the line** at every point. **bring into line** make conform. **come into line** conform. **end of the line 1** the point at which further effort is unproductive or one can go no further. **2** the terminus of a rail, subway, or bus route. **get a line on** *informal* learn something about. **in line 1** arranged or standing in a line. **2** under control. **in line for** likely to receive. **in the line of** in the course of (esp. duty). **in** (or **out of**) **line with** in (or not in) accordance with. **keep in line** control (*keep prices in line; kept ambitious backbenchers in line*). **lay** (or **put**) **it on the line 1** speak frankly. **2** pay money. **(draw) a line in the sand** (state that one has reached) a point beyond which one will not go. **line up 1** arrange or be arranged in a line or lines. **2** have ready; organize (*had a job lined up*). **on the line 1** at risk (*put my reputation on the line*). **2** speaking on the telephone. **3** immediately; at the time of the transaction (*pay cash on the line*). **out of line 1** not in alignment; discordant. **2** failing to conform to a rule or convention; behaving inappropriately. [Middle English *line*, *ligne* from Old French *ligne*, ultimately from Latin *linea* from *linum* flax, & from Old English *line* rope, series]

line[2] *transitive verb* **1 a** cover the inside surface of (a garment, box, etc.) with a layer of usu. different material. **b** serve as a lining for. **2** cover as if with a lining (*shelves lined with books*). **3** fill, esp. plentifully. □ **line one's pockets** make money, usu. by corrupt means. [Middle English from obsolete *line* flax, with reference to the use of linen for linings]

lin·eage /ˈlɪniɪdʒ/ *noun* lineal descent; ancestry, pedigree.

lin·eal /ˈlɪniəl/ *adjective* **1** in the direct line of descent or ancestry. **2** linear; of or in lines. □ **lin·eal·ly** *adverb*

linea·ment /ˈlɪniəmənt/ *noun* (usu. in *pl.*) **1** a distinctive feature or characteristic, esp. of the face. **2** a linear feature on the earth's surface, such as a fault. [Latin *lineamentum* from *lineare* make straight, from *linea* LINE[1]]

linear /ˈlɪniɜr/ *adjective* **1 a** of or in lines; in lines rather than masses (*linear development*). **b** of length (*linear extent*). **2** long and narrow and of uniform breadth. **3** involving one dimension only. **4** progressing in a single series of steps or stages; sequential (*linear thinking*). □ **linear·ity** /-ˈerɪti/ *noun* **linear·ize** /ˈlɪniəraɪz/ *transitive verb* (also esp. *Brit.* **-ise**). **linear·ly** *adverb* [Latin *linearis* from *linea* LINE[1]]

linear accelerator *noun Physics* an accelerator in which particles travel in straight lines, not in closed orbits.

Linear B *noun* a form of Bronze Age writing found in Crete and parts of Greece and recording a form of Mycenaean Greek: an earlier undeciphered form (**Linear A**) also exists.

linear equation *noun* an equation between two variables that gives a straight line when plotted on a graph.

linear measure *noun* (also **long measure**) a measure of length (metres, miles, etc.).

linear motor *noun* a motor producing straight-line (not rotary) motion by means of a magnetic field.

linear perspective *noun* a mathematically based form of perspective where the relative size of objects depicted is based on lines converging to a central viewpoint.

linear programming *noun* a mathematical technique for maximizing or minimizing a linear function of several variables, e.g. output or cost.

line art *noun* illustrative material composed of lines or areas of pure black and white, needing no screening for reproduction.

linea·tion /ˌlɪniˈeɪʃən/ *noun* **1** a marking with or drawing of lines. **2** a division into lines. **3** *Geol.* a linear feature observed in rock etc. [Latin *lineatio* from *lineare* make straight]

line·back·er *noun Football* a player or position just behind the defensive line. □ **line·back·ing** *noun*

line break *noun* the point at which one line of text, in print or on a computer screen, meets the margin.

Vowels: a *cat* ɑ *arm* e *bed* ɜr *her* ɜ: *deux* ə *ago* ɪ *sit* i *cosy* i: *feed* ɒ *hot* ɔ *pore* oː *no* ʌ *run* ʊ *put*

line-breeding *noun* selective breeding of animals for some desired feature by mating within a related line. □ **line-bred** *adjective*

line dancing *noun* a type of country-and-western dancing in which dancers line up in a row without partners and follow a choreographed pattern of steps to music. □ **line dance** *noun & intransitive verb* **line dancer** *noun*

line drawing *noun* a drawing in which images are produced from variations of lines.

line drive *noun Baseball* a ball hit straight and low above the ground.

line-feed *noun* **1** the action of advancing paper in a printing machine by the space of one line. **2** the analogous movement of text on a computer screen.

line fence *noun N Amer.* a boundary fence between two farms or ranches.

Line Islands a group of eleven islands in the central Pacific, straddling the equator south of Hawaii. Eight of the islands, including Kiritimati (Christmas Island) form part of Kiribati; the remaining three are uninhabited dependencies of the US.

line-item veto *noun* (also **item veto**) (in the US) the power of a state governor to veto certain items in a bill without vetoing the entire bill.

line-man *noun* (*pl.* **-men**) **1 a** a person who repairs and maintains telephone or electrical etc. lines. **b** a person who tests the safety of railway lines. **2** *Football* a centre, guard, tackle, or end.

line manager *noun* a manager to whom an employee is directly responsible. □ **line management** *noun*

line-mate *noun Hockey* a player who plays on the same line as another.

lin·en ● *noun* **1 a** cloth woven from flax. **b** a particular kind of such cloth. **2** (*collective*) articles made or originally made of linen, cotton, etc., as sheets, cloths, shirts, undergarments, etc. ● *adjective* made of linen or flax (*linen cloth*). □ **wash** (or **air**) **one's dirty linen in public** be indiscreet about one's domestic quarrels etc. [Old English *línen* from West Germanic, related to obsolete *line* flax]

linen closet *noun* (also **linen cupboard**) a closet for bed and table linen, towels, etc.

lin·en·fold *noun* (often *attributive*) a carved or moulded ornament representing a fold or scroll of linen (*linenfold panelling*).

line of credit *noun* an amount of credit extended to a borrower.

line of defence *noun* a strategy or argument for protecting one's position, opinion, etc.

line of fire *noun* **1** the expected path of gunfire, a missile, etc. **2** the intended direction of criticism, controversy, etc.

line of force *noun Physics* an imaginary line which represents the strength and direction of a magnetic, gravitational, or electric field at any point.

line of scrimmage *noun Football* the imaginary line separating two teams at the beginning of a scrimmage.

line of sight *noun* a straight line along which an observer has unobstructed vision or along which radio waves etc. may be transmitted directly.

line of vision *noun* the straight line along which an observer looks.

line-out *noun Rugby* parallel lines of opposing forwards at right angles to the touchline for the throwing in of the ball.

line printer *noun* a machine that prints output from a computer a line at a time rather than character by character.

line producer *noun* a person who supervises the production of a film or broadcast up to the post-production phase.

liner¹ *noun* **1** a ship or aircraft etc. carrying passengers on a regular line. **2** = EYELINER. **3** = LINE DRIVE.

liner² *noun* **1** a lining in an appliance, device, or container, esp. a removable one. **2** a lining of a garment, esp. one made of a synthetic fibre.

liner·board *noun* a paperboard used as a facing on fibreboard.

liner notes *plural noun* explanatory text about a record, cassette, etc., appearing on the cover or included inside the package.

line·score *noun Sport* a summary of the scoring by inning, period, etc. presented in the form of a horizontal table.

lines·man *noun* (*pl.* **-men**) **1** *Hockey* an on-ice official whose tasks include making offside and icing calls, breaking up fights, etc. **2** (in games played on a field or court) an umpire's or referee's assistant who decides whether a ball falls within the playing area or not. **3** *Football* an official who marks the distances won or lost on each play. **4** *Brit.* = LINEMAN 1.

line squall *noun* a squall, consisting of a violent straight blast of cold air with snow or rain, occurring along a cold front.

line-up *noun* **1** a line of people formed for a particular reason, e.g. to buy tickets etc. **2** the personnel or configuration of persons on a team, in a musical group, etc. **3** (in police work) a line of persons from whom a suspect is to be identified. **4** a schedule of television programs, events, etc. **5** a line of items or services offered by a company.

ling¹ *noun* **1** any of several long slender predacious fishes of the cod family of the genus *Molva*, esp. *M. molva*, an important food fish found chiefly in the E Atlantic. **2** a burbot. [Middle English *leng(e)*, prob. from Middle Dutch, related to LONG¹]

ling² *noun* any of various heathers, esp. *Calluna vulgaris*. [Old Norse *lyng*]

-ling¹ *suffix* **1** denoting a person or thing: **a** connected with (*hireling*; *sapling*). **b** having the property of being (*weakling*; *underling*) or undergoing (*starveling*). **2** denoting a diminutive (*duckling*), often derogatory (*princeling*). [Old English (as -LE¹ + -ING³): sense 2 from Old Norse]

-ling² *suffix* forming adverbs and adjectives (*darkling*; *grovelling*) (*compare* -LONG). [Old English from Germanic]

Lin·gala /lɪˈgɒlə/ *noun* a Bantu language used by over 8 million people as a lingua franca in northern parts of the Republic of the Congo and the Democratic Republic of the Congo (formerly Zaire). [a local name]

lin·gam /ˈlɪŋgəm/ *noun* (also **linga** /ˈlɪŋgə/) a phallus, esp. as the Hindu symbol of Shiva. [Sanskrit *lingam*, lit. 'mark']

ling cod *noun* a large food fish, *Ophiodon elongatus*, of the greenling family, found in the N Pacific.

lin·ger *intransitive verb* **1 a** be slow or reluctant to depart. **b** stay about. **c** (foll. by *over*, *on*, etc.) dally (*lingered over dinner*). **2** (foll. by *on*) (of an action or condition) be protracted; drag on (*his cold lingered on*; *the memory lingered on*). **3** (foll. by *on*) (of a dying person or custom) be slow in dying; drag on feebly. □ **lin·ger·er** *noun* **lin·ger·ing** *adjective* **lin·ger·ing·ly** *adverb* [Middle English *lenger*, frequentative of *leng* from Old English *lengan* from Germanic, related to LENGTHEN]

linge·rie /ˈlɔ̃ʒəˌreɪ, lɑ̃-, -riː/ *noun* women's underwear and nightclothes. [French from *linge* linen]

lingo *noun* (*pl.* **-gos** or **-goes**) *informal* **1** the vocabulary of a special subject or group of people. **2** a foreign language. [prob. from Portuguese *lingoa* from Latin *lingua* tongue]

lingon·berry *noun* (*pl.* **-berries**) **1** the cowberry, *Vaccinium vitis-idaea*, of northern regions, esp. typically in Scandinavia, where the berries are used in cooking. **2** an Arctic variety of this occurring in the former USSR and N America. [from Swedish *lingon* cowberry + BERRY]

lin·gua fran·ca /ˌlɪŋgwə ˈfraŋkə/ *noun* (*pl.* **lin·gua fran·cas**) **1** a language adopted as a common language between speakers whose native languages are different. **2** a system of communication providing mutual understanding. **3** *hist.* a mixture of Italian with French, Greek, Arabic, and Spanish, used in the Levant. [Italian, = Frankish tongue]

lin·gual /ˈlɪŋgwəl/ *adjective* **1** of or formed by the tongue. **2** of speech or languages. □ **lin·gual·ly** *adverb* [medieval Latin *lingualis* from Latin *lingua* tongue, language]

lin·gui·form /ˈlɪŋgwɪˌfɔrm/ *adjective Bot., Zool., & Anat.* tongue-shaped. [Latin *lingua* tongue + -FORM]

lin·gui·ne /lɪŋˈgwiːni/ *plural noun* (also **lin·gui·ni**) pasta in the form of narrow ribbons. [Italian, pl. of *linguina*, diminutive of *lingua* 'tongue']

lin·guist /ˈlɪŋgwɪst/ *noun* a person skilled in languages or linguistics. [Latin *lingua* language]

lin·guis·tic /lɪŋˈgwɪstɪk/ *adjective* of or relating to language or the study of languages. □ **lin·guis·tic·ally** *adverb*

lin·guis·tics /lɪŋˈgwɪstɪks/ *noun* the scientific study of language and its structure.

lin·hay *var. of* LINNY.

lini·ment /ˈlɪnəmənt/ *noun* a medicated lotion, usu. made with oil, for rubbing onto the body to relieve pain. [Late Latin *linimentum* from Latin *linire* smear]

lining *noun* **1** a layer of material used to line a surface etc. **2** an inside layer or surface etc. (*stomach lining*). **3** the technique of guiding or controlling a canoe or boat from the bank or shore of a stretch of inland water by means of a rope or ropes.

link¹ ● *noun* **1** one loop or ring of a chain etc. **2 a** a connecting part, esp. a thing or person that unites or provides continuity; one in a series. **b** a state or means of connection. **c** an instruction or code that serves as a connection between two parts of a computer program, or between consecutive elements of a computerized list. **d** = HYPERLINK. **3** a means of contact by radio, telephone, television, or computer between two points. **4** a means of travel or transport between two places (*a link to the mainland*). **5** = CUFFLINK. **6** a measure equal to one-hundredth of a surveying chain (20.12 cm or 7.92 inches). **7** (usu. in *pl.*) any of the divisions of a chain of sausages. ● *verb* **1** *transitive* (foll. by *together, to, with*) connect or join (two things or one to another). **2** *transitive* (foll by. *to, with*) connect causally, associate in speech, thought, etc. (*many diseases have been linked to smoking; her name was linked by gossip columnists with that of a cabinet minister*). **3** *transitive* clasp or intertwine (hands or arms). **4** *intransitive* (foll. by *on, to, in to*) be joined; attach oneself to (a system, company, etc.). **5** *transitive* connect by means of a hyperlink. □ **link up** (foll. by *with*) connect or combine. □ **link·er** *noun* [Old Norse from Germanic]

link² *noun hist.* a torch of pitch and tow for lighting the way in dark streets. [16th c.: perhaps from medieval Latin *li(n)chinus* wick, from Greek *lukhnos* light]

link·age *noun* **1** the action of linking; a link or system of links. **2** the linking of different issues in political negotiations. **3** *Genetics* the tendency of genes on the same chromosome to be inherited together. **4** an assembly of interconnected rods for transmitting or controlling the motion of a mechanism.

links *plural noun* (treated as *sing.* or *pl.*) a golf course, esp. one having undulating ground, coarse grass, etc. [pl. of *link* 'rising ground' from Old English *hlinc*]

link-up *noun* an act or result of linking up.

Lin·naean /lɪˈniːən, lɪˈneɪən/ *adjective* of or relating to Linnaeus or his system of binary nomenclature in the classification of plants and animals. ¶ This word is spelled *Linnean* in *Linnean Society*.

Lin·naeus /lɪˈneɪəs, -ˈniːəs/ **Caro·lus** (Latinized name of Carl von Linné, 1707–78), Swedish botanist, founder of modern systematic botany and zoology. He devised a classification system for flowering plants, introducing binomial Latin names, and describing over 7000 plants, although his classification was later superseded by that of Jussieu; his works include *Systema Naturae* (1735) and *Species Plantarum* (1753).

lin·net¹ *noun* a small common Eurasian songbird related to the finches, *Carduelis cannabina*, with brown and grey plumage, formerly kept as a cage bird. [Old French *linette* from *lin* flax (the bird feeding on flax seeds)]

lin·net² *noun Cdn (Nfld)* **1** twine used for making fishnets. **2** a completed net or seine. [perhaps from *lint*, a netting for fishnets]

linny *noun* (also **linhay, lin·ney**) *Cdn (Nfld)* a row of rooms across the back of a house, often containing a porch, kitchen, and pantry, usu. with a lean-to roof. [SW English and Irish dialect designating a shed with a lean-to roof]

lino /ˈlaɪnoʊ/ *noun* (*pl.* **linos**) esp. *Brit.* linoleum. [abbreviation]

lino·cut /ˈlaɪnoʊˌkʌt/ *noun* **1** a design or form carved in relief on a block of linoleum. **2** a print made from this. □ **lino·cut·ting** *noun*

Li·no·la /lɪˈnoʊlə/ *noun proprietary* **1** a variety of yellow flax seed bred so as to be low in linolenic acid, producing an oil that keeps longer than linseed oil, both the seed and the oil being used in food products. **2** flax grown from Linola seed. [as *linoleic* (see LINOLEIC ACID) + -A¹]

lino·leic acid /lɪnoʊˈliːɪk, -ˈleɪɪk/ *noun Chem.* a polyunsaturated fatty acid occurring as a glyceride in linseed and other oils and essential in the human diet. [Latin *linum* 'flax' + OLEIC ACID]

lino·len·ic acid /lɪnoʊˈlɛnɪk, -ˈliːnɪk/ *noun Chem.* a polyunsaturated fatty acid (with one more double bond than linoleic acid) occurring as a glyceride in linseed and other oils and essential in the human diet. [German *Linolensäure* from *Linolsäure* LINOLEIC ACID with *-ene-* inserted]

li·no·leum /lɪˈnoʊliəm/ *noun* a material consisting of a canvas backing thickly coated with a preparation of linseed oil and powdered cork etc., used esp. as a floor covering. □ **li·no·leumed** *adjective* [Latin *linum* flax + *oleum* oil]

Lino·type /ˈlaɪnoʊˌtaɪp/ *noun Printing proprietary* a typesetting machine, operated by a keyboard, that produces lines of words as single strips of metal, used esp. for newspapers before the introduction of electronic technology. [= *line o' type*]

Lin Piao see LIN BIAO.

lin·sang /ˈlɪnsaŋ/ *noun* any of various civet-like cats, esp. of the genus *Poiana* of Africa or *Prionodon* of SE Asia. [Javanese]

lin·seed *noun* the seed of flax. [Old English *līnsǣd* from *līn* flax + *sǣd* seed]

linseed oil *noun* oil extracted from linseed and used in paint and varnish.

linsey-woolsey *noun* a fabric of coarse wool woven on a cotton warp. [Middle English from *linsey* coarse linen, prob. from *Lindsey* in Suffolk + WOOL, with jingling ending]

lin·stock *noun hist.* a match holder used to fire cannon. [earlier *lintstock* from Dutch *lontstok* from *lont* match + *stok* stick, assimilated to LINT]

lint *noun* **1** tiny threads or fibres of fabric; fluff. **2** a soft material used esp. for dressing wounds, originally made by ravelling or scraping linen cloth. **3** an accumulation of dirt, dead skin cells, etc. in the navel. □ **linty** *adjective* [Middle English *lyn(n)et*, perhaps from Old French *linette* linseed, from *lin* flax]

lin·tel *noun Archit.* a horizontal supporting piece of timber, stone, concrete, etc., across the top of a door or window. [Old French *lintel* threshold, from Romanic *limitale* (unrecorded), influenced by Late Latin *liminare* from Latin *limen* threshold]

Linux /ˈlɪnəks, ˈlaɪnəks, ˈliːnəks/ *noun Computing* a freely available Unix-like operating system. [*Linus* Benedict Torvalds, Finnish software engineer b.1969, who wrote the first version of the system, + UNIX]

Linz /lɪnts/ an industrial city in N Austria, on the Danube River, capital of the state of Upper Austria; pop. (2001) 186,300.

lion *noun* **1** a large flesh-eating cat, *Panthera leo*, of Africa and S Asia, with a tawny coat and, in the male, a flowing shaggy mane. **2** (**the Lion**) the zodiacal sign or constellation Leo. **3** a brave or celebrated person. **4** the lion as a national emblem of Great Britain or as a representation in heraldry. **5** (**Lion**) a member of a Lions Club. □ **lion-like** *adjective* [Anglo-French *liun* and Latin *leo -onis* from Greek *leōn leontos*]

lion dance *noun* a traditional Chinese dance in which two dancers in an elaborate, multicoloured costume representing a lion, parade through the streets to the beating of a drum, bobbing and weaving, to symbolize the chasing away of evil spirits and invoke good fortune. □ **lion dancer** *noun*

lion·ess *noun* **1** a female lion. **2** (**Lioness**) a member of a Lioness Club.

Lioness Club *noun* a women's service club, affiliated with the Lions Club.

lion-hearted *adjective* brave and generous.

lion·ize *transitive verb* (also esp. *Brit.* **-ise**) treat as a celebrity. □ **lion·iz·a·tion** *noun* **lion·iz·er** *noun*

Lions Club *noun* any of numerous associated clubs devoted to social and international service, the first of which was founded in Chicago in 1917.

lion's mane *noun* a large toxic jellyfish, *Cyanea capillata*.

lion's share *noun* the largest or best part.

lip ● *noun* **1 a** either of the two fleshy parts forming the edges of the mouth. **b** a thing resembling these. **c** = LABIUM. **2 a** the edge of a cup, vessel, etc., esp. the part shaped for pouring from. **b** the edge of an opening or cavity, e.g. of a canyon, the crater of a volcano, etc. **3** *informal* impudent talk (*that's enough of your lip!*). ● *transitive verb* (**lipped, lip·ping**) **1 a** touch with the lips; apply the lips to. **b** touch lightly. **2** *Golf* **a** hit a ball just to the edge of (a hole). **b** (of a ball) reach the edge of (a hole) but fail to drop in. **3** *informal* insult, abuse; be impudent to (someone). □ **bite one's lip** repress an emotion; stifle laughter, a retort, etc. **curl one's lip** express scorn. **lick one's lips** see LICK. **pass a person's lips** be eaten, drunk, spoken, etc. **smack one's lips** open and close the lips noisily in relish or anticipation, esp. of food. □ **lip·less** *adjective* **lip·like** *adjective* **lipped** *adjective* (also in combination). [Old English *lippa* from Germanic]

lipa /ˈliːpə/ *noun* (*pl.* **lipa**) a monetary unit of Croatia, equal to one-hundredth of a kuna. [Serbo-Croat, literally 'lime tree']

Lip·ari Islands /ˈlɪpəri/ a group of seven volcanic islands in the Tyrrhenian Sea, off the northeast coast of Sicily, and in Italian possession. Believed by the ancient Greeks to be the home of Aeolus, the god of the winds, the islands were formerly known as the Aeolian Islands.

lip·ase /ˈlaɪpeɪs, ˈlɪp-, -peɪz/ *noun Biochem.* any enzyme that catalyzes the breakdown of fats. [Greek *lipos* fat + -ASE]

lip balm *noun* a greasy or waxy preparation to prevent or relieve chapped lips.

lip brush *noun* a small brush for applying lipstick or lip gloss.

Lip·chitz /ˈlɪpʃɪts/ **Jacques** (1891–1973), Lithuanian-born French sculptor. One of the first cubist sculptors, he is known for works such as *Man with a Guitar* (1916) and *Prometheus Strangling the Vulture* (1944–53).

Li·petsk /ˈlipetsk/ an industrial city in SW Russia, on the Voronezh River; pop. (est. 2002) 530,400. It is a major centre of the iron and steel industries.

lip gloss *noun* a glossy cosmetic applied to the lips.

Consonants: b *but* d *dog* f *few* g *get* h *her* j *yes* k *cat* l *leg* m *man* n *no* p *pen* r *red* s *sit*

lip·id /ˈlɪpɪd/ *noun Chem.* any of a group of organic compounds that are insoluble in water but soluble in organic solvents, including fatty acids, oils, waxes, and steroids. [French *lipide* (as LIPASE)]

lipid·o·sis /ˌlɪpɪˈdoːsɪs/ *noun* (also **lipoid·o·sis** /ˌlɪpɔɪ-/) (*pl.* **-o·ses** /-siːz/) any disorder of lipid metabolism in the body tissues.

Lip·iz·zan·er /ˌlɪpɪtˈsanɜr/ *noun* (also **Lip·pi·zan·er, Lip·pizan**) **1** a horse of a fine white breed used esp. in displays of dressage. **2** this breed. [German from *Lippíza* in Slovenia]

lip·liner *noun* a cosmetic applied as a line around the lips, to accentuate them and keep lipstick from bleeding.

lip-lock *informal* ● *noun* a kiss. ● *transitive & intransitive verb* kiss.

Li Po /liːˈboː/ (also **Li Bo, Li Tʼai Po** /taɪ/) (701–62), Chinese poet. He is considered one of China's greatest poets, his lyrics portray the themes of wine, women, and nature.

lipo- *combining form* fat. [Greek *lipos*]

lipo /ˈlɪpoː/ *noun informal* liposuction.

lip·oid /ˈlɪpɔɪd/ *adjective* resembling fat.

lipo·phil·ic /ˌlɪpoːˈfɪlɪk, ˌlaɪ-/ *adjective* tending to combine with or dissolve in lipids or fats. □ **lipo·phili·city** *noun*

lipo·pro·tein /ˌlɪpoːˈproːtiːn, ˌlaɪ-/ *noun Biochem.* any of a group of soluble proteins that combine with and transport fat or other lipids in the blood plasma.

lipo·sculp·ture *noun* a type of liposuction in which saline solution combined with local anaesthetic and adrenaline is introduced into the tissues before fat is removed, and which allows for greater sculpting of the tissue.

lipo·some /ˈlɪpoːˌsoːm, ˈlaɪ-, -pə-/ *noun Biochem.* a minute artificial spherical sac usu. of a phospholipid membrane enclosing an aqueous core, esp. used to carry drugs to specific tissues.

lipo·suc·tion /ˈlɪpoːsʌkʃən, ˈlaɪ-/ ● *noun* a technique in cosmetic surgery for removing excess fat from under the skin by suction. ● *transitive verb* remove (fat) by liposuction.

lip pencil *noun* lipliner in pencil form.

Lippi ▸ **1 Fil·ip·pi·no** (*c.*1457–1504), Italian painter, who is known for the fresco cycle on the life of St. Peter in the Brancacci Chapel, Florence (*c.*1481–3), the series of frescoes in the Carafa Chapel in Rome (1488–93), and the painting *The Vision of St. Bernard* (*c.*1486). **2** his father, **Fra Filip·po** (*c.*1406–69), Italian painter. In the early 1420s he became a pupil of Masaccio, whose influence can be seen in the fresco *The Relaxation of the Carmelite Rule* (*c.*1432); his characteristic later style is more decorative and less monumental than his early work, and often depicts the Madonna as the central feature, stressing the human aspect of the theme.

Lip·pi·zan·er *var.* of LIPIZZANER.

Lipp·mann, **Gab·riel (Jonas)** (1845–1921), French physicist. He designed a number of instruments, including an electrometer that was sensitive to potential changes of a thousandth of a volt, and is best known today for his production of the first fully orthochromatic colour photograph (1893).

lippy *adjective* (**lip·pi·er, lip·pi·est**) *informal* **1** insolent, impertinent. **2** having large lips.

lip-read *intransitive verb* (*past* and *past participle* **-read**) (esp. of a deaf person) understand (speech) entirely from observing a speaker's lip movements. □ **lip-reader** *noun* **lip-reading** *noun*

lip service *noun* an insincere expression of support etc.

lip-smacking *adjective* **1** (of food etc.) delicious. **2** tantalizing; tempting. □ **lip-smacking·ly** *adverb*

lip·stick *noun* coloured cosmetic applied to the lips from a small solid stick, usu. a shade of red or pink. □ **lip·sticked** *adjective*

lipstick lesbian *noun informal* a lesbian of glamorous or manifestly feminine appearance.

lip-synch (also **lip-sync**) ● *noun* (in film acting etc.) the movement of a performer's lips in synchronization with a pre-recorded soundtrack. ● *transitive & intransitive verb* perform (esp. a song) on film using this technique. □ **lip-syncher** *noun* **lip-synching** *noun*

li·que·fy *transitive & intransitive verb* (also **li·qui·fy**) (**-fies, -fied**) *Chem.* make or become liquid. □ **li·que·fac·tion** *noun* **li·que·fac·tive** *adjective* **li·que·fier** *noun* [French *liquéfier* from Latin *liquefacere* from *liquēre* be liquid]

li·ques·cent /lɪˈkwesənt/ *adjective* becoming or apt to become liquid. [Latin *liquescere* (as LIQUEFY)]

li·queur /lɪˈkjɜr, -kjʊr/ *noun* any of several strong sweet alcoholic spirits, variously flavoured, usu. drunk after a meal. [French, = LIQUOR]

li·quid ● *adjective* **1** (of a material substance) having a consistency like that of water or oil, flowing freely but of constant volume. **2** (of light, fire, the eyes, etc.) like water in appearance; clear, bright, translucent (*liquid blue*; *a liquid lustre*). **3** (of a gas, e.g. oxygen, hydrogen) reduced to a liquid state by intense cold or high pressure. **4 a** (of sounds) clear and pure; harmonious, fluent. **b** (of movement) unconstrained. **5 a** (of assets) easily converted into cash. **b** having ready cash or liquid assets (*prompting investors to stay liquid*). **6** not fixed; fluid (*liquid opinions*). ● *noun* **1 a** a liquid substance. **b** (usu. in *pl.*) liquid food. **2** *Phonetics* a voiced, frictionless, continuant consonant, esp. the sound of *l* or *r*. □ **li·quid·ly** *adverb* **li·quid·ness** *noun* **li·quidy** *adjective* [Latin *liquidus* from *liquēre* be liquid]

li·quid·am·bar /ˌlɪkwɪˈdambər/ *noun* **1** any tree of the genus *Liquidambar* yielding a resinous gum. **2** this gum. [modern Latin apparently from Latin *liquidus* (see LIQUID) + medieval Latin *ambar* amber]

li·quid·ate *verb* **1 a** *transitive* wind up the affairs of (a company or firm) by ascertaining liabilities and apportioning assets. **b** *intransitive* (of a company) be liquidated, go into liquidation. **2** *transitive* clear or pay off (a debt). **3** *transitive* put an end to or get rid of (esp. by violent means); wipe out, kill. [medieval Latin *liquidare* make clear (as LIQUID)]

li·quid·a·tion *noun* **1 a** the process of liquidating a company etc. **b** the state or condition of being wound up. **2** the action or process of abolishing or eliminating something or someone, esp. the doing away with or killing of unwanted people. □ **go into liquidation** (of a company etc.) be wound up and have its assets apportioned.

li·quid·ator *noun* **1** a person called in to wind up the affairs of a company etc. **2** a person who implements a policy of liquidation.

liquid-cooled *adjective* (of an engine, computer chip, etc.) cooled when in operation by circulating water or other fluid.

liquid crystal *noun* a turbid liquid that exhibits some degree of ordering in its molecular structure and exists as a distinct state of certain pure substances between the melting point and some higher temperature.

liquid crystal display *noun* a form of visual display in electronic devices, esp. of segmented numbers or letters, in which liquid crystals are made visible by temporarily modifying their capacity to reflect light. Abbr.: **LCD**.

li·quid·ity *noun* (*pl.* **-ities**) **1** the state of being liquid. **2** availability of liquid assets.

li·quid·ize *transitive verb* (also **-ise**) esp. *Brit.* reduce (esp. food) to a liquid or puréed state, esp. using an electric blender.

li·quid·izer *noun Brit.* = BLENDER 1.

liquid lunch *noun informal* a midday meal at which not food but alcoholic drinks are consumed.

liquid measure *noun* a unit for expressing the volume of liquids.

liquid smoke *noun* a liquid basted onto barbecued foods to impart a flavour of smoke.

liquid sunshine *noun jocular* rain.

li·qui·fy *var.* of LIQUEFY.

li·quor /ˈlɪkər/ ● *noun* **1** an alcoholic drink, esp. produced by distillation. **2** a liquid of a particular kind used or produced in a chemical or industrial process etc. **3** other liquid, esp. that produced in cooking. **4** *Pharm.* a solution of a specified drug in water. ● *verb* **1** *slang* (usu. foll. by *up*; usu. in *passive*) cause to drink alcoholic liquor. **2** *transitive* steep (malt etc.) in water. [Old French *lic(o)ur* from Latin *liquor -oris* (as LIQUID)]

liquor board *noun Cdn* = LIQUOR CONTROL BOARD.

liquor commission *noun Cdn* **1** (in the territories and certain provinces) a regulatory body controlling the sale and distribution of alcoholic beverages. **2** a liquor store operated by this body. Abbr.: **LC**.

liquor control board *noun Cdn* (in certain provinces) a regulatory body controlling the sale and distribution of alcoholic beverages.

li·quor·ice *var.* of LICORICE.

liquor licence *noun* a permanent licence allowing the sale and serving of liquor for consumption in a restaurant, bar, etc.

liquor permit *noun* a temporary, special-occasion permit allowing the sale or consumption of liquor in a place not generally open to the public.

LIRA /ˈliːrə/ *abbreviation Cdn* LOCKED-IN RETIREMENT ACCOUNT.

lira /ˈliːrə/ *noun* (*pl.* **lire** /ˈliːre, ˈliːri/) **1 a** the former chief monetary unit of Italy, used also in San Marino and the Vatican City, now replaced by the euro. **b** the chief monetary unit of Malta, equal to 100 cents. **2** the

t *top*   v *voice*   w *we*   z *zoo*   ʃ *she*   ʒ *vision*   θ *thin*   ð *this*   ŋ *ring*   x *loch*   tʃ *chip*   dʒ *jar*   (*see over for vowels*)

chief monetary unit of Turkey, equal to 100 kurush. [Italian from Provençal *liura* from Latin *libra* pound (weight etc.)]

Lis·bon /ˈlɪzbən/ the capital and chief port of Portugal, on the Atlantic coast at the mouth of the Tagus River; pop. (2001) 556,797. It flourished during the period of Portuguese colonial expansion, but was devastated by an earthquake in 1755, after which much of the city had to be rebuilt.

li·sente *pl. of* SENTE.

Lis·gar /ˈlɪzɡɑr/ **Sir John Young, Baron** (1807–76), British politician and colonial administrator. A supporter of Confederation, he was both Governor General of Canada and governor of PEI 1869–72; he helped diffuse the tensions caused by the Red River Rebellion, the creation of Manitoba, and the transfer of Rupert's Land, and encouraged BC to enter Confederation.

lisi·an·thus /lɪsiˈanθəs/ *noun* a plant, *Eustoma grandiflorum*, with delicate roselike white, purple, or pink flowers. [Modern Latin from Greek *lysis* 'breaking up, dissolving' + *anthos* 'flower', the original tropical American plant so called being used as a cathartic]

lisle /laɪl/ *noun* (in full **lisle thread**) (usu. *attributive*) a fine smooth cotton thread for stockings etc. [*Lisle*, former spelling of *Lille* in France, where originally made]

Lis·mer /ˈlɪzmər/ **Ar·thur** (1885–1969), English-born Canadian painter and educator who emigrated to Canada in 1911, a founding member of the Group of Seven in 1920. His paintings are characterized by raw colour, simplified form, and coarse brushwork. He devoted most of his life to teaching.

LISP /lɪsp/ *abbreviation Computing* a high-level programming language devised for list processing. [*list processor*]

lisp ● *noun* **1 a** a speech defect in which *s* is pronounced like *th* in *thick* and *z* is pronounced like *th* in *this*. **b** the action or act of lisping; a lisping pronunciation. **2** a sound resembling a lisp, e.g. the rippling of waters, rustling of leaves, etc. ● *verb intransitive & transitive* speak or utter with a lisp. □ **lisp·er** *noun* **lisp·ing** *adjective & noun* **lisp·ing·ly** *adverb* [Old English *wlispian* (recorded in *āwlyspian* from *wlisp* (adj.) lisping, of uncertain origin]

lis·some /ˈlɪsəm/ *adjective* (also **lis·som**) lithe, supple, agile. □ **lis·some·ly** *adverb* **lis·some·ness** *noun* [ultimately from LITHE + -SOME¹]

list¹ ● *noun* **1** a number of connected items, names, etc., written or printed together usu. consecutively to form a record or aid to memory (*shopping list*). **2 a** a catalogue of the titles of books published, or to be published, by a particular publisher. **b** the books in such a catalogue collectively (*Oxford has a very strong fall list*). **3** *Computing* a formalized representation of the concept of a list, used for the storage of data or in list processing. **4** (in *pl.*) **a** palisades enclosing an area for a tournament. **b** the scene of a contest. **5** LIST PRICE. ● *verb* **1** *transitive* make a list of. **2** *transitive* **a** enter in a list. **b** include as if in a list or catalogue; report, mention. **3** *transitive N Amer.* **a** place (a property) in the hands of a real estate agent for sale or rent. **b** add to the list or properties advertised by a real estate agent. **4** *transitive* enter (a name and address) in a telephone directory. **5** *transitive Computing* display or print out (a program, the contents of a file, etc.). **6** *transitive* (usu. in *passive*) approve (securities etc.) for dealings on a stock exchange. **7** *intransitive* (usu. foll. by *at, for*) be specified in a price list (*the fishing reel lists at $4.95*). □ **enter the lists** issue or accept a challenge. □ **list·able** *adjective* **list·er** *noun* [Old English *liste* border, strip, from Germanic]

list² ● *intransitive verb* **1** (of a ship etc.) lean over to one side, esp. owing to a leak or shifting cargo (*compare* HEEL²). **2** (of a building etc.) lean over, tilt. ● *noun* the process or an instance of listing. [17th c.: origin unknown]

list³ *intransitive verb archaic* listen. [Old English *hlystan* from *hlyst* 'hearing']

list⁴ *intransitive verb archaic* wish, desire, like, choose. [Old English *lystan* from Germanic]

list·ed *adjective* **1** included in a list, directory, or catalogue. **2** (of securities etc.) approved for dealings on a stock exchange. **3** (of a building in the UK) designated and protected as of architectural or historical importance.

lis·ten ● *intransitive verb* **1 a** make an effort to hear something. **b** pay attention to (a person speaking or some utterance). **2** (foll. by *to*) **a** give attention with the ear (*listened to my story*). **b** pay heed, respond, or yield to advice, a request, etc. (*Never listen to lawyers!; listen to your mother*). **3** (also **listen out**) (often foll. by *for*) be eager or make a careful effort to catch the sound of. ● *noun* an act or instance of listening. □ **listen in 1** listen secretly to or tap a private communication by telephone etc. **2** listen to a broadcast radio

program etc. **3** listen to the conversation of others, often covertly and usu. without contributing. **listen up** *informal* pay attention. [Old English *hlysnan* from West Germanic]

lis·ten·able *adjective* easy or pleasant to listen to. □ **lis·ten·abil·ity** *noun*

lis·ten·er *noun* **1** a person who listens. **2** a person receiving broadcast radio programs.

lis·ten·er·ship *noun* the estimated number of listeners to a broadcast program or to radio.

lis·ten·ing *noun* **1** *in senses of* LISTEN. **2** (with qualifying adj.) broadcast, recorded, or other matter for listening to, esp. with reference to its quality or kind (*easy listening*).

listening post *noun* **1 a** a point near an enemy's lines for detecting movements by sound. **b** a station for intercepting electronic communications. **2** a place for the gathering of information from reports etc.

Lis·ter, Jo·seph, 1st Baron (1827–1912), English surgeon, who invented antiseptic techniques in surgery, by using carbolic acid as a disinfectant on dressings and requiring strict hygiene.

lis·teria /lɪˈstiːriə/ *noun* any motile rod-like bacterium of the genus *Listeria*, esp. *L. monocytogenes* infecting humans and animals eating contaminated food. [modern Latin from LISTER]

lis·teri·osis /lɪˌstiːriˈoːsɪs/ *noun* infection with, or a disease caused by, listerias, contracted esp. by the ingestion of contaminated food or silage.

list·ing¹ *noun* **1** a list or catalogue (*see* LIST¹ 1). **2 a** the drawing up of a list. **b** an entry in a catalogue, telephone directory, or other list. **3** *N Amer.* **a** the placing of a property on the list of a real estate agent. **b** a real estate agent's register of properties available for sale. **c** a property so listed. **4** *Computing* a printed or displayed copy of a program or of the contents of a file.

list·ing² *adjective* (of a ship etc.) heeling, inclining to one side.

list·less *adjective* lacking energy or enthusiasm; disinclined for exertion. □ **list·lessly** *adverb* **list·less·ness** *noun* [Middle English from obsolete *list* inclination + -LESS]

Lis·towel /ˈlɪstəwʊl/ a former town in SW central Ontario, north of Stratford, now part of North Perth; pop. (2001) 5,905.

list price *noun* the price shown for an article in a printed list issued by the maker, or by the general body of makers of the particular class of goods.

list processing *noun Computing* the manipulation and use of chained lists and of data in them.

list·serv *noun Computing* an email system which automatically sends messages to all subscribers on specific mailing lists, in special interest groups, etc.

Lis·tu·guj /ˌlɪstəˈɡuːʃ/ an Indian reserve in E Quebec, situated on the Gaspé Peninsula at the mouth of the Restigouche River, opposite Campbellton, New Brunswick; pop. (2001) 1,442. The area was the scene in 1760 of the final battle between the British and the French during the Seven Years War. The British were victorious. The reserve was formerly known as Restigouche.

Liszt /lɪst/ **Franz** (1811–86), Hungarian composer and pianist. He was a key figure in the Romantic movement and a virtuoso pianist; his compositions include the Faust and Dante Symphonies (1854–7; 1855–6), 12 tone poems (1848–58), masses, and oratorios such as *Christus* (1862–7). □ **Liszt·ian** *adjective & noun*

lit¹ past and past participle of LIGHT¹,².

lit² *noun informal* literature. [abbreviation]

lit. *abbreviation* **1** literary. **2** literature.

Li T'ai Po see LI PO.

lit·any /ˈlɪtəni/ *noun* (*pl.* **-anies**) **1** a series of petitions for use in church services or processions, usu. recited by the clergy and responded to in a recurring formula by the people. **2 a** a continuous repetition or long enumeration; a repeated formula; a long series. **b** a tedious recital (*a litany of woes*). [Old French *letanie* from ecclesiastical Latin *litania* from Greek *litaneia* prayer, from *litē* supplication]

litas /ˈliːtas/ *noun* (*pl.* same) the basic monetary unit of Lithuania, equal to 100 cents.

litchi *var. of* LYCHEE.

lit crit *noun* literary criticism. [abbreviation]

lite ● *adjective* **1** applied to low-fat or low-sugar versions of manufactured food or drink products, esp. to low-calorie beer. **2** *N Amer. informal* lacking in substance; facile, over-simplified. ● *noun* **1** a light beer with relatively few calories. **2** a light, esp. a courtesy light in a motor vehicle. **3** a pane of glass, esp. in a door. [variant of LIGHT[1], [2], now usu. a deliberate respelling]

-lite *suffix* forming names of minerals (*rhyolite*; *zeolite*). [French from Greek *lithos* stone]

liter *esp. US var. of* LITRE.

lit·er·acy /ˈlɪtərəsi/ *noun* **1** the ability to read and write. **2** competence in some field of knowledge, technology, etc. (*computer literacy*; *economic literacy*).

lit·er·al /ˈlɪtərəl/ ● *adjective* **1** taking words in their usual or primary sense without metaphor or allegory (*literal interpretation*). **2 a** (of a translation, version, transcript, etc.) following the letter, text, or exact or original words. **b** (of a representation in art or literature) exactly copied, true to life, realistic. **3** (in full **literal-minded**) (of a person) apt to take what is spoken or written at face value, missing irony, humorous exaggeration, etc.; matter of fact. **4 a** without metaphor, exaggeration, or inaccuracy (*the literal truth*). **b** so called without exaggeration (*a literal extermination*). **5** *informal disputed* (as an intensifier) so called with some exaggeration or using metaphor (*a literal avalanche of mail*). ¶ The use of *literal* and *literally* simply as intensifiers is better avoided in writing or formal speech. This hyperbolic usage is often wordy. **6** of, in, or expressed by a letter or the letters of the alphabet. **7** *Algebra* denoted or expressed by a letter or letters; not numerical. ● *noun* a misprint of a letter; a typographical error. □ **lit·er·al·ity** /-ˈralɪti/ *noun* **lit·er·al·ize** *transitive verb* (also esp. *Brit.* **-ise**). **lit·er·al·ly** *adverb* **lit·er·al·ness** *noun* [Old French *literal* or Late Latin *litteralis* from Latin *littera* (as LETTER)]

lit·er·al·ism /ˈlɪtərəˌlɪzəm/ *noun* **1** insistence on a literal interpretation; adherence to the letter. **2** literal representation in art or literature. □ **lit·er·al·ist** *noun* **lit·er·al·is·tic** /-ˈlɪstɪk/ *adjective*

lit·er·ary /ˈlɪtərˌeri/ *adjective* **1** of, constituting, or occupied with books or literature or written composition, esp. of the kind valued for quality of form. **2** well informed about literature. **3** (of a word or idiom) used chiefly in literary works or other formal writing. **4** (of painting, sculpture, etc.) depicting or representing a story. □ **lit·er·ar·i·ly** *adverb* **lit·er·ar·i·ness** *noun* [Latin *litterarius* (as LETTER)]

literary agent *noun* a person who acts on behalf of authors in dealing with publishers etc. □ **literary agency** *noun*

literary criticism *noun* the art or practice of estimating the qualities and character of literary works. □ **literary critic** *noun* **literary-critical** *adjective*

literary device *noun* = DEVICE 4.

literary history *noun* **1** a history of the major literary traditions, movements, works, and authors of a country, region, etc. **2** the history of the treatment of, and references to, a specified subject in literature, e.g. a legend, historical person, event, etc. □ **literary historian** *noun*

lit·er·ate /ˈlɪtərət/ ● *adjective* **1** able to read and write. **2 a** well-read, cultured. **b** educated. **3** competent or well-versed in a specified area (*computer literate*). **4** (of a text etc.) lucid, articulate, polished; competently written, presented, etc. ● *noun* a literate person. □ **lit·er·ate·ly** *adverb* [Latin *litteratus* (as LETTER)]

lit·er·ati /ˌlɪtəˈrɒti/ *plural noun* educated and intelligent people who produce or are well-versed in literature. [Latin, pl. of *literatus* (as LETTER)]

lit·er·a·ture /ˈlɪtərətʃər, ˈlɪtrə-/ *noun* **1** written works, esp. those whose value lies in beauty of language or in emotional effect. **2** the realm of letters; literary work or production as a whole. **3** the body of writings produced in a particular country or period. **4** printed matter, leaflets, etc. **5** the material in print on a particular subject (*there is a considerable literature on geraniums*). [Middle English, = literary culture, from Latin *litteratura* (as LITERATE)]

-lith *suffix* denoting types of stone (*laccolith*; *monolith*). [Greek *lithos* stone]

lithe /laɪð/ *adjective* **1** moving or bending easily and gracefully; supple. **2** gracefully slim and muscled. □ **lithe·ly** *adverb* **lithe·ness** *noun* [Old English *lithe* from Germanic]

lith·ic /ˈlɪθɪk/ *adjective* **1** of, like, or made of stone. **2** of or pertaining to stone artifacts. [Greek *lithikos* (as LITHIUM)]

lith·i·fy /ˈlɪθɪfaɪ/ *transitive verb* (usu. as **lithi·fied** *adjective*) form into stone. □ **lithi·fi·ca·tion** *noun* [Greek *lithos* 'stone' + -FY]

lith·i·um /ˈlɪθiəm/ *noun Chem.* **1** a soft silver-white metallic element, the lightest metal, used in alloys and in batteries. Symbol: **Li**; at. no.: 3. **2** lithium carbonate. [modern Latin *lithia* lithium oxide, alteration of earlier *lithion* from Greek neuter of *litheios* from *lithos* stone, after *soda* etc. + -IUM]

lithium carbonate *noun* a compound of lithium and carbon used in treating manic depression.

litho /ˈlɪθəʊ/ *informal* ● *noun* **1** = LITHOGRAPHY. **2** = LITHOGRAPH. ● *transitive verb* (**lithoes**, **lithoed**) produce by lithography. [abbreviation]

litho- /ˈlɪθəʊ, ˈlaɪθəʊ/ *combining form* stone. [Greek *lithos* stone]

litho·graph /ˈlɪθəˌɡraf/ ● *noun* a lithographic print. ● *transitive verb* print by lithography. [back-formation from LITHOGRAPHY]

lith·og·raphy /lɪˈθɒɡrəfi/ *noun* (*pl.* **-ies**) a process of obtaining prints from a stone or metal surface so treated that what is to be printed can be inked but the remaining area rejects ink. □ **lith·og·raph·er** *noun* **litho·graph·ic** *adjective* **litho·graph·ic·ally** *adverb* [German *Lithographie* (as LITHO-, -GRAPHY)]

lith·ol·ogy /lɪˈθɒlədʒi/ *noun* **1** the general physical characteristics of a rock, esp. as discernible without a microscope. **2** the branch of geology that deals with these characteristics. □ **litho·logic** /-θəˈlɒdʒɪk/ *adjective* **litho·logic·al** /-θəˈlɒdʒɪkəl/ *adjective* **litho·logic·ally** /-θəˈlɒdʒɪkli/ *adverb*

litho·phyte /ˈlɪθəˌfaɪt/ *noun Bot.* a plant that grows on stone.

litho·sphere /ˈlɪθəˌsfɪər/ *noun* the rigid outer portion of the earth including the crust and the outermost mantle, above the asthenosphere. □ **litho·spher·ic** /-ˈsferɪk/ *adjective*

lith·ot·omy /lɪˈθɒtəmi/ *noun* (*pl.* **-omies**) the surgical removal of a stone from the urinary tract, esp. the bladder. [Late Latin from Greek *lithotomia* (as LITHO-, -TOMY)]

litho·tripsy /ˈlɪθəˌtrɪpsi/ *noun* (*pl.* **-sies**) a treatment using ultrasound to shatter a stone in the bladder into small particles that can be passed through the urethra. [LITHO- + Greek *tripsis* rubbing, from *tribo* rub]

litho·trip·ter /ˈlɪθəˌtrɪptər/ *noun* a machine which generates and focuses ultrasonic waves to shatter stones in the bladder or kidney.

Lithu·ania /ˌlɪθuːˈeɪniə/ a country on the southeast shore of the Baltic Sea; pop. (est. 2002) 3,601,138; capital, Vilnius. Medieval Lithuania was an independent grand duchy which at its zenith, in the 14th c., extended to the shores of the Black Sea.

Lithu·an·ian /ˌlɪθuːˈeɪniən, ˌlɪθjuː-/ ● *noun* **1 a** a native or inhabitant of Lithuania. **b** a person of Lithuanian descent. **2** the language of Lithuania. ● *adjective* of or relating to Lithuania or its people or language.

liti·gant /ˈlɪtɪɡənt/ ● *noun* a party to a lawsuit. ● *adjective* engaged in a lawsuit. [French (as LITIGATE)]

liti·gate /ˈlɪtɪˌɡeɪt/ *verb* **1** *intransitive* take a claim or dispute to a law court; be a party to a lawsuit. **2** *transitive* contest (a point) in a lawsuit. □ **lit·ig·able** /ˈlɪtɪɡəbəl/ *adjective* [Latin *litigare litigat-* from *lis litis* lawsuit]

liti·ga·tion /ˌlɪtɪˈɡeɪʃən/ *noun* **1** the action or process of carrying on a lawsuit; legal proceedings. **2** an instance of legal proceedings.

liti·ga·tor /ˈlɪtɪˌɡeɪtər/ *noun esp. N Amer.* a person who litigates, esp. a trial lawyer.

liti·gious /lɪˈtɪdʒəs/ *adjective* **1** fond of or given to litigation or carrying on lawsuits; unreasonably so. **2** disputable in a law court; liable to become the subject of a lawsuit. **3** of or pertaining to lawsuits. □ **liti·gious·ly** *adverb* **liti·gious·ness** *noun* [Old French *litigieux* or Latin *litigiosus* from *litigium* litigation: see LITIGATE]

lit·mus *noun* a dye obtained from lichens that is red under acid conditions and blue under alkaline conditions. [Old Norwegian *litmosi* from Old Norse *litr* dye + *mosi* moss]

litmus paper *noun* a paper stained with litmus to be used as a test for acids or alkalis.

litmus test *noun* **1** *informal* a circumstance, phenomenon, question, etc., one's reaction to which serves to establish decisively the true character of an individual etc. **2** a test for acids or alkalis using litmus paper.

li·to·tes /laɪˈtoːtiːz/ *noun* ironic understatement, esp. the expressing of an affirmative by the negative of its contrary, e.g. *no mean feat* for some great accomplishment. [Late Latin from Greek *litotēs* from *litos* plain, meagre]

litre /ˈliːtər/ *noun* (esp. *US* **liter**) a metric unit of capacity, formerly defined as the volume of one kilogram of water under standard conditions, now equal to 1 cubic decimetre (about 35 oz.). [French from *litron*, an obsolete measure of capacity, from medieval Latin from Greek *litra* a Sicilian monetary unit]

Litt.D. *abbreviation* Doctor of Letters. [Latin *Litterarum Doctor*]

lit·ter ● *noun* **1 a** garbage discarded in an open or public place. **b** odds and ends lying about. **c** (*attributive*) for disposing of litter (*litter bin*). **2** a state of untidiness, disorderly accumulation of papers etc. **3** a group of young mammalian animals comprising all those born at one birth. **4** decomposing but still recognizable vegetable debris from plants etc. forming a distinct layer above the soil, esp. in a forest. **5** esp. *hist.* a vehicle containing a couch shut in by curtains and carried on men's shoulders or by beasts of burden. **6** a stretcher or portable bed for transporting the sick and wounded. **7 a** straw, rushes, etc., as bedding, esp. for animals. **b** straw and dung in a farmyard. **8** = CAT LITTER. ● *verb* **1 a** *transitive* make (a place) untidy with litter. **b** *intransitive* leave paper, garbage, etc. lying about, esp. in a public place. **2** *transitive* **a** scatter (paper etc.) untidily and leave lying about. **b** (of things) lie about untidily on (*old car parts littered the premises*). **c** fill (a text, history, etc.) with examples of something unpleasant (*news pages have been littered with doom and gloom about company collapses*). **3** *transitive* (of an animal) give birth to (whelps etc.). **4** *transitive* (often foll. by *down*) **a** provide (a horse etc.) with litter as bedding. **b** spread litter or straw on (a floor) or in (a stable). □ **lit·ter·er** *noun* [Anglo-French *litere*, Old French *litiere* from medieval Latin *lectaria* from Latin *lectus* bed]

lit·té·ra·teur /ˌlɪtɜrɑˈtɜr/ *noun* a writer of literary or critical works; a literary person. [French]

litter box *noun* a tray for cat litter.

litter·bug *noun* a person who carelessly leaves litter in a public place.

litter·less *adjective* **1** (of a lunch, picnic, etc.) packed in reusable containers so as to create no litter. **2** *proprietary* designating a small reusable container for food and beverages suitable for packed lunches etc.

litter lout *noun Brit.* = LITTERBUG.

litter·mate *noun* a mammal which is one of a group born or reared together in a single litter.

lit·tle ● *adjective* (**lit·tler, lit·tlest; less** or **lesser; least**) **1 a** (of a material object, immaterial thing, area of space, etc.) small in size, amount, degree, etc.; not large, great, or big. **b** often used to convey affectionate or emotional overtones, or condescension, not implied by *small* (*a terrific little guy; a silly little fool; a nice little car*). **2 a** (of a person) short in stature. **b** of short distance or duration (*will go a little way with you; wait a little while*). **3** (prec. by *a*) a certain though small amount of (*I'll have a little cream*). **4** trivial; relatively unimportant (*exaggerates every little difficulty*). **5** not much; inconsiderable (*gained little advantage from it*). **6** operating on a small scale (*the little store owner*). **7** as a distinctive epithet: **a** of a smaller or the smallest size of the things or the class specified (*little auk*). **b** that is the smaller or smallest of the name, type, or kind (*little auk*). **c** (of a town, district, etc.) less large or important, later established, or suggestive of another or others of that name (*Little Italy; Little India*). **8** young or younger (*a little boy; my little sister*). **9** (of a collective unity) having few members, small in number (*a little group of students*). **10** as of a child, evoking tenderness, condescension, amusement, etc. (*we know their little ways*). **11** mean, paltry, contemptible (*you little sneak*). ● *noun* **1** not much; only a small amount (*got very little out of it; did what little I could*). **2** (usu. prec. by *a*) **a** a certain but no great amount (*knows a little of everything*). **b** a short time or distance (*after a little*). ● *adverb* (**less, least**) **1 a** to a small extent only (*little-known authors; is little more than speculation*). **b** infrequently, rarely. **2** (prec. by *a*) somewhat (*is a little deaf*). **3** not at all; hardly (*they little thought*). □ **a little 1** to a little or slight extent. **2** for or at a short time or distance. **in little** (esp. of a painting) on a small scale, in miniature. **little by little** by degrees; gradually. **little or nothing** hardly anything. **no little** considerable, a good deal of (*took no little trouble over it*). **not a little 1** much; a great deal. **2** extremely (*not a little concerned*). **quite a little** a lot, much, considerably. □ **little·ness** *noun* [Old English *lýtel* from Germanic]

Little Ararat see ARARAT, MOUNT.

little auk *noun* a small arctic auk, *Alle alle*. Also called (*N Amer. & Scot.*) DOVEKIE.

Little Bear *noun* = LITTLE DIPPER.

Little Big·horn the site in Montana of the defeat of General George Custer and his forces by Sioux warriors on 25 June 1876, popularly known as Custer's Last Stand.

little-bitty *adjective N Amer. informal* very small; tiny.

little black book *noun* a record or list of valuable information, esp. of names and addresses of sexual partners.

little black dress *noun* a simple but elegant, classically designed short black dress, suitable for a variety of social occasions.

little boys' room *noun jocular* a men's washroom.

Little Dipper *noun N Amer.* the constellation Ursa Minor, containing the North Star.

little finger *noun* the smallest finger, at the outer end of the hand.

little girls' room *noun jocular* a women's washroom.

little green man *noun* an imaginary person of peculiar appearance, esp. from outer space.

little guy *noun N Amer.* (prec. by *the*) the common man, esp. a weak or unimportant person in contrast to the wealthy and powerful.

little ice age *noun* any period of comparatively cold climate occurring outside the major glacial periods, esp. (**Little Ice Age**) such a period which reached its peak in the 18th c.

little Johnny *noun* an unspecified boy, esp. a schoolchild (*why little Johnny can't read*).

little known *adjective* (hyphenated when *attributive*) not widely known; obscure, not famous.

Little League *noun N Amer.* a baseball league for children between the ages of 8 and 12.

little magazine *noun* a magazine devoted to serious literary or artistic interests, usu. with experimental writing and in small format.

little man *noun* esp. *jocular* **1** the average 'man in the street'. **2** a person working or producing on a small scale. **3** (as a form of address) a boy.

Little Minch see MINCH, THE.

little·neck *noun* (in full **littleneck clam**) a small variety of quahog.

little ones *plural noun* young children or animals.

little people *plural noun* **1** fairies, elves, leprechauns, etc. **2** the poor, ordinary people. **3** children. **4** *pl.* OF LITTLE PERSON.

little person *noun* a person who is genetically of abnormally short stature; a dwarf.

little red schoolhouse *noun N Amer.* **1** a one-room schoolhouse, esp. one of red brick, of a design that was typical throughout N America, esp. in rural areas, from the 19th to the mid-20th c. **2** (prec. by *the*) this as a symbol of old-fashioned educational practice, with all grades taught in the same room, emphasis on basics, rote learning, etc.

Little Rock the state capital of Arkansas; pop. (2000) 183,133.

Little Russian *hist.* ● *noun* a Ukrainian. ● *adjective* Ukrainian.

Little St. Bernard Pass see ST. BERNARD PASS.

little slam *noun Bridge* = SMALL SLAM.

little theatre *noun* a small playhouse, esp. one used for experimental drama or for community, non-commercial productions.

Little Tibet an alternative name for BALTISTAN.

little toe *noun* either of the outermost and smallest toes.

little woman *noun informal offensive* (prec. by *the*) one's wife.

lit·toral /ˈlɪtərəl/ ● *adjective* **1** of or on the shore of the sea, a lake, etc. **2** = INTERTIDAL. ● *noun* a region lying along a shore. [Latin *littoralis* from *litus litoris* shore]

Lit·tré /liːˈtreɪ/ **(Maxi·mi·lien)** Paul Émile (1801–81), French lexicographer and philosopher. He was the author of the major *Dictionnaire de la langue française* (1863–77) and also wrote a history of the French language (1862); he became the leading exponent of positivism after Comte's death.

li·tur·gic·al /lɪˈtɜrdʒɪkəl/ *adjective* of or related to liturgies or public religious worship. □ **li·tur·gic·al·ly** *adverb* [medieval Latin from Greek *leitourgikos* (as LITURGY)]

li·tur·gics /lɪˈtɜrdʒɪks/ *plural noun* (usu. treated as *sing.*) the branch of knowledge that deals with liturgies, their form, origin, etc.

lit·urgy /ˈlɪtərdʒi/ *noun* (*pl.* **-gies**) **1 a** public worship, esp. in accordance with a prescribed form. **b** a collection of formularies for the conducting of divine services. **2** the Communion office of the Orthodox Church. □ **lit·ur·gist** *noun* [French *liturgie* or Late Latin *liturgia* from Greek *leitourgia* public worship, from *leitourgos* minister, from *leit-* public + *ergon* work]

liv·able *adjective* (also **liveable**) **1** (of a house, room, climate, etc.) fit to live in. **2** (of a life) bearable; worth living. **3** (of a person) companionable; easy to live with. □ **liv·abil·ity** *noun* **liv·able·ness** *noun*

live¹ /lɪv/ *verb* **1** *intransitive* be alive; have animal or vegetable life. **2** *intransitive* (foll. by *on*) subsist or feed (*lives on fruit*). **3** *intransitive* (foll. by *on, off*) depend on for a livelihood or subsistence (*lives off the family; lives on income from investments*). **4** *intransitive* (foll. by *on, by*) sustain one's position or repute (*live on their reputation; lives by his wits*). **5** *transitive* **a** spend, pass, experience (*lived a happy life*). **b** express in one's life (*was living a lie; Jan lives her faith*). **6** *intransitive* conduct oneself in a specified way, esp. with reference to moral behaviour, personal aims or principles, etc. (*lived in a perpetual state of anxiety*). **7** *intransitive* arrange one's habits, expenditure, feeding, etc. (*live modestly*). **8** *intransitive* **a** make or have one's abode (*lived in Brandon*). **b** *informal* (of an inanimate object) have as its usual storage place (*where does the kettle live?*).

9 *intransitive* (foll. by *in*) spend much non-working time, the daytime, etc. (*the room does not seem to be lived in*). **10** *intransitive* **a** (of a person etc.) continue in life, have one's life prolonged. **b** (of a thing, experience, etc.) continue in actuality (*the horrors of war live on*). **c** (of a thing, experience, etc.) continue in memory, escape obliteration or oblivion (*ideals live on*). **11** *intransitive* enjoy life intensely or to the full (*you haven't lived till you've seen Robert Tewsley dance*). □ **live and breathe** be utterly absorbed or consumed by (an interest). **live and learn** expressing surprise at some new or unexpected information. **live and let live** be tolerant towards others of different opinions, lifestyles, etc. **live dangerously** take risks habitually. **live down** (usu. with *neg.*) cause (past guilt, embarrassment, etc.) to be forgotten by different conduct over a period of time (*you'll never live that down!*). **live for** regard as the aim or purpose of one's life (*she lives for her work*). **live in** (of a domestic employee, student, etc.) reside on the premises of one's work, school, etc. **live in hope** remain hopeful. **live in the past** behave as though circumstances, values, etc. have not changed from what they were previously. **live it up** *informal* pursue pleasure, live extravagantly. **live off the land** subsist on the produce of the land. **live one's own life** follow one's own plans or principles; live independently. **live out 1** spend the rest of (one's life) (*will I live out my days as a lexicographer?*). **2** experience or execute in reality (one's fantasies, ideas, etc.). **3** (of a domestic employee etc.) reside away from one's place of work. **live through** survive; remain alive at the end of. **live to** survive and reach (*lived to a great age*). **live together** (esp. of an unmarried couple) share a home and have a sexual relationship. **live up to 1** honour or fulfill; put into practice (principles etc.). **2** reach and maintain an expected standard, either good or bad. **live well 1** thrive, survive. **2** have plenty; be in comfortable circumstances. **3** live a virtuous, satisfying life. **live with 1** share a home with. **2** share a home and have a sexual relationship with. **3** tolerate; endure. **live with oneself** retain one's self-respect. **long live …!** an exclamation of support, loyalty, or endorsement (to a person etc. specified). **where one lives** *N Amer.* at, to, or in the right, vital, or most vulnerable spot (*hits me where I live*). [Old English *libban, lifian*, from Germanic]

live² /laɪv/ ● *adjective* **1 a** (*attributive*) that is alive; living. **b** actual, genuine; not pretended or pictured as a toy (*real live musicians*). **2 a** (of a broadcast) heard or seen at the time of its performance, not from a recording. **b** (of a recording, film, etc.) made of a live performance. **c** taking place concurrently (*live telephone bidding*). **3 a** (of a person etc.) lively, alert, energetic; full of life. **b** (of a question, issue, etc.) of current interest, not obsolete or exhausted (*sustainable development is a live issue*). **4** *Sport* **a** (of a ball in baseball, football, etc.) in play. **b** (of a tennis ball etc.) having ample bounce or rebound. **5** expending or still able to expend energy in various forms, esp.: **a** (of coals) glowing, burning. **b** (of a shell) unexploded and capable of exploding. **c** (of a cartridge) containing a bullet; not a blank. **d** (of a wire etc.) connected to a source of electrical power. **e** (of a microphone) switched on, receptive to sound. **6 a** (of a volcano) not extinct. **b** (of a mineral or rock) still forming part of the earth's mass, unwrought. **7** (of a room, auditorium, etc.) having a relatively long reverberation time. **8** (of a wheel or axle etc. in machinery) moving or imparting motion. **9** (of a vaccine) containing living but weakened disease-causing micro-organisms. ● *adverb* in order to make a live broadcast; as a live performance (*going over live now to the House of Commons; the show went out live*). □ **go live** *Computing* (of a system) become operational. □ **live·ness** *noun* [apheptic form of ALIVE]

live·able *var. of* LIVABLE.

live-aboard ● *noun* **1** a yacht etc. equipped with basic facilities for daily, and often year-round, living. **2** a person who lives on a yacht etc. ● *adjective* (of a yacht etc.) equipped with the necessary facilities for daily living.

live action *noun* (often *attributive*) *Film* action involving real people or animals, as opposed to animation etc.

live bait *noun* a living worm, small fish, etc. used as bait.

live birth *noun* a birth in which the child is born alive.

lived-in *adjective* **1** (of a room etc.) showing signs of habitation. **2** *informal* (of a face) marked by experience.

live-in ● *attributive adjective* **1** (of a sexual partner) cohabiting. **2** (of a domestic employee etc.) residing on the premises of one's work (*a live-in nanny*). ● *noun* a live-in employee, lover, etc.

live·li·hood *noun* a way of earning a living; an occupation. [Old English *līflād* from *līf* LIFE + *lād* course (see LOAD): assimilated to obsolete *livelihood* liveliness]

live·long /ˈlɪvlɒŋ/ *adjective* in its entire length or apparently so (*the*

livelong day). [Middle English *lefe longe* (as LIEF, LONG¹): assimilated to LIVE¹]

live·ly *adjective* (**live·li·er, live·li·est**) **1** full of life; vigorous, energetic. **2** brisk (*a lively pace; a lively tune*). **3** vivid, stimulating (*a lively discussion; a lively imagination*). **4** (of a person, group, etc.) vivacious, jolly, sociable. **5** *jocular* exciting, dangerous, difficult (*the press is making things lively for them*). **6** (of a colour) bright and vivid. **7 a** (of an image, picture, etc.) lifelike, realistic, animated (*a lively description*). **b** (of feelings, impressions, memories, etc.) strong, intense, striking. **8** (of a ball) bouncy. **9** (of a narrative) full of action and incident. **10** (of food) tasty, esp. spicy. □ **step** (or **look**) **lively** move (more) quickly or energetically. □ **live·li·ness** *noun* [Old English *līflic* (as LIFE, -LY¹)]

liven /ˈlaɪvən/ *transitive & intransitive verb* (usu. foll. by *up*) *informal* **1** make or become more lively. **2** cheer; brighten.

live oak *noun* an American evergreen tree, *Quercus virginiana*.

live-out *adjective* (of a domestic employee etc.) residing away from one's place of work.

liver¹ *noun* **1 a** a large, lobed, glandular organ in the abdomen of vertebrates, functioning in many metabolic processes including the regulation of toxic materials in the blood, secreting bile, etc. **b** a similar organ in other animals. **2** the flesh of an animal's liver as food. **3** a dark reddish brown. [Old English *lifer* from Germanic]

liver² *noun* a person who lives in a specified way (*a clean liver*).

liver fluke *noun* either of two types of fluke, esp. *Fasciola hepatica*, the adults of which live within the liver tissues of vertebrates, and the larvae within snails.

liver·ish *adjective* **1** resembling liver in colour etc. **2** peevish, glum, bad-tempered. **3** suffering from a disorder of the liver. □ **liver·ish·ness** *noun*

Liver·pool a city and seaport in NW England, situated at the east side of the mouth of the Mersey; pop. (1998) 461,500.

Liver·pud·lian ● *noun* a native of Liverpool. ● *adjective* of or relating to Liverpool. [jocular from *Liverpool* + PUDDLE]

liver spots *plural noun* brown spots or patches of melanin on the skin, characteristic of any of several medical conditions. □ **liver·spotted** *adjective*

liver·wort /ˈlɪvər,wɜrt, -wɔrt/ *noun* any small leafy or thalloid bryophyte of the class Hepaticae, of which some have liver-shaped parts.

liver·wurst *noun N Amer.* (also **liver sausage**) a cooked sausage having a high proportion of esp. pork liver. [LIVER¹ + German *Wurst* sausage]

liv·ery /ˈlɪvəri/ *noun* (*pl.* **-eries**) **1 a** a distinctive uniform worn by servants in a particular household. **b** *hist.* distinctive attire worn by members of the London trade guilds. **2** a distinctive guise, marking, or outward appearance (*birds in their winter livery*). **3** an emblem, device, or distinctive colour scheme on a vehicle, product, etc. indicating its owner or manufacturer. **4** *N Amer.* a place where horses can be hired. **5** *hist.* a provision of food or clothing for retainers etc. **6** *Law* the legal delivery of property. □ **liv·er·ied** *adjective* (esp. in senses 1, 3). [Old French *livrée*, fem. past participle of *livrer* DELIVER]

livery company *noun Brit.* one of the London corporations descended from an ancient trade guild that formerly had a distinctive costume.

livery·man /ˈlɪvərimən/ *noun* (*pl.* **-men**) **1** *Brit.* a member of a livery company. **2** a keeper of or attendant in a livery stable.

livery stable *noun* (also **livery barn**) a stable where horses are kept for their owners in return for payment, or from which horses may be rented.

lives *pl. of* LIFE.

Live·say /ˈlaɪvsi/ **Dor·othy** (1909–96), Canadian poet and critic. Her first book, *Green Pitcher*, was published in 1928; it was followed by volumes such as *Day and Night* (1944) and *Collected Poems* (1972).

live·stock *noun* (usu. treated as *pl.*) animals kept esp. on a farm for use or profit, e.g. cattle, sheep, etc.

live trap ● *noun* a boxlike trap for catching esp. wild animals alive and without hurting them. ● *transitive verb* (**live-trap**) (**live-trapped, live-trapping**) catch (an animal) in such a trap for relocation, ear tagging, etc. □ **live trapping** *noun*

live weight *noun* the weight of an animal before it has been slaughtered and prepared as a carcass.

live·well *noun* a tub-like container of water in a fishing boat, often aerated and sunk flush with the deck, in which caught fish are kept alive and fresh.

live wire noun **1** an energetic and forceful person. **2** a wire conveying an electric current.

live·yer Cdn (Nfld) var. of LIVYER.

livid /ˈlɪvɪd/ adjective **1** informal furiously angry. **2** disputed of an intense reddish colour. ¶ Evolving from the association of 'livid' with an angry visage, this sense is contrary to the word's original meaning and is therefore often regarded as incorrect. It is, however, widely used. **3 a** of a bluish leaden colour. **b** discoloured as by a bruise. □ **livid·ity** /lɪˈvɪdɪti/ noun **livid·ly** adverb **livid·ness** noun [French livide or Latin lividus from livēre be bluish]

liv·ing ● noun **1 a** a means of keeping alive or living in a certain style (made my living as a journalist). **b** a way of earning this (what does she do for a living?). **2** the action of leading one's life in a particular moral, physical, etc. manner. **3** (prec. by the; treated as pl.) those who are alive. **4** Brit. a position as a vicar or rector with an income or property. ● adjective **1 a** that lives or has life; not dead or extinct. **b** contemporary; now existent (the greatest living poet). **2** (of a likeness or image of a person) exact. **3** (of a language) still in vernacular use. **4** (of water) perennially flowing. **5** (of rock etc.) = LIVE² 6b. **6** informal complete, entire (scared the living daylights out of him; a living hell). □ **within living memory** within the memory of people still living.

living area noun an area in a room or house for general use during the day.

living colour noun vivid or true-to-life colour.

living dead noun = ZOMBIE 2.

living death noun **1** an empty or miserable existence. **2** a zombie-like state, believed to be induced by voodoo, witchcraft, etc.

living fossil noun a plant or animal that has survived relatively unchanged since the extinction of others of its group, known only as fossils.

living legend noun a person widely celebrated, while still alive, as very famous (or notorious) in a particular field.

living museum noun (also **living history museum**) **1** a historic site, or a recreation of one, at which historical interpreters dress in period costume, perform period-specific tasks and trades, etc., to bring the period to life for tourists etc. **2** a site in which flora etc. no longer usu. found elsewhere is preserved in its natural state.

living room noun **1** a room in a private home for general use during the daytime. **2** = LEBENSRAUM.

living space noun **1** an area in a room or house for general use during the day. **2** space for accommodation.

living standard noun the level of consumption in terms of food, clothing, services, etc. estimated for a person, group, or nation.

Living·stone¹ /ˈlɪvɪŋstən/ the former name for MARAMBA.

Living·stone² /ˈlɪvɪŋstən/ **David** (1813–73), Scottish missionary and explorer. He first went to Bechuanaland as a missionary in 1841, and on his extensive travels in the interior he discovered Lake Ngami (1849), the Zambezi river (1851), and Victoria Falls (1855); in 1866 he led an expedition into central Africa in search of the source of the Nile, and was eventually found in poor health by the explorer Sir Henry Morton Stanley (1871).

living wage noun the lowest wage on which a person can afford a reasonable standard of living without undue hardship.

living will noun a written declaration, morally though in many jurisdictions not legally binding, by a person setting out the circumstances in which artificial means of maintaining his or her life should be withdrawn.

Li·vo·nia /lɪˈvoːniə/ a region on the east coast of the Baltic Sea, north of Lithuania, comprising most of present-day Latvia and Estonia. Formerly ruled by Teutonic Knights, the region was the scene of the Livonian War (1558–82), in which Russia unsuccessfully fought an alliance of Poland, Sweden, and Lithuania for control of the territory. □ **Li·vo·nian** adjective & noun

Li·vor·no /lɪˈvɔːrnoʊ/ (also **Leghorn** /ˈlɛghɔːrn/) a port in NW Italy, in Tuscany, on the Ligurian Sea; pop. (2001) 148,143. It is the site of the Italian Naval Academy.

livre /ˈliːvrə/ noun an old French monetary unit, worth one pound of silver. [French from Latin libra pound]

Livy /ˈlɪvi/ (Latin name Titus Livius) (59 BC–AD 17), Roman historian. His history of Rome from its foundation to his own time contained 142 books, of which 35 survive (including the earliest history of the war with Hannibal).

liv·yer /ˈlɪvjər/ noun (also **liveyer**) Cdn (Nfld) a resident or permanent settler in Newfoundland or Labrador. [prob. var. of LIVER²]

lix·ivi·ate /lɪˈksɪvɪˌeɪt/ transitive verb separate (a substance) into soluble and insoluble constituents by the percolation of liquid. □ **lix·ivi·ation** noun [Latin lixivius made into lye, from lix lye]

Lizard, the a promontory in SW England, in Cornwall. Its southern tip, Lizard Point, is the southernmost point of the British mainland.

liz·ard noun **1** any reptile of the suborder Lacertilia, having usu. a long body and tail, four legs, movable eyelids, and a rough or scaly hide. **2** leather made from lizard skin. [Old French lesard(e) from Latin lacertus]

Ljub·lja·na /luːˈbljɑnə/ the capital of Slovenia; pop. (2002) 257,338.

ll. abbreviation lines (in references).

'll verb **1** (usu. after pronouns) shall, will (I'll; that'll). **2** informal (usu. after verbs) till (wait'll they get a load of me!). [abbreviation]

llama /ˈlɑːmə, ˈlʌmə/ noun **1** a S American ruminant, Lama glama, kept as a beast of burden and for its soft woolly fleece. **2** the wool from this animal, or cloth made from it. [Spanish, prob. from Quechua]

llano /ˈlɑːnoʊ, ˈljɑ-/ noun (pl. **llanos**) a treeless grassy plain or steppe, esp. in S America. [Spanish from Latin planum plain]

LL.B. abbreviation Bachelor of Laws. [Latin legum baccalaureus]

LLBO abbreviation Cdn Liquor Licence Board of Ontario.

LL.D. abbreviation Doctor of Laws. [Latin legum doctor]

Llew·elyn /luːˈwɛlɪn/ (also **Llyw·elyn ap Gruf·fydd** /ˈluːwɛlɪn ap ˈɡrɪfɪð/) (d.1282), prince of Wales. He proclaimed himself prince of all Wales (1258) and later formed an alliance with Simon de Montfort, leader of the baronial opposition to Henry III (1262); his refusal to pay homage to Edward I led the latter to invade and subjugate Wales (1276–7), and Llewelyn died in an unsuccessful rebellion.

LL.M. abbreviation Master of Laws. [Latin legum magister]

Llosa see VARGAS LLOSA.

Lloyd 1 Gwen·eth (1901–1993), English-born Canadian ballet teacher, director and choreographer. Coming to Canada in 1938, she settled in Winnipeg and soon opened both a school and the Winnipeg Ballet Club, which grew into the Royal Winnipeg Ballet; she continued to choreograph and direct ballets for the company until 1952. She also founded ballet schools in Toronto and Kelowna, and in 1946 helped to establish the Banff Centre's summer dance program. **2 Har·old (Clay·ton)** (1893–1971), US film comedian. Performing his own hair-raising stunts, he used physical danger as a source of comedy in silent movies such as High and Dizzy (1920), Safety Last (1923), and The Freshman (1925). He received an honorary Academy Award in 1952.

Lloyd George, David, 1st Earl Lloyd George of Dwyfor (1863–1945), English Liberal politician, prime minister 1916–22. As Chancellor of the Exchequer (1908–15), he introduced old-age pensions (1908) and national insurance (1911); supported by the Conservatives, he took over from Asquith as prime minister (1916), and led the coalition government for the remainder of the First World War.

Lloyd·min·ster a city on the Alberta-Saskatchewan border, about 250 km east of Edmonton; pop. (2001) 20,988. [Rev. G. Exton Lloyd, who led two thousand settlers to the area from Britain c.1903]

Lloyd's noun an incorporated society of underwriters in London who undertake insurance, originally marine insurance only, with individual liability. [after the original meeting in a coffee house established in 1688 by Edward Lloyd]

Lloyd's Register noun **1** an annual alphabetical list of ships assigned to various classes. **2** an independent society that publishes this.

Lloyd Web·ber, Sir An·drew (b.1948), English composer. He has written many successful musicals, several of them in collaboration with the lyricist Tim Rice (b.1944); they include Jesus Christ Superstar (1970), Evita (1976), Cats (1981), and The Phantom of the Opera (1986).

Llyw·elyn ap Gruf·fydd SEE LLEWELYN.

LM abbreviation lunar module.

lm abbreviation lumen(s).

ln abbreviation natural logarithm. [modern Latin logarithmus naturalis]

LNB abbreviation low noise blocker (on a satellite dish).

LNG abbreviation liquefied natural gas.

lo¹ interjection archaic or jocular calling attention to an amazing sight. □ **lo and behold** a formula introducing a surprising or unexpected fact. [Old English lā interj. of surprise etc., & Middle English lō = lōke LOOK]

lo² adjective low, used esp. in advertising etc. (lo fi, lo-cal). [simplified spelling]

loach noun any of numerous small slender freshwater cyprinoid fishes of the family Cobitidae, found in Europe and Asia. [Old French loche from Gaulish leuka 'whiteness', with reference to the colour of its flesh]

load • *noun* **1 a** a thing that is being carried or to be carried, esp. if heavy. **b** (often in *combination*) an amount usu. or actually carried, esp. by a specified vehicle (*a busload of tourists; a truckload of grain*). **2 a** the quantity of a particular substance which it is customary to load at one time. **b** a unit of measure or weight based on this. **3 a** a burden of care, grief, affliction, etc. **b** an amount of work, teaching, responsibility, etc. to be done or borne by a person. **4** *informal* **a** (in *pl.*; often foll. by *of*) plenty; a lot. **b** (**a load of**) a quantity of (*a load of nonsense*). **5 a** the amount of electric power that a generating system is delivering or required to deliver at any moment. **b** the amount of power supplied by a generating system at any given time. **c** an impedance or circuit that receives or develops the output of a transistor or other device. **6** the weight or force borne by the supporting part of a structure. **7** a material object or force which acts or is conceived as a weight, clog, etc. **8** the resistance of machinery to motive power. **9** a quantity of items washed or to be washed in a washing machine or dishwasher at one time. **10** the charge of a firearm. **11** a commission charged on the purchase of mutual funds. • *verb* **1** *transitive* **a** put a load on or aboard (a person, vehicle, ship, etc.). **b** place (a load or cargo) aboard a ship, on a vehicle, etc. **2** *intransitive* (often foll. by *up*) **a** (of a ship, vehicle, or person) take a load aboard, pick up a load. **b** (of a vehicle) fill with passengers. **3** *transitive* (often foll. by *with*) **a** add weight to; be a weight or burden upon (*a stomach loaded with food*). **b** oppress with affliction, responsibility, etc. **4** *transitive* strain the bearing capacity of (*a table loaded with food*). **5** *transitive* (also **load up**) (foll. by *with*) **a** supply overwhelmingly (*loaded us with work*). **b** assail overwhelmingly (*loaded us with abuse*). **6** *transitive & intransitive* put a charge of ammunition into (a firearm). **7** *transitive* **a** insert a photographic film or plate in (a camera). **b** insert (a film) into a camera. **8** *transitive* transfer (a program or data) into memory, or into the central processing unit from a more remote part of memory. **9** *transitive Electricity* provide with a load consisting of any kind of impedance. **10** *transitive* add an extra charge to (an insurance premium) in the case of a poorer risk. **11** *transitive* give a bias to (dice, a roulette wheel, etc.) with weights. **12** *transitive* place items for washing in (a washing machine or dishwasher). □ **a load off one's mind** (or **back** etc.) a source of anxiety removed. **get a load of** *slang* listen attentively to; notice. **load the bases** *Baseball* place baserunners on all three bases. **take a load off (one's feet)** *informal* sit or lie down; take the body's weight off the feet. **under load** *Mech. & Electricity* subjected to a load. □ **load·able** *adjective* [Old English *lād* way, journey, conveyance, from Germanic: related to LEAD[1]]

load-bearing *adjective* (of a wall, beam, etc.) supporting much of the weight of a structure.

load cell *noun* an electronic device for weighing large quantities of material.

load·ed *adjective* **1 a** bearing or carrying a load. **b** (of a weapon) charged with ammunition. **2** *slang* **a** wealthy. **b** drunk. **c** *N Amer.* drugged. **3** (of dice etc.) weighted or given a bias. **4** (of a question or statement) charged with some hidden or improper implication. **5** *N Amer. informal* (of a car etc.) equipped with optional extras; containing more than the standard equipment. □ **loaded for bear** *slang* fully prepared, esp. for a fight, challenge, or confrontation.

load·er *noun* **1 a** a machine or device for loading things. **b** = FRONT-END LOADER. **2** *Computing* a program which controls the loading of other programs. **3** (in *combination*) a gun, machine, vessel, etc. that is loaded in a specified way (*hand-loader, breech-loader*). **4** a person who loads things, esp. guns. □ **-loading** *adjective* (in *combination*) (in sense 3).

load factor *noun* **1** the ratio of the average or actual amount of work, power, etc. to the maximum possible. **2 a** the ratio of seats occupied in an aircraft to the number available. **b** the weight of freight carried as a proportion of the maximum that can be carried. **c** the ratio of the weight of an aircraft to the maximum weight the wings can support.

load·ing *noun* **1 a** the act of one who loads. **b** the load or cargo of a vehicle, vessel, etc. **2** *Electricity* the maximum current or power taken by an appliance. **3** an increase in an insurance premium due to a factor increasing the risk involved (*see* LOAD *verb* 10). **4** *Archit. & Engin.* the loads collectively that act on a structure or part of one. **5** *Psych.* the extent to which a factor or variable contributes to or is correlated with some resultant quality or overall situation, usu. represented by a number arrived at by statistical analysis of test results. **6 a** the use of some added material for the purpose of adulteration or falsification. **b** the substance added. **7** *informal* massive consumption of a particular substance etc. to enhance one's performance (*carbo-loading*).

loading dock *noun* *N Amer.* a raised platform, e.g. at a warehouse etc., from which trucks or railway cars are loaded or unloaded.

load line *noun* a marking on a ship's side showing the limit of legal submersion under various conditions.

load·master *noun* the member of an aircraft's crew who is responsible for the cargo.

load·star *var. of* LODESTAR.

load·stone *var. of* LODESTONE.

loaf[1] *noun* (*pl.* **loaves**) **1** a portion of baked bread, usu. of a standard size or shape. **2** a quantity of other food formed into a particular, usu. oblong shape (*meat loaf*). **3** = LOAF CAKE. **4** *Brit. slang* the head, esp. as a source of common sense (*use your loaf*). □ **half a loaf is better than none** (or **no bread**) **1** having to accept less than one expects or feels entitled to is better than having nothing at all. **2** it is better to compromise in one's demands than to risk losing all. [Old English *hlāf* from Germanic]

loaf[2] *verb* **1** *intransitive* (often foll. by *about, around*) spend time idly; hang about. **2** *transitive* (foll. by *away*) waste (time) idly (*loafed away the morning*). **3** *intransitive* saunter. [prob. a back-formation from LOAFER]

loaf cake *noun* a plain cake, usu. including fruit or nuts, baked in an oblong shape.

loaf·er *noun* **1** an idle person. **2** a leather shoe shaped like a moccasin with a flat heel. [perhaps from German *Landläufer* vagabond]

loaf·ing *adjective* (*attributive*) designating a barn or part of one or an outdoor area in which cattle etc. are allowed to roam freely, rather than being tied, penned, or at pasture (*loafing barn; loafing area*).

loaf pan *noun* *N Amer.* (*Brit.* **loaf tin**) a deep, rectangular baking pan, typically 22×12 cm (9×5 inches), used for breads etc.

loam *noun* **1** a fertile soil of clay and sand containing decayed vegetable matter. **2** a paste of clay and water with sand, chopped straw, etc., used in making bricks, plastering, etc. □ **loamy** *adjective* **loam·i·ness** *noun* [Old English *lām* from West Germanic, related to LIME[1]]

loan • *noun* **1** something lent, esp. a sum of money to be returned, normally with interest. **2** the act of lending or state of being lent. **3** a word, custom, etc., adopted by one people from another. • *transitive verb* lend (esp. money). □ **on loan** acquired or given as a loan. □ **loan·able** *adjective* [Middle English *lan* from Old Norse *lán* from Germanic: compare LEND]

loan·er *noun* **1** a car, computer, etc. lent to a customer while the customer's is kept for repair or service. **2** a lender.

loan shark *noun* *informal* a person who lends money at exorbitant rates of interest. □ **loan·shark·ing** *noun*

loan translation *noun* = CALQUE.

loan word *noun* a word adopted, usu. with little modification, from a foreign language.

loath /loːθ/ *predicative adjective* (usu. foll. by *to* + infin.) disinclined, reluctant, unwilling (*was loath to admit it*). [Old English *lāth* from Germanic]

loathe /loːð/ *transitive verb* regard with disgust; abominate, detest. □ **loath·er** *noun* **loath·ing** *noun* [Old English *lāthian* from Germanic, related to LOATH]

loath·some /ˈloːðsəm, ˈloːθ-/ *adjective* arousing hatred or disgust; offensive, repulsive. □ **loath·some·ly** *adverb* **loath·some·ness** *noun* [Middle English from *loath* disgust from LOATHE]

loaves *pl.* of LOAF[1].

LOB *abbreviation Baseball* left on base.

lob • *transitive verb* (**lobbed, lobbing**) **1** hit or throw (a ball etc.) slowly or in a high arc. **2** fire (a rocket or other missile) in a high arc. **3** send (an opponent) a lobbed ball. **4** direct (questions, insults, accusations, etc.) at a person. • *noun* **1 a** a ball struck in a high arc. **b** a stroke producing this result. **2** *Cdn* (also **lob ball**) a question that is easy to answer, esp. one that is made intentionally so in order to make the respondent look competent, articulate, etc. [earlier as noun, prob. from Low German or Dutch]

Loba·chev·ski /ˌlɒbəˈtʃɛfski/ **Niko·lai Ivan·ovich** (1792–1856), Russian mathematician. At about the same time as Gauss in Germany and János Bolyai (1802–60) in Hungary, he independently discovered non-Euclidean geometry.

lobar /ˈloːbər/ *adjective* **1** of the lungs (*lobar pneumonia*). **2** of, relating to, or affecting a lobe.

lob·ate /ˈloːbeit/ *adjective Biol.* having a lobe or lobes; lobed. □ **lob·a·tion** /-ˈbeiʃən/ *noun*

lob·by • *noun* (*pl.* **-bies**) **1** a usu. large area inside the main entrance of a public building leading to other rooms, or to the auditorium in a theatre etc. **2 a** a body of persons seeking to influence legislators on behalf of a particular interest (*the anti-abortion lobby*). **b** an organized attempt by members of the public to influence legislators. **3 a** (also **division lobby**) each of two areas on either side of the Commons chamber in which MPs may relax or discuss party strategy and in which they assemble before a vote. **b** *Brit.* (in the House of Commons) a large hall used esp. for meetings between MPs and members of the public. ● *verb* (**-bies, -bied**) **1** *transitive* solicit the support of (an influential person). **2 a** *transitive* (of members of the public) seek to influence (the members of a legislature). **b** *intransitive* attempt to persuade a politician to support or oppose changes in the law (*fishermen lobbying for higher quotas*). □ **lob·by·ing** *noun & adjective* **lob·by·ist** *noun* [medieval Latin *lobia, lobium* LODGE]

lobe *noun* **1** a roundish and flattish projecting or pendulous part, often each of two or more such parts divided by a fissure (*lobes of the brain*). **2** = EARLOBE. □ **lobed** *adjective* **lobe·less** *adjective* [Late Latin from Greek *lobos* lobe, pod]

lob·ec·tomy /ləˈbɛktəmi/ *noun* (*pl.* **-mies**) *Surgery* the excision of a lobe of an organ such as the thyroid gland, lung, etc.

lo·belia /ləˈbiːliə/ *noun* any plant of the genus *Lobelia*, with blue, scarlet, white, or purple flowers having a deeply cleft corolla. [M. de *Lobel*, Flemish botanist in England d.1616]

Lobo *noun* N *Amer.* a large, yellow-green eating apple with red streaks.

lob·ot·om·ize /ləˈbɒtəmaɪz/ *transitive verb* (also esp. *Brit.* **-ise**) **1** perform a lobotomy on. **2** (usu. as **lob·ot·om·ized** *adjective*) make (a person) apathetic or zombie-like.

lob·ot·omy /ləˈbɒtəmi/ *noun* (*pl.* **-omies**) *Surgery* **1** surgical incision into a lobe, esp. the prefrontal lobe of the brain, formerly used to treat intractable psychiatric disorders. **2** an instance of this.

lob·scouse /ˈlɒbskaʊs/ *noun* a sailor's dish of meat stewed with vegetables and ship's biscuit. [18th c.: origin unknown: compare Dutch *lapskous*, Danish, Norwegian, German *Lapskaus*]

lob·ster ● *noun* **1** any large marine crustacean of the family Nephropidae, with stalked eyes and two pincer-like claws as the first pair of ten limbs. **2** its flesh as food. ● *intransitive verb* catch lobsters. □ **lob·ster·ing** *noun* [Old English *lopustre*, corruption of Latin *locusta* crustacean, locust]

lobster boat *noun* a boat used in lobster fishing, with a well in which to keep the lobsters alive.

lob·ster·man *noun* (*pl.* **-men**) N *Amer.* a person who traps lobster for a living.

lobster pot *noun* (also **lobster trap**) a device for trapping lobster, esp. one made of wooden slats.

lobster pound *noun* a place where lobsters trapped during the season are kept alive until they are sold and shipped.

lobster roll *noun* N *Amer.* (*Maritimes & New England*) a long bread roll with a filling of chopped lobster and mayonnaise.

lobster supper *noun* Cdn (*Maritimes*) a meal, usu. served in a community hall, featuring boiled lobster served with melted butter and accompanied by copious salads, bread rolls, clam chowder, and cake or pie.

lobster thermidor /ˈθɜːmɪdər/ *noun* a mixture of lobster meat, mushrooms, cream, egg yolks, and sherry, cooked in a lobster shell. [*thermidor* from the name of the 11th month of the French revolutionary calendar]

lobstick *noun* Cdn a tall, conspicuous coniferous tree that has had all but its uppermost branches lopped off, serving as a landmark, a monument, or a talisman. [LOP¹ + STICK¹]

lob·tail *intransitive verb* (of a whale) raise its tail in the air and beat the water with it. □ **lob·tail·ing** *noun*

lob·ule /ˈlɒbjuːl/ *noun* a small lobe or a subdivision of a lobe. □ **lob·ular** *adjective* **lob·ulate** /-lət/ *adjective* [LOBE]

local ● *adjective* **1** belonging to, existing in, or pertaining to a particular locality as opposed to the country as a whole. **2** limited, peculiar to, or only encountered in a particular place or places. **3 a** of or belonging to the neighbourhood (*the local doctor*). **b** (of a train, bus, etc.) serving a particular district or stopping at all or most stations or stops on the line or route. **4** of or affecting a part and not the whole, esp. of the body (*local pain; a local anaesthetic*). **5** (of a telephone call) to a nearby place and not subject to long-distance charges. ● *noun* **1** an inhabitant of a particular place regarded with reference to that place. **2** a local train, bus, etc. **3** N *Amer.* a local branch of a trade union. **4** a local anaesthetic. **5** (often prec. by *the*) *Brit. informal* a pub convenient to a person's home. □ **local·ly** *adverb* **local·ness** *noun* [Old French from Late Latin *localis* from Latin *locus* place]

local anaesthetic *noun* an anaesthetic that affects a restricted area of the body.

local area network *noun* a computer network in which computers in close proximity are able to communicate with each other and share resources. Abbr.: **LAN**.

local authority *noun* Brit. an administrative body in local government.

local bus *noun* **1** a bus service operating over short distances. **2** a computer connection directly from a microprocessor to an adjacent peripheral device such as a video system, allowing rapid transmission of data.

local colour *noun* **1** the detailed representation of the characteristic features of a place or period in order to convey a sense of actuality. **2** such features themselves in real life; picturesque qualities.

local content *noun* the part of a manufactured product that is made, supplied, or assembled locally.

lo·cale /loˈkal/ *noun* a scene or locality, esp. with reference to an event or occurrence taking place there. [French *local* (n.) (as LOCAL), respelt to indicate stress: compare MORALE]

local government *noun* **1** a system of administration of a city, municipality, etc. by the elected representatives of those who live there. **2** a governing body, e.g. a council, in such a system.

local group *noun* Astronomy the cluster of about twenty galaxies to which ours belongs.

local·ism *noun* **1** preference for what is local. **2** a local idiom, custom, etc. **3 a** attachment to a locality, esp. to the place where one lives. **b** a limitation of ideas, sympathies, and interests resulting from such attachment.

local·ity *noun* (*pl.* **-ities**) **1** an area or district considered as the site occupied by certain people or things or as the scene of certain activities; a neighbourhood. **2** the site or scene of something, esp. in relation to its surroundings. **3** the situation or position of an object, esp. the geographical place or situation of a plant, mineral, etc. [French *localité* or Late Latin *localitas* (as LOCAL)]

local·ize *verb* (also esp. *Brit.* **-ise**) **1 a** *transitive* restrict or assign to a particular place. **b** *Med. intransitive* (foll. by *in*) (of a disease or causative agent of disease) be confined to (a specified area of the body). **2** *transitive* invest with the characteristics of a particular place. **3** *transitive* attach to districts; decentralize. □ **local·iz·able** *adjective* **local·iz·a·tion** *noun* **local·ized** *adjective* **local·iz·er** *noun*

local municipality *noun* Cdn (Ont. & Que.) = URBAN MUNICIPALITY.

local paper *noun* a newspaper distributed only in a certain area and usu. featuring local, as distinct from national, news.

local talent *noun* the singers, artists, etc. from a given city, region, etc.

local time *noun* **1** the time as reckoned in a particular place. **2** time measured from the sun's transit over the meridian of a place.

Lo·car·no /ləˈkɑːrnoʊ/ a resort in S Switzerland, at the northern end of Lake Maggiore; pop. (est. 1998) 14,312.

Locarno Pact a series of agreements made in Locarno in 1925 between the UK, Germany, France, Belgium, Poland, and Czechoslovakia, which guaranteed the common borders of France, Germany, and Belgium and the demilitarization of the Rhineland, but did not fully resolve the question of Germany's eastern boundaries.

lo·cate /loˈkeit, ˈloː-/ *verb* **1** *transitive* discover the exact place or position of (*locate the enemy's camp*). **2** *transitive* establish in a place or in its proper place. **3** *transitive* state the locality of. **4** *transitive* (in *passive*) be situated. **5** *intransitive* (often foll. by *in*) N *Amer.* take up residence or business (in a place). □ **lo·cat·able** *adjective* **lo·ca·tor** *noun* [Latin *locare locat-* from *locus* place]

lo·ca·tion *noun* **1** a particular place; the place or position in which a person or thing is. **2** the act of locating or process of being located. **3** an actual place or natural setting featured in a film or broadcast, as distinct from a simulation in a studio (*filmed entirely on location*). **4** Computing = ADDRESS 1c, 1d. □ **lo·ca·tion·al** *adjective*

location ticket *noun* Cdn hist. a certificate entitling a settler to take possession of a piece of land as a homestead, but not conveying legal title.

loca·tive /ˈlɒkətɪv/ Grammar ● *noun* (in some languages) the case of nouns, pronouns, and adjectives, expressing location. ● *adjective* of or in the locative. [formed as LOCATE + -IVE, after *vocative*]

loc. cit. *abbreviation* in the passage already cited. [Latin *loco citato*]

loch /lɒk, lɒx/ *noun* Scot. **1** a lake. **2** an arm of the sea, esp. when narrow or partially landlocked. [Middle English from Gaelic]

loche /lɒʃ/ *noun* Cdn (North) = BURBOT. [French, as LOACH]

lochia /ˈlɒkiə, ˈloː-/ *noun* a discharge from the uterus after childbirth.

loch·ial *adjective* [modern Latin from Greek *lokhia* neuter pl. of *lokhios* of childbirth]

Loch Lo·mond /ˈlɒːmənd/ a lake in west central Scotland, to the northwest of Glasgow. It is the largest freshwater lake in Scotland.

Loch Morar /ˈmɔrɑr/ a lake in W Scotland. At 310 m (1,017 ft.), it is the deepest lake in the country.

Loch Ness a deep lake in NW Scotland, in the Great Glen. It is 38 km (24 miles) long, with a maximum depth of 230 m (755 ft.).

Loch Ness monster *noun* a large creature alleged since the 6th c. to live in the deep waters of Loch Ness; there is no proof of its existence.

loci[1] pl. *of* LOCUS.

loci[2] /ˈloːkiː/ *noun* (also **locie**) *Cdn informal* an engine used in logging or mining. [abbreviation of LOCOMOTIVE]

loci clas·sici pl. *of* LOCUS CLASSICUS.

Lock, Édouard (b.1954), Moroccan-born Canadian choreographer. In 1981 he founded the modern dance company now known as La La La Human Steps. His style aims more towards high energy and risk than to conventional aesthetics.

lock[1] ● *noun* **1** a device for fastening a door, lid, etc., which can only be opened by means of a key, combination, code, etc. **2** a confined section of a canal or river where the level can be changed for raising and lowering boats between adjacent sections by the use of gates and sluices. **3 a** the turning of the front wheels of a vehicle to change its direction of motion. **b** the maximum extent of this. **4** an interlocked or jammed state. **5** *Wrestling* a hold that keeps an opponent's limb fixed. **6** (in full **lock forward**) *Rugby* a player in the second row of a scrum. **7** an appliance to keep a wheel from revolving or slewing. **8** a mechanism for exploding the charge of a gun. **9** = AIRLOCK 2. **10** *N Amer. informal* a sure thing; a person or thing that is certain to succeed (*she is a lock to win the election*). ● *verb* **1 a** *transitive* fasten with a lock. **b** *intransitive* (of a door, window, box, etc.) have the means of being locked. **2** *transitive* (foll. by *up, in, into*) enclose (a person or thing) by locking or as if by locking. **3** *transitive* (often foll. by *up, away*) store or allocate inaccessibly (*capital locked up in land; lock away your jewels when you go on vacation*). **4** *transitive & intransitive* make or become rigidly fixed or immovable. **5** *intransitive & transitive* become or cause to become jammed or caught. **6** *transitive* (often in *passive*; foll. by *in*) entangle in an embrace or struggle. **7** *intransitive* interlace or intertwine (*the protesters locked arms*). **8** *intransitive* go through a lock on a canal etc. **9** *transitive Computing* make (a computer screen) inaccessible unless a password is entered. □ **lock down** *N Amer.* subject (a prisoner or prisoners) to a lockdown. **have a lock on** *N Amer. informal* have an unbreakable hold on or total control over (*she has a lock on her seat in the legislature*). **lock horns** come into conflict; engage in an argument. **be locked into** be irrevocably committed to (*am locked into going to this stupid party*). **lock in 1** (usu. in *passive*) convert (a mortgage) from a floating to a fixed rate of interest. **2** (of an investor) be unable to sell or convert (investments). **3** fix (a pension, investment, etc.) so that it cannot be transferred or sold. **lock lips** *informal* kiss. **lock on to** locate or cause to locate by radar, a heat-seeking device, etc., and then track. **lock oneself out** accidentally prevent oneself from entering a place, esp. by losing the key or locking it inside (*locked myself out of my car*). **lock out 1** keep (a person) out by locking the door. **2** (of an employer) submit (employees) to a lockout. **lock up 1** shut and secure (esp. a building) by locking (*you go ahead, and I'll lock up*). **2** imprison (*he should be locked up for life*). **3** commit to a psychiatric institution. **4** (of a computer or computer screen) cease to respond to input from the keyboard or mouse. **5** (esp. of a turning object) cease to move; seize (*slammed on the brakes and her wheels locked up*). **6** store; hold in reserve (*Canada's forests lock up huge amounts of carbon*). **7** *N Amer.* have complete control of; be assured of success in (*her party has locked up Ontario and will win almost every seat*). **under lock and key** securely locked up. □ **lock·able** *adjective* **lock·less** *adjective* [Old English *loc* from Germanic]

lock[2] *noun* **1 a** a portion of hair that coils or hangs together. **b** (in *pl.*) the hair of the head. **2** a tuft of wool or cotton. □ **-locked** *adjective* (in combination). [Old English *locc* from Germanic]

lock·box *noun* a small box with a locked lid which can be opened with a combination, usu. used to hold a house key.

lock·down *noun N Amer.* the confining of prisoners to their cells, esp. to gain control during a riot etc.

Locke, John (1632–1704), English philosopher, a founder of empiricism and political liberalism. In *Two Treatises of Government* (1690) he justified the Revolution of 1688 by arguing that the authority of rulers has a human origin, and is limited, and in his most famous work, *An Essay concerning Human Understanding* (1690), he denied that

any ideas are innate and argued that all knowledge is derived from sense-experience. □ **Lock·ean** *adjective*

locked-in retirement account *noun Cdn* a retirement savings account created with money transferred out of a registered pension plan and from which funds can only be transferred to a life income fund, a locked-in retirement income fund, or a life annuity. Abbr.: **LIRA**.

locked-in retirement income fund *noun Cdn* a tax-sheltered savings plan which provides retirement income. Abbr.: **LRIF**.

lock·er *noun* **1** a small lockable cupboard or compartment, esp. one of several in a school, bus station, locker room, etc. **2** *Naut.* a chest or compartment for clothes, stores, ammunition, etc. **3** a person or thing that locks.

Lock·er·bie /ˈlɒkɜrbiː/ a town in SW Scotland, in Dumfries and Galloway; pop. (est. 2001) 4,000. In 1988 the wreckage of an American airliner, destroyed by a terrorist bomb, crashed on the town. The disaster claimed the lives of all 259 people on the aircraft and eleven people on the ground.

locker room ● *noun* a change room at a swimming pool, fitness club, etc., with lockers for storing one's clothes etc. ● *adjective* (usu. **locker-room**) (of language, conversation, etc.) characteristic of or suited for a men's locker room; coarse, ribald (*locker-room humour*).

lock·et *noun* a small ornamental case holding a portrait, lock of hair, etc., and usu. hung from the neck. [Old French *locquet* diminutive of *loc* latch, lock, from West Germanic (as LOCK[1])]

lock·jaw *noun* a variety of tetanus with sustained contractions of the jaw muscles causing the mouth to remain tightly closed. *Also called* TRISMUS.

lock·nut *noun* **1** a nut screwed down on another to keep it tight. **2** a nut designed to prevent accidental loosening once it has been tightened.

lock·out *noun* the exclusion of employees by their employer from their place of work until certain terms are agreed to.

lock·smith *noun* a person who makes, repairs, and replaces locks. □ **lock·smith·ing** *noun*

lock·step ● *noun* marching with each person as close as possible to the one in front. ● *adjective* (usu. **lock-step**) rigid; inflexible. □ **in lockstep** exactly parallel; in exact synchronism.

lock stitch *noun* a stitch made by a sewing machine by firmly locking together two threads or stitches.

lock, stock, and barrel ● *noun* the whole of a thing. ● *adverb* completely.

lock-up *noun* **1** *informal* = JAIL *noun* 1. **2** *Cdn* a type of press conference where members of the media are allowed to examine a government budget in a locked room before it is brought down in the legislature, but are not allowed to leave the room or file any reports until the budget is officially brought down. **3** *Brit.* non-residential premises etc. that can be locked up, esp. a small shop or storehouse. **4 a** the locking up of premises for the night. **b** the time of doing this. **5 a** the unrealizable state of invested capital. **b** an amount of capital locked up.

Lock·yer, Sir Jo·seph Nor·man (1836–1920), English astronomer. His spectroscopic analysis of the sun led to his discovery of a new element, which he named *helium*.

loco[1] *noun* (pl. **locos**) *informal* a locomotive engine. [abbreviation]

loco[2] ● *adjective slang* crazy. ● *noun* (pl. **locos**) (in full **loco·weed**) a poisonous leguminous plant of N America causing brain disease in cattle eating it. [Spanish, = insane]

loco·motion *noun* motion or the power of motion from one place to another. [Latin *loco* ablative of *locus* place + *motio* MOTION]

loco·motive ● *noun* an engine, powered by diesel fuel or electricity, used for pulling trains. ● *adjective* **1** of or relating to or effecting locomotion (*locomotive power*). **2** having the power of or given to locomotion; not stationary.

loco·motor *adjective* of or relating to locomotion. [LOCOMOTION + MOTOR]

locu·lus /ˈlɒkjʊləs/ *noun* (pl. **loculi** /-ˌlaɪ/) *Zool., Anat., & Bot.* each of a number of small separate cavities. □ **locu·lar** *adjective* [Latin, diminutive of *locus*: see LOCUS]

lo·cum /ˈloːkəm/ *noun* (also **locum tenens** /ˌloːkəm ˈtiːnenz, ˈtenenz/) **1** a temporary substitute, esp. for a doctor, lawyer, minister, etc. **2** a position working as this. [medieval Latin *locum tenens*, one holding a place: see LOCUS, TENANT]

locus /ˈloːkəs/ *noun* (pl. **loci** /-saɪ/) **1** a position or point, esp. in a text, treatise, etc. **2** *Math.* a curve etc. formed by all the points satisfying a particular equation of the relation between coordinates, or by a point, line, or surface moving according to mathematically defined conditions. **3** *Biol.* the position of a gene, mutation, etc. on a chromosome. **4** the centre or source of something (*the locus of power has shifted*). [Latin, = place]

locus clas·si·cus /ˌloːkəs ˈklasıkəs/ *noun* (*pl.* **loci clas·si·ci** /ˌloːsai ˈklasɪˌsai/) the best-known or most authoritative passage on a subject. [Latin]

locus standi /ˌloːkəs ˈstandai/ *noun* a recognized or identifiable (esp. legal) status.

lo·cust /ˈloːkəst/ *noun* **1** any of various grasshoppers of the family Acrididae, migrating in swarms and destroying vegetation. **2** *N Amer.* a cicada. **3** (in full **locust bean**) a carob. **4** (in full **locust tree**) **a** a carob tree. **b** a tree, *Robinia pseudoacacia*, native to N America, bearing fragrant white flowers and black pods, grown for ornament. *Also called* BLACK LOCUST, FALSE ACACIA. **c** any of various other trees of the legume family. [Old French *locuste* from Latin *locusta* lobster, locust]

lo·cu·tion /ləˈkjuːʃən/ *noun* **1** a word or phrase, esp. considered in regard to style or idiom. **2** style of speech. □ **lo·cu·tion·ary** *adjective* [Old French *locution* or Latin *locutio* from *loqui locut-* speak]

lode *noun* **1** a vein of metal ore. **2** a rich source or plentiful supply (*your book is a lode of wisdom*). [var. of LOAD]

lo·den /ˈloːdən/ *noun* **1** a thick waterproof woollen cloth. **2** the dark olive-green colour in which this is often made. [German, originally woven by peasants living in *Loderers*, Austria]

lode·star *noun* (also **loadstar**) **1** a star that a ship etc. is steered by, esp. the pole star. **2 a** a guiding principle. **b** an object of pursuit. [LODE in obsolete sense 'way, journey' + STAR]

lode·stone *noun* (also **loadstone**) **1** magnetic oxide of iron, magnetite. **2 a** a piece of this used as a magnet. **b** a thing that attracts.

Lodge, Sir Oli·ver (Jo·seph) (1851–1940), English physicist. He made important contributions to the study of electromagnetic radiation, and was a pioneer of radio transmission; he also carried out intensive studies of psychic phenomena.

lodge ● *noun* **1** a hotel or inn, esp. in a resort area. **2** *N Amer.* the main building in a resort or summer camp, usu. containing a dining area etc. **3** *Cdn* (esp. in proper names) an old people's home. **4** a house occupied in the hunting or fishing season. **5** a N American Indian's tent or wigwam. **6** a small house at the gates of a park or in the grounds of a large house, occupied by a gatekeeper, gardener, etc. **7 a** the meeting place of a branch of a society such as the Freemasons. **b** the members of such a local branch. **8** a beaver's or otter's lair. **9** esp. *Brit.* a porter's room or quarters at the gate of a college or other large building. ● *verb* **1** *transitive* deposit in court or with an official a formal statement of (complaint or information). **2** *transitive* deposit (money etc.) for security. **3** *transitive* bring forward (an objection etc.). **4** *transitive* (foll. by *in*, *with*) place (power etc.) in a person or group. **5** *transitive & intransitive* make or become fixed or caught without further movement (*the bullet lodged in his brain; the tide lodges mud in the cavities*). **6** *transitive* **a** provide with sleeping quarters. **b** receive as a guest or inhabitant. **c** establish as a resident in a house or room or rooms. **7** *intransitive* reside or live, esp. as a guest paying for accommodation. **8** *transitive* serve as a habitation for; contain. **9** *transitive* (in *passive*; foll. by *in*) be contained in. **10** *transitive* (of wind or rain) flatten (crops). [Old French *loge* arbour, hut, from medieval Latin *laubia*, *lobia* (see LOBBY) from Germanic]

lodge·ment *noun* (also **lodg·ment**) **1** the act of lodging or process of being lodged. **2** the depositing or a deposit of money. **3** an accumulation of matter intercepted.

lodge·pole *noun* *N Amer.* **1** a pole used to support a teepee or wigwam. **2** a lodgepole pine.

lodgepole pine *noun* a pine native to mountainous regions of northwestern N America, *Pinus contorta* var. *latifolia*.

lodg·er *noun* a person receiving accommodation in another's house for payment.

lodg·ing *noun* **1** temporary accommodation (*a lodging for the night*). **2** (in *pl.*) a room or rooms rented for lodging in on a relatively long-term basis. **3** a dwelling place. **4** the flattening of standing crops by wind or rain.

lodging house *noun* = ROOMING HOUSE.

lodi·cule /ˈlɒdɪˌkjuːl/ *noun* *Bot.* a small green or white scale below the ovary of a grass flower. [Latin *lodicula* diminutive of *lodix* coverlet]

lods et ventes /lɒːz ei vãt/ *noun* *Cdn* (*Que.*) *hist.* a seigneurial right to one-twelfth of the purchase price of an estate changing hands by sale or transfer. [French *lods* 'consent' from Old French *los* from Latin *laudis* 'praise', + *ventes* 'sales']

Łódź /wʊtʃ/ an industrial city in central Poland, southwest of Warsaw, the second largest city in the country; pop. (est. 2002) 793,217.

loess /ˈloːes/ *noun* a deposit of fine light-coloured windblown dust found esp. in the basins of large rivers and very fertile when irrigated. [German *Löss* from Swiss German *lösch* loose, from *lösen* loosen]

Loewe /loː/ **Fred·erick** (1904–88), Austrian-born US composer, who wrote the music for a number of popular musicals with lyrics by Alan Jay Lerner; these include *Brigadoon* (1947), *Paint Your Wagon* (1951), *My Fair Lady* (1956), and *Camelot* (1960).

Loewi /ˈloːi/ **Otto** (1873–1961), German-born US pharmacologist and physiologist. He demonstrated that the passage of a nerve impulse is associated with the release of a chemical at the nerve endings, and later identified this as the substance acetylcholine; he shared a Nobel Prize with Sir Henry Dale in 1936.

lo-fi *adjective* (also **low-fi**) **1** of or employing sound reproduction of a lower quality than hi-fi. **2** (of popular music) recorded and produced with basic equipment and thus having a raw and unsophisticated sound.

Lo·fo·ten Islands /ləˈfoːtən/ an island group off the northwest coast of Norway. They are situated within the Arctic Circle, southwest of the Vesterålen group.

loft ● *noun* **1** a room or space directly under the roof of a house, used as storage or living space. **2** a space under the roof of a barn or stable etc., used esp. for storing hay and straw. **3** a gallery or upper level in a church or hall (*choir loft*). **4** *N Amer.* **a** an upper room or floor of a large building, factory, etc., sometimes converted into apartments, studios, etc. **b** = LOFT APARTMENT. **5** *N Amer.* the resiliency of a fabric, esp. wool. **6** *N Amer.* the thickness of insulating matter in something, e.g. a sleeping bag or down-filled coat. **7** *Golf* **a** a backward slope on the head of a club. **b** a lofting stroke. **8** a pigeon house. ● *transitive verb* **1 a** send (a ball etc.) high up. **b** clear (an obstacle) in this way. **2** (esp. as **loft·ed** *adjective*) give a loft to (a golf club). [Old English from Old Norse *lopt* air, sky, upper room, from Germanic (related to LIFT)]

loft apartment *noun* *N Amer.* a usu. open-concept apartment built into a converted warehouse, office building, etc.

lofty *adjective* (**loft·i·er**, **loft·i·est**) **1** (of things) of imposing height, towering, soaring (*lofty heights*). **2** consciously haughty, aloof, or dignified (*lofty contempt*). **3** exalted or noble; sublime (*lofty ideals*). □ **loft·i·ly** *adverb* **loft·i·ness** *noun* [Middle English from LOFT as in *aloft*]

log[1] ● *noun* **1 a** a part of the trunk of a tree or of a large branch that has fallen or been cut down. **b** something long and cylindrical like a log (*shape the dough into a log*). **2 a** *hist.* a float attached to a line wound on a reel for gauging the speed of a ship. **b** any other apparatus for the same purpose. **3** a record of events occurring during and affecting the voyage of a ship or aircraft (including the rate of a ship's progress shown by a log: *see* sense 2). **4** = LOGBOOK. **5** any systematic record of things done, experienced, etc. ● *verb* (**logged**, **log·ging**) **1** *transitive* clear (a region) of trees. **2** *transitive* cut (a tree) into logs. **3** *intransitive* fell timber and cut the wood into logs. **4** *transitive* **a** enter (the distance made or other details) in a ship's logbook. **b** enter details about (a person or event) in a logbook. **c** (of a ship) achieve (a certain distance). **5** *transitive* **a** enter (information) in a regular record. **b** attain (a cumulative total of time etc. recorded in this way) (*logged 50 hours on the computer*). □ **like a log** *informal* without stirring (*slept like a log*). **log off** (or **out**) go through the procedures to conclude use of a computer system. **log on** (or **in**) go through the procedures to begin use of a computer system. [Middle English: origin unknown]

log[2] *noun* a logarithm (esp. prefixed to a number or algebraic symbol whose logarithm is to be indicated). [abbreviation]

-log *US var. of* -LOGUE.

Logan /ˈloːgən/ a city in Queensland, Australia, forming part of the conurbation of Brisbane; pop. (est. 1998) 165,924.

Logan, Mount a peak in the St. Elias Mountains of SW Yukon Territory, near the border with Alaska. Rising to a height of 5 959 m, it is the highest mountain in Canada and the second highest in N America. [Sir W. E. Logan, Canadian geologist d.1875]

lo·gan /ˈloːgən/ *noun* *Cdn* (*Nfld*) a leather boot with a rubber foot, reaching to below the knee, worn in winter or when working in the bush. [origin unknown]

logan·berry /ˈloːgənˌberi/ *noun* (*pl.* **-berries**) **1** a hybrid, *Rubus loganobaccus*, between a blackberry and a raspberry, with dark red acid fruits. **2** the fruit of this plant. [J. H. *Logan*, US horticulturalist d.1928 + BERRY]

loga·rithm /ˈlɒgəˌrɪðəm/ *noun* a figure representing the power to which a fixed number or base must be raised to produce a given number (*the logarithm of 1,000 to base 10 is 3*), used to simplify calculations as the addition and subtraction of logarithms is equivalent to multiplication and division. □ **loga·rith·mic** /-ˈrɪðmɪk/ *adjective* **loga·rith·mic·ally** *adverb* [modern Latin *logarithmus* from Greek *logos* reckoning, ratio + *arithmos* number]

log barge *noun Cdn (BC)* a large barge used to transport logs from the log dump to the mill.

log·book *noun* **1** a book containing a detailed record of things done or experienced. **2** a book in which particulars of aircraft flights, flying hours, etc. are recorded.

log boom *noun N Amer.* = BOOM² 2.

log bronc *noun Cdn (BC)* a small tugboat used to direct a log boom or to gather logs together in the booming grounds.

log cabin *noun* **1** (also **log house**, **log home**) a house or cabin with walls made of logs. **2** (*attributive*) designating a quilt pattern in which square blocks are made up of a small square centre section surrounded by rectangular strips of increasing length, usu. with dark colours on two adjacent sides of the square and light colours on the two opposite adjacent sides.

log chute *noun Cdn* a chute constructed to allow logs being driven down a river to bypass a waterfall or rapids.

log drive *noun Cdn* the transporting of logs from the bush to the mills by floating them down rivers etc. □ **log driver** *noun*

log dump *noun N Amer.* = DUMP *noun* 6.

loge /loːʒ/ *noun* **1** a seating area in a theatre, usu. elevated above the orchestra level and on the side. **2** a private box or enclosure in a theatre. [French]

-loger *combining form* forming nouns, = -LOGIST. [after *astrologer*]

logged-over *attributive adjective* (also **logged-off**, **logged-out**) *N Amer.* (of a tract of forest) that has been logged (*some animals prefer to live in logged-over areas*).

log·ger *noun N Amer.* a person who fells trees and prepares timber for milling.

log·ger·head *noun* **1** an iron instrument with a ball at the end heated for melting pitch etc. **2** any of various large-headed animals, esp. a turtle (*Caretta caretta*) or shrike (*Lanius ludovicianus*). □ **at loggerheads** (often foll. by *with*) disagreeing or disputing (*has been at loggerheads with her for years*). [prob. from dial. *logger* block of wood for hobbling a horse + HEAD]

log·gia /ˈloːdʒə, ˈlɒ-/ *noun* **1** an open-sided gallery or arcade. **2** an open-sided extension of a house. [Italian, = LODGE]

log·ging *noun* the work of cutting and preparing forest timber.

logging chain *noun Cdn* a heavy-duty steel chain of the type used esp. in logging.

logging division *noun Cdn* a tract of forest being logged by loggers resident in a single logging camp.

logging road *noun* (also **lumber road**) *N Amer.* an unimproved road into a forest area, used for logging purposes.

logic /ˈlɒdʒɪk/ *noun* **1 a** the science of reasoning, proof, thinking, or inference. **b** a particular scheme of or treatise on this. **2 a** a chain of reasoning (*I don't follow your logic*). **b** the correct or incorrect use of reasoning (*your logic is flawed*). **c** ability in reasoning (*argues with great learning and logic*). **d** arguments (*is not governed by logic*). **3 a** the inexorable force or compulsion of a thing (*the logic of events*). **b** the necessary consequence of (an argument, decision, etc.). **4 a** a system or set of principles underlying the arrangements of elements in a computer or electronic device so as to perform a specified task. **b** logical operations collectively. □ **logi·cian** /ləˈdʒɪʃən/ *noun* [Old French *logique* from Late Latin *logica* from Greek *logikē* (*tekhnē*) (art) of reason: see LOGOS]

-logic *combining form* (also **-logical**) forming adjectives corresponding esp. to nouns in *-logy* (*geologic*; *theological*). [from or after Greek *-logikos*: see -IC, -ICAL]

logic·al *adjective* **1** of logic or formal argument. **2** not contravening the laws of thought, correctly reasoned. **3** deducible or defensible on the ground of consistency; reasonably to be believed or done. **4** capable of correct reasoning. □ **logic·al·ity** *noun* **logic·al·ly** *adverb*

logical positivism *noun* (also **logical empiricism**) a form of positivism regarding all valid philosophical problems as solvable by logical analysis. □ **logical positivist** *noun*

logic bomb *noun Computing* a set of instructions secretly incorporated into a program so that if a particular logical condition is satisfied they will be carried out, usu. with harmful effects.

log-in *noun Computing* **1** the action of logging in (also *attributive*: *log-in screen*). **2** a code, password, etc. used in logging in.

-logist *combining form* forming nouns denoting a person skilled or involved in a branch of study etc. with a name in *-logy* (*archaeologist*; *etymologist*).

logis·tics *plural noun* **1** the organization of moving, lodging, and supplying troops and equipment. **2** the detailed organization and implementation of a plan or operation. □ **logis·tic** *adjective* **logis·tic·al** *adjective* **logis·tic·ally** *adverb* [French *logistique* from *loger* lodge]

log·jam *noun* **1** a crowded mass of logs in a river. **2** a deadlock. **3** *Sport* a situation in which several contestants are tied at the same place in the standings.

logo *noun* (*pl.* **logos**) a symbol designed for and used by a company or organization as its special sign, e.g. in advertising and packaging. □ **logoed** *adjective* [abbreviation of LOGOTYPE]

logo·cen·tric /ˌloːɡoʊˈsentrɪk/ *noun* **1** centred on reason. **2** centred on language; regarding the word as a fundamental expression of reality. □ **logo·cen·trism** *noun* [Greek *logos* word + -CENTRIC]

logo·gram /ˈlɒɡəˌɡram/ *noun* a sign or character representing a word, e.g. the symbol & representing the word *and*. [Greek *logos* word + -GRAM]

log-on *noun* = LOG-IN.

log·or·rhea /ˌlɒɡəˈriə/ *noun* (also esp. *Brit.* **log·or·rhoea**) an excessive flow of words esp. in mental illness. [Greek *logos* word + *rhoia* flow]

Logos /ˈlɒɡɒs/ *noun* (in Christian theology) the Word of God, or Second Person of the Trinity. [Greek, = word, reason]

logo·type /ˈlɒɡəˌtaɪp/ *noun Printing* **1** a single piece of type that prints a word or group of separate letters. **2 a** = LOGO. **b** *Printing* a single piece of type that prints this. [Greek *logos* word + TYPE]

log-rolling *noun N Amer.* **1** *informal* the practice of exchanging favours, esp. (in politics) of exchanging votes to mutual benefit. **2** the action of causing a floating log to rotate by treading, esp. as a competitive sport; birling. □ **log-roll** *transitive & intransitive verb* **log-roller** *noun* [polit. sense from phr. *you roll my log and I'll roll yours*]

log scaler *noun Cdn* a person who measures cut logs and calculates the amount of lumber that they contain.

-logue *combining form* (also esp. *US* **-log**) **1** forming nouns denoting talk (*dialogue*) or compilation (*catalogue*). **2** = -LOGIST (*ideologue*). [from or after French *-logue* from Greek *-logos*, *-logon*]

log·wood *noun* **1** a Caribbean tree, *Haematoxylon campechianum*. **2** the wood of this, producing a substance used in dyeing.

logy /ˈloːɡi/ *adjective* (**logi·er**, **logi·est**) *N Amer.* dull and heavy in motion or thought. [origin uncertain: compare Dutch *log* heavy, dull]

-logy *combining form* forming nouns denoting: **1** (usu. as **-ology**) a subject of study or interest (*archaeology*; *zoology*). **2** a characteristic of speech or language (*tautology*). **3** discourse (*trilogy*). [French *-logie* or medieval Latin *-logia* from Greek (as LOGOS)]

loin *noun* **1** (in *pl.*) the part of the body on both sides of the spine between the false ribs and the hip bones. **2** (in *pl.*) *literary* the source of reproductive power (*fruit of his loins*). **3** a cut of meat that includes the loin vertebrae. □ **gird one's loins** see GIRD. [Old French *loigne* ultimately from Latin *lumbus*]

loin·cloth *noun* a cloth worn round the loins, esp. as a sole garment.

Loire River /lwɑr/ a river of west central France, which rises in the Massif Central and flows 1 015 km (630 miles) north and west to the Atlantic at Saint-Nazaire. Principal cities on its route are Orleans, Tours, and Nantes. The longest river in France, it is noted for the châteaux and vineyards that lie along its course.

loi·ter *intransitive verb* **1** hang about; linger idly. **2** linger indolently on the way when on an errand, journey, etc. □ **loi·ter·er** *noun* [Middle Dutch *loteren* wag about]

Loki /ˈloːki/ *Scand. Myth* a mischievous and sometimes evil god who contrived the death of Balder and was punished by being bound to a rock.

LOL *abbreviation* (in emails) laughing out loud.

Lo·lita *noun* a sexually precocious young girl. [from the name of a character in the novel *Lolita* (1958) by Vladimir Nabokov]

loll *intransitive verb* **1** (often foll. by *about*, *around*) stand, sit, or recline in a lazy attitude. **2** hang loosely. [Middle English: prob. imitative]

Lol·land /ˈloːlɒn/ a Danish island in the Baltic Sea, to the south of Zealand and west of Falster. [Danish, = low land]

lol·la·pa·looza *noun* (also **la·la·pa·looza** etc.) *N Amer. slang* an excellent or attractive person or thing. [fanciful formation]

Lol·lard *noun* any of a group of radical Christians in the Middle Ages who followed or held opinions similar to those of the 14th-c. religious reformer John Wyclif. The Lollards believed that the Church should aid people to live a life of evangelical poverty and imitate Christ. □ **Lol·lard·ism** *noun* [Middle Dutch *lollaerd* from *lollen* mumble]

lol·li·pop *noun* **1** a large flat or round candy on a small stick, held in the hand and sucked. **2** *Brit.* = ICE LOLLY. **3** a treat or reward (handed out like a lollipop to a child). [perhaps from dial. *lolly* tongue + POP¹]

lollipop man *noun* (*fem.* **lollipop lady** or **lollipop woman**) *Brit. informal* = CROSSING GUARD.

lol·lop *intransitive verb* (**lol·loped**, **lol·lop·ing**) *informal* move forward in bounds, esp. in a loose-limbed way. [prob. from LOLL, assoc. with TROLLOP]

lolly¹ *noun* (*pl.* **-lies**) **1** *informal* **a** *Brit.* = LOLLIPOP. **b** *Austral.* & *NZ* a candy. **2** *Brit., Austral.,* & *NZ slang* money. [abbreviation of LOLLIPOP]

lolly² *noun Cdn* (*Nfld* & *Maritimes*) = FRAZIL. [*Brit.* dial. *loblolly* 'thick soup or porridge']

lol·ly·gag *intransitive verb* (**lolly·gagged**, **lolly·gag·ging**) *N Amer. slang* **1** dawdle. **2** spend time aimlessly. [20th c.: origin unknown]

Lomas de Zam·ora /ˌlomasdəzaˈmorə/ a city in eastern Argentina, immediately south of Buenos Aires; pop. (est. 1999) 609,621.

Lom·bard¹, Peter (c.1100–60), Italian theologian and bishop of Paris 1159–60, who is noted for his influential *Sententiae* (1145–1150), a collection of opinions on the Church Fathers, dealing with God, the Redemption, the nature of the Sacraments, etc.

Lom·bard² ● *noun* **1** a native of Lombardy. **2** a member of a Germanic people who conquered Italy in the 6th c. **3** the dialect of Lombardy. ● *adjective* of or relating to the Lombards or Lombardy. □ **Lom·bard·ic** *adjective* [Italian *lombardo*, representing late Latin *Langobardus*, of Germanic origin, from the base of LONG¹ + the ethnic name *Bardi*]

Lom·bar·di /lombardi/ **Vin·cent Thom·as** (**'Vince'**) (1913–70), US football coach. As head coach of the Green Bay Packers (1959–67) he led the team to five NFL championships and victory in the first two Superbowls (1966 and 1967); the Superbowl trophy is named after him.

Lom·bar·do /lɒmˈbardoː/ **Guy** (Gaetano Alberto) (1902–77), Canadian bandleader and violinist. With his brothers Carmen and Lebert and other musicians from his hometown of London he formed the jazz band the Royal Canadians in 1924. The band played at the Roosevelt Hotel in New York from 1929 to 1959, and their New Year's Eve broadcasts (1929–62) were a major part of New Year's celebrations across N America.

Lom·bard Street a street in the City of London, formerly occupied by bankers from Lombardy and still containing many of the principal London banks.

Lom·bar·dy /lombardi/ a region of central N Italy, between the Alps and the Po River; capital, Milan.

Lombardy poplar /ˈlombardi/ *noun* a variety of poplar, *Populus nigra* var. *italica*, with an especially tall slender form.

Lom·bok /ˈlombɒk/ a volcanic island of the Lesser Sunda group in Indonesia, between Bali and Sumbawa; pop. (est. 2002) 3,600,000; chief town, Mataram.

Lomé /ˈlomeɪ/ the capital and chief port of Togo, on the Gulf of Guinea; pop. (est. 2002) 658,100.

lo mein /loːˈmeɪn/ *noun* a Chinese dish of boiled wheat noodles combined with stir-fried meat, fish, or vegetables in a sauce. [Chinese (Guangdong) *lòu* 'stirred' + *mihn*, noodles]

lo·men·tum /loːˈmentəm/ *noun* (also **loment** /ˈloːment/) *Bot.* the pod of some leguminous plants, breaking up when mature into one-seeded joints. □ **lomen·ta·ceous** /-ˈteɪʃəs/ *adjective* [Latin *lomentum* 'bean-meal' (originally a cosmetic) from *lavare* 'wash']

Lo·mond, Loch see LOCH LOMOND.

Lon·don¹ 1 the capital of the UK, situated in SE England on the Thames River; pop. (2001) 7,172,036. London is divided administratively into the City of London, known as the Square Mile, which is the country's financial centre, and thirty-two boroughs. **2** a city in SW Ontario, about 100 km southwest of Kitchener; pop. (2001) 336,539. □ **Lon·don·er** *noun* [sense 2 from sense 1, because it was considered a possible capital for Upper Canada]

Lon·don², Jack (pseudonym of John Griffith Chaney) (1876–1916), US novelist, who is best known for his depiction of individualistic struggle in novels such as *The Call of the Wild* (1903), *The Sea-Wolf* (1904), and *White Fang* (1906).

London broil *noun N Amer.* flank steak broiled and served cut into slices across the grain.

London Conference a conference held in London, England, in December 1866, at which delegates from the Province of Canada, New Brunswick, and Nova Scotia met with the British government; the major issue was that of Roman Catholic separate schools. Early in 1867 the London Resolutions were rewritten into the BNA Act.

Lon·don·derry 1 one of the Six Counties of Northern Ireland, formerly an administrative area. **2** its chief town (also known as Derry, formerly the official name), a city and port on the Foyle River near its outlet on the north coast; pop. (est. 2002) 84,100.

London gin *noun* (also **London dry gin**) a light, unsweetened variety of gin. [originally distilled in London]

lone *attributive adjective* **1** (of a person) solitary; without a companion or supporter. **2** single, only. **3** (of a place) unfrequented, uninhabited, lonely (*the lone prairie*). **4** unmarried, single (*lone parent*). [Middle English, from ALONE]

lone hand *noun* a hand played or a player playing against the rest in euchre. □ **play a lone hand** act on one's own.

lone·ly *adjective* (**lone·li·er, lone·li·est**) **1** solitary, isolated, without companions. **2** (of a place) unfrequented. **3** sad because without friends or company. **4** imparting a sense of loneliness; dreary. □ **lone·li·ness** *noun*

lonely heart *noun* (usu. in *pl.*) a lonely person, esp. one seeking companionship by advertising in a newspaper etc. (usu. *attributive: a lonely hearts column*).

loner *noun* a person who prefers not to associate with others.

lone·some *adjective* **1** solitary, lonely. **2** feeling lonely or forlorn. **3** causing such a feeling. □ **by** (or **on**) **one's lonesome** all alone. □ **lone·some·ly** *adverb* **lone·some·ness** *noun*

lone wolf *noun* a person who prefers to act alone.

Long, Craw·ford William·son (1815–78), US physician, who was the first to use ether as an anaesthetic in surgery.

long¹ ● *adjective* (**long·er; long·est**) **1** measuring much from end to end in space or time; not soon traversed or finished (*a long line; a long journey; a long time ago*). **2** (following a measurement) in length or duration (*2 metres long; their summer vacation is two months long*). **3** relatively great in extent or duration (*a long meeting*). **4 a** consisting of a large number of items (*a long list*). **b** seemingly more than the stated amount; tedious, lengthy (*ten long miles; tired after a long day*). **5** of elongated shape. **6 a** lasting or reaching far back or forward in time (*a long friendship*). **b** (of a person's memory) retaining things for a long time. **7** far-reaching; acting at a distance; involving a great interval or difference. **8** *Phonetics* & *Prosody* of a vowel or syllable: **a** having the greater of the two recognized durations. **b** stressed. **c** (of a vowel in English) having the pronunciation shown in the name of the letter (as in *pile* and *cute* which have a long *i* and *u*, as distinct from *pill* and *cut*) (compare SHORT *adjective* 6). **9** (of odds or a chance) reflecting or representing a low level of probability. **10** *Stock Exch.* **a** (of stocks, bonds, etc.) bought in large quantities in advance, with the expectation of a rise in price. **b** (of a broker etc.) buying etc. on this basis. **11** (of a bill of exchange) maturing at a distant date. **12** (of a mixed drink) containing a relatively large proportion of mixer to liquor. **13** *informal* (of a person) tall. **14** (foll. by *on*) *informal* well supplied with. **15** (of a thrown or hit ball) travelling a long distance. ● *noun* **1** a long interval or period (*shall not be away for long; it will not take long*). **2** *Phonetics* **a** a long syllable or vowel. **b** a mark indicating that a vowel is long. **3 a** long-dated stock. **b** a person who buys this. ● *adverb* (**long·er; long·est**) **1** by or for a long time (*long before; long ago; long live the king!*). **2** (following nouns of duration) throughout a specified time (*all day long*). **3** (in *comparative*; with *neg.*) after an implied point of time (*shall not wait any longer*). **4** esp. *Sport* at or to a great distance (*kick the ball long*). □ **as** (or **so**) **long as 1** during the whole time that. **2** provided that; only if. **at long last** see LAST¹. **before long** fairly soon (*we'll bring Maggie to see you before long*). **be long** (often foll. by pres. part. or *in* + verbal noun) take a long time; be slow (*was long finding it out; the chance was long in coming; I won't be long*). **by a long chalk** see CHALK. **in the long run 1** over a long period. **2** eventually; finally. **long ago** in the distant past. **the long and the short of it 1** all that can or need be said. **2** the eventual outcome. **long in the tooth** rather old (originally of horses, from the recession of the gums with age). **long time no see** *informal* (used as a greeting) it is a long time since we last met. □ **long·ish** *adjective* [Old English *long, lang*]

long² *intransitive verb* (foll. by *for* or *to* + infin.) have a strong wish or desire for. [Old English *langian* seem long to]

long. *abbreviation* longitude.

long- *combining form* forming adverbs meaning 'for or lasting for a long time' (*long-expected; long-lasting*).

-long *combining form* forming adjectives and adverbs: **1** for the duration of (*lifelong*). **2** = -LING[2] (*headlong*).

long-ago *adjective* that is in the distant past.

lon·gan /ˈlɒŋgən/ *noun* an edible juicy fruit from a plant (*Dimocarpus longan*) related to the lychee, cultivated in SE Asia. [Chinese lóngyǎn, lit. = 'dragon's eye']

long-awaited *adjective* that has been awaited for a long time.

Long Beach a port and resort in California, situated on the south side of the Los Angeles conurbation; pop. (2000) 461,522.

long·board *noun* a type of long surfboard.

Long·boat, Thom·as Charles (1887-1949), Onondaga long-distance runner from the Six Nations Reserve near Brantford. One of the premier runners of his age, he won the Boston Marathon in record time in 1907.

long·boat *noun* a sailing ship's largest boat.

long·bow *noun* a bow drawn by hand and shooting a long feathered arrow.

long car *noun* (also **long cart**) *Cdn* (*Nfld*) a long two-wheeled horse-drawn cart.

long-case clock *noun* = GRANDFATHER CLOCK.

long-chain *adjective* (of a molecule) containing a chain of many carbon atoms.

long-dated *adjective* (of securities) not due for early payment or redemption.

long-day *adjective* (of a plant) needing a long daily period of light to cause flowering.

long-dead *adjective* that has been dead for a long time.

long-distance ● *adjective* **1** (of a telephone call) made between places that are sufficiently far apart as to require extra payment. **2** of, relating to, or providing such service (*a long-distance company*). **3** covering relatively great distances (*long-distance race; long-distance trucker*). ● *adverb* (also **long distance**) between distant places (*phone long-distance*). ● *noun* (usu. **long distance**) **1** long-distance telephone service (*we pay a lot for long distance*). **2** a long-distance telephone call.

long division *noun* division of numbers with details of the calculations written down.

long-drawn-out *adjective* (also **drawn-out, long-drawn**) prolonged, esp. unduly.

longe *var. of* LUNGE[2].

long·er *noun* (usu. in *pl.*) *Cdn* (*Nfld & Maritimes*) a long pole, esp. from the trunk of a conifer, used for building fences, fishing stages, roofs, floors, etc. [LONG[1] + -ER[1]]

lon·ger·on /ˈlɒndʒərən/ *noun* a longitudinal member of a plane's fuselage. [French, = girder]

lon·gev·ity /lɒnˈdʒɛvɪti/ *noun* **1** long life. **2** duration of life (*am studying longevity*). **3** duration or length of service, employment, tenure, etc. (*holiday time is based on longevity*). [Late Latin *longaevitas* from Latin *longus* long + *aevum* age]

long face *noun* a dismal or disappointed expression. ☐ **long-faced** *adjective*

Long·fel·low, Henry Wads·worth (1807–82), US poet, who is best known for 'The Wreck of the Hesperus' (1841), 'The Village Blacksmith' (1841), and narrative poems such as *Evangeline* (1849) and *The Song of Hiawatha* (1855).

Long·ford 1 a county of the Republic of Ireland, in the province of Leinster. **2** its county town; pop. (est. 2002) 7,300.

long gone *adjective* (usu. *predicative*; with hyphen when *attributive*) that has been gone for a long time (*she was long gone by the time he got there*).

long·hair *noun* **1** an intellectual. **2** a person interested in the arts, esp. a classical musician. **3** a long-haired cat.

long·hand *noun* ordinary handwriting (as opposed to shorthand or typing or printing).

long haul *noun* **1** the transport of goods or passengers over a long distance (also *attributive*: *long-haul flights*). **2** a prolonged effort or task. ☐ **over the long haul** over a long period; in the long run.

long-headed *adjective* shrewd, far-seeing, sagacious. ☐ **long-headed·ness** *adjective*

long hop *noun* **1** the action of a ball that bounces several feet in front of a fielder and is therefore usu. easily caught. **2** a ball that bounces in this way.

long·horn *noun* **1** one of a breed of cattle with long horns. **2** any of numerous usu. elongate beetles of the family Cerambycidae, having very long, slender antennae, and found worldwide esp. in woodland.

long·house *noun* a dwelling shared by several nuclear families, esp. among the Iroquois and the Aboriginal peoples of the northwest coast of N America.

Longhouse religion *noun* an Iroquois religion established by the Seneca chief Ganiodaio ('Handsome Lake') in the late 18th c., incorporating a strict code of ethics, certain Christian elements such as heaven and hell, and traditional Iroquois beliefs.

long hundredweight *noun* see HUNDREDWEIGHT 2.

longi·corn /ˈlɒndʒɪˌkɔrn/ *noun* a longhorn beetle. [modern Latin *longicornis* from Latin *longus* long + *cornu* horn]

long·ing ● *noun* a feeling of intense desire. ● *adjective* having or showing this feeling. ☐ **long·ing·ly** *adverb*

Lon·gi·nus /lɒnˈdʒaɪnəs/ (fl. 1st c. AD), Greek scholar. He is the supposed author of a Greek literary treatise *On the Sublime*, a critical analysis of literary greatness, showing concern with the moral function of literature and impatience with pedantry.

Long Island an island on the coast of New York State. Its western tip, comprising the New York districts of Brooklyn and Queens, is separated from Manhattan and the Bronx by the East River and is linked to Manhattan by the Brooklyn Bridge. The island extends 210 km (118 miles) eastward roughly parallel to the coast of Connecticut, from which it is separated by Long Island Sound.

Long Island iced tea *noun* a mixed drink of vodka, tequila, rum, gin, orange liqueur, lime or lemon juice, and cola.

longi·tude /ˈlɒŋgɪˌtud, ˈlɒndʒ-, -ˌtjuːd/ *noun* **1** *Geog.* the angular distance east or west from a standard meridian such as Greenwich to the meridian of any place. Symbol: λ. **2** *Astronomy* the angular distance of a celestial body north or south of the ecliptic measured along a great circle through the body and the poles of the ecliptic. [Latin *longitudo -dinis* from *longus* long]

longi·tud·in·al /ˌlɒŋgɪˈtuːdɪnəl, ˌlɒndʒ-, -ˈtjuːd-/ *adjective* **1** of or in length. **2** running lengthwise. **3** of longitude. **4** (of research, a study, etc.) involving information about an individual or group at different times throughout a long period. ☐ **longi·tud·in·ally** *adverb*

longitudinal wave *noun* a wave vibrating in the direction of propagation.

long john *noun* **1** (in *pl.*) *informal* underpants with close-fitting legs that extend to the ankles. **2** *N Amer.* a long, cream-filled doughnut, usu. iced.

long jump *noun* an athletic contest of jumping as far as possible along the ground in one leap. ☐ **long-jumper** *noun*

long knives *plural noun* vindictive attacks.

long-lasting *adjective* that lasts, or has lasted, for a long time.

long-legged *adjective* **1** having long legs. **2** *informal* speedy.

long-life *adjective* **1** (of perishable foods etc.) treated to preserve freshness. **2** (esp. of batteries etc.) manufactured in such a way as to last for a long time.

long·line *noun* a deep-sea fishing line with a large number of baited hooks attached to it. ☐ **long·lining** *noun*

long·liner *noun* a fishing boat using longlines.

long-lived *adjective* having a long life; durable.

long-lost *attributive adjective* that has been lost or not seen for a long time.

long lot *noun Cdn* = RIVER LOT.

Long March *noun* **1** the epic withdrawal of the Chinese Communists from SE to NW China in 1934–35, over a distance of 9 600 km (6,000 miles). Of over 100,000 who began the march, only about 20,000 survived. **2** (**long march**) any long and arduous progression towards a goal.

long measure *noun* = LINEAR MEASURE.

long metre *noun* **1** a hymn stanza of four lines with eight syllables each. **2** a quatrain of iambic tetrameters with alternate lines rhyming.

long neck *noun N Amer. slang* **1** a beer bottle with a long neck. **2** a beer in such a bottle.

Long Parliament the Parliament summoned by Charles I which sat through the English Civil War, from November 1640 to March 1653, and during part of 1659 before finally voting its own dissolution in 1660.

long-playing *adjective* (of a microgroove record) designed to be played at 33⅓ revolutions per minute.

Long Point a 35-km-long narrow sand spit of SW Ontario, extending into Lake Erie, southeast of London.

long-range *adjective* **1** (of a missile, aircraft, etc.) having a long range. **2** of or relating to a period of time far into the future.

t top   v voice   w we   z zoo   ʃ she   ʒ vision   θ thin   ð this   ŋ ring   x loch   tʃ chip   dʒ jar   (*see over for vowels*)

Long Range Mountains a mountain range in NW Newfoundland, stretching from the Northern Peninsula of the island to Cape Ray. Part of the Appalachian system, they extend 500 km and reach a maximum elevation of 814 m.

long-run *adjective* occurring or running over a long period of time (*long-run costs*).

long-running *adjective* continuing for a long time.

Long·shan /lɒŋˈʃan/ an ancient civilization of the Yellow River valley in China *c.*2500–1700 BC, characterized by pottery kiln-fired to a uniform black colour, and by the establishment of towns.

long ship *noun hist.* a long narrow warship with many rowers, used esp. by the Vikings.

long·shore *adjective* **1** existing on or frequenting the shore. **2** directed along the shore. [for *along shore*]

long·shore·man *noun* (*pl.* **-men**) *N Amer.* a person employed to load and unload ships.

long shot *noun* **1** a competitor or team etc. that is unlikely to succeed. **2** an undertaking or venture that has great potential but little chance of success. **3** a wild guess. **4** a bet at long odds. **5** *Film* a shot including objects at a distance. □ **by a long shot** by any means (*it isn't over by a long shot*).

long-sighted *adjective* esp. *Brit.* = FAR-SIGHTED. □ **long-sighted·ly** *adverb* **long-sighted·ness** *noun*

long-sleeved *adjective* with sleeves reaching to the wrist.

long·spur *noun* a N American bunting of the genus *Calcarius*.

long-standing *adjective* that has long existed; not recent (*a long-standing purchase agreement*).

long-suffer·ing *adjective* bearing provocation patiently. □ **long-suffer·ing·ly** *adverb*

long suit *noun* **1** many cards of one suit in a hand (esp. more than 3 or 4 in a hand of 13). **2** a thing at which one excels (*car repair is not my long suit*).

long-term *adjective* **1** of or for a long period of time (*long-term plans*). **2** (of an investment, loan, etc.) maturing or coming down after a long period of time.

long-term care *noun* medical care provided on an ongoing basis to patients with chronic physical or mental disorders.

long-time *adjective* that has been such for a long time.

long ton *noun see* TON 2.

long-track *noun* (also **long-track speed skating**) speed skating done on a traditional 400 m oval.

Lon·gueuil /lɔˈɡɜːj/ a city in south central Quebec, located on the St. Lawrence, opposite Montreal; pop. (2001) 371,934. [*Longueuil*, France, birthplace of C. LE MOYNE]

lon·gueur /lɔˈɡɜːr/ *noun* **1** a tedious passage in a book etc. **2** a tedious stretch of time. [French, = length]

long vacation *noun Brit.* the summer vacation of law courts and universities.

long view *noun* (prec. by *the*) a broad and forward-looking assessment of circumstances etc. □ **take the long view** consider what is likely to happen, be relevant, etc. over the long term, rather than looking at the immediate situation.

long-waisted *adjective* (of a person's body or article of clothing) having a greater than average distance between the shoulders and the waist.

long wave *noun* a radio wave of frequency less than 300 kHz.

long·ways *adverb* (also **long·wise**) = LENGTHWISE.

long weekend *noun* a three-day weekend consisting of Saturday, Sunday, and a statutory holiday on the Friday or Monday.

long-winded *adjective* **1** (of speech or writing) tediously lengthy. **2** (of a person) verbose; given to long discourses. □ **long-winded·ly** *adverb* **long-winded·ness** *noun*

lo·ni·cera /ləˈnɪsərə/ *noun* = HONEYSUCKLE. [A. *Lonicerus*, German botanist d.1586]

loo *noun* esp. *Brit. informal* a toilet or washroom. [20th c.: origin uncertain]

loo·fah *noun* (also **loofa**) **1** a climbing gourd-like plant, *Luffa cylindrica*, native to Asia, producing edible marrow-like fruits. **2** the dried fibrous vascular system of this fruit used as a sponge. [Egyptian Arabic *lūfa*, the plant]

look ● *verb* **1 a** *intransitive* (often foll. by *at*) use one's sight; turn one's eyes in some direction. **b** *transitive* turn one's eyes on; contemplate or examine (*looked me in the eyes*). **2** *intransitive* **a** make a visual or mental

search (*I'll look in the morning*). **b** (foll. by *at*) consider, examine (*we must look at the facts*). **3** *intransitive* (foll. by *for*) **a** search for. **b** hope or be on the watch for. **c** expect. **4** *intransitive* inquire (*when one looks deeper*). **5** *intransitive* **a** have a specified appearance (*look foolish*). **b** seem; appear (*things don't look good for her; it looks to me as if you ought to go*). **6** *intransitive* (foll. by *to*) **a** consider; take care of; be careful about (*look to the future*). **b** rely on (a person or thing) (*you can look to me for support*). **c** expect; count on; aim at. **7** *intransitive* (foll. by *into*) investigate or examine. **8** *transitive* (foll. by *what, where*, etc. + clause) ascertain or observe by sight (*look where we are*). **9** *intransitive* (of a thing) face or be turned, or have or afford an outlook, in a specified direction. **10** *transitive* express, threaten, or show (an emotion etc.) by one's looks. **11** *intransitive* (foll. by *that* + clause) take care; make sure. **12** *intransitive* (foll. by *to* + infin.) expect (*am looking to finish this today*). **13** *intransitive informal* (foll. by *at*) be faced with an estimated expense, deficit, etc. (*you're looking at $40 to get to the airport; looking at a $2 million debt*). ● *noun* **1** an act of looking; the directing of the eyes to look at a thing or person; a glance (*a scornful look; let's have a look*). **2** (in *sing.* or *pl.*) the appearance of a face; a person's expression or personal aspect. **3** the (esp. characteristic) appearance of a thing (*the place has a European look*). **4** style, fashion (*this year's look; the wet look*). **5** (in *combination*) designating imitation fabrics etc. that have the appearance of a natural substance (*a linen-look suit*). ● *interjection* (also **look here!**) calling attention, expressing a protest, etc. □ **look after 1** attend to; take care of. **2** follow with the eye. **3** seek for. **look one's age** appear to be as old as one really is. **look alive** (or **lively**) *informal* be brisk and alert. **look around 1** look in every or another direction. **2** examine the objects of interest in a place (*you must come and look around sometime*). **3** examine the possibilities etc. with a view to deciding on a course of action. **look as if** suggest by appearance the belief that (*it looks as if she's gone*). **look back 1** (foll. by *on, upon, to*) turn one's thoughts to (something past). **2** (usu. with *neg.*) cease to progress (*since then we have never looked back*). **look before you leap** avoid precipitate action. **look daggers** see DAGGER. **look down on** (or **upon** or **look down one's nose at**) regard with contempt or a feeling of superiority. **look for trouble** see TROUBLE. **look forward to** await (an expected event) eagerly or with specified feelings. **look in** make a short visit or call. **look a person in the eye** (or **eyes** or **face**) look directly and unashamedly at him or her. **look like 1** have the appearance of. **2** indicate the presence of (*it looks like woodworm*). **3** threaten or promise (*it looks like rain*). **4** *Brit.* seem to be (*they look like winning*). **look on 1** (often foll. by *as*) regard (*looks on you as a friend; looked on them with disfavour*). **2** be a spectator; avoid participation. **look oneself** appear in good health (esp. after illness etc.). **look out 1** direct one's sight or put one's head out of a window etc. **2** (often foll. by *for*) be vigilant or prepared. **3** (foll. by *on, over*, etc.) have or afford a specified outlook. **4** search for and produce (*shall look one out for you*). **5** have someone's interests at heart (*a doting husband always looking out for his wife*). **look over 1** inspect or survey (*looked over the house*). **2** examine (a document etc.) esp. cursorily (*shall look it over*). **look sharp** (also esp. *Brit.* **look smart**) act promptly; make haste. **look small** see SMALL. **look through 1** examine the contents of, esp. cursorily. **2** penetrate (a pretense or pretender) with insight. **3** ignore by pretending not to see (*I waved, but you just looked through me*). **look up 1** search for (esp. information in a book). **2** *informal* go to visit (a person) (*had intended to look them up*). **3** raise one's eyes (*Mary Jane looked up when I went in*). **4** improve, esp. in price, prosperity, or well-being (*things are looking up all over*). **look a person up and down** scrutinize a person keenly or contemptuously. **look up to** respect or venerate. **not like the look of** find alarming or suspicious. □ **-looking** *adjective* (in *combination*). [Old English *lōcian* from West Germanic]

look-alike ● *noun* a person or thing closely resembling another (*an Elvis look-alike*). ● *adjective* closely similar, esp. in appearance; identical.

look·er *noun* **1** a person having a specified appearance (*a good-looker*). **2** *informal* an attractive person, esp. a woman. **3** a person who looks.

looker-on *noun* (*pl.* **lookers-on**) a person who is a mere spectator.

look-in *noun informal* **1** an informal call or visit. **2** *Brit.* a chance of participation or success (*never gets a look-in*).

look·ing glass *noun archaic* a mirror for looking at oneself.

look·ism *noun* prejudice or discrimination on the basis of looks or appearance. □ **look·ist** *adjective & noun*

lookit *interjection N Amer.* **1** demanding attention or expostulating. **2** look at (someone or something). [extension of LOOK]

look-off *noun N Amer.* a stopping place along a road etc. affording a good view of a scenic spot.

look·out *noun* **1** a watch or looking out (*on the lookout for bargains*). **2 a** a post of observation. **b** a person or party or boat stationed to keep watch. **3** a view over a landscape. **4** a prospect of luck (*it's a bad lookout for them*). **5** *informal* a person's own concern.

look-see *noun informal* a survey or inspection.

look·up *noun* **1** the action of systematic electronic information retrieval. **2** a facility for this.

looky *intransitive verb N Amer. informal* (in *imperative*; usu. as *looky here*) demanding attention. [extension of LOOK, perhaps reproducing *look ye*]

loom¹ *noun* an apparatus in which yarn or thread is woven into fabric by the crossing of vertical and horizontal threads. [Old English *gelōma* tool]

loom² ● *intransitive verb* (often foll. by *up*) **1** come into sight dimly, esp. as a vague and often magnified or threatening shape. **2** (of an event or prospect) be ominously close. **3** (often foll. by *over*) be ominously above (*the castle loomed over the village*). ● *noun* a vague often exaggerated first appearance of land at sea etc. □ **loom large** figure significantly. [prob. from Low German or Dutch: compare East Frisian *lōmen* move slowly, Middle High German *lüemen* be weary]

loon *noun* **1** *N Amer.* any aquatic diving bird of the family Gaviidae, with a long slender body and a sharp bill, esp. the common loon, *Gavia immer*, with a haunting yodel-like call, red eyes, bands of alternating black and white on the collar, and a checkered black and white back. **2** *informal* a crazy person (compare LOONY). **3** *Cdn* = LOONIE. [alteration of *loom* from Old Norse *lómr*]

loon·ie *noun Cdn* **1** the Canadian one-dollar coin. **2** *informal* the Canadian dollar. [LOON 1 (after the image on the coin) + -IE]

loony *slang* ● *noun* (*pl.* **-ies**) a mad or silly person; a lunatic. ● *adjective* (**loon·i·er, loon·i·est**) crazy, silly. □ **loon·i·ness** *noun* [abbreviation of LUNATIC]

loony bin *noun slang* a mental home or hospital.

loony-tune (also **looney tune**) *informal* ● *adjective* (also **-tunes**) crazy, silly; bizarre. ● *noun* a crazy or silly person. [from *Looney Tunes*, US animated cartoon series]

loop ● *noun* **1 a** the esp. oval or circular figure produced by a curve or string etc. that crosses itself. **b** anything forming this figure. **2** a similarly shaped attachment or ornament formed of cord or thread etc. and fastened at the crossing. **3** a ring or curved piece of material as a handle etc. **4** a contraceptive coil. **5 a** (in full **loop line**) a railway or telephone line etc. that diverges from a main line and joins it again. **b** a trail etc. that returns to its starting point. **c** a short circular stretch of track or roadway where a bus, streetcar, etc. turns at the end of its run. **6** a manoeuvre in which an airplane describes a vertical loop. **7** *Figure Skating* **a** a compulsory figure describing a curve that crosses itself, made on a single edge. **b** a jump from the back outside edge of one foot, landing on the back outside edge of the same foot, with rotation in the air. **8** *Electricity* a complete circuit for a current. **9** an endless strip of tape or film allowing continuous repetition. **10** *Computing* a programmed sequence of instructions that is repeated until or while a particular condition is satisfied. **11** *N Amer.* the circle of influential people or those keeping up to date (*has been out of the loop for a while now*). **12** any continuously-repeated process or routine. ● *verb* **1** *transitive* form (thread etc.) into a loop or loops. **2** *transitive* enclose with or as with a loop. **3** *transitive* (often foll. by *up, back, together*) fasten or join with a loop or loops. **4** *intransitive* **a** form a loop. **b** move in loop-like patterns. **5** *intransitive* (also **loop the loop**) perform the feat of circling in an aircraft in a vertical loop. □ **throw** (or **knock**) **one for a loop** *N Amer.* surprise, astonish; catch off-guard. [Middle English: origin unknown]

looped *adjective* **1** coiled or wreathed in loops. **2** consisting of a loop (*looped hiking trails*). **3** *N Amer. slang* drunk.

loop·er *noun* **1** a caterpillar of the geometer moth which progresses by arching itself into loops; inchworm. **2** a device for making loops.

loop·hole ● *noun* **1** a means of evading a rule etc. without infringing the letter of it. **2** a narrow vertical slit in a wall for shooting or looking through or to admit light or air. ● *transitive verb* make loopholes in (a wall etc.).

loop-the-loop *noun* the feat of circling in an aircraft in a vertical loop.

loopy *adjective* (**loop·i·er, loop·i·est**) **1** *slang* crazy. **2** having many loops.

loose ● *adjective* **1 a** not or no longer held by bonds or restraint. **b** (of an animal) not confined or tethered etc. **2** detached or detachable from its place (*has come loose*). **3** not held together or contained or fixed. **4** not specially fastened or packaged (*loose papers; had her hair loose*). **5** hanging partly free (*a loose end*). **6** slack, relaxed; not tense or tight. **7** (of a person's joints) easily moved. **8** not compact or dense

(*loose soil*). **9** (of language, concepts, etc.) inexact; conveying only the general sense. **10** (preceding an agent noun) doing the expressed action in a loose or careless manner (*a loose thinker*). **11** morally lax; dissolute (*loose living*). **12 a** (of talk) indiscreet. **b** (of the tongue) likely to speak indiscreetly. **13** (of the bowels) lax; afflicted with diarrhea. **14** *Sport* **a** (of a ball, puck, etc.) in play but not in any player's possession. **b** (of play etc.) with the players not close together. **15** (of a partnership, coalition, etc.) allowing for substantial independence among its members. ● *adverb* **1** (in *combination*) loosely (*loose-flowing; loose-fitting*). **2** without constraint (*let the dogs run loose*). **3** without attachment (*pried their fingers loose*). ● *transitive verb* **1** release; set free; free from constraint. **2** untie or undo (something that constrains). **3** detach from moorings. **4** relax (*loosed my hold on it*). **5** discharge (a gun or arrow etc.). □ **on the loose 1** escaped from captivity. **2** having a free enjoyable time. **stay loose** remain relaxed. □ **loose·ly** *adverb* **loose·ness** *noun* [Middle English *lōs* from Old Norse *lauss* from Germanic]

loose box *noun* a compartment for a horse in a stable or vehicle, in which it can move about.

loose cannon *noun* a reckless person or thing causing unintentional or misdirected damage.

loose change *noun* a relatively insignificant amount of money for casual use, as coins kept in a pocket.

loose cover *noun Brit.* = SLIPCOVER *noun*.

loose end *noun* an unfinished detail. □ **at loose ends** (*Brit.* **at a loose end**) (of a person) with nothing to do; unsettled, without a place or purpose.

loose-jointed *adjective* **1** having loose or ill-fitting joints. **2** limber, agile.

loose-leaf ● *adjective* **1** (of a notebook, manual, etc.) with each leaf separate and removable. **2** pertaining to or for use with a loose-leaf binder etc. (*loose-leaf paper*). ● *noun* loose-leaf paper.

loose-limbed *adjective* having supple limbs.

loose lips *noun* indiscreet talk. □ **loose-lipped** *adjective*

loos·en *verb* **1** *transitive & intransitive* make or become less tight or compact or firm. **2** *transitive* make (a regime etc.) less severe. **3** *transitive* release (the bowels) from constipation. **4** *transitive* relieve (a cough) from dryness. □ **loosen a person's tongue** make a person talk freely. **loosen up 1** limber up (see LIMBER¹ *verb*). **2** lighten up (see LIGHTEN¹). □ **loos·en·er** *noun*

loose·strife *noun* **1** any plant of the genus *Lysimachia*, e.g. the European garden loosestrife, *L. vulgaris*, naturalized in N America. **2** any plant of the genus *Lythrum*, esp. the purple loosestrife, *L. salicaria*, with racemes of star-shaped purple flowers. [LOOSE + STRIFE, taking the Greek name *lusimakhion* (from *Lusimakhos*, its discoverer) as if directly from *luō* undo + *makhē* battle]

loosey-goosey *adjective N Amer. informal* laid back; very relaxed. [fanciful reduplication]

loot ● *noun* **1** goods taken from an enemy; spoil. **2** booty; illicit gains made by an official. **3** *slang* money. **4** *informal* a collection or mass of recently-obtained goodies (*rummaging through their Halloween loot*). ● *transitive verb* **1** rob (premises) or steal (goods) left unprotected, esp. after riots or other violent events. **2** plunder or sack (a city, building, etc.). **3** carry off as booty. □ **loot·er** *noun* **loot·ing** *noun* [Hindi *lūṭ*]

loot bag *noun N Amer.* a small bag containing candy, trinkets, etc., given to each child at a birthday party etc.

lop¹ ● *verb* (**lopped, lop·ping**) **1** *transitive* **a** (often foll. by *off, away*) cut or remove (a part or parts) from a whole, esp. branches from a tree. **b** remove branches from a tree. **2** *transitive* (often foll. by *off, away*) remove (items) as superfluous. **3** *intransitive* (foll. by *at*) make lopping strokes on (a tree etc.). ● *noun* parts lopped off, esp. branches and twigs of trees. □ **lop·per** *noun* [Old English *loppian* (unrecorded): compare obsolete *lip* to prune]

lop² *verb* (**lopped, lop·ping**) **1** *intransitive & transitive* hang limply. **2** *intransitive* move with short bounds. □ **loppy** *adjective* [related to LOB]

lop³ *noun* a state of the sea in which the waves are short and choppy; the sea or its surface when in this condition. □ **loppy** *adjective* [imitative]

lope ● *intransitive verb* **1** run with a long bounding stride. **2** move with long, easy strides. ● *noun* a long bounding stride. [Middle English, var. of Scots *loup* from Old Norse *hlaupa* LEAP]

lop-ears *plural noun* drooping ears. □ **lop-eared** *adjective*

lopho- *combining form Zool.* crested. [Greek *lophos* crest]

lopho·phore /ˈlɒfəfɔr, ˈlɒf-/ *noun* a horseshoe-shaped structure bearing ciliated tentacles around the mouth of bryozoans, brachiopods, etc. □ **lo·phoph·or·ate** /ləˈfɒfəreɪt, loːfəˈfɔreit/ *noun & adjective*

Lop Nor /lɒp ˈnɔr/ (also **Lop Nur** /ˈnʊr/) a marshy depression in the arid basin of the Tarim River in NW China. The remote area has been used since 1964 for nuclear testing.

lop·pet *noun* a long-distance cross-country ski race in which all competitors start together. [Norwegian *løpet*, definite sing. of *løp* race, run, running (cognate with English *lope*)]

lop·sided *adjective* **1** with one side lower or smaller than the other; unevenly balanced. **2** *Sport* (of a score, victory, etc.) with one side greatly outscoring the other. □ **lop·sided·ly** *adverb* **lop·sided·ness** *noun* [LOP² + SIDE]

lo·qua·cious /loːˈkweɪʃəs/ *adjective* talkative. □ **lo·qua·cious·ly** *adverb* **lo·qua·cious·ness** *noun* **lo·quacity** /-ˈkwasɪti/ *noun* [Latin *loquax -acis* from *loqui* talk]

lo·quat /ˈloːkwɒt/ *noun* **1** a rosaceous tree, *Eriobotrya japonica*, bearing small yellow egg-shaped fruits. **2** this fruit. [Chinese dial. *luh kwat* rush orange]

lor *interjection* *Brit. slang* an exclamation of surprise or dismay. [abbreviation of LORD]

loran /ˈlɔran/ *noun* a system of long-distance navigation in which position is determined from the intervals between signal pulses received from widely spaced radio transmitters. [*long-range navigation*]

Lorca, Fede·rico Gar·cía (1898–1936), Spanish poet and dramatist. His works include the verse collection *Gypsy Ballads* (1928), which is strongly influenced by the folk poetry of his native Andalusia, and intense, poetic tragedies such as *Blood Wedding* (1933) and *The House of Bernarda Alba* (published posthumously in 1945).

lord ● *noun* **1 a** a master or ruler. **b** a powerful person in a specified field or group (*drug lord*). **2** *hist.* a feudal superior, esp. of a manor. **3** (**Lord**) (often prec. by *the*) **a** a name for God. **b** a name for Christ. **4** (in the UK) a peer of the realm or a person entitled to the title *Lord*, esp. a marquess, earl, viscount, or baron. **5** (**Lord**) (in the UK) **a** prefixed as the designation of a marquess, earl, viscount, or baron. **b** prefixed to the first name of the younger son of a duke or marquess. **c** (**the Lords**) = HOUSE OF LORDS. **6** *Astrology* the ruling planet (of a sign, house, or chart). **●** *interjection* (**Lord**) expressing surprise, dismay, etc. **●** *transitive verb* confer the title of Lord upon. □ **lord it over 1** domineer. **2** adopt an attitude of superiority over. **Lord knows** God knows (*see* GOD). **lord over** (*usu. in passive*) rule over. □ **lord·less** *adjective* **lord·like** *adjective* [Old English *hlāford* from *hlāfweard* = bread-keeper (as LOAF¹, WARD)]

lord and lady *noun* (*pl.* **lords and ladies**) esp. *Cdn* (*usu. in pl.*) the harlequin duck.

Lord Chamberlain *noun* (in full **Lord Chamberlain of the Household**) (in the UK) the official in charge of the Royal Household, formerly the licensor of plays.

Lord Chancellor *noun* (also **Lord High Chancellor**) (in the UK) the highest officer of the Crown, presiding in the House of Lords etc.

Lord Chief Justice *noun* (in the UK) the president of the Queen's Bench Division.

Lord Lieutenant *noun* **1** (in the UK) the chief executive authority and head of magistrates in each county. **2** *hist.* the viceroy of Ireland.

lord·ly *adjective* (**lord·li·er**, **lord·li·est**) **1** haughty, imperious. **2** suitable for a lord. □ **lord·li·ness** *noun* [Old English *hlāfordlic* (as LORD)]

Lord Mayor *noun* (in the UK) the title of the mayor in London and some other large cities.

lor·do·sis *noun* *Med.* inward curvature of the spine (*opp.* KYPHOSIS). □ **lor·dot·ic** *adjective* [modern Latin from Greek *lordōsis* from *lordos* bent backwards]

Lord Privy Seal *noun* (in the UK) a senior cabinet minister without official duties.

Lord Protector of the Commonwealth *noun see* PROTECTOR 4.

Lord's Day *noun* Sunday.

lord·ship *noun* **1** (foll. by *of*, *over*) dominion, rule, or ownership. **2** *archaic* the state of being a lord. □ **his** (or **your**) **Lordship** (or **lordship**) (*pl.* **their** (or **your**) **Lordships** or **lordships**) **1** *Brit.* a respectful form of reference or address to a Lord or a bishop. **2** *Cdn & Brit.* a respectful form of reference or address to a judge. **3** *ironic* a form of reference or address to a man thought to give himself airs. [Old English *hlāfordscipe* (as LORD, -SHIP)]

Lord's Prayer *noun* the prayer taught by Christ to his disciples, beginning with the words 'Our Father'.

Lords spiritual *plural noun* (in the UK) the bishops in the House of Lords.

Lord's Supper *noun* the Eucharist.

Lords temporal *plural noun* (in the UK) the members of the House of Lords other than the bishops.

Lordy *interjection* = LORD *interjection*.

lore¹ *noun* a body of traditions and knowledge on a subject or held by a particular group (*herbal lore*; *Acadian lore*). [Old English *lār* from Germanic, related to LEARN]

lore² *noun* *Zool.* a surface between the eye and upper mandible in birds, or between the eye and nostril in snakes. [Latin *lorum* strap]

Lore·lei /ˈlɔrəˌlaɪ/ **1** a rock on the right bank of the Rhine, in the Rhine gorge near Sankt Goarshausen. It is held by legend to be the home of a siren whose song lures boatmen to destruction. **2** the siren herself. **3** a dangerously fascinating woman; a temptress.

Loren /ləˈren/ **So·phia** (born Sophia Scicolone) (b.1934), Italian actress, whose films include the romantic melodrama *The Black Orchid* (1959), the slapstick comedy *The Millionairess* (1960), and the wartime drama *La Ciociara* (1961), for which she won an Oscar.

Lor·entz /ˈlɔrənts/ **Hen·drik An·toon** (1853–1928), Dutch theoretical physicist. He coined the word *electron*, and his name is applied to various concepts and phenomena which he described; for their work on electromagnetic theory, he and his pupil Pieter Zeeman shared the 1902 Nobel Prize for physics.

Lorentz-FitzGerald contraction *noun* (also **FitzGerald contraction**) *Physics* the relativistic shortening of a moving body in the direction of its motion, esp. at speeds close to that of light. [H.A. LORENTZ + G.F. FITZGERALD]

Lor·enz /ˈlɔrənts/ **Kon·rad Zach·a·rias** (1903–89), Austrian zoologist. He pioneered the science of ethology, emphasizing innate rather than learned behaviour or conditioned reflexes, and his popular books include *King Solomon's Ring* (1952) and *On Aggression* (1966); he shared a Nobel Prize in 1973 with von Frisch and Nikolaas Tinbergen.

Lo·ren·zo de' Med·ici /ləˈrenzo də ˈmeditʃi/ (known as 'Lorenzo the Magnificent') (1449–92), Italian statesman and scholar. A patron of the arts, he promoted humanist learning and Neoplatonic philosophy, and was a noted poet and scholar; Botticelli, Leonardo da Vinci, and Michelangelo were among the artists who enjoyed his patronage.

Lor·eto /ləˈreto/ a town in E Italy, near the Adriatic coast to the south of Ancona; pop. (1996) 10,780. It is the site of the 'Holy House', said to be the home of the Virgin Mary and to have been brought from Nazareth by angels in 1295.

Lorette·ville a former town in SE central Quebec, now part of the city of Québec; pop. (2001) 13,737. [ultimately after *Loreto*, Italy: see L'ANCIENNE-LORETTE]

lor·gnette /lɔrˈnjet/ *noun* (in *sing.* or *pl.*) a pair of eyeglasses or opera glasses held by a long handle. [French from *lorgner* to squint]

Lo·rient /lɔrˈjã/ a port in NW France, on the south coast of Brittany; pop. (1999) 63,238.

lori·keet *noun* any of various small brightly coloured parrots of the subfamily Loriinae, including the rainbow lorikeet. [diminutive of LORY, after *parakeet*]

loris *noun* (*pl.* **loris·es**) either of two small tailless nocturnal primates of the subfamily Lorisinae, with small ears, very short tails, and opposable thumbs, *Loris tardigradus* of S India (**slender loris**), and *Nycticebus coucang* of the E Indies (**slow loris**). [French perhaps from obsolete Dutch *loeris* clown]

lorn *adjective* *literary* desolate, forlorn, abandoned. [past participle of obsolete *leese* from Old English -*lēosan* lose]

Lorne, John Doug·las Suther·land Camp·bell, Mar·quess of (later 9th Duke of Argyll) (1845–1914), English politician and Governor General of Canada. A British Liberal MP 1868–78, he married Princess Louise, the fourth daughter of Queen Victoria, in 1871. During his term in Canada (1878–83) he helped reconcile BC to Confederation and founded both the Canadian Academy of Arts (a forerunner of the National Gallery) in 1880 and the Royal Society of Canada in 1882.

Lor·rain see CLAUDE LORRAIN.

Lor·raine /lɔrˈen, ləˈrein/ **1** a town in south central Quebec, situated on the Rivière des Mille-Îles, northwest of Montreal; pop. (2001) 9,476. **2** a region of NE France, between Champagne and the Vosges mountains. The modern region corresponds to the southern part of the medieval kingdom of Lorraine, which extended from the North Sea to Italy. [Latin *Lotharingia* from *Lothair* name of king (825–69); sense 1 from sense 2]

Consonants: b *but*   d *dog*   f *few*   g *get*   h *her*   j *yes*   k *cat*   l *leg*   m *man*   n *no*   p *pen*   r *red*   s *sit*

Lorraine, Cross of *noun* a cross with two parallel crosspieces, originally a heraldic device. It was the symbol of Joan of Arc, and in the Second World War was adopted by the Free French forces of General de Gaulle.

lorry *noun* (*pl.* **-ries**) **1** *Brit.* = TRUCK[1] 1. **2** *archaic* a long flat low wagon, esp. used on railways. [19th c.: origin uncertain]

Lor·tie /lɔrˈtiː/ **Louis** (b.1959), Canadian pianist. He won the Canadian Music Competitions five times (1968–72), the CBC Talent Festival (1975), and numerous other Canadian and international competitions.

lory *noun* (*pl.* **-ies**) any of various brightly coloured Australasian parrots of the subfamily Loriinae. [Malay *lūrī*]

Los Ala·mos /lɒs ˈaləˌmɒːs/ a town in N New Mexico; pop. (2000) 11,909. It has been a centre for nuclear research since the 1940s, when it was the site of the development of the first atomic and hydrogen bombs.

Los An·gel·es /lɒs ˈandʒələs/ a city on the Pacific coast of S California, the second largest city in the US; pop. (2000) 3,694,820. It is a major centre of industry, filmmaking, and television, its metropolitan area having expanded to include towns such as Beverley Hills, Hollywood, Santa Monica, and Pasadena.

lose *verb* (*past* and *past participle* **lost**) **1** *transitive* be deprived of or cease to have, esp. by negligence or misadventure. **2** *transitive* **a** be deprived of (a person, esp. a close relative or patient) by death. **b** suffer the death of (a baby) in childbirth or through miscarriage. **3** *transitive* become unable to find; fail to keep in sight or follow or mentally grasp (*lose one's way*). **4** *transitive* let or have pass from one's control or reach (*lose one's chance*; *lose one's bearings*). **5** *transitive & intransitive* be defeated in (a game, race, lawsuit, battle, etc.). **6** *transitive* evade; get rid of (*lost our pursuers*). **7** *transitive* fail to apprehend by sight or hearing; not catch (words etc.). **8** *transitive* forfeit (a stake, deposit, right to a thing, etc.). **9** *transitive* spend (time, efforts, etc.) to no purpose (*lost no time in raising the alarm*). **10 a** *intransitive* suffer loss or detriment; incur a disadvantage. **b** *intransitive* be worse off, esp. financially. **c** *transitive* experience a deficit of expenditure over income (*lost money on her house*; *the company's been losing money for years*). **11** *transitive* cause (a person) the loss of (*will lose you your job*). **12** (of a timepiece) **a** *intransitive* become slow. **b** *transitive* become slow by (a specified amount of time). **13** *transitive* (in *passive*) disappear, perish; be dead (*was lost in the war*; *is a lost art*). **14** *transitive informal* get rid of; discard. **15** *transitive* undergo a reduction of; shed (weight). **16** *transitive* vomit (*lose one's lunch*). □ **lose one's balance** fail to remain stable; fall. **lose one's cool** *informal* lose one's composure. **lose face** be humiliated; lose one's credibility. **lose ground** see GROUND[1]. **lose one's head** see HEAD. **lose heart** be discouraged. **lose one's heart** see HEART. **lose it** *informal* **1** lose one's composure suddenly and completely. **2** lose one's mind, sense of reality, sanity, etc. **3** cease to excel or be proficient in a specified field. **lose one's nerve** become timid or irresolute. **lose out** *informal* **1** (often foll. by *on*) be unsuccessful; not get a fair chance or advantage (in). **2** (foll. by *to*) be beaten in competition or replaced by. **lose one's rag** esp. *Brit.* become angry; lose one's temper. **lose one's temper** become angry. **lose time** allow time to pass with something not achieved etc. **lose touch** see TOUCH. **lose track of** see TRACK[1]. **lose the** (or **one's**) **way** become lost; fail to reach one's destination. □ **losing** *noun & adjective* [Old English *losian* 'perish, destroy' from *los* 'loss']

lose-lose *adjective* (esp. *attributive*) *informal* designating a condition, policy, settlement, etc. which is damaging or disadvantageous to everyone involved (*a lose-lose situation*).

loser *noun* **1** a person or thing that loses or has lost (esp. a contest or game) (*is a poor loser*; *the loser pays*). **2** *informal* **a** a person who regularly fails. **b** a socially awkward person; a misfit.

losing battle *noun* a contest or effort in which failure seems inevitable.

loss *noun* **1 a** the act or an instance of losing; the state of being lost. **b** the fact of being deprived of a person by death, estrangement, etc. **2** a person, thing, or amount lost. **3** the detriment or disadvantage resulting from losing (*that is no great loss*). □ **at a loss** (sold etc.) for less than was paid for it. **be at a loss** be puzzled or uncertain. **be at a loss for words** not know what to say. [Middle English *los*, *loss*, prob. a back-formation from *lost*, past participle of LOSE]

loss leader *noun* an item sold at a loss to attract customers.

loss-making *adjective Brit.* (of a business etc.) making a financial loss. □ **loss-maker** *noun*

lost ● *transitive & intransitive verb past* and *past participle* of LOSE. ● *adjective* **1** unable to find one's way; not knowing where one is. **2** confused or in difficulties. **3** that cannot be found or recovered. **4** damned, fallen

(*lost souls*). □ **be lost for words** be so surprised, confused, etc. that one cannot think what to say. **be lost in** be engrossed in. **be lost on** be wasted on, or not noticed or appreciated by. **be lost to** be no longer affected by or accessible to (*is lost to the world*). **be lost without** have great difficulty if deprived of (*am lost without my address book*). **get lost** (usu. in *imperative*) *slang* go away.

lost and found *noun* a place where misplaced items are collected for retrieval by their owners.

lost cause *noun* **1** an enterprise etc. with no chance of success. **2** a person one can no longer hope to influence.

lost generation *noun* the generation reaching maturity *c.*1915–25, a high proportion of whose men were killed in the First World War, characterized by disillusionment.

lost soul *noun* **1** a soul that is damned. **2** a person who is unable to cope with everyday life; a bewildered or pitiful person.

Lost Tribes the ten tribes of Israel taken away *c.*720 BC by Sargon II to captivity in Assyria (2 Kings 17:6), from which they are believed never to have returned, while the tribes of Benjamin and Judah remained.

lost wax *noun* a method of bronze-casting using a clay core and a wax coating placed in a mould: the wax is melted in the mould and bronze poured into the space left, producing a hollow bronze figure when the core is discarded (usu. *attributive*: *lost wax process*).

Lot (in the Bible) the nephew of Abraham, who was allowed to escape from the destruction of Sodom (Gen. 19); his wife, who disobeyed orders and looked back, was turned into a pillar of salt.

lot ● *noun* **1** *informal* (prec. by *a* or in *pl.*) **a** a large number or amount (*a lot of people*; *lots of chocolate*). **b** *informal* much (*a lot warmer*; *smiles a lot*; *is lots better*). **2 a** each of a set of objects used in making a chance selection. **b** this method of deciding (*chosen by lot*). **3** a share, or the responsibility resulting from it. **4** a person's destiny, fortune, or condition. **5** esp. *N Amer.* **a** a portion of land assigned to a particular owner; each of the portions into which a tract of land is divided when offered for sale. **b** land near a film studio where outside filming may be done. **c** a plot of land used for parking vehicles. **d** the area at a car dealership where cars for sale are kept (*depreciates the minute you drive it off the lot*). **6** an article or set of articles for sale at an auction etc. **7** a number or quantity of associated persons or things. ● *transitive verb* (**lot·ted**, **lot·ting**) divide into lots. □ **cast** (or **draw**) **lots** decide by means of lots. **throw in one's lot with** decide to share the fortunes of. **the** (or **the whole**) **lot** the whole number or quantity. **a whole lot** *informal* very much (*is a whole lot better*). [Old English *hlot* portion, choice, from Germanic]

Lo·thair I /lɒˈθeːr/ (795–855), Frankish ruler and Holy Roman emperor 823–30, 833–4, and 840–55.

Lo·thair II /lɒˈθeːr/ (1075–1137), German king 1125–37 and Holy Roman emperor 1133–7.

Lo·thario /ləˈθɑːriɔː, -ˈθeriɔː/ *noun* (*pl.* **-tharios**) a man known for many sexual conquests. [a character in Rowe's *Fair Penitent* (1703)]

Lo·thian /ˈlɒːðiən/ a former local government region in SE central Scotland, on the south shore of the Firth of Forth, now divided into four smaller jurisdictions.

loti /ˈlɒːti, ˈluːti/ *noun* (*pl.* **maloti** /məˈlɒːti, -ˈluːti/) the basic monetary unit of Lesotho, equal to 100 lisente. [Sesotho]

lo·tion /ˈlɒːʃən/ *noun* a medicinal or cosmetic liquid preparation applied externally. [Old French *lotion* or Latin *lotio* from *lavare lot-* wash]

Lot River /lɒt, lɔː/ a river of S France, which rises in the Auvergne and flows 480 km (300 miles) west to meet the Garonne southeast of Bordeaux.

lotsa *adverb informal* lots of. [corruption]

lotta *informal* a lot of. [corruption]

lot·tery *noun* (*pl.* **-ies**) **1 a** a means of raising money, usu. on a large scale and government-operated, by selling numbered tickets and giving prizes to the holders of numbers drawn at random. **b** any game of chance involving the sale of tickets. **c** a process of selection which relies on random drawing (*visas are awarded through a lottery*). **2** an enterprise, process, etc., whose outcome is governed by chance (*life is a lottery*). [prob. from Dutch *loterij* (as LOT)]

lot·to *noun* **1** *N Amer.* (also esp. *Que.* **loto**) a lottery. **2** a game of chance like bingo, but with numbers drawn by the players instead of being called. [Italian]

lotus *noun* **1** (in Greek mythology) a legendary plant inducing luxurious languor when eaten. **2 a** any water lily of the genus *Nelumbo*, esp. *N. nucifera* of India, with large pink flowers. **b** this flower used symbolically in Hinduism and Buddhism. **3** an Egyptian water lily,

Nymphaea lotus, with white flowers. **4** any plant of the genus *Lotus*, e.g. bird's-foot trefoil. [Latin from Greek *lōtos*, of Semitic origin]

lotus-eater *noun* **1** a member of a people represented by Homer as living on the fruit of the lotus in a state of dreamy forgetfulness and idleness. **2** a person given to indolent enjoyment.

lotus land *noun* **1** a place of indolent enjoyment. **2** (**Lotus Land**) *Cdn jocular* southern British Columbia.

lotus position *noun* a cross-legged position of meditation with the feet resting on the thighs.

Lotus Sutra /ˈlɒtəs ˈsuːtrə/ *noun Buddhism* one of the most important texts in Mahayana Buddhism, significant particularly in China and Japan and given special veneration by the Nichiren sect.

Louang·phra·bang see LUANG PRABANG.

louche /luːʃ/ *adjective* disreputable, shifty. [French, lit. 'squinting']

Lou·cheux /ˈluːʃuː/ *noun* (*pl. same*) = GWICH'IN. [French, 'squinting', translation of Gwich'in *Tukkuth*, lit. 'people of the slanting eyes', one of the Gwich'in bands]

loud ● *adjective* **1 a** strongly audible, esp. noisily or oppressively so. **b** able or liable to produce loud sounds (*a loud engine*). **c** clamorous, insistent (*loud complaints*). **2** (of colours, design, etc.) gaudy, obtrusive. **3** (of behaviour) aggressive and noisy. ● *adverb* in a loud manner. □ **loud and clear 1** loudly and clearly (*speak loud and clear*). **2** without misunderstanding (*got the hint loud and clear*). **out loud 1** aloud. **2** loudly (*laughed out loud*). □ **loud·en** *transitive & intransitive verb* **loud·ly** *adverb* **loud·ness** *noun* [Old English *hlūd* from West Germanic]

loud-hailer *noun* an electronic device for amplifying the sound of the voice so that it can be heard at a distance; a bullhorn.

loud·mouth *noun informal* a noisily self-assertive or vociferous person. □ **loud-mouthed** *adjective*

loud·speaker *noun* an apparatus that converts electrical impulses into sound, esp. music and voice.

Lou Gehrig's disease *noun* = AMYOTROPHIC LATERAL SCLEROSIS. [L. GEHRIG]

lough /lɒk, lɒx/ *noun Irish* = LOCH. [Irish *loch* LOCH, assimilated to the related obsolete Middle English form *lough*]

Lougheed /ˈlɒhiːd/ (**Edgar) Peter** (b.1928), Canadian lawyer and politician, Progressive Conservative premier of Alberta 1971–85. After two years playing with the CFL Edmonton Eskimos and a brief period practising law, he was elected leader of the Alberta Progressive Conservative Party in 1965. The party, which had not been a political force for over 40 years, became the opposition in 1967 and won 49 of 75 seats in 1971. As premier, he encouraged development of oil and gas in the province while increasing royalties paid to the province, and started the Alberta Heritage Fund.

Lough Neagh /lɒx ˈneɪ/ a lake in E Northern Ireland, about 32 km west of Belfast. With an area of 396 sq. km, it is the largest lake in the British Isles.

Louis /ˈluːɪs/ **1 Joe** (born Joseph Louis Barrow; known as the 'Brown Bomber') (1914–81), US boxer. He was world heavyweight champion (1937–49), defending his title 25 times during that period. **2 St.**, see LOUIS IX.

Louis VII /ˈluːi/ (known as 'Louis the Younger') (*c.*1120–80), king of France 1137–80, who led the Second Crusade (1147–9).

Louis IX /ˈluːi/ (canonized as St. Louis) (1214–70), son of Louis VIII, king of France 1226–70. His reign was dominated by two crusades to the Holy Land, neither of them successful: the first (1248–54) ended with his capture by the Egyptians, the second (1270–1) in his own death from plague in Tunis.

Louis XI /ˈluːi/ (1423–83), son of Charles VII, king of France 1461–83. His reign was dominated by his struggle with Charles the Rash, Duke of Burgundy; this ended with Charles's death in battle (1477) and France's absorption of much of Burgundy's former territory along her border.

Louis XIII /ˈluːi/ (1601–43), son of Henry IV of France, king of France 1610–43. During his minority, the country was ruled by his mother Marie de Médicis; Louis asserted his right to rule in 1617, but from 1624 he was heavily influenced in policy-making by his chief minister Cardinal Richelieu.

Louis XIV /ˈluːi/ (1638–1715), son of Louis XIII, king of France 1643–1715. He is known as the 'Sun King' from the magnificence of his reign, which represented the high point of the Bourbon dynasty and of French power in Europe, and during which French art and literature flourished; however, his almost constant wars of expansion united Europe against him, and gravely weakened France's financial position.

Louis XV /ˈluːi/ (1710–74), king of France 1715–74. His reign saw

France's entry into the War of the Austrian Succession (1740–8) and the Seven Years War (1756–63).

Louis XVI /ˈluːi/ (1754–93), grandson and successor of Louis XV, king of France 1774–92. He inherited a situation of growing political discontent and severe problems of debt in the state finances which contributed to the outbreak of the French Revolution; the monarchy was abolished in 1792 and he was executed.

Louis XVIII /ˈluːi/ (1755–1824), the younger brother of Louis XVI, king of France 1814–24. He became titular regent after the death of Louis XVI in 1793, declared himself king in 1814, and with the final defeat of Napoleon in 1815 he returned from exile in England.

louis /ˈluːi/ *noun* (*pl. same* /ˈluːiz/) *hist.* (in full **louis d'or** /-ˈdɔr/) a former French gold coin worth about 20 francs. [*Louis*, the name of kings of France]

Louis·bourg /ˈluːɪsbɜrg/ an urban community on Cape Breton Island, part of the regional municipality of Cape Breton. Situated on the Atlantic coast, about 30 km southeast of Sydney, it is the site of a reconstructed historic fortress founded by the French in 1713. The fortified settlement served as capital of the French colony of Île Royale and as a stronghold against the British in N America, protecting French trade routes and fishing rights. It was captured and destroyed by the British in 1758. [LOUIS XIV]

Louise, Lake see LAKE LOUISE.

Louise Falls a waterfall, 16 m high, in the southern NWT, situated on the Hay River, 2 km downstream from Alexandra Falls.

Lou·ise·ville a town in south central Quebec, southwest of Trois-Rivières; pop. (2001) 7,622. [Princess *Louise* Caroline Alberta, 4th daughter of Queen Victoria and wife of the Marquess of Lorne, d.1939]

Lou·isi·ana a state in the southern US, on the Gulf of Mexico; pop. (2000) 4,468,976; capital, Baton Rouge. Louisiana originally denoted the large region of the Mississippi basin claimed for France by the explorer La Salle in 1682. It was sold by the French to the US in the Louisiana Purchase of 1803. The smaller area now known as Louisiana became the 18th state in 1812. □ **Lou·isi·anan** *adjective & noun* (also **Lou·isi·an·ian**).

Louisiana Purchase the territory sold by France to the US in 1803, comprising the western part of the Mississippi valley.

Louis Napoleon see NAPOLEON III.

Louis Phi·lippe /ˌluːi fɪˈliːp/ (1773–1850), king of France 1830–48. His bourgeois-style regime was popular at first but it was gradually undermined by radical discontent and overthrown in a brief uprising in 1848, with Louis Philippe going into exile in England.

Louis·ville /ˈluːi,vɪl/ an industrial city and river port in N Kentucky, on the Ohio River just south of the border with Indiana; pop. (2000) 256,200. It is the site of the annual Kentucky Derby, which takes place on nearby Churchill Downs racetrack.

Lou Marsh Trophy *noun* a trophy awarded annually to Canada's best athlete, as chosen by a committee of sports journalists. [Louis Edwin *Marsh*, Toronto sports writer and editor d.1936]

lounge ● *intransitive verb* **1** recline comfortably and casually; loll. **2** (often foll. by *around, about*) stand or move about idly. ● *noun* **1** a place where people may sit and relax, esp.: **a** a public room or bar, e.g. in a hotel. **b** a place in an airport etc. with seats for waiting passengers. **c** a room where staff, students, etc. may congregate informally. **2** (*attributive*) designating live easy listening musical entertainment characteristic of lounges (*lounge singer*; *lounge music*). **3** a sitting room in a house. **4** *Brit.* an act or instance of lounging. [perhaps from obsolete *lungis* lout]

lounge chair *noun N Amer.* any chair for lounging or reclining in.

lounge·core *noun* any of a variety of musical styles which combine elements of lounge music and hardcore.

lounge lizard *noun informal* **1** an esp. smarmy or unctuous idler who frequents lounges. **2** an idler in fashionable society. **3** a singer or other performer of esp. pop songs in lounges.

loun·ger *noun* **1** a person who lounges. **2** a piece of furniture for relaxing on. **3** a casual garment for wearing when relaxing.

lounge·wear *noun* clothing for relaxing in, esp. at home.

loun·gey *adjective* **1** (of a place) conducive to lounging; comfortable (*a loungey bar with low seating*). **2** *informal* denoting or relating to easy-listening music.

loupe /luːp/ *noun* a small magnifying glass used by jewellers etc. [French]

loup-garou /ˌluːgəˈruː/ *noun* (*pl.* **loups-garous** /ˌluːgəˈruːz/) a werewolf. [French]

lour /laur/ *var. of* LOWER[3].

Lourdes /lʊrd/ a town in SW France, at the foot of the Pyrenees; pop. (1999) 15,203. It has been a major place of Roman Catholic pilgrimage since 1858, when a young peasant girl, Marie Bernarde Soubirous (St. Bernadette), claimed to have had a series of visions of the Virgin Mary.

Lou·ren·ço Marques /ləˌrensoː ˈmɑːks/ the former name (until 1976) of Maputo.

louse ● *noun* **1** (*pl.* **lice**) **a** a parasitic insect, *Pediculus humanus*, infesting the human hair and skin and transmitting various diseases. **b** any insect of the order Anoplura or Mallophaga parasitic on mammals, birds, fish, or plants. **2** (*pl.* **louses**) *slang* a contemptible or unpleasant person. ● *transitive verb* remove lice from. □ **louse up** *slang* mess up. [Old English *lūs*, pl. *lȳs*]

louse·wort /ˈlaʊswɜːt, -wɔːt/ *noun* any plant of the genus *Pedicularis* with purple-pink flowers found in marshes and wet places.

lousy *adjective* (**lous·i·er**, **lous·i·est**) **1** infested with lice. **2** *informal* very bad; disgusting (also as a term of general disparagement). **3** *informal* (often foll. by *with*) well supplied, teeming. □ **lous·i·ly** *adverb* **lous·i·ness** *noun*

lout *noun* a rough, crude, or ill-mannered person (usu. a man). □ **lout·ish** *adjective* **lout·ish·ly** *adverb* **lout·ish·ness** *noun* [perhaps from archaic *lout* to bow]

Louth /laʊθ/ a county of the Republic of Ireland, on the east coast in the province of Leinster; county town, Dundalk.

Lou·vain see LEUVEN.

louvre /ˈluːvər/ *noun* (also **louver**) **1** each of a set of overlapping slats, esp. in a door, designed to admit air and some light. **2** a domed structure on a roof with side openings for ventilation etc. □ **louvred** *adjective* [Old French *lover, lovier* skylight, prob. from Germanic]

lov·able *adjective* (also **loveable**) inspiring or deserving love or affection. □ **lov·abil·ity** *noun* **lov·able·ness** *noun* **lov·ably** *adverb*

lov·age /ˈlʌvɪdʒ/ *noun* **1** a S European herb, *Levisticum officinale*, used for flavouring etc. **2** a white-flowered umbelliferous plant, *Ligusticum scoticum*. [Middle English *loveache* alteration of Old French *levesche* from Late Latin *levisticum* from Latin *ligusticum* neuter of *ligusticus* Ligurian]

lovat /ˈlʌvət/ ● *noun* (also **lovat green**) a muted green colour found esp. in tweed and woollen garments. ● *adjective* (also **lovat green**; hyphenated when *attributive*) of this colour. [*Lovat*, a place in Highland Scotland]

love ● *noun* **1** an intense feeling of deep affection or fondness for a person or thing; great liking. **2** sexual passion. **3** sexual relations. **4 a** a beloved one; a sweetheart (often as a form of address). **b** *Brit. informal* a familiar form of address regardless of affection. **5** *informal* a person of whom one is fond. **6** affectionate greetings (*give him my love*). **7** (often **Love**) a representation of Cupid. **8** (in some sports) no score; nil. **9** a formula for ending an affectionate letter etc. ● *verb* **1** *transitive & intransitive* feel love or deep fondness (for). **2** *transitive* delight in; admire; greatly cherish. **3** *transitive* like very much (*loves books*). **4** *transitive* (foll. by verbal noun, or *to* + infin.) be inclined, esp. as a habit; greatly enjoy; find pleasure in (*children love dressing up; loves to find fault*). □ **fall in love** (often foll. by *with*) develop a great (esp. sexual) love (for). **for love** for pleasure not profit. **for the love of** for the sake of. **in love** (often foll. by *with*) deeply enamoured (of). **make love 1** (often foll. by *to, with*) have sexual intercourse (with). **2** (often foll. by *to*) *archaic* pay amorous attention (to). **no love lost between** mutual dislike between (two people etc.). **not for love or money** *informal* not in any circumstances. **out of love** no longer in love. [Old English *lufu* from Germanic: related to LEAVE², LIEF]

love·able *var. of* LOVABLE.

love affair *noun* **1** an esp. extramarital romantic or sexual relationship between two people in love. **2** an intense enthusiasm or liking for something.

love apple *noun archaic* a tomato.

love beads *plural noun* a necklace of coloured beads worn as a symbol of universal love.

love·bird *noun* **1** any of various African and Madagascan parrots, esp. *Agapornis personata*. **2** (in *pl.*) *informal* an affectionate couple; lovers.

love bite *noun* a red mark on the neck, caused by biting or sucking during lovemaking.

love child *noun* a child conceived during a love affair.

loved one *noun* a person whom one loves deeply.

love feast *noun* **1** a meal affirming brotherly love among early Christians. **2** a religious service imitating this.

love·fest *noun* **1** a gathering involving or celebrating free love. **2** = LOVE-IN 2.

love handles *plural noun esp. N Amer. slang* excess fat at the waist.

love-hate relationship *noun* **1** an intensely emotional relationship in which one or each party has ambivalent feelings of love and hate for the other. **2** a situation in which feelings of liking and disliking are combined (*Torontonians' love-hate relationship with raccoons*).

love-in *noun* (*pl.* **-ins**) *informal* **1** a gathering (esp. of hippies) expressing or advocating love and peace. **2** *jocular* a gathering of like-minded people.

love-in-a-mist *noun* a plant of the buttercup family with white, pink, mauve or purple cornflower-like flowers and delicate, feathery foliage.

love interest *noun* a person or character in a film etc. in whom another has a romantic or sexual interest.

Love·lace ▶ 1 (Au·gus·ta) Ada King, Countess of (1815–52), English mathematician. The daughter of Lord Byron, she became Charles Babbage's assistant (1833) and translated an Italian paper on Babbage's computer or 'difference engine', to which she added significant and detailed notations as to how the machine could be programmed (1843); the high-level computer programming language *Ada* is named after her. **2 Rich·ard** (1618–57), English poet. A Royalist soldier and courtier, he is known for the poem 'To Althea from Prison' (1642) and the lyrics in the volume *Lucasta* (1649).

love·less *adjective* without love; unloving or unloved or both. □ **love·less·ly** *adverb* **love·less·ness** *noun*

love letter *noun* a letter expressing feelings of romantic love.

love-lies-bleeding *noun* a plant with long drooping tassels of crimson flowers.

love life *noun* a person's life with regard to relationships with lovers.

Lov·ell /ˈlʌvəl/ **Sir (Al·fred Charles) Ber·nard** (b.1913), English radio astronomer and physicist. He founded the radio observatory at Jodrell Bank, England (1951), and directed the construction of the large radio telescope there, now named after him.

love·lorn *adjective* pining from or pertaining to unrequited love.

love·ly ● *adjective* (**love·li·er**, **love·li·est**) **1** exquisitely beautiful. **2** pleasing, delightful. ● *noun* (*pl.* **lovelies**) *informal* a pretty woman. □ **love·li·ness** *noun* [Old English *luflic* (as LOVE)]

love·making *noun* **1** amorous sexual activity, esp. sexual intercourse. **2** *archaic* courtship.

love match *noun* a marriage made for love's sake.

love nest *noun* a place of intimate lovemaking.

lover *noun* **1** a person in love with another. **2** a person with whom another is having sexual relations. **3** (in *pl.*) a couple in love or having sexual relations. **4** a person who likes or enjoys something specified (*a music lover; a lover of words*).

lovers' lane *noun* a road or other secluded spot in which lovers engage in amorous activity.

love·seat *noun* a small sofa for two.

love·sick *adjective* languishing with romantic love. □ **love·sick·ness** *noun*

love slave *noun* a person kept willingly or unwillingly in thrall to another to provide sexual favours.

love·struck *adjective* completely smitten by love.

love triangle *noun* a situation in which one person is romantically involved with two others.

lovey *informal* ● *noun* (*pl.* **loveys**) *esp. Brit.* love, sweetheart (esp. as a form of address). ● *adjective* (also **lovey-dovey**) fondly affectionate, esp. unduly sentimental.

lov·ing ● *adjective* feeling or showing love; affectionate. ● *noun* affection; active love. □ **loving·ly** *adverb* **loving·ness** *noun* [Old English *lufiende* (as LOVE)]

loving cup *noun* a two-handled often silver drinking cup, passed around at banquets or awarded as a trophy.

loving-kindness *noun* tenderness and consideration.

Low, Sir David (Alex·an·der Cecil) (1891–1963), New Zealand-born English political cartoonist, who is noted for his creation of the pompous, reactionary character Colonel Blimp.

low¹ ● *adjective* **1** of less than average height; not high or tall or reaching far up (*a low fence*). **2 a** situated close to ground or sea level etc.; not elevated in position (*low altitude*). **b** (of the sun) near the horizon. **c** (of latitude) near the equator. **3** of or in humble rank or position (*of low birth*). **4** of small or less than normal amount or extent or intensity (*low price; low temperature; low in calories*). **5** small or reduced in quantity (*supplies are low*). **6** coming below the normal level (*a dress with a low neck*). **7 a** dejected; lacking vigour (*feeling low; in low spirits*). **b** poorly nourished; indicative of poor nutrition. **8 a** (of a sound, voice, etc.) not high-pitched. **b** (of a sound) not loud. **9** *Phonetics* = OPEN

adjective 25. **10** not exalted or sublime; commonplace.
11 unfavourable (*a low opinion*). **12** vulgar; coarse (*low humour*).
13 contemptible; underhanded. **14** (of an oven etc.) warm but not hot
(*cook over low heat*). ● *noun* **1** a low or the lowest level, number, or thing
(*the dollar has reached a new low*). **2** an area of low barometric pressure; a
depression. **3** the lowest temperature reached during a specified
period (*overnight low of minus 36°*). **4** the lowest setting of a cooking
element, microwave oven, etc. ● *adverb* **1** in or to a low position or
state. **2** in a low tone (*speak low*). **3** at or to a low pitch (*I can't sing so
low*). **4** at or to a moral position considered contemptible (*how low can
you stoop?*). □ **low·ish** *adjective* **low·ness** *noun* [Middle English *lāh*
from Old Norse *lágr*, from Germanic]

low² ● *noun* a sound made by cattle; a moo. ● *transitive & intransitive verb*
utter (with) this sound. [Old English *hlōwan* from Germanic]

Low Arctic *noun* the part of the Canadian Arctic south of the Arctic
Circle.

low·ball ● *attributive adjective* **1** designating a deceptively or
unrealistically low price or estimate. **2** inexpensive. ● *verb* **1** *transitive &
intransitive* deceptively offer (someone) an unrealistically low price or
estimate. **2** *transitive* deceptively make (an offer, estimate, etc.) lower
than is realistic.

low beam *noun N Amer.* (usu. in *pl.*) a headlight beam used for
short-range illumination.

low blow *noun* **1** a cruel or unfair criticism or attack. **2** a punch below
the belt in boxing.

low-born *adjective* of humble birth.

low·boy *noun N Amer.* a low chest or table with drawers and short legs.

low·brow ● *adjective* not highly intellectual or cultured. ● *noun* a
lowbrow person.

low-budget *adjective* produced or operated with a limited amount of
money (*a low-budget film*).

low·bush *noun* **1** (in full **lowbush blueberry**) a low shrub of
northeastern N America, *Vaccinium angustifolium*, with sweet edible
blue berries. **2** (in full **lowbush cranberry**) a shrub of northern
N America, *Viburnum edule*, with lobed leaves and red, edible fruit; *also
called* SQUASHBERRY.

low-cal *adjective* (in full **low-calorie**) (of food, a diet, etc.) low in
calories.

Low Church *noun* a tradition within the Anglican Church stressing
evangelicalism and giving little emphasis to ritual, priestly authority,
and the sacraments.

low comedy *noun* comedy in which the subject and the treatment
border on farce.

Low Countries a region of NW Europe, comprising the Netherlands,
Belgium, and Luxembourg. (*See also* NETHERLANDS, THE.)

low-cut *adjective* **1** (of a dress etc.) made with a low neckline. **2** (of a
running shoe etc.) not covering the ankle.

low-density lipoprotein *noun* the form of lipoprotein in which
cholesterol is transported in the blood. Abbr.: **LDL**.

low·down ● *noun informal* (usu. foll. by *on*) the relevant information
(about). ● *adjective* dishonourable, contemptible.

low-E *adjective* (in full **low-emissivity**) *N Amer.* designating a window
which has been coated to prevent the escape or entry of heat, yet
which permits the passage of visible light.

Low·ell ▸ 1 Amy (Law·rence) (1874–1925), US poet. A leading
imagist poet, she is also known for her experiments in 'polyphonic
prose'; her volumes of poetry include *Men, Women and Ghosts* (1916), *Can
Grande's Castle* (1918), and *What's O'Clock* (Pulitzer Prize, 1925). **2 James
Rus·sell** (1819–91), US poet and critic. His works include volumes of
verse, the satirical *Biglow Papers* (1848 and 1867; prose and verse),
memorial odes after the American Civil War, and various volumes of
essays, including *Among my Books* (1870) and *My Study Window* (1871).
3 Per·ci·val (1855–1916), US astronomer, brother of Amy. He founded
an observatory in Flagstaff, Arizona, which now bears his name, and
predicted the existence of the planet Pluto. **4 Rob·ert (Traill
Spence)** (1917–77), US poet. His life was marked by recurring bouts of
manic illness, alcoholism, and marital discord, and his poetry is
notable for its intense confessional nature and for its ambiguous
complex imagery, as in the volumes *Life Studies* (1959), *For the Union Dead*
(1964), and *The Dolphin* (1973).

low-end *adjective* designating or pertaining to relatively cheap models
of consumer products, services, etc. (*bought low-end equipment*).

lower¹ ● *adjective* (*comparative of* LOW¹) **1** less high in position or status.
2 situated below another part (*lower lip; lower atmosphere*). **3 a** situated
on less high land (*the lower town*). **b** situated to the south (*Lower*

California). **c** situated along or pertaining to the downstream part of a
river, esp. the part closest to the mouth (*the Lower St. Lawrence; Lower
Canada*). **4** (of an animal or plant) showing relatively primitive
characteristics, e.g. a platypus or a fungus. **5** (often **Lower**) *Geol. &
Archaeology* designating an older, and hence usu. deeper, part of a
stratigraphic division, archaeological deposit, etc., or the period in
which it was formed or deposited. ● *adverb* in or to a lower position,
status, etc. □ **lower·most** *adjective*

lower² *verb* **1** *transitive* let or haul down. **2** *transitive & intransitive* make or
become lower. **3** *transitive* reduce the height or pitch or elevation of
(*lowered her eyes; lower your voice*). **4** *transitive* degrade. **5** *transitive & intransitive*
diminish. □ **lower the boom on** *N Amer. slang* **1** inflict a physical
defeat on (a person). **2** treat (a person) severely. **3** put a stop to (an
activity).

lower³ (also **lour**) ● *intransitive verb* **1** frown; look sullen. **2** (of the sky
etc.) look dark and threatening. ● *noun* **1** a scowl. **2** a gloomy look (of
the sky etc.). [Middle English *loure*, of unknown origin]

Lower Arrow Lake a long, narrow lake in south central BC, lying
in the Columbia River valley and part of the Columbia River system. It
curves southward some 100 km from Upper Arrow Lake to Castlegar.

Lower California an alternative name for BAJA CALIFORNIA.

Lower Canada *hist.* the mainly French-speaking region of Canada
around the lower St. Lawrence River, occupying what is now Labrador
and the southern portion of Quebec. It was a British colony from 1791
to 1841, when it was united with Upper Canada to form the Province of
Canada. □ **Lower Canadian** *noun & adjective*

Lower Canada Rebellion *see* REBELLIONS OF 1837.

lower case ● *adjective* designating the smaller characters most often
used in printing and writing, often differing in shape as well as size
from the capital forms. ● *noun* lower case letters. [originally
designating the lower of a typesetter's cases, which traditionally held
the type for such characters]

lower class ● *noun* working-class people and their families. ● *adjective*
(**lower-class**) of the lower class.

lower court *noun* a court of law that is not a court of appeal.

lower criticism *noun* (prec. by *the*) textual criticism of the Bible.

lower deck *noun* **1** the deck of a ship situated immediately over the
hold. **2** the petty officers and men of a ship collectively.

Lower Fort Garry a historic site in SE Manitoba, located on the Red
River, northeast of Winnipeg. Established during the 1830s by the
Hudson's Bay Co. as an administrative centre, it houses the largest
group of fur-trade buildings in Canada.

Lower Great Lakes Lakes Erie and Ontario (also usu. including
Lake St. Clair).

lower house *noun* the usu. larger and more representative body of a
bicameral legislature, esp. (in Canada) the House of Commons.

Lower Mainland the heavily-populated lowland region of
southwestern BC, around the city of Vancouver.

lower middle class ● *noun* the class of society between the lower
and middle classes. ● *adjective* (**lower-middle-class**) of the lower
middle class.

Lower Saxony a state of NW Germany; capital, Hanover. It
corresponds to the northwestern part of the former kingdom of
Saxony.

lower world *noun* (also **lower regions** *plural noun*) the realm of the
dead; hell.

lowest common denominator *noun* **1** the lowest common
multiple of the denominators of several fractions. **2** the least desirable
common feature of members of a group.

lowest common multiple *noun* the lowest quantity that is a
multiple of two or more given quantities.

low fi *adjective & noun* = LO FI.

low frequency *noun* (in radio) 30–300 kilohertz. Abbr.: **LF**.

low gear *noun* a gear such that the driven end of a transmission
revolves slower than the driving end.

Low German *noun* the group of dialects of Germany spoken in the
lowland areas of the north, most closely related to Dutch and Frisian.

low-grade *adjective* of low quality or strength.

low-impact *adjective* **1** designating esp. aerobic exercises designed to
put little or no potentially harmful stress on the body. **2** (of camping
etc.) affecting or altering the natural environment as little as possible.

low-income *attributive adjective* of or relating to the income group
comprising those earning relatively low wages (*low-income housing*).

low-inten·sity *attributive adjective* (of warfare, conflicts, etc.) relatively restrained, localized, or small-scale; involving weapons of limited potency.

low-key *adjective* (also **low-keyed**) lacking intensity or prominence; restrained.

low·land ● *noun* **1** (usu. in *pl.*) low-lying country. **2** (**Lowland**) (usu. in *pl.*) the region of Scotland lying south and east of the Highlands. ● *adjective* of or in lowland or the Scottish Lowlands. □ **low·land·er** *noun* (also **Lowlander**).

Low Latin *noun* medieval and later forms of Latin.

low latitudes *plural noun* regions near the equator.

low-level *adjective* **1** designating an activity conducted on or at a low level (*low-level negotiations*; *low-level flight*). **2** *Computing* (of a programming language) close in form to machine language.

low-life *noun* (*pl.* **-lifes**) (also **low-lifer**) **1** a degenerate person or a member of the underworld. **2** such people collectively.

low·light *noun* **1** a monotonous or dull period; a feature of little prominence (*one of the lowlights of the evening*). **2** (usu. in *pl.*) a dark tint in the hair produced by dyeing. [after HIGHLIGHT]

lowly *adjective* (**low·li·er**, **low·li·est**) **1** humble in feeling, behaviour, or status. **2** modest, unpretentious. □ **low·li·ness** *noun*

low-lying *adjective* (of land) at low altitude (above sea level etc.).

low maintenance *adjective* requiring little or infrequent maintenance, attention, etc. (*a low maintenance machine*).

low mass *noun Catholicism* mass with no music and a minimum of ceremony.

low-minded *adjective* vulgar or ignoble in mind or character. □ **low-minded·ness** *noun*

low·pass *adjective* designating a filter that attenuates only those components with a frequency greater than some cut-off frequency.

low-pitched *adjective* **1** (of a sound) low. **2** (of a roof) having only a slight slope.

low post *noun Basketball* the area below the opponent's basket (often, with hyphen, *attributive*: *low-post scorer*).

low-pressure ● *adjective* **1** characterized by or exerting below-average pressure. **2** (of a job, situation, etc.) not demanding or stressful. ● *noun* (**low pressure**) an atmospheric condition with pressure below 101.3 kilopascals.

low-pressure system *noun Meteorol.* a large expanse of air at low atmospheric pressure.

low profile *noun* an attitude or manner characterized by the avoidance of attention or publicity (often, with hyphen, *attributive*: *a low-profile position*).

low relief *noun see* RELIEF 6a.

low-rent *adjective* **1** (in full **low-rental**) designating housing or a neighbourhood for tenants with relatively low incomes. **2** *informal* inferior; second-rate; cheap.

low-rider *noun* (often *attributive*) *US* **1** a car customized with hydraulics, enabling the chassis to be lowered very close to the ground. **2** the usu. young owner or driver of such a car. **3** (in *pl.*) pants or underpants that are worn low on the hips. □ **low-riding** *noun*

low-rise ● *adjective* **1** (of a building) having few storeys. **2** (of trousers) cut so as to fit low on the hips rather than on the waist. ● *noun* a low-rise building.

low-risk *adjective* that does not constitute a troubling risk.

Lowry /ˈlauri/ (**Clar·ence**) **Mal·colm** (1909–57), English novelist. His experiences in Mexico during the 1930s provided the background for his symbolic semi-autobiographical novel *Under the Volcano* (1947), which traces the decline of an alcoholic British ex-consul.

low season *noun* the period during which the fewest people travel, book accommodation, etc.

low-slung *adjective* **1** suspended; sagging. **2 a** with a low and wide profile (*low-slung houses*). **b** close to the ground (*low-slung furniture*). **3** (of clothes, esp. trousers) cut to fit low on the hips rather than the waist.

low spirits *plural noun* dejection, depression. □ **low-spirited** *adjective* **low-spirited·ness** *noun*

Low Sunday *noun* the Sunday after Easter.

low-tech *noun* (in full **low-technology**) (usu. *attributive*) relatively unsophisticated tools, machines, procedures, etc. (*a low-tech kitchen*).

Low·ther /ˈlauθər/ **Pat·ri·cia Lou·ise** (1935–75), Canadian poet. She published four volumes of poetry, many of which reflect her dual interests in socialist politics and the politics of sex. Her husband Roy was found guilty of her murder in 1977.

low tide *noun* (also **low water**) the time or level of the tide at its ebb.

low-water mark *noun* **1** the level reached at low water. **2** a minimum recorded level or value etc.

lox[1] *noun* liquid oxygen. [abbreviation]

lox[2] *noun N Amer.* smoked salmon. [Yiddish *laks*]

loyal *adjective* **1** (often foll. by *to*) true or faithful (to duty, a friend, cause, etc.). **2** steadfast in allegiance; devoted to the sovereign or government of one's country. □ **loyal·ly** *adverb* [French from Old French *loial* etc. from Latin *legalis* LEGAL]

loyal·ist *noun* **1** a person who remains loyal to the existing sovereign, government, etc., esp. in the face of rebellion or usurpation. **2** (**Loyalist**) **a** any of the colonists of the American revolutionary period who supported the British cause, many of whom afterwards migrated to Canada. **b** *Cdn* a descendant of such a person. **3** (**Loyalist**) a supporter of Parliamentary union between Great Britain and Northern Ireland. **4** a person loyal to a specific person, cause, etc. □ **loyal·ism** *noun*

loyal Opposition *noun* = OFFICIAL OPPOSITION.

loyal·ty *noun* (*pl.* **-ties**) **1** the state of being loyal. **2** (often in *pl.*) a feeling or application of loyalty.

loyalty program *noun* a program operated by a store, airline, etc. which offers rewards to frequent customers, e.g. a frequent flyer program.

Loy·ola *see* IGNATIUS LOYOLA.

loz·enge /ˈlɒzɪndʒ/ *noun* **1** a rhombus or diamond figure. **2** a small candy or medicinal tablet, originally lozenge-shaped, for dissolving in the mouth. **3** a lozenge-shaped pane in a window. **4** *Heraldry* a lozenge-shaped device. **5** the lozenge-shaped facet of a cut gem. [Old French *losenge*, probably derived from the base of Spanish *losa*, Portuguese *lousa* 'slab', late Latin *lausia (lapides)* 'stone slabs']

LP *noun* a long-playing record. [abbreviation]

LPG *abbreviation* liquefied petroleum gas.

LPGA *abbreviation* Ladies Professional Golf Association.

LPN *abbreviation* LICENSED PRACTICAL NURSE.

Lr *symbol Chem.* the element lawrencium.

LRB *abbreviation* Labour Relations Board.

LRC *abbreviation* (of trains) light, rapid, comfortable.

LRIF /ˈɛlrɪf/ *abbreviation Cdn* LOCKED-IN RETIREMENT INCOME FUND.

LRT *abbreviation* light rail (or rapid) transit.

LS *abbreviation Cdn* LEADING SEAMAN.

LSAT /ˈɛlsæt/ *abbreviation* Law School Admission Test.

LSD *abbreviation* LYSERGIC ACID DIETHYLAMIDE.

l.s.d. *noun* (also **£.s.d.**) *Brit. dated* **1** pounds, shillings, and pence (in former British currency). **2** money, riches. [Latin *librae, solidi, denarii*]

LSI *abbreviation Computing* large-scale integration; the technology integrating several thousand circuits on one chip.

Lt *abbreviation* **1** (also **Lt.**) LIEUTENANT. **2** (**Lt.**) light.

Lt. Cdr. *abbreviation* LIEUTENANT COMMANDER. ¶ The Canadian Forces use the abbreviation *LCdr*.

Lt. Col. *abbreviation* LIEUTENANT COLONEL. ¶ The Canadian Forces use the abbreviation *LCol*.

Ltd. *abbreviation* Limited.

Lt. Gen. *abbreviation* LIEUTENANT GENERAL. ¶ The Canadian Forces use the abbreviation *LGen*.

Lt.-Gov. *abbreviation* Lieutenant-Governor.

Lu *symbol Chem.* the element lutetium.

Lua·laba River /ˌluːəˈlɑːbə/ a river of central Africa, which rises near the southern border of Congo (formerly Zaire) and flows northward for about 640 km (400 miles), joining the Lomami to form the Congo River.

Lu·an·da /luːˈandə/ the capital of Angola, a port on the Atlantic coast; pop. (est. 2002) 2,193,400. Founded by the Portuguese in 1575, it was a centre for the shipment of slaves to Brazil in the 17th and 18th c.

Luang Pra·bang /luːˌaŋ prəˈbaŋ/ (also **Louangphrabang**) a city in NW Laos, on the Mekong River; pop. (est. 2002) 26,300. It was the capital of a kingdom of the same name from 1707 until the reorganization of 1946–7, and remained the royal residence and Buddhist religious centre of Laos until the end of the monarchy in 1975.

luau /ˈluːau/ *noun* a Hawaiian party or feast usu. accompanied by some form of entertainment. [Hawaiian *lūʻau*]

Luba·vitch·er /ˈluːbə‚vɪtʃər, luːˈbɒ-/ ● *noun* a member of a group of Hasidic Jews founded in the 18th c., stressing piety and missionary work. ● *adjective* (also **Luba·vitch**) of or pertaining to Lubavitchers.

---

t *top*   v *voice*   w *we*   z *zoo*   ʃ *she*   ʒ *vision*   θ *thin*   ð *this*   ŋ *ring*   x *loch*   tʃ *chip*   dʒ *jar*   (*see over for vowels*)

[from *Lubavich*, a town in Russia near Smolensk, an important centre for the group in the 19th c.]

lub·ber *noun* **1** a big clumsy fellow; a lout. **2** = LANDLUBBER.
□ **lub·ber·ly** *adjective & adverb* [perhaps from Old French *lobeor* swindler, parasite from *lober* deceive]

lubber line *noun* (also **lubber's line**) *Naut.* a line marked on a compass, showing the ship's forward direction.

lube *esp. N Amer. & Austral. informal* ● *noun* **1** = LUBRICANT. **2** an application of lubricant (esp. to a motor vehicle). ● *transitive verb* = LUBRICATE. [abbreviation]

Lü·beck /ˈluːbek/ a port in N Germany, on the Baltic coast in Schleswig-Holstein, northeast of Hamburg; pop. (est. 2002) 213,200. Between the 14th and 19th c. it was an important city within the Hanseatic League.

Lubi·con /ˈluːbɪkɒn/ *noun* (also **Lubicon Cree**, **Lubicon Lake Cree**) **1** an Aboriginal group living near Peace River, Alberta. **2** the Algonquian language of the Lubicon.

Lu·bitsch /ˈluːbɪtʃ/ **Ernst** (1892–1947), German-born US film director, who is known for his witty and sophisticated comedies, such as *Trouble in Paradise* (1932), *Ninotchka* (1939), and *Heaven Can Wait* (1943).

Lub·lin /ˈlʊblɪn/ a manufacturing city in E Poland; pop. (est. 2000) 355,803.

lu·bri·cant /ˈluːbrɪkənt/ ● *noun* a substance used to reduce friction.
● *adjective* lubricating.

lu·bri·cate /ˈluːbrɪˌkeɪt/ *transitive verb* **1** reduce friction in (machinery etc.) by applying oil or grease etc. **2** make slippery or smooth; make smooth the motion or action of (something) by applying a fluid or unguent. **3** (usu. as **lu·bri·cat·ed** *adjective*) *informal* drunk.
□ **lu·bri·ca·tion** *noun* **lu·bri·ca·tor** *noun* [Latin *lubricare lubricat-* from *lubricus* slippery]

lu·bri·cious /luːˈbrɪʃəs/ *adjective* **1** lewd, prurient. **2** slippery, smooth, oily. □ **lu·bri·city** *noun* [Latin *lubricus* slippery]

Lubum·bashi /ˌluːbʊmˈbaʃi/ a copper-mining city in SE Congo (formerly Zaire), near the border with Zambia, capital of the region of Shaba; pop. (est. 2002) 1,074,600. Until 1966 it was called Elisabethville.

Luc /luːk/ **Frère** (born Claude François) (1614–85), French Récollet, painter, and architect. After earning the title 'king's painter' for his work in decorating the Louvre (1640–42) he joined the Récollets, and came to Canada in 1671, staying only for 15 months. In that time he designed the chapel for the Récollet monastery in Quebec City (now the oldest chapel in Canada) and a wing of the Séminaire de Québec. He also made many paintings for local churches, both while in the colony and after returning to France.

Lucan /ˈluːkən/ (Latin name Marcus Annaeus Lucanus) (AD 39–65), Roman poet, born in Spain. His major work, a hexametric epic in ten books known as the *Pharsalia*, deals with the civil war between Julius Caesar and Pompey.

Lu·ca·nia, Mount /luːˈkeɪniə, -jə/ a peak in the St. Elias Mountains of SW Yukon Territory, north of Mount Logan. Rising to a height of 5 226 m, it is the third highest mountain in Canada. [the name of a Cunard liner *c.*1897]

Lucas /ˈluːkəs/ **George** (b.1944), US film director, producer, and screenwriter, who is known for the science fiction adventure films *Star Wars* (1977), *The Empire Strikes Back* (1980), and *Return of the Jedi* (1983), as well as a number of films he produced with Steven Spielberg, including *Raiders of the Lost Ark* (1981).

Lucas van Ley·den /ˌluːkəs van ˈlaɪdən/ (*c.*1494–1533), Dutch engraver and painter. He was principally an engraver, and his works in this field include *Ecce Homo* (1510); his paintings include portraits, genre scenes, and religious subjects, such as the triptych *The Last Judgement* (1526–7).

lu·cent /ˈluːsənt/ *adjective literary* **1** shining, luminous. **2** translucent.
□ **lu·cen·cy** *noun* [Latin *lucēre* 'shine' (as LUX)]

Lu·cerne /luːˈsɜrn/ a resort on the western shore of Lake Lucerne, in central Switzerland; pop. (est. 2002) 57,100.

lu·cerne /luːˈsɜrn/ *noun* (also **lu·cern**) = ALFALFA. [French *luzerne* from modern Provençal *luzerno* glow-worm, with reference to its shiny seeds]

Lucerne, Lake (also **Lake of Lucerne**; also called the **Lake of the Four Cantons**) a lake in central Switzerland, surrounded by the four cantons of Lucerne, Nidwalden, Uri, and Schwyz.

Lu·cian /ˈluːʃən/ (*c.*115–*c.*80 BC), Greek rhetorician and satirist, who is known for his satirical *Dialogues of the Gods* and *Dialogues of the Dead*.

lucid /ˈluːsɪd/ *adjective* **1 a** expressing or expressed clearly; easy to understand. **b** (of a dream) vivid; clear. **2** of or denoting intervals of sanity between periods of insanity or dementia. **3** *poet.* bright.

□ **lu·cid·ity** /-ˈsɪdɪti/ *noun* **lu·cid·ly** *adverb* **lu·cid·ness** *noun* [Latin *lucidus* (perhaps through French *lucide* or Italian *lucido*) from *lucēre* shine (as LUX)]

Lu·ci·fer /ˈluːsɪfər/ *noun* **1** Satan. **2** *poet.* the morning star (the planet Venus). **3** (**lucifer**) *archaic* a friction match. [Old English from Latin, = light-bringing, morning star (as LUX, *-fer* from *ferre* bring)]

lu·cif·er·ase /luːˈsɪfəreɪz/ *noun* an enzyme which catalyzes a reaction by which a luciferin produces light.

lu·cif·er·in /luːˈsɪfərɪn/ *noun* a substance in an organism such as the firefly which can produce light when oxidized in the presence of a specific enzyme.

Lu·cite /ˈluːsaɪt/ *noun proprietary* a solid transparent plastic resin. [Latin *luc-, lux* light + -ITE¹]

luck ● *noun* **1** chance regarded as the bringer of good or bad fortune. **2** circumstances of life (beneficial or not) brought by this. **3** good fortune; success due to chance (*in luck*; *out of luck*). ● *intransitive verb informal* **1** (foll. by *into*) esp. *N Amer.* acquire by good fortune. **2** (foll. by *out*, *in*) esp. *N Amer.* achieve success or advantage by good luck. **3** (foll. by *out*) esp. *N Amer.* fail or be disadvantaged by bad luck. □ **as luck would have it** by chance; because of luck. **for luck** to bring good fortune. **no such luck** *informal* unfortunately not. **try one's luck** make a venture. **with luck** if all goes well. **worse luck** *informal* unfortunately. [Low German *luk* from Middle Low German *geluke*]

luck·i·ly *adverb* **1** (qualifying a whole sentence or clause) fortunately (*luckily there was enough food*). **2** in a lucky or fortunate manner.

luck·less *adjective* having no luck; unfortunate. □ **luck·less·ly** *adverb* **luck·less·ness** *noun*

Luck·now /ˈlʌknaʊ/ a city in N India, capital of the state of Uttar Pradesh; pop. (2001) 2,207,300.

lucky *adjective* (**luck·i·er**, **luck·i·est**) **1** having or resulting from good luck, esp. as distinct from skill or design or merit. **2** bringing good luck (*a lucky charm*). **3** fortunate, appropriate (*a lucky guess*). □ **get lucky** *informal* have sex, esp. with a date. **thank one's lucky stars** be extremely grateful to fate. □ **luck·i·ness** *noun*

lucky dip *noun Brit.* a tub containing different articles concealed in wrapping or bran etc., and chosen at random by participants.

lu·cra·tive /ˈluːkrətɪv/ *adjective* profitable, yielding financial gain.
□ **lu·cra·tive·ly** *adverb* **lu·cra·tive·ness** *noun* [Latin *lucrativus* from *lucrari* to gain]

lucre /ˈluːkər/ *noun derogatory* financial profit or gain. [French *lucre* or Latin *lucrum*]

Lu·cre·tius /luːˈkriːʃəs, -ʃiəs/ (full name Titus Lucretius Carus) (*c.*94–*c.*55 BC), Roman poet and philosopher. His didactic poem *On the Nature of Things* is an exposition of the atomist physics of Epicurus, and postulates that fear of the gods and of punishment after death is without foundation. □ **Lu·cre·tian** *adjective*

lucu·bra·tion /ˌluːkʊˈbreɪʃən/ *noun literary* **1** (usu. in *pl.*) literary writings, esp. of a pedantic or elaborate character. **2** study or meditation. [Latin *lucubratio* from *lucubrare* work by lamplight (as LUX)]

Lu·cul·lan /luːˈkʌlən/ *adjective* (esp. of food) profusely luxurious. [LUCULLUS]

Lu·cul·lus /luːˈkʌləs/ **Lu·cius Li·cin·ius** (*c.*117–*c.*56 BC), Roman general. He fought a series of campaigns against Mithridates VI from 74 to 66, and was known for his self-indulgence and luxurious tastes.

lud *noun Brit.* □ **m'lud** (or **my lud**) a form of address to a judge in a court of law. [corruption of LORD]

Luda /ˈluːdɒ/ an industrial conurbation and port in NE China, in the province of Liaoning at the southeastern tip of the Liaodong Peninsula; pop. (est. 2002) 1,737,800. It comprises the cities of Lushun and Dalian.

Lud·dite ● *noun* **1** *hist.* a member of any of the bands of English artisans who rioted against mechanization and destroyed machinery (1811–16). **2** a person opposed to increased industrialization or new technology. ● *adjective* of the Luddites or their beliefs. □ **Lud·dism** *noun* [perhaps from Ned *Lud*, who destroyed machinery *c.* 1779]

'lude *noun* (also **lude**) *N Amer. slang* a Quaalude. [abbreviation]

Luden·dorff /ˈluːdənˌdɔrf/ **Erich** (1865–1937), German general. Shortly after the outbreak of the First World War he was appointed chief of staff to General von Hindenburg and they jointly directed the war effort until the final offensive failed (Sept. 1918).

Ludhi·ana /ˌlʊdiˈɒnə/ a city in NW India, in Punjab southeast of Amritsar; pop. (2001) 1,395,100. Founded in 1480 by the rulers of the Muslim Lodi dynasty, it is now an industrial and agricultural centre and a major railway junction.

ludic /ˈluːdɪk/ *adjective* spontaneously playful. □ **ludic·ally** *adverb* [French *ludique*, from Latin *ludere* to play, from *ludus* sport]

ludi·crous /ˈluːdɪkrəs/ *adjective* absurd or ridiculous; laughable. □ **ludi·crous·ly** *adverb* **ludi·crous·ness** *noun* [Latin *ludicrus* prob. from *ludicrum* stage play]

ludo /ˈluːdəʊ/ *noun* esp. *Brit.* a simple board game in which counters are moved around according to the throw of dice. [Latin, = I play]

Lud·wig I /ˈlʊdvɪɡ/ (1786–1868), king of Bavaria 1825–48. His reactionary policies and lavish expenditure were the cause of radical protests in 1830; his domination by the dancer Lola Montez led to further unrest and he was forced to abdicate.

Lud·wig II /ˈlʊdvɪɡ/ (1845–86), king of Bavaria 1864–86. He came increasingly under Prussian influence and his country eventually joined the new German Empire in 1871. A patron of the arts, in particular of Wagner, he later became a recluse and concentrated on building a series of elaborate castles. He was declared insane and deposed in 1886.

Lud·wigs·hafen /ˈlʊdvɪɡz͵hɒfən/ an industrial river port in west central Germany, southwest of Mannheim, on the Rhine River in the state of Rhineland-Palatinate; pop. (est. 2002) 163,400.

luff *Naut.* ● *noun* the edge of the fore-and-aft sail next to the mast or stay. ● *verb* **1** *transitive & intransitive* steer (a ship) nearer the wind. **2** *transitive* turn (the helm) so as to achieve this. **3** *transitive* raise or lower (the jib of a crane or derrick). **4** *intransitive* (of a sail) flap from being set too close to the wind. [Old French *lof*, prob. from Low German]

Luft·waffe /ˈlʊft͵vɒfə/ *noun hist.* the German air force up to the end of the Second World War. [German from *Luft* air + *Waffe* weapon]

lug¹ ● *verb* (**lugged, lug·ging**) **1** *transitive* **a** drag or tug (a heavy object) with effort or violence. **b** (usu. foll. by *around, about*) carry (something heavy) around with one. **2** *transitive* (usu. foll. by *in, into*) introduce (a subject etc.) irrelevantly. **3** *intransitive* (usu. foll. by *at*) pull hard. ● *noun* a hard or rough pull. [Middle English, prob. from Scandinavian: compare Swedish *lugga* pull a person's hair, from *lugg* forelock]

lug² *noun* **1** a projection on an object by which it may be carried, fixed in place, etc. **2** a ridge on the sole of a shoe or boot, or on a tire, designed to provide traction. **3** *slang* an awkward or stupid person, esp. a man. **4** *Brit. informal* an ear. **5** either of two flaps of a hat, for covering the ears. **6** a wooden box for shipping fruit or vegetables. [prob. from Scandinavian origin: compare LUG¹]

lug³ *noun* = LUGWORM. [17th c.: origin unknown]

lug⁴ *noun* = LUGSAIL. [abbreviation]

Lu·gano /luːˈɡɒːnəʊ/ a town in S Switzerland, on the northern shore of Lake Lugano; pop. (est. 2002) 25,900. It is a centre of international finance and a health and holiday resort.

Lu·gansk see LUHANSK.

luge /luːʒ/ ● *noun* **1** a light sled with runners for one or two people, ridden in a sitting or supine position. **2** the sport in which these are raced. ● *intransitive verb* ride on a luge. □ **luger** *noun* [Swiss French]

Luger /ˈluːɡər/ *noun* a type of German automatic pistol. [G. *Luger*, German firearms expert d.1922]

lug·gage *noun* suitcases, bags, etc. to hold a traveller's belongings. [LUG¹ + -AGE]

luggage van *noun Brit.* = BAGGAGE CAR.

lug·ger *noun* a small ship carrying two or three masts with a lugsail on each. [LUGSAIL + -ER¹]

Lu·go·si /luːˈɡɒːsi/ **Bela** (born Béla Blasko) (1884–1956), Hungarian-born US actor, who became famous for his roles in horror films such as *Dracula* (1931), *Mark of the Vampire* (1935), and *The Wolf Man* (1941).

lug·sail /ˈlʌɡseɪl, -səl/ *noun Naut.* a quadrilateral sail which is bent on and hoisted from a yard. [prob. from LUG²]

lu·gu·bri·ous /luˈɡuːbrɪəs, lʊ-/ *adjective* doleful, mournful, dismal. □ **lu·gu·bri·ous·ly** *adverb* **lu·gu·bri·ous·ness** *noun* [Latin *lugubris* from *lugēre* mourn]

lug·worm *noun* any polychaete worm of the genus *Arenicola*, living in muddy sand and leaving characteristic worm castings on lower shores, and often used as bait by fishermen. [LUG³]

Lu·hansk /luːˈhɑnsk/ (Russian **Lugansk** /luːˈɡɑnsk/) an industrial city in E Ukraine, in the Donets Basin; pop. (est. 2001) 463,000. From 1935 until 1991 it was known as Voroshilovgrad.

Lu·kács /ˈluːkatʃ/ **Georg** (Hungarian name György Lukács) (1885–1971), Hungarian Marxist philosopher and literary critic. A major figure in Western Marxism, he is best known for his philosophical work *History and Class Consciousness* (1923); his literary criticism includes *The Theory of the Novel* (1916) and *The Historical Novel* (1955).

Luke ▸ **1 St.** (fl. 1st c. AD), an evangelist, closely associated with St. Paul and traditionally the author of the third Gospel and the Acts of the Apostles; a physician, he was possibly the son of a Greek freedman of Rome. Feast day, 18 Oct. **2** the third Gospel.

luke·warm *adjective* **1** moderately warm; tepid. **2** unenthusiastic, indifferent. □ **luke·warm·ly** *adverb* **luke·warm·ness** *noun* [Middle English from (now dial.) *luke, lew* from Old English]

lull ● *verb* **1** *transitive* soothe or send to sleep gently. **2** *transitive* (usu. foll. by *into*) deceive (a person) into confidence (*lulled into a false sense of security*). **3** *transitive* allay (suspicions etc.) usu. by deception. **4** *intransitive* (of noise, a storm, etc.) abate or fall quiet. ● *noun* a temporary quiet period in a storm or in any activity. □ **lull·ing** *adjective* **lull·ing·ly** *adverb* [Middle English, imitative of sounds used to quieten a child]

lul·la·by ● *noun* (*pl.* **-bies**) **1** a soothing song to send a child to sleep. **2** the music for this. ● *transitive verb* (**-bies, -bied**) sing to sleep. [as LULL + -*by* as in BYE-BYE²]

Lully /lʊˈliː/ **Jean-Baptiste** (Italian name Giovanni Battista Lulli) (1632–87), Italian-born French composer. In 1653 he entered the service of Louis XIV, and from 1664 collaborated with Molière, writing incidental music for a series of comedies; he turned to composing operas in 1673, and his works, which include *Alceste* (1674) and *Armide* (1686), mark the beginning of the French operatic tradition.

lulu *noun slang* a remarkable, incredible, or memorable person or thing, esp. for its unpleasantness (*a lulu of a nightmare*). [19th c., perhaps from *Lulu*, pet form of *Louise*]

Lulu Island an island in southwestern BC, forming in large part the Fraser River delta. The city of Richmond is situated on it. [*Lulu* Sweet, theatre company actress *c*.1862]

luma *noun* (*pl.* same or **lumas**) a monetary unit of Armenia, equal to one-hundredth of a dram. [Armenian]

lum·bago /lʌmˈbeɪɡəʊ/ *noun* rheumatic pain in the muscles of the lower back. [Latin from *lumbus* loin]

lum·bar /ˈlʌmbər, -bɑr/ *adjective Anat.* relating to the loin, esp. the lower back area. [medieval Latin *lumbaris* from Latin *lumbus* loin]

lumbar puncture *noun* the withdrawal of cerebrospinal fluid from the lower back with a hollow needle, usu. for diagnosis.

lum·ber¹ *intransitive verb* (usu. foll. by *along, past, by*, etc.) move in a slow clumsy noisy way. □ **lum·ber·ing** *adjective* **lum·ber·ing·ly** *adverb* [Middle English *lomere*, perhaps imitative]

lum·ber² ● *noun* **1** *N Amer.* partly or fully prepared timber. **2** *Brit.* disused articles of furniture etc. inconveniently taking up space. **3** *slang* a hockey stick. ● *verb* **1** *N Amer.* **a** *intransitive* perform the labour or carry on the business of cutting and preparing forest timber. **b** *transitive* (often foll. by *over*) go over (ground) cutting down timber. **2** *transitive* (usu. in *passive*; usu. foll. by *with*) burden or leave (a person etc.) with something unwanted or unpleasant (*I always get lumbered with the chores*). □ **lay on the lumber** *slang* check heavily with a hockey stick. [perhaps from LUMBER¹: later assoc. with obsolete *lumber* pawnbroker's shop]

lumber baron *noun N Amer.* a leading or wealthy timber merchant.

lumber camp *noun N Amer.* a camp in which loggers live.

lum·ber·ing *noun* esp. *N Amer.* **1** the lumber or timber trade. **2** the work of cutting and preparing forest timber.

lumber·jack *noun N Amer. esp. hist.* = LOGGER.

lumberjack jacket *noun N Amer.* (also **lumber·jacket**) a jacket, usu. of warm, red and black checked material, originally worn by loggers.

lumberjack shirt *noun* esp. *N Amer.* a long-sleeved shirt of brushed cotton or flannel, usu. in red and black check.

lumber·man *noun* (*pl.* **-men**) *N Amer.* **1** a lumber company owner or manager. **2** = LOGGER.

lumber mill *noun N Amer.* a factory where logs and lumber are dressed.

lumber road *noun N Amer.* = LOGGING ROAD.

lumber·yard *noun N Amer.* **1** a place where lumber is stored and sold. **2** a business operating such a place.

lumen /ˈluːmən/ *noun* **1** (*pl.* **lu·mens**) *Physics* the SI unit of luminous flux, equal to the amount of light emitted per second in a unit solid angle of one steradian from a uniform source of one candela. Abbr.: **lm. 2** (*pl.* **lumina** /-mɪnə/) *Anat.* a cavity within a tube, cell, etc. [Latin *lumen luminis* 'a light, an opening']

Lu·mière /luːˈmjɛr/ **Au·guste Marie Louis Nicho·las** (1862–1954), and his brother, **Louis Jean** (1864–1948), French inventors and pioneers of cinema, who patented their 'Cinématographe', a motion picture camera and projector in one, in 1895, and invented an improved process of colour photography.

---

uː m**oo**d   aɪ m**y**   əɪ p**i**pe   aʊ br**ow**n   ʌʊ h**ou**se   eɪ d**ay**   ɔɪ b**oy**   ɑ̃ fr**an**glais   ã Canadi**en**   ɔ̃ Br**ayon**   (*see over for consonants*)

lumin·aire /ˈluːmɪnɛr/ *noun* a unit consisting of an electric light and its fittings. [French]

lumin·ance /ˈluːmɪnəns/ *noun Physics* **1** the state or quality of reflecting light. **2** the intensity of light emitted from a surface per unit area in a given direction. [Latin *luminare* illuminate (as LUMEN)]

lumin·ary /ˈluːmɪnɛri/ *noun* (*pl.* **-aries**) **1** a prominent member of a group or gathering (*a host of show-business luminaries*). **2** a person as a source of intellectual light or moral inspiration. **3** *literary* a natural light-giving body, esp. the sun or moon. **4** a lamp, an artificial light. [Old French *luminarie* or Late Latin *luminarium* from Latin LUMEN]

lumin·es·cence /ˌluːmɪˈnɛsəns/ *noun* **1** the emission of light by a substance that has not been heated, as in fluorescence and phosphorescence. **2** the light emitted by a luminescent object or surface. □ **lumin·es·cent** *adjective* [as LUMEN + -ESCENCE (see -ESCENT)]

lumin·ous /ˈluːmɪnəs/ *adjective* **1** full of or shedding light; radiant, bright, shining. **2** phosphorescent, visible in darkness (*luminous paint*). **3** shedding intellectual, moral, or spiritual light. **4** of visible radiation (*luminous intensity*). □ **lumin·os·ity** *noun* **lumin·ous·ly** *adverb* **lumin·ous·ness** *noun* [Old French *lumineux* or Latin *luminosus*]

lum·mox *noun esp. N Amer. informal* a clumsy or stupid person. [19th c. in US & dial.: origin unknown]

lump¹ ● *noun* **1 a** a compact shapeless or unshapely mass (*a lump of coal*). **b** a cube of sugar for putting in tea or coffee. **2** *slang* a quantity or heap. **3** a tumour, swelling, or bruise. **4** a heavy, dull, or ungainly person. **5** (in *pl.*) *slang* hard knocks, attacks, defeats (esp. in phr. **take one's lumps**). **6** *Cdn* (*Nfld*) = LUMPFISH. ● *verb* **1** *transitive* (usu. foll. by *together, with, in with, under,* etc.) mass together or group indiscriminately. **2** *transitive & intransitive* make or become lumpy. **3** *intransitive* (usu. foll. by *along*) proceed heavily or awkwardly. □ **lump in the throat** a feeling of pressure there, caused by emotion. [Middle English, perhaps of Scandinavian origin]

lump² *transitive verb informal* endure or suffer (a situation); tolerate reluctantly. □ **like it or lump it** put up with something whether one likes it or not. [imitative: compare *dump, grump,* etc.]

lump·ec·tomy *noun* (*pl.* **-mies**) the surgical removal of a usu. cancerous lump from the breast.

lum·pen *derogatory* ● *adjective* ignorantly contented, boorish, stupid; uninterested in revolutionary advancement. ● *noun* the class of those who are lumpen. [back-formation from LUMPENPROLETARIAT]

lumpen·prole·tar·iat /ˈlʌmpənˌproʊləˈtɛriət/ *noun* (esp. in Marxist terminology) the unorganized and unpolitical lower orders of society, not interested in revolutionary advancement. [German from *Lumpen* rag, rogue: see PROLETARIAT]

lump·er *noun* **1** *N Amer.* a person employed in loading and unloading cargo; a longshoreman. **2** a person (esp. a taxonomist) who attaches importance to similarities rather than differences in classification or analysis and so favours inclusive categories (*compare* SPLITTER 2).

lump·fish *noun* (*pl.* **-fish·es** or **-fish**) a spiny-finned fish, *Cyclopterus lumpus*, of the N Atlantic with modified pelvic fins for clinging to objects, fished for its flesh and roe. [Middle Low German *lumpen*, Middle Dutch *lumpe* (perhaps = LUMP¹) + FISH¹]

lum·pia /ˈlʌmpiə/ *noun* an Indonesian spring roll served with a sauce for dipping. [Dutch *loempia* from Indonesian *lumpia*]

lump·ish *adjective* **1** heavy and clumsy. **2** stupid, lethargic. **3** shaped like a lump; lumpy. □ **lump·ish·ly** *adverb* **lump·ish·ness** *noun*

lump net *noun Cdn* (*Nfld*) a net for catching lumpfish, with a 10 ¹/₂-inch mesh.

lump·suck·er *noun* = LUMPFISH.

lump sum *noun* **1** a sum covering a number of items. **2** money paid down at once (opp. INSTALMENT 1).

lumpy *adjective* (**lump·i·er, lump·i·est**) **1** full of or covered with lumps. **2** (of water) cut up by the wind into small waves. **3** (of a person, style, etc.) heavy and clumsy. □ **lump·i·ly** *adverb* **lump·i·ness** *noun*

Lu·mum·ba /luˈmʊmbə/ **Pa·trice (Hem·ery)** (1925–61), Congolese leader, the first prime minister of the Democratic Republic of the Congo (subsequently Zaire, now Congo) 1960. He was deposed by the armed forces led by Mobutu, and later assassinated.

lun *noun Cdn* (*Nfld*) a lee; a sheltered spot. [British dialect, 'lull']

Luna /ˈluːnə/ *Rom. Myth* the goddess of the moon.

lunacy /ˈluːnəsi/ *noun* (*pl.* **-cies**) **1** insanity (originally of the intermittent kind attributed to changes of the moon); the state of being a lunatic. **2** great folly or eccentricity; a foolish act.

luna moth /ˈluːnə/ *noun* a N American moth, *Actias luna*, with crescent-shaped spots on its pale green wings. [Latin *luna,* = moon (from its markings)]

lunar /ˈluːnər/ *adjective* **1** of, relating to, resembling, or determined by the moon. **2** concerned with travel to the moon and related research. **3** crescent-shaped, lunate. **4** of or containing silver (from alchemists' use of *luna* (= moon) for 'silver'). [Latin *lunaris* from *luna* moon]

lunar calendar *noun* any calendar in which the year is divided into months determined by complete phases of the moon.

lunar cycle *noun* = METONIC CYCLE.

lunar eclipse *noun* an eclipse of the moon (see ECLIPSE *noun* 1).

lunar module *noun* a small craft used for travelling between the moon's surface and a spacecraft in orbit around the moon.

lunar month *noun* the period of the moon's revolution, esp. the interval between new moons of about 29¹/₂ days.

lunar orbit *noun* **1** the orbit of the moon around the earth. **2** an orbit around the moon.

lunar year *noun* a period of 12 lunar months.

lun·ate /ˈluːneɪt/ ● *adjective* crescent-shaped. ● *noun* a crescent-shaped prehistoric implement etc. [Latin *lunatus* from *luna* moon]

luna·tic /ˈluːnətɪk/ ● *noun* **1** an insane person. **2** someone foolish or eccentric. ● *adjective* mad, foolish. [Old French *lunatique* from Late Latin *lunaticus* from Latin *luna* moon]

lunatic asylum *noun hist.* or *offensive* a mental home or hospital.

lunatic fringe *noun* a fanatical, eccentric, or visionary minority of any group, society, etc.

lun·a·tion /luːˈneɪʃən/ *noun* the interval between new moons, about 29¹/₂ days. [medieval Latin *lunatio* (as LUNATIC)]

lunch ● *noun* **1** the meal eaten in the middle of the day. **2** a light meal eaten at any time. ● *intransitive verb* eat one's lunch. □ **do lunch** *informal* have lunch with a person, esp. a business associate. **out to lunch** *slang* out of touch with reality; unaware; crazy. □ **lunch·er** *noun* [LUNCHEON]

lunch box *noun* (also **lunch bucket**, *N Amer.* **lunch pail**) a plastic or metal container with a handle, for carrying a packed meal to school or work.

lunch break *noun* = LUNCH HOUR.

lunch bucket ● *noun* = LUNCH BOX. ● *adjective N Amer.* (**lunch-bucket**) = LUNCH-PAIL *adjective*.

lunch counter *noun N Amer.* **1** a counter in a department store etc., where light lunches and snacks are served. **2** = LUNCHEONETTE.

lunch·eon /ˈlʌntʃən/ *noun* a lunch, esp. a formal one. [17th c.: origin unknown]

lunch·eon·ette /ˌlʌntʃəˈnɛt/ *noun N Amer.* a small restaurant or snack bar serving light lunches.

luncheon meat *noun* a usu. tinned block of ground meat, usu. sliced and eaten cold in sandwiches etc.

luncheon plate *noun N Amer.* a plate larger than a side plate and smaller than a dinner plate, used for sandwiches etc.

lunch hour *noun* (also **lunch break**) a break from work, usually around the middle of the day, when lunch is eaten.

lunch kit *noun* = LUNCH BOX.

lunch meat *noun N Amer.* a type of cold meat suitable for sandwiches.

lunch pail *N Amer.* ● *noun* = LUNCH BOX. ● *adjective* (**lunch-pail**) working-class; blue-collar (*lunch-pail town*).

lunch·room *noun* **1** *N Amer.* a room in a school, office, etc. where lunch is served or where people may eat lunches brought from home. **2** = LUNCHEONETTE.

lunch·time *noun* the time around the middle of the day when lunch is usually eaten (often *attributive*: *lunchtime drinking*).

Lundy's Lane the site of a battle (1814), near Niagara Falls, fought between British forces (aided by a Canadian militia) and US troops, regarded as one of the bitterest encounters of the War of 1812. The British and Canadians eventually prevailed, but both sides suffered heavy losses.

Lunen·burg /ˈluːnənbɜrɡ/ a town on the southeastern coast of Nova Scotia, situated about 10 km southeast of Mahone Bay; pop. (2001) 2,568. The old town section is the best surviving example of a planned British colonial settlement in North America, and is a World Heritage Site. □ **Lunen·burg·er** *noun* [after the British royal house of Brunswick-*Lüneburg*]

Lunenburg bump *noun Cdn* a large bay window over the main entrance to a house, peculiar to houses in Lunenburg, NS.

lun·ette /luːˈnɛt/ *noun* **1** an arched aperture in a domed ceiling to admit light. **2 a** a crescent-shaped or semicircular space or alcove which contains a painting, statue, etc. **b** a piece of decoration filling

Consonants: **b** *but*   **d** *dog*   **f** *few*   **g** *get*   **h** *her*   **j** *yes*   **k** *cat*   **l** *leg*   **m** *man*   **n** *no*   **p** *pen*   **r** *red*   **s** *sit*

such a space. **3** any of various objects shaped like a crescent. [French, diminutive of *lune* moon, from Latin LUNA]

lung *noun* either of the pair of respiratory organs which bring air into contact with the blood in humans and many other vertebrates. □ **-lunged** *adjective* (in *combination*). **lung·ful** *noun* (*pl.* **-fuls**). **lung·less** *adjective* [Old English *lungen* from Germanic, related to LIGHT[2] (compare LIGHTS)]

lunge[1] ● *noun* **1** a sudden movement forward. **2** a thrust with a sword etc., esp. the basic attacking move in fencing. **3** a movement forward by bending the front leg at the knee while keeping the back leg straight. ● *intransitive verb* **1** make a lunge. **2** *Fencing* make a thrust with a foil or rapier. [earlier *allonge* from French *allonger* lengthen, from *à* to + *long* LONG[1]]

lunge[2] (also **longe**) (in full **lunge line**) ● *noun* a long rope on which a horse is held and made to move in a circle around its trainer. ● *transitive verb* (**lunge·ing**) exercise (a horse) with or in a lunge. [French *longe*, *allonge* (as LUNGE[1])]

lunge[3] *noun* = MUSKELLUNGE. [abbreviation]

lung·fish *noun* any freshwater fish of the order Dipnoi, having gills and a modified swim bladder used as lungs, and able to aestivate to survive drought.

lun·gi /ˈlʊŋgɪ/ *noun* (*pl.* **lun·gis**) a length of cotton cloth, usu. worn as a loincloth in India, or as a skirt in Burma (Myanmar) where it is the national dress for both sexes. [Urdu]

lung power *noun* the power of one's voice.

lung·worm *noun* a nematode parasitic in the lungs of mammals, esp. of farm and domestic animals.

lung·wort *noun* **1** any herbaceous plant of the genus *Pulmonaria*, esp. *P. officinalis* with white-spotted leaves likened to a diseased lung. **2** a lichen, *Lobaria pulmonaria*, formerly used as a remedy for lung disease.

luni·solar /ˌluːnɪˈsoʊlər/ *adjective* of or concerning the sun and moon. [Latin *luna* moon + *sol* sun]

lunk·er *noun* N Amer. slang an animal, esp. a fish, which is an exceptionally large example of its species; a whopper. [origin unknown]

lunk·head *noun* (also **lunk**) esp. N Amer. slang a slow-witted, unintelligent person. □ **lunk·head·ed** *adjective* [prob. from alteration of LUMP[1] *noun* + HEAD *noun*]

lun·ula /ˈluːnjʊlə/ *noun* (*pl.* **lun·ulae** /-ˌliː/) **1** a crescent-shaped mark, esp. the white area at the base of the fingernail. **2** a crescent-shaped Bronze Age ornament. [Latin, diminutive of *luna* moon]

Luo·yang /loːˈjæŋ/ (formerly called **Honan**) an industrial city in east central China, in Henan province on the Luo River; pop. (est. 2002) 1,492,400. It was founded in the 12th c. BC as the imperial capital of the Zhou dynasty and was the capital of several subsequent dynasties. Between the 4th and 6th c. AD the construction of cave temples to the south of the city made it an important Buddhist centre.

Luper·calia /ˌluːpərˈkeɪliə/ an ancient Roman festival of purification and fertility, held on 15 February at a cave called the Lupercal.

lu·pine[1] /ˈluːpɪn/ *noun* (also **lupin**) any plant of the genus *Lupinus*, with long tapering spikes of blue, purple, pink, white, or yellow flowers. [Latin *lupinus* '(grass) of the wolf']

lu·pine[2] /ˈluːpaɪn/ *adjective* of or like a wolf or wolves. [Latin *lupinus* from *lupus* wolf]

lu·pini bean /luːˈpiːniː/ *noun* the seed of a large-seeded bitter variety of lupin, eaten as food. [Italian, pl. of *lupino* 'lupin']

lupus /ˈluːpəs/ *noun* any of various ulcerous or erosive skin diseases, esp. lupus erythematosus. □ **lu·poid** *adjective* **lu·pous** *adjective* [Latin, = wolf]

lupus ery·thema·to·sus /ˌerəθiːməˈtoʊsəs/ *noun* an inflammatory disease of the skin giving rise to scaly red patches, esp. on the face, and sometimes also involving internal organs. [modern Latin, from Greek *eruthēma*: see ERYTHEMA]

lupus vul·garis /vʌlˈgeərɪs/ *noun* tuberculosis with dark red patches on the skin, usu. due to direct inoculation of the tuberculosis bacillus into the skin.

lurch[1] ● *noun* a sudden unsteady movement or leaning; a stagger. ● *intransitive verb* **1** (of a person etc.) stagger, move unsteadily. **2** (of a ship etc.) move suddenly to one side. [originally Nautical *lee-lurch* alteration of *lee-latch* drifting to leeward]

lurch[2] *noun* □ **leave in the lurch** desert (a friend etc.) in difficulties. [originally = a severe defeat in a game, from French *lourche* (also the game itself, like backgammon)]

lurch·er *noun* **1** Brit. a crossbred dog, usu. a retriever, collie, or

sheepdog crossed with a greyhound, used esp. for hunting and by poachers. **2** *archaic* a petty thief, swindler, or spy. [from obsolete *lurch* (v.) var. of LURK]

lure ● *transitive verb* **1** (usu. foll. by *away*, *into*) entice (a person, an animal, etc.) usu. with some form of bait. **2** attract back again or recall (a person, animal, etc.) with the promise of a reward. ● *noun* **1** a thing used to entice. **2** (usu. foll. by *of*) the attractive or compelling qualities (of a pursuit etc.). **3** live or esp. artificial bait used to entice fish or animals; a decoy. **4** a falconer's apparatus for recalling a hawk, consisting of a bunch of feathers attached to a thong, within which the hawk finds food while being trained. [Old English *luere* from Germanic]

Lurex *noun* **1** a type of yarn which incorporates a glittering metallic thread. **2** fabric made from this yarn.

lurid *adjective* **1** sensational, horrifying, or terrible (*lurid details*). **2** showy, gaudy (*paperbacks with lurid covers*). **3** vivid or glowing in colour (*lurid orange*). **4** of an unnatural glare (*lurid nocturnal brilliance*). **5** ghastly, wan (*lurid complexion*). □ **lurid·ly** *adverb* **lurid·ness** *noun* [Latin *luridus* from *luror* wan or yellow colour]

lurk *intransitive verb* **1** linger furtively or unobtrusively. **2 a** lie in ambush. **b** (usu. foll. by *in*, *under*, *about*, etc.) hide, esp. for sinister purposes. **3** exist latently or semi-consciously (*a lurking suspicion*). **4** *Computing* read messages on an online bulletin board without contributing messages oneself. □ **lurk·er** *noun* [Middle English perhaps from LOUR with frequentative *-k* as in TALK]

Lu·saka /luːˈsɑːkə/ the capital of Zambia; pop. (est. 2002) 1,218,200.

lus·cious /ˈlʌʃəs/ *adjective* **1 a** richly sweet in taste or smell. **b** *informal* delicious. **2** (of literary style, music, etc.) over-rich in sound, imagery, or voluptuous suggestion. **3** voluptuously attractive. □ **lus·cious·ly** *adverb* **lus·cious·ness** *noun* [Middle English perhaps alteration of obsolete *licious* from DELICIOUS]

lush[1] *adjective* **1 a** (of vegetation, esp. grass) luxuriant, abundant. **b** characterized by luxuriance of vegetation (*a lush forest*). **2** luxurious. **3** (of colour, sound, etc.) rich, voluptuous. □ **lush·ly** *adverb* **lush·ness** *noun* [Middle English, perhaps a variant of obsolete *lash* 'soft', from Old French *lasche* 'lax' (see LACHES): associated with LUSCIOUS]

lush[2] *slang* ● *noun* **1** an alcoholic, a drunkard. **2** alcohol, liquor. ● *transitive & intransitive verb* N Amer. drink (alcohol). [18th c.: perhaps jocular use of LUSH[1]]

Lu·shun /luːˈʃʊn/ a port on the Liaodong Peninsula in NE China, now part of the urban complex of Luda. It was leased by Russia for use as a Pacific naval port from 1898 until 1905, when it was known as Port Arthur. Between 1945 and 1955 it was jointly held by China and the Soviet Union.

Lusi·tania /ˌluːsɪˈteɪniə/ an ancient Roman province in the Iberian peninsula, corresponding to modern Portugal. □ **Lusi·tan·ian** *adjective & noun*

lust ● *noun* **1** strong sexual desire. **2 a** (usu. foll. by *for*, *of*) a passionate desire for (*a lust for power*). **b** (usu. foll. by *of*) a passionate enjoyment of (*the lust of battle*). **3** (usu. in *pl.*) a sensuous appetite regarded as sinful (*the lusts of the flesh*). ● *intransitive verb* (usu. foll. by *after*, *for*) have a strong or excessive (esp. sexual) desire. □ **lust·ful** *adjective* **lust·ful·ly** *adverb* **lust·ful·ness** *noun* [Old English from Germanic]

lus·ter esp. US var. of LUSTRE[1], [2].

lus·tra *pl.* of LUSTRUM.

lus·tra·tion /lʌsˈtreɪʃən/ *noun* purification by expiatory sacrifice, ceremonial washing, or other such rite. [Latin *lustrare* (as LUSTRUM)]

lustre[1] (also esp. US **luster**) ● *noun* **1** gloss, brilliance, or sheen. **2** a shiny or reflective surface. **3 a** a thin metallic coating giving an iridescent glaze to ceramics. **b** = LUSTREWARE. **4** a radiance or attractiveness; splendour, glory, distinction (of achievements etc.) (*add lustre to*; *shed lustre on*). **5 a** a prismatic glass pendant on a chandelier etc. **b** a cut-glass chandelier or candelabra. **6 a** Brit. a thin dress material with a cotton warp, woollen weft, and a glossy surface. **b** any fabric or yarn with a sheen or gloss. ● *transitive verb* put lustre on (pottery, a cloth, etc.). □ **lustre·less** *adjective* (esp. US **lusterless**). **lus·trous** *adjective* **lus·trous·ly** *adverb* **lus·trous·ness** *noun* [French from Italian *lustro* from *lustrare* from Latin *lustrare* illuminate]

lustre[2] *noun* (esp. US **luster**) = LUSTRUM. [Middle English, anglicized from LUSTRUM]

lustre·ware *noun* (esp. US **luster·ware**) ceramics with an iridescent glaze. [LUSTRE[1]]

lus·trum *noun* (*pl.* **lustra** or **lus·trums**) a period of five years. [Latin, an originally purificatory sacrifice after a quinquennial census]

lusty *adjective* (**lust·i·er**, **lust·i·est**) **1** healthy and strong. **2** vigorous

t **top** v **voice** w **we** z **zoo** ʃ **she** ʒ **vision** θ **thin** ð **this** ŋ **ring** x **loch** tʃ **chip** dʒ **jar**   *(see over for vowels)*

or lively. **3** lustful; full of sexual desire. **4** (of a meal etc.) hearty, abundant. □ **lust·i·ly** *adverb* **lust·i·ness** *noun*

lusus /ˈluːsəs/ *noun* (in full **lusus naturae** /nəˈtʊriː, -ˈtjʊriː/) a freak of nature. [Latin]

lute[1] *noun* a guitar-like instrument with a long neck and a pear-shaped body, much used in the 14th–17th c. [French *lut, leüt,* prob. from Provençal *laüt* from Arabic *al-ʿūd*]

lute[2] ● *noun* clay or cement used to stop a hole, make a joint airtight, etc. ● *transitive verb* apply lute to. [Old French *lut* from Latin *lutum* mud, clay]

lu·teal /ˈluːtɪəl/ *adjective* of or pertaining to the corpus luteum.

lu·tein /ˈluːtiːn/ *noun Chem.* a pigment of a deep yellow colour found in egg yolk etc. [Latin *luteum* yolk of egg, neuter of *luteus* yellow]

lu·tein·iz·ing hormone /ˈluːtənaiːzɪŋ/ *noun* (also esp. *Brit.* **luteinising hormone**) *Biochem.* a hormone secreted by the anterior pituitary gland that in females stimulates ovulation and in males stimulates the synthesis of androgen. Abbr.: **LH**.

lut·en·ist /ˈluːtənɪst/ *noun* a lute player. [medieval Latin *lutanista* from *lutana* LUTE[1]]

lu·tetium /luːˈtiːʃiəm/ *noun Chem.* a silvery metallic element of the lanthanide series. Symbol: **Lu**; at. no.: 71. [French *lutécium* from Latin *Lutetia* the ancient name of Paris, France, the home of its discoverer]

Lu·ther, Mar·tin (1483–1546), German Protestant theologian, the principal figure of the German Reformation. He preached the doctrine of justification by faith rather than by works, attacked the sale of indulgences with his 95 theses (1517), and was condemned and excommunicated at the Diet of Worms (1521); in 1530 he approved Melanchthon's Augsburg Confession, which laid down the Lutheran position, and his translation of the Bible into High German (1522–34) contributed significantly to the development of German literature in the vernacular.

Lu·ther·an ● *noun* **1** a member of the Church which accepts the Augsburg Confession of 1530, with justification by faith alone as a cardinal doctrine. **2** a follower of Martin Luther. ● *adjective* **1** of or relating to Lutherans or the Lutheran church. **2** of or characterized by the theology of Martin Luther. □ **Lu·ther·an·ism** *noun*

lu·thier /ˈluːtɪər/ *noun* a maker of stringed instruments, esp. those of the violin family and guitars. [French from *luth* LUTE[1]]

Lu·thu·li /luːˈtuːli/ **Al·bert (John Mvum·bi)** (also **Lutuli**) (1899–1967), South African political leader. He was president of the African National Congress (1952–60), and was awarded the Nobel Peace Prize in 1960 for his commitment to non-violence as a means of opposing apartheid.

lut·ing /ˈluːtɪŋ/ *noun* = LUTE[2] *noun*.

Luton /ˈluːtən/ an industrial town northwest of London, England; pop. (est. 2002) 179,100.

Lu·tu·li see LUTHULI.

Lutz *noun* (also **lutz**) *Figure Skating* a jump in which the skater takes off from the back outside edge of one skate, using the toe of the free foot to assist the takeoff, and lands, after at least one complete rotation in the air, on the back outside edge of the other skate. [prob. from the name of Gustave *Lussi* b.1898, who invented it]

luvvy *noun* (also **luv·vie**) (*pl.* **-vies**) *Brit. informal* **1** (as a form of address) = LOVEY. **2** an actor or actress, esp. one who is particularly effusive or affected.

lux *noun* (*pl.* same) *Physics* the SI unit of illumination, equivalent to one lumen per square metre. Abbr.: **lx**. [Latin *lux lucis* 'light']

luxe /lʌks, lʊks/ ● *noun* luxury (*compare* DELUXE). ● *adjective* deluxe, sumptuous. [French from Latin *luxus*]

Lux·em·bourg /ˈlʌksəmˌbɜrg/ **1** (also **Grand Duchy of Luxembourg**) a country in W Europe, situated between Belgium, Germany, and France; pop. (est. 2002) 448,569; capital, Luxembourg. **2** the capital of the Grand Duchy of Luxembourg; pop. (2001) 76,833. It is the seat of the European Court of Justice. **3** a province of SE Belgium, until 1839 a province of the Grand Duchy of Luxembourg; capital, Arlon. □ **Lux·em·bourg·er** *noun*

Lux·em·burg /ˈlʌksəmˌbɜrg/ **Rosa** (1871–1919), Polish-born German socialist and revolutionary leader. She co-founded what became the Polish Communist Party (1893), and with Karl Liebknecht founded the German revolutionary and pacifist group known as the Spartacus League (1915), and the German Communist Party (1918); in 1919 she and Liebknecht were assassinated after organizing an abortive Communist uprising in Berlin.

Lux·em·burg·ish /ˈlʌksəmˌbɜrgɪʃ/ ● *noun* a form of German spoken in Luxembourg. ● *adjective* of or relating to Luxemburgish.

Luxor /ˈlʌksɔr/ a city in E Egypt, on the east bank of the Nile; pop. (est. 2002) 412,300. It is the site of the southern part of ancient Thebes and contains the ruins of the temple built by Amenhotep III between 1411 and 1375 BC and of monuments erected by Ramses II in the 13th c. BC.

lux·uri·ant /lʌgˈʒʊriənt, lʌkˈʃʊr-/ *adjective* **1** (of vegetation, hair, etc.) lush, profuse in growth. **2** prolific, exuberant (*luxuriant imagination*). **3** (of literary or artistic style) florid, richly ornate. □ **lux·uri·ance** *noun* **lux·uri·ant·ly** *adverb* [Latin *luxuriare* grow rank, from *luxuria* LUXURY] ¶ *Luxuriant,* meaning 'growing profusely, exuberant' is sometimes confused with *luxurious,* the adjective relating to luxury.

lux·uri·ate /lʌgˈʒʊriˌeit, lʌkˈʃʊr-/ *intransitive verb* **1** (foll. by *in*) take self-indulgent delight in, enjoy in a luxurious manner. **2** take one's ease, relax in comfort. **3** (of a plant etc.) grow profusely.

lux·uri·ous /lʌgˈʒʊriəs, lʌkˈʃʊr-/ *adjective* **1** characterized by luxury; sumptuous, rich (*a luxurious estate*). **2** extremely comfortable. **3** self-indulgent, voluptuous. □ **lux·uri·ous·ly** *adverb* **lux·uri·ous·ness** *noun* ¶ See Usage Note at LUXURIANT.

lux·ury /ˈlʌkʃəri, ˈlʌgʒəri/ *noun* (*pl.* **-uries**) **1** choice or costly surroundings, possessions, food, etc.; luxuriousness (*a life of luxury*). **2** (often in *pl.*) something desirable for comfort or enjoyment, but not indispensable. **3** a means of indulging one's tastes and desires (*the luxury of only having to work when one wants to*). **4** (*attributive*) providing great comfort, expensive (*a luxury condo; a luxury holiday*). [Old French *luxurie, luxure* from Latin *luxuria* from *luxus* abundance]

Luzon /luːˈzɒn/ the most northerly and the largest island in the Philippines. Its chief towns are Quezon City and Manila, the country's capital.

Lviv /ləˈviv/ (Russian **Lvov** /ljvɒf/) an industrial city in W Ukraine, near the border with Poland; pop. (est. 2001) 732,000.

Lw *symbol Chem.* the element lawrencium.

lwei /ləˈwei/ *noun* a monetary unit of Angola, equal to one-hundredth of a kwanza. [Angolan name]

lx *abbreviation* lux.

LXX *symbol* Septuagint. [Roman numeral for 70]

-ly[1] *suffix* forming adjectives esp. from nouns, meaning: **1** having the qualities of (*princely; manly*). **2** recurring at intervals of (*daily; hourly*). [from or after Old English *-lic* from Germanic, related to LIKE[1]]

-ly[2] *suffix* forming adverbs from adjectives, denoting esp. manner or degree (*boldly; happily; miserably; deservedly; amusingly*). [from or after Old English *-lice* from Germanic (as -LY[1])]

Lyall·pur /ˌlaiəlˈpʊr/ the former name (until 1979) for FAISALABAD.

ly·can·thrope /ˈləikanˌθroːp/ *noun* **1** a werewolf. **2** an insane person who believes that he or she is an animal, esp. a wolf.

ly·can·thropy /laiˈkanθrəpi/ *noun* **1** the mythical transformation of a person into a wolf (*see also* WEREWOLF). **2** a form of madness involving the delusion of being a wolf, with changed appetites, voice, etc. □ **ly·can·throp·ic** /-ˈθrɒpɪk/ *adjective* [modern Latin *lycanthropia* from Greek *lukanthrōpia* from *lukos* wolf + *anthrōpos* man]

lycée /liːˈsei/ *noun* a public secondary school in France. [French from Latin (as LYCEUM)]

Ly·ceum /laiˈsiːəm/ *noun* **1 a** the garden at Athens in which Aristotle taught philosophy. **b** Aristotelian philosophy and its followers. **2** (**lyceum**) esp. *US hist.* a literary institution, lecture hall, or teaching place. **3** (esp. in the names of buildings) a concert hall or theatre. [Latin from Greek *Lukeion* neuter of *Lukeios* epithet of Apollo (from whose neighbouring temple the Lyceum was named)]

lychee /ˈliːtʃi/ *noun* (also **litchi, lichee**) **1** a sweet fleshy fruit with a thin spiny skin. **2** the tree, *Nephelium litchi,* originally from China, bearing this. [Chinese *lizhi*]

lych-gate /ˈlitʃgeit/ *noun* a roofed gateway to a churchyard. [Old English *líc* corpse, from Germanic + GATE[1], traditionally where a coffin was held until the arrival of the clergyman]

Lycia /ˈlisiə/ an ancient region on the coast of SW Asia Minor, between Caria and Pamphylia. Formerly under Persian and Syrian rule, it was annexed by Rome as part of Pamphylia in AD 43, becoming a separate province in the 4th c. □ **Ly·cian** *adjective & noun*

lyco·pene /ˈləikəˌpiːn/ *noun* a red carotenoid pigment and antioxidant present in tomatoes and some fruits. [from the variant *lycopin* (from modern Latin *Lycopersicon,* a genus name including the tomato) + -ENE]

lyco·pod /ˈləikəˌpɒd/ *noun* any of various clubmosses, esp. of the genus *Lycopodium.* [anglicized form of LYCOPODIUM]

lyco·po·dium /ˌləikəˈpoːdiəm/ *noun* **1** = LYCOPOD. **2** a fine powder of spores from this, formerly used as an absorbent in surgery, and in making fireworks etc. [modern Latin from Greek *lukos* wolf + *pous podos* foot]

Lycra /ˈlaɪkrə/ *noun* proprietary an elastic polyurethane fibre or fabric used esp. for close-fitting sports clothing and foundation garments.

Ly·cur·gus /laɪˈkɜːgəs/ (9th c. BC), Spartan lawgiver. He is traditionally held to be the founder of the constitution and military regime of ancient Sparta.

Lydia /ˈlɪdɪə/ an ancient region of W Asia Minor, south of Mysia and north of Caria. It became a powerful kingdom in the 7th c. BC and was probably the first realm to use coined money.

Lyd·ian /ˈlɪdɪən/ ● *noun* **1** a native or inhabitant of ancient Lydia. **2** the language of this people. ● *adjective* of or relating to the people of Lydia or their language.

Lydian mode *noun* Music the mode represented by the natural diatonic scale F–F.

lye *noun* **1** any strong alkaline solution, esp. of potassium hydroxide used for washing or cleansing. **2** water that has been made alkaline by lixiviation of vegetable ashes. [Old English *lēag* from Germanic]

Lyell, **Sir Charles** (1797–1875), Scottish geologist. His influential textbook *Principles of Geology* (1830–3) argued that the earth's features were shaped over a long period of time by natural processes, and not during short periodic upheavals as proposed by the catastrophist school of thought.

lying[1] *pres. part. of* LIE[1].

lying[2] ● *verb pres. part. of* LIE[2]. ● *adjective* deceitful, false.

Lyly /ˈlɪli/ **John** (c.1554–1606), English prose writer and dramatist. He is remembered for his prose romance in two parts: *Euphues, The Anatomy of Wit* (1578) and *Euphues and his England* (1580); both were written in an elaborate style that became known as *euphuism*.

Lyme disease *noun* a form of arthritis which mainly affects the large joints and is caused by spirochete bacteria transmitted by ticks. [*Lyme*, a town in Connecticut, US, where an outbreak occurred]

lyme grass *noun* (in full **sea lyme grass**) a blue-green grass of sandy coasts, *Elymus arenarius*, often planted to stabilize dunes. [perhaps from LIME[1]]

lymph *noun* Physiol. a colourless fluid containing white blood cells, drained from the tissues and conveyed through the body in the lymphatic system. □ **lymph·oid** *adjective* [French *lymphe* or Latin *lympha, limpa* water]

lymph·aden·op·athy /lɪmˌfadəˈnɒpəθi/ *noun* chronic swelling of the lymph nodes.

lymph·at·ic ● *adjective* **1** of or secreting or conveying lymph. **2** (of a person) pale, flabby, or sluggish. ● *noun* a veinlike vessel conveying lymph. [originally = frenzied, from Latin *lymphaticus* mad, from Greek *numpholēptos* seized by nymphs: now assoc. with LYMPH (on the analogy of *spermatic* etc.)]

lymphatic system *noun* a network of vessels conveying lymph.

lymph node *noun* (also **lymph gland**) a small mass of tissue in the lymphatic system where lymph is purified and lymphocytes are formed.

lymph·o·blast /ˈlɪmfəˌblast/ *noun* an abnormal cell resembling a large lymphocyte, produced in large numbers in a form of leukemia. □ **lymph·o·blast·ic** *adjective*

lymph·o·cyte /ˈlɪmfəˌsaɪt/ *noun* a form of leukocyte occurring in the blood, in lymph, etc. *See also* B LYMPHOCYTE, T LYMPHOCYTE. □ **lymph·o·cyt·ic** /-ˈsɪtɪk/ *adjective*

lymph·o·kine /ˈlɪmfəˌkaɪn/ *noun* any of various soluble substances released by lymphocytes which are thought to be involved in cell-mediated immunity but to lack the antigen-specificity of antibodies. [LYMPH + Greek *kinein* 'move']

lymph·oma /lɪmˈfəʊmə/ *noun* (pl. **lymph·omas**, **lymph·o·mata** /-mətə/) any malignant tumour of the lymph nodes, excluding leukemia.

Lynch ▶ **1 David (Keith)** (b.1946), American film director. Lynch uses compelling images in his films to emphasize a quality of subtle mystery or menace. He is noted for films including *Blue Velvet* (1986) and *Wild at Heart* (1990, for which he won an Oscar), and for his television series *Twin Peaks*. **2 John (Mary) ('Jack')** (1917–99), Irish politician, prime minister of Ireland 1966–73 and 1977–9. His first term of office saw Ireland's entry into the European Economic Community (1973).

lynch *transitive verb* (of a body of people) put (a person) to death, esp. by hanging, for an alleged offence without a legal trial. □ **lynch·er** *noun* **lynch·ing** *noun* [*Lynch's law*, after Capt. W. *Lynch* of Virginia c.1780]

lynch law *noun* the practice of summary punishment and esp. execution of an alleged offender carried out by a self-constituted illegal court.

lynch mob *noun* **1** a mob intent on lynching someone. **2** any unruly, angry crowd of people.

lynch·pin *var. of* LINCHPIN.

Lynn, Dame Vera (born Vera Margaret Lewis) (b.1917), English singer. She became known as the 'Forces' Sweetheart' during the Second World War, and is mainly remembered for songs such as 'We'll Meet Again' and 'White Cliffs of Dover'.

Lynx an obscure northern constellation lying between Auriga and Ursa Major.

lynx *noun* (pl. same) **1** any of various small to medium-sized members of the cat family typically having a short tail, tufted ears, and mottled or spotted fur, esp. *Lynx canadensis* of northern N America or the smaller *Lynx lynx*, which inhabits forest in NW Europe and northern Asia. **2** its fur. [Latin from Greek *lugx*]

Lyons /liːˈɔ̃/ (also **Lyon**) an industrial city and river port in SE France, situated at the confluence of the Rhone and Saône rivers; pop. (1999) 445,452. It was founded by the Romans in AD 43 as Lugdunum.

lyo·phil·ic /ˌlaɪəˈfɪlɪk/ *adjective* (of a colloid) readily dispersed by a solvent. [Greek *luō* loosen, dissolve + Greek *philos* loving]

lyo·phil·ize /laɪˈɒfɪˌlaɪz/ *transitive verb* (also esp. Brit. **-ise**) freeze-dry. □ **lyo·phil·iz·a·tion** *noun*

lyo·phob·ic /ˌlaɪəˈfəʊbɪk/ *adjective* (of a colloid) not lyophilic. [Greek *luō* loosen, dissolve + -PHOBIC (see -PHOBIA)]

Lyo·tard /ˈljɒtɑː/ **Jean-François** (1924–98), French philosopher and literary critic. He outlined his 'philosophy of desire', based on the politics of Nietzsche, in *L'Économie libidinale* (1974). In later books he adopted a postmodern quasi-Wittgensteinian linguistic philosophy.

Lyra /ˈlaɪrə/ a small but prominent constellation in the northern hemisphere. [Latin *lyra* (as LYRE)]

lyr·ate /ˈlaɪrət/ *adjective* Biol. lyre-shaped.

lyre /laɪr/ *noun* Gk Hist. an ancient stringed instrument like a small U-shaped harp, played usu. with a plectrum and accompanying the voice. [Old French *lire* from Latin *lyra* from Greek *lura*]

lyre·bird *noun* any Australian bird of the family Menuridae, the male of which has a lyre-shaped tail display.

lyric ● *adjective* **1** (of poetry) expressing the writer's emotions, usu. briefly and in stanzas or recognized forms. **2** (of a poet) writing in this manner. **3** of or for the lyre. **4** meant to be sung, fit to be expressed in song, song-like (*lyric drama*; *lyric opera*). **5** (of a singing voice) using a light register (*a lyric soprano*). ● *noun* **1** a lyric poem or verse. **2** (in *pl.*) lyric verses. **3** (usu. in *pl.*) the words of a song. [as LYRE]

lyric·al *adjective* **1** = LYRIC 1, 2, 5. **2** resembling, couched in, or using language appropriate to, lyric poetry. **3** informal highly enthusiastic (*wax lyrical about*). □ **lyric·ally** *adverb*

lyri·cism *noun* **1** the character or quality of being lyric or lyrical. **2** a lyrical expression. **3** high-flown sentiments.

lyri·cist *noun* a person who writes the words to a song.

lyr·ist *noun* **1** /ˈlaɪrɪst/ a person who plays the lyre. **2** /ˈlɪrɪst/ a lyric poet.

Lysan·der /laɪˈsandər/ (d.395 BC), Spartan general. He commanded the Spartan fleet that defeated the Athenian navy in 405 BC, and captured Athens in 404, bringing the Peloponnesian War to an end.

lyse /laɪz, laɪs/ *transitive & intransitive verb* bring about or undergo lysis. [back-formation from LYSIS]

Lysen·ko /lɪˈsɛŋkɔ/ **Tro·fim Denis·ovich** (1898–1976), Soviet biologist and geneticist. An adherent of Lamarck's theory of evolution by the inheritance of acquired characteristics, he was favoured by Stalin and dominated Soviet genetics for many years.

lys·ergic acid /laɪˈsɜːdʒɪk/ *noun* a crystalline acid extracted from ergot or prepared synthetically. [hydrolysis + *ergot* + -IC]

lys·ergic acid di·ethyl·amide /daɪˌeθəˈlamaɪd, daɪˈeθələˌmaɪd/ *noun* a powerful hallucinogenic drug. Abbr.: **LSD**.

Ly·sima·chus /laɪˈsɪməkəs/ (c.360–281 BC), Macedonian general under Alexander the Great, who was king of Thrace from 323 to 281.

lysin /ˈlaɪsɪn/ *noun* a protein in the blood able to cause lysis.

ly·sine /ˈlaɪsiːn/ *noun* Biochem. an amino acid present in protein and essential in the diet of vertebrates.

Ly·sip·pus /laɪˈsɪpəs/ (4th c. BC), Greek sculptor. He introduced naturalistic proportions for the human body into Greek sculpture with works such as the bronze Apoxyomenos (c.320–315), representing a young male athlete scraping and cleaning his oil-covered skin.

lysis /ˈləɪsɪs/ *noun* (*pl.* **lyses** /-siːz/) the disintegration of a cell. [Latin from Greek *lusis* loosening, from *luō* loosen]

-lysis /lɪsɪs/ *combining form* forming nouns denoting disintegration or decomposition (*electrolysis*; *hemolysis*).

Lysol /ˈləɪsɒl/ *noun* *proprietary* a mixture of cresols and soft soap, used as a disinfectant. [LYSIS + -OL²]

lyso·some /ˈləɪsə,səʊm/ *noun* a cytoplasmic organelle in eukaryotic cells containing degradative enzymes enclosed in a membrane. □ **lyso·som·al** *adjective* [LYSIS + -SOME³]

lyso·zyme /ˈləɪsə,zaɪm/ *noun* *Biochem.* an enzyme found in tears and egg white which catalyzes the destruction of cell walls of certain bacteria. [LYSIS + ENZYME]

lyth·rum /ˈlɪθrəm/ *noun* a genus of plants including among others the purple loosestrife. [Modern Latin from Greek *lythron* 'gore', from the colour of the flowers]

lytic /ˈlɪtɪk/ *adjective* of, relating to, or causing lysis.

-lytic /ˈlɪtɪk/ *combining form* forming adjectives corresponding to nouns in *-lysis*. [Greek *lutikos* (as LYSIS)]

Lyt·ton, **1st Baron** (born Edward George Earle Bulwer-Lytton) (1803–73), English writer. His prolific literary output includes *Pelham* (1828), a novel of fashionable society, historical romances such as *The Last Days of Pompeii* (1834), and plays.

Mm

M¹ *noun* (also **m**) (*pl.* **Ms** or **M's**) **1** the thirteenth letter of the alphabet. **2** (as a Roman numeral) 1,000. **3** *Printing* em.

M² *abbreviation* (also **M.**) **1** Monsieur. **2** (in sizes) medium. **3** *Chem.* molar. **4** Middle. **5** (in the UK in road designations) motorway. **6** Monday.

M³ *symbol* mega-.

m¹ *abbreviation* (also **m.**) **1 a** masculine. **b** male. **2** married. **3** mile(s). **4** million(s). **5** minute(s). **6** month. **7** mare.

m² *symbol* **1** metre(s). **2** milli-. **3** *Physics* mass.

m' *adjective* = MY (*m'lud*).

'm¹ *abbreviation informal* am (*I'm sorry*).

'm² *noun informal* madam (in *yes'm* etc.).

M-16 *noun* (*pl.* **M-16s**) a lightweight, automatic or semi-automatic magazine-fed rifle.

MA *abbreviation* Massachusetts (in official postal use).

M.A. *abbreviation* Master of Arts.

Ma, Yo-Yo (b.1955), US cellist. He performed at Carnegie Hall at age nine, and continued to gain great popularity, winning several Grammy awards, and collaborating with musicians and artists from different traditions.

ma *noun informal* mother. [abbreviation of MAMMA¹]

ma'am *noun* madam. [contraction]

ma-and-pa *adjective N Amer.* = MOM-AND-POP.

Maas·tricht /ˈmɒstrɪxt/ an industrial city in the Netherlands, capital of the province of Limburg, situated on the Maas River near the Belgian and German borders; pop. (est. 2002) 123,000.

Maat /mɒt/ *Egyptian Myth* the goddess of truth, justice, and cosmic order, daughter of Ra. She is depicted as a young and beautiful woman, standing or seated, with a feather on her head.

Ma Bell *noun informal* the Bell Telephone Company (*compare* BABY BELL).

Mac¹ *noun informal* **1** *N Amer.* a form of address to a male stranger. **2** a Scotsman. [*Mac-* as a patronymic prefix in many Scottish and Irish surnames]

Mac² *noun N Amer. informal* a McIntosh apple. [abbreviation]

mac *noun* (also **mack**) *Brit. informal* a raincoat. [abbreviation]

Mac- ¶ In this dictionary, surnames beginning *Mc-* are alphabetized with other words beginning *mc-*, separate from those surnames beginning *Mac-*.

ma·cabre /məˈkɒbrə, -ˈkɒb, -ˈkabrə/ *adjective* **1** grim, gruesome. **2** dealing with death. [Old French *macabré* perhaps from *Macabé* a Maccabee, with reference to a miracle play showing the slaughter of the Maccabees]

mac·ad·am *noun* **1** material for road building with successive layers of compacted broken stone. **2** = TARMACADAM. □ **mac·ad·am·ize** *transitive verb* (also esp. *Brit.* **-ise**). **mac·ad·am·iz·a·tion** *noun* (also esp. *Brit.* **-is·a·tion**). [J. L. *McAdam*, British surveyor d.1836, who advocated using this material]

maca·da·mia /ˌmakəˈdeɪmɪə/ *noun* any evergreen tree of the genus *Macadamia*, esp. *M. ternifolia*, bearing edible nutlike seeds. [J. *Macadam*, Australian chemist d.1865]

Mac·Alpin, Ken·neth, see KENNETH I.

mac and cheese *noun N Amer. informal* macaroni and cheese.

Macao see MACAU.

Maca·pá /ˌmakəˈpɒ/ a town in N Brazil, on the Amazon delta; pop. (est. 2002) 301,600.

ma·caque /məˈkak/ *noun* any monkey of the genus *Macaca*, including the rhesus monkey and Barbary ape, having prominent cheek pouches and usu. a long tail. [French from Portuguese *macaco* from Bantu *makaku* some monkeys, from *kaku* monkey]

Maca·rena /ˌmakəˈreɪnə/ *noun* a dance performed with hand and body language, including exaggerated hip motion, to 16 beats of music. [from a Spanish female given name, or from the name of a barrio of Seville]

maca·ro·ni *noun* **1** a tubular variety of pasta, usu. cut into short pieces. **2** (*pl.* **maca·ro·nies**) *hist.* an 18th-c. British dandy affecting Continental fashions. [Italian *maccaroni* from late Greek *makaria* 'food made from barley', from ancient Greek *makaarios* 'blessed' (because originally a funeral or charitable meal)]

macaroni and cheese *noun* (also *Brit.* **macaroni cheese**) a savoury dish consisting of macaroni baked or served with a cheese sauce.

maca·ron·ic /ˌmakəˈrɒnɪk/ ● *noun* (in *pl.*) verse in which vernacular words are introduced in the context of another language, esp. Latin. ● *adjective* (of verse) of this kind. [modern Latin *macaronicus* from obsolete Italian *macaronico*, jocularly formed as MACARONI]

maca·roon /ˌmakəˈruːn/ *noun* a small light cookie made with egg whites, sugar, and ground almonds or coconut. [French *macaron* from Italian (as MACARONI)]

Mac·Arthur, Doug·las (1880–1964), US general. He commanded US (later Allied) forces in the SW Pacific during the Second World War, formally accepted Japan's surrender (1945), and commanded the Allied occupation (1945–51) that followed; in 1950 he was put in charge of UN forces in Korea, but was relieved of his command in 1951.

Ma·cas·sar¹ see MAKASSAR.

Ma·cas·sar² /məˈkasər/ *noun* (in full **Macassar oil**) a kind of oil formerly used by men to make their hair shine and lie flat. [MACASSAR, from where its ingredients were said to come]

Macau /məˈkau/ (also **Macao**) a special administrative region of China, on the west side of the Pearl River estuary opposite Hong Kong; pop. (est. 2002) 457,100. It comprises the Macau peninsula and two nearby islands. It was a dependency of Portugal from 1887 to 1999. □ **Macan·ese** /makəˈniːz/ *adjective & noun*

Mac·aulay /məˈkɒli/ **1 Dame (Emilie) Rose** (1881–1958), English novelist and essayist. Her novels display her skill as a social satirist, and include *Dangerous Ages* (1921), *The World My Wilderness* (1950), and *The Towers of Trebizond* (1956). **2 Thom·as Bab·ing·ton, 1st Baron** (1800–59), English historian, essayist, and philanthropist. Among his best-known works are *The Lays of Ancient Rome* (1842) and his *History of England* (1849–61), which covers from a Whig standpoint the period from the accession of James II to the death of William III.

Mac·aulay, Mount /məˈkɒli/ a mountain (4 663 m) in the St. Elias mountain range of SW Yukon Territory. [C. D. *Macaulay*, territorial judge c.1958]

macaw /məˈkɔ/ *noun* any long-tailed brightly coloured parrot of the genus *Ara* or *Anodorhynchus*, native to S and Central America. [Portuguese *macao*, of unknown origin]

Mac·beth (c.1005–57), king of Scotland 1040–57. He came to the throne after murdering Duncan I, but was himself killed 17 years later by Malcolm III; he is chiefly remembered as the subject of one of Shakespeare's tragedies.

Mac·Bride, Sean (1904–88), Irish statesman, who served as

---

t top v voice w we z zoo ʃ she ʒ vision θ thin ð this ŋ ring x loch tʃ chip dʒ jar   *(see over for vowels)*

chairman of Amnesty International (1961–75), and UN commissioner for Namibia (1973–7); he was awarded the Nobel Peace Prize in 1974.

Macc. *abbreviation* Maccabees (Apocrypha).

Mac·ca·baeus see JUDAS MACCABAEUS.

Mac·ca·bean /ˌmakəˈbiːən/ *adjective* of, pertaining to, or reminiscent of Judas Maccabaeus or the Maccabees.

Mac·ca·bee /ˈmakəˌbiː/ *noun* **1** any of a Jewish family (or their supporters), members of which (esp. Judas Maccabaeus) led a religious revolt in Judea against the Seleucid king, Antiochus IV Epiphanes, from around 167 BC, thus stemming the threatened destruction of Judaism by the advance of Hellenism. **2** (**the Maccabees**) four books of Jewish history and theology, of which the first two (whose hero is Judas Maccabaeus) are included in the Apocrypha. [Latin *Maccabaeus* from Greek, epithet of Judas, perhaps from Hebrew *maqāb* hammer]

mac·chi·ato /makiˈatoː/ *noun* (*pl.* **-atos**) coffee served with a very small amount of hot milk or milk froth. [Italian (*caffè*) *macchiato*, from *caffè* 'coffee' + *macchiato* 'stained']

Mac·Don·ald ▸ **1 James Ed·ward Her·vey** (1873–1932), English-born Canadian painter, a key member of the Group of Seven. His paintings, often inspired by Algoma (north of Lake Superior), feature a dark palette and an elegant style. **2 (James) Ram·say** (1866–1937), Scottish Labour politician, prime minister 1924, 1929–31, and 1931–5. He became Britain's first Labour prime minister in 1924; elected prime minister again in 1929, but faced with economic crisis and dissent in his own party, he formed a national government with some Conservatives and Liberals, and was expelled from the Labour Party (1931).

Mac·don·ald ▸ **1 An·drew Archi·bald** (1829–1912), Canadian politician, Father of Confederation. He represented PEI at the Quebec Conference and served as PEI's Lieutenant-Governor 1884–1889. **2 Angus Lewis** (1890–1954), Canadian lawyer and politician, Liberal premier of Nova Scotia 1933–40 and 1945–54. As premier he implemented old-age pensions; during the Second World War he served as federal minister of naval services. **3 Brian** (b.1928), Canadian choreographer and theatre director. A founding member of the National Ballet of Canada in 1951, he subsequently devoted himself to teaching and choreography, and has directed many musical productions at Stratford. **4 James Wil·liam Gal·lo·way** ('Jock') (1897–1960), Scottish-born Canadian artist. In addition to becoming one of the first abstract painters in Canada, he was important as a teacher of art in Vancouver, Calgary and Toronto. **5 Sir John Alex·an·der** (1815–1891), Scottish-born Canadian lawyer, businessman and politician, first prime minister of Canada (1867–73 and 1878–91). He was the key architect of the British North America Act. His terms of office saw the entry of Manitoba, the North-West Territories, BC, and PEI into Confederation as well as the building of the CPR. **6 John Sand·field** (1812–72), Canadian lawyer and politician, first premier of Ontario (1867–71). An opponent of federalism, he recognized that it was inevitable and ran for provincial election with Sir John A. Macdonald on a joint federal-provincial platform.

Mac·Don·nell /ˌmakdəˈnel/ **Miles** (c.1767–1828), Scottish-born Canadian soldier and politician. He served as a captain in the Royal Canadian Volunteers 1796–1802, and was made the first governor of Assiniboia by Lord Selkirk in 1811, leading the initial settlers to Red River in 1812.

Mac·Don·nell Ranges /məkˈdɒnəl/ a series of mountain ranges extending westward from Alice Springs in Northern Territory, Australia. The highest peak is Mount Liebig, which rises to a height of 1 524 m (4,948 ft.). [Sir R. *MacDonnell*, British colonial governor d.1881]

mace¹ *noun* **1** a staff of office, esp. the symbol of the Speaker's authority in the House of Commons. **2** *hist.* a heavy club usu. having a metal head and spikes. **3** = MACE BEARER. [Old French *mace, masse* from Romanic *mattea* (unrecorded) club]

mace² *noun* an irritant chemical preparation used in aerosol form as a disabling weapon. ● *transitive verb* spray (a person) with mace. [US proprietary name, prob. from MACE¹]

mace³ *noun* the dried outer covering of the nutmeg, used as a spice. [Old French *macis* from Latin *macir* a red spicy bark]

mace bearer *noun* an official who carries a mace on ceremonial occasions.

macé·doine /ˈmasɪˌdwan/ *noun* **1** mixed vegetables or fruit, esp. cut up small or in jelly. **2** a medley or mixture. [French, = Macedonia, with reference to the mixture of peoples there]

Mace·donia /ˌmasəˈdɔːnɪə/ **1** (also **Mace·don** /ˈmasədən/) an ancient country in SE Europe, at the northern end of the Greek peninsula, including the coastal plain around Thessaloníki and the mountain ranges behind. In classical times it was a kingdom which under Philip II and Alexander the Great became a world power. The region is now divided between Greece, Bulgaria, and the republic of Macedonia (see sense 3). **2** a region in the northeast of modern Greece; capital, Thessaloníki. **3** a landlocked republic in the Balkans; pop. (est. 2002) 2,054,800; capital, Skopje. Formerly a constituent republic of Yugoslavia, Macedonia became independent after a referendum in 1991. □ **Mace·do·nian** *noun & adjective*

Macedonian Wars a series of four wars between Rome and Macedonia (214–148 BC), in which Philip V of Macedonia and his son Perseus were successively defeated by the Romans, resulting ultimately in Macedonia becoming a Roman Province.

Maceió /ˌmaseiˈoː/ a port in E Brazil, on the Atlantic coast; pop. (est. 2002) 850,500.

macer·ate /ˈmasəˌreit/ *transitive & intransitive verb* make or become soft by soaking. □ **macer·a·tion** *noun* **macer·ator** *noun* [Latin *macerare macerat-*]

Mac·Ewen /məˈkjuːən/ **Gwen·do·lyn** (1941–87), Canadian poet and novelist whose work celebrated her love of history, magic, and, above all, poetry. Her 1969 poetry collection, *The Shadow-Maker*, was awarded the Governor General's Award.

Mac·gil·li·cuddy's Reeks /məˌɡɪləˌkʌdiz ˈriːks/ a range of hills in County Kerry in SW Ireland.

Mac·Guffin *noun* = MCGUFFIN.

Mach¹ /ˈmɒk/ **Ernst** (1838–1916), Austrian physicist and philosopher of science. In commemoration of his work on aerodynamics, his name has been preserved in the Mach number.

Mach² /mɒk, mak/ *noun* (in full **Mach number**) the ratio of the speed of a body to the speed of sound in the surrounding medium. ¶ Often as *Mach 1, 2,* etc., indicating the speed of sound, twice the speed of sound, etc. [E. MACH¹]

ma·chaca /məˈtʃɒkə/ *noun* a Mexican dish consisting of strips of dried meat (esp. beef) shredded, pounded to a pulp, and fried with onions, egg, tomatoes, peppers, etc. [Mexican Spanish from Spanish *machacar* 'to pound, to crush']

mâche /mɒʃ/ *noun* = LAMB'S LETTUCE. [French]

mach·er /ˈmaxər/ *noun* esp. *N Amer.* usu. *derogatory* an important or overbearing person. [Yiddish *makher*, from Middle High German *Macher* 'doer, active person']

ma·chete /məˈʃeti/ *noun* a broad heavy knife, originally used in Central America and the W Indies as an implement and weapon. [Spanish from *macho* hammer, from Late Latin *marcus*]

Ma·chia·velli /ˌmakiəˈveli/ **Nic·colò di Ber·nar·do dei** (1469–1527), Italian political philosopher. His best-known work is *The Prince* (1532), a treatise on statecraft advising rulers that the acquisition and effective use of power may necessitate unethical methods that are not in themselves desirable.

Ma·chia·vel·lian /ˌmakiəˈveliən/ ● *adjective* **1** elaborately cunning; scheming, unscrupulous. **2** of, pertaining to, or characteristic of Machiavelli or his principles. ● *noun* **1** a person preferring expediency to morality. **2** a person who adopts the principles recommended by Machiavelli in his treatise on statecraft. □ **Ma·chia·vel·lian·ism** *noun* [MACHIAVELLI]

ma·chico·late /məˈtʃɪkəˌleit/ *transitive verb* furnish (a structure, parapet, etc.) with openings between supporting corbels for dropping stones etc. on attackers. □ **ma·chico·la·tion** *noun* [Old French *machicoler*, ultimately from Provençal *machacol* from *macar* crush + *col* neck]

ma·chico·lat·ed /məˈtʃɪkəˌleitəd/ *adjective* (of a structure, parapet, etc.) having openings between supporting corbels for dropping stones etc. on attackers.

ma·chin·able *adjective* capable of being cut by machine tools.

ma·chin·a·tion /maʃɪˈneiʃən, makɪ-/ *noun* (usu. in *pl.*) a cunning plot or scheme. [Latin *machinari* contrive (as MACHINE)]

ma·chine ● *noun* **1** an apparatus using or applying mechanical power, having several parts, each with a definite function which together perform certain kinds of work. **2** a particular kind of machine, e.g. a vehicle, piece of electrical or electronic apparatus, etc. **3** an instrument that transmits a force or directs its application. **4 a** the controlling system of a political party, a similar organization, etc. (*the Big Blue Machine*). **b** a well-organized group acting with often ruthless efficiency. **5** a person who acts mechanically and with apparent lack of emotion. **6** (esp. in *combination*) a coin-operated dispenser (*vending* *machine*; *pop machine*). ● *transitive verb* **1** cut, make, form, or operate on by means of a machine. **2** engrave, shape, print, or sew (a thing) by means of a machine. □ **ma·chin·ing** *noun & adjective* [Latin *machina* from Greek *makhana* from *mēkhos* contrivance]

machine age *noun* an era notable for its extensive use of mechanical devices, esp. the present age so considered.

machine code *noun* (also **machine language**) a language that a particular computer can handle or act on directly, without further translation (compare SOURCE CODE).

machine gun ● *noun* **1** a mounted or portable gun which is mechanically loaded and fired, giving continuous fire while the trigger is pressed. **2** (**machine-gun**) (*attributive*) like a machine gun, esp. in rapidly and usu. noisily repeated action. ● *transitive verb* (**machine-gun**) (**-gunned**, **-gun·ning**) shoot at with a machine gun. □ **machine gunner** *noun*

machine pistol *noun* an automatic pistol; a light machine gun.

machine-readable *adjective* (of data) in a form that a computer can process.

ma·chin·ery *noun* (*pl.* **-ies**) **1** machines collectively or in general. **2** the moving parts or mechanism of a machine. **3** (foll. by *of*) an organized system (*the machinery of government*). **4** (foll. by *for*) the means or procedures devised or available (*the machinery for decision-making*).

machine screw *noun* a small, threaded screw, usu. with a slotted or socket head, for fastening metal parts together.

machine shed *noun* *Cdn* (*West*) a small, auxiliary structure or outbuilding in which machines, equipment, implements, etc. are kept.

machine shop *noun* a workshop for making or repairing machines or parts of machines.

machine tool *noun* a mechanically operated tool for working on metal, wood, or plastics.

machine-tooled *adjective* **1** shaped by a machine tool. **2** (of artistic presentation etc.) precise, slick, esp. excessively so.

machine translation *noun* the translation of a text from one human, natural language to another by means of a computer.

machine washable *adjective* (of clothes etc.) able to be washed in a washing machine without damage. □ **machine wash** *transitive verb*

ma·chin·ist /məˈʃiːnɪst/ *noun* **1** a person who operates a machine, esp. a machine tool. **2** a person who makes, invents, or controls machines or machinery; an engineer.

ma·chis·mo /məˈtʃɪzmoː, -ˈkɪzmoː/ *noun* **1** exaggerated or aggressive pride in being male. **2** a show of such assertive manliness or masculinity. [Spanish from *macho* 'male' from Latin *masculus*]

Mach·meter /ˈmɒkˌmiːtər, ˈmak-/ *noun* an instrument indicating airspeed in the form of a Mach number.

Mach number *noun* see MACH².

macho /ˈmɒtʃoː, ˈmatʃoː/ ● *adjective* aggressively or ostentatiously masculine. ● *noun* = MACHISMO. [MACHISMO]

Machu Pic·chu /ˌmɒtʃuː ˈpiːktʃuː/ a fortified Inca town in the Andes in Peru, which the invading Spaniards never found; it was discovered in 1911. Not an important fortress but famous for its dramatic position, Machu Picchu is perched high on a steep-sided ridge. It contains a palace, a temple to the sun, and extensive cultivation terraces. [after the mountain that rises above it]

Ma·cias Nguema /məˌsiːəs əŋˈgweimə/ a former name (1973–9) for BIOKO.

mac·in·tosh *var.* of MACKINTOSH.

Mac·Isaac /məˈkaɪsɪk/ (**Ash·ley** (**Dwayne**) (b.1975), Canadian fiddler who blends traditional Celtic music with more modern styles. His energetic performances and creative music videos helped make his 1995 album, *Hi How Are You Today?* and the 1996 follow-up *Fine Thank You Very Much* national bestsellers.

mack¹ *var.* of MAC.

mack² *noun* *US informal* a pimp or playboy. [shortening of rare *mackerel* 'procurer']

mack daddy *noun* esp. *US informal* a successful pimp or criminal, esp. one who acts or dresses in a way regarded as characteristic of such a person.

Mac·ken·zie¹ a district municipality in NE central BC, situated on Williston Lake, about 180 km north of Prince George; pop. (2001) 5,206. [Sir A. MACKENZIE²]

Mac·ken·zie² ▸ **1** **Sir Alex·an·der** (1822–92), Scottish-born Canadian builder, newspaper editor, and politician, second prime minister of Canada (1873–78). A supporter of Confederation, he was elected to both the House of Commons and the Ontario legislature in

1867. As prime minister he formed the first Liberal Canadian government; his administration saw the creation of the Supreme Court, the office of the Auditor General, and the foundations of the modern electoral system. **2** **Sir Alex·an·der** (1764–1820), Scottish-born fur trader and explorer of Canada. In 1789 Mackenzie, working for the North West Company, travelled from Fort Chipewyan on Lake Athabasca northwest along the Mackenzie River to the Arctic Ocean. Four years later he travelled southwest from Fort Chipewyan to the Pacific, becoming the first European explorer to reach the Pacific. He returned to Britain in 1799. **3** **Sir Wil·liam** (1849–1923), Canadian railroad entrepreneur. In 1895 he began to assemble a network of prairie railroad lines that would eventually become the basis of the Canadian Northern Railway, which on completion in 1915 ran from Victoria to Halifax. **4** **Wil·liam Lyon** (1795–1861), Scottish-born Canadian journalist and politician, Upper Canada rebellion leader. First elected to the legislative assembly of Upper Canada in 1828, he visited England in 1832 to present the Reform movement's grievances to the imperial cabinet. In 1834 he was elected the first mayor of Toronto. In December 1837, he led an armed force down Yonge St. towards Toronto; the party was intercepted by the local militia and Mackenzie fled to the US, where he remained until pardoned in 1849.

Mackenzie, District of a former district (est. 1895) of the NWT, occupying the western and central mainland region.

Mackenzie King Island one of the Parry Islands in the Canadian High Arctic, situated south of Borden Island. [W. L. Mackenzie KING]

Mackenzie Mountains a mountain range straddling the border between the NWT and Yukon Territory, a northern extension of the Rocky Mountains. [Sir A. MACKENZIE²]

Mackenzie-Papineau Battalion a Canadian military formation of approximately 1300 volunteers which fought in the International Brigades against the Nationalist forces of General Franco during the Spanish Civil War. [W. L. MACKENZIE² and L.-J. PAPINEAU]

Mackenzie River the longest river in Canada, flowing 4 241 km (including its headwaters, the Finlay River, which rises in north central BC, and the Peace River), whose main stream flows generally northwestward approx. 1 700 km from Great Slave Lake to Mackenzie Bay, an inlet of the Beaufort Sea. [Sir A. MACKENZIE²]

mack·erel /ˈmakrəl/ *noun* (*pl.* same or **mack·erels**) any of various swift-swimming pelagic fishes of the family Scombridae, of which several are commercially important as food fishes, esp. *Scomber scombrus*, of the N Atlantic and Mediterranean, which approaches the shore in shoals in summer for spawning. [Old French *maquerel*]

mackerel shark *noun* a shark of the family Lamnidae, esp. the porbeagle.

mackerel sky *noun* a sky dappled with rows of small white fleecy clouds, like the pattern on a mackerel's back.

mack·i·naw /ˈmakɪnɒ/ *noun* *N Amer.* **1 a** a heavy, napped and felted woollen cloth, now usu. with a plaid design. **b** (in full **mackinaw coat** or **mackinaw jacket**) a thick, double-breasted jacket, usu. short and often belted, made of this cloth. **2** (in full **Mackinaw trout**) = LAKE TROUT. [*Mackinaw* City, Michigan, an important trading post]

Mack·in·tosh, Charles Ren·nie (1868–1928), Scottish architect and designer. A leading exponent of art nouveau, he pioneered the new concept of functionalism in architecture and interior design; his works include the Glasgow School of Art (1898–1909).

mack·in·tosh *noun* (also **macintosh**) **1** esp. *Brit.* a waterproof coat or cloak. **2** cloth waterproofed with rubber. [C. *Macintosh*, Scottish inventor d.1843, who originally patented the cloth]

macle /ˈmakəl/ *noun* a diamond or other crystal that is twinned. [French from Latin *macula* blemish: see MACULA]

Mac·lean /məˈkleɪn/ **1** **Don·ald** (**Duart**) (1913–83), English Foreign Office official and Soviet spy. After acting as a Soviet agent from the late 1930s, he fled to the USSR with Guy Burgess in 1951. **2** **John Bayne** (1862–1950), Canadian publisher. He founded *The Financial Post* (1907) and *Chatelaine* (1928); he purchased *Busy Man's Magazine* in 1905 and renamed it *Maclean's* in 1911. His company, named Maclean Hunter in 1933, became Canada's largest publisher of magazines.

Mac·leish /məˈkliːʃ/ **Archi·bald** (1892–1982), US poet and playwright.

Mac·Len·nan, (John) Hugh (1907–90), Canadian novelist and professor. He published his first successful novel, *Barometer Rising*, in 1941, and followed it with many others including *Two Solitudes* (1945) and *The Watch that Ends the Night* (1959). He won 5 Governor General's Awards, three for fiction and two for non-fiction, and is known as the first significant English-speaking author to attempt to define the Canadian character.

Mac·leod /məˈklaud/ **1 Alis·tair** (b.1936), Canadian writer. Many of his stories, including his 1999 novel *No Great Mischief*, are set in the Cape Breton of his youth. **2 James Far·quhar·son** (1836–94), Scottish-born Canadian police officer and judge. As commissioner of the NWMP 1876–80, he suppressed the whisky trade and negotiated a treaty with the Blackfoot. **3 John James Rick·ard** (1876–1935), Scottish-born physiologist. He came to the University of Toronto in 1918, and in 1921 gave F.G. Banting lab space and a student assistant to conduct research into the pancreas. He shared the 1923 Nobel Prize for the discovery of insulin, but his role was downplayed by Banting and Best.

Mac·Master, **Nat·alie** (b.1972), Canadian fiddler and step dancer. Her exuberant style, showcased on *Fit As a Fiddle* (1993) and *My Roots Are Showing* (1997), has generated new interest in Canadian Celtic music.

Mac·Mil·lan ▸ 1 Sir Er·nest Alex·an·der Camp·bell (1893–1973), Canadian conductor and educator. Internationally recognized as a conductor of symphonic and choral music, he served as principal of the Toronto (later Royal) Conservatory of Music (1926–42), dean of the Faculty of Music at the University of Toronto (1927–52), and conductor of the Toronto Symphony (1931–56) and Toronto Mendelssohn Choir (1942–56). **2 Har·vey Reg·in·ald** (1885–1976), Canadian businessman. In 1919 he formed H.R. MacMillan Export Co., which quickly became a major exporter of lumber. The company merged with Bloedel, Stewart and Welch in 1951 to become MacMillan Bloedel, Canada's largest forest-products company. **3 Sir Ken·neth** (1929–92), British dancer, choreographer, and ballet director. He choreographed many ballets for the Royal Ballet, of which he was director 1970–77, including *Manon* and *Elite Syncopations* (both 1974) and *Romeo and Juliet* (1965).

Mac·mil·lan, (Mau·rice) Har·old, 1st Earl of Stock·ton (1894–1986), English Conservative politician, prime minister 1957–63. He played an important part in the negotiation of the Nuclear Test Ban Treaty (1963) between the US and the USSR, and advocated the granting of independence to British colonies.

Mac·Neice /məkˈniːs/ **(Fred·erick) Louis** (1907–63), Northern Irish poet. His work is characterized by the use of assonance, internal rhymes, and ballad-like repetitions.

Mac·Neil /məkˈniːl/ **Rita** (b.1944), Canadian singer. Her songs blend folk, pop and country influences and have earned her several Juno awards, but she is perhaps best known as host of CBC television's *The Rita MacNeil Show* (1994–97).

Mac·phail /məkˈfeil/ **Agnes Camp·bell** (1890–1954), Canadian politician. The first woman MP, she was elected to the House of Commons in 1921, the first year in which women were allowed to vote, and sat until 1940; she was also an Ontario MPP from 1942–45 and 1948–51. An active supporter of disarmament, she also supported prison reform and women's rights.

Mac·pher·son /məkˈfɜrsən/ **James** (1736–96), Scottish poet and translator, who allegedly translated the poems of a 3rd-c. Gaelic poet, Ossian; these works were in fact compilations of his own writing and passages from existing Gaelic poems.

Mac·qua·rie River a river in New South Wales, Australia, rising on the western slopes of the Great Dividing Range and flowing 960 km (600 miles) northwest to join the Darling River, of which it is a headwater. [L. *Macquarie*, Scottish-born Australian colonial administrator d.1824]

mac·ramé /ˈmakrəmei/ *noun* **1** the art of knotting cord or string in patterns to make decorative articles. **2** articles made in this way. [Turkish *makrama* 'bedspread', from Arabic *miḵrama*]

macro • *noun* Computing a series of abbreviated instructions expanded automatically when required. **•** *adjective* **1** large-scale. **2** overall, comprehensive. [independent use of MACRO-]

macro- *combining form* **1** long, large, large-scale. **2** comprehensive. **3** *Med.* abnormally enlarged or elongated. [Greek *makro-* from *makros* long, large]

macro·biot·ic /ˌmakroʊbaiˈɒtɪk/ **•** *adjective* **1** relating to or following an originally Zen Buddhist dietary system intended to prolong life, usu. comprised of pure vegetable foods, brown rice, etc. **2** tending to prolong life; relating to the prolongation of life. **•** *noun* (in *pl.*) treated as *sing.*) the use or theory of such a dietary system.

macro·carpa /ˌmakroʊˈkɑrpə/ *noun* an evergreen tree, *Cupressus macrocarpa*, often cultivated for hedges or windbreaks. [modern Latin from Greek MACRO- + *karpos* fruit]

macro·ceph·alic /ˌmakroʊsəˈfalɪk/ *adjective* (also **macro·ceph·al·ous** /-ˈsefələs/) having a long or large head. □ **macro·ceph·aly** /-ˈsefəli/ *noun*

macro·cosm /ˈmakroʊˌkɒzəm/ *noun* **1** the universe; the whole of all nature. **2** a complex structure or whole, esp. one considered to be epitomized by some constituent portion or microcosm. □ **macro·cos·mic** *adjective*

macro·econom·ics *noun* the study of large-scale or general economic factors, e.g. national productivity (compare MICROECONOMICS). □ **macro·econom·ic** *adjective* **macro·econo·mist** *noun*

macro·evo·lu·tion *noun* Biol. major evolutionary change, esp. over a long period. □ **macro·evo·lu·tion·ary** *adjective*

macro lens *noun* a large lens used to focus on very near objects in close-up photography.

macro·mol·ecule *noun* a molecule containing a very large number of atoms and having a very high molecular weight, e.g. a molecule of a polymer, protein, or nucleic acid. □ **macro·molecu·lar** *adjective*

mac·ron /ˈmakrɒn/ *noun* a written or printed mark (ˉ) over a long or stressed vowel. [Greek *makron* neuter of *makros* large]

macro·nutri·ent *noun* a chemical required in relatively large amounts for the growth and development of living organisms.

macro·phage /ˈmakroʊˌfeidʒ/ *noun* a large phagocytic white blood cell usu. occurring at points of infection. □ **macroph·a·gous** *adjective*

macro·phyte /ˈmakroʊˌfəit/ *noun* any plant, esp. an aquatic plant, large enough to be discerned by the naked eye.

macro·pod /ˈmakroʊˌpɒd/ *noun* any plant-eating mammal of the family Macropodidae native to Australia and New Guinea, including kangaroos and wallabies. [MACRO- + Greek *pous podos* foot]

macro·scop·ic /ˌmakroʊˈskɒpɪk/ *adjective* **1** visible to the naked eye. **2** general, comprehensive; regarded in terms of large units. □ **macro·scop·ic·ally** *adverb*

mac·ula /ˈmakjʊlə/ *noun* (*pl.* **mac·ulae** /-ˌliː/) **1** a dark spot, esp. a permanent one, in the skin, e.g. a freckle. **2** (in full **macula lutea** /ˈluːtiə/) an oval yellowish area surrounding the fovea near the centre of the retina, where visual acuity is most pronounced. □ **macu·lar** *adjective* **macu·la·tion** /-ˈleiʃən/ *noun* [Latin, = spot, mesh]

MAD /mad/ *noun* = MUTUAL ASSURED DESTRUCTION.

mad *adjective* (**mad·der**, **mad·dest**) **1** insane; having a disordered mind. **2** (of a person, conduct, or an idea) wildly foolish. **3** (often foll. by *about*, *on*) carried away by enthusiasm or desire (*mad about football*; *is power-mad*). **4** *informal* **a** beside oneself with anger; furious. **b** annoyed, exasperated. **5** (of an animal) **a** suffering from rabies. **b** abnormally furious. **6 a** frantic, wild, desperate (*made a mad dash*). **b** wildly lighthearted. **7** (of a storm, wind, etc.) wild, violent. □ **like mad** *informal* with great energy, intensity, or enthusiasm. **mad as a hatter** see HATTER. [Old English *gemǣded* part. form from *gemād* mad]

Mada·gas·car /ˌmadəˈgaskɑr/ an island country in the Indian Ocean, off the east coast of Africa; pop. (est. 2002) 16,473,477; capital, Antananarivo. □ **Mada·gas·can** *adjective & noun*

Madagascar periwinkle *noun* a shrub native to Madagascar, *Catharanthus roseus*, widely grown in gardens and as a houseplant. Also called ROSY PERIWINKLE.

madam *noun* **1** a polite or respectful form of address or mode of reference to a woman. **2** a woman who keeps a brothel. **3** *Brit. informal* a conceited or precocious girl or young woman. [Old French *ma dame* my lady]

Ma·dame /məˈdam, ˈmadəm/ *noun* **1** (*pl.* **Mes·dames** /meiˈdam/) a title or form of address used of or to a French-speaking woman, corresponding to Mrs. or madam. **2** (**madame**) = MADAM 1. [French (as MADAM)]

Madame, Isle /məˈdam/ an island off the southern shore of Cape Breton Island. It lies to the north of Canso, at the entrance to Chedabucto Bay. [origin uncertain]

Mada·was·kan *Cdn* **•** *noun* a resident of the Madawaska region of NW New Brunswick. **•** *adjective* of or pertaining to Madawaskans.

Mada·was·ka River /ˌmadəˈwɒskə/ **1** a river in east central Ontario, which rises northeast of Huntsville and flows generally southeastward to join the Ottawa River at Arnprior. **2** a river in E Quebec and NW New Brunswick, issuing from Lac Témiscouata and flowing southeastward to join the Saint John River at Edmundston. [sense 1 possibly after the *Matouoüescarini*, an Algonquin band whose name means 'people of the shallows'; sense 2 from Maliseet *medaweskak* 'porcupine place', or 'murmuring at the mouth']

mad·cap • *adjective* **1** (of a person) reckless, wildly impulsive. **2** (of an endeavour etc.) undertaken without forethought. **•** *noun* a wildly impulsive person.

mad cow disease *noun informal* = BSE 1.

Consonants: b *but*   d *dog*   f *few*   g *get*   h *her*   j *yes*   k *cat*   l *leg*   m *man*   n *no*   p *pen*   r *red*   s *sit*

mad·den *verb* **1** *transitive & intransitive* make or become mad. **2** *transitive* irritate intensely. □ **mad·den·ing** *adjective* **mad·den·ing·ly** *adverb*

mad·der /'madər/ *noun* **1** a herbaceous plant, *Rubia tinctorum*, with yellowish flowers. **2** a reddish-purple dye obtained from the root of the madder, or its synthetic substitute. [Old English *mædere*]

mad·ding *adjective* □ **far from the madding crowd** (of a place) secluded, removed from public notice.

made ● *verb* past and past participle of MAKE. ● *adjective* **1** (usu. in *combination*) **a** (of a person or thing) built or formed artificially or in a specified manner (*well-made; strongly-made*). **b** successful (*a self-made man*). **2** *US slang* (of a person) formally inducted as a full member of the Mafia or other criminal organization. □ **be made for** be ideally suited to. **be made of** consist of. **have it made** *informal* be sure of success. **made to order** *see* ORDER.

made beaver *noun Cdn hist.* (*pl.* often same) **1** a unit of exchange formerly used among fur traders, equivalent to the value of the prepared skin of one adult beaver in prime condition. **2** a coin or token equivalent to this.

made-for-TV *adjective* (also **made-for-television**) **1** (of a film etc.) specially made for first showing on television, not in theatres. **2** (of a set, event, sound bite, etc.) ideally suited to television.

Ma·dei·ra[1] /mə'dɪːrə/ an island in the Atlantic Ocean off NW Africa, belonging to Portugal; pop. (2001) 242,600; capital, Funchal.
□ **Ma·deir·an** *noun & adjective*

Ma·dei·ra[2] *noun* **1** a fortified white wine from the island of Madeira. **2** (in full **Madeira cake**) *Brit.* = POUND CAKE.

Madeira River a river in NW Brazil, which rises on the Bolivian border and flows about 1 450 km (900 miles) to meet the Amazon east of Manaus. It is navigable to large ocean-going vessels as far as Pôrto Velho.

mad·el·eine /'madə‚len/ *noun* a small, shell-shaped sponge cake. [French]

Mad·el·eine, Îles de la /mad'len/ (also **Magdalen Islands** /'magdələn/) a group of sixteen islands belonging to Quebec, situated in the Gulf of St. Lawrence, about 100 km northwest of Cape Breton Island. [*Madeleine* Fontaine, wife of F. Doublet, early seigneur *c*.1663]

Made·lin·ot /madəli'no:/ *noun Cdn* a resident or native of the Magdalen Islands. [French, from 'Madeleine']

made man *noun* a man who has attained success or whose success in life is assured.

Ma·demoi·selle /‚madmwə'zel/ *noun* (*pl.* **Mes·demoi·selles** /‚meidm-/) **1** a title or form of address used of or to an unmarried French-speaking woman, corresponding to Miss or madam. **2** (**mademoiselle**) **a** a young Frenchwoman. **b** a French governess. [French from *ma* my + *demoiselle* DAMSEL]

mader·iza·tion /‚madərai'zeiʃən/ *noun* a form of oxidation which gives white wine a brownish colour and caramelized flavour like that of Madeira. □ **mader·ized** *adjective* [French *madérisation*, from *madériser*, from *Madère* 'Madeira']

made-to-measure *adjective* **1** (of clothing, draperies, etc.) made to a specific customer's measurements, specifications, etc. **2** conceived, designed, or particularly suited for a specific situation etc.

made up *adjective* (hyphenated when *attributive*) **1** invented, not true. **2** (of a person) wearing makeup. **3** (of a meal etc.) already prepared.

mad·house *noun* **1** *esp. hist.* a home or hospital for the mentally ill. **2** *informal* a scene of extreme confusion or uproar.

Madhya Pra·desh /‚mʌdjə prə'deʃ/ a large state in central India, formed in 1956; capital, Bhopal.

Madi·son[1] the state capital of Wisconsin; pop. (2000) 208,054. [J. MADISON[2]]

Madi·son[2], **James** (1751–1836), US Democratic Republican politician, 4th president of the US 1809–17. Before taking office, he played a leading part in drawing up the US Constitution (1787) and proposed the Bill of Rights (1791).

Madison Avenue *noun* **1** a street in New York where many American advertising agencies have their offices. **2 a** the American advertising industry. **b** the attitudes and methods characteristic of this industry. **c** American advertising agents collectively.

madly *adverb* **1** in a mad, insane, or foolish manner. **2 a** passionately, fervently. **b** extremely, very.

mad·man *noun* (*pl.* **-men**) an insane, wildly foolish, or furious man.

mad money *noun* **1** a small reserve of cash for use in an emergency, on petty extravagances, etc. **2** *dated* emergency cash carried by a woman on a date for bus fare etc. if needed.

mad·ness *noun* the quality or state of being mad.

Ma·donna[1] /mə'dɒnə/ *noun Christianity* **1** (prec. by *the*) a name for the Virgin Mary. **2** (usu. **madonna**) a picture or statue of the Madonna. [Italian from *ma* = *mia* my + *donna* lady, from Latin *domina*]

Ma·donna[2] (born Madonna Louise Veronica Ciccone) (b.1958), US pop singer and actress. She rose to international stardom in the mid-1980s through her records and accompanying videos.

ma·donna lily *noun* the white *Lilium candidum*, as shown in many pictures of the Madonna.

Ma·dras /mə'dras, -'drɒs/ **1** the former name (until 1995) for CHENNAI, a seaport on the east coast of India, capital of Tamil Nadu; pop. (2001) 4,298,600. **2** the former name (until 1968) for the state of Tamil Nadu.

ma·dras /mə'dras/ *noun* **1** a strong cotton fabric with brightly coloured or white stripes, checks, etc. **2** (**Madras**; in full **Madras curry**) a hot spiced curry dish usu. made with chicken or beef. [MADRAS]

madre·pore /'madrə‚pɔr/ *noun* **1** any perforated coral of the genus *Madrepora*. **2** the animal producing this. [Italian *madrepora* from *madre* mother + *poro* PORE[1]]

Ma·drid /mə'drɪd/ the capital of Spain; pop. (est. 2001) 2,957,058.

mad·rigal /'madrɪgəl/ *noun* **1** a usu. 16th-c. or 17th-c. part-song for several voices, usu. arranged in elaborate counterpoint and without instrumental accompaniment. **2** a short love poem. □ **mad·rigal·ist** *noun* [Italian *madrigale* from medieval Latin *matricalis* mother (church)]

ma·droño /mə'dro:njo:/ *noun* (*pl.* **-droños**) (also **ma·droña**, **ma·drone** /-njə/) an evergreen tree, *Arbutus menziesii*, of western N America, with white flowers, red berries, and glossy leaves. ¶ In Canada usu. called ARBUTUS. [Spanish]

mad scientist *noun* a wildly eccentric or dangerously insane scientist, esp. as a stock figure in melodramatic horror stories.

Mad Trapper *see* Albert JOHNSON.

Ma·dura /mə'dʊrə/ an island of Indonesia, off the northeast coast of Java. □ **Madur·ese** *adjective & noun*

Madu·rai /'madjʊ‚rai/ a city in Tamil Nadu in S India; pop. (2001) 922,900.

mad·woman *noun* (*pl.* **-women**) an insane, wildly foolish, or furious woman.

Mae·ce·nas /mai'si:nəs/ *noun* a generous patron of literature or art. [Gaius (Cilnius) Maecenas, Roman statesman d.8 BC, patron of poets such as Virgil and Horace]

M.A.Ed. *abbreviation* Master of Arts in Education.

mael·strom /'meilstrəm/ *noun* **1** a great whirlpool. **2** a state of turbulence or confusion. [early modern Dutch from *malen* grind, whirl + *stroom* STREAM]

mae·nad /'mi:nad/ *noun* **1** a bacchante. **2** a frenzied woman. □ **mae·nad·ism** *noun* [Latin *Maenas Maenad-* from Greek *Mainas -ados* from *mainomai* rave]

maes·toso /mai'sto:zo:/ *Music* ● *adjective & adverb* to be performed majestically. ● *noun* (*pl.* **-tosos**) a piece of music to be performed in this way. [Italian]

maes·tro /'maistro:/ *noun* (*pl.* **-tros**) (often as a respectful form of address) **1** a distinguished musician, esp. a conductor or performer. **2** a great performer in any sphere, esp. artistic. [Italian, = master]

Maeter·linck /'meitər‚lɪŋk/ **Mau·rice** (1862–1949), Belgian poet, dramatist, and essayist, a leading figure in the symbolist movement. His play *Pelléas et Mélisande* (1892) was the source of Debussy's opera of that name (1902); he was awarded the Nobel Prize for literature in 1911.

Mae West *noun* an inflatable life jacket. [M. WEST, noted for her large bust]

Mafe·king /'mafə‚kɪŋ/ (also **Mafi·keng**) a town in South Africa, in North-West Province. In 1899–1900, during the Second Boer War, a small British force under the command of Baden-Powell was besieged there by the Boers for 215 days. Although the town was of little strategic significance, its successful defence, at a time when the war was going very badly for the British, excited great interest, while its relief was hailed almost with a national sense of jubilation.

Mafia /'mɒfiə, 'ma-/ *noun* **1** an organized secret society of criminals, originating in Sicily but now operating internationally, esp. in the US. **2** (**mafia**) any closely united group regarded as exerting a secret and often sinister influence. [Italian dial. (Sicilian) = bragging]

mafic /'mafɪk/ *adjective* **1** of, pertaining to, or designating a group of dark coloured, mainly ferromagnesian minerals. **2** (of rocks) containing a high proportion of such minerals. [contraction of MAGNESIUM + FERRIC]

---

t *top*   v *voice*   w *we*   z *zoo*   ʃ *she*   ʒ *vision*   θ *thin*   ð *this*   ŋ *ring*   x *loch*   tʃ *chip*   dʒ *jar*   (*see over for vowels*)

Mafi·oso /ˌmafiˈoːsoː, ˌmɒ-/ *noun* (*pl.* **Mafi·osi** /-si/) **1** a member of the Mafia. **2** (**mafioso**) a member of a group regarded as exerting a hidden sinister influence. [Italian (as MAFIA)]

mag *noun* **1 a** *informal* a magazine (periodical). **b** *informal* a magazine (in a rifle, camera, etc.). **2** *informal* **a** magnesium. **b** magneto. **c** magnetic. **3** magnitude. [abbreviation]

Mag·adha /məˈɡʊdə/ an ancient kingdom situated in the valley of the River Ganges in NE India (modern Bihar) which was the centre of several empires, notably those of the Mauryan and Gupta dynasties, between the 6th c. BC and the 8th c. AD.

Mag·adi, Lake /məˈɡʊdi/ a salt lake in the Great Rift Valley, in S Kenya, with extensive deposits of sodium carbonate and other minerals.

mag·a·logue /ˈmaɡəlɒɡ/ *noun* a promotional catalogue or sales brochure designed to resemble a high-quality magazine. [blend of MAGAZINE + CATALOGUE]

maga·zine *noun* **1** a periodical publication containing articles, stories, etc. by various writers, usu. with photographs, illustrations, etc. **2** a chamber for holding a supply of cartridges to be fed automatically to the breech of a repeating rifle, machine gun, etc. **3** a similar device feeding a camera, slide projector, etc. **4 a** a building for the storage of arms, ammunition, and provisions for use in war. **b** a store for large quantities of explosives. **5** a regular television or radio broadcast format comprising a variety of entertainment or news items. [French *magasin* from Italian *magazzino* from Arabic *makāzin* pl. of *makzan* storehouse, from *kazana* store up]

mag·dalen /ˈmaɡdələn/ *noun* **1** *archaic* a reformed prostitute. **2** *hist.* a home for reformed prostitutes. [Mary *Magdalene* of Magdala in Galilee (Luke 8:2), identified (prob. wrongly) with the sinner of Luke 7:37]

Mag·da·lena /ˌmaɡdəˈleinə/ the principal river of Colombia, rising in the Andes and flowing northward for about 1 600 km (1,000 miles) to enter the Caribbean at Barranquilla.

Mag·dalen·ian /ˌmaɡdəˈliːniən/ ● *adjective* of the culture of the latest paleolithic period in Europe, characterized by fine horn and bone tools and a strong artistic tradition. ● *noun* the culture of this period. [French *Magdalénien* of La *Madeleine*, Dordogne, France, where remains were found]

Magdalen Islands see MADELEINE, ÎLES DE LA.

Mag·de·burg /ˈmaɡdəˌbɜrɡ/ an industrial city in Germany, the capital of Saxony-Anhalt, situated on the Elbe River and linked to the Rhine and Ruhr by the Mittelland Canal; pop. (est. 2002) 230,000.

mage /meidʒ/ *noun archaic* **1** a magician. **2** a wise and learned person. [Middle English, anglicized from MAGUS]

Magel·lan /məˈdʒelən, -ˈɡelən/ **Fer·di·nand** (*c.*1480–1521), Portuguese explorer in the service of Spain. In 1519 he sailed from Spain to S America, rounding the continent through the strait which now bears his name (1520), and reached the Philippines (1521), but was killed in a war on Cebu. The survivors sailed back to Spain around Africa, thereby completing the first circumnavigation of the globe (1522).

Magellan, Strait of a passage separating Tierra del Fuego and other islands from mainland S America, connecting the Atlantic and Pacific Oceans. [F. MAGELLAN]

Magel·lan·ic cloud /ˌmadʒɪˈlanɪk/ *noun* each of two small galaxies associated with the Milky Way and visible at night in the southern sky as cloudy spots. [F. MAGELLAN]

Magen David /mɒˈɡɪn dɒˈvid/ *noun* = STAR OF DAVID. [Hebrew, lit. 'shield of David']

ma·genta /məˈdʒentə/ ● *noun* **1** a brilliant mauvish-crimson shade. **2** an aniline dye of this colour; fuchsin. ● *adjective* of or coloured with magenta. [*Magenta* in N Italy, site of a battle (1859) fought shortly before the dye was discovered]

Mag·giore, Lake /ˌmadʒˈɔri/ the second largest of the lakes of N Italy, extending into S Switzerland.

mag·got *noun* any soft-bodied limbless larva, esp. that of a housefly, blowfly, or other dipteran fly, typically found in decaying organic matter. □ **mag·goty** *adjective* [Middle English, perhaps alteration of *maddock*, earlier *mathek*, from Old Norse *mathkr*: compare MAWKISH]

Magh·rib /ˈmaɡrɪb, ˈmʌɡrəb/ (also **Magh·reb**) a region of North and NW Africa between the Atlantic Ocean and Egypt, comprising the coastal plain and Atlas Mountains of Morocco, together with Algeria, Tunisia, and sometimes also Tripolitania, forming a well-defined zone bounded by sea or desert. It formerly included Moorish Spain (see BARBARY). [Arabic, = west]

Magi, the /ˈmeidʒai/ the three 'wise men' from the East who brought gifts to the infant Christ (Matt. 2:1); their names, Caspar, Melchior, and Balthasar, are first mentioned in the 6th c. [pl. of MAGUS]

magi *pl. of* MAGUS.

magic ● *noun* **1 a** the supposed art of influencing events by the occult control of nature or spirits. **b** witchcraft. **2** the art of producing by sleight of hand, optical illusion, etc. apparently inexplicable phenomena. **3** an inexplicable or remarkable influence producing surprising results. **4** an enchanting quality or phenomenon. **5** *informal* exceptional skill or talent. ● *adjective* **1 a** of, pertaining to, working, or produced by magic. **b** (of a material object) used or usable in magic rites; having supernatural powers (*magic wand*). **2** producing surprising results, like those attributed to magic. **3** *informal* wonderful, exciting, fantastic. ● *transitive verb* (**magicked, magicking**) change or create by magic, or apparently so. □ **like magic 1** very rapidly. **2** without any apparent explanation. [Old French *magique* from Late Latin *magica* n., from Greek *magikos* (as MAGUS)]

magic·al *adjective* **1** of or relating to magic. **2 a** resembling magic in action or effect. **b** produced as if by magic. **3** wonderful, enchanting. □ **magic·al·ly** *adverb*

magic bullet *noun informal* = SILVER BULLET.

magic carpet *noun* a mythical carpet able to transport a person on it to any desired place.

ma·gi·cian *noun* **1** a person skilled in or practising magic or sorcery. **2** a conjuror. **3** a person with exceptional skill.

magic lantern *noun* a simple optical device using slides to display a magnified image on a white screen, wall, etc. in a darkened room.

Magic Marker *noun proprietary* a felt-tipped indelible marker pen.

magic mushroom *noun* a mushroom with hallucinogenic properties, esp. one producing psilocybin.

magic number *noun* **1** a figure regarded as significant or momentous in a particular context. **2** *Baseball* the number which, at a given stage in the season, signifies the combination of wins for the first-place team and defeats for the second-place team which will assure the former of championship victory.

magic realism *noun* (also **magical realism**) a literary or artistic genre in which realism and narrative are combined with surreal, fantastic, dreamlike, or mythological elements. □ **magical realist** *noun & adjective*

magic square *noun* a square divided into smaller squares each containing a number such that the sums of all vertical, horizontal, or diagonal rows are equal.

magic word *noun* a word or phrase the utterance of which effects magic or creates a desired effect.

Magi·not line /ˈmaʒɪˌnoː/ *noun* **1** *hist.* a line of defensive fortifications completed in 1936 along France's northeastern frontier from Switzerland to Luxembourg as a defence against German invasion. When France was invaded in 1940, the Germans outflanked the line by advancing through Belgium. **2** a line of defence on which one relies excessively or blindly. [A. *Maginot*, French minister of war d.1932]

magis·ter·ial /ˌmadʒɪˈstiːriəl/ *adjective* **1** imperious, dictatorial. **2 a** (of a person) invested with authority. **b** of, pertaining to, or befitting a master, teacher, or someone qualified to speak with authority. **3** of or conducted by a magistrate. **4** (of a work, opinion, etc.) highly authoritative. □ **magis·ter·ial·ly** *adverb* [medieval Latin *magisterialis* from Late Latin *magisterius* from Latin *magister* MASTER]

magis·ter·iate /ˌmadʒɪˈstiːriət/ *noun Cdn* an alternative name for a master's degree. [as MAGISTERIAL]

magis·ter·ium /ˌmadʒɪˈstiːriəm/ *noun Catholicism* the teaching function and authority of the Church. [Latin, = the office of a master (as MAGISTERIAL)]

magis·tracy /ˈmadʒɪstrəsi/ *noun* (*pl.* **-cies**) **1** the office or authority of a magistrate. **2** magistrates collectively.

magis·trate /ˈmadʒɪstreit, -ˌstrət/ *noun* **1** an official conducting a court for minor cases and preliminary hearings. **2** a civil officer administering the law. □ **magis·trate·ship** *noun* **magis·tra·ture** /-trəˌtʃʊr/ *noun* [Latin *magistratus* from *magister* MASTER]

Magistrate's Court *noun Cdn* = PROVINCIAL COURT.

Mag·le·mo·sian /ˌmaɡəlˈmoːziən/ ● *noun* a N European mesolithic culture, characterized by bone and stone implements. ● *adjective* of or relating to this culture. [*Maglemose* in Denmark, where articles from it were found]

mag·lev /ˈmaɡlev/ *noun* (usu. *attributive*) magnetic levitation, a system in which magnetic repulsion supports a train above the rail or rails on which it runs, allowing it to glide along in a magnetic field. [abbreviation]

Vowels: a *cat* ɑ *arm* e *bed* ɜr *her* ɜː *deux* ə *ago* ɪ *sit* i *cosy* iː *feed* ɒ *hot* ɔ *pore* oː *no* ʌ *run* ʊ *put*

magma /ˈmagmə/ *noun* (*pl.* **mag·mata** /-mətə/ or **magmas**) **1** a hot fluid or semi-liquid material beneath the crust of the earth or other planet, which erupts as lava and from which igneous rock is formed by cooling. **2** a crude pasty mixture of mineral or organic matter. □ **mag·ma·tic** /-ˈmatɪk/ *adjective* **mag·ma·tic·ally** *adverb* [Greek *magma* from the root of *massō* knead]

magma chamber *noun* a reservoir of magma within the planetary crust, esp. below a volcano.

Magna Carta /ˌmagnə ˈkɑrtə/ *noun* (also **Magna Charta**) **1** an English political charter which King John was forced to sign by rebellious barons at Runnymede in 1215, effectively redefining the limits of royal power, and eventually coming to be seen as the seminal document of English constitutional practice. Among its provisions were that no freeman should be imprisoned or banished except by the law of the land. **2** any similar document of rights. [medieval Latin, = great charter]

magna cum laude /ˌmagnə kuːm ˈlaudei, -ˈlaudə/ *adverb & adjective* *N Amer.* (of a degree, diploma, etc.) with or of great distinction; of a higher standard than average, though not the highest (*compare* SUMMA CUM LAUDE). [Latin, lit. 'with great praise']

mag·nani·mous /magˈnanɪməs/ *adjective* nobly generous; not petty in feelings or conduct. □ **mag·na·nim·ity** /ˌmagnəˈnɪmɪti/ *noun* **mag·nani·mous·ly** *adverb* [Latin *magnanimus* from *magnus* great + *animus* soul]

mag·nate /ˈmagneit, -nət/ *noun* a wealthy and influential person, esp. in business (*shipping magnate*; *financial magnate*). [Late Latin *magnas -atis* from Latin *magnus* great]

mag·ne·sia /magˈniːʒə, -ʃə, -zjə/ *noun* **1** *Chem.* magnesium oxide, a white refractory solid used in ceramics etc. **2** (in general use) hydrated magnesium carbonate, a white powder used as an antacid and laxative. □ **mag·nes·ian** *adjective* [medieval Latin from Greek *Magnēsia* (*lithos*) (stone) of Magnesia in Asia Minor, originally referring to loadstone]

mag·nes·ite /ˈmagnɪˌsəit/ *noun* a white or grey mineral form of magnesium carbonate.

mag·ne·sium *noun* a silvery metallic element occurring naturally in magnesite and dolomite, used for making light alloys and important as an essential element in living organisms. Symbol: **Mg**; at. no.: 12.

magnesium flare *noun* an intense white light produced by burning magnesium wire.

mag·net *noun* **1** a piece of iron, steel, alloy, ore, etc., usu. in the form of a bar or horseshoe, having properties of attracting or repelling iron. **2** a person or thing that attracts. **3** = LODESTONE. [Latin *magnes magnetis* from Greek *magnēs = Magnēs -ētos* (*lithos*) (stone) of Magnesia: compare MAGNESIA]

mag·net·ic *adjective* **1 a** having the properties of a magnet. **b** pertaining to a magnet or magnetism. **c** producing, produced by, or acting by magnetism. **2** capable of being attracted by or acquiring the properties of a magnet. **3** very attractive or alluring (*a magnetic personality*). **4** (of a bearing, direction, etc.) measured relative to magnetic north. □ **mag·net·ic·ally** *adverb*

magnetic anomaly *noun* a local deviation from the general pattern of a magnetic field.

magnetic compass *noun* = COMPASS 1.

magnetic disk *noun* see DISK 1a.

magnetic equator *noun* an irregular line, passing round the earth near the geographical equator, on which the earth's magnetic field is horizontal so that a magnetic needle has no dip.

magnetic field *noun* a region of variable force around magnets, magnetic materials, or current-carrying conductors.

magnetic flux *noun* a measure of the quantity of magnetism, taking account of the strength and extent of a magnetic field.

magnetic moment *noun* the measured total intensity of magnetization of a magnet or current-carrying coil, irrespective of the volume or weight of the magnet or coil itself.

magnetic needle *noun* a piece of magnetized steel used as an indicator of direction, esp. on the dial of a compass or in magnetic and electrical apparatus in telegraphy etc.

magnetic north *noun* the north magnetic pole, usu. the point indicated by the north end of a compass needle.

magnetic pole *noun* **1** each of the points of the earth's surface, near to but not corresponding to the geographical poles, where the lines of force of the earth's magnetic fields are vertical. **2** a point at which magnetic force is concentrated, esp. either of two such opposite points or regions of a magnet.

magnetic resonance imaging *noun* a form of medical imaging using the nuclear magnetic resonance of protons in the body. Abbr.: **MRI**.

magnetic storm *noun* a large-scale disturbance of the earth's magnetic field caused by charged particles from the sun etc.

magnetic stripe *noun* (also **magnetic strip**) a dark strip of magnetized material on the back of a bank card, credit card, etc. containing electronically coded information.

magnetic tape *noun* a tape coated with magnetic material for recording sound or pictures or for the storage of information.

mag·net·ism *noun* **1 a** the characteristic properties of magnetic phenomena, esp. attraction. **b** the property of matter producing these phenomena. **2** the branch of knowledge that deals with magnetic phenomena. **3** an attractive power or influence, esp. personal charm.

mag·net·ite /ˈmagnəˌtəit/ *noun* magnetic iron oxide, an important ore of iron.

mag·net·ize *transitive verb* (also esp. *Brit.* **-ise**) **1** give magnetic properties to; make into a magnet. **2** attract as or like a magnet. □ **mag·net·iz·a·tion** *noun*

mag·neto /magˈniːtoː/ *noun* (*pl.* **-netos**) an electric generator using permanent magnets and producing high voltage, esp. for the ignition of an internal combustion engine. [abbreviation of MAGNETO-ELECTRIC]

magneto- /magˈniːtoː/ *combining form* indicating a magnet or magnetism. [Greek *magnēs*: see MAGNET]

magneto-electric /magˌniːtoːɪˈlektrɪk/ *adjective* of, pertaining to, or involving electric currents induced in a conducting material by its motion in a magnetic field. □ **magneto-electri·city** *noun*

mag·neto·graph /magˈniːtəˌgraf/ *noun* an instrument for recording measurements of magnetic quantities.

mag·neto·hydro·dynam·ic /magˌniːtoːhaidroːˈdainamɪk/ *adjective* of, pertaining to, or involving an electrically conducting fluid, as a plasma or molten metal, acted on by a magnetic field. □ **mag·neto·hydro·dynam·ics** *noun*

mag·net·om·eter /ˌmagnəˈtɒmɪtər/ *noun* an instrument measuring magnetic forces, esp. the earth's magnetism. □ **mag·neto·met·ric** /magniːˌtoːˈmetrɪk/ *adjective* **mag·net·om·etry** *noun*

mag·ne·ton /ˈmagnɪˌtɒn/ *noun* a unit of magnetic moment in atomic and nuclear physics.

magneto-optics *noun* the branch of physics that deals with the optical effects of magnetic fields. □ **magneto-optic** *adjective* **magneto-optical** *adjective*

mag·neto·sphere /magˈniːtəˌsfiːr/ *noun* the not necessarily spherical region surrounding a planet, star, etc. in which its magnetic field is effective and prevails over other magnetic fields. □ **mag·neto·spher·ic** /-ˈsfiːrɪk/ *adjective*

mag·ne·tron /ˈmagnəˌtrɒn/ *noun* an electron tube for amplifying or generating microwaves, with the flow of electrons controlled by an external magnetic field. [MAGNET + -TRON]

magnet school *noun* a public school specializing in a particular field or subject area to attract students from various neighbourhoods, regions, etc.

Mag·nifi·cat /magˈnɪfɪˌkat/ *noun* **1** the hymn of the Virgin Mary (Luke 1:46–55) used as a canticle. **2** a musical setting of this. [from the opening words *magnificat anima mea Dominum* my soul magnifies the Lord]

magni·fi·ca·tion *noun* **1 a** the act or an instance of magnifying by or as by a lens. **b** the process of being so magnified. **2** the amount or degree of magnification. **3** a magnified reproduction.

mag·nifi·cent *adjective* splendid; remarkable; impressive. □ **mag·nifi·cence** *noun* **mag·nifi·cent·ly** *adverb* [ultimately from Latin *magnus* great]

mag·nif·ico /magˈnɪfɪˌkoː/ ● *noun* (*pl.* **-icoes**) **1** *hist.* a magnate or grandee, esp. a Venetian one. **2** a high-ranking or much esteemed person. ● *adjective* magnificent. [Italian, = MAGNIFICENT]

mag·nify *transitive verb* (**-fies**, **-fied**) **1** make (a thing) appear larger than it is, as with a lens. **2** exaggerate. **3** intensify. **4** *archaic* extol, glorify, esp. render honour to (God). □ **magni·fi·able** *adjective* **magni·fi·er** *noun* [Old French *magnifier* or Latin *magnificare* (as MAGNIFICENT)]

magnifying glass *noun* a convex lens used to increase the apparent size of an object viewed through it.

mag·nilo·quent /magˈnɪləkwənt/ *adjective* grand or grandiose in speech. □ **mag·nilo·quence** *noun* **mag·nilo·quent·ly** *adverb* [Latin *magniloquus* from *magnus* great + *-loquus* -speaking]

Mag·nito·gorsk /ˌmagnɪtəˈgɔrsk/ an industrial city in S Russia, on the Ural River close to the border with Kazakhstan; pop. (est. 2002) 427,800. Founded in 1921 near deposits of iron and magnetite, it has developed into a leading centre of metallurgy.

mag·ni·tude /noun/ **1** great size or extent. **2 a** size (*electorates of less than average magnitude*). **b** a numerical quantity or value (*the magnitudes of all the economic variables could be determined*). **3** each of a set of classes into which stars are arranged according to their brilliance, stars of the first magnitude being the most brilliant, those of the sixth barely visible to the naked eye (*see also* ABSOLUTE MAGNITUDE, APPARENT MAGNITUDE). **b** the relative brightness of a star according to this scale. **4** the intrinsic size of an earthquake or underground explosion, as distinct from local intensity. □ **of the first magnitude** very important. [Latin *magnitudo* from *magnus* great]

mag·no·lia /mag'noːliə/ *noun* **1** any tree or shrub of the genus *Magnolia*, cultivated for its dark green foliage and large waxlike flowers in spring. **2** a pale, creamy pink colour. [modern Latin from P. *Magnol*, French botanist d.1715]

mag·nox *noun* any of various magnesium-based alloys used to enclose uranium fuel elements in a nuclear reactor. [*magnesium no oxidation*]

mag·num *noun* (*pl.* **mag·nums**) **1 a** a wine bottle of about twice the standard size, now usu. containing 1½ litres. **b** the quantity of liquor held by such a bottle. **2** (**Magnum**) *proprietary* **a** a cartridge or shell that is especially powerful or large. **b** (often *attributive*) a cartridge or gun adapted so as to be more powerful than its calibre suggests. [Latin, neuter of *magnus* great]

magnum opus /ˌmagnəm 'oːpəs/ *noun* **1** a great and usu. large work of art, literature, etc. **2** the most important work of an artist, writer, etc. [Latin, = great work: see OPUS]

Mag·nus·sen /'magnəsən/ **Karen Diane** (b.1952), Canadian figure skater. She won the Canadian women's championship in 1968 and 1970–73. In 1972 she took silver medals in the Olympics and world championships, and she won the world championship in 1973.

Magog[1] /ma'gɒg/ a town in S Quebec, situated at the northern end of Lac Memphrémagog, southwest of Sherbrooke; pop. (2001) 22,535. [shortening from Abenaki *memphrémagog*: see MEMPHRÉMAGOG, LAC]

Magog[2] *see* GOG AND MAGOG.

mag·pie *noun* **1** a European and N American bird of the crow family, *Pica pica*, with a long pointed tail, black and white plumage, and a noisy chattering call, proverbial for its habit of taking and hoarding bright objects. **2** any of various birds with plumage like a magpie, esp. *Gymnorhina tibicen* of Australia. **3** an idle chatterer. **4** a person who collects things indiscriminately. [*Mag*, abbreviation of *Margaret* + PIE[2]]

M.Agr. *abbreviation* Master of Agriculture.

Ma·gritte /ma'griːt/ **René (Fran·çois Ghis·lain)** (1898–1967), Belgian painter. His paintings are typical examples of surrealism, displaying startling or amusing juxtapositions of the ordinary, the strange, and the erotic, all depicted in a realist manner.

ma·guey /'magwei/ *noun* an agave plant, esp. one yielding pulque. [Spanish from Haitian]

magus /'meigəs/ *noun* (*pl.* **magi** /'madʒai, 'meidʒai/) **1** a member of a priestly caste of ancient Persia. **2** a sorcerer. **3** *see* MAGI, THE. [Latin from Greek *magos* from Old Persian *magus*]

mag wheel *noun* a lightweight, steel wheel for a motor vehicle, often with an intricate pattern of holes and spokes. [abbreviation of *magnesium steel*]

Mag·yar /'magjɑr/ ● *noun* **1** a member of a Ural-Altaic people now predominant in Hungary. **2** the language of this people; Hungarian. ● *adjective* **1** of or relating to this people or language. **2** designating a style of blouse, bodice, etc. in which the sleeves are cut in one piece with the main part of the garment. [Hungarian]

Maha·bad /ˌmɒhə'bad/ a city in NW Iran, near the Iraqi border, with a chiefly Kurdish population; pop. (est. 2002) 119,500. Occupied by Soviet troops in 1941, Mahabad became the centre of a short-lived Soviet-supported Kurdish republic, which was overthrown by the Iranians in 1946.

Maha·bhar·ata /mə'hɑːbʊrətə/ *noun* an ancient Hindu epic relating a dynastic feud between two great families, the Pandavas and the Kauravas. [Sanskrit, 'the great history of the Bharata dynasty']

maha·raja /ˌmɒhə'rɑːdʒə/ *noun* (also **maha·rajah**) *hist.* a title of some Indian princes of high rank. [Hindi *mahārājā* from *mahā* great + RAJA]

maha·ra·nee /ˌmɒhə'rɒni/ *noun* (also **maha·rani**) *hist.* the title of a maharaja's wife or widow. [Hindi *mahārānī* from *mahā* great + RANEE]

Maha·rash·tra /ˌmɒhə'raʃtrə/ a large state in W India bordering on the Arabian Sea, formed in 1960 from the southeastern part of the former Bombay State; capital, Bombay (Mumbai). □ **Maha·rash·trian** *adjective & noun*

maha·rishi /ˌmɒhə'riːʃi/ *noun* **1** a great Hindu sage or spiritual leader. **2** a popular leader of spiritual thought. [Hindi from *mahā* great + RISHI]

ma·hatma /mə'hatmə, -'hɒtmə/ *noun* **1** (in India etc.) a person regarded with reverence, love, and respect. **2 a** each of a class of persons in India and Tibet supposed by some to have preternatural powers. **b** a sage. [Sanskrit *mahātman* from *mahā* great + *ātman* soul]

Maha·weli /ˌmɒhə'weili/ the largest river in Sri Lanka. Rising in the central highlands, it flows 330 km (206 miles) to the Bay of Bengal near Trincomalee.

Maha·yana /ˌmɒhə'jɒnə/ *noun* a school of Buddhism with syncretistic features, practised in China, Japan, and Tibet. [Sanskrit from *mahā* great + *yāna* vehicle]

Mahdi /'mɒdi/ *noun* (*pl.* **Mahdis**) **1** a spiritual and temporal messiah expected by Muslims. **2** a leader claiming to be this Messiah. □ **Mahd·ism** *noun* **Mahd·ist** *noun* [Arabic *mahdīy* he who is guided right, past participle of *hadā* guide]

Mah·fouz /mɑː'fuːz/ **Na·guib** (b.1911), Egyptian novelist and short-story writer. His novels include the Cairo Trilogy (1956–7), which monitors the stages of Egyptian nationalism up to the revolution of 1952, *The Children of Gebelawi* (1959), and *Miramar* (1967); in 1988 he became the first Arabic writer to be awarded the Nobel Prize for literature.

Ma·hi·can ● *noun* **1** a member of an American Indian people formerly inhabiting the Upper Hudson Valley in New York State. **2** the extinct Algonquian language of this people. ● *adjective* of or relating to the Mahicans or their language.

Mahi·lyow /ˌmɒhɪ'ljɔː/ (Russian **Mogilev** /məgi'ljɔf/) an industrial city and railway centre in E Belarus, on the Dnieper River; pop. (est. 2002) 373,000.

mahi mahi /'mɒhiːˌmɒhi/ *noun* N *Amer.* the dorado, *Coryhaena hippurus*, eaten as food. [Hawaiian]

mah-jong /mɒ'dʒɒŋ/ *noun* (also **mah-jongg**) a Chinese game for four resembling rummy and played with 136 or 144 pieces called tiles. [Chinese dial. *ma-tsiang*, lit. 'sparrows']

Mah·ler /'mɒlər/ **Gus·tav** (1860–1911), Austrian composer, conductor, and pianist. His music forms a link between the romantic tradition of the 19th c. and 20th-c. composers such as Schoenberg, and includes nine complete symphonies (1888–1910) and the symphonic song-cycle *Das Lied von der Erde* (1908).

ma·hog·any /mə'hɒgəni/ ● *noun* (*pl.* **-ies**) **1** a rich, reddish-brown wood used for furniture. **2** any tropical tree of the genus *Swietenia*, esp. *S. mahagoni*, yielding this wood. **3** a deep rich reddish-brown. ● *adjective* of a rich reddish-brown colour. [17th c.: origin unknown]

Mahón /mə'hɒn/ (also **Mahon**, **Port Mahon**) the capital of the island of Minorca, a port on the southeast coast; pop. (est. 2002) 24,200.

Ma·hone Bay /mə'hoːn/ **1** an inlet of the N Atlantic Ocean, on the east central coast of Nova Scotia, southwest of Halifax. **2** a town situated on its western shore; pop. (2001) 991. □ **Ma·hone Bay·er** *noun* (in sense 2) [French *Mahonne* Venetian boat, after the long, low-lying pirate boats that once frequented the bay]

ma·ho·nia /mə'hoːniə/ *noun* any evergreen shrub of the genus *Mahonia*, with yellow bell-shaped or globular flowers. [scientific Latin from Bernard *McMahon*, US naturalist d.1816]

Ma·hore /mə'hɔr/ an alternative name for MAYOTTE.

ma·hout /mə'hʌut/ *noun* (in India etc.) an elephant driver or keeper. [Hindi *mahāut* from Sanskrit *mahāmātra* high official, lit. 'great in measure']

Mahov·lich /mə'hɒvəlitʃ/ **Fran·cis Wil·liam** ('Frank') (b.1938), Canadian hockey player. He joined the Toronto Maple Leafs in 1957 and won the Calder Trophy as best rookie. His powerful skating and strong slapshot made a major contribution to Toronto's four Stanley Cup victories in the 1960s.

Mah·ratta *var. of* MARATHA.

Mah·ratti *var. of* MARATHI.

ma huang *noun* = EPHEDRA. [Chinese]

Maia[1] /'maiə/ *Gk Myth* the daughter of Atlas and mother of Hermes. [Greek, = mother, nurse]

Maia[2] /'maiə/ *Rom. Myth* a goddess associated (for unknown reasons) with Vulcan and also (by confusion with MAIA[1]) with Mercury. She was worshipped on 1 May and 15 May; that month is named after her. [perhaps from Latin root *mag-* growth, increase]

Consonants: b *but*   d *dog*   f *few*   g *get*   h *her*   j *yes*   k *cat*   l *leg*   m *man*   n *no*   p *pen*   r *red*   s *sit*

maid *noun* **1** a female domestic servant. **2** *literary* a girl or young woman. [abbreviation of MAIDEN]

mai·dan /maiˈdɒn/ *noun Anglo-Indian* **1** an open space in or near a town. **2** a parade ground. [Urdu from Arabic *maydān*]

maid·en *noun* **1 a** *literary* a girl; a young unmarried woman. **b** (*attributive*) unmarried (*maiden aunt*). **2** (*attributive*) (of a female animal) unmated. **3** (often *attributive*) **a** a horse that has never won a race. **b** a race open only to such horses. **4** (*attributive*) being or involving the first attempt or occurrence (*maiden speech*; *maiden voyage*). **5** (*attributive*) **a** (of soil etc.) that has never been disturbed; unworked. **b** (of a plant or tree) grown from seed as opposed to a stock; not pruned or transplanted. □ **maiden·hood** *noun* **maiden·ly** *adjective* [Old English *mægden*, diminutive from *mægeth* from Germanic]

maiden·hair *noun* (in full **maidenhair fern**) a fern of the genus *Adiantum*, esp. *A. capillus-veneris*, with fine hairlike stalks and delicate fronds.

maidenhair tree *noun* = GINKGO.

Maiden·head a town in S England; pop. (est. 2002) 59,700. It is situated to the west of London on the Thames River.

maiden·head *noun* **1** virginity. **2** the hymen.

maiden name *noun* a wife's surname before marriage.

Maid Marian Robin Hood's sweetheart.

maid of honour *noun* **1** esp. *N Amer.* an unmarried woman who acts as a bride's principal bridesmaid (*compare* MATRON OF HONOUR). **2** an unmarried lady attending a queen or princess. **3** *Brit.* a kind of small custard tart.

maid·serv·ant *noun* a female domestic servant.

maid service *noun* light housework performed by a chambermaid, esp. in a hotel.

Maid·stone a town in SE England, on the Medway River, the county town of Kent; pop. (est. 2002) 93,500.

Mai·du·guri /ˌmaiˈduːɡuri/ a city in NE Nigeria; pop. (est. 1991) 618,278.

mai·eut·ic /meiˈuːtɪk/ *adjective* (of the Socratic mode of inquiry) serving to bring a person's latent ideas into clear consciousness. [Greek *maieutikos* from *maieuomai* act as a midwife, from *maia* midwife]

Mai·kop /maiˈkɒp/ a city in SW Russia, capital of the republic of Adygea; pop. (est. 2002) 167,900.

mail[1] ● *noun* **1 a** letters, parcels, etc. conveyed by the postal system. **b** the postal system. **c** one complete delivery or collection of mail. **d** one delivery of letters to one place, esp. to a business on one occasion. **2** electronic mail. **3** voice mail. **4** a vehicle carrying mail. **5** (*pl.*) (prec. by *the*) *N Amer.* the postal service, esp. serving remote areas as the North etc. ● *transitive verb* esp. *N Amer.* **1** send (a letter etc.) through the postal service. **2** send email to (a person). **3** send by email. [Old French *male* wallet, from West Germanic]

mail[2] ● *noun* **1** armour made of interlaced rings or chains, or overlapping plates, joined together flexibly. **2** the protective shell, scales, etc., of an animal. ● *transitive verb* clothe with or as if with mail. □ **mailed** *adjective* [Old French *maille* from Latin *macula* spot, mesh]

mail·able *adjective* acceptable for conveyance by post.

mail·bag *noun* **1** a large sack or bag for carrying mail. **2** the correspondence, comments, etc. received by a radio station, television program, etc.

mail bomb ● *noun* **1** an explosive device disguised as a letter or package and sent through the mail. **2** *Computing* a huge, useless file sent by electronic mail to take up a large amount of the recipient computer's memory, disk space, etc. ● *transitive verb* send a mail bomb of either the explosive or electronic variety.

mail·box *noun N Amer.* **1 a** a public receptacle into which letters are dropped for delivery by the postal service. **b** a private receptacle to which letters are delivered. **2** the file etc. in which electronic or voice mail is received and stored.

mail drop *noun N Amer.* **1** a receptacle for mail. **2** an often covert place where mail may be left to be collected by another person.

mailed fist *noun* the use of physical force to maintain control or impose one's will.

Mail·er /ˈmeilər/ **Nor·man** (b.1923), US novelist and essayist. The effects of war and violence on human relationships is a recurrent theme in his work, which also often includes an element of social criticism; his novels include *The Naked and the Dead* (1948), *The Executioner's Song* (1979), and *Harlot's Ghost* (1991).

mail·er *noun* **1** an advertising pamphlet, brochure, or catalogue sent out in the mail. **2** a container such as a cardboard tube etc. for sending items, esp. papers, by mail. **3** a person who or thing which dispatches

messages etc. by mail. **4** *Computing* a program which provides users with the facilities necessary for reading, storing, composing, and sending email.

mail-in ● *adjective* **1** (of an item, such as a rebate coupon etc.) that is or can be sent through the mail. **2** (of a ballot, survey, etc.) conducted through the mail. ● *noun* an item as a coupon etc. sent out or returned by mail.

mail·ing *noun* **1 a** the action or process of sending something by mail. **b** a letter or parcel sent by mail. **2** a batch of mail or a number of items mailed at one time, esp. as part of a publicity campaign, survey, etc.

mailing address *noun N Amer.* the address to which one has one's mail sent, esp. if different from one's street address.

mailing list *noun* **1** a list of people to whom advertising matter, information, etc. is to be mailed regularly. **2** a list of email addresses, or an email alias for such a list, that allows the same message to be sent to each address.

Mail·let /maiˈjei/ **An·to·nine** (b.1929), Canadian novelist. Beginning with the publication of *La Sagouine* in 1971, she has dominated contemporary Acadian literature. Her stories, including *Pélagie-la-charrette* (1979), set in an imaginary Acadian past, gave a new voice to the history of her people as well as a new interpretation of their history.

Mail·lol /maiˈjɒl/ **Aris·tide** (1861–1944), French sculptor and painter, who is noted for his monumental sculptures of nude female figures, often shown in repose, and modelled with simple gestures.

mail·lot /maiˈjoː/ *noun* a woman's one-piece bathing suit. [French]

mail·man *noun* (*pl.* **-men**) *N Amer.* a postman.

mail merge *noun Computing* **1** a program that draws on a file of names and addresses and a text file to produce multiple copies of a letter, each addressed to a different recipient. **2** the facility for doing this.

mail order ● *noun* **1** an order for goods sent by mail. **2 a** a system of buying and selling goods by mail. **b** (hyphenated when *attributive*) a company etc. offering mail-order goods (*mail-order catalogue*). ● *transitive verb* (**mail-order**) buy through mail-order catalogues, companies, etc.

mail-order bride *noun N Amer. slang* a woman whom a man courts and contracts to marry wholly though correspondence, e.g. through a matrimonial agency etc.

mail·room *noun* a room in a company etc. where mail is collected, sorted, or otherwise dealt with.

mail slot *noun N Amer.* a slit in the door of a house, apartment, etc. through which letters are delivered.

maim *transitive verb* **1** cripple, disable, mutilate. **2** harm, impair, render powerless or essentially incomplete (*emotionally maimed by neglect*). [Middle English *maime* from Old French *mahaignier*, of unknown origin]

Mai·moni·des /maiˈmɒnɪˌdiːz/ (born Moses ben Maimon) (1135–1204), Jewish philosopher and Rabbinic scholar, born in Spain. His influential writings include a codification of Jewish law in *Mishneh Torah* (1180), and the *Guide for the Perplexed* (1190), which endeavoured to reconcile Talmudic scripture with the philosophy of Aristotle.

main ● *adjective* **1** chief in size, importance, extent, etc.; principal (*the main part*; *the main point*). **2** (of strength etc.) exerted to the full; sheer (*by main force*). ● *noun* **1** a principal channel, duct, etc., for water, sewage, etc. (*water main*). **2** esp. *Brit.* (usu. in *pl.*; prec. by *the*) **a** the central distribution network for electricity, gas, water, etc. **b** a domestic electricity supply as distinct from batteries. **3** *literary* **a** the ocean or oceans (*the Spanish Main*). **b** the mainland. **4** (**the Main**) *Cdn informal* Saint-Laurent Boulevard in Montreal. □ **in the main** for the most part. **with might and main** with all one's strength. [Middle English, partly from Old Norse *megenn*, *megn* (adj.), partly from Old English *mægen-* from Germanic: (n.) originally = physical force]

main brace *noun Naut.* the brace attached to the main yard.

main chance *noun* something which is of principal importance, esp. the opportunity of enriching or otherwise benefiting oneself. □ **an eye for** (or **to**) **the main chance** consideration for one's own interests.

main clause *noun Grammar* a clause that alone forms a complete sentence (*compare* SUBORDINATE CLAUSE).

main course *noun* **1 a** the chief course of a meal. **b** any of a number of substantial dishes in a large menu. **2** *Naut.* the mainsail.

main deck *noun* the principal deck of a ship, usu. the uppermost enclosed one running the whole length of the ship.

main dish *noun* = MAIN COURSE 1.

main drag *noun N Amer. informal* = MAIN STREET.

Maine /mein/ a northeastern state of the US, on the Atlantic coast; pop. (2000) 1,274,923; capital, Augusta. □ **Main·er** noun

main floor noun esp. N Amer. = GROUND FLOOR.

main·frame noun **1** (often attributive) a large or general-purpose computer, esp. one supporting numerous peripherals etc. **2** the central processing unit and primary memory of a computer.

Main·land 1 the largest island in Orkney. **2** the largest island in Shetland.

main·land noun **1** a large continuous extent of land, including the greater part of a country or territory and excluding neighbouring islands, peninsulas, etc. **2** (**Mainland**) Cdn (Nfld) **a** the provinces of Canada other than Newfoundland. **b** (to those on the coastal islands) the coast of Labrador. **3** (**Mainland**) Cdn (BC) (usu. prec. by the) = LOWER MAINLAND. **4** (**Mainland**) Cdn (Cape Breton) peninsular Nova Scotia. □ **main·land·er** noun

main·line ● adjective (of an institution etc.) established, normative, and usu. moderate in opinions, attitudes, etc. (mainline churches). ● noun **1** (usu. **main line**) a principal railway line. **2** N Amer. Forestry the primary, heavy cable used to haul logs from the forest to the landing. **3** slang a principal vein, esp. as a site for a drug injection. ● verb slang **1** intransitive take drugs intravenously. **2** transitive inject (drugs) intravenously. □ **main·lin·er** noun

main·ly adverb for the most part; chiefly.

main man noun **1** a principal figure on a team, in a political campaign, etc. **2** the principal performer in a band. **3** slang a close and usu. trusted friend or companion.

main·mast noun the principal mast of a ship.

main memory noun random access memory (see RANDOM ACCESS).

Main River /main/ a river of SW Germany which rises in N Bavaria and flows 500 km (310 miles) westward, through Frankfurt, to meet the Rhine at Mainz.

main·sail /'meinseil, -səl/ noun **1** (in a square-rigged vessel) the lowest sail on the mainmast. **2** (in a fore-and-aft rigged vessel) a sail set on the after part of the mainmast.

main·sheet noun the rope which controls the boom of the mainsail when set.

main·spring noun **1** a chief motive, reason, or incentive. **2** the principal spring of a mechanical watch, clock, etc.

main squeeze noun N Amer. slang a lover.

main·stage noun the stage of the principal theatre operated by a theatrical company, usu. the one on which major works are performed.

main·stay noun **1** a chief support or principal element (a mainstay of the repertoire). **2** Naut. a stay from the maintop to the foot of the foremast.

main·stream ● adjective **1** belonging to or characteristic of an established field of activity. **2** of or pertaining to the mainstream. ● noun **1** the prevailing trend in opinion, fashion, etc. **2** the stream of education or a class at school etc. for students without special needs. **3** a type of jazz based on the swing style of the 1930s and consisting esp. of solo improvisation on chord sequences. **4** the principal current of a river. ● transitive & intransitive verb **1 a** place (a child with a disability) in a school or class for those without special needs for all or part of the school day. **b** educate in such an integrated environment. **2** incorporate into the mainstream. □ **main·stream·er** noun **main·stream·ing** noun

main street noun the principal street of a town or city.

main·street·ing noun Cdn political campaigning in main streets to win electoral support. □ **main·street** intransitive verb [perhaps coined by J. G. DIEFENBAKER]

main·tain transitive verb **1** cause to continue; keep up, preserve (a state of affairs, an activity, etc.) (maintained friendly relations). **2** (often foll. by in) support (life, a condition, etc.) by work, nourishment, expenditure, etc. (maintained him in comfort). **3** (often foll. by that + clause) support or uphold, esp. in speech or argument (maintained that she was the best; his story was true, he maintained). **4** preserve or provide for the preservation of (a building, machine, road, etc.) in good repair. **5** give aid to (a cause, party, etc.). **6** pay for the upkeep, repair, or equipping of (a garrison etc.). □ **main·tain·abil·ity** noun **main·tain·able** adjective **main·tain·er** noun [Old French maintenir, ultimately from Latin manu tenēre hold in the hand]

main·ten·ance noun **1 a** the action or process of maintaining or being maintained. **b** the state or fact of being maintained. **2 a** the provision of the means to support life, esp. by work etc. **b** a monetary provision for a spouse after separation or divorce. **3** (attributive) (of a drug, dosage, treatment, etc.) sufficient to sustain an esp. beneficial

effect on the body. **4** Law hist. the offence of aiding a party in litigation without lawful cause. [Old French from maintenir: see MAINTAIN]

maintenance man noun a man employed for caretaking and janitorial duties.

Main·te·non /mãtənͻ̃/ **Mar·quise de** (title of Françoise d'Aubigné) (1635–1719), mistress and later second wife (from 1683) of Louis XIV of France.

main·top /'meintɒp/ noun Naut. a platform above the head of the lower mainmast.

main·top·mast /mein'tɒpməst/ noun Naut. a mast above the head of the lower mainmast.

main yard noun Naut. the yard on which the mainsail is extended.

Mainz /maints/ a city in western Germany, capital of Rhineland-Palatinate, situated at the confluence of the Rhine and Main rivers; pop. (est. 2002) 190,600.

maiol·ica /mə'jɒlɪkə/ var. of MAJOLICA.

Mair /mer/ **Charles** (1838–1927), Canadian poet and civil servant. A founder of the Canada First nationalist movement (1868) and a staunch opponent of the Metis cause, he was imprisoned by Louis Riel in 1869, but escaped back to Ontario where he agitated for the suppression of the rebellion.

mai·son de la cul·ture /me'zɔ̃ də la kultyr/ noun (pl. **mai·sons de la cul·ture**) Cdn (Que.) a cultural centre, usu. containing a library, theatre, and exhibition space for visual arts. [French, lit. 'house of culture']

maison·ette /ˌmeizə'net/ noun (also **maison·nette**) a part of a house, apartment building, etc., forming separate living accommodation, usu. on two floors and having a separate entrance. [French maisonnette, diminutive of maison house]

Maison·neuve /'mezɒnɜv/ **Paul de Chome·dey de** (1612–76), French officer. Chosen to found a colony on Montreal Island, he arrived in New France in 1641, and began work on the fort and other buildings of Ville-Marie the following year.

mai tai /'maitai/ noun a cocktail of rum, curaçao, and fruit juices. [prob. from Tahitian maita'i, 'good, nice, pleasant']

maître d' /ˌmeitrə 'diː, ˌmeitɜr, ˌmetrə/ = MAÎTRE D'HOTEL. [abbreviation]

maître d'hotel /ˌmeitrə doː'tel, ˌmet-/ noun **1** the manager, head steward, etc., of a hotel. **2** a head waiter. [French, = master of (the) house]

maize /meiz/ noun esp. Brit. = CORN¹ 1. [French maïs or Spanish maíz, of Carib origin]

Maj abbreviation (also **Maj.**) = MAJOR noun 1.

ma·jes·tic adjective showing majesty; stately and dignified; grand, imposing. □ **ma·jes·tic·ally** adverb

maj·esty noun (pl. **-ties**) **1** impressive dignity or beauty. **2 a** royal power. **b** (**Majesty**) (prec. by your, her, his, their, etc.) a title used to refer to or address a sovereign or a sovereign's wife or widow. [Old French majesté from Latin majestas (as MAJOR)]

Maj. Gen. abbreviation MAJOR GENERAL. ¶ The Canadian Forces use the abbreviation MGen.

Maj·lis /'madʒlɪs/ noun **1** the parliament of Iran. **2** (in various N African and Middle Eastern countries) an assembly or council. [Persian, = assembly]

majol·ica /mə'dʒɒlɪkə, mə'jɒl-/ noun (also **maiolica**) a type of earthenware with coloured decoration on an opaque white glaze. [Italian from former name of Majorca]

Major, John (b.1943), English Conservative politician, prime minister 1990–97. He became the youngest British prime minister of the 20th c. following the resignation of Margaret Thatcher; his term saw the negotiations within the European Community leading to the signing of the Maastricht Treaty.

ma·jor ● adjective **1** important, large, serious, significant (a major road; a major war; the major consideration must be their health). **2** (of an operation) serious or life-threatening. **3** Music **a** (of a scale) having intervals of a semitone between the third and fourth, and seventh and eighth degrees. **b** (of an interval) greater by a semitone than a minor interval (major third). **c** (of a key) based on a major scale, tending to produce a bright or joyful effect (D major). **4** of full age. **5** Logic **a** (of a term) occurring in the predicate or conclusion of a syllogism. **b** (of a premise) containing a major term. ● noun **1** Military **a** (in the Canadian or US Army and Air Force and other armies) an officer of a rank next below lieutenant colonel and above captain. Abbr.: **Maj** Cdn or **Maj.** **b** an officer in charge of a section of band instruments (drum major; pipe major). **2** a person of full age. **3** Music a major key etc. **4** N Amer.,

Vowels: a cat   ɑ arm   e bed   ɜr her   ɜː deux   ə ago   ɪ sit   i cosy   iː feed   ɒ hot   ͻ pore   oː no   ʌ run   ʊ put

Austral. & NZ **a** the principal subject or course of a student at university or college. **b** a student specializing in a specified subject (*a philosophy major*). **5** *N Amer.* (in *pl.*) the major leagues. **6** *Hockey* = MAJOR PENALTY. **7** designating levels of amateur hockey for competitors between the ages of 18 and 21, or for younger players if their skills are adequate to compete with older players. **8** *Cdn Football informal* = TOUCHDOWN. **9** *Logic* a major term or premise. ● *intransitive verb* (foll. by *in*) *N Amer., Austral. & NZ* study or qualify in a subject (*majored in history*). □ **major·ship** *noun* [Latin, comparative of *magnus* great]

major axis *noun Geom.* the principal axis of an ellipse, passing through its foci.

Ma·jor·ca /məˈjɔːrkə/ (Spanish **Mallorca** /maˈjorka/) the largest of the Balearic Islands; pop. (2001) 676,516; capital, Palma.

major-domo /ˌmeɪdʒərˈdoːmoː/ *noun* (*pl.* **-domos**) **1** the chief official of an Italian or Spanish princely household. **2** a butler. [Italian *maggiordomo* from medieval Latin *major domus* highest official of the household (as MAJOR, DOME)]

major·ette *noun* = DRUM MAJORETTE. [abbreviation]

major general *noun* (in the Canadian or US Army and Air Force and other armies) an officer of a rank next below a lieutenant general and above brigadier general or brigadier. Abbr.: **MGen** *Cdn* or **Maj. Gen.**

ma·jori·tar·ian ● *adjective* **1** governed by or believing in majority rule. **2** of, relating to, or constituting a majority. ● *noun* a person who supports majority rule. □ **ma·jori·tar·ian·ism** *noun*

ma·jor·ity *noun* (*pl.* **-ities**) **1** (usu. foll. by *of*) the greater number or part. ¶ Some feel that *majority* in this sense should be used only with countable nouns, e.g. *a majority of people*, and not with mass nouns, e.g. *a majority of the work*, although use with mass nouns is both widespread and standard. To avoid wordiness and possible criticism, *most* may be used in such cases, e.g. *most of the work*. When *majority* is followed by a plural noun, a plural verb is used, e.g. *The majority of her books are bestsellers*. **2** *Politics* **a** = MAJORITY GOVERNMENT. **b** the number by which the votes cast for one party, candidate, etc. exceed those of the next in rank (*won by a majority of 151*) (compare PLURALITY 3). **3** full legal age (*attained her majority*). **4** the rank of major. □ **in the majority** belonging to or constituting a majority party etc. [medieval Latin *majoritas* (as MAJOR)]

majority government *noun Cdn, Brit., Austral., & NZ* a government that has more than half of the total number of parliamentary seats.

majority leader *noun* (in the US) the floor leader of the party having the majority in a legislature.

majority rule *noun* the principle that the greater number should exercise greater power.

major junior *noun Cdn* the highest level of junior amateur hockey competition.

major league *N Amer.* ● *noun* **1** either of the two principal professional baseball leagues in N America, the American League and the National League. **2** a similar league in other sports. **3** a category in any field considered to be the most demanding, most professional, or of the highest calibre. ● *adjective* (usu. **major-league**) **1** of or relating to a major league (*set a major-league record*). **2** of the highest order. □ **major-leaguer** *noun*

major·ly *adverb slang* to a great extent.

major penalty *noun Hockey* a five minute penalty, given esp. for fighting.

major planet *noun see* PLANET 1a.

major prophet *noun* each of the prophets (Isaiah, Jeremiah, and Ezekiel) for whom the longer prophetic books of the Bible are named and whose prophecies they record.

major suit *noun Bridge* spades or hearts.

Ma·juro /məˈdʒuroː/ the capital of the Marshall Islands, situated on several islets in the eastern Ratak chain; pop. (est. 1999) 23,676.

maj·us·cule /ˈmadʒəˌskjuːl/ ● *noun* **1** a large letter, whether capital or uncial. **2** large lettering. ● *adjective* of, written in, or concerning majuscules. [French from Latin *majuscula* (*littera* letter), diminutive of MAJOR]

Ma·kar·ios III /məˈkɑriˌɒs/ (born Mikhail Christodolou Mouskos) (1913–77), Greek Cypriot archbishop and political leader. He was primate and archbishop of the Greek Orthodox Church in Cyprus from 1950, reorganized the movement for union of Cyprus with Greece, and was elected first president of an independent Cyprus (1960–77).

Ma·kas·sar /məˈkasər/ (also **Macassar** or **Ma·kas·ar**) the former name (until 1973) for UJUNG PANDANG.

Makassar Strait a stretch of water separating the islands of Borneo

and Sulawesi (Celebes) and linking the Celebes Sea in the north with the Java Sea in the south.

make ● *verb* (*past* and *past participle* **made**) **1** *transitive* construct; create; form from parts or other substances (*made a table; made it out of cardboard; made him a sweater*). **2** *transitive* (foll. by *to* + infin.) cause or compel (a person etc.) to do something (*make her repeat it; was made to confess*). **3** *transitive* **a** cause to exist; create; bring about (*made a noise; making enemies*). **b** cause to become or seem (*made an exhibition of myself; made him angry*). **c** appoint; designate (*made her a senator*). **4** *transitive* compose; prepare; draw up (*made her will; made a march of the Arctic*). **5** *transitive* constitute; amount to (*makes a difference; 2 and 2 make 4; this makes the tenth time*). **6** *transitive* **a** undertake or agree to (an aim or purpose) (*made a promise; make an effort*). **b** execute or perform (a bodily movement, a speech, etc.) (*made a face; making a bow*). **7** *transitive* gain, acquire, procure (money, a profit, etc.) (*made $20,000 on the deal*). **8** *transitive* prepare (tea, coffee, a dish, etc.) for consumption (*make yourself a sandwich*). **9** *transitive* **a** arrange bedclothes tidily on (a bed) ready for use. **b** arrange and light materials for (a fire). **10** *intransitive* **a** proceed (*made towards the river*). **b** (foll. by *to* + infin.) begin an action (*she made to go*). **11** *transitive informal* **a** arrive at (a place) or in time for (a train etc.) (*made the town before dark; made the six o'clock train*). **b** manage to attend; manage to attend on (a certain day) or at (a certain time) (*couldn't make the meeting last week; can make any day except Friday*). **c** achieve a place in (*made the top ten; made the six o'clock news*). **d** esp. *N Amer.* achieve the rank of (*made colonel in three years*). **12** *transitive* establish or enact (a distinction, rule, law, etc.). **13** *transitive* consider to be; estimate as (*what do you make the time?; do you make that a 1 or a 7?*). **14** *transitive* secure the success or advancement of (*his mother made him; it made my day*). **15** *transitive* accomplish (a distance, speed, score, etc.) (*made 120 km/h on the highway*). **16** *transitive* **a** become by development or training (*made a great leader*). **b** serve as (*a log makes a useful seat*). **17** *transitive* (usu. foll. by *out*) represent as; cause to appear as (*makes him out a liar*). **18** *transitive* form in the mind; feel (*I make no judgment*). **19** *transitive* **a** determine, establish, or choose (*let's make it Tuesday; made it my business to know*). **b** bring to (a chosen value etc.) (*decided to make it a dozen*). **20** *transitive slang* have sexual relations with. **21** *transitive Cards* **a** win (a trick). **b** play (a card) to advantage. **c** win the number of tricks that fulfills (a contract). **d** shuffle (a pack of cards) for dealing. **22** *transitive Electricity* complete or close (a circuit) (*opp.* BREAK 10). **23** *intransitive* (of the tide) begin to flow or ebb. **24** *transitive Cdn* (esp. *Nfld*) preserve (fish) by drying and salting. ● *noun* **1** (esp. of a product) a type, origin, brand, etc. of manufacture (*different make of car; our own make*). **2** a kind of mental, moral, or physical structure or composition. **3** an act of shuffling cards. **4** *Electricity* **a** the making of contact. **b** the position in which this is made. □ **make after** *archaic* pursue. **make against** be unfavourable to. **make as if** (or **though**) (foll. by *to* + infin. or conditional) act as if the specified circumstances applied (*made as if to leave; made as if he would hit me; made as if she had not noticed*). **make away** (or **off**) depart hastily. **make believe** *see* BELIEVE. **make a clean breast of** *see* BREAST. **make conversation** *see* CONVERSATION. **make a day** (or **night** etc.) **of it** devote a whole day (or night etc.) to an activity. **make difficulties** *see* DIFFICULTY. **make do 1** manage with the limited or inadequate means available. **2** (foll. by *with*) manage with (something) as an inferior substitute. **make an example of** *see* EXAMPLE 3. **make eyes** *see* EYE. **make a fool of** *see* FOOL[1]. **make for 1** tend to result in (happiness etc.). **2** proceed towards (a place). **3** assault; attack. **4** confirm (an opinion). **make friends (with)** *see* FRIEND. **make fun of** *see* FUN. **make good** *see* GOOD. **make a habit of** *see* HABIT. **make a hash of** *see* HASH[1]. **make hay** *see* HAY. **make head(s) or tail(s) of** *see* HEAD. **make it** *informal* **1** succeed in reaching, esp. in time. **2** be successful. **3** (usu. foll. by *with*) *slang* have sexual intercourse (with). **4** (usu. with *neg.*) survive (*she's in intensive care and they don't think she'll make it*). **make it up 1** be reconciled, esp. after a quarrel. **2** fill in a deficit. **make it up to** remedy negligence, an injury, etc. to (a person). **make light of** *see* LIGHT[2]. **make like** *informal* pretend to be; imitate (*let's make like monkeys*). **make love** *see* LOVE. **make a meal of** *see* MEAL[1]. **make merry** *see* MERRY. **make the most of** *see* MOST. **make much** (or **little**) **of 1** derive much (or little) advantage from. **2** give much (or little) attention, importance, etc., to. **make a name for oneself** *see* NAME. **make no bones about** *see* BONE. **make nothing of** *see* NOTHING. **make of 1** construct from. **2** conclude to be the meaning or character of (*can you make anything of it?*). **make off** = MAKE AWAY. **make off with** carry away; steal. **make oneself scarce** *see* SCARCE. **make or break** (or *Brit.* **mar**) cause the success or ruin of. **make out 1 a** distinguish by sight or hearing. **b** decipher (handwriting etc.). **2** understand (*can't make him out*). **3** assert; pretend (*made out she liked it*). **4** *informal* make progress; fare (*how did you make out?*). **5** (usu. foll. by *to, in favour of*) draw up; write out (*made out a cheque to her*). **6** *N Amer. informal* indulge in sexual activity usu. stopping short of intercourse; neck, pet. **7** prove or try to prove (*how do you make that out?*). **make over 1** transfer the possession of (a thing) to a person. **2** refashion (a garment etc.). **3** change (a person, an institution) to fit a new image. **make a point of** see POINT. **make sail** see SAIL. **make shift** see SHIFT. **make so bold as to** see BOLD. **make time** see TIME. **make up 1** serve or act to overcome (a deficiency). **2** complete (an amount, a party, etc.). **3** compensate. **4** be reconciled. **5** put together; compound; prepare (*made up the prescription*). **6** sew (parts of a garment etc.) together. **7** get (a sum of money, a company, etc.) together. **8** concoct (a story). **9** (of parts) compose (a whole). **10 a** apply cosmetics. **b** apply cosmetics to. **11** settle (a dispute). **12** prepare (a bed) for use with fresh sheets etc. **13** *Printing* arrange (type) in pages. **14** compile (a list, an account, a document, etc.). **15** arrange (a marriage etc.). **make up one's mind** see MIND. **make up to** curry favour with; court. **make water** see WATER. **make way** see WAY. **make one's way** see WAY. **make with** *US informal* supply; perform; proceed with (*made with the feet and left in a hurry*). **on the make** *informal* **1** intent on gain. **2** looking for sexual partners. □ **mak·able** *adjective* [Old English *macian* from West Germanic: related to MATCH[1]]

make-believe ● *noun* pretense. ● *adjective* pretended.

make-do *adjective* makeshift.

make·over *noun* a complete transformation or remodelling.

mak·er *noun* **1** (often in *combination*) a person or thing that makes. **2** a manufacturer. **3** (**our, the,** etc. **Maker**) God. **4** a person who executes a legal document, esp. a promissory note. **5** *archaic* a poet. □ **meet one's maker** *informal* die.

make·shift ● *adjective* temporary; serving for the time being (*a makeshift arrangement*). ● *noun* a temporary substitute or device.

make·up *noun* **1** cosmetics for the face etc., either generally or to create a performer's appearance or disguise. **2** the appearance of the face etc. when cosmetics have been applied (*his makeup was not convincing*). **3** *Printing* the making up of a type. **4** *Printing* the type made up. **5** a person's character, temperament, etc. **6** the composition or constitution (of a thing). **7** *N Amer.* a supplementary test or assignment given to a student who missed or failed the original one (also *attributive*: *makeup exam*).

make·weight *noun* **1** a small quantity or thing added to make up the full weight, esp. on a scale. **2** an unimportant extra person. **3** an unimportant point added to make an argument seem stronger.

make-work *noun* **1** esp. *N Amer.* work or activity of little or no value, devised mainly to keep someone busy (also *attributive*: *a make-work project*). **2** esp. *Cdn* (*attributive*) designating an esp. government-sponsored project, program, grant, etc. intended to create jobs (*slashed funding to make-work programs*).

Makh·ach·ka·la /ˌmaxətʃkəˈlɑ/ a port in SW Russia, on the Caspian Sea, capital of the autonomous republic of Dagestan; pop. (est. 2002) 336,500. It was known as Port Petrovsk until 1922. [*Makhach*, Dagestani revolutionary d.1918]

maki /ˈmaki/ *noun* (in full **maki sushi**) a dish consisting of sushi and raw vegetables wrapped in a sheet of seaweed. [Japanese, from *maku* 'to roll (up)' + SUSHI]

mak·ing *noun* **1** in senses of MAKE *verb*. **2** (in *pl.*) **a** earnings; profit. **b** (usu. foll. by *of*) essential qualities or ingredients (*has the makings of a general*; *we have the makings of a meal*). **c** *N Amer. & Austral. informal* paper and tobacco for rolling a cigarette. □ **be the making of** ensure the success or favourable development of a person. □ **in the making** in the course of being made or formed. [Old English *macung* (as MAKE)]

Ma·kiyiv·ka /məˈkijəvkə/ a city in E Ukraine, just northeast of Donetsk; pop. (est. 1998) 394,800.

mako[1] /ˈmɑːkoː/ *noun* (*pl.* **makos**) a large blue mackerel shark of the genus *Isurus*, of tropical and temperate oceans worldwide. [Maori]

mako[2] /ˈmɑːkoː/ *noun* (*pl.* **makos**) a small New Zealand tree, *Aristotelia serrata*, with clusters of dark red berries and large racemes of pink flowers. *Also called* WINEBERRY. [Maori]

ma·kuta *pl.* of LIKUTA.

Mal. *abbreviation* Malachi.

mal- /mal/ *combining form* **1 a** bad, badly (*malpractice*; *maltreat*). **b** faulty, faultily (*malfunction*). **2** not (*maladroit*). [French *mal* badly, from Latin *male*]

Mala·bar Christians /ˈmaləˌbɑr/ *noun* a group of Christians of SW India, tracing their origin to St. Thomas, who according to their tradition landed on the Malabar Coast.

Mala·bar Coast /ˈmaləˌbɑr/ the southern part of the west coast of India, including the coastal region of Karnataka and most of the state of Kerala.

Mal·abo /məˈlɒboː/ the capital of Equatorial Guinea, on the island of Bioko; pop. (est. 2002) 112,800.

mal·ab·sorp·tion *noun* imperfect absorption of food material by the small intestine.

Ma·lac·ca see MELAKA.

Ma·lac·ca, Strait of the channel between the Malay Peninsula and the Indonesian island of Sumatra, an important sea passage linking the Indian Ocean to the South China Sea. The ports of Melaka and Singapore lie on this strait.

ma·lac·ca /məˈlakə/ *noun* (in full **malacca cane**) a cane from the stem of the palm tree *Calamus scipionum* having a rich brown colour, used for walking sticks etc. [MALACCA var. of MELAKA]

Mal·achi /ˈmaləˌkai/ the last book of the Old Testament in the English versions, belonging to a period before Ezra and Nehemiah. [Hebrew *mālāki* my messenger]

mal·ach·ite /ˈmaləˌkait/ *noun* a bright green mineral of hydrous copper carbonate, taking a high polish and used ornamentally. [Greek *molokhitis* from *molokhē* = *malakhē* mallow]

malaco- /ˈmaləkoː/ *combining form* soft. [Greek *malakos* soft]

mala·col·ogy /ˌmaləˈkɒlədʒi/ *noun* the study of molluscs. □ **mala·co·logic·al** *adjective* **mala·col·o·gist** *noun*

mala·cos·tra·can /ˌmaləˈkɒstrəkən/ ● *noun* any crustacean of the class Malacostraca, including crabs, shrimps, lobsters, and krill. ● *adjective* of or relating to this class. [MALACO- + Greek *ostrakon* shell]

mal·adapt·ive *adjective* (of an individual, species, etc.) failing to adjust adequately to the environment, and undergoing emotional, behavioural, physical, or mental repercussions. □ **mal·adap·ta·tion** *noun* **mal·adapt·ed** *adjective*

mal·adjust·ed *adjective* **1** not correctly adjusted. **2** (of a person) unable to adapt to or cope with the demands of a social environment. □ **mal·adjust·ment** *noun*

mal·adroit /ˌmaləˈdrɔit/ *adjective* clumsy; bungling. □ **mal·adroit·ly** *adverb* **mal·adroit·ness** *noun* [French (as MAL-, ADROIT)]

mal·ady *noun* (*pl.* **-adies**) **1** an ailment; a disease. **2** a morbid or depraved condition; something requiring a remedy. [Old French *maladie* from *malade* sick, ultimately from Latin *male* ill + *habitus* past participle of *habēre* have]

Mal·aga[1] /ˈmaləgə/ a seaport on the Andalusian coast of S Spain; pop. (est. 2001) 534,207.

Mal·aga[2] *noun* a sweet fortified wine from Malaga.

Mala·gasy /ˌmaləˈgasi/ ● *adjective* of or relating to Madagascar. ● *noun* **1** the language of Madagascar. **2** a native or inhabitant of Madagascar. [originally *Malegass, Madegass* from *Madagascar*]

mal·aise /məˈleiz/ *noun* **1** a non-specific bodily discomfort not associated with the development of a disease. **2** a feeling of uneasiness. [Old French *mal* bad + *aise* EASE]

Mal·amud /ˈmaləməd/ **Ber·nard** (1914–86), US novelist and short-story writer. One of the leading Jewish writers to emerge in the US during the 1950s, he is known for novels such as *The Natural* (1952), *The Fixer* (1967), and *Dubin's Lives* (1979).

mala·mute /ˈmaləˌmjuːt/ *noun* (also **malemute**) a dog of a breed developed in Alaska, with a thick grey or black and white coat, pointed ears, and a plumed tail curling over the back. [Inupiaq *malimiut*, a people of the Kolzebue Sound, Alaska, who developed the breed]

Ma·lang /məˈlɒŋ/ a city in SE Java, Indonesia; pop. (est. 1995) 716,862.

mala·prop·ism /ˈmaləˌprɒˌpizəm/ *noun* (also **mala·prop** /ˈmaləˌprɒp/) the use of a word in mistake for one sounding similar, to comic effect, e.g. *consummated* for *consommé*. [Mrs. *Malaprop* (from MALAPROPOS) in R. B. Sheridan's *The Rivals* (1775)]

mal·apro·pos /ˌmaləprəˈpoː/ *adjective* inopportune; inappropriate. [French *mal à propos* from *mal* ill: see APROPOS]

ma·lar /ˈmeilər/ ● *adjective* of the cheek. ● *noun* a bone of the cheek. [modern Latin *malaris* from Latin *mala* jaw]

Mäl·aren /ˈmeləˌren/ a lake in SE Sweden, extending inland from the Baltic Sea. The city of Stockholm is situated at its outlet.

mal·aria /məˈleriə/ *noun* an intermittent and remittent fever caused by a protozoan parasite of the genus *Plasmodium*, introduced by the bite of a mosquito. □ **mal·arial** *adjective* [Italian *mal'aria* 'bad air', because the disease was formerly believed to be caused by the unwholesome condition of the atmosphere in marshy districts of Italy and other hot countries]

Consonants: b *but* d *dog* f *few* g *get* h *her* j *yes* k *cat* l *leg* m *man* n *no* p *pen* r *red* s *sit*

ma·lar·key /məˈlɑːki/ *noun informal* humbug; nonsense. [20th c.: origin unknown]

Mala·spina, Mount /ˈmaləˌspiːnə/ a peak (3 886 m) in SW Yukon Territory, part of the St. Elias mountain range. [A. *Malaspina*, Italian-born navigator and explorer d.1810]

mala·thion /ˌmaləˈθaiən/ *noun* an insecticide containing phosphorus, with low toxicity to other animals. [diethyl *maleate* + *thio-* acid + -ON]

Mala·tya /ˌmɒləˈtiːə/ a city in east central Turkey; pop. (est. 1997) 400,248.

Ma·lawi /məˈlɒwi/ a landlocked country in south central Africa, in the Great Rift Valley; pop. (est. 2002) 10,701,824; capital, Lilongwe.
□ **Ma·lawi·an** *adjective & noun*

Malawi, Lake an alternative name for Lake Nyasa (see NYASA, LAKE).

Ma·lay /məˈlei/ ● *noun* **1 a** a member of a people inhabiting Malaysia and Indonesia. **b** a person of Malay descent. **2** the language of this people, the official language of Malaysia. ● *adjective* of or relating to this people or language. [Malay *malāyu*]

Ma·laya /məˈleiə/ a former country in SE Asia, consisting of the southern part of the Malay Peninsula and some adjacent islands (originally including Singapore), now forming the western part of the federation of Malaysia, and known as West Malaysia.

Ma·lay·alam /ˌmaləˈjɒləm/ *noun* the Dravidian language of the state of Kerala in S India. [Malayalam, from *mala* 'mountain' + *āḷ* 'man']

Ma·lay·an /məˈleiən/ ● *noun* = MALAY noun 1. ● *adjective* of or relating to Malays or Malaya (now part of Malaysia).

Malay Archipelago a very large group of islands, including Sumatra, Java, Borneo, the Philippines, and New Guinea, lying between SE Asia and Australia. They constitute the bulk of the area formerly known as the East Indies.

Malayo- /məˈleiɔː/ *combining form* Malayan and (*Malayo-Chinese*). [MALAY]

Malayo-Polynes·ian /məˌleiɔːˌpɒliˈniːʒən/ ● *adjective* of or relating to the Malays and the Polynesians, or to Malayo-Polynesian. ● *noun* a family of languages (also called **Austronesian**) extending from Madagascar in the west to the Pacific islands in the east.

Malay Peninsula a peninsula in SE Asia separating the Indian Ocean from the South China Sea. It extends approximately 1 100 km (700 miles) southward from the Isthmus of Kra and comprises the southern part of Thailand and the whole of Malaya (West Malaysia).

Ma·lay·sia /məˈleiʒə/ a country in SE Asia; pop. (est. 2002) 22,662,365; capital, Kuala Lumpur. Malaysia is a federation consisting of **East Malaysia** (the northern part of Borneo, including Sabah and Sarawak) and **West Malaysia** (the southern part of the Malay Peninsula). The two parts of Malaysia are separated from each other by 650 km (400 miles) of the South China Sea. (*See also* MALAYA.)
□ **Ma·lay·sian** *adjective & noun*

Mal·bec /ˈmalbek/ *noun* **1** a variety of black grape, native to areas of SW France, but now also widely cultivated elsewhere, esp. in Latin America. **2** a wine made from this grape. [19th c.: origin unknown]

Mal·colm III /ˈmalkəm/ (known as 'Malcolm Canmore' from Gaelic *Ceann-mor* great head) (*c*.1031–93), son of Duncan I, king of Scotland 1058–93. He came to the throne after killing Macbeth in battle (1057), and spent a large part of his reign involved in intermittent border warfare with the new Norman regime in England; he was killed in battle.

Mal·colm IV (known as 'the Maiden') (*c*.1141–65), grandson of David I, king of Scotland 1153–65. His reign witnessed a progressive loss of power to Henry II of England; he died young and without an heir.

Mal·colm Island an island in Queen Charlotte Strait, situated off the northeastern coast of Vancouver Island, southeast of Port Hardy.

Mal·colm X /ˈmalkəm ˈeks/ (born Malcolm Little) (1925–65), US political activist. He converted to the Black Muslim faith (Nation of Islam) in 1946 and during the 1950s and early 1960s became a vigorous campaigner against the exploitation of blacks; he broke away from the Black Muslims and moderated his views on black separatism in 1964, and was assassinated the following year.

mal·con·tent /ˈmalkənˌtent/ ● *noun* a discontented person; a rebel. ● *adjective* discontented or rebellious.

mal·dis·tri·bu·tion *noun* faulty or imperfect distribution.
□ **mal·dis·trib·ut·ed** *adjective*

Mal·dives, the /ˈmɔldaivz, -diːv/ a country consisting of a chain of coral islands in the Indian Ocean southwest of Sri Lanka; pop. (est. 2002) 320,165; capital, Male. □ **Mal·div·ian** *noun & adjective*

Male /ˈmɔlei/ the capital of the Maldives; pop. (2000) 74,069.

male ● *adjective* **1** of the sex that can beget offspring by fertilization or insemination (*male child*; *male dog*). **2** of men or male animals, plants, etc.; masculine (*playing a male role*; *male voice choir*). **3** (of plants or their parts) containing only fertilizing organs. **4** (of parts of machinery etc.) designed to enter or fill the corresponding female part (*a male plug*). ● *noun* a male person, animal, or plant. □ **male·ness** *noun* [Old French *ma(s)le*, from Latin *masculus* from *mas* a male]

male bonding *noun* the formation of friendship and loyalty between males, esp. between a particular pair of male associates.

male chauvinist *noun* a man who is prejudiced against women or regards women as inferior. □ **male chauvinism** *noun*

male chauvinist pig *noun derogatory* = MALE CHAUVINIST.

Mal·ecite *var. of* MALISEET.

mal·edic·tion /ˌmaləˈdikʃən/ *noun* **1** a curse. **2** the utterance of a curse. [Latin *maledictio* from *maledicere* speak evil of, from *male* ill + *dicere dict-* speak]

mal·efac·tor /ˈmaləˌfaktər/ *noun* a criminal; an evildoer.
□ **mal·efac·tion** /-ˈfakʃən/ *noun* [Latin *malefacere malefact-* from *male* ill + *facere* do]

mal·efic /məˈlefik/ *adjective literary* (of magical arts etc.) harmful; baleful. [Latin *maleficus* from *male* ill]

mal·efi·cent /məˈlefisənt/ *adjective literary* hurtful; malicious.
□ **mal·efi·cence** *noun* [*maleficence* formed as MALEFIC after *malevolence*]

ma·leic acid /məˈleiik/ *noun* a colourless crystalline organic acid used in making synthetic resins. [French *maléique* (AS MALIC ACID)]

male menopause *noun* a crisis of potency, confidence, etc., supposed to afflict men in middle life.

mal·emute *var. of* MALAMUTE.

Mal·evich /ˈmaliˌvitʃ/ **Kaz·i·mir (Sev·erin·ovich)** (1878–1935), Russian painter and designer. His abstract works use only basic geometrical shapes and a severely restricted range of colour.

ma·levo·lent /məˈlevələnt/ *adjective* wishing evil to others.
□ **ma·levo·lence** *noun* **ma·levo·lent·ly** *adverb* [Latin *malevolens* from *male* ill + *volens* willing, part. of *velle*]

mal·feas·ance /malˈfiːzəns/ *noun Law* evildoing; illegal action.
□ **mal·feas·ant** *noun & adjective* [Anglo-French *malfaisance* from Old French *malfaisant* (as MAL-, *faisant* part. of *faire* do, from Latin *facere*): compare MISFEASANCE]

mal·for·ma·tion *noun* faulty formation. □ **mal·formed** *adjective*

mal·func·tion ● *noun* a failure to function in a normal or satisfactory manner. ● *intransitive verb* fail to function normally or satisfactorily.

Mali /ˈmɒli/ a landlocked country in West Africa, south of Algeria; pop. (est. 2002) 11,340,480; capital, Bamako. □ **Mali·an** *adjective & noun* [after a mercantile empire which dominated the region from the 13th to the 16th c.]

Mal·ibu a resort on the Pacific coast of S California, to the west of Los Angeles. The home of a number of movie stars, it is noted for its beaches and for the J. Paul Getty art museum.

malic acid /ˈmalik/ *noun* an organic acid found in apples and other fruits. [French *malique* from Latin *malum* apple]

malice /ˈmalis/ *noun* **1** the intention to do evil or to injure another person. **2** *Law* wrongful intention, esp. as increasing the guilt of certain offences. [Latin *malitia* from *malus* bad]

malice aforethought *noun Law* (also **malice prepense**) the intention to commit a crime, esp. murder.

ma·li·cious *adjective* characterized by malice; intending or intended to do harm. □ **ma·li·cious·ly** *adverb* **ma·li·cious·ness** *noun*

ma·lign /məˈlain/ ● *adjective* **1** (of a thing) injurious. **2** malevolent. ● *transitive verb* speak ill of; slander. □ **ma·lign·er** *noun* **ma·lig·nity** /məˈligniti/ *noun* (*pl.* **-ties**). **ma·lign·ly** *adverb* [Latin *malignus* from *malus* bad: compare BENIGN]

ma·lig·nant /məˈlignənt/ *adjective* **1 a** (of a disease) very virulent or infectious (*malignant cholera*). **b** (of a tumour) tending to invade normal tissue and recur after removal; cancerous. **2** harmful; feeling or showing intense ill will. □ **ma·lig·nancy** *noun* (*pl.* **-cies**).
ma·lig·nant·ly *adverb* [as MALIGN]

Ma·ligne Lake /məˈlain/ a lake in W Alberta, situated in Jasper National Park. [French, lit. 'bad']

Ma·lines /malin/ the French name for MECHELEN.

ma·lin·ger /məˈliŋgər/ *intransitive verb* exaggerate or feign illness in order to escape duty, work, etc. □ **ma·lin·ger·er** *noun* [back-formation from *malingerer* apparently from French *malingre*, perhaps formed as MAL- + *haingre* weak]

Mali·now·ski /ˌmaliˈnɒfski/ **Bron·is·law (Kas·par)** (1884–1942), Polish-born English anthropologist. He sought to explain social phenomena in terms of their functional significance, esp. in his studies of the Pueblo Indians in Mexico and Bantu tribes in Africa.

Mali·seet /'malə,siːt/ (also **Malecite** /-,səit/) (*pl.* same) ● *noun* **1** a member of an Aboriginal people now occupying northwestern New Brunswick and eastern Quebec. **2** the Algonquian language of this people. ● *adjective* of or relating to this people or their language or culture. [French *Malecite*, from Mi'kmaq *malisit*, lit. 'a person who speaks poorly or incomprehensibly']

mall *noun* **1** a retail complex containing several stores, restaurants, etc., in a single building or in two or more adjacent buildings. **2** a sheltered walk or promenade. **3** *hist.* **a** = PALL-MALL. **b** an alley used for this. [var. of MAUL: applied to *The Mall* in London (originally a pall-mall alley)]

mal·lard *noun* (*pl.* same or **mal·lards**) a common wild duck or drake, *Anas platyrhynchos*, of the northern hemisphere, the male of which has a green head, narrow white collar, chestnut breast, and a blue patch on the wings. [Old French prob. from *maslart* (unrecorded, as MALE)]

Mal·lar·mé /,malar'mei/ **Sté·phane** (1842–98), French poet. A symbolist who experimented with rhythm and syntax by transposing words and omitting grammatical elements, he is known for poems such as 'Hérodiade' (*c.*1871), 'L'Après-midi d'un faune' (1876), and 'Un Coup de dés jamais n'abolira le hasard' (1897).

mall crawl *noun N Amer. slang* the act of visiting a large number of stores in a shopping mall.

Malle /mal/ **Louis** (1932–95), French film director. His films *Ascenseur pour l'échafaud* (1958) and the erotic *Les Amants* (1959) are considered seminal examples of the French *nouvelle vague*. Other films include *Pretty Baby* (1978) and *Au Revoir les enfants* (1987).

mal·le·able /'maliəbəl/ *adjective* **1** (of metal etc.) able to be hammered or pressed permanently out of shape without breaking or cracking. **2** (of a person) adaptable; pliable, flexible. □ **malle·abil·ity** *noun* [medieval Latin *malleabilis* from Latin *malleare* to hammer, from *malleus* hammer]

mal·lee /'mali/ *noun Austral.* **1** any of several types of eucalyptus, esp. *Eucalyptus dumosa*, that flourish in arid areas. **2** a scrub or undergrowth formed by such trees, typical of some arid parts of Australia. [prob. from Wemba-wemba *mali*]

mallee fowl *noun* (also **mallee hen**) a mottled grey, brown, and white bird, *Leipoa ocellata*, of southern inland Australia, which builds its nest in large mounds.

mal·lei *pl.* of MALLEUS.

mal·leo·lus /mə'liːələs/ *noun* (*pl.* **mal·leo·li** /-,lai/) a bony protuberance of the tibia or fibula on either side of the ankle. [Latin, diminutive of *malleus* hammer]

mal·let *noun* **1** a type of hammer, usu. made of wood and having a relatively large head, used for driving chisels, beating metal, etc. **2** a light hammer used for playing the vibraphone, xylophone, etc. **3** a long-handled wooden hammer for striking a croquet or polo ball. [Old French *maillet* from *mailler* to hammer, from *mail* hammer, from Latin *malleus*]

mal·leus /'maliəs/ *noun* (*pl.* **mallei** /-lɪ,ai/) a small bone in the middle ear transmitting the vibrations of the tympanum to the incus. [Latin, = hammer]

mall·ing *noun* the process or result of the extensive building of large, self-contained shopping centres, esp. in the suburbs.

Mal·lor·ca *see* MAJORCA.

mal·low *noun* **1** any plant of the genus *Malva*, esp. *M. sylvestris*, naturalized in N America with pink or purple flowers. **2** any of several other plants of the family Malvaceae, including marsh mallow. [Old English *meal(u)we* from Latin *malva*]

mall rat *noun N Amer. informal* a person, esp. a teenager, who frequents malls to socialize in.

Malmö /'mɒlmə/ a port and fortified city in SW Sweden, situated on the Øresund opposite Copenhagen; pop. (2000) 259,579.

malm·sey /'mɑːmzi/ *noun* a strong sweet wine originally from Greece, now chiefly from Madeira. [Middle Dutch *malemeseye* via Old French from *Monemvasia* in S Greece]

mal·nour·ished *adjective* suffering from malnutrition.

mal·nour·ish·ment *noun* = MALNUTRITION.

mal·nutri·tion *noun* a dietary condition resulting from the absence of some foods or essential elements necessary for health; insufficient nutrition.

mal·occlu·sion /malə'kluːʒən/ *noun* imperfect positioning of the teeth when the jaws are closed.

mal·odor·ous /mal'oːdərəs/ *adjective* foul smelling.

malo·lac·tic /malo'laktɪk/ *adjective* designating bacterial fermentation which converts malic acid (in wine) to lactic acid. [MALIC (ACID) + -O- + LACTIC]

Mal·ory /'maləri/ **Sir Thom·as** (d. *c.*1470), English writer. His major work, *Le Morte d'Arthur* (printed 1483), is a prose translation of a collection of the legends of King Arthur, selected from French and other sources; it was one of the earliest works to be printed by Caxton.

Mal·peque Bay /'mɒlpek/ a small inlet of the Gulf of St. Lawrence, situated on the north central shore of PEI, northwest of Cavendish. [from Mi'kmaq *makpaak* big bay]

Malpeque oyster *noun Cdn* a large edible oyster raised in Malpeque Bay.

Mal·pighi /mal'piːgi/ **Mar·cello** (1628–94), Italian microscopist. He began the study of embryology, and discovered the alveoli and capillaries in the lungs, the fibres and red cells of clotted blood, and demonstrated the pathway of blood from arteries to veins.

Mal·pighi·an layer /mal'pɪgiən/ *noun* a layer of proliferating cells in the epidermis. [MALPIGHI]

Mal·pla·quet /,malpla'kei/ a village in N France, on the border with Belgium about 16 km (10 miles) south of Mons, scene of the victory in 1709 of allied British and Austrian troops over the French during the War of the Spanish Succession.

mal·prac·tice *noun* **1** improper or negligent professional treatment, esp. by a medical practitioner. **2 a** criminal wrongdoing; misconduct. **b** an instance of this.

Mal·raux /mal'rɔː/ **André (Georges)** (1901–76), French novelist, art critic, and politician. His works include the novels *La Condition humaine* (1933) and *L'Espoir* (1937), and the history of art, *Les Voix du silence* (1951).

malt ● *noun* **1** barley or other grain that is steeped, germinated, and dried, esp. for brewing or distilling and vinegar making. **2 a** = MALT WHISKY. **b** = MALT LIQUOR. **3** (also **malted**) *N Amer.* = MALTED MILK. ● *verb* **1** *transitive* convert (grain) into malt. **2** *intransitive* (of seeds) become malt when germination is checked by drought. [Old English *m(e)alt* from Germanic, related to MELT]

Malta /'mɒltə/ an island country in the central Mediterranean, about 100 km (60 miles) south of Sicily; pop. (est. 2002) 397,499; capital, Valletta. The country also includes two other inhabited islands, Gozo and Comino.

malt·ed ● *adjective* **1** converted into malt. **2** mixed with malt or a malt extract. ● *noun N Amer.* = MALTED MILK.

malted milk *noun* **1** a powder made from dried milk and malted cereals. **2** a drink made of this and milk, usu. with ice cream and flavouring.

Mal·tese /mɒl'tiːz/ ● *noun* **1** (*pl.* same) **a** a native or national of Malta. **b** a person of Maltese descent. **2** the Semitic language of Malta, heavily influenced by Italian. ● *adjective* of or relating to Malta or its people or language.

Maltese cross *noun* a cross with arms of equal length broadening from the centre, often indented at the ends.

Maltese dog *noun* (also **Maltese terrier**) a small breed of spaniel or terrier.

Mal·thus /'malθəs/ **Thom·as Rob·ert** (1766–1834), English economist and clergyman. In his *Essay on the Principle of Population* (1798) he asserted that the rate of increase of the population tends to be out of proportion to the increase of its means of subsistence, and argued that controls on population (by sexual abstinence or birth control) are therefore necessary to prevent catastrophe. □ **Mal·thu·sian** /mal'θuːziən/ *adjective* **Mal·thu·sian·ism** *noun*

malt liquor *noun* alcoholic liquor made from malt by fermentation as opposed to distillation, e.g. beer, ale, etc.

malt·ose /'mɒltoːz/ *noun Chem.* a sugar produced by the hydrolysis of starch under the action of the enzymes in malt, saliva, etc. [MALT + -OSE²]

mal·treat /mal'triːt/ *transitive verb* ill-treat. □ **mal·treat·er** *noun* **mal·treat·ment** *noun*

malt whisky *noun* whisky made from malted barley.

malty *adjective* (**malt·i·er**, **malt·i·est**) of, containing, or resembling malt. □ **malt·i·ness** *noun*

Mal·va·sia /malvə'siːə/ *noun* a variety of grape used to make white and red wines, esp. in Italy. [Italian form of *Monemvasia*: see MALMSEY]

Mal·vern Hills /'mɒlvərn/ (also **the Mal·verns**) a range of limestone hills in W England, in Herefordshire and Worcestershire. The highest point is Worcestershire Beacon (425 m; 1,394 ft.).

mal·ver·sa·tion /,malvɜr'seiʃən/ *noun formal* **1** corrupt behaviour in a

Vowels: a *cat* ɑ *arm* e *bed* ɜr *her* ɜː *deux* ə *ago* ɪ *sit* i *cosy* iː *feed* ɒ *hot* ɔ *pore* oː *no* ʌ *run* ʊ *put*

position of trust. **2** (often foll. by *of*) corrupt administration (of public money etc.). [French from *malverser* from Latin *male* badly + *versari* behave]

mam /mam/ *noun* esp. *Brit. informal* mother. [formed as MAMA]

mama *noun informal* **1** (esp. as a child's term) mother. **2** *informal* a woman (*she's one hot mama*). [imitative of child's *ma, ma*]

mama's boy *noun N Amer. informal* a boy or man who is excessively influenced by or devoted to his mother.

mama·teek *noun hist.* a type of wigwam used by the Beothuk. [Beothuk]

mam·ba /'mambə/ *noun* any large venomous African snake of the genus *Dendroaspis*. [Zulu *imamba*]

mambo /'mamboː/ ● *noun* (*pl.* **-bos**) **1** a Latin American dance like the rumba. **2** the music for this. ● *intransitive verb* (**-boes, -boed**) perform the mambo. [Latin American Spanish prob. from Haitian]

Mam·eluke /'maməˌluːk/ *noun* a member of a group of Turkoman warriors. Originally brought to Egypt as slaves, they became a powerful group, ruling as sultans in Egypt and Syria from the mid-13th c. until conquered by the Ottoman Turks in 1517; in Egypt the Mamelukes continued to rule under Ottoman sovereignty until they were finally defeated and massacred by the viceroy Muhammad Ali in 1811. [ultimately from Arabic *mamlūk* slave from *malaka* possess]

Mamet /'mamət/ **David** (b.1947), US dramatist, director, and screenwriter. His works are noted for their radical approach to social issues, and include the plays *Glengarry Glen Ross* (1984) and *Oleanna* (1992), whose portrayal of a case involving false accusations of sexual harassment caused much controversy.

mam·il·la /məˈmɪlə/ *noun* (*pl.* **mam·il·lae** /-liː/) **1** the nipple of a woman's breast. **2** a nipple-shaped organ etc. □ **mam·il·lary** /'mamɪləri/ *adjective* [Latin, diminutive of MAMMA²]

mamma¹ (also esp. *N Amer.* **momma**) *informal var. of* MAMA.

mamma² /'mamə/ *noun* (*pl.* **mam·mae** /-miː/) **1** a milk-secreting organ of female mammals. **2** a corresponding non-secretory structure in male mammals. □ **mammi·form** *adjective* [Old English from Latin]

mam·mal *noun* any warm-blooded animal of the vertebrate class Mammalia, members of which are characterized by the possession of mammary glands in the female and a four-chambered heart, including human beings, carnivores, ungulates, rodents, whales, etc. □ **mam·mal·ian** /-'meilien/ *adjective & noun* **mam·mal·o·gist** *noun* **mam·mal·ogy** /-'malədʒi/ *noun* [modern Latin *mammalia* neuter pl. of Latin *mammalis* (as MAMMA²)]

mam·mary /'maməri/ *adjective* of the human female breasts or milk-secreting organs of other mammals. [MAMMA² + -ARY¹]

mammary gland *noun* the milk-producing gland of female mammals.

mam·mee /ma'miː/ *noun* a tropical American tree, *Mammea americana*, with large red-rinded yellow-pulped fruit. [Spanish *mamei* from Haitian]

mam·mo·gram *noun* an image obtained by mammography.

mam·mog·raphy /ma'mɒɡrəfi/ *noun Med.* an X-ray technique of diagnosing and locating abnormalities (esp. tumours) of the breasts. [MAMMA² + -GRAPHY]

Mam·mon /'mamən/ *noun* **1** an early name for the god of covetousness, used in the Greek text of the New Testament in Matt. 6:24 and Luke 16:9–13, and retained in the Vulgate. **2** wealth regarded as an idol or as an evil influence. [Aramaic *māmōn* 'riches']

mam·moth ● *noun* any large extinct elephant of the genus *Mammuthus*, with a hairy coat and curved tusks. ● *adjective* huge. [Russian *mamo(n)t*]

Mammoth Cave National Park a national park in west central Kentucky, site of the largest known cave system in the world. It consists of over 480 km (300 miles) of charted passageways and contains some spectacular rock formations.

mammy *noun* (*pl.* **-mies**) *dated* **1** a child's word for mother. **2** *US* a black nursemaid or nanny in charge of white children. [formed as MAMMA¹]

Man. *abbreviation* Manitoba.

man ● *noun* (*pl.* **men**) **1** an adult human male, esp. as distinct from a woman or boy. **2 a** a human being; a person (*no man is perfect*). **b** human beings in general; the human race (*man is mortal*). ¶ The generic use of *man* to mean 'a human being' or 'the human race' is regarded by many as sexist. **3** a person showing characteristics associated with males (*she's more of a man than he is*). **4 a** a worker; an employee (*the manager spoke to the men*). **b** a manservant or valet. **c** *hist.* a vassal. **5 a** (usu. in *pl.*) soldiers, sailors, etc., esp. non-officers (*was in

command of 200 men*). **b** an individual, usu. male, person (*fought to the last man*). **c** (usu. prec. by *the*, or *possessive adj.*) a person regarded as suitable or appropriate in some way; a person fulfilling requirements (*I'm your man; not the man for the job*). **6 a** a husband (*man and wife*). **b** *informal* a boyfriend or lover. **7 a** a human being of a specified historical period or character (*Renaissance man*). **b** a type of prehistoric man named after the place where the remains were found (*Peking man*). **8** any one of a set of pieces used in playing chess, checkers, etc. **9** (as second element in *combination*) a man of a specified nationality, profession, skill, etc. (*Dutchman; clergyman; horseman; gentleman*). **10 a** an expression of impatience etc. used in addressing a male (*nonsense, man!*). **b** *informal* a general mode of address (*blew my mind, man!*). **11** (prec. by *a*) a person; one (*what can a man do?*). **12** a person pursued; an opponent etc. (*the Mounties always get their man*). **13** (**the Man**) *US slang* **a** the police. **b** *Black slang* a person or group with power or authority. **14** (in *combination*) a ship of a specified type (*merchantman*). ● *transitive verb* (**manned, man·ning**) **1** supply (a ship, fort, factory, etc.) with a person or people for work or defence etc. **2** work or service or defend (a specified piece of equipment, a fortification, etc.) (*man the pumps*). **3** *Naut.* place men at (a part of a ship). **4** fill (a post or office). ● *interjection* esp. *N Amer. informal* expressing surprise, admiration, etc. (*Man! Was that ever a great meal!*). □ **as one man** in unison; in agreement. **be a man** be courageous; not show fear. **be one's own man 1** be free to act; be independent. **2** be in full possession of one's faculties etc. **man to man** with candour; honestly. **my** (or **my good**) **man** a patronizing mode of address to a man. **separate** (or **sort out**) **the men from the boys** *informal* find those who are truly virile, competent, etc. **to a man** all without exception. □ **man·less** *adjective* [Old English *man(n)*, pl. *menn, mannian*, from Germanic]

Man, Isle of see ISLE OF MAN.

mana /'mɒnə/ *noun* (esp. in Polynesian, Melanesian, and Maori belief) an impersonal supernatural power which can be associated with people or objects and which can be transmitted or inherited. [Maori]

man about town *noun* a sophisticated man who frequently goes to fashionable clubs, parties, theatres, etc.

man·acle /'manəkəl/ ● *noun* (usu. in *pl.*) **1** a fetter or shackle for the hand; a handcuff. **2** a restraint. ● *transitive verb* fetter with manacles. [Old French *manicle* handcuff, from Latin *manicula* diminutive of *manus* hand]

man·age *verb* **1** *transitive* organize; regulate; be in charge of (a business, household, team, a person's career, etc.). **2** *transitive* (often foll. by *to* + *infin.*) succeed in achieving; contrive (*managed to arrive on time; managed a smile; managed to ruin the day*). **3** *intransitive* **a** (often foll. by *with*) succeed in one's aim, esp. against heavy odds (*managed with one assistant*). **b** meet one's needs with limited resources etc. (*just about manages on her pension*). **4** *transitive* gain influence with or maintain control over (a person etc.) (*cannot manage their teenage son*). **5** *transitive & intransitive* (often prec. by *can, be able to*) **a** cope with; make use of (*couldn't manage another bite; can you manage by yourself?*). **b** be free to attend on (a certain day) or at (a certain time) (*can you manage Thursday?*). **6** *transitive* handle or wield (a tool, weapon, etc.). [orig. in sense 'put (a horse) through the paces of the manège', from Italian *maneggiare, maneggio* ultimately from Latin *manus* hand]

man·age·able *adjective* able to be easily managed, controlled, and accomplished etc. □ **man·age·abil·ity** *noun* **man·age·able·ness** *noun* **man·age·ably** *adverb*

managed care *noun* esp. *US* a system of health care emphasizing preventative medicine and home treatment.

man·age·ment *noun* **1** the process or an instance of managing or being managed. **2 a** the professional administration of business concerns, public undertakings, etc. **b** the people engaged in this. **c** (prec. by *the*) a governing body; a board of directors or the people in charge of running a business, regarded collectively. **3** (usu. foll. by *of*) *Med.* the technique of treating a disease etc.

management buyout *noun* the purchase of at least a controlling share in a company by its directors.

man·ager *noun* **1** a person controlling or administering a business or part of a business. **2** a person controlling the affairs, training, etc. of a person or team in sports, entertainment, etc. **3** a person regarded in terms of skill in household or financial or other management (*a good manager*). □ **man·ag·er·ial** /ˌmanɪˈdʒiːriəl/ *adjective* **man·ag·er·ial·ly** /-ˈdʒiːriəli/ *adverb*

man·ager·ess *noun* a woman manager, esp. of a shop, hotel, theatre, etc.

man·ag·ing *adjective* (in *combination*) having executive control or authority (*managing director*).

uː mood ai my əi pipe au brown ʌu house ei day ɔi boy ā franglais ã Canadien ɔ̃ Brayon   (*see over for consonants*)

Ma·na·gua /məˈnɒgwə/ the capital of Nicaragua; pop. (est. 2002) 1,106,600. The city was almost completely destroyed by an earthquake in 1972.

mana·kin /ˈmanəkɪn/ *noun* any small bird of the family Pipridae of Central and S America, the males of which are often brightly coloured. [var. of MANIKIN]

Ma·nama /məˈnɒmə/ the capital of Bahrain; pop. (est. 2002) 148,000.

ma·ñana /manˈjɒnə/ ● *adverb* in the indefinite future (esp. to indicate procrastination). ● *noun* an indefinite future time. [Spanish, = tomorrow]

Ma·nas·seh /məˈnasi, -ˈnasə/ **1** a Hebrew patriarch, son of Joseph (Gen. 48:19). **2** the tribe of Israel traditionally descended from him.

manat /ˈmanat/ *noun* (*pl.* same) the basic monetary unit of Azerbaijan and Turkmenistan, equal to 100 gopik in Azerbaijan and 100 tenesi in Turkmenistan. [Azerbaijani and Turkmen]

man-at-arms *noun* (*pl.* **men-at-arms**) *archaic* a soldier, esp. when heavily armed and mounted.

mana·tee /ˌmanəˈtiː/ *noun* any large aquatic plant-eating mammal of the genus *Trichechus*, with paddle-like forelimbs, no hind limbs, and a powerful tail. [Spanish *manati* from Carib *manattouí*]

Ma·naus /məˈnʌus/ a city in NW Brazil; pop. (2000) 1,394,724. It is the principal commercial centre of the upper Amazon region.

Mana·watu River /ˌmanəˈwɒtuː/ a river of North Island, New Zealand, flowing into Cook Strait.

Mance /mɑ̃s/ **Jeanne** (1606–73), founder of the first hospital in New France, the Hôtel-Dieu in Montreal (completed 1645).

Man·ches·ter an industrial city and metropolitan district in NW England; pop. (2001) 392,819. It developed in the 18th and 19th c. as a centre of the English cotton industry.

man·chi·neel /ˌmantʃɪˈniːl/ *noun* a Caribbean tree, *Hippomane mancinella*, with a poisonous and caustic milky sap and acrid apple-like fruit. [French *mancenille* from Spanish *manzanilla* diminutive of *manzana* apple]

Man·chu /manˈtʃuː/ ● *noun* **1** a member of a people in China, descended from a Tartar people, who formed the last imperial dynasty (1644-1912). **2** the language of the Manchus, now spoken in parts of NE China. ● *adjective* of or relating to the Manchu people or their language. [Manchu, = pure]

Man·chu·ria /manˈtʃʊriə/ a mountainous region forming the northeastern portion of China, now comprising the provinces of Jilin, Laoning, and Heilongjiang. □ **Man·chu·rian** *noun & adjective*

Man·cini /manˈsiːni/ **En·rico 'Henry'** (1924–94), US composer. He wrote over 80 film scores; his best-known composition is the theme for the *Pink Panther* series.

man·ciple /ˈmansɪpəl/ *noun* an officer or steward who buys provisions for a college, monastery, etc. [Latin *mancipium* purchase, from *manceps* buyer, from *manus* hand + *capere* take]

Man·cu·nian /manˈkjuːniən/ ● *noun* a native of Manchester, England. ● *adjective* of or relating to Manchester. [Latin *Mancunium* Manchester]

-mancy *combining form* forming nouns meaning 'divination by' (*geomancy*; *necromancy*). □ **-mantic** *combining form*. [Greek *manteia* divination]

M&A *abbreviation* mergers and acquisitions.

Man·dae·an /manˈdiːən/ ● *noun* **1** a member of a Gnostic sect surviving in Iraq and claiming descent from John the Baptist. **2** the language of this sect. ● *adjective* of or concerning the Mandaeans or their language. [Aramaic *mandaiia* Gnostics, from *manda* knowledge]

man·dala /ˈmandələ/ *noun* **1** a symbolic circular figure representing the universe in Hinduism and Buddhism. **2** *Psych.* such a symbol in a dream, representing the dreamer's search for completeness and self-unity. [Sanskrit *máṇḍala* disc]

Man·da·lay /ˌmandəˈlei/ a port on the Irrawaddy River in central Burma (Myanmar); pop. (est. 2002) 1,057,600. It is an important Buddhist religious centre.

man·da·mus /manˈdeiməs/ *noun* *Law* a judicial writ issued as a command to an inferior court, or ordering a person to perform a public or statutory duty. [Latin, = we command]

man·da·rin¹ /ˈmandrɪn/ *noun* **1** (**Mandarin**) the most widely spoken form of Chinese and the official language of China. **2** *hist.* a Chinese official in any of nine grades of the pre-Communist civil service. **3 a** a bureaucrat. **b** a powerful member of the establishment. □ **man·da·rin·ate** *noun* [Portuguese *mandarim* from Malay from Hindi *mantrī* from Sanskrit *mantrin* counsellor]

man·da·rin² /ˈmandrɪn/ *noun* (in full **mandarin orange**) **1** a small flattish deep-coloured orange with a loose skin. **2** the tree, *Citrus reticulata*, yielding this. *Also called* TANGERINE 1. [French *mandarine* (perhaps as MANDARIN¹ 2, with reference to the official's yellow robes)]

mandarin collar *noun* a narrow collar standing up from a close-fitting neckline and not quite meeting in front.

mandarin duck *noun* a small Chinese duck, *Aix galericulata*, noted for its bright plumage.

man·date ● *noun* **1** an order given to a person, organization, etc. to carry out a certain task. **2 a** a support for a policy or course of action, regarded by a victorious party, candidate, etc., as derived from the wishes of the people in an election. **b** *Cdn* the period during which a government is in power. **3** a commission to act for another. **4** *Law* a commission by which a party is entrusted to perform a service, often gratuitously and with indemnity against loss by that party. **5** *hist.* a commission from the League of Nations to a member nation to administer a territory. ● *transitive verb* **1** require, esp. by law; make mandatory. **2** instruct (a delegate) to act or vote in a certain way. **3** (usu. foll. by *to*) *hist.* assign (territory) under a mandate from the League of Nations. [Latin *mandatum*, neuter past participle of *mandare* command, from *manus* hand + *dare* give]

man·da·tory *adjective* **1** compulsory. **2** of or conveying a command. □ **man·da·tor·ily** *adverb* [as MANDATE]

mandatory supervision *noun* *Cdn Law* supervision by a parole officer of a convict serving the last part of a sentence in the community after being released from prison, usu. because of good behaviour in the first two-thirds of the sentence.

man-day *noun* a day of work etc. by one person, as a unit of measure.

Man·dela /manˈdelə/ **Nel·son (Ro·lih·lahla)** (b.1918), South African political activist, president of South Africa 1994–9. His long imprisonment (1962–1990) for activism with the African National Congress made him an international symbol of the struggle against apartheid; after his release he resumed leadership of the ANC, and was elected president in South Africa's first open election. He shared the Nobel Peace Prize with President F. W. de Klerk in 1993.

Man·del·stam /ˈmandəlˌʃtam/ **Osip (Emily·evich)** (also **Man·del·shtam**) (1891–*c.*1938), Russian poet. In volumes such as *Kamen* (1913) and *Tristiya* (1922) he favoured concrete detail, clarity, and precision of language in reaction to the mysticism of symbolist poetry; he was sent into internal exile (1934–7) and eventually died in a prison camp.

man·dible /ˈmandɪbəl/ *noun* **1** the jaw, esp. the lower jaw in mammals and fishes. **2** the upper or lower part of a bird's beak. **3** either half of the crushing organ in an arthropod's mouthparts. □ **man·dibu·lar** /-ˈdɪbjʊlər/ *adjective* **man·dibu·late** /-ˈdɪbjʊlət/ *adjective* [Old French *mandible* or Late Latin *mandibula* from *mandere* chew]

man·do·lin /ˌmandəˈlɪn, ˈman-/ *noun* **1** a musical instrument resembling a lute, having paired metal strings plucked with a plectrum. **2** (also **man·do·line**) a kitchen utensil fitted with cutting blades and used for slicing vegetables. □ **man·do·lin·ist** *noun* [French *mandoline* from Italian *mandolino* diminutive of *mandola*, an early form of mandolin]

man·dor·la /manˈdɔrlə/ *noun* *Art* a pointed oval used as an aureole in medieval sculpture and painting. [Italian, = almond]

man·drake /ˈmandreik/ *noun* a poisonous plant, *Mandragora officinarum*, with white or purple flowers and large yellow fruit, having emetic and narcotic properties and possessing a root once thought to resemble the human form and to shriek when plucked. [medieval Latin: assoc. with MAN + *drake* dragon (compare DRAKE)]

man·drel /ˈmandrəl/ *noun* **1** a shaft inserted into a workpiece to secure it to a lathe (compare CHUCK² 2). **2** a cylindrical rod round which metal or other material is forged or shaped. [16th c.: origin unknown]

man·drill /ˈmandrɪl/ *noun* a large W African baboon, *Mandrillus sphinx*, with a brightly coloured red and blue face, the male having a blue rump. [prob. from MAN + DRILL³]

man·du·cate /ˈmandjʊˌkeit/ *transitive verb* *literary* chew; eat. [Latin *manducare* chew, from *manduco* guzzler, from *mandere* chew]

mane *noun* **1** long hair growing in a line on the neck of a horse, lion, etc. **2** a person's long, thick hair. □ **maned** *adjective* (also in *combination*). [Old English *manu* from Germanic]

man-eater *noun* **1** an animal, esp. a shark or tiger, that eats or has a propensity for eating human flesh. **2** *informal* a woman who has many men as lovers and is perceived as using them for her own advantage.

manège /maˈneiʒ/ *noun* (also **manege**) **1** a riding school. **2** the movements of a trained horse. **3** horsemanship. [French *manège* from Italian (as MANAGE)]

Consonants: b *but* d *dog* f *few* g *get* h *her* j *yes* k *cat* l *leg* m *man* n *no* p *pen* r *red* s *sit*

Manes /'meɪniːz/ see MANI.

manes /'mɒneɪz, 'meɪniːz/ *plural noun* the deified souls of dead ancestors in ancient Roman belief. [Latin]

Manet /ma'neɪ/ **Édouard** (1832–83), French painter. His work greatly influenced the Impressionists and several of his paintings aroused controversy because of the frank and unidealized treatment of their subject matter; notable works include *Déjeuner sur l'herbe* (1863), *Olympia* (1865), and *A Bar at the Folies-Bergère* (1882).

man·eu·ver *var. of* MANOEUVRE.

man Friday *noun* a male helper or follower; a right-hand man. [from *Man Friday* in Defoe's novel *Robinson Crusoe* (1719)]

man·ful *adjective* brave; resolute. □ **man·ful·ly** *adverb*

manga *noun* an orig. Japanese genre of cartoons, comic books, etc. usu. featuring characters with distinctive large, staring eyes, and typically having a science-fiction or fantasy theme.

man·ga·bey /'maŋɡə,beɪ/ *noun* any small long-tailed W African monkey of the genus *Cercocebus*. [*Mangabey*, a region of Madagascar]

man·ga·nese /'maŋɡə,niːz/ *noun* **1** *Chem.* a grey brittle metallic transition element used with steel to make alloys. Symbol: **Mn**; at. no.: 25. **2** (in full **manganese oxide**) the black mineral oxide of this used in the manufacture of glass. [Italian *manganese*, alteration of MAGNESIA]

mange /meɪndʒ/ *noun* a skin disease in hairy and woolly animals, caused by an arachnid parasite and occasionally communicated to humans. [Old French *manjue, mangeue* itch, from *mangier* eat, from Latin *manducare* chew]

man·gel /'maŋɡəl/ *noun* (also **mangold** /'maŋɡəld/) (in full **mangel-wurzel, mangold-wurzel** /-'wɜːrzəl/) a large kind of beet, *Beta vulgaris*, used as cattle food. [German *Mangoldwurzel* from *Mangold* beet + *Wurzel* root]

man·ger /'meɪndʒɜːr/ *noun* a long open box or trough in a barn etc. for livestock to eat from. [Old French *mangeoire*, ultimately from Latin (as MANDUCATE)]

manger scene *noun N Amer.* = NATIVITY SCENE.

mange-tout /'mɑ̃ʒtuː, -'tuː/ *noun* the sugar-pea. [French, = eat-all]

mangia-cake /'mʌndʒə,keɪk/ *noun Cdn derogatory* or *jocular* (among Italian-Canadians) a non-Italian white person, esp. of British stock, with characteristically North American traits or customs. [Italian from *mangiare* 'eat' + CAKE]

man·gle[1] *transitive verb* **1** crush, bend, break, or mutilate (something), esp. so that it is difficult to ascertain its original form. **2** spoil (a quotation, text, etc.) by misquoting, mispronouncing, etc. **3** cut roughly so as to disfigure. ● **man·gler** *noun* [Anglo-French *ma(ha)ngler* apparently frequentative of *mahaignier* MAIM]

man·gle[2] ● *noun* **1** esp. *Brit. hist.* a machine having two or more cylinders usu. turned by a handle, between which wet clothes etc. are squeezed and pressed. **2** *US* a large machine for ironing usu. damp sheets etc. using heated rollers. ● *transitive verb* press (clothes etc.) in a mangle. [Dutch *mangel(stok)* from *mangelen* to mangle, ultimately from Greek *magganon* + *stok* staff, STOCK]

mango *noun* (*pl.* **man·goes** or **man·gos**) **1** a fleshy yellowish-red fruit, eaten ripe or used green for pickles etc. **2** the Indian evergreen tree, *Mangifera indica*, bearing this. [Portuguese *manga* from Malay *mangā* from Tamil *mānkāy* from *mān* mango tree + *kāy* fruit]

man·gold (also **mangold-wurzel**) *var. of* MANGEL.

man·gonel /'maŋɡənəl/ *noun hist.* a military engine for throwing stones etc. [Old French *mangonel(le)*, from medieval Latin *manganellus* diminutive of Late Latin *manganum* from Greek *manganon*, axis of a pulley]

man·go·steen /'maŋɡə,stiːn/ *noun* **1** a white juicy-pulped fruit with a thick reddish-brown rind. **2** the E Indian tree, *Garcinia mangostana*, bearing this. [Malay *manggustan*]

man·grove /'maŋɡroʊv/ *noun* **1** any tropical tree or shrub of the genus *Rhizophora*, growing in shore mud with many tangled roots above ground. **2** any of various other trees or shrubs resembling this. [17th c.: origin uncertain: assimilated to GROVE]

mangy /'meɪndʒi/ *adjective* (**mangi·er, mangi·est**) **1** (esp. of a domestic animal) having mange. **2** squalid; shabby. □ **mangi·ness** *noun*

man·handle *transitive verb* **1** move (heavy objects) by human effort. **2** *informal* handle (a person) roughly.

Man·hat·tan an island near the mouth of the Hudson River forming part of the city of New York. The site of the original Dutch settlement of New Amsterdam, it is now a borough containing the commercial and cultural centre of New York City. □ **Man·hat·tan·ite** *noun* [after the Algonquin people from whom the Dutch settlers claimed to have bought the island in 1626]

man·hat·tan *noun* a cocktail made of vermouth, whisky, etc. [MANHATTAN]

Manhattan clam chowder *noun N Amer.* a soup of clams, tomatoes, onion, and potatoes.

Manhattan Project *noun* the code name for the American project set up in 1942 to develop an atom bomb.

man·hole *noun* a covered opening allowing access to a sewer, tunnel, boiler, etc.

man·hood *noun* **1** the state of being a man rather than a child or woman. **2 a** manliness; courage. **b** a man's sexual potency. **c** *informal euphemism* the penis. **3** men collectively. **4** the state of being human.

man-hour *noun* an hour regarded in terms of the amount of work that could be done by one person within this period.

man·hunt *noun* an organized search for a person, esp. a criminal.

Mani /'mɒni/ (also **Manes** or **Mani·chae·us**) (216–*c.*274), Persian prophet, who was the founder of Manichaeism.

mania *noun* **1** *Psych.* mental illness marked by periods of great excitement and violence. **2** (often foll. by *for*) an extreme or abnormal desire or enthusiasm (*has a mania for jogging*). [Late Latin from Greek, = madness, from *mainomai* be mad, related to MIND]

-mania *combining form* **1** *Psych.* denoting a special type of mental abnormality or obsession (*megalomania; nymphomania*). **2** denoting extreme enthusiasm or admiration (*bibliomania; Trudeaumania*).

ma·niac ● *noun* **1** a person exhibiting extreme symptoms of wild behaviour etc.; an insane person. **2** an obsessive enthusiast. ● *adjective* of or behaving like a maniac. □ **man·iac·al** /mə'naɪəkəl/ *adjective* **man·iac·al·ly** /mə'naɪəkəli/ *adverb* [Late Latin *maniacus* from late Greek *maniakos* (as MANIA)]

-maniac *combining form* forming adjectives and nouns meaning 'affected with -mania' or 'a person affected with -mania' (*nymphomaniac*).

manic /'manɪk/ *adjective* **1** of or affected by mania. **2** frenzied, elated, or abnormally energetic as if affected by a manic disorder. □ **man·ic·ally** *adverb*

manic-depres·sive *Psych.* ● *adjective* affected by or relating to a mental disorder with alternating periods of elation and depression. ● *noun* a person having such a disorder. □ **manic depression** *noun*

Mani·chae·an /ˌmanɪ'kiːən/ (also **Mani·che·an**) ● *noun* **1** an adherent of a religious system of the 3rd–5th c., representing Satan in a state of everlasting conflict with God. **2** *Theol. & Philos.* a dualist (see DUALISM 2, 3a). ● *adjective* of or relating to Manichaeans. □ **Mani·chae·ism** /-'kiːɪzəm/ *noun* (also **Mani·che·ism**). [MANICHAEUS]

Mani·chae·us /ˌmanɪ'kiːəs/ *see* MANI.

Mani·chee /ˌmanɪ'kiː/ *noun* = MANICHAEAN *noun*.

mani·cotti /ˌmanɪ'kɒti/ *noun* large tubular pasta, usu. served stuffed with ricotta cheese and covered with tomato sauce. [Italian, pl. of *manicotto* 'sleeve, muff']

Mani·cou·agan River /manikuːa'ɡɑ̃/ a river in east central Quebec, flowing 455 km southward to empty into the St. Lawrence at Baie-Comeau. [Montagnais, = where birch bark is gathered (for repairing canoes), or place where they get a drink]

mani·cure /'manɪ,kjʊr/ ● *noun* a usu. professional cosmetic treatment of the hands and fingernails. ● *transitive verb* **1** apply a manicure to (the hands or a person). **2** trim or cut neatly (*spent all her time manicuring the lawn*). □ **mani·cured** *adjective* [French from Latin *manus* hand + *cura* care]

mani·cur·ist /'manɪ,kjʊrɪst/ *noun* a person who manicures hands and fingernails professionally.

mani·fest[1] ● *adjective* clear or obvious to the eye or mind (*her distress was manifest*). ● *verb* **1** *transitive* display or show (a quality, feeling, etc.) by one's acts etc. **2** *transitive* show plainly to the eye or mind. **3** *transitive* be evidence of; prove. **4** *intransitive & reflexive* (of a thing) reveal itself. **5** *intransitive* (of a ghost) appear. □ **mani·fest·a·tion** *noun* **mani·fest·ly** *adverb* [Latin *manifestus, manifestare* from *manus* hand + *festus* (unrecorded) struck]

mani·fest[2] ● *noun* a list of the cargo or passengers carried by a ship, truck, aircraft, etc. ● *transitive verb* record (names, cargo, etc.) in a manifest. [Italian *manifesto*: see MANIFESTO]

manifest destiny *noun* the esp. 19th c. belief that the US was intended by God to expand to the Pacific coast, and (among some politicians etc.) eventually to cover all of N America.

M
NO

t *top*   v *voice*   w *we*   z *zoo*   ʃ *she*   ʒ *vision*   θ *thin*   ð *this*   ŋ *ring*   x *loch*   tʃ *chip*   dʒ *jar*   (*see over for vowels*)

mani·festo *noun* (*pl.* **-festos** or **-toes**) a public declaration of principles, intentions, purposes, etc. [Italian from *manifestare* from Latin (as MANIFEST[1])]

mani·fold ● *adjective literary* **1** many and various (*manifold vexations*). **2** having various forms, parts, applications, etc. **3** performing several functions at once. ● *noun* **1** a thing with many different forms, parts, applications, etc. **2** *Mech.* a pipe or chamber branching into several openings. [Old English *manigfeald* (as MANY, -FOLD)]

mani·kin /'manɪkɪn/ *noun* (also **mannikin**) **1** a little person; a dwarf. **2** an artist's lay figure. **3** an anatomical model of the body. [Dutch *manneken*, diminutive of *man* MAN]

Man·ila /mə'nɪlə/ the capital and chief port of the Philippines, on the island of Luzon; pop. (est. 2002) 1,350,320.

man·ila *noun* (also **man·illa**) **1** (in full **manila hemp**) the strong fibre of a Philippine tree, *Musa textilis*, used for rope etc. **2** a strong brown paper made from manila hemp or other material and used for wrapping paper, envelopes, etc. [MANILA]

man in the moon *noun* the semblance of a face seen on the surface of a full moon.

man in the street *noun* (also **man on the street**) an ordinary average person, as distinct from an expert.

man·ioc /'manɪˌɒk/ *noun* = CASSAVA. [Tupi *mandioca*]

man·iple /'manɪpəl/ *noun* **1** *Rom. Hist.* a subdivision of a legion, containing 120 or 60 men. **2** *Christianity* a Eucharistic vestment consisting of a strip hanging from the left arm. [Latin *manipulus* handful, troop, from *manus* hand]

ma·nipu·late *transitive verb* **1** handle, treat, or use, esp. skilfully (a tool, question, material, etc.). **2** manage (a person, situation, etc.) to one's own advantage, esp. unfairly or unscrupulously. **3** manually examine and treat (a part of the body). **4** *Computing* alter, edit, or move (text, data, etc.). □ **ma·nipu·la·bil·ity** *noun* **ma·nipu·lable** *adjective* **ma·nipu·la·tion** *noun* **ma·nipu·la·tor** *noun* [modern Latin *manipulatio* (as MANIPLE)]

ma·nipu·la·tive *adjective* **1** characterized by unscrupulous exploitation of a situation, person, etc., for one's own ends. **2** of, concerning, or causing manipulation. □ **ma·nipu·la·tive·ness** *noun*

Mani·pur /ˌmʌnɪ'pʊr/ a small state in the far east of India, east of Assam, on the border with Burma (Myanmar); capital, Imphal. □ **Mani·puri** *adjective & noun*

Mani·toba a province of west central Canada, with a coastline on Hudson Bay; pop. (2001) 1,119,583; capital, Winnipeg. The area was part of Rupert's Land from 1670 until it was transferred to Canada by the Hudson's Bay Co. and became a province in 1870. □ **Mani·toban** *adjective & noun* [prob. from Ojibwa *manito-bah* or Cree *manito-wapow* strait of the spirit, with reference to The Narrows of Lake Manitoba]

Manitoba, Lake a large lake in south central Manitoba, situated about 75 km northwest of Winnipeg. It occupies an area of 4 624 sq. km.

Manitoba Escarpment see RIDING MOUNTAIN.

Manitoba maple *noun Cdn* a fast-growing N American maple, *Acer negundo*, with pinnate leaves, found east of the Rockies. *Also called* ASH-LEAVED MAPLE, BOX ELDER.

mani·tou /'manɪˌtuː/ *noun* (esp. among the Cree and Ojibwa) **1** a good or evil spirit as an object of reverence. **2** something regarded as having supernatural power. [Algonquian *manito*, *-tu* 'he has surpassed']

Mani·tou·lin Island /ˌmanɪ'tuːlɪn/ an island of north central Ontario, situated off the northern shore of Lake Huron and separated from the mainland by the North Channel. A popular tourist and recreation area, it is the world's largest island in a freshwater lake. [see MANITOU]

Mani·waki /ˌmanɪ'wɒki/ a town in SW central Quebec, situated on the Gatineau River, about 100 km north of Gatineau; pop. (1996) 3,571. [Algonquin, = place of Mary, with reference to the Oblate mission established there in 1849]

man·kind *noun* **1** the human species. ¶ Some people consider the use of *mankind* in this sense sexist and prefer where possible to use *humankind* or *the human race* instead. **2** male people, as distinct from female.

manky /'maŋki/ *adjective* (**mank·i·er, mank·i·est**) *Brit. informal* **1** bad, inferior, defective. **2** dirty. [obsolete *mank* mutilated, defective]

man·like *adjective* **1** having the qualities of a man. **2** (of an animal, shape, etc.) resembling a human being.

manly *adjective* (**man·li·er, man·li·est**) **1** having qualities regarded as admirable in a man, such as courage, frankness, etc. **2** (of things, qualities, etc.) befitting a man. □ **man·li·ness** *noun*

man-made *adjective* made by humans; artificial, synthetic.

Mann /man/ **Thom·as** (1875–1955), German novelist and essayist. The role and character of the artist in relation to society is a recurrent theme in his works, which include *Buddenbrooks* (1901), the novella *Death in Venice* (1912), and *Dr. Faustus* (1947); he was awarded the Nobel Prize for literature in 1929.

manna /'manə/ *noun* **1** *Bible* the substance miraculously supplied as food to the Israelites in the wilderness (Exod. 16). **2** (also **manna from heaven**) an unexpected benefit. **3** spiritual nourishment, esp. the Eucharist. **4** the sweet dried juice from the manna ash and other plants, used as a mild laxative. [Aramaic *mannā* from Hebrew *mān*, explained as = *mān hū?* what is it?, but prob. = Arabic *mann* exudation of common tamarisk (*Tamarix gallica*)]

manna ash *noun* an ash tree native to S Europe, *Fraxinus ornus*.

Man·nar /ma'nɑr/ **1** an island off the northwest coast of Sri Lanka, linked to India by the chain of coral islands and shoals known as Adam's Bridge. **2** a town on this island; pop. (est. 2002) 42,000.

Mannar, Gulf of an inlet of the Indian Ocean lying between NW Sri Lanka and the southern tip of India. It lies to the south of Adam's Bridge, which separates it from the Palk Strait.

Mann Cup *noun* a trophy awarded annually to the Canadian senior amateur lacrosse champions, first presented in 1910 (*compare* MINTO CUP). [Sir D. Mann, Canadian railway builder d.1934, who donated the trophy]

manned *adjective* (of an aircraft, spacecraft, etc.) having a human crew.

man·ne·quin /'manəkɪn/ *noun* **1** a three-dimensional model of a human body, used when making clothes or esp. for displaying them in stores. **2** a model employed by a couturier etc. to show clothes to customers. [French, = MANIKIN]

man·ner *noun* **1** a way a thing is done or happens (*always dresses in that manner*). **2** (in *pl.*) **a** the social habits and customs, esp. of a particular group (*18th-century aristocratic manners*). **b** polite or well-bred behaviour (*she has no manners*). **3** a person's outward bearing, way of speaking, etc. (*has an imperious manner*). **4 a** a style in literature, art, etc. (*in the manner of Leacock*). **b** = MANNERISM 2. **5** a kind or sort (*what manner of man is he?*). □ **all manner of** many different kinds of. **in a manner of speaking** in some sense; to some extent; so to speak. **manner of means** see MEANS. **to the manner born 1** *informal* naturally at ease in a specified job, situation, etc. **2** destined by birth to follow a custom or way of life. [Anglo-French *manere*, ultimately from Latin *manuarius* of the hand (*manus*)]

man·nered *adjective* **1** (in *combination*) behaving in a specified way (*ill-mannered; well-mannered*). **2** (of a style, artist, writer, etc.) showing idiosyncratic mannerisms. **3** (of a person) eccentrically affected in behaviour.

man·ner·ism *noun* **1** a habitual gesture or way of speaking etc.; an idiosyncrasy. **2** excessive addiction to a distinctive style in art or literature. **3** (usu. **Mannerism**) a style of Italian art preceding the Baroque, characterized by unusual and often bizarre effects of scale, lighting, and perspective, and the use of bright colours. □ **man·ner·ist** *noun* **man·ner·is·tic** *adjective*

man·ner·ly *adjective* well-mannered; polite. □ **man·ner·li·ness** *noun*

Mann·heim /'manhaɪm/ an industrial port at the confluence of the Rhine and the Neckar in Baden-Württemberg, SW Germany; pop. (est. 2002) 305,900.

man·ni·kin *var.* of MANIKIN.

Man·ning ▸ 1 Er·nest Charles (1908–1996), Canadian politician, Social Credit premier of Alberta 1943–1968. His premiership was marked by financial prosperity gained from Alberta's oil resources. **2** his son, **(Er·nest) Pres·ton** (b.1942), Canadian politician. Instrumental in the formation of the Reform Party in 1987, he was its leader until it became part of the Canadian Alliance in 2000.

manning depot *noun Cdn hist.* (during World War II) a training depot for recruits to the RCAF.

man·nish *adjective* **1** usu. *derogatory* (of a woman) masculine in appearance or manner. **2** characteristic of a man. □ **man·nish·ly** *adverb* **man·nish·ness** *noun*

mano-a-mano /ˌmanoː ə 'manoː/ *adverb & adjective* hand-to-hand; one-on-one. [Spanish, = hand-to-hand]

man·oeuvre /mə'nuːvər/ (also **man·eu·ver, man·oeu·ver**) ● *noun* **1** a planned and controlled movement or series of moves. **2** (in *pl.*) a large-scale exercise of troops, warships, etc. **3 a** an often deceptive planned or controlled action designed to gain an objective. **b** a skilful plan. ● *verb* **1** *intransitive & transitive* perform or cause to perform a manoeuvre (*manoeuvred the car into the space*). **2** *intransitive & transitive* perform or cause (troops etc.) to perform military manoeuvres.

3 a *transitive* (usu. foll. by *into*, *out*, *away*) force, drive, or manipulate (a person, thing, etc.) by scheming or adroitness. **b** *intransitive* use artifice. □ **man·oeuv·rabil·ity** *noun* **man·oeuv·rable** *adjective*

man·oeuv·rer *noun* [French *manœuvre* from medieval Latin *manuoperare* from Latin *manus* hand + *operari* to work]

man of God *noun* **1** a clergyman. **2** a male saint.

man of honour *noun* a man whose word can be trusted.

man of letters *noun* a scholar or author.

man of straw *noun* = STRAW MAN.

man of the cloth *noun* a clergyman.

man of the house *noun* the male head of a household.

man of the world *noun* see WORLD.

man-of-war *noun* an armed ship.

man·om·eter /məˈnɒmɪtər/ *noun* a pressure gauge for gases and liquids. □ **mano·met·ric** /ˌmanəˈmetrɪk/ *adjective* **man·om·etry** *noun* [French *manomètre* from Greek *manos* thin]

man on the street *var. of* MAN IN THE STREET.

ma non troppo *see* TROPPO.

manor *noun* **1** (also **manor house**) a large house with lands. **2** *Brit.* **a** a unit of land consisting of a lord's demesne and lands rented to tenants etc. **b** *hist.* a feudal lordship over lands. **3** *Brit. informal* the district covered by a police station. □ **manor·ial** /məˈnɔːriəl/ *adjective* [Old French *maneir*, from Latin *manēre* remain]

Mano River /ˈmɑːnəʊ/ a river of West Africa. It rises in NW Liberia and flows to the Atlantic, forming for part of its length the boundary between Liberia and Sierra Leone.

man·power *noun* **1** the power generated by a person working, as opposed to by a machine etc. **2** people available for work, service, etc. **3** *Cdn* (often **Manpower**) a government department offering job referral services for the unemployed (also *attributive*: *manpower centre*). ¶ *Canada Manpower* is no longer in official use.

man·qué /ˈmɒŋkeɪ/ *adjective* (placed after noun) that might have been but is not; unfulfilled (*a comic actor manqué*). [French, past participle of *manquer* miss]

Man Ray see RAY 2.

Mans, Le see LE MANS.

man·sard /ˈmansɑːd/ *noun* a roof which has four sloping sides, each of which becomes steeper halfway down. □ **man·sard·ed** *adjective* [French *mansarde* from F. MANSART]

Man·sart /mɑːˈsɑːr/ **Fran·çois** (1598–1666), French architect. His first major work was the rebuilding of part of the château of Blois, which incorporated the type of roof now named after him (see MANSARD).

manse /mans/ *noun* the house, owned by a congregation, of an esp. Presbyterian or United Church minister. □ **son** (or **daughter**) **of the manse** a child of an esp. Presbyterian minister. [medieval Latin *mansus* house, from *manēre* remain]

Man·sel Island /ˈmansəl/ an island at the mouth of Hudson Bay, southeast of Coats Island. It is part of Nunavut. [Sir R. *Mansell*, English admiral d.1656]

Man·sell /ˈmansəl/ **Nigel** (b.1954), English racing driver. He won the Formula One world championship in 1992 and the Indy car championship in 1993, becoming the only driver to win both titles.

man·serv·ant *noun* (*pl.* **men·serv·ants**) a male servant.

Mans·field, Kath·er·ine (pseudonym of Kathleen Mansfield Beauchamp) (1888–1923), New Zealand short-story writer. Her stories show the influence of Chekhov and range from extended Impressionistic evocations of family life to short sketches.

-manship *suffix* forming nouns denoting skill in a subject or activity (*craftsmanship*; *gamesmanship*).

man·sion *noun* a large house. [Latin *mansio* 'a staying' (as MANSE)]

man-sized *adjective* (also **man-size**) **1** of the size of a man. **2** big enough for a man (*a man-sized sandwich*). **3** *informal* very large (*a man-sized project*).

man·slaugh·ter *noun* **1** the killing of a human being. **2** *Law* the unlawful killing of a human being without malice aforethought.

Man·son ▶ 1 Charles (b.1934), US cult leader. In 1967 he founded a commune based on free love and complete subordination to him. Two years later its members carried out a series of murders, including that of the American actress Sharon Tate for which he and some followers received the death sentence (later commuted to life imprisonment). **2 Sir Pat·rick** (1844–1922), Scottish physician. A pioneer of tropical medicine, he discovered the organism responsible for elephantiasis and established that it was spread by the bite of a mosquito; he later suggested a similar role for the mosquito in spreading malaria.

man·sue·tude /ˈmanswɪˌtjuːd/ *noun archaic* meekness, docility, gentleness. [Latin *mansuetudo* from *mansuetus* gentle, tame, from *manus* hand + *suetus* accustomed]

Man·sur /manˈsʊr/ **Abu Ja'far al-** (c.709–75), the second caliph of the Abbasid dynasty 754–75, who founded Baghdad as his capital city (762–3).

manta /ˈmantə/ *noun* any large ray of the family Mobulidae, esp. *Manta birostris*, having wing-like pectoral fins and a whip-like tail. [Latin American Spanish, = large blanket]

man-tailored *adjective N Amer.* (of a style of women's clothing) tailored after the conventional fashion of a man's garment (*a man-tailored jacket*).

Man·tegna /manˈtenjə/ **An·drea** (c.1431–1506), Italian painter and engraver. He is noted esp. for his frescoes, which include those painted for the bridal chamber of the Ducal Palace in Mantua (c.1474); here the illusionistic painting style appears to extend the interior space and gives the impression that the room is open to the sky.

man·tel *noun* (also **mantel·piece**) **1** a structure of wood, marble, etc. above and around a fireplace. **2** (also **mantel·shelf**) a shelf above a fireplace. [var. of MANTLE]

man·tel·et /ˈmantələt/ *noun* (also **mant·let** /ˈmantlət/) **1** *hist.* a woman's short loose sleeveless mantle. **2** a bulletproof screen for gunners. [Old French, diminutive of *mantel* MANTLE]

man·tic /ˈmantɪk/ *adjective formal* of or concerning divination or prophecy. [Greek *mantikos* from *mantis* prophet]

man·ti·core /ˈmantɪkɔr/ *noun* **1** a fabulous monster having the body of a lion, the head of a man, porcupine's quills, and the tail or sting of a scorpion. **2** *Heraldry* a monster represented with the body of a beast of prey, the head of a man, sometimes with spiral or curved horns, and sometimes the feet of a dragon. [Latin *manticora* representing Greek *mantikhōras*, corrupt reading in Aristotle for *martikhoras* from an Old Persian word for 'man-eater']

man·tid /ˈmantɪd/ *noun* = MANTIS.

man·tilla /manˈtɪlə/ *noun* a lace scarf worn by Spanish women over the hair and shoulders. [Spanish, diminutive of *manta* MANTLE]

man·tis /ˈmantɪs/ *noun* (*pl.* same or **man·tis·es**) any insect of the family Mantidae, feeding on other insects etc. [Greek, = prophet]

man·tissa /manˈtɪsə/ *noun* the part of a logarithm after the decimal point. [Latin, = makeweight]

Man·tle, Mick·ey (Charles) (1931–95), US baseball player. He was an outfielder with the New York Yankees (1951–68) and hit 536 career home runs.

man·tle ● *noun* **1** a loose sleeveless cloak. **2** a covering (*a mantle of snow*). **3** a spiritual influence or authority. **4** a fragile lace-like tube fixed around a gas jet to give an incandescent light. **5** an outer fold of skin enclosing a mollusc's viscera. **6** the plumage of the back and folded wings of a bird, esp. if distinct in colour. **7** the region between the crust and the core of the earth. ● *verb* **1** *transitive* clothe in or as if in a mantle; cover, conceal, envelop. **2** *intransitive* **a** (of the blood) suffuse the cheeks. **b** (of the face) glow with a blush. **3** *intransitive* (of a liquid) become covered with a coating or scum. [Latin *mantellum* cloak]

mant·let *var. of* MANTELET.

man·tra /ˈmantrə/ *noun* **1** *Hinduism & Buddhism* a word or sound repeated to aid concentration in meditation. **2** a Vedic hymn. **3** a frequently repeated word, phrase, etc; a slogan. [Sanskrit, = instrument of thought, from *man* think]

man·trap *noun* a trap for catching poachers, trespassers, etc.

man·tua /ˈmantjʊə/ *noun hist.* a woman's loose gown of the 17th–18th c. [corruption of *manteau* (French, as MANTLE) after *Mantua* in Italy]

Manu /ˈmɑːnuː/ the archetypal first man of Hindu mythology, survivor of the great flood, and father of the human race. He is also the legendary author of one of the most famous codes of Hindu religious law, the *Manusmriti* (*The Laws of Manu*), composed in Sanskrit and dating in its present form from the 1st c. BC. [Sanskrit, = man]

manu·al ● *adjective* **1** of or relating to the hand or hands. **2** done or performed with the hands. **3** involving physical rather than mental effort (*manual labour*). **4** worked by hand, not by automatic equipment or with electronic assistance etc. (*manual transmission*). **5** not involving computers or electronic transmission of data etc. ● *noun* **1 a** a book of instructions, esp. for operating a machine or learning a subject; a handbook (*a computer manual*). **b** any small book. **2** an organ keyboard played with the hands not the feet. **3** *Military* an exercise in handling a rifle etc. □ **manu·al·ly** *adverb* [Latin *manualis* from *manus* hand]

manual alphabet *noun* a system of manual signs for communicating with the deaf.

manu·fac·tory /ˌmanjʊˈfaktɜri/ *noun* (*pl.* **-ies**) *archaic* = FACTORY 1. [MANUFACTURE, after *factory*]

manu·fac·ture ● *noun* **1 a** the making of articles esp. in a factory etc. **b** a branch of an industry (*woollen manufacture*). **2** a manufactured item or product. ● *transitive verb* **1** make (articles), esp. on an industrial scale. **2** invent or fabricate (evidence, a story, etc.). **3** esp. *derogatory* make or produce (literature, art, etc.) in a mechanical way. □ **manu·fac·tur·abil·ity** *noun* **manu·fac·tur·able** *adjective* **manu·fac·tur·er** *noun* [French from Italian *manifattura* & Latin *manufactum* made by hand]

man·uka /ˈmɒnʊkə, maˈnuːkə/ *noun* a small tree, *Leptospermum scoparium*, native to New Zealand and Tasmania, yielding aromatic leaves which are sometimes used for tea and nectar which produces a honey which has antibiotic properties. [Maori]

Manu·kau /maˈnuːkau/ a city on the north island of New Zealand, just south of Auckland; pop. (est. 1999) 281,800.

manu·mat·ic /ˌmanjʊˈmatɪk/ *adjective* (of a motor vehicle or its transmission) using gears that are changed manually by the driver but without the need of a clutch pedal. [blend of MANUAL + AUTOMATIC]

manu·mit /ˌmanjʊˈmɪt/ *transitive verb* (**manu·mit·ted**, **manu·mit·ting**) *hist.* set (a slave) free. □ **manu·mis·sion** *noun* [Latin *manumittere* from *manus* hand + *emittere* send forth]

ma·nure /məˈnʊr, -ˈnjʊr/ ● *noun* **1** animal dung used for fertilizing land. **2** any compost or artificial fertilizer. *See also* GREEN MANURE. ● *transitive verb* apply manure to (land etc.). [Anglo-French *mainoverer* = Old French *manouvrer* MANOEUVRE]

manure spreader *noun* a farm implement used for spreading manure on fields.

manu·script ● *noun* **1** a book, document, etc. written by hand. **2** an author's text submitted for publication. **3** handwritten form (*produced in manuscript*). ● *adjective* written by hand. [medieval Latin *manuscriptus* from *manu* by hand + *scriptus* past participle of *scribere* write]

manuscript paper *noun* paper printed with staffs for writing music on.

Manu·tius see ALDUS MANUTIUS.

Manx /maŋks/ ● *adjective* of or relating to the Isle of Man. ● *noun* **1** *Language hist.* the now extinct Celtic language formerly spoken in the Isle of Man. **2** (prec. by *the*; treated as *pl.*) the Manx people. [Old Norse from Old Irish *Manu* Isle of Man]

Manx cat *noun* a breed of cat with no tail and hind legs longer than the front legs.

Manx shearwater *noun* a brownish-black and white shearwater, *Puffinus puffinus*, of Atlantic and Mediterranean waters.

many ● *adjective* (**more**; **most**) great in number; numerous (*many times; many people; many a person; her reasons were many*). ● *noun* (as *pl.*) **1** a large number (*many like skiing; many went*). **2** (prec. by *the*) the majority of people. □ **have one too many** become drunk. **as many** the same number of (*six mistakes in as many lines*). **as many again** the same number additionally (*sixty here and as many again there*). **be too** (or **one too**) **many for** outwit, baffle. **a good** (or **great**) **many** a large number. **many's the time** often (*many's the time we saw it*). **many a time** many times. [Old English *manig*, ultimately from Germanic]

many·fold *adverb* by many times.

many-sided *adjective* having many sides, aspects, interests, capabilities, etc. □ **many-sided·ness** *noun*

man·za·nilla /ˌmanzəˈnɪlə/ *noun* **1** a pale very dry Spanish sherry. **2** a variety of olive, distinguished by small thin-skinned fruit. [Spanish, lit. 'camomile']

man·za·nita /ˌmanzəˈniːtə/ *noun* any of several evergreen shrubs of the genus *Arctostaphylos*, of the southwestern US. [Spanish, diminutive of *manzana* apple]

Man·zoni /manˈzoːni/ **Ales·san·dro** (1785–1873), Italian novelist, dramatist, and poet. He is remembered chiefly as the author of the historical novel *I promessi sposi* (1825–42).

Mao·ism /ˈmauɪzəm/ *noun* the Communist doctrines of Mao Zedong as formerly practised in China, having as a central idea permanent revolution and stressing the importance of the peasantry, of small-scale industry, and of agricultural collectivization. □ **Mao·ist** *noun & adjective*

Maori /ˈmauri/ ● *noun* (*pl.* same or **Mao·ris**) **1** a member of the Polynesian aboriginal people of New Zealand. **2** the language of the Maori. ● *adjective* of or concerning the Maori or their language. [Maori]

Maori Wars a series of wars fought intermittently in 1845–8 and 1860–72 between Maoris and the colonial government of New Zealand over the enforced sale of Maori lands to Europeans, which was forbidden by the Treaty of Waitangi.

Mao Ze·dong /ˌmau dzəˈdɒŋ/ (also **Mao Tse-tung** /ˌmau tseiˈtʊŋ/) (1893–1976), Chinese leader, chairman of the Communist Party of the People's Republic of China 1949–76 and head of state 1949–59. In 1921 he co-founded the Chinese Communist Party, became its effective leader following the Long March (1934–5), and defeated both the occupying Japanese and rival Kuomintang nationalist forces to form the People's Republic of China, becoming its first head of state (1949).

MAP *abbreviation* N Amer. MODIFIED AMERICAN PLAN.

map ● *noun* **1 a** a usu. flat representation of the earth's surface, or part of it, showing physical features, cities, etc. (compare GLOBE 2). **b** a diagrammatic representation of a route etc. (*drew a map of the journey*). **2** a two-dimensional representation of the stars, the heavens, etc., or of the surface of a planet, the moon, etc. **3** a diagram showing the arrangement or components of a thing, esp. (*Biol.*) of the sequence of genes on a chromosome or of bases in a DNA or RNA molecule. **4** *Math.* a correspondence by which each element of a given set has associated with it one or more elements of a second set. ● *transitive verb* (**mapped**, **map·ping**) **1** represent (a country etc.) on a map. **2** *Math.* associate each element of (a set) with one element of another set. □ **all over the map** *N Amer.* disorganized; lacking a central focus (*the presentation was all over the map*). **map out** arrange in detail; plan (a course of conduct etc.). **put on the map** *informal* establish as prominent or important. **wipe off the map** *informal* obliterate. □ **map·pable** *adjective* **map·per** *noun* [Latin *mappa* napkin: in medieval Latin *mappa* (*mundi*) map (of the world)]

maple *noun* **1** any tree or shrub of the genus *Acer*, with usu. lobed leaves, frequently grown for shade, ornament, wood, or its sugar. **2** the wood of the maple. **3** (also *attributive*) the flavour of maple syrup or maple sugar. [Middle English *mapul* etc. from Old English *mapeltrēow*, *mapulder*]

maple bush *noun* Cdn = SUGAR BUSH.

maple butter *noun* Cdn **1** a spread made by heating maple syrup, then rapidly cooling it while stirring until it has a creamy consistency. **2** butter blended with maple syrup or maple sugar.

maple leaf *noun* **1** the leaf of the maple, used as an emblem of Canada. **2** (**Maple Leaf**) the Canadian flag. **3** (**Maple Leaf**) (*pl.* **Maple Leafs**) a one ounce gold coin, bearing the image of a maple leaf, produced by the Royal Canadian Mint.

Maple Leaf Card *noun* Cdn a plastic, wallet-sized Permanent Resident Card issued by the Canadian government from 2002 onwards.

Maple Ridge a district municipality in southwestern BC, about 40 km east of Vancouver; pop. (2001) 63,169.

maple sugar *noun* a sugar produced by evaporating the sap of the sugar maple etc.

maple syrup *noun* a syrup produced from the sap of the sugar maple etc.

map-maker *noun* a person who makes maps; a cartographer. □ **map-making** *noun*

map-reading *noun* the inspection and interpretation of a map. □ **map-reader** *noun*

map reference *noun* a set of numbers and letters specifying a location as represented on a map.

Ma·puto /məˈpuːtoː/ the capital and chief port of Mozambique, on the Indian Ocean in the south of the country; pop. (est. 2002) 1,639,600. It was known as Lourenço Marques until 1976.

ma·quette /məˈket/ *noun* **1** a sculptor's or architect's small preliminary model. **2** a preliminary sketch. [French from Italian *machietta* diminutive of *macchia* spot]

ma·quila·dora /ˌmakiːlaˈdɔrə/ *noun* a Mexican factory taking advantage of cheap labour, run by a foreign company and exporting its products to the country of that company. [Latin American Spanish from *maquilar* assemble]

ma·quil·lage /ˌmakiːˈjɔʒ/ *noun* **1** makeup; cosmetics. **2** the application of makeup. [French from *maquiller* make up, from Old French *masquiller* stain]

Ma·quis /maˈkiː/ *noun* **1** the French resistance movement during the German occupation (1940–45). **2** a member of this. [French, = brushwood, from Corsican Italian *macchia* thicket]

Mar. *abbreviation* March.

mar *transitive verb* (**marred**, **mar·ring**) **1** ruin. **2** impair the perfection of; spoil; disfigure. [Old English *merran* hinder]

mara·bou /ˈmarəˌbuː/ *noun* (also **mara·bout**) **1** a large W African stork, *Leptoptilos crumeniferus*. **2** N Amer. a lead head jig used in freshwater fishing, with a marabou feather or something resembling it attached to simulate the appearance of a small fish. **3** a tuft of down from the wing or tail of the marabou used as a trimming for hats etc. [French from Arabic *murābiṭ* holy man (see MARABOUT), the stork being regarded as holy]

mara·bout /ˈmarəˌbuːt/ *noun* **1** a Muslim hermit or monk, esp. in N Africa. **2** a shrine marking a marabout's burial place. [French from Portuguese *marabuto* from Arabic *murābiṭ* holy man, from *ribāṭ* frontier station, where he acquired merit by combat against the infidel]

ma·raca /məˈrɒkə, -rakə/ *noun* a hollow gourd or gourd-shaped container filled with beans, pebbles, etc. and usu. shaken in pairs as a percussion instrument. [Portuguese *maracá*, prob. from Tupi]

Mara·caibo /ˌmarəˈkaɪboː/ a city and port in NW Venezuela, situated on the channel linking the Gulf of Venezuela with Lake Maracaibo; pop. (est. 2002) 1,799,900.

Maracaibo, Lake a large lake in NW Venezuela, linked by a narrow channel to the Gulf of Venezuela and the Caribbean Sea.

Mara·dona /ˌmerəˈdɒnə/ **Diego (Ar·man·do)** (b.1960), Argentinian soccer player. He was captain of the victorious Argentinian team in the 1986 World Cup, and retired in 1997.

Ma·ram·ba /məˈrambə/ a city in S Zambia, situated about 5 km (3 miles) from the Zambezi River and Victoria Falls; pop. (est. 2002) 108,100. Formerly called Livingstone.

Mara·ñón River /ˌmarəˈnjɒn/ a river of N Peru, which rises in the Andes and forms one of the principal headwaters of the Amazon.

mara·schi·no /ˌmerəˈʃiːnoː, -ˈskiːnoː, ˌmarə-/ *noun* (*pl.* **-nos**) a strong sweet liqueur made from a small black Dalmatian cherry. [Italian from *marasca* small black cherry, from *amaro* bitter, from Latin *amarus*]

maraschino cherry *noun* a cherry preserved in maraschino or maraschino-flavoured syrup and used esp. as a garnish.

mar·as·mus /məˈrazməs/ *noun* severe loss of weight in a person, esp. an undernourished child. □ **mar·as·mic** *adjective* [modern Latin from Greek *marasmos* from *marainō* wither]

Marat /maˈrɒ/ **Jean Paul** (1743–93), French revolutionary and journalist. He was prominent during the early days of the French Revolution as a virulent critic of the moderate Girondins, and was instrumental in their fall from power (1793); he was murdered in his bath by the Girondin Charlotte Corday.

Ma·ra·tha /məˈrɒtə, -ˈratə/ *noun* (also **Mahratta**) a member of a Hindu people native to the Indian state of Maharashtra. In the 17th c. the Marathas rose in rebellion against the Muslim Moguls and established their own kingdom, which in the early 18th c. came to dominate much of southern and central India. [Hindi *Marhaṭṭa* from Sanskrit *Māhārāṣṭra* great kingdom]

Ma·ra·thi /məˈrɒti, -ˈrati/ *noun* (also **Mahratti**) the Indic language of the Marathas. [MARATHA]

Mara·thon a town in north central Ontario, located on the north shore of Lake Superior, east of Thunder Bay; pop. (2001) 4,416. [after *Marathon* Paper Mills, parent company of the General Timber Company (which built a paper mill on the townsite in 1936)]

mara·thon *noun* **1** a long-distance running race, usu. of 26 miles 385 yards (42.195 km). **2** a long-lasting or difficult task, operation, etc. (often *attributive*: *a marathon shopping expedition*). □ **mara·thon·er** *noun* [*Marathon* in Greece, scene of a victory over the Persians in 490 BC: a messenger was said to have run to Athens with the news, but the account has no authority]

ma·raud *verb* **1** *intransitive* go about in search of things to steal, people to attack, etc. **2** *transitive* plunder (a place). □ **ma·raud·er** *noun* [French *marauder* from *maraud* rogue]

Mar·bella /marˈbeɪjə/ a resort town on the Costa del Sol of S Spain, in Andalusia; pop. (est. 2001) 110,847.

mar·ble ● *noun* **1** limestone in a metamorphic crystalline (or granular) state, and capable of taking a polish, used in sculpture and architecture. **2** (often *attributive*) **a** anything made of marble (*a marble clock*). **b** anything resembling marble in hardness, coldness, durability, etc. (*her features were marble*). **3 a** a small ball of marble, glass, clay, etc., used as a toy. **b** (in *pl.*; treated as *sing.*) a game using these. **4** (in *pl.*) *slang* one's mental faculties (*he's lost his marbles*). **5** (*attributive*) (esp. of a food) made with two or more colours swirled together (*marble cake*; *marble cheese*). **6** a marble sculpture. ● *transitive verb* stain or colour (paper, the edges of a book, soap, etc.) to look like variegated marble. □ **mar·bly** *adjective* [Old French *marbre*, *marble*, from Latin *marmor* from Greek *marmaros* shining stone]

mar·bled *adjective* **1** (of meat) streaked with alternating layers of lean and fat. **2** stained or coloured to look like variegated marble.

marbled murrelet *noun* a murrelet, *Brachyramphus marmoratus* of the N Pacific, with mottled brown and white underparts.

marble·ize *transitive verb* (also esp. *Brit.* **-ise**) **1** stain or colour to look like variegated marble. **2** give a variegated appearance to, esp. by an artificial process.

mar·bling *noun* **1** colouring or marking like marble. **2** streaks of fat in lean meat.

Mar·burg¹ /ˈmɑrbʊrk/ a city in the state of Hesse in west central Germany; pop. (est. 2002) 78,600.

Mar·burg² /ˈmɑrbɜrg/ *noun* (usu. *attributive*) designating the virus of an acute, often fatal, hemorrhagic febrile disease originally transmitted to humans from the green monkey. [MARBURG¹, where the first major outbreak occurred (1967)]

marc *noun* **1** the residue of pressed grapes etc. **2** a brandy made from this. [French from *marcher* tread, MARCH¹]

marca·site /ˈmɑrkəˌsaɪt/ *noun* **1** a yellowish crystalline iron sulphide mineral. **2** these bronze-yellow crystals used in jewellery. [medieval Latin *marcasita*, from Arabic *markaṣīta* from Persian]

mar·cato /mɑrˈkɒtoː/ *adverb & adjective* Music played with emphasis. [Italian, = marked]

Mar·ceau /mɑrˈsoː/ **Mar·cel** (b.1923), French mime artist. He developed his white-faced character Bip from the French 19th-c. Pierrot; he created a number of mime-dramas, including *Don Juan* (1964).

mar·cel /mɑrˈsel/ ● *noun* (in full **marcel wave**) a deep wave in the hair created with a hot curling iron, popular as a hairstyle esp. in the twenties and thirties. ● *transitive verb* (**mar·celled**, **mar·cel·ling**) wave (hair) with a deep wave. [*Marcel* Grateau, Paris hairdresser d.1936, who invented the method]

Mar·cel·lus /mɑrˈseləs/ **Mar·cus Claud·ius** (*c.*268–208 BC), Roman general and consul. He campaigned successfully against the Gauls, and captured Syracuse (211) during the Second Punic War.

March *noun* the third month of the year. [Latin *Martius* (*mensis*) (month) of Mars]

march¹ ● *verb* **1** *intransitive* (usu. foll. by *away*, *off*, *out*, etc.) walk in a military manner with a regular measured tread. **2** *transitive* (often foll. by *away*, *on*, *off*, etc.) cause to march or walk (*marched the cadets back to camp*; *marched him out of the room*). **3** *intransitive* **a** walk and proceed steadily, esp. across country. **b** (of events etc.) continue unrelentingly (*time marches on*). **4** *intransitive* take part in a protest march. ● *noun* **1 a** the act or an instance of marching. **b** the uniform step of troops etc. (*a slow march*). **2** a long difficult walk. **3** a procession as a protest or demonstration. **4** (usu. foll. by *of*) progress or continuity (*the march of events*). **5 a** a piece of music composed to accompany a march. **b** a composition of similar character and form. □ **march on 1** advance towards (a military objective). **2** proceed. **on the march 1** marching. **2** in steady progress. [French *marche* (n.), *marcher* (v.), from Late Latin *marcus* hammer]

march² ● *noun* hist. **1** (usu. in *pl.*) a boundary, a frontier (esp. of the borderland between England and Scotland or Wales). **2** a tract of often disputed land between two countries. ● *intransitive verb* (foll. by *upon*, *with*) (of a country, an estate, etc.) have a common frontier with, border on. [Old French *marche*, *marchir* ultimately from Germanic]

Mar·chand /mɑrˈʃɑ̃/ **Jean** (1918–88), Canadian union leader and politician. A member of the Royal Commission on Bilingualism and Biculturalism (1963–65), he was persuaded to enter the federal Liberal cabinet in 1965, bringing Pierre Trudeau and Gérard Pelletier with him.

March break *noun* Cdn a school holiday, usu. about a week long, in March.

march·er¹ *noun* a person who marches or takes part in a march.

march·er² *noun* an inhabitant of a march or border district.

March·es, the 1 the parts of England along the borders with Wales and (formerly) Scotland. **2** a region of east central Italy, between the Apennines and the Adriatic Sea; capital, Ancona. [MARCH²]

March hare *noun* a hare in the breeding season, characterized by excessive leaping, strange behaviour, etc. (*mad as a March hare*).

march·ing band *noun* a usu. brass band which performs while marching in parades etc.

march·ing orders *plural noun* **1** a dismissal (*gave him his marching orders*). **2** instructions or directions given authoritatively. **3** *Military* the direction for troops to depart for war etc.

mar·chion·ess /ˌmɑrʃəˈnes, ˈmɑr-/ *noun* **1** the wife or widow of a marquess. **2** a woman holding the rank of marquess in her own right

---

t top   v voice   w we   z zoo   ʃ she   ʒ vision   θ thin   ð this   ŋ ring   x loch   tʃ chip   dʒ jar   (*see over for vowels*)

(*compare* MARQUISE 1b). [medieval Latin *marchionissa* from *marchio* captain of the marches (as MARCH[2])]

march·pane /'mɑːtʃpeɪn/ *archaic var. of* MARZIPAN.

march past *noun* the marching of troops past a saluting point at a review.

Mar·ci·ano /ˌmɑːsɪˈɒnoː/ **Rocky** (born Rocco Francis Marchegiano) (1923–69), US boxer. In 1952 he became world heavyweight champion and successfully defended his title six times until he retired, undefeated, in 1956.

Mar·coni /mɑːˈkoːni/ **Gu·gliel·mo** (1874–1937), Italian electrical engineer and pioneer of radio. He transmitted a signal across the Atlantic from Cornwall to Newfoundland (1901), and in 1912 produced a continuously oscillating wave, essential for the transmission of sound; he went on to develop shortwave transmission over long distances, and was awarded the Nobel Prize for physics in 1909.

mar·coni *noun* *Cdn* (*Nfld*) *informal* a radio, esp. one used for two-way communications (also *attributive*: marconi station). [G. MARCONI]

Marco Polo (c.1254–c.1324), Italian traveller. In 1271 he journeyed east from Acre into central Asia, eventually reaching China and the court of Kublai Khan (1275); he returned to Venice (1295) via Sumatra, India, and Persia, and his book recounting his travels gave considerable impetus to the European quest to discover the riches of the East.

Marcos /'mɑːkoːs/ **Fer·di·nand (Edra·lin)** (1917–89), Philippine leader, president of the Philippines 1966–86. His authoritarian regime was characterized by government corruption; he was deposed in 1986 and went into exile in Hawaii with his wife Imelda (b.1930).

Mar·cus Aurel·ius see AURELIUS.

Mar·cuse ▸ 1 /mɑːˈkuːzə/ **Her·bert** (1898–1979), German-born US philosopher. His works include *Eros and Civilization* (1955), *Soviet Marxism* (1958), and *One-Dimensional Man* (1964), in which he contends that modern industrial society satisfies material needs and allows certain freedoms while ignoring fundamental needs and restricting true liberty. **2** /mɑːˈkjuːz/ **Jud·ith Rose** (born Judith Rose Margolick) (b.1947), Canadian modern dancer, choreographer and teacher. She choreographs for companies in Canada and around the world.

Mar del Plata /ˌmɑːr del ˈplɒtə/ a fishing port and resort in Argentina, on the Atlantic coast south of Buenos Aires; pop. (est. 1999) 579,483.

Mardi Gras /'mɑːdi ˌɡrɒ/ *noun* **1** the last Tuesday before Lent, celebrated in some areas (esp. New Orleans) as a day of great revelry. **2** the period of festivities culminating in this. **3** *Austral.* a carnival or fair at any time. [French, = fat Tuesday, from the custom of consuming all animal products before beginning the fast of Lent]

Mar·duk /'mɑːdʊk/ *Babylonian Myth* the chief god of Babylon, who became lord of the gods of heaven and earth after conquering Tiamat, the monster of primeval chaos.

Mare see DE LA MARE.

mare[1] /mer/ *noun* the female of any equine animal, esp. the horse. [Old English *mearh* horse, from Germanic: compare MARSHAL]

mare[2] /'mɒreɪ, -ri/ *noun* (*pl.* **maria** /'mɒriə/ or **mares**) **1** (in full **mare clausum** /'klaʊsʊm/) *Law* the sea under the jurisdiction of a particular country. **2** (in full **mare liberum** /'liːbəˌrʊm/) *Law* the sea open to all nations. **3 a** any of a number of large dark flat areas on the surface of the moon, once thought to be seas. **b** a similar area on Mars. [Latin, = sea]

Ma·ren·go, Battle of /məˈrɛŋɡoː/ a decisive French victory of Napoleon's campaign in Italy in 1800, close to the village of Marengo near Turin. Napoleon crossed the Alps to defeat and capture an Austrian army, a victory which led to Italy coming under French control again.

mare's nest *noun* **1** an illusory discovery; a fraud. **2** a complex situation or muddle.

mare's tail *noun* **1** a tall slender marsh plant with whorled leaves of the genus *Hippuris*. **2** (in *pl.*) long straight streaks of cirrus cloud.

Mar·garet, Princess Margaret Rose (1930–2002), only sister of Elizabeth II.

mar·gar·ine *noun* a butter substitute made from vegetable oils or animal fats with milk etc. [French, misapplication of a chemical term, from *margarique*, from Greek *margaron* pearl]

Mar·ga·rita /ˌmɑːɡəˈriːtə/ an island in the Caribbean Sea, off the coast of Venezuela. Visited by Columbus in 1498, it was used as a base by Simón Bolívar in 1816 in the struggle for independence from Spanish rule.

mar·ga·rita /mɑːɡəˈriːtə/ *noun* a cocktail made with tequila, lime juice, and orange liqueur, typically served in a glass with a salt-coated rim. [Spanish equivalent of female first name Margaret]

mar·gay /'mɑːɡeɪ/ *noun* a small wild S American cat, *Felis wiedii*. [French from Tupi *mbaracaïa*]

marge[1] *noun* *Brit. informal* margarine. [abbreviation]

marge[2] *noun* *literary* a margin or edge. [French from Latin *margo* (as MARGIN)]

mar·ghe·rita /mɑːɡəˈriːtə/ *adjective* designating a pizza topped with cheese, tomatoes, and traditionally also basil. [Italian *margherita* from the name of *Margherita* Teresa Giovanna of Savoy (d.1926), Queen of Italy 1878–1900, the colours of mozzarella, tomatoes, and basil being white, red, and green like the Italian flag]

mar·gin ● *noun* **1 a** the edge or border of a surface. **b** (in *pl.*) the ignored or unimportant sections of a group etc. **2 a** the blank border on each side of the print on a page etc. **b** a line ruled esp. on exercise paper, marking off a margin. **3** an amount (of time, money, etc.) by which a thing exceeds, falls short, etc. (*won by a narrow margin*; *a margin of profit*). **4** the lower limit of possibility, success, etc. **5** a sum deposited with a stockbroker to cover the risk of loss on a transaction on account. **●** *transitive verb* (**mar·gined**, **mar·gin·ing**) **1** provide with a margin or marginal notes. **2** deposit an amount of money with a broker as security for (an account or transaction). [Latin *margo -ginis* edge]

mar·gin·al ● *adjective* **1 a** of or written in a margin. **b** having marginal notes. **2 a** of or at the edge; not central. **b** not significant or decisive (*the work is of merely marginal interest*). **3** *Cdn*, *Brit.*, *Austral.*, & *NZ* (of a parliamentary seat or constituency) having a small majority at risk in an election. **4** close to the limit, esp. of profitability. **5** (of the sea) adjacent to the shore of a country. **6** (of land) that cannot produce enough to be profitable except when prices of farm products are high. **7** barely adequate; unprovided for (*living a marginal existence*). **8** (of a person) not fitting into the mainstream. **9** (of a rate of taxation) imposed on the portion of income exceeding the limit of a tax bracket, rather than on the total income. **●** *noun* *Brit.* a marginal constituency or seat. □ **mar·gin·al·ity** *noun* **mar·gin·al·ly** *adverb*

marginal cost *noun* the cost added by making one extra item of a product.

mar·gin·alia /ˌmɑːdʒɪˈneɪliə/ *plural noun* marginal notes. [medieval Latin, neuter pl. of *marginalis*]

mar·gin·al·ize *transitive verb* (also esp. *Brit.* **-ise**) make or treat as insignificant. □ **mar·gin·al·iz·a·tion** *noun*

margin call *noun* a demand by a broker that an investor deposit further cash or securities to guarantee the margin on an investment.

margin of error *noun* a usu. small difference allowed for miscalculation, change of circumstances, etc.

Mar·gi·son /'mɑːdʒɪsən/ **Rich·ard Charles** (b.1953), Canadian opera singer, celebrated for his dramatic-lyric tenor roles, including Pinkerton in *Madama Butterfly*, and for his performances of Verdi.

mar·grave /'mɑːɡreɪv/ *noun* *hist.* the hereditary title of some princes of the Holy Roman Empire (originally of a military governor of a border province). [Middle Dutch *markgrave* border count (as MARK[1], *grave* COUNT[2] from Old Low German *grēve*)]

mar·grav·ine /'mɑːɡrəˌviːn/ *noun* *hist.* the wife of a margrave. [Dutch *markgravin* (as MARGRAVE)]

Mar·grethe II /mɑːˈɡreɪtə/ (full name Margrethe Alexandrine Thorhildur Ingrid) (b.1940), queen of Denmark from 1972.

mar·guer·ite /ˌmɑːɡəˈriːt/ *noun* a daisy, esp. the ox-eye daisy, *Chrysanthemum leucanthemum*. [French from Latin *margarita* from Greek *margaritēs* from *margaron* pearl]

Mari /'mɑːri/ an ancient city on the Euphrates, in Syria. Its period of greatest importance was from the late 19th to the mid-18th c. BC. The palace of the last king, Zimri-lin, has yielded an archive of 25,000 cuneiform tablets, which are the principal source for the history of N Syria and Mesopotamia at that time.

maria pl. of MARE[2].

mari·achi /meriˈatʃi, -ˈɒtʃi/ *noun* **1** an itinerant Mexican folk band. **2** a member of such a band. [Mexican Spanish *mariache, mariachi* street singer]

Maria de' Medici see MARIE DE MÉDICIS.

Mar·ian /'meriən/ *adjective* of or relating to the Virgin Mary (*Marian devotion*). [Latin *Maria* Mary]

Mari·ana Islands /ˌmeriˈɒnə/ (also **Marianas**) a group of islands in the W Pacific, comprising Guam and the Northern Marianas. (*See also* NORTHERN MARIANAS.) [originally named *Las Marianas*, in honour of *Maria Anna*, widow of Philip IV]

Mari·ana Trench an ocean trench to the southeast of the Mariana Islands in the W Pacific, with the greatest known ocean depth (11 034 m, 36,200 ft. at the Challenger Deep).

Maria Ther·esa /məˌriːə təˈreizə/ (1717–80), daughter of emperor Charles VI, archduchess of Austria, queen of Hungary and Bohemia 1740–80. Her accession to the Hapsburg dominions triggered the War of the Austrian Succession (1740–8), during which Silesia was lost to Prussia; she attempted but failed to regain it in the Seven Years War (1756–63).

mari·cul·ture /ˈmerəˌkʌltʃər/ *noun* the cultivation of the living resources of the sea (such as algae, shellfish, or esp. fish).

Marie An·toin·ette /maˈriːˌantwəˈnet/ (1755–93), French queen, wife of Louis XVI. A daughter of Maria Theresa and the Emperor Francis I, she became a centre of opposition to reform and was unpopular because of her extravagance; she was imprisoned during the French Revolution and eventually executed.

Marie Byrd Land /ˌmɑri ˈbɜrd/ a region of Antarctica bordering the Pacific, between Ellsworth Land and the Ross Sea. [after the wife of US naval commander R. E. *Byrd*, who explored it in 1929]

Marie de l'Incarna·tion /maˈriː də lãkɑrnaˈsjõ/ (born Marie Guyart) (1599–1672), French-born Canadian mystic and writer. She came to Canada in 1639, and founded a convent and boarding school for girls at Ville-Marie (Montreal).

Marie de Médicis /maˌri də ˌmeidiːˈsiːs/ (Italian name Maria de' Medici) (1573–1642), queen of France (1600–10) as the second wife of Henry IV of France, and regent during the minority of her son Louis XIII (1610–17). Her influence continued after her son came to power, and she plotted against Richelieu, her former protege, but was eventually exiled in 1631.

Mari El /ˌmɑri ˈel/ (also called **Mari Autonomous Republic**) an autonomous republic in European Russia, east of Nizhni Novgorod and north of the Volga; pop. (est. 2002) 743,300; capital, Yoshkar-Ola.

Marie Lou·ise /ˌmeri luːˈiːz/ (1791–1847), Austrian archduchess, who became empress of France (1811–15) as the second wife of Napoleon I.

Marie-Victorin /mɑriː viːktʊˈrã/ **Frère** (born Conrad Kirouac) (1885–1944), Canadian monk, botanist, and teacher, who devoted his life to the study and classification of N American plants.

Marie·ville /mɑriˈvil/ a town in south central Quebec, northeast of Saint-Jean-sur-Richelieu; pop. (2001) 7,240. [ultimately after the seigneury, Saint-Nom de *Marie* de Monnoir]

mari·gold /ˈmeriˌɡoːld/ *noun* any plant of the genus *Calendula* or *Tagetes*, with golden or bright yellow flowers. [Middle English from *Mary* (prob. the Virgin) + dial. *gold*, Old English *golde*, prob. related to GOLD]

ma·ri·juana /ˌmeriˈwɒnə/ *noun* **1** the dried leaves, flowering tops, and stems of the hemp, used as an intoxicating drug usu. smoked in cigarettes; cannabis. **2** the plant yielding these (*compare* HEMP). [Latin American Spanish]

ma·rim·ba /məˈrɪmbə/ *noun* a kind of deep-toned xylophone, originating in Africa and consisting of wooden keys on a frame with a tuned resonator beneath each key. [Congolese]

mar·ina /məˈriːnə/ *noun* a specially designed harbour with moorings for pleasure boats etc. [Italian & Spanish fem. adj. from *marino* from Latin (as MARINE)]

mar·in·ade /ˈmerineid, -ˈneid/ ● *noun* **1** a mixture of wine, vinegar, oil, spices, etc., in which meat, fish, etc., is soaked before cooking. **2** meat, fish, etc., in such a mixture. ● *transitive verb* = MARINATE. [French from Spanish *marinada*, via *marinar* 'pickle in brine' from *marino* (as MARINA)]

mar·in·ara /ˌmerəˈnerə, mɑrəˈnɑrə/ *adjective* designating a sauce made from tomatoes, onions, herbs, etc., usu. served with pasta. [Italian *alla marinara* sailor-fashion]

mar·in·ate /ˈmeriˌneit/ *transitive verb* soak (meat, fish, etc.) in a marinade. □ **mar·in·a·tion** *noun* [Italian *marinare* or French *mariner* (as MARINE)]

mar·ine ● *adjective* **1 a** of, found in, or produced by the sea. **b** of, found in, or produced by any esp. large body of water. **2 a** of or relating to shipping or naval matters (*marine insurance*). **b** for use at sea. ● *noun* **1** a country's shipping, fleet, or navy (*mercantile marine; merchant marine*). **2 a** a member of a body of troops trained to serve on land or sea. **b** (**Marine**) (in the US) a member of the Marine Corps. **3** a picture of a scene at sea. [Latin *marinus*, from *mare* 'sea']

marine architecture *noun* = NAVAL ARCHITECTURE.

Marine Corps *noun* a branch of the US armed forces trained to attack land targets from the sea.

marine park *noun* **1** an area of an ocean or other body of water set aside as an ecological preserve. **2** a theme park featuring marine wildlife.

mar·in·er /ˈmerɪnər/ *noun* a sailor. [as MARINE]

marine railway *noun* a structure consisting of inclined rails and a cradle drawn by cables, used for launching or landing boats or for moving them between bodies of water of different levels.

Mari·netti /ˌmɑriˈneti/ **Filip·po Tom·maso (Emilio)** (1876–1944), Italian poet and dramatist. He launched the futurist movement, exalting technology, glorifying war, and demanding revolution and innovation in the arts; his plays include *The Feasting King* (1909) and *Anti-Neutrality* (1912).

Mari·ol·atry /ˌmeriˈɒlətri/ *noun derogatory* idolatrous worship of the Virgin Mary. [Latin *Maria* Mary + -LATRY, after *idolatry*]

Mari·ol·ogy /ˌmeriˈɒlədʒi/ *noun* the study of the Virgin Mary in Christian belief. [Latin *Maria* Mary + -OLOGY]

marion·berry *noun* (*pl.* **-berries**) a large black berry produced by crossing loganberry and blackberry cultivars. [*Marion* County, Oregon, where the variety was tested]

mar·ion·ette /ˌmeriəˈnet/ *noun* a puppet worked from above by strings. [French *marionnette* from *Marion* diminutive of *Marie* Mary]

mari·posa lily *noun* any of various lilies of western N America of the genus *Calochortus* with showy flowers of three petals. [Spanish, = 'butterfly']

Mar·ist /ˈmerɪst/ *noun* **1** a member of a Roman Catholic religious order of priests, the Society of Mary. **2** a member of a Roman Catholic religious order of brothers engaged in teaching, the Little Brothers of Mary. [French *Mariste* from *Marie* Mary]

mari·tal /ˈmerɪtəl/ *adjective* of marriage or the relations between spouses. □ **mari·tal·ly** *adverb* [Latin *maritalis* from *maritus* husband]

marital status *noun* a person's situation as regards being single, married, divorced, separated, or in a common-law relationship.

mari·time *adjective* **1** connected with the sea or seafaring (*maritime insurance*). **2** living or found near the sea. **3** (**Maritime**) *Cdn* of or relating to the Maritime provinces. [Latin *maritimus* from *mare* sea]

Maritime Command *noun Cdn* the official name for the Canadian navy.

maritime pine *noun* = CLUSTER PINE.

Maritime provinces *plural noun* see MARITIMES.

Mari·tim·er *noun Cdn* a native or resident of the Maritime provinces.

Mari·times *plural noun* (also **Maritime provinces**) New Brunswick, Nova Scotia, and Prince Edward Island. These provinces, together with Newfoundland and Labrador, are also known as the Atlantic provinces.

Ma·ritsa River /məˈritsə/ a river of S Europe, which rises in the Rila Mountains of SW Bulgaria and flows 480 km (300 miles) south to the Aegean Sea. It forms the border between Bulgaria and Greece and then, for about 185 km (115 miles), that between Greece and Turkey.

Ma·riu·pol /ˌmɑriˈuːpɒl/ an industrial port on the south coast of Ukraine, on the Sea of Azov; pop. (est. 2001) 492,000.

Mar·ius /ˈmeriəs, ˈmɑ-/ **Gaius** (*c.*157–86 BC), Roman general and politician. Elected consul seven times, he established his dominance by victories over Jugurtha and invading Germanic tribes, and was expelled from Italy (88) in a struggle for power with Sulla; in 87 he returned and took Rome by force.

Ma·ri·vaux /ˌmɑriˈvo/ **Pierre (Car·let de Cham·blain de)** (1688–1763), French playwright and novelist, whose comedies depict love frustrated by social and psychological obstacles; they include *Arlequin poli par l'amour* (1723) and *Le Jeu de l'amour et du hasard* (1730).

mar·jor·am /ˈmɑrdʒərəm/ *noun* **1** either of two aromatic herbaceous plants, (in full **wild marjoram**) *Origanum vulgare*, or (in full **sweet marjoram**) *Origanum marjorana*. **2** the fresh or dried leaves of sweet marjoram used as a flavouring in cooking. [Old French *majorane* from medieval Latin *majorana*, of unknown origin]

Mark ▸ **1 St.**, an Apostle, companion of St. Peter and St. Paul, traditional author of the second Gospel. Feast day, 25 April. **2** the second Gospel (the earliest in date).

mark¹ ● *noun* **1** a trace, sign, stain, scar, etc., on a surface, face, page, etc. **2** (esp. in *combination*) **a** a written or printed symbol (*check mark; question mark*). **b** a numerical or alphabetical award denoting a degree of excellence, conduct, proficiency, etc. (*got good marks for effort; how are your marks?*). **3** (usu. foll. by *of*) a sign or indication of quality, character, feeling, etc. (*took off his hat as a mark of respect*). **4 a** a sign, seal, etc., used for distinction or identification. **b** a cross etc. made in place of a signature by an illiterate person. **5 a** a target, object, goal, etc. (*missed the mark with his first play*). **b** a standard for attainment (*his work falls below the mark*). **c** a level considered important or critical (*sales have reached the million mark*). **d** a point in time (*scored at the three-minute mark in the first period*). **e** a record (*broke her own world mark of 30.48 metres*). **6** a line etc. indicating a position; a marker. **7** (usu. **Mark**) (followed by a numeral) a particular design, model, etc., of a car, aircraft, etc. (*this is the Mark 2 model*). **8** a runner's starting point in a race. **9** *Naut.* a piece of material etc. used to indicate a position on a sounding line. **10** *Rugby* a heel mark on the ground made by a player who has caught the ball direct from a kick, knock-on, or forward throw by an opponent. **11** *slang* the intended victim of a swindler etc. **12** *Boxing* the pit of the stomach. ● *transitive verb* **1 a** make a mark on (a thing or person), esp. by writing, cutting, scraping, etc. **b** put a distinguishing or identifying mark, initials, name, etc., on (clothes etc.) (*marked the tree with their initials*). **c** (of an animal) leave a scent mark on. **2 a** allot marks to; correct (a student's work etc.). **b** record (the points gained in games etc.). **3** attach a price to (goods etc.) (*marked the doll at $5*). **4** (often foll. by *by*) show or manifest (displeasure etc.) (*marked his anger by leaving early*). **5** notice or observe (*she marked his agitation*). **6 a** characterize or be a feature of (*the day was marked by storms*). **b** acknowledge, recognize, celebrate (*marked the occasion with a toast*). **c** constitute (a significant event) (*this year marks the hundredth anniversary of our foundation*). **7** name or indicate (a place on a map, the length of a syllable, etc.) by a sign or mark. **8** characterize (a person or a thing) as (*marked them as weak*). **9** keep close to so as to prevent the free movement of (an opponent in sport); cover. **10** (of a graduated instrument) show, register (so many degrees etc.). **11** perform (a series of dance steps, a sung passage, etc.) with minimal exertion, to save one's strength while rehearsing. □ **hit** (or **miss**) **the mark** succeed (or fail) in an attempt to do something. **one's mark** *Brit. informal* **1** what one prefers. **2** an opponent, object, etc., of one's own size, calibre, etc. (*the little one's more my mark*). **leave** (or **make**) **one's mark on** have a long-lasting (often harmful) effect on. **make one's mark** attain distinction. **mark down 1** mark (goods etc.) at a lower price. **2** make a written note of. **3** choose (a person) as one's victim. **4** reduce the examination marks of. **mark off** (often foll. by *from*) separate (one thing from another) by a boundary etc. (*marked off the subjects for discussion*). **mark out 1** plan (a course of action etc.). **2** destine (*marked out for success*). **3** trace out boundaries, a course, etc. **mark time** *Military* march on the spot, without moving forward. **2** act routinely; go through the motions. **3** await an opportunity to advance. **mark up 1** mark (goods etc.) at a higher price. **2** mark or correct (text etc.) for typesetting or alteration. **mark you** *Brit.* please note (*without obligation, mark you*). **off the mark 1** having made a start. **2** (also **wide of the mark**) not accurate. **quick** (or **slow**) **off the mark** fast (or slow) in responding to a situation or understanding something. **on the mark 1** accurate. **2** ready to start. **on your mark** (or **marks**) (as an instruction) get ready to start (esp. a race). **up to the mark** reaching the usual or normal standard, esp. of health. [Old English *me(a)rc* (n.), *mearcian* (v.), from Germanic]

mark² *noun* **1 a** = DEUTSCHMARK. **b** *hist.* = OSTMARK. **2** *hist.* **a** a denomination of weight for gold and silver. **b** a monetary unit equal to thirteen shillings and fourpence in the (English and Scottish) currency of the day. [Old English *marc*, prob. related to medieval Latin *marca*, *marcus*]

marka *noun* (*pl.* same or **markas**) the basic monetary unit of Bosnia and Herzegovina, equal to one hundred fenning. [Bosnian]

Mark Antony see ANTONY.

mark·down *noun* a reduction in price.

marked *adjective* **1** having a visible mark. **2** clearly noticeable; evident (*a marked difference*). **3** (of playing cards) having distinctive marks on their backs to assist cheating. **4** designating a person whose conduct is watched with suspicion or hostility (*marked man*). □ **mark·ed·ly** *adverb* **mark·ed·ness** *noun*

mark·er *noun* **1** a stone, post, etc., used to mark a position, place reached, etc. **2** a person or thing that marks. **3** a felt-tipped pen with a broad tip. **4** a person who records a score, esp. in billiards. **5** a flare etc. used to direct a pilot to a target. **6** a bookmark. **7** = GENETIC MARKER. **8** any distinguishing characteristic or mark. **9** a person who marks school assignments or examination papers. **10** *Linguistics* a word, affix, etc., which distinguishes or determines the class or function of the form, construction, etc. with which it is used (*s is a common plural marker in English*). **11** *N Amer. slang* a promissory note; an IOU.

mar·ket ● *noun* **1** the gathering of people for the purchase and sale of provisions, livestock, etc., esp. with a number of different vendors. **2** an open space or covered building used for this. **3 a** (often foll. by *for*) a demand for a commodity or service (*goods find a ready market*). **b** a place or group providing such a demand (*Canada is a small market*). **4** conditions as regards, or opportunity for, buying or selling. **5** the rate of purchase and sale, market value (*the market fell*). **6** (prec. by *the*) the trade in a specified commodity (*the market in soft drinks*). **7** = STOCK MARKET. ● *verb* (**mar·ket·ed, mar·ket·ing**) **1** *transitive* sell. **2** *transitive*

a offer for sale. **b** promote an item for sale. **3** *intransitive* buy or sell goods in a market. □ **be in the market for** wish to buy. **be on** (or **come into**) **the market** be offered for sale. **put on the market** offer for sale. [ultimately from Latin *mercatus* from *mercari* 'buy': see MERCHANT]

market·able *adjective* **1** able or fit to be sold. **2** (of an attribute, skill, etc.) in demand. □ **market·abil·ity** *noun*

market-driven *adjective* determined solely by consumer demand (*market-driven economics; a market-driven program*).

market economy *noun* an economy subject to and determined by free competition.

mar·ket·eer /ˌmɑːkəˈtiːr/ *noun* **1** a person involved in or promoting a usu. specified market (*free marketeer; black marketeer*). **2** = MARKETER. □ **mar·ket·eer·ing** *noun*

mar·ket·er *noun* a person trained in the marketing of products etc.

market garden *noun* esp. *Brit. & Cdn* a place where vegetables and fruit are grown for the market etc. □ **market gardener** *noun* **market gardening** *noun*

mar·ket·ing *noun* **1** the action or business of promoting and selling products and services, including market research and advertising. **2** in senses of MARKET *verb*.

marketing board *noun* *Cdn & Brit.* an association of agricultural producers controlling the marketing of a specific commodity, often setting prices and imposing production quotas.

market leader *noun* **1** the company that sells the largest quantity of a particular product. **2** a product which sells more than all its competitors.

market-maker *noun* *Brit.* a member of the Stock Exchange granted certain privileges and trading to prescribed regulations.

market·place *noun* **1** an open space where a market is held in a town. **2** the world of commerce or trade. **3** any place or environment where ideas etc. are exchanged or evaluated.

market price *noun* the current price which a commodity or service fetches in the market.

market research *noun* the study of consumers' needs and preferences. □ **market researcher** *noun*

market share *noun* a single company's or product's proportion of the total sales of a commodity or service.

market town *noun* *Brit.* a town where a market is held.

market value *noun* the value of a product or service as determined by consumer demand (*opp.* BOOK VALUE).

Mark·ham /ˈmɑːkəm/ a town in S Ontario, located on the northeastern edge of Toronto; pop. (2001) 208,615. [Rt. Rev. W. Markham, archbishop of York d.1806]

mark·hor /ˈmɑːkɔːr/ *noun* a large spiral-horned wild goat, *Capra falconeri*, of N India. [Persian *mār-kwār* from *mār* serpent + *kwār* -eating]

mark·ing *noun* (usu. in *pl.*) **1** an identification mark, esp. a symbol on an aircraft. **2** the colouring of an animal's fur, feathers, skin, etc. **3** the action of MARK¹ *verb*.

mark·ka /ˈmɑːkə/ *noun* (*pl.* **mark·kaa** *pronunc.* same) the former chief monetary unit of Finland, now replaced by the euro. [Finnish]

Mar·kova /mɑːˈkɔːvə/ **Dame Ali·cia** (born Lilian Alicia Marks) (b.1910), the first British prima ballerina, with a career spanning 1925 to 1962, particularly known for her performance of *Giselle*.

marks·man *noun* (*pl.* **-men**) a person skilled in shooting, esp. with a pistol or rifle. □ **marks·man·ship** *noun*

mark·up *noun* **1** the amount added to the cost price of goods to cover overhead charges, profit, etc. **2** an act or instance of increasing the price of goods. **3** the corrections made in marking up text. **4** a system of tagging used to identify the structure of a text held electronically.

marl¹ ● *noun* soil consisting of clay and lime, with fertilizing properties. ● *transitive verb* apply marl to (the ground). □ **marly** *adjective* [Old French *marle* from medieval Latin *margila* from Latin *marga*]

marl² *noun* *Brit.* **1** a mottled yarn of differently coloured threads. **2** the fabric made from this. □ **marled** *adjective* [shortening of *marbled*: see MARBLE]

Marl·bor·ough /ˈmɑːlbrə, -bərə/ **1st Duke of** (title of John Churchill) (1650–1722), English general. As commander of British and Dutch troops in the War of the Spanish Succession he defeated the French armies of Louis XIV (notably at Blenheim in 1704), effectively ending Louis' attempts to dominate Europe.

Mar·ley /ˈmɑːli/ **Rob·ert Nesta ('Bob')** (1945–81), Jamaican reggae singer, guitarist, and songwriter. A devout Rastafarian and supporter of

Black Power, he formed the trio The Wailers in 1965 and they went on to become the first reggae musicians to gain international recognition.

mar·lin *noun* any of several large marine game fishes and food fishes of the swordfish family (genera *Makaira* and *Tetrapterus*) with the upper jaw elongated to form a pointed snout. [MARLINSPIKE, with reference to its pointed snout]

mar·line /ˈmɑrlɪn/ *noun Naut.* a thin line of two strands. [Dutch *marlijn* from *marren* bind + *lijn* LINE¹]

mar·lin·spike /ˈmɑrlɪnˌspəɪk/ *noun* (also **mar·line·spike**) *Naut.* a pointed iron tool used to separate strands of rope or wire. [originally apparently *marling spike* from *marl* fasten with marline (from Dutch *marlen* frequentative of Middle Dutch *marren* bind) + -ING¹ + SPIKE¹]

Mar·lowe /ˈmɑrloʊ/ **Chris·to·pher** (1564–93), English dramatist and poet. He brought a new strength and vitality to blank verse in plays such as *Tamburlaine the Great* (1587–8) and *Doctor Faustus* (*c.*1590); his poems include 'Come live with me and be my love' (published 1599).

mar·mal·ade ● *noun* **1** a preserve of citrus fruit, usu. bitter oranges, made like jam. **2** a preserve made of other fruits or vegetables, esp. onions stewed with sugar and vinegar. ● *attributive adjective* (esp. of a cat) orange tabby; ginger. [French *marmelade* from Portuguese *marmelada* quince jam, from *marmelo* quince, from Latin *melimelum* from Greek *melimēlon* from *meli* honey + *mēlon* apple]

Mar·mara, Sea of /ˈmɑrmərə/ a small sea in NW Turkey. Connected by the Bosporus to the Black Sea and by the Dardanelles to the Aegean, it separates European Turkey from Asian Turkey.

Mar·mite /ˈmɑrmaɪt/ *noun* **1** *Brit. proprietary* a preparation made from yeast extract and vegetable extract, used in sandwiches and for flavouring. **2** (**marmite**) (also /mɑrˈmiːt/) an earthenware cooking vessel. [French, = cooking pot]

mar·mor·eal /mɑrˈmɔrɪəl/ *adjective literary* of or like marble. □ **mar·mor·eal·ly** *adverb* [Latin *marmoreus* (as MARBLE)]

mar·mo·set /ˈmɑrməˌzet/ *noun* any of several small tropical American monkeys of the family Callitricidae, having a long bushy tail. [Old French *marmouset* grotesque image, of unknown origin]

mar·mot /ˈmɑrmət/ *noun* any burrowing rodent of the genus *Marmota*, with a heavy-set body and short bushy tail. [French *marmotte* prob. from Romansh *murmont* from Latin *murem montis* mountain mouse]

Marne River /mɑrn/ a river of east central France, which rises in the Langres plateau north of Dijon and flows 525 km (328 miles) north and west to join the Seine near Paris. Its valley was the scene of two important battles in the First World War. The first battle (Sept. 1914) halted and repelled the German advance on Paris; the second (July 1918) ended the final German offensive.

Maro·nite /ˈmerənəɪt, ˈma-/ ● *noun* a member of a Christian church of Syrian origin, living chiefly in Lebanon and in communion with the Roman Catholic Church. ● *adjective* of or relating to the Maronites. [medieval Latin *Maronita* from *Maro*, the name of the 5th-c. Syrian founder]

ma·roon¹ ● *adjective* brownish crimson. ● *noun* this colour. [French *marron* chestnut, from Italian *marrone* from medieval Greek *maraon*]

ma·roon² ● *transitive verb* **1** leave (a person) isolated in a desolate place (esp. an island). **2** (of a person or a natural phenomenon) cause (a person) to be unable to leave a place. ● *noun* (**Maroon**) a person descended from a group of fugitive slaves in the remoter parts of Suriname and the W Indies. [French *marron* from Spanish *cimarrón* wild, from *cima* peak]

Mar·quand /mɑrˈkwɒnd/ **John Phil·lips** (1893–1960), US novelist, who is known for his detective stories about the Japanese sleuth, Mr. Moto, and satires such as *The Late George Apley* (1937).

marque /mɑrk/ *noun* a make or brand, esp. of motor vehicle. [French, = MARK¹]

mar·quee /mɑrˈkiː/ *noun* **1** esp. *N Amer.* a canopy over the entrance to a large building. **2 a** a usu. brightly-lit sign over the entrance to a theatre etc., listing the names of featured performers. **b** (*attributive*) *N Amer.* popular enough to be listed on a marquee; famous (*a marquee player*; *achieved marquee status*). **3** a large tent used for social or commercial functions. [MARQUISE, taken as pl. & assimilated to -EE]

marquee value *noun* the drawing power of a star attraction.

Mar·ques·as Islands /mɑrˈkeɪsəs/ a group of volcanic islands in the S Pacific, forming part of French Polynesia; pop. (est. 2002) 9,400.

mar·quess /ˈmɑrkwɪs/ *noun* a British nobleman ranking between a duke and an earl (*compare* MARQUIS). [var. of MARQUIS]

mar·quet·ry /ˈmɑrkɪtri/ *noun* (also **mar·quet·erie**) inlaid work in wood, ivory, etc., esp. as used for the decoration of furniture. [French *marqueterie* from *marqueter* variegate, from MARQUE]

Mar·quette /mɑrˈket/ **Jacques** (known as Père Marquette) (1637–75), French Jesuit missionary and explorer. He was active in missions, esp. among the Odawa; in 1673 he joined Jolliet's expedition to explore the Mississippi River.

Már·quez see GARCÍA MÁRQUEZ.

Mar·quis /ˈmɑrkwɪs/ **Don·ald Rob·ert Perry ('Don')** (1878–1937), US journalist and humorist, who is best known for his stories featuring the characters Archy the cockroach and Mehitabel the cat.

mar·quis /ˈmɑrkiː/ *noun* a European nobleman ranking between a duke and a count (*compare* MARQUESS). [Old French *marchis* from Romanic (as MARCH², -ESE)]

mar·quise /mɑrˈkiːz/ *noun* **1 a** the wife or widow of a marquis. **b** a woman holding the rank of marquis in her own right (*compare* MARCHIONESS). **2** a pointed oval shape cut of diamond, usu. with 58 facets. **3** a chilled chocolate mousse-like dessert. **4** *archaic* =MARQUEE. [French, fem. of MARQUIS]

Mar·quis wheat /ˈmɑrkwɪs/ *noun* a variety of wheat which ripens in a relatively short growing season, allowing wheat to be grown further north in Canada. [possibly in honour of the Marquess of DUFFERIN AND AVA, Governor General of Canada 1872–8]

Mar·ra·kesh /ˌmærəˈkeʃ/ (also **Mar·ra·kech**) a city in W Morocco, in the foothills of the High Atlas Mountains; pop. (est. 2002) 745,800.

mar·ram /ˈmerəm, ˈma-/ *noun* a coarse shore grass, *Ammophila brevigulata* or *A. arenaria*, that binds sand with its tough rhizomes. [Old Norse *marálmr* from *marr* sea + *hálmr* HAULM]

mar·riage *noun* **1** the legal or religious union of two people. **2** an act or ceremony establishing this union. **3** one particular union of this kind (*by a previous marriage*). **4** a close association or intimate union (*the marriage of true minds*). **5** a combination of different elements. □ **by marriage** as a result of a marriage (*related by marriage*). **in marriage** as a spouse (*give in marriage*; *take in marriage*).

mar·riage·able *adjective* **1** (of a person) fit for marriage, esp. of an appropriate age. **2** (of age) fit for marriage. □ **mar·riage·abil·ity** *noun*

marriage bed *noun* the sexual relationship of a married couple.

marriage broker *noun* **1** *jocular* a matchmaker. **2** (in cultures in which arranged marriages are the norm) a person who arranges marriages for a fee.

marriage certificate *noun* a certificate certifying the completion of a marriage ceremony.

marriage commissioner *noun Cdn* (in some provinces) an official who conducts civil marriages.

marriage encounter *noun* an esp. religious encounter group aimed at improving marital relationships.

marriage licence *noun* a licence to marry.

marriage of convenience *noun* a marriage concluded to achieve some practical purpose, esp. financial or political.

Marriage of the Adriatic a former Ascension Day ceremony symbolizing the sea power of Venice, during which the doge dropped a ring into the water from his official barge.

marriage settlement *noun* an arrangement securing property between spouses.

mar·ried ● *adjective* **1** united in marriage. **2** of or relating to marriage (*married name*; *married life*; *the married residence*). **3** bound by strong, almost irrevocable ties (*she is married to her job*; *I am not married to the idea*). ● *noun* (usu. in pl.) a married person (*young marrieds*).

married quarters *plural noun* housing provided to married military personnel and their families by the armed forces, usu. for a low rent.

Mar·ri·ner /ˈmerɪnər/ **Sir Nev·ille** (b.1924), English conductor and violinist. He was the founder (1956) and director (1956–78) of the Academy of St. Martin-in-the-Fields, a chamber orchestra specializing in baroque music.

mar·ron glacé /ˌmaˌrɒ̃ glaˈseɪ/ *noun* (pl. **mar·rons glacés** *pronunc.* same) a chestnut preserved in and coated with sugar. [French, = iced chestnut: compare GLACÉ]

mar·row *noun* **1** = BONE MARROW. **2** the essential part. **3** (in full **vegetable marrow**) **a** a large usu. white-fleshed gourd used as food. **b** the plant, *Cucurbita pepo*, yielding this. □ **marrow·less** *adjective* **mar·rowy** *adjective* [Old English *mearg*, *mærg* from Germanic]

marrow bone *noun* a bone containing edible marrow.

marrow·fat *noun* a kind of large pea.

marry¹ *verb* (**-ries**, **-ried**) **1** *transitive* **a** take as one's spouse in marriage. **b** (of a person authorized to perform marriages) join (persons) in marriage. **c** (of a parent or guardian) give (a son, daughter, etc.) in

---

t *top*   v *voice*   w *we*   z *zoo*   ʃ *she*   ʒ *vision*   θ *thin*   ð *this*   ŋ *ring*   x *loch*   tʃ *chip*   dʒ *jar*   (*see over for vowels*)

marriage. **2** *intransitive* **a** enter into marriage. **b** (foll. by *into*) become a member of (a family, a social group) by marriage. **3** *transitive* **a** unite intimately. **b** correlate (things) as a pair. **c** *Naut.* splice (rope-ends) together without increasing their girth. **4** *transitive & intransitive* combine or be combined successfully with something else. ☐ **marry money** marry a rich person. **marry off** find a wife or husband for. [Old French *marier* from Latin *maritare* from *maritus* husband]

marry² *interjection archaic* expressing surprise, asseveration, indignation, etc. [Middle English, = (the Virgin) *Mary*]

Mars 1 *Rom. Myth* the god of war and the most important Roman god after Jupiter. He is identified with Ares and was probably originally an agricultural god; the month of March is named after him. **2** *Astronomy* the fourth planet from the sun in the solar system, orbiting between earth and Jupiter at an average distance of 228 million km from the sun, with an equatorial diameter of 6 787 km.

Mar·sala /mɑrˈsɑlə, -ˈsɒlə/ *noun* a dark sweet fortified dessert wine. [*Marsala* in Sicily, where originally made]

Mar·salis /mɑrˈsɑlɪs/ **1 Bran·ford** (b.1960), US jazz and classical saxophonist, who has performed with noted jazz musicians and pop stars, including Miles Davis and Sting; his albums include *Scenes in the City* (1983). **2** his brother, **Wyn·ton** (b.1961), US jazz and classical trumpet player. Noted as an outstanding virtuoso, he has played with established jazz and classical musicians and toured with his own quintet.

Mar·seil·laise /ˌmɑrseiˈjez/ *noun* the national anthem of France. [French, fem. adj. from *Marseille* Marseilles, the anthem having first been sung by patriots from there]

Mar·seilles /mɑrˈsei/ (French **Mar·seille**) a city and port on the Mediterranean coast of S France; pop. (1999) 798,430.

Marsh, Dame (Edith) Ngaio (1899–1982), New Zealand writer of detective fiction. Many of her novels feature Inspector Roderick Alleyn of Scotland Yard.

marsh *noun* **1** low land flooded in wet weather and usu. watery at all times. **2** (*attributive*) of or inhabiting marshland. ☐ **marshed** *adjective* **marsh·i·ness** *noun* **marshy** *adjective* (**marsh·i·er, marsh·i·est**). [Old English *mer(i)sc* from West Germanic]

mar·shal ● *noun* **1 a** (in titles of ranks) a high-ranking officer in the armed forces of some countries (*Marshal of the Royal Air Force*; *Field Marshal*). **b** an officer of the highest rank in the armies of some countries (*Marshal of France*). **c** a high-ranking officer of state (*Earl Marshal*). **2** a person arranging ceremonies, controlling procedure at parades, races, etc. **3** *US* **a** a federal or municipal law officer. **b** the head of a fire department. **4** (in full **judge's marshal**) (in the UK) an official accompanying a judge on circuit, with secretarial and social duties. ● *verb* (**mar·shalled, mar·shal·ling**; *US* **mar·shaled, mar·shal·ing**) **1** *transitive* **a** arrange or draw up (armed forces) in order for fighting, exercise, or review. **b** arrange (people) in a body or procession or for a race etc. **c** dispose, arrange, or set (things, material or immaterial) in methodical order, esp. in preparation for something (*marshalling her arguments for the case*; *marshalling my thoughts*). **2** *transitive* conduct (a person) ceremoniously. **3** *transitive Heraldry* combine (coats of arms). **4** *intransitive* take up positions in due arrangement.
☐ **mar·shal·ler** *noun* **marshal·ship** *noun* [Middle English via Old French *mareschal* and Late Latin *mariscalcus* from Germanic, literally 'horse servant']

Mar·shall ▶ **1 George Cat·lett** (1880–1959), US general. As US secretary of state (1947–9), he initiated the program of economic aid to European countries known as the Marshall Plan; he was awarded the Nobel Peace Prize in 1953. **2 John** (1755–1835), US jurist and statesman, who was chief justice of the US Supreme Court (1801–35) and helped devise the principles of US constitutional law. **3 Lois Cath·er·ine** (1924–97), Canadian soprano. She began voice lessons at the age of 12, and had her first major solo performance in 1947. Subsequently she toured extensively, performing and recording with the world's leading orchestras. **4 Thur·good** (1908–93), US jurist, who was the first black member of the US Supreme Court (1967–91); he was noted for his liberal views and as a champion of civil rights.

marshalling yard *noun* a railway yard in which freight trains etc. are assembled.

Marshall Islands (also **Mar·shalls**) a country consisting of two chains of islands in the NW Pacific; pop. (est. 2002) 73,630; capital, Majuro. They were administered by the US as part of the Pacific Islands Trust Territory from 1947 until 1986, when they became a republic in free association with the US. [J. *Marshall*, English adventurer, who visited the islands in 1788]

Marshall Plan *noun* a US plan to supply financial assistance to

certain western European countries after the Second World War to further their recovery. [G. C. MARSHALL]

marshal of the Royal Air Force *noun* (also **Marshal of the Royal Air Force**) an officer of the highest rank in the Royal Air Force.

marsh·berry *noun* (*pl.* **-berries**) *Cdn* (*Nfld*) a small bog cranberry, *Vaccinium oxycoccos*.

marsh gas *noun* methane.

marsh grass *noun* any of various grasses growing in marshy ground or salt marshes, esp. (*N Amer.*) cordgrass.

marsh harrier *noun* a European harrier, *Circus aeruginosus* (see HARRIER³).

marsh hawk *noun* *N Amer.* = NORTHERN HARRIER.

marsh·land *noun* land consisting of marshes.

marsh·mal·low *noun* **1** a very soft, fluffy, usu. white candy made of sugar, egg white, gelatin, etc. **2** an excessively tender-hearted or unassertive person.

marsh mallow *noun* a shrubby herbaceous plant, *Althaea officinalis*, the roots of which were formerly used to make marshmallow.

marsh marigold *noun* a golden-flowered herbaceous plant of the buttercup family, *Caltha palustris*, growing in moist meadows etc. Also called KINGCUP.

marsh pennywort *noun see* PENNYWORT 2.

Mars·ton Moor, Battle of the largest battle of the English Civil War, fought in 1644 on Marston Moor near York. The combined Royalist armies of Prince Rupert and the Duke of Newcastle were defeated by the English and Scottish Parliamentary armies, a defeat which destroyed Royalist power in the north of England and fatally weakened Charles I's cause.

mar·sup·ial /mɑrˈsuːpiəl/ ● *noun* any mammal of the order Marsupialia, characterized by being born incompletely developed and usu. carried and suckled in a pouch on the mother's belly. ● *adjective* **1** of or belonging to this order. **2** of or like a pouch (*marsupial muscle*). [modern Latin *marsupialis* from Latin *marsupium* from Greek *marsupion* pouch, diminutive of *marsipos* purse]

Mar·sy·as /ˈmɑrsiəs/ *Gk Myth* a satyr who took to flute-playing. He challenged Apollo to a musical contest and was flayed alive when he lost.

mart *noun* **1** *N Amer.* (usu. in proper names) a store (*Drug Mart*). **2** *archaic* a market. [obsolete Dutch *mart*, var. of *markt* MARKET]

Mar·ta·ban, Gulf of /ˌmɑrtəˈbɒn/ an inlet of the Andaman Sea, a part of the Indian Ocean, on the coast of SE Burma (Myanmar) east of Rangoon.

mar·ta·gon /ˈmɑrtəɡən/ *noun* a lily, *Lilium martagon*, with small purple turban-like flowers. [French from Turkish *martagān* a form of turban]

Mar·tel /mɑrˈtel/ **1** see CHARLES MARTEL. **2 Yann** (b.1963), Canadian novelist. His novel *The Life of Pi* (2001) won the Booker Prize in 2002.

Mar·tel·lo tower /mɑrˈtelo/ *noun* a small circular fort, often built on the coast to prevent a hostile landing, esp. any of those erected by British forces during the Napoleonic Wars. [alteration of Cape *Mortella* in Corsica, where such a tower proved difficult for the British to capture in 1794]

mar·ten *noun* **1** any weasel-like carnivore of the genus *Martes* found in forests of Eurasia and N America, esp. the pine marten. **2** the pelt or fur of the marten. [Middle Dutch *martren* from Old French (*peau*) *martrine* marten (fur), from *martre* from West Germanic]

mar·tens·ite /ˈmɑrtənˌzaɪt/ *noun* a hard, very brittle solid solution of carbon in iron, the chief constituent of hardened steel, formed when steel is quenched very rapidly. ☐ **mar·ten·sit·ic** /-ˈzɪtɪk/ *adjective* [A. *Martens*, German metallurgist d.1914 + -ITE¹]

Mar·tha (in the New Testament) the sister of Lazarus and Mary and friend of Jesus (Luke 10:40), who is depicted as being concerned with domestic affairs while her sister preferred to listen to Jesus' teachings; in Christian allegory she symbolizes the active life.

Martha's Vineyard a resort island off the coast of Massachusetts, to the south of Cape Cod. It was an important centre of fishing and whaling in the 18th and 19th c.

Mar·tial /ˈmɑrʃəl/ (Latin name Marcus Valerius Martialis) (AD *c*.40–*c*.104), Roman epigrammatist, born in Spain. His fifteen books of epigrams, mostly satirical, reflect all facets of Roman life.

mar·tial /ˈmɑrʃəl/ *adjective* **1** of or appropriate to warfare or the military. **2** warlike, brave; fond of fighting. ☐ **mar·tial·ly** *adverb* [Latin *martialis* of the Roman god Mars: see MARS]

martial art *noun* any of various fighting techniques or sports including judo and karate.

martial law *noun* military government, involving the suspension of ordinary law.

Mar·tian /ˈmɑrʃən/ ● *adjective* of the planet Mars. ● *noun* a hypothetical inhabitant of Mars. [Latin *Martianus* from *Mars*: see MARS]

Mar·tin ▸ **1 Ar·cher John Por·ter** (1910–2002), English biochemist, who developed partition chromatography and gas chromatography; he shared the Nobel Prize for chemistry in 1952. **2 Dean** (born Dino Paul Crocetti) (1917–95), US singer and actor. He became known originally for his comedy and singing act with Jerry Lewis from 1946, appearing on television and then in a series of films, such as *Hollywood or Bust* (1956). He joined with Frank Sinatra and Sammy Davis, Jr. — forming the 'Rat Pack' — in a number of films including *Bells are Ringing* (1960). **3 Paul Edgar Phil·lipe** (b.1938), Canadian business executive and politician, who succeeded Jean Chrétien as Liberal prime minister in 2004. As minister of finance (1993–2002), Martin was credited with significantly reducing the federal deficit. **4 Paul Jo·seph James** (1903–1992), Canadian politician and diplomat. First elected to the House of Commons as a Liberal in 1935, he became a member of the cabinet in 1945 as secretary of state. As minister of health and welfare from 1946, he introduced national government health insurance. **5 St.** (known as St. Martin of Tours) (d.397), French bishop, a patron saint of France. As a Roman soldier, he once cut his cloak in half to clothe a naked beggar. Soon afterwards, he was baptized a Christian and went on to found monasteries. Feast day, 11 November. **6 Steve** (b.1945), US actor and comedian. He successfully moved from zany stand-up comedy to farcical film comedies with *The Jerk* (1979), which he co-wrote. He went on to write, produce, and star in *Roxanne* (1987) and *LA Story* (1991), and also starred in *Sgt Bilko* (1996). **7 Wil·liam Mel·ville** (1876–1970), Canadian lawyer and politician, Liberal premier of Saskatchewan 1916–1922.

Martin V (born Oddone Colonna) (1368–1431), pope 1417–31. His election as pope at the Council of Constance brought an end to the Great Schism in the Western Church (1378–1417).

mar·tin *noun* any of several birds belonging to the swallow family Hirundinidae, e.g. the purple martin. [prob. from St. MARTIN]

Mar·tin du Gard /mɑrˈtɛ̃ ˌduː ˈɡɑr/ **Roger** (1881–1958), French novelist, who depicted the French bourgeoisie in his eight-part novel series *Les Thibault* (1922–40); he was awarded the Nobel Prize for literature in 1937.

Mar·ti·neau /ˈmɑrtɪˌnoː/ **Har·riet** (1802–76), English novelist, journalist, and writer on political economy. Her works include the series of instructive tales *Illustrations of Political Economy* (1832–34), the novel *Deerbrook* (1839), and a condensed translation of Comte, *The Positive Philosophy of Comte* (1853).

mar·ti·net /ˌmɑrtɪˈnet/ *noun* a strict (originally military or naval) disciplinarian. [J. *Martinet*, 17th-c. French drill master]

mar·tin·gale /ˈmɑrtɪnˌɡeɪl/ *noun* **1** a strap, or set of straps, fastened at one end to the noseband of a horse and at the other end to the girth, to prevent rearing etc. **2** a gambling system in which a player who is losing doubles the stake after each loss in the hope of eventual recoupment. [French, of uncertain origin]

Mar·tini /mɑrˈtiːni/ **Paul** (b.1960), Canadian figure skater, gold medallist along with his partner Barbara Underhill at the 1984 World Championships in Ottawa.

mar·tini *noun* a cocktail made of dry vermouth and usu. gin. [*Martini & Rossi*, Italian firm selling vermouth]

Mar·ti·nique /ˌmɑrtəˈniːk/ a French island in the W Indies, in the Lesser Antilles group; pop. (est. 2002) 422,277; capital, Fort-de-France. Its former capital, St. Pierre, was completely destroyed by an eruption of Mount Pelée in 1902. ☐ **Mar·tin·iquan** *noun*

Martin Luther King Day *noun* (in some US states) a holiday on the third Monday in January, commemorating Martin Luther King Jr.

Mar·tin·mas /ˈmɑrtɪnməs/ *noun* St. Martin's day, 11 Nov. [Middle English from St. MARTIN + MASS[2]]

mart·let /ˈmɑrtlət/ *noun* **1** *Heraldry* an imaginary footless bird borne as a charge. **2** *archaic* **a** a swift. **b** a house martin. [French *martelet* alteration of *martinet* diminutive from MARTIN]

mar·tyr /ˈmɑrtɜr/ ● *noun* **1 a** a person who is put to death for refusing to renounce a faith or belief. **b** a person who suffers for adhering to a principle, cause, etc. **c** a person who suffers or pretends to suffer in order to obtain sympathy or pity. **2** (foll. by *to*) a constant sufferer from (an ailment etc.). ● *transitive verb* **1** put to death as a martyr. **2** torment. ☐ **mar·tyr·ish** *adjective* [ecclesiastical Latin *martyr* from Greek *martur, martus -uros* witness]

mar·tyr·dom /ˈmɑrtɜrdəm/ *noun* **1** the sufferings or death of a martyr. **2** torment.

mar·tyr·ol·ogy /ˌmɑrtəˈrɒlədʒi/ *noun* (*pl.* **-gies**) **1** a list or register of martyrs. **2** the history of martyrs. ☐ **mar·tyr·o·logic·al** /-rəˈlɒdʒɪkəl/ *adjective* **mar·tyr·ol·o·gist** *noun*

Mar·uts /ˈmɒruts/ *Hinduism* (also called the **Rudras**) the sons of Rudra. In the Rig-Veda they are the storm gods, Indra's henchmen.

mar·vel ● *noun* **1** a wonderful thing. **2** (foll. by *of*) a wonderful example of (a quality). ● *intransitive verb* (**mar·velled**, **mar·vel·ling**; US **mar·veled**, **mar·vel·ing**) **1** (foll. by *at*, or *that* + clause) feel or express surprise or wonder. **2** (foll. by *how*, *why*, etc. + clause) wonder. ☐ **mar·vel·ler** *noun* [Old French *merveille, merveiller* from Late Latin *mirabilia* neuter pl. of Latin *mirabilis* from *mirari* wonder at: see MIRACLE]

Mar·vell /mɑrˈvel, ˈmɑrvəl/ **An·drew** (1621–78), English metaphysical poet. Most of his poetry was published posthumously (1681) and did not achieve recognition until the early 20th c.; his best-known poems include 'To his Coy Mistress' and 'The Garden'.

mar·vel·lous *adjective* (also esp. US **mar·vel·ous**) **1** astonishing. **2** excellent. **3** extremely improbable. ☐ **mar·vel·lous·ly** *adverb* **mar·vel·lous·ness** *noun*

marvel of Peru *noun* a showy garden plant, *Mirabilis jalapa*, with flowers opening in the afternoon. *Also called* FOUR O'CLOCK.

marvy /ˈmɑrvi/ *adjective* *slang* marvellous.

Marx /mɑrks/ **Karl (Hein·rich)** (1818–83), German political philosopher and economist, resident in England from 1849. The founder of modern communism with Engels, he collaborated with him in the writing of the *Communist Manifesto* (1848); his other works include the three-volume *Das Kapital* (1867; 1885; 1894), which develops his theories on the eventual 'withering away' of the state and the establishment of a communist society.

Marx Brothers /mɑrks/ a family of US comedians, consisting of **'Chico'** (Leonard, 1886–1961) and his brothers **'Harpo'** (Adolph Arthur, 1888–1964), **'Groucho'** (Julius Henry, 1890–1977), and **'Zeppo'** (Herbert, 1901–79). Their films, which are characterized by their anarchic humour, include *Horse Feathers* (1932), *Duck Soup* (1933), and *A Night at the Opera* (1935).

Marx·ism *noun* the political and economic theories based on the writings of Karl Marx, predicting the overthrow of capitalism, the taking over of the means of production by the proletariat, and the eventual attainment of a classless society, in accordance with scientific laws determined by dialectical materialism. ☐ **Marx·ist** *noun & adjective*

Marxism-Leninism *noun* Marxism as developed by Lenin and as implemented in the Soviet Union and subsequently in China. ☐ **Marxist-Leninist** *noun & adjective*

Mary ▸ **1** (known as the '(Blessed) Virgin Mary', or 'St. Mary', or 'Our Lady'), mother of Jesus. According to the Gospels, she was a virgin betrothed to Joseph at the time of the Annunciation; the doctrines of her Immaculate Conception and Assumption are taught by some Churches. Feast days, 1 Jan. (Mary, Mother of God), 25 Mar. (Annunciation), 15 Aug. (Assumption), 8 Sept. (Nativity of the Blessed Virgin), 8 Dec. (Immaculate Conception). **2** (in the New Testament) a woman of Bethany, the sister of Lazarus and Martha and friend of Jesus (Luke 10:40), who is depicted as preferring to listen to Jesus' teachings while her sister busied herself with domestic affairs.

Mary I (known as Mary Tudor) (1516–58), daughter of Henry VIII, queen of England 1553–8. As queen she attempted to re-establish Catholicism; she married Philip II of Spain, and after putting down several revolts, began a series of religious persecutions which earned her the name 'Bloody Mary'.

Mary II (1662–94), daughter of James II, queen of England 1689–94. Although her father converted to Catholicism, Mary remained a Protestant, and was invited to replace him on the throne after his deposition in 1689; she insisted that her husband, William III, be crowned along with her.

Mary, Queen of Scots (known as Mary Stuart) (1542–87), daughter of James V, queen of Scotland 1542–67. A devout Catholic, she was unable to control her Protestant lords, and after the defeat of her supporters she fled to England in 1567; she was imprisoned, became the centre of several Catholic plots against Elizabeth I, and was eventually beheaded.

Mary Jane *noun* esp. *N Amer.* **1** a flat, low-cut shoe for girls, with a single strap across the top. **2** *slang* marijuana.

Mary·land /ˈmerəˌlænd/ a state of the eastern US, on the Atlantic coast, surrounding Chesapeake Bay; pop. (2000) 5,296,486; capital, Annapolis. □ **Mary·land·er** noun [Queen Henrietta *Maria*, wife of Charles I]

Mary Mag·da·lene, St. /ˈmaɡdəˌliːn, -lən/ (also **Mary Mag·da·len**) *New Testament* a woman of Magdala in Galilee. She was a follower of Jesus, who cured her of evil spirits (Luke 8:2); she is also traditionally identified with the 'sinner' of Luke 7:37. Feast day, 22 July.

Marys·town /ˈmeriːzˌtaʊn/ a town in SE Newfoundland, on the east coast of the Burin Peninsula; pop. (2001) 5,908. [possibly after MARY 1]

Mary Stuart see MARY, QUEEN OF SCOTS.

Mary Tudor see MARY I.

mar·zi·pan /ˈmɑrzɪˌpan, -ˈpan/ ● noun a paste of ground almonds, sugar, etc., moulded into decorative shapes or used to coat large cakes. ● transitive verb (**mar·zi·panned**, **mar·zi·pan·ning**) cover with or as with marzipan. [German from Italian *marzapane*]

mas /mas/ noun (in Trinidad, and subsequently elsewhere), a masquerade, esp. one held as part of an annual carnival parade. [abbreviation of MASQUE]

masa /ˈmasə/ noun a type of dough made from cornmeal and used to make tortillas etc. [Spanish]

Ma·sac·cio /məˈsatʃiˌoː/ (born Tommaso Giovanni di Simone Guidi) (1401–28), Italian painter. He was the first artist to develop the laws of perspective (which he learned from Brunelleschi) and apply them to painting, and is remembered particularly for his frescoes in the Brancacci Chapel (1424–7), Florence.

Ma·sada /məˈsɑdə/ the site, on a steep rocky hill on the southwest shore of the Dead Sea, of the ruins of a palace and fortification built by Herod the Great in the 1st c. BC. It was a Jewish stronghold in the Zealots' revolt against the Romans (AD 66–73) and was the scene in AD 73 of mass suicide by the Jewish defenders when the Romans breached the citadel after a siege of nearly two years.

Masai /ˈmasai/ ● noun (pl. same or **Mas·ais**) **1 a** a pastoral people living in Kenya and Tanzania. **b** a member of this people. **2** the Nilotic language of the Masai. ● adjective of or relating to the Masai or their language. [Bantu]

ma·sala /məˈsɑlə/ noun **1** any of various spice mixtures ground into a paste or powder for use in Indian cooking. **2** a dish flavoured with this. [Urdu *maṣālah*, ultimately from Arabic *maṣāliḥ* 'ingredients, materials']

Mas·aryk /ˈmasərɪk/ (**Tomáš (Garrigue)**) (1850–1937), Czechoslovak leader, president 1918–35. A founder of Czechoslovakia, he promoted the cause of his country's independence in London during the First World War, and became Czechoslovakia's first president in 1918.

Mas·bate /masˈbɒti/ **1** an island in the central Philippines; pop. (2000) 707,688. **2** its chief town.

M.A.Sc. abbreviation Master of Applied Science.

masc. abbreviation = MASCULINE.

mas·cara /maˈskerə/ noun a cosmetic applied to the eyelashes to make them look darker and thicker. □ **mas·car·aed** /maˈskerəd/ adjective [Italian *mascara*, *maschera* MASK]

Mas·car·ene Islands /ˌmaskəˈriːn/ (also **Mas·car·enes**) a group of three islands in the W Indian Ocean, east of Madagascar, comprising Réunion, Mauritius, and Rodrigues. [P. de *Mascarenhas*, 16th-c. Portuguese navigator]

mas·car·pone /maskɑrˈpoːni/ noun a soft mild Italian cream cheese. [Italian]

mas·con /ˈmaskɒn/ noun Astronomy a concentration of dense matter below parts of the moon's surface, producing a gravitational pull. [*mass concentration*]

mas·cot noun **1** a person, animal, or thing that is supposed to bring good luck to or represent a team, school, etc. **2** N Amer. a costumed figure representing a sports team, usu. leading cheers among the spectators watching games. [French *mascotte* from modern Provençal *mascotto* fem. diminutive of *masco* witch]

Mas·couche /maˈskuːʃ/ a town in south central Quebec, north of Montreal; pop. (2001) 29,556. [Algonquin, = little bear]

mas·cu·line ● adjective **1** of or characteristic of men. **2** manly, vigorous. **3** (of a woman) having qualities considered appropriate to a man. **4** *Grammar* of or denoting the gender proper to certain words or grammatical forms, including those referring to males. ● noun Grammar the masculine gender; a masculine word. □ **mas·cu·lin·ity** noun **mas·cu·lin·ize** transitive verb (also esp. Brit. **-ise**). [Old French *masculin* -ine from Latin *masculinus* (as MALE)]

masculine rhyme noun Prosody a rhyme between final stressed syllables, e.g. *blow/flow*, *confess/suppress* (compare FEMININE RHYME).

mas·cu·lin·ist ● noun an advocate of the rights of men. ● adjective of or relating to the advocacy of the rights of men.

Mase·field /ˈmeisfiːld/ (**John (Ed·ward)**) (1878–1967), English poet and novelist. His fascination with the sea is reflected in his first published book of poetry, *Salt-Water Ballads*; his other works include narrative poems, novels, and the children's story *The Midnight Folk* (1927), and he was appointed Poet Laureate in 1930.

maser /ˈmeizər/ noun a device using the stimulated emission of radiation by excited atoms to amplify or generate coherent monochromatic electromagnetic radiation in the microwave range (compare LASER). [*m*icrowave *a*mplification by the *s*timulated *e*mission of *r*adiation]

Ma·seru /məˈseruː/ the capital of Lesotho; pop. (est. 2002) 169,200. It is situated on the Caledon River near the border with the province of Free State in South Africa.

mash ● noun **1** a soft mixture. **2** a mixture of boiled grain, bran, etc., given warm to horses etc. **3** *Brit. informal* mashed potatoes (*sausage and mash*). **4** a mixture of malt grains and hot water used esp. to form wort for brewing. **5** a soft pulp made by crushing, mixing with water, etc. ● transitive verb **1** reduce (potatoes etc.) to a uniform mass by crushing. **2** crush or pound to a pulp. **3** mix (malt) with hot water to form wort. □ **mash·er** noun [Old English *māsc* from West Germanic: perhaps related to MIX]

Mash·had /maʃˈhad/ (also **Meshed** /məˈʃed/) a city in NE Iran, close to the border with Turkmenistan; pop. (est. 2002) 2,040,700. The burial place in AD 809 of the Abbasid caliph Harun ar-Rashid and in 818 of the Shiite leader Ali ar-Rida, it is a holy city of the Shiite Muslims.

mash·ie /ˈmaʃi/ noun Golf an iron formerly used for lofting or for medium distances. [perhaps from French *massue* club]

mash note noun N Amer. informal a letter gushing with affection or praise; a love letter. [archaic slang *mash*, an infatuation]

Ma·shona·land /məˈʃɒnəˌland/ an area of N Zimbabwe, occupied by the Shona people. A former province of Southern Rhodesia, it is now divided into the three provinces of Mashonaland East, West, and Central.

mas·jid /ˈmasdʒɪd/ noun a mosque. [Arabic, lit. 'place of prostration']

mask ● noun **1** a covering for all or part of the face: **a** worn as a disguise, as part of a costume, or to amuse or terrify. **b** made of wire, gauze, paper, etc., and worn for protection, e.g. by an athlete, or by a medical practitioner to prevent infection of a patient. **c** worn to conceal the face at balls etc. and usu. made of velvet or silk. **2** a respirator used to filter inhaled air or to supply gas for inhalation. **3** a likeness of a person's face, esp. one made by taking a mould from the face (*death mask*). **4** a disguise or pretense (*mask of respectability*). **5** a hollow model of a human head worn by ancient Greek and Roman actors. **6** *Photog.* a screen used to exclude part of an image. **7** the face or head of an animal, esp. a fox. **8** = FACE MASK 2. **9** archaic a masked person. ● transitive verb **1** cover (the face etc.) with a mask. **2** disguise or conceal (a taste, one's feelings, etc.). **3** protect from a process. **4** *Military* **a** conceal (a battery etc.) from the enemy's view. **b** hinder (an army etc.) from action by observing with adequate force. **c** hinder (a friendly force) by standing in its line of fire. □ **mask·er** noun [French *masque* from Italian *maschera* from Arabic *maskara* buffoon, from *sakira* to ridicule]

masked adjective **1** wearing a mask; disguised or hidden by or as by a mask. **2** (of an animal etc.) having facial markings or features suggesting a mask.

masked ball noun a ball at which masks are worn.

masking tape noun usu. cream coloured adhesive tape used in painting to cover areas on which paint is not wanted, and in various household tasks.

mas·kin·onge /ˈmaskɪnɒndʒ, -ˈnɒndʒi/ noun = MUSKELLUNGE. [ultimately from Ojibwa, = great fish]

maso·chism /ˈmasəˌkɪzəm/ noun **1** the condition or state of deriving (esp. sexual) gratification from one's own pain or humiliation (compare SADISM). **2** the enjoyment of what appears to be painful or tiresome. □ **maso·chist** noun **maso·chis·tic** adjective **maso·chis·tic·ally** adverb [L. von Sacher-*Masoch*, Austrian novelist d.1895, who described cases of it]

Mason▸ 1 (**James (Nev·ille)**) (1909–84), English actor. He made his film debut in 1935 and went on to act in over one hundred films, receiving Oscar nominations for his performances in *A Star is Born* (1954), *Georgy Girl* (1966), and *The Verdict* (1982). **2** (**John**) (1586–1635), English colonial administrator. The second governor of the English colony in Newfoundland (1615–21), he explored much of the island,

---

Consonants: b *but*   d *dog*   f *few*   g *get*   h *her*   j *yes*   k *cat*   l *leg*   m *man*   n *no*   p *pen*   r *red*   s *sit*

creating the first English map of the territory. In 1621 he left for New England, and founded New Hampshire.

mason ● *noun* **1** a person who builds with stone or brick. **2** (**Mason**) a Freemason. ● *transitive verb* build or strengthen with masonry. [Old French *masson*, *maçonner*, Old Northern French *machun*, prob. ultimately from Germanic]

Mason-Dixon Line *noun* (also **Mason and Dixon Line**) the boundary line between Pennsylvania and Maryland. The name was later applied to the entire southern boundary of Pennsylvania, and in the years before the American Civil War it represented the division between the northern states and the slave-owning states of the South. [after surveyors C. *Mason* and J. *Dixon*]

Ma·son·ic /məˈsɒnɪk/ *adjective* of or relating to Freemasons.

Ma·son·ite /ˈmeɪsənaɪt/ *noun* esp. N Amer. proprietary fibreboard made from wood fibre pulped under steam at high pressure. [from *Mason* Fibre Co., Laurel, Mississippi + -ITE[1]]

Mason jar *noun* N Amer. a wide-mouthed glass jar with an airtight screw top, used in home canning. [John *Mason*, 19th-c. US inventor]

ma·son·ry /ˈmeɪsənri/ *noun* **1 a** the work of a mason. **b** stonework or brickwork. **2** (**Masonry**) Freemasonry. [Old French *maçonerie* (as MASON)]

Ma·sor·ah /məˈsɔːrə, masəˈrɒ/ *noun* (also **Massorah**) a body of traditional information and comment on the correct text of the Hebrew Bible. [Hebrew *māsōreṯ*, perhaps = bond]

Mas·or·ete /ˈmasəˌriːt/ *noun* (also **Massorete**) any of the Jewish scholars who contributed to the formation of the Masorah.
□ **Mas·or·etic** /-ˈretɪk/ *adjective* [French *Massoret* & modern Latin *Massoreta*, originally a misuse of Hebrew (see MASORAH), assimilated to -ETE]

masque /mask/ *noun* **1** a dramatic and musical entertainment esp. of the 16th and 17th c., originally of pantomime, later with metrical dialogue. **2** a dramatic composition for this. □ **mas·quer** *noun* [var. of MASK]

mas·quer·ade /ˌmaskəˈreɪd/ ● *noun* **1** a false show or pretense. **2** a masked ball. ● *intransitive verb* (often foll. by *as*) have or assume a false appearance. □ **mas·quer·ad·er** *noun* [French *mascarade* from Spanish *mascarada* from *máscara* mask]

Mass. *abbreviation* Massachusetts.

mass¹ ● *noun* **1** a coherent body of matter of indefinite shape. **2** a dense aggregation of objects (*a mass of fibres*). **3** (in *sing.* or *pl.*; foll. by *of*) a large number or amount. **4** (usu. foll. by *of*) an unbroken expanse (of colour etc.). **5** (foll. by *of*) a person or thing covered or abounding in something (*was a mass of cuts and bruises*). **6** a main portion (of a painting etc.) as perceived by the eye. **7** (prec. by *the*) **a** the majority. **b** (in *pl.*) the ordinary people. **8** *Physics* the quantity of matter a body contains. **9** (*attributive*) relating to, done by, or affecting large numbers of people or things; large-scale (*mass audience*; *mass communications*; *mass murder*). ● *transitive & intransitive verb* (usu. as **massed** *adjective*) **1** assemble into a mass or as one body (*massed bands*; *massed rain clouds*). **2** *Military* (with reference to troops) concentrate or be concentrated. □ **in the mass** in the aggregate; collectively. □ **mass·less** *adjective* [Old French *masse*, *masser* from Latin *massa* from Greek *maza* barley-cake: perhaps related to *massō* knead]

mass² *noun* (usu. **Mass**) **1** the Eucharist, esp. in the Roman Catholic Church. **2** a celebration of this. **3** the liturgy used in the Mass. **4** a musical setting of parts of this. [Old English *mæsse* from ecclesiastical Latin *missa* from Latin *mittere miss-* dismiss, perhaps from the concluding dismissal *Ite, missa est* 'Go, it is the dismissal']

Mas·sa·chu·setts /ˌmasəˈtʃuːsəts/ a state in the northeastern US, on the Atlantic coast; pop. (2000) 6,349,097; capital, Boston.

mas·sacre ● *noun* **1** a general slaughter (of persons, occasionally of animals). **2** *informal* an utter defeat or destruction. ● *transitive verb* **1** murder (esp. a large number of people) cruelly or violently. **2** *informal* defeat heavily; destroy. [Old French, of unknown origin]

Massacre of the Innocents *noun* New Testament the killing of all male infants in Bethlehem on Herod's orders (Matt. 2:16–18).

mas·sage /məˈsɒʒ/ ● *noun* **1** the rubbing, kneading, etc., of muscles and joints of the body esp. with the hands, for relaxation, to stimulate circulation, increase suppleness, etc. **2** an instance of this. ● *transitive verb* **1** apply massage to. **2** (usu. foll. by *into*, *onto*) apply (a lotion etc.) by rubbing. **3** manipulate (statistics etc.) to give an acceptable result. **4** flatter (a person's ego etc.). □ **mas·sa·ger** *noun* [French, from *masser* 'treat with massage', perhaps via Portuguese *amassar* 'knead', from *massa* 'dough': see MASS¹]

massage parlour *noun* an establishment at which massages and often sexual services are provided.

massage therapy *noun* the therapeutic use of massage.
□ **massage therapist** *noun*

mas·sa·sau·ga /ˌmasəˈsɒgə/ *noun* (also **massasauga rattlesnake**) a small spotted venomous N American rattlesnake, *Sistrurus catenatus*. [Ojibwa = 'great river mouth']

Mas·sa·soit /ˈmasəˌsɔɪt/ (c.1590–1661), Wampanoag chief, who established peaceful relations (1621) with the Pilgrim settlers of the Plymouth colony.

Mas·sawa /məˈsɒwə/ (also **Mitsiwa** /mɪˈtsiːwə/) the chief port of Eritrea, on the Red Sea; pop. (est. 2002) 29,700.

mass defect *noun* the difference between the mass of an isotope and its mass number.

mass-energy *noun* mass and energy regarded as interconvertible manifestations of the same phenomenon, according to the laws of relativity.

Mas·senet /ˈmasəˌneɪ/ **Jules (Émile Fré·dé·ric)** (1842–1912), French composer, known for his operas, which include *Manon* (1884), *Werther* (1892), and *Don Quichotte* (1910).

mas·seter /maˈsiːtər/ *noun* either of two chewing muscles which run from the temporal bone to the lower jaw. [Greek *masētēr* from *masaomai* chew]

mas·seur /maˈsɜːr/ *noun* a person who provides massage professionally. [French from *masser*: see MASSAGE]

mas·seuse /məˈsuːs, -ˈsɜːz/ *noun* a woman who provides massage professionally. [French from *masser*: see MASSAGE]

Mas·sey /ˈmasi/ **1 Charles Vin·cent** (1887–1967), Canadian politician and diplomat, first native-born Governor General of Canada 1952–59. He served as Canada's first minister to the US (1926–30), and then as high commissioner to Britain (1935–46), and chaired the Royal Commission on National Development in the Arts, Letters and Sciences (1951). **2** his great-grandfather, **Dan·iel** (1798–1856), American-born Canadian farmer and manufacturer. He developed an interest in farm machinery during the 1830s, and in 1849 opened the Newcastle Foundry and Machine Manufactory. **3** Daniel's son, **Hart Almer·rin** (1823–1896), Canadian manufacturer and philanthropist. He transformed his father's Newcastle Foundry into a large and successful farm machinery corporation, incorporating it in 1870 as the Massey Manufacturing Company, and ultimately, after several mergers, as the Massey-Harris Company (1891). He donated the money to build Massey Hall; his estate built both Hart House and Massey College at the University of Toronto. **4 Ray·mond Hart** (1896–1983), brother of Vincent, Canadian actor. After numerous amateur appearances while a student and a soldier, he turned professional in 1922. He made his Broadway and film debuts in 1931, and in the 1950s and 1960s he starred in the TV series *Dr Kildare*, playing Dr Gillespie.

mas·si·cot /ˈmasɪˌkɒt/ *noun* yellow lead monoxide, used as a pigment. [French, perhaps related to Italian *marzacotto* unguent, prob. from Arabic *mashaqūnyā*]

mas·sif /maˈsiːf, ˈmasɪf/ *noun* a large mountain mass; a compact group of mountain heights. [French *massif* used as noun: see MASSIVE]

Mas·sif Cen·tral /maˈsiːf sɑ̃ˈtral/ a mountainous plateau in south central France. Covering almost one-sixth of the country, it rises to a height of 1 887 m (6,188 ft.) at Puy de Sancy in the Auvergne. It is bounded to the southeast by the Cévennes.

Mas·sine /maˈsiːn/ **Léo·nide (Fedor·ovich)** (born Leonid Fëdorovich Myassin) (1896–1979), Russian-born French choreographer and dancer. He created ballets such as *Le Tricorne* (1919) and the first symphonic ballet, *Les Présages* (1933), set to Tchaikovsky's Fifth Symphony.

mas·sive *adjective* **1** large and heavy or solid. **2** (of the features, head, etc.) relatively large in scale; of solid build. **3** exceptionally large, substantial, or far-reaching (*took a massive overdose*; *massive amounts of alcohol*; *a massive heart attack*). **4** (of a mineral) not visibly crystalline. **5** *Geol.* (of a rock formation) without structural divisions. **6** (of architectural or artistic style) presenting great, solid masses.
□ **mas·sive·ly** *adverb* **mas·sive·ness** *noun* [French *massif* -*ive* from Old French *massiz*, ultimately from Latin *massa* MASS¹]

massively parallel *adjective* of or relating to a computer which consists of many individual processing units, and which is thus able to carry out simultaneous calculations on a substantial scale.

mass market ● *noun* the market for mass-produced goods. ● *adjective* (**mass-market**) designed for or appealing to a large segment of the

---

t *top*   v *voice*   w *we*   z *zoo*   ʃ *she*   ʒ *vision*   θ *thin*   ð *this*   ŋ *ring*   x *loch*   tʃ *chip*   dʒ *jar*   (*see over for vowels*)

population. ● *transitive verb* (**mass-market**) market (a product) on a mass scale. □ **mass-market·ed** *adjective* **mass marketing** *noun*

mass media *noun* = MEDIA¹ 2.

mass meeting *noun* a meeting of a large body of people, esp. of all or most of the members of a workforce, community, etc.

mass murder *noun* the killing of several people, esp. at once by one person. □ **mass murderer** *noun*

mass noun *noun* *Grammar* a noun that is not countable and cannot be used with the indefinite article or in the plural, e.g. *luggage, china, happiness*.

mass number *noun* the total number of protons and neutrons in an atomic nucleus.

Masson-Angers /maˈsɔ̃ˈʒei/ a former city in W Quebec, now part of the city of Gatineau; pop. (2001) 9,799. [in honour of Louis Masson, lieutenant-governor of Quebec 1884–87, and ANGERS¹]

Mas·so·rah *var. of* MASORAH.

Mas·sor·ete *var. of* MASORETE.

mass-produce *transitive verb* manufacture by mass production. □ **mass-produced** *adjective*

mass production *noun* the production of large quantities of a standardized article, esp. by a standardized mechanical process.

mass society *noun* a society in which the population is largely homogeneous and is strongly influenced by the mass media.

mass spectrograph *noun* an apparatus separating isotopes, molecules, and molecular fragments by their passage in ionic form through electric and magnetic fields.

mass spectrometer *noun* an apparatus which ionizes material and separates the ions by deflecting them in a magnetic field or accelerating them in an electric field, and detects them electrically in order to produce a mass spectrum.

mass spectrometry *noun* the use of a mass spectrometer to analyze substances.

mass spectrum *noun* the distribution of ions shown by the use of a mass spectrograph or mass spectrometer.

mass transit *noun* *N Amer.* public transportation, esp. in urban areas.

mast¹ ● *noun* **1** a long upright post of timber, iron, etc., set up on a ship's keel, esp. to support sails. **2** a post or latticework upright for supporting a radio or television antenna. **3** a flagpole (*half-mast*). ● *transitive verb* furnish (a ship) with masts. □ **before the mast** serving as an ordinary seaman (quartered in the forecastle). □ **mast·ed** *adjective* (also in *combination*). **mas·ter** *noun* (also in *combination*). [Old English *mæst* from West Germanic]

mast² *noun* the fruit of the beech, oak, chestnut, and other forest trees, esp. as food for pigs. [Old English *mæst* from West Germanic, prob. related to MEAT]

mas·taba /ˈmastəbə/ *noun* **1** *Archaeology* an ancient Egyptian tomb with sloping sides and a flat roof. **2** a bench, usu. of stone, attached to a house in Islamic countries. [Arabic *maṣṭabah*]

mast cell *noun* a cell in connective tissue which releases histamine etc. during inflammatory and allergic reactions. [*mast* from German *Mast* 'fattening, feeding']

mas·tec·tomy /masˈtektəmi/ *noun* (*pl.* **-mies**) the surgical removal of all or part of a breast. [Greek *mastos* breast + -ECTOMY]

mas·ter ● *noun* **1 a** a person having control of persons or things. **b** an employer, esp. of domestic servants. **c** a male head of a household (*master of the house*). **d** the owner of a pet, horse, etc. **e** the owner of a slave. **f** *Naut.* the captain of a merchant ship. **g** *Cdn* (*Nfld*) the person in charge of a fishing crew. **h** *Hunting* the person in control of a pack of hounds etc. **2** esp. *Brit.* a male teacher or tutor, esp. a schoolmaster. **3 a** the head of a college, school, etc. **b** the head or presiding officer of a society, institution, Masonic lodge, etc. **4** a person who has or gets the upper hand (*we shall see which of us is master*). **5 a** a person skilled in a particular trade and able to teach others (often *attributive*: *master carpenter*). **b** a person highly accomplished in a particular skill, activity, etc. (*Italian violin masters; a master of manipulation*). **6 a** (in full **master's degree**) a graduate degree, usu. awarded after at least one full year of study beyond the undergraduate level. **b** a holder of such a university degree, originally giving authority to teach in the university (*Master of Arts; Master of Science*). **7 a** a revered teacher in philosophy etc. **b** (**the Master**) *Christianity* Christ. **8 a** an artist of great skill, esp. one regarded as a model of excellence. **b** a work of painting or sculpture by such an artist. **9 a** *Chess etc.* a player of proven ability at international level. **b** *Sport* (in *pl.*) (usu. *attributive*) a class for competitors over the usual age for the highest level of competition (*Masters tournament*). **10** the original copy of a sound recording, film, data file, etc. from which a series of copies can be made. **11** (**Master**) **a** a title prefixed to the name of a boy not old enough to be called *Mr* (*Master D. Barber; Master Steve*). **b** *archaic* a title for a man of high rank, learning, etc. **12 a** (in Ontario) a judicial officer with jurisdiction over interlocutory matters. **b** (in England and Wales) an official of the Supreme Court. **13** *Mech.* a machine, device, or component directly controlling another (*compare* SLAVE 5). **14** (**Master**) a courtesy title of the eldest son of a Scottish viscount or baron (*the Master of Falkland*). ● *adjective* **1** main, principal (*master bedroom*). **2 a** (of a material or immaterial thing) main, principal; controlling, supreme (*master plan*). **b** designating a device or component which directly controls the action of others (*master switch*). **3** designating the copy of a tape, disc, file, etc. which is the authoritative source for copies. **4** commanding, superior, great, leading (*a master spirit*). ● *transitive verb* **1** overcome, defeat, get the better of in a contest or struggle. **2** break, tame, reduce to subjection, or compel to obey. **3** acquire complete knowledge of (a subject), facility in using (an instrument etc.), or skill at (performing a task). **4** rule as a master. **5 a** record the master disc or tape for (a sound recording). **b** make a recording of (a performance) from which a master can be created. □ **be master of 1** know how to control. **2** have at one's disposal. **be one's own master** be independent or free to do as one wishes. □ **mas·ter·less** *adjective* [Latin *magister*, prob. related to *magis* more]

master-at-arms *noun* (*pl.* **masters-at-arms**) the chief police officer on a man-of-war or a merchant ship.

master bedroom *noun* the largest bedroom in a dwelling, usu., in a family dwelling, the one intended for the parents.

master bombardier *noun* (**Master Bombardier**) *Cdn* a non-commissioned officer in the artillery of a rank equivalent to master corporal. Abbr.: **MBdr**.

master class *noun* **1** an advanced class given by a person of distinguished skill, esp. in music. **2** the most powerful or influential class in a society.

master corporal *noun* (also **Master Corporal**) *Cdn* (in the Canadian Army and Air Force) a non-commissioned officer of a rank above corporal and below sergeant. Abbr.: **MCpl**.

mas·ter·ful *adjective* **1** powerful and able to control others (*he looked masculine and masterful*). **2** highly skilled (*a masterful assessment of the difficulties*). ¶ Some people maintain that *masterful* should be used of a person, whereas *masterly* should be used of achievements, abilities, etc. □ **mas·ter·ful·ly** *adverb* **mas·ter·ful·ness** *noun*

master hand *noun* **1** a person having commanding power or great skill. **2** the action or agency of such a person.

master key *noun* a key that opens several locks, each of which also has its own key that will not open any of the rest.

mas·ter·ly *adjective* worthy of a master; very skilful (*a masterly piece of work*). □ **mas·ter·li·ness** *noun*

master mariner *noun* **1** the commander of a ship, esp. the captain of a merchant ship. **2** a seaman certified competent to be captain.

master mason *noun* **1** a skilled mason, or one in business on his or her own account. **2** (**Master Mason**) a fully qualified Freemason, who has passed the third degree.

master·mind ● *noun* **1** the person directing an intricate operation. **2** a person with an outstanding intellect. ● *transitive verb* plan and direct (a scheme or enterprise).

master of ceremonies *noun* **1** a person introducing speakers at a banquet, entertainers in a variety show, etc. **2** a person in charge of ceremonies at a state or public occasion. Abbr.: **MC**.

master·piece *noun* **1** an outstanding piece of artistry or workmanship. **2** a person's best work.

master plan *noun* **1** a large-scale or comprehensive plan of action. **2** a general plan of a building, installation, subdivision, etc., esp. one made prior to construction.

master race *noun* a race of people considered or considering themselves pre-eminent in greatness or power, esp. the Germans or Aryans during the Nazi period.

master seaman *noun* (also **Master Seaman**) *Cdn* (in the Canadian Navy) a non-commissioned officer of a rank above leading seaman and below petty officer second class, equivalent to a master corporal in the other commands. Abbr.: **MS**.

master·sing·er *noun* = MEISTERSINGER.

master stroke *noun* an outstandingly skilful act of policy etc.

master switch *noun* a switch controlling the supply of electricity etc. to an entire system.

master warrant officer *noun* (also **Master Warrant Officer**)

Cdn (in the Canadian Army and Air Force) a non-commissioned officer of a rank above warrant officer and below chief warrant officer. Abbr.: **MWO**.

mas·ter·work *noun* = MASTERPIECE.

mas·tery *noun* **1** (often foll. by *of*) comprehensive knowledge or use of a subject or instrument. **2** masterly skill. **3** dominion, sway. **4** (prec. by *the*) superiority or ascendancy in competition or strife; the upper hand.

mast·head *noun* **1 a** the title of a newspaper etc. at the head of the front or editorial page. **b** *N Amer.* a box in a newspaper or magazine listing the names of owners and staff, etc. **2** the highest part of a ship's mast, esp. that of a lower mast as a place of observation or punishment.

mas·tic /ˈmastɪk/ *noun* **1** a gum or resin exuded from the bark of the mastic tree, used in making varnish. **2** (in full **mastic tree**) the evergreen tree, *Pistacia lentiscus*, yielding this. **3** a waterproof, putty-like filler and sealant used in building. [Old French from Late Latin *mastichum* from Latin *mastiche* from Greek *mastikhē*, perhaps from *mastikhaō* (see MASTICATE) with reference to its use as chewing gum]

mas·ti·cate /ˈmastɪˌkeɪt/ *transitive verb* grind or chew (food) with one's teeth. □ **mas·ti·ca·tion** *noun* **mas·ti·ca·tor** *noun* **mas·ti·ca·tory** *adjective* [Late Latin *masticare masticat-* from Greek *mastikhaō* gnash the teeth]

mas·tiff /ˈmastɪf/ *noun* a dog of a large strong breed with drooping ears and pendulous lips. [ultimately from Old French *mastin*, ultimately from Latin *mansuetus* tame; see MANSUETUDE]

mas·titis /maˈstaɪtɪs/ *noun* an inflammation of the mammary gland (the breast or udder). [Greek *mastos* breast + -ITIS]

mas·to·don /ˈmastəˌdɒn/ *noun* a large extinct mammal of the genus *Mammut*, resembling the elephant but having nipple-shaped tubercles on the crowns of its molar teeth. [modern Latin from Greek *mastos* breast + *odous odontos* tooth]

mas·toid /ˈmastɔɪd/ ● *adjective* **1** shaped like a woman's breast. **2** of or pertaining to the mastoid process or bone. ● *noun* = MASTOID PROCESS. [French *mastoïde* or modern Latin *mastoides* from Greek *mastoeidēs* from *mastos* breast]

mas·toid·itis *noun* inflammation of the mastoid process.

mastoid process *noun* a conical prominence on the temporal bone behind the ear, to which muscles are attached.

mas·tur·bate /ˈmastərˌbeɪt/ *transitive & intransitive verb* arouse oneself sexually or cause (another person) to be aroused by manual stimulation of the genitals. □ **mas·tur·ba·tion** *noun* **mas·tur·ba·tor** *noun* **mas·tur·ba·tory** *adjective* [Latin *masturbari masturbat-*]

Ma·suria /məˈsjʊriə/ (also **Ma·sur·ian Lakes**) a low-lying and forested lakeland region of NE Poland. Extending from the Vistula to Poland's eastern borders, it contains some 2,700 lakes.

M.A.T. *abbreviation* Master of Arts in Teaching.

mat¹ ● *noun* **1** a small piece of carpeting or other heavy material, used as a covering on a floor. **2** a usu. thin piece of cork, rubber, plastic, etc., to protect a surface from the heat or moisture of an object placed on it. **3** a piece of padded, resilient material for landing on in gymnastics, wrestling, etc. **4** a piece of coarse fabric of braided rushes, straw, etc. **5** a thick tangled mass of hair, vegetation, etc., esp. forming a layer. ● *verb* (**mat·ted**, **mat·ting**) **1** *intransitive* become matted. **2** *transitive* cover or furnish with mats. □ **go to the mat** vigorously engage in an argument or contention, esp. on behalf of a particular person or cause. [Old English *m(e)att(e)* from West Germanic from Late Latin *matta*]

mat² (also esp. *Brit.* **matt**) ● *noun* **1** a sheet of cardboard forming a margin around a picture inside a frame. **2** a sheet of cardboard on which a picture etc. is mounted. ● *transitive verb* (**mat·ted**, **mat·ting**) **1** mount (a print etc.) on a cardboard backing. **2** provide (a print etc.) with a border. [French *mat*, *mater*]

mat³ *noun* = MATRIX 2. [abbreviation]

mata·dor /ˈmatəˌdɔr/ *noun* a bullfighter whose task is to kill the bull. [Spanish from *matar* kill, from Persian *māt* dead]

Mata Hari /ˌmɒtə ˈhɑri/ (born Margaretha Geertruida Zelle) (1876–1917), Dutch dancer and secret agent. She probably worked for both French and German intelligence services before being executed by the French in 1917; her name derives from Malay *mata* 'eye' and *hari* 'day'.

Ma·tane /məˈtan/ a town in E Quebec, situated on the south shore of the St. Lawrence, opposite Baie-Comeau; pop. (2001) 14,933. [ultimately from Mi'kmaq *mtctan* beaver pond]

Mata·pédia River /ˌmatəˈpeɪdjə/ a river in E Quebec, 70 km long, which rises south of Matane and flows southeastward to join the Restigouche near its mouth. [Mi'kmaq, = river that forks]

match¹ ● *noun* **1** a person, thing, action, etc. equal to another in some quality (*we shall never see his match; this river is a match for the most skilled anglers*). **2** a person or thing exactly like or corresponding to another (*this vase is an exact match for the one that was broken*). **3** a person or thing that associates or combines well with another (*ginger and peaches are a wonderful match; I believe that this candidate is an excellent match for your company*). **4** a contest or game of skill etc. in which persons or teams compete against each other. **5 a** a marriage. **b** a close association of two people (*as partners they are a perfect match*). **6** a person viewed in regard to his or her eligibility for marriage, esp. as to rank or fortune (*an excellent match*). **7** *Computing* a record, string, etc. that matches the requirements of a search or is identical with a given record etc. **8** an incident in which the participants vie to outdo each other (*slanging match*). ● *verb* **1 a** *transitive* combine well with, esp. in colour (*the curtains match the wallpaper*). **b** *intransitive* (often foll. by *with*) correspond; harmonize (*his socks do not match; the records didn't match with the certificates in his possession*). **2** *transitive* (foll. by *against, with*) place (a person, aptitudes etc.) in competition with (another) (*match your skill against the experts*). **3** *transitive* find material etc. that matches (another) (*can you match this paint chip?*). **4** *transitive* find a person or thing suitable for another (*matching unemployed workers with vacant positions*). **5** *transitive* be equal to (*the players are well matched*). **6** *transitive* find or provide something equal to (*can you match that story?; no one can match their offer*). **7** *transitive Electronics* produce or have an adjustment of (circuits) such that maximum power is transmitted between them. **8** *transitive* (usu. foll. by *with*) *archaic* join (a person) with another in marriage. □ **match up** (often foll. by *with*) pair up; fit to form a coherent whole or relation. **match up to** be as good as or equal to. **meet one's match** meet someone who has as much skill, determination, etc. as oneself, and perhaps more. **to match** corresponding in some essential respect with what has been mentioned (*yellow dress with gloves to match*). [Old English *gemæcca* mate, companion, from Germanic]

match² *noun* **1** a short thin piece of wood, paper, etc., tipped with a composition that can be ignited by friction. **2** a piece of wick, cord, etc., designed to burn at a uniform rate, for firing a cannon, igniting a trail of gunpowder, etc. □ **put a match to** set fire to. [Old French *mesche, meiche*, perhaps from Latin *myxa* wick]

match·board *noun* a board with a tongue cut along one edge and a groove along another, so as to fit with similar boards.

match·book *noun N Amer.* a small cardboard folder, usu. with a striking surface on the back, containing paper matches.

match·box *noun* **1** a small box for holding matches. **2** (often *attributive*) something very small, esp. a very small house or apartment.

match·ing *adjective* **1** that matches (*shoes and matching gloves*). **2** (of financial grants) of an amount based on the amount raised from other sources (*they received a $1-million matching grant from the government*).

match·less *adjective* without an equal, incomparable. □ **match·less·ly** *adverb*

match·lock *noun hist.* **1** an old type of gun with a lock in which a match was placed for igniting the powder. **2** such a lock.

match·mak·er *noun* **1 a** a person who schemes to bring couples together. **b** a person who arranges marriages. **2** a person who arranges matches between employers and prospective employees, corporate deal makers, etc. □ **match·make** *intransitive verb* **match·making** *noun & adjective*

match penalty *noun Hockey* = GAME MISCONDUCT.

match play *noun Golf* play in which the score is reckoned by counting the holes won by each side (*compare STROKE PLAY*).

match point *noun* **1** *Tennis etc.* **a** the state of a game when one side needs only one more point to win the match. **b** this point. **2** *Bridge* a unit of scoring in matches and tournaments.

match·stick ● *noun* the stick or stem of a match. ● *adjective* **1** something likened to a matchstick in being long and thin (*matchstick potatoes*). **2** made of or as though of matchsticks.

match·up *noun* **1** the action of pairing or setting in opposition. **2** (esp. in sports or politics) **a** two suited or equal persons, teams, or things. **b** a pair so matched. **c** a contest between such a pair.

match·wood *noun* **1** wood suitable for matches. **2** minute splinters. □ **make matchwood of** smash utterly.

mate¹ ● *noun* **1** (in *combination*) a fellow member or joint occupant of (*teammate; roommate*). **2** a partner in marriage or a lover. **3** either of a pair of mated animals. **4** either of a pair of things, a counterpart or parallel (*I have the left shoe, but I can't find its mate*). **5** *Naut.* **a** an officer on a merchant ship subordinate to the master, the rank being divided into *first, second, third*, etc. *mate* according to seniority. **b** an assistant to an officer on board ship (*boatswain's mate*). **6** an assistant to a skilled worker (*plumber's mate*). **7** esp. *Brit. & Austral.* **a** a friend or fellow worker. **b** *informal* a general form of address, esp. by one man to another. ● *verb* (often foll. by *with*) **1 a** *transitive* bring (animals or birds) together for breeding. **b** *intransitive* (of animals or birds) come together for breeding. **2 a** *transitive* join (persons) in marriage. **b** *intransitive* (of persons) be joined in marriage. **c** *intransitive* copulate. **3** *intransitive Mech.* (of a part) fit well, make a good or proper fit. □ **mate·less** *adjective* [Middle Low German *mate* from *gemate* messmate, from West Germanic, related to MEAT]

mate² *noun & transitive verb Chess* = CHECKMATE. [French *mat(er)*: see CHECKMATE]

mate /ˈmateɪ/ *noun* (in full **yerba maté**) **1** an infusion of the leaves of a S American shrub, *Ilex paraguariensis*. **2** this shrub, or its leaves. [Spanish *mate* from Quechua *mati*]

mate·lot /ˈmatloː/ *noun Cdn & Brit. slang* a sailor. [French]

mate·lote /ˈmatəˌloːt/ *noun* a dish of fish etc. with a sauce of wine and onions. [French (as MATELOT)]

mater /ˈmeɪtɜr/ *noun Brit. slang* mother. ¶ Now only in jocular or affected use. [Latin]

mater·famil·ias /ˌmeɪtɜrfəˈmɪliˌas/ *noun* the female head of a family or household (compare PATERFAMILIAS). [Latin from *mater* mother + *familia* FAMILY]

ma·teri·al ● *noun* **1** the matter from which a thing is made. **2** cloth, fabric. **3** (in *pl.*) things needed for an activity (*building materials; cleaning materials; writing materials*). **4** a person or thing suitable for a specific role or purpose (*officer material*). **5** (in *sing.* or *pl.*) information, ideas, evidence, etc. to be used in creating an artistic or literary work, drawing a conclusion, etc. (*experimental material; materials for a biography*). **6** (in *sing.* or *pl.*, often foll. by *of*) the elements or constituent parts of a substance. ● *adjective* **1** formed or consisting of matter; corporeal. **2 a** concerned with bodily comfort etc. (*material well-being*). **b** relating to the physical, not intellectual or spiritual, aspect of things. **3** (of conduct, points of view, etc.) not elevated or spiritual. **4 a** (often foll. by *to*) pertinent, essential, relevant (*at the material time*). **b** serious, important, of consequence. **5** *Law* (of evidence, a fact, etc.) significant, influential, esp. to the extent of determining a cause, affecting a judgment, etc. (*a material witness*). **6 a** *Logic* concerned with the matter, not the form, of reasoning. **b** *Philos.* of or pertaining to matter, as opposed to form. □ **ma·teri·al·ity** *noun* [Old French *materiel, -al*, from Late Latin *materialis* from Latin (as MATTER)]

material culture *noun* the physical objects (tools, articles of domestic and religious use, dwelling places, etc.) which give evidence of the type of culture developed by a social group.

ma·teri·al·ism *noun* **1 a** a tendency to prefer material possessions and physical comfort to spiritual values. **b** a way of life based on material interests. **2** *Philos.* **a** the doctrine that nothing exists but matter and its movements and modifications. **b** the doctrine that consciousness and will are wholly due to material agencies. **3** *Art* a tendency to lay stress on the material aspect of objects represented. □ **ma·teri·al·ist** *noun & adjective* **ma·teri·al·is·tic** *adjective* **ma·teri·al·is·tic·ally** *adverb*

ma·teri·al·ize *verb* (also esp. *Brit.* **-ise**) **1** *intransitive* become actual fact. **2** *intransitive* appear, arrive, or be present when expected. **3 a** *transitive* cause (a spirit) to appear in bodily form. **b** *intransitive* (of a spirit) appear in this way. **4** *transitive* represent or express in material form. **5** *transitive* make materialistic. □ **ma·teri·al·iz·a·tion** *noun*

ma·teri·al·ly *adverb* **1** substantially, considerably. **2** with respect to matter.

ma·teria med·ica /məˌtiːriə ˈmedikə/ *noun* **1** the remedial substances used in the practice of medicine. **2** the study of the origin and properties of these substances. [modern Latin, translation of Greek *hulē iatrikē* healing material]

ma·téri·el /məˌtiːriˈel/ *noun* available means or resources, esp. materials and equipment used in warfare (*opp.* PERSONNEL 1). [French (as MATERIAL)]

mater·nal /məˈtɜrnəl/ *adjective* **1** of or like a mother. **2** motherly, having the instincts of motherhood. **3 a** related through the mother (*maternal uncle*). **b** inherited from the mother (*maternal chromosome*). **4** of or pertaining to the mother in pregnancy and childbirth. □ **mater·nal·ly** *adverb* [Old French *maternel* or Latin *maternus* from *mater* mother]

mater·nity /məˈtɜrnɪti/ *noun* **1** (attributive) **a** for women during and just after childbirth (*maternity hospital; maternity leave*). **b** designed for a pregnant woman (*maternity dress; maternity wear*). **2** a maternity ward or hospital. **3 a** motherhood. **b** motherliness. [medieval Latin *maternitas -tatis* from *maternus* from *mater* mother]

mate's bed *noun N Amer.* = CAPTAIN'S BED.

matey ● *adjective* (**mati·er, mati·est**) *informal* (often foll. by *with*) sociable; familiar and friendly. ● *noun* esp. *Brit.* (*pl.* **mateys**) *informal* (usu. as a form of address) mate, companion. □ **matey·ness** *noun* (also **mati·ness**).

math *noun N Amer. informal* mathematics. □ **do the math** make calculations based on the figures implicit in a given situation, esp. to determine profitability, feasibility, etc. [abbreviation]

math·emat·ical *adjective* **1** of or relating to mathematics. **2 a** (of a concept, object, etc.) as understood or defined in mathematics. **b** (of a proof etc.) rigorously precise. □ **math·emat·ical·ly** *adverb* [Greek *mathēmatikos* from *mathēma -matos* science, from *manthanō* learn]

math·emat·ics *noun* **1** the abstract, deductive science of number, quantity, space, and arrangement studied in its own right (**pure mathematics**), or as applied to other disciplines such as physics, engineering, etc. (**applied mathematics**). **2** (as *pl.*) the use of mathematics in calculation etc. □ **math·em·at·ician** /-məˈtɪʃən/ *noun* [see MATHEMATICAL]

Mathe·son /ˈmaθəsən/ **Alex·an·der Wal·lace** (1903–76), Canadian lawyer and politician, Liberal premier of PEI 1953–59.

Mathie·son /ˈmaθəsən/ **John Alex·an·der** (1863–1947), Canadian lawyer, politician, and judge, Conservative premier of PEI 1911–1917. As premier he negotiated a constitutional guarantee that PEI would always have at least 4 MPs.

maths *noun Brit. informal* mathematics (compare MATH). [abbreviation]

-matic /ˈmatɪk/ *combining form* forming nouns, usu. proprietary names, denoting a device which works automatically or mechanically. [from AUTOMATIC]

Ma·tilda¹, (known as 'the Empress Maud') (1102–67), English princess, daughter of Henry I. In 1135 her father died and Matilda was forced to flee when his nephew Stephen seized the throne; her claim as heir was supported by King David I of Scotland, and she waged an unsuccessful civil war against Stephen (1139–48). Her son succeeded Stephen as Henry II.

Ma·tilda² *noun Austral. slang* a bushman's bundle; a swag. □ **waltz** (or **walk**) **Matilda** carry a swag. [the name *Matilda*]

mati·nee /ˈmatɪˌneɪ/ *noun* an afternoon performance at a theatre, concert hall, etc. [French, = 'what occupies a morning' (extended in fashionable French society to the dinner hour, 6 or 7 p.m.), from *matin* morning (as MATINS)]

matinee coat *noun* (also **matinee jacket**) a baby's short coat.

matinee idol *noun* esp. *dated* a handsome actor.

mat·ing ● *noun* an act or instance of matching, marrying, or pairing (of animals etc.) for breeding purposes. ● *adjective* of or pertaining to the act of mating (*mating ritual; mating season*).

matins /ˈmatɪnz/ *noun* (also **mat·tins**) (as *sing* or *pl.*) **1 a** a service of morning prayer in the Anglican Church. **b** *Catholicism* the office of one of the canonical hours of prayer, properly a night office, but also recited with lauds at daybreak or on the previous evening. **2** (also **matin**) *archaic* the morning song of birds. [Old French *matines* from ecclesiastical Latin *matutinas*, accusative fem. pl. adj. from Latin *matutinus* of the morning, from *Matuta* dawn goddess]

Ma·tisse /maˈtiːs/ **Henri (Emile Be·noît)** (1869–1954), French painter and sculptor. A leader of Fauvism, he heralded a new style based on simple reductive line, giving a rhythmic decorative pattern on a flat ground of rich colour.

mat leave *noun Cdn, Brit., & Austral. informal* maternity leave.

Mato Gros·so /ˌmatoː ˈɡrɒsoː/ a high plateau region of SW Brazil, forming a watershed between the Amazon and Plate river systems. The region is divided into two states: **Mato Grosso** and **Mato Grosso do Sul**.

matri·arch /ˈmeɪtriˌɑrk/ *noun* **1 a** a woman who is the head of a family or tribe. **b** a woman who dominates an organization. **2** an elderly woman who is highly respected. □ **matri·arch·al** *adjective* [Latin *mater* mother, after PATRIARCH]

matri·archy *noun* (*pl.* **-ies**) **1** a form of social organization in which the mother is the head of the family and descent is reckoned through the female line. **2 a** a society, organization, etc. governed by a woman or women. **b** government by a woman or women.

ma·tric /məˈtrɪk/ *noun* esp. *Brit. informal* matriculation. [abbreviation]

matri·ces *pl.* of MATRIX.

matri·cide /ˈmatrɪˌsaɪd/ *noun* **1** the killing of one's mother. **2** a person who does this. □ **matri·cid·al** *adjective* [Latin *matricida, matricidium* from *mater matris* mother]

ma·tric·u·late /məˈtrɪkjʊˌleɪt/ *verb* **1** *intransitive* be enrolled at a college or university. **2** *transitive* admit (a student) to membership of a college or university. [medieval Latin *matriculare matriculat-* enrol, from Late Latin *matricula* register, diminutive of Latin MATRIX]

ma·tric·u·la·tion *noun* **1** the act or an instance of matriculating, esp. formal admission into a university, college, etc. **2** esp. *Brit.* an examination to qualify for this. **3** *Cdn see* JUNIOR MATRICULATION, SENIOR MATRICULATION.

matri·lin·eal /ˌmatrɪˈlɪnɪəl/ *adjective* of or based on kinship with the mother or the female line. □ **matri·lin·eage** *noun* **matri·lin·eal·ly** *adverb* [Latin *mater matris* mother + LINEAL]

matri·local /ˌmatrɪˈloːkəl/ *adjective* of or denoting a custom in marriage where the married couple goes to live with the wife's community. □ **matri·local·ity** /matrɪloːˈkalɪti/ *noun* [Latin *mater matris* mother + LOCAL]

matrimonial cake *noun Cdn (Prairies)* = DATE SQUARE.

matrimonial home *noun* the residence occupied by both spouses as the family home during a marriage.

matri·mony /ˈmatrɪˌmoːni/ *noun (pl.* **-ies**) **1** the rite or institution of marriage. **2 a** the state of being married. **b** the relation between married persons. □ **matri·mon·ial** *adjective* **matri·mon·ial·ly** *adverb* [Anglo-French *matrimonie* from Latin *matrimonium* from *mater matris* mother]

mat·rix /ˈmeɪtrɪks/ *noun (pl.* **matri·ces** /-ˌsiːz/ or **matrix·es**) **1** an environment or substance in which a thing is developed. **2 a** a mould in which a thing is cast or shaped, such as printing type, an engraved die to strike coins, etc. **b** a positive or negative copy of an original disc recording used in making other copies. **3 a** the rock material in which a gem, fossil, etc. is embedded. **b** any relatively fine or homogeneous substance in which coarser or larger particles are embedded. **4** *Math.* a rectangular array of symbols, elements, etc. in rows and columns that is treated as a single element. **5 a** *Zool.* the formative tissue from which a tooth, hair, feather, nail, etc. arises. **b** *Bot.* the substrate on which a fungus, lichen, etc. grows. **6** *Computing* a grid-like array of interconnected circuit elements. **7** an organizational structure in which two or more lines of command, responsibility, or communication run through the same individual. [Latin, = breeding female, womb, from *mater matris* mother]

ma·tron /ˈmeɪtrən/ *noun* **1** a middle-aged or elderly married woman, esp. a dignified, staid, or portly one of high social standing. **2** esp. *N Amer.* a female prison officer. **3** esp. *Brit.* a woman managing the domestic arrangements of a boarding school or other institution. **4** esp. *hist.* a woman in charge of the nurses in a hospital. [Latin *matrona* from *mater matris* mother]

ma·tron·ly *adjective* like or characteristic of a matron, esp. as regards staidness or portliness.

matron of honour *noun* a married woman attending the bride at a wedding.

matry·oshka /maˈtrɪɒʃkə/ *noun* (also **matri·oshka**) (often *attributive*) = RUSSIAN DOLL. [Russian *matrëshka*]

Mats·qui /ˈmatskwiː/ *noun (pl.* same) a member of a Salishan Aboriginal people, a subgroup of the Halq'emeylem, living in the Lower Fraser valley of BC. [Halkomelem, = 'easy portage, easy travelling', in reference to the ease of ascending creeks from the Fraser and portaging over a nearby height of land]

mat·su·take /ˌmatsuːˈtɒkeɪ/ *noun* = PINE MUSHROOM. [Japanese *matsu* 'pine' + *take* 'mushroom']

Mat·su·yama /ˌmatsuːˈjɒmə/ a city in Japan, the capital and largest city of the island of Shikoku; pop. (est. 2002) 461,700.

Matt. *abbreviation New Testament* Matthew.

matt esp. *Brit. var. of* MATTE[1].

Matta·gami River /məˈtɒgəmi/ a river in NE central Ontario, 443 km long, which rises in Mattagami Lake northwest of Sudbury and flows northward through Timmins to join the Missinaibi River, together with which it forms the Moose River. [the name of the lake, from Ojibwa and Cree, = forked lake]

matte[1] /mat/ ● *adjective* **1** (of a colour, surface, etc.) dull, without lustre. **2** (of lipstick, face powder, paint, etc.) having a flat, not shiny or glossy, finish. ● *noun* paint formulated to give a dull flat finish (*compare* GLOSS[1] 3, SEMIGLOSS). [French *mat*]

matte[2] /mat/ *noun* an impure product of the smelting of sulphide ores, esp. those of copper or nickel. [French]

matte[3] /mat/ *noun Film* a mask to obscure part of an image and allow another image to be superimposed, giving a combined effect. [French]

mat·ted *adjective* **1** (esp. of plants, hair, etc.) tangled and interlaced. **2** covered with a dense growth. **3** (of a picture) provided with a mat.

mat·ter ● *noun* **1 a** a physical substance in general, as distinct from mind and spirit. **b** that which has mass and occupies space. **2** a constituent substance, esp. of a particular kind (*colouring matter*). **3** (prec. by *the*; often foll. by *with*) the thing that is amiss (*what is the matter?*; *there is something the matter with him*). **4** fact or thought as material for expression. **5 a** the content of a book, speech, etc., as distinct from its stylistic manner or form. **b** *Logic* the particular content of a proposition or syllogism, as distinct from its form. **6** a thing or things collectively of a specified kind or relating to a specified thing (*printed matter*; *reading matter*). **7 a** an affair or situation being considered, esp. in a specified way (*a serious matter*; *a matter for concern*; *the matter of your overdraft*). **b** (in *pl.*) events, circumstances, etc. generally which are objects of consideration or practical concern. **8 a** any substance in or discharged from the body (*fecal matter*; *grey matter*). **b** pus. **9** (foll. by *of, for*) a ground, reason, or what is or may be a good reason for (complaint, regret, etc.). **10** *Art* the body of a printed work, as type or as printed sheets, distinct from titles, headings, etc. **11** *Law* **a** a thing which is to be tried or proved. **b** statements or allegations which come under the consideration of a court. ● *intransitive verb* **1** (often foll. by *to*) be of importance; have significance (*it does not matter to me when it happened*). **2** secrete or discharge pus. □ **as a matter of course** as a regular habit or usual procedure. **be another** (or **a different**) **matter** be completely different. **for that matter 1** as far as that is concerned. **2** and indeed also. **in the matter of** as regards. **make matters worse** make an already difficult situation more difficult. **a matter of 1** approximately (*a matter of hours*). **2** a thing that relates to, depends on, or is determined by (*dealing with such problems is all a matter of experience*; *it's simply a matter of knowing when to take a chance*). **a matter of life and death** a matter of vital importance. **it's all** (or **only**) **a matter of time** (**before...**) this consequence is inevitable though it may not happen immediately. **no matter 1** (foll. by *when, how,* etc.) regardless of (*will do it no matter what the consequences*). **2** it is of no importance. **take matters into one's own hands** act decisively and independently. **what is the matter with** surely there is no objection to. **what matter?** that need not worry us. [Old French *matiere* from Latin *materia* timber, substance, subject of discourse]

Matter·horn a mountain in the Alps, on the border between Switzerland and Italy. Rising to 4 477 m (14,688 ft.), it was first climbed in 1865 by the English mountaineer Edward Whymper.

matter of fact ● *noun* **1** what belongs to the sphere of fact as distinct from opinion etc. **2** *Law* the part of a judicial inquiry concerned with the truth of alleged facts. ● *adjective* (**matter-of-fact**) **1** unimaginative, prosaic. **2** unemotional. **3** pertaining to, having regard to, or depending on actual fact as distinct from what is speculative or fanciful. □ **as a matter of fact** actually, in reality (esp. to correct a falsehood or misunderstanding). □ **matter-of-factly** *adverb* **matter-of-factness** *noun*

matter of form *noun* **1** a point of correct procedure. **2** a mere routine.

matter of law *noun Law* the part of a judicial inquiry concerned with the interpretation of the law and correctness of procedure.

matter of record *noun see* RECORD.

Mat·thew ▶ **1** *St.*, an Apostle, a tax collector from Capernaum in Galilee, traditional author of the first Gospel. Feast day, 21 Sept. **2** the first Gospel, written after AD 70 and based largely on the Gospel of Mark.

Matthew Paris *see* PARIS[2] 2.

Mat·thias, St. /məˈθaɪəs/ an Apostle, chosen by lot after the Ascension to take the place left by Judas. Feast day (in the Western Church) 14 May; (in the Eastern Church) 9 August.

mat·ting *noun* **1** fabric of hemp, bast, grass, etc., for mats (*coconut matting*). **2** in senses of MAT[1], [2] *verb*.

mat·tins *var. of* MATINS.

mat·tock /ˈmatək/ *noun* an agricultural tool shaped like a pickaxe, with an adze and a chisel edge as the ends of the head. [Old English *mattuc*, of unknown origin]

mat·tress *noun* a large fabric case stuffed with soft, firm, or springy material, or a similar case filled with air or water, used on or as a bed. [Old French *materas* from Italian *materasso* from Arabic *almaṭrah* 'the place, the cushion', from *ṭaraḥa* throw]

mat·ur·a·tion /ˌmatʃʊˈreɪʃən/ *noun* **1** the act or an instance of maturing. **2** the state of being matured. □ **mat·ur·a·tion·al** *adjective*

[French *maturation* or medieval Latin *maturatio* from Latin (as MATURE *verb*)]

ma·ture ● *adjective* (**ma·tur·er**, **ma·tur·est**) **1 a** with fully developed powers of body and mind; adult. **b** sensible, wise. **c** middle aged or elderly. **2 a** complete in natural development or growth. **b** (of wine, cheese, etc.) ready for consumption. **c** (of fruit) ripe. **3** (of thought, intentions, etc.) duly careful and adequate. **4** fully developed or established; at a point after which further development, expansion, or improvement is unlikely or impossible (*mature technology; a mature market*). **5** (of a bond etc.) due for payment. **6 a** (in Alberta) a film classification which requires that viewers under 14 years of age be accompanied by an adult. **b** (in BC) a film classification which advises of content which may be inappropriate for young viewers, without indicating an age restriction. ● *verb* **1 a** *transitive & intransitive* bring to or reach a mature state; develop fully. **b** *transitive & intransitive* ripen. **c** *intransitive* come to maturity. **2** *transitive* perfect (a plan etc.). **3** *intransitive* (of a bond etc.) become due for payment. □ **ma·ture·ly** *adverb* **ma·tur·ity** *noun* [Latin *maturus* timely, early]

mature student *noun* a person, usu. an adult, who undertakes a course of study at a later age than normal.

matu·tinal /ˌmatjuːˈtaɪnəl, məˈtjuːtɪnəl/ *adjective* **1** of or occurring in the morning. **2** early. [Late Latin *matutinalis* from Latin *matutinus*: see MATINS]

matzo /ˈmɒtsəʊ/ *noun* (also **mat·zoh**, **mat·zah** /ˈmɒtsə/) (*pl.* **-zos**, **-zohs**, **-zahs** or **mat·zoth** /-oːt/) **1** a flat, crisp, unleavened bread for the Passover. **2** a slab of this. [Yiddish from Hebrew *maṣṣāh*]

matzo ball *noun* a small dumpling made of seasoned matzo meal bound together with egg and chicken fat, typically served in chicken soup.

maud·lin /ˈmɔːdlɪn/ *adjective* **1** foolishly sentimental or self-pitying. **2** tearful and effusive from drunkenness. [Old French *Madeleine* from ecclesiastical Latin *Magdalena* MAGDALEN, with reference to pictures of Mary Magdalen weeping]

Maugham /ˈmɔːm/ **Wil·liam Somer·set** (1874–1965), English novelist, short-story writer, and dramatist. His life and wide travels often provide the background to his writing, which includes the novels *Of Human Bondage* (1915) and *The Razor's Edge* (1944).

Maui /ˈmaʊi/ the second largest of the Hawaiian islands, lying to the northwest of the island of Hawaii.

maul ● *transitive verb* **1** (of an animal) tear and mutilate (a person, prey etc.). **2 a** beat and bruise (a person). **b** handle roughly or carelessly; damage by rough handling. **3** subject to damaging criticism; injure by criticizing. ● *noun* **1** a special heavy hammer, commonly of wood, esp. for driving piles. **2** a wooden club. **3** *Rugby* a loose scrum with the ball off the ground. □ **maul·er** *noun* **maul·ing** *noun* [Old French *mail* from Latin *malleus* hammer]

Mau Mau /ˈmaʊmaʊ/ ● *noun* (*pl.* same) **1** an African secret society active in the 1950s, originating among the Kikuyu, and working to expel European settlers and end British rule in Kenya. **2** (treated as *pl.*) members of this society. ● *adjective* of or pertaining to the Mau Mau or a member of it. [Kikuyu]

Mauna Kea /ˌmaʊnə ˈkeɪə/ an extinct volcano on the island of Hawaii, in the central Pacific. Rising to 4 205 m (13,796 ft.), it is the highest peak in the Hawaiian islands. The summit area is the site of several large astronomical telescopes.

Mauna Loa /ˌmaʊnə ˈloːə/ an active volcano on the island of Hawaii, to the south of Mauna Kea, rising to 4 169 m (13,678 ft.). The volcano Kilauea is situated on its flanks.

maun·der /ˈmɔːndər/ *intransitive verb* **1** talk in a dreamy or rambling manner. **2** move or act listlessly or idly. [perhaps from obsolete *maunder* beggar, to beg]

Maun·dy Thursday *noun* the Thursday before Easter. [Old French *mandé* from Latin *mandatum* MANDATE, commandment (see John 13:34), from the custom of the British sovereign distributing money on this day.]

Mau·pas·sant /ˈmoːpaˌsɑ̃/ **(Henri René Al·bert) Guy de** (1850–93), French short-story writer and novelist. His short stories, such as *Boule de Suif* (1880) and *The Necklace* (1884), are notable for their use of irony and portray a broad spectrum of French society; his best-known novels include *Une Vie* (1883) and *Bel-Ami* (1885).

Maure·tania /ˌmɒrɪˈteɪniə/ an ancient region of North Africa, corresponding to the northern part of Morocco and western and central Algeria. It was annexed by Claudius in the mid-1st c. AD and divided into two Roman provinces. It was conquered by the Arabs in the 7th c. □ **Maure·tan·ian** *adjective & noun* [from Latin *Mauri* Moors, the original inhabitants of the region]

Maur·iac /ˈmɒriˌak/ **Fran·çois** (1885–1970), French novelist, dramatist, and critic. In novels such as *Thérèse Desqueyroux* (1927) and *Le Noeud de vipères* (1932), he addresses the conflict between religion and passion, and the narrowness and oppression of rural French life. He won the Nobel Prize for literature in 1952.

Mauri·tania /ˌmɒrɪˈteɪniə/ a country in West Africa with a coastline on the Atlantic Ocean; pop. (est. 2002) 2,828,858; capital, Nouakchott. The north of the country is desert, while the south lies in the Sahel. □ **Mauri·tan·ian** *adjective & noun*

Maur·itius /məˈrɪʃəs/ an island country in the Indian Ocean, about 850 km (550 miles) east of Madagascar; pop. (est. 2002) 1,200,206; capital, Port Louis. □ **Maur·itian** *adjective & noun*

Mau·rois /mɔːˈrwɒ/ **André** (pseudonym of Émile Herzog) (1885–1967), French biographer, novelist, and essayist, who is noted for his biographies, esp. of Shelley, Byron, Proust, and Balzac.

Maury /ˈmɒri/ **Mat·thew Fon·taine** (1806–73), US oceanographer. He conducted the first systematic survey of oceanic winds and currents, and published charts which enabled voyages to be considerably shortened.

Mau·rya /ˈmauriə/ a dynasty which ruled northern India 321– *c.*184 BC. It was founded by Chandragupta Maurya, who introduced a centralized government and script and developed a highway network which led to Mauryan control of most of the Indian subcontinent. □ **Mau·ryan** *adjective*

Mau·ser /ˈmauzər/ *noun proprietary* a type of firearm, originally a repeating rifle, now also a pistol. [P. von *Mauser*, German inventor d.1914]

mau·so·leum /ˌmɔːzəˈliːəm/ *noun* **1** a large and grand tomb. **2** a building in which are entombed the bodies or remains of several people, often of one family. **3** a very large and sombre building. [Latin from Greek *Mausōleion* from *Mausōlos* Mausolus king of Caria (4th c. BC), to whose tomb the name was originally applied]

mauve /məʊv/ ● *adjective* pale purple. ● *noun* **1** this colour. **2** a bright but delicate pale purple dye from coal tar aniline. [French, lit. 'mallow', from Latin *malva*]

mauzy /ˈmɒzi/ *adjective* (also **mausy**) *Cdn (Nfld)* (of weather) foggy, damp, or misty, esp. producing condensation on objects. [English dialect *mosey* 'muggy, foggy']

maven /ˈmeɪvən/ *noun N Amer. informal* an expert or connoisseur. [Hebrew *mēbīn*]

mav·er·ick /ˈmavrɪk/ *noun* **1** an unorthodox or independent-minded person (also *attributive*: *maverick politicians*). **2** *N Amer.* an unbranded calf or yearling. [S. A. *Maverick*, Texas engineer and rancher d.1870, who did not brand his cattle]

maw *noun* **1 a** the stomach of an animal. **b** the jaws or throat of a voracious animal or *jocular* person. **2** a thing perceived as a consuming mouth or entrance (*consumed by the voracious maw of the publicity machine*). [Old English *maga* from Germanic]

mawk·ish *adjective* **1** sentimental in a feeble or sickly way. **2** having a faint sickly flavour. □ **mawk·ish·ly** *adverb* **mawk·ish·ness** *noun* [obsolete *mawk* maggot, from Old Norse *mathkr* from Germanic]

max *N Amer. slang* ● *noun* maximum. ● *adjective* maximal. ● *adverb* maximally; at most. ● *verb* **1** *intransitive* (foll. by *out*) achieve or attain a maximum in something (*prices start in the low thirties and max out at fifty thousand*). **2** *transitive* (foll. by *out*) *informal* spend to the limit of (a credit card). □ **to the max 1** completely. **2** to the furthest possible extreme.

max. *abbreviation* maximum.

maxi *noun* (*pl.* **maxis**) *informal* **1** a maxi-coat, -skirt, etc. **2** = MAXI-PAD. [abbreviation]

maxi- *combining form* very large or long (*maxi-coat*). [abbreviation of MAXIMUM: compare MINI-]

max·illa /makˈsɪlə/ *noun* (*pl.* **max·il·lae** /-liː/) **1** the jaw or jawbone, esp. the upper jaw in most vertebrates. **2** the mouthpart of many arthropods used in chewing. □ **max·il·lary** *adjective* [Latin, = jaw]

Maxim /ˈmaksɪm/ **Sir Hiram (Ste·vens)** (1840–1916), US-born English inventor, who designed and manufactured the first automatic machine gun (1884).

max·im /ˈmaksɪm/ *noun* a general truth or rule of conduct expressed in a sentence. [medieval Latin *maxima* (*propositio*), fem. adj. (as MAXIMUM)]

max·ima *pl.* of MAXIMUM.

max·imal /ˈmaksɪməl/ *adjective* **1** being or relating to a maximum. **2** the greatest possible in size, duration, etc. □ **max·imal·ly** *adverb*

max·imal·ist /ˈmaksɪməlɪst/ *noun* a person who rejects compromise and expects a full response to (esp. political) demands.

Max·imil·ian /ˌmaksəˈmɪlɪən/ (full name Ferdinand Maximilian Joseph) (1832–67), emperor of Mexico 1864–7. He was established as emperor of Mexico under French auspices in 1864; in 1867 Napoleon III was forced to withdraw his support as a result of US pressure, and a popular uprising led by Juárez resulted in Maximilian's execution.

Maximilian I /ˌmaksəˈmɪlɪən/ (1459–1519), king of Germany 1486–93, and Holy Roman emperor 1493–1519, whose reign saw the expansion of the Hapsburg territories.

maxi·mize *transitive verb* (also esp. *Brit.* **-mise**) increase or enhance to the utmost. □ **maxi·miz·a·tion** *noun* **maxi·miz·er** *noun*

max·imum *noun* (pl. **max·imums** or **max·ima**) the highest possible or attainable amount or magnitude. ● *adjective* of or pertaining to a maximum; that is a maximum. [modern Latin, neuter of Latin *maximus*, superlative of *magnus* great]

maximum-security *adjective* (of a correctional institution) intended for offenders who require the greatest degree of physical security and so usu. having not only bars on the windows, but high walls, double fences, security posts with armed guards, electronic monitoring systems, etc. (compare MEDIUM-SECURITY, MINIMUM-SECURITY).

maxi-pad *noun* a sanitary pad designed to absorb heavy menstrual flow.

Max·well, **James Clerk** (1831–79), Scottish physicist. He extended the ideas of Faraday and Kelvin into his field equations of electromagnetism, thus unifying electricity and magnetism, identified the electromagnetic nature of light, and predicted the existence of other electromagnetic radiation.

max·well *noun* a unit of magnetic flux in the cgs system, equal to that induced through one square centimetre by a perpendicular magnetic field of one gauss. [MAXWELL]

May *noun* **1** the fifth month of the year. **2** (**may**) the hawthorn or its blossom. [Old French *mai* from Latin *Maius* (*mensis*) (month) of the goddess *Maia*]

may *auxiliary verb* (3rd sing. present **may**; past **might**) **1** (often foll. by *well* for emphasis) expressing possibility (*it may be true*; *I may have been wrong*; *you may well lose your way*). **2** expressing permission (*you may not go*; *may I come in?*). ¶ Both *can* and *may* are used to express permission; in more formal contexts *may* is usual since *can* also denotes capability (*can I move?* = am I physically able to move?; *may I move?* = am I allowed to move?). **3** expressing a wish (*may he live to regret it*). **4** expressing uncertainty or irony in questions (*who may you be?*; *who are you, may I ask?*). **5** in purpose clauses and after *wish, fear*, etc. (*take such measures as may avert disaster*; *hope she may succeed*). □ **be that as it may** (or **that is as may be**) despite the fact that it may be so (*be that as it may, I still want to go*). **may as well** = MIGHT AS WELL (see MIGHT[1]). [Old English *mæg* from Germanic, related to MAIN, MIGHT[2]]

Maya /ˈmaɪjə/ ● *noun* **1** (pl. same or **Mayas**) a member of an ancient Indian people of Central America. **2** the language of this people. ● *adjective* of or relating to this people or language. □ **Mayan** *adjective & noun* [Spanish from Maya]

maya /ˈmaɪjə/ *noun* **1** *Hindu Philos.* illusion, magic, the supernatural power wielded by gods and demons. **2** *Hinduism & Buddhism* the power by which the universe becomes manifest, the illusion or appearance of the phenomenal world. [Sanskrit *māyā* from *mā* create]

may·apple *noun* a herbaceous plant, *Podophyllum peltatum*, bearing a yellow egg-shaped fruit and flowering in May.

maybe ● *adverb* perhaps, possibly. ● *noun* an uncertain response, a possibility; what may be. [Middle English from *it may be*]

May bug *noun* = JUNE BUG.

May Day *noun* 1 May esp. as a festival with dancing, or as an international holiday in honour of workers.

may·day *noun* an international radio distress signal used esp. by ships and aircraft. [French *m'aidez* help me]

May-December *adjective* (of a romance, marriage, etc.) involving two people of widely disparate ages, usu. a young woman and a much older man.

Mayer /ˈmeɪər/ **Louis Burt** (born Eliezer Mayer) (1885–1957), Russian-born US film executive. He joined with Samuel Goldwyn to form the Metro-Goldwyn-Mayer (MGM) film studio in 1924, and was head of MGM until 1951; he also helped to establish the Academy of Motion Picture Arts and Sciences (1927).

may·est /ˈmeɪəst/ *archaic* = MAYST.

may·flower *noun* any of various flowers that bloom in May, esp. the trailing arbutus, *Epigaea repens*, the floral emblem of Nova Scotia. See also CANADA MAYFLOWER.

may·fly *noun* (pl. **-flies**) **1** any insect of the order Ephemeroptera,

living briefly in spring in the adult stage. **2** an imitation mayfly used by anglers.

may·hap /ˈmeɪhap, ˈmeɪ-/ *adverb archaic* perhaps, possibly. [Middle English from *it may hap*]

may·hem /ˈmeɪhem/ *noun* **1** violent or damaging action. **2** *hist.* the crime of maiming a person so as to render him or her partly or wholly defenceless. [Old French *mayhem* (as MAIM)]

may·ing *noun* participation in May Day festivities. [MAY]

Mayne Island one of the Gulf Islands in the Strait of Georgia, BC, lying to the east of Saltspring Island. [R. C. *Mayne*, British admiral d.1892]

mayn't *contraction* may not.

Mayo[1] /ˈmeɪoʊ/ a county in the Republic of Ireland, in the northwest in the province of Connacht; county town, Castlebar.

Mayo[2] /ˈmeɪoʊ/ **Charles Hor·ace** (1865–1939), US surgeon, who with his brother, William James (1861–1939), founded the Mayo Clinic in Rochester, Minnesota (1903), and pioneered group practice.

mayo /ˈmeɪoʊ/ *noun* esp. *N Amer. informal* mayonnaise. [abbreviation]

mayon·naise /ˈmeɪəˌneɪz/ *noun* **1** a thick creamy dressing made of egg yolks, oil, vinegar, etc. **2** *Brit.* a (usu. specified) dish of meat etc. dressed with this (*chicken mayonnaise*). [French, perhaps from *mahonnais -aise* of Port *Mahon* on Minorca]

may·or /ˈmeɪr, mer/ *noun* the head of a municipal corporation, esp. of a city or town. □ **mayor·al** *adjective* **mayor·ship** *noun* [Old French *maire* from Latin (as MAJOR)]

mayor·alty /ˈmeɪrəlti, ˈmer-/ *noun* (pl. **-ties**) **1** the office of mayor. **2** a mayor's period of office.

mayor·ess /ˈmeɪrəs/ *noun* **1** a woman holding the office of mayor. **2** the wife of a mayor. **3** a woman fulfilling the ceremonial duties of a mayor's wife.

May·otte /maˈjɒt/ (also called **Ma·hore**) an island to the east of the Comoros in the Indian Ocean; pop. (est. 2002) 170,879; capital, Mamoutzu. When the Comoros became independent in 1974, Mayotte elected to remain an overseas territory of France.

may·pole *noun* a tall pole painted and decked with flowers and ribbons, for dancing around on May Day.

Mays /meɪz/ **Wil·lie (How·ard)** (b.1931), US baseball player. He was noted for both his fielding and hitting, and scored 660 home runs in his lengthy career (1951–73).

mayst *archaic* 2nd sing. present of MAY.

May Two-Four *noun Cdn informal* Victoria Day. [punningly after May 24th, the official date of the holiday, and after TWO-FOUR in reference to copious consumption of beer over the holiday]

may·weed *noun* the stinking camomile, *Anthemis cotula*. [earlier *maidwede* from the same Germanic source as MAIDEN, the herb being used to relieve menstrual cramps]

maz·ard /ˈmazrd/ *noun* (also **maz·zard**) the wild sweet cherry, *Prunus avium*, of Europe. [alteration of MAZER]

Mazar-e-Sharif /maˌzɑːriˈʃəˈriːf/ a city in N Afghanistan; pop. (est. 2002) 239,800. The city is the reputed burial place of Ali, son-in-law of Muhammad. [Arabic, = tomb of the saint]

Maza·rin /mazaˈrɑ̃/ **Jules** (Italian name Giulio Mazzarino) (1602–61), Italian-born French statesman. He succeeded Richelieu as chief minister of France (1642) under Louis XIII; his administration aroused such opposition as to provoke the civil wars of the Fronde (1648–53).

Maz·at·lán /ˌmazətˈlan/ a seaport and resort in Mexico, on the Pacific coast in the state of Sinaloa; pop. (est. 2002) 335,900.

Maz·da·ism /ˈmazdəˌɪzəm/ *noun* Zoroastrianism. [Avestan *mazda*, the supreme god (AHURA MAZDA) of ancient Persian religion]

maze *noun* **1 a** a network of paths and passages arranged in bewildering complexity, usu. with a correct path concealed by blind alleys etc. **b** such a pattern, represented on paper by a pattern of lines, designed as a puzzle. **2** any complex system, arrangement, process, etc. that bewilders, confuses, or perplexes. □ **mazed** *adjective* **mazy** *adjective* (**mazi·er, mazi·est**). [Middle English, originally as *mased* (adj.): related to AMAZE]

mazel tov /ˈmɒzəltɒv, -tɒf, -toːv/ *interjection* good luck, congratulations. [modern Hebrew *mazzāl ṭōb*, lit. 'good star', from Hebrew *mazzāl* 'star']

mazer /ˈmeɪzr/ *noun hist.* a hardwood drinking bowl, usu. silver-mounted. [Old French *masere* from Germanic]

ma·zuma /məˈzuːmə/ *noun* esp. *US & Austral. slang* money, cash. [Yiddish from Hebrew *mĕzummān*, from *zimmēn* 'prepare']

ma·zurka /məˈzɜːrkə/ *noun* **1** a usu. lively Polish dance in triple time, usu. with a slide and hop. **2** a piece of music for this dance or composed in its rhythm, usu. with accentuation of the second or third beat. [French *mazurka* or German *Masurka*, from Polish *mazurka* denoting a woman from the province of Mazovia]

Maz·zini /mat'si:ni/ **Giu·seppe** (1805–72), Italian nationalist leader. He founded the patriotic movement Young Italy (1831) and became a leader of the Risorgimento, planning attempted insurrections during the 1850s; he continued to campaign for a republic following Italy's unification as a monarchy in 1861.

MB *abbreviation* **1** (also **Mb**) *Computing* megabyte. **2** Manitoba (in official postal use). **3** *Cdn* MEDAL OF BRAVERY. **4** Mennonite Brethren.

M.B.A. ● *abbreviation* Master of Business Administration. ● *noun* a person who holds this degree.

Mba·bane /ˌəmbɒˈbɒni/ the capital of Swaziland; pop. (est. 2002) 67,200.

mba·qanga /bɒˈkɒŋɡə, ˌəmbɒ-/ *noun* an upbeat form of South African popular music blending the influences of Zulu rhythms, blues, rock, and jazz. [Zulu *umbaqanga* 'steamed corn bread']

MBdr *abbreviation Cdn* MASTER BOMBARDIER.

MBE *abbreviation* Member of the Order of the British Empire.

Mbps *abbreviation Computing* megabytes per second.

Mbyte *abbreviation* megabyte.

MC¹ *abbreviation* **1** (in the UK) Military Cross. **2** (in the US) Member of Congress.

MC² ● *noun* **1** a master of ceremonies. **2** a person who provides entertainment at a club or party by instructing the DJ and performing rap. ● *transitive verb* (**MCs, MCd, MCing**) **1** act as master of ceremonies for. **2** perform as an MC.

Mc *abbreviation* megacycle(s).

Mc- ¶ In this dictionary, surnames beginning *Mac-* are alphabetized with other words beginning *mac-*, separate from those surnames beginning *Mc-*.

Mc·Arthur Peak a peak (4 344 m) in the St. Elias Mountains of SW Yukon Territory, situated north of Mount Logan. [J. J. *McArthur*, Canadian surveyor and Yukon commissioner d.1925]

Mc·Bride, Rich·ard (1870–1917), Canadian lawyer and politician, Conservative premier of BC 1903–15. The first party-based BC government, his administration initially led BC to a period of prosperity fuelled by provincially-supported railway expansion.

Mc·Cain, H. Har·ri·son (1927–2004), Canadian businessman. With his brother Wallace he opened the first frozen french fry plant in the Maritimes. The company rapidly expanded into overseas markets, and now owns a variety of enterprises.

Mc·Carthy, 1 Doris (b.1910), Canadian artist who is best known for her Canadian landscape paintings. **2 Jo·seph Ray·mond** (1908–57), US Republican politician. Between 1950 and 1954 he was the instigator of widespread investigations into alleged Communist infiltration in US public life.

Mc·Carthy·ism *noun* **1** *hist.* (esp. in the US) the policy of hunting out suspected Communists and removing them from government departments or other positions, esp. as pursued by Joseph McCarthy. **2** any use of unfair or unsubstantiated accusations to hound, harass, or investigate. □ **Mc·Carthy·ite** *adjective & noun* [MCCARTHY]

Mc·Cart·ney, Sir (James) Paul (b.1942), English pop and rock singer, songwriter and bass guitarist. A founding member of the Beatles (1961–70), he wrote most of their songs in collaboration with John Lennon; he later formed the band Wings (1971–81) and has produced solo albums, film scores, and a classical composition, the *Liverpool Oratorio* (1991), co-written with Carl Davis (b.1936).

Mc·Clel·land, John Gor·don ('Jack') (b.1922), Canadian publisher. Under his leadership the McClelland and Stewart publishing company published many well-known Canadian authors.

Mc·Clung, Nel·lie Leti·tia (born Nellie Letitia Mooney) (1873–1951), Canadian suffragist, author, and legislator. Living in Winnipeg and Edmonton 1911–33, she campaigned for women's suffrage, prohibition, factory safety laws, and other reforms; she was a Liberal MLA for Edmonton 1921–26. She was a Canadian delegate to the League of Nations (1938).

Mc·Cor·mack, John (1884–1945), Irish-born US operatic tenor, who was noted for his performances as Don Ottavio in *Don Giovanni* and Rodolfo in *La Bohème*.

McCoy *noun informal* □ **the** (or **the real**) **McCoy** the real thing; the genuine article. [19th c.: origin uncertain]

Mc·Crae, John (1872–1918), Canadian physician and poet. As a

member of the Canadian Expeditionary Force in Belgium (1914-18), he wrote his most famous poem, 'In Flanders Fields' (1915).

Mc·Cul·lers, Car·son (Smith) (1917–67), US novelist and short-story writer. Her works frequently address the theme of social isolation, and include the novels *The Heart is a Lonely Hunter* (1940) and *The Member of the Wedding* (1946), and the collection *The Ballad of the Sad Café* (1951).

Mc·Cully, Jona·than (1809–77), Canadian lawyer, politician and judge, Father of Confederation. Appointed to the Nova Scotia legislative council in 1847, he was a delegate to all three Confederation conferences.

Mc·Doug·all, Wil·liam (1822–1905), Canadian lawyer and politician, Father of Confederation. A member of the legislative assembly of the province of Canada (1858–67), he attended all three Confederation conferences, and then served as minister of public works in the 1867 Macdonald government. He was appointed Lieutenant-Governor of Rupert's Land in 1869, but was prevented by Louis Riel's supporters from entering the territory.

Mc·Enroe /ˈmakənˌroː/ **John (Pat·rick)** (b.1959), US tennis player, who won the singles (1981, 1983, and 1984) and doubles (1979, 1981, 1983, and 1984) titles at Wimbledon, and the singles (1979, 1980, 1981, and 1984) and doubles (1979 and 1981) titles at the US Open championships.

McEwan, Ian (Rus·sell) (b.1948), British novelist. His most notable works include *Black Dogs* (1992), the Booker Prize-winning *Amsterdam* (1998), and *Atonement* (2001).

Mc·Gar·rigle /məˈɡerɪɡəl/ **Kate** (b.1946) and her sister **Anna** (b.1944), Canadian singers and songwriters. They released their debut album together in 1976, and it has been followed by several other albums including *Dancer With Bruised Knees* (1977) and *Lover Over and Over* (1982).

McGee /məˈɡiː/ **Thom·as D'Arcy** (1825–68), Irish-born Canadian politician and Father of Confederation. He was elected to the legislative assembly of the province of Canada in 1858, and after a brief time in the Reform Party of George Brown joined the Great Coalition of Macdonald and Cartier. He attended the Charlottetown and Quebec Confederation conferences and was elected to the House of Commons in 1867, but was assassinated by a Fenian in 1868.

Mc·Gill /məˈɡɪl/ **James** (1744–1813), Scottish-born Canadian businessman and philanthropist. One of the Montreal merchants involved in the fur trade south of the Great Lakes from 1770, he diversified his activities into land speculation and by 1810 had abandoned the fur trade altogether. Rumoured to be the richest man in Montreal, he left a great deal of money to charity, including an estate and £10,000 to found McGill University.

Mc·Guffin *noun* (also **MacGuffin**) (in a film, novel, or other form of narrative fiction) a particular event, object, factor, etc., initially presented as being of great significance to the story, but often having little actual importance for the plot as it develops. [prob. from the surname *McGuffin*, allegedly borrowed by A. HITCHCOCK from a humorous story involving a diversion of this kind]

mCi *abbreviation* millicurie(s).

Mc·Intosh /ˈmakˌɪntɒʃ/ *noun N Amer.* a medium-sized, deep red, cooking and eating apple with green blotches. [J. McIntosh (1777–1845), Canadian farmer and apple breeder, who first discovered it]

McJob *noun informal* a low paying, low status, and usu. unstimulating job with few benefits and little possibility for advancement, esp. in a service industry. [from the name of the *McDonald's* chain of restaurants, fast-food restaurants being considered a typical source of such employment, + JOB, after the chain's general practice of using *Mc-* as a preformative element in a range of proprietary product names]

Mc·Kenna, Frank Jo·seph (b.1948), Canadian lawyer and politician, Liberal premier of New Brunswick (1987–1997). In 1987 he led the party to a stunning sweep of all 58 seats in the legislature, ending the 17-year reign of Richard Hatfield.

Mc·Ken·nitt, Lor·eena (b.1957), Canadian singer and harpist whose songs blend traditional Celtic music with more contemporary influences. Her 1991 album, *The Visit*, sold more than 500,000 copies and earned her a Juno award.

Mc·Kin·ley, Wil·liam (1843–1901), US Republican politician, 25th president of the US 1897–1901. He supported US expansion into the Pacific, fighting the Spanish-American War (1898), which resulted in the acquisition of Puerto Rico, Cuba, and the Philippines, as well as the annexation of Hawaii; he was assassinated by an anarchist.

Mc·Kinley, Mount a mountain in south central Alaska. Rising to

6 194 m (20,320 ft.), it is the highest mountain in N America. *Also called* DENALI. [W. McKINLEY]

Mc·Kin·ney, Louise (born Louise Crummy) (1868–1931), Canadian women's rights activist and legislator. One of the five appellants in the Persons Case, in 1903 she helped organize the North-West Territories Branch (later the Alberta and Saskatchewan Union) of the Woman's Christian Temperance Union, serving as its president until 1923. She also sat as a member of the Alberta legislature 1917–21.

Mc·Lach·lan /məˈɡlɒklən/ **Sarah** (b.1968), Canadian singer and songwriter. The haunting vocals and deeply personal lyrics on her albums, including her debut *Touch* (1988) and the more recent *Surfacing* (1997), have gained her fans across North America. She was awarded a Grammy in 2000 for the song 'I Will Remember You.'

Mc·Laren /məˈklɛrən/ **Nor·man** (1914–87), Scottish-born Canadian director of animated films. Boldly innovative in technique, he was Canada's leading director of animated film, producing 72 films in all, mostly with the NFB.

Mc·Lauch·lan /məˈɡlɒklən/ **Mur·ray Ed·ward** (b.1948), Scottish-born Canadian singer, songwriter, and guitarist. His 1972 'Farmer's Song' established his reputation with Canadian folk and country audiences.

M'Clin·tock Channel /məˈklɪntək, -ˌtɒk/ a sea passage in the Canadian Arctic, separating Prince of Wales Island from Victoria Island. [Sir F. L. *McClintock*, English naval officer and explorer who discovered the fate of Sir John Franklin's expedition d.1907]

Mc·Luhan /məˈkluːən/ **(Her·bert) Mar·shall** (1911–80), Canadian communications theorist. He is known for his theories on the role of the media and technology in society, claiming that the world had become a 'global village' in its electronic interdependence, and that 'the medium is the message', because it is the characteristics of a particular medium rather than the information it disseminates which influence and control society. □ **Mc·Luhan·esque** *adjective*

Mc·Mahon /məkˈmæn/ **Fran·cis Mur·ray Pat·rick** (1902–1986), Canadian petroleum industrialist. He founded a drilling firm in 1927, and eventually founded Pacific Petroleum, which became one of the most successful oil and gas companies in the west before being purchased by Petro-Canada in 1979.

Mc·Master, Wil·liam (1811–87), Irish-born Canadian businessman. In 1867 he helped to found the Canadian Bank of Commerce; as president he made the bank the largest in Ontario. His will left nearly $1,000,000 to found a Baptist university in Toronto; founded in 1890, McMaster University moved to Hamilton in 1930.

Mc·Millan, Edwin Matti·son (1907–91), US nuclear physicist, who shared the Nobel Prize for chemistry in 1951 with Seaborg for their discovery of transuranic elements.

Mc·Nair /məkˈnɛr/ **John Bab·bitt** (1889–1968), Canadian lawyer, politician, and judge, premier of New Brunswick 1940–52.

Mc·Naugh·ten rules /məkˈnɔːtən/ *plural noun* (also **M'Naghten rules**) *Brit.* rules governing the decision as to the criminal responsibility of an insane person. [*McNaughten* or *McNaughtan*, name of a 19th-c. accused person]

m-commerce *noun* commercial transactions conducted electronically by cellphone. [MOBILE]

MCP *abbreviation informal* = MALE CHAUVINIST PIG.

Mc·Pher·son, Aimee Sem·ple (born Aimee Semple Kennedy) (1890–1944), Canadian-born evangelist. She became the most publicized revivalist in the world, and in 1923 opened the $1.25 million Angelus Temple of the Foursquare Gospel in Los Angeles. From 1926 on she was increasingly involved in scandal.

MCpl *abbreviation Cdn* MASTER CORPORAL.

M.C.S. *abbreviation* Master of Computer Science.

Mc/s *abbreviation* megacycles per second.

Mc·Tavish, Simon (c.1750–1804), Scottish-born Canadian fur trader and businessman. From the 1770s he began financing trading missions as far west as the Saskatchewan River. He was instrumental in the formation of the North West Company in 1779.

MD *abbreviation* **1** Doctor of Medicine. **2** Mini Disc. **3** Maryland (in official postal use). **4** *Cdn* (*Prairies & North*) MUNICIPAL DISTRICT. **5** musical director. [sense 1 from Latin *Medicinae Doctor*]

Md *symbol Chem.* the element mendelevium.

Md. *abbreviation* Maryland.

MDA *abbreviation* methylenedioxyamphetamine, a synthetic hallucinogenic drug.

MDF *abbreviation* medium density fibreboard.

M.Div. *abbreviation* Master of Divinity.

MDMA *abbreviation* methylenedioxymethamphetamine, an amphetamine-based drug that causes euphoric and hallucinatory effects, originally produced as an appetite suppressant (*see* ECSTASY 3).

MDT *abbreviation* MOUNTAIN DAYLIGHT TIME.

ME *abbreviation* **1** Maine (in official postal use). **2** myalgic encephalomyelitis, an obscure disease with symptoms like those of influenza and prolonged periods of tiredness and depression.

Me. *abbreviation* **1** Maine. **2** *Maître* (title of a French-speaking lawyer).

me¹ ● *pronoun* **1** objective case of I² (*he saw me*). **2** *N Amer. informal* myself, to or for myself (*I got me a gun*). **3** *informal* used in exclamations (*dear me!; silly me!*). ● *adjective* of or displaying an excessive preoccupation with personal fulfillment and gratification (*the me generation*). ● *noun* one's personality, the ego (*the real me*). [Old English *me*, *mē* accusative & dative of I² from Germanic] ¶ See Usage Note at HER.

me² *var. of* MI.

mea culpa /meɪə ˈkʊlpə, -ˈkʌlpə/ ● *noun* an acknowledgement of one's fault or error. ● *interjection* expressing such an acknowledgement. [Latin, = by my fault]

Mead /miːd/ **Mar·garet** (1901–78), US anthropologist and social psychologist. She studied non-literate societies in Samoa and the New Guinea area, and the role of culture in character development; her books include *Coming of Age in Samoa* (1928) and *Male and Female* (1949).

mead¹ /miːd/ *noun* an alcoholic drink of fermented honey and water. [Old English *me(o)du* from Germanic]

mead² /miːd/ *noun literary* or *archaic* = MEADOW. [Old English *mæd* from Germanic, related to MOW¹]

Meade /miːd/ **George Gor·don** (1815–72), US general, who fought for the Union during the American Civil War, and defeated the Confederate Army at Gettysburg (1863).

mead·ow *noun* **1** a piece of grassland, esp. one used for hay or for grazing animals. **2** a piece of low well-watered ground, esp. near a river. □ **mead·owy** *adjective* [Old English *mædwe*, oblique case of *mæd*: see MEAD²]

meadow grass *noun* a perennial creeping grass, *Poa pratensis*.

meadow·land *noun* land used for the cultivation of grass, esp. for hay.

meadow·lark *noun* any of several N American songbirds of the genus *Sturnella* related to the blackbirds but speckled brown with yellow underparts, esp. the eastern meadowlark, *S. magna*, or western meadowlark, *S. neglecta*, which has a characteristic bubbling song.

meadow rue *noun* any plant of the genus *Thalictrum* of the buttercup family, with delicate leaves and flowers without petals.

meadow saffron *noun* a perennial plant, *Colchicum autumnale*, abundant in meadows, with lilac flowers. *Also called* AUTUMN CROCUS.

meadow·sweet *noun* **1** a rosaceous plant, *Filipendula ulmaria*, common in meadows and damp places, with creamy-white fragrant flowers. **2** any of several rosaceous plants of the genus *Spiraea*, native to N America.

Mea·ford /ˈmiːfərd/ a town in south central Ontario, situated on the west shore of Nottawasaga Bay, about 25 km east of Owen Sound, pop. (2001) 10,381. □ **Mea·ford·ite** *noun* [*Meaford Hall* in Staffordshire, England, birthplace of J. Jervis, admiral of the fleet d.1823]

mea·gre /ˈmiːɡər/ *adjective* **1** lacking in amount or quality (*a meagre salary*). **2** (of literary composition, ideas, etc.) lacking fullness, unsatisfying. **3** (of a person or animal) lean, thin. □ **meagre·ly** *adverb* **meagre·ness** *noun* [Anglo-French *megre* from Latin *macer*]

meal¹ *noun* **1** an occasion when food is eaten. **2** the food eaten on one occasion. □ **make a meal of 1** *Brit.* treat (a task etc.) too laboriously or fussily. **2** consume as a meal. [Old English *mæl* mark, fixed time, meal, from Germanic]

meal² *noun* **1** the edible part of any grain or pulse (usu. other than wheat) ground to powder. **2** any powdery substance made by grinding. [Old English *melu* from Germanic]

Meals on Wheels *plural noun* (usu. treated as *sing.*) a service by which meals are delivered to old people, invalids, etc.

meal ticket *noun* **1** a ticket entitling one to a meal, esp. at a specified place with reduced cost. **2** *informal* a person or thing that is a source of food or income.

meal·time *noun* any of the usual times of eating.

meal·worm *noun* the larva of any of several beetles of the genus *Tenebrio*, infesting cereal products, and often raised as food for pet fish or reptiles.

mealy *adjective* (**meal·i·er**, **meal·i·est**) **1 a** of or like meal; soft and powdery. **b** containing meal. **c** covered with or as with meal, flour, or any fine dust or powder. **2** (of a complexion) pale. **3** (of a horse) spotty. □ **meal·i·ness** *noun*

mealy bug *noun* any insect of the genus *Pseudococcus*, infesting vines etc., whose body is covered with white powder, a pest of citrus trees and greenhouses.

mealy-mouthed *adjective* not willing to speak in a direct or open way.

mean¹ *transitive verb* (*past* and *past participle* **meant**) **1 a** (often foll. by *to* + infin.) have as one's purpose or intention; have in mind (*they really mean mischief; I didn't mean to break it*). **b** (foll. by *by*) have as a motive in explanation (*what do you mean by that?*). **2** (often in *passive*) design or destine for a purpose (*mean it to be used; is meant to be a gift*). **3** intend to convey or indicate or refer to (a particular thing or notion) (*I mean we cannot go; I mean London in Ontario*). **4** entail, involve (*it means catching the early flight*). **5** (often foll. by *that* + clause) portend, signify (*this means trouble; your refusal means that we must look elsewhere*). **6** (of a word) have as its explanation in the same language or its equivalent in another language. **7** (foll. by *to*) be of some specified importance to (a person), esp. as a source of benefit or object of affection etc. (*that means a lot to me*). □ **mean it** not be joking or exaggerating. **mean to say** really admit (usu. in *interrogative*: *do you mean to say you have lost it?*). **mean well** (often foll. by *by*) have good intentions. [Old English *mænan* from West Germanic, related to MIND]

mean² *adjective* **1** uncooperative, unkind or unfair. **2** stingy; not generous. **3 a** malicious, ill-tempered. **b** *N Amer.* vicious or aggressive in behaviour. **4 a** low in the social hierarchy; humble (*mean origins*). **b** (of housing etc.) shabby; characterized by poverty. **5** (of a person's capacity, understanding, etc.) inferior, poor. **6** *informal* **a** (of a person) skilful, formidable (*is a mean fighter*). **b** (of a thing) excellent, impressive (*a mean batch of chili*). □ **no mean** a very good (*that is no mean achievement*). □ **mean·ly** *adverb* **mean·ness** *noun* [Old English *mǽne*, *gemǽne* from Germanic]

mean³ ● *noun* **1** a condition, quality, virtue, or course of action equally removed from two opposite (usu. unsatisfactory) extremes. **2** *Math.* **a** the term or one of the terms midway between the first and last terms of an arithmetical or geometrical etc. progression (*2 and 8 have the arithmetic mean 5 and the geometric mean 4*). **b** the quotient of the sum of several quantities and their number; the average. ● *adjective* **1** (of a quantity) equally far from two extremes. **2** calculated as a mean. [Anglo-French *meen* from Old French *meien*, *moien* from Latin *medianus* MEDIAN]

me·an·der /miˈandər/ ● *intransitive verb* **1** wander randomly. **2** (of a stream) wind about. ● *noun* **1** (often in *pl.*) a curve in a winding river. **2** a crooked or winding path or passage. **3** a circuitous journey. **4** an ornamental pattern of lines winding in and out; a fret. □ **me·an·der·ing** *adjective & noun* [Latin *maeander* from Greek *Maiandros*, the name of a winding river in Phrygia]

mean free path *noun* the average distance travelled by a gas molecule etc. between collisions.

mean·ie *noun* (also **meany**) (*pl.* **-ies**) *informal* a mean, stingy, or ill-tempered person.

mean·ing ● *noun* **1** what is meant by a word, action, idea, etc. **2** significance. **3** importance. ● *adjective* expressive, significant (*a meaning glance*). □ **mean·ing·ly** *adverb*

mean·ing·ful *adjective* **1** full of meaning; significant. **2** able to be interpreted. **3** intended to communicate something not directly expressed (*a meaningful look*). □ **mean·ing·ful·ly** *adverb* **mean·ing·ful·ness** *noun*

mean·ing·less *adjective* having no meaning or significance. □ **mean·ing·less·ly** *adverb* **mean·ing·less·ness** *noun*

means *plural noun* **1** (often treated as *sing.*) an action, object, system, etc. by which a result is brought about; a method or methods (*an effective means of communication*). **2 a** money resources (*live beyond one's means*). **b** wealth (*a man of means*). □ **by all means** certainly. **by any means** in any way (*not by any means rich*). **by means of** by the agency or instrumentality of (a thing or action). **by no means** (or **not by any manner of means**) not at all; certainly not. [pl. of MEAN³, in the sense 'an intermediary']

mean sea level *noun* the sea level halfway between the mean levels of high and low water.

means of production *noun* (in Marxist doctrine) the raw materials and means of labour (machines, implements, etc.) used in the production process.

mean-spirit·ed *adjective* petty; spiteful; selfish. □ **mean-spirit·ed·ly** *adverb* **mean-spirit·ed·ness** *noun*

means test ● *noun* an official inquiry to establish need before financial assistance from public funds is given. ● *transitive verb* (**means-test**) **1** assess (a grant etc.) by a means test. **2** subject (a person) to a means test.

mean streets *plural noun* **1** streets where the poor or socially deprived live or work. **2** streets noted for violence and crime.

mean sun *noun* an imaginary sun moving in the celestial equator at the mean rate of the real sun, used in calculating solar time.

meant *past and past participle of* MEAN¹.

mean·time ● *noun* the intervening period (*in the meantime*). ● *adverb* = MEANWHILE. [MEAN³ + TIME] ¶ As an adverb, *meantime* is less common than *meanwhile*.

mean time *noun* the time based on the movement of the mean sun.

mean·while ● *adverb* **1** in the intervening period of time. **2** at the same time. ● *noun* the intervening period (esp. in phr. **in the meanwhile**). [MEAN³ + WHILE]

meany *var. of* MEANIE.

Meares Island /miːrz/ an island off the west central coast of Vancouver Island, west of Port Alberni. [J. Meares, English naval commander and voyager d.1809]

measles *plural noun* (also treated as *sing.*) **1 a** an acute infectious viral disease marked by red spots on the skin. **b** the spots of measles. **2** a disease of pigs etc. caused by infestation with encysted larvae of the human tapeworm. [Middle English *masele(s)* prob. from Middle Low German *masele*, Middle Dutch *masel* pustule (compare Dutch *mazelen* measles), Old High German *masala*: change of form prob. due to assimilation to Middle English *meser* leper]

meas·ly /ˈmiːzli/ *adjective* (**meas·li·er**, **meas·li·est**) **1** *informal* ridiculously small in size, amount, or value. **2** *informal* inferior, contemptible, worthless. **3** of or affected with measles. **4** (of pork etc.) infested with encysted larvae of the human tapeworm.

meas·ur·able *adjective* **1** that can be measured. **2** noticeable; definite (*a measurable improvement*). □ **meas·ur·abil·ity** *noun* **meas·ur·ably** *adverb*

meas·ure ● *noun* **1** a size or quantity found by measuring. **2** a system of measuring (*liquid measure; linear measure*). **3** a rod or tape etc. for measuring. **4** a vessel of standard capacity for transferring or determining fixed quantities of liquids etc. (*a pint measure*). **5 a** the degree, extent, or amount of a thing. **b** (foll. by *of*) some degree of (*she gained a measure of acceptance*). **6** a unit of capacity, e.g. a bushel (*20 measures of wheat*). **7** a factor by which a person or thing is reckoned or evaluated (*their success is a measure of their determination*). **8** suitable action to achieve some end (*a stopgap measure; take drastic measures to conserve fuel*). **9** a legislative enactment. **10** a quantity contained in another an exact number of times. **11** a prescribed extent or quantity. **12** *Printing* the width of a page or column of type. **13 a** a poetical rhythm; metre. **b** a metrical group of a dactyl or two iambs, trochees, spondees, etc. **14** *N Amer.* a bar of music. **15** *archaic* a dance. **16** a mineral stratum (*coal measures*). ● *verb* **1 a** *transitive* ascertain the extent or quantity of (a thing) by comparison with a fixed unit or with an object of known size. **b** *intransitive* take measurements; use a measuring instrument. **2** *intransitive* be of a specified size (*it measures six centimetres*). **3** *transitive* ascertain the size and proportion of (a person) for clothes. **4** *transitive* estimate (a quality, person's character, etc.) by some standard or rule. **5** *transitive* (often foll. by *off*) mark (a line etc. of a given length). **6** *transitive* (foll. by *out*) deal or distribute (a thing) in measured quantities. **7** *transitive* (foll. by *with*, *against*) bring (oneself or one's strength etc.) into competition with. **8** *transitive archaic* traverse (a distance). □ **beyond measure** very greatly. **for good measure** as something beyond the minimum; as a finishing touch. **have** (or **get**) **the measure of** have an accurate opinion of the abilities or character of. **in a** (or **some**) **measure** partly. **measure up 1 a** determine the size etc. of by measurement. **b** take comprehensive measurements. **2** (often foll. by *to*) have the necessary qualifications (for). □ **meas·ur·er** *noun* [Old French *mesure* from Latin *mensura* from *metiri mens-* measure]

meas·ured *adjective* **1** ascertained by measurement. **2** rhythmical; regular in movement (*a measured pace*). **3** (of language) carefully considered; restrained.

meas·ure·less *adjective* not measurable; infinite. □ **meas·ure·less·ly** *adverb*

meas·ure·ment *noun* **1** the act or an instance of measuring. **2** a size, quantity, or extent determined by measuring. **3** (in *pl.*) **a** detailed dimensions. **b** the measured circumference or length of the parts of a person's body used in fitting clothes, esp. the chest, waist, and hips. **4** a system of measuring or of measures (*metric measurement*).

Vowels: a *cat* ɑ *arm* e *bed* ɜr *her* ɜː *deux* ə *ago* ɪ *sit* i *cosy* iː *feed* ɒ *hot* ɔ *pore* oː *no* ʌ *run* ʊ *put*

measuring cup *noun* a cup used for measuring, esp. one marked with gradations, or in a standard size (*a half-cup measuring cup*).

measuring tape *noun* a tape marked to measure length.

measuring worm *noun* = INCHWORM.

meat *noun* **1** the flesh of animals (esp. mammals) as food. **2 a** (foll. by *of*) the essence or chief part of. **b** significant content; substance. **3** the edible part of fruits, nuts, eggs, shellfish, etc. **4 a** *informal* human flesh. **b** *coarse slang* the penis. **5** *archaic* **a** food of any kind. **b** a meal. □ **meat·less** *adjective* [Old English *mete* food, from Germanic]

meat and potatoes esp. *N Amer.* ● *noun* basics; ordinary but fundamental things. ● *adjective* (**meat-and-potatoes**) basic, fundamental, down-to-earth (*meat-and-potatoes rock'n'roll*).

meat axe *noun* a butcher's cleaver.

meat·ball *noun* **1** minced meat compressed into a small round ball. **2** *N Amer.* a stupid, clumsy, or ineffectual person.

meat cutter *noun N Amer.* a butcher.

Meath /miːθ/ a county in the eastern part of the Republic of Ireland, in the province of Leinster; county town, Navan.

meat·head *noun* a stupid person.

meat·hook *noun* **1** a hook on which to hang meat carcasses etc. **2** *slang* an arm or hand.

meat loaf *noun* esp. *N Amer.* a dish of ground meat mixed with onion, bread crumbs, egg, etc., baked in a loaf pan.

meat market *noun* **1** a butcher's shop. **2** *slang* a place, esp. a bar, club, etc. where people seek to meet others for sexual encounters.

meat-packing *noun* the business of processing and packing meat and distributing it to retailers. □ **meat packer** *noun*

me·atus /miˈeɪtəs/ *noun* (*pl.* same or **me·atus·es**) *Anat.* a tubular channel or passage in the body, esp. that leading into the ear. [Latin, = passage from *meare* flow, run]

meaty *adjective* (**meat·i·er**, **meat·i·est**) **1** full of meat; fleshy. **2** of or like meat. **3** full of substance. □ **meat·i·ly** *adverb* **meat·i·ness** *noun*

Mecca /ˈmekə/ a city in W Saudi Arabia, an oasis town in the Red Sea region of Hejaz; pop. (est. 2002) 1,541,800. The birthplace in AD 570 of the prophet Muhammad, it was the scene of his early teachings and his expulsion to Medina in 622 (see HEGIRA 1). On Muhammad's return to Mecca in 630 it became the centre of the new Muslim faith. Considered by Muslims to be the holiest city of Islam, it is the site of the Great Mosque and the Kaaba, and is a centre of Islamic ritual, including the hajj pilgrimage which leads thousands of visitors to the city each year. □ **Mec·can** *adjective & noun*

mec·ca *noun* (also **Mecca**) **1** a place which attracts people of a particular group (*a mecca for gardeners; a tourist mecca*). **2** the birthplace of a policy, pursuit, etc. [MECCA]

Mec·cano /məˈkɑːno/ *noun proprietary* a construction set of reusable metal components, for making model machines, vehicles, etc. [invented word, after *mechanic* etc.]

mech·an·ic *noun* a skilled worker who makes or uses or repairs machinery, esp. engines. [Old French *mecanique* or Latin *mechanicus* from Greek *mēkhanikos* (as MACHINE)]

mech·an·ic·al ● *adjective* **1** of or relating to machines or mechanisms. **2** working or produced by machinery. **3** (of a person or action) like a machine; automatic; lacking originality. **4 a** (of an agency, principle, etc.) belonging to mechanics. **b** (of a theory etc.) explaining phenomena by the assumption of mechanical action. **5** of or relating to mechanics as a science. ● *noun* **1** (in *pl.*) the working parts of a machine, esp. of an automobile. **2** (usu. in *pl.*) *archaic* a manual worker. □ **mech·an·ic·al·ly** *adverb* [Latin *mechanicus* (as MECHANIC)]

mechanical advantage *noun* the ratio of exerted to applied force in a machine.

mechanical drawing *noun* a scale drawing of machinery etc. done with precision instruments.

mechanical engineering *noun* the branch of engineering that deals with the design, construction, and maintenance of machines. □ **mechanical engineer** *noun*

mechanical excavator *noun* a machine for removing soil from the ground by means of a crane to which a scoop is attached.

mechanical pencil *noun* a pencil having a mechanism by means of which a lead can be extended as it wears down, or retracted after use.

mech·an·ician /ˌmekəˈnɪʃən/ *noun* a person skilled in constructing machinery.

mech·an·ics *plural noun* **1** (treated as *sing.*) the branch of applied mathematics dealing with motion and tendencies to motion. **2** (treated as *sing.*) the science of machinery. **3** (usu. treated as *pl.*) **a** the

construction, workings, or routine operation of a thing (*mechanics of a lawn mower*). **b** the practicalities or details of a thing (*mechanics of how money is laundered*).

mech·an·ism *noun* **1** the structure or adaptation of parts of a machine. **2** a system of mutually adapted parts working together in or as in a machine. **3** the mode of operation of a process. **4** a means (*no mechanism for complaints*). **5** *Philos.* the doctrine that all natural phenomena, including life, allow mechanical explanation by physics and chemistry. **6** an unconscious, structured set of mental processes underlying a person's behaviour or responses (*defence mechanism*). [modern Latin *mechanismus* from Greek (as MACHINE)]

mech·an·ist /ˈmekənɪst/ *noun* **1** a mechanician. **2** *Philos.* a person who holds the doctrine of mechanism. □ **mech·an·is·tic** *adjective* **mech·an·is·tic·ally** *adverb*

mech·an·ize *transitive verb* (also esp. *Brit.* **-ise**) **1** make mechanical; give a mechanical character to. **2** introduce machines or machinery in or into (a factory, process, etc.). **3** *Military* equip with tanks, armoured cars, etc. □ **mech·an·iz·a·tion** *noun* **mech·an·iz·er** *noun*

mechano- /ˈmekəno/ *combining form* mechanical. [Greek *mēkhano-* from *mēkhanē* machine]

mech·ano·recep·tor /ˌmekənoʊrɪˈseptər/ *noun Biol.* a sensory receptor that responds to mechanical stimuli such as touch or sound. □ **mech·ano·recep·tion** *noun* **mech·ano·recep·tive** *adjective*

mecha·tron·ics /ˌmekəˈtrɒnɪks/ *plural noun* (treated as *sing.*) technology combining electronics and mechanical engineering, esp. in developing new manufacturing techniques. [blend of MECHANICS + ELECTRONICS]

Me·che·len /ˈmexələn/ (called in French **Malines**) a city in N Belgium, north of Brussels; pop. (est. 2000) 75,438. It was formerly known in English as Mechlin, lending its name to the Mechlin lace made there.

Mech·lin /ˈmeklɪn/ *noun* (in full **Mechlin lace**) lace made at Mechlin (now Mechelen or Malines) in Belgium.

me·choui /ˈmeiʃwi/ *noun Cdn* (*Que.*) **1** a meal of meat, esp. lamb or mutton, roasted on a spit over a fire. **2** a party, usu. outdoors and for large numbers of people, at which meat, usu. a whole animal, is cooked in this way and served. [French from North African Arabic *mashwi*, 'grilled foods']

Meck·len·burg /ˈmeklənˌbɜrɡ/ a former state of NE Germany, on the Baltic coast, now part of Mecklenburg-West Pomerania.

Meck·lenburg-West Pom·er·ania a state of NE Germany, on the coast of the Baltic Sea; capital, Schwerin. The modern state consists of the former state of Mecklenburg and the western part of Pomerania.

meco·nium /mɪˈkoːniəm/ *noun Med.* a dark substance forming the first feces of a newborn infant. [Latin, lit. 'poppy juice', from Greek *mēkōnion* from *mēkōn* poppy]

M.Ed. *abbreviation* Master of Education.

Med *noun informal* the Mediterranean Sea. [abbreviation]

med esp. *N Amer. informal* ● *adjective* medical (*med school*). ● *noun* (usu. in *pl.*) medication (*take your meds!*).

med. *abbreviation* medium.

medal ● *noun* **1** a piece of metal, usu. in the form of a disc, struck or cast with an inscription or device to commemorate an event etc., or awarded as a distinction to a soldier, scholar, athlete, etc., for services rendered, for proficiency, etc. **2** a similar object marked with a religious image, inscription, etc. **3** (*attributive*) designating the part of a competition that will determine the medal winners or a sport eligible for medals (*lost in the medal round; curling is now a medal sport*). ● *verb* (**med·alled**, **medal·ling**; also esp. *US* **med·aled**, **medal·ing**) **1** *transitive* (usu. in *passive*) decorate or honour with a medal. **2** *intransitive* (esp. of an athlete) receive a medal (*the team hasn't medalled in years*). □ **med·alled** *adjective* [French *médaille* from Italian *medaglia*, ultimately from Latin *metallum* METAL]

med·al·lion *noun* **1** a large medal. **2** a thing shaped like this, e.g. a decorative panel or tablet, portrait, etc. **3** a small, flat, round or oval cut of meat or fish. [French *médaillon* from Italian *medaglione* augmentative of *medaglia* (as MEDAL)]

med·al·list *noun* (also esp. *US* **medal·ist**) **1** a recipient of a (specified) medal (*gold medallist*). **2** an engraver or designer of medals.

Medal of Bravery *noun* Canada's third highest decoration for bravery. Abbr.: **MB**. See also CROSS OF VALOUR, STAR OF COURAGE.

medal play *noun Golf* = STROKE PLAY.

Medan /ˈmedan/ a city in Indonesia, in NE Sumatra near the coast of the Strait of Malacca; pop. (est. 2000) 2,059,300.

Med·awar /ˈmedəwər/ **Sir Peter Brian** (1915–87), Brazilian-born

English immunologist. He showed that the rejection of grafts was the result of an immune mechanism; he shared a Nobel Prize in 1960.

med·dle *intransitive verb* (often foll. by *with*, *in*) interfere in or busy oneself unduly with others' concerns. □ **med·dler** *noun* [Old French *medler*, var. of *mesler*, ultimately from Latin *miscēre* mix]

meddle·some *adjective* fond of meddling; interfering. □ **meddle·some·ly** *adverb* **meddle·some·ness** *noun*

Mede /miːd/ *noun hist.* a member of an Indo-European people which established an empire in Media in Persia (modern Iran) in the 7th c. BC. □ **Med·ian** *adjective* [Latin *Medi* (pl.) from Greek *Mēdoi*]

Medea /mə'diːə/ *Gk Myth* a sorceress, daughter of Aeetes king of Colchis. She helped Jason to obtain the Golden Fleece, and married him, but was deserted in Corinth and avenged herself by killing their two children. [Greek, = cunning]

Me·del·lín /ˌmedei'jiːn/ a city in E Colombia, the second largest city in the country; pop. (est. 2002) 1,932,400.

med·evac /'medəvak/ (also **medivac**) ● *noun* the transportation of sick or wounded patients by air to hospital, esp. from a remote location, a battlefield, etc. ● *transitive verb* (**med·evaced**, **med·evac·ing**; also **med·evacked**, **med·evack·ing**) transport by medevac. [from MED(ICAL) + EVAC(UATION)]

Media /'miːdiə/ an ancient region of Asia to the southwest of the Caspian Sea, corresponding approximately to present-day Azerbaijan, NW Iran, and NE Iraq. Originally inhabited by the Medes, the region was conquered in 550 BC by Cyrus the Great of Persia.

media[1] *plural noun* **1** pl. of MEDIUM. **2** (usu. prec. by *the*; treated as *pl.* or *sing.*) the main means of mass communication (esp. newspapers and broadcasting) regarded collectively (often *attributive: media coverage*; *media studies*). ¶ Although considerable opposition has been expressed to the use of *media* as a mass noun with a singular verb, e.g. *the media is on our side*, this usage is fairly well established.

media[2] *noun* (*pl.* **mediae** /-diiː/) *Anat.* a middle layer of the wall of an artery or other vessel. [Latin, fem. of *medius* 'middle']

medi·aev·al esp. *Brit.* var. of MEDIEVAL.

media event *noun* an event primarily intended to attract publicity.

med·ial /'miːdiəl/ *adjective* **1 a** situated in the middle. **b** (of a letter etc.) occurring in the middle of a word or between words. **2** of average size. □ **med·ial·ly** *adverb* [Late Latin *medialis* from Latin *medius* middle]

media literacy *noun* the ability to analyze and interpret critically the messages conveyed by the media, esp. the visual media.

med·ian /'miːdiən/ ● *adjective* **1** situated in the middle. **2** *Statistics* designating or pertaining to the midpoint of a frequency distribution, such that the variable has an equal probability of falling above or below it. **3** *Anat., Bot., & Zool.* of, pertaining to, or designating the plane which divides a body, organ, or limb into roughly symmetrical halves. ● *noun* **1** *Math.* the middle value of a series of values arranged in order of size. **2** (also **median strip**) *N Amer.* a paved or landscaped strip of ground, or a physical barrier such as a raised curb, dividing a street or highway. **3** *Math.* a straight line drawn from any vertex of a triangle to the middle of the opposite side. [French *médiane* or Latin *medianus* (as MEDIAL)]

medi·ant /'miːdiənt/ *noun Music* the third note of a diatonic scale of any key. [French *médiante* from Italian *mediante* part. of obsolete *mediare* come between, from Latin (as MEDIATE)]

medi·as·tin·um /ˌmiːdiə'stainəm/ *noun* (*pl.* **medi·as·tina** /-nə/) *Anat.* a membranous middle septum, esp. between the lungs. □ **medi·as·tin·al** *adjective* [modern Latin from medieval Latin *mediastinus* medial, after Latin *mediastinus* drudge, from *medius* middle]

medi·ate ● *verb* /'miːdiˌeit/ **1** *intransitive* (often foll. by *between*) intervene (between parties in a dispute) to produce agreement or reconciliation. **2** *transitive* be the medium for bringing about (a result) or for conveying (a gift etc.). **3** *transitive* form a connecting link between. ● *adjective* /'miːdiət/ **1** connected not directly but through some other person or thing. **2** involving an intermediate agency. □ **medi·ate·ly** /-ətli/ *adverb* **medi·ator** *noun* **medi·atory** /'miːdiətɔri/ *adjective* [Late Latin *mediare mediat-* from Latin *medius* middle]

medi·a·tion *noun Law* the process or action of mediating between parties in a dispute to produce agreement or reconciliation (*compare* ARBITRATION, CONCILIATION 1).

med·ic[1] *noun informal* a doctor or medical student. [Latin *medicus* physician, from *medēri* heal]

med·ic[2] var. of MEDICK.

med·ic·able /'medikəbəl/ *adjective* able to be treated or cured medically. [Latin *medicabilis* (as MEDICATE)]

Medic·aid /'mediˌkeid/ *noun* (in the US) a federal and state system of health insurance for those requiring financial assistance. [MEDICAL + AID]

med·ic·al ● *adjective* **1** of or relating to the science or practice of medicine in general. **2** of or relating to conditions requiring medical and not surgical treatment (*medical ward*). **3** of or relating to the condition of one's health (*medical leave*). ● *noun informal* a medical examination. □ **med·ic·al·ly** *adverb*

medical certificate *noun* a certificate of fitness or unfitness to work etc., usu. issued by a doctor.

medical doctor *noun* a qualified practitioner of medicine; a physician.

medical examination *noun* an examination to determine the state of a person's physical health or fitness.

medical examiner *noun* **1** *N Amer.* a medically qualified public officer who investigates unusual or suspicious deaths, performs post-mortems, and initiates inquests. **2** a doctor who performs medical examinations.

medical history *noun* **1** the medically significant events and phenomena in a person's life. **2** a record of these.

med·ic·al·ize *transitive verb* (also esp. *Brit.* **-ise**) involve medicine in; view in medical terms, esp. unnecessarily (*medicalize menopause*). □ **med·ic·al·iz·a·tion** *noun*

medical officer *noun* a doctor appointed by a company or public authority to attend to matters relating to health.

medical officer of health *noun Cdn & Brit.* a person in charge of a public health department, responsible for enforcing public health regulations. Abbr.: **MOH**.

medical practitioner *noun* a physician or surgeon.

med·ica·ment /mə'dikəmənt, 'medikəmənt/ *noun* a substance used for medical treatment. [French *médicament* or Latin *medicamentum* (as MEDICATE)]

medi·care /'mediker/ *noun* **1** (in Canada) a national health care program financed by taxation and administered by the provinces and territories. **2** (**Medicare**) (in the US) a federal system of health insurance for persons over 65 years of age. [MEDICAL + CARE]

medi·cate *transitive verb* **1** treat medically; administer medication to. **2** impregnate with a medicinal substance (*medicated shampoo*). [Latin *medicari medicat-* administer remedies to, from *medicus*: see MEDIC[1]]

medi·ca·tion *noun* **1** a substance used for medical treatment. **2** treatment using drugs.

Med·ici /'meditʃi/ a powerful and influential Italian family of bankers and merchants whose members effectively ruled Florence for much of the 15th c. and from 1569 were grand dukes of Tuscany. Cosimo and Lorenzo de' Medici (see separate entries) were notable rulers and patrons of the arts in Florence; four members of the family (including Leo X and Clement VII) became pope, while two others (Catherine de' Medici and Marie de Médicis) were married to kings of France. □ **Medi·cean** /ˌmedi'tʃiːən, -siːən, mə'diːtʃiən/ *adjective*

medi·cin·al /mə'disənəl/ ● *adjective* **1** (of a substance) having healing properties. **2** (of a taste, smell, etc.) resembling that of medicine. ● *noun* a medicinal substance. □ **medi·cin·al·ly** *adverb* [Old French from Latin *medicinalis* (as MEDICINE)]

medi·cine *noun* **1** the science or practice of the diagnosis, treatment, and prevention of disease, esp. as distinct from surgical methods. **2** any drug or preparation used for the treatment or prevention of disease, esp. one taken by mouth. **3** a spell, charm, or fetish which is thought to cure afflictions. **4** (*attributive*) (in Aboriginal societies) used to designate the healing power that may reside in physical objects or in the knowledge and techniques of healing rites. □ **a taste** (or **dose**) **of one's own medicine** treatment such as one is accustomed to giving others. **take one's medicine** submit to something disagreeable. [Old French *medecine* from Latin *medicina* from *medicus*: see MEDIC[1]]

medicine ball *noun* a large heavy stuffed usu. leather ball thrown and caught for exercise.

medicine bundle *noun* a collection of objects, often wrapped in hide, which have sacred and personal power for the owner, used by Plains Aboriginal peoples as a religious object.

medicine cabinet *noun* (also **medicine chest**) a small cupboard containing medicines, items for first aid, etc.

Medicine Hat a city in SE Alberta, located on the South Saskatchewan River, southeast of Calgary; pop. (2001) 51,249. [origin uncertain: possibly from a translation of Blackfoot *saamis* 'headdress of a medicine man', with reference to the shape of a nearby hill]

Medicine Line *noun Cdn (West)* esp. *hist.* the Canada–US border, esp. from Ontario westward.

medicine man *noun* a person believed to have magical powers of healing, esp. among some N American Aboriginal peoples.

medicine show *noun N Amer.* **1** *hist.* a travelling show in which entertainers attract customers to whom medicine can be sold. **2** any event, spectacle, etc. designed to lure customers.

medicine wheel *noun* a wheel-shaped arrangement of stones at which acts of ritual and meditation were or are performed by certain Aboriginal peoples, located at various places throughout N America.

Mé·di·cis see MARIE DE MÉDICIS.

med·ick /'medɪk/ *noun* (also **medic**) any leguminous plant of the genus *Medicago*, esp. alfalfa. [Latin *medica* from Greek *Mēdikē poa* Median grass]

med·ico /'medɪˌkoː/ *noun* (*pl.* **-icos**) *informal* a doctor or medical student. [Italian from Latin (as MEDIC¹)]

medico- /'medɪkoː/ *combining form* medical; medical and (*medico-legal*). [Latin *medicus* (as MEDIC¹)]

medi·ev·al /mɪd'iːvəl, med-, ˌmedi-/ *adjective* (also esp. *Brit.* **medi·aev·al**) **1** of, or in the style of, the Middle Ages. **2** *informal* old-fashioned, archaic. □ **medi·ev·al·ism** *noun* **medi·ev·al·ist** *noun* **medi·ev·al·ize** *transitive & intransitive verb* (also esp. *Brit.* **-ise**). **medi·ev·al·ly** *adverb* [modern Latin *medium aevum* from Latin *medius* middle + *aevum* age]

medieval Latin *noun* Latin of about AD 600–1500.

Me·dina /meˈdiːnə/ a city in W Saudi Arabia, an oasis some 320 km (200 miles) north of Mecca; pop. (est. 2002) 818,800. In AD 622 it became the refuge of Muhammad's infant Muslim community after its expulsion from Mecca. It was Muhammad's burial place and the site of the first Islamic mosque. It is considered by Muslims to be the second most holy city after Mecca and a visit to the prophet's tomb at Medina forms a frequent sequel to the formal pilgrimage to Mecca. [Arabic, = the city]

me·dina /məˈdiːnə/ *noun* the old Arab or non-European quarter of a N African town. [Arabic, literally 'town']

medi·ocre /ˌmiːdiˈoːkər/ *adjective* **1** of middling quality, neither good nor bad. **2** second-rate. [French *médiocre* or from Latin *mediocris* of middle height or degree, from *medius* middle + *ocris* rugged mountain]

medi·oc·rity /ˌmiːdiˈɒkrɪti/ *noun* (*pl.* **-ties**) **1** the state of being mediocre. **2** a mediocre person or thing.

medi·tate *verb* **1** *intransitive* **a** exercise the mind in (esp. religious) contemplation. **b** (usu. foll. by *on, upon*) focus on a subject in this manner. **2** *transitive* plan mentally; design. □ **medi·ta·tion** *noun* **medi·ta·tion·al** *adjective* **medi·ta·tor** *noun* [Latin *meditari* contemplate]

medi·ta·tive /'medɪtətɪv, -ˌteɪtɪv/ *adjective* **1** inclined to meditate. **2** indicative of meditation. □ **medi·ta·tive·ly** *adverb*

Medi·ter·ran·ean /ˌmedɪtəˈreɪniən/ ● *noun* **1** (prec. by *the*) **a** the Mediterranean Sea. **b** the countries bordering on the Mediterranean Sea. **2** a native of a country bordering on the Mediterranean Sea. ● *adjective* **1** of or characteristic of the Mediterranean, countries bordering it, or their inhabitants (*Mediterranean cooking; of Mediterranean appearance*). **2** (of climate) characterized by hot dry summers and warm wet winters. [Latin *mediterraneus* inland, from *medius* middle + *terra* land]

Mediterranean Sea an almost landlocked sea between S Europe, the north coast of Africa, and SW Asia. It is connected with the Atlantic by the Strait of Gibraltar, with the Red Sea by the Suez Canal, and with the Black Sea by the Dardanelles, the Sea of Marmara, and the Bosporus.

med·ium ● *noun* (*pl.* **media** or **med·iums**) **1** the middle quality, degree, etc. between extremes (*find a happy medium*). **2** the means by which something is communicated (*the medium of sound; the medium of television*). **3** the intervening substance through which impressions are conveyed to the senses etc. (*light passing from one medium into another*). **4** *Biol.* the physical environment or conditions of growth, storage, or transport of a living organism (*the shape of a fish is ideal for its fluid medium; growing mould on the surface of a medium*). **5** an agency or means of doing something (*the medium through which money is raised*). **6** the material or form used by an artist, composer, etc. (*language as an artistic medium*). **7** the liquid, e.g. oil or gel, with which pigments are mixed for use in painting. **8** (*pl.* **mediums**) a person claiming to be in contact with the spirits of the dead and to communicate between the dead and the living. **9** (*pl.* **mediums**) **a** a garment size designed to fit the average figure. **b** an article of clothing in this size. ● *adjective*

1 between two qualities, degrees, etc. **2** average; moderate (*of medium height*). □ **medium·is·tic** *adjective* **medium·ship** *noun* (both in sense 8 of *noun*). [Latin, = middle, neuter of *medius*]

medium dry *adjective* (of sherry, wine, etc.) having a flavour intermediate between dry and sweet.

medium frequency *noun* a radio frequency between 300 kHz and 3 MHz.

medium of exchange *noun* something that serves as an instrument of commercial transactions, e.g. coin.

medium-range *adjective* (of an aircraft, missile, etc.) able to travel a medium distance.

medium-security *adjective* (of a correctional institution) having perimeter security, ranging from fences to armed posts (*compare* MAXIMUM-SECURITY, MINIMUM-SECURITY).

medium-sized *adjective* of average size.

medi·vac *var. of* MEDEVAC.

med·lar /'medlər/ *noun* **1** a rosaceous tree, *Mespilus germanica*, bearing small brown apple-like fruits. **2** the fruit of this tree which is eaten when very ripe. [Old French *medler* from Latin *mespila* from Greek *mespilē, -on*]

med·ley ● *noun* (*pl.* **-leys**) **1** a varied mixture; a miscellany. **2** a collection of musical items from one work or various sources arranged as a continuous whole. **3** a dish of assorted vegetables. **4** (in full **medley relay**) a relay race between teams in which each team member runs a different distance, swims a different stroke, etc. ● *adjective archaic* mixed; motley. [Old French *medlee* var. of *meslee* from Romanic (as MEDDLE)]

Medoc /meiˈdɒk, 'medɒk/ *noun* a fine red claret from the Médoc region of SW France.

me·dul·la /məˈdʌlə/ *noun* **1** *Anat.* the inner region of certain organs or tissues usu. when it is distinguishable from the outer region or cortex, as in hair or a kidney. **2** = MEDULLA OBLONGATA. **3** *Bot.* the soft internal tissue of plants. □ **me·dul·lary** *adjective* [Latin, = pith, marrow, prob. related to *medius* 'middle']

me·dul·la ob·lon·gata /ˌɒblɒŋˈɡɑːtə/ *noun* the continuation of the spinal cord within the skull, forming the lowest part of the brain stem.

Me·dusa /məˈdjuːsə, -ˈdjuːsə/ *Gk Myth* one of the gorgons, the only mortal one, slain by Perseus, who cut off her head.

me·dusa /məˈdjuːsə, -ˈdjuː-/ *noun* (*pl.* **me·du·sae** /-siː/ or **me·du·sas**) **1** a jellyfish. **2** a free-swimming form of any coelenterate, having tentacles round the edge of a usu. umbrella-shaped jellylike body, e.g. a jellyfish. □ **me·du·san** *adjective* **me·dus·oid** *noun & adjective* [MEDUSA]

Meech *noun* (also **Meech Lake**) *Cdn* the Meech Lake Accord.

Meech Lake a small lake in SW Quebec, about 15 km northwest of Gatineau. [A. *Meech*, congregational minister d.1849]

Meech Lake Accord *noun Cdn* the 1987 agreement between Ottawa and the provinces that accepted Quebec's conditions for signing the Constitution Act of 1982. The deal lapsed when the legislatures of Newfoundland and Manitoba failed to ratify it by the June 23, 1990 deadline. [MEECH LAKE, site of negotiations]

meed *noun literary* or *archaic* **1** reward. **2** merited portion (of praise etc.). [Old English *mēd* from West Germanic, related to Gothic *mizdō*, Greek *misthos* reward]

meek *adjective* **1** humble and submissive; suffering injury etc. tamely. **2** piously gentle in nature. □ **meek·ly** *adverb* **meek·ness** *noun* [Middle English *me(o)c* from Old Norse *mjúkr* soft, gentle]

Meel·paeg Lake /'miːlpəeɡ/ a lake in south central Newfoundland, situated southeast of Red Indian Lake. [Mi'kmaq *makpaq* lake of many bays]

meer·kat /'miːrkat/ *noun* a South African burrowing mongoose, *Suricata suricatta*, with grey and black stripes. [Dutch, = sea cat]

meer·schaum /'miːrʃəm, -ʃɒm/ *noun* **1** a soft white form of hydrated magnesium silicate, chiefly found in Turkey, which resembles clay. **2** a tobacco pipe with the bowl made from this. [German, = seafoam, from *Meer* sea + *Schaum* foam, translation of Persian *kef-i-daryā*, with reference to its frothiness]

Mee·rut /'miːrət/ a city in N India, in Uttar Pradesh northeast of Delhi; pop. (2001) 1,074,200.

meet¹ ● *verb* (*past* and *past participle* **met**) **1 a** *transitive* encounter (a person or persons) by accident or design; come face to face with. **b** *intransitive* (of two or more people) come into each other's company by accident or design (*decided to meet at the restaurant*). **c** *transitive* come to the notice of; confront (*an amazing sight met their eyes*). **2** *transitive* go to a place to be present at the arrival of (a person, train, etc.). **3 a** *transitive* (of a moving object, line, feature of landscape, etc.) come together or into contact with (*where the road meets the bridge*). **b** *intransitive* come together or into contact (*where the lake and the sky meet; their eyes met*). **c** *transitive & intransitive* (of an artistic style, a culture, etc.) influence or be influenced by another (*where jazz meets hip hop*). **4 a** *transitive* make the acquaintance of (*delighted to meet you*). **b** *intransitive* (of two or more people) make each other's acquaintance. **5** *intransitive & transitive* come together or come into contact with for the purposes of conference, business, worship, etc. (*the committee meets every week; the union met management yesterday*). **6** *transitive* **a** (of a person or a group) deal with or answer (a demand, objection, etc.) (*met the original proposal with hostility*). **b** satisfy or conform with (proposals, deadlines, a person, etc.) (*agreed to meet the new terms; did my best to meet them on that point; it's a challenge we can meet*). **7** *transitive* pay (a bill etc.); provide the funds required by (a cheque etc.) (*meet the cost of the move*). **8** *transitive & intransitive* experience, encounter, or receive (success, disaster, a difficulty, etc.) (*met their death; met with many problems*). **9** *transitive* oppose in battle, contest, or confrontation. **10** *intransitive* (of clothes, curtains, etc.) join or fasten correctly (*my jacket won't meet*). ● *noun* the assembly of competitors for various sporting activities (*track meet*). □ **make ends meet** *see* END. **meet the eye** (or **the ear**) be visible (or audible). **meet a person's eye** check if another person is watching and look into his or her eyes in return. **meet a person halfway** make a compromise; respond in a friendly way to the advances of another person. **meet up** (often foll. by *with*) *informal* meet or make contact, esp. by chance. **meet with 1** *see* sense 8 of *verb* **2** receive (a reaction) (*met with the committee's approval*). **3** esp. *N Amer.* = sense 1a of *verb*. **more (to it) than meets the eye** hidden qualities or complications. [Old English *mētan* from Germanic: compare MOOT]

meet² *adjective archaic* suitable, fit, proper. [Middle English (*i*)*mete* representing Old English *gemǣte* from Germanic, related to METE¹]

meet-and-greet *noun* an organized event during which a person, esp. a celebrity, author, etc., meets and talks with members of the public.

meet·ing *noun* **1** *in senses of* MEET¹. **2** an assembly of people, esp. the members of a society, committee, etc., for discussion or entertainment. **3** *Brit.* = RACE MEETING. **4** an assembly (esp. of Quakers) for worship. **5** the persons assembled (*address the meeting*).

meeting house *noun* **1** a place of worship for Quakers. **2** *hist.* a Protestant place of worship.

meeting of minds *noun* a close understanding between people, esp. as soon as they meet for the first time.

meeting place *noun* a place where people often meet.

meg *noun* Computing slang megabyte(s). [abbreviation]

mega /ˈmegə/ *slang* ● *adjective* of enormous size, importance, etc. ● *adverb* extremely (*mega famous*). [independent use of MEGA-]

mega- /ˈmegə/ *combining form* **1** large. **2** denoting a factor of one million (10^6) in the metric system of measurement. Abbr.: **M**. **3** to a great degree, extent, etc. [Greek from *megas* great]

mega·bit *noun* Computing 1,048,576 (i.e. 2^{20}) bits as a measure of data capacity, or loosely 1,000,000 bits.

mega·buck *noun informal* **1** a million dollars (also *attributive*: *megabuck salary*). **2** (*in pl.*) a huge sum of money.

mega·byte *noun* Computing 1,048,576 (i.e. 2^{20}) bytes as a measure of data capacity, or loosely 1,000,000 bytes. Abbr.: **MB**, **Mb**.

mega·city *noun* (*plural* **mega·cities**) **1** a large city formed by combining separate cities in a metropolitan area into one corporate entity. **2** a very large city, esp. one with a population of over 10 million.

mega·cycle *noun* a unit of frequency equal to one million cycles.

mega·deal *noun* a business transaction involving large amounts of money, property, etc.

mega·death *noun* the death of one million people (esp. as a unit in estimating the casualties of war).

mega·dose *noun* a very large dose, esp. of a vitamin, medicine, etc.

Me·gaera /mɪˈdʒɛrə/ *Gk Myth* one of the Furies.

mega·fauna *noun* the large animals, esp. the large vertebrates, of a given area, habitat, or epoch.

mega·flop *noun* **1** Computing a unit of computing speed equal to one million floating-point operations per second. **2** *slang* a complete failure.

mega·hertz *noun* (*pl.* same) one million hertz, esp. as a measure of frequency of radio transmissions. Abbr.: **MHz**.

mega·hit *noun* a highly successful enterprise, product, etc.

mega·lith /ˈmegəlɪθ/ *noun Archaeology* a large stone, esp. one placed upright as a monument or part of one. [MEGA- + Greek *lithos* stone]

mega·lith·ic *adjective Archaeology* made of or marked by the use of large stones.

megalo- /ˈmegəloː/ *combining form* great (*megalomania*). [Greek from *megas megal-* great]

meg·alo·mania /ˌmegələˈmeɪniə/ *noun* **1** a mental disorder producing delusions of grandeur. **2** a passion for grandiose schemes. **3** lust for power. □ **meg·alo·maniac** *adjective & noun* **meg·alo·man·iacal** /-məˈnaɪəkəl/ *adjective*

meg·alop·olis /ˌmegəˈlɒpəlɪs/ *noun* **1** a very large city. **2** an urban region consisting of a city and its environs. □ **meg·alo·pol·itan** /-ləˈpɒlɪtən/ *adjective & noun* [MEGA- + Greek *polis* city]

meg·alo·saur /ˌmegəˈlɔːr/ *noun* (also **meg·alo·saur·us** /ˌmegələˈsɔːrəs/) a large flesh-eating dinosaur of the genus *Megalosaurus*, with stout hind legs and small forelimbs. [MEGALO- + Greek *sauros* lizard]

mega·mall *noun* an extremely large shopping mall, usu. including elaborate entertainment facilities.

mega-musical *noun N Amer.* a musical theatrical production characterized by spectacular scenery, costumes, and special effects, and a large cast.

Mé·gan·tic Hills /meɪgɑ̃ˈtiːk/ a highland region of southern and SE Quebec, part of the Appalachian mountain system that is bounded by the St. Lawrence River, the Canada-US border, and the Gulf of St. Lawrence. [as LAC-MÉGANTIC]

mega·phone ● *noun* a large funnel-shaped device for amplifying the sound of the voice. ● *intransitive verb* speak through or as through a megaphone. □ **mega·phon·ic** *adjective*

mega·pixel *noun* Computing 1,048,576 or 2^{20} pixels, esp. as a unit of graphic resolution.

mega·pode /ˈmegəˌpoːd/ *noun* (also **mega·pod** /-ˌpɒd/) any bird of the family Megapodidae, native to Australasia, that builds a mound of debris for the incubation of its eggs, e.g. a mallee fowl. [modern Latin *Megapodius* (genus name) formed as MEGA- + Greek *pous podos* foot]

mega·project *noun* a very large-scale, costly construction or engineering project e.g. the building of a dam, the development of a transportation infrastructure, etc.

mega·spore *noun* the larger of the two kinds of spores produced by some ferns (*compare* MICROSPORE).

mega·star *noun* a very famous person, esp. in the world of entertainment. □ **mega·star·dom** *noun*

mega·store *noun* a large store, selling many different types of goods, usu. situated on the outskirts of a town or city.

mega·ton *noun* **1** a unit of explosive power equal to one million tons of TNT. **2** *informal* a very large or heavy amount (*sold megatons of albums*). □ **mega·ton·nage** *noun*

mega·volt *noun* one million volts, esp. as a unit of electromotive force. Abbr.: **MV**.

mega·watt *noun* one million watts, esp. as a measure of electrical power as generated by power stations. Abbr.: **MW**.

Megha·laya /ˌmegəˈleɪə/ a small state in the extreme northeast of India, on the northern border of Bangladesh; capital, Shillong.

Me·giddo /məˈgɪdoː/ an ancient city of NW Palestine, situated to the southeast of Haifa in present-day Israel. Founded in the 4th millennium BC, the city controlled an important route linking Syria and Mesopotamia with the Jordan valley, Jerusalem, and Egypt. Its commanding location made the city the scene of many early battles, and from its name the word *Armageddon* ('hill of Megiddo') is derived.

meg·ohm /ˈmegoːm/ *noun* Electricity one million ohms. [MEGA- + OHM]

me·grim /ˈmiːgrɪm/ *noun* **1** *archaic* migraine. **2** a whim, a fancy. **3** (*in pl.*) depression; low spirits. [Middle English *mygrane* from Old French MIGRAINE]

Me·hem·et Ali /mɪˈhemɪt ˈɒli/ *see* MUHAMMAD ALI 1.

Mehta /ˈmeɪtə/ **1 Deepa** (b.1950), Indian-born Canadian screenwriter and filmmaker. Her films, including *Fire* and *Bollywood/Hollywood*, explore themes and characters inspired by her youth in India, though screenings of her films have often occasioned violent protests in her native country. **2 Zubin** (b.1936), Indian conductor, music director of the Los Angeles Philharmonic Orchestra (1961–77), the New York Philharmonic (1978–91), and the Israel Philharmonic Orchestra (since 1977). He conducted the world-famous 'Three Tenors' concerts in Rome (1990) and Los Angeles (1994).

Meigh·en /ˈmiːən/ **Arthur** (1874–1960), Canadian lawyer and politician. Serving as an MP from 1908 to 1926, he was leader of the

Conservative Party 1920–26 and 1941–42, and prime minister 1920–21 and 1926.

Meiji /'meidʒi/ ● *noun* the period of the rule of the Japanese emperor Meiji Tenno. ● *adjective* pertaining to or characteristic of this period. [Japanese, lit. 'enlightened government']

Meiji Tenno /ˌmeidʒi: 'tenoː/ (born Mutsuhito) (1852–1912), emperor of Japan 1867–1912. He restored imperial power after centuries of control by the shoguns, encouraged Japan's rapid modernization and political reform, and laid the foundations for the country's emergence as a major world power.

mei·o·sis /mai'ɔːsɪs/ *noun* (*pl.* **mei·o·ses** /-siːz/) **1** *Biol.* a type of cell division that results in daughter cells with half the chromosome number of the parent cell (*compare* MITOSIS). **2** = LITOTES. □ **mei·otic** /-'ɒtɪk/ *adjective* **mei·otic·al·ly** *adverb* [modern Latin from Greek *meiōsis* from *meioō* lessen, from *meiōn* less]

Meir /mei'iːr/ **Golda** (born Goldie Mabovich) (1898–1978), Russian-born Israeli Labour stateswoman, prime minister 1969–74. Following Israel's independence she served in ministerial posts (1949–66), and was elected prime minister in 1969, retaining her position through coalition rule until her retirement in 1974.

Meis·sen¹ /'maisən/ a city in eastern Germany, in Saxony, on the Elbe River northwest of Dresden; pop. (1998) 30,486. It is famous for its porcelain, known as Dresden china, which has been made there since 1710.

Meis·sen² /'maisən/ *noun* Dresden china. [MEISSEN¹]

-meister /maist3r/ *combining form* often *jocular* a person skilled in or famous for something specified by the initial element (*schlockmeister*; *funkmeister*). [German, = MASTER]

Meister·singer /'maist3r,siŋ3r/ *noun* (*pl.* same) a member of one of the 14th–16th-c. German guilds for lyric poets and musicians. [German from *Meister* MASTER + *Singer* SINGER]

Meit·ner /'maitn3r/ **Lise** (1878–1968), Austrian-born Swedish physicist. She worked in Germany with Otto Hahn, discovering the element protactinium with him in 1917, but fled the Nazis in 1938 to continue her research in Sweden; she later formulated the concept of nuclear fission with her nephew Otto Frisch.

meit·ner·ium *noun* a very unstable chemical element made by high-energy atomic collisions. Symbol: **Mt**; at. no. 109. [modern Latin, from MEITNER]

Me·kele /mɪ'keili/ the capital of Tigray province in Ethiopia; pop. (est. 2002) 122,700.

Mek·nès /mek'nes/ a city in N Morocco, in the Middle Atlas mountains west of Fez; pop. (est. 2002) 562,000.

Me·kong River /miː'kɒŋ/ a river of SE Asia, which rises in Tibet and flows southeast and south for 4 180 km (2,600 miles) through S China, Laos, Cambodia, and Vietnam to its extensive delta on the South China Sea. For part of its course it forms the boundary between Laos and its western neighbours Burma (Myanmar) and Thailand.

Me·laka /mə'lakə/ (also **Malacca**) **1** a state of Malaysia, on the southwest coast of the Malay Peninsula, on the Strait of Malacca. **2** its capital and chief port; pop. (2000) 149,518. It played an important role in the development of trade between Europe and the East, esp. China.

mel·amine /'melə,miːn/ *noun* **1** a white crystalline compound that can be copolymerized with formaldehyde to give thermosetting resins. **2** (in full **melamine resin**) a plastic made from melamine and used esp. for laminated coatings and for moulded items, e.g. dishes, utensils, etc. [*melam* (arbitrary) + AMINE]

mel·an·cholia /melən'koːliə/ *noun* **1** a mental illness marked by depression and ill-founded fears. **2** = MELANCHOLY *noun* 1.
□ **mel·an·chol·ic** *adjective & noun* **mel·an·chol·ic·al·ly** *adverb* [Late Latin: see MELANCHOLY]

mel·an·choly /'melənkɒli/ ● *noun* (*pl.* **-ies**) **1 a** a pensive sadness. **b** a tendency to this. **2** *hist.* one of the four humours; black bile (*see* HUMOUR *noun* 5). **3** *Med. archaic* = MELANCHOLIA 1. ● *adjective* (of a person) sad, gloomy; (of a thing) saddening, depressing; (of words, a tune, etc.) expressing sadness. [Old French *melancolie* and Late Latin *melancholia* from Greek *melagkholia*, from *melas melanos* 'black' + *kholē* 'bile']

Me·lanch·thon /mə'laŋkθən/ **Phil·ipp** (born Philipp Schwartzerd) (1497–1560), German Protestant reformer. He succeeded Luther as leader of the Reformation movement in Germany (1521), helped to systematize Luther's teachings in the *Loci Communes* (1521), and drew up the Augsburg Confession (1530).

Mela·nesia /ˌmelə'niːʒə/ a region of the W Pacific to the south of Micronesia and west of Polynesia. Lying south of the equator, it contains the Bismarck Archipelago, the Solomon Islands, Santa Cruz, Vanuatu, New Caledonia, Fiji, and the intervening islands. [Greek *melas* black + *nēsos* island]

Mela·nes·ian /ˌmelə'niːʒən/ ● *noun* **1** a native or inhabitant of Melanesia. **2** any of the Malayo-Polynesian languages of this people. ● *adjective* of or relating to this people or their language.

mé·lange /mei'lɑ̃ʒ/ ● *noun* a mixture, a medley. ● *adjective* (of a fabric) made of a blend of fibres (*mélange flannel*). [French from *mêler* mix (as MEDDLE)]

mel·an·in /'melənɪn/ *noun* a dark brown to black pigment occurring in the hair, skin, and iris of the eye, that is responsible for tanning of the skin when exposed to sunlight. [Greek *melas melanos* black + -IN]

mel·an·ism /'melənɪzəm/ *noun* the unusual darkening of body tissues caused by excessive production of melanin, esp. as a form of colour variation in animals. □ **mel·an·ic** /mɪ'lanɪk/ *adjective*

mel·an·oma /ˌmelə'noːmə/ *noun* a usu. malignant tumour of melanin-forming cells, usu. in the skin. [MELANIN + -OMA]

mel·an·o·sis /ˌmelə'nɔːsɪs/ *noun* **1** = MELANISM. **2** a disorder in the body's production of melanin. □ **mel·an·otic** /-'nɒtɪk/ *adjective* [modern Latin from Greek (as MELANIN)]

mela·to·nin /melə'toːnɪn/ *noun* an indole derivative formed in the pineal gland of various mammals, which inhibits melanin formation and is thought to be concerned with regulating the reproductive cycle. [MELANIN + SEROTONIN]

Melba¹, **Dame Nel·lie** (born Helen Porter Mitchell) (1861–1931), Australian operatic soprano. She was born near Melbourne, from which city she took her professional name, and gained worldwide fame with her coloratura singing.

Melba² *noun Cdn* an early, sweet, yellow cooking and eating apple with pink and red stripes. [MELBA¹]

Melba toast *noun* very thin crisp toast. [MELBA¹]

Mel·bourne¹ /'melbərn/ the capital of Victoria, in SE Australia, on the Bass Strait opposite Tasmania; pop. (2001) 3,466,000. It became state capital in 1851 and was capital of Australia from 1901 until 1927. It is a major port and the second largest city in Australia. [MELBOURNE²]

Mel·bourne² /'melbərn, -bɔrn/ **Wil·liam Lamb, 2nd Vis·count** (1779–1848), English Whig politician, prime minister 1834 and 1835–41. He became chief political adviser to Queen Victoria after her accession in 1837, and his term was marked by Chartist and anti-Corn-Laws agitation.

Mel·chior /'melki,ɔr/ one of the three Magi.

Mel·chite /'melkəit/ *noun* a Christian of the eastern Orthodox or Catholic Churches originating in Syria and Egypt, following the Byzantine rite, which historically accepted the Orthodox faith of the ecumenical Councils of Ephesus and Chalcedon, as did the Emperor. [ecclesiastical Latin *Melchitae* from Byzantine Greek *Melkhitai* representing Syriac *malkāyā* royalists, from *malkā* king]

Mel·chiz·edek /mel'kɪzə,dek/ *Bible* a priest and king of Salem (which is usually identified with Jerusalem). When Abraham returned victorious from battle, Melchizedek blessed him (Gen. 14:18).

meld¹ ● *transitive & intransitive verb* (in rummy, canasta, etc.) lay down or declare (one's cards) in order to score points. ● *noun* a completed set or run of cards in any of these games. [German *melden* announce]

meld² ● *transitive & intransitive verb* merge, blend, combine. ● *noun* a thing formed by merging or blending. [perhaps from MELT + WELD¹]

Mele·ager /ˌmelɪ'eigər/ *Gk Myth* a hero at whose birth the Fates declared that he would die when a brand then on the fire was consumed. His mother Althaea seized the brand and kept it, but threw it back into the fire when he quarrelled with and killed her brothers in a hunting expedition, whereupon he died.

melee /'meilei, 'melei, me'lei/ *noun* **1** a confused fight, skirmish, or scuffle. **2** a muddle. [French (as MEDLEY)]

Mel·fort /'melfɔrt/ a city in central Saskatchewan, about 80 km southeast of Prince Albert; pop. (2001) 5,559. [*Melfort House* in Argyllshire, Scotland, family home and birthplace of Mrs. R. Beatty, first female settler in the area *c.*1892]

Me·lilla /me'liːjə/ a Spanish enclave on the Mediterranean coast of Morocco; pop. (2001) 66,400 (with Ceuta).

meli·lot /'meləlɒt/ *noun* a leguminous plant of the genus *Melilotus*, with trifoliate leaves, long spikes of small flowers, and a scent of hay when dried. [(Old) French *mélilot* via Latin *melilotus* from Greek *melilōtos* 'honey lotus']

melior·ate /'miːliə,reit/ *transitive & intransitive verb literary* improve.
□ **melior·a·tion** *noun* **melior·a·tive** /-rətɪv/ *adjective* [Late Latin *meliorare* (as MELIORISM)]

melior·ism /ˈmiːliəˌrɪzəm/ *noun* a doctrine that the world may be made better by properly directed human effort. □ **melior·ist** *noun* **melior·is·tic** *adjective* [Latin *melior* better + -ISM]

me·lis·ma /məˈlɪzmə/ *noun* (*pl.* **me·lis·mas** or **me·lis·mata** /-mətə/) *Music* the prolongation of one syllable of text over a number of notes. □ **me·lis·mat·ic** *adjective* [Greek, lit. 'song']

mel·lif·er·ous /məˈlɪfɜrəs/ *adjective* yielding or producing honey. [Latin *mellifer* from *mel* honey]

mel·lif·lu·ous /məˈlɪfluːəs/ *adjective* (of a voice, words, etc.) pleasing, musical, flowing. □ **mel·lif·lu·ent** *adjective* **mel·lif·lu·ous·ly** *adverb* **mel·lif·lu·ous·ness** *noun* [Late Latin *mellifluus* from *mel* honey + *fluere* flow]

mel·low ● *adjective* **1** (of sound, colour, light) soft and rich, free from harshness. **2** (of character) softened or matured by age or experience. **3** good-humoured, relaxed, genial. **4** *informal* partly intoxicated, esp. pleasantly. **5** (of fruit) soft, sweet, and juicy with ripeness. **6** (of wine, cheese, etc.) well-matured, smooth. **7** (of earth) rich, loamy. ● *transitive & intransitive verb* **1** make or become mellow. **2** *N Amer. informal* (often foll. by *out*) relax, become less intense. □ **mel·low·ly** *adverb* **mel·low·ness** *noun* [Middle English, perhaps from attributive use of Old English *melu*, *melw-* MEAL²]

Mel·mac /ˈmelmak/ *noun proprietary* melamine.

melo·deon /məˈloːdiən/ *noun* **1** a small organ popular in the 19th c., similar to the harmonium. **2** a small German accordion, played esp. by folk musicians. [MELODY + HARMONIUM with Graecized ending]

mel·od·ic /məˈlɒdɪk/ *adjective* **1** of or relating to melody. **2** having or producing melody. □ **mel·od·ic·ally** *adverb*

melo·di·ous /məˈloːdiəs/ *adjective* **1** of, producing, or having melody. **2** sweet-sounding. □ **melo·di·ous·ly** *adverb* **melo·di·ous·ness** *noun*

melo·dist /ˈmelədɪst/ *noun* **1** a composer of melodies. **2** a singer.

melo·dize /ˈmeləˌdaɪz/ *verb* (also esp. *Brit.* **-dise**) **1** *intransitive* make melody, produce sweet music. **2** *transitive* make melodious.

melo·drama *noun* **1** a sensational dramatic piece with crude appeals to the emotions and usu. a happy ending. **2** the genre of drama of this type. **3** language, behaviour, or an occurrence suggestive of this. **4** *hist.* a play with songs interspersed and with orchestral music accompanying the action. □ **melo·dramat·ic** *adjective* **melo·dramat·ic·ally** *adverb* **melo·drama·tize** *transitive verb* (also esp. *Brit.* **-tise**). [French *mélodrame* from Greek *melos* music + French *drame* DRAMA]

melo·dramat·ics *plural noun* melodramatic behaviour, action, or writing.

mel·ody *noun* (*pl.* **-odies**) **1** an arrangement of single notes in a musically expressive succession. **2** the principal part in harmonized music. **3** a musical arrangement of words; a song. **4** sweet music, either vocal or instrumental (*the haunting melody of the meadowlark*). [Old French *melodie* from Late Latin *melodia* from Greek *melōidia* from *melos* song]

melon *noun* **1** the sweet fruit of various gourds. **2** the gourd producing this. **3** *Zool.* **a** a mass of waxy material in the head of some toothed whales, thought to focus acoustic signals. **b** the dome this forms on the forehead. **4** a yellowish pink colour. **5** *slang* (in *pl.*) a woman's (esp. large) breasts. □ **mel·ony** *adjective* [Old French from Late Latin *melo -onis* abbreviation of Latin *melopepo* from Greek *mēlopepōn* from *mēlon* apple + *pepōn* gourd, from *pepōn* ripe]

melon baller *noun* a scoop for making small balls of melon.

Melos /ˈmiːlɒs/ a Greek island in the Aegean Sea, in the southwest of the Cyclades group. It was the centre of a flourishing civilization in the Bronze Age and is the site of the discovery in 1820 of the Hellenistic marble statue of Aphrodite known as the Venus de Milo.

Mel·pom·ene /melˈpɒmɪni/ *Gk & Rom. Myth* the Muse of tragedy. [Greek, = singer]

melt ● *verb* **1** *intransitive* become liquefied by heat. **2** *transitive* change to a liquid condition by heat (*see also* MOLTEN). **3** *intransitive & transitive* soften, disintegrate, or liquefy, esp. by the action of moisture; dissolve. **4** *intransitive* **a** (of a person, feelings, the heart, etc.) be softened as a result of pity, love, etc. **b** dissolve into tears. **5** *transitive* soften (a person, feelings, the heart, etc.) (*a look to melt a heart of stone*). **6** *intransitive* (usu. foll. by *into*) change or merge imperceptibly into another form or state (*night melted into dawn*). **7** *intransitive* (often foll. by *away*) (of a person) leave or disappear unobtrusively (*melted into the background*; *melted away into the crowd*). **8** *intransitive informal* (of a person) perspire excessively, suffer extreme heat (*I'm melting in this parka*). ● *noun* **1** the process or an instance of melting. **2** *N Amer.* **a** a period of melting, esp. of the snow in spring. **b** = MELTWATER. **3** *N Amer.* a sandwich, hamburger, or other dish

having melted cheese on top (*tuna melt*). **4** metal etc. in a melted condition. **5** an amount of a substance melted at any one time. □ **melt away** disappear or make disappear by or as if by liquefaction.

melt down 1 melt (esp. metal articles) in order to reuse the raw material. **2** become liquid and lose structure. **3** (of a part of a nuclear reactor) lose structural integrity, creating a potential for the catastrophic release of radiation (*compare* MELTDOWN 1). **melt in the mouth** (of food) be delicious and esp. very light. □ **melt·able** *adjective* **melt·er** *noun* [Old English *meltan*, *mieltan* from Germanic, related to MALT]

melt·down *noun* **1** the melting of (and consequent damage to) a structure, esp. the overheated core of a nuclear reactor. **2 a** any uncontrolled and usu. disastrous transformation with far-reaching repercussions. **b** a collapse or reversal of fortune, esp. a sudden rapid drop in the value of assets, shares, a specified currency, etc. **3** *informal* a total loss of emotional control; a breakdown.

melt·ing *adjective* **1** that melts or is in the process of melting. **2** (of a person, a mood, etc.) yielding to emotion, esp. feeling or showing pity, love, etc. **3** (of sound) be soft and liquid (*melting chords*). □ **melt·ing·ly** *adverb*

melting point *noun* the temperature at which any given solid will melt.

melting pot *noun* **1** a place where races, ethnic groups, etc. are integrated and mixed together. **2** an imaginary pool where theories, ideas, etc. are mixed together. **3** a pot in which metals etc. are melted and mixed.

melt-in-the-mouth *adjective* (also **melt-in-your-mouth**) (of food) delicious and of a very fine texture.

mel·ton /ˈmeltən/ *noun* (also **melton cloth**) cloth with a close-cut nap, used for jackets, overcoats, etc. [Melton Mowbray in central England]

melt·water *noun* water formed by the melting of snow and ice, esp. from a glacier.

Mel·ville¹ /ˈmelvɪl/ a city in SE central Saskatchewan, about 130 km northeast of Regina; pop. (2001) 4,453. □ **Mel·vill·ite** *noun* [C. *Melville* Hays, general manager and president of the Grand Trunk Pacific Railway d.1912]

Mel·ville², **Her·man** (1819–91), US novelist and short-story writer. His novel *Moby Dick* (1851), about the conflict between the obsessive Captain Ahab and a great white whale, was drawn from his experiences aboard a whaler in the South Seas.

Melville, Lake a lake in central Labrador, situated just northeast of Happy Valley-Goose Bay. It is part of Hamilton Inlet. [H. Dundas, 1st Viscount *Melville*, British politician d.1811]

Melville Island the largest of the Parry Islands in the Canadian High Arctic, situated between Prince Patrick and Bathurst islands. [R. S. Dundas, 2nd Viscount *Melville*, English statesman d.1851]

Melville Peninsula a large peninsula of the northeastern coast of mainland Nunavut, separating Foxe Basin from the Gulf of Boothia. It is separated from Baffin Island by Fury and Hecla Strait. [as MELVILLE ISLAND]

mem·ber *noun* **1** a person or thing belonging to or member of an association, team, etc. **2** (**Member**) a person formally elected to take part in the proceedings of certain organizations (*Member of Parliament*; *Member of Congress*). **3** (also *attributive*) a part or branch of a political, social, etc. body (*member nation*; *a member of NATO*; *member agencies*). **4** a constituent part of a complex structure. **5** a part of a sentence, equation, group of figures, mathematical set, etc. **6 a** any part or organ of the body, esp. a limb. **b** *slang* = PENIS. **c** *Biol.* any part of a plant or animal viewed with regard to its form and position. **7** used in the title awarded to a person admitted to (usu. the lowest grade of) certain honours (*Member of the Order of Canada*). □ **mem·bered** *adjective* **mem·ber·less** *adjective* [Old French *membre* from Latin *membrum* limb]

mem·ber·ship *noun* **1** the state or condition of being a member. **2** the number of members in a particular body. **3** the body of members collectively.

mem·brane *noun* **1** any pliable sheet-like structure acting as a boundary, lining, or partition in an organism. **2** a thin pliable sheet or skin of various kinds. □ **mem·bran·ous** /ˈmembrənəs/ *adjective* [Latin *membrana* skin of body, parchment (as MEMBER)]

meme /miːm/ *noun Biol.* an element of a culture or system of behaviour that is passed from one individual to another by non-genetic means, esp. imitation. [Greek *mimēma* 'that which is imitated', after GENE]

Memel /ˈmeiməl/ **1** the German name for KLAIPEDA. **2** a former district of East Prussia, centred on the city of Memel (Klaipeda).

Memel River the Neman River in its lower course (see NEMAN RIVER).

me·men·to *noun* (*pl.* **-mentoes** or **-mentos**) an object kept as a reminder or a souvenir of a person or an event. [Latin, imperative of *meminisse* remember]

memento mori /mə,mentoː 'mɔri, -rai/ *noun* a warning or reminder of death, e.g. a skull or other symbolic object. [Latin, = 'remember you must die']

Mem·ling /'memlɪŋ/ **Hans** (also **Mem·linc** /'memlɪŋk/) (*c*.1430–94), Flemish painter, who is known for his portraits and religious paintings, which include the *Passion Triptych* (1491).

Mem·non /'memnɒn/ *Gk Myth* an Ethiopian king who went to Troy to help Priam, his uncle, and was killed by Achilles.

memo *noun* (*pl.* **memos**) a memorandum. [abbreviation]

mem·oir *noun* **1** (in *pl.*) an autobiography or a written account of one's memory of certain events or people. **2** a historical account or biography written from personal knowledge or special sources. **3** an essay on a learned subject specially studied by the writer. □ **mem·oir·ist** *noun* [French *mémoire* (masc.), special use of *mémoire* (fem.) MEMORY]

mem·ora·bil·ia *plural noun* souvenirs of memorable events, people, periods, etc. [Latin, neuter pl. (as MEMORABLE)]

mem·or·able *adjective* **1** worth remembering, not to be forgotten. **2** easily remembered. □ **mem·or·abil·ity** *noun* **mem·or·able·ness** *noun* **mem·or·ably** *adverb* [French *mémorable* or Latin *memorabilis* from *memorare* bring to mind, from *memor* mindful]

memo·ran·dum *noun* (*pl.* **memo·ran·da** or **memo·ran·dums**) **1 a** a written note or communication esp. in business between people working for the same organization. **b** an informal diplomatic message, esp. summarizing the state of a question etc. **2** a note or record made for future use. **3** *Law* a document summarizing or embodying the terms of a contract or other legal details. [Latin neuter sing. gerundive of *memorare*: see MEMORABLE]

memorandum of understanding *noun* a formal document embodying the firm commitment of two or more parties to an undertaking, and setting out its general principles, but falling short of constituting a detailed contract or agreement. Abbr.: **MOU**.

me·mor·ial ● *noun* **1** an object, institution, or custom established in memory of a person or event (*the Terry Fox Memorial*). **2** (often in *pl.*) *hist.* a statement of facts as the basis of a petition etc.; a record; an informal diplomatic paper. ● *adjective* intending to commemorate a person or thing (*memorial service*). □ **me·mor·ial·ist** *noun* [Old French *memorial* or Latin *memorialis* (as MEMORY)]

Memorial Cup *noun* a trophy awarded annually to the Canadian major junior amateur hockey champions, in memory of the Canadian hockey players who died in the First World War.

Memorial Day *noun* **1** *Cdn* (*Nfld*) a statutory holiday, 1 July, commemorating losses to the Newfoundland Regiment at the battle of the Somme. **2** *US* a day on which those who died on active service are remembered, usu. the last Monday in May.

me·mor·ial·ize *transitive verb* (also esp. *Brit.* **-ise**) **1** commemorate. **2** address a memorial to (a person or body). □ **me·mor·ial·iz·a·tion** *noun* **me·mor·ial·iz·er** *noun*

memorial park *noun* *N Amer.* a cemetery.

memorial service *noun* a service of commemoration of the dead, usu. without the body or bodies being present.

mem·or·ize *verb* (also esp. *Brit.* **-ise**) **1** *transitive* commit to memory, learn by heart. **2** *intransitive* learn things by heart. □ **mem·or·iz·a·tion** *noun* **mem·or·iz·er** *noun* **mem·or·iz·ing** *noun*

mem·ory *noun* (*pl.* **-ories**) **1 a** the faculty by which things are recalled to or kept in the mind. **b** an individual's capacity to remember things (*my memory is beginning to fail*). **2** one's store of things remembered (*buried deep in my memory*). **3** a recollection or remembrance (*the memory of better times*). **4 a** the capacity of a computer or other electronic machinery to store data or program instructions in such a way that they may be retrieved when required. **b** a device in which data or program instructions may be stored and from which they may be retrieved when required. **c** = MEMORY BOARD. **5** the remembrance of a person or thing (*his mother's memory haunted him*). **6 a** the reputation of a dead person (*his memory lives on*). **b** in formulaic phrases used of a dead sovereign etc. (*of blessed memory*). **7** the length of time over which the memory or memories of any given person or group extends (*within living memory*; *within the memory of anyone still working here*). **8 a** the capacity of a substance etc. for manifesting effects of its previous state, behaviour, or treatment. **b** the capacity of a substance etc. for returning to a previous state when the cause of the transition from that state is removed. **c** such effects or such a state. □ **commit to**

memory learn (a thing) so as to be able to recall it at will. **down memory lane** through a succession of sentimental memories deliberately pursued. **from memory** without reading from or referring to books etc. **in memory of** to keep alive the remembrance of. [Old French *memorie* from Latin *memoria* from *memor* mindful, remembering, related to MOURN]

memory bank *noun* **1** the memory device of a computer etc. **2** *informal* the store of memories of an individual or group.

memory board *noun* a detachable storage device, containing additional memory capacity, which can be installed in a computer.

memory card *noun* *Computing* a memory chip housed in a rectangular plastic case which plugs into a computer enabling data storage and retrieval.

memory cell *noun* **1** *Med.* a long-lived lymphocyte capable of responding to a particular antigen on its reproduction, long after the exposure that prompted its production. **2** *Computing* an identifiable or addressable unit of memory or data storage, esp. one with a capacity of one byte or one word. **3** *jocular* a nerve cell concerned with memory.

memory chip *noun* a semiconductor chip made as a memory, e.g. a ROM or a RAM, containing many separately addressable locations.

memory trace *noun* *Psych.* a hypothetical trace left in the nervous system by the act of memorizing. (*Compare* ENGRAM).

Mem·phis /'memfɪs/ **1** an ancient city of Egypt, whose ruins are situated on the Nile about 15 km (nearly 10 miles) south of Cairo. It is thought to have been founded as the capital of the Old Kingdom of Egypt *c*.3100 BC. It is the site of the pyramids of Saqqara and Giza and the Sphinx. **2** a river port on the Mississippi in the extreme southwest of Tennessee; pop. (2000) 659,100. It was the home in the late 19th c. of blues music, the scene in 1968 of the assassination of Martin Luther King, and the childhood home and burial place of Elvis Presley. [sense 2 after the ancient city on the Nile because of its river location]

Mem·phré·ma·gog, Lac /mãfreima'gɒg/ a small, narrow lake in S Quebec, situated southwest of Sherbrooke. Its southern tip straddles the border with Vermont. [Abenaki, = at the great stretch of water]

mem·sahib /'mem,saɪb, -sɒɪb/ *noun hist.* a European married woman in India, as spoken of or to by Indians. [MA'AM + SAHIB]

men *pl.* of MAN.

men·ace ● *noun* **1** a dangerous thing or person. **2** *jocular* a pest, a nuisance. **3** a threat. ● *transitive & intransitive verb* threaten, esp. in a malignant or hostile manner. □ **mena·cing** *adjective* **mena·cing·ly** *adverb* [ultimately from Latin *minax -acis* threatening, from *minari* threaten]

mé·nage /mei'naʒ, -ɒʒ/ *noun* **1** a domestic establishment, a household. **2** the members of a household. [Old French *manaige*, ultimately from Latin (as MANSION)]

mé·nage à trois /mei,naʒ a 'trwa/ *noun* a sexual relationship involving three people, esp. in one household. [French, = household of three (as MÉNAGE)]

men·ager·ie /mə'naʒɜri, -'nadʒ-, -'nɒʒ-/ *noun* **1 a** a collection of wild animals in captivity for exhibition etc. **b** the place where these are housed. **2** a heterogeneous collection of animals. **3** a collection of strange or outlandish people etc. [French *ménagerie* (as MÉNAGE)]

Menai Strait /'menai/ a channel separating Anglesey from the mainland of NW Wales.

Me·nan·der /mə'nandər/ (*c*.342–292 BC), Greek dramatist. His comic plays, set in contemporary Greece, deal with domestic situations, and were adapted by Plautus and Terence; the *Dyskolos* is his sole complete extant play.

mena·quin·one /,menə'kwɪnoːn/ *noun* one of the K vitamins, produced by bacteria found in the large intestine, essential for the blood clotting process. *Also called* VITAMIN K$_2$. [chemical derivative of *methyl-naphthoquinone*]

men·arche /me'nɑrki/ *noun* the onset of first menstruation. [modern Latin formed as MENO- + Greek *arkhē* beginning]

Men·cius /'menʃiəs/ **1** (Latinized name of Meng-tzu or Mengzi = 'Meng the Master') (*c*.371–*c*.289 BC), Chinese philosopher, who developed Confucianism; two of his central doctrines were that rulers should provide for the welfare of the people and that human nature is intrinsically good. **2** one of the Four Books of Confucianism, containing the teachings of Mencius, which formed the basis of primary and secondary education in imperial China from the 14th c.

Men·cken /'meŋkən/ **Henry Louis** (1880–1956), US journalist and literary critic. From 1908 he boldly attacked the political and literary establishment, and strongly opposed the dominance of European culture in the US; his book *The American Language* (1919) defended the vigour and versatility of colloquial American usage.

mend ● *verb* **1** *transitive* restore to a sound condition; repair (a broken article, a damaged road, torn clothes, etc.). **2** *intransitive* regain health; heal. **3** *transitive* improve or put right (a fault, something wrong, etc.) (*mend matters*). **4** *transitive* add fuel to (a fire). ● *noun* a darn or repair in material etc. (*a mend in my shirt*). □ **mend (one's) fences** make peace with a person; reconcile differences. **mend one's manners** improve one's behaviour. **mend one's ways** reform, improve one's habits. **mend or end** improve or abolish. **on the mend** improving in health or condition. □ **mend·able** *adjective* **mend·er** *noun* [Anglo-French *mender* from *amender* AMEND]

men·da·cious /men'deɪʃəs/ *adjective* lying, untruthful; false. □ **men·da·cious·ly** *adverb* **men·da·city** /-'dasɪtɪ/ *noun* (*pl.* **-ties**). [Latin *mendax -dacis* lying, perhaps from *mendum* fault]

Men·del /'mendəl/ **Gregor (Jo·hann)** (1822–84), Moravian monk, the father of genetics. From his experiments with peas, he demonstrated that parent plants showing different characters produced hybrids exhibiting the dominant parental character, and that the hybrids themselves produced offspring in which the parental characters re-emerged unchanged and in precise ratios. □ **Men·del·ian** /-'diːlɪən/ *adjective & noun*

Men·de·leev /,mendə'leief/ **Dmitri Ivan·ovich** (1834–1907), Russian chemist. He developed the periodic table, in which the chemical elements are classified according to their atomic weights in groups with similar properties.

men·de·lev·ium /,mendə'liːvɪəm/ *noun Chem.* an artificially made transuranic radioactive metallic element. Symbol: **Md**; at. no.: 101. [MENDELEEV]

Men·del·ism /'mendə,lɪzəm/ *noun* the theory of heredity based on the recurrence of certain inherited characteristics transmitted by genes. [MENDEL]

Men·dels·sohn /'mendəlsən/ **Felix** (full name Jakob Ludwig Felix Mendelssohn-Bartholdy) (1809–47), German composer. His music is known for its elegance and lightness, as well as its melodic inventiveness, and includes *A Midsummer Night's Dream* (1826), *Fingal's Cave* (1830–2), the *Italian Symphony* (1833), and the oratorio *Elijah* (1846). □ **Men·dels·sohn·ian** /,mendəl'soːnɪən/ *adjective*

men·di·cant /'mendɪkənt/ ● *adjective* **1** begging. **2** designating or belonging to any of the religious orders, e.g. the Franciscans, Dominicans, etc., whose members support themselves by work and charitable contributions. ● *noun* **1** a beggar. **2** a mendicant friar. □ **men·di·cancy** *noun* [Latin *mendicare* beg, from *mendicus* beggar, from *mendum* fault]

mend·ing *noun* **1** the action of a person who mends. **2** things, esp. clothes, to be mended.

Men·dip Hills /'mendɪp/ (also **Men·dips**) a range of limestone hills in SW England.

Men·doza /men'doːzə/ a city in W Argentina, situated in the foothills of the Andes at the centre of a noted wine-producing region; pop. (est. 1999) 119,681.

Mene·laus /,menə'leɪəs/ *Gk Myth* king of Sparta, husband of Helen and brother of Agamemnon.

Men·elik II /'menəlɪk/ (born Sahle Miriam) (1844–1913), emperor of Ethiopia 1889–1913, who expanded and modernized the empire, and defeated an Italian invasion (1896).

Menes /'miːniːz/ Egyptian pharaoh, reigned *c.*3100 BC. He founded the first dynasty that ruled ancient Egypt and is traditionally held to have united Upper and Lower Egypt with Memphis as its capital.

men·folk *plural noun informal* **1** men in general. **2** the men of one's family.

M.Eng. *abbreviation* Master of Engineering.

Meng-tzu /meŋ'tsuː/ see MENCIUS 1.

Meng·zi /meŋ'ziː/ see MENCIUS 1.

men·haden /men'heɪdən/ *noun* any large herring-like fish of the genus *Brevoortia*, of the E coast of N America, yielding valuable oil and used for fertilizer. [Algonquian: compare Narragansett *munnawhatteaûg*]

men·hir /'menhiːr/ *noun Archaeology* a single, tall, upright usu. prehistoric monumental stone. [Breton *men* stone + *hir* long]

menial ● *adjective* (esp. of unskilled work) of the nature of drudgery; servile, degrading. ● *noun* **1** a domestic servant. **2** a servile person. □ **menial·ly** *adverb* [Old French *meinee* household]

Mé·nière's disease /mein'jers/ *noun* a disease of the membranous labyrinth of the ear associated with tinnitus, progressive deafness, and intermittent vertigo. [Prosper *Ménière*, French physician d.1862]

me·nin·ges /mɪ'nɪndʒiːz/ *plural noun* (*sing.* **me·ninx** /'miːnɪŋks/) (usu. in *pl.*) the three membranes that line the skull and vertebral canal and enclose the brain and spinal cord (dura mater, arachnoid, pia mater). □ **me·nin·geal** /mɪ'nɪndʒɪəl/ *adjective* [modern Latin from Greek *mēninx -iggos* membrane]

men·in·gi·tis /,menɪn'dʒaɪtɪs/ *noun* an inflammation of the meninges of the brain or spinal cord due to infection by viruses or bacteria.

me·nin·go·coc·cus /me,nɪŋgə'kɒkəs, -,nɪndʒə-/ *noun* (*pl.* **me·nin·go·coc·ci** /-'kɒkaɪ, -'kɒksiː/) a bacterium, *Neisseria meningitidis*, involved in some forms of meningitis and cerebrospinal infection. □ **me·nin·go·coc·cal** *adjective*

me·nis·cus /mə'nɪskəs/ *noun* (*pl.* **me·nisci** /-saɪ/) **1** *Physics* the curved upper surface of a liquid in a tube etc., caused by surface tension or capillarity. **2** a lens that is convex on one side and concave on the other, esp. one thickest in the middle, with a crescent-shaped section. **3** *Anat.* a thin fibrous cartilage between the surfaces of some joints, e.g. the knee. **4** a crescent-shaped figure. □ **me·nis·coid** *adjective* [modern Latin from Greek *mēniskos* crescent, diminutive of *mēnē* moon]

Men·non·ite /'menə,naɪt/ ● *noun* a member of a Protestant denomination originating in Friesland in the 16th c., emphasizing adult baptism and rejecting the taking of oaths, military service, and the holding of public office. ● *adjective* of or pertaining to Mennonites. □ **Men·non·it·ism** *noun* [Menno Simons, its founder, d.1561]

meno /'meino/ *adverb Music* less (*meno forte*). [Italian]

meno- /'meino/ *combining form* menstruation. [Greek *mēn mēnos* month]

men·ol·ogy /mɪ'nɒlədʒɪ/ *noun* (*pl.* **-gies**) a calendar, esp. that of the Greek Church, with biographies of the saints. [modern Latin *menologium* from ecclesiastical Greek *mēnologion* from *mēn* month + *logos* account]

meno mosso /meino 'mɒso/ *adverb Music* more slowly. [Italian, MENO + *mosso*, past participle of *muovere* move]

meno·pause /'menə,pɔːz/ *noun* **1** the final cessation of menstruation. **2** the period in a woman's life, usu. between 45 and 50, when this occurs (*see also* MALE MENOPAUSE). □ **meno·paus·al** *adjective* [modern Latin *menopausis* (as MENO-, PAUSE)]

me·nor·ah /mə'nɔrə/ *noun Judaism* **1** a candelabrum with usu. seven branches, used at home and in the synagogue on Sabbaths and holidays. **2** a candelabrum used during Hanukkah, having eight branches and a holder for the candle used to light the others. **3** a representation of either as a symbol of Judaism. [Hebrew, = candlestick]

men·or·rhagia /,menə'reidʒɪə/ *noun* abnormally heavy bleeding at menstruation. [MENO- + stem of Greek *rhēgnumi* burst]

men·or·rhea /,menə'riːə/ *noun* (also **men·or·rhoea**) ordinary flow of blood at menstruation. [MENO- + Greek *rhoia* from *rheō* flow]

Me·notti /mə'nɒti/ **Gian Carlo** (b.1911), Italian-born US composer and librettist, whose highly acclaimed operas include *The Medium* (1945), *Amahl and the Night Visitors* (1951), and *Goya* (1986).

Menou d'Aul·nay /mə'nuː doː'nei/ **Charles de** (*c.*1604–1650), French sea captain and colonial administrator. First coming to Acadia in 1632, he succeeded as governor in 1635. His most notable achievement was the establishment of an Acadian settlement at Port-Royal (Annapolis Royal) in present-day Nova Scotia.

mensch /menʃ/ *noun* an admirable or honourable person. [Yiddish from German 'person']

men·ser·vants *pl.* of MANSERVANT.

men·ses /'mensiːz/ *plural noun* **1** blood and mucosal tissue etc. discharged from the uterus at menstruation. **2** the time of menstruation. [Latin, pl. of *mensis* month]

Men·she·vik /'menʃə,vɪk/ *noun* a member of a minority faction of the Russian Socialist Party who opposed the Bolshevik policies of non-cooperation with more moderate reformers as well as disagreeing with their advocacy of revolutionary action by a small political elite. The Mensheviks and other revolutionary groups were defeated by the Bolsheviks in the power struggle following the overthrow of the czar in 1917. [Russian *Men'shevik* a member of the minority (*men'she* less)]

mens rea /menz 'riːə/ *noun* criminal intent; the state of mind or knowledge of wrongdoing accompanying an illegal act which makes the act a crime (*compare* ACTUS REUS). [Latin, = guilty mind]

men's room *noun* (also **men's**) esp. *N Amer.* a public washroom for men.

men·stru·al /'menstrəl, -struəl/ *adjective* of or relating to the menses or menstruation. [Latin *menstrualis* from *mensis* month]

menstrual cycle *noun* the process of ovulation and menstruation in sexually mature women and female primates.

men·stru·ant /ˈmenstrʊənt/ *noun* a woman who is menstruating.

men·stru·ate /ˈmenstreɪt/ *intransitive verb* undergo menstruation.
☐ **men·stru·at·ing** *adjective* [Late Latin *menstruare menstruat-* (as MENSTRUAL)]

men·stru·a·tion /ˌmenstrɪˈeɪʃən/ *noun* the process of discharging blood and mucosal tissue etc. from the uterus through the vagina that occurs in sexually mature, non-pregnant women, normally at intervals of about one lunar month, until menopause.

men·stru·um /ˈmenstrʊm/ *noun* (*pl.* **men·strua** /-strʊ/) a solvent. [Latin, neuter of *menstruus* monthly, from *mensis* month, from the alchemical parallel between transmutation into gold and the supposed action of menses on the ovum]

men·sur·a·tion /ˌmensjʊˈreɪʃən/ *noun* **1** the act or action of measuring. **2** *Math.* the part of geometry that deals with the measurement of lengths of line, areas of surfaces, and volumes of solids. [Late Latin *mensuratio*]

mens·wear *noun* clothes for men.

-ment *suffix* **1** forming nouns expressing the means, product, or result of the action of a verb (*abridgement; embankment*). **2** forming nouns from adjectives (*merriment*). [from French, or from Latin *-mentum*]

men·tal *adjective* **1** of or pertaining to the mind. **2** carried on or performed by, or taking place in, the mind. **3** *informal derogatory* insane, crazy (*this is driving me mental*). **4** designating a medical establishment for the care and treatment of the mentally ill (*mental hospital; mental institution*). ☐ **men·tal·ly** *adverb* [Old French *mental* or Late Latin *mentalis* from Latin *mens mentis* mind]

mental age *noun* the degree of a person's mental development expressed as an age at which the same degree is attained by an average person.

mental arithmetic *noun* arithmetic performed in the mind, without the use of written figures or other visible symbols.

mental block *noun* a sudden and temporary inability to continue a thought process or mental link, esp. due to subconscious emotional factors.

mental case *noun* *informal derogatory* a person suffering from some kind of mental impairment, esp. one under or requiring medical care for mental illness.

mental cruelty *noun* *Law* conduct which inflicts suffering on the mind of another person, rendering continued relations impossible, esp. as grounds for divorce.

mental handicap *noun* **1** the condition of being of such low intelligence, or having the intellectual capacities so underdeveloped, esp. through illness or injury, as to inhibit normal social functioning. **2** an instance of this.

mental health *noun* the condition of a person or a group in respect to the functioning of the mind, emotions, etc.

mental health day *noun* *N Amer.* a day taken off school or work as a sick day, spent in relaxation or enjoyable activities, on the pretext that this is necessary for one's mental health.

mental illness *noun* **1** disordered functioning of the mind. **2** an instance of this.

men·tal·ism *noun* *Philos.* the theory that physical and psychological phenomena are ultimately only explicable in terms of a creative and interpretative mind. ☐ **men·tal·ist** *noun* **men·tal·is·tic** *adjective*

men·tal·ity /menˈtalɪti/ *noun* (*pl.* **-ities**) **1** mental character or disposition. **2** outlook; what is in or of the mind. **3** kind or degree of intelligence.

mentally handicapped *adjective* (of a person) having a mental handicap.

mentally ill *adjective* (of a person) having a mental illness.

mentally incompetent *adjective* (of a person) mentally ill or mentally handicapped to an extent that care, supervision, and control are required.

mentally retarded *adjective* (of a person) suffering from mental retardation.

mental note *noun* a fixing of something in one's mind, to be remembered subsequently.

mental patient *noun* a sufferer from mental illness, esp. while in a hospital or under active treatment.

mental reservation *noun* a qualification, limitation, or exemption tacitly added in making a statement etc.

mental retardation *noun* a developmental disorder in which a person has impaired learning ability and a lower than normal IQ.

men·ta·tion /menˈteɪʃən/ *noun* **1** mental activity. **2** state of mind. [Latin *mens -ntis* mind]

men·thol /ˈmenθɒl/ *noun* a mint-tasting organic alcohol found in oil of peppermint etc., used as a flavouring and to relieve local pain. [German from Latin *mentha* MINT¹]

men·thol·at·ed /ˈmenθəˌleɪtəd/ *adjective* treated with or containing menthol.

men·tion ● *transitive verb* **1** refer to or remark on incidentally. **2** specify by name or otherwise. **3** reveal or disclose (*do not mention this to anyone*). **4** (in dispatches) award (a person) a minor honour for meritorious, usu. gallant, military service. ● *noun* **1** an incidental reference, esp. by name, to a person or thing. **2** (in dispatches) a military honour awarded for outstanding conduct. ☐ **don't mention it** said in polite dismissal of an apology or thanks. **make mention** (or **no mention**) **of** refer (or not refer) to. **not to mention** introducing a fact or thing of secondary or (as a rhetorical device) of primary importance.
☐ **men·tion·able** *adjective & noun* [Latin *mentio -onis* from the root of *mens* mind]

men·tor ● *noun* an experienced and trusted adviser or guide.
● *transitive verb* act as a mentor to (a person). ☐ **men·tor·ing** *noun & adjective* **men·tor·ship** *noun* [Greek *Mentōr*, adviser of the young Telemachus in Homer's *Odyssey*]

menu *noun* **1 a** a list of dishes to be served at a meal, available in a restaurant, etc. **b** a card, folder, etc. on which such a list is written or printed. **c** the food served or available. **2** a list of available commands, options, etc., displayed on a television or computer screen, for selection by the operator. [French, = detailed list, from Latin *minutus* MINUTE²]

menu bar *noun* *Computing* a graphically represented bar in which the primary menus and menu options for a software program are displayed and from which these can be accessed.

menu-driven *adjective* (of a program or computer) used by making selections from menus.

Men·uhin /ˈmenjuːɪn/ **Sir Ye·hudi** (1916–99), US-born English violinist. As a child prodigy he became known for his interpretations of Bach, Beethoven, and Mozart.

Men·zies /ˈmenzɪz/ **Sir Rob·ert Gor·don** (1894–1978), Australian Liberal politician, prime minister 1939–41 and 1949–66. Australia's longest-serving prime minister, he implemented a policy of fast industrial growth in the 1950s.

meow /miːˈaʊ/ ● *noun* one of the characteristic sounds made by a domestic cat. ● *intransitive verb* make this sound. [imitative]

MEP *abbreviation* (in Britain) Member of the European Parliament.

me·peri·dine /meˈperɪdiːn/ *noun* esp. *N Amer.* a narcotic analgesic used for moderate to severe pain, the generic name for Demerol. [METHYL + PIPERIDINE]

Meph·is·toph·eles /ˌmefɪˈstɒfɪˌliːz/ *noun* **1** an evil spirit to whom Faust, in the German legend, sold his soul. **2** a fiendish person.
☐ **Meph·is·to·phe·lean** /-ˈliːən/ *adjective* **Meph·is·to·phe·lian** /-ˈfiːlɪən/ *adjective* [German (16th c.), of unknown origin]

meph·itis /mɪˈfaɪtɪs/ *noun* **1** a noxious emanation, esp. from the earth. **2** a foul or poisonous stench. ☐ **meph·itic** /-ˈfɪtɪk/ *adjective* [Latin]

-mer *combining form* denoting a substance of a specified class, esp. a polymer (*dimer; isomer; tautomer*). [Greek *meros* part, share]

mer·bromin /merˈbroːmɪn/ *noun* a fluorescein derivative containing bromine and mercury, obtained as greenish iridescent scales which dissolve in water to give a red solution used as an antiseptic. [from MER(CURY) n. + BROM(O-) + -IN]

mer·can·tile /ˈmɜrkənˌtaɪl/ *adjective* **1** of or pertaining to trade, traders, or trading. **2** concerned with the exchange of merchandise; commercial. **3** mercenary, having payment or gain as the motive. [French from Italian from *mercante* MERCHANT]

mer·can·til·ism /ˈmɜrkəntɪˌlɪzəm/ *noun* *hist.* the economic theory that trade generates wealth and is stimulated by the accumulation of bullion, which a government should encourage by promoting exports and restricting imports. ☐ **mer·can·til·ist** *noun* **mer·can·til·is·tic** *adjective*

mer·cap·tan /mɜrˈkaptən/ *noun* = THIOL. [modern Latin *mercurium captans* capturing mercury]

Mer·cator /mɜrˈkeɪtər/ **Ger·ar·dus** (Latinized name of Gerhard Kremer) (1512–94), Flemish geographer and cartographer. He is best known for inventing the system of map projection that is named after him, and is also credited with introducing the term *atlas*, following the publication of his *Atlas* of part of Europe (1585).

Mercator projection *noun* (also **Mercator's projection**) a cylindrical map projection in which all parallels of latitude have the same length and meridians are represented by equidistant straight lines at right angles to the equator and any course that follows a constant compass bearing is represented by a straight line.

mer·cen·ary /ˈmɜrsəˌneri/ ● *adjective* primarily concerned with money or other material reward (*mercenary motives*). ● *noun* (*pl.* **-ies**) **1** a professional soldier serving a foreign power for money. **2** a hireling; a person whose services are available for money (*intellectual mercenaries with knowledge for sale*). □ **mer·cen·ari·ness** *noun* [Latin *mercenarius* from *merces -edis* reward]

mer·cer·ized /ˈmɜrsəˌraizd/ *adjective* (also esp. *Brit.* **-ised**) (of cotton fabric or thread) treated under tension with caustic alkali to give greater strength and impart lustre. [J. *Mercer*, alleged inventor of the process d.1866]

mer·chan·dise ● *noun* /ˈmɜrtʃənˌdais, -daiz/ the commodities of commerce, goods to be bought and sold. ● *transitive verb* /ˈmɜrtʃənˌdaiz/ (also **-ize**) **1** put on the market, promote the sale of (goods etc.). **2** advertise, publicize (an idea or person). □ **mer·chan·dis·er** *noun* **mer·chan·dis·ing** *noun & adjective* [Old French *marchandise* from *marchand*: see MERCHANT]

Mer·chant /ˈmɜrtʃənt/ **Ismail** (b.1936), Indian film producer. A partner with James Ivory in Merchant Ivory Productions, he has produced many films, esp. period pieces.

mer·chant ● *noun* **1** a person whose occupation is the purchase and sale of goods for profit. **2** a wholesale trader, esp. with foreign countries. **3** esp. *N Amer. & Scot.* a retail trader, a storekeeper. **4** *informal usu.* derogatory a person showing a partiality for a specified activity or practice (*speed merchant*). **5** *Cdn (Nfld)* an entrepreneur involved in the fish trade, usu. purchasing and exporting salt cod, financing fishing operations, etc. ● *adjective* **1 a** connected with or relating to trade or commerce. **b** connected with merchandise. **2** (of a ship, fleet, etc.) serving for or involved in the transport of merchandise. [Old French *marchand*, *marchant*, ultimately from Latin *mercari* trade, from *merx mercis* merchandise]

mer·chant·able *adjective* suitable or prepared for purchase or sale; marketable. □ **mer·chant·abil·ity** *noun*

Merchant Adventurers an English trading guild involved in trade overseas (1407–1806), principally with the Netherlands (and later Germany). Engaged mainly in the lucrative business of exporting woollen cloth, it reached its peak in the 16th c. as one of the most wealthy and influential trading guilds.

merchant bank *noun* esp. *Brit.* a bank dealing primarily in long-term commercial loans and financing. □ **merchant banker** *noun* **merchant banking** *noun*

mer·chant·man *noun* (*pl.* **-men**) esp. *hist.* = MERCHANT SHIP.

merchant marine *noun* *N Amer.* a fleet or number of ships used in trade and not for purposes of war; a nation's commercial shipping. □ **merchant mariner** *noun*

merchant navy *noun* = MERCHANT MARINE.

merchant prince *noun* a wealthy merchant.

merchant seaman *noun* a sailor serving on a merchant ship or in the merchant marine.

merchant ship *noun* a ship conveying merchandise.

Mer·cia /ˈmɜrʃiə, ˈmɜrsiə/ a former kingdom of central England. Established by invading Angles in the 6th c. AD between the new Anglo-Saxon settlements in the east and the Celtic regions in the west, it had expanded by the 8th c. to cover an area stretching from the Humber River to the south coast. □ **Mer·cian** *adjective & noun* [Latin from Old English, = people of the marches (i.e. borders, with reference to the border with Wales)]

Mer·cier¹ /mɛrˈsjei/ a town in south central Quebec, south of Châteauguay; pop. (2001) 9,442. [MERCIER²]

Mer·cier² /mɛrˈsjei/ **Hon·oré** (1840–94), Canadian lawyer and politician, premier of Quebec 1887–91. As a founder of the short-lived Parti national (1872), he was the first Quebec politician to state that the Quebec government was a national government for the Québécois, and so is considered a father of nationalism in Quebec.

merci·ful *adjective* having, showing, or feeling mercy. □ **merci·ful·ness** *noun*

merci·ful·ly *adverb* **1** in a merciful manner. **2** (qualifying a whole sentence) fortunately (*mercifully, the sun came out*).

merci·less *adjective* **1** pitiless, unrelenting. **2** showing no mercy. □ **merci·less·ly** *adverb* **merci·less·ness** *noun*

Merco·sur /ˈmɜrkəsur/ *noun* the *Mercado del Sur*, a common market agreement permitting the movement of goods and services between Argentina, Brazil, Paraguay, and Uruguay.

Mer·credi /ˈmerkrədi/ **Ovide Wil·liam** (b.1946), Canadian lawyer and Aboriginal leader. From 1991–97 he was national chief of the Assembly of First Nations.

Mer·cure /merˈkjuːr/ **Pierre** (1927–66), Canadian composer. A bassoonist, he wrote among other pieces the electronic composition *Structures métalliques* (1962) and *Psaume pour abri* (1963) for choir and orchestra.

mer·cur·ial /mɜrˈkjuriəl/ ● *adjective* **1** (of a person) lively, quick to react and often changing. **2** of or containing mercury. **3** (**Mercurial**) of or pertaining to the planet Mercury. ● *noun* a drug containing mercury. □ **mer·cur·ial·ly** *adverb*

Mer·curo·chrome /merˈkjurəkroːm/ *noun* *N Amer.* proprietary merbromin. [from MERCURY + -o- + Greek *khrōma* 'colour']

Mer·cury /ˈmɜrkjuri/ **1** *Rom. Myth* the god of eloquence, skill, trading, and thieving, herald and messenger of the gods, who was identified with the Greek god Hermes. **2** *Astronomy* the innermost planet of the solar system, orbiting 57.9 million km from the sun; with a diameter of 4 878 km, it is somewhat larger than the moon. □ **Mer·cur·ian** *adjective* [Latin *Mercurius* from *merx mercis* merchandise]

mer·cury *noun* **1** *Chem.* a toxic silvery-white heavy liquid metallic element used in barometers, thermometers, and amalgams. Symbol: **Hg**; at. no.: 80. **2 a** the column of mercury in a thermometer or barometer. **b** the temperature or barometric pressure indicated by this, esp. as rising or falling. **3** any plant of the genus *Mercurialis*. □ **mer·cur·ic** /mɜrˈkjurik/ *adjective* **mer·cur·ous** *adjective* [MERCURY]

mercury vapour *noun* (often *attributive*) a vapour of mercury atoms or ions above liquid mercury or at low pressure.

mercury vapour lamp *noun* (also **mercury vapour light**) a lamp in which bluish light is produced by an electric discharge through mercury vapour.

mercy ● *noun* (*pl.* **-cies**) **1** compassion or forbearance shown to a powerless person, esp. an offender or one with no claim to kindness. **2** the disposition to forgive or show compassion; mercifulness. **3** an act of mercy. **4** (*attributive*) administered or performed out of mercy or pity for a suffering person (*mercy killing*). **5** something to be thankful for (*small mercies*). ● *interjection* expressing surprise or fear. □ **at the mercy of 1** wholly in the power of. **2** liable to danger or harm from. **have mercy on** (or **upon**) show mercy to. [Old French *merci* from Latin *merces -edis* reward, in Late Latin pity, thanks]

mercy flight *noun* *Cdn, Brit., Austral., & NZ* the transporting by air of an injured or sick person from a remote area to a hospital.

mercy killing *noun* = EUTHANASIA.

mercy seat *noun* **1** the throne of God in heaven. **2** *Bible* the golden covering placed upon the Ark of the Covenant, regarded as the resting place of God.

mere¹ /miːr/ *attributive adjective* (**merest**) **1** having no greater extent, range, value, power, or importance than the designation implies (*a mere child; no mere theory*). **2** insignificant, ordinary. □ **mere·ly** *adverb* [Anglo-French *meer* from Latin *merus* unmixed]

mere² /miːr/ *noun* esp. *literary* a lake or pond. [Old English from Germanic]

Mere·dith /ˈmerəˌdiθ/ **George** (1828–1909), English novelist and poet. He is noted for his sharp psychological characterization and deliberately intricate style in novels such as *The Egoist* (1879); he is also known for the semi-autobiographical verse collection *Modern Love* (1862).

mere mortal *noun* a person with no outstanding skills or characteristics; an average person.

mer·en·gue /məˈreŋgei/ *noun* **1** a dance of Dominican and Haitian origin, with alternating long and stiff-legged steps. **2** a piece of music for this dance, usu. in duple and triple time. [probably American Spanish; compare perhaps with the sense 'upheaval, disorder,' attested in Argentina, Paraguay, and Uruguay]

mere·tri·cious /ˌmerəˈtriʃəs/ *adjective* (of decorations, literary style, etc.) showily attractive but valueless. □ **mere·tri·cious·ly** *adverb* **mere·tri·cious·ness** *noun* [Latin *meretricius* from *meretrix -tricis* prostitute, from *merēri* be hired]

mer·gan·ser /mɜrˈgansər/ *noun* any of various diving fish-eating northern ducks of the genus *Mergus*, with a long narrow serrated hooked bill, esp. the common merganser, *M. merganser*, the male of which has a glossy green head and black and white body, and the female of which has a conspicuous crest, and the red-breasted merganser, *M. serrator*. *Also called* SAWBILL. [modern Latin from Latin *mergus* diver, from *mergere* dive + *anser* goose]

merge ● *verb* **1** *transitive & intransitive* (often foll. by *with*) **a** combine or be combined. **b** join or blend gradually. **2** *intransitive & transitive* (foll. by *in*) lose or cause to lose character and identity by absorption in (something else). **3** *transitive Computing* combine (multiple files, sets of data, etc.) to produce only one file, set, etc., usu. in an ordered sequence. **4** *intransitive* **a** (of lanes of traffic etc.) be gradually integrated into fewer lanes. **b** (of a vehicle) join a lane of traffic. ● *noun* **1** an act or instance of merging, esp. a merger. **2 a** *Computing* (often *attributive*) a function that enables file or data merging (*merge facility*). **b** = MAIL MERGE. **3** an instance or the site of a traffic merge. □ **merged** *adjective* **mer·ging** *noun & adjective* [Latin *mergere mers-* dip, plunge, partly via legal Anglo-French *merger*]

mer·ger *noun* **1** the combining of two commercial companies etc. into one. **2** a merging, esp. of one estate in another. **3** *Law* the absorbing of a minor offence in a greater one.

mer·guez /mɜrˈɡez/ *noun* a spicy sausage made of beef and lamb, and coloured with red peppers, originally made in parts of North Africa. [French *merguez* from Arabic *mirkās, mirqās*]

Mér·ida /ˈmerɪdə/ **1** a city in W Spain, on the Guadiana River, capital of Extremadura region; pop. (est. 2002) 50,400. **2** a city in SE Mexico, capital of the state of Yucatán; pop. (2000) 662,500, founded in 1542 on the site of an ancient Mayan city.

me·rid·ian /məˈrɪdiən/ *noun* **1 a** a great circle passing through the celestial poles and zenith of a given place on the earth's surface. **b** the circle of the earth which lies on the same plane. **2 a** half the circle of the earth which extends from pole to pole through a place, corresponding to a line of longitude. **b** a line on a map, globe, etc. representing one of these. **3** any of the pathways in the body along which energy is said to flow, esp. each of twelve associated with specific organs for acupuncture etc. **4 a** any great circle of a sphere that passes through the poles. **b** any line on a surface of revolution that is in a plane with its axis. [Old French *meridien* or Latin *meridianus* (adj.) from *meridies* midday, from *medius* middle + *dies* day]

meridian circle *noun Astronomy* a telescope mounted so as to move only on a north-south line, for observing the transit of celestial objects across the meridian. *Also called* TRANSIT INSTRUMENT.

me·rid·ion·al /məˈrɪdiənəl/ ● *adjective* **1 a** of or in the south (esp. of Europe). **b** characteristic of the inhabitants of S Europe. **2** of or relating to a meridian. ● *noun* an inhabitant of the south (esp. of France). [Old French from Late Latin *meridionalis* irreg. from Latin *meridies*: see MERIDIAN]

Méri·mée /ˈmerɪmeɪ/ **Pros·per** (1803–70), French novelist, playwright, and short-story writer, who is noted for the short stories *Colomba* (1840) and *Carmen* (1845), which inspired Bizet's opera.

mer·ingue /məˈraŋ/ *noun* **1** a mixture of stiffly beaten egg white and sugar. **2** this used as a topping for pies or cakes, browned on top but still soft inside. **3** a round of this mixture, baked until crisp, usu. decorated or filled with whipped cream etc. [French, of unknown origin]

me·rino /məˈriːnoʊ/ *noun* (*pl.* **-rinos**) **1** (in full **merino sheep**) a variety of sheep with long fine wool. **2** a soft woollen or wool-and-cotton material like cashmere, originally of merino wool. **3** a fine woollen yarn. [Spanish *merino*, probably from Arabic *Marīnī* member of the Banū Marīn, a Berber people and former dynasty of Morocco, from whose territory sheep were imported to Spain]

meri·stem /ˈmerɪˌstem/ *noun* a plant tissue consisting of actively dividing cells forming new tissue. □ **meri·stem·at·ic** /-stəˈmatɪk/ *adjective* [Greek *meristos* divisible, from *merizō* divide, from *meros* part, after *xylem*]

merit ● *noun* **1** the quality of being entitled to reward or gratitude. **2** excellence, worth. **3** (usu. in *pl.*) **a** a thing that entitles one to reward or gratitude. **b** claim or title to commendation or esteem. **4** esp. *Law* intrinsic rights and wrongs or excellences and defects (*the merits of a case*). **5** *Theol.* **a** good deeds viewed as entitling a person to a future reward from God. **b** *Buddhism* the quality of actions in one of a person's states of existence which helps determine a better succeeding state. ● *transitive verb* (**merit·ed**, **merit·ing**) deserve or be worthy of (reward, punishment, consideration, etc.). □ **on its merits** with regard only to its intrinsic worth. [Latin *meritum* price, value, = past participle of *merēri* earn, deserve]

merit increase *noun* an increase in pay for personal ability or achievement.

merit·oc·racy /ˌmerɪˈtɒkrəsi/ *noun* (*pl.* **-cies**) **1** government or the holding of power by persons selected competitively according to merit. **2** a group of persons selected in this way. **3** a society governed by meritocracy. □ **merit·o·crat·ic** /-təˈkratɪk/ *adjective*

merit·or·ious /ˌmerɪˈtɔːriəs/ *adjective* **1** (of a person or act) having merit; deserving reward, praise, or gratitude. **2** deserving commendation for thoroughness etc.

merit pay *noun* pay awarded as a merit increase.

merit system *noun* the system of hiring and promoting, esp. in the public service, according to the competence of the candidates rather than because of political affiliations, personal connections, etc.

merle /mɜrl/ ● *noun* a dog, esp. a collie, having a light-coloured coat with dark markings, esp. blue-grey fur speckled or streaked with black. ● *adjective* (of a dog) having such a colour pattern. [from *merled, mirled* variants of *marled*, perhaps from Old French *merelé* from *merelle*, 'counter']

Mer·lin /ˈmɜrlɪn/ (in Arthurian legend) a magician who guides the destinies of Arthur and his predecessor Uther.

mer·lin /ˈmɜrlɪn/ *noun* a small European or N American falcon, *Falco columbarius*, that hunts small birds. [Anglo-French *merilun* from Old French *esmerillon* augmentative of *esmeril* from Frankish]

mer·lon /ˈmɜrlɒn/ *noun* the solid part of an embattled parapet between two embrasures. [French from Italian *merlone* from *merlo* battlement]

Mer·lot /mɜrˈloʊ, mer-/ *noun* **1** a variety of black grape used in winemaking. **2** the vine on which this grape grows. **3** a red wine made from Merlot grapes. [French from *merle* blackbird, with allusion to the colour of the grapes]

mer·maid *noun* an imaginary half-human sea creature, with the head and trunk of a woman and the tail of a fish. [Middle English from MERE² in obsolete sense 'sea' + MAID]

mermaid's purse *noun* the horny egg case of a skate, ray, or shark.

Mer·man /ˈmɜrmən/ **Ethel** (born Ethel Agnes Zimmerman) (1909–84), US singer and actress. Known for her stridently powerful voice, she appeared in a number of Broadway musicals, including *Anything Goes* (1934), *Annie Get Your Gun* (1946), and *Gypsy* (1959).

mer·man /ˈmɜrmən/ *noun* (*pl.* **-men**) an imaginary half-human sea creature, with the head and trunk of a man and the tail of a fish.

mero- /ˈmeroʊ/ *combining form* partly, partial. [Greek *meros* part]

Meroe /ˈmeroʊi/ an ancient city on the Nile, in present-day Sudan northeast of Khartoum. Founded in *c.*750 BC, it was the capital of the ancient kingdom of Cush from *c.*590 BC until it fell to the invading Aksumites in the early 4th c. AD.

-merous /mɜrəs/ *combining form* esp. *Bot.* having esp. a specified number of parts (*dimerous; 5-merous*). [Greek (as MERO-)]

Mero·vin·gian /ˌmeroʊˈvɪndʒiən/ ● *adjective* of or relating to the Frankish dynasty founded by Clovis and reigning in Gaul and Germany *c.*500–750. ● *noun* a member of this dynasty. [French *mérovingien* from medieval Latin *Merovingi* from Latin *Meroveus* name of the reputed founder]

mer·ri·ment *noun* **1** exuberant enjoyment; being merry. **2** mirth, fun.

Mer·ritt /ˈmerɪt/ a city in south central BC, situated at the junction of the Nicola and Coldwater rivers, south of Kamloops; pop. (2001) 7,088. [W. H. *Merritt*, promoter of the Nicola, Kamloops, and Similkameen Railway, the company that laid out the city in 1906]

merry *adjective* (**mer·ri·er, mer·ri·est**) **1 a** joyous. **b** full of laughter or gaiety. **2** *Brit. informal* slightly drunk. □ **make merry** be festive; enjoy oneself. **play merry hell with** *see* HELL. □ **mer·ri·ly** *adverb* [Old English *myrige* from Germanic]

merry an·drew *noun archaic* a comic entertainer; a clown or buffoon.

merry-go-round /ˈmerɪɡoʊˌraʊnd/ *noun* **1** a revolving platform with wooden horses, cars, etc. for people to ride on at a fair etc.; a carousel. **2** a cycle of bustling activities.

merry·making *noun* festivity, fun. □ **merry·maker** *noun*

merry widow *noun* a waist-length, usu. lace-trimmed corselette, with attached stocking garters.

Mer·sey River /ˈmɜrzi/ a river in NW England, which rises in the Peak District and flows 112 km (70 miles) to the Irish Sea near Liverpool.

Mer·sey·side /ˈmɜrziˌsaɪd/ a former metropolitan county of NW England, encompassing the conurbation of Liverpool.

Mer·sin /mɜrˈsiːn/ an industrial port in S Turkey, on the Mediterranean southwest of Adana; pop. (est. 2002) 559,400.

Mer·ton /ˈmɜrtən/ **Thom·as (Fev·erel)** (1915–68), US writer and Trappist monk. He is known for his works on spiritual and social issues, which include *The Seven Storey Mountain* (1948) and *No Man is an Island* (1955).

M.E.S. *abbreviation* Master of Environmental Studies.

mesa /'meɪsə/ *noun N Amer.* an isolated flat-topped hill with steep sides, found in landscapes with horizontal strata. [Spanish, lit. 'table', from Latin *mensa*]

Mesa a city in south central Arizona, part of the conurbation of Phoenix; pop. (est. 2000) 396,375.

més·alli·ance /meɪ'zali,ɑ̃s, meɪzali'ɑ̃s/ *noun* **1** a marriage with a person thought to be of a lower social position. **2** an inappropriate association. [French (as MIS-², ALLIANCE)]

mes·cal /'meskal/ *noun* **1 a** any of several plants of the genus *Agave* found in Mexico and the southwestern US, used as sources of fermented liquor, food, or fibre, esp. the American aloe, *Agave americana*. **b** a strong liquor distilled from this (compare TEQUILA). **2 a** a peyote cactus. **b** a preparation of this used as a hallucinogenic drug (compare MESCALINE, PEYOTE). [Spanish *mezcal* from Nahuatl *mexcalli*]

mescal button *noun* the disc-shaped dried top from the peyote cactus, eaten or chewed for its hallucinogenic effects.

mes·ca·line /'meskə,li:n/ *noun* (also **mes·ca·lin** /-lɪn/) a hallucinogenic alkaloid present in mescal buttons.

mes·clun /'mesklən/ *noun* a kind of green salad made from a selection of lettuces, typically with other edible leaves and flowers. [Provençal 'mixture,' from *mesclar* 'mix,' from Old French *mes(c)ler*, from medieval Latin *misculare* 'to mix thoroughly' from Latin *miscēre*]

Mes·dames *pl. of* MADAME.

Mes·demoi·selles *pl. of* MADEMOISELLE.

mes·em·bry·an·the·mum /mɪ,zembrɪ'anθɪməm/ *noun* any of various succulent plants esp. of the genus *Mesembryanthemum* of S Africa, having daisy-like flowers in a wide range of bright colours that fully open in sunlight. [modern Latin from Greek *mesembria* noon + *anthemon* flower]

mes·en·ceph·alon /,mesɛn'sefə,lɒn/ *noun* the part of the brain developing from the middle of the primitive or embryonic brain. *Also called* MIDBRAIN. [Greek *mesos* middle + *encephalon* brain: see ENCEPHALIC]

mesen·tery /'mesən,teri/ *noun* (*pl.* **-ies**) a double layer of peritoneum attaching the stomach, small intestine, pancreas, spleen, and other abdominal organs to the posterior wall of the abdomen.
□ **mes·en·ter·ic** /-'terɪk/ *adjective* **mes·en·ter·itis** /-'raɪtɪs/ *noun* [medieval Latin *mesenterium* from Greek *mesenterion* (as MESO-, *enteron* intestine)]

mesh ● *noun* **1** an interlaced fabric or structure; netting. **2 a** each of the open spaces or interstices between the strands of a net or sieve etc. **b** (in *pl.*) the strands between the interstices of a net etc. **3** a network. **4 a** the coarseness or spacing of the strands of a grid, net, or screen. **b** (with preceding numeral) a measure of this (representing the number of openings per unit length), or of the size of particles which will just pass through such a grid etc. **5 a** *Math.* a set of discrete ordered points, which can be chosen arbitrarily, at which a numerical function or mathematical model is evaluated. **b** (in computer graphics and computer-aided design) a set of finite elements used to represent a geometric object for modelling or analysis. **6** (in *pl.*) *Physiol.* an interlaced structure. ● *verb* **1 a** *intransitive* (often foll. by *with*, *together*) fit in, be harmonious, combine. **b** *transitive* bring together, harmonize, reconcile. **2** *intransitive* (often foll. by *with*) (of the teeth of a wheel) be engaged (with another piece of machinery). **3** *transitive* entangle, catch in or as in a net. □ **in mesh** (of the teeth of wheels) engaged.
□ **meshed** *adjective* **mesh·ing** *noun & adjective* [Middle Dutch *maesche* from Germanic]

Me·shach /'mi:ʃak/ *see* SHADRACH.

Me·shed *see* MASHHAD.

me·shuga /mə'ʃʌgə/ *adjective* (also **me·shug·ga**, **me·shug·gah**) *slang* mad, crazy; stupid. [Yiddish *meshuge* from Hebrew *mĕshuggā'*]

me·sial /'mi:zɪəl/ *adjective Anat.* of, in, or directed towards the middle line of a body. □ **me·sial·ly** *adverb* [irreg. from Greek *mesos* middle]

mesic /'mezɪk, 'mi:zɪk/ *adjective* (of a habitat) containing a moderate amount of moisture. [Greek *mesos* 'middle' + -IC]

Mes·mer /'mezmər/ **Franz Anton** (1734–1815), Austrian physician. He had a successful practice in Vienna, where he used a number of novel treatments, and is chiefly remembered for introducing hypnotism, formerly known as *mesmerism*, as a therapeutic technique.

mes·mer·ism /'mezmə,rɪzəm/ *noun* **1** the process or practice of inducing a hypnotic state by the influence of an operator over the will and nervous system of the patient. **2** the state so induced.

□ **mes·mer·ic** /mez'merɪk/ *adjective* **mes·mer·ic·ally** *adverb* **mes·mer·ist** *noun*

mes·mer·ize /'mezmə,raɪz/ *transitive verb* (also esp. *Brit.* **-ise**) **1** fascinate, hold spellbound. **2** *Psych.* hypnotize; exercise mesmerism on.

mesne /mi:n/ *adjective Law* intermediate. [var. of Anglo-French *meen*, MEAN³: compare DEMESNE]

mesne lord *noun Brit. hist.* a lord holding an estate from a superior feudal lord.

meso- /'mezo:, 'mi:z-/ *combining form* middle, intermediate. [Greek *mesos* middle]

Meso-America the central region of America, from central Mexico to Nicaragua, esp. as a region of ancient civilizations and Aboriginal cultures before the arrival of the Spanish settlers.
□ **Meso-Americ·an** *adjective & noun*

meso·blast /'mezo:,blast/ *noun* = MESODERM.

meso·derm /'mezo:,dɜrm/ *noun Biol.* the middle germ layer of an embryo. □ **meso·derm·al** *adjective* [MESO- + Greek *derma* skin]

meso·lith·ic /,mezo:'lɪθɪk/ *Archaeology* (also **Mesolithic**) ● *adjective* of or concerning the part of the Stone Age between the paleolithic and neolithic periods. ● *noun* the mesolithic period. [MESO- + Greek *lithos* stone]

meso·morph /'mezo:,mɔrf/ *noun* a person with a compact and muscular build of body (compare ECTOMORPH, ENDOMORPH 1).
□ **meso·morph·ic** *adjective* [MESO- + Greek *morphē* form]

meson /'mezɒn, 'mi:zɒn/ *noun Physics* any of a class of elementary particles believed to participate in the forces that hold nucleons together in the atomic nucleus. □ **meson·ic** /mɪ'zɒnɪk/ *adjective* [earlier *mesotron*: compare MESO-, -ON]

meso·pause /'mezo:pɒz, 'mi:z-/ *noun* the boundary in the atmosphere between the mesosphere and the thermosphere, at which the temperature stops decreasing with increasing height and begins to increase.

meso·phyll /'mezo:fɪl/ *noun* the inner tissue of a leaf. [MESO- + Greek *phullon* leaf]

meso·phyte /'mezo:,faɪt/ *noun* a plant needing only a moderate amount of water.

Meso·po·tamia /,mesəpə'teɪmɪə/ an ancient region of SW Asia in present-day Iraq, lying between the Tigris and Euphrates rivers. Its alluvial plains were the site of the civilizations of Akkad, Sumer, Babylonia, and Assyria. □ **Meso·po·ta·mian** *adjective & noun* [Greek, from *mesos* middle + *potamos* river]

meso·sphere /'mezo:,sfɪr/ *noun* the region of the atmosphere extending from the top of the stratosphere to an altitude of about 50 miles. □ **meso·spher·ic** *adjective*

meso·theli·oma /,mezo:θi:li:'o:mə/ *noun* a tumour of the lungs, or of the lining of the pleural or abdominal cavities, associated esp. with exposure to asbestos. [MESO- + (EPI)THELIUM + -OMA]

Meso·zoic /,mezo:'zo:ɪk, ,mes-/ *Geol.* ● *adjective* of or relating to the geological era between the Paleozoic and Cenozoic, comprising the Triassic, Jurassic, and Cretaceous periods. The Mesozoic lasted from about 248 to 65 million years BP, and was a time of abundant vegetation. ● *noun* this geological era. [MESO- + Greek *zōē* life]

mes·quite /'meskiːt/ *noun* **1** any N American leguminous tree of the genus *Prosopis*, esp. *P. juliflora*. **2** the wood of this used for grilling food in a barbecue etc. [Latin American Spanish *mezquite* from Nahuatl *mizquitl*]

mess ● *noun* **1 a** a dirty, untidy state of things (*the room is a mess*; *the renovations made such a mess*). **b** a bungled state of affairs. **2** a state of confusion, embarrassment, or trouble (*the country's in a mess*; *my life's a mess*). **3** something causing a mess, e.g. spilled liquid etc. **4 a** a person whose life or affairs are confused. **b** a dirty or unkempt person. **5** excrement, esp. of a domestic animal or child. **6 a** a company of persons who take meals together, esp. in the armed forces. **b** a place where such meals or recreation take place communally. **c** a meal taken there. **7** esp. *US* **a** a prepared dish (of a specified kind of food). **b** a quantity of food sufficient to make a dish. **8** *N Amer. informal* a large quantity of something (*approached the position with a whole mess of preconceptions*). **9** *archaic* a portion of liquid or pulpy food. ● *verb* **1** *intransitive informal* (foll. by *with*) interfere or get involved with. **2** *intransitive* take one's meals, esp. as the member of a mess. **3** *intransitive & transitive informal* (esp. of an animal or infant) defecate or soil by defecating. □ **make a mess of** bungle (an undertaking). **mess around** (or **about**) **1** act desultorily; putter. **2** *informal* make things awkward for; cause arbitrary inconvenience to (a person). **3** esp. *N Amer. informal* **a** engage in sexual activity. **b** engage in adulterous sexual activity. **mess up 1** make a mess of; dirty. **2** muddle; make a mess of a situation. **3** make unhappy, confused, or dysfunctional (*the world is full of messed-up kids*). **4** ruin or damage. [Old French *mes* 'portion of food', from Late Latin *missus* 'course at dinner', past participle of *mittere* 'send']

mes·sage ● *noun* **1** a usu. brief oral or written communication. **2** an inspired or significant communication from a prophet, writer, or preacher. **3** the central import of something; an implicit esp. polemical meaning in an artistic work etc. **4** *N Amer.* a television or radio advertisement. ● *transitive verb* **1** send a message to (a person) (*message me tomorrow*). **2** transmit (a plan etc.) by email etc. (*messaged the examples*). □ **get the message** *informal* understand what is meant. **send a message** make a significant statement, esp. implicitly or by one's actions (*the Supreme Court's decision sends a clear message to the government on gay rights*). □ **mes·sa·ging** *noun* [Old French, ultimately from Latin *mittere miss-* send]

message board *noun N Amer.* **1** = BULLETIN BOARD 1. **2** a computerized bulletin board on the Internet for the posting of electronic messages. **3** an electronic board in an arena, train station, etc., which displays instructions to fans, information to travellers, etc.

Mes·sei·gneurs *pl. of* MONSEIGNEUR.

mes·sen·ger *noun* **1** a person who carries a message. **2** a person employed to carry messages. **3** *Biol.* a molecule or substance that carries (esp. genetic) information. □ **shoot** (or **kill** etc.) **the messenger** treat the bearer of bad news as if they were to blame for it. [Old French *messager* (as MESSAGE): *-n-* as in *harbinger, passenger*, etc.]

messenger RNA *noun* the form of RNA in which genetic information transcribed from DNA as a sequence of bases is transferred to a ribosome. Abbr.: **mRNA**.

Mes·ser, Don·ald Charles Fred·erick ('Don') (1909–73), Canadian musician. In 1939 he formed the group 'The Islanders', which appeared on CBC television from 1959–69. With over 30 LPs, his radio and television shows, and his numerous concerts, he introduced traditional fiddle and dance music to many Canadians.

mess hall *noun* a military dining area.

Mes·siaen /mesˈjã/ **Oli·vier (Eu·gène Pros·per Charles)** (1908–1992), French composer and organist. His music is rhythmically complex and harmonically unusual, influenced by Hindu rhythms, birdsong, Impressionism in the style of Debussy, and Catholicism.

Mes·siah /məˈsaiə/ *noun* **1 a** the promised deliverer of the Jews, as prophesied in the Hebrew Bible. **b** (usu. prec. by *the*) (in Christian theology) Jesus Christ regarded as fulfilling this prophecy, and as saviour of humankind. **2** (usu. **messiah**) a liberator or would-be liberator of an oppressed people, group, country, etc.
□ **Messiah·ship** *noun* [ultimately from Hebrew *māšīaḥ* anointed]

mes·si·anic /ˌmesiˈanɪk/ *adjective* (also **Messianic**) **1** of, pertaining to, or characteristic of the Messiah or a messiah. **2** inspired by hope or belief in the Messiah or a messiah. **3** fervent or passionate.
□ **mes·si·an·ism** /məˈsaiəˌnizəm/ *noun* [French *messianique* (as MESSIAH) after *rabbinique* rabbinical]

Mes·sieurs *pl. of* MONSIEUR.

Mes·sina /meˈsiːnə/ a city in NE Sicily; pop. (2001) 236,621.

Mes·sina, Strait of a channel separating the island of Sicily from the 'toe' of Italy. It forms a link between the Tyrrhenian and Ionian seas. The strait, which is 32 km (20 miles) in length, is noted for the strength of its currents. It is traditionally identified as the location of the legendary sea monster Scylla and the whirlpool Charybdis.

mess jacket *noun* a short close-fitting coat worn by members of the armed forces, esp. in the mess.

mess kit *noun* **1** a soldier's cooking and eating utensils. **2** *Cdn & Brit.* a dress military uniform worn at formal meals, balls, etc. in the mess.

mess·mate *noun* a person with whom one regularly takes meals, esp. in the armed forces.

mess of pottage *noun* a material comfort etc. for which something higher is sacrificed. [with reference to the story of how Jacob tricks his brother Esau into exchanging his birthright for a helping of food (Gen. 25:29–34)]

Messrs. /ˈmesərz/ *pl. of* MR. [abbreviation of MESSIEURS]

mes·suage /ˈmeswɪdʒ/ *noun Law* a dwelling with outbuildings and land assigned to its use. [Anglo-French: perhaps an alternative form of *mesnage* dwelling]

mess-up *noun* a mess, a muddle; a confused situation.

messy *adjective* (**mess·i·er, mess·i·est**) **1** untidy or dirty. **2** causing or accompanied by a mess. **3** difficult to deal with; full of awkward complications (*a messy divorce*). □ **mess·i·ly** *adverb* **mess·i·ness** *noun*

mes·tiza /meˈstiːzə/ *noun* (*pl.* **-tizas**) a woman who is a mestizo.

mes·tizo /meˈstiːzo/ *noun* (*pl.* **-tizos**) a person of mixed ancestry, esp. (in Latin and South America), the offspring of a European and an American Indian. [Spanish, ultimately from Latin *mixtus*, past participle of *miscēre* mix]

met[1] *past and past participle of* MEET[1].

met[2] *adjective informal* **1** meteorological. **2** metropolitan. **3** (**the Met**) **a** the Metropolitan Opera House in New York. **b** *Brit.* the Metropolitan Police in London, England. [abbreviation]

meta- /ˈmetə/ *combining form* (usu. **met-** before a vowel or *h*) **1** denoting change of position or condition (*metabolism*). **2** denoting position: **a** behind. **b** after or beyond (*metaphysics*; *metacarpus*). **c** of a higher or second-order kind (*metalanguage*). **3** *Chem.* **a** relating to two carbon atoms separated by one other in a benzene ring. **b** relating to a compound formed by dehydration (*metaphosphate*). [Greek *meta-*, *met-*, *meth-* from *meta* with, after]

metabolic rate *noun* the rate at which energy is used up by an organism or tissue, usu. measured in terms of oxygen consumption.

metab·ol·ism /məˈtabəˌlizəm/ *noun* all the chemical processes that occur within a living organism, resulting in energy production (**destructive metabolism**) and growth (**constructive metabolism**). □ **meta·bol·ic** /ˌmetəˈbɒlɪk/ *adjective* **meta·bol·ic·ally** *adverb* [Greek *metabolē* change (as META-, *bolē* from *ballō* throw)]

metab·ol·ite /məˈtabəˌlait/ *noun Physiol.* a substance formed in or necessary for metabolism.

metab·ol·ize /məˈtabəˌlaiz/ *transitive & intransitive verb* (also esp. *Brit.* **-ise**) process or be processed by metabolism. □ **metab·ol·iz·able** *adjective*

meta·car·pus /ˌmetəˈkɑrpəs/ *noun* (*pl.* **meta·carpi** /-pai/) **1** the set of five bones of the hand that connects the wrist to the fingers. **2** this part of the hand. □ **meta·car·pal** *adjective* [as META-, CARPUS]

meta·centre *noun* (also esp. *US* **meta·center**) the point of intersection between a line (vertical in equilibrium) through the centre of gravity of a floating body and a vertical line through the centre of pressure after a slight angular displacement, which must be above the centre of gravity to ensure stability. □ **meta·cen·tric** *adjective*

Meta·com·et see PHILIP 1.

meta·data *noun* a set of data that describes and gives information about other data.

meta·fic·tion *noun* a work of fiction in which the author self-consciously alludes to the artificiality or literariness of a work by parodying or departing from novelistic conventions (esp. naturalism) and traditional narrative techniques. □ **meta·fic·tion·al** *adjective* **meta·fic·tion·ist** *noun*

meta·gen·esis /ˌmetəˈdʒenəsɪs/ *noun* the alternation of generations between sexual and asexual reproduction. □ **meta·gen·etic** *adjective*

Meta Incognita Peninsula /ˈmetə ˌɪnkɒɡˈniːtə/ a large peninsula at the southern end of Baffin Island. It is separated from the Ungava Peninsula of Quebec by Hudson Strait. [Latin, lit. 'limits unknown', with reference to a 16th-c. royal description of Martin Frobisher's new-found lands]

meta key *noun* a key on some computer keyboards which activates a particular function when held down simultaneously with another key.

metal ● *noun* **1 a** any of a class of substances (including many chemical elements) which are in general lustrous, malleable, fusible, ductile solids and good conductors of heat and electricity, e.g. gold, silver, iron, brass, steel. **b** a material of this kind. **2** material used for making glass, in a molten state. **3** = HEAVY METAL 1. ● *adjective* made of metal. ● *transitive verb* (**met·alled, metal·ling; met·aled, metal·ing**) provide or fit with metal. [Old French *metal* or Latin *metallum* from Greek *metallon* mine]

meta·lan·guage *noun* **1** a language used for the description or analysis of another language. **2** a system of propositions about propositions.

met·alde·hyde /məˈtaldəˌhaid/ *noun Chem.* a solid that is a low polymer of acetaldehyde and is used to kill slugs and snails and as a fuel for cooking and heating. [from META- + ALDEHYDE]

metal detector *noun* an electronic device giving a signal when it locates metal.

metal fatigue *noun* fatigue (*see* FATIGUE *noun* 2) in metal.

metal·head *noun slang* a fan of heavy metal music.

meta·lin·guis·tics *noun* the branch of linguistics that deals with metalanguages. □ **meta·lin·guis·tic** *adjective*

me·tal·lic ● *adjective* **1** of, consisting of, or characteristic of metal or metals. **2** sounding sharp and ringing, like struck metal. **3** having the sheen or lustre of metals. ● *noun* (usu. in *pl.*) **1** an article or substance made of or containing metal, esp. a fabric. **2** a paint or colour having the sheen or lustre of metal. □ **me·tal·lic·al·ly** *adverb* **metal·lic·ity** /mɛtəˈlɪsɪti/ *noun* [Latin *metallicus* from Greek *metallikos* (as METAL)]

metallic thread *noun* thread or yarn made from metal or a synthetic material resembling metal.

metal·lize /ˈmɛtəˌlaɪz/ *transitive verb* (also esp. *Brit.* **-lise**; *US* **metal·ize**) **1** render metallic. **2** coat with a thin layer of metal. □ **metal·liz·a·tion** *noun*

metallo- /məˈtæloː/ *combining form* metal.

metal·log·ra·phy /ˌmɛtəˈlɒɡrəfi/ *noun* the descriptive science of the structure and properties of metals. □ **me·tal·lo·graph·ic** *adjective* **me·tal·lo·graph·ic·al·ly** *adverb*

metal·loid /ˈmɛtəˌlɔɪd/ ● *adjective* having the form or appearance of a metal. ● *noun* any element intermediate in properties between metals and non-metals, e.g. boron, silicon, and germanium.

metal·lurgy /ˈmɛtəˌlɜrdʒi, məˈtælɜrdʒi/ *noun* the science concerned with the production, purification, and properties of metals and their application. □ **metal·lur·gic** /mɛtəˈlɜrdʒɪk/ *adjective* **metal·lur·gic·al** *adjective* **metal·lur·gic·al·ly** *adverb* **metal·lur·gist** *noun* [Greek *metallon* metal + *-ourgia* working]

metal·ware *noun* utensils or other articles made of metal.

metal wood *noun* *Golf* a driver made out of metal.

metal·work *noun* **1** the art of working in metal. **2** metal objects collectively. □ **metal·work·er** *noun* **metal·work·ing** *noun & attributive adjective*

meta·mere /ˈmɛtəˌmɪr/ *noun* *Zool.* each of several similar body segments containing the same internal structures e.g. in an earthworm. [META- + Greek *meros* part]

meta·mer·ic /ˌmɛtəˈmɛrɪk/ *adjective* **1** *Chem.* having the same proportional composition and molecular weight, but different functional groups and chemical properties. **2** *Zool.* of or relating to metameres. □ **meta·mer** /ˈmɛtəmər/ *noun* **meta·mer·ism** /məˈtæməˌrɪzəm/ *noun*

meta·morph·ic /ˌmɛtəˈmɔrfɪk/ *adjective* **1** of or marked by metamorphosis. **2** *Geol.* (of rock) that has undergone transformation by natural agencies such as heat and pressure. □ **meta·morph·ism** *noun* [META- + Greek *morphē* form]

meta·morph·ose /ˌmɛtəˈmɔrfoːz/ *verb* **1** *transitive* change in form. **2** *transitive* (foll. by *to*, *into*) **a** turn (into a new form). **b** change the nature of. **3** *intransitive* undergo metamorphosis.

meta·morph·o·sis /ˌmɛtəˈmɔrfəsɪs, ˌmɛtəmərˈfoːsɪs/ *noun* (*pl.* **meta·morph·o·ses** /-ˌsiːz/) **1** a change of form (by natural or supernatural means). **2** a changed form. **3** a change of character, conditions, etc. **4** *Zool.* the transformation between an immature form and an adult form, e.g. from a pupa to an insect, or from a tadpole to a frog. [Latin from Greek *metamorphōsis* from *metamorphoō* transform (as META-, *morphoō* from *morphē* form)]

meta·phase /ˈmɛtəˌfeɪz/ *noun* *Biol.* the stage of meiotic or mitotic cell division when the chromosomes become attached to the spindle fibres.

meta·phor /ˈmɛtəfər/ *noun* **1 a** the application of a name or descriptive term or phrase to an object or action to which it is imaginatively but not literally applicable, e.g. *a glaring error*. **b** an instance of this. **2** (often foll. by *of* or *for*) a symbol of a usu. abstract thing (*the lark was a metaphor for release*). □ **meta·phor·ic** /-ˈfɔrɪk/ *adjective* **meta·phor·ic·al** *adjective* **meta·phor·ic·al·ly** *adverb* [Greek *metaphora*, from *metapherō* 'transfer']

meta·phrase /ˈmɛtəˌfreɪz/ ● *noun* a literal translation. ● *transitive verb* put into other words. □ **meta·phras·tic** /-ˈfrastɪk/ *adjective* [Greek *metaphrasis* from *metaphrazō* 'word differently']

meta·phys·ic /ˌmɛtəˈfɪzɪk/ *noun* a system of metaphysics.

meta·phys·ic·al /ˌmɛtəˈfɪzɪkəl/ ● *adjective* **1** of or relating to metaphysics. **2** based on abstract general reasoning. **3** excessively subtle or theoretical. **4** incorporeal; supernatural. **5** (of certain 17th-c. English poets or their poetry) exhibiting subtlety of thought and complex imagery. ● *noun* (**the Metaphysicals**) the metaphysical poets. □ **meta·phys·ic·al·ly** *adverb*

meta·phys·ics *plural noun* (usu. treated as *sing.*) **1** the branch of philosophy that deals with the first principles of things, including such concepts as being, knowing, substance, essence, cause, identity, time, and space. **2** the philosophy of mind. **3** *informal* abstract or subtle talk; mere theory. □ **meta·physi·cian** *noun* [medieval Latin

metaphysica, ultimately from Greek *ta meta ta phusika* the things after the Physics, from the sequence of Aristotle's works]

meta·plasia /ˌmɛtəˈpleɪʒə, -ziə/ *noun* *Physiol.* an abnormal change in the nature of a tissue. □ **meta·plas·tic** /-ˈplastɪk/ *adjective* [modern Latin from German *Metaplase* from Greek *metaplasis* (as META-, *plasis* from *plassō* to mould)]

meta·psych·ol·ogy *noun* the study of the nature and functions of the mind beyond what can be studied experimentally. □ **meta·psych·o·logic·al** *adjective*

meta·stable *adjective* **1** (of a state of equilibrium) stable only under small disturbances. **2** (of a substance etc.) technically unstable but so long-lived as to be stable for practical purposes. □ **meta·stabil·ity** *noun*

me·tas·ta·sis /məˈtastəsɪs/ *noun* (*pl.* **me·tas·ta·ses** /-ˌsiːz/) *Physiol.* **1** the transfer of a disease, etc. from one part of the body to another; esp. the development of secondary tumours at a distance from a primary site of cancer. **2** a secondary tumour. □ **me·tas·ta·size** *intransitive verb* (also esp. *Brit.* **-sise**). **meta·stat·ic** /ˌmɛtəˈstatɪk/ *adjective* [Late Latin from Greek from *methistēmi* change]

meta·tar·sus /ˌmɛtəˈtɑrsəs/ *noun* (*pl.* **meta·tarsi** /-saɪ/) **1** the part of the human foot between the ankle and the toes. **2** the set of bones in this. **3** the corresponding bones in other vertebrates. □ **meta·tar·sal** *adjective*

me·tath·esis /məˈtaθəsɪs/ *noun* (*pl.* **me·tath·eses** /-ˌsiːz/) **1** *Grammar* the transposition of sounds or letters in a word. **2** *Chem.* the interchange of atoms or groups of atoms between two molecules; double decomposition. **3** an instance of either of these. □ **meta·thet·ic** /ˌmɛtəˈθɛtɪk/ *adjective* **meta·thet·ic·al** /ˌmɛtəˈθɛtɪkəl/ *adjective* [Late Latin from Greek *metatithēmi* transpose]

meta·zoan /ˌmɛtəˈzoːən/ ● *noun* any animal of the subkingdom Metazoa, having multicellular and differentiated tissues and comprising all animals except protozoa and sponges. ● *adjective* of or relating to the Metazoans. [*Metazoa* from Greek META- + *zōia* pl. of *zōion* animal]

Met·calf, John (b.1938), English-born Canadian writer. At his best in his short stories, he continually pokes fun at the Canadian literary establishment.

Met·calfe, Charles The·oph·ilus, 1st Baron (1785–1846), Governor General of British North America in 1843–45. Inflexible in opposition to Responsible Government, he moved the capital to Montreal and negotiated pardons for the exiled rebels of 1837–38 before returning to England in 1845.

Metch·ni·koff /ˈmɛtʃˌnɪkɒf/ **Élie** (1845–1916), Russian zoologist and microbiologist, who shared a Nobel Prize in 1908 with Paul Ehrlich for their discovery of phagocytosis.

mete[1] /miːt/ *transitive verb* **1** (usu. foll. by *out*) apportion or allot (a punishment or reward). **2** *archaic* measure. [Old English *metan* from Germanic, related to MEET[1]]

mete[2] *noun* esp. *hist.* a boundary or limit (esp. in phr. **metes and bounds**). [Old French from Latin *meta* boundary, goal]

metem·psych·o·sis /ˌmɛtəmsaɪˈkoːsɪs/ *noun* (*pl.* **-psych·o·ses** /-ˌsiːz/) **1** the supposed transmigration of the soul of a human being or animal at death into a new body of the same or a different species. **2** an instance of this. [Greek *metempsukhōsis* (as META-, EN-[2], *psukhē* soul)]

me·teor *noun* a small body of matter from outer space that becomes incandescent as a result of friction with the earth's atmosphere and is visible as a streak of light. [modern Latin *meteorum* from Greek *meteōron* neuter of *meteōros* lofty, (as META-, *aeirō* raise)]

me·teor·ic /ˌmiːtiˈɒrɪk/ *adjective* **1** of meteors or meteorites. **2** rapid like a meteor; dazzling, transient (*meteoric rise to fame*). **3** of or relating to the atmosphere. □ **me·teor·ical·ly** *adverb*

me·teor·ite *noun* a rock or metal fragment formed from a meteor of sufficient size to reach the earth's surface without burning up completely in the atmosphere. □ **me·teor·it·ic** *adjective*

me·teor·o·graph /ˈmiːtiərəˌɡraf, ˌmiːtiˈɒrəˌɡraf/ *noun* an apparatus that records several meteorological phenomena at the same time.

me·teor·oid *noun* any small body moving in the solar system that becomes visible as it passes through the earth's atmosphere as a meteor. □ **me·teor·oid·al** *adjective*

me·teor·ol·ogy /ˌmiːtiəˈrɒlədʒi/ *noun* **1** the study of the processes and phenomena of the atmosphere, esp. as a means of forecasting the weather. **2** the atmospheric character of a region. □ **me·teor·o·logic·al** /-rəˈlɒdʒɪkəl/ *adjective* **me·teor·o·logic·al·ly** *adverb* **me·teor·ol·o·gist** *noun* [Greek *meteōrologia* (as METEOR)]

Consonants: b *but* d *dog* f *few* g *get* h *her* j *yes* k *cat* l *leg* m *man* n *no* p *pen* r *red* s *sit*

meteor shower *noun* a group of meteors appearing to come from one point in the sky, esp. around a particular date each year.

me·ter¹ ● *noun* **1** a thing that measures, esp. an instrument for recording a quantity of gas, electricity, etc. supplied, present, or needed, or a device in a taxi measuring the time and distance travelled and the fare payable. **2** = PARKING METER. ● *verb* **1** *transitive & intransitive* measure by means of a meter. **2** *transitive* provide with a meter or meters. [Middle English from METE¹ + -ER¹]

me·ter² *var. of* METRE¹.

me·ter³ *var. of* METRE².

-meter /mɪtɜr, miːtɜr/ *combining form* **1** forming nouns denoting measuring instruments (*barometer*). **2** *Prosody* forming nouns denoting lines of poetry with a specified number of measures (*pentameter*).

meth *noun slang* methamphetamine. [abbreviation]

meth·adone /ˈmeθəˌdoːn/ *noun* a potent narcotic analgesic drug used to relieve severe pain, and as a substitute for morphine or heroin. [6-dimethylamino-4,4-diphenyl-3-heptanone]

meth·am·pheta·mine /ˌmeθamˈfetəmiːn, -mɪn/ *noun* an amphetamine derivative with quicker and longer action, used as a stimulant. [METHYL + AMPHETAMINE]

meth·ane /ˈmeθein/ *noun* a colourless odourless inflammable gaseous hydrocarbon, the simplest in the alkane series, and the main constituent of natural gas. *Also called* MARSH GAS. Chem. formula: CH_4. [METHYL + -ANE²]

methanoic acid /ˌmeθəˈnoːɪk/ *noun* = FORMIC ACID. [METHANE + -IC]

meth·an·ol /ˈmeθənɒl/ *noun* a colourless volatile inflammable liquid, used as a solvent (*also called* METHYL ALCOHOL). Chem. formula: CH_3OH. [METHANE + -OL¹]

meth·aqua·lone /meˈθakwəloːn/ *noun* a hypnotic and sedative drug derived from quinazoline. ¶ A proprietary name for this drug is QUAALUDE. [METHYL + -a- + QUININE + AZO- + -ONE]

Methe·drine /ˈmeθədriːn, -drɪn/ *noun proprietary* = METHAMPHETAMINE. [METHYL + BENZEDRINE]

me·thinks *intransitive verb* (*past* **me·thought**) *archaic* or *jocular* it seems to me. [Old English *mē thyncth* from *mē* dative of ME¹ + *thyncth* 3rd sing. of *thyncan* seem, THINK]

me·thio·nine /meˈθaiəˌniːn/ *noun Biochem.* an amino acid which contains sulphur and is an important constituent of proteins. [METHYL + Greek *theion* sulphur]

meth·od *noun* **1** a mode of procedure; a defined or systematic way of doing a thing. **2** orderliness; regular habits. **3** the orderly arrangement of ideas etc. **4** = METHOD ACTING. □ **method in one's madness** sense in what appears to be foolish or strange behaviour. [French *méthode* or Latin *methodus* from Greek *methodos* pursuit of knowledge (as META-, *hodos* way)]

method acting *noun* an acting theory and technique based on the ideas of Konstantin Stanislavsky, in which an actor aspires to complete emotional identification with a part. □ **method-act** *intransitive verb* **method actor** *noun*

mé·thode cham·pe·noise /ˈmeitɒd ʃɑ̃pənˈwɒz/ *noun* **1** the method of introducing a sparkle into wine by allowing the last stage of fermentation to take place in the bottle. **2** a sparkling wine made in this way. [French. = champagne method]

meth·od·ic·al /məˈθɒdɪkəl/ *adjective* (also **meth·od·ic**) characterized by method or order. □ **meth·od·ic·al·ly** *adverb*

Meth·od·ist /ˈmeθədɪst/ ● *noun* a member of any of various branches of a Protestant denomination originating in the 18th-c. evangelistic movement of Charles and John Wesley and George Whitefield. ● *adjective* of or relating to Methodists or Methodism. □ **Meth·od·ism** *noun* [modern Latin *methodista* (as METHOD): sense 1 prob. from following a specified 'method' of devotional study]

Me·tho·dius, St. /məˈθoːdiəs/ the brother of St. Cyril (see CYRIL, ST.).

meth·od·ol·ogy /ˌmeθəˈdɒlədʒi/ *noun* (*pl.* **-gies**) **1** a body of methods used in a particular branch of activity. **2** the branch of knowledge that deals with method and its application in a particular field. □ **meth·odo·logic·al** /-dəˈlɒdʒɪkəl/ *adjective* **meth·odo·logic·al·ly** *adverb* **meth·od·ol·o·gist** *noun*

metho·trex·ate /meθəˈtrekseit/ *noun Pharm.* a cytotoxic orange-brown powder which is a folic acid antagonist used to treat certain cancers. [from *meth-* + elements of unknown origin]

me·thought *past of* METHINKS.

meths /meθs/ *noun esp. Brit. informal* methylated spirits. [abbreviation]

Me·thu·selah¹ /məˈθuːzələ, -ˈθjuːzələ/ *Bible* a patriarch, grandfather of Noah, said to have lived 969 years (Gen. 5:27).

Me·thu·selah² *noun* **1** a very old person or thing. **2** (**methuselah**) a wine bottle of about eight times the standard size. [METHUSELAH¹]

methyl /ˈmeθəl/ *noun Chem.* the monovalent hydrocarbon radical $-CH_3$, present in many organic compounds. □ **methy·lic** /məˈθɪlɪk/ *adjective* [see METHYLENE]

methyl alcohol *noun* = METHANOL.

methyl·ate /ˈmeθəˌleit/ *transitive verb* **1** mix or impregnate with methanol. **2** introduce a methyl group into (a molecule or compound). □ **methyl·a·tion** *noun*

methylated spirits *noun* (also **methylated spirit**) alcohol impregnated with methanol to make it unfit for drinking and exempt from duty.

methyl benzene *noun* = TOLUENE.

methyl·ene /ˈmeθəˌliːn/ *noun* the highly reactive divalent group of atoms CH_2. [French *méthylène* from Greek *methu* wine + *hulē* wood + -ENE]

methyl·phenid·ate /ˌmeθɪlˈfenideit/ *noun* a synthetic drug that stimulates the sympathetic and central nervous systems and is used to improve mental activity in attention deficit disorder and other conditions.

met·ic·al /ˌmetiˈkɒl/ *noun* the basic monetary unit of Mozambique, equal to 100 centavos. [Portuguese *matical*, from Arabic *miṭkāl* Arabian unit of weight, from *ṯakala* weigh]

me·ticu·lous /məˈtɪkjuləs/ *adjective* **1** giving great or excessive attention to details. **2** very careful and precise. □ **me·ticu·lous·ly** *adverb* **me·ticu·lous·ness** *noun* [Latin *meticulosus* from *metus* fear]

mé·tier /ˈmeiˈtjei, ˈmei-/ *noun* **1** one's trade, profession, or department of activity. **2** one's forte. [French, ultimately from Latin *ministerium* service]

Metis /meiˈtiː/ *noun* (*pl.* same) (esp. in Canada) a person of mixed Aboriginal and European descent. [French *métis*, Old French *mestis*, from Romanic: related to MESTIZO]

Me·ton·ic cycle /mɪˈtɒnɪk/ *noun* a period of 19 years (235 lunar months) covering all the changes of the moon's position relative to the sun and the earth. [Greek *Metōn*, Athenian astronomer of the 5th c. BC]

meto·nym /ˈmetənɪm/ *noun* a word used in metonymy. [back-formation from METONYMY, after *synonym*]

me·tony·my /mɪˈtɒnəmi/ *noun* the substitution of the name of an attribute or adjunct for that of the thing meant, e.g. *Crown* for *monarch*, *pigskin* for *football*. □ **meto·nym·ic** /metəˈnɪmɪk/ *adjective* **meto·nym·ic·al** *adjective* **meto·nym·ic·ally** *adverb* [Greek *metōnumia* (as META-, *onoma*, *onuma* 'name')]

me-too *adjective* **1** (of a person or course of action) adopting or acquiescing in the views, policies, etc. of someone else, often those of one's political or other opponents. **2** (of a product) designed to emulate or rival another which has already been commercially successful. **3** (of policies, techniques, or companies) emulating a rival in this way.

met·ope /ˈmetəpi, ˈmetoːp/ *noun Archit.* a square space between triglyphs in a Doric frieze. [Greek *metopē* (as META-, *opē* hole for a beam end)]

metre¹ *noun* (also **meter**) a metric unit and the base SI unit of linear measure, equal to about 39.4 inches, and reckoned as the length of the path travelled by light in a vacuum during $^1/_{299{,}792{,}458}$ of a second. Symbol: **m**. [French *mètre* from Greek *metron* measure]

metre² *noun* (also **meter**) **1 a** any form of poetic rhythm, determined by the number and length of feet in a line. **b** a metrical group or measure. **2** the basic pulse and rhythm of a piece of music. [Old French *metre* from Latin *metrum* from Greek *metron* MEASURE]

metre-kilogram-second *adjective* denoting a system of measure using the metre, kilogram, and second as the basic units of length, mass, and time. Abbr.: **mks**.

met·ric ● *adjective* **1** of or pertaining to the metre or metric system. **2** of or relating to measurement; metrical. ● *noun* **1** = METRIC SYSTEM. **2** a system or standard of measurement. **3** a mathematical function based on distances, or on quantities treated as analogous to distances for the purpose of analysis. [French *métrique* (as METRE¹)]

-metric /ˈmetrɪk/ *combining form* (also **-metrical**) forming adjectives corresponding to nouns in *-meter* and *-metry* (*thermometric*; *geometric*). □ **-metric·al·ly** *combining form.* [from or after French *-métrique* from Latin (as METRICAL)]

met·ric·al *adjective* **1** of, relating to, or composed in metre (*metrical psalms*). **2** of or involving measurement (*metrical geometry*). □ **met·ric·al·ly** *adverb* [Latin *metricus* from Greek *metrikos* (as METRE²)]

met·ri·cate /ˈmetrɪˌkeit/ *transitive & intransitive verb* change or adapt to a metric system of measurement. □ **metri·ca·tion** *noun*

metric hundredweight *noun see* HUNDREDWEIGHT 1.

metric system *noun* the decimal measuring system with the metre, litre, and gram (or kilogram) as units of length, volume, and mass. *See also* INTERNATIONAL SYSTEM OF UNITS.

metric ton *noun* (also **metric tonne**) 1,000 kilograms (2205 lb.).

me·tritis /məˈtraɪtɪs/ *noun* inflammation of the womb. [Greek *mētra* womb + -ITIS]

Metro *noun* **1** *hist* an informal name for the former municipal entity of Metropolitan Toronto. **2** an informal name for the urban area of Halifax-Dartmouth. [abbreviation]

met·ro¹ *noun* (pl. **-ros**) a subway system in some cities, e.g. Montreal and Paris. [French *métro*, abbreviation of *métropolitain* METROPOLITAN]

met·ro² *adjective* N Amer. metropolitan (*metro council*). [abbreviation]

met·rol·ogy /mɪˈtrɒlədʒi/ *noun* the scientific study of measurement. □ **metro·log·ic·al** *adjective* [Greek *metron* measure + -LOGY]

metro·nome /ˈmetrəˌnoːm/ *noun* Music an instrument marking time at a selected rate by giving a regular tick. □ **metro·nom·ic** /-ˈnɒmɪk/ *adjective* **metro·nom·ic·ally** *adverb* [Greek *metron* measure + *nomos* law]

metro·nym·ic /ˌmetrəˈnɪmɪk/ ● *adjective* (of a name) derived from the name of a mother or female ancestor. ● *noun* a metronymic name. [Greek *mētēr mētros* mother, after *patronymic*]

me·trop·olis /məˈtrɒpəlɪs/ *noun* **1** a large, busy city, esp. the main city of a country or region. **2** a city or town which is a local centre of activity. **3** a metropolitan bishop's see. [Greek *mētropolis* parent state, from *mētēr mētros* mother + *polis* city]

metro·pol·itan /ˌmetrəˈpɒlɪtən/ ● *adjective* **1** of or relating to a metropolis. **2** encompassing a city and its suburbs (*metropolitan Toronto*). **3** belonging to, forming or forming part of, a mother country as distinct from its colonies etc. (*metropolitan France*). **4** of an ecclesiastical metropolis. ● *noun* **1** (in full **metropolitan bishop**) a bishop having authority over the bishops of a province, in the Western Church equivalent to archbishop, in the Orthodox Church ranking above archbishop and below patriarch. **2** an inhabitant of a metropolis. □ **metro·pol·itan·ism** *noun* [Late Latin *metropolitanus* from Greek *mētropolitēs* (as METROPOLIS)]

Metropolitan Toronto *hist.* a municipal entity consisting of the city of Toronto proper and the municipalities of East York, Etobicoke, North York, Scarborough, and York surrounding it.

me·tror·rha·gia /ˌmiːtrəˈreidʒiə/ *noun* abnormal bleeding from the uterus. [modern Latin from Greek *mētra* uterus + *-rrhage* as HEMORRHAGE]

-metry /mɪtri/ *combining form* forming nouns denoting procedures and systems corresponding to instruments in *-meter* (*calorimetry*; *thermometry*). [on the pattern of *geometry* etc. from Greek *-metria* from *-metrēs* measurer]

Met·ter·nich /ˈmetɜrnɪx/ **Klem·ens (Wenzel Nepo·muk Lo·thar), Prince of Metternich-Winneburg-Beilstein** (1773–1859), Austrian statesman. As Foreign Minister (1809–48), he was one of the organizers of the Congress of Vienna (1815), which devised the settlement of Europe after the Napoleonic Wars.

met·tle *noun* **1** the quality of a person's disposition or temperament (*a chance to show your mettle*). **2** spirit, courage. **3** the natural vigour of an animal, esp. a horse. □ **on one's mettle** incited to do one's best. □ **mettle·some** *adjective* [var. of METAL *noun*]

Metz /mets/ a city in Lorraine, NE France, on the Mosel River; pop. (1999) 123,776. Formerly the capital of the medieval Frankish kingdom of Austrasia, the city grew to prosperity in the 13th c. when it was a free town within the Holy Roman Empire, ruled by a virtually independent bishop.

Meulles /məl/ **Jacques de** (d.1703), French soldier and colonial administrator. Appointed Intendant of New France in 1682, de Meulles quarrelled with the Governor, La Barre, throughout his term. Finding himself with no cash with which to pay his soldiers in 1685, de Meulles used playing cards as currency, promising to convert them to cash the next year.

meu·nière /mʊnˈjer/ *adjective* (esp. of fish) cooked or served in lightly browned butter with lemon juice and parsley (*sole meunière*). [French (*à la*) *meunière* (in the manner of) a miller's wife]

Meur·sault /mɜrˈsoː/ *noun* a (usu. white) burgundy wine produced near Beaune, France. [*Meursault*, in the Côte d'Or]

Meuse River /mɜːz/ a river of W Europe, which rises in NE France

and flows 950 km (594 miles) through Belgium and the Netherlands to the North Sea south of Dordrecht.

MeV *abbreviation* mega-electron volt(s).

mew¹ /mjuː/ ● *intransitive verb* (of a cat, gull, etc.) utter its characteristic cry. ● *noun* this sound, esp. of a cat. [Middle English: imitative]

mew² *noun* a gull. [Old English *mæw* from Germanic]

mew³ ● *noun* a cage for hawks, esp. while moulting. ● *transitive verb* **1** put (a hawk) in a cage. **2** (often foll. by *up*) shut up; confine. [Old French *mue* from *muer* moult, from Latin *mutare* change]

mew gull *noun* esp. N Amer. a small gull, *Larus canus*.

mewl /mjuːl/ *intransitive verb* cry feebly; whimper. [imitative]

mews /mjuːz/ *noun* esp. Brit. **1** a set of stables around an open yard or along a lane. **2** such a set of buildings converted into dwellings; a row of houses in the style of a mews. [pl. (now used as sing.) of MEW³, originally referring to the royal stables on the site of hawks' mews at Charing Cross, London]

Mexi·cali /ˌmeksɪˈkɒli/ the capital of Baja California Norte, in NW Mexico; pop. (1999) 549,900.

Mex·ican ● *noun* **1 a** a native or national of Mexico. **b** a person of Mexican descent. **2** an indigenous language of Mexico, esp. Nahuatl. ● *adjective* **1** of or relating to Mexico or its people or indigenous languages. **2** of Mexican descent. [Spanish *mexicano*]

Mexican standoff *noun* a situation in which there is no clear winner; an impasse. [originally in poker]

Mex·ico 1 a country in N America, with extensive coastlines on the Gulf of Mexico and the Pacific Ocean, bordered by the US to the north; pop. (est. 2002) 103,400,165; capital, Mexico City. **2** a state of central Mexico, to the west of Mexico City; capital, Toluca de Lerdo. [*Mextili*, Aztec war god]

Mexico, Gulf of a large extension of the W Atlantic Ocean. Bounded in a sweeping curve by the US to the north, by Mexico to the west and south, and by Cuba to the southeast, it is linked to the Atlantic by the Straits of Florida and to the Caribbean Sea by the Yucatán Channel.

Mexico City the capital of Mexico; pop. (2000) 18,327,000.

Meyer·beer /ˈmaɪərˌbiːr/ **Gia·como** (born Jakob Liebmann Beer) (1791–1864), German composer. He is noted for such operas as *Robert le diable* (1831) and *Les Huguenots* (1836), which established him as a leading exponent of French grand opera.

Meyer·hof /ˈmaɪərˌhɒf/ **Otto (Fritz)** (1884–1951), German-born US biochemist. He studied the biochemical processes involved in muscle action, including the production of lactic acid and heat as by-products, and provided the basis for understanding the process by which glucose is broken down to provide energy; he shared a Nobel Prize in 1922.

meze /ˈmeizei/ *noun* (pl. same or **mezes**) (in Turkish, Greek, and Middle Eastern cooking) a selection of hot and cold dishes, typically served as an hors d'oeuvre. [Turkish, lit. 'appetizer', from Persian *maza* 'to relish']

me·zer·eon /məˈziːriən/ *noun* a small European and Asian shrub, *Daphne mezereum*, with fragrant purplish-red flowers and red berries. [medieval Latin from Arabic *māzaryūn*]

me·zu·zah /məˈzuːzə/ *noun* (pl. **me·zu·zahs** or **me·zu·zoth** /-zoːθ/) a parchment inscribed with religious texts and attached in a case to the doorpost of a Jewish house as a sign of faith. [Hebrew *mᵉzūzāh* doorpost]

Mézy /meiˈziː/ **Au·gus·tin de Saf·fray de** (d.1665), French colonial administrator. Appointed the first governor of New France under direct royal rule in 1663, he reorganized the administration of the colony and came into conflict with the church, in the person of Bishop Laval.

mezza·nine /ˈmezəniːn, mezəˈniːn/ ● *noun* (also *attributive*) **1** a low storey between two others (usu. between the ground floor and the second floor). **2 a** N Amer. the lowest balcony or foremost part of a single balcony in a theatre. **b** Brit. a floor or space beneath the stage of a theatre. ● *adjective* Commerce designating or relating to unsecured, higher-yielding loans that are subordinate to bank and secured loans but rank above equity. [French from Italian *mezzanino*, diminutive of *mezzano* 'middle', from Latin *medianus* MEDIAN]

mezza voce /ˌmetsə ˈvoːtʃei/ *adverb* Music with half of the possible vocal or instrumental power; restrained. [Italian, = half voice]

mez·zo /ˈmetsoː/ Music ● *adverb* half, moderately. ● *noun* (in full **mezzo-soprano**) (pl. **-zos**) **1 a** a female singing voice between soprano and contralto. **b** a singer with this voice. **2** a part written for mezzo-soprano. [Italian, from Latin *medius* middle]

mezzo-forte *adjective & adverb* fairly loud. Abbr.: **mf**.

Mezzo·gior·no /ˌmetsɔːˈdʒɔrnɔː/ the southern part of Italy, including Sicily and Sardinia. [Italian, = midday (compare MIDI)]

mezzo-piano *adjective & adverb* fairly soft. Abbr.: **mp**.

mezzo·tint /ˈmetsɔːtɪnt, ˈmezɔː-/ ● *noun* **1** a method of printing or engraving in which the surface of a plate is roughened by scraping so that it produces tones and halftones. **2** a print produced by this process. ● *transitive verb* engrave in mezzotint. [Italian *mezzotinto* from *mezzo* half + *tinto* tint]

MF *abbreviation* **1** medium frequency. **2** milk fat.

M.F. *abbreviation* Master of Forestry.

mf *abbreviation* mezzo-forte.

M.F.A. *abbreviation* Master of Fine Arts.

mfg. *abbreviation* manufacturing.

MFN *abbreviation* MOST FAVOURED NATION.

mfr. *abbreviation* manufacturer's.

Mg *symbol Chem.* the element magnesium.

mg *abbreviation* milligram(s).

MGen *abbreviation Cdn* MAJOR GENERAL.

Mgr. *abbreviation* **1** Manager. **2** Monseigneur. **3** Monsignor.

MHA *abbreviation* (in Newfoundland and Labrador and in Australia) Member of the House of Assembly.

M.H.A. *abbreviation* Master of Health Administration.

mho /mɔː/ *noun* (*pl.* **mhos**) *Electricity* the reciprocal of an ohm, a former unit of conductance. [OHM reversed]

MHR *abbreviation* (in the US and Australia) Member of the House of Representatives.

M.H.S.A. *abbreviation* Master of Health Services Administration.

M.H.Sc. *abbreviation* Master of Health Sciences.

MHz *abbreviation* megahertz.

MI *abbreviation* **1** Michigan (in official postal use). **2** Military Intelligence.

mi /miː/ *noun* (also **me**) *Music* **1** (in tonic sol-fa) the third note of a major scale. **2** the note E in the fixed-do system. [Latin *mira*: see GAMUT]

mi. *abbreviation* mile(s).

MI5 *abbreviation* (in the UK) the department of Military Intelligence concerned with state security. ¶ The official term for MI5 is the *Security Service*.

MI6 *abbreviation* (in the UK) the department of Military Intelligence concerned with espionage. ¶ The official term for MI6 is the *Secret Intelligence Service*.

MIA *abbreviation* missing in action.

Miami /maiˈami/ a city and port on the coast of SE Florida; pop. (2000) 362,470. □ **Mi·ami·an** *noun & adjective*

miaow *Brit. var. of* MEOW.

mi·asma /maiˈazmə, miː-/ *noun* (*pl.* **mi·as·mas** or **mi·as·mata** /-mətə/) **1** an infectious or noxious vapour, esp. from putrescent organic matter, which pollutes the atmosphere. **2** a polluting, oppressive or foreboding atmosphere or influence. □ **mi·as·mal** *adjective* **mi·as·mat·ic** /-ˈmatɪk/ *adjective* **mi·as·mic** *adjective* [Greek, = defilement, from *miainō* pollute]

Mic. *abbreviation* Micah (Old Testament).

mic /maik/ *noun* microphone. [abbreviation]

mica /ˈmaikə/ *noun* any of a group of silicate minerals with a layered structure, esp. muscovite. [Latin, = crumb]

mi·ca·ceous /maiˈkeiʃəs/ *adjective* containing or resembling mica.

Micah /ˈmaikə/ **1** a Hebrew minor prophet. **2** a book of the Bible bearing his name, foretelling the destruction of Samaria and of Jerusalem.

mica-schist *noun* a fissile rock containing quartz and mica.

mice *pl. of* MOUSE.

mi·celle /mɪˈsel, maiˈsel/ *noun Chem.* an aggregate of molecules in a colloidal solution, as formed e.g. by detergents. [modern Latin *micella* diminutive of Latin *mica* crumb]

Mich. *abbreviation* Michigan.

Mi·chael /ˈmaikəl/ **1** (b.1921), king of Romania 1927–30 and 1940–7. He overthrew the fascist dictator Ion Antonescu (1882–1946) in 1944, and was forced to abdicate by the Communist government in 1947. **2 St.**, one of the archangels, usually represented slaying a dragon (see Rev. 12:7). Feast day, 29 Sept. (Michaelmas).

Michael·mas /ˈmɪkəlməs/ *noun* the feast of St. Michael, 29 September. [Old English *sancte Micheles mæsse* Saint Michael's mass: see MASS²]

Michaelmas daisy *noun* an autumn-flowering aster.

Michaelmas term *noun Brit.* (in some universities) the autumn term.

Michel·angelo /ˌmaikəlˈandʒəˌloː, ˌmɪk-/ (full name Michelangelo Buonarroti) (1475–1564), Italian sculptor, painter, architect, and poet. His best-known works are the statues of the *Pietà* (c.1497–1500) and *David* (1501–4), the ceiling of the Sistine Chapel in Rome (1508–12) and accompanying fresco, *The Last Judgement* (1536–41); he also designed the Laurentian Library in Florence (1524–34) and the dome of St. Peter's in Rome (1546–64).

Mi·che·let /ˌmiːʃəˈlei/ **Jules** (1798–1874), French historian, whose principal work is the 17-volume *Histoire de France* (1833–67).

Mi·chel·son /ˈmaikəlsən/ **Al·bert Abra·ham** (1852–1931), German-born US physicist. He performed a number of accurate determinations of the velocity of light, and, with E. W. Morley, demonstrated that the hypothetical ether did not exist (1887). He was awarded a Nobel Prize in 1907.

Mich·ener /ˈmɪtʃnər/ **1 (Dan·iel) Ro·land** (1900–1991), Canadian lawyer and politician, Governor General 1967–74. Born in Alberta, he practised law in Toronto from 1924, and sat as an Ontario MPP 1945–48. Elected to the House of Commons as a Progressive Conservative in 1953, he was Speaker (1957–62), and served as high commissioner to India (1964–67). **2 James** (1907–1997), US novelist, traveller, and philanthropist. He won a Pulitzer Prize for his first novel, *Tales of the South Pacific* (1947), and wrote more than 20 successful books, often donating royalties to charities and schools. In Canada, earnings from his novel *Journey* help to fund the Journey Prize, an award for emerging writers.

Mich·igan a state in the northern US, bordered on the west, north, and east by Lakes Michigan, Superior, Huron, and Erie; pop. (est. 2002) 9,938,444; capital, Lansing. □ **Michi·gan·der** /ˌmɪʃɪˈgandər/ *noun*

Michigan, Lake one of the five Great Lakes, bordered by Michigan, Wisconsin, Illinois, and Indiana, the only one of the Great Lakes to lie wholly within the US. The cities of Milwaukee and Chicago are on its shores.

Mich·ili·mack·inac /ˌmɪʃɪlɪˈmakinak/ a place on the shores of the Mackinac Strait connecting Lake Huron and Lake Michigan, the site of an American fort which was captured by Sir Isaac Brock's forces at the outset of the War of 1812 and held for the duration of the war, securing the northwest frontier.

Mi·cho·acán /ˌmiːtʃoːəˈkɒn/ a state of W Mexico, on the Pacific coast; capital, Morelia.

mick *noun* (also **Mick**) *slang offensive* **1** an Irishman. **2** a Roman Catholic. [pet form of the name *Michael*]

mick·ey¹ *noun* (*pl.* **-eys**) **1** *Cdn* a half bottle of liquor, usu. 375 ml. **2** = MICKEY FINN. [20th c.: origin uncertain]

mick·ey² *noun* (also **micky**) □ **take the mickey** (often foll. by *out of*) *Brit. slang* tease, mock, ridicule. □ **mickey-taking** *noun* [20th c.: origin uncertain]

Mickey Finn *noun* (also **mickey, Mickey**) *slang* **1** a strong alcoholic drink, esp. adulterated with a narcotic or laxative. **2** the adulterant itself. [20th c.: origin uncertain]

Mickey Mouse *adjective informal* **1** of inferior quality. **2** ridiculous, trivial. **3** (of a university course etc.) requiring little work or intellectual ability. [mouselike cartoon character created by Walt DISNEY]

mickle /ˈmɪkəl/ (also **muckle** /ˈmʌkəl/) *archaic* or *Scot.* ● *adjective* much, great. ● *noun* a large amount. [Old Norse *mikell* from Germanic]

micky *var. of* MICKEY².

Mic·mac *var. of* MI'KMAQ.

micro /ˈmaikroː/ *informal* ● *noun* (*pl.* **micros**) **1** = MICROCOMPUTER. **2** = MICROPROCESSOR. **3** = MICROWAVE. ● *adjective* **1** microscopic; very small. **2** small-scale. [abbreviation]

micro- /ˈmaikroː/ *combining form* **1** small (*microchip*). **2** denoting a factor of one millionth (10⁻⁶) (*microgram*). Symbol: μ. **3** *Med.* involving arrested development or underdevelopment of a part (*microencephaly*). **4** (in names of instruments, techniques, and disciplines) dealing with small effects or small quantities. **5** involving the use of a microscope (*microanalyzer*). **6** containing or pertaining to something in minute form, quantity, or degree (*microvascular*). **7** pertaining to or obtained by micrography (*microtext*). [Greek *mikro-* from *mikros* small]

micro·analy·sis *noun* (*pl.* **-analy·ses**) the quantitative analysis of chemical compounds using a sample of a few milligrams. □ **micro·ana·lytic** *adjective*

micro·array *noun Genetics* a set of DNA sequences representing the entire set of genes of an organism, arranged in a grid pattern for use in genetic testing.

mi·crobe /ˈmaɪkrəʊb/ *noun* a minute living being; a micro-organism (esp. a bacterium causing disease or fermentation). □ **mi·crob·ial** *adjective* **mi·crob·ic** *adjective* [French from Greek *mikros* small + *bios* life]

micro·biol·ogy *noun* the scientific study of micro-organisms, e.g. bacteria, viruses, and fungi. □ **micro·bio·logic·al** *adjective* **micro·bio·logic·al·ly** *adverb* **micro·biol·o·gist** *noun*

micro·brew·ery *noun* esp. *N Amer.* a brewery which produces beer on a small scale, and which usu. specializes in high-quality brands made with natural ingredients. □ **micro·brew** *noun & transitive verb* **micro·brew·er** *noun*

micro·brows·er *noun* an Internet browser for use with cellphones and other hand-held devices with small screens.

micro·burst *noun* a particularly violent wind shear, esp. during a thunderstorm.

micro·cas·sette *noun* a small audio cassette for use in a tape recorder, answering machine, etc.

micro·ceph·aly /ˌmaɪkrəʊˈsefəli/ *noun* an abnormal smallness of the head in relation to the rest of the body. □ **micro·ceph·alic** /-səˈfalɪk/ *adjective & noun*

micro·chip *noun* ● *noun* a tiny wafer of semiconducting material used to make an integrated circuit. ● *transitive verb* implant a microchip under the skin of (a pet) for identification purposes.

micro·cir·cuit *noun* a minute electric circuit, esp. an integrated circuit. □ **micro·cir·cuit·ry** *noun*

micro·cli·mate *noun* the climate of a small local area or enclosed space, esp. as differing from the surroundings. □ **micro·climat·ic** *adjective* **micro·climat·ic·al·ly** *adverb*

micro·code *noun* **1** = MICROINSTRUCTION. **2** = MICROPROGRAM.

micro·com·put·er *noun* a small computer that contains a microprocessor as its central processing unit.

micro·control·ler *noun* *Computing* a control device which incorporates a microprocessor.

micro·cosm /ˈmaɪkrəˌkɒzəm/ *noun* **1** (often foll. by *of*) a miniature representation. **2** humankind viewed as the epitome of the universe. **3** any community or complex unity viewed in this way. □ **micro·cos·mic** /-ˈkɒzmɪk/ *adjective* **micro·cos·mic·ally** *adverb* [French *microcosme* or medieval Latin *microcosmus* from Greek *mikros kosmos* little world]

micro·dot *noun* **1** a microphotograph of a document etc. reduced to the size of a dot. **2** a tiny capsule or tablet of LSD.

micro·econom·ics *noun* the branch of economics that deals with small-scale economic factors such as individual commodities, producers, consumers, etc. (*compare* MACROECONOMICS). □ **micro·econom·ic** *adjective*

micro·elec·tron·ics *noun* the design, manufacture, and use of microchips and microcircuits. □ **micro·elec·tron·ic** *adjective*

micro·environ·ment *noun* *Biol. & Bot.* the immediate small-scale environment of a thing, esp. as a distinct part of a larger environment. □ **micro·environ·ment·al** *adjective*

micro·evolu·tion *noun* *Biol.* evolutionary change within a species or small group of organisms, esp. over a short period. □ **micro·evolu·tion·ary** *adjective*

micro·fibre *noun* a lightweight, water-resistant polyester used esp. for outerwear, swimsuits, etc.

micro·fiche /ˈmaɪkrəʊˌfiːʃ/ *noun* (*pl.* same or **microfiches**) a flat rectangular piece of film bearing microphotographs of the pages of a printed text or document.

micro·film *noun* ● *noun* a length of film bearing microphotographs of documents etc. ● *transitive verb* photograph (a document etc.) on microfilm.

micro·fine *adjective* **1** (of a powder etc.) ground to a very fine consistency. **2** (of a tool, instrument, etc.) very precise in its measurements, readings, etc.

micro·form *noun* microphotographic reproduction on film or paper of a manuscript etc.

micro·gram *noun* one-millionth of a gram.

micro·graph *noun* a photograph taken by means of a microscope.

micro·grav·ity *noun* very weak gravity, as in an orbiting spacecraft.

micro·groove *noun* a very narrow groove on a long-playing record.

micro·habi·tat *noun* *Ecology* a habitat which is of small or limited extent and which differs in character from some surrounding more extensive habitat.

micro·instruc·tion *noun* a machine-code instruction that effects a basic operation in a computer system.

micro·lepi·dop·tera /ˌmaɪkrəʊlepɪˈdɒptərə/ *plural noun* the numerous small moths that are of interest only to specialists. ¶ The term *microlepidoptera* is not used in formal classification. [MICRO- + modern Latin *Lepidoptera*: see LEPIDOPTEROUS]

micro·light *noun* *Brit.* = ULTRALIGHT *noun.*

micro·lith /ˈmaɪkrəʊˌlɪθ/ *noun* *Archaeology* a minute worked flint usu. as part of a composite tool. □ **micro·lith·ic** *adjective*

micro·manage *transitive verb* supervise or control with excessive attention to small details. □ **micro·man·age·ment** *noun* **micro·man·ag·er** *noun*

mi·crom·eter /maɪˈkrɒmɪtər/ *noun* a gauge for accurately measuring small distances, thicknesses, etc. □ **mi·crom·etry** *noun*

micro·metre /ˈmaɪkrəʊˌmiːtər/ *noun* one-millionth of a metre.

micro·mini ● *adjective* **1** (of a skirt etc.) very short. **2** (of a car, computer, etc.) very small. ● *noun* an object that is very short in length or very small in size.

micro·mini·atur·iz·a·tion *noun* (also esp. *Brit.* **-isation**) the manufacture of very small electronic devices by using integrated circuits.

mi·cron /ˈmaɪkrɒn/ *noun* one-millionth of a metre. Symbol: μ. [Greek *mikron* neuter of *mikros* small: compare MICRO-]

Micro·nesia /ˌmaɪkrəʊˈniːʒiə/ **1** a region of the W Pacific to the north of Melanesia and north and west of Polynesia. It includes the Mariana, Caroline, and Marshall island groups and Kiribati. **2** (in full **Federated States of Micronesia**) a group of associated island states comprising the 600 islands of the Caroline Islands, in the W Pacific to the north of the equator; pop. (est. 2002) 135,869; capital, Palikir (on Pohnpei). The group, which includes the islands of Yap, Kosrae, Truk, and Pohnpei, was administered by the US as part of the Pacific Islands Trust Territory from 1947 until 1986, when it entered into free association with the US as an independent state. [MICRO- + Greek *nēsos* island]

Micro·nes·ian /ˌmaɪkrəʊˈniːʒən, -ziən/ ● *adjective* of or relating to Micronesia, its people or their languages. ● *noun* **1** a native of Micronesia. **2** the group of Austronesian languages spoken in Micronesia.

micro·nutri·ent *noun* a chemical element or substance required in trace amounts for the growth and development of living organisms.

micro·organ·ism *noun* any of various microscopic organisms, esp. a bacterium or virus.

micro·phone *noun* an instrument for converting sound waves into electrical energy variations which may be reconverted into sound after transmission by wire or radio or after recording. □ **micro·phon·ic** /ˌmaɪkrəʊˈfɒnɪk/ *adjective*

micro·photo·graph *noun* **1** a photograph reduced to a very small size. **2** a photograph of a microscopic object on a magnified scale. □ **micro·photo·graph·ic** *adjective* **micro·photog·raphy** *noun*

micro·proces·sor *noun* an integrated circuit that contains all the functions of a central processing unit of a computer.

micro·pro·gram *noun* a microinstruction program that controls the functions of a central processing unit of a computer.

micro·proof *adjective* (of a dish, container, etc.) able to be used in a microwave oven.

micro·pyle /ˈmaɪkrəʊˌpaɪl/ *noun* *Bot.* a small opening in the surface of an ovule, through which pollen passes. [MICRO- + Greek *pulē* gate]

micro·sat·el·lite *noun* **1** *Genetics* a set of short repeated DNA sequences at a particular locus on a chromosome, which vary in number in different individuals and so can be used for genetic fingerprinting. **2** a very small man-made satellite.

micro·scoot·er *noun* a small two-wheeled foldable aluminum scooter for both children and adults.

micro·scope *noun* an instrument magnifying small objects by means of a lens or lenses so as to reveal details invisible to the naked eye. □ **under the microscope** examined in great detail. [modern Latin *microscopium* (as MICRO-, -SCOPE)]

micro·scop·ic *adjective* **1** so small as to be visible only with a microscope. **2** extremely small. **3** regarded in terms of small units; concerned with minute detail. **4** of the microscope. □ **micro·scop·ic·al** *adjective* (in sense 4). **micro·scop·ic·ally** *adverb*

mi·cros·copy /maɪˈkrɒskəpi/ *noun* the use of the microscope. □ **mi·cro·scop·ist** *noun*

micro·sec·ond *noun* one-millionth of a second.

micro·some /ˈmaɪkrəʊˌsoʊm/ *noun* *Biol.* a small particle of organelle

Consonants: b *but*   d *dog*   f *few*   g *get*   h *her*   j *yes*   k *cat*   l *leg*   m *man*   n *no*   p *pen*   r *red*   s *sit*

fragments obtained by centrifugation of homogenized cells. □ **micro·som·al** adjective [MICRO- + -SOME³]

micro·sphere noun a minute sphere, esp. one obtained by cooling a solution of a proteinoid.

micro·spore noun the smaller of the two kinds of spore produced by some ferns.

micro·struc·ture noun (in a metal or other material) the arrangement of crystals etc. which can be made visible and examined with a microscope. □ **micro·struc·tur·al** adjective

micro·sur·gery noun intricate surgery performed using microscopes, enabling the tissue to be operated on with miniaturized precision instruments. □ **micro·sur·geon** noun **micro·sur·gical** adjective

micro·switch noun a switch that can be operated rapidly by a small movement.

micro·tome noun an instrument for cutting extremely thin sections of material for examination under a microscope.

micro·tone noun Music an interval smaller than a semitone. □ **micro·tonal** adjective **micro·tonal·ity** noun **micro·tonal·ly** adverb

micro·tubule noun Biol. a minute protein filament occurring in cytoplasm and involved in forming the spindles during cell division etc.

micro·vil·lus /ˌmaɪkroʊˈvɪləs/ noun (pl. **micro·villi** -laɪ/) Biol. any of a number of minute projections from the surface of some cells. □ **micro·vil·lar** adjective **micro·vil·lous** adjective

micro·wave ● noun **1** an electromagnetic wave with a wavelength in the range 0.001–0.3 m. **2** (in full **microwave oven**) an oven that uses microwaves to cook or heat food. ● transitive verb cook in a microwave oven. □ **micro·wave·able** adjective (also **micro·wav·able**).

microwave background noun = BACKGROUND RADIATION 2.

micro·winery noun a winery which produces wine on a small scale, and which usu. specializes in high-quality or natural wines.

mic·tur·ition /ˌmɪktʃʊˈrɪʃən/ noun formal urination. □ **mic·tur·ate** /ˈmɪktʃʊreɪt/ intransitive verb [Latin micturire micturit-, desiderative from mingere mict- urinate]

mid¹ attributive adjective **1** (usu. in combination) that is the middle of (in mid-air; from mid-June to mid-July). **2** that is in the middle; medium, half. **3** Phonetics (of a vowel) pronounced with the tongue neither high nor low. [Old English midd (recorded only in oblique cases), related to Latin medius, Greek mesos]

mid² preposition poet. = AMID. [abbreviation from AMID]

mid-air noun some part or section of the air above ground level or above another surface (suspended in mid-air; also attributive: mid-air collision).

Midas /ˈmaɪdəs/ Gk Myth a king of Phrygia, who, according to one story, was given by Dionysus the power of turning everything he touched into gold. Unable to eat or drink, he prayed to be relieved of the gift and was instructed to wash in the Pactolus River, which since then has had golden sands.

Midas touch noun the ability to turn one's activities to esp. financial advantage. [MIDAS]

Mid-Atlantic Ridge a submarine ridge system extending the length of the Atlantic Ocean from the Arctic to the Antarctic. It is seismically and, in places, volcanically active; the islands of Iceland, the Azores, Ascension, St. Helena, and Tristan da Cunha are situated on it. See also MIDOCEAN RIDGE.

mid·brain noun the part of the brain developing from the middle of the primitive or embryonic brain.

mid·day noun the middle of the day; noon.

mid·den /ˈmɪdən/ noun **1** a dunghill. **2** a refuse heap near a dwelling. **3** = KITCHEN MIDDEN. [Middle English myddyng, of Scandinavian origin: compare Danish mødding muck heap]

mid·dle ● attributive adjective **1** at an equal distance from the extremities of a thing. **2** (of a member of a group) so placed as to have the same number of members on each side. **3** intermediate in rank, quality, order, etc. **4** average (of middle height). **5** (of a language) of the period between the old and modern forms. **6** Grammar designating the voice of (esp. Greek) verbs that expresses reciprocal or reflexive action. ● noun **1** (often foll. by of) the middle point or position or part. **2** a person's waist. **3** Grammar the middle form or voice of a verb. **4** = MIDDLE TERM. **5** a position between two rivals, subject to attack from both (caught in the middle). □ **in the middle of** (often foll. by verbal noun) in the process of; during. **up the middle** Baseball (of a ground ball or line drive) (hit) down the centre of the field, past the pitcher and second baseman. [Old English middel from Germanic]

middle age noun the period between youth and old age, about 40 to 60. □ **middle-aged** adjective

Middle Ages plural noun the period of European history generally considered as beginning either with the fall of the Roman Empire in the West (5th c.) or with the end of the Dark Ages (c. 1000), and ending either with the start of the Renaissance in Italy (14th c.) or with the fall of Constantinople (1453).

middle-age spread noun (also **middle-aged spread**) the increased bodily girth often associated with middle age.

Middle America noun **1** the middle class in the US, esp. seen as having conventional attitudes, tastes, etc. **2** Mexico and Central America.

middle·brow informal ● adjective claiming to be or regarded as only moderately intellectual. ● noun a middlebrow person.

middle C noun Music the C near the middle of the piano keyboard, the note between the treble and bass staffs, at about 260 Hz.

middle class ● noun the class of society between the upper and the lower, including professional and business workers and their families. ● adjective (**middle-class**) of the middle class.

Middle Congo see CONGO 2.

middle course noun a compromise between two extremes.

middle distance noun **1** (in a painted or actual landscape) the part between the foreground and the background. **2** Athletics a race distance of esp. 400, 800, or 1500 metres (also attributive: middle-distance runner).

middle ear noun the cavity of the central part of the ear behind the drum.

Middle East a term loosely applied to an extensive area of SW Asia and northern Africa, stretching from the Mediterranean to Pakistan, including the Arabian peninsula, and having a predominantly Muslim population. □ **Middle Eastern** adjective

middle eight noun the eight bars in the middle of a conventionally structured popular song, often of a different character from the other parts of the song.

Middle English noun the English language from c.1150 to 1500.

middle finger noun the finger between the index finger and the ring finger.

middle·game noun the central phase of a chess game, when strategies are developed.

middle ground noun **1** the thought, area, or path, tending to moderation and compromise. **2** the people regarded as holding moderate views.

middle-income attributive adjective of or relating to the group of people earning average salaries.

Middle Kingdom noun a period of ancient Egyptian history (c.2040–1640 BC, 11th–14th dynasty) considered to be the classical age of ancient Egyptian culture.

middle·man noun (pl. **-men**) **1** any of the traders who handle a commodity between its producer and the retailer or consumer. **2** an intermediary. **3** Cdn hist. any of several canoemen positioned in the middle of a canoe, between the bowman and the steersman.

middle management noun **1** the level in an organization between senior and junior management. **2** the managers at this level (compare SENIOR MANAGEMENT, JUNIOR MANAGEMENT).

middle name noun **1** a person's name placed after the first name and before the surname. **2** a characteristic quality of a person or thing (punctuality is my middle name).

middle-of-the-road adjective **1** (of a person, course of action, etc.) moderate; avoiding extremes. **2** (of music) intended to appeal to a wide audience; unadventurous. Abbr.: MOR. □ **middle-of-the-roader** noun **middle-of-the-roadism** noun

middle passage noun the sea journey between W Africa and the W Indies (with reference to the slave trade).

middle power noun a nation with average political or military influence on world affairs.

middle school noun **1** N Amer. = JUNIOR HIGH SCHOOL. **2** Brit. a school for children from about 9 to 13 years old.

Middle·sex /ˈmɪdəlˌseks/ a former county of SE England, situated to the north of London. In 1965 it was divided between Hertfordshire, Surrey, and Greater London.

middle-sized adjective of medium size.

Middle Temple noun one of the two Inns of Court on the site of the Temple in London (compare INNER TEMPLE).

middle term noun Logic the term common to both premises of a syllogism.

---

t *top*   v *voice*   w *we*   z *zoo*   ʃ *she*   ʒ *vision*   θ *thin*   ð *this*   ŋ *ring*   x *loch*   tʃ *chip*   dʒ *jar*   (*see over for vowels*)

middle·ware noun software that acts as a bridge between an operating system and applications, esp. among networked clients or a distributed system.

middle watch noun Naut. the watch from midnight to 4 a.m.

middle way noun = MIDDLE COURSE.

middle·weight noun **1** a weight in certain sports intermediate between welterweight and light heavyweight, in the amateur boxing scale 71·5 kg but differing for professionals and wrestlers. **2** an athlete of this weight.

Middle West noun = MIDWEST.

mid·dling /ˈmɪdlɪŋ/ ● adjective **1 a** moderately good (fair to middling). **b** informal (of a person's health) fairly good. **c** second-rate. **2** (of goods) of the second of three grades. ● noun (in pl.) middling goods, esp. flour of medium fineness. ● adverb fairly or moderately (middling good). [Middle English, of Scots origin: prob. from MID¹ + -LING²]

middy /ˈmɪdi/ noun (pl. **-dies**) **1** informal a midshipman. **2** (in full **middy blouse**) a woman's or child's loose blouse with a sailor collar.

Mid·east noun N Amer. = MIDDLE EAST.

Mi·de·wiwin /mɪˈdeɪwɪwɪn/ noun (also **Mide·win** /mɪˈdeɪwɪn/) a shamanic society among the Ojibwa and Algonquin, devoted to the understanding of herbal remedies and spiritual knowledge. [Ojibwa]

mid·field noun **1** (in football, soccer, etc.) the central part of the playing field, away from the goals or end zones. **2** (in soccer) the players positioned in the midfield. □ **mid·field·er** noun

Mid·gard /ˈmɪdɡɑrd/ Scand. Myth the region, encircled by the sea, in which human beings live; the earth.

Midgard serpent noun a monstrous serpent, the offspring of Loki, thrown by Odin into the sea, where, with its tail in its mouth, it encircled the earth.

midge noun **1** informal **a** a gnat-like insect. **b** a small person. **2 a** any small dipterous non-biting insect of the family Chironomidae, accumulating in swarms. **b** any similar insect of the family Ceratopogonidae with piercing mouthparts for sucking blood or eating smaller insects. [Old English mycg(e) from Germanic]

midget noun **1** an extremely small person or thing. **2** (attributive) very small. **3** Cdn **a** a level of amateur sport, usu. involving players aged 16 to 17. **b** a player in this age group. [MIDGE + -ET¹]

Mid Glamorgan /ɡləˈmɔrɡən/ a former county of S Wales, formed in 1974 from parts of Breconshire, Glamorgan, and Monmouthshire and dissolved in 1996.

mid·gut noun the middle part of the alimentary canal, including the small intestine.

MIDI /ˈmɪdi/ noun a standard system for transferring data between electronic musical instruments, synthesizers, computers, etc., allowing them to be used simultaneously (also attributive: MIDI keyboard). [acronym from musical instrument digital interface]

Midi /ˈmiːdi/ the south of France. [French, = midday (compare MEZZOGIORNO)]

midi /ˈmɪdi/ noun (pl. **midis**) a garment of medium length, usu. reaching to mid-calf. [MID¹ after MINI]

midi- /ˈmɪdi/ combining form medium-sized; of medium length.

Midi-Pyrénées /miːdiːpiːreɪˈneɪ/ a region of S France, between the Pyrenees and the Massif Central, centred on Toulouse.

mid-iron noun Golf an iron giving medium lift.

Mid·land a town in south central Ontario, located on an inlet of Georgian Bay, northwest of Barrie; pop. (2001) 16,214. [Midland Railway of Canada, the company that developed the town c.1872–3]

mid·land ● noun **1** (**the Midlands**) the inland counties of central England. **2** the middle part of a country. ● adjective of or in the midland or Midlands. □ **mid·land·er** noun

mid-life noun middle age (often attributive: mid-life planning).

mid-life crisis noun an emotional crisis of self-confidence that can occur in early middle age.

mid·line ● noun a median line, or plane of bilateral symmetry. ● adjective (**mid-line**) designating or pertaining to consumer products or services that are of a general quality, neither expensive nor cheap; mid-range.

Mid·lo·thian /mɪdˈloːðiən/ an administrative region of central Scotland. It was part of Lothian region from 1975 to 1996.

mid·night noun **1** 12 o'clock at night. **2** the middle of the night.

midnight blue ● noun a very dark blue. ● adjective of this colour.

midnight Mass noun esp. Catholicism a Mass beginning at midnight on Christmas Eve.

midnight sun noun the sun visible at midnight during the summer in polar regions.

mid·ocean ridge noun Geol. a long seismically active submarine ridge system rising in the middle of an ocean basin and marking the site of the upwelling of magma associated with sea floor spreading. See also MID-ATLANTIC RIDGE.

mid-off noun Cricket the fielder or fielding position near the bowler on the off side.

mid-on noun Cricket the fielder or fielding position near the bowler on the on side.

mid·point noun the middle point.

mid-range ● adjective (esp. of a consumer product etc.) mid-priced; of average cost, capability, etc. ● noun the middle part of the range of audible frequencies (also attributive: mid-range speakers).

Mid·rash /ˈmɪdrɑʃ/ noun (pl. **Mid·rash·im** /-ˈʃɪm/) an ancient commentary on part of the Hebrew scriptures. □ **Mid·rash·ic** /mɪdˈrɑʃɪk/ adjective [Biblical Hebrew midrāš commentary]

mid·rib noun the central rib of a leaf.

mid·riff noun **1 a** the region of the front of the body between the chest and the waist. **b** the diaphragm. **2** a garment or part of a garment covering the abdomen. **3** a garment exposing the midriff. [Old English midhrif (as MID¹, hrif belly)]

mid-rise adjective (of an apartment building) of a height between low-rise and high-rise; having an intermediate number of storeys.

mid·sec·tion noun **1** the middle part of something. **2** the middle part of the human torso; midriff.

mid·ship noun the middle part of a ship or boat.

mid·ship·man noun (pl. **-men**) **1** (in the Royal Navy and hist. in the Royal Canadian Navy) a naval officer ranking above naval cadet and below sub-lieutenant. **2** US a naval cadet.

mid·ships adverb = AMIDSHIPS.

mid·shore attributive adjective Cdn designating the fishery an intermediate distance from shore, between the inshore and the offshore fisheries.

mid-size ● adjective (also **mid-sized**) **1** N Amer. (of a car) of a size between compact and full-size, usu. having a wheelbase of 100 to 105 inches and a four- or six-cylinder engine from 2 to 3.5 litres in size. **2** of intermediate size. ● noun N Amer. a mid-size car.

mid·sole noun a shock-absorbing layer in the sole of a running shoe etc.

midst ● preposition poet. amidst. ● noun middle (now only in phrases as below). □ **in the midst of** among; in the middle of. **in our** (or **your** or **their**) **midst** among us (or you or them). [Middle English middest, middes from in middes, in middan (as IN, MID¹)]

mid·stream ● noun the middle of a stream, river, etc. ● adverb (also **in midstream**) in the middle of an action etc. (abandoned the project midstream).

mid·sum·mer noun the period of or near the summer solstice, about 21 June.

Midsummer Day noun (also **Midsummer's Day**) 24 June.

mid-term ● adjective occurring in the middle of a term. ● noun N Amer. a mid-term exam.

mid·town noun N Amer. an area of a city at a moderate distance from the downtown area.

mid·way ● adverb in or towards the middle of the distance or interval between two points. ● noun N Amer. a fair or an area with amusements, sideshows, rides, etc.

Midway Islands two small islands with a surrounding coral atoll, in the western part of the Hawaiian chain, in the central Pacific. The islands, which lie outside the state of Hawaii, are a US territory and naval base. They were the scene in 1942 of the decisive Battle of Midway, in which the US navy repelled a Japanese invasion fleet, sinking four aircraft carriers. This defeat marked the end of Japanese expansion in the Pacific during the Second World War.

mid-week ● noun the middle of the week. ● adjective occurring at mid-week. ● adverb at mid-week.

Mid·west noun (in the US) the region of northern states from Ohio west to the Missouri valley. □ **Mid·west·ern** adjective **Mid·west·ern·er** noun

mid·wife noun (pl. **-wives**) **1** a person (usu. a woman) trained to assist women in childbirth. **2** a person or thing that brings about change (act as a midwife to emergent culture). □ **mid·wif·ery** /mɪdˈwɪfəri/ noun [Middle English, prob. from obsolete prep. mid 'with' + WIFE 'woman', in the sense of 'a person who is with the mother']

Vowels: a cat ɑ arm e bed ɜr her ɜː deux ə ago ɪ sit i cosy iː feed ɒ hot ɔ pore ɔː no ʌ run ʊ put

midwife toad *noun* a European toad, *Alytes obstetricans*, in which the male carries the developing eggs on his hind legs.

mid-winter *noun* **1** the middle of the winter (also *attributive: mid-winter blues*). **2** the period of or near the winter solstice, about 22 Dec.

mien /miːn/ *noun* a person's look or bearing, as showing character or mood. [prob. from obsolete *demean* from DEMEAN², assimilated to French *mine* expression]

Mies van der Rohe /ˈmiːz van dər ˈrojə/ **Lud·wig** (1886–1969), German-born US architect and designer. A major proponent of functionalism, he succeeded Gropius as director of the Bauhaus 1930–3; his designs include the Seagram Building in New York (1954–58) and the Toronto-Dominion Centre in Toronto (1963–69). □ **Mies·ian** *adjective*

mife·pris·tone /mɪfeˈprɪstoːn/ *noun* a synthetic norsteroid, C₂₉H₃₅NO₂, which inhibits the action of progesterone and may be given orally in early pregnancy to induce abortion. [prob. adapted from Dutch *mifepriston* from *mefi-* (representing *aminophenol*, from AMINO + PHENOL) + *-pri-* (representing PROPYNE) + *-st-* (representing ESTRADIOL) + *-ONE*]

miffed *adjective informal* put out of humour; offended. [originally as *miff*, v.; perhaps imitative: compare German *muff*, exclamation of disgust]

MiG *noun* any of various Russian-designed fighter aircraft. [Russian *MIG*, from A. I. Mikoyan and M. I. Gurevich, Russian aircraft designers]

mi·gawd /mɪˈɡɒd/ *interjection* expressing (often exaggerated) surprise etc. [corruption of *my God*]

might¹ *auxiliary verb* (3rd. sing. **might**) *past of* MAY, used esp.: **1** in reported speech, expressing possibility (*said he might come*) or permission (*asked if I might leave*) (compare MAY 1, 2). **2** (foll. by perfect infin.) expressing a possibility based on a condition not fulfilled (*if you'd looked you might have found it; but for the radio we might not have known*). **3** (foll. by present infin. or perfect infin.) expressing complaint that an obligation or expectation is not or has not been fulfilled (*he might offer to help; they might have asked; you might have known they wouldn't come*). **4** expressing a request (*you might give them a call*). **5** *informal* **a** = MAY 1 (*it might be true*). **b** (in tentative questions) = MAY 2 (*might I have the pleasure of this dance?*). **c** = MAY 4 (*who might you be?*). □ **might as well** expressing that it is probably at least as desirable to do a thing as not to do it (*finished the work and decided they might as well go to lunch; won't win but might as well try*).

might² *noun* **1** great bodily or mental strength. **2** power to enforce one's will (usu. in contrast with *right*). □ **with all one's might** to the utmost of one's power. **with might and main** see MAIN. [Old English *miht, mieht* from Germanic, related to MAY]

might-have-been *noun informal* **1** a past possibility that no longer applies. **2** a person or thing that could have been more eminent.

mightn't *contraction* might not.

mighty ● *adjective* (**might·i·er, might·i·est**) **1** powerful or strong, in body, mind, or influence. **2** massive, bulky. **3** *informal* great, considerable. ● *adverb informal* very (*a mighty difficult task*). □ **might·i·ly** *adverb* **might·i·ness** *noun*

mignon·ette /ˌmɪnjəˈnɛt/ *noun* any of various plants of the genus *Reseda*, esp. *R. odorata*, with fragrant grey-green flowers. [French *mignonnette*, diminutive of *mignon* small]

mi·graine /ˈmaɪɡreɪn/ *noun* a recurrent throbbing headache that usually affects one side of the head, often accompanied by nausea and disturbance of vision. [French from Late Latin *hemicrania* from Greek *hēmikrania* (as HEMI-, CRANIUM): originally of a headache confined to one side of the head]

mi·grant ● *adjective* that migrates. ● *noun* a migrant person or animal, esp. a bird.

mi·grate *intransitive verb* **1** (of people) move from one place of residence to another, esp. in a different country. **2** (of an animal, esp. a bird or fish) change its area of habitation with the seasons. **3** (of a cell, atom, molecule, etc.) move in a non-random manner from one position or region to another or in a particular direction. **4** *transitive* transfer (data, programs, etc.) from one environment to another. **b** *intransitive* move from the use of one kind of computer, software, database, or programming language to another. □ **mi·gra·tion** *noun* **mi·gra·tion·al** *adjective* **mi·gra·tor** *noun* **mi·gra·tory** /ˈmaɪɡrəˌtɔri/ *adjective* [Latin *migrare migrat-*]

Migua·sha Park /mɪɡˈwɒʃə/ a provincial park and UNESCO World Heritage Site on the southern coast of the Gaspé peninsula which has the greatest number and best-preserved fossil specimens of the lobe-finned fishes of the Devonian Period.

mih·rab /ˈmiːrab/ *noun* a niche or slab in a mosque, used to show the direction of Mecca. [Arabic *miḥrāb* praying place]

mi·kado /mɪˈkɒdoː/ *noun* (*pl.* **-kados**) *hist.* the emperor of Japan. [Japanese from *mi* august + *kado* door]

Mike *noun slang* □ **for the love of Mike** an exclamation of entreaty or dismay. [abbreviation of the name *Michael*]

mike *informal* ● *noun* **1** a microphone. **2** a microwave oven. ● *transitive verb* put a microphone near, in, or on (a person, place, etc.) in order to transmit, amplify, or record sounds. [abbreviation]

Mi'kmaq /ˈmɪkmak, ˈmɪɡmə, ˈmiːmɒ/ (also **Micmac**) ● *noun* **1** a member of an Aboriginal people living in Nova Scotia, New Brunswick, PEI, and the Gaspé Peninsula. **2** the Algonquian language of this people. ● *adjective* of or relating to this people or their culture or language. [Mi'kmaq]

mik·veh /ˈmɪkvə/ *noun* (also **mik·vah, mikva**) a bath in which certain Jewish ritual purifications are performed. [Yiddish *mikve* from Hebrew *miqweh*, lit. 'collection, mass, esp. of water']

mil¹ /mɪl/ *noun* one thousandth of an inch (0.0254 mm), as a unit of measure for the diameter of wire, thickness of a film, etc. [Latin *millesimum* thousandth, from *mille* thousand]

mil² *noun* (*pl.* same) (usu. in *pl.*) esp. *N Amer. informal* a million dollars (or pounds). [abbreviation]

mi·lady /mɪˈleɪdi/ *noun* (*pl.* **-ladies**) **1** an English noblewoman. **2** a form used in speaking of or to such a person. [French from English *my lady*: compare MILORD]

Milan /mɪˈlan/ an industrial city in NW Italy, capital of Lombardy region; pop. (2001) 1,182,693. It is a leading financial, commercial, and fashion centre and is known for its large opera house, La Scala. □ **Milan·ese** /ˌmɪləˈniːz/ *adjective & noun*

Mil·banke Sound an arm of the sea off the coast of British Columbia, between Hecate Strait and Queen Charlotte Strait.

milch /mɪltʃ/ *adjective* (of a domestic mammal) giving or kept for milk. [Middle English *m(i)elche* representing Old English *mielce* (unrecorded) from Germanic: see MILK]

milch cow *noun* a source of easy profit, esp. a person.

mild ● *adjective* **1** (esp. of a person) gentle and conciliatory. **2** moderate; not severe or harsh. **3** (of the weather, esp. in winter) moderately warm. **4** (of food, tobacco, etc.) not sharp or strong in taste etc. **5** (of medicine, soap, etc.) operating gently; not harsh. **6** tame, feeble; lacking energy or vivacity. ● *noun Brit.* a beer not strongly flavoured with hops (compare BITTER 2). □ **mild·ish** *adjective* **mild·ness** *noun* [Old English *milde* from Germanic]

mil·dew /ˈmɪlduː, -djuː/ ● *noun* **1** a destructive growth of minute fungi on plants. **2** a similar growth on paper, leather, etc. exposed to damp. ● *transitive & intransitive verb* taint or be tainted with mildew. □ **mil·dewed** *adjective* **mil·dewy** *adjective* [Old English *mildēaw* from Germanic]

mildew·cide *noun* a substance used to destroy mildew.

mild·ly *adverb* in a mild fashion; to a limited extent. □ **to put it mildly** as an understatement (implying the reality is more extreme).

mild-mannered *adjective* = MILD *adjective* 1.

mild steel *noun* steel containing a small percentage of carbon, strong and tough but not readily tempered.

mile *noun* **1** (also **statute mile**) a unit of linear measure equal to 1,760 yards (approx. 1.609 kilometres). **2** *hist.* a Roman measure of 1,000 paces (approx. 1.481 kilometres, or 1,620 yards). **3** (in *pl.*) *informal* a great distance or amount (*miles better; beat them by miles*). **4** a race extending over a mile. □ **the mile-high club** used in reference to having sex on an aircraft. **miles away** *informal* lost in thought; preoccupied. (*talk* etc.) **a mile a minute** (talk etc.) very quickly. **go the extra mile** extend or exert oneself for another's benefit, esp. beyond what is strictly necessary. [Old English *mīl*, ultimately from Latin *mīl(l)ia*, pl. of *mille* 'thousand' (see sense 2)]

mile·age /ˈmaɪlɪdʒ/ *noun* **1 a** the distance travelled. **b** the distance a vehicle is capable of travelling per unit of fuel. **2** expenses per distance travelled. **3** *informal* use, benefit, profit, advantage (*got good mileage out of that suit*).

miler *noun informal* a person or horse qualified or trained specially to run a mile.

mile·stone *noun* (also *N Amer. & Austral.* **mile·post**) **1** a stone (or post) set up beside a road to mark a distance in miles. **2** a significant event or stage in a life, history, project, etc.

Mi·le·tus /maɪˈliːtəs/ an ancient city of the Ionian Greeks in SW Asia Minor. In the 7th and 6th c. BC it was a powerful port, from which more than 60 colonies were founded on the shores of the Black Sea and in Italy and Egypt.

mil·foil /ˈmɪlfɔɪl/ *noun* **1** the common yarrow, *Achillea millefolium*, with

---

uː m**oo**d   aɪ m**y**   əi p**i**pe   au br**ow**n   ʌu h**ou**se   ei d**ay**   ɔi b**oy**   ã fr**an**glais   ā C**a**nadien   ɔ̃ Br**ay**on   (*see over for consonants*)

small white flowers and finely divided leaves. **2** (in full **water milfoil**) an aquatic plant of the genus *Myriophyllum* with whorls of fine leaves. [Middle English via Old French from Latin *millefolium* from *mille* thousand + *folium* leaf, suggested by Greek *muriophullon*]

Mil·haud /miˈjo/ **Dar·ius** (1892–1974), French composer. A member of the group known as Les Six, he composed the music to Cocteau's ballet *Le Boeuf sur le toit* (1919), and his contact with Latin American music formed the inspiration for his two dance suites *Saudades do Brasil* (1920–1).

mili·ary /ˈmɪliˌeri, ˈmɪliəri/ *adjective* **1** like a millet seed in size or form. **2** (of a disease) having as a symptom a rash with lesions resembling millet seed. [Latin *miliarius* from *milium* millet]

mi·lieu /mɪlˈjuː, mɪlˈjɜː/ *noun* (*pl.* **milieux** or **milieus** /-ljuːz/) one's environment or social surroundings. [French from *mi* MID[1] + *lieu* place]

mil·itant ● *adjective* **1** combative; aggressively active esp. in support of a (usu. political) cause. **2** engaged in warfare. ● *noun* a militant person, esp. a political activist. □ **mil·itan·cy** *noun* **mil·itant·ism** *noun* **mil·itant·ly** *adverb* [Old French from Latin (as MILITATE)]

mil·itar·ia /ˌmɪlɪˈteriə/ *plural noun* military articles of historical interest.

mil·itar·ism /ˈmɪlɪtəˌrɪzəm/ *noun* **1** the policy of maintaining a strong military capability. **2** the attachment of undue importance to military values and military strength. **3** the spirit or tendencies of a professional soldier. □ **mil·itar·is·tic** *adjective* **mil·itar·is·tic·ally** *adverb*

mil·itar·ist ● *noun* **1** a person dominated by militaristic ideas. **2** a student of military science. ● *adjective* militaristic.

mil·itar·ize /ˈmɪlɪtəˌraɪz/ *transitive verb* (also esp. *Brit.* **-ise**) **1** equip with military resources. **2** make military or warlike. **3** imbue with militarism. □ **mil·itar·iz·a·tion** *noun*

mil·itary ● *adjective* of, relating to, or characteristic of soldiers or armed forces. ● *noun* (as *sing.* or *pl.*; prec. by *the*) members of the armed forces, as distinct from civilians and the police. □ **mil·itar·i·ly** *adverb* [French *militaire* or Latin *militaris* from *miles militis* soldier]

military honours *noun* marks of respect paid by troops at the burial of a soldier, to royalty, etc.

military-industri·al complex *noun* esp. *N Amer.* a nation's military and the industries supplying it, esp. as a single powerful influence on public policy.

military police *noun* (treated as *pl.*) a corps responsible for police and disciplinary duties in the armed forces.

military policeman *noun* a member of the military police. Abbr.: **MP.**

mil·itate /ˈmɪlɪˌteɪt/ *intransitive verb* (usu. foll. by *against*) (of facts or evidence) have force or effect (*what you say militates against our opinion*). ¶ See Usage note at MITIGATE. [Latin *militare militat-* from *miles militis* soldier]

mil·itia /mɪˈlɪʃə/ *noun* **1** a military force raised from the civilian population and supplementing a regular army in an emergency. **2** any usu. small military force not sanctioned by a nation or government. [Latin, = military service, from *miles militis* soldier]

mil·itia·man *noun* (*pl.* **-men**) a member of a militia.

milk ● *noun* **1** an opaque white fluid secreted by female mammals for the nourishment of their young. **2** the milk of cows, goats, or sheep as food. **3** the milk-like juice of plants, e.g. in the coconut. **4** a milk-like preparation of herbs, drugs, etc. ● *verb* **1** *transitive* draw milk from (a cow, ewe, goat, etc.). **2** *transitive* **a** exploit (a person or thing) esp. financially. **b** get all possible advantage from (a situation or thing). **3** *transitive* extract sap, venom, etc. from. **4** *intransitive* (of a cow etc.) yield milk. □ **cry over spilt milk** lament an irremediable loss or error. [Old English *milc, milcian* from Germanic]

milk and honey *noun* abundance, comfort, prosperity.

milk and water ● *noun* a feeble or insipid or mawkish discourse or sentiment. ● *attributive adjective* (**milk-and-water**) feeble, insipid.

milk chocolate *noun* chocolate made with milk (*compare* DARK CHOCOLATE).

milk·er *noun* **1** an animal, esp. a cow, yielding milk or kept for milking. **2** a person who, or a machine which, milks.

milk fat *noun* = BUTTERFAT. Abbr.: **MF.**

milk fever *noun* an acute illness in female cows, goats, etc. that have just produced young, caused by calcium deficiency.

milk float *noun Brit.* a small usu. electric motor vehicle used in delivering milk.

milk glass *noun* a semi-translucent glass, whitened by the addition of various ingredients.

milk house *noun* a room or building on a dairy farm where milk is cooled and stored.

milking parlour *noun* = PARLOUR 3.

milk·maid *noun* a girl or woman who milks cows or works in a dairy.

milk·man *noun* (*pl.* **-men**) a person who sells or delivers milk.

milk of human kindness *noun* kindness regarded as natural to humanity.

milk of magnesia *noun* a white suspension of magnesium hydroxide usu. in water as an antacid or laxative.

milk paint *noun* a durable paint containing milk protein, quicklime, clay, and earth pigments.

milk powder *noun* milk dehydrated by evaporation.

milk pudding *noun* a dessert made of flavoured milk thickened with cornstarch.

Milk River a river which rises in NW Montana and, flowing northeastward in an arc, enters SE Alberta, then flows southeastward back into Montana to join the Missouri River. [so called because its waters resembled the colour of tea with milk]

milk round *noun* **1** = MILK RUN. **2** esp. *Brit.* a regular tour or trip with several stops, esp. to recruit students for businesses.

milk run *noun* **1** the regular route followed by a person delivering milk. **2** a routine trip or train route with many regular stops. **3** a routine or easy task, expedition, etc.

milk·shake *noun* a frothy drink, usu. cold, of milk, flavouring, and usu. ice cream, mixed in a blender.

milk snake *noun* a harmless, usu. brightly coloured N American snake, *Lampropeltis triangulum*, formerly thought to suck milk from cows.

milk·sop *noun* a spiritless or ineffectual person.

milk store *noun Cdn* = CONVENIENCE STORE.

milk sugar *noun* lactose.

milk tooth *noun* a temporary tooth in young mammals; a baby tooth.

milk train *noun* a train chiefly transporting milk, usu. very early in the morning.

milk vetch *noun* any of various leguminous plants of the genus *Astragalus*, some of which are edible and some poisonous to cattle.

milk·weed *noun* **1** any of various N American plants of the genus *Asclepias*, which have milky juice and seeds plumed with long silky hairs. **2** any of various other plants with milky juice.

milk-white *adjective* (usu. *attributive*) white like milk.

milk·wort /ˈmɪlkwɜːt, -wɔːt/ *noun* any plant of the genus *Polygala*, formerly supposed to increase women's milk.

milky *adjective* (**milk·i·er**, **milk·i·est**) **1** of, like, or mixed with milk. **2** (of a gem, liquid, etc.) cloudy; not clear. **3** weak, compliant. □ **milk·i·ness** *noun*

Milky Way *noun* **1** (in full **Milky Way Galaxy**) the galaxy of which the solar system is part. **2** this viewed as a faintly luminous band of light encircling the heavens, formed of countless indistinguishable stars.

Mill ▸ 1 James (1773–1836), Scottish philosopher, economist, and historian, whose works include the *History of British India* (1817), the *Elements of Political Economy* (1821), and the *Analysis of the Phenomena of the Human Mind* (1829), in which he provided a psychological basis for Bentham's utilitarianism. **2** his son, **John Stuart** (1806–73), English philosopher and economist. In *On Liberty* (1859) he argued for the importance of individuality, and *Utilitarianism* (1861) developed Bentham's theory; his other works include *System of Logic* (1843) and *The Subjection of Women* (1869).

mill[1] ● *noun* **1 a** a building fitted with a mechanical apparatus for grinding grain. **b** such an apparatus. **2** an apparatus for grinding any solid substance to powder or pulp (*pepper mill*). **3 a** a building fitted with machinery for manufacturing processes etc. (*paper mill; steel mill*). **b** such machinery. **4 a** any group etc. generating something specified (*rumour mill*). **b** any institution etc. operating impersonally or inhumanely and concerned solely with output (*puppy mill*). **5 a** a boxing match. **b** a fist fight. ● *verb* **1** *transitive* **a** grind (grain), produce (flour), or hull (seeds) in a mill. **b** extract (a mineral) from rock by crushing the rock in a mill. **2** *transitive* produce regular ribbed markings on the edge of (a coin). **3** *transitive* cut or shape (metal) with a rotating tool. **4** *intransitive* (often foll. by *about, around*) (of people or animals) move in an aimless manner, esp. in a confused mass. **5** *transitive* beat (chocolate etc.) to froth. **6** *transitive slang* beat, strike, fight. □ **go** (or **put**, or **run**) **through the mill** undergo (or cause to undergo) intensive work or a difficult ordeal. □ **mill·able** *adjective* [Old English

Consonants: b *but* d *dog* f *few* g *get* h *her* j *yes* k *cat* l *leg* m *man* n *no* p *pen* r *red* s *sit*

mylen, ultimately from Late Latin *molinum* from Latin *mola* grindstone, mill, from *molere* grind]

mill² *noun N Amer.* one thousandth of a dollar as money of account. [Latin *millesimum* thousandth: compare CENT]

Mil·lais /'mɪleɪ/ **Sir John Ever·ett** (1829–96), English painter. A founding member of the Pre-Raphaelite Brotherhood, he gradually departed from the Pre-Raphaelite principles, and produced lavishly painted portraits, landscapes, and sentimental genre pictures; his works include *Christ in the House of his Parents* (1850), *The Blind Girl* (1856), and *Bubbles* (1886).

Mil·lay /mɪ'leɪ/ **Edna Saint Vin·cent** (1892–1950), US poet and playwright, who was noted for her technical virtuosity and directness; her verse collections include *Renascence and Other Poems* (1917) and the sonnet cycle *Fatal Interview*.

mill·board *noun* stout pasteboard for bookbinding etc.

mill dam *noun* a dam put across a stream to make it usable by a mill.

mille feuille /miːl 'fɜɪ/ *noun* **1** a dessert comprised of thin layers of puff pastry and a filling of cream, custard, etc. **2** a similar savoury dish of layers of pastry alternating with filling. [French, = thousand leaf]

mil·len·ar·ian /ˌmɪlɪ'neriən/ ● *adjective* **1** of or related to the millennium. **2** believing in the imminence of the millennium or a millennium. ● *noun* a person who believes in the imminence of the millennium or a millennium. □ **mil·len·ar·ian·ism** *noun* [as MILLENARY]

mil·len·ary /'mɪlən,eri, mɪ'lenəri/ ● *noun* (*pl.* **-aries**) **1** a period of 1,000 years. **2** the festival of the 1,000th anniversary of a person or thing. **3** a person who believes in the imminence of the millennium or a millennium. ● *adjective* of or relating to a millenary. [Late Latin *millenarius* consisting of a thousand, from *milleni* distributive of *mille* thousand]

mil·len·nial·ism /mɪ'leniəlɪzm/ *noun* the belief in the imminence of the millennium or a millennium; millenarianism. □ **mil·len·nial·ist** *noun* [as MILLENNIUM]

mil·len·nium /mɪ'leniəm/ *noun* (*pl.* **mil·len·niums** or **mil·len·nia** /-niə/) **1 a** a period of 1,000 years. **b** any millennium reckoned from the supposed date of the birth of Christ (*dawn of the third millennium*). **2** *Christianity* the period of 1,000 years during which (according to one interpretation of Rev. 20:1–5) Christ will reign in person on earth. **3** a period of good government, great happiness, and prosperity. □ **mil·len·nial** *adjective* [modern Latin from Latin *mille* 'thousand', on the pattern of BIENNIUM]

Mil·ler ▸ 1 (Alton) Glenn (1904–44), US jazz trombonist and bandleader. From 1938 he led his celebrated swing big band, with whom he recorded his signature tune 'Moonlight Serenade'; he joined the US Army in 1942 and died when his aircraft disappeared on a routine flight across the English Channel. **2 Ar·thur** (b.1915), US dramatist. He established his reputation with *Death of a Salesman* (1949), before writing *The Crucible* (1953), which used the witch trials of 1692 in Salem, Massachusetts as an allegory for McCarthyism in the 1950s. **3 Henry (Val·en·tine)** (1891–1980), US novelist, whose works achieved notoriety for their use of sexually explicit and obscene language; they include *Tropic of Cancer* (1934) and *Tropic of Capricorn* (1939).

mil·ler *noun* **1** the proprietor or tenant of a grain mill. **2** a person who works or owns a mill.

Mil·let /mɪ'leɪ/ **Jean Fran·çois** (1814–75), French painter, who is primarily known for his scenes of peasant life, which include *The Winnower* (1848), *The Gleaners* (1857), and *The Angelus* (1859).

mil·let /'mɪlət/ *noun* **1** any of various cereal plants, esp. *Panicum miliaceum*, bearing a large crop of small nutritious seeds. **2** the seed of this. [French, diminutive of *mil* from Latin *milium*]

Mil·lett /'mɪlət/ **Kath·er·ine Mur·ray ('Kate')** (b.1934), US feminist theorist and literary critic, whose influential *Sexual Politics* (1970) was one of the first works to apply the principles of feminist practice to literary criticism.

mill hand *noun* a worker in a mill or factory.

Mill·haven /'mɪlheɪvən/ part of Loyalist township in SE Ontario, located southeast of Napanee. It is the site of a penitentiary. [so called because it was originally the location of a government mill]

milli- /'mɪli/ *combining form* a thousand, esp. denoting a factor of one thousandth. Abbr.: **m**. [Latin *mille* thousand]

milli·am·meter /ˌmɪli'amɪtər/ *noun* an instrument for measuring electrical current in milliamperes.

milli·am·pere *noun* (also **milli·amp**) one thousandth of an ampere, a measure for small electrical currents.

milli·bar *noun* one thousandth of a bar, the cgs unit of atmospheric pressure equivalent to 100 pascals.

Milli·gan /'mɪlɪɡən/ **Ter·ence Alan 'Spike'** (1918–2002), British comedian and writer, born in India. He came to prominence in the cult radio program *The Goon Show* (1951–9), and thereafter appeared regularly on stage and television, and in minor film roles.

milli·gram *noun* one thousandth of a gram.

Mil·li·kan /'mɪlɪkən/ **Rob·ert An·drews** (1868–1953), US physicist. He was the first to give an accurate figure for the electric charge on an electron, and in studying the photoelectric effect, he confirmed the validity of Einstein's equation and gave an accurate figure for Planck's constant; he was awarded the Nobel Prize for physics in 1923.

milli·litre *noun* (also esp. *US* **milli·liter**) one thousandth of a litre (0.002 pint).

milli·metre *noun* (also esp. *US* **milli·meter**) one thousandth of a metre (0.039 in.).

mil·lin·er /'mɪlɪnər/ *noun* a person who makes or sells women's hats. □ **mil·lin·ery** *noun* [originally = vendor of goods from *Milan*]

mill·ing frolic *noun Cdn* (*NS*) **1** *hist.* a gathering at which participants pound new wool to raise the nap, usu. with singing, dancing, etc. **2** a cultural event at which songs traditionally sung at these are performed.

mil·lion ● *noun* (*pl.* same or (in sense 2) **mil·lions**) (in *sing.* prec. by *a* or *one*) **1** a thousand thousand. **2** (often in *pl.*) *informal* a very large number (*millions of years*; *thanks a million*). **3** (prec. by *the*) the bulk of the population. **4** a million dollars, pounds, etc. ● *adjective* that amount to a million. □ **look** (or **feel** etc.) (**like**) **a million bucks** (**dollars** etc.) look (or feel) extremely good. □ **mil·lion·fold** *adjective & adverb*

mil·lionth *adjective & noun* [Old French, prob. from Italian *millione* from *mille* thousand + *-one* augmentative suffix]

mil·lion·aire *noun* **1** a person whose assets are worth at least one million dollars, pounds, etc. **2** a person of great wealth. □ **mil·lion·air·ess** *noun*

milli·pede /'mɪli,piːd/ *noun* any arthropod of the class Diplopoda, having a long segmented body with two pairs of legs on each segment. [Latin *millepeda* wood louse, from *mille* thousand + *pes pedis* foot]

milli·sec·ond *noun* one thousandth of a second.

milli·volt *noun* one thousandth of a volt. Abbr.: **mV**.

mill·pond *noun* a pool of water retained by a mill dam for the operation of a mill. □ **like a millpond** (of a stretch of water) very calm.

mill·race *noun* a current of water that drives a mill wheel.

mill rate *noun N Amer.* the rate at which a property is taxed, expressed as the number of mills of tax for every dollar of assessed property value (*see* MILL²).

mill·stone *noun* **1** each of two circular stones used for grinding grain. **2** a heavy burden or responsibility.

mill·stream *noun* = MILLRACE.

mill wheel *noun* a wheel used to drive a water mill.

mill·work *noun* **1** work done in a mill. **2** wood products manufactured in a mill, e.g. trim or mouldings.

mill worker *noun* a worker in a factory or mill.

mill·wright *noun* **1** a person who maintains or repairs mill machinery. **2** a person who designs or builds mills.

Milne /mɪln/ **1 Alan Alex·an·der** (1882–1956), English writer of stories and poems for children. His works include the stories *Winnie-the-Pooh* (1926) and *The House at Pooh Corner* (1928), and the verse collections *When We Were Very Young* (1924) and *Now We Are Six* (1927). **2 David Brown** (1882–1953), Canadian painter. As well as working in oils and watercolours, he developed his own technique of painting in colour drypoints. His landscapes, city scenes, and still lifes give great beauty and stature to the simplest of subjects.

milo /'maɪloː/ *noun* a drought-resistant variety of sorghum grown esp. in the central US. [Sesotho *maili*]

mi·lord /mɪ'lɔrd/ *noun hist.* an Englishman travelling in Europe in aristocratic style. [French from English *my lord*: compare MILADY]

Milos·evic /mɪ'lɒsəvɪtʃ/ **Slo·bo·dan** (b.1941) Serbian politician, president of Serbia 1989-97 and of Yugoslavia 1997-2000. His nationalist policies accelerated the breakup of Yugoslavia and led to war in Bosnia-Herzegovina, Croatia, and Kosovo.

Mi·łosz /'miːlɒʃ/ **Czes·ław** (b.1911), Lithuanian-born US poet and writer. He was a member of the Polish literary avant-garde in the 1930s, and his works include *The Captive Mind* (1953), about the effect of communism on Polish writers; he was awarded the Nobel Prize for literature in 1980.

milpa /ˈmɪlpə/ *noun* (in Central America and Mexico) a small cultivated field, usu. of corn. [Latin American Spanish]

milque·toast /ˈmɪlktoːst/ *noun* a timid, submissive person. [Caspar *Milquetoast*, a cartoon character created by H. T. Webster, US cartoonist, in 1924]

milt *noun* **1 a** a sperm-filled reproductive gland of a male fish. **b** the semen of a male fish. **2** the spleen in mammals. **3** an analogous organ in other vertebrates. [Old English *milt(e)* from Germanic, perhaps related to MELT]

Mil·tia·des /mɪlˈtaɪəˌdiːz/ (c.540–489 BC), Athenian general, who led the defeat of Persian invaders at the Battle of Marathon (490).

Mil·ton[1] a town in S Ontario, situated between Oakville and Guelph; pop. (2001) 31,471. □ **Mil·ton·ian** *noun* [so called in honour of J. MILTON[2], as well as with reference to the town's numerous mills]

Mil·ton[2], **John** (1608–74), English poet and pamphleteer. His three major poems, all completed after he had gone blind (1652), are *Paradise Lost* (1667, revised 1674), an epic on the fall of man, *Paradise Regained* (1671), on Christ's temptations, and *Samson Agonistes* (1671), on Samson's final years.

Milton Keynes /ˌmɪltən ˈkiːnz/ a town in south central England, formerly in Buckinghamshire; pop. (est. 2002) 174,630. It was established as a new town in the late 1960s, and is the site of the headquarters of the Open University.

Mil·wau·kee /mɪlˈwɒki/ an industrial port and city in SE Wisconsin, on the west shore of Lake Michigan; pop. (2000) 586,974. It is noted for its brewing industry and is an important port on the St. Lawrence Seaway. □ **Mil·wau·kee·an** *noun & adjective*

Mimas /ˈmaɪmas, -məs/ **1** *Gk Myth* one of the giants, killed by Mars. **2** *Astronomy* satellite I of Saturn, the seventh closest to the planet, discovered by W. Herschel in 1789 (diameter 390 km). It is probably composed mainly of ice and is heavily cratered, with one crater a third the size of the whole satellite.

MIME *noun* a protocol for transmitting different types of data by email, whereby special characters, formatted text, and non-textual data (e.g. graphics, audio, and video) are encoded so that they can be sent and received by a standard email program. [acronym from Multi-purpose Internet Mail Extensions]

mime ● *noun* **1** the theatrical technique of suggesting action, character, etc. by gesture and expression without using words. **2** a theatrical performance using this technique. **3** (also **mime artist**) a practitioner of mime. **4** *Gk & Rom. Hist.* a simple farcical drama including mimicry. **●** *transitive & intransitive verb* **1** convey (an idea or emotion) by gesture without words. **2** (often foll. by *to*) (of singers etc.) mouth (the words of a song etc.) along with a soundtrack (*miming the latest song; mime to a record*). □ **mimer** *noun* [Latin *mimus* from Greek *mimos*]

mimeo /ˈmɪmiəʊ/ *informal* **●** *noun* (*pl.* **mimeos**) = MIMEOGRAPH *noun*. **●** *verb* (**mimeoed, mimeo·ing**) = MIMEOGRAPH *verb*. [abbreviation]

mimeo·graph /ˈmɪmiəˌɡraf/ **●** *noun* **1** (often *attributive*) a duplicating machine which produces copies from a stencil. **2** a copy produced in this way. **●** *transitive verb* reproduce (text or diagrams) by this process. [irreg. from Greek *mimeomai* imitate: see -GRAPH]

mi·mesis /mɪˈmiːsɪs, maɪ-/ *noun* **1** *Biol.* = MIMICRY 3. **2** the representation of the real world in art, poetry, etc. [Greek *mimēsis* from *mimeisthai* to imitate]

mi·met·ic /mɪˈmɛtɪk/ *adjective* **1** relating to or habitually practising mimesis or mimicry. **2** *Biol.* of or exhibiting mimicry. □ **mi·met·ic·ally** *adverb* [Greek *mimētikos* imitation (as MIMESIS)]

mimic ● *transitive verb* (**mim·icked, mim·ick·ing**) **1** imitate (a person, gesture, manner of speech, etc.) esp. to entertain or ridicule. **2** copy minutely or servilely. **3** (of a thing) resemble closely. **●** *noun* a person skilled in imitation. **●** *adjective* having an aptitude for mimicry; imitating; imitative, esp. for amusement. □ **mim·ick·er** *noun* [Latin *mimicus* from Greek *mimikos* (as MIME)]

mim·ic·ry *noun* (*pl.* **-ries**) **1** the act or art of mimicking. **2** a thing that mimics another. **3** *Biol.* a close external resemblance of an animal (or part of one) to another animal or to a plant or inanimate object; a similar resemblance in a plant.

Mimir /ˈmiːmɪːr/ *Scand. Myth* a giant who guarded the well of wisdom at the roots of the tree Yggdrasil.

Mi·mosa /mɪˈmoːzə, -ə/ a giant star, the second-brightest in the constellation Crux. [as MIMOSA]

mi·mosa *noun* **1** any leguminous shrub of the genus *Mimosa*, esp. the

sensitive plant, *M. pudica*, having globular flowers and sensitive leaves which droop when touched. **2** any of various acacia plants with showy yellow flowers. **3** a drink of champagne and orange juice. [modern Latin, apparently from Latin (as MIME, from being as sensitive as animals) + *-osa* fem. suffix]

mimu·lus /ˈmɪmjʊləs/ *noun* any flowering plant of the genus *Mimulus*, including the N American plants musk and the monkey flower. [modern Latin, apparently diminutive of Latin (as MIME, perhaps with reference to its mask-like flowers)]

Min /mɪn/ *noun* any of the Chinese languages or dialects spoken in the Fukien province in SE China and in parts of Taiwan. [Chinese]

Min. *abbreviation* **1** Minister. **2** Ministry.

min *abbreviation* **1** minute(s). **2** minim (fluid measure).

min. *abbreviation* minimum.

Mina·mata disease /mɪnəˈmɒtə/ *noun* chronic poisoning by alkyl mercury compounds, characterized by (usu. permanent) impairment of brain functions such as speech, sight, and muscular coordination. [*Minamata* bay in Japan, where residents consumed fish contaminated by industrial effluent and developed the ailment]

mina·ret /ˌmɪnəˈrɛt, ˈmɪnəˌrɛt/ *noun* a slender turret connected with a mosque and having a balcony from which the muezzin calls at hours of prayer. □ **mina·ret·ed** *adjective* [French *minaret* or Spanish *minarete* from Turkish *minare* from Arabic *manār(a)* lighthouse, minaret, from *nār* fire, light]

Minas Basin /ˈmaɪnəs/ a large inlet of the Bay of Fundy, extending into central Nova Scotia and connected to the bay via the Minas Channel. The basin is known for its daily tides, measuring 15–16 m, among the highest in the world. [originally French *Bassin des Mines* Mines' Basin, after the discovery of copper on the north shore of Minas Channel]

mina·tory /ˈmɪnəˌtɔri/ *adjective* threatening, menacing. [Late Latin *minatorius* from *minari minat-* threaten]

mince ● *verb* **1** *transitive* **a** cut up into very small pieces. **b** grind (meat). **2** *transitive* (usu. with *neg.*) restrain (one's words etc.) within the bounds of politeness. **3** *intransitive* speak or walk with an affected delicacy. **●** *noun* esp. *Brit.* minced meat. □ **min·cer** *noun* **min·cing** *adjective* (in sense 3 of *verb*). **min·cing·ly** *adverb* [Old French *mincier*, ultimately from Latin (as MINUTIA)]

mince·meat *noun* a mixture of currants, raisins, sugar, apples, candied peel, spices, and often suet. □ **make mincemeat of** utterly defeat (a person, argument, etc.).

mince pie *noun* a pie containing mincemeat.

Minch, the /mɪntʃ/ (also **the Minch·es**) a channel of the Atlantic, between the mainland of Scotland and the Outer Hebrides. The northern stretch is called the **North Minch**, the southern stretch, northwest of Skye, is called the **Little Minch**.

mincha /ˈmɪnxə/ *noun* the Jewish daily afternoon worship. [Hebrew *minḥāh*, lit. 'gift, offering']

mind ● *noun* **1 a** the seat of consciousness, awareness, thought, volition, and feeling. **b** attention, concentration (*my mind keeps wandering*). **2** the intellect; intellectual powers. **3** remembrance, memory (*it went out of my mind; I can't call it to mind*). **4** one's opinion (*we're of the same mind*). **5** a way of thinking or feeling (*shocking to the Victorian mind*). **6** the focus of one's thoughts or desires (*put one's mind to it*). **7** the state of normal mental functioning (*lose one's mind; in one's right mind*). **8** a person as embodying mental faculties (*a great mind*). **●** *verb* **1** (usu. with *neg.* or *interrogative*) **a** *transitive* object to (*do you mind if I smoke?; I don't mind your being late*). **b** *intransitive* object, be annoyed (*do you think they'd mind?*). **2** *transitive* remember; take care to (*mind you come on time*). **3** *transitive* have charge of temporarily (*mind the house while I'm away*). **4** *transitive* apply oneself to, concern oneself with (business, affairs, etc.) (*I try to mind my own business*). **5** *transitive* **a** be careful about (*mind the step; mind your mouth!; mind you don't drop it*). **b** pay attention to; concern oneself with (*don't mind the expense*). **6** *transitive N Amer. & Irish* be obedient to (*mind what your mother says*). **7** *transitive N Amer. & Scot.* recall, recollect. □ **bear** (or **keep**) **in mind** retain an awareness of; remember. **be of one mind** be in agreement; share an opinion. **be of** (or esp. *Brit.* **in**) **two minds** be undecided. **change one's mind** adopt a different opinion or plan. **come into a person's mind** be remembered. **come** (or **spring**) **to mind** (of a thought, idea, etc.) suggest itself. **don't mind me 1** often *ironic* do as you please. **2** do not let yourself be disturbed by me. **do you mind!** *ironic* an expression of annoyance. **give a person a piece of one's mind** scold or reproach a person. **give one's mind to** concentrate on or direct all one's attention to. **have a good** (or **half a**) **mind to** (often as a threat, usu. unfulfilled) feel tempted to (*I've a good mind to report you*).

Vowels: a *cat* ɑ *arm* e *bed* ɜr *her* ɜː *deux* ə *ago* ɪ *sit* i *cosy* iː *feed* ɒ *hot* ɔ *pore* oː *no* ʌ *run* ʊ *put*

have (it) in mind intend. **have in mind** be considering as suitable (*who do you have in mind for the job?*). **have a mind of one's own** be capable of independent opinion or action. **have on one's mind** be troubled by the thought of. **I don't mind if I do** used when accepting something offered. **make up one's mind** decide, resolve. **mind out for** *Brit.* guard against, avoid. **mind over matter** the power of the mind asserted over the physical universe. **mind one's Ps & Qs** be careful in one's behaviour. **mind the store** have charge of affairs temporarily. **mind you** an expression used to qualify a previous statement (*I found it quite quickly; mind you, it wasn't easy*). **never mind 1** an expression used to comfort or console. **2** (also **never you mind**) an expression used to evade a question. **3** not to mention; let alone. **open** (or **close**) **one's mind to** be receptive (or unreceptive) to (changes, new ideas, etc.). **out of one's mind 1** insane. **2** to a great extent (*I was bored out of my mind*). **not pay a person any mind** *N Amer.* not pay any attention to a person. **put a person in mind of** remind a person of. **put** (or **set**) **a person's mind at rest** (or **ease**) reassure a person. **put a person or thing out of one's mind** deliberately forget. **read a person's mind** discern a person's thoughts. **spring to mind** = COME TO MIND. **take a person's mind off** help a person not to think or worry about. **to my mind** in my opinion. [Old English *gemynd*, from Germanic]

mind-altering *adjective* (of a drug) hallucinogenic.

Min·da·nao /ˌmɪndəˈnaʊ/ the second largest island in the Philippines, in the southeast of the group. Its chief town is Davao.

mind-bending *adjective informal* (esp. of a psychedelic drug) influencing or altering one's state of mind.

mind-blowing *adjective slang* **1** overwhelming, bewildering. **2** (esp. of drugs etc.) inducing hallucinations. □ **mind-blowing·ly** *adverb*

mind-boggling *adjective informal* overwhelming, startling.
□ **mind-boggling·ly** *adverb*

mind candy *noun N Amer. slang* enjoyable but intellectually undemanding entertainment.

mind·ed *adjective* **1** (*in combination*) **a** inclined to think in some specified way (*mathematically minded; fair-minded*). **b** having a specified kind of mind (*high-minded*). **c** interested in or enthusiastic about a specified thing (*car-minded*). **2** (usu. foll. by *to* + infin.) disposed or inclined (to an action). □ **mind·ed·ly** *adverb* **mind·ed·ness** *noun*

mind·er *noun* **1** a person whose job it is to attend to a person or thing (often in *combination*: *netminder*). **2** esp. *Brit.* **a** a person employed to accompany or assist another person, either to provide protection or advice, or to monitor that person's movements, esp. a bodyguard. **b** a political adviser, esp. an experienced politician assigned to help a candidate during an election campaign.

mind-expand·ing *adjective* giving a sense of heightened or broader awareness.

mind·fuck esp. *N Amer. coarse slang* ● *transitive verb* manipulate or disturb (someone) psychologically. ● *noun* an instance of this.
□ **mind·fuck·er** *noun*

mind·ful *adjective* (often foll. by *of*) taking heed or care; being conscious. □ **mind·ful·ly** *adverb* **mind·ful·ness** *noun*

mind game *noun* **1** (usu. in *pl.*) *informal* an instance of psychological manipulation. **2** a game designed to test or exercise the intellect.

mind·less *adjective* **1** lacking intelligence; stupid. **2** not requiring thought or skill (*totally mindless work*). **3** (of an action, condition, thing, etc.) characterized by a lack of thought. **4** (usu. foll. by *of*) heedless of (advice etc.). □ **mind·less·ly** *adverb* **mind·less·ness** *noun*

mind-meld *noun* **1** (in science fiction) **a** (supposed) technique for the psychic fusion of two or more minds, permitting unrestricted communication or deep understanding. **2** a meeting of minds. [originally from the television series *Star Trek*]

mind-numbing *adjective* (esp. of tedium) that numbs the mind.
□ **mind-numbing·ly** *adverb*

Min·doro /mɪnˈdɔːroʊ/ an island in the Philippines. It is situated to the southwest of Luzon.

mind reader *noun* a person capable of discerning the thoughts of another. □ **mind reading** *noun*

mind·scape *noun* reality as imagined in one's mind, and often as portrayed in art. [after LANDSCAPE]

mind·set *noun* a frame of mind, a mental attitude.

mind's eye *noun informal* the mind as viewer of memories or things imagined. □ **in one's mind's eye** in one's imagination or mental view.

mine¹ *possessive pronoun* **1** the one or ones belonging to or associated with me (*it is mine; mine are over there*). **2** (*attributive* before a vowel) *archaic*

= MY (*mine eyes have seen*). □ **of mine** of or belonging to me (*a friend of mine*). [Old English *mīn* from Germanic]

mine² ● *noun* **1** an excavation in the earth for extracting metal, coal, salt, etc. **2** an abundant source (of information etc.). **3** a receptacle filled with explosive and placed in the ground or in the water for destroying enemy personnel, ships, etc. **4 a** a subterranean gallery in which explosive is placed to blow up fortifications. **b** *hist.* a subterranean passage under the wall of a besieged fortress. ● *transitive verb* **1** *transitive* obtain (metal, coal, etc.) from a mine. **2** *transitive & intransitive* (often foll. by *for*) dig in (the earth etc.) for ore etc. **3** *transitive* **a** dig or burrow in (usu. the earth). **b** make (a hole, passage, etc.) underground. **4** *transitive* lay explosive mines under or in. **5** *transitive* = UNDERMINE. □ **min·able** *adjective* [Old French *mine, miner*, perhaps from Celtic]

mine·field *noun* **1** an area planted with explosive mines. **2** a subject or situation presenting unseen hazards.

mine·lay·er *noun* a ship or aircraft for laying mines.

min·er *noun* **1** a person who works in a mine. **2** any burrowing insect or grub.

min·eral ● *noun* **1** a substance that occurs naturally in the earth and is not formed from animal or vegetable matter. **2** a solid, inorganic substance of homogeneous composition and usu. a crystalline structure, having distinctive chemical and physical properties. **3** a substance obtained by mining. **4** any of the elements, e.g. calcium, iron, etc., that are essential for good nutrition. **5** (often in *pl.*) *Brit.* an artificial mineral water or other effervescent drink. ● *adjective* **1** of or containing a mineral or minerals. **2** obtained by mining. [medieval Latin *minerale*, neuter of *mineralis* from *minera* ore]

min·eral·ize *verb* (also esp. *Brit.* **-ise**) **1** *transitive & intransitive* change wholly or partly into a mineral. **2** *transitive* impregnate (water etc.) with a mineral substance. **3** *transitive* change (a metal) into an ore.
□ **min·eral·iz·a·tion** *noun*

min·eral·ogy /ˌmɪnəˈrɒlədʒi, -ˈalədʒi/ *noun* the scientific study of minerals. □ **min·eral·ogi·cal** *adjective* **min·eral·ogi·cal·ly** *adverb* **min·eral·o·gist** *noun*

mineral oil *noun* **1** a colourless odourless oily liquid obtained from petroleum and used as a lubricant, laxative, etc. **2** *Brit.* petroleum or one of its distillation products.

mineral rights *plural noun* ownership rights to the minerals located on or below a property.

mineral spirits *plural noun N Amer.* a volatile liquid distilled from petroleum and used esp. as a paint thinner.

mineral water *noun* **1** water found in nature with some dissolved salts present. **2** *Brit.* any effervescent non-alcoholic drink.

mineral wool *noun* = ROCKWOOL.

miner's lettuce *noun* any of various edible plants of the genus *Montia* of moist places of western N America.

Min·erva /mɪˈnɜːrvə/ *Rom. Myth* the goddess of handicrafts, widely worshipped and regularly identified with Athene, which led to her being regarded also as the goddess of war.

mine shaft *noun* a shaft giving access to a mine.

min·es·trone /ˌmɪnɪˈstroʊni/ *noun* a soup containing vegetables and pasta, beans, or rice. [Italian]

mine·sweep·er *noun* a ship for clearing away floating and submarine mines.

mine·work·er *noun* = MINER 1.

Ming *noun* **1** the Chinese dynasty founded in 1368 by Zhu Yuanzhang after the collapse of Mongol authority in China, and ruling until succeeded by the Manchus in 1644 (*see* QING). **2** Chinese porcelain made during the rule of this dynasty. [Chinese, = 'bright, clear']

Min·gan Archipelago National Park Reserve /mãˈgã/ a park reserve in E Quebec, situated along the north shore of the Gulf of St. Lawrence, opposite Anticosti Island. Established in 1984, it encompasses close to fifty islands, islets and reefs. [prob. from Breton, = white stone]

min·gle *verb* (often foll. by *with*) **1** *transitive & intransitive* mix, blend. **2** *intransitive* socialize, esp. at a party etc. □ **mingle with** go about among. □ **ming·ler** *noun* [Middle English *mengel* from obsolete *meng* from Old English *mengan*, related to AMONG]

Min·gus /ˈmɪŋgəs/ **Charles ('Charlie')** (1922–79), US jazz bassist and composer. A leading figure of the 1940s jazz scene, he experimented with atonality and was influenced by gospel and blues; his compositions include 'Goodbye Porkpie Hat'.

mingy /ˈmɪndʒi/ *adjective* (**min·gi·er, min·gi·est**) *informal* **1** mean, stingy. **2** small. □ **min·gi·ly** *adverb* [perhaps from MEAN² and STINGY]

---

uː mood aɪ my əɪ pipe aʊ brown ʌʊ house eɪ day ɔɪ boy ɑ̃ franglais ã Canadien ɔ̃ Brayon   (*see over for consonants*)

mini *noun* (*pl.* **minis**) **1** *informal* **a** a miniskirt. **b** a garment, e.g. a dress, with a miniskirt. **2** a minicomputer. [abbreviation]

mini- *combining form* miniature; very small or minor of its kind (*minibus; mini-budget*). [abbreviation of MINIATURE]

min·ia·ture /ˈmɪnɪtʃər, ˈmɪnɪətʃər/ ● *adjective* **1** much smaller than normal. **2** represented on a small scale. ● *noun* **1** any object reduced in size. **2** a small-scale minutely finished portrait. **3** this branch of painting (*portrait in miniature*). **4** a picture or decorated letters in an illuminated manuscript. □ **in miniature** on a small scale.
□ **mini·atur·ist** *noun* (in senses 2 and 3 of *noun*). [Italian *miniatura* from medieval Latin *miniatura* from Latin *miniare* from Latin *minium* red lead, vermilion]

miniature golf *noun* a game patterned on golf, but played on a small obstacle course.

mini·atur·ize *transitive verb* (also esp. *Brit.* **-ise**) produce in a smaller version; make small. □ **mini·atur·iz·a·tion** *noun*

mini·bar *noun* a small fridge containing mainly alcoholic drinks and snacks placed in a hotel room for the use of guests, the contents being charged to the bill if used.

mini·blind *noun* *N Amer.* a type of venetian blind with narrow slats.

mini·budget *noun* an interim budget, usu. limited in scope, brought down by a government.

mini·bus *noun* a small bus for about twelve passengers.

mini·cab *noun* *Brit.* a taxi available for hire only by phone.

mini·cam *noun* a hand-held video camera.

mini·camp *noun* *N Amer.* *Sport* a short training camp, held esp. in addition to the regular training camp, to which players are invited to try out for a team or prepare for the coming season.

mini·com·put·er *noun* a computer of medium power, more than a microcomputer but less than a mainframe.

Mini·coy Islands /ˈmɪnɪˌkɔɪ/ one of the groups of islands forming the Indian territory of Lakshadweep in the Indian Ocean.

Mini Disc /ˈmɪnɪdɪsk/ *noun proprietary* a small recordable version of a compact disc.

mini·dress *noun* a very short dress.

mini·golf *noun* = MINIATURE GOLF.

min·im /ˈmɪnɪm/ *noun* **1** *Music* = HALF NOTE. **2** one-sixtieth of a fluid drachm, about a drop. **3** an object or portion of the smallest size or importance. **4** a single downstroke of the pen. [Latin *minimus* smallest]

min·ima *pl.* of MINIMUM.

min·imal *adjective* **1** as small as possible; minimum. **2 a** *Art etc.* characterized by the use of simple or primary forms or structures etc., often geometric or massive (*huge minimal forms in a few colours*). **b** *Music* characterized by the repetition of short phrases which change very gradually as the music proceeds. □ **min·imal·ly** *adverb* [Latin *minimus* smallest]

min·imal·ist ● *adjective* **1** (esp. of an aesthetic style) constituting or characterized by the minimum required; not elaborate. **2** advocating moderate policies. **3** of or relating to minimal art or music. ● *noun* **1** (also *attributive*) a person advocating minor or moderate reform in politics (*opp.* MAXIMALIST). **2** a person who advocates or practises minimal art or music. □ **min·imal·ism** *noun* **min·imal·is·tic** *adjective*

mini·mall *noun* *N Amer.* a mall containing a relatively small number of stores etc. and with access to each store from the outdoors rather than from an interior hallway.

mini·mart *noun* *N Amer.* = CONVENIENCE STORE.

mini·max *noun* **1** *Math.* the lowest of a set of maximum values. **2** (usu. *attributive*) **a** a strategy that minimizes the greatest risk to a participant in a game etc. **b** the theory that in a game with two players, a player's smallest possible maximum loss is equal to the same player's greatest possible minimum gain. [MINIMUM + MAXIMUM]

mini·mill *noun* a small steel plant, esp. one that produces steel by melting down scrap.

mini·mize *transitive verb* (also esp. *Brit.* **-mise**) **1** reduce to, or estimate at, the smallest possible amount or degree. **2** estimate or represent at less than the true value or importance. □ **mini·miz·a·tion** *noun* **mini·miz·er** *noun*

min·imum (*pl.* **-imums** or **min·ima**) ● *noun* **1** the least possible or attainable amount (*reduced to a minimum*). **2** the lowest amount of a varying quality, e.g. temperature, pressure, etc., attained or recorded within a particular period. ● *adjective* that is a minimum. [Latin, neuter of *minimus* least]

minimum-security *adjective* (of a correctional institution) having no extraordinary security measures such as perimeter fences, barred windows, etc. (*compare* MAXIMUM-SECURITY, MEDIUM-SECURITY).

minimum wage *noun* the lowest wage permitted by law or special agreement.

min·ing *noun* the process or industry of removing metals, coal, etc. from a mine.

mining recorder *noun* *Cdn* a government official who registers mining claims.

min·ion /ˈmɪnjən/ *noun derogatory* a follower or underling of a powerful person, esp. a servile or unimportant one. [French *mignon*, Old French *mignot*, of Gaulish origin]

mini·pill *noun* a contraceptive pill containing a progestin only (not estrogen).

mini·putt *noun* *Cdn* = MINIATURE GOLF.

mini·series *noun* a film shown on television in several segments broadcast within a few days of each other.

mini·skirt *noun* a very short skirt. □ **mini·skirt·ed** *adjective*

min·is·ter ● *noun* **1** *Parl.* (in Canada, the UK, and other Commonwealth countries) a head of a government department. **2** (in full **minister of religion**) a member of the clergy, esp. in some Protestant denominations. **3** a diplomatic agent, usu. ranking below an ambassador. **4** (in full **minister general**) the superior of some religious orders. **5** *archaic* (usu. foll. by *of*) a person employed in the execution of (a purpose, will, etc.). ● *verb* **1** *intransitive* (usu. foll. by *to*) render aid or service (to a person, cause, etc.). **2** *intransitive* serve as or perform the functions of a minister of religion (*ministered there for 17 years*). □ **min·is·trable** *adjective* [Old French *ministre* from Latin *minister* servant, from *minus* less]

min·is·ter·ial /ˌmɪnɪˈstiːriəl/ *adjective* **1** of a government minister. **2** of a minister of religion or a minister's office. **3** instrumental or subsidiary in achieving a purpose (*ministerial in bringing about a settlement*). □ **min·is·ter·ial·ly** *adverb*

ministering angel *noun* a kind-hearted person, esp. a woman, who nurses or comforts others. [with reference to Mark 1:13, where angels are said to minister to Jesus during his 40 days in the wilderness]

minister of state *noun* (in Canada) a federal government minister having responsibility for a certain policy area but without direct control over a department established by statute with a dedicated budget (*Minister of State for Fitness and Amateur Sport*). ¶ In Canada, this position was superseded in 1993 by the creation of that of SECRETARY OF STATE.

Minister of the Crown *noun* (in Canada, the UK, and other Commonwealth countries) a member of the Cabinet.

Minister's Permit *noun* *Cdn* a permit issued by a visa or immigration officer that allows a person not otherwise eligible to immigrate to Canada to enter or remain in Canada for a period of up to three years.

minister without portfolio *noun* a government minister who has Cabinet status, but is not in charge of a specific department or ministry. ¶ This position no longer exists in Canada.

min·is·trant /ˈmɪnɪstrənt/ *noun* a person who ministers to another's needs.

min·is·tra·tion /ˌmɪnɪˈstreɪʃən/ *noun* **1** (usu. in *pl.*) aid or service (*the kind ministrations of her neighbours*). **2** ministering, esp. in religious matters. **3** (usu. foll. by *of*) the supplying (of help, justice, etc.). [Old French *ministration* or Latin *ministratio* (as MINISTER)]

min·is·try *noun* (*pl.* **-tries**) **1 a** a government department headed by a minister. **b** the building or buildings which it occupies. **2 a** (prec. by *the*) the vocation or profession of a religious minister (*called to the ministry*). **b** the office of a religious minister, priest, etc. **c** the period of tenure of this. **d** a form of Christian service effected by a lay person. **3** (prec. by *the*) the body of ministers of a government or of a religion. **4** a period of government under one prime minister. **5** ministering, ministration. [Latin *ministerium* (as MINISTER)]

mini·van *noun* a small passenger van, usu. having side windows and removable rear seats.

min·iver /ˈmɪnɪvər/ *noun* plain white fur used in ceremonial robes of state. [Anglo-French *menuver*, Old French *menu vair* (as MENU, VAIR)]

mink *noun* **1** either of two small semi-aquatic ermine-like animals of the genus *Mustela*, *M. vison* of N America and *M. intreola* of Europe. **2** the thick brown fur of these. **3** a coat made of this. [Middle Low German *menk*]

minke /ˈmɪŋkə/ *noun* a small baleen whale, *Balaenoptera acutorostrata*, with a pointed snout. [prob. from *Meincke*, the name of a Norwegian whaler]

Min·kow·ski /mɪŋˈkɒfski/ **Her·mann** (1864–1909), Russian-born

German mathematician. He studied the theory of quadratic forms, contributed to the understanding of the geometrical properties of sets in multi-dimensional space, and was the first to suggest the concept of four-dimensional space-time, which was the basis for Einstein's later work on the general theory of relativity.

Minn. *abbreviation* Minnesota.

Min·ne·ap·olis /ˌmɪnɪˈapəlɪs/ an industrial city and port on the Mississippi in SE Minnesota; pop. (2000) 382,618. □ **Min·nea·pol·itan** /ˌmɪniəˈpəlɪtən/ *noun*

min·neo·la /ˌmɪnɪˈoːlə/ *noun* a thin-skinned, deep-reddish variety of tangelo. [*Minneola*, a town in Florida]

minne·singer /ˈmɪnɪˌsɪŋər/ *noun* a German lyric poet and singer of the 12th–14th c. [German, = love singer]

Min·ne·sota /ˌmɪnəˈsoːtə/ a state in the north central US, on the Canadian border; pop. (2000) 4,919,479; capital, St. Paul. □ **Min·ne·so·tan** *noun & adjective*

min·now *noun* any of various small freshwater fish, esp. of the carp family. [late Middle English *menow*, perhaps representing Old English *mynwe* (unrecorded), *myne*: influenced by Middle English *menuse, menise* from Old French *menuise*, ultimately related to MINUTIA]

Min·oan /mɪˈnoːən/ ● *adjective* **1** lesser or relating to the Bronze Age civilization centred on Crete (*c*.3000–1100 BC). ● *noun* **1** an inhabitant of Minoan Crete or the Minoan world. **2** the language or scripts associated with the Minoans. [MINOS, to whom the palace excavated at Knossos was attributed]

min·or /ˈmaɪnər/ ● *adjective* **1** lesser or comparatively small in size or importance (*minor poet; minor operation*). **2** *Music* **a** (of a scale) having intervals of a semitone between the second and third, fifth and sixth, and seventh and eighth degrees. **b** (of an interval) less by a semitone than a major interval. **c** (of a key) based on a minor scale, tending to produce a melancholy effect. **3** *Cdn* designating organized amateur team sport for children (*minor hockey; minor soccer*). **4** *Logic* **a** (of a term) occurring as the subject of the conclusion of a categorical syllogism. **b** (of a premise) containing the minor term in a categorical syllogism. **5** *Brit.* (in schools) indicating the younger of two children from the same family or the second to enter the school (usu. put after the name). ● *noun* **1** a person under the legal age limit or majority (*no unaccompanied minors*). **2** *Music* a minor key etc. **3** *N Amer., Austral., & NZ* a student's subsidiary subject or course (*compare* MAJOR 4). **4** *Hockey* = MINOR PENALTY. **5** (in *pl.*) *N Amer.* the minor leagues. **6** *Logic* a minor term or premise. ● *intransitive verb* (foll. by *in*) *N Amer., Austral., & NZ* (of a student) undertake study in (a subject) as a subsidiary to a main subject. □ **in a minor key** (of novels, events, people's lives, etc.) understated, subdued, often with a melancholy tinge. [Latin, = smaller, less, related to *minuere* lessen]

minor axis *noun* the axis of an ellipse which passes through the centre at right angles to the major axis.

Min·orca /mɪˈnɔːkə/ the most easterly and second largest of the Balearic Islands; pop. (2001) 75,296; capital, Mahón. □ **Min·or·can** *adjective & noun*

Min·or·ite /ˈmaɪnəˌraɪt/ *noun* a Franciscan friar or Friar Minor, so called because the Franciscans regarded themselves as of humbler rank than members of other orders.

min·or·ity /maɪˈnɒrɪti, mɪ-/ *noun* (pl. **-ities**) **1** (often foll. by *of*) a smaller number or part, esp. within a political party or structure. **2** the state of having less than half the votes or of being supported by less than half of the body of opinion (*in the minority*). **3 a** (also **minority group**) a relatively small group of people differing from others in the society of which they are a part in race, religion, language, political persuasion, etc. **b** a member of such a group. **4** (*attributive*) relating to or done by the minority (*minority interests*). **5 a** the state of being under full legal age. **b** the period of this. [French *minorité* or medieval Latin *minoritas* from Latin *minor*: see MINOR]

minority government *noun Cdn, Brit., Austral., & NZ* a government that has fewer seats in parliament than the total number held by all other parties.

minority leader *noun* (in the US) the floor leader of the party having a minority in a legislature.

Miño River /ˈmiːnjoː/ a river which rises in NW Spain and flows south to the Portuguese border, which it follows before entering the Atlantic north of Viana do Castelo.

minor-key *adjective* subdued, understated.

minor league *N Amer.* ● *noun* **1** (esp. in hockey and baseball) a league of professional clubs other than the major leagues. **2** *Cdn* an amateur league for children and youth, esp. in hockey, football, etc. ● *adjective* (usu. **minor-league**) **1** of or relating to a minor league (*set a*

minor-league record). **2** of inferior quality; small-time. □ **minor-leaguer** *noun*

minor orders *plural noun Catholicism hist.* the grades of members of the clergy below that of deacon.

minor penalty *noun Hockey* a two minute penalty given for lesser infractions.

minor planet *noun see* PLANET 1b.

minor prophet *noun Bible* any of the Hebrew prophets from Hosea to Malachi, whose surviving writings are not lengthy.

minor suit *noun Bridge* diamonds or clubs.

Minos /ˈmaɪnɒs/ *Gk Myth* a legendary king of Crete, son of Zeus and Europa. According to one story, Poseidon revenged himself on Minos by causing his wife Pasiphaë to give birth to the Minotaur; a cruel tyrant, Minos later exacted tribute from Athens in the form of youths and maidens to be devoured by the monster.

Mino·taur /ˈmɪnəˌtɔːr, ˈmaɪn-/ *noun* (in Greek mythology) a man with a bull's head, kept in a Cretan labyrinth and fed with human flesh; it was eventually slain by Theseus. [Greek *Minōtauros* from MINOS + *tauros* bull]

min·oxid·il /mɪˈnɒksɪˌdɪl/ *noun* a pyrimidine derivative used to treat hypertension, which can also promote hair growth when applied topically. [AMINO + OXIDE + *-il*, of unknown origin]

Minsk /mɪnsk/ the capital of Belarus, an industrial city in the central region of the country; pop. (est. 2002) 1,764,700.

min·ster /ˈmɪnstər/ *noun Brit.* a large or important church, esp. a cathedral. [Old English *mynster* from ecclesiastical Latin *monasterium* from Greek *monastērion* MONASTERY]

min·strel /ˈmɪnstrəl/ *noun* **1** a medieval singer or musician, esp. singing or reciting poetry. **2** *hist.* a person who entertained patrons with singing, buffoonery, etc. **3** (usu. in *pl.*) a member of a minstrel show. [Old French *menestral* entertainer, servant, from Provençal *menest(ai)ral* officer, employee, musician, from Late Latin *ministerialis* official, officer]

minstrel show *noun* an entertainment popular in the late 19th and early 20th c., featuring usu. whites in blackface performing comedy routines, songs, and dances based on stereotypes of black culture.

min·strel·sy /ˈmɪnstrəlsi/ *noun* (pl. **-sies**) **1** the minstrel's art. **2** a body of minstrels. **3** minstrel poetry.

mint¹ ● *noun* **1** any aromatic plant of the genus *Mentha*. **2** a mint-flavoured candy. **3** the flavour or scent of mint. ● *adjective* having the flavour of mint (*mint icing*). □ **minty** *adjective* (**mint·i·er**, **mint·i·est**). [Old English *minte* ultimately from Latin *ment(h)a* from Greek *minthē*]

mint² ● *noun* **1** a place where money is coined under governmental control. **2** a vast sum of money (*making a mint*). **3** a source of invention etc. (*a mint of ideas*). ● *adjective* in perfect condition; as new (*the bike was in mint condition*). ● *transitive verb* **1** make (coin) by stamping metal. **2** invent, coin (a word, phrase, etc.). □ **mint·age** *noun* [Old English *mynet* from West Germanic from Latin *moneta* MONEY]

mint·ed¹ *adjective* flavoured with mint.

mint·ed² *adjective* recently created (*newly minted MBAs*).

mint green ● *noun* a pale pastel green. ● *adjective* of this colour.

mint julep *noun N Amer.* a sweet iced alcoholic drink of bourbon flavoured with mint.

mint mark *noun* a mark on a coin to indicate the mint at which it was struck.

mint master *noun* the superintendent of coinage at a mint.

Minto¹ a town in SW Ontario, northwest of Waterloo; pop. (2001) 8,164. [in honour of the 1st Earl of *Minto* (1751–1814)]

Minto² /ˈmɪntoː/ **Gil·bert John Mur·ray Kynyn·mond El·liot, 4th Earl of** (1845–1914), British soldier, Governor General of Canada 1898–1904. Although he attempted to foster closer relations between English and French Canadians, his distrust of politicians and his frequent criticism of the government caused a great deal of tension.

Minto Cup *noun Cdn* a trophy awarded annually to the Canadian junior amateur lacrosse champions, first presented in 1901 (*compare* MANN CUP). [Lord MINTO², who donated it]

Min·ton /ˈmɪntən/ **Thom·as** (1765–1836), English pottery and china manufacturer. He founded his own business in Stoke-on-Trent (1789) and built a pottery works in Stoke in 1793, where he popularized the willow pattern. In 1820 he started producing bone china.

mint sauce *noun* chopped mint in vinegar and sugar, usu. eaten with lamb.

minu·end /ˈmɪnjʊˌend/ *noun Math.* a quantity or number from which another is to be subtracted. [Latin *minuendus* gerundive of *minuere* diminish]

minu·et /ˌmɪnjʊˈet/ *noun* **1** a slow stately dance for two in triple time, popular esp. in the 17th and 18th c. **2** the music for this, or music in the same rhythm and style, often as a movement in a suite, sonata, or symphony. [French *menuet*, originally adj. = fine, delicate, diminutive of *menu*: see MENU]

minus ● *preposition* **1** with the subtraction of (*7 minus 4 equals 3*). Symbol: –. **2** (of temperature) below zero (*minus 2°*). **3** lacking; deprived of (*Stephen returned minus the dog*). ● *adjective* **1** *Math.* negative. **2** *Electronics* having a negative charge. **3** (after a grade etc.) of a standard slightly lower than the one stated (*got a B minus on the exam*). ● *noun* **1** = MINUS SIGN. **2** *Math.* a negative quantity. **3** a disadvantage. [Latin, neuter of *minor* less]

min·us·cule /ˈmɪnəˌskjuːl/ ● *adjective* **1** extremely small or unimportant. **2** lower case. ● *noun* **1** a lower case letter. **2** a kind of cursive script developed in the 7th c. □ **min·us·cu·lar** /mɪˈnʌskjʊlər/ *adjective* [French from Latin *minuscula* (*littera* letter) diminutive of *minor*: see MINOR]

minus sign *noun* the symbol –, indicating subtraction or a negative value.

min·ute¹ /ˈmɪnɪt/ ● *noun* **1** the sixtieth part of an hour. **2** a distance covered in one minute (*ten minutes from the subway*). **3 a** a moment; an instant; a point of time (*Shannon will be home any minute; stop it this minute!; one minute she's happy and the next she's depressed*). **b** a short time (*I'll be there in a minute; do you have a minute?; just be quiet for a minute*). **c** (prec. by *the*) *informal* the present time (*what are you doing at the minute?*). **d** (foll. by clause) as soon as (*call me the minute you get back*). **4** the sixtieth part of an angular degree. **5** (in *pl.*) a brief summary of the proceedings at a meeting. **6** a note or memorandum authorizing or recommending a course of action. ● *transitive verb* **1** record (proceedings) in the minutes. **2** esp. *Brit.* send the minutes to (a person). □ **in a minute 1** very soon (*I'll get up in a minute*). **2** very readily (*she'd marry him in a minute*). **just** (or **wait**) **a minute 1** a request to wait for a short time. **2** as a prelude to a query or objection. **not for a minute** not at all (*I never thought for a minute that you would refuse*). [Old French from Late Latin *minuta* (n.), from fem. of *minutus* MINUTE²: senses 1 & 4 of noun from medieval Latin *pars minuta prima* first minute part (compare SECOND²): senses 5 & 6 perhaps from medieval Latin *minuta scriptura* draft in small writing]

min·ute² /maɪˈnjuːt, -ˈnuːt/ *adjective* (**minut·est**) **1** very small. **2** trifling, petty. **3** (of an inquiry, inquirer, etc.) accurate, detailed, precise. □ **mi·nute·ly** *adverb* **mi·nute·ness** *noun* [Latin *minutus* past participle of *minuere* lessen]

minute hand *noun* the hand on an analog watch or clock which indicates minutes.

Minute·man *noun* (*pl.* **-men**) *US* **1** a type of three-stage intercontinental ballistic missile. **2** *hist.* an American militiaman of the revolutionary period (ready to march at a minute's notice).

minute steak *noun* a thin slice of steak to be cooked quickly, esp. one that has been tenderized.

minu·tia /mɪˈnuːʃə, -ˈʃɪə, -ˈjuː-, mai-/ *noun* (*pl.* **-tiae** /-ʃiaɪ, -ʃiə, -ʃə/) (usu. in *pl.*) a precise, trivial, or minor detail. [Latin, = smallness, in pl. trifles, from *minutus*: see MINUTE²]

minx /mɪŋks/ *noun* a mischievous or pert girl. □ **minx·ish** *adjective* [16th c.: origin unknown]

min·yan /ˈmɪnjən, mɪnˈjɒn/ *noun* the quorum of ten males over thirteen years of age required for traditional Jewish public worship. [Hebrew *minyān* count, reckoning]

Mio·cene /ˈmaɪəˌsiːn/ *Geol.* ● *adjective* of or relating to the fourth epoch of the Tertiary period, between the Oligocene and the Pliocene. The Miocene lasted from about 24.6 to 5.1 million years ago, and was a period of great earth movements during which the Alps and Himalayas were being formed. ● *noun* this geological epoch or system. [irreg. from Greek *meiōn* less + *kainos* new]

mi·o·sis /maɪˈoʊsɪs/ *noun* (also **myosis**) excessive constriction of the pupil of the eye. □ **mi·otic** /maɪˈɒtɪk/ *adjective* [Greek *muō* shut the eyes + -OSIS]

MIPS /mɪps/ *noun* a unit of computing speed equivalent to a million instructions per second. [acronym]

Mi·que·lon see SAINT-PIERRE AND MIQUELON.

Mira·beau /ˈmɪrəˌboʊ/ **Hon·oré Gab·riel Ri·queti, Comte de** (1749–91), French revolutionary politician. A deputy of the Third Estate in the Estates General, and a political moderate, he pressed for a form of constitutional monarchy; he was made president of the National Assembly in 1791.

Mira·bel /ˈmɪrəbel/ a town in south central Quebec, northwest of Montreal; pop. (2001) 27,330. It is the site of an international airport serving charter and cargo flights. [origin uncertain: perhaps a blend of *Miriam* and *Isabelle*, daughters of an early Scottish settler, or perhaps from MIRABELLE]

mira·belle /ˌmɪrəˈbel/ *noun* **1 a** a European variety of plum tree, bearing small round yellow fruit. **b** a fruit from this tree. **2** a liqueur distilled from this fruit. [French]

mir·ab·ile dictu /mɪˈrabɪleɪ ˈdɪktuː/ *adverb* wonderful to relate. [Latin]

mir·acle *noun* **1** an extraordinary event attributed to some supernatural agency. **2 a** any remarkable occurrence. **b** a remarkable development in some specified area (*an economic miracle*). **3** (usu. foll. by *of*) a remarkable or outstanding specimen (*the plan was a miracle of ingenuity*). [Old French from Latin *miraculum* object of wonder, from *mirari* wonder, from *mirus* wonderful]

miracle drug *noun* a drug which represents a breakthrough in medical science.

miracle play *noun* a medieval play based on the Bible or the lives of the saints.

mir·acu·lous *adjective* **1** of the nature of a miracle; supernatural. **2** remarkable, surprising. **3** having the power to work miracles. □ **mir·acu·lous·ly** *adverb* **mir·acu·lous·ness** *noun* [French *miraculeux* or medieval Latin *miraculosus* from Latin (as MIRACLE)]

mira·dor /ˌmɪrəˈdɔr/ *noun* a turret or tower etc. attached to a building, and commanding an excellent view. [Spanish from *mirar* to look]

mir·age /mɪˈrɒʒ/ *noun* **1** an optical illusion caused by atmospheric conditions, esp. the appearance of a sheet of water in a desert or on a hot road from the reflection of light. **2** an illusory thing. [French from *se mirer* be reflected, from Latin *mirare* look at]

Mira·michi /ˌmɪrəməˈʃi/ a city in NE New Brunswick, situated on the Miramichi River near its mouth, 72 km (45 miles) south of Bathurst; pop. (2001) 18,508. □ **Mira·michi·er** *noun* [the name of the bay, possibly from Montagnais *Maissimeu Assi* Mi'kmaq land]

Miramichi River a river in NE New Brunswick, rising in three main branches (the Southwest, Little Southwest, and Northwest Miramichi rivers) in the north and central parts of the province, and flowing through the city of Miramichi into Miramichi Bay, an inlet of the Gulf of St. Lawrence. [see MIRAMICHI]

Mir·anda /mɪˈrandə/ *adjective* *US Law* designating or pertaining to the duty of the police to inform a person taken into custody of his or her right to legal counsel and the right to remain silent under questioning (*Miranda rights*). [*Miranda* versus Arizona, the case that led to the US Supreme Court ruling on the matter]

Mir·an·dize /mɪˈrandaɪz/ *transitive verb* *US Law* inform (a person under arrest) of the right to remain silent and to have legal counsel. [as MIRANDA + -IZE]

mire ● *noun* **1** a stretch of swampy or boggy ground. **2** wet or soft mud; muck. **3** a difficult situation from which it is difficult to extricate oneself. ● *verb* **1** *transitive & intransitive* plunge or sink in a mire. **2** *transitive* (usu. in *passive*) involve in difficulties. □ **miry** *adjective* [Old Norse *mýrr* from Germanic, related to MOSS]

mire·poix /mɪrəˈpwɒ/ *noun* sautéed chopped vegetables, usu. including carrots and onions, used in sauces etc. [French, from Duc de *Mirepoix*, French general d.1757]

mirex /ˈmaɪreks/ *noun* an organochlorine insecticide used esp. against ants. [origin unknown]

Mir·fak /ˈmɪrfak/ a yellow super giant star, the brightest in the constellation Perseus. [Arabic, lit. 'the elbow']

mir·id /ˈmɪrɪd, ˈmaɪrɪd/ ● *noun* a heteropteran bug of the family Miridae (formerly Capsidae), which includes numerous plant pests. *Also called* CAPSID¹. ● *adjective* of or relating to this family. [modern Latin *Miris* genus name, from *mirus* 'wonderful']

mirin /ˈmiːrɪn/ *noun* a sweet, golden coloured Japanese rice wine, used esp. in cooking. [Japanese, from *mi*- taste + *-rin* to remove astringency, both from Middle Chinese]

mir·li·ton /ˈmɜrlɪtən/ *noun* = CHAYOTE. [French, = 'reed pipe', of unknown origin]

Miró /mɪˈroʊ/ **Joan** (1893–1983), Spanish painter. One of the most prominent figures of surrealism, he painted a brightly coloured fantasy world of variously spiky and amoebic calligraphic forms against plain backgrounds; major works include *Harlequinade* (1924–5).

mir·ror ● *noun* **1** a polished surface, usu. of amalgam-coated glass or metal, which reflects an image. **2** anything regarded as giving an accurate reflection or description of something else. **3** *Computing* (in full **mirror site**) a site on a network which stores some or all of the contents from another site. ● *transitive verb* **1** reflect as in a mirror. **2** *Computing* keep a copy of some or all of the contents of (a network site) at another site, esp. in order to improve accessibility. [Old French *mirour* ultimately from Latin *mirare* look at]

mirror ball *noun* a large ball covered with small pieces of mirror glass, suspended esp. above dance floors to reflect light in revolving patterns.

mir·rored *adjective* **1** fitted with a mirror or mirrors (*a mirrored wall in the bedroom*). **2** having a reflective surface (*mirrored sunglasses*).

mirror finish *noun* a smooth or highly-polished reflective surface.

mirror image *noun* **1** an identical image, but with the structure reversed, as in a mirror. **2** a phenomenon or occurrence which is identical to another. □ **mirror-image** *adjective*

mirror symmetry *noun* symmetry as of an object and its reflection.

mirror writing *noun* backwards writing, like ordinary writing reflected in a mirror.

mirth *noun* merriment, laughter. □ **mirth·ful** *adjective* **mirth·ful·ness** *noun* **mirth·less** *adjective* **mirth·less·ly** *adverb* **mirth·less·ness** *noun* [Old English *myrgth* (as MERRY)]

MIRV /mɜrv/ *noun* a missile containing several independently guided warheads. [acronym from *multiple independently-targeted re-entry vehicle*]

Mir·vish /ˈmɜrvɪʃ/ **Edwin** 'Honest Ed' (b.1914), American-born Canadian entrepreneur and theatrical producer who came to Canada in 1923. In 1962 he purchased the Royal Alexandra Theatre in Toronto, and in 1982 he acquired and restored the Old Vic Theatre in London, England.

Mir·zam /ˈmiːrzam/ a giant star, the second-brightest in the constellation Canis Major. [Arabic *al murzim* 'the announcer', because its appearance in the sky heralded that of Sirius]

MIS *abbreviation Computing* management information systems.

mis-¹ *prefix* added to verbs and verbal derivatives: meaning 'amiss', 'badly', 'wrongly', 'unfavourably' (*mislead*; *misshapen*; *mistrust*). [Old English from Germanic]

mis-² *prefix* occurring in a few words adopted from French meaning 'badly', 'wrongly', 'amiss', 'ill-', or having a negative force (*misadventure*; *mischief*). [Old French *mes-* ultimately from Latin *minus* (see MINUS): assimilated to MIS-¹]

mis·adven·ture *noun* **1** a misfortune. **2** bad luck. **3** *Law* an accident without concomitant crime or negligence (*death by misadventure*). [Old French *mesaventure* from *mesavenir* turn out badly (as MIS-², ADVENT: compare ADVENTURE)]

mis·align *transitive verb* give the wrong alignment to. □ **mis·aligned** *adjective* **mis·align·ment** *noun*

mis·alli·ance *noun* an unsuitable alliance, esp. an unsuitable marriage. □ **mis·ally** *transitive verb* (**-allies, -allied**).

mis·allo·ca·tion *noun* inappropriate or wrongful allocation, esp. of money.

mis·andry /mɪˈsandri/ *noun* the hatred of men. [Greek *misos* 'hatred' + *andr- aner* 'man', on the pattern of MISOGYNY]

mis·an·thrope /ˈmɪsənˌθrəʊp, mɪz-/ *noun* (also **mis·an·throp·ist** /mɪˈsanθrəpɪst, -ˈzan-/) **1** a person who hates humans. **2** a person who avoids human society. □ **mis·an·throp·ic** /-ˈθrɒpɪk/ *adjective* **mis·an·thropy** /mɪˈzanθrəpi/ *noun* [French from Greek *misanthrōpos* from *misos* hatred + *anthrōpos* man]

mis·apply *transitive verb* (**-plies, -plied**) apply (a theory, a term, funds, etc.) wrongly. □ **mis·appli·ca·tion** *noun*

mis·ap·pre·hend *transitive verb* misunderstand (words, a person). □ **mis·ap·pre·hen·sion** *noun*

mis·ap·pro·pri·ate *transitive verb* apply (usu. another's money) to one's own use, or to a wrong use. □ **mis·ap·pro·pri·a·tion** *noun*

mis·begot·ten *adjective* **1** badly conceived, designed, or planned: (*someone's misbegotten idea of an English country house*). **2** contemptible (used as a term of abuse): (*you misbegotten hound!*). **3** *archaic* (of a child) illegitimate.

mis·behave *intransitive verb & reflexive* (of a person, machine, etc.) behave badly. □ **mis·behav·iour** *noun*

misc. *abbreviation* miscellaneous.

mis·cal·cu·late *transitive & intransitive verb* calculate (amounts, results, etc.) wrongly. □ **mis·cal·cu·la·tion** *noun*

mis·call *transitive verb* = MISNAME.

mis·car·ri·age *noun* **1** /ˈmɪsˌkerɪdʒ/ the expulsion of a fetus from the womb before it can survive independently, esp. before the 28th week of pregnancy; a spontaneous abortion. **2** /mɪsˈkerɪdʒ/ the failure (of a plan etc.) to reach completion.

miscarriage of justice *noun* any failure of the judicial system to attain the ends of justice.

mis·carry *verb* (**-ries, -ried**) **1 a** *intransitive* (of a woman or female animal) have a miscarriage. **b** *transitive* suffer the miscarriage of (a fetus). **2** *transitive* (of a business, plan, etc.) fail, be unsuccessful.

mis·cast *transitive verb* (*past* and *past participle* **-cast**) assign an unsuitable role to (a performer).

mis·ce·gen·a·tion /mɪsˈedʒɪˌneɪʃən, ˌmɪsɪdʒɪˈneɪʃən/ *noun* **1** the interbreeding of races, esp. of whites and non-whites. **2** marriage between people of different races. [irreg. from Latin *miscēre* mix + *genus* race]

mis·cel·la·nea /ˌmɪsəˈleɪniə/ *plural noun* **1** a collection of miscellaneous items. **2** a literary miscellany. [Latin neuter pl. (as MISCELLANEOUS)]

mis·cel·lan·eous /ˌmɪsəˈleɪniəs/ *adjective* **1** of mixed composition or character. **2** (foll. by pl. noun) of various kinds. [Latin *miscellaneus* from *miscellus* mixed, from *miscēre* mix]

mis·cel·lany /ˈmɪsəˌleɪni, -ˈseləni/ *noun* (*pl.* **-ies**) **1** a mixture, a medley. **2** a book containing a collection of stories etc., or various literary compositions. [French *miscellanées* (fem. pl.) or Latin MISCELLANEA]

mis·chance *noun* **1** bad luck. **2** an instance of this.

mis·chief *noun* **1** conduct which is troublesome, but not malicious, esp. in children. **2** pranks, scrapes (*get into mischief*; *keep out of mischief*). **3** playful malice, archness (*eyes full of mischief*). **4** harm or injury caused by a person or thing. **5** a person or thing responsible for harm or annoyance (*that loose connection is the mischief*). □ **do a person a mischief** wound or kill a person. **get up to** (or **make**) **mischief** create discord. [Old French *meschief* from *meschever* (as MIS-², *chever* come to an end, from *chef* head: see CHIEF)]

mischief-maker *noun* a person who encourages discord, esp. by gossip etc. □ **mischief-making** *noun*

mis·chiev·ous /ˈmɪstʃɪvəs, disputed mɪsˈtʃiːvɪəs, -ˈtʃiːvəs/ *adjective* **1** (of a person) disposed to mischief. **2** (of conduct etc.) teasing; playfully malicious. **3** (of a thing) having harmful effects. □ **mis·chiev·ous·ly** *adverb* **mis·chiev·ous·ness** *noun* ¶ Although the pronunciation /mɪsˈtʃiːvɪəs/ is very common, it is not considered standard by many people. [Anglo-French *meschevous* from Old French *meschever*: see MISCHIEF]

misch metal /mɪʃ/ *noun* an alloy of lanthanide metals, usu. added to iron to improve its malleability. [German *mischen* mix + *Metall* metal]

mis·cible /ˈmɪsɪbəl/ *adjective* (often foll. by *with*) capable of being mixed. □ **misci·bil·ity** *noun* [medieval Latin *miscibilis* from Latin *miscēre* mix]

mis·com·muni·ca·tion *noun* **1** failure to communicate adequately. **2** an instance of this.

mis·con·ceive *verb* **1** *intransitive* (often foll. by *of*) have a wrong idea or conception. **2** *transitive* misunderstand (a word, person, etc.). □ **mis·con·ceiv·er** *noun*

mis·con·ceived *adjective* badly planned, organized, etc.

mis·con·cep·tion *noun* a misunderstanding; a wrong idea.

mis·con·duct ● *noun* /mɪsˈkɒndʌkt/ **1** improper or unprofessional behaviour. **2** bad management. **3** *Hockey* a penalty, usu. lasting for five minutes or more, called against a player for fighting or arguing with the referee etc. (*game misconduct*). ● *verb* /ˌmɪskənˈdʌkt/ *transitive* mismanage.

mis·con·strue *transitive verb* (**-con·strues, -con·strued, -constru·ing**) **1** interpret (a word, action, etc.) wrongly. **2** mistake the meaning of (a person). □ **mis·con·struc·tion** *noun*

Mis·cou Island /ˈmɪskuː/ an island of NE New Brunswick, situated in the Gulf of St. Lawrence at the entrance to Chaleur Bay, just north of Île Lamèque. [Mi'kmaq *susqu* wet bog]

mis·count ● *transitive & intransitive verb* count wrongly. ● *noun* a wrong count.

mis·cre·ant /ˈmɪskriənt/ ● *noun* **1** an immoral or criminal person. **2** *archaic* a heretic. ● *adjective* **1** depraved, villainous. **2** *archaic* heretical. [Old French *mescreant* (as MIS-², *creant* part. of *croire* from Latin *credere* believe)]

mis·cue ● *noun* **1** an error or blunder. **2** (in pool etc.) the failure to strike the ball properly with the cue. ● *intransitive verb* (**-cues, -cued, -cue·ing** or **-cu·ing**) make a miscue.

mis·deal ● *transitive & intransitive verb* (*past* and *past participle* **-dealt**) make a mistake in dealing (cards). ● *noun* **1** a mistake in dealing cards. **2** a misdealt hand.

mis·deed *noun* an evil deed, a wrongdoing; a crime. [Old English *misdǣd* (as MIS-¹, DEED)]

mis·demean·our /ˌmɪsdəˈmiːnər/ *noun* (also **mis·demean·or**) **1** a minor wrongdoing. **2** *Law* a minor criminal offence, esp. (in the US) one less serious than a felony. ¶ Not used in Canadian law, where the term *summary conviction offence* is used to refer to such offences.

mis·de·scribe *transitive verb* describe inaccurately. □ **mis·de·scrip·tion** *noun*

mis·diag·nose *transitive verb* diagnose incorrectly. □ **mis·diag·no·sis** *noun*

mis·dial *transitive & intransitive verb* (-**dialed**, -**dial·ing**; also -**dialled**, -**dial·ling**) dial (a telephone number etc.) incorrectly.

mis·direct *transitive verb* **1** direct (a person, letter, blow, etc.) wrongly. **2** (of a judge) instruct (the jury) wrongly. □ **mis·direc·tion** *noun*

mis·direct·ed *adjective* **1** sent in the wrong direction (*a misdirected pass*). **2** used or applied wrongly or inappropriately (*misdirected energies*). **3** undeserved by its target or victim (*misdirected anger*).

mis·doing *noun archaic* a misdeed.

mis·doubt *transitive verb* **1** have doubts or misgivings about the truth or existence of. **2** be suspicious about; suspect that.

mise en scène /ˌmiːz ɑ̃ ˈsɛn/ *noun* **1** *Theatre* **a** the scenery and properties of a play. **b** the way in which these are arranged. **2** *Film* the disposition of all the visual elements in a frame. **3** the setting or surroundings of an event. [French]

mis·em·ploy *transitive verb* employ or use wrongly or improperly.

miser /ˈmaɪzər/ *noun* **1** a person who hoards wealth and lives miserably. **2** an avaricious person. [Latin, = wretched]

mis·er·able /ˈmɪzrəbəl, ˈmɪzər-/ *adjective* **1** wretchedly unhappy or uncomfortable (*felt miserable; a miserable hovel*). **2** contemptible, mean. **3** causing wretchedness or discomfort (*miserable weather*). **4** *informal* (of a person) gloomy, morose. **5** *Scot., Austral., & NZ* stingy, mean. □ **mis·er·able·ness** *noun* **mis·er·ably** *adverb* [French *misérable* from Latin *miserabilis* pitiable, from *miserari* to pity, from *miser* wretched]

mi·seri·cord /mɪˈzɛrɪˌkɔrd/ *noun hist.* a shelving projection on the underside of a hinged seat in a choir stall serving (when the seat is turned up) to help support a person standing. [Old French *misericorde* from Latin *misericordia* from *misericors* compassionate, from stem of *miserēri* pity + *cor cordis* heart]

miser·ly *adjective* like a miser, stingy. □ **miser·li·ness** *noun*

mis·ery *noun* (*pl.* -**eries**) **1** great discomfort of mind or body. **2** a thing causing this. **3** *Brit. informal* a constantly depressed or discontented person. □ **put out of its** etc. **misery 1** release (a person, animal, etc.) from suffering or suspense. **2** kill (an animal in pain). [Old French *misere* or Latin *miseria* (as MISER)]

mis·feas·ance /mɪsˈfiːzəns/ *noun Law* a transgression, esp. the wrongful exercise of lawful authority. [Old French *mesfaisance* from *mesfaire* misdo (as MIS-², *faire* do, from Latin *facere*): compare MALFEASANCE]

mis·fire ● *intransitive verb* **1** (of a gun, motor engine, etc.) fail to go off or start or function regularly. **2** (of an action etc.) fail to have the intended effect. ● *noun* a failure of function or intention.

mis·fit *noun* **1** a person unsuited to a particular kind of environment, occupation, etc. **2** something that does not fit or suit well.

mis·for·tune *noun* **1** bad luck. **2** an instance of this.

mis·giv·ing *noun* (usu. in *pl.*) a feeling of mistrust or apprehension.

mis·gov·ern *transitive verb* govern (a country etc.) badly. □ **mis·govern·ment** *noun*

mis·guide *transitive verb* mislead, misdirect. □ **mis·guid·ance** *noun*

mis·guid·ed *adjective* mistaken in thought or action (*a misguided attempt to rescue the hostages*). □ **mis·guid·ed·ly** *adverb* **mis·guid·ed·ness** *noun*

mis·handle *transitive verb* **1** deal with incorrectly or ineffectively. **2** handle (a person or thing) roughly or rudely; ill-treat.

mis·hap /ˈmɪshap/ *noun* an unlucky accident.

mis·hear /mɪsˈhɪr/ *transitive verb* (*past* and *past participle* -**heard**) hear incorrectly or imperfectly.

Mish·ima /ˈmɪʃɪmə/ **Yukio** (pseudonym of Hiraoka Kimitake) (1925–70), Japanese writer. His books include *Confessions of a Mask* (1949), in which he describes coming to terms with his homosexuality, and the four-volume *The Sea of Fertility* (1965–70), which looks at reincarnation and the sterility of modern life. An avowed imperialist, he committed hara-kiri after failing to incite soldiers against the postwar regime.

mis-hit ● *transitive verb* (-**hit·ting**; *past* and *past participle* -**hit**) hit (a ball etc.) faultily. ● *noun* a faulty or bad hit.

mish·mash *noun* a confused mixture. [Middle English, reduplication of MASH]

Mish·nah /ˈmɪʃnə/ *noun* an authoritative collection of exegetical material embodying the oral tradition of Jewish law, which forms the first part of the Talmud. □ **Mish·naic** /-ˈneɪɪk/ *adjective* [Hebrew *mišnāh* (teaching by) repetition]

mis·iden·tify *transitive verb* (-**fies**, -**fied**) identify erroneously. □ **mis·iden·ti·fi·ca·tion** *noun*

mis·in·form *transitive verb* give wrong information to, mislead. □ **mis·infor·ma·tion** *noun*

mis·in·formed *adjective* **1** (of a person) incorrectly informed; having an incorrect or imperfect knowledge of or acquaintance with the facts. **2** (of an argument etc.) based on incorrect information.

mis·in·ter·pret *transitive verb* (-**in·ter·pret·ed**, -**in·ter·pret·ing**) interpret wrongly; draw a wrong inference from. □ **mis·in·ter·pret·a·tion** *noun* **mis·in·ter·pret·er** *noun*

mis·judge *transitive & intransitive verb* **1** judge wrongly. **2** have a wrong opinion of. □ **mis·judg·ment** *noun* (also **misjudgement**).

Mis·kito /mɪˈskiːtoʊ/ ● *noun* (*pl.* same or -**tos**) **1** a member of an Aboriginal people of the Atlantic coast of Nicaragua and Honduras. **2** the language of this people. ● *adjective* of or relating to the Miskito or their language. [the name in Miskito]

Mis·kolc /ˈmiːʃkolts/ a city in NE Hungary; pop. (est. 2002) 181,200. It is one of Hungary's major industrial centres.

mis·label *transitive verb* (-**labelled**, -**label·ling**) **1** attach an incorrect label to. **2** describe or designate wrongly.

mis·lay *transitive verb* (*past* and *past participle* -**laid**) **1** unintentionally put (a thing) where it cannot readily be found. **2** lose.

mis·lead /mɪsˈliːd/ *transitive verb* (*past* and *past participle* -**led** /-ˈled/) **1** cause (a person) to have a wrong idea or impression about something. **2** *archaic* lead in the wrong direction. □ **mis·lead·er** *noun*

mis·lead·ing /mɪsˈliːdɪŋ/ *adjective* giving the wrong idea or impression. □ **mis·lead·ing·ly** *adverb* **mis·lead·ing·ness** *noun*

mis·man·age *transitive verb* manage badly or dishonestly. □ **mis·manage·ment** *noun*

mis·match ● *transitive verb* match unsuitably or incorrectly. ● *noun* a bad match.

mis·meas·ure *transitive verb* measure or estimate incorrectly. □ **mis·measure·ment** *noun*

mis·name *transitive verb* call by a wrong or inappropriate name.

mis·nomer /mɪsˈnoʊmər/ *noun* **1** a name or term used wrongly. **2** the wrong use of a name or term. [Anglo-French from Old French *mesnom(m)er* (as MIS-², *nommer* name, from Latin *nominare* formed as NOMINATE)]

miso /ˈmiːsoʊ/ *noun* a paste made from fermented soybeans and barley or rice malt, used in Japanese cooking. [Japanese]

mis·ogyny /mɪˈsɒdʒɪni/ *noun* the hatred of women. □ **mis·ogyn·ist** *noun* **mis·ogyn·is·tic** *adjective* **mis·ogyn·ous** *adjective* [Greek *misos* hatred + *gunē* woman]

mis·per·ceive *transitive verb* perceive wrongly or incorrectly; mistake.

mis·per·cep·tion *noun* a wrong or incorrect perception.

mis·place *transitive verb* (usu. as **mis·placed** *adjective*) **1** put in the wrong place. **2** bestow (affections, confidence, etc.) on an inappropriate object. □ **mis·place·ment** *noun*

misplaced modifier *noun* a word, phrase, or clause which is intended to modify a noun or pronoun but is placed in an ambiguous grammatical relationship to it, e.g. *as a single woman, he found her very interesting.*

mis·play ● *transitive verb* play (a ball, card, etc.) in a wrong or ineffective manner. ● *noun* an instance of this.

mis·print ● *noun* a mistake in printing. ● *transitive verb* print wrongly.

mis·pri·sion /mɪsˈprɪʒən/ *noun Law* **1** (in full **misprision of a felony** or **of treason**) the deliberate concealment of one's knowledge of a crime, treason, etc. **2** a wrong action or omission. **3** a misreading, misunderstanding, etc. **4** (usu. foll. by *of*) a failure to appreciate the value of a thing. [Anglo-French *mesprisioun* from Old French *mesprison* error, from *mesprendre* to mistake (as MIS-², *prendre* take)]

mis·prize *transitive verb literary* despise, scorn; fail to appreciate. [Old French *mesprisier* (as MIS-¹, PRIZE¹)]

mis·pro·nounce *transitive verb* pronounce (a word etc.) wrongly. □ **mis·pro·nun·ci·a·tion** *noun*

mis·quote *transitive verb* quote wrongly. □ **mis·quo·ta·tion** *noun*

Consonants: b *but* d *dog* f *few* g *get* h *her* j *yes* k *cat* l *leg* m *man* n *no* p *pen* r *red* s *sit*

mis·read *transitive verb* (*past* and *past participle* **-read** /-'red/) read or interpret (text, a situation, etc.) wrongly. □ **mis·read·ing** *noun*

mis·remem·ber *transitive verb* remember imperfectly or incorrectly.

mis·report *transitive verb* give a false or incorrect report of.

mis·repre·sent *transitive verb* represent wrongly; give a false or misleading account or idea of. □ **mis·repre·sen·ta·tion** *noun* **mis·repre·sent·a·tive** *adjective*

mis·rule ● *noun* **1** bad government. **2** disorder. ● *transitive verb* govern badly.

Miss. *abbreviation* Mississippi.

miss¹ ● *verb* **1** *transitive & intransitive* fail to hit, reach, find, capture, etc. (an object or goal). **2** *transitive* fail to catch (a bus, train, etc.). **3** *transitive* fail to experience, see, or attend (an occurrence or event). **4** *transitive* fail to meet (a person), keep (an appointment), etc. **5** *transitive* fail to take advantage of (an opportunity etc.) (*I missed my chance*). **6** *transitive* fail to hear, observe, or understand (*I'm sorry, I missed what you said*). **7** *transitive* **a** regret the loss or absence of (a person or thing) (*did you miss me while I was away?*). **b** notice the loss or absence of (an object) (*bound to miss the key if it isn't there*). **8** *transitive* avoid (*go early to miss the traffic*). **9** (often foll. by *out*) **a** *transitive* omit, leave out (*you missed my name*). **b** *transitive & intransitive* fail to get or experience (*always misses out on the good times*). **10** *intransitive* (of an engine etc.) fail, misfire. **11** *transitive* fail to take (medication, food, etc.), either intentionally or unintentionally. **12** *intransitive* fail (*you can't miss if you serve veal scaloppine*). ● *noun* a failure to hit, reach, attain, connect, etc. □ **be missing** not have (see also MISSING *adjective*). **give** (**a thing**) **a miss** avoid, leave alone (*gave the party a miss*). **miss a beat** (usu. with *neg.*) hesitate in making a transition from one activity to another or in conversation (*she carried on without missing a beat*). **miss the boat 1** lose an opportunity. **2** fail to understand the point. **a miss is as good as a mile** the fact of failure, escape, or success is not affected by the narrowness of the margin. **not miss much** be alert. **not miss a trick** never fail to seize an opportunity, advantage, etc. □ **miss·able** *adjective* [Old English *missan* from Germanic]

miss² *noun* **1** (**Miss**) **a** the title of an unmarried woman or girl without a higher, honorific, or professional title. **b** the title of a married woman retaining her maiden name for professional purposes. **2** (**Miss**) **a** the title of a young woman representing a country, group, etc., esp. in a beauty contest (*Miss Canada*). **b** *ironic* or *jocular* a mock title of a young woman supposedly personifying a particular state, condition, etc. (*little Miss Innocent*). **3 a** a girl or unmarried woman. **b** usu. *derogatory* or *jocular* a girl, esp. a schoolgirl, with implications of silliness etc. **4** used as a term of address to a waitress, female schoolteacher, sales clerk, etc. **5** *N Amer.* (in *pl.*) = MISSY 1. [abbreviation of MISTRESS]

mis·sal /'misəl/ *noun Catholicism* **1** a book containing the texts used in the service of the Mass throughout the year. **2** a book of prayers, esp. an illuminated one. [medieval Latin *missale* neuter of ecclesiastical Latin *missalis* of the Mass, from *missa* MASS²]

mis·sal·ette /misə'let/ *noun* a small booklet containing the liturgy, prayers, readings, hymns, etc. for Masses for a week or a month.

mis·shape *transitive verb* give a bad, ugly, or wrong shape or form to; distort.

mis·shapen *adjective* ill-shaped, deformed, distorted. □ **mis·shapen·ly** *adverb* **mis·shapen·ness** *noun*

mis·sile /'misəl, 'misail/ *noun* **1** a destructive, self-propelling projectile, esp. a nuclear weapon, that is directed automatically or by remote control. **2** an object or weapon suitable for throwing at a target or discharging from a machine. □ **mis·sil·eer** *noun* **mis·sil·ery** /-lri/ *noun* [Latin *missilis* from *mittere miss-* send]

mis·sing *adjective* **1** not in its place; lost. **2** not present, absent. **3** (of a person) not yet traced or confirmed as alive but not known to be dead.

missing link *noun* **1** a thing lacking to complete a series. **2** a hypothetical intermediate animal assumed to be an evolutionary link between humans and apes.

Mis·sion a district municipality in southwestern BC, situated on the Fraser River, about 70 km east of Vancouver; pop. (2001) 31,272. □ **Mis·sion·ite** *noun* [St. Mary's Indian *Mission*, established there in 1861]

mis·sion ● *noun* **1 a** a particular task or goal assigned to a person or group. **b** a journey with a purpose. **c** a person's duty, vocation, or work, esp. that enthusiastically accepted or assumed (*mission in life*). **2 a** a military or scientific operation or expedition for a particular purpose. **b** the dispatch of an aircraft or spacecraft on an operational flight. **3 a** a body of persons sent, esp. to a foreign country, to conduct negotiations, establish political or commercial relations, etc. **b** *US* a

permanent diplomatic establishment, embassy, or legation. **4 a** members of a religious organization sent to propagate their faith abroad. **b** a field of missionary activity. **c** a missionary post or organization. **d** a place of worship attached to a mission. **e** a body of people established to do missionary, evangelical, or humanitarian work in their own country, esp. among the poor or disadvantaged. **f** (in *pl.*) organized missionary activities (*world missions*). **5** a particular, usu. intensive, course or period of preaching, services, etc., undertaken to stimulate interest in the work of a parish, a community, the faith, etc. **6** (often **Mission**) *N Amer.* (*attributive*) (of furniture) of a plain, solid style modelled originally on the furniture of Spanish missions in N America. ● *transitive verb* (usu. in *passive*) send on a mission; give (a person) a mission to perform. [French *mission* or Latin *missio* from *mittere miss-* send]

mis·sion·ary ● *adjective* **1** of, concerned with, or characteristic of, religious missions. **2** characteristic of a person engaged in a religious mission (*missionary zeal*). ● *noun* (*pl.* **-aries**) a person doing missionary work.

missionary position *noun informal* a position for sexual intercourse with the woman lying on her back and the man lying on top and facing her.

mission boat *noun Cdn* (*BC*) *hist.* a vessel carrying spiritual and medical services to isolated villages on coastal inlets, inland rivers, etc.

mission control *noun* a group or organization responsible for directing a spacecraft, its crew, and mission.

mission creep *noun slang* a gradual shift in political or strategic objectives during the course of a military campaign, frequently resulting in an unresolved conflict or open-ended commitment.

mission-critical *adjective* designating equipment (esp. a computer system or software application) the correct functioning of which is essential for the fulfillment of a particular task.

mission impossible *noun* a difficult or impossible assignment. [after the name of *Mission: Impossible*, a US television series, first broadcast in 1966]

mis·sion·ize *verb* (also esp. *Brit.* **-ise**) **1** *intransitive* conduct a mission. **2** *transitive* do missionary work among. □ **mis·sion·iz·a·tion** *noun*

mission statement *noun* a declaration made by a company etc. of its general principles of operation.

mis·sis *var. of* MISSUS.

Mis·sis·sauga¹ /misi'sɔgə/ a city in S Ontario, situated on Lake Ontario, just southwest of Toronto; pop. (2001) 612,925. □ **Mis·sis·saugan** *noun* [MISSISSAUGA²]

Mis·sis·sauga² /misi'sɔgə/ *noun* (*pl.* same or **-gas**) **1** a member of an Ojibwa Aboriginal people living in S Ontario. **2** the Algonquian language of this people. [Ojibwa *misizaagii* 'inhabitant of the large river outlet' (referring to the *Mississagi* river draining into Lake Huron, where the group was first encountered by the French]

Mis·sis·sip·pi /misi'sipi/ a state of the southern US, on the Gulf of Mexico, bounded to the west by the lower Mississippi River; pop. (2000) 2,844,658; capital, Jackson.

Mis·sis·sip·pian /misi'sipiən/ ● *noun* **1** a native or resident of Mississippi. **2** *Geol.* **a** the Mississippian period. **b** the system of rocks dating from this time. ● *adjective* **1** of or pertaining to the state of Mississippi or its inhabitants. **2** designating or pertaining to the period of the Paleozoic era in N America following the Devonian and preceding the Pennsylvanian, from about 360 to 320 million years BP and corresponding to the Lower Carboniferous in Europe. **3** designating a culture which flourished in the Mississippi basin from about AD 800 until the arrival of the Europeans, based on intensive agriculture, esp. of corn, and characterized by large towns in river valleys.

Mississippi Mills a town in NE Ontario, west of Ottawa, incorporating the former town of Almonte and surrounding townships; pop. (2001) 11,647. [after MISSISSIPPI RIVER 2]

Mississippi River 1 a major river of N America, which rises in Minnesota near the Canadian border and flows south to a delta on the Gulf of Mexico. With its chief tributary, the Missouri, it is 5 970 km (3,710 miles) long. From the 1830s onwards it was famous for the sternwheeler steamboats which plied between New Orleans, St. Louis, and other northern cities. **2** a river in E Ontario, rising west of Perth and flowing generally northeastward through Carleton Place to join the Ottawa River just east of Arnprior. [Cree, = big river]

mis·sive *noun* **1** an esp. official letter. **2** *jocular* a letter, esp. a long and serious one. [medieval Latin *missivus* from Latin (as MISSION)]

Misso·lon·ghi /misə'lɒŋgi/ a city in W Greece, on the north shore of the Gulf of Patras; pop. (est. 2002) 9,000. It resisted the Turkish forces in the War of Greek Independence (1821–9) and it was there that the poet Byron, who had joined the fight, died of malaria in 1824.

Mis·souri /mɪˈzʊri/ **1** a major river of N America, one of the main tributaries of the Mississippi. It rises in the Rocky Mountains in Montana and flows 3 736 km (2,315 miles) to meet the Mississippi just north of St. Louis. **2** a state of the US, bounded on the east by the Mississippi River; pop. (2000) 5,595,211; capital, Jefferson City. □ **Mis·sour·ian** noun & adjective

mis·speak verb (past **-spoke**; past participle **-spoken**) N Amer. **1** intransitive speak wrongly or improperly. **2** intransitive & reflexive fail to convey the meaning one intends by one's words.

mis·spell transitive verb (past and past participle **-spelled** or **-spelt**) spell wrongly. □ **mis·spelled** adjective **mis·spell·ing** noun

mis·spend transitive verb (past and past participle **-spent**) spend amiss or wastefully.

mis·spent adjective wastefully or irresponsibly spent, passed, etc. (misspent money; misspent youth).

mis·state transitive verb state wrongly or inaccurately. □ **mis·state·ment** noun

mis·step noun an inappropriate or clumsy action.

mis·sus /ˈmɪsəz/ noun (also **mis·sis** /-sɪz/) **1** a form of address to a woman. **2** slang or jocular a wife. □ **the missus** the wife of the person speaking, addressed, or referred to. [corruption of MISTRESS: compare MRS.]

missy noun (pl. **-ies**) **1** N Amer. (also **mis·ses'** /ˈmɪsəs/) a standard size of clothing designed for well-proportioned and well-developed women, usu. around 5 feet 6 inches. **2** an affectionate or derogatory form of address to a young girl.

mist ● noun **1 a** a diffuse cloud of water droplets on or near the ground that limits visibility, but to a lesser degree than fog. **b** any condensed vapour settling in fine droplets on a surface and obscuring glass etc. **2** dimness or blurring of the sight caused by tears etc. **3 a** a diffuse cloud of small particles resembling mist. **b** a haze or haziness produced by distance, time, etc. (lost in the mists of time). ● verb (usu. foll. by up, over) **1** transitive & intransitive cover or become covered with mist or as with mist. **2** transitive spray (a plant, one's hair, etc.) with vaporized moisture. [Old English from Germanic]

mis·take ● noun **1 a** a misconception about the meaning of something; an incorrect idea or opinion. **b** a thing incorrectly done or thought. **2** an error of judgment. ● transitive verb (past **mis·took**; past participle **mis·taken**) **1** misunderstand the meaning or intention of (a person, a statement, etc.). **2** (foll. by for) wrongly take or identify (mistook me for you). **3** choose wrongly (mistake one's vocation). □ **and** (or **make**) **no mistake** informal undoubtedly; have no doubt about. **by mistake** accidentally; in error. **there is no mistaking** one is sure to recognize (a person or thing). □ **mis·tak·able** adjective [Old Norse mistaka (as MIS-¹, TAKE)]

mis·taken adjective **1** wrong in opinion or judgment. **2** based on or resulting from an error, misapprehension, etc. (mistaken loyalty; mistaken identity). □ **mis·taken·ly** adverb

Mis·tas·sini /ˌmɪstəˈsiːni/ a former town in NE central Quebec, immediately north of Lac Saint-Jean, now part of Dolbeau-Mistassini; pop. (2001) 6,873. [see MISTASSINI, LAC]

Mistassini, Lac a large, elongated lake in north central Quebec, situated over 200 km northwest of Lac Saint-Jean. [Cree, = big rock]

Mistassini Cree noun a member of a Cree people living on the shores of Lac Mistassini.

mis·ter¹ noun **1** = MR. **2** slang or jocular a form of address to an adult male stranger. [weakened form of MASTER in unstressed use before a name]

mis·ter² noun device for producing or dispensing mist, esp. for misting plants, hair, etc.

mis·time transitive verb say or do at the wrong time. □ **mis·tim·ing** noun

mis·title transitive verb give the wrong title or name to.

mis·tle thrush /ˈmɪsəl/ noun a large greyish Eurasian thrush, Turdus viscivorus, with a spotted breast, that feeds on mistletoe berries. [Old English mistel basil, mistletoe, of unknown origin]

mistle·toe /ˈmɪsəlˌtoʊ/ noun **1** a parasitic plant, Viscum album, growing on apple and other trees and bearing white glutinous berries in winter. **2** a similar plant, Phoradendron flavescens, native to N America. [Old English misteltān (as MISTLE THRUSH, tān twig)]

mist net ● noun a net made of very fine threads, used to trap birds for tagging or examination. ● transitive verb trap (birds) in a mist net.

mis·took past of MISTAKE.

Mis·tral /mɪˈstral/ **1 Fré·dé·ric** (1830–1914), French poet. He was one of the leaders of the 19th-c. movement to revive Provençal language and literature, and his works include Mirèio (1859) and Calendau (1867); he shared the Nobel Prize for literature in 1904. **2 Gab·ri·ela** (pseudonym of Lucila Godoy Alcayaga) (1889–1957), Chilean poet and diplomat. Her works include Desolación (1922) and Tala (1938); she was awarded the Nobel Prize for literature in 1945.

mis·tral /ˈmɪstral, mɪˈstral/ noun a cold north wind that blows down the Rhone valley and southern France into the Mediterranean. [French & Provençal]

mis·trans·late transitive verb translate incorrectly. □ **mis·trans·lat·ion** noun

mis·treat transitive verb treat wrongly, badly, or abusively. □ **mis·treat·ment** noun

mis·tress noun **1** a woman (other than his wife) with whom a married man has a (usu. prolonged) sexual relationship. **2** (often foll. by of) a woman with power to control, use, or dispose of something at will (mistress of the situation). **3** a female head of a household. **4 a** a woman in authority over others. **b** the female owner of a pet. **5** esp. Brit. **a** a female teacher (music mistress). **b** a female head of a college etc. **6 a** literary a woman loved and courted by a man. **b** archaic (as a title) = MRS. [Old French maistresse from maistre MASTER]

mis·trial noun **1** a trial rendered invalid through some error in the proceedings. **2** US a trial in which the jury cannot agree on a verdict.

mis·trust ● transitive verb **1** be suspicious of; doubt the truth, validity, or genuineness of. **2** feel no confidence in (a person, oneself, one's powers, etc.). ● noun **1** suspicion. **2** lack of confidence.

mis·trust·ful adjective **1** (foll. by of) distrustful, suspicious. **2** lacking confidence or trust. □ **mis·trust·ful·ly** adverb

Mis·try, Ro·hin·ton (b.1952), Indian-born Canadian novelist whose novels tell stories set in, and inspired by, the India of his youth. Such a Long Journey, his first novel (1991), won the Governor General's Award, as well as the Commonwealth Writers Prize, and was later adapted for film. His second novel, A Fine Balance, won the 1995 Giller Prize.

misty adjective (**mist·i·er**, **mist·i·est**) **1 a** clouded, obscured, or accompanied by mist. **b** consisting of or covered with mist or fine particles resembling mist. **2** indistinct or dim in outline. **3** obscure, vague. □ **mist·i·ly** adverb **mist·i·ness** noun

misty-eyed adjective **1** emotional; sentimental, maudlin. **2** having eyes blurred by tears.

mis·type transitive verb type wrongly.

mis·under·stand transitive verb (past and past participle **-under·stood**) fail to understand correctly.

mis·under·stand·ing noun **1** a failure to understand correctly. **2** a slight disagreement or quarrel.

mis·under·stood adjective **1** (of word, actions, etc.) misinterpreted. **2** (of a person) unappreciated, not valued sympathetically.

mis·usage noun **1** wrong or improper usage. **2** ill-treatment.

mis·use ● transitive verb /mɪsˈjuːz/ **1** use wrongly or improperly; apply to the wrong purpose. **2** subject to ill-treatment; maltreat. ● noun /mɪsˈjuːs/ **1 a** wrong or improper use or application of power, a word, etc. **b** the non-therapeutic use of a drug. **2** an instance of misuse. □ **mis·user** noun

Mitch·ell /ˈmɪtʃəl/ **1 Joni** (born Roberta Joan Anderson) (b.1943), Canadian singer and songwriter. Her many albums, often highly personal in their lyrics, reflect her move from a folk style to a fusion of folk, jazz, and rock; her hit songs include such titles as 'The Circle Game' and 'Both Sides Now'. **2 Mar·garet** (1900–49), US novelist. She wrote the bestselling novel Gone with the Wind (1936), set during the American Civil War; it was awarded the Pulitzer Prize, as well as being made into a successful film (1939). **3 Peter** (1824–99), Canadian lawyer and politician, Conservative premier of New Brunswick 1866–67, and strong supporter of Confederation. As minister of fisheries 1867–73, he created an international incident by ordering the seizure of US fishing boats fishing in Canadian waters. **4 Wil·liam Or·mond** (1914–98), Canadian novelist and dramatist. He achieved rapid success with the publication of the novel Who Has Seen the Wind in 1947. Much of his writing deals with life and mortality, and is set on the prairies.

mite¹ noun **1** any small arachnid of the order Acarina, having four pairs of legs when adult. **2** N Amer. **a** an initiation level of sports competition for young children, usu. between the ages of 5 and 8. **b** a player at this level. [Old English mīte from Germanic]

mite² ● adverb (usu. prec. by a) informal somewhat (is a mite shy). ● noun **1** a small object or person, esp. a child. **2** a modest contribution; the best one can do (*offered my mite of comfort*). **3** any small monetary unit (*compare* WIDOW's MITE). **4** *hist.* a Flemish copper coin of small value. [Middle Low German, Middle Dutch *mīte* from Germanic: prob. the same as MITE¹]

miter esp. *US var. of* MITRE.

Mith·ras /ˈmɪθras/ *Rom. Myth* a god of light and truth, of Persian origin; the Roman cult, centred on bull-sacrifice and also associated with merchants and the protection of warriors, was the principal rival of Christianity in the first three centuries AD. □ **Mith·ra·ic** /mɪθˈreɪɪk/ *adjective* **Mith·ra·ism** /ˈmɪθreiˌizəm/ *noun* **Mith·ra·ist** *noun*

Mith·ri·dates VI /ˌmɪθrɪˈdeitiːz/ (*also* **Mith·ra·dates VI**; known as 'Mithridates the Great') (c.132–63 BC), king of Pontus 120–63. His expansionist policies led to three wars with Rome (88–85; 83–82; 74–66); he was defeated by Pompey (in 66) and later committed suicide.

miti·gate /ˈmɪtɪˌgeit/ *transitive verb* make milder or less intense or severe; moderate or give relief from (*how can we mitigate the suffering?*). □ **miti·ga·ble** *adjective* **miti·ga·tion** *noun* **miti·ga·tor** *noun* **miti·ga·tory** *adjective* [Latin *mitigare mitigat-* from *mitis* mild] ¶ Care should be taken not to confuse *mitigate* 'make less intense or severe' with *militate* 'have force or effect' as is often done in the phrase *mitigate against*, which attracts criticism. Appropriate use of both words is illustrated by the sentence *The heavy rains militated against their attempts to mitigate the problem of flooding.*

miti·gat·ing circumstances *noun Law* extenuating circumstances which, while not excusing a crime etc., permit greater leniency in sentencing or imposing penalties.

Mitla /ˈmiːtlə/ an ancient city in S Mexico, to the east of the city of Oaxaca, now a noted archaeological site. Believed to have been established as a burial site by the Zapotecs, it was eventually overrun by the Mixtecs in about AD 1000. [Nahuatl, = place of the dead]

mito·chon·drion /ˌmaitəˈkɒndriən/ *noun* (*pl.* **mito·chon·dria** /-driə/) *Biol.* an organelle found in most eukaryotic cells, containing enzymes for respiration and energy production. □ **mito·chon·drial** *adjective* [modern Latin from Greek *mitos* thread + *khondrion* diminutive of *khondros* granule]

mito·gen /ˈmaitədʒən/ *noun Biol.* a substance or agent that induces or stimulates mitosis. □ **mito·genic** *adjective*

mi·to·sis /maiˈtoːsɪs/ *noun Biol.* a type of cell division that results in two daughter cells each having the same number and kind of chromosomes as the parent nucleus (*compare* MEIOSIS). □ **mi·tot·ic** /-ˈtɒtɪk/ *adjective* **mi·tot·ic·ally** *adverb* [modern Latin from Greek *mitos* thread]

mi·tral /ˈmaitrəl/ *adjective* **1** designating or pertaining to the mitral valve. **2** of or like a mitre. [modern Latin *mitralis* from Latin *mitra* girdle]

mitral valve *noun* a two-cusped valve between the left atrium and the left ventricle of the heart.

mitre /ˈmaitər/ (*also esp. US* **miter**) ● *noun* **1** a tall, deeply-cleft headdress worn by bishops and abbots, forming in outline the shape of a pointed arch. **2 a** (in full **mitre joint**) the joint of two pieces of wood or other material at an angle of 90°, such that the line of junction bisects this angle. **b** either of the shaped ends or edges which form such a joint. **c** a 45° angle such as these ends or edges have. **3** a diagonal join of two pieces of fabric that meet at a corner, made by folding. ● *verb* **1 a** *transitive & intransitive* join with a mitre or mitre joint. **b** *transitive* make a mitre joint in. **c** *transitive* cut or shape to a mitre. **2** *transitive* bestow or confer a mitre on (a bishop or abbot). □ **mitred** *adjective* [Old French from Latin *mitra* from Greek *mitra* girdle, turban]

mitre box *noun* a block or frame of wood with slits for guiding a saw when cutting mitre joints.

mitre·wort /ˈmaitərwɜːrt, -wɔːrt/ *noun* **1** a woodland plant of the genus *Mitella*, found east of the Rockies, with small white fringed flowers. **2** (in full **false mitrewort**) = FOAMFLOWER.

Mit·siwa *see* MASSAWA.

mitt *noun* **1** a covering for the hand with two sections, one for the thumb and the other for all four fingers. **2** *Baseball* a protective glove worn by the catcher or first baseman for catching the ball. **3** *N Amer.* a padded cloth mitten worn as protection from heat etc. (*oven mitt*). **4** *slang* a hand or fist. **5** *slang* (in *pl.*) boxing gloves. [abbreviation of MITTEN]

Mittel·eur·opa /ˌmɪtəljuˈroːpə/ *noun* central Europe. □ **Mittel·euro·pean** *adjective* [German]

Mittel·land Canal /ˈmɪtəlˌland/ a canal in NW Germany, which was constructed between 1905 and 1930. It is part of an inland waterway network linking the Rhine and Elbe rivers.

mit·ten *noun* **1** = MITT 1. **2** a glove leaving the tips of the fingers and thumb exposed. □ **mit·tened** *adjective* [Old French *mitaine*, ultimately from Latin *medietas* half: see MOIETY]

Mit·ter·rand /miːteˈrɑ̃/ **Fran·çois (Mau·rice Marie)** (1916–96), French socialist politician, president 1981–95. As president he initially moved to raise basic wages, increase social benefits, nationalize key industries, and decentralize government; after his Socialist Party lost its majority vote in the 1986 general election, he asked the right-wing politician Jacques Chirac to serve as prime minister, and was re-elected president in 1988.

mitz·vah /ˈmɪtsvɑ/ *noun* (*pl.* **mitz·voth** /-vɒt/) in Judaism: **1 a** a precept or commandment. **b** a religious obligation. **2** a good deed or considerate act. [Hebrew *miṣwāh* commandment]

-miut /ˈmiːʊt/ *suffix* meaning 'the people of' (*Sadlermiut*). [Inuktitut]

mix ● *verb* **1** *transitive* **a** combine or put together (two or more substances or things) so that the constituents of each are diffused among those of the other(s). **b** combine or blend (different principles, qualities, etc.). **2** *transitive* prepare (a cocktail etc.) by combining various ingredients. **3** *transitive* combine an activity etc. with another simultaneously (*mix business and pleasure*). **4** *intransitive* **a** join, be mixed, or combine, esp. readily (*oil and water will not mix*). **b** be compatible. **c** be sociable, esp. at a party. **5** *intransitive* **a** (foll. by *with*) of (a person) be harmonious or sociable with; have regular dealings with. **b** (foll. by *in*) participate in. **6** *transitive* drink different kinds of (alcoholic liquor) in close succession. **7** *Film* **a** *transitive* blend (two pictures or sounds) temporarily by fading one out as the other is faded in. **b** *transitive* combine (two or more sound signals) into one, with or without modulation, in a mixer. **c** *intransitive* (foll. by *from*, *to*) pass from one picture or sound to another by fading one out as the other is faded in. **8** *transitive* produce (a recording) by combining a number of separate recordings or soundtracks. **9** *transitive* (foll. by *down*) convert (a multi-track sound recording or multiple signal) to one consisting of fewer tracks or components. **10** *transitive & intransitive* crossbreed (animals etc.). ● *noun* **1** the result of mixing or combining, esp. disparate elements; a mixture. **2 a** a number of ingredients mixed together (*trail mix*). **b** the proportion or combination of different components that make up a product, plan, policy, or other integrated whole. **3** a group of persons or things of different types (*a good mix of businessmen and blue-collar workers*; *a mix of housing types*). **4 a** a commercially prepared mixture of ingredients for making a cake, etc., or for a process such as making concrete. **5 a** the action or process of combining or merging film pictures or soundtracks. **b** a transition between two pictures or sounds in which one fades out as the other fades in; a dissolve. **6** *Music* **a** a version of a recording in which the component tracks are mixed in a different way. **b** a recording made by mixing other recordings. **7** the soft drink, fruit juice, etc. with which an alcoholic drink is diluted. **8** a crossbred animal (*a Labrador-collie mix*). □ **be** (or **get**) **mixed up in** be or become involved in (esp. something undesirable). **be** (or **get**) **mixed up with** be or become associated with (esp. someone dishonest). **mix in 1** combine, blend. **2** (of a person) blend sociably or harmoniously with a group. **mix and match** select from a range of alternative combinations. **mix it up** *informal* **1** fight, argue; cause trouble. **2** interact vigorously, boisterously, or roughly. **mix up 1** mix thoroughly. **2** confuse; mistake the identity of. □ **mix·able** *adjective* [back-formation from MIXED (taken as past participle)]

mix-and-match ● *adjective* **1** suitable for or selected by mixing and matching. **2** complementary, coordinating; assorted. ● *noun* **1** an instance of mixing and matching. **2** a combination of complementary or coordinating items.

mix·down *noun* **1** the process of mixing down a multi-track sound recording etc. **2 a** an instance of this. **b** a recording so produced.

mixed *adjective* **1 a** consisting of diverse qualities or elements. **b** formed by mingling, blending, or combining different substances, individuals, etc. **2** containing persons from various backgrounds etc. **3** for or involving persons of both sexes (*a mixed school*; *mixed curling*). **4** (of wooded land) consisting of several species of trees. **5 a** (of reactions, reviews, results, etc.) having both negative and positive aspects. **b** (of a message, a signal, etc.) ambiguous, unclear. [Middle English *mixt* from Old French *mixte* from Latin *mixtus* past participle of *miscēre* mix]

mixed bag *noun* a diverse assortment of things or persons.

mixed bill *noun* = MIXED PROGRAM.

mixed blessing *noun* a thing having advantages and disadvantages.

mixed-blood ● *adjective* (of a person) having parents or ancestors from two or more races. ● *noun* (**mixed blood**) a person having parents or ancestors from two or more races.

mixed breed *noun* a crossbreed.

mixed company *noun* company comprising both men and women.

mixed doubles *plural noun Tennis* a doubles game with a man and a woman as partners on each side.

mixed drink *noun* an alcoholic beverage consisting of several ingredients, usu. liquor with fruit juice or a soft drink etc.

mixed economy *noun* an economic system combining private and government enterprise.

mixed farming *noun* farming of both crops and livestock. □ **mixed farm** *noun* **mixed-farm** *attributive adjective*

mixed feelings *plural noun* (also **mixed emotions**) a mixture of pleasure and dismay about something; conflicting emotions.

mixed grass *noun* (hyphenated when *attributive*) grass combining a variety of species, esp. blue grama and wheat grass (*mixed-grass prairie*).

mixed greens *plural noun* assorted lettuces, salad vegetables, etc.

mixed grill *noun* a dish of various grilled meats and vegetables etc.

mixed marriage *noun* a marriage between persons of different races or religions.

mixed media ● *noun* the use of a variety of mediums in a work of art, public performance, show, etc. ● *attributive adjective* (also **mixed-media**) = MULTIMEDIA *adjective*.

mixed metaphor *noun* a combination of inconsistent metaphors, e.g. *this tower of strength will forge ahead*.

mixed number *noun* an integer and a proper fraction.

mixed program *noun* a performance by a dance company, choir, etc. featuring several short works.

mixed race *adjective* = MIXED-BLOOD.

mixed train *noun* a railway train made up of cars carrying passengers as well as boxcars, flatcars, etc. hauling goods.

mixed-up *adjective informal* **1** mentally or emotionally confused. **2** socially ill-adjusted.

mixed-use *adjective* (of a building, development, etc.) designed to accommodate diverse functions, usu. including residential units, work places, public areas, etc.

mixer *noun* **1 a** a kitchen appliance for mixing or beating foods, usu. one with two rotating beaters. **b** a machine or device for mixing or processing other materials. **2 a** a person who manages socially in a specified way (*a good mixer*). **b** *N Amer.* a social gathering to enable people to get to know one another. **3** = MIX *noun* 7. **4 a** a device for merging input signals to produce a combined output in the form of sound or pictures. **b** a person who operates this.

mixing desk *noun* a console where sound signals are mixed during recording or broadcasting.

Mix·master *noun* **1** *proprietary* a type of electric food mixer. **2** (**mixmaster**) a person or thing constantly on the move. **3** (**mixmaster**) *informal* a sound-recording engineer who is an accomplished mixer of music, during recording or as a disc jockey.

Mix·tec /miːˈstek/ ● *noun* **1** a member of an Aboriginal people of Central America. **2** the language of this people. ● *adjective* of or pertaining to the Mixtecs or their language. [Spanish from Nahuatl *mixtecah* 'person from a cloudy place']

mix·ture *noun* **1** the result of mixing; something mixed; a combination. **2** *Chem.* the product of the mechanical mixing of substances without chemical change, as opposed to a chemical compound. **3** a medicinal or other preparation consisting of two or more ingredients mixed together, esp. a liquid medicine as opposed to pills, powders, etc. (*cough mixture*). **4 a** a gas, vaporized gasoline, or oil mixed with air, forming an explosive charge in an internal combustion engine. **b** a combination of gasoline with a small proportion of oil, used as a combined fuel and lubricant in some two-stroke engines. **5** the process of mixing or being mixed. [French *mixture* or Latin *mixtura* (as MIXED)]

mix-up *noun* a confusion, misunderstanding, or mistake.

Miz·oram /mɪˈzɔːrəm/ a state in the far northeast of India, lying between Bangladesh and Burma (Myanmar); capital, Aizawl.

miz·zen /ˈmɪzən/ *noun* (also **mizen**) *Naut.* (in full **mizzen-sail**) the lowest fore-and-aft sail of a fully rigged ship's mizzen-mast. [French *misaine* from Italian *mezzana* mizzen-sail, fem. of *mezzano* middle: see MEZZANINE]

mizzen-mast *noun* the mast next aft of the mainmast on a sailing ship.

miz·zle /ˈmɪzəl/ *noun & intransitive verb* drizzle. □ **miz·zling** *adjective* **miz·zly** *adjective* [Middle English, prob. from Low German *miseln*: compare Middle Dutch *miezelen*]

Mk. *abbreviation* **1** the German mark. **2** *New Testament* Mark. **3** (also **Mk**) mark (*the Mk III version*).

mks *abbreviation* metre-kilogram-second.

Mkt. *abbreviation* Market.

ml *abbreviation* **1** (also **mL**) millilitre(s). **2** mile(s).

MLA *abbreviation* **1** *Cdn & Ind.* Member of the Legislative Assembly. **2** Modern Language Association (of America). **3** (**M.L.A.**) Master of Landscape Architecture.

MLB *abbreviation* Major League Baseball.

MLD *abbreviation* minimum lethal dose.

M.L.I.S. *abbreviation* Master of Library and Information Studies.

M.Litt. *abbreviation* Master of Letters. [Latin *Magister Litterarum*]

Mlle *abbreviation* (*pl.* **Mlles**) Mademoiselle.

MLM *abbreviation* multi-level marketing.

MLS *abbreviation* **1** *proprietary* = MULTIPLE LISTING SERVICE. **2** (**M.L.S.**) Master of Library Sciences. **3** *Aviation* microwave landing system.

MM *abbreviation* **1** Messieurs. **2** (in Canada and the UK) Military Medal.

mm *abbreviation* millimetre(s).

M.Math. *abbreviation* Master of Mathematics.

Mme *abbreviation* (*pl.* **Mmes**) Madame.

m.m.f. *abbreviation* magnetomotive force.

MMM *abbreviation Cdn* Member of the Order of Military Merit.

mmm *interjection* expressing hesitation or inarticulate interrogation, assent, reflection, or satisfaction. [imitative]

MMR *abbreviation* measles, mumps, and rubella (vaccine).

MMS *abbreviation* Multimedia Messaging Service, a system that enables cellphones to send and receive colour pictures and sound clips as well as text messages.

MMT *abbreviation* methylcyclopentadienyl manganese tricarbonyl, an octane-boosting gasoline additive.

M.Mus. *abbreviation* Master of Music.

MN *abbreviation* **1** Minnesota (in official postal use). **2** (**M.N.**) Master of Nursing.

Mn *symbol Chem.* the element manganese.

MNA *abbreviation Cdn* (in Quebec) Member of the National Assembly.

M'Naghten rules *var.* of McNAUGHTEN RULES.

mne·mon·ic /nɪˈmɒnɪk/ ● *adjective* **1** of or designed to aid the memory. **2** of or pertaining to mnemonics. **3** (of a formula, code, etc.) easy to remember or understand. ● *noun* a mnemonic device, formula, or code. □ **mne·mon·ic·ally** *adverb* [medieval Latin *mnemonicus* from Greek *mnēmonikos* from *mnēmōn* mindful]

mne·mon·ics /nɪˈmɒnɪks/ *plural noun* (usu. treated as *sing.*) **1** the art of improving memory, esp. by artificial aids. **2** a system of precepts and rules intended to aid or improve the memory.

Mne·mo·syne /niːˈmɒzɪni/ *Gk Myth* the mother of the Muses. [Greek *mnēmosunē* memory]

MNR *abbreviation Cdn* (in Ontario) Ministry of Natural Resources.

MO *abbreviation* **1** Missouri (in official postal use). **2** *Computing* magneto-optical. **3** = MODUS OPERANDI. **4** Medical Officer. **5** money order.

Mo *symbol Chem.* the element molybdenum.

Mo. *abbreviation* Missouri.

mo /moʊ/ *noun* (*pl.* **mos**) esp. *Brit. informal* a moment (*wait a mo*). [abbreviation]

mo. *abbreviation N Amer.* month.

-mo /moʊ/ *suffix* forming nouns denoting a book size by the number of leaves into which a sheet of paper has been folded. [the final syllable of terms derived from the ablative sing. masc. of Latin ordinal numbers, e.g. DUODECIMO]

moa /ˈmoʊə/ *noun* (*pl.* **moas**) any extinct flightless New Zealand bird of the family Dinornithidae, resembling the ostrich. [Maori]

Moab·ite /ˈmoʊəˌbaɪt/ ● *adjective* of Moab, an ancient region by the Dead Sea, or its people. ● *noun* a member of a Semitic people traditionally descended from Lot, living in Moab.

Moabite Stone a monument erected by Mesha, king of Moab, *c.*850 BC which describes (in an early form of the Hebrew language) the campaign between Moab and ancient Israel (2 Kings 3), and furnishes an early example of an inscription in the Phoenician alphabet.

moan ● *noun* **1** a long, low mournful sound expressing physical or mental suffering etc. **2** a low plaintive sound made by wind etc. **3** a complaint or grievance. ● *verb* **1** *intransitive* make a moan. **2** *intransitive* *informal* complain or grumble. **3** *transitive* utter with moans. □ **moan·er** *noun* [Old English *mān* (unrecorded) from Germanic]

moat ● *noun* a deep defensive ditch round a castle, town, etc., usu. filled with water. ● *transitive verb* surround with or as with a moat. [Old French *mote*, *motte* mound]

mob ● *noun* **1 a** a disorderly crowd; a rabble. **b** an assembly of people; a crowd or group. **2** (prec. by *the*) usu. *derogatory* the ordinary people; the populace. **3** (**the Mob**) the Mafia or a similar criminal organization. ● *transitive & intransitive verb* (**mobbed, mob·bing**) **1** *transitive* **a** crowd round in order to attack or admire. **b** (of a mob) attack. **c** *N Amer.* crowd into (a building). **2** *intransitive* assemble in a mob. □ **mob·ber** *noun & adjective* [abbreviation of *mobile*, short for Latin *mobile vulgus* excitable crowd: see MOBILE]

mob·cap *noun hist.* a woman's large indoor cap covering all the hair, worn in the 18th and early 19th c. [obsolete (18th-c.) *mob*, originally = slut + CAP]

Mo·bile /moːˈbiːl/ an industrial city and port on the coast of S Alabama; pop. (2000) 198,915. It is situated at the head of Mobile Bay, an inlet of the Gulf of Mexico.

mo·bile ● *adjective* /ˈmoːbail/ **1 a** movable; not fixed; free or able to move or flow easily. **b** (of troops, police patrols, etc.) that may be easily and rapidly moved from place to place. **2 a** (of a person) able to move into different social levels or change environments, fields of employment, etc. **b** (of a society) not rigidly stratified, able to accommodate social or professional movement. **3** (of the face etc.) readily changing its expression. **4** (of a service, library, etc.) accommodated in a vehicle so as to serve various places. ● *noun* /ˈmoːbail/ a decorative structure, usu. consisting of pieces of metal, plastic, etc., hung so as to turn freely. [French from Latin *mobilis* from *movēre* move]

-mobile /-məˈbiːl/ *combining form* (of specialized vehicles etc.) having a function pertaining to, or being an imitation of, an automobile or other form of transport (*bookmobile*).

Mobile Command *noun Cdn* the division of the Armed Forces encompassing all combat-ready land forces, including land reserves.

mobile home *noun* a large, transportable structure equipped with living accommodations, permanently parked, and used as a residence.

mobile phone *noun* (also **mobile telephone**) = CELLPHONE.

mo·bil·ity *noun* **1** the ability to move or be moved freely or easily. **2** the ability to move between different levels in society or employment. **3** *Cdn* (esp. in names of companies) mobile telecommunications systems, e.g. cellphones, pagers, etc. (*Telus Mobility*).

mo·bil·ize /ˈmoːbɪˌlaiz/ *verb* (also esp. *Brit.* **-ise**) **1 a** *transitive* organize or make ready for service or action (originally troops in time of war). **b** *intransitive* be organized or made ready for action. **2** *transitive* render movable or capable of movement; bring into circulation. □ **mo·bil·iz·able** *adjective* **mo·bil·iz·a·tion** *noun* **mo·bil·iz·er** *noun*

Mö·bius strip /ˈmɜːbiəs, moː-/ *noun* (also **Möbius loop**) **1** *Math.* a surface with only one side and one edge, formed by twisting a long, narrow, rectangular strip through 180° and joining the ends. **2** a stylized version of this used as a symbol for recycling, recyclable, etc. [A. F. *Möbius*, German mathematician d.1868]

mob·oc·racy /mɒˈbɒkrəsi/ *noun* (*pl.* **-cies**) *informal* **1** rule or government by a mob. **2** a ruling mob.

mob rule *noun* rule imposed and enforced by a mob.

mob·ster *noun slang* a gangster.

Mo·butu /məˈbuːtuː/ **Sese Seko** (full name Mobutu Sese Seko Koko Ngbendu Wa Za Banga) (1930–97), president of Zaire (now Congo) 1965–97. After seizing power in a military coup, he changed his original name (Joseph-Désiré Mobutu) and that of his country (then known as the Belgian Congo) as part of his policy of Africanizing names. He was deposed in 1997.

moc·ca·sin *noun* **1** a type of soft leather slipper or shoe with combined sole and heel, as originally worn by some N American Aboriginal peoples. **2** a hard-soled shoe with a low heel resembling this. **3** *N Amer.* a venomous N American snake of the genus *Agkistrodon*, esp. (also **water moccasin**) the semi-aquatic *A. piscivorus* of the southern US. □ **moc·ca·sined** *adjective* [Virginia Algonquian and other N American Aboriginal languages *mockasin*, *makisin*]

moccasin flower *noun* = LADY'S SLIPPER.

moccasin telegraph *noun* esp. *Cdn* (esp. *North*) *informal* **1** a means of transmitting rumours or unofficial information by word of mouth; the grapevine. **2** information so relayed.

mocha /ˈmoːkə/ *noun* **1** a coffee of fine quality. **2 a** a flavouring made from this, often with chocolate added, used in cakes, ice cream, etc.

b a chocolate-flavoured coffee drink. **3** a dark brown colour as that of mocha coffee. **4** a soft kind of sheepskin. [*Mocha*, a port on the Red Sea, from where the coffee first came]

moch·ac·cino /ˌmɒkəˈtʃiːnoː/ *noun* (*pl.* **-cinos**) a cappuccino flavoured with chocolate syrup. [blend of MOCHA + CAPPUCCINO]

mock ● *verb* **1 a** *transitive* ridicule; scoff at. **b** *intransitive* (foll. by *at*) act or speak with scorn or contempt for; use ridicule. **2** *transitive* mimic contemptuously. **3** *transitive* jeer or defy contemptuously. ● *attributive adjective* **1** sham, imitation (esp. without intention to deceive). **2** pretended, fake (*a mock battle; mock chicken*). ● *noun* (in *pl.*) *Brit. informal* mock examinations. □ **mock·able** *adjective* **mock·er** *noun* **mock·ing** *adjective* **mock·ing·ly** *adverb* [Old French *mo(c)quer* deride, from Romanic]

mock·ery *noun* (*pl.* **-eries**) **1 a** derision, ridicule. **b** a subject or occasion of this. **2** (often foll. by *of*) a counterfeit or absurdly inadequate representation. **3 a** a ludicrously futile action. **b** something insultingly unfitting. □ **make a mockery of something** make something appear foolish or worthless.

mock-heroic ● *adjective* (of a literary style) burlesquing a heroic style. ● *noun* such a style.

mock·ing·bird *noun* a bird, esp. the American songbird *Mimus polyglottos*, that mimics the notes of other birds.

mock moon *noun* = PARASELENE.

mock orange *noun* any of various white-flowered, heavy-scented shrubs, esp. *Philadelphus coronarius*.

mock·tail *noun N Amer.* a non-alcoholic drink consisting of the same mixes etc. as the various cocktail recipes and usu. served in the same glasses, but without the alcohol.

mock turtleneck *noun N Amer.* **1** a high close-fitting neck on a knitted garment, similar to a turtleneck but not folded over. **2** a garment having this style of neck.

mock turtle soup *noun* soup made from a calf's head etc. to resemble turtle soup.

mocku·men·tary /ˌmɒkjuːˈmentəri/ *noun* (*pl.* **-ies**) a film, radio drama, etc. written and presented as a straightforward documentary, which is actually a spoof or parody of the profiled subject. [blend of MOCK + DOCUMENTARY]

mock-up *noun* an experimental model or replica of a proposed structure, page layout, etc.

mod[1] *informal* ● *adjective* modern, esp. in style of dress. ● *noun Brit.* a young person (esp. in the 1960s) of a group aiming at sophistication and fashionable modern dress. [abbreviation]

mod[2] *preposition Math.* = MODULO. [abbreviation]

mod[3] *noun* (in Scotland and areas of Scottish settlement, e.g. Cape Breton) an event at which Gaelic music, poetry, and dancing are performed, often with a competitive element. [Gaelic *mōd*]

mod[4] *noun* (usu. **mods**) *informal* modification. [shortening]

mod·acryl·ic /mɒdəˈkrɪlɪk/ ● *noun* a synthetic, acrylic-based fibre. ● *adjective* (of a carpet etc.) made of this. [from 'modified acrylic']

modal /ˈmoːdəl/ ● *adjective* **1** of or relating to mode or form as opposed to substance. **2** *Grammar* **a** of or denoting the mood of a verb. **b** (of an auxiliary verb, e.g. *would*) used to express the mood of another verb. **3** *Statistics* of, pertaining to, or of the nature of a mode. **b** (of a value etc.) occurring most frequently in a sample or population. **4** *Music* denoting a style of music using a particular mode. **5** *Logic* **a** (of a proposition) in which the predicate is affirmed of the subject with some qualification, or which involves the affirmation of possibility, impossibility, necessity, or contingency. **b** (of an argument) containing a modal proposition as a premise. **6** *Geol.* of or pertaining to the mode of a rock. ● *noun* **1** *Grammar* a modal verb. **2** *Logic* a modal proposition. □ **mo·dal·ly** *adverb*

mo·dal·ity /məˈdaliti/ *noun* (*pl.* **-ities**) **1 a** the state of being modal. **b** a modal quality or circumstance. **2** (in *sing.* or *pl.*) a prescribed method or technique of procedure, treatment, behaviour, etc.

mod cons *plural noun Brit.* = MODERN CONVENIENCES. [abbreviation]

mode *noun* **1** a way or manner in which a thing is done; a method of procedure. **2** a prevailing fashion, custom, or style, esp. of a particular place or period. **3 a** any of a number of distinct ways in which a machine, computer system, etc. operates (*print mode*). **b** *informal* or *jocular* a specified way in which a person functions, behaves, etc., esp. by conscious choice (*as soon as this is over I'm switching into holiday mode; I see her in her executive mode and she's a completely different person*). **4** *Statistics* the value or range of values that occurs most frequently in a given set of data etc. **5** *Music* **a** each of the scale systems that result when the white notes of the piano are played consecutively over an octave (*Lydian* *mode*). **b** each of the two main modern scale systems, the major and minor (*minor mode*). **6** *Logic* **a** the character of a modal proposition. **b** = MOOD² 2. **7** *Physics* any of the distinct kinds or patterns of vibration that an oscillating system can sustain. **8** *N Amer. Grammar.* = MOOD² 1. **9** *Geol.* the quantitative mineral, as distinct from chemical, composition of a rock sample. **10** *Philos.* **a** a manner or state of being of a thing. **b** a thing considered as possessing certain non-essential attributes. [French *mode* and Latin *modus* measure]

model ● *noun* **1** (often *attributive*) a representation in three dimensions of an existing person or thing or of a proposed structure, esp. in smaller scale (*a model airplane; architect's model*). **2** a simplified description of a system, process, etc. put forward as a basis for theoretical or empirical understanding; a conceptual or mental representation of a thing. **3** a figure in clay, wax, etc. to be reproduced in another, usu. more durable material. **4 a** a car etc. of a particular design or produced in a specified year. **b** each of a series of varying designs of the same type of structure, commodity, or object. **5** an exemplary person or thing (*a model of self-discipline*). **6** (often foll. by *for*) a person or thing used, or for use, as an example to copy or imitate (*an unlikely model for emulation; the Canadian model of federalism*). **7 a** a person employed to pose for an artist, photographer, etc. **b** a person employed to display clothes etc. by wearing them. **8** an actual person, place, etc. on which a fictional character, location, etc. is based. **9** esp. *Brit.* a garment etc. by a well-known designer, or a copy of this. ● *adjective* **1** serving as an example; exemplary, ideally perfect. **2** designating a small-scale model of the object or kind of object specified. ● *verb* (**mod·elled, model·ling**; also **mod·eled, model·ing**) **1 a** *intransitive* act or pose as an esp. fashion or photographic model. **b** *transitive* (of a person acting as a model) display (a garment). **2** *transitive* **a** fashion or shape (a figure) in clay, wax, etc. **b** (foll. by *after, on,* etc.) form, frame, or give shape to (a document, argument, other immaterial object, etc.), esp. in imitation of another. **3** *transitive* devise a (usu. mathematical) model or simplified description of (a phenomenon, system, etc.). **4** *transitive Art* (in drawing, painting, etc.) form with or assume the appearance of natural relief; cause to appear three-dimensional. □ **mod·el·ler** *noun* **mod·el·ling** *noun & adjective* [French *modelle* from Italian *modello*, ultimately from Latin *modulus*: see MODULUS]

model home *noun N Amer.* a finished house, sometimes furnished and decorated, in a subdivision under construction, used to give potential buyers an idea of what other houses of its type would look like when finished.

mo·dem *noun* a combined device for modulation and demodulation, e.g. between a computer and a telephone line, used for converting digital electrical signals to analog or audio ones and vice versa. [*modulator* + *demodulator*]

Mod·ena /ˈmɒdenə/ a city in N Italy, northwest of Bologna; pop. (2001) 175,442.

mod·er·ate ● *adjective* /ˈmɒdərət/ **1** avoiding extremes in conduct, opinions, or expression. **2** of medium quantity, quality, size, or extent. **3** (of a process, condition, or agency) intermediate in strength or degree; not intense, violent, or severe. **4** (of a wind) of medium strength. **5** (of prices, charges, etc.) reasonable, fairly low. **6** (of an oven temperature for baking) between 350° and 375° F. ● *noun* /ˈmɒdərət/ a person who holds moderate views, esp. in politics, religion, etc. ● *verb* /ˈmɒdəˌreɪt/ **1** *transitive & intransitive* make or become less violent, intense, rigorous, etc. **2** *transitive* preside over (a deliberative body) or at (a debate etc.). **3** *transitive Physics* retard (neutrons), esp. with a moderator. □ **mod·er·ate·ly** *adverb* **mod·er·ate·ness** *noun* **mod·er·at·ism** *noun* [Latin *moderatus* past participle of *moderare* reduce, control: related to MODEST]

mod·er·a·tion *noun* **1** the process or an instance of moderating. **2** the quality of being moderate, esp. in conduct, opinion, etc. **3** *Physics* the action or process of slowing down neutrons by the use of a moderator (*see* MODERATOR 5). □ **in moderation** in a moderate manner or degree.

mod·er·ato /ˌmɒdəˈrɑːtoʊ/ *Music* ● *adjective & adverb* performed at a moderate pace. ● *noun* (*pl.* **-atos**) a piece of music to be performed in this way. [Italian (as MODERATE)]

mod·er·ator *noun* **1** *N Amer.* a chairperson of a discussion on television or radio. **2** a person chosen to preside over a meeting or assembly and conduct its business. **3** (in the Presbyterian Church) **a** a person elected by the General Assembly to moderate the Assembly. **b** a person appointed or elected by a synod or presbytery to preside over meetings, officiate at services, etc. **4** (in the United Church) a person elected by the General Council to serve as the head of the church. **5** *Physics* a substance used in a nuclear reactor to retard neutrons and control the

rate of fission. **6** an arbitrator or mediator. □ **mod·er·ator·ial** *adjective* (in senses 3, 4).

mod·ern ● *adjective* **1** of the present and recent times. **2** in current fashion; not antiquated. **3** (of a person) up-to-date in lifestyle, outlook, opinions, etc. **4** designating the form of a language currently used, or the form representing the most recent significant stage of development (*modern Greek; modern Hebrew*). **5** designating or pertaining to art, architecture, etc. of the 20th c. marked by a departure from traditional styles and values. **6** *Zool., Geol., etc.* belonging to a comparatively recent period in the history of the earth. ● *noun* **1** (usu. in *pl.*) a person living in or belonging to modern times. **2** a person with modern tastes or opinions. **3** = MODERN DANCE. □ **mod·ern·ity** /mɒˈdɜrnɪti, -dər-/ *noun* **mod·ern·ly** *adverb* **mod·ern·ness** *noun* [French *moderne* or Late Latin *modernus* from Latin *modo* just now]

modern conveniences *plural noun* gadgets, amenities, labour-saving devices, etc. typical of a well-equipped modern home.

modern dance *noun* a style of theatrical dance developed in the 20th c., not constrained by the rules and techniques of classical ballet.

modern-day *adjective* of the present; contemporary.

modern dress *noun* costuming for a theatrical production which reflects current styles rather than those in fashion at the time the play etc. was written or depicts.

mod·erne *noun* a style of architecture and interior design originating in the US in the late 1920s as an adaptation of European art deco, and similarly characterized by austere geometrical shapes, strong colours, and frequent use of chrome, enamel, bronze, and polished stone.

modern English *noun* English from about 1500 onward.

modern history *noun* history from the end of the Middle Ages, or after the fall of the Western Roman Empire, to the present day.

mod·ern·ism *noun* **1** (**Modernism**) the methods, style, or attitudes of modern artists, writers, architects, composers, etc., esp. a style of art etc. rejecting classical and traditional methods of expression. **2** a movement towards modifying traditional religious beliefs and doctrines in accordance with modern ideas. **3 a** a modern character or quality of thought, expression, etc. **b** a modern term or expression. □ **mod·ern·ist** *noun* **mod·ern·is·tic** *adjective* **mod·ern·is·tic·ally** *adverb*

mod·ern·ize *verb* (also esp. *Brit.* **-ise**) **1** *transitive* make modern; adapt to modern needs, habits, standards, or styles. **2** *intransitive* adopt modern ways, views, styles, etc. □ **mod·ern·iz·a·tion** *noun* **mod·ern·iz·er** *noun*

modern jazz *noun* jazz as developed in the 1940s and 1950s, esp. bebop.

modern language *noun* a language that is spoken or written currently, esp. a European language.

modern Latin *noun* Latin since 1500, used esp. in scientific classification.

modern pentathlon *noun* an athletic competition in which participants engage in five different events usu. in a single day or over two days, including fencing, shooting, swimming, riding, and cross-country running.

mod·est *adjective* **1 a** having or expressing a humble or moderate estimate of one's own merits or achievements. **b** (of an action, attribute, etc.) proceeding from or indicating such a quality. **2** diffident, bashful, not bold or forward. **3 a** decorous in manner and conduct, avoiding impropriety or indecency. **b** reserved in sexual matters. **4** moderate or restrained in amount, extent, severity, etc.; not excessive or exaggerated (*a modest sum*). **5** (of a thing) unpretentious in appearance etc.; unostentatious. □ **mod·est·ly** *adverb* [French *modeste* from Latin *modestus* keeping due measure]

mod·esty *noun* the quality of being modest.

mod·icum /ˈmɒdɪkəm/ *noun* (foll. by *of*) a small quantity. [Latin, = short distance or time, neuter of *modicus* moderate, from *modus* measure]

modi·fi·ca·tion *noun* **1** the act or an instance of modifying or being modified. **2** a change made. **3** *Biol.* **a** the development of non-heritable changes in an organism. **b** the non-heritable changes produced in an organism in response to a particular environment. [French or from Latin *modificatio* (as MODIFY)]

modified American plan *noun N Amer.* (in hotels etc.) a method of charging a fixed rate that covers bed and breakfast, plus one other meal (*compare* AMERICAN PLAN, EUROPEAN PLAN). Abbr.: **MAP**.

modi·fi·er *noun* **1** a person or thing that modifies or alters something. **2** *Grammar* a word, esp. an adjective or noun used attributively, that qualifies the sense of another word, e.g. *good* and *family* in *a good family house.*

mod·ify *transitive verb* (**-fies, -fied**) **1** make partial or minor changes in; alter without radical transformation. **2** make less severe or extreme; tone down (*modify one's demands*). **3** *Grammar* limit, qualify, or expand the sense of (a word, phrase, etc.). **4** *Phonetics* change (a vowel) by umlaut. **5** *Chem.* change or replace all the substituent radicals of a polymer, thereby changing its physical properties such as solubility etc. (*modified starch*). **6** *Bot. & Zool.* transform (part of a plant or animal body) from its original anatomical form during development or evolution. □ **mod·i·fi·able** *adjective* [Old French *modifier* from Latin *modificare* (as MODE)]

Modi·gliani /ˌmoːdiˈljɒni/ **Ame·deo** (1884–1920), Italian painter and sculptor, resident in France from 1906. His portraits and nudes are noted for their elongated forms, linear qualities, and earthy colours.

modil·lion /məˈdiljən/ *noun* a projecting bracket placed in series under the corona of a cornice in the Corinthian and other orders. [French *modillon* from Italian *modiglione*, ultimately from Latin *mutulus* mutule]

mod·ish /ˈmoːdiʃ/ *adjective* fashionable. □ **mod·ish·ly** *adverb* **mod·ish·ness** *noun*

mod·ular /ˈmɒdjʊlər, -ʒʊlər/ *adjective* **1** of or pertaining to modules or moduli. **2 a** employing or involving a module or modules as the basis of design, measurement, or construction. **b** part of a system so designed or constructed. **3 a** (of an educational course) designed as a series of units or discrete sections. **b** (of a facility, service, etc.) provided in a number of discrete stages. □ **mod·ular·ity** /-ˈlɛriti/ *noun* **mod·ular·iz·a·tion** *noun* (also esp. *Brit.* **-isation**). [modern Latin *modularis* from Latin *modulus*: see MODULUS]

modu·late /ˈmɒdjʊˌleit, ˈmɒdʒəˌleit/ *verb* **1** *transitive* **a** regulate or adjust. **b** moderate, temper. **2** *transitive* adjust or vary the tone or pitch of (the speaking voice etc.). **3** *transitive* alter the amplitude or frequency of (a wave) by a wave of a lower frequency to convey a signal. **4** *intransitive & transitive Music* (often foll. by *from, to*) change or cause to change from one key to another. □ **modu·la·tion** *noun* **modu·la·tor** *noun* **modu·la·tory** *adjective* [Latin *modulari modulat-* to measure, from *modus* measure]

mod·ule /ˈmɒdjuːl, ˈmɒdʒuːl/ *noun* **1** a standardized part or independent unit used in construction or assembly, esp. of furniture, a building, or an electronic system. **2** an independent self-contained unit of a spacecraft (*lunar module*). **3** a distinct unit or period of training or education which can be combined with others to make up a course. **4** *Computing* any of a number of distinct but interrelated units from which a program may be built up or into which a complex activity may be analyzed. **5 a** a standard or unit of measurement. **b** *Archit.* a length chosen as a basis for the dimension of parts of a building, items of furniture, etc. so that all lengths are integral multiples of it. [French *module* or Latin *modulus*: see MODULUS]

mod·ulo /ˈmɒdjʊˌloː/ *preposition & adjective Math.* using, or with respect to, a modulus (*see* MODULUS 2). [Latin, ablative of MODULUS]

mod·ulus /ˈmɒdjʊləs/ *noun* (pl. **mod·uli** /-ˌlai/) *Math.* **1 a** the magnitude of a real number without regard to its sign. **b** the positive square root of the sum of the squares of the real and imaginary parts of a complex number. **2** a constant factor or ratio. **3** (in number theory) a number by which another number may be divided leaving a remainder. **4** a constant indicating the relation between a physical effect and the force producing it. [Latin, = measure, diminutive of *modus*]

modus op·er·an·di /ˌmoːdəs ˌɒpəˈrandi/ *noun* (pl. **modi operandi** /ˌmoːdiː/) **1** the particular way in which a person performs a task or action. **2** the way a thing operates. [Latin, = way of operating: see MODE]

modus vi·ven·di /ˌmoːdəs viˈvendi/ *noun* (pl. **modi vivendi** /ˌmoːdiː/) **1** a way of living or coping. **2 a** an arrangement whereby those in dispute can carry on pending a settlement. **b** an arrangement between people who agree to differ. [Latin, = way of living: see MODE]

MOE *abbreviation Cdn* (in Ontario) Ministry of the Environment.

Moga·dishu /ˌmoːɡəˈdiʃuː/ the capital of Somalia, a port on the Indian Ocean; pop. (est. 2002) 1,183,100.

mog·gie *noun Brit. slang* a cat. [20th c.: of dial. origin]

Mogi·lev see MAHILYOW.

mo·gul[1] /ˈmoːɡəl/ *noun* **1** *informal* an important or influential person. **2** (**Mogul**) *hist.* **a** = MUGHAL. **b** (often **the Great Mogul**) any of the emperors of Delhi in the 16th–19th c. [Persian *muǵul*: see MUGHAL]

mo·gul[2] *noun* **1** a mound of hard snow on a ski slope. **2** (in pl.) a freestyle skiing event in which skiers negotiate the moguls on a run

with as much speed and élan as possible. [prob. from southern German dialect *Mugel, Mugl*]

MOH *abbreviation* MEDICAL OFFICER OF HEALTH.

Mo·hács /ˈmoːhɒtʃ/ a river port and industrial town on the Danube in S Hungary, close to the borders with Croatia and Serbia; pop. (est. 2002) 20,100. It was the site of a battle in 1526 in which the Hungarians were defeated by a Turkish force, as a result of which Hungary became part of the Ottoman Empire.

mo·hair /ˈmoːher/ ● *noun* **1** the hair of the angora goat. **2** a yarn or fabric from this, either pure or mixed with wool or cotton. ● *adjective* made or consisting of mohair. [ultimately from Arabic *mukayyar*, lit. 'choice, select']

Moham·med see MUHAMMAD.

Moham·med II see MUHAMMAD II.

Moham·med Ali see MUHAMMAD ALI 1.

Moham·med·an *noun & adjective* = MUSLIM. ¶ A term not used or favoured by Muslims, and often regarded as *offensive*.

Mo·have Desert see MOJAVE DESERT.

Mo·hawk *noun* **1 a** a member of an Iroquois people, one of the five of the original Iroquois federation, now inhabiting parts of southern Ontario and northern New York. **b** the Iroquoian language of this people. **2** *Figure Skating* a step from either edge of the skate to the same edge on the other foot in the opposite direction (compare CHOCTAW 2). **3** (**mohawk**) (also **mohawk haircut**) esp. *N Amer.* a haircut, supposedly resembling that worn by the Mohawk, in which the head is shaved except for a brushlike strip of hair over the top of the head to the back of the neck. [Narragansett *mohowawog*, lit. 'man-eaters']

Mo·hegan /moˈhiːɡən/ ● *noun* **1** a member of an Algonquian people formerly inhabiting part of Connecticut. **2** the language of this people. ● *adjective* designating or pertaining to this people or their language. [Mohegan]

mohel /mɒˈhel, ˈmoːhəl/ *noun* a person trained to perform ritual circumcisions according to Jewish law. [Hebrew *mōhēl*]

Mohenjo-Daro /məˌhendʒoːˈdɑːroː/ an ancient city of the civilization of the Indus valley (*c.*2600–1700 BC), now a major archaeological site in Pakistan, southwest of Sukkur.

Mo·hi·can /moːˈhiːkən/ ● *noun* **1** = MAHICAN *noun*. **2** *Brit.* a Mohawk haircut. ● *adjective* = MAHICAN *adjective*. [Mohegan]

moho /ˈmoːhoː/ *noun* (pl. **mohos**) *Geol.* a boundary of discontinuity separating the earth's crust and mantle. [A. *Mohorovičić*, Yugoslav seismologist d.1936]

Moholy-Nagy /məˈhoːliˈnɒdʒ, ˌmoːhoːi-/ **László** (1895–1946), Hungarian-born US painter, sculptor, and photographer. He pioneered the experimental use of plastic materials, light, photography, and film; he headed the new Bauhaus school in Chicago from 1937.

moi /mwɒ/ *pronoun jocular* as a tongue-in-cheek rejoinder to being accused of something of which one knows one is guilty; what, me? (*pretentious? moi?*). [French]

moi·dore /ˈmɔidɔːr/ *noun hist.* a Portuguese gold coin, current in England in the 18th c. [Portuguese *moeda d'ouro* money of gold]

moi·ety /ˈmɔiəti/ *noun* (pl. **-ies**) **1** *Law* or *literary* a half, either of two equal parts. **2** *Law* or *literary* each of the two parts into which a thing is divided. **3** *Anthropology* either of two primary social divisions of a tribe. [Old French *moité, moitié* from Latin *medietas -tatis* middle, from *medius* (adj.) middle]

moil /mɔil/ ● *intransitive verb* **1** toil, work hard, drudge, esp. *toil and moil.* **2** swirl, mill about; move around in agitation or confusion. ● *noun* **1** turmoil, confusion, trouble. **2** drudgery. [Old French *moillier* moisten, paddle in mud, ultimately from Latin *mollis* soft]

Moi·rai /ˈmɔirai/ *Gk Myth* the Greek name for the Fates (see FATES, THE).

moiré /ˈmɔrei, mwɔr-/ ● *noun* **1** a fabric, often silk, having a pattern of glossy wavy bars. **2** a variegated or clouded appearance like that of this fabric, esp. as an ornamental finish applied to metal. **3** (in full **moiré pattern**) light and dark fringes observed when a pattern of lines, dots, etc. is visually superimposed on another similar or identical pattern slightly out of alignment with the first. ● *adjective* having a moiré pattern. [French, past participle of *moirer* (earlier *mouaire*) from MOHAIR]

Mois·san /mwɒsɑ̃/ (**Fer·di·nand Fré·dé·ric**) **Henri** (1852–1907), French chemist and educator. He succeeded in isolating the very reactive element fluorine (1886), and invented the electric arc furnace that bears his name (1892); he was awarded the Nobel Prize for chemistry in 1906.

moist *adjective* **1** slightly wet; damp. **2 a** (of the season, climate, etc.) rainy; having some or considerable rainfall. **b** (of the eyes) wet with tears, ready to shed tears. □ **moist·ly** *adverb* **moist·ness** *noun* [Old French *moiste*, ultimately from or related to Latin *mucidus* (see MUCUS) and *musteus* fresh (see MUST²)]

mois·ten *transitive & intransitive verb* make or become moist; wet superficially or moderately.

mois·ture *noun* water or other liquid diffused in a small quantity as vapour, or within a solid, or condensed on a surface.
□ **mois·ture·less** *adjective*

mois·tur·ize *transitive verb* (also esp. *Brit.* **-ise**) make less dry (esp. the skin by use of a cosmetic). □ **mois·tur·iz·er** *noun* **mois·tur·iz·ing** *adjective*

Mo·jave Des·ert /mo'hɒvi/ (also **Mohave**) a desert in S California, to the southeast of the Sierra Nevada and north and east of Los Angeles.

mo·ji·to /mo'hi:to:, mo:'dʒi:to:/ *noun* a cocktail originating in Cuba and consisting of white rum, lime or lemon juice, sugar, fresh mint, ice, and carbonated or soda water. [Cuban Spanish from stem of Spanish *mojado* wet + diminutive *-ito*]

mojo /'mo:dʒo:/ *noun* (pl. **mojos**) **1** magic, voodoo. **2** a charm or amulet. **3** *informal* a power, force, or influence of any kind (often with sexual connotations). [prob. of African origin]

mok·sha /'mɒkʃə/ *noun* Hinduism the final release of the soul from the cycle of reincarnations. [Sanskrit *mokṣa*]

mol /mo:l/ *abbreviation* = MOLE⁴.

mol. *abbreviation* **1** molecular. **2** molecule.

molal /'mo:ləl/ *adjective* Chem. (of a solution) containing one mole, or a specified number of moles, of solute per kilogram of solvent (compare MOLAR³). □ **molal·ity** /mə'laliti/ *noun* [MOLE⁴ + -AL]

molar¹ ● *adjective* **1** (of a tooth) serving to grind, esp. designating any of the back teeth of mammals. **2** of or pertaining to a molar tooth.
● *noun* a molar tooth. [Latin *molaris* from *mola* millstone]

molar² *adjective* **1** of or relating to mass. **2** acting on or by means of large masses or units. [Latin *moles* mass]

molar³ *adjective* Chem. **1** of a mass of substance usu. per mole (*molar latent heat*). **2** (of a solution) containing one mole, or a specified number of moles, of solute per litre of solvent (compare MOLAL). □ **mo·lar·ity** /mə'leriti/ *noun* [MOLE⁴ + -AR¹]

mo·las·ses /mə'lasis, -siz/ *noun* **1** a thick, dark, uncrystallized syrup drained from raw sugar during refining, often used in animal feed etc. **2** N Amer. a lighter, sweeter version of this substance combined with invert sugar and corn syrup for use as a table syrup, in baking, etc. [Portuguese *melaço* from Late Latin *mellaceum* MUST² from *mel* honey]

Mold /mɒld/ a town in NE Wales; pop. (est. 2001) 9,200.

mold *var.* of MOULD¹, MOULD², MOULD³.

Mol·dau /'mɒldau/ the traditional English name for the VLTAVA RIVER.

Mol·davia /mɒl'deiviə/ **1** a former principality of SE Europe. In 1859 Moldavia united with Wallachia to form Romania. **2** see MOLDOVA.

mold·er *var.* of MOULDER.

mold·ing *var.* of MOULDING.

Mol·dova /mɒl'do:və, 'mɒldəvə/ (also **Moldavia**) a landlocked country in SE Europe, between Romania and Ukraine; pop. (est. 2002) 4,434,547; capital, Chișinău. A former constituent republic of the USSR, Moldova was formed from territory ceded by Romania in 1940.
□ **Mol·do·van** *adjective & noun*

moldy *var.* of MOULDY.

mole¹ *noun* **1** any small burrowing insect-eating mammal of the family Talpidae, with dark velvety fur and very small eyes. **2** *informal* **a** a spy established deep within an organization and usu. dormant for a long period while attaining a position of trust. **b** a betrayer of confidential information. **3** a remotely operated or automatic machine capable of tunnelling through rock. [prob. from Middle Dutch *moll(e)*, *mol*, Middle Low German *mol*, *mul*]

mole² *noun* a small often slightly raised dark blemish on the skin caused by a high concentration of melanin. [Old English *māl* from Germanic]

mole³ *noun* **1** a massive structure serving as a pier, breakwater, or causeway. **2** an artificial harbour. [French *môle* from Latin *moles* mass]

mole⁴ *noun* Chem. the SI unit of amount of substance equal to the quantity containing as many elementary units as there are atoms in 0.012 kg of carbon-12. In other words, one mole of a substance has a mass equal to its molecular weight expressed in grams and contains 6.02×10^{23} molecules of the substance. Abbr.: **mol**. [German *Mol* from *Molekül* MOLECULE]

mole⁵ *noun* Med. an abnormal mass of tissue in the uterus. [French *môle* from Latin *mola* millstone]

mole⁶ /'mo:lei/ *noun* a highly spiced Mexican sauce made chiefly from chili peppers and chocolate, served with meat. [Mexican Spanish from Nahuatl *molli* sauce, stew]

mole cricket *noun* a large burrowing nocturnal cricket-like insect of the family Gryllotalpidae.

mo·lec·u·lar /mə'lekjulər/ *adjective* of, relating to, or consisting of molecules. □ **mo·lec·u·lar·ity** /-'leriti/ *noun* **mo·lec·u·lar·ly** *adverb*

molecular biology *noun* the study of the structure and function of large molecules associated with living organisms. □ **molecular biologist** *noun*

molecular electronics *plural noun* (treated as *sing.*) a branch of electronics in which individual molecules perform the same function as microelectronic devices such as diodes.

molecular sieve *noun* a crystalline substance with pores of molecular dimensions which permit the passage of molecules below a certain size.

molecular weight *noun* the ratio of the average mass of one molecule of an element or compound to one twelfth of the mass of an atom of carbon-12. *Also called* RELATIVE MOLECULAR MASS.

mol·ec·ule *noun* **1** Chem. the smallest fundamental unit (usu. a group of atoms) of a chemical compound that can take part in a chemical reaction. **2** (in general use) a small particle. [French *molécule* from modern Latin *molecula* diminutive of Latin *moles* mass]

mole·hill *noun* a small mound thrown up by a mole in burrowing.
□ **make a mountain out of a molehill** exaggerate the importance of a minor difficulty.

mole rat *noun* any of various rat-like rodents with reduced eyes, esp. of the African family Bathyergidae, which live underground, often communally.

mole·skin *noun* **1** the skin of a mole used as fur. **2 a** a kind of cotton fustian with its surface shaved before dyeing. **b** (in *pl.*) clothes, esp. trousers, made of this. **3** an adhesive-backed felt put on parts of the feet to reduce abrasion from shoes.

mo·lest *transitive verb* **1** attack or interfere with (a person), esp. sexually. **2** annoy or pester (a person) in a hostile or injurious way.
□ **mo·lest·a·tion** *noun* **mo·lest·er** *noun* [Old French *molester* or Latin *molestare* annoy, from *molestus* troublesome]

Mo·lière /mɒli'er, mɒl'jer/ (pseudonym of Jean-Baptiste Poquelin) (1622–73), French playwright. The creator of French classical comedy, he depicted the vices and follies of contemporary France, simultaneously adopting and developing stock characters from Italian *commedia dell'arte*; his works include *Le Tartuffe* (1664), *Don Juan* (1665), and *Le Misanthrope* (1666).

Mol·i·nari /ˌmɒli'nɑri/ **Guido** (1933–2004), Canadian painter. Born in Montreal, he was a founding member of the Association des Artistes Non-Figuratifs de Montréal in 1956. After early work in the formal abstract style, his painting evolved into an analytic style utilizing large vertical bands of colour.

mo·line /mə'lain/ *adjective* Heraldry (of a cross) having each extremity broadened and curved back. [prob. from Anglo-French *moliné* from *molin* MILL¹, because of the resemblance to the iron support of a millstone]

Mo·lise /mə'li:zei/ a region of E Italy, on the Adriatic coast; capital, Campobasso.

moll /mɒl/ *noun* slang **1** a gangster's female companion. **2** *archaic* a prostitute. [pet form of the name *Mary*]

mol·li·fy /'mɒlə,fai/ *transitive verb* (**-fies**, **-fied**) **1** appease, pacify. **2** reduce the severity of; soften. □ **mol·li·fi·ca·tion** *noun* **mol·li·fi·er** *noun* [French *mollifier* or Latin *mollificare* from *mollis* soft]

mol·lusc *noun* (also esp. *US* **mol·lusk**) any invertebrate of the phylum Mollusca, with a soft body and usu. a hard shell, including limpets, snails, cuttlefish, oysters, mussels, etc. □ **mol·lusc·an** /mə'lʌskən/ *adjective* [modern Latin *mollusca* neuter pl. of Latin *molluscus* from *mollis* soft]

molly /'mɒli/ *noun* (also **mol·lie**) a small killifish bearing live young, esp. *Poecilia sphenops*, bred in many colours for aquariums. [from modern Latin *Mollienisia* (former genus name), from Count *Mollien*, French statesman (d.1850)]

molly·cod·dle /'mɒli,kɒdəl/ *transitive verb* coddle, pamper. [as MOLL + CODDLE]

Mol·och /'mo:lɒk, 'mɒlək/ *noun* **1 a** a Canaanite idol to whom children were sacrificed. **b** a tyrannical object of sacrifices. **2** (**moloch**) the spiny slow-moving grotesque Australian reptile, *Moloch horridus*. [Late Latin from Greek *Molokh* from Hebrew *mōlek*]

Molo·tov¹ /ˈmɒləˌtɒf/ a former name (1940–57) for PERM.

Molo·tov² /ˈmɒləˌtɒf/ **Vya·che·slav Mik·hail·ovich** (born Vyacheslav Mikhailovich Skryabin) (1890–1986), Soviet leader. As Commissar (later Minister) for Foreign Affairs (1939–49; 1953–6), he negotiated the non-aggression pact with Nazi Germany (1939) and after 1945 represented the Soviet Union at meetings of the United Nations, where his frequent exercise of the veto helped to prolong the Cold War.

Molotov cocktail noun a homemade incendiary device, usu. consisting of a bottle filled with inflammable liquid, usu. with a rag stuffed in the neck that is ignited just before throwing. [MOLOTOV²]

Mol·son ▸ 1 John (1763–1836), English-born Canadian brewer and entrepreneur. Orphaned as a child, he emigrated to Montreal in 1782 and purchased a small brewery in 1786. He invested in a steamship line between Quebec City and Montreal, built Lower Canada's first distillery (1821), established the Champlain and Saint Lawrence Railroad (the first railway into Canada), and introduced steam power to Montreal industry. **2** his son **John Jr.** (1787–1860), Canadian brewer and entrepreneur. After his father's death he sold his share in the Molson brewing operation to his two brothers and concentrated on transportation and utilities. He served as president of the Champlain and Saint Lawrence Railroad and of City Gas Co., which introduced gas lighting to Montreal, and was a director of the Bank of Montreal 1824–53.

Molson muscle noun *Cdn slang* a beer belly. [*Molson*, a popular brand of beer]

molt esp. *US var. of* MOULT.

mol·ten adjective melted, esp. made liquid by heat. [archaic past participle of MELT]

molto /ˈmɒltoː/ adverb *Music* very (*molto sostenuto*; *allegro molto*). [Italian from Latin *multus* much]

Mo·luc·ca Islands /məˈlʌkə/ (also **Moluccas**) an island group in Indonesia, between Sulawesi and New Guinea; capital, Amboina. The islands were taken in the 17th c. by the Dutch, who controlled the lucrative trade in the spices produced on the islands, which were formerly known as the Spice Islands.

moly /ˈmoːli/ noun (pl. **-ies**) **1** an alliaceous plant, *Allium moly*, with small yellow flowers. **2** a mythical herb with white flowers and black roots, endowed with magic properties. [Latin from Greek *mōlu*]

mo·lyb·den·ite /məˈlɪbdəˌnaɪt/ noun molybdenum disulphide as an ore.

mo·lyb·den·um /məˈlɪbdənəm/ noun *Chem.* a silver-white brittle metallic transition element occurring naturally in molybdenite and used in steel to give strength and resistance to corrosion. Symbol: **Mo**; at. no.: 42. [modern Latin, earlier *molybdena*, originally = molybdenite, lead ore: Latin *molybdena* from Greek *molubdaina* 'plummet', from *molubdos* 'lead']

mom /mɒm, mʌm/ noun *N Amer. informal* mother. [abbreviation of MOMMA]

mom-and-pop attributive adjective *N Amer.* (also **ma-and-pa**) designating a store, restaurant, etc. run by a married couple or other members of a family.

Mom·basa /mɒmˈbasə/ a seaport and industrial city in SE Kenya, on the Indian Ocean; pop. (est. 2002) 707,400. It is the leading port and second largest city of Kenya.

mo·ment noun **1** a very brief portion of time; an instant. **2** a short period of time (*wait a moment*) (see also MINUTE¹ 3a). **3 a** an exact or particular point of time (*at last the moment arrived; I came the moment you called*). **b** a brief period of time marked by a particular quality or experience (*a TV moment; a revolutionary moment*). **4** importance (*of no great moment*). **5** *Physics & Mech. etc.* **a** the turning effect produced by a force acting at a distance on an object. **b** this effect expressed as the product of the force and the distance from its line of action to a point. □ **at the moment** at this time; now. **have one's moments** be impressive, happy, etc., on occasions. **in a moment 1** very soon. **2** instantly. **man** (or **woman** etc.) **of the moment** the one of importance at the time in question. **not for a** (or **one**) **moment** never; not at all. **this moment** immediately; at once (*come here this moment*). **live** (or **be**) **in the moment** live or act without worrying about the future or past. [Old French from Latin *momentum*]

mo·men·ta pl. of MOMENTUM.

mo·men·tar·i·ly adverb **1** for a moment; fleetingly. **2 a** *N Amer.* at any moment; very soon. **b** instantly.

mo·men·tary adjective **1** lasting only a moment. **2** short-lived; transitory.

moment of inertia noun *Physics* the quantity by which the angular acceleration of a body must be multiplied to give corresponding torque.

moment of truth noun a crisis or turning point; a testing situation. [Spanish *el momento de la verdad*, the time of the final sword thrust in a bullfight]

mo·men·tous adjective having great importance. □ **mo·men·tous·ly** adverb **mo·men·tous·ness** noun

mo·men·tum /moːˈmentəm/ noun (pl. **mo·men·ta** /-tə/) **1** *Physics* the quantity of motion of a moving body, measured as a product of its mass and velocity. **2** the impetus gained by movement. **3** strength or continuity derived from an initial effort. [Latin from *movimentum* from *movēre* move]

momentum investing noun an investment strategy in which stocks or shares that are rising in price are bought while those that are falling in price are sold. □ **momentum investor** noun

mom·ma /ˈmɒmə/ noun esp. *N Amer. var. of* MAMMA¹.

Momm·sen /ˈmɒmsən/ **(Chris·tian Mat·thias) Theo·dor** (1817–1903), German historian. Noted for his *History of Rome* (1854–6; 1885) and his treatises on Roman constitutional law (1871–88), he was awarded the Nobel Prize for literature in 1902.

mommy /ˈmɒmi, ˈmʌmi/ noun (pl. **-mies**) *N Amer. informal* mother.

mommy track noun esp. *N Amer. informal* a career path for women who sacrifice some promotions and pay raises in order to devote more time to raising their children. □ **mommy tracker** noun **mommy tracking** noun

Momus /ˈmoːməs/ *Gk Myth* the god of blame.

Mon. abbreviation Monday.

Mon·aco /ˈmɒnəˌkoː/ a principality forming an enclave within French territory, on the Mediterranean coast near the Italian frontier; pop. (est. 2002) 31,987. The smallest sovereign state in the world apart from the Vatican, it includes the resort of Monte Carlo.

mon·ad /ˈmɒnad, ˈmoː-/ noun **1** the number one; a unit. **2** (esp. in the philosophy of Leibniz) any ultimate unit of being, e.g. a soul, an atom, a person, God. **3** *Biol.* a simple organism, e.g. one assumed to be the first in the genealogy of living beings. □ **mon·ad·ic** /məˈnadɪk/ adjective [French *monade* or Late Latin *monas monad-* from Greek *monas -ados* unit, from *monos* alone]

mo·nad·nock /məˈnadnɒk/ noun a steep-sided isolated hill resistant to erosion and rising above a plain. [Mount *Monadnock* in New Hampshire, US]

Mona·ghan /ˈmɒnəhən/ **1** a county of the Republic of Ireland, part of the old province of Ulster. **2** its county town; pop. (est. 2002) 6,100.

Mona Lisa /ˈmoːnə ˈliːsə/ ● noun a woman having an enigmatic smile or expression. ● adjective (of a smile etc.) enigmatic. [*Mona Lisa*, a painting of a young woman with an enigmatic smile, painted by Leonardo da Vinci 1503-6]

mon·andry /məˈnandri/ noun **1** the custom of having only one husband at a time. **2** *Bot.* the state of having a single stamen. □ **mon·an·drous** adjective [MONO- after *polyandry*]

mon·arch noun **1** a sovereign with the title of king, queen, emperor, empress, or the equivalent. **2** a powerful or pre-eminent person. **3** (in full **monarch butterfly**) a large migrating orange and black butterfly, *Danaus plexippus*, found mainly in the Americas. **4** (in full **monarch flycatcher**) a flycatcher of the Old World family Monarchidae. □ **mon·arch·al** /məˈnɑrkəl/ adjective **mon·arch·ic** /məˈnɑrkɪk/ adjective **mon·arch·ic·al** adjective [Greek *monarkhēs, -os*, from *monos* 'alone' + *arkhō* 'to rule']

mon·arch·ism noun the advocacy of or the principles of monarchy. □ **mon·arch·ist** noun & adjective

mon·archy noun (pl. **-ies**) **1** a form of government with a monarch at the head. **2** a state with this. □ **mon·arch·ial** /məˈnɑrkɪəl/ adjective

Mona·shee Mountains /ˈmɒnəʃi/ the most westerly range of the Columbia mountain system, situated in SE central BC. [Scots Gaelic *monadh sith* mountain of peace]

mon·as·tery /ˈmɒnəˌsteri/ noun (pl. **-ies**) **1** the residence of a religious community, esp. of monks living in seclusion. **2** the community itself. [ecclesiastical Latin *monasterium* from ecclesiastical Greek *monastērion* from *monazō* live alone, from *monos* alone]

mon·as·tic /məˈnastɪk/ ● adjective **1** of or relating to monasteries or the religious communities living in them. **2** resembling these or their way of life; solitary and celibate. ● noun a monk or other follower of a monastic rule. □ **mon·as·tic·al·ly** *adverb* **mon·as·ti·cism** /-ˌsɪzəm/ *noun* [as MONASTERY]

mon·atom·ic /ˌmɒnəˈtɒmɪk/ *adjective Chem.* (esp. of a molecule) consisting of one atom.

mon·aural /mɒˈnɔːrəl/ *adjective* **1** = MONOPHONIC 1. **2** of or involving one ear.

mona·zite /ˈmɒnəˌzaɪt/ *noun* a phosphate mineral containing rare-earth elements and thorium. [German *Monazit* from Greek *monazō* 'live alone' (because of its rarity)]

Mön·chen·glad·bach /ˌmʊnxənˈɡladbax/ a city in NW Germany; pop. (est. 2002) 266,400. It is the site of the NATO headquarters for N Europe.

Monck /mʌŋk/ **1 Charles Stan·ley, 4th Vis·count** (1819–94), Irish-born colonial administrator, appointed Governor General of British North America in 1861. A strong supporter of Confederation, he was one of the architects of the Great Coalition. In 1867 he was named the first Governor General of Canada and PEI; he returned to Ireland in 1868. **2 George, 1st Duke of Albe·marle** (also **Monk**) (1608–70), English general. Although initially a Royalist in the English Civil War, he became a supporter of Cromwell, and completed the suppression of the Royalists in Scotland (1651); he was later instrumental in restoring the monarchy (1660).

Monck·ton /ˈmʌŋktən/ **Rob·ert** (1726–82), British army officer. Arriving in Nova Scotia in 1752, he helped to found Lunenburg in 1753 and supervised the deportation of the Acadians two years later. He was Wolfe's second-in-command in the siege of Quebec, but was wounded in the Battle of the Plains of Abraham and left Canada shortly after.

Monc·ton /ˈmʌŋktən/ a city in E New Brunswick, located on the Petitcodiac River, 152 km (94 miles) northeast of Saint John; pop. (2001) 61,046. □ **Monc·ton·ian** /ˌmʌŋkˈtoːnɪən/ *noun* [R. MONCKTON]

mon·daine /mɔ̃ˈden/ ● *adjective* **1** of the fashionable world. **2** worldly. ● *noun* a worldly or fashionable woman. [French, fem. of *mondain*: see MUNDANE]

Mon·day ● *noun* the second day of the week, following Sunday. ● *adverb* **1** on Monday. **2** (**Mon·days**) on Mondays; each Monday. [Old English *mōnandæg* day of the moon, translation of Late Latin *lunae dies*]

Monday-morning quarterback *noun N Amer. informal* a person who, having the advantage of hindsight, criticizes the actions of another. [from the fact of football games being commonly televised on Sunday afternoons]

mondo /ˈmɒndoː/ *slang* ● *adjective* big, large, considerable (*mondo waves*). ● *adverb* very, extremely (*mondo cool*). [from Italian *Mondo Cane*, lit. 'world for a dog', title of a 1961 film showing bizarre behaviour]

Mon·dri·an /ˈmɒndriˌɒn/ **Piet** (born Pieter Cornelis Mondriaan) (1872–1944), Dutch abstract painter. A co-founder of the De Stijl movement, he is noted for his use of vertical and horizontal lines, rectangular shapes, and primary colours in paintings such as *Composition with Red, Yellow, and Blue* (1921).

Mone·gasque /mɒnəˈɡask/ ● *noun* a native or inhabitant of Monaco. ● *adjective* pertaining to or characteristic of Monaco or its inhabitants. [French]

Monet /mɒˈnei/ **Claude** (1840–1926), French painter. One of the first Impressionists, he was fascinated with the play of light on objects, executing a series of paintings of single subjects at different times of day and under different weather conditions, notably the *Haystacks* series (1890–1) and the *Water lilies* sequence (1899–1906; 1916 onward).

mon·et·ar·ism /ˈmɒnətəˌrɪzəm/ *noun* the theory or practice of controlling the supply of money as the chief method of stabilizing the economy. □ **mon·et·ar·ist** *noun & adjective*

mon·et·ary /ˈmɒnətəri/ *adjective* **1** of or pertaining to coinage or currency. **2** of or pertaining to money. □ **mon·et·ar·i·ly** *adverb* [French *monétaire* or Late Latin *monetarius* from Latin (as MONEY)]

monetary policy *noun* the means by which a government tries to affect macroeconomic conditions by increasing or decreasing the supply of money.

monetary unit *noun* a standard unit of currency in a country, related to monetary units of other countries by a foreign exchange rate.

mon·et·ize /ˈmɒnəˌtaɪz/ *transitive verb* (also esp. *Brit.* **-ise**) **1** give a fixed value as currency. **2** put (a metal) into circulation as money. □ **mon·et·iz·a·tion** *noun* [French *monétiser* from Latin (as MONEY)]

Mon·ette /mɒˈnet/ **Rich·ard Jean** (b.1944), Canadian stage actor and director who, since 1994, has been artistic director of the Stratford Festival.

money *noun* **1 a** a current medium of exchange in the form of coins and banknotes. **b** a particular form of this (*paper money*). **2** (*pl.* **-ies** or

-eys) (in *pl.*) sums of money. **3 a** wealth; property etc. viewed as convertible into money. **b** wealth as giving power or influence (*money speaks*). **c** a rich person or family (*has married into money*). **4 a** money as a resource (*time is money*). **b** profit, remuneration (*in it for the money*). **c** a salary, wage (*makes good money*). **5** money earmarked for a particular purchase or purpose (*pin money*; *beer money*). □ **for my money** in my opinion or judgment; for my preference (*is too aggressive for my money*). **have money to burn** see BURN¹. **in the money** *informal* having or winning a lot of money. **made of money** *informal* very rich. **put one's money where one's mouth is** produce, bet, or pay out money to support one's statements or opinions. **put money into** invest in. (**right**) **on the money 1** on target; carried out with skill and precision. **2** correct in a prediction, observation, etc. □ **money·less** *adjective* [Old French *moneie* from Latin *moneta* mint, money, originally a title of Juno, in whose temple at Rome money was minted]

money-back guarantee *noun* a guarantee by a manufacturer, retailer, etc. to refund the full purchase price of a product or service which the purchaser finds to be defective or unsatisfactory.

money·bags *plural noun* (treated as *sing.*) usu. *derogatory* a wealthy person.

money·belt *noun* a belt with a compartment for carrying money, passports, etc., worn underneath clothing esp. by tourists.

money bill *noun* a government bill to impose, change, or regulate taxation, to supply government monetary requirements, etc.

money-changer *noun* a person whose business it is to change money, esp. at an official rate. □ **money-changing** *noun & adjective*

moneyed *adjective* (also **monied**) **1** having much money; wealthy. **2** consisting of money.

money-grubber *noun informal* a person greedily intent on amassing money. □ **money-grubbing** *adjective & noun*

money laundering *noun* the practice or system of transferring funds to conceal a dubious or illegal origin (also *attributive*: *money-laundering operation*). □ **money launderer** *noun*

money·lend·er *noun* a person who lends money, esp. as a business, at interest. □ **money·lend·ing** *noun & adjective*

money-loser *noun* an unprofitable business venture etc. □ **money-losing** *adjective*

money-maker *noun* **1** a person who earns much money. **2** a thing, idea, etc. that produces much money. □ **money-making** *noun & adjective*

money man *noun informal* a financier or financial expert.

money manager *noun* a person who manages mutual funds and other investments at a brokerage firm, mutual fund company, etc. □ **money management** *noun*

money market *noun* the market in short-term debt instruments issued by governments, corporations, etc. such as treasury bills, short-term bonds, commercial paper, etc.

money market fund *noun* a mutual fund that invests in the money market, usu. highly liquid, very secure, and offering higher interest than bank accounts.

money of account *noun* denominations of money used in reckoning, but not current as coins.

money order *noun* an order for payment of a specified sum, issued by a bank or post office.

money pit *noun informal* **1** a project, program, etc. that eats up large amounts of money and is often perceived as wasteful and unnecessary. **2** = PIT¹ *noun* 6.

money player *noun N Amer. informal* a player who performs well at decisive or crucial times.

money-spinner *noun* esp. *Brit. informal* a thing that brings in a profit.

money supply *noun* the total amount of money in circulation or in being in a country.

money's worth *noun* (prec. by *your*, *my*, *one's*) good value for one's money.

money·wort /ˈmʌniˌwɜrt, -ˌwɔrt/ *noun* a trailing evergreen plant, *Lysimachia nummularia*, with round glossy leaves and yellow flowers. Also called CREEPING JENNY.

mon·ger /ˈmɒŋɡər, ˈmʌŋɡər/ *noun* (usu. in *combination*) **1** a dealer or trader (*fishmonger*). **2** usu. *derogatory* a person who promotes or deals in something specified (*warmonger*; *scaremonger*). □ **-monger·ing** *combining form*. [Old English *mangere* from *mangian* to traffic, from Germanic, ultimately from Latin *mango* dealer]

Vowels: a c*a*t ɑ *ar*m e b*e*d ɜr h*er* ɜː *deux* ə *ago* ɪ s*i*t i c*o*sy iː f*ee*d ɒ h*o*t ɔ p*o*re oː n*o* ʌ r*u*n ʊ p*u*t

mon·go /ˈmɒŋɡoː/ *noun* (*pl.* **-gos** or same) a monetary unit of Mongolia, equal to one-hundredth of a tugrik. [Mongolian *möngö* silver]

Mon·gol /ˈmɒŋɡəl/ ● *adjective* **1** of or relating to the Asian people now inhabiting Mongolia or their language. **2** resembling this people, esp. in appearance. **3** (**mongol**) *offensive* suffering from Down's syndrome. ● *noun* **1 a** a Mongolian. **b** the Mongolian language. **2** (**mongol**) *offensive* a person suffering from Down's syndrome. [Mongolian, said to be from *mong* brave]

Mon·go·lia /mɒŋˈɡoːliə/ a large and sparsely populated country of E Asia, bordered by Siberian Russia and China; pop. (est. 2002) 2,694,432; capital, Ulan Bator. Mongolia was formerly known as **Outer Mongolia** to distinguish it from Inner Mongolia, which is a province of China.

Mon·go·lian ● *noun* **1** a native or inhabitant of Mongolia. **2** the language of Mongolia, usu. considered a member of the Altaic family. ● *adjective* of or relating to Mongolia or its people or language.

mon·gol·ism /ˈmɒŋɡəˌlɪzəm/ *noun offensive* = DOWN'S SYNDROME. [MONGOL + -ISM, because its physical characteristics were thought to be reminiscent of Mongolians]

Mon·gol·oid /ˈmɒŋɡəˌlɔɪd/ ● *adjective* **1** of or relating to the division of humankind including the indigenous peoples of E Asia, SE Asia, and the Arctic region of N America, characteristically having dark eyes, straight hair, pale ivory to dark skin, and little facial or body hair. **2** (**mongoloid**) *offensive* affected with Down's syndrome. ● *noun* **1** a person of Mongoloid physical type. **2** *offensive* a person affected with Down's syndrome.

mon·goose /ˈmɒŋɡuːs/ *noun* (*pl.* **mon·goos·es**) any of various short-legged carnivorous mammals of the family Viverridae (which also includes the civets and genets), native to southern Asia and Africa, and noted for the ability to kill venomous snakes. [Marathi *maṅgūs*]

mon·grel ● *noun* **1** a dog of no definable type or breed. **2** any other animal or plant resulting from the crossing of different breeds or types. **3** *offensive* a person of mixed race. ● *adjective* of mixed origin, nature, or character. □ **mon·grel·ism** *noun* **mon·grel·ize** *transitive verb* (also esp. *Brit.* **-ise**). **mon·grel·iz·a·tion** *noun* [earlier *meng-, mang-* from Germanic: prob. related to MINGLE]

'mongst *literary var. of* AMONGST (*see* AMONG).

mon·ied *var. of* MONEYED.

mon·ies *see* MONEY 2.

mon·ik·er /ˈmɒnɪkər/ *noun* (also **mon·ick·er**) *slang* a name. [19th c.: origin unknown]

mon·ism /ˈmɒnɪzəm, ˈmoːn-/ *noun* **1** any theory denying the duality of matter and mind. **2** *Philos. & Theol.* the doctrine that only one ultimate principle or being exists (*compare* PLURALISM 3). □ **mon·ist** *noun* **mon·is·tic** *adjective* [modern Latin *monismus* from Greek *monos* single]

mon·ition /məˈnɪʃən/ *noun* **1** (foll. by *of*) *literary* a warning (of danger). **2** *Christianity* a formal notice from a bishop or ecclesiastical court admonishing a person not to commit an offence. [Old French from Latin *monitio -onis* (as MONITOR)]

mon·itor ● *noun* **1** any of various persons or devices for observing, checking, or warning about a situation, operation, etc. (*fetal monitor*; *baby monitor*). **2** a school pupil with disciplinary or other special duties. **3 a** a television receiver used in a studio to select or verify the picture being broadcast. **b** a loudspeaker used in a studio for listening to what is being recorded. **c** any large or powerful speaker, esp. one used on stage by a band. **4** *Computing* **a** a component displaying data as characters on a screen. **b** a computer program which monitors the running of other programs or the operation of a system. **5** a detector of radioactive contamination. **6** any tropical lizard of the genus *Varanus*, supposed to give warning of the approach of crocodiles. **7** *hist.* a heavily armed warship of shallow draft. ● *transitive verb* **1** watch and check something over a period of time. **2** maintain regular surveillance over. **3** regulate the strength of (a recorded or transmitted signal). □ **mon·itor·ial** *adjective* **mon·itor·ing** *noun & adjective* [Latin from *monēre monit-* warn]

mon·itory /ˈmɒnɪtəri/ ● *adjective literary* giving or serving as a warning. ● *noun* (*pl.* **-ies**) *Christianity* a letter of admonition from the Pope or a bishop. [Latin *monitorius* (as MONITION)]

Monk ▸ **1** George, *see* MONCK. **2 Thelo·nious (Sphere)** (1917–82), US jazz pianist and composer. One of the founders of bebop in the 1940s, he became popular in the late 1950s, as the new style of 'cool' jazz reached a wider audience.

monk *noun* a member of a religious community of men living under certain vows esp. of poverty, chastity, and obedience. □ **monk·ish**

adjective **monk·ish·ly** *adverb* **monk·ish·ness** *noun* [Old English *munuc*, ultimately from Greek *monakhos* solitary, from *monos* alone]

mon·key ● *noun* (*pl.* **-keys**) **1** any of various mainly long-tailed agile tree-dwelling primates of the families *Cebidae*, *Callithricidae*, and *Cercopithecidae*. **2** a mischievous person, esp. a child (*young monkey*). ● *intransitive verb* (**-keys**, **-keyed**) **1** (often foll. by *with*) tamper or play mischievous tricks. **2** (foll. by *around*, *about*) fool around. □ **have a monkey on one's back** *slang* **1** be a drug addict. **2** have a burdensome problem. **make a monkey of** humiliate by making appear ridiculous. □ **monkey·ish** *adjective* [16th c.: origin unknown (perhaps Low German)]

monkey bars *plural noun N Amer.* a playground structure of joined bars for children to climb on.

monkey business *noun informal* **1** mischief; tomfoolery. **2** suspicious or dishonest activities or behaviour.

monkey flower *noun* a mimulus, esp. *M. guttatus*, with bright yellow flowers.

monkey in the middle *noun N Amer.* **1** a children's game in which two people throw a ball over the head of a third person standing in the middle, who tries to catch it. **2** a person who is placed in an awkward situation between two others.

monkey puzzle *noun* a coniferous evergreen tree, *Araucaria araucana*, native to Chile, with small close-set leaves. *Also called* CHILE PINE.

monkey·shine *noun* (usu. in *pl.*) *N Amer. informal* = MONKEY BUSINESS 1.

monkey suit *noun informal* **1** a tuxedo. **2** any uniform.

monkey trail *noun Cdn* (*West*) a narrow trail, in a park, field, along a riverbank, etc. created by the passage of walkers, cyclists, etc.

monkey wrench ● *noun* a wrench with an adjustable jaw. ● *transitive verb* (**monkey·wrench**) sabotage, esp. as a means of environmentalist protest. □ **throw a monkey wrench into** (**the works** etc.) *N Amer.* cause confusion or disruption. □ **monkey·wrench·er** *noun* **monkey·wrench·ing** *noun*

monk·fish *noun* **1** an anglerfish, esp. *Lophius americanus*. **2** a large bottom-dwelling shark, *Squatina squatina*, with a flattened body and large pectoral fins. *Also called* ANGEL SHARK.

monks·hood /ˈmʌŋkshʊd/ *noun* an aconite, esp. the cultivated *Aconitum napellus*, with hood-shaped blue or purple flowers.

Mon·mouth·shire /ˈmɒnməθˌʃɪr/ a county of SE Wales, on the border with England; administrative centre, Cwmbran. Most of the county was part of Gwent 1974–96.

Mon·net /mɒˈneɪ/ **Jean** (1888–1979), French economist and politician, who was a leading figure in the formation of the EEC.

Mono a town in S central Ontario, just northwest of Caledon; pop. (2001) 6,922. [origin uncertain]

mono¹ *informal* ● *adjective* monophonic. ● *noun* (*pl.* **monos**) a monophonic record, reproduction, etc. [abbreviation]

mono² *noun N Amer.* = MONONUCLEOSIS. [abbreviation]

mono³ *noun N Amer.* = MONOFILAMENT 2. [abbreviation]

mono- *combining form* (usu. **mon-** before a vowel) **1** one, alone, single. **2** *Chem.* (forming names of compounds) containing one atom or group of a specified kind. [Greek from *monos* alone]

mono·amine /ˌmɒnoːˈeɪmiːn, -ˈamiːn/ *noun Biochem.* any compound having a single amine group in its molecule.

monoamine oxidase *noun Biochem.* an enzyme which catalyzes the oxidation (and hence the inactivation) of monoamine neurotransmitters.

monoamine oxidase inhibitor *noun Biochem.* any of a class of antidepressant drugs which inhibit the activity of monoamine oxidase (so allowing the accumulation of serotonin and noradrenaline in the brain).

mono·bloc /ˈmɒnəblɒk/ *adjective* made as, contained in, or involving a single casting (*a monobloc chair*). [French, from MONO- + *bloc* block]

mono·car·pic /ˌmɒnəˈkɑːrpɪk/ *adjective Bot.* bearing fruit only once. [MONO- + Greek *karpos* fruit]

mono·caus·al /ˌmɒnəˈkɒzəl/ *adjective* in terms of a sole cause.

Mon·ocer·os /məˈnɒsərəs/ a faint constellation straddling the celestial equator next to Orion. [Latin *monocerōs* unicorn]

mono·chro·mat·ic /ˌmɒnəkrəˈmatɪk/ *adjective* **1** *Physics* (of light or other radiation) of a single wavelength or frequency. **2** containing only one colour. **3** (of a musical performance etc.) lacking any distinguishing or inspiring characteristics. □ **mono·chro·mat·ic·ally** *adverb*

mono·chroma·tism /ˌmɒnəˈkroːməˌtɪzəm/ *noun* complete colour-blindness in which all colours appear as shades of one colour.

mono·chrome /ˈmɒnəˌkrəʊm/ ● *noun* **1** a photograph or picture done in one colour or different tones of this, or in black and white only. **2** *Photog. etc.* black and white. ● *adjective* having or using only one colour or in black and white only. □ **mono·chrom·ic** *adjective* [ultimately from Greek *monokhrōmatos* (as MONO-, *khrōmatos* from *khrōma* colour)]

mon·ocle /ˈmɒnəkəl/ *noun* a single eyeglass, kept in position by the muscles around the eye. □ **mon·ocled** *adjective* [French, originally adj. from Late Latin *monoculus* one-eyed (as MONO-, *oculus* eye)]

mono·cline /ˈmɒnəˌklaɪn/ *noun Geol.* a bend in rock strata that is otherwise uniformly dipping or horizontal. □ **mono·clinal** *adjective* [MONO- + Greek *klinō* lean, dip]

mono·clin·ic /ˌmɒnəˈklɪnɪk/ *adjective* (of a crystal) having one axial intersection oblique. [MONO- + Greek *klinō* lean, slope]

mono·clon·al /ˌmɒnəˈkləʊnəl/ *adjective* forming a single clone; derived from a single individual or cell.

monoclonal antibodies *plural noun* antibodies produced artificially by a single clone of cells or cell line and consisting of identical antibody molecules.

mono·coque /ˈmɒnəˌkɒk/ *noun* (also *attributive*) an aircraft or vehicle structure in which the chassis is integral with the body. [French (as MONO-, *coque* shell)]

mono·cot /ˈmɒnəˌkɒt/ *noun* = MONOCOTYLEDON. [abbreviation]

mono·coty·ledon /ˌmɒnəˌkɒtɪˈliːdən/ *noun Bot.* any flowering plant with a single cotyledon. □ **mono·coty·ledon·ous** *adjective*

mon·oc·racy /məˈnɒkrəsi/ *noun* (*pl.* **-cies**) government by one person only. □ **mono·crat·ic** *adjective*

mono·crop·ping *noun* the practice of planting the same crop in the same field year after year. □ **mono·crop** *noun*

mon·ocu·lar /məˈnɒkjʊlər/ ● *adjective* of or pertaining to one eye only. ● *noun* a field glass or microscope for use with one eye. [Late Latin *monoculus* having one eye]

mono·cul·ture /ˈmɒnəˌkʌltʃər/ *noun* **1 a** the cultivation of a single crop to the exclusion of others. **b** an area in which such a practice prevails. **2** a society which is ethnically or culturally homogeneous. □ **mono·cultur·al** *adjective*

mono·cycle /ˈmɒnəˌsaɪkəl/ *noun* = UNICYCLE.

mono·cyte /ˈmɒnəˌsaɪt/ *noun Biol.* a large leukocyte with a simple nucleus, developing into a macrophage. □ **mono·cyt·ic** /-ˈsɪtɪk/ *adjective*

mono·drama /ˈmɒnəˌdrɑːmə, -ˌdrɒmə/ *noun* a dramatic piece for one performer.

mon·ody /ˈmɒnədi/ *noun* (*pl.* **-ies**) **1** an ode sung by a single actor in a Greek tragedy. **2** a poem lamenting a person's death. **3** *Music* a composition with only one melodic line. □ **mon·od·ic** /məˈnɒdɪk/ *adjective* **mon·od·ist** *noun* [Late Latin *monodia* from Greek *monōidia* from *monōidos* singing alone (as MONO-, ODE)]

mon·oe·cious /məˈniːʃəs/ *adjective* **1** *Bot.* with unisexual male and female organs on the same plant. **2** *Zool.* hermaphrodite. [modern Latin *Monoecia* the class of such plants (Linnaeus), from Greek *monos* single + *oikos* house]

mono·fila·ment /ˈmɒnəˌfɪləmənt/ *noun* **1** a single strand of synthetic fibre. **2** a type of fishing line using this.

mon·og·amy /məˈnɒɡəmi/ *noun* **1 a** the practice or state of being married to one person at a time. **b** the practice or state of having only one sexual partner at a time. **2** *Zool.* the habit of having only one mate at a time. □ **mon·og·am·ist** *noun* **mon·og·am·ous** *adjective* **mon·og·am·ous·ly** *adverb* [French *monogamie* from ecclesiastical Latin from Greek *monogamia* (as MONO-, *gamos* marriage)]

mono·gen·esis /ˌmɒnəˈdʒenəsɪs/ *noun* (also **mon·ogeny** /məˈnɒdʒəni/) **1** the theory of the development of all beings from a single cell. **2** the theory that mankind descended from one pair of ancestors. □ **mono·gen·etic** *adjective*

mono·glot /ˈmɒnəˌɡlɒt/ ● *adjective* speaking, writing, or understanding only one language. ● *noun* a monoglot person. [Greek *monoglōttos* (as MONO- *glōtta* tongue)]

mono·gram /ˈmɒnəˌɡræm/ *noun* two or more letters, esp. a person's initials, combined in one design and marked on items of clothing etc. □ **mono·grammed** *adjective* [as MONO-, -GRAM]

mono·graph /ˈmɒnəˌɡrɑːf/ ● *noun* a separate treatise on a single subject or an aspect of it. ● *transitive verb* write a monograph on. □ **mon·og·raph·er** /məˈnɒɡrəfər/ *noun* **mono·graph·ic** *adjective* [earlier *monography* from modern Latin *monographia* from *monographus* writer on a single genus or species (as MONO-, -GRAPH, -GRAPHY)]

mono·hull /ˈmɒnəˌhʌl/ *noun* a boat with a single hull.

mono·hybrid /ˌmɒnəˈhaɪbrɪd/ ● *noun Biol.* a hybrid that is heterozygous for alleles of one gene. ● *adjective* of or relating to inheritance of alleles of one gene.

mono·kini /ˌmɒnəˈkiːni/ *noun* a woman's one-piece bathing suit equivalent to the lower half of a bikini. [MONO- + BIKINI, by false association with BI-]

mono·layer /ˈmɒnəˌleɪər/ *noun* **1** *Chem.* a layer only one molecule in thickness. **2** *Biol. & Med.* a cell culture in a layer one cell thick.

mono·lin·gual /ˌmɒnəˈlɪŋɡwəl, -lɪŋɡjuːəl/ ● *adjective* **1** knowing or using only one language. **2** written in a single language. ● *noun* a person who knows only one language. □ **mono·lin·gual·ism** *noun*

mono·lith /ˈmɒnəlɪθ/ *noun* **1** a single block of stone, esp. shaped into a pillar or monument. **2 a** a person or thing like a monolith in being massive, immovable, or solidly uniform. **b** a large impersonal political or corporate body. **3** a large block of concrete, brickwork, etc., sunk in water, e.g. in the building of a dock. □ **mono·lith·ic** *adjective* **mono·lith·ic·ally** *adverb* [French *monolithe* from Greek *monolithos* (as MONO-, *lithos* stone)]

mono·logue /ˈmɒnəˌlɒɡ/ *noun* **1 a** a long speech in a play, film, etc. spoken by one actor, esp. when alone. **b** a dramatic composition, esp. in verse, told or performed by one person. **2** a long speech by one person in a conversation etc. **3** a stand-up comedy routine, esp. one performed at the beginning of a late-night talk show by the host. □ **mono·logic** *adjective* **mono·logic·al** *adjective* **mon·ol·o·gist** /ˈmɒnəˌlɒɡɪst, məˈnɒlədʒɪst/ *noun* (also **-loguist** /-ɡɪst/). **mon·ol·o·gize** /məˈnɒləˌdʒaɪz/ *intransitive verb* (also esp. *Brit.* **-gise**). [French from Greek *monologos* speaking alone (as MONO-, -LOGUE)]

mono·mania /ˌmɒnəˈmeɪniə/ *noun* obsession of the mind by one idea or interest. □ **mono·maniac** *noun* **mono·man·iacal** /-məˈnaɪəkəl/ *adjective*

mono·mer /ˈmɒnəmər/ *noun Chem.* **1** a unit in a dimer, trimer, or polymer. **2** a molecule or compound that can be polymerized (*compare* DIMER). □ **mono·mer·ic** /-ˈmerɪk/ *adjective*

mo·nom·ial /məˈnəʊmiəl/ *Math.* ● *adjective* (of an algebraic expression) consisting of one term. ● *noun* a monomial expression. [MONO- after *binomial*]

mono·molecu·lar /ˌmɒnəʊməˈlekjʊlər/ *adjective Chem.* (of a layer) only one molecule in thickness.

mono·morph·ic /ˌmɒnəˈmɔːfɪk/ *adjective* (also **mono·morph·ous**) *Biochem.* not changing form during development. □ **mono·morph·ism** *noun* [MONO- + Greek *morphē* form]

mono·nuclear /ˌmɒnəˈnjuːkliər, -ˈnjuːk-/ *adjective Biol.* having one nucleus.

mono·nucle·o·sis /ˌmɒnəʊˌnjuːkliˈəʊsɪs, -ˌnjuːk-/ *noun* an abnormally high proportion of monocytes in the blood, esp. = GLANDULAR FEVER. [MONO- + NUCLEO- + -OSIS]

mono·phon·ic /ˌmɒnəˈfɒnɪk/ *adjective* **1** (of sound reproduction) using only one channel of transmission (*compare* STEREOPHONIC). **2** *Music* having a simple melodic line predominating over other parts. □ **mono·phon·ic·ally** *adverb* [MONO- + Greek *phōnē* sound]

mon·oph·thong /ˈmɒnəfˌθɒŋ/ *noun Phonetics* a single vowel sound. □ **mon·oph·thong·al** *adjective* [Greek *monophthoggos* (as MONO-, *phthoggos* sound)]

mono·phylet·ic /ˌmɒnəʊfaɪˈletɪk/ *adjective Biol.* (of a group of organisms) descended from a common evolutionary ancestor or ancestral group, esp. one not shared with any other group.

Mon·ophy·site /məˈnɒfəˌsaɪt/ *noun* a person who holds that there is only one nature (partly divine, partly and subordinately human) in the person of Christ. [ecclesiastical Latin *monophysita* from ecclesiastical Greek *monophusitēs* (as MONO-, *phusis* nature)]

mono·plane /ˈmɒnəˌpleɪn/ *noun* an airplane with one set of wings (*compare* BIPLANE).

mono·pole[1] /ˈmɒnəˌpəʊl/ *noun* **1** *Physics* a single electric charge or magnetic pole, esp. a hypothetical isolated magnetic pole. **2** a radio antenna, pylon, etc. consisting of a single pole or rod.

mono·pole[2] /ˈmɒnəˌpəʊl/ *noun* (also **Monopole**) a champagne exclusive to one shipper. [French *monopole* MONOPOLY]

mon·opol·ist /məˈnɒpəlɪst/ *noun* a person who has or advocates a monopoly. □ **mon·op·o·lis·tic** *adjective* **mon·op·o·lis·tic·ally** *adverb*

mon·op·ol·ize /məˈnɒpəˌlaɪz/ *transitive verb* (also esp. *Brit.* **-ise**) **1** obtain exclusive possession or control of (a trade or commodity etc.). **2** dominate or prevent others from sharing in (a conversation, person's attention, etc.). □ **mon·op·ol·iz·a·tion** *noun* **mon·op·ol·iz·er** *noun*

Mon·op·oly /məˈnɒpəli/ *noun proprietary* a board game in which players use imitation money to engage in simulated property and financial dealings, the board representing streets and other locations in a large city which can be acquired and developed.

mon·op·oly *noun* (*pl.* **-ies**) **1 a** the exclusive possession or control of the trade in a commodity or service. **b** this conferred as a privilege by the state. **2 a** a commodity or service that is subject to a monopoly. **b** a company etc. that possesses a monopoly. **3** (foll. by *of*, *on*) exclusive possession, control, or exercise. [Latin *monopolium* from Greek *monopōlion* (as MONO-, *pōleō* sell)]

Monopoly money *noun* **1** imitation money used in the game of Monopoly. **2** money that has no real existence or value.

mono·print *noun* = MONOTYPE *noun* 2a.

mono·rail /ˈmɒnəˌreɪl/ *noun* a railway in which the track consists of a single rail, usu. elevated with the train units suspended from it.

mono·sac·char·ide /ˌmɒnəˈsakəˌraɪd/ *noun Chem.* a sugar that cannot be hydrolyzed to give a simpler sugar, e.g. glucose.

mono·sodium gluta·mate /ˌmɒnəˈsoːdiəm ˈɡluːtəˌmeɪt/ *noun Chem.* a sodium salt of glutamic acid used in foods as a flavour enhancer (*compare* GLUTAMATE). Abbr.: **MSG.**

mono·sperm·ous /ˌmɒnəˈspɜːməs/ *adjective Bot.* having one seed. [MONO- + Greek *sperma* seed]

mono·syllab·ic /ˌmɒnəsɪˈlabɪk/ *adjective* **1** (of a word) having one syllable. **2** (of a person or statement) using or expressed in monosyllables. □ **mono·syllab·ic·ally** *adverb*

mono·sylla·ble /ˈmɒnəˌsɪləbəl/ *noun* a word of one syllable. □ **in monosyllables** in simple direct words.

mono·theism /ˈmɒnəˌθiːɪzəm/ *noun* the doctrine or belief that there is only one God. □ **mono·theist** *noun* **mono·theis·tic** *adjective* **mono·theis·tic·ally** *adverb* [MONO- + Greek *theos* god]

mono·tint /ˈmɒnətɪnt/ *noun* = MONOCHROME *noun*.

mono·tone /ˈmɒnəˌtoʊn/ ● *noun* **1** a sound or utterance continuing or repeated on one note without change of pitch. **2** sameness of style in writing, expression, etc. ● *adjective* **1** without change of pitch or tone. **2** containing only one tone of one colour.

mono·ton·ic /ˌmɒnəˈtɒnɪk/ *adjective* **1** uttered in a monotone. **2** *Math.* (of a function or quantity) varying in such a way that it either never decreases or never increases. □ **mono·ton·ic·ally** *adverb*

mon·ot·on·ous /məˈnɒtənəs/ *adjective* **1** lacking in variety; tedious through sameness. **2** (of a sound or utterance) without variation in tone or pitch. □ **mon·ot·on·ous·ly** *adverb*

mon·ot·ony /məˈnɒtəni/ *noun* **1** lack of interesting variety; dull or tedious routine. **2** sameness of tone or pitch; lack of variety in cadence or inflection.

mono·treme /ˈmɒnəˌtriːm/ *noun* any mammal of the order Monotremata, native to Australia and New Guinea, including the duckbill and echidna, laying large yolky eggs through a common opening for urine, feces, etc. [MONO- + Greek *trēma* -*matos* hole]

mono·type /ˈmɒnəˌtaɪp/ *noun* **1** (**Monotype**) *Printing proprietary* a typesetting machine that casts and sets up types in individual characters. **2 a** an impression on paper made from an inked design painted on glass or metal. **b** the process for making such an impression.

mono·typ·ic /ˌmɒnəˈtɪpɪk/ *adjective* having only one type or representative.

mono·unsatur·at·ed *adjective Chem.* (of a compound, esp. a fat or oil molecule) containing one double bond.

mono·valent *adjective Chem.* having a valence of one; univalent.

mon·ox·ide *noun Chem.* an oxide containing one oxygen atom (*carbon monoxide*). [MONO- + OXIDE]

mono·zygot·ic /ˌmɒnəzaɪˈɡɒtɪk/ *adjective* (of twins, triplets, etc.) derived from a single ovum; identical. [MONO- + ZYGOTE + -IC]

Mon·roe /mənˈroʊ/ **1 James** (1758–1831), US Democratic Republican politician, 5th president of the US 1817–25. In 1803, while minister to France under President Jefferson, he negotiated and ratified the Louisiana Purchase; he is chiefly remembered, however, as the originator of the Monroe doctrine. **2 Mari·lyn** (born Norma Jean Mortenson, later Baker) (1926–62), US actress. She starred in a series of comedy films, including *Gentlemen Prefer Blondes* (1953) and *Some Like it Hot* (1959), emerging as the definitive Hollywood sex symbol; she died of an apparent overdose of sleeping pills.

Monroe doctrine *noun* a principle of US foreign policy that any intervention by external powers in the politics of the Americas is a potentially hostile act against the US. [J. MONROE]

Mon·rovia /mɒnˈroʊviə/ the capital and chief port of Liberia; pop. (est. 2002) 543,000.

Mons /mɒnz/ a town in S Belgium, capital of the province of Hainaut; pop. (est. 2002) 90,300. In August 1914 it was the scene of the first major battle between Allied and German forces during the First World War.

Mon·sei·gneur /ˌmɔ̃senˈjɜːr/ *noun* (*pl.* **Mes·sei·gneurs** /ˌmesenˈjɜːr/) a title given to an eminent French person, esp. a prince, cardinal, archbishop, or bishop. [French from *mon* my + *seigneur* lord]

Mon·sieur /məˈsjuː/ *noun* (*pl.* **Mes·sieurs** /meˈsjuː/) the title or form of address used of or to a French-speaking man, corresponding to Mr. or sir. [French from *mon* my + *sieur* lord]

Mon·signor /mʌnˈsiːnjɔːr, mɒn-/ *noun* (*pl.* **Mon·signori** /-ˈnjɔːri/) **1** a title in the Roman Catholic Church bestowed by the Pope on priests, either in conjunction with an office or as an honorary title for distinguished service. **2** a person holding this title. [Italian, after MONSEIGNEUR: see SIGNOR]

mon·soon *noun* **1** a wind in S Asia, esp. in the Indian Ocean, blowing from the southwest in summer (**wet monsoon**) and the northeast in winter (**dry monsoon**). **2** a rainy season accompanying a wet monsoon. **3** any other wind with periodic alternations. □ **mon·soon·al** *adjective* [obsolete Dutch *monssoen* from Portuguese *monção* from Arabic *mawsim* fixed season, from *wasama* to mark]

mons pubis /mɒnz ˈpjuːbɪs/ *noun* a rounded mass of fatty tissue lying over the joint of the pubic bones, esp. = MONS VENERIS. [Latin, = mount of the pubes]

mon·ster *noun* **1** an imaginary creature, usu. large and frightening, often compounded of incongruous elements. **2** an inhumanly cruel or wicked person. **3** a misshapen or ugly person, animal, or plant. **4** a large animal or thing. **5** (*attributive*) **a** huge; extremely large of its kind (*monster home*; *monster truck*). **b** very successful (*had a monster season*). [Old French *monstre* from Latin *monstrum* portent, monster, from *monēre* warn]

mon·stera /mɒnˈstiːrə/ *noun* any climbing plant of the genus *Monstera*, including Swiss cheese plant. [modern Latin, perhaps from Latin *monstrum* monster (from the odd appearance of its leaves)]

mon·strance /ˈmɒnstrəns/ *noun Catholicism* a receptacle, usu. of gold or silver, with an open or transparent compartment in which the consecrated Host is exposed for veneration. [Middle English, = demonstration, from medieval Latin *monstrantia* from Latin *monstrare* show]

mon·stros·ity /mɒnˈstrɒsɪti/ *noun* (*pl.* **-ities**) **1** a huge, hideous, or outrageous thing, esp. an unsightly building. **2** the condition or fact of being monstrous. **3** = MONSTER 3. [Late Latin *monstrositas* (as MONSTROUS)]

mon·strous /ˈmɒnstrəs/ *adjective* **1** of or like a monster in appearance, fearsomeness, etc. **2** huge. **3 a** outrageously wrong or absurd. **b** atrocious; horrible (*a monstrous crime*). □ **mon·strous·ly** *adverb* **mon·strous·ness** *noun* [Old French *monstreux* or Latin *monstrosus* (as MONSTER)]

mons Ven·eris /mɒnz ˈvenərɪs/ *noun* a rounded mass of fatty tissue on a woman's lower abdomen above the vulva. [Latin, = mount of Venus]

Mont. *abbreviation* Montana.

mon·tage /mɒnˈtɑːʒ/ ● *noun* **1** *Film* **a** a combination of images in quick succession to compress background information or provide atmosphere. **b** a system of editing in which the narrative is modified or interrupted to include images that are not necessarily related to the dramatic development. **2 a** the technique of producing a new composite whole from fragments of pictures, words, music, etc. **b** a composition produced in this way. ● *transitive verb* make or integrate into a montage. [French from *monter* MOUNT[1]]

Mon·ta·gnais /ˈmɒntənˌjeɪ/ ● *noun* **1** a member of an Innu people living in the barrens between Hudson Bay and the Labrador coast. **2** the Cree language of this people. ● *adjective* of or relating to this people or their culture or language. [French, = mountaineer]

Mon·tagnais-Naskapi *noun* = INNU *noun*.

Mon·tagu /ˈmɒntəɡjuː/ **Lady Mary Wort·ley** (1689–1762), English writer. She is principally remembered for her *Turkish Letters* (1716–18; published 1763), recording her responses to Turkish life and culture as the wife of the ambassador to Turkey.

Mon·taigne /mɒnˈteɪn/ **Michel (Ey·quem) de** (1533–92), French essayist. Often regarded as the originator of the modern essay, he wrote about prominent personalities and ideas of his age in his skeptical *Essays* (1580; 1588).

t top   v voice   w we   z zoo   ʃ she   ʒ vision   θ thin   ð this   ŋ ring   x loch   tʃ chip   dʒ jar   (*see over for vowels*)

Mon·tana /mɒnˈtanə/ a state in the western US, on the Canadian border to the east of the Rocky Mountains; pop. (2000) 902,195; capital, Helena. □ **Mon·tan·an** *adjective & noun*

mon·tane /ˈmɒntein/ *adjective* **1** of or inhabiting mountainous country. **2** designating or pertaining to the belt of upland vegetation below the timberline. [Latin *montanus* (as MOUNT², -ANE¹)]

Mont Blanc /mɔ̃ blɑ̃/ a peak in the Alps on the border between France and Italy, rising to 4 807 m (15,771 ft.). It is the highest peak in the Alps and the highest in W Europe.

mont·bre·tia /mɒnˈbriːʃə/ *noun* a hybrid plant of the genus *Crocosmia*, with bright orange-yellow trumpet-shaped flowers. [modern Latin from A. F. E. Coquebert de *Montbret*, French botanist d.1801]

Mont·calm /mɒntˈkɒm/ **Louis-Joseph de, Marquis de Montcalm** (1712–59), French army officer. He was sent to Quebec in 1756 as the commander of French troops in N America. After some initial successes against the British, his army was defeated on the Plains of Abraham by the British under James Wolfe, and Montcalm died the day after the battle.

monte /ˈmɒnti/ *noun Cards* **1** a Spanish game of chance, played with 40 cards. **2** (in full **three-card monte**) a game of Mexican origin played with three cards, similar to three-card trick. [Spanish, = mountain, heap of cards]

Monte Albán /ˌmɒnte alˈbɒn/ an ancient city, now in ruins, in Oaxaca, S Mexico. Occupied from the 8th c. BC, it became a centre of the Zapotec culture from about the 1st c. BC to the 8th c. AD, after which it was occupied by the Mixtecs until the Spanish conquest in the 16th c.

Monte·bello /ˌmɒntəˈbeloː/ a village in SW Quebec, about halfway between Gatineau and Montreal; pop. (2001) 1,039. [the name of the residence of L.-J. Papineau, after N.-A. Lannes, Duc de *Montebello*, French minister of foreign affairs d.1874]

Monte Carlo /ˌmɒnti ˈkɑrloː/ a resort in Monaco, forming one of the four communes of the principality; pop. (est. 2002) 15,300. It is famous as a gambling resort and as the terminus of the annual Monte Carlo car rally.

Monte Carlo method *noun Statistics* a method of using the random sampling of numbers in order to estimate the solution to a numerical problem. [MONTE CARLO]

Monte Cas·si·no /ˌmɒnti kəˈsiːnoː/ a hill in central Italy near the town of Cassino, midway between Rome and Naples. It is the site of the principal monastery of the Benedictines, founded by St. Benedict *c.*529. The monastery, demolished and rebuilt several times in its history, was almost totally destroyed during the Second World War, but has since been restored.

Mon·tego Bay /mɒnˈtiːgoː/ a port and tourist resort on the north coast of Jamaica; pop. (est. 2002) 92,000.

Monte·negro /ˌmɒntəˈneigroː/ a mountainous republic in the Balkans along the Adriatic Sea; pop. (est. 2003) 676,000; capital, Podgorica. In 1918 Montenegro became part of the federation of Yugoslavia, the remains of which became in 2003 the Union of Serbia and Montenegro. □ **Monte·neg·rin** *adjective & noun*

Monteregian Hills /ˌmɒntəˈriːdʒən/ a series of hills rising abruptly from the plain to the east of Montreal formed by the intrusion of igneous rock into sedimentary layers that have subsequently been removed by erosion and glaciation, including Mount Royal, Mont Saint-Bruno, and Mont Saint-Hilaire. [French *Montérégie* from Latin *montis* 'mount' + *regius* 'royal']

Mon·terey /ˌmɒntəˈrei/ a city and fishing port on the coast of California; pop. (2000) 29,700.

Monterey Jack *noun* a mild, white cheddar cheese. [*Monterey* County, California, where it was first made]

Mon·ter·rey /ˌmɒntəˈrei/ an industrial city in NE Mexico, capital of the state of Nuevo León; pop. (est. 2002) 3,468,200.

Mon·tes·quieu /ˈmɒntə‚skjuː/ **Baron de la Brède et de** (title of Charles Louis de Secondat) (1689–1755), French political philosopher. His works include *Lettres persanes* (1721) and the influential *L'Esprit des lois* (1748), a comparative study of political systems in which he championed the separation of judicial, legislative, and executive powers, holding up the English state as a model.

Mon·tes·sori¹ /ˌmɒntəˈsɒri/ **Maria** (1870–1952), Italian physician and educator. She revolutionized the teaching of infants through her child-centred educational system, in which the pace is largely set by the child and play is free but guided, using a variety of sensory materials; her books include *The Montessori Method* (1909).

Mon·tes·sori² /ˌmɒntəˈsɒri/ *noun* (usu. *attributive*) the system of education (esp. of young children) propounded by Maria Montessori that seeks to develop natural interests and activities rather than use formal teaching methods.

Monte·verdi /ˌmɒntəˈverdi/ **Claudio** (1567–1643), Italian composer. An influential composer of madrigals and sacred music, he introduced, in innovative operas such as *Orfeo* (1607), a sustained dramatic focus and more fully defined characters, interweaving the music with the drama.

Monte·video /ˌmɒntəvɪˈdeioː/ the capital and chief port of Uruguay, on the Plate River; pop. (est. 2002) 1,449,900.

Monte·zuma II /ˌmɒntəˈzuːmə/ (1466–1520), Aztec emperor 1502–20. The last ruler of the Aztec Empire in Mexico, he was defeated and imprisoned by the Spanish conquistadors under Cortés in 1519, and was killed while trying to pacify some of his former subjects during the Aztec uprising against his captors.

Montezuma's revenge *noun slang* or *jocular* diarrhea suffered by travellers, esp. visitors to Mexico. [MONTEZUMA II]

Mont·fort /ˈmɒntfərt/ **Simon de, Earl of Leices·ter** (*c.*1208–65), English soldier, born in Normandy. He led the baronial opposition to Henry III, defeated the king at Lewes, Sussex (1264), and summoned a parliament (1265); he was defeated and killed by Henry's son (later Edward I).

Mont·gol·fier /mɔ̃ˈgɒlfi‚ei/ **Joseph Michel** (1740–1810) and **Jacques Étienne** (1745–99), French inventors, who pioneered experiments in hot-air ballooning, successfully lifting a number of animals in 1782 and conducting the first human ascents in 1783.

Mont·gom·ery¹ /mɒntˈgʌməri/ the state capital of Alabama; pop. (2000) 201,568.

Mont·gom·ery² /mɒntˈgʌməri/ **1 Ber·nard Law, 1st Viscount Montgomery of Alamein ('Monty')** (1887–1976), English Field Marshal. In 1942 he commanded the 8th Army in the Western Desert; he was later given command of the Allied ground forces in the invasion of Normandy (1944) and accepted the German surrender on 7 May, 1945. **2 Lucy Maud** (1874–1942), Canadian writer. Born and raised in PEI, she published her first and most successful novel, *Anne of Green Gables*, in 1908; it was immediately successful. She eventually published 7 sequels to *Anne* as well as other novels set in PEI, a book of poetry and over 500 short stories.

Mont·gom·ery·shire /mɒntˈgʌməri‚ʃɪr, -ˈgɒməri-/ a former county of central Wales. It became a part of Powys in 1974.

month /mʌnθ/ *noun* **1 a** (in full **calendar month**) each of usu. twelve periods into which a year is divided. **b** a period of time between the same dates in successive calendar months. **2** a period of 30 days or of four weeks. **3** = LUNAR MONTH. **4** the period of a woman's menstrual cycle. □ **month of Sundays** a very long period. [Old English *mōnath* from Germanic, related to MOON]

month·ly /ˈmʌnθli/ ● *adjective* done, produced, or occurring once a month. ● *adverb* once a month; from month to month. ● *noun* (pl. **-lies**) **1** a monthly periodical. **2** (in pl.) *informal* a menstrual period.

Mont-Joli /mɔ̃ʒɒˈliː/ a town in E Quebec, situated on the south shore of the St. Lawrence, northeast of Rimouski; pop. (2001) 6,579. [French, lit. 'pretty mountain', with reference to the town's picturesque location on a hilltop]

Mont-Laurier /mɔ̃lɒrˈjei/ a town in SW central Quebec, situated on the Rivière du Lièvre, north of Gatineau; pop. (2001) 13,517. [LAURIER]

Mont·magny¹ /mɔ̃maˈnjiː/ a town in SE central Quebec, situated on the south shore of the St. Lawrence, northeast of Lévis; pop. (2001) 11,654. [MONTMAGNY²]

Mont·magny² /mɔ̃maˈnjiː/ **Charles Huault de** (*c.*1583–*c.*1653), French colonial administrator. Succeeding Champlain in 1636 he served as governor and lieutenant-general of New France until 1648. He expanded the fortifications at Quebec and Trois-Rivières and built Fort Richelieu at Sorel.

Mont·martre /mɔ̃ˈmartrə/ a district in N Paris, on a hill above the Seine, much frequented by artists in the late 19th and early 20th c. when it was a village separated from Paris. Many of its buildings have artistic associations, e.g. the Moulin de la Galette, which was painted by Renoir.

Mont·moren·cy, Chute /mɔ̃mɔrɑ̃ˈsiː/ (also **Montmorency Falls** /ˌmɒntməˈrensi/) a waterfall in SE central Quebec, 85 m high, situated on the Rivière Montmorency at the St. Lawrence, just northeast of Quebec City. It is the highest waterfall in Quebec. [Henri II, duc de *Montmorency*, French admiral d.1632]

mont·moril·lon·ite /ˌmɒntməˈrɪləneit/ *noun* any of a group of clay minerals which undergo reversible expansion on absorbing water, including the main constituents of fuller's earth and bentonite. [*Montmorillon*, a town in France]

Mont·par·nasse /ˌmɔ̃nparˈnas/ a district of Paris, on the left bank of the Seine River. Noted for its cafés, it was frequented in the late 19th c. by writers and artists and is traditionally associated with Parisian cultural life.

Mont·pe·lier /mɒntˈpiːljər/ the state capital of Vermont; pop. (2000) 8,035.

Mont·pel·lier /mɔ̃pelˈjei/ a city in S France, near the Mediterranean coast, capital of Languedoc-Roussillon; pop. (1999) 225,392.

Mont·ra·chet /mɔ̃raˈʃei/ *noun* **1** a white burgundy made from Chardonnay grapes from a single vineyard in the Côte de Beaune district of the Côte d'Or. **2** a kind of goat cheese produced in this area.

Mont·real /mɒntriːˈɒl, mɒn-/ a city and port in south central Quebec, occupying the Île de Montréal, at the confluence of the Ottawa and St. Lawrence rivers; pop. (2001) 1,812,723. □ **Mont·real·er** *noun* [from an Italian mistranslation of the French *Mont-Royal*, the words *royal* and *real* having the same meaning in the 16th c.: see MOUNT ROYAL]

Montréal, Île de /mɔ̃reiˈal/ an island in south central Quebec, located in the St. Lawrence River, at its confluence with the Ottawa River. The city of Montreal is situated on it. [see MONTREAL]

Montreal bagel *noun* Cdn a type of bagel, originally made in Montreal, which is lighter, thinner, and sweeter than other kinds of bagel.

Montreal canoe *noun* Cdn = CANOT DU MAÎTRE.

Montreal Lake a lake in central Saskatchewan, situated about 100 km north of Prince Albert.

Montréal-Nord /mɔ̃reialˈnɔr/ a former city in south central Quebec, located on the Rivière des Prairies, at the northern part of the Island of Montreal, now part of the city of Montreal; pop. (2001) 83,600. [French, lit. 'Montreal North']

Montréal-Ouest /mɔ̃reialˈwest/ a former town in south central Quebec, in the southwest part of the Island of Montreal, now part of the city of Montreal; pop. (2001) 5,172. [French, lit. 'Montreal West']

Montreal smoked meat *noun* Cdn = SMOKED MEAT 2.

Mon·treux /mɒnˈtrɜː/ a resort town in SW Switzerland, at the east end of Lake Geneva; pop. (est. 2002) 22,300.

Mon·trose /mɒnˈtroːz/ **James Gra·ham, 1st Marquis of** (1612–50), Scottish general. A supporter of Charles I in the English Civil War, he inflicted a dramatic series of defeats on the stronger Covenanter forces in the north (1644–5) before being defeated at Philiphaugh; he was later betrayed to the Covenanters and hanged.

Mont-Royal /mɔ̃rwaˈjal/ a former city located on the northwest side of Mount Royal, now part of the city of Montreal; pop. (2001) 18,682. [French, = MOUNT ROYAL]

Monts see DE MONTS.

Mont Saint-Bruno /mɔ̃sãbruːˈnoː/ an isolated mountain 210 m high east of Montreal, formed by the intrusion of igneous rock into sedimentary layers that have subsequently been removed by erosion and glaciation. [as SAINT-BRUNO-DE-MONTARVILLE]

Mont Saint-Hilaire /mɔ̃sãtiːˈler/ **1** an isolated mountain 400 m high, near the Richelieu River, 35 km east of Montreal, formed by the intrusion of igneous rock into sedimentary layers that have subsequently been removed by erosion and glaciation.
2 (**Mont-Saint-Hilaire**) a town in south central Quebec, situated on the Richelieu, east of Montreal; pop. (2001) 14,270. [ultimately after the mission of *Saint-Hilaire c.1799*]

Mont Saint-Michel /mɔ̃ sã miːˈʃel/ a rocky islet off the coast of Normandy, NW France. An island only at high tide, it is surrounded by sandbanks and linked to the mainland by a causeway. It is crowned by a magnificent medieval Benedictine abbey-fortress.

Mont·ser·rat /ˌmɒntsəˈrat/ an island in the W Indies, one of the Leeward Islands; pop. (est. 2002) 8,436; capital, Plymouth. [after a Benedictine monastery on the mountain of Montserrat in Catalonia, NE Spain]

Mont-Tremblant /mɔ̃trãˈblã/ a city in south central Quebec, situated over 100 km northwest of Montreal; pop. (2001) 8,352. It is a popular ski resort and winter sports centre. [French, lit. 'trembling mountain', ultimately adapted from Algonquin *manitou ewitchi saga* the mountain of the formidable spirit (capable of making mountains tremble)]

monty *noun* Brit. □ **the full monty** everything necessary or appropriate; to the utmost (*insisted on nothing less than the full monty*; *promised to go the full monty in fighting crime*). [origin unknown]

monu·ment *noun* **1** anything enduring that serves to commemorate or make celebrated, esp. a structure or building. **2** a stone or other

structure placed over a grave or in a church etc. in memory of the dead. **3** an ancient building or site etc. that has survived or been preserved. **4** (foll. by *of*, *to*) a typical or outstanding example (*a monument of indiscretion*). **5** a lasting reminder. **6** a written record. [French from Latin *monumentum*, from *monēre* 'remind']

monu·men·tal *adjective* **1 a** extremely great; stupendous (*a monumental achievement*). **b** (of a literary work etc.) impressive and of lasting importance. **2** of or serving as a monument. **3** *informal* (as an intensifier) very great; calamitous (*a monumental blunder*). □ **monu·men·tal·ity** *noun* **monu·men·tal·ly** *adverb*

monu·men·tal·ize *transitive verb* (also esp. Brit. **-ise**) record or commemorate by or as by a monument.

-mony /mɒni/ *suffix* forming nouns esp. denoting an abstract state or quality (*acrimony*; *testimony*). [Latin *-monia*, *-monium*, related to -MENT]

moo ● *intransitive verb* (**moos**, **mooed**) make the characteristic vocal sound of cattle. ● *noun* (pl. **moos**) this sound. [imitative]

mooch /muːtʃ/ *informal* ● *verb* **1** *transitive* **a** (often foll. by *off*) beg, scrounge. **b** esp. *N Amer.* steal. **2** *intransitive* loiter or saunter desultorily. **3** *transitive & intransitive N Amer.* fish with light tackle allowed to drift. ● *noun* a person who mooches. □ **mooch·er** *noun* [prob. from Old French *muchier* hide, skulk]

moo-cow *noun* a childish name for a cow.

mood[1] *noun* **1** a state of mind or feeling. **2** a fit of melancholy or bad temper. **3** (*attributive*) inducing a particular mood (*mood music*). **4** the atmosphere or pervading tone of a place, event, composition, etc. □ **in the** (or **no**) **mood** (foll. by *for*, or *to* + infin.) inclined (or disinclined) (*was in no mood to go dancing*). [Old English *mōd* mind, thought, from Germanic]

mood[2] *noun* **1** *Grammar* **a** a form or set of forms of a verb serving to indicate whether it is to express fact, command, wish, etc. (*subjunctive mood*). **b** the distinction of meaning expressed by different moods. **2** *Logic* any of the classes into which each of the figures of a valid categorical syllogism is subdivided. [var. of MODE, assoc. with MOOD[1]]

Mood·ie, Su·san·na (born Susanna Strickland) (1803–85), English-born Canadian settler and author, younger sister of Catharine Parr Traill. Her most famous work, *Roughing It in the Bush* (1852), tells of her struggles as a settler in Upper Canada from 1832, and contains strong pro-British and equally strong anti-American sentiment.

mood swing *noun* Psych. an abrupt and unaccountable change of mood.

Moody, Dwight Lyman (1837–99), US evangelist, who initiated popular revivalist campaigns in the US and Britain with the hymn writer Ira David Sankey (1840–1908).

moody *adjective* (**mood·i·er**, **mood·i·est**) given to changes of mood; gloomy, sullen. □ **mood·i·ly** *adverb* **mood·i·ness** *noun*

Moog /moːg, muːg/ *noun* (in full **Moog synthesizer**) *proprietary* an electronic instrument with a keyboard, for producing a wide variety of musical sounds: see SYNTHESIZER. [R. A. *Moog*, US engineer b.1934, who invented it]

moo juice *noun slang* milk.

moo·lah /ˈmuːlə/ *noun* (also **moola**) *slang* money. [20th c.: origin unknown]

Moon, Sun Myung (b.1920), Korean industrialist and religious leader. In 1954 he founded the Holy Spirit Association for the Unification of World Christianity, which became known as the Unification Church.

moon ● *noun* **1 a** the natural satellite of the earth, orbiting it monthly, illuminated by the sun and reflecting some light to the earth. **b** this regarded in terms of its waxing and waning in a particular month (*new moon*). **c** moonlight (*there is no moon tonight*). **2** a satellite of any planet. **3** (prec. by *the*) something desirable but unattainable (*promised them the moon*). **4** a month. ● *verb* **1** *intransitive* (often foll. by *about*, *around*, etc.) move or look listlessly. **2** *transitive* (foll. by *away*) spend (time) in a listless manner. **3** *intransitive* (foll. by *over*) act aimlessly or inattentively from infatuation for (a person). **4** *slang* **a** *transitive* expose one's buttocks to (another person) (*turned around and mooned the crowd*). **b** *intransitive* expose one's buttocks. □ **many moons ago** a long time ago. **once in a blue moon** see BLUE[1]. **over the moon** extremely happy or delighted. □ **moon·less** *adjective* [Old English *mōna* from Germanic, related to MONTH]

moon·beam *noun* a ray of moonlight.

moon boot *noun* a thickly-padded boot designed for low temperatures.

moon·calf *noun* (pl. **moon·calves**) *informal* a fool; dolt.

moon-faced *adjective* having a round face. □ **moon face** *noun*

moon·fish *noun* any of various pale or silver-coloured marine fishes with round, usu. thin bodies, esp. the opah, a sunfish, *Mola mola*, or the crappie.

moon·flower *noun* a white-flowered morning glory.

Moon·ie *noun slang* a member of the Unification Church. [MOON]

moon·light ● *noun* **1** the light of the moon. **2** (*attributive*) lighted by the moon. ● *intransitive verb* (**-light·ed**) *informal* have a second job, esp. at night, in addition to one's regular day job. □ **moon·light·er** *noun*

moon·lit *adjective* lighted by the moon.

moon·quake *noun* a tremor of the moon's surface.

moon·rise *noun* **1** the rising of the moon. **2** the time of this.

moon·roof *noun* = SUNROOF.

moon·scape *noun* **1** the surface or landscape of the moon. **2** an area resembling this; a wasteland.

moon·seed *noun* a vine of moist places east of the Rockies, *Menispermum canadense*, with fruit like wild grapes.

moon·set *noun* **1** the setting of the moon. **2** the time of this.

moon·shine *noun* **1** *slang* illicitly distilled alcoholic liquor. **2** foolish or unrealistic talk or ideas.

moon·shin·er *noun N Amer. slang* an illicit distiller of alcoholic liquor.

moon shot *noun* the launching of a spacecraft to the moon.

moon·stone *noun* any of various milky, opalescent varieties of albite and other minerals, used in jewellery.

moon·struck *adjective* **1** romantically captivated. **2** mentally deranged.

moon·walk *noun* **1** a walk by an astronaut on the surface of the moon. **2** a dance step in which a person moves backwards while making the motions of walking forwards. □ **moon·walk** *intransitive verb*

moony *adjective* (**moon·i·er**, **moon·i·est**) **1** listless; stupidly dreamy. **2** of or like the moon.

Moor /mʊr, mɔr/ *noun* a member of a Muslim people of mixed Berber and Arab descent inhabiting NW Africa, who conquered the Iberian peninsula in the 8th c. and retained control of portions of Spain until the 15th c., leaving behind an important architectural legacy. [Old French *More* from Latin *Maurus* from Greek *Mauros* inhabitant of Mauretania, a region of N Africa]

moor[1] /mʊr, mɔr/ *noun* a tract of open, uncultivated, usu. poorly drained upland. □ **moor·ish** *adjective* **moory** *adjective* [Old English *mōr* waste land, marsh, mountain, from Germanic]

moor[2] *verb* **1** *transitive* make fast (a boat, buoy, etc.) by attaching a cable etc. to a fixed object. **2** *intransitive* (of a boat) be moored. □ **moor·age** *noun* [Middle English *more*, prob. from Low German or Middle Low German *mōren*]

Moore /mʊr, mɔr/ **1 Brian** (1921–99), Irish-born Canadian writer. Each of his many novels explores the meeting of past and present from the perspective of individual characters. He won the Governor General's Award for fiction twice, once for *The Luck of Ginger Coffey* (1960) and once for *The Great Victorian Collection* (1975). **2 Dora Mavor** (1888–1979), Scottish-born Canadian actress and teacher. After making her professional debut in Ottawa in 1912, she performed in New York and London and then returned to Toronto. In 1938 she founded the Village Players; it was succeeded by the New Play Society, which performed 72 plays between 1946–56. She was also involved in the founding of the Stratford Festival; Toronto's annual theatre awards are named in her honour. **3 Clem·ent (Clarke)** (1779–1863) US writer, best known for his poem 'A Visit from St. Nicholas' (1823). **4 Henry (Spen·cer)** (1898–1986), English sculptor. His work is characterized by abstract and semi-abstract organic forms in bronze and stone, and prominent themes for the postwar period include monumental upright figures, family groups, and two and three-piece reclining forms, such as those for the UNESCO building in Paris (1957–8). **5 Mari·anne (Craig)** (1887–1972), US poet, a leading figure in the US avant-garde literary scene of the mid-20th c. **6 Thom·as** (1779–1852), Irish poet and musician. He wrote patriotic and nostalgic songs, which he set to Irish tunes, and collected in *Irish Melodies* (1807–34); his other works include the narrative poem *Lalla Rookh* (1817).

Moores /mʊrz/ **Frank Duff** (b.1933), Canadian businessman and politician, Conservative premier of Newfoundland 1972–79. He emphasized rural development and management of natural resources.

moor·hen *noun* a small aquatic bird, *Gallinula chloropus*, with long legs and a short red-yellow bill.

moor·ing *noun* **1 a** a fixed object to which a boat, buoy, etc., is moored. **b** (often in *pl.*) a place where a boat etc. is moored. **2** (in *pl.*) a set of permanent anchors and chains laid down for ships to be moored

to. **3** (in *pl.*) a source of stability or security (*drifted away from her spiritual moorings*).

Moor·ish *adjective* of or relating to the Moors.

moor·land *noun* esp. *Brit.* an extensive area of moor.

moose *noun* (*pl.* same) esp. *N Amer.* **1** the largest living deer, *Alces alces*, found in northern parts of N America, Europe, and Asia, and having a growth of skin hanging from the neck and (in males) very large antlers. **2** (also **moose meat**) the flesh of the moose as food. [Abenaki *mos*]

moose·hair *noun* stiff, pale hair from the shoulders, back, rump, and chest of a moose, dyed and used by some Aboriginal peoples to form decorative patterns on garments.

moose·hide *noun* esp. *N Amer.* the skin of a moose, esp. when tanned (also *attributive*: *moosehide leggings*).

Moose Jaw an industrial city in south central Saskatchewan, located on the Moose Jaw River, 71 km west of Regina; pop. (2001) 32,131. □ **Moose Jav·ian** /ˈdʒeɪviən/ *noun* [the name of the river, prob. so called because of its moose head configuration, flowing first northwestward to the city, then turning sharply eastward, and gradually curving northward to join the Qu'Appelle River]

moose milk *noun Cdn* **1** a drink including alcoholic liquor (usu. rum), milk, and often other ingredients, esp. eggs. **2** home-distilled liquor. **3** any alcoholic drink.

moose pasture *noun Cdn slang* **1** a piece of land promoted as having mining potential but in fact unproductive. **2** worthless land, useful only for grazing moose.

Moose River a river in NE Ontario, 104 km long, formed by the confluence of several tributaries, mainly the Missinaibi and Mattagami rivers. It flows northeastward through Moosonee into Hannah Bay, an inlet of James Bay. [after *Monsoni*, a name given by French explorers to an Algonquian people whose totem was the moose: compare MOOSONEE]

moose·wood *noun* **1** see STRIPED MAPLE. **2** a N American viburnum, *Viburnum alnifolium*, with clusters of white flowers and purple-black berries. *Also called* HOBBLEBUSH. **3** leatherwood.

moo shu pork /ˈmuː ʃuː/ *noun* a Chinese dish consisting of shredded pork, mushrooms, bean sprouts, etc. stir-fried together and wrapped in a thin pancake. [Chinese]

Mooso·nee /ˌmuːsəˈniː/ an unincorporated place in NE Ontario, situated on the northwest bank of the Moose River near its mouth; pop. (2001) 936. [blend of *Moose River* + *Rivière des Monsonis*, both after *Monsoni* (see MOOSE RIVER)]

moot ● *adjective* **1** debatable, undecided. **2** having little or no practical significance. **3** *N Amer. Law* (of a case etc.) hypothetical. ● *transitive verb* raise (a question) for discussion. ● *noun* **1** *Brit. hist.* an assembly. **2** *Law* a discussion of a hypothetical case as an academic exercise. [Old English *mōt* assembly or meeting, and *mōtian* converse, from Germanic, related to MEET[1]]

moot court *noun N Amer.* **1** a simulation trial, used esp. for training law students. **2** the room in which this is conducted.

moot point *noun* **1** a statement or question that is not or is no longer of any practical purpose. **2** a statement or question that is undecided or debatable.

mop ● *noun* **1** a tool for cleaning floors etc., consisting of a bunch of thick strings or soft material fastened to a long handle. **2** a similarly-shaped large or small implement for various purposes. **3** anything resembling a mop, esp. a thick mass of hair. **4** an act of mopping or being mopped (*gave it a mop*). ● *transitive verb* (**mopped**, **mop·ping**) **1** wipe or clean with or as with a mop. **2 a** wipe tears or sweat etc. from (one's face or brow etc.). **b** wipe away (tears etc.). □ **mop up 1** wipe up with or as with a mop. **2** *informal* absorb (profits etc.). **3** dispatch; make an end of. **4** *Military* **a** complete the occupation of (a district etc.) by capturing or killing enemy troops left there. **b** capture or kill (stragglers). [Middle English *mappe*, perhaps ultimately related to Latin *mappa* napkin]

mope ● *intransitive verb* **1** be gloomily depressed or listless; behave sulkily. **2** wander about listlessly. ● *noun* **1** a person who mopes. **2** (**the mopes**) low spirits. □ **moper** *noun* **mopey** *adjective* (also **mopy**) (**mopi·er, mopi·est**). **mopi·ly** *adverb* **mopi·ness** *noun* [16th c.: prob. related to *mope, mopp(e)* fool]

mo·ped /ˈmoʊpɛd/ *noun* a small motorcycle equipped with both a low-powered engine and pedals. [Swedish (as MOTOR, PEDAL[1])]

mop·head *noun* **1** a person with thick matted hair. **2** a plant or flower resembling the head of a mop (also *attributive*: *huge white mophead flowers*). □ **mop·head·ed** *adjective*

Consonants: b *but*   d *dog*   f *few*   g *get*   h *her*   j *yes*   k *cat*   l *leg*   m *man*   n *no*   p *pen*   r *red*   s *sit*

mop·pet *noun informal* (esp. as a term of endearment) a baby or small child. [obsolete *moppe* baby, doll]

MOR *abbreviation* MIDDLE-OF-THE-ROAD.

mor *noun* humus formed under acid conditions. [Danish]

Mor·ada·bad /ˌmɔrədəˈbad/ a city in N India, in Uttar Pradesh; pop. (2001) 641,200.

mor·aine /məˈrein/ *noun* a ridge or mound of rock debris etc. carried and deposited by a glacier. □ **mor·ain·al** *adjective* **mor·ain·ic** *adjective* [French from Italian dial. *morena* from French dial. *mor(re)*, from Romanic]

moral ● *adjective* **1 a** concerned with goodness or badness of human character or behaviour, or with the distinction between right and wrong. **b** concerned with accepted rules and standards of human behaviour. **2 a** conforming to accepted standards of general conduct. **b** capable of moral action (*humans are moral creatures*). **3** (of rights or duties etc.) founded on moral law. **4 a** concerned with morals or ethics (*moral philosophy*). **b** (of a literary work etc.) dealing with moral conduct. **5** concerned with or leading to a psychological effect associated with confidence in a right action (*moral courage; moral support; moral victory*). ● *noun* **1 a** a moral lesson (esp. at the end) of a fable, story, event, etc. **b** a moral maxim or principle. **2** (in *pl.*) moral behaviour, e.g. in sexual conduct. □ **mor·al·ly** *adverb* [Latin *moralis* from *mos moris* custom, pl. *mores* morals]

moral certainty *noun* probability so great as to allow no reasonable doubt.

mor·ale /məˈral/ *noun* the amount of confidence, enthusiasm, determination, etc. that a person or group has at a particular time (*morale is at an all-time high*). [French *moral* respelt to preserve the pronunciation]

mor·al·ism *noun* the practice of moralizing, esp. showing a tendency to make judgments about others' morality (*the patriotic moralism of many political leaders*).

mor·al·ist *noun* **1** a person who practises or teaches morality. **2** a person who follows a natural system of ethics.

mor·al·is·tic *adjective* **1** pertaining to or characteristic of a moralist. **2** fond of moralizing. **3** having or showing definite but narrow beliefs and judgments about what is right and wrong. □ **mor·al·is·tic·ally** *adverb*

mor·al·ity *noun* (*pl.* **-ities**) **1** the degree of conformity of an idea, practice, etc., to moral principles. **2** right moral conduct. **3** a lesson in morals. **4** a particular system of morals (*commercial morality*). **5** *hist.* = MORALITY PLAY.

morality play *noun hist.* a kind of drama with personified abstract qualities as the main characters and inculcating a moral lesson, popular in the 16th c.

morality squad *noun Cdn* a police unit dealing with infractions of legislation concerning prostitution, pornography, drugs, gambling, etc.

mor·al·ize *verb* (also esp. *Brit.* **-ise**) **1** *intransitive* (often foll. by *on*) indulge in moral reflection or talk. **2** *transitive* interpret morally; explain the moral meaning of. **3** *transitive* make moral or more moral. □ **mor·al·iza·tion** *noun* **mor·al·iz·er** *noun* **mor·al·iz·ing·ly** *adverb*

Moral Majority *noun* (in the US) a right-wing conservative political movement composed mainly of Protestant fundamentalists.

moral philosophy *noun* the branch of philosophy concerned with ethics.

moral pressure *noun* persuasion by appealing to a person's moral sense.

moral sense *noun* the ability to distinguish right and wrong.

Morar, Loch *see* LOCH MORAR.

mo·rass /məˈras/ *noun* **1** an entanglement; a disordered situation, esp. one impeding progress. **2** a bog or marsh. [Dutch *moeras* (assimilated to *moer* MOOR¹) from Middle Dutch *marasch* from Old French *marais* marsh, from medieval Latin *mariscus*]

mora·tor·ium /ˌmɔrəˈtɔriəm/ *noun* (*pl.* **mora·tor·iums** or **mora·toria**) **1** (often foll. by *on*) a temporary prohibition or suspension (of an activity). **2 a** a legal authorization to debtors to postpone payment. **b** the period of this postponement. [modern Latin, neuter of Late Latin *moratorius* delaying, from Latin *morari morat-* to delay, from *mora* delay]

Mor·avia /məˈreiviə/ a region of the Czech Republic, situated between Bohemia in the west and the Carpathians in the east; chief town, Brno. Traversed by the Morava River, it is a fertile agricultural region and is rich in mineral resources.

Mor·avian /məˈreiviən/ ● *noun* **1** a native of Moravia. **2** a member of a Protestant denomination founded in Saxony by emigrants from Moravia, holding views derived from the Hussites and accepting the Bible as the only source of faith. ● *adjective* **1** of, relating to, or characteristic of Moravia or its people. **2** of or relating to the Moravian Church.

Mor·avian·town /məˈreiviəntaun/ a place on the Moravian Indian reserve in SW Ontario, situated on the Thames River, near Chatham. It was the scene in 1813 of a battle between British troops, aided by Indians under Tecumseh, and an American force. The British retired early, abandoning the Indians in the midst of battle and effectively handing victory to the US. It was here that Tecumseh was killed. [with reference to the denomination of its early settlers]

Moray /ˈmʌri/ (also **Moray·shire** /ˈmʌriˌʃɪr/) a council area and former county of N Scotland, bordered on the north by the Moray Firth; administrative centre, Elgin.

moray /ˈmɒrei/ *noun* any tropical eel-like fish of the family Muraenidae. [Portuguese *moreia* from Latin from Greek *muraina*]

Moray Firth a deep inlet of the North Sea on the northeast coast of Scotland. The city of Inverness is near its head.

mor·bid *adjective* **1** (of the mind, ideas, etc.) having or showing an unusual interest in sad or unpleasant things, esp. death. **2** gruesome, grisly. **3** *Med.* of the nature of or indicative of disease. □ **mor·bid·ity** *noun* **mor·bid·ly** *adverb* [Latin *morbidus* from *morbus* disease]

morbid anatomy *noun* the anatomy of diseased organs, tissues, etc.

mor·dant /ˈmɔrdənt/ ● *adjective* **1** (of sarcasm etc.) caustic, biting. **2** pungent, smarting. **3** corrosive or cleansing. **4** (of a substance) serving to fix colouring matter or gold leaf on another substance. ● *noun* a mordant substance (in senses 3, 4 of *adjective*). □ **mor·dan·cy** *noun* **mor·dant·ly** *adverb* [French, part. of *mordre* bite, from Latin *mordēre*]

Mor·den /ˈmɔrdən/ a town in S Manitoba, southwest of Winnipeg, near the border with N Dakota; pop. (2001) 6,142. □ **Mor·den·ite** *noun* [A. Morden, local settler d.1891]

mor·dent /ˈmɔrdənt/ *noun Music* an ornament consisting of one rapid alternation of a written note with the note immediately below or above it. [German from Italian *mordente* part. of *mordēre* bite]

Mor·dred /ˈmɔrdrəd/ (in Arthurian legend) the nephew of King Arthur.

Mord·vinia /mɔrˈdvɪniə/ (also called **Mord·vin·ian Autonomous Republic**) an autonomous republic in European Russia, south of Nizhni Novgorod; pop. (est. 2002) 901,700; capital, Saransk.

More /ˈmɔr/ **Sir Thom·as** (canonized as St. Thomas More) (1478–1535), English scholar and statesman, Lord Chancellor 1529–32. His opposition to Henry VIII's divorce from Catherine of Aragon led to his resignation, imprisonment, and execution. One of the leading humanists of the Renaissance, he described an ideal city state in his *Utopia* (1516). Feast day, 22 June.

more ● *adjective* **1** existing in a greater or additional quantity, amount, or degree (*more problems than last time; bring some more water*). **2** greater in degree (*more's the pity; the more fool you*). ● *noun* a greater quantity, number, or amount (*more than three people; more to it than meets the eye*). ● *adverb* **1** in a greater degree (*do it more carefully*). **2** to a greater extent (*people like to walk more these days*). **3** forming the comparative of adjectives and adverbs, esp. those of more than one syllable (*more absurd; more easily*). **4** again (*once more; never more*). **5** moreover. □ **more and more** in an increasing degree. **more like it** *see* LIKE¹. **more of** to a greater extent (*more of a poet than a musician*). **more or less 1** in a greater or less degree. **2** approximately; as an estimate. **more so** of the same kind to a greater degree. [Old English *māra* from Germanic]

Mo·reau /mɒˈroː/ **Jeanne** (b.1928), French actress. She portrayed isolated and autonomous women in films such as *Ascenseur pour l'échafaud* (1958), *Les Liaisons dangereuses* (1959), and *Jules et Jim* (1961). Her more recent films include *Nikita* (1990).

more·ish /ˈmɔriʃ/ *adjective* (also **morish**) *Brit. informal* pleasant to eat, causing a desire for more.

morel /məˈrel/ *noun* an edible fungus, *Morchella esculenta*, with a honeycombed cap. [French *morille* from Dutch *morilje*]

Mor·elia /məˈreiliə/ a city in central Mexico, capital of the state of Michoacán; pop. (2000) 550,000. Founded in 1541, it was known as Valladolid until 1828. [J. M. *Morelos* y Pavón, revolutionary priest and leader of the Mexican independence movement d.1815]

mor·ello /məˈreloː/ *noun* (*pl.* **-ellos**) a sour kind of dark cherry. [Italian *morello* blackish, from medieval Latin *morellus*, diminutive of Latin *Maurus* Moor]

Mor·elos /məˈreilɒs/ a state of central Mexico, to the west of Mexico City; capital, Cuernavaca.

Mor·enz /ˈmɔrenz/ **How·arth Wil·liam** ('Howie') (1902–37), Canadian hockey player. After joining the Montreal Canadiens in 1923, he quickly became known for his skating, stickhandling, and scoring. He scored the most goals in the NHL in 1928 and 1931, and won the Hart Trophy for most valuable player in 1928, 1931, and 1932. He died of complications from injuries sustained in a game.

more·over *adverb* (introducing or accompanying a new statement) further, besides.

mores /ˈmɔreiz, -riːz/ *plural noun* customs or conventions regarded as essential to or characteristic of a community. [Latin, pl. of *mos* custom]

Mores·by Island /ˈmɔrzbi/ the second largest of the Queen Charlotte Islands off the west coast of BC. It is separated from Graham Island to the north by a narrow channel. [Sir F. *Moresby*, British admiral of the fleet d.1877]

Mor·esque /mɒˈresk/ *adjective* (of art or architecture) Moorish in style or design. [French from Italian *moresco* from *Moro* MOOR]

Mor·gan¹ ▶ **1 Sir Henry** (1635–88), Welsh buccaneer, who raided Spanish settlements and shipping in the Caribbean during the late 17th c. **2 John Pier·pont** (1837–1913), US financier, philanthropist, and art collector. He built up one of the leading art collections of his day, bequeathing it to the Museum of Modern Art in New York. **3 Thom·as Hunt** (1866–1945), US zoologist. In his studies with the rapidly-reproducing fruit fly *Drosophila* he established the chromosome theory of heredity, showing that the genetic information was carried by genes arranged along the length of the chromosomes; he was awarded the Nobel Prize for medicine in 1933.

Mor·gan² *noun* a breed of light saddle and carriage horse. [Justin *Morgan* (1747–98), US teacher, owner of a stallion from which the breed descends]

mor·gan·atic /ˌmɔrgəˈnatɪk/ *adjective* of or relating to a marriage between a person of high rank and another of lower rank, the spouse and children having no claim to the possessions or title of the person of higher rank. □ **mor·gan·atic·al·ly** *adverb* [French *morganatique* or German *morganatisch* from medieval Latin *matrimonium ad morganaticam* 'marriage with a morning gift', the husband's gift to the wife after consummation being his only obligation in such a marriage]

Morgan le Fay /ˌmɔrgən lə ˈfei/ (in Arthurian legend) 'Morgan the Fairy', a magician, sister of King Arthur.

Mor·gen·taler /ˈmɔrgənˌtɒlər/ **Henry** (b.1923), Polish-born Canadian physician and abortionist. He began campaigning for the repeal of the anti-abortion laws in 1967, and after numerous court cases the Supreme Court legalized abortion and finally acquitted him of any criminal charges in 1988.

morgue /mɔrg/ *noun* **1** a mortuary. **2** (esp. in a newspaper office or television studio) a room or file of miscellaneous cuttings, photographs, videotape, etc. for future use. [French, originally the name of a Paris mortuary]

mori·bund /ˈmɔrɪˌbʌnd/ *adjective* **1** at the point of death. **2** lacking vitality. [Latin *moribundus* from *mori* die]

Morin /mɔrˈã/ **Claude** (b.1929), Canadian professor and politician, one of the key intellectual forces behind the Quiet Revolution. He served as an adviser to Jean Lesage from 1960, and was a deputy minister from 1963–71. He joined the PQ in 1972, won a seat in 1976, and served as intergovernmental affairs minister until 1981. He was the main architect of the plan that brought the PQ to power, and also of the party's strategy for the first referendum on sovereignty-association.

Morin·ville /ˈmɔrənvɪl/ a town in central Alberta, about 30 km north of Edmonton; pop. (2001) 6,540. [Fr. J.-B. *Morin*, founder of the area's francophone community d.1911]

Moris·sette, Alanis (Na·dine) (b.1974), Canadian singer and songwriter who gained international fame following the release of her third album, *Jagged Little Pill* (1995), which sold more than 25 million copies worldwide.

mor·ish *var. of* MOREISH.

Mori·sot /mɒriˈzoː/ **Berthe (Marie Pau·line)** (1841–95), French painter. The first woman to join the Impressionists, she exhibited with them from 1874; her works typically depict women and children, as in *The Cradle* (1872), and waterside scenes, notably *A Summer's Day* (1879).

Mori·yama /ˌmɒriːˈjɒmə/ **Ray·mond** (b.1929), Canadian architect and planner. Noted for his designs of large public buildings, including the Ontario Science Centre (1969), he was made an Officer of the Order of Canada in 1985.

Mor·ley /ˈmɔrli/ **1 Ed·ward Wil·liams** (1838–1923), US chemist. He specialized in accurate quantitative measurements, such as those of the combining weights of hydrogen and oxygen, and collaborated with A. A. Michelson in an 1887 experiment to determine the speed of light. **2 Thom·as** (*c*.1557–1602), English organist and composer, who is best known for his madrigals.

Mor·mon /ˈmɔrmən/ ● *noun* a member of the Church of Jesus Christ of Latter-day Saints, a millenary religion founded in 1830 by Joseph Smith. The central scripture (apart from the Bible) is the Book of Mormon, which tells the history of a group of Hebrews who migrated to America *c*.600 BC; Smith claimed to have found and translated the book through divine revelation. ● *adjective* of or relating to the Mormons or their beliefs. □ **Mor·mon·ism** *noun*

morn *noun literary* morning. [Old English *morgen* from Germanic]

mor·nay /ˈmɔrnei/ *noun* a cheese-flavoured white sauce. [named after *Mornay*, the French cook and eldest son of Joseph Voiron, 19th c. inventor of the sauce]

mor·ning ● *noun* **1** the early part of the day, esp. from sunrise to noon (*this morning*; *during the morning*; *morning coffee*). **2** sunrise, daybreak. **3** a time compared with the morning, esp. the early part of one's life etc. ● *interjection* = GOOD MORNING *interjection*. □ **in the morning** during or in the course of the morning. [Middle English *mor(we)ning* from *morwen* MORN + -ING¹ after *evening*]

morning after *noun* (also **morning after the night before**) *informal* a morning when one feels the effects of previous overindulgences, esp. with alcohol.

morning-after pill *noun* a contraceptive pill effective when taken some hours after intercourse.

morning coat *noun* a coat with tails, and with the front cut away below the waist.

morning dress *noun* a man's morning coat and striped trousers.

morning glory *noun* any of various twining plants of the genus *Ipomoea* or related genera of the bindweed family, with trumpet-shaped flowers which fade in the afternoon.

morning glory muffin *noun N Amer.* a muffin containing grated carrots, apples, raisins, and cinnamon, and sometimes other ingredients such as coconut, pineapple, and nuts.

morning paper *noun* a newspaper published early in the morning.

morning person *noun N Amer.* a person who likes to get up early in the morning (*I'm a morning person, but my wife isn't*).

morning room *noun* a sitting room for the morning.

morning sickness *noun* nausea experienced during early pregnancy, often (but not necessarily) in the morning.

morning star *noun* a planet, usu. Venus, seen in the east before sunrise.

Moro /ˈmɔroː/ *noun* (pl. **Moros**) a member of a group of Muslim peoples of the Philippines. [Spanish, = MOOR]

Mo·roc·co /məˈrɒkoː/ a country in NW Africa, with coastlines on the Mediterranean Sea and Atlantic Ocean; pop. (est. 2002) 31,167,783; capital, Rabat. □ **Mo·roc·can** *adjective & noun*

mo·roc·co *noun* (pl. **-cos**) **1** a fine flexible leather made (originally in Morocco) from goatskins tanned with sumac, used esp. in bookbinding and shoemaking. **2** an imitation of this in grained calf etc.

moron *noun* **1** *informal* a very stupid or foolish person. **2** an adult with a mental age of about 8–12. □ **mor·on·ic** /məˈrɒnɪk/ *adjective* **mor·on·ic·al·ly** *adverb* **mor·on·ism** *noun* [Greek *mōron*, neuter of *mōros* foolish]

Mor·oni /məˈroːni/ the capital of Comoros, on the island of Grande Comore; pop. (est. 2002) 42,200.

mor·ose /məˈroːs/ *adjective* sullen and ill-tempered. □ **mor·ose·ly** *adverb* **mor·ose·ness** *noun* [Latin *morosus* peevish etc., from *mos moris* manner]

Mor·peth /ˈmɔrpəθ/ a town in NE England, the county town of Northumberland; pop. (est. 1998) 14,200.

morph¹ /mɔrf/ *noun* = ALLOMORPH. [back-formation]

morph² *noun* a variant form of an animal or plant. [Greek *morphē* 'form']

morph³ *verb* **1** *transitive* alter or transform (an image) by computer. **2** *intransitive slang* be transformed. [extracted from METAMORPHOSIS]

mor·pheme /ˈmɔrfiːm/ *noun Linguistics* **1** a morphological element considered with respect to its functional relations in a linguistic system. **2** a meaningful morphological unit of a language that cannot be further divided (e.g. *in*, *come*, *-ing*, forming *incoming*). □ **mor·phem·ic** *adjective* **mor·phem·ic·al·ly** *adverb* [French *morphème* from Greek *morphē* form, after PHONEME]

Vowels: a cat ɑː arm e bed ɜr her ɜː deux ə ago ɪ sit i cosy iː feed ɒ hot ɔ pore ɔː no ʌ run ʊ put

Mor·phe·us /ˈmɔrfiəs/ *Rom. Myth* the son of Somnus (god of sleep), god of dreams, and, in later writings, also god of sleep.

mor·phia /ˈmɔrfiə/ *noun* (not in technical use) = MORPHINE.

mor·phine /ˈmɔrfiːn/ *noun* an analgesic and narcotic drug obtained from opium and used medicinally to relieve pain. [German *Morphin* & modern Latin *morphia* from *Morpheus* god of sleep]

mor·phing *noun* a technique that changes a film image into a numerical code, enabling it to be manipulated by a computer so that the effect can be created of transforming an image smoothly into a different one. [MORPH³]

morph·o·gen·e·sis /ˌmɔrfəˈdʒɛnɪsɪs/ *noun Biol.* the development of form in organisms. □ **morph·o·gen·et·ic** *adjective* **morph·o·gen·ic** *adjective* [modern Latin from Greek *morphē* form + GENESIS]

mor·phol·o·gy /mɔrˈfɒlədʒi/ *noun* **1** *Biol.* the study of the forms of organisms. **2** *Linguistics* **a** the study of the forms of words. **b** the system of forms in a language. **3** the shape, form, or external arrangement of something, esp. as an object of study. □ **morph·o·logic** *adjective* **morph·o·logic·al** *adjective* **morph·o·logic·al·ly** *adverb* **mor·phol·o·gist** *noun* [Greek *morphē* form + -LOGY]

Mor·rice /ˈmɒrɪs/ **James Wil·son** (1865–1924), Canadian painter. One of the earliest Canadian modernists and the first Canadian painter to earn widespread acclaim abroad, his paintings include such traditional Canadian scenes as *The Ice Bridge* as well as many more modernistic European works.

Mor·ris /ˈmɒrɪs/ **1 Ed·ward Pat·rick, 1st Baron Morris** (1859–1939), Newfoundland politician, prime minister of Newfoundland 1909–18. First elected to the Newfoundland Assembly in 1885, he joined the Liberal Cabinet in 1889 and formed his own party, the People's Party, in 1908. **2 Wil·liam** (1834–96), English designer, craftsman, poet, and writer. A leading figure in the Arts and Crafts movement, he established Morris & Company (1861) to produce handcrafted goods, and the Kelmscott Press (1890) to print limited editions of fine books; his writings include *News from Nowhere* (1891), which expresses his socialist ideals.

Morris chair *noun* a type of armchair with large, removable cushions and an adjustable back. [W. MORRIS]

morris dance *noun* a lively traditional English dance performed by groups of people in distinctive costume, often using bells, handkerchiefs, or sticks. □ **morris dancer** *noun* **morris dancing** *noun* [*morys*, var. of MOORISH]

Mor·ri·son /ˈmɒrɪsən/ **1 Jim** (full name James Douglas Morrison) (1943–71), US rock singer and songwriter. The lead singer (1965–71) of The Doors, he is remembered for songs such as 'Light my Fire' (1967), 'Hello, I Love You' (1968), and 'Riders on the Storm' (1971), and gained a cult following after his death. **2 Toni** (full name Chloe Anthony Morrison) (b.1931), US novelist. She is noted for her novels depicting the black American experience and heritage, often focusing on rural life in the South; her works include *The Bluest Eye* (1970), *Tar Baby* (1979), and the Pulitzer Prize-winning *Beloved* (1987). She was awarded the Nobel Prize for literature in 1993. **3 Van** (full name George Ivan Morrison) (b.1945), Northern Irish singer, instrumentalist, and songwriter. He has developed a distinctive personal style from a background of blues, soul, folk music, and rock; his albums include *Astral Weeks* (1968), *Moondance* (1970), and *Irish Heartbeat* (1989).

mor·row /ˈmɒroʊ/ *noun* (usu. prec. by *the*) *literary* the following day. [Middle English *morwe*, *moru* (as MORN)]

Morse¹ /ˈmɔrs/ **Sam·uel Fin·ley Breese** (1791–1872), US inventor and painter. He pioneered the use of the electric telegraph, conceiving the idea in 1832, and by 1838 had extended the range and capabilities of his working model by means of electromagnetic relays, and developed the Morse code.

Morse² *noun* (in full **Morse code**) an alphabet or code in which letters are represented by combinations of long and short light or sound signals. [MORSE¹]

mor·sel *noun* a small amount or piece of something, esp. food. [Old French, diminutive of *mors* a bite, from *mordēre mors-* to bite]

mor·ta·del·la /ˌmɔrtəˈdɛlə/ *noun* a large spiced sausage usu. made of pork and pork fat and eaten cold. [Italian diminutive, irreg. from Latin *murtatum* seasoned with myrtle berries]

mor·tal ● *adjective* **1** subject to death. **2** causing death; fatal. **3** (of a battle) fought to the death. **4** associated with death (*mortal agony*). **5** (of an enemy) implacable. **6** (of pain, fear, an affront, etc.) intense, very serious. **7** *informal* **a** very great (*in a mortal hurry*). **b** long and tedious (*for two mortal hours*). **8** *informal* conceivable, imaginable (*every mortal thing*; *of no mortal use*). ● *noun* **1** a mortal being, esp. a human. **2** *jocular* a person

described in some specified way (*a thirsty mortal*). □ **mor·tal·ly** *adverb* [Old French *mortal*, *mortel* or Latin *mortalis* from *mors mortis* death]

mor·tal·i·ty *noun* (*pl.* **-ies**) **1** the state of being subject to death. **2** loss of life on a large scale. **3 a** the number of deaths in a given period etc. **b** (in full **mortality rate**) = DEATH RATE.

mortal sin *noun* a grave sin that is regarded as depriving the soul of divine grace.

mor·tar ● *noun* **1** a mixture of lime with cement, sand, and water, used in building to bond bricks or stones. **2** a short large-bore cannon for firing shells at high angles (also *attributive*: *mortar fire*). **3** a contrivance for firing a lifeline or firework. **4** a vessel made of hard material, in which ingredients are pounded with a pestle. ● *transitive verb* **1** plaster or join with mortar. **2** attack or bombard with mortar shells. [Old French *mortier*, originally in sense 4, with transference from the vessel to the substance made in it, from Latin *mortarium*: partly from Low German]

mor·tar·board *noun* **1** an academic cap with a stiff flat square top. **2** a flat board with a handle on the undersurface, for holding mortar in bricklaying etc.

mort·gage /ˈmɔrgɪdʒ/ ● *noun* **1 a** an agreement by which money is lent by a bank, trust company, etc. for buying a house or other property, the property itself being the security. **b** a deed effecting this (*burned our mortgage*). **2 a** a debt secured by a mortgage. **b** a loan resulting in such a debt. **3** *see* CHATTEL MORTGAGE. ● *transitive verb* **1** give a bank, trust company, etc. the legal right to take possession of (a house or some other property) as a security for money lent. **2** pledge; place under an obligation (*have mortgaged our future to foreign investment*). □ **mort·gage·able** *adjective* [Old French, = dead pledge, from *mort* from Latin *mortuus* dead + *gage* GAGE¹]

mort·ga·gee /ˌmɔrgɪˈdʒiː/ *noun* the creditor in a mortgage, e.g. a bank, trust company, etc.

mortgage rate *noun* the rate of interest charged by a mortgagee.

mort·ga·gor /ˈmɔrgɪdʒɔr/ *noun* (also **mort·ga·ger** /-ˈdʒɜr/) the debtor in a mortgage.

mor·tice *var. of* MORTISE.

mor·ti·cian /mɔrˈtɪʃən/ *noun N Amer.* an undertaker. [Latin *mors mortis* death + -ICIAN]

mor·ti·fy /ˈmɔrtɪˌfaɪ/ *verb* (**-fies, -fied**) **1** *transitive* **a** cause (a person) to feel shamed or humiliated. **b** wound (a person's feelings). **2** *transitive* bring (the body, the flesh, the passions, etc.) into subjection by self-denial or discipline. **3** *intransitive* (of flesh) be affected by gangrene or necrosis. □ **mor·ti·fi·ca·tion** *noun* **mor·ti·fy·ing** *adjective* **mor·ti·fy·ing·ly** *adverb* [Old French *mortifier* from ecclesiastical Latin *mortificare* kill, subdue from *mors mortis* death]

Mor·ti·mer /ˈmɔrtɪmər/ **1 John (Clif·ford)** (b.1923), English writer, creator of the slovenly, clever barrister Horace Rumpole in the popular television series *Rumpole of the Bailey*; his novels include *Paradise Postponed* (1985). **2 Roger de, 8th Baron of Wig·more and 1st Earl of March** (*c.*1287–1330), English noble. In 1326 he invaded England with his lover Isabella of France, forcing her husband Edward II to abdicate in favour of her son, the future Edward III; Mortimer and Isabella acted as regents for the young Edward until 1330, when the monarch assumed royal power and had Mortimer executed.

mor·tise /ˈmɔrtɪs/ (also **mor·tice**) ● *noun* a hole in a piece of wood etc. designed to receive the end of another part, esp. a tenon. ● *transitive verb* **1** join securely, esp. by mortise and tenon. **2** cut a mortise in. □ **mor·tis·er** *noun* [Old French *mortoise* from Arabic *murtazz* fixed in]

mortise lock *noun* a lock recessed into a mortise in the frame of a door or window etc.

mort·main /ˈmɔrtmeɪn/ *noun Law hist.* the status of lands or tenements held inalienably by an ecclesiastical or other corporation. [Old French *mortemain* from medieval Latin *mortua manus* dead hand, prob. in allusion to impersonal ownership]

Mor·ton /ˈmɔrtən/ **'Jelly Roll'** (born Ferdinand Joseph La Menthe Morton) (1885–1941), US jazz pianist, composer, and bandleader. He was one of the principal links between ragtime and New Orleans jazz, and formed his own band, the Red Hot Peppers, in 1926.

mor·tu·ar·y /ˈmɔrtʃuˌɛri/ ● *noun* (*pl.* **-aries**) a room or building in which dead bodies may be kept until burial or cremation. ● *adjective* of or concerning death or burial. [Anglo-French *mortuarie* from medieval Latin *mortuarium* from Latin *mortuarius* from *mortuus* dead]

mortuary pole *noun* (among the Haida) a tall pole, elaborately carved with family crests, at the top of which the bodies of dead people of high status were placed.

mor·u·la /ˈmɔrʊlə/ *noun* (*pl.* **morulae** /-ˌliː/) a fully segmented ovum from which a blastula is formed. [modern Latin, diminutive of Latin *morum* mulberry]

Mo·saic /mɔːˈzeɪɪk/ *adjective* of or associated with Moses. [French *mosaïque* or modern Latin *Mosaicus* from MOSES]

mo·saic ● *noun* **1 a** a picture or pattern produced by an arrangement of small variously coloured pieces of glass or stone etc. **b** the process of producing such a work. **2** something that resembles a mosaic, esp. in its diversity of composition (*the Canadian cultural mosaic*). **3** an arrangement of photosensitive elements in a television camera. **4** *Biol.* = CHIMERA 3. **5** (in full **mosaic disease**) a virus disease causing mottled leaves in plants, esp. tobacco, corn, and sugar cane. **6** (*attributive*) **a** of or like a mosaic. **b** diversified. ● *transitive verb* (**mo·saicked**, **mo·saick·ing**) **1** adorn with mosaics. **2** combine into or as into a mosaic. □ **mo·sai·cist** /mɔːˈzeɪɪsɪst/ *noun* [French *mosaïque* from Italian *mosaico* from medieval Latin *mosaicus*, *musaicus* from Greek *mous(e)ion* mosaic work, from *mousa* MUSE¹]

Mosaic Law *noun* the laws attributed to Moses and listed in the Pentateuch.

mosa·saur /ˌmɔːsəˈsɔːr/ *noun* (also **mosa·saur·us**) any large extinct marine reptile of the genus *Mosasaurus*, with a long slender body and flipper-like limbs. [modern Latin from *Mosa*, Meuse River (near which it was first discovered) + Greek *sauros* lizard]

Mos·cow /ˈmɒskaʊ, -kɔː/ the capital of Russia, situated at the centre of the vast plain of European Russia, on the Moskva River; pop. (est. 2002) 8,376,000. After the Bolshevik Revolution of 1917 it was made the capital of the USSR and seat of the new Soviet government, with its centre in the Kremlin, the ancient citadel of the 15th-c. city.

Mose·ley /ˈmoʊzli/ **Henry Gwyn Jef·freys** (1887–1915), English physicist. He determined the atomic numbers of elements from their X-ray spectra, demonstrated that an element's chemical properties are determined by this number, and showed that there are only ninety-two naturally occurring elements.

mo·selle /moʊˈzel/ *noun* a light medium-dry white wine produced in the valley of the Mosel River in Germany.

Mosel River /ˈmoʊzəl/ (also **Mo·selle** /moʊˈzel/) a river of W Europe, which rises in the Vosges mountains of NE France and flows 514 km (321 miles) northeast through Luxembourg and Germany to meet the Rhine at Koblenz.

Moses /ˈmoʊzəs/ **1** (*fl. c.*14th–13th c. BC), Hebrew prophet and lawgiver. According to the Biblical account, he was born in Egypt and led the Jews away from servitude there, across the desert toward the Promised Land; during the journey he was inspired by God on Mount Sinai to write down the Ten Commandments on tablets of stone (Exod. 20). **2 Anna Mary Rob·ert·son** (known as 'Grandma Moses') (1860–1961), US painter. She took up painting after the death of her husband in 1927, and produced more than a thousand naive paintings, principally colourful scenes of US rural life. **3 Edwin Cor·ley** (b.1955), US athlete. He won Olympic gold medals for the 400-metres hurdles in the 1976 and 1984 Olympics. He finished first in 122 consecutive races between 1977 and 1987 and set four successive world records.

Moses ben Mai·mon /ben maiˈmɒn/ see MAIMONIDES.

mosey *intransitive verb* (**moseys**, **moseyed**) *informal* walk in a leisurely or aimless manner. [19th c.: origin unknown]

mosh *intransitive verb* dance in a violent manner, involving jumping up and down and deliberately colliding with other dancers, esp. at a rock concert. □ **mosh·er** *noun* **mosh·ing** *noun* [20th c.: origin unknown: perhaps from MASH *verb*]

mo·shav /moʊˈʃɒv/ *noun* (*pl.* **mo·shav·im**) a co-operative association of Israeli smallholders. [Hebrew *mošāb*, lit. 'dwelling']

mosh pit *noun* the area in front of the stage at a rock concert, where moshing usually takes place.

Mos·lem *var. of* MUSLIM.

Mos·ley /ˈmoʊzli/ **Sir Os·wald (Er·nald), 6th Bar·on·et** (1896–1980), English Fascist leader. He founded and led the British Union of Fascists (1932), also known as the Blackshirts; the party was effectively destroyed by the Public Order Act of 1936 and in 1948 Mosley founded the right-wing Union Movement.

mosque /mɒsk/ *noun* a Muslim place of worship. [French *mosquée* from Italian *moschea* from Arabic *masjid*]

mos·quito *noun* (*pl.* **-toes** or **-tos**) **1** any of various slender biting insects, esp. of the genus *Culex*, *Anopheles*, or *Aedes*, the female of which punctures the skin of humans and other animals with a long proboscis to suck their blood and transmits diseases such as malaria and encephalitis. **2** *Cdn* **a** an initiation level of sports competition for young children. **b** a player at this level. [Spanish & Portuguese, diminutive of *mosca* from Latin *musca* fly]

Mosquito Coast a sparsely populated coastal strip of swamp, lagoon, and tropical forest comprising the Caribbean coast of Nicaragua and NE Honduras. [MISKITO]

mosquito coil *noun* a slowly-burning spiral made with a dried paste of pyrethrum powder, which produces a smoke that inhibits mosquitos from biting.

mosquito net *noun* (also **mosquito netting**) a net to keep off mosquitoes. □ **mosquito-netted** *adjective*

moss ● *noun* **1** any small cryptogamous plant of the class Musci, growing in dense clusters on the surface of the ground, in bogs, on trees, stones, etc. **2** a mass or growth of moss. **3** (in full **Irish moss**) = CARRAGEEN. ● *transitive verb* cover with moss. □ **moss·like** *adjective* **mossy** *adjective* [Old English *mos* bog, moss, from Germanic]

Mos·sad /mɒˈsad, ˈmɒs-/ *noun* the principal intelligence service of Israel. [Hebrew *mōsād* institution]

moss agate *noun* agate with mosslike dendritic markings.

moss·back *noun* N Amer. **1** *informal* an old-fashioned or extremely conservative person. **2** a large and old fish. □ **moss·backed** *adjective*

moss berry *noun* the cranberry, *Vaccinium oxycoccus*.

moss campion *noun* a pink flowered, almost stemless campion, *Silene acaulis*, found on mountains and on northern coasts.

moss·er *noun* a person who harvests Irish moss.

moss green *noun* a yellowish-green colour resembling that of moss.

moss-grown *adjective* overgrown with moss.

moss heather *noun* = CASSIOPE.

moss stitch *noun* alternate plain and purl in knitting.

most ● *adjective* **1** existing in the greatest quantity or degree (*you have made the most mistakes; see who can make the most noise*). **2** the majority of; nearly all of (*most people think so*). ● *noun* **1** the greatest quantity or number (*this is the most I can do*). **2** (**the most**) *slang* the best of all. **3** the majority (*most of them are missing*). ● *adverb* **1** in the highest degree (*this is most interesting; what most annoys me*). **2** forming the superlative of adjectives and adverbs, esp. those of more than one syllable (*most certain; most easily*). **3** N Amer. *informal* almost. □ **at most** no more or better than (*this is at most a makeshift*). **at the most 1** as the greatest amount. **2** not more than. **for the most part 1** as regards the greater part. **2** usually. **make the most of 1** employ to the best advantage. **2** represent at its best or worst. [Old English *mǣst* from Germanic]

-most *suffix* forming superlative adjectives and adverbs from prepositions and other words indicating relative position (*foremost; uttermost*). [Old English *-mest* from Germanic]

Most Favoured Nation *noun* a country which is afforded beneficial trade terms with another, e.g. lower import tariffs than others.

Most High *noun* (prec. by *the*) God.

most·ly *adverb* **1** as regards the greater part. **2** usually.

Mós·to·les /ˈmɒstɒles/ a city in central Spain, just southeast of Madrid; pop. (est. 1998) 195,311.

Most Reverend *noun* the official title of certain high-ranking clergy, e.g. archbishops and bishops.

Mosul /ˈmoʊsʊl/ a city in N Iraq, on the Tigris River, opposite the ruins of Nineveh; pop. (est. 2002) 1,739,800. It gives its name to muslin, a cotton fabric first produced there.

MOT *abbreviation* **1** (*hist.* in the UK) Ministry of Transport. **2** *Brit.* (in full **MOT test**) a compulsory annual test of motor vehicles of more than a specified age.

mot /moʊ/ *noun* (*pl.* **mots** *pronunc.* same) a witty saying. [French, = word, ultimately from Latin *muttum* uttered sound, from *muttire* murmur]

mote /moʊt/ *noun* a speck of dust. [Old English *mot*, corresponding to Dutch *mot* dust, sawdust, of unknown origin]

mo·tel *noun* a hotel designed for motorists, usu. having direct access from each room to the parking lot. [blend of MOTOR + HOTEL]

mo·tet /moʊˈtet/ *noun* a short sacred choral composition. [Old French, diminutive of *mot*: see MOT]

moth *noun* **1** any of the large group of insects (including clothes moths) which together with butterflies constitute the order Lepidoptera and are distinguished from butterflies (in most instances) by nocturnal activity, hairlike or slender antennae that are not clubbed, thicker bodies, the usu. folded position of the wings when at rest, and duller colouring. **2** any small lepidopterous insect of the family Tineidae breeding in cloth etc., on which its larva feeds. [Old English *moththe*]

moth·ball ● *noun* a ball of naphthalene etc. placed in stored clothes to keep away moths. ● *transitive verb* **1** place in mothballs. **2 a** take out of use or active service. **b** put in storage for an indefinite time. □ **in mothballs** stored unused for a considerable time.

moth-eaten *adjective* **1** damaged or destroyed by moths. **2** antiquated, time-worn.

moth·er[1] ● *noun* **1 a** a woman in relation to a child or children to whom she has given birth. **b** a woman who serves as a mother, e.g. a stepmother, adoptive mother, or foster mother. **2** any female animal in relation to its offspring. **3** a quality or condition etc. that gives rise to another (*necessity is the mother of invention*). **4** (in full **Mother Superior**) the head of a female religious community. **5** *archaic* (esp. as a form of address) an elderly woman. **6** (*attributive*) **a** designating an institution etc. regarded as having maternal authority (*Mother Church; mother earth*). **b** designating the main ship, spacecraft, etc., in a convoy or mission (*the mother craft*). ● *adjective* **1** that is a mother (*a mother bird*). **2** characteristic of a mother (*mother love*). **3** inherited or learned from, or as if from, one's mother; native (*mother tongue*). ● *transitive verb* **1** give birth to; be the mother of. **2** protect as a mother. **3** give rise to; be the source of. □ **every mother's son** *informal* every man; everyone. **the mother of all …** the largest … of all. ¶ This phrase, which experienced a vogue in the early nineties, has been condemned as an overworked cliché. □ **mother·less** *adjective* **mother·less·ness** *noun* **mother·like** *adjective & adverb* [Old English *mōdor* from Germanic]

moth·er[2] *noun* esp. *N Amer.* **1** *slang* a person or thing that is very large, powerful, etc. **2** *coarse slang* = MOTHERFUCKER. [abbreviation]

moth·er[3] *noun* (in full **mother of vinegar**) a ropy mucilaginous substance produced on the surface of liquids during fermentation, and used to ferment other liquids, as in changing wine to vinegar. [prob. a use of MOTHER[1]]

mother·board *noun Computing* a printed circuit board containing the principal components of a microcomputer etc.

Mother Carey's chicken *noun* = STORM PETREL.

Mother Corp. *noun* (also **Mother Corporation**) *Cdn informal* the CBC.

mother country *noun* **1** the country which colonized or settled a particular place. **2** one's native country.

mother figure *noun* an older woman who is regarded as a source of nurture, support, etc.

mother·fucker *noun* esp. *N Amer. coarse slang* an obnoxious or very unpleasant person or thing. □ **mother·fuck·ing** *adjective*

mother goddess *noun* (also called **Great Mother**) a mother-figure deity, goddess of the entire complex of birth and growth, commonly a central figure of early nature cults where maintenance of fertility was of prime religious importance.

Mother Goose *noun* the fictitious author of a collection of nursery rhymes first published in England in the late 18th c.

mother hen *noun* **1** a person who sees to the needs of others, esp. in a fussy or annoying way. **2** a hen with a brood of chicks.

mother·hood *noun* **1** the state or condition of being a mother. **2** the qualities or attributes characteristic of a mother. **3** *N Amer.* (*attributive*) having an inherent goodness or justness that is obvious or cannot be disputed (*a motherhood issue*).

mother house *noun* a convent or monastery having authority over other houses of the same order.

Mother Hubbard /ˈhʌbərd/ *noun* **1** *Cdn* (in full **Mother Hubbard parka**) a type of woman's parka, worn esp. in the Western Arctic, consisting of an inner duffle shell covered in a bright print fabric, edged with fur at the hood and cuffs and having a deep ruffle around the bottom. **2** a woman's long unfitted dress. [Old *Mother Hubbard*, a character in a nursery rhyme]

Moth·er·ing Sunday *noun Brit.* the fourth Sunday in Lent, traditionally a day for honouring mothers with gifts.

mother-in-law *noun* (*pl.* **mothers-in-law**) the mother of one's spouse.

mother-in-law's tongue *noun* a plant, *Sansevieria trifasciata*, with long erect pointed leaves.

mother-in-law suite *noun N Amer.* = IN-LAW SUITE.

mother·land *noun* **1** one's native country. **2** the land in which one's ancestors lived.

mother·lode *noun* **1** *Mining* the main vein of a system. **2** a rich or important source of something.

mother·ly *adjective* **1** like or characteristic of a mother in affection, care, etc. **2** of or relating to a mother. □ **mother·li·ness** *noun*

mother-naked *adjective* stark naked.

Mother of Parliaments *noun* (prec. by *the*) the British parliament.

mother-of-pearl *noun* a smooth iridescent substance forming the inner layer of the shell of some molluscs.

mother's allowance *noun Cdn hist.* = FAMILY ALLOWANCE 1.

Mother's Day *noun* **1** *N Amer.* the second Sunday in May, set aside as a day to honour mothers. **2** *Brit.* = MOTHERING SUNDAY.

mother ship *noun* **1** a ship escorting or having charge of a number of other, smaller, vessels. **2** an aircraft or spacecraft from which another aircraft or spacecraft is launched or controlled.

mother's ruin *noun informal* gin.

Mother Superior *noun see* MOTHER[1] *noun* 4.

Mother Teresa see TERESA, MOTHER.

mother-to-be *noun* a woman who is expecting a baby.

mother tongue *noun* **1** one's native language. **2** a language from which others have evolved.

Moth·er·well, Rob·ert (1915–91), US painter. A pioneer and principal exponent of abstract expressionism, he often retained a suggestion of figuration in the amorphous shapes and bold austere colours of his paintings; his works include the series entitled *Elegy to the Spanish Republic*.

mother wit *noun* native wit; common sense.

moth·proof ● *adjective* (of clothes) treated so as to repel moths. ● *transitive verb* treat (clothes) in this way.

mothy *adjective* (**moth·i·er**, **moth·i·est**) infested with moths.

mo·tif /moːˈtiːf/ *noun* **1** a distinctive feature or dominant idea in artistic or literary composition. **2** *Music* = FIGURE *noun* 12. **3** a decorative design or pattern. **4** an ornament of lace etc. sewn separately on a garment. [French (as MOTIVE)]

mo·tile /ˈmoːtail/ *adjective Zool. & Bot.* capable of motion. □ **mo·til·ity** /-ˈtɪlɪti/ *noun* [Latin *motus* motion (as MOVE)]

mo·tion ● *noun* **1** the act or process of moving or of changing position. **2** a particular manner of moving the body in walking etc. **3** a change of posture. **4** a gesture. **5** a formal proposal put to a committee, legislature, etc. **6** *Law* an application for a rule or order of court. **7** *Brit.* **a** an evacuation of the bowels. **b** (in *sing.* or *pl.*) feces. **8** a piece of moving mechanism. ● *verb* (often foll. by *to* + infin.) **1** *transitive* direct (a person) by a sign or gesture. **2** *intransitive* (often foll. by *to* a person) make a gesture directing (*motioned to me to leave*). □ **go through the motions 1** make a pretense; do something perfunctorily or superficially. **2** simulate an action by gestures. **in motion** moving; not at rest. **put** (or **set**) **in motion** set going or working. □ **mo·tion·al** *adjective* **mo·tion·less** *adjective* **mo·tion·less·ly** *adverb* [Old French from Latin *motio -onis* (as MOVE)]

motion detector *noun* (also **motion sensor**) a security device, usu. emitting an infrared beam which triggers an alarm when interrupted by any movement through it.

motion picture *noun* a continuous picture of events obtained by projecting a sequence of photographs taken at very short intervals (also *attributive*: *the motion picture industry*).

motion sickness *noun* nausea induced by motion, esp. by travelling in a vehicle.

mo·tiv·ate *transitive verb* **1** supply a motive to; be the motive of. **2** cause (a person) to act in a particular way. **3** stimulate the interest of (a person in an activity). □ **mo·tiv·a·tion** *noun* **mo·tiv·a·tion·al** *adjective* **mo·tiv·a·tion·al·ly** *adverb* **mo·tiv·a·tor** *noun*

motivational speaker *noun* a person whose profession is to make speeches to groups, esp. to motivate them to personal or professional improvement.

mo·tive ● *noun* **1** a factor or circumstance that induces a person to act in a particular way. **2** a motif in art, literature, or music. ● *adjective* **1** tending to initiate movement. **2** concerned with movement. **3** motivating. □ **mo·tive·less** *adjective* [Old French *motif* (adj. & n.) from Late Latin *motivus* (adj.) (as MOVE)]

motive power *noun* a moving or impelling power, esp. a source of energy used to drive machinery.

motiv·ic /ˈmoːtɪvɪk/ *adjective Music* of or relating to a motif or motifs.

mot juste /moːˈʒuːst/ *noun* (*pl.* **mots justes** *pronunc.* same) the most appropriate expression.

mot·ley ● *adjective* (**mot·li·er**, **mot·li·est**) **1** of varied character (*a motley crew*). **2** diversified in colour. ● *noun* **1** an incongruous mixture. **2** *hist.* the parti-coloured costume of a jester. [Middle English *mottelay*, perhaps ultimately related to MOTE]

mot·mot /ˈmɒtmɒt/ *noun* a bird of the tropical American family

Momotidae, some members of which have two long tail feathers like racquets. [Latin American Spanish, imitative]

mo·to·cross /ˈmoʊtoʊˌkrɒs/ *noun* cross-country racing on motorcycles. □ **moto·cross·er** *noun* [blend of MOTOR + CROSS-COUNTRY]

mo·tor ● *noun* **1** a thing that imparts motion. **2** a machine (esp. one using electricity or internal combustion) supplying motive power for a vehicle etc. or for some other device with moving parts. **3** *Brit. informal* a car. ● *adjective* **1** giving, imparting, or producing motion. **2** driven by a motor. **3** of or for motor vehicles. **4** of or for motorists (*motor hotel*). **5** *Anat.* relating to muscular movement or the nerves activating it (*motor skills*). ● *verb* **1** *intransitive* travel by or in a motor vehicle. **2** *transitive Brit.* convey in a motor vehicle. **3** *intransitive* move under motor power in a boat. [Latin, = mover (as MOVE)]

motor area *noun* a part of the central nervous system associated with the initiation of muscular action, esp. the motor cortex.

motor·bike *noun informal* **1** = MOTORCYCLE. **2** = DIRT BIKE.

motor·boat ● *noun* a motor-driven boat. ● *intransitive verb* travel in or by motorboat.

motor·cade *noun* a procession of motor vehicles. [MOTOR, after *cavalcade*]

motor car *noun* esp. *Brit.* = CAR 1.

motor·coach *noun* a bus that is comfortably equipped for long journeys.

motor cortex *noun* the part of the cerebral cortex in the brain in which originate the nerve impulses that initiate voluntary muscular activity.

motor·cycle *noun* a two-wheeled motor-driven road vehicle without pedal propulsion. □ **motor·cyc·ling** *noun* **motor·cyc·list** *noun*

motor drive *noun* a battery-driven motor in a camera used to wind the film rapidly between exposures.

motor·home *noun* esp. *N Amer.* a large motor vehicle equipped as a self-contained home for camping or long trips.

motor·ist *noun* the driver of a car.

motor·ize *transitive verb* (also esp. *Brit.* **-ise**) **1** provide with a motor. **2** equip (troops etc.) with motor transport. □ **motor·iz·a·tion** *noun*

motor·man *noun* (pl. **-men**) *dated* the driver of a subway, streetcar, etc.

motor·mouth *noun N Amer. slang* a person who talks incessantly and trivially. □ **motor-mouthed** *adjective*

motor nerve *noun* a nerve carrying impulses from the brain or spinal cord to a muscle.

motor neurone disease *noun Med.* esp. *Brit.* = AMYOTROPHIC LATERAL SCLEROSIS.

motor·sail·er *noun* a boat equipped with both sails and an engine.

motor scooter *noun see* SCOOTER 1.

motor·sport *noun* (also **motor racing**) the racing of motorized vehicles, esp. cars, as a sport.

motor vehicle *noun* a road vehicle powered by an internal combustion engine.

motor·way *noun Brit.* a main road with divided lanes and limited access, specially constructed and controlled for fast traffic.

motor yacht *noun* a motor-driven yacht.

Mo·town /ˈmoʊtaʊn/ *noun* music with rhythm and blues and soul elements, associated with Detroit. [abbreviation of *Tamla Motown*, the proprietary name of a record label, *Motown* being a name for Detroit, a shortening of *Motor Town*, from its car manufacturing industry]

motte /mɒt/ *noun* a mound forming the site of a castle, camp, etc. [Old French *mote* (as MOAT)]

mot·tle /ˈmɒtl/ ● *transitive verb* (esp. as **mot·tled** *adjective*) mark with spots or smears of colour. ● *noun* **1** an irregular arrangement of spots or patches of colour. **2** any of these spots or patches. □ **mot·tling** *noun* [prob. back-formation from MOTLEY]

motto *noun* (pl. **-toes, -tos**) **1** a short sentence or phrase chosen and used as a guide or rule of behaviour or as an expression of the aims or ideals of a family, country, institution, etc. **2** a phrase or sentence accompanying a coat of arms or crest. **3** *Music* a recurrent phrase having some symbolical significance. [Italian (as MOT)]

MOU *abbreviation* MEMORANDUM OF UNDERSTANDING.

moue /muː/ *noun* = POUT[1] *noun*. [French]

mouf·lon /ˈmuːflɒn/ *noun* (also **mouf·flon**) **1** a wild mountain sheep with chestnut-brown wool, *Ovis orientalis*, found in mountainous regions from Iran to Asia Minor, and thought to be the closest relation of the domestic sheep. **2** a soft double-faced coating fabric of wool or a wool blend. [French *mouflon* from Italian *muflone* from Romanic]

mouillé /muːˈjeɪ/ *adjective* (of a consonant, esp. *ll* in Spanish or French, *gl* and *gn* in Italian, etc.) palatalized, pronounced with a /j/ sound. [French, = wetted]

mou·jik *var. of* MUZHIK.

mould[1] (also **mold**) ● *noun* **1** a hollow container into which molten metal etc. is poured or soft material is pressed to harden into a required shape. **2** a metal, earthenware, or plastic vessel used to give shape to puddings, jellies, etc. **3** something formed in a mould. **4** *Archit.* a moulding or group of mouldings. **5** a frame or template for producing mouldings. **6** a usual or expected type of something (*Martha doesn't fit into the traditional mould of a university professor*). ● *verb* **1** *transitive* make (an object) in a required shape or from certain ingredients (*was moulded out of clay*). **2** *transitive* give a shape to. **3** *transitive* influence the formation or development of (*consultation helps to mould policies*). **4** *transitive* (esp. of clothing) fit closely to (*the gloves moulded his hands*). **5** *intransitive* (foll. by *to*) conform to the shape of (*the shoe moulds to my foot*). □ **break the mould 1** (also **break out of the mould**) change people's expectations of something, esp. in a dramatic or challenging way. **2** make impossible the repetition of a certain type of creation (*they broke the mould when Alex was born*). □ **mould·able** *adjective* **mould·er** *noun* [Middle English *mold(e)*, apparently from Old French *modle* from Latin *modulus*: see MODULUS]

mould[2] *noun* (also **mold**) a woolly, furry, or staining growth of minute fungi, as that which forms on food, textiles, etc., esp. in moist conditions. [Middle English prob. from obsolete *mould* adj.; past participle of *moul* grow mouldy, from Old Norse *mygla*]

mould[3] *noun* (also **mold**) **1** loose earth. **2** the upper soil of cultivated land, esp. when rich in organic matter. [Old English *molde* from Germanic, related to MEAL[2]]

mould·board *noun* (also **moldboard**) the curved board or blade in a plow that turns over the furrow.

mould·ed *adjective* (also **molded**) **1** formed, shaped. **2** made from a mould.

mould·er *intransitive verb* (also esp. *US* **molder**) **1** decay to dust. **2** (foll. by *away*) rot or crumble. **3** deteriorate. [perhaps from MOULD[3], but compare Norwegian dial. *muldra* crumble]

mould·ing *noun* (also **molding**) **1 a** an ornamentally shaped outline as an architectural feature, esp. in a cornice. **b** a strip of material in wood or stone etc. for use as moulding. **2** similar material in wood or plastic etc. used for other decorative purposes, e.g. in picture framing.

mouldy *adjective* (also **moldy**) (**-ier, -iest**) **1** covered with mould; smelling of mould. **2** old and decaying. **3** old-fashioned. □ **mould·i·ness** *noun*

moult (also esp. *US* **molt**) ● *verb* **1** *intransitive* shed feathers, hair, a shell, etc., in the process of renewing plumage, a coat, etc. **2** *transitive* (of an animal) shed (feathers, hair, etc.). ● *noun* the act or an instance of moulting (*is in moult once a year*). [Middle English *moute* from Old English *mutian* (unrecorded) from Latin *mutare* change: -*l*- after *fault* etc.]

mound ● *noun* **1** a raised mass of earth, stones, or other compacted material. **2** a heap or pile. **3** a hillock. **4** *Baseball* a slight elevation on which the pitcher stands. ● *transitive verb* heap up in a mound or mounds. □ **take the mound** *Baseball* (of a pitcher) start or enter a game. [16th c. (originally = hedge or fence): origin unknown]

mound builder *noun* a member of a prehistoric N American Aboriginal people whose culture was characterized by the erection of mounds for burial and other purposes.

mount[1] ● *verb* **1** *transitive* ascend or climb (a hill, stairs, etc.). **2** *transitive* **a** get up on (an animal, esp. a horse) to ride it. **b** set (a person) on horseback. **c** provide (a person) with a horse. **3** *transitive* go up or climb on to (a raised surface). **4** *intransitive* **a** move upwards. **b** (often foll. by *up*) increase, accumulate. **c** (of a feeling) become stronger or more intense (*excitement was mounting*). **5** *transitive* (esp. of a male animal) get on to (a female) to copulate. **6** *transitive* (often foll. by *on*) place (an object) on an elevated support. **7** *transitive* **a** set in or attach to a backing, setting, or other support. **b** attach (a picture etc.) to a mount or frame. **c** fix (an object for viewing) on a microscope slide. **8** *transitive* **a** arrange (a play, exhibition, etc.) or present for public view or display. **b** conduct or take action to initiate (a program, campaign, etc.). **9** *transitive* prepare (specimens) for preservation. **10** *transitive* **a** bring into readiness for operation. **b** put (a gun, missile, etc.) into position for use. **c** (usu. in *passive*; foll. by *with*) fit (a military vehicle etc.) with a weapon. ● *noun* **1** a backing or setting on which a photograph, work of art, gem, etc. is set for display. **2** a support for a gun, camera, etc. **3** a glass microscope slide for securing a specimen etc. to be viewed. **4** a small piece of gummed transparent paper for fixing postage stamps in an album etc. **5 a** a horse available for riding. **b** an opportunity to ride a horse, esp. as a jockey. □ **mount guard** (often foll. by *over*) perform the duty of guarding; take up sentry duty. □ **mount·able** *adjective* **mount·er** *noun* [Old French *munter*, *monter*, ultimately from Latin (as MOUNT²)]

mount² *noun* mountain, hill (*Mount Everest*; *Mount of Olives*). [Old English *munt* & Old French *mont* from Latin *mons montis* mountain]

Mount Adams *see* ADAMS, MOUNT.

moun·tain *noun* **1** a large natural elevation of the earth's surface rising abruptly from the surrounding level; a large or high and steep hill. **2** a large heap or pile; a huge quantity (*a mountain of work*). **3** (esp. in the EEC) a large surplus stock of a commodity (*butter mountain*). □ **make a mountain out of a molehill** *see* MOLEHILL. **move mountains 1** achieve spectacular results. **2** make every possible effort. □ **moun·tainy** *adjective* [Old French *montaigne*, ultimately from Latin (as MOUNT²)]

mountain ash *noun* **1** any of various small trees of the genus *Sorbus*, with delicate pinnate leaves and scarlet berries. *Also called* ROWAN, DOGBERRY. **2** any of several Australian eucalypts.

mountain avens *noun* a rosaceous alpine plant of the genus *Dryas*, bearing white or yellow flowers. One species, *D. octopetala*, is the floral emblem of the Northwest Territories.

mountain bike *noun* a bicycle with a light sturdy frame, broad deep-treaded tires, and multiple gears, originally designed for riding on mountainous terrain. □ **mountain biker** *noun* **mountain biking** *noun*

mountain·board *noun* a type of skateboard resembling a snowboard with wheels, for use on downhill slopes and designed to emulate the action of a snowboard. □ **mountain·board·er** *noun* **mountain·board·ing** *noun*

mountain chain *noun* a connected series of mountains.

mountain climber *noun* a person who climbs mountains, esp. as a sport. □ **mountain climbing** *noun*

mountain cranberry *noun* the cowberry.

Mountain Daylight Time *noun* daylight time in the Mountain Time zone. Abbr.: **MDT**.

moun·tain·eer ● *noun* **1** a person skilled in mountain climbing. **2** a person living in an area of high mountains. ● *intransitive verb* climb mountains as a sport. □ **moun·tain·eer·ing** *noun*

mountain goat *noun* **1** (in full **Rocky Mountain goat**) a white goat-antelope, *Oreamnos americanus*, of mountains in western N America. **2** a goat which lives on mountains, proverbial for agility.

mountain laurel *noun* a shrub of the eastern and central US, *Kalmia latifolia*.

mountain lion *noun* a cougar.

mountain man *noun* **1** a person who inhabits or frequents mountains or mountainous country. **2** (in N America) an early European pioneer, esp. living in the wilderness.

mountain maple *noun* a shrub or small tree, *Acer spicatum*, with three-lobed leaves, found from Newfoundland to Saskatchewan.

moun·tain·ous *adjective* **1** (of a region) having many mountains. **2** huge.

mountain oyster *noun* N Amer. slang the testicle of a lamb or calf, eaten as food.

mountain range *noun* a line of mountains connected by high ground.

moun·tain·scape *noun* a landscape including mountains.

mountain sheep *noun* a sheep native to mountain regions, esp. a bighorn sheep or a Dall sheep.

mountain sickness *noun* = ALTITUDE SICKNESS.

moun·tain·side *noun* the side of a mountain; slope.

Mountain Standard Time *noun* standard time in the Mountain Time zone. Abbr.: **MST**.

Mountain Time *noun* the time in a zone including Alberta, the US states in or near the Rocky Mountains, and Mexico. Mountain Standard Time is seven hours behind Greenwich Mean Time; Mountain Daylight Time is six hours behind Greenwich Mean Time. Abbr.: **MT**.

moun·tain·top *noun* the top of a mountain.

Mount Alberta *see* ALBERTA, MOUNT.

Mount Alverstone *see* ALVERSTONE, MOUNT.

Mount Ararat *see* ARARAT, MOUNT.

Mount Assiniboine *see* ASSINIBOINE, MOUNT.

Mount Athos *see* ATHOS, MOUNT.

Mount Augusta *see* AUGUSTA, MOUNT.

Mount Badham *see* BADHAM, MOUNT.

Mount·bat·ten /maunt'batən/ **Louis (Fran·cis Al·bert Vic·tor Nicho·las), 1st Earl Mountbatten of Burma** (1900–79), English admiral and administrator. A great-grandson of Queen Victoria, he became the supreme Allied commander in SE Asia (1943–5), and the last viceroy (1947) and first Governor General of India (1947–8); he was killed by an IRA bomb.

Mount Blackcomb *see* BLACKCOMB, MOUNT.

Mount Carmel *see* CARMEL, MOUNT.

Mount Clemenceau *see* CLEMENCEAU, MOUNT.

Mount Columbia *see* COLUMBIA, MOUNT.

Mount Cook *see* COOK, MOUNT.

Mount Craig *see* CRAIG, MOUNT.

moun·te·bank /'mauntə,baŋk/ *noun* **1** a swindler; a charlatan. **2** *hist.* an itinerant quack appealing to an audience from a platform. [Italian *montambanco* = *monta in banco* climb on bench: see MOUNT¹, BENCH]

mount·ed ● *adjective* **1** in senses of MOUNT¹ *verb*. **2** serving on horseback (*mounted police*). ● *noun* Cdn a mounted police force (*officers of the mounted*).

Mount Edith Cavell *see* EDITH CAVELL, MOUNT.

Mount Egmont *see* EGMONT, MOUNT.

Mount Elbert *see* ELBERT, MOUNT.

Mount Elgon *see* ELGON, MOUNT.

Mount Erebus *see* EREBUS, MOUNT.

Mount Etna *see* ETNA, MOUNT.

Mount Everest *see* EVEREST, MOUNT.

Mount Forbes *see* FORBES, MOUNT.

Mount Fuji *see* FUJI, MOUNT.

Mount Godwin-Austen *see* GODWIN-AUSTEN, MOUNT.

Mount Helicon *see* HELICON, MOUNT.

Mount Hubbard *see* HUBBARD, MOUNT.

Moun·tie *noun* informal a member of the RCMP.

Mountie hat *noun* Cdn the characteristic tan hat of the RCMP, with a broad flat encircling brim.

mount·ing *noun* **1** = MOUNT¹ *noun* 1, 2. **2** in senses of MOUNT¹ *verb*.

mounting block *noun* a block of stone placed to help a rider mount a horse.

Mount Kennedy *see* KENNEDY, MOUNT.

Mount Kenya *see* KENYA, MOUNT.

Mount Kinabalu *see* KINABALU, MOUNT.

Mount Kosciusko *see* KOSCIUSKO, MOUNT.

Mount Logan *see* LOGAN, MOUNT.

Mount Lucania *see* LUCANIA, MOUNT.

Mount Macaulay *see* MACAULAY, MOUNT.

Mount Malaspina *see* MALASPINA, MOUNT.

Mount McKinley *see* McKINLEY, MOUNT.

Mount Musala *see* MUSALA, MOUNT.

Mount Newton *see* NEWTON, MOUNT.

Mount Ngaliema *see* NGALIEMA, MOUNT.

Mount Olympus *see* OLYMPUS, MOUNT.

Mount Ossa *see* OSSA, MOUNT.

Mount Palomar *see* PALOMAR, MOUNT.

Mount Parnassus *see* PARNASSUS, MOUNT.

Mount Pearl a city in SE Newfoundland, located on the Avalon Peninsula, near St. John's; pop. (2001) 24,964. [Sir J. *Pearl*, British naval officer d.1840]

Mount Pelée *see* PELÉE, MOUNT.

Mount Pinatubo *see* PINATUBO, MOUNT.

Mount Queen Mary *see* QUEEN MARY, MOUNT.

Mount Quincy Adams *see* QUINCY ADAMS, MOUNT.

Mount Rainier *see* RAINIER, MOUNT.

Mount Revelstoke National Park a park in the Selkirk Mountains of SE central BC, located immediately northeast of Revelstoke. It was established in 1914. [as REVELSTOKE]

Mount Robson *see* ROBSON, MOUNT.

Mount Root *see* ROOT, MOUNT.

Mount Roraima *see* RORAIMA, MOUNT.

Mount Royal 1 a small mountain in south central Quebec, situated at the southwestern end of the city of Montreal. Despite its size (only

250 m high), it dominates the city's landscape. **2** = MONT-ROYAL. Mont-Royal is commonly known in English as the Town of Mount Royal. Abbr.: **TMR**. [in honour of FRANCIS I: compare MONTREAL]

Mount Rundle *see* RUNDLE, MOUNT.

Mount Rushmore *see* RUSHMORE, MOUNT.

Mount St. Elias *see* ST. ELIAS, MOUNT.

Mount St. Helens *see* ST. HELENS, MOUNT.

Mount Slaggard *see* SLAGGARD, MOUNT.

Mount Snowdon *see* SNOWDON, MOUNT.

Mount Stanley *see* STANLEY, MOUNT.

Mount Steele *see* STEELE, MOUNT.

Mount Strickland *see* STRICKLAND, MOUNT.

Mount Tiedemann *see* TIEDEMANN, MOUNT.

Mount Tongariro *see* TONGARIRO, MOUNT.

Mount Vancouver *see* VANCOUVER, MOUNT.

Mount Waddington *see* WADDINGTON, MOUNT.

Mount Walsh *see* WALSH, MOUNT.

Mount Washington *see* WASHINGTON, MOUNT.

Mount Whistler *see* WHISTLER, MOUNT.

Mount Whitney *see* WHITNEY, MOUNT.

Mount Wood *see* WOOD, MOUNT.

mourn *verb* **1** *transitive & intransitive* feel or show deep sorrow or regret for (a dead person, a lost thing, a past event, etc.). **2** *intransitive* show conventional signs of grief after a person's death. [Old English *murnan*]

mourn·er *noun* a person who mourns, esp. at a funeral.

mourn·ful *adjective* **1** doleful, sad, sorrowing. **2** expressing or suggestive of mourning. □ **mourn·ful·ly** *adverb* **mourn·ful·ness** *noun*

mourn·ing *noun* **1** the expression of deep sorrow, esp. for a loss, death, etc. **2** the wearing of solemn clothing as a convention to indicate sorrow after a death. **3** the clothes worn in mourning. □ **in mourning** assuming the signs of mourning, esp. in dress.

mourning cloak *noun* N Amer. a butterfly, *Nymphalis antiopa*, with deep purple yellow-bordered wings.

mourning dove *noun* a small slender N American dove, *Zenaida macroura*, with a long pointed tail and a plaintive call.

mour·vèdre /muːrˈvedrə/ *noun* **1** a variety of vine of the species *Vitis vinifera*, yielding black grapes used in winemaking, widely grown in Spain, Southern France, California, and elsewhere. **2** the grape of this variety, noted for its intense fruity flavour and often used in blends. **3** the red wine made from this grape. [French, perhaps from *Murviedro*, the name of a town in Valencia, Spain, where the grape is grown]

Mou·sal·la *see* MUSALA, MOUNT.

mouse ● *noun* (*pl.* **mice**) **1 a** any of various small rodents of the family Muridae, esp. of the genus *Mus*, usu. having a pointed snout and relatively large ears and eyes. **b** any of several similar rodents such as a small shrew or vole. **2** a timid or feeble person. **3** *Computing* a small hand-held device moved over a flat surface to produce a corresponding movement of a cursor or arrow on a computer screen, usu. having fingertip controls for selecting a function or entering a command. ● *intransitive verb* **1** (esp. of a cat, owl, etc.) hunt for or catch mice. **2** (foll. by *around, about*) search industriously; prowl about as if searching. **3** *Computing* use a mouse to control an application, browse through data, etc. □ **mouse·like** *adjective & adverb* **mous·er** *noun* [Old English *mūs*, pl. *mȳs* from Germanic]

mouse pad *noun* a flat pad across which a computer mouse is moved.

mouse·trap ● *noun* **1** a trap with bait for catching and usu. killing mice. **2** (often *attributive*) cheese of poor quality. ● *transitive verb* N Amer. entice (a person) to destruction or defeat.

mousey *var. of* MOUSY.

mous·saka /muˈsɒkə/ *noun* a Greek and eastern Mediterranean baked dish of ground meat, eggplant, etc. with white sauce. [modern Greek or Turkish]

mousse /muːs/ ● *noun* **1 a** a dessert of whipped cream, eggs, etc., usu. flavoured with fruit or chocolate. **b** a meat or fish purée made with whipped cream etc. **2** a foamy preparation applied to the hair enabling it to be styled more easily. ● *transitive verb* apply mousse to (hair). □ **moussed** *adjective* [French, = moss, froth]

mousse·line /ˈmuːsliːn, muːˈsliːn/ *noun* **1** a muslin-like fabric of silk etc. **2 a** a soft light mousse. **b** hollandaise sauce made frothy with whipped cream or egg white. [French: see MUSLIN]

Mous·sorg·sky *see* MUSSORGSKY.

mous·tache /ˈmʌstaʃ, məˈstaʃ/ *noun* (also **mustache**) **1 a** the hair on the upper lip, esp. as left to grow by men. **b** something on the upper lip resembling this (*a milk moustache*). **2** a similar growth around the mouth of some animals. □ **mous·tached** *adjective* [French from Italian *mostaccio* from Greek *mustax -akos*]

moustache cup *noun* a cup with a partial cover to protect the moustache when drinking.

mous·tach·io *var. of* MUSTACHIO.

Mous·ter·ian /muːˈstiːrɪən/ *Archaeology* ● *adjective* of or relating to the main culture of the middle paleolithic period, associated with Neanderthal peoples and dated to *c.*80,000–35,000 BC. ● *noun* this culture. [French *moustiérien* from *Le Moustier* a cave in SW France, where remains were found]

mousy *adjective* (**mous·i·er**, **mous·i·est**) **1** of or like a mouse. **2** (of a person) shy or timid; ineffectual. **3** (esp. of hair) nondescript light brown. **4** dark grey with a yellow tinge. □ **mous·i·ly** *adverb* **mous·i·ness** *noun*

mouth ● *noun* /maʊθ/ (*pl.* **mouths** /maʊðz, maʊθs/) **1 a** an external opening in the head, through which most animals admit food and emit communicative sounds. **b** (in humans and some animals) the cavity behind it containing the means of biting and chewing and the vocal organs. **2 a** the opening of a container such as a bag or sack. **b** the opening of a cave, volcano, etc. **c** the muzzle of a gun. **3 a** the place where a river enters a sea or lake. **b** the expanse of water connecting a bay or harbour with a lake or the sea. **4** *informal* **a** talkativeness. **b** impudent talk; cheek. **c** boastful talk. **5** an individual regarded as needing sustenance (*an extra mouth to feed*). **6** a horse's readiness to feel and obey the pressure of the bit. ● *verb* /maʊð, maʊθ/ **1** *transitive & intransitive* utter or speak solemnly or with affectations; rant, declaim (*mouthing platitudes*). **2** *transitive* say (words) with movement of the mouth but no sound. **3** *transitive* utter very distinctly. **4** *intransitive* **a** move the lips silently. **b** grimace. **5** *transitive* take (food) in the mouth. **6** *transitive* touch with the mouth. **7** *transitive* train the mouth of (a horse). □ **have a big mouth** talk indiscreetly. **keep one's mouth shut** *informal* refrain from saying something inappropriate. **mouth off 1** (often foll. by *at*) talk insolently or disrespectfully. **2** talk loudly; express one's opinions forcefully. **put words into a person's mouth** inaccurately represent a person as having said something. **take the words out of a person's mouth** say what another was about to say. **watch one's mouth** be careful not to say something offensive. □ **mouthed** /maʊðd, maʊθd/ *adjective* (also in *combination*). **mouth·less** *adjective* [Old English *mūth*, from Germanic]

mouth-breath·er *noun* **1** a person who inhales through the mouth instead of the nose. **2** a stupid or inept person; an oaf.

mouth feel *noun* the sensation produced in the mouth by the texture of food, wine, etc., regardless of the taste.

mouth·ful *noun* (*pl.* **-fuls**) **1** a quantity, esp. of food, that fills or is in the mouth. **2** a small quantity. **3** a long or complicated word or phrase. □ **say a mouthful** N Amer. say something important.

mouth·guard *noun* a piece of esp. sports equipment protecting the mouth, teeth, etc.

mouth music *noun* an originally Gaelic style of singing without the utterance of distinct words.

mouth organ *noun* (also **mouth harp**) = HARMONICA.

mouth·part *noun* any of the (usu. paired) organs surrounding the mouth of an insect or other arthropod and adapted for feeding.

mouth·piece *noun* **1 a** the part of a musical instrument placed between or against the lips. **b** the part of a telephone for speaking into. **c** the part of a tobacco pipe placed between the lips. **2** any apparatus or part of one that fits into the mouth, e.g. of scuba equipment, a bridle, etc. **3 a** a person, organization, etc. that speaks for another or others. **b** *informal* a lawyer.

mouth-to-mouth *noun* a method of resuscitation in which a person breathes into a subject's lungs through the mouth (also *attributive*: *mouth-to-mouth resuscitation*).

mouth·wash *noun* a liquid antiseptic etc. for rinsing the mouth or gargling.

mouth-watering *adjective* **1** (of food etc.) having a delicious smell or appearance; appetizing. **2** tempting, alluring.

mouthy *adjective* (**mouth·i·er**, **mouth·i·est**) *informal* inclined to talk a lot, esp. in a cheeky way.

mov·able (also **moveable**) ● *adjective* **1** that can be moved. **2** *Law* (of property) of the nature of a chattel, as distinct from land or buildings. **3** (of a religious feast or festival) variable in date from year to year. ● *noun* **1** an article of furniture that may be removed from a house, as distinct from a fixture. **2** (in *pl.*) personal property. □ **mov·abil·ity** *noun*

movable-do *attributive adjective* applied to a system of sight-singing in which do is the keynote of any major scale (*compare* FIXED-DO).

movable feast *noun* **1** a religious feast day, e.g. Easter, that occurs on a different date each year. **2** a meal that is transported before consumption, e.g. a picnic.

move ● *verb* **1** *intransitive & transitive* **a** shift one's position or posture, or cause to do this. **b** change (*Russia moved toward a market economy; let's move the meeting to Wednesday*). **2** *transitive & intransitive* **a** put or keep in motion; rouse, stir. **b** maintain a fairly quick pace or tempo. **3** *intransitive* (often foll. by *about, around*, etc.) go or pass from place to place. **4** *intransitive* take action, esp. promptly (*moved to reduce unemployment*). **5** *intransitive* **a** (often foll. by *ahead*) make progress (*the project is moving fast; share prices moved ahead today*). **b** (foll. by *on*) advance, progress (*moved on to the quarter-finals*). **6** *intransitive* change (one's place of residence or work). **7 a** *intransitive* make a move in a board game. **b** *transitive* change the position of (a piece) in a board game. **8** *intransitive* (foll. by *in*) live or be socially active in (a specified place or group etc.) (*moves in the best circles*). **9** *transitive* affect (a person) with (usu. tender or sympathetic) emotion. **10** *transitive* (foll. by *to*) provoke (a person to laughter etc.). **11** *transitive* (foll. by *to, or to + infin.*) prompt or incline (a person to a feeling or action). **12** *transitive & intransitive* (cause to) change in attitude or opinion (*nothing can move me on this issue*). **13 a** *transitive* cause (the bowels) to be emptied. **b** *intransitive* (of the bowels) be emptied. **14** *transitive* (often foll. by *that* + clause) propose in a meeting, deliberative assembly, etc. **15** *intransitive* (foll. by *for*) make a formal request or application. **16 a** *intransitive* (of merchandise) be sold. **b** *transitive* sell. ● *noun* **1** the act or an instance of moving. **2** a change of house, business premises, etc. **3** a step taken to secure some action or effect; an initiative. **4 a** the changing of the position of a piece in a board game. **b** a player's turn to do this. **5** *Sport* a manoeuvre employed by a single player esp. to avoid or deceive an opponent. □ **get a move on** *informal* **1** hurry up. **2** make a start. **get moving** *informal* begin, leave, etc. quickly (*it's late - we'd better get moving*). **get something moving** *informal* cause something to make vigorous progress. **make a move** take action. **move along** (or **on**) change to a new position, esp. to avoid crowding, getting in the way, etc. **move away** go to live in another area. **move heaven and earth** *see* HEAVEN. **move house** esp. *Cdn & Brit.* transfer one's furniture, goods, etc. from one residence to another. **move in 1** take possession of a new house etc. **2** get into a position of influence, interference, etc. **3** (often foll. by *on*) get into a position of readiness or proximity (for an offensive action etc.). **move in with** start to share accommodation with (an existing resident). **move mountains** *see* MOUNTAIN. **move off** (esp. of a vehicle) to start a journey. **move on** move to another place, topic, job, etc. **move out 1** leave one's home; change one's place of residence. **2** leave a position, job, etc. **move over** adjust one's position to make room for another. **move up 1** improve one's position or condition, esp. in a career. **2** *Baseball* (of a baserunner) move to the next base. **on the move 1** progressing. **2** moving around. **put the move** (or **moves**) **on** make sexual advances toward. [Old French *moveir* from Latin *movēre mot-*]

move·able *var. of* MOVABLE.

move·ment *noun* **1 a** the act or an instance of moving or being moved. **b** an act of changing position, esp. as a planned and controlled act by armed forces (*large-scale troop movements*). **2** (usu. in *pl.*) a person's activities and whereabouts, esp. at a particular time. **3 a** a body of persons with a common object (*the peace movement*). **b** a campaign undertaken by such a body. **4** a direction of thought or opinion; a social trend (*the movement toward smoke-free public places*). **5** a change in amount. **6 a** the moving parts of a mechanism (esp. a clock or watch). **b** a particular group of these. **7** *Music* **a** a principal division of a longer musical work, self-sufficient in terms of key, tempo, structure, etc. **b** rhythmical or accentual character in music; tempo. **8** the progressive development of a poem, story, etc. **9** (of the bowels) the action of discharging feces. **10 a** an activity in a market for some commodity. **b** a rise or fall in price. **11** *Baseball* the deviation of a pitched ball from a straight trajectory.

mov·er *noun* **1** a person or thing that moves. **2** *N Amer.* a person or company that transports furniture etc. for clients changing residence or business location. **3** a person who makes a motion in a formal meeting etc. **4** (esp. in **movers and shakers**) a person who incites or instigates to action; an enterprising person.

mov·ie *noun* esp. *N Amer. informal* **1** a motion picture film. **2** (in *pl.*) the motion picture industry. **3** (also *pl.*) a showing of a motion picture film (*were at a movie; went to the movies*).

movie·goer *noun* esp. *N Amer.* a person who attends movies. □ **movie-going** *adjective*

movie·land *noun informal* the motion picture industry.

movie·maker *noun* esp. *N Amer.* a filmmaker. □ **movie·making** *noun*

movie theatre *noun* (also **movie house**) esp. *N Amer.* a theatre where motion picture films are shown.

mov·ing *adjective* **1** that moves or causes to move. **2** affecting with emotion. □ **mov·ing·ly** *adverb* (in sense 2).

moving picture *noun* = MOTION PICTURE.

moving sidewalk *noun* a structure like a conveyor belt for pedestrians.

moving target *noun* **1** a target that is in motion when aimed at. **2** a person, thing, or phenomenon that changes character so frequently as to be difficult to assess, deal with, etc.

mow[1] /moː/ *transitive verb* (*past participle* **mowed** or **mown**) **1** cut down (grass, hay, etc.) with a machine or scythe. **2** cut down the grass etc. of (a lawn) or the produce of (a field) by mowing. □ **mow down** kill or destroy randomly or in great numbers. □ **mow·er** *noun* [Old English *māwan* from Germanic, related to MEAD[2]]

mow[2] /mau/ *noun* **1** a pile or heap of hay, grain, etc. **2** a place in a barn where hay or straw is stored. [Old English *mūga*]

Mowat /ˈmoːwət/ **Far·ley** (b.1921), Canadian author. His publication list is wide-ranging in subject, though many of his books, including *A Whale for the Killing* (1972) and *Sea of Slaughter* (1984), deal with environmental and animal welfare issues.

moxa /ˈmɒksə/ *noun* a downy substance from the dried leaves of *Artemisia moxa* etc., burned on the skin in oriental medicine as a counterirritant. [Japanese *mogusa* from *moe kusa* burning herb]

moxi·bus·tion /ˌmɒksɪˈbʌstʃən/ *noun* the burning of moxa on or near the skin. [MOXA + COMBUSTION]

moxie /ˈmɒksi/ *noun N Amer. slang* force of character, energy, ingenuity. [proprietary name of a soft drink]

Mo·zam·bique /ˌmoʊzamˈbiːk/ a country on the east coast of southern Africa; pop. (est. 2002) 19,607,519; capital, Maputo. □ **Mo·zam·bi·can** *adjective & noun*

Mozambique Channel an arm of the Indian Ocean separating the eastern coast of mainland Africa from the island of Madagascar.

Moz·art /ˈmoːtsɑrt/ **(Jo·hann Chrys·os·tom) Wolf·gang Ama·deus** (1756–91), Austrian composer. A child prodigy as a harpsichordist, pianist, and composer, he came to epitomize classical music in its purity of form and melody; his works include operas, symphonies, piano concertos, string quartets, and the unfinished *Requiem* (1791). □ **Moz·art·ian** /moːˈtsɑrˌtiən/ *adjective* (also **Moz·art·ean**).

moz·za·rella /ˌmɒtsəˈrelə, ˌmʌt-/ *noun* a white Italian cheese originally made of buffalo milk. [Italian, diminutive of *mozza*, a kind of cheese, from *mozzare*, 'cut off']

MP *abbreviation* **1** Member of Parliament. **2 a** military police. **b** military policeman.

MP3 *noun* a digital audio compression format which, by limiting bandwidth and exploiting stereo effects, reduces sound data by a factor of 12 without sacrificing humanly audible sound quality, much used in music files to be downloaded over the Internet. [from the filename extension *.mp3* used for such files, derived from the name of the Moving Picture Experts Group, the name of the committee who devised the standard]

mp *abbreviation* mezzo-piano.

m.p. *abbreviation* melting point.

M.P.A. *abbreviation* Master of Public Administration.

MPD *abbreviation* multiple personality disorder.

M.P.E. *abbreviation* Master of Physical Education.

mpg *abbreviation* miles per gallon.

mph *abbreviation* miles per hour.

M.Phil. *abbreviation* Master of Philosophy.

M.P.M. *abbreviation* Master of Public Management.

MPP *abbreviation Cdn* (Ont.) Member of Provincial Parliament.

Mpuma·langa /mˌpuːməˈlaŋgə/ a province of NE South Africa, formerly called Eastern Transvaal; capital, Nelspruit.

MPV *abbreviation* multi-purpose vehicle, a minivan.

Mr. /ˈmɪstər/ *noun* (*pl.* **Messrs.**) **1** a title prefixed to the name of a man not having a higher, honorific, or professional title (*Mr. Hubert*). **2** a title prefixed to a designation of office etc. (*Mr. President; Mr. Speaker*).

3 a title prefixed to a characteristic of a certain man (*Mr. Nice Guy*). [abbreviation of MISTER¹]

MRC *abbreviation* **1** *Cdn* (in Quebec) *Municipalité Régionale de Comté.* **2** (in the UK) Medical Research Council.

M.R.E. *abbreviation* Master of Religious Education.

MRI *abbreviation* MAGNETIC RESONANCE IMAGING.

mRNA *abbreviation Biol.* messenger RNA.

Mr. Right *noun jocular* the man who would make the ideal husband for a particular woman.

Mrs. /ˈmɪsɪz/ *noun* (*pl.* same or **Mes·dames**) a title prefixed to the name of a married woman not having a higher, honorific, or professional title (*Mrs. Hubert*). [abbreviation of MISTRESS: compare MISSIS]

MS *abbreviation* **1** manuscript. **2** Mississippi (in official postal use). **3** MULTIPLE SCLEROSIS. **4** *Cdn* MASTER SEAMAN. **5** *US* motor ship.

M.S. *abbreviation* **1** Master of Science. **2** Master of Surgery.

Ms. /mɪz, məz/ *noun* a title prefixed to the name of a woman regardless of her marital status. [combination of Mrs., MISS²]

ms *abbreviation* millisecond(s).

M.Sc. *abbreviation* Master of Science.

M.Sc.F. *abbreviation* Master of Science in Forestry.

MS-DOS /ˌeməsˈdɒs/ *noun proprietary* an operating system for personal computers. [abbreviation of Microsoft disk operating system]

MSG *abbreviation* MONOSODIUM GLUTAMATE.

Msgr. *abbreviation* **1** Monseigneur. **2** Monsignor.

MSRP *abbreviation* manufacturer's suggested retail price.

MSS /emˈesɪz/ *abbreviation* manuscripts.

MST *abbreviation* MOUNTAIN STANDARD TIME.

M.S.W. *abbreviation* Master of Social Work.

MT *abbreviation* **1** Montana (in official postal use). **2** MOUNTAIN TIME.

Mt. *abbreviation* **1** Mount (*Mt. Logan*). **2** Mountain.

MTB *abbreviation* **1** motor torpedo boat. **2** mountain bike.

MTBF *abbreviation esp. Computing* mean time between failures.

M.Th. *abbreviation* Master of Theology.

Mtl. *abbreviation* Montreal.

M.T.S. *abbreviation* Master of Theological Studies.

mu /mju:/ *noun* **1** the twelfth Greek letter (M, μ). **2** (μ, as a symbol) = MICRO- 2. [Greek]

Mu·bar·ak /mu:ˈbarak/ (**Muham·mad**) **Hosni (Said)** (b.1928), Egyptian leader, president since 1981. Although he attempted to ally Egypt more closely with the other Arab nations, he risked division by aligning Egypt against Saddam Hussein in the Gulf war of 1991; after the resurgence of militant Islamic fundamentalism in Egypt in 1992, his government adopted harsh measures to suppress activists.

MUC *abbreviation* Montreal Urban Community.

much ● *adjective* **1** existing or occurring in a great quantity (*much trouble; not much rain; too much noise*). **2** (prec. by *as, how, that,* etc.) with relative rather than distinctive sense (*I don't know how much money you want*). ● *noun* **1** a great quantity (*much of that is true*). **2** (prec. by *as, how, that,* etc.) with relative rather than distinctive sense (*we do not need that much*). **3** (usu. in *neg.*) a noteworthy or outstanding example (*not much to look at; not much of a party*). ● *adverb* **1 a** in a great degree (*much to my surprise; is much the same*). **b** (qualifying a verb or past participle) greatly (*they much regret the mistake; I was much annoyed*). **c** qualifying a comparative or superlative adjective (*much better; much the most likely*). **2** for a large part of one's time (*is much away from home*). ● *interjection informal* expressing strong disagreement. □ **as much** the extent or quantity just specified; the idea just mentioned (*I thought as much; as much as that?*). **a bit much** *informal* somewhat excessive or immoderate. **make much of** *see* MAKE. **much as** even though (*cannot come, much as I would like to*). **much less** *see* LESS. **much obliged** *see* OBLIGE. **too much** *informal* an intolerable situation etc. (*that really is too much*). **too much for 1** more than a match for. **2** beyond what is endurable by. □ **much·ly** *adverb jocular*. [Middle English from *muchel* MICKLE: for loss of *el* compare BAD, WENCH]

Mu·chin·ga Mountains /mu:ˈtʃɪŋɡə/ a range of mountains in E Zambia.

much·ness *noun* greatness in quantity or degree. □ (**much**) **of a muchness** very nearly the same or alike.

mucho /ˈmu:tʃo/ *adjective & adverb jocular* much. [Spanish]

mucho di·nero /ˈmu:tʃo di:ˈnero/ *noun slang* much money. [Spanish]

muci·lage /ˈmju:sɪlɪdʒ/ *noun* **1** a solution of gum or glue in water, used as an adhesive. **2** a viscous or gelatinous solution obtained from plant roots, seeds, etc., used in medicines and adhesives. **3** any viscous or gummy solution or secretion, e.g. mucus. □ **muci·la·gin·ous** /-ˈlædʒɪnəs/ *adjective* [French from Late Latin *mucilago -ginis* musty juice (MUCUS)]

muck ● *noun* **1** mud. **2** very dark and highly organic soil. **3** *informal* dirt or filth; anything disgusting. **4** farmyard manure. **5** *informal* an untidy state; a mess. **6** waste material removed during mining or civil engineering operations. ● *verb* **1** *transitive* (usu. foll. by *up*) *informal* ruin, spoil, mess up. **2** *transitive* make dirty. **3** *transitive* manure with muck. **4** *intransitive* (in hockey) play tenaciously and physically, esp. along the boards in an attempt to gain control of the puck. □ **muck about** (or **around**) *informal* **1** putter or fool about. **2** (foll. by *with*) fool or interfere with. **muck in** *Brit.* (often foll. by *with*) share tasks etc. equally. **muck out** clean (a barn etc.) of manure. [Middle English *muk* prob. from Scandinavian: compare Old Norse *myki* dung, related to MEEK]

muck·a·muck /ˈmʌkə,mʌk/ (also **muckety-muck** /ˈmʌkəti,mʌk/) *var. of* MUCKY-MUCK.

muck·er *noun slang* **1** a person or machine that removes mining waste. **2** *N Amer.* a person, esp. a hockey player, known more for tenacity and hard work than for remarkable talent; a grinder, a digger. **3** *Brit.* a friend or companion.

muckle *var. of* MICKLE.

muck·rake *intransitive verb* search out and reveal scandal, esp. among famous people. □ **muck·rak·er** *noun* **muck·rak·ing** *noun*

mucky *adjective* (**muck·i·er**, **muck·i·est**) **1** covered with muck. **2** dirty. □ **muck·i·ness** *noun*

mucky-muck /ˈmʌki,mʌk/ *noun N Amer. slang* a person of great self-importance. [Chinook *muckamuck*, = 'food']

muco- /ˈmju:ko:/ *combining form Biochem.* mucus, mucous.

muco·poly·sac·char·ide /ˌmju:ko:ˌpɒlɪˈsakə,raid/ *noun* any of a group of polysaccharides whose molecules contain sugar residues and are often found as components of connective tissue.

mu·cosa /mju:ˈko:sə/ *noun* (*pl.* **mu·co·sae** /-si:/) a mucous membrane. □ **mu·co·sal** *adjective* (modern Latin, fem. of *mucosus*: see MUCOUS)

mu·cous /ˈmju:kəs/ *adjective* of, resembling, secreting, or covered with mucus. □ **mu·cos·ity** /-ˈkɒsɪti/ *noun* [Latin *mucosus* (as MUCUS)]

mucous membrane *noun* a mucus-secreting epithelial tissue lining many body cavities and tubular organs.

mucro /ˈmju:kro:/ *noun* (*pl.* **mu·cro·nes** /-ˈkro:ni:z/) *Bot. & Zool.* a sharp-pointed part or organ. [Latin *mucro -onis* sharp point]

mucus /ˈmju:kəs/ *noun* **1** a slimy substance, usu. not miscible with water, secreted by a mucous membrane or gland. **2** a gummy substance found in plants. [Latin]

mud *noun* **1** wet soft earthy matter. **2** hard ground from the drying of an area of this. □ **as clear as mud** *informal* not at all clear. **drag through the mud** denigrate publicly. **fling** (or **sling** or **throw**) **mud** speak disparagingly or slanderously. **here's mud in your eye!** *informal* a drinking toast. **one's name is mud** one is unpopular or in disgrace. [prob. from Middle Low German *mudde*]

mud·bank *noun* a bank of mud, esp. on the bed of a river or the bottom of the sea.

mud bath *noun* **1** a bath in the mud of mineral springs, esp. to relieve rheumatism etc. **2** a muddy scene or occasion.

mud brick *noun* a brick made from baked mud (also *attributive*: *mud-brick huts*).

mud·cat *noun* **1** *Cdn* = BULLHEAD 1. **2** *N Amer.* a large N American catfish, *Pylodictis olivaris*, with a long slender body and a flat head.

mud·dle ● *verb* **1** *transitive* (often foll. by *up*) bring into disorder. **2** *transitive* bewilder, confuse. **3** *transitive* mismanage (an affair). **4** *intransitive* (often foll. by *with*) busy oneself in a confused and ineffective way. **5** *transitive US* crush and mix (the ingredients for a drink). ● *noun* **1** a state of disorder. **2** mental confusion. □ **make a muddle of 1** bring into disorder. **2** bungle. **muddle along** (or **on**) progress in a haphazard way. **muddle through** succeed by perseverance rather than skill or efficiency. □ **mud·dler** *noun* **mud·dling·ly** *adverb* [perhaps from Middle Dutch *moddelen*, frequentative of *modden* dabble in mud]

muddle-headed *adjective* stupid, confused. □ **muddle-headed·ness** *noun*

mud·dler *noun N Amer.* a type of fly used in trout fishing.

muddy ● *adjective* (**mud·di·er**, **mud·di·est**) **1** like mud. **2** covered in or full of mud. **3** (of liquid) turbid. **4** mentally confused. **5** obscure. **6** (of light) dull. **7** (of colour) impure. ● *transitive verb* (**-dies**, **-died**) make muddy. □ **muddy the waters** confuse matters. □ **mud·di·ly** *adverb* **mud·di·ness** *noun*

Mu·dé·jar /muːˈðeihɑr/ ● *noun* (pl. **Mu·dé·jar·es** /-hɑres/) a subject Muslim during the Christian reconquest of the Iberian peninsula from the Moors (11th–15th c.) who until 1492 was allowed to retain Islamic laws and religion in return for loyalty to a Christian monarch. ● *adjective* of or relating to a style of architecture and decorative art of the 12th–15th c. produced by Mudéjares. The style combines Islamic and Gothic elements; examples can be seen in the churches and palaces of the Spanish cities Toledo, Cordoba, Seville, and Valencia. [Spanish from Arabic *mudajjan* permitted to remain]

mud·fish *noun* any fish that burrows in mud.

mud flap *noun* a flap hanging behind the wheel of a vehicle, to catch mud and stones etc. thrown up from the road.

mud flat *noun* a stretch of muddy land left uncovered at low tide.

mud·flow *noun* **1** a fluid or hardened stream or avalanche of mud. **2** the flow or motion of such a stream.

mud·guard *noun* a curved strip or cover over a wheel of a bicycle, motorcycle, etc. to reduce the amount of mud etc. thrown up from the road.

mud·hole *noun* **1** a water hole dried so as to become mud. **2** a muddy hole in a road.

mud·pack *noun* a cosmetic paste applied thickly to the face.

mud pie *noun* **1** mud made into a pie shape by a child. **2** *N Amer.* a rich chocolate ice cream pie.

mud puppy *noun* a large nocturnal salamander, *Necturus maculosus*, of central N America.

mud room *noun N Amer.* a small room, often a vestibule, in a house, in which wet or muddy footwear and outer clothes are removed.

mud skipper *noun* any of various gobies of the family Periophthalmidae, able to leave the water and leap on the mud.

mud·slide *noun* an avalanche of mud etc.

mud·sling·ing *noun informal* abuse, slander, or malevolent criticism. □ **mud·sling·er** *noun*

mud·stone *noun* a dark clay rock.

mud trout *noun* (Cdn (*Nfld*) the eastern brook trout, *Salvelinus fontinalis*.

mud wrestling *noun* an activity in which usu. female contestants wrestle in a mud-filled ring for the amusement of spectators. □ **mud-wrestle** *transitive & intransitive verb* **mud wrestler** *noun*

Muen·ster /ˈmʊnstər/ *noun* a fairly strong soft-ripened cheese, having a washed rind cured in a solution of brine or seasoned wine or beer. [*Munster* in Alsace, France]

muesli /ˈmjuːzli/ *noun* a breakfast food of crushed cereals (usu. oats), dried fruits, nuts, etc., eaten with milk. [Swiss German]

muez·zin /muːˈezɪn/ *noun* a Muslim crier who proclaims the hours of prayer usu. from a minaret. [Arabic *mu'addin* part. of *'addana* proclaim]

muff[1] *noun* a fur or other covering, usu. in the form of a tube with an opening at each end for the hands to be inserted for warmth. **2** = EARMUFF. [Dutch *mof*, Middle Dutch *moffel*, *muffel* from medieval Latin *muff(u)la*, of unknown origin]

muff[2] ● *transitive verb* **1** bungle; deal clumsily with. **2** fail to catch or receive (a ball etc.). **3** blunder in (a theatrical part etc.). ● *noun* **1** esp. *Brit.* a person who is awkward or stupid, originally in some athletic sport. **2** a failure, esp. to catch a ball. [19th c.: origin unknown]

muf·fin *noun* **1** *N Amer.* a quick bread made of flour, milk, eggs, and fat, often also with oats or bran, etc., leavened with baking powder or baking soda, and baked in a small cup-shaped pan. **2** *Brit.* = ENGLISH MUFFIN. [18th c.: origin unknown]

muffin tin *noun N Amer.* a baking pan having a series of small round wells, for cooking muffins.

muf·fle[1] ● *transitive verb* **1** (often foll. by *up*) wrap or cover for warmth. **2** cover or wrap up (a source of sound) to reduce its loudness. **3** (usu. as **muf·fled** *adjective*) stifle (an utterance, e.g. a curse). **4** prevent from speaking. ● *noun* **1** a receptacle in a furnace where substances may be heated without contact with combustion products. **2** a similar chamber in a kiln for baking painted pottery. **3** muffled sound. [Middle English: (n.) from Old French *moufle* thick glove; (v.) perhaps from Old French *enmoufler* from *moufle*]

muf·fle[2] *noun* the thick part of the upper lip and nose of ruminants and rodents. [French *mufle*, of unknown origin]

muf·fler *noun* **1** *N Amer.* a device attached to a motor vehicle's exhaust system to reduce noise. **2** a scarf worn for warmth. **3** any of various devices used to deaden sound in musical instruments.

muf·ti[1] /ˈmʌfti/ *noun* a Muslim legal expert empowered to give rulings on religious matters. [Arabic *muftī*, part. of *'aftā* decide a point of law]

muf·ti[2] *noun* plain clothes worn by a person who also wears (esp. military) uniform (*in mufti*). [19th c.: perhaps from MUFTI[1]]

mug[1] ● *noun* **1 a** a drinking vessel, usu. cylindrical and with a handle and used without a saucer. **b** its contents. **2** *slang* the face or mouth of a person. **3** *Brit. slang* **a** a simpleton. **b** a gullible person. **4** *US slang* a hoodlum or thug. ● *verb* (**mugged**, **mug·ging**) **1** *transitive* rob (a person) with violence esp. in a public place. **2** *intransitive slang* make faces, esp. before an audience, camera, etc. □ **a mug's game** *informal* a foolish or unprofitable activity. □ **mug·ful** *noun* (pl. **-fuls**)

mug·ging *noun* (in sense 1 of *verb*). [prob. from Scandinavian: sense 2 of *n.* prob. from the representation of faces on mugs, and sense 3 prob. from this]

mug[2] *transitive verb* (**mugged**, **mug·ging**) esp. *Brit. slang* (usu. foll. by *up*) learn (a subject) by concentrated study. [19th c.: origin unknown]

Mu·gabe /muˈɡɒbi/ **Rob·ert (Gab·riel)** (b.1924), Zimbabwean leader, prime minister 1980–7, president since 1987. He became Prime Minister in Zimbabwe's first post-independence elections. In 1987 his party ZANU merged with ZAPU and he became executive President of a one-party state.

mug·ger[1] *noun* a person who robs people violently, esp. in public.

mug·ger[2] *noun* a broad-nosed Indian crocodile, *Crocodylus palustris*, venerated by many Hindus. [Hindi *magar*]

mug·gins *noun* (pl. same or **mug·gins·es**) *Brit. informal* **1** a simpleton. **2** a person who is easily outwitted (often with allusion to oneself: *so muggins had to pay*). [perhaps the surname *Muggins*, with allusion to MUG[1]]

muggy *adjective* (**mug·gi·er**, **mug·gi·est**) (of the weather, a day, etc.) oppressively damp and warm; humid. □ **mug·gi·ness** *noun* [dial. *mug* mist, drizzle, from Old Norse *mugga*]

Mu·ghal /ˈmuːɡɒl/ *noun* **1** a Mongolian. **2** (*attributive*) denoting the Muslim dynasty in India in the 16th–19th c. (*compare* MOGUL[1] 2b). [Persian *mugūl* MONGOL]

mugho pine /mjuːɡoː, muː-/ *noun* (also **mugo pine**) a dwarf pine, *Pinus mugo*, of the mountains of central and southern Europe, much used in landscaping. [French *mugho* from Italian *mugo*]

mug shot *noun slang* a photograph of a face, esp. for official purposes.

mug-up *noun Cdn* (esp. *Nfld*) a break for a hot drink (esp. tea) and snacks, esp. while on a hike, journey, etc.

mug·wort /ˈmʌɡwɔːt, -wɔrt/ *noun* any of various plants of the genus *Artemisia*, esp. *A. vulgaris*, with silver-grey aromatic foliage. [Old English *mucgwyrt* (as MIDGE, WORT)]

mug·wump /ˈmʌɡwʌmp/ *noun* esp. *N Amer.* **1** *jocular* a great man; a boss. **2** a person who holds aloof, esp. from party politics; an independent politician. [Algonquian *muggquomp* great chief]

Muham·mad /məˈhɒməd, -ˈhaməd/ (also **Mo·ham·med**) (c.570–632), Arab prophet and founder of Islam. Born in Mecca, he began his teaching after visions in which he received from God the words of the Quran. Rejected and exiled from Mecca, he later returned to begin the conversion of the Arabian peninsula to Islam. He replaced the tribal and pagan society with a new social and monotheistic religious structure. Muslims call him the Prophet, last in the line of Abraham, Moses, and Jesus.

Muhammad II /moːˈhaməd/ (also **Mohammed II**) (1432–81), Ottoman sultan of Turkey 1451–81, who captured Constantinople (1453), thereby uniting the European and Asian parts of the Ottoman Empire.

Muhammad Ali /məˌhɒməd ɒˈliː, -ˌhaməd-/ **1** (also **Mehemet Ali**, **Mohammed Ali**) (1769–1849), Ottoman viceroy and pasha of Egypt 1805–49, possibly of Albanian descent. He modernized Egypt's infrastructure, making it the leading power in the eastern Mediterranean, and established a dynasty that survived until 1952. **2** (born Cassius Marcellus Clay) (b.1942), US boxer. He first won the world heavyweight title in 1964 and regained it in 1974 and 1978, becoming the only boxer to be world champion three times.

mu·ja·he·deen /ˌmuːdʒəhəˈdiːn/ *plural noun* (also **mu·ja·hi·deen**, **-din**) guerrilla fighters in Islamic countries, esp. supporting Muslim fundamentalism. [Persian & Arabic *mujāhidīn* pl. of *mujāhid* one who fights a jihad]

Mukh·er·jee /ˈmʊkərdʒi/ **Bhar·ati** (b.1940), Indian-born Canadian novelist and short-story writer. She emigrated to the US and then to Canada (1966). Her first novel, *The Tiger's Daughter* (1972), deals with the cultural tension of her East Indian characters both in Canada and in India. She returned to the US in 1980, citing increasing racial intolerance in Canada, esp. of East Indian women.

muk·luk /ˈmʌklʌk/ *noun N Amer.* **1** a winter boot with a heavy rubber sole and a high fabric upper, usu. with laces. **2** a traditional Inuit boot, usu. made from seal or caribou skin. [Yupik *maklak* bearded seal]

muk·tuk *noun* a traditional Inuit food consisting of the skin and surface blubber of a whale, esp. a beluga or narwhal, either dried, cooked, or eaten raw. [Inuit]

mu·lat·to /məˈlatoː, -ˈlɒtoː, mjuː-/ *noun* (*pl.* **-toes** or **-tos**) a person of mixed white and black parentage. [Spanish *mulato* young mule or mulatto, irreg. from *mulo* MULE¹]

mul·berry /ˈmʌlˌberi, ˈmʌlbəri/ ● *noun* (*pl.* **-berries**) **1** (also **mulberry tree** or **mulberry bush**) any deciduous tree of the genus *Morus* (family Moraceae), esp. *M. alba* (**white mulberry**), grown originally for feeding silkworms, and *M. rubra* of eastern N America (**red mulberry**), with juicy edible fruit. **2** the dark red or white berry of such a tree. **3** a dark red or purple colour. ● *adjective* of this colour. [Middle English *mol-, mool-, mulberry*, with dissimilation from *murberie* from Old English *mōrberie*, from Latin *morum*: see BERRY]

mulch ● *noun* a mixture usu. of vegetable matter spread around or over a plant to enrich or insulate the soil or suppress weeds. ● *transitive verb* treat with mulch. [prob. used as noun of *mulsh* soft: compare dial. *melsh* mild, from Old English *melsc*]

mulch·ing mower *noun* a lawn mower which converts the clippings into mulch for the lawn.

mulct /mʌlkt/ *transitive verb* **1** extract money from by fine or taxation. **2 a** (often foll. by *of*) deprive by fraudulent means; swindle. **b** obtain by swindling. [French *mulcter* from Latin *mulctare*]

mule¹ *noun* **1** the offspring (usu. sterile) of a male donkey and a female horse, or (in general use) of a female donkey and a male horse (compare HINNY¹), used as a beast of burden. **2** a stupid or obstinate person. **3** (often *attributive*) a hybrid and usu. sterile plant or animal (*mule canary*). **4** esp. *N Amer. slang* a person acting as a courier for illicit drugs. **5** (in full **spinning mule**) a kind of spinning machine producing yarn on spindles. [Old French *mul(e)* from Latin *mulus mula*]

mule² *noun* a light shoe or slipper without a back. [French, = 'slipper', 'a chilblain on the heel']

mule deer *noun* a long-eared black-tailed deer of prairies and mountains of western N America, *Odocoileus hemionus.* [MULE¹]

mule skinner *noun* N Amer. hist. a muleteer.

mule·teer /ˌmjuːlɪˈtɪːr/ *noun* a mule driver. [French *muletier* from *mulet* diminutive of Old French *mul* MULE¹]

muley *noun* (also **mulie**) N Amer. informal = MULE DEER. [abbreviation]

Mul·ha·cén /ˌmuːləˈsen/ a mountain in S Spain, southeast of Granada, in the Sierra Nevada range. Rising to 3 482 m (11,424 ft.), it is the highest mountain in the country.

Mül·heim /ˈmuːlhaɪm/ (in full **Mülheim an der Ruhr** /an der ˈrʊr/) an industrial city in western Germany, in North Rhine-Westphalia southwest of Essen; pop. (est. 2002) 174,000.

mul·ish *adjective* **1** like a mule. **2** stubborn. □ **mul·ish·ly** *adverb* **mul·ish·ness** *noun*

Mull /mʌl/ an island of the Inner Hebrides, off the west coast of Scotland; chief town, Tobermory. It is separated from the mainland by the Sound of Mull.

mull¹ *transitive & intransitive verb* (often foll. by *over*) ponder or consider. [perhaps from *mull* grind to powder, Middle English *mul* dust, from Middle Dutch]

mull² *transitive verb* (esp. as **mulled** *adjective*) warm (wine or beer) with added sugar, spices, etc. [17th c.: origin unknown]

mull³ *noun* Scot. a promontory. [Middle English: compare Gaelic *maol*, Icelandic *múli*]

mull⁴ *noun* a thin soft plain muslin, used in bookbinding for joining the spine of a book to its cover. [abbreviation of *mulmull* from Hindi *malmal*]

mull⁵ *noun* humus formed under non-acid conditions. [Danish *muld* 'soil']

mul·lah /ˈmʌlə, ˈmʊlə/ *noun* a Muslim learned in Islamic theology and sacred law. [Persian, Turkish, Urdu *mullā* from Arabic *mawlā*]

mul·lein /ˈmʌlən/ *noun* any herbaceous plant of the genus *Verbascum*, with woolly leaves and yellow flowers. [Old French *moleine* from Gaulish]

Mul·ler /ˈmʌlər/ **Her·mann Jo·seph** (1890–1967), US geneticist, who discovered that X-rays could induce mutations in the genetic material of living cells; he was awarded a Nobel Prize in 1946.

Mül·ler /ˈmʊlər/ **1** (**Frie·drich) Max** (1823–1900), German-born English philologist. He published an edition of the Sanskrit *Rig-Veda* (1849–75) and promoted the comparative study of Indo-European

languages, as well as exploring comparative mythology and religion. **2 Jo·hann**, see REGIOMONTANUS. **3 Jo·han·nes Peter** (1801–58), German anatomist and zoologist. A pioneer of comparative and microscopical methods in biology, he investigated respiration in the fetus, the nervous and sensory systems, the glandular system, and locomotion. **4 Paul Her·mann** (1899–1965), Swiss chemist. He synthesized DDT in 1939 and soon patented it as an insecticide; he was awarded a Nobel Prize in 1948.

mul·ler /ˈmʌlər/ *noun* a stone or other heavy weight used for grinding material on a slab. [Middle English, perhaps from Anglo-French *moldre* grind]

mul·let¹ /ˈmʌlət/ *noun* any fish of the family Mullidae (**red mullet**) or Mugilidae (**grey mullet**), usu. with a thick body and a large blunt-nosed head, commonly used as food. [Old French *mulet* diminutive of Latin *mullus* red mullet, from Greek *mollos*]

mul·let² *noun* a hairstyle, worn esp. by men, in which the hair is cut short at the front and sides, and left long at the back. [origin unknown]

mul·li·gan /ˈmʌlɪɡən/ *noun* (in full **mulligan stew**) N Amer. a stew made from odds and ends of food. [apparently from the surname *Mulligan*]

mul·li·ga·taw·ny /ˌmʌlɪɡəˈtɔːni/ *noun* a highly seasoned soup originally from India. [Tamil *milagutannir*, lit. 'pepper water']

mul·lion /ˈmʌljən/ *noun* a vertical bar dividing the panes of glass in a window (compare TRANSOM 1). □ **mul·lioned** *adjective* [prob. an altered form of Middle English *monial*, from Old French *moinel* middle, from *moien* MEAN³]

Mul·ro·ney /mʌlˈruːni/ (**Mar·tin) Brian** (b.1939), Canadian Progressive Conservative politician, prime minister 1984–93. After becoming leader of the Progressive Conservative Party in 1983, he won a landslide victory in the 1984 election. He was re-elected in 1988 on a platform of free trade with the US, but resigned in 1993.

Mul·tan /mʊlˈtɒn/ a commercial city in Punjab province, east central Pakistan; pop. (1998) 1,182,400.

multi- *combining form* many; more than one. [Latin from *multus* much, many]

multi·axial *adjective* of or involving several axes.

multi·billion *attributive adjective* costing or involving several billion (dollars, pounds, etc.) (*multi-billion dollar lawsuits*).

multi·cellu·lar *adjective* Biol. having or involving many cells. □ **multi·cellu·lar·ity** *noun*

multi-channel *adjective* employing or possessing many communication or television channels.

multi·col·oured *adjective* (also **multi·colour**) of many colours.

multi·cult *adjective* Cdn informal = MULTICULTURAL.

multi·culti *adjective* informal = MULTICULTURAL.

multi·cul·tur·al *adjective* **1** designating or pertaining to a society consisting of many culturally distinct groups. **2 a** (of a person etc.) advocating or receptive to the establishment of a multicultural society. **b** (of a group etc.) consisting of individuals from various, culturally distinct groups. □ **multi·cul·tur·al·ism** *noun* **multi·cul·tur·al·ist** *noun & adjective* **multi·cul·tur·al·ly** *adverb*

multi-dimension·al *adjective* of or involving more than three dimensions. □ **multi-dimension·al·ity** *noun*

multi·direc·tion·al *adjective* of, involving, or operating in several directions.

multi·disci·plin·ary *adjective* combining or involving many separate disciplines or fields of endeavour.

multi-ethnic *adjective* composed of or involving several ethnic groups.

multi·faceted *adjective* having several facets, aspects, etc.

multi·factor·ial *adjective* involving or dependent on a number of factors, esp. genes or causes.

multi·family *adjective* (esp. of housing) designed for or occupied by more than one family.

multi·far·ious /ˌmʌltɪˈferiəs/ *adjective* **1** (foll. by pl. noun) many and various. **2** having great variety or diversity. □ **multi·far·ious·ly** *adverb* **multi·far·ious·ness** *noun* [Latin *multifarius*]

multi·flora *noun* (also **multiflora rose**) a rose, *Rosa multiflora*, with clusters of small, fragrant flowers. [Late Latin, fem. of *multiflorus*, as MULTI- + *flor-, flos*, flower]

multi·focal *adjective* having or pertaining to several foci, or a range of focal lengths.

multi·form *noun* (usu. *attributive*) **1** having many forms. **2** of many kinds.

multi-function *adjective* (also **multi-functional**) having or fulfilling several functions.

multi-genera·tion·al *adjective* **1** (of a family or other group) including more than two generations. **2** lasting over several generations (*multi-generational poverty*).

multi·grade *noun* (usu. *attributive*) **1** an engine oil, paper, etc. meeting the requirements of several standard grades. **2** *N Amer.* (of a class or classroom) having students from more than one academic year studying together.

multi·grain *adjective* (of baked goods, cereals, etc.) incorporating many grains.

multi·hull *noun* a boat having more than one hull.

multi·lane *adjective* (of a road) having many lanes, usu. more than two in each direction.

multi·lat·eral *adjective* **1 a** (of an agreement, treaty, conference, etc.) in which three or more parties participate. **b** performed by more than one party (*multilateral disarmament*). **2** having many sides. □ **multi·lat·eral·ism** *noun* **multi·lat·eral·ist** *noun & adjective* **multi·lat·eral·ly** *adverb*

multi·layered *adjective* (also **multi-layer**) composed of, occurring in, or having many layers.

multi·level *adjective* **1** having, involving, or operating on many levels. **2** designating a method of direct selling in which buyers at each level of a hierarchy secure the participation of further buyers at a level below them. □ **multi-levelled** *adjective*

multi·lin·gual *adjective* **1** in or using several languages. **2** (of a person) speaking several languages fluently. □ **multi·lin·gual·ism** *noun*

multi·media ● *attributive adjective* (of art, education, etc.) using more than one medium of expression, communication, etc. ● *noun* an extension of hypertext allowing the provision of audio and video material cross-referenced to a computer text (also *attributive*: *multimedia applications*). *Also called* HYPERMEDIA.

multi·meter *noun* an instrument designed to measure voltage, current, and usu. resistance, often over several different ranges of value.

multi·million *attributive adjective* costing or involving several million (dollars, pounds, etc.) (*multi-million dollar fraud*).

multi·million·aire *noun* a person with a fortune of several million dollars, pounds, etc.

multi·nation·al ● *adjective* **1** (of a business organization) operating in several countries. **2** relating to or including several nationalities or ethnic groups. ● *noun* a multinational company.

multi·nom·ial /ˌmʌltiˈnoːmiəl/ *adjective & noun Math.* = POLYNOMIAL. [MULTI-, after *binomial*]

multi·pack *noun* a composite package containing several units of a product, sold at a lower price than the equivalent number of units sold separately.

mul·tip·ar·ous /mʌlˈtɪpɜrəs/ *adjective* **1** bringing forth many young at a birth. **2** having borne more than one child. [MULTI- + -PAROUS]

multi·part·ite /ˌmʌltiˈpɑrtəit/ *adjective* divided into many parts.

multi·party *attributive adjective* **1 a** comprising members of several esp. political parties (*multi-party talks*). **b** sponsored by or involving more than one person, interest group, etc. (*multi-party lawsuit*). **2** designating or pertaining to an electoral system in which the interests of the electorate are represented by three or more political parties. □ **multi-party·ism** *noun*

mul·tiple ● *adjective* **1** having many parts, elements, or individual components. **2** (foll. by pl. noun) many and various. **3** *Med.* (of a disease or symptom) affecting several parts, organs, etc. ● *noun* **1** a number that may be divided by another a certain number of times without a remainder (*56 is a multiple of 7*). **2** *Business* a number expressing the current market price of a company share divided by the earnings per share of the company. **3** an inexpensive work of art able to be mass-produced by industrial methods. □ **multi·ply** *adverb* [French from Late Latin *multiplus* from Latin (as MULTIPLEX)]

multiple-choice *adjective* **1** (of a question in an examination) accompanied by several possible answers from which the correct one is to be chosen. **2** (of a test, questionnaire, etc.) consisting of multiple-choice questions.

multiple exposure *noun* **1** the exposure of the same frame of film more than once. **2** a multiple image resulting from this.

Multiple Listing Service *noun N Amer. proprietary* a co-operative real estate market system in which the seller signs an agreement with one vendor and broker allowing other brokers to sell the property for part of the agreed upon commission, to create a broader market for the property. Abbr.: **MLS**.

multiple personality *noun Psych.* (in full **multiple personality disorder**) (usu. *attributive*) a dissociative condition in which an individual's personality is apparently split into two or more distinct sub-personalities, each of which may become dominant at different times. Abbr.: **MPD**.

multiple sclerosis *noun* a chronic, progressive disease of the nervous system, in which sclerosis occurs in patches in the brain and spinal cord, resulting in tremor, paralysis, speech and sight defects, etc. Abbr.: **MS**.

multiple star *noun* a group of three or more associated stars rotating around a common centre.

multi·plex ● *adjective* **1** manifold; of many elements; having many related features. **2** involving simultaneous transmission of several messages along a single channel of communication. **3** of or relating to a single-site complex of two or more cinemas. ● *noun* **1** a multiplex cinema. **2** a multiplex system or signal. ● *transitive verb* incorporate into a multiplex signal or system. □ **multi·plex·er** *noun* (also **multi·plex·or**). **multi·plex·ing** *noun & adjective* [Latin (as MULTI-, -*plex* -*plicis* -fold)]

multi·pli·cand /ˌmʌltɪpliˈkand/ *noun* a quantity to be multiplied by a multiplier. [medieval Latin *multiplicandus* gerundive of Latin *multiplicare* (as MULTIPLY)]

multi·pli·ca·tion *noun* **1** the arithmetical process of multiplying. **2** the act or process of multiplying. **3** the reproduction of people or animals, or the propagation of plants. □ **multi·plic·a·tive** *adjective* [Old French *multiplication* or Latin *multiplicatio* (as MULTIPLY)]

multiplication sign *noun* the sign (×) to indicate that one quantity is to be multiplied by another, as in 2 × 3 = 6.

multiplication table *noun* a list of multiples of a particular number, usu. from 1 to 12.

multi·pli·city *noun* (*pl.* **-ties**) **1** manifold variety. **2** (foll. by *of*) a great number. [Late Latin *multiplicitas* (as MULTIPLEX)]

multi·pli·er *noun* **1 a** a thing which or person who multiplies or causes something to increase. **b** a quantity by which a given number is multiplied. **2** *Econ.* a factor by which an increment of income exceeds the resulting increment of saving or investment. **3** *Electricity* an instrument for increasing by repetition the intensity of a current, force, etc.

multi·ply *verb* (**-plies**, **-plied**) **1** *transitive & intransitive* obtain from (a number) another that is a specified number of times its value (*multiply 6 by 4 and you get 24*). **2** *intransitive* **a** increase in number by accumulation or repetition. **b** increase in number by reproduction or procreation. **3** *transitive* produce a large number of (instances etc.). **4** *transitive* **a** breed (animals). **b** propagate (plants). [Old French *multiplier* from Latin *multiplicare* (as MULTIPLEX)]

multi-point *adjective* having or serving several points.

multi·polar *adjective* **1** having or pertaining to many poles (*see* POLE²). **2** consisting of or divided into more than two esp. political alliances, parties, etc. □ **multi·polar·ity** /ˌmʌltipəˈlerɪti/ *noun*

multi·pro·cess·ing *noun Computing* processing by a number of processors sharing a common memory and common peripherals.

multi·pro·ces·sor *noun* a computer capable of performing multiprocessing.

multi·pro·gram·ming *noun Computing* the execution of two or more independent programs concurrently.

multi-purpose *adjective* having many purposes.

multi·racial *adjective* relating to or made up of many human races. □ **multi·racial·ism** *noun*

multi·sensory *adjective* pertaining to or affecting more than one of the five senses.

multi·skilled *adjective* (of a person, workforce, etc.) trained in a number of distinct jobs, skills, etc., allowing a flexible response to the shifting demands of the economy, workplace, etc. □ **multi-skilling** *noun*

multi·stage *attributive adjective* consisting of, occurring in, or involving many stages.

multi·storey *attributive adjective* (of a building) having many esp. similarly designed storeys.

multi-tasking *Computing* ● *noun* the execution of a number of tasks at the same time. ● *adjective* capable of multi-tasking. □ **multi-task** *transitive & intransitive verb*

multi-thread·ing *noun Computing* a programming technique whereby several processes can use the same applications software concurrently without interference. ▢ **multi-thread·ed** *adjective*

multi-track ● *attributive adjective* **1** relating to or made by the mixing of separately recorded soundtracks. **2** (of a school) having students divided into several groups on overlapping schedules esp. to ease overcrowding. ● *noun* a multi-track recording. ● *transitive & intransitive verb* **1** record using multi-track recording. **2** divide a student body into several groups on overlapping schedules to ease overcrowding etc. ▢ **multi-tracked** *adjective* **multi-tracking** *noun*

multi·tude /ˈmʌltɪˌtuːd, -ˌtjuːd/ *noun* **1** (often foll. by *of*) a great number. **2** a large gathering of people; a crowd. **3** (**the multitude**) the common people. **4** the state of being numerous. [Old French from Latin *multitudo -dinis* from *multus* many]

multi·tud·in·ous /ˌmʌltɪˈtuːdɪnəs, -ˈtjuːdɪnəs/ *adjective* **1** very numerous. **2** consisting of many individuals or elements.

multi-use *adjective* serving many uses.

multi-user *attributive adjective* **1** having many users. **2** (of a computer system) able to be used by more than one person and accessed from more than one terminal concurrently.

multi·valent /ˌmʌltɪˈveɪlənt/ *adjective* **1** having or susceptible of many applications, interpretations, meanings, or values. **2** *Chem.* **a** having a valence of more than two. **b** having a variable valence. ▢ **multi·valence** *noun* **multi·valen·cy** *noun*

multi·valve *attributive adjective* **1** *Electronics* having several thermionic valves. **2** (of a shell, shelled animal, etc.) having several valves.

multi·vari·ate /mʌltiˈveriət/ *adjective* *Statistics* involving or having two or more variable quantities.

multi·vita·min ● *noun* a nutritional supplement, esp. a pill, incorporating several vitamins. ● *adjective* designating a nutritional supplement of this sort.

multi·vocal *adjective* having many meanings or interpretations.

multi-way *attributive adjective* having several paths of communication etc.

multi-year *adjective* lasting or covering many years.

multi-year ice *noun* polar ice that is more than two years old.

mum[1] *noun Cdn & Brit. informal* mother. [abbreviation of MUMMY[1]]

mum[2] *adjective informal* silent (*keep mum*). ▢ **mum's the word** say nothing. [Middle English: imitative of closed lips]

mum[3] *intransitive verb* (**mummed, mum·ming**) play as a mummer. [compare MUM[2] and Middle Low German *mummen*]

mum[4] *noun informal* = CHRYSANTHEMUM. [abbreviation]

Mum·bai /mʊmˈbaɪ/ the Hindi name (official from 1995) for BOMBAY.

mum·ble ● *verb* **1** *intransitive & transitive* speak or utter indistinctly. **2** *transitive* bite or chew with or as with toothless gums. ● *noun* an indistinct utterance. ▢ **mum·bler** *noun* **mum·bling** *noun & adjective* **mum·bling·ly** *adverb* [Middle English *momele*, as MUM[2]: compare Low German *mummelen*]

mumbo-jumbo *noun* (*pl.* **-jumbos**) **1** meaningless or ignorant ritual. **2** obscure language or action intended to mystify or confuse. **3** an object of superstitious veneration. [*Mumbo Jumbo*, a supposed African idol]

mu-meson *noun* = MUON.

Mum·ford /ˈmʌmfərd/ **Lewis** (1895–1990), US sociologist, architectural critic, and urban theorist, whose works, including *The City in History* (1961) and *The Myth of the Machine* (1967–70), assess the effect of architecture and technology on human society and the environment.

mum·mer ● *noun* **1** an actor in a traditional masked mime. **2** *jocular* or *derogatory* an actor in the theatre. **3** (in Newfoundland) (also *attributive*) a person participating in Christmas mumming. ● *intransitive verb* (in Newfoundland) participate in mumming activities. [Old French *momeur* from *momer* MUM[3]]

mum·mer·ing *noun* = MUMMING.

mum·mery *noun* (*pl.* **-ies**) **1** ridiculous ceremonial, esp. religious ritual regarded as silly or hypocritical. **2** a performance by mummers. [Old French *momerie* (as MUMMER)]

mum·mi·chog /ˈmʌmiːtʃɒɡ/ *noun* a black and silver killifish, *Fundulus heteroclitus*, common in marshy coastal waters of N America. [Narragansett *moammitteaug*]

mum·mi·fy *transitive verb* (**-fies, -fied**) **1** embalm and preserve (a body) in the form of a mummy (*see* MUMMY[2]). **2** shrivel or dry up (tissues etc.). ▢ **mum·mi·fi·ca·tion** *noun* **mum·mi·fied** *adjective*

mum·ming *noun* **1** a performance, esp. of a folk play, by disguised actors, often accompanied by an outdoor procession or visits to private

houses. **2** (in Newfoundland) the visiting of private houses by disguised merrymakers during the twelve days of Christmas.

mummy[1] *noun* (*pl.* **-mies**) *Cdn & Brit. informal* mother. [imitative of a child's pronunciation: compare MAMMA[1]]

mummy[2] *noun* (*pl.* **-mies**) **1** a body of a human being or animal embalmed for burial, esp. in ancient Egypt. **2** a dried-up body. [French *momie* from medieval Latin *mumia* from Arabic *mūmiyā* from Persian *mūm* wax]

mummy bag *noun N Amer.* a snugly fitting sleeping bag in which the space for the feet is narrower than that for the shoulders, usu. having a pillowed hood.

mumps *plural noun* (treated as *sing.*) an acute contagious and infectious viral disease, esp. of children, characterized by fever and swelling of the parotid salivary glands in the face. [archaic *mump* be sullen]

mumsy /ˈmʌmzi/ *Brit. informal* ● *adjective* maternal; homely; unfashionable. ● *noun* = MUMMY[1]. [jocular variant of MUMMY[1]]

Munch /mʊŋk/ **Ed·vard** (1863–1944), Norwegian painter and engraver. A major influence on German expressionism, he infused his subjects with an intense emotionalism and used violent colour and linear distortion to express feelings about life and death; his works include the *Frieze of Life* sequence, incorporating *The Scream* (1893).

munch *transitive & intransitive verb* eat steadily and usu. audibly with a marked action of the jaws, esp. with great enjoyment. ▢ **munch on** eat. ▢ **munch·er** *noun* **munchy** *adjective* [Middle English, imitative: compare CRUNCH]

Munch·ausen's syndrome /ˈmʌntʃhauzənz/ *noun Med.* a mental illness in which a person repeatedly feigns severe illness so as to obtain hospital treatment. [Baron *Munchausen*, hero of a book of fantastic tales (1785) by R.E. Raspe]

Munchausen's syndrome by proxy *noun* (also **Munchausen by proxy**) a mental condition in which a person seeks attention by inducing illness in another person, esp. a child.

munch·ies *plural noun informal* **1** snacks; food suitable for snacks. **2** (prec. by *the*) hunger, esp. desire for snack food.

munch·kin *noun N Amer. informal* **1** a small or dwarf-like person, animal, etc. **2** a child. [the *Munchkins*, a race of small childlike creatures depicted in L. Frank Baum's *The Wonderful Wizard of Oz* (1900)]

mun·dane /mʌnˈdeɪn/ *adjective* **1** dull, routine; of or pertaining to everyday life. **2** of this world; worldly. ▢ **mun·dane·ly** *adverb* **mun·dane·ness** *noun* **mun·dan·ity** /-ˈdanɪti/ *noun* (*pl.* **-ities**). [Old French *mondain* from Late Latin *mundanus* from Latin *mundus* world]

Mun·dell, **Rob·ert Alex·an·der** (b.1932), Canadian economist. He was awarded the Nobel Prize for economics in 1999 for his work in the field of international monetary dynamics which paved the way for the introduction of the euro in 1999.

mung /mʌŋ/ *noun* the seed of either of two widely cultivated, originally Asian leguminous plants: **1** (in full **mung bean**) the green gram, *Vigna radiata*. **2** the black gram, *V. mungo*. [Hindi *mūng*]

Mun·ich /ˈmjuːnɪk/ a city in SE Germany, capital of Bavaria; pop. (est. 2002) 1,161,100.

Munich Agreement (also called **Munich Pact**) an agreement between Britain, France, Germany, and Italy, signed at Munich on 29 Sept. 1938, under which part of Czechoslovakia was ceded to Germany. It is remembered as an act of appeasement, illustrating the inadequacy of such action in the face of the fiercely expansionist and powerful German state.

mu·ni·ci·pal /mjuːˈnɪsɪpəl, ˌmjuːnɪˈsɪpəl/ *adjective* of, concerning, or operated by a municipality or its government. ▢ **mu·ni·ci·pal·ly** *adverb* [Latin *municipalis* from *municipium* free city, from *municeps -cipis* citizen with privileges, from *munia* civic offices + *capere* take]

municipal court *noun N Amer.* a lower court with limited jurisdiction, usu. extending to bylaw infractions, certain civil matters, etc.

municipal district *noun Cdn* (*Prairies & North*) a large, lightly populated rural area administered by a regional municipal government. Abbr.: **MD**.

mu·ni·ci·pa·li·té ré·gio·nale de com·té /muːniːsiːpaliːˈtei reiʒiʊˈnal də kɔˈtei/ *noun Cdn* (*Que.*) = REGIONAL COUNTY MUNICIPALITY.

mu·ni·ci·pal·ity /mjuːˌnɪsɪˈpalɪti/ *noun* (*pl.* **-ities**) **1** a city, town, or district having local government. **2** the governing body of this area.

muni·fi·cent /mjuːˈnɪfɪsənt/ *adjective* (of a giver or a gift) splendidly generous, bountiful. ▢ **muni·fi·cence** *noun* **muni·fi·cent·ly** *adverb* [Latin *munificent-*, var. stem of *munificus* from *munus* gift]

mu·ni·ment /ˈmjuːnɪmənt/ *noun* (usu. in *pl.*) **1** a document kept as evidence of rights or privileges etc. **2** an archive. [Old French from

Latin *munimentum* defence, in medieval Latin 'title deed,' from *munire* *munit-* fortify]

mu·ni·tion /mjuˈnɪʃən/ ● *noun* (usu. in *pl.*) military weapons, ammunition, equipment, and stores. ● *transitive verb* supply with munitions. [French from Latin *munitio -onis* fortification (as MUNIMENT)]

Munro /mənˈroː/ **1 Alice** (b.1931), Canadian short-story writer. Her fiction is characterized by her use of narrators and by her regional southwestern Ontario settings. Two of her books, *Dance of the Happy Shades* (1968) and *Who Do You Think You Are* (1978), have won the Governor General's Award. **2 Hec·tor Hugh**, see SAKI.

Munsch /mʌntʃ/ **Rob·ert** (b.1945), Canadian children's writer and storyteller. His more than 35 books, including *Love You Forever* (1986), *Thomas' Snowsuit* (1985) and *The Paper Bag Princess* (1988), have sold more than 31 million copies worldwide.

Mun·see /ˈmʌnsiː/ ● *noun* **1** a member of either of two groups of Aboriginal people living esp. in New Jersey and New York, but with a small population near St. Thomas, Ont. **2** either of the Algonquian languages of these peoples. ● *adjective* of or relating to this people or their culture or language. [corruption of an Algonquian word of uncertain meaning]

Mun·ster /ˈmʌnstər/ a province of the Republic of Ireland, in the southwest of the country.

Mün·ster /ˈmʊnstər/ a city in NW Germany; pop. (est. 2002) 265,500. It was formerly the capital of Westphalia; the Treaty of Westphalia, ending the Thirty Years War, was signed simultaneously there and at Osnabrück in 1648.

munt·jac /ˈmʌntdʒak/ *noun* (also **munt·jak**) any small deer of the genus *Muntiacus* native to SE Asia, the male having tusks and small antlers. [local name in W Java]

muon /ˈmjuːɒn/ *noun* Physics an unstable elementary particle like an electron, but with a much greater mass. □ **muon·ic** *adjective* [μ (MU), as the symbol for it]

M.U.P. *abbreviation* Master of Urban Planning.

mur·age /ˈmjʊrɪdʒ/ *noun hist.* a tax levied for building or repairing the walls of a town. [Old French *mur* from Latin *murus* wall]

mural ● *noun* a painting executed directly on a wall. ● *adjective* **1** of or like a wall. **2** placed or painted on a wall. **3** *Anat. & Med.* of or pertaining to the wall of a body cavity or vessel. □ **mural·ist** *noun* [French from Latin *muralis* from *murus* wall]

Mura·saki Shi·kibu /ˌmʊrəˈsɒki ˈʃiːkiˌbuː/ (c.978–c.1014), Japanese court lady and writer, whose work, *The Tale of Genji* (c.1010), is considered to be the oldest complete novel.

Murat /mʊˈrɒ/ **Joa·chim** (1767–1815), French general, king of Naples 1808–15. One of Napoleon's marshals, he was made king of Naples in 1808 and attempted to become king of all Italy in 1815, but was captured in Calabria and executed.

MURB *abbreviation Cdn* multiple unit residential building.

Mur·chi·son Falls /ˈmɜrtʃɪsən/ the former name for KABALEGA FALLS.

Mur·cia /ˈmʊrsiə/ **1** an autonomous region in SE Spain. **2** its capital city; pop. (est. 2001) 367,189.

mur·der[1] ● *noun* **1 a** the unlawful premeditated killing of a human being by another (*compare* MANSLAUGHTER). **b** an instance of this. **2** *informal* an unpleasant, troublesome, or dangerous state of affairs (*it was murder here on Saturday*). **3** something very damaging (*chlorine is murder on hair*). ● *transitive verb* **1** kill (a human being) unlawfully, esp. wickedly or inhumanly. **2** *Law* kill (a human being) with malice and a premeditated motive. **3** *informal* **a** put an end to or destroy. **b** spoil by bad execution, performance, mispronunciation, etc. (*murdered the soliloquy in the second act*). **4** *slang* conclusively defeat (an opponent etc.), esp. at a game or sport. □ **scream** (or **shout, yell,** etc.) **bloody** (or **blue**) **murder** *slang* shout loudly. **get away with murder** *informal* do whatever one wishes and escape punishment. **murder will out** murder cannot remain undetected. □ **mur·der·er** *noun* **mur·der·ess** *noun* [Old English *morthor* & Old French *murdre* from Germanic]

mur·der[2] *noun* a flock (of crows). [origin uncertain; probably the same word as MURDER[1], perhaps alluding to the crow's traditional association with violent death]

murder·ball *noun Cdn* a game in which players in opposing teams attempt to hit their opponents with a large, inflated ball.

murder mystery *noun* a novel, play, etc. about a murder in which the murderer's identity is concealed by a complicated plot until the denouement.

murder one *noun N Amer. slang* first-degree murder.

mur·der·ous *adjective* **1** (of a person, weapon, action, etc.) capable of, intending, or involving murder or great harm. **2** *informal* extremely arduous or unpleasant. □ **mur·der·ous·ly** *adverb* **mur·der·ous·ness** *noun*

Mur·doch /ˈmɜrdɒk/ **1 Dame (Jean) Iris** (1919–99), Irish-born English novelist and philosopher. The author of several philosophical works, she is primarily known for her novels, which often portray complex sexual relationships and the quest for the spiritual life; they include *The Red and the Green* (1965), *The Sea, The Sea* (1978), and *The Book and the Brotherhood* (1987). **2 (Keith) Ru·pert** (b.1931), Australian-born US publisher and media entrepreneur. As the founder and head of the News International Communications empire, he owns major newspapers in Australia, Britain, and the US, together with film and television companies and a multinational publishing company.

mure /mjʊr/ *transitive verb archaic* **1** immure. **2** (foll. by *up*) wall up or shut up in an enclosed space. [Old French *murer* from *mur*: see MURAGE]

murex /ˈmjʊrəks/ *noun* (*pl.* **mur·ex·es** or **mur·ices** /-rɪˌsiːz/) any of various spiny-shelled predatory gastropod molluscs of the genus *Murex* and related genera, of tropical and temperate seas, from some of which the dye Tyrian purple was formerly obtained. [Latin]

muri·at·ic acid /mjʊriˈatɪk/ *noun* = HYDROCHLORIC ACID. □ **muri·ate** /ˈmjʊriət, -ieit/ *noun* [Latin *muriaticus* from *muria* 'brine']

Mur·illo /mʊˈriːjoː/ **Bar·tolo·mé Este·ban** (c.1618–82), Spanish painter. He is noted both for his genre scenes of beggar children and for his devotional pictures.

mur·ine /ˈmjʊˌrain/ *adjective* of or like a mouse or mice. [Latin *murinus* from *mus muris* mouse]

murk ● *noun* **1** darkness, gloom; poor visibility. **2 a** air obscured by fog, dense vapour, etc. **b** confusion, obscurity, vagueness, or incomprehensibility. ● *adjective archaic* (of night, day, place, etc.) = MURKY. [prob. from Scandinavian: compare Old Norse *myrkr*]

murky *adjective* (**-ier, -iest**) **1** dark, gloomy. **2** (of darkness) thick, dense. **3** suspiciously obscure (*a murky past*). **4** indistinct, confused, not easily understood. □ **murk·i·ly** *adverb* **murk·i·ness** *noun*

Mur·mansk /mʊrˈmansk/ a port in NW Russia, on the northern coast of the Kola Peninsula, in the Barents Sea; pop. (est. 2001) 361,000. It is the largest city north of the Arctic Circle and its port is ice-free throughout the year.

mur·mur ● *noun* **1** a softly spoken or nearly inarticulate utterance. **2** a subdued expression of discontent. **3** *Med.* a recurring sound heard in the auscultation of the heart and usu. indicating abnormality. **4** a subdued continuous sound, as made by waves, a brook, etc. ● *verb* **1** *transitive* utter (words) in a low voice. **2** *intransitive* make a subdued continuous sound. **3** *intransitive* (usu. foll. by *at, against*) complain in low tones, grumble. □ **mur·mur·er** *noun* **mur·mur·ing** *adjective & noun* **mur·mur·ous** *adjective* [Old French *murmurer* from Latin *murmurare*: compare Greek *mormurō* (of water) roar, Sanskrit *marmaras* noisy]

Mur·nau /ˈmʊrnau/ **F. W.** (born Frederick Wilhelm Plumpe) (1888–1931), German film director. His revolutionary use of the camera to record and interpret human emotion resulted in films such as *Nosferatu* (1922). Other films include *Der letzte Mann* (1924) and the Hollywood-made *Sunrise* (1927), which won three Oscars.

Mur·phy, Emily (born Emily Ferguson) (1868–1933), Canadian journalist, magistrate and reformer. Writing under the pseudonym Janey Canuck, she contributed articles to newspapers and magazines as well as writing four books, including *The Impressions of Janey Canuck Abroad* (1901) and *Janey Canuck in the West* (1910).

Murphy bed *noun N Amer.* a folding bed, esp. one that fits vertically into a cupboard and can be pulled down when needed. [W. L. *Murphy*, US manufacturer d.1959]

Murphy's Law *noun jocular* any of various maxims about the apparent perverseness of things, esp. the principle that if anything can go wrong, it will.

mur·rain /ˈmʌrin/ *noun* **1** an infectious disease of cattle, carried by parasites. **2** *archaic* a plague, esp. the potato blight during the Irish famine in the mid-19th c. [Anglo-French *moryn*, Old French *morine* from *morir* from Latin *mori* die]

Mur·ray /ˈmʌri/ **1 Sir James (Au·gus·tus Henry)** (1837–1915), Scottish lexicographer, who was the chief editor (1879–1915) of the *Oxford English Dictionary* (1933). **2 (Morna) Anne** (b.1945), Canadian singer and songwriter. Songs like 'Snowbird' (1970) and 'You Needed Me' (1978) made her the most successful Canadian pop singer of the 1970s, and she enjoys continued popularity.

Murray River /ˈmʌri/ the principal river of Australia, which rises in the Great Dividing Range in New South Wales and flows 2 590 km

uː mood   ai my   əi pipe   au brown   ʌu house   ei day   ɔi boy   ā franglais   ã Canadien   ɔ̃ Brayon   (*see over for consonants*)

(1,610 miles) generally northwestward, forming part of the border between the states of Victoria and New South Wales, before turning southward in South Australia to empty into the Indian Ocean southeast of Adelaide.

murre /mɜr/ *noun esp. N Amer.* an auk or guillemot. [16th c.: origin unknown]

murre·let /ˈmɜrlət/ *noun* any of several small auks of the N Pacific, of the genera *Brachyramphus* and *Synthliboramphus*.

Mur·rum·bidg·ee River /ˌmʌrəmˈbɪdʒi/ a river of SE Australia, in New South Wales. Rising in the Great Dividing Range, it flows 1 759 km (1,099 miles) westward to join the Murray, of which it is a major tributary.

mur·ther /ˈmɜrðər/ *archaic var. of* MURDER[1].

Mur·u·roa /ˌmʊruˈroːə/ a remote S Pacific atoll in the Tuamotu archipelago, in French Polynesia, used as a nuclear testing site since 1966.

Mu·sala, Mount /muˈsɒlə/ (also **Mousalla**) the highest peak in Bulgaria, in the Rila Mountains, rising to 2 925 m (9,596 ft.).

Mus·ca·det /ˈmʌskəˌdeɪ/ *noun* **1** a white wine from the Loire region of France. **2** a variety of grape from which the wine is made. [French from *muscade* 'nutmeg' from *musc* MUSK + -ET[1]]

mus·ca·dine /ˈmʌskədɪn, -ˌdaɪn/ *noun* any of a group of species and varieties of wine grape native to Mexico and the southeastern US, typically having thick skins and a musky flavour. [prob. alteration of MUSCATEL]

mus·ca·rine /ˈmʌskərɪn/ *noun* a poisonous alkaloid from the fungus *Amanita muscaria*. □ **mus·ca·rin·ic** *adjective* [Latin *muscarius* from *musca* fly]

Mus·cat /ˈmʌskat/ the capital of Oman, a port on the southeast coast of the Arabian peninsula; pop. (est. 2002) 60,110.

mus·cat /ˈmʌskat/ *noun* **1** a variety of white, red, or black grape with a musky scent, grown in warm climates for wine or raisins or as table grapes. **2** a sweet fortified white wine made from muscat grapes. [French from Provençal *muscat muscade* (adj.) from *musc* MUSK]

Muscat and Oman the former name (until 1970) for OMAN.

mus·ca·tel /ˌmʌskəˈtel/ *noun* **1** = MUSCAT. **2** a raisin from a muscadine grape. [Old French from Provençal diminutive of *muscat*: see MUSCAT]

muscat raisin *noun* a large, dark, sweet raisin with the seeds removed, made by drying muscat grapes in the sun.

muscle ● *noun* **1** a fibrous tissue with the ability to contract, producing movement in or maintaining the position of an animal body. **2** the part of an animal body that is composed of muscles. **3 a** physical power or strength. **b** force, influence (*the members have banded together to give them more marketing muscle*). **4** *slang* a person employed to threaten or use violence. **5** (*attributive*) *N Amer.* designating an exceptionally powerful vehicle (*muscle boat; muscle sled*). ● *verb* **1** *informal* **a** *transitive N Amer.* move by the exercise of physical power (*muscling a snowmobile over rough terrain*). **b** *intransitive* make one's way by the exercise of physical power (*muscled through the crowds*). **c** *transitive Baseball* (of a batter) propel (the ball) forcefully with the part of the bat nearest the hands, relying more on muscle strength than on swing momentum. **2** *transitive slang* coerce by violence, intimidation, etc., esp. by economic or political pressure. □ **not move a muscle** be completely motionless. **muscle in (on)** *informal* involve oneself in something when one has no right to do so, for one's own advantage. □ **muscled** *adjective* (usu. in *combination*). **muscle·less** *adjective* **muscly** *adjective* [French from Latin *musculus* diminutive of *mus* mouse, from the fancied mouselike form of some muscles]

muscle-bound *adjective* **1** with muscles stiff and inelastic through excessive exercise or training. **2** *informal* usu. *derogatory* (of a person) very, esp. excessively muscular.

muscle car *noun esp. N Amer. informal* a powerful car, esp. a hot rod.

muscle fibre *noun* each of the elongated contractile cells of which muscular tissue is composed.

muscle-flexing *noun* an assertion of strength or power.

muscle·man *noun* (pl. **-men**) **1** a man with highly developed muscles. **2** a person who employs or threatens violence on behalf of another, esp. a professional criminal.

muscle memory *noun* the capacity of a muscle or set of muscles to function in a certain way in response to a stimulus, acquired through frequent repetition.

muscle pull *noun N Amer.* a pulled muscle.

muscle shirt *noun N Amer.* a man's tight-fitting, sleeveless T-shirt, usu. with a low scoop neck in front and back.

muscle·wood *noun* = BLUE BEECH .

mus·co·vado /ˌmʌskəˈvɑːdoʊ/ *noun* an unrefined sugar made from the juice of sugar cane by evaporation and draining off the molasses. [Spanish *mascabado* (sugar) of the lowest quality]

Mus·co·vite /ˈmʌskəˌvaɪt/ ● *noun* **1** a native or citizen of Moscow. **2** *archaic* a Russian. ● *adjective* **1** of or relating to Moscow. **2** *archaic* of or relating to Russia. [modern Latin *Muscovita* from *Muscovia* = MUSCOVY]

mus·co·vite *noun* a silver-grey form of mica with a sheet-like crystalline structure that is used in the manufacture of electrical equipment etc. [obsolete MUSCOVY *glass* (in the same sense) + -ITE[1]]

Mus·covy /ˈmʌskəvi/ a medieval principality in west central Russia, centred on Moscow, which formed the nucleus of modern Russia. [obsolete French *Muscovie* from modern Latin *Moscovia* from Russian *Moskva* Moscow]

Muscovy duck *noun* a tropical American duck, *Cairina moschata*, having a small crest and red markings on its head.

mus·cu·lar *adjective* **1** having well-developed muscles. **2** of or affecting the muscles. **3** robust, vigorous. □ **mus·cu·lar·ity** *noun* **mus·cu·lar·ly** *adverb* [earlier *musculous* (as MUSCLE)]

muscular dystrophy *noun* a hereditary progressive weakening and wasting of the muscles.

mus·cu·la·ture /ˈmʌskjʊlətʃər/ *noun* **1** the muscular system of a body or organ. **2** a person's or animal's muscles collectively, esp. if well-developed (*you could tell by his musculature that Jeremy had been working out*). [French from Latin (as MUSCLE)]

mus·cu·lo·skel·etal /ˌmʌskjuloˈskelətəl/ *adjective* of or relating to the musculature and skeleton together.

Mus.D. *abbreviation* (also **Mus. Doc.**) Doctor of Music. [Latin *Musicae Doctor*]

muse[1] *noun* **1** (**Muse**) *Gk & Rom. Myth* any of the goddesses who presided over the arts and sciences. They were the daughters of Zeus and Mnemosyne, traditionally nine in number (Calliope, Clio, Euterpe, Terpsichore, Erato, Melpomene, Thalia, Polyhymnia, and Urania), though their functions and names vary considerably between different sources. **2** (usu. prec. by *the*) **a** a poet's inspiring goddess. **b** a poet's genius. **3** a source of inspiration for creativity. [Old French *muse* or Latin *musa* from Greek *mousa*]

muse[2] *literary* ● *verb* **1** *intransitive* **a** (usu. foll. by *on, upon*) ponder, reflect. **b** (usu. foll. by *on*) gaze meditatively (on a scene etc.). **2** *transitive* say or murmur meditatively. ● *noun archaic* a fit of abstraction. [Old French *muser* to waste time, from Romanic perhaps from medieval Latin *musum* muzzle]

mu·seol·ogy /ˌmjuːziˈɒlədʒi/ *noun* the science or practice of organizing and managing museums. □ **mu·seo·logic·al** *adjective* **mu·seol·o·gist** *noun*

mu·sette /mjuːˈzet/ *noun* **1 a** a kind of small bagpipe with bellows, common in the French court in the 17th–18th c. **b** a tune imitating the sound of this. **2** a small oboe-like double-reed instrument in 19th-c. France. **3** a popular dance in the courts of Louis XIV and XV. **4** *US* (in full **musette bag**) a small knapsack. [Old French, diminutive of *muse* bagpipe]

mu·seum *noun* a building used for storing, preserving, and exhibiting objects considered to be of lasting historical, scientific, or cultural interest. [Latin from Greek *mouseion* seat of the Muses: see MUSE[1]]

museum piece *noun* **1** a specimen of art etc. fit for a museum. **2** *derogatory* an old-fashioned or quaint person or object.

mush[1] ● *noun* **1** a soft pulpy or formless mass. **2** feeble sentimentality. **3** *US* porridge, esp. cornmeal boiled in water until it thickens. ● *transitive verb* reduce to mush; mash. [apparently var. of MASH]

mush[2] *N Amer.* ● *intransitive verb* **1 a** travel through snow with a dogsled. **b** (of dogs) pull a sled. **2** (in *imperative*) used as a command to dogs pulling a sled to urge them forward. ● *noun* a journey across snow with a dogsled. □ **mush·er** *noun* **mush·ing** *noun* [prob. corruption of French *marchons* imperative of *marcher* advance]

mush·room ● *noun* **1** the usu. edible spore-producing body of various fungi, esp. *Agaricus campestris*, with a stem and domed cap, proverbial for its rapid growth. **2** the pinkish-brown colour of this. **3** any item resembling a mushroom in shape. **4** (usu. *attributive*) something that appears or develops suddenly or is ephemeral; an upstart. ● *intransitive verb* **1** appear or develop rapidly. **2** expand and flatten like a mushroom cap. **3** gather mushrooms. □ **mush·room·ing** *adjective* & *noun* **mush·roomy** *adjective* [Old French *mousseron* from Late Latin *mussirio -onis*]

mushroom cloud *noun* a cloud of smoke, vapour, etc. suggesting the shape of a mushroom, esp. from a nuclear explosion.

Consonants: b *but* d *dog* f *few* g *get* h *her* j *yes* k *cat* l *leg* m *man* n *no* p *pen* r *red* s *sit*

mushy *adjective* (**mush·i·er**, **mush·i·est**) **1** like mush, soft and pulpy. **2** feebly sentimental. □ **mush·i·ly** *adverb* **mush·i·ness** *noun*

music *noun* **1** the art of combining vocal or instrumental sounds (or both) to produce beauty of form, harmony, and expression of emotion. **2** the sounds so produced. **3** musical compositions collectively. **4** the written or printed score of a musical composition. **5** certain pleasant sounds, e.g. birdsong, the sound of a stream, etc. □ **face the music** *informal* put up with or stand up to unpleasant consequences, esp. criticism. **music of the spheres** *see* SPHERE. **music to one's ears** something very pleasant to hear. [Old French *musique* from Latin *musica* from Greek *mousikē* (*tekhnē* art) of the Muses (*mousa* Muse: see MUSE[1])]

music·al ● *adjective* **1** of or relating to music. **2** (of sounds, a voice, etc.) melodious, harmonious. **3** fond of or skilled in music (*the musical one of the family*). **4** set to or accompanied by music. ● *noun* a musical comedy or music theatre. □ **music·al·ize** *transitive verb* (also esp. *Brit.* **-ise**). **music·al·ly** *adverb*

musical box *noun Brit.* = MUSIC BOX.

musical chairs *plural noun* **1** a party game in which the players compete in successive rounds for a decreasing number of chairs, sitting down on a chair whenever the music stops. **2** a series of esp. minor changes, political manoeuvres, etc. after the manner of the game.

musical comedy *noun* a light drama on stage or film, consisting of dialogue, songs, and dancing.

musi·cale /ˌmjuːzɪ'kal/ *noun N Amer.* a concert or musical social evening. [French fem. adj. (as MUSICAL)]

musical instrument *noun see* INSTRUMENT *noun* 2.

musi·cal·ity /mjuːzɪ'kalɪti/ *noun* **1** the quality or character of being musical. **2** (of a dancer, choreographer, etc.) the ability to suit or fit dance steps to music particularly pleasingly.

musical ride *noun* an exhibition in which riders on horseback (usu. members of a mounted police force) perform choreographed manoeuvres to music.

musical saw *noun* a bent saw played with a violin bow.

music box *noun* **1** a mechanical instrument playing a tune by causing a toothed cylinder to strike a comb-like metal plate within a box. **2** a figurine, toy, or other decorative item incorporating a music box.

music director *noun* (also **musical director**) the person responsible for the musical aspects of a performance, production, arts organization, etc., usu. the conductor of an orchestra, band, etc.

music drama *noun* Wagnerian-type opera without formal arias etc. and governed by dramatic considerations.

music hall *noun* **1** a public hall or theatre used for musical performances. **2** variety entertainment, popular c.1850–1914, consisting of singing, dancing, and novelty acts; vaudeville.

musi·cian *noun* a person who performs esp. instrumental music, esp. professionally. □ **musi·cian·ly** *adjective* **musi·cian·ship** *noun* [Old French *musicien* from *musique* (as MUSIC, -ICIAN)]

music man *noun Cdn* (*Man.*) a disc jockey who plays recorded music at a dance etc.

music·ol·ogy /ˌmjuːzɪ'kɒlədʒi/ *noun* the branch of knowledge that deals with music as a subject of study rather than as a skill or performing art; esp. academic research in music. □ **musico·logic·al** *adjective* **music·ol·o·gist** *noun*

music room *noun* a room in which music is performed, practised, etc.

music stand *noun* a rest or frame on which sheet music or a score is supported.

music theatre *noun* in late 20th-c. music, the combination of elements from music and drama in new forms distinct from traditional opera, esp. as designed for small groups of performers.

music therapy *noun* the therapeutic use of music in the treatment of certain (esp. mental) conditions. □ **music therapist** *noun*

music video *noun* a dramatization of a song or piece of music on videotape, esp. for broadcast on television.

mus·ing *noun* **1** an act or instance of being absorbed in thought. **2** (often in *pl.*) an expression of one's thoughts or opinions. □ **mus·ing·ly** *adverb*

mu·sique con·crète /mjuːˌziːk kɔ̃'krɛt/ *noun* = CONCRETE MUSIC. [French]

musk *noun* **1 a** a strong-smelling reddish-brown substance produced by a gland in the male musk deer and used as an ingredient in perfumes. **b** any of various similar odorous substances secreted by other animals, esp. for scent-marking. **2 a** a substance designed to imitate musk, esp.

for use in perfumes. **b** an aromatic odour resembling that of musk, esp. worn as a fragrance. **3** the plant, *Mimulus moschatus*, with pale-green ovate leaves and yellow flowers (originally with a smell of musk which is no longer perceptible in modern varieties). □ **musky** *adjective* (**musk·i·er**, **musk·i·est**). **musk·i·ness** *noun* [Late Latin *muscus* from Persian *mušk*, perhaps from Sanskrit *muṣka* scrotum (from the shape of the musk deer's gland)]

musk deer *noun* any small Asian deer of the genus *Moschus*, having no antlers and in the male having long protruding canine teeth.

mus·keg /'mʌskeg/ *noun* **1** a swamp or bog in northern N America, consisting of a mixture of water and partly dead vegetation, often covered by a layer of sphagnum or other mosses. **2** terrain characterized by such swamps. [Cree *maske:k*]

mus·kel·lunge /'mʌskəˌlʌndʒ/ *noun* a large N American pike, *Esox masquinongy*, esp. of the Great Lakes. *Also called* MUSKIE, LUNGE[3]. [Algonquian]

mus·ket *noun hist.* an infantryman's usu. smoothbore light gun, fired from shoulder level. [French *mousquet* from Italian *moschetto* crossbow bolt, from *mosca* fly]

mus·ket·eer *noun hist.* **1** a soldier armed with a musket. **2** a member of either of two bodies forming part of the household troops of the French king in the 17th and 18th c.

mus·ket·ry *noun hist.* **1** the knowledge of handling muskets. **2** muskets, or soldiers armed with muskets, referred to collectively.

musket shot *noun hist.* **1** a shot fired from a musket. **2** the range of this shot.

mus·kie *noun N Amer.* = MUSKELLUNGE.

musk mallow *noun* a perennial herbaceous plant, *Malva moschata*, with pink or white flowers, naturalized in eastern N America and cultivated as an ornamental.

musk·mel·on *noun* the common yellow or green melon, *Cucumis melo*, usu. with a raised network of markings on the skin.

Mus·ko·gean /ˌmʌskə'giːən, mʌ'skoːgiən/ ● *noun* a language family of southeastern N America, including Creek, Seminole, Choctaw, and Chickasaw. ● *adjective* of or pertaining to this language family or the peoples belonging to it. [MUSKOGEE + -AN]

Mus·ko·gee /mʌ'skoːgiː/ ● *noun* **1** a member of a N American Aboriginal people forming part of the Creek Confederacy. **2** the Muskogean language of this people. ● *adjective* of or relating to this people or their culture or language. [Creek *ma:skó:ki*]

Mus·koka /mə'skoːkə/ *noun* a region of south central Ontario, situated off the southeastern end of Georgian Bay and north of Lake Simcoe. It is centred on the Muskoka Lakes (Rosseau, Joseph, and Muskoka) and is a popular area for summer cottages. [see MUSKOKA, LAKE]

Muskoka, Lake a lake in south central Ontario, southeast of Parry Sound. [adapted from Ojibwa *Mesqua Ukie* Yellowhead, Ojibwa chief c.1817, from *mesqua* red + *ahkees* ground]

Muskoka chair *noun Cdn* a slatted wooden lawn chair with a fan-shaped back and broad arms. *Also called* ADIRONDACK CHAIR.

Muskoka room *noun Cdn* (*S Ont.*) a glassed (or screened) room on the side of a house, cottage, etc.

musk·ox *noun* (*pl.* same or **musk·oxen**) **1** a large goat-antelope, *Ovibos moschatus*, of the tundra, esp. in Canada and Greenland, with a thick shaggy coat and small curved horns, the male of which emits a strong odour during rutting. **2** the flesh of this used as food.

musk·rat *noun* **1** a large semi-aquatic rodent, *Ondatra zibethicus*, native to N America, having a musky smell. **2** the fur of this.

musk rose *noun* a rambling rose, *Rosa moschata*, with large white flowers smelling of musk.

Mus·lim /'mʌzlɪm, -ləm/ (also *hist.* **Moslem** /'mɒzləm/) ● *noun* a follower of the Islamic religion. ● *adjective* of or relating to Muslims or their religion. [Arabic *muslim*, part. of *aslama*: see ISLAM]

Muslim Brotherhood *noun* a Islamic religious and political organization, founded in Egypt in 1928 and dedicated to the establishment of a nation based on Islamic principles.

mus·lin /'mʌzlɪn/ *noun* a cotton or cotton blend fabric of a plain weave. [French *mousseline* from Italian *mussolina* from *Mussolo* Mosul in Iraq, where it was made]

muso /'mjuːzoː/ *noun* (*pl.* **musos**) *Brit. slang* a musician, esp. a professional. [abbreviation]

mus·quash /'mʌskwɒʃ/ *noun* **1** *archaic* = MUSKRAT. **2** *Brit.* the fur of the muskrat. [Algonquian]

muss *N Amer. informal* ● *transitive verb* (often foll. by *up*) mess, make untidy (*don't muss my hair*). ● *noun* a mess; a state of confusion or untidiness. □ **mussy** *adjective* [apparently var. of MESS]

mus·sel *noun* **1** any bivalve mollusc of the genus *Mytilus*, living in sea water and often used for food. **2** any similar freshwater mollusc of the genus *Margaritifer* or *Anodonta*, forming pearls. [Old English *mus(c)le* & Middle Low German *mussel*, ultimately related to Latin *musculus* (as MUSCLE)]

mussel mud *noun Cdn* (*Maritimes*) thick sea mud, rich in lime from the remains of mussels etc., used as fertilizer.

Mus·set /mjuː'seɪ/ (**Louis Charles**) **Al·fred de** (1810–57), French poet and playwright. A leading poet of the French romantic movement, he is remembered for the poems such as 'Les Nuits' (1835–37) and plays such as *Lorenzaccio* (1834).

Mus·so·lini /ˌmʊsə'liːni/ **Ben·ito** (**Amil·care An·drea**) (known as 'Il Duce' = the leader) (1883–1945), Italian Fascist leader, prime minister 1922–43. He founded the Italian Fascist Party (1919) and, assuming dictatorial powers, he annexed Abyssinia (1936) and entered the Second World War on Germany's side (1940); he was forced to resign after the Allied invasion of Sicily (1943) and was executed by Italian Communist partisans (1945).

Mus·sorg·sky /mə'sɔrgski/ **Mo·dest (Petro·vich)** (also **Moussorgsky**) (1839–81), Russian composer, who is known for the opera *Boris Godunov* (1874), the piano suite *Pictures at an Exhibition* (1874), and song cycles such as *Songs and Dances of Death* (1875–7).

Mus·sul·man /'mʌsəlmən/ *archaic* ● *noun* (*pl.* **-mans** or **-men**) a Muslim. ● *adjective* of or concerning Muslims. [Persian *musulmān* originally adj. from *muslim* (as MUSLIM)]

must[1] ● *auxiliary verb* (*3rd sing. present* **must**; *past* **had to** or in indirect speech **must**) (foll. by infin., or *absol.*) **1 a** be obliged or required to (*you must go to school*; *must we leave now?*; *said he must go*). **b** be necessary that (*it must be done now*). **2** used in ironic questions (*must you slam the door?*). **3** be certain to (*we must win in the end*; *you must be her sister*; *he must be mad*; *they must have left by now*; *seemed as if the roof must blow off*). **4** should, ought to (*we must see what can be done*; *it must be said that*). **5** expressing insistence (*I must ask you to leave*). **6** (foll. by *not* + infin.) **a** not be permitted to, be forbidden to (*you must not smoke*). **b** ought not; need not (*you mustn't think he's angry*; *you must not worry*). **c** expressing insistence that something should not be done (*they must not be told*). ● *noun informal* (also *attributive*) a thing that cannot or should not be overlooked or missed (*if you go to Halifax the Citadel is a must*; *a must-read*). □ **I must say** often *ironic* I cannot refrain from saying (*I must say he made a good attempt*; *a fine way to behave, I must say*). **must needs** see NEEDS. [Old English *mōste* past of *mōt* may]

must[2] *noun* grape juice before or during fermentation. [Old English from Latin *mustum* neuter of *mustus* new]

must[3] *noun* mustiness, mould. [back-formation from MUSTY]

must[4] /mʌst/ (also **musth**) ● *adjective* (of a male elephant or camel) in a state of dangerous frenzy, associated with the rutting season. ● *noun* this state. [Urdu from Persian *mast* intoxicated]

mus·tache *var. of* MOUSTACHE.

mus·tach·io /mə'staʃɪəʊ/ *noun* (*pl.* **-ios**) (often in *pl.*) a moustache, esp. a large one. □ **mus·tach·ioed** *adjective* [Spanish *mostacho* & Italian *mostaccio* (as MOUSTACHE)]

mus·tang *noun* a small wild horse of the American plains. [Spanish *mestengo* (from *mesta* 'company of graziers') & Spanish *mostrenco*, both meaning 'wild or masterless cattle']

mustang grape *noun* a grape from the wild vine *Vitis candicans*, of the southern US, used for making wine.

mus·tard ● *noun* **1 a** any of various plants of the genus *Brassica* with slender pods and yellow flowers, esp. *B. nigra*. **b** any of various plants of the genus *Sinapis*, esp. *S. alba*, eaten at the seedling stage. **c** any of various other plants, esp. of the mustard family (*Cruciferae, Brassicaceae*), resembling these in appearance, pungency, etc. **2** a paste made from the crushed seeds of these and used as a spicy condiment. **3** (also **mustard yellow**) the brownish-yellow colour of this condiment. ● *adjective* of a brownish-yellow colour. □ **mus·tardy** *adjective* [Old French *mo(u)starde*: originally the condiment as prepared with MUST[2]]

mustard gas *noun* a colourless oily liquid, whose vapour causes severe irritation and blistering of the skin, used in chemical warfare.

mustard plaster *noun* a poultice made with mustard.

mus·te·lid /'mʌstəlɪd, mʌ'stelɪd/ ● *noun* a mammal of the family *Mustelidae*, including weasels, otters, badgers, skunks, martens, etc. ● *adjective* of or relating to this family. [modern Latin *Mustelidae* from Latin *mustela* 'weasel']

mus·ter ● *verb* **1** *transitive & intransitive* collect, gather together. **2** *transitive*

collect or assemble (originally soldiers) for inspection, to check numbers, etc. **3** *transitive* (often foll. by *up*) summon up (courage, strength, etc.). ● *noun* **1 a** the assembly of persons for inspection. **b** an act of mustering soldiers, sailors, etc. **2** an assembly, a collection. □ **muster out** *US* discharge (soldiers etc.). **pass muster** come up to the required standard. [Old French *mo(u)stre*, ultimately from Latin *monstrare* show]

muster roll *noun* an official list of officers and other ranks in a regiment or ship's company.

musth *var. of* MUST[4].

must-have ● *noun* an item regarded as indispensable. ● *adjective* indispensable.

Mus·tique /mʊ'stiːk/ a small resort island in the N Grenadines, in the Caribbean to the south of St. Vincent.

mustn't *contraction* must not.

must-see ● *noun* a site, event, film, etc. that must be seen. ● *adjective* that must be seen.

musty *adjective* (**must·i·er**, **must·i·est**) **1** mouldy; having a smell or taste indicative or suggestive of mouldiness or decay. **2** stale-smelling or fusty. **3** having lost newness, interest, or liveliness. □ **must·i·ly** *adverb* **must·i·ness** *noun* [perhaps alteration of *moisty* (MOIST) by assoc. with MUST[2]]

Mut /'mʊt/ *Egyptian Myth* a goddess who was the wife of Amun and mother of Khonsu. Her name means 'the mother'.

mut·able /'mjuːtəbəl/ *adjective literary* **1** liable or subject to change or alteration. **2** fickle. **3** *Biol.* able or liable to undergo esp. frequent mutation. □ **mut·abil·ity** *noun* [Latin *mutabilis* from *mutare* change]

muta·gen /'mjuːtədʒən, -dʒen/ *noun* an agent causing or promoting mutation, e.g. radiation. □ **muta·gen·esis** *noun* **muta·gen·ic** *adjective* **muta·gen·icity** *noun* **muta·gen·ized** *adjective* [MUTATION + -GEN]

mu·tant /'mjuːtənt/ ● *adjective* **1** resulting from mutation. **2** having the characteristics or attributes of a mutant. ● *noun* **1** an individual, gene, etc. which has arisen by or undergone mutation. **2** (esp. in science fiction) an individual with freak or grossly abnormal anatomy, abilities, etc. [Latin *mutant-* part. from *mutare* change]

mu·tate *transitive & intransitive verb* undergo or cause to undergo mutation. □ **mu·tat·ed** *adjective* [back-formation from MUTATION]

muta·tion *noun* **1** the process or an instance of change or alteration. **2 a** a genetic change which, when transmitted to offspring, gives rise to heritable variations. **b** the process by which such changes arise. **3** a distinct form produced by genetic change; a mutant. **4 a** an umlaut. **b** (in a Celtic language) a change of a consonant etc. determined by a preceding word. □ **muta·tion·al** *adjective* [Latin *mutatio* from *mutare* change]

mu·ta·tis mu·tan·dis /mjuː,tatɪs mjuː'tandɪs/ *adverb* (in comparing cases) making the necessary alterations. [Latin 'things being changed that have to be changed']

mute ● *adjective* **1** silent, refraining from, or temporarily bereft of speech. **2** (of a person) lacking the faculty of speech. **3** (of an animal) naturally lacking the power of articulate speech. **4 a** not expressed in speech (*mute protest*). **b** characterized by an absence of sound; quiet, still (*the mute forest*). **5** (of a letter) not pronounced. ● *noun* **1** a person who cannot or will not speak (*a deaf mute*). **2** *Music* **a** a clip placed over the bridge of a violin etc. to dampen the resonance without affecting the vibration of the strings. **b** a pad or cone inserted into the bell of a wind instrument to soften the sound. **3** an unsounded consonant. **4** = MUTE BUTTON 2. ● *transitive verb* **1 a** deaden, muffle, or soften the sound of (a thing, esp. a musical instrument). **b** suppress the volume of (a loudspeaker) or the output of (an amplifier or other circuit component). **2** tone down, make less intense. □ **mutely** *adverb* **mute·ness** *noun* [Old French *muet*, diminutive of *mu* from Latin *mutus*, assimilated to Latin]

mute button *noun* **1** a device on a telephone etc. to temporarily prevent the caller from hearing what is being said at the receiver's end. **2** a device on a television etc. that temporarily suppresses all sound.

muted *adjective* **1** (of colours etc.) subdued (*a muted green*). **2** (of a musical instrument) having a muffled tone or employing a mute. **3 a** silent, quiet, muffled. **b** understated.

mute swan *noun* the common white swan, *Cygnus olor*, native to Eurasia.

muti·late *transitive verb* **1** injure or damage (a person or animal or a part of the body) very severely, e.g. by removal of a limb or organ. **2** render (a book etc.) imperfect by excision or some act of destruction.

muti·la·tion noun **muti·la·tor** noun [Latin mutilare from mutilus maimed]

mu·tin·eer /ˌmjuːtɪˈnɪːr/ noun a person who mutinies. [French mutinier from mutin rebellious, from muete movement, ultimately from Latin movère move]

mu·tin·ous /ˈmjuːtɪnəs/ adjective (of a person or their conduct) rebellious, tending to mutiny. □ **mu·tin·ous·ly** adverb [obsolete mutine rebellion, from French mutin: see MUTINEER]

mu·tiny ● noun (pl. **-ies**) an open revolt against constituted authority, esp. by soldiers or sailors against their officers. ● intransitive verb (**-ies**, **-ied**) (often foll. by against) revolt; engage in mutiny. [obsolete mutine (as MUTINOUS)]

mut·ism /ˈmjuːtɪzəm/ noun **1** the state or condition of being mute. **2** Psych. the inability or unwillingness to speak, esp. for psychological rather than physiological reasons.

Mutsu /ˈmʌtsuː/ noun = CRISPIN. [Japanese]

Mut·su·hito /ˌmuːtsuˈhiːtoː/ see MEIJI TENNO.

mutt noun **1** derogatory or jocular a dog, esp. a mongrel. **2** slang an ignorant, stupid, or blundering person. [abbreviation of muttonhead]

Mutt and Jeff noun a seemingly ill-matched pair of people. [from two cartoon characters, one tall and one short, created by H.C. Fisher, US cartoonist d.1954]

Mut·ter /ˈmuːtər/ **Anne-Sophie** (b.1963), German violinist. She has played with many orchestras worldwide, and released more than forty recordings of standard and contemporary pieces, often working closely with conductor André Previn, whom she married in 2002.

mut·ter ● verb **1** transitive & intransitive speak in a barely audible manner. **2** intransitive murmur or grumble about. **3** transitive say or express (complaints etc.), esp. in secret. **4** intransitive make a low rumbling sound. ● noun **1** low, indistinct muttered words or sounds. **2** an act of muttering. □ **mut·ter·er** noun **mut·ter·ing** noun & adjective **mut·ter·ing·ly** adverb [Middle English, related to MUTE]

mut·ton noun the flesh of sheep used for food. □ **mutton dressed as lamb** informal a usu. middle-aged or elderly woman dressed or made up to appear younger. □ **mut·tony** adjective [Old French moton from medieval Latin multo -onis, prob. from Gaulish]

mutton busting noun N Amer. a children's rodeo event in which a child attempts to remain on the back of a moving sheep for four seconds while gripping the animal with his or her hands and knees.

mutton chop noun **1** (usu. in pl.) (in full **mutton chop whisker**) a side whisker, narrow at the top and broad and rounded at the bottom. **2** a piece of mutton, usu. the rib and half vertebra to which it is attached.

mutton·head noun informal a dull, stupid person. □ **mutton·head·ed** adjective

mu·tual /ˈmjuːtʃuəl/ ● adjective **1** (of feelings, actions, etc.) experienced or done by each of two or more parties with reference to the other or others; reciprocal (mutual affection). **2** held in common or shared between two or more persons (a mutual friend; a mutual interest). **3** (of people) having the same specified relationship to each other (mutual well-wishers). ● noun = MUTUAL FUND. □ **mu·tual·ity** /-ˈalɪti/ noun **mu·tual·ly** adverb [Old French mutuel from Latin mutuus mutual, borrowed, related to mutare change]

mutual admiration society noun two or more people who think very highly of one another, even to the extent of overestimating one another's merits.

mutual assured destruction noun a US military scenario in which nuclear war is deterred by each side knowing that the other is capable of inflicting unacceptable damage if attacked. Abbr.: **MAD**.

mutual fund noun N Amer. a fund in which contributions from many persons combined are invested in various securities and in which dividends are paid in proportion to the contributors' holdings.

mutual inductance noun the property of an electric circuit that causes an electromotive force to be generated in it by change in the current flowing through a magnetically linked circuit.

mutual induction noun the production of an electromotive force between adjacent circuits that are magnetically linked.

mutual insurance noun insurance in which some or all of the profits are divided among the policyholders.

mu·tual·ism noun **1 a** the doctrine that mutual dependence is necessary to social well-being. **b** a system based on this. **2** mutually beneficial symbiosis. □ **mu·tual·ist** noun & adjective **mu·tual·is·tic** adjective

mu·tuel /ˈmjuːtʃuəl/ noun N Amer. = PARIMUTUEL. [abbreviation]

mu·tule /ˈmjuːtʃuːl/ noun a block derived from the ends of wooden beams projecting under a Doric cornice. [French from Latin mutulus]

muu·muu /ˈmuːmuː/ noun a woman's usu. brightly coloured and patterned loose-fitting dress. [Hawaiian]

Muy·bridge /ˈmaɪbrɪdʒ/ **Ead·weard** (born Edward James Muggeridge) (1830–1904), English-born US photographer. A pioneer of motion photography, he is known for his studies of the movement of animals and humans.

Muzak /ˈmjuːzak/ noun **1** proprietary a system for transmitting background music for playing in public places. **2** (**muzak**) recorded light background music. **3** (**muzak**) bland, undemanding music. [alteration of MUSIC]

mu·zhik /ˈmuːʒɪk/ noun (also **moujik**) hist. a Russian peasant. [Russian muzhik]

Muz·tag /muːsˈtɒg/ a mountain in W China, on the N Tibetan border close to the Karamiran Shankou pass. Rising to 7 723 m (25,338 ft.), it is the highest peak in the Kunlun Shan range.

muz·zle ● noun **1** the projecting part of an animal's face, including the nose and mouth. **2** a guard, usu. made of straps or wire, fitted over an animal's nose and mouth to stop it biting or feeding. **3** the open end of a firearm. ● transitive verb **1** put a muzzle on (an animal etc.). **2** impose silence upon. □ **muz·zler** noun [Old French musel, ultimately from medieval Latin musum: compare MUSE[2]]

muzzle·load·er noun a gun that is loaded through the muzzle. □ **muzzle·load·ing** adjective & noun

muzzle velocity noun the velocity with which a projectile leaves the muzzle of a gun.

muzzy adjective (**muz·zi·er**, **muz·zi·est**) **1 a** mentally hazy; dull, spiritless. **b** dazed or fuddled from drinking alcohol. **2** blurred, indistinct. □ **muz·zi·ly** adverb **muz·zi·ness** noun [18th c.: origin unknown]

MV abbreviation **1** motor vessel. **2** megavolt(s).

mV abbreviation millivolt(s).

MVA abbreviation Cdn market value assessment (of property values for tax purposes).

MVD the Ministry of Internal Affairs, the secret police in the Soviet Union from 1946 to 1953. [Russian abbreviation]

MVP abbreviation N Amer. Sport most valuable player.

MW abbreviation megawatt(s).

mW abbreviation milliwatt(s).

MWO abbreviation Cdn MASTER WARRANT OFFICER.

Mx. abbreviation **1** maxwell(s). **2** Middlesex (a former county in England).

my ● possessive adjective (attributive) **1** of or belonging to me or myself (my house; my own business). **2** as a form of address in affectionate, sympathetic, respectful, jocular, or patronizing contexts (my dear boy). **3** in various expressions of surprise (my God!). ● interjection expressing surprise, admiration, etc. (my oh my, he's beautiful!) [Middle English mī, reduced from mīn MINE[1]]

my- var. of MYO-.

my·al·gia /maɪˈaldʒə, -dʒɪə/ noun a pain in a muscle or group of muscles. □ **my·al·gic** adjective [modern Latin from Greek mus muscle]

My·an·mar /ˌmaɪanˈmɑr/ the official name (since 1989) for BURMA.

my·as·the·nia /ˌmaɪəsˈθiːnɪə/ noun a condition causing abnormal weakness of certain muscles. □ **my·as·then·ic** adjective [modern Latin from Greek mus muscle: compare ASTHENIA]

myasthenia gravis /ˈɡravɪs/ noun a rare chronic autoimmune disease marked by muscular weakness without atrophy.

my·celi·um /maɪˈsiːlɪəm/ noun (pl. **mycelia** /-lɪə/) the vegetative part of a fungus, consisting of microscopic threadlike hyphae. □ **my·celi·al** adjective [modern Latin from Greek mukēs mushroom, after EPITHELIUM]

My·ce·nae /maɪˈsiːniː/ an ancient city in Greece, situated near the coast in the NE Peloponnese, on a site dominating various land and sea routes. The capital of King Agamemnon, it was the centre of the late Bronze Age Mycenaean civilization. Its period of greatest prosperity was c.1400–1200 BC, which saw construction of the palace and the massive walls of cyclopean masonry, including the 'Lion Gate,' the entrance to the citadel (c.1250 BC). The city was destroyed in about 1100 BC by invading Dorians.

My·ce·nae·an /ˌmaɪsəˈniːən/ ● adjective of or relating to the late Bronze Age civilization in Greece depicted in the Homeric poems and represented by finds at Mycenae and elsewhere. ● noun an inhabitant of Mycenae or the Mycenaean world.

-mycin /ˈməɪsɪn/ combining form used to form the names of antibiotic compounds derived from fungi. [as MYCO-]

myco- /ˈmaɪkəʊ/ *combining form* fungus. [Greek *mukēs* 'fungus, mushroom']

my·co·bac·ter·ium /maɪkəʊbakˈtɪəriəm/ *noun* (*pl.* **my·co·bac·teria**) any of various Gram-positive, aerobic, filament-forming bacteria of the genus *Mycobacterium* or the family Mycobacteriaceae, including the causative agents of tuberculosis and leprosy. □ **myco·bac·ter·ial** *adjective*

my·col·ogy /maɪˈkɒlədʒi/ *noun* the study of fungi. □ **myco·logic·al** *adjective* **myco·logic·al·ly** *adverb* **my·col·o·gist** *noun*

myco·plasma /maɪkəʊˈplazmə/ *noun* (*pl.* **myco·plas·mas**, **myco·plas·mata** /-mətə/) any of a group of mainly parasitic micro-organisms smaller than bacteria and without a cell wall.

mycor·rhiza /ˌmaɪkəˈraɪzə/ *noun* (*pl.* **mycor·rhi·zae** /-ziː/ or **mycor·rhi·zas**) a symbiotic association of a fungus and the roots of a plant. □ **mycor·rhi·zal** *adjective* [MYCO- + Greek *rhiza* root]

my·co·sis /maɪˈkəʊsɪs/ *noun* (*pl.* **-co·ses** /-ˈkəʊsiːz/) any disease caused by a fungus, e.g. ringworm. □ **my·cot·ic** /-ˈkɒtɪk/ *adjective*

myco·toxin /ˌmaɪkəˈtɒksɪn/ *noun* any toxic substance produced by a fungus.

my·dria·sis /mɪˈdraɪəsɪs/ *noun* excessive dilation of the pupil of the eye. [Latin from Greek *mudriasis*]

my·el·in /ˈmaɪəlɪn/ *noun* a white substance which forms a sheath around certain nerve fibres. □ **my·el·in·a·tion** *noun* **my·el·in·ated** *adjective* [Greek *muelos* marrow + -IN]

my·el·itis /maɪəˈlaɪtɪs/ *noun* inflammation of the spinal cord. [modern Latin from Greek *muelos* marrow + -ITIS]

my·el·oid /ˈmaɪəlɔɪd/ *adjective* of or relating to bone marrow or the spinal cord. [Greek *muelos* marrow]

my·el·oma /ˌmaɪəˈləʊmə/ *noun* (*pl.* **my·el·omas** or **my·elo·mata** /-mətə/) a malignant tumour of the bone marrow. [modern Latin, as MYELITIS + -OMA]

Myers, **Mi·chael** ('Mike') (b.1963), Canadian comedian. He created and starred in the spoof film *Austin Powers* (1997) and its sequels, as well as the comedy *Wayne's World* (1992).

Myko·lay·iv /ˌmɪkəˈlaiɛf/ (Russian **Nikolaev** /ˌnikaˈlajɪf/) an industrial city in S Ukraine, on the Southern Bug River near its confluence with the Dnieper and their joint estuaries on the northern shores of the Black Sea; pop. (est. 2001) 514,000.

My·ko·nos /ˈmiːkəˌnɒs/ a Greek island in the Aegean, one of the Cyclades.

Mylar /ˈmaɪlɑr/ *noun proprietary* a polyester film used to make audiotapes, insulation, etc. [arbitrary]

my·lo·don /ˈmaɪlədɒn/ *noun* an extinct gigantic ground sloth of the genus *Mylodon*, with cylindrical teeth, remains of which are found in deposits formed during the ice age of the Pleistocene epoch in S America. [modern Latin from Greek *mulē* mill, molar + *odous odontos* tooth]

My·men·singh /ˌmaɪmənˈsɪŋ/ a port on the Brahmaputra River in central Bangladesh; pop. (est. 2002) 334,400.

myna /ˈmaɪnə/ *noun* (also **mynah**) any of various SE Asian starlings, esp. *Gracula religiosa* able to mimic the human voice. [Hindi *mainā*]

myo- /ˈmaɪəʊ/ *combining form* (also **my-** before a vowel) muscle. [Greek *mus muos* muscle]

myo·car·di·um /maɪəʊˈkɑːdiəm/ *noun* (*pl.* **myo·car·dia** /-diə/) the muscular tissue of the heart. □ **myo·car·di·al** *adjective*

myo·car·ditis /-ˈdaɪtɪs/ *noun* [MYO- + Greek *kardia* heart]

myo·fib·ril /maɪəʊˈfaɪbrɪl/ *noun* any of the elongated contractile threads found in striated muscle cells.

myo·genic /ˌmaɪəˈdʒɛnɪk/ *adjective* originating in muscle tissue.

myo·glo·bin /ˌmaɪəʊˈɡləʊbɪn/ *noun* an oxygen-carrying protein containing iron and found in muscle cells.

my·ol·ogy /maɪˈɒlədʒi/ *noun* the study of the structure and function of muscles.

my·opia /maɪˈəʊpiə/ *noun* **1** short-sightedness. **2** lack of imagination or intellectual insight. □ **my·op·ic** /-ˈɒpɪk/ *adjective* **my·op·ic·ally** *adverb* [modern Latin from French from Late Latin *myops* from Greek *muōps* from *muō* shut + *ōps* eye]

myo·sin /ˈmaɪəsɪn/ *noun* a protein which with actin forms the contractile filaments of muscle. [MYO- + -OSE² + -IN]

my·o·sis *var. of* MIOSIS.

myo·tonia /ˌmaɪəˈtəʊniə/ *noun* an inability to relax or delay in relaxing a voluntary muscle. □ **myo·ton·ic** /-ˈtɒnɪk/ *adjective* [MYO- + Greek *tonos* tone]

myr·iad /ˈmɪriəd/ ● *noun* **1** an indefinitely great number. **2** *archaic* ten thousand. ● *adjective* **1** of an indefinitely great number. **2** having countless phases or aspects. [Late Latin *mirias miriad-* from Greek *murias -ados* from *murioi* 10,000]

myr·ia·pod /ˈmɪriəˌpɒd/ ● *noun* any land-living arthropod of the group Myriapoda, with numerous leg-bearing segments, e.g. centipedes and millipedes. ● *adjective* of or relating to this group. [modern Latin *Myriapoda* (as MYRIAD, Greek *pous podos* foot)]

myr·mi·don /ˈmɜːmɪdɒn/ *noun* an unquestioning follower or servant etc. [Latin *Myrmidones* (pl.) from Greek *Murmidones*, warlike Thessalian people who went with Achilles to Troy]

my·roba·lan /maɪˈrɒbələn/ *noun* **1** (in full **myrobalan plum**) = CHERRY PLUM. **2** (in full **myrobalan nut**) the fruit of an Asian tree, *Terminalia chebula*, used in medicines, for tanning leather, and to produce inks and dyes. [French *myrobolan* or Latin *myrobalanum* from Greek *murobalanos* from *muron* unguent + *balanos* acorn]

Myron /ˈmaɪrən/ (*fl. c.*480–440 BC), Greek sculptor. Only two certain copies of his work survive, the best known being the *Discobolus* (c.450 BC), a figure of a man throwing the discus which demonstrates Myron's interest in symmetry and movement.

myrrh¹ /mɜr/ *noun* **1** a gum resin from several trees of the genus *Commiphora* used, esp. in the Near East, in perfumery, medicine, incense, etc. **2** *Cdn* (*Nfld*) fir or spruce resin, often used as a component of home remedies. □ **myr·rhic** *adjective* **myr·rhy** *adjective* [Old English *myrra*, *myrre* from Latin *myrr(h)a* from Greek *murra*, of Semitic origin]

myrrh² /mɜr/ *noun* = SWEET CICELY. [Latin *myrris* from Greek *murris*]

myr·tle /ˈmɜːtəl/ *noun* **1** an evergreen shrub of the genus *Myrtus* with aromatic foliage and white flowers, esp. *M. communis*, bearing purple-black ovoid berries. **2** *N Amer.* the periwinkle, *Vinca minor*. [medieval Latin *myrtilla*, *-us* diminutive of Latin *myrta*, *myrtus* from Greek *murtos*]

my·self *pronoun* **1** *emphatic form of* I² or ME¹ (*I saw it myself*; *I like to do it myself*). **2** *reflexive form of* ME¹ (*I was angry with myself*; *able to dress myself*; *as bad as myself*). **3** in my normal state of body and mind (*I'm not myself today*). □ **by myself** *see* BY ONESELF (*see* BY). **I myself** I for my part (*I myself am doubtful*). [ME¹ + SELF: *my-* partly after *herself* with *her* regarded as possess. adj.]

Mysia /ˈmɪsiə/ an ancient region of NW Asia Minor, on the Mediterranean coast south of the Sea of Marmara. □ **Mys·ian** *adjective & noun*

My·sore /maɪˈsɔr/ **1** a city in the Indian state of Karnataka; pop. (2001) 742,300. It was the former capital of the princely state of Mysore and is noted for the production of silk, incense and sandalwood oil. **2** the former name (until 1973) for KARNATAKA.

mys·teri·ous *adjective* **1** full of or wrapped in mystery. **2** puzzling; enigmatic. □ **mys·teri·ous·ly** *adverb* **mys·teri·ous·ness** *noun*

mys·tery¹ *noun* (*pl.* **-ies**) **1** a secret, hidden, or inexplicable matter (*the reason remains a mystery*). **2** secrecy or obscurity (*wrapped in mystery*). **3** (*attributive*) secret, undisclosed (*mystery guest*). **4** the practice of making a secret of (esp. unimportant) things (*engaged in mystery and intrigue*). **5** a fictional work dealing with a puzzling event, esp. a crime (also *attributive*: *a well-known mystery writer*). **6 a** a religious truth divinely revealed, esp. one beyond human reason. **b** *Catholicism* a decade of the rosary. **7** (in *pl.*) **a** the secret religious rites of the ancient Greeks, Romans, etc. **b** *archaic* the Eucharist. □ **make a mystery of** treat as an impressive secret. [Old French *mistere* or Latin *mysterium* from Greek *mustērion*, related to MYSTIC]

mys·tery² *noun* (*pl.* **-ies**) *archaic* a handicraft or trade, esp. as referred to in indentures etc. [medieval Latin *misterium* contraction of *ministerium* MINISTRY, assoc. with MYSTERY¹]

mystery play *noun* a miracle play.

mystery shopper *noun* a person, such as a consumer representative etc., who visits a store or restaurant incognito in order to assess the quality of the goods or services provided.

mys·tic ● *noun* a person who seeks by contemplation and self-surrender to obtain unity or identity with or absorption into the Deity or the ultimate reality, or who believes in the spiritual apprehension of truths that are beyond the understanding. ● *adjective* **1** mysterious and awe-inspiring. **2** spiritually allegorical or symbolic. **3** occult, esoteric. **4** of hidden meaning. □ **mysti·cism** *noun* [Old French *mystique* or Latin *mysticus* from Greek *mustikos* from *mustēs* initiated person, from *muō* close the eyes or lips, initiate]

mys·tic·al *adjective* **1** of mystics or mysticism. **2** mystic. □ **mys·tic·al·ly** *adverb*

mys·tify *transitive verb* (**-fies**, **-fied**) **1** bewilder, confuse. **2** wrap up in

mystery. □ **mysti·fi·ca·tion** *noun* **mysti·fy·ing** *adjective*
mysti·fy·ing·ly *adverb* [French *mystifier* (irreg. formed as MYSTIC or MYSTERY¹)]

mys·tique /mɪˈstiːk/ *noun* an atmosphere of mystery and importance evoking admiration, surrounding some activity or person; charisma. [French (as MYSTIC)]

myth *noun* **1** a traditional narrative usu. involving supernatural or imaginary persons and embodying popular ideas on natural or social phenomena etc. **2** such narratives collectively. **3** a widely held but false notion. **4** a fictitious person, thing, or idea. **5** an idealized version of the past, esp. as embodying significant cultural realities. **6** an allegory (*the Platonic myth*). □ **myth·ic** *adjective* **myth·ic·al** *adjective*
myth·ic·al·ly *adverb* [modern Latin *mythus* from Late Latin *mythos* from Greek *muthos*]

mythi·cize /ˈmɪθɪˌsaɪz/ *transitive verb* (also esp. *Brit.* **-cise**) treat (a story etc.) as a myth; interpret mythically. □ **mythi·ciz·a·tion** *noun*

myth·maker *noun* a creator of myths or folklore. □ **myth·making** *noun*

mytho- /ˈmɪθoː/ *combining form* myth.

myth·og·raph·er /mɪˈθɒɡrəfər/ *noun* a compiler or collector of myths.

myth·og·raphy /mɪˈθɒɡrəfi/ *noun* **1** the representation of myths in the plastic arts. **2** a collection of myths.

myth·ol·ogy *noun* (*pl.* **-ies**) **1** a body of myths (*Greek mythology*). **2** the study of myths. **3** myths collectively. **4** a body of traditions or stories, usu. somewhat idealized, concerning a particular person, institution, event, etc. (*the mythology of the settlement of the prairies*). □ **mytho·logic** *adjective* **mytho·logic·al** *adjective* **mytho·logic·al·ly** *adverb*

myth·ol·o·gist *noun* **myth·olo·giz·a·tion** *noun* **myth·ol·o·gize** *transitive & intransitive verb* (also esp. *Brit.* **-gise**). **myth·ol·o·giz·er** *noun*

mytho·mania /ˌmɪθoːˈmeɪnɪə/ *noun* an abnormal tendency to exaggerate or tell lies. □ **mytho·maniac** *noun & adjective*

mytho·poeia /ˌmɪθoːˈpiːə/ *noun* the making of myths.
□ **mytho·poeic** *adjective*

mytho·poet·ic /ˌmɪθoːpoːˈetɪk/ *adjective* **1** of or relating to the making of a myth or myths. **2** relating to or denoting a movement for men that uses activities such as storytelling and poetry reading as a means of self-understanding.

myth·os /ˈmɪθɒs, ˈmaɪθɒs/ *noun* (*pl.* **mythoi** /-θɔɪ/) **1** *literary* a myth; a body of myths. **2** a narrative theme or pattern. [Late Latin: see MYTH]

myx·edema /ˌmɪksəˈdiːmə/ *noun* (also esp. *Brit.* **myx·oedema**) a syndrome caused by hypothyroidism, resulting in thickening of the skin, weight gain, mental dullness, loss of energy, and sensitivity to cold. [MYXO- + EDEMA]

myxo- /ˈmɪksoː/ *combining form* (also **myx-** before a vowel) mucus. [Greek *muxa* mucus]

myx·oma /mɪkˈsoːmə/ *noun* (*pl.* **myx·omas** or **myx·omata** /-mətə/) a benign tumour of mucous or gelatinous tissue. □ **myxo·ma·tous** /-ˈsɒmətəs/ *adjective* [modern Latin (as MYXO-, -OMA)]

myxo·ma·to·sis /ˌmɪksəməˈtoːsɪs/ *noun* an infectious usu. fatal viral disease in rabbits, causing swelling of the mucous membranes.

myxo·my·cete /ˌmɪksoːmaɪˈsiːt/ *noun* = SLIME MOULD.

myxo·virus /ˈmɪksoːˌvaɪrəs/ *noun* any of a group of viruses including the influenza virus.

Nn

N¹ *noun* (also **n**) (*pl.* **Ns** or **N's**) **1** the fourteenth letter of the alphabet. **2** *Printing* en.

N² *abbreviation* (also **N.**) **1 a** North. **b** Northern. **2** *Chess* knight. **3** New. **4** nuclear.

N³ *symbol* **1** the element nitrogen. **2** newton(s).

n¹ *abbreviation* (also **n.**) **1** name. **2** neuter. **3** noon. **4** note. **5** noun.

n² *symbol* **1** *Math.* an indefinite number. **2** nano-. □ **to the nth** (or **nth degree**) **1** *Math.* to any required power. **2** to any extent; to the utmost.

'n *conjunction* (also **'n'**) *informal* and. [abbreviation]

-n¹ *suffix see* -EN².

-n² *suffix see* -EN³.

NA *abbreviation* **1** North America. **2** North American.

Na *symbol* the element sodium. [modern Latin *natrium*]

na /nə/ *adverb Scot.* (in *combination*; usu. with an auxiliary verb) = NOT (*I canna do it; they didna go*).

n/a *abbreviation* **1** not applicable. **2** not available.

NAACP *abbreviation* (in the US) National Association for the Advancement of Colored People.

NAAFI /'nafi/ *abbreviation Brit.* Navy, Army, and Air Force Institutes, an organization providing stores and places to eat for British soldiers etc. in the UK and abroad.

naan *var. of* NAN².

NAB *abbreviation* NEW AMERICAN BIBLE.

nab *transitive verb* (**nabbed, nab·bing**) *informal* **1** arrest; catch in wrongdoing. **2** capture, catch. [17th c., also *napp*, as in KIDNAP: origin unknown]

Nab·lus /'nɒbləs/ a town in the West Bank; pop. (est. 2002) 112,800. It is close to the site of the Canaanite city of Shechem, important in ancient times because of its position on an east-west route through the mountains of Samaria.

na·bob /'neibɒb/ *noun* **1** *informal* a very rich or influential person. **2** *hist.* = NAWAB. **3** *Brit. hist.* a person returning from India with a large fortune acquired there. [Portuguese *nababo* or Spanish *nabab*, from Urdu (as NAWAB)]

Nabo·kov /'nabə,kɒf, nə'bɒkɒf/ **Vlad·i·mir (Vlad·imor·ovich)** (1899–1977), Russian-born US novelist and poet. He wrote in both Russian and English. His novel *Lolita* (1958) recounts a middle-aged European man's obsession with a 12-year-old American girl. □ **Nabo·kov·ian** /,nabə'ko:viən/ *adjective*

NAC *abbreviation* (in Canada) **1** National Action Committee (on the Status of Women). **2** National Archives of Canada.

na·celle /nə'sel/ *noun* **1** a streamlined housing or tank for something on the outside of an aircraft or motor vehicle. **2** the outer casing of an aircraft engine. **3** *hist.* the car of an airship. [French, from Late Latin *navicella* diminutive of Latin *navis* ship]

naches /'nʌxəs/ *noun informal* **1** pride or gratification, esp. at the achievements of one's children. **2** congratulations (*naches to Miriam on her acceptance into rabbinic school*). [Yiddish *nakhes*, from Hebrew *naḥaṭ* contentment]

nacho /'nɒtʃo:/ *noun* (*pl.* **nachos**) (usu. in *pl.*) a tortilla chip topped with cheese, salsa, peppers, etc. and broiled. [20th c.: origin uncertain]

nacre /'neikər/ *noun* = MOTHER-OF-PEARL. □ **na·cre·ous** /'neikriəs/ *adjective* [French]

NAD *abbreviation Biochem.* nicotinamide adenine dinucleotide, a coenzyme important in many biological oxidation reactions.

nada /'nɒdə/ *noun informal* nothing (*has said nada all evening*). [Spanish]

Nader /'neidər/ **Ralph** (b.1934), US lawyer and reformer. A leading figure in the US consumer protection movement, he has been a moving force behind legislation concerning automobile safety standards, radiation hazards, food packaging, and the use of insecticides; his books include *Unsafe at Any Speed* (1965). □ **Nader·ite** *noun*

na·dir /'neidi:r/ *noun* **1** the part of the celestial sphere directly below an observer (opp. ZENITH). **2** the lowest point in one's fortunes; a time of deep despair. [Old French from Arabic *naẓir* (*as-samt*) opposite (to the zenith)]

nae /nei/ *adverb Scot.* not. [variant of NA]

nae·vus *var. of* NEVUS. [Latin]

naff¹ /naf/ *intransitive verb Brit. slang* **1** (in *imperative*, foll. by *off*) go away. **2** (as **naff·ing** *adjective*) used as an intensive to express annoyance etc. [prob. euphemism for FUCK: compare EFF]

naff² *adjective Brit. slang* **1** unfashionable; socially awkward. **2** worthless, rubbishy. **3** in poor taste; tacky. [20th c.: origin unknown]

NAFTA /'naftə/ *abbreviation* North American Free Trade Agreement.

nag¹ ● *verb* (**nagged, nag·ging**) **1 a** *transitive* annoy or irritate (a person) with persistent fault-finding or continuous urging. **b** *intransitive* (often foll. by *at*) find fault, complain, or urge, esp. persistently. **2** *intransitive* (of a pain) ache dully but persistently. **3 a** *transitive* worry or preoccupy (a person, the mind, etc.) (*his mistake nagged him*). **b** *intransitive* (often foll. by *at*) worry or gnaw. ● *noun* a persistently nagging person. □ **nag·ger** *noun* [of dial., perhaps Scandinavian or Low German, origin: compare Norwegian & Swedish *nagga* gnaw, irritate, Low German (g)*naggen* provoke]

nag² *noun* **1** an old or broken-down horse. **2** *informal* a horse, esp. a racehorse. [Middle English: origin unknown]

naga /'nɒgə/ *noun Hinduism* a member of a race of semi-divine creatures, half-snake half-human. [Sanskrit, = serpent]

Naga·land /'nɒgə,land/ a state in the far northeast of India, on the border with Burma (Myanmar); capital, Kohima.

Naga·saki /,nagə'saki, ,nɒgə'sɒki/ a city and port in SW Japan, on the west coast of Kyushu island; pop. (est. 2002) 431,900. It was the target of the second atomic bomb, dropped by the US on 9 Aug. 1945, which resulted in the deaths of about 75,000 people and devastated one-third of the city.

nag·ging ● *noun* the action of persistent fault-finding or urging. ● *adjective* **1** worrying or preoccupying (*a nagging feeling we've forgotten something*). **2** aching dully and persistently (*a nagging headache*). □ **nag·ging·ly** *adverb*

Nagorno-Karabakh /nə,gɔrno:,karə'bax/ a region of Azerbaijan in the southern foothills of the Caucasus, which has long had a majority Armenian population; pop. (est. 2002) 143,100; capital, Xankändi.

Na·goya /nə'gɔiə/ a city in central Japan, on the south coast of the island of Honshu, capital of Chubu region; pop. (est. 2002) 2,186,200.

Nag·pur /nag'pur/ a city in central India, in the state of Maharashtra; pop. (2001) 2,051,300.

Nagy /'nɒdʒ/ **Imre** (1896–1958), Hungarian Communist leader, prime minister 1953–5 and 1956. During his second term in office he announced Hungary's withdrawal from the Warsaw Pact and sought a neutral status for his country; when the Red Army moved in to crush the Hungarian uprising (1956), he was removed from office and executed.

Nah. *abbreviation Bible* Nahum.

nah /na/ *adverb informal* no. [casual pronunciation of NO²]

Naha /ˈnnhə/ a port in S Japan, capital of Okinawa island; pop. (est. 2002) 321,500.

Na·han·ni National Park Reserve /nəˈhani/ a park reserve in the southwestern corner of mainland NWT, surrounding the area of the South Nahanni River. Known for its varied and spectacular landscape, it is a designated World Heritage Site. [as SOUTH NAHANNI RIVER]

Na·huatl /nɒˈwɒtəl, ˈnɒ-/ ● *noun* **1** a member of a group of Aboriginal peoples of S Mexico and Central America, including the Aztecs. **2** the language of these people. ● *adjective* of or concerning the Nahuatl peoples or language. □ **Na·huat·lan** *adjective* [Spanish from Nahuatl]

Nahum /ˈneihəm/ **1** a Hebrew minor prophet. **2** a book of the Bible containing his prophecy of the fall of Nineveh (early 7th c. BC).

naiad /ˈnaiad/ *noun* (*pl.* **naiads** or **nai·ades** /-əˌdiːz/) **1** *Gk Myth* a water nymph. **2** the larva of a dragonfly etc. **3** any aquatic plant of the genus *Najas*, with narrow leaves and small flowers. [Latin *Naïas Naïad-* from Greek *Naias -ados* from *naō* flow]

naïf /nɒˈiːf/ ● *adjective* = NAIVE *adjective*. ● *noun* a naive person. [French: see NAIVE]

nail ● *noun* **1** a small usu. sharpened metal spike with a broadened flat head, driven in esp. with a hammer to join things together. **2 a** a horny covering on the upper surface of the tip of the human finger or toe. **b** a claw or talon. **3** *hist.* a measure of cloth length (equal to 2¹⁄₄ inches). ● *transitive verb* **1** fasten with a nail or nails (*nail it to the wall; nailed the planks together*). **2** fix or hold (one's eyes, attention, etc.) on something. **3** hit, strike, or punch (a person, ball, etc.). **4 a** secure, catch, or get hold of (a person or thing). **b** arrest (a person). **5** *Baseball* put (a runner) out (*nailed him at first*). **6** complete or perform (something) well or perfectly (*nailed a triple somersault*). □ **hard as nails 1** callous; unfeeling. **2** in good physical condition. **hit the nail on the head** *see* HIT. **nail one's colours to the mast** persist; refuse to give in. **nail down 1** bind (a person) to a promise etc. **2** define precisely. **3** fasten (a thing) with nails. **nail in the coffin** something to make imminent a person's death or the end or failure of something. **nail up 1** close (a door etc.) with nails. **2** fix (a thing) at a height with nails. **on the nail** *Brit.* (esp. of payment) without delay (*cash on the nail*). □ **nailed** *adjective* (also in *combination*). **nail·less** *adjective* [Old English *nægel, næglan* from Germanic]

nail-biter *noun* **1** something that causes anxiety or tension (*the game was a real nail-biter right up to the last second*). **2** a person who habitually bites his or her fingernails.

nail-biting ● *adjective* **1** causing severe anxiety or tension. **2** (of a person) having a tendency to bite his or her fingernails, esp. habitually. ● *noun* the act or an instance of biting one's fingernails.

nail brush *noun* a small brush for cleaning the nails.

nail enamel *noun N Amer.* = NAIL POLISH.

nail·er *noun* **1** a tool used to drive nails; a nail gun. **2** an additional joist or support inside a wall, used for fastening a cabinet, shelf, etc. to.

nail file *noun* a roughened metal or emery strip used for smoothing the nails.

nail gun *noun* a tool that uses electric power or an explosive charge to drive nails into wood.

nail·head *noun* **1** the flat head of a nail. **2** *Archit.* an ornament like the head of a nail.

nail polish *noun* a varnish applied to the nails to colour them or make them shiny.

nail scissors *plural noun* small curved scissors for trimming the nails.

nail set *noun* (also **nail punch**) a tool for sinking the head of a nail below a surface.

nail varnish *noun Brit.* = NAIL POLISH.

Nain /nein/ a town situated on the northeastern coast of Labrador; pop. (2001) 936.

nain·sook /ˈneinsʊk/ *noun* a fine soft cotton fabric, used esp. for baby clothes. [Hindi *nainsukh* from *nain* eye + *sukh* pleasure]

Nai·paul /ˈnaipɒl/ **Sir Vidi·ad·har Suraj·pra·sad** (b.1932), Trinidadian-born English novelist and travel writer, of Indian descent. His novels often address the Indian subculture of the West Indies with a satirical but sympathetic eye, and include *A House for Mr. Biswas*

(1961), *In a Free State* (1971), which won the Booker Prize, and *The Enigma of Arrival* (1987). He won the Nobel Prize for literature in 2001.

naira /ˈnairə/ *noun* the chief monetary unit of Nigeria, equal to 100 kobo. [contraction of *Nigeria*]

Nai·ro·bi /naiˈroːbi/ the capital of Kenya; pop. (est. 2002) 2,510,800. It is situated on the central Kenyan plateau at an altitude of 1 680 m (5,500 ft.).

Nai·smith /ˈneismɪθ/ **James A.** (1861–1939), Canadian-born educator, who invented basketball in Springfield, Massachusetts, in 1891 to meet his own needs for a competitive, indoor team sport.

naive /naiˈiːv/ *adjective* **1** artless; innocent; unaffected. **2** foolishly credulous. **3** (of art etc.) produced in a sophisticated society but deliberately rejecting conventional expertise. □ **naive·ly** *adverb* **naive·ness** *noun* [French, fem. of *naïf* from Latin *nativus* NATIVE]

naïv·eté /naiˌiːvəˈtei, naiˈiːvəti/ *noun* (also **naiv·ety** /naiˈiːvəti/) **1** the state or quality of being naive. **2** a naive action. [French (as NAIVE)]

Najaf /ˈnadʒaf/ (also **An Najaf** /an/) a city in S Iraq, on the Euphrates; pop. (est. 2002) 563,000. It contains the shrine of Ali, the prophet Muhammad's son-in-law, and is a holy city of the Shiite Muslims.

naked *adjective* **1** unclothed; nude. **2** plain; undisguised; exposed (*the naked truth; naked ambition*). **3 a** (of a flame etc.) unprotected from the wind etc. **b** (of a light bulb) unshaded. **4** defenceless. **5 a** (of landscape) barren; treeless. **b** (of rock) exposed; without soil etc. **6** (of a sword etc.) unsheathed. **7** without leaves, hairs, scales, shell, etc. **8** (of a room, wall, etc.) without decoration, furnishings, etc.; empty, plain. □ **naked·ly** *adverb* **naked·ness** *noun* [Old English *nacod* from Germanic]

naked eye *noun* unassisted vision, e.g. without a telescope, microscope, etc.

nakfa *noun* (*pl.* same or **nakfas**) the basic monetary unit of Eritrea, equal to one hundred cents. [*Nakfa*, the name of the town where the country's armed struggle against the Ethiopian regime was launched]

Nakhi·che·van *see* NAXÇIVAN.

Na·kota /naˈkoːtə/ *noun & adjective* = ASSINIBOINE. [Sioux, = 'allies']

Na·kuru /naˈkuːruː/ an industrial city in W Kenya; pop. (est. 2002) 337,200. Nearby is Lake Nakuru, which is famous for its spectacular flocks of flamingos.

Nal·chik /ˈnaltʃɪk/ a city in the Caucasus, SW Russia, capital of the republic of Kabardino-Balkaria; pop. (est. 2002) 233,900.

na·lox·one /nəˈlɒksoːn/ *noun Med.* a synthetic drug, similar to morphine, which blocks opiate receptors in the nervous system. [contraction of *N-allylnoroxymorphone*]

nal·trex·one /nalˈtreksoːn/ *noun Med.* a synthetic drug, similar to morphine, which blocks opiate receptors in the nervous system and is used chiefly in the treatment of heroin addiction. [contraction of *N-allylnoroxymorphone*, with the insertion of the arbitrary element *-trex-*]

Nam /nam, nɒm/ an informal name for Vietnam. [abbreviation]

Nama /ˈnɒmə/ ● *noun* (*pl.* same or **Namas**) **1** a member of a people of South Africa and Namibia. *Also called* KHOIKHOI. **2** the language of this people. ¶ The term *Hottentot* is sometimes used for this people and language, but it is often considered to be *offensive*. ● *adjective* of or relating to this people or their language. [Nama]

Nam·an·gan /ˌnamənˈɡɒn/ a city in E Uzbekistan, near the border with Kyrgyzstan; pop. (est. 2002) 442,700.

Na·ma·qua·land /nəˈmɒkwəˌland/ a region of SW Africa, the homeland of the Nama people of SW Namibia and South Africa. **Little Namaqualand** lies immediately to the south of the Orange River and is in the South African province of Northern Cape, while **Great Namaqualand** lies to the north of the river and is in Namibia.

namby-pamby ● *adjective* **1** lacking vigour or drive; weak. **2** insipidly pretty or sentimental. ● *noun* (*pl.* **-pambies**) a namby-pamby person. [fanciful formulation on name of *Ambrose* Philips, English pastoral writer d.1749]

name ● *noun* **1 a** the word by which an individual person, animal, place, or thing is known, spoken of, etc. (*mentioned you by name; her name is Sandra*). **b** all who go under one name; a family, clan, or people in terms of its name (*brought dishonour to his name*). **2 a** a usu. abusive term used of a person etc. (*called me names*). **b** a word denoting an object or esp. a class of objects, ideas, etc. (*what is the name of that kind of vase?; that sort of behaviour has no name*). **3** a famous person (*some of the biggest names in the art world*). **4** a reputation, esp. a good one (*has a name for honesty; their name is guarantee enough*). **5** something existing only nominally (*opp.* FACT, REALITY). ● *transitive verb* **1** give a usu. specified name to (*what will we name her?*). **2** call (a person or thing) by the right name (*named the child in the photograph*). **3** mention; specify;

cite (*named her requirements; named a time for the meeting*). **4** nominate, appoint, etc. (*was named the new director*). **5** specify as something desired (*named it as her dearest wish*). **6** *Cdn & Brit. Parl.* (of the Speaker) mention (a member of a legislative assembly) as disobedient to the chair, thus banning her or him from the House. ● *attributive adjective* **1** famous; widely-known (*a name band*). **2** designating the person that gives his or her name to a firm, theatrical production, etc. (*one of the name partners*). □ **by name 1** called (*Gordon by name*). **2** using the name or names of someone (*knows all her students by name*). **by the name of** called (*a young girl by the name of Beth*). **enter one's name** apply to enter an educational institution, competition, course, etc. **give a bad name** cause disrepute to (*this kind of behaviour gives students a bad name*). **give one's name to something** invent or originate something which then becomes known by one's own name. **have one's name on a thing** be destined or particularly suited to receive that thing (*a bullet out there with my name on it*). (**have**) **to one's name** (possess) as one's own. **in all but name** virtually. **in name** (or **in name only**) as a mere formality; hardly at all (*was the manager in name only*). **in the name of 1** calling to witness; invoking (*in the name of goodness; in God's name, what are you doing?*). **2** by the authority of (*stop in the name of the law*). **3** for the sake of (*they did it all in the name of friendship*). **in one's own name** independently; without authority. **lend one's name to** see LEND. **make a name for oneself** (also **make one's name**) become famous. **name after** (also *N Amer.* **name for**) call (a person) by the name of (a specified person) (*named him Robert after his grandfather*). **name the day** arrange a date for one's wedding. **name names** mention specific names, esp. in accusation. **name of the game** *informal* the purpose or essence of an action etc. **put a name to a person or a thing** know or remember what a person or thing is called (*I know that tune but I can't put a name to it*). **put one's name down for 1** apply for. **2** promise to subscribe (a sum). **take a person's name in vain** see VAIN. **under the name** using as a pseudonym. **what's in a name?** names are arbitrary labels. **you name it** *informal* no matter what; whatever you like. □ **name·able** *adjective* **nam·er** *noun* [Old English *nama*, *noma*, (*ge*)*namian* from Germanic, related to Latin *nomen*, Greek *onoma*]

name brand *noun* (also *attributive*) = BRAND NAME.

name-calling *noun* abusive language.

name day *noun* the feast day of a saint after whom a person is named.

name-dropping *noun* the practice of casually mentioning the names of famous people one knows or pretends to know in order to impress others. □ **name-drop** *intransitive verb* (**-dropped**, **-drop·ping**). **name-dropper** *noun*

name·less *adjective* **1** having no name or inscription. **2** inexpressible; indefinable (*a nameless sensation*). **3** unnamed; anonymous, esp. deliberately (*our informant, who shall be nameless*). **4** too loathsome or horrific to be named (*nameless vices*). **5** obscure; inglorious. □ **name·less·ly** *adverb* **name·less·ness** *noun*

name·ly *adverb* that is to say; in other words.

name·plate *noun* **1** a plate or panel bearing the name of an occupant of a room etc. **2 a** a plate attached to a car, computer, etc. bearing the name of the manufacturer or model. **b** a line of products produced under a single name.

name recognition *noun* the extent to which a name, as of a politician, company, etc., is familiar to members of the public.

name·sake *noun* a person or thing having the same name as another (*was her aunt's namesake*). [prob. from phr. *for the name's sake*]

name tag *noun* **1** a label, sticker, etc. bearing a person's name and often other relevant information and worn as identification. **2** a label sewn inside a garment etc. and bearing the name of the owner.

Namib Desert /ˈnɒmɪb/ a desert of SW Africa, extending 1 900 km (1,200 miles) along the Atlantic coast, from the Curoca River in SW Angola through Namibia to the border between Namibia and South Africa.

Na·mib·ia /nəˈmɪbɪə/ a country in southern Africa, with a coastline on the Atlantic Ocean; pop. (est. 2002) 1,820,916; capital, Windhoek. Namibia is an arid country, with large tracts of desert along the coast and in the east. □ **Na·mib·ian** *adjective & noun*

nam pla /ˈnam plɑ/ *noun* a pungent, salty fish sauce used in Thai cooking. [Thai, from *naam* water + *plaa* fish]

Nampo /ˈnampoː/ a city on the west coast of North Korea, southwest of Pyongyang; pop. (est. 1993) 731,448.

Namur /nəˈmʊr/ **1** a province in central Belgium. It was the scene of the last German offensive in the Ardennes in 1945. **2** the capital of this province, at the junction of the Meuse and Sambre rivers; pop. (est. 2002) 106,100.

nan[1] /nan/ *noun Brit. & Cdn* (*Nfld*) *informal* grandmother. [childish pronunciation]

nan[2] /nan/ *noun* (also **naan**) (in Indian cooking) a type of flat, oval, leavened bread cooked esp. in a clay oven. [Persian & Urdu *nān*]

nana /ˈnanə/ *noun* (also esp. *Brit.* **nanna**) *informal* grandmother. [childish pronunciation]

Na·naimo /nəˈnaɪmoː/ a city and port on the east coast of Vancouver Island, located 113 km northwest of Victoria, across the Strait of Georgia from Vancouver; pop. (2001) 73,000. □ **Na·naimo·ite** *noun* [ultimately after SNE NAY MUXW]

Na·naimo bar *noun Cdn* a dessert consisting of a crust of chocolate and cookie crumbs, usu. also including coconut and nuts, covered with a usu. vanilla buttercream filling and a chocolate glaze, served cut into squares. [NANAIMO]

Nanak /ˈnɒnək/ (known as 'Guru Nanak') (1469–1539), Indian religious leader and founder of Sikhism. He travelled widely as a wandering preacher and settled in Kartarpur, in what is now Punjab province, Pakistan; there he built the first Sikh temple. His teachings are contained in a number of hymns which form part of the Adi Granth.

Nan·chang /nanˈtʃaŋ/ the capital of Jiangxi province in SE China; pop. (est. 2002) 1,613,500.

Nancy /ˈnansi/ a city in NE France, capital of Lorraine; pop. (1999) 103,605.

nancy (also **nance**) *slang offensive* ● *noun* (*pl.* **-cies**) (in full **nancy boy**) an effeminate man, esp. a homosexual. ● *adjective* effeminate. [from the female given name *Nancy*]

Nandi /ˈnʌndi/ *Hinduism* a bull which serves as the mount of Shiva and symbolizes fertility. [Sanskrit, = the happy one]

Nanga Par·bat /ˌnʌŋə ˈpʊrbʌt/ a mountain in N Pakistan, in the W Himalayas. It rises to 8 126 m (26,660 ft.).

Nan·jing /nanˈdʒɪŋ/ (also **Nan·king** /-ˈkɪŋ/) a city in E China, on the Yangtze River, capital of Jiangsu province; pop. (est. 2002) 3,034,500. It was the capital of various ruling dynasties and capital of China from 1368 until replaced by Beijing in 1421.

nan·keen /nanˈkiːn, nan-/ ● *noun* **1** a yellowish cotton cloth. **2** a yellowish-buff colour. **3** (in *pl.*) trousers of nankeen. ● *adjective* **1** made of nankeen. **2** of the yellowish-buff colour of nankeen. [*Nankin(g)* in China, where originally made]

Nan·king cherry *noun* a cherry tree, *Prunus tomentosa*, native to east Asia, with sweet edible fruit.

nanna *Brit. var. of* NANA.

Nan·ning /nanˈnɪŋ/ the capital of Guangxi Zhuang autonomous region in S China; pop. (est. 2002) 1,437,000.

nanny ● *noun* (*pl.* **-nies**) **1 a** a person employed, esp. on a full-time basis, to care for a child, usu. in the child's home. **b** an unduly protective person, institution, etc. **2** = NAN[1]. **3** (in full **nanny goat**) a female goat. ● *transitive verb* (**-nies**, **-nied**) be unduly protective towards. [pet form of the female given name *Ann*]

nanny·berry *noun* (*pl.* **-berries**) a large shrub, *Viburnum lentago*, found east of the Rockies, with dark blue sweet edible fruit.

nanny cam *noun informal* a (usu. hidden) wireless video camera sending a signal to a television monitor, often used by parents for surveillance of young children in their rooms, or of caregivers.

nanny state *noun* a derogatory nickname for the collective government institutions and practices of the welfare state, perceived as either overprotective or too authoritarian.

nanny suite *noun* a self-contained apartment within a house, as for a live-in nanny.

nano- /ˈnanoː/ *combining form* **1** denoting a factor of 10⁻⁹ (*nanosecond*). **2** very small; minute. [Latin from Greek *nanos* dwarf]

nano·metre /ˈnanoːˌmiːtər/ *noun* (also **nano·meter**) one billionth of a metre. Abbr.: **nm**.

nano·sec·ond /ˈnanoːˌsekənd/ *noun* **1** one billionth of a second. **2** an extremely short interval.

nano·tech·nol·ogy /ˌnanoːtekˈnɒlədʒi/ *noun* the branch of technology that deals with dimensions and tolerances of less than 100 nanometres, esp. the manipulation of individual atoms and molecules. □ **nano·techno·logic·al** *adjective* **nano·tech·nol·o·gist** *noun*

Nan·sen /ˈnansən/ **Fridt·jof** (1861–1930), Norwegian Arctic explorer and statesman. In 1888 he led the first expedition to cross the Greenland icefields, and in 1893 he set out for the North Pole, reaching a latitude of 86° 14′, the furthest north anyone had been at that time. In 1922 he was awarded the Nobel Peace Prize for organizing relief work among victims of the Russian famine.

Consonants:　b *but*　d *dog*　f *few*　g *get*　h *her*　j *yes*　k *cat*　l *leg*　m *man*　n *no*　p *pen*　r *red*　s *sit*

Nantes /nɑ̃t/ a city in W France, on the Loire, chief town of Pays de la Loire region; pop. (1999) 270,251. *See also* EDICT OF NANTES.

Nan·ti·coke /'nantɪˌkoːk/ a former city in S Ontario, located on Lake Erie, southwest of Hamilton, now part of Haldimand; pop. (2001) 23,588. [from an Aboriginal language, perhaps meaning 'crooked creek', with reference to a creek nearby]

Nan·tuck·et /nan'tʌkət/ an island off the coast of Massachusetts, south of Cape Cod and east of Martha's Vineyard.

Naoise /'niːʃə/ *Irish Myth* the husband of Deirdre, who was slain by Conchobar.

Naomi /neiˈoːmi/ *Bible* the mother-in-law of Ruth (Ruth 1:2).

nap¹ ● *intransitive verb* (**napped**, **nap·ping**) sleep lightly or briefly. ● *noun* a short sleep or doze, esp. by day. □ **catch a person napping 1** find a person asleep or off guard. **2** detect in negligence or error. [Old English *hnappian*, related to Old High German (*h*)*naffezan* to slumber]

nap² ● *noun* **1** the raised pile on textiles, esp. velvet. **2** a soft downy surface. ● *transitive verb* (**napped**, **nap·ping**) raise a nap on (cloth). □ **nap·less** *adjective* **napped** *adjective* [Middle Dutch, Middle Low German *noppe* nap, *noppen* trim nap from]

nap³ *transitive verb* (**napped**, **napping**) (usu. in *passive*) cover (food) with a sauce (*clams napped with a white wine cream sauce*). [French *napper* coat]

nap⁴ ● *noun* **1 a** a form of whist in which players declare the number of tricks they expect to take, up to five. **b** a call of five in this game. **2** *Brit.* **a** the betting of all one's money on one horse etc. **b** a tipster's choice for this. ● *transitive verb* (**napped**, **napping**) *Brit.* name (a horse etc.) as a probable winner. □ **go nap 1** attempt to take all five tricks in nap. **2** risk everything in one attempt. **3** win all the matches etc. in a series. [abbreviation of *napoleon*, the original name of the card game]

napa¹ /'napə/ *noun* (also **nappa**) a soft leather made by a special process from the skin of sheep or goats. [Napa in California]

napa² *noun* (also **nappa**) a plant, *Brassica rapa pekinensis*, with a long, dense head of whitish, broad leaves used in salads and Oriental cooking. [Japanese]

na·palm /'neipɑm/ ● *noun* **1** a thickening agent produced from naphthenic acid, other fatty acids, and aluminum. **2** a jellied gasoline made from this, used in incendiary bombs. ● *transitive verb* attack with napalm bombs. [NAPHTHENIC (see NAPHTHENE) + *palmitic acid* in coconut oil]

Napa·nee /napənˈiː, 'napəni/ a former town in SE Ontario, west of Kingston, now part of Greater Napanee; pop. (2001) 5,351. [*Appanea*, the original name of the Napanee River (meaning unknown)]

nape *noun* the back of the neck. [Middle English: origin unknown]

nap·ery /'neipəri/ *noun* *N Amer.* & *Scot.* household linen, esp. table linen. [Old French *naperie* from *nape* (as NAPKIN)]

Naph·ta·li /'naftəˌlai/ **1** a Hebrew patriarch, son of Jacob and Bilhah (Gen. 30:7-8). **2** the tribe of Israel traditionally descended from him.

naph·tha /'nafθə, 'naf-/ *noun* a colourless, flammable petroleum distillate used as a fuel and solvent. [Latin from Greek, = 'flammable volatile liquid issuing from the earth']

naph·tha·lene /'nafθəˌliːn/ *noun* a white crystalline aromatic substance produced by the distillation of coal tar and used in mothballs and the manufacture of dyes etc. □ **naph·thal·ic** /-'θalɪk/ *adjective* [NAPHTHA + -ENE]

naph·thene /'nafθiːn/ *noun* any of a group of cycloalkanes. □ **naph·then·ic** /naf'θiːnɪk/ *adjective* [NAPHTHA + -ENE]

Na·pier ► **1 Sir Charles James** (1782–1853), English general and colonial administrator, who was the conqueror (1843) and governor (1843-7) of Sind, now a province of Pakistan. **2 John** (1550–1617), Scottish mathematician. He was the inventor (independently of the German Joost Bürgi (1552-1632)) of logarithms; his tables, modified and republished by Henry Briggs, had an immediate and lasting influence on mathematics.

Napier·ian logarithm /neipiˈɜrɪən/ *noun* = NATURAL LOGARITHM. [J. NAPIER]

nap·kin *noun* **1** (in full **table napkin**) a square piece of linen, paper, etc. used for wiping the lips, fingers, etc. at meals; a serviette. **2** *Brit.* = DIAPER. [Old French *nappe* from Latin *mappa* MAP]

napkin ring *noun* a ring used to hold a rolled table napkin.

Na·ples /'neipəlz/ a city and port on the west coast of Italy, capital of Campania region; pop. (2001) 993,386.

Napo·leon I /nəˈpoːliən/ (full name Napoleon Bonaparte) (1769–1821), emperor of the French 1804–14 and 1815. A Corsican by birth, he experienced a meteoric rise through the French Revolutionary Army, taking power in 1799. As First Consul and then as emperor, he founded the modern French legal, administrative, and educational systems and established a French empire stretching from Spain to Poland. After the failure of his attack on Russia (1812) he was forced into exile (1814), and, returning to power a year later, was defeated at Waterloo (1815) and exiled to the island of St. Helena.

Napo·leon II (full name François Charles Joseph Bonaparte) (1811–32), son of Napoleon I and Marie Louise. Named Napoleon II by Bonapartists following his father's death (1821), he remained politically powerless.

Napo·leon III (full name Charles Louis Napoleon Bonaparte; known as 'Louis-Napoleon') (1808–73), nephew of Napoleon I, emperor of the French 1852–70. He was elected president of the Second Republic (1848), and as emperor he was noted for his aggressive foreign policy, which included intervention in Mexico, participation in the Crimean War, and war against Austria in Italy; he abdicated in 1870 after the French defeat at Sedan in the Franco-Prussian War.

napo·leon *noun* **1** *N Amer.* = MILLE FEUILLE 1. **2** *hist.* a gold twenty-franc piece minted in the reign of Napoleon I. **3** = NAP⁴ *noun* 1a. [French *napoléon* from *Napoléon*, name of 19th-c. French emperors]

Napo·leon·ic /nəˌpoːliˈɒnɪk/ *adjective* of, relating to, or characteristic of Napoleon I or his time.

Napoleonic Wars a series of campaigns (1800-15) of French armies under Napoleon I against Austria, Russia, Great Britain, Portugal, Prussia, and other European powers. They ended with Napoleon's defeat at the battle of Waterloo.

nap·pa *var. of* NAPA¹, NAPA².

nappe /nap/ *noun* *Geol.* a sheet of rock that has moved sideways over neighbouring strata, usu. as a result of overthrust. [French *nappe* tablecloth]

nappy¹ *noun* (pl. **-pies**) *Brit.* = DIAPER.

nappy² *noun* (pl. **-pies**) *N Amer.* a small, shallow, glass or ceramic bowl for serving fruit, ice cream, etc. [19th c.: origin unknown]

na·prox·en /ne'prɒksen/ *noun* an anti-inflammatory analgesic substance, $C_{14}H_{14}O_3$, given orally as a painkiller and in the treatment of some forms of arthritis. [*naphthyl* (as NAPHTHALENE + -YL) + PROPIONIC ACID + OXY-² + -*en*]

Nara /'nɑrə/ a city in central Japan, on the island of Honshu; pop. (est. 2002) 384,800. It was the first capital of Japan (710-84) and an important centre of Japanese Buddhism.

Na·ra·yan·ganj /nəˈrɒjən̩ˌɡʌndʒ/ a river port in Bangladesh, on the Ganges delta southeast of Dhaka; pop. (est. 2002) 351,000.

Nar·bonne /nɑr'bɒn/ a city in S France, in Languedoc-Roussillon, just inland from the Mediterranean; pop. (1999) 46,500. It was the capital of the Roman province of Gallia Narbonensis and a prosperous port of medieval France until its harbour silted up in the 14th c.

narc *noun* (also **nark**) esp. *N Amer. slang* a narcotics officer in a police force. [abbreviation of NARCOTIC]

nar·cis·sism /'nɑrsɪˌsɪzəm/ *noun* *Psych.* excessive or erotic interest in oneself, one's physical features, etc. □ **nar·cis·sist** *noun* **nar·cis·sis·tic** /-'sɪstɪk/ *adjective* [NARCISSUS]

Nar·cis·sus /nɑr'sɪsəs/ *Gk Myth* a beautiful youth who rejected the nymph Echo and fell in love with his own reflection in a pool, eventually pining away and being changed into the flower that bears his name.

nar·cis·sus /nɑr'sɪsəs/ *noun* (pl. **nar·cis·si** /-sai/ or **nar·cis·sus·es**) any bulbous plant of the genus *Narcissus*, esp. *N. poeticus* bearing a heavily scented single flower with an undivided corona edged with crimson and yellow. [Latin from Greek *narkissos*, perhaps from *narkē* numbness, with reference to its narcotic effects]

narco- /'nɑrkoː/ *combining form* **1** of or relating to the use of or trade in illegal narcotics (*narcoterrorism*). **2** of or involving the therapeutic use of narcotic drugs (*narco-analysis*). [Greek *narkē* 'numbness, deadness', or extracted from NARCOTIC]

narco·lepsy /'nɑrkəˌlepsi/ *noun* a disease with fits of sleepiness and drowsiness. □ **narco·lep·tic** /-'leptɪk/ *adjective & noun* [Greek *narkē* numbness, after EPILEPSY]

narco·sis /nɑr'koːsɪs/ *noun* a state of drowsiness or unconsciousness induced by a narcotic drug. [Greek *narkōsis* from *narkoun* make numb]

narco·terror·ism /ˌnɑrkoːˈterərɪzəm/ *noun* terrorism associated with illicit drugs, esp. directed against law enforcement. □ **narco·terror·ist** *noun*

nar·cot·ic /nɑr'kɒtɪk/ ● *adjective* **1** (of a substance) inducing drowsiness, sleep, stupor, or insensibility. **2** (of a drug) affecting the

t top   v voice   w we   z zoo   ʃ she   ʒ vision   θ thin   ð this   ŋ ring   x loch   tʃ chip   dʒ jar   (*see over for vowels*)

mind. **3** of or involving narcosis. **4** soporific. ● *noun* a narcotic substance, drug, or influence. □ **nar·cot·ic·al·ly** *adverb* [Old French *narcotique* or medieval Latin from Greek *narkōtikos* (as NARCOSIS)]

narco·tize /ˈnɑːkəˌtaɪz/ *transitive verb* (also esp. *Brit.* **-tise**) **1** stupefy or make insensible with a narcotic. **2** deaden, make dull.

nard /nɑːd/ *noun* **1** any of various plants yielding an aromatic balsam used by the ancients. **2** = SPIKENARD. [Old English, via Latin from Greek *nardos*; related to Sanskrit *nalada*, *narada*]

nar·doo /ˈnɑːduː/ *noun* **1** a clover-like plant, *Marsilea drummondii*, native to Australia. **2** a food made from the spores of this plant. [various Aboriginal languages *ngardu*, *nhaadu*]

nares /ˈneəriːz/ *plural noun Anat.* the nostrils. [pl. of Latin *naris*]

Nares Strait /neəz/ the sea channel situated between Ellesmere Island and Greenland, providing a northern route from Baffin Bay to the Arctic Ocean. It comprises Smith Sound, Kane Basin and Hall Basin. [Sir G. S. *Nares*, English admiral and Arctic explorer d.1915]

nar·ghi·le /ˈnɑːɡəli/ *noun* (also **nar·gi·leh**) an oriental tobacco pipe with the smoke drawn through water; a hookah. [Persian *nārgīleh* (*nārgīl* coconut)]

nark¹ *slang* ● *noun* **1** *Brit.* a police informer or decoy. **2** *Austral.* an annoying person or thing. ● *transitive verb* (usu. in *passive*) *Brit.* annoy; infuriate (*was narked by their attitude*). □ **nark it!** *Brit.* stop that! [Romany *nāk* nose]

nark² *var. of* NARC.

narky *adjective* (**nark·i·er**, **nark·i·est**) *Brit. slang* bad-tempered, irritable. [NARK¹]

Nar·mada River /ˈnɜːmədə/ a river which rises in Madhya Pradesh, central India, and flows generally westward for 1 245 km (778 miles) to the Gulf of Cambay. It is regarded by Hindus as sacred.

Nar·ra·gan·sett /narəˈɡansət/ *noun* an Algonquian language of Rhode Island, now virtually extinct. [Algonquian, ≈ people of the small point (of land)]

nar·rate /ˈnareit, nəˈreit/ *verb* **1** *transitive* give a continuous story or account of. **2** *transitive* provide a spoken commentary or accompaniment for (a film etc.). **3** *intransitive* recount or relate a story, events, experiences, etc. □ **nar·rat·able** *adjective* **nar·ra·tion** /nəˈreiʃən/ *noun* [Latin *narrare narrat-*]

nar·ra·tive /ˈnarətɪv/ ● *noun* **1** a spoken or written account of connected events in order of happening. **2** the practice or art of narration. ● *adjective* in the form of, or concerned with, narration (*narrative verse*). □ **nar·ra·tive·ly** *adverb*

nar·ra·tol·ogy /narəˈtɒlədʒi/ *noun* the branch of knowledge that deals with the structure and function of narrative. □ **nar·ra·to·logic·al** *adjective* **nar·ra·tol·o·gist** *noun*

nar·ra·tor /ˈnar.eitər, nəˈreit-/ *noun* **1** a character in a play, film, etc., who relates part of the plot to the audience. **2** a person who speaks a commentary in a film, broadcast, etc. **3** a character who recounts the events in a plot, esp. that of a novel or narrative poem. **4** the imagined voice recounting a story in a novel, etc., as distinct from the author (*the omniscient narrator*). □ **nar·ra·tor·ial** *adjective*

nar·row /ˈnaroʊ/ ● *adjective* (**narrow·er**, **narrow·est**) **1 a** of small width in proportion to length; lacking breadth. **b** confined or confining; constricted (*within narrow bounds*). **2** of limited scope; restricted (*in the narrowest sense*). **3** with little margin (*a narrow escape*). **4** searching; precise; exact (*a narrow examination*). **5** = NARROW-MINDED. **6** (of a vowel) pronounced with the vocal muscles relatively tense. **7** of small size. ● *noun* **1** (usu. in *pl.*) the narrow part of a strait, river, sound, etc. **2** a narrow pass or street. ● *verb* **1** *intransitive* become narrow; diminish; contract; lessen. **2** *transitive* make narrow; constrict; restrict. □ **narrow down** reduce the number of possibilities or choices, esp. by eliminating those that are less appropriate or desirable (*narrowing down the list of applicants for the job*). □ **narrow·ish** *adjective* **narrow·ly** *adverb* **narrow·ness** *noun* [Old English *nearu nearw-* from Germanic]

narrow·boat *noun Brit.* a canal boat, esp. one less than 7 ft. (2.1 metres) wide.

narrow·cast *esp. N Amer.* ● *transitive & intransitive verb* (*past* and *past participle* **narrow·cast** or **narrow·cast·ed**) transmit (a television program etc.), esp. by cable, to an audience targeted by interests or location. ● *noun* **1** transmitting in this way. **2** a transmission or program of this kind. □ **narrow·cast·er** *noun* **narrow·cast·ing** *noun*

narrow gauge ● *noun* a railway track that has a smaller gauge than the standard one. ● *adjective* (usu. **narrow-gauge**) of or relating to a railway with a narrow gauge.

narrow-minded *adjective* rigid or restricted in one's views; intolerant,

prejudiced. □ **narrow-minded·ly** *adverb* **narrow-minded·ness** *noun*

narrow squeak *noun* **1** a narrow escape. **2** a success barely attained.

nar·thex /ˈnɑːθeks/ *noun* a lobby inside the main entrance to a church building. [Latin from Greek *narthēx*]

nar·whal /ˈnɑːwəl/ *noun* a white Arctic whale, *Monodon monoceros*, the male of which has a long straight spirally fluted tusk developed from one of its teeth. [Dutch *narwal* from Danish *narhval* from *hval* whale: compare Old Norse *náhvalr* (perhaps from *nár* corpse, with reference to its pale colour)]

nary /ˈneri/ *adjective informal* or *jocular* not a; no (*nary a one*). [from *ne'er a*]

NASA /ˈnasə, ˈnasə/ *abbreviation* (in the US) National Aeronautics and Space Administration.

nasal /ˈneizəl/ ● *adjective* **1** of, for, or relating to the nose. **2** *Phonetics* (of a letter or a sound) pronounced with the breath passing through the nose, e.g. *m*, *n*, *ng*, or French *en*, *un*, etc. **3** (of the voice or speech) having an intonation caused by breathing through the nose. ● *noun Phonetics* a nasal letter or sound. □ **na·sal·ity** /-ˈzaliti/ *noun* **nasal·ize** *transitive & intransitive verb* (also esp. *Brit.* **-ise**). **nasal·iz·a·tion** *noun* **nasal·ly** *adverb* [French *nasal* or medieval Latin *nasalis* from Latin *nasus* nose]

NASCAR *abbreviation* National Association for Stock Car Auto Racing.

nas·cent /ˈneisənt, ˈnas-/ *adjective* **1** just beginning to be; not yet mature (*nascent talents*). **2** in the act of being born. **3** *Chem.* just being formed and therefore unusually reactive (*nascent hydrogen*). □ **nas·cency** /ˈnasənsi/ *noun* [Latin *nasci nascent-* be born]

NASDAQ /ˈnasdak, ˈnaz-/ *noun* (in the US) National Association of Securities Dealers Automated Quotations, a system for quoting prices on over-the-counter securities. [acronym]

nase·berry /ˈneizberi/ *noun* (*pl.* **-berries**) a sapodilla. [Spanish & Portuguese *néspera* medlar, from Latin (see MEDLAR): assimilated to BERRY]

Nase·by, Battle of /ˈneizbi/ a major battle of the English Civil War, taking place in 1645 near the village of Naseby in Northamptonshire. The last Royalist army, commanded by Prince Rupert and Charles I himself, was decisively defeated by the larger and better organized New Model Army under General Fairfax and Oliver Cromwell.

Nash, (Fred·eric) Ogden (1902–71), US poet. His sophisticated light verse, characterized by puns, epigrams, wildly asymmetrical lines, and other verbal eccentricities, appeared in many collections from 1931 onward.

Nash·ville the state capital of Tennessee, the main centre of the country music industry; pop. (2000) 545,524.

nasi gor·eng /ˈnasi ˌɡɒˈrɛŋ/ *noun* (in Malaysian and Indonesian cooking) a dish of savoury fried rice with a variety of ingredients including meat (and sometimes fish) and a sliced omelette or fried egg. [Malay *nasi*]

Nasik /ˈnɒsɪk/ a city in W India, in Maharashtra, on the Godavari River northeast of Bombay (Mumbai); pop. (2001) 1,077,000.

Nas·kapi /nəˈskapi/ ● *noun* **1** a member of an Innu people living along the north shores of the Gulf of St. Lawrence and the St. Lawrence River. **2** the Cree language of this people. ● *adjective* of or relating to this people or their culture or language. [Naskapi]

Na·smyth /ˈneismɪθ/ **James** (1808–90), Scottish-born engineer, whose invention of the steam hammer was a major innovation for the forging industry.

naso- /ˈneizoʊ/ *combining form* nose. [Latin *nasus* nose]

naso·gas·tric /ˌneizoʊˈɡastrɪk/ *adjective Med.* supplying the stomach via the nose (*nasogastric tube*).

Nas·sau 1 /ˈnasaʊ/ a former duchy of western Germany, centred on the small town of Nassau, from which a branch of the House of Orange arose. It corresponds to parts of the present-day states of Hesse and Rhineland-Palatinate. **2** /ˈnasɔː/ a port on the island of New Providence, capital of the Bahamas; pop. (est. 2002) 179,300.

Nas·ser /ˈnasər, ˈnɒs-/ **Gamal Abdel** (1918–70), Egyptian colonel, prime minister 1954–6 and president 1956–70. He deposed King Farouk in a military coup (1952), and became president of the new Republic of Egypt (1956); his nationalization of the Suez Canal brought war with Britain, France, and Israel (1956), and he also led Egypt in two unsuccessful wars against Israel (1956 and 1967). □ **Nas·ser·ist** *noun & adjective*

Nasser, Lake a lake in SE Egypt created in the 1960s by the building of the two dams on the Nile at Aswan. [NASSER]

Nass-Gitksan /ˌnasɡɪtˈksan/ *noun* a Tsimshian language comprising

---

Vowels: a *cat*　ɑ *arm*　e *bed*　ɜː *her*　ɜː *deux*　ə *ago*　ɪ *sit*　i *cosy*　iː *feed*　ɒ *hot*　ɔ *pore*　oː *no*　ʌ *run*　ʊ *put*

the mutually intelligible dialects spoken by the Nisga'a and Gitksan. [NASS RIVER]

Nass River /nas/ a river in western BC, 380 km long, rising in the Skeena Mountains and flowing southward in a jagged line to a point north of Terrace, then turning westward to drain into Portland Inlet, an arm of the Pacific Ocean. [Tlingit, = stomach, so called because the river provided an ample source of food, esp. salmon and eulachon]

nas·tur·tium /nə'stɜrʃəm/ noun **1** a trailing plant, *Tropaeolum majus*, with rounded edible leaves and bright orange, yellow, or red flowers. **2** any cruciferous plant of the genus *Nasturtium*, including watercress. [Latin]

nasty ● adjective (**nas·ti·er**, **nas·ti·est**) **1 a** highly unpleasant (*a nasty experience*). **b** annoying; objectionable (*the car has a nasty habit of breaking down*). **2** difficult to negotiate; dangerous, serious (*a nasty fence; a nasty question; a nasty illness*). **3** (of a person or animal) ill-natured, ill-tempered, spiteful; violent, offensive (*nasty to her mother*). **4** (of the weather) unpleasant because of cold, wind, precipitation, etc. **5 a** disgustingly dirty, filthy. **b** unpalatable; disagreeable (*nasty smell*). **6** obscene. ● noun (pl. **-ties**) *informal* a nasty person, animal, thing, etc. □ **a nasty bit** (or **piece**) **of work** *informal* an unpleasant or contemptible person. □ **nas·ti·ly** adverb **nas·ti·ness** noun [Middle English: origin unknown]

Nat. abbreviation **1** National. **2** Natural.

Natal /nə'tal, -'tɒl/ **1** a former province on the east coast of South Africa, now called KwaZulu-Natal. **2** a port on the Atlantic coast of NE Brazil; pop. (2002) 709,442.

natal /'neɪtəl/ adjective **1** of or pertaining to one's birth. **2** (of a place) native; connected with one from birth. [Latin *natalis* (as NATION)]

Natal Day noun (in Nova Scotia) a day celebrating the founding of a town or city, usu. now observed on the first Monday in August.

natch adverb *informal* = NATURALLY. [abbreviation]

nates /'neɪtiːz/ plural noun *Anat.* the buttocks. [Latin]

Nathan /'neɪθən/ *Bible* a prophet during the reigns of David and Solomon.

nath·less /'neɪθləs/ adverb (also **nathe·less**) *archaic* nevertheless. [Old English *nā* not (from *ne* not + *ā* ever) + THE + *læs* LESS]

nation noun **1 a** a community of people of mainly common descent, history, language, etc., forming a country or inhabiting a territory. **b** the state or territory itself. **2** *N Amer.* a group of Aboriginal people with common ancestry who are socially, culturally, and linguistically united. □ **na·tion·hood** noun [Latin *natio -onis* from *nasci nat-* be born]

na·tion·al ● adjective **1** of or pertaining to a nation or the nation, esp. as a whole. **2** peculiar to or characteristic of a particular nation. **3** owned, controlled, or financially supported by the federal government (*a national library*). ● noun **1** a citizen of a specified country, usu. entitled to hold that country's passport (*French nationals*). **2** (in pl.) a national tournament or competition. **3** *Brit.* a national newspaper. □ **na·tion·al·ly** adverb

National Acadian Day n. *Cdn* August 15, on which Acadians celebrate their culture and heritage.

national anthem noun a song adopted by a nation, expressive of its identity etc. and intended to inspire patriotism.

National Assembly noun **1** *Cdn* the provincial legislature of Quebec. **2** an elected house of legislature in various countries. **3** *hist.* the elected legislature in France 1789-91.

national bank noun **1** *US* a bank chartered under the federal government and required to be a member of the Federal Reserve System. **2** a bank owned and operated by the state.

National Capital Region an area of E Ontario and SW Quebec encompassing the cities of Ottawa and Gatineau and surrounding areas.

National Child Benefit noun *Cdn* a joint program of the federal, provincial, and territorial governments and First Nations to increase income support and child-welfare services for low-income working families. Abbr.: **NCB**.

national convention noun *US* a convention of each major political party, nominating candidates for the presidency etc.

National Curriculum noun (in the UK) a common program of study laid down for pupils in the publicly-funded schools of England and Wales with tests at specified ages.

national day noun **1** (usu. **National Day**) a national holiday celebrating a country's or people's nationhood. **2** a day designated by the government of a nation for the nationwide observance or recognition of something (*a national day of mourning*).

national debt noun the money owed by a central government, including both internal and overseas debts.

national dream noun a vision of a unified nation, esp. (in Canada) one created by a national transportation network, e.g. a railway. [from the title of Pierre Berton's book about the creation of the Canadian Pacific Railway]

National Energy Program noun *Cdn* a controversial federal program which aimed to achieve oil self-sufficiency and greater Canadian ownership of the oil industry, brought into effect by the Liberals in 1980 and dismantled by the Conservatives after their 1984 election victory. Abbr.: **NEP**.

national forest noun (in the US) a tract of forestland under federal supervision, set aside for conservation and recreation.

National Front noun a UK political party with extreme reactionary views on immigration etc.

National Guard noun (in the US) a militia recruited on a state-by-state basis but serving as the primary reserve force of the US army, and available for federal use in emergencies.

National Health Service noun (also **National Health**) (in the UK) a system of national medical care paid for mainly by taxation and started in 1948.

National Historic Site noun (in Canada) a place designated by the federal government as historically significant, identified by an associated building, archaeological remains, or commemorative statue, cairn or plaque.

national holiday noun a holiday commemorating the creation or celebrating the existence of a nation.

national income noun the total annual money value of the goods and services produced by a country.

National Insurance noun (in the UK) the system of compulsory payments by employed persons (supplemented by employers) to provide state assistance in sickness, unemployment, retirement, etc.

na·tion·al·ism noun **1 a** patriotic feeling, principles, etc. **b** an extreme form of this. **2** a policy of national independence. □ **na·tion·al·ist** noun & adjective **na·tion·al·is·tic** adjective **na·tion·al·is·tic·ally** adverb

na·tion·al·ity noun (pl. **-ities**) **1 a** the status of belonging to a particular nation (*what is your nationality?*). **b** a nation. **2** the condition of being national; distinctive national qualities. **3** an ethnic group forming a part of one or more political nations. **4** existence as a nation; nationhood. **5** patriotic sentiment.

na·tion·al·ize transitive verb (also esp. *Brit.* **-ise**) **1** take over (an industry, transportation service, land, etc.) from private ownership on behalf of the state. **2 a** make national. **b** make into a nation. □ **na·tion·al·iz·a·tion** noun [French *nationaliser* (as NATION)]

national monument noun a natural landmark or historic site maintained by a national government, esp. in the US.

national park noun an area of natural beauty or ecological or historical significance, protected by the nation for the use of the general public.

National Policy noun *Cdn hist.* a policy of tariff protection for Canadian manufacturers brought into effect in 1879 by Sir John A. Macdonald and espoused by subsequent Conservative prime ministers such as Robert Borden and R.B. Bennett.

national service noun service in the armed forces under conscription for a specified period.

National Socialism noun *hist.* the doctrines of nationalism, racial purity, etc., adopted by the Nazis. □ **National Socialist** noun & adjective

National Trust noun (in the UK, Australia, etc.) an organization for maintaining and preserving historic buildings etc.

National Wildlife Area noun *Cdn* an area of public land owned or leased by the federal government to conserve habitat for migratory birds or rare or endangered plants or animals. Abbr.: **NWA**.

nation building noun the creation of a unified nation, esp. out of diverse populations or regions.

Nation of Islam noun a black Islamic organization founded *c*.1930 in Detroit, which became prominent under the influence of Malcolm X, who joined in 1946.

nation-state noun a sovereign state of which most of the citizens or subjects are united also by factors such as language, common descent, etc., which define a nation.

na·tion·wide adjective & adverb extending over the whole nation.

native ● noun **1 a** (usu. foll. by *of*) a person born in a specified place (*a* *native of Kamloops).* **b** a local inhabitant. **2** a member of an indigenous people of a country, region, etc., as distinguished from settlers, immigrants, etc. or their descendants. **3** (usu. foll. by *of*) an indigenous animal or plant. ● *adjective* **1** (usu. foll. by *to*) belonging to a person or thing by nature; inherent; innate (*native intelligence*). **2** of one's birth or birthplace (*our home and native land*). **3** belonging to one by right of birth (*native language*). **4** (usu. foll. by *to*) belonging to a specified place (*the anteater is native to South America*). **5** (also **Native**) **a** (of a person) indigenous; descended from the original inhabitants of a region or country. **b** of, pertaining to, or characteristic of the indigenous people of a place (*native customs*). **6** unadorned; simple; artless. **7** *Geol.* (of metal etc.) found in a pure or uncombined state. **8** *Computing* designed for or built into a given system. □ **go native** (of a settler, traveller, etc.) adopt the way of life of the indigenous inhabitants of a place. □ **na·tive·ly** *adverb* **na·tive·ness** *noun* [Latin *nativus* from *nasci* nat- 'be born']

Native American *noun* an American Indian, esp. of the US. ¶ The term *Native American* is now often preferred to *American Indian.* However, when used to include the Indian peoples of Canada as well as of the US, it can cause offence. Ambiguity can be avoided by using *American Indian* or *Canadian Indian* as appropriate. See also Usage Note at INDIAN.

native-born *adjective* belonging to a particular place or country by birth.

Native Canadian *noun* an Aboriginal Canadian; a Canadian Indian, Inuit, or Metis.

native friendship centre *noun Cdn* = FRIENDSHIP CENTRE.

native son *noun N Amer.* a male native of a particular city, province or state, etc.

native speaker *noun* a person who has spoken a specified language from early childhood.

na·tiv·ism *noun* **1** the attitude, practice, or policy of protecting the interests of native-born or existing inhabitants against those of immigrants. **2** *Anthropology* a return to or emphasis on a way of life or customs under threat from outside influences. **3** *Philos.* the doctrine of innate ideas. □ **na·tiv·ist** *adjective & noun*

na·tiv·ity /nəˈtɪvɪti/ *noun* (*pl.* **-ities**) **1** (esp. **the Nativity**) **a** the birth of Christ. **b** the festival of Christ's birth; Christmas. **2** a picture of the Nativity. **3** birth. **4 a** the birth of the Virgin Mary or St. John the Baptist. **b** the festival of the nativity of the Virgin (8 Sept.) or St. John (24 June). [Late Latin *nativitas* from Latin (as NATIVE)]

nativity play *noun* a play usu. performed by children at Christmas dealing with the birth of Christ.

nativity scene *noun* a usu. three-dimensional depiction of Christ's birth in a stable, with Mary and Joseph, farm animals, visiting shepherds, etc.

NATO /ˈneɪtoʊ/ *abbreviation* (also esp. *Brit.* **Nato**) North Atlantic Treaty Organization.

na·tron /ˈneɪtrɒn, -trən/ *noun* a mineral form of hydrated sodium salts found in dried lake beds. [French from Spanish *natrón* from Arabic *naṭrūn* from Greek *nitron* NITRE]

Na·tron, Lake /ˈneɪtrən/ a lake in N Tanzania, on the border with Kenya, containing large deposits of salt and soda.

nat·ter *informal* ● *intransitive verb* **1** chatter idly. **2** grumble; talk fretfully. ● *noun* **1** aimless chatter. **2** grumbling talk. [originally Scots, imitative]

natty *adjective* (**nat·ti·er, nat·ti·est**) *informal* **1 a** smartly or neatly dressed, dapper. **b** spruce; trim; smart (*a natty suit*). **2** deft. □ **nat·ti·ly** *adverb* **nat·ti·ness** *noun* [originally slang, perhaps related to NEAT[1]]

nat·ural ● *adjective* **1 a** existing in or caused by nature; not artificial (*natural landscape*). **b** uncultivated; wild (*existing in its natural state*). **2** in the course of nature; not exceptional or miraculous (*died of natural causes; a natural occurrence*). **3** (of human nature etc.) not surprising; to be expected (*natural for her to be upset*). **4 a** (of a person or a person's behaviour) unaffected, easy, spontaneous. **b** (foll. by *to*) spontaneous, easy (*friendliness is natural to him*). **5 a** (of qualities etc.) inherent; innate (*a natural talent for music*). **b** (of a person) having such qualities (*a natural comedian*). **6** not disguised or altered (as by makeup, hair dye etc.). **7** lifelike; as if in nature (*the portrait looked very natural*). **8** likely by its or their nature to be such (*natural enemies; the natural antithesis*). **9** having a physical existence as opposed to what is spiritual, intellectual, etc. (*the natural world*). **10 a** having genetically the specified familial relationship; actually begotten, not adopted (*her natural son*). **b** *archaic* illegitimate (*a natural child*). **11** based on the innate moral sense; instinctive (*natural justice*). **12** *Music* **a** (of a note) not sharpened or flattened (*B natural*). **b** (of a scale) not containing any sharps or flats. **c** (of a key) having no sharps or flats. **13** without

spiritual enlightenment (*the natural man*). **14** (of cotton, silk, etc.) having a colour characteristic of the unbleached and undyed state; off-white, creamy beige. **15** not refined or treated (*natural wood*). **16** containing no additives, preservatives, or other artificial ingredients (*natural foods*). ● *noun* **1** (usu. foll. by *for*) *informal* a person or thing naturally suitable, adept, expert, etc. (*a natural for the championship*). **2** *archaic* a person mentally deficient from birth. **3** *Music* **a** a sign (♮) denoting a return to natural pitch after a sharp or a flat. **b** a natural note. **c** a white key on a piano. **4** a pale fawn colour. □ **nat·ur·al·ness** *noun* [Latin *naturalis* (as NATURE)]

natural-born *adjective* (usu. *attributive*) having a character or position by birth.

natural childbirth *noun* childbirth with minimal medical or technological intervention.

natural classification *noun* a scientific classification according to natural features.

natural death *noun* death by age or disease, not by accident, poison, violence, etc.

natural family planning *noun* methods of birth control based on recognition of natural signs of ovulation rather than on the use of artificial contraceptives.

natural food *noun* food without preservatives etc.

natural gas *noun* an inflammable mainly methane gas found in the earth's crust, not manufactured.

natural history *noun* **1** the study of animals or plants, esp. as set forth for popular use. **2** an aggregate of the facts concerning the flora and fauna etc. of a particular place or class (*a natural history of Vancouver Island*). □ **natural historian** *noun*

natural ice *noun* an ice surface created by the freezing of water naturally in sub-zero temperatures, not by mechanical refrigeration.

natural increase *noun* population growth resulting from births exceeding deaths.

nat·ur·al·ism *noun* **1** the theory or practice in art and literature of representing nature, character, etc. realistically and in great detail. **2 a** *Philos.* a theory of the world that excludes the supernatural or spiritual. **b** any moral or religious system based on this theory. **3** action based on natural instincts. **4** indifference to conventions.

nat·ur·al·ist ● *noun* **1** an expert or student of natural history. **2** a person who believes in or practises naturalism. ● *adjective* = NATURALISTIC.

nat·ur·al·is·tic *adjective* **1** imitating nature closely; lifelike. **2** of or according to naturalism. **3** of natural history. □ **nat·ur·al·is·tic·ally** *adverb*

nat·ur·al·ize *verb* (also esp. *Brit.* **-ise**) **1** *transitive* admit (a person of foreign birth) to the citizenship of a country. **2 a** *transitive* introduce (an animal, plant, etc.) into another region so that it flourishes in the wild. **b** *intransitive* (of a cultivated plant) become established and spread in a natural situation. **3** *transitive* adopt (a foreign word, custom, etc.). **4** *intransitive* become naturalized. □ **nat·ur·al·iz·a·tion** /-ˈzeɪʃən/ *noun* [French *naturaliser* (as NATURAL)]

natural language *noun* a language used natively by people, as opposed to an artificial language or code.

natural law *noun* **1** *Philos.* unchanging moral principles common to all people by virtue of their nature as human beings. **2 a** an observable law relating to natural phenomena. **b** these collectively (*where they saw chance, we see natural law*).

natural life *noun* the duration of one's life on earth.

natural logarithm *noun* a logarithm to the base *e* (2.71828...).

nat·ur·al·ly *adverb* **1** in a natural manner (*spoke very naturally*). **2** as a natural result. **3** (qualifying a whole sentence) as might be expected; of course. **4** by nature; instinctively (*a naturally talented actor*). **5** without artificial help, special treatment, etc. (*her hair curls naturally*).

natural note *noun Music* a note that is neither sharp nor flat.

natural numbers *noun* the integers 1, 2, 3, etc., sometimes with the addition of 0.

natural philosophy *noun hist.* natural science, esp. physical science. □ **natural philosopher** *noun*

natural religion *noun* a religion based on reason (*opp.* REVEALED RELIGION); deism.

natural resources *noun* materials or conditions occurring in nature and capable of economic exploitation.

natural science *noun* **1** the sciences used in the study of the physical world, e.g. physics, chemistry, geology, biology, botany. **2** any one of these sciences.

Consonants: b *but*   d *dog*   f *few*   g *get*   h *her*   j *yes*   k *cat*   l *leg*   m *man*   n *no*   p *pen*   r *red*   s *sit*

natural selection *noun* the Darwinian theory of the survival and propagation of organisms best adapted to their environment.

natural theology *noun* theology based on reasoning from natural facts apart from revelation.

natural uranium *noun* uranium that has not been enriched.

na·ture *noun* **1** a thing's or person's innate or essential qualities or character (*not in their nature to be cruel*; *is the nature of iron to rust*). **2** (often **Nature**) **a** the physical power causing all the phenomena of the material world (*Nature is the best physician*). **b** these phenomena, including plants, animals, landscape, etc. **3** a kind, sort, or class (*things of this nature*). **4** = HUMAN NATURE. **5** a specified element of human character (*the rational nature*; *our animal nature*). **6 a** an uncultivated or wild area, condition, community, etc. **b** the countryside, esp. when picturesque. **7** inherent impulses determining character or action. **8** heredity as an influence on or determinant of personality (*opp.* NURTURE *noun* 3). **9** a living thing's vital functions or needs (*such a diet will not support nature*). □ **against nature** unnatural; immoral. **back to nature** returning to a pre-industrial or natural state. **by nature** innately. **from nature** *Art* using natural objects as models. **in nature 1** actually existing. **2** anywhere; at all. **3** in the natural world. **in** (or **of**) **the nature of** characteristically resembling or belonging to the class of (*the answer was in the nature of an excuse*). **in the nature of things** inevitably. **in a state of nature** in an uncivilized or uncultivated state. **one's better nature** the good side of one's character; one's capacity for tolerance, generosity, etc. [Latin *natura*, from *nasci nat-* 'be born']

na·tured *adjective* (in *combination*) having a specified disposition (*good-natured*; *ill-natured*).

nature reserve *noun* a tract of land managed so as to preserve its flora, fauna, physical features, etc.

nature's call *noun* a need to urinate or defecate.

nature spirit *noun* a spirit supposed to reside in some natural element or object.

nature study *noun* the practical study of plant and animal life etc., esp. as a school subject.

nature trail *noun* a signposted path through the countryside designed to draw attention to natural phenomena.

nature walk *noun* (also **nature hike**) *N Amer.* a walk through woods, marshland, etc. to observe plants, animals, physical phenomena, etc.

na·tur·ism /ˈneɪtʃərɪzm/ *noun* **1** nudism. **2** naturalism in religion or philosophy. **3** the worship of natural objects. □ **na·tur·ist** *noun* & *adjective*

nat·ur·op·athy /ˌneɪtʃəˈrɒpəθi/ *noun* **1** the treatment of disease etc. without drugs, usu. involving diet, exercise, massage, etc. **2** this regimen used preventively. □ **nat·uro·path** /ˈneɪtʃɜrə,paθ/ *noun* **nat·uro·path·ic** /ˌneɪtʃɜrə'paθɪk/ *adjective*

Nauga·hyde /ˈnɒɡəhaɪd/ *noun* proprietary a material used in upholstery, consisting of a fabric base coated with a layer of rubber or vinyl resin and finished with a leather-like grain. [from *Naugatuk*, a town in Connecticut where rubber is manufactured + *-hyde* alteration of HIDE²]

naught *archaic* or *literary* ● *noun* nothing, nought. ● *adjective* (usu. *predicative*) worthless; useless. □ **come to naught** be ruined or baffled. **set at naught** disregard; despise. [Old English *nāwiht, -wuht* from *nā* (see NO²) + *wiht* WIGHT]

naugh·ty *adjective* (**naugh·ti·er, naugh·ti·est**) **1** (esp. of children) disobedient; badly behaved. **2** *informal jocular* connected with sex in a rude or funny way (*a naughty postcard*). □ **naugh·ti·ly** *adverb* **naugh·ti·ness** *noun* [Middle English from NAUGHT + -Y¹]

Nault /noʊ/ **Fer·nand** (born Fernand-Noël Boissonneault) (b.1921), Canadian dancer, choreographer, and director. He danced with American Ballet Theatre 1944–65, and then joined Les Grands Ballets Canadiens, where he has served as associate director (1967–74), director of schools (1974–76) and resident choreographer.

naup·lius /ˈnɒpliəs/ *noun* (*pl.* **naup·lii** /-pli,aɪ/) the first larval stage of some crustaceans. [Latin, = a kind of shellfish, or from Greek *Nauplios* son of Poseidon]

Nauru /naʊˈuːruː/ an island country in the SW Pacific, near the equator; pop. (est. 2002) 12,329; capital Yaren.

Nau·ru·an /naʊˈruːən/ ● *noun* **1** a native or inhabitant of Nauru. **2** the Malayo-Polynesian language of Nauru. ● *adjective* of or relating to Nauru or Nauruan.

nau·sea /ˈnɒziə, ˈnɒʒə/ *noun* **1** a feeling of sickness with an inclination to vomit. **2** loathing; revulsion. [Latin from Greek *nausia* seasickness, from *naus* ship]

nau·se·ate /ˈnɒzi,eɪt/ *transitive verb* **1** affect with nausea; cause to feel sick (*was nauseated by the smell*). **2** disgust; appall. □ **nau·se·at·ed** *adjective* **nau·se·at·ing** *adjective* **nau·se·at·ing·ly** *adverb*

nau·seous /ˈnɒʃəs, ˈnɒʒəs, ˈnɒziəs/ *adjective* **1** affected with nausea, sick (*felt nauseous all day*). ¶ Objections to the use of *nauseous* in this sense on the grounds that *nauseated* should be used instead are ill-founded. This is in fact by far the most common sense of *nauseous*. **2** causing nausea, offensive to the taste or smell. **3** disgusting; loathsome.

-naut *combining form* designating a person who navigates a vehicle, esp. one used for space travel (*astronaut*; *cosmonaut*). [from Greek *nautēs* sailor]

nautch /nɒtʃ/ *noun* a performance of professional Indian dancing girls. [Urdu (Hindi) *nāch* from Prakrit *nachcha* from Sanskrit *nṛitja* dancing]

nautch girl *noun* a professional Indian dancing girl.

naut·ical *adjective* of or concerning sailors or ships; naval; maritime. □ **naut·ical·ly** *adverb* [French *nautique* or from Latin *nauticus* from Greek *nautikos* from *nautēs* sailor from *naus* ship]

nautical mile *noun* a unit of approx. 1 852 metres (2,025 yards).

naut·ilus /ˈnɒtɪləs/ *noun* (*pl.* **naut·ilus·es** or **naut·ili** /-,laɪ/) **1** any cephalopod of the genus *Nautilus* with a light brittle spiral shell, esp. (**pearly nautilus**) one having a chambered shell with nacreous septa. **2** (in full **paper nautilus**) any small floating octopus of the genus *Argonauta*, of which the female has a very thin shell and webbed sail-like arms. **3 Nautilus** proprietary a type of weightlifting machine on which, with one's arms or legs, one lifts padded bars that are attached by pulleys to removable weights that give variable resistance. [Latin from Greek *nautilos*, lit. sailor (as NAUTICAL)]

NAV *abbreviation* net asset value.

nav. *abbreviation* **1** navigation. **2** naval.

nav *noun informal* **1** (usu. *attributive*) navigation (*nav lights*). **2** navigator.

nav·aid *noun* a navigational device in an aircraft, ship, etc. [from *nav(igational* + AID *noun*]

Nav·ajo /ˈnavəhoʊ/ (also **Nav·aho**) ● *noun* (*pl.* same or **-ajos** or **-ahos**) **1** a member of an Athapaskan people of Arizona, Utah, and New Mexico. **2** the Athapaskan language of this people. ● *adjective* of this people or their language. [Spanish, = pueblo]

naval *adjective* **1** of, in, for, etc. the navy or a navy. **2** of or concerning ships or boats (*a naval battle*). [Latin *navalis* from *navis* ship]

naval architecture *noun* the designing of ships and boats. □ **naval architect** *noun*

naval base *noun* a securely held seaport from which naval operations can be carried out.

naval cadet *noun* (also **Naval Cadet**) an officer cadet in the Canadian navy. Abbr.: **NCdt**.

Navan /ˈnavən/ the county town of Meath, in the Republic of Ireland; pop. (2002) 3,415.

Nava·nagar /ˌnʌvəˈnʌgɜr/ a former princely state of NW India, centred on the city of Jamnagar. It is now part of the modern state of Gujarat.

nava·rin /ˈnavə,rã/ *noun* a casserole of mutton or lamb with vegetables. [French, possibly after the battle of NAVARINO]

Nava·rino, Battle of /ˌnavəˈriːnoʊ/ a decisive naval battle in the Greek struggle for independence from the Ottoman Empire, fought in 1827 in the Bay of Navarino off Pylos in the Peloponnese, in which Britain, Russia, and France sent a combined fleet which destroyed the Egyptian and Turkish fleet.

Na·varre /nəˈvɑr/ an autonomous region of N Spain, on the border with France; capital, Pamplona.

Nav·Can *abbreviation* Nav Canada, a corporation responsible for providing air traffic control, flight information, weather briefings, airport advisory services and electronic aids to navigation for civil aviation in Canada.

nave¹ *noun* the central longitudinal part of a church, usu. from the main entrance to the chancel and excluding the side aisles. [medieval Latin *navis* from Latin *navis* ship]

nave² *noun* the hub of a wheel. [Old English *nafu, nafa* from Germanic, related to NAVEL]

navel *noun* **1** a rounded depression in the centre of the belly caused by the detachment of the umbilical cord; the umbilicus. **2** a central point. [Old English *nafela* from Germanic, related to NAVE²]

navel-gazing *noun* usu. profitless meditation; complacent introversion; self-absorption.

navel orange *noun* a large seedless orange with a navel-like formation at the top.

nav·icu·lar /nə'vɪkjʊlər/ ● *adjective* boat-shaped. ● *noun* (in full **navicular bone**) a boat-shaped bone in the foot or hand. [Latin *navicula* diminutive of *navis* ship]

navicular disease *noun* an inflammatory disease of the navicular bone in horses, causing lameness.

nav·ig·able /'navɪgəbəl/ *adjective* (of a river, the sea, etc.) affording a passage for ships. □ **nav·ig·abil·ity** *noun* [as NAVIGATE]

navi·gate *verb* **1 a** *transitive* manage or direct the course of (a ship, aircraft, etc.). **b** *intransitive* find one's way; steer the correct course. **2** *transitive* sail on or across (a sea, river, etc.). **b** travel or fly through (the air). **3** *intransitive* (of a passenger in a vehicle) assist the driver by map-reading etc. **4** *transitive informal* steer (oneself, a course, etc.) through a crowd etc. [Latin *navigare*, from *navis* 'ship' + *agere* 'drive']

navi·ga·tion *noun* **1** the act or process of navigating. **2** any of several methods of determining or planning a ship's or aircraft's position and course by geometry, astronomy, radio signals, etc. **3** *Computing* the action or process of moving around a file, file system, website, etc. □ **navi·ga·tion·al** *adjective*

navigation light *noun* a light on a ship or aircraft, indicating its position and direction.

navi·ga·tor *noun* **1** a person skilled or engaged in navigation. **2** an explorer by sea.

Nav·ra·ti·lova /na,vratɪ'loːvə/ **Mar·tina** (b.1956), Czech-born US tennis player, winner of twenty Wimbledon titles, including nine singles titles (1978–9; 1982–7; 1990), in addition to two world championships (1980; 1984) and many other grand slam titles.

navvy *noun* (*pl.* **-vies**) *Brit. & Cdn informal* a labourer employed in excavating or constructing roads, canals, railways, etc. [abbreviation of NAVIGATOR, in obsolete sense 'canal builder']

navy ● *noun* (*pl.* **-ies**) **1 a** the whole body of a nation's ships of war, including crews, maintenance systems, and related material such as aircraft etc. **b** the officers and other ranks of a navy. **2** (in full **navy blue**) a dark blue colour as used in naval uniform. **3** *archaic* a fleet of ships. ● *adjective* (in full **navy blue**) dark blue. [Middle English, = fleet, via Old French *navie* 'ship, fleet' and Romanic & popular Latin *navia* 'ship' from Latin *navis*]

navy bean *noun* = HARICOT.

navy yard *noun* US a government shipyard with civilian labour.

naw *adverb slang* = NO[2] interjection.

nawab /nə'wab, -'wɒb/ *noun hist.* the title of a governor or nobleman in India. [Urdu *nawwāb* pl. from Arabic *nā'ib* deputy: compare NABOB]

Naxa·lite /'naxə,ləɪt/ *noun* (in the Indian subcontinent) a member of an armed revolutionary group advocating Maoist communism.

Nax·çi·van /,naxtʃə'vɒn/ (Russian **Nakhichevan** /nəxɪtʃə'van/) **1** a predominantly Muslim Azerbaijani autonomous republic, situated on the borders of Turkey and N Iran and separated from the rest of Azerbaijan by a narrow strip of Armenia; pop. (est. 2000) 363,000. **2** the capital city of this republic; pop. (est. 2002) 68,600.

Naxos /'naksɒs/ a Greek island in the S Aegean, the largest of the Cyclades.

nay ● *adverb* **1** or rather; and even; and more than that (*impressive, nay, magnificent*). **2** *Parl.* or *archaic* = NO[2] interjection 1. ● *noun* **1** the word 'nay'. **2** a negative vote (*counted 16 nays*). [Old Norse *nei* from *ne* not + *ei* AYE[2]]

Naya·rit /,nɒjɒ'riːt/ a state of W Mexico, on the Pacific coast; capital, Tepic.

nay·say·er *noun N Amer.* **1** a person who expresses negative, cynical, or gloomy views. **2** a person who does this habitually. □ **nay·say·ing** *noun*

Naza·rene /nazə'riːn, 'nazə-/ ● *noun* **1** (prec. by *the*) Christ. **2** a native or inhabitant of Nazareth. **3 a** a member of an early Jewish-Christian sect living in Syria. **b** a Protestant denomination called the Church of the Nazarene. ● *adjective* of or concerning Nazareth, the Nazarenes, etc. [Greek *Nazarēnos*, from *Nazaret* 'Nazareth']

Naza·reth /'nazərəθ/ a historic town in lower Galilee in present-day N Israel; pop. (2000) 59,600. It was mentioned in the Gospels as the home of Mary and Joseph, is closely associated with the childhood of Jesus, and is a centre of Christian pilgrimage.

Nazi /'nɒtsi, 'natsi/ ● *noun* (*pl.* **Nazis**) **1** *hist.* a member of the German National Socialist party, led by Adolf Hitler. **2** *derogatory* a person holding extreme racist or authoritarian views or behaving brutally. **3** a person belonging to any organization similar to the Nazis. ● *adjective* of or concerning the Nazis, Nazism, etc. □ **Nazi·fi·ca·tion** *noun* **Nazi·fy** *transitive verb* (**-fies**, **-fied**). **Nazi·ism** /-iː,ɪzəm/ *noun* **Naz·ism** /'natsɪzəm/ *noun* [representing pronunciation of *Nati-* in German *Nationalsozialist*, 'National Socialist']

Nazir·ite /'nazə,rəɪt/ *noun* (also **Nazar·ite**) *hist.* a Hebrew who had taken certain vows of abstinence; an ascetic. [Late Latin *Nazaraeus* from Hebrew *nāzîr* from *nāzar* to separate or consecrate oneself]

NB *abbreviation* **1** New Brunswick. **2** *nota bene*.

Nb *symbol Chem.* the element niobium.

NBA *abbreviation* National Basketball Association.

NBC *abbreviation* (of armaments or warfare) nuclear, biological, and chemical.

NC *abbreviation* **1** North Carolina (also in official postal use). **2** network computer, a personal computer with reduced functionality intended to be used to access services on a network.

NC-17 *abbreviation US* no children under 17: a movie rating from the Motion Picture Association of America advising that persons under the age of 17 will not be admitted to the film.

NCAA *abbreviation* (in the US) National Collegiate Athletic Association.

NCC *noun* (in Canada) National Capital Commission.

NCdt *abbreviation Cdn* NAVAL CADET.

NCM *abbreviation Cdn* non-commissioned member.

NCO *abbreviation* non-commissioned officer.

NCR *abbreviation proprietary* no carbon required, designating paper chemically treated so that the pressure of writing or typing alone produces duplicate copies without the use of carbon paper between the sheets.

ND *abbreviation* North Dakota (also in official postal use).

Nd *symbol Chem.* the element neodymium.

n.d. *abbreviation* no date.

N.Dak. *abbreviation* North Dakota.

NDB *abbreviation* nondirectional beacon, a radio beacon for the assistance of aircraft pilots in navigation.

NDE *abbreviation* near-death experience.

Nde·bele /əndə'biːli, -'beili/ ● *noun* **1** (*pl.* same or **Nde·beles**) a member of a Nguni people. **2** the Bantu language of this people. ● *adjective* of or relating to this people or their language. [the name in the Nguni languages]

NDHQ *abbreviation Cdn* National Defence Headquarters.

N'Dja·mena /,əndʒa'meinə/ the capital of Chad; pop. (est. 2002) 601,500. Founded by the French in 1900, it was known (until 1973) as Fort Lamy.

Ndola /ən'doːlə/ a city in the Copperbelt region of central Zambia; pop. (est. 2002) 347,900.

NDP *abbreviation Cdn* NEW DEMOCRATIC PARTY. □ **NDPer** *noun*

NDT *abbreviation* NEWFOUNDLAND DAYLIGHT TIME.

NE *abbreviation* **1** northeast. **2** northeastern. **3** Nebraska (in official postal use).

Ne *symbol Chem.* the element neon.

né /nei/ *adjective* born (indicating a man's previous name) (*Lord Beaconsfield, né Benjamin Disraeli*). [French, past participle of *naître* be born: compare NÉE]

NEA *abbreviation* (in the US): **1** National Endowment for the Arts. **2** National Education Association.

Neagh, Lough /lɒx 'nei/ *see* LOUGH NEAGH.

Ne·an·der·thal /ni'andər,θɒl, -,tɒl/ ● *adjective* **1** of or belonging to the type of human widely distributed in paleolithic Europe, with a retreating forehead and massive brow ridges. **2** (also **neanderthal**) *jocular* or *derogatory* **a** primitive, uncivilized, uncouth. **b** reactionary; extremely conservative. ● *noun* **1** a Neanderthal hominid. **2** (also **neanderthal**) *jocular* or *derogatory* **a** a primitive, uncivilized, or uncouth person. **b** a reactionary or extremely conservative person. [*Neanderthal*, a region in Germany where remains were found]

neap *noun* (in full **neap tide**) a tide just after the first and third quarters of the moon when there is least difference between high and low water. [Old English *nēpflōd* (compare FLOOD), of unknown origin]

Nea·pol·itan /niə'pɒlɪtən/ ● *noun* a native or citizen of Naples in Italy. ● *adjective* of or relating to Naples. [Latin *Neapolitanus* from Latin *Neapolis* Naples, from Greek from *neos* new + *polis* city]

Neapolitan ice cream *noun* ice cream made in layers of chocolate, vanilla, and strawberry.

neap tide *noun see* NEAP.

near ● *adverb* **1** (often foll. by *to*) to or at a short distance in space or time; close by (*the time drew near; dropped near to them*). **2** closely (*as near as one can guess*). **3** *informal* almost, nearly (*damn near died*). ● *preposition* (comparative & superlative also used) **1** to or at a short distance (in space, time, condition, or resemblance) from (*stood near the back; occurs*

---

nearer the end; the sun is near setting). **2** (in combination) **a** that is almost (near-hysterical; a near-alcoholic). **b** intended as a substitute for; resembling (near-beer). ● adjective **1** close at hand; close to, in place or time (the end is near; in the near future). **2 a** closely related (a near relation). **b** intimate (a near friend). **3** close; narrow (a near escape; a near guess). **4** similar (to) (is nearer the original). **5** niggardly, mean. ● verb **1** transitive approach; draw near to (neared the harbour). **2** intransitive draw near (could distinguish them as they neared). □ **come near** (foll. by verbal noun, or to + verbal noun) be on the point of, almost succeed in (came near to falling). **near at hand 1** within easy reach. **2** in the immediate future. **nearest and dearest** one's closest friends and relatives collectively. □ **near·ish** adjective **near·ness** noun [Old Norse nær, originally comparative of ná = Old English néah NIGH]

near bank noun (in Canada) a financial institution, e.g. a credit union or caisse populaire, that provides banking services but does not have the status or privileges of a chartered bank.

near-beer noun a drink resembling beer; beer with a very low alcohol content.

near·by ● adjective situated in a near position (a nearby hotel). ● adverb (also **near by**) close; not far away.

Ne·arc·tic /niːˈɑrktɪk, -ˈɑrtɪk/ ● adjective of or relating to the Arctic and the temperate parts of N America as a zoogeographical region. ● noun the Nearctic region. [NEO- + ARCTIC]

near-death experience noun an out-of-body experience taking place on the brink of death, recounted by a person on recovery.

Near East (prec. by the) **1** = MIDDLE EAST. **2** hist. the Balkans. □ **Near Eastern** adjective

near·ly adverb **1** almost (we are nearly there). **2** closely (they are nearly related). **3** with a close degree of approximation. □ **not nearly** nothing like; far from (not nearly enough).

near miss noun **1** a bomb etc. falling close to the target. **2** a narrowly avoided collision. **3** an attempt that is almost but not quite successful.

Near North noun Cdn the southern edge of the Subarctic, extending across Canada in a band just north of the heavily settled areas of the Fraser Valley, the Prairies, and Southern Ontario and the St. Lawrence Valley.

near·shore adjective situated or occurring close to a shore (nearshore ecosystem).

near·sight·ed adjective esp. N Amer. **1** unable to distinguish objects clearly at a distance; myopic. **2** = SHORT-SIGHTED 2. □ **near·sight·ed·ly** adverb **near·sight·ed·ness** noun

near-term adjective occurring in or pertaining to the near future.

near thing noun a narrow escape.

neat¹ ● adjective **1 a** (of a room etc.) tidy; clean; in an orderly condition. **b** (of a person) liking to keep things in order; fastidious (a neat worker). **2** elegantly simple in form etc.; well-proportioned. **3** (of language, style, etc.) brief, clear, and pointed; epigrammatic. **4** cleverly executed (a neat piece of work). **b** deft; dexterous. **5** (of esp. alcoholic liquor) undiluted. **6** N Amer. slang (as a general term of approval) good, pleasing, excellent. ● adverb informal neatly. ● noun (in pl.) a small pattern or design of dots, geometrics, etc. found esp. on ties, socks, etc. □ **neat·ly** adverb **neat·ness** noun [French net from Latin nitidus shining, from nitēre shine]

neat² noun archaic **1** a bovine animal. **2** (as pl.) cattle. [Old English néat from Germanic]

neat·en transitive verb make neat.

neat freak noun slang an obsessively tidy person.

'neath preposition (also **neath**) literary beneath. [BENEATH]

neat·nik noun N Amer. slang a person who is excessively neat in his or her personal habits. [from NEAT¹ adjective 1b + -NIK, after BEATNIK]

neat-o adjective N Amer. slang = NEAT¹ adjective 6.

neat's-foot oil noun oil made from boiled cow-heel and used to dress leather.

NEB abbreviation **1** NEW ENGLISH BIBLE. **2** (in Canada) National Energy Board.

Neb. abbreviation Nebraska.

Neb·bi·olo /nebiˈoːloː/ ● noun **1** a black wine grape grown in Piedmont in northern Italy. **2** red wine made from this grape. ● adjective of or pertaining to this grape or this wine. [Italian]

neb·bish /ˈnebɪʃ/ informal ● noun an ineffectual or timid person. ● adjective ineffectual; timid. □ **neb·bishy** adjective [Yiddish nebach poor thing!]

Neb·lina, Pico da see PICO DA NEBLINA.

Nebr. abbreviation Nebraska.

Neb·raska a state in the central US to the west of the Missouri; pop. (2000) 1,711,263; capital, Lincoln. □ **Neb·ras·kan** adjective & noun

Nebu·chad·nez·zar /ˌnebʊkədˈnezər, ˌnebjʊ-/ (c.630–562 BC), king of Babylon 605–562 BC. He rebuilt the city with massive fortifications and extended his rule over neighbouring countries; in 586 BC he captured and destroyed Jerusalem and deported its leaders.

nebu·chad·nez·zar /ˌnebʊkədˈnezər, ˌnebjʊ-/ noun a wine bottle of about 20 times the standard size. [NEBUCHADNEZZAR]

neb·ula /ˈnebjʊlə/ noun (pl. **neb·ulae** /-ˌliː, -ˌlaɪ/ or **neb·ulas**) **1** Astronomy a cloud of gas and dust in space, sometimes glowing and sometimes appearing as a dark silhouette against other glowing matter. **2** Med. a clouded spot on the cornea causing defective vision. [Latin, = mist]

nebu·lar /ˈnebjʊlər/ adjective of or relating to a nebula or nebulae.

nebular theory noun (also **nebular hypothesis**) the theory that the solar and stellar systems were developed from a primeval nebula.

nebu·liz·er /ˈnebjʊlaɪzər/ noun (also esp. Brit. **-iser**) a device for producing a fine spray of liquid. □ **nebu·lize** transitive verb (also esp. Brit. **-ise**).

nebu·lous /ˈnebjʊləs/ adjective **1** hazy, indistinct, vague (put forward a few nebulous ideas). **2** Astronomy of or like a nebula or nebulae. □ **nebu·los·ity** /-ˈlɒsɪti/ noun **nebu·lous·ly** adverb **nebu·lous·ness** noun [Latin nebulosus (as NEBULA)]

ne·ces·sar·ily adverb **1** as a necessary result; inevitably. **2** by force of necessity (we don't necessarily have to leave now).

ne·ces·sary ● adjective **1** requiring to be done, achieved, etc.; requisite, essential (it is necessary to work; lacks the necessary documents). **2** determined, existing, or happening by natural laws, predestination, etc., not by free will; inevitable (a necessary evil). **3** Philos. (of a concept or a mental process) inevitably resulting from or produced by the nature of things etc., so that the contrary is impossible. **4** Philos. (of an agent) having no independent volition. ● noun (pl. **-ies**) (usu. in pl.) any of the basic requirements of life, such as food, warmth, etc. □ **the necessary** an action, item, etc., needed for a purpose (they will do the necessary). [Latin necessarius from necesse needful]

necessary condition noun Logic a condition without which another condition cannot exist, but which in itself is not sufficient for the other condition to exist.

ne·ces·si·tar·ian /nəˌsesɪˈteriən/ Philos. ● noun a person who holds that all action is predetermined and free will is impossible (opp. LIBERTARIAN noun 2). ● adjective of or concerning such a person or theory. □ **ne·ces·si·tar·ian·ism** noun

ne·ces·si·tate /nəˈsesɪˌteɪt/ transitive verb make necessary (esp. as a result) (will necessitate some sacrifice).

ne·ces·si·tous /nəˈsesɪtəs/ adjective poor; needy.

ne·ces·si·ty noun (pl. **-ties**) **1 a** (often in pl.) an indispensable thing (central heating is a necessity; the necessities of life). **b** (usu. foll. by of) indispensability (the necessity of a warm overcoat). **2** a state of things or circumstances enforcing a certain course (there was a necessity to hurry). **3** imperative need (necessity is the mother of invention). **4** want; poverty; hardship (stole because of necessity). **5** constraint or compulsion regarded as a natural law governing all human action. □ **of necessity** unavoidably. [Latin necessitas -tatis from necesse needful]

Ne·chako Reservoir /nəˈtʃakoː/ a series of lakes (Natalkuz, Eutsuk, Ootsa, Whitesail and Tetachuck) in west central BC, formed by the damming of the Nechako River's headwaters. [NECHAKO RIVER]

Ne·chako River /nəˈtʃakoː/ a river in central BC, which flows generally northeastward from the Coast Mountains to join the Fraser River at Prince George. [Carrier, = big river]

neck ● noun **1 a** the part of the body connecting the head to the shoulders. **b** the part of a shirt, dress, etc. around or close to the neck. **c** = NECKLINE. **2 a** something resembling a neck, such as the narrow part of a cavity or vessel, a passage, channel, pass, isthmus, etc. **b** the narrow part of a bottle, vase, etc. near the mouth. **3** the part of a violin, guitar, etc. bearing the fingerboard. **4** the length of a horse's head and neck as a measure of its lead in a race. **5** Geol. solidified lava or igneous rock in an old volcano crater or pipe. **6** Archit. the lower part of a capital. ● verb **1** intransitive informal kiss and caress amorously. **2 a** transitive form a narrowed part in. **b** intransitive form a narrowed part. □ **get it in the neck** informal **1** receive a severe reprimand or punishment. **2** suffer a fatal or severe blow. **neck and neck** very close in a race, competition, etc. **up to one's neck** (often foll. by in) informal very deeply involved; very busy. □ **necked** adjective (also in combination). **neck·er** noun (in sense 1 of verb). **neck·less** adjective [Old English hnecca, ultimately from Germanic]

Neck·ar River /ˈnekɑr/ a river of western Germany, which rises in the Black Forest and flows 367 km (228 miles) north and west through Stuttgart to meet the Rhine at Mannheim.

neck·band noun a strip of material around the neck of a garment.

neck·cloth noun hist. = CRAVAT 1.

Neck·er /ˈnekər/ **Jacques** (1732–1804), Swiss banker, director general of French finances 1777–81 and 1788–9. During his second term he recommended summoning the Estates General; his resulting dismissal on 11 July 1789 was one of the factors which resulted in the storming of the Bastille three days later.

neck·er·chief /ˈnekərtʃɪf, -tʃiːf/ noun a square of cloth worn around the neck.

neck guard noun a piece of equipment worn by hockey players to protect the neck area.

neck·lace /ˈnekləs/ ● noun **1** a chain or string of beads, precious stones, links, etc., worn as an ornament around the neck. **2** South Africa a tire soaked or filled with gasoline, placed round a victim's neck, and set alight. **3** a series of towns, buildings, objects, etc., spread over an area. ● transitive verb South Africa kill with a 'necklace'.

neck·let noun = NECKLACE noun 1.

neck·line noun the edge or shape of the opening of a garment at the neck (a square neckline).

neck of the woods noun informal a community or locality.

neck pillow noun a pillow specially designed to support the neck, esp. one with a raised ridge of foam along one long edge or an inflatable cushion with a hole for the neck.

neck·tie noun esp. N Amer. = TIE noun 2.

necktie party noun slang a lynching or hanging.

neck·wear noun collars, ties, etc.

necro- /ˈnekrəʊ/ combining form forming nouns and adjectives concerning death, corpses, or dead tissue. [from or after Greek nekro- from nekros corpse]

necro·bio·sis /ˌnekrəʊbaɪˈəʊsɪs/ noun decay in the tissues of the body, esp. swelling of the collagen bundles in the dermis. □ **necro·biot·ic** /-ˈtɪk/ adjective

necrol·ogy /nəˈkrɒlədʒi/ noun (pl. **-gies**) **1** a list of recently dead people. **2** an obituary notice. □ **necro·logic·al** /-rəˈlɒdʒɪkəl/ adjective **necrol·o·gist** noun

necro·mancy /ˈnekrəˌmansi/ noun **1** the prediction of the future by the supposed communication with the dead. **2** witchcraft. □ **necro·man·cer** noun **necro·man·tic** /-ˈmantɪk/ adjective [Old French nigromancie from medieval Latin nigromantia changed (by assoc. with Latin niger nigri black) from Late Latin necromantia from Greek nekromanteia (as NECRO-, -MANCY)]

necro·philia /nekrəˈfɪliə/ noun a morbid and esp. erotic attraction to corpses. □ **necro·phile** /ˈnekrəfaɪl/ noun **necro·phil·iac** /-ˈfɪliak/ noun **necro·phil·ic** adjective **ne·croph·il·ism** /-ˈkrɒfɪlɪzəm/ noun

necro·phobia /ˌnekrəˈfəʊbiə/ noun an abnormal fear of death or dead bodies.

ne·crop·olis /nəˈkrɒpəlɪs/ noun **1** an ancient cemetery or burial place. **2** a cemetery, esp. a large one in or near a city. [Greek, formed as NECRO- + polis city]

nec·ropsy /ˈnekrɒpsi/ noun (pl. **-sies**) = AUTOPSY 1. [NECRO- after AUTOPSY, or +-SCOPY]

ne·cro·sis /nəˈkrəʊsɪs/ noun the death or decay of part or all of an organ or tissue due to disease, injury, or deficiency of nutrients, esp. as one of the symptoms of gangrene or pulmonary tuberculosis. □ **ne·crot·ic** /-ˈkrɒtɪk/ adjective **ne·cro·tize** /ˈnekrətaɪz/ intransitive verb (also esp. Brit. **-tise**). [modern Latin from Greek nekrōsis (as NECRO-, -OSIS)]

nec·ro·tiz·ing fasci·itis noun a severe infection caused by Streptococcus pyogenes, in which inflammation of the superficial and deep fascia produces thrombosis of subcutaneous vessels and gangrene of underlying tissue.

nec·tar noun **1** a sugary substance produced by plants to attract pollinating insects and made into honey by bees. **2 a** (in Greek and Roman mythology) the drink of the gods. **b** a drink compared to this. **3** a drink of usu. undiluted fruit juice or a blend of fruit juices. [Latin from Greek nektar]

nec·tar·ine /nektəˈriːn, ˈnek-/ noun **1** a variety of peach with a thin brightly coloured smooth skin and firm flesh. **2** the tree bearing this. [originally as adj., = nectar-like, from NECTAR + -INE⁴]

nec·tary /ˈnektəri/ noun (pl. **-ies**) the nectar-secreting organ of a flower or plant.

née /neɪ/ adjective (also **nee**) (used in adding a married woman's maiden name after her surname) born (Mrs. Patricia Barber, née Clarke). [French, fem. past participle of naître be born]

need ● verb **1** transitive stand in want of; require (needs a new coat; this needs revising). **2** transitive **a** (foll. by to + infin.) (esp. in positive and declarative contexts) be under a necessity or obligation (it needs to be done carefully). **b** (3rd sing. present **need**) (without to) (esp. in neg. or interrog. contexts) be under the necessity or obligation (he need not come; she need only ask). **3** intransitive N Amer. informal must get (I need in there, now!). **4** intransitive archaic be necessary. ● noun **1 a** a want or requirement (my needs are few; the need for greater freedom). **b** a thing wanted (my greatest need is a car). **2** circumstances requiring some course of action; necessity (there is no need to worry; if need arise). **3 a** a condition of lacking or requiring some necessary thing, either physically or psychologically. **b** destitution; poverty. **4** a crisis, time of difficulty, distress, or trouble; an emergency (failed them in their need). □ **at need** in time of need. **had need** archaic ought to (had need remember). **have need of** require; want. **have no need to** not be obliged to (I have no need to prove my manhood). **if need be** if necessary. **in need** requiring help. **in need of** requiring. **need not have** did not need to (but did). [Old English nēodian, nēd from Germanic]

need·ful ● adjective **1** requisite; necessary; indispensable. **2** having a need or needs. ● noun **1** (prec. by the) what is necessary. **2** informal money or action needed for a purpose. □ **need·ful·ly** adverb **need·ful·ness** noun

nee·dle ● noun **1 a** a very thin small piece of smooth steel etc. pointed at one end and with a slit (eye) for thread, used in sewing. **b** a larger plastic, wooden, etc. slender stick without an eye, used in knitting. **2 a** a slender, usu. pointed, indicator on a dial or other measuring instrument, esp. a speedometer. **b** = MAGNETIC NEEDLE. **3** any of several small thin pointed instruments, esp.: **a** a surgical instrument for stitching. **b** the end of a hypodermic syringe. **c** a thin metal rod used in acupuncture. **d** = STYLUS 3. **e** an etching tool. **f** a steel pin exploding the cartridge of a breech-loading rifle. **4 a** a hypodermic syringe. **b** an injection of a drug, vaccine, etc. through the needle of such a syringe. **5 a** an obelisk or pillar (Cleopatra's Needle). **b** a pointed peak or mass of rock. **c** a long narrow pointed crystal or spicule. **6** any of the sharp, stiff, slender leaves characteristic of a coniferous tree. **7** a beam used as a temporary support during underpinning. ● transitive verb **1** informal **a** incite or irritate; provoke (the silence needled him). **b** tease, harass. **2** sew, pierce, or operate on with a needle. □ **needle in a haystack** something almost impossible to find because it is concealed by so many other things etc. □ **nee·dled** adjective (also in combination). **need·ler** noun **need·ling** noun [Old English nǣdl from Germanic]

needle-and-thread grass noun a tall bunchgrass, Stipa comata, with long, twisted awns and a spiky seed, common in the western grasslands of North America.

needle biopsy noun Med. removal of tissue with a hollow needle for analysis and diagnosis.

needle·craft noun = NEEDLEWORK.

needle exchange noun **1** a public health service making sterile hypodermic needles available to drug users. **2** a place or building in which such a service is based.

needle·fish noun any of various elongated fishes, e.g. a gar.

needle lace noun lace made with needles not bobbins (compare BOBBIN LACE, PILLOW LACE).

needle-nose attributive adjective (of pliers) having long, thin pincers suitable for gripping in very narrow spaces.

needle·point ● noun **1** embroidery worked over canvas etc., esp. PETIT POINT or GROS POINT. **2** = NEEDLE LACE. ● transitive & intransitive verb work or create through needlepoint.

Nee·dles, the a group of rocks in the sea off the west coast of the Isle of Wight, in S England.

need·less adjective unnecessary, uncalled for, not needed or wanted. □ **needless to say** of course; it goes without saying. □ **need·less·ly** adverb **need·less·ness** noun

needle stick noun (often attributive) an act or instance of being, usu. accidentally, stuck by a hypodermic needle, esp. if possibly contaminated by HIV etc. (needle-stick injury).

needle tracks plural noun rows of scars, usu. on the arms, left by hypodermic injections, esp. by drug addicts.

needle trade noun (usu. prec. by the; usu. in pl.) a business, occupation, or organization involved in clothing manufacturing.

needle·woman noun (pl. **-women**) **1** a seamstress. **2** a woman or girl with specified sewing skill (a good needlewoman).

Consonants: b but   d dog   f few   g get   h her   j yes   k cat   l leg   m man   n no   p pen   r red   s sit

needle·work *noun* **1** the action of producing something with a needle, esp. by embroidery, tapestry, etc. **2** a piece of work so produced (also *attributive: needlework cushion*). □ **needle·work·er** *noun*

needn't *contraction* need not.

needs *adverb* (usu. prec. or foll. by *must*) of necessity (*must needs decide*). [Old English *nēdes* (as NEED, -S³)]

need-to-know *adjective* designating the principle or practice of telling people only what is necessary for them to carry out a task effectively.

needy *adjective* (**need·i·er**, **need·i·est**) **1** (of a person) a poor; destitute. **b** lacking some essential emotional or psychological quality, experience, etc. **2** (of circumstances) characterized by poverty or need. **3** needing emotional support; insecure. □ **need·i·ness** *noun*

Néel /neɪˈel/ **Louis Eugène Félix** (1904–2000), French physicist, who was noted for his studies of magnetism and solid state physics; he shared the Nobel Prize for physics in 1970.

neem *noun* a tree, *Azadirachta indica* (mahogany family), whose leaves and bark are used medicinally in the Indian subcontinent. [Hindi *nīm*]

neep *noun Scot. & Northern England* a turnip. [Old English *nǣp* from Latin *napus*]

Nee·pa·wa /ˈniːpəwɒ/ a town in south central Manitoba, about 90 km northwest of Portage la Prairie, birthplace of the writer Margaret Laurence; pop. (2001) 3,325. □ **Nee·pa·wan** *noun* [Ojibwa *nibiwa* abundance, plenty]

ne'er /ner/ *adverb* **1** *literary* = NEVER. **2** *Cdn (Nfld)* not one, not a; no. [Middle English contraction of NEVER]

ne'er-do-well ● *noun* a good-for-nothing person. ● *adjective* good-for-nothing.

ne·fari·ous /nəˈferiəs/ *adjective* wicked; iniquitous. □ **ne·fari·ous·ly** *adverb* **ne·fari·ous·ness** *noun* [Latin *nefarius* from *nefas* wrong, from *ne-* not + *fas* divine law]

Nefer·titi /ˌnefərˈtiːti/ (also **Nofretete** /ˈnɒfrə-/) (*fl.* 14th c. BC), Egyptian queen, wife of Akhenaten. She initially supported her husband's religious reforms, but it is a matter of dispute whether she continued her support or withdrew it in favour of the new religion promoted by her half-brother Tutankhamen.

neg *noun informal* a photographic negative.

neg. *abbreviation* negative.

neg·ate /nəˈgeɪt/ *transitive verb* **1** nullify, make ineffective, invalidate. **2** imply, involve, or assert the non-existence of; deny. **3** *Grammar* make (a clause, sentence, etc.) negative in meaning. [Latin *negare* (as NEGAT- deny]

neg·a·tion /nəˈgeɪʃən/ *noun* **1** (often foll. by *of*) **a** the act of refusing, or of contradicting or denying a statement or allegation. **b** an instance of this; a contradiction, denial, or refusal. **c** a negative statement or doctrine. **2** the absence or opposite of something actual or positive (*death is the negation of life*). **3** *Grammar* **a** the grammatical process by which the truth of a clause or sentence is denied, involving the use of a negative word, e.g. *not, no, never*. **b** an instance of this. **4** a negative or unreal thing; a nonentity. **5** *Logic* the assertion that a certain proposition is false. [French *negation* or Latin *negatio* (as NEGATE)]

nega·tive /ˈnegətɪv/ ● *adjective* **1** expressing or implying denial, prohibition, or refusal (*a negative vote; a negative answer*). **2 a** (of a person, attitude, etc.) unhelpful, critical, or destructive; pessimistic, defeatist. **b** not having or showing an interested attitude, aiming to improve something, etc.; uncooperative. **3** (of an effect) harmful (*eliminate the negative side effects of the drug*). **4 a** (of the results of a test or an experiment) indicating that a substance or condition is not present (*the biopsy was negative*). **b** (in *combination*) (of a person, blood, etc.) not having a specified condition, substance, etc. (*relieved to find he was HIV-negative*). **5** marked by the absence rather than the presence of qualities. **6** of the opposite nature to a thing regarded as positive (*debt is negative capital*). **7** *Grammar* (of a word, clause, etc.) expressing negation. **8** *Algebra* (of a quantity) less than zero, to be subtracted from others or from zero (*opp.* POSITIVE *adjective* 9). **9** *Electricity* **a** of the kind of charge carried by electrons (*opp.* POSITIVE *adjective* 10a). **b** containing or producing such a charge. **10** *Logic* expressing negation or denial of a proposition. **11** *Photog.* (of a visual image, esp. a photograph) showing the lights, shades, and colour values reversed from those of the original. ● *noun* **1** a negative statement or reply. **2** *Photog.* **a** an image with black and white reversed or colours replaced by complementary ones, from which positive pictures are obtained. **b** a developed film or plate bearing such an image. **3** *Grammar* = NEGATOR. **4** (prec. by *the*) the side or aspect of a question which is opposed to the affirmative or positive. **5 a** a negative quality or characteristic. **b** an absence of something. **6** *Logic* = NEGATION 5. **7** a negative result on a medical test, experiment, etc. ● *interjection* esp. *N Amer.* no. ● *transitive verb* **1** refuse to accept or countenance; veto; reject. **2** disprove (an inference or

hypothesis). **3** contradict (a statement). **4** neutralize (an effect). □ **in the negative** in rejection of a proposal or suggestion, with negative effect; no (*the answer was in the negative*). □ **nega·tive·ly** *adverb* **nega·tive·ness** *noun* **nega·tiv·ity** *noun* [Late Latin *negativus* (as NEGATE)]

negative equity *noun* the indebtedness arising when the market value of a property falls below the outstanding amount of a mortgage secured on it.

negative evidence *noun* evidence of the non-occurrence of something.

negative feedback *noun* **1** the return of part of an output signal to the input, tending to decrease the amplification etc. **2** esp. *Biol.* the diminution or counteraction of an effect by its own influence on the process giving rise to it. **3** a negative response to a questionnaire, an experiment, etc.

negative option *noun* a method of selling whereby the customer's failure to indicate actively that the product, service, etc., is not wanted is taken as consent to purchase it.

negative pole *noun* the south-seeking pole of a magnet.

nega·tiv·ism *noun* **1 a** the tendency to be negative in attitude, action, or position. **b** extreme skepticism, criticism, etc. **2** denial of accepted beliefs. □ **nega·tiv·ist** *noun* **nega·tiv·is·tic** *adjective*

neg·ator /nəˈgeɪtər/ *noun* **1** a person who denies something. **2** *Grammar* a word or particle expressing negation, e.g. *not, don't*.

Negev, the /ˈnegev/ an arid region forming most of S Israel, between Beersheba and the Gulf of Aqaba, on the Egyptian border. Large-scale irrigation projects have greatly increased the fertility of the region.

neg·lect ● *transitive verb* **1** fail to care for or to do; be remiss about (*neglected their duty; neglected his children*). **2** (foll. by *to* + infin.) fail; overlook or forget the need to (*neglected to inform them*). **3** not pay due attention to; disregard (*this area of research has been largely neglected*). ● *noun* **1** lack of caring; negligence (*the house suffered from neglect*). **2 a** the act or fact of neglecting. **b** the state or condition of being neglected (*the house fell into neglect*). **3** (usu. foll. by *of*) disregard. □ **neg·lect·ed** *adjective* **neg·lect·ful** *adjective* **neg·lect·ful·ly** *adverb* **neg·lect·ful·ness** *noun* [Latin *neglegere* neglect- from *neg-* not + *legere* choose, pick up]

neg·li·gee /ˈneglɪˌʒeɪ/ *noun* a woman's light dressing gown, usu. made of delicate, semi-transparent fabric and trimmed with lace etc. [French, past participle of *négliger* NEGLECT]

neg·li·gence /ˈneglɪdʒəns/ *noun* **1 a** a lack of reasonable or proper care and attention; carelessness. **b** an act or instance of carelessness or inattention. **2** *Law* **a** = CONTRIBUTORY NEGLIGENCE. **b** = CRIMINAL NEGLIGENCE. □ **neg·li·gent** *adjective* **neg·li·gent·ly** *adverb* [Latin *negligentia* from *negligere* = *negligere*: see NEGLECT]

neg·li·gible /ˈneglɪdʒɪbəl/ *adjective* not worth considering or noticing; insignificant. □ **neg·li·gibly** *adverb* [obsolete French from *négliger* NEGLECT]

Ne·gom·bo /nəˈgɒmboʊ/ a port and resort on the west coast of Sri Lanka; pop. (est. 2002) 123,300.

ne·go·ti·able /nəˈgoʊʃəbəl/ *adjective* **1 a** able to be decided or arranged by negotiation or mutual agreement. **b** subject to modification of meaning or interpretation. **2** (of a bill, draft, cheque, etc.) transferable or assignable in the course of business from one person to another simply by delivery. **3** (of an obstacle) that may be crossed or got over, around, or through.

negotiable instrument *noun* a freely negotiable legal document such as a cheque, promissory note, etc. that is payable to the bearer.

ne·go·ti·ate /nəˈgoʊʃiˌeɪt/ *verb* **1** *intransitive* (usu. foll. by *with*) confer with others in order to reach a compromise or agreement. **2** *transitive* arrange or settle (a matter) or bring about (a result) by negotiating (*negotiated a settlement; negotiate a loan*). **3** *transitive* find a way over, through, etc. (an obstacle, difficulty, etc.). **4** *transitive* **a** transfer or assign (a cheque etc.) to another. **b** convert (a cheque etc.) into cash or banknotes. **c** get or give value for (a cheque etc.) in money. □ **ne·go·ti·at·ed** *adjective* **ne·go·ti·at·ing** *noun* **ne·go·ti·a·tion** /-ʃiˈeɪʃən, -sɪˈeɪʃən/ *noun* **ne·go·ti·ator** *noun* [Latin *negotiari* from *negotium* business, from *neg-* not + *otium* leisure]

negotiating table *noun* a place or meeting etc. at which disputes, esp. labour disputes, armed conflicts, constitutional matters, etc., are negotiated.

Ne·gress /ˈniːgres/ *noun hist.*, now *offensive* a Black woman.

Ne·gril·lo /nəˈgrɪloʊ/ *noun* (*pl.* **-los**) a member of a very small Negroid people native to Central and S Africa. [Spanish, diminutive of NEGRO]

Negri Sem·bi·lan /ˌnegri semˈbiːlən/ a state of Malaysia, on the southwest coast of the Malay Peninsula; capital, Seremban.

Ne·gri·to /nəˈɡriːtəʊ/ noun (pl. **-tos**) a member of a small Negroid people native to the Malayo-Polynesian region. [as NEGRILLO]

Ne·gri·tude /ˈniːɡrɪˌtuːd, -tjuːd/ noun **1** the affirmation or consciousness of the value of Black or African culture. **2** the quality or state of being a Black person. [French négritude]

Negro /ˈniːɡrəʊ/ ¶ now usu. considered offensive ● noun (pl. **-groes**) a member of the black or dark-skinned group of human populations that exist or originated in Africa south of the Sahara, now distributed around the world. ● adjective of or concerning this people. [Spanish & Portuguese, from Latin niger nigri black]

Ne·groid /ˈniːɡrɔɪd/ ● adjective **1** denoting, concerning, or belonging to one of the group of human populations having dark skin, tightly curled hair, and a broad flattish nose, indigenous to sub-Saharan Africa and parts of Melanesia. **2** (of features etc.) characteristic of these peoples. ● noun a member of one of these peoples. [NEGRO]

Ne·gros /ˈneɪɡrɒs/ an island in the Visayan group, the fourth largest island of the Philippines; pop. (2000) 3,692,000; chief city, Bacolod.

Negro spiritual noun = SPIRITUAL noun.

Negus /ˈniːɡəs/ noun hist. the title of the supreme ruler of Ethiopia. [Amharic n'gus king]

negus /ˈniːɡəs/ noun hist. a hot drink of port or sherry mixed with water, sugar, lemon, and spice. [Col. F. Negus d.1732, its inventor]

Neh. abbreviation Nehemiah (Bible).

Nehe·miah /niːˈmaɪə/ **1** a Hebrew leader (5th c. BC) who supervised the rebuilding of the walls of Jerusalem (c.444) and introduced moral and religious reforms (c.432); his work was continued by Ezra. **2** a book of the Bible telling of this rebuilding and of the reforms.

Nehru /ˈneɪruː/ **Jawa·har·lal** (known as 'Pandit Nehru') (1889–1964), Indian leader, prime minister 1947–64. An early associate of Mahatma Gandhi, he was elected leader of the Indian National Congress, succeeding his father 'Pandit' Motilal Nehru (1861–1931), in 1929. He was a leading figure in the campaign for independence during the 1930s and 1940s and became the first prime minister of independent India. □ **Neh·ru·vian** /neɪˈruːvɪən/ adjective

Nehru jacket noun a long, narrow jacket with a high stand-up collar. [NEHRU]

neigh /neɪ/ ● noun **1** the high whinnying sound of a horse. **2** any similar sound, e.g. a laugh. ● verb **1** intransitive make such a sound. **2** transitive utter with such a sound. [Old English hnægan, of imitative origin]

neigh·bour (also **neigh·bor**) ● noun **1** a person, institution, etc., resident or established next door to or near or nearest another (my next-door neighbour; his nearest neighbour is 12 miles away; they are neighbours). **2 a** a person or thing near or next to another (my neighbour at dinner). **b** a country etc. adjacent to or near another (Canada and the US are neighbours). **c** (in pl.) a resident of such a country etc. (our neighbours to the South). **3** a person regarded as a fellow human being, esp. as entitled to kindness, compassion, consideration, etc. **4** (attributive) **a** neighbouring (a neighbour nation). **b** living in the vicinity or next door (used to play with two neighbour kids). ● verb **1** transitive border on; adjoin. **2** intransitive (often foll. by on, upon) border; adjoin. □ **neigh·bour·ing** adjective [Old English nēahgebūr (as NIGH: gebūr, compare BOOR)]

neigh·bour·hood noun (also **neigh·bor·hood**) **1 a** a district, esp. considered in reference to the character or circumstances of its inhabitants. **b** a small, but relatively self-contained section of a larger urban area. **2** the people of a district; one's neighbours. **3** (often foll. by of) the nearby or surrounding area, the vicinity. **4** (attributive) belonging to or serving a particular neighbourhood (neighbourhood eatery). □ **in the neighbourhood of** roughly; about (paid in the neighbourhood of $100). **your friendly neighbourhood ...** often ironic the well-known and popular ....

neighbourhood watch noun systematic local vigilance by householders to discourage crime, esp. against property.

neigh·bour·ly adjective (also **neigh·bor·ly**) characteristic of a good neighbour; friendly; kind. □ **neigh·bour·li·ness** noun

Neisse River /ˈnaɪsə/ **1** a river in central Europe which rises in the north of the Czech Republic and flows over 225 km (140 miles) generally northward, forming the southern part of the border between Germany and Poland, joining the Oder River northeast of Cottbus. **2** a river of S Poland, which rises near the border with the Czech Republic and flows 195 km (120 miles) generally northeastward, through the town of Nysa, joining the Oder River southeast of Wrocław.

nei·ther /ˈnaɪðər, ˈniːð-/ ● adjective & pronoun (foll. by sing. verb) **1** not the one nor the other (of two things); not either (neither of the accusations is true; neither of them knows; neither wish was granted; neither went to the fair). **2** Cdn (Nfld) no, none, not any. ● adverb **1** not either; not on the one hand (foll. by nor; introducing the first of two or more things in the negative: neither knowing nor caring; would neither come in nor go out; neither the teachers nor the parents nor the children). **2** not either; also not (if you do not, neither shall I). ● conjunction nor yet; nor (I do not know, neither can I guess). [Middle English naither, neither from Old English nowther contraction of nōhwæther (as NO², WHETHER): assimilated to EITHER] ¶ As a pronoun, neither is singular: Neither of us likes tennis; however, in informal English, it is often treated as a plural: Neither of them are good players. When two subjects are linked by neither...nor, either a singular or a plural verb is permissible: Neither the television nor the radio works properly; Neither the television nor the radio work properly; some people feel, however, that singular subjects require a singular verb.

Nejd /nedʒd/ an arid plateau region in central Saudi Arabia, north of the Rub' al Khali desert, at an altitude of about 1 500 m (5,000 ft.).

nek·ton /ˈnektən/ noun Zool. free-swimming aquatic animals collectively. □ **nek·ton·ic** /nekˈtɒnɪk/ adjective [German from Greek nēkton neuter of nēktos swimming, from nēkhō swim]

Nel·li·gan /ˈnelɪɡən/ **1 Émile** (1879–1941), Canadian poet. Born in Montreal, he began writing symbolist poetry at age 16 and produced some 170 poems, sonnets, and songs. He was institutionalized for depression from 1899 until his death. His poetry, which is sad and nostalgic, includes such notable pieces as 'Romance du vin' and 'Vaisseau d'or'. **2 Kate** (b.1951), Canadian actress. After studying in Toronto and London, England, she made her London debut as Jenny in David Hare's Knuckle, and has continued to be associated with Hare's work. She played Rosalind in the Stratford Festival production of As You Like It (1977), and has performed in television and movies (including Eye of the Needle (1980)).

Nel·lore /neˈlɔːr/ a city and river port in SE India, in Andhra Pradesh, on the Penner River; pop. (2001) 378,900. Situated close to the mouth of the river, it is one of the chief ports of the Coromandel Coast.

nelly noun (pl. **-lies**) a silly or effeminate person. □ **not on your nelly** Cdn & Brit. slang certainly not. [perhaps from the name Nelly: idiom from rhyming slang Nelly Duff = puff = breath: compare not on your life]

Nel·son[1] a city in southern BC, located 41 km northeast of Castlegar, about 50 km north of the border with Washington state; pop. (2001) 9,298. □ **Nel·son·ite** noun [after Hugh Nelson, Lieutenant-Governor of the province d.1893]

Nel·son[2] ▶ **1 Hor·atio, Viscount Nelson, Duke of Bronte** (1758–1805), English admiral. He became a national hero after he defeated a Spanish fleet off Cape St. Vincent (1797) and virtually destroyed the French fleet in the Battle of Aboukir Bay (1798); he defeated a combined French and Spanish fleet decisively at the Battle of Trafalgar (1805), in which he was mortally wounded. **2 Wil·lie** (b.1933), US country singer and songwriter, whose best-known songs include 'On the Road Again' (1980) and 'Always on My Mind' (1982). □ **Nel·son·ian** adjective

nel·son noun a wrestling hold in which one arm is passed under the opponent's arm from behind and the hand is applied to the neck (**half nelson**), or both arms and hands are applied (**full nelson**). [apparently from the name Nelson]

Nelson River a river in NE central Manitoba, 644 km long, flowing generally northeastward from Playgreen Lake, situated at the northeastern end of Lake Winnipeg, to Hudson Bay. [R. Nelson, captain of the Resolution c.1612]

ne·lum·bo /nɪˈlʌmbəʊ/ noun (pl. **-bos**) either of two water lilies of the genus Nelumbo, the sacred lotus of the East, N. nucifera, bearing red flowers, and the yellow-flowered American lotus, N. lutea. [modern Latin from Sinhalese nelum(bu)]

Neman River /ˈnemən/ (also **Ne·mu·nas** /ˈnjamʊnəs/) a river of E Europe, which rises south of Minsk in Belarus and flows 955 km (597 miles) west and north to the Baltic Sea. Its lower course, which forms the boundary between Lithuania and the Russian enclave of Kaliningrad, is called the Memel.

nem·atic /nɪˈmatɪk/ ● adjective designating or involving a state of a liquid crystal in which the molecules are oriented in parallel but not arranged in well-defined planes (compare SMECTIC). ● noun a nematic substance. [Greek nēma nēmat- 'thread' + -IC]

nem·ato·cyst /nɪˈmatəsɪst, ˈnemə-/ noun a specialized cell in a jellyfish

Vowels: a cat ɑː arm e bed ɜr her ɜː deux ə ago ɪ sit i cosy iː feed ɒ hot ɔ pore ɔː no ʌ run ʊ put etc. containing a coiled thread that can be projected as a sting. [as NEMATODE + CYST]

nema·tode /'nemə,təʊd/ *noun* any parasitic or free-living worm of the phylum Nematoda, with a slender unsegmented cylindrical shape. *Also called* ROUNDWORM. [Greek *nēma -matos* thread + -ODE¹]

Nem·bu·tal /'nembjʊ,tɒl/ *noun proprietary* a sodium salt of pentobarbital, used as a sedative and anticonvulsant. [Na (= sodium) + 5-ethyl-5-(1-methylbutyl) barbiturate + -AL]

ne·mer·tean /nɪ'mɜːtɪən/ (also **ne·mer·tine** /-taɪn/) ● *noun* any marine ribbon worm of the phylum Nemertea, often very long and brightly coloured, found in tangled knots in coastal waters of Europe and the Mediterranean. ● *adjective* of or relating to this class. [modern Latin *Nemertes* from Greek *Nēmertēs* name of a sea nymph]

nem·esia /nɪ'miːʒə/ *noun* any chiefly S African plant of the genus *Nemesia*, cultivated for its variously coloured and irregular flowers. [modern Latin from Greek *nemesion*, the name of a similar plant]

Nem·esis /'neməsɪs/ *Gk Myth* a goddess usually portrayed as the agent of divine punishment for wrongdoing or presumption (hubris). [Greek: see NEMESIS]

nem·esis /'neməsɪs/ *noun* (*pl.* **nem·eses** /-,siːz/) **1** esp. *N Amer.* a long-standing or persistent rival, enemy, or tormentor. **2** retributive justice. **3 a** a downfall caused by this. **b** an agent of such a downfall. [Greek, = righteous indignation, from *nemō* give what is due]

neo- /'niːəʊ/ *combining form* **1** new, modern. **2** a new or revived form of. [Greek from *neos* new]

neo·classic·al *adjective* (also **neo·classic**) **1** of or relating to a revival or development of a classical style or treatment in art, literature, music, etc. **2** *Econ.* of, pertaining to, or characteristic of a body of theory primarily concerned with supply and demand rather than with the source and distribution of wealth. □ **neo·classi·cism** *noun* **neo·classi·cist** *noun*

neo-colonial·ism *noun* the use of economic, political, or other pressures to control or influence other countries, esp. former dependencies. □ **neo-colonial·ist** *noun & adjective*

neo-con = NEO-CONSERVATIVE.

neo-conserv·a·tive ● *adjective* of or pertaining to a form of political conservatism advocating a moderate type of democratic capitalism. ● *noun* an advocate or supporter of neo-conservative principles or beliefs. □ **neo-conserv·a·tism** *noun*

neo·cor·tex *noun* (*pl.* **-ti·ces** /-tɪsəs/) the most recently evolved part of the cerebral cortex, involved in sight and hearing in advanced reptiles and in mammals. □ **neo·corti·cal** *adjective*

Neo-Darwin·ian ● *adjective* of or relating to the modern version of Darwin's theory of evolution by natural selection, incorporating the findings of genetics. ● *noun* an adherent of this theory. □ **Neo-Darwin·ism** *noun* **Neo-Darwin·ist** *noun*

neo·dym·ium /,niːə'dɪmɪəm/ *noun Chem.* a silver-grey naturally occurring metallic element of the lanthanide series used in colouring glass etc. Symbol: **Nd**; at. no.: 60. [NEO- + DIDYMIUM]

neo-fascist ● *adjective* of or relating to a political belief, movement, etc. based on, inspired by, or emulating fascism, Nazism, etc. ● *noun* **1** an adherent or advocate of a fascist belief or movement. **2** a person belonging to an organization based on the Italian Fascist movement of the early 20th c. □ **neo-fascism** *noun*

neo-Georgian *adjective* of or relating to a revival of a Georgian style in architecture. [GEORGIAN¹]

neo-Gothic *adjective* of or relating to a revival of the medieval Gothic style in art or architecture.

neo-hippie ● *noun* a person who resembles or behaves like a hippie, or subscribes to an ideology like that of the hippies of the 1960s, such as espousing pacifism, use or tolerance of recreational drugs, etc. ● *adjective* of, relating to, or characteristic of neo-hippies.

neo-liberal ● *adjective* of or designating a modern political belief or movement that modifies certain doctrines of classical liberalism, esp. attitudes toward trade unions, big business, and military spending. ● *noun* an adherent or advocate of such a belief or movement. □ **neo-liberal·ism** *noun*

neo·lith·ic /,niːə'lɪθɪk/ (also **Neolithic**) ● *adjective* of or relating to the later Stone Age, when ground or polished stone weapons and implements prevailed. ● *noun* the neolithic period. [NEO- + Greek *lithos* stone]

neolo·gism /niː'ɒlədʒ,ɪzəm/ *noun* **1** a new word or expression. **2** the coining or use of new words. □ **neolo·gist** *noun* **neolo·gis·tic** *adjective* **neolo·gize** *intransitive verb* (also esp. *Brit.* **-gise**). [French *néologisme* (as NEO-, -LOGY, -ISM)]

neo·mycin /,niːə'maɪsɪn/ *noun* an antibiotic, related to streptomycin, used to treat a wide variety of bacterial infections. [NEO- + -MYCIN]

neon ● *noun* **1** (often *attributive*) an inert gaseous element occurring in traces in the atmosphere and giving an orange glow when electricity is passed through it in a sealed low-pressure tube, used in lights and illuminated advertisements (*neon light; neon sign*). Symbol: **Ne**; at. no.: 10. **2** a neon lamp or tube; neon lighting. ● *adjective* **1** of, pertaining to, or involving neon. **2 a** resembling a neon light in colour or brilliance. **b** harshly bright, gaudy, or glowing. [Greek, neuter of *neos* new]

neo·nate /'niːə,neɪt/ *noun* **1** a newborn child, esp. an infant less than four weeks old. **2** *Zool.* a newly born animal, bird, etc. □ **neo·natal** /-'neɪtəl/ *adjective* [modern Latin *neonatus* (as NEO-, Latin *nasci nat-* be born)]

neo·natol·ogy /,niːənə'tɒlədʒi/ *noun* the branch of medicine that deals with the disorders and problems of newly born infants. □ **neo·natol·o·gist** *noun*

neo-Nazi /,niːəʊ'nɒtsi, -'natsi/ ● *noun* (*pl.* **neo-Nazis**) a person belonging to an organization based on or deriving from the German National Socialist Party, or holding extreme racist views. ● *adjective* of or relating to neo-Nazis or neo-Nazism. □ **neo-Nazism** *noun*

neo·phobia /,niːə'fəʊbɪə/ *noun* a fear or dislike of what is new. □ **neo·phob·ic** *adjective*

neo·phyte /'niːə,faɪt/ *noun* **1** a beginner; a novice (also *attributive*: *neophyte sailor*). **2** a convert, esp. to a religious faith. **3** *Catholicism* **a** a novice of a religious order. **b** a newly ordained priest. [ecclesiastical Latin *neophytus* from New Testament Greek *neophutos* newly planted (as NEO- *phuton* plant)]

neo·plasm /'niːə,plazəm/ *noun* a new and abnormal growth of tissue in some part of the body, esp. a tumour. □ **neo·plas·tic** /-'plastɪk/ *adjective* [NEO- + Greek *plasma* formation: see PLASMA]

Neo·platon·ism /,niːəʊ'pleɪtə,nɪzəm/ *noun* a philosophical and religious system based on Platonic ideas and developed by the followers of Plotinus in the 3rd c., which emphasizes the distinction between a supposed eternal world and the changing physical world, and combines this with a mystic possibility of union with the supreme being from which all reality is supposed to derive. □ **Neo·platon·ic** /-plə'tɒnɪk/ *adjective* **Neo·platon·ist** *noun*

neo·prene /'niːə,priːn/ *noun* any of various strong synthetic rubbers which are resistant to oil, heat, and weathering. [NEO- + *chloroprene* etc. (perhaps from PROPYL + -ENE)]

Neop·tol·emus /,niːɒp'tɒləməs/ *Gk Myth* the son of Achilles and killer of Priam after the fall of Troy. [Greek, = young warrior]

neo-realism *noun* the doctrine of realism in philosophy, art, literature, etc. revived at the beginning of the 20th c. to refute certain tenets of idealism. □ **neo-realist** *noun*

neot·eny /ni'ɒtəni/ *noun* **1** the retention of juvenile features in the adult form of some animals, e.g. an axolotl. **2** the possession of precocious sexual maturity by an animal still in its larval stage. □ **neo·ten·ic** /-'tenɪk/ *adjective* **neo·ten·ous** *adjective* [German *Neotenie* (as NEO- + Greek *teinō* extend)]

neo-tradition·al·ism *adjective* a revival of traditional styles, customs, etc., esp. in architecture, urban design, music, etc.

neo·trop·ical *adjective* of or relating to tropical and S America as a biogeographical region.

NEP *abbreviation Cdn* NATIONAL ENERGY PROGRAM.

Nepal /nə'pɒl/ a mountainous landlocked country in S Asia, in the Himalayas; pop. (est. 2002) 25,873,917; capital, Kathmandu.

Nepal·ese /,nepə'liːz/ *adjective & noun* (*pl.* same) = NEPALI.

Nepali /nə'pɒli/ ● *noun* (*pl.* same or **Nep·alis**) **1 a** a native or national of Nepal. **b** a person of Nepali descent. **2** the language of Nepal. ● *adjective* of or relating to Nepal or its language or people.

nephew *noun* a son of one's brother or sister, or of one's brother-in-law or sister-in-law. [Old French *neveu* from Latin *nepos nepotis* grandson, nephew]

neph·rec·tomy /nə'frektəmi/ *noun* (*pl.* **-mies**) **1** the surgical removal of a kidney. **2** an instance of this. [NEPHRO- + -ECTOMY]

neph·rite /'nefraɪt/ *noun* a green, yellow, or white calcium magnesium silicate form of jade. [German *Nephrit* from Greek *nephros* kidney, with reference to its supposed efficacy in treating kidney disease]

neph·rit·ic /nɪ'frɪtɪk/ *adjective* **1** of, in, or affecting the kidneys; renal. **2** of or relating to nephritis. [Late Latin *nephriticus* from Greek *nephritikos* (as NEPHRITIS)]

neph·ritis /nɪ'fraɪtɪs/ *noun* inflammation of the kidneys. [Late Latin from Greek *nephros* kidney + -ITIS]

---

uː m**oo**d   ai m**y**   əi p**i**pe   au br**ow**n   ʌu h**ou**se   ei d**ay**   ɔi b**oy**   ā fr**an**glais   â C**an**adien   õ Br**ay**on   (*see over for consonants*)

nephro- /'nefrɔː/ *combining form* (usu. **nephr-** before a vowel) kidney. [Greek from *nephros* kidney]

neph·ron /'nefrɒn/ *noun* each of the functional units in the kidney, through which filtrate passes before emerging as urine.

Ne·pisi·guit River /nə'pɪzɪgwɪt/ a river in NE central New Brunswick, which rises in the Nepisiguit Lakes about 70 km south of Campbellton and flows first eastward, then northward, to empty into Nepisiguit Bay at Bathurst. [Mi'kmaq *winpegijooik* river that dashes roughly along]

ne plus ultra /ˌneɪ plʊs 'ʊltrɑ/ *noun* **1** the culmination, acme, or perfection. **2** the furthest attainable point. [Latin, = not further beyond, the supposed inscription on the Pillars of Hercules (the Strait of Gibraltar) prohibiting passage by ships]

nepo·tism /'nepəˌtɪzəm/ *noun* favouritism shown to relatives in bestowing employment or conferring privileges. □ **nepo·tist** *noun* **nepo·tis·tic** /-'tɪstɪk/ *adjective* [French *népotisme* from Italian *nepotismo* from *nepote* NEPHEW: originally with reference to popes with illegitimate sons called nephews]

Nep·tune ▶ **1** *Rom. Myth* the god of water and of the sea, identified with the Greek god Poseidon. **2** *Astronomy* the eighth planet from the sun in the solar system, orbiting between Uranus and Pluto at an average distance of 4 497 million km from the sun (but temporarily outside the orbit of Pluto 1979–99); it is the fourth largest planet (but third in mass), with an equatorial diameter of 48,600 km. □ **Nep·tun·ian** *adjective*

nep·tun·ium /nep'tjuːnɪəm/ *noun* a radioactive transuranic metallic element produced when uranium atoms absorb bombarding neutrons. Symbol: **Np**; at. no.: 93. [NEPTUNE, as the next planet beyond Uranus, + -IUM]

nerd *noun* esp. *N Amer. slang* a foolish, feeble, or uninteresting person, esp. one ridiculed as studious, puny, or unfashionable. □ **nerd·i·ness** *noun* **nerd·ish** *adjective* **nerdy** *adjective* [20th c.: origin uncertain]

ner·eid /'nɪːrɪɪd/ *noun* **1** *Gk Myth* any of the sea nymphs, daughters of Nereus. They include Thetis, mother of Achilles. **2** *Fauna* a carnivorous marine polychaete worm of the ragworm family *Nereidae*. [Latin *Nereis Nereïd-* from Greek *Nērēis -idos* daughter of Nereus]

Ner·eus /'nɪːrɪəs/ *Gk Myth* an old sea god, the father of the nereids. Like Proteus he had the power of assuming various forms.

Nerf *noun* *proprietary* a type of foam rubber used esp. in the manufacture of children's toys and sports equipment (*Nerf ball*).

Neri /'neri/ **St. Phil·ip** (1515–1622), Italian priest and mystic. He founded the Congregation of the Oratory (1564), and helped to secure papal absolution for Henry IV of France (1593). Feast day, 26 May.

Nernst /'nɜrnst/ **Wal·ther Her·mann** (1864–1941), German physical chemist. Among his contributions to electrochemistry and thermodynamics is his discovery of the third law of thermodynamics; he was awarded the Nobel Prize for chemistry in 1920.

Nero /'nɪːrɔː/ (full name Nero Claudius Caesar Augustus Germanicus) (AD 37–68), Roman emperor 54–68. The adopted son and successor of Claudius, he became infamous for his cruelty; during his reign a fire destroyed half of Rome (64), and a wave of uprisings (68) led to his flight from the city and his eventual suicide.

ner·oli /'nɪːrəli/ *noun* (in full **neroli oil**) an essential oil from the flowers of the Seville orange, used in perfumery. [Italian *neroli*, from the name of Anna-Maria de la Tremoille, the wife of the Prince of Nerola in Italy, who is said to have discovered the oil *ca.* 1670]

Ne·ruda /nə'ruːdə/ **Pablo** (born Neftalí Ricardo Reyes Basoalto) (1904–73), Chilean poet and diplomat. His major work *Canto General* (completed 1950) was originally conceived as an epic on Chile and was later expanded to cover the history of all the Americas from their ancient civilizations to their modern wars of liberation; he was awarded the Nobel Prize for literature in 1971.

nerve ● *noun* **1 a** a fibre or bundle of fibres that transmits impulses of sensation or motion between the brain or spinal cord and other parts of the body. **b** the material constituting these. **2 a** coolness in danger; bravery; assurance. **b** *informal* impudence, audacity (*they've got nerve*). **3** (in *pl.*) **a** the bodily state in regard to physical sensitiveness and the interaction between the brain and other parts. **b** a state of heightened nervousness or sensitivity; a condition of mental or physical stress (*need to calm my nerves*). **4** a rib of a leaf, esp. the midrib. **5** *archaic* a sinew or tendon. ● *transitive verb* **1** (usu. *reflexive*) brace (oneself) to face danger, suffering, etc. **2** *archaic* give strength, vigour, or courage to. □ **get on a person's nerves** irritate or annoy a person. **have nerves of steel** (of a person etc.) be not easily upset or frightened. **hit** (or **touch**) **a nerve** remark on or draw attention to a sensitive subject or point. □ **nerved** *adjective* (also in *combination*). [Middle English, = sinew, from Latin *nervus*, related to Greek *neuron*]

nerve agent *noun* = NERVE GAS.

nerve block *noun* inactivation of the nerve supplying a particular area of the body, esp. by use of a local anaesthetic.

nerve cell *noun* an elongated branched cell transmitting impulses in nerve tissue.

nerve centre *noun* **1** a group of closely connected nerve cells associated in performing some function. **2** the centre of control of an organization etc.

nerve cord *noun* esp. *Zool.* a major nerve, esp. the main axis of a nervous system.

nerve ending *noun* the branched or specialized end of a nerve fibre.

nerve gas *noun* a poisonous gas or vapour that disrupts the functioning of the nervous system, esp. for use in warfare.

nerve impulse *noun* a signal transmitted along a nerve fibre, consisting of a wave of electrical depolarization.

nerve·less *adjective* **1** inert, lacking vigour or spirit. **2** confident; not nervous. **3** *Bot. & Entomol.* without nervures. **4** *Anat. & Zool.* without nerves. □ **nerve·less·ly** *adverb* **nerve·less·ness** *noun*

nerve-racking *adjective* (also **nerve-wracking**) stressful, frightening; straining the nerves.

Nervi /'nervi/ **Pier Luigi** (1891–1979), Italian engineer and architect, a pioneer of new technology and materials, esp. reinforced concrete; he co-designed the UNESCO building in Paris (1953) and the Pirelli skyscraper in Milan (1958).

nervo- *combining form* (also **nerv-** before a vowel) nerve or the nerves.

nerv·ous *adjective* **1 a** worried, anxious. **b** timid, reluctant, afraid. **c** resulting from or reflecting these feelings (*nervous smile*). **2 a** excitable; highly strung; easily agitated. **b** resulting from this temperament, from a disorder of the nervous system, etc. (*nervous tension*; *a nervous headache*). **3** pertaining to or affecting the nerves (*the nervous system*; *a nervous disorder*). □ **nerv·ous·ly** *adverb* **nerv·ous·ness** *noun*

nervous breakdown *noun* a period of incapacitating mental and emotional disturbance, severe depression, etc.

nervous Nel·lie *noun* *informal* an excessively timid or anxious person.

nervous system *noun* the body's network of specialized cells which transmit nerve impulses between parts of the body (*compare* CENTRAL NERVOUS SYSTEM, PERIPHERAL NERVOUS SYSTEM).

nervous wreck *noun* *informal* a person suffering from mental stress, emotional exhaustion, etc.

nerv·ure /'nɜrvjʊr/ *noun* **1** each of the hollow tubes that form the framework of an insect's wing; a venule. **2** the principal vein of a leaf. [French, from *nerf* nerve]

nervy *adjective* (**nerv·i·er**, **nerv·i·est**) **1** *N Amer.* impudent, audacious. **2** *Brit.* anxious or easily disturbed; uneasy. **3** *archaic* sinewy, strong. □ **nerv·i·ly** *adverb* **nerv·i·ness** *noun*

Ness, Loch see LOCH NESS.

ness /nes/ *noun* *archaic* (except in place names) a headland or promontory. [Old English *næs*, related to Old English *nasu* NOSE]

-ness *suffix* forming nouns from adjectives, and occasionally other words, expressing: **1** state or condition, or an instance of this (*bitterness*; *conceitedness*; *happiness*; *a kindness*). **2** something in a certain state (*wilderness*). [Old English *-nes, -ness* from Germanic]

nest ● *noun* **1** a structure or place where a bird lays eggs and shelters its young. **2** an animal's or insect's breeding ground or lair. **3** a snug or secluded retreat, shelter, home, etc. **4** (often foll. by *of*) a place fostering something undesirable (*a nest of vice*). **5** a number of birds, insects, etc. occupying the same nest or habitation; a brood or swarm. **6** a group or set of similar objects, often of different sizes and fitting together for storage (*a nest of tables*). **7** a group of machine guns, snipers, etc. **8** a set of nested procedures, subroutines, syntactic units, etc. ● *verb* **1** *intransitive* use or build a nest. **2** *intransitive* take or collect wild birds' nests or eggs. **3 a** *intransitive* (of objects) fit together or one inside another. **b** *transitive* place or fit (a thing) inside another, similar one, esp. in a hierarchical arrangement. □ **nest·er** *noun* **nest·like** *adjective* [Old English *nest*]

nest·ed *adjective* placed or fitted inside another, similar object etc., esp. in a hierarchical arrangement.

nest egg *noun* **1** a sum of money saved for the future. **2** *hist.* a real or artificial egg left in a nest to induce hens to lay eggs there.

nesting box *noun* (also **nest box**) a box provided for a bird to make its nest in.

Consonants: b *but* d *dog* f *few* g *get* h *her* j *yes* k *cat* l *leg* m *man* n *no* p *pen* r *red* s *sit*

nes·tle *verb* **1** *transitive & intransitive* (often in *passive*; often foll. by *in*, *against*, *among*) place or lie in a partly hidden, snug, or sheltered position. **2** *intransitive* (often foll. by *down*, *in*, etc.) settle down in a snug or comfortable manner. **3** *transitive* (foll. by *in*, *into*, etc.) rest or settle (a head, shoulder, etc.) in a snug or affectionate manner. **4** *intransitive* draw or press close to a person or thing, esp. in an affectionate manner. [Old English *nestlian* (as NEST)]

nest·ling /'neslɪŋ, 'nest-/ *noun* a bird that is too young to leave its nest.

nest·mate *noun* a bird, animal, etc. sharing a nest with another.

nest of vipers *noun* = VIPER'S NEST.

Nes·tor /'nestər/ *Gk Myth* a king of Pylos in the Peloponnese, who in old age led his subjects to the Trojan War, where his wisdom and eloquence were proverbial.

Nes·tor·ian /ne'stɔriən/ ● *adjective* of or relating to an early Christian doctrine that there were distinct divine and human persons in Christ, maintained by some ancient Churches of the Middle East. ● *noun* a member of such a Church. □ **Nes·tor·ian·ism** *noun* [NESTORIUS]

Nes·tor·ius /ne'stɔriəs/ (died *c*.451), Syrian-born patriarch of Constantinople 428–31, who was deposed for heresy by the Council of Ephesus (431) and banished; his followers in Syria and Persia gradually constituted themselves into a separate Nestorian Church.

Net *noun* (also **net**) (usu. prec. by *the*) the Internet. [abbreviation]

net¹ ● *noun* **1** an open-meshed fabric of cord, rope, fibre, etc. **2** a piece of net used esp. to restrain, contain, or to catch fish or other animals. **3 a** a structure backed by a net, forming the goal in hockey, lacrosse, etc. **b** a structure from which a net is suspended dividing the court in tennis etc. **4** a system or procedure for catching or entrapping a person or persons. **5 a** a network of spies. **b** a broadcasting network. **c** *Computing* a network of interconnected computers. **6** a number of lines, veins, fibres, etc. arranged like or resembling the threads of a net. **7** = SAFETY NET 2. ● *transitive verb* (**net·ted**, **net·ting**) **1 a** cover, confine, or catch with a net. **b** procure as with a net. **2** *Sport* hit or shoot etc. (a puck or ball) into a net. **3** cover or confine with or as with a net or nets. **4** fish (a river etc.) with nets; set or use nets in. **5** make (a purse, hammock, etc.) by knotting etc. threads together to form a net. **6** mark with a netlike pattern; reticulate. □ **net·like** *adjective* **net·ted** *adjective* (also in *combination*). **net·ter** *noun* [Old English *net*, *nett*]

net² ● *adjective* **1** (esp. of money) remaining after all necessary deductions, or free from deductions (*net income; net loss*). **2** (of a price) to be paid in full; not reducible. **3** (of a weight) excluding that of the packaging or container etc. **4** (of an effect, result, etc.) ultimate. **5** after all factors have been calculated (*a net importer of oil*). ● *noun* a net sum, income, result, etc. ● *transitive verb* (**net·ted**, **net·ting**) gain or yield (a sum) as net profit. [French *net* NEAT¹]

Net·an·ya·hu /ˌnetənˈjɔhu/ **Ben·ja·min** (b.1949), Israeli Likud politician, prime minister 1996–1999. Leader of the right-wing Likud coalition 1993–1999, he narrowly defeated Shimon Peres in the elections of 1996.

net·ball *noun* a team game, esp. for women, similar to basketball, in which players cannot run or walk with the ball but must throw or hand it to each other.

net-cam *noun* a small, remote-controlled camera with a wide-angle lens, mounted inside a hockey net. [NET¹ + CAMERA]

Net·head *noun informal* a frequent user of the Internet.

neth·er *adjective esp. literary or jocular* = LOWER¹ *adjective* 1, 2. □ **nether·most** *adjective* [Old English *nithera* etc. from Germanic]

Neth·er·lands, the **1** a country in W Europe, on the North Sea, often called **Holland**; pop. (est. 2002) 16,067,754; capital, Amsterdam; seat of government, The Hague. The name **Holland** strictly refers to the western coastal provinces of the country. **2** *hist.* the Low Countries. □ **Neth·er·land·er** /-ˌlandər/ *noun* **Neth·er·land·ish** *adjective* [Dutch (as NETHER, LAND)]

Neth·er·lands An·til·les two widely separated groups of Dutch islands in the Caribbean, in the Lesser Antilles; capital, Willemstad, on Curaçao; pop. (est. 2002) 214,258. The southernmost group, situated just off the north coast of Venezuela, comprises the islands of Bonaire and Curaçao. The other group, about 800 km (500 miles) to the north, situated at the northern end of the Lesser Antilles, comprises the islands of St. Eustatius, St. Martin, and Saba. Until 1986 the islands also included Aruba.

nether regions *plural noun* **1** *jocular* the parts of the human body below the waist, esp. the buttocks and genitals. **2** hell; the abode of the dead. **3** a place or situation viewed as an unpleasant exile.

nether·world *noun* **1** the infernal regions; hell. **2** the world of the criminal underground. **3** a state of neglect or oblivion; limbo.

net·iquette /'netɪˌkət/ *noun informal* the informal code of conduct governing effective and polite use of the Internet. [blend of NET + ETIQUETTE]

net·izen *noun* a user of the Internet, esp. a habitual or avid one. [blend of NET¹ + CITIZEN]

net·mind·er *noun* a goaltender. □ **net·mind·ing** *noun*

net profit *noun* the effective profit; the actual gain after working expenses have been paid.

Net·si·ling·miut /netsɪˈlɪŋmiʊt/ *plural noun* (also **Net·silik Inuit**) an Inuit people inhabiting an area of Nunavut around the Boothia Peninsula and Pelly Bay. [Inuit, = 'people of the seal']

net·su·ke /'netsʊki/ *noun* (*pl.* same or **net·su·kes**) (in Japan) a carved button-like ornament, esp. of ivory or wood, formerly worn to suspend articles from a girdle. [Japanese]

net·surf·er *noun* a person who uses the Internet, esp. habitually. □ **net·surf** *intransitive verb* **net·surf·ing** *noun & adjective*

Net·til·ling Lake /nəˈtɪlɪŋ/ a lake in south central Baffin Island, extending across the Arctic Circle. [origin uncertain: possibly from Inuktitut *netsek* ringed seal, because the lake is its only permanent freshwater habitat]

net·ting *noun* **1** netted fabric. **2** a piece of this. **3** the action of fishing with a net or nets. **4 a** the action or process of making a net, nets, or a network. **b** the act of enclosing an area etc. with nets, wire, etc.

net·tle ● *noun* **1** any plant of the genus *Urtica*, esp. *U. dioica*, with leaves covered with stinging hairs. **2** any of various plants resembling this. ● *transitive verb* **1** irritate, provoke, annoy. **2** sting with nettles. [Old English *netle*, *netele*]

nettle·some *adjective* causing annoyance or difficulty.

net ton *noun* see TON *noun* 5b.

net·work ● *noun* **1** a group of interconnected or intercommunicating things, points, or people. **2** an arrangement of intersecting horizontal and vertical lines, like the structure of a net. **3** a complex system of railways, roads, telephone lines, etc. **4** a group of people who exchange information, contacts, and experience for professional or social purposes. **5** a chain of interconnected computers, machines, or operations. **6** a system of connected electrical conductors. **7 a** a group of broadcasting stations connected for a simultaneous broadcast of a program. **b** a nationwide broadcasting company or broadcasting companies collectively. ● *verb* **1** *intransitive* communicate or foster relationships with a network of people, esp. for personal advantage. **2** *transitive & intransitive* **a** link (machines, esp. computers) together to allow the sharing of data and efficient utilization of resources. **b** incorporate (a computer, data, etc.) into a computer network. □ **net·work·able** *adjective* **net·worked** *adjective* **net·work·ing** *noun*

network computer *noun* a low-cost personal computer without local disk storage, designed to be connected to the Internet, a local area network, etc., from which it would access applications and data.

net·work·er *noun* **1** *Computing* a member of an organization or computer network who operates from home or from an external office. **2** a member of a professional or social network.

net worth *noun* the monetary value of a person's or organization's holdings when liabilities have been deducted from the value of assets.

Neu·châ·tel, Lake /nɜːʃaˈtel/ the largest lake lying wholly within Switzerland, situated at the foot of the Jura Mountains in W Switzerland.

neume /nuːm, njuːm/ *noun Music* a sign in plainsong indicating a note or group of notes to be sung to a syllable. [Old French *neume* from medieval Latin *neu(p)ma* from Greek *pneuma* breath]

neur·al /'njʊrəl, 'nɜrəl/ *adjective* of or relating to a nerve or the central nervous system. □ **neur·al·ly** *adverb* [Greek *neuron* nerve]

neur·al·gia /njʊˈraldʒə, nəˈral-/ *noun* an intense intermittent pain along the course of a nerve, esp. in the head or face. □ **neur·al·gic** *adjective* [as NEURAL + -ALGIA]

neural network *noun* (also **neural net**) **1** a system of interconnections which resembles or is based on the arrangement of neurons in the brain and nervous system. **2** a configuration of computers designed to simulate this.

neural tube *noun* a hollow structure from which the brain and spinal cord develop.

neural tube defect *noun* any of a range of congenital abnormalities, including spina bifida, resulting from incomplete fusion of the neural tube.

neur·as·thenia /ˌnjʊrəsˈθiːniə, ˌnɜrəs-/ *noun* an ill-defined medical condition characterized by lassitude, fatigue, headache, and irritability, associated chiefly with emotional disturbance.

□ **neur·as·then·ic** /-ˈθenɪk/ *adjective & noun* [Greek *neuron* nerve + ASTHENIA]

neur·itis /njʊˈraɪtɪs, nəˈraɪt-/ *noun* inflammation of a nerve or nerves, usu. with pain and loss of function. □ **neur·itic** /-ˈrɪtɪk/ *adjective* [formed as NEURO- + -ITIS]

neuro- /ˈnjʊrɔː, ˈnɜrɔː-/ *combining form* a nerve or the nerves. [Greek *neuron* nerve]

neuro·anat·omy /ˌnjʊrɔːˈnatəmi, ˌnɜrɔː-/ *noun* the anatomy of the nervous system. □ **neuro·ana·tom·ical** /-anəˈtɒmɪkəl/ *adjective* **neuro·anat·o·mist** *noun*

neuro·biol·ogy /ˌnjʊrɔːbaɪˈɒlədʒi, ˌnɜrɔː-/ *noun* the biology of the nervous system. □ **neuro·bio·logic·al** /-baɪəˈlɒdʒɪkəl/ *adjective* **neuro·biol·o·gist** *noun*

neuro·blas·toma /ˌnjʊrɔːblasˈtoʊmə, ˌnɜrɔː-/ *noun* a tumour composed of embryonic cells from which nerve fibres originate, esp. a malignant tumour originating in the adrenal gland.

neuro·chem·ical /ˌnjʊrɔːˈkemɪkəl, ˌnɜrɔː-/ ● *adjective* of or pertaining to the chemistry of the nervous system. ● *noun* a drug, chemical, or other substance that acts on the nervous system. □ **neuro·chem·ist** *noun* **neuro·chem·istry** *noun*

neuro·de·gener·a·tive /ˌnjʊrɔːdəˈdʒenərɑtɪv, ˌnɜrɔː-/ *adjective adjective* (of a disease) causing degeneration of the nervous system.
□ **neuro·de·gener·a·tion** *noun*

neuro·genic /ˌnjʊrɔːˈdʒenɪk, ˌnɜrɔː-/ *adjective* caused by or arising in nervous tissue.

neuro·hor·mone /ˌnjʊrɔːˈhɔrmoʊn, ˌnɜrɔː-/ *noun* a hormone produced by nerve cells and secreted into the circulation.
□ **neuro·hor·mon·al** *adjective*

neuro·lep·tic /ˌnjʊrɔːˈleptɪk, ˌnɜrɔː-/ ● *adjective* **1** tending or able to reduce nervous tension by depressing nerve function. **2** effective against psychosis. ● *noun* a neuroleptic drug; a major tranquilizer.

neurolinguistic programming *noun* a system of alternative therapy intended to educate people in self-awareness and effective communication, and to model and change their patterns of mental and emotional behaviour.

neuro·lin·guis·tics /ˌnjʊrɔːlɪŋˈgwɪstɪks, ˌnɜrɔː-/ *noun* the branch of linguistics dealing with the relationship between language and the structure and functioning of the brain. □ **neuro·lin·guis·tic** *adjective*

neur·ol·ogy /njʊˈrɒlədʒi, nəˈrɒ-/ *noun* the branch of biology or esp. medicine that deals with the anatomy, functions, and organic disorders of nerves and the nervous system. □ **neuro·logic** /-rəˈlɒdʒɪk/ *adjective* **neuro·logic·al** /-rəˈlɒdʒɪkəl/ *adjective* **neuro·logic·al·ly** /-rəˈlɒdʒɪkəli/ *adverb* **neur·ol·o·gist** *noun* [modern Latin *neurologia* from modern Greek (as NEURO-, -LOGY)]

neur·oma /njʊˈroʊmə, nəˈroː-/ *noun* (*pl.* **neur·omas** or **neuro·mata** /-mətə/) a tumour on a nerve or in nerve tissue. [Greek *neuron* nerve + -OMA]

neuro·muscu·lar /ˌnjʊrɔːˈmʌskjʊlər, ˌnɜrɔː-/ *adjective* pertaining to, consisting of, or resembling both nerves and muscle tissue.

neur·on /ˈnjʊrɒn, ˈnɜrɒn/ *noun* (*Brit.* also **neur·one** /-roːn/) a specialized cell transmitting nerve impulses; a nerve cell. □ **neur·on·al** /-ˈroːnəl/ *adjective* [Greek *neuron* nerve]

neuro·path·ol·ogy /ˌnjʊrɔːpəˈθɒlədʒi, ˌnɜrɔː-/ *noun* the branch of pathology that deals with diseases and disorders of the nervous system. □ **neuro·patho·logic·al** /-θəˈlɒdʒɪkəl/ *adjective* **neuro·path·ol·o·gist** *noun*

neur·op·athy /njʊˈrɒpəθi, nəˈrɒ-/ *noun* a disease or dysfunction of one or more peripheral nerves, typically causing numbness or weakness.

neuro·pep·tide /ˌnjʊrɔːˈpeptaɪd, ˌnɜrɔː-/ *noun* any short-chain protein in the nervous system which is capable of acting as a neurotransmitter. [NEURO- + PEPTIDE]

neuro·physi·ol·ogy /ˌnjʊrɔːˌfɪziˈɒlədʒi, ˌnɜrɔː-/ *noun* the physiology of the nervous system. □ **neuro·physio·logic·al** *adjective* **neuro·physi·ol·o·gist** *noun*

neuro·psych·ol·ogy /ˌnjʊrɔːsaɪˈkɒlədʒi, ˌnɜr-/ *noun* the study of the relationship between the nervous system (esp. the brain) and behaviour. □ **neuro·psych·o·logic·al** *adjective* **neuro·psych·o·logist** *noun*

neur·op·ter·an /njʊˈrɒptərən, nəˈrɒ-/ *noun* any insect of the order Neuroptera, including lacewings, having four finely-veined membranous leaflike wings. □ **neur·op·ter·ous** *adjective* [NEURO- + Greek *pteron* wing]

neuro·sci·ence /ˈnjʊrɔːsaɪəns, ˈnɜr-/ *noun* any or all of the sciences dealing with the structure and function of the nervous system and brain. □ **neuro·scien·tist** *noun*

neur·o·sis /njuˈroːsɪs, nəˈroː-/ *noun* (*pl.* **neur·o·ses** /-siːz/) **1** a mild mental illness, not attributable to organic cause, characterized by symptoms of stress such as anxiety, depression, obsessive behaviour, hypochondria, etc., without loss of contact with reality. **2** any more or less specific anxiety or malaise experienced by an individual, group, nation, etc. [modern Latin (as NEURO-, -OSIS)]

neuro·sur·gery /ˌnjʊrɔːˈsɜrdʒəri, ˌnɜr-/ *noun* surgery performed on the nervous system, esp. the brain and spinal cord.
□ **neuro·sur·geon** *noun* **neuro·sur·gical** *adjective*

neur·otic /njʊˈrɒtɪk, nəˈrɒ-/ ● *adjective* **1** caused by or relating to neurosis. **2** (of a person) suffering from neurosis. **3** *informal* abnormally sensitive or obsessive. ● *noun* a neurotic person. □ **neur·otic·ally** *adverb* **neur·oti·cism** /-ˌsɪzəm/ *noun*

neuro·toxin /ˌnjʊrɔːˈtɒksɪn, ˌnɜrɔː-/ *noun* any poison which acts on the nervous system. □ **neuro·toxic** *adjective* **neuro·tox·icity** /-tɒkˈsɪsɪti/ *noun*

neuro·trans·mit·ter /ˌnjʊrɔːˈtransmɪtər, ˌnɜr-/ *noun Biochem.* a chemical substance released from a nerve fibre that effects the transfer of an impulse to another nerve or muscle.
□ **neuro·trans·mis·sion** *noun*

Neu·sied·ler See /ˈnɔɪˌziːdlər ˌzeɪ/ a shallow lake straddling the frontier between E Austria and NW Hungary.

neut. *abbreviation* neuter.

neu·ter /ˈnuːtər, ˈnjuː-/ ● *adjective* **1** *Grammar* (of a noun etc.) neither masculine nor feminine. **2** (of a plant) having neither pistils nor stamen. **3** (of an insect) having no functional sexual organs, sterile. **4** having no sexual characteristics, being neither male nor female; asexual. ● *noun* **1** *Grammar* **a** the neuter gender. **b** a neuter word. **2 a** a non-fertile insect, esp. a worker bee or ant. **b** a castrated animal. **3** an asexual or genderless person. ● *transitive verb* **1** castrate or spay (an animal). **2** deprive of potency, vigour, or force. □ **neu·tered** *adjective* **neu·ter·ing** *noun* [Latin *neuter* neither from *ne-* not + *uter* either]

Neu·tral /ˈnuːtrəl, ˈnjuː-/ *noun* a member of an Iroquoian people formerly living on the shores of Lake Erie; attacked by the Seneca in the mid-17th c., they dispersed or were absorbed into the Iroquois. [from the name given them by French explorers, because they were not involved in the Huron–Iroquois wars]

neu·tral /ˈnuːtrəl, ˈnjuː-/ ● *adjective* **1** not helping or supporting either of two opposing sides, esp. countries at war or in dispute; impartial. **2** belonging to a neutral party, nation, etc. (*neutral ships*). **3** indistinct, vague, indeterminate. **4** occupying a middle position with regard to two extremes. **5** (of colours, esp. white, beige, or grey) not strong or intense; harmonizing well with most other colours. **6** *Chem.* neither acid nor alkaline. **7** having neither a positive nor a negative electrical charge. **8** *Biol.* having either no sexual characteristics or no functional sexual organs; asexual, neuter. **9** *Physics* designating or situated at a point, on a line or plane, etc. where opposing forces are in equilibrium. **10** (in *combination*) having neither a positive nor a negative effect (*revenue-neutral*). **11** (in *combination*) specifying neither male nor female characteristics (*gender-neutral*). ● *noun* **1 a** a neutral country or person. **b** a citizen of a neutral country. **2** a position of the driving and driven parts in a gear mechanism in which no power is transmitted. **3** a state in which no progress is made (*this government seems to be stuck in neutral on this issue*). **4** a neutral colour. □ **neu·tral·ity** *noun* **neu·tral·ly** *adverb* [Latin *neutralis* of neuter gender (as NEUTER)]

neutral corner *noun* **1** either of the two corners of a boxing ring not allocated to a boxer as a base between rounds etc. **2** any similar position removed from a scene of battle, confrontation, argument, etc.

neu·tral·ism *noun* a policy of political neutrality. □ **neu·tral·ist** *noun*

neu·tral·ize *transitive verb* (also esp. *Brit.* **-ise**) **1** counterbalance; render ineffective by an opposite force or effect. **2 a** make (an acidic or alkaline solution etc.) chemically neutral. **b** eliminate a charge difference in; make electrically neutral. **3** exempt or exclude (a place) from the sphere of hostilities. **4** *euphemism* kill or make (a person) harmless or ineffective. □ **neu·tral·iz·a·tion** /-ˈzeɪʃən/ *noun* **neu·tral·iz·er** *noun* [French *neutraliser* from medieval Latin *neutralizare* (as NEUTRAL)]

neutral zone *noun* **1** *Hockey* the central area of a rink, extending from blue line to blue line. **2** an esp. demilitarized area acting as a buffer between two belligerents.

neutral-zone trap *noun Hockey* a conservative, defensive strategy in which a team positions all its skaters in the neutral zone to challenge their opponents' rush, rather than send players into the opponents' end to forecheck.

neu·tri·no /nuːˈtriːnoʊ, njuː-/ *noun* (*pl.* **-nos**) any of a group of stable elementary particles with zero electric charge and probably zero mass, which travel at the speed of light. [Italian, diminutive of *neutro* neutral (as NEUTER)]

neu·tron /'nuːtrɒn, 'njuː-/ *noun* an elementary particle of about the same mass as a proton but without an electric charge, present in all atomic nuclei except those of ordinary hydrogen. [NEUTRAL + -ON]

neutron bomb *noun* a kind of atomic bomb producing large numbers of neutrons but little blast, so causing great damage to life but little destruction to property.

neutron star *noun* a very small, dense star composed mainly of closely packed neutrons.

neutro·phil /'nuːtrɒfɪl, 'njuː-/ ● *adjective* (esp. of a cell or tissue) that can be stained with natural dyes, but usu. not readily with either acidic or basic dyes. ● *noun* a neutrophil cell. □ **neutro·phil·ic** /-'fɪlɪk/ *adjective*

Nev. *abbreviation* Nevada.

Nev·ada¹ /nəˈvadə/ a state of the western US; pop. (2000) 1,988,257; capital, Carson City. It lies on an arid plateau, almost totally in the Great Basin area. □ **Nev·ad·an** *adjective & noun*

Nev·ada² /nəˈvadə/ *noun* (in full **Nevada ticket**) *Cdn* = BREAK-OPEN.

Neva River /'niːvə/ a river in NW Russia which flows 74 km (46 miles) westward from Lake Ladoga to the Gulf of Finland, passing through St. Petersburg.

névé /'neivei/ *noun* an expanse of crystalline or granular snow on the upper part of a glacier, not yet compressed into ice. [Swiss French, = glacier, ultimately from Latin *nix nivis* snow]

never *adverb* **1 a** at no time; on no occasion; not ever (*have never been to Charlottetown*; *never saw them again*). **b** *informal* as an emphatic negative (*I never heard you come in*). **2** not at all, in no way (*never fear*). **3** *informal* (expressing surprise or incredulity) surely not (*you never left the key in the lock!*). □ **never ever** (also **never, ever**) never at all, absolutely never. **never mind** *see* MIND. **never say die** *see* DIE¹. **well I never!** expressing great surprise. [Old English *næfre* from *ne* not + *æfre* EVER]

never-ending *adjective* never coming to an end, endless.

never·more *adverb* at no future time; never again.

Never-Never 1 the unpopulated desert country of the interior of Australia; the remote outback. **2** (**Never-Never Land** (or **Country**)) a region of Northern Territory, Australia, southeast of Darwin; chief town, Katherine.

never-never *noun Brit. informal* (prec. by *the*) instalment plan (*buying on the never-never*).

never-never land *noun* an imaginary, utopian or illusory place.

Ne·vers /nəˈveːr/ a city in central France, on the Loire; pop. (1999) 40,932. It was capital of the former province of Nivernais.

never·the·less *adverb* in spite of that; notwithstanding; all the same.

Nevis /'niːvɪs, 'nevɪs/ one of the Leeward Islands in the W Indies, part of St. Kitts and Nevis; capital, Charlestown (*see also* ST. KITTS AND NEVIS).

Nev·ski *see* ALEXANDER NEVSKI.

nevus /'niːvəs/ *noun* (*pl.* **nevi** /-vai/) (also **naevus**) **1** a birthmark in the form of a raised red patch on the skin. **2** = MOLE². [Latin]

new ● *adjective* **1 a** of recent origin or arrival. **b** made, invented, discovered, acquired, or experienced recently or now for the first time (*a new star*; *has many new ideas*). **2** in original condition; not worn or used. **3** a renewed or reformed (*a new life*; *the new order*). **b** reinvigorated (*felt like a new person*). **4** different from a recent previous one (*has a new job*). **5** in addition to others already existing (*have you been to the new supermarket?*). **6** (often foll. by *to*) unfamiliar or strange (*a new sensation*; *the idea was new to me*). **7** (often foll. by *at*) (of a person) inexperienced, unaccustomed (to doing something) (*am new at this business*). **8** (usu. prec. by *the*) often *derogatory* **a** later, modern. **b** newfangled. **c** given to new or modern ideas (*the new woman*). **d** recently affected by social change (*the new rich*). **9** (often prec. by *the*) advanced in method or theory (*the new formula*). **10** (in place names) discovered or founded later than and named after (*New Brunswick*; *New Zealand*). **11** (of vegetables, esp. potatoes or carrots) recently harvested and usu. small, with a thin light skin. ● *adverb* (usu. in *combination*) newly, recently (*new-found*). □ **a new one** (often foll. by *on*) *informal* an account or idea not previously encountered (by a person). □ **new·ish** *adjective* **new·ness** *noun* [Old English *nīwe* from Germanic]

New Age *noun* a broad movement characterized by alternative approaches to traditional Western culture, with interest in spiritual matters, mysticism, holistic ideas, environmentalism, etc. (often *attributive*: *New Age philosophy*). □ **New Ager** *noun* **New Agey** *adjective*

New Age music *noun* a style of chiefly instrumental music characterized by light melodic harmonies, improvisation, and the

reproduction of sounds from the natural world, intended to promote serenity.

New American Bible *noun* a translation of the Bible published in 1970 and used esp. in Roman Catholic churches. Abbr.: **NAB**.

New Amsterdam the original name (until 1664) for NEW YORK.

New·ark /'nuːɜrk, njuː-/ an industrial city in New Jersey; pop. (2000) 273,456.

new·bie *noun slang* a novice on the Internet. [arbitrary formation from NEW]

new·born ● *adjective* **1** (of a child etc.) recently born. **2** spiritually reborn; regenerated. ● *noun* a newborn child.

New Britain a mountainous island in the S Pacific, administratively part of Papua New Guinea, lying off the northeast coast of New Guinea; pop. (est. 2002) 445,600; capital, Rabaul.

new broom *noun* a newly appointed person eager to make changes. [from the proverb 'the new broom sweeps clean']

New Brunswick a Maritime province on the southeast coast of Canada; pop. (2001) 729,498; capital, Fredericton. It was one of the original four provinces in the Dominion of Canada in 1867. □ **New Bruns·wick·er** *noun* [after the British royal family's House of Brunswick]

New Caledonia /ˌkalə'doːniə/ **1** an island in the S Pacific, east of Australia; pop. (est. 2002) 207,858; capital, Nouméa. Since 1946 it has formed, with its dependencies, a French overseas territory. **2** the former name (1806–58) for the central interior region of BC. [Latin *Caledonia* (see CALEDONIAN)]

new Canadian *noun Cdn* a person who has recently immigrated to Canada.

New·castle an industrial port on the southeast coast of Australia, in New South Wales; pop. (est. 2002) 477,100.

Newcastle disease *noun* an acute infectious viral fever affecting birds, esp. poultry. [NEWCASTLE-UPON-TYNE]

Newcastle-under-Lyme an industrial town in Staffordshire, central England, just southwest of Stoke-on-Trent; pop. (est. 1998) 123,300.

Newcastle-upon-Tyne an industrial city and metropolitan district in NE England, a port on the Tyne River; pop. (est. 2002) 187,200.

New·comb /'nuːkəm, 'njuː-/ **Simon** (1835–1909), Canadian-born US astronomer and mathematician, known for his astronomical tables indicating the positions of celestial bodies.

New·comen /'nuːˌkʌmən, 'njuː-/ **Thom·as** (1663–1729), English engineer. He developed the first practical steam engine, which operated a pump removing water from mines; it was later greatly improved by James Watt.

new·com·er *noun* **1** a person who has recently arrived. **2** a beginner in some activity.

new country *noun* a style of country music blending traditional country and western elements with elements of rock music, including elaborate production values, and a more urban focus.

New Criticism *noun* an approach to the analysis of literary texts which concentrates on the organization of the text itself, with particular emphasis on irony, ambiguity, paradox, etc., rather than on its historical or biographical context. □ **New Critic** *noun* **New Critical** *adjective*

new deal *noun* **1** new arrangements or conditions, esp. when better than the earlier ones. **2** (**New Deal**) the economic measures introduced by Franklin D. Roosevelt as President of the US in 1933 to counteract the effects of the Great Depression. The New Deal depended largely on a massive public works program, complemented by the large-scale granting of loans, and succeeded in reducing unemployment by between 7 and 10 million. □ **New Dealer** *noun*

New Delhi *see* DELHI.

New Democrat *noun Cdn* a member or supporter of the New Democratic Party.

New Democratic *adjective Cdn* of, belonging to or constituted by the New Democratic Party.

New Democratic Party *noun* (in Canada) a left-of-centre political party, more successful provincially than federally, formed from the Co-operative Commonwealth Federation in 1961. Abbr.: **NDP**.

new economy *noun* the economic sector consisting of new, high-tech industries.

newel /'nuːəl, 'njuː(ə)l/ *noun* **1** the supporting central post of winding stairs. **2** (in full **newel post**) a post at the head or foot of a staircase supporting a handrail. [Old French *nouel*, knob, from medieval Latin *nodellus* diminutive of Latin *nodus* knot]

New England an area on the northeast coast of the US, comprising the states of Maine, New Hampshire, Vermont, Massachusetts, Rhode Island, and Connecticut.

New English Bible *noun* a translation of the Bible published in 1976 using colloquial language. Abbr.: **NEB**.

new·fan·gled *adjective derogatory* different from what one is used to; objectionably new. [Middle English *newfangle* liking what is new, from *newe* NEW *adverb* + *-fangel* from Old English *fangol* (unrecorded) inclined to take]

Newf·ie[1] (also **Newf**) *informal* ● *noun* **1** a Newfoundlander. **2** Newfoundland. **3** a Newfoundland dog. ● *adjective* (esp. *attributive*) of or relating to Newfoundland or Newfoundlanders. [from NEWFOUNDLAND[1] + -IE]

Newfie joke *noun Cdn* a joke in which the humour is derived from the purported lack of sophistication or intelligence of Newfoundlanders.

New Forest an area of heath and woodland in southern Hampshire, in S England. It has been reserved as Crown property since 1079, originally by William I as a royal hunting area. William II was killed by an arrow when hunting there in 1100.

new-found *adjective* newly discovered.

New·found·land[1] /ˌnuːˈfændlənd, ˈnuːfəndlənd, ˈnuːfəndland, njuːˈfaundlənd/ a large island of E Canada, situated in the N Atlantic, at the entrance to the Gulf of St. Lawrence. In 1949 it was united with Labrador (as Newfoundland and Labrador) to form a province of Canada. □ **New·found·land·er** /ˌnuːfəndˈlandər, ˈnuːfəndlandər, njuː-/ *noun*

Newfoundland[2] *noun* (in full **Newfoundland dog**) a very large breed of dog with a thick coarse coat and webbed feet, noted for its intelligence, strength, and swimming ability. [NEWFOUNDLAND[1]]

Newfoundland and Labrador a province of Canada, comprising the island of Newfoundland and the eastern part of the Labrador-Ungava Peninsula; pop. (2001) 512,930; capital, St. John's. It joined the confederation of Canada in 1949.

Newfoundland Daylight Time *noun* daylight time in the Newfoundland Time zone. Abbr.: **NDT**.

Newfoundland pony *noun* a breed of pony found in Newfoundland that has adapted to conditions there by developing a thick winter coat and powerful teeth to eat coarse grasses and shrubs.

Newfoundland Standard Time *noun* standard time in the Newfoundland Time zone. Abbr.: **NST**.

Newfoundland Time *noun* the time in a zone including the island of Newfoundland. Newfoundland Standard Time is three and a half hours behind Greenwich Mean Time; Newfoundland Daylight Time is two and a half hours behind Greenwich Mean Time.

New France *hist.* the former colonies and possessions of France (until 1763) in N America, including Quebec, Acadia and Louisiana.

new-genera·tion *attributive adjective* designating the latest model, type, etc. of a thing (*new-generation audio equipment*).

New Glasgow a town in north central Nova Scotia, about 60 km northeast of Truro; pop. (2001) 9,432.

new guard *noun* the new or progressive members of a group (*compare* OLD GUARD).

New Guinea an island in the western S Pacific, off the north coast of Australia, the second largest island in the world (following Greenland). It is divided into two parts; the western half comprises part of Irian Jaya, a province of Indonesia, the eastern half forms part of the country of Papua New Guinea.

New Hampshire a state in the northeastern US, on the Atlantic coast; pop. (2001) 1,235,786; capital, Concord. □ **New Hamp·shir·ite** *noun*

New Hebrides the former name (until 1980) for VANUATU.

New International Version *noun* a version of the Bible completed in the 1970s and used esp. by conservative Protestant churches. Abbr.: **NIV**.

New Ireland an island in the S Pacific, administratively part of Papua New Guinea, lying to the north of New Britain; pop. (est. 2002) 120,900; capital, Kavieng.

new jack *adjective* of or relating to new jack swing, or the clothes, culture, etc. associated with it.

new jack swing *noun* a form of dance music combining elements from rhythm and blues, soul, hip hop, and rap music. [NEW + the

name of Michael JACKSON, whose producer, Teddy Riley, developed the style, + SWING *noun* 7]

New Jersey a state in the northeastern US, on the Atlantic coast; pop. (2000) 8,414,350; capital, Trenton. □ **New Jerseyan** *noun & adjective* **New Jer·sey·ite** *noun & adjective*

New Jerusalem *noun* **1** *Christianity* the abode of the saints in heaven. **2** *informal* an ideal place or situation.

New Jerusalem Church a Christian sect instituted by followers of Emanuel Swedenborg. It was founded in London in 1787.

New Kingdom *noun* a period of ancient Egyptian history (*c.*1550–1070 BC, 18th–20th dynasty), with its capital at Thebes, marked by imperial expansion in Syria, Palestine, and Nubia.

New Left *noun* a movement initiated in the 1960s by young left-wing radicals opposed to the philosophy of the old liberal society. □ **New Leftist** *noun*

New Lis·keard /nuː ˈlɪskərd, njuː/ a town in NE Ontario, situated at the northwestern end of Lake Timiskaming, near the border with Quebec; pop. (2001) 4,906. [*Liskeard* in Cornwall, England]

new look ● *noun* **1** a new or revised appearance or presentation, esp. of something familiar. **2** (often **New Look**) a style of women's clothing introduced after the Second World War, featuring long full skirts and a generous use of material in contrast to wartime austerity. ● *attributive adjective* (**new-look**) having a new image; restyled.

newly *adverb* **1** recently. **2** afresh, anew (*newly painted*). **3** in a new or different manner (*newly arranged*).

newly·wed *noun* a recently married person.

New·man ► **1 Bar·nett** (1905–70), US painter. A leading abstract expressionist painter, he is noted for his vast canvases, on which large blocks of uniform colour are dramatically juxtaposed with narrow marginal strips of contrasting colours. **2 John Henry** (1801–91), English clergyman and theologian. An Anglican minister, he founded the Oxford Movement with Keble and Pusey in 1833, and in 1845 converted to Roman Catholicism, becoming a cardinal in 1879; his works include the autobiographical *Apologia pro Vita Sua* (1864), the poem *The Dream of Gerontius* (1865), and the essay *The Idea of a University* (1852). **3 Paul** (b.1925), US actor and film director. Among his many films are *Butch Cassidy and the Sundance Kid* (1969), *The Sting* (1973), and *The Colour of Money* (1987), for which he won an Oscar; he has also directed several films, including *Rachel, Rachel* (1968). **4 Peter Charles** (born Peta Karel Neuman) (b.1929), Austrian-born Canadian journalist, writer and editor. He has had a distinguished career as a journalist, notably as editor of *Maclean's* (1971-1982). He has also published numerous books, including *Renegade in Power: The Diefenbaker Years* (1963) and a multi-volume history of the Hudson's Bay Company, *Company of Adventurers* (1985) and *Caesars of the Wilderness* (1987).

new man *noun* (usu. prec. by *the*) a man who rejects the traditional male role in favour of more caring or sensitive attitudes.

New·mar·ket 1 a town in south central Ontario, 25 km north of Toronto; pop. (2001) 65,788. **2** a town in E England, in Suffolk; pop. (est. 1998) 16,970. It is a noted horse racing centre. [sense 1 so called because a 'new market' was established there *c.*1816 for Aboriginal peoples to trade and sell their furs and other goods]

New Maryland a community in south central New Brunswick, just south of Fredericton; pop. (2001) 4,284.

new math *noun* a system of teaching mathematics to children, with emphasis on investigation by them and on set theory.

new media *plural noun* electronic forms of media, e.g. the Internet, CD-ROMs, etc.

New Mexico a state in the southwestern US, on the border with Mexico; pop. (2000) 1,819,046; capital, Santa Fe. □ **New Mexican** *adjective & noun*

New Model Army *noun hist.* a disciplined and well-trained army created in 1645 by Oliver Cromwell and led by Thomas Fairfax to fight for the Parliamentary cause in the English Civil War.

new money *noun informal* **1** recently acquired money or wealth. **2** the recently wealthy (*a neighbourhood of new money*).

new moon *noun* **1 a** the moon when first seen as a crescent after conjunction with the sun. **b** the time of its appearance. **2** *Astronomy* the time at which the moon is in conjunction with the sun.

New Or·leans /nuː ɔːrˈliːnz, -ˈɔːrlənz, njuː-/ a city and port in SE Louisiana, on the Mississippi; pop. (2000) 484,674. It is noted for its annual Mardi Gras celebrations and for its association with the development of blues and jazz. □ **New Or·lean·ian** *noun & adjective*

New·port 1 an industrial town and port in S Wales, on the Bristol Channel; pop. (est. 2002) 115,400. **2** a historic port city in southern

---

Consonants: b *but*   d *dog*   f *few*   g *get*   h *her*   j *yes*   k *cat*   l *leg*   m *man*   n *no*   p *pen*   r *red*   s *sit*

Rhode Island, on the island of Rhode Island, noted as a resort for the very wealthy in the late 19th c.

Newport News a city in SE Virginia, at the mouth of the James River on the Hampton Roads estuary; pop. (2000) 180,200. It is a major seaport and shipbuilding centre.

New Revised Standard Version *noun* a 1991 revision of the Revised Standard Version of the Bible. Abbr.: **NRSV**.

New Right *noun* a political movement characterized by rejection of all forms of socialism and an emphasis on traditional conservative values. □ **New Right·ist** *noun*

news *noun* **1** information about important or interesting recent events, esp. when published or broadcast. **2** (prec. by *the*) a broadcast report of news. **3** newly received or noteworthy information. **4** (foll. by *to*) *informal* information not previously known (to a person) (*that's news to me*). **5** a person or thing much in the news. [Middle English, pl. of NEW after Old French *noveles* or medieval Latin *nova* neuter pl. of *novus* new]

news agency *noun* an organization that collects and distributes news items.

news·agent *noun Brit.* a seller of or store selling newspapers and usu. related items, e.g. stationery.

news·boy *noun* esp. *hist.* a boy who sells or delivers newspapers.

news bulletin *noun* a short broadcast or published news item or collection of news items.

news·cast *noun* a radio or television broadcast of news reports.

news·cast·er *noun* a person who reads news broadcasts.

news conference *noun* a press conference.

news flash *noun* a single item of important news broadcast separately and often interrupting other programs.

news·gather·ing *noun* the process of researching news items, esp. those for broadcast or publication.

news·group *noun* (on the Internet or other network) a forum for the discussion of, and exchange of information about, a particular subject.

news·hound *noun* (also **news·hawk**) *informal* a newspaper reporter, esp. an aggressive one.

news·letter *noun* a usu. informal printed report issued periodically by a society, business, organization, etc.

news·maga·zine *noun N Amer.* **1** a publication reporting and commenting on current events, usu. issued weekly on glossy paper, typically with many photographs. **2** a television news program consisting of in-depth reports on selected current events.

news·maker *noun* a person or thing at the centre of newsworthy events. □ **news·making** *noun*

news·man *noun* (pl. **-men**) a reporter, newscaster, or journalist.

New South Wales a state of SE Australia; pop. (2001) 6,609,304; capital, Sydney.

New Spain a former Spanish viceroyalty established in Central and N America in 1535, centred on present-day Mexico City. It comprised all the land under Spanish control north of the Isthmus of Panama, including parts of the southern US. It also came to include the Spanish possessions in the Caribbean and the Philippines. It was abolished in 1821, when Mexico achieved independence.

news·paper *noun* **1** a printed publication (usu. daily or weekly) containing news, advertisements, correspondence, etc. **2** the sheets of paper forming this (*wrapped in newspaper*).

news·paper·ing *noun* the business etc. of producing newspapers.

news·paper·man *noun* (pl. **-men**) a journalist. □ **news·paper·woman** (pl. **-women**) *noun*

New·speak *noun* ambiguous euphemistic language used esp. in political propaganda. [an artificial official language in George Orwell's *Nineteen Eighty-Four* (1949)]

news·print *noun* a type of low-quality paper on which newspapers are printed.

news reader *noun* = NEWSCASTER.

news·reel *noun hist.* a short motion picture of recent events.

news release *noun* = PRESS RELEASE.

news·room *noun* a room in a newspaper or broadcasting office where news is processed.

news service *noun* = NEWS AGENCY.

news·stand *noun* a stall for the sale of newspapers.

New Style *noun* dating reckoned by the Gregorian Calendar (*compare* OLD STYLE).

new-style *attributive adjective* having a new style (*new-style contracts*).

news·weekly *noun* (pl. **-lies**) *N Amer.* a weekly newspaper or newsmagazine.

news wire *noun* a service transmitting the latest news stories, e.g. via teleprinter, satellite, or the Internet.

news·worthy *adjective* of sufficient interest to the public to warrant mention in the news; topical. □ **news·worthi·ness** *noun*

newsy *informal* ● *adjective* (**news·i·er**, **news·i·est**) **1** (of a newspaper etc.) full of esp. gossipy news. **2** (of a news item) light, gossipy. ● *noun* (pl. **-ies**) *US* a person who sells newspapers.

newt *noun* any of various small rough-skinned amphibians, esp. of the genus *Notophthalmus* or *Taricha*, having a well-developed tail. [Middle English from *ewt*, with *n* from *an* (compare NICKNAME): var. of *evet* EFT]

New Tecum·seth a town in S central Ontario, just west of Bradford-West Gwillimbury; pop. (2001) 26,141. [variant of TECUMSEH²]

New Territories part of the territory of Hong Kong on the south coast of mainland China, lying to the north of the Kowloon peninsula and including the islands of Lantau, Tsing Yi, and Lamma.

New Testament *noun* the second part of the Christian Bible concerned with the life and teachings of Christ and his earliest followers.

New·ton ▶ 1 Chris·to·pher (b.1936), British-born Canadian actor and theatre director. In an over forty-year career in Canadian theatre, his most significant contribution has been as artistic director of the Shaw Festival (1980–2002), which he developed into one of the most respected theatre companies in the English-speaking world. **2 Sir Isaac** (1642–1727), English mathematician and physicist, the greatest single influence on theoretical physics until Einstein. He discovered the binomial theorem and differential calculus, and in his major treatise, *Principia Mathematica* (1687), he gave a mathematical description of the laws of mechanics and gravitation, and applied these to planetary and lunar motion; he also discovered that white light is made up of a mixture of colours. □ **New·ton·ian** /-ˈtoːniən/ *adjective*

Newton, Mount a peak in the St. Elias Mountains of SW Yukon Territory (4 210 m). [H. *Newton*, US geologist *c.*1890]

new·ton *noun Physics* the SI unit of force that, acting on a mass of one kilogram, increases its velocity by one metre per second every second along the direction that it acts. Abbr.: **N**. [NEWTON]

Newtonian mechanics *plural noun* (usu. treated as *sing.*) the system of mechanics which relies on Newton's laws of motion concerning the relations between forces acting and motions occurring.

New·town /ˈnuːtən, ˈnjuː-/ *noun* a medium-sized greenish-yellow eating and cooking apple. [*Newtown* (now part of Queens), Long Island, where first introduced]

new town *noun Brit.* a town planned and established as a completely new settlement with government sponsorship.

New Urbanism *noun* a movement in urban planning aiming to reduce urban sprawl and create housing developments along a traditional pattern, with residential, shopping, and business areas integrated and less reliance on the automobile. □ **New Urbanist** *noun & adjective*

New Waterford an urban community on Cape Breton Island, northeast of Sydney; pop. (1996) 10,713.

new wave *noun* (also *attributive*) **1** a recent trend in a given field (*the new wave in fitness; a new wave diet*). **2** (often prec. by *the*) a movement in French cinema of the late 1950s and early 1960s, characterized by frequent use of jump-cuts, on-location shooting, hand-held cameras, etc. **3** a style of pop music of the late 1970s and early 1980s, influenced by punk but characterized by a greater use of synthesizers and a more mainstream sound.

New Westminster a city in southwestern BC, located on the Fraser River just southeast of Vancouver; pop. (2001) 54,656. □ **New West·min·ster·ite** *noun* [after WESTMINSTER, so called by Queen Victoria because the site was originally selected to be the provincial capital]

New World *noun* North and South America regarded collectively in relation to Europe. The term was first applied to the Americas (also to other areas, e.g. Australia) after the early voyages of European explorers (*compare* OLD WORLD).

new world order *noun* often *ironic* a state of co-operation, peace, and justice among all nations.

new year *noun* the calendar year just begun or about to begin.

New Year's *noun* **1** (in full **New Year's Eve**) the evening of 31 December. **2** (in full **New Year's Day**) the first day of the year, 1 January.

---

t *top*   v *voice*   w *we*   z *zoo*   ʃ *she*   ʒ *vision*   θ *thin*   ð *this*   ŋ *ring*   x *loch*   tʃ *chip*   dʒ *jar*   (*see over for vowels*)

New York 1 a state in the northeastern US; pop. (2000) 18,976,046; capital, Albany. It stretches from the Canadian border and Lake Ontario in the northwest to the Atlantic in the east, with the Adirondacks in the north and the Catskills in the south. **2** a city in the southeast of New York State, a major port of the US, situated on the Atlantic coast at the mouth of the Hudson River; pop. (2000) 8,008,278. It is situated mainly on islands, linked by bridges, in New York harbour and comprises five boroughs: Manhattan, Brooklyn, the Bronx, Queens and Staten Island. Manhattan is the economic and cultural heart of the city, containing the country's financial centre, the Stock Exchange in Wall Street. New York is the country's leading commercial and industrial city and is the headquarters of the United Nations. □ **New York·er** noun [the Duke of *York*, third son of Charles I, later king of England as James II d.1701]

New York steak noun (also **New York strip**) *N Amer.* a steak cut from the outer side of a T-bone.

New Zea·land an island country in the S Pacific about 1 900 km (1,200 miles) east of Australia; pop. (est. 2002) 3,908,037; capital, Wellington. New Zealand consists of two major islands (North and South Islands) separated by Cook Strait, and several smaller islands. □ **New Zea·land·er** noun

next ● adjective **1** (often foll. by *to*) being or positioned or living nearest (*in the next house*; *the chair next to the fire*). **2 a** the nearest in order of time; the first or soonest encountered or considered (*next Friday*; *ask the next person you see*). **b** following the nearest in order of time; the second to be encountered or considered (*not this Friday, but next Friday*). ● adverb **1** (often foll. by *to*) in the nearest place or degree (*put it next to mine*; *came next to last*). **2** on the first or soonest occasion (*when we next meet*). **3** subsequently, afterwards (*next beat in the eggs*). **4** (with superlatives) following in the specified order (*the next oldest building is the church*). **5** expressing surprise (*whatever next!*). ● noun the next person or thing. ● preposition *informal* next to. □ **as good** (or **well** or **much** etc.) **as the next person** as good, well, etc. as the average person (*I can take a joke as well as the next guy, but this is going too far*). **next to 1** adjacent to. **2** almost (*next to nothing left*). **3** following in order after (*next to skiing her favourite sport was skating*). [Old English *nēhsta* superlative (as NIGH)]

next door adverb & adjective (as adj. often hyphenated) in or to the next house, room, etc. □ **next door to 1** in the next house etc. to. **2** nearly, almost, near to.

next-genera·tion attributive adjective designating an imminent technology, style, model, etc.

next of kin noun the closest living relative or relatives.

next-to-last adjective penultimate.

next world noun a supposed life after death.

nexus noun (pl. **nex·us·es**) **1** a connected group, series, or network. **2** a bond; a connection. [Latin from *nectere nex-* bind]

Ney /'neɪ/ **Michel** (1769–1815), French marshal. One of Napoleon's leading generals, he commanded the French cavalry at Waterloo (1815), and after Napoleon's defeat and final overthrow was executed by the Bourbons.

Neza·hual·có·yotl /ˌnesəwalˈkɔːjɒtəl/ a city in central Mexico, forming part of the Mexico City conurbation; pop. (est. 2000) 1,224,500.

NF abbreviation **1** Newfoundland (formerly in official postal use). **2** (in the UK) National Front.

NFB abbreviation National Film Board of Canada.

NFC abbreviation (in the US) National Football Conference.

NFL abbreviation (in the US) National Football League.

Nfld. abbreviation Newfoundland.

Ngali·ema, Mount /əŋˌgɒliˈeɪmə/ the Congolese name for Mount Stanley (see STANLEY, MOUNT).

Ng·bandi /əŋˈbandi/ ● noun a Niger-Congo language of N Congo (formerly Zaire) (compare SANGO). ● adjective of or relating to this language or its speakers. [Ngbandi]

NGO abbreviation non-governmental organization.

Ngoro·ngoro /əŋˌɡɒrəŋˈɡɔːroː/ a huge extinct volcanic crater in the Great Rift Valley in NE Tanzania, 326 sq. km (126 sq. miles) in area. It is the centre of a wildlife conservation area, established in 1959, which includes the Olduvai Gorge.

ngul·trum /əŋˈɡʊltrəm/ (pl. same) noun the basic monetary unit of Bhutan, equal to 100 chetrum. [Dzongkha]

Nguni /əŋˈɡuːni/ ● noun **1** (pl. same) a member of a group of Bantu-speaking peoples living mainly in southern Africa. **2** the group of closely related Bantu languages spoken by these peoples. ● adjective of or relating to these peoples or this group of languages. [Zulu]

NGV abbreviation natural gas vehicle.

ngwee /əŋˈɡwiː/ noun a monetary unit of Zambia, equal to one-hundredth of a kwacha. [a local word]

NH abbreviation New Hampshire (also in official postal use).

NHL abbreviation National Hockey League. □ **NHLer** noun

NHS abbreviation (in the UK) National Health Service.

NI abbreviation **1** (in the UK) National Insurance. **2** Northern Ireland.

Ni symbol *Chem.* the element nickel.

nia·cin /'naɪəsɪn/ noun a vitamin of the B complex, found in milk, liver, and yeast, a deficiency of which causes pellagra. Also called NICOTINIC ACID, VITAMIN B₃. [*nicotinic acid* + -IN]

nia·cin·amide /naɪəˈsɪnəmaɪd/ noun the amide of niacin, which is interconvertible with niacin in living organisms, providing a source of vitamin B₃.

Ni·ag·ara /naɪˈaɡrə/ noun **1** = NIAGARA PENINSULA. **2** = NIAGARA-ON-THE-LAKE. **3** (also **niagara**; usu. foll. by *of*) an outpouring, a deluge (*a Niagara of fan mail*). □ **Ni·ag·aran** noun & adjective (in sense 1)

Niagara Escarpment a ridge extending over 1 000 km in an arc from the Door Peninsula of E Wisconsin, through Manitoulin Island and the Bruce and Niagara peninsulas. It is a remnant of the shore of an ancient body of water. [see NIAGARA RIVER]

Niagara Falls 1 the waterfall on the Niagara River, consisting of two principal parts separated by Goat Island: the Horseshoe Falls adjoining the west (Canadian) bank, which fall 57 m, and the American Falls adjoining the east (American) bank, which fall 59 m, representing the world's greatest waterfall by volume. **2** a city in S Ontario, situated on the west bank of the Niagara River beside the falls; pop. (2001) 78,815. **3** a city in upper New York state situated on the east bank of the Niagara River beside the falls; pop. (2000) 55,600. [see NIAGARA RIVER]

Niagara-on-the-Lake a town in S Ontario, situated northeast of St. Catharines, on Lake Ontario and the Niagara River; pop. (2001) 13,839. [see NIAGARA RIVER]

Niagara Peninsula a region in S Ontario, bounded by Lake Ontario to the north, Lake Erie to the south, and the Niagara River to the east. [see NIAGARA RIVER]

Niagara River a river in S Ontario, 55 km long, flowing northward from Lake Erie to Lake Ontario. [prob. from Neutral *onghiara* neck]

Nia·mey /njɒˈmeɪ/ the capital of Niger, a port on the Niger River; pop. (est. 2002) 732,200.

nib ● noun **1** the point of a pen, which touches the writing surface. **2** (in *pl.*) shelled and crushed coffee or cocoa beans. **3** the point of a tool etc. ● transitive verb (**nibbed**, **nib·bing**) provide with a nib. [prob. from Middle Dutch *nib* or Middle Low German *nibbe*, var. of *nebbe* nose, snout]

nib·ble ● verb **1** transitive & intransitive **a** take small bites (at). **b** eat in small amounts. **c** bite (at) gently or cautiously or playfully. **2** intransitive (often foll. by *at*) show cautious interest in. ● noun **1** an instance of nibbling. **2 a** a very small amount of food. **b** (also **nib·bly** pl. **-blies**) esp. *Cdn* & *Austral.* (usu. in pl.) a small food item. **3** *Computing* half a byte, i.e. 4 bits. **4** a tentative display of interest. □ **nib·bler** noun [prob. of Low German or Dutch origin: compare Low German *nibbeln* gnaw]

Nibel·ung /'niːbəlʊŋ/ noun (pl. **-ungs**, **Nibel·ung·en** /'niːbəlʊŋən/) *Germanic Myth* **1** a member of a Scandinavian race of dwarfs, owners of a hoard of gold and magic treasures, who were ruled by Nibelung, king of Nibelheim (the land of mist). **2** (in the *Nibelungenlied*) any of the supporters of Siegfried, the subsequent possessor of the hoard; any of the Burgundians who stole it from him.

Nibel·ung·en·lied /'niːbəˌlʊŋənliːd/ noun a 13th-c. German poem, embodying a story found in the Edda, telling of the life and death of Siegfried, a prince of the Netherlands. Siegfried kills the dragon Fafner to seize the treasure of the Nibelungs; he then marries the Burgundian princess Kriemhild and uses trickery to help her brother Gunther win Brunhild, but is killed by Gunther's retainer Hagen. Kriemhild agrees to marry Etzel (Attila the Hun) in order to be revenged, and beheads Hagen herself.

nib·let noun a small piece of food, e.g. a kernel of corn. [prob. from NIBBLE + -LET]

nib·lick noun *Golf dated* an iron with a large round heavy head, used esp. for playing out of bunkers. [19th c.: origin unknown, perhaps an alteration of Scottish *neb laigh* a broken nose, with reference to the short club face]

nibs noun □ **his nibs** *jocular informal* a mock title used with reference to an important or self-important person. [19th c.: origin unknown]

NIC /ˌenaɪˈsiː, nɪk/ abbreviation newly industrialized (or industrializing) country.

nicad /ˈnaɪkad/ *noun* (often *attributive*) a battery, often rechargeable, with a nickel anode and a cadmium cathode. [NICKEL + CADMIUM]

Ni·caea /naɪˈsiːə/ an ancient city in Asia Minor, on the site of modern Iznik, which was important in Roman and Byzantine times. It was the site of two ecumenical councils of the early Christian Church. The first, the Council of Nicaea in 325, condemned Arianism and produced the Nicene Creed. The second, in 787, condemned the iconoclasts.

Nic·ar·a·gua /ˌnɪkəˈrɒgwə, -ˈrag-/ the largest country in Central America, with a coastline on both the Atlantic and the Pacific Ocean; pop. (est. 2002) 5,023,818; capital, Managua. ☐ **Nic·ar·a·guan** *adjective & noun*

Nicaragua, Lake a lake near the west coast of Nicaragua, the largest lake in Central America.

Nice /niːs/ a resort city on the French Riviera, near the border with Italy; pop. (1999) 342,738.

nice *adjective* **1** pleasant, agreeable, satisfactory. **2** (of a person) kind, good-natured. **3** *ironic* bad or awkward (*a nice mess you've made*). **4 a** fine or subtle (*a nice distinction*). **b** requiring careful thought or attention (*a nice problem*). **5** fastidious; delicately sensitive. **6** punctilious, scrupulous (*were not too nice about their methods*). **7** (foll. by an adj., often with *and*) satisfactory or adequate in terms of the quality described (*a nice long bath*; *nice and warm*). ☐ **make nice** (also **make nice-nice**) *N Amer. informal* be pleasant when one would rather not. **nice one** *informal* expressing approval or commendation. ☐ **nice·ly** *adverb* **nice·ness** *noun* [Middle English originally = stupid, wanton: via Old French, = silly, simple, from Latin *nescius* ignorant, from *ne-* not + *scire* know]

nice-guy *attributive adjective N Amer.* characteristic of a nice, agreeable person (*a nice-guy image*).

Ni·cene Creed /ˈnaɪsiːn, ˈnaɪ-, -ˈsiːn/ *noun* (also **Ni·caean** /-ˈsiːən/) a formal statement of Christian belief based on that adopted at the first Council of Nicaea in 325. [Late Latin *Nicenus* of Nicaea]

nicety /ˈnaɪsəti/ *noun* (*pl.* **-ies**) **1** a subtle distinction or detail. **2** precision, accuracy. **3** (in *pl.*) a minor aspect of polite social behaviour; a detail of etiquette.

nicey-nice *adjective* (also **nicey-nicey**) *informal* irritatingly or disingenuously pleasant or agreeable.

niche /niːʃ/ ● *noun* **1** a shallow recess, esp. in a wall to contain a statue etc. **2** a comfortable or suitable position in life or employment. **3** a specialized but profitable corner of the market (also *attributive: niche marketing*). **4** *Ecology* a position or role taken by a kind of organism within its community. ● *transitive verb* (often as **niched** *adjective*) place in a niche. ☐ **carve (out) a niche** *see* CARVE. [French from *nicher* 'make a nest', ultimately from Latin *nidus* nest]

Nich·iren /ˈnɪʃərən/ *noun* (also **Nichiren Buddhism**) a Japanese Buddhist sect founded by the religious teacher Nichiren (1222–82).

Nichol, Bar·rie Phil·ip ('bp Nichol') (1944–88), Canadian writer, poet, and teacher. He is known esp. for his sound poetry; his works include the long poem *The Martyrology* (1972–88).

Nicho·las, Cyn·thia ('Cindy') (b.1957), Canadian swimmer. In her first marathon swimming achievement, she crossed Lake Ontario in 1974, beating all previous female and male records. In 1977 she became the first woman to make a double crossing of the English Channel; by 1982 she had swum the Channel 19 times, including five double crossings. She was the world champion women's marathon swimmer in 1976.

Nicholas I (1796–1855), brother of Alexander I, czar of Russia 1825–55. He pursued rigidly conservative policies, maintaining serfdom and building up a large secret police force to suppress radical reformers; his expansionist policies in the Near East led to the Crimean War.

Nicholas II (1868–1918), son of Alexander III, czar of Russia 1894–1917. After a disastrous war with Japan (1904–5) he became more open to reform, but the czarist regime disintegrated under the strain of fresh military disasters during the First World War; he was forced to abdicate after the Russian Revolution in 1917 and was shot along with his family a year later.

Nicholas, St. (4th c.), Christian clergyman. Bishop of Myra in Lycia, he became the subject of many legends and is patron saint of children, sailors, and the countries of Greece and Russia; the cult of Santa Claus (a corruption of his name) arose in N America from the Dutch custom of giving gifts to children on his feast day (6 Dec.), a practice now usually transferred to Christmas.

Nichol·son, Jack (b.1937), US actor. He gained wide recognition with *Easy Rider* (1969); he won Oscars for *One Flew Over the Cuckoo's Nest* (1975), *Terms of Endearment* (1983), and *As Good as it Gets* (1997).

Ni·chrome /ˈnaɪkroʊm/ *noun proprietary* a group of nickel-chromium alloys used for making wire in heating elements etc. [NICKEL + CHROME]

nick ● *noun* **1 a** a small cut or notch. **b** a scratch or light wound. **2** *Brit. slang* **a** a prison. **b** a police station. **3** (prec. by *in* with adj.) *Brit. informal* condition (*in reasonable nick*). ● *transitive verb* **1** make a nick or nicks in. **2** *Brit. slang* **a** steal. **b** arrest, catch. ☐ **in the nick of time** only just in time; just at the right moment. **nick (someone) for** *informal* defraud someone of (a sum). [Middle English: origin uncertain]

nick·el ● *noun* **1** a malleable ductile silver-white metallic transition element, occurring naturally in various minerals and used in special steels, in magnetic alloys, and as a catalyst. Symbol: **Ni**; at. no.: 28. **2** *N Amer.* **a** a five-cent coin. **b** five cents. ● *transitive verb* (**nick·elled**, **nick·el·ling**; also esp. *US* **nick·eled**, **nick·el·ing**) coat with nickel. ☐ **it's your nickel** (or **dime**) you may use your time or money as you see fit, or talk as long as you like (said esp. to someone who is paying for a long-distance telephone call). [abbreviation of German *Kupfernickel* copper-coloured ore from which nickel was first obtained, from *Kupfer* copper + *Nickel* demon, with reference to the ore's failure to yield copper]

nickel and dime ● *transitive verb* (**nickel-and-dimed** or **nickelled and dimed**, **nickel-and-diming** or **nickelling and diming**) put a financial strain on (someone) by charging small amounts for many minor services etc. ● (**nickel-and-dime**) *attributive adjective* petty, insignificant.

Nick·el Belt a nickel-rich region surrounding the city of Sudbury in north central Ontario.

Nick·el Cen·tre a former town in north central Ontario, now part of Greater Sudbury; pop. (2001) 12,672.

nickel·odeon /ˌnɪkəˈloʊdiən/ *noun N Amer. hist.* **1** *informal* a jukebox. **2** a movie theatre with an admission fee of one nickel. [NICKEL + MELODEON]

nickel silver *noun* = GERMAN SILVER.

nick·er *intransitive verb* neigh. [imitative]

Nick·laus /ˈnɪkləs/ **Jack (Wil·liam)** (b.1940), US golfer. Since the start of his professional career in 1962, he has won more than 80 tournaments, including six wins in the PGA championship, four in the US Open, and three in the British Open.

nick·name ● *noun* **1** a familiar or humorous name given to a person or thing instead of or as well as the real name. **2** a familiar or abbreviated form of a first name. ● *transitive verb* give a nickname to; call (a person or thing) by a nickname. [Middle English from *eke-name*, with *n* from *an* (compare NEWT): *eke* = addition, from Old English *ēaca* (as EKE)]

nicky nicky nine doors *noun Cdn* a children's game involving knocking on a door or ringing a doorbell and running away before the door is answered.

Nico·bar Islands *see* ANDAMAN AND NICOBAR ISLANDS.

ni·çoise /niːˈswɒz/ *adjective* designating food (esp. a salad) garnished with tomatoes, capers, anchovies, etc. [French, = of Nice]

Nico·let /niːkɒˈle/ a town in south central Quebec, situated on Lac Saint-Pierre at the mouth of the Rivière Nicolet, about 15 km southwest of Bécancour; pop. (2001) 7,928. [J. *Nicolet* (or Nicollet) de Belleborne, French explorer d.1642]

Nico·sia /ˌnɪkəˈsiːə/ the capital of Cyprus; pop. (2001) 200,548. Since 1974 it has been divided into Greek and Turkish sectors. (Greek name **Lef·ko·sia**; Turkish name **Lef·koşa**)

nico·ti·ana /ˌnɪkɒtiˈanə, -ʃiˈanə/ *noun* = TOBACCO PLANT. [modern Latin *nicotiana (herba)* 'tobacco plant', named after J. *Nicot*, 16th-c. French diplomat who introduced tobacco to France]

nico·tin·a·mide /ˌnɪkəˈtiːnəmaɪd, -ˈtɪnə-/ *noun Biochem.* the amide of niacin, having a similar role in the diet, and important as a constituent of NAD.

nico·tine /ˈnɪkətiːn, ˌnɪkəˈtiːn/ *noun* a colourless poisonous alkaloid present in tobacco. ☐ **nico·tin·ic** *adjective* [French from NICOTIANA + -INE⁴]

nicotine patch *noun* a patch applied to the skin of those addicted to nicotine, releasing a measured amount of the drug into the bloodstream in order to break the addiction.

nicotinic acid /ˌnɪkəˈtɪnɪk/ *noun* = NIACIN.

nic·ti·tat·ing membrane *noun* a clear membrane forming a third eyelid in amphibians, birds, and some other animals, that can be drawn across the eye to give protection without loss of vision. [medieval Latin *nictitare* frequentative of Latin *nictare* blink]

nidus /ˈnaɪdəs/ *noun* (*pl.* **nidi** /-daɪ/) **1** a place in which an insect etc.

deposits its eggs, or in which spores or seeds develop. **2** a place in which something is nurtured or developed. [Latin, related to NEST]

Nie·buhr /ˈniːbʊr/ **Rein·hold** (1892–1971), US Protestant theologian, whose works, such as *Moral Man and the Immoral Society* (1932) and *Christianity and Power Politics* (1969), are primarily concerned with the issue of morality in contemporary society.

niece *noun* a daughter of one's brother or sister, or of one's brother-in-law or sister-in-law. [Old French, ultimately from Latin *neptis* granddaughter]

ni·ello /niˈelɔː/ *noun* (*pl.* **-los**) **1** a black composition of sulphur with silver, lead, or copper, for filling engraved lines in silver or other metal. **2 a** such ornamental work. **b** an object decorated with this. □ **ni·el·loed** *adjective* [Italian from Latin *nigellus* diminutive of *niger* black]

Niel·sen ▸ 1 Carl (Aug·ust) (1865–1931), Danish composer. A major figure in the development of modern Scandinavian music, he gained his first success in 1888 with his *Little Suite* for string orchestra; his major works include six symphonies (1890–1925), the opera *Maskerade* (1906), concertos, and an organ work, *Commotio* (1931). **2 Les·lie** (b.1926), Canadian actor. Appearing in over one hundred Hollywood films (originally in serious roles but subsequently in comic ones) since the 1950s, he is perhaps best known for the disaster spoof *Airplane!* (1980) and the series of *Naked Gun* movies (1988, 1991, 1994).

Nielsen ratings *plural noun* (also **Niel·sens**) popularity ratings for television programs provided by A. C. Nielsen Co. and calculated from figures obtained from a sample survey of receiving sets fitted with a device to record automatically listening or viewing patterns. [A. C. Nielsen, US market researcher d.1980]

Nie·meyer /ˈniːˌmaɪər/ **(So·ares Filho) Oscar** (b.1907), Brazilian architect. An early exponent of modernist architecture in Latin America, he designed the main public buildings of Brasilia (1950–60) within the master plan drawn up by Lúcio Costa.

Nietz·sche /ˈniːtʃə/ **Frie·drich (Wil·helm)** (1844–1900), German philosopher, poet, and critic. He is known for repudiating Christianity's compassion for the weak, exalting the 'will to power', and formulating the idea of the *Übermensch* (superman), who can rise above the restrictions of ordinary morality. □ **Nietz·sche·an** /ˈniːtʃiən/ *noun* & *adjective*

niff *Brit. informal* ● *noun* a smell, esp. an unpleasant one. ● *intransitive verb* smell, stink. □ **niffy** *adjective* (**nif·fi·er, nif·fi·est**). [originally dial., perhaps from SNIFF]

Nifl·heim /ˈnɪvəlheɪm, -haɪm/ *Scand. Myth* the underworld, a place of eternal cold, darkness, and mist inhabited by those who died of old age or illness. [Old Norse *Niflheimr*, = world of mist]

nifty *adjective* (**nif·ti·er, nif·ti·est**) *informal* **1** cleverly designed, executed, etc. **2** clever, adroit. **3** smart, stylish. □ **nif·ti·ly** *adverb* **nif·ti·ness** *noun* [19th c.: origin uncertain]

Niger /ˈnaɪdʒər/ a landlocked country in West Africa, on the southern edge of the Sahara; pop. (est. 2002) 10,639,744; capital, Niamey.

Niger-Congo *adjective* denoting or belonging to a large phylum of languages in Africa, named after the Niger and Congo rivers. It comprises most of the languages spoken by the indigenous peoples of Africa south of the Sahara and includes the Bantu and Kwa families.

Ni·geria /naɪˈdʒɪəriə/ a country on the coast of West Africa, bordered by the Niger River to the north; pop. (est. 2002) 129,934,911; capital, Abuja. □ **Ni·ger·ian** *adjective* & *noun*

Niger River a river in NW Africa, which rises on the northeast border of Sierra Leone and flows in a great arc for 4 100 km (2,550 miles) northeast to Mali, then southeast through W Niger and Nigeria, before turning southward to empty through a great delta into the Gulf of Guinea.

niger seed /ˈnaɪdʒər/ *noun* the seeds of *Guizotia abyssinica*, an African composite plant, used as bird seed and for their oil. [NIGER]

nig·gard /ˈnɪgərd/ ● *noun* a mean or stingy person. ● *adjective archaic* = NIGGARDLY. [Middle English, alteration of earlier (obsolete) *nigon*, prob. of Scandinavian origin: compare NIGGLE]

nig·gard·ly /ˈnɪgərdli/ ● *adjective* **1** stingy, parsimonious. **2** meagre, scanty. ● *adverb* in a stingy or meagre manner. □ **nig·gard·li·ness** *noun*

nig·ger *noun offensive* **1** a black person. **2** a dark-skinned person. □ **a nigger in the woodpile** a hidden cause of trouble or inconvenience. [earlier *neger* from French *nègre* from Spanish *negro* NEGRO]

nig·gle ● *verb* **1** *intransitive* be over-attentive to details. **2** *intransitive* find fault in a petty way. **3** *transitive informal* irritate; nag pettily. ● *noun* a

trifling complaint or criticism; a worry or annoyance. [apparently of Scandinavian origin: compare Norwegian *nigla*]

nig·gling *adjective* **1** troublesome or irritating in a petty way. **2** trifling or petty. □ **nig·gling·ly** *adverb*

nigh /naɪ/ *often jocular* ● *adjective* (esp. of a momentous event) near; approaching. ● *adverb* almost (*nigh impossible*). □ **nigh on** almost. [Old English *nēh, nēah*]

night ● *noun* **1** the period of darkness between one day and the next; the time from sunset to sunrise. **2** nightfall (*shall not reach home before night*). **3** the darkness of night (*as black as night*). **4** a night or evening appointed for some activity, or spent or regarded in a certain way (*parent-teacher night; a great night out*). ● *interjection informal* = GOOD NIGHT *interjection* 1. □ **night and day** all the time; unceasingly. □ **night·less** *adjective* [Old English *neaht, niht*, from Germanic]

night blindness *noun* the inability to see in dim light or at night. Also called NYCTALOPIA.

night·cap *noun* **1** *hist.* a cap worn in bed. **2** a hot or alcoholic drink taken at bedtime. **3** *Baseball* the second game of a doubleheader when played in the evening.

night·clothes *noun* clothes for wearing in bed.

night·club *noun* a club that is open at night for drinking, eating, dancing, entertainment, etc.

night·club·bing *noun* the frequenting of nightclubs. □ **night·club·ber** *noun*

night crawler *noun N Amer.* an earthworm.

night·dress *noun* = NIGHTGOWN.

night·fall *noun* the onset of night; the end of daylight.

night·gown *noun* **1** a woman's or girl's loose garment worn in bed. **2** *hist.* a dressing gown.

night·hawk *noun* **1** a nocturnal insectivorous N American bird of the genus *Chordeiles*. **2** a person who is active at night.

night·ie *noun informal* a nightgown. [abbreviation]

Night·in·gale, Flor·ence (known as 'the Lady of the Lamp') (1820–1910), English nurse and medical reformer. She became famous during the Crimean War for her work improving the medical procedures and standard of care in army hospitals, thereby achieving a dramatic reduction in the mortality rate.

night·in·gale *noun* any small reddish-brown bird of the genus *Luscinia*, esp. *L. megarhynchos*, of which the male sings melodiously, esp. at night. [Old English *nihtegala* (whence obsolete *nightgale*) from Germanic: for *-n-* compare FARTHINGALE]

night·jar *noun* a nocturnal insectivorous migratory bird, *Caprimulgus europaeus*, with grey-brown cryptic plumage and a distinctive churring call.

Night Journey *Islam* the journey through the air made by Muhammad, guided by the archangel Gabriel. They flew first to Jerusalem, where Muhammad prayed with earlier prophets including Abraham, Moses, and Jesus, before ascending to heaven and entering the presence of Allah.

night·life *noun* activity or entertainment occurring at night in a city, as in nightclubs etc.

night light *noun* **1** a dim light kept on in a bedroom or hallway at night. **2** any light at night, e.g. a street light.

night-long *attributive adjective* throughout the night.

night·ly ● *adjective* **1** happening, done, or existing in the night. **2** recurring every night. ● *adverb* every night.

night·mare *noun* **1** a frightening or unpleasant dream. **2** a terrifying or very unpleasant experience or situation. **3** a haunting or obsessive fear. □ **night·mar·ish** *adjective* **night·mar·ish·ly** *adverb* [an evil spirit (incubus) once thought to lie on and suffocate sleepers: Old English *mære* incubus]

night night *interjection* (also **nighty night**) = GOOD NIGHT *interjection* 1.

night nurse *noun* a nurse on duty during the night.

night of the long knives *noun* **1** the massacre of Ernst Röhm and his Brownshirt associates by Hitler on 29–30 June 1934. **2** a similar ruthless or decisive action.

night owl *noun* a person active at night.

night person *noun* a person who functions best (esp. late) at night.

night·scape *noun* **1** a scene or landscape viewed by night. **2** a picture representing a scene or landscape at night.

night school *noun* an institution providing evening classes for those working by day.

night·shade *noun* **1** any of various poisonous plants, esp. of the genus

Solanum, including *S. nigrum* (**black nightshade**) with black berries, and *S. dulcamara* (**woody nightshade**) with red berries. **2** (in full **deadly nightshade**) = BELLADONNA 1. [Old English *nihtscada* apparently formed as NIGHT + SHADE, prob. with reference to its poisonous properties]

night shift *noun* a shift of workers employed during the night.

night·shirt *noun* a long shirt worn in bed.

night side *noun* **1** the side of a planet or satellite that is facing away from the sun and is therefore in darkness. **2** the dark or bad aspect of a person or thing.

night sight *noun* a sight on a gun etc. enabling one to see in the dark.

night soil *noun* human excrement used as manure.

night·spot *noun* a nightclub.

night·stand *noun* N Amer. a night table.

night·stick *noun* N Amer. a police officer's truncheon.

night sweats *plural noun* profuse perspiration occurring during the night, symptomatic of some diseases and conditions.

night table *noun* N Amer. a small low bedside table, often with drawers.

night terror *noun* (also **night terrors** *plural noun*) a sudden great fear experienced during the night, esp. by children, and causing wakening.

night·time *noun* the time between evening and morning; the time of night or darkness.

night vision *noun* **1** the faculty of seeing during the night or in the dark. **2** (**night-vision**) (*attributive*) designating equipment enabling one to see in the dark (*night-vision goggles*).

night watchman *noun* a person whose job is to keep watch by night.

night·wear *noun* clothing suitable for wearing in bed.

nighty-night ● *interjection* = GOOD NIGHT *interjection* 1. ● *noun* an instance of saying 'nighty-night'.

NIH *abbreviation* (in the US) National Institutes of Health.

nihil·ism /ˈnaɪɪlɪzəm, ˈniː-/ *noun* **1** the rejection of all moral and religious principles. **2** an extreme form of skepticism maintaining that nothing has a real existence. □ **nihil·ist** *noun* **nihil·is·tic** *adjective* [Latin *nihil* nothing]

nihil ob·stat /ˌnaɪhɪl ˈɒbstat, ˌniː-/ *noun* **1** *Catholicism* a certificate that a book is not open to objection on doctrinal or moral grounds. **2** an authorization or official approval. [Latin, = nothing hinders]

Nii·gata /ˌniːˈɡɒtə/ an industrial port in central Japan, on the northwest coast of the island of Honshu; pop. (est. 2002) 593,200.

Ni·jin·sky /nɪˈdʒɪnski/ **Vas·lav Fom·ich** (1890–1950), Russian dancer and choreographer, considered one of the greatest artists in ballet history, celebrated especially for his spectacular leaps and sensitive characterizations. From 1909 he was the leading dancer with Diaghilev's Ballets Russes, giving celebrated performances in the classics and Fokine's ballets, including *Le Spectre de la rose* (1911); he also choreographed *L'Après-midi d'un faune* (1912), *Jeux* (1913), and *The Rite of Spring* (1913). His career ended in 1919 as he lapsed into schizophrenia.

Nij·megen /ˈnaɪˌmeɪɡən/ an industrial town in the E Netherlands, south of Arnhem; pop. (est. 2002) 154,800.

-nik *suffix* forming nouns denoting a person associated with a specified thing or quality (*beatnik*; *refusenik*). [Russian (as SPUTNIK) and Yiddish]

Nike /ˈnaɪki/ *Gk Myth* the goddess of victory. [Greek *nikē* victory]

Nik·kei /ˈniːkeɪ/ *noun* (in full **Nikkei index**, **Nikkei average**) a figure indicating the relative price of representative shares on the Tokyo Stock Exchange. [*Nikkei* from Japanese abbreviation of the name of a financial newspaper]

Niko·laev see MYKOLAYIV.

nil *noun* nothing; no number or amount (often as a score in games). [Latin, = *nihil* nothing]

nil des·per·an·dum /nɪl dɛspəˈrandəm/ *interjection* do not despair, never despair. [Latin *nil desperandum (Teucro duce)* 'no need to despair (with Teucer as your leader)', from Horace *Odes*]

Nile, Battle of the *see* ABOUKIR BAY, BATTLE OF.

Nile River a river in eastern Africa, the longest river in the world, which rises in east central Africa near Lake Victoria and flows 6 695 km (4,160 miles) generally northward through Uganda, Sudan, and Egypt to empty through a large delta into the Mediterranean. It flows from Lake Victoria to Lake Albert, in Uganda, as the **Victoria Nile**. As the **Albert Nile** it flows onward to the Ugandan–Sudanese border, where it is known as the **White Nile**. At Khartoum, after its confluence with the **Blue Nile** (which arises in NW Ethiopia), it continues northward as the Nile.

nil·gai /ˈniːlɡaɪ/ *noun* a large short-horned Indian antelope, *Boselaphus tragocamelus*. [Hindi *nīlgāī* from *nīl* blue + *gāī* cow]

Nil·giri Hills /ˈnɪlɡəri/ a range of hills in S India, in W Tamil Nadu. They form a branch of the Western Ghats.

Nil·ot·ic /naɪˈlɒtɪk/ *adjective* **1** of or relating to the Nile or the Nile region of Africa. **2** of or relating to a group of E African Negroid peoples, or the languages spoken by them. [Latin *Niloticus* from Greek *Neilōtikos* from *Neilos* Nile]

Nils·son /ˈnɪlsən/ **(Märta) Bir·git** (b.1918), Swedish operatic soprano. Particularly noted for her interpretation of Wagnerian roles, she also performed the operas of Richard Strauss and Verdi.

nim·ble *adjective* (**nim·bler**, **nim·blest**) **1** quick and light in movement or action; agile. **2** (of the mind) quick to comprehend; clever, versatile. □ **nimble·ness** *noun* **nim·bly** *adverb* [Old English *næmel* quick to seize, from *niman* take, from Germanic, with -*b*- as in THIMBLE]

nimbo·strat·us /ˌnɪmboʊˈstratəs/ *noun* cloud forming a low diffuse dark grey layer, often with falling rain or snow. [modern Latin, from NIMBUS + STRATUS]

nim·bus *noun* (pl. **nim·bus·es** or **nimbi** /-baɪ/) **1 a** a bright cloud or halo investing a deity or person or thing. **b** the halo of a saint etc. **2** a rain cloud. □ **nim·bused** *adjective* [Latin, = cloud, aureole]

NIMBY *noun* (pl. **NIMBYs**) (often *attributive*) a person who objects to unwanted groups or developments appearing in his or her neighbourhood. □ **Nimby·ism** *noun* [not in my back yard]

Nîmes /niːm/ a city in S France; pop. (1999) 133,242. It is noted for its many well-preserved Roman remains.

niminy-piminy /ˌnɪmɪniˈpɪmɪni/ *adjective* feeble, affected; lacking in vigour. [compare NAMBY-PAMBY]

Nim·itz /ˈnɪmɪts/ **Ches·ter Wil·liam** (1885–1966), US admiral, who was the commander of the US Pacific fleet during the Second World War.

Nim·rod *noun* **1** *Bible* a hunter noted for his exceptional skill (Gen. 10:8–12). **2** (often **nimrod**) a skilled hunter. **3** (**nimrod**) N Amer. slang an inept person.

Nim·rud /ˈnɪmrʊd/ an ancient Mesopotamian city, situated on the eastern bank of the Tigris south of Nineveh, near the modern city of Mosul. Palaces of the Assyrian kings with monumental sculptured reliefs, carved ivory furniture inlays and metalwork have been discovered there. The city was known in biblical times as Calah (Gen. 10:11).

Nin /nɪn/ **Anaïs** (1903–77), French-born US novelist and short-story writer. She is primarily known for her erotic stories collected as *Delta of Venus: Erotica* (1977) and for the eight-volume *Diary of Anaïs Nin 1931–66* (1966–80).

nin·com·poop *noun* a simpleton; a fool. [17th c.: origin unknown]

nine ● *noun* **1** one more than eight, or one less than ten; the sum of five units and four units. **2** a symbol for this (9, ix, IX). **3 a** a size etc. denoted by nine. **b** a shoe, garment, etc., of such a size. **4** a set or team of nine individuals. **5** nine o'clock. **6** a playing card with nine pips. ● *adjective* that amount to nine. □ **dressed to** (or *Brit.* **up to**) **the nines** dressed very elaborately or elegantly. **have nine lives** appear to recover repeatedly from disastrous circumstances. **nine days' wonder** a person or thing that is briefly famous. **nine-tenths** nearly all (*possession is nine-tenths of the law*). **nine times out of ten** nearly always. **the whole nine yards** see WHOLE. [Old English *nigon*, from Germanic]

nine·bark *noun* a shrub of the rose family, of the genus *Physocarpus*, with showy clusters of white flowers and peeling bark, found on the Pacific coast and the shores of the Great Lakes.

9/11 *noun* = SEPTEMBER 11.

nine·fold *adjective & adverb* **1** nine times as much or as many. **2** consisting of nine parts.

900 number *noun* N Amer. a telephone number, with the digits '900' in place of an area code, used to access information or entertainment provided for a fee charged by the minute.

nine·pin *noun* **1** (in *pl.*; usu. treated as *sing.*) a game in which nine pins are set up at the end of an alley and bowled at in an attempt to knock them down. **2** a pin used in this game. □ **go down** (or **drop** or **fall**) **like ninepins** topple or succumb in large numbers.

niner *noun* Cdn (esp. Ont.) *slang* a student in grade nine, the first year of high school.

nine·teen ● *noun* **1** one more than eighteen, nine more than ten. **2** the symbol for this (19, xix, XIX). **3** a size etc. denoted by nineteen.

● *adjective* that amount to nineteen. □ **talk nineteen to the dozen** see DOZEN. □ **nine·teenth** *adjective, adverb & noun* [Old English *nigontȳne*]

nineteenth hole *noun* Golf slang the bar at a golf club (as reached after a standard round of 18 holes).

nine-to-five *attributive adjective* of or involving standard office hours (typically 9 a.m. to 5 p.m.). □ **nine-to-fiver** *noun*

nine·ty ● *noun* (*pl.* **-ties**) **1** the product of nine and ten. **2** a symbol for this (90, xc, XC). **3** (in *pl.*) the numbers from 90 to 99, esp. the years of a century or of a person's life. ● *adjective* that amount to ninety. □ **ninety-first, -second**, etc. the ordinal numbers between ninetieth and a hundredth. **ninety-one, -two**, etc. the cardinal numbers between ninety and a hundred. □ **nine·ti·eth** *adjective, adverb & noun* **ninety·fold** *adjective & adverb* [Old English *nigontig*]

Nin·eveh /ˈnɪnəvə/ an ancient city located on the east bank of the Tigris, opposite the modern city of Mosul. It was the oldest city of the ancient Assyrian Empire and its capital during the reign of Sennacherib until it was destroyed by a coalition of Babylonians and Medes in 612 BC. A famous archaeological site, it is noted for its monumental Neo-Assyrian palace, library and statuary as well as for its crucial sequence of prehistoric pottery.

Ning·xia /nɪŋˈʃjɒ/ (also **Ning·sia**) an autonomous region of north central China; capital, Yinchuan.

ninja /ˈnɪndʒə/ *noun* **1** a person skilled in an originally Japanese martial art characterized by stealthy movement and camouflage. **2** *informal* any fanciful warrior using acrobatics and various bladed weapons. [Japanese]

ninny *noun* (*pl.* **-nies**) a foolish or simple-minded person. [perhaps from *innocent*]

ninth ● *noun* **1** the position in a sequence corresponding to the number 9 in the sequence 1–9. **2** something occupying this position. **3** each of nine equal parts of a thing. **4** *Music* **a** an interval or chord spanning nine consecutive notes in the diatonic scale, e.g. C to D an octave higher. **b** a note separated from another by this interval. **5** *Baseball* the ninth inning. ● *adjective* that is the ninth. ● *adverb* in the ninth place; ninthly. □ **ninth·ly** *adverb*

Niobe /ˈnaɪəbi/ *Gk Myth* the daughter of Tantalus. Apollo and Artemis, enraged because she boasted herself superior to their mother Leto, slew her children; Niobe herself was turned into a stone, and her tears into streams that trickled from it.

nio·bium /naɪˈoːbiəm/ *noun Chem.* a rare grey-blue metallic transition element occurring naturally in several minerals and used in alloys for superconductors. Symbol: **Nb**; at. no.: 41. [*Niobe* daughter of Tantalus: so called because first found in TANTALITE]

Nip *noun slang offensive* a Japanese person. [abbreviation of NIPPONESE]

nip[1] ● *verb* (**nipped, nip·ping**) **1** *transitive* pinch, squeeze, or bite sharply. **2** *transitive* (often foll. by *off*) remove by pinching etc. **3** *transitive* (of the cold, frost, etc.) cause pain or harm to. **4** *intransitive* (foll. by *in, out,* etc.) *informal* go quickly. **5** *transitive N Amer. informal* (of an athlete, team, etc.) overtake or defeat (an opponent) by a narrow margin. **6** *transitive US slang* steal, snatch. **7** *transitive* make (the waist of a garment) very narrow in comparison to the shoulders, bust, and hips. ● *noun* **1 a** a pinch, a sharp squeeze. **b** a bite. **2 a** biting cold. **b** a check to vegetation caused by this. **3** *Cdn* (*Man. & NW Ont.*) a hamburger. □ **nip at someone's heel** (or **heels**) pursue someone very closely. **nip in the bud** suppress or destroy (esp. an idea) at an early stage. □ **nip·ping** *adjective* [Middle English, prob. of Low German or Dutch origin]

nip[2] ● *noun* a small quantity of an alcoholic beverage. ● *transitive verb* (**nipped, nip·ping**) drink (alcohol). [prob. abbreviation of *nipperkin* small measure: compare Low German, Dutch *nippen* to sip]

nipa /ˈniːpə/ *noun* an E Indian palm tree, *Nypa fruticans*, with a creeping trunk and large feathery leaves. [Spanish & Portuguese from Malay *nipah*]

nip and tuck ● *noun* (*pl.* **nips and tucks**) *informal* **1** a cosmetic surgical operation. **2** a minor renovation or improvement. ● *adjective* (of a competition) not decided until the last possible moment.

Nip·igon, Lake /ˈnɪpɪˌɡɒn/ a lake in NW Ontario (4 848 sq. km), situated northeast of Thunder Bay. [Ojibwa *anemebegong* continuous water, with reference either to its size or its river route southward to Lake Superior]

Nip·is·sing, Lake /ˈnɪpɪˌsɪŋ/ a lake in NE central Ontario, situated southeast of Sudbury. The city of North Bay lies on its shore. [Algonquin, = little body of water]

nip·per *noun* **1** a person or thing that nips. **2** *Cdn* (*Maritimes & Nfld*) a glove worn while handling lines to protect the hands from friction.

3 *Cdn* (*Nfld*) a large mosquito. **4** the claw of a crab, lobster, etc. **5** *Brit. informal* a young child. **6** (in *pl.*) any tool for gripping or cutting, e.g. forceps or pincers.

nip·ple *noun* **1 a** a small projection in which the mammary ducts of female mammals terminate and from which milk is secreted for the young. **b** an analogous structure in the male. **2** a rubber device shaped like this on a baby's or animal's feeding bottle. **3** a device like a nipple in function, e.g. the tip of a grease gun. **4** a nipple-like protuberance. **5** *N Amer.* a short section of pipe with a screw thread at each end for coupling. □ **nip·ple·less** *adjective* [16th c., also *neble, nible*, perhaps diminutive from *neb*]

Nip·pon·ese /ˌnɪpɒˈniːz/ ● *noun* (*pl.* same) a Japanese person. ● *adjective* Japanese. [Japanese *Nippon* Japan, lit. 'land of the rising sun']

nippy *adjective* (**nip·pi·er, nip·pi·est**) *informal* **1** chilly, cold. **2** *Cdn* (of food, esp. cheese) piquant, sharp. **3** quick, nimble, active. □ **nip·pi·ly** *adverb*

Niro see DE NIRO.

nir·vana /nɜːrˈvɑːnə, -ˈvɒnə/ *noun* **1** (in Buddhism) perfect bliss and release from karma, attained by the extinction of individuality. **2** *informal* a state of perfection. □ **nir·van·ic** *adjective* [Sanskrit *nirvāṇa* from *nirvā* be extinguished, from *nis* out + *vā-* to blow]

Niš /niːʃ/ (also **Nish**) an industrial city in SE Serbia, on the Nišava River near its confluence with the Morava; pop. (est. 2002) 185,200. The city, commanding the principal route by river between Europe and the Aegean, was for centuries a strategic stronghold. It was the birthplace of Constantine the Great (*c.*274 AD).

Nisei /niːˈseɪ/ *N Amer.* (*pl.* same) ● *noun* a Canadian or American whose parents were immigrants from Japan. ● *adjective* of or relating to the Nisei. [Japanese, lit. 'second generation']

Nisga'a /ˈnɪsɡə/ *noun* (also **Nish·ga** /ˈnɪʃɡə/) **1** a member of a Tsimshian Aboriginal people living in the Skeena River valley in northwestern BC. **2** the language of this people, a dialect of Nass-Gitksan. [Nisga'a, = 'people of the mighty river']

Nishnawbe-Aski /nɪʃˈnɒbeiˈaski/ *noun* an Aboriginal political organization representing bands within the area of NW Ontario covered by Treaty number 9.

nisi /ˈnaɪsaɪ/ *adjective Law* that takes effect only on certain conditions (*decree nisi*). [Latin, = 'unless']

Nis·sen hut /ˈnɪsən/ *noun Brit.* a tunnel-shaped hut of corrugated iron with a cement floor; a Quonset hut. [P. N. *Nissen*, Canadian engineer d.1930, its inventor]

nit *noun* **1** the egg or young form of a louse or other parasitic insect, esp. of human head lice or body lice. **2** esp. *Brit. slang* a stupid person. □ **pick nits** search for and criticize small, esp. insignificant faults or errors; nitpick. [Old English *hnitu* from West Germanic]

nite *noun N Amer. informal* night.

niter esp. *US var.* of NITRE.

Niti·nat /ˈnɪtənat/ *noun* the former name of the DITIDAHT. [Nuu-chah-nulth *nitinaht*, from Ditidaht *ditidaht*]

nit·pick·ing *noun & adjective informal* searching for and criticizing small, esp. insignificant faults or errors. □ **nit·pick** *intransitive verb* **nit·pick·er** *noun* **nit·picky** *adjective*

ni·trate /ˈnaɪtreɪt/ ● *noun* **1** any salt or ester of nitric acid. **2** potassium or sodium nitrate when used as a fertilizer. ● *transitive verb Chem.* treat, combine, or impregnate with nitric acid. □ **ni·tra·tion** /-ˈtreɪʃən/ *noun* [French (as NITRE, -ATE[1])]

nitre /ˈnaɪtər/ *noun* (also esp. *US* **niter**) saltpetre, potassium nitrate. [Old French from Latin *nitrum* from Greek *nitron*, of Semitic origin]

ni·tric /ˈnaɪtrɪk/ *adjective* of or containing nitrogen, esp. in the quinquevalent state.

nitric acid *noun* a colourless corrosive poisonous liquid. Chem. formula: HNO_3.

nitric oxide *noun* a colourless toxic gas, involved in physiological processes in minute quantities, and forming nitrogen dioxide in air. Chem. formula: NO.

ni·tride /ˈnaɪtraɪd/ *noun* a binary compound of nitrogen with a more electropositive element.

nitri·fy /ˈnaɪtrɪˌfaɪ/ *transitive verb* (**-fies, -fied**) **1** impregnate with nitrogen. **2** convert (nitrogen, usu. in the form of ammonia) into nitrites or nitrates. □ **nitri·fi·ca·tion** *noun*

ni·trile /ˈnaɪtraɪl/ *noun Chem.* an organic compound consisting of an alkyl radical bound to a cyanide compound.

ni·trite /ˈnaɪtraɪt/ *noun* any salt or ester of nitrous acid.

nitro /ˈnaɪtroː/ *noun informal* nitroglycerine. [abbreviation]

Vowels: a cat ɑ arm e bed ɜr her ɜː deux ə ago ɪ sit i cosy iː feed ɒ hot ɔ pore ɔː no ʌ run ʊ put

nitro- /'nəitrəʊ/ *combining form* **1** of or containing nitric acid, nitre, or nitrogen. **2** made with or by use of any of these. **3** of or containing the monovalent -NO₂ group (*the nitro groups in TNT*). [Greek (as NITRE)]

nitro·ben·zene /ˌnəitrəʊ'benziːn/ *noun* a yellow oily liquid made by the nitration of benzene and used to make aniline etc.

nitro·cellu·lose /ˌnəitrəʊ'seljʊˌləʊs, -ˌləʊz/ *noun* a highly flammable material made by treating cellulose with concentrated nitric acid, used in the manufacture of explosives and celluloid. *Also called* CELLULOSE NITRATE.

nitro·gen /'nəitrədʒən/ *noun* a colourless odourless unreactive gaseous element that forms four-fifths of the earth's atmosphere and is an essential constituent of proteins, nucleic acids, and other biological molecules. Symbol: **N**; at. no.: 7. □ **nitro·gen·ous** /-'trɒdʒɪnəs/ *adjective* [French *nitrogène* (as NITRO-, -GEN)]

nitrogen cycle *noun* the interconversion of nitrogen and its compounds, usu. in the form of nitrates, in nature.

nitrogen dioxide *noun* a reddish brown poisonous gas. Chem. formula: NO₂.

nitrogen fixation *noun* a chemical process in which atmospheric nitrogen is assimilated into organic compounds in living organisms and hence into the nitrogen cycle. □ **nitrogen-fixing** *adjective*

nitro·glycer·ine /ˌnəitrəʊ'glɪsərɪn/ *noun* (also **nitro·glycer·in**) an explosive yellow liquid made by reacting glycerol with a mixture of concentrated sulphuric and nitric acids, used as an explosive and medically as a vasodilator.

nitro·sa·mine /nəi'trəʊsəmiːn, -'sæmiːn, -main/ *noun* any of a group of carcinogenic substances containing the chemical group :N·N:O.

ni·trous /'nəitrəs/ *adjective* of, like, or impregnated with nitrogen, esp. in the trivalent state.

nitrous acid *noun* a weak acid existing only in solution and in the gas phase. Chem. formula: HNO₂.

nitrous oxide *noun* a colourless gas used as an anaesthetic (= LAUGHING GAS) and as an aerosol propellant. Chem. formula: N₂O.

nitty-gritty *noun slang* the realities or practical details of a matter. [20th c.: origin uncertain]

nit·wit *noun informal* a stupid person. [perhaps from NIT + WIT[1]]

Niue /nɪ'uːeɪ/ an island territory in the S Pacific to the east of Tonga; pop. (est. 2002) 2,134; capital, Alofi. Niue is the largest coral island in the world.

NIV *abbreviation* NEW INTERNATIONAL VERSION.

Niver·nais /ˌniːver'neɪ/ a former duchy and province of central France. Its capital was the city of Nevers.

nix *slang* ● *noun* **1** nothing. **2** a denial or refusal. ● *transitive verb* **1** cancel. **2** reject. ● *adverb* no. [German, informal var. of *nichts* nothing]

Nixon, Rich·ard Mil·hous (1913–1994), US Republican politician, 37th president of the US 1969–74. He served as vice-president under Eisenhower (1953–61), and in his first term as president restored Sino-American diplomatic relations by his visit to China (1972), and initiated the withdrawal of US forces from Vietnam; elected for a second term (1972), he was soon implicated in the Watergate scandal and became the first president to resign from office, taking this action before impeachment proceedings began. □ **Nixon·ian** /-'səʊniən/ *adjective* **Nixon·ite** *noun & adjective*

Nizhni Novgorod /ˌniːʒnɪ 'nɒvgəˌrɒd/ a river port in European Russia on the Volga; pop. (est. 2002) 1,346,400. Between 1932 and 1991 it was named Gorky after the writer Maxim Gorky, who was born there.

Nizhni Tagil /ˌniːʒnɪ tə'giːl/ an industrial and metal-mining city in central Russia, in the Urals north of Yekaterinburg; pop. (est. 2002) 385,400.

NJ *abbreviation* New Jersey (also in official postal use).

Nkru·mah /əŋ'kruːmə/ **Kwame** (1909–72), Ghanaian leader, prime minister 1957–60, president 1960–66. He led the non-violent struggle for the Gold Coast's independence, declared Ghana a republic in 1960, and proclaimed himself president for life in 1964; his dictatorial methods eventually led to his overthrow in a military coup.

NKVD the secret police agency in the USSR responsible from 1934 for internal security and the labour prison camps. Mainly concerned with political offenders, it was notably used for Stalin's purges, and merged with the MVD in 1946. [Russian abbreviation, = People's Commissariat of Internal Affairs]

NL *abbreviation* **1** (in official postal use) Newfoundland and Labrador. **2** *Baseball* National League.

Nlaka'pamux /ˌənθləʊ'kɒpəm/ ● *noun* **1** a member of an Aboriginal people living near the Thompson River in the Fraser River Valley of BC.

Also called THOMPSON. **2** the Salishan language of this people. ● *adjective* of or relating to this people or their culture or language. [Nlaka'pamux, = 'people of the mighty canyon']

NLCS *abbreviation Baseball* National League Championship Series.

NLP *abbreviation* NEUROLINGUISTIC PROGRAMMING.

NM *abbreviation* New Mexico (in official postal use).

nm *abbreviation* **1** nanometre. **2** nautical mile.

NMR *abbreviation* nuclear magnetic resonance.

NNE *abbreviation* north-northeast.

NNW *abbreviation* north-northwest.

No¹ *symbol Chem.* the element nobelium.

No² *noun var. of* NOH.

No. *abbreviation* **1** number. **2** *US* North. [sense 1 from Latin *numero*, ablative of *numerus* number]

no¹ *adjective* **1** not any (*there is no excuse; no circumstances could justify it; no two of them are alike*). **2** not a, quite other than (*is no fool; is no part of my plan; caused no slight inconvenience*). **3** hardly any (*is no distance; did it in no time*). **4** used elliptically as a slogan, notice, etc., to forbid, reject, or deplore the thing specified (*no parking; no surrender*). □ **by no means** see MEANS. **no contest** see CONTEST. **no dice** see DICE. **no doubt** see DOUBT. **no end** see END. **no fair** see FAIR¹. **no great shakes** see SHAKE. **no joke** see JOKE. **no joy** see JOY *noun* 3. **no little** see LITTLE. **no man** no person, nobody. **no small** see SMALL. **no sweat** *informal* no bother, no trouble. **no two ways about it** (or **that**) *informal* there is no question; undoubtedly. **no way** (also **no way, José**) *informal* **1** it is impossible. **2** I will not agree etc. **3** you're kidding. **no whit** see WHIT. **no wonder** see WONDER. **... or no ...** regardless of the ... (*rain or no rain, I shall go out*). **there is no ...ing** it is impossible to ... (*there is no accounting for tastes; there was no mistaking what they meant*). [Middle English from *nān, nōn* NONE¹, originally only before consonants]

no² ● *interjection* equivalent to a negative sentence: the answer to your question is negative, your request or command will not be complied with, the statement made or course of action intended or conclusion arrived at is not correct or satisfactory, the negative statement made is correct. ● *adverb* **1** (foll. by *comparative*) by no amount; not at all (*no better than before*). **2** *Scot.* not (*will ye no come back again?*). ● *noun* (pl. **noes**) **1** an utterance of the word *no*. **2** a denial or refusal. **3** a negative vote. □ **is no more** has died or ceased to exist. **no can do** *informal* I am unable to do it. **the noes have it** the negative voters are in the majority. **no less** (often foll. by *than*) **1** as much (*gave me $50, no less; gave me no less than $50; is no less than a scandal; a no less fatal victory*). **2** as important (*no less a person than the prime minister*). **3** disputed no fewer (*no less than ten people have told me*). **no longer** not now or henceforth as formerly. **not take no for an answer** persist in spite of refusals. **or no** or not (*pleasant or no, it is true*). [Old English *nō, nā* from *ne* not + *ō, ā* ever]

NOAA *abbreviation* (in the US) National Oceanic and Atmospheric Administration.

no-account ● *adjective* unimportant, worthless. ● *noun* an unimportant or worthless person or thing.

Noah /'nəʊə/ *Bible* a Hebrew patriarch represented as tenth in descent from Adam. According to the story in Genesis he made the ark which saved his family and specimens of every animal from the flood sent by God to destroy the world, and his sons Ham, Shem, and Japheth were regarded as ancestors of all the races of humankind (Gen. 5–10).

Noah's ark *noun* **1** the ship in which Noah, his family, and the animals were saved. **2** an imitation of this as a child's toy.

nob¹ *noun esp. Brit. slang* a person of wealth or high social position. [originally Scots *knabb, nab*; 18th c., of unknown origin]

nob² *noun* **1** *slang* the head. **2** *Cdn* (*Nfld*) a round, usu. mint-flavoured hard candy. [perhaps var. of KNOB]

no-bake *attributive adjective* designating a recipe or food item (esp. a dessert) requiring no baking (*no-bake treat*).

nob·ble *transitive verb Brit. slang* **1** tamper with (a racehorse) to prevent its winning. **2** get hold of (money etc.) dishonestly. **3** catch (a criminal). **4** secure the support of or weaken (a person) esp. by underhand means. **5** seize, grab. [prob. = dial. *knobble, knubble* knock, beat, from KNOB]

Nobel¹ /nəʊ'bel/ **Al·fred Bern·hard** (1833–96), Swedish chemist and engineer. He invented dynamite as a substitute for the more dangerous nitroglycerine; his large fortune enabled him to endow the prizes that bear his name.

Nobel² /nəʊ'bel/ *noun* = NOBEL PRIZE.

Nobel·ist /nəʊ'belɪst/ *noun N Amer.* a winner of a Nobel Prize.

uː m**oo**d   ai m**y**   əi p**i**pe   au br**ow**n   ʌu h**ou**se   ei d**ay**   ɔi b**oy**   ã fr**an**glais   ã C**an**adien   ɔ̃ Br**ay**on   (*see over for consonants*)

nobel·ium /noʊˈbiːliəm/ *noun Chem.* an artificially produced radioactive transuranic metallic element. Symbol: **No**; at. no.: 102. [NOBEL[1] + -IUM]

Nobel Prize /ˈnoʊbel/ *noun* any of six international prizes awarded annually for physics, chemistry, physiology or medicine, literature, economics, and the promotion of peace. [NOBEL[1]]

no·bil·iary /nəˈbɪljəri/ *adjective* of the nobility. [French *nobiliaire* (as NOBLE)]

nobiliary particle *noun* a preposition forming part of a title of nobility (e.g. French *de*, German *von*).

no·bil·ity /noʊˈbɪlɪti/ *noun* (*pl.* **-ities**) **1** nobleness of character, mind, birth, or rank. **2** (*prec. by a, the*) a class of nobles, an aristocracy. [Old French *nobilité* or Latin *nobilitas* (as NOBLE)]

noble ● *adjective* (**nobler**, **nob·lest**) **1** belonging by rank, title, or birth to the aristocracy. **2** of excellent character; having lofty ideals; free from pettiness and meanness, magnanimous. **3** of imposing appearance, splendid, magnificent, stately. **4** (of a metal or chemical element) unreactive; inert. **5** excellent, admirable. ● *noun* **1** a nobleman or noblewoman. **2** *hist.* a former English gold coin first issued in 1351. □ **noble·ness** *noun* **nobly** *adverb* [Old French from Latin (g)*nobilis*, related to KNOW]

noble gas *noun* any gaseous element of a group that almost never combine with other elements.

noble·man *noun* (*pl.* **-men**) a man of noble rank or birth; an aristocrat.

noble metal *noun* a metal (e.g. gold, silver, or platinum) that resists chemical action, does not corrode or tarnish in air or water, and is not easily attacked by acids.

noble rot *noun* **1** the condition of grapes affected by the mould *Botrytis cinerea* (see BOTRYTIS). **2** the mould itself.

noble savage *noun* an idealized concept, prevalent esp. in Romantic literature, of an innately good humanity uncorrupted by exposure to civilization.

no·blesse oblige /noʊˈbles ɒˈbliːʒ/ *noun* the moral obligation incumbent upon rich or noble people to act generously and honourably. [French]

noble·woman *noun* (*pl.* **-women**) a woman of noble rank or birth.

no·body ● *pronoun* no person. ● *noun* (*pl.* **-ies**) a person of no importance, authority, or position. □ **like nobody's business** see BUSINESS. **nobody's fool** see FOOL[1].

no-brainer *noun* esp. *N Amer. informal* something that requires a minimum of thought or mental effort.

nock ● *noun* **1** a notch at either end of a bow for holding the string. **2 a** a notch at the butt-end of an arrow for receiving the bowstring. **b** a notched piece of metal or plastic etc. serving this purpose. ● *transitive verb* set (an arrow) on the string. [Middle English, perhaps = *nock* forward upper corner of some sails, from Middle Dutch *nocke*]

no-confidence motion *noun* a non-confidence motion.

noc·tam·bu·list /nɒkˈtambjʊlɪst/ *noun* a sleepwalker. □ **noc·tam·bu·lism** *noun* [Latin *nox noctis* night + *ambulare* walk]

noctilucent cloud *noun* a high-altitude cloud that is luminous at night, esp. in summer in high latitudes. [from Latin *nox, noct-* 'night' + *lucere* 'to shine' + -ENT]

noc·tule /ˈnɒktjuːl/ *noun* a large bat, *Nyctalus noctula*, of temperate and subtropical Eurasia and N Africa. [French from Italian *nottola* bat]

noc·turn /ˈnɒktɜːn/ *noun Catholicism* a part of matins originally said at night. [see NOCTURNAL]

noc·tur·nal /nɒkˈtɜːnəl/ *adjective* **1** of or relating to the night. **2** done at night. **3** active at night. □ **noc·tur·nal·ly** *adverb* [Late Latin *nocturnalis* from Latin *nocturnus* of the night, from *nox noctis* night]

nocturnal emission *noun* involuntary emission of semen during sleep.

noc·turne /ˈnɒktɜːn/ *noun* **1** *Music* a short composition of a romantic nature, usu. for piano. **2** a picture of a night scene. [French (as NOCTURN)]

nod ● *verb* (**nodded**, **nod·ding**) **1** *intransitive* incline one's head slightly and briefly in greeting, assent, or command. **2** *intransitive* let one's head fall forward in drowsiness; be drowsy. **3** *transitive* incline (one's head). **4** *transitive* signify (assent etc.) by a nod. **5** *intransitive* (of flowers, plumes, etc.) bend downwards and sway, or move up and down. **6** *intransitive* make a mistake due to a momentary lack of alertness or attention. ● *noun* **1** a nodding of the head. **2** an indication of approval, acceptance, or merit. **3** a passing or superficial reference, allusion, or acknowledgement (*a folk festival with a nod to the 1960s*). □ **get the nod** *N Amer. informal* be chosen or approved. **nod off** *informal* fall asleep. [Middle English *nodde*, of unknown origin]

nodal /ˈnoʊdəl/ *adjective* of or pertaining to a node or nodes.

nodding acquaintance *noun* (usu. foll. by *with*) a very slight acquaintance with a person or subject.

nod·dle *noun informal* the head. [Middle English *nodle*, of unknown origin]

noddy *noun* (*pl.* **-dies**) **1** a simpleton. **2** any of various tropical seabirds of the genus *Anous*, resembling terns. **3** *Cdn* (*Nfld*) the Atlantic fulmar, *Fulmaris glacialis glacialis*. **4** *Cdn* (*Nfld*) *derogatory* = BAYMAN 1a. [prob. from obsolete *noddy* foolish, which is perhaps from NOD]

node *noun* **1** *Bot.* **a** the part of a plant stem from which one or more leaves emerge. **b** a knob on a root or branch. **2** *Anat.* a natural swelling or bulge in an organ or part of the body. **3** *Astronomy* either of two points at which a planet's orbit intersects the plane of the ecliptic or the celestial equator. **4** *Physics* a point of minimum disturbance in a standing wave system. **5** *Math.* **a** a point at which a curve intersects itself. **b** a vertex in a graph. **6** a point in a computer network where information is received and distributed among various communication lines, such as telephone lines, optical fibres, and electric cables. **7** a central or connecting point. □ **nod·ical** *adjective* (in sense 3). [Latin *nodus* knot]

nod·ule /ˈnɒdjuːl/ *noun* **1** a small rounded lump of anything. **2** a small swelling or aggregation of cells, e.g. a small tumour, node, or ganglion, or a swelling on a root of a legume containing bacteria. □ **nodu·lar** *adjective* **nodu·lat·ed** *adjective* **nodu·la·tion** *noun* [Latin *nodulus* diminutive of *nodus* 'knot']

Noel /noʊˈel/ *noun* (also **Noël**, *archaic* **Nowel**, **Nowell**) Christmas. [French from Latin *natalis (dies)* 'day of birth']

noes *pl.* of NO[2] *noun*.

Noe·ther /ˈnɜːtər/ (**Ama·lie**) **Emmy** (1882–1935), German mathematician. She simplified and extended the work of her predecessors on the properties of rings, and inaugurated the modern period in algebraic geometry and abstract algebra. □ **Noe·ther·ian** *adjective*

no·etic /noʊˈetɪk, noʊˈiːtɪk/ *adjective* **1** of the intellect. **2** purely intellectual or abstract. **3** given to intellectual speculation. [Greek *noētikos* from *noētos* intellectual, from *noeō* apprehend]

no-fault *attributive adjective* esp. *N Amer.* **1** (of automobile insurance) valid regardless of the allocation of blame for an accident etc. **2** not assigning responsibility to either party (*a no-fault divorce*).

no-fly zone *noun* an area where esp. military aircraft are forbidden to fly.

Nofre·tete see NEFERTITI.

no-frills *adjective* **1** providing only the strict minimum necessary (*no-frills flights*). **2** lacking ornament or embellishment.

nog *noun* = EGGNOG. [17th c.: origin unknown]

nog·gin *noun* **1** *informal* the head. **2** a small mug. **3** a small measure, usu. ¼ pint, of hard liquor. [17th c.: origin unknown]

no go ● *noun* **1** a project, proposal, etc. that cannot proceed. **2** an athlete who cannot play, esp. because of injury. ● *adjective* impossible. ● *interjection* indicating impossibility, inadvisability, etc.

no-go area *noun* (also **no-go zone**) an area forbidden to unauthorized people.

no-good *informal* ● *attributive adjective* useless. ● *noun* a useless person or thing.

no·good·nik *noun slang* a no-good person.

No·guchi /noʊˈɡuːtʃi/ **Hi·deyo** (born Noguchi Seisaku) (1876–1928), Japanese-born US bacteriologist, who is noted for his research into the causes and treatment of syphilis and yellow fever.

Noh (also **No**) traditional Japanese drama with dance and song, evolved from Shinto rites. [Japanese *nō*]

no-hitter *noun Baseball* a game in which a team's pitchers yield no hits. □ **no-hit** *adjective*

no-holds-barred *adjective* with all restrictions relaxed.

no-hoper *noun slang* a useless person; a person who has no chance of succeeding.

nohow *adverb N Amer.* in no way; by no means. ¶ Not used in standard English.

noir /nwɑːr/ ● *adjective* having the characteristics of film noir. ● *noun* film noir as a genre. □ **noir·ish** *adjective* [French]

noise ● *noun* **1** a sound, esp. a loud or unpleasant or undesired one. **2** a series of loud sounds, esp. shouts; a confused sound of voices and movements. **3 a** irregular fluctuations accompanying a transmitted signal but not relevant to it. **b** *Computing* a signal that interrupts a program, usu. causing an error. **4** (in *pl.*) remarks expressing a specified feeling, which may or may not be genuine (*made sympathetic noises; made all the right noises*). ● **verb 1** *transitive* (usu. in *passive*) make public; spread abroad (a person's fame or a fact). **2** *intransitive archaic* make much noise. □ **make noises** (usu. foll. by *about*) speak indirectly about one's attitude or intentions (*management is making noises about layoffs*). **noises off** sounds made offstage to be heard by the audience of a play. [Old French, = outcry, disturbance, from Latin *nausea*: see NAUSEA]

noise·less *adjective* **1** silent. **2** making no avoidable noise.
□ **noise·less·ly** *adverb* **noise·less·ness** *noun*

noise·maker *noun* a device for making a loud noise at a party, celebration, etc.

noise pollution *noun* harmful or annoying noise in public places.

noi·sette /nwɒˈzet/ *noun* a small round piece of meat etc. [French, diminutive of *noix* nut]

noi·some /ˈnɔɪsəm/ *adjective literary* **1** harmful, noxious. **2** evil-smelling. **3** objectionable, offensive. □ **noi·some·ness** *noun* [Middle English from obsolete *noy* from ANNOY]

noisy *adjective* (**nois·i·er**, **nois·i·est**) **1** full of or attended with noise. **2** making or given to making much noise. **3** clamorous, turbulent.
□ **nois·i·ly** *adverb* **nois·i·ness** *noun*

Nok /nɒk/ *noun* an ancient civilization of northern Nigeria *c*.400 BC–AD 200, characterized by the production of distinctive terracotta figurines and significant for its development of ironworking.

no·lens vo·lens /ˌnoʊlenz ˈvoʊlenz/ *adverb literary* willy-nilly, perforce. [Latin participles, = unwilling, willing]

nolle pro·se·qui /ˌnɒli ˈprɒsɪˌkwaɪ/ *noun Law* **1** the relinquishment by a plaintiff or prosecutor of all or part of a suit. **2** the entry of this on record. [Latin, = refuse to pursue]

no-load *adjective N Amer.* (of a mutual fund share) sold without a commission being charged to the buyer.

nolo con·ten·dere /ˈnoʊloʊ kɒnˈtendəreɪ/ *noun US Law* a plea by which a defendant in a criminal prosecution accepts conviction as in the case of a plea of guilty but does not admit guilt. [Latin, = 'I do not wish to contend']

nom. *abbreviation* nominal.

no·mad /ˈnoʊmad/ ● *noun* **1** a member of a people roaming from place to place for food or fresh pasture. **2** a wanderer. ● *adjective* **1** living as a nomad. **2** wandering. □ **no·mad·ic** /-ˈmadɪk/ *adjective* **no·mad·ic·al·ly** /-ˈmadɪkli/ *adverb* **nomad·ism** *noun* [Latin *nomas nomad-* from Greek *nomas -ados* from *nemō* to pasture]

no man's land *noun* **1** *Military* the space between two opposing armies. **2** an area not assigned to any owner. **3** an area not clearly belonging to any one subject etc.

nom de /ˌnɒm də, ˈnɔ̃ də/ *noun jocular* an assumed name in a specified field or activity (*her nom de Net was Jungle Goddess*). [after NOM DE PLUME]

nom de guerre /ˌnɒm də ˈger, nɔ̃ -/ *noun* (pl. **noms de guerre** *pronunc.* same) an assumed name under which a person fights, plays, writes, etc. [French, = war name]

nom de plume /ˌnɒm də ˈpluːm, nɔ̃ -/ *noun* (pl. **noms de plume** *pronunc.* same) an assumed name under which a person writes. [formed in English of French words, = pen name, after NOM DE GUERRE]

Nome /noʊm/ a city in W Alaska, on the south coast of the Seward Peninsula. Founded in 1896 as a gold-mining camp, it became a centre of the Alaskan gold rush at the turn of the century.

nom·en /ˈnoʊmen/ *noun* an ancient Roman's second name, indicating the gens, as in Marcus *Tullius* Cicero. [Latin, = name]

nom·en·cla·ture /ˈnoʊmənˌkleɪtʃər, ˈnɒm-, noʊˈmenklətʃər/ *noun* a set or system of names, esp. as used in a particular science etc.
□ **nom·en·cla·tur·al** *adjective* [Latin *nomenclatura* from *nomen* + *calare* call]

nom·en·kla·tura /ˌnoʊmənkləˈtʊrə/ *noun* (in the former Soviet Union) a select list or group of people from whom upper-level government positions were filled. [Russian from Latin *nomenclatura*: see NOMENCLATURE]

Nomex *noun proprietary* a type of artificial fibre which is exceptionally heat-resistant and fire-resistant.

nom·in·al /ˈnɒmɪnəl/ *adjective* **1** existing in name only; not real or actual (*nominal and real prices; nominal ruler*). **2** (of a sum of money, rent, etc.) virtually nothing; much below the actual value of a thing. **3** of or in names (*nominal and essential distinctions*). **4** consisting of or giving the names (*nominal list of officers*). **5** of or as or like a noun. □ **nom·in·al·ly** *adverb* [Latin *nominalis* from *nomen -inis* name]

nom·in·al·ism /ˈnɒmɪnəˌlɪzəm/ *noun Philos.* the doctrine that universals or abstract concepts are mere names without any corresponding reality (*opp.* REALISM). □ **nom·in·al·ist** *noun* **nom·in·al·is·tic** *adjective*

nom·in·al·ize /ˈnɒmɪnəˌlaɪz/ *transitive verb* (also esp. *Brit.* **-ise**) form a noun from (a verb, adjective, etc.), e.g. *output, truth,* from *put out, true.* □ **nom·in·al·iz·a·tion** *noun*

nominal value *noun* the face value (of a coin, shares, etc.).

nom·in·ate /ˈnɒmɪˌneɪt/ *transitive verb* **1 a** propose (a candidate) for election. **b** propose (a person or thing) formally for an honour, office, or task (*the film was nominated for six Genies*). **2** appoint to an office (*a board of six nominated and six elected members*). **3** name or appoint (a date or place). **4** mention by name. **5** call by the name of, designate. □ **nom·in·ator** *noun* [Latin *nominare nominat-* (as NOMINAL)]

nom·in·a·tion /ˌnɒmɪˈneɪʃən/ *noun* **1** the act or an instance of nominating; the state of being nominated. **2** the right of nominating for an appointment (*have a nomination at your disposal*).

nomination day *noun Cdn* a day on which nominations for esp. municipal offices are closed.

nom·in·a·tive /ˈnɒmɪnətɪv/ ● *noun Grammar* the case of nouns, pronouns, and adjectives, expressing the subject of a verb. ● *adjective* **1** *Grammar* of or in this case. **2** /-ˈneɪtɪv/ of, or appointed by, nomination (as distinct from election). [Latin *nominativus* (as NOMINATE)]

nom·inee /ˌnɒmɪˈniː/ *noun* **1 a** a person who is nominated for an office. **b** a person, creative work, etc. nominated for an award. **2** *Commerce* a person (not necessarily the owner) in whose name a stock etc. is registered. [NOMINATE]

nomo·gram /ˈnɒməˌgram, ˈnoʊm-/ *noun* (also **nomo·graph** /-ˌgraf/) a graphical presentation of relations between quantities whereby the value of one may be found by simple geometrical construction (e.g. drawing a straight line) from those of others. □ **nomo·graph·ic** *adjective* **nomo·graph·ic·al·ly** *adverb* **nom·og·raphy** *noun* [Greek *nomo-* from *nomos* law + -GRAM]

no more ● *noun* nothing further (*have no more to say; want no more of it*). ● *adjective* not any more (*no more wine?*). ● *adverb* **1** no longer. **2** never again. **3** to no greater extent (*could no more do it than fly in the air*). **4** just as little, neither (*you did not come, and no more did she*).

nomo·thet·ic /ˌnɒməˈθetɪk, ˌnoʊm-/ *adjective* of or relating to the study or discovery of general scientific laws. [obsolete *nomothete* legislator, from Greek *nomothetēs*]

-nomy *combining form* denoting an area of knowledge or the laws governing it (*aeronomy; economy*). [Greek *-nomia*, related to *nomos* 'law' and *nemein* 'distribute']

non- *prefix* giving the negative sense of words with which it is combined, esp.: **1** not doing or having or involved with (*non-attendance; nonpayment; non-productive*). **2 a** not of the kind or class described (*non-alcoholic; non-member; non-event*). **b** forming terms used adjectivally (*non-union; non-party*). **3** a lack of. **4** (with adverbs) not in the way described (*non-aggressively*). **5** forming adjectives from verbs, meaning 'that does not' or 'that is not meant to (or to be)' (*non-skid*). **6** used to form a neutral negative sense when a form in *in-* or *un-* has a special sense or (usu. unfavourable) connotation (*non-controversial; non-effective; non-human*). ¶ The number of words that can be formed with this prefix is unlimited; consequently only a selection, considered the most current or semantically noteworthy, can be given here. [Latin *non* not]

nona- /ˈnɒnə/ *combining form* nine. [Latin from *nonus* ninth]

non-Aborig·in·al ● *adjective* (of a person, community, etc.) not Aboriginal. ● *noun* a non-Aboriginal person.

non-addict·ive *adjective* (of a drug, habit, etc.) not causing addiction.

non-age /ˈnoʊnɪdʒ, ˈnɒn-/ *noun* **1** *hist.* the state of being under full legal age, minority. **2** a period of immaturity. [Old French *nonage* (as NON-, AGE)]

nona·gen·ar·ian /ˌnɒnədʒəˈneriən, ˌnoʊn-/ ● *noun* a person from 90 to 99 years old. ● *adjective* of this age. [Latin *nonagenarius* from *nonageni* distributive of *nonaginta* ninety]

non-aggres·sion *noun* a lack of or restraint from aggression (often *attributive*: *non-aggression pact*). □ **non-aggres·sive** *adjective* **non-aggres·sive·ly** *adverb*

nona·gon /ˈnɒnəgɒn/ *noun* a plane figure with nine sides and angles. [Latin *nonus* ninth, after HEXAGON]

non-alcohol·ic *adjective & noun* (of a drink etc.) not containing alcohol.

non-aligned *adjective* (of a country etc.) not aligned with another (esp. major) power. □ **non-align·ment** *noun*

non-allerg·ic *adjective* not causing allergy or an allergic reaction.

no-name ● *adjective* (*attributive*) **1** designating a person or thing that is not well known or famous (*a movie starring no-name actors*). **2** not having a well-known brand name (*no-name computers*). ● *noun* a no-name person or thing (*a team of no-names*).

non-A, non-B hepatitis *noun* = HEPATITIS C.

non-appear·ance *noun* failure to appear or be present.

non·ary /ˈnoːnɜri/ ● *adjective Math.* (of a scale of notation) having nine as its base. ● *noun* (*pl.* **-aries**) a group of nine. [Latin *nonus* ninth]

non-attend·ance *noun* failure to attend.

non-believ·er *noun* a person who does not believe or has no (esp. religious) faith.

non·bel·liger·ency *noun* a lack of belligerency.

non·bel·liger·ent ● *adjective* not engaged in hostilities. ● *noun* a nonbelligerent nation, state, etc.

non-binding *adjective* (of arbitration, a vote, an agreement, etc.) not legally binding on any of the parties involved.

non-biodegrad·able *adjective* not able to be decomposed by bacteria or other living organisms. □ **non-biodegrad·abil·ity** *noun*

non-biolog·ic·al *adjective* not relating to biology or living organisms.

non-Canadian ● *adjective* not Canadian. ● *noun* a person who is not a Canadian.

non-capital *adjective* **1** (of an offence) not punishable by death. **2** not relating to capital.

non-Catholic ● *adjective* not Roman Catholic. ● *noun* a non-Catholic person.

nonce /nɒns/ *noun* (*attributive*) designating a word or phrase etc. coined for one specific occasion (*nonce word*; *nonce formation*). □ **for the nonce** for the time being; for the present occasion. [Middle English *than anes* = for the one, altered by wrong division (compare NEWT)]

non·cha·lant /ˈnɒnʃəˌlɒnt, ˈnɒnʃəˌlɒnt, -lənt/ *adjective* calm and casual, unmoved, unexcited, indifferent. □ **non·cha·lance** *noun* **non·cha·lant·ly** *adverb* [French, part. of *nonchaloir* from *chaloir* be concerned]

non-Christian ● *adjective* not Christian. ● *noun* a non-Christian person.

non-citizen *noun* a person who is not a citizen (of a particular country, region, etc.).

non-com *noun informal* a non-commissioned officer. [abbreviation]

non-combat·ant /nɒnˈkɒmˈbatənt, nɒnkəm-, -ˈkɒmbatənt, -ˈkʌm-/ *noun* **1** a member of a military force who is not engaged in combat, e.g. a doctor, chaplain, etc. **2** a person not fighting in a war, esp. a civilian.

non-commer·cial *adjective* not commercial (*approved for non-commercial use*).

non-commis·sioned *adjective Military* (of an officer) not holding a commission.

non·com·mit·tal /ˌnɒnkəˈmɪtəl/ *adjective* avoiding commitment to a definite opinion or course of action. □ **non·com·mit·tal·ly** *adverb*

non-commun·ist (also **non-Commun·ist** with reference to a particular party) ● *adjective* not advocating or practising communism. ● *noun* a non-communist person.

non-competi·tive *adjective* not competitive.

non-compli·ance *noun* failure to comply; a lack of compliance. □ **non-compli·ant** *adjective*

non compos mentis /ˌnɒn kɒmpəs ˈmentɪs/ *adjective* (also **non compos**) not in one's right mind. [Latin, = not having control of one's mind]

non-conduct·or *noun* a substance that does not conduct heat or electricity. □ **non-conduct·ing** *adjective* **non-conduct·ive** *adjective*

non-confidence *noun Cdn* a lack of majority support for a government, policy, etc. expressed by a legislature (also *attributive: a non-confidence motion*).

non·con·form·ist ● *noun* **1** a person who does not conform to a prevailing principle. **2** (usu. **Nonconformist**) (in the United Kingdom) a Protestant belonging to a denomination other than the established church (in England and Wales the Church of England, in Scotland the Church of Scotland). ● *adjective* of or relating to a nonconformist or to Nonconformism. □ **non·con·form·ism** *noun* **Non·con·form·ism** *noun*

non·con·form·ity *noun* **1 a** nonconformists or (**Nonconformity**) Nonconformists as a body. **b** the principles or practice of nonconformists or (**Nonconformity**) of Nonconformists. **2** (usu. foll. by *to*) failure to conform to a rule etc. **3** lack of correspondence between things.

non-contribu·tory *adjective* **1** not contributing. **2** (esp. of a pension plan) not supported by contributions made by the beneficiary.

non-contro·ver·sial *adjective* not controversial. ¶ Neutral in sense: see NON- 6, UNCONTROVERSIAL.

non-custod·ial *adjective* **1** (of a parent) not having custody of a child or children, e.g. after a divorce. **2** (of a criminal sentence) served outside of a traditional correctional institution.

non-dairy *adjective* containing no milk products (*a non-dairy creamer*).

non-delivery *noun* failure to deliver.

non-denomin·a·tion·al *adjective* not restricted as regards religious denomination.

non·de·script /ˈnɒndɪskrɪpt/ *adjective* lacking distinctive characteristics; uninteresting, dull. □ **non·de·script·ly** *adverb* **non·de·script·ness** *noun* [NON- + *descript* described, from Latin *descriptus* (as DESCRIBE)]

non-destruc·tive *adjective* that does not involve destruction or damage.

non-drinker *noun* a person who does not drink alcoholic liquor.

non-drowsy *adjective* (of a medication) that does not cause drowsiness.

none¹ ● *pronoun* **1** (foll. by *of*) **a** not any of (*none of this concerns me; none of them have found it; none of your impudence!*). **b** not any one of (*none of them has come*). ¶ The verb following none in this sense can be singular or plural according to the sense. **2 a** no persons (*none but fools have ever believed it*). **b** no person (*none can tell*). ● *adjective* (usu. with a preceding noun implied) **1** no; not any (*you have money and I have none; would rather have a bad reputation than none at all*). **2** not to be counted in a specified class (*my understanding is none of the clearest; if a linguist is wanted, I am none*). ● *adverb* (foll. by *the* + comparative, or *so*, *too*) by no amount; not at all (*am none the wiser; are none too fond of it*). □ **none other** (usu. foll. by *than*) no other person. [Old English *nān* from *ne* not + *ān* ONE]

none² /noːn/ *noun* (also in *pl.*) **1** the office of the fifth of the canonical hours of prayer, originally said at the ninth hour (3 p.m.). **2** this hour. [Latin *nona* fem. sing. of *nonus* ninth: compare NOON]

non·entity /nɒnˈentɪti/ *noun* (*pl.* **-ties**) **1** a person or thing of no importance. **2 a** a non-existence. **b** a non-existent thing, a figment. [medieval Latin *nonentitas* non-existence]

nones /noːnz/ *plural noun* in the ancient Roman calendar, the ninth day before the ides by inclusive reckoning, i.e. the 7th day of March, May, July, October, the 5th of other months. [Old French *nones* from Latin *nonae* fem. pl. of *nonus* ninth]

non-essential ● *adjective* not essential. ¶ Neutral in sense: see NON- 6, INESSENTIAL. ● *noun* a non-essential thing.

none·such *var.* of NONSUCH.

no·net /noːˈnet/ *noun* **1** *Music* **a** a composition for nine voices or instruments. **b** the performers of such a piece. **2** a group of nine. [Italian *nonetto* from *nono* ninth, from Latin *nonus*]

none·the·less *adverb* (also **none the less**) nevertheless.

non-Euclid·ean *adjective* denying or going beyond Euclidean principles in geometry.

non-European ● *adjective* not European. ● *noun* a non-European person.

non-event *noun* an unimportant or anticlimactic occurrence.

non-exist·ent *adjective* not existing. □ **non-exist·ence** *noun*

non-fat *adjective* (of a food) containing little or no fat (*non-fat yogourt*).

non-feas·ance /nɒnˈfiːzəns/ *noun* failure to perform an act required by law. [NON-: see MISFEASANCE]

non-ferrous *adjective* (of a metal) other than iron or steel.

non-fiction *noun* literary work other than fiction, including biography and reference books. □ **non-fiction·al** *adjective*

non-flammable *adjective* not flammable. ¶ See Usage Note at FLAMMABLE.

non-flower·ing *adjective* (of a plant) reproducing by means of spores rather than with flowers and seeds, as in ferns, mosses, algae, etc.

non-fulfill·ment *noun* failure to fulfill (an obligation).

non-function·al *adjective* **1** not having a function. **2** not functioning; out of order.

non-govern·ment·al *adjective* not belonging to or associated with a government.

non-Hodgkin's lymphoma *noun* a form of malignant lymphoma distinguished from Hodgkin's disease only by the absence of binucleate giant cells.

non-human ● *adjective* (of a being) not human. ● *noun* a non-human being. ¶ Neutral in sense: see NON- 6, INHUMAN, UNHUMAN.

non-import *noun Cdn Football* a player who trained only in Canada or who lived in Canada for five years before the age of fifteen.

Vowels: a *cat* ɑ *arm* e *bed* ɜr *her* ɜː *deux* ə *ago* ɪ *sit* i *cosy* iː *feed* ɒ *hot* ɔ *pore* oː *no* ʌ *run* ʊ *put*

non-infectious *adjective* (of a disease) not infectious.

non-insulin-dependent *adjective* relating to or denoting a type of diabetes in which there is some insulin secretion. Such diabetes typically develops in adulthood and can frequently be managed by diet and hypoglycemic agents.

non-interfer·ence *noun* a lack of interference.

non-interven·tion *noun* the principle or practice of not becoming involved in others' affairs, esp. by one country in regard to another. □ **non-interven·tion·ist** *adjective & noun*

non-invasive *adjective* **1** (of a medical procedure) not requiring incision into the body or the removal of tissue. **2** (of an infection etc.) not tending to spread.

non-issue *noun* something that is of little or no importance (*the debate was a non-issue*).

non-Jew *noun* a person who is not Jewish. □ **non-Jewish** *adjective*

non-judgment·al *adjective* not judgmental; avoiding moral judgments.

non-jury *adjective* (of a trial) without a jury.

non-linear *adjective* not linear; not pertaining to, involving, or arranged in a straight line.

non-literary *adjective* (of writing, a text, etc.) not literary in character.

non-literate *adjective* (of a person or culture etc.) having no written language.

non·logic·al *adjective* not involving logic. ¶ Neutral in sense: *see* NON-6, ILLOGICAL. □ **non·logic·al·ly** *adverb*

non-magnet·ic *adjective* (of a substance) not magnetic.

non-member *noun* a person who is not a member (of a particular association, club, etc.). □ **non-member·ship** *noun*

non-metal *adjective* not made of metal. □ **non-metal·lic** *adjective*

non-militant *adjective* not militant.

non-military *adjective* not military; not involving armed forces; civilian.

non-moral *adjective* not concerned with morality. ¶ Neutral in sense: *see* NON-6, AMORAL, IMMORAL.

non-native ● *adjective* **1** (of a person, plant, or animal) not indigenous or native to a particular place. **2** (of a speaker) not having spoken the language in question from early childhood. ● *noun* a non-native person.

non-natural *adjective* not involving natural means or processes. ¶ Neutral in sense: *see* NON-6, UNNATURAL.

non-negoti·able *adjective* that cannot be negotiated.

non-nuclear *adjective* **1** not involving nuclei or nuclear energy. **2** (of a country etc.) not having nuclear weapons.

no-no *noun* (pl. **-nos**) *informal* something that is not possible or acceptable.

non-object·ive *adjective* **1** not objective. **2** *Art* abstract.

non-observ·ance *noun* failure to observe (esp. an agreement, requirement, etc.).

no-nonsense *adjective* serious, sensible; without flippancy.

non-operation·al *adjective* **1** that does not operate. **2** out of order.

non-organic *adjective* not organic. ¶ Neutral in sense: *see* NON-6, INORGANIC.

non·par·eil /ˌnɒnpəˈreɪ, -aɪ/ ● *adjective* unrivalled or unique. ● *noun* such a person or thing. [French from *pareil* equal, from popular Latin *pariculus* diminutive of Latin *par*]

non-partisan *adjective* not partisan.

non-party *adjective* independent of political parties.

non·pay·ment *noun* failure to pay; a lack of payment.

non-penetra·tive *adjective* (of sexual activity) in which penetration does not take place.

non-perform·ing *adjective* (of an investment, loan, etc.) producing no income.

non-perishable ● *adjective* not subject to significant deterioration or quality when stored without refrigeration etc. ● *noun* a product, esp. a food, of this description.

non-person *noun* a person regarded as non-existent or insignificant (compare UNPERSON).

non-person·al *adjective* not personal. ¶ Neutral in sense: *see* NON-6, IMPERSONAL.

non-physic·al *adjective* not physical.

non·plussed *adjective* (also *US* **non·plused**) **1** perplexed. **2** *N Amer.* unfazed. [Latin *non plus* not more]

non-poison·ous *adjective* (of a substance, plant, etc.) not poisonous.

non-politic·al *adjective* not political; not involved in politics.

non-porous *adjective* (of a substance) not porous.

non-prescrip·tion *adjective* (of medication) available without a prescription.

non-product·ive *adjective* not productive. ¶ Neutral in sense: *see* NON-6, UNPRODUCTIVE. □ **non-product·ive·ly** *adverb*

non-profes·sion·al ● *adjective* not professional (esp. in status). ¶ Neutral in sense: *see* NON-6, UNPROFESSIONAL. ● *noun* a non-professional person.

non-profit ● *adjective* (of an organization, institution, event, etc.) not involving or making a profit. ● *noun* a non-profit organization.

non-prolifer·a·tion *noun* the prevention of an increase in something, esp. possession of nuclear weapons (also *attributive*: *nuclear non-proliferation treaty*).

non-racial *adjective* not involving race or racial factors.

non-react·ive *adjective* (of a substance, container, etc.) that does not react or cause a reaction.

non-reader *noun* a person who cannot or does not read.

non-refund·able *adjective* that cannot be refunded.

non-renew·able *adjective* (esp. of a resource) not renewable.

non-resident ● *adjective* (of a person) not residing in a particular place. ● *noun* a non-resident person. □ **non-residence** *noun* **non-residen·tial** *adjective*

non·resist·ance *noun* failure to resist; a lack of resistance. □ **non·resist·ant** *adjective*

non-restrict·ive *adjective* *Grammar* (of a clause or phrase) not delimiting the meaning of a reference of a modified noun phrase or element. ¶ In the phrase 'Peter, who is my brother', 'who is my brother' is a non-restrictive clause; it is set off by commas; the subject it modifies has already been defined, that is we already know which Peter we are talking about, and the phrase just adds some further descriptive information about him.

non-return·able *adjective* that may or need or will not be returned.

non-scientif·ic *adjective* not involving science or scientific methods. ¶ Neutral in sense: *see* NON-6, UNSCIENTIFIC. □ **non-scientist** *noun*

non-sectar·ian *adjective* not sectarian.

non·sense *noun* **1** spoken or written words that have no meaning, or make no sense. **2** foolish talk, ideas, etc. **3** unacceptable behaviour (*she tolerates a lot of nonsense from her staff*). **4** (often *attributive*) a form of literature meant to amuse by absurdity (*nonsense verse*). □ **non·sens·ical** *adjective* **non·sens·ical·ity** *noun* (pl. **-ities**). **non·sens·ical·ly** *adverb*

non sequi·tur /nɒn ˈsɛkwɪtər/ *noun* **1** a conclusion that does not logically follow from the premises. **2** a remark, response, etc. not logically following from what has gone before. [Latin, = it does not follow]

non-sexist *adjective* (of language, an attitude, etc.) not sexist.

non-sexual *adjective* not based on or involving sex. □ **non-sexual·ly** *adverb*

non-skid *adjective* **1** that does not skid. **2** that inhibits skidding.

non-slip *adjective* **1** that does not slip. **2** that inhibits slipping.

non-smoker *noun* a person who does not smoke. □ **non-smoking** *adjective & noun*

non-special·ist *noun* a person who is not a specialist (in a particular subject).

non-specif·ic *adjective* that cannot be specified.

non-standard *adjective* **1** not standard. **2** (of language) containing features which are widely used but generally considered incorrect.

non-starter *noun* **1** a person or animal that does not start in a race. **2** *informal* a person or thing that is unlikely to succeed or be effective.

non-status *adjective* (in Canada) designating a person of Indian ancestry who is not registered as an Indian under the Indian Act.

non-steroid·al *adjective* of or relating to a drug etc. that is not a steroid but which has similar effects.

non-stick *adjective* **1** that does not stick. **2** that does not allow things to stick to it.

non-stop ● *adjective* **1** (of a train, flight, journey, etc.) without any stops (*a non-stop flight to Victoria*). **2** without any breaks or pauses (*a non-stop meeting*). ● *adverb* without stopping or pausing (*cried non-stop for three hours*). ● *noun* a non-stop train, flight, etc.

non·such /ˈnʌnsʌtʃ/ *noun* (also **none·such**) a person or thing that is unrivalled, a paragon. [NONE[1] + SUCH, usu. now assimilated to NON-]

non-surgical *adjective* (of a medical procedure) performed without surgery (*a non-surgical treatment for varicose veins*).

non-swimmer *noun* a person who cannot swim.

non-tariff barrier *noun* something, such as a system of grants to domestic manufacturers, that has the effect of limiting imports without the use of tariffs.

non-techni·cal *adjective* **1** not technical. **2** without technical knowledge.

non-toxic *adjective* not toxic.

non-traditional *adjective* not traditional.

non-transfer·able *adjective* that may not be transferred.

non-treaty *adjective* designating status or non-status Indian people who have not signed a treaty with the Canadian government.

non-U *adjective Brit. informal* not characteristic of the upper class. [NON- + U²]

non-uniform *adjective* not uniform.

non-union *adjective* **1** not belonging to a trade union. **2** not done or produced by members of a trade union. □ **non-union·ized** *adjective*

non-use *noun* failure to use. □ **non-user** *noun*

non-verbal *adjective* not involving words or speech. □ **non-verbal·ly** *adverb*

non-vintage *adjective* (of wine etc.) not vintage.

non-violence *noun* the avoidance of violence, esp. as a principle. □ **non-violent** *adjective* **non-violent·ly** *adverb*

non-volatile *adjective* (esp. of a substance) not volatile.

non-voting *adjective* not having or using a vote. □ **non-voter** *noun*

non-white ● *adjective* **1** (of a person) not white. **2** of or relating to non-white people. ● *noun* a non-white person.

non-word *noun* an unrecorded or unused word.

noo·dle¹ *noun* **1** a thin, flat strip of pasta used in soups etc. **2** (also **pool noodle**) a long solid cylinder of polystyrene foam, used as a flotation toy. [German *Nudel*]

noo·dle² *noun* (**noo·dled**, **nood·ling**) *informal* **1** a foolish person. **2** the head (*use your noodle!*). [18th c.: origin unknown]

noo·dle³ *intransitive verb* **1** improvise or play esp. jazz music in a casual or desultory manner. **2** do or say something in an unproductive or undirected way (*I wish he'd stop noodling around and get to work*). □ **nood·ling** *noun* [origin unknown]

noodle house *noun* an Oriental restaurant serving noodle dishes.

noog·ie /ˈnʊgi/ *noun slang* the act or an instance of rubbing esp. a person's head with one's knuckles, either as a prank or to express affection. [origin unknown, perhaps diminutive of KNUCKLE]

nook /nʊk/ *noun* **1** a corner or recess; a secluded place. **2** a small or inaccessible place (*searched every nook and cranny*). [Middle English *nok(e)* corner, of unknown origin]

nook·ie /ˈnʊki/ *noun* (also **nooky**) *slang* sexual activity. [20th c.: perhaps from NOOK]

noon *noun* twelve o'clock in the day, midday. [Old English *nōn* from Latin *nona* (*hora*) ninth hour: originally = 3 p.m. (compare NONE²)]

noon·day *noun* midday (also *attributive: noonday meal*).

no one *noun* (also **no-one**) no person; nobody.

noon hour *noun* the time around midday when students, workers, etc. are given a lunch break.

noon·tide *noun archaic* noontime.

noon·time *noun* midday (also *attributive: noontime concert*).

noose /nuːs/ ● *noun* **1** a loop with a running knot, tightening as the rope or wire is pulled, esp. in a snare, lasso, or hangman's halter. **2** a snare or bond. ● *transitive verb* **1** catch with or enclose in a noose, ensnare. **2 a** make a noose on (a cord). **b** (often foll. by *round*) arrange (a cord) in a noose. □ **put one's head in a noose** bring about one's own downfall. [perhaps from Old French *no(u)s* from Latin *nodus* knot]

Noot·ka /ˈnuːtkə/ *noun* = NUU-CHAH-NULTH. □ **Noot·kan** *adjective* [NOOTKA SOUND]

Noot·ka Sound /ˈnuːtkə/ an inlet of the N Pacific, situated on the western coast of Vancouver Island, northwest of Clayoquot Sound. It was the site of the Nootka Sound Controversy (1789–94), in which Britain contested Spain's claim to sole right of trade, settlement and navigation along the northwest coast of N America and in the Pacific. The controversy was settled in Britain's favour, i.e. each nation was granted equal right to the area.

no·otrop·ic /ˌnoːəˈtrɒpɪk/ ● *adjective* (of a drug) used to enhance memory or other cognitive functions. ● *noun* a drug of this kind. [French *nootrope* from Greek *noos* 'mind' + *tropē* 'turning' + -IC]

no·pal /ˈnoːpəl/ *noun* any American cactus of the genus *Nopalea*, esp. *N. cochinellifera* grown in plantations for breeding cochineal. [French & Spanish from Nahuatl *nopalli* cactus]

nope *interjection informal* = NO² *interjection* 1. [NO²]

no place *adverb N Amer.* nowhere.

nor *conjunction* **1** and not; and not either (*neither one thing nor the other; not a man nor a child was to be seen; I said I had not seen it, nor had I; all that is true, nor must we forget ...; can neither read nor write*). **2** and no more; neither (*'I cannot go' — 'Nor can I'*). □ **nor ... nor ...** *literary* or *archaic* neither ... nor ... [Middle English, contraction from obsolete *nother* from Old English *nawther*, *nāhwæther* (as NO², WHETHER)]

nor- *prefix* **1** denoting the contraction of a chain or ring of carbon atoms by one methylene group, or the replacement of one or (esp. in terpenes) all the (methyl) side chains by hydrogen atoms (*noradrenalin*). **2** denoting a normal (unbranched) isomer of a compound. [abbreviation of NORMAL]

nor' (esp. in compounds) = NORTH (*nor'ward; nor'wester*). [abbreviation]

NORAD *abbreviation* North American Aerospace Defence Command.

nor·adren·a·lin /ˌnɔrəˈdrɛnəlɪn/ *noun* (also **nor·adren·a·line**) a hormone released by the adrenal medulla and by sympathetic nerve endings as a neurotransmitter. *Also called* NOREPINEPHRINE. [NOR- + ADRENALIN]

Nor-Am *adjective esp. Skiing* North American (*Nor-Am circuit*). [abbreviation]

Nor·dau /ˈnɔrdau/ **Max Simon** (born Max Simon Südfeld) (1849–1923), Hungarian-born German writer, who was a leading figure in the Zionist movement; his works include *The Conventional Lies of Our Civilization* (1883).

Nor·den·skjöld /ˈnʊrdənʃɔːld/ **(Nils) Adolf Erik, Baron** (1823–1901), Finnish-born Swedish geologist and Arctic explorer, who was the first to navigate the Northeast Passage (1878–80).

Nor·dic ● *adjective* **1** of or relating to a physical type of northern Germanic peoples characterized by tall stature and fair colouring. **2** of or relating to Scandinavia or Finland. **3** of or relating to cross-country skiing or ski jumping (*compare* ALPINE *adjective* 3). ● *noun* a Nordic person, esp. a native of Scandinavia or Finland. [French *nordique* from *nord* north]

Nordic combined *noun* a sporting discipline in which participants compete in ski jumping and subsequently in cross-country skiing.

nor·di·city /nɔrˈdɪsɪti/ *noun Cdn* a measure of the degree of northernness of a high-latitude place, calculated by assigning values to ten criteria, including latitude, summer heat, and annual cold.

Nord·kyn /ˈnʊrtʃʊn/ a promontory on the north coast of Norway, to the east of North Cape. At 71° 8′ N, it is the northernmost point of the European mainland.

Nord-Pas-de-Calais /ˌnɔrpɒdəkaˈlei/ a region of N France, on the border with Belgium.

nor'easter *noun N Amer.* = NORTHEASTER. [contraction]

nor·epi·neph·rine /ˌnɔrɛpəˈnɛfrɪn/ *noun* = NORADRENALIN. [NOR- + EPINEPHRINE]

nor·ethin·drone /nɔrˈɛθɪnˌdrɔːn/ *noun* a progestin used in oral contraceptives, often in combination with an estrogen. [alteration and rearrangement of chemical name]

Nor·folk /ˈnɔrfək/ **1** a county on the east coast of England, east of the Wash; county town, Norwich. **2** (also /ˈnɔrfɔːk/) a seaport and naval base in Virginia; pop. (2000) 234,403.

Norfolk County a city in SW Ontario, just west of Haldimand County, between Brant and Lake Erie, including the former town of Simcoe; pop. (2001) 60,847. [after NORFOLK 1]

Norfolk Island an island in the Pacific Ocean, off the east coast of Australia, administered since 1913 as an external territory of Australia; pop. (est. 2002) 1,866. Occupied from 1788 to 1814 as a penal colony, the island was settled in 1856 by some of the descendants of the mutineers from the *Bounty*, to ease overcrowding on Pitcairn Island.

Norfolk Island pine *noun* (also **Norfolk pine**) a large pyramidal coniferous tree, *Araucaria heterophylla*, with tiered branches and small needles, grown as a pot-bound houseplant. [NORFOLK ISLAND]

Norfolk jacket /ˈnɔrfək/ *noun* a man's loose belted jacket, with box pleats. [NORFOLK, England]

nori /ˈnɔri/ *noun* edible seaweed of the genus *Porphyra*, eaten either fresh or dried in sheets. [Japanese]

Nori·ega /ˌnɔriˈeigə/ **Man·uel (An·tonio Mor·ena)** (b.1940), Panamanian leader and general, head of state 1983–9. He was charged with drug trafficking by a US grand jury in 1988, and in 1989 President

Bush authorized a US invasion of Panama to arrest him; Noriega eventually surrendered and was tried and convicted in 1992.

Nor·land *noun* a large red and green cooking and eating apple, orig. developed in Saskatchewan. [probably from 'Northland', with reference to the cultivar's suitability for northern climates]

norm *noun* **1** a standard or pattern or type (*dual-income families have become the norm*). **2** a standard quantity to be produced or amount of work to be done. **3** customary behaviour, appearance, etc. (*social norms*). **4** the average or general level (*temperature well below the season's norm*). [Latin *norma* carpenter's square]

nor·mal ● *adjective* **1** constituting or conforming to a standard; regular, usual, typical. **2 a** physically or mentally sound; healthy. **b** about average in intelligence, emotional development, ability, etc. **3** *Geom.* (of a line) at right angles, perpendicular. **4** *Chem.* (of a solution) containing one gram-equivalent of solute per litre. ● *noun* **1 a** the normal value of a temperature etc., esp. blood heat. **b** the usual state, level, etc. (*things have returned to normal*). **2** *Geom.* a line at right angles. **3** a person or thing that is normal. □ **nor·malcy** *noun* esp. *N Amer.*

nor·mal·ity /-'malɪti/ *noun* [French *normal* or Latin *normalis* (as NORM)]

normal distribution *noun Statistics* a function that represents the distribution of many random variables as a symmetrical bell-shaped graph.

nor·mal·ize *verb* (also esp. *Brit.* **-ise**) **1** *transitive* make normal or regular. **2** *transitive* make (relations) normal or standard between countries etc. **3** *intransitive* become normal. **4** *transitive* cause to conform to a standard. □ **nor·mal·iza·tion** *noun* **nor·mal·iz·er** *noun*

nor·mally *adverb* **1** in a normal manner. **2** usually.

normally aspirated *adjective* (of an engine) not turbocharged or supercharged.

normal school *noun hist.* (in Canada, the US, etc.) a school or college for training teachers.

Nor·man¹ ● *noun* **1** a native or inhabitant of Normandy. **2** a descendant of the people of mixed Scandinavian and Frankish origin established there in the 10th c., who conquered England in 1066. **3** Norman French. **4** *Archit.* the style of Romanesque architecture found in Britain under the Normans. **5** any of the English kings from William I to Stephen. ● *adjective* **1** of or relating to the Normans or Normandy. **2** of or relating to the Norman style of architecture. □ **Nor·man·ize** *transitive & intransitive verb* (also esp. *Brit.* **-ise**). [Old French *Normans* pl. of *Normant* from Old Norse *Northmathr* (as NORTH, MAN)]

Nor·man² ▸ **1 Greg·ory John ('Greg')** (b.1955), Australian golfer, who won the world match-play championship three times (1980; 1983; 1986) and the British Open twice (1986; 1993). **2 Jes·sye** (b.1945), US operatic soprano. Her repertoire includes both opera and concert music and she has given notable interpretations of the works of Wagner, Schubert, and Mahler.

Norman Conquest (also **the Conquest**) the conquest of England by William of Normandy (William the Conqueror) after the Battle of Hastings in 1066. William was crowned William I, founding a Norman dynasty that ruled until 1154, having crushed most Saxon resistance by 1071. Norman institutions and customs (such as feudalism) were imported, and Anglo-French and Latin became the languages of literature, law, and government.

Nor·man·dy a former province of NW France with its coastline on the English Channel, now divided into the two regions of Lower Normandy (Basse-Normandie) and Upper Normandy (Haute-Normandie); chief city, Rouen.

Norman English *noun* English as spoken or influenced by the Normans.

Norman French *noun* French as spoken by the Normans or (after 1066) in English law courts.

nor·ma·tive /'nɔrmətɪv/ *adjective* of or establishing a norm. □ **nor·ma·tive·ly** *adverb* **nor·ma·tiv·ity** *noun* [French *normatif -ive* from Latin *norma* (see NORM)]

normo·ten·sive /ˌnɔrmoʊ'tensɪv/ ● *adjective* having or designating a normal blood pressure. ● *noun* a person who has a normal blood pressure.

Norn /nɔrn/ ● *noun* a form of Norwegian formerly spoken in the Orkney and Shetland Islands. ● *adjective* of or relating to this language. [Old Norse *norroen* from *norðr* north]

Norns /'nɔrnz/ *plural noun* the three goddesses of destiny in Scandinavian mythology (Urd or Urdar, Verdandi, and Skuld), who sit by the well of fate at the base of the ash tree Yggdrasil and spin the web of fate. [Old Norse: origin unknown]

Norse /nɔrs/ ● *noun* **1 a** the Norwegian language. **b** the Scandinavian language group. **2** (prec. by *the*; treated as *pl.*) **a** the Norwegians. **b** the Vikings. ● *adjective* **1** of or relating to Norway or the Norse language. **2** of or relating to ancient Scandinavia or its inhabitants. □ **Norse·man** *noun* (*pl.* **-men**). [Dutch *noor(d)sch* from *noord* 'north']

nor·ster·oid /nɔr'steroɪd/ *noun* a steroid lacking a methyl side chain or having one of its rings contracted by one methylene group. [NOR- + STEROID]

North, Fred·erick, Lord (1732–92), English Whig politician, prime minister 1770–82. He sought to avoid the American Revolution, but was regarded as responsible for the loss of the American colonies; this, together with allegations that his ministry was dominated by the influence of George III, brought his resignation in 1782.

north ● *noun* **1 a** the point of the horizon 90° counter-clockwise from east. **b** the compass point corresponding to this. **c** the direction in which this lies. **2** (usu. **the North**) **a** the Arctic. **b** (in Canada) (from Labrador to the west) the northern part of a province. **c** the part of the world or a country or a town lying to the north, esp. = NORTH COUNTRY 1 or NORTHERN STATES. **d** the industrialized nations. **3** (**North**) *Bridge* a player occupying the position designated 'north'. ● *adjective* **1** towards, at, near, or facing north. **2** coming from the north (*north wind*). ● *adverb* **1** towards, at, or near the north. **2** (foll. by *of*) further north than. **3** *informal* (foll. by *of*) more than (*paid him north of $40,000*). □ **north by east** (or **west**) between north and north-northeast (or north-northwest). **up north** to or in the north. [Old English from Germanic]

North America a continent comprising the northern half of the American land mass, connected to S America by the Isthmus of Panama. It contains Canada, the US, Mexico, and the countries of Central America. □ **North American** *adjective & noun*

North American Free Trade Agreement *noun* an agreement which came into effect in January 1994 between Canada, the US, and Mexico to remove barriers to trade between the three countries over a ten-year period. Abbr.: **NAFTA**.

North Americanism *noun* **1** a word or expression originating in Canada and the US. **2** a word or expression used only in Canada and the US.

North·amp·ton /nɔr'θamptən/ a town in SE central England, on the Nene River, the county town of Northamptonshire; pop. (2001) 194,477.

North·amp·ton·shire /nɔr'θamptənˌʃɪr/ a county of central England; county town, Northampton.

North·ants /nɔr'θants/ *abbreviation* Northamptonshire.

North Atlantic Drift a continuation of the Gulf Stream across the Atlantic Ocean and along the coast of NW Europe, where it has a significant warming effect on the climate.

North Atlantic Ocean see ATLANTIC OCEAN.

North Atlantic Treaty Organization *noun* an association of European and North American states, formed in 1949 for the defence of Europe and the North Atlantic against the perceived threat of Soviet aggression. Abbr.: **NATO**, esp. *Brit.* **Nato**.

North Battle·ford /'batəlfərd/ a city in west central Saskatchewan, located on the North Saskatchewan River, 138 km northwest of Saskatoon; pop. (2001) 13,692. [*Battleford*, a town on the opposite (south) bank of the river *c.*1875, after the *Battle* River, which refers to a number of battles between local Blackfoot and Cree]

North Bay a city in NE central Ontario, situated on Lake Nipissing, about 360 km north of Toronto; pop. (2001) 52,771. □ **North Bay·ite** *noun* [so called because its location was identified as being on the 'north bay' of Lake Nipissing *c.*1881]

north·bound *adjective* travelling or leading northwards.

north canoe *noun Cdn* = CANOT DU NORD.

North Cape a promontory on Magerøya, an island off the north coast of Norway. Situated on the edge of the Barents Sea, North Cape is the northernmost point of the world accessible by road.

North Carolina /ˌkerə'laɪnə/ a state of the east central US, on the Atlantic coast; pop. (2000) 8,049,313; capital, Raleigh. [from *Carolus*, the Latin name of Charles I]

North Channel a narrow channel of northern Lake Huron, connecting Lake Superior with Georgian Bay and separating Manitoulin Island from the mainland of north central Ontario.

North·cliffe, 1st Vis·count (title of Alfred Charles William Harmsworth) (1865–1922), English newspaper proprietor. With his younger brother Harold (later Lord Rothermere, 1868–1940), he built up a large newspaper empire in the years preceding the First World War, including *The Times*, the *Daily Mail*, and the *Daily Mirror*.

North Country *noun* (also **north country**) **1** the northern part of England (north of the Humber). **2** the northern part of any country.

North Cowichan /ˈkauwɪtʃən/ a district municipality situated on the east coast of Vancouver Island, north of Duncan; pop. (2001) 26,148. [COWICHAN]

North Dakota an agricultural state in the north central US, on the border with Canada; pop. (2000) 642,200; capital, Bismarck. □ **North Dakotan** *noun & adjective*

north·east ● *noun* **1** the point of the horizon midway between north and east. **2** the compass point corresponding to this. **3** the direction in which this lies. **4** (**Northeast**) the part of a country, city, etc. lying to the northeast. ● *adjective* of, towards, or coming from the northeast. ● *adverb* towards, at, or near the northeast. □ **north·east·ern** *adjective*

north·east·er *noun* a northeast wind.

north·east·er·ly ● *adjective & adverb* = NORTHEAST. ● *noun* (*pl.* **-lies**) a northeast wind.

Northeast Passage a passage for ships along the northern coast of Europe and Asia, from the Atlantic to the Pacific via the Arctic Ocean, sought for many years as a possible trade route to the East. It was first navigated in 1878–9 by the Swedish Arctic explorer Baron Nordenskjöld (1832–1901).

north·east·ward *adjective & adverb* (also **north·east·wards**) towards the northeast.

north·er *noun US* a strong cold north wind blowing in autumn and winter over Texas, Florida, and the Gulf of Mexico.

north·er·ly ● *adjective & adverb* **1** in a northern position or direction. **2** (of wind) blowing from the north. ● *noun* (*pl.* **-lies**) (usu. in *pl.*) a wind blowing from the north.

north·ern ● *adjective* **1** of or in the north; inhabiting the north. **2** lying or directed towards the north. **3** (of a wind) blowing from the north. ● *noun N Amer.* = NORTHERN PIKE. □ **north·ern·most** *adjective*

north·ern·ness *noun* [Old English *northerne* (as NORTH, -ERN)]

northern allowance *noun Cdn* a supplementary allowance in addition to the basic income for a position, paid to people who work in the North to compensate for higher costs, isolation, etc.

Northern Cape a province of W South Africa, formerly part of Cape Province; capital, Kimberley.

North·ern Cir·cars /ˈsɜrkɑrz/ a former name for the coastal region of E India between the Krishna River and Orissa, now in Andhra Pradesh.

Northern Dancer (1961–1990), the first Canadian-bred horse to win the Kentucky Derby (1964).

north·ern·er *noun* a native or inhabitant of the north.

northern fulmar *noun* a fulmar, *Fulmarus glacialis*, breeding in immense colonies along the North Atlantic and Arctic coasts.

Northern Games *noun Cdn* a festival of arts and crafts, dancing, and games held in a different Arctic community every year.

northern gannet *noun see* GANNET.

northern harrier *noun* a common harrier, *Circus cyaneus*, having a partial facial disk reminiscent of an owl's, and a conspicuous white rump patch.

northern hemisphere *noun* **1** the half of the earth north of the equator. **2** the half of the celestial sphere north of the celestial equator.

Northern Ireland a part of the UK occupying the northeastern part of Ireland; pop. (2001) 1,685,267; capital, Belfast. Northern Ireland, which comprises six of the counties of Ulster, was established as a self-governing province in 1920, having refused to be part of the Irish Free State. It has always been dominated by Unionist parties, which represent the Protestant majority.

northern lights *plural noun* a northern occurrence of aurora (*see* AURORA 1). *Also called* AURORA BOREALIS.

Northern Marianas a self-governing territory in the W Pacific, comprising the Mariana Islands with the exception of the southernmost, Guam; pop. (est. 2002) 77,311; capital, Capital Hill (on Saipan). (*See also* MARIANA ISLANDS.)

northern oriole *noun* a N American oriole, *Icterus galbula*, with black and orange or yellowish-orange plumage.

Northern Peninsula (also called **Great Northern Peninsula**) a large and long extension of the northwestern coast of the island of Newfoundland, stretching northward from the head of White Bay to L'Anse aux Meadows.

northern pike *noun* a large species of pike, *Esox lucius*, found in northern waters and valued as a game fish.

northern pintail *noun see* PINTAIL.

Northern Rhodesia the former name (until 1964) for ZAMBIA.

northern sea lion *noun* = STELLER'S SEA LION.

Northern Spy *noun N Amer.* a large bright red apple streaked with green, used esp. in cooking.

Northern States *plural noun* the states in the north of the US, esp. those lying roughly north of the Mason-Dixon Line and the Ohio river forming the Union side in the Civil War.

Northern Territory a state of north central Australia; pop. (2001) 200,019; capital, Darwin.

North Germanic ● *noun* the northern group of Germanic languages, comprising the Scandinavian languages. ● *adjective* of or relating to North Germanic.

north·ing /ˈnɔrθɪŋ/ *noun Naut.* the distance travelled or measured northward.

North Island the northernmost of the two main islands of New Zealand, separated from South Island by Cook Strait.

North Korea (official name **Democratic People's Republic of Korea**) a country in the Far East, occupying the northern part of the peninsula of Korea; pop. (est. 2002) 22,224,195; capital, Pyongyang. North Korea was formed in 1948 when Korea was partitioned along the 38th parallel. In 1950 North Korean forces invaded the south, but were forced back to more or less the previous border (see KOREAN WAR).

north·land *noun* (also **north·lands**) the northern lands; the northern part of a country.

north light *noun* good natural light without direct sun, esp. as desired by painters and in factory design.

North·man *noun* (*pl.* **-men**) **1** a Viking. **2** *Cdn hist.* = HOMME DU NORD.

North Minch see MINCH, THE.

north-northeast ● *noun* the point or direction midway between north and northeast. ● *adjective & adverb* in, from, or towards this direction. Abbr.: **NNE**.

north-northwest ● *noun* the point or direction midway between north and northwest. ● *adjective & adverb* in, from, or towards this direction. Abbr.: **NNW**.

north of 60 *noun Cdn informal* the areas of Canada north of 60 degrees latitude, esp. the Yukon, Northwest Territories, and Nunavut.

North Ossetia an autonomous republic of Russia, in the Caucasus on the border with Georgia; pop. (est. 2002) 689,200; capital, Vladikavkaz. (See also OSSETIA.)

North Pender Island one of the Gulf Islands in the Strait of Georgia, BC, situated south of Mayne Island. [D. *Pender*, master of the survey vessel *Plumper c.*1859]

North Perth a town in SW Ontario, north of Stratford, incorporating the former town of Listowel; pop. (2001) 12,055. [in honour of its Scottish settlers from PERTHSHIRE]

North Pole *noun* **1** the northernmost point of the earth's axis of rotation. **2** (**north pole**) the northernmost point about which the stars appear to revolve.

North Rhine-Westphal·ia /ˌrainwestˈfeiliə/ a state of western Germany; capital, Düsseldorf.

North Saanich /ˈsanɪtʃ/ a district municipality on the Saanich Peninsula of Vancouver Island, south of Sidney; pop. (2001) 10,436. [SAANICH¹]

North Saskatchewan River a river in central Alberta and west central Saskatchewan, 1 287 km long, rising in the Columbia Icefield of the Rocky Mountains and flowing generally eastward through Edmonton, North Battleford, and Prince Albert, 45 km east of which it joins the South Saskatchewan River to form the Saskatchewan River. [see SASKATCHEWAN RIVER]

North Sea an arm of the Atlantic Ocean lying between the mainland of Europe and the east coast of Britain. Its seabed is an important source of oil and natural gas.

North Slavey *noun & adjective* = SAHTU DENE.

north-south *attributive adjective* of or relating to countries of the north and south (*north-south divide*).

North Star *noun* = POLARIS¹.

North Sydney an urban community on Cape Breton Island, north of Sydney.

North Twin a peak in the Rocky Mountains, Alberta (3 733 m).

North·um·ber·land /nɔrˈθʌmbərlənd/ a county in NE England, on the Scottish border; county town, Morpeth.

Northumberland Strait a southern channel of the Gulf of St. Lawrence, separating PEI from New Brunswick and Nova Scotia. [HMS

Northumberland, flagship of Admiral Lord Colville, who surveyed the coast of Nova Scotia in 1764]

North·um·bria /nɔrˈθʌmbriə/ **1** an ancient Anglo-Saxon kingdom in NE England extending from the Humber to the Forth. **2** (loosely) an area of NE England comprising Northumberland, Durham, and Tyne and Wear. [obsolete *Northumber*, persons living beyond the Humber, from Old English *Northhymbre*]

North·um·brian /nɔrˈθʌmbriən/ ● *adjective* of or relating to ancient Northumbria or modern Northumberland. ● *noun* **1** a native of ancient Northumbria or modern Northumberland. **2** the dialect of ancient Northumbria or modern Northumberland.

North Vancouver a city in southwestern BC, located on the north side of Burrard Inlet, opposite Vancouver; pop. (2001) 44,303.

North Vietnam *see* VIETNAM.

north·ward ● *adverb* (also **north·wards**) towards the north. ● *adjective* **1** situated or directed towards the north. **2** moving or facing towards the north. ● *noun* a northward direction or region.

North Warning System *noun* N Amer. a network of 52 radar stations along the Arctic coast designed to detect low-flying aircraft and missiles.

north·west ● *noun* **1** the point of the horizon midway between north and west. **2** the compass point corresponding to this. **3** the direction in which this lies. **4** (**Northwest**) the part of a country, city, etc. lying to the northwest. ● *adjective* of, towards, or coming from the northwest. ● *adverb* towards, at, or near the northwest. □ **north·west·ern** *adjective* **north·west·ern·most** *adjective*

Northwest Angle a small part of Minnesota extending north of the 49th parallel, including the southwestern corner of Lake of the Woods and the promontory of land extending into it.

North West Company *noun* Cdn hist. a fur-trading syndicate formed in Montreal in the late 18th c. and absorbed by the Hudson's Bay Company in 1821. Abbr.: **NWC**.

north·west·er *noun* **1** a northwest wind. **2** (**Northwester**) Cdn hist. **a** a wintering partner or employee of the North West Company. **b** (in pl.) the North West Company collectively.

north·west·er·ly ● *adjective & adverb* = NORTHWEST. ● *noun* (pl. **-lies**) a northwest wind.

North-Western Territory hist. a region of Canada, under British rule, originally occupying what is now Yukon Territory, the western and northern portions of the NWT and Nunavut, and parts of northern BC, Alberta, and Saskatchewan. In 1870, together with Rupert's Land, it was transferred to Canada and designated the North-West Territories.

North-West Frontier Province a province of NW Pakistan, on the border with Afghanistan; capital, Peshawar.

North West Mounted Police *noun* Cdn hist. a federal police force established in 1873, renamed the Royal North West Mounted Police in 1904 and the Royal Canadian Mounted Police in 1920. Abbr.: **NWMP**.

Northwest Passage a sea passage along the northern coast of the N American continent, through the Canadian Arctic from the Atlantic to the Pacific. It was sought for centuries as a possible trading route by many explorers, including Sebastian Cabot, Sir Francis Drake, Martin Frobisher, and Henry Hudson. In 1850–4 it was first completed on foot by the Irish naval officer Robert McClure (1807–73), and was finally successfully navigated in 1903–6 by Roald Amundsen.

North-West Province a province of N South Africa, formed in 1994 from the northeastern part of Cape Province and SW Transvaal; capital, Mmabatho.

Northwest Rebellion *noun* Cdn an armed uprising of Metis, Indians, and white settlers in Saskatchewan in 1885, led by Louis Riel, who proclaimed a provisional government for Western Canada with the capital at Batoche. The rebellion was put down by troops sent from Eastern Canada.

Northwest Territories *plural noun* a territory of N Canada north of Saskatchewan and Alberta, and between Yukon and Nunavut; pop. (2001) 37,360; capital, Yellowknife.

North-West Territories *plural noun* hist. a region (1870–1905) of Canada formed by the union of the North-Western Territory and Rupert's Land.

Northwest Territory a region and former territory of the US lying between the Mississippi and Ohio rivers and the Great Lakes. It was acquired in 1783 after the American Revolution and now forms the states of Indiana, Ohio, Michigan, Illinois, and Wisconsin.

north·west·ward *adjective & adverb* (also **north·west·wards**) towards the northwest.

north woods *plural noun* N Amer. the vast regions of forest in northern Canada and parts of the northern US.

North York a former city in S Ontario, one of six municipalities of Metropolitan Toronto, now part of the city of Toronto; pop. (2001) 608,288. [ultimately after YORK in England]

North Yorkshire a county in NE England; administrative centre, Northallerton. It was formed in 1974 from parts of the former North, East, and West Ridings of Yorkshire.

Nor·walk virus *noun* a virus which can cause epidemics of gastroenteritis in humans, with severe vomiting and diarrhea usu. lasting 24 to 48 hours. [*Norwalk*, Ohio, where, in 1968, an outbreak of gastroenteritis occurred from which the virus was isolated]

Nor·way a mountainous European country on the northern and western coastline of Scandinavia; pop. (est. 2002) 4,525,116; capital, Oslo.

Norway lobster *noun* a small European lobster, *Nephrops norvegicus*.

Norway maple *noun* a European maple tree with leaves similar to the sugar maple, *Acer platanoides*, with many cultivated varieties, frequently planted in eastern N America.

Norway rat *noun* the common brown rat, *Rattus norvegicus*.

Norway spruce *noun* a large Eurasian spruce, *Picea abies*, with many cultivated varieties planted both as a forest tree and as an ornamental.

Nor·we·gian /nɔrˈwiːdʒən/ ● *noun* **1 a** a native or national of Norway. **b** a person of Norwegian descent. **2** the language of Norway. ● *adjective* of or relating to Norway or its people or language. [medieval Latin *Norvegia* from Old Norse *Norvegr* (as NORTH, WAY), assimilated to *Norway*]

nor'wester *noun* **1** a northwester. **2** an oilskin hat, a sou'wester. **3** (**Nor'Wester**) Cdn hist. = NORTHWESTER 2. [contraction]

Nor·wich /ˈnɒrɪtʃ/ a city in E England, the county town of Norfolk; pop. (est. 2002) 173,300.

Nos. *abbreviation* (also **nos.**) numbers. [compare No.]

nose ● *noun* **1** an organ above the mouth on the face or head of a human or animal, containing nostrils and used for smelling and breathing. **2 a** the sense of smell (*dogs have a good nose*). **b** the ability to detect a particular thing (*a nose for scandal*). **3** the odour or perfume of wine, tea, tobacco, hay, etc. **4** the open end or nozzle of a tube, pipe, etc. **5** the front end or projecting part of a thing, e.g. of a car or aircraft. **6** Cdn the northeast portion of the Grand Banks of Newfoundland, lying outside Canada's 320-km (200-mile) fishing zone (compare TAIL 10). ● *verb* **1** *transitive* (often foll. by *out*) **a** perceive the smell of, discover by smell. **b** detect. **2** *transitive* **a** thrust or rub one's nose against or into, esp. in order to smell. **b** smell or sniff (wine etc.). **3** *intransitive* (usu. foll. by *about*, *around*, *through*, etc.) pry or search. **4 a** *intransitive* (often foll. by *out*) move forward slowly and cautiously. **b** *transitive* make (one's or its way) forward slowly and cautiously. □ **as plain as the nose on your face** easily seen. **by a nose** by a very narrow margin (*won the race by a nose*). **count noses** count those present, one's supporters, etc.; decide a question by mere numbers. **cut off one's nose to spite one's face** disadvantage oneself in the course of trying to disadvantage another. **get up a person's nose** esp. Brit. slang annoy a person. **have one's nose in** (**a book etc.**) informal read intently. **keep one's nose clean** slang stay out of trouble, behave properly. **keep one's nose to the grindstone** see GRINDSTONE. **nose out** defeat by a narrow margin. **nose to tail** Brit. (of vehicles) moving or stationary one close behind another, esp. in heavy traffic. **on the nose** N Amer. slang precisely. **poke** (or **stick**) **one's nose into** informal pry or intrude into (esp. a person's affairs). **put a person's nose out of joint** informal upset or annoy a person. **rub a person's nose in it** see RUB. **see no further than one's nose** be short-sighted, esp. in foreseeing the consequences of one's actions etc. **turn up one's nose** (usu. foll. by *at*) informal show disdain. **under a person's nose** informal right before a person (esp. of defiant or unnoticed actions). **with one's nose in the air** haughtily. □ **nosed** *adjective* (also in *combination*) [Old English *nosu*]

nose·bag *noun* = FEED BAG.

nose·band *noun* the lower band of a bridle, passing over the horse's nose.

nose·bleed ● *noun* an instance of bleeding from the nose. ● *adjective* N Amer. slang **1** (of seats in an arena, theatre, etc.) situated in a high level. **2** (of a price etc.) very high.

nose candy *noun* N Amer. slang cocaine.

nose cone *noun* the cone-shaped nose of a rocket etc.

nose·dive ● *noun* **1** a steep downward plunge by an aircraft. **2** a sudden plunge, drop, or decline (*his career took a nosedive*). ● *intransitive verb* make a nosedive.

no-see-um *noun N Amer.* a small bloodsucking insect, esp. a midge of the family Ceratopogonidae.

nose flute *noun* a musical instrument blown with the nose, popular in Fiji etc.

nose·gay *noun* a small bunch of flowers; a posy. [NOSE + GAY in obsolete use = ornament]

nose job *noun informal* = RHINOPLASTY.

nose leaf *noun* a fleshy part on the nostrils of some bats, used for echolocation.

nose·piece *noun* **1** the part of eyeglass frames that goes over the bridge of the nose. **2** = NOSEBAND. **3** the part of a helmet etc. protecting the nose. **4** the part of a microscope to which the objective lenses are attached.

nose ring *noun* a ring fixed in the nose of an animal (esp. a bull) for leading it, or of a person for ornament.

nose tackle *noun Football* **1** the defensive player who lines up in the centre of the linemen in formation. **2** this field position.

nose-thumbing ● *noun* behaviour meant to show one's contempt (for a person, establishment, etc.) ● *adjective* derisory; contemptuous.

nose wheel *noun* a landing wheel under the nose of an aircraft.

nosey *var. of* NOSY.

nosh *slang* ● *transitive & intransitive verb* **1** eat or drink. **2** *N Amer.* eat between meals; snack. ● *noun* **1** food or drink. **2** *N Amer.* a snack. □ **nosh·er** *noun* [Yiddish]

no-show *noun* a person who is expected at an event, has a ticket reserved for a trip, etc. but does not appear for it.

nosh-up *noun Brit.* a large meal.

nos·ing /ˈnoʊzɪŋ/ *noun* a rounded edge of a step, moulding, etc., or a metal shield for it.

nos·og·ra·phy /nəˈsɒɡrəfi/ *noun* the systematic description of diseases. [Greek *nosos* disease + -GRAPHY]

nos·ol·ogy /nəˈsɒlədʒi/ *noun* the branch of medical science dealing with the classification of diseases. □ **noso·logic·al** /ˌnɒsəˈlɒdʒɪkəl/ *adjective* **noso·log·ic·al·ly** /-ɪkli/ *adverb* **nos·ol·o·gist** *noun* [Greek *nosos* disease + -LOGY]

nos·tal·gia /nɒˈstaldʒə, -dʒɪə, nə-/ *noun* **1** (often foll. by *for*) sentimental yearning for a period of the past; regretful or wistful memory of an earlier time. **2** a thing or things which evoke a former era. **3** severe homesickness. □ **nos·tal·gic** *adjective* **nos·tal·gic·al·ly** *adverb* **nos·tal·gist** *noun* [modern Latin, from Greek *nostos* 'return home']

nos·toc /ˈnɒstɒk/ *noun* any gelatinous blue-green alga of the genus *Nostoc*, that can fix nitrogen from the atmosphere. [name invented by Paracelsus]

Nos·tra·da·mus /ˌnɒstrəˈdɑːməs/ (Latinized name of Michel de Nostredame) (1503–66), French astrologer and physician. His cryptic and apocalyptic predictions, in rhymed quatrains, appeared in two collections (1555; 1558).

nos·tril *noun* either of two external openings of the nasal cavity in vertebrates that admit air to the lungs and smells to the olfactory nerves. [Old English *nosthyrl, nosterl* from *nosu* NOSE + *thȳr(e)l* hole: compare THRILL]

nos·trum /ˈnɒstrəm/ *noun* **1** a quack remedy, a patent medicine, esp. one prepared by the person recommending it. **2** a pet scheme, esp. for political or social reform. [Latin, neuter of *noster* our, used in sense 'of our own make']

nosy *adjective* (also **nosey**) (**nosi·er, nosi·est**) *informal* inquisitive, prying. □ **nosi·ly** *adverb* **nosi·ness** *noun*

Nosy Parker *noun* (also **Nosey Parker**) *informal* a busybody; a nosy person. [20th c.: used as a postcard caption 'The Adventures of Nosey Parker', referring to a peeping Tom in Hyde Park in London.]

not *adverb* expressing negation, esp.: **1** (also **n't** joined to a preceding verb) following an auxiliary verb or *be* or (in a question) the subject of such a verb (*I cannot say; she isn't there; didn't you tell me?; am I not right?; aren't we smart?*). **2** used elliptically for a negative sentence or verb or phrase (*Is she coming? — I hope not; Do you want it? — Certainly not!*). **3** used to express the negative of other words (*not a single one was left; Are they pleased? — Not they; he is not my cousin, but my nephew*). **4** *informal* following and emphatically negating an affirmative statement (*great party . . . not!*). □ **not at all** (in polite reply to thanks) there is no need for thanks. **not but what** *archaic* **1** all the same; nevertheless (*I cannot do it; not but what a stronger man might*). **2** not such . . . or so . . . that . . . not (*not such a fool but what he can see it*). **not half** *see* HALF. **not least** with considerable importance, notably. **not quite 1** almost (*am not quite there*). **2** noticeably not (*not quite proper*). **not in the slightest**

not at all. **not a thing** nothing at all. **not that** (foll. by clause) it is not to be inferred that (*if he said so — not that he ever did — he lied*). **not very** *see* VERY. [Middle English contraction of NOUGHT]

nota bene /ˌnoʊtə ˈbeneɪ/ *transitive verb* (as imperative) observe what follows, take notice. [Latin, = note well]

nota·bil·ity *noun* (*pl.* **-ities**) **1** the state of being notable (*names of no historical notability*). **2** a prominent person.

nota·ble ● *adjective* worthy of note; striking, remarkable, eminent. ● *noun* **1** an eminent person. **2** a noteworthy fact or thing. □ **nota·bly** *adverb*

no·tar·ize /ˈnoʊtəˌraɪz/ *transitive verb* (also **-ise**) *N Amer.* certify (a document) as a notary.

no·tary /ˈnoʊtəri/ *noun* (*pl.* **-ies**) **1** (in full **notary public**, *pl.* **notaries public**) a person authorized to perform certain legal formalities, esp. to draw up or certify contracts, deeds, etc. **2** *Cdn (Que.)* a member of the legal profession not authorized to plead in court but qualified to draft deeds, contracts, and other legal documents, e.g. wills, real estate transactions, etc. □ **no·tar·ial** /noʊˈtɛriəl/ *adjective* **no·tar·ial·ly** /noʊˈtɛriəli/ *adverb* [Latin *notarius* secretary (as NOTE)]

no·tate /noʊˈteɪt/ *transitive verb* write in notation. □ **no·tat·ed** *adjective* **no·ta·tor** *noun* [back-formation from NOTATION]

no·ta·tion /noʊˈteɪʃən/ *noun* **1 a** the representation of numbers, quantities, pitch, and duration etc. of musical notes, dance movements, chess moves, etc. by symbols. **b** any set of such symbols. **2** esp. *N Amer.* **a** a note or annotation. **b** a record. □ **no·ta·tion·al** *adjective* [French *notation* or Latin *notatio* (as NOTE)]

notch ● *noun* **1** a V-shaped indentation on an edge or surface. **2** one of a series of holes for the tongue of a buckle on a belt, shoe, etc. **3** each of a series of indentations marking graduated points on a regulating dial etc. **4** a nick made on a stick etc. in order to keep count. **5** *informal* a step or degree (*move up a notch*). **6** *N Amer.* a deep gorge. ● *transitive verb* **1** make notches in. **2** (often foll. by *up*) record or score with or as with notches. **3** secure or insert by notches. □ **notched** *adjective* **notch·er** *noun* **notchy** *adjective* (**notch·i·er, notch·i·est**). [probably from Anglo-French *noche*, variant of Old French *osche* hole in an object, or *oche* incised mark used to keep a record, of uncertain origin]

note ● *noun* **1** a brief record of facts, topics, thoughts, etc., as an aid to memory, for use in writing, public speaking, etc. (often in *pl.*: *make notes; spoke without notes*). **2** an observation, usu. unwritten, of experiences etc. (*compare notes*). **3** a short or informal letter. **4** a formal diplomatic or parliamentary communication. **5** a short annotation or additional explanation in a book etc.; a footnote. **6 a** = BANKNOTE (*a five-pound note*). **b** a written promise or notice of payment of various kinds. **7 a** notice, attention (*worthy of note*). **b** distinction, eminence (*a person of note*). **8 a** a written sign representing the pitch and duration of a musical sound. **b** a single tone of definite pitch made by a musical instrument, the human voice, etc. **c** a key of a piano etc. **9 a** a bird's song or call. **b** a single tone in this. **10** a quality or tone of speaking, expressing mood or attitude etc.; a hint or suggestion (*sound a note of warning; ended on a note of optimism*). **11** a characteristic; a distinguishing feature. **12** any of the basic components of the fragrance of a perfume which give it its character. ● *transitive verb* **1** observe, notice; give or draw attention to. **2** (often foll. by *down*) record as a thing to be remembered or observed. **3** (in *passive*; often foll. by *for*) be famous or well known (for a quality, activity, etc.) (*were noted for their generosity*). □ **hit** (or **strike**) **the right** (or **a false**) **note** speak or act in an appropriate (or inappropriate) manner. **of note** important, distinguished (*a person of note*). **take note** (often foll. by *of*) observe; pay attention (to). □ **noted** *adjective* (in sense 3 of verb). **note·less** *adjective* [Latin *nota* mark]

note·book *noun* **1** a small book for making or taking notes. **2** (in full **notebook computer**) a portable computer smaller than a laptop.

note·card *noun* a decorative card with a blank space for a short message.

note·let *noun* a small folded sheet of paper, usu. with a decorative design, for an informal letter.

note·pad *noun* **1** a pad of paper for writing notes on. **2** a small hand-held computer taking input from an electronic stylus rather than a keyboard.

note·paper *noun* paper for writing letters.

note·worthy *adjective* worthy of attention; remarkable. □ **note·worthi·ness** *noun*

not-for-profit *adjective* = NON-PROFIT.

noth·ing ● *noun* **1** not anything (*nothing has been done; have nothing to do*). **2** no thing (often foll. by complement: *I see nothing that I want; can* *find nothing useful*). **3 a** a person or thing of no importance or concern; a trivial event or remark (*was nothing to me; murmured sweet nothings in her ear*). **b** (*attributive*) *informal* of no value; indeterminate (*a nothing sort of day*). **4** no part, share, etc., of some thing (*the singer had nothing of his former power*). **5** non-existence; what does not exist. **6** (in calculations) no amount; nought (*a third of nothing is nothing*). ● *adverb* **1** not at all, in no way (*is nothing like enough*). **2** *informal* not at all (*Is he ill? — Ill nothing, he's dead.*). ☐ **be nothing to 1** not concern. **2** not compare with. **3** have no claim on a person's affections. **be** (or **have**) **nothing to do with 1** have no connection with. **2** not be involved or associated with. **for nothing 1** at no cost; without payment. **2** with no reward or result; to no purpose (*did all that work for nothing*). **have nothing on 1** be naked. **2** have no engagements. **have nothing on a person 1** have much less of a certain quality or ability than something else (*today's pop music has nothing on the old Broadway musicals*). **2** (of the police etc.) have no information that could show a person to be guilty of something. **make nothing of 1** do without hesitation. **2** treat as a trifle. **3** be unable to understand, use, or deal with. **no nothing** *informal* (concluding a list of negatives) nothing at all. **nothing doing** *informal* **1 a** there is no prospect of success or agreement. **b** I refuse. **2** nothing is happening. **nothing** (or **nothing else**) **for it** (often foll. by *but* to + infin.) no alternative (*nothing for it but to pay up*). **nothing less than** at least (*nothing less than a disaster*). **nothing** (or **not much**) **to it** (or *Brit.* **in it**) **1** untrue or unimportant. **2** simple to do. **think nothing of it** do not apologize or feel bound to show gratitude. [Old English *nān thing* (as NO¹, THING)]

nothing game *noun* N Amer. *Sport* a league game the outcome of which has no effect upon the final standings in the league.

noth·ing·ness *noun* **1** non-existence; the non-existent. **2** worthlessness, triviality, insignificance.

no·tice ● *noun* **1** attention, observation (*it escaped my notice*). **2** a displayed sheet etc. bearing an announcement or other information. **3 a** an intimation or warning, esp. a formal one to allow preparations to be made (*give notice; at a moment's notice*). **b** (often foll. by *to* + infin.) a formal announcement or declaration of intention to end an agreement or leave employment at a specified time (*hand in one's notice; notice to quit*). **4 a** a short published review or comment about a new play, book, etc. **b** a small advertisement or announcement in a newspaper or magazine (*birth and death notices*). ● *transitive verb* **1** (often foll. by *that, how*, etc. + clause) perceive, observe; take notice of. **2** remark upon; speak of. **3** treat (a person) with some degree of attention, favour, or politeness; recognize or acknowledge (a person) (*a young actor trying desperately to be noticed*). ☐ **at short** (or **a moment's**) **notice** with little warning. **put on notice** alert or warn (a person). **take notice** (or **no notice**) show signs (or no signs) of interest. **take notice of 1** observe; pay attention to. **2** act upon. [Old French from Latin *notitia* being known, from *notus* past participle of *noscere* know]

no·tice·able *adjective* **1** easily seen or noticed; perceptible. **2** worthy or deserving notice. ☐ **no·tice·ably** *adverb*

notice board *noun* a board for displaying notices.

noti·fi·able /ˈnoʊtɪˌfaɪəbəl/ *adjective* (of a disease, crop, pest, etc.) requiring that the appropriate authorities be notified.

noti·fy /ˈnoʊtɪˌfaɪ/ *transitive verb* (**-fies, -fied**) **1** (often foll. by *of*, or *that* + clause) inform or give notice to (a person). **2** *Brit.* make known; announce or report (a thing). ☐ **noti·fi·ca·tion** /-fɪˈkeɪʃən/ *noun* [Old French *notifier* from Latin *notificare* from *notus* known: see NOTICE]

no-till *noun* a method of farming in which seed is sown in unplowed ground, with herbicides being used to kill or control any existing vegetation.

no·tion *noun* **1 a** a concept or idea; a conception (*it was an absurd notion*). **b** an opinion (*has the notion that people are honest*). **c** a vague view or understanding (*have no notion what you mean*). **2** an inclination, impulse, or intention (*has no notion of conforming*). **3** (in *pl.*) esp. *N Amer.* small articles related to sewing, such as thread, ribbons, buttons, etc. [Latin *notio* idea, from *notus* past participle of *noscere* know]

no·tion·al *adjective* **1 a** existing only in the mind; imaginary. **b** (of knowledge etc.) speculative; not based on experiment etc. **2** *Grammar* of or pertaining to semantic content as opposed to grammatical structure or behaviour. ☐ **no·tion·al·ly** *adverb*

noto·chord /ˈnoʊtəˌkɔrd/ *noun* a cartilaginous skeletal rod supporting the body in all embryo and some adult chordate animals. [Greek *nōton* back + CHORD²]

no·tori·ous /noʊˈtɔːriəs, nə-/ *adjective* well known, esp. unfavourably (*a notorious criminal; notorious for its climate*). ☐ **no·tori·ety** /-təˈraɪəti/ *noun*

no·tori·ous·ly *adverb* [medieval Latin *notorius* from Latin *notus* (as NOTION)]

Notre-Dame, Monts /nɔtrəˈdam/ a mountain range in E Quebec, a northern outcrop of the Appalachian Mountains. They extend northeastward for some 800 km from Sherbrooke in S Quebec to Gaspé. [French, lit. 'Our Lady', so named on the feast day of the Assumption of the Virgin Mary]

Notre Dame Bay /ˈnoʊtɜr ˌdeɪm/ a large bay of the N Atlantic, indenting the coastline of N Newfoundland. [French, lit. 'Our Lady', in honour of the Virgin Mary]

no trump *noun* (also **no trumps**) *Bridge* a declaration or bid involving playing without a trump suit.

Not·ta·wa·saga Bay /ˌnɒtəwəˌsɒɡə/ a bay at the southern end of Georgian Bay in south central Ontario. [ultimately from Ojibwa *nahdowasaga* outlet of the river of the Iroquois]

Not·ta·way River /ˈnɒtəweɪ/ a river in W Quebec, 776 km long, rising northeast of Val-d'Or and flowing generally northwestward into James Bay south of Eastmain. [possibly Algonquin, = (river of) the enemy]

Not·ting·ham /ˈnɒtɪŋəm/ a town in east central England, the county town of Nottinghamshire; pop. (est. 2002) 271,400.

Not·ting·ham·shire /ˈnɒtɪŋəmˌʃɪːr/ a county in central England; county town, Nottingham.

Notts. *abbreviation* Nottinghamshire.

not·with·stand·ing ● *preposition* in spite of; without prevention by (*notwithstanding your objections; this fact notwithstanding*). ● *adverb* nevertheless; all the same. ● *conjunction* (usu. foll. by *that* + clause) although.

notwithstanding clause *noun* Cdn Section 33 of the Canadian Charter of Rights and Freedoms, which allows Parliament and the provincial legislatures to override Charter clauses covering fundamental freedoms and legal and equality rights.

Nou·ak·chott /nwakˈʃɒt/ the capital of Mauritania, situated on the Atlantic coast; pop. (est. 2000) 611,833.

nou·gat /ˈnuːɡət/ *noun* a candy made from sugar or honey, nuts, and egg white. [French from Provençal *nogat* from *noga* nut]

nought *noun* **1** *Brit.* the digit 0; a cipher. **2** *literary* or *archaic* (in certain phrases) nothing (*compare* NAUGHT). [Old English *nōwiht* from *ne* not + *ōwiht* var. of *āwiht* AUGHT¹]

noughts and crosses *noun* Brit. = TIC-TAC-TOE 1.

Nou·méa /nuːˈmeɪə/ the capital of the island of New Caledonia; pop. (est. 2002) 84,900. It was formerly called Port de France.

noun *noun* Grammar a word (other than a pronoun) or group of words used to name or identify any of a class of persons, places, or things (**common noun**), or a particular one of these (**proper noun**). [Anglo-French from Latin *nomen* name]

nour·ish /ˈnɜrɪʃ/ *transitive verb* **1 a** sustain with food. **b** enrich; promote the development of (the soil etc.). **c** provide with intellectual or emotional sustenance or enrichment. **2** foster or cherish (a feeling etc.). ☐ **nour·ish·er** *noun* [Old French *norir* from Latin *nutrire*]

nour·ish·ing /ˈnɜrɪʃɪŋ/ *adjective* (esp. of food) containing much nourishment; sustaining. ☐ **nour·ish·ing·ly** *adverb*

nour·ish·ment /ˈnɜrɪʃmənt/ *noun* **1** something that nourishes; sustenance, food. **2** the action, process, or fact of nourishing someone or something.

nous /naʊs/ *noun* **1** *Brit. informal* common sense; gumption. **2** *Philos.* the mind or intellect. [Greek]

nou·veau /ˈnuːvoʊ, nuːˈvoʊ/ *adjective* **1** *derogatory* or *jocular* (of a person) having recently become the thing specified (*nouveau gentry*). **2** modern; up-to-date (*nouveau chic*). [French, = new]

nouveau riche /ˌnuːvoʊ ˈriːʃ/ ● *noun* (pl. **nou·veaux riches** pronunc. same) a person who has recently acquired (usu. ostentatious) wealth. ● *adjective* of, pertaining to, or characteristic of a nouveau riche. [French, = new rich]

nouveau roman /ˌnuːvoʊ rɔːˈmɑ̃/ *noun* a style of avant-garde French novel that came to prominence in the 1950s, rejecting the plot, characters, and omniscient narrator central to the traditional novel in an attempt to reflect more faithfully the sometimes random nature of existence. [French, = new novel]

nou·velle /nuːˈvel/ *adjective* of, pertaining to, or characteristic of nouvelle cuisine. [French, = new]

nouvelle cuisine /nuːˌvel kwɪˈziːn/ *noun* a modern style of (esp. French) cooking that avoids traditional rich sauces and emphasizes the freshness of the ingredients and attractive presentation. [French, = new cooking]

nouvelle vague /nuːvel ˈvɑːɡ/ *noun* = NEW WAVE 2. [French, fem. of *nouveau* new + *vague* wave]

Nov. *abbreviation* November.

nova *noun* (*pl.* **novae** /-viː/ or **novas**) a star showing a sudden large increase of brightness and then subsiding. [Latin, fem. of *novus* new, because originally thought to be a new star]

Nova Lis·boa /ˌnɒːvə lizˈbɔːə/ the former name (until 1978) for HUAMBO.

Nova Sco·tia /ˌnɒːvə ˈskɔːʃə/ **1** a peninsula on Canada's southeast coast, separating the Bay of Fundy from the Atlantic Ocean. **2** a province of E Canada, comprising the peninsula of Nova Scotia and the adjoining Cape Breton Island; pop. (2001) 908,007; capital, Halifax. It was one of the original four provinces in the Dominion of Canada in 1867. □ **Nova Sco·tian** *adjective & noun* [Latin, lit. 'New Scotland']

Nova Scotia duck tolling retriever *noun* a reddish dog of a breed created by crossing black Labradors with red cocker spaniels, trained to attract ducks along a shoreline and then retrieve them. [from *toll*, v. = lure or decoy]

Nov·aya Zem·lya /ˌnɒːvəjə zemˈljɒ/ two large uninhabited islands in the Arctic Ocean off the north coast of Siberian Russia. [Russian, = new land]

novel[1] *noun* **1** a fictitious prose story of considerable length and complexity, esp. one representing character and action with some degree of realism. **2** (prec. by *the*) this type of literature. [Italian *novella* (*storia* story) fem. of *novello* new, from Latin *novellus* from *novus*]

novel[2] *adjective* of a new kind or nature; strange; previously unknown. □ **novel·ly** *adverb* [Old French from Latin *novellus* from *novus* new]

novel·ette *noun* **1** a short novel. **2** esp. *Brit. derogatory* a light romantic novel.

novel·et·tish *adjective derogatory* in the style of a light romantic novel; sentimental.

novel food *noun* a genetically modified or radically altered food, or a substance sold as a food that does not have a history of safe use as a food.

novel·ist *noun* a writer of novels. □ **novel·is·tic** *adjective*

novel·ize *transitive verb* (also esp. *Brit.* **-ise**) make into a novel. □ **novel·iz·a·tion** *noun*

novel·la /nəˈvelə/ *noun* (*pl.* **novel·las**) a short novel or narrative story. [Italian: see NOVEL[1]]

novel·ty ● *noun* (*pl.* **-ties**) **1 a** newness; new character. **b** originality. **2** a new or unusual thing or occurrence. **3** a small toy or decoration etc. of novel design. **4** (*attributive*) having novelty; appealing through newness; faddish (*novelty song*). [Old French *novelté* (as NOVEL[2])]

Nov·em·ber *noun* the eleventh month of the year. [Latin *November* from *novem* nine (originally the ninth month of the Roman year)]

nov·ena /nɒːˈviːnə/ *noun Catholicism* a devotion consisting of special prayers or services on nine successive days. [medieval Latin from Latin *novem* nine]

No·verre /nɒˈver/ **Jean-Georges** (1727–1810), French choreographer and dance theorist. He stressed the importance of dramatic motivation and criticized overemphasis on technical virtuosity; his work, esp. as set out in *Lettres sur la danse et sur les ballets* (1760), had a significant influence on the development of ballet.

Nov·go·rod /ˈnɒvɡəˌrɒd/ a city in NW Russia, on the Volkhov River at the northern tip of Lake Ilmen; pop. (est. 2002) 227,900. Russia's oldest city, first chronicled in 859, it became the first Russian principality in 862. It was a major commercial and cultural centre of medieval E Europe, developing important trading links with Constantinople, the Baltic, Asia, and the rest of Europe.

nov·ice /ˈnɒvɪs/ *noun* **1** a beginner; an inexperienced person (also *attributive*: *novice programmer*). **2** a probationary member of a religious order, before the taking of vows. **3** a horse, dog, etc. that has not won a major prize in a competition. **4** *Cdn* **a** a level of children's sports, usu. involving children aged 8 to 9. **b** a player in this age group. [Latin *novicius* from *novus* new]

Novi Sad /ˌnɒːviˈsad/ an industrial city in Serbia, on the Danube River, capital of the autonomous province of Vojvodina; pop. (est. 2002) 175,400.

novi·ti·ate /nɒːˈvɪʃiət/ *noun* **1** the period of being a novice. **2** a religious novice. **3** novices' quarters. [French *noviciat* or medieval Latin *noviciatus* (as NOVICE)]

novo·caine /ˈnɒːvəˌkeɪn/ *noun* a local anaesthetic derived from benzoic acid. [Latin *novus* new + -CAINE]

Novo·kuz·netsk /ˌnɒːvəkʊzˈnjetsk/ an industrial city in the Kuznets Basin in south central Siberian Russia; pop. (est. 2002) 556,800.

Novo·si·birsk /ˌnɒːvəsəˈbiːrsk/ a city in central Siberian Russia, to the west of the Kuznets Basin, on the Ob River; pop. (est. 2002) 1,396,800.

no vote *noun* a vote in opposition to a proposal etc.

now ● *adverb* **1** at the present or mentioned time. **2** immediately (*I must go now*). **3** by this or that time (*it was now clear*). **4** under the present circumstances (*I cannot now agree*). **5** on this further occasion (*what do you want now?*). **6** in the immediate past (*just now*). **7** in these times; nowadays. **8** (esp. in a narrative or discourse) then, next (*now to consider the next point*). **9** (without reference to time, giving various tones to a sentence) surely, I insist, I wonder, etc. (*now what do you mean by that?*; *oh come now!*). ● *conjunction* (often foll. by *that* + clause) as a consequence of the fact (*now that I am older*; *now you mention it*). ● *noun* this time; the present (*should be there by now*; *has happened before now*). ● *adjective informal* modern, fashionable. □ **as of now** from or at this time. **for now** until a later time (*goodbye for now*). **now and again** (or **then**) from time to time; intermittently. **now now** used to reprimand or pacify a person. **now or never** an expression of urgency. □ **now·ness** *noun* [Old English *nū*]

now·a·days *adverb* at the present time or age; in these times.

noway *adverb* (also **noways**) in no manner; not at all (*compare no way* (NO[1])).

Nowel *noun* (also **Nowell**) *archaic var.* of NOEL.

no·where ● *adverb* in, at, or to no place; not anywhere. ● *noun* **1** no place. **2** a remote, dull, or nondescript place. ● *adjective slang* **1** remote, insignificant. **2** unsatisfactory, dull (*a nowhere job*). □ **come out of** (or **from**) **nowhere** be suddenly evident or successful. **get nowhere** make or cause to make no progress. **in the middle of nowhere** *informal* remote from urban life. **nowhere near** not nearly. [Old English *nāhwǣr* (as NO[1], WHERE)]

no·wheres·ville *noun informal* **1** a remote or insignificant town or village. **2** a job or position that lacks prestige, recognition, or the opportunity for advancement. **3** anything that is impractical, unrealistic, or fruitless.

no win *attributive adjective* of or designating a situation in which success is impossible.

no·wise *adverb* = NOWAY.

nowt /naut/ *noun Brit. informal* or *dialect* nothing. [var. of NOUGHT]

NOx *noun* oxides of nitrogen, esp. as atmospheric pollutants.

nox·ious /ˈnɒkʃəs/ *adjective* **1** harmful, injurious (*noxious fumes*). **2** morally harmful; unwholesome. □ **nox·ious·ly** *adverb* **nox·ious·ness** *noun* [from Latin *noxius* from *noxa* harm]

noxious weed *noun* a plant considered harmful to animals or the environment.

noz·zle *noun* **1** a spout on a hose etc. through which a stream of air or liquid issues. **2** a duct in a jet or rocket engine in which the speed of the ejected fuel is increased. [NOSE + -LE[2]]

NP *abbreviation* **1** Notary Public. **2** noun phrase. **3** NURSE PRACTITIONER.

Np *symbol Chem.* the element neptunium.

n.p. *abbreviation* **1** new paragraph. **2** no place of publication.

NPT *abbreviation* Non-Proliferation Treaty.

nr. *abbreviation* near.

NRA *abbreviation* **1** (in the US) National Rifle Association. **2** (in the UK) National Rivers Authority.

NRC *abbreviation* **1** (in Canada) National Research Council of Canada. **2** (in the US) Nuclear Regulatory Commission.

NRSV *abbreviation* NEW REVISED STANDARD VERSION.

NS *abbreviation* Nova Scotia.

ns *abbreviation* nanosecond.

NSA *abbreviation* (in the US) National Security Agency.

NSAID /ˈensed/ *abbreviation* non-steroidal anti-inflammatory drug.

NSC *abbreviation* (in the US) National Security Council.

NSERC /ˈensɜrk/ *abbreviation* (in Canada) Natural Sciences and Engineering Research Council.

NSF *abbreviation* **1** not sufficient funds. **2** (in the US) National Science Foundation.

NST *abbreviation* NEWFOUNDLAND STANDARD TIME.

NSW *abbreviation* New South Wales.

NT *abbreviation* **1** New Testament. **2** NEWFOUNDLAND TIME. **3** Northwest Territories (in official postal use). **4** Northern Territory (of Australia).

n't *adverb* (in combination) = NOT 1 (usu. with *is*, *are*, *have*, *must*, and the auxiliary verbs *can*, *do*, *should*, *would*, *might*, *ought*: *isn't*; *mustn't*) (*see also* CAN'T, DON'T, WON'T). [contraction]

NTD *abbreviation* neural tube defect.

nth /enθ/ *see* N².

NTSC *abbreviation* National Television Standards Committee.

NU *abbreviation* (in postal use) Nunavut.

nu /nju:/ *noun* the thirteenth letter of the Greek alphabet (N, *ν*). [Greek]

nu- *combining form* informal respelling of 'new', used esp. in names of new or revived genres of popular music (*nu-metal bands*).

nuance /ˈnuːɒns, ˈnjuː-/ ● *noun* a subtle difference in or shade of meaning, feeling, colour, etc. ● *transitive verb* give a nuance or nuances to. □ **nu·anced** *adjective* [French from *nuer* to shade, ultimately from Latin *nubes* cloud]

nub *noun* **1** the point or gist (of a matter or story). **2** a small lump or chunk. **3** a stub; a protuberance. **4** a knot or irregularity in fabric. □ **nubby** *adjective* [apparently var. of *knub*, from Middle Low German *knubbe*, *knobbe* KNOB]

nub·bin *noun* N Amer. a small lump or stub. [diminutive of NUB]

nub·ble *noun* a small knob or lump. □ **nub·bly** *adjective* [diminutive of NUB]

Nubia /ˈnuːbiə, ˈnjuː-/ an ancient region of S Egypt and N Sudan, including the Nile valley between Aswan and Khartoum and the surrounding area. Much of Nubia is now drowned by the waters of Lake Nasser, formed by the building of the two dams at Aswan. Nubians constitute an ethnic minority group in Egypt. □ **Nu·bian** *adjective & noun*

nu·bile /ˈnuːbaɪl, ˈnjuː-/ *adjective* (of a woman) sexually attractive. □ **nu·bil·ity** /-ˈbɪlɪti/ *noun* [Latin *nubilis* from *nubere* become the wife of]

nu·buck /ˈnuːbʌk/ *noun* a type of cow, pig, or lamb skin which is brushed to give it the feel and look of suede. [origin obscure: perhaps from respelling of NEW + BUCK¹]

nu·chal /ˈnuːkəl, ˈnjuː-/ *adjective* of or relating to the nape of the neck. [*nucha* nape, from medieval Latin *nucha* medulla oblongata, from Arabic *nuka'* spinal marrow]

nu·cle·ar /ˈnuːkliər, ˈnjuː-/ *adjective* **1** of, relating to, or constituting a nucleus. **2** using, producing, or resulting from nuclear energy (*nuclear reactor*). **3** of, involving, or possessing nuclear weapons.

nuclear bomb *noun* a bomb using the release of energy by nuclear fission or fusion or both.

nuclear club *noun* the nations possessing nuclear weapons.

nuclear disarmament *noun* the gradual or total reduction by a state of its nuclear weapons.

nuclear energy *noun* = ATOMIC ENERGY.

nuclear family *noun* a couple and their children, regarded as a basic social unit.

nuclear fission *noun* a nuclear reaction in which a heavy nucleus splits spontaneously or on impact with another particle, with the release of energy.

nuclear force *noun* a strong attractive force between nucleons in the atomic nucleus that holds the nucleus together.

nuclear-free *adjective* (of a country or region) free from nuclear weapons, power, etc.

nuclear fuel *noun* a substance that will sustain a fission chain reaction so that it can be used as a source of nuclear energy.

nuclear fusion *noun* a nuclear reaction in which atomic nuclei of low atomic number fuse to form a heavier nucleus with the release of energy.

nuclear magnetic resonance *noun* the absorption of electromagnetic radiation by a nucleus having a magnetic moment when in an external magnetic field, used mainly as an analytical technique and in body imaging for diagnosis. Abbr.: **NMR**.

nuclear medicine *noun* the branch of medicine that deals with the use of radioactive substances in research, diagnosis, and treatment.

nuclear physics *noun* the physics of atomic nuclei and their interactions, esp. in the generation of nuclear energy. □ **nuclear physicist** *noun*

nuclear power *noun* **1** electric or motive power generated by a nuclear reactor. **2** a country that has nuclear weapons. □ **nuclear-powered** *adjective*

nuclear reactor *noun see* REACTOR 2.

nuclear umbrella *noun* supposed protection afforded by an alliance with a country possessing nuclear weapons.

nuclear warfare *noun* warfare in which nuclear weapons are used.

nuclear waste *noun* radioactive waste material e.g. from the use or reprocessing of nuclear fuel.

nuclear weapon *noun* a missile, bomb, etc., using the release of energy by nuclear fission or fusion or both.

nuclear winter *noun* a period of abnormal cold and darkness predicted to follow a nuclear war, caused by a layer of smoke and dust in the atmosphere blocking the sun's rays.

nu·cle·ase /ˈnuːklieɪz, ˈnjuː-/ *noun* any enzyme that catalyzes the breakdown of nucleic acids.

nu·cle·ate ● *adjective* /ˈnuːkliət, ˈnjuː-/ having a nucleus. ● *transitive & intransitive verb* /ˈnuːklieɪt, ˈnjuː-/ form or form into a nucleus. □ **nu·cle·a·tion** /-ˈeɪʃən/ *noun* [Late Latin *nucleare nucleat-* form a kernel (as NUCLEUS)]

nu·clei *pl.* of NUCLEUS.

nu·cle·ic acid /nuːˈkleɪɪk, -ˈkliːɪk, njuː-/ *noun* either of two complex organic substances (DNA and RNA) present in living cells, whose molecules consist of many nucleotides linked in a long chain.

nucleo- /ˈnuːklɪo, ˈnjuː-/ *combining form* nucleus; nucleic acid (*nucleoprotein*).

nu·cle·olus /nuːˈkliːˈoːləs, ˌnjuː-/ *noun* (*pl.* **nu·cle·oli** /-laɪ/) a small dense spherical structure in the nucleus of a cell during interphase. □ **nu·cle·olar** *adjective* [Late Latin, diminutive of Latin *nucleus*: see NUCLEUS]

nu·cle·on /ˈnuːklɪɒn, ˈnjuː-/ *noun* Physics a proton or neutron.

nu·cle·on·ics /ˌnuːkliˈɒnɪks, ˌnjuː-/ *plural noun* (treated as *sing.*) the branch of science and technology concerned with atomic nuclei and nucleons, esp. the exploitation of nuclear power. □ **nu·cle·on·ic** *adjective* [NUCLEAR, after *electronics*]

nu·cleo·pro·tein /ˌnuːklɪoˈprɒtiːn, ˌnjuː-/ *noun* a complex of nucleic acid and protein.

nu·cleo·side /ˈnuːkliəˌsaɪd, ˈnjuː-/ *noun* Biochem. an organic compound consisting of a purine or pyrimidine base linked to a sugar, e.g. adenosine.

nu·cleo·synth·e·sis /ˌnuːklɪoˈsɪnθəsɪs, ˌnjuː-/ *noun* Astronomy the cosmic formation of atoms more complex than the hydrogen atom. □ **nu·cleo·syn·thet·ic** /-ˈθetɪk/ *adjective*

nu·cleo·tide /ˈnuːkliəˌtaɪd, ˈnjuː-/ *noun* Biochem. an organic compound consisting of a nucleoside linked to a phosphate group.

nu·cle·us /ˈnuːkliəs, ˈnjuː-/ *noun* (*pl.* **nu·clei** /-li,aɪ/) **1 a** the central part or thing around which others are collected. **b** the kernel of an aggregate or mass. **2** an initial part meant to receive additions. **3** Astronomy the solid part of a comet's head. **4** Physics the positively charged central core of an atom that contains most of its mass. **5** Biol. a large dense organelle of eukaryotic cells, containing the genetic material. **6** a discrete mass of grey matter in the central nervous system. **7** Chem. a ring structure or other arrangement of atoms which is characteristic of a group of compounds. **8** the most prominent syllable or syllables in a word or utterance. [Latin, = kernel, inner part, diminutive of *nux nucis* nut]

nu·clide /ˈnuːklaɪd, ˈnjuː-/ *noun* Physics a distinct kind of atom or nucleus characterized by a specific number of protons and neutrons. [NUCLEUS + Greek *eidos* form]

nude ● *adjective* **1 a** (of a person, body part, etc.) naked, unclothed, bare. **b** (of performance etc.) involving a naked or scantily clad person or persons. **c** (of a thing) lacking natural coverage, foliage, etc. **2** (of hosiery etc.) flesh-coloured and very sheer. **3** (of beaches etc.) used by nudists. ● *noun* **1** a painting, sculpture, photograph, etc. of a nude human figure. **2** a nude person. **3** (prec. by *the*) an unclothed state (*sleeps in the nude*). [Latin *nudus*]

nudge ● *verb* **1** *transitive* prod gently esp. with the elbow to attract attention. **2** *transitive* push gently or gradually. **3** *transitive* coax or give a gentle reminder or encouragement to (a person). **4** *intransitive* move slightly or slowly, esp. by gradual pushing (*we nudged through the lily pads*). **5** *transitive & intransitive* increase or approach (an age, figure, or level) very closely. ● *noun* **1 a** the act or an instance of nudging. **b** a gentle push. **2** a gentle reminder. □ **nudge, nudge, wink, wink** used to imply a sexual innuendo in the preceding phrase or clause. □ **nudg·er** *noun* [17th c.: origin unknown: compare Norwegian dial. *nugga*, *nyggja* to push, rub]

nudi·branch /ˈnuːdɪbraŋk, ˈnjuː-/ ● *noun* a marine gastropod of the order Nudibranchia, with exposed gills and a vestigial shell; a sea slug. ● *adjective* of or relating to this order. □ **nudi·bran·chi·ate**

/-ˈbraŋkiət/ *noun & adjective* [modern Latin *Nudibranchia*, from Latin *nudus* NUDE + BRANCHIA]

nud·ie *noun informal* **1** (usu. *attributive*) a film, photograph, etc. featuring nudity (*a nudie magazine*). **2** a nude person.

nud·ist *noun* a person who advocates or practises going unclothed. □ **nud·ism** *noun*

nud·ity *noun* the state or condition of being nude; nakedness.

nud·nik /ˈnuːdnɪk/ *noun slang* a pestering, nagging, or irritating person. [Yiddish from Russian *nudnyĭ* 'tedious, boring' + -NIK]

Nu·el·tin Lake /nuːˈeltɪn/ an irregularly-shaped lake straddling the border between Nunavut and NE Manitoba. Many islands dot its elaborately indented shoreline. [Chipewyan, = sleeping island lake]

Nuer /ˈnuːər/ ● *noun* **1** (*pl.* same or **Nuers**) a member of an African people of southeastern Sudan and Ethiopia, traditionally rearers of cattle. **2** the Nilotic language of these people. ● *adjective* of or relating to this people or their language. [the name in Dinka]

Nuevo León /ˌnweivo ˈleiɒn/ a state of NE Mexico, on the border with the US; capital, Monterrey.

nuevo sol /ˈnweivo sɒl/ *noun* = SOL³.

nuff *noun slang* enough (*nuff said*). [representing pronunciation of ENOUGH]

nug *noun Cdn* (*Nfld*) a chunk or rough mass of wood sawn from a log for use as fuel. [origin unknown]

nu·ga·tory /ˈnuːgəˌtɔri, ˈnjuː-/ *adjective* **1** futile, trifling, worthless. **2** inoperative; not valid. [Latin *nugatorius* from *nugari* to trifle, from *nugae* jests]

nug·get *noun* **1 a** a lump of gold, platinum, etc., as found in the earth. **b** a lump of anything compared to this. **2** a valuable idea or fact (*a little nugget of information*). **3** *N Amer.* a small piece of chicken etc. covered with batter and deep-fried. [apparently from dial. *nug* lump etc.]

nuis·ance /ˈnuːsəns, ˈnjuː-/ *noun* **1** a person, thing, or circumstance causing trouble, annoyance, or inconvenience. **2** anything harmful or offensive to the community or a member of it and for which a legal remedy exists. [Old French, = hurt, from *nuire nuis-* from Latin *nocēre* to hurt]

nuisance grounds *plural noun Cdn* (*West*) *informal* a garbage dump.

nuisance value *noun* an advantage resulting from the capacity to harass or frustrate.

nuke *informal* ● *noun* **1** a nuclear weapon. **2** a nuclear power station. ● *transitive verb* **1** bomb or destroy with nuclear weapons. **2** *informal* cook (food) in a microwave. **3** *slang* destroy. [abbreviation]

Nuku'alofa /ˌnuːkuːəˈlɒfə/ the capital of Tonga, situated on the island of Tongatapu; pop. (est. 2002) 24,300.

null ● *adjective* **1** (esp. **null and void**) invalid; having no legal or binding force. **2 a** associated with, producing, or having the value zero. **b** designating or pertaining to a point or region in which no effect or force occurs or in which effects or forces cancel each other out. **3** (of a class or set) **a** empty; having no elements (*null list*). **b** all the elements of which are zeros (*null matrix*). **4** without distinctive character or expression. ● *noun* **1 a** *Computing* (in full **null character**) a character denoting nothing, usu. represented by a zero. **b** a dummy letter in a cipher. **2** a zero; nothing. ● *transitive verb* annul, cancel, make void. [French *nul nulle* or Latin *nullus* none, from *ne* not + *ullus* any]

nul·lah /ˈnʌlə/ *noun* a dry riverbed or ravine, esp. in the Indian subcontinent. [Hindi *nālā*]

Null·ar·bor Plain /ˈnʌlərˌbɔr/ a vast arid plain in SW Australia, stretching inland from the Great Australian Bight. It contains no surface water and is sparsely vegetated and almost uninhabited. [Latin *nullus arbor* no tree]

null hypothesis *noun* a hypothesis suggesting that the difference between statistical samples does not imply a difference between populations, any apparent difference being due to sampling or experimental error.

nul·li·fy *transitive verb* (-**fies**, -**fied**) **1** make legally null and void; annul, invalidate. **2** make of no value or use; cancel out, neutralize. □ **nul·li·fi·ca·tion** *noun*

nul·lip·ara /nʌˈlɪpərə/ *noun* a female who has never borne a child. □ **nul·lip·ar·ous** *adjective* [modern Latin from Latin *nullus* none + -*para* fem. of -*parus* from *parere* bear children]

nul·li·pore /ˈnʌlɪˌpɔr/ *noun* any of various seaweeds able to secrete lime. [Latin *nullus* none + PORE¹]

nul·lity *noun* (*pl.* -**ties**) **1** *Law* **a** the fact of being null and void; invalidity, esp. of marriage. **b** an act, document, etc., that is null. **c** a fact or circumstance causing nullity. **2 a** nothingness; the condition of being non-existent. **b** a mere nothing; a nonentity. [French *nullité* from Latin *nullus* none]

Num. *abbreviation* Numbers (Bible).

Numa Pom·pil·ius /ˌnuːmə pɒmˈpɪliəs/ the legendary second king of Rome, successor to Romulus, revered by the ancient Romans as the founder of nearly all their religious institutions.

numb ● *adjective* **1** (often foll. by *with*) deprived of feeling or the power of motion (*numb with cold*). **2** unable to experience emotion (*I felt numb after his death*). ● *transitive verb* **1** make numb. **2** stupefy, paralyze. □ **numb·ing** *adjective* (also in *combination*). **numb·ing·ly** *adverb* **numb·ly** *adverb* **numb·ness** *noun* [Middle English *nome(n)* past participle of *nim* take: for -*b* compare THUMB.]

num·bat /ˈnʌmbat/ *noun* a small termite-eating Australian marsupial, *Myrmecobius fasciatus*, with a bushy tail and black and white striped back. [Nyungar *numbad*]

num·ber ● *noun* **1 a** an arithmetical value representing a particular quantity and used in counting and making calculations. **b** a word, symbol, or figure representing this; a numeral. **c** an arithmetical value showing position in a series esp. for identification, reference, etc. (*registration number*). **d** = TELEPHONE NUMBER 1. **2** (often foll. by *of*) the total count or aggregate (*the number of accidents has decreased; twenty in number*). **3 a** (in *pl.*) arithmetic (*not good at numbers*). **b** the study of the behaviour of numbers; numerical reckoning (*the laws of number*). **4 a** (in *sing.* or *pl.*) a quantity or amount; a total; a count (*a large number of people; only in small numbers*). **b** (**a number of**) several (of), some (of). ¶ In this sense, *a number of* is normally used with a plural verb, e.g. *a number of problems remain*. **c** (in *pl.*) numerical preponderance (*force of numbers; there is safety in numbers*). **5 a** a person or thing having a place in a series, esp. a single issue of a magazine, an item in a program, etc. **b** a song, dance, musical item, etc. **6** company, collection, group (*among our number*). **7** *Grammar* **a** the classification of words by their singular or plural forms. **b** a particular such form. **8** *informal* a person or thing regarded familiarly or affectionately (usu. qualified in some way: *an attractive little number*). **9** *informal* a garment. ● *transitive verb* **1** count or class among people or things of a specified category (*I number you among my friends*). **2** assign a number or numbers to. **3** have, equal, or amount to (a specified number). **4 a** count or ascertain the number of. **b** include or comprise in a specified number. □ **any number of** **1** *informal* a large unspecified number of. **2** any particular whole quantity of. **by** (**the**) **numbers** following simple instructions (as if) identified by numbers. **one's days are numbered** one does not have long to live, prosper, etc. **do a number on** (**a person**) *N Amer. slang* **1** disparage, speak, or write of with contempt. **2** deceive. **have a person's number** *informal* understand a person's real motives, character, etc. **have a person's number on it** (of a bomb, bullet, etc.) be destined to hit a specified person. **one's number is up** *informal* one is finished or doomed to die. **without number** innumerable. □ **num·bered** *adjective* **num·ber·ing** *adjective & noun* [Old French *nombre* (n.), *nombrer* (v.) from Latin *numerus, numerare*]

number cruncher *noun slang* **1** *Computing & Math.* a machine capable of complex calculations etc. **2** a person, esp. an accountant or statistician, whose primary concern is with numbers, statistics, budgets, the bottom line, etc. □ **number crunching** *noun* (usu. hyphenated when *attributive*)

numbered company *noun Cdn* a corporation the name of which is simply its registration number followed by the province in which it is registered.

numbered treaty *noun* any of a number of land cession treaties signed from 1871 to 1921 between the Canadian government and Aboriginal nations throughout the north and west of Canada.

number·less *adjective* **1** innumerable, countless. **2** without a number or numbers.

number one *informal* ● *noun* **1** oneself, one's own person and interests (*always takes care of number one*). **2** the best; the finest quality (*we're number one!*). **3** *euphemism* an act of urination. ● *adjective* **1** leading; most important (*the number one priority; the number one album in Canada*). **2** best; finest quality (*number one Northern wheat*).

number plate *noun Brit.* = LICENCE PLATE.

Num·bers the fourth book of the Bible, relating the experiences of the Israelites under Moses during their wanderings in the desert; the English title is explained by its two records of a census; its Hebrew title means 'in the wilderness'.

numbers game *noun* **1** *N Amer.* (also **numbers, numbers racket**) a lottery based on the occurrence of unpredictable numbers in the results of races etc. **2** a comparison, contest, etc. regarded merely in terms of numerical statistics.

number sign *noun* the sign #, esp. on a telephone keypad or computer keyboard.

Number 10 *noun* (also **Number Ten**) (in the UK) 10 Downing Street, the official London home of the British prime minister.

number theory *noun* the branch of mathematics that deals with the properties and relationships of numbers, esp. the positive integers.

number two *noun* **1** (often *attributive*) something second-rate. **2** a second-in-command. **3** *euphemism* an act of defecation.

num·bles /ˈnʌmbəlz/ *plural noun Brit. archaic* a deer's entrails. [Old French *numbles, nombles* loin etc., from Latin *lumbulus* diminutive of *lumbus* loin: compare UMBLES]

numb·nuts *noun N Amer. slang* a stupid or contemptible person.

numb·skull *noun* (also **num·skull**) a stupid or foolish person.

num·dah /ˈnʌmdə/ *noun* (in full **numdah rug**) an embroidered felt rug from India etc. [Urdu *namdā* from Persian *namad* carpet]

numen /ˈnuːmen, ˈnjuː-/ *noun* (*pl.* **nu·mina** /-mɪnə/) a local or presiding deity or spirit. [Latin *numen -minis*]

num·er·able /ˈnuːmərəbəl, ˈnjuː-/ *adjective* that can be counted. [Latin *numerabilis* from *numerare* NUMBER *verb*]

num·er·al /ˈnuːmərəl, ˈnjuː-/ ● *noun* a word, figure, or group of figures denoting a number. ● *adjective* expressing or denoting a number or numbers. [Late Latin *numeralis* from Latin (as NUMBER)]

num·er·ate /ˈnuːmərət, ˈnjuː-/ *adjective* acquainted with the basic principles of mathematics, esp. arithmetic. □ **num·er·acy** *noun* [Latin *numerus* number + -ATE[2] after *literate*]

num·er·a·tion /ˌnuːməˈreɪʃən, ˌnjuː-/ *noun* **1 a** a method or process of numbering or computing. **b** calculation. **2** the expression in words of a number written in figures.

num·er·a·tor /ˈnuːmərˌeɪtər, ˈnjuː-/ *noun* **1** the number above the line in a vulgar fraction showing how many of the parts indicated by the denominator are taken (e.g. 2 in $^2/_3$). **2** a person or device that numbers.

num·er·i·cal /nuːˈmerɪkəl, njuː-/ *adjective* (also **num·er·ic**) **1** of, pertaining to, or characteristic of a number or numbers (*numerical superiority*). **2** (of a figure, symbol, etc.) expressing a number. □ **num·er·i·cal·ly** *adverb* [medieval Latin *numericus* (as NUMBER)]

num·er·ol·ogy /ˌnuːməˈrɒlədʒi, ˌnjuː-/ *noun* (*pl.* **-gies**) the study of the supposed occult or esoteric significance of numbers. □ **num·ero·logic·al** /-rəˈlɒdʒɪkəl/ *adjective* **num·er·ol·o·gist** *noun* [Latin *numerus* number + -LOGY]

num·ero uno /ˌnuːməroːˈuːnoː/ *noun informal* = NUMBER ONE *noun* 1, 2. [Italian]

num·er·ous /ˈnuːmərəs, ˈnjuː-/ *adjective* **1** (with *pl.*) great in number (*received numerous gifts*). **2** consisting of many (*a numerous family*). **3** *Cdn* (*Nfld*) plentiful, abundant, copious; comprising many separate things. □ **num·er·ous·ly** *adverb* **num·er·ous·ness** *noun* [Latin *numerosus* (as NUMBER)]

Nu·midia /nuːˈmɪdiə, njuː-/ an ancient kingdom, later a Roman province, situated in North Africa in an area north of the Sahara corresponding roughly to present-day Algeria. □ **Nu·mid·ian** *adjective & noun*

nu·mina *pl.* of NUMEN.

nu·min·ous /ˈnuːmɪnəs, ˈnjuː-/ *adjective* **1 a** spiritual. **b** indicating the presence of a divinity. **2 a** awe-inspiring, uplifting. **b** aesthetically appealing. □ **nu·min·os·ity** /-ˈnɒsɪti/ *noun* [Latin *numen*: see NUMEN]

nu·mis·mat·ic /ˌnuːmɪzˈmatɪk, ˌnjuː-/ *adjective* of or relating to coins or medals. □ **nu·mis·mat·ic·ally** *adverb* [French *numismatique* from Latin *numisma* from Greek *nomisma -atos* current coin, from *nomizō* use currently]

nu·mis·mat·ics /ˌnuːmɪzˈmatɪks, ˌnjuː-/ *plural noun* (usu. treated as *sing.*) the study of coins or medals, esp. from an archaeological or historic standpoint. □ **nu·mis·ma·tist** /-ˈmɪzmətɪst/ *noun*

nummy *adjective N Amer. informal* delicious. [perhaps childish alteration of YUMMY]

num·nah /ˈnʌmnə/ *noun* a saddle cloth or pad placed under a saddle. [Urdu *namdā*: see NUMDAH]

num·skull *var.* of NUMBSKULL.

nun *noun* a member of a Christian community of women living under vows of poverty, chastity, and obedience, according to the rule of a particular order. □ **nun·like** *adjective* **nun·nish** *adjective* [Old English *nunne* and Old French *nonne* from ecclesiastical Latin *nonna* fem. of *nonnus* monk, originally a title given to an elderly person]

nuna·tak /ˈnʌnəˌtak/ *noun* an isolated peak of rock projecting above a surface of inland ice or snow. [Greenlandic]

Nuna·vik *noun* Arctic Quebec. [Inuit, = 'great land']

Nuna·vum·miut /ˌnʌnəˈvʊmiːət/ *plural noun* the people inhabiting the territory of Nunavut.

Nuna·vut /ˈnʌnəˌvʊt, ˈnuːnəvuːt/ a territory of N Canada extending northward from Manitoba, then northwestward to the Arctic Ocean, together with most of the Arctic Archipelago; pop. (2001) 26,745. [Inuktitut, = our land]

Nunavut Day *noun Cdn* (in Nunavut) July 9, observed as a holiday in commemoration of the final signing of the Nunavut Land Claim on July 9, 1993.

nun·buoy /ˈnʌnbɔɪ/ *noun* a buoy circular in the middle and tapering to each end. [obsolete *nun* child's top + BUOY]

Nunc Di·mit·tis /ˌnʌŋk dɪˈmɪtɪs/ *noun* the Song of Simeon (Luke 2:29-32) used as a canticle. [from the opening words *nunc dimittis* now let (your servant) depart]

nun·cha·ku /nʌnˈtʃaku/ *noun* (also **nunchaku stick, nun·chuk** /nʌnˈtʃʌk/) (usu. *pl.*) a Japanese martial arts weapon consisting of two usu. hardwood sticks joined together with a strap, chain, etc. [Japanese]

nun·ci·a·ture /ˈnʌnsiəˌtʃər/ *noun Catholicism* the office or tenure of a nuncio. [Italian *nunziatura* (as NUNCIO)]

nun·cio /ˈnʌnsioː, nʊn-/ *noun* (*pl.* **-cios**) *Catholicism* a papal ambassador to a foreign court or government. [Italian from Latin *nuntius* messenger]

Nunki /ˈnʊnki/ the second-brightest star in the constellation Sagittarius. [Babylonian]

nun·nery *noun* (*pl.* **-ies**) *hist.* a convent.

nunny bag *noun Cdn* (*Nfld*) a knapsack of sealskin, burlap, or canvas, used to carry supplies when hunting, sealing, etc. [English dialect *noony* 'meal at noon' + BAG]

Nuns' Island = SOEURS, ÎLE DES.

nuoc mam /nwɒkˈmam/ *noun* a spicy Vietnamese fish sauce. [Vietnamese]

nup·tial /ˈnʌpʃəl/ ● *adjective* **1** of or relating to marriage or weddings. **2** *Zool.* of or pertaining to mating or the breeding season, esp. designating characteristic breeding coloration or behaviour. ● *noun* (usu. in *pl.*) a wedding. [Latin *nuptialis* from *nuptiae* wedding, from *nubere nupt-* wed]

Nur·em·berg /ˈnɜrəmˌbɜrg, ˈnjɜr-/ a city in S Germany, in Bavaria; pop. (est. 2002) 486,800. In the 1930s the Nazi Party congresses and the annual Nazi Party rallies were held there and in 1945-6 it was the scene of the Nuremberg war trials, in which Nazi war criminals were tried by international military tribunal.

Nur·eyev /ˈnʊriev, nʊˈreief, njʊ-/ **Ru·dolf (Hamet·ovich)** (1938–93), Russian-born dancer and choreographer renowned for his virtuosity. After defecting to the West (1961), he joined the Royal Ballet in London (1962) and began a famous partnership with Margot Fonteyn; among other works he choreographed *The Sleeping Beauty* (1972) for The National Ballet of Canada.

nurse[1] ● *noun* **1** a person professionally trained to care for the sick or infirm, assist in surgery, treat minor medical problems, and give advice on health matters. **2** (formerly) a person employed or trained to take charge of young children. **3** *archaic* = WET NURSE. **4** *Forestry* (also **nurse tree, nurse crop,** etc.) a tree, crop, etc. planted as a shelter to others. **5** *Zool.* a sexually imperfect bee, ant, etc., caring for a young brood; a worker. ● *verb* **1 a** *intransitive* work as a nurse. **b** *transitive* care for (a person) during sickness or infirmity. **c** *transitive* give medical attention to (an illness or injury). **2 a** *transitive & intransitive* (of a woman) breastfeed (a baby). **b** *intransitive* feed or be fed at the breast or teat; suckle. **3** *transitive* harbour or nurture (a grievance, hatred, etc.). **4** *transitive* **a** foster; promote the development of. **b** tend or cultivate (a plant) carefully. **5** *transitive* consume (a drink) slowly. **6** *transitive* hold or treat carefully or caressingly (*he sat nursing my feet; Melissa stood nursing the teapot*). **7** *transitive archaic* (in *passive*; foll. by *in*) be reared or brought up in (a specified place, condition, etc.) (*nursed in poverty*). [Old French *norice, nurice* from Late Latin *nutricia* fem. of Latin *nutricius* from *nutrix -icis* from *nutrire* NOURISH]

nurse[2] *noun* any of various dogfishes and sharks. [originally *nusse*, perhaps derived by wrong division of *an huss* (compare ADDER)]

nurse·maid *noun* a woman hired to care for a child or children.

nurse practitioner *noun* a specially trained registered nurse who is qualified to diagnose and treat common diseases, minor injuries, etc.

nurs·ery *noun* (*pl.* **-eries**) **1 a** a room or place equipped for young children. **b** = DAYCARE 3. **2 a** a place where plants, trees, etc., are reared for sale or transplantation. **b** a place which breeds or supports animals, esp. a pond etc. where young fry are reared. **3** any sphere or place in or by which qualities or types of people are fostered or bred.

nursery·man *noun* (*pl.* **-men**) an owner of or worker in a plant nursery.

nursery rhyme *noun* a simple traditional song or story in rhyme for children.

nursery school *noun* a school for children below the age for compulsory education, usu. between the ages of three and five.

nursery slope *noun Brit. Skiing* a gentle slope suitable for beginners; a bunny run.

nurse's aide *noun* a person who assists registered nurses in hospital or home care by performing basic tasks such as making beds, serving meals, giving baths, etc.

nurs·ing *noun* **1 a** the practice or profession of providing health care as a nurse. **b** the duties of a nurse. **2** (*attributive*) concerned with or suitable for nursing the sick or infirm etc. (*nursing care*). **3** the action of breastfeeding.

nursing assistant *noun* a person who is trained to provide nursing care for patients who are not acutely ill, and to assist nurses in the care of the acutely ill.

nursing home *noun* an institution providing long-term health care, esp. for the elderly.

nursing mother *noun* a mother who is breastfeeding her baby.

nursing station *noun* **1** *Cdn* a clinic or small hospital in a remote community, staffed by nurses and visited regularly by a doctor. **2** the central desk on a hospital floor or ward where nurses complete paperwork, store medications, etc.

nurs·ling *noun* an infant or baby animal that is being suckled.

nur·tur·ance *noun* **1** emotional and physical nourishment and care given to someone. **2** the ability to provide such care. □ **nur·tur·ant** *adjective*

nur·ture ● *noun* **1** the process of bringing up or training (esp. children). **2** that which nurtures; food, nourishment. **3** the social environment as an influence on or determinant of personality (*opp.* NATURE 8). ● *transitive verb* **1** foster the development of; encourage. **2** bring up to maturity. **3** feed, nourish. □ **nur·tur·er** *noun* [Old French *nour(e)ture* (as NOURISH)]

Nut /nʊt/ *Egyptian Myth* the sky goddess, thought to swallow the sun at night and give birth to it in the morning. She is usually depicted as a naked woman, with her body arched above the earth which she touches with her feet and hands.

nut ● *noun* **1 a** a fruit consisting of a hard or tough shell around an edible kernel. **b** this kernel. **2** a small usu. square or hexagonal flat piece of metal or other material with a threaded hole through it for screwing on the end of a bolt to secure it. **3** *slang* **a** an obsessive enthusiast or devotee (*a health food nut*). **b** a crazy or eccentric person. **4** (in *pl.*) *coarse slang* the testicles. **5** *slang* a person's head. **6** esp. *Brit.* a small lump of coal, butter, etc. **7 a** a device fitted to the bow of a violin for adjusting its tension. **b** the fixed ridge on the neck of a stringed instrument over which the strings pass. ● *verb* (**nut·ted**, **nut·ting**) *intransitive* seek or gather nuts (*go nutting*). □ **do one's nut** esp. *Brit. slang* be extremely angry or agitated. **off one's nut** *slang* crazy. **a tough** (or **hard**) **nut to crack** a problem resisting easy solution. □ **nut·like** *adjective* [Old English *hnutu* from Germanic]

nu·tant /ˈnuːtənt, ˈnjuː-/ *adjective Bot.* nodding, drooping. [Latin *nutare* nod]

nu·ta·tion /nuːˈteɪʃən, njuː-/ *noun* **1** *Astronomy* a periodic oscillation of the earth's poles. **2** oscillation of the axis of a spinning body. **3** the act or an instance of nodding the head. **4** the spiral movement of a plant organ during growth. [Latin *nutatio* (as NUTANT)]

nut·bar *noun* **1** *N Amer. informal* an eccentric or crazy person. **2** (also **nut bar**) a bar made from chopped nuts and other vegetarian ingredients.

nut brown ● *noun* a dark brown colour. ● *adjective* (hyphenated when attributive) of this colour.

nut·case *noun slang* a crazy, eccentric, or foolish person.

nut·crack·er *noun* **1** a device for cracking the shell of a nut to reach the edible kernel. **2** a crow of the genus *Nucifraga*.

nut cutlet *noun Brit.* a cutlet-shaped savoury patty of chopped nuts and other ingredients.

nut·gall *noun* a gall found on dyer's oak, used as a dyestuff.

nut·hatch *noun* any small bird of the family Sittidae, climbing up and down tree trunks and feeding on nuts, insects, etc. [NUT + *hatch* related to HATCH²]

nut·house *noun slang* a mental home or hospital.

nut·let *noun* a small nut or nutlike fruit.

nut·meg *noun* **1** an evergreen E Indian tree, *Myristica fragrans*, yielding a hard aromatic spheroidal seed. **2** the seed of this grated or ground and used as a spice. □ **nut·meggy** *adjective* [Middle English: partial translation of Old French *nois mug(u)ede* ultimately from Latin *nux* nut + Late Latin *muscus* MUSK]

nutra·ceut·ical *noun* a food containing health-giving additives and having medicinal benefit. [blend of NUTRITION + PHARMACEUTICAL]

nu·tria /ˈnuːtrɪə, ˈnjuː-/ *noun* **1** the skin or fur of a coypu. **2** *N Amer.* the coypu. [Spanish, = otter]

nutri·ent /ˈnuːtrɪənt, ˈnjuː-/ ● *noun* any substance that provides essential nourishment for the maintenance of life. ● *adjective* serving as or providing nourishment. [Latin *nutrire* nourish]

nutri·ment /ˈnuːtrɪmənt, ˈnjuː-/ *noun* a nourishing substance. [Latin *nutrimentum* (as NUTRIENT)]

nu·tri·tion /nuːˈtrɪʃən, njuː-/ *noun* **1** the process by which humans or animals utilize food for the proper functioning of the organism. **2** the scientific study of this and of dietary requirements. □ **nu·tri·tion·al** *adjective* **nu·tri·tion·al·ly** *adverb* [French *nutrition* or Late Latin *nutritio* (as NUTRIENT)]

nu·tri·tion·ist /nuːˈtrɪʃənɪst, njuː-/ *noun* a person who studies or is an expert on the processes of esp. human nourishment.

nu·tri·tious /nuːˈtrɪʃəs, njuː-/ *adjective* rich in nutrients. □ **nu·tri·tious·ly** *adverb* **nu·tri·tious·ness** *noun*

nutri·tive /ˈnuːtrɪtɪv, ˈnjuː-/ *adjective* **1** of, pertaining to, or concerned in nutrition. **2** serving as nutritious food. [medieval Latin *nutritivus* (as NUTRIENT)]

nuts ● *adjective informal* crazy, mad, eccentric. ● *interjection informal* an expression of contempt or derision (*nuts to you*). □ **be nuts about** *informal* be enthusiastic about or very fond of.

nuts and bolts ● *plural noun* the practical details. ● *adjective* (usu. **nuts-and-bolts**) pertaining to the practical details.

nut·sedge *noun* any of various plants of the sedge family, esp. *Cyperus esculenta*, cultivated in the southwestern US for its edible tuber, a weed in other parts of N America.

nut·shell *noun* the hard exterior covering of a nut. □ **in a nutshell** in a few words; concisely stated.

nut·so *N Amer. informal* ● *noun* (*pl.* **-sos**) a crazy or eccentric person. ● *adjective* crazy, eccentric. [NUTS + -O]

nutsy *adjective* (**nuts·i·er**, **nuts·i·est**) *N Amer. informal* = NUTSO *adjective*.

nut·ter *noun* esp. *Brit. slang* a crazy or eccentric person.

nut tree *noun* any tree bearing nuts, esp. a hazel.

nutty *adjective* (**nut·ti·er**, **nut·ti·est**) **1 a** tasting like nuts. **b** having a rich mellow flavour. **2** *informal* crazy, eccentric. **3** enthusiastic (*nutty about boats*). **4** full of or having many nuts. □ **nutty as a fruitcake** *informal* crazy, extremely eccentric. □ **nut·ti·ly** *adverb* **nut·ti·ness** *noun*

Nuu-chah-nulth /nuːˈtʃɒnʊlθ/ ● *noun* **1** a member of a major linguistic group of the Wakashan living on the west coast of Vancouver Island. **2** the Wakashan language of this people. ● *adjective* of or relating to this people or their culture or language. [Nuu-chah-nulth, = 'all along the mountains']

Nuuk /nuːk/ the capital of Greenland, a port on the Davis Strait; pop. (est. 2002) 13,650. It was known by the Danish name Godthåb until 1979.

Nuxalk /nuːˈxɒlk/ ● *noun* **1** a member of a Salishan Aboriginal people of the central BC coast. **2** the Salishan language of this people. ● *adjective* of or relating to this people or their culture or language. ¶ Formerly known as BELLA COOLA. [Nuxalk *nuxalk*, the name for the Bella Coola Valley]

nux vom·ica /nʌks ˈvɒmɪkə/ *noun* **1** an E Indian tree, *Strychnos nux-vomica*, yielding a poisonous fruit. **2** the seeds of this tree, containing strychnine and used in homeopathic remedies etc. [Latin *nux* nut + *vomicus* from *vomere* vomit]

nuz·zle *verb* **1** *transitive* touch or rub gently with the nose. **2** *intransitive* (foll. by *against*, *up*) press the nose or mouth gently. **3** *transitive & intransitive* (foll. by *up to*, *against*, *into*) move so as to touch; snuggle. [Middle English from NOSE + -LE⁴]

NV *abbreviation* Nevada (in official postal use).

NW *abbreviation* **1** northwest. **2** northwestern.

NWA *noun Cdn* NATIONAL WILDLIFE AREA.

NWC *abbreviation Cdn hist.* = NORTH WEST COMPANY.

NWMP *abbreviation Cdn hist.* = NORTH WEST MOUNTED POLICE.

NWO *abbreviation* Northwestern Ontario.

N-word *noun* the word 'nigger'.

NWT *abbreviation* (also **N.W.T.**) **1** Northwest Territories. **2** *Cdn hist.* North-West Territories.

NY *abbreviation* New York (also in official postal use).

nyah *interjection* (also **nyah-nyah**) used to express the speaker's feeling of superiority or contempt for another. [imitative of a child's reduplicated phrase used in taunting]

nyala /ˈnjɑlə/ *noun* (*pl.* same) a large antelope, *Tragelaphus angasi*, native to southern Africa, with curved horns having a single complete turn. [Zulu]

Nyasa, Lake /naiˈɑsə/ (also called **Lake Malawi**) a lake in east central Africa, the third largest lake in Africa. About 580 km (360 miles) long, it forms most of the eastern border of Malawi with Mozambique and Tanzania. [lit. 'lake']

Ny·asa·land /naiˈɑsə,land/ the former name of Malawi until it gained independence in 1966.

NYC *abbreviation* New York City.

nyc·tal·opia /ˌnɪktəˈloːpiə/ *noun* = NIGHT BLINDNESS. [Late Latin from Greek *nuktalōps* from *nux nuktos* night + *alaos* blind + *ōps* eye]

nycti·trop·ic /ˌnɪktɪˈtroːpɪk/ *adjective Bot.* (of plant movements) occurring at night and caused by changes in light and temperature. [Greek *nukti-* combining form of *nux nuktos* night + *tropos* turn]

Nye·rere /njeˈreri/ **Jul·ius Kam·bar·age** (1922–99), Tanzanian leader, president of Tanganyika 1962–4 and of Tanzania 1964–85. The first prime minister of independent Tanganyika, he was also its first president; in 1964 he successfully negotiated union with Zanzibar. He was one of the founders of the Organization of African Unity.

ny·lon *noun* **1** any of various synthetic polyamide fibres having a protein-like structure, with tough, lightweight, elastic properties, used for textiles, cord, etc. **2** a nylon fabric. **3** (in *pl.*) pantyhose or stockings made of nylon. ☐ **ny·loned** *adjective* (in sense 3). [invented word, after *cotton*, *rayon*]

nymph ● *noun* **1** any of various mythological semi-divine spirits regarded as maidens and associated with aspects of nature, esp. rivers and woods. **2** esp. *literary* a beautiful young woman. **3 a** an immature form of some insects. **b** a young dragonfly or damselfly. **4** a fishing fly made to resemble the aquatic larva of a mayfly. ● *intransitive verb* fish using a nymph. ☐ **nymph·al** *adjective* **nymph·ean** /-ˈfiːən/ *adjective* [Latin *nympha* from Greek *numphē*]

nym·phae /ˈnɪmfiː/ *plural noun Anat.* the labia minora. [Latin, pl. of *nympha*: see NYMPH]

nym·phal·id /nɪmˈfalɪd/ ● *adjective* of or relating to the large family Nymphalidae of butterflies with degenerate forelegs. ● *noun* a butterfly of this family. [modern Latin genus name *Nymphalis*, from Latin *nympha* NYMPH]

nymph·et /nɪmˈfet, ˈnɪmfət/ *noun informal* a sexually attractive girl or young woman.

nym·pho *noun* (*pl.* **-phos**) *informal* a nymphomaniac. [abbreviation]

nym·pho·lepsy /ˈnɪmfə,lepsi/ *noun* ecstasy or frenzy caused by desire of the unattainable. [NYMPHOLEPT after *epilepsy*]

nym·pho·lept /ˈnɪmfə,lept/ *noun* a person afflicted with nympholepsy. ☐ **nym·pho·lep·tic** /-ˈleptɪk/ *adjective* [Greek *numpholēptos* caught by nymphs (as NYMPH, *lambanō* take)]

nym·pho·mania /ˌnɪmfəˈmeiniə/ *noun* excessive or uncontrollable sexual desire in women. ☐ **nym·pho·maniac** *noun & adjective* [modern Latin (as NYMPH, -MANIA)]

NYSE *abbreviation* New York Stock Exchange.

nys·tag·mus /nɪˈstagməs/ *noun* a rapid, involuntary, and usu. lateral movement of the eyeball. ☐ **nys·tag·mic** *adjective* [Greek *nustagmos* nodding]

ny·sta·tin /ˈnəistətɪn, ˈnɪs-/ *noun* an antibiotic used esp. to treat fungal infections. [New York *State* (where developed) + -IN]

Nyun·gar /ˈnjuŋɡr/ *noun* an Aboriginal language of SW Australia, now extinct.

Nyx /nɪks/ *Gk Myth* the female personification of Night, daughter of Chaos, a primeval deity seldom worshipped.

NZ *abbreviation* New Zealand.

Oo

O¹ *noun* (also **o**) (*pl.* **Os** or **O's**) **1** the fifteenth letter of the alphabet. **2** (**0**) = OH². **3** a human blood type of the ABO system. **4** a round thing, as a circle, spot, etc.

O² *abbreviation* (also **O.**) Old.

O³ *symbol Chem.* the element oxygen.

O⁴ *interjection* **1** *var.* of OH¹. **2** prefixed to a name in the vocative (*O Canada*).

O' *prefix* of Irish patronymic names (*O'Connor*). [Irish ó, ua, descendant]

o' *preposition* of, on (esp. in phrases: *o'clock*; *will-o'-the-wisp*). [abbreviation]

-o *suffix* forming usu. *slang* or *informal* variants or derivatives (*wacko*; *wino*). [perhaps OH¹ as jocular suffix]

-o- *suffix* the terminal vowel of combining forms (*spectro-*; *chemico-*; *Franco-*). ¶ Often elided before a vowel, as in *neuralgia*. [originally Greek]

OAC *abbreviation* **1** (also **o.a.c.**) on approved credit. **2** *Cdn* (*Ont.*) *hist.* Ontario Academic Credit, a senior level high school course, undertaken after Grade 12, usu. as preparation for university.

oaf *noun* (*pl.* **oafs**) **1** an awkward lout. **2** a stupid person. □ **oaf·ish** *adjective* **oaf·ish·ly** *adverb* **oaf·ish·ness** *noun* [originally = elf's child, var. of obsolete *auf* from Old Norse *álfr* elf]

Oahu /oːˈɒhuː/ the third largest of the Hawaiian islands; pop. (2000) 836,207. Its principal town, Honolulu, is the state capital of Hawaii. It is the site of Pearl Harbor, a US naval base (see PEARL HARBOR).

oak *noun* **1** any tree or shrub of the genus *Quercus* usu. having lobed leaves and bearing acorns. **2** the durable wood of this tree, used esp. for furniture and in building. **3** (*attributive*) made of oak (*oak table*). □ **oaken** *adjective* [Old English āc from Germanic]

oak apple *noun* (also **oak gall**) an apple-like gall containing larvae of certain wasps, found on oak trees.

Oak Bay 1 a small bay on the southeastern tip of Vancouver Island, just northeast of Victoria. **2** a district municipality on Victoria's east side, adjacent to the bay; pop. (2001) 17,798. □ **Oak Bayer** *noun* (in sense 2)

oaked *adjective* (of wines) matured in an oak container; flavoured by oak-aging.

oak fern *noun* any fern of northeastern N America of the genus *Gymnocarpium*.

Oak Island a small island off the east central coast of Nova Scotia, situated on the west side of Mahone Bay. According to legend, it is the site of a buried treasure that has been attributed to numerous pirates, such as William Kidd and Blackbeard. [so called because an oak tree apparently marks the spot of the lost treasure]

Oak·land an industrial port on the east side of San Francisco Bay in California; pop. (2000) 399,500.

oak·leaf lettuce *noun* a red or green variety of lettuce that has leaves with serrated edges and a slightly bitter taste.

Oak·ley, Annie (full name Phoebe Anne Oakley Moses) (1860–1926), US sharpshooter. She joined Buffalo Bill's Wild West Show in 1885 and became its star attraction for the next 17 years.

oakum /ˈoːkəm/ *noun* a loose fibre obtained by picking old rope to pieces and used esp. in caulking. [Old English ǣcumbe, ācumbe, lit. 'off-combings']

Oak·ville a town in S Ontario, on Lake Ontario, northeast of Burlington; pop. (2001) 144,738. □ **Oak·vil·lian** *noun* [after the area's great white oak trees and the local oak-stave industry]

oaky *adjective* (of wine etc.) having the coconut-like aroma or flavour of oak, acquired from the wood of the barrel in which it is aged. □ **oak·i·ness** *noun*

OAP *abbreviation* **1** *Cdn* Old Age Pension. **2** *Brit.* old-age pensioner.

oar *noun* **1** a pole with a wide, flat blade at one end used for rowing or steering a boat by leverage against the water. **2** a rower. □ **put one's oar in** interfere, meddle. **rest on one's oars** relax one's efforts. □ **oared** *adjective* (also in *combination*). [Old English ār from Germanic, perhaps related to Greek *eretmos* oar]

oar·fish *noun* a ribbonfish, *Regalecus glesne.*

oar·lock *noun N Amer.* a device on a boat's gunwale, esp. a pair of thole-pins, serving as a fulcrum for an oar and keeping it in place.

oars·man *noun* (*pl.* **-men**) a rower. □ **oars·man·ship** *noun*

oars·woman *noun* (*pl.* **-women**) a female rower.

OAS *abbreviation* **1** Organization of American States. **2** *Cdn* OLD AGE SECURITY.

oasis /oːˈeɪsɪs/ *noun* (*pl.* **oases** /-siːz/) **1** a fertile spot in a desert, where water is found. **2** an area or period of calm in the midst of turbulence. **3** (**Oasis**) *proprietary* a type of rigid, absorbent foam into which the stems of flowers can be secured in flower arranging. [Late Latin from Greek, apparently of Egyptian origin]

oast /oːst/ *noun* a kiln for drying hops. [Old English āst from Germanic]

oast·house /ˈoːsthaʊs/ *noun* a building containing a kiln for drying hops.

oat *noun* **1 a** a cereal plant, *Avena sativa*, cultivated in cool climates. **b** (in *pl.*) the grain yielded by this, used as food. **2** any other cereal of the genus *Avena*, esp. the wild oat, *A. fatua.* □ **feel one's oats** *informal* **1** be lively or frisky. **2** *N Amer.* revel in one's own power. **sow one's oats** (or **wild oats**) indulge in youthful excess or promiscuity. □ **oaten** *adjective* **oaty** *adjective* [Old English āte, pl. ātan, of unknown origin]

oat·cake *noun* a thin, unleavened, biscuit-like food made of oatmeal, common in Scotland and northern England.

oater *noun informal* a western movie or television show. [derivative of OAT, with allusion to horse feed]

Oates, 1 Joyce Carol (b.1938), US writer noted esp. for her realistic short stories and novels which focus on dysfunctional characters in modern society; her works include *A Garden of Earthly Delights* (1967) and *Them* (1969). **2 Titus** (1649–1705), English Protestant clergyman. He fabricated the Popish Plot (1678), a fictitious Jesuit plot to kill Charles II, massacre Protestants, and put the Catholic Duke of York on the English throne; the 'discovery' of the plot led to widespread panic and the execution of a number of Catholics.

oat grass *noun* any of various grasses, esp. of the genus *Arrhenatherum.*

oath /oːθ/ *noun* (*pl.* **oaths** /oːθs, oːðz/) **1** a solemn declaration or undertaking (often naming God) as to the truth of something or as a commitment to future action. **2** a statement or promise contained in an oath (*oath of allegiance*). **3** a profane or blasphemous utterance; a curse. □ **under** (or **on**) **oath** having sworn a solemn oath. **take** (or **swear**) **an oath** make such a declaration or undertaking. [Old English āth from Germanic]

oat·meal ● *noun* **1 a** rolled oats (also *attributive*: *oatmeal cookies*). **b** meal

---

Consonants: b *but* d *dog* f *few* g *get* h *her* j *yes* k *cat* l *leg* m *man* n *no* p *pen* r *red* s *sit*

made from ground oats. **2** *N Amer.* porridge made from oats. **3** a greyish-fawn colour flecked with brown. ● *adjective* of this colour.

OAU *abbreviation* Organization of African Unity.

Oax·a·ca /wəˈhɒkə/ **1** a state of S Mexico. **2** (in full **Oaxaca de Juárez** /dei ˈhwɑrez/) its capital city; pop. (2000) 257,000.

OB *abbreviation* *N Amer.* **1** obstetric. **2** obstetrics. **3** obstetrician.

Ob /ɒb/ the principal river of the W Siberian lowlands and one of the largest rivers in Russia. Rising in the Altai Mountains, it flows generally north and west for 5 410 km (3,481 miles) before entering the Gulf of Ob (or Ob Bay), an inlet of the Kara Sea, a part of the Arctic Ocean.

ob. *abbreviation* he or she died. [Latin *obiit*]

ob- *prefix* (also **oc-** before *c*, **of-** before *f*, **op-** before *p*) occurring mainly in words of Latin origin, meaning: **1** exposure, openness (*object*; *obverse*). **2** meeting or facing (*occasion*; *obvious*). **3** direction (*oblong*; *offer*). **4** opposition, hostility, or resistance (*obstreperous*; *opponent*; *obstinate*). **5** hindrance, blocking, or concealment (*obese*; *obstacle*; *occult*). **6** finality or completeness (*obsolete*; *occupy*). **7** (in technical words) inversely; in a direction or manner contrary to the usual (*obconical*; *obovate*). [Latin from *ob* towards, against, in the way of]

O/B *abbreviation* (also **o/b**) outboard.

Obad. *abbreviation* Obadiah (Bible).

Oba·diah /ˌoːbəˈdaiə/ **1** a Hebrew minor prophet. **2** the shortest book of the Bible, bearing his name.

ob·li·ga·to /ˌɒblɪˈɡɑːtoː/ *noun* (also **ob·li·ga·to**) (*pl.* **-tos**) *Music* an accompaniment, usu. special and unusual in effect, forming an integral part of a composition (*with violin obbligato*). [Italian, = obligatory, from Latin *obligatus* past participle (as OBLIGE)]

ob·con·i·cal /ɒbˈkɒnɪkəl/ *adjective* (also **ob·con·ic**) in the form of an inverted cone.

ob·cor·date /ɒbˈkɔrdeit/ *adjective* *Biol.* in the shape of a heart and attached at the pointed end.

ob·dur·ate /ˈɒbdjurət, -dɜr-/ *adjective* **1** stubborn, unyielding. **2** hardened against esp. moral persuasion or influence.

□ **ob·dur·acy** *noun* **ob·dur·ate·ly** *adverb* **ob·dur·ate·ness** *noun* [Latin *obduratus* past participle of *obdurare* (as OB-, *durare* harden, from *durus* hard)]

OBE *abbreviation* (in the UK) Officer of the Order of the British Empire.

obeah /ˈoːbiə/ *noun* a kind of sorcery or witchcraft practised esp. in the W Indies. [Twi *ɔbayifo* sorcerer, from *bayi* sorcery]

obedi·ence /oːˈbiːdiəns/ *noun* **1** the act or practice of obeying. **2** submission to another's rule or authority. **3** compliance with a law or command. **4** (*attributive*) designating courses, trials, etc. pertaining to the training of dogs to obey orders. □ **in obedience to** actuated by or in accordance with. [Latin *obedientia* (as OBEY)]

obedi·ent /oːˈbiːdiənt/ *adjective* obeying or ready to obey.

□ **obedi·ent·ly** *adverb* [Latin *obediens -entis* (as OBEY)]

obedient plant *noun* a plant of the mint family, *Physostegia virginiana*, whose flowers, if moved sideways, remain in their new position.

obei·sance /oːˈbeisəns, -biː-/ *noun* **1** homage, submission, deference (*pay obeisance*). **2** a bow, curtsy, or other respectful or submissive gesture. □ **obei·sant** *adjective* [Old French *obeissance* (as OBEY)]

obeli *pl.* of OBELUS.

ob·el·isk /ˈɒbəlɪsk/ *noun* **1** a tapering usu. four-sided stone pillar set up as a monument or landmark etc. **2** = OBELUS. **3** a roughly pyramidal arrangement of metal rods used as a free-standing structure in a garden for vines to grow up. [Greek *obeliskos* diminutive of *obelos* SPIT²]

ob·el·us /ˈɒbələs/ *noun* (*pl.* **obeli** /-lai, -liː/) **1** a symbol (†) used as a reference mark in printed matter or to indicate that a person is deceased. **2** a mark (− or ÷) used in ancient manuscripts to mark a word or passage, esp. as spurious. [Latin from Greek *obelos* SPIT²]

Ober·am·mer·gau /ˌoːbərˈaməˌɡau/ a village in the Bavarian Alps of SW Germany; pop. (1997) 5,225. It is the site of the most famous of the few surviving Passion plays, which has been performed every tenth year (with few exceptions) from 1634 as a result of a vow made during an epidemic of plague. It is entirely amateur, the villagers dividing the parts among themselves and being responsible also for the production, music, costumes and scenery.

Ober·hau·sen /ˈoːbərˌhauzən/ an industrial city in western Germany, in the Ruhr valley of North Rhine-Westphalia; pop. (est. 2002) 221,900.

Ober·on /ˈoːbəˈrɒn/ **1** (in medieval folklore) the king of the fairies and husband of Titania. **2** *Astronomy* satellite IV of Uranus, the furthest from the planet, discovered by William Herschel in 1787 (diameter 1 550 km).

obese /oːˈbiːs/ *adjective* very fat; corpulent. □ **obes·ity** *noun* [Latin *obesus* (as OB-, *edere* eat)]

obey *verb* **1** *transitive* **a** carry out the command of (*you will obey me*). **b** carry out (a command) (*obey orders*). **2** *intransitive* do what one is told to do. **3** *transitive* be actuated by, respond to (a force or impulse).

□ **obey·er** *noun* [Old French *obeir* from Latin *obedire* (as OB-, *audire* hear)]

ob·fus·cate /ˈɒbfʌˌskeit/ *transitive verb* **1** obscure or confuse (a mind, topic, etc.). **2** stupefy, bewilder. □ **ob·fus·ca·tion** /-ˈkeiʃən/ *noun* **ob·fus·ca·tory** *adjective* [Late Latin *obfuscare* (as OB-, *fuscus* dark)]

OB/GYN /ˌoːbiːdʒiːwaiˈen/ *abbreviation* (also **ob-gyn**) *N Amer.* **1** obstetrics and gynecology. **2** obstetrician-gynecologist.

obi /ˈoːbi/ *noun* (*pl.* **obis**) a sash worn with a Japanese kimono. [Japanese *obi* belt]

obit *noun* *informal* an obituary. [abbreviation]

obi·ter dic·tum /ˌɒbitər ˈdiktəm/ *noun* (*pl.* **obiter dicta** /-tə/) **1** a judge's expression of opinion uttered in court or giving judgment, but not essential to the decision and therefore without binding authority. **2** an incidental remark. [Latin from *obiter* by the way + *dictum* a thing said]

obitu·ary /oːˈbitʃuːri, əˈbit-/ *noun* (*pl.* **-aries**) **1** a notice of a death, esp. in a newspaper, usu. comprising a brief biographical sketch of the deceased. **2** (*attributive*) of, relating to, or serving as an obituary.

□ **obitu·ar·ist** *noun* [medieval Latin *obituarius* from Latin *obitus* death, from *obire obit-* die (as OB-, *ire* go)]

object ● *noun* **1** a material thing that can be seen or touched. **2** (foll. by *of*) a person or thing to which action or feeling is directed (*the object of attention*; *the object of our study*). **3** a thing sought or aimed at; a purpose. **4** *Grammar* a noun or its equivalent governed by an active transitive verb or by a preposition. **5** *Philos.* **a** a thing external to the thinking mind or subject. **b** a thing or being of which a person thinks or has cognition. **6** *derogatory* a person or thing of esp. a pathetic or ridiculous appearance. **7** *Computing* a package of information, containing both data and a description of its manipulation, that can perform specific tasks. ● *verb* **1** *intransitive* **a** (often foll. by *to*, *against*) express or feel opposition, disapproval, or reluctance; protest (*I object to being treated like this*; *objecting against government policies*). **b** have an objection (*I object, your honour!*). **2** *transitive* (foll. by *that* + clause) state as an objection (*objected that they were kept waiting*). □ **no object** not forming an important or restricting factor (*money is no object*). **object of the exercise** the main point of an activity. □ **ob·ject·or** *noun* [medieval Latin *objectum* thing presented to the mind, past participle of Latin *objicere* (as OB-, *jacere ject-* throw)]

object ball *noun* *Billiards etc.* the ball at which a player aims the cue ball.

object glass *noun* the lens in a telescope etc. nearest to the object observed.

object·ify *transitive verb* (**-fies**, **-fied**) **1** make into or present as an object of perception. **2** embody, make objective, or express in an external or concrete form. **3** reduce to the status of an object.

□ **ob·jecti·fi·ca·tion** *noun*

ob·jec·tion *noun* **1** an expression or feeling of opposition, disapproval, or protest. **2** the act of objecting. **3** an adverse reason or statement.

□ **ob·jec·tion·al** *adjective*

ob·jec·tion·able *adjective* **1** unpleasant, offensive, undesirable, disapproved of. **2** open to objection. □ **ob·jec·tion·ably** *adverb*

ob·jec·tive ● *adjective* **1** (of a person, an opinion, etc.) not influenced by feelings or personal bias (compare SUBJECTIVE 1). **2 a** (of writing, art, etc.) concerned with outward things or events; dealing with or laying stress on what is external to the mind. **b** external to or independent of the mind. **3** *Grammar* (of a case or word) constructed as or appropriate to the object of a transitive verb or preposition (compare ACCUSATIVE). **4** (of symptoms) observed by another and not only felt by the patient. **5** (of a lens) that is an object glass. ● *noun* **1** something sought or aimed at; a target, goal, or aim. **2** *Grammar* **a** the objective case. **b** a word or form in this case. **3** = OBJECT GLASS. □ **ob·jec·tiv·al** /ˌɒbdʒekˈtaivəl/ *adjective* **ob·ject·ive·ly** *adverb* **ob·ject·ive·ness** *noun* **ob·jec·tiv·ity** /ˌɒbdʒekˈtiviti/ *noun* **ob·jec·tiv·ize** *transitive verb* (also esp. *Brit.* **-ise**). **ob·jec·tiv·iz·a·tion** *noun* [medieval Latin *objectivus* (as OBJECT)]

objective correlative *noun* the artistic technique of representing or evoking a particular emotion by means of symbols which become indicative of that emotion and are associated with it.

ob·jec·tiv·ism *noun* **1** the tendency to lay stress on what is external to or independent of the mind. **2** *Philos.* the belief that certain things, esp.

moral truths, exist apart from human knowledge or perception of them. □ **ob·jec·tiv·ist** *noun* **ob·jec·tiv·is·tic** *adjective*

object language *noun* **1** a language described by means of another language (*see* METALANGUAGE 1). **2** *Computing* a language into which a program is translated by means of a compiler or assembler.

object lesson *noun* a practical example or illustration of some principle.

object-orient·ed *adjective Computing* designating a component-based form of computer programming in which objects communicate with other objects to order a program.

objet /ɒbˈʒeɪ/ *noun* an object displayed as an ornament. [French, lit. 'object']

objet d'art /ˌɒbʒeɪ ˈdɑr/ *noun* (*pl.* **objets d'art** *pronunc.* same) a small decorative or artistic object. [French, lit. 'object of art']

ob·lan·ceo·late /ɒbˈlansɪələt/ *adjective Bot.* (esp. of leaves) lanceolate with the more pointed end at the base.

ob·last /ˈɒblast/ *noun* an administrative division or region in Russia and the former Soviet Union, and in some constituent republics of the former Soviet Union. [Russian]

Oblate /ˈɒbleɪt, ɔː-/ ● *noun* a member of the Oblates of Mary Immaculate. ● *adjective* of or pertaining to the Oblates of Mary Immaculate.

ob·late¹ /ˈɒbleɪt/ *noun* a person dedicated to a monastic or religious life or work. [French from medieval Latin *oblatus* from *offere oblat-* offer (as OB-, *ferre* bring)]

ob·late² /ˈɒbleɪt/ *adjective Math.* (of a spheroid) flattened at the poles (*compare* PROLATE). [modern Latin *oblatus* (as OBLATE¹)]

Oblates of Mary Immaculate *plural noun* a Roman Catholic missionary order of priests and brothers founded in France in 1816 and very active in Canada from 1841, esp. in the west and north. Abbr.: **OMI**.

ob·la·tion /ɔːˈbleɪʃən/ *noun* **1** a thing offered to a divine being. **2** *Christianity* the presentation of bread and wine to God in the Eucharist. [Late Latin *oblatio* (as OBLATE¹)]

ob·li·gate ● *transitive verb* /ˈɒblɪˌɡeɪt/ **1** (usu. in *passive*; foll. by *to* + infin.) bind (a person) legally or morally. **2** *US* commit (assets) as security. ● *adjective* /ˈɒblɪɡət/ *Biol.* that has to be as described, esp. (of an organism) restricted to a particular, specified function (*obligate parasite*). [Latin *obligare obligat-* (as OBLIGE)]

ob·li·ga·tion /ˌɒblɪˈɡeɪʃən/ *noun* **1** a duty, what one is morally or legally required to do. **2** the constraining power of a law, precept, duty, contract, etc. **3** a binding agreement, esp. one enforceable under legal penalty; a written contract or bond. **4 a** a service, benefit, or kindness done or received (*repay an obligation*). **b** indebtedness for this (*be under an obligation*). □ **day of obligation** *Catholicism* a day on which all are required to attend Mass or Communion. □ **obli·ga·tion·al** *adjective*

ob·li·ga·to *var. of* OBBLIGATO.

ob·liga·tory /əˈblɪɡətɔri/ *adjective* **1** required by rule, law, or custom. **2** legally or morally binding. **3** creating or constituting an obligation. □ **ob·liga·tor·i·ly** *adverb* [Late Latin *obligatorius* (as OBLIGE)]

ob·lige *verb* **1** *transitive* (foll. by *to* + infin.) constrain, compel. **2** *transitive* be binding on. **3 a** *transitive* make indebted by conferring a favour. **b** *transitive* (foll. by *with*, or by + verbal noun) gratify (*oblige me by leaving*). **c** *transitive & intransitive* perform a service for (*will you oblige?*). **4** *transitive* (in *passive*; foll. by *to*) be indebted (*am obliged to you for your help*). **5** *intransitive informal* (foll. by *with*) make a contribution of a specified kind (*Beth obliged with a song*). **6** *transitive archaic* (foll. by *to*, or *to* + infin.) bind by oath, promise, contract, etc. □ **much obliged** an expression of thanks. □ **ob·liger** *noun* [Old French *obliger* from Latin *obligare* (as OB-, *ligare* bind)]

ob·li·gee /ˌɒblɪˈdʒiː/ *noun Law* a person to whom another is bound by contract or other legal procedure (*compare* OBLIGOR).

ob·liging *adjective* courteous, accommodating; ready to do a service or kindness. □ **ob·liging·ly** *adverb* **ob·liging·ness** *noun*

ob·ligor /ˌɒblɪˈɡɔr/ *noun Law* a person who is bound to another by contract or other legal procedure (*compare* OBLIGEE).

ob·lique /əˈbliːk, ɔː-/ ● *adjective* **1 a** slanting; declining from the vertical or horizontal. **b** diverging from a straight line or course. **2** not going straight to the point; roundabout, indirect. **3** *Math.* **a** (of a line, plane figure, or surface) inclined at other than a right angle. **b** (of an angle) acute or obtuse. **c** (of a cone, cylinder, etc.) with an axis not perpendicular to the plane of its base. **4** *Anat.* neither parallel nor perpendicular to the long axis of a body or limb. **5** *Bot.* (of a leaf) with unequal sides. **6** *Grammar* denoting any case other than the nominative

or vocative. ● *noun* **1** an oblique stroke (/). **2** an oblique muscle. ● *intransitive verb* (**ob·liques**, **ob·liqued**, **ob·liquing**) esp. *Military* advance obliquely. □ **ob·lique·ly** *adverb* **ob·lique·ness** *noun* **ob·liqui·ty** /əˈblɪkwɪti/ *noun* [French from Latin *obliquus*]

ob·liter·ate /əˈblɪtəˌreɪt/ *transitive verb* **1** blot out; efface, erase, destroy. **2** leave no clear traces of. □ **ob·liter·a·tion** /-ˈreɪʃən/ *noun* **ob·liter·a·tive** /-rətɪv/ *adjective* **ob·liter·ator** *noun* [Latin *obliterare* (as OB-, *litera* LETTER)]

ob·liv·ion /əˈblɪvɪən/ *noun* **1** a state in which one is no longer aware or conscious of what is happening (*drink oneself into oblivion*). **2** the state of being forgotten or disregarded (*this composer was rescued from oblivion in the 20th century*). [Old French from Latin *oblivio -onis* from *oblivisci* forget]

ob·livi·ous /əˈblɪvɪəs/ *adjective* **1** (foll. by *to*, *of*) unaware or unconscious of. **2** (often foll. by *of*) forgetful, unmindful. □ **ob·livi·ous·ly** *adverb* **ob·livi·ous·ness** *noun*

ob·long ● *adjective* **1** deviating from a square form by having one long axis, esp. rectangular with adjacent sides unequal. **2** greater in breadth than in height. ● *noun* an oblong figure or object. [Latin *oblongus* longish (as OB-, *longus* long)]

ob·lo·quy /ˈɒbləkwi/ *noun* (*pl.* **-quies**) **1** the state of being generally ill spoken of. **2** abuse, detraction. [Late Latin *obloquium* contradiction, from Latin *obloqui* deny (as OB-, *loqui* speak)]

ob·nox·ious /ɒbˈnɒkʃəs, əb-/ *adjective* annoying, irritating, disliked, offensive. □ **ob·nox·ious·ly** *adverb* **ob·nox·ious·ness** *noun* [originally = vulnerable (to harm), from Latin *obnoxiosus* or *obnoxius* (as OB-, *noxa* harm: assoc. with NOXIOUS)]

OBO *abbreviation N Amer.* or best offer.

oboe /ˈoʊboʊ/ *noun* **1 a** a woodwind double-reed instrument of treble pitch and a plaintive tone. **b** its player. **2** an organ stop with a quality resembling an oboe. □ **obo·ist** /ˈoʊboʊɪst/ *noun* [Italian *oboe* or French *hautbois* from *haut* high + *bois* wood]

oboe d'amore /ˌoʊboʊ daˈmɔreɪ/ *noun* (*pl.* **oboes d'amore**) an oboe with a pear-shaped bell and mellow tone, pitched a minor third below a normal oboe, commonly used in baroque music. [Italian, literally 'oboe of love']

obol /ˈɒbəl/ *noun* an ancient Greek coin, equal to one-sixth of a drachma. [Greek *obolos*, var. of *obelos* OBELUS]

Obote /əˈboʊti/ **(Apol·lo) Mil·ton** (b.1924), Ugandan leader, prime minister 1962–6, president 1966–71 and 1980–5. After founding the Uganda People's Congress in 1960, he became the first prime minister of independent Uganda; overthrown by Idi Amin in 1971, he was re-elected president in 1980, but was removed in a second military coup in 1985.

ob·ovate /ɒbˈoʊveɪt/ *adjective Biol.* (of a leaf) ovate with the narrower end at the base.

O'Brien /oʊˈbraɪən/ **1 Edna** (b.1932), Irish novelist and short-story writer. Her novels include the trilogy *The Country Girls* (1960), *The Lonely Girl* (1962), and *Girls in Their Married Bliss* (1964), which follows the fortunes of two Irish girls from their rural, convent-educated early years to new lives in Dublin and later in London. **2 Lu·cius Rich·ard** (1832–99), Canadian painter. One of Canada's leading landscape artists of the late 19th c., he painted widely throughout Ontario, Quebec, and the Atlantic provinces, and was sponsored by the CPR to paint in the Rockies and on the Pacific coast.

ob·scene /ɒbˈsiːn, əb-/ *adjective* **1** offensively or repulsively indecent, esp. by offending accepted sexual morality. **2** *informal* highly offensive or repugnant (*an obscene accumulation of wealth*). □ **ob·scene·ly** *adverb* [French *obscène* or Latin *obsc(a)enus* ill-omened, abominable]

ob·scen·ity /ɒbˈsenɪti, əb-/ *noun* (*pl.* **-ities**) **1** an obscene word, action, etc. **2** the state or quality of being obscene.

ob·scur·ant·ism /ˌɒbskjʊərənˌtɪzəm, əb-/ /ˌɒbskjuːˈrantɪzəm/ *noun* opposition to knowledge and enlightenment. □ **ob·scur·ant** /əbˈskjʊərənt/ *noun & adjective* **ob·scur·ant·ist** *noun & adjective* [*obscurant* from German from Latin *obscurans* from *obscurare*: see OBSCURE]

ob·scure /ɒbˈskjʊr, əb-/ ● *adjective* **1** not clearly expressed or easily understood. **2** unexplained, doubtful. **3** dark, dim. **4** indistinct; not clear. **5** hidden; remote from observation. **6 a** unnoticed. **b** undistinguished, hardly known. **7** (of a colour) dingy, dull, indefinite. ● *transitive verb* **1** prevent from being seen, heard, detected, understood, etc. **2** make indistinct. **3** conceal from sight. □ **ob·scur·a·tion** /-ˈreɪʃən/ *noun* **ob·scure·ly** *adverb* [Old French *obscur* from Latin *obscurus* dark]

ob·scur·ity /ɒbˈskjʊrɪti, əb-/ *noun* (*pl.* **-ities**) **1** the state of not being well-known. **2** an obscure thing, esp. one that is difficult to understand. **3** darkness; poor light.

ob·se·quies /ˈɒbsɪkwiːz/ *plural noun* **1** funeral rites. **2** a funeral. [Anglo-French *obsequie* from medieval Latin *obsequiae* from Latin *exsequiae* funeral rites (see EXEQUIES): assoc. with *obsequium* (see OBSEQUIOUS)]

ob·se·qui·ous /ɒbˈsiːkwiəs, əb-/ *adjective* servilely obedient or attentive. □ **ob·se·qui·ous·ly** *adverb* **ob·se·qui·ous·ness** *noun* [Latin *obsequiosus* from *obsequium* compliance (as OB-, *sequi* follow)]

ob·serv·ance /ɒbˈzɜrvəns, əb-/ *noun* **1** the act or process of keeping or performing a law, duty, custom, ritual, etc. **2** an act of a religious or ceremonial character; a customary rite. **3** the rule of a religious order. **4** *archaic* respect, deference.

ob·serv·ant /ɒbˈzɜrvənt, əb-/ *adjective* **1** acute or diligent in taking notice. **2** attentive in esp. religious observances (*an observant few*). □ **ob·serv·ant·ly** *adverb* [French (as OBSERVE)]

ob·ser·va·tion /ɒbzɜrˈveɪʃən/ *noun* **1 a** the act or an instance of noticing; the condition of being noticed. **b** an observed truth or fact; a thing learned by observing. **2** perception; the faculty of taking notice. **3** a remark or statement, esp. one that is of the nature of a comment. **4 a** the accurate watching and noting of a phenomenon etc. for the purpose of scientific investigation. **b** a measurement or other result so obtained. **c** the noting of the symptoms of a patient, the behaviour of a suspect, etc. **5** the taking of the sun's or another celestial body's altitude to find a latitude or longitude. **6** *Military* the watching of a fortress or hostile position or movements. □ **under observation** being watched or monitored. □ **ob·ser·va·tion·al** *adjective* **ob·ser·va·tion·al·ly** *adverb*

observation deck *noun* a platform or area designed for viewing e.g. aircraft at an airport, animals at a wildlife sanctuary, etc.

ob·serv·a·tory /ɒbˈzɜrvətɔri, əb-/ *noun* (*pl.* **-ies**) a room or building equipped for the observation of natural, esp. astronomical or meteorological, phenomena.

ob·serve *transitive verb* **1** (often foll. by *that, how* + clause) perceive, note; take notice of; become conscious of. **2** watch carefully. **3 a** follow or adhere to (a law, command, method, principle, etc.). **b** keep or adhere to (an appointed time). **c** maintain (silence). **d** duly perform (a rite). **e** celebrate (an anniversary). **4** examine and note (phenomena) without the aid of experiment. **5** (often foll. by *that* + clause) say, esp. by way of comment. □ **ob·serv·able** *adjective* **ob·serv·ably** *adverb* [Latin *observare* watch (as OB-, *servare* keep)]

ob·serv·er *noun* **1** a person who observes. **2** a person who attends a conference etc. to note the proceedings but does not participate. **3** a person posted to an area in an official capacity to monitor political or military events (*a UN Military Observer Group; elections scrutinized by international observers*). **4** (in science or art) a real or hypothetical person whose observation is regarded as having a particular viewpoint or effect. **5** a person who follows events, esp. political ones, closely and comments publicly on them (*some observers expect interest rates to rise*).

ob·sess *verb* **1** *transitive* (often in *passive*) preoccupy, haunt; fill the mind of (a person) continually. **2** *intransitive N Amer.* (foll. by *about, on, over*) be continually preoccupied with. □ **ob·sessed** *adjective* (also in *combination*). **ob·ses·sive** *adjective & noun* **ob·ses·sive·ly** *adverb* **ob·ses·sive·ness** *noun* [Latin *obsidēre obsess-* (as OB-, *sedēre* sit)]

ob·ses·sion *noun* **1** the act of obsessing or the state of being obsessed. **2** a persistent idea or thought dominating a person's mind. **3** a condition in which such ideas are present. □ **ob·ses·sion·al** *adjective* **ob·ses·sion·al·ism** *noun* **ob·ses·sion·al·ity** *noun* **ob·ses·sion·al·ly** *adverb* [Latin *obsessio* (as OBSESS)]

ob·sessive-compul·sive ● *adjective* designating or pertaining to a disorder in which a person has an obsessive compulsion to perform meaningless acts repeatedly. ● *noun* a person characterized by such obsessive behaviour.

ob·sid·ian /ɒbˈsɪdiən, əb-/ *noun* a dark glassy volcanic rock formed from hardened lava. [Latin *obsidianus*, error for *obsianus* from *Obsius*, the name (in Pliny) of the discoverer of a similar stone]

ob·so·les·cent /ˌɒbsəˈlesənt/ *adjective* becoming obsolete; going out of use or date. □ **ob·so·les·cence** *noun* [Latin *obsolescere obsolescent-* (as OB-, *solēre* be accustomed)]

ob·so·lete /ˌɒbsəˈliːt, ˈɒbsəˌliːt/ *adjective* **1** disused, discarded, antiquated, outmoded, out of date. **2** *Biol.* less developed than formerly or than in a cognate species; rudimentary. □ **ob·so·lete·ly** *adverb* **ob·so·lete·ness** *noun* [Latin *obsoletus* past participle (as OBSOLESCENT)]

ob·sta·cle /ˈɒbstəkəl/ *noun* a person or thing that obstructs progress. [Old French from Latin *obstaculum* from *obstare* impede (as OB-, *stare* stand)]

obstacle course *noun* (also **obstacle race**) **1** a course or race in which various obstacles have to be negotiated. **2** an endeavour in which there are many problems to overcome.

ob·stet·ric /ɒbˈstetrɪk, əb-/ *adjective* (also **ob·stet·ric·al**) of or relating to childbirth and associated processes. □ **ob·stet·ric·al·ly** *adverb* [modern Latin *obstetricus* for Latin *obstetricius* from *obstetrix* midwife, from *obstare* be present (as OB-, *stare* stand)]

ob·stet·ri·cian /ˌɒbstəˈtrɪʃən/ *noun* a physician specializing in obstetrics.

ob·stet·rics /ɒbˈstetrɪks, əb-/ *noun* the branch of medicine and surgery concerned with pregnancy and childbirth.

ob·stin·ate /ˈɒbstənət/ *adjective* **1** stubborn, intractable. **2** firmly adhering to one's chosen course of action or opinion despite dissuasion. **3** inflexible, self-willed. **4** not readily responding to treatment etc. □ **ob·stin·acy** *noun* **ob·stin·ate·ly** *adverb* [Latin *obstinatus* past participle of *obstinare* persist (as OB-, *stare* stand)]

ob·strep·er·ous /ɒbˈstrepərəs, əb-/ *adjective* **1** unruly; resisting control. **2** noisy, vociferous. □ **ob·strep·er·ous·ly** *adverb* **ob·strep·er·ous·ness** *noun* [Latin *obstreperus* from *obstrepere* (as OB-, *strepere* make a noise)]

ob·struct *transitive verb* **1** block up; make hard or impossible to pass along or through. **2** prevent or retard the progress of; impede. **3** block (a view). □ **ob·struct·or** *noun* [Latin *obstruere obstruct-* (as OB-, *struere* build)]

ob·struc·tion *noun* **1** the act or an instance of blocking; the state of being blocked. **2** the act of making or the state of becoming more or less impassable. **3** an obstacle or blockage. **4** the retarding of progress by deliberate delays. **5** *Sport* the act of unlawfully obstructing another player. **6** *Med.* a blockage in a bodily passage, esp. in an intestine. □ **ob·struc·tion·ism** *noun* (in sense 4). **ob·struc·tion·ist** *noun* (in sense 4).

obstruction of justice *noun* interference with the course of justice by influencing jurors, intimidating witnesses, being influenced by bribes or threats as a juror or witness, etc.

ob·struct·ive *adjective* causing or intended to cause an obstruction. □ **ob·struct·ive·ly** *adverb* **ob·struct·ive·ness** *noun*

ob·tain *verb* **1** *transitive* acquire, secure; have granted to one. **2** *intransitive* be prevalent or established or in vogue; apply, hold good. □ **ob·tain·able** *adjective* **ob·tain·abil·ity** *noun* **ob·tain·er** *noun* **ob·tain·ment** *noun* [Old French *obtenir* from Latin *obtinēre* keep (as OB-, *tenēre* hold)]

ob·trude *verb* **1** *intransitive* be or become obtrusive. **2** *transitive* (often foll. by *on, upon*) thrust forward (oneself, one's opinion, etc.) importunately. □ **ob·trud·er** *noun* **ob·tru·sion** *noun* [Latin *obtrudere obtrus-* (as OB-, *trudere* push)]

ob·tru·sive *adjective* unpleasantly or unduly noticeable. □ **ob·tru·sive·ly** *adverb* **ob·tru·sive·ness** *noun* [as OBTRUDE]

ob·tuse /ɒbˈtuːs, əb-, -tjuːs/ *adjective* **1 a** dull-witted; slow to understand. **b** difficult to understand; obscure. **2** of blunt form; not sharp-pointed or sharp-edged. **3** (of an angle) more than 90° and less than 180°. **4** (of pain or the senses) dull; not acute. □ **ob·tuse·ly** *adverb* **ob·tuse·ness** *noun* [late Middle English (in the sense 'blunt') from Latin *obtusus* past participle of *obtundere* 'beat against']

ob·verse /ˈɒbvɜrs, ɒbˈvɜrs/ ● *noun* **1 a** the side of a coin or medal etc. bearing the head or principal design. **b** this design (compare REVERSE 7). **2** the front or proper or top side of a thing. **3** the counterpart of a fact or truth. ● *adjective* **1** *Biol.* narrower at the base or point of attachment than at the apex or top (see OB- 7). **2** answering as the counterpart to something else. **3** of or denoting the obverse of a coin or medal. □ **ob·verse·ly** *adverb* [Latin *obversus* past participle (as OBVERT)]

ob·vert /ɒbˈvɜrt, əb-/ *transitive verb Logic* alter (a proposition) so as to infer another proposition with a contradictory predicate, e.g. *no men are immortal* to *all men are mortal*. □ **ob·ver·sion** *noun* [Latin *obvertere obvers-* (as OB-, *vertere* turn)]

ob·vi·ate /ˈɒbviˌeɪt/ *transitive verb* get around or do away with (a need, inconvenience, etc.). □ **ob·vi·a·tion** *noun* [Late Latin *obviare* oppose (as OB-, *via* way)]

ob·vi·ous *adjective* **1** easily seen or recognized or understood; palpable, indubitable. **2** not subtle; revealing sentiments, intentions, etc. clearly. □ **ob·vi·ous·ly** *adverb* **ob·vi·ous·ness** *noun* [Latin *obvius* from *ob viam* in the way]

OC *abbreviation* Officer of the Order of Canada.

oc- /ɒk/ *prefix* assimilated form of OB- before *c*.

oca·ri·na /ˌɒkəˈriːnə/ *noun* a small egg-shaped wind instrument with finger holes. [Italian from *oca* goose (from its shape)]

O'Casey /oːˈkeisi/ **Sean** (1880–1964), Irish dramatist. Many of his plays deal realistically with the lives of the Irish poor before and during the civil war that followed the establishment of the Irish Free State; they include *Juno and the Paycock* (1924) and *The Plough and the Stars* (1926).

Occam see WILLIAM OF OCCAM.

Occam's razor /ˌɒkəmz/ *noun* the principle, attributed to the English philosopher William of Occam, that in explaining a thing no more assumptions should be made than are necessary.

oc·ca·sion ● *noun* **1 a** a special or noteworthy event or happening (*dressed for the occasion*). **b** the time or occurrence of this (*on the occasion of their marriage*). **2** (often foll. by *for*, or *to* + infin.) a reason, ground, or justification (*there is no occasion to be angry*). **3** a juncture suitable for doing something; an opportunity. **4** an immediate but subordinate or incidental cause (*the assassination was the occasion of the war*). ● *transitive verb* **1** be the occasion or cause of; bring about esp. incidentally. **2** (foll. by *to* + infin.) cause (a person or thing to do something). □ **on occasion** now and then; when the need arises. **rise to the occasion** produce the necessary will, energy, ability, etc., in unusually demanding circumstances. **take the** (or **this** etc.) **occasion** (foll. by *to* + infin.) make use of the opportunity. [Old French *occasion* or Latin *occasio* juncture, reason, from *occidere occas-* go down (as OB-, *cadere* fall)]

oc·ca·sion·al *adjective* **1** happening, done, consumed, etc. infrequently; not regular. **2** made or meant for, or associated with, a special occasion. **3** acting on a special occasion. **4** constituting or serving as the occasion or incidental cause of something. **5** (of furniture etc.) used from time to time and for various purposes. □ **oc·ca·sion·al·ly** *adverb*

Oc·ci·dent /ˈɒksɪdənt/ *noun literary* **1** (prec. by *the*) the West. **2** western Europe. **3** Europe, the Americas, or both, as distinct from the Orient. **4** European in contrast to Oriental civilization. [Latin *occidens -entis* setting, sunset, west (as OCCASION)]

oc·ci·dent·al /ɒksɪˈdentəl/ ● *adjective* **1** of the Occident, as distinct from oriental. **2** western. **3** of western Europe. **4** relating to European or Western (in contrast to oriental) civilization. ● *noun* (**Occidental**) a native or inhabitant of the Occident.

oc·cip·i·tal /ɒkˈsɪpɪtəl/ *adjective* belonging to or situated in or on the occiput. [as OCCIPUT]

occipito- /ɒkˈsɪpɪtoː/ *combining form* the back of the head. [as OCCIPUT]

oc·ci·put /ˈɒksɪˌpʌt/ *noun* the back of the head. [Latin *occiput* (as OB-, *caput* head)]

Oc·ci·tan /ˈɒksɪtan/ *noun* (also *attributive*) **1** the group of Romance dialects spoken south of the Loire (*compare* LANGUE D'OC). **2** the Occitan dialect spoken in Provence; Provençal. □ **Oc·ci·tan·ian** /-ˈteɪniən/ *noun & adjective* [French: compare LANGUE D'OC]

oc·clude /əˈkluːd/ *transitive verb* **1** stop up or close (pores, an orifice, a passage, etc.). **2** *Chem.* absorb and retain (gases or impurities). [Latin *occludere occlus-* (as OB-, *claudere* shut)]

occluded front *noun Meteorol.* a front resulting from occlusion.

oc·clu·sion /əˈkluːʒən/ *noun* **1** the act or process of occluding. **2** *Meteorol.* a phenomenon in which the cold front of a depression overtakes the warm front, causing upward displacement of warm air between them. **3** *Dentistry* the position of the teeth when the jaws are closed. **4** the blockage or closing of a hollow organ etc. (*coronary occlusion*). □ **oc·clu·sive** *adjective*

oc·cult /ɒˈkʌlt/ ● *adjective* **1** involving the supernatural; mystical, magical. **2** kept secret; esoteric. **3** mysterious; beyond the range of ordinary knowledge. **4** *Med.* not obvious on inspection. ● *noun* (prec. by *the*) supernatural phenomena. ● *transitive verb Astronomy* (of a celestial body) conceal (an apparently smaller body) from view by passing or being in front of it. □ **oc·cul·ta·tion** /-ˈteɪʃən/ *noun* **oc·cult·ism** *noun* **oc·cult·ist** *noun* **oc·cult·ly** *adverb* [Latin *occulere occult-* (as OB-, *celare* hide)]

oc·cu·pan·cy *noun* (*pl.* **-cies**) **1** the act, condition, or fact of occupying something or of being occupied. **2** *N Amer.* the number of people occupying or meant to be occupying a room, vehicle, etc. (*double occupancy*; *high-occupancy vehicle*).

oc·cu·pant *noun* **1** a person who occupies, resides in, or is in a place etc. (*both occupants of the car were unhurt*). **2** a person holding property, esp. land, in actual possession. **3** a person who establishes a title by taking possession of something previously without an established owner.

oc·cu·pa·tion *noun* **1** what occupies one; a means of passing one's time. **2** a person's temporary or regular employment; a business, calling, or pursuit. **3** the act of occupying or state of being occupied. **4 a** the act of taking or holding possession of (a country, district, etc.) by military force. **b** the state or time of this. **5** tenure, occupancy.

oc·cu·pa·tion·al *adjective* **1** of or in the nature of an occupation or occupations. **2** (of a disease, etc.) rendered more likely by one's occupation.

occupational hazard *noun* **1** a risk or danger connected with a particular job. **2** an unpleasant but not necessarily dangerous consequence of one's job, hobby, etc.

occupational therapy *noun* mental or physical activity designed to assist recovery from disease or injury; therapy in which one occupies oneself with various activities. Abbr.: **OT**. □ **occupational therapist** *noun*

oc·cupy *transitive verb* (**-pies**, **-pied**) **1** reside in; be the tenant of. **2** take up or fill (space or time or a place). **3** hold (a position or office). **4** take military possession of (a country, region, town, strategic position). **5** place oneself in (a building etc.) forcibly or without authority. **6** (usu. in *passive*; often foll. by *in*, *with*) keep busy or engaged. □ **oc·cu·pi·er** *noun* [Latin *occupare* seize (as OB-, *capere* take)]

occur *intransitive verb* (**oc·curred**, **oc·cur·ring**) **1** come into being as an event or process at or during some time; happen. **2** exist or be encountered in some place or conditions (*fossils occur throughout this area*). **3** (foll. by *to*; usu. foll. by *that* + clause) come into the mind of, esp. as an unexpected or casual thought (*it occurred to me that you were right*). [Latin *occurrere* go to meet, present itself (as OB-, *currere* run)]

oc·cur·rence *noun* **1** the act or an instance of occurring. **2** an incident or event. **3** the rate or measure of occurring; incidence.

OCD *abbreviation* obsessive-compulsive disorder (*see* OBSESSIVE-COMPULSIVE).

OCdt *abbreviation Cdn* OFFICER CADET.

ocean /ˈoːʃən/ *noun* **1 a** a large expanse of sea, esp. each of the main areas called the Atlantic, Pacific, Indian, Arctic, and Antarctic Oceans. **b** these regarded cumulatively as the body of water surrounding the land of the globe. **2** (usu. prec. by *the*) the sea. **3** (often in *pl.*) a very large expanse or quantity of anything (*oceans of time*). □ **ocean·ward** *adverb & adjective* [Latin *oceanus* from Greek *ōkeanos* stream encircling the earth's disc]

ocean·arium /ˌoːʃəˈneriəm/ *noun* (*pl.* **ocean·ariums** or **-aria** /-riə/) a large sea water aquarium for keeping sea animals. [OCEAN + -ARIUM, after *aquarium*]

ocean·front ● *attributive adjective* on the shore of an ocean (*oceanfront cottages*). ● *noun* a property or land on the shore of an ocean.

ocean-going *adjective* (of a ship) able to cross oceans.

Oce·an·ia /ˌoːʃiˈaniə, ˌoːsi-/ *noun* the islands of the Pacific and adjacent seas, sometimes including Australasia and the Malay archipelago. □ **Oce·an·ian** *adjective & noun*

ocean·ic /ˌoːʃiˈanɪk, ˌoːsi-/ *adjective* **1** of, like, or near the ocean. **2** (of a climate) governed by the ocean. **3** *Biol. & Geol.* of the part of the ocean beyond the edge of the continental shelf. **4** immense, vast. **5** (**Oceanic**) of Oceania.

Ocean·id /ˈoːsiːənɪd/ *noun* (*pl.* **Ocean·ids** or **-ides** /ˌoːsɪˈanɪˌdiːz/) *Gk Myth* an ocean nymph. [Greek *ōkeanis -ides* daughter of Oceanus]

Ocean Island an alternative name for BANABA.

ocean·og·raphy /ˌoːʃəˈnɒɡrəfi/ *noun* the study of the oceans. □ **ocean·og·raph·er** *noun* **ocean·o·graph·ic** /-nəˈɡrafɪk/ *adjective*

ocean perch *noun* **1** the flesh of various species of redfish marketed as food. **2** any of various fish of the scorpion fish family.

ocean·side *attributive adjective* near, by, on or along the shore of an ocean (*oceanside resort*).

Oce·a·nus /oːˈsiːənəs, oːˈʃiː-/ *Gk Myth* the son of Uranus (Heaven) and Gaia (Earth), and father of the ocean nymphs (Oceanids) and river gods. He is the personification of the river encircling the whole world.

ocean·view *attributive adjective* designating a room etc. with a view of an ocean.

ocel·lus /ɒˈseləs/ *noun* (*pl.* **ocel·li** /-laɪ/) **1** each of the simple, as opposed to compound, eyes of insects etc. **2** a spot of colour surrounded by a ring of a different colour on the wing of a butterfly etc. □ **ocel·lar** *adjective* **ocel·lat·ed** /ˈɒsɪˌleɪtɪd/ *adjective* [Latin, diminutive of *oculus* eye]

oce·lot /ˈɒsəˌlɒt, ˈoː-/ *noun* **1** a medium-sized cat, *Felis pardalis*, native to South and Central America, having a deep yellow or orange coat with black striped and spotted markings. **2** its fur. [French from Nahuatl *ocelotl* jaguar]

Consonants: b *but* d *dog* f *few* g *get* h *her* j *yes* k *cat* l *leg* m *man* n *no* p *pen* r *red* s *sit*

och /ɒx/ *interjection* Scot. & Irish expressing surprise or regret. [Gaelic & Irish]

oche /ˈɒki/ *noun* Darts the line behind which the players stand when throwing. [20th c.: origin uncertain (perhaps connected with Old French *ochen* cut a deep notch in)]

ocher US var. of OCHRE.

och·loc·racy /ɒkˈlɒkrəsi/ *noun* (pl. **-cies**) mob rule. □ **ochlo·crat** /ˈɒkləˌkrat/ *noun* **ochlo·crat·ic** /ˌɒkləˈkratɪk/ *adjective* [French *ochlocratie* from Greek *okhlokratia* from *okhlos* mob]

ochre /ˈoʊkər/ (US also **ocher**) ● *noun* **1** a mineral of clay and ferric oxide, used as a pigment varying from light yellow to brown or red. **2** a pale brownish yellow. ● *adjective* of the colour of ochre, esp. pale brownish yellow. □ **ocher·ous** /ˈoʊkərəs/ *adjective* **och·re·ous** /ˈoʊkriəs/ *adjective* **och·rous** /ˈoʊkrəs/ *adjective* [Greek *ōkhra* 'yellow ochre']

-ock /ək/ *suffix* forming nouns originally with diminutive sense (*hillock*; *bullock*). [from or after Old English *-uc*, *-oc*]

ocker *noun* Austral. slang a boorish or aggressive Australian (esp. as a stereotype). [20th c.: origin uncertain]

Ock·ham see WILLIAM OF OCCAM.

o'clock *adverb* **1** of the clock (used to specify the hour) (*6 o'clock*). **2** used following a numeral to indicate direction or bearing with reference to an imaginary clock face, twelve o'clock being directly above or in front of the observer or at the top of a circular target etc.

O'Con·nor ▸ 1 (Mary) Flan·nery (1925–64), US novelist and short-story writer. Her works, set in the southern US, explore issues of alienation and the absurd; they include the novels *Wise Blood* (1952) and *The Violent Bear it Away* (1960) and short-story collections such as *A Good Man is Hard to Find* (1955). **2 Thom·as Power** (known as Tay Pay) (1848–1929), Irish journalist and politician.

oco·til·lo /ˌoʊkəˈtiːljoʊ/ *noun* (pl. **-los**) esp. US a spiny scarlet-flowered desert shrub, *Fouquieria splendens*, of Mexico and the southwestern US. [Latin American Spanish, diminutive from Nahuatl *ocotl* 'torch']

OCR *abbreviation* optical character recognition.

-ocracy *combining form* = -CRACY.

Oct. *abbreviation* October.

oct. *abbreviation* octavo.

oct- /ɒkt/ *combining form* assimilated form of OCTA-, OCTO- before a vowel.

octa- /ˈɒktə/ *combining form* (also **oct-** before a vowel) eight. [Greek *okta-* from *oktō* eight]

oct·ad /ˈɒktad/ *noun* a group of eight. [Late Latin *octas octad-* from Greek *oktas -ados* from *oktō* eight]

octa·gon /ˈɒktəgɒn/ *noun* **1** a plane figure with eight sides and angles. **2** an object or building with this cross-section. □ **oct·ag·on·al** /-ˈtagənəl/ *adjective* **oct·ag·on·al·ly** /-ˈtagənəli/ *adverb* [Latin *octagonos* from Greek *oktagōnos* (as OCTA-, -GON)]

octa·hed·ron /ˌɒktəˈhiːdrən, -ˈhedrən/ *noun* (pl. **-hed·rons** or **-hed·ra** /-drə/) **1** a solid figure contained by eight (esp. triangular) plane faces. **2** a body, esp. a crystal, in the form of a regular octahedron. □ **octa·hed·ral** *adjective* [Greek *oktaedron* (as OCTA-, -HEDRON)]

octal /ˈɒktəl/ *adjective* pertaining to or designating a system of numerical notation in which the base is 8, using digits 0 through 7.

oct·am·er·ous /ɒkˈtamərəs/ *adjective* **1** esp. Bot. having eight parts. **2** Zool. having organs arranged in eights.

oc·tane *noun* a colourless inflammable hydrocarbon of the alkane series. Chem. formula: C_8H_{18}. [OCT- + -ANE²]

octane number *noun* (also **octane rating**) a figure indicating the anti-knock properties of a fuel.

oct·ant /ˈɒktənt/ *noun* **1** an arc of a circle equal to one eighth of the circumference. **2** such an arc with two radii, forming an area equal to one eighth of the circle. **3** each of eight parts into which three planes intersecting (esp. at right angles) at a point divide the space or the solid body round it. **4** an instrument in the form of a graduated eighth of a circle, used in astronomy and navigation. [Latin *octans octant-* half-quadrant from *octo* eight]

octa·valent /ˌɒktəˈveɪlənt/ *adjective* Chem. having a valence of eight. [OCTA- + VALENCE]

oc·tave /ˈɒktɪv/ *noun* **1** Music **a** a series of eight notes occupying the interval between (and including) two notes, one having twice or half the frequency of vibration of the other. **b** this interval. **c** each of the two notes at the extremes of this interval. **d** these two notes sounding together. **2** a group or stanza of eight lines; an octet. **3 a** the seventh day after a church festival. **b** a period of eight days including a festival and its octave. **4** a group of eight. [Old French from Latin *octava dies* eighth day (reckoned inclusively)]

Oc·tav·ian /ɒkˈteivian/ see AUGUSTUS.

oc·tavo /ɒkˈtɑːvoʊ, ɒkˈteivoʊ/ *noun* (pl. **-tavos**) **1** a size of book or page given by folding a standard sheet three times to form a quire of eight leaves. **2** a book or sheet of this size. Abbr.: **8vo**. [Latin *in octavo* in an eighth, from *octavus* eighth]

oc·ten·nial /ɒkˈteniəl/ *adjective* **1** lasting eight years. **2** occurring every eight years. [Late Latin *octennium* period of eight years (as OCT-, *annus* year)]

oc·tet /ɒkˈtet/ *noun* **1** Music **a** a composition for eight voices or instruments. **b** the performers of such a piece. **2** a group of eight. **3** the first eight lines of a sonnet. **4** Chem. a stable group of eight electrons. [Italian *ottetto* or German *Oktett*: assimilated to OCT-, DUET, QUARTET]

octo- /ˈɒktoʊ/ *combining form* (also **oct-** before a vowel) eight. [Latin *octo* or Greek *oktō* eight]

Oc·to·ber *noun* the tenth month of the year. [Old English from Latin (as OCTO-): originally the eighth month of the Roman year]

October Crisis *noun* Cdn the kidnapping of the British diplomat James Cross and the Quebec labour and immigration minister Pierre Laporte by separate cells of the Front de Libération du Québec in October of 1970, resulting in the federal government's invoking of the War Measures Act to allow for the detention of some 450 suspected FLQ members; Laporte was murdered by his kidnappers, who were arrested and convicted; Cross was released in exchange for the safe passage of his captors to Cuba.

October Revolution see RUSSIAN REVOLUTION.

October War see YOM KIPPUR WAR.

Oc·to·brist *noun* hist. a member of the moderate party in the Russian Duma, supporting the Imperial Constitutional Manifesto of 30 Oct. 1905. [OCTOBER, after Russian *oktyabríst*]

octo·deci·mo /ˌɒktoʊˈdesɪˌmoʊ/ *noun* (pl. **-mos**) **1** a size of book or page given by folding a standard sheet into eighteen leaves. **2** a book or sheet of this size. Abbr.: **18mo**. [in *octodecimo* from Latin *octodecimus* eighteenth]

octo·gen·ar·ian /ˌɒktədʒəˈneriən/ ● *noun* a person from 80 to 89 years old. ● *adjective* **1** of this age. **2** of octogenarians. [Latin *octogenarius* from *octogeni* distributive of *octoginta* eighty]

octo·pod *noun* any cephalopod of the order Octopoda, with eight arms usu. having suckers, and a round sacklike body, including octopuses. [Greek *oktōpous -podos* from *oktō* eight + *pous* foot]

octo·pus *noun* (pl. **octo·puses**, **octo·pi** /-pai/) any cephalopod mollusc of the genus *Octopus* having eight suckered arms, a soft sacklike body, and strong beaklike jaws. [Greek *oktōpous*: see OCTOPOD]

octo·roon /ˌɒktəˈruːn/ *noun* esp. hist. the offspring of a quadroon and a white person, a person of one-eighth black ancestry. [OCTO- after QUADROON]

octo·sylla·ble /ˈɒktəˌsiləbəl/ ● *noun* a verse or word with eight syllables. ● *adjective* having eight syllables. □ **octo·syllab·ic** /-sɪˈlabɪk/ *adjective* [Late Latin *octosyllabus* (as OCTO-, SYLLABLE)]

oc·troi /ˈɒktrwɒ/ *noun* **1** a duty levied in some countries on goods entering a town. **2 a** the place where this is levied. **b** the officials by whom it is levied. [French from *octroyer* grant, from medieval Latin *auctorizare*: see AUTHORIZE]

oc·tu·ple /ˈɒktʌpəl/ ● *adjective* eightfold. ● *noun* an eightfold amount. ● *transitive & intransitive verb* multiply by eight. [French *octuple* or Latin *octuplus* (adj.) from *octo* eight: compare DOUBLE]

ocu·lar /ˈɒkjulər/ ● *adjective* of or connected with the eyes or sight; visual. ● *noun* the eyepiece of an optical instrument. □ **ocu·lar·ly** *adverb* [Late Latin *ocularis* from Latin *oculus* eye]

ocu·list /ˈɒkjulɪst/ *noun* dated a person who specializes in the medical treatment of eye disorders or defects. [French *oculiste* from Latin *oculus* eye]

oculo- /ˈɒkjuloʊ/ *combining form* eye (*oculo-nasal*). [Latin *oculus* eye]

OD¹ *abbreviation* outer diameter.

OD² /oʊˈdiː/ esp. N Amer. slang ● *noun* an overdose, esp. of a narcotic drug. ● *intransitive verb* (**ODs**, **OD'd**, **ODing**) take an overdose. [abbreviation]

O.D. *abbreviation* Doctor of Optometry.

od *noun* (as interjection or in oaths) archaic God (see GOD 5). [corruption]

odal·isque /ˈoʊdəlɪsk/ *noun* hist. an Eastern female slave or concubine, esp. in the Turkish Sultan's seraglio. [French from Turkish *odalik* from *oda* chamber + *lik* function]

Odawa /oʊˈdɒwə/ ● *noun* **1** a member of an Aboriginal people formerly living along the Ottawa River, and now living esp. on Manitoulin

Island. **2** the Ojibwa dialect of this people. ● *adjective* of or relating to this people or their language. [Ojibwa, self-designation]

odd *adjective* **1** strange, queer, eccentric. **2** casual, occasional, unconnected (*odd jobs; odd moments*). **3** not normally noticed or considered; unpredictable (*in some odd corner; picks up odd bargains*). **4** additional; beside the reckoning (*earned the odd dollar*). **5 a** (of numbers such as 3 and 5) not integrally divisible by two. **b** (of things or persons numbered consecutively) bearing such a number (*no parking on odd dates*). **6** left over when the rest have been distributed or divided into pairs (*I've got an odd sock*). **7** detached from a set or series (*a few odd volumes*). **8** (appended to a number, sum, weight, etc.) somewhat more than (*forty odd; forty-odd people*). **9** by which a round number, given sum, etc., is exceeded (*we have 102 – what'll we do with the odd 2?*). □ **oddly** *adverb* **odd·ness** *noun* [Old Norse *odda-* in *odda-mathr* 'third man, odd man', from *oddi* angle, triangle, whence 'third or odd number']

odd·ball *informal* ● *noun* an odd or eccentric person. ● *adjective* strange, bizarre.

odd bod *noun Brit. slang* a strange or eccentric person.

odd couple *noun* two apparently incompatible people who live, work, etc. together.

Odd·fellow *noun* a member of a fraternal society similar to the Freemasons.

odd·ity *noun* (*pl.* **-ities**) **1** a strange person, thing, or occurrence. **2** a peculiar trait. **3** the state of being odd.

odd-job man *noun* (also **odd jobber**) a person who does odd jobs.

odd jobs *plural noun* small, esp. domestic, jobs of various types, usu. done for others.

odd man out *noun* (also **odd one out**) **1** a person or thing differing from all the others in a group in some respect. **2** a method of selecting one of three or more persons e.g. by tossing a coin.

odd-man rush *noun Hockey* a situation in which the players leading an offensive rush outnumber the skaters defending against it.

odd·ment *noun* **1** an odd article; something left over. **2** (in *pl.*) miscellaneous articles.

odds *plural noun* **1** the ratio between the amounts staked by the parties to a bet, based on the expected probability either way. **2 a** the chances or balance of probability in favour of or against some result (*the odds are against it; the odds are that it will rain*). **b** this probability expressed as a ratio (*the odds against winning the raffle are 500 to 1*). **3** the balance of advantage (*the odds are in your favour; won against all the odds*). **4** an equalizing allowance to a weaker competitor; a handicap. **5** a difference giving an advantage (*it makes no odds*). □ **at odds** (often foll. by *with*) in conflict or at variance. **by all odds** certainly. **over the odds** *Brit.* above a generally agreed price etc. **take odds** accept a bet. [apparently pl. of ODD *noun* 'unequal things': compare NEWS]

odds and ends *plural noun* miscellaneous articles or remnants.

odds·maker *noun* a person who sets the odds offered to gamblers betting on sports etc.

odds-on *attributive adjective* designating the outcome or chance most favoured by the odds (*odds-on favourite*).

ode *noun* **1** a lyric poem, usu. rhymed and in the form of an address, in varied or irregular metre. **2** *hist.* a poem meant to be sung. **3** an artistic or literary creation praising or exalting something (*this film is an ode to fly fishing*). [French from Late Latin *oda* from Greek *ōidē* Attic form of *aoidē* song, from *aeidō* sing]

-ode[1] *suffix* forming nouns meaning 'thing of the nature of' (*geode; trematode*). [Greek *-ōdēs* adj. ending]

-ode[2] *combining form Electricity* forming names of electrodes, or devices having them (*cathode; diode*). [Greek *hodos* way]

Oden·se /'oːdənsə/ a port in E Denmark, on the island of Fyn; pop. (1998) 145,296.

Oder River /'oːdər/ a river of central Europe which rises in the mountains in the west of the Czech Republic and flows 907 km (567 miles) northward through W Poland to meet the Neisse River, then continues northward forming the northern part of the border between Poland and Germany before emptying into the Baltic Sea. This frontier, known as the Oder-Neisse Line, was adopted at the Potsdam Conference in 1945.

Odes·sa /oː'desə/ a city and port on the south coast of Ukraine, on the Black Sea; pop. (est. 2001) 1,029,000.

Odets /oː'dets/ **Clif·ford** (1906–63), US dramatist. He was a founding member in 1931 of the avant-garde Group Theatre, which followed the naturalistic methods of the Moscow Art Theatre and staged his

best-known political play, *Waiting for Lefty* (1935); other works include *Golden Boy* (1937) and *The Country Girl* (1950).

odeum /'oːdiəm, -'diːm/ *noun* (*pl.* **ode·ums** or **odea** /-diə/) (also **odeon** /'oːdiən/) a building for musical performances, esp. among the ancient Greeks and Romans. [French *odéum* or Latin *odeum* from Greek *ōideion* (as ODE)]

Odin /'oːdin/ (also called **Woden, Wotan**) *Scand. Myth* the supreme god and creator, god of victory and the dead, married to Frigga and usually represented as a one-eyed old man of great wisdom. Wednesday is named after him.

odi·ous /'oːdiəs/ *adjective* hateful, repulsive. □ **odi·ous·ly** *adverb* **odi·ous·ness** *noun* [Latin *odiosus* (as ODIUM)]

odium /'oːdiəm/ *noun* **1** a general or widespread dislike or reprobation incurred by a person or associated with an action. **2** hatred. [Latin, = hatred, from *odi* to hate]

Odo·acer /ˌoːdoː'eisər/ (also **Odo·vacar** /oːdoː'veikər/) (*c.*433–93), Germanic chieftain. In 476 he led an uprising against the emperor Romulus Augustus (reigned 475–6) and became the first Germanic ruler of Italy (476–93); he was assassinated by Theodoric.

odom·eter /oː'dɒmɪtər/ *noun* an instrument for measuring the distance travelled by a vehicle. □ **odom·etry** *noun* [French *odomètre* from Greek *hodos* way: see -METER]

-odontics /oː'dɒntɪks/ *combining form* treatment of the teeth. [Greek *odous odont-* tooth]

odonto- /oː'dɒntoː/ *combining form* tooth. [Greek *odous odont-* tooth]

odont·oid /oː'dɒntɔɪd/ *adjective* toothlike. [Greek *odontoeidēs* (as ODONTO- + Greek *eidos* form)]

odontoid process *noun* a projection from the second cervical vertebra.

odon·tol·ogy /ˌoːdɒn'tɒlədʒi/ *noun* the scientific study of the structure and diseases of teeth. □ **odon·to·logic·al** *adjective* **odon·tol·o·gist** *noun*

odor *var. of* ODOUR.

odor·ant *noun* a substance giving off a smell, esp. one used to give a particular scent or odour to a product.

odor·if·er·ous /ˌoːdə'rɪfərəs/ *adjective* diffusing an intense odour, esp. an unpleasant one. □ **odor·if·er·ous·ly** *adverb*

odor·ous /'oːdərəs/ *adjective* having a scent or odour. □ **odor·ous·ly** *adverb*

odour *noun* (also **odor**) **1** a distinctive, usu. unpleasant smell. **2** a lasting esp. unpleasant quality or trace attaching to something (*an odour of intolerance*). **3** regard, repute (*in bad odour*). □ **odour·less** *adjective* (in sense 1). [Anglo-French *odour* from Latin *odor -oris* smell, scent]

Odo·vacar *var. of* ODOACER

Odys·seus /oː'dɪsiəs/ *Gk Myth* a king of Ithaca, called Ulysses by the Romans. Renowned for his cunning and resourcefulness, he survived the Trojan War but was kept from home by Poseidon for ten years; his adventures during his wanderings around the Mediterranean are recounted in Homer's *Odyssey*. □ **Odys·sean** *adjective*

odys·sey /'ɒdɪsi/ *noun* (*pl.* **-seys**) a series of wanderings; a long adventurous journey. [The *Odyssey* (see ODYSSEUS)]

OE *abbreviation* Old English.

OECD *abbreviation* Organization for Economic Co-operation and Development.

OED *abbreviation* Oxford English Dictionary.

oedema /ɪ'diːmə/ *noun Brit. var. of* EDEMA. [Late Latin from Greek *oidēma -atos* from *oideō* swell]

Oedi·pus /'iːdɪpəs/ *Gk Myth* the son of Jocasta and of Laius, king of Thebes. Left to die on a mountain by Laius, who had been told by an oracle that he would be killed by his own son, the infant Oedipus was saved by a shepherd; returning eventually to Thebes, Oedipus unwittingly killed his father and married Jocasta. On discovering the truth he blinded himself in a fit of madness, and Jocasta killed herself. [Greek = swollen foot, from the story that Laius ran a spike through the infant's feet before leaving it to die]

Oedipus complex /'iːdɪpəs/ *noun Psych.* (according to Freud etc.) the complex of emotions aroused in a young (esp. male) child by a subconscious sexual desire for the parent of the opposite sex and wish to exclude the parent of the same sex. □ **Oedi·pal** *adjective* [OEDIPUS]

OEM *abbreviation* original equipment manufacturer.

oen·ol·ogy /iː'nɒlədʒi/ *noun* the study of wines. □ **oeno·logic·al** *adjective* **oen·ol·o·gist** *noun* [Greek *oinos* wine]

Oeno·ne /iːˈnoːni/ *Gk Myth* a nymph of Mount Ida and lover of Paris, who deserted her for Helen.

oeno·phile /ˈiːnəˌfaɪl/ *noun* a connoisseur of wines. □ **oeno·phil·ic** /-ˈfɪlɪk/ *adjective* **oen·oph·il·ist** /iːˈnɒfɪlɪst/ *noun* [as OENOLOGY]

o'er /ˈoːr/ *adverb & preposition literary* = OVER. [contraction]

Oer·sted /ˈɜrsted/ **Hans Chris·tian** (1777–1851), Danish physicist, who discovered the magnetic effect of an electric current (1820).

oer·sted /ˈɜrsted/ *noun* a unit of magnetic field strength equivalent to 79.58 amperes per metre. [OERSTED]

oesopha·gus esp. *Brit. var. of* ESOPHAGUS. [Greek *oisophagos*]

oestradiol *Brit. var. of* ESTRADIOL.

oes·tro·gen *Brit. var. of* ESTROGEN.

oes·trus *Brit. var. of* ESTRUS.

oeuvre /ˈɜːvrə/ *noun* (pl. **oeuvres** *pronunc.* same) **1** the works of an author, painter, composer, filmmaker, etc., esp. regarded collectively. **2** a work of art, music, literature, etc. [French, = work, from Latin *opera*]

OF *abbreviation Baseball* outfielder.

of *preposition* connecting a noun (often a verbal noun) or pronoun with a preceding noun, adjective, adverb, or verb, expressing a wide range of relations broadly describable as follows: **1** origin, cause, or authorship (*paintings of Thomson; people of Rome; died of malnutrition*). **2** the material or substance constituting or identifying a thing (*a house of cards; was built of bricks*). **3** belonging, connection, or possession (*a thing of the past; articles of clothing; the head of the business; the tip of the iceberg*). **4** identity or close relation (*the city of Rome; a pound of apples; a fool of a man*). **5** removal, separation, or privation (*north of the city; got rid of them; robbed us of $1000*). **6** reference, direction, or respect (*beware of dog; suspected of lying; very good of you; short of money; the selling of goods*). **7** objective relation (*love of music; in search of peace*). **8** partition, classification, or inclusion (*no more of that; part of the story; a friend of mine; this sort of book; some of us will stay*). **9** description, quality, or condition (*the hour of prayer; a person of tact; a girl of ten; on the point of leaving*). **10** *N Amer.* time in relation to the following hour (*a quarter of three*). □ **be of** possess intrinsically; give rise to (*is of great interest*). **of all** designating the (nominally) least likely or expected example (*you of all people!*). **of all the nerve** (or **cheek** etc.) an exclamation of indignation at a person's impudence etc. **of an evening** (or **morning** etc.) *informal* **1** on most evenings (or mornings etc.). **2** at some time in the evenings (or mornings etc.). **of it** *informal* concerning what is being discussed (*had a hard time of it; that's the truth of it*). [Old English, unaccented form of *æf*, from Germanic]

of- *prefix* assimilated form of OB- before *f*.

ofay /ˈoːfeɪ/ *noun esp. US slang offensive* a white person (esp. used by blacks). [20th c.: prob. of African origin]

Off. *abbreviation* **1** Office. **2** Officer.

off ● *adverb* **1 a** away; at or to a distance in time or space (*drove off; is three miles off; summer is not far off*). **b** distant or remote in fact, nature, likelihood, etc. **2** out of position; not on or touching or attached; loose, separate, gone (*has come off; take your coat off*). **3** so as to be rid of (*sleep it off*). **4** so as to break continuity or continuance; discontinued, stopped, cancelled (*turn off the radio; take a day off; the wedding is off*). **5** starting a journey, race, etc. (*she's off to Hong Kong tomorrow*). **6** to the end; entirely; so as to be clear (*clear off; finish off; pay off*). **7** situated as regards money, supplies, etc. (*is badly off; is not very well off*). **8** offstage (*noises off*). **9** esp. *Brit.* (with preceding numeral) denoting a quantity produced or made at one time (esp. *one-off*). **10** taken from the price (*all shirts are 10 per cent off*). **11** into operation; activated (*the alarm went off at 6:30*). **12** (of crops) harvested (*we have to get the wheat off before it rains*). ● *preposition* **1 a** from; away or down or up from (*fell off the chair; took something off the price; jumped off the edge*). **b** not on (*was already off the ice*). **2 a** (temporarily) relieved of or abstaining from (*off duty; am off my diet*). **b** not attracted by for the time being (*off their food; off smoking*). **c** not achieving or doing one's best in (*off form; off one's game*). **3** using as a source or means of support (*live off the land*). **4** leading from; not far from (*a laneway off King Street*). **5** at a short distance to sea from (*sank off Cape Horn*). **6** *informal* from (a specified source) (*bought it off my neighbour*). ● *adjective* **1** (predicative) *informal* **a** strange, eccentric (*she's a little off*). **b** *Brit.* & *Cdn* unwell (*am feeling a bit off*). **c** (of food etc.) unfit for consumption; no longer fresh. **2** not up to par; disappointing, weak (*his game was off*). **3** not on; no longer in operation or effect (*the radio is off; our agreement is off*). **4** decreased in price, quantity etc. (*tourism is off this summer*). ● *transitive verb N Amer. slang* kill, murder. ● *noun* **1** *N Amer.* (in combination) a competition (*cook-off; weigh-off*). **2** *Brit. informal* the start of a race; the beginning, the departure. □ **off and on** intermittently; now and then. **off one's feet** see FOOT. **off form** see FORM. **off guard**

see GUARD. **off one's hands** see HAND. **off one's head** see HEAD. **off of** *slang disputed* = OFF *preposition* 1a (*picked it up off of the floor*). ¶ The use of *off of* for the preposition *off* (sense 1a), e.g. *lifted it up off of the table*, is non-standard and should be avoided in writing. **off the record** see RECORD. [originally variant of OF, to distinguish the sense]

Offa /ˈɒfə/ (d.796), king of Mercia 757–96. After seizing power in Mercia in 757, he expanded his territory to become overlord of most of England south of the Humber, and constructed the earthwork along the Welsh border (see OFFA'S DYKE).

off-air *adjective & adverb* **1** involving or by the transmission of programs by broadcasting. **2** associated with a radio or television program but not broadcast (*off-air comments*).

of·fal /ˈɒfəl/ *noun* **1** the less valuable edible parts of a carcass, esp. the entrails and internal organs. **2** refuse or waste stuff. [Middle Dutch *afval* from *af* OFF + *vallen* FALL]

Of·faly /ˈɒfəli/ a county in the central part of the Republic of Ireland, in the province of Leinster; county town, Tullamore.

Offa's Dyke a series of earthworks running from near the mouth of the Wye to near the mouth of the Dee, originally built or repaired by Offa in the second half of the 8th c. to mark the boundary established by his wars with the Welsh.

off·beat ● *adjective* **1** eccentric, unconventional. **2** *Music* not coinciding with the beat. ● *noun Music* any of the normally unaccented beats in a bar.

off-brand *noun* (often *attributive*) an unknown, unpopular, or inferior brand of item.

off-Broad·way ● *noun* (often *attributive*) New York City theatres, theatrical productions, or theatre life outside the area of Broadway, characteristically being more experimental and less commercial. ● *adverb* occurring outside New York City's main theatre district.

off-camera *adjective & adverb* out of the range of a film or television camera.

off-campus *adjective & adverb* away from a university or college campus (*off-campus housing*).

off-centre ● *adjective* **1** slightly away from the centre; not quite coinciding with a central position. **2** unconventional, eccentric (*off-centre ideas*). ● *adverb* positioned away from the centre.

off chance *noun* (prec. by *the*) the slight possibility.

off-colour *adjective* **1** esp. *N Amer.* slightly indecent or obscene (*an off-colour joke*). **2** esp. *Brit.* slightly unwell; not in the best health.

off·cut *noun* a remnant of wood, paper, etc., after cutting.

off-day *noun* **1** a day when one is not at one's best. **2** *N Amer.* a day off from work, sports training, etc.

off-dry *adjective* (of wine) having an almost dry flavour, with just a trace of sweetness.

off-duty *adjective* **1** not engaged in one's regular work (*an off-duty police officer*). **2** pertaining to or during the time when one is not at work (*off-duty activities*).

Of·fen·bach /ˈɒfənˌbɒx/ **Jacques** (born Jacob Offenbach) (1819–80), German-born French composer. Best known for operettas such as *Orpheus in the Underworld* (1858), he also wrote the opera *The Tales of Hoffmann* (1881).

of·fence /əˈfens/ *noun* (also **of·fense**) **1** an illegal act; a transgression or misdemeanour. **2** a wounding of the feelings; resentment or umbrage (*no offence was meant*). **3** the act of attacking or taking the offensive; aggressive action. **4** a cause of annoyance or disgust; an offensive person or thing. **5** esp. *N Amer. Sport* /ˈɒfens/ **a** the role of scoring points, goals, etc. for one's team (*he plays offence*). **b** the plays, moves, or tactics for achieving this. **c** the players on a team who perform this role. □ **give offence** cause hurt feelings. **take offence** suffer hurt feelings. [originally = stumbling, stumbling block: Middle English & Old French *offens* from Latin *offensus* annoyance, and Middle English & French *offense* from Latin *offensa* a striking against, hurt, displeasure, both from *offendere* (as OB-, *fendere fens*- strike)]

of·fend *verb* **1** *transitive* cause offence to or resentment in; wound the feelings of. **2** *transitive* displease or anger. **3** *intransitive* commit an illegal act. **4** *intransitive* (often foll. by *against*) do wrong; transgress. □ **of·fend·er** *noun* **of·fend·ing** *adjective* [Old French *offendre* from Latin (as OFFENCE)]

of·fense *var. of* OFFENCE.

of·fen·sive ● *adjective* **1** giving or meant or likely to give offence; insulting (*offensive language*). **2** disgusting, foul-smelling, nauseating, repulsive. **3 a** aggressive, attacking. **b** (of a weapon) meant for use in attack. **4** esp. *N Amer. Sport* of or relating to a team in possession of the ball, puck, etc. (*offensive line*). ● *noun* **1** (usu. prec. by *the*) an aggressive action or attitude (*take the offensive*). **2** an attack, an offensive campaign or stroke. **3** aggressive or forceful action in pursuit of a cause (*a peace offensive*). □ **of·fen·sive·ly** *adverb* **of·fen·sive·ness** *noun*

of·fer ● *verb* **1** *transitive* present for acceptance or refusal or consideration (*offered me a drink*; *was offered a lift*; *offer one's services*; *offer no apology*). **2** *intransitive* (foll. by *to* + infin.) express readiness or show intention (*offered to take the children*). **3** *transitive* provide; give an opportunity for. **4** *transitive* **a** make available for sale. **b** propose as payment; bid (*offered $30 for the table*). **5** *transitive* (of a thing) present to one's attention or consideration (*each day offers new opportunities*). **6** *transitive* present (a sacrifice, prayer, etc.) to a deity. **7** *intransitive* present itself; occur (*as opportunity offers*). **8** *transitive* give an opportunity for (battle) to an enemy. **9** *transitive* attempt, or try to show (violence, resistance, etc.). **10** *transitive* (with direct speech as object) say tentatively or helpfully (*'It's a nice day,' she offered*). ● *noun* **1** an expression of readiness to do or give if desired, or to buy or sell (for a certain amount). **2** an amount offered. **3** a proposal (esp. of marriage). **4** a bid. **5** *Law* a proposal made by one party that will establish a binding contract if accepted unconditionally by the party to whom it is made. □ **on offer** *Brit.* for sale at a certain (esp. reduced) price.
□ **of·fer·ee** *noun* **of·fer·or** *noun* [Old English *offrian* in religious sense, from Latin *offerre* (as OB-, *ferre* bring)]

of·fer·ing *noun* **1** a contribution, esp. of money, to a church. **2** a thing offered as a religious sacrifice or token of devotion. **3** anything contributed or offered.

of·fer·tory /ˈɒfərˌtɔri, ˈɒfrə-/ *noun* (*pl.* **-ies**) **1** *Christianity* **a** the offering of the bread and wine at the Eucharist. **b** a hymn accompanying this. **2 a** the collection of money at a religious service. **b** music played or sung while this is collected. **c** the money collected.

off-field *adjective Sport* situated or taking place away from a playing field.

off-flavour *noun* a stale, rancid, or unnatural flavour in food.

off-gas ● *noun* a gas which is given off, esp. one emitted as the by-product of a chemical process. ● *intransitive verb* emit a chemical, esp. a harmful one, in the form of a gas. □ **off-gassing** *noun*

off·hand ● *adjective* curt or casual in manner. ● *adverb* **1** in an offhand manner. **2** without preparation or premeditation. □ **off·hand·ed** *adjective* **off·hand·ed·ly** *adverb* **off·hand·ed·ness** *noun*

off-hour ● *noun* an hour when one is not working. ● *adjective* of, pertaining to, or taking place during an off-hour.

off-ice *adjective & adverb Hockey etc.* not occurring or positioned on the ice (*off-ice training*; *off-ice official*).

of·fice *noun* **1 a** a room or building used as a place of business, esp. for clerical or administrative work. **b** the employees who work in such a place of business (*called the office together to make an announcement*). **2** a room or department or building for a particular kind of business (*ticket office*; *post office*). **3** the local centre of a large business (*our London office*). **4** *N Amer.* **a** a suite of rooms in which a doctor, dentist, etc. treats patients. **b** the staff of this. **5** a position with duties attached to it; a place of authority or trust or service, esp. of a public nature. **6** tenure of an official position, esp. that of a government minister or of the party forming the government (*hold office*; *out of office for 13 years*). **7** (**Office**) **a** a government agency, or a subdivision of such an agency (*Land Titles Office*; *Federal Provincial Relations Office*). **b** *Brit.* the quarters or staff or collective authority of a department of the national government (*Foreign Office*). **8** a duty attaching to one's position; a task or piece of kindness or attention; a service (esp. *through the good offices of*). **10** *Christianity* **a** an authorized form of worship (*Office for the Dead*). **b** (in full **divine office**) the daily service of the Roman Catholic breviary (*say the office*). **11** a ceremonial duty. [Old French from Latin *officium* performance of a task (in medieval Latin also office, divine service), from *opus* work + *facere* fic- do]

office-bearer *noun* esp. *Brit.* = OFFICE-HOLDER.

office boy *noun* a young man employed to do minor jobs in a business office.

office building *noun* (also **office block**) a large building designed to contain business offices.

office girl *noun* a young woman employed to do minor jobs in a business office.

office-holder *noun* (also esp. *Brit.* **office-bearer**) a person who holds office; an esp. elected official.

office hours *noun* the hours during which business is normally conducted.

office·mate *noun* a person who shares an office with another or others.

of·fi·cer ● *noun* **1** a person holding a position of authority or trust, esp. one with a commission in the armed services, in the mercantile marine, or on a passenger ship. **2** a policeman or policewoman. **3** a holder of a post in a society or organization, e.g. the president or secretary. **4** a holder of a public, civil, or ecclesiastical office; a sovereign's minister; an appointed or elected functionary (usu. with a qualifying word: *medical officer*; *probation officer*; *returning officer*). **5** a person who acts in an official capacity in a company. **6** a bailiff (*the sheriff's officer*). **7** (**Officer**) **a** a member of the grade below Companion in the Order of Canada. **b** a member of the grade below commander in the Order of the British Empire. ● *transitive verb* **1** provide with officers. **2** act as the commander of. [Anglo-French *officer*, Old French *officier* from medieval Latin *officiarius* from Latin *officium*: see OFFICE]

officer cadet *noun Cdn & Brit.* a person training to be an officer in the armed forces. Abbr.: **OCdt**.

officer commanding *noun* (also **Officer Commanding**) an officer commanding a sub-unit (usu. an army company or equivalent) of a military unit. Abbr.: **OC**.

office tower *noun* a tall building housing business offices.

office worker *noun* an employee in a business office.

of·fi·cial ● *adjective* **1** of or relating to an office (*see* OFFICE *noun* 5, 6) or its tenure or duties. **2** (often *derogatory*) characteristic of officials and bureaucracy. **3** emanating from or attributable to a person in office; properly authorized. **4** holding office; employed in a public capacity. **5** formal; ceremonial (*an official reception*). ● *noun* a person holding office or engaged in official duties. □ **of·fi·cial·dom** *noun* **of·fi·cial·ism** *noun* **of·fi·cial·ly** *adverb* [Middle English (as noun) from Old French from Latin *officialis* (as OFFICE)]

official birthday *noun* (in the UK) a day in June chosen for the observance of the sovereign's birthday.

of·fi·cial·ese *noun derogatory* turgid or pedantic language supposedly characteristic of official documents and correspondence.

official language *noun* the language or languages under which government services etc. must be provided to citizens upon their request.

official opposition *noun Cdn & Brit.* (in a legislature) the opposition party which has the most seats and is thereby granted certain parliamentary privileges.

official receiver *noun see* RECEIVER 3.

official secrets *plural noun* (esp. in phr. **Official Secrets Act**) *Cdn & Brit.* confidential information involving national security.

of·fi·ciant /əˈfɪʃiənt/ *noun* a person who officiates at a religious ceremony.

of·fi·ci·ate /əˈfɪʃiˌeit/ *verb* **1** *intransitive* act in an official capacity, esp. on a particular occasion. **2** *intransitive* perform a religious service or ceremony. **3 a** *intransitive* act as a referee, umpire, etc. at a competition or game. **b** *transitive* act as a referee at (a game). □ **of·fi·ci·a·tion** *noun* **of·fi·ci·ator** *noun* [medieval Latin *officiare* perform a divine service (*officium*): see OFFICE]

of·fi·cious /əˈfɪʃəs/ *adjective* **1** asserting one's authority aggressively; domineering. **2** intrusive or excessively enthusiastic in offering help etc.; meddlesome. □ **of·fi·cious·ly** *adverb* **of·fi·cious·ness** *noun* [Latin *officiosus* obliging, from *officium*: see OFFICE]

of·fing *noun* the more distant part of the sea in view. □ **in the offing** not far away; likely to appear or happen soon. [perhaps from OFF + -ING¹]

off·ish *adjective informal* inclined to be aloof. [OFF: compare *uppish*]

off-island ● *adjective* situated or occurring away from an island, esp. (in Canada) Prince Edward Island. ● *adverb* on an island, esp. (in Canada) Prince Edward Island (*travelled off-island last summer*).

off-key *adjective* **1** out of tune. **2** not suitable or appropriate; incongruous.

off-kilter *adjective* **1** out of alignment, off-centre. **2** offbeat, bizarre.

off-licence *noun Brit.* **1** a shop selling alcoholic drink for consumption elsewhere. **2** a licence for this.

off-line ● *adjective* **1** *Computing* (of a computer terminal or process) not directly controlled by or connected to a central processing unit. **2** designating or relating to the initial stage of video editing, in which the material is viewed and the desired selections are made, frequently with a rough copy being made on a videotape, prior to being re-recorded onto a master tape or disc in the final editing stage. ● *adverb* **1** with a delay between the production of data and its processing; while not directly controlled by or connected to a central

---

Consonants: b *but*   d *dog*   f *few*   g *get*   h *her*   j *yes*   k *cat*   l *leg*   m *man*   n *no*   p *pen*   r *red*   s *sit*

processing unit. **2** while not surfing the Internet or otherwise connected to a computer network (*purchases products off-line*).

off·load *transitive verb* **1** get rid of (esp. something unpleasant) by giving it to someone else. **2** unload (cargo etc.)

off·message *adjective & adverb* not in accordance with a planned or intended message, esp. in a way which departs from official party policy.

off-off Broadway *adjective & adverb* denoting or relating to avant-garde, experimental theatrical productions in New York City taking place in small or informal venues.

off·peak ● *adjective* used or for use at times other than those of greatest demand. ● *adverb* at times other than those of greatest demand.

off·piste *attributive adjective & adverb Skiing* away from prepared ski runs.

off·price *adjective N Amer.* involving merchandise sold at a lower price than that recommended by the manufacturer.

off·print *noun* a printed copy of an article etc. originally forming part of a larger publication.

off·putting *adjective* **1** disconcerting; disturbing. **2** repellent; unpleasant. □ **off-putting·ly** *adverb*

off·ramp *noun N Amer.* a sloping one-way road leading off a highway.

off·reserve *Cdn* ● *adjective* located on or inhabiting land which is not part of a designated reserve for Aboriginal people (*off-reserve housing*). ● *adverb* not on a reserve (*lives off-reserve*).

off·road ● *attributive adjective* (of a vehicle etc.) designed for rough terrain or for cross-country driving. ● *adverb* away from the road, on rough terrain.

off·roading *noun* the activity of driving over rough terrain, esp. as a sport. □ **off-roader** *noun*

off·sale *Cdn (BC, Alta., & North)* ● *noun* **1** the sale of liquor for consumption elsewhere than at the place of sale. **2** (usu. in *pl.*) an alcoholic drink sold for consumption elsewhere. ● *adjective* designating a place where liquor is sold in this manner (*an off-sale outlet*).

off·screen ● *adjective* **1** not appearing on a movie, television, or computer screen. **2** (*attributive*) in private life or in real life as opposed to a film or television role. ● *adverb* **1** outside the view presented by a movie, television, or computer screen. **2** in private life or in real life as opposed to a film or television role.

off·season *noun* **1** *Sport* the period following the conclusion of the regular season and playoffs, during which no competition takes place. **2** a time when business etc. is slack (often *attributive*: *off-season prices*).

off·set ● *noun* **1** a side shoot from a plant serving for propagation. **2** an offshoot or scion. **3** a compensation; a consideration or amount diminishing or neutralizing the effect of a contrary one. **4** (often *attributive*) a method of printing in which ink is transferred from a plate or stone to a uniform rubber surface and from there to paper etc. (*offset litho*). **5** a mountain spur. **6** a bend in a pipe etc. to carry it past an obstacle. **7** *Archit.* a sloping ledge in a wall etc. where the thickness of the part above is diminished. **8** *Surveying* a short distance measured perpendicularly from the main line of measurement. **9** a small deviation from a correct or normal voltage, current, etc. ● *transitive verb* (**-set·ting**; *past* and *past participle* **-set**) **1** counterbalance, compensate. **2** place out of line. **3** print by the offset process.

off·shoot *noun* **1** a side shoot or branch. **2** a thing which originated as a branch of something else; a derivative.

off·shore ● *adjective* **1 a** situated at sea some distance from the shore. **b** of or pertaining to fishing conducted from large vessels at some distance from the shore. **2** (of the wind) blowing seawards. **3 a** (of goods, funds, etc.) made or registered abroad. **b** (of a person) living abroad (*offshore investors*). ● *adverb* **1** at some distance from the shore. **2** in a direction away from the shore. **3** abroad.

off·side ● *adjective* **1** *Hockey, Soccer, etc.* **a** (of a player) in a position, usu. ahead of the ball or puck, that is not allowed if it affects play. **b** of or relating to such a position (*offside pass*). **2** not in agreement with. ● *adverb* in an offside position (*caught offside*). ● *noun* the infraction of being offside.

off·site *adjective & adverb* away from a site; removed from the premises (*off-site storage*).

off·speed *adjective Baseball* (of a pitch or ball) delivered at less than full speed.

off·spring *noun* (*pl.* same) **1** a person's child or children or descendant(s). **2** an animal's young or descendant(s). **3** something

derived or descended from another (*ringette is an offspring of hockey*). [Old English *ofspring* from OF 'from' + *springan* SPRING *verb*]

off·stage *attributive adjective & adverb* **1** not on the stage and so not visible or audible to the audience. **2** in private life or real life as opposed to a theatre, ballet, etc. role.

off·street *adjective* (esp. of parking facilities) other than on a street.

off-the-cuff *adjective* without preparation, extempore.

off-the-rack *adjective N Amer.* (esp. of clothes) ready-made.

off-the-shelf ● *attributive adjective* (of goods) supplied ready-made; available from existing stock. ● *adverb* (**off the shelf**) ready-made; from existing stock.

off-the-shoulder *attributive adjective* (of a dress etc.) leaving the shoulders bare.

off-the-wall *adjective slang* crazy, absurd, outlandish.

off·track *adjective* **1** situated or taking place away from a racetrack (*off-track betting*). **2** (of skiing, hiking, etc.) not performed on a groomed trail. **3** situated or taking place away from a railway track. **4** (**off track**) away from the subject, goal, etc.

off·trail ● *adjective* (of hiking, horseback riding, etc.) not performed on a groomed trail. ● *adverb* away from a groomed trail.

off·white ● *noun* a white colour with a grey or yellowish tinge. ● *adjective* of this colour.

off·world esp. *US* ● *noun* (esp. in science fiction) any place away from earth, or from that world which serves as the location of a given narrative or which is regarded in a given context as the native world; another world or planet. ● *adjective* involving, located in, inhabiting, or coming from a place outside the native world. ● *adverb* away from the native world; on or towards another world or planet. □ **off-worlder** *noun*

off-year election *noun* (in the US) an election held in a year when there is not a presidential election.

oft *adverb* (in *combination*) often (*oft-recurring; oft-quoted*). [Old English]

often /ˈɒfən, ˈɒftən/ *adverb* (**often·er, often·est**) **1 a** frequently; many times. **b** at short intervals. **2** in many instances. □ **as often as not** in roughly half the instances. **more often than not** in more than (roughly) half the instances. [Middle English: extended from OFT, prob. after *selden* = SELDOM]

often·times /ˈɒfəntaɪmz, ˈɒftən-/ *adverb* often.

Oga·den, the /ˌɒɡəˈdɛn/ a desert region in SE Ethiopia, largely inhabited by Somali nomads. It has been claimed by successive governments of neighbouring Somalia.

ogam *var. of* OGHAM.

Og·bo·mo·sho /ˌɒɡbəˈmoːʃoː/ a city and agricultural market in SW Nigeria, north of Ibadan; pop. (est. 2002) 726,300.

ogee /ˈoːdʒiː, -ˈdʒiː/ *Archit.* ● *adjective* showing in section a double continuous S-shaped curve. ● *noun* an S-shaped line or moulding. [apparently from OGIVE, as being the usual moulding in groin ribs]

ogee arch *noun* an arch with two ogee curves meeting at the apex.

og·ham /ˈɒɡəm/ *noun* (also **ogam**) **1** an ancient British and Irish alphabet of twenty characters formed by parallel strokes on either side of or across a continuous line. **2** an inscription in this alphabet. **3** each of its characters. [Old Irish *ogam*, referred to *Ogma*, its supposed inventor]

Ogil·vie Mountains /ˈoːɡəlvi/ a mountain range in west central Yukon Territory, situated north of Dawson. [W. *Ogilvie*, Canadian surveyor d.1912]

ogive /ˈoːdʒaɪv, -ˈdʒaɪv/ *noun* **1** a pointed or Gothic arch. **2** one of the diagonal groins or ribs of a vault. **3** *Statistics* a cumulative frequency graph. □ **ogiv·al** *adjective* [French, of unknown origin]

ogle /ˈoːɡəl/ ● *verb* **1** *transitive* eye amorously, lecherously, or covetously. **2** *intransitive* look amorously. **3** *transitive* stare at; keep an eye on. ● *noun* an amorous or lecherous look. □ **og·ler** *noun* [prob. Low German or Dutch: compare Low German *oegeln*, frequentative of *oegen* look at]

Ogle·thorpe /ˈoːɡəl,θɔrp/ **James Ed·ward** (1696–1785), English general, colonial administrator, and philanthropist, who founded the colony of Georgia (1732) as a refuge for persecuted European Protestants and unemployed English debtors.

Ogo·po·go /ˌoːɡoːˈpoːɡoː/ an aquatic monster alleged to live in Okanagan Lake, BC. [invented word, said to be from a British music hall song]

ogre /ˈoːɡər/ *noun* **1** a man-eating giant in folklore etc. **2** a cruel, irascible, or ugly person. □ **ogre·ish** *adjective* [French, from classical Latin *Orcus*, the god of the infernal regions]

t top   v voice   w we   z zoo   ʃ she   ʒ vision   θ thin   ð this   ŋ ring   x loch   tʃ chip   dʒ jar   (*see over for vowels*)

ogress /ˈoːgres/ *noun* a man-eating giantess in folklore etc.

OH *abbreviation* Ohio (in official postal use).

oh[1] *interjection* (also **O**) expressing surprise, pain, entreaty, etc. (*oh, what a mess; oh for a holiday*). □ **oh boy** expressing surprise, excitement, etc. **oh well** expressing resignation. [variant of O[4]]

oh[2] *noun* (also **O**) zero (*turned the big four oh; the Jays are five and oh*).

OHC *abbreviation* overhead camshaft.

O'Hig·gins, Ber·nar·do (*c.*1778–1842), Chilean revolutionary leader, head of state (supreme director) 1817–23. He led the Chilean independence movement and, with the help of José de San Martín, liberator of Argentina, led the army which triumphed over Spanish forces in 1817 and won independence for Chile.

Ohio /oʊˈhaɪoʊ/ a state in the northeastern US, bordering on Lake Erie; pop. (2000) 11,353,140; capital, Columbus. □ **Ohio·an** *adjective & noun*

Ohio buckeye *noun* a tree of the horse chestnut family, *Aesculus glabra*, native to the US, with palmate leaves and yellowish-green flowers, planted as an ornamental.

OHIP /ˈoːhɪp/ *abbreviation Cdn* Ontario Health Insurance Plan.

Ohm /ˈoːm/ **Georg Simon** (1789–1854), German physicist. He formulated the law named after him (**Ohm's law**) (1826), which states that the electric current flowing in a conductor is directly proportional to the potential difference (voltage), and inversely proportional to the resistance; the units *ohm* and *mho* are also named after him.

ohm /oːm/ *noun Electricity* the SI unit of resistance, transmitting a current of one ampere when subjected to a potential difference of one volt (symbol Ω). □ **ohmic** *adjective* [OHM]

ohm·meter /ˈoːmˌmiːtɜr/ *noun* an instrument for measuring electrical resistance.

OHMS *abbreviation* On Her (or His) Majesty's Service.

oho *interjection* expressing surprise or exultation.

-oholic *combining form* -AHOLIC.

OHOSP /ˈoːhɒsp/ *abbreviation Cdn* Ontario Home Ownership Savings Plan.

Ohrid, Lake /ˈɒxrɪd/ a lake in SE Europe, on the border between Macedonia and Albania.

oi *var. of* OY.

-oid *suffix* forming adjectives and nouns, denoting form or resemblance (*asteroid; rhomboid; thyroid*). □ **-oidal** *suffix*. **-oidally** *suffix*. [modern Latin *-oides* from Greek *-oeidēs* from *eidos* form]

oidium /oʊˈɪdiəm/ *noun* (*pl.* **oidia** /-diə/) any of several kinds of fungal spore, formed by the breaking up of fungal hyphae into cells. [modern Latin from Greek *ōion* egg + *-idion* diminutive suffix]

oil ● *noun* **1** any of various thick, viscous, usu. inflammable liquids insoluble in water but soluble in organic solvents, obtained from animal, plant, or mineral sources (*see also* ESSENTIAL OIL, FIXED OIL, MINERAL OIL). **2** petroleum. **3** (*in combination*) using oil as fuel (*oil furnace*). **4** = COOKING OIL. **5 a** (usu. in *pl.*) = OIL PAINT. **b** a picture painted in oil paints. **6** any of various thick liquids used on the hair, skin, etc. as a cosmetic (*suntan oil; bath oil*). **7** (in *pl.*) shares in an oil company. ● *transitive verb* **1** apply oil to; moisten, smear, cover, or lubricate with oil. **2** impregnate or treat with oil (*oiled silk*). □ **oil the wheels** help make things go smoothly. [Old French *oile* from Latin *oleum* '(olive) oil', from *olea* 'olive']

oil and water *noun* two elements or factors which do not agree or blend together.

oil-based *adjective* (esp. of paint etc.) having oil as the main ingredient.

oil·bird *noun* a nocturnal fruit-eating bird, *Steatornis caripensis*, resembling a nightjar and living in caves in Central and S America.

oil cake *noun* a mass of compressed linseed etc. left after oil has been extracted, used as fodder or fertilizer.

oil can *noun* a can containing oil, esp. one with a long nozzle for oiling machinery.

oil·cloth *noun* **1** a fabric waterproofed with oil. **2** a canvas coated with linseed or other oil and used to cover a table or floor.

oil colour *noun* = OIL PAINT.

oil drum *noun* a metal drum used for transporting oil.

oil·er *noun* **1** an oil can for oiling machinery. **2** an oil tanker. **3** a person who oils machinery. **4** *N Amer.* **a** an oil well. **b** (in *pl.*) oilskins.

oil field *noun* an area of land or seabed underlain by strata which contain oil, usu. in amounts that justify commercial exploitation.

oil-fired *adjective* using oil as fuel.

oil lamp *noun* a lamp using oil as fuel.

oil·man *noun* (*pl.* **-men**) an owner or employee of an oil company.

oil of turpentine *noun* = TURPENTINE 1.

oil paint *noun* (also **oil colour**) a mix of ground colour pigment and oil.

oil painting *noun* **1** the art of painting in oils. **2** a picture painted in oils. □ **is no oil painting** *Brit.* is physically unattractive. □ **oil painter** *noun*

oil palm *noun* either of two trees, *Elaeis guineensis* of W Africa, or *E. oleifera* of the US, from which palm oil is extracted.

oil pan *noun* (in an internal combustion engine) the bottom part of the crankcase, in which the oil used to lubricate the engine collects.

oil paper *noun* a paper made transparent or waterproof by soaking in oil.

oil patch *noun* esp. *N Amer. slang* **1** a petroleum-rich region in a country etc. **2** the petroleum industry.

oil rig *noun* a structure with equipment for drilling an oil well. □ **oil rigger** *noun*

oil sand *noun* (usu. in *pl.*) a deposit of loose sand or partially consolidated sandstone containing bitumen.

oil·seed *noun* any of various seeds from cultivated crops yielding oil, e.g. rape, peanut, or cotton.

oil shale *noun* a fine-grained rock from which oil can be extracted.

oil·skin *noun* **1** cloth waterproofed with oil. **2** (often in *pl.*) a garment made of this.

oil slick *noun* a smooth patch of floating oil, esp. one on the sea.

oil·stone *noun* a fine-grained flat stone used with oil for sharpening flat tools, e.g. chisels, planes, etc.

oil tanker *noun* a ship designed to carry oil in bulk.

oil well *noun* a well from which petroleum is drawn.

oily *adjective* (**oil·i·er**, **oil·i·est**) **1** of, like, or containing much oil. **2** covered or soaked with oil. **3** (of a manner etc.) fawning, insinuating, unctuous. □ **oil·i·ness** *noun*

oink ● *intransitive verb* **1** (of a pig) make its characteristic grunt. **2** (of a person) grunt like a pig. ● *noun* the grunt of a pig or a sound resembling this. [imitative]

oint·ment *noun* a smooth greasy healing or cosmetic preparation for the skin. [Middle English *oignement*, *ointment*, from Old French *oignement*, ultimately from Latin (as UNGUENT): *oint-* after obsolete *oint* anoint, from Old French, past participle of *oindre* ANOINT]

Oire·ach·tas /ˈɜrəktəs/ *noun* the legislature of the Irish Republic: the President, Dáil, and Seanad. [Irish]

Oirot-Tura /ˌɔɪrɒtˈtuːrə/ a former name (1932–48) for GORNO-ALTAISK.

Oisin /ˈoːʃiːn/ *see* OSSIAN.

OJ *noun N Amer. informal* (also **O.J.**) orange juice. [abbreviation]

Ojib·wa /oʊˈdʒɪbweɪ/ ● *noun* (also **Ojib·way, Ojib·we**) (*pl.* same or **-s**) **1** a member of an Algonquian people living esp. around Lake Superior and certain adjacent areas. **2** the Algonquian language of this people. ● *adjective* of or relating to the Ojibwa or their language. [Ojibwa, from a root meaning 'puckered', with reference to their moccasins]

Oji-Cree /ˈɒdʒɪkriː/ *noun* a mixture of the Cree and Ojibwa languages spoken in NW Ontario and Manitoba. [OJIBWA + CREE]

OK[1] *var. of* OKAY.

OK[2] *abbreviation* Oklahoma (in official postal use).

Oka[1] /ˈoːkə/ a municipality in south central Quebec, located on Lac des Deux Montagnes, west of Montreal; pop. (2001) 3,194. In 1990 the Mohawks on a reserve near there blockaded a road to protest the expansion of a golf course on disputed land; a police officer was killed and a 78-day armed standoff followed. [from the name of an Algonquian chief, after a type of pike]

Oka[2] *noun Cdn* a variety of semi-soft cured cheese originally made by Trappist monks. [from OKA[1], where this cheese is made]

Oka·nag·an[1] /ˌoːkəˈnɒgən/ *noun* (also called **Okanagan Valley**) a region of south central BC, lying between the Cascade and Columbia mountain systems and extending southward into N Washington state. [as OKANAGAN LAKE]

Oka·nag·an[2] /ˌoːkəˈnɒgən/ *noun* **1** a member of an Aboriginal people living in southern BC. **2** the Salishan language of this people. [OKANAGAN LAKE]

Okanagan Lake a long, narrow lake in southern BC, situated in the Okanagan Valley, southwest of Kamloops. [Okanagan *ookanawgan* farthest point, perhaps with reference to the head of the Okanagan River, near Okanagan Falls, the farthest point upstream that salmon could swim]

okapi /oːˈkɑːpi/ *noun* (*pl.* same or **oka·pis**) a ruminant mammal, *Okapia johnstoni*, native to central Africa, with a head resembling that of a giraffe and a body resembling that of a zebra, having a dark chestnut coat and transverse stripes on the hindquarters and upper legs only. [local word]

Okara /oːˈkɑːrə/ a commercial city in NE Pakistan, in Punjab province; pop. (1998) 258,300.

Oka·van·go River /ˌoːkəˈvaŋɡoː/ (also **Cu·bango** /kuːˈbaŋɡoː/) a river of SW Africa which rises in central Angola and flows 1 600 km (1,000 miles) southeastward to Namibia, where it turns eastward to form part of the border between Angola and Namibia before entering Botswana, where it drains into the extensive Okavango marshes of Ngamiland.

okay (also **OK**) *informal* ● *adjective* all right; satisfactory. ● *adverb* well, satisfactorily (*that worked out okay*). ● *noun* (*pl.* **okays** or **OKs**) approval, sanction. ● *interjection* all right, yes. ● *transitive verb* (**okays** or **OK's**, **okayed** or **OK'd**, **okay·ing** or **OK'ing**) give an okay to; approve, sanction. □ **be okay with 1** be acceptable to (*that's okay with me*). **2** be content with (*I'm okay with that*). [written-out form of *OK*, prob. abbreviation of *orl* (or *oll*) *korrect*, jocular form of 'all correct']

Oka·yama /ˌoːkəˈjɒmə/ an industrial city and major railway junction in SW Japan, on the southwest coast of the island of Honshu; pop. (est. 2002) 631,600.

Okee·cho·bee, Lake /ˌoːkəˈtʃoːbiː/ a lake in S Florida. Fed by the Kissimmee River from the north, it drains into the Everglades in the south, this drainage being controlled by embankments and canals. It forms part of the Okeechobee Waterway, which crosses the Florida peninsula from west to east, linking the Gulf of Mexico with the Atlantic.

O'Keefe /oːˈkiːf/ **Eu·gene** (1827–1913), Irish-born Canadian brewer. In 1861 he founded the Victoria Brewery in Toronto and by 1891, when the company was incorporated as O'Keefe Brewing Company Ltd., it was the largest brewer of lager beer in Canada.

O'Keeffe /oːˈkiːf/ **Geor·gia** (1887–1986), US painter. A pioneer of American modernism, she is best known for her figurative paintings of the 1920s and 1930s, depicting enlarged studies, particularly of flowers, which are often regarded as being sexually symbolic, e.g. *Black Iris*, 1926; she also painted notable landscapes of New Mexico.

Oke·fen·okee Swamp /ˌoːkəfəˈnoːkiː/ an area of swampland in SE Georgia and NE Florida. It extends over 1 555 sq. km (600 sq. miles).

okey-doke *adjective, interjection, & adverb* (also **okey-dokey**) *slang* = OKAY. [reduplication]

Okhotsk, Sea of /oːˈxɒtsk/ an inlet of the N Pacific Ocean on the east coast of Russia, between the Kamchatka peninsula and the Kurile Islands.

Okie *noun informal* **1** a native or inhabitant of Oklahoma. **2** a migrant agricultural worker, esp. one from Oklahoma who was forced to leave a farm during the Great Depression. [OKLAHOMA + -IE]

Oki·nawa /ˌoːkəˈnɒwə/ **1** a region in S Japan, in the S Ryukyu Islands; capital, Naha. **2** the largest of the Ryukyu Islands, S Japan. It was captured from the Japanese in the Second World War by a US assault in April–June 1945. With its bases commanding the approaches to Japan, it was a key objective, defended by the Japanese almost to the last man, with kamikaze air attacks inflicting substantial damage on US ships. After the war it remained under US administration until 1972.

Okla. *abbreviation* Oklahoma.

Okla·ho·ma /ˌoːkləˈhoːmə/ a state in the south central US, north of Texas; pop. (2000) 3,450,654; capital, Oklahoma City. □ **Okla·ho·man** *noun & adjective*

Oklahoma City the state capital of Oklahoma; pop. (2000) 506,132.

Oko·toks /ˈoːkətoːks/ a town in SW Alberta, about 40 km south of Calgary; pop. (2001) 11,664. [from the Blackfoot word for a nearby erratic block known as 'Big Rock']

okra /ˈoːkrə/ *noun* **1** a plant, *Abelmoschus esculentus*, yielding long ridged seed pods. **2** the seed pods eaten as a vegetable and used to thicken soups and stews. *Also called* GUMBO. [apparently West African: compare Ibo *okuro* okra, Twi *nkrakra* broth]

Ok·tober·fest *noun* **1** an annual beer festival celebrated in Munich, Germany in late September and early October. **2** a similar autumn festival held elsewhere. [German, *Oktober* October + *Fest* festivity, celebration]

-ol[1] *suffix Chem.* the termination of *alcohol*, used in names of alcohols or analogous compounds (*methanol*; *phenol*).

-ol[2] *combining form* = -OLE. [Latin *oleum* oil]

-ola *combining form* forming nouns, as *granola*, *payola*. [prob. from PIANOLA]

Olaf I /ˈoːlaf/ (known as Olaf Tryggvason) (*c*.964–*c*.1000), king of Norway 995–*c*.1000. According to legend he was brought up in Russia, being converted to Christianity and carrying out extensive Viking raids before returning to Norway to be accepted as king; his exploits as a warrior and his popularity as sovereign made him a national legend.

Olaf II /ˈoːlaf/ (known as Olaf Haraldsson; canonized as St. Olaf) (*c*.995–1030), king of Norway 1016–30. Notable for his attempts to spread Christianity in his kingdom, he was forced into exile by a rebellion in 1028 and killed in battle while attempting to return; he is the patron saint of Norway. Feast day, 29 July.

Öland /ˈɜːland/ a narrow island in the Baltic Sea off the southeast coast of Sweden, separated from the mainland by Kalmar Sound.

old *adjective* (**older**, **old·est**) (*compare* ELDER[1], ELDEST). **1 a** advanced in age; far on in the natural period of existence. **b** not young or near its beginning. **2 a** (often in *combination*) of a particular age (*Hermione is two years old*; *a two-year-old girl*; *how old is this building?*). **b** (in *combination*, as noun) a person or animal of the age specified (*our four-year-old is ill*). **3** made long ago. **4** long in use. **5 a** worn or dilapidated or shabby from the passage of time. **b** familiar through repetition (*an old joke*; *the same old story*). **6** having the characteristics (experience, wisdom, etc.) of age (*the child is old beyond her years*). **7** practised, inveterate (*an old offender*). **8** belonging only or chiefly to the past; lingering on; former (*old times*; *haunted by old memories*). **9** dating from far back; long established or known; ancient, primeval (*old as the hills*; *old friends*; *an old family*). **10** (of language) as used in former or earliest times. **11** *informal* as a term of affection or casual reference (*good old Charlie*; *let's fire up the old barbecue!*). **12** the former or first of two or more similar things (*our old house*; *wants his old job back*). **13** used as an intensifier (*we'll have a grand old time*; *any old thing will do*). **14** *Cdn* (of cheddar) aged 10-24 months. □ **of old** formerly; long ago. □ **old·ish** *adjective* **old·ness** *noun* [Old English *ald* from West Germanic]

old age *noun* the later part of normal life.

old-age home *noun* = OLD PEOPLE'S HOME.

old-age pension *noun* a pension paid by the state to citizens above a certain age. □ **old-age pensioner** *noun*

old age security *noun Cdn* a system of government-funded pensions for those over 65. Abbr.: **OAS**.

Old Bailey *noun* the Central Criminal Court in London.

old bat *noun derogatory* an older woman, esp. one regarded as unattractive or unpleasant.

Old Believer *noun* a member of a Russian Orthodox group which refused to accept the liturgical reforms of the patriarch Nikon (1605-81).

Old Bill *noun Brit. slang* the police.

old bird *noun slang* a wary, astute person.

Old Blighty *see* BLIGHTY.

old boy *noun* **1** esp. *Brit.* a former male pupil of a school. **2** *informal* **a** an elderly man. **b** an affectionate form of address to a boy or man.

old boys' network *noun informal* (also **old boy network**) an informal network through which men from the same social background, profession, school, etc. help each other in business, politics, etc.

Old Church Slavonic *noun* the earliest written Slavic language, surviving as a liturgical language in the Orthodox Church.

old country *noun* (prec. by *the*) the native country of an immigrant, settler, etc.

old dear *noun informal* an elderly woman.

Old Delhi *see* DELHI.

old economy *noun* the economic sector consisting of traditional, non high-tech industries (also *attributive*: *old economy stocks*).

olden *adjective archaic* or *literary* of old; of a former age (esp. *in the olden days*).

Ol·den·burg /ˈoːldənbɜːrɡ/ **Claes (Thure)** (b.1929), Swedish-born US sculptor. A leader of the pop art movement, he is known for his 'soft sculptures' of normally hard objects, such as *Soft Typewriter* (1963).

Old English *noun* **1** the English language up to *c*.1150. **2** *Typography* a form of black letter resembling that used by early English printers.

Old English sheepdog *noun* a breed of large sheepdog with a shaggy blue-grey and white coat.

olde worlde /ˌoːldi ˈwɜːldi/ *adjective jocular* old and quaint, often in a mock old style.

old-fashioned ● *adjective* **1** in or according to the style, fashion, or tastes of an earlier period; antiquated. **2** believing in old ways, customs, etc.; conservative. ● *noun N Amer.* a cocktail consisting chiefly of whisky, bitters, water, and sugar. □ **old-fashioned·ness** *noun*

old-fashioned glass *noun N Amer.* a low tumbler holding approximately 300 ml (11 oz.).

old folks' home *noun informal* = OLD PEOPLE'S HOME.

Old French *noun* the French language of the period before *c.*1400.

old girl *noun* **1** *esp. Brit.* a former female pupil of a school. **2** *informal* **a** an elderly woman. **b** an affectionate term of address to a girl or woman.

Old Glory *noun* the US national flag.

old-growth *adjective* (of a tree, forest, etc.) mature, never felled.

old guard *noun* the original or past or conservative members of a group.

Old·ham /ˈɒldəm/ an industrial town in NW England, near Manchester; pop. (est. 2002) 103,700.

old hand *noun* a person with much experience.

old hat *adjective informal* tediously familiar or out of date.

Old Hickory *see* Andrew JACKSON.

Old High German *noun* High German up to *c.*1200.

old home week *noun N Amer. informal* **1** a week-long festival during which former residents of a town return home for the festivities. **2** any event attended by people who have not seen each other for a long time.

Old Icelandic *noun* Icelandic up to the 16th c., a form of Old Norse.

old·ie *noun informal* **1** a thing that is old or familiar, esp. an old song or film. **2** an elderly person.

Old Kingdom a period of ancient Egyptian history (*c.*2575–2134 BC, 4th–8th dynasty), the 'Pyramid Age', characterized by strong central government based at Memphis.

old lady *noun informal* or *offensive* one's mother, wife, or girlfriend.

old lag *see* LAG³.

old-line *adjective N Amer.* **1** conservative; traditional. **2** long established; venerable.

old maid *noun* **1** *derogatory* an elderly unmarried woman. **2** a prim and fussy person. **3** a card game in which players try not to be left with an unpaired queen. □ **old-maidish** *adjective*

old man *noun informal* **1** one's father, husband, or boyfriend. **2** an affectionate form of address to a boy or man.

Old·man River /ˈoːldmən/ a river in S Alberta, 362 km long, which rises in the Rocky Mountains north of Crowsnest Pass and flows eastward to join the Bow River west of Medicine Hat, where the two form the South Saskatchewan River. [ultimately after the 'Old man' trickster figure of Blackfoot and Cree mythology, because a point near the river's head marked the Old man's playground]

old man's beard *noun* any of various plants with plumed seeds esp. fringetree, *Chionanthus virginica*, and species of clematis. *Also called* TRAVELLER'S JOY.

Old Master *noun* **1** a great artist of former times, esp. of the 13th–17th c. in Europe. **2** a painting by such a painter.

old money *noun* **1** wealth accumulated in a family over several generations. **2** people endowed with this.

old moon *noun* the moon in its last quarter, before the new moon.

Old Nick *noun informal* the Devil.

Old Norse *noun* the North Germanic language of Norway and its colonies until the 14th c., from which the Scandinavian languages are derived.

Old Order *adjective* of or relating to various sects of the Mennonite church in N America, which strictly observe the oldest forms of worship and preserve the most conservative codes of behaviour, dress, etc. (*Old Order Amish*).

old people's home *noun* (also **old-age home**, *informal* **old folks' home**) an institution providing accommodation and nursing care for the elderly, esp. for those too infirm to live alone.

Old Pretender James Stuart, son of James II of England, Ireland, and Scotland (*see* STUART 3).

Old Prussian *noun* the Baltic language spoken in Prussia until the 17th c.

old retainer *see* RETAINER 2b.

Olds /ɒldz/ a town in south central Alberta, about 90 km north of Calgary; pop. (2001) 6,607. [G. *Olds*, CPR traffic manager *c.*1892]

Old Sarum /ˈsɛrəm/ a hill in S England 3 km (2 miles) north of

Salisbury, the site of an ancient Iron Age settlement and hill fort and subsequently a Norman cathedral town, deserted in the 13th c.

Old Saxon *noun* = SAXON *noun* 1b.

old school *noun* **1** traditional attitudes. **2** people having such attitudes.

old school tie *noun esp. Brit.* **1** a necktie with a characteristic pattern worn by the pupils of a particular (usu. private) school. **2** the principle of excessive loyalty to traditional values.

old soldier *noun* an experienced person, esp. in an arduous activity.

old·squaw *noun N Amer.* a duck, *Clangula hyemalis*, the male of which has a very long tail.

old stager *noun* an experienced person, an old hand.

old·ster *noun* an old person. [OLD + -STER, after *youngster*]

old-stock *adjective* designating people whose ancestors have lived in a certain place for several generations.

Old Style *noun* dating reckoned by the Julian calendar (*compare* NEW STYLE).

old-style *attributive adjective* of an old style, outmoded (*old-style communists*).

old sweat *noun Cdn & Brit. informal* **1** an old soldier; a veteran. **2** a person who has had long experience in an activity.

Old Testament *noun* the first part of the Christian Bible containing the scriptures of the Hebrews.

old-time *attributive adjective* belonging to or typical of former times (*old-time rock'n'roll*). □ **old-timey** *adjective*

old-timer *noun* **1** a person who has lived in a place or been associated with an organization, job, etc. for a long time. **2** an elderly person. **3** *N Amer. Sport* **a** a retired professional player, esp. one who participates in sports charity events (*NHL old-timers*). **b** a member of a team of middle-aged or elderly amateur players.

Ol·du·vai Gorge /ˈɒlduˌvaɪ/ a gorge in N Tanzania, 48 km (30 miles) long and up to 90 metres (300 ft.) deep. The exposed strata contain numerous fossils spanning the full range of the Pleistocene period.

Old West *noun* the western US and Canada before the influx of settlers and the establishment of stable government.

old wives' tale *noun* a foolish or unscientific tradition or belief.

old woman *noun informal* or *offensive* **1** one's wife, mother, or girlfriend. **2** a fussy or timid man. □ **old-woman·ish** *adjective*

Old World *noun* Europe, Asia, and Africa, regarded collectively as the part of the world known before the European discovery of the Americas (*compare* NEW WORLD).

old-world *adjective* belonging to or associated with old times.

old year *noun* the year just ended or about to end.

-ole *combining form* forming names of esp. heterocyclic compounds (*indole*). [Latin *oleum* oil]

ole·agin·ous /ˌoːliˈadʒənəs/ *adjective* **1** having the properties of or producing oil. **2** oily, greasy. **3** obsequious, ingratiating. [French *oléagineux* from Latin *oleaginus* from *oleum* oil]

ole·an·der /ˌoːliˈandər/ *noun* an evergreen poisonous shrub, *Nerium oleander*, native to the Mediterranean and bearing clusters of white, pink, or red flowers. [medieval Latin]

ole·as·ter /ˌoːliˈastər/ *noun* any of various sometimes thorny trees of the genus *Elaeagnus*, esp. *E. angustifolia* bearing olive-shaped yellowish fruits. *Also called* RUSSIAN OLIVE. [Latin from *olea* olive tree: see -ASTER]

ole·ate /ˈoːliːeɪt/ *noun* a salt or ester of oleic acid.

olec·ra·non /oːˈlɛkrəˌnɒn, ˌoːliˈkreɪnən/ *noun* a bony prominence on the upper end of the ulna at the elbow. [Greek *ōle(no)kranon* from *ōlenē* elbow + *kranion* head]

ole·fin /ˈoːləfɪn/ *noun* (also **ole·fine**) /-fɪn, -fiːn/ *Chem.* = ALKENE. [French *oléfiant* oil-forming (with reference to oily ethylene dichloride)]

oleic acid /oːˈliːɪk/ *noun* an unsaturated fatty acid present in many fats and soaps. [Latin *oleum* oil]

oleo¹ /ˈoːlio/ *adjective Aviation* designating a system containing a telescopic strut, used esp. in aircraft undercarriages, which absorbs shocks by causing oil to be forced through a small valve into a hollow piston where the strut is compressed. [Latin *oleum* oil]

oleo² /ˈoːlio/ *noun esp. US dated informal* margarine. [abbreviation of OLEOMARGARINE]

oleo- /ˈoːlio/ *combining form* oil. [Latin *oleum* oil]

oleo·graph /ˈoːlioˌɡrɑːf/ *noun* a print made to resemble an oil painting. □ **oleo·graph·ic** *adjective* **ole·og·raphy** /-ˈɒɡrəfi/ *noun*

oleo·mar·gar·ine /ˌoːlioˌmɑːdʒəˈriːn/ *noun N Amer. dated* = MARGARINE.

Consonants: b *but*   d *dog*   f *few*   g *get*   h *her*   j *yes*   k *cat*   l *leg*   m *man*   n *no*   p *pen*   r *red*   s *sit*

oleo·res·in /ˌɔːliːˈrezɪn/ noun a natural or artificial mixture of essential oils and a resin, e.g. balsam.

Oles·tra /ɒˈlestrə/ noun proprietary a synthetic sucrose polyester used as a calorie-free substitute for fat in various foods because of its ability to pass through the body without being absorbed. [from polyester + -a]

oleum /ˈɔːliəm/ noun concentrated sulphuric acid containing excess sulphur trioxide in solution forming a dense corrosive liquid. [Latin, = oil]

O level /ɔː/ noun Brit. hist. (in full **ordinary level**) (in the UK except Scotland) the lower of the two main levels of the GCE examination. [abbreviation]

ol·fac·tion /ɒːlˈfakʃən, ɒl-/ noun the act or capacity of smelling; the sense of smell. [Latin olfactus a smell, from olēre to smell + facere fact-make]

ol·fac·tory /ɒːlˈfaktəri, ɒl-/ adjective of or relating to the sense of smell (olfactory nerves). [Latin olfactare frequentative of olfacere (as OLFACTION)]

olib·anum /ɒːˈlɪbənəm/ noun an aromatic gum resin from any tree of the genus Boswellia, used as incense. [Late Latin libanus from Greek libanos frankincense, of Semitic origin]

oli·garch /ˈɒlɪˌɡɑːk/ noun a member of an oligarchy. [Greek oligarkhēs from oligoi few + arkhō to rule]

oli·garchy /ˈɒlɪˌɡɑːki/ noun (pl. **-ies**) **1** government by a small group of people. **2** a state governed in this way. **3** the members of such a government. □ **oli·garch·ic** /-ˈɡɑːkɪk/ adjective **oli·garch·ic·al** /-ˈɡɑːkɪkəl/ adjective **oli·garch·ic·al·ly** /-ˈɡɑːkɪkli/ adverb

oligo- /ˈɒlɪɡɔː/ combining form few, slight. [Greek oligos small, oligoi few]

Oligo·cene /ˈɒlɪɡəˌsiːn/ Geol. ● adjective of or relating to the third epoch of the Tertiary period, between the Eocene and the Miocene. The Oligocene lasted from about 38 to 24.6 million years ago, and was a time of falling temperatures. ● noun this geological epoch or system. [as OLIGO- + Greek kainos new]

oligo·chaete /ˈɒlɪɡɔːˌkiːt/ ● noun an annelid worm of the division Oligochaeta, which includes the earthworms. ● adjective of or relating to this division. [OLIGO- + Greek khaitē 'long hair' (taken as 'bristle'), so called as having fewer bristles than polychaetes]

oligo·nucleo·tide /ˌɒlɪɡɔːˈnuːkliɔːˌtaɪd, -ˈnjuː-/ noun a polynucleotide whose molecules contain a relatively small number of nucleotides.

oli·gop·oly /ˌɒlɪˈɡɒpəli/ noun (pl. **-ies**) a state of limited competition between a small number of producers or sellers. □ **oli·gop·ol·ist** noun **oli·gop·o·lis·tic** /-ˈlɪstɪk/ adjective [OLIGO-, after MONOPOLY]

oligo·sac·char·ide /ˌɒlɪɡɔːˈsakəˌraɪd/ noun any carbohydrate whose molecules are composed of a relatively small number of monosaccharide units.

oligo·troph·ic /ˌɒlɪɡɔːˈtrɒfɪk, -ˈtrɒfɪk/ adjective (of a lake etc.) relatively poor in plant nutrients. □ **oli·got·rophy** /ˌɒlɪˈɡɒtrəfi/ noun

O-line noun Football offensive line.

Oli·phant /ˈɒlɪfənt/ **Betty** (b.1918), Canadian dance teacher. She emigrated to Canada from England in 1947 and founded the National Ballet School in Toronto in 1959. She was its director until 1989, establishing it as one of the best ballet schools in the world.

oli·va·ceous /ˌɒlɪˈveɪʃəs/ adjective olive green; of a dusky yellowish green.

ol·ive ● noun **1** (in full **olive tree**) any evergreen tree of the genus Olea, having dark green lance-shaped leathery leaves with silvery undersides, esp. O. europaea of the Mediterranean, and O. africana native to S Africa. **2** the small oval fruit of this, having a hard stone and bitter flesh, green when unripe and bluish black when ripe. **3** (in full **olive green**) the greyish-green colour of an unripe olive. **4** the wood of the olive tree. **5 a** any olive-shaped gastropod of the genus Oliva. **b** the shell of this. ● adjective **1** (in full **olive green**) coloured like an unripe olive. **2** (of the complexion) yellowish brown, sallow. [Latin oliva from Greek elaia, from elaion 'oil']

olive branch noun **1** the branch of an olive tree as a symbol of peace. **2** a gesture of reconciliation or friendship.

olive drab ● noun the dull olive green colour used in certain army uniforms. ● adjective of this colour.

olive green noun & adjective see OLIVE noun 3, adjective 1.

olive oil noun a faintly scented oil extracted from olives, used esp. in cooking.

Oli·ver ▸ **1 John** (1856–1927), English-born Canadian politician, Liberal premier of BC 1918–27. As premier, he encouraged the growth of fruit farming in the Okanagan Valley. **2 Jo·seph** (known as 'King Oliver') (1885–1938), US jazz cornetist, composer, and bandleader, who was a leading figure in early jazz history; his compositions include 'Just Gone' (1923), 'New Orleans Stomp' (1924), and 'Too Late' (1929).

Ol·ives, Mount of the highest point in the range of hills to the east of Jerusalem. It is a holy place for both Judaism and Christianity and frequently mentioned in the Bible. The Garden of Gethsemane is located nearby. Its slopes have been a sacred Jewish burial ground for centuries.

Oliv·ier /əˈlɪviˌeɪ/ **Lau·rence (Kerr), Baron Olivier of Brighton** (1907–89), English actor and director. Considered one of the greatest actors of the 20th c., he performed in all the major Shakespearean roles and was the director of the National Theatre (1963–73); his films include Wuthering Heights (1939), Rebecca (1940), Henry V (1944), Hamlet (1948), and Richard III (1955).

oliv·ine /ˈɒlɪˌviːn/ noun a naturally occurring form of magnesium-iron silicate, usu. olive green and found in igneous rocks.

ollie ● noun (in skateboarding and snowboarding) a jump performed without the aid of a takeoff ramp, executed by pushing the back foot down on the tail of the board, bringing the board off the ground. ● intransitive verb (**ollie·ing**) perform an ollie. [20th c.: origin unknown]

Olmec /ˈɒlmek/ noun (pl. same or **Ol·mecs**) **1** a member of a prehistoric people inhabiting the coast of Veracruz and western Tabasco on the Gulf of Mexico (c.1200-400 BC) who established what was probably the first Meso-American civilization. **2** a native people living in the same general area during the 15th and 16th centuries. [Nahuatl Olmecatl, literally 'inhabitants of the rubber country']

-ology combining form see -LOGY.

olo·ro·so /ˌɒləˈrɔːsɔː/ noun (pl. **-sos**) a heavy dark medium-sweet sherry. [Spanish, lit. 'fragrant']

Ol·sztyn /ˈɒlʃtɪn/ a city in N Poland, in the lakeland area of Masuria; pop. (est. 2000) 174,271.

Olym·pia /əˈlɪmpiə/ **1** a plain in Greece, in the W Peloponnese. In ancient Greece it was the site of the chief sanctuary of the god Zeus, the place where the original Olympic Games were held, after which the site is named. **2** the capital of the state of Washington, a port on Puget Sound; pop. (2000) 42,500.

Olym·pi·ad /əˈlɪmpiˌad/ noun **1 a** a period of four years between Olympic Games, used by the ancient Greeks in dating events. **b** a four-yearly celebration of the ancient Olympic Games. **2** a celebration of the modern Olympic Games. **3** a regular international contest in chess, bridge, etc. [Latin Olympias Olympiad- from Greek Olumpias Olumpiad- from Olumpios: see OLYMPIC]

Olym·pi·an /əˈlɪmpiən/ ● adjective **1 a** of or associated with Mount Olympus in Greece, traditionally the home of the Greek gods. **b** celestial, godlike. **2** (of manners etc.) magnificent, condescending, superior (Olympian detachment). **3 a** of or relating to ancient Olympia in southern Greece. **b** = OLYMPIC. ● noun **1** any of the pantheon of twelve gods regarded as living on Olympus. **2** a competitor in the Olympic Games.

Olym·pic /əˈlɪmpɪk/ ● adjective **1** of or pertaining to the modern Olympic Games. **2** of ancient Olympia or the ancient Olympic Games. ● noun (**the Olympics**) the Olympic Games. [Latin Olympicus from Greek Olumpikos of OLYMPUS or OLYMPIA]

Olympic Games 1 a modern international sports competition, traditionally held every four years since 1896 in different venues. Since 1992, the Summer and Winter Games have alternated every second year. **2** hist. an ancient Greek festival held at Olympia every four years, with athletic, literary, and musical competitions.

Olympic-sized adjective (also **Olympic-size**) of the dimensions prescribed for modern Olympic competitions (an Olympic-sized pool is 50 m × 25 m).

Olym·pus /əˈlɪmpəs/ Gk Myth the home of the twelve greater gods and the court of Zeus, identified in later antiquity with Mount Olympus in Greece.

Olympus, Mount /əˈlɪmpəs/ **1** a mountain in N Greece, at the eastern end of the range dividing Thessaly from Macedonia; height 2 917 m (9,570 ft.). (See also OLYMPUS.) **2** a mountain in Cyprus, in the Troodos range. Rising to 1 951 m (6,400 ft.), it is the highest peak on the island.

OM abbreviation (in the UK) Order of Merit.

om /ɔːm/ noun Hinduism & Buddhism a mystic syllable used as a mantra and at the beginning and end of prayers etc. [Sanskrit om, om, sometimes regarded as composed of three sounds, a-u-m, symbolizing the three major Hindu deities]

oma /ˈɔːmə/ noun (among people of German descent) grandmother; grandma. [German]

-oma *noun* forming nouns denoting tumours and other abnormal growths (*carcinoma*). [modern Latin from Greek *-ōma* suffix denoting the result of verbal action]

oma·dhaun /ˈɒmədɒn/ *noun* a foolish person. [Irish *amadán*]

Omagh /ˈoːmɑ, ˈoːmə/ a town in Northern Ireland, principal town of County Tyrone; pop. (est. 2002) 18,100.

Omaha[1] /ˈoːmə,hɒ/ a city in E Nebraska, on the Missouri River; pop. (2000) 390,000.

Omaha[2] /ˈoːmɑhɒ/ ● *noun* (*pl.* same or **-has**) **1** a member of an Aboriginal people of NE Nebraska. **2** the Siouan language of this people. ● *adjective* of or pertaining to the Omaha or their language. [Omaha *umonhon*, upstream people]

Oman /oːˈmɑn/ a country at the eastern corner of the Arabian peninsula; pop. (est. 2002) 2,713,462; capital, Muscat. The economy is dependent on oil, discovered in 1964. □ **Oma·ni** *adjective & noun*

Oman, Gulf of an inlet of the Arabian Sea, connected by the Strait of Hormuz to the Persian Gulf.

Omar Khay·yám /ˌoːmɑr kaiˈjɑm/ (d.1123), Persian poet, mathematician, and astronomer. He is remembered for his *rubáiyát* (quatrains), translated and adapted by Edward Fitzgerald in *The Rubáiyát of Omar Khayyám* (1859).

oma·sum /oːˈmeisəm/ *noun* (*pl.* **omasa** /-sə/) the third stomach of a ruminant. [Latin, = steer's tripe]

Omay·yad *var. of* UMAYYAD.

ombré /ˈɔbrei/ *adjective* (of a fabric etc.) having gradual shading of colour from light to dark. [French, past participle of *ombrer* to shadow (as UMBER)]

ombro- /ˈɒmbrɒ/ *combining form* rain. [Greek *ombros* rain shower]

om·buds·man /ˈɒmbʌdzmən, -bʊdz-, -ˈbʌdz-/ *noun* (*pl.* **-men**) (also **om·buds·person** /ˈɒmbʌdz,pɜrsən/) **1** an official appointed by a government to investigate individuals' complaints against public authorities etc. **2** *N Amer.* an official within an institution who investigates complaints from employees, students, newspaper readers, etc. [Swedish, = legal representative]

Om·dur·man /ˌɒmdərˈmɑn/ a city in central Sudan, on the Nile opposite Khartoum; pop. (est. 2002) 1,670,000.

-ome *suffix* forming nouns denoting objects or parts of a specified nature (*rhizome*; *trichome*). [var. of -OMA]

omega /oːˈmeigə, -megə/ *noun* **1** the last (24th) letter of the Greek alphabet (Ω, ω). **2** the last of a series; the final development. [Greek, *ō mega* = great O]

omega-3 fatty acid *noun* a long-chain polyunsaturated fatty acid found esp. in fish oil, believed to help reduce blood cholesterol levels.

ome·lette /ˈɒmlət/ *noun* (also **ome·let**) a dish of beaten eggs cooked in a frying pan and served plain or filled with cheese, meat, vegetables, etc. [French *omelette*, obsolete *amelette* by metathesis from *alumette* var. of *alumelle* from *lemele* knife blade, from Latin *lamella*: see LAMELLA]

omen ● *noun* **1** an occurrence or object regarded as portending good or evil. **2** prophetic significance (*of good omen*). ● *transitive verb* (usu. in *passive*) portend; foreshow. □ **omened** *adjective* (also in *combination*). [Latin *omen ominis*]

omen·tum /oːˈmentəm/ *noun* (*pl.* **omen·ta** /-tə/) a fold of peritoneum connecting the stomach with other abdominal organs. □ **omen·tal** *adjective* [Latin]

omer·tà /oːˈmertɑ/ *noun* a code of silence, esp. as practised by the Mafia. [Italian, = conspiracy of silence]

OMI *abbreviation* OBLATES OF MARY IMMACULATE.

omi·cron /ˈɒmɪkrɒn, ˈoː-/ *noun* the fifteenth letter of the Greek alphabet (O, o). [Greek, *o mikron* = small o]

omin·ous /ˈɒmɪnəs/ *adjective* **1** threatening; indicating disaster or difficulty. **2** of evil omen; inauspicious. **3** giving or being an omen. □ **omin·ous·ly** *adverb* **omin·ous·ness** *noun* [Latin *ominosus* (as OMEN)]

omis·sion /oːˈmɪʃən/ *noun* **1** the act or an instance of omitting or being omitted. **2** something that has been omitted or overlooked. □ **sin of omission** *see* SIN OF OMISSION.

omit *transitive verb* (**omit·ted**, **omit·ting**) **1** leave out; not insert or include. **2** (foll. by verbal noun or *to* + infin.) fail or neglect (*omitted saying anything*; *omitted to say*). □ **omis·sible** *adjective* [Latin *omittere omiss-* (as OB-, *mittere* send)]

OMM *abbreviation* Cdn Officer of the Order of Military Merit.

om·ma·tid·ium /ˌɒməˈtɪdiəm/ *noun* (*pl.* **om·ma·tidia** /-diə/) a structural element in the compound eye of an insect. [modern Latin from Greek *ommatidion* diminutive of *omma ommat-* eye]

omni- /ˈɒmni/ *combining form* **1** all; of all things. **2** in all ways or places. [Latin from *omnis* all]

omni·bus /ˈɒmnibʌs/ ● *noun* (*pl.* **-es**) **1** *hist.* = BUS *noun* 1. **2** a volume containing several novels etc. previously published separately. ● *adjective* **1** serving several purposes at once. **2** comprising several items (*an omnibus anti-terrorism law*). [French from Latin (dative pl. of *omnis*), = for all]

omni·compe·tent /ˌɒmniˈkɒmpətənt/ *adjective* **1** able to deal with all matters. **2** having jurisdiction in all cases. □ **omni·compe·tence** *noun*

omni·direc·tion·al /ˌɒmnidɪˈrekʃənəl/ *adjective* of equal sensitivity or power in all (esp. horizontal) directions (*omnidirectional microphone*; *omnidirectional antenna*).

omni·far·ious /ˌɒmniˈferiəs/ *adjective* of all sorts or varieties. [Late Latin *omnifarius* (as OMNI-): compare MULTIFARIOUS]

OMNI·MAX /ˈɒmni,maks/ *noun* proprietary (often *attributive*) a technique of widescreen cinematography in which 70mm film is projected through a fish-eye lens onto a hemispherical screen. [OMNI- + MAXIMUM *noun*, after IMAX]

om·nipo·tent /ɒmˈnɪpətənt/ *adjective* **1** having great or absolute power. **2** having great influence. □ **om·nipo·tence** *noun* **om·nipo·tent·ly** *adverb* [Latin *omnipotens* (as OMNI-, POTENT)]

omni·pres·ent /ˌɒmniˈprezənt/ *adjective* **1** present everywhere at the same time. **2** widely or constantly encountered. □ **omni·pres·ence** *noun* [medieval Latin *omnipraesens* (as OMNI-, PRESENT[1])]

om·nis·cient /ɒmˈnɪsiənt, -ʃənt/ *adjective* having infinite or very extensive knowledge. □ **om·nis·cience** *noun* **om·nis·cient·ly** *adverb* [medieval Latin *omnisciens -entis* (as OMNI-, *scire* know)]

omnium-gatherum /ˌɒmniəm ˈgaðərəm/ *noun* jocular a miscellany or strange mixture. [mock Latin from Latin *omnium* of all + GATHER]

om·niv·or·ous /ɒmˈnɪvrəs/ *adjective* **1** feeding on many kinds of food, esp. on both plants and flesh. **2** making use of everything available. □ **omni·vore** /ˈɒmni,vɔr/ *noun* **om·niv·or·ous·ly** *adverb* **om·niv·or·ous·ness** *noun* [Latin *omnivorus* (as OMNI-, -VOROUS)]

om·phal·os /ˈɒmfə,lɒs/ *noun* **1** *Gk Hist.* a conical stone (esp. that at Delphi) representing the navel of the earth. **2** *literary* the navel. **3** a centre or hub. [Greek, = navel, hub]

Omsk /ɒmsk/ a city in south central Russia, on the Irtysh River; pop. (est. 2002) 1,137,900.

ON *abbreviation* Ontario (in official postal use).

on ● *preposition* **1** (so as to be) supported by or attached to or covering or enclosing (*sat on a chair*; *stuck on the wall*; *rings on her fingers*; *leaned on his elbow*). **2** carried with; about the person of (*do you have a pen on you?*). **3** (of time) exactly at; during; contemporaneously with (*on March 28*; *on the hour*; *on schedule*; *working on Sunday*). **4** immediately after or before (*I saw them on my return*). **5** as a result of (*on further examination I found this*). **6** (so as to be) having membership etc. of or residence at or in (*she is on the board of directors*; *lives on Cape Breton Island*). **7** supported financially by (*lives on $200 a week*; *lives on her wits*). **8** close to; just by (*a cabin on the lake*; *lives on the main road*). **9** in the direction of; against. **10** so as to threaten; touching or striking (*advanced on them*; *pulled a knife on me*; *a punch on the nose*). **11** having as an axis or pivot (*turned on his heels*). **12** having as a basis or motive (*works on a ratchet*; *arrested on suspicion*). **13** having as a standard, confirmation, or guarantee (*had it on good authority*; *did it on purpose*; *I promise on my word*). **14** concerning or about (*writes on Maritime folklore*). **15** using or engaged with (*is on the pill*; *here on business*). **16** so as to affect (*walked out on me*). **17** at the expense of (*the drinks are on me*; *the joke is on him*). **18** added to (*disaster on disaster*; *five cents on a litre of gas*). **19** in a specified manner or style (often foll. by *the* + adj. or noun: *on the cheap*; *on the run*). ● *adverb* **1** (so as to be) covering or in contact with something, esp. of clothes (*put your boots on*). **2** in the appropriate direction; towards something (*look on*). **3** further forward; in an advanced position or state (*time is getting on*; *it happened later on*). **4** with continued movement or action (*went plodding on*; *keeps on complaining*). **5** in operation or activity (*the light is on*; *the chase was on*). **6** due to take place as planned (*is the party still on?*). **7** *informal* **a** (of a person) willing to participate or approve, or make a bet. **b** esp. *Brit.* (of an idea, proposal, etc.) practicable or acceptable (*that's just not on*). **8** being shown or performed (*a good movie on tonight*). **9 a** (of a performer) on stage; performing. **b** (of a radio or television host etc.) on the air (*we're on in 5 minutes*). **10** (of an employee) on duty. **11** forward (*head on*). □ **be on about** refer to or discuss esp. tediously or persistently (*what are they on about?*). **be on at** *informal* nag or grumble at. **be on to 1** realize the significance or intentions of. **2** get in touch with (esp. by telephone). **on and off** intermittently; now and then. **on and on** continually; at tedious length. **on side** *see* ONSIDE.

Vowels: a *cat* ɑ *arm* e *bed* ɜr *her* ɜː *deux* ə *ago* ɪ *sit* i *cosy* iː *feed* ɒ *hot* ɔ *pore* oː *no* ʌ *run* ʊ *put*

on time punctual, punctually. **on to** to a position or state on or in contact with (*compare* ONTO). [Old English *on, an* from Germanic]

-on *suffix Physics, Biochem.,* & *Chem.* forming nouns denoting: **1** elementary particles (*meson; neutron*). **2** quanta (*photon*). **3** molecular units (*codon*). **4** substances (*interferon; parathion*). [ION, originally in *electron*]

on-again, off-again *adjective* operating or occurring at irregular and often unpredictable intervals (*their on-again, off-again relationship*).

on·ager /ˈɒnəgər/ *noun* **1** a wild ass, esp. *Equus hemionus* of Central Asia. **2** *hist.* a type of catapult for throwing rocks. [ultimately from Greek *onagros* from *onos* ass + *agrios* wild]

on-air *adjective* on the air; broadcasting.

onan·ism /ˈoʊnəˌnɪzəm/ *noun* **1** masturbation. **2** coitus interruptus. □ **onan·ist** *noun* **onan·is·tic** /-ˈnɪstɪk/ *adjective* [from the Biblical story of *Onan* (Gen. 38:9), who 'wasted his seed on the ground']

Ona·ping Falls /ˈɒnəpɪŋ/ a former town in north central Ontario, northwest of Sudbury, now part of Greater Sudbury; pop. (2001) 4,877. [perhaps from Ojibwa *onapina* I harness it, with reference possibly to the nearby dam]

Onas·sis /oʊˈnɑsɪs/ **1 Aris·totle (Soc·ra·tes)** (1906–75), Turkish-born Greek shipping magnate. The owner of a substantial shipping empire, he was also the founder of the Greek national airline, Olympic Airways (1957). **2** his wife, **Jacque·line (Lee Bou·vier Ken·nedy)** (known as 'Jackie O') (1929–94), First Lady of the US (1961–63) as the wife of President John F. Kennedy; she married Aristotle Onassis in 1968 and after his death in 1975 pursued a career in publishing.

on-base percentage *noun Baseball* a statistic indicating the number of times a player reaches base in relation to his or her at-bats.

on-board *attributive adjective* provided or situated on board a vehicle, ship, etc. (*on-board computer*). Compare ON BOARD (*see* BOARD).

on-camera *adjective* & *adverb* within the range of a film or television camera (*an on-camera interview; the shooting occurred on-camera*).

once ● *adverb* **1** on one occasion or for one time only (*did not once say please; have read it once*). **2** at some point or period in the past (*could once play chess*). **3** ever or at all (*if you once forget it*). **4** by one degree (*a cousin once removed*). ● *conjunction* as soon as (*once they have gone we can relax*). ● *noun* one time or occasion (*just the once*). □ **all at once 1** without warning; suddenly. **2** all together. **at once 1** immediately. **2** simultaneously. **for once** on this (or that) occasion, even if at no other. **once again** (or **more**) another time. **once or for all** (or **once for all**) (done) in a final or conclusive manner, esp. so as to end hesitation or uncertainty. **once and future** that has been in the past and will be again. **once** (or **every once**) **in a while** from time to time; occasionally. **once or twice** a few times. **once upon a time 1** at some vague time in the past. **2** formerly. [Middle English *ānes, ōnes,* genitive of ONE]

once-in-a-lifetime *adjective* (of an experience, opportunity, etc.) so extraordinary that it is not likely to be repeated in one's lifetime (*the trip was a once-in-a-lifetime opportunity*).

once-over *noun informal* a rapid preliminary inspection or piece of work.

onco- *combining form Med.* tumour. [Greek *ogkos* mass]

onco·gene /ˈɒŋkəˌdʒiːn/ *noun* a gene which can transform a cell into a tumour cell.

onco·gen·ic /ɒŋkoʊˈdʒɛnɪk/ *adjective Med.* causing development of a tumour or tumours. □ **onco·gen·icity** /-ˈnɪsɪti/ *noun*

onc·ol·ogy /ɒŋˈkɒlədʒi/ *noun Med.* the branch of medicine dealing with the diagnosis and treatment of cancerous tumours. □ **on·col·o·gist** *noun*

on·com·ing ● *adjective* approaching from the front. ● *noun* an approach or onset.

On·daatje /ɒnˈdɒtjə/ **(Phil·ip) Mi·chael** (b.1943), Sri-Lankan born Canadian writer. He uses unusual settings and thematic and stylistic shifts to compel the reader to see reality as transient and uncertain. His works include an autobiography *Running in the Family* (1982), poetry, and novels such as *The English Patient* (Booker Prize, 1992).

on-deck circle *noun Baseball* a circular area outside the team's dugout where the next batter warms up etc.

101 *adjective N Amer.* **1** designating an introductory university course (*French 101*). **2** designating something regarded as being at an elementary or introductory level (*it's Negotiation 101 to hold on to all your bargaining chips until you get to the table*).

one ● *adjective* **1** single and integral in number. **2** (with a noun implied) a single person or thing of the kind expressed or implied (*one of the best; a nasty one*). **3 a** particular but undefined, esp. as contrasted with another (*that is one view; one thing after another*). **b** *informal* (as an emphatic) a noteworthy example of (*that is one difficult question*). **4** only such (*the one person who can do it*). **5** forming a unity (*one and undivided*). **6** identical; the same (*of one opinion*). **7** a certain (*the RCMP have issued a warrant for one Donald Smith*). ● *noun* **1 a** the lowest cardinal number. **b** a symbol for this (1, i, I). **c** a thing numbered with it. **2** unity; a unit (*one is half of two; came in ones and twos*). **3** a single thing or person or example (often referring to a noun previously expressed or implied: *the big dog and the small one*). **4** *informal* an alcoholic drink (*have a quick one; have one on me*). **5** a story or joke (*the one about the frog*). **6** one o'clock. ● *pronoun* **1** a person of a specified kind (*loved ones; like one possessed*). **2** any person, as representing people in general (*one is bound to lose in the end*). ¶ The use of the pronoun *one* in this sense is usually regarded as a formal usage. It is useful in cases where *you* is inappropriate and where one wishes to avoid the passive. Where a sentence requires that the pronoun be repeated, either *one* or *he, she,* or *they* (or *his, her, their,* or *theirs*) may be used, but it is important to avoid ambiguity, e.g. *One can never tell how she will react.* **3** *Brit.* I, me (*one would like to help*). ¶ Often regarded as an affectation. □ **at one** in agreement. **for one** being one, even if the only one (*I for one do not believe it*). **for one thing** as a single consideration, ignoring others. **one and all** everyone. **one and only 1** unique. **2** superb, unequalled. **one by one** singly, successively. **one day 1** on an unspecified day. **2** at some unspecified future date. **one or two** *see* OR¹. **one thing and another** *informal* various events, items, matters, tasks, etc. (*always complaining about one thing and another*). [Old English *ān* from Germanic]

-one *suffix Chem.* forming nouns denoting various compounds, esp. ketones (*acetone*). [Greek *-ōnē* fem. patronymic]

one-and-a-half *noun Cdn* (*Que.*) an apartment having one room plus a bathroom.

one another *pronoun* each the other or others (esp. as a formula of reciprocity) (*love one another*).

one-armed bandit *noun informal* a slot machine worked by a long handle at the side.

one-dimension·al *adjective* **1** having or pertaining to a single dimension. **2** lacking depth or scope; superficial (*the characters in her books are very one-dimensional*). □ **one-dimension·al·ity** *noun*

one-eighty *noun informal* **1** a turn of 180 degrees; a U-turn. **2** a complete reversal in attitude or opinion.

Onega, Lake /əˈnjeɪgə/ a lake in NW Russia, near the border with Finland, the second largest European lake.

one-handed ● *adjective* **1** having only one hand, or only one hand capable of use. **2** used, worked, or performed with one hand. ● *adverb* using only one hand (*can do it one-handed*).

one-hit wonder *noun* a performer etc. who gains only one popular success before returning to relative anonymity.

one-horse *adjective* **1** using a single horse. **2** *informal* small, unimportant; obscure (*a one-horse town*).

On·eida /oʊˈnaɪdə/ ● *noun* **1** a member of an Iroquois people formerly living in New York State, and now living esp. along the Thames River near London, Ont. **2** the Iroquoian language of this people. ● *adjective* of or relating to this people or their culture or language. [Oneida, lit. 'people of the stone']

O'Neill /oʊˈniːl/ **Eu·gene Glad·stone** (1888–1953), US playwright. His plays portray the struggle between self-destruction, self-deception, and redemption, and include *Mourning Becomes Electra* (1931), *The Iceman Cometh* (1946), and the semi-autobiographical tragedy *Long Day's Journey into Night* (published posthumously in 1956); he was awarded the Nobel Prize for literature in 1936.

oneir·ic /əˈnaɪrɪk/ *adjective* of or relating to dreams or dreaming. [Greek *oneiros* dream]

oneiro- /əˈnaɪroʊ/ *combining form* dream. [Greek *oneiros* dream]

onei·ro·mancy /əˈnaɪrəˌmænsi/ *noun* the interpretation of dreams.

one-liner *noun informal* a short witty remark; a joke consisting of only one sentence.

one-lunger /ˌwʌnˈlʌŋər/ *noun informal* a boat or other vehicle powered by a one-cylinder engine.

one-man *adjective* **1** involving, done, or operated by only one man. **2** committed or attached to one man only (*Katherine is a one-man woman*).

one-man band *noun* **1** an entertainer who plays a number of musical instruments at the same time. **2** a person who does everything personally or operates without assistance.

one·ness *noun* **1** the fact or state of being one; singleness. **2** uniqueness. **3** agreement; unity of opinion. **4** identity, sameness.

one-night stand *noun* **1** *informal* a sexual liaison lasting only one night. **2** a single performance of a play etc. in a place.

one-off *informal* ● *attributive adjective* made or happening only once; not repeated. ● *noun* a thing that is made or happens only once.

one-on-one ● *adjective* involving direct communication, competition, confrontation, etc. between two people; person-to-person. ● *adverb* in direct communication, confrontation, etc. (*spoke one-on-one for the first time*). ● *noun* a one-on-one meeting, encounter, confrontation, etc.

one per cent *noun* (also **1 per cent**, **1%**) *N Amer.* partly skimmed milk containing one per cent milk fat.

one-piece ● *adjective* **1** (of a bathing suit, snowsuit, etc.) made as a single garment. **2** made or consisting of a single piece. ● *noun* a thing that is made or consists of one piece.

one-room schoolhouse *noun* (also **one-room school**) *N Amer.* esp. *hist.* a school in which all grades are taught by one teacher in a single classroom.

oner·ous /ˈoːnərəs, ˈɒn-/ *adjective* **1** burdensome; causing or requiring trouble. **2** *Law* involving heavy obligations. □ **oner·ous·ly** *adverb* **oner·ous·ness** *noun* [Old French *onereus* from Latin *onerosus* from *onus oneris* burden]

one·self *pronoun* the reflexive and (in apposition) emphatic form of *one* (*hurt oneself; one has to do it oneself*).

one-shot *adjective* **1** achieved or done with a single attempt, stroke, etc. **2** occurring, produced, used, etc. only once (*a one-shot deal*).

one-sided *adjective* **1** favouring one side in a dispute; unfair, partial. **2** having or occurring on one side only. **3** larger or more developed on one side. □ **one-sidedly** *adverb* **one-sidedness** *noun*

one-size-fits-all *adjective* **1** (of clothing) available in one size only. **2** *informal* suitable for or used in all circumstances (*attempted to impose a one-size-fits-all solution*).

one-step *adjective* done or made etc. in a single step (*one-step installation process*).

one-stop *attributive adjective* (of a store etc.) capable of supplying all a customer's needs within a particular range of goods or services (*a one-stop building supply centre*).

one-time ● *adjective* **1** former (*the one-time champ*). **2** done or occurring etc. only once (*a one-time payment*). ● *transitive verb Hockey* shoot (a moving puck) without stopping it first.

one-timer *noun Hockey* a shot that has been one-timed.

one-to-one *adjective* **1** with each member of a group corresponding to a member of another group. **2** = ONE-ON-ONE *adjective*.

one-touch *adjective* (of an electrical device or facility, e.g. a telephone), that can be operated simply at the touch of a single button, esp. as a shortcut replacing a series of keystrokes or button pushes.

one-track mind *noun* a mind preoccupied with one subject.

one-trick pony *noun* a person or thing with only one special feature, talent, or area of expertise.

one-two *informal* ● *noun Boxing* the delivery of two punches in quick succession. ● *adjective* (of two teams, competitors, etc.) holding first and second place (*our two teams were one-two at the end of the season*).

one-two punch *noun* a double blow, disaster, etc.

one-up *informal* ● *adjective* having a particular advantage. ● *transitive verb* (**one-upped**, **one-upping**) do better than (someone) (*always trying to one-up me*).

one-upmanship *noun informal* the art or practice of maintaining an advantage in a competitive relationship.

one-way *adjective* **1** allowing movement or travel in one direction only (*a one-way ticket to St. John's*). **2** characterized by or entailing no reciprocal feeling, communication, responsibility, etc. (*a one-way relationship*). **3** (of a window, mirror, etc.) permitting vision from one side only.

one-way street *noun* **1** a street on which vehicular travel is allowed in only one direction. **2** a situation, relationship, etc., in which there is no reciprocity or possibility of returning to a previous state.

one-woman *adjective* **1** involving, done, or operated by only one woman (*a one-woman show*). **2** committed or attached to one woman only.

on·going *adjective* **1** continuing to exist or be operative etc. **2** that is or are in progress (*ongoing discussions*). □ **on·going·ness** *noun*

on-ice *adjective & adverb Hockey & Curling* occurring or positioned on the ice (*on-ice violence; the rink's only on-ice triumph*).

on·ion /ˈʌnjən/ *noun* **1** a liliaceous plant, *Allium cepa*, having a short stem and bearing greenish-white flowers. **2** the swollen bulb of this, used as a vegetable. □ **know one's onions** *Brit.* be fully knowledgeable or experienced. □ **on·iony** *adjective* [Old French *oignon* ultimately from Latin *unio -onis*]

onion dome *noun* a bulbous dome, esp. on an Eastern Orthodox church etc. □ **onion-domed** *adjective*

onion ring *noun* a ring of onion coated in batter and deep-fried.

On·ions /ˈʌnjənz/ **Charles Tal·but** (1873–1965), English grammarian and lexicographer, who was co-editor of the *Oxford English Dictionary* (1914–33).

onion skin *noun* **1** the brown outermost skin or any outer skin of an onion. **2** thin smooth translucent paper.

Onley /ˈɒnli/ **Nor·man An·tony** ('Toni') (b.1928), Canadian painter. Born on the Isle of Man, he immigrated to Canada with his family in 1948. His landscapes, painted in a very sparse and formal style, have been very successful. His watercolours are painted on location, usually in very broad washes, and are then used as the basis for studio oil paintings and silkscreen prints.

on·line *Computing* ● *adjective* **1** (of an operation or a process) carried out while connected to a computer and under its direct control. **2** (of a device) directly connected to a computer and receiving input from it and sending an output to it as soon as it is generated. **3** designating or relating to a service, resource, etc., available or performed using a computer network (esp. the Internet), or a person or organization that can operate or accesses this (*online dictionaries; online shoppers*). ● *adverb* **1** with processing of data carried out simultaneously with its production; while connected to a computer, or under direct computer control. **2** by means of or over a computer network, esp. the Internet. □ **go online 1** establish connection with the Internet. **2** begin using the Internet. **3** in or into operation, production, or existence (*as new recycling facilities come online*).

on·look·er *noun* a non-participating observer; a spectator. □ **on·look·ing** *adjective*

only ● *adverb* **1** solely, merely, exclusively; and no one or nothing more besides (*I only want to sit down; will only make matters worse; needed six only; is only a child*). **2** no longer ago than (*saw them only yesterday*). **3** not until (*arrives only on Tuesday*). **4** with no better result than (*hurried home only to find her gone*). ¶ In informal English *only* is usually placed between the subject and verb regardless of what it refers to (e.g. *I only want to talk to you*); in more formal English it is often placed more exactly, esp. to avoid ambiguity (e.g. *I want to talk only to you*). In speech, intonation usually serves to clarify the sense. ● *attributive adjective* **1** existing alone of its or their kind (*their only son*). **2** best or alone worth knowing (*the only place to eat*). ● *conjunction informal* **1** except that; but for the fact that (*I would go, only I feel ill*). **2** but then (as an extra consideration) (*he always makes promises, only he never keeps them*). □ **only too** extremely (*is only too willing*). [Old English *ānlic, ǣnlic*, Middle English *onliche* from ONE, -LY²]

on-message *adjective & adverb* in accordance with a planned or intended message, esp. reinforcing official party policy.

Ono /ˈoːnoʊ/ **Yoko** (b.1933), US musician and artist, born in Japan. An established avant-garde performance artist when she married John Lennon in 1969, she collaborated with him on experimental recordings such as *Unfinished Music No. 1: Two Virgins* (1969). Ono also recorded her own albums, such as *Approximately Infinite Universe* (1973) and *Season of Glass* (1981).

o.n.o. *abbreviation Brit.* or near offer.

on-off *adjective* **1** (of a switch) having two positions, 'on' and 'off'. **2** = ON AND OFF (see on).

ono·mas·tic /ˌɒnəˈmastɪk/ *adjective* relating to names or nomenclature. [Greek *onomastikos* from *onoma* name]

ono·mas·tics /ˌɒnəˈmastɪks/ *plural noun* (treated as *sing.*) the study of the origin and formation of (esp. personal) proper names.

ono·mato·poeia /ˌɒnəˌmatəˈpiːə/ *noun* **1** the formation of a word from a sound associated with what is named (e.g. *cuckoo, sizzle*). **2** the use of such words. □ **ono·mato·poeic** *adjective*

ono·mato·poeic·ally *adverb* [Late Latin from Greek *onomatopoiia* word-making, from *onoma -matos* name + *poieō* make]

Onon·daga /ˌɒnɒnˈdɒɡə/ ● *noun* **1** a member of an Iroquois people now living esp. on the Six Nations reserve near Brantford, Ont. **2** the Iroquoian language of this people. ● *adjective* of or relating to this people or their culture or language. [Onondaga *onó:taʼke*, the name of the main Onondaga village, lit. 'on the hill']

on-ramp *noun N Amer.* a sloping one-way road leading onto a highway.

Consonants:　b *but*　d *dog*　f *few*　g *get*　h *her*　j *yes*　k *cat*　l *leg*　m *man*　n *no*　p *pen*　r *red*　s *sit*

on-reserve *Cdn* ● *adjective* located on or inhabiting land which is part of a designated reserve for Aboriginal people (*on-reserve housing*). ● *adverb* on a reserve (*works on-reserve*).

on·rush *noun* an onward rush. □ **on·rush·ing** *adjective*

on·screen ● *adjective* appearing on a movie, television, or computer screen. ● *adverb* **1** on or by means of a screen. **2** within the view presented by a motion picture scene.

onset *noun* **1** the beginning of some esp. unpleasant operation, situation, condition, etc. **2** an attack.

on-set *attributive adjective* taking place or occurring on the set of a play or film.

on·shore ● *adjective* **1** on the shore. **2** (of the wind) blowing from the sea towards the land. ● *adverb* on or towards the land.

on·side *adjective & adverb* **1** *Sport* (of a player) in a legal position; not offside. **2** (also **on side**) in or into a position of agreement with (another person or thing) (*the Maritime provinces have now come onside*).

on-site *attributive adjective* taking place or available on a site or premises.

on·slaught /ˈɒnslɒt/ *noun* a fierce attack. [earlier *anslaight* from Middle Dutch *aenslag* from *aen* on + *slag* blow, assimilated to obsolete *slaught* slaughter]

on·stage *adjective & adverb* on the stage; visible to the audience.

on stream *adverb* in or into industrial production or useful operation.

Ont. *abbreviation* Ontario.

-ont *combining form Biol.* denoting an individual of a specified type (*symbiont*). [Greek *ōn ont-* being]

On·tario a province of central Canada, between Hudson Bay and the Great Lakes; pop. (2001) 11,410,046; capital, Toronto. It became one of the original four provinces in the Dominion of Canada in 1867. □ **On·tar·ian** *adjective & noun* [see ONTARIO, LAKE]

Ontario, Lake the smallest (19 001 sq. km) and most easterly of the Great Lakes, lying on the US–Canada border between Ontario and New York State. It is linked to Lake Erie in the south by the Niagara River and to the Atlantic Ocean by the St. Lawrence River. [Huron *ontare* lake]

Ontario Court *noun Cdn* (also **Ontario Court of Justice**) (in Ontario) a provincial court with two divisions, the **General Division**, which has jurisdiction over all indictable offences and most civil cases, and the **Provincial Division**, which has jurisdiction over cases involving family law and also acts as a youth court and small claims court.

Ontario Scholar *noun hist.* a student who obtained an average higher than 80% in Grade 13 or OAC.

on-the-job *adjective* done or occurring while a person is at work.

onto *preposition* to a position or state on or in contact with.

onto·gen·esis /ˌɒntəˈdʒɛnɪsɪs/ *noun* the origin and development of an individual (*compare* PHYLOGENY). □ **onto·gen·etic** /-dʒɪˈnɛtɪk/ *adjective* **onto·gen·etic·al·ly** /-dʒɪˈnɛtɪkli/ *adverb* [formed as ONTOGENY + Greek *genesis* birth]

onto·geny /ɒnˈtɒdʒəni/ *noun* = ONTOGENESIS. □ **onto·gen·ic** /-təˈdʒɛnɪk/ *adjective* **onto·gen·ic·al·ly** /-təˈdʒɛnɪkli/ *adverb* [Greek *ōn ont-* being, pres. part. of *eimi* be + -GENY]

on·tol·ogy /ɒnˈtɒlədʒi/ *noun* the branch of metaphysics dealing with the nature of being. □ **onto·logic·al** /-təˈlɒdʒɪkəl/ *adjective* **onto·logic·al·ly** /-təˈlɒdʒɪkli/ *adverb* **on·tol·o·gist** *noun* [modern Latin *ontologia* from Greek *ōn ont-* being + -LOGY]

onus /ˈɒnəs/ *noun* (*pl.* **onus·es**) a burden, duty, or responsibility. [Latin]

on·ward ● *adverb* (also **on·wards**) **1** further on. **2** towards the front. **3** with advancing motion. **4** into the future (*from 1998 onward*). ● *adjective* directed onward.

onyx /ˈɒnɪks/ *noun* a semi-precious variety of agate with different colours in layers. [Old French *onix* from Latin from Greek *onux* fingernail, onyx]

oo- /ˈoːə/ *combining form Biol.* egg, ovum. [Greek *ōion* egg]

oo·cyte /ˈoːəˌsʌɪt/ *noun* an immature ovum in an ovary.

oo·dles *plural noun informal* a very great amount. [19th-c. US: origin unknown]

oog·am·ous /oːˈɒɡəməs/ *adjective* reproducing by the union of mobile male and immobile female cells. □ **oog·amy** *noun*

oo·gen·esis /ˌoːəˈdʒɛnɪsɪs/ *noun* the production or development of an ovum.

ooh ● *interjection* expressing surprise, delight, pain, etc. ● *noun* an exclamation of 'ooh'. ● *intransitive verb* (**oohed**, **ooh·ing**) (in phr. **ooh and aah**) express delight, a favourable reaction, etc.

Ook·pik /ˈuːkpɪk/ *noun Cdn* a doll resembling an owl, originally handcrafted of sealskin by Inuit artisans, now mass-produced and sold as a souvenir. [Inuktitut *ukpik* snowy owl]

ooli·chan *var. of* EULACHON.

oo·lite /ˈoːəˌlʌɪt/ *noun* a sedimentary rock, usu. limestone, consisting of rounded grains made up of concentric layers. □ **oo·lit·ic** /-ˈlɪtɪk/ *adjective* [French *oölithe* (as OO-, -LITE)]

ool·ogy /oːˈɒlədʒi/ *noun* the study or collecting of birds' eggs. □ **oo·log·ic·al** /ˌoːəˈlɒdʒɪkəl/ *adjective* **oolo·gist** *noun*

oo·long /ˈuːlɒŋ/ *noun* a dark kind of tea, grown esp. in China, that is partially fermented before it is dried. [Chinese *wulong* black dragon]

oo·miak *var. of* UMIAK.

oom·pah *noun* (also **oom·pah·pah**) a representation of the repetitive rhythmical playing of lower brass instruments, esp. in German and E European dance music. [imitative]

oomph *noun* (also **umph**) *slang* **1** energy, liveliness. **2** attractiveness, esp. sexual appeal. [20th c.: origin uncertain]

-oon *suffix* forming nouns, originally from French words in stressed *-on* (*balloon*; *buffoon*). ¶ Replaced by *-on* in recent borrowings and those with unstressed *-on* (*baron*). [Latin *-o -onis*, sometimes via Italian *-one*]

oophor·ec·tomy /ˌoːəfəˈrɛktəmi/ *noun* (*pl.* **-mies**) *Med.* the surgical removal of one or both ovaries. [modern Latin *oophoron* 'ovary' (from Greek *ōophoros* 'egg-bearing') + -ECTOMY]

oops *interjection informal* expressing surprise or apology, esp. on making an obvious mistake.

oopsy daisy *var. of* OOPS.

Oort /ɔːt/ **Jan Hen·drik** (1900–92), Dutch astronomer. His early measurements of the proper motion of stars enabled him to prove that the Milky Way is rotating, and to determine the position and orbital period of our sun within it; he also proposed the existence of a cloud of incipient comets beyond the orbit of Pluto, now named after him.

ooze¹ ● *verb* **1** *intransitive* (of fluid) pass slowly through the pores of a body. **2** *intransitive* trickle or leak slowly out. **3** *intransitive* (of a substance) exude moisture. **4** *transitive* exude or exhibit (a feeling, an ambience) liberally (*oozed sympathy; the town oozes history*). ● *noun* **1** a sluggish flow or exudation. **2** an infusion of oak bark or other vegetable matter, used in tanning. □ **oozy** *adjective* [originally as noun (sense 2), from Old English *wōs* juice, sap]

ooze² *noun* **1** a deposit of wet mud or slime, esp. at the bottom of a river, lake, or estuary. **2** a bog or marsh; soft muddy ground. □ **oozy** *adjective* [Old English *wāse*]

OP *abbreviation* **1** *Catholicism* Order of Preachers (used after the name of a member of the Dominican order). **2** *Military* observation post. **3** out of print. [sense 1 from Latin *Ordo Praedicatorum*]

Op. *abbreviation Music* opus.

op *noun informal* operation (in surgical and military senses).

o.p. *abbreviation* overproof.

op- *prefix* assimilated form of OB- before p.

opa /ˈoːpə/ *noun* (among people of German descent) grandfather; grandpa. [German]

opaci·fy /oːˈpasɪˌfʌɪ/ *transitive & intransitive verb* (**-fies**, **-fied**) make or become opaque. □ **opaci·fi·ca·tion** *noun* **opaci·fi·er** *noun*

opa·city /əˈpasɪti/ *noun* **1** the state of being opaque. **2** the degree to which a substance is opaque. **3** obscurity of meaning. **4** obtuseness of understanding. [French *opacité* from Latin *opacitas -tatis* (as OPAQUE)]

opah /ˈoːpə/ *noun* a large rare deep-sea fish, *Lampris guttatus*, usu. having a silver-blue back with white spots and crimson fins. Also called MOONFISH. [West African name]

opal /ˈoːpəl/ *noun* a quartz-like form of hydrated silica, usu. white or colourless and sometimes showing changing colours, often used as a gemstone. [French *opale* or Latin *opalus* prob. ultimately from Sanskrit *upalas* precious stone]

opal·es·cent /ˌoːpəˈlɛsənt/ *adjective* showing changing colours like an opal. □ **opal·esce** *intransitive verb* **opal·es·cence** *noun*

opal glass *noun* a semi-translucent white glass.

opal·ine /ˈoːpəˌlʌɪn/ ● *adjective* opal-like, opalescent, iridescent. ● *noun* opal glass.

opaque /oːˈpeɪk/ ● *adjective* (**opaquer**, **opaquest**) **1** not transmitting light. **2** impenetrable to sight. **3** obscure; not lucid. **4** obtuse, dull-witted. ● *noun* **1** an opaque thing or substance. **2** a substance for producing opaque areas on negatives. □ **opaque·ly** *adverb*

opaque·ness *noun* [Middle English *opak* from Latin *opacus*: spelling now assimilated to French]

op art *noun informal* = OPTICAL ART. [abbreviation]

op. cit. /ˈɒp sɪt/ *abbreviation* in the work already quoted. [Latin *opere citato*]

OPEC /ˈoːpek/ *abbreviation* Organization of Petroleum Exporting Countries.

op-ed *noun* a newspaper page usu. located opposite the editorial page and containing signed opinion pieces, letters to the editor, etc. (also *attributive: printed on the op-ed page; wrote an op-ed article*). [abbreviation of *opposite editorial page*]

open ● *adjective* **1** not closed or locked or blocked up; allowing entrance or passage or access. **2 a** (of a room, field, or other area) having its door or gate in a position allowing access, or part of its confining boundary removed. **b** (of a container) not fastened or sealed; in a position or with the lid etc. in a position allowing access to the inside part. **3 a** unconfined, unobstructed (*the open road; open views*). **b** unenclosed or unprotected on at least one side (*cooked over an open fire*). **4** uncovered, bare, exposed (*open drain; open wound*). **5** *Sport* **a** (of a goal or other object of attack) unprotected, vulnerable. **b** (of a player) not guarded by a member of the opposing team. **6** undisguised, public, manifest; not exclusive or limited (*open scandal; open hostilities; an open disregard for the law*). **7** expanded, unfolded, or spread out (*had the map open on the table*). **8** (of land etc.) having few trees, buildings, etc. (*a tract of open farmland*). **9** (of a fabric) not close; with gaps or intervals. **10 a** (of a person) frank and communicative. **b** (of the mind) accessible to new ideas; unprejudiced or undecided. **11 a** (of an exhibition, store, etc.) accessible to visitors or customers; ready for business. **b** (of a meeting) admitting all, not restricted to members etc. **12 a** (of a race, competition, scholarship, etc.) unrestricted as to who may compete. **b** (of a champion, scholar, etc.) having won such a contest. **13** *Cdn* (of a mortgage etc.) that may be paid off in full without penalty before the expiry of the stated term. **14** (of government) conducted in an informative manner receptive to inquiry, criticism, etc., from the public. **15** (foll. by *to*) **a** willing to receive (*is open to offers*). **b** (of a choice, offer, or opportunity) still available (*there are three courses open to us*). **c** likely to suffer from or be affected by (*open to abuse*). **16 a** relating to that part of a body of water which is not surrounded by headlands, etc. (*sailed into open water; lost on the open lake*). **b** designating water on a river, lake, etc. that has not frozen over. **17 a** (of the mouth) with lips apart, esp. in surprise or incomprehension. **b** (of the ears or eyes) eagerly attentive. **18** (of a compound word) written as separate words, e.g. *garbage truck*. **19** *Music* **a** (of a string) allowed to vibrate along its whole length. **b** (of a pipe) unstopped at each end. **c** (of a note) sounded from an open string or pipe. **20** (of an electrical circuit) having a break in the conducting path. **21** (of the bowels) not constipated. **22** (of a return ticket) not restricted as to day of travel. **23** (of a boat) without a deck. **24** (of the weather or winter) mild. **25** *Phonetics* **a** (of a vowel) produced with a relatively wide opening of the mouth. **b** (of a syllable) ending in a vowel. **26** (of a sandwich etc.) = OPEN-FACED 2. **27** (of a town, city, etc.) not defended even if attacked. ● *verb* **1** *transitive & intransitive* make or become open or more open. **2 a** *transitive* change from a closed or fastened position so as to allow access (*opened the door; opened the box*). **b** *intransitive* (of a door, lid, etc.) have its position changed to allow access (*the door opened slowly*). **3** *transitive* remove the sealing or fastening element of (a container) to get access to the contents (*opened the envelope*). **4** *intransitive* (foll. by *into, onto*, etc.) (of a door, room, etc.) afford access as specified (*opened onto a large garden*). **5 a** *transitive* start or establish or set going (a business, activity, etc.). **b** *intransitive* be initiated; make a start (*the session opens tomorrow; the story opens with a murder*). **c** *transitive* (of a counsel in a law court) make a preliminary statement in (a case) before calling witnesses. **6 a** *transitive* spread out or unfold (a map, newspaper, etc.). **b** *transitive & intransitive* refer to the contents of (a book). **7** *intransitive* (often foll. by *with*) (of a person) begin speaking, writing, etc. (*he opened with a warning*). **8** *intransitive* (of a prospect) come into view; be revealed. **9** *transitive* reveal or communicate (one's feelings, intentions, etc.). **10** *transitive* make (one's mind, heart, etc.) more sympathetic or enlightened. **11** *transitive* ceremonially declare (a building etc.) to be completed and in use. **12** *intransitive* *Cards* play the first card, or make the first bid, in a hand; lead. **13** *transitive* break up (ground) with a plow etc. **14** *transitive* cause (the bowels) to empty. **15** *Naut.* **a** *transitive* get a view of by change of position. **b** *intransitive* come into full view. ● *noun* **1** (prec. by *the*) **a** open space or country or air. **b** public notice or view; general attention (*brought the affair into the open*). **2** an open championship, competition, or scholarship. □ **be open with** speak frankly to. **open-and-shut** (of an argument, case,

etc.) straightforward and conclusive. **open the door to** see DOOR. **open a person's eyes** see EYE. **open fire** start shooting (*the police opened fire on the gunman*). **open out 1** unfold; spread out. **2** develop, expand. **3** *Brit.* become communicative. **4** accelerate. **open up 1** unlock (premises). **2** make accessible. **3** reveal; bring to notice. **4** accelerate esp. a motor vehicle. **5** begin shooting or sounding. **6** talk or speak openly. **with open arms** see ARM[1]. □ **open·able** *adjective* **open·ness** *noun* [Old English *open*]

open air ● *noun* (usu. prec. by *the*) a free or unenclosed space outdoors. ● *attributive adjective* (**open-air**) **1** out of doors. **2** open to the air; having no covering (*an open-air vehicle*).

open bar *noun* *N Amer.* a bar, e.g. at a reception etc., where the drinks are paid for by the host or through an admission fee rather than purchased directly by the guests (*compare* CASH BAR).

open book ● *noun* a person or thing that is easily understood. ● *adjective* (usu. **open-book**) (of an examination etc.) written with the use of a textbook, one's notes, etc. (*the final mark is based on an open-book exam*).

open·cast *adjective* *Brit.* (of a mine or mining) with removal of the surface layers and working from above, not from shafts.

open cluster *noun* an open or loose grouping of stars.

open concept *adjective* *Cdn* (of a house, office, etc.) having few or no internal walls or partitions.

open custody *noun* *Cdn* custody in a correctional facility that has relatively little supervision or security, e.g. a group home etc. (also *attributive: open-custody institution*).

open day *noun* *Brit. & Austral.* = OPEN HOUSE 2.

open door *noun* **1** a policy or practice of allowing trade with all nations on an equal basis. **2** free or unrestricted admittance, esp. for immigration etc. (also *attributive: open door policies*).

open-ended *adjective* **1** having no predetermined limit or boundary. **2** (of a question etc.) not limiting the respondent in the range of his or her answer. □ **open-endedness** *noun*

open·er *noun* **1** a person or thing that opens (something). **2** a device for opening cans, bottles, etc. **3** the first item in a program, series, season, etc. □ **for openers** *informal* to start with.

open-eyed *adjective* **1** with the eyes open. **2** alert, watchful.

open-faced *adjective* **1** having a frank or ingenuous expression. **2** (also **open-face**) (of a sandwich etc.) without an upper layer of bread etc.

open flame *noun* a source of combustion, esp. when exposed to combustible gases (*should be kept away from open flame*).

open-handed *adjective* generous. □ **open-handed·ly** *adverb* **open-handed·ness** *noun*

open-heart *adjective* of or relating to surgery in which the heart has been temporarily bypassed and opened.

open-hearted *adjective* **1** frank; candid. **2** kindly. □ **open-hearted·ness** *noun*

open-hearth *adjective* of or relating to a process of steel manufacture using a shallow reverberatory furnace.

open house *noun* **1** *N Amer.* a reception or party during which guests are invited to drop in to a person's home. **2** a time during which an institution, such as a school, is open to visitors. **3** *N Amer., Austral., & NZ* a time during which a house or apartment that is for sale may be viewed by prospective buyers without an appointment. □ **keep open house** provide general hospitality.

open ice *noun* *Hockey* ice that is free of opposing players and away from the boards (also *attributive: open-ice play*).

open·ing ● *noun* **1** an aperture or gap, esp. one allowing access. **2** a favourable situation or opportunity. **3** an available position or opportunity in a business or company etc. **4** a beginning; an initial part. **5** the process of becoming open or making something open (*the long-awaited opening of a new library*). **6** a ceremony to celebrate a new building, facility, etc. being ready for use. **7** esp. *N Amer.* the first performance of a theatrical production etc.; a premiere (also *attributive: opening night*). **8** *N Amer.* a tract of land that is thinly wooded in comparison to the surrounding forest. **9** *Cdn* a period of fixed length determined by the government during which herring fishing may be undertaken. **10** a counsel's preliminary statement of a case in a law court. **11** *Chess* a recognized sequence of moves at the beginning of a game. ● *adjective* initial, first.

opening line *noun* **1** the first line of a book, movie, etc. **2** a phrase or sentence initiating a conversation, esp. with someone to whom one is sexually attracted.

Vowels: a cat ɑ arm e bed ɜr her ɜː deux ə ago ɪ sit i cosy iː feed ɒ hot ɔ pore oː no ʌ run ʊ put

opening time noun esp. Brit. the time at which bars etc. may legally begin to serve alcohol.

open letter noun a letter, esp. of protest, addressed to an individual and published in a newspaper or magazine.

open-line adjective Cdn designating a radio or television program in which the public can participate by telephone.

open-liner noun Cdn the host of an open-line radio or television program.

open·ly adverb **1** frankly, honestly. **2** publicly; without concealment. [Old English openlice (as OPEN, -LY²)]

open market noun an unrestricted market with free competition of buyers and sellers.

open mike noun **1** a microphone that is in use. **2** a session in a club during which anyone is welcome to sing or perform stand-up comedy.

open-minded adjective accessible to new ideas; unprejudiced. □ **open-minded·ly** adverb **open-minded·ness** noun

open-mouthed adjective with the mouth open, esp. in surprise.

open-necked adjective (of a shirt) worn with the top button unfastened.

open-pit mine noun a large pit excavated in the ground from which minerals are mined. □ **open-pit mining** noun

open-plan adjective (usu. attributive) = OPEN CONCEPT.

open question noun a matter on which differences of opinion are legitimate.

open-reel adjective (of a tape recorder) having reels of tape requiring individual threading, as distinct from a cassette.

open season noun **1** the season when restrictions on the killing of game etc. are lifted. **2** (often foll. by on) a period when all restrictions on a particular activity, esp. on attacking and criticizing a particular group, are abandoned or ignored (appears to be open season on unions).

open secret noun a supposed secret that is known to many people.

open sesame interjection see SESAME.

open shop noun **1** a business etc. where employees do not have to be members of a labour union (opp. CLOSED SHOP). **2** this system.

open skies noun a system allowing unrestricted access to the airspace over a country (also attributive: open skies agreement).

open society noun a society with wide dissemination of information and freedom of belief.

open-source adjective Computing denoting software for which the original source code is made freely available.

open stock noun N Amer. merchandise, e.g. dishes or silverware, which may be purchased as individual pieces rather than as a set.

open system noun (often in pl.) a computer system in which the components conform to non-proprietary standards rather than to the standards of a specific supplier of hardware or software, thus allowing greater compatibility.

open-toed adjective (of shoes) leaving a toe or toes exposed.

open university noun (often **Open University**) a university that teaches mainly by broadcasting and correspondence, and is open to those without formal academic qualifications.

open·work noun a pattern with intervening spaces in metal, leather, lace, etc.

opera¹ noun **1 a** a dramatic work in one or more acts, set to music for singers (usu. in costume) and instrumentalists. **b** this as a genre. **c** the score for an opera. **d** a performance of an opera. **2** a building for the performance of opera. **3** a company performing opera. [Italian from Latin, = labour, work]

opera² pl. of OPUS.

oper·able /ˈɒpərəbəl/ adjective **1** that can be operated. **2** suitable for treatment by surgical operation. □ **oper·abil·ity** /-ˈbɪlɪti/ noun [Late Latin operabilis from Latin (as OPERATE)]

opera buffa /ˌɒpərə ˈbuːfə/ noun (esp. Italian) comic opera, esp. with characters drawn from everyday life. [Italian]

opéra comique /ˌɒpeˌrɒ kɒˈmiːk/ noun (esp. French) opera on a lighthearted theme, with spoken dialogue. [French]

opera glasses plural noun small binoculars for use in a theatre.

opera·goer noun a person who attends opera performances, esp. habitually.

opera hat noun a man's tall collapsible hat.

opera house noun **1** a theatre for the performance of opera, also often used for ballet performances. **2** N Amer. a theatre, esp. in a small town.

oper·and /ˈɒpəˌrand/ noun Math. the quantity etc. on which an operation is to be done. [Latin operandum neuter gerundive of operari: see OPERATE]

opera seria /ˌɒpərə ˈsiːriə/ noun (esp. 18th-c. Italian) opera on a serious, usu. classical or mythological theme. [Italian]

oper·ate verb **1** transitive manage, work, control; put or keep in a functional state. **2** intransitive be in action; function. **3** intransitive produce an effect; exercise influence (the tax operates to our disadvantage). **4** intransitive (often foll. by on) **a** perform a surgical operation. **b** conduct a military or naval action. **c** be active in business etc., esp. dealing in stocks and shares. **5** intransitive (foll. by on) influence or affect (feelings etc.). **6** transitive bring about; accomplish. [Latin operari to work, from opus operis work]

oper·at·ic /ˌɒpəˈratɪk/ adjective **1** of, relating to, or characteristic of opera. **2** extravagantly theatrical, overly dramatic. □ **oper·at·ic·ally** adverb [irreg. from OPERA¹, after dramatic]

operating profit noun gross profit before deduction of expenses.

operating room noun (also **operating theatre**) a room for surgical operations.

operating system noun the basic software that enables the running of a computer program. Abbr.: **OS**.

operating table noun a table on which surgical operations are performed.

oper·ation noun **1 a** the action or process or method of working or operating. **b** the state of being active or functioning (not yet in operation). **c** the scope or range of effectiveness of a thing's activity. **2** an active process; a discharge of a function (the operation of breathing). **3** a piece of work, esp. one in a series (often in pl.: begin operations). **4** an act of surgery performed on a patient. **5 a** a strategic movement of troops, ships, etc. for military action. **b** preceding a code name for such a movement (Operation Overlord). **6** a financial transaction. **7** a business or enterprise (owned a dairy operation near Goderich). **8** Math. the subjection of a number or quantity or function to a process affecting its value or form, e.g. multiplication, differentiation.

oper·ation·al adjective **1 a** of or used for operations. **b** engaged or involved in operations. **2** able or ready to function. □ **oper·ation·al·ly** adverb

operations room noun a room etc. from which military or police operations are directed.

oper·ative ● adjective **1** in operation; having effect. **2** having the principal relevance ('may' is the operative word). **3** of or by surgery. **4** Law expressing an intent to perform a transaction. ● noun **1** a worker, esp. a skilled one. **2** esp. N Amer. a secret service agent; a spy. **3** US a private investigator. □ **oper·ative·ly** adverb **oper·ative·ness** noun

oper·ator noun **1** a person operating a machine etc., esp. one who operates a telephone switchboard. **2** a person operating or engaging in business. **3** informal a person acting in a specified way (a smooth operator). **4** Math. a symbol or function denoting an operation (e.g. ×, +). **5** a segment of chromosomal DNA believed to control the activity of the structural genes of an operon.

oper·cu·lum /əˈpɜrkjʊləm, ɔːˈp-/ noun (pl. **oper·cula** /-lə/) **1** Zool. **a** a flap-like structure covering the gills in a fish. **b** a plate-like structure closing the aperture of a gastropod mollusc's shell when the organism is retracted. **c** any of various other parts covering or closing an aperture, such as a flap over the nostrils in some birds. **2** Bot. a lid-like structure of the spore-containing capsule of mosses. □ **oper·cu·lar** adjective **oper·cu·late** /-lət/ adjective **operculi-** combining form. [Latin from operire cover]

oper·etta /ˌɒpəˈretə/ noun a theatrical production, usu. of a comic nature, combining songs with spoken dialogue. [Italian, diminutive of opera: see OPERA¹]

op·eron /ˈɒpərɒn/ noun Biol. a unit made up of linked genes thought to regulate other genes responsible for protein synthesis. [from French opérer 'effect, work' + -ON]

ophi·cleide /ˈɒfɪˌklaɪd/ noun an obsolete usu. bass brass wind instrument developed from the serpent. [French ophicléide from Greek ophis serpent + kleis kleidos key]

ophid·ian /oʊˈfɪdiən/ noun any reptile of the suborder Serpentes (formerly Ophidia), including snakes. ● adjective **1** of or relating to this group. **2** snakelike. [modern Latin Ophidia from Greek ophis snake]

ophio- /ˈɒfɪɒ/ combining form snake. [Greek ophis snake]

Ophir /ˈoːfər/ (in the Bible) an unidentified region, perhaps in SE Arabia, famous for its fine gold and precious stones.

Ophiu·chus /ɒˈfjuːkəs/ a large constellation straddling the celestial equator, traditionally seen as representing a serpent bearer. [Latin from Greek *Ophioukhos*, from *ophis* snake + *ekhein* to hold]

oph·thal·mia /ɒfˈθalmɪə, ɒp-/ *noun* an inflammation of the eye, esp. conjunctivitis. [Late Latin from Greek *ophthalmos* eye]

oph·thal·mic /ɒfˈθalmɪk, ɒp-/ *adjective* of or relating to the eye and its diseases. [Latin *ophthalmicus* from Greek *ophthalmikos* (as OPHTHALMIA)]

ophthalmo- /ɒfˈθalmɔː, ɒp-/ *combining form* denoting the eye. [Greek *ophthalmos* eye]

oph·thal·mol·ogy /ˌɒfθalˈmɒlədʒɪ, ɒp-/ *noun* the scientific study of the eye. □ **oph·thal·mo·logic·al** /-məˈlɒdʒɪkəl/ *adjective* **oph·thal·mol·o·gist** *noun*

oph·thal·mo·scope /ɒfˈθalmə,skəʊp, ɒp-/ *noun* an instrument for inspecting the retina and other parts of the eye. □ **oph·thal·mo·scop·ic** /-ˈskɒpɪk/ *adjective* **oph·thal·mos·copy** *noun*

-opia /ˈəʊpɪə/ *combining form* denoting a visual disorder (*myopia*). [Greek from *ōps* eye]

opi·ate ● *noun* /ˈəʊpɪət/ **1** a drug containing or derived from opium, usu. to ease pain or induce sleep. **2** a thing which soothes or stupefies. ● *adjective* /ˈəʊpɪət/ **1** containing opium. **2** narcotic, soporific. ● *transitive verb* /ˈəʊpɪ,eɪt/ **1** mix with opium. **2** stupefy. [medieval Latin *opiatus, -um, opiare* from Latin *opium*: see OPIUM]

opine /əʊˈpaɪn/ *verb* **1** *transitive* (often foll. by *that* + clause) hold or express as an opinion. **2** *intransitive* express an opinion. [Latin *opinari* think, believe]

opin·ion /əˈpɪnjən/ *noun* **1** a belief or assessment based on grounds short of proof. **2** a view held as probable. **3** (often foll. by *on*) what one thinks about a particular topic or question (*my opinion on capital punishment*). **4 a** a formal statement of professional advice (*will get a second opinion*). **b** *Law* a formal statement of reasons for a judgment given. **5** an estimation (*had a low opinion of it*). □ **be of the opinion that** believe or maintain that. **in one's opinion** according to one's view or belief. **a matter of opinion** a disputable point. [Latin *opinio -onis* (as OPINE)]

opin·ion·at·ed /əˈpɪnjə,neɪtəd/ *adjective* conceitedly assertive or dogmatic in one's opinions. [obsolete *opinionate* in the same sense, from OPINION]

opinion poll *noun* = GALLUP POLL.

opi·oid /ˈəʊpiɔɪd/ *Pharm. & Biochem.* ● *noun* any compound resembling cocaine and morphine in its addictive properties or physiological effects. ● *adjective* of or relating to such a compound. [OPIUM + -OID]

opium /ˈəʊpɪəm/ *noun* **1** a reddish-brown heavy-scented addictive drug prepared from the juice of the opium poppy, used in medicine as an analgesic and narcotic; it is the source of both morphine and heroin. **2** anything regarded as soothing or stupefying. [Greek *opion* poppy juice, from *opos* juice]

opium den *noun* a place where opium may be purchased and used.

opium poppy *noun* a poppy, *Papaver somniferum*, native to Europe and E Asia, with white, red, pink, or purple flowers.

Opium War either of two wars, that between Britain and China (1839–42) and that involving Britain and France against China (1856–60), following China's attempt to prohibit the illegal importation of opium from British India into China. Defeat of the Chinese resulted in the ceding of Hong Kong to Britain and the opening of five 'treaty ports' to traders.

opop·anax /əʊˈpɒpə,naks/ *noun* **1 a** an umbelliferous plant, *Opopanax chironium*, with yellow flowers. **b** a resinous gum obtained from the roots of this plant and used in perfume. **2** = SPONGE TREE. [Greek from *opos* juice + *panax* formed as PANACEA]

Opor·to /əʊˈpɔːtəʊ/ *see* PORTO.

opos·sum /əˈpɒsəm/ *noun* **1** any mainly tree-living marsupial of the family Didelphidae, having a prehensile tail and hind feet with an opposable thumb, esp. (in full **Virginia opossum**) the common N. American species, *Didelphis virginiana*, which is the size of a cat. **2** an opossum, *Chironectes minimus*, suited to an aquatic habitat and having webbed hind feet. *Also called* YAPOK. [Virginia Algonquian *āpassūm*]

OPP *abbreviation* (in Canada) Ontario Provincial Police.

opp. *abbreviation* opposite.

Op·pen·heim·er /ˈɒpən,haɪmər/ **Jul·ius Rob·ert** (1904–67), US theoretical physicist. He was the director of the laboratory at Los Alamos which designed and built the first atomic bomb (1943–5); after the war he opposed development of the hydrogen bomb and his security clearance was withdrawn (1953).

op·pon·ent /əˈpəʊnənt/ ● *noun* a person who opposes or belongs to an opposing side. ● *adjective* opposing, contrary, opposed. □ **op·pon·ency** *noun* [Latin *opponere opponent-* (as OB-, *ponere* place)]

opponent muscle *noun* a muscle enabling the thumb to be placed front to front against a finger of the same hand.

op·por·tune /ˌɒpərˈtjuːn, -ˈtjuːn/ *adjective* **1** (of a time) well-chosen or especially favourable or appropriate (*an opportune moment*). **2** (of an action or event) well-timed; done or occurring at a favourable or useful time. □ **op·por·tune·ly** *adverb* **op·por·tune·ness** *noun* [Latin *opportunus* (as OB-, *portus* harbour), originally of the wind driving towards the harbour]

op·por·tun·ism /ˌɒpərˈtjuːnɪzəm, ˈɒpər-, -ˈtjuːn-/ *noun* **1** the adaptation of policy or judgment to circumstances or opportunity, esp. regardless of principle. **2** the seizing of opportunities when they occur. □ **op·por·tun·ist** *noun*

op·por·tun·is·tic /ˌɒpərtjuːˈnɪstɪk/ *adjective* **1** of or relating to opportunism. **2** *Ecology* (of a species) able to spread quickly in a previously unexploited habitat. **3** *Med.* **a** (of a micro-organism) rarely causing disease except in unusual circumstances, e.g. in patients with depressed immune systems. **b** (of an infection) caused by such a micro-organism. □ **op·por·tun·is·tic·ally** /-ˈnɪstɪkli/ *adverb*

op·por·tun·ity /ˌɒpərˈtjuːnəti, -ˈtjuːn-/ *noun* (*pl.* **-ities**) **1** a good chance; a favourable occasion. **2** a chance or opening offered by circumstances. **3** good fortune. □ **opportunity knocks** an opportunity occurs.

opportunity cost *noun* *Econ.* **1** the loss of other alternatives when one alternative is chosen. **2** an alternative lost in this way.

op·pos·able *adjective* **1** able to be opposed. **2** *Zool.* (of the thumb in primates) capable of facing and touching the other digits on the same hand.

op·pose *verb* **1** *transitive & intransitive* resist; set oneself against; argue against. **2** *transitive & intransitive* be hostile (to). **3** *transitive* take part in a game, sport, etc., against (another competitor or team). **4** *transitive* (foll. by *to*) place in opposition or contrast. □ **as opposed to** in contrast with. □ **op·pos·er** *noun* **op·pos·ing** *adjective* [Old French *opposer* from Latin *opponere*: see OPPONENT]

op·pos·ite /ˈɒpəzɪt/ ● *adjective* **1** (often foll. by *to*) having a position on the other or further side, facing or back to back. **2** (often foll. by *to, from*) **a** of a contrary kind; diametrically different. **b** being the other of a contrasted pair. **3** (of angles) between opposite sides of the intersection of two lines. **4** *Bot.* (of leaves etc.) placed at the same height on the opposite sides of the stem, or placed straight in front of another organ. ● *noun* an opposite thing or person or term. ● *adverb* **1** in an opposite position (*the tree stands opposite*). **2** (of a leading theatrical etc. part) in a complementary role to (another performer). ● *preposition* in a position opposite to (*opposite the house is a tree*). □ **op·pos·ite·ly** *adverb* **op·pos·ite·ness** *noun* [Latin *oppositus* past participle of *opponere*: see OPPONENT]

opposite field *noun* *Baseball* the part of the diamond on the opposite side of the plate from the batter, e.g. right field for right-handed hitters (who stand on the left side of the plate) (also with hyphen) *attributive: opposite-field home run*).

opposite number *noun* a person holding an equivalent position in another group or organization.

opposite sex *noun* women in relation to men or vice versa.

op·pos·ition /ˌɒpəˈzɪʃən/ *noun* **1** resistance, antagonism. **2** the state of being hostile or in conflict or disagreement. **3** contrast or antithesis. **4** a group or party of opponents or competitors. **5** *Cdn, Brit., Austral. & NZ* **a** (**the Opposition**) the principal parliamentary party opposed to that in office (*see also* OFFICIAL OPPOSITION). **b** (often **Opposition**) all the members of a parliament who are not of the governing party (often *attributive: opposition parties*). **6** the act of opposing or placing opposite. **7 a** diametrically opposite position. **b** *Astrology & Astronomy* the position of two heavenly bodies when their longitude differs by 180°, as seen from the earth. □ **op·pos·ition·al** *adjective* **op·pos·ition·ist** *noun* [Latin *oppositio* (as OB-, POSITION)]

Opposition Day *noun* *Parl.* one of a number of designated days in each parliamentary session during which Opposition members can choose subjects for discussion.

op·press *transitive verb* **1** keep in subservience by coercion. **2** govern or treat harshly or with cruel injustice. **3** weigh down (with cares or unhappiness). □ **op·pressed** *adjective* **op·pres·sor** *noun* [medieval Latin *oppressare* (as OB-, PRESS¹)]

op·pres·sion *noun* **1** the act or an instance of oppressing; the state of being oppressed. **2** prolonged harsh or cruel treatment or control. **3** mental distress.

op·pres·sive *adjective* **1** oppressing; harsh or cruel. **2** difficult to endure. **3** (of weather) close and sultry. □ **op·pres·sive·ly** *adverb* **op·pres·sive·ness** *noun*

op·pro·bri·ous /ə'prəʊbrɪəs/ *adjective* (of language) severely scornful; abusive. □ **op·pro·bri·ous·ly** *adverb*

op·pro·bri·um /ə'prəʊbrɪəm/ *noun* **1** disgrace or bad reputation attaching to some act or conduct. **2** a cause of this. [Latin from *opprobrium* (as OB-, *probrum* disgraceful act)]

opsi·math /'ɒpsɪˌmaθ/ *noun literary* a person who learns only late in life. [Greek *opsimathēs* from *opse* late + *math-* learn]

op·son·in /'ɒpsənɪn/ *noun* a substance (often an antibody) in blood plasma which combines with foreign cells and makes them more susceptible to phagocytosis. □ **op·son·ic** /ɒp'sɒnɪk/ *adjective* [Greek *opsōnion* victuals + -IN]

op·son·ize /'ɒpsəˌnaɪz/ *transitive verb* (also esp. *Brit.* **-ise**) make more susceptible to phagocytosis. □ **op·son·iz·a·tion** /-'zeɪʃən/ *noun* [as OPSONIN]

ops room *noun* = OPERATIONS ROOM.

opt *intransitive verb* (usu. foll. by *for* or *to* + infin.) exercise an option; make a choice. □ **opt out** (often foll. by *of*) **1** choose not to participate (*opted out of the race*). **2** (in Canada) (of a doctor, health clinic, etc.) operate with private rather than government funding. **3** (in the UK) (of a school or hospital) decide to withdraw from local authority control. **opt in** choose to participate. [French *opter* from Latin *optare* choose, wish]

opt·a·tive /'ɒptətɪv, ɒp'teɪtɪv/ *Grammar* ● *adjective* expressing a wish. ● *noun* **1** the optative mood. **2** a verb in the optative mood. □ **opt·a·tive·ly** *adverb* [French *optatif -ive* from Late Latin *optativus* (as OPT)]

optative mood *noun* a set of verb forms expressing a wish etc., distinct esp. in Sanskrit and Greek.

opted-out *attributive adjective* designating a person or thing that has opted out (*an opted-out clinic*).

op·tic ● *adjective* of or relating to the eye, vision, or light (*optic nerve*). ● *noun* **1** a lens etc. in an optical instrument. **2** *archaic* the eye. [French *optique* or medieval Latin *opticus* from Greek *optikos* from *optos* seen]

op·tic·al *adjective* **1** of sight; visual. **2 a** of or concerning sight or light in relation to each other. **b** belonging to optics. **3** (esp. of a lens) constructed to assist sight or on the principles of optics. **4** designating a part of a computer requiring infrared, visible, or ultraviolet radiation for its operation. □ **op·tic·al·ly** *adverb*

optical art *noun* a style of painting that gives the illusion of movement by the precise use of pattern and colour.

optical brightener *noun* any fluorescent substance used to produce a whitening effect on laundry.

optical character recognition *noun* the identification of printed characters using photoelectric devices. Abbr.: **OCR**.

optical disk *noun* see DISK *noun* 1b.

optical fibre *noun* thin glass fibre through which signals can be transmitted as modulated light.

optical glass *noun* a very pure kind of glass used for lenses etc.

optical illusion *noun* **1** a thing having an appearance so resembling something else as to deceive the eye. **2** an instance of mental misapprehension caused by this.

optical isomer *noun Chem.* each of two or more forms of a chemical substance which have the same structure but a different spatial arrangement of atoms, and so usu. differ in optical activity. □ **optical isomerism** *noun*

optical microscope *noun* a microscope using the direct perception of light (*compare* ELECTRON MICROSCOPE). □ **optical microscopy** *noun*

optical scanning *noun* = OPTICAL CHARACTER RECOGNITION. □ **optical scanner** *noun*

optic axis *noun* **1** a line passing through the centre of curvature of a lens or spherical mirror and parallel to the axis of symmetry. **2** the direction in a doubly refracting crystal for which no double refraction occurs.

op·ti·cian /ɒp'tɪʃən/ *noun* a maker or seller of optical instruments, esp. eyeglasses and contact lenses. [French *opticien* from medieval Latin *optica* (as OPTIC)]

optic nerve *noun* each of the second pair of cranial nerves, transmitting impulses to the brain from the retina at the back of the eye.

op·tics *plural noun* **1** (treated as *sing.*) the scientific study of sight and the behaviour of light, or of other radiation or particles (*electron optics*).

2 the optical components of an instrument or apparatus. **3** *N Amer.* the way in which something is perceived by the public (*a CBC spokeswoman said that because of optics, the part of Trudeau had to be played by a Canadian*).

op·tima *pl.* of OPTIMUM.

opti·mal /'ɒptɪməl/ *adjective* best or most favourable, esp. under a particular set of circumstances. □ **opti·mal·ity** /-'malɪtɪ/ *noun* **opti·mal·ly** *adverb* [Latin *optimus* best]

opti·mism /'ɒptɪˌmɪzəm/ *noun* **1** an inclination to hopefulness and confidence; a tendency to take a favourable view of circumstances or prospects. **2** *Philos.* **a** the doctrine, esp. as set forth by Leibniz, that this world is the best of all possible worlds. **b** the theory that good must ultimately prevail over evil in the universe (*opp.* PESSIMISM 2). [French *optimisme* from Latin OPTIMUM]

opti·mist /'ɒptɪmɪst/ *noun* **1** a person inclined to or professing optimism. **2** (**Optimist**) a member of an international social and charitable association founded in 1911, dedicated esp. to helping children and youth, e.g. by sponsoring sports clubs etc. □ **opti·mis·tic** *adjective* **opti·mis·tic·ally** *adverb*

opti·mize /'ɒptɪˌmaɪz/ *verb* (also esp. *Brit.* **-mise**) **1** *transitive* **a** make the best or most effective use of (a situation, an opportunity, etc.). **b** make optimal; improve to the utmost. **2** *transitive* make (a computer program) as efficient as possible. **3** *intransitive* be an optimist. □ **opti·miz·a·tion** *noun* **opti·miz·er** *noun* [Latin *optimus* best]

opti·mum /'ɒptɪməm/ ● *noun* (*pl.* **op·tima** /-mə/ or **opti·mums**) **1 a** the most favourable conditions (for growth, reproduction, etc.). **b** the best or most favourable situation. **2** the best possible compromise between opposing tendencies. ● *adjective* = OPTIMAL. [Latin, neuter (as n.) of *optimus* best]

op·tion ● *noun* **1 a** the act or an instance of choosing; a choice. **b** a thing that is or may be chosen; an alternative (*those are the options*). **2** the liberty of choosing; freedom of choice. **3 a** the right to buy, sell, etc. specified stocks etc. at a specified price within a set time. **b** the provision in a contract allowing one to extend the terms of the contract for a specified time (also *attributive*: *option year*). **4** (in full **option play**) *Football* a play in which a player, esp. the quarterback, has the option of throwing the ball or running with it himself. ● *transitive verb N Amer.* buy or sell under option; have an option on. □ **have no option but to** must. **keep** (or **leave**) **one's options open** not commit oneself. [French or from Latin *optio*, stem of *optare* choose]

op·tion·al *adjective* being an option only; not obligatory. □ **op·tion·al·ity** /-'nalɪtɪ/ *noun* **op·tion·al·ly** *adverb*

option year *noun N Amer. Sport* an optional one-year extension to a player's contract (*decided to play out his option year*).

opto·elec·tron·ics *noun* the branch of technology concerned with the combined use of electronics and light. □ **opto·elec·tron·ic** *adjective*

op·tomet·rist /ɒp'tɒmətrɪst/ *noun esp. N Amer.* a person who practises optometry.

op·tom·etry /ɒp'tɒmətrɪ/ *noun* the science or profession of measuring eyesight, detecting eye disease, and prescribing corrective lenses (but not drugs or medicines). □ **opto·met·ric** /-'metrɪk/ *adjective* [Greek *optos* seen, visible + -METRY]

opt-out *noun* **1** (*attributive*) designating a provision in a contract etc. allowing one to opt out (*opt-out clause*). **2** esp. *Brit.* the act or an instance of opting out of something, esp. of a school or hospital opting out of local-authority control.

opu·lent /'ɒpjʊlənt/ *adjective* **1** ostentatiously rich; wealthy. **2** luxurious (*opulent surroundings*). **3** abundant; profuse. □ **opu·lence** *noun* **opu·lent·ly** *adverb* [Latin *opulens, opulent-* from *opes* wealth]

opun·tia /ɒ'pʌnʃiə/ *noun* any cactus of the genus *Opuntia*, with jointed cylindrical or elliptical stems and barbed bristles. *Also called* PRICKLY PEAR. [Latin plant name from *Opus -untis* in Locris in ancient Greece]

opus /'əʊpəs/ *noun* (*pl.* **opus·es** or **opera** /'ɒpərə/) **1** *Music* **a** a separate musical composition or set of compositions of any kind. **b** used before a number given to a composer's work, usu. indicating the order of publication. Abbr.: **Op. 2** any artistic or creative work (*compare* MAGNUM OPUS). [Latin, = work]

opus·cule /ə'pʌskjuːl/ *noun* (also **opus·cu·lum** /ə'pʌskjʊləm/) (*pl.* **opus·cules** or **opus·cula** /-lə/) a minor (esp. musical or literary) work. [French from Latin *opusculum* diminutive of OPUS]

Opus Dei /'deɪiː/ *Christianity* **1** a Roman Catholic organization esp. of lay people founded in Spain in 1928 with the aim of re-establishing

t *top*   v *voice*   w *we*   z *zoo*   ʃ *she*   ʒ *vision*   θ *thin*   ð *this*   ŋ *ring*   x *loch*   tʃ *chip*   dʒ *jar*   (*see over for vowels*)

Christian ideals in society. **2** (**opus Dei**) liturgical worship regarded as man's primary duty to God. [Latin, lit. 'the work of God']

OR *abbreviation* **1** operations research. **2** Oregon (in official postal use). **3** other ranks.

O.R. *abbreviation* N Amer. operating room.

or¹ *conjunction* **1 a** introducing the second of two alternatives (*white or black*). **b** introducing all but the first, or only the last, of any number of alternatives (*white or grey or black; white, grey, or black*). **2** (often prec. by *either*) introducing the only remaining possibility or choice given (*take it or leave it; either come in or go out*). **3** (prec. by *whether*) introducing the second part of an indirect question or conditional clause (*ask him whether he was there or not; must go whether I like or dislike it*). **4** introducing a synonym or explanation of a preceding word etc. (*suffered from vertigo or giddiness*). **5** introducing a significant afterthought (*he must know — or is he bluffing?*). **6** = OR ELSE (*run or you'll be late*). **7** *archaic* each of two; either (*or in the heart or in the head*). □ **not A or B** not A, and also not B. **one or two** (or **two or three** etc.) *informal* a few. **or else 1** otherwise (*do it now, or else you will have to do it tomorrow*). **2** *informal* expressing a warning or threat (*hand over the money or else*). **or rather** introducing a rephrasing or qualification of a preceding statement etc. (*he was there, or rather I heard that he was*). **or so** (after a quantity or a number) or thereabouts (*send me ten or so*). [reduced form of obsolete *other* conj. (which superseded Old English *oththe* or), of uncertain origin]

or² *Heraldry* ● *noun* a gold or yellow colour. ● *adjective* (usu. following noun) gold or yellow (*a crescent or*). [French from Latin *aurum* gold]

-or¹ *suffix* forming nouns denoting a person or thing performing the action of a verb, or an agent more generally (*actor; escalator; tailor*) (*see also* -ATOR, -ITOR). [Latin *-or, -ator*, etc., sometimes via Anglo-French *-eour*, Old French *-ĕor, -ĕur*]

-or² *suffix* forming nouns denoting state or condition (*error; horror*). [Latin *-or -oris*, sometimes via (or after) Old French *-or, -ur*]

-or³ *suffix* forming adjectives with comparative sense (*major; senior*). [Anglo-French *-our* from Latin *-or*]

-or⁴ *suffix* esp. *US* = -OUR¹.

or·ache /ˈɒrɪtʃ/ *noun* (also **orach**) any of various plants of the genus *Atriplex* of the goosefoot family, with red, yellow, or green leaves, esp. garden orache, *A. hortensis*, cultivated for its edible leaves. *Also called* SALTBUSH. [Anglo-French *arasche* from Latin *atriplex* from Greek *atraphaxus*]

or·acle /ˈɒrəkəl, ˈɒ-/ *noun* **1 a** a place at which advice or prophecy was sought from the gods in classical antiquity. **b** the usu. ambiguous or obscure response given at an oracle. **c** a prophet or prophetess at an oracle. **2 a** a person or thing regarded as an infallible guide to future action etc. **b** a saying etc. regarded as infallible guidance. **3** divine inspiration or revelation. [Latin *oraculum* from *orare* speak]

or·acu·lar /əˈrakjʊlər/ *adjective* **1** of or concerning an oracle or oracles. **2** (esp. of advice etc.) mysterious or ambiguous. **3** prophetic. □ **or·acu·lar·ly** *adverb* [Latin (as ORACLE)]

oracy /ˈɒrəsi/ *noun* the ability to express oneself fluently in speech and to understand a spoken language. [Latin *os oris* mouth, after *literacy*]

Ora·dea /ɒˈradiə/ an industrial city in W Romania, near the border with Hungary; pop. (est. 2002) 220,100.

oral ● *adjective* **1 a** by word of mouth; spoken; not written (*the oral tradition*). **b** designating a society or culture which has not reached the stage of literacy. **2** done or taken by the mouth (*oral contraceptive*). **3** of the mouth. **4** *Psych.* of or concerning a supposed stage of infant emotional and sexual development, in which the mouth is of central interest. ● *noun* (usu. in *pl.*) *informal* a spoken examination, test, etc. □ **oral·ly** *adverb* [Late Latin *oralis* from Latin *os oris* mouth]

oral history *noun* **1** the study of tape-recorded historical information drawn from the speaker's personal knowledge of past events or from stories handed down from generation to generation. **2** a record of this kind.

oral·ism /ˈɔːrəlɪzəm/ *noun* the principle that profoundly deaf people should learn to communicate by speech and lip-reading without the use of sign language. □ **oral·ist** *adjective & noun*

oral·ity /ɔˈralɪti/ *noun* **1** the quality of being spoken or verbally communicated. **2** preference for or tendency to use spoken forms of language.

oral sex *noun* sexual activity in which the genitals of one partner are stimulated by the mouth of the other.

oral tradition *noun* the passing on of knowledge, stories, etc. from one generation to another by word of mouth.

-orama *combining form* = -RAMA.

Oran /ɔːˈran/ a port on the Mediterranean coast of Algeria; pop. (est. 2002) 732,000.

or·ang /ɔːˈraŋ/ *noun* = ORANGUTAN. [abbreviation]

Or·ange¹ /ɒˈrɑ̃ʒ/ a town in S France, on the Rhone. It was a small principality in the 16th c. in the possession of the House of Orange, whose descendants became rulers of the Netherlands (*see* ORANGE, HOUSE OF). It has an exceptionally well preserved Roman theatre.

Or·ange² /ˈɒrɪndʒ, ˈɒ-/ *adjective* **1** of or relating to Orangemen or their activities. **2** of or relating to the House of Orange (*see* ORANGE, HOUSE OF). □ **Orange·ism** *noun*

Orange, House of /ˈɒrɪndʒ, ˈɒ-/ the Dutch royal house. Originally a princely dynasty of the principality centred on the town of Orange in France, after a marital alliance with the duchy of Nassau the family became a major force in the politics of the Netherlands.

Orange, William of *see* WILLIAM III.

or·ange ● *noun* **1 a** a large round juicy citrus fruit with a bright reddish-yellow tough rind. **b** any of various trees or shrubs of the genus *Citrus*, esp. *C. sinensis* or *C. aurantium*, bearing fragrant white flowers and yielding this fruit. **2** a fruit or plant resembling this. **3 a** the reddish yellow colour of an orange. **b** orange pigment. ● *adjective* **1** orange coloured; reddish yellow. **2** tasting like an orange; orange flavoured. □ **oran·gey** *adjective* (also **orangy**). [Old French *orenge*, ultimately from Arabic *nāranj* from Persian *nārang*]

or·ange·ade /ˌɒrɪndʒˈeid, ˈɒ-/ *noun* a non-alcoholic drink flavoured with orange.

Orange Day *noun* = GLORIOUS TWELFTH.

orange flower water *noun* a solution of neroli in water, used esp. in flavouring desserts.

Orange Free State a former province in central South Africa, situated to the north of the Orange River; now called FREE STATE. [*House of Orange* (see ORANGE, HOUSE OF)]

Orange·man *noun* (*pl.* **-men**) a member of the Orange Order.

Orangeman's Day *noun* = GLORIOUS TWELFTH.

Orange Order *noun* (also **Orange Lodge**) a fraternal society formed in 1795 to support Protestantism in Ireland, established in Canada in the 19th c., where its anti-Catholic and conservative attitudes had a considerable social and political influence, esp. in Ontario. [after William of *Orange* (William III)]

orange peel *noun* **1** the skin of an orange. **2** (**orange-peel**) (*attributive*) designating a rough surface resembling this.

orange pekoe *noun* a black tea made from very small leaves. [prob. after the Dutch Royal House of Orange, so named by Dutch tea-traders who dominated the tea market in the 1700s.]

Orange River the longest river in South Africa, which rises in the Drakensberg Mountains in NE Lesotho and flows generally westward for 1 859 km (1,155 miles) to the Atlantic across almost the whole breadth of the continent, forming the border between Namibia and South Africa in its lower course.

orange roughy *noun* an orange-coloured fish, *Hoplostethus atlanticus*, much prized for food.

oran·gery /ˈɒrɪndʒəri, -dʒri, ˈɒ-/ *noun* (*pl.* **-ies**) a place, esp. a special structure, where orange trees are cultivated.

orange squash *noun* Brit. a soft drink made from oranges and other ingredients, often sold in concentrated form.

orange stick *noun* a thin stick, pointed at one end and usu. of orangewood, for manicuring the fingernails.

Orange·ville a town in south central Ontario, about 60 km northwest of Mississauga; pop. (2001) 25,248. [*Orange* Lawrence, miller and first postmaster d.1861]

orange·wood *noun* the wood of the orange tree.

or·an·gu·tan /ɔːˈraŋə.tan, -ˌtaŋ/ *noun* a large red long-haired tree-living ape, *Pongo pygmaeus*, native to Borneo and Sumatra, with characteristic long arms and hooked hands and feet. [Malay *ōrang ūtan* wild man]

Or·anje·stad /ɒˈranjə.stɒt/ the capital of the Dutch island of Aruba in the W Indies; pop. (est. 2002) 20,700.

Ora·şul Stal·in /ɒˌraʃul ˈstɒlɪn/ a former name for BRAŞOV.

orate /ɔˈreit, ˈɔː-/ *intransitive verb* make a speech or speak, esp. pompously or at length. [back-formation from ORATION]

ora·tion /ɔˈreifən, ə-/ *noun* **1** a formal speech, discourse, etc., esp. when ceremonial. **2** *Grammar* a way of speaking; language. [Latin *oratio* discourse, prayer, from *orare* speak, pray]

ora·tor /ˈɔːrətər, ˈɒ-/ *noun* **1** a person making a speech. **2** an eloquent public speaker. [Latin *orator -oris* speaker, pleader (as ORATION)]

Vowels: a cat ɑ arm e bed ɜr her ɜː deux ə ago ɪ sit i cosy iː feed ɒ hot ɔ pore ɔː no ʌ run ʊ put

Ora·tor·ian /ɒrəˈtɔːrɪən, ɒ-/ ● *noun* a member of the Institute of the Oratory of St. Philip Neri, a Roman Catholic society of priests. ● *adjective* of or relating to this society.

ora·torio /ˌɒrəˈtɔːrɪəʊ, ˌɒ-/ *noun* (*pl.* **-torios**) a semi-dramatic work for orchestra and voices esp. on a sacred theme, performed without costume, scenery, or action. [Italian from ecclesiastical Latin *oratorium* ORATORY, originally of musical services at the church of the Oratory of St. Philip Neri in Rome]

ora·tory /ˈɒrəˌtɔːri, ˈɒ-/ *noun* (*pl.* **-ies**) **1** the art or practice of formal speaking, esp. in public. **2** exaggerated, eloquent, or highly coloured language. **3** a small chapel, esp. for private worship. **4** (**Oratory**) *Catholicism* **a** (in full **Institute of the Oratory of St. Philip Neri**) a religious society of priests living in community without vows. **b** a church, branch, or house of this society. □ **ora·tor·ical** /-ˈtɒrɪkəl/ *adjective* [senses 1 and 2 from Latin *ars oratoria* art of speaking; sense 3 Anglo-French *oratorie* from ecclesiastical Latin *oratorium*: both from Latin *oratorius* from *orare* pray, speak]

ora·ture /ˈɒrətʃər/ *noun* a body of poetry, tales, etc. preserved through oral transmission as part of a particular culture, esp. a pre-literate one. [blend of ORAL + LITERATURE]

orb ● *noun* **1** a globe surmounted by a cross esp. carried by a sovereign at a coronation. **2** a sphere; a globe. **3** *literary* **a** a heavenly body, esp. the sun or moon. **b** *hist.* = SPHERE *noun* 3e. **4** *literary* an eyeball; an eye. ● *verb* **1** *transitive* enclose in (an orb); encircle. **2** *intransitive* form or gather into an orb. [Latin *orbis* ring]

or·bic·u·lar /ɔːˈbɪkjʊlər/ *adjective formal* **1** circular and flat; disc-shaped; ring-shaped. **2** spherical; globular; rounded. [Late Latin *orbicularis* from Latin *orbiculus* diminutive of *orbis* ring]

Orbi·son /ˈɔːbɪsən/ **Roy (Kel·ton)** (1936–88), US singer and songwriter. He began by writing country music songs for other artists, establishing himself as a singer with the ballad 'Only the Lonely' (1960); other notable songs include 'Crying' (1961), 'Blue Bayou' (1963), and 'Oh, Pretty Woman' (1964).

or·bit ● *noun* **1 a** the regularly repeated elliptical course of a celestial object, spacecraft, satellite, etc. about a star or a planet. **b** (prec. by *in*, *into*, *out of*, etc.) the state of motion in an orbit. **c** one complete passage around an orbited body. **2** the path of an electron around an atomic nucleus. **3** a range or sphere of action or influence. **4 a** the eye socket. **b** the area around the eye of a bird or insect. ● *verb* (**or·bit·ed**, **or·bit·ing**) **1** *intransitive* **a** (of a satellite etc.) go around in orbit. **b** fly in a circle. **2** *transitive* move in orbit around. **3** *transitive* put into orbit. □ **into orbit** into a state of heightened performance, frenzy, etc. (*our response sent him into orbit*; *sales went into orbit*). [Latin *orbita* course, track (in medieval Latin eye cavity): fem. of *orbitus* circular, from *orbis* ring]

or·bit·al ● *adjective* of an orbit or orbits. ● *noun Physics* each of the actual or potential patterns of electron density which may be formed around an atomic nucleus by one or more electrons, represented as a wave function.

orbital sander *noun* a sander having a circular and not oscillating motion.

or·bit·er *noun* a spacecraft designed to remain in orbit without landing.

orca *noun* the killer whale. [French *orque* or Latin *orca* a kind of whale]

Or·cadi·an /ɔːˈkeɪdiən/ ● *adjective* of or relating to the Orkney Islands off the north coast of Scotland. ● *noun* a native of the Orkney Islands. [Latin *Orcades* Orkney Islands]

orch. *abbreviation* **1** orchestrated by. **2** orchestra.

or·chard *noun* a piece of enclosed land with fruit trees. □ **or·chard·ist** *noun* [Old English *ortgeard* from Latin *hortus* garden + YARD²]

or·chard·ing *noun* the cultivation of fruit trees.

or·ches·tra /ˈɔːkɪstrə/ *noun* **1** a usu. large group of instrumentalists, esp. combining strings, woodwinds, brass, and percussion (*symphony orchestra*). **2 a** (in full **orchestra pit**) the part of a theatre, opera house, etc., where the orchestra plays, usu. in front of the stage and on a lower level. **b** *N Amer.* the seats on the ground floor in a theatre. **3** the semicircular space in front of an ancient Greek theatre stage where the chorus danced and sang. □ **or·ches·tral** *adjective* **or·ches·tral·ly** *adverb* [Latin from Greek *orkhēstra* from *orkheomai* to dance (see sense 3)]

orchestra stalls *noun Brit.* the front section of orchestra seating in a theatre.

or·ches·trate /ˈɔːkəˌstreɪt/ *transitive verb* **1** arrange, score, or compose (music) for orchestral performance. **2** combine, arrange, or build up (elements of a situation etc.) for maximum effect. □ **or·ches·tra·tion** *noun* **or·ches·tra·tor** *noun*

or·chid /ˈɔːkɪd/ *noun* **1** any epiphytic or terrestrial plant of the family Orchidaceae, bearing flowers in fantastic shapes and brilliant colours, usu. having one petal larger than the others and variously spurred, lobed, pouched, etc. **2** a flower of any of these plants. □ **orchid·ist** *noun* [modern Latin *Orchid(ac)eae* irreg. from Latin *orchis*: see ORCHIS]

orchid·aceous /ˌɔːkɪˈdeɪʃəs/ *adjective* **1** of or pertaining to orchids. **2** resembling an orchid, esp. in flamboyancy or exoticness.

orchido- /ˈɔːkɪdəʊ/ *combining form* (also **orchid-** before a vowel) *Med.* of a testicle or the testicles (*orchidectomy*). [modern Latin, from Greek *orkhis* 'testicle']

or·chil /ˈɔːtʃɪl/ *noun* (also **or·chil·la** /ɔːˈtʃɪlə/, **ar·chil** /ˈɑːtʃɪl/) **1** a red or violet dye from lichen, esp. from *Roccella tinctoria*, often used in litmus. **2** the tropical lichen yielding this. [Old French *orcheil* etc., perhaps ultimately from Latin *herba urceolaris* a plant for polishing glass pitchers]

or·chis /ˈɔːkɪs/ *noun* **1** any orchid of the genus *Orchis*, with a tuberous root and an erect fleshy stem having a spike of usu. purple or red flowers. **2** any of various wild orchids. [Latin from Greek *orkhis*, originally = testicle (with reference to the shape of its tuber)]

or·chi·tis /ɔːˈkaɪtɪs/ *noun* inflammation of the testicles. [modern Latin from Greek *orkhis* testicle + -ITIS]

orcin /ˈɔːsɪn/ *noun* (also **or·cin·ol** /ˈɔːsɪˌnɒl/) a crystalline substance, becoming red in air, extracted from any of several lichens and used to make dyes. [modern Latin *orcina* from Italian *orcello* orchil]

Orcus /ˈɔːkəs/ *Rom. Myth* a synonym of Pluto, the god of the underworld, or the underworld itself.

Orczy /ˈɔːtsi/ **Baron·ess Em·mus·ca** (1865–1947), Hungarian-born English novelist. Her best-known novel, *The Scarlet Pimpernel* (1905), tells of the adventures of an English nobleman smuggling aristocrats out of France during the French Revolution.

ord. *abbreviation* ordinary.

or·dain /ɔːˈdeɪn/ *transitive verb* **1** bestow the office of minister, priest, or deacon on (a person). **2** (in the Presbyterian church) bestow the office of elder on (a person). **3 a** (often foll. by *that* + clause) decree (*ordained that he should go*). **b** (of God, fate, etc.) destine; appoint (*has ordained us to die*). □ **or·dain·er** *noun* [Anglo-French *ordeiner*, Old French *ordein-* stressed stem of *ordener* from Latin *ordinare* from *ordo -inis* order]

or·deal *noun* **1** a painful or trying experience; a severe trial. **2** *hist.* an ancient esp. Germanic test of guilt or innocence by subjection of the accused to severe pain or torture, survival of which was taken as divine proof of innocence. [Old English *ordāl, ordēl* from Germanic: compare DEAL¹]

or·der ● *noun* **1 a** the condition in which every part, unit, etc. is in its right place; tidiness (*restored some semblance of order*). **b** a usu. specified sequence, succession, etc. (*alphabetical order*; *the order of events*). **2** (in *sing.* or *pl.*) an authoritative command, direction, instruction, etc. (*only obeying orders*; *gave orders for it to be done*; *the judge made an order*). **3** a state of peaceful harmony under a constituted authority (*peace, order, and good government*; *law and order*). **4 a** rank, class, kind, sort (*an engine of a higher order*). **b** (esp. in *pl.*) *Brit.* a social class, rank, etc., constituting a distinct group in society (*the lower orders*; *the order of baronets*). **5** a kind; a sort (*talents of a high order*). **6 a** a direction to a manufacturer, seller, waiter, etc. to supply something. **b** the quantity of goods etc. supplied. **7** the constitution or nature of the world, society, etc. (*the moral order*; *the order of things*). **8** *Biol.* a taxonomic rank below a class and above a family. **9** a body or society of persons living by common consent under the same religious, moral, or social regulations and discipline (*the Franciscan order*; *the order of Templars*). **10 a** any of the grades of the Christian ministry. **b** (in *pl.*) the status of a member of the clergy (*Anglican orders*). **11 a** any of the five classical styles of architecture (Doric, Ionic, Corinthian, Tuscan, and Composite) based on the proportions of columns, amount of decoration, etc. **b** any style or mode of architecture subject to uniform established proportions. **12** (esp. **Order**) **a** a company of distinguished people to which appointments are made as an honour or reward (*Order of Canada*; *Order of Merit*). **b** the insignia worn by members of an order. **13** *Math.* **a** a degree of complexity of a differential equation (*equation of the first order*). **b** the order of the highest derivative in the equation. **14** *Math.* **a** the size of a matrix. **b** the number of elements of a finite group. **15** *Christianity* the stated form of divine service (*the order of confirmation*). **16** the principles of procedure, decorum, etc., accepted by a meeting, legislative assembly, etc. or enforced by its president. **17** *Military* **a** a style of dress and equipment (*review order*). **b** (prec. by *the*) the position of a company etc. with arms ordered (*see order arms*). **18 a**

Masonic or similar fraternity. **19** *Christianity* any of the nine ranks of angelic beings (seraphim, cherubim, thrones, dominations, principalities, powers, virtues, archangels, angels). ● *verb* **1** *transitive* (usu. foll. by *to* + infin., or *that* + clause) command; bid; prescribe (*ordered him to go*; *ordered that they should be sent*). **2** *transitive* command or direct (a person) to a specified destination (*was ordered to Singapore*; *ordered them home*). **3** *transitive & intransitive* direct a manufacturer, waiter, seller, etc. to supply (*ordered a new suit*; *ordered dinner*; *are you ready to order?*). **4** *transitive* put in order; regulate (*ordered her affairs*). **5** *transitive* (of God, fate, etc.) ordain (*fate ordered it otherwise*). **6** *transitive N Amer.* command (a thing) done or (a person) dealt with (*ordered it settled*; *ordered him expelled*). □ **by order** according to the proper authority. **in bad** (or **good** etc.) **order** not working (or working properly etc.). **in order 1** one after another according to some principle. **2** ready or fit for use. **3** according to the rules (of procedure at a meeting etc.). **in order that** with the intention; so that. **in order to** with the purpose of doing; with a view to. **keep order** enforce orderly behaviour. **made to order 1** made according to individual requirements, measurements, etc. (*opp.* READY-MADE 1). **2** exactly what is wanted. **of** (or **in** or **on**) **the order of 1** approximately. **2** having the order of magnitude specified by (*of the order of one in a million*). **on order** (of goods etc.) ordered but not yet received. **order about 1** dominate; command officiously. **2** send hither and thither. **order arms** *Military* hold a rifle with its butt on the ground close to one's right side. **Order! Order!** *Parl.* a call for silence or calm, esp. by the Speaker of a legislative assembly. **order out** (or **in**) *N Amer.* order food to be delivered to one's home etc. **out of order 1** not working properly. **2** not in the correct sequence. **3** not according to the rules (of a meeting, organization, etc.). **4** *informal* **a** not behaving in an acceptable fashion. **b** (of behaviour) not acceptable. **take orders 1** accept commissions. **2** accept and carry out commands. **3** (also **take holy orders**) be ordained. □ **or·der·er** *noun* [Old French *ordre* from Latin *ordo ordinis* row, array, degree, command, etc.]

order book *noun* **1** a listing or record of orders for a product etc. **2** the level of incoming orders.

order form *noun* a printed form on which customers enter details concerning their orders.

order-in-council *noun* (*pl.* **orders-**) *Cdn & Brit.* an administrative order determined by the cabinet and formally issued by the sovereign or the sovereign's representative, usu. to deal with routine matters or to establish detailed regulations concerning acts passed by Parliament.

or·der·ly ● *adjective* **1** methodically arranged; regular. **2** obedient to discipline; well-behaved; not unruly. **3** *Military* **a** of or concerned with orders. **b** charged with the conveyance or execution of orders. ● *noun* (*pl.* **-ies**) **1** an attendant in a hospital responsible for the non-medical care of patients and the maintenance of order and cleanliness. **2** a soldier who carries orders for an officer etc. □ **or·der·li·ness** *noun*

orderly room *noun Military* a room in a barracks used for company business.

order of business *noun N Amer.* a subject or task requiring attention, esp. in a series (*move to the next order of business*).

Order of Canada *noun* an order of merit established in 1967 to honour Canadians for exemplary achievement, awarded in three ranks: Companion (CC), Officer (OC), and Member (CM).

order of magnitude *noun* **1** a class in a system of classification determined by size, usu. by powers of 10. **2** size or quantity.

Order of Merit *Brit.* an order founded in 1902, for distinguished achievement.

Order of Military Merit *noun* an order of merit established in 1972 to honour members of the Canadian Forces in recognition of special achievement, awarded in three grades: Commander (CMM), Officer (OMM), and Member (MMM).

Order of the Bath *noun* (in the UK) an order of knighthood. [so called from the ceremonial bath which originally preceded installation.]

order of the day *noun* **1** the prevailing state of things. **2** a principal topic of action or a procedure decided upon. **3** business set down for treatment; a program. **4** what is called for by necessity, fashion, etc.

Order of the Eastern Star *noun* a social and charitable organization for female relatives of Master Masons.

Order of the Garter *noun* the highest order of English knighthood. [so called from the traditional story of the order's founding, that the garter was that of the Countess of Salisbury which Edward III placed on his own leg after it fell off while she was dancing]

Order Paper *noun* esp. *Parl.* an agenda, esp. a daily list of topics etc. to be discussed or voted on in a legislature. □ **die on the Order Paper** *Cdn* (of a bill) fail to be voted on before the end of a legislative session.

or·din·al /ˈɔrdɪnəl/ ● *noun* **1** (in full **ordinal number**) a number defining a thing's position in a series, e.g. 'first', 'second', 'third', etc. (*compare* CARDINAL NUMBER). **2** *Christianity* a service book, esp. one with the forms of service used at ordinations. ● *adjective* **1 a** of or relating to an ordinal number. **b** defining a thing's position in a series etc. **2** *Biol.* of or concerning an order (*see* ORDER *noun* 8). [Late Latin *ordinalis* from Latin (as ORDER)]

or·din·ance /ˈɔrdɪnəns/ *noun* **1** an authoritative order; a decree. **2** an enactment by a local authority. **3** a religious rite. [medieval Latin *ordinantia* from Latin *ordinare*: see ORDAIN]

or·din·and /ˈɔrdɪnand/ *noun Christianity* a candidate for ordination. [Latin *ordinandus*, gerundive of *ordinare* ORDAIN]

or·din·ary ● *adjective* **1 a** regular, normal, customary, usual (*in the ordinary course of events*). **b** boring; commonplace (*an ordinary little man*). **2** *Law* (esp. of a judge) having immediate or *ex officio* jurisdiction, not deputed. ● *noun* (*pl.* **-aries**) **1** *Law* a person, esp. a judge, having immediate or *ex officio* jurisdiction. **2** (**the Ordinary**) a person who has immediate jurisdiction in ecclesiastical cases, as the archbishop in a province, or the bishop in a diocese. **3** usu. (**Ordinary**) *Catholicism* those parts of a service, esp. the Mass, which do not vary from day to day. **4** *Heraldry* a charge of the earliest, simplest, and commonest kind (esp. chief, pale, bend, fess, bar, chevron, cross, saltire). **5** *Brit. hist.* **a** a public meal provided at a fixed time and price at an inn etc. **b** an establishment providing this. □ **in ordinary** *Brit.* by permanent appointment (esp. to the royal household) (*physician in ordinary*). **out of the ordinary** unusual. □ **or·din·ar·ily** *adverb* **or·din·ar·i·ness** *noun* [Latin *ordinarius* orderly (as ORDER)]

ordinary level *noun see* O LEVEL.

ordinary seaman *noun* a sailor of the lowest rank, that below able seaman. Abbr.: **OS**.

ordinary share *noun Brit.* = COMMON SHARE.

Ordinary Time *noun* (in some Christian denominations) those parts of the liturgical year that are not part of one of the seasons of Advent, Christmas, Lent, or Easter (*10th Sunday in Ordinary Time*).

or·din·ate /ˈɔrdɪnət/ *noun Math.* **1** a straight line from any point drawn parallel to one coordinate axis and meeting the other, usually a coordinate measured parallel to the vertical. **2** the distance of a point from the horizontal axis measured parallel to the vertical axis (*compare* ABSCISSA 1). [Latin *linea ordinata applicata* line applied parallel, from *ordinare*: see ORDAIN]

or·din·a·tion /ˌɔrdɪˈneɪʃən/ *noun* **1 a** the act of ordaining or conferring holy orders on a priest, minister, etc. **b** the admission of a priest etc. to church ministry. **2** the arrangement of things etc. in ranks; classification. **3** the act of decreeing or ordaining. [Latin *ordinatio* (as ORDAIN)]

ord·nance /ˈɔrdnəns/ *noun* **1** mounted guns; cannon. **2** a branch of government service or the military dealing esp. with military stores and materials. [Middle English var. of ORDINANCE]

Ordnance Survey *Brit.* (in the UK) an official survey organization, originally under the Master of the Ordnance, preparing large-scale detailed maps of the whole country.

Or·do·vi·cian /ˌɔrdəˈvɪsɪən, ˌɔrdəˈvɪʃən/ *Geol.* ● *adjective* of or relating to the second period of the Paleozoic era, lasting from about 505 to 438 million years ago, between the Cambrian and Silurian periods. It saw the diversification of many invertebrate groups and the appearance of the first vertebrates. ● *noun* this geological period or system. [Latin *Ordovices* ancient British tribe in N Wales]

ord·ure /ˈɔrdjʊr/ *noun* **1** excrement; dung. **2** obscenity; filth; foul language. [Old French from *ord* foul, from Latin *horridus*: see HORRID]

Or·dzho·ni·kidze /ˌɔrdʒɒnəˈkɪdzi/ the former name (1931–44 and 1954–93) for VLADIKAVKAZ.

Ore. *abbreviation* Oregon.

ore¹ *noun* a naturally occurring solid material from which metal or other valuable minerals may be extracted. [Old English *ōra* unwrought metal, *ār* bronze, related to Latin *aes* crude metal, bronze]

ore² /ˈuːrə, ˈɜːrə/ *noun* (also **øre**, **öre**) (*pl.* same) a Scandinavian monetary unit equal to one-hundredth of a krona or krone. [Danish, Norwegian *øre*, Swedish *öre*]

ore·ad /ˈɔːriˌad/ *noun* (in Greek and Roman mythology) a mountain nymph. [Latin *oreas -ados* from Greek *oreias* from *oros* mountain]

ore body *noun* a large mass of mineral-bearing rock etc.

orec·chiet·te /ɔrəˈkjɛtɪ/ *plural noun* a pasta dish of small ear-shaped noodles. [Italian, lit. 'little ears']

Consonants: b *but* d *dog* f *few* g *get* h *her* j *yes* k *cat* l *leg* m *man* n *no* p *pen* r *red* s *sit*

Oreg. *abbreviation* Oregon.

oreg·ano /ɔˈrɛɡənoː/ *noun* **1** the dried leaves of wild marjoram used as a culinary herb (*compare* MARJORAM). **2** the plant, *Origanum vulgare*, bearing these. [Spanish, = ORIGANUM]

Ore·gon /ˈɔrəɡən/ a state in the northwestern US, on the Pacific coast; pop. (2000) 3,421,399; capital, Salem. □ **Ore·gon·ian** /ˌɒrəˈɡoːnɪən/ *adjective & noun*

Oregon grape *noun* **1** a N American evergreen shrub, *Mahonia aquifolium*, of the barberry family, with spiny-toothed leaves and racemes of yellow flowers. **2** the dark blue-black berry of this plant.

Oregon Trail a route across the central US, from Missouri to Oregon, some 3 000 km (2,000 miles) in length, used in the mid-1800s by settlers moving west.

Orel /ɒˈrel, aˈrjəl/ an industrial city in SW Russia; pop. (est. 2002) 343,700.

Ore Mountains an alternative name for the ERZGEBIRGE.

Oren·burg /ˈɒrənˌbɜrɡ/ a city in S Russia, on the Ural River; pop. (est. 2002) 522,200. It was known as Chkalov from 1938 to 1957.

Oreo /ˈɔrioː/ *noun esp. US slang derogatory* a black person who is considered, esp. by other blacks, to have adopted values of the white establishment. [proprietary term for a cookie consisting of two dark biscuits with a white filling]

Ores·tes /ɒˈrestiːz/ *Gk Myth* the son of Agamemnon and Clytemnestra. He killed his mother and her lover Aegisthus to avenge the murder of Agamemnon.

Øre·sund /ˌɜrəˈsʊnd/ (also called **the Sound**) a narrow channel between Sweden and the Danish island of Zealand.

Orff /ˈɔrf/ **Carl** (1895–1982), German composer, known for his operas and his innovative approach to musical education; his works include the secular cantata *Carmina Burana* (1937) and the opera *Antigone* (1949).

org *noun* organization. [abbreviation]

or·gan *noun* **1 a** a usu. large musical instrument having pipes supplied with air from bellows, sounded by keys, and distributed into sets or stops which form partial organs, each with a separate keyboard (*choir organ*; *pedal organ*). **b** a smaller instrument without pipes, producing similar sounds electronically. **c** a smaller keyboard wind instrument with metal reeds; a harmonium. **d** = BARREL ORGAN. **2 a** a usu. self-contained part of an organism having a special vital function (*vocal organs*; *digestive organs*). **b** esp. *jocular* the penis. **3** a medium of communication, esp. a newspaper, sectarian periodical, etc. **4** a means of action or operation; an instrument. [Old English *organa* & Old French *organe*, from Latin *organum* from Greek *organon* tool]

or·gan·dy /ˈɔrɡəndi/ *noun* (esp. *Brit.* **or·gan·die**) (*pl.* **-dies**) a fine translucent cotton muslin, usu. stiffened. [French *organdi*, of unknown origin]

or·gan·elle /ˌɔrɡəˈnel/ *noun Biol.* any of various organized or specialized structures which form part of a cell. [modern Latin *organella* diminutive; see ORGAN, -LE]

organ grinder *noun* the player of a barrel organ.

or·gan·ic /ɔrˈɡanɪk/ ● *adjective* **1** of or relating to plants or animals. **2 a** *Physiol.* of or relating to a bodily organ or organs. **b** *Med.* (of a disease) affecting the structure of an organ. **3** (of a plant or animal) having organs or an organized physical structure. **4** produced or involving production without the use of chemical fertilizers, pesticides, etc. (*organic crop*; *organic farming*). **5** *Chem.* (of a compound etc.) containing carbon (*opp.* INORGANIC). **6 a** structural, inherent. **b** constitutional, fundamental. **7** organized, systematic, coordinated (*an organic whole*). **8** characterized by or designating continuous or natural development (*the company expanded through organic growth rather than acquisitions*). ● *noun* (esp. in *pl.*) an organic substance, esp. a fertilizer, pesticide, etc. □ **or·gan·ic·al·ly** *adverb*

organic chemistry *noun* the chemistry of carbon compounds.

or·gani·cism /ɔrˈɡanɪˌsɪzəm/ *noun* **1** the doctrine that everything in nature has an organic basis or is part of an organic whole. **2** the use or advocacy of literary or artistic forms in which the parts are connected or coordinated in the whole. **3** the use or advocacy of organic farming methods. □ **or·gani·cist** *noun & adjective*

organic law *noun* a law stating the formal constitution of a country.

or·gan·ism *noun* **1** a living individual consisting of a single cell or of a group of interdependent parts sharing the life processes; an individual plant or animal. **2** a whole with interdependent parts compared to a living being. [French *organisme* (as ORGANIZE)]

or·gan·ist *noun* the player of an organ.

or·gan·iz·a·tion *noun* (also esp. *Brit.* **-isation**) **1** the act or an instance of organizing; the state of being organized. **2** an organized body, esp. a business, government department, charity, etc. **3** systematic arrangement; tidiness. □ **or·gan·iz·a·tion·al** *adjective* **or·gan·iz·a·tion·al·ly** *adverb*

organization man *noun* a man who subordinates his individuality and his personal life to the organization he serves.

or·gan·ize *verb* (also esp. *Brit.* **-ise**) **1** *transitive* **a** give an orderly structure to, systematize. **b** bring the affairs of (another person or oneself) into order; make arrangements for (a person). **2** *transitive* **a** arrange for or initiate (a scheme etc.). **b** provide; take responsibility for (*organized some sandwiches*). **3 a** *transitive* enrol (new members) in a trade union, political party, etc. **b** *transitive* form (a trade union or other political group). **c** *intransitive* form a trade union etc. **4** *transitive* **a** form (different elements) into an organic whole. **b** form (an organic whole). **5** *transitive* (esp. as **or·gan·ized** *adjective*) make organic; make into a living being or tissue. □ **or·gan·iz·able** *adjective* ¶ For the spelling with *-ize*, please see the usage note at the entry for *-IZE*. [medieval Latin *organizare* from Latin (as ORGAN)]

or·gan·ized *adjective* **1** arranged in a systematic way, esp. on a large scale (*organized sports*). **2** having one's affairs in order so as to deal with them efficiently. **3** having formed a labour union, political group, etc.

organized crime *noun* widespread criminal activity organized under powerful leadership.

organized religion *noun* any structured system of faith or worship, usu. one followed by a large number of people, esp. when in contrast to a personal or individual faith, spirituality, etc.

or·gan·iz·er *noun* **1** a person who organizes an event, the creation of a trade union, a political party, etc. **2** a thing used for organizing objects, such as a handbag or folder with many compartments. **3** = PERSONAL ORGANIZER.

organ loft *noun* a gallery in a church or concert hall for an organ.

organ meat *noun* an animal's liver, kidneys, etc., eaten as food.

organo- /ˈɔrɡənoː, ɔrˈɡanoː-/ *combining form* **1** esp. *Biol.* organ. **2** *Chem.* organic, esp. in naming classes of organic compounds containing a particular element (*organochlorine*; *organophosphorus*). [Greek (as ORGAN)]

or·gano·chlor·ine /ˌɔrɡənoːˈklɔriːn, ɔrˈɡanoː-/ *noun* any of a large group of pesticides and other synthetic organic compounds with chlorinated aromatic molecules.

organ of Corti /ˈkɔrti/ *noun Anat.* a structure in the inner ear of mammals, responsible for converting sound signals into nerve impulses. [A. *Corti*, Italian anatomist d.1876]

or·gano·gen·esis /ˌɔrɡənoːˈdʒenɪsɪs, ɔrˈɡanoː-/ *noun* the production or development of the organs of an animal or plant.

or·gano·lep·tic /ˌɔrɡənoːˈleptɪk, ɔrˈɡanoː-/ *adjective* affecting the organs of sense. [ORGANO- + Greek *lēptikos* disposed to take, from *lambanō* take]

or·gano·met·al·lic /ˌɔrɡənoːməˈtalɪk, ɔrˌɡanoː-/ *adjective* (of a compound) organic and containing a metal.

or·ga·non /ˈɔrɡəˌnɒn/ *noun* (also **or·gan·um**) an instrument of thought, esp. a means of reasoning or a system of logic. [Greek *organon* & Latin *organum* (as ORGAN): *Organon* was the title of Aristotle's logical writings, and *Novum* (new) *Organum* that of Bacon's]

or·gano·phos·phor·us /ˌɔrɡənoːˈfɒsfərəs, ɔrˌɡanoː-/ *noun* an organic compound that contains phosphorus. □ **or·gano·phos·phate** *noun* **or·gano·phos·phor·ous** *adjective*

organ pipe cactus *noun* any of several large cacti of the southwestern US with columnar stems or branches esp. *Lemairocereus marginatus*.

organ stop *noun* **1** a set of pipes of a similar tone in an organ. **2** the handle of the mechanism that brings it into action.

or·gan·um /ˈɔrɡənəm/ *noun* (*pl.* **or·gana** /-nə/) **1** (in medieval music) a part sung as an accompaniment below or above a melody, usu. at an interval of a fourth or fifth. **2** = ORGANON.

or·gan·za /ɔrˈɡanzə/ *noun* a thin stiff transparent silk or synthetic dress fabric. [prob. from French *organsin* strong silk thread, from Italian *organzino*, from *Organzi*, the European name of *Urgench*, a town in Uzbekistan, known in the Middle Ages for its silk trade]

or·gasm /ˈɔrɡazəm/ ● *noun* **1 a** the culmination or climax of sexual excitement, arousing an intensely pleasurable sensation in both sexes, and accompanied in the male by ejaculation of semen. **b** an instance of this. **2** violent excitement. ● *intransitive verb* experience a sexual orgasm. □ **or·gas·mic** /-ˈɡazmɪk/ *adjective* **or·gas·mic·ally** /-ˈɡazmɪkli/ *adverb* [Greek *orgasmos* from *orgaō* swell, be excited]

---

t *top*   v *voice*   w *we*   z *zoo*   ʃ *she*   ʒ *vision*   θ *thin*   ð *this*   ŋ *ring*   x *loch*   tʃ *chip*   dʒ *jar*   (*see over for vowels*)

or·geat /ˈɔːdʒɪət, -ʒat/ *noun* a cooling drink made from barley or almonds and orange flower water. [French from Provençal *orjat* from *ordi* barley, from Latin *hordeum*]

orgi·as·tic /ˌɔːdʒiˈastɪk/ *adjective* of or resembling an orgy. □ **orgi·as·tic·ally** *adverb* [Greek *orgiastikos* from *orgiazō* hold an orgy]

or·gu·lous /ˈɔːɡjʊləs/ *adjective archaic* haughty, proud. [Old French *orguillus* from *orguill* 'pride', from Frankish]

orgy /ˈɔːdʒi/ *noun* (*pl.* **-gies**) **1** a wild festivity esp. with much drinking and indiscriminate sexual activity. **2** excessive indulgence in an activity (*an orgy of gluttony*). **3** (usu. in *pl.*) *Gk & Rom. Hist.* secret rites used in the worship of esp. Bacchus, celebrated with dancing, drunkenness, singing, etc. [originally pl., from French *orgies* from Latin *orgia* from Greek *orgia* secret rites]

oribi /ˈɒrɪbi/ *noun* (*pl.* same or **ori·bis**) a small S African grazing antelope, *Ourebia ourebi*, having a reddish-fawn back and white underparts. [prob. Khoisan]

oriel /ˈɔːrɪəl/ *noun* (in full **oriel window**) a window built out from the wall of a building, usu. supported by corbels. [Old French *oriol* gallery, of unknown origin]

ori·ent ● *noun* **1** (**the Orient**) **a** the Far East. **b** (formerly) the Middle East. **2 a** the special lustre of a high-quality pearl. **b** a pearl having this lustre. **3** (**the Orient**) *literary* the east. ● *adjective* **1** (of a pearl or other precious stone, originally from the East) of superior value and brilliancy; lustrous, sparkling. **2** *archaic* situated in or belonging to the east; oriental. ● *transitive verb* **1 a** (also *reflexive*) establish one's position in relation to one's surroundings, the points of the compass, etc. (*took a while to get oriented*; *tried to orient themselves with the help of the stars*). **b** bring (oneself, different elements, etc.) into a clearly understood position or relationship, esp. to known facts or principles. **c** place, align, or determine exactly the position of (a structure etc.), esp. with the aid of a compass; find the bearings of. **2** direct (a person) towards a particular interest, action, career, etc. **3** direct or aim (something) at; design (something) specifically for (*programs oriented toward the immigrant community*). **4** place or build (a church, building, etc.) facing towards the East. [Old French *orient*, *orienter* from Latin *oriens -entis* rising, sunrise, east, from *oriri* rise]

ori·ent·al ● *adjective* **1** (often **Oriental**) of, relating to, or characteristic of E Asia, or Asiatic countries generally. **2** (often **Oriental**) of or characteristic of Eastern civilizations etc. generally. **3** (often **Oriental**) designating a person of E Asian origin. **4** (of a pearl etc.) orient. ● *noun* (esp. **Oriental**) *offensive* a person of East Asian origin. □ **ori·ent·al·ize** *transitive & intransitive verb* (also esp. *Brit.* **-ise**). **ori·ent·al·iz·ing** *adjective & noun* **ori·ent·al·ly** *adverb* [Latin *orientalis* (as ORIENT)]

ori·ent·al·ism *noun* **1** (often **Orientalism**) **a** the representation, image, or concept of the Orient, esp. the Middle East, in Western academic writing, art, or literature. **b** this representation perceived as romanticized, idealized, or stereotyped, esp. as embodying a colonialist attitude. **2** the study or knowledge of Oriental languages, literatures, etc. □ **ori·ent·al·ist** *noun*

oriental poppy *noun* a perennial garden poppy, *Papaver orientale*, with showy usu. scarlet flowers, native to SW Asia.

oriental rug *noun* (also **oriental carpet**) a rug or carpet hand-knotted in or as in the Orient.

orien·tate *transitive & intransitive verb* = ORIENT *verb*. [prob. back-formation from ORIENTATION]

orien·ta·tion *noun* **1 a** a person's esp. political or psychological attitude or adjustment in relation to circumstances, ideas, etc. **b** = SEXUAL ORIENTATION. **2** an introduction to a subject or situation; a briefing. **3** the position of a building, object, etc. relative to specific defined data, the points of the compass, etc. **4 a** the act or an instance of orienting. **b** the state of being oriented. **5** the faculty by which birds etc. find their way home from a distance. □ **orien·ta·tion·al** *adjective* [apparently from ORIENT]

orientation program *noun* esp. *N Amer.* (also **orientation course** etc.) a course giving information to newcomers to a university, organization, etc.

ori·ent·ed *adjective* **1** (with preceding n. or adv.) having a specified emphasis, bias, or interest (*job-oriented*; *future-oriented*). **2** having a particular orientation.

ori·en·teer·ing *noun* a competitive sport in which participants have to find their way on foot, skis, etc. across rough country with the aid of map and compass. □ **ori·en·teer** *noun & intransitive verb* [Swedish *orientering*]

ori·fice /ˈɒrɪfɪs, ˈɒr-/ *noun* a usu. small opening or aperture, esp. the mouth of a bodily organ or other cavity. [French from Late Latin *orificium* from *os oris* mouth + *facere* make]

ori·flamme /ˈɒrɪˌflam, ˈɒr-/ *noun* **1** *hist.* the sacred scarlet silk banner of St. Denis given to early French kings by the abbot of St. Denis on setting out for war. **2** a banner, a principle, or an ideal as a rallying point in a struggle. **3** a bright conspicuous object, colour, etc. [Old French from Latin *aurum* gold + *flamma* flame]

ori·gami /ˌɒrɪˈɡami, ˌɒr-/ *noun* the Japanese art of folding paper into decorative shapes and figures. [Japanese from *ori* fold + *kami* paper]

ori·ganum /ɒˈrɪɡənəm, ɒ-/ *noun* any plant of the genus *Origanum*, esp. wild marjoram (*see* MARJORAM, OREGANO). [Latin *origanum* from Greek *origanon*]

Ori·gen /ˈɒrɪdʒən/ (*c.*185–*c.*254), Christian scholar and theologian, probably born in Alexandria. His writings include the *Hexapla*, an edition of the Old Testament with six or more parallel versions; he introduced Neoplatonist elements into Christianity but these teachings were later rejected by Church orthodoxy.

ori·gin *noun* **1 a** a beginning, cause, or ultimate source of something. **b** that from which a thing is derived, a source, or starting point (*a word of Latin origin*). **2** (often in *pl.*) a person's social background, family, etc. (*middle-class origins*). **3** *Anat.* **a** a place at which a muscle is firmly attached. **b** a place where a nerve or blood vessel begins or branches from a main nerve or blood vessel. **4** *Math.* **a** a fixed point from which measurement or motion begins. **b** the point of intersection of axes in Cartesian coordinates. [French *origine* from Latin *origo -ginis* from *oriri* rise]

ori·gin·al ● *adjective* **1** existing from the beginning or earliest stages. **2** novel; inventive; creative (*has an original mind*; *original ways to cook chicken*). **3 a** that is the origin or source of something. **b** (of a picture, text, etc.) from which another is copied, translated, etc. (*in the original Greek*; *has an original Rembrandt*). **c** not derivative or imitative, esp. made, composed, etc. by a person himself or herself (*an original poem*). ● *noun* **1 a** an original model, pattern, picture, etc. from which another is copied or translated (*kept the copy and destroyed the original*). **b** a person represented in a picture or upon whom a literary character is based. **2** an unusual or eccentric person. **3 a** a garment specially designed for a fashion collection. **b** a copy of such a garment made to order. □ **ori·gin·al·ly** *adverb*

original instrument *noun* a musical instrument, or a copy of one, dating from the time the music played on it was composed.

ori·gin·al·ity *noun* (*pl.* **-ities**) **1** the quality or fact of being original, esp. the power of creating or thinking creatively. **2** newness or freshness, esp. of literary or artistic style. **3** an original act, thing, trait, etc.

original print *noun* a print made directly from an artist's own woodcut, etching, etc., and printed under the artist's supervision.

original sin *noun* (in Christian theology) the innate tendency to evil or depravity of all humans, held to be inherited from Adam as a consequence of the Fall.

ori·gin·ary /əˈrɪdʒɪˌneri/ *adjective* that is the origin or source of a person or thing.

ori·gin·ate *verb* **1** *intransitive* (usu. foll. by *from*, *in*, *with*) begin, arise, be derived, take its origin. **2** *transitive* cause to begin; initiate. **3** *N Amer.* (of an aircraft, bus, etc.) begin a scheduled trip at a particular place. □ **ori·gin·a·tion** *noun* **ori·gin·ator** *noun*

Oril·lia /əˈrɪljə/ a city in south central Ontario, located at the northern end of Lake Simcoe and the southern end of Lake Couchiching, about 40 km northeast of Barrie; pop. (2001) 29,121. □ **Oril·lian** *noun* [Spanish *orilla* bank or shore]

O-ring *noun* a gasket in the form of a ring with a circular cross-section.

Ori·noco River /ˌɒrəˈnoːkoː, ˌɒr-/ a river in northern S America, which rises in SE Venezuela and flows 2 060 km (1,280 miles) in a great arc through Venezuela, entering the Atlantic Ocean through a vast delta. For part of its length it forms the border between Colombia and Venezuela.

ori·ole /ˈɔːrɪəl, -oːl/ *noun* **1** any New World bird of the genus *Icterus*, esp. the northern oriole. **2** any Old World bird of the genus *Oriolus*, many of which have brightly coloured plumage (*see* GOLDEN ORIOLE). [Old French *oriol* from Latin *aureolus* diminutive of *aureus* golden, from *aurum* gold]

Orion /əˈraɪən/ *noun* **1** *Gk Myth* a giant and hunter who was changed into a constellation at his death. **2** *Astronomy* a conspicuous constellation (the Hunter), said to represent a hunter holding a club and shield. It contains many bright stars, including Rigel and Betelgeuse, and a prominent line of three forms **Orion's Belt**. Others form the **Sword**

Vowels: a *cat*   ɑ *arm*   e *bed*   ɜr *her*   ɜː *deux*   ə *ago*   ɪ *sit*   i *cosy*   iː *feed*   ɒ *hot*   ɔ *pore*   ɔː *no*   ʌ *run*   ʊ *put*

of Orion, which contains the Great Nebula and the multiple star Theta Orionis.

Ori·sha /ˈɒrɪˌʃə/ *noun* (in southern Nigeria) any of several minor gods or spirits. The term is also used in various religious cults of South America and the Caribbean. [Yoruba]

ori·son /ˈɒrɪzən, -ɒr-/ *noun* (usu. in *pl.*) *literary* a prayer. [Old French *oreison* from Latin (as ORATION)]

Oris·sa /əˈrɪsə/ a state in E India, on the Bay of Bengal; capital, Bhubaneswar.

-orium *suffix* forming nouns denoting a place for a particular function (*auditorium*; *crematorium*). [Latin, neuter of adjectives in *-orius*: see -ORY[1]]

Oriya /ɔˈriːə/ *noun* **1** a native of the State of Orissa in India. **2** the Indo-European language of this people. [Hindi]

Ork·ney Islands (also **Ork·neys**, **Ork·ney**) a group of more than 70 islands off the northeast tip of Scotland, constituting an administrative region of Scotland; pop. (1991) 19,245; chief town, Kirkwall.

Ork·ney·man *noun* (*pl.* **-men**) *Cdn hist.* a native or inhabitant of the Orkney Islands working in the N American fur trade, esp. with the Hudson's Bay Company.

Or·lan·do a city in central Florida; pop. (2000) 185,951. A popular tourist resort, it is situated near the John F. Kennedy Space Center and Disney World.

Or·lean·ist /ˈɔːrliənɪst, ɔːrˈliːə-/ *noun hist.* a supporter of the claim to the French throne of the branch of the Bourbon dynasty descended from the Duc d'Orléans, younger brother of Louis XIV, whose members included Louis Philippe, king of France 1830–48.

Or·léans /ɔːrleiˈɑ̃/ a city in central France, on the Loire; pop. (1999) 113,126. In 1429 it was the scene of Joan of Arc's first victory over the English during the Hundred Years War.

Orléans, Île d' an island in SE central Quebec, located in the St. Lawrence River, just northeast of Quebec City. [Henri II, Duc d'*Orléans*: see HENRY II, king of France]

Orlon /ˈɔːrlɒn/ *noun proprietary* a synthetic fibre and fabric for textiles and knitwear. [invented word, after NYLON]

or·lop /ˈɔːrlɒp/ *noun* the lowest deck of a ship with three or more decks. [Middle Dutch *overloop* covering, from *overloopen* run over (as OVER-, LEAP)]

Orly /ɔːrˈliː/ *noun* a Parisian suburb in which one of Paris's two international airports is located.

Or·man·dy /ˈɔːrməndi/ **Eu·gene** (born Jenő Ormandy Blau) (1899–1985), Hungarian-born US conductor, who was noted as the director of the Philadelphia Orchestra (1938–80).

Or·mazd /ˈɔːrməzd/ (also **Or·muzd**) see AHURA MAZDA.

or·molu /ˈɔːrməluː/ *noun* **1** (often *attributive*) gilded bronze; a gold-coloured alloy of copper, zinc, and tin used to decorate furniture, make ornaments, etc. **2** articles made of or decorated with this. [French *or moulu* 'powdered gold' (for use in gilding)]

Ormuz see HORMUZ.

orna·ment ● *noun* **1 a** a thing used or serving to adorn, esp. a small trinket, vase, figure, etc. (*a mantelpiece crowded with ornaments; her only ornament was a brooch*). **b** a person who adds honour or distinction to his or her sphere, time, etc. (*an ornament to her profession*). **c** a quality or circumstance that confers beauty, grace, or honour. **2** decoration added to embellish esp. a building (*a tower rich in ornament*). **3** (in *pl.*) *Music* embellishments and decorations made to a melody. ● *transitive verb* adorn, beautify, provide with ornaments. □ **orna·men·ta·tion** *noun* [Latin *ornamentum* equipment, from *ornare* adorn]

orna·ment·al ● *adjective* serving as an ornament; decorative. ● *noun* a thing considered to be ornamental rather than essential, esp. a cultivated plant. □ **orna·ment·al·ism** *noun* **orna·ment·al·ly** *adverb*

or·nate /ɔːrˈneit/ *adjective* **1** elaborately adorned; highly decorated. **2** (of literary style etc.) convoluted; flowery. □ **or·nate·ly** *adverb* **or·nate·ness** *noun* [Latin *ornatus* past participle of *ornare* adorn]

or·nery /ˈɔːrnəri/ *adjective* N Amer. informal **1** grumpily stubborn. **2** crotchety, cantankerous. □ **or·neri·ness** *noun* [var. of ORDINARY]

or·nith·ic /ɔːrˈnɪθɪk/ *adjective* of or relating to birds. [Greek *ornithikos* birdlike (as ORNITHO-)]

or·nith·is·chian /ɔːrnɪˈθɪskiən, -ˈθɪʃən/ ● *adjective* of or relating to the order Ornithischia, including dinosaurs with a pelvic structure like that of birds. ● *noun* a dinosaur of this order. [modern Latin, from Greek *ornis ornithos* 'bird' + *iskhion* 'hip joint']

ornitho- /ˈɔːrnɪθoː/ *combining form* bird. [Greek from *ornis ornithos* bird]

orni·thol·ogy /ˌɔːrnɪˈθɒlədʒi/ *noun* the branch of zoology that deals

with the study of birds. □ **orni·tho·logic·al** *adjective*

orni·thol·o·gist *noun* [modern Latin *ornithologia* from Greek *ornithologos* treating of birds (as ORNITHO-, -LOGY)]

or·nitho·pod /ˈɔːrnɪθəpɒd/ ● *noun* a bipedal herbivorous ornithischian dinosaur of the suborder Ornithopoda. ● *adjective* of or relating to this suborder. [modern Latin, from Greek *ornis ornith-* 'bird' + *pous pod-* 'foot']

or·nith·opter /ˈɔːrnɪˌθɒptər/ *noun* a machine designed to achieve flight by means of flapping wings. [French, as ORNITHO- + Greek *ptero* wing]

oro- /ˈɔːroː/ *combining form* mountain. [Greek *oros* mountain]

or·ogeny /ɔːˈrɒdʒɪni/ *noun* (*pl.* **-ies**) **1** (also **or·ogen·esis** /ˌɔːroːˈdʒɛnɪsɪs/) the process of the formation of mountains. **2** a geological period of mountain building. □ **oro·gen·ic** /ˌɔːrəˈdʒɛnɪk/ *adjective*

oro·graph·ic /ˌɔːrəˈɡrafɪk/ *adjective* **1** of or relating to mountains, esp. with regard to their position and form. **2** (of clouds or rainfall) resulting from the effects of mountains in forcing moist air to rise.

orog·raphy /ɒˈrɒɡrəfi/ *noun* the branch of physical geography dealing with the formation and features of mountains.

Oro·moc·to /ɔːrəˈmɒktoː/ a town in south central New Brunswick, situated at the confluence of the Oromocto and Saint John rivers, southeast of Fredericton; pop. (2001) 8,843. □ **Oro·moc·ton·ian** *noun* [ultimately from Maliseet *welamooktook* fine river or deep water, with reference to the river's good conditions for canoeing]

Oron·tes River /əˈrɒntiːz/ a river in SW Asia which rises near Baalbek in N Lebanon and flows 571 km (355 miles) through western and N Syria before turning west through S Turkey to enter the Mediterranean. It is an important source of water for irrigation, esp. in Syria.

oro·tund /ˈɒrəˌtʌnd, ˈɔːr-/ *adjective* **1** (of the voice or phrasing) full, resonant; imposing. **2** (of writing, style, expression, etc.) pompous; pretentious. □ **oro·tund·ity** /-ˈtʌndɪti/ *noun* **oro·tund·ly** *adverb* [Latin *ore rotundo* with rounded mouth]

Oroz·co /ɔːˈrɒskoː/ **José Cle·mente** (1883–1949), Mexican painter, who is noted for his monumental murals depicting the life and history of the Mexican people, such as *Hidalgo and the Liberation of Mexico* (1949).

or·phan ● *noun* (often *attributive*) **1 a** a child or young animal deprived by death of one or usu. both parents. **b** a child bereft of parental care, esp. through abandonment or neglect. **2** a person, country, policy, etc. bereft of previous protection, advantages, etc. **3** *Printing* the first line of a paragraph at the foot of a page or column (*compare* WIDOW *noun* 3). ● *transitive verb* **1** bereave (a child etc.) of its parents or a parent. **2** abandon or deprive of previously provided assistance, support, etc. □ **or·phaned** *adjective* **or·phan·hood** *noun* [Late Latin *orphanus* from Greek *orphanos* 'bereaved']

or·phan·age *noun* **1** a usu. residential institution for the care and education of orphans. **2** orphanhood.

orphan drug *noun* a drug that is useful but not commercially viable for the pharmaceutical company producing it unless it is granted tax credits and other special status.

Or·pheus /ˈɔːrfijəs/ *Gk Myth* a poet who sang and played with his lyre so wonderfully that wild beasts were spellbound by his music. He persuaded the god of the underworld to release his wife Eurydice from the dead, but, by looking back at her before they had reached the world of the living, lost her once again. □ **Or·phean** *adjective*

Or·phic /ˈɔːrfɪk/ *adjective* **1 a** of or concerning Orpheus or the mysteries, doctrines, etc. associated with him. **b** oracular; mysterious. **2** melodious; entrancing. [Latin *Orphicus* from Greek *Orphikos* from *Orpheus*]

Or·phism /ˈɔːrfɪzəm/ *noun* a mystic religion of ancient Greece, originating in the 7th or 6th c. BC and based on poems (now lost) attributed to Orpheus, emphasizing the mixture of good and evil in human nature and the necessity for individuals to rid themselves of the evil part by ritual and moral purification throughout a series of reincarnations.

or·phrey /ˈɔːrfri/ *noun* (*pl.* **-phreys**) an ornamental stripe or border or separate piece of ornamental needlework, esp. on ecclesiastical vestments. [Middle English *orfreis* (taken as pl.) (gold) embroidery, from Old French from medieval Latin *aurifrisium* etc. from Latin *aurum* gold + *Phrygius* Phrygian, also 'embroidered']

or·pi·ment /ˈɔːrpɪmənt/ *noun* a mineral form of arsenic trisulphide, formerly used as a dye and artist's pigment. [Old French from Latin *auripigmentum* from *aurum* gold + *pigmentum* pigment]

or·pine /ˈɔːrpɪn/ *noun* (also **orpin**) a succulent herbaceous purple-flowered plant, *Sedum telephium*. Also called LIVELONG[2]. [Old

French *orpine*, prob. alteration of ORPIMENT, originally of a yellow-flowered species of the same genus]

Orr, **Rob·ert Gor·don** ('Bobby') (b.1948), Canadian hockey player. He joined the NHL Boston Bruins in 1967, and revolutionized the role of the defenceman. He is the only defenceman ever to win the Art Ross Trophy as leading scorer.

or·rery /ˈɒrəri/ *noun* (*pl.* **-ies**) a mechanical, usu. clockwork, model of the solar system. [the fourth Earl of *Orrery* d.1731, for whom one was made]

orris *noun* **1** any plant of the genus *Iris*, esp. *I. florentina*. **2** = ORRISROOT. [16th c.: apparently an unexplained alteration of IRIS]

orris·root *noun* the fragrant rootstock of the orris, used as a flavouring and in perfumery.

Orser, **Brian** (b.1961), Canadian figure skater. The Canadian senior men's champion from 1981–8, he won the world figure skating championship in 1987. He won the silver medal at the 1984 and 1988 Olympics, and turned professional in 1988.

Orsk a city in S Russia, in the Urals on the Ural River near the border with Kazakhstan; pop. (est. 2002) 273,400.

or·ta·nique /ˈɔrtəˌniːk/ *noun* a citrus fruit produced by crossing an orange and a tangerine. [*orange* + *tangerine* + un*ique*]

Or·tega /ɔrˈteigə/ **Dan·iel** (full surname Ortega Saavedra) (b.1945), Nicaraguan Sandinista leader, president 1985–90. As the leader of the Sandinista National Liberation Front (FSLN) he played a major role in the revolution which overthrew Anastasio Somoza (1979); his government was constantly under attack from the US-backed Contras, and he lost power to an opposition coalition following elections in 1990.

Or·tega y Gas·set /ɔrˈteigə iː gaˈset/ **José** (1883–1955), Spanish philosopher. In his best-known work, *The Rebellion of the Masses* (1929), he argued that democracy could lead to tyranny and proposed leadership by an intellectual elite.

ortho- *combining form* **1 a** straight, rectangular, upright. **b** normal, proper, correct. **2** *Chem.* **a** denoting substitution in a benzene ring at adjacent carbon atoms. **b** forming names of acids and salts containing one molecule of water more than a corresponding *meta*-compound (*orthophosphates*). **3** *Physics & Chem.* denoting the fact of having parallel spins. [Greek *orthos* straight]

ortho·chro·mat·ic /ˌɔrθəkrəˈmatik/ *adjective* giving fairly correct relative intensity to colours in photography by being sensitive to all except red.

ortho·clase /ˈɔrθəˌkleis/ *noun* a common alkali feldspar usu. occurring as variously coloured crystals, used in ceramics and glass-making. [ORTHO- + Greek *klasis* breaking]

ortho·don·tics /ˌɔrθəˈdɒntiks/ *plural noun* (treated as *sing.*) (also **ortho·don·tia** /-ˈdɒntiə/) the branch of dentistry that deals with treatment of irregular alignment of the teeth and jaws. □ **ortho·don·tic** *adjective* **ortho·don·tist** *noun* [ORTHO- + Greek *odous odont-* tooth]

ortho·dox *adjective* **1 a** holding correct or currently accepted opinions, esp. on religious doctrine, morals, etc. **b** conventional, not independent-minded. **2 a** (of opinion, doctrine, etc.) right, correct, in accordance with what is generally accepted or authoritatively established. **b** (of standards of morality etc.) approved, in accordance with what is regarded as proper or usual. **3** (usu. **Orthodox**) (of Judaism or Jews) adhering strictly to the rabbinical interpretation of Jewish law and its traditional observances. **4** (**Orthodox**) of or relating to the Orthodox Church. □ **ortho·dox·ly** *adverb* [Greek *orthodoxos* (as ORTHO-, *doxa* 'opinion')]

Orthodox Church *noun* the family of Eastern Churches, separated from the Western Church in the 11th c., having the Patriarch of Constantinople as its head, and including the national Churches of Russia, Romania, Greece, etc.

ortho·doxy *noun* (*pl.* **-ies**) **1 a** the quality or character of being orthodox. **b** belief in or agreement with what is, or is currently held to be, right, esp. in religious matters. **c** the body of orthodox doctrine. **2** an authorized or generally accepted theory, doctrine, etc. **3** (also **Orthodoxy**) **a** the Orthodox practice of Judaism. **b** the body of Orthodox Jews. **4 a** the Orthodox Church or Churches. **b** the body of Orthodox Christians.

or·tho·epy /ˈɔrθəʊˌepi, ɔrˈθəʊɪpi/ *noun* the scientific study of the correct pronunciation of words. □ **or·tho·epic** /-ˈepik/ *adjective* **or·tho·epist** *noun* [Greek *orthoepeia* correct speech (as ORTHO-, *epos* word)]

ortho·gen·esis /ˌɔrθəʊˈdʒenisis/ *noun* evolutionary change in a

defined direction, esp. as supposedly caused by internal tendency rather than external influence. □ **ortho·gen·etic** /-dʒɪˈnetik/ *adjective*

orth·og·onal /ɔrˈθɒgənəl/ *adjective* of, involving, or at right angles; rectangular. □ **orth·og·onal·ity** /-ˈnaliti/ *noun* [French from *orthogone* (as ORTHO-, -GON)]

orth·og·raphy /ɔrˈθɒgrəfi/ *noun* (*pl.* **-ies**) **1 a** correct or conventional spelling. **b** spelling with reference to its correctness (*dreadful orthography*). **c** the branch of grammar which deals with letters and their combinations to represent sounds and words; the subject of spelling. **2 a** perspective projection used in maps and elevations in which the projection lines are parallel. **b** a map etc. so projected. □ **orth·og·raph·er** *noun* **ortho·graph·ic** /-ˈgrafik/ *adjective* **ortho·graph·ic·al** /-ˈgrafikəl/ *adjective* **ortho·graph·ic·al·ly** /-ˈgrafikli/ *adverb* [Greek *orthographia* (as ORTHO-, -GRAPHY)]

ortho·paed·ic /ˌɔrθəˈpiːdik/ *adjective* (also **ortho·ped·ic**) **1** pertaining to or concerned with orthopaedics. **2 a** (of a bed etc.) designed to relieve back problems, usu. having a very firm mattress or board. **b** (of footwear etc.) designed to ease or correct deformities of the feet.

ortho·paed·ics /ˌɔrθəˈpiːdiks/ *plural noun* (treated as *sing.*) (also **ortho·ped·ics**) the branch of medicine dealing with the correction of deformities of bones or muscles or the treatment of impairments of the skeletal system. □ **ortho·paed·ist** *noun* [French *orthopédie* (as ORTHO-, *pédie* from Greek *paideia* rearing of children, the treatment being originally for children)]

orth·op·ter·an /ɔrˈθɒptərən/ *noun* any insect of the order Orthoptera, with straight narrow forewings, and hind legs modified for jumping etc., including grasshoppers and crickets. □ **orth·op·ter·ous** *adjective* [ORTHO- + Greek *pteros* wing]

orth·op·tic /ɔrˈθɒptik/ *adjective* relating to the correct or normal use of the eyes. □ **orth·op·tist** *noun* [ORTHO- + Greek *optikos* of sight: see OPTIC]

orth·op·tics /ɔrˈθɒptiks/ *noun* *Med.* the branch of medicine that deals with the treatment of defective binocular vision by means of eye exercises.

ortho·rhom·bic /ˌɔrθəʊˈrɒmbik/ *adjective* *Mineral.* (of a crystal) characterized by three mutually perpendicular axes which are unequal in length, as in topaz and talc.

orth·ot·ic /ɔrˈθɒtik/ ● *noun* (usu. in *pl.*) **1** a moulded insert for a shoe etc. designed to improve posture and gait. **2** an artificial external device, as a brace or splint, serving to prevent or assist relative movement in the limbs. ● *adjective* related to orthotics. □ **orth·ot·ist** /ˈɔrθətist/ *noun* [Greek *orthoun* 'set straight' + -OTIC]

orto·lan /ˈɔrtələn/ *noun* (in full **ortolan bunting**) a small European bird, *Emberiza hortulana*, eaten as a delicacy. [French from Provençal, lit. 'gardener', from Latin *hortulanus* from *hortulus* diminutive of *hortus* garden]

Oruro /əˈruroː/ a city in W Bolivia; pop. (2001) 201,230. It is the centre of an important mining region, with rich deposits of tin, zinc, silver, copper, and gold.

Or·vi·eto /ɔrˈvjetoː/ a town in Umbria, central Italy; pop. (2001) 20,692. It lies at the centre of a wine-producing area.

Or·well, **George** (pseudonym of Eric Arthur Blair) (1903–50), English novelist and essayist, born in India. His work is characterized by his concern with social injustice, and includes *Animal Farm* (1945), a satire on Communism under Stalin, and *Nineteen Eighty-four* (1949), a futuristic dystopia under the control of Big Brother.

Or·well·ian /ɔrˈweliən/ *adjective* of or characteristic of the writings of George Orwell, esp. with reference to the totalitarian development of the state as depicted in *Nineteen Eighty-four* and *Animal Farm*.

-ory[1] *suffix* forming nouns denoting a place for a particular function (*dormitory*; *refectory*). □ **-orial** *suffix* [Latin *-oria*, *-orium*, sometimes via Old Northern French and Anglo-French *-orie*, Old French *-oire*]

-ory[2] *suffix* forming adjectives (and occasionally nouns) relating to or involving a verbal action (*accessory*; *compulsory*; *directory*). [Latin *-orius*, sometimes via Anglo-French *-ori(e)*, Old French *-oir(e)*]

oryx /ˈɒriks/ *noun* any large straight-horned antelope of the genus *Oryx*, native to Africa and Arabia. [Greek *orux* stonemason's pickaxe, from its pointed horns]

orzo *noun* a variety of pasta shaped like grains of rice or barley. [Italian 'barley']

OS *abbreviation* **1** *Computing* operating system. **2** old style. **3** ORDINARY SEAMAN. **4** outsize. **5** out of stock.

Os *symbol* *Chem.* the element osmium.

Osage /oːˈseidʒ, ˈoː-/ ● *noun* **1** a member of a N American Indian people formerly inhabiting the Osage river valley, Missouri. **2** the

Siouan language of this people. ● *adjective* of or pertaining to the Osages or their language [Osage *Wazhazhe*, one of the three bands composing this people]

Osage orange *noun* **1** a hardy thorny tree, *Maclura pomifera*, of the US, bearing inedible wrinkled orange-like fruit. **2** the durable orange-coloured timber from this.

Osaka /oːˈsakə/ a port and commercial city in central Japan, on the island of Honshu, capital of Kinki region; pop. (est. 2002) 2,602,600.

Os·borne, John (James) (1929–1994), English playwright. His first play, *Look back in Anger* (1956), ushered in a new era of kitchen-sink drama, and its hero, Jimmy Porter, was seen as the archetype of the 'angry young man'.

OSC *abbreviation Cdn* (*Ont.*) Ontario Securities Commission.

Oscan /ˈɒskən/ ● *noun* the ancient language of Campania in Italy, related to Latin and surviving only in inscriptions. ● *adjective* relating to or written in Oscan. [Latin *Oscus*]

Os·car *noun* any of the statuettes awarded by the US Academy of Motion Picture Arts and Sciences for excellence in film acting, directing, etc. *Also called* ACADEMY AWARD. [one of the several speculative stories of its origin claims that the statuette reminded Margaret Herrick, an executive director of the Academy, of her uncle Oscar]

Oscar II (full name Oscar Fredrik) (1829–1907), king of Sweden 1872–1907 and Norway 1872–1905.

os·cil·late /ˈɒsɪˌleɪt/ *verb* **1** *intransitive & transitive* **a** swing to and fro like a pendulum. **b** move to and fro between points. **2** *intransitive* vacillate; vary between extremes of opinion, action, etc. **3** *intransitive Physics* move with periodic regularity. **4** *intransitive Electricity* (of a current) undergo high-frequency alternations as across a spark-gap or in a valve-transmitter circuit. **5** *intransitive* (of a radio receiver) radiate electromagnetic waves owing to faulty operation. **6** *intransitive Math.* (of a series or function) increase and decrease alternately as successive items are taken or as the variable tends to infinity. □ **os·cil·lat·ing** *adjective* **os·cil·la·tion** *noun* **os·cil·la·tor** *noun* **os·cil·la·tory** /ɒˈsɪlətɔri, ˈɒsɪˌleɪtəri/ *adjective* [Latin *oscillare oscillat-* swing]

oscillo- /əˈsɪloː/ *combining form* oscillation, esp. of electric current.

os·cil·lo·gram /əˈsɪləˌgram/ *noun* a record obtained from an oscillograph.

os·cil·lo·graph /əˈsɪləˌgraf/ *noun* **1** a device for displaying or recording oscillations as a continuous curve. **2** = OSCILLOGRAM. □ **os·cil·lo·graph·ic** /-ˈgrafɪk/ *adjective* **os·cil·log·raphy** /-ˈlɒgrəfi/ *noun*

os·cil·lo·scope /əˈsɪləˌskoːp/ *noun* a device for viewing oscillations by a display on the screen of a cathode ray tube. □ **os·cil·lo·scop·ic** /-ˈskɒpɪk/ *adjective*

os·cine /ˈɒsɪn/ *adjective* (also **os·cin·ine** /ˈɒsɪˌniːn/) of or relating to the suborder Oscines of passerine birds including many of the songbirds. [Latin *oscen -cinis* songbird (as OB-, *canere* sing)]

os·cula *pl.* of OSCULUM.

os·cu·lar /ˈɒskjʊlər/ *adjective* **1** of or relating to the mouth. **2** of or relating to kissing. [Latin *osculum* mouth, kiss, diminutive of *os* mouth]

os·cu·late /ˈɒskjʊˌleɪt/ *verb* **1** *Math.* **a** *transitive* (of a curve or surface) touch (another curve or surface) without crossing, so as to have a common tangent. **b** *intransitive* (of two curves or surfaces) have a common tangent. **2** *transitive & intransitive verb jocular* kiss. □ **os·cu·la·tion** /-ˈleɪʃən/ *noun* **os·cu·la·tory** /ˈɒskjʊlətɔri/ *adjective* [Latin *osculari* kiss (as OSCULAR)]

os·cu·lum /ˈɒskjʊləm/ *noun* (*pl.* **os·cula** /-lə/) *Zoology* a mouth-like aperture, esp. of a sponge. [Latin: see OSCULAR]

-ose[1] *suffix* forming adjectives denoting possession of a quality, esp. in sense of 'full of', 'abounding in' (*grandiose*; *verbose*). □ **-osely** *suffix.* **-oseness** *suffix.* [from or after Latin *-osus*]

-ose[2] *suffix Chem.* forming names of sugars and other carbohydrates (*cellulose*; *sucrose*). [after GLUCOSE]

Osh /ɒʃ/ a city in W Kyrgyzstan, near the border with Uzbekistan; pop. (est. 2002) 221,300. It was, until the 15th c., an important post on an ancient trade route to China and India.

Osh·awa /ˈɒʃəwɒ, -wə/ a city in S Ontario, located on Lake Ontario, 50 km east of Toronto; pop. (2001) 139,051. [ultimately from Mississauga *ajawi* crossing to the other side (or, shore of lake)]

osier /ˈoːziːr/ *noun* **1** any of various willows, esp. *Salix viminalis*, with long flexible shoots used in basketwork. **2** a shoot of a willow. [Old French: compare medieval Latin *auseria* 'osier bed']

Os·iris /oːˈsaɪrɪs/ *Egyptian Myth* a god originally connected with fertility,

husband of Isis and father of Horus. He was killed by his brother Seth but subsequently restored to a new life as ruler of the afterlife.

-osis *suffix* (*pl.* **-oses**) denoting a process or condition (*apotheosis*; *metamorphosis*), esp. a pathological state (*acidosis*; *neurosis*; *thrombosis*). [Latin from Greek *-ōsis* suffix of verbal nouns]

-osity *suffix* forming nouns from adjectives in *-ose* (see -OSE[1]) and *-ous* (*verbosity*; *curiosity*). [French *-osité* or Latin *-ositas -ositatis*: compare -ITY]

Osler /ˈɒzlər, ˈoːs-/ **Sir Wil·liam** (1849–1919), Canadian physician, writer, and teacher. He taught at McGill University, the University of Pennsylvania (1884–89), Johns Hopkins University, where he was the first professor of medicine (1889–1905), and Oxford (from 1905). The best-known physician in the English-speaking world at the turn of the century, he was an extremely wide-ranging practitioner.

Oslo /ˈɒzloː/ the capital and chief port of Norway, on the south coast at the head of Oslofjord; pop. (est. 2002) 787,400. Founded in the 11th c., it was known as Christiania from 1624 until 1924 in honour of Christian IV of Norway and Denmark (1577–1648), who rebuilt the city after it had been destroyed by fire in 1624.

Osman I /ˈɒzmən/ (also **Oth·man I** /ˈɒθmən/) (1259–1326), Turkish conqueror, founder of the Ottoman (Osmanli) Dynasty and Empire. After succeeding his father as leader of the Seljuk Turks in 1288, Osman reigned as sultan, conquering NW Asia Minor; he assumed the title of emir in 1299.

Os·man·li /ɒzˈmanli, ɒs-/ *adjective & noun* = OTTOMAN. [Turkish from *Osman* from Arabic *'utmān* (see OTTOMAN) + *-li* adj. suffix]

osmic /ˈɒzmɪk/ *adjective Chem.* containing osmium, esp. in one of its higher oxidation states.

os·mium /ˈɒzmiəm/ *noun Chem.* a hard bluish-white transition element, the heaviest known metal, occurring naturally in association with platinum and used in certain alloys. Symbol: **Os**; at. no.: 76. [Greek *osmē* smell (from the pungent smell of its tetroxide)]

osmo·regu·la·tion /ˌɒzmoːˌregjʊˈleɪʃən/ *noun Biol.* the maintenance of constant osmotic pressure in the fluids of an organism by control of water and salt levels etc.

os·mo·sis /ɒzˈmoːsɪs, ɒs-/ *noun* **1** *Biochem.* the passage of a solvent through a semi-permeable partition into a more concentrated solution, so as to make the concentration on the two sides more nearly equal. **2** gradual, usu. unconscious assimilation or absorption of ideas, knowledge, etc. □ **os·mot·ic** /-ˈmɒtɪk/ *adjective* **os·mot·ic·ally** /-ˈmɒtɪkli/ *adverb* [originally *osmose*, after French from Greek *ōsmos* push]

os·mun·da /ɒzˈmʌndə/ *noun* (also **os·mund** /ˈɒzmənd/) any fern of the genus *Osmunda*, esp. the royal fern, having large divided fronds. [of uncertain origin]

Osna·brück /ˈɒznəˌbrʊk/ a city in NW Germany, in Lower Saxony; pop. (est. 2002) 164,200. In 1648 the Treaty of Westphalia, ending the Thirty Years War, was signed there and in Münster.

os·prey /ˈɒspreɪ, -pri/ *noun* (*pl.* **-preys**) a large bird of prey, *Pandion haliaetus*, with a brown back and white markings, feeding on fish, which it catches in its claws after making a spectacular dive from the air. *Also called* FISH HAWK. [Old French *ospres*, apparently ultimately from Latin *ossifraga* osprey, from *os* bone + *frangere* break]

Ossa, Mount /ˈɒsə/ **1** a mountain in Thessaly, NE Greece, south of Mount Olympus, rising to a height of 1 978 m (6,489 ft.). In Greek mythology the giants were said to have piled Mount Olympus and Mount Ossa onto Mount Pelion in an attempt to reach heaven and destroy the gods. **2** the highest mountain on the island of Tasmania, rising to a height of 1 617 m (5,305 ft.).

os·sein /ˈɒsɪn/ *noun* the collagen of bones. [Latin *osseus* (as OSSEOUS)]

os·seous /ˈɒsiəs/ *adjective* of, pertaining to, consisting of, or resembling bone. [Latin *osseus* from *os ossis* bone]

Os·se·tia /ɒˈsiːʃə/ a region of the central Caucasus. It is divided by the boundary between Russia and Georgia into two parts, North Ossetia and South Ossetia. □ **Os·se·tian** *adjective & noun*

Ossi /ˈɒsi/ (also **Os·sie**) *informal* ● *noun* a person from East Germany (the former German Democratic Republic) (*compare* WESSI). ● *adjective* being or pertaining to an Ossi. [German from *Ost* east]

Os·sian /ˈɒʃən, ˈɒsiən/ the anglicized form of Oisin, a legendary Irish warrior and bard; see MACPHERSON.

os·sicle /ˈɒsɪkəl/ *noun* **1** *Anat.* any small bone, esp. of the middle ear. **2** a small skeletal plate, joint, etc., esp. each of the calcareous plates forming the skeleton of an echinoderm. [Latin *ossiculum* diminutive (as OSSEOUS)]

Os·sie *noun* **1** var. of AUSSIE. **2** var. of OSSI.

Os·sietz·ky /ˌɒsiˈetski/ **Carl von** (1888–1938), German journalist and pacifist, who was imprisoned (1931–2 and 1933–6) for his articles describing Germany's rearmament during the 1920s and 1930s; he was awarded the Nobel Peace Prize in 1935.

os·sify /ˈɒsɪˌfaɪ/ *transitive & intransitive verb* (**-fies, -fied**) **1** turn into bone or bony tissue; harden. **2 a** make or become emotionally callous. **b** make or become rigid, fixed, or unprogressive in attitude. □ **os·si·fi·ca·tion** /-fɪˈkeɪʃən/ *noun* [French *ossifier* from Latin *os ossis* bone]

osso bucco /ˌɒsəʊ ˈbʊkəʊ/ *noun* (also **osso buco**) an Italian dish of veal shanks containing marrow bone stewed in wine with vegetables. [Italian, 'marrow bone']

os·suary /ˈɒsjʊˌeri/ *noun* (*pl.* **-ies**) **1** a receptacle for the bones of the dead; a charnel house. **2** a cave in which ancient bones are found. [Late Latin *ossuarium* irreg. from *os ossis* bone]

oste·itis /ˌɒstiˈaɪtɪs/ *noun* inflammation of the substance of a bone. [Greek *osteon* bone + -ITIS]

Os·tend /ɒˈstend/ a port on the North Sea coast of NW Belgium, in West Flanders; pop. (est. 2000) 67,279. It is a major ferry port.

os·ten·sible /ɒˈstensɪbəl/ *adjective* **1** apparent, but not necessarily real (*his brother's ostensible detachment*). **2** declared, professed, esp. while concealing the actual or genuine (*her ostensible function was that of interpreter*). □ **os·ten·sibly** *adverb* [French from medieval Latin *ostensibilis* from Latin *ostendere ostens-* stretch out to view (as OB-, *tendere* stretch)]

os·ten·ta·tion /ˌɒstenˈteɪʃən/ *noun* **1** a pretentious and vulgar display esp. of wealth and luxury. **2** the attempt or intention to attract notice; showing off. □ **os·ten·ta·tious** *adjective* **os·ten·ta·tious·ly** *adverb* [Latin *ostentatio -onis* from *ostentare* frequentative of *ostendere*: see OSTENSIBLE]

osteo- /ˈɒstiəʊ/ *combining form* bone. [Greek *osteon*]

osteo·arth·ritis /ˌɒstiəʊɑːrˈθraɪtɪs/ *noun* a degenerative disease of joint cartilage causing pain and stiffness esp. in those middle aged and older.

osteo·blast /ˈɒstiəˌblast/ *noun* a mesodermal cell which secretes the substance of bone. □ **osteo·blas·tic** /-ˈblastɪk/ *adjective*

osteo·clast /ˈɒstiəˌklast/ *noun* a large cell which absorbs bone tissue during growth and healing. □ **osteo·clas·tic** /-ˈklastɪk/ *adjective*

osteo·gen·esis /ˌɒstiəʊˈdʒenɪsɪs/ *noun* the formation of bone. □ **osteo·gen·etic** /-dʒɪˈnetɪk/ *adjective*

oste·ol·ogy /ˌɒstiˈɒlədʒi/ *noun* the study of the structure and function of the skeleton and bony structures. □ **osteo·logic·al** /-əˈlɒdʒɪkəl/ *adjective* **osteo·logic·al·ly** /-əˈlɒdʒɪkli/ *adverb* **oste·ol·o·gist** *noun*

osteo·mal·acia /ˌɒstiəʊməˈleɪʃə/ *noun* softening of the bones, often through a deficiency of vitamin D and calcium (*compare* RICKETS). □ **osteo·mal·acic** /-ˈlasɪk/ *adjective* [modern Latin (as OSTEO-, Greek *malakos* soft)]

osteo·myel·itis /ˌɒstiəʊmaɪˈlaɪtɪs/ *noun* inflammation of the bone or bone marrow, usu. due to infection.

oste·op·athy /ˌɒstiˈɒpəθi/ *noun* a system of healing based on the theory that some disorders can be alleviated by treatment of the skeleton and musculature using manipulation and massage. □ **osteo·path** /ˈɒstiəˌpaθ/ *noun* **osteo·path·ic** /ˌɒstiəˈpaθɪk/ *adjective*

osteo·por·osis /ˌɒstiəʊpəˈrəʊsɪs/ *noun* a condition of fragile, porous bones caused by loss of the protein and mineral content of bone tissue, esp. as a result of hormonal changes, or deficiency of calcium or vitamin D. □ **osteo·por·otic** /-ˈrɒtɪk/ *adjective & noun* [OSTEO- + Greek *poros* passage, pore]

osteo·sar·coma /ˌɒstiəʊsɑːrˈkəʊmə/ *noun* (*pl.* **-comas**) *Med.* a malignant tumour of bone, esp. one involving proliferation of osteoblasts. [OSTEO- + SARCOMA]

osteo·tomy /ˌɒstiˈɒtəmi/ *noun* the surgical cutting of a bone, esp. to allow realignment.

Ostia /ˈɒstiə/ an ancient city and harbour which was situated on the western coast of Italy at the mouth of the Tiber River. It was the first colony founded by ancient Rome and was a major port and commercial centre. Now located about 6 km (4 miles) inland, the original city was buried, its ruins preserved by the gradual silting up of the Tiber.

os·tin·ato /ˌɒstɪˈnatəʊ/ *noun* (*pl.* **-atos** or **-ati**) (often *attributive*) *Music* a persistent phrase or rhythm repeated through all or part of a piece. [Italian, = OBSTINATE]

os·tium /ˈɒstiəm/ *noun* (*pl.* **ostia** /ˈɒstiə/) *Anat. & Zool.* an opening into a vessel or body cavity. [Latin, = door, opening]

ostler /ˈɒslər/ *noun Brit. hist.* = HOSTLER. [from earlier HOSTLER, *hosteler* from Anglo-French *hostiler*, Old French *(h)ostelier* (as HOSTEL)]

Ost·mark /ˈɒstmɑːrk/ *noun hist.* the chief monetary unit of the German Democratic Republic. [German, = east mark: see MARK²]

os·tomy /ˈɒstəmi/ *noun* (*pl.* **-mies**) *Med.* **1** an operation that involves making a permanent artificial opening in the body. **2** an opening so made. [extracted from *colostomy*, *ileostomy*, etc.]

Ost·polit·ik /ˈɒstpɒliˌtiːk/ *noun hist.* the foreign policy, esp. of détente, of many western European countries with reference to the Communist bloc. [German from *Ost* east + *Politik* politics]

os·tra·cize /ˈɒstrəˌsaɪz/ *transitive verb* (also esp. *Brit.* **-cise**) **1** exclude (a person) from a society, favour, privileges, etc. by common consent; refuse to associate with. **2** (esp. in ancient Athens) banish (a too powerful or unpopular citizen) for five or ten years by popular vote. □ **os·tra·cism** /-ˌsɪzəm/ *noun* [Greek *ostrakizō* from *ostrakon* shell, potsherd (used to write a name on in voting)]

Os·trava /ˈɒstrəvə/ an industrial city in the NE Czech Republic; pop. (2001) 312,293.

os·trich *noun* **1** a large African swift-running flightless bird, *Struthio camelus*, with long legs and two toes on each foot. **2** a person who refuses to accept facts (from the false belief that ostriches bury their heads in the sand when pursued). □ **os·trich·like** *adjective* [Old French *ostric(h)e* from Latin *avis* bird + Late Latin *struthio* from Greek *strouthiōn* ostrich, from *strouthos* sparrow, ostrich]

ostrich fern *noun* a fern, *Matteucia struthiopteris*, with separate fertile fronds, and sterile fronds shaped like ostrich feathers.

Os·tro·goth /ˈɒstrəˌgɒθ/ *noun hist.* a member of the Eastern branch of the Goths, who conquered Italy in the 5th–6th c. (*compare* VISIGOTH) □ **Os·tro·goth·ic** /-ˈgɒθɪk/ *adjective* [Late Latin *Ostrogothi* (pl.) from Germanic *austro-* (unrecorded) east + Late Latin *Gothi* Goths: see GOTH]

Ost·wald /ˈɒstvalt/ **(Frie·drich) Wil·helm** (1853–1932), German physical chemist. He conducted pioneering research on catalysis, and developed a new quantitative colour theory; he was awarded the Nobel Prize for chemistry in 1909.

Os·wald /ˈɒzwɒld/ **Lee Har·vey** (1939–63), alleged assassin of John F. Kennedy. In Nov. 1963 he was arrested in Dallas, Texas shortly after Kennedy's assassination and charged with his murder; he denied the charge, but was murdered by Jack Ruby (1911–67), a Dallas nightclub owner, before he could be brought to trial.

Os·wego tea /ɒsˈwiːgəʊ/ *noun* a N American bergamot, *Monarda didyma*, grown for its showy heads of scarlet flowers. [*Oswego* river and town in the northern part of New York State]

OT *abbreviation* **1 a** overtime. **b** *Football* offensive tackle. **2 a** occupational therapy. **b** occupational therapist. **3** Old Testament.

-ot¹ *suffix* forming nouns, originally diminutives (*ballot*; *chariot*; *parrot*). [French]

-ot² *suffix* **1** forming nouns denoting persons of a particular type of character (*patriot*; *zealot*; *idiot*). **2** forming nouns denoting persons from or native to a particular place (*Cypriot*). [French *-ote*, Latin *-ota*, Greek *-ōtēs*]

Otago /ɒˈtaːgəʊ/ a region of New Zealand, on the southeast coast of South Island. Formerly a province, it was centred on the settlement of Dunedin. [the name of a Maori village]

OTC *abbreviation* **1** = OVER-THE-COUNTER. **2** (in the UK) Officers' Training Corps.

other ● *adjective* **1** not the same as one or some already mentioned or implied; separate in identity or distinct in kind (*other people*; *use other means*; *revealed a quite other side of her personality*). **2 a** further; additional (*a few other examples*). **b** alternative of two (*open your other eye*) (*compare every other*; *see* EVERY). **3** (*prec. by the*) that remains after all except the one or ones in question have been considered, eliminated, etc. (*must be in the other pocket*; *where are the other two?*; *the other three men left*). **4** (foll. by *than*) **a** apart from; excepting (*any person other than you*). **b** different in kind or quality (*might be other than what she seemed*). ● *noun or pronoun* **1** an additional, different, or extra person, thing, example, etc. (*one or other of us will be there*; *some others have come*) (*see also* ANOTHER, EACH OTHER). **2** (in *pl.*; *prec. by the*) the ones remaining, the different ones (*where are the others?*). **3** (usu. **Other** or in quotation marks, *prec. by the*) *Philos. & Sociol.* that which is distinct, different from, or opposite to something or oneself (*fear of the 'other'*). ● *adverb* (usu. foll. by *than*) disputed otherwise (*cannot react other than angrily*). □ **no other** *archaic* nothing else (*I can do no other*). **of all others** out of the many possible or likely (*on this night of all others*). **on the other hand** *see* HAND. **the other day** (or **night** or **week** etc.) a few days etc. ago (*heard from him the other day*). **other things being equal** if conditions are or were alike in all but the point in question. **someone** (or **something** or **somehow** etc.). **or other** some unspecified person, thing, manner, etc. [Old English *ōther*, from Germanic]

other-direct·ed *adjective* governed by external circumstances and trends. □ **other-direct·ed·ness** *noun*

other half *noun* **1** *jocular* one's spouse. **2** *informal* (prec. by *the*) a group of people having different, esp. markedly superior or inferior, social, cultural, or economic standing (*how the other half lives*). **3** the rest, the remainder, or esp. the second of two equal parts.

other·ness *noun* **1** the state or fact of being other or different. **2** a thing or existence separate from or other than the thing mentioned and the thinking subject.

other place *noun* (prec. by *the*) *jocular* **1** hell (as opposed to heaven). **2 a** *Cdn* the Senate as regarded by the House of Commons and vice versa. **b** *Brit.* the House of Lords as regarded by the House of Commons and vice versa. **3** *Brit.* Oxford University as regarded by Cambridge, and vice versa.

other ranks *plural noun Cdn, Brit., Austral.*, & *NZ* non-commissioned officers and ordinary soldiers, sailors, etc.

other side *noun* the afterlife; the abode of the dead.

other·where *adjective archaic* elsewhere.

other·wise ● *adverb* **1** else; or else; in the circumstances other than those considered etc. (*bring your umbrella, otherwise you will get wet*). **2** in other respects (*he is untidy, but otherwise very suitable*). **3** (often foll. by *than*) in another way, differently (*could not have acted otherwise*). **4** as an alternative (*otherwise known as Josh*). ● *adjective* (*predicative*) different, other (*the matter is quite otherwise*). □ **and** (or **or**) **otherwise** the negation or opposite (of a specified thing) (*the merits or otherwise of the bill*; *experiences pleasant and otherwise*). [Old English *on ōthre wisan* (as OTHER, WISE²)]

other woman *noun* a married man's mistress.

other world *noun* **1** = NEXT WORLD. **2** (also **other·world**) **a** an alternate reality or state of consciousness. **b** (esp. in science fiction etc.) a fantastic or extraterrestrial planet or culture.

other·world·ly *adjective* **1** concerned with spiritual matters, life after death, etc. **2** of or pertaining to an imaginary, ideal, or fantastic world. **3** unworldly; impractical. □ **other·world·li·ness** *noun*

Othman I see OSMAN I.

Otho /ˈoʊθoʊ/ **Mar·cus Sal·vius** (AD 32–69), Roman emperor Jan.–Apr. 69. He was proclaimed emperor after he had procured the death of Galba in a conspiracy of the Praetorian Guard; Otho's troops were subsequently defeated by the German legions under a rival candidate, Vitellius, and Otho committed suicide.

Otho I /ˈoʊθoʊ/ *var. of* OTTO I.

otic *adjective* of or relating to the ear. [Greek *ōtikos* from *ous ōtos* ear]

-otic *suffix* forming adjectives and nouns corresponding to nouns in *-osis*, meaning 'affected with or producing or resembling a condition in *-osis*' or 'a person affected with this' (*narcotic*; *neurotic*; *osmotic*). □ **-otically** *suffix* [from or after French *-otique* from Latin from Greek *-ōtikos* adj. suffix]

oti·ose /ˈoʊtɪoʊs, ˈoʊʃ-, -oʊz/ *adjective* serving no practical purpose; not required; functionless. □ **oti·ose·ness** *noun* [Latin *otiosus* from *otium* leisure]

ot·itis /oʊˈtaɪtɪs/ *noun* inflammation of the ear. [modern Latin (as OTO-)]

ot·itis media *noun* inflammation of the middle ear.

oto- /ˈoʊtoʊ/ *combining form* ear. [Greek *ōto-* from *ous ōtos* ear]

oto·laryn·gol·ogy /ˌoʊtəˌlærɪnˈɡɒlədʒi/ *noun* the study of diseases of the ear and throat. □ **oto·laryn·go·logic·al** *adjective* **oto·laryn·gol·o·gist** *noun*

oto·lith /ˈoʊtəlɪθ/ *noun* any of the small particles of calcium carbonate found in the inner ear of vertebrates, important as sensors of gravity and acceleration. □ **oto·lith·ic** /-ˈlɪθɪk/ *adjective*

otol·ogy /oʊˈtɒlədʒi/ *noun* the study of the anatomy, functions, and diseases of the ear. □ **oto·logic·al** /-təˈlɒdʒɪkəl/ *adjective* **otol·o·gist** *noun*

O'Toole, **Peter Seamus** (b.1932), Irish-born British actor. He came to international prominence in *Lawrence of Arabia* (1962). Other films include *Goodbye Mr Chips* (1969) and *The Last Emperor* (1987); he is especially noted for his polished portrayals of unpredictable or eccentric characters.

oto·rhino·laryn·gol·ogy /ˌoʊtəˌraɪnoʊˌlærɪnˈɡɒlədʒi/ *noun* the study of diseases of the ear, nose, and throat. □ **oto·rhino·laryn·gol·o·gist** *noun*

oto·scope /ˈoʊtəˌskoʊp/ *noun* an apparatus for examining the eardrum

and the passage leading to it from the ear. □ **oto·scop·ic** /-ˈskɒpɪk/ *adjective*

Ot·ran·to, Strait of /ɒˈtrantoʊ/ a channel linking the Adriatic Sea with the Ionian Sea and separating the 'heel' of Italy from Albania.

OTT *abbreviation Brit.* = OVER THE TOP 2 (see TOP¹).

ottava rima /ɒˌtavə ˈriːmə/ *noun* a stanza of eight lines of 10 or 11 syllables, rhyming *abababcc*. [Italian, lit. eighth rhyme]

Ot·tawa¹ /ˈɒtəwɒ, -wə/ the federal capital of Canada, situated in E Ontario on the Ottawa River, opposite Gatineau; pop. (2001) 774,072. □ **Ot·ta·wan** *noun & adjective* [after the ODAWA, to honour the bicentennial of fur trading between them and the French *c.*1854]

Ot·tawa² /ˈɒtəwɒ, -wə/ *noun* = ODAWA.

Ottawa River /ˈɒtəwɒ, -wə/ a river, 1 271 km long, which rises in the Laurentian Highlands of SW Quebec, and flows generally southeastward, forming the southern boundary between Quebec and Ontario, to join the St. Lawrence just southwest of Montreal. [perhaps Algonquian *adawe* trade or buy and sell]

Otter, **Sir Wil·liam Dil·lon** (1843–1929), Canadian soldier. Commander of the Battleford column in the North-West Campaign of 1885, he became the first commanding officer of the Royal Canadian Regiment of Infantry in 1893 and led the first Canadian contingent to the South African War in 1899. In 1908 he served as the first Canadian-born chief of the general staff, and he was knighted after his retirement in 1912.

ot·ter *noun* **1 a** any of several semi-aquatic fish-eating mammals of the family Mustelidae, esp. of the genus *Lutra*, having strong claws and webbed feet and noted for the agility of its swimming. **b** its fur or pelt. **2** = SEA OTTER. [Old English *otr*, *ot(t)or* from Germanic]

otter board *noun* a device, usu. consisting of two boards or metal plates attached to the ends of a trawl net, for keeping the mouth of the net open.

Otter·burn Park a town in S Quebec, situated on the Richelieu, south of Mont-Saint-Hilaire; pop. (2001) 7,866. □ **Otter·burn·er** *noun* [after *Otterburn*, in Northumberland, England]

otter trawl *noun* a cone-shaped net, the mouth held open with an otter board, that is dragged along the ocean floor to catch groundfish, esp. cod and haddock.

Otto, **Niko·laus Aug·ust** (1832–91), German engineer, whose name is given to the four-stroke cycle on which most internal combustion engines work.

Otto I (known as 'Otto the Great') (912–73), king of the Germans 936–73, Holy Roman emperor 962–73. As king of the Germans he carried out a policy of eastward expansion and defeated the invading Hungarians (955), and as Holy Roman emperor he established a strong imperial presence in Italy to rival that of the papacy.

otto *noun var. of* ATTAR.

Otto·man /ˈɒtəmən/ ● *adjective hist.* **1** of or concerning the dynasty of Osman or Othman I, the branch of the Turks to which he belonged, or the empire ruled by his descendants (see OTTOMAN EMPIRE). **2** Turkish. ● *noun* an Ottoman person; a Turk. [French from Arabic *'utmānī* adj. of Othman (*'utmān*)]

otto·man /ˈɒtəmən/ *noun* a footstool or low upholstered seat, usu. square and without a back or arms, sometimes serving as a box. [French *ottomane* fem. (as OTTOMAN)]

Ottoman Empire the Turkish Empire, established in northern Anatolia by Osman or Othman at the end of the 13th c. and expanded by his successors to include all of Asia Minor and much of SE Europe. Having captured Constantinople in 1453, the empire reached its zenith under Suleiman in the mid-16th c., dominating the eastern Mediterranean and threatening central Europe. Thereafter it began to decline, though it remained powerful in the 17th c.; the empire collapsed after the First World War.

Oua·ga·dou·gou /ˌwɒɡəˈduːɡuː/ the capital of Burkina Faso; pop. (est. 2002) 839,800.

oua·na·niche /ˈwɒnənɪʃ/ *noun Cdn* a landlocked lake variety of Atlantic salmon, found in Newfoundland and Labrador, Quebec, and Ontario. [Canadian French from Montagnais *wananish* 'little salmon']

oubli·ette /ˌuːbliˈet/ *noun* a secret dungeon with access only through a trap door. [French from *oublier* forget]

ouch *interjection* expressing pain or annoyance. [imitative: compare German *autsch*]

Ouden·arde, Battle of /ˈuːdəˌnɑrd/ a battle which took place in 1708 during the War of the Spanish Succession, near the town of Oudenarde in eastern Flanders, Belgium, in which allied British and

Austrian troops under the Duke of Marlborough and the Austrian general Prince Eugene defeated the French.

Oudh /aud/ (also **Audh, Awadh** /ˈʌwəd/) a region of N India. After annexation by Britain in 1856 it became the centre of the Indian Mutiny of 1857–8. In 1877 it joined with Agra and formed the United Provinces of Agra and Oudh in 1902. This was renamed Uttar Pradesh in 1950.

ought[1] *auxiliary verb* (usu. foll. by *to* + infin.; present and past indicated by the following infin.) **1** expressing duty or rightness (*we ought to love our neighbours*). **2** expressing shortcoming (*it ought to have been done long ago*). **3** expressing advisability or prudence (*you ought to go for your own good*). **4** expressing esp. strong probability (*he ought to be there by now*). [Old English *āhte*, past of *āgan* OWE]

ought[2] *noun* (also **aught**) *informal* a figure denoting nothing; nought. [perhaps from *an ought* for a NOUGHT; compare ADDER]

ought[3] *var. of* AUGHT[1].

oughtn't *contraction* ought not.

ou·guiya /uːˈɡiːjə/ *noun* (also **ou·giya**) the basic monetary unit of Mauritania, equal to five khoums. [French from Mauritanian Arabic *ūgiyya*, ultimately from Latin *uncia* ounce]

Ouiat·chou·ane, Chute /wiatʃuˈɒn/ a waterfall in NE central Quebec, 79 m high, situated on the south shore of Lac Saint-Jean at the mouth of the Rivière Ouiatchouane.

Ouija /ˈwiːdʒiː, -dʒə/ *noun* (in full **Ouija board**) *proprietary* a board having letters or signs at its rim to which a planchette points under supposedly spiritualistic influence in answer to questions from attenders at a seance etc. [French *oui* yes + German *ja* yes]

Oulu /ˈaulu/ a city in central Finland, on the west coast, capital of a province of the same name; pop. (2001) 123,374.

ounce[1] *noun* **1 a** a unit of weight of one-sixteenth of a pound avoirdupois (approx. 28 grams). Abbr.: **oz. b** a unit of one-twelfth of a pound troy or apothecaries' measure, equal to 480 grains (approx. 31 grams). **2** = FLUID OUNCE. **3** a small quantity. [Old French *unce* from Latin *uncia* twelfth part of pound or foot: compare INCH[1]]

ounce[2] /auns/ *noun* = SNOW LEOPARD. [Old French *once* (earlier *lonce*) = Italian *lonza*, ultimately from Latin *lynx*: see LYNX]

oun·cer *noun* (in *combination*) a thing that weighs or consists of a specified number of ounces (*a forty-ouncer of rye whisky*).

our *possessive adjective* (*attributive*) **1** of or belonging to us or ourselves (*our house; our own business*). **2** of or belonging to all people (*our children's future*). **3** (esp. as **Our**) of Us the king or queen, emperor or empress, etc. (*given under Our seal*). **4** of us, the editorial staff of a newspaper etc. (*a foolish adventure in our view*). **5** *Brit. informal* indicating a relative, acquaintance, or colleague of the speaker (*our Barry works there*). [Old English *ūre* originally genitive pl. of 1st person pronoun = of us, later treated as possessive adj.]

-our[1] *suffix var. of* -OR[2] surviving in some nouns (*ardour; colour; valour*).

-our[2] *suffix var. of* -OR[1] (*saviour*).

Our Fath·er *noun Christianity* **1** the Lord's Prayer. **2** God.

Our Lady *noun Christianity* **1** the Virgin Mary. **2** an image or representation of the Virgin Mary.

Our Lady's bedstraw *noun* a yellow-flowered European plant, *Galium verum*, of dry grassland.

Our Lord *noun* **1** *Christianity* Jesus Christ. **2** God.

ours *possessive pronoun* the one or ones belonging to or associated with us (*it is ours; ours are over there*). □ **of ours** of or belonging to us (*a friend of ours*).

our·self *pronoun* **1** *archaic* a word formerly used instead of *myself* by a sovereign, newspaper editorial staff, etc. (compare OUR 3, 4). **2** *disputed* = OURSELVES. ¶ The use of *ourself* rather than *ourselves* in contexts such as *We see ourself as the biggest club in Canada*, is considered incorrect by some people.

our·selves *pronoun* **1 a** *emphatic form of* WE or US (*we ourselves did it; made it ourselves; for our friends and ourselves*). **b** *reflexive form of* US (*are pleased with ourselves*). **2** in our normal state of body or mind (*not quite ourselves today*). □ **be ourselves** act in our normal unconstrained manner. **by ourselves** *see* by oneself (*see* BY).

-ous *suffix* **1** forming adjectives meaning 'abounding in, characterized by, of the nature of' (*envious; glorious; mountainous; poisonous*). **2** *Chem.* denoting a state of lower valence than the corresponding word in *-ic* (*ferrous*). □ **-ously** *suffix*. **-ousness** *suffix*. [from or after Anglo-French *-ous*, Old French *-eus*, from Latin *-osus*]

ousel *noun var. of* OUZEL.

Ouse River /uːz/ **1** (also **Great Ouse**) a river of E England, which

rises in Northamptonshire and flows 257 km (160 miles) eastward then northward through East Anglia to the Wash near King's Lynn. **2** a river of NE England, formed at the confluence of the Ure and Swale in North Yorkshire and flowing 92 km (57 miles) southeastward through York to the Humber estuary.

oust /aust/ *transitive verb* **1** remove (a person) from a job or position of power, esp. by forcing oneself in. **2** (usu. foll. by *of*) *Law* put (a person) out of possession; deprive. □ **oust·ed** *adjective* [Anglo-French *ouster*, Old French *oster* take away, from Latin *obstare* oppose, hinder (as OB-, *stare* stand)]

oust·er /ˈaustər/ *noun* **1** a removal (of a person), esp. from a position of power, as a result of physical action, judicial process, or political upheaval. **2** esp. *N Amer.* dismissal, expulsion.

out ● *adverb* **1 a** away from or not in or at a place etc. (*keep her out; get out of here*). **b** *Cdn* (*North*) in or to the more southern or heavily populated part of the country. **2** (forming part of phrasal verbs) **a** indicating dispersal away from a centre etc. (*hire out; share out; board out*). **b** indicating a progression to a conclusion or resolution (*die out; fight it out*). **c** indicating coming or bringing into the open for public attention etc. (*call out; send out; shine out; stand out*). **d** indicating a need for attentiveness (*watch out; look out*). **3 a** not in one's house, office, etc. (*went out for a walk*). **b** occupied elsewhere, esp. socially (*out with friends*). **c** no longer detained in prison. **4 a** completely; thoroughly (*tired out*). **b** in its entirety (*typed it out*). **5** (of a fire, candle, etc.) not burning. **6** in error (*was 3 per cent out in my calculations*). **7** *informal* unconscious (*she was out for five minutes*). **8** (of a tooth) extracted. **b** (of a joint, bone, etc.) dislocated (*put his shoulder out*). **9** (of a party, politician, etc.) not in office. **10** (of a jury) considering its verdict in secrecy. **11** (of workers) on strike. **12 a** (of a secret) revealed. **b** *informal* (of a person) having declared to other people that one is homosexual (*I always knew I was gay, but I've only been out for two years*). **13** (of a flower) blooming, open. **14** (of a book etc.) **a** published; on the market (*my third novel will be out this fall; their new CD is just out*). **b** not in the library; currently on loan to someone else. **15** (of a star) visible after dark. **16** unfashionable (*wide ties are out*). **17 a** *Baseball* (of a batter) having failed to get on base. **b** *Baseball* (of a runner) having failed to advance from one base to another. **c** (of a shot, serve, etc.) outside the boundary of the playing area. **18** not worth considering; rejected (*that idea is out*). **19** *informal* (prec. by *superlative*) known to exist (*the best game out*). **20** (of a stain, mark, etc.) not visible, removed (*painted out the sign*). **21** (of time) not spent working (*took five minutes out*). **22** having lost in a transaction (*am out $50 on the deal*). **23** (of the tide) at the lowest point. **24** *Boxing* unable to rise from the floor (*out for the count*). **25 a** at an end; over (*before the week is out*). **b** (in a radio conversation etc.) indicating that a transmission has come to an end (*over and out*). **26** *archaic* (of a young upper-class woman) introduced into society. ● *preposition* **1** out of (*looked out the window*). **2** *archaic* outside; beyond the limits of. ● *noun* **1** *informal* a way of escape; an excuse. **2** *Baseball* the action or an act of putting a player out. ● *adjective* **1** *informal* (of a person) openly homosexual (*an out lesbian*). **2** *Brit.* (of a game) played away. **3** (of an island) away from the mainland. ● *interjection* a peremptory dismissal, reproach, etc. (*out, you scoundrel!*). ● *verb* **1** *transitive* **a** put out. **b** *informal* eject forcibly. **2** *intransitive* come or go out; emerge (*murder will out*). **3** *transitive informal* **a** reveal the homosexuality of (esp. a prominent person). **b** reveal a previously unknown fact about (a person). **4** *transitive Boxing* knock out. □ **on the outs** *N Amer.* at variance or enmity. **out and about** (of a person, esp. after an illness) engaging in normal activity. **out and away** by far. **out at elbows** *see* ELBOW. **out for** having one's interest or effort directed to; intent on. **out in left field** *see* LEFT FIELD. **out like a light** *see* LIGHT[1]. **out of 1** from within (*came out of the house*). **2** not within (*I was never out of the province*). **3** from among (*nine people out of ten; must choose out of these*). **4** beyond the range of (*is out of reach*). **5** without or so as to be without (*was swindled out of her money; out of breath; out of sugar*). **6** from (*get the money out of your parents*). **7** owing to (*asked out of curiosity*). **8** by the use of (material) (*what did you make it out of?*). **9** at a specified distance from (a town, port, etc.) (*seven miles out of Moncton*). **10** beyond (*something out of the ordinary*). **11** *Racing* (of an animal, esp. a horse) born of. **12** as depicted in (a fictional work) (*a scene straight out of Dickens*). **out of bounds** *see* BOUND[2]. **out of doors** *see* DOOR. **out of hand** *see* HAND. **out of it** *N Amer. informal* **1** dazed, dopey. **2** out of touch; not up to date. **out of the loop** *see* LOOP *noun* 11. **out of order** *see* ORDER. **out of pocket** *see* POCKET. **out of the question** *see* QUESTION. **out of sorts** *see* SORT. **out of temper** *see* TEMPER. **out of this world** *see* WORLD. **out of the way** *see* WAY. **out of the woods** *see* WOODS. **out there** *informal* avant-garde, offbeat. **out to** keenly striving to do. **out with** an exhortation to expel or dismiss (an unwanted person). **out with it** say what you are thinking. [Old English *ūt*, Old High German *ūz*, related to Sanskrit *ud-*]

out- *prefix* added to verbs and nouns, meaning: **1** so as to surpass or exceed (*outdo*; *outnumber*). **2** external, separate (*outline*; *outhouse*; *outdoors*). **3** out of; away from; outward (*outspread*; *outgrowth*).

outa *var. of* OUTTA.

out·age *noun* **1** an interruption in supply, esp. of electricity. **2** a period of time during which this happens.

out-and-out ● *adjective* in every respect; complete (*an out-and-out crook*). ● *adverb* completely; totally (*out-and-out lying*).

Outa·ouais /ˈuːtaweɪ/ *noun* a region in SW Quebec along the Ottawa River valley, encompassing the city of Gatineau and surrounding towns. [French name of the Ottawa River]

Ou·tardes, Ri·vière aux /uːˈtɑrd/ a river in NE central Quebec, about 400 km long, which rises northeast of Lac Mistassini and flows southeastward to empty into the St. Lawrence just southwest of Baie-Comeau. [French, = bustard river, with reference to Canada geese]

out·back *noun* esp. *Austral.* the remote and usu. uninhabited inland districts. □ **out·back·er** *noun*

out basket *noun N Amer.* a tray or basket, esp. on a person's desk, for outgoing documents etc.

out·bid *transitive verb* (**-bid·ding**; *past* and *past participle* **-bid**) bid higher than (another person) at an auction etc.

out·board ● *adjective* **1** (of a motor) portable and attachable to the outside of the stern of a boat. **2** (of a boat) having an outboard motor. **3** located on, near, or towards the outside of an aircraft, ship, etc. ● *adverb* on, towards, or near the outside of a ship, aircraft, etc. ● *noun* **1** an outboard engine. **2** a boat with an outboard engine.

out·bound *adjective* outward bound.

out·break *noun* a usu. sudden eruption of emotion, war, disease, rebellion, etc.

out·breed *transitive & intransitive verb* (*past* and *past participle* **-bred**) breed from parents not closely related.

out·build·ing *noun* a detached building, e.g. a shed, barn, garage, etc., that is separate from but within the grounds of a main building.

out·burst *noun* **1** an explosion of anger etc., expressed in words. **2** a sudden eruption or explosion of activity etc.

out·call *noun* a visit by an escort, prostitute, etc., to the address of the caller.

out·cast ● *noun* **1** a person cast out from or rejected by his or her home, country, society, etc. **2** a tramp or vagabond. ● *adjective* rejected; homeless; friendless.

out·caste ● *noun* /ˈaʊtkɑst/ (also *attributive*) **1** a person who has no caste, esp. in Hindu society. **2** a person who has lost his or her caste. ● *transitive verb* /-ˈkɑst/ cause (a person) to lose his or her caste.

out·class *transitive verb* **1** belong to a higher class than. **2** defeat easily. **3** (usu. in *passive*) be superior to.

out·come *noun* a result; a visible effect.

out·crop ● *noun* (also **out·crop·ping**) **1 a** the emergence of a stratum, vein, or rock, at the surface. **b** a stratum etc. emerging. **2** a noticeable manifestation or occurrence. ● *intransitive verb* (**-cropped**, **-crop·ping**) appear as an outcrop; crop out.

out·cross ● *transitive & intransitive verb* cross (an animal, plant, breed, or stock) with one not closely related. ● *noun* a cross with an unrelated breed or race.

out·cry *noun* (pl. **-cries**) **1** a vehement or prolonged public protest. **2** an uproar. **3** the act or an instance of crying out.

out·dated *adjective* out of date; obsolete.

out·dis·tance *transitive verb* **1** leave (a competitor) behind completely. **2** be vastly superior to.

outdo *transitive verb* (*3rd sing. present* **-does**; *past* **-did**; *past participle* **-done**) exceed or surpass in doing or performance.

out·door *adjective* **1** done, existing, or used out of doors. **2** fond of the open air (*an outdoor type*).

out·doors ● *adverb* in or into the open air; out of doors. ● *adjective* = OUTDOOR *adjective* 2. ● *noun* the world outside buildings; the open air.

out·doors·man *noun* (pl. **-men**) a person who enjoys or frequently participates in outdoor activities.

out·doors·woman *noun* (pl. **-women**) a woman who enjoys or frequently participates in outdoor activities.

out·doorsy *adjective* **1** associated with or characteristic of the outdoors. **2** (of a person) fond of an outdoor life or outdoor activities.

out·er ● *adjective* **1** outside; external (*pierced the outer layer*). **2** farther from the centre or inside; relatively far out. **3** objective or physical, not subjective. ● *noun Brit.* **1 a** the division of a target furthest from the bull's eye. **b** a shot that strikes this. **2** an outer container for transport or display.

outer garment *noun* an article of clothing worn over other clothes or outdoors.

Outer Heb·ri·des see HEBRIDES, THE.

Outer Mon·go·lia see MONGOLIA.

outer·most *adjective* furthest from the inside; the most far out.

outer planet *noun* any of the five planets Jupiter, Saturn, Uranus, Neptune, and Pluto, whose orbits are beyond the asteroid belt.

outer space *noun* the universe beyond the earth's atmosphere.

outer·wear *noun* clothing, such as a coat, that is worn over other clothing to provide warmth or protection while outdoors.

out·face *transitive verb* **1** disconcert or defeat by or as if by staring. **2** face boldly or defiantly; defy.

out·fall *noun* the outlet of a river, drain, sewer, etc.

out·field *noun* **1** the part of a baseball field that lies outside of the baseline. **2** the positions in this space, i.e. right, left, and centre field. **3** the players who occupy these positions. □ **out·field·er** *noun*

out·fight *transitive verb* (*past* and *past participle* **-fought**) fight better than; beat in a fight.

out·fit ● *noun* **1** a set of clothes worn or esp. designed to be worn together. **2** a complete set of equipment etc. for a specific purpose. **3** a business or company engaged in a particular type of work (*owns a construction outfit*). **4** a military unit (*my outfit was sent overseas for peacekeeping duty*). **5** a group of musicians (*joined a jazz outfit*). ● *transitive verb* (also *reflexive*) (**-fit·ted**, **-fit·ting**) provide with an outfit, e.g. of clothes or equipment.

out·fit·ter *noun* **1** *N Amer.* **a** a supplier of equipment for outdoor activities such as hiking trips etc. **b** a person who acts as guide on wilderness trips etc. **2** *Brit.* a supplier of conventional styles of clothing.

out·flank *transitive verb* **1 a** extend one's flank beyond that of (an enemy). **b** outmanoeuvre (an enemy) in this way. **2** get the better of; confound (an opponent).

out·flow *noun* **1** an outward flow. **2** the amount that flows out.

out·fly *transitive verb* (**-flies**; *past* **-flew**; *past participle* **-flown**) **1** surpass in flying. **2** fly faster or farther than.

out·fox *transitive verb informal* outwit.

out·gas *verb* (**out·gas·es**, **outgassed**, **out·gas·sing**) **1** *intransitive* release or give off a dissolved or adsorbed gas or vapour. **2** *transitive* **a** release or give off (a substance) as a gas or vapour. **b** drive off a gas or vapour from.

outgo *noun* (pl. **-goes**) expenditure of money, effort, etc.

out·going ● *adjective* **1** friendly; sociable; extrovert. **2** retiring from office. **3** going out or away. ● *noun* **1** (in *pl.*) expenditure. **2** the act or an instance of going out.

out·gross *transitive verb* surpass (another film, etc.) in gross earnings or profit.

out·group *noun* a group perceived as outsiders by members of an in-group.

out·grow *transitive verb* (*past* **-grew**; *past participle* **-grown**) **1** grow too big for (one's clothes). **2** leave behind (a childish habit, taste, ailment, etc.) as one matures. **3** grow faster or taller than (a person, plant, etc.).

out·growth *noun* **1** something that grows out. **2** an offshoot; a natural product. **3** the process of growing out.

out·guess *transitive verb* guess correctly what is intended by (another person).

out·gun *transitive verb* (**-gunned**, **-gun·ning**) **1** surpass in military or other power or strength. **2** shoot better than.

out·harbour *noun Cdn* (*Nfld*) = OUTPORT 1.

out·house *noun* **1** *N Amer.* an outdoor toilet that is enclosed but separate from the main building. **2** an outbuilding.

out·hustle *transitive verb* surpass in hustling.

out·ing *noun* **1** a short holiday away from home, esp. of one day or part of a day; a pleasure trip, an excursion. **2** any brief journey from home. **3** a public appearance in a game, race, etc. **4** *informal* the practice or policy of revealing the homosexuality of a prominent person.

out·jump *transitive verb* surpass in jumping.

out·land·er *noun* a foreigner, alien, or stranger.

out·land·ish *adjective* **1** bizarre, strange, unfamiliar. **2** *archaic* looking

t top   v voice   w we   z zoo   ʃ she   ʒ vision   θ thin   ð this   ŋ ring   x loch   tʃ chip   dʒ jar   (*see over for vowels*)

or sounding foreign. □ **out·land·ish·ly** *adverb* **out·land·ish·ness** *noun* [Old English *útlendisc* from *útland* foreign country, from OUT + LAND]

out·last *transitive verb* last longer than or beyond; survive (*outlasted its usefulness*).

out·law ● *noun* **1** a fugitive from the law. **2** *hist.* a person deprived of the protection of the law. **3** a person who does not conform to traditional or established practices. ● *transitive verb* **1** make illegal; prohibit (a practice etc.). **2** declare (a person) an outlaw. □ **out·lawry** *noun* [Old English *útlaga, útlagian* from Old Norse *útlagi* from *útlagr* outlawed, related to OUT, LAW]

out·lay *noun* **1** an amount of money spent; an expenditure. **2** an act or instance of spending money.

out·let *noun* **1** a means of exit or escape. **2** *N Amer.* a socket in a wall etc. for connecting an electrical appliance to a wiring system. **3** (usu. foll. by *for*) a means of expression (of a talent, emotion, etc.) (*find an outlet for tension*). **4 a** a place that sells merchandise made by a particular company or of a particular type; a store (*opened a new clothing outlet in Victoria*). **b** = FACTORY OUTLET. **5 a** a stream, river, or channel flowing out of and draining a larger body of water, e.g. a lake. **b** the mouth of a river.

outlet box *noun* **1** an electrical outlet. **2** a small metal box inserted in a wall etc., for containing an electrical outlet.

outlet pass *noun* Basketball a pass from a defending player to begin a fast break, usu. after the player has caught a rebound from a shot by the opposing team.

out·lier /ˈʌutˌlair/ *noun* **1** (also *attributive*) an outlying part or member. **2** *Geol.* a younger rock formation isolated in older rocks. **3** *Statistics* a result differing greatly from others in the same sample.

out·line ● *noun* **1** a rough statement of the main facts or points to be presented in a piece of writing, etc.; a summary. **2** a sketch containing only contour lines. **3** (in *sing.* or *pl.*) **a** lines enclosing or indicating an object (*the outline of a shape under the blankets*). **b** a contour. **c** an external boundary. **4** (in *pl.*) the main features or general principles (*the outlines of a plan*). ● *transitive verb* **1** describe the main features of; summarize. **2** draw in outline. **3** draw a line around (*the passage was outlined in red*). □ **in outline** sketched or represented as an outline.

out·live *transitive verb* **1** live longer than (another person). **2** live beyond (a specified date or time). **3** live through (an experience).

out·look *noun* **1** the prospect for the future (*the outlook is bleak*). **2** one's mental attitude or point of view (*narrow in their outlook*). **3** a view on which one looks out (*the house has a pleasant outlook over the valley*).

out·lying *adjective* situated far from a centre; remote.

out·man·oeuvre *transitive verb* (also **-man·eu·ver**) **1** use skill and cunning to secure an advantage over (a person). **2** outdo in manoeuvring.

out·match *transitive verb* be more than a match for (an opponent etc.); surpass.

out·migration *noun* the action of migrating from one place to another, esp. in the same country.

out·moded *adjective* **1** no longer in fashion. **2** obsolete.

out·most *adjective* **1** outermost, furthest. **2** uttermost. [Middle English, var. of *utmest* UTMOST]

out·muscle *transitive verb* surpass in strength.

out·num·ber *transitive verb* exceed in number.

out-of-body experience *noun* a sensation of being outside one's body, esp. of floating and being able to observe oneself from a distance.

out-of-court *attributive adjective* (esp. of a settlement) made or done outside or without the intervention of a court.

out of date *adjective* (hyphenated when *attributive*) old-fashioned, obsolete.

out-of-pocket *adjective* (of costs or expenses) paid out in cash (*out-of-pocket expenses*).

out of print *adjective* (of a book) no longer available from the publisher.

out-of-province *adjective Cdn* in, from, or pertaining to another province (*an out-of-province visitor; out-of-province health insurance*).

out-of-sight *adjective* **1** not visible. **2** *informal* excellent; delightful.

out-of-the-way *adjective* **1** remote; far from a main road or centre of population. **2** unusual; extraordinary.

out-of-town *attributive adjective* **1** originating from outside of a particular place (*had some out-of-town visitors*). **2** occurring in another place (*an out-of-town hockey tournament*). □ **out-of-towner** *noun*

out-of-work *adjective* unemployed.

out·pace *transitive verb* **1** go faster than. **2** outdo in a contest.

out·patient *noun* a person who receives treatment at a hospital without being hospitalized.

out·per·form *transitive verb* **1** perform better than. **2** surpass in a specified field or activity. □ **out·per·form·ance** *noun*

out·place·ment *noun* the act or process of finding new employment for esp. executive workers who have been dismissed or made redundant (also *attributive*: *outplacement consultant*).

out·play *transitive verb* surpass in playing; play better than.

out·point *transitive verb* (in various sports, esp. boxing) score more points than.

out·poll *transitive verb* receive more votes than (an opponent) in an election, opinion poll, etc. (*outpolled her closest competitor three to one*).

out·port *noun* **1** *Cdn* **a** (*Nfld*) any port other than St. John's, esp. a small, isolated fishing village. **b** (*Maritimes*) a coastal fishing village. **2** a subsidiary port.

out·port·er *noun Cdn* (*Nfld*) an inhabitant or native of an outport.

out·post *noun* **1** a detachment set at a distance from the main body of an army, esp. to prevent surprise. **2** a distant branch or settlement.

outpost camp *noun Cdn* a remote hunting or fishing camp.

out·pour·ing *noun* **1** a large amount of something produced in a short time (*a remarkable outpouring of new ideas*). **2** (usu. in *pl.*) an expression of very strong feelings (*outpourings of public grief*). **3** something that pours out (*an outpouring of water from the lake*).

out·put ● *noun* **1** the product of a process, esp. of manufacture, or of mental or artistic work. **2** the quantity or amount of this. **3** the printout, results, etc. supplied by a computer. **4** the power etc. delivered by an apparatus. **5** a place where energy, information, etc. leaves a system. ● *transitive verb* (**-put·ting**; past and past participle **-put** or **-put·ted**) **1** put or send out. **2** (of a computer) supply (results etc.).

out·rage ● *noun* **1** an extreme or shocking violation of others' rights, sentiments, etc. **2** a gross offence or indignity. **3** fierce anger or resentment (*a feeling of outrage*). ● *transitive verb* **1** subject to outrage. **2** injure, insult, etc. flagrantly. **3** shock and anger. □ **out·raged** *adjective* [Old French *outrage* from *outrer* exceed, from *outre* from Latin *ultra* beyond]

out·ra·geous /ʌutˈreidʒəs/ *adjective* **1** deeply shocking and unacceptable. **2** grossly cruel. **3** immoral, offensive. **4** highly unusual or unconventional. □ **out·ra·geous·ly** *adverb* **out·ra·geous·ness** *noun*

out·ran past of OUTRUN.

out·rank *transitive verb* **1** be superior in rank to. **2** take priority over.

outré /ˈuːtrei/ *adjective* outside the bounds of what is usual or proper. [French, past participle of *outrer*: see OUTRAGE]

out·reach ● *transitive verb* **1** reach further than. **2** surpass. **3** *literary* stretch out (one's arms etc.). ● *noun* **1** the activity of an organization in contacting, educating, and providing services, advice, etc. to people in the community, esp. outside its usual centres. **2** the extent or length of reaching out (*an outreach of 38 metres*).

Outre·mont /ˈuːtrəmɔ̃/ a former city in south central Quebec, located on the northern side of Mount Royal, now part of the city of Montreal; pop. (2001) 22,933. [French, lit. 'beyond the mountain']

out·ride *transitive verb* (past **-rode**; past participle **-rid·den**) **1** ride better, faster, or further than. **2** (of a ship) come safely through (a storm etc.).

out·rid·er *noun* **1** a mounted attendant riding ahead of, or with, a carriage etc. **2** a motorcyclist acting as a guard in a similar manner. □ **out·rid·ing** *noun*

out·rig·ger *noun* **1** a beam, spar, or framework, rigged out and projecting from or over a ship's side for various purposes. **2** a similar projecting beam etc. in a building. **3** a log etc. fixed parallel to a canoe to stabilize it. **4** a chassis extension supporting the body of a motor vehicle. **5 a** an iron bracket bearing an oarlock attached horizontally to a boat's side to increase the leverage of the oar. **b** a boat fitted with these. [OUT- + RIG: perhaps partly after obsolete (Naut.) *outligger*]

out·right ● *adverb* **1** altogether, entirely (*proved outright*). **2** not gradually, nor by degrees, nor by instalments (*bought it outright*). **3** without reservation, openly (*denied the charge outright*). ● *adjective* **1** downright, direct, complete (*their resentment turned to outright anger*). **2** undisputed, clear (*the outright winner*). □ **out·right·ness** *noun*

outro /ˈʌutroʊ/ *noun* (pl. **outros**) *informal* a concluding section, esp. of a broadcast program or a piece of music. [OUT, on the pattern of INTRO]

out·rode past of OUTRIDE.

out·run *transitive verb* (**-run·ning**; past **-ran**; past participle **-run**) **1 a** run

Vowels: a cat ɑ arm e bed ɜr her ɜː deux ə ago ɪ sit i cosy iː feed ɒ hot ɔ pore oː no ʌ run ʊ put

faster or farther than. **b** escape from. **2** go beyond (a specified point or limit).

out·score *transitive verb* score more than (an opponent) in a game etc.

out·sell *transitive verb* (*past* and *past participle* **-sold**) **1** sell more than. **2** be sold in greater quantities than.

out·set *noun* the start, beginning. □ **at** (or **from**) **the outset** from the beginning.

out·shine *transitive verb* (*past* and *past participle* **-shone**) **1** shine brighter than. **2** surpass in ability, excellence, etc.

out·shoot *transitive verb* (*past* and *past participle* **-shot**) **1** shoot better or further than (another person). **2** esp. *N Amer.* (in hockey, etc.) make more shots on (an opposing team) than the opposing team is able to make.

out·side ● *noun* **1** the external side or surface; the outer parts (*painted blue on the outside*). **2** the external appearance; the outward aspect of a building etc. **3** (of a path) the side away from the wall or next to the road. **4** (also *attributive*) all that is without; the world as distinct from the thinking subject (*learn about the outside world*; *viewed from the outside the problem is simple*). **5** a position on the outer side (*the gate opens from the outside*). **6** *informal* the highest computation (*it is a mile at the outside*). **7** *Cdn* (*North*) the rest of the world, esp. a more heavily populated or urban area. **8** *Brit.* an outside player in soccer etc. ● *adjective* **1** of or on or nearer the outside; outer. **2** not of or belonging to some circle or institution (*outside help*; *outside work*). **3** (of a chance etc.) remote; very unlikely. **4** (of an estimate etc.) the greatest or highest possible (*the outside price*). **5** (of a player in football etc.) positioned nearest to the edge of the field. **6** *Baseball* **a** (of a pitched ball) missing the plate on the side opposite the batter. **b** (of the strike zone) furthest away from the batter. **7** *Cdn* (*North*) of or relating to the rest of the world, esp. to a more heavily populated or urban area. ● *adverb* **1** on or to the outside. **2** in or to the open air. **3** not within or enclosed or included. **4** *Cdn* (*North*) in or to the rest of the world, esp. a more heavily populated or urban area. **5** *slang* not in prison. ● *preposition* **1** not in; to or at the exterior of (*meet me outside the post office*). **2** external to, not included in, beyond the limits of (*outside the law*). ¶ The use of *outside of* as a preposition, e.g. *There is nothing like it outside of Newfoundland*, is considered incorrect by some people, but is acceptable in both written and spoken English. □ **at the outside** (of an estimate etc.) at the most. **get outside of** *slang* eat or drink. **outside and in** outside and inside. **outside in** = INSIDE OUT. **outside of** esp. *N Amer. informal* apart from.

outside interest *noun* a hobby; an interest not connected with one's work or normal way of life.

out·sider *noun* **1 a** a non-member of some circle, party, profession, etc. **b** an uninitiated person, a layman. **2** a competitor, applicant, etc. thought to have little chance of success.

outsider art *noun* art produced by self-taught artists who are not part of the artistic establishment. □ **outsider artist** *noun*

out·size ● *adjective* **1** unusually large. **2** (of garments etc.) of an exceptionally large size. ● *noun* an exceptionally large person or thing, esp. a garment. □ **out·sized** *adjective*

out·skate *transitive verb* skate better, faster, etc. than.

out·skirts *plural noun* the outer border or fringe of a town, district, subject, etc.

out·smart *transitive verb* outwit, be cleverer than.

out·sold *past* and *past participle* of OUTSELL.

out·sole *noun* the outer sole of a boot or shoe, esp. a sports shoe.

out·source *transitive verb* esp. *N Amer. Commerce* **1** obtain (goods etc.) by contract from an outside source. **2** contract (work) out. □ **out·sourcer** *noun* **out·sourcing** *noun*

out·spend *transitive verb* (*past* and *past participle* **-spent**) spend more than (one's resources or another person).

out·spoken *adjective* given to or involving plain speaking; frank in stating one's opinions. □ **out·spoken·ly** *adverb* **out·spoken·ness** *noun*

out·spread ● *adjective* spread out; fully extended or expanded. ● *transitive & intransitive verb* (*past* and *past participle* **-spread**) spread out; expand.

out·stand·ing *adjective* **1 a** conspicuous, eminent, esp. because of excellence. **b** (usu. foll. by *at*, *in*) remarkable in (a specified field). **2** (esp. of a debt) not yet settled (*$200 still outstanding*). □ **out·stand·ing·ly** *adverb*

out·station *noun* **1** a branch of an organization, enterprise, or business in a remote area or at a considerable distance from

headquarters. **2** esp. *Austral. & NZ* part of a farming estate separate from the main estate.

out·stay *transitive verb* **1** stay beyond the limit of (one's welcome, invitation, etc.). **2** stay or endure longer than (another person etc.).

out·step *transitive verb* (**-stepped**, **-step·ping**) step outside or beyond.

out·stretch *transitive verb* **1** (usu. as **out·stretched** *adjective*) reach out or stretch out (esp. one's hands or arms). **2** reach or stretch further than.

out·strip *transitive verb* (**-stripped**, **-strip·ping**) **1** pass in running etc. **2** surpass in competition or relative progress or ability. **3** be or become faster than (*demand is outstripping supply*).

outta *preposition* (also **outa**) esp. *N Amer. informal* out of (*Quick! Let's get outta here!*). [reproducing a pronunciation of *out of*]

out·take *noun* a length of film or tape rejected in editing.

out·talk *transitive verb* outdo or overcome in talking.

out·think *transitive verb* (*past* and *past participle* **-thought**) outwit; outdo in thinking.

out·thrust ● *adjective* extended; projected (*ran forward with out-thrust arms*). ● *transitive verb* (*past* and *past participle* **-thrust**) thrust out. ● *noun* **1** the act or an instance of thrusting forcibly outward. **2** the act or an instance of becoming prominent or noticeable.

out to lunch *adjective* *informal* out of touch with reality; unaware; crazy.

out tray *noun* = OUT BASKET.

out-turn *noun* **1** *Curling* **a** an inward turn of the elbow and an outward turn of the hand made in delivering a stone, giving it a clockwise rotation. **b** a stone delivered with such a motion. **2** *Brit.* the result of a process or sequence of events.

out·vote *transitive verb* defeat by a majority of votes.

out·ward ● *adjective* **1** situated on or directed towards the outside. **2** going out (*on the outward voyage*). **3** bodily, external, apparent, superficial (*in all outward respects*). **4** *archaic* outer (*the outward man*). ● *adverb* (also **out·wards**) in an outward direction; towards the outside. ● *noun* the outward appearance of something; the exterior. □ **out·ward·ly** *adverb* **out·ward·ness** *noun*

outward bound *adjective* **1** (of a ship, passenger, etc.) going away from home. **2** (**Outward Bound**) a movement to provide adventure training, naval training, and other outdoor activities for young people.

out·wards *var.* of OUTWARD *adverb*.

out·wash *noun* the material carried from a glacier by meltwater and deposited beyond the moraine.

out·wear *transitive verb* (*past* **-wore**; *past participle* **-worn**) **1** exhaust; wear out; wear away. **2** live or last beyond the duration of.

out·weigh *transitive verb* exceed in weight, value, importance, or influence.

out·wit *transitive verb* (**-wit·ted**, **-wit·ting**) be too clever or crafty for; deceive by greater ingenuity.

out·with *preposition* *Scot.* outside, beyond.

out·wore *past* of OUTWEAR.

out·work ● *transitive verb* work harder or faster than. ● *noun* **1** an advanced or detached part of a fortification. **2** *Brit.* work done outside the shop or factory which supplies it. □ **out·work·er** *noun* (in sense 2 of *noun*).

out·worn ● *verb past participle* of OUTWEAR. ● *adjective* **1** obsolete; out of date. **2** worn out.

ouzel /ˈuːzəl/ *noun* (also **ousel**) **1** = WATER OUZEL. **2** *archaic* a blackbird. [Old English *ōsle* blackbird, of unknown origin]

ouzo /ˈuːzəʊ/ *noun* (*pl.* **ouzos**) a Greek aniseed-flavoured spirit. [modern Greek]

ova *pl.* of OVUM.

oval /ˈəʊvəl/ ● *adjective* **1** egg-shaped, ellipsoidal. **2** having the outline of an egg, elliptical. ● *noun* **1** an egg-shaped or elliptical closed curve. **2** any object with an oval outline. **3** an oval speed skating rink, racetrack, etc. [medieval Latin *ovalis* (as OVUM)]

Oval Office *noun* **1** the office of the US President in the White House. **2** this seen as representing the executive power of the US presidency (*the Oval Office is looking for a solution to the dispute*).

Ovam·bo /ɒˈvambəʊ/ ● *noun* (*pl.* same or **Ovam·bos**) **1** a member of a Bantu-speaking people inhabiting N Namibia. **2** the language of the Ovambo. ● *adjective* of or relating to the Ovambo or their language. [a local name, from *ova-* (prefix denoting a plural) + *ambo* 'man of leisure']

Ovam·bo·land /oːˈvamboˌland/ a semi-arid region of N Namibia, the homeland of the Ovambo people.

ovary /ˈoːvəri/ *noun* (*pl.* **-ies**) **1** each of the female reproductive organs in which ova are produced. **2** the hollow base of the carpel of a flower, containing one or more ovules. □ **ovar·ian** /əˈveriən/ *adjective*
ovari·ec·tomy /-rɪˈektəmi/ *noun* (*pl.* **-mies**) (in sense 1). [modern Latin *ovarium* (as OVUM)]

ovate /ˈoːveit/ *adjective* Biol. egg-shaped as a solid or in outline; oval. [Latin *ovatus* (as OVUM)]

ova·tion /oːˈveiʃən/ *noun* **1** an enthusiastic reception, esp. spontaneous and sustained applause. **2** Rom. Hist. a processional entrance into Rome by a victorious commander, of lesser honour than a triumph. □ **ova·tion·al** *adjective* [Latin *ovatio* from *ovare* exult]

oven /ˈʌvən/ *noun* **1** an enclosed compartment, e.g. as part of a stove, used for baking, roasting, heating, etc. **2** a small furnace or kiln used in chemistry, metallurgy, etc. [Old English *ofen* from Germanic]

oven·bird *noun* any of various birds that build a domed or globular nest of grass or mud, esp. the N American warbler *Seiurus aurocapillus* or a bird of the S American family Furnariidae.

oven mitt *noun* N Amer. an insulated mitten (usu. one of a pair) for handling hot pans etc.

oven·proof *adjective* suitable for use in an oven; heat-resistant.

oven-ready *adjective* (of food) prepared before sale so as to be ready for immediate cooking in the oven.

oven·ware *noun* dishes that can be used for cooking food in the oven.

over ● *adverb* expressing movement or position or state above or beyond something stated or implied: **1** outward and downward from a brink or from any erect position (*knocked the lamp over*). **2** so as to cover or touch a whole surface (*paint it over*). **3** so as to produce a fold, or reverse a position; with the effect of being upside down. **4 a** across a street or other space (*decided to cross over; came over from Europe*). **b** for a visit etc. (*invited them over last night*). **5** with transference or change from one hand or part to another (*went over to the Tories; handed them over*). **6** with motion above something; so as to pass across something (*climb over; fly over; boil over*). **7** from beginning to end with repetition or detailed concentration (*think it over; did it six times over*). **8** in excess; more than is right or required (*had one left over*). **9** for or until a later time (*held over*). **10** at an end; settled (*the crisis is over; all is over between us*). ● *preposition* **1** above, in, or to a position higher than; upon. **2** out and down from; down from the edge of (*fell over the cliff*). **3** so as to cover (*a hat over her eyes*). **4** above and across; so as to clear (*flew over Lake Huron; a bridge over the South Saskatchewan*). **5** concerning; as a result of; (*laughing over a good joke; had an argument over money*). **6** while engaged or occupied with (*fell asleep over the newspaper*). **7 a** superior to (*a victory over the enemy; it was Calgary over Toronto 6–5 in overtime*). **b** in charge of (*ruled over three kingdoms*). **c** in preference to (*I'd choose you over her any day*). **8** divided by. **9 a** throughout; covering the extent of (*travelled over most of the southern prairies; a blush spread over his face*). **b** so as to deal with completely (*went over the plans*). **10 a** for the duration of (*stay over Saturday night*). **b** at any point during the course of (*I'll do it over the weekend*). **11** beyond; more than (*bids of over $50; travelled over 60 miles to get here; are you over 18?*). **12** transmitted by (*heard it over the radio*). **13** in comparison with (*gained 20 per cent over last year*). **14** having recovered from (*am now over my cold; will get over it in time*). ● *adjective* (see also OVER-). **1** upper, outer. **2** superior. **3** extra. ● *interjection* (in full **over to you**) (in radio conversations etc.) said to indicate that it is the other person's turn to speak. □ **not over** not very; not at all (*not over friendly*). **over again** once again, again from the beginning. **over against** in an opposite situation to; adjacent to, in contrast with. **over all** taken as a whole. **over and above** in addition to; not to mention (*$100 over and above the asking price*). **over and over** so that the same thing or the same point comes up again and again (*said it over and over; rolled it over and over*). **over one's head** see HEAD. **over the hill** see HILL. **over the moon** see MOON. **over the top** see TOP¹. **over with** (also **over and done with**) (esp. of an unpleasant or disagreeable task, experience, etc.) finished, completed (*let's get it over with; glad to have that over with*). **start** (or **begin** etc.) **over** N Amer. begin again. [Old English *ofer* from Germanic]

over- *prefix* added to verbs, nouns, adjectives, and adverbs, meaning: **1** excessively; to an unwanted degree (*overheat; overdue*). **2** upper, outer, extra (*overcoat; overtime*). **3** 'over' in various senses (*overhang; overshadow*). **4** completely, utterly (*overawe; overjoyed*).

over·abun·dant *adjective* in excessive quantity.
□ **over·abun·dance** *noun* **over·abun·dant·ly** *adverb*

over·achieve *verb* **1** *intransitive* do more than might be expected (esp.

scholastically). **2** *transitive* achieve more than (an expected goal or objective etc.). □ **over·achieve·ment** *noun* **over·achiev·er** *noun*

over·act *transitive & intransitive verb* act in an exaggerated manner.

over·active *adjective* excessively active. □ **over·activ·ity** *noun*

over·age /ˈoːvəridʒ/ *noun* a surplus or excess, esp. an amount greater than estimated.

over·age *adjective* over a certain age limit; too old.

over·all ● *adjective* **1** total, inclusive of all (*overall cost*). **2** taking everything into account, general (*overall improvement*). **3** from end to end (*overall length*). ● *adverb* **1** in all parts; taken as a whole (*overall, the performance was excellent*). **2** when everything is included (*finished second in their division and eighth overall*). ● *noun* **1** (in *pl.*) = BIB OVERALLS. **2** esp. Brit. = COVERALL. □ **over·alled** *adjective*

over·ambitious *adjective* excessively ambitious. □ **over·ambition** *noun* **over·ambitious·ly** *adverb*

over·anxious *adjective* excessively anxious. □ **over·anxiety** *noun* **over·anxious·ly** *adverb*

over·arch *transitive verb* form an arch over.

over·arch·ing *adjective* **1** all-embracing; comprehensive. **2** forming an arch over.

over·arm *adjective & adverb* **1** = OVERHAND 1. **2** Swimming with one or both arms lifted out of the water during a stroke.

over·ate past of OVEREAT.

over·awe *transitive verb* cause (a person) to feel a great deal of fear, respect, etc.

over·bal·ance ● *verb* **1** *transitive* cause (a person or thing) to lose its balance and fall. **2** *intransitive* fall over, capsize. **3** *transitive* outweigh. ● *noun* **1** an excess. **2** the amount of this.

over·bear *transitive verb* (past **-bore**; past participle **-borne**) **1** bear down; upset by weight, force, or emotional pressure. **2** put down or repress by power or authority. **3** surpass in importance etc.; outweigh.

over·bear·ing *adjective* **1** domineering, masterful. **2** overpowering. □ **over·bear·ing·ly** *adverb* **over·bear·ing·ness** *noun*

over·bid ● *verb* (**-bid·ding**; past and past participle **-bid**) **1** *transitive* make a higher bid than. **2** *transitive & intransitive* Bridge **a** bid more on (one's hand) than warranted. **b** overcall. ● *noun* a bid that is higher than another, or higher than is justified. □ **over·bid·der** *noun*

over·bite *noun* the overlapping of the lower teeth by the upper.

over·blouse *noun* a garment like a blouse, but worn without tucking it into a skirt or trousers.

over·blown *adjective* **1** excessively inflated or pretentious. **2** (of a flower etc.) past its prime.

over·board *adverb* from on a ship into the water (*fall overboard*). □ **go overboard 1** be highly enthusiastic. **2** behave immoderately; go too far. **throw overboard** abandon, discard.

over·book *transitive verb* accept too many bookings or reservations for (an aircraft, hotel, etc.).

over·bore past of OVERBEAR.

over·borne past participle of OVERBEAR.

over·bought past and past participle of OVERBUY.

over·build *transitive verb* (past and past participle **-built**) **1** build over or upon. **2** place too many buildings on (land etc.). □ **over·build·ing** *noun*

over·bur·den ● *transitive verb* burden (a person, thing, etc.) to excess. ● *noun* **1** rock etc. that must be removed prior to mining the mineral deposit beneath it. **2** an excessive burden. □ **over·bur·den·some** *adjective*

over·busy *adjective* excessively busy.

over·buy *transitive & intransitive verb* (past and past participle **-bought**) buy (a commodity etc.) in excess of immediate need.

over·call ● *transitive & intransitive verb* Bridge **1** make a higher bid than a previous bid or opponent). **2** Brit. = OVERBID verb 2a. ● *noun* an act or instance of overcalling.

over·came past of OVERCOME.

over·capa·city /ˌoːvərkəˈpasɪti/ *noun* the resources to produce more goods, handle more business, etc. than is needed at a particular time.

over·capit·al·ize /ˌoːvərˈkapɪtəˌlaɪz/ *transitive verb* (also esp. Brit. **-ise**) fix or estimate the capital of (a company etc.) too high.

over·cast ● *adjective* **1** (of the sky, weather, etc.) covered with cloud; dull and gloomy. **2** (in sewing) edged with stitching to prevent fraying. ● *transitive verb* (past and past participle **-cast**) **1** cover (the sky etc.) with clouds or darkness. **2** stitch over (a raw edge etc.) to prevent fraying. ● *noun* a covering, esp. of clouds.

over·cautious *adjective* excessively cautious. □ **over·caution** *noun* **over·cautious·ly** *adverb* **over·cautious·ness** *noun*

over·charge ● *verb* **1** *transitive & intransitive* charge too high a price to (a person) or for (a thing). **2** *transitive* put too much charge into (a battery, gun, etc.). **3** *transitive* put exaggerated or excessive detail into (a description, picture, etc.). ● *noun* an excessive charge (of explosive, money, etc.).

over·class *noun* a privileged, wealthy, or powerful subgroup in society.

over·clock *transitive verb* run (the processor of a computer) at a speed higher than that intended by the manufacturers.

over·cloud *transitive verb* **1** cover with cloud. **2** mar, spoil, or dim, esp. as the result of anxiety etc. (*overclouded by uncertainties*). **3** make obscure.

over·coat *noun* **1** a heavy coat, esp. one worn over indoor clothes for warmth outdoors in cold weather. **2** a protective coat of paint etc.

over·come ● *verb* (*past* **-came**; *past participle* **-come**) **1** *transitive* prevail over, master, conquer. **2** *intransitive* be victorious. ● *adjective* (usu. foll. by *with, by*) **1** exhausted, made helpless. **2** affected by (emotion etc.). [Old English *ofercuman* (as OVER-, COME)]

over·commit *transitive verb* (**over·commit·ted**, **over·commit·ting**) (usu. *reflexive*) commit (esp. oneself) to an excessive degree. □ **over·commit·ment** *noun*

over·compen·sate *verb* **1** *transitive* (usu. foll. by *for*) compensate excessively for (something). **2** *intransitive* *Psych.* strive for power etc. in an exaggerated way, esp. to make allowance or amends for a real or fancied grievance, defect, handicap, etc. □ **over·compen·sa·tion** *noun*

over·confi·dent *adjective* excessively confident. □ **over·confi·dence** *noun* **over·confi·dent·ly** *adverb*

over·cook *transitive verb* cook too much or for too long. □ **over·cooked** *adjective*

over·critic·al *adjective* excessively critical; quick to find fault.

over·crowd *transitive verb* fill (a space, object, etc.) beyond what is usual or comfortable. □ **over·crowd·ed** *adjective* **over·crowd·ing** *noun*

over·cut·ting *noun* the act or an instance of cutting too many trees in an area of forest at one time. □ **over·cut** *transitive verb*

over·deter·mine *transitive verb* **1** determine, account for, or cause in more than one way, or with more conditions than are necessary. **2** (in *passive*) have more determining factors than the minimum necessary, have more than one cause. **3** *Psych.* give expression to more than one need or desire. □ **over·deter·min·a·tion** *noun*

over·devel·op *transitive verb* (**-devel·oped**, **-devel·op·ing**) **1** develop too much. **2** *Photog.* treat with developer for too long. □ **over·devel·op·ment** *noun*

over·do *transitive verb* (*3rd sing. present* **-does**; *past* **-did**; *past participle* **-done**) carry to excess, go too far, exaggerate (*I think you overdid the sarcasm*). □ **overdo it** (or **things**) exhaust oneself. [Old English *oferdōn* (as OVER-, DO[1])]

over·done *adjective* **1** overcooked. **2** excessive, exaggerated.

over·dose ● *noun* an excessive dose (of a drug, sensation, etc.). ● *verb* **1** *intransitive* (often foll. by *on*) take an overdose of a drug etc. **2** *transitive* give an excessive dose of (a drug etc.) or to (a person). □ **over·dosage** *noun*

over·draft *noun* **1** a deficit in a bank account caused by drawing more money than is credited to it. **2** the amount of this.

over·drama·tize *transitive & intransitive verb* (also esp. *Brit.* **-tise**) express or react to in an excessively dramatic way. □ **over·dramat·ic** *adjective*

over·draw *verb* (*past* **-drew**; *past participle* **-drawn**) **1** *transitive* draw a sum of money in excess of the amount credited to (one's bank account). **2** *intransitive* overdraw one's account. **3** *transitive* exaggerate in describing or depicting. □ **over·draw·er** *noun* (in senses 1 & 2).

over·drawn *adjective* **1** (of a bank account) having an overdraft. **2** (of a person) having overdrawn one's bank account.

over·dress ● *verb* **1** *transitive* dress (a person, esp. a child) too warmly. **2** *transitive* dress with too much display or formality. **3** *intransitive* overdress oneself. ● *noun* a dress worn over another dress or a blouse etc. □ **over·dressed** *adjective*

over·drive *noun* **1 a** a mechanism in a motor vehicle providing a gear ratio higher than that of the usual gear. **b** an additional speed-increasing gear. **2** (usu. prec. by *in, into*) a state of high or excessive activity (*when she heard about it she went into overdrive*).

over·dub ● *transitive & intransitive verb* (**-dubbed**, **-dub·bing**) impose (additional sounds) on an existing recording. ● *noun* the act or an instance of overdubbing.

over·due *adjective* **1** past the time when due or ready. **2** not yet paid, arrived, etc., though after the expected time. **3** (of a library book etc.) retained longer than the period allowed. **4 a** (of a baby) not yet born, though past the due date. **b** (of a pregnant woman) having passed her due date without having given birth.

over·eager *adjective* excessively eager. □ **over·eager·ly** *adverb* **over·eager·ness** *noun*

over easy *adjective* N Amer. (of a fried egg) flipped when almost cooked and fried lightly on the other side, so that the yolk remains slightly liquid.

over·eat *intransitive verb* (*past* **-ate**; *past participle* **-eaten**) eat too much. □ **over·eat·er** *noun* **over·eat·ing** *noun*

over-educate *transitive verb* provide (a person) with more education than they need. □ **over-educat·ed** *adjective*

over-elabor·ate *adjective* excessively elaborate. □ **over-elabor·ate·ly** *adverb*

over-emotion·al *adjective* excessively emotional. □ **over-emotion·al·ly** *adverb*

over·empha·sis *noun* excessive emphasis. □ **over·empha·size** *transitive & intransitive verb* (also esp. *Brit.* **-sise**)

over·enthusi·asm *noun* excessive enthusiasm. □ **over·enthusi·as·tic** *adjective* **over·enthusi·as·tic·ally** *adverb*

over·esti·mate ● *transitive & intransitive verb* form too high an estimate of (a person, ability, cost, etc.). ● *noun* too high an estimate. □ **over·esti·ma·tion** *noun*

over·excite *transitive verb* excite excessively. □ **over·excit·ed** *adjective* **over·excite·ment** *noun*

over-exercise ● *verb* **1** *transitive* use or exert (a part of the body, one's authority, etc.) too much. **2** *intransitive* take too much exercise; overexert oneself. ● *noun* excessive exercise.

over·exert *transitive verb & reflexive* exert too much. □ **over·exer·tion** *noun*

over·expand *transitive & intransitive verb* expand too much or too quickly. □ **over·expan·sion** *noun*

over·expose *transitive & intransitive verb* **1** expose too much, esp. to the public eye. **2** *Photog.* expose (film) for too long a time. □ **over·expo·sure** *noun*

over·extend *transitive verb* **1** extend (a thing) too far. **2** *reflexive* take on (oneself) an excessive burden of work etc. □ **over·exten·sion** *noun*

over·extend·ed *adjective* **1** extended too far. **2** (of a person etc.) having too many commitments etc.

over·famil·iar *adjective* excessively familiar. □ **over·famili·ar·ity** *noun*

over·feed *transitive verb* (*past and past participle* **-fed**) feed excessively.

over·fill *transitive & intransitive verb* fill to excess or to overflowing.

over·fine *adjective* excessively fine; too precise.

over·fish *transitive verb* deplete (a body of water) by too much fishing. □ **over·fish·ing** *noun*

over·flight *noun* an instance of overflying.

over·flow ● *verb* **1** *transitive* **a** flow over (the brim, limits, etc.). **b** flow over the brim or limits of. **c** cause to overflow; fill (a container) so full that the contents spill out. **2** *intransitive* **a** (of a receptacle etc.) be so full that the contents overflow it (*until the cup was overflowing*). **b** (of contents) overflow a container. **3** *transitive* (of a crowd etc.) extend beyond the limits of (a room etc.). **4** *transitive* flood (a surface or area). **5** *intransitive* (foll. by *with*) be full of. **6** *intransitive* (of kindness, a harvest, etc.) be very abundant. ● *noun* (also *attributive*) **1** what overflows or is superfluous (*mop up the overflow*; *an overflow crowd*). **2** an instance of overflowing (*overflow occurs when both systems are run together*). **3** (esp. in a bathtub or sink) an outlet for excess water etc. **4** an excess; a superabundance (*an overflow of ideas*). **5** *Computing* the generation of a number having more digits than the assigned location. **6** esp. *Cdn* an overflow of water from beneath the frozen surface of a river, lake, etc. □ **to overflowing** so as to be more than full; so as to overflow (*the auditorium was packed to overflowing*). [Old English *oferflōwan* (as OVER-, FLOW)]

over·fly *transitive verb* (**-flies**; *past* **-flew**; *past participle* **-flown**) fly over or beyond (a place or territory).

over·fond *adjective* (often foll. by *of*) having too great an affection or liking (for a person or thing) (*overfond of chocolate*; *an overfond parent*). □ **over·fond·ness** *noun*

over·fulfill *transitive verb* (also **-fulfil**) (**-ful·filled**, **-fulfil·ling**) fulfill (a plan, quota, etc.) beyond expectation or before the appointed time. □ **over·fulfill·ment** *noun*

over·full *adjective* filled excessively or to overflowing.

over·gener·al·ize *verb* (also esp. *Brit.* **-ise**) **1** *intransitive* draw general conclusions from inadequate data etc. **2** *intransitive* argue more widely than is justified by the available evidence, by circumstances, etc. **3** *transitive* draw an overly general conclusion from (data, circumstances, etc.). □ **over·gener·al·iza·tion** *noun*

over·gener·ous *adjective* excessively generous. □ **over·gener·ous·ly** *adverb*

over·glaze ● *noun* **1** a second glaze applied to ceramic ware. **2** decoration on a glazed surface. ● *adjective* (of painting etc.) done on a glazed surface.

over-govern *transitive verb* **1** subject to too much government interference. **2** provide with too many layers of government, too many elected representatives, etc. □ **over-governed** *adjective* **over-govern·ment** *noun*

over·graze *transitive verb* allow (grassland) to be so heavily grazed, or (of livestock) feed on (grassland) so heavily, that the vegetation is damaged and ground becomes liable to erosion. □ **over·grazed** *adjective* **over·graz·ing** *noun*

over·ground *adjective & adverb* raised above or on the ground.

over·grow *transitive verb* (*past* **-grew**; *past participle* **-grown**) **1** grow over, overspread, esp. so as to choke (*the weeds have overgrown the pathway*). **2** grow too big for (one's strength etc.).

over·grown *adjective* **1** abnormally large (*treated her husband like an overgrown child*). **2** wild; grown over with vegetation (*an overgrown cemetery*).

over·growth *noun* **1** growth that is excessive or too rapid; an instance of this. **2** a growth over or on something; an accretion.

over·hand *adjective & adverb* **1** (in tennis, baseball, etc.) thrown or played with the hand above the shoulder. **2** *Swimming* = OVERARM 2. **3 a** with the palm of the hand downward or inward. **b** with the hand above the object held.

overhand knot *noun* a simple knot made by forming a loop and passing the free end through it.

over·hang ● *verb* (*past* and *past participle* **-hung**) *transitive & intransitive* project or hang over. ● *noun* **1** the overhanging part of a structure or rock formation. **2** the amount by which this projects. **3** an excess or buildup of any factor in an economy or market which has, or is likely to have, an undesirable effect upon it. □ **over·hang·ing** *adjective*

over·harvest·ing *noun* the act or an instance of killing too many trees, animals, fish, etc., by logging, hunting, fishing, etc. (*cod stocks have been depleted by decades of overharvesting*). □ **over·harvest** *transitive verb & noun*

over·hasty *adjective* excessively hasty. □ **over·hasti·ly** *adverb*

over·haul ● *transitive verb* **1 a** take to pieces in order to examine. **b** examine the condition of (and improve or repair as necessary). **2** *Brit.* overtake. ● *noun* a thorough examination, with adjustments or repairs as necessary. [originally *Naut.*, = release (rope tackle) by slackening]

over·head ● *adverb* above one's head. ● *adjective* /ˈoːvərhed/ **1** placed overhead. **2** (of a driving mechanism etc.) above the object driven. **3** (of expenses) arising from general running costs, as distinct from particular business transactions. ● *noun* **1** (also in *pl.*) overhead expenses. **2** = OVERHEAD PROJECTOR. **3** a transparency for use on an overhead projector. **4** an overhead compartment, e.g. on an airplane.

overhead projector *noun* a device that projects an enlarged image of a transparency onto a screen or wall.

over·hear *transitive & intransitive verb* (*past* and *past participle* **-heard**) hear as an eavesdropper or as an unperceived or unintentional listener.

over·heat *transitive & intransitive verb* **1** make or become too hot; heat to excess. **2** suffer, or cause to suffer, from marked inflation as a result of placing excessive pressure on resources at a time of expanding demand. □ **over·heat·ing** *noun*

over·heat·ed *adjective* **1** excessively hot (*a car with an overheated engine*). **2** excessively passionate about a matter (*an overheated editorial*). **3** (of an economy etc.) suffering from marked inflation.

over·hype *transitive verb* promote with excessive hype. □ **over·hyped** *adjective*

Over·ijssel a province of the east central Netherlands, north of the IJssel River, on the border with Germany; capital, Zwolle.

over·indulge *transitive & intransitive verb* indulge to excess. □ **over·indul·gence** *noun* **over·indul·gent** *adjective*

over·inflat·ed *adjective* excessively large or aggrandized; exaggerated.

over·issue ● *transitive verb* (**-issues**, **-issued**, **-issu·ing**) issue (notes, shares, etc.) beyond the authorized amount, or the ability to pay. ● *noun* the notes, shares, etc., or the amount so issued.

over·joyed *adjective* (often foll. by *at*, *to hear*, etc.) filled with great joy.

over·kill *noun* **1** an excess of what is necessary or appropriate. **2** the amount by which destruction or the capacity for destruction exceeds what is necessary for victory or annihilation.

over·laden *adjective* bearing or carrying too large a load.

over·laid *past and past participle of* OVERLAY¹.

over·lain *past participle of* OVERLIE.

over·land *adjective & adverb* over the surface of the land.

Over·land·er *noun Cdn hist.* one of a group of people who journeyed overland from Ontario to the Cariboo goldfields in British Columbia in 1862.

over·lap ● *verb* (**-lapped**, **-lap·ping**) **1** *transitive* (of part of an object) partly cover (another object). **2** *transitive* cover and extend beyond. **3** *intransitive* (of two things) partly coincide; not be completely separate (*where psychology and philosophy overlap*). ● *noun* **1** an instance of overlapping. **2** the amount of this. □ **over·lap·ping** *noun & adjective*

over·large *adjective* too large.

over·lay¹ ● *transitive verb* (*past* and *past participle* **-laid**) **1** lay over. **2** (foll. by *with*) cover the surface of (a thing) with (a coating etc.). **3** overlie. ● *noun* **1** a thing laid over another. **2** (in printing, map-reading, etc.) a transparent sheet to be superimposed on another sheet. **3** *Computing* **a** the process of transferring a block of data etc. to replace what is already stored. **b** a section so transferred. **4** a coverlet, small tablecloth, etc.

over·lay² *past of* OVERLIE.

over·leaf *adverb* on the other side of the leaf (of a book) (*see the diagram overleaf*).

over·leap *transitive verb* (*past* and *past participle* **-leaped** or **-leapt**) leap over, surmount.

over-lever·aged /ˌoːvərˈlevrɪdʒd, -liːvɜrˈɪdʒd/ *adjective* designating a company, national economy, or individual having assets insufficient to repay borrowed capital, esp. owing to the failure of anticipated return on an investment. □ **over-lever·age** *transitive verb*

over·lie *transitive verb* (**-lying**; *past* **-lay**; *past participle* **-lain**) lie on top of.

over·load ● *transitive verb* (esp. in *passive*) **1** put too great a load on or into something. **2** (often foll. by *with*) give (a person or thing) too much of something. **3** put too great a demand on a computer, electrical system, etc., causing it to fail. ● *noun* an excessive load or amount.

over·long *adjective & adverb* too or excessively long.

over·look ● *transitive verb* **1 a** miss or fail to see or notice (a thing) (*a fact that is often overlooked*). **b** see (a mistake, wrongdoing, etc.) but decide officially to ignore it (*we have overlooked your persistent lateness*). **c** consider (a person or thing) not good or important enough and so ignore them or it (*despite her qualifications she has been repeatedly overlooked for promotion*). **2** have a view from above, be higher than. **3** supervise, oversee. **4** *archaic* bewitch with the evil eye. ● *noun N Amer.* a place giving a view of the scene below.

over·lord *noun* **1** a lord superior to other lords or rulers. **2** a person in a position of superiority or supreme power. □ **over·lord·ship** *noun*

over·ly *adverb* excessively; too.

over·lying ● *pres. part. of* OVERLIE. ● *adjective* that overlies.

over·man ● *transitive verb* (**-manned**, **-man·ning**) provide with too large a crew, staff, etc. ● *noun* (*pl.* **-men**) **1** an overseer or foreman. **2** *Philos.* = SUPERMAN 1. □ **over·man·ning** *noun*

over·mantel *noun* ornamental shelves etc. over a mantelpiece.

over-many *adjective* too many; an excessive number.

over·master *transitive verb* master completely, conquer. □ **over·master·ing** *adjective*

over·match *transitive verb* esp. *N Amer.* **1** be more than a match for; defeat by superior strength etc. **2** match (a person) against a superior opponent.

over·medi·cate *transitive verb* prescribe too many drugs for. □ **over·medi·cated** *adjective*

over·much ● *adverb* to too great an extent; excessively. ● *adjective* excessive; superabundant.

over·night ● *adverb* **1** for the duration of a night (*stay overnight*). **2** during the course of a night. **3** suddenly, immediately (*the situation changed overnight*). ● *adjective* **1** done, happening, operating, etc. overnight (*an overnight stop*). **2** staying for one night (*an overnight guest*).

3 for use overnight (*an overnight bag*). **4** lasting or valid for one night. **5** (of a delivery etc.) occurring before opening time the next business day. **6** sudden, instant (*an overnight success*). ● *verb* **1** *transitive* send (a package etc.) by overnight delivery. **2** *intransitive* stay for the night at or in (*overnighted at Kingston*). ● *noun* a stop or stay lasting one night.

overnight bag *noun* a piece of luggage large enough to hold clothing and toiletries etc. for an overnight trip.

over·night·er *noun* **1** *N Amer.* an overnight trip, stay, etc. **2** a person who stays at a place overnight. **3** an overnight bag.

over-optimis·tic *adjective* excessively or unjustifiably optimistic. □ **over-optimism** *noun*

over·pack·aging *noun* excessive packaging of a product, e.g. consisting of several layers of wrapping. □ **over·pack·aged** *adjective*

over·paid *past and past participle of* OVERPAY.

over·paint *transitive verb* cover with another colour or layer of paint.

over-particu·lar *adjective* excessively particular or fussy.

over·pass *noun* a road or railway line that passes over another by means of a bridge.

over·pay *transitive verb* (*past and past participle* **-paid**) **1** recompense (a person etc.) too highly. **2** pay more than (an amount owing). □ **over·pay·ment** *noun*

over·play *transitive verb* **1** play (a part) to excess. **2** give undue importance to; overemphasize. □ **overplay one's hand 1** be unduly optimistic about one's capabilities. **2** spoil a good case by exaggerating its value.

over·plus *noun* a surplus, a superabundance. [Middle English, partial translation of Anglo-French *surplus* or medieval Latin *su(pe)rplus*]

over·popu·lat·ed *adjective* having too large a population. □ **over·popu·la·tion** *noun*

over·power *transitive verb* **1** reduce to submission, subdue. **2** make (a thing) ineffective or imperceptible by greater intensity. **3** (of heat, emotion, etc.) be too intense for, overwhelm. □ **over·power·ing** *adjective* **over·power·ing·ly** *adverb*

over-prescribe *transitive & intransitive verb* prescribe an excessive amount of (a drug) or too many (drugs). □ **over-prescrip·tion** *noun*

over·price *transitive verb* price (a thing) too highly. □ **over·priced** *adjective*

over·print ● *transitive verb* **1** print further matter on (a surface already printed, esp. a postage stamp). **2** print (further matter) in this way. ● *noun* **1** the words etc. overprinted. **2** an overprinted postage stamp.

over·produce *transitive & intransitive verb* **1** produce more of (a commodity) than is wanted. **2** produce to an excessive degree. □ **over·produc·tion** *noun*

over·proof *adjective* containing more alcohol than proof spirit does.

over·protect·ive *adjective* excessively protective, esp. of a person in one's charge. □ **over·protect·ed** *adjective*

over·quali·fied *adjective* too highly qualified (esp. for a particular job etc.).

over·ran *past of* OVERRUN.

over·rate *transitive verb* rate or esteem too highly. □ **over·rat·ed** *adjective*

over·reach *transitive verb* **1** exceed (the limits of a person's authority etc.). **2** (*usu. reflexive*) **a** strain oneself by reaching too far. **b** defeat one's object by attempting what is beyond one's abilities. **3** circumvent, outwit; get the better of by cunning or artifice. □ **over·reach·er** *noun* **over·reach·ing** *noun & adjective*

over·react *intransitive verb* respond more forcibly etc. than is justified. □ **over·reac·tion** *noun*

over·refine *transitive & intransitive verb* **1** refine too much. **2** make too subtle distinctions in (an argument etc.). □ **over·refine·ment** *noun*

over·reli·ance *noun* excessive reliance.

over·repre·sent *transitive verb* (*usu. in passive*) cause to be present in numbers higher than would be expected statistically (*women are overrepresented in this group*).

over·ride ● *transitive verb* (*past* **-rode**; *past participle* **-rid·den**) **1** have or claim precedence or superiority over. **2** intervene and make ineffective. **3** interrupt the action of (an automatic device) esp. to take manual control. **4** extend over, esp. (of a part of a fractured bone) overlap (another part). **5** ride over (enemy country). **6** exhaust (a horse etc.) by hard riding. ● *noun* **1** the action or process of suspending an automatic function. **2** a device for this.

over·rid·ing *adjective* foremost; taking precedence (*accuracy is our overriding concern*).

over·ripe *adjective* (esp. of fruit etc.) past its best; excessively ripe. □ **over·ripe·ness** *noun*

over·rode *past of* OVERRIDE.

over-rotate *verb* **1** *intransitive* (of a figure skater, diver, etc.) rotate too much on a turn, jump, etc. **2** *transitive* rotate too far on (a turn, jump, etc.) (*over-rotated his double Axel*). □ **over-rotation** *noun*

over·ruff ● *transitive & intransitive verb* overtrump. ● *noun* an instance of this.

over·rule *transitive verb* **1** set aside (a decision, argument, proposal, etc.) by exercising a superior authority. **2** annul a decision by or reject a proposal of (a person) in this way.

over·run ● *transitive verb* (**-run·ning**; *past* **-ran**; *past participle* **-run**) **1** (esp. of something undesirable) swarm or spread over. **2** conquer or ravage (territory) by force. **3** (of time, expenditure, production, etc.) exceed (a fixed limit). **4** *Printing* carry over (a word etc.) to the next line or page. **5** *Mech.* rotate faster than. **6** flood (land). ● *noun* **1** an instance of overrunning. **2** the amount of this. **3** the movement of a vehicle at a speed greater than is imparted by the engine.

over·sam·pling *noun Electronics* a process used in CD players by which each component of the digital signal is repeated electronically so as to increase the apparent sampling frequency, making it easier to remove spurious signals introduced by the original sampling process.

over·saw *past of* OVERSEE.

over·sched·ule *transitive verb* schedule too many activities for (a person).

over-scrupu·lous *adjective* excessively scrupulous or particular.

over·seas ● *adverb* abroad (*was sent overseas for training; came back from overseas*). ● *adjective* (also **over·sea**) **1** foreign; across or beyond the sea. **2** of or connected with movement or transport over the sea (*overseas postage rates*).

over·see *transitive verb* (**-sees**; *past* **-saw**; *past participle* **-seen**) officially supervise (workers, work, etc.).

over·seer *noun* a person who supervises others, esp. workers.

over·sell *transitive & intransitive verb* (*past and past participle* **-sold**) **1** sell more of (a commodity etc.) than one can deliver. **2** exaggerate the merits of.

over-sensitive *adjective* excessively sensitive; easily hurt by, or too quick to react to, outside influences. □ **over-sensitive·ness** *noun* **over-sensitiv·ity** *noun*

over·set *transitive verb* (**-set·ting**; *past and past participle* **-set**) **1** overturn, upset. **2** *Printing* set up (type) in excess of the available space.

over·sew *transitive verb* (*past participle* **-sewn** or **-sewed**) sew (two edges) with every stitch passing over the join.

over·sexed *adjective* having unusually strong sexual desires.

over·shadow *transitive verb* **1** appear much more prominent or important than. **2** cast into the shade; shelter from the sun. **3** (usu. in *passive*) make an occasion less happy than it should be (*the victory was overshadowed by the terrible loss of life*). [Old English *ofersceadwian* (as OVER-, SHADOW)]

over·shirt *noun* a shirt worn over another shirt or without being tucked in.

over·shoe *noun* a shoe worn over another as protection from wet, cold, etc.

over·shoot ● *transitive & intransitive verb* (*past and past participle* **-shot**) **1** pass or send beyond (a target or limit). **2** (of an aircraft) fly beyond or taxi too far along (the runway) when landing or taking off. ● *noun* **1** the act of overshooting. **2** the amount of this. □ **overshoot the mark** go beyond what is intended or proper; go too far.

over·shot *adjective* (of a water wheel) operated by the weight of water falling into buckets attached to its periphery.

over·side *adverb* over the side of a ship (into a smaller boat, or into the sea).

over·sight *noun* **1** a failure to notice something. **2** an inadvertent mistake. **3** supervision.

over·simpli·fy *transitive & intransitive verb* (**-fies**, **-fied**) distort (a problem etc.) by stating it in too simple terms. □ **over·simpli·fi·ca·tion** *noun* **over·simpli·fied** *adjective*

over·sized *adjective* (also **over·size**) of more than the usual size.

over·skate *verb* (of a hockey player) **1** *transitive* skate faster than or past (the puck). **2** *intransitive* overskate the puck.

over·skirt *noun* an outer or second skirt, esp. one that is draped etc. to reveal a decorative underskirt.

uː mood ai my əi pipe au brown ʌu house ei day ɔi boy ɑ̃ franglais ã Canadien ɔ̃ Brayon   (*see over for consonants*)

over·sleep *intransitive verb* (*past* and *past participle* **-slept**) continue sleeping beyond the intended time of waking; sleep too long.

over·sold *past and past participle of* OVERSELL.

over-solici·tous *adjective* excessively worried, anxious, eager, etc.

over·soul *noun* (in transcendentalism) the absolute spirit which includes and animates the universe.

over·special·ize *intransitive verb* (also esp. *Brit.* **-ise**) concentrate too much on one aspect or area. □ **over·special·iz·a·tion** *noun*

over·spend *verb* (*past* and *past participle* **-spent**) **1** *intransitive & reflexive* spend too much. **2** *transitive* spend more than (a specified amount). □ **over·spend·er** *noun* **over·spend·ing** *noun*

over·spill *noun* **1** what is spilled over or overflows. **2** the surplus population leaving a country or city to live elsewhere.

over·spread ● *transitive verb* (*past* and *past participle* **-spread**) **1** become spread or diffused over. **2** cover or occupy the surface of. ● *adjective* (usu. foll. by *with*) covered (*high mountains overspread with trees*).

over·staff *transitive verb* provide with too large a staff.

over·state *transitive verb* **1** state (esp. a case or argument) too strongly. **2** exaggerate. □ **over·state·ment** *noun*

over·stay *transitive verb* stay longer than (one's welcome, a time limit, etc.).

over·steer ● *intransitive verb* (of a motor vehicle) have a tendency to turn more sharply than was intended. ● *noun* this tendency.

over·step *transitive verb* (**-stepped**, **-step·ping**) **1** pass beyond (a boundary or mark). **2** violate (certain standards of behaviour etc.). □ **overstep the mark** (also **overstep the bounds**) violate conventions of behaviour.

over·stimu·late *transitive verb* stimulate or excite excessively. □ **over·stimu·la·tion** *noun*

over·stock ● *transitive verb* stock excessively. ● *noun* esp. *N Amer.* a supply in excess of demand or requirement.

over·storey *noun* (also **over·story** *pl.* **-stories**) the uppermost canopy level of a forest ecosystem, formed by the taller trees.

over·strain *transitive verb* strain too much.

over·stress ● *transitive verb* stress too much. ● *noun* an excessive degree of stress.

over·stretch ● *transitive verb* **1** stretch too much. **2** (esp. as **over·stretched** *adjective*) make excessive demands on (resources, a person, etc.). ● *noun* the fact or an instance of overstretching.

over·stuff *transitive verb* stuff more than is necessary.

over·stuffed *adjective* (of furniture) made soft and comfortable by thick upholstery.

over·sub·scribe *transitive verb* (usu. as **over·sub·scribed** *adjective*) subscribe for more than the amount available of (a commodity offered for sale etc.) (*the offer was oversubscribed*).

over·subtle *adjective* excessively subtle; not plain or clear.

over·supply ● *transitive verb* (**-supplies**, **-supplied**) supply with too much. ● *noun* an excessive supply.

overt /oʊˈvɜrt, ˈoʊvɜrt/ *adjective* unconcealed; done openly. □ **overt·ly** *adverb* **overt·ness** *noun* [Old French past participle of *ovrir* open, from Latin *aperire*]

over·take *transitive verb* (*past* **-took**; *past participle* **-taken**) **1** catch up with and pass in the same direction. **2** (of a storm, misfortune, etc.) come suddenly or unexpectedly upon. **3** become level with and exceed (a compared value etc.).

over·task *transitive verb* **1** give too heavy a task to. **2** be too heavy a task for.

over·tax *transitive verb* **1** make excessive demands on (a person's strength etc.). **2** tax too heavily.

over-the-counter *attributive adjective* **1** obtainable from a store, esp. (of drugs) without a prescription. *See also* over the counter (*see* COUNTER[1]). **2 a** (of stocks and other securities) not listed on or traded in an organized stock exchange. **b** (of a market) trading in such securities. Abbr.: **OTC**.

over-the-top *adjective informal* (esp. of behaviour, dress, etc.) outrageous, excessive.

over·throw ● *transitive verb* (*past* **-threw**; *past participle* **-thrown**) **1** remove forcibly from power. **2** put an end to (an institution etc.). **3** conquer, overcome. **4** knock down, upset. **5 a** throw (a ball) too far. **b** throw a ball past or over (a person, base, spot, etc.). ● *noun* **1** a defeat or downfall. **2** the act or an instance of overthrowing.

over·thrust *noun Geol.* the thrust of esp. lower strata on one side of a fault over those on the other side.

over·time ● *noun* **1** the time during which a person works at a job in addition to the regular hours. **2** payment for this. **3** *N Amer. Sport* a further period of play at the end of a game when the score is tied. ● *adjective* **1** pertaining to overtime (*overtime pay*). **2** happening in overtime (*an overtime goal*). ● *adverb* in addition to regular hours.

over·tire *transitive verb & reflexive* exhaust or wear out (a person).

over·tired *adjective* excessively tired.

over·tone *noun* **1** a subtle or elusive quality or implication (*sinister overtones*). **2** *Music* any of the tones above the lowest in a harmonic series.

over·took *past of* OVERTAKE.

over·top ● *transitive verb* (**-topped**, **-top·ping**) **1** be or become higher than. **2** surpass. ● *preposition* above. ● *adverb* over the top of.

over·train *transitive & intransitive verb* subject to or undergo too much (esp. athletic) training with a consequent loss of proficiency.

over·trick *noun Bridge* a trick taken in excess of one's contract.

over·trump *transitive & intransitive verb* play a higher trump than (another player).

over·ture *noun* **1** an orchestral piece opening an opera, musical, ballet, etc. **2** a one-movement composition in this style. **3** (usu. in *pl.*) an approach or proposal made to a person with the aim of starting a discussion, establishing a relationship, etc. **4** something that serves as an introduction. **5** (in the Presbyterian church) a formal motion presented by a lower to a higher court proposing or calling for legislation on a particular issue. [Old French from Latin *apertura* APERTURE]

over·turn *verb* **1** *transitive* cause to fall down or over; upset. **2** *transitive* overthrow; destroy. **3** reverse; invalidate (*the Supreme Court overturned the verdict*). **4** *intransitive* turn over; capsize.

over·use ● *transitive verb* use too much or too frequently. ● *noun* excessive use.

over·value *transitive verb* (**-values**, **-valued**, **-valu·ing**) value too highly; have too high an opinion of.

over·view *noun* a general review or summary of a subject.

over·water ● *transitive & intransitive verb* water (a plant etc.) too much. ● *attributive adjective* situated above the water.

over·ween·ing *adjective* **1** arrogant, presumptuous, conceited. **2** (of an opinion, emotion, etc.) excessive, exaggerated; immoderate. [OVER- + WEEN]

over·weight ● *adjective* **1** in excess of a weight considered normal or desirable. **2** beyond an allowed or suitable weight. ● *noun* excessive or extra weight; preponderance. ● *transitive verb* **1** (usu. foll. by *with*) load unduly. **2** *Finance* invest in (a market sector, industry, etc.) to a greater than normal degree.

over·whelm *transitive verb* **1** overpower with emotion. **2** (usu. foll. by *with*) overpower with an excess of work, responsibility, etc. **3** bring to sudden ruin or destruction; crush. **4** bury or drown beneath a huge mass, submerge utterly. [OVER- + WHELM]

over·whelm·ing *adjective* **1** very great or very strong; overpowering (*your affection is overwhelming; an overwhelming urge*). **2** complete; total, or nearly so (*an overwhelming success; the overwhelming majority*). □ **over·whelm·ing·ly** *adverb* **over·whelm·ing·ness** *noun*

over·wind *transitive verb* (*past* and *past participle* **-wound**) wind (a mechanism, esp. a watch) beyond the proper stopping point.

over·winter *verb* **1** *intransitive* (usu. foll. by *at*, *in*, etc.) spend the winter. **2** *intransitive* (of insects, fungi, etc.) live through the winter. **3** *transitive* keep (animals, plants, etc.) alive through the winter.

over·work ● *verb* **1** *intransitive* work too hard. **2** *transitive* cause (another person) to work too hard. **3** *transitive* weary or exhaust with too much work. **4** *transitive* make excessive use of. ● *noun* excessive work. □ **over·worked** *adjective*

over·wound *past and past participle of* OVERWIND.

over·write *verb* (*past* **-wrote**; *past participle* **-writ·ten**) **1** *transitive* write on top of (other writing). **2** *transitive Computing* destroy (data) in (a file etc.) by entering new data. **3** *transitive* (usu. as **over·writ·ten** *adjective*) write too elaborately or too ornately. **4** *intransitive & reflexive* write too much; exhaust oneself by writing. **5** *transitive* write too much about. **6** *intransitive* (esp. as **over·writ·ing** *noun*) in shipping insurance, accept more risk than the premium income limits allow.

over·wrought *adjective* **1** overexcited, nervous, distraught. **2** overdone; too elaborate.

over·zeal·ous /ˌoʊvɜrˈzeləs/ *adjective* too zealous in one's attitude, behaviour, etc.; excessively enthusiastic.

ovi- /ˈoʊvi/ *combining form* egg, ovum. [Latin *ovum* egg]

Consonants: **b** *but* **d** *dog* **f** *few* **g** *get* **h** *her* **j** *yes* **k** *cat* **l** *leg* **m** *man* **n** *no* **p** *pen* **r** *red* **s** *sit*

Ovid /ˈɒvɪd/ (full name Publius Ovidius Naso) (43 BC–AD *c.* 17), Roman poet. His best-known works include elegiac love poems (such as the *Amores* and the *Ars Amatoria*) and the *Metamorphoses*, a hexametric epic retelling Greek and Roman myths; in AD 8 he was exiled by Augustus. □ **Ovid·ian** *adjective*

ovi·duct /ˈoːvɪˌdʌkt/ *noun* the tube through which an ovum passes from the ovary. ● **ovi·duct·al** *adjective*

Oviedo /ˌɒvˈjeidoː/ a city in NW Spain, capital of the Asturias; pop. (est. 2001) 201,005.

ovi·form /ˈoːvɪˌfɔrm/ *adjective* egg-shaped.

ovine /ˈoːvain/ *adjective* of or like sheep. [Late Latin *ovinus* from Latin *ovis* sheep]

ovip·ar·ous /oːˈvɪpɜrəs/ *adjective Zool.* producing young by means of eggs expelled from the body before they are hatched (compare VIVIPAROUS 1, OVOVIVIPAROUS). □ **ovi·par·ity** /-ˈperɪti/ *noun* **ovip·ar·ous·ly** *adverb*

ovi·posit /ˌoːvɪˈpɒzɪt/ *intransitive verb* (**ovi·posit·ed, ovi·posit·ing**) lay an egg or eggs, esp. with an ovipositor. □ **ovi·pos·ition** *noun* [OVI- + Latin *ponere posit-* to place]

ovi·posit·or /ˌoːvɪˈpɒzɪtər/ *noun* a pointed tubular organ with which a female insect deposits her eggs. [modern Latin from OVI- + Latin *positor* from *ponere posit-* to place]

ovoid /ˈoːvɔid/ ● *adjective* **1** (of a solid or of a surface) egg-shaped. **2** oval, with one end more pointed than the other. ● *noun* an ovoid body or surface. [French *ovoïde* from modern Latin *ovoides* (as OVUM)]

ovolo /ˈoːvəˌloː/ *noun* (*pl.* **ovoli** /-ˌliː/) *Archit.* = QUARTER-ROUND. [Italian diminutive of *ovo* egg from Latin OVUM]

ovo·tes·tis /ˌoːvəˈtestɪs/ *noun* (*pl.* **-testes** /-tiːz/) *Zool.* an organ producing both ova and spermatozoa. [OVUM + TESTIS]

ovo·vi·vip·ar·ous /ˌoːvoːvɪˈvɪpɜrəs/ *adjective Zool.* producing young by means of eggs hatched within the body (compare OVIPAROUS, VIVIPAROUS). □ **ovo·vivi·par·ity** /-ˈperɪti/ *noun* [OVUM + VIVIPAROUS]

ovu·late /ˈɒvjuˌleit/ *intransitive verb* produce ova or ovules, or discharge them from the ovary. □ **ovu·la·tion** *noun* **ovu·la·tory** *adjective* [modern Latin *ovulum* (as OVULE)]

ovule /ˈoːvjuːl/ *noun* the part of the ovary of seed plants that contains the germ cell; an unfertilized seed. □ **ovu·lar** *adjective* [French from medieval Latin *ovulum*, diminutive of OVUM]

ovum /ˈoːvəm/ *noun* (*pl.* **ova** /ˈoːvə/) **1** a mature reproductive cell of female animals, produced by the ovary. **2** the egg cell of plants. [Latin, = egg]

ow *interjection* expressing sudden pain.

owe /oː/ *verb* **1 a** *transitive* be under obligation (to a person etc.) to pay or repay (money etc.) (*we owe you five dollars; owe more than I can pay*). **b** *intransitive* (usu. foll. by *for*) be in debt (*still owe for my car*). **2** *transitive* (often foll. by *to*) render (gratitude etc., a person honour, gratitude, etc.) (*owe grateful thanks to my father*). **3** *transitive* (usu. foll. by *to*) be indebted to a person or thing for (*we owe the discovery of insulin to Banting and Best*). **4** esp. *Law* be under an obligation to fulfill (a duty). □ **owe it to oneself** (often foll. by *to* + infin.) need (to do) something in order to avoid unfairness to oneself. **owe someone (one)** *informal* feel indebted to someone for a favour done. **owe someone a living** used to express disapproval of someone who expects to receive financial support or other benefits without doing any work (*they think the world owes them a living*). [Old English *āgan* (see OUGHT¹) from Germanic]

Owen /ˈoːən/ **1 Sir Rich·ard** (1804–92), English anatomist and paleontologist. He made important contributions to the study of the evolution and taxonomy of monotremes and marsupials, flightless birds, and fossil reptiles, coined the word *dinosaur* in 1841, and is chiefly remembered for his opposition to Darwinism and to its defender T. H. Huxley. **2 Rob·ert** (1771–1858), Welsh social reformer and industrialist. A pioneer socialist thinker, he founded a model industrial community centred on his cotton mills at New Lanark, Scotland, which was organized on principles of mutual co-operation, with improved working conditions, housing, and educational institutions provided for workers and their families. **3 Wil·fred** (1893–1918), English poet. His experiences in the First World War inspired his best-known work, which is characterized by its bleak realism and its indignation at the horrors of war, and includes 'Strange Meeting' and 'Anthem for Doomed Youth'; he was killed in action.

Owens /ˈoːənz/ **Jesse** (born James Cleveland Owens) (1913–80), US track-and-field athlete. In 1935 he equalled or broke six world records in 45 minutes, and in 1936 won four gold medals at the Olympic Games in Berlin; the success in Berlin of Owens, as a black man, outraged Hitler, who was conspicuously absent when Owens's medals were presented.

Owen Sound 1 a deep inlet of the southwestern shore of Georgian Bay, forming the eastern base of the Bruce Peninsula. **2** a city at its head, situated in south central Ontario, almost 200 km northwest of Toronto; pop. (2001) 21,431. [Sir E. C. Rich *Owen*, British admiral d.1849]

owing /ˈoːɪŋ/ *predicative adjective* **1** owed; yet to be paid (*the balance owing*). **2** (foll. by *to*) **a** caused by; attributable to (*the cancellation was owing to lack of public interest*). **b** (foll. by *to*) because of (*the bus was delayed owing to bad weather*).

owl *noun* **1** any nocturnal bird of prey of the order Strigiformes, with large eyes and a hooked beak, including barn owls, snowy owls, etc. **2** *informal* a person compared to an owl, esp. in looking solemn or wise. □ **owl·ery** *noun* (*pl.* **-ies**). **owl-like** *adjective* [Old English *ūle* from Germanic]

owlet *noun* a small or young owl.

owl·ish *adjective* like an owl, esp. in acting or appearing wise and solemn. □ **owl·ish·ly** *adverb* **owl·ish·ness** *noun*

owly *adjective* **1** irritable. **2** like an owl.

own ● *adjective* (prec. by possessive) **1 a** belonging to oneself or itself; not another's (*saw it with my own eyes*). **b** individual, peculiar, particular (*a charm all of its own*). **2** used to emphasize identity rather than possession (*cooks his own meals*). ● *pronoun* **1** private property (*is it your own?*). **2** kindred (*among my own*). ● *verb* **1** *transitive* have as property; possess. **2 a** *transitive* confess; admit as valid, true, etc. (*own their faults; owns he did not know*). **b** *intransitive* (foll. by *to*) confess to (*owned to a prejudice*). **3** *transitive* acknowledge paternity, authorship, or possession of. □ **come into one's own 1** receive one's due. **2** achieve recognition. **get one's own back** (often foll. by *on*) *informal* get revenge. **hold one's own** maintain one's position; not be defeated or lose strength. **of one's own** belonging to oneself alone. **on one's own 1** alone. **2** independently, without help. **own up** (often foll. by *to*) confess frankly. □ **-owned** *adjective* (in *combination*). [Old English *āgen, āgnian*: see OWE]

owner *noun* a person who owns something. □ **owner·less** *adjective* **owner·ship** *noun*

own goal *noun Brit.* **1** a goal scored (usu. by mistake) against the scorer's own side. **2** an act or initiative that has the unintended effect of harming one's own interests.

owt *noun Brit. informal* or *dialect* anything. [var. of AUGHT¹]

ox *noun* (*pl.* **oxen**) **1** any bovine animal, esp. a large usu. horned domesticated ruminant used for draft, for supplying milk, and for eating as meat. **2** a castrated male of a domesticated species of cattle, *Bos taurus.* **3** a foolish, clumsy person. [Old English *oxa* from Germanic]

ox- *var.* of OXY-².

oxalic acid /ɒkˈsalɪk/ *noun Chem.* a very poisonous and sour acid found in sorrel and rhubarb leaves. Chem. formula: $(COOH)_2$. □ **ox·al·ate** /ˈɒksəˌleit/ *noun* [Greek *oxalis* wood sorrel]

ox·al·is /ˈɒksəlɪs/ *noun* any plant of the genus *Oxalis*, with trifoliate leaves. [Latin from Greek from *oxus* sour]

ox·blood ● *noun* a dull, deep reddish-brown colour. ● *adjective* of this colour.

ox·bow *noun* **1** a U-shaped collar of an ox yoke. **2 a** a loop formed by a horseshoe bend in a river. **b** (also **oxbow lake**) a lake formed when the river cuts across the narrow end of the loop.

Ox·bridge *noun* **1** (also *attributive*) Oxford and Cambridge universities regarded together, esp. in contrast to newer institutions. **2** (often *attributive*) the characteristics of these universities or of their students (*an Oxbridge accent*). [blend of Ox(ford) + (Cam)bridge]

ox cart *noun* a cart pulled by an ox or oxen.

oxen *pl.* of OX.

oxer *noun* **1** a strong fence for keeping in cattle, consisting of railings, a hedge, and often a ditch. **2** a similar fence used in show jumping.

ox-eye *noun* a plant with a flower like the eye of an ox. □ **ox-eyed** *adjective*

ox-eye daisy *noun* a daisy, *Chrysanthemum leucanthemum*, having flowers with white petals and a yellow centre.

Ox·ford a city in central England, on the Thames River, the county town of Oxfordshire; pop. (2001) 134,248.

ox·ford *noun* (in full **oxford shoe**) a low, sturdy shoe laced over the instep. [OXFORD]

Oxford blue ● *noun* **1** a dark blue, sometimes with a purple tinge. **2** = BLUE¹ *noun* 5. ● *adjective* (hyphenated when *attributive*) of this colour. [adopted by *Oxford* University]

oxford cloth *noun* a heavy cotton or cotton blend fabric used esp. for dress shirts.

Oxford Group *noun* a Christian movement founded at Oxford in 1921, with discussion of personal problems by groups.

Oxford Movement *noun* a Christian movement (*c.*1833–45) based at Oxford and led by Keble, Newman, and Pusey, which aimed at restoring traditional Catholic teaching within the Church of England. It eventually formed the basis for the development of Anglo-Catholicism.

Ox·ford·shire /ˈɒksfərd,ʃɪr/ a county of south central England; county town, Oxford.

Oxford shirt *noun* a dress shirt made of oxford cloth.

oxford shoe *noun* = OXFORD.

ox-hide *noun* **1** the hide of an ox. **2** leather made from this.

oxi·dant /ˈɒksɪdənt/ *noun* an oxidizing agent.

oxi·dase /ˈɒksɪ,deɪs, -,deɪz/ *noun* any of a class of enzymes that react with molecular oxygen to form water or hydrogen peroxide. [French *oxydase*, from *oxyde* OXIDE]

oxi·da·tion /ɒksɪˈdeɪʃən/ *noun* the process or result of oxidizing or being oxidized. □ **oxi·da·tion·al** *adjective* **oxi·da·tive** *adjective*

oxidation state *noun* (also **oxidation number**) *Chem.* **1** a number indicating the number of electrons actually or notionally lost or gained by an atom of an element when chemically combined. **2** the state represented by a value of this.

ox·ide *noun* a binary compound of oxygen. [French from *oxygène* OXYGEN + *-ide* after *acide* ACID]

oxi·dize *verb* (also esp. *Brit.* **-dise**) **1** *intransitive & transitive* combine or cause to combine with oxygen. **2** *transitive & intransitive* cover (metal) or (of metal) become covered with a coating of oxide etc.; make or become rusty or tarnished. **3** *intransitive & transitive Chem.* undergo or cause to undergo a loss of electrons (*opp.* REDUCE 12b). □ **oxi·diz·able** *adjective* **oxi·diz·a·tion** *noun* **oxi·dized** *adjective* **oxi·diz·er** *noun*

oxidizing agent *noun Chem.* a substance that brings about oxidation by being reduced and gaining electrons.

ox·lip *noun* **1** a woodland primula, *Primula elatior.* **2** (in general use) a natural hybrid between a primrose and a cowslip.

Oxon. /ˈɒksən/ *abbreviation* **1** Oxfordshire. **2** of Oxford University. [abbreviation of medieval Latin *Oxoniensis* from *Oxonia*: see OXONIAN]

Ox·on·ian /ɒkˈsoʊnɪən/ ● *adjective* of or relating to Oxford or Oxford University. ● *noun* **1** a member of Oxford University. **2** a native or inhabitant of Oxford. [*Oxonia* Latinized name of *Ox(en)ford*]

ox·peck·er *noun* any African bird of the genus *Buphagus*, feeding on skin parasites living on animals.

ox·tail *noun* the tail of an ox, esp. as an ingredient in soup.

ox·ter *noun Scot., Northern Engl., & Irish* the armpit. [Old English *ōhsta, ōxta*]

ox tongue *noun* **1** the tongue of an ox, esp. cooked as food. **2** any composite plant of the genus *Picris*, with bright yellow flowers.

Oxus River /ˈɒksəs/ the ancient name for the AMU DARYA RIVER.

oxy-¹ *combining form* denoting sharpness (*oxytone*). [Greek *oxu-* from *oxus* sharp]

oxy-² *combining form* (also **ox-** /ɒks/) *Chem.* oxygen (*oxyacetylene*). [abbreviation]

oxy·acetyl·ene /ɒksɪəˈsetɪ,liːn/ *adjective* of or using a mixture of oxygen and acetylene, esp. in cutting or welding metals (*oxyacetylene torch*).

oxy·acid /ˈɒksɪ,asɪd/ *noun Chem.* an acid containing oxygen.

Oxy·Cont·in *noun proprietary* a synthetic painkiller which is similar to morphine in its effects. [*oxy-²* + *co-* as in CODEINE]

oxy·gen /ˈɒksɪdʒən/ *noun Chem.* a colourless tasteless odourless gaseous element, occurring naturally in air, water, and most minerals and organic substances, and essential to plant and animal life. Symbol: **O**; at. no.: 8. □ **oxy·gen·ic** /-ˈdʒenɪk/ *adjective* **oxy·gen·ous** /ɒkˈsɪdʒənəs/ *adjective* [French *oxygène* acidifying principle (as *oxy-¹*): it was at first held to be the essential principle in the formation of acids]

oxy·gen·ate /ˈɒksɪdʒə,neɪt, ɒkˈsɪ-/ *transitive verb* **1** supply, treat, or mix with oxygen; oxidize. **2** charge (blood) with oxygen by respiration. □ **oxy·gen·a·tion** *noun* [French *oxygéner* (as OXYGEN)]

oxy·gen·ator /ˈɒksɪdʒə,neɪtər/ *noun* **1** an apparatus for oxygenating the blood. **2** an aquatic plant which enriches the surrounding water with oxygen.

oxygen bar *noun* a place where customers pay to inhale oxygen for therapeutic effects.

oxygen debt *noun* (also **oxygen deficit**) *Physiol.* the condition or degree of temporary oxygen shortage in the tissues arising from exercise.

oxygen mask *noun* a mask placed over the nose and mouth through which oxygen or oxygen-enriched air is supplied to relieve breathing difficulties.

oxygen tent *noun* a tent-like enclosure containing oxygen-enriched air, placed over a patient to aid breathing.

oxy·hemo·glo·bin /ˌɒksɪ,hiːməˈgloʊbɪn/ *noun* (also esp. *Brit.* **oxy·haemo·glo·bin**) *Biochem.* a bright red complex formed when hemoglobin combines with oxygen.

oxy·mor·on /ˌɒksɪˈmɔrɒn/ *noun* a figure of speech in which apparently contradictory terms appear in conjunction, e.g. *faith unfaithful kept him falsely true.* □ **oxy·mor·on·ic** /ˌɒksɪməˈrɒnɪk/ *adjective* **oxy·mor·on·ic·ally** *adverb* [Greek *oxumōron* neuter of *oxumōros* pointedly foolish, from *oxus* sharp + *mōros* foolish]

oxy·tetra·cy·cline /ˌɒksɪtetrəˈsaɪklɪn/ *noun* an antibiotic related to tetracycline.

oxy·to·cin /ˌɒksɪˈtoːsɪn/ *noun* **1** a hormone released by the pituitary gland that causes increased contraction of the uterus during labour and stimulates the ejection of milk into the ducts of the breasts. **2** a synthetic form of this used to induce labour etc. [*oxytocic* accelerating parturition, from Greek *oxutokia* sudden delivery (as *oxy-¹, tokos* childbirth)]

oxy·tone /ˈɒksɪ,toːn/ ● *adjective* (esp. in ancient Greek) having an acute accent on the last syllable. ● *noun* a word of this kind. [Greek *oxutonos* (as *oxy-¹, tonos* tone)]

oxy·trope /ˈɒksɪ,troːp/ *noun* any of various leguminous plants of the genus *Oxytropis*, with pinnate leaves and racemes of flowers, some cultivated, some poisonous to livestock. [Greek *oxy* 'sharp' + *tropis* 'keel']

oy *interjection* (also **oi**) calling attention or expressing alarm, dismay, exasperation, etc. [var. of HOY¹]

oya·mel fir /ˈɔɪjəmel/ *noun* a large fir tree, *Abies religiosa*, of mountainous regions in Mexico, forests of which provide the wintering grounds of the monarch butterfly. [Mexican Spanish from Aztec *oyametl*]

oyer and terminer /ˌɔɪər ənd ˈtɜrmənər/ *noun hist.* a commission issued to judges on a circuit to hold courts. [Anglo-French *oyer et terminer* from Latin *audire* hear + *et* and + *terminare* determine]

oyez /oːˈjes, -ˈjez/ *interjection* (also **oyes**) uttered, usu. three times, by a public crier or a court officer to command silence and attention. [Old French *oiez, oyez,* imperative pl. of *oïr* hear, from Latin *audire*]

oys·ter ● *noun* **1** any of various bivalve molluscs of the family Ostreidae or Aviculidae. **2** (in full **oyster white**) (often *attributive*) a white colour with a grey tinge. **3** something regarded as containing all that one desires (*the world is my oyster*). **4** an oyster-shaped morsel of meat in a fowl's back. ● *intransitive verb* fish for or gather oysters. □ **oys·ter·ing** *noun* [Old French *oistre* from Latin *ostrea, ostreum* from Greek *ostreon*]

oyster bar *noun* **1** a bar or counter in a restaurant where patrons gather to eat oysters and drink. **2** a restaurant having an oyster bar.

oyster bed *noun* a part of the sea bottom where oysters breed or are bred.

oyster·catch·er *noun* any usu. coastal wading bird of the genus *Haematopus*, with a strong orange-coloured bill, feeding on shellfish.

oyster leaf *noun* a blue-flowered plant, *Mertensia maritima*, growing on beaches.

oyster·man *noun* (*pl.* **-men**) a person who fishes for oysters for a living.

oyster mushroom *noun* an edible fungus, *Pleurotus ostreatus*, which grows on trees.

oyster plant *noun* = SALSIFY.

oyster sauce *noun* a dark brown sauce made from soy sauce and oyster extract, used in Asian cooking.

oy vey /ɔɪ veɪ/ *interjection* (also **oy vey is mir** /ɔɪ 'veɪ ɪz ,miːr/) an exclamation of dismay, grief, etc. [Yiddish *vey* woe]

Oz¹ *slang* ● *noun* **1** Australia. **2** an Australian. ● *adjective* Australian. [abbreviation of the pronunciation]

Oz² *noun* any place thought to resemble the land or city of Oz, esp. any fantastic, ideal, or imaginary domain. [the name of the fictional city and land in the children's fantasy *The Wonderful Wizard of Oz*, by L. Frank Baum (1856-1919), U.S. writer]

oz. *abbreviation* ounce(s). [Italian from *onza* ounce]

Ozark Mountains /ˈoːzɑrk/ (also **Ozarks**) a heavily forested highland plateau dissected by rivers, valleys, and streams, lying between the Missouri and Arkansas rivers and within the states of Missouri, Arkansas, Oklahoma, Kansas, and Illinois.

Ozawa /oːˈzɒwə/ **Seiji** (b.1935), Japanese conductor, who specializes in the symphonic music of the 19th and 20th c.; he was the conductor of the Toronto Symphony Orchestra (1965–70) and in 1973 became music director and conductor of the Boston Symphony Orchestra, a position he held until 2002.

ozo·cer·ite /oːˈzoːkəˌrəit, -sərəit, oːzoːˈsiːrəit/ *noun* (also **ozo·ker·ite**) a waxlike fossil paraffin used for candles, insulation, etc. [German *Ozokerit* from Greek *ozō* smell + *kēros* wax]

ozone *noun* **1** *Chem.* a colourless unstable toxic gas with a pungent odour and powerful oxidizing properties, formed from normal oxygen by electrical discharges or ultraviolet light. Chem. formula: O₃. **2** = OZONE LAYER. □ **ozon·ic** /oːˈzɒnɪk/ *adjective* **ozon·ize** *transitive verb* (also esp. *Brit.* **-ise**). **ozon·iz·a·tion** *noun* **ozon·iz·er** *noun* [German *Ozon* from Greek, neut. pres. part. of *ozō* 'smell']

ozone depletion *noun* a reduction of ozone concentration in the stratosphere, believed to be due to atmospheric pollution. □ **ozone depleter** *noun*

ozone-friend·ly *adjective* (of manufactured articles) not containing chemicals that are destructive to the ozone layer.

ozone hole *noun* a region of marked thinning of the ozone layer, esp. above each pole.

ozone layer *noun* a layer of ozone in the stratosphere that absorbs most of the sun's ultraviolet radiation.

Oz·zie *var. of* AUSSIE.

Pp

P¹ *noun* (also **p**) (*pl.* **Ps** or **P's**) the sixteenth letter of the alphabet.

P² *abbreviation* (also **P.**) **1 a** (on road signs) parking. **b** (on an automatic transmission display) park. **2** *Chess* pawn. **3** (also Ⓟ) proprietary. **4** (of a grade) pass. **5** *Baseball* pitcher. **6** president. **7** pareve.

P³ *symbol* **1** *Chem.* the element phosphorus. **2** *Physics* **a** poise (unit). **b** proton.

p *abbreviation* (also **p.**) **1** (*pl.* **pp**) page. **2** *Brit.* penny, pence. **3** pico-. **4** piano (softly).

PA¹ *abbreviation* **1** Pennsylvania (in official postal use). **2** (also **P.A.**) production assistant. **3** (also **P.A.**) *Cdn* (*Sask. & Man.*) PARENTAL ACCOMPANIMENT.

PA² *noun* **1** a public address system. **2** *Brit.* personal assistant. [abbreviation]

P.A. *abbreviation* Prince Albert (Saskatchewan).

Pa *symbol Chem.* the element protactinium.

pa *noun informal* father. [abbreviation of PAPA]

p.a. *abbreviation* per annum.

paan /pɑn/ *noun* the leaf of the betel palm wrapped around a preparation of betel nuts and lime and chewed. [Hindi *pān* betel leaf, from Sanskrit *parṇà*, feather, leaf]

pa'anga /pɑˈɑŋɡə/ *noun* the basic monetary unit of Tonga, equal to 100 seniti. [Tongan]

Paarl /pɑrl/ a town in southwestern S Africa, northeast of Cape Town; pop. (est. 2002) 156,100. It is at the centre of a noted wine-producing region.

PABA /ˈpɑbə/ *abbreviation* para-aminobenzoic acid, a substance widely distributed in plant and animal tissue, and used in sunscreens, in manufacturing folic acid, dyes, etc. and in laboratories as a sulphonamide antagonist.

Pab·lum *noun* **1** *proprietary* a soft cereal for infants. **2** (**pablum**) bland or insipid intellectual fare, entertainment, etc. [from PABULUM]

pab·ulum /ˈpæbjələm/ *noun* **1** food, esp. for the mind (*mental pabulum*). **2** = PABLUM 2. [Latin 'food', from *pascere* feed]

PABX *abbreviation Brit.* private automatic branch exchange.

PAC *abbreviation* **1** *US* political action committee. **2** (in South Africa) Pan-Africanist Congress. **3** pre-authorized chequing.

paca /ˈpækə/ *noun* either of two rodents of Mexico and northern S America related to the agoutis and cavies and constituting the genus *Agouti*, esp. *A. paca*, hunted locally for food. [Spanish & Portuguese, from Tupi]

pace¹ ● *noun* **1 a** a single step in walking or running. **b** the distance covered in this (about 75 cm or 30 in.). **c** the distance between two successive stationary positions of the same foot in walking. **2** speed in walking or running. **3** speed or tempo in theatrical or musical performance. **4 a** the rate at which something progresses (*the pace of technological change*; *learn at your own pace*). **b** the speed at which life is led (*the pace of city life*). **5 a** a manner of walking or running. **b** any of various gaits, esp. of a trained horse etc. (*rode at an ambling pace*). ● *verb* **1** *intransitive* **a** walk (esp. repeatedly or methodically) with a slow or regular pace (*pacing up and down*). **b** (of a horse) = AMBLE *verb* 2. **2** *transitive* traverse by pacing. **3** *transitive* set the pace for (a rider, runner, etc.). **4** *transitive* (often foll. by *off*) measure (a distance) by pacing. **5** *reflexive* distribute one's energy, efforts, etc. equally over the time allotted for a task, so as not to exhaust oneself too soon. □ **change of pace** a change from what one is used to. **keep pace** (often foll. by *with*) advance at an equal rate (as). **off the pace 1** slower than the leading horse in the early part of a race. **2** behind the leader in any race or contest; not performing satisfactorily. **put a person through his** (or **her**) **paces** test a person's qualities in action etc. **set the pace** determine the speed, esp. by leading. **stand** (or **stay**) **the pace** be able to keep up with others. □ **-paced** *adjective* [Old French *pas* from Latin *passus*, from *pandere pass-* 'stretch']

pace² /ˈpɑtʃeɪ/ *preposition* (in stating a contrary opinion) with due deference to (the person named). ¶ *Pace* means 'despite (someone's) opinion', e.g. *I was not* (*pace Mr. Smith*) *defending the legalization of drugs*. It does not mean 'according to (someone)' or 'notwithstanding (something)'. [Latin, ablative of *pax* peace]

pace car *noun Motorsport* a car that sets the pace for the competing vehicles during the pace lap and leaves the track before the race begins.

pace lap *noun Motorsport* a lap made before a race by all participating cars, motorcycles, etc. to warm up the engines.

pace·maker *noun* **1** a device which supplies electrical signals to the heart, stimulating it to beat at an appropriate rate. **2** the part of the heart which determines the rate at which it contracts and where the contractions begin (in humans and other mammals normally the sino-atrial node). **3** a competitor who sets the pace for another in racing or training for a race. **4** = PACESETTER 1.

pa·cer *noun* **1** a horse bred to take part in harness racing. **2** a person who paces or sets the pace.

pace·set·ter *noun* **1** a person, institution, etc. that serves as a model for others; a leader. **2** = PACEMAKER 3. □ **pace-setting** *adjective & noun*

pacey *var.* of PACY.

pa·cha *var.* of PASHA 1.

Pach·el·bel /ˈpɒkəlbɛl/ **Jo·hann** (1653–1706), German organist and composer, who is best known for the popular *Canon in D Major*.

pa·chin·ko /pəˈtʃɪŋkoʊ/ *noun* a Japanese form of pinball. [Japanese]

pa·chi·si /pəˈtʃiːzi/ *noun* a four-handed Indian board game with six cowries used like dice. [Hindi, = of 25 (the highest throw)]

Pa·chu·ca de Soto /pəˌtʃuːkə deɪ ˈsoːtoː/ (also **Pa·chu·ca**) a city in Mexico, capital of the state of Hidalgo; pop. (2000) 261,400.

pachy·derm /ˈpækɪdɜrm/ *noun* any thick-skinned mammal, esp. an elephant or rhinoceros. □ **pachy·der·ma·tous** /-ˈdɜrmətəs/ *adjective* [French *pachyderme* from Greek *pakhudermos* from *pakhus* thick + *derma -matos* skin]

pachy·san·dra /pækɪˈsændrə/ *noun* any of various N American and eastern Asian evergreen shrubs of the genus *Pachysandra*, of the box family, esp. the Japanese *P. terminalis*, grown as ground cover. [Greek *pakhus* thick + *andr-* man (with reference to the thick stamens]

pachy·tene /ˈpækɪtiːn/ *noun Biol.* a stage during the prophase of meiosis when the chromosomes thicken and may exchange genes by crossing over. [Greek *pakhus* 'thick' + *tainia* 'band']

pa·cif·ic /pəˈsɪfɪk/ ● *adjective* **1** characterized by or tending to peace; tranquil. **2** (**Pacific**) of or adjoining the Pacific. ● *noun* (**the Pacific**) = PACIFIC OCEAN. □ **pa·cif·ic·ally** *adverb* [French *pacifique* or Latin *pacificus* from *pax pacis* peace]

paci·fi·ca·tion /ˌpæsəfɪˈkeɪʃən/ *noun* the act of pacifying or the process of being pacified. [French from Latin *pacificatio -onis* (as PACIFY)]

Pacific Daylight Time *noun* daylight time in the Pacific Time zone. Abbr.: **PDT**.

Consonants: b *but*   d *dog*   f *few*   g *get*   h *her*   j *yes*   k *cat*   l *leg*   m *man*   n *no*   p *pen*   r *red*   s *sit*

Pacific dogwood *noun* a dogwood tree, *Cornus nuttallii*, of the west coast of N America, with showy white floral bracts and bright red fruits, planted as an ornamental; it is the floral emblem of BC.

Pacific loon *noun* a loon, *Gavia pacifica*, which breeds in the Arctic and winters on the coast of BC, similar in appearance to the common loon but smaller, with a grey crown and back of the neck.

Pacific Ocean the world's largest ocean, covering one-third of the earth's surface. It separates Asia and Australia from North and South America and extends from Antarctica in the south to the Bering Strait (which links it to the Arctic Ocean) in the north. It was named by its first European navigator, Ferdinand Magellan, in the hope of experiencing calm weather there.

Pacific Rim *noun* (usu. prec. by *the*) the countries and regions bordering the Pacific Ocean, esp. regarded collectively as a group with shared political, economic, and environmental interests.

Pacific Rim National Park Reserve a park reserve encompassing a portion of the west coast of Vancouver Island. Established in 1970, it covers over 100 km along the rim of the Pacific, from Tofino to Port Renfrew.

Pacific salmon *noun* any of the five species constituting the genus *Oncorhynchus*, of the N Pacific: the pink salmon, chum salmon, coho salmon, sockeye salmon, and chinook salmon.

Pacific sardine *noun* a sardine, *Sardinops sagax caerulea*, of the Pacific coast of N America.

Pacific Scandal *noun Cdn hist.* a political scandal surrounding the issue of financial contributions to Sir John A. Macdonald's 1872 election campaign by businessmen who were subsequently granted the charter to build the Canadian Pacific Railway.

Pacific Standard Time *noun* standard time in the Pacific Time zone. Abbr.: **PST**.

Pacific Time *noun* the time in a zone including British Columbia and the Pacific states of the US. Pacific Standard Time is eight hours behind Greenwich Mean Time; Pacific Daylight Time is seven hours behind Greenwich Mean Time. Abbr.: **PT**.

Pacific yew *noun* a small yew tree of the west coast of N America, *Taxus brevifolia*. *Also called* WESTERN YEW.

paci·fi·er /ˈpasəˌfaɪr/ *noun* **1** a person or thing that pacifies. **2** *N Amer.* a baby's soother.

paci·fism /ˈpasəˌfɪzəm/ *noun* the belief that war and violence are morally unjustified and that all disputes should be settled by peaceful means. □ **paci·fist** *noun & adjective* **paci·fis·tic** *adjective* [French *pacifisme* from *pacifier* PACIFY]

paci·fy /ˈpasəˌfaɪ/ *transitive verb* (**-fies**, **-fied**) **1** appease (a person, anger, etc.). **2** bring (a country etc.) to a state of peace. [Old French *pacifier* or Latin *pacificare* (as PACIFIC)]

pa·cing *noun* **1** in senses of PACE¹ *verb*. **2** the apparent speed at which the events in a film, play, etc. take place. **3** the tempos and overall rhythm, taken as a whole, selected by a conductor for a performance of a work.

Pa·cino /pəˈtʃiːnoʊ/ **Al** (full name Alfredo James Pacino) (b.1939), US actor. Nominated for an Oscar eight times and winning one for *Scent of a Woman* (1992), he first achieved recognition with *The Godfather* (1972) and *The Godfather Part II* (1974). Other notable films: *Scarface* (1983) and *Dick Tracy* (1990).

pack¹ ● *noun* **1 a** a collection of things wrapped up or tied together for carrying. **b** = BACKPACK *noun*. **2 a** a set of items packaged for sale, use, or disposal together. **b** a package, esp. of cigarettes. **3** usu. *derogatory* **a** a lot or set (of similar things or persons) (*a pack of lies*; *a pack of thieves*). **b** a group of journalists regarded as a predatory mob which hounds those in the news (also *attributive*: *pack journalism*). **4** a set of playing cards. **5 a** a group of wild animals, esp. wolves, hunting together. **b** a group of hounds esp. for fox hunting. **6** *Cdn & Brit.* an organized group of Cubs, Brownies, etc. **7 a** *Rugby* a team's forwards. **b** *Sport* the main body of competitors following the leader or leaders esp. in a race. **c** any group of competitors. **8 a** a medicinal or cosmetic substance applied to the skin; = FACE MASK 2. **b** a hot or cold pad of absorbent material for treating a wound etc. **9** (also **ice pack**) an area of pack ice. **10** a quantity of fish, fruit, etc., packed in a season etc. **11** *Med.* **a** the wrapping of a body or part of a body in a wet sheet etc. **b** a sheet etc. used for this. ● *verb* **1** (often foll. by *up*) **a** *transitive* fill (a suitcase, bag, box, etc.) with clothes or other items for transport or storage. **b** *transitive* put (things) together in a bag, suitcase, box, etc. esp. for travelling or moving. **c** *intransitive* pack clothes etc. for travelling or moving. **2** *intransitive & transitive* come or put closely together; crowd or cram (*packed a lot into a few hours*; *passengers packed like sardines*). **3** *transitive* (in *passive*; often foll. by *with*) be filled (with); contain

extensively (*the restaurant was packed*; *the book is packed with information*). **4** *transitive* fill (a hall, theatre, etc.) with an audience etc. **5** *transitive* cover (a thing) with something pressed tightly around (*pack a wound*). **6** *intransitive* be suitable for packing (*these skirts pack well*). **7** *transitive informal* **a** carry (a gun etc.). **b** be capable of delivering (a punch, impression, etc.) with skill or force. **8** *N Amer.* **a** *transitive* carry (goods, equipment, etc.), esp. on the back. **b** *intransitive* = BACKPACK *verb*. **9** *transitive Computing* compress (stored data) in a way that permits subsequent recovery. **10** *transitive* place (food items) in a bag or box for later consumption, e.g. at work or school or while travelling. **11** *transitive* store (food items) in a preservative substance (*peaches packed in sugar syrup*). **12** *transitive* form a hard thick mass (*the wind had packed the snow against the door*). ● *adjective* (of an animal) used for carrying a load (*pack dog*). □ **pack a punch 1** be capable of hitting with skill or force. **2** have a powerful effect. **pack heat** *N Amer. informal* carry a gun. **pack in** *informal* stop, give up (*packed in his job*). **pack it in** (or **up**) *informal* end or stop it. **pack off** *informal* send (a person) away, esp. abruptly or promptly. **pack one's bags** prepare to leave. **pack up** *Brit. informal* **1** (esp. of a machine) stop functioning; break down. **2** retire from an activity, contest, etc. **send packing** *informal* dismiss (a person) summarily. □ **pack·able** *adjective* [Middle Dutch, Middle Low German *pak*, *pakken*, of unknown origin]

pack² *transitive verb* select (a jury etc.) or fill (a meeting) so as to secure a decision in one's favour. [prob. from obsolete verb *pact* from PACT]

pack·age ● *noun* **1 a** an object or objects wrapped in paper or packed in a box; a parcel. **b** a box, container, etc., in which things are packed. **2** (also **package deal**) a set of proposals or items offered or agreed to as a whole. **3** a portfolio, folder, etc., containing printed matter or other multimedia materials for publicity purposes etc. (*information package*). **4** a group of related objects viewed or organized as a unit. **5** *Computing* a piece of software suitable for various applications rather than one which is custom-built. **6** *informal* = PACKAGE TOUR. ● *transitive verb* **1** make up into or enclose in a package. **2** present (a product, person, or message) so as to appeal to the public. □ **pack·ager** *noun* [PACK¹ + -AGE]

package tour *noun* (also **package holiday**) a tour, vacation, etc. with all arrangements made at an inclusive price.

pack·aging *noun* **1** a wrapping or container for goods. **2** the action or process of packing goods. **3** the creation of an image for promotional purposes; the style and context in which a particular product, person, or idea is marketed.

pack animal *noun* an animal for carrying packs.

pack drill *noun* esp. *Brit.* a military punishment of marching up and down carrying full equipment.

packed *adjective* **1** full to capacity (*a packed auditorium*). **2** filled with something packed in. **3 a** (*predicative*) (of a person) having finished one's packing for a trip. **b** (of a box, suitcase, etc.) that has been packed. **4** having a specified quality in abundance (*packed with features*) (also in *combination*: *an action-packed movie*). **5** compressed into a hardened mass (*the packed snow squeaked underfoot*). **6** (of a food) packed in a specified substance for preservation (*oil-packed tuna*).

packed lunch *noun* a lunch carried in a bag, box, etc., esp. to work, school, etc.

pack·er *noun* **1** a person or thing that packs, esp. a dealer who prepares and packs food for transportation and sale. **2** *N Amer.* **a** a pack animal. **b** a person who transports goods by means of pack animals. **c** a person who carries goods on his or her back.

pack·et ● *noun* **1** a small package. **2** esp. *Brit. informal* a large sum of money won, lost, or spent. **3** *Computing* a unit of data transmitted over a network. **4** = PACKAGE *noun* 3. **5** (in full **packet boat**) *hist.* a mail boat or passenger ship. ● *transitive verb* make up into or wrap up in a packet. [PACK¹ + -ET¹]

packet·ize *transitive verb* (also esp. *Brit.* **-ise**) partition or separate (data) into units for transmission in a packet switching network.

packet sniffer *noun* a sniffer program which targets packets of data transmitted over the Internet.

packet switching *noun* a method of data transmission in which parts of a message are sent independently by the optimum route for each part and then reassembled. □ **packet-switched** *adjective*

Pack·ham pear /ˈpakəm/ *noun* a large, bumpy green pear with smooth white sweet and juicy flesh, grown esp. in the southern hemisphere. [C.H. *Packham* Australian fruit grower d.1909]

pack horse *noun* a horse for carrying loads.

pack ice *noun* an area of large crowded pieces of floating ice in the sea. *Also called* ICE PACK.

pack·ing *noun* **1** the act or process of packing. **2** material used to fill up space around or in something, esp. to protect a fragile article in transit. **3** material used to seal a joint or assist in lubricating an axle.

packing case *noun* a usu. wooden box or case for storing or transporting goods.

packing house *noun* a factory where meat, produce, etc. is processed and packaged for shipping and sale.

packing parka *noun Cdn (North)* = AMAUTIK.

packing plant *noun* a factory where meat or fish is processed and packaged for shipping and sale.

packing snow *noun* wet snow that holds together when compressed, good for making snowballs etc.

pack rat *noun* **1** a N American woodrat of the genus *Neotoma cinerea*, which accumulates hoards of litter in its den. *Also called* BUSHY-TAILED WOODRAT. **2** *N Amer.* a person who hoards things.

pack·sack *noun N Amer.* a knapsack.

pack·saddle *noun* a saddle adapted for supporting packs.

pack train *noun N Amer.* a train of pack animals with their loads.

pack trip *noun N Amer.* a hiking or horseback trip in which all supplies and equipment are carried in packs.

pact *noun* an agreement or treaty between two or more people, groups, or countries. [Old French *pact(e)* from Latin *pactum*, neuter past participle of *pacisci* agree]

pacy /ˈpeisi/ *adjective* (also **pacey**) (**paci·er**, **paci·est**) *Brit.* fast-moving.

pacz·ki /ˈpʊnʃki/ *noun* a round doughnut with a filling of jam, prunes, lemon, custard, etc., traditionally eaten by Poles on Shrove Tuesday. [Polish]

pad[1] ● *noun* **1 a** a piece of material to reduce friction or jarring, fill out hollows, hold or absorb liquid, etc. **b** = SANITARY PAD. **2** a number of sheets of blank or printed paper fastened together at one edge. **3** = STAMP PAD. **4** the fleshy underpart of an animal's foot or of a human finger. **5** a guard for the leg, elbow, etc. in sports. **6 a** a flat surface for helicopter takeoff or rocket launching. **b** a broad, flat expanse of concrete etc. used as a floor or foundation. **7** *informal* a person's living quarters, esp. an apartment. **8** the floating leaf of a water lily. **9** = CUSHION *noun* 3. **10** = TOUCHPAD. **11** *Cdn* = ICE PAD. ● *transitive verb* (**pad·ded**, **pad·ding**) **1** provide with a pad or padding; stuff. **2** lengthen or fill out (a book etc.) with unnecessary material. **3** inflate or falsify figures in an expense account, budget, etc. [prob. of Low German or Dutch origin]

pad[2] ● *intransitive verb* (**pad·ded**, **pad·ding**) **1** (often foll. by *around*, *over*, etc.) walk with a soft dull steady step. **2** travel on foot. ● *noun* the sound of soft steady steps. [Low German *padden* tread, *pad* PATH]

Pa·dang /pɑ'dɑŋ/ a seaport of Indonesia, the largest city on the west coast of Sumatra; pop. (est. 2002) 586,400.

PA day *abbreviation Cdn* = PROFESSIONAL DEVELOPMENT DAY. [abbreviation of *professional activity*]

padded cell *noun* a room in a psychiatric hospital etc. with padded walls to prevent patients from injuring themselves.

pad·ding *noun* **1** soft material used to pad or stuff with. **2** superfluous matter introduced simply to lengthen or expand a book, essay, etc. **3** inflated or fraudulent entries in an expense account, budget, etc. **4** fat (*many women carry extra padding over the hips*).

pad·dle[1] ● *noun* **1** a short broad-bladed oar used without a rowlock. **2** a paddle-shaped instrument or part of a machine, esp. one used for beating or mixing food. **3 a** a short-handled bat used in various ball games, esp. table tennis. **b** (also **bidding paddle**) a numbered bat shaped like this, used to signal bids in an auction. **4** *Zool.* a fin or flipper. **5** each of the boards fitted around the circumference of a paddlewheel or mill wheel. **6** the action of paddling; a period spent paddling. **7** a plastic-covered electrode used in cardiac stimulation. ● *verb* **1** *intransitive & transitive* move on water or propel a boat by means of paddles. **2** *intransitive & transitive* row gently. **3** *transitive* transport (a person) by paddling (*we paddled her to the island*). **4** *transitive* esp. *N Amer. informal* spank. **5** *transitive* stir or mix with or as with a paddle. **6** *transitive* dog-paddle. □ **paddle one's own canoe** *N Amer.* manage one's own affairs. □ **pad·dler** *noun* **pad·dling** *noun* [15th c.: origin unknown]

pad·dle[2] ● *intransitive verb* **1** *Brit. & Cdn* walk, esp. barefoot, in shallow water. **2** dabble the feet or hands in shallow water. ● *noun* the action of paddling; a period spent paddling. □ **pad·dler** *noun* [prob. of Low German or Dutch origin: compare Low German *paddeln* tramp about]

paddle·ball *noun* a game played with a light ball and wooden bat in a four-walled handball court.

paddle·boat *noun* **1** (also **paddle steamer** etc.) a boat, steamer,

etc., propelled by a paddlewheel. **2** = PEDAL BOAT. □ **pad·dle boat·ing** *noun*

paddle·fish *noun* (*pl.* same or **-fishes**) a large, mainly freshwater fish related to the sturgeon, with an elongated snout, of which there are two species, *Polyodon spathula* of the Mississippi basin and *Psephurus gladius* of the Yangtze River.

paddle tennis *noun* a racquet sport combining elements of tennis and handball, played on a small court with a rubber ball and a wooden or plastic bat.

paddle·wheel *noun* a wheel with blades fitted around its circumference, which provides impetus to a boat when revolved so that the blades push backwards against the water.

paddle·wheel·er *noun N Amer.* a steamer propelled by paddlewheels.

paddling pool *noun* = WADING POOL.

pad·dock ● *noun* **1** a small field, esp. for keeping horses in. **2** an enclosure adjoining a racecourse or racetrack where horses or cars are assembled before a race. **3** *Austral. & NZ* a field; a plot of land. ● *transitive verb* keep or enclose in a paddock. [apparently variant of (now dialect) *parrock* from Old English *pearruc*: see PARK]

Paddy *noun* (*pl.* **-dies**) *informal often offensive* an Irishman. [pet form of the Irish name *Padraig* (= Patrick)]

paddy[1] *noun* (*pl.* **-dies**) **1** (in full **paddy field**) a field where rice is grown. **2** rice before threshing or in the husk. [Malay *pādi*]

paddy[2] *noun* (*pl.* **-dies**) *Brit. informal* a rage; a fit of temper. [PADDY]

paddy wagon *noun N Amer., Austral., & NZ slang* a police van for transporting prisoners or people who have been arrested. [PADDY, perhaps because formerly many American police officers were of Irish descent]

pade·mel·on /ˈpadə,melən/ *noun* any small wallaby of the genus *Thylogale*, inhabiting the coastal scrub of Australia. [earlier *paddymelon*, prob. alteration of Dharuk *badimaliyan*]

Pade·rew·ski /,padə'refski/ **Ig·nacy (Jan)** (1860–1941), Polish pianist, composer, and statesman, first prime minister of independent Poland 1919. One of the most famous international pianists of his time, he was also acclaimed for his compositions. After only ten months in office as prime minister, he resigned and resumed his musical career.

pad·lock ● *noun* a detachable lock hanging by a pivoted hook on the object fastened. ● *transitive verb* secure with a padlock. [Middle English from LOCK[1]: first element unexplained]

Padlock Law *noun Cdn hist.* a 1937 Quebec statute which allowed the Attorney General to close any premises suspected of being a location used to propagate communism.

Padma River /ˈpadmə/ a river of S Bangladesh, formed by the confluence of the Ganges and the Brahmaputra near Rajbari.

pa·douk /pə'duːk/ *noun* **1** any hardwood tree of the genus *Pterocarpus*, esp. *P. indicus* (also called AMBOYNA) or *P. soyauxii* (also called CAMWOOD). **2** the wood of this tree, resembling rosewood. [Burmese]

padre /ˈpɒdrei, 'pad-/ *noun* **1** a Christian clergyman, esp. a Roman Catholic priest. **2** a chaplain in any of the armed services. [Italian, Spanish, & Portuguese, = father, priest, from Latin *pater patris* father]

pa·drone /pə'droːni, -nei/ *noun* **1** a boss, a manager. **2** an exploitative employer of unskilled immigrant workers. **3** the proprietor of an inn or hotel in Italy. [Italian]

pad Thai *noun* a spicy Thai dish of rice noodles and shrimp, chicken, vegetables, etc. [Thai]

Padua /ˈpadjʊə/ a city in NE Italy; pop. (2001) 203,350.

Padua, Antony of see ANTHONY OF PADUA.

paean /ˈpiːən/ *noun* **1** a song of praise or triumph. **2** a written or spoken attribution of praise. [Latin from Doric Greek *paian* 'hymn of thanksgiving to Apollo' (invoked by the name *Paian*, originally the Homeric name for the physician of the gods)]

paedi·at·rics esp. *Brit. var.* of PEDIATRICS.

paedo- esp. *Brit. var.* of PEDO-.

paedo·phile esp. *Brit. var.* of PEDOPHILE.

paedo·philia esp. *Brit. var.* of PEDOPHILIA.

pael·la /pai'eiə, -elə/ *noun* a Spanish dish of rice, saffron, chicken, seafood, etc. [Catalan from Old French *paele* from Latin *patella* pan]

paeon /ˈpiːən/ *noun* a metrical foot of one long syllable and three short syllables in any order. [Latin from Greek *paiōn*, the Attic form of *paian* PAEAN]

Pagan /pə'gɒn/ a town in Burma, situated on the Irrawaddy southeast of Mandalay. It is the site of an ancient city, founded in about AD 849, which was the capital of a powerful Buddhist dynasty from the 11th to the end of the 13th c.

pa·gan /ˈpeɪɡən/ ● *noun* **1** a person holding religious beliefs other than those of any of the main religions of the world, esp. formerly regarded by Christians as unenlightened or heathen. **2** a person considered to be hedonistic or irreligious. ● *adjective* **1 a** of or relating to or associated with pagans. **b** irreligious. **2** identifying divinity or spirituality in nature; pantheistic. □ **pa·gan·ism** *noun* [Latin *paganus* villager, rustic, from *pagus* country district: in Christian Latin = civilian, heathen]

Paga·nini /ˌpaɡəˈniːni/ **Nic·co·lò** (1782–1840), Italian violinist and composer. His virtuoso violin recitals established him as an almost legendary figure of the romantic movement and radically changed the violin technique of the day.

Page, **Pa·tri·cia Kath·leen** (ʹP.K.ʹ) (b.1916), English-born Canadian poet, writer, and artist.

page[1] ● *noun* **1 a** a leaf of a book, periodical, etc. **b** each side of this. **c** what is written or printed on this. **2** *Computing* **a** a section of stored data, esp. that can be displayed on a screen at one time. **b** a hypertext document containing text and/or images which can be accessed by users of a network, esp. the Internet (compare HOME PAGE, WEB PAGE). **3 a** an episode that might fill a page in written history etc.; a record. **b** a memorable event. ● *verb* **1** *transitive* paginate. **2** *intransitive* **a** (foll. by *through*) leaf through (a book etc.). **b** (foll. by *through, up, down*) *Computing* display (text etc.) one page at a time. □ **on the same page** (of two or more people) in agreement. **take** (or **borrow**) **a page from** (or **out of**) **a person's book** imitate a person. [French from Latin *pagina*, from *pangere* ʹfastenʹ]

page[2] ● *noun* **1 a** a boy employed as a personal attendant of a person of rank, a bride, etc. **b** *N Amer.* a person employed in a legislative assembly to deliver members' messages. **2** a boy or man, usu. in livery, employed to run errands, attend to a door, etc. **3** *hist.* a boy in training for knighthood and attached to a knight's service. ● *transitive verb* **1** (in hotels, airports, etc.) summon by making an announcement or by sending a messenger. **2** summon by means of a pager. □ **paging** *noun* [Old French, perhaps from Italian *paggio* from Greek *paidion*, diminutive of *pais paidos* boy]

pa·geant /ˈpadʒənt/ *noun* **1 a** a brilliant spectacle, esp. an elaborate parade. **b** a procession or play illustrating historical events (*Christmas pageant*). **c** a contest or show (*beauty pageant*). **2** a tableau etc. on a fixed stage or moving vehicle. **3** something resembling a pageant in its grandeur, sweep, etc. (*the pageant of history*). [Middle English *pagyn*, of unknown origin]

pa·geant·ry /ˈpadʒəntri/ *noun* (*pl.* **-ries**) **1 a** elaborate or sumptuous show or display. **b** empty or specious show or display. **2** an instance of this.

page·boy *noun* **1** a woman's hairstyle with the hair reaching to the shoulder and rolled under at the ends. **2** a youth employed as a page.

page break *noun* **1** the point in a piece of continuous text where a page ends and its successor begins. **2** *Computing* a special character or other distinctive marker which, inserted into a text, causes a computer to display or print a new page.

page description language *noun* *Computing* a programming language, designed for use with typesetting equipment, visual displays, etc., which allows users to specify the typographical form of documents. Abbr.: **PDL**.

page proof *noun* a proof taken from type printed in pages, usu. after galley corrections have been made.

pager *noun* a radio device with a beeper, activated from a central point to alert the person wearing it.

Paget /ˈpadʒət/ **Sir James, 1st Baronet** (1814–99), English surgeon and pathologist, who discovered the cause of trichinosis (1834), and the forms of breast cancer (1874) and bone disease (1877) which are named after him.

page-turner *noun* **1** a book so exciting or engrossing that one is compelled to read it quickly. **2** a person who turns the pages of a musical score for a pianist, organist, etc. □ **page-turning** *adjective*

page wire *noun* smooth wiring in a grid pattern, used as fencing material to enclose fields etc. (often *attributive*: *page-wire fence*).

pagin·ate /ˈpadʒɪˌneɪt/ *transitive verb* assign numbers to the pages of a book etc. □ **pagin·a·tion** *noun* [French *paginer* from Latin *pagina* PAGE[1]]

Pag·lia /ˈpaɡliə/ **Ca·mille (Anna)** (b.1947), US cultural critic. Her first book *Sexual Personae* (1990), with its controversial pro-capitalist

and anti-feminist examination of art and decadence through the ages, brought her to public attention.

Pa·gnol /paˈnjɒl/ **Mar·cel** (1895–1974), French dramatist, film director, and writer who depicted especially life in the south of France. He is best known for the humorous film trilogy *Marius* (1931), *Fanny* (1932), and *César* (1936), cinematic adaptations of his own plays. In 1946 he became the first filmmaker to be elected to the Académie française.

pa·goda /pəˈɡoːdə/ *noun* **1** a Hindu or Buddhist temple or sacred building, esp. a many-tiered tower, in India and the Far East. **2** an ornamental imitation of this. [Portuguese *pagode*, prob. ultimately from Persian *butkada* idol temple]

pagoda dogwood *noun* a dogwood tree of eastern N America, with clusters of white flowers, dark blue fruit, and tiered branches.

PAH *abbreviation* polycyclic aromatic hydrocarbon.

pah *interjection* expressing disgust or contempt.

Pa·hang /pəˈhaŋ/ a mountainous, forested state of Malaysia, on the east coast of the Malay Peninsula; capital, Kuantan.

Pah·lavi[1] /ˈpɒləvi/ **1 Muham·mad Reza** (1919–80), shah of Iran 1941–79. After 1953 he assumed direct control over all aspects of Iranian life and, with US support, embarked on a national development plan; opposition to his regime culminated in the Islamic revolution of 1979 under Ayatollah Khomeini, and Pahlavi was forced into exile and died in the US. **2** his father, **Reza** (born Reza Khan) (1878–1944), shah of Iran 1925–41. An army officer, he took control of the Persian government after a coup in 1921, and was elected shah by the National Assembly in 1925; he abdicated in 1941, following the occupation of Iran by British and Soviet forces, passing the throne to his son.

Pah·lavi[2] /ˈpɒləvi/ *noun* **1** an Aramaic-based writing system used in Persia from the 2nd c. BC to the advent of Islam in the 7th c. AD. **2** the form of the Middle Persian language written in this. [Persian *pahlawi*, via *pahlav* from *parthava* ʹParthiaʹ]

pa·hoe·hoe /pəˈhoːɪhoːi/ *noun* *Geol.* lava forming smooth undulating or ropy masses (compare AA). [Hawaiian]

paid ● *verb* past and past participle of PAY[1]. ● *adjective* recompensed or reimbursed (*paid vacation*).

paid-up member *noun* **1** a member of an association, union, etc. who has paid the membership dues in full. **2** (also **fully paid-up member**) *informal* a fully committed supporter of a cause, organization, etc.

Paige, **Leroy Rob·ert** (known as ʹSatchelʹ) (c.1906–82), US baseball player, who was the first black pitcher to play in the American League (1948).

pail *noun* **1** a bucket. **2** an amount contained in this. □ **pail·ful** *noun* (*pl.* **-fuls**). [Old English *pægel* (compare Middle Dutch *pegel* gauge), assoc. with Old French *paelle*: see PAELLA]

pail·lasse *var.* of PALLIASSE.

pail·lette /palˈjet, paiˈjet/ *noun* **1** a spangle. **2** a piece of bright metal used in enamel painting. [French, diminutive of *paille* from Latin *palea* straw, chaff]

pain ● *noun* **1 a** a strongly unpleasant bodily sensation such as is produced by illness, injury, or other harmful physical contact etc.; the condition of hurting. **b** a particular kind or instance of this (often in *pl.*: *suffering from stomach pains*). **c** contractions of the uterus during labour. **2** mental suffering or distress. **3** (in *pl.*) careful effort; trouble taken (*take pains; got nothing for my pains*). **4** (also **pain in the neck** etc.) *informal* a troublesome person or thing; a nuisance. ● *verb* **1** *transitive* cause pain to. **2** *intransitive* (of a part of the body) ache; be painful. □ **be at** (or **take**) **pains** (usu. foll. by *to* + infin.) take great care in doing something. **in pain** suffering pain. **no pain, no gain** one cannot make progress (esp. in physical activity) without experiencing some pain. **on** (or **under**) **pain of** with (death etc.) as the penalty. [Old French *peine* from Latin *poena* ʹpenaltyʹ]

Paine, **Thom·as** (1737–1809), English-born political writer. After emigrating to the US in 1774, he wrote the pamphlet *Common Sense* (1776), which called for American independence and laid the ground for the Declaration of Independence; other works include *The Rights of Man* (1791), defending the French Revolution, and *The Age of Reason* (1794), an attack on orthodox Christianity.

pained *adjective* expressing pain (*a pained expression*).

Paine Towers /ˈpaɪni/ a group of spectacular granite peaks in S Chile, rising to a height of 2 668 m (8,755 ft.).

pain·ful *adjective* **1** causing bodily or mental pain or distress. **2** (esp. of part of the body) suffering pain. **3** causing trouble or difficulty;

laborious (*a painful climb*). **4** very bad (*painful jokes*). □ **pain·ful·ly** *adverb* **pain·ful·ness** *noun*

pain·kill·er *noun* a medicine or drug for alleviating pain. □ **pain·kill·ing** *adjective*

pain·less *adjective* **1** not causing or suffering pain. **2** effortless; easy. □ **pain·less·ly** *adverb* **pain·less·ness** *noun*

pains·tak·ing *adjective* careful, industrious, thorough. □ **pains·tak·ing·ly** *adverb* **pains·tak·ing·ness** *noun*

paint ● *noun* **1 a** colouring matter, esp. in liquid form for imparting colour to a surface. **b** this as a dried film or coating (*the paint peeled off*). **2** *jocular* or *archaic* cosmetic makeup, esp. rouge or nail polish. **3** *N Amer.* (often *attributive*) a piebald horse. **4** *Basketball* the rectangular area marked out around the basket at each end of the court. ● *verb* **1** *transitive* **a** cover the surface of (a wall, object, etc.) with paint. **b** apply paint of a specified colour to (*paint the door green*). **2** *transitive* depict (an object, scene, etc.) with paint; produce (a picture) by painting. **3** *transitive* describe vividly as if by painting (*painted the scene in vivid terms*). **4** *transitive* **a** apply a liquid or cosmetics to (the face, skin, etc.). **b** apply nail polish to (fingernails or toenails). **5** *transitive* apply (a liquid) to a surface with a brush etc. **6** *intransitive* practise the art of painting. **7** *transitive* cause (text, images, etc.) to be displayed or represented on a computer screen. □ **paint a picture** describe in vivid detail. **paint into a corner** force (a person, oneself) into a situation from which it is not easy to escape. **paint over** (or **out**) efface with paint. **paint the town red** *informal* enjoy oneself flamboyantly. □ **paint·able** *adjective* [Middle English, via *peint*, past participle of Old French *peindre*, from Latin *pingere pict-* 'paint']

paint·ball *noun* a game in which participants simulate military combat using air guns to shoot capsules of paint at each other. □ **paint·ball·er** *noun*

paint·box *noun* a box holding dry paints for painting pictures.

paint·brush *noun* **1** a brush for applying paint. **2** any of various plant species of the chiefly western N American genus *Castilleja*, with showy, brightly coloured bracts. *Also called* INDIAN PAINTBRUSH. **3** = HAWKWEED.

paint-by-number *adjective* **1** designating a type of painting set or book in which the pictures are divided into sections containing numbers indicating the colour to be used. **2** unoriginal; lacking individuality.

paint chip *noun* **1** *N Amer.* a card showing a colour or a range of related colours available in a type of paint. **2** a small area on a painted surface where the paint has been chipped away.

paint·ed *adjective* **1** that has been painted. **2** (of a plant or animal) brightly coloured; variegated.

painted lady *noun* any of several orange-red butterflies, esp. *Vanessa cardui* or *V. virginiensis*, with black and white spots.

painted trillium *noun* a trillium with red and white petals, *Trillium undulatum*, found east of the Rockies.

painted turtle *noun* a small freshwater turtle of N America, *Chrysema picta*, that is black or olive with red and yellow markings on the head and shell.

paint·er¹ *noun* **1** a person who paints pictures. **2** a person who applies paint for decoration and protection to walls, doors, etc.

paint·er² *noun* a rope attached to the bow of a boat for tying it to a quay etc. [Old French *penteur* rope from a masthead: compare German *Pentertakel* from *pentern* fish the anchor]

paint·er·ly *adjective* **1** like, characteristic of, or pertaining to a painter or paintings; artistic. **2** (of a painting or style of painting) characterized by qualities of colour, stroke, and texture rather than of contour or line. □ **paint·er·li·ness** *noun*

Painters Eleven a group of abstract artists, founded in 1953, who banded together to exhibit and promote Canadian abstract art. Through exhibitions in New York and Toronto between 1954–1960, the group launched the careers of several Canadian abstract artists, including Kazuo Nakamura and J.W.G. Macdonald.

paint·ing *noun* **1** the process or art of using paint. **2** a painted picture.

paint shop *noun* the part of a factory where goods are painted, esp. by spraying.

paint stick *noun* a stick of water-soluble paint used like a crayon.

paint stripper *noun* a heating device or a solvent for removing paint.

paint thinner *noun* a volatile liquid, e.g. turpentine, mineral spirits, etc., used to dilute paint, clean paintbrushes, etc.

paint·work *noun* **1** a painted surface or area in a building, on a car, etc. **2** the work of painting.

pair ● *noun* **1** a set of two persons or things used together or regarded

as a unit (*a pair of scoundrels; a pair of gloves; a pair of eyes*). **2** an article, e.g. scissors, trousers, or tights, consisting of two joined or corresponding parts not used separately. **3 a** a dating, engaged, cohabiting, or married couple. **b** a mated couple of animals. **4** two horses harnessed side by side (*a coach and pair*). **5** the second member of a pair in relation to the first (*cannot find its pair*). **6** two playing cards of the same denomination. **7** *Parl.* **a** either or both of two members of a legislative assembly on opposite sides absenting themselves from voting by mutual arrangement. **b** an agreement to do this. **8** (in *pl.*) = PAIRS SKATING. **9** (in *pl.*) a sporting event, e.g. in synchronized swimming or rowing, performed by teams of two. ● *transitive & intransitive verb* **1** (often foll. by *off*) arrange or be arranged in couples. **2** match or be matched together (*pair a wool vest with a silk shirt*). **3 a** join or be joined in marriage, close friendship, etc. **b** (of animals) mate. **4** *Parl.* form a pair (see sense 7 of *noun*). □ **in pairs** in twos. [Old French *paire* from Latin *paria* neuter pl. of *par* equal]

pair bond *noun* the relationship formed during courtship and mating of a pair of animals or two people. □ **pair bond** *intransitive verb* **pair bonding** *noun*

paired *adjective* occurring in pairs or as a pair.

pair·ing *noun* an arrangement or match resulting from organizing or forming into pairs.

pair production *noun* *Physics* the conversion of a radiation quantum into an electron and a positron.

pairs skating *noun* a type of figure skating in which a couple perform together a choreographed routine of jumps, lifts, throws, etc. to music. □ **pairs skater** *noun*

pair·wise ● *adjective* of, pertaining to, or forming a pair or pairs. ● *adverb* in or by pairs.

paisa /ˈpaizə/ *noun* (*pl.* same or **paise** /-zei or -zə/) a coin and monetary unit of India, Pakistan, and Nepal, equal to one-hundredth of a rupee. [Hindi]

Pais·ley¹ /ˈpeizli/ a town in central Scotland, to the west of Glasgow, administrative centre of Renfrewshire; pop. (est. 2002) 70,900, famous for its distinctive handwoven shawls imitating those imported from Kashmir in India in the late 18th and early 19th c.

Pais·ley² /ˈpeizli/ **Ian (Rich·ard Kyle)** (b.1926), Northern Irish politician and Presbyterian minister. As a co-founder of the Ulster Democratic Unionist Party (1972), he has been a vociferous and outspoken supporter of the Protestant Unionist position in Northern Ireland.

pais·ley /ˈpeizli/ *noun* (often *attributive*) **1** a distinctive detailed pattern of curved feather-shaped figures. **2** a soft woollen fabric having this pattern. **3** a garment, esp. a shawl, made from this fabric. [PAISLEY¹]

pa·ja·mas *N Amer. var. of* PYJAMAS.

pak *noun* (esp. in combination) = PACK¹ *noun* 2a (*econo-pak*). [variant of PACK¹, now usu. a deliberate respelling]

pa·keha /ˈpakɪhə/ *NZ* ● *noun* a white person as opposed to a Maori. ● *adjective* of or relating to white people. [Maori]

Paki /ˈpaki/ *noun* (*pl.* **Pakis**) *slang offensive* a Pakistani, esp. an immigrant. [abbreviation]

Pak·istan /ˌpakəˈstan, ˈpak-/ a Muslim country in the Indian subcontinent; pop. (est. 2002) 147,663,429; capital, Islamabad. Pakistan was created as a separate country in 1947, following the British withdrawal from India. It originally comprised two territories, respectively to the east and west of India, in which the population was predominantly Muslim. Civil war in East Pakistan over local claims for autonomy led to Indian intervention in 1971 and the establishment of the independent state of Bangladesh in 1972. □ **Pak·istani** *adjective & noun* [Punjab, Afghan Frontier, Kashmir, Baluch*istan*, lands where Muslims predominated]

pa·kora /pəˈkɔrə/ *noun* a piece of cauliflower, carrot, or other vegetable, coated in seasoned batter and deep-fried. [Hindi]

Pakse /ˈpaksei/ (also **Pakxe**) a town in S Laos, on the Mekong river; pop. (est. 1990) 25,000. The 7th-c. ruins of the ancient Khmer capital of Wat Phou lie to the south.

PAL *abbreviation* phase alternation line, the television broadcast format used in Europe and many other countries.

pal ● *noun* *informal* **1** a friend. **2** a form of address to an esp. male stranger. ● *intransitive verb* (**palled**, **pal·ling**) (usu. foll. by *around*) associate; form a friendship. [Romany = brother, mate, ultimately from Sanskrit *bhrātr* BROTHER]

pal·ace *noun* **1** the official residence of a sovereign, president, archbishop, or bishop. **2** a splendid mansion; a spacious building. **3** a spacious building used for exhibitions, concerts, etc. (*cow palace*). **4** an

Consonants: **b** *but* **d** *dog* **f** *few* **g** *get* **h** *her* **j** *yes* **k** *cat* **l** *leg* **m** *man* **n** *no* **p** *pen* **r** *red* **s** *sit*

establishment noted for the provision of a specified thing (*movie palace*; *gaming palace*). [Old French *palais* from Latin *Palatium* Palatine (hill) in Rome where the house of the emperor was situated]

palace coup *noun* (also **palace revolution**) the (usu. non-violent) overthrow of a sovereign, government, etc. at the hands of senior officials.

pala·csin·ta /ˌpalɑˈtʃɪntə/ *noun* (also **pala·cin·ke** /-ˈsɪŋkə/) (in Hungarian cuisine) a thin pancake eaten as a dessert, filled esp. with jam, cottage cheese, nuts, or chocolate. [Hungarian *palacsinta* pancake]

pal·adin /ˈpalədɪn/ *noun* **1** *hist.* any of the twelve peers of Charlemagne's court, of whom the Count Palatine was the chief. **2** *hist.* a knight errant; a champion. **3** a dedicated advocate or supporter of a cause. [French *paladin* from Italian *paladino* from Latin *palatinus*: see PALATINE¹]

palaeo- esp. *Brit.* var. of PALEO-.

Palaeo·cene esp. *Brit.* var. of PALEOCENE.

Palaeo·zoic esp. *Brit.* var. of PALEOZOIC.

pa·laestr·a esp. *Brit.* var. of PALESTRA.

pal·ais /ˈpaleɪ/ *noun* esp. *Brit. informal* a public hall for dancing. [French *palais* (*de danse*) (dancing) hall]

pal·an·quin /ˌpalənˈkiːn/ *noun* (also **pal·an·keen**) (in India and the East) a covered litter for one passenger. [Portuguese *palanquim*: compare Hindi *pālkī* from Sanskrit *palyanka* bed, couch]

pal·at·able /ˈpalətəbəl/ *adjective* **1** pleasant to taste. **2** (of an idea, suggestion, etc.) acceptable, satisfactory. □ **pal·at·abil·ity** *noun* **pal·at·able·ness** *noun* **pal·at·ably** *adverb*

pal·at·al /ˈpalətəl/ ● *adjective* **1** of the palate. **2** (of a sound) made by placing the surface of the tongue against the hard palate, e.g. *y* in *yes.* ● *noun* a palatal sound. □ **pal·at·al·ize** *transitive verb* (also esp. *Brit.* **-ise**). **pal·at·al·iz·a·tion** *noun* [French (as PALATE)]

pal·ate /ˈpalət/ *noun* **1** a structure closing the upper part of the mouth cavity in vertebrates. **2** the sense of taste. **3** flavour, taste, esp. of wine or beer. **4** a mental taste or inclination; liking. [Latin *palatum*]

pa·la·tial /pəˈleɪʃəl/ *adjective* (of a building) like a palace, esp. spacious and splendid. □ **pa·la·tial·ly** *adverb* [Latin (as PALACE)]

pal·at·in·ate /pəˈlatɪˌnət/ *noun* territory under the jurisdiction of a Count Palatine.

pal·at·ine¹ /ˈpaləˌtaɪn, -tɪn/ *adjective* (also **Palatine**) *hist.* **1** (of an official or feudal lord) having local authority that elsewhere belongs only to a sovereign (*Count Palatine*). **2** (of a territory) subject to this authority. [French *palatin -ine* from Latin *palatinus* of the PALACE]

pal·at·ine² /ˈpaləˌtaɪn, -tɪn/ ● *adjective* of or connected with the palate. ● *noun* (in full **palatine bone**) each of two bones forming the hard palate. [French *palatin -ine* (as PALATE)]

Palau /pəˈlaʊ/ (also **Belau** /bə-/) a group of islands in the W Pacific Ocean, part of the US Trust Territory of the Pacific Islands from 1947 and internally self-governing since 1980; pop. (est. 2002) 19,409; capital, Koror.

pa·lav·er /pəˈlavər/ ● *noun* **1** fuss and bother, esp. prolonged. **2** profuse or idle talk. **3** flattery, cajolery. **4** *informal* a prolonged or tiresome affair or business. **5** *hist.* a parley between African or other Aboriginal peoples and traders. ● *verb* **1** *intransitive* talk profusely. **2** *transitive* flatter, wheedle. **3** *intransitive* confer. [Portuguese *palavra* word, from Latin (as PARABLE)]

Pa·law·an /pəˈlɒwən/ a long, narrow island in the W Philippines, separating the Sulu Sea from the South China Sea. Its chief town is Puerto Princesa.

pa·laz·zo /pəˈlatsoː, -ˈlɒtsoː/ ● *noun* (pl. **-zos**) **1** a palatial mansion; a large imposing building. **2** loose, wide-legged pants worn by women. ● *adjective* designating a loose, wide-legged garment. [Italian from Latin *palatium*, palace]

Pale, the see ENGLISH PALE.

pale¹ ● *adjective* **1** (of a person or complexion) of a whitish or ashen appearance. **2 a** (of a colour) faint; not dark or deep. **b** faintly coloured. **3** of faint lustre; dim. **4** feeble; weak (*a pale imitation*). ● *verb* **1** *intransitive & transitive* grow or make pale. **2** *intransitive* (often foll. by *before, beside*) become feeble in comparison (with). □ **pale·ly** *adverb* **pale·ness** *noun* **pal·ish** *adjective* [Old French *pale, palir* from Latin *pallidus* from *pallēre* be pale]

pale² *noun* **1** a pointed piece of wood for fencing etc.; a stake. **2** a boundary. **3** an enclosed or delimited area, e.g. the areas of Russia to which Jewish residence was historically restricted. **4** *Heraldry* a vertical stripe in the middle of a shield. □ **beyond the pale** outside the bounds of acceptable behaviour. [Old French *pal* from Latin *palus* stake]

palea /ˈpeɪliə/ *noun* (pl. **pa·leae** /-liˌiː/) *Bot.* the upper bract of the floret of a grass. [Latin, = chaff]

Pale·arc·tic /ˌpeɪliˈɑrktɪk, ˌpali-, -ˈɑrtɪk/ *adjective* (also esp. *Brit.* **Palae·arc·tic**) *Zool.* of the Arctic and temperate parts of the Old World. [PALEO- + ARCTIC]

pale·face *noun* a name supposedly used by the N American Indians for the white man.

Pa·lem·bang /pɒˈlembɒŋ, ˌpɒləmˈbɒŋ/ a city in Indonesia, in the southeastern part of the island of Sumatra, a river port on the Musi river; pop. (est. 2002) 1,462,300. Formerly the capital of the Buddhist kingdom of Srivijaya, it became a sultanate in the late 15th c. From 1616 it was developed as a trading post by the Dutch, who abolished the sultanate in 1825.

Pa·len·que /pəˈleŋkeɪ/ the site of a former Mayan city in SE Mexico, southeast of present-day Villahermosa. The well-preserved ruins of the city, which existed from about AD 300 to 900, include notable examples of Mayan architecture and extensive hieroglyphic texts.

paleo- /ˈpeɪlioː, ˈpalioː/ *combining form* (esp. *Brit.* **palaeo-**) ancient, old; of ancient (esp. prehistoric) times. [Greek *palaios* ancient]

paleo·anthro·pol·ogy /ˌpeɪlioːˌanθrəˈpɒlədʒi, ˌpalioː-/ *noun* (esp. *Brit.* **palaeo·anthro·pol·ogy**) the branch of anthropology concerned with fossil hominids. □ **paleo·anthro·po·logic·al** *adjective* **paleo·anthro·pol·o·gist** *noun*

paleo·botany /ˌpeɪlioːˈbɒtəni, ˌpalioː-/ *noun* (esp. *Brit.* **palaeo·botany**) the study of fossil plants. □ **paleo·botan·ic·al** *adjective* **paleo·botan·ist** *noun*

Paleo·cene /ˈpeɪlioːˌsiːn, ˈpali-/ (esp. *Brit.* **Palaeo·cene**) *Geol.* ● *adjective* of or relating to the earliest epoch of the Tertiary period, between the Cretaceous period and the Eocene epoch, lasting from about 65 to 55 million years BP, characterized by a sudden diversification of mammals. ● *noun* this geological epoch or system. [PALEO- + Greek *kainos* new]

paleo·clima·tol·ogy /ˌpeɪlioːˌklaɪməˈtɒlədʒi, ˌpalioː-/ *noun* (esp. *Brit.* **palaeo·clima·tol·ogy**) the study of the climate in geologically past times. □ **paleo·clima·tol·o·gist** *noun*

paleo·ecol·ogy /ˌpeɪlioːɪˈkɒlədʒi, ˌpalioː-/ *noun* (esp. *Brit.* **palaeo·ecol·ogy**) the ecology of extinct and prehistoric organisms. □ **paleo·eco·logic·al** *adjective* **paleo·ecolo·gist** *noun*

paleo·geog·raphy /ˌpeɪlioːdʒiˈɒɡrəfi, ˌpalioː-/ *noun* (esp. *Brit.* **palaeo·geog·raphy**) the study of the geographical features at periods in the geological past. □ **paleo·geog·raph·er** *noun*

paleog·raphy /ˌpeɪliˈɒɡrəfi/ *noun* (esp. *Brit.* **palaeog·raphy**) the study of writing and documents from the past. □ **paleog·raph·er** *noun* **paleo·graph·ic** *adjective* **paleo·graph·ic·al** *adjective* **paleo·graph·ic·al·ly** *adverb*

paleo·lith·ic /ˌpeɪlioːˈlɪθɪk, ˌpalioː-/ (esp. *Brit.* **palaeo·lith·ic**) *Archaeology* ● *adjective* of or relating to the early phase of the Stone Age, lasting for about 2.5 million years until the end of the last ice age. ● *noun* the paleolithic period. [PALEO- + Greek *lithos* 'stone']

paleo·magnet·ism /ˌpeɪlioːˈmaɡnɪˌtɪzəm, ˌpalioː-/ *noun* (esp. *Brit.* **palaeo·magnet·ism**) the study of the magnetism remaining in rocks. □ **paleo·magnet·ic** *adjective*

paleon·tol·ogy /ˌpeɪlionˈtɒlədʒi, ˌpali-/ *noun* (esp. *Brit.* **palaeon·tol·ogy**) the branch of science that deals with extinct and fossil animals and plants. □ **paleon·to·logic·al** *adjective* **paleon·tol·o·gist** *noun* [PALEO- + Greek *onta* neuter pl. of *ōn* being, part. of *eimi* be + -LOGY]

Paleo·zoic /ˌpalioːˈzoːɪk/ (also esp. *Brit.* **Palaeo·zoic**) *Geol.* ● *adjective* of or relating to the geological era between the Precambrian and the Mesozoic, comprising the Cambrian, Ordovician, Silurian, Devonian, Carboniferous, and Permian periods, and lasting from about 590 to 248 million years ago. The earliest hard-shelled fossils are from this era. ● *noun* this geological era (*compare* CENOZOIC, MESOZOIC). [PALEO- + Greek *zōē* life, *zōos* living]

Pa·ler·mo /pəˈlermoː/ the capital of the Italian island of Sicily, a port on the north coast; pop. (2001) 652,640.

Pal·es·tine /ˈpaləˌstaɪn/ a territory in the Middle East on the eastern coast of the Mediterranean Sea. In Biblical times Palestine comprised the kingdoms of Israel and Judea. The land was in Muslim hands from AD 634 until the First World War, when Turkish and German forces were defeated by the British. The name Palestine was used as the official political title for the land west of the Jordan mandated to Britain in 1920. Jewish immigration was encouraged, and in 1948 the state of Israel was established. The name Palestine continues to be used, particularly in the context of the struggle for territory and political rights of Palestinian Arabs displaced when Israel was established. [Greek *Palaistinē* (used in early Christian writing), Latin (*Syria*) *Palaestina* (name of Roman province), from *Philistia* land of the Philistines]

Pal·es·tin·ian /ˌpaləˈstɪniən/ ● *adjective* of or relating to Palestine. ● *noun* **1** a native of Palestine in ancient or modern times. **2** an Arab, or a descendant of one, born or living in the area formerly called Palestine.

pa·les·tra /pəˈlestrə/ *noun* (also esp. *Brit.* **pal·aes·tra** /-ˈliːstrə, -ˈlaɪstrə/) *Gk & Rom. Hist.* a wrestling school or gymnasium. [Latin *palaestra* from Greek *palaistra* from *palaiō* wrestle]

Pal·es·tri·na /ˌpaləˈstriːnə/ **Gio·van·ni Pier·luigi da** (*c.*1525–94), Italian composer. His unaccompanied church music, including 105 masses and 250 motets, is remarkable for the beauty of its smooth vocal lines and masterly counterpoint; major works include the *Missa Papae Marcelli* (1567).

pal·ette /ˈpalət/ *noun* **1** a thin board or slab or other surface, usu. with a hole for the thumb, on which an artist lays and mixes colours. **2** a range of colours esp. that used by an artist, interior or fashion designer, etc. **3** the range or variety of tonal or instrumental colour in a musical piece, composer's work, etc. **4** *Computing* the range of colours or shapes available to a user of a computer graphics card. [French, diminutive of *pale* shovel, from Latin *pala* spade]

pal·ette knife *noun* **1** a thin steel blade with a handle for mixing colours or applying or removing paint. **2** a kitchen knife with a long blunt round-ended flexible blade.

pal·frey /ˈpɒlfri/ *noun* (*pl.* **-freys**) *archaic* a horse for ordinary riding, esp. for women. [Old French *palefrei* from medieval Latin *palefredus*, Late Latin *paraveredus* from Greek *para* beside, extra, + Latin *veredus* light horse, of Gaulish origin]

Pal·grave /ˈpɒlgreɪv, ˈpal-/ **Fran·cis Tur·ner** (1824–97), English critic and poet, who is chiefly known as the editor of the poetry anthology *The Golden Treasury* (1861).

Pali /ˈpɑːli/ ● *noun* an Indic language used in the canonical books of Buddhists. ● *adjective* of or relating to this language. [Pali *pāli-bhāsā*, from *pāli* 'line, canon' + *bhāsā* 'language']

Pal·ik·ir /ˌpaliˈkɪr/ the capital of Micronesia, situated on the island of Pohnpei; pop. (est. 2000) 8,600.

pali·mony /ˈpalɪmɔːni/ *noun* esp. *N Amer. informal* an allowance made by one member of an unmarried couple to the other after separation. [blend of PAL + ALIMONY]

pal·imp·sest /ˈpalɪmpˌsest/ *noun* **1** a piece of writing material or manuscript on which the original writing has been effaced to make room for other writing. **2** a place, experience, etc., in which something new is superimposed over traces of something preceding it. □ **pal·imp·ses·tic** *adjective* [Latin *palimpsestus* from Greek *palimpsēstos* from *palin* again + *psēstos* rubbed smooth]

pal·in·drome /ˈpalɪnˌdroːm/ *noun* a word or phrase that reads the same backwards as forwards, e.g. *rotator*, or *nurses run*. □ **pal·in·drom·ic** /-ˈdrɒmɪk/ *adjective* **pal·in·drom·ist** *noun* [Greek *palindromos* running back again, from *palin* again + *drom-* run]

pal·ing /ˈpeɪlɪŋ/ *noun* **1** a fence of pales. **2** a pale.

pal·in·gen·esis /ˌpalɪnˈdʒenɪsɪs/ *noun* **1** regeneration, rebirth. **2** *Biol.* the exact reproduction of ancestral characteristics in ontogenesis. □ **pal·in·gen·etic** /-dʒəˈnetɪk/ *adjective* [Greek *palin* again + *genesis* birth, GENESIS]

pali·sade /ˌpalɪˈseɪd/ ● *noun* **1 a** a fence of pales or iron railings. **b** a strong pointed wooden stake used in a close row for defence. **2** *US* (in *pl.*) a line of high cliffs. ● *transitive verb* enclose or provide with a palisade. [French *palissade* from Provençal *palissada* from *palissa* paling, ultimately from Latin *palus* stake]

palisade layer *noun Bot.* a layer of elongated cells below the epidermis.

Palisades, the /ˌpaləˈseɪdz/ a ridge of high basalt cliffs on the west bank of the Hudson River, in NE New Jersey.

Palk Strait /pɒlk/ an inlet of the Bay of Bengal separating N Sri Lanka from the coast of Tamil Nadu in India. It lies to the north of Adam's Bridge, which separates it from the Gulf of Mannar.

pall¹ /pɔːl/ *noun* **1** a cloth spread over a coffin, hearse, or tomb. **2** a narrow circular shoulder band with pendants, worn as an ecclesiastical vestment and sign of authority. **3** a dark or gloomy covering (*a pall of darkness*; *a pall of smoke*). **4** *Heraldry* a Y-shaped bearing charged with crosses representing the front of an ecclesiastical pall. [Old English *pæll*, from Latin *pallium* cloak]

pall² /pɔːl/ *verb* **1** *intransitive* (often foll. by *on*) become uninteresting (to). **2** *transitive* satiate, cloy. [Middle English, from APPALL]

pal·la·dia *pl.* of PALLADIUM².

Pal·la·dian /pəˈleɪdiən/ *adjective Archit.* in the neoclassical style of Palladio. □ **Pal·la·dian·ism** *noun* [A. PALLADIO]

Palladian window *noun* a large window consisting of a central arched section flanked by two narrow rectangular sections.

Pal·la·dio /pəˈleɪdiˌoː, ˈpalɪo-/ **An·drea** (1508–80), Italian architect. He led a revival of classical architecture in 16th-c. Italy, in particular promoting the Roman ideals of harmonic proportions and symmetrical planning; major buildings include the church of San Giorgio Maggiore in Venice (1566 onward). His theoretical work *Four Books on Architecture* (1570) was highly influential.

pal·la·dium¹ /pəˈleɪdiəm/ *noun Chem.* a white ductile metallic element occurring naturally in various ores and used in chemistry as a catalyst and for making jewellery. Symbol: **Pd**; at. no.: 46. [modern Latin from PALLAS 2, which was discovered just before the element, + -IUM; compare CERIUM]

pal·la·dium² /pəˈleɪdiəm/ *noun* (*pl.* **pal·la·dia** /-diə/) a safeguard or source of protection. [Latin from Greek *palladion* image of Pallas (Athene), a protecting deity]

Pal·las /ˈpaləs/ **1** *Gk Myth* one of the names (of unknown meaning) of Athene. **2** *Astronomy* asteroid 2, discovered in 1802. It is the second largest (diameter 523 km), and its surface appears to be rich in carbon.

pall·bear·er /ˈpɔːlˌberər/ *noun* a person helping to carry or officially escorting a coffin at a funeral.

pal·let¹ /ˈpalət/ *noun* **1** a straw mattress. **2** a makeshift or small, uncomfortable bed. [Anglo-French *paillete* straw, from Old French *paille* from Latin *palea*]

pal·let² /ˈpalət/ *noun* **1** a portable platform for transporting and storing loads. **2** = PALETTE. **3** a flat wooden blade with a handle, used in ceramics to shape clay. **4** a projection transmitting motion from an escapement to a pendulum etc. **5** a projection on a machine part, serving to change the mode of motion of a wheel. □ **pal·let·ize** *transitive verb* (also esp. *Brit.* **-ise**) (in sense 1). [French *palette*: see PALETTE]

pal·lia *pl.* of PALLIUM.

pal·li·asse /ˈpaliˌas/ *noun* (also **pail·lasse**) a straw mattress. [French *paillasse* from Italian *pagliaccio*, ultimately from Latin *palea* straw]

pal·li·ate /ˈpaliˌeɪt/ *transitive verb* **1** alleviate (disease or its symptoms) without curing it. **2** excuse, extenuate. □ **pal·li·a·tion** *noun* [Late Latin *palliare* to cloak, from *pallium* cloak]

pal·li·a·tive /ˈpaliətɪv/ ● *noun* anything used to alleviate pain, anxiety, etc., esp. without eliminating its source. ● *adjective* serving to palliate or alleviate. □ **pal·li·a·tive·ly** *adverb* [as PALLIATE]

palliative care *noun* medical care provided for the terminally ill, aimed at relieving symptoms.

pal·lid /ˈpalɪd/ *adjective* **1** pale. **2** lacking intensity or vitality. □ **pal·lid·ly** *adverb* **pal·lid·ness** *noun* [Latin *pallidus* PALE¹]

Pal·liser /ˈpaləsər/ **1 Hugh** (*c.*1722–1796), English naval officer. After serving at the siege of Quebec (1759), he was appointed governor of Newfoundland in 1764. Primarily concerned with the English migratory fishery, he attempted both to limit settlement and to restrict French fishing to the limits set by the Treaty of Paris (1763). He was the first administrator of Newfoundland to establish relations with the Aboriginal peoples of the region. **2 John** (1817–1887), Irish sportsman and explorer. He spent 3 years (1857–60) exploring the southern prairies and mountains of western British North America for the British Colonial Office and the Royal Geographical Society.

Palliser Triangle an unofficial name for a large, roughly triangular area of semi-arid land lying south of the Saskatchewan River in SW Saskatchewan and SE Alberta. [John PALLISER]

pal·lium /ˈpaliəm/ *noun* (*pl.* **pal·liums** or **pal·lia** /-liə/) **1** an ecclesiastical pall, esp. that sent by the Pope to an archbishop as a symbol of authority. **2** *hist.* a man's large rectangular cloak esp. as worn in antiquity. **3** *Zool.* the mantle of a mollusc or brachiopod. [Latin]

pall-mall /palˈmal, pelˈmel/ *noun hist.* a game in which a ball was driven through an iron ring suspended in a long alley. [obsolete French *pallemaille* from Italian *pallamaglio* from *palla* ball + *maglio* mallet]

pal·lor /ˈpalər/ *noun* pallidness, paleness. [Latin from *pallēre* be pale]

pally /ˈpali/ *adjective* (**pal·li·er**, **pal·li·est**) *informal* like a pal; friendly.

palm¹ /pɑːm/ *noun* **1** any usu. tropical tree of the family Palmae, with no branches and a mass of large pinnate or fan-shaped leaves at the top. **2** the leaf of this tree as a symbol of victory. **3 a** supreme excellence. **b** a prize for this. **4 a** a palm leaf or cross woven from palm leaves used in celebrating Palm Sunday. **b** a branch of various trees used instead of a palm in non-tropical countries in celebrating Palm Sunday. [Old English *palm(a)* from Germanic from Latin *palma* PALM², its leaf being likened to a spread hand]

palm² /pɒm/ ● *noun* **1** the inner surface of the hand between the wrist and fingers. **2** the part of a glove that covers this. **3** the palmate part of an antler. ● *transitive verb* **1** conceal in the hand. **2** take or pass on stealthily. **3** touch, move, etc. with the palm. **4** *Basketball* illegally grip (the ball) with the hand while dribbling. □ **in the palm of one's hand** under one's control or influence. **palm off 1** (often foll. by *on*) **a** impose or thrust fraudulently (on a person). **b** cause a person to accept unwillingly or unknowingly (*palmed my old typewriter off on him*). **2** (often foll. by *with*) cause (a person) to accept unwillingly or unknowingly (*palmed him off with my old typewriter*). □ **pal·mar** /ˈpalmər/ *adjective* **palm·ful** *noun* (*pl.* **-fuls**). [Old French *paume* from Latin *palma*: later assimilated to Latin]

Palma /ˈpalmə/ (in full **Palma de Mallorca**) the capital of the Balearic Islands, an industrial port and resort on the island of Majorca; pop. (est. 2001) 346,189.

pal·ma·ceous /palˈmeiʃəs/ *adjective Bot.* of or pertaining to the Palmae or palm family.

pal·mate /ˈpalmeit/ *adjective* (also **pal·mat·ed**) **1** *Botany* (of a leaf) having several lobes (typically 5–7) whose midribs all radiate from one point. **2** *Zool.* (of an antler) in which the angles between the tines are partly filled in to form a broad flat surface, as in fallow deer and moose. **3** web-footed. □ **pal·mate·ly** *adverb* **pal·ma·tion** /pɒlˈmeiʃən/ *noun* [Latin *palmatus* (as PALM²)]

Palm Beach a resort town in SE Florida, situated on an island just off the coast; pop. (2000) 10,648.

palm·corder *noun* a small, hand-held camcorder. [blend of PALM² & RECORDER]

Palme /ˈpɒlmə/ **(Sven) Olof (Jo·a·chim)** (1927–86), Swedish Social Democratic politician, prime minister 1969–76 and 1982–6. During his first term of office he criticized US intervention in the Vietnam War and granted asylum to US Army deserters; he was shot by an unknown assassin.

Palme d'Or /pɒmˈdɔr/ *noun* a prize awarded to the best film at the Cannes International Film Festival each year. [French, = golden palm]

Palmer /ˈpɒmər/ **1 Ar·nold (Dan·iel)** (b.1929), US golfer. His many championship victories include the Masters (1958; 1960; 1962; 1964), the US Open (1960), and the British Open (1961–2). **2 Ed·ward** (1809–89), Canadian lawyer, land agent, and politician. He was premier of Prince Edward Island 1859–63, and resigned from the Cabinet in 1865 as an attempt to prevent union with the other British colonies. In 1872 he was elected as a Liberal on an anti-Confederation platform, but resigned to become a judge after PEI entered Confederation in 1873, and served as chief justice of the province from 1874 until his death.

palmer *noun* **1** *hist.* **a** a pilgrim returning from the Holy Land with a palm branch or leaf. **b** an itinerant monk under a vow of poverty. **2** a hairy artificial fly used in angling. [Anglo-French *palmer* from medieval Latin *palmarius* pilgrim]

Palmer·ston /ˈpɒmərstən/ **Henry John Tem·ple, 3rd Vis·count** (1784–1865), English Whig politician, foreign secretary 1830–4, 1835–41, and 1846–51, prime minister 1855–8 and 1859–65. He single-mindedly promoted British interests abroad, declaring the second Opium War against China in 1856, and overseeing the successful conclusion of the Crimean War in 1856 and the suppression of the Indian Mutiny in 1858.

pal·mette /palˈmet/ *noun Archaeology* an ornament of radiating petals like a palm leaf. [French, diminutive of *palme* PALM¹]

pal·metto /palˈmetɔ, pɒl-/ *noun* (*pl.* **-mettos**) a small palm tree, e.g. any of various fan palms of the genus *Sabal* or *Chamaerops*. [Spanish *palmito*, diminutive of *palma* PALM¹, assimilated to Italian words in *-etto*]

pal·mier /ˈpalmiei/ *noun* (*pl.* **pal·miers** pronunc. same) a sweet crisp pastry shaped like a palm leaf. [French, = palm tree]

palm·is·try *noun* supposed divination from lines and other features on the palm of the hand. □ **palm·ist** *noun*

palmi·tate /ˈpalmiteit, ˈpɒl-/ *noun* a salt or ester of palmitic acid.

palmi·tic acid /palˈmitik, pɒl-/ *noun Chem.* a saturated fatty acid, solid at room temperature, found in palm oil and other vegetable and animal fats. [French *palmitique*, from *palme* PALM¹]

palm oil *noun* oil from the fruit of any of various palms.

palm·print *noun* an impression made on a surface by the palm of the hand.

palm reader *noun* a person who practises palmistry.

Palm Springs a popular resort city in the desert area of S California, east of Los Angeles, noted for its hot mineral springs; pop. (2000) 42,800.

Palm Sunday *noun Christianity* the Sunday before Easter, celebrating Christ's entry into Jerusalem.

palm·top *noun* a computer small and light enough to be held in one hand.

palm wine *noun* an alcoholic drink made from fermented palm sap.

palmy *adjective* (**palm·i·er**, **palm·i·est**) **1** of or like or abounding in palms. **2** triumphant, flourishing, prosperous (*palmy days*).

Pal·myra /palˈmairə/ an ancient city of Syria, an oasis in the Syrian desert northeast of Damascus on the site of present-day Tadmur. [Greek translation of pre-Semitic Tadmur or Tadmor 'city of palms']

pal·myra /palˈmairə/ *noun* an Asian palm, *Borassus flabellifer*, with fan-shaped leaves used for matting etc. [Portuguese *palmeira* palm tree, assimilated to PALMYRA]

Palo Alto /ˌpaloʊ ˈaltoʊ/ a city in W California, south of San Francisco; pop. (2000) 58,600. It is a noted centre for electronics and computer technology, and Stanford University is located near it.

Palo·mar, Mount /ˈpaləˌmɑr/ a mountain in S California, northeast of San Diego, which rises to a height of 1 867 m (6,126 ft.). It is the site of an astronomical observatory. [Spanish, = 'place of the pigeons']

palo·mino /ˌpaləˈmiːnoʊ/ *noun* (*pl.* **-minos**) a golden or tan-coloured horse with a light-coloured mane and tail, originally bred in the southwestern US. [Latin American Spanish from Spanish *palomino* young pigeon, from *paloma* dove, from Latin *palumba*]

pa·loo·ka /pəˈluːkə/ *noun* esp. *N Amer. slang* an oaf or lout. [origin unknown]

palo·verde /ˌpaloʊˈvɜrdi/ *noun* any yellow-flowered thorny tree of the genus *Cercidium*. [Latin American Spanish, = green tree]

palp /palp/ *noun* (also **pal·pus** /ˈpalpəs/) (*pl.* **palps** or **palpi** /-pai/) a segmented sense organ at the mouth of an arthropod; a feeler. □ **palp·al** *adjective* [Latin *palpus* from *palpare* feel]

palp·able /ˈpalpəbəl/ *adjective* **1** that can be touched or felt. **2** readily perceived by the senses or mind; obvious. □ **palp·abil·ity** *noun* **palp·ably** *adverb* [Late Latin *palpabilis* (as PALPATE)]

pal·pate /ˈpalpeit/ *transitive verb* examine (esp. medically) by touch. □ **pal·pa·tion** /-ˈpeiʃən/ *noun* [Latin *palpare palpat-* touch gently]

pal·pe·bral /palˈpiːbrəl/ *adjective* of or relating to the eyelids. [Late Latin *palpebralis* from Latin *palpebra* eyelid]

pal·pi·tate /ˈpalpɪˌteit/ *intransitive verb* **1** pulsate, throb. **2** tremble, quiver. □ **pal·pi·tant** *adjective* [Latin *palpitare* frequentative of *palpare* touch gently]

pal·pi·ta·tion /ˌpalpɪˈteiʃən/ *noun* **1** throbbing, trembling, quivering, fluttering. **2** (often in *pl.*) increased beating or fluttering of the heart due to exertion, excitement, agitation, or disease.

pal·pus *var. of* PALP.

palsa /ˈpalsə/ *noun* a landform of subarctic regions, consisting of a mound or ridge of peat covered with vegetation and containing a core of frozen peat or mineral soil. [Swedish *palse* (pl. *palsar*) from Finnish and Lappish *palsa*]

pals·grave /ˈpɒlzgreiv/ *noun* a German Count Palatine. [Dutch *paltsgrave* from *palts* palatinate + *grave* count]

palsy /ˈpɒlzi/ ● *noun* (*pl.* **-sies**) paralysis, esp. with involuntary tremors. ● *transitive verb* (**-sies**, **-sied**) affect with palsy. □ **pal·sied** *adjective* [Middle English *parlesi* from Old French *paralisie*, ultimately from Latin *paralysis*: see PARALYSIS]

palsy-walsy /ˌpalzi ˈwalzi/ *adjective* = CHUMMY. [reduplication of PAL]

pal·try /ˈpɒltri/ *adjective* (**pal·tri·er**, **pal·tri·est**) **1** trifling, meagre. **2** worthless, contemptible. □ **pal·tri·ness** *noun* [16th c.: from *paltry* trash, apparently from *palt*, *pelt* rubbish + -RY (compare *trumpery*); compare Low German *paltrig* ragged]

paly·nol·ogy /ˌpali'nɒlədʒi/ *noun* the study of pollen, spores, etc., esp. from archaeological or geological deposits, e.g. for carbon dating and the investigation of past environments. □ **paly·no·logic·al** /-nəˈlɒdʒɪkəl/ *adjective* **paly·nol·o·gist** *noun* [Greek *palunō* sprinkle + -LOGY]

Pamir Mountains /pəˈmiːr/ (also **Pamirs**) a mountain system of central Asia, centred in Tajikistan and extending into Kyrgyzstan, Afghanistan, Pakistan, and W China. It is here that the Karakoram, Hindu Kush, Tien Shan, and Kunlun Shan mountain ranges meet. The system's highest peak, in Tajikistan, rises to 7 495 m (24,590 ft.).

pam·pas /ˈpampəs/ *plural noun* (*sing.* **pampa**) large treeless plains in S America. [Spanish from Quechua *pampa* plain]

pampas grass *noun* a tall grass, *Cortaderia selloana*, from S America, with silky flowering plumes.

pam·per *transitive verb* (also *reflexive*) treat (a person or animal) with abundant or excessive kindness, attention, or comfort. □ **pam·pered** *adjective* **pam·per·ing** *noun* [Middle English, prob. of Low German or Dutch origin]

pamph·let ● *noun* **1** a small, usu. unbound booklet or leaflet containing information. **2** a short treatise on a controversial, esp. political subject. ● *intransitive verb* (**pamph·let·ed**, **pamph·let·ing**) distribute pamphlets. [Middle English from *Pamphilet*, the familiar name of the 12th-c. Latin love poem *Pamphilus seu de Amore*]

pamph·let·eer ● *noun* a writer or issuer of (esp. political) pamphlets. ● *intransitive verb* write or issue pamphlets. □ **pamph·let·eer·ing** *noun*

Pam·phyl·ia /pam'fɪliə/ an ancient coastal region of S Asia Minor, between Lycia and Cilicia, to the east of the modern port of Antalya. It became a Roman province in the reign of Augustus, between 31 BC and AD 14. □ **Pam·phyl·ian** *adjective & noun*

Pam·plona /pam'plɔːnə/ a city in N Spain, capital of the former kingdom and modern region of Navarre; pop. (est. 2001) 186,245. The fiesta of San Fermin, held there in July, is celebrated with the running of bulls through the streets of the city.

Pan *Gk Myth* a god of flocks and herds usually represented with the horns, ears, and legs of a goat on a man's body.

pan¹ ● *noun* **1 a** a container of metal, earthenware, heat-resistant glass, etc. used for cooking. **b** the contents of this. **2** a panlike vessel in which substances are heated etc. **3** any similar shallow container such as the bowl of a pair of scales or that used for washing gravel etc. to separate gold. **4** *N Amer.* = ICE PAN. **5** part of the lock that held the priming in old guns. **6** a hollow in the ground (*salt pan*). **7** *US slang* the face. **8** a hard substratum of soil. **9 a** a metal drum in a steel band. **b** steel-band music and the associated culture. ● *verb* (**panned**, **pan·ning**) **1** *transitive informal* criticize severely. **2** *transitive slang* hit or punch (a person). **3 a** *transitive* (often foll. by *off, out*) wash (gold-bearing gravel) in a pan. **b** *intransitive* search for gold by panning gravel. **c** *intransitive* (foll. by *out*) (of gravel) yield gold. □ **pan out** (of an action etc.) turn out well or in a specified way. □ **pan·ful** *noun* (pl. **-fuls**). **pan·like** *adjective* [Old English *panne*, perhaps ultimately from Latin *patina* 'dish']

pan² ● *verb* (**panned**, **pan·ning**) **1** *transitive* swing (a movie camera) horizontally to give a panoramic effect or to follow a moving object. **2** *intransitive* (of a movie camera) be moved in this way. ● *noun* a panning movement. [abbreviation of PANORAMA]

pan³ *noun* **1** a leaf of the betel. **2** this enclosing lime and areca-nut parings for chewing. [Hindi from Sanskrit *parna* feather, leaf]

pan- *combining form* **1** all; the whole of. **2** relating to the whole or all the parts or members of (*pan-American*; *pan-African*; *pan-Hellenic*). [Greek from *pan* neuter of *pas* all]

pana·cea /ˌpanə'siːə/ *noun* a universal remedy; a cure for all ills. □ **pana·cean** *adjective* [Latin from Greek *panakeia* from *panakēs* all-healing (as PAN-, *akos* remedy)]

pa·nache /pə'naʃ/ *noun* **1** assertiveness or flamboyance of style or manner. **2** *hist.* a tuft or plume of feathers, esp. as a headdress or on a helmet. [French from Italian *pennacchio* from Late Latin *pinnaculum* diminutive of *pinna* feather]

pan-African *adjective* of or relating to all people of African birth or descent.

pan-Africanism *noun* the principle or advocacy of the political union of all the indigenous inhabitants of Africa. □ **pan-Africanist** *noun*

Pa·naji /pa'nɒdʒi/ (also **Pan·jim** /'pɒndʒɪm/) a city in W India, a port on the Arabian Sea and the capital of the state of Goa; pop. (est. 2002) 100,800.

Pan-Am *adjective* Pan-American.

Pan·ama /'panə,mɒ/ a country in Central America, occupying the isthmus connecting N and S America; pop. (est. 2002) 2,882,329; capital, Panama City. □ **Pan·ama·nian** /ˌpanə'meɪnɪən/ *adjective & noun*

Panama Canal a canal about 80 km (50 miles) long, across the Isthmus of Panama, connecting the Atlantic and Pacific Oceans. The surrounding territory, the Panama Canal Zone or Canal Zone, was administered by the US until 1979, when it was returned to the control of Panama. The canal itself was ceded to Panama in 1999.

Panama City the capital of Panama, situated on the Pacific coast close to the Panama Canal; pop. (2000) 416,000.

panama hat *noun* (also **panama**) a hat of straw-like material made from the leaves of a palm-like plant. [PANAMA]

Pan-American *adjective* of, relating to, representing, or involving all of the countries of North and South America.

pan and scan *noun* (**pans and scans**, **panned and scanned**, **panning and scanning**) a technique for narrowing the aspect ratio of a widescreen film by eliminating part of the image on both sides, to fit the squarer shape of a television screen (also *attributive*: *pan-and-scan video*) (compare LETTER BOX 3). □ **pan and scan** *verb*

pan-Arabism *noun* the principle or advocacy of the political alliance or union of all the Arab states. □ **pan-Arab** *adjective* **pan-Arabist** *adjective*

pana·tela /ˌpanə'telə/ *noun* (also **pana·tella**) a long thin cigar. [Latin American Spanish *panatela*, = long thin biscuit, from Italian *panatella* diminutive of *panata*, ultimately from Latin *panis* bread]

Panay /pa'naɪ/ an island in the central Philippines; chief town, Iloilo.

pan-broil *transitive verb* heat (meat) in a pan with little or no fat.

pan·cake ● *noun* **1 a** any of various thin, flat, usu. round cakes of batter, beaten eggs, grated potatoes, etc., fried on both sides. **b** a flat round fried cake made of flour, milk, eggs, and leavening, usu. served with butter and maple syrup. Also called GRIDDLE CAKE, HOTCAKE, FLAPJACK. **2** (also **pancake makeup**) a thick layer of makeup, esp. foundation. **3** (in full **pancake landing**) an emergency landing in which an aircraft levels out close to the ground and drops vertically with its undercarriage still retracted. ● *verb* **1 a** *intransitive* make a pancake landing. **b** *transitive* cause (an aircraft) to pancake. **2** *N Amer. informal* **a** *transitive* flatten. **b** *intransitive* be flattened. □ **flat as a pancake** completely flat.

pancake breakfast *noun* *N Amer.* a breakfast, usu. for large numbers of people and often as a fundraiser, at which pancakes and usu. sausages or bacon are served.

Pancake Day *noun* Shrove Tuesday (on which pancakes are traditionally eaten).

pancake house *noun* *N Amer.* a fast-food restaurant or diner specializing in pancakes.

pancake syrup *noun* *N Amer.* a maple- or caramel-flavoured syrup used for pouring on pancakes.

pan-Canadian *adjective* embracing or relating to the whole of Canada.

pan·cetta /pan'tʃetə/ *noun* cured belly of pork, usu. in a long casing. [Italian, dim. of *pancia* belly]

pan·chayat /pən'tʃaɪət/ *noun* a village council in India. [Hindi from Sanskrit *pancha* five]

Pan·chen lama /'pantʃən ˌlɒmə/ *noun* a Tibetan lama ranking next after the Dalai lama. [Tibetan *panchen* great learned one]

pan·chro·mat·ic /ˌpankrəʊ'matɪk/ *adjective Photog.* (of a film etc.) sensitive to all visible colours of the spectrum.

pan·creas /'paŋkrɪəs/ *noun* a gland near the stomach supplying the duodenum with digestive fluid and secreting insulin into the blood. □ **pan·creat·ic** /-'atɪk/ *adjective* **pan·crea·titis** /-'taɪtɪs/ *noun* [modern Latin from Greek *pagkreas* (as PAN-, *kreas -atos* flesh)]

pan·crea·tin /'paŋkrɪətɪn/ *noun* a digestive extract containing pancreatic enzymes, prepared from animal pancreases.

panda *noun* **1** (also **giant panda**) a bearlike mammal, *Ailuropoda melanoleuca*, native to China and Tibet, having characteristic black and white markings. **2** (also **red panda**) a Himalayan raccoon-like mammal, *Ailurus fulgens*, about the size of a large cat, with reddish-brown fur and a long bushy tail. [Nepali name]

panda car *noun* *Brit.* a police patrol car (originally black and white or blue and white).

pan·danus /pan'deɪnəs, -'dan-/ *noun* (also **pan·dan** /'pandən/) **1** a tropical tree or shrub of the genus *Pandanus*, with a twisted stem, aerial roots, and spiral tufts of long narrow leaves at the top; *also called* SCREW PINE. **2** fibre from the leaves of such a plant, or material woven from this. [modern Latin from Malay *pandan*]

Pan·darus /'pandərəs/ *Gk Myth* a Lycian fighting on the side of the Trojans, described in the *Iliad* as breaking the truce with the Greeks by wounding Menelaus with an arrow; his role as the lovers' go-between in Chaucer's (and later Shakespeare's) story of Troilus and Cressida originated with Boccaccio and is also the origin of the word *pander*.

pan·dect /'pandekt/ *noun* (usu. in *pl.*) **1** a complete body of laws. **2** *hist.* a compendium in 50 books of the Roman civil law made by order of Justinian in the 6th c. [French *pandecte* or Latin *pandecta pandectes* from Greek *pandektēs* all-receiver (as PAN-, *dektēs* from *dekhomai* receive)]

pan·dem·ic /pan'demɪk/ ● *adjective* (of a disease) prevalent over a whole country or the world. ● *noun* a pandemic disease. [Greek *pandēmos* (as PAN-, *dēmos* people)]

pan·de·mon·ium /ˌpandəˈmoːniəm/ *noun* **1** uproar; utter confusion. **2** a scene of this. [modern Latin (place of all demons in Milton's *Paradise Lost*) from PAN- + Greek *daimōn* DEMON]

pan·der ● *noun* **1** a go-between in illicit love affairs; a procurer. **2** a person who provides another with a means of gratifying lust; a pimp. ● *intransitive verb* **1** (foll. by *to*) gratify or indulge a person, a desire or weakness, etc. **2** act as a pimp. □ **pan·der·er** *noun* **pan·der·ing** *noun* [PANDARUS]

P & H *abbreviation* postage and handling.

Pan·dit /ˈpʌndɪt/ **Vi·jaya (Lak·shmi)** (1900–90), Indian politician and diplomat. After joining the Indian National Congress, led by her brother Jawaharlal Nehru, she was imprisoned three times by the British (1932; 1941; 1942) for her nationalist activities; following independence, she led the Indian delegation to the United Nations (1946–8; 1952–3) and was the first woman to serve as president of the United Nations General Assembly (1953–4).

pan·dit *noun* (also **pun·dit**) a Hindu learned in Sanskrit and in the philosophy, religion, and jurisprudence of India.

P & L *abbreviation* profit and loss.

Pan·dora /panˈdɔːrə/ *Gk Myth* the first mortal woman. She was created by Zeus and sent to earth with a jar or box of evils in revenge for Prometheus' having brought the gift of fire back to the world. Pandora opened it out of curiosity, and all the evils flew out; Hope alone remained to assuage the lot of humankind. [Greek *Pandōra* all-gifted (as PAN-, *dōron* gift)]

Pandora's box *noun* a process that once activated will generate many unmanageable problems. [PANDORA]

pane *noun* **1** a single sheet of glass in a window or door. **2** a rectangular division of a checkered pattern etc. **3** a sheet or page of stamps. □ **paned** *adjective* [Old French *pan* from Latin *pannus* piece of cloth]

pa·neer /paˈniːr/ *noun* a mild milk curd cheese similar to cottage cheese, originally from N India, Iran, and Afghanistan. [from Hindi or Persian *panīr*, cheese]

pan·egyr·ic /ˌpanɪˈdʒɪrɪk, -ˈdʒai-/ *noun* a laudatory or praising discourse, speech, etc. □ **pan·egyr·ic·al** *adjective* [French *panégyrique* from Latin *panegyricus* from Greek *panēgurikos* of public assembly (as PAN-, *ēguris* = *agora* assembly)]

pan·egyr·ize /ˈpanɪdʒɪˌraɪz/ *transitive verb* (also esp. *Brit.* **-ise**) speak or write in praise of. □ **pan·egyr·ist** /-ˈdʒɪrɪst, -ˈdʒai-/ *noun* [Greek *panēgurizō* (as PANEGYRIC)]

panel ● *noun* **1 a** a distinct, usu. rectangular, section of a surface, e.g. of a wall, door, or vehicle. **b** a usu. rectangular box, sheet of metal, etc., containing a number of electrical or electronic switches. **c** = INSTRUMENT PANEL. **2** a strip of material as part of a garment. **3** a group of people invited to act as judges, discuss a topic, etc. esp. for the benefit of an audience. **4** a list of available jurors; a jury. ● *transitive verb* (**pan·elled**, **pan·el·ling**; also esp. *US* **pan·eled**, **pan·el·ing**) **1** fit or provide with panels. **2** cover or decorate with panels. [Old French, = piece of cloth, ultimately from Latin *pannus*: see PANE]

panel beater *noun Brit.* & *South Africa* a person whose job is to beat out the metal panels of motor vehicles. □ **panel beating** *noun*

pan·el·ling *noun* (also esp. *US* **pan·el·ing**) **1** panels collectively, esp. wooden panels used for a decorative wall covering. **2** wood or other material made or for making into a panel or panelling.

pan·el·list *noun* (also esp. *US* **pan·el·ist**) a member of a panel (esp. in broadcasting).

panel truck *noun N Amer.* a robust small truck capable of carrying heavy loads, with an enclosed rear compartment behind the driver's cab.

panel van *noun N Amer.* & *Austral.* a van designed for carrying fairly light loads.

pan·et·tone /panəˈtoːni/ *noun* (*pl.* **pan·et·toni** /-ni/) a usu. tall bread-like cake made with eggs and raisins, candied fruit, etc. [Italian, from *panetto*, diminutive of *pane* bread, from Latin *panis*]

pan·fish *noun N Amer.* any small freshwater fish suitable for frying whole in a pan, esp. one caught by an angler rather than bought. □ **pan·fish·ing** *noun*

pan·forte /panˈfɔrtei/ *noun* a hard, spicy, Sienese cake containing nuts, candied peel, and honey. [Italian, from *pane* 'bread', and *forte* 'strong']

pan-fry *transitive verb* fry in a pan in shallow fat. □ **pan-fried** *adjective*

pang *noun* (often in *pl.*) a sudden sharp pain or painful emotion. [16th c.: var. of earlier *prange* pinching, from Germanic]

panga /ˈpaŋgə/ *noun* a bladed African tool like a machete. [Swahili]

Pan·gaea /panˈdʒiːə/ a vast continental area or supercontinent comprising all the continental crust of the earth, which is postulated to have existed in late Paleozoic and Mesozoic times before breaking up into Gondwanaland and Laurasia. [PAN- + GAIA]

Pan·glos·sian /panˈɡlɒsiən/ *adjective* unrealistically optimistic. [from *Pangloss*, the philosopher and tutor in Voltaire's *Candide* (1759)]

Pang·nir·tung /ˈpaŋnɪrtʌŋ/ a hamlet on Baffin Island, situated on the south coast of the Cumberland Peninsula; pop. (2001) 1,276. [Inuktitut, = place of many buck deer]

Pangnirtung hat *noun Cdn* (*North*) a knitted wool hat in bright colours, with a tassel at the crown and earflaps, traditional in the E Arctic. [PANGNIRTUNG]

pan·go·lin /paŋˈɡoːlɪn/ *noun* any scaly anteater of the genus *Manis*, native to Asia and Africa, having a small head with elongated snout and tongue, and a tapering tail. [Malay *peng-gōling* roller (from its habit of rolling itself up)]

pan·gram /ˈpaŋɡram/ *noun* an often quizzical sentence, rhyme, joke, etc., usu. with poor syntax, including every letter of the alphabet.

pan·handle *N Amer.* ● *noun* a narrow strip of territory surrounded on three sides by the territory of another state etc. ● *transitive & intransitive verb informal* beg for money in the street. □ **pan·hand·ler** *noun*

panic¹ ● *noun* **1** sudden uncontrollable fear or alarm leading to unreasoned behaviour, esp. that which may suddenly spread through a crowd of people. **2** a condition of widespread apprehension in relation to financial and commercial matters leading to hasty measures to guard against possible loss (also *attributive*: panic selling). **3** an agitated busyness as when making hurried preparations for something. ● *transitive & intransitive verb* (**pan·icked**, **pan·ick·ing**) affect or be affected with panic (*was panicked into buying*). □ **panicky** *adjective* [French *panique* via modern Latin *panicus* from Greek *panikos*, from PAN, reputed to cause terror]

panic² *noun* any grass of the genus *Panicum*, including millet and other cereals. [Old English from Latin *panicum* from *panus* thread on bobbin, millet ear, from Greek *pēnos* web]

panic attack *noun* a sudden overwhelming feeling of intense and disabling anxiety.

panic button *noun* a button for summoning help in an emergency. □ **push** (or **press**) **the panic button** react in an unduly alarmed manner.

panic disorder *noun* a psychiatric disorder in which debilitating anxiety and fear arise frequently and without reasonable cause.

pan·icle /ˈpanɪkəl/ *noun Bot.* a loose branching cluster of flowers, as in oats. □ **pan·icled** *adjective* [Latin *paniculum* diminutive of *panus* thread]

panic-strick·en *adjective* (also **panic-struck**) affected with panic; very apprehensive or anxious.

pan·ino /pəˈniːnoː/ *noun* (also **pan·ini** /-ni/) (*pl.* **pan·ini** or **pan·inis**) **1** a crusty, originally Italian, white, elongated bread roll. **2** a sandwich made with such a roll. [Italian, diminutive of *pane* bread]

Pan·jabi *noun* var. of PUNJABI.

pan·jan·drum /panˈdʒandrəm/ *noun* **1** a mock title for an important person. **2** a pompous or pretentious official etc. [apparently invented in nonsense verse by S. Foote 1755]

Pan·jim see PANAJI.

Pank·hurst, Em·me·line (1858–1928), and her daughters **Chris·ta·bel** (1880–1958), and **(Es·telle) Syl·via** (1882–1960), English suffragists. In 1903 they founded the Women's Social and Political Union, with the motto 'Votes for Women'; following the imprisonment of Christabel in 1905 after an altercation with police, Emmeline initiated the militant suffragist campaign and kept the cause in the public eye until the outbreak of the First World War.

pan·leuk·o·penia /ˌpanluːkəˈpiːniə/ *noun* (also **pan·leuc·o·penia**) feline distemper. [PAN- + LEUKOPENIA]

Pan·mun·jom /ˌpanmʊnˈdʒɒm/ a village in the demilitarized zone between North and S Korea, site of the signing of the armistice ending the Korean War on 27 July 1953.

pan·na·cotta /ˌpanəˈkɒtə/ *noun* an Italian dessert made with flavoured sweetened cream set with gelatin, usu. in a mould. [Italian, lit. 'cooked cream']

panne /pan/ *noun* (in full **panne velvet**) a velvet-like fabric of silk or rayon with a flattened pile. [French]

Panne·ton /panˈtɔ̃/ **Phil·ippe** (pen name **Ring·uet**) (1895–1960), Canadian physician, diplomat, and writer. His novel *Trente Arpents* (1938), tells the story of three generations of Québécois peasants who farm the family's 30 acres of land. This book, which won a Governor

General's Award and many other prizes, was followed by five other novels and a collection of short stories.

pan·nier /'panjər/ *noun* **1** a basket, esp. one of a pair carried by a beast of burden. **2** each of a pair of bags or boxes on either side of the rear wheel of a bicycle or motorcycle. **3** *hist.* **a** part of a skirt looped up round the hips. **b** a frame supporting this. [Old French *panier* from Latin *panarium* breadbasket, from *panis* bread]

Pan·non·ia /pə'noːniə/ an ancient country of S Europe lying south and west of the Danube, in present-day Austria, Hungary, Slovenia, and Croatia. It was occupied by the Romans from 35 BC, becoming a province in AD 6. It lost its separate identity after the Romans withdrew at the end of the 4th c.

pan·oply /'panəpli/ *noun* (*pl.* **-lies**) **1** a complete or splendid array. **2** a complete suit of armour. □ **pan·op·lied** *adjective* [French *panoplie* or modern Latin *panoplia* full armour, from Greek (as PAN-, *oplia* from *hopla* arms)]

pan·op·tic /pan'ɒptɪk/ *adjective* showing or seeing the whole at one view. [Greek *panoptos* seen by all, *panoptēs* all-seeing]

pan·op·tic·on /pan'ɒptɪkɒn/ *noun hist.* a circular prison with cells arranged around a central well, from which prisoners could at all times be observed. [as PANOPTIC]

pan·orama /ˌpanə'ramə/ *noun* **1** an unbroken view of a surrounding region. **2** a complete survey or presentation of a subject, sequence of events, etc. **3** a picture or photograph containing a wide view. **4** a continuous passing scene. □ **pan·oram·ic** *adjective* **pan·oram·ic·ally** *adverb* [PAN- + Greek *horama* view, from *horaō* see]

pan pipe *noun* (in *sing.* or *pl.*) a musical instrument originally associated with the Greek rural god Pan, made of a series of short pipes graduated in length and fixed together with the mouthpieces in line.

pan·sexual *adjective* not limited or inhibited in sexual choice. □ **pan·sexual·ity** *noun*

pansy *noun* (*pl.* **-sies**) **1** any garden plant of the genus *Viola*, with flowers of various rich colours. **2** *informal derogatory* **a** an effeminate man. **b** a male homosexual. [French *pensée* thought, pansy, from *penser* think, from Latin *pensare* frequentative of *pendere* pens- weigh]

pant¹ ● *verb* **1** *intransitive* breathe with short quick breaths, as from exertion or excitement. **2** *transitive* utter breathlessly. **3** *intransitive* (often foll. by *for*) yearn or crave. **4** *intransitive archaic* (of the heart etc.) throb violently. ● *noun* **1** a panting breath. **2** *archaic* a throb. □ **pant·ing·ly** *adverb* [Old French *pantaisier*, ultimately from Greek *phantasioō* cause to imagine (as FANTASY)]

pant² *noun esp. N Amer.* = PANTS (often *attributive*: *pant leg*). [back-formation from PANTS]

pan·ta·lets /ˌpantə'lets/ *plural noun* (also **pan·ta·lettes**) *hist.* long underpants worn by women and girls in the 19th c., with a frill at the bottom of each leg. [diminutive of PANTALOON]

pan·ta·loon *noun* **1** (in *pl.*) **a** *hist.* men's close-fitting breeches fastened below the calf or at the foot. **b** *informal* pants. **c** baggy pants (esp. for women) gathered at the ankles. **2** (**Pantaloon**) a character in Italian comedy wearing pantaloons (in sense 1a). [French *pantalon* from Italian *Pantalone*]

Panta·nal /ˌpantə'nɒl/ a vast region of tropical swampland in the upper reaches of the Paraguay River in SW Brazil.

pan·tech·nicon /pan'teknɪkən/ *noun Brit.* a large van for transporting furniture. [PAN- + *technic* (as TECHNICS) originally as the name of a bazaar and then a furniture warehouse]

Pan·tel·le·ria /ˌpantelə'riːə/ a volcanic Italian island in the Mediterranean, situated between Sicily and the coast of Tunisia.

pan·the·ism /'panθiˌɪzəm/ *noun* **1** the belief or philosophical theory that God and the universe are identical (implying a denial of the personality and transcendence of God); the identification of God with the forces of nature and with natural substances. **2** worship that admits or tolerates all gods. □ **pan·the·ist** *noun* **pan·the·is·tic** *adjective* **pan·the·is·tic·al** *adjective* **pan·the·is·tic·al·ly** *adverb* [PAN- + Greek *theos* god]

pan·the·on /'panθiɒn/ *noun* **1** a building in which illustrious dead are buried or have memorials. **2** the deities of a people collectively. **3** a temple dedicated to all the gods, esp. (**the Pantheon**) the circular one at Rome. **4** a group of individuals who are admired, respected, or distinguished. [Greek *pantheion* (as PAN-, *theion* 'holy' from *theos* 'god')]

pan·ther *noun* **1** *N Amer.* a cougar. **2** a leopard, esp. with black fur. [Old French *pantere* from Latin *panthera* from Greek *panthēr*]

Panther Falls a waterfall in SW Alberta, 183 m high, situated on

Nigel Creek in Banff National Park; the fourth highest waterfall in Canada.

pant·ies *plural noun informal* legless underpants worn by women and girls. [diminutive of PANTS]

pan·tile /'pantaɪl/ *noun* **1** a roof tile curved to form an S-shaped section, fitted to overlap. **2** a simply curved tile laid so that a convex one overlaps the joined edges of two concave ones. □ **pan·tiled** *adjective* [PAN¹ + TILE]

panti·liner *noun* a very thin adhesive pad attached to women's underwear to absorb light menstrual flow, spotting, discharge, etc.

panto *noun* (*pl.* **pantos**) *Brit. informal* = PANTOMIME 2. [abbreviation]

panto- *combining form* all, universal. [Greek *pas pantos* all]

panto·graph /'pantəˌgraf/ *noun* **1** *Art* an instrument for copying a plan or drawing etc. on a different scale by a system of jointed rods. **2** a jointed framework conveying a current to an electric vehicle from overhead wires. □ **panto·graph·ic** *adjective* [PANTO- + Greek *-graphos* writing]

panto·mime /'pantəˌmaɪm/ ● *noun* **1 a** the use of gestures and facial expression to convey meaning, esp. in drama and dance. **b** an act or a performance of this. **2** an esp. British theatrical entertainment based on a fairy tale, with music, topical jokes, etc., usu. produced around Christmas. **3** *informal* an absurd or outrageous piece of behaviour. ● *verb* **1** *intransitive* express oneself in or as in a pantomime. **2** *transitive* express or represent by pantomime. □ **panto·mim·ic** /-'mɪmɪk/ *adjective* [French *pantomime* or Latin *pantomimus* from Greek *pantomimos* (as PANTO-, MIME)]

Pan·tone *noun proprietary* a system for matching colours used in specifying printing inks (*Pantone colours*).

pan·to·then·ic acid /ˌpantə'θenɪk/ *noun* a vitamin of the B complex, found in rice, bran, and many other foods, and essential for the oxidation of fats and carbohydrates. [Greek *pantothen* from every side]

pan·try *noun* (*pl.* **-tries**) a small room or cupboard in which food, dishes, cutlery, table linen, etc., are kept. [Old French *paneterie* from *panetier* baker, ultimately from Late Latin *panarius* bread seller, from Latin *panis* bread]

pants *plural noun* **1** esp. *N Amer.* any of various outer garments reaching from the waist at least as far as the thighs, but usu. to the ankles, divided into two parts to cover each leg separately; trousers. **2** *Brit.* underpants. □ **scare** (or **beat** etc.) **the pants off** *informal* scare, beat, etc., thoroughly or to an intolerable degree. **wear the pants** see WEAR¹. **with one's pants down** *informal* in an embarrassingly unprepared state. [abbreviation of *pantaloons* (see PANTALOON)]

pant·suit *noun esp. N Amer.* a women's suit of pants and a matching jacket.

panty *noun* (often *attributive*) = PANTIES.

panty girdle *noun* a woman's girdle with a crotch.

panty·hose *plural noun N Amer.* very thin or sheer usu. nylon tights for women. [PANTY + HOSE]

panty raid *noun N Amer.* a prank in which a group of usu. male students breaks into a females' room or dormitory to steal their underwear.

panty·waist *N Amer. informal* ● *noun* a childish, effeminate, or cowardly man or boy. ● *adjective* week, feeble, ineffectual. [originally a child's outfit consisting of pants and a top joined with buttons at the waist]

pan·zer *noun* **1** (in *pl.*) armoured troops. **2** (*attributive*) heavily armoured (*panzer division*). **3** an armoured vehicle, esp. a tank. [German, = coat of mail]

pan·zerot·to /panzə'rɒtoː/ *noun* (*pl.* **pan·zerot·ti**) *Cdn* a baked pizza-like turnover, consisting of dough folded into a sealed pocket, filled with tomato sauce, cheese, etc. [Italian *panzarotto* from *panza*, obsolete form of *pancia* belly, from its shape]

pap¹ *noun* **1 a** soft or semi-liquid food for infants or invalids. **b** a mash or pulp. **2** intellectually unchallenging or trivial reading matter, ideas, entertainment, etc.; nonsense. □ **pappy** *adjective* [prob. ultimately from Latin *pappare* eat]

pap² *noun archaic* or *dialect* the nipple of a breast. [Middle English, of Scandinavian origin:, ultimately imitative of sucking]

papa *noun archaic* father (esp. as a child's word). [French from Late Latin from Greek *papas*]

pap·acy /'peɪpəsi/ *noun* (*pl.* **-acies**) **1** a pope's office or tenure. **2** the papal system. [medieval Latin *papatia* from *papa* pope]

Papa·dop·oul·os /ˌpapə'dɒpələs/ **George** (1919–99), Greek army officer who headed the military junta that ruled Greece from 1967 to 1973, becoming prime minister (1967–73) and president (1973).

Vowels: a *cat* ɑ *arm* e *bed* ɜr *her* ɜː *deux* ə *ago* ɪ *sit* i *cosy* iː *feed* ɒ *hot* ɔ *pore* oː *no* ʌ *run* ʊ *put*

papa·dum *var. of* PAPPADUM.

Pap·ago /ˈpapəgoː, ˈpɒ-/ ● *noun* **1** a member of an American Indian people of the southwestern US and northern Mexico. **2** the Uto-Aztecan language of this people. ● *adjective* of or relating to the Papago or their language. [Spanish from American Indian name]

pa·pain /pəˈpeɪɪn/ *noun* a protein-digesting enzyme obtained from unripe papayas, used to tenderize meat and as a food supplement to aid digestion. [PAPAYA + -IN]

papal /ˈpeɪpəl/ *adjective* of or relating to a pope or to the papacy. □ **papal·ly** *adverb* [medieval Latin *papalis* from ecclesiastical Latin *papa* POPE¹]

Papal States a part of central Italy held between 756 and 1870 by the Catholic Church, corresponding to the modern regions of Emilia-Romagna, Marche, Umbria, and Lazio. Their annexation to the newly-unified Italy in 1870 deprived the papacy of its temporal powers until the Lateran Treaty of 1929 recognized the sovereignty of the Vatican City.

Pap·an·dreou /ˌpapənˈdreiu/ **An·dreas (George)** (1919–1996), Greek prime minister 1981–9. Founder of the Pan-Hellenic Socialist Movement (PASOK) he was defeated at the polls in 1989 after charges of implication in a massive embezzlement scandal.

pap·ar·azzo /ˌpapəˈratso/ *noun* (*pl.* **pap·ar·azzi** /-tsi/) (usu. in *pl.*) a freelance photographer who pursues celebrities to get photographs of them. [Italian, from the name of a character in Fellini's film *La Dolce Vita* (1960)]

papaw *var. of* PAWPAW.

pa·paya /pəˈpaijə/ *noun* **1** an elongated melon-shaped fruit with edible orange flesh and small black seeds. **2** a tropical tree, *Carica papaya*, bearing this and producing a milky sap from which papain is obtained. [from Spanish & Portuguese, of Carib origin]

Pape·ete /ˌpɒpiˈeiti, -pəˈiːti/ the capital of French Polynesia, situated on the northwest coast of Tahiti; pop. (est. 2002) 29,500.

paper ● *noun* **1** a material manufactured in thin sheets from the pulp of wood or other fibrous substances, used for writing or drawing or printing on, or as wrapping material etc. **2** (*attributive*) **a** made of or using paper. **b** flimsy like paper. **3** = NEWSPAPER. **4 a** a document printed on paper. **b** (in *pl.*) documents attesting identity or credentials. **c** (in *pl.*) documents belonging to a person or relating to a matter. **5** *Commerce* **a** negotiable documents, e.g. bills of exchange. **b** (*attributive*) recorded on paper though not existing (*paper profits*). **6** = WALLPAPER 1. **7** an essay or dissertation, esp. one read to a learned society, published in a learned journal, or written as an assignment at university. **8** a piece of paper, esp. as a wrapper etc. **9** *Theatre slang* free tickets or the people admitted by them (*the house is full of paper*). **10 a** a set of questions to be answered at one session in an examination. **b** the written answers to these. ● *transitive verb* **1** apply paper to, esp. decorate (a wall etc.) with wallpaper. **2** (foll. by *over*) **a** cover (a hole or blemish) with paper. **b** disguise or try to hide (a fault etc.). **3** *Theatre* fill (a theatre) by giving free tickets. □ **on paper 1** in writing. **2** in theory; to judge from written or printed evidence. **push paper** engage in office work. □ **paper·er** *noun* [Anglo-French *papir*, = Old French *papier* from Latin *papyrus*: see PAPYRUS]

paper·back ● *adjective* (of a book) bound in stiff paper not boards. ● *noun* a paperback book.

paper·bark *noun* any of various trees with flaking bark, esp. the paperbark maple.

paperbark maple *noun* a maple, *Acer griseum*, with flaky, light brown bark.

paper birch *noun* = WHITE BIRCH.

paper·board *noun* a sheet of stiff material made by pasting and pressing together sheets of paper.

paper boy *noun* (or **paper girl**) a boy or girl who delivers or sells newspapers.

paper carrier *noun* a person who delivers newspapers.

paper chase *noun* **1** *informal* any process involving much paperwork, writing, etc. **2** a cross-country run in which the runners follow a trail marked by torn-up paper.

paper clip ● *noun* a clip of bent wire or of plastic for holding several sheets of paper together. ● *transitive verb* (**paper-clip**) attach with a paper clip.

paper·hang·er *noun* a person who decorates with wallpaper, esp. professionally.

paper knife *noun* = LETTER OPENER.

paper·less *adjective* using computers rather than paper to record or exchange information (*the paperless office has turned out to be a myth*).

paper·maker *noun* a person who makes paper for a living. □ **paper·making** *noun* & *adjective*

paper mill *noun* a mill in which paper is made.

paper money *noun* money in the form of banknotes.

paper mulberry *noun* a small Asiatic tree, *Broussonetia papyrifera*, of the mulberry family, whose bark is used for making paper and cloth.

paper nautilus *noun* see NAUTILUS 2.

paper-pusher *noun* *informal* a menial clerical or office worker. □ **paper-pushing** *noun*

paper route *noun* N *Amer.* **1** a job of regularly delivering newspapers. **2** a route taken doing this.

paper shuffler *noun* *informal* & *derogatory* a person whose job involves routine or excessive paperwork, esp. a menial clerical worker or a bureaucrat. □ **paper shuffling** *noun*

paper tape *noun* *Computing* tape made of paper, esp. that on which data or instructions are represented by means of holes punched in it, for conveying to a processor etc.

paper-thin ● *adjective* very thin; of no substance (*paper-thin slices*). ● *adverb* very thinly.

paper tiger *noun* an apparently threatening but ineffectual person or thing.

paper towel *noun* N *Amer.* **1** absorbent paper for drying hands, wiping up spills, or other domestic tasks. **2** (in *pl.*) a roll of this in perforated sheets.

paper trail *noun* N *Amer.* documentation linking a person or group to an esp. incriminating event or series of events.

paper wasp *noun* a social wasp that forms a small, umbrella-shaped nest made from wood pulp.

paper·weight *noun* a small heavy object for keeping loose papers in place.

paper·work *noun* **1** routine clerical or administrative work. **2** paper documents collectively.

paper·work·er *noun* a person employed in the pulp and paper industry.

papery *adjective* like paper in thinness or texture.

Paph·la·gonia /ˌpaflʌˈgoːniə/ an ancient region of N Asia Minor, on the Black Sea coast between Bithynia and Pontus, to the north of Galatia. It was incorporated into Roman Bithynia and Galatia between 65 and 6 BC. □ **Paph·la·gon·ian** *adjective* & *noun*

papier mâché /ˌpeɪpər maˈʃei, -məˈʃei, ˌpapjei ˈmaʃei/ *noun* paper reduced to a pulp mixed with glue etc., or sheets of paper pasted together, used for making moulded boxes, trays, figures, etc. [French, = chewed paper]

pa·pil·ion·aceous /pəˌpɪljəˈneiʃəs/ *adjective* (of a plant) with a corolla like a butterfly. [modern Latin *papilionaceus* from Latin *papilio -onis* butterfly]

pap·il·la /pəˈpɪlə/ *noun* (*pl.* **pap·il·lae** /-liː/) **1** a small nipple-like protuberance in a part or organ of the body. **2** *Bot.* a small fleshy projection on a plant. □ **pap·il·lary** /ˈpapɪˌeri, pəˈpɪləri/ *adjective* **pap·il·late** /ˈpapɪˌleit/ *adjective* **pap·il·lose** /ˈpapɪˌlos/ *adjective* [Latin, = nipple, diminutive of *papula*: see PAPULE]

pap·il·loma /ˌpapɪˈloːmə/ *noun* (*pl.* **pap·il·lomas** or **pap·il·lo·mata** /-mətə/) a wart-like usu. benign tumour.

pap·il·lon /pəˈpɪljən/ *noun* a breed of toy spaniel with ears suggesting the form of a butterfly. [French, = butterfly, from Latin *papilio -onis*]

Pap·ineau /ˌpapiˈnoː/ **Louis-Joseph** (1786–1871), Canadian lawyer, seigneur, and politician. First elected to the legislative assembly of Lower Canada in 1809, he emerged as the leader of a nationalistic party, the Parti Canadien (later the Parti Patriote). Made Speaker in 1815, he began working for the reform of Lower Canada's political institutions. An address to a rally at Saint-Charles in 1837 after the British rejected his list of demands for reform led to open rebellion; Papineau fled to the US and then to France, where he remained until pardoned in 1844. He then returned from exile in 1845.

Papineau-Couture /ˈpapino kuːˈtur/ **Jean** (1916–2000), Canadian composer and teacher. After studying in both Canada and the US, he began teaching in Montreal, and served as dean of the faculty of music at the Université de Montréal (1968–73); his compositions include *Psaume CL* and *Étude in B-flat Minor*.

pap·ist /ˈpeɪpɪst/ *offensive* ● *noun* a Roman Catholic. ● *adjective* of or relating to Roman Catholics. □ **pap·ism** *noun* **pap·is·try** *noun* [French *papiste* or modern Latin *papista* from ecclesiastical Latin *papa* POPE¹]

pa·poose /pəˈpuːs/ *noun* a young N American Indian child. [Algonquian *papoos*]

pap·pa·dum /ˈpɒpədəm/ *noun* (also **pap·pa·dam**, **papa·dum**, **poppa·dum**) a thin, crisp, spiced roasted or fried chip made from lentil flour and eaten with Indian food. [Tamil *pappaḍam*]

pap·par·delle /ˌpɑːpərˈdelei/ *plural noun* pasta in the form of broad flat ribbons, usu. served with a meat sauce. [Italian from *pappare* eat greedily]

Pap·pus /ˈpapəs/ (known as Pappus of Alexandria) (*fl. c.*300–350 AD), Greek mathematician. His *Collection* of six books (another two are missing) is the principal source for our knowledge of the mathematics of his predecessors, particularly in geometry.

pap·pus /ˈpapəs/ *noun* (*pl.* **pappi** /-pai/) a group of hairs on the fruit of thistles, dandelions, etc. □ **pap·pose** *adjective* [Latin from Greek *pappos*]

pappy *noun* (*pl.* **-pies**) esp. *US* father.

pap·rika /pəˈpriːkə/ *noun* a condiment made from the dried ground fruits of certain (esp. red) varieties of the sweet pepper, *Capsicum annuum*. [Magyar]

pap·ri·kash /ˈpaprikaʃ/ *noun* (also **pap·rikas**) a Hungarian stew of usu. chicken or veal with tomato, green pepper, and paprika, thickened with sour cream. [Hungarian]

Pap smear *noun* (also **Pap test**) a procedure for detecting cervical cancer involving the scraping and microscopic examination of cells from the cervix. [abbreviation of G. N. *Papanicolaou*, US scientist d.1962]

Papua /ˈpapuə/ the southeastern part of the island of New Guinea, now part of the independent state of Papua New Guinea. *See also* PAPUA NEW GUINEA. [Malay, = woolly-haired]

Pap·uan /ˈpapuən/ ● *noun* 1 a native or inhabitant of Papua. 2 a language group consisting of around 750 languages spoken by some 3 million people in New Guinea and neighbouring islands. ● *adjective* of or relating to Papua or its people or to Papuan.

Papua New Guinea a country in the W Pacific comprising the eastern half of the island of New Guinea together with some neighbouring islands; pop. (est. 2002) 5,172,033; capital, Port Moresby. □ **Papua New Guinean** *adjective & noun*

pap·ule /ˈpapjuːl/ *noun* (also **pap·ula** /-jʊlə/; *pl.* **papu·lae** /-juliː/ or **papu·las**) 1 a pimple. 2 a small fleshy projection on a plant. □ **papu·lar** *adjective* [Latin *papula*]

papyr·ol·ogy /ˌpapɪˈrɒlədʒi/ *noun* the study of ancient papyri. □ **papyr·o·logic·al** *adjective* **papyr·ol·o·gist** *noun*

pa·pyr·us /pəˈpairəs/ *noun* (*pl.* **pa·pyri** /-rai/) 1 an aquatic plant, *Cyperus papyrus*, with dark green stems topped with fluffy inflorescences. 2 a a writing material prepared in ancient Egypt from the pithy stem of this. b a document written on this. [Latin *papyrus* from Greek *papuros*]

par ● *noun* 1 the average or normal amount, degree, condition, etc. (*feel below par; be up to par*). 2 equality; an equal status or footing (*on a par with*). 3 *Golf* the number of strokes a first-class player should normally require for a hole or course. 4 the face value of stocks, shares, currencies, etc. (*at par*). 5 the recognized value of one country's currency in terms of another's. ● *transitive verb Golf* complete (a hole or course) with a score equal to par. □ **par for the course** *informal* what is normal or expected in any given circumstances. [Latin (adj. & n.) = equal, equality]

par. *abbreviation* (also **para.**) paragraph.

par- *prefix* var. of PARA-[1] before a vowel or *h* (*paraldehyde; parody; parhelion*).

para[1] *noun informal* 1 a paratrooper. 2 a paragraph. [abbreviation]

para[2] /ˈparə/ *noun* (*pl.* same or **paras**) a monetary unit of Serbia and Montenegro, equal to one-hundredth of a dinar. [Turkish, from Persian *pāra* 'piece']

para-[1] *prefix* (also **par-**) 1 beyond or distinct from, but analogous or parallel to (*paramilitary; paranormal*). 2 *Chem.* a modification of. b relating to diametrically opposite carbon atoms in a benzene ring (*paradichlorobenzene*). [from or after Greek *para-* from *para* beside, past, beyond]

para-[2] *combining form* protect, ward off (*parachute; parasol*). [French from Italian from Latin *parare* defend]

para-[3] *combining form* using or pertaining to parachutes (*paragliding; parasailing; paratrooper*). [from PARACHUTE]

para·bio·sis /ˌparəbaiˈoːsɪs/ *noun Biol.* 1 the anatomical union of a pair of organisms, either naturally (as in Siamese twins) or surgically. 2 the state of being so joined. □ **para·biot·ic** /-ˈbɒtɪk/ *adjective* [modern Latin, formed as PARA-[1] + Greek *biōsis* mode of life, from *bios* life]

par·able /ˈparəbəl, ˈpa-/ *noun* 1 a narrative of imagined events used to illustrate a moral or spiritual lesson. 2 an allegory. [Old French

parabole from Late Latin sense 'allegory, discourse' of Latin *parabola* comparison]

para·bola /pəˈrabələ/ *noun* an open plane curve formed by the intersection of a cone with a plane parallel to its side, resembling the path of a projectile under the action of gravity. [modern Latin from Greek *parabolē* placing side by side, comparison (as PARA-[1], *bolē* a throw, from *ballō*)]

para·bol·ic /ˌparəˈbɒlɪk, ˌpa-/ *adjective* 1 of or expressed in a parable. 2 of or like a parabola; having a shape whose cross-section is a parabola. □ **para·bol·ic·ally** *adverb*

para·bol·oid /pəˈrabəˌlɔɪd/ *noun* 1 (in full **paraboloid of revolution**) a solid generated by the rotation of a parabola about its axis of symmetry. 2 a solid having two or more non-parallel parabolic cross-sections. □ **para·bol·oid·al** *adjective*

Para·cel Islands /ˌparəˈsel/ (also **Para·cels**) a group of about 130 small barren coral islands and reefs in the South China Sea to the southeast of the Chinese island of Hainan. The islands, which lie close to deposits of oil, are claimed by both China and Vietnam.

Para·cel·sus /ˌparəˈselsəs/ (born Theophrastus Phillipus Aureolus Bombastus von Hohenheim, 1493–1541), Swiss physician. He developed a new approach to medicine and philosophy condemning medical teaching that was not based on observation and experience, introduced chemical remedies to replace traditional herbal ones, and gave alchemy a wider perspective. □ **Para·cel·sian** *adjective*

para·ceta·mol /ˌparəˈsiːtəˌmɒl/ *noun Brit.* 1 = ACETAMINOPHEN. 2 a tablet of this. [*para-acetylaminophenol*]

para·chute /ˈparəˌʃuːt, ˈpa-/ ● *noun* 1 a device allowing a person or object to fall (esp. from an airplane) at a safe rate, or retarding other motion, by increasing air resistance, consisting of a fabric sheet along whose perimeter are attached ropes secured to the person or object. 2 (*attributive*) dropped or to be dropped by parachute; involving a parachute (*parachute troops; parachute flare*). ● *transitive & intransitive verb* 1 convey or descend by parachute. 2 appoint or be appointed as an outsider to a position, candidacy, etc. □ **para·chut·ist** *noun* [French (as PARA-[2], CHUTE[1])]

Para·clete /ˈparəˌkliːt, ˈpa-/ *noun Christianity* the Holy Spirit as advocate or counsellor. [Old French *paraclet* from Late Latin *paracletus* from Greek *paraklētos* called in aid (as PARA-[1], *klētos* from *kaleō* call)]

pa·rade ● *noun* 1 a a public march or procession that is conducted in a formal, ceremonial, or celebratory manner. b a progression of people or things, esp. in quick succession (*a parade of players to the penalty box*). 2 an ostentatious display (*made a parade of their wealth*). 3 a an esp. formal or ceremonial assembling or mustering of troops for inspection, display, etc. b = PARADE GROUND. 4 *Brit.* (esp. in names) a public square, promenade, or row of shops. ● *verb* 1 a *intransitive* go or march ceremonially or in a parade. b *transitive* march through (streets etc.) in procession. 2 *transitive* make (a person, thing, etc.) appear in public, esp. so as to be admired or treated with contempt. 3 *intransitive* (often foll. by *around, through*) walk up and down, esp. in a public place, so as to be seen. 4 *transitive* make an ostentatious display of; reveal, expose. 5 *transitive & intransitive* pass by or cause to pass by in procession. 6 *intransitive* assemble for parade, go or march on parade. □ **on parade** 1 on display. 2 taking part in a parade. **rain on a person's parade** *see* RAIN. □ **pa·rad·er** *noun* [French, = show, from Spanish *parada* and Italian *parata*, ultimately from Latin *parare* prepare, furnish]

parade ground *noun* (also **parade square** *Cdn*) an outdoor area where soldiers etc. gather for inspection, roll call, etc.

para·di·chloro·ben·zene /ˌparədaiˌklɔːrəˈbenziːn/ *noun* a crystalline compound, $C_6H_4Cl_2$, used as a mothproofing agent.

para·did·dle /ˈparəˌdidəl/ ● *noun* a basic drum roll produced by alternate beating of sticks. ● *intransitive verb* perform a paradiddle. [imitative]

para·digm /ˈparəˌdaim/ *noun* 1 an example or pattern followed; a typical instance. 2 *Philos.* a mode of viewing the world which underlies the theories and methodology of science etc. in a particular period of history. 3 a list serving as an example or pattern of the inflections of a noun, verb, etc. □ **para·dig·mat·ic** /-dɪɡˈmatɪk/ *adjective* [Late Latin *paradigma* from Greek *paradeigma* from *paradeiknumi* show side by side (as PARA-[1], *deiknumi* show)]

paradigm shift *noun* a fundamental change (in approach, philosophy, etc.).

Para·dise a town in SE Newfoundland, west of St. John's; pop. (2001) 9,598.

para·dise /ˈparəˌdais/ *noun* 1 (in some religions) heaven as the ultimate abode of the just. 2 a a place or state of surpassing beauty and delight,

supreme bliss, etc. **b** an ideal or perfect place (*a paradise for pickpockets*). **3** (in full **earthly paradise**) the original abode of Adam and Eve in the Biblical account of the Creation; the garden of Eden.
□ **para·dis·aical** /-dɪˈseɪ̯ɪkəl/ *adjective* **para·disal** /ˈperəˌdəɪsəl/ *adjective* **para·dis·iacal** /-dɪˈsaɪ̯əkəl/ *adjective* **para·dis·ical** /-ˈdɪsɪkəl/ *adjective* [Old French *paradis* from Late Latin *paradisus* from Greek *paradeisos* from Avestan *pairidaēza* park]

para·dox /ˈperəˌdɒks/ *noun* **1 a** a seemingly absurd or self-contradictory statement which, when investigated or explained, may prove to be well-founded or true. **b** a statement that is actually self-contradictory, absurd, or false. **2 a** a phenomenon that exhibits some contradiction or conflict with preconceived notions of what is reasonable or possible. **b** a person of perplexingly inconsistent life or behaviour. **3** a paradoxical quality, condition, or character. [originally = a statement contrary to accepted opinion, from Late Latin *paradoxum* from Greek *paradoxon* neuter adj. (as PARA-¹, *doxa* opinion)]

para·dox·ical /ˌperəˈdɒksɪkəl/ *adjective* **1** of, like, or involving paradox, esp. apparently inconsistent with itself or with reason, though in fact true. **2** (of a person etc.) characterized by or fond of paradox. **3** (of sleep) characterized by increasing physiological and mental activity, e.g. rapid eye movements and dreaming in humans, and normally alternating with longer periods of orthodox sleep.
□ **para·dox·ical·ly** *adverb*

par·aes·the·sia esp. *Brit.* var. of PARESTHESIA.

par·af·fin /ˈperəfɪn/ *noun* **1 a** a translucent, inflammable, waxy or oily substance obtained by distillation from petroleum and shale and used esp. in candles, cosmetics, and polishes, and for coating and sealing. **b** esp. *Brit.* (also **paraffin oil**) = KEROSENE. **2** *Chem.* = ALKANE. [German (1830) from Latin *parum* little + *affinis* related, from the small affinity it has for other substances]

paraffin wax *noun* paraffin in its solid form.

para·glid·ing *noun* a sport resembling hang-gliding, using a wide, parachute-like canopy attached to the body by a harness, allowing a person to glide after jumping from or being hauled to a height.
□ **para·glide** *intransitive verb* **para·glid·er** *noun*

para·goge /ˌperəˈɡoːdʒi/ *noun* the addition of a letter or syllable to a word in some contexts or as a language develops, e.g. *t* in *peasant*.
□ **para·gogic** /-ˈɡɒdʒɪk/ *adjective* [Late Latin from Greek *paragōgē* derivation (as PARA-¹, *agōgē* from *agō* lead)]

para·gon /ˈperəɡɒn/ *noun* **1 a** a model of excellence. **b** a supremely excellent person or thing. **2** (foll. by *of*) a model (of virtue etc.). [obsolete French from Italian *paragone* touchstone, from medieval Greek *parakonē* whetstone]

para·graph ● *noun* **1 a** a distinct passage of a text, dealing with one particular point of the subject, the words of one speaker, etc., and beginning on a new, usu. indented line. **b** a distinct, usu. numbered, article or section of a legal document. **2** a symbol (usu. ¶) used to mark a new paragraph or section of a text, introduce an editorial comment, or as a reference mark. **3** a short item in a newspaper or periodical, usu. of only one paragraph. ● *transitive verb* arrange (a piece of writing) in paragraphs. [French *paragraphe* or medieval Latin *paragraphus* from Greek *paragraphos* short stroke marking a break in sense (as PARA-¹, *graphō* write)]

Para·guay /ˈperəˌɡwei, ˈperəˌɡwai/ a landlocked country in central S America; pop. (est. 2002) 5,884,491; capital, Asunción.
□ **Para·guay·an** /ˌperəˈɡwaiən/ *adjective & noun*

para·keet /ˈperəˌkiːt/ *noun* any of various small usu. long-tailed parrots. [Old French *paroquet*, Italian *parrocchetto*, Spanish *periquito*, perhaps ultimately from diminutive of *Pierre* etc. Peter: compare PARROT]

para·lan·guage *noun* elements or factors in communication that are ancillary to language proper, e.g. intonation and gesture.

par·alde·hyde /pəˈraldəˌhaid/ *noun* a colourless liquid cyclic polymer of acetaldehyde, used formerly as a narcotic and sedative. [PARA-¹ + ALDEHYDE]

para·legal esp. *N Amer.* ● *noun* a person trained in subsidiary legal matters, but not fully qualified as a lawyer; a legal aide. ● *adjective* of or relating to auxiliary aspects of the law. [PARA-¹ + LEGAL]

para·li·pom·ena /ˌperəlɪˈpɒmənə/ *plural noun* (also **para·lei·pom·ena** /-lai-ˈpɒmənə/) *Bible* (usu. **Paralipomena**) the books of Chronicles in the Hebrew Bible, containing particulars omitted from Kings. [ecclesiastical Latin from Greek *paraleipomena* from *paraleipō* omit (as PARA-¹, *leipō* leave)]

para·lip·sis /ˌperəˈlɪpsɪs/ *noun* (also **-leipsis** /-ˈlaipsɪs/) (*pl.* **-ses** /-siːz/) *Rhetoric* **1** the device of giving emphasis by professing to say little or nothing of a subject, as in *not to mention their unpaid debts of several*

millions. **2** an instance of this. [Late Latin from Greek *paraleipsis* passing over (as PARA-¹, *leipsis* from *leipō* leave)]

par·al·lax /ˈperəˌlaks/ *noun* **1 a** the apparent difference in the position or direction of an object caused when the observer's position is changed. **b** such a difference or change in the position of a celestial object as seen from different points on the earth's surface or opposite points in its orbit. **2** the angular amount of such a difference or change. □ **par·al·lac·tic** /-ˈlaktɪk/ *adjective* [Greek *parallaxis* change, from *parallassō* to alternate (as PARA-¹, *allassō* exchange, from *allos* other)]

par·al·lel ● *adjective* **1 a** (of lines or planes) side by side and having the same distance continuously between them. **b** (foll. by *to*, *with*) (of a line or plane) having this relation (to another). **2** (of circumstances etc.) precisely similar, analogous, or corresponding. **3** running through the same period of time, contemporary in duration (*parallel universe*). **4** *Computing* **a** involving the concurrent or simultaneous performance of multiple operations (*parallel processing*). **b** of, relating to, or involving the simultaneous transmission of data over separate wires (*parallel port*; *parallel printer*). **5** (of a text etc.) having two or more translations etc. printed in a format which allows direct comparison, usu. on facing or consecutive pages (*a parallel Bible*). ● *noun* **1** a comparison (*drew a parallel between the two situations*). **2** a person or thing precisely analogous or equal to another in essential particulars. **3** (in full **parallel of latitude**) **a** each of the imaginary parallel circles of constant latitude on the earth's surface. **b** a corresponding line on a map. **4** *Printing* two parallel lines (‖) used as a reference mark. ● *transitive verb* (**par·al·leled**, **par·al·lel·ing**) **1** be parallel to; correspond to. **2** represent as similar; compare. **3** esp. *N Amer.* run parallel with or alongside of, go or tend to go in the same direction as. ● *adverb* in a parallel direction or manner (*main streets ran parallel to the shoreline*).
□ **in parallel 1** (of electric circuits) arranged so as to join at common points at each end. **2** concurrently, simultaneously, contemporaneously. [Greek *parallēlos* (as PARA-¹, *allēlos* one another)]

parallel bars *plural noun* **1** a pair of parallel rails on posts for gymnastics. **2** a gymnastics event in which participants perform feats on the parallel bars.

parallel·epi·ped /ˌperəlelˈepɪˌped -ləˈpaipɪd/ *noun Math.* a solid figure bounded by six parallelograms, of which opposite pairs are parallel. [Greek *parallēlepipedon* (as PARALLEL, *epipedon* plane surface)]

par·al·lel·ism *noun* **1 a** the state, position or character of being parallel. **b** an instance of this. **c** a parallel case, passage, etc. **2 a** correspondence, in sense or construction, of successive clauses or passages in writing. **b** a sentence or passage exemplifying this. **3** *Computing* **a** the execution of operations concurrently by separate parts of a computer, esp. separate microprocessors. **b** the capability of a computer to operate in this way. **4** *Biol.* the development of similar characteristics by two related groups of plants or animals in response to similar environmental pressures.

par·al·lelo·gram /ˌperəˈlelaˌɡram/ *noun Math.* a four-sided plane rectilinear figure with opposite sides parallel. [Greek *parallēlogrammon* (as PARALLEL, *grammē* line)]

parallel parking *noun* the parking of a vehicle or vehicles parallel to the roadside. □ **parallel park** *transitive & intransitive verb*

parallel port *noun Computing* a connector for a device that sends or receives several bits of data simultaneously by using more than one wire.

parallel structure *noun* a correspondence in grammatical construction of successive clauses or phrases in a sentence.

parallel turn *noun* a turn in skiing with the skis kept parallel to each other.

Para·lym·pics /perəˈlɪmpɪks/ *plural noun* (also **Paralympic Games**) an international athletic competition for disabled athletes.
□ **Para·lym·pi·an** *noun* **Para·lym·pic** *attributive adjective* [PARAPLEGIC (see PARAPLEGIA) + OLYMPIC]

par·aly·sis /pəˈralɪsɪs/ *noun* (*pl.* **par·aly·ses** /-ˌsiːz/) **1** loss of the ability to move a part of the body, usu. as a result of disease or injury to the nervous system. **2** a state of utter powerlessness, inability to act, or suspension of activity. [Latin from Greek *paralusis* from *paraluō* disable (as PARA-¹, *luō* loosen)]

para·lytic /ˌperəˈlɪtɪk/ ● *adjective* **1 a** affected by, suffering from, or subject to paralysis. **b** of the nature of, pertaining to, characterized by, or causing paralysis. **2** *Brit. slang* very drunk. ● *noun* a person affected by paralysis. □ **para·lytic·ally** *adverb* [Latin *paralyticus* from Greek *paralutikos* (as PARALYSIS)]

para·lyze /ˈperəˌlaiz/ *transitive verb* (also **para·lyse**) **1** affect with paralysis. **2** render powerless or incapable of action. **3** bring to a standstill. □ **para·lyzed** *adjective* **para·lyz·ing·ly** *adverb* [French *paralyser* from *paralysie*: compare PALSY]

para·magnet·ic *adjective* (of a body or substance) tending to become weakly magnetized so as to lie parallel to a magnetic field force. □ **para·magnet·ism** *noun*

Para·mar·ibo /ˌparəˈmarɪˌboː/ the capital of Suriname, a port on the Atlantic coast; pop. (est. 2002) 216,200.

para·meci·um /ˌpɛrəˈmiːsɪəm/ *noun* (*pl.* **para·mecia**) any freshwater protozoan of the genus *Paramecium*, of a characteristic slipper-like shape covered with cilia. [modern Latin from Greek *paramēkēs* oval (as PARA-¹, *mēkos* length)]

para·med·ic *noun* a paramedical worker, esp. one who works in ambulances and is trained in first aid, emergency care, etc.

para·medic·al *adjective* (of services etc.) supplementing and supporting medical work.

par·am·eter /pəˈramətər/ *noun* **1 a** a distinguishing or defining characteristic or feature, esp. one that may be measured or quantified. **b** a constant element or aspect, esp. serving as a limit or boundary. **2** *Math.* a quantity constant in the case considered but varying in different cases. □ **para·met·ric** /ˌpɛrəˈmetrɪk/ *adjective* [modern Latin from Greek *para* beside + *metron* measure]

param·eter·ize /pəˈramətərˌaɪz/ *transitive verb* (also **param·et·rize**, esp. *Brit.* **-ise**) describe or represent in terms of a parameter or parameters. □ **param·eter·iz·a·tion** *noun*

para·mil·itary ● *adjective* (of an organization, unit, etc.) not a professional military force, but having an ancillary or analogous function, organization, or status. ● *noun* (*pl.* **-ies**) **1** a paramilitary force or organization. **2** a member of such a force or organization.

par·amo /ˈpɛrəˌmoː/ *noun* (*pl.* **-amos**) a high treeless plateau in tropical S America. [Spanish & Portuguese from Latin *paramus*]

para·mount *adjective* **1** pre-eminent, requiring first consideration; superior to others in importance, influence, etc. (*of paramount importance*). **2** (of a person, people, nation, etc.) above others in rank or order; highest in power or jurisdiction (*the paramount chief*). □ **para·mount·cy** *noun* **para·mount·ly** *adverb* [Anglo-French *paramont* from Old French *par* by + *amont* above: compare AMOUNT]

par·amour /ˈpɛrəˌmʊr/ *noun* **1** an illicit lover of a married person. **2** any lover, a sweetheart. [Old French *par amour* by love]

Paraná /ˌparəˈnɑ/ a river port in E Argentina, on the Paraná River; pop. (est. 1999) 256,602. It was the capital of Argentina between 1853 and 1862.

Paraná River a river of S America, which rises in SE Brazil and flows some 3 300 km (2,060 miles) southward to the Plate River estuary in Argentina. For part of its length it forms the southeastern border of Paraguay.

par·ang /ˈpɛraŋ/ *noun* a large heavy Malayan knife used for clearing vegetation etc. [Malay]

para·noia /ˌpɛrəˈnɔɪə/ *noun* **1** a mental illness characterized by delusions of persecution, unwarranted jealousy, or exaggerated self-importance. **2** a tendency to suspect and mistrust others or to believe oneself unfairly used. □ **para·noiac** *adjective & noun* **para·noiac·ally** *adverb* **para·noic** /-ˈnoːɪk, -ˈnɔɪk/ *adjective* **para·noid** /ˈpɛrəˌnɔɪd/ *adjective & noun* [modern Latin from Greek from *paranoos* distracted (as PARA-¹, *noos* mind)]

para·normal *adjective* designating, pertaining to, or involving phenomena or powers such as telekinesis, clairvoyance, etc., whose operation is outside the scope of known laws of nature or normal objective investigation.

para·pente /ˈpɛrəˌpɒnt/ *noun* **1** the activity (sometimes practised as an organized sport) of gliding by means of an airfoil parachute launched from high ground. **2** the parachute used in parapente. [French *parapente* from PARA-² + *pente* 'slope, incline, gradient, sloping flight path']

para·pet /ˈpɛrəpət/ *noun* **1** a low wall at the edge of a roof, balcony, etc., or along the sides of a bridge, pier, etc. **2** a bank of earth or stone erected to provide protection from the enemy's observation and fire, esp. one on top of a wall or rampart, or in front of a trench. [French *parapet* or Italian *parapetto* breast-high wall (as PARA-², *petto* breast, from Latin *pectus*)]

par·aph /ˈpɛrəf/ *noun* a flourish after a signature, originally as a precaution against forgery. [French *paraphe* from medieval Latin *paraphus* for *paragraphus* PARAGRAPH]

para·pher·nalia /ˌpɛrəfəˈneɪljə/ *plural noun* (also treated as *sing.*) miscellaneous belongings, items of equipment, accessories, etc. [originally = property owned by a married woman, from medieval Latin *paraphernalia* from Late Latin *parapherna* from Greek *parapherna* property apart from a dowry (as PARA-¹, *pherna* from *phernē* dower)]

para·phrase ● *noun* a free rendering or rewording of a passage. ● *transitive & intransitive verb* express the meaning of (a passage) in other words; render or translate freely. □ **para·phras·able** *adjective* **para·phras·tic** /-ˈfrastɪk/ *adjective* [Greek *paraphrasis* from *paraphrazō* (as PARA-¹ *phrazō* tell)]

para·plegia /ˌpɛrəˈpliːdʒə/ *noun* paralysis of the legs and part or the whole of the trunk. □ **para·plegic** *adjective & noun* [modern Latin from Greek *paraplēgia* from *paraplēssō* (as PARA-¹, *plēssō* strike)]

para·profes·sion·al ● *noun* a person without professional training to whom a particular aspect of a professional task is designated. ● *adjective* of, designating, or pertaining to such a person.

para·psych·ol·ogy /ˌpɛrəsaɪˈkɒlədʒi/ *noun* the study of mental phenomena outside the sphere of the ordinary, e.g. hypnosis, telepathy, etc. □ **para·psycho·logic·al** *adjective* **para·psych·ol·o·gist** *noun*

para·quat /ˈpɛrəˌkwɒt/ *noun* a quick-acting, highly toxic herbicide that is rendered inactive on contact with the soil. [PARA-¹ + QUATERNARY (from the position of the bond between the two parts of the molecule relative to quaternary nitrogen atom)]

para·sail·ing *noun* a sport in which participants wearing open parachutes glide through the air while being towed by a speedboat. □ **para·sail** *intransitive verb & noun*

para·selene /ˌpɛrəsɪˈliːni/ *noun* (*pl.* **para·sel·enae** /-niː/) a bright spot, esp. an image of the moon, on a lunar halo. *Also called* MOCK MOON. [modern Latin (as PARA-¹, Greek *selēnē* moon)]

para·site /ˈpɛrəˌsaɪt/ *noun* **1** an organism living in or on another and benefiting at the expense of the other. **2** a person who lives off or exploits another or others. □ **para·sit·ic** /-ˈsɪtɪk/ *adjective* **para·sit·ic·al** /-ˈsɪtɪkəl/ *adjective* **para·sit·ic·ally** *adverb* **para·siti·cide** /-ˈsɪtɪˌsaɪd/ *noun* **para·sit·o·logic·al** *adjective* **para·sit·ol·o·gist** *noun* **para·sit·ol·ogy** *noun* [Greek *parasitos* one who eats at another's table (as PARA-¹, *sitos* food)]

parasitic jaeger *noun* a medium-sized jaeger, *Stercorarius parasiticus*, which breeds in the Canadian Arctic.

para·sit·ism *noun* the condition of living or acting as a parasite.

para·sit·ize *transitive verb* (also esp. *Brit.* **-ise**) infest as a parasite. □ **para·sit·iz·a·tion** *noun*

para·sit·oid /ˈpɛrəsɪtɔɪd/ ● *noun* an insect whose larvae live as parasites which eventually kill their hosts, e.g. an ichneumon wasp. ● *adjective* of, relating to, or designating such an insect.

para·sol *noun* **1** a light umbrella used to give shade from the sun. **2** (in full **parasol mushroom**) a tall fungus of the genus *Lepiota* with a broad shaggy domed cap, esp. the edible *L. procera*. [French from Italian *parasole* (as PARA-², *sole* 'sun' from Latin *sol*)]

para·statal /pɛrəˈsteɪtəl/ ● *adjective* (of an industrial organization etc.) having some political authority and serving the nation indirectly, esp. in some African countries. ● *noun* a parastatal organization.

para·sympa·thet·ic /ˌpɛrəˌsɪmpəˈθetɪk/ *adjective Anat.* relating to one of the major divisions of the autonomic nervous system, whose nerves leave the spinal cord in the cranial or sacral region, and which is associated more with calmness and rest than with alertness (*compare* SYMPATHETIC 8). [PARA-¹ + SYMPATHETIC, because some of these nerves run alongside sympathetic nerves]

para·synth·esis /ˌpɛrəˈsɪnθəsɪs/ *noun Linguistics* a derivation from a compound, e.g. *black-eyed* from *black eye(s)* + *-ed*. □ **para·syn·thet·ic** /-ˈθetɪk/ *adjective* [Greek *parasunthesis* (as PARA-¹, SYNTHESIS)]

para·taxis /ˌpɛrəˈtaksɪs/ *noun Grammar* the placing of clauses etc. one after another, without words to indicate coordination or subordination, e.g. *Tell me, how are you?* □ **para·tac·tic** /-ˈtaktɪk/ *adjective* **para·tac·tic·ally** /-ˈtaktɪkli/ *adverb* [Greek *parataxis* (as PARA-¹, *taxis* arrangement, from *tassō* arrange)]

pa·ratha /pəˈrɒtə/ *noun* (in esp. Indian cookery) a piece of flat unleavened bread fried in butter, ghee, etc. on a griddle. [Hindi *parāṭhā*]

para·thion /ˌpɛrəˈθaɪən/ *noun* a sulphur-containing organophosphorous agricultural insecticide which is also highly toxic to mammals. [PARA-¹ + THIO- + -ON]

para·thyroid /ˌpɛrəˈθaɪrɔɪd/ ● *noun* a gland next to the thyroid, secreting a hormone that regulates calcium and phosphate levels in the body. ● *adjective* of or associated with this gland.

para·troop·er *noun* a member of a body of paratroops.

para·troops *plural noun* troops equipped to be dropped by parachute

Vowels: a *cat* ɑ *arm* e *bed* ɜr *her* ɜ: *deux* ə *ago* ɪ *sit* i *cosy* iː *feed* ɒ *hot* ɔ *pore* oː *no* ʌ *run* ʊ *put*

from aircraft. □ **para·troop** *attributive adjective* [contraction of PARACHUTE + TROOP]

para·typhoid ● *noun* a fever resembling typhoid but less severe and caused by different, though related, bacteria. ● *adjective* of, relating to, or caused by this fever.

para·vane /ˈperəˌveɪn/ *noun* a device attached by wire to a ship, esp. one used to cut the moorings of submerged mines, having vanes or planes to keep it at a desired depth.

par·boil *transitive verb* partly cook by boiling. [Old French *parbo(u)illir* from Late Latin *perbullire* boil thoroughly (as PER-, *bullire* boil: confused with PART)]

par·buckle /ˈpɑrˌbʌkəl/ ● *noun* a rope arranged like a sling, for raising or lowering casks and cylindrical objects. ● *transitive verb* raise or lower with this. [earlier *parbunkle*, of unknown origin: assoc. with BUCKLE]

Par·cae /ˈpɑrkaɪ, ˈpɑrsiː/ *Rom. Myth* the Roman name for the Fates.

par·cel ● *noun* **1** an item or quantity of goods etc. wrapped up in a single package. **2** a piece of land. **3** (esp. in **part and parcel**) an integral part. ● *transitive verb* (**par·celled, par·cel·ling**; also esp. *US* **par·celed, par·cel·ing**) **1** (foll. by *up*) wrap as a parcel. **2** (foll. by *out*) divide into portions. **3** cover (rope) with strips of canvas. [Old French *parcelle*, ultimately from Latin *particula* (as PART)]

parcel post *noun N Amer.* a postal rate, slightly cheaper than that for first class mail, for packages weighing over 500g (or one pound in the US).

parch *verb* **1** *transitive & intransitive* make or become hot and dry; shrivel up with heat. **2** *transitive* roast (peas, grain, etc.) lightly. [Middle English *perch, parche*, of unknown origin]

parched *adjective* **1** dried out, esp. by heat. **2** *informal* thirsty.

Par·chee·si *proprietary var. of* PACHISI.

parch·ment *noun* **1 a** an animal skin, esp. that of a sheep or goat, prepared as a writing or painting surface. **b** a manuscript written on this. **2** (in full **parchment paper**) **a** high-grade paper made to resemble parchment. **b** (also **baking parchment**) a tough, translucent, glossy, waterproof and greaseproof paper made by soaking ordinary unsized paper in dilute sulphuric acid. **3** *N Amer.* a diploma. [Old French *parchemin*, ultimately a blend of Late Latin *pergamina* writing material from Pergamum (in Asia Minor) with *Parthica pellis* Parthian skin (leather)]

pard *noun esp. archaic* a leopard. [Old French from Latin *pardus* from Greek *pardos*]

pard·ner *noun N Amer. jocular* a partner or comrade. [corruption]

par·don ● *noun* **1 a** the act of excusing or forgiving an offence, error, sin, etc. **b** courteous forbearance or indulgence. **2 a** a remission of the legal consequences of a crime or conviction. **b** a document conveying a legal pardon. **3** *Catholicism hist.* an indulgence. ● *transitive verb* **1 a** release from the consequences of an offence, error, sin, etc. **b** duly authorize remission of the legal consequences of (a crime etc.). **2** forgive or excuse a person for (an offence etc.). **3** make esp. courteous allowances for, excuse (a person, fact, or action). ● *interjection* (also **pardon me** or **I beg your pardon** or **beg pardon**) **1** a formula of apology or disagreement. **2** a request to repeat something said. □ **pardon me for living** an ironic rejoinder to someone who feels imposed upon. □ **par·don·able** *adjective* **par·don·ably** *adverb* [Old French *pardun, pardoner* from medieval Latin *perdonare* concede, remit (as PER-, *donare* give)]

par·don·er *noun hist.* a person licensed to sell papal pardons or indulgences.

pare *transitive verb* **1 a** trim by cutting away the surface or edge (*pared his nails*). **b** cut away the skin or outer covering of (esp. fruit or vegetables). **c** (often foll. by *off, away*) cut off (the surface or edge). **2** (often foll. by *away, down*) reduce, diminish little by little, make gradual reductions in. **3** (foll. by *down*) remove all superfluous matter from so as to arrive at the essentials. □ **parer** *noun* [Old French *parer* adorn, peel (fruit), from Latin *parare* prepare]

pared-down *adjective* simplified, reduced esp. to a minimum (*pared-down companies*).

pare·gor·ic /ˌperɪˈɡɒrɪk/ *noun hist.* a camphorated tincture of opium used to reduce pain. [Late Latin *paregoricus* from Greek *parēgorikos* soothing (as PARA-¹, *-agoros* speaking, from *agora* assembly)]

par·en·chyma /pəˈreŋkɪmə/ *noun* **1** *Anat. & Zool.* the functional part of a gland or organ as distinguished from the connective and supporting tissue. **2** *Bot.* the cellular material, usu. soft and succulent, found esp. in the softer parts of leaves, pulp of fruits, bark and pith of stems, etc. □ **par·en·chym·al** *adjective* **par·en·chyma·tous** /-ˈkɪmətəs/ *adjective*

[Greek *paregkhuma* something poured in besides (as PARA-¹, *egkhuma* infusion, from *egkheō* pour in)]

par·ens pat·riae /ˌperenz ˈpatriː/ *noun Law* the power of the monarch, superior court, or other authority to act on behalf of citizens unable to act for or protect themselves because of mental incapacity etc. [modern Latin, lit. 'parent of the country']

Pa·rent /pəˈrɑ̃/ **Simon-Napoleon** (1855–1920), Canadian businessman, lawyer, and politician, Liberal premier of Quebec 1900–05. As mayor of Quebec City (1894–1906), he promoted economic development and city planning. As provincial minister of lands and forests he encouraged the exploitation of the province's timber and hydro resources. Succeeding Félix-Gabriel Marchand as premier in 1900, he was removed in 1905, partly by a younger group of nationalists who disagreed with his promotion of outside capitalist investment.

par·ent ● *noun* **1** a person who has begotten or borne offspring; a biological father or mother. **2** a person who holds the position or exercises the function of such a parent, e.g. by adopting a child; a protector or guardian. **3** an ancestor. **4** (also *attributive*) an animal or plant considered in relation to its offspring. **5** (also *attributive*) a thing from which another is derived or has its existence; a source or origin. **6 a** (also *attributive*) an initiating organization or enterprise (*the St. John's Maple Leafs' parent club in the NHL*). **b** = PARENT COMPANY. ● *verb* **1** *transitive* **a** be or act as a parent to, rear (a child). **b** beget, produce. **2** *intransitive* be a parent; take care of one's children. □ **par·ent·al** *adjective* **par·ent·al·ly** *adverb* **parent·hood** *noun* [Old French from Latin *parens parentis* from *parere* bring forth]

par·ent·age *noun* lineage; descent from or through parents (*their parentage is unknown*).

Parental Accompaniment *noun hist* **1** (in Manitoba) a former film classification recommending that viewers under 15 years of age be accompanied by a parent or guardian. **2** (in Saskatchewan) a former film classification requiring that viewers under 14 years of age be accompanied by a parent or guardian. Abbr.: **PA**.

Parental Guidance *noun* **1** (in Alberta, Saskatchewan, and Ontario) a film classification which advises of content that should be subject to parental discretion, without specifying an age restriction. **2** (in Manitoba and the Maritimes) a film classification which advises of content most suitable for mature viewers over 12 years of age. Abbr.: **PG**.

parental leave *noun* a paid or unpaid leave from work afforded to either parent to care for a child, esp. a newborn.

parent company *noun* a company of which other companies are subsidiaries.

par·en·ter·al /pəˈrentərəl/ *adjective Med.* involving or designating the introduction of a substance into the body other than by the mouth or intestine, esp. by injection. □ **par·en·ter·al·ly** *adverb* [PARA-¹ + Greek *enteron* intestine]

par·en·the·sis /pəˈrenθəsɪs/ *noun* (pl. **par·en·the·ses** /-ˌsiːz/) **1 a** a word, clause, or sentence inserted as an explanation or afterthought into a passage which is grammatically complete without it, usu. marked off by brackets, dashes, or commas. **b** (in *pl.*) a pair of round brackets ( ) used for this. **c** either of a pair of round brackets. **2** an interlude or interval. □ **in parentheses** (or **in parenthesis**) by way of explanation, digression, or afterthought. [Greek *parenthesis* from *parentithēmi* put in beside]

par·en·the·size /pəˈrenθəˌsaɪz/ *verb* (also esp. *Brit.* **-ise**) **1** *transitive & intransitive* insert or express as a parenthesis. **2** *transitive* put (a word, expression, etc.) into brackets or similar punctuation.

par·en·thet·ic·al /ˌperənˈθetɪkəl/ *adjective* **1** of or by way of a parenthesis. **2** interposed. □ **par·en·thet·ic** *adjective* **par·en·thet·ic·al·ly** *adverb* [PARENTHESIS after *synthesis, synthetic*, etc.]

par·ent·ing *noun* the occupation or concerns of parents, esp. taking care of one's children.

parent-in-law *noun* (pl. **parents-in-law**) a father-in-law or mother-in-law.

parent-teacher association *noun* a local organization of parents and teachers for promoting closer relations and improving educational facilities at a school. Abbr.: **PTA**.

par·esis /pəˈriːsɪs, ˈperɪsɪs/ *noun* (pl. **par·eses** /-ˌsiːz/) *Med.* **1** partial paralysis. **2** chronic inflammation of the brain and meninges, occurring in tertiary syphilis and causing progressive dementia and general paralysis. □ **par·etic** /-ˈretɪk/ *adjective* [modern Latin from Greek from *pariēmi* let go (as PARA-¹, *hiēmi* let go)]

par·es·the·sia /ˌperəsˈθiːziə/ *noun* (also esp. *Brit.* **par·aes·the·sia**) (pl.

-siae /-zɪiː/ (in *sing.* or *pl.*) *Med.* abnormal sensations caused esp. by pressure on or damage to peripheral nerves. [PARA-¹ + Greek *aisthēsis* 'sensation' + -IA¹]

Par·eto /pəˈreitoː/ **Vil·fredo (Fred·erico Damaso)** (1848–1923), Italian economist, mathematician, and sociologist, whose work formed the foundation of modern welfare economics; his *Mind and Society* (1916) is said to have formed the basis of Italian Fascism.

par·eve /ˈpɑrəvə, ˈpɑrvə/ *adjective* (also **parve** /ˈpɑrvə/) *Judaism* (of food) being or containing neither meat nor dairy and so kosher for use with either according to the dietary laws (includes fruit, vegetables, fish, many synthetic products, etc.). [Yiddish *parev(e)*, lit. 'neutral']

par excellence /ˌpɑr eksəˈlɑ̃s, pɑr ˈeksəˌlɑ̃s/ *adjective* as having special excellence; being the supreme example of its kind (*the short story par excellence*). [French, = by excellence]

par·fait /pɑrˈfei/ *noun* **1** a layered dessert consisting of ice cream, sauces, crushed fruit, etc. served in a tall glass. **2** a frozen dessert made with egg whites, sugar, whipped cream, and flavouring. [French *parfait*, perfect]

parfait glass *noun* a tall, narrow, short-stemmed glass used to serve parfaits.

par·fleche /ˈpɑrfleʃ/ *N Amer.* ● *noun* **1** an esp. buffalo hide from which the hair has been removed and which has been dried on a frame. **2** an article made of this. ● *adjective* made of parfleche. [Canadian French *parflèche* from French *parer* from Italian *parare* 'ward off' + French *flèche* 'arrow']

parge /pɑrdʒ/ (also **par·get** /ˈpɑrdʒət/) ● *transitive verb* (**par·get·ed**, **par·get·ing**) **1** apply parging to (a wall, brickwork, etc.) **2** plaster (a wall etc.) esp. with an ornamental pattern. ● *noun* **1** plaster applied in this way; ornamental plasterwork. **2** roughcast. [Old French *pargeter*, *parjeter* from *par* all over + *jeter* throw]

par·ging /ˈpɑrdʒɪŋ/ *noun* **1** a thin layer of mortar, roughcast, etc. covering a wall, brickwork, etc. for protection or to create a smooth surface. **2** the mortar used for parging.

par·heli·on /pɑrˈhiːliən/ *noun* (*pl.* **par·helia** /pɑrˈhiːliə/) = SUN DOG. □ **par·helic** *adjective* [Latin *parelion* from Greek (as PARA-¹, *hēlios* sun)]

pa·riah /pəˈraiə/ *noun* **1** a social outcast. **2** a despised person. **3** (also **pariah state**) a country against which political or diplomatic sanctions are in force. **4** *hist.* a member of a low caste or of no Hindu caste in S India. [Tamil *paṛaiyar* pl. of *paṛaiyan* hereditary drummer, from *paṛai* drum]

pariah dog *noun* = PYE-DOG.

pa·ri·et·al /pəˈraiətəl/ *adjective* **1** *Anat.* **a** of the wall of the body or the lining of any of its cavities. **b** of or near the parietal bones. **2** *Bot.* of the wall of a hollow structure, esp. an ovary. [French *pariétal* from Latin *paries -etis* wall]

parietal bone *noun* either of a pair of bones, right and left, forming the central part of the sides and top of the skull.

parietal lobe *noun* either of the paired lobes of the brain at the top of the head, including areas concerned with the reception and correlation of sensory information.

pa·ri·mutu·el /ˌpɑrɪˈmjuːtʃuˌel/ *noun* **1** a form of betting in which those backing the first three places divide the losers' stakes (less the operator's commission). **2** a booth, machine, etc. for placing bets under this system. [French, = mutual stake]

paring *noun* **1** (often in *pl.*) a thin portion cut or peeled from the surface of a thing; a shaving. **2** an act of cutting, shaving, or peeling such a strip.

paring knife *noun* a kitchen knife with a short, firm, pointed blade used for paring fruit, vegetables, etc.

pari passu /ˌpɑrɪ ˈpɑsuː, ˌperi/ *adverb* **1** with equal speed, side by side, simultaneously and equally. **2** on equal footing, without preference. [Latin]

Paris¹ 1 the capital of France, on the Seine River; pop. (1999) 2,125,246. **2** a former town in SW central Ontario, situated about 50 km west of Hamilton, now part of the city of Brant; pop. (2001) 8,987. [sense 2 so called because of the area's extensive gypsum beds, from which plaster of *Paris* is derived]

Paris² ▸ 1 *Gk Myth* a Trojan prince, the son of Priam and Hecuba. Appointed by the gods to decide who among the three goddesses Hera, Athene, and Aphrodite should win a prize for beauty, he awarded it to Aphrodite, who promised him the fairest woman in the world, Helen, wife of Menelaus king of Sparta; he abducted Helen, bringing about the Trojan War, in which he killed Achilles but was later himself killed. **2 Mat·thew** (*c.*1199–1259) English chronicler and Benedictine

monk, who is known for his *Chronica Majora* (1235–59), a history of the world from the Creation to the mid-13th c.

Paris, Peace of *noun* (also **Treaty of Paris**) the collection of treaties signed by Great Britain, the US, France, and Spain in 1783 that concluded the American Revolution.

Paris, Treaty of *noun* **1** a treaty signed by France, Britain, and Spain in 1763, ending the Seven Years War and ceding the following territories to Britain: from Spain, Florida; from France, Île Royale (now Prince Edward Island) and Canada, including the Great Lakes Basin and the east bank of the Mississippi River. **2** = PARIS, PEACE OF.

Paris Commune *see* COMMUNE, THE.

Paris green *noun* a vivid green toxic crystalline salt of copper and arsenic, used as a preservative, pigment and insecticide. [PARIS¹ 1]

par·ish *noun* **1 a** an area of ecclesiastical jurisdiction having a church and clergy. **b** the people who are members of a parish. **2** *Cdn* **a** (*Que.*) a county subdivision functioning as both a political and an ecclesiastical unit. **b** (*NB*) a county subdivision, the unit of representation at county councils. **3** (in the UK) a district constituted for various purposes of local civil administration or government. **4** *US* a county in Louisiana. [Old French *paroche*, *paroisse* from ecclesiastical Latin *parochia*, *paroechia* from Greek *paroikia* sojourning, from *paroikos* (as PARA-¹, -*oíkos* -dwelling, from *oikeō* dwell)]

parish council *noun* **1** the council of a church parish. **2** *Brit.* the administrative body in a civil parish.

parish hall *noun* **1** a large meeting room, usu. part of or connected to a parish church, in which social events, meetings, etc. are held. **2** the building in which this is housed, if separate from the church.

pa·rish·ion·er /pəˈrɪʃənər/ *noun* **1** a member of or someone who attends a particular church. **2** an inhabitant of a parish. [obsolete *parishen* from Middle English from Old French *parossien*, formed as PARISH]

parish priest *noun* a priest in charge of a parish.

parish pump *noun* (often *attributive*) a symbol of parochialism or a limited scope, outlook, or knowledge (*parish-pump politics*).

Paris·ian /pəˈrɪːʒən, -ˈriːziən/ ● *adjective* of, relating to, or typical of Paris or the people of Paris. ● *noun* **1** a native or inhabitant of Paris. **2** the kind of French spoken in Paris. [French *parisien*]

Paris·ienne /pəriˈziːen/ *noun* a Parisian girl or woman. [French feminine of *Parisien* Parisian]

par·ity¹ /ˈperiti/ *noun* **1** equality or equal status. **2** equality of nature, character, or tendency; parallelism or analogy (*parity of reasoning*). **3 a** equivalence of pay for jobs or categories of work perceived as being comparable or analogous. **b** the practice or system of setting pay levels according to such perceived comparability. **4** *Math. & Computing* **a** the property of an integer by virtue of which it is odd or even. **b** the property of employing odd or even numbers. **5** *Computing* (in full **parity bit**) a bit that is automatically made 1 or 0 as to make the parity of the word or set containing it either odd or even, as previously determined. **6** *Physics* (of a quantity) the fact of changing its sign or remaining unaltered under a given transformation of coordinates etc. **7** equivalence of one currency with another; being at par. [French *parité* or Late Latin *paritas* (as PAR)]

par·ity² /ˈperiti/ *noun Med.* **1** the fact or condition of having borne children or offspring. **2** the number of children or offspring previously borne. [formed as -PAROUS + -ITY]

Pari·zeau /pɑriˈzoː/ **Jacques** (b.1930), Canadian economist and politician, PQ premier of Quebec 1994–96. Chosen as leader of the Parti Québécois in 1987, he was elected premier in 1994. He resigned in 1996 after a provincial referendum narrowly rejected Quebec sovereignty.

Park, Mungo (1771–1806), Scottish explorer. He undertook a series of explorations in W Africa (1795–7), among them the navigation of the Niger; he drowned while on a second expedition to the Niger (1805–6).

park ● *noun* **1** a piece of land usu. with lawns, gardens, etc. in a town or city, maintained at public expense for recreational use. **2** a large area of government land kept in its natural state for recreational use, wildlife conservation, etc. **3** a large enclosed area of land etc., either public or private, used to accommodate wild animals in captivity (*wildlife park*). **4** (usu. in *combination*) **a** an area devoted to a specified purpose (*industrial park*). **b** an area developed for a particular form of recreation (*snowboard park*; *water park*; *theme park*). **5** *N Amer.* an enclosed arena, area, stadium, etc. for sports events (esp. *ballpark*). **6** an area for motor vehicles etc. to be left in (*trailer park*). **7** the gear position or function in an automatic transmission in which the gears are locked, preventing the vehicle's movement. **8** a large enclosed piece of ground, usu. with woodland and pasture, attached to a stately home etc.

● **1** *transitive & intransitive verb* **a** leave (a vehicle) usu. temporarily, in a parking lot, by the side of the road, etc. **b** manoeuvre (a vehicle) into a particular position of this kind. **2** *transitive informal* leave, deposit, or settle (a person or thing) in a convenient place, usu. temporarily. **3** *intransitive N Amer. slang* kiss, pet, etc. in a parked car. **4** *transitive Computing* register (an Internet domain name) without making a website available at the relevant URL. □ **park oneself** *informal* sit down. □ **park-like** *adjective* [Old French *parc* from medieval Latin *parricus* of Germanic origin, related to *pearruc*]

par·ka *noun* a warm, hooded coat extending to the thighs or calves. [Aleut]

park·ade *noun Cdn* a parking garage.

park-and-ride ● *noun* a system whereby commuters, shoppers, etc. travel by car to parking lots on the outskirts of a city and continue into the city by public transportation. ● *adjective* designating or pertaining to such a system.

park belt *noun Cdn (West)* = PARKLAND 1b.

Park Chung Hee /ˌpɑrk tʃʊŋ ˈhiː/ (1917–79), South Korean leader, president 1963–79. He assumed dictatorial powers in 1971, and under his presidency, South Korea emerged as a leading industrial nation, with one of the world's highest rates of economic growth; he was assassinated.

Par·ker ▶ **1 Charles Chris·to·pher ('Char·lie**'; known as 'Bird' or 'Yardbird') (1920–55), US jazz saxophonist. He played with Thelonious Monk and Dizzy Gillespie, and became one of the key figures of the bebop movement; he is noted for his recordings with Miles Davis in 1945. **2 Dor·o·thy (Roths·child)** (1893–1967), US humorist, literary critic, short-story writer, and poet. She was a leading member of the Algonquin Round Table, a circle of New York writers and humorists that met in the 1920s, and is known for her book reviews and short stories for the *New Yorker* magazine, and the verse collection *Enough Rope* (1927).

Parker House roll *noun N Amer.* an oval bread roll formed by folding a flat disk of dough in half. [after the *Parker House* hotel in Boston, Mass., where originally served in the 19th c.]

Par·ker·iz·ing *noun proprietary* a process for rust-proofing iron or steel by brief immersion in a hot acidic solution of a metal phosphate. □ **Par·ker·ized** *adjective* [*Parker* Rust-Proof Company of America (which introduced the process)]

park·ette *noun Cdn (S Ont.)* a small park in a city, usu. less than a block and containing a grassy area, small gardens, benches, etc.

par·kin *noun Brit.* a kind of bread or cake made with molasses, usu. oatmeal, and sometimes ginger. [perhaps from the name *Parkin*, diminutive of *Peter*]

park·ing *noun* **1** (also *attributive*) the act of stopping a motor vehicle at a place and leaving it there for a time (*valet parking; parking attendant*). **2** a space or area for leaving vehicles (*ample underground parking; angle parking*). **3** *N Amer. slang* the act of kissing, petting, etc. in a parked car.

parking brake *noun* = EMERGENCY BRAKE.

parking garage *noun* a structure with space for parking vehicles.

parking light *noun* a small light on either side of a vehicle, front and rear, for use when the vehicle is parked at night.

parking lot *noun N Amer.* a usu. outdoor area for parking vehicles.

parking meter *noun* a machine next to a parking space in a street, by means of which the use of the parking space for a specific period is paid for.

parking space *noun* (also **parking spot**) a space for the parking of a single vehicle.

parking stall *noun Cdn (West) & US* a parking space in a parking garage or parking lot.

parking ticket *noun* a notice of a fine etc. imposed for parking illegally.

Par·kin·son Cyril North·cote (1909–1993), English historian. He formulated a number of pithy jocular maxims, the most famous being 'Parkinson's law'.

Par·kin·son·ism *noun* = PARKINSON'S DISEASE.

Parkinson's disease *noun* a progressive disease of the nervous system which produces tremor, muscular rigidity, as well as slowness and imprecision of movements. *Also called* PARKINSONISM. □ **par·kin·son·ian** /pɑrkɪnˈsoːniən/ *adjective* [J. *Parkinson*, English surgeon d.1824]

Parkinson's law *noun jocular* the idea, facetiously expounded as a law akin to that of physics, that work will always take as long as the time available for its completion. [C.N. PARKINSON]

park·land *noun* **1 a** open grassland scattered with clumps of trees etc. **b** *Cdn* the lightly wooded grasslands between the open prairie and the northern forests in Manitoba, Saskatchewan, and Alberta. **c** *Cdn* the grassy region between the Prairies and the foothills of the Rockies. **2** a piece of land set aside by the government for public recreation, wildlife conservation, etc.

parks officer *noun Cdn* = PARK WARDEN.

Parks·ville a city located on the east shore of Vancouver Island, about 35 km northwest of Nanaimo; pop. (2001) 10,323. [N. *Parks*, first postmaster and settler in the area *c*.1887]

park warden *noun* (also **park ranger**) an official responsible for patrolling and maintaining a national, provincial, etc. park, having the powers of a peace officer in matters of park regulations.

park·way *noun* **1** *N Amer.* a highway or main road with trees, grass, etc. planted alongside. **2** *Brit.* a railway station with extensive parking facilities, serving as an interchange between the road and rail systems.

parky *adjective* (**park·i·er**, **park·i·est**) *Brit. informal* chilly. [19th c.: origin unknown]

Parl. *abbreviation* **1** Parliament. **2** Parliamentary.

par·lance /ˈpɑrləns/ *noun* a particular way of speaking, esp. as regards choice of words, idiom, etc. [Old French from *parler* speak, ultimately from Latin *parabola* (see PARABLE): in Late Latin = 'speech']

par·lay /pɑrˈleɪ, ˈpɑrleɪ, ˈpɑrli/ *N Amer.* ● *transitive verb* **1** (foll. by *into*) exploit (a circumstance), transform (an advantage etc.) into something greater. **2** use (money won on a bet) as a further stake. **3** increase (capital) by gambling. ● *noun* **1** an act of parlaying. **2** a bet made by parlaying. [French *paroli* from Italian from *paro* like, from Latin *par* equal]

Parl·by, Mary Irene (born Mary Irene Marryat) (1868–1965), English-born Canadian farm women's leader and politician. She helped found the first women's local (1913) of the United Farmers of Alberta, and reorganized the UFA Women's Auxiliary into the United Farm Women of Alberta. A UFA member of the Alberta legislature 1921–35, she was Alberta's first female cabinet minister and a Canadian delegate to the League of Nations (1930).

par·ley /ˈpɑrli/ ● *noun* (pl. **-leys**) an informal conference, under truce, with an enemy, for discussing the mutual arrangement of matters such as terms for armistice, exchange of prisoners, etc. ● *intransitive verb* (**-leys**, **-leyed**) (often foll. by *with*) hold a parley. [perhaps from Old French *parlee*, fem. past participle of *parler* speak: see PARLANCE]

par·lia·ment /ˈpɑrləmənt/ *noun* **1** (usu. **Parliament**) the highest legislative body in certain countries, including Canada. In Canada the federal parliament consists of the Sovereign, the House of Commons, and the Senate. **2** a legislative body of a province, state, etc. (*provincial parliament*). **3** the members of a parliament. **4** a period during which the members of a parliament are assembled, following a general election and until dissolution. **5** a place where parliament meets. **6** the House of Commons. [Old French *parlement* speaking (as PARLANCE)]

par·lia·men·tar·ian /ˌpɑrləmənˈteriən/ ● *noun* **1** a member of a parliament, esp. one well-versed in its procedures. **2** *hist.* an adherent of Parliament in the English Civil War of the 17th c. ● *adjective* = PARLIAMENTARY.

par·lia·men·tary /ˌpɑrləˈmentri, -ˈmentəri/ *adjective* **1** of or relating to a parliament. **2** enacted or established by a parliament. **3** according to the constitution of a parliament (*parliamentary democracy*). **4** (of language) admissible in a parliament; polite, civil, courteous.

parliamentary committee *noun see* COMMITTEE 2.

parliamentary government *noun* a government in which a prime minister (or premier) chooses Members of Parliament, usu. from his or her own party, to be Ministers of the Crown who will form the Cabinet and be responsible to Parliament for the conduct of the government.

parliamentary secretary *noun* a Member of Parliament belonging to the party in government, appointed by the prime minister to assist a senior cabinet minister.

parliament building *noun* **1** a building in which a parliament meets. **2** a complex of buildings housing the parliament and offices of its members and staff, esp. in Canada (**Parliament Buildings**), those in Ottawa.

Parliament Hill *noun Cdn* **1** the hill in Ottawa on which the Parliament Buildings stand. **2** the federal government of Canada.

par·lour *noun* (also **parlor**) **1** a sitting room in a private house. **2 a** esp. *N Amer.* a business providing specified goods or services (*beauty parlour; funeral parlour*). **b** *Cdn* = BEER PARLOUR. **3** (in full **milking parlour**) a room or building equipped for milking cows. **4** a room in a hotel, club, etc. for the private use of guests. **5** a room set aside for conversation with visitors in a convent, priest's house, etc. **6** (attributive) derogatory denoting support for political views by those who do not try to practise them (parlour socialist). [Anglo-French parlur, Old French parleor, parleur: see PARLANCE]

parlour car noun N Amer. a luxuriously fitted railway passenger car, usu. with individually reserved seats etc.

parlour game noun a game, e.g. charades, played by a number of people indoors.

parlour·maid noun hist. a female domestic servant who waits at table.

par·lous /ˈpɑːləs/ adjective dangerous or difficult. □ **par·lous·ly** adverb **par·lous·ness** noun [Middle English, = PERILOUS]

Parma 1 a province of N Italy, south of the Po River in Emilia-Romagna. **2** its capital; pop. (2001) 156,172.

Parma ham /ˈpɑːmə/ noun a type of smoked ham which is eaten uncooked. [PARMA]

Par·meni·des /pɑːˈmenɪˌdiːz/ (fl. 5th c. BC), Greek philosopher. In On Nature, he maintained that the apparent motion and changing forms of the universe are in fact manifestations of an unchanging and indivisible reality.

Par·me·san /ˈpɑːmɪˌzɒn, -zən, -zan, -ʒɒn, -ʒan, -ˈzɒn, -ˈʒɒn/ noun (also **parmi·giano** /pɑːmɪˈdʒiːˈanoʊ/) a kind of hard dry cheese made originally at Parma and used esp. in grated form. [French from Italian parmigiano of Parma]

parmi·giana /pɑːmɪˈdʒɒnə, -ʒɒnə, -ʒanə, -dʒiˈanə/ adjective made or served with Parmesan cheese. [Italian, feminine of parmigiano (see PARMESAN)]

Parmi·gian·ino /ˌpɑːmɪdʒəˈniːnoʊ/ (also **Parmi·giano** /ˌpɑːmɪˈdʒɒnoʊ/) (born Girolamo Francesco Maria Mazzola) (1503–40), Italian painter. A follower of Correggio, he made an important contribution to early mannerism with the graceful figure style of his frescoes and portraits; his works include Self-Portrait in a Convex Mirror (1524) and Madonna with the Long Neck (1534).

Par·nas·sian /pɑːˈnasiən/ ● adjective **1** of Parnassus in Greece. **2** poetic. **3** of or relating to a group of French poets in the late 19th c., emphasizing strictness of form, named from the anthology Le Parnasse contemporain (1866). ● noun a member of this group.

Par·nas·sus, Mount /pɑːˈnasəs/ a mountain in central Greece, just north of Delphi, rising to a height of 2 457 m (8,064 ft.). Held to be sacred by the ancient Greeks, as was the spring of Castalia on its southern slopes, it was associated with Apollo and the Muses and regarded as a symbol of poetry.

Par·nell /pɑːˈnel/ **Charles Stew·art** (1846–91), Irish nationalist leader. Elected to the British Parliament in 1875, he became leader of the Irish Home Rule faction in 1880, and, through his obstructive parliamentary tactics, successfully raised the profile of Irish affairs; he was forced to retire from public life in 1890 after the public exposure of his adultery with Mrs. Katherine O'Shea (1840–1905). □ **Par·nell·ite** adjective & noun

pa·roch·ial /pəˈroʊkiəl/ adjective **1** of or concerning a parish. **2** (of affairs, views, etc.) merely local, narrow or restricted in scope. □ **pa·roch·ial·ism** noun **pa·roch·ial·ity** /-ˈalɪti/ noun **pa·roch·ial·ly** adverb [ecclesiastical Latin parochialis (as PARISH)]

parochial school noun N Amer. a primary or secondary school established and maintained by a religious body.

par·ody /ˈperədi, ˈpa-/ ● noun (pl. **-ies**) **1 a** humorous exaggerated imitation of an author, literary work, style, etc., esp. for purposes of ridicule. **b** a work of this kind. **2** a thing done so badly that it seems to be an intentional mockery of what it should be; a travesty. **3** a comic or satirical imitation of a person, event, etc. ● transitive verb (**-ies, -ied**) **1** compose a parody of. **2** mimic humorously. **3** imitate in a poor or feeble manner. □ **par·od·ic** /pəˈrɒdɪk/ adjective **par·od·ic·ally** /pəˈrɒdɪkli/ adverb **par·od·ist** noun **par·od·is·tic** /-ˈdɪstɪk/ adjective [Late Latin parodia or Greek parōidia 'burlesque poem' (as PARA-¹, ōidē 'ode')]

par·ol /pəˈroʊl/ Law ● adjective **1** expressed or given orally; not in writing. **2** (of a contract, lease, etc.) made by word of mouth or in a writing not under seal. ● noun an oral declaration. [Old French parole (as PAROLE)]

par·ole /pəˈroʊl/ ● noun **1 a** the release of a prisoner, temporarily for a special purpose or completely, before the expiry of a sentence, on the promise of good behaviour. **b** the system or practice of granting or accepting such a conditional release. **2** the actual linguistic behaviour or performance of an individual, in contrast to the linguistic system. ● transitive verb put (a prisoner) on parole. □ **on parole** released esp.

from a custodial sentence on the terms of parole. □ **pa·rolee** noun [French, = word: see PARLANCE]

par·ono·masia /ˌperənəˈmeɪziə/ noun a play on words; a pun. [Latin from Greek paronomasia (as PARA-¹, onomasia naming, from onoma a name)]

paro·nym /ˈperənɪm/ noun **1** a word cognate with another. **2** a word formed by partial translation of a foreign word. □ **par·onym·ous** /pəˈrɒnɪməs/ adjective [Greek parōnumon, neuter of parōnumos (as PARA-¹, onuma name)]

Paros /ˈpeərɒs/ a Greek island in the S Aegean, in the Cyclades. A translucent white marble has been quarried there since the 6th c. BC.

par·otid /pəˈrɒtɪd/ ● adjective **1** situated near the ear. **2** of or pertaining to the parotid glands or the surrounding region. ● noun (in full **parotid gland**) a salivary gland in front of the ear. [French parotide or Latin parotis parotid- from Greek parōtis -idos (as PARA-¹, ous ōtos ear)]

par·ot·itis /ˌperəˈtaɪtɪs/ noun **1** inflammation of the parotid gland. **2** = MUMPS. [PAROTID + -ITIS]

-parous /pərəs/ combining form bearing offspring of a specified number or kind (multiparous; viviparous). [Latin -parus -bearing, from parere bring forth]

Par·ou·sia /pəˈruːziə/ noun Theol. = SECOND COMING 1. [Greek, 'presence, coming']

par·ox·ysm /ˈperəkˌsɪzm, pəˈrɒk-/ noun **1** (often foll. by of) a sudden attack or outburst (of rage, laughter, etc.). **2 a** a sudden fit or convulsion. **b** a sudden attack, recurrence, or worsening of disease etc. □ **par·oxys·mal** /-ˈsɪzməl/ adjective [medieval Latin paroxysmus from Greek paroxusmos from paroxunō exasperate (as PARA-¹, oxunō sharpen, from oxus sharp)]

par·oxy·tone /pəˈrɒksɪˌtoʊn/ ● adjective (esp. in ancient Greek) having an acute accent on the last syllable but one. ● noun a word of this kind. [as PARA-¹, OXYTONE]

par·quet /pɑːˈkeɪ, ˈpɑː-/ ● noun (often attributive) a flooring of short strips or blocks of wood arranged in an esp. geometric pattern, usu. sold in square, interlocking tiles. ● transitive verb (**parqueted** /-keɪd/; **parquet·ing** /-keɪɪŋ/) furnish (a room) with a parquet floor. [French, = small compartment, floor, diminutive of parc PARK]

par·quet·ry /ˈpɑːkɪtri/ noun inlaid work of blocks of various woods arranged in a geometric pattern, esp. for furniture or flooring.

Parr ► 1 Cath·er·ine (1512–48), sixth wife of Henry VIII. Having married the king in 1543, she influenced his decision to restore the succession to his daughters Mary and Elizabeth (later Mary I and Elizabeth I respectively). **2 John** (1725–91), Irish-born soldier and Canadian colonial administrator. He was appointed governor of Nova Scotia in 1782, just as some 30,000 Loyalists arrived in the Maritimes. Forced to mediate between the demands of the new settlers and the claims of the existing populace, he was fairly successful but won little admiration or popularity.

parr noun a young salmon between the stages of fry and smolt, distinguished by dark rounded patches evenly spaced along its sides. [18th c.: origin unknown]

parri·cide /ˈpɑːrɪsaɪd/ noun **1** the killing of a near relative, esp. of a parent. **2** a person who commits parricide. ¶ Parricide, the killing of a near relative, especially of a parent, is sometimes confused with patricide, the killing of one's father. □ **parri·cid·al** /-ˈsaɪdəl/ adjective [French parricide or Latin parricida (= sense 2), parricidium (= sense 1), of uncertain origin, associated in Latin with pater 'father' and parens 'parent']

par·rot ● noun **1** any of various mainly tropical birds of the order Psittaciformes, with a short hooked bill, often having vivid plumage and able to mimic the human voice. **2** a person who mindlessly and mechanically repeats the words or actions of another. ● transitive verb (**parroted, parroting**) repeat mindlessly or mechanically. [prob. from obsolete or dial. French perrot parrot, diminutive of Pierre Peter: compare PARAKEET]

parrot·fish noun any fish of the genus Scarus, with a mouth like a parrot's bill and forming a protective mucous cocoon against predators.

Parry /ˈperi/ **Sir Wil·liam Ed·ward** (1790–1855), English naval officer and Arctic explorer. He served in Arctic expeditions in 1818, 1819, 1821, 1824, and 1827 (commanding the last four). He demonstrated that ships and their crews could survive an Arctic winter, and penetrated further north in 1827 than any European would go until 1876.

parry ● transitive verb (**-ries, -ried**) **1** avert or ward off (a weapon or attack), esp. with a countermove. **2** deal skilfully with (an awkward question etc.). ● *noun* (*pl.* **-ries**) an act of parrying. [prob. representing French *parez* imperative of *parer* from Italian *parare* ward off]

Parry Channel /ˈpɛri/ a sea channel through the Arctic Archipelago, connecting Baffin Bay and the Arctic Ocean. It comprises (from east to west) Lancaster Sound, Barrow Strait, Viscount Melville Sound and M'Clure Strait. The islands to the north of the channel constitute the Queen Elizabeth Islands. [Sir W.E. PARRY]

Parry Islands /ˈpɛri/ a group of islands in the NW Arctic Archipelago, including (from east to west) Cornwallis, Bathurst, Melville, Mackenzie King and Prince Patrick islands. Together with the Sverdrup Islands, they form the group known as the Queen Elizabeth Islands. [Sir W.E. PARRY, who discovered and named each of the islands]

Parry Sound /ˈpɛri/ **1** an inlet of the east central shore of Georgian Bay, separating Parry Island from the mainland of south central Ontario. **2** a town situated on its shore, about 125 km north of Barrie; pop. (2001) 6,124. □ **Parry Sounder** *noun* (in sense 2) [Sir W.E. PARRY]

parse /pɑrs, pɑrz/ *transitive verb* **1** describe (a word in context) grammatically, stating its inflection, relation to the sentence, etc. **2** resolve (a sentence) into its component parts and describe them grammatically. **3** *Computing* analyze (a string) into syntactic components, esp. to test conformability to a grammar. □ **pars·er** *noun* (esp. in sense 3). [perhaps from Middle English *pars* 'parts of speech' from Old French *pars*, pl. of *part* PART, influenced by Latin *pars* 'part']

par·sec /ˈpɑrsɛk/ *noun* a unit of stellar distance, equal to about 3.25 light years (3.08×10^{16} metres), the distance at which the mean radius of the earth's orbit subtends an angle of one second of arc. [PARALLAX + SECOND^2]

Par·si /ˈpɑrsiː/ *noun* (also **Parsee**) an adherent of Zoroastrianism, esp. a descendant of the Zoroastrian Persians who fled to India in the 7th–8th c. to escape Muslim persecution. [Persian *pārsī* Persian, from *pārs* Persia]

parsi·mony /ˈpɑrsɪˌmoʊni/ *noun* extreme or excessive carefulness in the use of money or other resources; miserliness, stinginess. □ **parsi·moni·ous** /-ˈmoʊniəs/ *adjective* **parsi·moni·ous·ly** /-ˈmoʊniəsli/ *adverb* **parsi·moni·ous·ness** /-ˈmoʊniəsnəs/ *noun* [Latin *parsimonia, parcimonia* from *parcere* pars- spare]

pars·ley *noun* a biennial herb, *Petroselinum crispum*, with white flowers and flavourful leaves, used for seasoning and garnishing food. [Old French *peresil*, and Old English *petersilie*, ultimately from Latin *petroselinum* from Greek *petroselinon*]

pars·leyed *adjective* flavoured or garnished with parsley (*parsleyed potatoes*).

pars·nip *noun* **1** a biennial umbelliferous plant, *Pastinaca sativa*, with yellow flowers and a large pale-yellow tapering root. **2** this root eaten as a vegetable. [Middle English *pas(se)nep* (assimilated to *nep* turnip) from Old French *pasnaie* from Latin *pastinaca*]

par·son *noun* **1** any (esp. Protestant) member of the clergy. **2** an Anglican parish priest. □ **par·son·ical** /pɑrˈsɒnɪkəl/ *adjective* [Old French *persone* from Latin *persona* PERSON (in medieval Latin 'rector')]

par·son·age /ˈpɑrsənɪdʒ/ *noun* a church house provided for a parson; a rectory.

parson's nose *noun Brit.* = POPE'S NOSE.

part ● *noun* **1** some but not all of a thing or number of things. **2** an essential member or constituent of anything (*part of the family; a large part of the job*). **3** a component of a machine etc. (*spare parts; needs a new part*). **4 a** a portion of a human or animal body. **b** (in *pl.*) *informal* = PRIVATE PARTS. **5** a division of a book, broadcast serial, etc., esp. as much as is issued or broadcast at one time. **6 a** each of several equal portions of a whole (*the recipe has 3 parts sugar to 2 parts flour*). **b** (prec. by ordinal number) a specified fraction of a whole (*each received a fifth part*). **7 a** a portion allotted; a share. **b** a person's share in an action or enterprise (*will have no part in it*). **c** one's duty (*was not my part to interfere*). **8 a** a character assigned to an actor. **b** the words spoken by an actor. **c** a copy of these. **9** *Music* **a** a melody or other constituent of harmony assigned to a particular voice or instrument (often in combination; *four-part harmony*). **b** a copy of the music for a particular musician. **10** each of the sides in an agreement or dispute. **11** (often in *pl.*) a region or district (*am not from these parts*). **12** (in *pl.*) abilities (*a man of many parts*). **13** esp. *N Amer.* the dividing line of combed hair. ● *verb* **1** *transitive & intransitive* divide or separate into parts (*the crowd parted to let them through*). **2** *intransitive* **a** leave one another's company (*they parted the best of friends*). **b** (foll. by *from*) say goodbye to. **3** *transitive* cause to separate (*they fought hard and had to be parted*). **4** *intransitive* (foll. by *with*) give up possession of; hand over. **5** *transitive* separate (the hair of

the head on either side of the part) with a comb. ● *adverb* to some extent; partly (*is part iron and part wood; a lie that is part truth*). □ **for the most part** see MOST. **for one's part** as far as one is concerned. **in part** (or **parts**) to some extent; partly. **look the part** have an appearance or wear clothes suitable for a role, job, or position. **on the part of** proceeding from (*a long struggle on the part of the scholars; no objection on my part*). **part and parcel** (usu. foll. by *of*) an essential part. **part company** see COMPANY. **play a part 1** be significant or contributory. **2** perform a dramatic role. **take in good part** see GOOD. **take part** (often foll. by *in*) assist, participate, or have a share (in). **take the part of** support; back up. [Middle English via Old French from Latin *pars partis* (n.), *partire, partiri* (v.)]

par·take *intransitive verb* (past **par·took**; past participle **par·taken**) **1** (foll. by *in, of*) take a share or part; participate in (*partook in the festivities*). **2** (foll. by *of*) eat or drink a part or amount (of a thing). **3** (foll. by *of*) have some (of a quality etc.). □ **par·taker** *noun* [16th c.: back-formation from *partaker, partaking* = part-taker etc.]

part·er *combining form* something having a specified number of parts, esp. a radio or television production in a specified number of episodes.

par·terre /pɑrˈtɛr/ *noun* a level space in a garden occupied by flower beds arranged formally. [French, = *par terre* on the ground]

par·theno·gen·esis /ˌpɑrθənoʊˈdʒɛnəsɪs/ *noun Biol.* reproduction from an ovum without fertilization, esp. as a normal process in invertebrates and lower plants. □ **par·theno·gen·etic** /-dʒəˈnɛtɪk/ *adjective* **par·theno·gen·etic·ally** /-dʒəˈnɛtɪkli/ *adverb* [modern Latin from Greek *parthenos* virgin + *genesis* as GENESIS]

Par·the·non /ˈpɑrθənɒn/ *noun* the temple of Athene Parthenos built on the Acropolis at Athens in 447–432 BC by Pericles. [Greek *parthenos* virgin]

Par·thia /ˈpɑrθiə/ an ancient Asian kingdom which lay southeast of the Caspian Sea in present-day Iran, the centre of an empire stretching from the Euphrates to the Indus, with Ecbatana as its capital (*c*.250 BC to AD *c*.230). The empire peaked around the 2nd c. BC, with a culture that contained a mixture of Greek and Persian elements. □ **Par·thian** *noun & adjective*

Parthian shot *noun* = PARTING SHOT. [PARTHIA, from the custom of a retreating Parthian horseman firing a shot at the enemy]

par·tial ● *adjective* **1** not complete; forming only part (*a partial success*). **2** biased, unfair. **3** (foll. by *to*) having a liking for. ● *noun* **1** *Music* any of the constituents of a musical sound. **2** a denture replacing some but not all of the teeth. □ **par·tial·ly** *adverb* **par·tial·ness** *noun* [Late Latin *partialis* (as PART)]

partial derivative *noun Math.* a derivative of a function of two or more variables with respect to one variable, the other(s) being treated as constant.

partial differential equation *noun Math.* an equation containing a partial derivative.

partial eclipse *noun* an eclipse in which only part of the sun or moon is covered or darkened.

par·tial·ity /ˌpɑrʃiˈæliti/ *noun* **1** bias, favouritism. **2** (foll. by *for*) fondness.

partial pressure *noun Physics* the pressure that would be exerted by one of the gases in a mixture if it occupied the same volume on its own.

Par·tici·pac·tion *noun Cdn* **1** a private, non-profit organization which promotes physical fitness through regular exercise. **2** (**participaction**) *informal* physical activity; exercise. [PARTICIPATE + ACTION]

par·tici·pant /pɑrˈtɪsəpənt/ *noun* a person who participates in something.

participant observation *noun* (in the social sciences) a method of research involving the use of a researcher who, while appearing to be a member of the group under observation, is in fact gathering information on it. □ **participant observer** *noun*

par·tici·pate /pɑrˈtɪsəpeɪt/ *intransitive verb* (usu. foll. by *in*) share or take part (in). □ **par·tici·pa·tion** /-ˈpeɪʃən/ *noun* **par·tici·pa·tive** *adjective* **par·tici·pa·tor** *noun* **par·tici·pa·tory** /pɑrˈtɪsəpəˌtɔri/ *adjective* [Latin *participare* from *particeps -cipis* 'taking part' (as PART + *-cip-* = *cap-*, stem of *capere* 'take')]

participatory democracy *noun* involvement of citizens in the political decision-making process.

par·ti·ciple /ˈpɑrtɪˌsɪpəl, pɑrˈtɪsəpəl/ *noun Grammar* a word formed from a verb, e.g. *going, gone, being, been*, and used in compound verb forms, e.g. *is going, has been*, or as an adjective, e.g. *working woman, burnt toast*.

□ **par·ti·cip·ial** /-'sɪpɪəl/ adjective **par·ti·cip·ial·ly** adverb [Old French, by-form of particip from Latin participium (as PARTICIPATE)]

par·ticle noun **1** a very small bit or piece of something (dirt particles). **2** Physics any of numerous subatomic constituents of the physical world that interact with each other, including electrons, neutrinos, photons, and alpha particles. **3** the least possible amount (not a particle of sense). **4** Grammar **a** a minor part of speech, esp. a short indeclinable one. **b** a common prefix or suffix such as in-, -ness. [Latin particula (as PART)]

particle accelerator noun an apparatus for accelerating subatomic particles to high velocities by means of electric or electromagnetic fields.

particle beam noun a stream of subatomic particles produced by a particle accelerator, used for studying nuclear structure, crystal structure, etc., or as a military weapon.

par·ticle·board noun a rigid sheet or panel made from compressed wood chips, splinters, sawdust, and resin.

particle physics noun the branch of physics concerned with the properties and interactions of subatomic particles. □ **particle physicist** noun

parti-coloured adjective (also **parti-colored**) partly of one colour, partly of another or others. [PARTY² + COLOURED]

par·ticu·lar ● adjective **1** relating to or considered as one thing or person as distinct from others; individual (in this particular instance). **2** more than is usual; special, noteworthy (took particular trouble). **3** scrupulously exact; fastidious. **4** detailed (a full and particular account). **5** Logic (of a proposition) in which something is asserted of some but not all of a class (opp. UNIVERSAL adjective 2). ● noun **1** a detail; an item. **2** (in pl.) points of information; a detailed account. □ **in particular** especially, specifically. [Latin particularis (as PARTICLE)]

par·ticu·lar·ism noun **1** exclusive devotion to one party, sect, etc. **2** the principle of leaving political independence to each state in an empire or federation. **3** the theological doctrine of individual election or redemption. □ **par·ticu·lar·ist** noun & adjective **par·ticu·lar·is·tic** adjective

par·ticu·lar·ity /pɑr,tɪkjʊ'lerɪti, pɜr-, pə-/ noun (pl. **-ities**) **1** the quality of being individual or particular. **2** fullness or minuteness of detail in a description. **3** (usu. in pl.) **a** a particular point or circumstance; a detail. **b** a special or distinctive quality or feature; a peculiarity.

par·ticu·lar·ize verb (also esp. Brit. **-ise**) **1** transitive mention or describe particularly; name specially or one by one. **2** intransitive go into detail. □ **par·ticu·lar·iz·a·tion** noun

par·ticu·lar·ly adverb **1** especially, very. **2** specifically (they particularly asked for you). **3** in a particular or fastidious manner.

par·ticu·late /pɑr'tɪkjʊˌlət, pɜr-, pə-, -leit/ ● adjective in the form of separate particles. ● noun matter in this form. [Latin particula PARTICLE]

parti·er noun (also **party·er**) **1** a person who parties. **2** slang a person who drinks or uses drugs on a recreational basis.

part·ing noun **1** a leave-taking or departure (often attributive: parting words). **2** a division; an act of separating. **3** a point at which things part or are parted (the parting of the ways). **4** Brit. = PART noun 13.

parting shot noun a remark or glance etc. reserved for the moment of departure.

parti pris /,parti 'priː/ ● noun a preconceived view; a bias. ● adjective prejudiced, biased. [French, = side taken]

Parti Québécois /pɑr'tiː keibek'wɒ/ noun Cdn a political party in Quebec, founded in 1968 and dedicated to achieving Quebec sovereignty. Abbr.: **PQ**. [French]

Parti Rouge /,parti 'ruːʒ/ noun Cdn hist. a radical French-Canadian political party founded about 1848 and first led by Louis-Joseph Papineau. [French, = 'red party']

par·ti·san /'pɑrtɪˌzan, -ən, -'zan/ ● noun **1** an adherent or supporter of a party, person, or cause, esp. a zealous supporter. **2** a member of an armed group formed to fight secretly against an occupying force, in particular one operating in enemy-occupied Yugoslavia, Italy, and parts of eastern Europe in World War II. ● adjective **1** of or characteristic of partisans. **2** loyal to a particular cause; biased. □ **par·ti·san·ship** noun [French from Italian dial. partigiano etc. from parte PART]

par·tita /pɑr'tiːtə/ noun (pl. **par·titas** or **par·tite** /-tei/) Music = SUITE 3a. [Italian, fem. past participle of partire divide, formed as PART]

par·tite /'pɑrtəit/ adjective **1** divided (esp. in combination: tripartite). **2** Bot. & Zool. divided to or nearly to the base. [Latin partitus past participle of partiri PART verb]

par·tition /pɑr'tɪʃən/ ● noun **1** division into parts, esp. of a country with separate areas of government. **2** a structure dividing a space into two parts, esp. a light interior wall. **3** Computing **a** a self-contained part of a program, or a group of programs within a program library. **b** each of a number of blocks into which some operating systems divide memory in order to facilitate storage and retrieval of information. ● transitive verb **1** divide into parts. **2** (foll. by off) separate (part of a room etc.) with a partition. **3** Computing divide (memory) into partitions. □ **par·ti·tioned** adjective **par·ti·tion·ist** noun [Latin partitio -onis (as PARTITE)]

par·ti·tive /'pɑrtɪtɪv/ Grammar ● adjective (of a word, form, etc.) denoting part of a collective group or quantity. ● noun a partitive word, e.g. some, any, or form. □ **par·ti·tive·ly** adverb [French partitif -ive or medieval Latin partitivus (as PARTITE)]

part·ly adverb **1** with respect to a part or parts. **2** to some extent.

part·ner ● noun **1 a** a person, company, etc. who shares or takes part with another or others in some activity. **b** a person who is associated with another or others in the carrying on of a business with shared risks and profits. **2** a colleague or associate. **3** a person who dances or figure skates with another. **4** a player (esp. one of two) on the same side in a game. **5 a** either member of a married couple or an established unmarried couple. **b** a person with whom one has sexual relations. **6** a country, organization, etc. that has an agreement with another or others (Canada's trading partners). ● verb **1** transitive be or act as the partner of. **2 a** intransitive associate as partners. **b** intransitive join with as a partner. □ **partner in crime 1** an accomplice, esp. a habitual one. **2** one of a pair of persons or things often associated or seen together. □ **part·ner·ing** noun **part·ner·less** adjective [Middle English, alteration of parcener joint heir, after PART]

part·ner·ship noun **1** the state of being a partner or partners. **2** a joint business. **3** a pair or group of partners.

part of speech noun each of the categories to which words are assigned in accordance with their grammatical and semantic functions (in English esp. noun, pronoun, adjective, adverb, verb, preposition, conjunction, and interjection).

par·took past of PARTAKE.

part owner noun a person who owns something jointly with another. □ **part ownership** noun

par·tridge noun (pl. same or **par·tridges**) **1** any game bird of the genus Perdix, esp. the grey partridge, P. perdix native to Europe and Asia and also introduced in N America. **2** any other of various similar birds of the family Phasianidae, esp. the ruffed grouse or the ptarmigan. [Middle English partrich etc. from Old French perdriz etc. from Latin perdix -dicis: for -dge compare CABBAGE]

par·tridge·berry noun (pl. **-berries**) **1** either of two N American plants with edible red berries, Mitchella repens or Gaultheria procumbens. **2** the fruit of either of these plants.

Partridge Island an island off the southern coast of New Brunswick, at the mouth of Saint John Harbour. Twice designated a national historic site it was, in the mid-19th c., an immigrant quarantine station, as well as home to the world's first steam-operated fog alarm.

part-skim adjective (of cheeses) made partly with skim milk.

part-song noun a song with three or more voice parts, often without accompaniment, and harmonic rather than contrapuntal in character.

part-time ● adjective employed, occurring, or lasting less than full-time (a part-time student; a part-time job). ● adverb on a part-time basis (he works part-time). □ **part-timer** noun

par·turi·ent /pɑr'tʊriənt, -'tjʊr-, -tʃʊr/ adjective about to give birth. [Latin parturire be in labour, inceptive of parere part- bring forth]

par·tur·ition /,pɑrtʊ'rɪʃən, -tjʊr-, -tʃʊr/ noun formal the act of bringing forth young; childbirth. [Late Latin parturitio (as PARTURIENT)]

part·way adverb **1** part of the way. **2** partly.

party¹ ● noun (pl. **-ties**) **1** a social gathering, usu. of invited guests (often attributive: party clothes; party food). **2** a body of persons engaged in an activity or travelling together (fishing party; search party). **3** a group of people united in a cause, opinion, etc., esp. a political group organized to campaign for election (often attributive: party leaders; party policy). **4** a person or persons forming one side in an agreement or dispute. **5** (foll. by to) Law an accessory (to an action). **6** informal a person. ● intransitive verb (**-ties, -tied**) **1** go to parties frequently. **2** revel, carouse (partied all night long). □ **party·ing** noun [Old French partie, ultimately from Latin partire: see PART]

party² adjective Heraldry divided into parts of different colours. [Old French parti from Latin (as PARTY¹)]

party animal *noun informal* a person who attends many parties.

party boat *noun N Amer.* a boat for hire by people who want to go fishing.

party·er *var. of* PARTIER.

party·goer *noun* a person who attends a party or who frequents parties.

party line *noun* **1** the official policies adopted by a political party. **2** an official position or interpretation of events etc. put forth publicly by members of an organization, institution, etc. **3** a telephone line shared by two or more subscribers.

party man *noun* a man belonging to or loyally supporting a certain political party.

party piece *noun* **1** a musical or other performance intended to be performed on a special occasion. **2** a trick, feat, or other entertaining speciality for which one is renowned.

party politics *plural noun* (also treated as *sing.*) political activity carried out through, by, or for political parties.

party-pooper *noun* (also **party-poop**) esp. *N Amer. slang* a person whose manner or behaviour inhibits other people's enjoyment; a killjoy. □ **party-pooping** *noun*

party wall *noun* a wall common to two adjoining buildings or rooms.

par·ure /pəˈrʊr/ *noun* a set of jewels or other ornaments intended to be worn together. [Old French from *parer* (see PARE) + -URE]

Par·vati /ˈpɑrvəti/ *Hinduism* a benevolent goddess, wife of Shiva, mother of Ganesha and Skanda. She is often identified with Sati, Devi, and Sakti, and in her malevolent aspect with Durga and Kali. [Sanskrit, = daughter of the mountain]

parve /ˈpɑrvə/ *adjective var. of* PAREVE.

par·venu /ˈpɑrvə,nuː/ ● *noun* **1** a person of obscure origin who has gained wealth or position. **2** an upstart. ● *adjective* **1** associated with or characteristic of such a person. **2** upstart. [French, past participle of *parvenir* arrive, from Latin *pervenire* (as PER-, *venire* come)]

par·vis /ˈpɑrvɪs/ *noun* (also **par·vise**) **1** an enclosed area in front of a cathedral, church, etc. **2** a room over a church porch. [Old French, ultimately from Late Latin *paradisus* PARADISE, a court in front of St. Peter's, Rome]

parvo·virus /ˈpɑrvoˌvairəs/ *noun* (also **parvo**) any of a class of small viruses affecting vertebrate animals, esp. one which causes contagious disease in dogs. [Latin *parvus* 'small' + VIRUS]

pas /pɒ/ *noun (pl.* same) a step in dancing, esp. in ballet. [French, = step]

Pasa·dena /ˌpɑsəˈdiːnə/ a city in California, in the San Gabriel Mountains northeast of Los Angeles; pop. (2000) 141,700.

Pas·cal /paˈskal/ **Blaise** (1623–62), French mathematician, physicist, and religious philosopher. He discovered that air has weight, confirmed that a vacuum could exist, and derived the principle that the pressure of a fluid at rest is transmitted equally in all directions; he also founded the theory of probabilities, and developed a forerunner of integral calculus. His philosophical works include *Lettres Provinciales* (1656–7), directed against the casuistry of the Jesuits, and *Pensées* (1670), a defence of Christianity. □ **Pas·cal·ian** *adjective*

pas·cal *noun* **1** /ˈpaskəl/ the SI unit of pressure, equal to one newton per square metre. **2** (**Pascal**) /pasˈkal/ *Computing* a programming language esp. used in education. [B. PASCAL: in sense 2 because he built a calculating machine]

Pascal's wager *noun* the argument that it is in one's own best interest to behave as if God exists, since the possibility of eternal punishment in hell outweighs any advantage of believing otherwise.

pas·chal /ˈpaskəl/ *adjective* **1** of or relating to Easter. **2** of or relating to the Jewish Passover. [ecclesiastical Latin *paschalis* from *pascha* from Greek *paskha* from Aramaic *pasḥa*, related to Hebrew *pesaḥ* PASSOVER]

paschal lamb *noun* **1** a lamb sacrificed at Passover. **2** Christ.

pas de chat /pɒ də ˈʃɒ/ *noun (pl.* same) *Dance* a jump in which each foot in turn is raised to the opposite knee. [French, = (dance) step of a cat]

pas de deux /pɒ də ˈdə/ *noun (pl.* same; /-də, -dəz/) *Dance* **1** a dance for two persons. **2** a dance for a ballerina and danseur, in 19th-c. ballet usu. consisting of an introductory adagio part for the couple followed by solos for each and a coda for both partners, but not following a set structure in contemporary ballet. [French, = dance (lit. 'step') of two]

pas de quatre /pɒ də ˈkatr/ *noun Dance* a dance for four people, usu. two men and two women. [French, = dance (lit. 'step') of four]

pas de trois /pɒ də ˈtwɒ/ *noun (pl.* same; /-twɒ, -twɒz/) *Dance* a dance for three persons. [French, = dance (lit. 'step') of three]

pa·sha /ˈpɑʃə/ *noun* **1** *hist.* (also **pacha**) the title (placed after the name) of a Turkish officer of high rank, e.g. a military commander, the governor of a province, etc. **2** *informal* a wealthy, powerful person. [Turkish *paşa*, prob. = *başa* from *baş* head, chief]

pashm /ˈpaʃəm/ *noun* the under-fur of some Tibetan animals, esp. that of goats as used for cashmere shawls. [Persian *pašm* wool]

pash·mina /paʃˈmiːnə/ *noun* **1** fine quality material made from goat's wool; a fine cashmere. **2** a garment, esp. a shawl, made from pashmina or a blend of pashmina and silk. [Persian *pashmīn* 'woollen']

Pash·to /ˈpaʃtoː/ ● *noun* the Indo-Iranian language of the Pashtuns, an official language of Afghanistan, and spoken also in NW Pakistan. ● *adjective* of or in this language. [Pashto]

Pash·tun /paʃˈtuːn/ *noun* a member of a Pashto-speaking people inhabiting NW Pakistan and SE Afghanistan. [name in Pashto]

Pasi·phaë /pəˈsɪfə,iː/ *Gk Myth* the wife of Minos and mother of the Minotaur.

paska /ˈpɒskə, ˈpaskə/ *noun* **1** *Cdn* a rich, usu. decorated, egg bread, often containing dried fruits, traditional at Easter among people of Ukrainian origin. **2** (also **pas·kha, pash·ka**) a rich dessert containing curd cheese and dried fruit, traditionally eaten at Easter by people of Slavic descent. [Ukrainian and Russian, = Easter]

paso doble /ˌpasoː ˈdoːbleɪ/ *noun* **1** a quick ballroom dance based on a Latin American style of marching. **2** a piece of music for this dance, usu. in 2/4 time. [Spanish, = double step]

Paso·lini /pazoˈliːniː/ **Pier Paolo** (1922–75), Italian film director, poet, and novelist. The body of his work is characterized by an idiosyncratic combination of Marxist, Christian, and bawdy themes; his films include *Mamma Roma* (1962), *The Gospel According to St. Matthew* (1964), and *The Canterbury Tales* (1973).

pasque flower /pask/ *noun* either of two spring flowering anemones with plumed seeds, the prairie crocus, *Anemone* (*Pulsatilla*) *patens*, of N America or *A. vulgaris* of Europe. [earlier *passe-flower* from French *passe-fleur*: assimilated to *pasque* = obsolete *pasch* (as PASCHAL), Easter]

pas·quin·ade /ˌpaskwɪˈneɪd/ *noun* a lampoon or satire, originally one displayed in a public place. [Italian *pasquinata* from *Pasquino*, a statue in Rome on which abusive Latin verses were annually posted]

pass¹ ● *verb (past participle* **passed**) *(see also* PAST). **1** *intransitive* (often foll. by *along, by, down, on*, etc.) move onward; proceed, esp. past some point of reference (*saw the procession passing*). **2** *transitive* **a** go past; leave (a thing etc.) on one side or behind in proceeding. **b** overtake, esp. in a vehicle. **c** go across (a frontier, mountain range, etc.). **3** *intransitive & transitive* be transferred or cause to be transferred from one person or place to another (*pass the butter; the title passes to his son*). **4** *transitive* surpass; be too great for (*it passes my comprehension*). **5** *transitive* get through; effect a passage. **6** *intransitive* **a** be accepted as adequate; go uncensured (*let the matter pass*). **b** (foll. by *as, for*) be accepted or currently known as. **7** *transitive* move; cause to go (*passed her hand over her face; passed a rope round it*). **8 a** *intransitive* (of a student in a course, or writing a test) be successful. **b** *transitive* be successful in (a course, test, etc.). **c** *transitive* (of a teacher, examiner) judge the performance of (a student) to be satisfactory. **9 a** *transitive* (of a bill) be examined and approved by (a parliamentary body or process). **b** *transitive* cause or allow (a bill) to proceed to further legislative processes. **c** *intransitive* (of a bill or proposal) be approved. **10** *intransitive* **a** occur, elapse (*the remark passed unnoticed; time passes slowly*). **b** happen; be done or said (*heard what passed between them*). **11 a** *intransitive* circulate; be current. **b** *transitive* put into circulation (*was passing forged cheques*). **12** *transitive* spend or use up (a certain time or period) (*passed the afternoon reading*). **13** *transitive & intransitive* (in hockey, football, etc.) send (the puck or ball) to another player on one's own side. **14** *intransitive* **a** forgo one's turn or chance in a game etc. **b** (often foll. by *on*) decline an offer etc. **15** *intransitive* (foll. by *to, into*) change from one form (to another). **16** *intransitive* come to an end. **17** *transitive* discharge (urine, feces, a kidney stone etc.) from the body. **18** *transitive* (foll. by *on, upon*) **a** utter (criticism) about. **b** pronounce (a judicial sentence) on. **19** *intransitive* (often foll. by *on, upon*) adjudicate. **20** *transitive* not declare or pay (a dividend). **21** *transitive* cause (troops etc.) to go by esp. ceremonially. ● *noun* **1** an act or instance of passing. **2 a** a success in an examination, course, etc. **b** *Brit. & Cdn* the status of a university degree without honours. **3** written permission to pass into or out of a place, or to be absent from quarters. **4 a** a ticket or permit giving free entry or access etc. **b** a purchased ticket giving unlimited usage, access, etc. for a certain period (*bus pass*). **5 a** (in hockey, football, etc.) a transference of the puck or ball to another player on the same side. **b** *Baseball* = WALK *noun* 7. **6 a** an act of declining to make a bid in a game of cards. **b** any act of declining or being unable to act in one's turn in a game etc. **7** a thrust in fencing. **8** a juggling trick. **9** an act of passing the hands over anything, as in conjuring or hypnotism. **10** a critical position; a state of affairs (*how have things come to such a pass?*). **11** a short sweeping movement or dive made by an aircraft. **12** an act of passing something through or over a piece of equipment in order to subject it to a mechanical, chemical, or other process. □ **in passing 1** by the way. **2** in the course of speech, conversation, etc. **make a pass at** *informal* make amorous or sexual advances to. **pass around** (or esp. *Brit.* **round**) **1** distribute. **2** send or give to each of a number in turn. **pass away 1** *euphemism* die. **2** cease to exist; come to an end. **pass by 1** go past. **2** disregard, omit. **pass one's eye over** read (a document etc.) cursorily. **pass muster** *see* MUSTER. **pass off 1** (foll. by *as*) misrepresent (a person or thing) as something else. **2** (of feelings etc.) disappear gradually. **3** (of proceedings) be carried through (in a specified way). **4** evade or lightly dismiss (an awkward remark etc.). **pass on 1** transmit to the next person in a series. **2** *euphemism* die. **3** proceed on one's way. **pass out 1** become unconscious. **2** complete one's training as a cadet. **3** distribute. **pass over 1** omit, ignore, or disregard. **2** ignore the claims of (a person) to promotion or advancement. **3** *euphemism* die. **pass through 1** experience. **2** be in a place temporarily while on the way to somewhere else. **pass the buck** *see* BUCK³. **pass the time of day** *see* TIME. **pass up** *informal* refuse or neglect (an opportunity etc.). **pass water** urinate. □ **pass·er** *noun* [Old French *passer*, ultimately from Latin *passus* PACE¹]

pass² *noun* **1** a narrow passage through mountains. **2** a navigable channel, esp. at the mouth of a river. **3** a way by which to pass or get through; a road or route. **4** *Cdn* a migration route followed by animals (*deer pass*). □ **head** (or **cut**) **off at the pass** deter (a person) or prevent (a problem) early on. [Middle English, var. of PACE¹, influenced by French *pas* and by PASS¹]

pass·able *adjective* **1** barely satisfactory; just adequate. **2** (of a road, pass, etc.) that can be passed. □ **pass·ably** *adverb*

pas·sa·caglia /ˌpasəˈkaliə/ *noun* Music an instrumental piece usu. with a ground bass. [Italian from Spanish *pasacalle* from *pasar* pass + *calle* street: originally often played in the streets]

pas·sage¹ *noun* **1** the process, action, or means of passing (*the passage of time; a passage through the crowd*). **2 a** a sea route around a large land mass, usu. between two oceans (*Northwest Passage*). **b** a narrow strait between islands or other land masses. **3** the liberty or right to pass through. **4 a** the right of conveyance as a passenger, esp. by sea. **b** a journey, esp. by sea. **5 a** a short extract from a book etc. **b** a section of a piece of music. **6** = PASSAGEWAY. **7** a transition from one state to another. **8** the passing of a bill etc. into law. **9** *Anat.* a duct etc. in the body (*nasal passages*). □ **work one's passage** work aboard a ship in exchange for the voyage. [Old French (as PASS¹)]

pas·sage² *Riding* ● *noun* a slow collected trot in which the feet are momentarily held high before striking the ground. ● *verb* **1** *intransitive* (of a horse or rider) move sideways, by the pressure of the rein on the horse's neck and of the rider's leg on the opposite side. **2** *transitive* make (a horse) do this. [French *passager*, earlier *passéger* from Italian *passeggiare* to walk, pace, from *passeggio* walk, from Latin *passus* PACE¹]

pas·sage·way *noun* a narrow way for passing along, esp. with walls on either side; a corridor.

pas·sage·work *noun* music of interest chiefly for the scope it gives for virtuosic display.

Pas·sama·quoddy /ˌpasəməˈkwɒdi/ ● *noun* **1** a member of a N American Aboriginal people inhabiting parts of SE Maine and (formerly) SW New Brunswick. **2** the Algonquian language of this people. ● *adjective* of or pertaining to this people or their language. [Passamaquoddy or Mi'kmaq *peskutumaquadik* place where there are pollock]

Pas·sama·quoddy Bay an inlet of the Bay of Fundy, situated near its mouth, indenting the shores of SW New Brunswick and E Maine.

pas·sant /ˈpasənt/ *adjective* Heraldry (of an animal) walking and looking to the dexter side, with three paws on the ground and the right forepaw raised. [Old French, part. of *passer* PASS¹]

pass·band *noun* a frequency band within which signals are transmitted by a filter without attenuation.

pass·book *noun* a small book issued by a financial institution to an account holder recording sums deposited and withdrawn.

pass card *noun* a plastic card with an encoded magnetic strip, which, when passed through a scanner, acts as a key to open a locked door, lift a parking garage gate, etc.

Pas·schen·daele, Battle of /ˈpaʃənˌdeɪl/ the third Battle of Ypres during the First World War, a period of trench warfare from July to November in 1917 near the village of Passchendaele in W Belgium. The village was the furthest point of an Allied advance that saw appallingly

heavy loss of life in a sea of mud. The village was eventually captured by Canadian troops after a two-week assault with Canadian losses of over 15,000 dead and wounded. The battle brought the Allies no eventual strategic gain, however.

passé /paˈseɪ/ *adjective* **1** no longer fashionable or topical; out of date. **2** past one's prime. [French, past participle of *passer* PASS¹]

passed ball *noun* Baseball a pitched baseball that the catcher can reasonably be expected to field but misses, allowing a runner to advance one or more bases.

passed pawn *noun* Chess a pawn that has advanced beyond the pawns on the other side.

pas·sel /ˈpasəl/ *noun* esp. *US informal* an indeterminate number or quantity; a group (*a passel of reporters*). [representing a pronunciation of PARCEL]

passe·ment·erie /pasˈmentri/ *noun* a trimming of gold or silver lace, braid, beads, etc. [French from *passement* gold lace etc. from *passer* PASS¹]

pas·sen·ger *noun* **1** a traveller in or on a public or private conveyance (other than the driver, pilot, crew, etc.). **2** (*attributive*) for the use of passengers (*passenger train*). [Old French *passager* (adj.) passing (as PASSAGE¹): -*n*- as in *messenger* etc.]

pas·senger-mile *noun* one mile travelled by one passenger, as a unit of traffic.

passenger pigeon *noun* an extinct wild pigeon of N America, noted for migrating in huge flocks and hunted to extinction by 1914.

passe-partout /ˌpaspɑrˈtuː/ *noun* **1** a master key. **2** a simple picture frame (esp. for mounted photographs), esp. one consisting of a piece of glass stuck to a backing by adhesive tape along the edges. **3** adhesive tape or paper used for this. [French, = passes everywhere]

passer·by *noun* (*pl.* **passers·by**) a person who goes past, esp. by chance.

pas·ser·ine /ˈpasəˌriːn/ ● *noun* any perching bird of the order Passeriformes, having feet with three toes pointing forward and one pointing backwards, including sparrows and most land birds. ● *adjective* of or relating to this order. [Latin *passer* sparrow]

pas·sible *adjective* Theol. capable of feeling or suffering. □ **pas·si·bil·ity** *noun* [Old French *passible* or Late Latin *passibilis* from Latin *pati* pass- suffer]

pas·sim /ˈpasɪm/ *adverb* (of allusions or references in a published work) to be found at various places throughout the text. [Latin from *passus* scattered, from *pandere* spread]

pass·ing ● *adjective* **1** in senses of PASS¹ *verb*. **2** transient, fleeting (*a passing glance*). **3** cursory, incidental (*a passing reference*). **4** (of a resemblance or similarity) slight. ● *noun* **1** in senses of PASS¹ *verb*. **2** *euphemism* the death of a person (*mourned his passing*). □ **pass·ing·ly** *adverb*

passing lane *noun* **1** N Amer. a traffic lane on a highway in which a driver may pass other vehicles. **2** Basketball any open space on the court through which players attempt to pass the ball.

passing note *noun* (also **passing tone**) Music a note not belonging to the harmony but interposed to secure a smooth transition.

passing shot *noun* Tennis a shot aiming the ball beyond and out of reach of the other player.

pas·sion *noun* **1** strong barely controllable emotion. **2 a** intense sexual love or desire. **b** a person arousing this. **3** an outburst of anger (*flew into a passion*). **4 a** strong enthusiasm (*has a passion for football*). **b** a thing arousing this. **5** (**the Passion**) **a** Christianity the suffering of Christ during his last days. **b** a narrative of this from the Gospels. **c** a musical setting of any of these narratives. □ **pas·sion·less** *adjective* [Late Latin *passio -onis* from Latin *pati* pass- suffer]

pas·sion·al /ˈpaʃənəl/ ● *adjective* literary of or marked by passion. ● *noun* a book of the sufferings of saints and martyrs.

pas·sion·ate *adjective* **1** dominated by or easily moved to strong feeling, esp. love or anger. **2** showing or caused by passion. □ **pas·sion·ate·ly** *adverb* **pas·sion·ate·ness** *noun*

passion flower *noun* any climbing plant of the genus *Passiflora*, with a flower that was supposed to suggest the instruments of the Crucifixion.

passion fruit *noun* the edible fruit of some species of passion flower, esp. *Passiflora edulis*. *Also called* GRENADILLA.

passion pit *noun* N Amer. slang a place where people engage in sexual activity.

Passion play *noun* (also **passion play**) a play depicting the events of Christ's Passion, usu. performed during Lent.

Vowels: a *cat* ɑ *arm* e *bed* ɜr *her* ɜː *deux* ə *ago* ɪ *sit* i *cosy* iː *feed* ɒ *hot* ɔ *pore* ɔː *no* ʌ *run* ʊ *put*

Passion Sunday noun the fifth Sunday in Lent.

Pas·sion·tide noun the last two weeks of Lent.

pas·siv·ate /ˈpasəˌveɪt/ transitive verb make (esp. metal) passive (see PASSIVE 3b). □ **pas·siv·a·tion** /-ˈveɪʃən/ noun

pas·sive ● adjective **1** suffering action; acted upon. **2** offering no opposition; submissive. **3 a** not active; inert. **b** (of a metal) abnormally unreactive owing to a surface coating of oxide. **4** Grammar designating the voice in which the subject undergoes the action of the verb, e.g. in they were killed. **5** of, pertaining to, or designating a system in which energy for heating or other purposes is obtained by the absorption of existing radiant energy, usu. sunlight. **6** (of radar, a satellite, etc.) not generating its own signal; receiving or reflecting radiation from a transmitter, target, etc. ● noun Grammar the passive voice or form of a verb. □ **pas·sive·ly** adverb **pas·sive·ness** noun **pas·siv·ity** /-ˈsɪvɪti/ noun [Latin passivus (as PASSION)]

passive-aggres·sive adjective (of a person or his or her behaviour) exhibiting or characterized by anger, manipulation, etc. expressed in passive ways, such as procrastination, sulking, etc.

passive obedience noun **1** surrender to another's will without co-operation. **2** compliance with commands irrespective of their nature.

passive resistance noun a non-violent refusal to comply esp. with legal requirements, as a form of political protest.

passive smoking noun the involuntary inhaling, esp. by a non-smoker, of smoke from others' cigarettes etc. □ **passive smoke** noun **passive smoker** noun

pass-key noun **1** a private key to a door, gate etc. given to people who have a right to enter. **2** a master key.

pass laws plural noun hist. (in South Africa) laws (now repealed) which determined the passes to be carried by Africans, and restricted the free movement of African citizens.

Pas·sos see DOS PASSOS.

Pass·over noun **1** the Jewish spring festival commemorating the liberation of the Israelites from slavery in Egypt, held from the 14th to the 21st day of the seventh month of the Jewish year. **2** = PASCHAL LAMB. [pass over = pass without touching, with reference to the exemption of the Israelites from the death of the first-born (Exod. 12)]

pass·port noun **1** an official document issued by a government certifying the holder's identity and citizenship, and entitling the holder to travel under its protection to and from foreign countries. **2** (foll. by to) a thing that ensures admission or attainment (a passport to success). [French passeport (as PASS¹, PORT¹)]

pass rush noun Football the elements of a team's defensive play aimed at thwarting the quarterback's attempts to pass. □ **pass rusher** noun **pass-rushing** adjective

pass the parcel noun Brit. a children's game in which a wrapped parcel is passed between participants while music plays, the one left holding it when the music stops being allowed to unwrap a layer. The person who unwraps the final layer wins the prize.

pass-through N Amer. ● noun an opening in a wall between two rooms, esp. a kitchen and a dining area, through which dishes etc. are passed. ● adjective (of costs) chargeable to the customer.

pass·word noun **1** a selected word or phrase securing recognition, admission, etc., when used by those to whom it is disclosed. **2** Computing a confidential sequence of characters that has to be typed in order to gain access to a particular computer, network, etc.

Passy /paˈsiː/ **Fré·dé·ric** (1822–1912), French economist, who advocated international arbitration as a means to prevent war, and shared the first Nobel Peace Prize with Jean Henri Dunant in 1901.

past ● adjective **1** gone by in time and no longer existing (in past years; the time is past). **2** recently completed or gone by (the past month; for some time past). **3** relating to a former time (past president). **4** Grammar expressing a past action or state. ● noun **1** (prec. by the) **a** past time. **b** what has happened in past time (cannot undo the past). **2** a person's past life or career, esp. if discreditable (a man with a past). **3** a past tense or form. ● preposition **1** beyond in time or place (is past two o'clock; ran past the house). **2** beyond the range, duration, or compass of (past belief; past endurance). ● adverb so as to pass by (hurried past). □ **not put it past a person** believe it possible of a person. **past it** informal old and useless. □ **past·ness** noun [past participle of PASS¹ verb]

pasta /ˈpastə, ˈpɒstə/ noun **1** a type of dough extruded or stamped into various shapes for cooking, e.g. lasagna or spaghetti, and used fresh or dried. **2** a dish made from this. [Italian, = PASTE]

paste ● noun **1** a moist fairly stiff mixture, esp. of powder and liquid. **2** an adhesive of flour, water, etc., esp. for sticking paper and other light materials. **3** a dough of flour with fat, water, etc., used in baking. **4** a puréed preparation of ground meat, fish, vegetable, etc. (anchovy paste; tomato paste). **5 a** a hard vitreous composition used in making imitation gems. **b** imitation jewellery made of this. **6 a** a mixture of clay, water, etc., used in making ceramic ware, esp. a mixture of low plasticity used in making porcelain. ● transitive verb **1** fasten or coat with paste. **2** Computing insert or reproduce (already existing text) at a new location in a document, file, etc. **3** slang **a** beat or thrash. **b** bomb or bombard heavily. □ **past·ing** noun (esp. in sense 3 of verb). [Late Latin pasta 'small, square medicinal lozenge' from Greek pastē, from pastos 'sprinkled']

paste·board noun **1** a sheet of stiff material made by pasting together sheets of paper. **2** (attributive) **a** flimsy, unsubstantial. **b** fake.

pasted-on adjective (of a smile) artificial, forced.

pas·tel /paˈstel/ ● noun **1** a crayon consisting of powdered pigments bound with a gum solution. **2 a** the art or technique of drawing with pastels. **b** a work of art in pastel. **3** a light and subdued shade of a colour. ● adjective of a light and subdued shade or colour. □ **pastel·ist** noun **pastel·list** noun [French pastel or Italian pastello, diminutive of pasta PASTE]

pas·tern /ˈpastɜrn/ noun **1** the part of a horse's foot between the fetlock and the hoof. **2** a corresponding part in other animals. [Middle English pastron from Old French pasturon from pasture hobble, ultimately from Latin pastorius of a shepherd from PASTOR]

Pas·ter·nak /ˈpastɜrˌnak/ **Boris (Leonid·ovich** (1890–1960), Russian poet, novelist, and translator, who is best known for his novel Doctor Zhivago (1957), a testament to the experience of the Russian intelligentsia before, during, and after the Russian Revolution; he was awarded the Nobel Prize for literature in 1958, but was forced to turn it down under pressure from the Soviet authorities.

paste-up noun a document prepared for copying etc. by combining and pasting various sections on a backing.

Pas·teur /paˈstɜr/ **Louis** (1822–95), French chemist and bacteriologist. He proved that each fermentation process was caused by a specific living micro-organism, and introduced the process of pasteurization; he also isolated the bacteria causing anthrax and chicken cholera, made vaccines against them, and pioneered vaccination against rabies using attenuated virus.

pas·teur·ize /ˈpastʃəˌraɪz, -təˌraɪz/ transitive verb (also esp. Brit. **-ise**) subject (milk etc.) to the process of partial sterilization by heating. □ **pas·teur·iz·a·tion** noun **pas·teur·iz·er** noun [L. PASTEUR]

pas·tic·cio /paˈstiːtʃoʊ/ noun (pl. **-cios**) a musical pastiche. [Italian: see PASTICHE]

pas·tiche /paˈstiːʃ/ ● noun **1** a medley, esp. a picture or a musical composition, made up from or imitating various sources. **2** a literary or other work of art composed in the style of a well-known writer, artist, etc. ● transitive verb copy or imitate the style of (an artist, author, time period, etc.) □ **pas·ti·cheur** /pastiˈʃɜr/ noun [French from Italian pasticcio, ultimately from Late Latin pasta PASTE]

pas·tille /paˈstiːl/ noun **1** a small candy, lozenge, or chocolate. **2** a small roll of aromatic paste burned as a room deodorizer etc. [French from Latin pastillus little loaf, lozenge, from panis loaf]

pas·time noun **1** a pleasant recreation or hobby. **2** a sport or game. [PASS¹ + TIME]

pas·tis /paˈstiːs/ noun (pl. same) an aniseed-flavoured aperitif. [French]

pas·tit·sio /paˈstiːtsioʊ/ noun (pl. **-sios**) a Greek dish consisting of a layer of ground meat in a tomato sauce between two layers of macaroni in a cheese cream sauce. [Greek]

past master noun **1** a person who is especially adept or expert in an activity, subject, etc. **2** a person who has been a master in a guild, Freemason's lodge, etc.

pas·tor ● noun **1** (also **Pastor**) (often as a title or form of address) a minister or priest in charge of a church or a congregation. **2** a person exercising spiritual guidance. **3** a pink starling, Sturnus roseus, of E Europe and Asia. ● verb **1** transitive **a** be minister of (a church). **b** have the spiritual care of (a congregation). **2** intransitive be a pastor. □ **pas·tor·ship** noun [Old French pastour from Latin pastor -oris 'shepherd', from pascere past- 'feed, graze']

pas·tor·al /ˈpastərəl/ ● adjective **1 a** of, relating to, or associated with shepherds or flocks and herds (pastoral nomads). **b** of or pertaining to the country; rural. **2** (of a poem, picture, etc.) portraying country life, usu. in a romantic or idealized form. **3** (of land) used for pasture. **4** of or pertaining to a pastor or the spiritual care of a congregation. ● noun **1** a pastoral poem, play, picture, etc. **2** (in full **pastoral letter**) a letter from a pastor (esp. a bishop) to the clergy or people.

☐ **pas·tor·al·ism** noun **pas·tor·al·ly** adverb [Middle English from Latin pastoralis (as PASTORAL)]

pastoral charge noun the congregation or congregations for which a minister is responsible, esp. in the United Church.

pas·tor·ale /ˌpastəˈral, -ˌralɪ/ noun (pl. **pas·tor·ales** or **pas·tor·ali** /-liː/) **1** a slow instrumental composition, usu. with drone notes in the bass suggestive of a shepherd's bagpipes. **2** a simple musical play with a rural subject. [Italian (as PASTORAL)]

pas·tor·al·ist /ˈpastərəlɪst/ ● noun a farmer of sheep or cattle.
● adjective = PASTORAL adjective 1a.

pastoral theology noun theology that considers religious truth in relation to spiritual needs.

pas·tor·ate /ˈpastərət/ noun **1** the office or tenure of a pastor. **2** a body of pastors; pastors collectively.

past perfect noun = PLUPERFECT.

pas·trami /pəˈstrɒmi/ noun seasoned smoked beef brisket, usu. cut in thin slices for sandwiches. [Yiddish from Romanian pastramă cured meat, prob. of Turkish origin]

pas·try noun (pl. **-tries**) **1** a dough of flour, fat, and water baked and used as a base and covering for pies etc. **2 a** food made wholly or partly of this. **b** a piece or item of this food. **3** a sweet bread or cake. [PASTE after Old French pastaierie]

pastry bag noun a cloth funnel through which icing, food paste, etc. is squeezed to decorate the top of a cake, canapé, etc.

pastry blender noun a kitchen utensil with a curved body of stiff wires for cutting butter etc. into flour etc.

pastry chef noun (also **pastry cook**) a cook who specializes in pastry, esp. for public sale.

pas·tur·age /ˈpastʃərɪdʒ/ noun **1** land for pasture. **2** the process of pasturing cattle etc.

pas·ture /ˈpastʃər/ ● noun **1 a** land covered with grass etc. suitable for grazing animals, esp. cattle or sheep. **b** a specific piece of such land. **2** herbage for animals. **3** the circumstances of a person's life, work, etc. (find greener pastures). ● verb **1** transitive put (animals) to graze in a pasture. **2** intransitive & transitive (of animals) graze. ☐ **out to pasture 1** out to graze. **2** informal **a** (of a person) in retirement. **b** (of a thing) no longer used; closed down. [Old French from Late Latin pastura (as PASTOR)]

pasture land noun = PASTURE noun 1.

pasty¹ /ˈpasti/ noun (pl. **-ies**) esp. Brit. a piece of pastry folded around a usu. savoury filling, baked without a dish to shape it. [Old French pasté, ultimately from Late Latin pasta PASTE]

pasty² /ˈpeɪsti/ ● adjective (**pasti·er**, **pasti·est**) **1** unhealthily pale (esp. in complexion) (pasty-faced). **2** of or like or covered with paste.
● noun (pl. **-ies**) (usu. in pl.) a decorative covering for the nipple worn by a stripper. ☐ **pas·ti·ly** adverb **pas·ti·ness** noun

PA system noun = PUBLIC ADDRESS SYSTEM.

pat¹ ● verb (**pat·ted**, **pat·ting**) **1** transitive strike gently with the hand or a flat surface. **2** transitive flatten or mould by patting. **3** transitive strike gently with the inner surface of the hand, esp. as a sign of affection, sympathy, or congratulation. **4** transitive & intransitive (foll. by on, upon) tap or beat lightly on (a surface), esp. so as to produce a gentle sound.
● noun **1** a light stroke or tap, esp. with the hand in affection etc. **2** the sound made by this, or by light footsteps. **3** a small mass (esp. of butter) formed by patting. ☐ **pat on the back** see BACK. **pat a person on the back** see BACK. [Middle English, prob. imitative]

pat² ● adjective **1** known thoroughly and ready for any occasion. **2** apposite or opportune, esp. unconvincingly so (gave a pat answer).
● adverb **1** in a pat manner. **2** appositely, opportunely. ☐ **have down** (or Brit. **off**) **pat** know or have memorized perfectly. **stand pat** esp. N Amer. **1** stick stubbornly to one's opinion or decision. **2** Poker retain one's hand as dealt; not draw other cards. ☐ **patly** adverb **pat·ness** noun [16th c.: related to PAT¹]

pat. abbreviation patent.

pa·ta·ca /pəˈteɪkə/ noun the basic monetary unit of Macao, equal to 100 avos. [Spanish and Portuguese]

pat-a-cake noun Brit. var. of PATTY CAKE.

pata·gium /pəˈteɪdʒɪəm/ noun (pl. **pata·gia** /-ˈdʒaɪə/) Zool. **1** the wing membrane of a bat or similar animal. **2** a scale covering the wing joint in moths and butterflies. [medieval Latin use of Latin patagium from Greek patageion gold edging]

Pata·gonia /ˌpatəˈɡoʊniə/ a region of S America, in S Argentina and Chile. Consisting largely of a dry barren plateau, it extends from the Colorado River in central Argentina to the Strait of Magellan and from

the Andes to the Atlantic coast. ☐ **Pata·gon·ian** adjective & noun [obsolete Patagon, a member of a S American Aboriginal people alleged by travellers of the 17th and 18th c. to be the tallest known people]

Pa·tali·putra /pəˌtʊlɪˈpuːtrə/ the ancient name for PATNA.

pata·phys·ics noun the branch of philosophy that deals with an imaginary realm additional to metaphysics. ☐ **pata·physic·al** adjective [from Greek ta epi ta metaphusika, literally 'the works imposed on the Metaphysics'. The concept was introduced by Alfred Jarry, French writer of the Absurd]

patch ● noun **1** a piece of material or metal etc. used to mend a hole or as reinforcement. **2** a pad or shield worn over an eye or eye socket. **3** a dressing etc. put over a wound. **4** a small area or expanse, esp. one that contrasts with a surrounding area (a patch of ice). **5** a piece of ground. **6** a number of plants growing in one place (brier patch). **7** a small scrap, piece, or remnant (fog patches). **8** an adhesive patch worn on the skin, which releases measured amounts of a drug into the bloodstream, used in hormone replacement therapy, the treatment of nicotine addiction, motion sickness, etc. **9** Cdn (Nfld) a herd of seals. **10** informal a period of time in terms of its characteristic quality (went through a bad patch). **11** Brit. informal an area assigned to or patrolled by an authorized person, esp. a police officer. **12 a** a temporary electrical connection. **b** Computing a small piece of code inserted to correct or enhance a program. **13** hist. a small disc etc. of black silk attached to the face, worn esp. by women in the 17th–18th c. for adornment. **14** Military a piece of cloth on a uniform as the badge of a unit. ● verb **1** transitive (often foll. by up) repair with a patch or patches; put a patch or patches on. **2** transitive (of material) serve as a patch to. **3** transitive (often foll. by up) put together, esp. hastily or in a makeshift way. **4** transitive (foll. by up) settle (a quarrel etc.) esp. hastily or temporarily. **5** transitive & intransitive (often foll. by through, into) connect or be connected by a temporary electrical, radio, etc. connection. **6** transitive Computing correct or enhance (a routine, program, etc.) by inserting a patch. ☐ **not a patch on** informal greatly inferior to. ☐ **patch·er** noun [Middle English pacche, patche, perhaps variant of peche, from Old French pieche a dialect variant of piece PIECE]

patch cord noun a short electrical cord with a plug at each end, for linking electronic equipment or circuits.

patch·ouli /pəˈtʃuːli/ noun **1** a strongly scented E Indian plant, Pogostemon cablin. **2** the perfume obtained from this. [Tamil pacculi]

patch pocket noun a pocket made of a piece of cloth sewn on a garment.

patch test noun **1** a test for allergies by applying to the skin patches containing allergenic substances, and then examining the area for signs of redness, swelling, etc. **2** an application of a cosmetic, hair dye, etc. to a small area of skin before using the product for its intended purpose, to determine if it will cause an allergic reaction.

patch·work ● noun **1** needlework in which small pieces of cloth in different designs are sewn together to form one article such as a quilt. **2** a thing composed of different pieces, fragments, or elements.
● attributive adjective **1** composed of patchwork pieces. **2 a** resembling patchwork (patchwork fields). **b** pieced together with lack of uniformity (patchwork political philosophy). ● transitive verb make as patchwork (patchwork a quilt).

patchy adjective (**patch·i·er**, **patch·i·est**) **1** uneven in quality. **2** having or existing in patches. ☐ **patch·i·ly** adverb **patch·i·ness** noun

pat-down noun (also **pat-down search**) a search for concealed weapons, drugs, etc. conducted by running the hands over the body of a clothed person.

pate noun jocular the head, esp. if bald. [Middle English: origin unknown]

pâte /pɑt/ noun the paste of which porcelain is made. [French, = PASTE]

pâté /pɑˈteɪ, ˈpɑteɪ/ noun a rich paste or spread of ground or puréed and seasoned meat or fish etc., usu. served as an appetizer. [French from Old French pasté (as PASTY¹)]

pâté de foie gras noun see FOIE GRAS.

pa·tel·la /pəˈtelə/ noun (pl. **pa·tel·las** or **pa·tel·lae** /-liː/) the kneecap. ☐ **pa·tel·lar** adjective **pa·tel·late** /-lət/ adjective [Latin, diminutive of patina: see PATEN]

paten /ˈpatən/ noun **1** a shallow dish used for the bread at the Eucharist. **2** a thin circular plate of metal. [Old French patene or Latin patena, patina shallow dish, from Greek patanē a plate]

pat·ent /ˈpatənt, ˈpeɪt-/ ● noun **1** a government authority to an individual or organization conferring a right or title, esp. the sole right to make or use or sell some invention. **2** a document granting this authority. **3** an invention or process protected by it. **4** *N Amer.* the right or title to an area of public land granted to an individual by the government. ● *adjective* **1** /ˈpeɪtənt/ obvious, plain. **2** conferred or protected by patent. **3** made and marketed under a patent; proprietary. **4** concerning patents (*patent law*). **5** made of patent leather. **6** (of a bodily passage etc.) unobstructed. ● *transitive verb* **1** obtain a patent for (an invention). **2** *N Amer.* grant (an area of public land) by a patent. □ **pat·ent·abil·ity** *noun* **pat·en·cy** *noun* **pat·ent·able** *adjective* **pat·ent·ly** /ˈpeɪtntli/ *adverb* (in sense 1 of *adjective*). [Old French *patent* and Latin *patēre* lie open]

pat·en·tee /ˌpatənˈtiː, ˌpeɪt-/ *noun* a person, company, etc. that takes out or holds a patent.

patent leather *noun* leather with a glossy varnished surface, used for shoes and accessories (often *attributive: patent-leather pumps*).

patent medicine *noun* medicine made and marketed under a patent and available without prescription.

patent office *noun* an office from which patents are issued.

pat·ent·or /ˈpatəntər, ˈpeɪt-/ *noun* a person or body that grants a patent.

Pater /ˈpeɪtər/ **Wal·ter (Hor·atio)** (1839–94), English essayist and critic. His *Studies in the History of the Renaissance* (1873) had a major impact on the development of the Aesthetic movement; his other works include *Marius the Epicurean* (1885), which develops his ideas on 'art for art's sake'.

pater /ˈpeɪtər/ *noun Brit. slang* father. ¶ *Pater* is now only found in jocular or affected use. [Latin]

pater·famil·ias /ˌpatərfəˈmɪliəs, -ˌas, ˌpeɪtər-/ *noun* the male head of a family or household. [Latin, = father of the family]

pa·ter·nal /pəˈtɜːrnəl/ *adjective* **1** of or like or appropriate to a father. **2** fatherly. **3** related through the father (*paternal grandmother*). **4** inherited from the male parent (*paternal chromosome*). **5** (of an organization, government etc.) limiting freedom and responsibility by well-meant regulations. □ **pa·ter·nal·ly** *adverb* [Late Latin *paternalis* from Latin *paternus* from *pater* father]

pa·ter·nal·ism /pəˈtɜːrnəˌlɪzəm/ *noun* the policy of governing in a paternal way, or behaving paternally to one's associates or subordinates. □ **pa·ter·nal·ist** *adjective & noun* **pa·ter·nal·is·tic** *adjective* **pa·ter·nal·is·tic·al·ly** *adverb*

pa·ter·nity /pəˈtɜːrnɪti/ *noun* **1** fatherhood. **2** one's paternal origin. **3** the source or authorship of a thing. [Late Latin *paternitas*]

paternity leave *noun* a leave of absence taken by a father to care for a new baby.

paternity suit *noun* a lawsuit held to determine whether a certain man is the father of a certain child.

paternity test *noun* a blood test to determine whether a man may be or cannot be the father of a particular child.

pater·noster /ˌpatərˈnɒstər/ *noun* **1 a** the Lord's Prayer, esp. in Latin. **b** a rosary bead indicating that this is to be said. **2** an elevator consisting of a series of linked doorless compartments moving continuously on a circular belt. [Old English from Latin *pater noster* our father]

path *noun* (*pl.* **paths**) **1 a** a way or track laid down for walking or made by continual treading. **b** a specially laid track for cyclists or for machinery to run on (*bike path*). **2** the line along which a person or thing moves (*flight path*). **3** a course of action or conduct (*career path*). **4** *Computing* a sequence of movements or operations taken by a system. □ **path·less** *adjective* [Old English *pæth* from West Germanic]

-path *combining form* forming nouns denoting: **1** a practitioner of curative treatment (*homeopath; osteopath*). **2** a person who suffers from a disease (*psychopath*). [back-formation from -PATHY, or from Greek *-pathēs* -sufferer (as PATHOS)]

Pa·than /pəˈtɑːn/ *noun var. of* PASHTUN. [Hindi]

path-breaking *adjective* (of a person, invention, etc.) pioneering in some subject. □ **path-breaker** *noun*

Pathé /ˈpaθeɪ/ **Charles** (1863–1957), French film pioneer. In 1896 he and his brothers founded a company which dominated the production and distribution of films in the early 20th c.; the firm also became internationally known for its newsreels, which were first introduced in France in 1909.

pa·thet·ic /pəˈθetɪk/ *adjective* **1** arousing pity or sadness or contempt. **2** *informal* miserably inadequate; useless or worthless (*a pathetic performance*). **3** *archaic* of the emotions. □ **pa·thet·ic·al·ly** *adverb* [Late Latin *patheticus* from Greek *pathētikos* (as PATHOS)]

pathetic fallacy *noun* the attribution of human feelings and responses to inanimate things, esp. in art and literature.

path·find·er *noun* **1** a person who explores new territory, investigates a new subject, etc. **2** an aircraft or its pilot sent ahead to locate and mark the target area for bombing. **3** (**Pathfinder**) *Cdn* a member of the branch of the Girl Guides for 12- to 15-year-olds.

patho- *combining form* disease. [Greek *pathos* suffering: see PATHOS]

patho·gen /ˈpaθədʒən/ *noun* an agent causing disease. □ **patho·gen·ic** /-ˈdʒenɪk/ *adjective* **patho·gen·icity** /-ˈnɪsɪti/ *noun* [PATHO- + -GEN]

patho·gen·esis /ˌpaθəˈdʒenəsɪs/ *noun* (also **patho·geny** /pəˈθɒdʒəni/) the manner of development of a disease. □ **patho·gen·etic** /-dʒɪˈnetɪk/ *adjective*

patho·logic·al /ˌpaθəˈlɒdʒɪkəl/ *adjective* (also **patho·logic**) **1** of pathology. **2** of or caused by a physical or mental disorder (*pathological depression*). **3** *informal* **a** not reasonable or sensible (*a pathological fear of spiders*). **b** compulsive (*a pathological liar*). □ **patho·logic·al·ly** *adverb*

patho·lo·gize /pəˈθɒlədʒaɪz/ *transitive verb* (also *esp. Brit.* **-gise**) cause (someone or something) to be considered abnormal or ill.

path·ol·ogy /pəˈθɒlədʒi/ *noun* (*pl.* **-gies**) **1** the science of bodily diseases. **2** the symptoms of a disease. **3** any abnormal or unhealthy condition. □ **path·ol·o·gist** *noun* [as PATHO-, -LOGY]

patho·physio·logy *noun* the disordered physical processes associated with disease or injury. □ **patho·physio·logic·al** *adjective*

pa·thos /ˈpeɪθɒs/ *noun* a quality in speech, writing, events, etc. that excites pity or sadness. [Greek *pathos* suffering, related to *paskhō* suffer, *penthos* grief]

path·way *noun* **1** a path or its course. **2** *Biochem. etc.* a sequence of reactions undergone in a living organism.

-pathy *combining form* forming nouns denoting: **1** curative treatment (*allopathy; homeopathy*). **2** disease (*psychopathy*). **3** feeling (*telepathy*). [Greek *patheia* suffering]

pa·tience /ˈpeɪʃəns/ *noun* **1** calm endurance of hardship, provocation, pain, delay, etc. **2** tolerant perseverance or forbearance. **3** the capacity for calm self-possessed waiting. **4** *esp. Brit.* = SOLITAIRE 1. □ **have no patience with** (or **for**) **1** be unable to tolerate. **2** be irritated by. [Old French from Latin *patientia* (as PATIENT)]

pa·tient /ˈpeɪʃənt/ ● *adjective* having or showing patience. ● *noun* a person receiving or registered to receive medical treatment. □ **pa·tient·ly** *adverb* [Old French from Latin *patiens -entis* pres. part. of *pati* suffer]

pa·tina /pəˈtiːnə, ˈpatɪnə/ *noun* (*pl.* **pa·tinas**) **1** a film, usu. green, formed on the surface of old bronze. **2** a similar film on other surfaces. **3** a gloss produced by age on woodwork etc. **4** a superficial appearance (*a patina of respectability*). □ **pat·in·ated** /ˈpatɪˌneɪtəd/ *adjective* **pat·in·a·tion** /ˈpatɪˈneɪʃən/ *noun* [Italian from Latin *patina* dish]

pat·io *noun* (*pl.* **-ios**) **1** a paved usu. roofless area adjoining and belonging to a house, used for outdoor recreation. **2** an inner court open to the sky in a Spanish or Latin American house. [Spanish]

patio door *noun* (often in *pl.*) a set of sliding glass doors.

pa·tis·ser·ie /pəˈtiːsəri/ *noun* **1** a bakeshop where fancy, esp. French, pastries are made, sold, and usu. served. **2** esp. French pastries collectively. [French *pâtisserie* from medieval Latin *pasticium* pastry, from *pasta* PASTE]

Pat·mos /ˈpatmɒs/ a Greek island in the Aegean Sea, in the Dodecanese. It is believed that St. John was living there in exile (from AD 95) when he had the visions described in Revelation.

Patna /ˈpatnə/ a city in NE India, on the Ganges, capital of the state of Bihar; pop. (2001) 1,377,000. Known as Pataliputra, it was the capital between the 5th and 1st c. BC of the Magadha kingdom and in the 4th c. AD of the Gupta dynasty.

Patna rice /ˈpatnə/ *noun* a variety of rice with long firm grains. [PATNA, where it was originally grown]

pa·tois /ˈpatwɒ, ˈpat-/ *noun* (*pl.* same /-wɒz/) a non-standard local dialect. [French, = rough speech, perhaps from Old French *patoier* treat roughly, from *patte* paw]

Paton /ˈpeɪtən/ **Alan (Stew·art)** (1903–88), South African writer and politician. He is best known for his novel *Cry, the Beloved Country* (1948), a passionate indictment of the apartheid system; he helped found the South African Liberal Party in 1953, later serving as its president until it was banned in 1968.

pa·toot·ie /pəˈtuːti/ *noun* (also **pa·toot** /pəˈtuːt/) *N Amer. slang* the buttocks. [perhaps alteration of POTATO]

Pat·ras /ˈpatrəs/ an industrial port in the NW Peloponnese, on the Gulf of Patras; pop. (est. 2002) 173,900. It was the site in 1821 of the outbreak of the Greek war of independence.

patri·arch /ˈpeɪtriˌɑːrk/ *noun* **1** the male head of a family or tribe.

2 (often in *pl.*) *Bible* **a** each of the twelve sons of Jacob, from whom the tribes of Israel were descended. **b** Abraham, Isaac, and Jacob, and their forefathers. **3** *Christianity* **a** the title of a chief bishop, esp. those presiding over the Churches of Antioch, Alexandria, Constantinople, Jerusalem, and Rome; now also the title of the heads of certain autocephalous Orthodox Churches. **b** (in the Roman Catholic Church) a bishop ranking next above primates and metropolitans, and immediately below the pope. **c** the head of a Uniate community. **4** **a** founder of an order, science, etc. **b** a venerable old man. **c** the oldest member of a group. [Old French *patriarche* from ecclesiastical Latin *patriarcha* from Greek *patriarkhēs* from *patria* family, from *patēr* father + *-arkhēs* -ruler]

patri·arch·al /ˌpeɪtriˈɑrkəl/ *adjective* of or pertaining to a patriarch or to patriarchy. □ **patri·arch·al·ist** *noun* **patri·arch·al·ly** *adverb*

patri·arch·ate /ˈpeɪtriˌɑrkət/ *noun* **1** the office, see, or residence of an ecclesiastical patriarch. **2** the rank of a tribal patriarch.

patri·archy /ˈpeɪtriˌɑrki/ *noun* (*pl.* **-ies**) **1** a system of society, government, etc., ruled by a man and with descent through the male line. **2** the attitudes, structures, etc. of a society seen as ensuring male dominance. □ **patri·arch·ism** *noun*

patri·ate /ˈpeɪtriˌeɪt/ *transitive verb Cdn* bring (legislation, esp. a constitution) under the authority of the autonomous country to which it applies, used with reference to laws passed on behalf of that country by its former mother country. □ **patri·a·tion** *noun* [from REPATRIATE]

patri·cian /pəˈtrɪʃən/ ● *noun* **1** *hist.* a member of the ancient Roman nobility (*compare* PLEBEIAN *noun* 1). **2** *hist.* a nobleman in some Italian republics. **3** an aristocrat. **4** *N Amer.* a refined or well-bred person. ● *adjective* **1** noble, aristocratic. **2** *hist.* of the ancient Roman nobility. **3** *N Amer.* refined, well-bred. [Old French *patricien* from Latin *patricius* 'having a noble father', from *pater patris* 'father']

Pat·ri·cias *plural noun Cdn* an informal name for the Princess Patricia's Canadian Light Infantry regiment.

pa·trici·ate /pəˈtrɪʃət/ *noun* **1** a patrician order; an aristocracy. **2** the rank of patrician. [Latin *patriciatus* (as PATRICIAN)]

patri·cide /ˈpatrɪsaɪd/ *noun* **1** the killing of one's father. **2** a person who commits patricide. □ **patri·cid·al** *adjective* [Late Latin *patricida*, *patricidium*, alteration of Latin *parricida*, *parricidium* (see PARRICIDE) by association with *pater* 'father']

Patrick, St. (5th c.), patron saint of Ireland. Of Romano-British parentage, he was captured at the age of 16 by raiders and shipped to Ireland as a slave, where he experienced a religious conversion; escaping after six years, probably to Gaul, he was ordained and returned to Ireland in about 432. Feast day, 17 March.

patri·lin·eal /ˌpatrɪˈlɪniəl/ *adjective* of or relating to, or based on kinship with, the father or descent through the male line. □ **patri·lin·eal·ly** *adverb* [Latin *pater patris* father + LINEAL]

patri·local /ˌpatrɪˈloʊkəl/ *adjective* designating or pertaining to a pattern of marriage in which the couple settles in the husband's home or community. □ **patri·local·ity** /ˌpatriloʊˈkalɪti/ *noun*

patri·mony /ˈpatrɪˌmoʊni/ *noun* (*pl.* **-ies**) **1** a heritage. **2** property inherited from one's father or ancestor. **3** the endowment of a church etc. □ **patri·mon·ial** /-ˈmoʊniəl/ *adjective* [Old French *patrimoine* from Latin *patrimonium* from *pater patris* father]

pa·tri·ot /ˈpeɪtriət/ *noun* **1** a person who is ardently devoted to the well-being or interests of his or her country. **2** (**Patriot**) an automated surface-to-air missile designed for early detection and interception of incoming missiles or aircraft. □ **patri·ot·ic** /-ˈɒtɪk/ *adjective* **patri·ot·ic·ally** *adverb* **pa·triot·ism** *noun* [French *patriote* from Late Latin *patriota* from Greek *patriōtēs* from *patrios* of one's fathers, from *patēr patros* father]

Pa·triote /patriˈɒt/ *noun Cdn hist.* a supporter of Papineau in the Rebellion of Lower Canada.

Patriotes Day *noun Cdn* (*Que.*) the official name in Quebec from 2003 onwards for VICTORIA DAY.

pa·tris·tic /pəˈtrɪstɪk/ *adjective* of the early Christian theologians or their writings. [German *patristisch* from Latin *pater patris* father]

pa·tris·tics /pəˈtrɪstɪks/ *plural noun* (usu. treated as *sing.*) the branch of Christian theology that deals with the early Christian theologians or their writings. [as PATRISTIC]

Pa·troc·lus /pəˈtrɒkləs/ *Gk Myth* a Greek hero of the Trojan War, the close friend of Achilles. The *Iliad* describes how Patroclus' death at the hands of Hector led Achilles to return to battle.

pa·trol ● *noun* **1** the act of walking or travelling around an area, esp. at regular intervals, in order to protect or supervise it. **2** one or more persons or vehicles assigned or sent out on patrol, esp. a detachment

of guards, police, etc. **3** **a** a detachment of troops sent out to reconnoitre. **b** such reconnaissance. **4** a routine operational voyage of a ship or aircraft. **5** a routine monitoring of astronomical or other phenomena. **6** **a** = SCHOOL PATROL. **b** *Brit.* a crossing guard. **7** a unit of six to eight Scouts or Guides. ● *verb* (**pa·trolled**, **pa·trol·ling**) **1** *transitive* carry out a patrol of. **2** *intransitive* act as a patrol. □ **pa·trol·ler** *noun* [French *patrouiller* paddle in mud, from *patte* paw: (n.) from German *Patrolle* from French *patrouille*]

patrol car *noun N Amer.* a police car used in patrolling roads and streets.

patrol·man *noun* (*pl.* **-men**) *N Amer.* a police officer on a patrol.

pa·tron *noun* **1** a person who gives financial or other support to a person, cause, arts organization, work of art, etc. **2** a usu. regular customer of a store etc. **3** *Rom. Hist.* **a** the former owner of a freed slave. **b** the protector of a client. **4** *Brit.* a person who has the right of presenting a member of the clergy to a benefice. **5** = PATRON SAINT. □ **pa·tron·ess** *noun* [Old French from Latin *patronus* protector of clients, defender, from *pater patris* father]

pa·tron·age /ˈpeɪtrənɪdʒ, pat-/ *noun* **1** the support, promotion, or encouragement given by a patron. **2** **a** the control of appointments to office, privileges, etc., esp. in public service. **b** the appointing of friends, supporters, etc. to offices or privileges, esp. in public service. **3** a customer's support for a store etc. **4** a patronizing or condescending manner. **5** *Rom. Hist.* the rights and duties or position of a patron.

pa·tron·al /pəˈtroʊnəl/ *adjective* of or relating to a patron saint (*the parish's patronal festival*).

pa·tron·ize /ˈpeɪtrəˌnaɪz, pat-/ *transitive verb* (also esp. *Brit.* **-ise**) **1** treat condescendingly. **2** act as a patron towards (a person, cause, artist, etc.); support; encourage. **3** frequent (a store etc.) as a customer. □ **pa·tron·iz·er** *noun* **pa·tron·iz·ing** *adjective* **pa·tron·iz·ing·ly** *adverb*

patron saint *noun* a saint to whose intercession and protection a person, place, occupation, etc., is specially entrusted.

patro·nym·ic /ˌpatrəˈnɪmɪk/ ● *noun* a name derived from the name of a father or ancestor, e.g. *Johnson, O'Brien, Ivanovich, Fitzgerald.* ● *adjective* **1** (of a name) so derived. **2** (of an affix) indicating such a derivation. [Late Latin *patronymicus* from Greek *patrōnumikos* from *patrōnumos* from *patēr patros* father + *onuma, onoma* name]

pa·troon /pəˈtruːn/ *noun US hist.* a landowner with manorial privileges under the Dutch governments of New York and New Jersey. [Dutch, = PATRON]

patsy *noun* (*pl.* **-sies**) esp. *N Amer. slang* a person who is deceived, ridiculed, tricked, etc. [20th c.: origin unknown]

Pat·taya /paˈtaɪə/ a resort on the coast of S Thailand, southeast of Bangkok.

pat·ten /ˈpatən/ *noun hist.* a shoe or clog with a raised sole or set on an iron ring, for walking in mud etc. [Old French *patin* from *patte* paw]

pat·ter¹ ● *verb* **1** *intransitive* make a rapid succession of taps, as of rain on a windowpane. **2** *intransitive* run with quick short steps. **3** *transitive* cause (water etc.) to patter. ● *noun* a rapid succession of taps, short light steps, etc. [PAT¹]

pat·ter² ● *noun* **1** **a** the rapid speech used by a comedian or introduced into a song. **b** the words of a comic song. **2** the words used by a person selling or promoting a product; a sales pitch. **3** the special language or jargon of a profession, class, etc. ● *verb* **1** *transitive* repeat in a rapid mechanical way. **2** *intransitive* talk glibly or mechanically. [Middle English from *pater* = PATERNOSTER]

pat·tern ● *noun* **1** a repeated decorative design on fabric, paper, etc. **2** an esp. regular or logical form, order, or arrangement (*behaviour pattern; the pattern of one's daily life*). **3** **a** a model or design from which copies can be made. **b** a paper plan from which a garment may be made. **4** an example of excellence; an ideal; a model (*a pattern of elegance*). **5** a wooden or metal figure from which a mould is made for a casting. **6** a sample (of cloth, wallpaper, etc.). **7** the marks made by shots, bombs, etc. on a target or target area. **8** a random combination of shapes or colours. ● *transitive verb* **1** (usu. foll. by *after, on*) model (a thing) on a design etc. **2** decorate with a pattern. □ **pat·terned** *adjective* **pat·tern·ing** *noun* **pat·tern·less** *adjective* [Middle English *patron* (see PATRON): differentiated in sense and spelling since the 16th–17th c.]

patterned ground *noun Geography* ground showing a definite pattern of stones, fissures, vegetation, etc. (commonly polygons, rings, or stripes), typical of periglacial regions.

Pat·ter·son ▸ **1** **Wal·ter** (*c.*1735–1798), Irish-born army officer and

Canadian colonial administrator. After serving briefly in N America during the Seven Year's War, he was sent to Charlottetown in 1769 as governor of what was then called the Isle of St. John. The colony was inhabited by only a few hundred people, and had no reliable financial basis; Patterson established a House of Assembly (1773) and arranged for an annual grant of £3,000 from the crown in 1777. He was dismissed in 1787 due to land speculation, and returned to England. **2 Wil·liam John** (1886–1976), Canadian politician, Liberal premier of Saskatchewan 1935–44. His declining popularity matched the rise of the CCF, and he was defeated in 1944, resigning as party leader in 1946; he served as Lieutenant-Governor 1951–58.

patter song *noun* a humorous song in which many words are fitted to a few notes and sung rapidly.

Patti /ˈpati/ **Adel·ina** (born Adela Juana Maria Patti) (1843–1919), Spanish-born Italian operatic soprano, who was noted for her coloratura singing, esp. in the operas of Rossini and Bellini.

Pat·ti·son, James Allan (b.1928), Canadian businessman. His commercial empire has now grown to over 50 companies, including airlines, soft-drink bottlers, magazine distributors, and a neon sign corporation. The success of Expo 86 was largely due to his management.

Pat·ton, George Smith (1885–1945), US general, who led the US 3rd Army in its sweep across France following the Allied invasion of Normandy during the Second World War.

Pat·tul·lo /pəˈtuːloː/ **Thom·as Duf·fer·in** (1873–1956), Canadian businessman, civil servant, and politician, Liberal premier of BC 1933–41. After a varied career that included work as a newspaper editor, gold commissioner, real estate agent, and mayor of Prince Rupert, he was elected to the BC legislature as a Liberal in 1916. Becoming leader of the opposition in 1928, he reorganized the party and led it to victory in 1933. His frustration with the limited role of provincial governments led to battles with Ottawa which eventually resulted in the restructuring of Canadian federalism.

patty *noun* (*pl.* **-ties**) (also **pat·tie**) **1** a small, round or oval flat cake of ground meat etc. **2** *esp. N Amer.* a small round flat candy. **3** a quantity of any substance formed into a disc shape. **4 a** a little pie or pastry. **b** = JAMAICAN PATTY. [French *pâté* PASTY¹]

patty cake *noun N Amer.* (*Brit.* **pat-a-cake**) a child's game in which partners clap their own and each other's hands to the rhythm of a recited rhyme or song.

patty·pan squash *noun* = SCALLOP SQUASH. [from earlier *pattypan* pan for baking a patty]

patu·lous /ˈpatjuləs/ *adjective* (of branches etc.) spreading. [Latin *patulus* from *patēre* be open]

paua /ˈpauə/ *noun* **1** a large edible New Zealand shellfish of the genus *Haliotis.* **2** its ornamental shell. [Maori]

pau·city /ˈpɔːsɪti/ *noun* smallness of number or quantity. [Latin *paucitas* from *paucus* few]

Paul ▸ 1 Les (born Lester Polfus) (b.1915), US jazz guitarist. In 1946 he invented the solid-body electric guitar for which he is best known, which was first promoted in 1952 as the Gibson Les Paul guitar; in the 1950s he wrote and recorded a number of hit songs with his wife, Mary Ford (1928–77), such as 'Mockin' Bird Hill' (1951). **2 St.** (known as Paul the Apostle, or Saul of Tarsus, or 'the Apostle of the Gentiles') (died *c.*64), missionary of Jewish descent. Originally a persecutor of Christians, he was converted to Christianity after a vision he experienced on the way to Damascus, and became one of the first major Christian missionaries and theologians. His missionary journeys are described in the Acts of the Apostles, and his letters form part of the New Testament; he was martyred in Rome. Feast day, 29 June.

Paul I ▸ 1 (Russian name Pavel Petrovich) (1754–1801), emperor of Russia 1796–1801, the son of Catherine II. His despotic reign was marked by war against Napoleonic France (1798–1800); he was assassinated. **2** (1901–64), king of Greece 1947–64.

Paul III (born Alessandro Farnese) (1468–1549), Italian pope 1534–49. He excommunicated Henry VIII of England (1538), instituted the order of the Jesuits (1540), and initiated the Council of Trent (1545); a noted patron of the arts, he commissioned Michelangelo to paint the fresco of the *Last Judgement* for the Sistine Chapel and to design the dome of St. Peter's.

Paul VI (born Giovanni Battista Montini) (1897–1978), Italian pope 1963–78, who undertook the process of modernization of the Catholic Church initiated by the Second Vatican Council (1962–65).

Paula Red *noun* an early, red-and-green striped apple, used for cooking and eating.

Pauli /ˈpauli/ **Wolf·gang** (1900–58), Austrian-born US physicist who worked chiefly in Switzerland. He is best known for the *exclusion principle*; he also postulated the existence of the neutrino, which was later discovered by Fermi. He was awarded the Nobel Prize for physics in 1945.

Pauli exclusion principle /ˈpauli/ *noun Physics* the assertion that no two fermions can have the same quantum number. [W. PAULI]

Paul·ine /ˈpɔliːn/ *adjective* of or relating to St. Paul (*the Pauline epistles*).

Paul·ing, Linus (Carl) (1901–1994), US chemist. He is particularly renowned for his study of molecular structure and chemical bonding, esp. of complex biological macromolecules, for which he received the 1954 Nobel Prize for chemistry; after the Second World War he became increasingly involved with attempts to ban nuclear weapons, for which he was awarded the Nobel Peace Prize in 1962.

Paul·ist *noun* a member of the Missionary Society of St. Paul the Apostle, founded in New York in 1858 as a Roman Catholic order of priests. [St. PAUL]

pau·low·nia /pɔˈloːnɪə/ *noun* any Chinese tree of the genus *Paulownia*, with fragrant purple flowers. [Anna *Paulovna*, Russian princess d.1865]

paunch *noun* the belly or stomach, esp. when protruding. □ **paunchy** *adjective* (**paunch·i·er, paunch·i·est**). **paunch·i·ness** *noun* [Anglo-French *pa(u)nche*, ultimately from Latin *pantex panticis* bowels]

pau·per /ˈpɔpər/ *noun* a very poor person. □ **pau·per·dom** *noun* **pau·per·ism** *noun* **pau·per·ize** *transitive verb* (also esp. *Brit.* **-ise**). **pau·per·iz·a·tion** *noun* [Latin, = poor]

pau·piette /pɔːˈpjet/ *noun* a long thin slice of fish, meat, etc., esp. rolled and stuffed with a filling. [French, prob. from Italian *polpetta*, from Latin *pulpa* pulp]

Pau·san·ias /pɔˈseɪnɪəs/ (2nd c.), Greek geographer and historian. His *Description of Greece* (also called the *Itinerary of Greece*) is a guide to the topography and remains of ancient Greece and is still considered an invaluable source of information.

pause ● ** *noun* **1 an interval of inaction; a temporary stop. **2** a break in speaking or reading; a silence. **3** *Music* a mark (⌢) over a note or rest that is to be lengthened by an unspecified amount. **4** (also **pause button**) a control allowing the interruption of the operation of a VCR, CD player, etc. ● *intransitive verb* **1** make a pause; wait. **2** (usu. foll. by *upon*) linger over (a word etc.). □ **give pause to** cause (a person) to hesitate. [Latin *pausa* from Greek *pausis*, from *pauō* 'stop']

pa·vane /pəˈvan, -vɒn/ *noun* (also **pav·an** /ˈpavən/) *hist.* **1** a stately dance in elaborate clothing. **2** the music for this. [French *pavane* from Spanish *pavana*, perhaps from *pavon* peacock]

Pa·va·rotti /ˌpavəˈrɒti/ **Lu·ciano** (b.1935), Italian operatic tenor. Widely acclaimed for his bel canto singing, he has appeared in concerts throughout the world, and has made many recordings.

pave *transitive verb* **1** cover (a street, playground, etc.) with asphalt, concrete, or other densely packed material. **2** cover or strew (a floor etc.) with anything (*paved with flowers*). □ **pave the way for** make things ready for; facilitate or lead on to (an event etc.) (*paved the way for her arrival*). □ **pav·ior** /ˈpeɪvjər/ *noun* (also **pav·iour**). [Middle English from Old French *paver*, back-formation (as PAVEMENT)]

pavé /ˈpaveɪ/ *noun* a setting of jewels placed closely together so that no metal is visible. [French, past participle of *paver*: see PAVE]

pave·ment *noun* **1 a** a paved area or surface, as a roadway, playground, etc. **b** the asphalt, concrete, or densely packed stones etc. used to pave a surface. **2** *esp. Brit.* = SIDEWALK. [Old French from Latin *pavimentum* from *pavire* beat, ram]

pav·er *noun* **1** a person or machine that paves roads etc. **2** a stone, brick, etc. used in paving a surface.

pa·vil·ion /pəˈvɪljən/ ● *noun* **1** a summer house or other decorative building in a garden or park. **2** *N Amer.* a building in a park providing services such as refreshments, washrooms, change rooms, skate rental, etc. for park visitors. **3** a tent, esp. a large one with crenellated decorations at a show, fair, etc. **4** a building at a fair, exposition, multicultural festival, etc. housing displays or exhibits esp. on a common theme. **5** a detached building at a hospital. **6** a usu. highly decorated subdivision of a building. **7** the part of a cut gemstone below the girdle. **8** *Brit.* a building at a cricket or other sports ground used for changing, refreshments, etc. ● *transitive verb* enclose in or provide with a pavilion. □ **pa·vil·ioned** *adjective* [Old French *pavillon* from Latin *papilio -onis* butterfly, tent]

pav·ing *noun* **1** *in senses of* PAVE. **2** the material used to pave a surface.

paving stone *noun* a large flat usu. rectangular piece of stone etc. for paving.

Pav·lov /ˈpavlɒf/ **Ivan (Petro·vich)** (1849–1936), Russian physiologist. He was awarded a Nobel Prize in 1904 for his work on digestion, but is best known for his later studies on the conditioned reflex; he showed by experiment with dogs how the secretion of saliva can be stimulated not only by food but also by the sound of a bell associated with the presentation of food, and that this sound comes to elicit salivation when presented alone.

Pav·lo·va /pav'lo:və, ˈpavləvə/ **Anna (Pav·lov·na)** (1881–1931), Russian ballet dancer. She was the prima ballerina of the Russian Imperial Ballet (1906–13), and her highly acclaimed solo dance *The Dying Swan* was created for her by Fokine (1905); on settling in Britain (1912), she formed her own company and embarked on numerous tours all over the world.

pav·lova /pav'lo:və/ *noun esp. Austral. & NZ* a large round meringue shell filled with whipped cream and fruit. [A. PAVLOVA]

Pav·lov·ian /pav'lo:viən/ *adjective* **1** of or relating to I. P. Pavlov or his work, esp. on conditioned reflexes. **2** of the nature of a reaction or response made unthinkingly or under the influence of others.

Pavo /ˈpavo:/ a southern constellation, traditionally seen as being in the shape of a peacock. [Latin *pavo* peacock]

pavo·nine /ˈpavə,nain/ *adjective* of or like a peacock. [Latin *pavoninus* from *pavo -onis* peacock]

paw ● *noun* **1** a foot of an animal having claws or nails. **2** *informal* a person's hand. ● *verb* **1** *transitive* strike or scrape with a paw or foot. **2** *intransitive* scrape the ground with a paw or hoof. **3** *transitive informal* fondle awkwardly or indecently. [Old French *poue* etc., ultimately from Frankish]

pawky *adjective* (**pawk·i·er**, **pawk·i·est**) **1** drily humorous. **2** shrewd. □ **pawk·i·ly** *adverb* **pawk·i·ness** *noun* [Scots & Northern English dial. *pawk* trick, of unknown origin]

pawl *noun* a pivoted, usu. curved, bar or lever whose free end engages with the teeth of a cogwheel or ratchet so that it can only turn or move one way. [perhaps from Low German & Dutch *pal*, related to *pal* fixed]

Paw·ley, How·ard Rus·sell (b.1934), Canadian politician, NDP premier of Manitoba 1981–88.

pawn¹ *noun* **1** *Chess* a piece of the smallest size and value. **2** a person used by others for their own purposes. [Anglo-French *poun*, Old French *peon* from medieval Latin *pedo -onis* foot soldier, from Latin *pes pedis* foot: compare PEON]

pawn² ● *transitive verb* **1** deposit an object, esp. with a pawnbroker, as security for money lent. **2** pledge or wager (one's life, honour, word, etc.). ● *noun* an object left as security for money etc. lent. □ **in pawn** (of an object etc.) held as security. **pawn off** pass off (a responsibility, something unwanted). [Old French *pan*, *pand*, *pant*, 'pledge, security', from West Germanic]

pawn·brok·er *noun* a person who lends money at interest on the security of personal property pawned. □ **pawn·brok·ing** *noun*

Paw·nee /pɔ'ni:/ ● *noun* (pl. same or **Paw·nees**) **1** a member of a confederacy of N American Indians formerly inhabiting the valleys of the Loup, Platte, and Republican Rivers in Nebraska. **2** the Caddoan language of the Pawnee. ● *adjective* of or relating to the Pawnee or their language.

pawn·shop *noun* a shop where pawnbroking is conducted and often where property collected from defaulted loans is sold.

paw·paw *noun* (also **papaw** /pə'pɔ:/) **1** esp. *US* a N American tree, *Asimina triloba*, with purple flowers and edible fruit. **2** = PAPAYA. [earlier *papay(a)* from Spanish & Portuguese *papaya*, of Carib origin]

pax *noun* **1** (often **Pax**; usu. foll. by Latin or Modern Latin adj.) the peace or political stability due to the dominance of one state or power (*Pax Romana*; *Pax Americana*). **2** the kiss of peace. [Latin, = peace]

pay¹ ● *verb* (past and past participle **paid**) **1** *transitive & intransitive* give (a person etc.) what is due for services done, goods received, debts incurred, etc. (*paid him in full*; *I assure you I have paid*). **2** *transitive* **a** give (a usu. specified amount) for work done, a debt, a ransom, etc. (*they pay $12 an hour*). **b** (foll. by *to*) hand over the amount of (a debt, wages, recompense, etc.) to (*paid the money to the cashier*). **c** (of a stock etc.) yield (a specified return). **3** *transitive* **a** give, bestow, or express (attention, respect, a compliment, etc.) (*paid them no heed*). **b** make (a visit, a call, etc.) (*paid a visit to their uncle*). **4** *intransitive* (of a business, undertaking, attitude, etc.) be profitable or advantageous. **5** *transitive & intransitive* suffer or account for a fault etc. (*you'll pay!*; *paid the penalty*). **6** *transitive* (usu. foll. by *out*, *away*) let out (a rope etc.) by slackening it. ● *noun* wages; payment. ● *attributive adjective* designating a service or object the use of which requires payment (*pay phone*). □ **in the pay of** employed by. **pay back 1** return (money). **2** take revenge on (a person).

3 recompense (*I can never pay you back for your kindness*). **pay dearly** (usu. foll. by *for*) **1** obtain at a high cost, great effort, etc. **2** suffer for a wrongdoing etc. **pay down** reduce (debt etc.) by repayment. **pay one's dues** esp. *N Amer.* **1** fulfill one's obligations. **2** undergo hardship to succeed or gain experience. **pay for 1** hand over the price of. **2** bear the cost of. **3** suffer or be punished for (a fault etc.). **pay into** pay (money) into a bank account, savings plan, etc. **pay one's (own) way** cover costs; not be indebted. **pay one's last respects** show respect towards a dead person by attending the funeral home or funeral. **pay off 1** *informal* yield good results; succeed. **2** pay (a debt) in full. **3** dismiss (workers) with a final payment. **4** (of a ship) turn to leeward through the movement of the helm. **pay out** pay (money) from funds under one's control; spend. **pay the piper** pay the cost of an activity or undertaking. **he who pays the piper calls the tune** the person who pays the cost of an activity or undertaking has the right to control it. **pay a** (or **the**) **price** suffer a disadvantage or loss in return for a gain. **pay one's respects** make a polite visit. **pay through the nose** *informal* pay much more than a fair price. **pay up** pay the full amount. **put paid to** *informal* **1** eliminate. **2** terminate; negate. **3** deal effectively with (a person). □ **pay·ee** *noun* **pay·er** *noun* [Old French *paie*, *payer* from Latin *pacare* 'appease', from *pax pacis* 'peace']

pay² *transitive verb* (past and past participle **payed**) *Naut.* smear (a ship) with pitch, tar, etc. to make it watertight. [Old French *peier* from Latin *picare* from *pix picis* PITCH²]

pay·able ● *adjective* **1** that must be paid; due (*payable in April*). **2** that may be paid. **3** (of a mine etc.) profitable. ● *noun* (in *pl.*) debts owed by a business; liabilities.

pay-as-you-earn *noun* (often *attributive*) *Brit.* the deduction of income tax from wages at source.

pay-as-you-go *noun* (often *attributive*) a system or the practice of paying debts and meeting costs as they arise.

pay·back *noun* **1** a financial return; a reward. **2** the profit from an investment etc., esp. one equal to the initial outlay. **3** (in full **payback period**) the length of time required for an investment to pay for itself in terms of profits or savings. **4** an act of revenge or retaliation.

pay·cheque *noun* (*US* **pay·check**) **1** an esp. regular payment given to an employee. **2** a cheque for this.

pay·day *noun* **1** a day on which payment, esp. of wages, is collected or expected to be collected. **2** *N Amer. informal* the winning or gaining of a large sum, as from gambling, a contest, etc. (*a $7500 payday for her second-place finish*).

pay dirt *noun N Amer. Mining* ground worth working for ore. □ **hit** (or **strike**) **pay dirt** find or reach a source of profit or reward.

pay·down *noun* the reduction of debt through repayment.

PAYE *abbreviation Brit.* pay-as-you-earn.

pay envelope *noun N Amer.* = PAY PACKET.

pay equity *noun* the practice of ensuring that male and female employees in occupations of equal or comparable value receive equal pay.

pay·load *noun* **1 a** the part of a transport vehicle's load from which revenue is derived. **b** cargo; goods transported. **2 a** the explosive warhead carried by an aircraft or rocket. **b** the instruments etc. carried by a spaceship.

pay·master *noun* **1** an official who pays troops, workers, etc. **2** a person, organization, etc., to whom another owes duty or loyalty because of payment given.

pay·ment *noun* **1** the act or an instance of paying. **2** an amount paid. **3** reward, recompense.

pay·nim /ˈpeinim/ *noun archaic* **1** a pagan. **2** a non-Christian, esp. a Muslim. [Old French *pai(e)nime* from ecclesiastical Latin *paganismus* heathenism (as PAGAN)]

pay·off *noun informal* **1** an act of payment. **2** a deserved benefit, reward, or punishment. **3** a bribe.

pay·ola /pei'o:lə/ *noun esp. N Amer.* **1** a bribe offered in return for unofficial promotion of a product etc. in the media, esp. paid to radio disc jockeys in return for the playing of specific recordings. **2** the practice of such bribery. [PAY¹ + -OLA]

pay·out *noun* an instance of money being paid out, esp. compensation or dividends.

pay packet *noun* **1** a packet or envelope containing an employee's wages. **2** an employee's wages.

pay period *noun* the period between one payday and the next.

pay-per-view *noun* (usu. *attributive*) a television service requiring viewers to pay a fee in order to watch a specific broadcast (*a pay-per-view concert*).

pay phone *noun* a telephone operated by the insertion of coins, credit cards, phone cards, etc.

pay·roll *noun* **1** a list of employees receiving regular pay. **2** the personnel costs of a company etc.

payroll tax *noun* a tax paid by an employer calculated as a percentage of employees' salaries, the percentage being determined by the size of the payroll.

Pays Basque /peiˈi bask/ see BASQUE COUNTRY.

Pays de la Loire /peiˈi də la lwar/ a region of W France, centred on the Loire valley.

pay stub *noun* (also **pay slip**, **pay statement**) a note given to an employee when paid detailing the amount of pay, the tax, pension payments, and insurance deducted, etc.

pay-TV *noun* (also **pay television**) any television service requiring payment from viewers, esp. one in which viewers subscribe to a specific channel (compare CABLE TELEVISION; PAY-PER-VIEW).

Paz /ˈpaz/ **Oc·tavio** (1914–98), Mexican poet and essayist. His poems are noted for their preoccupation with Aztec mythology, as in *Sun Stone* (1957), and he is also known for his essays, which include *The Labyrinth of Solitude* (1950), a critique of Mexican culture, and *Postscript* (1970); he was awarded the Nobel Prize for literature in 1990.

PB *noun N Amer. informal* peanut butter. [abbreviation]

Pb *symbol Chem.* the element lead. [Latin *plumbum*]

pb. *abbreviation* paperback.

PBS *abbreviation* (in the US) Public Broadcasting System.

PBX *abbreviation* private branch exchange (a private telephone switchboard, as used by a company).

PC *abbreviation* **1** PERSONAL COMPUTER. **2** *Cdn* Progressive Conservative. **3** politically correct; political correctness. **4** *Cdn* postal code. **5** *Cdn & Brit.* privy councillor. **6** police constable. **7** protective custody.

pc *abbreviation* (in prescriptions) after food. [abbreviation of Latin *post cibum*]

pc. *abbreviation* (also **pce.**) piece (3 *pc. bath*).

p.c. *abbreviation* **1** per cent. **2** postcard.

PCB *abbreviation Chem.* polychlorinated biphenyl, any of several toxic aromatic compounds containing two benzene molecules in which hydrogens have been replaced by chlorine atoms, formed as waste in industrial processes.

PCC *abbreviation* The Presbyterian Church in Canada.

PCM *abbreviation* pulse code modulation.

PCMCIA *abbreviation Computing* Personal Computer Memory Card International Association, denoting a standard specification for memory cards and interfaces in small portable computers.

PCO *abbreviation Cdn* PRIVY COUNCIL OFFICE.

PCP *abbreviation* **1** = PHENCYCLIDINE. **2** *Med.* pneumocystis carinii pneumonia, a fatal lung infection esp. of immunodeficient patients.

PCR *abbreviation* polymerase chain reaction, a means of detecting and reproducing nucleic acid.

PCS *noun* personal communications service, a service supporting a network of compatible digital telephone and data communication facilities and devices, providing better sound quality, longer battery life, and more digital features than an analog cellular phone.

pct. *abbreviation N Amer.* per cent.

PD *abbreviation US* Police Department.

Pd *symbol Chem.* the element palladium.

pd. *abbreviation* paid.

PDA *abbreviation* PERSONAL DIGITAL ASSISTANT.

PD day *noun Cdn* PROFESSIONAL DEVELOPMENT DAY.

PDF *abbreviation* portable document format, a file format which allows documents including text, graphics, and images, to be displayed on a computer independent of the application software, hardware or operating system used to create the document.

PDL *abbreviation* PAGE DESCRIPTION LANGUAGE.

PDQ *abbreviation informal* pretty damn quick.

PDT *abbreviation* PACIFIC DAYLIGHT TIME.

PE *abbreviation* **1** physical education. **2** (in official postal use) Prince Edward Island.

p/e *abbreviation* price/earnings (ratio).

pea *noun* **1 a** a hardy climbing plant, *Pisum sativum*, of the legume family, with seeds growing in pods and used for food. **b** its seed. **2** any

of several similar leguminous plants or seeds (*sweet pea*; *chickpea*).
□ **peas in a pod** very similar or identical things, people, etc. [back-formation from PEASE (taken as pl.: compare CHERRY)]

Pea·body /ˈpiːˌbɒdi/ **George** (1795–1869), US financier and philanthropist. He amassed a fortune in banking in the US and England, and endowed a number of museums, art institutions, and libraries.

pea brain *noun informal* a stupid or dim-witted person.
□ **pea-brained** *adjective*

peace *noun* **1 a** quiet; tranquility (*needs peace to work well*). **b** mental calm; serenity (*peace of mind*). **2 a** (often *attributive*) freedom from or the cessation of war (*peace talks*). **b** (esp. **Peace**) a treaty of peace between two countries etc. at war. **3 a** freedom from civil disorder (*peace, order, and good government*). **b** freedom from quarrels or dissension between individuals; a state of friendliness. **4** *Christianity* a ritual liturgical greeting. □ **at peace 1** in a state of friendliness. **2** serene. **3** *euphemism* dead. **hold one's peace** keep silence. **keep the peace** prevent, or refrain from, strife. **make one's peace** (often foll. by *with*) re-establish friendly relations. **make peace** bring about peace; reconcile. [Anglo-French *pes*, Old French *pais* from Latin *pax pacis*]

peace·able *adjective* **1** disposed to peace; unwarlike. **2** free from disturbance; peaceful. □ **peace·able·ness** *noun* **peace·ably** *adverb* [Old French *peisible*, *plaisible* from Late Latin *placibilis* pleasing, from Latin *placēre* please]

peace bond *noun N Amer.* a written undertaking to a court of law to keep the peace, esp. to refrain from damaging property or inflicting personal injury.

Peace Corps *noun US* an organization sending young people to work as volunteers in developing countries.

peace dividend *noun* public money which becomes available when spending on defence is reduced.

peace·ful *adjective* **1** characterized by peace; tranquil. **2** not violating or infringing peace (*peaceful coexistence*). **3** pertaining to a state of peace. □ **peace·ful·ly** *adverb* **peace·ful·ness** *noun*

peace·keep·ing *noun* the active maintenance of a truce between nations or communities, esp. by international military forces (also *attributive*: *peacekeeping mission*). □ **peace·keep·er** *noun*

peace·maker *noun* a person, group, or nation who brings about peace, esp. by reconciling adversaries. □ **peace·making** *noun & adjective*

peace·nik *noun informal* a member of a pacifist movement, esp. in the 1960s and 1970s. [PEACE + -NIK]

peace offering *noun* **1** a propitiatory or conciliatory gift. **2** *Bible* an offering presented as a thanksgiving to God.

peace officer *noun* a civil officer appointed to preserve the public peace.

peace pipe *noun* CALUMET.

peace process *noun* a process of negotiation toward a peace treaty.

Peace River 1 a river in northeastern BC and N Alberta, 1 923 km long, flowing first eastward from Williston Lake to the town of Peace River, then generally northeastward to join the Slave River north of Fort Chipewyan on Lake Athabasca. **2** a town in NW central Alberta, situated at the confluence of the Peace and Smoky rivers, about 185 km northeast of Grande Prairie; pop. (2001) 6,240. □ **Peace River·ite** *noun* (in sense 2) [so called because of a peace treaty formed between the Cree and the Beaver at a point near the river's mouth]

peace sign *noun* **1** a sign of peace made by holding up the hand with the palm turned outwards and the first two fingers extended in a V-shape. **2** a symbol consisting of a circle divided into thirds by lines, with the central line extended to cover the whole diameter of the circle.

peace·time *noun* a period without war (usu. *attributive*: *peacetime troop levels*).

Peace Tower *noun* the central tower of the Centre Block of the Canadian Parliament Buildings in Ottawa, dedicated in 1927 as a memorial to Canadians who died in the First World War.

peach¹ ● *noun* **1 a** a round juicy stone fruit with downy cream or yellow skin flushed with red. **b** (in full **peach tree**) the tree, *Prunus persica*, bearing it. **2** the orange-pink colour of a peach. **3** *informal* an impressive or attractive person or thing. ● *adjective* of an orange-pink colour. [Old French *peche*, *pesche*, and medieval Latin *persica* from Latin *persicum* (*malum*), literally 'Persian apple']

peach² *verb* **1** *intransitive* (usu. foll. by *against*, *on*) *informal* turn informer;

inform. **2** *transitive archaic* inform against. [Middle English from *appeach* from Anglo-French *enpecher*, Old French *empechier* IMPEACH]

peaches and cream *noun* **1** *N Amer.* (usu. with *neg.*) an excellent or desirable situation (*it wasn't all peaches and cream*). **2** (often, with hyphens, *attributive*) a fair complexion characterized by creamy skin and pink cheeks (*Hermione's fair hair and peaches-and-cream complexion*). **3** a variety of corn with alternating white and yellow kernels.

peach fuzz *noun N Amer. informal* the down on the chin of an adolescent boy whose beard has not yet developed.

pea·chick *noun* a young peafowl. [formed as PEACOCK + CHICK]

peach Melba *noun* a dish of ice cream and peaches with raspberry sauce. [MELBA¹]

peachy *adjective* (**peach·i·er**, **peach·i·est**) **1** like a peach in colour or flavour. **2** (also **peachy-keen**) *N Amer. informal* attractive, outstanding, marvellous. □ **peach·i·ness** *noun*

pea·coat *noun* = PEA JACKET.

Pea·cock¹, **Thom·as Love** (1785–1866), English novelist and poet. He is chiefly remembered for his prose satires, including *Nightmare Abbey* (1818) and *Crotchet Castle* (1831), lampooning the romantic poets.

Pea·cock² the brightest star in the constellation Pavo. [translation of Latin *pavo*: see PAVO]

pea·cock *noun* **1** a male peafowl, having brilliant plumage and a tail (with eyelike markings) that can be expanded erect in display like a fan. **2** an ostentatious strutting person. [Middle English *pecock* from Old English *pēa* from Latin *pavo* + COCK¹]

peacock blue ● *noun* the lustrous greenish blue of a peacock's neck. ● *adjective* (hyphenated when *attributive*) of this colour.

peacock throne *noun* **1** the former throne of the Kings of Delhi, subsequently in the possession of the Shah of Persia (later Iran), adorned with precious stones forming an expanded peacock's tail. **2 (Peacock Throne)** the office of Shah of Iran (formerly Persia); the Iranian monarchy.

pea·fowl *noun* a pheasant of the genus *Pavo*, a peacock or peahen.

pea gravel *noun* gravel consisting of pea-sized particles.

pea green ● *noun* a bright green colour. ● *adjective* (hyphenated when *attributive*) of this colour.

pea·hen *noun* a female peafowl.

pea jacket *noun* a short, usu. navy blue double-breasted overcoat of coarse woollen cloth, originally worn by sailors. [prob. from Dutch *pijjakker* from *pij* coat of coarse cloth + *jekker* jacket: assimilated to JACKET]

peak¹ ● *noun* **1** a projecting usu. pointed part, esp.: **a** the pointed top of a mountain. **b** a mountain with a peak. **c** a stiff brim at the front of a cap; a visor. **d** the narrow part of a ship's hold at the bow or stern (*forepeak*; *after-peak*). **e** *Naut.* the upper outer corner of a sail extended by a gaff. **f** the highest point of a roof. **2 a** the highest point in a curve (*on the peak of the wave*). **b** the time of greatest success (in a career etc.). **c** the highest point on a graph etc. **3** (usu. in *pl.*) a pointed mass of beaten egg white, whipped cream, etc. ● *intransitive verb* reach the highest value, quality, etc. (*output peaked in September*). ● *attributive adjective* of or at the highest value, quality, frequency, rate, level, etc. (*peak shopping times*). [prob. a back-formation from *peaked*, variant of dialect *picked* 'pointed' (PICK²)]

peak² *intransitive verb* waste away; look sickly or emaciated. [16th c.: origin unknown]

Peak District a limestone plateau in Derbyshire, central England, at the southern end of the Pennines. It rises to 636 m (2,088 ft.) at Kinder Scout.

peaked¹ *adjective* having a peak. [PEAK¹]

peaked² /ˈpiːkəd/ *adjective* = PEAKY.

peaky *adjective* (**peak·i·er**, **peak·i·est**) **1** sickly. **2** white-faced. □ **peak·i·ness** *noun* [PEAK²]

peal ● *noun* **1 a** the loud ringing of a bell or bells, esp. a series of changes. **b** a set of bells. **2** a loud repeated sound, esp. of thunder, laughter, etc. ● *verb* **1** *intransitive* sound forth in a peal. **2** *transitive* utter sonorously. **3** *transitive* ring (bells) in peals. [Middle English *pele* from *apele* APPEAL]

Peale, **Nor·man Vin·cent** (1898–1993), US evangelist. Through stirring sermons, radio and television broadcasts, and publications, he attempted to bring about a spiritual renewal in the US. His bestselling book *The Power of Positive Thinking* was read by millions.

pea·meal bacon *noun Cdn* back bacon rolled in a coating of fine cornmeal. [from the former practice of coating cured meats in a meal of ground dried peas]

pea·nut *noun* **1** a leguminous plant, *Arachis hypogaea*, bearing pods that ripen underground and contain seeds used as food and yielding oil. **2** the seed of this plant. **3** (in *pl.*) *informal* a paltry or trivial thing or amount, esp. of money. **4** a piece of polystyrene foam the shape and size of a peanut, used in quantity as a packaging material. □ **pea·nutty** *adjective*

peanut butter *noun* a paste of ground roasted peanuts.

peanut gallery *noun N Amer. slang* **1** the uppermost balcony in a theatre, where the cheapest seats are. **2** a group of hecklers or rowdy spectators.

pear *noun* **1** a yellowish or brownish-green fleshy fruit, tapering towards the stalk. **2** any of various trees of the genus *Pyrus* bearing it, esp. *P. communis*. [Old English *pere*, *peru*, ultimately from Latin *pirum*]

pearl¹ ● *noun* **1 a** (often *attributive*) a usu. white or bluish-grey hard mass formed within the shell of a pearl oyster or other bivalve mollusc, highly prized as a gem for its lustre (*pearl necklace*). **b** an imitation of this. **c** (in *pl.*) a necklace of pearls. **d** (usu. *attributive*) = MOTHER-OF-PEARL. **2** a precious thing; the finest example. **3** anything resembling a pearl, e.g. a dewdrop, tear, etc. **4** an iridescent off-white colour. ● *adjective* of the colour of pearl. ● *verb* **1** *transitive poet.* **a** sprinkle with pearly drops. **b** make pearly in colour etc. **2** *transitive* reduce (barley etc.) to small rounded grains. **3** *intransitive* fish for pearl oysters. **4** *intransitive* form pearl-like drops. □ **cast pearls before swine** offer a treasure to a person unable to appreciate it. □ **pearl·er** *noun* [Old French *perle*, prob. from Latin *perna* 'leg' (applied to leg-of-mutton-shaped bivalve)]

pearl² *noun Brit.* = PICOT. [var. of PURL¹]

pearl ash *noun* commercial potassium carbonate.

pearl barley *noun* barley reduced to small round grains by grinding.

pearled *adjective* **1** adorned with pearls. **2** formed into pearl-like drops or grains. **3** pearl-coloured.

pearl·es·cent /pɜrˈlesənt/ *adjective* having or producing the appearance of mother-of-pearl. □ **pearl·es·cence** *noun*

Pearl Harbor a harbour on the island of Oahu, in Hawaii, the site of a major American naval base, where a surprise attack on 7 Dec. 1941 by Japanese carrier-borne aircraft inflicted heavy damage and brought the US into the Second World War. [translation of Hawaiian *Wai Momi*, lit. 'pearl waters']

pearl·ized *adjective* (also esp. *Brit.* **-ised**) treated so as to resemble mother-of-pearl; iridescent.

pearl millet *noun* a tall cereal, *Pennisetum americanum*.

pearl onion *noun* a very small onion, usu. pickled.

pearl oyster *noun* any of various marine bivalve molluscs of the genus *Pinctada*, esp. *P. margaritifera*, a major commercial source of pearls.

Pearl River a river of S China, flowing from Guangzhou (Canton) southward to the South China Sea and forming part of the delta of the Xi river. Its lower reaches widen to form the Pearl River estuary, the inlet between Hong Kong and Macau.

pearl tapioca *noun* a form of tapioca in small round pellets.

pearl·ware *noun* a fine white glazed earthenware.

pearly ● *adjective* (**pearl·i·er**, **pearl·i·est**) **1** resembling a pearl; lustrous. **2** containing pearls or mother-of-pearl. **3** adorned with pearls. ● *noun* (*pl.* **-ies**) (in *pl.*) *Brit. slang* teeth. □ **pearl·i·ness** *noun*

pearly everlasting *noun* a plant of the daisy family, *Anaphalis margaritacea*, covered with fine hairs and with showy flat-topped clusters of round white flower heads.

Pearly Gates *plural noun informal* the gates of Heaven.

pearly king *noun* (also **pearly queen**) *Brit.* a London costermonger wearing clothes covered with buttons made of mother-of-pearl or an imitation of it.

pearly nautilus *noun see* NAUTILUS 1.

pearly whites *plural noun informal* the teeth.

Pears /pɪərz/ **Sir Peter** (1910–86), English operatic tenor. In his lifelong partnership with Benjamin Britten he created the title roles in all Britten's operas, including those of *Peter Grimes* (1945) and *Gloriana* (1953), and founded the Aldeburgh Festival in 1948.

Pearse /pɪərs/ **Pat·rick (Henry)** (1879–1916), Irish nationalist and poet, who was a leader of the Easter Rising (1916); he was tried and executed by the British.

pear-shaped *adjective* **1** shaped like a pear; tapering towards the top. **2** (of a person) having hips that are disproportionately wide in relation to the upper body. □ **go pear-shaped** *Brit. slang* go amiss; go wrong.

Pear·son /ˈpɪərsən/ **1 John An·drew** (1867–1940), English-born

Canadian architect. Working with J. Omer Marchand, he designed the new Centre Block of Parliament (1916–24); he also designed the Peace Tower (1927). **2 Karl** (1857–1936), English mathematician, and the principal founder of 20th-c. statistics. He applied statistical analysis to the fields of heredity and evolution, defined the concept of standard deviation, and devised the chi-square test. **3 Les·ter Bowles** ('Mike') (1897–1972), Canadian diplomat and politician. He became Canada's first ambassador to the US in 1945 and deputy minister of external affairs in 1946. Made minister of external affairs in 1948, he was president of the UN assembly in 1952, and was awarded the 1957 Nobel Peace Prize for his role in mediating the Suez Crisis (1956). Chosen Liberal leader in 1958, he was prime minister 1963–68; his government oversaw the adoption of the Canada Pension Plan, universal medicare, and the Maple Leaf flag.

Peary /ˈpɪri/ **Rob·ert Edwin** (1856–1920), US explorer. He made eight Arctic voyages before becoming the first person to reach the North Pole on 6 Apr. 1909.

Peary caribou noun a small caribou of the Arctic islands of Canada. [R.E. PEARY]

Peary Land a mountainous region on the Arctic coast of N Greenland. [R.E. PEARY, who explored it in 1892 and 1900.]

peas·ant /ˈpezənt/ ● noun **1** a usu. poor farmer of low social status who owns or rents a small piece of land for cultivation (chiefly in historical use or with reference to subsistence farming in poorer countries). **2** derogatory an ignorant, stupid, or unsophisticated person. ● adjective **1** of, pertaining to, or characteristic of peasants. **2** (of a style of dress, art, etc.) inspired by Western folk traditions (a peasant dress). □ **peas·anty** adjective [Anglo-French paisant, Old French paisent, from pais 'country', ultimately from Latin pagus 'canton']

peas·ant·ry /ˈpezəntri/ noun peasants collectively.

Peasants' Revolt an uprising in England (1381). Poor economic conditions and repressive legislation led to public unrest which culminated in revolt among the peasant and artisan classes, a mass of whom marched on London and executed unpopular ministers. After the death of their leader, Wat Tyler, the rebels were persuaded to disperse by Richard II, who granted some of their demands. Afterwards the government went back on its promises and rapidly re-established control.

pease /piːz/ noun (pl. same) archaic = PEA. [Old English pise pea, pl. pisan, from Late Latin pisa from Latin pisum from Greek pison: compare PEA]

pease pudding noun **1** Brit. boiled split peas (served esp. with boiled ham). **2** (also **pease-souper**) N Amer. a thick yellowish fog. **3** Cdn (also **pea-souper**) dated slang offensive (also, with hyphen, attributive) a French Canadian.

pea·shoot·er noun a toy weapon consisting of a small tube through which peas, rolled paper, or other pellets are propelled by blowing.

pea soup noun **1** a thick soup, usu. dull yellow or green, made from dried split peas. **2** (also **pea-souper**) informal a thick yellowish fog. **3** Cdn (also **pea-souper**) dated slang offensive (also, with hyphen, attributive) a French Canadian.

peat noun **1** vegetable matter partly decomposed in wet acid conditions to form a brown deposit like soil, used for fuel, in gardening, etc. **2** a cut piece of this. □ **peaty** adjective [Anglo-Latin peta, perhaps from Celtic: compare PIECE]

peat bog noun a bog composed of peat.

peat·land noun land consisting largely of peat.

peat moss noun **1** any of various mosses of the genus Sphagnum, which grow in damp conditions and form peat as they decay. **2** such moss when dried, used in gardening as a mulch, soil conditioner, etc.

peau de soie /ˌpoʊdəˈswɒ/ noun a smooth finely-ribbed satiny fabric of silk or rayon. [French, = skin of silk]

pea·vey /ˈpiːvi/ noun (also **peavy**) (pl. **pea·veys, pea·vies**) N Amer. a logging implement consisting of a long pole ending in a metal spike and hinged hook. [J. Peavey, its US inventor]

pea vine noun **1** any of various leguminous plants esp. of the genus Lathyrus. **2** the climbing stem and leaves of the pea, esp. when dried as hay.

peb·ble ● noun **1** a small smooth stone worn by the action of water. **2** a dimpled texture, as of leather, the ice surface in curling, etc. **3** an agate or other gem, esp. when found as a pebble in a stream etc. ● verb **1** transitive give a dimpled texture to (leather, the ice surface in curling, etc.) **2** intransitive (of the skin etc.) assume a dimpled texture. □ **peb·bled** adjective **peb·bly** adjective [Old English papel-stān 'pebble-stone', pyppelripig 'pebble-stream', of unknown origin]

pebble-dash noun mortar with pebbles in it used as a coating for external walls. □ **pebble-dashed** adjective

pec noun (usu. in pl.) informal a pectoral muscle. [abbreviation]

pe·can /ˈpiːkan, piˈkan, pəˈkɒn/ noun **1** a pinkish-brown smooth nut with an edible kernel. **2** a hickory, Carya illinoensis, of the southern US, producing this. [earlier paccan, of Algonquian origin]

pec·ca·dillo /ˌpekəˈdɪloː/ noun (pl. **-loes** or **-los**) a trifling offence; a minor sin. [Spanish pecadillo, diminutive of pecado sin, from Latin (as PECCANT)]

pec·cant /ˈpekənt/ adjective formal sinning; guilty of an offence. □ **pec·can·cy** noun [French peccant or Latin peccare sin]

pec·cary /ˈpekəri/ noun (pl. **-ies**) any of several dark-furred gregarious pig-like mammals of the family Tayassuidae, which inhabit forest and forest scrub in Central and S America. [Carib pakira]

Pe·chen·ga /ˈpetʃɪŋgə/ a region of NW Russia, lying west of Murmansk on the border with Finland. Formerly part of Finland, it was ceded to the Soviet Union in 1940. It was known by its Finnish name, Petsamo, from 1920 until 1944.

Pe·chora River /pəˈtʃɔrə/ a river of N Russia, which rises in the Urals and flows some 1 800 km (1,125 miles) north and east to the Barents Sea.

Peck, (El·dred) Greg·ory (1916–2003), US actor. His many films ranged from the Hitchcock thriller Spellbound (1945) to the western The Big Country (1958); his most celebrated role was as the lawyer Atticus, defending a black man charged with rape, in To Kill a Mockingbird (1962).

peck[1] ● verb **1** transitive strike or bite (something) with a beak or pointed instrument. **2** transitive kiss (esp. a person's cheek) hastily or perfunctorily. **3** transitive **a** make (a hole) by pecking. **b** (foll. by out, off) remove or pluck out by pecking. **4** intransitive informal (foll. by at) eat (food) listlessly; nibble (at). **5** transitive (also foll. by away, out) type at a keyboard. ● noun **1 a** a stroke or bite with a beak or pointed instrument. **b** a mark made by this. **2** a hasty or perfunctory kiss. □ **peck at 1** eat (food) listlessly; nibble. **2** carp at; nag. **3** strike (a thing) repeatedly with a beak. [prob. from Middle Low German pekken, of unknown origin]

peck[2] noun **1 a** (in Britain and other Commonwealth countries) a measure of capacity for dry goods, equal to 2 imperial gallons (9.09 litres). **b** (in the US) a measure of capacity for dry goods, equal to 8 US quarts (8.81 litres). **2** a vessel used to contain this amount. □ **a peck of** a large number or amount of (troubles, dirt, etc.). [Anglo-French pek, of unknown origin]

peck·er noun **1** esp. N Amer. coarse slang the penis. **2** a bird that pecks (woodpecker). □ **keep your pecker up** Brit. informal remain cheerful.

pecker·head noun N Amer. coarse slang an aggressive objectionable person.

pecker·wood noun US derogatory a white person, esp. a poor one. [from WOODPECKER with reversal of the elements]

Peck·ford, Al·fred Brian (b.1942), Canadian politician, Progressive Conservative premier of Newfoundland 1979–89.

pecking order noun **1** a hierarchy based on rank or status. **2** a pattern of behaviour first observed in hens and later recognized in other groups of social animals, in which those of high rank within the group are able to attack those of lower rank without provoking an attack in return.

peck·ish adjective informal moderately hungry.

pec·or·ino /ˌpekəˈriːnoː/ noun (pl. **-inos**) an Italian cheese made from ewes' milk. [Italian from pecorino (adj.) of ewes, from pecora sheep]

Pécs /peitʃ/ an industrial city in SW Hungary; pop. (est. 2002) 163,100.

pec·ten /ˈpektɪn/ noun (pl. **pec·tens** or **pec·tines** /-tɪˌniːz/) Zool. **1** a comb-like structure of various kinds in animal bodies. **2** any bivalve mollusc of the genus Pecten. Also called SCALLOP. □ **pec·tin·ate** /-nət/ adjective (in sense 1). [Latin pecten pectinis comb]

pec·tin /ˈpektɪn/ noun any of various soluble gelatinous polysaccharides found in ripe fruits etc. and used as a setting agent in jams and jellies. □ **pec·tic** adjective [Greek pēktos congealed, from pēgnumi make solid]

pec·tor·al /ˈpektərəl/ ● adjective **1** of or relating to the breast or chest; thoracic (pectoral fin; pectoral muscle). **2** worn on the chest (pectoral cross). ● noun **1** (esp. in pl.) a pectoral muscle. **2** a pectoral fin. **3** an ornamental breastplate esp. of a Jewish high priest. [Latin pectorale pectus pectoris breast, chest]

pectoral sandpiper noun a migratory Arctic-breeding sandpiper, Calidris melanotos, which often has dark streaked markings on the breast.

pecu·late /ˈpekjʊˌleɪt/ transitive & intransitive verb embezzle (money).

uː mood aɪ my əɪ pipe aʊ brown ʌʊ house eɪ day ɔɪ boy ã franglais ã Canadien ɔ̃ Brayon   (see over for consonants)

□ **pecu·la·tion** noun **pecu·la·tor** noun [Latin *peculari* related to *peculium*: see PECULIAR]

pe·cu·liar /pəˈkjuːliːər/ ● adjective **1** strange; odd; unusual (*a peculiar flavour*; *is a little peculiar*). **2 a** (usu. foll. by *to*) belonging exclusively (*a fashion peculiar to the time*). **b** belonging to the individual (*their own peculiar brand of art*). **3** particular; special (*a point of peculiar interest*). **4** designating the motion of an individual star etc. relative to the system of which it is a part, esp. that component of its proper motion which is not due to parallax. ● noun *Brit.* a parish or church exempt from the jurisdiction of the diocese in which it lies. [Latin *peculiaris* of private property, from *peculium* from *pecu* cattle]

pe·cu·li·ar·ity /pəˌkjuːliˈerɪti/ noun (pl. **-ities**) **1 a** idiosyncrasy; unusualness; oddity. **b** an instance of this. **2** a distinguishing characteristic or habit (*meanness is his peculiarity*). **3** the state of being peculiar.

pe·cu·liar·ly adverb **1** more than usually; especially (*peculiarly annoying*). **2** oddly. **3** as regards an individual or a group of individuals alone (*that peculiarly Canadian political animal, the red Tory*).

pe·cu·ni·ary /pəˈkjuːniˌeri/ adjective **1** of, concerning, or consisting of, money (*pecuniary aid*; *pecuniary considerations*). **2** (of an offence) entailing a money penalty or fine. □ **pe·cu·ni·ar·ily** adverb [Latin *pecuniarius* from *pecunia* money, from *pecu* cattle]

peda·gogue /ˈpedəˌɡɒɡ/ noun a teacher. [Latin *paedagogus* from Greek *paidagōgos* from *pais paidos* boy + *agōgos* guide]

peda·gogy /ˈpedəˌɡɒdʒi/ noun (pl. **-gies**) the art or science of teaching. □ **peda·gogic** /-ˈɡɒdʒɪk/ adjective **peda·go·gics** /-ˈɡɒdʒɪks/ noun **peda·gog·ic·al** /-ˈɡɒdʒɪkəl/ adjective **peda·gog·ic·ally** /-ˈɡɒdʒɪkli/ adverb [French *pédagogie* from Greek *paidagōgia* (as PEDAGOGUE)]

pedal¹ /ˈpedəl/ ● noun **1** any of several types of foot-operated levers or controls for mechanisms, esp.: **a** either of a pair of levers for transmitting power to a bicycle or tricycle wheel etc. **b** any of the foot-operated controls in a motor vehicle. **c** any of the foot-operated keys of an organ used for playing notes, or for drawing out several stops at once etc. **d** each of the foot-levers on a piano etc. for making the tone fuller or softer. **e** any foot-operated lever on various other musical instruments, as a harpsichord, kettledrum, etc. **f** a foot-operated device for producing any of various sound effects on an electric guitar. **2** a note sustained in one part, usu. the bass, through successive harmonies, some of which are independent of it. ● verb (**ped·alled**, **ped·al·ling**; esp. *US* **ped·aled**, **ped·al·ing**) **1** intransitive operate a bicycle, organ, etc. by using the pedals. **2** transitive work (a bicycle etc.) with the pedals. □ **pedal to the metal** *N Amer.* **1** full speed, full out. **2** with the gas pedal of a vehicle pressed completely to the floor. □ **ped·al·ler** noun (also **ped·al·er**). [French *pédale* via Italian *pedale* from Latin (as PEDAL²)]

pedal² /ˈpedəl, ˈpiːdəl/ adjective *Zool.* of the foot or feet (esp. of a mollusc). [Latin *pedalis* from *pes pedis* foot]

pedal boat noun a small recreational pontoon boat usu. with paddlewheels, propelled by means of pedals.

pedal car noun a toy car big enough for a child to sit in, propelled by means of pedals.

ped·alo /ˈpedəˌloʊ/ noun (pl. **-alos**) *Brit.* = PEDAL BOAT.

pedal-pusher noun (in *pl.*) women's calf-length trousers.

pedal steel noun (in full **pedal steel guitar**) an electric guitar played like the Hawaiian guitar, but fixed on a stand and connected to pedals for altering the string tension.

ped·ant /ˈpedənt/ noun **1** a person excessively concerned with trifling details or who insists on strict adherence to formal rules or literal meaning at the expense of a wider view. **2** a person who parades or reveres academic learning or technical knowledge above everything. **3** a person obsessed by a theory; a doctrinaire. □ **ped·an·tic** /pəˈdæntɪk/ adjective **ped·an·tic·ally** /pəˈdæntɪkli/ adverb **ped·ant·ry** noun (pl. **-ries**). [French *pédant* from Italian *pedante*: apparently formed as PEDAGOGUE]

ped·ate /ˈpedeɪt/ adjective **1** *Zool.* having feet. **2** *Bot.* (of a leaf) having divisions like toes or a bird's claws. [Latin *pedatus* from *pes pedis* foot]

ped·dle verb **1** transitive sell (goods), esp. in small quantities, as a peddler. **2** transitive sell (goods). **3** transitive advocate or promote (ideas, a philosophy, a way of life, etc.). **4** intransitive engage in selling as a peddler. **5** transitive sell (drugs) illegally. [back-formation from PEDDLER]

ped·dler noun (also **ped·lar**) **1** a travelling seller of small items esp. carried in a pack etc. **2 a** a person who sells drugs illegally. **b** (usu. foll. by *of*) a retailer of gossip etc. [Middle English *pedlere* alteration of *pedder* from *ped* pannier, of unknown origin]

ped·er·ast /ˈpedəˌrast/ noun a man who engages in pederasty.

ped·er·asty /ˈpedəˌrasti/ noun sexual relations between a man and a boy, esp. anal intercourse. [modern Latin *paederastia* from Greek *paiderastia* from *pais paidos* boy + *erastēs* lover]

ped·es·tal /ˈpedəstəl/ noun **1** a base supporting a column or pillar. **2** the stone etc. base of a statue etc. **3** either of the two supports at either end of the writing surface of a desk, usu. containing drawers. **4** (often *attributive*) an upright, column-like support for a seat, machine, etc. (*pedestal seat*; *pedestal sink*). □ **put** (or **set**) **on a pedestal** admire disproportionately, idolize. [French *piédestal* via Italian *piedestallo*, from *piè* 'foot' (from Latin *pes pedis*) + *di* 'of' + *stallo* STALL¹]

pedestal table noun a table with a single central support.

ped·es·trian /pəˈdestrɪən/ ● noun a person on foot rather than in a vehicle. ● adjective **1** (esp. of writing) prosaic; dull; uninspired. **2** of, pertaining to, reserved for, or adapted for walkers or walking (*pedestrian mall*; *pedestrian traffic*). [French *pédestre* or Latin *pedester -tris*]

pedestrian crossing noun a demarcated area of a road where pedestrians have the right of way to cross.

ped·es·trian·ize /pəˈdestrɪənaɪz/ transitive verb (also esp. *Brit.* **-ise**) close (part of an urban area) to vehicular traffic and make accessible only to pedestrians. □ **ped·es·trian·iz·a·tion** noun

pedi·at·rics /ˌpiːdiˈatrɪks/ plural noun (treated as *sing.*) (also esp. *Brit.* **paedi·at·rics**) the branch of medicine dealing with children and their diseases. □ **pedi·at·ric** adjective **pedia·tri·cian** /-əˈtrɪʃən/ noun [PEDO- + Greek *iatros* physician]

pedi·cab /ˈpediˌkab/ noun a small pedal-operated vehicle, usu. a rickshaw-like tricycle, serving as a taxi.

pedi·cel /ˈpedɪsəl/ noun a small (esp. subordinate) stalklike structure in a plant or animal, esp. each stalk bearing an individual flower in a branched inflorescence (*compare* PEDUNCLE 1). □ **pedi·cel·late** /-səˌleɪt/ adjective [modern Latin *pedicellus* & Latin *pediculus* diminutive of *pes pedis* foot]

ped·icle /ˈpedɪkəl/ noun **1** *Anat.* & *Zool.* a small stalklike structure, esp. one supporting a seed, gland, tumour, etc. (*compare* PEDICEL). **2** *Med.* part of a graft, esp. a skin graft, left temporarily attached to its original site. □ **pe·dicu·lat·ed** /pɪˈdɪkjuleɪtəd/ adjective [Latin *pediculus*, diminutive of *ped pedis* 'foot']

pe·dicu·li·cide /ˌpedɪˈkjuːləˌsaɪd/ noun a substance that kills lice. [from Latin *pediculus* louse]

pe·dicu·lo·sis /pəˌdɪkjʊˈloʊsɪs/ noun an infestation with lice. [from Latin *pediculus* louse]

pedi·cure /ˈpediˌkjʊr/ ● noun **1** treatment of the feet, either remedial, as in the removal of corns and bunions, or cosmetic, as in the trimming, painting, etc. of the toenails. **2** a session of such treatment. ● transitive verb treat (the feet) by removing corns etc. □ **pedi·cur·ist** noun [French *pédicure* from Latin *pes pedis* foot + *curare*: see CURE]

pedi·gree /ˈpediˌɡriː/ noun **1** (often *attributive*) a recorded line of descent of a person or esp. a purebred domestic or pet animal. **2** *informal* the history of a person, thing, idea, etc., esp. a list of achievements. **3** the derivation of a word etc. **4** a genealogical table. □ **pedi·greed** adjective [Middle English *pedegru* etc. from Anglo-French from Old French *pie de grue* (unrecorded) crane's foot, a mark denoting succession in pedigrees]

pedi·ment /ˈpedɪmənt/ noun **1 a** the triangular part crowning the front of a building in the classical style. **b** a similar part of a building in other styles, irrespective of shape. **c** a similar feature surmounting and abutting on a niche, door, window, etc. **2** *Geol.* a broad flattish rock surface at the foot of a mountain slope. □ **pedi·men·tal** /-ˈmentəl/ adjective **pedi·ment·ed** adjective [earlier *pedament*, *periment*, perhaps corruption of PYRAMID]

ped·lar noun var. of PEDDLER.

pedo- /ˈpiːdoː, ˈpedoː/ combining form (also esp. *Brit.* **paedo-**) child. [Greek *pais paid-* child]

pe·dol·ogy /pəˈdɒlədʒi/ noun the scientific study of soil, esp. its formation, nature, and classification. □ **pedo·logic·al** /ˌpedəˈlɒdʒɪkəl/ adjective **pedo·ol·o·gist** noun [Russian *pedologiya* from Greek *pedon* ground]

ped·om·eter /pəˈdɒmɪtər/ noun an instrument for estimating the distance travelled on foot by recording the number of steps taken. [French *pédomètre* from Latin *pes pedis* foot]

pedo·phile /ˈpedəˌfaɪl, ˈpiːd-/ noun (also esp. *Brit.* **paedo·phile**) a person who displays pedophilia.

pedo·philia /ˌpedəˈfɪliə/ noun (also esp. *Brit.* **paedo·philia**) sexual desire directed towards children. □ **pedo·phil·iac** adjective

Pedro I /ˈpeɪdroː, ˈped-/ (1798–1834), first emperor of Brazil 1822–31. He declared Brazilian independence from Portugal in 1822, and was subsequently crowned emperor; he abdicated in favour of his son Pedro II.

Pedro II /ˈpeidrɔː, ˈped-/ (1825–91), second and last emperor of Brazil 1831–89, son of Pedro I. He oversaw the abolition of slavery, and was forced to abdicate in 1889.

Pedro Ximen·ez /ˈpeidrɔː hiˈmeineθ/ *noun* **1** a large sweet white Andalusian grape esp. from the Jerez region, used in making sherry or an extremely sweet, raisin-flavoured wine. **2** the wine itself. [the name of its Spanish originator]

ped·uncle /pəˈdʌŋkəl/ *noun* **1** *Bot.* the stalk of a flower, fruit, or cluster, esp. a main stalk bearing a solitary flower or subordinate stalks (compare PEDICEL). **2** *Zool.* a stalklike projection in an animal body, e.g. an eye-stalk of a crustacean, the pedicle of a tumour, a bundle of nerve fibres connecting two parts of the brain, etc. □ **ped·un·cu·lar** /-kjʊlər/ *adjective* [modern Latin *pedunculus* from Latin *pes pedis* foot: see -UNCLE]

ped·un·cu·late /pəˈdʌŋkjʊlət/ *adjective* (also **ped·un·cu·lat·ed** /pəˈdʌŋkjʊleitəd/) *Bot. & Zool.* having a peduncle or peduncles.

ped·way *noun* esp. *N Amer.* a walkway designed to separate pedestrians from urban traffic. [PEDESTRIAN + WAY]

pee *informal* ● *verb* (**pees, peed**) **1** *intransitive* urinate. **2** *transitive* pass (urine etc.) from the bladder. **3** *reflexive* urinate into one's clothes. **4** *transitive* wet (esp. bedclothes, one's clothing) by urinating. ● *noun* **1** an act of urination. **2** urine. □ **peed off** annoyed. [initial letter of PISS]

Peebles·shire /ˈpiːbəlz, ʃɪr/ a former county of S Scotland. It became a part of Borders region (now Scottish Borders) in 1975.

peek ● *intransitive verb* (usu. foll. by *in, out, at*) look quickly or slyly; peep, esp. through a crevice, out of or into a recess, etc. ● *noun* a quick or furtive look. [Middle English *pike, pyke*, of unknown origin]

peek·a·boo ● *noun* the game of hiding one's face and suddenly revealing it, as played by an older person with a young child. ● *interjection* the utterance made when doing this. ● *adjective* (of a garment etc.) transparent or having a pattern of small holes so as to reveal the skin etc. beneath. [PEEK + BOO]

Peel ▶ **1 Paul** (1860–92), Canadian painter. Born in London, Canada West, he spent most of his working life in Paris and was one of the first Canadian painters to paint nudes. His works, such as *A Venetian Bather* and *After the Bath* (1890), demonstrate great skill in using light and colour. **2 Sir Rob·ert** (1788–1850), English Conservative politician, prime minister 1834–5 and 1841–6. During his second term as Home Secretary (1828–30), he established the London Metropolitan Police (and gave his name to the nicknames *bobby* and *peeler*); his repeal of the Corn Laws in 1846 split the Conservatives and forced his resignation.

peel¹ ● *verb* **1** *transitive* **a** strip the skin, rind, bark, wrapping, etc. from (a fruit, vegetable, tree, etc.). **b** (usu. foll. by *off*) strip (skin, peel, wrapping, etc.) from a fruit etc. **2** *intransitive* **a** (of a tree, an animal's or person's body, a painted surface, etc.) have the outer layer of bark, skin, paint, etc. flake off. **b** (often foll. by *off*) (of bark, a person's skin, paint, etc.) flake off. **3 a** *transitive* remove or separate (a label, a banknote, etc.) from the outside or top of something. **b** *transitive* turn back so as to expose something underneath (*lips peeled back*). **4** *intransitive* separate from a body of people, vehicles, etc. (*the flagship peeled away from the smaller ships*). **5 a** *transitive* (often foll. by *off*) *informal* (of a person) take off (one's outer or all one's clothes). **b** *intransitive* (foll. by *down*) undress. **6** *intransitive* *N Amer.* (usu. foll. by *out, away*, etc.) (of a vehicle etc.) move quickly, leave a place, etc. suddenly (*peeled out of her driveway; the police peeled after him*). **7** *transitive & intransitive* *Curling* remove (a rock) from play with a rock that itself also goes out of play. ● *noun* **1** the outer covering of a fruit, vegetable, shrimp, etc.; rind. **2** the chemical removal of superficial layers of skin on the face, usu. to remove scars etc. **3** *Curling* an instance of peeling a rock (also *attributive: peel game*). □ **keep one's eyes peeled** see EYE. **peel off** veer away and detach oneself from a group of marchers, a formation of aircraft, etc. □ **peel·able** *adjective* [earlier *pill, pele* (originally = plunder) from Middle English *pilien* etc. from Old English *pilian* (unrecorded) from Latin *pilare* from *pilus* hair]

peel² *noun* a pole with a broad flat disc at one end by means of which loaves, pizzas, etc. are placed in and removed from an oven. [Old French *pele* from Latin *pala*, related to *pangere* fix]

peel³ *noun* (also **pele**) *hist.* a small square tower built in the 16th c. in the border counties of England and Scotland for defence against raids. [Middle English *pel* stake, palisade, from Old French *pel* from Latin *palus* stake: compare PALE²]

peel·er¹ *noun* **1 a** a kitchen utensil for peeling fruit etc. **b** a person who or thing which peels trees etc. **2** *US slang* a cowboy. **3** (in full **peeler crab**) a crab when it casts its shell. **4** *N Amer. informal* a stripper.

peel·er² *noun Brit. slang* a police officer. [Sir R. PEEL]

peel·ing *noun* a strip of the outer skin of a vegetable, fruit, etc. (*potato peelings*).

Peel River a river in N Yukon and the northwestern NWT, 684 km long, rising north of the Mackenzie Mountains and flowing first eastward, then northward into the NWT to join the Mackenzie River south of Inuvik. [Sir R. PEEL]

peen ● *noun* the wedge-shaped or thin or curved end of a hammer-head (opp. FACE *noun* 5a). ● *transitive verb* **1** hammer with a peen. **2** (usu. as **peen·ing** *noun*) treat (sheet metal) with a stream of metal shot in order to shape it. [17th c.: also *pane*, apparently from French *panne* from Dutch *pen* from Latin *pinna* point]

Peene·munde /ˌpeinəˈmʊndə/ a village in NE Germany, on a small island just off the Baltic coast. It was the chief site during the Second World War of German rocket research and testing.

peep¹ ● *intransitive verb* **1** (usu. foll. by *at, in, out, into*) look quickly and secretly, esp. through a small opening. **2** (usu. foll. by *out*) **a** come slowly into view; emerge. **b** (of a quality etc.) show itself unconsciously. ● *noun* **1** a furtive or peering glance. **2** the first appearance. [Middle English: compare PEEK, PEER¹]

peep² ● *intransitive verb* make a shrill feeble sound as of young birds, mice, etc.; squeak; chirp. ● *noun* **1** such a sound. **2** a slight sound, utterance, or complaint (*not a peep out of them*). **3** *N Amer.* any of several sandpipers. [imitative: compare CHEEP]

pee-pee *noun informal* **1** urine. **2** the penis. [childish reduplication of PEE]

peep·er¹ *noun* **1** a person who peeps. **2** *informal* (usu. in *pl.*) an eye. **3** *N Amer. slang* a private investigator.

peep·er² *noun* = SPRING PEEPER.

peep·hole *noun* a small hole that may be looked through.

peeping Tom *noun* a person who surreptitiously observes others, esp. women undressing. [in the story of Lady Godiva, the only person who looked out as she rode by naked]

peep show *noun* **1** a show of live nudes or an erotic film viewed from a coin-operated booth. **2** an exhibition of small pictures viewed through a magnifying lens placed in a small opening of a box etc.

peep sight *noun* a back sight for rifles with a slit for bringing the foresight into line with the object aimed at.

peep-toe *adjective* (also **peep-toed**) *Brit.* (of a shoe) leaving the toes partly bare; open-toed.

pee·pul /ˈpiːpəl/ *noun* (also **pipal**) = BO TREE. [Hindi *pipal* from Sanskrit *pippala*]

peer¹ *intransitive verb* **1** (usu. foll. by *into, at*, etc.) look keenly or with difficulty (*peered into the fog*). **2** peep out. **3** *archaic* come into view. [var. of *pire*, Low German *piren*; perhaps partly from APPEAR]

peer² *noun* **1** a person who is equal in ability, standing, rank, or value (*tried by a jury of his peers*). **2 a** a member of one of the degrees of the nobility in Britain, i.e. a duke, marquess, earl, viscount, or baron. **b** a noble or person of high rank of any country. □ **without peer** unequalled, unrivalled. □ **peer·less** *adjective* [Old French *peer* from Latin *par* equal]

peer·age *noun* **1** peers as a class; the nobility. **2** the rank of peer or peeress (*was given a life peerage*). **3** a book containing a list of peers with their genealogy etc.

peer·ess /ˈpiːrəs/ *noun* **1** the wife or widow of a peer. **2** a woman having the rank of a peer by creation or descent.

peer group *noun* a group of people of the same age, status, interests, etc.

peer of the realm *noun* (also **peer of the United Kingdom**) *Brit.* any of the class of hereditary peers whose adult members may all sit in the House of Lords.

peer pressure *noun* influence from members of one's peer group.

peer review *noun* **1** the evaluation by (other) experts of a research project for which a grant is sought, a paper received for publication, etc. **2** a review of commercial, professional, or academic efficiency, competence, etc. by others in the same occupation. □ **peer review** *transitive verb* **peer-reviewed** *adjective* **peer reviewer** *noun*

peer-to-peer *adjective Computing* designating or relating to a network in which each computer can act as a server for the others, allowing shared access to files and peripherals without the need for a central server.

peeve *informal* ● *noun* a cause of annoyance. ● *transitive verb* (usu. in passive) annoy. [back-formation from PEEVISH]

peev·ish *adjective* **1** easily annoyed, esp. by unimportant things;

---

t *top*   v *voice*   w *we*   z *zoo*   ʃ *she*   ʒ *vision*   θ *thin*   ð *this*   ŋ *ring*   x *loch*   tʃ *chip*   dʒ *jar*   (*see over for vowels*)

bad-tempered. **2** (of a quality, action, etc.) characterized by or exhibiting petty vexation or spite. □ **peev·ish·ly** *adverb* **peev·ish·ness** *noun* [Middle English, = foolish, mad, spiteful, etc., of unknown origin]

pee·wee ● *noun* **1** *Cdn* **a** a level of amateur sport, usu. involving children aged 12–13 (also *attributive*: peewee hockey). **b** a player in this age group. **2** *US* **a** a level of amateur sport, usu. involving children aged 8 or 9 (also *attributive*: peewee hockey). **b** a player in this age group. **3** *N Amer.* a very small or young person or thing. ● *adjective* very small. [reduplication of WEE[1]]

pee·wit *noun* (also **pewit**) **1** a lapwing. **2** its cry. [imitative]

Peg *noun Cdn* (prec. by *the*) a nickname for Winnipeg. [abbreviation]

peg ● *noun* **1 a** a usu. cylindrical pin or bolt of wood, metal, etc., often tapered at one end, and used for holding esp. two things together. **b** such a peg attached to a wall etc. and used for hanging garments etc. on. **c** a peg driven into the ground and attached to a rope for holding up a tent. **d** a piton etc. to attach a rope to. **e** each of several pegs used to tighten or loosen the strings of a violin etc. **f** a small peg, matchstick, etc. stuck into holes in a board for calculating the scores at cribbage. **2** *Baseball informal* a strong, long, low throw, esp. at a base. **3** an occasion, pretext, excuse, theme, etc. (*used the incident as a peg for the article*). **4** *Brit.* = CLOTHES PEG. **5** *Brit.* a measure of liquor or wine. **6** a short blunt structure or outgrowth in a plant, animal, etc. ● *transitive verb* (**pegged**, **peg·ging**) **1 a** (usu. foll. by *down, in, out*, etc.) fix (a thing) with a peg. **b** drive or insert a peg or pegs into. **2** esp. *N Amer. informal* identify, categorize, form an opinion of (a person etc.). **3** *N Amer. informal* **a** throw (a ball) hard and low. **b** *Baseball* stop or put out (a runner) with such a throw. **4** *informal* measure, mark, set (*construction value was pegged at $5.5 million*). **5** *Econ.* **a** fix (prices, wages, exchange rates, etc.) at a certain level or in line with a certain standard. **b** prevent the price of (stock etc.) from falling or rising by freely buying or selling at a given price. **6** mark (the score etc.) with pegs, as on a cribbage board. □ **off the peg** *Brit.* (of clothes) ready-made. **peg out 1** *slang* die. **2** measure, extend, or mark the boundaries of (land etc.). **3** score the winning point at cribbage. **4** *Croquet* hit the peg with the ball as the final stroke in a game. **a round** (or **square**) **peg in a square** (or **round**) **hole** a person in a situation unsuited to his or her capacities, disposition, etc.; a misfit. **take a person down a peg or two** humble a person. [Middle English, prob. of Low German or Dutch origin: compare Middle Dutch *pegge*, Dutch dialect *peg*, Low German *pigge*]

Peg·a·sus /ˈpɛɡəsəs/ **1** *Gk Myth* a winged horse which sprang from the blood of Medusa when Perseus cut off her head. Pegasus was ridden by Perseus in his rescue of Andromeda, and by Bellerophon when he fought the Chimera. **2** *Astronomy* a large northern constellation, said to represent a winged horse. The three brightest stars, together with one star of Andromeda, form the prominent 'Square of Pegasus'.

peg·board *noun* a type of perforated board having a regular pattern of small holes for pegs.

pegged *adjective* **1** in senses of the verb. **2** (*attributive*) *N Amer.* (of a garment) wide at the top and narrow at the bottom.

Peggys Cove a fishing community on the east central coast of Nova Scotia, situated about 45 km southwest of Halifax. [prob. after *Peggy* Rodgers, Irish immigrant *c.*1770]

peg leg *informal* ● *noun* **1** an artificial leg. **2** *offensive* a person with an artificial leg. ● *adjective* **1** (also **peg-legged**) *informal* having a peg leg. **2** = PEGGED 2.

peg·ma·tite /ˈpɛɡməˌtaɪt/ *noun* a coarsely crystalline type of granite commonly occurring in igneous intrusions. □ **peg·ma·tit·ic** /-ˈtɪtɪk/ *adjective* [Greek *pēgma -atos* thing joined together, from *pēgnumi* fasten]

Pegu /peˈɡuː/ a city and river port of S Burma, on the Pegu river northeast of Rangoon; pop. (est. 2002) 228,100. Founded in 825 as the capital of the Mon kingdom, it is a centre of Buddhist culture.

Peguis /ˈpɛɡwɪs/ (*c.*1774–1864), Canadian Saulteaux chief. A prominent leader among his people in southern Manitoba, he befriended the Selkirk settlers, defending them and helping them learn how to survive in the Red River area, but later grew disillusioned by the settlers' infractions of his 1817 treaty with Lord Selkirk.

PEI *abbreviation* Prince Edward Island.

Pei /ˈpeɪ/ **Ieoh Ming** (b.1917), Chinese-born US architect. In his monumental public buildings, simple geometric forms are dramatically juxtaposed; major works include the east wing of the National Gallery of Art, Washington, DC (1971–8), and the controversial glass and steel pyramid in the forecourt of the Louvre, Paris (1989).

Pei·gan /piːˈɡan/ (also **Pie·gan**) ● *noun* **1** a member of an Aboriginal

people, a part of the Blackfoot Confederacy, living in S Alberta and NW Montana. **2** the Algonquian language of this people. ● *adjective* of or relating to this people or their culture or language. [Blackfoot *piikániwa* Peigan]

pei·gnoir /ˈpeɪnwɑr/ *noun* a woman's loose dressing gown or bathrobe. [French from *peigner* to comb]

Peirce /ˈpiːrs/ **Charles San·ders** (1839–1914), US philosopher and logician. One of the founders of American pragmatism, he proposed a theory of meaning in which the meaning of a belief or an idea is to be understood by the actions, uses, and habits to which it gives rise; he also pioneered the logic of relations, in which he argued that induction is an indispensable correlative of deduction.

Pei·sis·tra·tus see PISISTRATUS.

pe·jor·a·tive /pɪˈdʒɔrətɪv/ ● *adjective* (of a word, an expression, etc.) expressing contempt and criticism or disapproval. ● *noun* a word, derivative, phrase, etc. which by its form or context expresses contempt for the thing named; a derogatory word or form. □ **pe·jor·a·tion** /pedʒəˈreɪʃən/ *noun* **pe·jor·a·tive·ly** *adverb* [French *péjoratif -ive* from Late Latin *pejorare* make worse (*pejor*)]

pekan /ˈpɛkən/ *noun* = FISHER 1. [Canadian French from Abenaki *pékané*]

Peke *noun informal* a Pekingese dog. [abbreviation]

Pe·king see BEIJING.

Peking duck *noun* a Chinese dish consisting of duck prepared by being hung to dry, coated with honey so that it turns a deep-reddish brown, dried again, and then roasted, and served in shredded strips accompanied by vegetables, sauce, and small pancakes.

Pe·king·ese (also **Pe·kin·ese**) ● *noun* (*pl.* same) **1** a lapdog of a short-legged breed with long hair and a snub nose. **2** a citizen of Peking (Beijing). **3** the form of the Chinese language used in Beijing. ● *adjective* of or concerning Beijing or its language or citizens.

Peking man *noun* a fossil hominid described in 1926 from the remains found in caves in China and now usu. classified as *Homo erectus*.

Peking opera *noun* a stylized Chinese form of opera dating from the late 18th c., in which speech, singing, mime, and acrobatics are performed to an instrumental accompaniment.

pekoe /ˈpiːkoː/ *noun* a high-quality black tea, made from leaves picked when very young. [Chinese dial. *pek-ho* from *pek* white + *ho* down, the leaves being so young as to have down on them]

pel·age /ˈpɛlɪdʒ/ *noun* the fur, hair, wool, etc. of a mammal. [French from *poil* hair]

pela·gic /pəˈladʒɪk/ *adjective* **1** of or performed on the open sea (*pelagic whaling*). **2** (of marine life) belonging to the upper layers of the open sea (compare DEMERSAL). **3** (of a species of bird) inhabiting the open sea beyond the continental shelf and returning to shore only to breed. **4** (of sea floor material) formed within the sea, not transported from the land. [Latin *pelagicus* from Greek *pelagikos* of the sea (*pelagos*)]

pelagic cormorant *noun* a cormorant, *Phalacrocorax pelagicus*, found in Canada along the BC coast.

Pela·gius /pəˈleɪdʒəs/ (*c.*360–*c.*420), British or Irish monk. He denied the doctrines of original sin and predestination, defending innate human goodness and free will; his beliefs were opposed by St. Augustine of Hippo and condemned as heretical by the Synod of Carthage in about 418. □ **Pela·gian** *noun & adjective* **Pela·gian·ism** *noun*

pel·ar·gon·ium /ˌpɛlərˈɡoːniəm/ *noun* any plant of the genus *Pelargonium*, with red, pink, or white flowers and fragrant leaves. *Also called* GERANIUM. [modern Latin from Greek *pelargos* stork: compare GERANIUM]

Pelé /ˈpeleɪ/ (born Edson Arantes do Nascimento) (b.1940), Brazilian soccer player. Regarded as one of the greatest soccer players of all time, he played for Brazil in three World Cup championships (1958, 1962, and 1970); he ended his career with the New York Cosmos (1975–7).

pele *var. of* PEEL[3].

Pelée, Mount /pəˈleɪ/ a volcano on the island of Martinique, in the W Indies. Its eruption in 1902 destroyed the town of St. Pierre, which was at that time the island's capital, killing its population of some 30,000.

Pelee, Point /ˈpiːli/ a point in SW Ontario, southeast of Windsor. Its peninsula extends southward into Lake Erie, making it the most southerly point of the Canadian mainland. It is also the site of Point Pelee National Park. [from French *pelée* bare, with reference to its stark eastern face]

Vowels: a *cat*   ɑ *arm*   e *bed*   ɜr *her*   ɜ: *deux*   ə *ago*   ɪ *sit*   i *cosy*   iː *feed*   ɒ *hot*   ɔ *pore*   oː *no*   ʌ *run*   ʊ *put*

Pelee Island /ˈpiːli/ an island in SW Ontario, situated in Lake Erie, southwest of Point Pelee. [see PELEE, POINT]

Pel·eus /ˈpiːljəs/ Gk Myth a king of Phthia in Thessaly, who is the subject of a number of legends. His wife was the sea nymph Thetis, and their child was Achilles.

pelf noun derogatory or jocular money or riches, esp. dishonestly acquired. [Old Northern French from Old French pelfre, peufre spoils, of unknown origin: compare PILFER]

Pel·ham¹ /ˈpeləm/ a town in S Ontario, about 15 km south of St. Catharines; pop. (2001) 15,272. □ **Pel·ham·ite** noun [H. F. Pelham Clinton, 9th Earl of Lincoln and 2nd Duke of Newcastle-under-Lyme d.1794]

Pel·ham² /ˈpeləm/ noun a horse's bit combining a curb and a snaffle. [the surname Pelham]

peli·can noun any large gregarious waterfowl of the family Pelecanidae with a large bill and a pouch in the throat for storing fish. [Old English pellican & Old French pelican from Late Latin pelicanus from Greek pelekan prob. from pelekus axe, with reference to its bill]

pelican crossing noun (in the UK) a pedestrian crossing with traffic lights operated by pedestrians. [Pedestrian Light Controlled, with alteration]

Pel·ion /ˈpiːliən/ a wooded mountain in Greece, near the coast of SE Thessaly, rising to 1 548 m (5,079 ft.). In Greek mythology it was held to be the home of the centaurs, and the giants were said to have piled Mounts Olympus and Ossa on its summit in their attempt to reach heaven and destroy the gods.

pel·isse /pəˈliːs/ noun hist. **1** a woman's cloak with armholes or sleeves, reaching to the ankles. **2** a fur-lined cloak, esp. as part of a hussar's uniform. [French from medieval Latin pellicia (vestis) (garment) of fur, from pellis skin]

pel·ite /ˈpiːləɪt/ noun a sediment or sedimentary rock composed of very fine clay or mud particles. □ **pel·it·ic** /pəˈlɪtɪk/ adjective [Greek pēlos clay, mud]

pel·lagra /pəˈlagrə, -ˈleɪgrə, -ˈlɒgrə/ noun a disease caused by niacin deficiency, characterized by dermatitis, diarrhea, and mental disturbance. □ **pel·lag·rous** adjective [Italian from pelle skin, after PODAGRA]

Pel·latt /ˈpelət/ **Sir Henry Mill** (1859–1939), Canadian entrepreneur. Active in the development of hydro projects at Niagara Falls and in the transmission and distribution of electricity in Toronto, he was also involved in several transportation companies and helped to found the Canadian General Electric Co. Casa Loma, his eccentric stone mansion, has become a Toronto landmark and tourist attraction.

pel·let ● noun **1** a small, hard, compressed mass of something. **2 a** a bullet or piece of small shot. **b** an imitation bullet for a toy gun (also attributive: pellet gun). **3 a** a small mass of bones, feathers, etc. regurgitated by a bird of prey. **b** a small hard piece of animal excreta. ● transitive verb (**pel·let·ed**, **pel·let·ing**) **1** make into a pellet or pellets. **2** hit with pellets. □ **pel·let·ize** transitive verb (also esp. Brit. **-ise**).
pel·let·iz·a·tion noun **pel·let·iz·er** noun **pel·let·iz·ing** noun & adjective [Middle English from Old French pelote from Latin pila ball]

Pel·le·tier /ˈpeltjeɪ/ **1** Gérard (1919–97), Canadian journalist and politician. He was a reporter with Le Devoir (1947–50) and editor of La Presse (1961–64). With Pierre Trudeau and others, he founded Cité Libre to denounce the regressive and oppressive tactics of the Duplessis government. An opponent of separatism, he was secretary of state for external affairs (1968–72) and minister of communications (1972–75) in the federal government before becoming ambassador to France (1975–81) and ambassador to the UN (1981–84). **2** Pierre-Joseph (1788–1842), French chemist. He specialized in plant products, and is best known as the founder of alkaloid chemistry, having isolated a number of alkaloids for the first time with his friend J.-B. Caventou (1795–1877); he and Caventou also isolated the green pigment of leaves and gave it the name chlorophyll. **3** Wil·fred (or Baibomsey) (1927–2000), Canadian Odawa philosopher and author. Especially interested in education, he was active in experiments in alternative learning and in the application of Native wisdom to problems affecting all people.

pel·licle /ˈpelɪkəl/ noun a thin skin, membrane, or film covering a surface, enclosing a cavity, etc. □ **pel·licu·lar** /-ˈlɪkjʊlər/ adjective [French pellicule from Latin pellicula, diminutive of pellis skin]

pel·li·tory /ˈpelɪˌtɒri/ noun (pl. **-ies**) any of several wild plants, esp.:
1 (in full **pellitory of Spain**) a composite plant, Anacyclus pyrethrum, with a pungent-flavoured root, used as a local irritant etc. **2** (in full **pellitory of the wall**) a low bushy plant, Parietaria judaica, with greenish flowers growing on or at the foot of walls. [(sense 1) alteration of Middle English from Old French peletre, peretre from Latin

pyrethrum from Greek purethron feverfew: (sense 2), ultimately from Old French paritaire from Late Latin parietaria from Latin paries -etis wall]

pell-mell ● adverb **1** headlong, recklessly (rushed pell-mell out of the room). **2** in disorder or confusion (stuffed the papers together pell-mell). ● adjective confused, tumultuous. ● noun confusion; a mixture. [French pêle-mêle, Old French pesle mesle, mesle pesle, etc., reduplication of mesle from mesler mix]

pel·lu·cid /pəˈluːsɪd, -ˈljuːsɪd/ adjective **1 a** (of water, light, etc.) transparent, clear. **b** (of sound, esp. music) clear, pure, uncluttered. **2** (of style, speech, etc.) not confused; clear. **3** mentally clear. □ **pel·lu·cid·ity** /-ˈsɪdɪti/ noun **pel·lu·cid·ly** adverb [Latin pellucidus from perlucēre (as PER-, lucēre shine)]

Pelly Bay 1 a small bay on the southwest side of the Gulf of Boothia, in northeastern mainland Nunavut. **2** the former name of a hamlet situated on its southeastern shore, now called Kugaaruk; pop. (1996) 496. [Sir J. H. Pelly, Hudson's Bay Co. governor d.1852]

Pelly River a river in south central Yukon Territory, 608 km long, which rises in the Mackenzie Mountains at the border with the NWT and flows generally westward to join the Yukon River southeast of Dawson. [Sir J. H. Pelly, a governor of the Hudson's Bay Co. c.1840]

pel·met noun a narrow border of cloth, wood, etc. above esp. a window, concealing the curtain rail; a valance. [prob. from French PALMETTE]

Pelo·pon·nese, the /ˌpeləpəˈniːs/ (also **Pelo·pon·nes·us** /-ˈniːsəs/) the mountainous southern peninsula of Greece, connected to central Greece by the isthmus of Corinth. Its Greek name means 'island of Pelops'.

Pelo·pon·nes·ian War /ˌpeləpəˈniːʒən/ the war of 431–404 BC fought between Athens and Sparta, occasioned largely by Spartan opposition to the Athenian Empire (see DELIAN LEAGUE). It ended in the total defeat of Athens and the transfer, for a brief period, of the leadership of Greece to Sparta.

Pe·lops /ˈpiːlɒps/ Gk Myth son of Tantalus, brother of Niobe, and father of Atreus. He was killed by his father and served up as food to the gods, but only one shoulder was eaten, and he was restored to life with an ivory shoulder replacing the one that was missing.

pe·lorus /pəˈlɔːrəs/ noun a sighting device like a ship's compass for taking bearings of a distant object. [perhaps from Pelorus, reputed name of Hannibal's pilot]

pe·lota /pəˈlɒtə, -ˈlɔːtə/ noun **1** a Basque or Spanish game played in a walled court with a ball and basket-like racquets attached to the hand. **2** the ball used in this. [Spanish, = ball, augmentative of pella, from Latin pila]

pe·lo·ton /ˈpelətɒn/ noun the main field or group of cyclists in a race. [French, lit. 'small ball' (because of the concentrated grouping of the pack)]

pelt¹ verb **1** transitive (usu. foll. by with) **a** hurl many small objects at. **b** strike repeatedly with esp. many small things. **c** assail (a person etc.) with insults, abuse, etc. **2** intransitive (usu. foll. by down) (of rain etc.) fall quickly and torrentially. **3** intransitive move or run fast or vigorously. □ **(at) full pelt** as fast as possible. [16th c.: origin unknown]

pelt² noun **1** the dressed or undressed skin of a fur-bearing mammal with hair, wool, etc. still on. **2** the raw skin of an animal, esp. a sheep, stripped ready for tanning. [Middle English from obsolete pellet skin, diminutive of Old French pel 'skin', or back-formation from PELTRY, ultimately from Latin pellis skin]

pelt·ry noun (pl. **-ries**) **1** undressed skins, esp. of animals valuable for their furs; pelts collectively. **2** (in pl.) kinds or varieties of pelts. [Anglo-French pelterie from peletier furrier, ultimately from Latin pellis skin]

pel·vic adjective of, relating to, or contained in the pelvis.

pelvic floor noun the muscular base of the abdomen, attached to the pelvis.

pelvic girdle noun the bony or cartilaginous structure in vertebrates to which the posterior limbs are attached.

pelvic inflammatory disease noun an inflammation of the female reproductive organs, caused by bacterial infection. Abbr.: **PID**.

pel·vis noun (pl. **pel·vis·es** or **pel·ves** /ˈpelviːz/) **1 a** a basin-shaped cavity at the lower end of the torso of most vertebrates, formed from the innominate bone with the sacrum and other vertebrae. **b** these bones collectively, constituting the pelvic girdle. **c** the part of the abdomen containing the pelvis. **2** the basin-like cavity of the kidney. [Latin, = basin]

Pemba 1 a seaport in N Mozambique, on the Indian Ocean; pop. (est. 2002) 95,600. **2** an island off the coast of Tanzania, in the W Indian Ocean north of Zanzibar. It is noted for the production of cloves.

Pem·bi·na River a river rising in southern Manitoba and flowing east, joining the Red River at the border town of Pembina. [Ojibwa *nepemenah* 'summer berry']

Pem·broke /'pembrʊk/ **1** a port in SW Wales; pop. (est. 2002) 16,000. **2** a city in E Ontario, located on the Ottawa River, northwest of Arnprior; pop. (2001) 13,490. □ **Pem·brok·ian** *noun* (in sense 2) [sense 2 from G. A. Herbert, 11th Earl of *Pembroke* d.1827]

Pem·broke·shire /'pembrʊk.ʃɪr/ a county of SW Wales; administrative centre, Haverfordwest. It was part of Dyfed from 1974 to 1996.

pem·mi·can /'pemɪkən/ *noun* pounded, dried meat (usu. buffalo) mixed to a paste with melted fat, berries, etc. originally made by N American Indians and adapted by fur traders etc. [Cree *pimecan* from *pime* fat]

pem·phig·us /'pemfɪgəs/ *noun* any of several skin diseases characterized by the formation of watery blisters or eruptions on the skin. □ **pem·phig·oid** *adjective* [modern Latin from Greek *pemphix -igos* bubble]

PEN *abbreviation* International Association of Poets, Playwrights, Editors, Essayists, and Novelists.

Pen. *abbreviation* Peninsula.

pen[1] ● *noun* **1** an instrument for writing or drawing with ink, consisting of a nib, ball, felt tip, etc., fixed into a metal or plastic holder. **2** (usu. prec. by *the*) the occupation or practice of writing. **3** an instrument resembling a pen in form or function. **4** an electronic pen-like device used in conjunction with a writing surface to enter commands or data into a computer. **5** *Zool.* the internal feather-shaped cartilaginous shell of certain cuttlefish, esp. squid. ● *transitive verb* (**penned, pen·ning**) **1** write. **2** compose and write. □ **the pen is mightier than the sword** persuasion, legislation, and education can achieve more than the use of armed force. **put pen to paper** begin writing. [Old French *penne* from Latin *penna* feather]

pen[2] ● *noun* **1 a** a small enclosure for cows, sheep, poultry, etc. **b** a number of animals in a pen or sufficient to fill a pen. **2** a place of confinement. **3** an enclosure for sheltering submarines. **4** a Jamaican farm or plantation. ● *transitive verb* (**penned, pen·ning**) (often foll. by *in*, *up*) enclose or shut in a pen. [Old English *penn*, of unknown origin]

pen[3] *noun* a female swan. [16th c.: origin unknown]

pen[4] *noun* N Amer. slang = PENITENTIARY *noun* 1. [abbreviation]

penal /'piːnəl/ *adjective* **1 a** of or concerning punishment or its infliction (*penal laws*; *a penal sentence*; *a penal colony*). **b** (of an act or offence) punishable, esp. by law. **2** extremely severe (*penal taxation*). □ **penal·ly** *adverb* [Old French *penal* or Latin *poenalis* from *poena* PAIN]

penal code *noun* a system of laws relating to crime and its punishment (*compare* CRIMINAL CODE).

penal·ize /'piːnə.laɪz, pen-/ *transitive verb* (also esp. *Brit.* **-ise**) **1 a** subject (a person) to a penalty for breaking a rule etc. **b** put (a person, group, etc.) at a comparative disadvantage; handicap unfairly. **2** make or declare (an action) penal. □ **penal·iz·a·tion** *noun*

Penal Laws *plural noun* various statutes passed in Britain and Ireland during the 16th and 17th c. imposing restrictions on Roman Catholics. Participants in Catholic services could be fined and imprisoned, and Catholics were banned from voting, holding public office, owning land, and teaching. Hardly enforced by the 18th c., the laws were repealed by various Acts 1791–1926. *See also* CATHOLIC EMANCIPATION, TEST ACTS.

penal servitude *noun hist.* imprisonment with compulsory labour.

pen·al·ty /'penəlti/ *noun* (pl. **-ties**) **1** a punishment, esp. a fine, for a breach of law, contract, etc. **2** a disadvantage, loss, etc., as a result of one's own actions (*paid the penalty for his carelessness*). **3 a** a disadvantage imposed on a competitor or side in a game etc. for a breach of the rules etc. **b** (*attributive*) awarded against a side incurring a penalty (*penalty kick*; *penalty shot*). **4** *Bridge etc.* points gained by opponents when a contract is not fulfilled. □ **under** (or **on**) **penalty of** under the threat of (dismissal etc.). [French *pénalité* from medieval Latin *penalitas* (as PENAL)]

penalty area *noun Soccer* the ground in front of the goal in which a foul by defenders involves the award of a penalty kick.

penalty box *noun Hockey & Lacrosse* an area of seating reserved for players temporarily withdrawn from play as a penalty.

penalty clause *noun* a clause in a contract stipulating a penalty for failure to fulfill any of its obligations.

penalty kick *noun Soccer* a free kick at the goal, given after a foul in the penalty area.

penalty killer *noun Hockey* a player who plays while his or her own team's strength is reduced through a penalty, esp. one skilled at preventing the opposing team from scoring. □ **penalty killing** *noun*

penalty shootout *noun* = SHOOTOUT 2.

penalty shot *noun Hockey* **1** a shot by an offensive player on a goal defended only by the goaltender, allowed as a penalty for certain infractions. **2** such a shot used esp. to decide the outcome of a tied game.

pen·ance /'penəns/ *noun* **1** an act of self-punishment as reparation for guilt. **2 a** (in the Roman Catholic and Orthodox Churches) a sacrament including confession of and contrition and absolution for a sin. *Also called* RECONCILIATION. **b** a punishment or discipline imposed esp. by a priest, or undertaken voluntarily, in expiation of a sin. **3** an unpleasant task or situation, esp. one regarded as a punishment for something. [Old French from Latin *paenitentia* (as PENITENT)]

pen and ink ● *noun* **1** the instruments of writing or drawing. **2** writing. **3** a drawing made using pen and ink. ● *adjective* (**pen-and-ink**) (esp. of a drawing) done in ink.

Pen·ang /pə'naŋ/ (also **Pin·ang**) **1** an island of Malaysia, situated off the west coast of the Malay Peninsula. **2** a state of Malaysia, consisting of this island and a coastal strip on the mainland; capital, George Town (on Penang Island). **3** see GEORGE TOWN 2.

pe·na·tes /pə'natiːz, -teɪz/ *plural noun* (in Roman mythology) the household gods, esp. the protectors of the storeroom (*see* LARES). [Latin from *penus* provision of food]

pen-based *adjective* (of a computer etc.) taking input from a hand-held electronic stylus rather than a keyboard.

pence *noun Brit.* **1** pl. of PENNY. **2** *informal* a penny, esp. in British decimal currency.

pen·chant /'penʃənt/ *noun* an inclination; a strong or habitual liking (*has a penchant for old films*). [French, pres. part. of *pencher* incline]

pen·cil ● *noun* **1 a** an instrument for writing or drawing, usu. consisting of a thin rod of graphite etc. enclosed in a wooden cylinder. **b** a similar instrument with a metal or plastic cover and retractable lead. **c** (usu. with a qualifying word) a cosmetic or medication in pencil form (*eyebrow pencil*; *styptic pencil*). **2** (*attributive*) **a** resembling a pencil in shape (*pencil bomb*; *pencil neck*). **b** for, with, or of a pencil (*pencil cup*; *pencil sketch*; *pencil stub*). **3** *Optics* a set of rays converging to or diverging from a single point. **4** *Math.* a figure formed by a set of straight lines meeting at a point. **5** esp. *literary* an artist's, draftsman's, etc. art or style. ● *transitive verb* (**pen·cilled, pen·cil·ling**; esp. US **pen·ciled, pen·cil·ing**) **1** write, sketch, draw, or outline with or as if with a pencil. **2** (usu. foll. by *in*) **a** note down or arrange tentatively or provisionally (*have pencilled in the 29th for our meeting*). **b** fill (an area) with thin or delicate pencil strokes (*pencilled in her eyebrows*). [Old French *pincel*, ultimately from Latin *penicillum* paintbrush, diminutive of *peniculus* brush, diminutive of *penis* tail]

pencil case *noun* a small bag, box, etc. for holding pencils, pens, etc.

pencil crayon *noun Cdn* a pencil with a coloured core used for art, colouring, etc.

pen·cilled *adjective* (esp. US **pen·ciled**) **1** written in pencil (*she read the pencilled queries and suggestions*). **2** (of an area) filled in with pencil strokes (*she had pencilled eyebrows*).

pencil line *noun* **1** a line drawn with or resembling one drawn with a pencil. **2** (also **pencil-line**) (*attributive*) (of a moustache) very thin.

pencil-pusher *noun N Amer. informal derogatory* a person, esp. a clerk, whose job involves a lot of boring paperwork. □ **pencil-pushing** *noun & adjective*

pencil-thin *adjective* very thin or narrow.

pen computer *noun* a computer capable of interpreting handwritten script input and which is controlled by an electronic pen rather than a keyboard.

pen·dant /'pendənt/ *noun* **1 a** a hanging jewel etc., esp. one attached to a necklace, bracelet, etc. **b** (*attributive*) designating such a jewel etc. (*pendant earring*; *pendant bracelet*). **2** a light fixture, ornament, etc., hanging from a ceiling. **3** *Naut.* a short rope hanging from the head of a mast etc., used for attaching tackles. **4** /'pendənt, 'pɒd\ʒ/ (usu. foll. by *to*) a match, companion, parallel, complement, etc. [Old French from *pendre* hang, from Latin *pendere*]

pen·dent /'pendənt/ *adjective* **1** hanging. **2** overhanging. □ **pen·den·cy** *noun* [Middle English (as PENDANT)]

pen·den·tive /pen'dentɪv/ *noun Archit.* a curved triangle of vaulting formed by the intersection of a dome with its supporting arches. [French *pendentif -ive* (adj.) (as PENDANT)]

Pender Islands *see* NORTH PENDER ISLAND *or* SOUTH PENDER ISLAND.

Consonants: b *but*   d *dog*   f *few*   g *get*   h *her*   j *yes*   k *cat*   l *leg*   m *man*   n *no*   p *pen*   r *red*   s *sit*

pend·ing ● *adjective* **1** awaiting decision or settlement, undecided (*a settlement was pending*). **2** about to come into existence (*patent pending*). ● *preposition* **1** until (*pending his return*). **2** during (*pending these negotiations*). [after French *pendant* (see PENDANT)]

pen·dragon /pɛnˈdragən/ *noun hist.* an ancient British or Welsh prince (often as a title). [Welsh, = chief war leader, from *pen* head + *dragon* standard]

pen·du·lous /ˈpɛndjʊləs/ *adjective* **1** (of a part of the body) tending to droop heavily, lacking firmness. **2** (of flowers, bird's nests, branches, etc.) hanging down, drooping, and esp. swinging. □ **pen·du·lously** *adverb* [Latin *pendulus* from *pendēre* hang]

pen·du·lum /ˈpɛndjʊləm/ *noun* **1** a weight suspended so as to swing freely, esp. a rod with a weighted end regulating the movement of a clock's works. **2** popular opinion etc. characterized by oscillation or regular movement from one extreme to another. [Latin neuter adj. (as PENDULOUS)]

Pe·nel·ope /pəˈnɛləpi/ *Gk Myth* the wife of Odysseus, who was besieged by suitors when her husband did not return after the fall of Troy. She put them off by saying that she would marry only when she had finished the piece of weaving on which she was engaged, every night unravelling the work she had done during the day.

pene·plain /ˈpiːnəˌpleɪn/ *noun* (also **pene·plane**) a low, nearly featureless tract of land produced esp. by erosion. [Latin *paene* almost + PLAIN[1]]

Pene·tan·gui·shene /ˌpɛnəˈtaŋwəˌʃiːn/ (also *informal* **Pene·tang** /ˈpɛnəˌtaŋ/) a town in south central Ontario, located on an inlet of Georgian Bay, just northwest of Midland; pop. (2001) 8,316. [Ojibwa, = place of the white rolling sands]

pene·tra·lia /ˌpɛnəˈtreɪlɪə/ *plural noun* **1** innermost shrines or recesses. **2** secret or hidden parts; mysteries. [Latin, neuter pl. of *penetralis* interior (as PENETRATE)]

pene·trate /ˈpɛnəˌtreɪt/ *verb* **1** *transitive* **a** find access into or through, esp. forcibly. **b** (usu. foll. by *with*) imbue (a person or thing) with; permeate. **2** *transitive* see into, find out, or discern (a person's mind, the truth, a meaning, etc.). **3** *transitive* see through (darkness, fog, etc.) (*could not penetrate the gloom*). **4** *intransitive* be understood, fully realized, or absorbed by the mind (*my hint did not penetrate*). **5** *transitive Sport* breach or get through (an opponent's defence). **6** *transitive Business* enter (a market) to establish a new brand, product, etc. **7** *intransitive* (usu. foll. by *into, through, to*) make a way. **8** *transitive* (of a male) put the penis into the vagina or anus of (a sexual partner). □ **pene·trable** /-trəbəl/ *adjective*
pene·tra·bil·ity /-trəˈbɪlɪti/ *noun* **pene·trant** *adjective & noun*
pene·tra·tion /-ˈtreɪʃən/ *noun* **pene·tra·tive** /-ˌtreɪtɪv/ *adjective*
pene·tra·tor *noun* [Latin *penetrare* place or enter within, from *penitus* interior]

pene·trat·ing /ˈpɛnəˌtreɪtɪŋ/ *adjective* **1** that permeates, gets or forces a way into or through something. **2** having or suggesting sensitivity or insight (*a penetrating remark*). **3 a** (of a voice etc.) easily heard through or above other sounds; piercing. **b** (of a smell) sharp, pungent. **4** *Sport* capable of penetrating an opponent's defence. □ **pene·trat·ing·ly** *adverb*

Pen·field, Wil·der Graves (1891–1976), US-born Canadian neurosurgeon and scientist. In 1934 he founded the Montreal Neurological Institute, serving as its director until 1960; through his research he developed a surgical treatment for epilepsy. During the last 15 years of his life he enjoyed what he called his 'second career' as a writer of historical fiction, medical biography, and essays.

pen·friend *noun* = PEN PAL.

pen·guin *noun* any flightless seabird of the family Spheniscidae of the southern hemisphere, with black upper parts and white underparts, and wings developed into scaly flippers for swimming underwater. [16th c., originally = great auk: origin unknown]

penguin suit *noun informal* a tuxedo.

peni·cil·late /ˈpɛnɪsɪlət, -ˈsɪlət/ *adjective Biol.* having or forming a small tuft or tufts. [Latin *penicillum*: see PENCIL]

peni·cil·lin /ˌpɛnɪˈsɪlən/ *noun* any of various antibiotics produced naturally by moulds of the genus *Penicillium*, or synthetically, and able to prevent the growth of certain disease-causing bacteria. [modern Latin *Penicillium* genus name from Latin *penicillum*: see PENCIL]

penile /ˈpiːnaɪl/ *adjective* of or concerning the penis. [modern Latin *penilis*]

pen·in·sula /pəˈnɪnsələ, -sjə-/ *noun* a piece of land almost surrounded by water or projecting far into a sea or lake etc. □ **pen·in·su·lar** *adjective* [Latin *paeninsula* from *paene* almost + *insula* island]

Peninsular War the campaign waged on the Iberian peninsula

between the French and the British, Spanish and Portuguese, from 1808 to 1814 during the Napoleonic Wars. Although an early British expedition was forced to evacuate the peninsula in 1809, a second expedition, led by Wellington, finally drove the French back over the Pyrenees in early 1814 after a long and bloody campaign.

penis /ˈpiːnəs/ *noun* (*pl.* **penis·es** or **penes** /-niːz/) the male genital organ which carries the duct for the emission of sperm, in mammals consisting largely of erectile tissue and serving also for the elimination of urine. [Latin, = tail, penis]

penis envy *noun Psych.* the supposed female envy of the male's possession of a penis, postulated by Freud to account for various behavioural characteristics or problems in women.

peni·tent /ˈpɛnɪtənt/ ● *adjective* regretting and wishing to atone for sins etc.; repentant. ● *noun* **1** a person who repents, a repentant sinner. **2** a person doing penance under the direction of a confessor. □ **peni·tence** *noun* **peni·tent·ly** *adverb* [Old French from Latin *paenitens* from *paenitēre* repent]

peni·ten·tial /ˌpɛnɪˈtɛnʃəl/ *adjective* of or concerning penitence or penance. □ **peni·ten·tial·ly** *adverb* [Old French *penitencial* from Late Latin *paenitentialis* from *paenitentia* penitence (as PENITENT)]

peni·ten·tiary /ˌpɛnɪˈtɛnʃəri/ ● *noun* (*pl.* **-ies**) **1 a** *Cdn* a federal corrections institution for convicted offenders serving a sentence of two years or more. **b** *US* a state or federal prison, esp. for serious offenders. **2** an office in the papal court deciding questions of penance, dispensations, etc. ● *adjective* **1** intended for or pertaining to the penal and reformatory treatment of criminals. **2** *N Amer.* (of an offence) making a culprit liable to a prison sentence. **3** of or concerning penance. [medieval Latin *paenitentiarius* (adj. & n.) (as PENITENT)]

pen·knife *noun* a small folding knife, esp. for carrying in a pocket.

pen·light *noun* a small, pen-shaped flashlight.

pen·man *noun* (*pl.* **-men**) **1** a person who writes by hand with a specified skill (*a good penman*). **2** a scribe.

penman·ship *noun* **1** handwriting. **2** the skill or art of handwriting.

Penn, Wil·liam (1644–1718), English Quaker, founder of Pennsylvania. He was granted a charter to land in N America by Charles II (1682), using it to found the colony of Pennsylvania as a sanctuary for Quakers and other Nonconformists in the same year.

Penn. *abbreviation* (also **Penna.**) Pennsylvania.

pen name *noun* a literary pseudonym.

pen·nant *noun* **1 a** *Naut.* a tapering flag, esp. that flown at the masthead of a vessel in commission. **b** *N Amer.* such a flag identifying a team, club, cause, etc. **2** *N Amer. Sport* **a** a flag symbolizing a league championship, esp. in professional baseball. **b** such a championship itself. [blend of PENDANT and PENNON]

pennant race *noun N Amer. Baseball* an esp. close competition among professional teams for the league pennant.

penne /ˈpɛneɪ/ *noun* pasta in the form of short tubes with the ends cut diagonally. [Italian, pl. of *penna* 'quill']

Pen·ner, Fred·erick Ralph Cor·nel·ius ('Fred') (b.1946), children's entertainer, best known for his album *The Cat Came Back* (1979) and for hosting *Fred Penner's Place* on CBC television since 1985.

penni·less *adjective* having no money; poor, destitute. □ **penni·less·ly** *adverb* **penni·less·ness** *noun*

Pen·nines /ˈpɛnaɪnz/ (also **Pennine Chain**) a range of hills in N England, extending from the Scottish border southward to the Peak District in Derbyshire. Its highest peak is Cross Fell in Cumbria, which rises to 893 m (2,930 ft.).

pen·non /ˈpɛnən/ *noun* **1** a long narrow flag, triangular or swallow-tailed, esp. as the military ensign of lancer regiments. **2** a flag or banner. **3** *Naut.* a long pointed pennant or streamer on a ship. [Old French from Latin *penna* feather]

Penn·syl·va·nia /ˌpɛnsəlˈveɪnjə/ a state in the northeastern US; pop. (2000) 12,281,054; capital, Harrisburg. Founded in 1682 by William Penn, it became one of the original 13 states of the US in 1787.

Pennsylvania Dutch (also **Pennsylvania German**) ● *noun* **1** a dialect of High German spoken by 17th–18th-c. German and Swiss immigrants to Pennsylvania, still spoken by some of their descendants in Pennsylvania and nearby areas and S Ontario, esp. the Amish. **2** (as *pl.*) these settlers or their descendants. ● *adjective* of, pertaining to, or designating these people or their dialect. [Dutch from German *Deutsch* 'German']

Penn·syl·va·nian /ˌpɛnsɪlˈveɪnjən/ ● *noun* **1** a native or inhabitant of Pennsylvania. **2** (prec. by *the*) esp. *N Amer. Geol.* the upper Carboniferous period or system. ● *adjective* **1** of or relating to Pennsylvania. **2** esp. *N Amer. Geol.* of or relating to the upper Carboniferous period or system.

penny *noun* (*pl.* for separate coins **pen·nies**, *Brit.* for a sum of money **pence**) **1** *N Amer.* a one-cent coin. **2** a British bronze coin and monetary unit equal to one-hundredth of a pound. Abbr.: **p. 3** *hist.* a former British coin and monetary unit equal to one-two-hundred-and-fortieth of a pound. Abbr.: **d. 4** a usu. small sum of money; a very little or the least amount of wealth, money, etc. (*plan for every penny you expect to spend; worth every penny*). **5** *Bible* a denarius. □ **in for a penny, in for a pound** an exhortation to total commitment to an undertaking. **like a bad penny** continually returning when unwanted. **pennies from heaven** unexpected esp. financial benefits. **the penny drops** esp. *Brit. informal* one begins to understand at last. **a penny for your thoughts** a request to a thoughtful person to confide in the speaker. **a pretty penny** a considerable sum of money. **two a penny** *Brit.* almost worthless though easily obtained. [Old English *penig*, *penning* from Germanic, perhaps related to PAWN²]

-penny *combining form Brit.* forming attributive adjectives meaning 'costing .. pence' (esp. in pre-decimal currency) (*fivepenny*).

penny ante *N Amer.* ● *noun* **1** poker played for small, esp. penny, stakes. **2** a matter, concern, business transaction, etc. involving an insignificant amount of money. ● *adjective* (**penny-ante**) contemptible, trivial.

penny arcade *noun dated* = ARCADE 3.

penny auction *noun* **1** a fundraising auction where items are sold for very small amounts. **2** an auction of goods repossessed or seized as collateral on a loan, in which the bidders collude to pay absurdly low prices so that the repossessor sees no financial benefit from the sale and the owner can regain the property at little or no cost.

Penny Black *noun* the first adhesive postage stamp in the UK, issued in 1840 and costing one penny.

penny candy *noun N Amer. hist.* any one of many varieties of candy costing a penny and displayed in large, glass jars usu. on the front counter of a general store etc.

penny·cress *noun* a herbaceous plant of the mustard family, *Thlaspi arvense*, with flat round pods.

penny dreadful *noun* a cheap sensational comic or novelette.

penny farthing *noun Cdn & Brit. hist.* an early type of bicycle with one large and one small wheel.

penny loafer *noun N Amer.* a low-heeled, usu. leather casual shoe with a slot in the vamp in which a coin, esp. a penny, is placed for decoration.

penny-pinching ● *noun* stinginess, miserliness. ● *adjective* stingy, miserly. □ **penny-pincher** *noun*

penny post *noun Brit. hist.* the system of carrying letters etc. at a standard charge of one penny regardless of distance within the British Empire.

penny·royal *noun* **1** a creeping mint, *Mentha pulegium*, cultivated for its supposed medicinal properties. **2** *N Amer.* an aromatic plant, *Hedeoma pulegioides*. [apparently from earlier *puliol(e) ryall* from Anglo-French *puliol*, Old French *pouliol* (ultimately from Latin *pulegium* 'thyme'), + *real* ROYAL]

penny stock *noun* esp. *N Amer.* common stock valued at less than one dollar a share, and therefore highly speculative.

penny·weight *noun* a unit of weight, 24 grains or one-twentieth of an ounce troy.

penny·whistle *noun* a tin pipe with six holes, which may be variously covered to give different notes.

penny-wise *adjective* careful, esp. overly careful, in saving small amounts or in small expenditures. □ **penny-wise and pound foolish** thrifty in small expenditures but careless or wasteful in large ones.

penny·wort /ˈpeni͵wɜrt, -wɔrt/ *noun* any of several wild plants with rounded leaves, esp.: **1** (**wall pennywort**) *Umbilicus rupestris*, growing in crevices. **2** (**marsh** or **water pennywort**) *Hydrocotyle vulgaris*, growing in marshy places. [from PENNY + WORT]

penny·worth /ˈpeni͵wɜrθ/ *noun* esp. *Brit.* **1** as much as can be bought for a penny. **2** a very small or the least amount. □ **not a pennyworth** not the least bit.

Pen·ob·scot /pəˈnɒbskɒt/ ● *noun* **1** (*pl.* same) a member of an Algonquian people of the Penobscot River valley in Maine. **2** the language of this people, a dialect of Eastern Abenaki. ● *adjective* of or pertaining to this people or their language. [Abenaki]

penol·ogy /piːˈnɒlədʒi/ *noun* the study of the prevention and

punishment of crime and of the penal system. □ **peno·logic·al** /-nəˈlɒdʒɪkəl/ *adjective* **penol·o·gist** *noun* [Latin *poena* penalty + -LOGY]

pen pal *noun* esp. *N Amer.* a person with whom one builds a friendship by exchanging letters, esp. someone in a foreign country whom one has never met.

pen-pusher *noun informal derogatory* = PENCIL-PUSHER. □ **pen-pushing** *noun*

pen·sée /pɑ̃ˈsei/ *noun* a thought or reflection put into literary form; an aphorism. [French]

pen·sile /ˈpensail/ *adjective* **1** hanging down, suspended; pendulous. **2** (of a bird etc.) building a pensile nest. [Latin *pensilis* from *pendēre pens-* hang]

pen·sion¹ /ˈpenʃən/ ● *noun* **1** a regular payment made by a government to people above a specified age, to the disabled, or to such a person's surviving dependants. **2** a similar payment made by an employer etc. to a retired employee. **3** a regular payment from a fund etc. to which the recipient has contributed (usu. with an employer) as an investment during his or her working life in order to realize a return upon retirement (also *attributive*: pension plan). ● *transitive verb* grant a pension to. □ **pension off 1** dismiss with a pension. **2** cease to employ or use. [Old French from Latin *pensio -onis* payment, from *pendere pens-* pay]

pension² /pɑ̃ˈsjɔ̃/ *noun* a European, esp. French, boarding house providing full or half board at a fixed rate. [French: see PENSION¹]

pen·sion·able *adjective* **1** entitled to a pension. **2** (of a service, job, etc.) entitling an employee to a pension. **3** of, pertaining to, or affecting a person's pension (*pensionable earnings*). □ **pen·sion·abil·ity** *noun*

pen·sion·er *noun* a recipient of a pension, esp. a retirement pension.

pen·sive /ˈpensɪv/ *adjective* **1** deep in thought. **2** sorrowfully thoughtful. □ **pen·sive·ly** *adverb* **pen·sive·ness** *noun* [Old French *pensif*, *-ive* from *penser* think, from Latin *pensare* frequentative of *pendere pens-* weigh]

pen·ste·mon /penˈstiːmən, ˈpenstəmən/ *noun* (also **pent·ste·mon** /pentˈstiːmən/) any N American herbaceous plant of the genus *Penstemon*, with showy flowers and five stamens, one of which is sterile. [modern Latin, irreg. from PENTA- + Greek *stēmōn* warp, used for 'stamen']

pen·stock *noun* **1** *N Amer.* a channel for conveying water to a turbine, water wheel, etc. **2** a sluice; a floodgate. [PEN² in sense 'mill dam' + STOCK]

pent *adjective* esp. *literary* = PENT-UP. [past participle of *pend* var. of PEN² verb]

penta- *combining form* **1** five. **2** *Chem.* (forming the names of compounds) containing five atoms or groups of a specified kind (*pentachloride*; *pentoxide*). [Greek from *pente* five]

penta·chloro·phenol /͵pentə͵klɔːrəˈfiːnɒl/ *noun* a colourless crystalline acidic solid, C_6Cl_5OH, used in insecticides, fungicides, weed killers, wood preservatives, etc.

pent·acle /ˈpentəkəl/ *noun* a figure used as a symbol, esp. in magic, e.g. a pentagram. [medieval Latin *pentaculum* (as PENTA-)]

pent·ad /ˈpentad/ *noun* **1** the number five. **2** a group or series of five. [Greek *pentas -ados* from *pente* five]

penta·dac·tyl /͵pentəˈdaktɪl/ *adjective Zool.* having five toes or fingers.

penta·gon /ˈpentəgɒn/ *noun* **1** a plane figure with five sides and angles. **2** (**the Pentagon**) **a** a pentagonal building in Arlington, Virginia, containing the headquarters of the US armed forces. **b** the leaders of the US armed forces. □ **pent·ag·on·al** /-ˈtagənəl/ *adjective*

penta·gram /ˈpentə͵gram/ *noun* a five-pointed star formed by extending the sides of a pentagon both ways until they intersect, formerly used as a mystic symbol. [Greek *pentagrammon* (as PENTA-, -GRAM)]

penta·hed·ron /͵pentəˈhiːdrən/ *noun* (*pl.* **-hed·rons** or **-hedra** /-drə/) a solid figure with five faces. □ **penta·hed·ral** *adjective*

pent·am·er·ous /penˈtamərəs/ *adjective* **1** *Bot.* having five parts in a flower whorl. **2** *Zool.* having five joints or parts.

pent·am·eter /penˈtamətər/ *noun* **1** a verse of five feet, e.g. English iambic verse of ten syllables. **2** a form of Greek or Latin dactylic verse composed of two halves each of two feet and a long syllable, used in elegiac verse.

pent·amid·ine /penˈtamɪ͵diːn/ *noun* a drug used to treat protozoal infections, esp. in AIDS patients. [PENTANE + *amidine* (as AMIDE + -INE⁴)]

pent·ane /ˈpentein/ *noun* a hydrocarbon of the alkane series. Chem. formula: C_5H_{12}. [Greek *pente* five + ALKANE]

pent·angle /ˈpenˌtaŋgəl/ noun = PENTAGRAM. [Middle English perhaps from medieval Latin *pentaculum* PENTACLE, assimilated to Latin *angulus* ANGLE¹]

Penta·teuch /ˈpentəˌtuːk, -ˌtjuːk/ noun the first five books of the Bible (Genesis, Exodus, Leviticus, Numbers, and Deuteronomy), called the Torah by Jews, and traditionally ascribed to Moses. □ **Penta·teuch·al** /-ˈtuːkəl, -ˈtjuːkəl/ adjective [ecclesiastical Latin *pentateuchus* from ecclesiastical Greek *pentateukhos* (as PENTA-, *teukhos* implement, book)]

pent·ath·lon /penˈtaθlɒn/ noun **1** = MODERN PENTATHLON. **2** any athletic event comprising five different events. □ **pent·ath·lete** /-ˈtaθliːt/ noun [Greek from *pente* five + *athlon* contest]

penta·ton·ic /ˌpentəˈtɒnɪk/ adjective Music **1** (of a scale) consisting of five notes, usu. without semitones, equivalent to an ordinary major scale with the fourth and seventh omitted. **2** relating to such a scale.

penta·valent /ˌpentəˈveɪlənt/ adjective Chem. having a valence of five; quinquevalent.

Pente·cost /ˈpentəˌkɒst/ noun **1** a Christian festival observed on the seventh Sunday after Easter, commemorating the descent of the Holy Spirit on the disciples. **2 a** the Jewish harvest festival, on the fiftieth day after the second day of Passover. **b** a synagogue ceremony on the anniversary of the giving of the Law on Mount Sinai. **3** (in some Christian denominations) the liturgical season extending from Pentecost to the beginning of Advent. [ecclesiastical Latin *pentecoste* from Greek *pentēkostē (hēmera)* fiftieth (day)]

Pente·cost·al /ˌpentəˈkɒstəl/ ● adjective (also **pentecostal**) **1** of or relating to Pentecost. **2** of or designating Christian denominations and individuals who emphasize charismatic forms of worship, e.g. speaking in tongues, healing, and uninhibited expressions of praise, and are often fundamentalist in outlook. ● noun a member of a Pentecostal denomination. □ **Pente·cost·al·ism** noun **Pente·cost·al·ist** adjective & noun

Pen·the·si·lea /ˌpenθesɪˈliːə/ Gk Myth the queen of the Amazons, who came to the help of Troy after the death of Hector and was killed by Achilles.

pent·house noun **1** an apartment or suite on the roof or top floor of a tall building. **2** a structure on the roof of a building to house elevator machinery, etc. **3** a sloping roof, esp. of a structure built on to another building. [Middle English *pentis* from Old French *apentis, -dis*, from medieval Latin *appendicium*, in Late Latin = appendage, from Latin (as APPEND): influenced by HOUSE]

Pen·tic·ton /penˈtɪktən/ a city in southern BC, located at the southern end of Okanagan Lake, 68 km south of Kelowna; pop. (2001) 30,985. [origin uncertain: possibly from Okanagan *pentaktin* always place, because the site was continually occupied, or possibly from Nicola-Similkameen (an extinct Athapaskan language) *snpnpiniyatn* place where the deer net was used]

penti·mento /ˌpentɪˈmentɔː/ noun (pl. **penti·menti** /-tiː/) a visible trace of an earlier composition or alteration, seen through later layers of paint on a canvas. [Italian, = repentance, correction]

Pent·land Firth /ˈpentlənd/ a channel separating the Orkney Islands from the northern tip of mainland Scotland. It links the North Sea with the Atlantic.

pento·barbi·tal /ˌpentəˈbɑːrbɪˌtɒl/ noun (Brit. also **pento·barbi·tone** /-ˌtɔːn/) a narcotic and sedative barbiturate drug formerly used to relieve insomnia. [PENTA- + BARBITAL]

pent·ose /ˈpentɔːs, -ɔːz/ noun Biochem. any monosaccharide containing five carbon atoms, including ribose. [PENTA- + -OSE²]

Pento·thal /ˈpentəθɒl/ noun proprietary = THIOPENTAL SODIUM.

pent·ste·mon var. of PENSTEMON.

pent-up adjective closely confined or held back (*pent-up demand*).

pentyl /ˈpentɪl/ noun = AMYL. [PENTANE + -YL]

pen·ult /pəˈnʌlt, ˈpiːnʌlt/ noun the last but one (esp. syllable). [abbreviation of PENULTIMATE]

pen·ul·tim·ate /pəˈnʌltɪmət/ ● adjective last but one; second-last. ¶ *Penultimate* is often mistakenly used and understood to mean 'absolutely ultimate; unsurpassable'. ● noun **1** the last but one. **2** the last syllable but one. [Latin *paenultimus* from *paene* almost + *ultimus* last, after *ultimate*]

pen·umbra /pəˈnʌmbrə/ noun (pl. **penumbrae** /-briː/ or **penumbras**) **1 a** the partly shaded region around the shadow of an opaque body, esp. that around the total shadow of the moon or earth in an eclipse. **b** the less dark outer part of a sunspot. **2** a partial shadow. □ **pen·um·bral** adjective [modern Latin from Latin *paene* almost + UMBRA shadow]

pen·uri·ous /pəˈnjʊəriəs/ adjective **1** poor; destitute. **2** stingy; grudging.

3 scanty. □ **pen·uri·ous·ly** adverb **pen·uri·ous·ness** noun [medieval Latin *penuriosus* (as PENURY)]

pen·ury /ˈpenjʊri/ noun (pl. **-ies**) **1** destitution; poverty. **2** a lack; scarcity. [Latin *penuria*, perhaps related to *paene* almost]

Penza /ˈpjenzə/ a city in south central Russia, on the Sura River; pop. (est. 2002) 530,400.

Pen·zance /penˈzans/ a resort town in SW England, on the south coast of Cornwall near Land's End; pop. (est. 2002) 20,300.

Pen·zias /ˈpentsiəs, ˈpenz-/ **Arno (Allan)** (b.1933), German-born US astrophysicist, who shared the Nobel Prize for physics in 1978 for his discovery of cosmic microwave background radiation.

peon /ˈpiːɒn/ noun **1** N Amer. a menial or drudge. **2 a** a Spanish American day labourer or farm worker. **b** a poor or destitute S American. **3** /ˈpiːən, pjuːn/ an Indian office messenger, attendant, or orderly. **4** a bullfighter's assistant. **5** hist. a worker held in servitude in the southern US. □ **peon·age** noun [Portuguese *peão* & Spanish *peon* from medieval Latin *pedo -onis* walker, from Latin *pes pedis* foot: compare PAWN¹]

peony /ˈpiːəni/ noun (pl. **-ies**) any herbaceous plant of the genus *Paeonia*, with large globular red, pink, or white flowers, often double in cultivated varieties. [Old English *peonie* from Latin *peonia* from Greek *paiōnia* from *Paiōn*, physician of the gods]

people /ˈpiːpəl/ ● noun **1** (treated as pl.) **a** human beings, esp. as opposed to animals etc. **b** persons in general (*people do not like rudeness*). **2** (usu. as pl.) **a** persons composing a community, tribe, race, nation, etc. (*the Canadian people; a warlike people; the peoples of the Commonwealth*). **b** a group of persons of a usu. specified kind (*the chosen people; these people here; right-thinking people*). **3** (prec. by *the*; treated as pl.) **a** the mass of people in a country etc. not having special rank or position. **b** these considered as an electorate (*the people will reject it*). **4** (treated as pl.) family (*my people came from Scotland*). **5** (treated as pl.) employees. **6** (treated as pl.) **a** subjects, armed followers, a retinue, etc. **b** a congregation of a parish priest etc. ● transitive verb (usu. foll. by *with*) **1** fill with people; populate. **2** (esp. as **peopled** adjective) inhabit; occupy as inhabitants, fictional characters etc. (*a novel peopled with unlovable characters*). [Anglo-French *poeple, people*, Old French *pople, peuple*, from Latin *populus*]

people·hood /ˈpiːpəlˌhʊd/ noun the condition, state, or awareness of being a people.

people meter noun an electronic device used to record the television viewing habits of a family etc. for use in compiling ratings.

people mover noun any of various forms of transportation over a fixed and relatively short route, e.g. a moving sidewalk or driverless vehicle.

people person noun a person who enjoys or is particularly good at interacting with other people.

people power noun **1** political or other pressure applied by the people, esp. through the public demonstration of popular organization. **2** physical power exerted by people as opposed to machines etc.

people's democracy noun a political system, esp. (formerly) in E Europe, with power regarded as invested in the people.

people skills plural noun character traits that allow one to deal effectively with other people.

Peoples of the Sea see SEA PEOPLES.

people-watch·ing noun the action of observing people as they pass by, esp. noting idiosyncrasies, styles, etc. □ **people-watch** intransitive verb **people-watch·er** noun

Peoria /piːˈɔːriə/ a river port and industrial city in central Illinois, on the Illinois River; pop. (2000) 112,936.

pep informal ● noun liveliness; energy and enthusiasm. ● transitive verb (**pepped, pep·ping**) (usu. foll. by *up*) fill with energy or liveliness. [abbreviation of PEPPER]

Pepin the Short /ˈpepɪn/ (also **Pepin III**) (c.714–68), son of Charles Martel, king of the Franks 751–68. A close ally of the papacy, he defended it from Lombard attacks and made the Donation of Pepin which was the basis for the Papal States.

pep·lum /ˈpepləm/ noun a short flounce etc. at waist level, esp. of a blouse or jacket over a skirt. [Latin from Greek *peplos* woman's outer garment]

pepo /ˈpiːpɔː/ noun (pl. **pepos**) any fleshy fruit of the melon or cucumber type, with numerous seeds and surrounded by a hard skin. [Latin, = pumpkin, from Greek *pepōn* abbreviation of *pepōn sikuos* ripe gourd]

uː mood   ai my   ɔi pipe   au brown   ʌu house   ei day   ɔi boy   ã franglais   ã Canadien   ɔ̃ Brayon   (see over for consonants)

pep·per ● *noun* **1 a** a hot aromatic condiment from the dried berries of certain plants used whole or ground. **b** any climbing vine of the genus *Piper*, esp. *P. nigrum*, yielding these berries. **2 a** the bell-shaped, smooth-skinned, mildly pungent fruit of certain varieties of the plant *Capsicum annuum*, eaten in salads or as a vegetable. **b** the plant of the nightshade family bearing this fruit. **3** = CAYENNE. **4** a style of skipping rope in which the rope is rotated very quickly. ● *transitive verb* **1** sprinkle or treat with or as if with pepper. **2** sprinkle liberally; dot (*the speech was peppered with quotations from Shakespeare*). **3** pelt with missiles. [Old English *piper*, *pipor* from Latin *piper* from Greek *peperi* from Sanskrit *pippalī-* berry, peppercorn]

pepper·corn *noun* **1** the dried berry of *Piper nigrum* as a condiment. **2** (in full **peppercorn rent**) *Brit.* a nominal rent.

pepper grass *noun* any of various peppery tasting cruciferous plants, esp. of the genus *Lepidium*.

pepper mill *noun* (also **pepper grinder**) a device for grinding pepper by hand.

pepper·mint *noun* **1 a** a mint plant, *Mentha piperita*, grown for the strong-flavoured oil obtained from its leaves. **b** the oil from this. **2** a candy flavoured with peppermint. □ **pepper·minty** *adjective*

peppermint knob *noun Cdn* (*Nfld*) a hard, usu. spherical, peppermint candy.

pep·per·oni /ˌpepəˈroːni/ *noun* a hard, highly-seasoned sausage made with beef and pork. [Italian *peperone* chili]

pepper pot *noun* **1** *Brit.* = PEPPER SHAKER. **2** a W Indian dish of meat etc. stewed with cayenne pepper.

pepper root *noun* = TOOTHWORT 1.

pepper shaker *noun N Amer.* a small container with a perforated lid for sprinkling pepper.

pepper spray ● *noun* an aerosol spray of oils derived from cayenne pepper, used to overcome an assailant, or by police to subdue protesters etc. ● (**pepper-spray**) *transitive & intransitive verb* spray (someone) with pepper spray.

pepper squash *noun Cdn* a variety of winter squash with dark green to orange ridged skin and yellow flesh. *Also called* ACORN SQUASH.

pepper steak *noun* **1** a dish of beef steak coated in coarsely crushed peppercorns before cooking. **2** steak coated with peppercorns as a basis for this dish. **3** a stew-like dish of steak with bell peppers.

pep·pery *adjective* **1** of, like, or containing much, pepper. **2** hot-tempered. **3** pungent; stinging. □ **pep·per·i·ness** *noun*

pep pill *noun informal* a pill containing a stimulant drug.

peppy *adjective* (**pep·pi·er**, **pep·pi·est**) *informal* vigorous, energetic. □ **pep·pi·ly** *adverb* **pep·pi·ness** *noun*

pep rally *noun* (*pl.* **-lies**) *N Amer.* a meeting or gathering to inspire enthusiasm, esp. before a sports event.

pepsi *noun* (*pl.* **-sis**) *Cdn informal derogatory* a French Canadian. [from the perceived Québécois preference for Pepsi-Cola]

pep·sin *noun* an enzyme contained in the gastric juice, which hydrolyzes proteins. [German from Greek *pepsis* digestion]

pep talk *noun* a usu. short talk intended to enthuse, encourage, etc.

pep·tic *adjective* concerning or promoting digestion. [Greek *peptikos* able to digest (as PEPTONE)]

peptic ulcer *noun* an ulcer in the stomach or duodenum.

pep·tide *noun Biochem.* any of a group of organic compounds consisting of two or more amino acids bonded in sequence. [German *Peptid*, back-formation (as POLYPEPTIDE)]

pep·tone *noun* a protein fragment formed by hydrolysis in the process of digestion. [German *Pepton* from Greek *peptos*, neuter *pepton* cooked]

Pepys /ˈpiːps/ **Sam·uel** (1633–1703), English diarist and naval administrator. His *Diary* (1660–9) is an important document of his times, covering events such as the Great Plague (1665–6), the Fire of London (1666), and the sailing of the Dutch fleet up the Thames (1665–67).

Pé·quiste /peiˈkiːst/ *noun Cdn* a supporter or member of the Parti Québécois. [Canadian French, from the initial letters of Parti Québécois + *-iste* -IST]

per *preposition* **1** for each; for every (*two dollars per person*; *five miles per hour*). **2** by means of; by; through (*per rail*). **3** (in full **as per**) in accordance with (*as per instructions*). □ **as per usual** *informal* as usual. [Latin]

per- *prefix* **1** forming verbs, nouns, and adjectives meaning: **a** through; all over (*perforate*; *perforation*; *pervade*). **b** completely; very (*perfervid*; *perturb*). **c** to destruction; to the bad (*pervert*; *perdition*). **2** *Chem.* having the maximum of some element in combination, esp.: **a** in the names

of binary compounds in *-ide* (*peroxide*). **b** in the names of oxides, acids, etc. in *-ic* (*perchloric*; *permanganic*). **c** in the names of salts of these acids (*perchlorate*; *permanganate*). [Latin *per-* (as PER)]

per·adven·ture /pɜːrədˈventʃər, ˌper-/ *archaic* ● *adverb* perhaps. ● *noun* uncertainty; chance; conjecture; doubt. [Old French *per* or *par auenture* by chance (as PER, ADVENTURE)]

Perak /ˈperə, peˈrak/ a state of Malaysia, on the west side of the Malay Peninsula; capital, Ipoh.

per·ambu·late /pəˈrambjʊˌleit/ *verb* **1** *transitive* walk through, over, or about (streets, the country, etc.). **2** *intransitive* walk from place to place. **3** *transitive* **a** travel through and inspect (territory). **b** formally establish the boundaries of (a territory) by walking around them. □ **per·ambu·la·tion** *noun* **per·ambu·la·tory** *adjective* [Latin *perambulare perambulat-* (as PER-, *ambulare* walk)]

per·ambu·la·tor /pəˈrambjʊˌleitər/ *noun Brit. formal* = BABY CARRIAGE. [PERAMBULATE]

per annum *adverb* for each year. [Latin]

perc *noun informal* perchloroethylene. [abbreviation]

per·cale /pɜːrˈkeil/ *noun* a closely woven cotton fabric used esp. for bedsheets. [French, of uncertain origin]

per cap·ita /pɜːr ˈkapitə/ *adverb & adjective* for each person. [Latin, = by heads]

Percé /perˈsei/ a town in E Quebec, situated at the eastern end of the Gaspé Peninsula, on the shore of the Gulf of St. Lawrence; pop. (2001) 3,614. It is a popular tourist destination, in large part because of the offshore presence of Rocher Percé. [see PERCÉ, ROCHER]

Percé, Rocher /perˈsei/ (also **Percé Rock**) a high-tide island and noted bird sanctuary of the Gaspé Peninsula, near the town of Percé, Quebec. An enormous monolith resembling an ocean liner, it rises to a height of over 70 m and is some 500 m in length. Its form, pierced by the sea, bears a large archway in its side (60 m high and 30 m wide). [French, lit. 'pierced rock']

per·ceive /pɜːrˈsiːv/ *transitive verb* **1** become aware or conscious of (something); come to realize or understand. **2** become aware of (something) by the use of one of the senses. **3** interpret or look on (someone or something) in a particular way; regard as. □ **per·ceiv·able** *adjective* **per·ceived** *adjective* **per·ceiv·er** *noun* [Old French *perçoivre*, from Latin *percipere* (as PER-, *capere* take)]

per cent (also **per·cent**) ● *adverb* in every hundred. ● *noun* **1** percentage. **2** one part in every hundred (*half a per cent*). **3** (in *pl.*) *Brit.* public securities yielding interest of so much per cent (*three per cents*).

per·cent·age *noun* **1** a rate or proportion per cent. **2** a proportion. **3** *informal* personal benefit or advantage.

per·cent·ile /pɜːrˈsentail/ *noun Statistics* one of 99 values of a variable dividing a population into 100 equal groups as regards the value of that variable.

per·cept /ˈpɜːrsept/ *noun Philos.* **1** an object of perception. **2** a mental concept resulting from perceiving, esp. by sight. [Latin *perceptum* perceived (thing), neuter past participle of *percipere* PERCEIVE, after *concept*]

per·cep·tible /pɜːrˈseptibəl/ *adjective* capable of being perceived by the senses or intellect. □ **per·cep·ti·bil·ity** /-ˈbɪliti/ *noun* **per·cep·tibly** *adverb* [Old French *perceptible* or Late Latin *perceptibilis* from Latin (as PERCEIVE)]

per·cep·tion /pɜːrˈsepʃən/ *noun* **1 a** the faculty of perceiving. **b** an instance of this. **2** (often foll. by *of*) **a** the intuitive recognition of a truth, aesthetic quality, etc. **b** an instance of this (*a sudden perception of the true position*). **3** an interpretation or impression based on one's understanding of something. **4** *Philos.* the ability of the mind to refer sensory information to an external object as its cause. □ **per·cep·tion·al** *adjective* **per·cep·tual** /pɜːrˈseptʃʊəl/ *adjective* **per·cep·tual·ly** *adverb* [Latin *perceptio* (as PERCEIVE)]

per·cep·tive /pɜːrˈseptiv/ *adjective* **1** capable of perceiving. **2** sensitive; discerning; observant (*a perceptive remark*). □ **per·cep·tive·ly** *adverb* **per·cep·tive·ness** *noun* **per·cep·tiv·ity** *noun* [medieval Latin *perceptivus* (as PERCEIVE)]

perch¹ ● *noun* **1** a usu. horizontal bar, branch, etc. used by a bird to rest on. **2** a usu. high or precarious place for a person or thing to rest on. **3** esp. *Brit. hist.* a measure of length, esp. for land, of 5½ yards (see also ROD 6). ● *transitive & intransitive verb* (usu. foll. by *on*) settle or rest, or cause to settle or rest on or as if on a perch etc. (*the bird perched on a branch*; *a town perched on a hill*). □ **knock something off its perch 1** vanquish, destroy. **2** make less confident or secure. [Old French *perche*, *percher* from Latin *pertica* pole]

perch² *noun* (*pl.* same or **perch·es**) **1** any spiny-finned freshwater edible fish of the genus *Perca*, esp. *P. flavescens* of N America or *P. fluviatilis* of Europe. **2** = WHITE PERCH. **3** = OCEAN PERCH. [Old French *perche* from Latin *perca* from Greek *perkē*]

per·chance /pərˈtʃɑːns/ *adverb archaic* or *literary* **1** by chance. **2** possibly; maybe. [Anglo-French *par chance* from *par* by, CHANCE]

perch·er *noun* any bird with feet adapted for perching; a passerine.

Per·che·ron /ˈpɜːtʃəˌrɒn/ *noun* a breed of heavy draft horse combining strength with agility and speed. [French, originally bred in le *Perche*, a district of N France]

per·chlor·ate /pərˈklɔːreɪt/ *noun Chem.* a salt or ester of perchloric acid.

per·chlor·ic acid /pərˈklɒrɪk/ *noun Chem.* a colourless toxic liquid acid, HClO₄, that contains chlorine in its highest oxidation state and is a powerful oxidizing agent.

per·chloro·ethyl·ene /pərˌklɔːrəˈɛθɪliːn/ *noun* an inert colourless liquid, C₂Cl₄, used as a dry-cleaning fluid.

per·cipi·ent /pərˈsɪpiənt/ ● *adjective* **1** able to perceive; conscious. **2** discerning; observant. ● *noun* a person who perceives, esp. something outside the range of the senses. □ **per·cipi·ence** *noun* **per·cipi·ent·ly** *adverb* [Latin (as PERCEIVE)]

Per·cod·an *noun proprietary* a semi-synthetic opioid analgesic and sedative drug combined with ASA.

per·co·late /ˈpɜːkəˌleɪt/ *verb* **1** *intransitive* (often foll. by *through*) **a** (of liquid etc.) filter or ooze gradually (esp. through a porous surface). **b** (of an idea etc.) permeate gradually. **2 a** *transitive* prepare (coffee) by repeatedly passing boiling water through ground beans. **b** *intransitive* (of coffee) be or become made by percolating. **3** *transitive* ooze through; permeate. **4** *transitive* strain (a liquid, powder, etc.) through a fine mesh etc. □ **per·co·la·tion** *noun* [Latin *percolare* (as PER-, *colare* strain, from *colum* strainer)]

per·co·la·tor /ˈpɜːkəˌleɪtər/ *noun* a machine for making coffee by circulating boiling water through ground beans.

per con·tra /pər ˈkɒntrə/ *adverb* on the opposite side (of an account, assessment, etc.); on the contrary. [Italian]

per·cuss /pərˈkʌs/ *transitive verb Med.* tap (a part of the body) gently with a finger or an instrument as part of a diagnosis. [Latin *percutere percuss-* strike (as PER-, *cutere* = *quatere* shake)]

per·cus·sion /pərˈkʌʃən/ *noun* **1** *Music* **a** (often *attributive*) the playing of music by striking instruments with sticks etc. (*a percussion ensemble*). **b** the section of such instruments in an orchestra (*asked the percussion to stay behind*). **2** *Med.* the act or an instance of percussing. **3** the forcible striking of one esp. solid body against another. □ **per·cus·sion·ist** *noun* **per·cus·sive** *adjective* **per·cus·sive·ly** *adverb* **per·cus·sive·ness** *noun* [as PERCUSS]

percussion cap *noun see* CAP *noun* 5.

per·cuta·neous /ˌpɜːkjuˈteɪniəs/ *adjective* esp. *Med.* made or done through the skin. [Latin *per cutem* through the skin]

Percy, **Sir Henry** (known as 'Hotspur' and 'Harry Hotspur') (1364–1403), English soldier. Son of the 1st Earl of Northumberland (1342–1408), he was killed at the battle of Shrewsbury during his father's revolt against Henry IV.

per diem /pər ˈdiːɛm/ ● *adverb* & *adjective* for each day. ● *noun* an allowance or payment for each day. [Latin]

per·di·tion /pərˈdɪʃən/ *noun* eternal death; damnation. [ecclesiastical Latin *perditio* from Latin *perdere* destroy (as PER-, *dere dit-* = *dare* give)]

per·dur·able /pərˈdjʊərəbəl/ *adjective formal* permanent; eternal; durable. □ **per·dur·abil·ity** *noun* **per·dur·ably** *adverb* [Old French from Late Latin *perdurabilis* (as PER-, DURABLE)]

père /pɛr/ *noun* (added to a surname to distinguish a father from a son) the father, senior. [French, = father]

Père David's deer /ˌpɛr ˈdeɪvɪdz/ *noun* a large slender-antlered deer, *Elaphurus davidianus*. [after Father A. *David*, French missionary d.1900]

pere·grin·ate /ˈpɛrəgrɪˌneɪt/ *intransitive verb archaic* or *jocular* travel; journey, esp. extensively or at leisure. □ **pere·grin·a·tion** *noun* **pere·grin·ator** *noun* [Latin *peregrinari* (as PEREGRINE)]

pere·grine /ˈpɛrəgrən/ *noun* (in full **peregrine falcon**) a falcon, *Falco peregrinus*, much prized for hawking on account of its fast and accurate flight. [Latin *peregrinus* from *peregre* abroad, from *per* through + *ager* field]

Perel·man /ˈpɛrəlmən/ **Sid·ney Jo·seph** (1904–79), US humorist and writer. He wrote most of his humorous short stories and sketches for the *New Yorker*, and was also a Hollywood scriptwriter.

per·emp·tory /pəˈrɛmptəri/ *adjective* **1** (of a statement or command) admitting no denial or refusal. **2** (of a person, a person's manner, etc.) dogmatic; imperious; dictatorial. **3** *Law* not open to appeal or

challenge; final. **4** absolutely fixed; essential. □ **per·emp·tor·i·ly** *adverb* **per·emp·tor·i·ness** *noun* [Anglo-French *peremptorie*, Old French *peremptoire* from Latin *peremptorius* deadly, decisive, from *perimere perempt-* destroy, cut off (as PER-, *emere* take, buy)]

peremptory challenge *noun Law* a defendant's objection to a proposed juror, made without needing to give a reason.

per·en·nial /pəˈrɛniəl/ ● *adjective* **1** (of a plant) lasting several years (*compare* ANNUAL 3). **2** constantly occurring; recurring (*a perennial problem*). **3** lasting for a long time (*a perennial source of hope*). **4** (of a stream) flowing through all seasons of the year. ● *noun* a perennial plant (*a herbaceous perennial*). □ **per·en·nial·ly** *adverb* [Latin *perennis* (as PER-, *annus* year)]

Peres /ˈpɛrɛz/ **Shi·mon** (Polish name Szymon Perski) (b.1923), Polish-born Israeli politician, prime minister 1984–6 and 1995–6. He became interim leader of the Opposition in 2003. As Foreign Minister under Yitzhak Rabin he played a major role in negotiating the PLO–Israeli peace accord (1993). He shared the 1994 Nobel Peace Prize with Rabin and Yasser Arafat.

pere·stroi·ka /ˌpɛrəˈstrɔɪkə/ *noun* (in the former Soviet Union) the policy or process of restructuring or reforming the economic and political system, esp. under the leadership of Mikhail Gorbachev during the period 1985–91. [Russian *perestroika* = restructuring]

Pérez de Cuél·lar /ˌpɛrɛz də ˈkweɪjɑr/ **Ja·vier** (b.1920), Peruvian diplomat. He served as Secretary-General of the United Nations from 1982 to 1991, and played a key role in ending the Iran-Iraq War (1980–88); his efforts to avert the Gulf War in 1990 raised his international standing, as did his part in negotiating the release of Western hostages held in the Middle East.

per·fect ● *adjective* **1** complete; not deficient. **2** flawless; without defect (*a perfect diamond*). **3** very satisfactory (*a perfect evening*). **4** exact; precise (*a perfect circle*). **5** entire; unqualified (*a perfect stranger*). **6** *Grammar* (of a tense) denoting a completed action or event in the past, formed in English with *have* or *has* and the past participle, as in *they have eaten*. **7** *Bot.* **a** (of a flower) having all four types of whorl. **b** (of a fungus) in the stage where the sexual spores are formed. **8** *Baseball* **a** designating a game or inning in which no member of the opposing team has reached first base safely. **b** designating a pitcher who has not allowed an opposing batter to reach first base safely (*has been perfect over four innings*). **9** eminently suitable (*spicy sausage is perfect in this dish*). ● *transitive verb* **1** make perfect; improve. **2** carry through; complete. **3** complete (a sheet) by printing the other side. ● *noun Grammar* the perfect tense. □ **per·fect·ible** *adjective* **per·fect·ibil·ity** *noun* **per·fect·ness** *noun* [Old French *parfit*, *perfet* from Latin *perfectus* past participle of *perficere* complete (as PER-, *facere* do)]

per·fecta /pərˈfɛktə/ *noun US* = EXACTOR. [Latin American Spanish *quiniela perfecta* perfect quinella]

perfect binding *noun* a form of bookbinding in which the leaves are attached to the spine by gluing rather than sewing. □ **perfect-bound** *adjective*

perfect interval *noun Music* an interval that is a fourth, fifth, or octave.

per·fec·tion *noun* **1** the act or process of making perfect. **2** the state of being perfect; faultlessness, excellence. **3** a perfect person, thing, or example. **4** full development; completion. □ **to perfection** exactly; completely.

per·fec·tion·ism *noun* **1** the uncompromising pursuit of perfection. **2** *Philos.* the belief that religious or moral perfection is attainable. □ **per·fec·tion·ist** *noun* & *adjective* **per·fec·tion·is·tic** *adjective*

per·fec·tive /pərˈfɛktɪv/ *Grammar* ● *adjective* (of an aspect of a verb etc.) expressing the completion of an action (*opp.* IMPERFECTIVE). ● *noun* the perfective aspect or form of a verb. [medieval Latin *perfectivus* (as PERFECT)]

per·fect·ly *adverb* **1** completely; absolutely (*I understand you perfectly*). **2** quite, completely (*is perfectly capable of doing it*). **3** in a perfect way.

perfect number *noun Math* a number equal to the sum of its positive divisors, e.g. the number 6, whose divisors (1, 2, 3) also add up to 6.

per·fecto /pərˈfɛktoʊ/ *noun* (pl. **-tos**) a large thick cigar pointed at each end. [Spanish, = perfect]

perfect pitch *noun* a non-technical name for ABSOLUTE PITCH 1.

perfect square *noun* = SQUARE NUMBER.

per·fer·vid /pərˈfɜːvɪd/ *adjective literary* impassioned; very intense. □ **per·fer·vid·ly** *adverb* **per·fer·vid·ness** *noun* [modern Latin *perfervidus* (as PER-, FERVID)]

per·fidy /ˈpɜːfɪdi/ *noun* breach of faith; treachery. □ **per·fidi·ous**

/-ˈfɪdɪəs/ *adjective* **per·fidi·ous·ly** /-ˈfɪdɪəsli/ *adverb* [Latin *perfidia* from *perfidus* treacherous (as PER-, *fidus* from *fides* faith)]

per·foli·ate /pərˈfoːliət/ *adjective* (of a plant) having the stalk apparently passing through the leaf. [modern Latin *perfoliatus* (as PER-, FOLIATE)]

per·for·ate ● *verb* /ˈpɜrfəˌreɪt/ **1** *transitive* make a hole or holes through; pierce. **2** *transitive* make a row of small holes in (paper etc.) so that a part may be torn off easily. **3** *transitive* make an opening into; pass into or extend through. **4** *intransitive* (usu. foll. by *into, through,* etc.) penetrate. ● *adjective* /ˈpɜrfərət/ perforated. □ **per·for·a·tion** *noun* **per·for·at·ed** *adjective* **per·for·a·tor** *noun* [Latin *perforare* (as PER-, *forare* pierce)]

per·force *adverb* unavoidably; necessarily. [Old French *par force* by FORCE]

per·form *verb* **1 a** *transitive* carry out, execute, or do (something). **b** *intransitive* carry out or do something. **2** *transitive & intransitive* fulfill or carry into effect (a promise, etc.). **3** *transitive* act in an official way; conduct (a ceremony etc.) (*performed the marriage*). **4** *transitive* **a** act or stage (a play, role, etc.). **b** play or sing (a piece of music etc.) for an audience. **c** accomplish (a feat, act of skill, etc.), esp. for an audience (*performed a card trick*). **5** *intransitive* **a** give a performance to entertain an audience (*is performing in Saint John all next week*). **b** be engaged in the performing arts, esp. as a professional. **6** *intransitive* function, esp. in a specified way (*the car performs well*). **7** *intransitive* (of an investment) yield a return; be profitable. **8** *intransitive slang* have sexual intercourse (esp. satisfactorily). □ **per·form·able** *adjective* **per·form·er** *noun* **per·form·ing** *adjective* [Anglo-French *parfourmer* from Old French *parfournir* (assimilated to *forme* FORM) from *par* PER-, *fournir* FURNISH]

per·form·ance *noun* **1** (usu. foll. by *of*) **a** the act or process of performing or carrying out. **b** the execution or fulfillment (of a duty etc.). **2 a** a staging or production (of a drama, piece of music, etc.) (*he danced in the afternoon performance*). **b** the action of performing a part, a piece of music, etc. **3** a person's achievement (*put up a good performance*). **4** *informal* a fuss; a scene; a public exhibition (*made such a performance about leaving*). **5 a** the capabilities of a machine, esp. a car or aircraft. **b** (*attributive*) of high capability (*a performance car*). **6** the return on an investment, esp. in stocks and shares etc.

performance art *noun* a kind of visual art in which the activity of the artist forms a central feature. □ **performance artist** *noun*

performance-enhancing *adjective* designating or relating to a substance (esp. one proscribed from competition) which improves athletic performance.

per·forma·tive /pərˈfɔrmətɪv/ ● *adjective* denoting an utterance that effects an action by being spoken or written (e.g. *I bet, I apologize*). ● *noun* a performative utterance.

performing arts *plural noun* the arts, such as drama, music, and dance, that require performance for their realization.

per·fume /ˈpɜrfjuːm, pɜrˈfjuːm/ ● *noun* **1** a sweet smell. **2** fluid containing the essence of flowers etc. ● *transitive verb* (usu. as **per·fumed** *adjective*) impart a sweet scent to; impregnate with a sweet smell. □ **per·fumy** *adjective* [French *parfum, parfumer* from obsolete Italian *parfumare, perfumare* (as PER-, *fumare* smoke, FUME): originally of smoke from a burning substance]

per·fum·er /pɜrˈfjuːmər/ *noun* a maker or seller of perfumes. □ **per·fum·ery** *noun* (*pl.* **-eries**).

per·func·tory /pɜrˈfʌŋktəri/ *adjective* **1** done merely for the sake of getting through a duty; superficial; mechanical. **2** dull, unenthusiastic, unemotional. □ **per·func·tor·i·ly** *adverb* **per·func·tor·i·ness** *noun* [Late Latin *perfunctorius* careless, from Latin *perfungi perfunct-* (as PER-, *fungi* perform)]

per·fuse /pɜrˈfjuːz/ *transitive verb* **1** *Med.* cause a fluid to pass through (an organ etc.). **2** (often foll. by *with*) **a** besprinkle (with water etc.). **b** cover or suffuse (with radiance etc.). **3** pour or diffuse (water etc.) through or over. □ **per·fu·sion** *noun* [Latin *perfundere perfus-* (as PER-, *fundere* pour)]

Per·ga·mum /ˈpɜrgəməm/ a city of ancient Mysia, in W Asia Minor, situated to the north of Izmir on a rocky hill close to the Aegean coast. It was one of the greatest and most beautiful of the Hellenistic cities, and was famed for its cultural institutions, esp. its library, which was second only to that at Alexandria. The city, and the extensive kingdom of Pergamum, later became a province of Rome. □ **Per·ga·mene** /-ˌmiːn/ *adjective & noun*

per·go·la /ˈpɜrgələ/ *noun* an arbour or covered walk, formed of growing plants trained over trellises. [Italian from Latin *pergula* projecting roof, from *pergere* proceed]

Per·go·lesi /pɜrgəˈleizi/ **Gio·van·ni Bat·tis·ta** (1710–36), Italian

composer, whose best-known works include his *Stabat Mater* (1729) and comic operas such as *La serva padrona* (1733).

per·haps *adverb* **1** it may be; possibly (*perhaps it is lost*). **2** introducing a polite request (*perhaps you would open the window?*). [PER + HAP]

peri /ˈpiːri/ *noun* (*pl.* **peris**) **1** any of a group of fairy-like beings in Persian mythology. **2** a beautiful or graceful being. [Persian *parī*]

peri- /ˈperi/ *prefix* **1** around, about. **2** *Astronomy* the point nearest to (*perigee; perihelion*). [Greek *peri* around, about]

peri·anth /ˈperiˌanθ/ *noun* the outer part of a flower. [French *périanthe* from modern Latin *perianthium* (as PERI- + Greek *anthos* flower)]

Péri·bon·ka, Ri·vière /ˌpeiriˈbɔ̃kə/ a river in NE central Quebec, which rises northeast of Lac Mistassini and flows southward to Lac Saint-Jean. [Montagnais, = river cutting through sand]

peri·car·di·um /ˌperɪˈkardiəm/ *noun* (*pl.* **peri·car·dia**) the membranous sac enclosing the heart. □ **peri·car·di·al** *adjective* **peri·car·ditis** *noun* [modern Latin from Greek *perikardion* (as PERI- + *kardia* heart)]

peri·carp /ˈperiˌkarp/ *noun* the part of a fruit formed from the wall of the ripened ovary. [French *péricarpe* from Greek *perikarpion* pod, shell (as PERI-, *karpos* fruit)]

peri·chon·drium /ˌperɪˈkɒndriəm/ *noun* the membrane enveloping cartilage tissue (except at the joints). [PERI- + Greek *khondros* cartilage]

Peri·cles /ˈperəˌkliːz/ (*c.*495–429 BC), Athenian statesman and general during the period of Athenian artistic, intellectual, and cultural supremacy. A champion of Athenian democracy, he promoted an imperialist policy and masterminded Athenian strategy in the Peloponnesian War. He commissioned the building of the Parthenon in 447 BC. □ **Peri·clean** /-ˈkliːən/ *adjective*

per·ico·pe /pəˈrɪkəpi/ *noun* a short passage or paragraph, esp. a portion of Scripture read in public worship. [Late Latin from Greek *perikopē* (as PERI-, *kopē* cutting, from *koptō* cut)]

peri·dot /ˈperiˌdɒt/ *noun* a green variety of olivine, used esp. as a semi-precious stone. [Old French *peritot*, of unknown origin]

peri·dot·ite /ˌperiˈdoːtaɪt/ *noun* any of a group of plutonic rocks containing little or no feldspar but much olivine. □ **peri·dot·itic** /-ˈtɪtɪk/ *adjective* [as PERIDOT]

peri·gee /ˈperiˌdʒiː/ *noun* the point in the orbit of a celestial body or satellite where it is nearest the earth (*opp.* APOGEE). □ **peri·gean** /ˌperiˈdʒiːən/ *adjective* [French *périgée* from modern Latin from Greek *perigeion* round the earth (as PERI-, *gē* earth)]

peri·glacial /ˌperiˈgleiʃəl, -siəl/ *adjective* of or relating to a region adjoining a glacier.

Péri·gord /peiriˈgɔr/ an area of SW France, in the southwestern Massif Central.

peri·gyn·ous /pəˈrɪdʒɪnəs/ *adjective* (of stamens) situated around the pistil or ovary. [modern Latin *perigynus* (as PERI-, -GYNOUS)]

peri·heli·on /ˌperiˈhiːliən/ *noun* (*pl.* **peri·helia**) the point of a planet's or comet's orbit nearest to the sun's centre. [Graecized from modern Latin *perihelium* (as PERI-, Greek *hēlios* sun)]

peril ● *noun* **1** serious and immediate danger. **2** something that causes or has the potential to cause damage or loss, esp. as covered by an insurance policy. ● *transitive verb* (**per·illed, per·il·ling**; *US* **per·iled, per·il·ing**) threaten; endanger. □ **at one's peril** at one's own risk. [Old French from Latin *peric(u)lum*, experiment, risk, danger, from base of *experiri* 'try' + *-culum, -CLE*]

per·illa /pəˈrɪlə/ *noun* any of several plants of the genus *Perilla*, comprising annual herbs native to eastern Asia, esp. *P. frutescens*, grown in Asia as an oilseed, medicinal, and culinary plant, and sometimes elsewhere as an ornamental plant on account of its coloured (often purple) leaves. [18th c.: origin unknown]

per·il·ous *adjective* full of risk; dangerous; hazardous. □ **per·il·ous·ly** *adverb* **per·il·ous·ness** *noun*

peri·lune /ˈperiˌluːn/ *noun* the point in a body's lunar orbit where it is closest to the moon's centre (*opp.* APOLUNE). [PERI- + Latin *luna* moon, after *perigee*]

peri·lymph /ˈperilɪmf/ *noun* the fluid in the labyrinth of the ear.

peri·meno·pause /ˌperiˌmenəpɒz/ *noun* the time of life occurring in the years just before menopause. □ **peri·meno·paus·al** *adjective*

per·im·eter /pəˈrɪmɪtər/ *noun* **1 a** the circumference or outline of a closed figure. **b** the length of this. **2** the outer edges of an area, away from the centre of activity, population, interest, etc. **3 a** the outer boundary of an enclosed area. **b** a defended boundary. **4** an instrument for measuring a field of vision. □ **peri·met·ric**

/ˌperɪˈmetrɪk/ *adjective* [Greek *perimetros* (as PERI-, *metros* from *metron* measure)]

peri·natal /ˌperɪˈneɪtəl/ *adjective* of or relating to the time immediately before and after birth. □ **peri·natal·ly** *adverb*

peri·neum /ˌperɪˈniːəm/ *noun* the region of the body between the anus and the scrotum or vulva. □ **peri·neal** *adjective* [Late Latin from Greek *perinaion*]

per·iod ● *noun* **1** a length or portion of time (*mostly sunny with cloudy periods*). **2** a distinct portion of history, a person's life, etc. (*the pre-Confederation period; Picasso's Blue Period*). **3** *Geol.* a time forming part of a geological era (*the Quaternary period*). **4 a** an interval between recurrences of an astronomical or other phenomenon. **b** the time taken by a planet to rotate about its axis. **5** a division of an academic day allotted to a particular subject, course, etc. (*I have history in third period*). **6** each of the intervals into which the playing time of a sporting event, game, etc. is divided (*scored twice in the second period*). **7** an occurrence of menstruation. **8** esp. *N Amer.* **a** a punctuation mark (.) used at the end of a sentence or an abbreviation. **b** used at the end of a sentence etc. to indicate finality, absoluteness, etc. (*we want the best, period*). **9 a** a set of figures marked off in a large number to assist in reading. **b** a set of figures repeated in a recurring decimal. **c** the smallest interval over which a function takes the same value. **10** *Chem.* a sequence of elements between two noble gases forming a row in the periodic table. ● *adjective* belonging to or characteristic of some past period (*period furniture*). □ **of the period** of the era under discussion (*the custom of the period*). [Old French *periode* from Latin *periodus* from Greek *periodos* (as PERI-, *odos* = *hodos* way)]

per·iod·ate /pəˈraɪəˌdeɪt/ *noun Chem.* a salt or ester of periodic acid.

peri·od·ic /ˌpiːriˈɒdɪk/ *adjective* **1** appearing or occurring at regular intervals. **2** intermittent; appearing or occurring at irregular intervals (*periodic outbreaks of meningitis*). **3** of or concerning the period of a celestial body (*periodic motion*). □ **peri·od·ic·al·ly** *adverb* **period·icity** /-riəˈdɪsɪti/ *noun*

periodic acid /ˌpɜːraɪˈɒdɪk/ *noun Chem.* a hygroscopic solid acid containing heptavalent iodine. [PER- + IODINE]

peri·od·ic·al /ˌpiːriˈɒdɪkəl/ ● *noun* a magazine etc. that is published at regular intervals, e.g. monthly or weekly. ● *adjective* **1** published at regular intervals. **2** of or relating to periodicals (*a periodical article*). **3** periodic, occasional.

periodic function *noun Math.* a function returning to the same value at regular intervals.

periodic table *noun* an arrangement of chemical elements in order of increasing atomic number and in which elements of similar chemical properties appear at regular intervals.

period·iz·a·tion /ˌpiːriədaɪˈzeɪʃən/ *noun* (also esp. *Brit.* **-isation**) the division of history into periods.

periodontal disease *noun* = PYORRHEA 1.

peri·odon·tics /ˌperiəˈdɒntɪks/ *plural noun* (treated as *sing.*) the branch of dentistry concerned with the gums and other structures surrounding and supporting the teeth. □ **peri·odon·tal** *adjective* **peri·odon·tist** *noun* [PERI- + Greek *odous odont-* tooth]

peri·odon·tol·ogy /ˌperiədɒnˈtɒlədʒi/ *noun* = PERIODONTICS.

period piece *noun* a work of art, furniture, literature, etc., considered in relation to its associations with or evocativeness of a past period.

peri·os·teum /ˌperiˈɒstiəm/ *noun* (pl. **peri·os·tea** /-tiə/) a membrane enveloping the bones where no cartilage is present. □ **peri·os·teal** *adjective* **peri·os·titis** /-ˈstaɪtɪs/ *noun* [modern Latin from Greek *periosteon* (as PERI-, *osteon* bone)]

peri·pa·tet·ic /ˌperɪpəˈtetɪk/ ● *adjective* **1** (of a teacher) working in more than one school or college etc. **2** going from place to place; itinerant. **3** (**Peripatetic**) Aristotelian (from Aristotle's habit of walking in the Lyceum while teaching). ● *noun* a peripatetic person, esp. a teacher. □ **peri·pa·tet·ic·ally** *adverb* **peri·pa·teti·cism** /-ˌsɪzəm/ *noun* [Greek *peripatētikos* from *peripateō* (as PERI-, *pateō* walk)]

peri·pet·eia /ˌperɪpəˈtaɪə, -ˈtiːə/ *noun* (esp. in a literary work) a sudden change of fortune. [Greek (as PERI-, *pet-* from *piptō* fall)]

per·iph·eral /pəˈrɪfərəl/ ● *adjective* **1** of minor importance; marginal. **2** of the periphery; on the fringe. **3** *Anat.* near the surface of the body, with special reference to the circulation and nervous system. **4** (of equipment) used with a computer etc. but not an integral part of it. ● *noun* a peripheral device or piece of equipment, e.g. a keyboard, printer, disk or tape drive, etc. □ **per·iph·eral·ly** *adverb*

peripheral nervous system *noun Anat.* the nervous system outside the brain and spinal cord.

peripheral vision *noun* that which is visible to the eye outside of the main area of focus.

per·iph·ery /pəˈrɪfəri/ *noun* (pl. **-eries**) **1** the boundary of an area or surface. **2** an outer or surrounding region (*built on the periphery of the old town*). [Late Latin *peripheria* from Greek *periphereia* circumference (as PERI-, *phereia* from *phero* bear)]

peri·phras·is /pəˈrɪfrəsɪs/ *noun* (pl. **peri·phras·es** /-ˌsiːz/) **1** a roundabout way of speaking; circumlocution. **2** a roundabout phrase. [Latin from Greek from *periphrazō* (as PERI-, *phrazō* declare)]

peri·phras·tic /ˌperɪˈfrastɪk/ *adjective Grammar* **1** of or involving periphrasis. **2** (of a case, tense, etc.) formed by combination of words rather than by inflection (e.g. *did go*, *of the people* rather than *went*, *the people's*). □ **peri·phras·tic·ally** *adverb* [Greek *periphrastikos* (as PERIPHRASIS)]

per·ip·ter·al /pəˈrɪptərəl/ *adjective* (of a classical temple) surrounded by a single row of columns. [Greek *peripteron* (as PERI-, Greek *pteron* wing)]

peri·scope /ˈperəˌskoʊp/ *noun* an apparatus with mirrors or prisms arranged in a tube so that the user can view the area above, e.g. the surface of the sea from a submerged submarine.

peri·scop·ic /ˌperəˈskɒpɪk/ *adjective* of a periscope. □ **peri·scop·ic·ally** *adverb*

periscopic lens *noun* a lens allowing distinct vision over a wide angle.

per·ish *verb* **1** *intransitive* be destroyed; suffer death or ruin. **2** *intransitive* fade away; disappear. **3** *intransitive Brit.* (esp. of rubber, a rubber object, etc.) lose its normal qualities; deteriorate, rot. **4** *transitive* (usu. in passive) *Brit.* suffer from cold or exposure (*we were perished standing outside*). □ **perish the thought** an exclamation of horror against an unwelcome idea. [Old French *perir* from Latin *perire* pass away (as PER-, *ire* go)]

per·ish·able ● *adjective* liable to perish; subject to decay. ● *noun* (in pl.) a thing, esp. a foodstuff, subject to speedy decay. □ **per·ish·abil·ity** *noun* **per·ish·able·ness** *noun*

per·ish·er *noun Brit. slang* an annoying person.

per·ish·ing *adjective* esp. *Brit. informal* freezing cold, extremely chilly. □ **per·ish·ing·ly** *adverb*

peri·sperm /ˈperəˌspɜːrm/ *noun* a mass of nutritive material outside the embryo sac in some seeds. [PERI- + Greek *sperma* seed]

per·isso·dac·tyl /pəˌrɪsoʊˈdaktɪl/ ● *adjective* of or relating to the order Perissodactyla of ungulate mammals with one main central toe, or a single toe, on each foot, including horses, rhinoceroses, and tapirs. ● *noun* an animal of this order. [modern Latin *Perissodactyla*, from Greek *perissos* 'uneven' + *daktulos* 'finger, toe']

peri·stal·sis /ˌperəˈstalsɪs/ *noun* the involuntary muscular wavelike movements by which the contents of the alimentary canal etc. are propelled along. □ **peri·stal·tic** *adjective* **peri·stal·tic·ally** *adverb* [modern Latin from Greek *peristellō* wrap around (as PERI-, *stellō* place)]

peri·stome /ˈperəˌstoʊm/ *noun* **1** *Bot.* a fringe of small teeth around the mouth of a capsule in mosses and certain fungi. **2** *Zool.* the parts surrounding the mouth of various invertebrates. [modern Latin *peristoma* from PERI- + Greek *stoma* mouth]

peri·style /ˈperəˌstaɪl/ *noun* a row of columns surrounding a temple, court, cloister, etc.; a space surrounded by columns. [Latin *peristylum* from Greek *peristulon* (as PERI-, *stulos* pillar)]

peri·ton·eum /ˌperɪtəˈniːəm/ *noun* (pl. **peri·ton·eums** or **peri·tonea** /-ˈniːə/) the serous membrane lining the cavity of the abdomen. □ **peri·ton·eal** *adjective* [Late Latin from Greek *peritonaion* (as PERI-, *tonaion* from *-tonos* stretched)]

peri·ton·itis /ˌperɪtəˈnaɪtɪs/ *noun* an inflammatory disease of the peritoneum.

peri·vascu·lar /ˌperɪˈvaskjʊlər/ *adjective* situated or occurring around a blood vessel.

peri·wig /ˈperiˌwɪg/ *noun* esp. *hist.* a wig. [alteration of PERUKE, with *-wi-* for French *-u-* sound]

peri·winkle¹ /ˈperiˌwɪŋkəl/ ● *noun* **1** any plant of the genus *Vinca*, esp. an evergreen trailing plant with blue or white flowers. **2** a tropical shrub, *Catharanthus roseus*, native to Madagascar. **3** a purple-blue colour like that of the periwinkle flower. ● *adjective* of the colour of a periwinkle. [Anglo-French *pervenke*, Old French *pervenche* from Late Latin *pervinca*, assimilated to PERIWINKLE²]

peri·winkle² /ˈperiˌwɪŋkəl/ *noun* = WINKLE. [16th c.: origin unknown]

per·jure /ˈpɜːrdʒər/ *reflexive verb Law* wilfully tell an untruth when under oath. □ **per·jur·er** *noun* [Old French *parjurer* from Latin *perjurare* (as PER-, *jurare* swear)]

uː mood   aɪ my   əi pipe   au brown   ʌu house   ei day   ɔi boy   ɑ̃ franglais   ã Canadien   ɔ̃ Brayon   (*see over for consonants*)

per·jured /ˈpɜrdʒərd/ *adjective* guilty of or involving perjury.

per·jury /ˈpɜrdʒəri/ *noun* (*pl.* **-ies**) *Law* **1** a breach of an oath, esp. the act of wilfully telling an untruth when on oath. **2** the practice of this.
□ **per·juri·ous** /-ˈdʒʊriəs/ *adjective*

perk¹ *transitive verb* (often foll. by *up*) raise (esp. one's ears) briskly.
□ **perk up 1** recover confidence, courage, life, or zest. **2** restore confidence or courage or liveliness in (esp. another person). **3** smarten up (*perk up an outfit with some new jewellery*). [Middle English, perhaps from var. of PERCH¹]

perk² *noun informal* a perquisite. [abbreviation]

perk³ *informal* ● *verb* **1** *intransitive* (of coffee) percolate, make a bubbling sound in the percolator. **2** *transitive* percolate (coffee). ● *noun Cdn* a coffee percolator. [abbreviation of PERCOLATE]

Per·kin, **Sir Wil·liam Henry** (1838–1907), English chemist and pioneer of the synthetic organic chemical industry. At the age of 18 he prepared the first synthetic dyestuff, mauve, which is made from aniline.

perky *adjective* (**perk·i·er**, **perk·i·est**) **1** lively; cheerful. **2** bright, jaunty, attractive (*a perky blouse*). **3** self-assertive; saucy; pert.
□ **perk·i·ly** *adverb* **perk·i·ness** *noun*

Perl *noun* a high-level interpreted programming language widely used for a variety of tasks and esp. for applications running on the World Wide Web. [from PEARL, arbitrarily chosen for its positive connotations, with omission of *-a-* to differentiate it from an existing programming language called *PEARL*]

Per·lis /ˈpɜrlɪs/ the smallest state of Malaysia and the most northerly of those on the Malay Peninsula; capital, Kangar.

perl·ite *noun* a glassy type of vermiculite, expandable to a solid form by heating, used for insulation, as a plant growth medium, etc. [French from *perle* pearl]

Perl·man, **It·zhak** (b.1945), Israeli-born US violinist, who is an acclaimed virtuoso.

Perm /pɜrm/ an industrial city of Russia, in the western foothills of the Ural Mountains; pop. (est. 2002) 1,002,500. It was known from 1940 to 1957 as Molotov.

perm ● *noun* a permanent wave. ● *transitive verb* give a permanent wave to (a person or person's hair). [abbreviation]

perma- *combining form* permanent or permanently (*wore a perma-smile*).

perma·cul·ture *noun* the development of agricultural ecosystems intended to be complete and self-sustaining. □ **perma·cul·tur·al** *adjective* **perma·cul·tur·ist** *noun* [PERMANENT + AGRICULTURE]

perma·frost *noun* subsoil which remains below freezing point throughout the year, as in polar regions. [PERMANENT + FROST]

perma·nent ● *adjective* **1** lasting, or intended to last or function, indefinitely without change (*his permanent address*). **2** persistent, enduring (*developed a permanent stoop*). **3 a** (of hair dye) producing colour that lasts until the hair grows out. **b** (of ink etc.) indelible. **4** (of an employee or position) not having a specified date of termination; not contractual. ● *noun* = PERMANENT WAVE. □ **perma·nence** *noun* **perma·nency** *noun* **perma·nent·ly** *adverb* [Old French *permanent* or Latin *permanēre* (as PER-, *manēre* remain)]

permanent magnet *noun* a magnet retaining its magnetic properties in the absence of an inducing field or current.

permanent population *noun* the population of a resort or university town etc. which resides there permanently, as opposed to the population during the season when tourists, students, etc. are in residence.

permanent press *noun* **1** a process for producing fabrics which retain their crease, press, shape, etc. **2** a fabric treated by this process (also *attributive*: *permanent-press slacks*).

permanent resident *noun* an immigrant to a country deemed to have settled there permanently and entitled to all privileges of citizenship except the right to vote; a landed immigrant.
□ **permanent residence** *noun*

permanent revolution *noun* the state or condition, envisaged by Leon Trotsky, of a country's continuing revolutionary progress being dependent on a continuing process of revolution in other countries.

Permanent Secretary *noun Brit.* a senior civil servant, usu. a permanent adviser to a minister.

permanent tooth *noun* a tooth succeeding a milk tooth in a mammal, and lasting most of the mammal's life.

permanent wave *noun* a long-lasting wave or curl set into the hair by the application of chemicals, heat, etc.

per·man·gan·ate /pərˈmaŋgəˌneit, -nət/ *noun Chem.* any salt of permanganic acid, esp. potassium permanganate.

per·man·gan·ic acid /ˌpərmaŋˈganɪk/ *noun Chem.* an acid containing heptavalent manganese. [PER- + *manganic* (as MANGANESE)]

perma-press *noun* = PERMANENT PRESS.

per·mea·bil·ity /ˌpɜrmiəˈbɪlɪti/ *noun* **1** the state or quality of being permeable. **2** a quantity measuring the influence of a substance on the magnetic flux in the region it occupies.

per·me·able /ˈpɜrmiəbəl/ *adjective* capable of being permeated. [Latin *permeabilis* (as PERMEATE)]

per·me·ate /ˈpɜrmiˌeit/ *verb* **1** *transitive* penetrate throughout; pervade; saturate. **2** *transitive* pass through (a membrane etc.) by osmosis or diffusion. **3** *intransitive* (usu. foll. by *through*) diffuse itself.
□ **per·me·a·tion** *noun* [Latin *permeare permeat-* (as PER-, *meare* pass, go)]

per·meth·rin /pɜrˈmiːθrɪn/ *noun* a synthetic pyrethroid used as an insecticide, esp. against disease-carrying insects. [from PER- + *-m-* + PYRETHRIN]

Per·mian /ˈpɜrmiən/ *Geol.* ● *adjective* of or relating to the final period of the Paleozoic era, lasting from about 286 to 248 million years ago, between the Carboniferous and Triassic periods. The climate was hot and dry in many parts of the world during this period, which saw the extinction of many marine animals and the proliferation of reptiles. ● *noun* this geological period or system. [PERM]

per mil /pɜr ˈmɪl/ *adverb* (also **per mill**) in every thousand. [Latin]

per·mis·sible *adjective* allowable. □ **per·mis·si·bil·ity** *noun* **per·mis·sibly** *adverb* [French or from medieval Latin *permissibilis* (as PERMIT)]

per·mis·sion *noun* (often foll. by *to* + infin.) consent; authorization. [Latin *permissio* (as PERMIT)]

per·mis·sive *adjective* allowing or characterized by great or excessive freedom of behaviour (*the permissive society*). □ **per·mis·sive·ly** *adverb* **per·mis·sive·ness** *noun* [medieval Latin *permissivus* (as PERMIT)]

per·mit ● *verb* (**per·mit·ted**, **per·mit·ting**) **1** *transitive* give permission or consent to; authorize (*permit me to say*). **2 a** *transitive* allow; give an opportunity to (*the new design permits easier storage*). **b** *intransitive* give an opportunity (*circumstances permitting*). **3** *intransitive* (foll. by *of*) admit; allow for. ● *noun* **1 a** a document granting legal permission (*building permit*; *liquor permit*). **b** a document etc. which allows entry into a specified zone. **2** *formal* permission. □ **per·mit·tee** *noun* **per·mit·ter** *noun* [Latin *permittere* (as PER-, *mittere miss-* let go)]

permit book *noun Cdn* a document issued annually by the Canadian Wheat Board to a farmer to record deliveries of and payments for the farmer's wheat and barley.

per·mit·tiv·ity /ˌpɜrmɪˈtɪvɪti/ *noun Electricity* a quantity measuring the ability of a substance to store electrical energy in an electric field.

per·mu·tate /ˈpɜrmjʊˌteit/ *transitive verb* change the order or arrangement of.

per·mu·ta·tion /ˌpɜrmjʊˈteiʃən/ *noun* **1 a** an ordered arrangement or grouping of a set of numbers, items, etc. **b** any one of the range of possible groupings (*the permutations of x, y, and z are xyz, xzy, yxz, yzx, zxy, and zyx*). **2** any combination or selection of a specified number of things from a larger group. □ **per·mu·ta·tion·al** *adjective*

per·mute /pɜrˈmjuːt/ *transitive verb* alter the sequence or arrangement of. [Latin *permutare* (as PER-, *mutare* change)]

Per·nam·buco /ˌpɜrnamˈbuːkoː/ the former name of RECIFE.

per·ni·cious /pɜrˈnɪʃəs/ *adjective* having a harmful effect, esp. in a gradual or subtle way. □ **per·ni·cious·ly** *adverb* **per·ni·cious·ness** *noun* [Latin *perniciosus* from *pernicies* ruin, from *nex necis* death]

pernicious anemia *noun* a defective formation of red blood cells through a lack of vitamin B_{12} or folic acid.

per·nick·ety *adjective informal* = PERSNICKETY. [19th-c. Scots: origin unknown]

Per·nod /perˈnoː, pɜr-/ *noun proprietary* an aniseed-flavoured aperitif from France. [*Pernod Fils*, the manufacturing firm]

per·ogy /pəˈroːgi/ *noun* (*pl.* **-ogies**) (also **per·ogie**, **per·ogi**, **pier·ogi**, **pir·ogi**, **pyr·ogy**, **pyr·ohy** /piˈroːhi/) *N Amer.* a dough dumpling stuffed with potato, cheese, etc., boiled and then optionally fried, and usu. served with onions, sour cream, etc. [Polish *pierogi* (singular *pieróg*) or Ukrainian *pyrohy*]

Perón /peˈroːn, -ˈrɒn/ **1 Eva** (full name Maria Eva Duarte de Perón; known as 'Evita') (1919–52), Argentinian politician. The second wife of Juan Perón, she became de facto Minister of Health and Labour, organized female workers, secured the vote for women, and earmarked

---

Consonants: b *but*   d *dog*   f *few*   g *get*   h *her*   j *yes*   k *cat*   l *leg*   m *man*   n *no*   p *pen*   r *red*   s *sit*

substantial government funds for social welfare; she was nominated for the vice-presidency in 1951, but was forced by the army to withdraw. **2** her husband, **Juan (Do·min·go)** (1895–1974), Argentinian leader, president 1946–55 and 1973–4. As president he assumed dictatorial powers and won popular support with his program of social reform, but, after the death of his second wife Eva, the faltering economy and his conflict with the Roman Catholic Church led to his removal and exile in 1955; he returned to power in 1973, but died in office. **3** his third wife, **Maria Es·tela** (known as 'Isabel') (b.1930), president of Argentina 1974–6. She succeeded her husband as president during a period of increasing political and economic turmoil; placed under house arrest in 1976, she went into exile in Spain in 1981. □ **Peron·ism** /ˈperəˌnɪzəm/ *noun* **Peron·ist** *adjective & noun*

pero·neal /ˌperəˈniːəl/ *adjective Anat.* relating to or near the fibula. [modern Latin *peronaeus* peroneal muscle, from *perone* fibula, from Greek *peronē* pin, fibula]

per·or·ate /ˈperəˌreɪt/ *intransitive verb* **1** sum up and conclude a speech. **2** speak at length. [Latin *perorare perorat-* (as PER-, *orare* speak)]

per·or·a·tion /ˌperəˈreɪʃən/ *noun* **1** the concluding part of a speech, forcefully summing up what has been said. **2** a long, often rhetorical speech.

per·oxi·dase /pəˈrɒksɪˌdeɪz, -ˌdeɪs/ *noun Biochem.* any of a class of enzymes found esp. in plants, which catalyze the oxidation of a substrate by hydrogen peroxide.

per·ox·ide /pəˈrɒksaɪd/ ● *noun Chem.* **1 a** = HYDROGEN PEROXIDE. **b** (often *attributive*) a solution of hydrogen peroxide used to bleach the hair or as an antiseptic. **2** a compound of oxygen with another element containing the greatest possible proportion of oxygen. **3** any salt or ester of hydrogen peroxide. ● *transitive verb* bleach (the hair) with peroxide. [PER- + OXIDE]

perp *noun* esp. *N Amer. slang* the perpetrator of a crime. [abbreviation]

per·pen·dicu·lar /ˌpɜːpənˈdɪkjʊlər/ ● *adjective* **1 a** at right angles to the plane of the horizon. **b** (usu. foll. by *to*) *Geom.* at right angles (to a given line, plane, or surface). **2** upright, vertical. **3** (of a slope etc.) very steep. **4** (**Perpendicular**) *Archit.* of the third stage of English Gothic (15th–16th c.) with vertical tracery in large windows. **5** *jocular* in a standing position. ● *noun* **1** a perpendicular line. **2** a plumb rule or a similar instrument. **3** (prec. by *the*) a perpendicular line or direction (*is out of the perpendicular*). □ **per·pen·dicu·lar·ity** /-ˈlerɪti/ *noun* **per·pen·dicu·lar·ly** *adverb* [Latin *perpendicularis* from *perpendiculum* plumb line, from PER- + *pendēre* hang]

perpe·trate /ˈpɜːpəˌtreɪt/ *transitive verb* commit or perform (a crime, blunder, or anything outrageous). □ **perpe·tra·tion** *noun* **perpe·tra·tor** *noun* [Latin *perpetrare perpetrat-* (as PER-, *patrare* effect)]

per·pet·ual /pərˈpetʃʊəl/ *adjective* **1** eternal; lasting forever or indefinitely. **2** continuous, uninterrupted. **3** frequent, much repeated (*perpetual interruptions*). **4** permanent during life (*perpetual secretary*). □ **perpetu·al·ly** *adverb* [Latin *perpetualis* from *perpetuus* from *perpes -etis* continuous]

perpetual calendar *noun* a calendar which can be adjusted to show any combination of day, month, and year.

perpetual motion *noun* the motion of a hypothetical machine which once set in motion would run forever unless subject to an external force or to wear.

per·petu·ate /pərˈpetʃʊeɪt/ *transitive verb* **1** make perpetual; cause to endure or continue indefinitely. **2** preserve from oblivion. □ **perpetu·a·tion** *noun* **perpetu·ator** *noun* [Latin *perpetuare* (as PERPETUAL)]

perpe·tu·ity /ˌpɜːpəˈtjuːɪti, -ˈtjuː-, -ˈtuː-/ *noun* (*pl.* **-ities**) **1** the state or quality of being perpetual. **2** a perpetual annuity. □ **in perpetuity** forever. [Old French *perpetuité* from Latin *perpetuitas -tatis* (as PERPETUAL)]

Per·pignan /perpiˈnjã/ a city of S France, in the northeastern foothills of the Pyrenees, close to the border with Spain; pop. (1999) 105,115. A former fortress town, it was the capital of the old province of Roussillon.

per·plex *transitive verb* **1** puzzle, bewilder, or disconcert (a person, a person's mind, etc.). **2** complicate or confuse (a matter). □ **per·plexed** *adjective* **per·plex·ing** *adjective* **per·plex·ing·ly** *adverb* [back-formation from *perplexed*, from obsolete adj. *perplex*, from Old French *perplexe* or Latin *perplexus* (as PER-, *plexus*, past participle of *plectere* 'plait')]

per·plex·ity *noun* (*pl.* **-ities**) **1** bewilderment; the state of being perplexed. **2** a thing which perplexes.

per·quis·ite /ˈpɜːkwəzɪt/ *noun* **1** an incidental benefit attached to employment etc., e.g. the use of a company car. **2** a customary extra right or privilege. **3** an extra profit or allowance additional to a main income etc. [medieval Latin *perquisitum* from Latin *perquirere* search diligently for (as PER-, *quaerere* seek)]

Per·rault /peˈroː/ **Charles** (1628–1703), French writer, author of *Mother Goose Tales* (1697), containing such fairy tales as 'The Sleeping Beauty', 'Little Red Riding Hood', 'Puss in Boots', and 'Cinderella'.

Per·rier /ˈperiˌeɪ/ *noun proprietary* an effervescent natural mineral water. [the name of a spring at Vergèze, France, its source]

Per·rin /peˈrã/ **Jean Bap·tiste** (1870–1942), French physical chemist. His investigations into Brownian motion led to a number of mathematical proofs and determinations, and it was accepted that he had provided the definitive proof of the existence of atoms; he was awarded the Nobel Prize for physics in 1926.

per·ron /ˈperən/ *noun* an exterior staircase leading up to a main entrance to a church or other (usu. large) building. [Old French, ultimately from Latin *petra* stone]

Perry, 1 Mat·thew Cal·braith (1794–1858), US naval officer, who negotiated the treaty opening Japan to Western trade (1854). **2** his brother **Oli·ver Haz·ard** (1785–1819), US naval officer, whose victory at the Battle of Put-In-Bay (1813) ensured American control of Lake Erie until the end of the War of 1812.

perry *noun* (*pl.* **-ries**) a drink like cider, made from the fermented juice of pears. [Old French *peré*, ultimately from Latin *pirum* pear]

Perse /pɜːs/ **Saint-John** (pseudonym of Marie René Auguste Alexis Saint-Léger), (1887–1975), French poet and diplomat, born in the W Indies. His works include the epic poem *Anabase* (1924) and prose poems such as *Exil* (1942); he was awarded the Nobel Prize for literature in 1960.

per se /pɜː ˈseɪ/ *adverb* by or in itself; intrinsically. [Latin]

per·se·cute /ˈpɜːsəˌkjuːt/ *transitive verb* **1** subject (a person etc.) to hostility or ill-treatment, esp. on the grounds of race or political or religious belief. **2** harass; annoy persistently. □ **per·se·cu·tor** *noun* **per·se·cu·tory** *adjective* [ultimately from Late Latin *persecutor* from Latin *persequi* (as PER-, *sequi secut-* follow, pursue)]

per·se·cu·tion /ˌpɜːsəˈkjuːʃən/ *noun* the act or an instance of persecuting; the state of being persecuted.

persecution complex *noun* (also **persecution mania**) an irrational obsessive fear that others are scheming against one.

Per·seid /ˈpɜːsiːɪd/ *adjective* designating or pertaining to the Perseids (*Perseid meteor shower*).

Per·seids /ˈpɜːsiːɪdz/ *plural noun* an annual meteor shower in August, radiating from the constellation Perseus and apparently derived from the comet Swift-Tuttle. [PERSEUS]

Per·seph·one /pɜːˈsefəni/ *Gk Myth* a goddess, the daughter of Zeus and Demeter, called Proserpine by the Romans. She was carried off by Hades and made queen of the underworld; Demeter, vainly seeking her, refused to let the earth produce its fruits until her daughter was restored to her, but Persephone was obliged to spend part of every year with Hades.

Per·sep·olis /pɜːˈsepəlɪs/ a city of ancient Persia, situated to the northeast of Shiraz, founded in the late 6th c. BC by Darius I as the ceremonial capital of Persia. Its impressive ruins include functional and ceremonial buildings and cuneiform inscriptions in Old Persian.

Per·seus /ˈpɜːsiəs, -sjuːs/ **1** *Gk Myth* the son of Zeus and Danae, a hero celebrated for many accomplishments. He cut off the head of the gorgon Medusa and gave it to Athene; he also rescued and married Andromeda, and became king of Tiryns in Greece. **2** *Astronomy* a large northern constellation which includes a dense part of the Milky Way. It contains several star clusters and the variable star Algol.

per·sev·er·ate /pɜːˈsevəˌreɪt/ *intransitive verb Psych.* tend to prolong or repeat an action, thought, or utterance after the original stimulus has ceased. □ **per·sev·er·a·tion** *noun* [as PERSEVERE]

perse·vere /ˌpɜːsɪˈvɪər/ *intransitive verb* (often foll. by *in, at, with*) continue steadfastly or determinedly; persist. □ **perse·ver·ance** *noun* [Latin *perseverare* persist, from *perseverus* very strict (as PER-, *severus* severe)]

Per·shing, John Jo·seph (known as 'Black Jack') (1860–1948), US general, who commanded the US Expeditionary Force in the First World War.

Per·sia /ˈpɜːʒə/ a country of SW Asia, now known as Iran. In ancient times, the kingdom of Persia dominated a powerful empire, including at its height all of W Asia, Egypt, and parts of E Europe.

Per·sian /ˈpɜːʒən/ ● *noun* **1 a** a native or inhabitant of ancient or modern Persia (now Iran). **b** a person of Persian descent. **2** the

t *top*   v *voice*   w *we*   z *zoo*   ʃ *she*   ʒ *vision*   θ *thin*   ð *this*   ŋ *ring*   x *loch*   tʃ *chip*   dʒ *jar*   (*see over for vowels*)

language of ancient Persia or modern Iran. ¶ The preferred terms for the language are *Iranian* and *Farsi* respectively. **3** (in full **Persian cat**) **a** a cat of a breed with a broad round head, long silky hair and a thick tail. **b** this breed. **4** *Cdn (NW Ont.)* an oblong doughnut covered with pink or white icing. ● *adjective* of or relating to Persia or its people or language.

Persian carpet *noun* (also **Persian rug**) a carpet or rug of a traditional pattern, made by hand in the Near East from silk or wool.

Persian Gulf (also called **the Gulf** and the **Arabian Gulf**) an arm of the Arabian Sea, to which it is connected by the Strait of Hormuz and the Gulf of Oman. It extends northwestward between the Arabian peninsula and the coast of SW Iran.

Persian lamb *noun* the silky tightly curled fur of a young karakul, used in clothing.

Persian Wars the wars fought between Greece and Persia in the 5th c. BC, in which the Persians sought to extend their territory over the Greek world. In 490 BC the Persians under Darius were defeated by a small force of Athenians at Marathon. Ten years later Darius' son Xerxes I attempted an invasion with a land and sea force, winning a land battle at Thermopylae and devastating Attica, but Persian forces were defeated on land at Plataea and in a sea battle at Salamis (480 BC), and retreated.

persi·flage /'pɜrsə,flɒʒ/ *noun* light raillery, banter. [French *persifler* banter, formed as PER- + *siffler* whistle]

per·sim·mon /pɜr'sɪmən/ *noun* **1** any evergreen tree of the genus *Diospyros* bearing edible orange pulpy fruits. **2** the fruit of this. **3** the colour of persimmon fruit, reddish orange. [corruption of Algonquian *pessemmins*]

per·sist *intransitive verb* **1** (often foll. by *in*) continue firmly or obstinately (in an opinion or a course of action) esp. despite obstacles, remonstrance, etc. **2** (of an institution, custom, phenomenon, etc.) continue in existence; survive. **3** be insistent with a statement or question. [Latin *persistere* (as PER-, *sistere* stand)]

per·sis·tent *adjective* **1** continuing in spite of obstacles, attempts at control, etc.; persisting. **2** enduring. **3** constantly repeated (*persistent nagging*). **4** *Biol.* (of horns, leaves, etc.) remaining instead of falling off in the normal manner. **5** (of a chemical) remaining within the environment for a long time after its introduction. □ **per·sis·tence** *noun* **per·sis·tency** *noun* **per·sis·tent·ly** *adverb*

persistent organic pollutant *noun* any of a number of hazardous organic chemicals, such as DDT, dioxin, and PCBs, that remain in the environment for a long period of time without breaking down.

persistent vegetative state *noun Med.* the state of a person whose body is kept functioning by medical means but who manifests no sign of higher brain functions.

per·snick·ety *adjective N Amer. informal* **1** fussy; fastidious. **2** requiring tact or careful handling. [alteration of PERNICKETY]

per·son *noun* **1** an individual human being (*a cheerful and forthright person*). **2** the living body of a human being (*hidden about your person*). **3** *Philos.* a self-conscious or rational being. **4** *Grammar* a category used in the classification of pronouns, verb forms, etc., according to whether they indicate the speaker (**first person**); the addressee (**second person**); a third party (**third person**). **5** (in *combination*) used to replace *-man* in offices open to either sex (*salesperson*). **6** (in Christianity) God as Father, Son, or Holy Spirit (*three persons in one God*). **7** an individual or a group of individuals as a corporation regarded as having rights and duties recognized by law. **8** *archaic* a character in a play or story. **9** an individual characterized by a preference or liking for a specified thing (*not a party person*). **10** (in *combination*) used as a unit of measure of work etc. (*person-day; person-year*). **11** an individual as distinguished from a thing, a type, or an animal, esp. an individual regarded as having human dignity, personality, or responsibility. □ **in one's own person** oneself; as oneself. **in person** physically present. [Latin *persona* 'actor's mask, character in a play, human being']

per·so·na /pɜr'soʊnə/ *noun* (pl. **per·so·nas** or **per·so·nae** /-naɪ, -niː/) **1** an aspect of the personality as shown to or perceived by others (*opp.* ANIMA 1). **2** a character assumed by an author, performer, etc. in his or her writing, work, etc. **3** a character in a fictional work. [Latin (as PERSON)]

per·son·able /'pɜrsənəbəl/ *adjective* pleasing in appearance and behaviour; agreeable, likeable. □ **per·son·able·ness** *noun* **per·son·ably** *adverb*

per·son·age /'pɜrsənɪdʒ/ *noun* **1** a person, esp. of rank or importance. **2** a character in a play etc. [Middle English from PERSON + -AGE, influenced by medieval Latin *personagium* effigy & French *personnage*]

per·sona grata /'grɑtə/ *noun* (pl. **personae gratae** /'grɑtaɪ, -tiː/) a person, esp. a diplomat, acceptable to certain others. [Latin, as PERSONA + *grata*, fem. of *gratus* pleasing]

per·son·al ● *adjective* **1** one's own; individual; private. **2** done or made in person (*made a personal appearance; my personal attention*). **3** directed to or concerning an individual (*a personal letter*). **4 a** referring (esp. in a hostile way) to an individual's private life or concerns (*making personal remarks; no need to be personal*). **b** close, intimate (*a personal friend*). **5** of the body and clothing (*personal hygiene; personal appearance*). **6** existing as a person, not as an abstraction or thing (*a personal God*). **7** *Grammar* of or denoting one of the three persons (*personal pronoun*). **8** intended for a particular person rather than a group (*my personal coach; a personal favour*). ● *noun* esp. *N Amer.* an advertisement or notice in the personal column of a newspaper, on a computer bulletin board, etc.

personal ad *noun* esp. *N Amer. informal* = PERSONAL *noun*.

personal best *noun* a person's best achievement in a sporting endeavour.

personal column *noun* a part of a newspaper in which personal messages, advertisements for companions, etc. are published.

personal computer *noun* a general-purpose microcomputer designed for use by one person at a time, esp. in a home or office environment. Abbr.: **PC**. □ **personal computing** *noun*

personal digital assistant *noun* a small hand-held computer, often pen-based, used as a personal organizer. Abbr.: **PDA**.

personal flotation device *noun* a life jacket or other buoyant or inflatable device for keeping a person afloat in water, esp. in an emergency. Abbr.: **PFD**.

personal foul *noun* a foul called in a basketball, football, etc. game for illegal body contact with, or roughing of, an opponent.

personal identification number *noun* a number allocated to an individual, serving as a password esp. for a bank machine, automatic debit terminal, etc. Abbr.: **PIN**.

per·son·al·ism *noun* any of various systems of thought which maintain the primacy of the (human or divine) person on the basis that reality has meaning only through the conscious minds of people. □ **per·son·al·ist** *adjective & noun*

per·son·al·ity *noun* (pl. **-ities**) **1 a** the assemblage of qualities or characteristics which makes a person a distinctive individual (*an attractive personality*). **b** socially attractive qualities (*was clever but had no personality*). **c** the unique characteristics of a place, situation, or thing. **2** a famous person; a celebrity (*a TV personality*). **3** a person who stands out from others by virtue of his or her character (*is a real personality*). **4** personal existence or identity; the condition of being a person. [Late Latin *personalitas -tatis* (as PERSONAL)]

personality cult *noun* the extreme adulation of an individual, esp. a politician.

personality disorder *noun* any of several psychiatric disorders characterized by a disposition to behave in certain abnormal ways that cause harm to oneself or others.

personality type *noun* a classification of personality according to the preponderant features or traits found in a person.

per·son·al·ize *transitive verb* (also esp. *Brit.* **-ise**) **1** make personal; adapt to individual persons' needs etc. **2** mark or inscribe (stationery, belongings, etc.) with a particular person's name, initials, etc. **3** cause (a discussion etc.) to become concerned with personal matters or feelings rather than with general issues. **4** personify. □ **per·son·al·iz·a·tion** *noun*

personal loan *noun* a loan to a private person by a bank or trust company for buying a car, renovating a home, etc.

per·son·al·ly *adverb* **1** in person (*see to it personally*). **2** for one's own part (*speaking personally*). **3** as a person (*I don't know him personally, but I've read his books*). □ **take personally** be offended by, as directed at one's own person.

personal organizer *noun* **1** a loose-leaf notebook with sections for various kinds of information, such as appointments, addresses, etc. **2** a hand-held microcomputer serving the same purpose.

personal pension plan *noun* a pension plan that is independent of the contributor's employer.

personal pronoun *noun* each of the pronouns (*I, you, he, she, it, we, they, me, him, her, us, them*) comprising a set that shows contrast of person, gender, number, and case. ¶ Reflexive pronouns (*myself, ourselves*, etc.) and possessive pronouns (*my, your*, etc.) are sometimes included in the category of personal pronouns.

personal property *noun Law* all one's property except land and those interests in land that pass to one's heirs (compare REAL[1] adjective 6).

personal service noun individual service given to a customer.

personal shopper noun an individual who is paid to help another to purchase goods, either by accompanying them while shopping or by shopping on their behalf.

personal space noun **1** the immediate area around an individual where any encroachment is considered threatening or uncomfortable. **2** space for the use of an individual.

personal stereo noun a small portable audio cassette player, often with radio, or compact disc player, used with lightweight headphones.

personal touch noun **1** a characteristic or individual approach to a situation. **2** a personal element added to something otherwise impersonal.

personal trainer noun a fitness expert who is hired to come to a person's house etc. to plan and supervise their workout regimen.

per·son·al·ty /ˈpɜrsənəlti/ noun (pl. **-ties**) Law one's personal property or estate (opp. REALTY).

personal video recorder noun a device that records television programs on to a hard disk and allows manipulation of programs while they are being transmitted.

personal watercraft noun N Amer. a jet-propelled recreational boat for one or two persons, ridden like a motorcycle. Abbr.: **PWC**.

per·so·na non gra·ta /nɒn ˈgrɑtə/ noun (pl. **per·so·nae non gra·tae** /ˈgrɑtaɪ, -tiː/) an unacceptable or unwelcome person. [Latin, as PERSONA GRATA + non not]

per·son·ate /ˈpɜrsəˌneɪt/ transitive verb **1** play the part of (a character in a drama etc.; another type of person). **2** pretend to be (another person), esp. for fraudulent purposes; impersonate. □ **per·son·a·tion** noun **per·son·ator** noun [Late Latin personare personat- (as PERSON)]

per·son·hood noun the quality or condition of being an individual person.

per·son·i·fi·ca·tion /pɜr ˌsɒnəfɪˈkeɪʃən/ noun **1** the act of personifying. **2** (foll. by of) a person or thing viewed as a striking example of (a quality etc.) (the personification of ugliness).

per·son·i·fy /pɜrˈsɒnəˌfaɪ/ transitive verb (**-fies, -fied**) **1** attribute a human nature or characteristics to (an abstraction or thing). **2** symbolize (a quality etc.) by a figure in human form. **3** (usu. as **per·son·i·fied** adjective) embody (a quality) in one's own person; exemplify typically (has always been kindness personified). □ **per·son·i·fi·er** noun [French personnifier (as PERSON)]

per·son·nel /ˌpɜrsəˈnel/ noun **1** a body of employees, persons involved in a public undertaking, armed forces, etc. **2** = PERSONNEL DEPARTMENT. [French, originally adj. = personal]

personnel carrier noun an armoured vehicle for transporting troops etc.

personnel department noun the part of an organization concerned with the hiring, training, and welfare of employees.

Persons Case the 1928 ruling by the Supreme Court of Canada that women were not 'persons' eligible to hold public office as senators; the case was appealed to the British Privy Council which overturned the ruling.

person-to-person ● attributive adjective **1** involving personal contact between individuals. **2** (of a phone call) booked through the operator to a specified person. **●** adverb in person; face to face.

per·spec·tive noun **1 a** the art of drawing solid objects on a two-dimensional surface so as to give the right impression of relative positions, size, etc. **b** a picture drawn in this way. **2** the apparent relation between visible objects as to position, distance, etc. **3 a** a point of view; a way of regarding a matter (a Marxist perspective). **b** a mental view of the relative importance of things (keep the right perspective). **4** a geographical or imaginary prospect. □ **in** (or **out of**) **perspective 1** drawn or viewed according (or not according) to the rules of perspective. **2** correctly (or incorrectly) regarded in terms of relative importance. □ **per·spec·tiv·al** /-ˈtaɪvəl/ adjective ¶ Do not confuse perspective with prospective in phrases like prospective buyer. [medieval Latin perspectiva (ars art) from perspicere perspect- (as PER-, specere spect- look)]

Per·spex /ˈpɜrspeks/ noun Brit. proprietary = PLEXIGLAS. [Latin perspicere look through (as PER-, specere look)]

per·spi·ca·cious /ˌpɜrspɪˈkeɪʃəs/ adjective having or showing discernment or insight; perceptive. □ **per·spi·ca·cious·ly** adverb **per·spi·ca·cious·ness** noun **per·spi·ca·city** /-ˈkasɪti/ noun [Latin perspicax -acis (as PERSPEX)]

per·spic·u·ous /pɜrˈspɪkjuːəs/ adjective easily understood; clearly

expressed. □ **per·spi·cu·ity** /-ˈkjuːɪti/ noun **per·spic·u·ous·ly** adverb **per·spic·u·ous·ness** noun [Middle English, = transparent, from Latin perspicuus (as PERSPECTIVE)]

per·spi·ra·tion /ˌpɜrspəˈreɪʃən/ noun **1** = SWEAT noun 1. **2** sweating.

per·spire verb **1** intransitive sweat or exude perspiration, esp. as the result of heat, exercise, anxiety, etc. **2** transitive sweat or exude (fluid etc.). [Latin perspirare (as PER-, spirare breathe)]

per·suade /pɜrˈsweɪd/ transitive verb & reflexive **1** (often foll. by that + clause, or of) cause (another person or oneself) to believe; convince (persuaded them that it would be helpful; tried to persuade me of its value). **2** (often foll. by to + infin.) induce (another person or oneself) (persuaded us to join them; managed to persuade them at last). □ **per·suad·able** adjective **per·suad·er** noun **per·sua·sible** adjective [Latin persuadēre (as PER-, suadēre suas- advise)]

per·sua·sion /pɜrˈsweɪʒən/ noun **1** persuading (yielded to persuasion). **2** persuasiveness (use all your persuasion). **3** a belief or conviction (my private persuasion). **4** a religious or political belief, or the group holding it (of a different persuasion). **5** informal or jocular **a** any group or party (the male persuasion). **b** kind or type. [Latin persuasio (as PERSUADE)]

per·sua·sive /pɜrˈsweɪsɪv/ adjective able to persuade; convincing. □ **per·sua·sive·ly** adverb **per·sua·sive·ness** noun [French persuasif -ive or medieval Latin persuasivus, (as PERSUADE)]

PERT abbreviation program evaluation and review technique.

pert adjective **1** saucy or impudent, esp. in speech or conduct. **2** (of clothes etc.) neat and suggestive of jauntiness. □ **pert·ly** adverb **pert·ness** noun [Old French apert from Latin apertus past participle of aperire 'open', & from Old French aspert from Latin expertus EXPERT]

per·tain intransitive verb **1** (foll. by to) relate or have reference to (evidence pertaining to the case). **2** belong to as a part or appendage or accessory. [Old French partenir from Latin pertinēre (as PER-, tenēre hold)]

Perth 1 the capital of the state of Western Australia, on the Indian Ocean; pop. (est. 2002) 1,360,000 (including the port of Fremantle). **2** a town in E Scotland, at the head of the Tay estuary; pop. (est. 2002) 41,100. It was the capital of Scotland from 1210 until 1452. **3** a town in SE central Ontario, situated on the Tay River, about 70 km southwest of Ottawa; pop. (2001) 6,003. □ **Perth·ite** noun (in sense 3). [sense 3 after sense 2]

Perth and Kinross an administrative region of central Scotland, formerly part of Tayside Region; administrative centre, Perth.

Perth·shire /ˈpɜrθʃɪr/ a former county of central Scotland. It became a part of Tayside region in 1975, and of Perth and Kinross in 1996.

per·ti·na·cious /ˌpɜrtɪˈneɪʃəs/ adjective stubborn; persistent; obstinate (in a course of action etc.). □ **per·ti·na·cious·ly** adverb **per·ti·na·cious·ness** noun **per·ti·na·city** /-ˈnasɪti/ noun [Latin pertinax (as PER-, tenax tenacious)]

per·ti·nent /ˈpɜrtɪnənt/ adjective (often foll. by to) relevant to the matter in hand; apposite. □ **per·ti·nence** noun **per·ti·nent·ly** adverb [Old French pertinent or Latin pertinēre (as PERTAIN)]

per·turb transitive verb **1** (usu. in passive) disturb mentally; agitate. **2** throw into confusion or disorder. **3** Physics & Math. subject (a physical system, or a set of equations, or its solution) to a perturbation. □ **per·turb·able** adjective **per·turb·ing·ly** adverb [Old French pertourber from Latin (as PER-, turbare disturb)]

per·tur·ba·tion /ˌpɜrtərˈbeɪʃən/ noun **1** the act or an instance of perturbing; the state of being perturbed. **2** a cause of disturbance or agitation. **3** Physics a slight alteration of a physical system, e.g. of the electrons in an atom, caused by a secondary influence. **4** Astronomy a minor deviation in the course of a celestial body, caused by the attraction of a neighbouring body.

per·tus·sis /pɜrˈtʌsɪs/ noun whooping cough. [modern Latin from PER- + Latin tussis cough]

Peru /pəˈruː/ a country in S America on the Pacific coast, traversed throughout its length by the Andes; pop. (est. 2002) 27,949,639; capital, Lima. □ **Peru·vian** /pəˈruːviən/ noun & adjective

Peru·gia /pəˈruːdʒə/ a city in central Italy, the capital of Umbria; pop. (2001) 148,575.

Peru·gino /peruˈdʒiːnoː/ **il** (born Pietro Vannucci) (c.1450–1523), Italian painter. He is best known for his altarpieces and frescoes such as Christ Delivering the Keys to St. Peter, in the Sistine Chapel, Rome.

per·uke /pəˈruːk/ noun hist. a wig. [French perruque from Italian perrucca parrucca, of unknown origin]

per·use /pəˈruːz/ transitive verb **1** read or study thoroughly or carefully. **2** read in a casual manner. **3** examine (a person's face etc.) carefully. □ **per·usal** noun **per·us·er** noun [Middle English, originally = use up, prob. from Anglo-Latin from Romanic (as PER-, USE)]

---

uː m**oo**d   ai m**y**   əi p**i**pe   au br**ow**n   ʌu h**ou**se   ei d**ay**   ɔi b**oy**   ã fr**an**glais   ã Canad**ien**   ɔ̃ Bray**on**   (see over for consonants)

Per·utz /pəˈruts/ **Max Fer·di·nand** (1914–2002), Austrian-born English biochemist, who discovered the molecular structure of hemoglobin, and shared the Nobel Prize for chemistry in 1962 with Sir John Kendrew.

Per·uzzi /pəˈruːtsi/ **Bal·das·sare (Tomas·so)** (1481–1536), Italian architect and painter, who became architect of St. Peter's, Rome, following the death of Raphael; his designs include the Villa Farnesina in Rome (1500–11).

perv noun slang **1** a sexual pervert. **2** Austral. an erotic gaze. □ **pervy** adjective [abbreviation]

per·vade transitive verb **1** spread throughout, permeate. **2** (of influences etc.) become widespread among or in. **3** be rife among or through. □ **per·va·sion** noun [Latin pervadere (as PER-, vadere vas- go)]

per·va·sive adjective **1** able to pervade. **2** able to pervade. □ **per·va·sive·ly** adverb **per·va·sive·ness** noun

per·verse adjective **1** (of a person or action) deliberately or stubbornly departing from what is reasonable or required. **2** persistent in error. **3** wayward; intractable; peevish. **4** perverted; wicked. **5** (of a verdict etc.) against the weight of evidence or the judge's direction. □ **per·verse·ly** adverb **per·verse·ness** noun **per·vers·ity** noun (pl. **-ities**). [Latin perversus (as PERVERT)]

per·ver·sion noun **1** an act of perverting; the state of being perverted. **2** a perverted form of an act or thing. **3 a** a preference for an abnormal form of sexual activity. **b** such an activity. [Latin perversio (as PERVERT)]

per·vert ● transitive verb /pərˈvərt/ **1** turn (a person or thing) aside from its proper use or nature (pervert the course of justice). **2** misapply or misconstrue (words etc.). **3** lead astray (a person, a person's mind, etc.) from right opinion or conduct; corrupt. ● noun /ˈpərvərt/ a person showing sexual perversion. □ **per·vert·er** /-ˈvərtər/ noun [Latin pervertere (as PER-, vertere vers- turn): compare CONVERT]

per·vert·ed /pərˈvərtəd/ adjective showing or practising perversion. □ **per·vert·ed·ly** adverb

per·vious /ˈpərviəs/ adjective permeable. □ **per·vious·ness** noun [Latin pervius (as PER-, vius from via way)]

Pe·sach /ˈpeisax/ noun the Passover festival. [Hebrew Pesah]

pes·eta /pəˈseitə/ noun the former basic monetary unit of Spain, now replaced by the euro. [Spanish, diminutive of pesa weight, from Latin pensa pl. of pensum: see POISE[1]]

pe·sewa /pəˈseiwə/ noun a monetary unit of Ghana, equal to one-hundredth of a cedi. [Fanti, = PENNY]

Pe·sha·war /pəˈʃɒwər/ the capital of North-West Frontier Province, in Pakistan; pop. (1998) 988,000. Situated near the Khyber Pass on the border with Afghanistan, it is of strategic and military importance.

Pe·shitta /pəˈʃitə/ the ancient Syriac version of the Bible, used in Syriac-speaking Christian countries from the early 5th c. and still the official Bible of the Syrian Christian Churches. [Syriac, = simple, plain]

pesh·merga /peʃˈmərgə/ noun a member of a Kurdish nationalist revolutionary army established in the early 1960s. [Kurdish pêšmerge from pêš in front of + merg death]

pesky adjective (**pesk·i·er**, **pesk·i·est**) esp. N Amer. informal troublesome; confounded; annoying. □ **pesk·i·ly** adverb **pesk·i·ness** noun [18th c.: perhaps from PEST]

peso /ˈpeisoʊ/ noun (pl. **pesos**) the basic monetary unit of several Latin American countries and of the Philippines, equal to 100 centésimos in Uruguay and 100 centavos elsewhere. [Spanish, = weight, from Latin pensum: see POISE[1]]

pes·sary /ˈpesəri/ noun (pl. **-ies**) Med. **1** a device worn in the vagina to support the uterus or as a contraceptive. **2** a vaginal suppository. [Late Latin pessarium, pessulum from pessum, pessus from Greek pessos oval stone]

pes·sim·ism /ˈpesəˌmizəm/ noun **1** a tendency to take a gloomy view of circumstances or expect the worst outcome. **2** Philos. a belief that this world is as bad as it could be or that all things tend to evil (opp. OPTIMISM 2). □ **pes·sim·ist** noun **pes·sim·is·tic** /-ˈmistik/ adjective **pes·sim·is·tic·ally** /-ˈmistikli/ adverb [Latin pessimus worst, after OPTIMISM]

pest noun **1** a troublesome or annoying person or thing; a nuisance. **2** a destructive animal, esp. an insect which attacks crops, livestock, etc. **3** archaic a pestilence; a plague. [French peste or Latin pestis plague]

Pesta·lozzi /ˌpestəˈlɒtsi/ **Jo·hann Hein·rich** (1746–1827), Swiss educational reformer. He pioneered education for poor children and had a major impact on the development of primary education; his theory and method are set out in How Gertrude Teaches Her Children (1801).

pes·ter transitive verb trouble or annoy, esp. with frequent or persistent requests. [prob. from impester from French empestrer encumber: influenced by PEST]

pester power noun the power exercised by children to pressure parents into buying them things, esp. items advertised on television.

pest·house noun hist. a hospital for sufferers from plague or other infectious disease.

pesti·cide noun a chemical preparation for destroying insects or other organisms harmful to cultivated plants or to animals. □ **pesti·cid·al** adjective

pest·ifer·ous /peˈstifərəs/ adjective **1** informal irritating, annoying. **2** noxious; pestilent. **3** harmful; pernicious; bearing moral contagion. [Latin pestifer, -ferus (as PEST)]

pesti·lence /ˈpestiləns/ noun **1** a fatal epidemic disease, esp. bubonic plague. **2** something evil or destructive. [Old French from Latin pestilentia (as PESTILENT)]

pesti·lent /ˈpestilənt/ adjective **1** destructive to life, deadly. **2** harmful or morally destructive. **3** informal troublesome; annoying. □ **pesti·lent·ly** adverb [Latin pestilens, pestilentus from pestis plague]

pesti·len·tial /ˌpestiˈlenʃəl/ adjective **1** of or relating to pestilence. **2** dangerous. **3** troublesome, annoying. □ **pesti·len·tial·ly** adverb

pestle /ˈpesəl/ ● noun **1** a club-shaped instrument for pounding substances in a mortar. **2** an appliance for pounding etc. ● transitive verb pound with a pestle or in a similar manner. [Old French pestel from Latin pistillum from pinsare pist- to pound]

pesto noun an Italian sauce of crushed basil leaves, pine nuts, garlic, Parmesan cheese, and olive oil, usu. served with pasta. [Italian, from pestare 'pound, crush']

PET abbreviation **1** POSITRON EMISSION TOMOGRAPHY. **2** (also **PETE**) polyethylene terephthalate, a plastic used in recyclable packaging.

Pet. abbreviation Peter (New Testament).

pet[1] ● noun **1** a domestic or tamed animal kept for pleasure or companionship. **2** a darling, a favourite (often as a term of endearment). ● attributive adjective **1** kept as a pet (pet lamb). **2** of or for pet animals (pet food). **3** often jocular favourite or particular (pet peeve). **4** expressing fondness or familiarity (pet name). ● transitive & intransitive verb (**pet·ted**, **pet·ting**) **1** transitive treat as a pet. **2** transitive stroke (an animal). **3** intransitive engage in erotic caressing. [16th-c. Scots & Northern English dial.: origin unknown]

pet[2] noun a feeling of petty resentment or ill-humour (be in a pet). [16th c.: origin unknown]

peta- /ˈpetə/ combining form denoting a factor of 10^{15}. [perhaps from PENTA-]

peta·byte /ˈpetəˌbait/ noun Computing 1,125,899,906,842,624 (i.e. 2^{50}) bytes (a million gigabytes).

Pé·tain /peiˈtã/ **(Henri) Phi·lippe (Omer)** (1856–1951), French general and political leader, head of state 1940–2. A national hero in the First World War for halting the German advance at Verdun (1916), he concluded an armistice with Nazi Germany in 1940 and established the French government at Vichy (effectively a puppet regime for the Third Reich) until German occupation in 1942; after the war he received a death sentence for collaboration, but this was commuted to life imprisonment.

petal noun each of the parts of the corolla of a flower. □ **pet·alled** adjective (also in combination). **petal-like** adjective **petal·oid** adjective [modern Latin petalum, in Late Latin metal plate, from Greek petalon leaf, from petalos outspread]

pé·tanque /peiˈtãk/ noun a French game similar to boule. [French]

pe·tard /piˈtɑrd/ noun hist. **1** a small bomb used to blast down a door etc. **2** a kind of firework or cracker. □ **hoist with one's own petard** adversely affect oneself by one's schemes against others. [French pétard from péter break wind]

Pe·tare /pəˈtɒri/ a city in N Venezuela, part of the conurbation of Caracas; pop. (est. 2000) 520,982.

pet·asus /ˈpetəsəs/ noun **1** an ancient Greek hat with a low crown and broad brim, esp. (in Greek mythology) as worn by Hermes. **2** the winged hat of Hermes. [Latin from Greek petasos]

Peta·wawa /ˈpetəˌwɒwɒ/ a town in NE Ontario, about 150 km northwest of Ottawa on the Ottawa River; pop. (2001) 14,398. [as PETAWAWA RIVER]

Petawawa River a river in E Ontario, a major tributary of the Ottawa River. [Algonquin, = a noise is heard far away]

pet·cock noun a small valve positioned in the pipe of a steam boiler or cylinder of a steam engine for drainage or testing. [possibly from French pet a fart, + COCK[1] noun 6]

Consonants: b but   d dog   f few   g get   h her   j yes   k cat   l leg   m man   n no   p pen   r red   s sit

PETE noun var. of PET 2.

Pete noun □ **for Pete's sake** (also **for the love of Pete**) a mild exclamatory phrase expressing exasperation or annoyance. [abbreviation of the name *Peter*]

pe·techia /pɪˈtiːkiə/ noun (pl. **pe·tech·iae** /-ki,iː/) Med. a small red or purple spot as a result of bleeding into the skin. □ **pe·tech·ial** adjective [modern Latin from Italian *petecchia* a freckle or spot on one's face]

Peter ▸ **1** St. (born Simon), an Apostle. 'Peter' (from *petros* = stone) is the Greek form of the name given him by Jesus, signifying the rock on which he would establish his church. He is regarded by Roman Catholics as the founder and first bishop of the Church at Rome, where he is said to have been martyred in about AD 67. He is often represented as the keeper of the door of heaven; his attribute is a set of keys. Feast day, 29 June. **2** either of the two letters in the New Testament ascribed to St. Peter.

Peter I (known as Peter the Great) (1672–1725), czar of Russia 1682–1725. After the death of his half-brother Ivan in 1689, he assumed sole authority and launched a policy of expansion along the Baltic coast; in 1703 he made St. Petersburg his capital, and his introduction of extensive government and administration reforms were instrumental in transforming Russia into a significant European power.

peter[1] intransitive verb (foll. by *out*) decrease, diminish, or fade gradually before coming to an end. [19th c.: origin unknown]

peter[2] noun slang the penis. [perhaps from the name *Peter*]

Peter·bor·ough /ˈpiːtər,bɜro, -bɜrə/ noun **1** an industrial city in east central England, formerly in Cambridgeshire; pop. (est. 2002) 144,800. **2** a city in south central Ontario, northeast of Oshawa; pop. (2001) 71,446. [sense 2 after *Peter* Robinson, Upper Canadian politician who helped with the settlement of over two thousand Irish immigrants in the area d.1838]

Peterborough canoe noun Cdn a type of all-wood canoe originally built at Peterborough, Ontario.

Peter·head noun Cdn (North) a decked launch or large whaleboat with a sail and a small motor, used in the E Arctic. [*Peterhead*, Scotland, where early boats of this type were made]

Peter·loo (also **Peterloo massacre**) an attack by yeomanry on 16 Aug. 1819 against a large but peaceable crowd which was gathered in St. Peter's Field, Manchester, in support of political reform. Eleven civilians were killed, and more than 500 injured. The event was named Peterloo in ironical reference to the Battle of Waterloo.

Peter Pan noun a person who retains youthful features, or who is immature. [hero of J. M. Barrie's play of the same name (1904)]

Peter Pan collar noun a flat collar with rounded points.

Peter Prin·ciple noun jocular the principle that members of a hierarchy are promoted until they reach the level at which they are no longer competent. [L. J. *Peter*, its propounder, b.1919]

Peters ▸ **1** Ar·thur (1854–1908), Canadian lawyer and politician, Liberal premier of PEI 1901–08. Throughout his premiership he defended PEI's position and status within Confederation. **2** his brother Fred·erick (1852–1919), Canadian lawyer and politician. Elected to the PEI Assembly as a Liberal in 1890, he was premier 1891–97; during his premiership the two chambers of the PEI legislature were merged into a single assembly.

peter·sham /ˈpiːtər,ʃəm/ noun thick corded silk ribbon used for stiffening in dressmaking etc. [Lord *Petersham*, English army officer d.1851]

Peter·son, Oscar Em·man·uel (b.1925), Canadian jazz pianist and composer. He has had a distinguished international career since the 1940s, often appearing with Ella Fitzgerald, and usually leading a trio with bass and guitar. He has recorded over 130 albums.

Peter's pence plural noun Catholicism **1** hist. an annual tax of one penny, formerly paid to the papal see. **2** (since 1860) a voluntary payment to the papal treasury. [St. PETER, as first pope]

Peter the Hermit (c.1050–1115), French monk. His preaching on the First Crusade was a rallying cry for thousands of peasants throughout Europe to journey to the Holy Land; most were massacred by the Turks in Asia Minor.

pethi·dine /ˈpeθɪ,diːn/ noun a synthetic soluble analgesic used esp. in childbirth. [perhaps from PIPERIDINE (from which the drug is derived) + ETHYL]

peti·ole /ˈpeti,oːl/ noun **1** Bot. the slender stalk joining a leaf to a stem. **2** Zool. a slender stalk between two structures, as that connecting the abdomen and thorax in wasps, ants, and other insects. □ **peti·olar**

peti·o·late /-lət/ adjective [French *pétiole* from Latin *petiolus* little foot, stalk]

Pe·tipa /ˈpeti:pp/ **Mar·ius (Ivan·ovich)** (1818–1910), French ballet dancer and choreographer, resident in Russia from 1847. He choreographed more than 50 ballets, many of which still constitute the mainstay of the classical ballet repertoire, such as *The Sleeping Beauty* (1890), *The Nutcracker* (1892), and *Swan Lake* (1895).

petit /ˈpeti/ adjective esp. Law petty; small; of lesser importance. [Old French, = small, from Romanic, perhaps imitative of child's speech]

petit bourgeois /ˌpeti ˈbʊrʒwʌ, pəˈtiː/ ● noun (pl. **pet·its bour·geois** pronunc. same) a member of the lower middle class. ● adjective pertaining to or characteristic of the lower middle class. [French]

Petit·co·di·ac River /ˌpetɪˈkoːdiak/ a river in E New Brunswick, flowing northeastward through Moncton and Dieppe, then bending sharply southeastward to empty into Shepody Bay, an inlet of Chignecto Bay on the Bay of Fundy. [Mi'kmaq *epetkutogoyek* river that bends around back]

pe·tite /pəˈtiːt/ ● adjective **1** (of a woman) of small and dainty build. **2** (of a thing) small in size. **3** designating a small size in women's clothing. ● noun a petite size in women's clothing. [French, fem. of PETIT]

petite bourgeoisie /ˈpeti ,bʊrʒwɒˈziː/ noun the lower middle class.

petit four /ˌpeti ˈfɔr/ noun (pl. **pet·its fours** /ˈfɔrz/) a small fancy cake or biscuit, esp. a small square cake covered with fondant icing. [French, = little oven]

petit grain /peˈtiː,grã/ noun any of various essential oils used in perfumery, distilled from the leaves and shoots of particular citrus plants, esp. the orange, and having a sweet floral scent. [French, lit. 'small grain']

pe·ti·tion /pəˈtɪʃən/ ● noun **1** a supplication or request. **2** a formal written request, esp. one signed by many people, appealing to authority in some cause. **3** Law an application to a court for a writ etc. ● verb **1** transitive make or address a petition to (*petition your MP*). **2** intransitive (often foll. by *for, to*) appeal earnestly or humbly. □ **pe·ti·tion·er** noun [Latin *petitio -onis*, from *petit-*, past participle stem of *petere*, aim at, lay claim to, ask, seek]

pe·ti·tio prin·cipii /pəˌtɪʃioː prɪnˈkɪpi,aɪ/ noun a logical fallacy in which a conclusion is taken for granted in the premise; begging the question. [Latin, = assuming a principle: see PETITION]

petit jeté /pəˌtiː ʒəˈteɪ/ noun Dance a jump in which the dancer brushes one leg outwards from the body and then lands on it with the other leg bent so that the foot is raised slightly off the floor and tucked in against the first leg's ankle. [French *petit* 'small' + *jeté* past participle of *jeter* 'throw']

petit mal /ˌpeti ˈmal, ˌpəti/ noun (also, with hyphen, attributive) a mild form of epilepsy with only momentary loss of consciousness (compare GRAND MAL). [French, = little sickness]

petit point /ˈpeti pɔint/ noun **1** embroidery on canvas using small stitches. **2** = TENT STITCH. [French, = little point]

pet·its pois /ˌpeti ˈpwɒ, pəˌtiː/ plural noun small green peas. [French]

pet name noun N Amer. an affectionate nickname.

Petra /ˈpetrə/ an ancient city of SW Asia, in present-day Jordan. Its extensive ruins include temples and tombs hewn from the rose-red sandstone cliffs.

Pe·trarch /ˈpetrɑrk/ (Italian name Francesco Petrarca) (1304–74), Italian poet, whose work had a great influence on later Renaissance writers (e.g. in its choice of themes from classical antiquity); he is best known for his love poems inspired by an idealized woman he called Laura.

Pe·trarch·an /peˈtrɑrkən/ adjective of, pertaining to, or characteristic of Petrarch, esp. denoting a sonnet of the kind used by him, with an octave rhyming *abbaabba*, and a sestet usu. rhyming *cdcdcd* or *cdecde*.

pet·rel /ˈpetrəl/ noun any of various seabirds of the family Procellariidae or Hydrobatidae, with mainly black (or brown) and white plumage and usu. a hooked bill, usu. flying far from land. [17th c. (also *pitteral*), of uncertain origin: later assoc. with St. Peter, from the bird's habit of flying low with the legs dangling, giving the appearance of walking on water (Matt. 14:30)]

petri dish /ˈpiːtri/ noun a shallow covered dish used for the culture of bacteria etc. [J. R. *Petri*, German bacteriologist d.1921]

Pet·rie /ˈpiːtri/ **Sir (Wil·liam Mat·thew) Flin·ders** (1853–1942), English archaeologist and Egyptologist. After fieldwork at Stonehenge in the 1870s, he began excavating the great pyramid at Giza in 1880, pioneering the use of mathematical calculation and precise measurement in field archaeology.

petri·fac·tion /ˌpetrɪˈfakʃən/ *noun* **1** the process of fossilization whereby organic matter is turned into a stony substance. **2** a petrified substance or mass. **3** a state of extreme fear or terror.

pet·ri·fy /ˈpetrɪfaɪ/ *verb* (**-fies, -fied**) (usu. as **petri·fied** *adjective*) **1** *transitive* paralyze with fear, astonishment, etc. **2** *transitive* change (organic matter) into a stony substance. **3** *intransitive* become like stone. **4** *transitive* deprive (the mind, a doctrine, etc.) of vitality; deaden. [French *pétrifier* from medieval Latin *petrificare* from Latin *petra* rock, from Greek]

Pet·rine /ˈpiːtraɪn/ *adjective* **1** of or relating to St. Peter or his teachings or writings. **2** of or relating to the authority of the pope over the church, in his role as successor of St. Peter. **3** of or relating to Peter I of Russia.

petro- *combining form* **1** petroleum (*petrochemistry*). **2** rock. [Greek *petros* stone or *petra* rock]

petro·chem·ical /ˌpetroˈkemɪkəl/ ● *noun* a substance industrially obtained from petroleum or natural gas. ● *adjective* of or relating to petrochemistry or petrochemicals.

petro·chem·istry /ˌpetroˈkemɪstri/ *noun* **1** the branch of chemistry dealing with petroleum and natural gas. **2** the branch of chemistry dealing with rocks.

petro·dollar *noun* a unit of currency earned by a country etc. from petroleum exports.

petro·glyph /ˈpetroˌɡlɪf/ *noun* a rock carving, esp. a prehistoric one. [PETRO- + Greek *glyphē* carving]

Petro·grad /ˈpetroˌɡrad/ a former name (1914–24) of ST. PETERSBURG 1.

pet·rog·raphy /peˈtrɒɡrəfi/ *noun* the scientific description of the composition and formation of rocks. □ **pet·rog·raph·er** *noun* **petro·graph·ic** *adjective* **petro·graph·ic·al·ly** *adverb*

pet·rol /ˈpetrəl/ *noun Brit.* = GASOLINE [French *pétrole* from medieval Latin *petroleum*: see PETROLEUM]

pet·rol·atum /ˌpetrəˈlɒtəm/ *noun N Amer.* petroleum jelly. [modern Latin from PETROL + -*atum*]

petrol bomb *Brit.* ● *noun* a simple bomb made of a gasoline-filled bottle and a wick; a Molotov cocktail. ● *transitive verb* (**petrol-bomb**) attack or destroy with a petrol bomb.

pet·rol·eum /pəˈtroːliəm/ *noun* a dark viscous hydrocarbon oil found in the upper strata of the earth, refined for use as a fuel for heating and in internal combustion engines, for lighting, as a solvent, etc. [medieval Latin from Latin *petra* rock, from Greek + Latin *oleum* oil]

petroleum jelly *noun* a soft, greasy, translucent semi-solid mixture of hydrocarbons used as a lubricant, ointment, etc.

Pet·rolia /pəˈtroːliə/ a town in SW Ontario, about 30 km southeast of Sarnia; pop. (2001) 4,849. □ **Pet·rol·ian** *noun* [corruption of *Petrolea*, the town's original name, so called because of the discovery of oil in the area]

pet·rol·ogy /pɪˈtrɒlədʒi/ *noun* the study of the origin, structure, composition, etc., of rocks. □ **petro·logic** /ˌpetrəˈlɒdʒɪk/ *adjective* **petro·logic·al** /ˌpetrəˈlɒdʒɪkəl/ *adjective* **pet·rol·o·gist** *noun*

Pe·tron·ius /pəˈtroːniəs/ **Gaius** (known as 'Petronius Arbiter') (d. AD 66), Roman writer. He is generally accepted as the author of the *Satyricon*, a work in prose and verse satirizing the excesses of Roman society.

Petro·pav·lovsk /ˌpetrəˈpavlɒfsk/ a city in N Kazakhstan pop. (est. 2001) 203,500.

Petro·pavlovsk-Kamchat·sky /ˌpetrəˈpavlɒfsk kamˈtʃatski/ a Russian fishing port and naval base on the east coast of the Kamchatka peninsula in E Siberia; pop. (est. 2002) 188,500.

pet·rous /ˈpetrəs/ *adjective Anat.* denoting the hard part of the temporal bone protecting the inner ear. [Latin *petrosus* from Latin *petra* rock, from Greek]

Petro·za·vodsk /ˌpetrəzaˈvɒdsk/ a city in NW Russia, on Lake Onega, capital of the Republic of Karelia; pop. (est. 2002) 281,500.

Pet·sa·mo /ˈpetsəˌmɔː/ the former name (1920–44) of PECHENGA.

petti·coat *noun* **1** a woman's or girl's undergarment in the form of a skirt or a skirt and bodice. **2** *slang* a woman or girl. □ **petti·coat·ed** *adjective* [Middle English from *petty coat*]

petti·fog *intransitive verb* (**petti·fogged, petti·fog·ging**) **1** quibble or wrangle about petty points. **2** practise legal deception or trickery. □ **petti·fog·ger** *noun* **petti·fog·gery** *noun* **petti·fog·ging** *adjective* **petti·fog·ging·ly** *adverb* [back-formation from *pettifogger*, from PETTY

+ *fogger* underhand dealer, prob. from *Fugger* family of merchants in Augsburg in the 15th–16th c.]

petting zoo *noun* (also **petting farm**) *N Amer.* a collection of wild or farm animals displayed so that visitors, esp. children, may walk among the animals to pet them, feed them, etc.

pet·tish *adjective* peevish, petulant; easily put out. □ **pet·tish·ly** *adverb* **pet·tish·ness** *noun* [PET² + -ISH¹]

petty *adjective* (**pet·ti·er, pet·ti·est**) **1** unimportant; trivial. **2** mean, small-minded; contemptible. **3** minor; inferior; on a small scale (*petty princes*). **4** (of a crime) of lesser importance (*compare* COMMON 8, GRAND 8). □ **pet·ti·ly** *adverb* **pet·ti·ness** *noun* [Middle English *pety*, var. of PETIT]

petty bourgeois *noun* = PETIT BOURGEOIS.

petty bourgeoisie *noun* = PETITE BOURGEOISIE.

petty cash *noun* a small amount of money kept from or for small payments.

petty officer *noun* (also **Petty Officer**) **1** *Cdn* (in the Canadian navy) an officer of either of two ranks: petty officer first class (Abbr.: **PO1**), ranking below chief petty officer second class, equivalent to warrant officer in the other commands, or petty officer second class (Abbr.: **PO2**), ranking next below it, equivalent to sergeant in the other commands. **2** a non-commissioned officer in other navies.

petu·lant /ˈpetjulənt, ˈpetʃulənt/ *adjective* peevishly impatient or irritable. □ **petu·lance** *noun* **petu·lant·ly** *adverb* [French *pétulant* from Latin *petulans -antis* from *petere* seek]

Petun /pəˈtuːn/ ● *noun* **1** a member of an Aboriginal people living in SW Ontario; defeated by the Iroquois in the mid 17th c., they were absorbed into neighbouring Aboriginal groups. **2** the Iroquoian language of this people. ● *adjective* of or relating to this people or their culture or language. [French from Tupi-Guarani *petȳ* tobacco]

pe·tu·nia /pəˈtuːnjə, -tjuːn-/ *noun* any plant of the genus *Petunia* with white, purple, red, etc., funnel-shaped flowers. [modern Latin from French *petun* from Tupi-Guarani *petȳ* tobacco]

pew *noun* **1** (in a church) a long bench with a back. **2** an enclosed compartment or section in a church, for a family or other group. □ **take a pew** have a seat. [Middle English *pywe, puwe* from Old French *puye* balcony, from Latin *podia* pl. of PODIUM]

pe·wee /ˈpiːwiː/ *noun* a N American tyrant flycatcher of the genus *Contopus*. [imitative of the bird's call]

pe·wit *var. of* PEEWIT.

pew·ter ● *noun* **1** a grey alloy of tin, antimony and copper (formerly, tin and lead). **2** utensils made of this. **3** a bluish or silvery grey. ● *adjective* of a bluish or silvery grey colour. □ **pew·ter·er** *noun* **pew·tery** *adjective* [Old French *peutre, peualtre* from Romanic, of unknown origin]

pewter·smith *noun* a worker in pewter; a manufacturer of pewter articles.

pey·ote /peɪˈoːti/ *noun* **1** any Mexican cactus of the genus *Lophophora*, esp. *L. williamsii* having no spines and button-like tops when dried. **2** a hallucinogenic drug containing mescaline prepared from this, taken sacramentally by some American Indians. □ **pey·ot·ism** /ˈpeɪoˌtɪzəm/ *noun* [Latin American Spanish from Nahuatl *peyotl*]

P.F. *abbreviation Military* permanent force.

Pf. *abbreviation* pfennig.

pf *abbreviation* (of a stock) preferred.

Pfc. *abbreviation US* Private First Class.

PFD *abbreviation N Amer.* PERSONAL FLOTATION DEVICE.

pfen·nig /ˈpfenɪɡ, ˈfen-/ *noun* **1** a former German monetary unit, equal to one-hundredth of a mark. **2** a coin of this value. [German, related to PENNY]

pfft *interjection* used to represent a dull abrupt sound as of a slight impact or explosion or the escaping of air under pressure.

PFRA *abbreviation* (in Canada) Prairie Farm Rehabilitation Administration.

PG *abbreviation* (of films) classified as suitable for children subject to parental guidance.

pg. *abbreviation* (*pl.* **pgs.**) page.

PGA *abbreviation* Professional Golfers' Association.

PGP *abbreviation* 'Pretty Good Privacy', a computer program which encrypts and decrypts messages for secure transmission over digital circuits.

pH /piːˈeɪtʃ/ *noun Chem.* the acidity or alkalinity of a solution, soil, skin, etc., expressed numerically as the logarithm to the base 10 of the reciprocal of the activity of hydrogen ions in moles per litre. A pH of 7

Vowels: a *cat* ɑ *arm* e *bed* ɜr *her* ɜː *deux* ə *ago* ɪ *sit* i *cosy* iː *feed* ɒ *hot* ɔ *pore* oː *no* ʌ *run* ʊ *put*

corresponds to a neutral solution, one less than 7 to an acidic solution, and one greater than 7 to an alkaline solution. [German, from *Potenz* power + *H* (symbol for hydrogen)]

ph. *abbreviation* phone (number).

Phae·dra /ˈfiːdrə/ *Gk Myth* the wife of Theseus. She fell in love with her stepson Hippolytus, who rejected her, whereupon she hanged herself, leaving behind a letter which accused him of raping her; Theseus would not believe his son's protestations of innocence and banished him.

Phae·drus /ˈfiːdrəs/ **Gaius Jul·ius** (c.15 BC–AD 50), Roman fabulist, who wrote five books of fables based on those of Aesop.

Phae·thon /ˈfeɪəθən/ *Gk Myth* the son of Helios the sun god. He asked to drive his father's solar chariot for a day, but could not control the immortal horses and the chariot plunged too near the earth until Zeus, to save the earth from destruction, killed Phaethon with a thunderbolt.

phae·ton /ˈfeɪtən, ˈfeɪətən/ *noun* **1** a light open four-wheeled carriage, usu. drawn by a pair of horses. **2** *US* a vintage touring car. [French *phaéton* from PHAETHON]

phage /feɪdʒ/ *noun* = BACTERIOPHAGE. [abbreviation]

phago·cyte /ˈfagəˌsəɪt/ *noun* a type of cell capable of engulfing and absorbing foreign matter, esp. a leukocyte ingesting bacteria in the body. □ **phago·cyt·ic** /-ˈsɪtɪk/ *adjective* [Greek *phag-* eat + -CYTE]

phago·cyt·o·sis /ˌfagəsəɪˈtoːsɪs/ *noun* the ingestion of bacteria etc. by phagocytes. □ **phago·cyt·ize** /ˈfagə-/ *transitive verb* (also esp. *Brit.* **-ise**). **phago·cyt·ose** /ˈfagə-/ *transitive verb*

-phagous /fəgəs/ *combining form* that eats (as specified) (*ichthyophagous*). [Latin *-phagus* from Greek *-phagos* from *phagein* eat]

-phagy /fədʒi/ *combining form* the eating of (specified food) (*ichthyophagy*). [Greek *-phagia* (as -PHAGOUS)]

phal·ange /ˈfaləndʒ, fəˈlandʒ/ *noun Anat.* = PHALANX 3. [French from Latin *phalanx*: see PHALANX]

pha·lan·geal /fəˈlandʒiəl/ *adjective Anat.* of or relating to a phalanx.

pha·lan·ger /fəˈlandʒər/ *noun* any of various marsupials of the family Phalangeridae. [French from Greek *phalaggion* spider's web, from the webbed toes of its hind feet]

phal·anx /ˈfalaŋks, ˈfeɪlaŋks/ *noun* (*pl.* **phal·anx·es** or **phal·an·ges** /ˈfalanˌdʒiːz/) **1** *Gk Hist.* a line of battle, esp. a body of Macedonian infantry drawn up in close order. **2** a set of people etc. forming a compact mass, or banded for a common purpose. **3** a bone of the finger or toe. **4** *Bot.* a bundle of stamens united by filaments. [Latin from Greek *phalagx -ggos*]

phala·rope /ˈfaləˌroːp/ *noun* any small wading or swimming bird of the subfamily Phalaropodinae, with a straight bill and lobed feet. [French from modern Latin *Phalaropus*, irreg. from Greek *phalaris* coot + *pous podos* foot]

phal·lic *adjective* **1** of, relating to, or resembling a phallus. **2** *Psych.* denoting the stage of male sexual development characterized by preoccupation with the genitals. □ **phal·lic·ally** *adverb*

phallo·cen·tric /ˌfaloːˈsentrɪk/ *adjective* **1** centred on a belief in male superiority. **2** centred on the phallus. □ **phallo·cen·tri·city** *noun* **phallo·cen·trism** *noun*

phall·oc·racy /faˈlɒkrəsi/ *noun* (*pl.* **-cies**) a society or system that is dominated by men and in which the male sex is thought superior. □ **phallo·crat·ic** /ˌfaloːˈkratɪk/ *adjective*

phal·lus /ˈfaləs/ *noun* (*pl.* **phal·lus·es** or **phal·li** /-laɪ/) **1** the (esp. erect) penis. **2** an image of this as a symbol of generative power in nature. □ **phal·li·cism** /-lɪˌsɪzəm/ *noun* [Late Latin from Greek *phallos*]

phan·ero·gam /ˈfanərəˌgam/ *noun Bot.* a plant that has stamens and pistils, a flowering plant (compare CRYPTOGAM). □ **phan·ero·gam·ic** /-ˈgamɪk/ *adjective* **phan·er·og·am·ous** /-ˈrɒgəməs/ *adjective* [French *phanérogame* from Greek *phaneros* visible + *gamos* marriage]

Phan·ero·zoic /ˌfanərəˈzoːɪk/ ● *adjective* designating or pertaining to the whole of geological time since the beginning of the Cambrian, as contrasted with the Precambrian. ● *noun* the Phanerozoic eon. [Greek *phaneros* 'visible' + *zoē* 'life']

phan·tasm /ˈfanˌtazəm/ *noun* **1** an illusion, a phantom. **2** (usu. foll. by *of*) an illusory likeness. **3** a supposed vision of an absent (living or dead) person. □ **phan·tas·mal** /-ˈtazməl/ *adjective* **phan·tas·mic** /-ˈtazmɪk/ *adjective* [Greek *phantasma* from *phantazō* make visible, from *phainō* show]

phan·tas·ma·goria /fanˌtazməˈgɔriə/ *noun* a shifting series of real or imaginary figures as seen in a dream or as created as an effect in a film etc. □ **phan·tas·ma·gor·ic** *adjective* **phan·tas·ma·gor·ic·al**

adjective [prob. from French *fantasmagorie* (as PHANTASM + fanciful ending)]

phan·tast *var.* of FANTAST.

phan·tasy *archaic* or *Psych. var.* of FANTASY.

phan·tom ● *noun* **1** a ghost; an apparition; a spectre. **2** a form without substance or reality; a mental illusion. ● *adjective* merely apparent; illusory. [Old French *fantosme*, ultimately from Greek *phantasma* (as PHANTASM)]

phantom limb *noun* a continuing sensation of the presence of a limb which has been amputated.

phar·aoh /ˈferoː/ *noun* **1** the ruler of ancient Egypt. **2** the title of this ruler. □ **phara·onic** /ˌfereɪˈɒnɪk/ *adjective* [Old English from ecclesiastical Latin *Pharao* from Greek *Pharaō* from Hebrew *par'ōh* from Egyptian *pr·'o* great house]

Phari·see /ˈferɪsiː/ *noun* **1** a member of an ancient Jewish sect, distinguished by strict observance of the traditional and written law, and commonly held to have pretensions to superior sanctity. **2** a self-righteous person; a hypocrite. □ **Phari·saic** /ˌferɪˈseɪɪk/ *adjective* **Phari·saic·al** /ˌferɪˈseɪɪkəl/ *adjective* **Phari·saism** /ˈferɪseɪˌɪzəm/ *noun* (also **Phari·see·ism** /-siˌɪzəm/). [ecclesiastical Latin *pharisaeus* from Greek *Pharisaios* from Aramaic *p'rišayyâ* pl. from Hebrew *pārûš* separated]

pharma *noun* a pharmaceutical company.

pharma·care *noun Cdn* (in some provinces) a system of subsidization of drug costs, esp. by the government. [PHARMACEUTICAL + CARE, after MEDICARE]

phar·ma·ceut·ical /ˌfarməˈsuːtɪkəl, -sjuːt-/ ● *adjective* **1** of or engaged in pharmacy. **2** pertaining to the preparation, use, or sale of medicinal drugs. ● *noun* a pharmaceutical preparation; a medicinal drug. □ **phar·ma·ceut·ical·ly** *adverb* [Late Latin *pharmaceuticus* from Greek *pharmakeutikos* from *pharmakeutēs* druggist, from *pharmakon* drug]

phar·ma·cist /ˈfarməsɪst/ *noun* a person qualified to prepare and dispense drugs and to give expert advice on their use and effects.

pharmaco- /ˈfarməkoː/ *combining form* forming words pertaining to drugs. [from Greek *pharmakon* drug, medicine, poison]

phar·ma·cog·nosy /ˌfarməˈkɒgnəsi/ *noun* the science of drugs, esp. relating to medicinal products in their natural or unprepared state. [Greek *pharmakon* drug + *gnōsis* knowledge]

phar·ma·co·kin·et·ics /ˌfarməkoːkɪˈnetɪks/ *plural noun* (treated as *sing.*) the branch of pharmacology that deals with the movement of drugs within the body. □ **phar·ma·co·kin·etic** *adjective* **phar·ma·co·kin·etic·ally** *adverb*

phar·ma·col·ogy /ˌfarməˈkɒlədʒi/ *noun* the branch of medicine that deals with the uses, effects, and modes of action of drugs. □ **phar·ma·co·logic** *adjective* **phar·ma·co·logic·al** *adjective* **phar·ma·co·logic·al·ly** *adverb* **phar·ma·col·o·gist** *noun*

phar·ma·co·poeia /ˌfarməkəˈpiːə/ *noun* **1** a book, esp. one officially published, containing a list of pharmaceutical drugs with directions for use. **2** a stock of drugs. [modern Latin from Greek *pharmakopoiia* from *pharmakopoios* drug maker (PHARMACO- + -poios making)]

phar·macy /ˈfarməsi/ *noun* (*pl.* **-cies**) **1** the preparation and the dispensing of (esp. medicinal) drugs. **2** a pharmacist's store or dispensary. [medieval Latin *pharmacia* from Greek *pharmakeia* practice of the druggist, from *pharmakeus* from *pharmakon* drug]

pharm·ing *noun* **1** the process of genetically modifying plants and animals so that they produce substances which may be used as pharmaceuticals. **2** the growing or keeping of animals and plants for this purpose. □ **pharm·er** *noun* [from PHARMACEUTICAL, punningly after FARMING]

phar·os /ˈferɒs/ *noun* a lighthouse or a beacon to guide sailors. [Latin from Greek *Pharos* island off Alexandria where a famous lighthouse stood]

pharyn·geal /fəˈrɪndʒiəl/ *adjective* of, pertaining to, or involving the pharynx.

pharyngo- /fəˈrɪŋgoː/ *combining form* denoting the pharynx.

pharynx /ˈferɪŋks/ *noun* (*pl.* **pha·ryn·ges** /-rɪnˌdʒiːz/) a cavity, with enclosing muscles and mucous membrane, behind the nose and mouth, and connecting them to the esophagus. □ **pharyn·gitis** /-ˈdʒəɪtɪs/ *noun* [modern Latin from Greek *pharugx -ggos*]

phase ● *noun* **1** a distinct period or stage in a process of change or development. **2** each of the aspects of the moon or a planet, according to the amount of its illumination, esp. the new moon, the first quarter, the last quarter, and the full moon. **3** *Physics* a particular stage or point in the cycle of a periodic phenomenon, esp. an alternating current or a light wave. **4** a difficult or unhappy period, esp. in adolescence. **5** a genetic or seasonal variety of an animal's coloration etc. **6** *Chem.* a distinct and homogeneous form of matter separated by its surface from other forms. ● *transitive verb* **1** carry out (a program etc.) in phases or stages. **2** adjust the phase of; bring into phase, synchronize. □ **in phase** having the same phase at the same time. **out of phase** not in phase. **phase in** (or **out**) bring gradually into (or out of) use. □ **phas·ic** *adjective* [ultimately from Greek *phasis* appearance, from *phainō* phan- show]

phase-in *noun* (often *attributive*) the process of bringing something into use or availability gradually (*two-year phase-in*; *phase-in period*).

phase-out *noun* (often *attributive*) the gradual removal of something from use or availability (*the phase-out of the tax*; *phase-out schedule*).

phas·er *noun* (esp. in science fiction) a usu. hand-held weapon incorporating a laser beam whose 'phase' can supposedly be altered to create different effects (such as stunning, annihilation, etc.) on the target.

phat /fat/ *adjective* (**phat·ter**, **phat·test**) *slang* excellent; cool. [20th c.: origin unknown]

phat·ic /'fatɪk/ *adjective* (of speech etc.) used to convey general sociability rather than to communicate a specific meaning, e.g. 'nice morning, isn't it?'. [Greek *phatos* spoken]

Ph.D. *abbreviation* Doctor of Philosophy. [Latin *philosophiae doctor*]

pheas·ant /'fezənt/ *noun* any of several long-tailed game birds of the family Phasianidae, originally from Asia. [Anglo-French *fesaunt* from Old French *faisan* from Latin *phasianus* from Greek *phasianos* (bird) of the river *Phasis* in Asia Minor]

pheas·ant·ry /'fezəntri/ *noun* (*pl.* **-ries**) a place where pheasants are reared or kept.

phen·cycli·dine /fen'saɪklɪˌdiːn/ *noun* a piperidine derivative used as a veterinary anaesthetic and a hallucinogenic drug (abbr.: **PCP**).

pheno- /'fiːnɔ/ *combining form* **1** *Chem.* derived from benzene (*phenol*; *phenyl*). **2** showing (*phenocryst*). [Greek *phainō* shine (with reference to substances used for illumination), show]

pheno·barbi·tal /ˌfiːnɔ'bɑːrbɪˌtɒl/ *noun* (*Brit.* **pheno·barbi·tone**, **pheno·barb** *informal*) a narcotic and sedative barbiturate drug used esp. to treat epilepsy. [PHENO- + BARBITAL]

pheno·cryst /'fiːnɔkrɪst, 'fen-/ *noun* a large or conspicuous crystal in porphyritic rock. [French *phénocryste* (as PHENO-, CRYSTAL)]

phe·nol /'fiːnɒl/ *noun Chem.* **1** a white hygroscopic mildly acidic crystalline solid, used in dilute form as an antiseptic and disinfectant (*also called carbolic*). Chem. formula: C_6H_5OH. **2** any hydroxyl derivative of an aromatic hydrocarbon. [French *phénole* from *phène* 'benzene' (formed as PHENO-) + -OL¹]

phe·nol·ic /fə'nɒlɪk/ ● *adjective* **1** of the nature of, derived from, or containing a phenol, esp. containing or designating a hydroxyl group bonded directly to a benzene ring. **2 a** designating a large class of usu. thermosetting polymeric materials that have wide industrial applications as plastics or resins and are prepared from phenols by condensation with aldehydes. **b** made of such a material. ● *noun* **1** a phenolic plastic or resin. **2** any compound containing a hydroxyl group bonded directly to a benzene ring, esp. in plants.

phenol·phthal·ein /ˌfiːnɒl'θeɪliːn/ *noun Chem.* a white crystalline solid used in solution as an acid-base indicator and medicinally as a laxative. [PHENOL + phthal from NAPHTHALENE + -IN]

phe·nom /'fiːnɒm/ *noun N Amer. informal* an unusually gifted person, a prodigy. [abbreviation of PHENOMENON 2]

phe·nom·ena *pl. of* PHENOMENON.

phe·nom·en·al /fə'nɒmənəl/ *adjective* **1** extraordinary, remarkable, prodigious. **2** of the nature of a phenomenon. **3** perceptible by, or perceptible only to, the senses. □ **phe·nom·en·al·ize** *transitive verb* (also esp. *Brit.* **-ise**). **phe·nom·en·al·ly** *adverb*

phe·nom·en·al·ism /fə'nɒmənəlɪzəm/ *noun Philos.* **1** the doctrine that human knowledge is confined to the appearances presented to the senses. **2** the doctrine that appearances are the foundation of all our knowledge. □ **phe·nom·en·al·ist** *noun & adjective* **phe·nom·en·al·is·tic** /-'lɪstɪk/ *adjective*

phe·nom·en·ol·ogy /fəˌnɒmə'nɒlədʒi/ *noun Philos.* **1** the science of phenomena as distinct from that of being (ontology). **2** a philosophical approach concentrating on the study of consciousness and the objects of direct experience. □ **phe·nom·eno·logic·al** /-nə'lɒdʒɪkəl/ *adjective* **phe·nom·eno·logic·al·ly** /-nə'lɒdʒɪkli/ *adverb* **phe·nom·en·ol·o·gist** *noun*

phe·nom·en·on /fə'nɒmə‚nɒn, -nən/ *noun* (*pl.* **phe·nom·ena**) **1** a fact, circumstance, or occurrence that appears or is perceived, esp. one of which the cause is in question. **2** a renowned, remarkable person or

thing. **3** *Philos.* the object of a person's perception (as distinguished from substance, or the thing in itself); what the senses or the mind notice. [Late Latin from Greek *phainomenon* neuter pres. part. of *phainomai* appear, from *phainō* show]

pheno·thia·zine /ˌfiːnɔ'θaɪəziːn/ *noun* **1** a heterocyclic compound which is used to treat parasitic infestations of animals. Chem. formula: $C_{12}H_9NS$. **2** any of various derivatives of this, which constitute an important class of tranquilizing drugs used esp. in the treatment of mental illnesses. [PHENO- + THIO- + AZINE]

pheno·type /'fiːnɔ‚taɪp/ *noun Biol.* a set of observable characteristics of an individual or group as determined by its genotype and environment. □ **pheno·typ·ic** /-'tɪpɪk/ *adjective* **pheno·typ·ic·ally** /-'tɪpɪkli/ *adverb* [German *Phaenotypus* (as PHENO-, TYPE)]

phenyl /'fenəl/ *noun Chem.* the monovalent radical formed from benzene by the removal of a hydrogen atom. [PHENO- + -YL]

phenyl·alan·ine /ˌfenəl'alə‚niːn/ *noun Biochem.* an amino acid widely distributed in plant proteins and essential in the human diet. [PHENYL + ALANINE]

phenyl·but·az·one /ˌfenəl'bjuː'təzoːn/ *noun* a white or cream-coloured crystalline solid which was formerly used as an analgesic, esp. for the relief of rheumatic pain and inflammation, and as an antipyretic, but now largely restricted to veterinary use. [PHENYL + BUTYL + AZO- + -ONE]

phenyl·ephr·ine /ˌfenəl'efriːn/ *noun* a compound related to adrenalin which is used (usu. in the form of its crystalline hydrochloride) as a vasoconstrictor and as a nasal decongestant. [PHENYL + EPINEPHRINE]

phenyl·keton·uria /ˌfenəlˌkiːtə'nʊriə, -'njʊriə/ *noun* an inherited inability to metabolize phenylalanine, ultimately leading to mental deficiency if untreated. Abbr.: **PKU**. [PHENYL + KETONE + -URIA]

pheny·toin /ˌfeni'toːɪn/ *noun* an anticonvulsant used to treat epilepsy. [PHENYL + hydantoin, a cyclic derivative of urea]

phero·mone /'ferə‚moːn/ *noun* a chemical substance secreted and released by an animal for detection and response by another usu. of the same species. □ **phero·mon·al** /-'moːnəl/ *adjective* [Greek *pherō* convey + HORMONE]

phew *interjection* an expression of relief, discomfort, astonishment, or disgust. [imitative of puffing]

phi /faɪ/ *noun* the twenty-first letter of the Greek alphabet (Φ, φ). [Greek]

phial /'faɪəl/ *noun* a small glass bottle, esp. for liquid medicine. [Latin *phiola phiala* from Greek *phialē*, a broad flat vessel: compare VIAL]

Phi Beta Kap·pa *noun* (in the US) **1** an intercollegiate honorary society to which distinguished scholars may be elected. **2** a member of this society. [from the initial letters of a Greek motto, *philosophia biou kubernētēs*, lit. 'philosophy the guide to life']

Phid·ias /'fɪdɪˌas, 'faɪd-/ (5th c. BC), Athenian sculptor. He planned and supervised public building on the Acropolis in Athens (*c.*447), contributing the colossal gold-and-ivory statue of Athene Parthenos for the Parthenon (*c.*438) and the Elgin Marbles; he is also noted for his vast statue of Zeus at Olympia (*c.*430), one of the Seven Wonders of the World.

Phil. *abbreviation* **1** Philosophy. **2** Philadelphia. **3** Philharmonic. **4** Philippians (New Testament).

phil- *combining form var. of* PHILO-.

-phil *combining form var. of* -PHILE.

Phila·del·phia /ˌfɪlə'delfɪə/ the chief city of Pennsylvania, on the Delaware River; pop. (2000) 1,517,550. It was the site in 1776 of the signing of the Declaration of Independence and in 1787 of the adoption of the Constitution of the United States and was the US capital from 1790 to 1800. □ **Phila·del·phian** *noun & adjective* [Greek *philadelphia* brotherly love]

phila·del·phus /ˌfɪlə'delfəs/ *noun* any highly-scented deciduous flowering shrub of the genus *Philadelphus*, esp. the mock orange. [modern Latin from Greek *philadelphon*]

phi·lan·der /fɪ'landər/ *intransitive verb* have casual affairs with many women; womanize. □ **phi·lan·der·er** *noun* [*philander* (n.) used in Greek literature as the proper name of a lover, from Greek *philandros* fond of men, from *anēr* male person: see PHIL-]

phil·an·thrope /'fɪlan‚θroːp/ *noun* = PHILANTHROPIST (*see* PHILANTHROPY).

phil·an·throp·ic /ˌfɪlan'θrɒpɪk/ *adjective* **1** loving humankind. **2** benevolent towards others, esp. in giving charity on a large scale. □ **phil·an·throp·ic·ally** *adverb* [French *philanthropique* from Greek *philanthrōpos* (as PHIL-, *anthrōpos* human being)]

phil·an·thropy /fɪ'lanθrəpi/ *noun* **1** a love of humankind. **2** the disposition or effort to promote the happiness and well-being of one's fellow people, esp. by gifts of money, work, etc. **3** a philanthropic institution. □ **phil·an·throp·ist** *noun* [Late Latin *philanthropia* from Greek *philanthrōpia* (as PHILANTHROPIC)]

phil·ately /fɪˈlatəli/ *noun* the collection and study of postage stamps. □ **phila·tel·ic** /ˌfɪləˈtelɪk/ *adjective* **phila·tel·ic·ally** /ˌfɪləˈtelɪkli/ *adverb* **phil·atel·ist** *noun* [French *philatélie* from Greek *ateleia* exemption from payment, from *a-* not + *telos* toll, tax]

Phil·by /ˈfɪlbi/ **Har·old Ad·rian Rus·sell ('Kim')** (1912–88), English Foreign Office official and spy. The chief liaison officer at the British Embassy in Washington, DC (1949–51), he defected to the USSR in 1963 and in the same year was officially revealed to have spied for the Soviets from 1933.

-phile /faɪl/ *combining form* (also **-phil** /fɪl/) forming nouns and adjectives with the sense 'lover of, that loves' something specified, designating either a fondness or affection (*bibliophile*; *francophile*), or an esp. sexual obsession (*pedophile*). [Greek *philos* dear, loving]

Philem. *abbreviation* Philemon (New Testament).

Phi·le·mon /fɪˈliːmən, faɪ-/ **1** *Gk Myth* an old countryman living with his wife Baucis in Phrygia who offered hospitality to Zeus and Hermes when the two gods came to earth, without revealing their identities, to test people's piety; Philemon and Baucis were subsequently saved from a flood which covered the district. **2** a book of the New Testament, an epistle of St. Paul to a well-to-do Christian living probably at Colossae in Phrygia.

phil·harmon·ic /ˌfɪlhɑrˈmɒnɪk, ˌfɪlər-/ *adjective* **1** fond of music. **2** used characteristically in the names of orchestras, choirs, etc. (*Winnipeg Philharmonic Choir*). [as PHIL-, HARMONIC]

-philia /ˈfiːliə/ *combining form* **1** denoting (esp. abnormal) fondness or love for what is specified (*necrophilia*). **2** denoting undue inclination (*hemophilia*). □ **-philiac** /-li,ak/ *combining form.* **-philic** /ˈfɪlɪk/ *combining form.* **-philous** *combining form.* [Greek from *philos* loving]

Phil·ip ▶ 1 King (also **Meta·comet**) (*c.*1638–76), Wampanoag chief, son of Massasoit. He led the raids on white settlements in New England known as King Philip's War (1675–6). **2 Prince, Duke of Edinburgh** (b.1921), husband of Elizabeth II. The son of Prince Andrew of Greece and Denmark, he married Princess Elizabeth in 1947; on the eve of his marriage he was created Duke of Edinburgh. **3 St.**, an Apostle. He is commemorated with St. James the Less on 1 May. **4 St.** (known as 'St. Philip the Evangelist'), one of seven deacons appointed to superintend the secular business of the Church at Jerusalem (Acts 6:5–6).

Philip I (known as Philip the Handsome) (1478–1506), king of Spain 1504–6. Son of the Holy Roman emperor Maximilian I of Hapsburg (1459–1519), Philip married the infanta Joanna, daughter of Ferdinand of Aragon and Isabella of Castile, in 1496; after Isabella's death, he ruled Castile jointly with Joanna, establishing the Hapsburgs as the ruling dynasty in Spain.

Philip II ▶ 1 (known as Philip of Macedon) (382–336 BC), father of Alexander the Great, king of Macedonia 359–336. He unified and expanded ancient Macedonia; his victory over Athens and Thebes at the battle of Chaeronea in 338 established his hegemony over Greece. **2** (known as Philip Augustus) (1165–1223), son of Louis VII, king of France 1180–1223. He succeeded in regaining Normandy (1204), Anjou (1204), and most of Poitou (1204–5) from the English; towards the end of his reign, after success in the crusade (1209–31) against the Albigenses, he added territories in the south to his kingdom. **3** (1527–98), son of Charles I, king of Spain 1556–98. He married the second of his four wives, Mary I of England, in 1554, and his reign came to be dominated by an anti-Protestant crusade which exhausted the Spanish economy; although he conquered Portugal in 1580, his attempted invasion of England was thwarted by the defeat of the Armada in 1588.

Philip IV (known as Philip the Fair) (1268–1314), king of France 1285–1314. In 1303 he imprisoned Pope Boniface VIII and, in 1305, his influence secured the appointment of the French Clement V as pope; Philip's domination of the papacy was further consolidated when Clement moved the papal seat to Avignon (1309), where it remained until 1377.

Philip V ▶ 1 (238–179 BC), king of Macedonia 221–179. His expansionist policies led to a series of confrontations with Rome, culminating in his defeat in Thessaly in 197 and his resultant loss of control over Greece. **2** (1683–1746), grandson of Louis XIV, king of Spain 1700–24 and 1724–46. The selection of Philip, a Bourbon, as successor to Charles II, and Louis XIV's insistence that Philip remain an heir to the French throne, gave rise to the War of the Spanish Succession (1701–14).

Philip VI (known as Philip of Valois) (1293–1350), king of France 1328–50, founder of the Valois dynasty. English disputes over his claim to the throne developed into the Hundred Years War; Philip was defeated by Edward I of England at the Battle of Crécy (1346).

Philip Augustus *see* PHILIP II 2.

Philip of Valois *see* PHILIP VI.

Phil·ippi /ˈfɪlɪˌpaɪ, fɪˈlɪpaɪ/ a city of ancient Macedonia, the scene in 42 BC of two battles in which Mark Antony and Octavian defeated Brutus and Cassius. The ruins lie close to the Aegean coast in NE Greece, near the port of Kaválla (ancient Neapolis).

Phil·ip·pi·ans /fɪˈlɪpiənz/ a book of the New Testament, an epistle of St. Paul to the Church at Philippi in Macedonia.

phil·ip·pic /fɪˈlɪpɪk/ *noun* a bitter verbal attack or denunciation. [Latin *philippicus* from Greek *philippikos* the name of Demosthenes' speeches against Philip II of Macedon and Cicero's against Mark Antony]

Phil·ip·pine /ˈfɪləˌpiːn/ *adjective* of or relating to the Philippines or their people; Filipino. [PHILIP II of Spain]

Phil·ip·pines /ˈfɪləˌpiːnz/ a country in SE Asia consisting of an archipelago of over 7,000 islands separated from the Asian mainland by the South China Sea; pop. (est. 2002) 84,525,639; capital, Manila.

Phil·ipps, Rich·ard (*c.*1661–1750), British colonial administrator. Although governor of Nova Scotia from 1717 to 1749, he was resident in the colony only briefly (1720–22 and 1729–31). Sent out with a mandate to force the Acadians to pledge alliance to the British but without sufficient military support to do so, he instead administered a modified oath and promised the Acadians that they would not be required to bear arms against France. While this allowed the Acadians to maintain neutrality for some 25 years, it left them unprepared for the ultimatum and subsequent deportation of 1755.

Philip the Fair *see* PHILIP IV.

Philip the Handsome *see* PHILIP I.

Phil·is·tine /ˈfɪlɪˌstaɪn, -stiːn/ ● *noun* **1** a member of a people opposing the Israelites in ancient Palestine. **2** (usu. **philistine**) a person who is hostile or indifferent to culture, the arts, etc., or one whose interests or tastes are commonplace or material. ● *adjective* hostile or indifferent to culture; commonplace, prosaic. □ **phil·is·tin·ism** /-stɪnɪzəm/ *noun* [French *Philistin* or Late Latin *Philistinus* from Greek *Philistinos* = *Palaistinos* from Hebrew *p'lištî*]

Phil·lips *noun* (usu. *attributive*) *proprietary* denoting a screw with a cross-shaped slot for turning, or a corresponding screwdriver. [name of the original US manufacturer]

Philly a nickname for Philadelphia. [abbreviation]

philo- /ˈfɪloː/ *combining form* (also **phil-** before a vowel or *h*) denoting a liking for what is specified.

philo·den·dron /ˌfɪləˈdendrən/ *noun* (*pl.* **philo·den·drons** or **philo·den·dra** /-drə/) any tropical American climbing plant of the genus *Philodendron*, with bright foliage, often grown as a houseplant. [PHILO- + Greek *dendron* tree]

phil·ol·ogy /fɪˈlɒlədʒi/ *noun* **1** the branch of language that deals with the structure, historical development, and relationships of a language or languages. **2** the branch of knowledge that deals with the linguistic, historical, interpretative, and critical aspects of literature. □ **phil·ol·o·gist** *noun* **philo·logic·al** *adjective* [French *philologie* from Latin *philologia* love of learning, from Greek (as PHILO-, -LOGY)]

Philo·mel /ˈfɪləˌmel/ (also **Philo·mela** /ˌfɪləˈmiːlə/) *Gk Myth* the daughter of Pandion, king of Athens. She was turned into a swallow (or, in Latin versions, a nightingale) when being pursued by the cruel Tereus, who had raped her; the name is sometimes used in poetry for the nightingale. [Latin *philomela* nightingale, from Greek *philomēla*]

philo-Semitism *noun* an attitude supporting or favouring Jews. □ **philo-Semite** *noun* **philo-Semitic** *adjective*

philo·sophe /ˈfɪləˌsɒf/ *noun* a philosopher, esp. any of the humanistic French philosophers of the 18th c. [French]

phil·oso·pher /fɪˈlɒsəfər/ *noun* **1** a person engaged or learned in philosophy or a branch of it. **2** a person who shows philosophic calmness in trying circumstances. [Anglo-French *philosofre* var. of Old French *philosophe* from Latin *philosophus* from Greek *philosophos* (as PHILO-, *sophos* wise)]

philosopher's stone *noun* (also **philosophers' stone**) the supreme object of alchemy, a substance supposed to change other metals into gold or silver.

philo·soph·ic·al /ˌfɪləˈsɒfɪkəl/ *adjective* (also **philo·soph·ic**) **1** of or according to philosophy. **2** skilled in or devoted to philosophy. **3** wise; serene; temperate. **4** calm in adverse circumstances. □ **philo·soph·ic·al·ly** *adverb*

---

t top   v voice   w we   z zoo   ʃ she   ʒ vision   θ thin   ð this   ŋ ring   x loch   tʃ chip   dʒ jar   (*see over for vowels*)

phil·oso·phize /fɪˈlɒsəˌfaɪz/ *verb* (also esp. *Brit.* **-phise**) **1** *intransitive* reason like a philosopher. **2** *intransitive* speculate; theorize. **3** *transitive* explain, treat, or argue (a point, idea, etc.) philosophically. □ **phil·oso·phiz·er** *noun*

phil·oso·phy /fɪˈlɒsəfi/ *noun* (pl. **-phies**) **1** the use of reason and argument in seeking truth and knowledge of reality, esp. of the causes and nature of things and of the principles governing existence, the material universe, perception of physical phenomena, and human behaviour. **2 a** a particular system or set of beliefs reached by this. **b** a personal rule of life. **3 a** serenity; calmness. **b** conduct governed by a particular philosophy. **4** the branch of knowledge that deals with the principles of a particular field or subject (*philosophy of art*; *philosophy of science*). [Latin *philosophia* from Greek (as PHILO-, *sophos* wise)]

phil·tre /ˈfɪltər/ *noun* (also esp. *US* **phil·ter**) a drink supposed to excite sexual love in the drinker; a love potion. [French *philtre* from Latin *philtrum* from Greek *philtron* from *phileō* to love]

-phily /ˈfɪli/ *combining form* = -PHILIA.

Phin·ti·as /ˈfɪntiˌəs/ *see* DAMON.

Phiz /fɪz/ (pseudonym of Hablot Knight Browne) (1815–82), English illustrator. In 1836 he was chosen to illustrate Dickens's *Pickwick Papers*, and took his pseudonym to complement Dickens's 'Boz'. He illustrated many of Dickens's works, including *Martin Chuzzlewit* and *Bleak House*.

phiz /fɪz/ *noun* (also **phizz**) *informal* **1** the face. **2** the expression on a face. [abbreviation of *phiznomy* = PHYSIOGNOMY]

phleb·itis /fləˈbaɪtɪs/ *noun* inflammation of the walls of a vein. □ **phleb·itic** /-ˈbɪtɪk/ *adjective* [modern Latin from Greek from *phleps phlebos* vein + -ITIS]

phleb·ot·omy /fləˈbɒtəmi/ *noun* **1** the surgical opening or puncture of a vein. **2** esp. *hist.* bloodletting as a medical treatment. □ **phleb·ot·o·mist** *noun* **phleb·ot·o·mize** *transitive verb* (also esp. *Brit.* **-mise**). [Greek *phleps phlebos* vein + -TOMY]

phlegm /flem/ *noun* **1** the thick viscous substance secreted by the mucous membranes of the respiratory passages, discharged by coughing. **2 a** coolness and calmness of disposition. **b** sluggishness or apathy (supposed to result from too much phlegm in the constitution). **3** *archaic* phlegm regarded as one of the four bodily humours. □ **phlegmy** *adjective* [Old French *fleume* from Late Latin *phlegma* from Greek *phlegma -atos* inflammation, from *phlegō* burn]

phleg·mat·ic /flegˈmatɪk/ *adjective* **1** stolidly calm; unexcitable, unemotional. **2** dull, sluggish, apathetic. □ **phleg·mat·ic·ally** *adverb*

phloem /ˈfloʊem/ *noun Bot.* the tissue conducting food material in plants (*compare* XYLEM). [Greek *phloos* bark]

phlo·gis·ton /floʊˈdʒɪstən, -stɒn/ *noun* a substance formerly supposed to exist in all combustible bodies, and to be released in combustion. [modern Latin from Greek *phlogizō* set on fire, from *phlox phlogos* flame]

phlox /flɒks/ *noun* any cultivated plant of the genus *Phlox*, with scented clusters of esp. white, blue, and red flowers. [Latin from Greek *phlox*, the name of a plant (lit., 'flame')]

Phnom Penh /nɒm ˈpen/ the capital of Cambodia, a port at the junction of the Mekong and Tonlé Sap rivers; pop. (est. 2002) 1,133,800. Controlled between 1975 and 1979 by the Khmer Rouge, who forced its population of 2.5 million to leave the city and resettle in the country, the city was repopulated after the arrival of the Vietnamese in 1979.

pho /fɒ/ *noun* a Vietnamese soup of rice noodles and vegetables in usu. beef broth. [Vietnamese]

-phobe *combining form* forming nouns and adjectives denoting a person having a fear or dislike of what is specified (*xenophobe*). [French from Latin *-phobus* from Greek *-phobos* from *phobos* fear]

pho·bia *noun* an abnormal or morbid fear or aversion. □ **phob·ic** *adjective & noun* [-PHOBIA used as a separate word]

-phobia *combining form* forming abstract nouns denoting a fear of or aversion to what is specified (*agoraphobia*; *xenophobia*). □ **-phobic** *combining form.* [Latin from Greek]

Phoe·be /ˈfiːbi/ **1** *Gk Myth* a Titan, daughter of Uranus (Heaven) and Gaia (Earth). She became the mother of Leto and thus the grandmother of Apollo and Artemis; in the later Greek writers her name was often used for Selene (Moon). **2** *Astronomy* satellite IX of Saturn, the furthest from the planet, discovered in 1898 (average diameter 220 km). [Greek *Phoibē* bright one]

phoe·be /ˈfiːbi/ *noun* any small N American tyrant flycatcher of the genus *Sayornis*. [imitative: influenced by the name]

Phoe·bus /ˈfiːbəs/ *Gk Myth* an epithet of Apollo, used in contexts where the god was identified with the sun. [Greek *Phoibos* bright one]

Phoe·ni·cia /fəˈniːʃə/ an ancient country on the shores of the E Mediterranean, corresponding to modern Lebanon and the coastal plains of Syria. It consisted of a number of city states, including Tyre and Sidon, and was a flourishing centre of Mediterranean trade and colonization during the early part of the first millennium BC.

Phoe·ni·cian /fəˈniːʃən/ ● *noun* **1** a member of a people of ancient Phoenicia in S Syria or of its colonies. **2** the Semitic language of the Phoenicians. ● *adjective* of or relating to Phoenicia, its colonies, its people, or their language.

Phoe·nix /ˈfiːnɪks/ the state capital of Arizona; pop. (2000) 1,321,045.

phoe·nix /ˈfiːnɪks/ *noun* **1** a mythical bird, the only one of its kind, that after living for five or six centuries in the Arabian desert, burned itself on a funeral pyre and rose from the ashes with renewed youth to live through another cycle. **2** a thing which is renewed after apparent destruction. [Latin *phoenix* from Greek *phoinix* Phoenician, purple, phoenix]

Phoenix Islands a group of eight islands lying just south of the equator in the W Pacific. They form a part of Kiribati.

phon·ate /ˈfoʊneɪt/ *intransitive verb* utter a vocal sound. □ **phon·a·tion** /ˈneɪʃən/ *noun* **phona·tory** /ˈfoʊnəˌtɔri/ *adjective* [Greek *phōnē* voice]

phone¹ ● *noun* = TELEPHONE. ● *verb* **1** *transitive* speak to (a person) by telephone. **2** *transitive* send (a message) by telephone. **3** *intransitive* make a telephone call. **4** *transitive* dial (a telephone number). **5** *transitive* make a telephone call to (a place) (*phone the store*; *phone England*). □ **phone in** call a radio show etc. on the telephone to participate in a broadcast discussion. **phone up** call (somebody) on the telephone. □ **phon·er** *noun* [abbreviation]

phone² *noun* a simple vowel or consonant sound. [formed as PHONEME]

-phone *combining form* forming nouns and adjectives meaning: **1** an instrument using or connected with sound (*telephone*; *xylophone*). **2** a person who uses a specified language (*anglophone*). **3** a sound with a specific quality (*homophone*). [Greek *phōnē* voice, sound]

phone bank *noun* esp. *US* a large number of telephones in one location used for telemarketing, election campaigning, etc.

phone book *noun* a book listing telephone subscribers in a particular area, their telephone numbers, and usu. their addresses.

phone booth *noun* = TELEPHONE BOOTH.

phone card *noun* a prepaid card for use with a public telephone.

phone-in *noun* a broadcast program during which the listeners or viewers phone the studio etc. and participate (also *attributive*: *phone-in show*).

phon·eme /ˈfoʊniːm/ *noun* any of the units of sound in a specified language that distinguish one word from another, e.g. *p*, *b*, *d*, *t* as in pad, pat, bad, bat, in English. □ **phon·emic** /-ˈniːmɪk/ *adjective* **phon·em·ics** /-ˈniːmɪks/ *noun* [French *phonème* from Greek *phōnēma* sound, speech, from *phōneō* speak]

phone phreak *noun see* PHREAK.

phone sex *noun* (also, with hyphen, *attributive*) an activity, often conducted as a commercial service, in which participants engage in sexually explicit telephone conversation or listen to recorded messages for the purpose of sexual gratification.

phon·etic /fəˈnetɪk/ *adjective* **1** representing vocal sounds. **2 a** designating the difference between any two sounds, often regardless of whether the difference distinguishes one word from another, e.g. in English the *b* of *bin*, the aspirated *p* of *pin*, and the unaspirated *p* of *spin* are phonetically different. **b** (of a system of spelling etc.) reflecting phonetic differences; having a direct correspondence between symbols and sounds. **3** of or relating to phonetics. □ **phon·etic·ally** *adverb* [modern Latin *phoneticus* from Greek *phōnētikos* from *phōneō* speak]

phon·et·ics /fəˈnetɪks/ *plural noun* (usu. treated as *sing.*) **1** vocal sounds and their classification. **2** the study of these. □ **phon·et·ician** /ˌfoʊnəˈtɪʃən/ *noun*

phoney *var.* of PHONY.

phon·ic /ˈfɒnɪk/ *adjective* **1** of sound; acoustic; of vocal sounds. **2** of, designating, or pertaining to phonics. □ **phon·ic·ally** *adverb* [Greek *phōnē* voice]

phon·ics /ˈfɒnɪks/ *plural noun* (treated as *sing.*) a method of teaching reading by associating letters or groups of letters with particular sounds.

phono /ˈfoʊnoʊ/ ● *noun* = PHONOGRAPH (esp. on a button or as a setting on a stereo system). ● *attributive adjective* designating a type of plug (and the corresponding socket) used with audio and video equipment, in which one conductor is cylindrical and the other is a central part that extends beyond it. [abbreviation of PHONOGRAPH]

phono- /ˈfoːnoː/ *combining form* denoting sound. [Greek *phōnē* voice, sound]

phono·gram /ˈfoːnəˌgram/ *noun* a symbol representing a spoken sound.

phono·graph /ˈfoːnəˌgraf/ *noun* **1** *N Amer.* a record player. **2** *Brit.* an early form of gramophone using cylinders and able to record as well as reproduce sound.

phon·ol·ogy /fəˈnɒlədʒi/ *noun* **1** the study of sounds in a language. **2** the system of sounds in a specific language. □ **phono·logic·al** /ˌfoːnəˈlɒdʒɪkəl, ˌfɒn-/ *adjective* **phono·logic·al·ly** /ˌfoːnəˈlɒdʒɪkli, ˌfɒn-/ *adverb* **phon·ol·o·gist** *noun*

phon·on /ˈfoːnɒn/ *noun* Physics a quantum of sound or elastic vibrations. [Greek *phōnē* sound, after PHOTON]

phony (also **phon·ey**) *informal* ● *adjective* (**phon·i·er, phon·i·est**) **1** sham; counterfeit; fake. **2** insincere. ● *noun* (*pl.* **-ies** or **-eys**) a phony person or thing. □ **phon·i·ly** *adverb* **phon·i·ness** *noun* [20th c.: origin unknown]

phony-baloney *adjective & noun N Amer. slang* = PHONY.

phony war the period of comparative inaction at the beginning of the Second World War between the German invasions of Poland (Sept. 1939) and Norway (Apr. 1940).

phooey *interjection* an expression of disgust or contempt. [imitative]

-phore *combining form* forming nouns meaning 'bearer' (*ctenophore; semaphore*). □ **-phorous** /fɜrəs/ *combining form.* [modern Latin from Greek *-phoros -phoron* bearing, bearer, from *pherō* bear]

phor·esy /ˈfɔrəsi/ *noun Biol.* an association in which one organism is carried by another, without being a parasite. □ **phor·etic** /fɔrˈɛtɪk/ *adjective* [French *phorésie* from Greek *phorēsis* being carried]

phos·gene /ˈfɒzdʒiːn/ *noun* a colourless poisonous gas (carbonyl chloride), formerly used in warfare. Chem. formula: $COCl_2$. [Greek *phōs* light + -GEN, with reference to its original production by the action of sunlight on chlorine and carbon monoxide]

phos·phat·ase /ˈfɒsfəˌteɪs, -teɪz/ *noun Biochem.* any enzyme that catalyzes the synthesis or hydrolysis of an organic phosphate.

phos·phate /ˈfɒsfeɪt/ *noun* any salt or ester of phosphoric acid. □ **phos·phat·ic** /-ˈfatɪk/ *adjective* [French from *phosphore* PHOSPHORUS]

phos·phene /ˈfɒsfiːn/ *noun* (usu. in *pl.*) the sensation of light patterns produced by irritation of the retina, as by pressure on the eyeball. [irreg. from Greek *phōs* light + *phainō* show]

phos·phide /ˈfɒsfaɪd/ *noun Chem.* a binary compound of phosphorus with another element or group.

phos·phine /ˈfɒsfiːn/ *noun* a colourless foul-smelling poisonous gaseous compound of phosphorus and hydrogen. Chem. formula: PH_3. □ **phos·phin·ic** /-ˈfɪnɪk/ *adjective* [PHOSPHO- + -INE⁴, after *amine*]

phospho- /ˈfɒsfoː/ *combining form* denoting phosphorus. [abbreviation]

phos·pho·lipid /ˌfɒsfəˈlɪpɪd/ *noun Biochem.* any lipid consisting of a phosphate group and one or more fatty acids, including those forming cell membranes.

phos·pho·pro·tein /ˌfɒsfoːˈproːtiːn/ *noun* any protein that contains phosphorus other than in a nucleic acid or a phospholipid.

phos·phor /ˈfɒsfər/ *noun* **1** a synthetic fluorescent or phosphorescent substance esp. used in cathode ray tubes. **2** (in *combination*) = PHOSPHORUS. [German from Latin *phosphorus* PHOSPHORUS]

phosphor bronze *noun* a tough hard bronze alloy containing a small amount of phosphorus.

phos·phor·es·cence /ˌfɒsfəˈrɛsəns/ *noun* **1** radiation similar to fluorescence but detectable after excitation ceases. **2** the emission of light without combustion or perceptible heat. □ **phos·phor·esce** *intransitive verb* **phos·phor·es·cent** *adjective* **phos·phor·es·cent·ly** *adverb*

phos·phor·ic /fɒsˈfɔrɪk/ *adjective Chem.* containing phosphorus, esp. in its higher valence of five.

phosphoric acid *noun* a crystalline solid which has many commercial uses, e.g. in fertilizer and soap manufacture and food processing. Chem. formula: H_3PO_4.

phos·phor·ite /ˈfɒsfəˌraɪt/ *noun* a non-crystalline form of apatite.

phos·phor·ous /ˈfɒsfɜrəs/ *adjective Chem.* containing phosphorus, esp. in its lower valence of three (*phosphorous acid*).

phos·phor·us /ˈfɒsfɜrəs/ *noun Chem.* a non-metallic element occurring naturally in various phosphate rocks and existing in allotropic forms, esp. as a poisonous whitish waxy substance burning slowly at ordinary temperatures and so appearing luminous in the dark, and a reddish form used in matches, fertilizers, etc. Symbol: **P**; at. no.: 15. [Latin, = morning star, from Greek *phōsphoros* from *phōs* light + *-phoros* -bringing]

phos·phoryl·ate /fɒsˈfɔriˌleɪt/ *transitive verb Chem.* introduce a phosphate group into (an organic molecule etc.). □ **phos·phoryl·a·tion** /-ˈleɪʃən/ *noun*

phot /fɒt, foːt/ *noun* a unit of illumination equal to one lumen per square centimetre. [Greek *phōs phōtos* light]

phot·ic /ˈfoːtɪk/ *adjective* **1** of or relating to light. **2** designating parts of the oceans penetrated by sufficient sunlight for the growth of plants.

photo *noun* (*pl.* **photos**) = PHOTOGRAPH *noun.* [abbreviation]

photo- *combining form* denoting: **1** light (*photosensitive*). **2** photography (*photocomposition*). [Greek *phōs phōtos* light, or as abbreviation of PHOTOGRAPH]

photo-aging *noun* skin damage such as wrinkles, brown spots, changes in texture, etc. caused by the ultraviolet light of the sun.

photo·biol·ogy *noun* the study of the effects of light on living organisms.

photo·call *noun Brit.* an occasion on which theatrical performers, famous personalities, etc., pose for photographers by arrangement.

Photo CD *noun proprietary* **1** a compact disc from which still photographs can be displayed on a television screen. **2** the technology for storing and reproducing photographs in this way.

photo·cell *noun* = PHOTOELECTRIC CELL.

photo·chem·ical *adjective* of or relating to the chemical action of light. □ **photo·chem·ical·ly** *adverb*

photochemical smog *noun* a condition of the atmosphere caused by the action of sunlight on pollutants, resulting in haze and high levels of ozone and nitrogen oxide.

photo·chem·istry *noun* the study of the chemical effects of light.

photo·chrom·ic /ˌfoːtoːˈkroːmɪk/ *adjective* changing colour or shade reversibly in light of a particular frequency or intensity (*photochromic lens*). [PHOTO- + Greek *khrōma* 'colour']

photo·col·lage /ˌfoːtoːˈkɒlɒʒ/ *noun* **1** a technique of collage using photographs, parts of photographs, or photographic negatives. **2** a work of art or display made this way.

photo·compos·ition *noun* typesetting using characters on photographic film or directly from a photographic image.

photo·copi·er *noun* an electrical machine for producing immediate photographic copies of text or graphic matter by a process usu. involving the electrical or chemical action of light.

photo·copy ● *noun* (*pl.* **-ies**) a copy made by a photocopier. ● *transitive verb* (**-ies, -ied**) **1** make a photocopy of. **2** *intransitive* make a photocopy or photocopies. □ **photo·copi·able** *adjective* **photo·cop·ied** *adjective*

photo·degrad·able /ˌfoːtoːdəˈgreɪdəbəl/ *adjective* capable of being decomposed by the action of light, esp. sunlight.

photo·diode /ˌfoːtoːˈdaɪoːd/ *noun* a semiconductor diode the resistance of which depends on the degree of illumination.

photo·dynam·ic *adjective* involving or causing a toxic response to light, esp. ultraviolet light.

photo·elec·tric *adjective* marked by or using emissions of electrons from substances exposed to light. □ **photo·elec·tri·city** *noun*

photoelectric cell *noun* a device which generates an electric current or voltage dependent on the degree of illumination.

photo·elec·tron *noun* an electron released from an atom by the action of a photon, esp. one emitted from a solid surface by the action of light.

photo·emis·sion *noun* the emission of electrons from a surface by the action of light incident on it.

photo essay *noun* an essay consisting of text matter and numerous photographs.

photo finish *noun* a close finish of a race or contest, esp. one where the winner is only distinguishable on a photograph.

photo·finish·ing *noun* the commercial development and printing of films. □ **photo·finish·er** *noun*

pho·tog /fəˈtɒg/ *noun N Amer. informal* photographer.

photo·gen·ic /ˌfoːtoːˈdʒɛnɪk/ *adjective* **1** (esp. of a person) having an appearance that looks pleasing in photographs. **2** *Biol.* producing or emitting light. □ **photo·gen·ic·ally** *adverb*

photo·gram·metry /ˌfoːtoːˈgramətri/ *noun* the use of photography for surveying and mapping. □ **photo·gram·met·ric** /-ˈmɛtrɪk/ *adjective* **photo·gram·met·rist** *noun*

photo·graph ● *noun* a picture formed by means of the chemical action of light or other radiation on sensitive film. ● *verb* **1** *transitive* take a photograph of (a person etc.). **2** *intransitive* appear (in a particular way) when in a photograph (*she photographs well*).

☐ **pho·to·graph·able** *adjective* **pho·tog·raph·er** *noun* **pho·to·graph·ic** *adjective* **pho·to·graph·ic·ally** *adverb*

photographic memory *noun* a memory allowing the precise recall of visual images with the accuracy of a photograph.

pho·tog·raphy *noun* **1** the process or art of taking photographs. **2** the business of producing and printing photographs. **3** a collection of photographs.

photo·grav·ure /ˌfoːtoːɡrəˈvjʊr/ *noun* **1** an image, plate, or print produced from a photographic negative transferred to a metal plate and etched in. **2** this process. [French (as PHOTO-, *gravure* engraving)]

photo ID *noun* identification containing a photograph of the bearer.

photo·jour·nal·ism *noun* the art or practice of relating news through the use of photographs, with or without an accompanying text, esp. in magazines etc. ☐ **photo·jour·nal·ist** *noun* **photo·jour·nal·is·tic** *adjective*

photo·lith·og·raphy /ˌfoːtoːlɪˈθɒɡrəfi/ *noun* **1** lithography in which the image is photographically transferred to the printing surface. **2** *Electronics* an analogous process for making integrated circuits and printed circuit boards. ☐ **photo·lith·og·raph·er** *noun* **photo·litho·graph·ic** *adjective*

pho·tol·y·sis /foːˈtɒlɪsɪs/ *noun* decomposition or dissociation of molecules by the action of light. ☐ **photo·lytic** /-təˈlɪtɪk/ *adjective*

photo·mechan·ical *adjective* relating to or denoting processes in which photography is involved in the making of a printing plate.

pho·tom·eter /foːˈtɒmətər/ *noun* an instrument for measuring light or for comparing the intensities of light from different sources. ☐ **photo·met·ric** /ˌfoːtoːˈmetrɪk/ *adjective* **pho·tom·etry** /-ˈtɒmɪtri/ *noun*

photo·micro·graph /ˌfoːtoːˈmaɪkrəˌɡrɑːf/ *noun* a photograph of an image produced by a microscope. ☐ **photo·microg·raphy** /-ˈkrɒɡrəfi/ *noun*

photo·mon·tage /ˌfoːtoːmɒnˈtɒʒ/ *noun* **1** the technique of constructing a montage from photographic images. **2** a composite picture so produced.

photo·multi·plier *noun* an instrument containing a photocell and a series of electrodes, used to detect and amplify the light from very faint sources.

pho·ton /ˈfoːtɒn/ *noun* a quantum of light or other electromagnetic radiation, the energy of which is proportional to the frequency of radiation. ☐ **pho·ton·ic** /-ˈtɒnɪk/ *adjective* [Greek *phôs phôtos* light, after *electron*]

pho·ton·ics /foːˈtɒnɪks/ *noun* the branch of technology concerned with the properties and transmission of photons, e.g. in fibre optics.

photo-offset *noun* offset printing with plates made photographically.

photo op *noun* esp. *N Amer. informal* = PHOTO OPPORTUNITY.

photo opportunity *noun* an opportunity provided for press and television photographers to take photographs of a politician, celebrity, etc.

photo·period *noun* the period of daily illumination which an organism receives. ☐ **photo·period·ic** *adjective*

photo·period·ism *noun* the phenomenon whereby many plants and animals are stimulated or inhibited in reproduction and other functions by the lengths of the daily periods of light and darkness to which they are subjected.

photo·phobia *noun* **1** an abnormal sensitivity of the eyes to light. **2** an abnormal fear of light, esp. as a result of such sensitivity. ☐ **photo·phob·ic** *adjective*

photo·phore *noun* a light-producing organ in certain fishes and other animals. [from Greek *phôtophoros* 'light-bearing']

photo radar *noun* a computer-operated radar system which takes a photograph of the licence plate of a speeding car, the picture and a ticket being subsequently delivered in the mail to the car's owner.

photo·real·ism *noun* detailed and unidealized representation in art, esp. of banal, mundane, or sordid aspects of life. ☐ **photo·real·ist** *noun* **photo·real·is·tic** *adjective*

photo·recep·tor *noun* any living structure that responds to incident light, esp. a cell in which light is converted to a nervous or other signal.

photo-reconnais·sance *noun* reconnaissance by means of aerial photography.

photo·refrac·tive kera·tec·tomy *noun* = PRK.

photo·sensi·tive *adjective* reacting chemically, electrically, etc., to light. ☐ **photo·sensi·tiv·ity** *noun*

photo·sphere *noun* the luminous surface layer of the sun or other

star, below the chromosphere, from which its light and heat radiate. ☐ **photo·spher·ic** *adjective*

photo·stat *dated* ● *noun* **1** a photocopier. **2** a photocopy. ● *transitive verb* (**photostat**) (**-stat·ted, -stat·ting**) make a photostat of. ☐ **photo·stat·ic** *adjective*

photo·syn·the·sis /ˌfoːtoːˈsɪnθəsɪs/ *noun* the process in which the energy of sunlight is used by organisms, esp. green plants to synthesize carbohydrates from carbon dioxide and water. ☐ **photo·syn·the·size** *transitive & intransitive verb* (also esp. *Brit.* **-sise**). **photo·syn·thet·ic** /-ˈθetɪk/ *adjective* **photo·syn·thet·ic·ally** /-ˈθetɪkli/ *adverb*

photo·sys·tem *noun* either of the two biochemical mechanisms in plants by which light is converted into useful energy.

photo·tran·sis·tor *noun* a transistor that responds to incident light by generating and amplifying an electric current.

photo·trop·ism /ˌfoːtoːˈtrɒpɪzəm, fəˈtɒtrəˌpɪzəm/ *noun* the tendency of a plant etc. to bend or turn towards or away from a source of light. ☐ **photo·troph·ic** *adjective* **photo·trop·ic** /-ˈtrɒpɪk/ *adjective*

photo·vol·taic /ˌfoːtoːvɒlˈteɪɪk/ ● *adjective* relating to the production of electric current at the junction of two substances exposed to light. Abbr.: **PV**. ● *noun* a photovoltaic device.

photo·vol·taics /ˌfoːtoːvɒlˈteɪɪks/ *noun* the branch of science and technology that deals with photovoltaic effects and devices.

phr. *abbreviation* phrase.

phras·al /ˈfreɪzəl/ *adjective Grammar* of the nature of or consisting of a phrase. ☐ **phras·al·ly** *adverb*

phrasal verb *noun* an idiomatic phrase consisting of a verb and an adverb, e.g. *break down* or a verb and a preposition, e.g. *see to*.

phrase ● *noun* **1** a small group of words forming a conceptual unit, but not a sentence, esp. such a group without a predicate or finite verb. **2** an idiomatic or short pithy expression. **3** a manner or mode of expression (*a nice turn of phrase*). **4** *Music* a group of notes forming a more or less distinct unit within a larger passage or piece. ● *transitive verb* **1** express in words (*phrased the reply badly*). **2** (esp. when reading aloud or speaking) divide (sentences etc.) into units so as to convey the meaning of the whole. **3** *Music* divide (music) into phrases etc. in performance; play so as to give due expression to phrasing. ☐ **phras·ing** *noun* [earlier *phrasis* from Latin from Greek *phrazō* declare, tell]

phrase book *noun* a book for tourists etc. listing useful expressions with their equivalent in another language.

phrase·ol·ogy /ˌfreɪziˈɒlədʒi/ *noun* (pl. **-ies**) **1** a choice or arrangement of words. **2** a mode of expression. ☐ **phrase·o·logic·al** /-ziəˈlɒdʒɪkəl/ *adjective* [modern Latin *phraseologia* from Greek *phraseōn* genitive pl. of *phrasis* PHRASE]

phreak /friːk/ ● *noun* (in full **phone freak**) a person who makes fraudulent use of a telephone system by electronic means, esp. for computer hacking etc. ● *transitive & intransitive verb* use an electronic device to obtain (a telephone call) without payment. ☐ **phreak·ing** *noun* [alteration of FREAK]

phre·atic /friˈatɪk/ *adjective* **1** (of water) situated underground in the zone of saturation. **2** (of a volcanic eruption or explosion) caused by the heating and expansion of underground water. [Greek *phrear phreatos* well]

phren·ic /ˈfrenɪk/ *adjective Anat.* of or relating to the diaphragm. [French *phrénique* from Greek *phrēn phrenos* diaphragm]

phren·ol·ogy /frəˈnɒlədʒi/ *noun hist.* the study of the shape and size of the cranium as a supposed indication of character and mental faculties. ☐ **phren·o·logic·al** /-nəˈlɒdʒɪkəl/ *adjective* **phren·ol·o·gist** *noun* [Greek *phrēn phrenos* diaphragm, mind (once thought to be located in the diaphragm) + -OLOGY]

Phry·gia /ˈfrɪdʒiə/ an ancient region of west central Asia Minor, to the south of Bithynia. It dominated Asia Minor after the decline of the Hittites in the 12th c. BC, reaching the peak of its power in the 8th c. under King Midas. ☐ **Phry·gian** *noun & adjective*

Phrygian cap *noun* a soft felt or wool conical cap with a pointed crown turned over in front, worn by the ancient Phrygians and emancipated Roman slaves, used as an emblem of liberty during the French Revolution and subsequent revolutionary movements in the 19th c.

Phrygian mode *noun Music* the church mode represented by the natural diatonic scale E–E.

phthal·ic acid /ˈfθalɪk/ *noun Chem.* a crystalline acid derived from benzene, with two carboxylic acid groups attached to the benzene ring. □ **phthal·ate** /-leɪt/ *noun* [abbreviation of NAPHTHALIC: see NAPHTHALENE]

phthis·is /'fθəɪsɪs, 'θəɪ-/ *noun archaic* any progressive wasting disease, esp. pulmonary tuberculosis. □ **phthis·ic** *adjective* **phthis·ic·al** *adjective* [Latin from Greek from *phthinō* to decay]

Phu·ket /puːˈket/ **1** an island of Thailand, situated at the head of the Strait of Malacca off the west coast of the Malay Peninsula. **2** a port at the south end of Phuket island, a major resort centre and outlet to the Indian Ocean.

phut /fʌt/ *noun esp. Brit.* a dull abrupt sound as of an impact or explosion. □ **go phut** *informal* (esp. of a scheme or plan) collapse, break down. [perhaps from Hindi *phaṭnā* to burst]

phy·col·ogy /faɪˈkɒlədʒi/ *noun* the study of algae. □ **phyco·logic·al** *adjective* **phy·col·o·gist** *noun* [Greek *phukos* seaweed + -LOGY]

phyco·my·cete /ˌfaɪkoʊˈmaɪsiːt/ *noun* any of various fungi which typically form non-septate mycelium. [Greek *phukos* seaweed + pl. of Greek *mukēs* mushroom]

Phyfe /'faɪf/ **Dun·can** (also **Fife**) (1768–1854), Scottish-born US furniture designer, who was one of the first to use factory methods of furniture production; his best-known design is a drop-leaf table with a central pedestal supported by four curved legs.

phyla *pl. of* PHYLUM.

phy·lac·tery /fɪˈlaktəri/ *noun* (*pl.* **-ies**) **1** either of two small leather boxes containing Biblical texts in Hebrew, worn by Jewish men during morning prayer on all days except the Sabbath as a reminder to keep the law. **2** an amulet; a charm. [Old French from Late Latin *phylacterium* from Greek *phulaktērion* amulet, from *phulassō* guard]

phy·let·ic /faɪˈletɪk/ *adjective Biol.* of or relating to the development of a species or other group. □ **phy·let·ic·ally** *adverb* [Greek *phuletikos* from *phuletēs* tribesman, from *phulē* tribe]

phyl·lo /'faɪloː, 'fiːloː/ *noun* (also **filo**) **1** a kind of dough capable of being stretched into very thin leaves which may then be layered together to make sweet and savoury pastries, e.g. baklava. **2** pastry made this way. [Greek *phullo-* from *phullon* leaf]

phyllo- /'fɪloː/ *combining form* leaf. [Greek *phullo-* from *phullon* leaf]

phyl·lode /'fɪloːd/ *noun* a flattened leaf stalk resembling and functioning as a leaf. [modern Latin *phyllodium* from Greek *phullōdēs* leaflike (as PHYLLO-)]

phyllo·quin·one /ˌfaɪloːˈkwɪnoːn/ *noun* one of the K vitamins, found in cabbage, spinach, and other leafy green vegetables, and essential for the blood clotting process. *Also called* VITAMIN K₁.

phyllo·taxis /ˌfɪloːˈtaksɪs/ *noun* the arrangement of leaves on an axis or stem. □ **phyllo·tac·tic** *adjective*

phyl·lox·era /ˌfɪlɒkˈsiːrə, fɪˈlɒksərə/ *noun* any plant louse of the genus *Phylloxera*, esp. of a species attacking vines. [modern Latin from Greek *phullon* leaf + *xēros* dry]

phylo- /'faɪloː/ *combining form Biol.* denoting a race or tribe. [Greek *phulon*, *phulē*]

phy·logeny /faɪˈlɒdʒəni/ *noun* (also **phylo·gen·esis** /ˌfaɪloːˈdʒenəsɪs/) **1** the evolutionary development and diversification of groups of organisms, or particular features of organisms. **2** a history of this (*compare* ONTOGENESIS). □ **phylo·gen·etic** /-dʒɪˈnetɪk/ *adjective* **phylo·gen·etic·ally** /-dʒɪˈnetɪkəli/ *adverb*

phy·lum /'faɪləm/ *noun* (*pl.* **phyla** /-lə/) **1** *Biol.* a taxonomic rank below kingdom comprising a class or classes and subordinate taxa. **2** *Linguistics* a group of languages related to each other less closely than those of a family. [modern Latin from Greek *phulon* 'race']

phys. ed. *noun N Amer.* = PHYSICAL EDUCATION.

phys·ia·trist /fəˈzaɪətrɪst/ *noun* a person who uses physical agents such as light, heat, etc. to diagnose or treat deformity, disease, or injury.

physic *archaic* ● *noun* **1** a medicine (*a dose of physic*). **2** the art or practice of healing. ● *transitive verb* (**phys·icked**, **phys·ick·ing**) dose or treat with medicine, esp. a purgative. [Old French *fisique* medicine, from Latin *physica* from Greek *phusikē* (*epistēmē*) (knowledge) of nature]

phys·ic·al ● *adjective* **1** **a** of or concerning the body (*physical exercise*; *physical abuse*). **b** of or concerning observable aspects or features of the environment. **2** of or pertaining to matter, the world of the senses, or things material as opposed to things mental or spiritual (*both mental and physical force*). **3** **a** of or in accordance with the laws of nature (*a physical impossibility*). **b** of or pertaining to physics (*physical science*). **4** **a** (of a person or action) inclined to be aggressive or violent, making frequent use of bodily contact, etc. (*a tough, physical playing style*). **b** (of an attribute etc.) involving the body rather than the mind; carnal (*physical charms*). **5** **a** (of a commodity) actually existing and deliverable.

b (of a market) involving the immediate delivery of a commodity rather than a notional or future delivery. ● *noun* (in full **physical examination**) a medical examination to determine health or physical fitness. □ **get physical 1** become violent or physically aggressive. **2** become sexually involved. **3** exercise, become physically fit or toned. □ **phys·ic·al·ity** *noun* **phys·ic·al·ly** *adverb* **phys·ic·al·ness** *noun* [medieval Latin *physicalis* from Latin *physica* (as PHYSIC)]

physical chemistry *noun* the application of the techniques and theories of physics to the study of chemical systems, behaviour, etc.

physical education *noun* instruction in physical exercise and sports, esp. in schools.

physical force *noun* **1** material or corporal rather than moral means of persuasion, coercion, etc. **2** the use of armed power to effect or repress political changes.

physical geography *noun* the branch of geography encompassing geomorphology, climatology, and meteorology.

phys·ic·al·ism *noun Philos.* the theory that all reality must eventually be expressible in the language of physics. □ **phys·ic·al·ist** *noun & adjective* **phys·ic·al·is·tic** *adjective*

physically challenged *adjective N Amer. euphemism* (of a person) having a physical disability.

physical object *noun Philos.* an object that exists in space and time and that can be perceived.

physical plant *noun* = PLANT 2c.

physical science *noun* any branch of the sciences that deals with inanimate matter and energy, e.g. physics, chemistry, geology, astronomy, etc.

physical therapy *noun esp. US* = PHYSIOTHERAPY. □ **physical therapist** *noun*

physical training *noun* the systematic use of exercises to promote bodily fitness and strength. *Abbr.*: **PT**.

phys·ician *noun* **1** a person legally qualified to practise medicine, esp. a specialist in non-surgical medical diagnosis and treatment. **2** a healer (*work is the best physician*). [Old French *fisicien* (as PHYSIC)]

physician-assisted suicide *noun* suicide carried out with the assistance of a doctor (whose role is typically to provide a lethal dose of a drug at the explicit request of the patient).

phys·ic·ist *noun* an expert in or student of physics.

physico- *combining form* **1** physical (and). **2** of physics (and).

phys·ico·chem·ical *adjective* of or relating to physics and chemistry or to physical chemistry.

phys·ics *noun* the science dealing with the properties and interactions of matter and energy. [pl. of *physic* (thing), after Latin *physica*, Greek *phusika* natural things, from *phusis* nature]

physio *noun Cdn & Brit. informal* **1** (*pl.* **physios**) a physiotherapist. **2** physiotherapy. [abbreviation]

physio- *combining form* **1** nature; what is natural. **2** physiology, physiological. [Greek *phusis* nature]

physi·oc·racy /ˌfɪziˈɒkrəsi/ *noun* (*pl.* **-cies**) *hist.* **1** government according to a supposed natural order, esp. as advocated by the French physiocrats. **2** a society based on this. [French *physiocratie* (as PHYSIO-, -CRACY)]

physio·crat /'fɪziəˌkrat/ *noun* a member of an 18th-c. group of French economists who held that agriculture, rather than manufacturing or trade, was the source of all wealth and that agricultural products should be highly priced. They stressed the necessity of free trade and coined the term *laissez-faire*. □ **physio·crat·ic** /-iəˈkratɪk/ *adjective*

physi·ognomy /ˌfɪziˈɒnəmi/ *noun* (*pl.* **-ies**) **1** **a** a person's face or expression, esp. viewed as indicative of the mind or character. **b** the art of supposedly judging character from facial characteristics etc. **2** the external features of a landscape, plant community, etc. **3** the ideal, mental, moral, or political aspect of anything as an indication of its character. □ **physio·gnom·ic** /-ziəˈnɒmɪk/ *adjective* **physio·gnom·ic·al** /-ziəˈnɒmɪkəl/ *adjective* **physi·ognom·ist** *noun* [Old French *phisonomie* from medieval Latin *phisonomia* from Greek *phusiognōmonia* judging of a person's nature (by the features) (as PHYSIO-, *gnōmōn* judge)]

physi·og·raphy /ˌfɪziˈɒɡrəfi/ *noun* physical geography; geomorphology. □ **physi·og·raph·er** *noun* **physio·graph·ic** *adjective* **physio·graph·ic·al** *adjective* [French *physiographie* (as PHYSIO-, -GRAPHY)]

physio·logic·al /ˌfɪziəˈlɒdʒɪkəl/ *adjective* (also **physio·logic**) of or concerning physiology. □ **physio·logic·al·ly** *adverb*

physi·ol·ogy /ˌfɪzɪˈɒlədʒɪ/ *noun* **1** the science that deals with the normal functioning of living organisms and their parts. **2** the physiological features of a thing. □ **physi·ol·o·gist** *noun* [as PHYSIO-, -LOGY]

physio·ther·apy *noun esp. Cdn & Brit.* the treatment of disease, injury, deformity, etc., by physical methods including manipulation, massage, infrared heat treatment, remedial exercise, etc., rather than by drugs. □ **physio·ther·apist** *noun*

phy·sique /fɪˈziːk/ *noun* the form, size, and development of a person's body. [French, originally adj. as PHYSIC)]

-phyte /faɪt/ *combining form* forming nouns denoting a vegetable or plantlike organism (*saprophyte*; *zoophyte*). □ **-phytic** /ˈfɪtɪk/ *combining form*. [Greek *phuton* plant, from *phuō* come into being]

phyto- /ˈfaɪtəʊ/ *combining form* denoting a plant.

phyto·chem·istry /ˌfaɪtəʊˈkemɪstrɪ/ *noun* the chemistry of plants and plant products. □ **phyto·chem·ical** *adjective* **phyto·chem·ist** *noun*

phyto·chrome /ˈfaɪtəʊˌkrəʊm/ *noun Biochem.* a blue-green pigment found in many plants, and regulating various developmental processes according to the nature and timing of the light it absorbs. [PHYTO- + Greek *khrōma* colour]

phyto·estro·gen /ˌfaɪtəʊˈestrədʒen/ *noun* an estrogen found in plants.

phyto·gen·esis /ˌfaɪtəʊˈdʒenəsɪs/ *noun* (also **phy·togeny** /-ˈtɒdʒɪnɪ/) the science of the origin or evolution of plants.

phyto·geog·raphy /ˌfaɪtəʊdʒɪˈɒɡrəfɪ/ *noun* the geographical distribution of plants. □ **phyto·geog·raph·er** *noun* **phyto·geo·graph·ic** *adjective*

phyto·nutri·ent *noun* a substance found in certain plants which is believed to be beneficial to human health and help prevent various diseases.

phyto·path·ol·ogy /ˌfaɪtəʊpəˈθɒlədʒɪ/ *noun* the study of plant diseases. □ **phyto·patho·logic·al** *adjective* **phyto·path·ol·o·gist** *noun*

phy·toph·a·gous /faɪˈtɒfəɡəs/ *adjective* (esp. of an insect or other invertebrate) feeding on plants.

phyto·plank·ton /ˌfaɪtəʊˈplaŋktən/ *noun* plankton consisting of microscopic plants.

phyto·toxin /ˌfaɪtəʊˈtɒksɪn/ *noun* **1** a substance poisonous or injurious to plants, esp. one produced by a parasite. **2** any toxin derived from a plant. □ **phyto·toxic** *adjective* **phyto·tox·icity** /-tɒˈksɪsɪtɪ/ *noun*

PI *abbreviation* private investigator.

pi /paɪ/ *noun* **1** the sixteenth letter of the Greek alphabet (Π, π). **2** (as π) the symbol of the ratio of the circumference of a circle to its diameter (approx. 3.14159). [Greek: sense 2 from Greek *periphereia* circumference]

Piaf /piːˈaf/ **Edith** (born Edith Giovanna Gassion) (1915–63), French singer, who is best known for her defiant and nostalgic songs, which include 'La Vie en rose' and 'Je ne regrette rien'.

pi·affe /piːˈaf/ ● *intransitive verb* (of a horse) move esp. on the spot with a high, slow, trotting step. ● *noun* an act of piaffing. [French *piaffer* to strut]

Pia·get /pɪaˈʒei/ **Jean** (1896–1980), Swiss psychologist, whose studies of the development of perception, reason, and logic in children changed the current views of children's intelligence and greatly influenced methods of child education, esp. in the US. □ **Pia·get·ian** /pɪəˈdʒetɪən, -ˈdʒeɪən/ *adjective*

pia mater /ˌpaɪə ˈmeɪtər, ˌpiːə/ *noun* the delicate, fibrous, and highly vascular innermost membrane enveloping the brain and spinal cord (*see* MENINGES). [medieval Latin, = tender mother, translation of Arabic *al-'umm al-raḳīḳa*: compare DURA MATER]

piani *pl.* of PIANO².

pian·ism /ˈpiːəˌnɪzəm/ *noun* **1** the art or technique of piano playing. **2** the skill or style of a composer of piano music. □ **pian·is·tic** *adjective* **pian·is·tic·ally** *adverb*

pian·is·simo /ˌpiəˈnɪsɪˌməʊ/ *Music* ● *adjective* performed very softly. ● *adverb* very softly. ● *noun* (*pl.* **-simos** or **pian·is·simi** /-mɪ/) a passage to be performed very softly. [Italian, superlative of PIANO²]

pian·ist /ˈpiːənɪst, piˈanɪst, ˈpjanɪst/ *noun* a person who plays the piano, esp. professionally.

piano¹ *noun* (*pl.* **pianos**) **1** a large musical instrument played by pressing down keys on a keyboard and causing hammers to strike metal strings, the vibration from which is stopped by dampers when the keys are released. **2** an instrument operated in the same way and producing the same tone by electronic means. [Italian, abbreviation of PIANOFORTE]

piano² ● *adjective* **1** *Music* performed softly. **2** subdued. ● *adverb* **1** *Music* softly. **2** in a subdued manner. ● *noun* (*pl.* **pianos** or **piani**) *Music* a piano passage. [Italian from Latin *planus* flat, (of sound) soft]

piano-accordion *noun* an accordion with the melody played on a small vertical keyboard like that of a piano, instead of on buttons.

piano bar *noun* a cocktail lounge having a piano and featuring live entertainment.

piano bench *noun* a low rectangular bench, often of adjustable height and with a hinged seat serving as a lid for a compartment for music.

piano·forte /ˌpiano:ˈfɔːteɪ/ *noun formal* a piano. [Italian, earlier *piano e forte* soft and loud, expressing its gradation of tone]

pian·ola /pɪəˈnəʊlə/ *noun* a kind of automatic piano; a player piano. [apparently diminutive of PIANO¹]

piano·less /pɪˈanɒləs/ *adjective* (of a group of esp. jazz musicians or music) not including a piano.

piano no·bile /ˌpjano: ˈnoːbɪˌleɪ/ *noun Archit.* **1** the main floor of a large house, containing the principal rooms, when this is the floor above the ground floor. **2** a mezzanine floor, usu. above the main lobby, in a theatre, concert hall, etc. [Italian, = noble floor]

piano reduction *noun* an arrangement of orchestral music for performance on the piano.

piano roll *noun* a roll of perforated paper which controls the movement of the keys in a player piano.

piano stool *noun* a low round stool with a seat that may be raised or lowered, usu. by means of a screw mechanism.

piano trio *noun* a trio for piano and two stringed instruments, usu. violin and cello.

piano tuner *noun* a person who tunes pianos for a living.

piano wire *noun* a special kind of strong steel wire used for the strings of pianos.

pias·sava /ˌpiːəˈsɒvə/ *noun* **1** a stout fibre obtained from the leaf stalks of various American and African palm trees. **2** any of these trees. [Portuguese from Tupi *piaçába*]

pi·astre /pɪˈastər/ *noun* (also esp. US **pi·aster**) a small coin and monetary unit of Egypt, Lebanon, and Syria, equal to one-hundredth of a pound. [French *piastre* from Italian *piastra (d'argento)* plate (of silver), formed as PLASTER]

piaz·za /pɪˈatsə, pɪˈɒtsə/ *noun* a public square or marketplace esp. in an Italian town. [Italian, formed as PLACE]

pi·broch /ˈpiːbrɒx, -brɒk/ *noun* a series of esp. martial or funerary variations on a theme for the bagpipes. [Gaelic *piobaireachd* art of piping, from *piobair* piper, from *piob* from English PIPE]

pic *noun* (*pl.* **pix** or **pics**) *informal* **1** a motion picture. **2** a picture, painting, or photograph. [abbreviation]

pica¹ /ˈpaɪkə/ *noun Printing* **1** a unit of type size equal to 12 points (approximately ¹/₆ inch). **2** a size of letters in typewriting (10 per inch). [origin obscure]

pica² /ˈpaɪkə/ *noun Med.* a tendency or craving to eat substances other than normal food, occurring during childhood or pregnancy, or as a symptom of disease. [modern Latin or medieval Latin, = magpie]

pica·dor /ˈpɪkəˌdɔr/ *noun* a mounted person with a lance who goads the bull in a bullfight. [Spanish from *picar* prick]

pi·can·te /pɪˈkɒnteɪ/ *adjective* (of food) hot, spicy, sharply seasoned. [Spanish, present participle of *picar* 'prick, bite']

Pi·card /piːˈkar/ **Jean** (1620–82), French astronomer, who was the first to measure the length of a longitude line, and thereby calculate the size of the earth.

Pic·ardy /ˈpɪkərdɪ/ a region (formerly a province) of N France, centred on the city of Amiens. It was the scene of heavy fighting in the First World War.

picar·esque /ˌpɪkəˈresk/ *adjective* **1** (of a style of fiction) dealing with the episodic adventures of rogues etc. **2** drifting, wandering. [French from Spanish *picaresco* from *pícaro* rogue]

picar·oon¹ /ˌpɪkəˈruːn/ *noun* a rogue, thief, or scoundrel. [Spanish *picarón* (as PICARESQUE)]

picar·oon² /ˌpɪkəˈruːn/ *noun N Amer.* a long pole fitted with a spike or hook, used in logging and fishing. [perhaps from French *piqueron* 'little pike, dart, goad' from *pique* 'pike']

Pi·cas·so /pɪˈkasoː, pɪˈkɒsoː/ **Pablo (Ruiz y)** (1881–1973), Spanish painter, resident in France from 1904. The dominant figure in avant-garde art in the first half of the 20th c., he was known for his prolific inventiveness and technical versatility; his painting *Les Demoiselles d'Avignon* (1907) signalled the emergence of cubism, and the 1920s and 1930s saw the evolution of semi-surrealist paintings using increasingly violent imagery, notably *The Three Dancers* (1935) and *Guernica* (1937).

pic·ay·une /ˌpɪkəˈjuːn/ esp. *N Amer.* ● *adjective* **1** contemptible; petty. **2** insignificant. ● *noun* **1** an insignificant person or thing. **2** *US (South) informal* a small coin of little value, esp. a 5-cent piece. [French *picaillon* a Piedmontese coin, cash, from Provençal *picaioun*, of unknown origin]

Pic·ca·dilly /ˌpɪkəˈdɪli/ a street in central London, England, extending from Hyde Park eastward to Piccadilly Circus, noted for its fashionable shops, hotels, and restaurants.

pic·ca·lilli /ˌpɪkəˈlɪli/ *noun* (pl. **pic·ca·lillis**) a condiment of pickled, chopped vegetables, mustard, and hot spices. [18th c.: perhaps from PICKLE + CHILI]

pic·ca·ninny *var. of* PICKANINNY.

pic·cata *noun* a dish of sautéed esp. veal cutlets with a sauce of lemon juice and parsley, sometimes with white wine and capers. [Italian]

pic·colo /ˈpɪkəˌlo/ *noun* (pl. **-colos**) **1** a small flute sounding an octave higher than the ordinary flute. **2** its player in an orchestra etc. [Italian, = small (flute)]

pick¹ ● *verb* **1** *transitive & intransitive* choose carefully from a number of alternatives (*picked the pink one; picked a team; picked the right moment to intervene; picked wisely*). **2** *transitive* detach or pluck (a flower, fruit, etc.) from a stem, tree, etc. **3** *transitive* **a** probe (the teeth, nose, ears, a pimple, etc.) with the finger, an instrument, etc. to remove unwanted matter. **b** clear (a bone, carcass, etc.) of scraps of meat etc. **c** make (a hole) by piercing or probing with a pointed instrument. **4** *transitive & intransitive* (of a person) eat (food, a meal, etc.) fastidiously, in small mouthfuls, or without interest. **5** *transitive & intransitive* esp. *N Amer.* play (a guitar etc.) by plucking the strings. **6** *transitive* remove stalks etc. from (esp. soft fruit) before cooking. **7** *transitive* **a** select (a route or path) carefully over difficult terrain on foot. **b** place (one's steps etc.) carefully. **8** *transitive* pull apart the strands of (wool etc.) (*pick oakum*). **9** *transitive* (of a bird) take up (grains etc.) in the beak. ● *noun* **1** the act or an instance of picking. **2 a** that which is picked. **b** *N Amer.* a person chosen as a member of a team etc. **c** *informal* the favourite to win a game, race, or competition. **d** the right to select (*had first pick of the prizes*). **3** (usu. foll. by *of*) the best (*the pick of the bunch*). **4** *Basketball* a permissible block. □ **pick and choose** select carefully or fastidiously. **pick apart** esp. *N Amer.* **1** find fault, criticize harshly. **2** break up or dismantle. **pick at 1** eat (food) without interest; nibble. **2** = PICK ON 1 (see below). **pick a person's brains** extract ideas, information, etc., from a person for one's own use. **pick a fight** start an argument or a fight deliberately. **pick holes in** *Brit.* = POKE HOLES IN (see POKE¹). **pick a lock** open a lock with an instrument other than the proper key, esp. with intent to steal. **pick off 1** pluck (leaves etc.) off. **2** shoot (people etc.) one by one without haste. **3** eliminate (opposition etc.) singly. **4** *Baseball* put out (a runner) by throwing the ball to a base. **pick on 1** find fault with; nag at. **2** single out (a person) for criticism, victimization, etc. **pick out 1** take from a larger number, esp. with care and deliberation (*picked him out from the others*). **2** distinguish from surrounding objects or at a distance (*can just pick out the church spire*). **3** play (a tune) by ear on the piano etc. **4** accentuate (decoration etc.) with a contrasting colour (*trim picked out in diamonds*). **5** make out (the meaning of a passage etc.). **pick over** select the best from. **pick a person's pockets** steal the contents of a person's pockets. **pick a quarrel** = PICK A FIGHT. **pick to pieces** = PICK APART. **pick up 1** grasp and raise (from the ground etc.) (*picked up his hat*). **2 a** learn or acquire with little effort (*picked up French easily*). **b** catch (an illness) (*picked up a cold*). **c** buy (a thing) cheaply or luckily (*picked up a first edition at the book sale*). **d** hear or learn (news etc.) (*he picked up the latest gossip*). **3 a** fetch (a person, animal, or thing) left in another person's charge. **b** stop for and take along with one, esp. in a vehicle (*pick me up on the corner*). **4** make the acquaintance of (a person) casually, esp. as a sexual overture. **5** (of one's health, the weather, share prices, etc.) recover, prosper, improve. **6 a** gather (speed); accelerate (a pace). **b** (of the wind) become stronger. **7** (of the police etc.) take into charge; arrest. **8** detect by scrutiny or with a telescope, searchlight, radio, etc. (*picked up most of the mistakes; picked up a distress signal*). **9 a** (often foll. by *with*) form or renew a friendship. **b** resume, take up anew (*pick up where we left off*). **10** (esp. in phr. **pick up the tab**) accept the responsibility of paying (a bill etc.). **11** (*reflexive*) raise or recover (oneself etc.) after a fall, setback, etc. **12** (esp. in phrase **pick up your feet**) raise (the feet) clear of the ground so as to walk without stumbling. **13** esp. *N Amer. informal* tidy or clean up (a room etc.). **14** *Golf* pick up one's ball, esp. when conceding a hole. **15** pick up the receiver to answer the telephone while someone is leaving a message on the answering machine. **16** reprint or rebroadcast (a story originally run by another media outlet). **pick up on** become aware of.

pick up the gauntlet = TAKE UP THE GAUNTLET (see TAKE). **pick up the pieces** restore to normality or make better (a situation, one's life, etc.), esp. after a setback, shock, or disaster. **pick up the slack** = TAKE UP THE SLACK (see SLACK¹). **take one's pick** make a choice. [Middle English, earlier *pike*, of unknown origin]

pick² *noun* **1** (in full **pick·axe**) a long-handled tool having a usu. curved iron bar pointed at one or both ends, used for breaking up hard ground, masonry, etc. **2** a plectrum. **3** (usu. in *combination*) an instrument with a sharp point, used for a specified purpose (*toothpick; ice pick; cocktail pick*). **4** a comb with long, widely spaced teeth used esp. for curly hair. **5** *Figure Skating* = TOE PICK. [Middle English, apparently var. of PIKE²]

picka·back esp. *Brit.* var. of PIGGYBACK.

picka·ninny *noun* (also **picca·ninny**) (pl. **-nies**) *offensive* a small Black or Australian Aboriginal child. [Caribbean creole from Spanish *pequeño* or Portuguese *pequeno* little]

pick·axe (*US* **pick·ax**) ● *noun* = PICK² *noun* 1. ● *verb* **1** *transitive* break (the ground etc.) with a pickaxe. **2** *intransitive* work with a pickaxe. [Middle English *pikois* from Old French *picois*, related to PIKE²: assimilated to AXE]

pick·er *noun* **1** a person or thing that picks. **2** (often in *combination*) a person who gathers or collects (*berry-picker; tree picker*).

pick·er·el *noun* (pl. same or **pick·er·els**) **1** *N Amer.* a walleye. **2** *N Amer.* **a** a northern pike. **b** any of various other small pikes of the genus *Esox*. **3** a sauger. **4** *Brit.* a young pike. [Middle English, diminutive of PIKE¹]

pick·erel·weed *noun* an aquatic plant of eastern N America, *Pontederia cordata*, with a spike of blue flowers and large arrowhead-shaped leaves.

Pick·er·ing¹ a town in S Ontario, situated on Lake Ontario, about 25 km east of Toronto; pop. (2001) 87,139. [*Pickering* in North Yorkshire, England]

Pick·er·ing², **Wil·liam Hay·ward** (b.1910), New Zealand-born US engineer. As director of the Jet Propulsion Laboratory at the California Institute of Technology in Pasadena (1954–76), he carried out early work on the telemetry, guidance, and communications systems of rockets, and went on to develop the first US satellite, Explorer I, which was launched in 1958.

pick·et ● *noun* **1 a** a person or group of people outside a place of work, intending to persuade esp. workers not to enter during a strike etc. **b** a person or group of people standing outside a place as a protest. **c** an occasion on which people act as pickets (*organized a mass picket of the embassy*). **2** a pointed stake or peg driven into the ground to form a fence or palisade, to tether a horse, etc. **3** *Military* a small body of troops sent out to watch for the enemy, held in readiness, etc. ● *verb* (**pick·et·ed, pick·et·ing**) **1** *transitive* form a picket outside (a place of work etc.). **b** *intransitive* demonstrate as a picket. **2** *transitive & intransitive* post or station (soldiers) as a picket. **3** *transitive* enclose or fence (a place) with stakes. **4** *transitive* tether (an animal). □ **pick·et·er** *noun* [French *piquet* pointed stake, from *piquer* prick, from *pic* PICK²]

picket fence *noun* *N Amer.* **1** a fence consisting of vertical pickets nailed to horizontal rails between fence posts. **2** (also **white picket fence**) this as a symbol of conventional middle-class esp. suburban domesticity and contentment (also *attributive: the ideal white-picket-fence life in the quiet town of Port Perry*).

picket line *noun* a boundary established by workers on strike, esp. at the entrance to the place of work, which others are asked not to cross.

Pick·ford, **Mary** (born Gladys Mary Smith) (1893–1979), Canadian-born US actress. She was a star of silent films, usually playing the innocent young heroine, as in *Rebecca of Sunnybrook Farm* (1917) and *Pollyanna* (1920); in 1919 she co-founded the film production company United Artists.

pick·ings *plural noun* **1** profits or gains that are easily or dishonestly earned or obtained (*rich pickings*). **2** remaining scraps; gleanings.

pickle ● *noun* **1 a** *N Amer.* a small cucumber preserved in brine, vinegar, etc. **b** (often in *pl.*) any other vegetable similarly preserved. **c** a condiment of chopped vegetables preserved in brine, vinegar, mustard, etc. **d** the brine, vinegar, etc. in which food is preserved. **2** *informal* a difficult or unpleasant predicament or situation (*we're in a pretty pickle!*). ● *transitive verb* **1** preserve (food) in brine, vinegar, etc. **2** steep (metal, wood, etc.) in or treat with an acid or other chemical solution for cleaning, bleaching, etc. **3** *Cdn (Nfld)* esp. *hist.* treat (cod, sealskins, etc.) with brine or, sometimes, salt for curing. [Middle English *pekille, pykyl*, from Middle Dutch, Middle Low German *pekel*, of unknown origin]

pickled *adjective* **1** (of food) preserved in brine or vinegar. **2** *slang* drunk.

---

uː m**oo**d   ai m**y**   əi p**i**pe   au br**ow**n   ʌu h**ou**se   ei d**ay**   ɔi b**oy**   ɑ̃ fr**an**glais   ã C**an**adien   ɔ̃ Br**ay**on   (*see over for consonants*)

3 (of wooden furniture etc.) artificially aged with acid or other chemicals.

pick·ler *noun* **1** a vegetable grown or suitable for pickling. **2** a person who pickles vegetables etc.

pickling spice *noun* a combination of herbs and spices, usu. bay leaves, mustard seed, coriander, dill seed, fenugreek, cinnamon, ginger, allspice, red pepper flakes, black peppercorns, and cloves, used in pickling.

pick·lock *noun* **1** a person who picks locks. **2** an instrument for this.

pick-me-up *noun* **1** a drink taken as a tonic or restorative when feeling weak, tired, ill, etc., esp. an alcoholic drink. **2** a good experience, good news, etc. that cheers.

pick·off *noun* (often *attributive*) *Baseball* a play in which a runner is caught off the base and tagged out by an infielder.

pick·pocket ● *noun* a person who steals from the pockets of others. ● *transitive & intransitive verb* steal from the pockets of (a person). □ **pick·pocket·ing** *noun*

pick·up *noun* **1** (in full **pickup truck**) a light truck having a usu. open bed with low sides. **2** a device that produces an electrical signal in response to some other kind of signal or change, esp.: **a** a device on a musical instrument which converts sound vibrations into electrical signals for amplification. **b** the part of a record player carrying the stylus. **c** an analogous part of a compact disc player. **3** *slang* a person met casually, esp. for sexual purposes. **4 a** the act or action of picking up (*free pickup and delivery*). **b** something picked up. **5 a** *N Amer.* the capacity for increasing speed; acceleration. **b** an increase in or recovery of health, prosperity, etc. **6** (*attributive*) **a** impromptu, done on the spur of the moment or with whatever components, people, etc. are at hand (*play pickup ball; pickup hockey*). **b** (of a performing group, esp. musicians or dancers) assembled for a particular performance, tour, etc. rather than as a permanent ensemble. **7** the tendency to pick up or absorb a substance (*prevents excessive wear and dirt pickup*). **8** *Music* a note or series of notes before a bar line, esp. as the beginning of a phrase. **9** *Fishing* a semicircular loop of metal for guiding the line back on to the spool as it is reeled in.

pick-up sticks *noun* a game in which players use two small thin sticks to attempt to remove other sticks from a jumbled pile without disturbing the pile itself.

Pick·wick·ian /pɪkˈwɪkɪən/ *adjective* **1** of or like Mr. Pickwick in Dickens's *Pickwick Papers*, esp. in being jovial, plump, etc. **2** (of words or their sense) misunderstood or misused, esp. to avoid offence.

picky *adjective* (**pick·i·er**, **pick·i·est**) *informal* excessively choosy; finicky. □ **pick·i·ness** *noun*

pick-your-own *noun* (usu. *attributive*) (of commercially grown fruit and vegetables) dug or picked by the customer at the place of production.

pic·nic ● *noun* **1** an outing or excursion including a packed meal eaten out of doors (also *attributive*: *picnic basket*). **2** any meal eaten out of doors or without preparation, tables, chairs, etc. **3** (usu. with *neg.*) *informal* something agreeable or easily accomplished etc. (*it was no picnic organizing the meeting*). **4** *N Amer.* = PICNIC SHOULDER. ● *intransitive verb* (**pic·nicked, pic·nick·ing**) go on or take part in a picnic. □ **pic·nick·er** *noun* **pic·nicky** *adjective* *informal* [French *pique-nique*, of unknown origin]

picnic area *noun* (also **picnic ground** or **grounds**) a piece of land set aside for picnics.

picnic shelter *noun* a usu. open-sided shelter at a picnic area, campground, etc. to protect picnickers from the elements.

picnic shoulder *noun* (also **picnic ham**) a cut of meat taken from the shoulder and upper foreleg of a pig, with most of the butt removed, often smoked.

picnic table *noun* a rectangular table with benches attached along each long side.

pico- /ˈpaɪkoʊ, ˈpiːkoʊ/ *combining form* denoting a factor of 10^{-12} (*picometre*). [Spanish *pico* beak, peak, little bit]

Pico da Neb·lina /ˌpiːkoʊ dɐ nɛˈbliːnə/ a mountain in NW Brazil, close to the border with Venezuela. Rising to 3 014 m (9,888 ft.), it is the highest peak in Brazil.

Pico della Miran·dola /ˈpiːkoʊ ˌdɛlə mɪˈrandələ/ **Gio·van·ni, Count** (1463–94), Italian humanist and Platonist philosopher, whose work attempted to synthesize classical, Christian, and Judaic thought; he is best known for his collection of 900 theses, prefaced by the oration *De dignitate hominis* (1486).

Pico de Ori·zaba /ˌpiːkoʊ dei ˌɒrɪˈzɒbə/ the Spanish name for CITLALTÉPETL.

picot /ˈpiːkoʊ/ *noun* any of a series of small loops worked in lace or

embroidery forming an ornamental edging etc. [French, diminutive of *pic* peak, point]

picric acid /ˈpɪkrɪk/ *noun* a yellow crystalline acid obtained by nitrating phenol, used in dyeing and in the manufacture of explosives. [Greek *pikros* bitter]

Pict *noun* a member of an ancient people of N Britain who fought against the Roman invaders and eventually amalgamated with the Scots before the Middle Ages. □ **Pict·ish** *adjective* [Late Latin *Picti* perhaps from *pingere pict-* paint, tattoo]

picto·graph *noun* (also **picto·gram**) **1 a** a pictorial symbol or sign. **b** an ancient record consisting of pictorial symbols, as in cave paintings etc. **2** a pictorial representation of statistics etc. on a chart, graph, etc. □ **picto·graph·ic** *adjective* [Latin *pingere pict-* paint]

pic·tor·ial ● *adjective* **1** of or expressed in a picture or pictures. **2** containing or illustrated by a picture or pictures. ● *noun* **1** a periodical, magazine article, etc. having pictures or photographs as the main feature. **2** a usu. commemorative postage stamp printed with a picture or scene. □ **pic·tor·ial·ly** *adverb* [Late Latin *pictorius* from Latin *pictor* painter (as PICTURE)]

Pic·tou /ˈpɪktoʊ/ a town in N Nova Scotia, situated off the Northumberland Strait on the north shore of Pictou Harbour, about 56 km northeast of Truro; pop. (2001) 3,875. □ **Pic·to·nian** *noun* [the name of the harbour, from Mi'kmaq *piktook* explosion of gas]

pic·ture ● *noun* **1 a** a painting, drawing, photograph, etc. (also *attributive*: *picture frame*). **b** a portrait, esp. a photograph, of a person (*does not like to have her picture taken*). **c** a beautiful or picturesque person or thing. **2 a** a total esp. mental impression or image. **b** a scene, situation, or state of affairs (*the picture looks bleak*). **c** a written or spoken description (*drew a vivid picture of moral decay*). **3 a** a film. **b** esp. *Brit.* dated (in *pl.*; prec. by *the*) a showing of films at a movie theatre (*went to the pictures*). **c** *Brit.* (in *pl.*) films in general. **4** a visible image produced by an optical or electronic system, esp. the image on a television or radar screen. **5** *informal* **a** a person or thing exemplifying something (*he was the picture of innocence*). **b** a person or thing resembling another closely (*the picture of her aunt*). **c** *ironic* or *informal* a striking expression, pose, etc.; a comic or striking sight (*her face was a picture*). ● *transitive verb* **1** represent in a picture or pictorial form. **2** (also *reflexive*; often foll. by *to*) imagine, esp. visually or vividly (*pictured it to herself*; *picture yourself hiking along ocean trails*). **3** describe graphically. □ **get the picture** *informal* grasp or become aware of a particular situation, drift of circumstances, information, etc. **in the picture 1** actively involved. **2** fully informed or noticed. **out of the picture** no longer involved, inactive; irrelevant. [Latin *pictura*, from *pingere pict-* 'paint']

picture book ● *noun* a book containing many illustrations, usu. for children. ● *adjective* (**picture-book**) characteristic of a children's picture book, esp. excessively or sentimentally pretty.

picture frame *noun* a frame made to hold a picture.

picture hat *noun* a woman's wide-brimmed hat.

picture-in-picture *noun* a feature of some television sets which allows viewers to see, on a small inset box, what is being shown on another channel.

picture-perfect *adjective* **1** ideal, perfectly ordered in every detail. **2** precisely accurate.

picture plane *noun* an imaginary plane lying at the front edge of a painting where its perspective meets that of the viewer.

picture postcard ● *noun* a postcard with a picture or view on one side and space for both a message and address on the other. ● *adjective* (**picture-postcard**) (of a view etc.) conventionally attractive or pretty.

picture rail *noun* a horizontal rail on a wall for hanging pictures from.

pic·tur·esque /ˌpɪktʃəˈrɛsk/ *adjective* **1 a** (of landscape, buildings, etc.) beautiful or striking, esp. in a quaint way. **b** (of a route etc.) affording views of this kind. **2** (of language etc.) strikingly graphic; vivid. **3** *informal* (of a person, appearance, manner, etc.) unique, strange, or unusual; eccentric. □ **pic·tur·esque·ly** *adverb* **pic·tur·esque·ness** *noun* [French *pittoresque* from Italian *pittoresco* from *pittore* painter, from Latin (as PICTORIAL): assimilated to PICTURE]

picture tube *noun* the cathode ray tube of a television set.

picture window *noun* a large window, esp. one consisting of one pane of glass without mullions.

picture-writing *noun* a mode of recording events etc. by pictorial symbols as in early hieroglyphics etc.

PID *abbreviation* pelvic inflammatory disease.

pid·dle ● *intransitive verb* **1** *informal* urinate. **2 a** work or act in a petty or

trifling way. **b** while or fritter away time etc. ● *noun informal*
1 urination. **2** urine. □ **pid·dler** *noun* [sense 1 of v. prob. from PISS +
PUDDLE: sense 2 of v. perhaps from PEDDLE]

pid·dling *adjective* (also **pid·dly**) *informal* trivial; trifling.

pid·dock /ˈpɪdək/ *noun* any rock-boring bivalve mollusc of the family
Pholadidae, used for bait. [18th c.: origin unknown]

pid·gin /ˈpɪdʒɪn/ *noun* a form of a language simplified or altered by
non-native speakers and containing vocabulary from two or more
languages, used for communication between people not having a
common language. □ **pidgin·iz·a·tion** *noun* (also esp. *Brit.* **-isation**).
pidgin·ize *transitive verb* (also esp. *Brit.* **-ise**). [corruption of *business*]

pidgin English *noun* a pidgin in which the chief language is English,
used originally between Chinese and Europeans.

pie[1] ● *noun* **1** any of various dishes with a pastry crust or topping or
both, with a filling of fruit, meat, custard, etc. **2** anything resembling
a pie in form (*a mud pie*). **3 a** *informal* wealth, market share, etc.
considered as something to be shared out (*the executives each claimed a
piece of the pie*). **b** *N Amer. slang* political favour or patronage. ● *transitive
verb* throw or push a cream pie into the face of (a public figure, etc.),
usu. as a means of political protest. □ **easy as pie** *informal* very easy.
pie in the sky *informal* **1** an extravagant promise unlikely to be
fulfilled. **2** an unrealistic prospect of future happiness, esp. after
present suffering. □ **pie·ing** *noun* [Middle English, perhaps = PIE[2],
from miscellaneous contents compared to objects collected by a
magpie]

pie[2] *noun archaic* a magpie. [Old French from Latin *pica*]

pie[3] /paɪ/ *noun hist.* a former monetary unit of India equal to one-twelfth
of an anna. [Hindustani etc. *pāʼī* from Sanskrit *pad, padī* quarter]

pie·bald /ˈpaɪbɔld/ ● *adjective* **1** (usu. of an animal, esp. a horse) having
irregular patches of two colours, esp. black and white. **2** motley;
mongrel. ● *noun* a piebald animal, esp. a horse. [from PIE[2] (because of
the magpie's black-and-white plumage + BALD in the obsolete sense
'streaked with white']

piece ● *noun* **1 a** (often foll. by *of*) one of the distinct portions forming
part of or broken off from a larger object; a bit; a part (*a piece of string*).
b a single, usu. small sample, instance, or quantity of a substance or
non-material thing (*a piece of paper; a new piece of software*). **c** each of the
parts of which a set or category is composed (*a five-piece band; a piece of
furniture*). **d** any of the irregular sections of a jigsaw or similar puzzle.
2 a coin of specified value (*50-cent piece*). **3 a** a usu. short literary or
musical composition or a picture. **b** an essay or article for a magazine,
newspaper, etc. **c** a work of art, esp. a painting, statue, or play. **4** an
item, instance, or example (*a piece of impudence; a piece of news*). **5 a** any
of the objects used to make moves in board games. **b** a chessman
(strictly, other than a pawn). **6** a definite quantity in which a thing is
sold, e.g. cloth etc. **7** (often foll. by *of*) an enclosed portion (of land etc.).
8 (also **piece of ass, piece of tail**) esp. *N Amer. coarse slang* **a** a
woman regarded as an object of sexual gratification. **b** sexual
intercourse with a woman. **9** (foll. by *of*) *N Amer. informal* involvement or
a share or esp. financial interest in (a business, project, etc.) (*has a piece
of the new production*). **10 a** esp. *N Amer. slang* a small portable firearm,
esp. a handgun. **b** a large but still portable gun, cannon, etc. (*artillery
pieces*). **11** *N Amer. informal* a short distance, part of the way (*down the road
a piece*). **12** *N Amer. hist.* a package in the fur trade weighing about 90
pounds (approximately 41 kg). **13** *slang* (in full **masterpiece**) a
particularly elaborate graffito. ● *transitive verb* **1** (usu. foll. by *together*)
a join together to form one thing, mend or make by putting pieces
together (*pieced together a parliamentary majority*). **b** infer or construct
from previously unrelated facts (*finally pieced his story together*). **2** (usu.
foll. by *out*) **a** eke out. **b** form (a theory etc.) by combining parts etc.
3 (usu. foll. by *up*) patch, mend, make whole, or complete by adding a
piece. □ **break to pieces** break into fragments. **by the piece**
(paid) according to the quantity of work done. **go to pieces 1** break
up, lose cohesion. **2** collapse emotionally or mentally; suffer a
breakdown. **in one piece 1** (of a thing) unbroken; consisting of a
single piece or mass. **2** (of a person etc.) whole, unharmed, without
injury or loss. **in pieces** broken, asunder, in fragments. **(all) of a
piece** (often foll. by *with*) uniform, consistent, in keeping. **piece by
piece** with one piece or part after another in succession; gradually. **a
piece of the action** *slang* **1** a share in the profits accruing from
something. **2** a share in the excitement. **a piece of cake** *see* CAKE. **a
piece of one's mind** a sharp rebuke or lecture. **a piece of the
puzzle** an item of information that helps to understand a larger
problem. **say one's piece** give one's opinion or make a prepared
statement. **take to pieces** = PICK APART (*see* PICK[1]). [Old French *piece*
from Romanic, prob. of Gaulish origin]

pièce de ré·sis·tance /ˌpjes də reizɪsˈtɑ̃s/ *noun* (pl. **pièces de**

résistance *pronunc.* same) **1** the most important or remarkable item.
2 the most substantial dish at a meal. [French]

piece·meal ● *adverb* piece by piece; gradually; separately. ● *adjective*
consisting of pieces; done bit by bit; gradual; unsystematic. [Middle
English from PIECE + -*meal* from Old English *mǣlum* in the sense
'measure, quantity taken at one time')]

piece of eight *noun hist.* a Spanish dollar, equivalent to 8 reals.

piece of work *noun* **1** a thing made by working. **2 a** a task, a
difficult thing. **b** *informal* a commotion, a to-do. **3** a person of a
specified and usu. unpleasant kind (*he's a nasty piece of work*).

piece rate *noun* (usu. *pl.*) the rate of payment for piecework.

piece·work *noun* work paid for by the amount produced.
□ **piece·work·er** *noun*

pie chart *noun* a circle divided into sectors to represent relative
quantities.

pie crust *noun* **1** the crust of a pie, made of pastry or a mixture of
crushed cookies and fat. **2** pie pastry.

pie·crust table *noun* a round table with a carved, fluted edge
resembling the crimped design of a pie crust.

pied /paɪd/ *adjective* parti-coloured. [Middle English from PIE[2]]

pied-à-terre /ˌpjeɪdaˈteʀ/ *noun* (pl. **pieds-à-terre** *pronunc.* same) a
usu. small apartment, house, etc. kept for occasional use. [French, lit.
'foot to earth']

Pied·mont /ˈpiːdmɒnt/ a region of NW Italy, in the foothills of the
Alps; capital, Turin. □ **Pied·mont·ese** *noun & adjective* [Italian *piemonte*
mountain foot]

pied·mont /ˈpiːdmɒnt/ *noun* a gentle slope leading from the foot of
mountains to a region of flat land (also *attributive*: *piedmont ice*). [as
PIEDMONT]

pie-dog *var. of* PYE-DOG.

Pied Piper 1 (in German legend) a piper who rid the town of
Hamelin (Hameln) in Brunswick of rats by enticing them away with his
music; when refused the promised payment he lured away all the
children. **2** a person enticing followers esp. to their doom.

pie-eyed *adjective slang* drunk.

pie-faced *adjective* having a very round, flat face.

Pie·gan *var. of* PEIGAN.

pie plate *noun* (also **pie pan**) a shallow metal or glass dish with
sloping sides, in which pies are baked.

pier /pɪər/ *noun* **1** a structure of iron, wood, concrete, etc., raised on piles
and leading out into the sea, a lake, etc., used as a landing stage and
promenade. **2** a long narrow structure projecting from the main body
of an airport terminal, along which passengers walk to and from their
aircraft. **3 a** a support of an arch or of the span of a bridge; a pillar.
b solid masonry between windows etc. [Middle English *per* from
Anglo-Latin *pera*, of unknown origin]

Pierce, Frank·lin (1804–69), US Democratic politician, 14th president
of the US 1853–7. His presidency saw the rise of divisions within the
country over slavery and the encouragement of settlement in the
northwest.

pierce *verb* **1** *transitive* **a** (of a sharp instrument etc.) penetrate the
surface of. **b** (often foll. by *with*) prick with a sharp instrument, esp. to
make a hole in. **c** make a hole, opening, or tunnel into or through
(something), bore through. **d** make (a hole etc.) (*pierced a hole in the belt*).
e (of cold, grief, etc.) affect keenly or sharply. **f** (of a light, glance,
sound, etc.) penetrate keenly or sharply. **2** *transitive* force (a way etc.)
through or into (something) (*pierced their way through the undergrowth*).
3 *intransitive* (usu. foll. by *through, into*) penetrate. □ **pier·cer** *noun* [Old
French *percer* from Latin *pertundere* bore through (as PER-, *tundere tus-
thrust*)]

pierced *adjective* **1** having a hole or holes. **2** (of a part of the body)
having a hole in which a ring etc. is worn (*pierced ears*). **3** (of an earring)
designed to be worn in a pierced ear.

pier·cing ● *adjective* **1** (of voices, sounds, etc.) very high and loud;
shrill. **2 a** (of eyes) very bright and seeming to see through the person
they are looking at. **b** (of a look) very direct; searching. **3** (of a feeling,
comment, etc.) very perceptive. **4** (of wind, cold, etc.) bitter;
penetrating. ● *noun* a hole pierced in a body part in which a ring etc. is
worn. □ **pier·cing·ly** *adverb*

pier glass *noun* a large mirror, used originally to fill wall space
between windows.

Piero della Francesca /ˌpjerɔ ˌdelə franˈtʃeskə/ (*c.*1420–92), Italian
painter. He used perspective, proportion, and geometrical
relationships to create ordered and harmonious pictures in which the

figures appear to inhabit real space; his major works include a fresco cycle in Arezzo depicting the story of the True Cross (begun 1452).

pier·ogi *var. of* PEROGY.

Pierre /piːr/ the state capital of S Dakota, situated on the Missouri River; pop. (2000) 13,876.

Pierre·fonds /pjɛrˈfɔ̃/ a former city in south central Quebec, on the south bank of the Rivière des Prairies opposite Île Bizard, now part of the city of Montreal; pop. (2001) 54,963. [the name of a residence, so called because its design was inspired by a castle in *Pierrefonds*, north central France]

Pier·rot /ˈpjɛroʊ/ *noun* a male figure in French pantomime, typically white-faced with a sad expression and dressed in a loose white clown's costume. [French, diminutive of *Pierre* Peter]

pie-shaped *adjective N Amer.* shaped like a triangular piece cut out of a round pie, having one curved side.

Pietà /ˌpiːeɪˈtɑː/ *noun* a picture or sculpture of the Virgin Mary holding the dead body of Christ on her lap or in her arms. [Italian from Latin (as PIETY)]

Pieter·maritz·burg /ˌpiːtərˈmærɪtsˌbɜːrɡ/ a city in eastern South Africa, the capital of KwaZulu-Natal; pop. (est. 2002) 420,500.

piet·ism /ˈpaɪəˌtɪzəm/ *noun* **1 a** pious sentiment. **b** an exaggerated or affected piety. **2** (esp. as **Pietism**) *hist.* a movement for the revival of piety in the Lutheran Church in the 17th c. □ **piet·ist** *noun* **piet·is·tic** *adjective* **piet·is·tic·al** *adjective* [German *Pietismus* (as PIETY)]

piety /ˈpaɪəti/ *noun* (*pl.* **-ies**) **1** the quality of being pious. **2** a pious act, remark, etc. [Old French *pieté* from Latin *pietas -tatis* dutifulness (as PIOUS)]

piezo *adjective* piezoelectric.

piezo·elec·tri·city /paɪˌiːzoʊˌɪlekˈtrɪsɪti/ *noun* electric polarization in a substance resulting from the application of mechanical stress, esp. in certain crystals. □ **piezo·elec·tric** *adjective* **piezo·elec·tric·ally** *adverb* [Greek *piezō* press + ELECTRIC]

piez·om·eter /ˌpaɪɪˈzɒmɪtər/ *noun* an instrument for measuring the magnitude or direction of pressure.

pif·fle *informal* ● *noun* nonsense; empty speech. ● *intransitive verb* talk or act feebly; trifle. □ **pif·fler** *noun* [imitative]

pif·fling *adjective informal* trivial; worthless.

pig ● *noun* **1 a** a domesticated even-toed ungulate derived from the wild boar *Sus scrofa*, with a large head, a broad flat snout, and a stout often almost hairless body, raised as a source of bacon, ham, pork, etc. **b** *N Amer.* a young pig; a piglet. **2** the flesh of esp. a young or sucking pig as food (*roast pig*). **3** *informal* **a** a selfish and greedy person. **b** an ill-mannered, insensitive, or vulgar person. **c** a fat person. **4** *Brit. informal* an unpleasant, awkward, or difficult thing, task, etc. **5** an oblong mass of metal (esp. iron or lead) from a smelting furnace. **6** *slang derogatory* a police officer. ● *transitive & intransitive verb* (**pigged**, **pig·ging**) (of a sow) bring forth (piglets). □ **bleed like a stuck pig** bleed copiously. **buy a pig in a poke** buy, accept, etc. something without knowing its value or esp. seeing it. **happy as a pig in shit** *coarse slang* very happy. **in pig** (of a sow) pregnant. **in a pig's eye** *informal* certainly not. **make a pig of oneself** overeat. **make a pig's ear of** *informal* make a mess of; bungle. **pig out** esp. *N Amer. informal* eat gluttonously (*pigging out on cookies; really pigged out last night*). **pigs might fly** *ironic* an expression of disbelief. □ **pig·like** *adjective* [Middle English *pigge* from Old English *pigga* (unrecorded)]

pi·geon /ˈpɪdʒən/ *noun* **1** any of several large usu. grey and white birds of the family Columbidae, esp. *Columba livia*, often domesticated and bred and trained to carry messages etc. **2** *informal* a person easily swindled; a simpleton. □ **pi·geon·ry** *noun* (*pl.* **-ries**). [Middle English from Old French *pijon* from Late Latin *pipio -onis* (imitative)]

pigeon chest *noun* (also **pigeon breast**) a deformed human chest with a projecting breastbone. □ **pigeon-chested** *adjective* (also **pigeon-breasted**).

pigeon fancier *noun* a person who keeps and breeds fancy pigeons. □ **pigeon fancying** *noun*

pigeon guillemot *noun* a guillemot of the N Pacific, *Cepphus columba*, similar to the black guillemot.

pigeon hawk *noun* = MERLIN.

pigeon·hole ● *noun* **1** each of a set of compartments in a cabinet or on a wall for papers, letters, etc. **2** a small recess for a pigeon to nest in. ● *transitive verb* **1** deposit (a document) in a pigeonhole. **2** put (a matter) aside for future consideration or to forget it. **3** assign (a person or thing) to a preconceived category.

Pigeon River a river in NW Ontario. Forming part of the border between Ontario and Minnesota, it flows eastward to empty into Lake

Superior southwest of Thunder Bay. [formerly French *Rivière aux Tourtes* wild pigeon river]

pigeon-toed *adjective* (of a person) having the toes turned inwards.

pig·gery *noun* (*pl.* **-ies**) **1** = PIGSTY. **2** piggishness.

pig·gish *adjective* **1** of or relating to pigs. **2** having a quality associated with pigs, esp. greedy, dirty, or stubborn. □ **pig·gish·ness** *noun*

piggy ● *noun* (also **pig·gie**) (*pl.* **pig·gies**) *informal* **1** a little pig. **2** a child's word for a pig. ● *adjective* (**pig·gi·er**, **pig·gi·est**) **1** like a pig; piggish. **2** (of features etc.) like those of a pig (*little piggy eyes*).

piggy·back ● *noun* (also **piggyback ride**) a ride on the back and shoulders of another person. ● *verb* **1** *intransitive* ride (as if) on a person's back and shoulders. **2** *transitive* **a** give a piggyback ride to. **b** carry or mount on top of another thing. **3** *intransitive* (usu. foll. by *on*) use an already established situation as a basis so as to gain an advantage. ● *adverb & adjective* **1** on the back and shoulders of another person. **2** on the back or top of a larger object. [16th c.: origin unknown]

piggy bank *noun* a container, esp. in the shape of a pig with a slot in the top, used for saving coins in.

piggy in the middle *noun* esp. *Brit.* = MONKEY IN THE MIDDLE.

pig·head·ed *adjective* obstinate. □ **pig·headed·ly** *adverb* **pig·headed·ness** *noun*

pig-ignorant *adjective informal* extremely ignorant.

pig in a blanket *noun* (*pl.* **pigs in a blanket**) a small sausage wrapped in dough and baked.

pig iron *noun* crude iron from a smelting furnace.

pig Latin *noun* a version of language formed from English by transferring the initial consonant or consonant cluster of each word to the end of the word and adding a vocalic syllable (usu. /eɪ/).

pig·let *noun* a young pig.

pig·ment ● *noun* **1** colouring matter used as paint or dye, usu. as an insoluble suspension. **2** the natural colouring matter of animal or plant tissue, e.g. chlorophyll, hemoglobin. ● *transitive verb* colour with or as if with pigment. □ **pig·men·tary** *adjective* [Latin *pigmentum* from *pingere* paint]

pig·men·ta·tion *noun* **1** the natural colouring of plants, animals, etc. **2** the colouring of tissue by the deposition of pigment.

pigmy *var. of* PYGMY.

pig·noli *plural noun* pine nuts. [Italian]

pig-out *noun N Amer. slang* an instance of eating to excess.

pig·pen *noun N Amer.* = PIGSTY.

pig·skin *noun* **1** the hide of a pig. **2** leather made from this. **3** *N Amer.* a football.

pig·stick·er *noun* a long sharp knife.

pig·sty /ˈpɪɡstaɪ/ *noun* (*pl.* **-sties**) **1** a pen or enclosure for a pig or pigs. **2** a filthy house, room, etc.

pig swill *noun* kitchen refuse and scraps fed to pigs.

pig·tail *noun* **1** the tail of a pig. **2** a braid of hair hanging from the back of the head, or either of a pair at the sides. **3** a thin twist of tobacco. □ **pig·tailed** *adjective* (in sense 2).

Pig War a boundary dispute between Britain and the US over the ownership of the islands located off the SE tip of Vancouver Island. It was provoked by an American farmer on San Juan Island who, in 1859, shot a pig owned by the Hudson's Bay Company. The incident was resolved twelve years later by a mediator who awarded the island to the US and decided on the location of the border between what is now BC and Washington State.

pig·weed *noun* **1** any herb of the genus *Amaranthus*, grown for grain or fodder. **2** = GOOSEFOOT.

pika /ˈpaɪkə/ *noun* any small rabbit-like mammal of the genus *Ochotona*, with small ears and no tail, found in the mountains and deserts of western N America. Also called ROCK RABBIT. [Tungus *piika*]

pike¹ *noun* (*pl.* same) **1** a large voracious freshwater fish, *Esox lucius*, with a long narrow snout and sharp teeth. **2** any other fish of the family Esocidae. [Middle English, = PIKE² (because of its pointed jaw)]

pike² ● *noun* **1** *hist.* an infantry weapon with a pointed steel or iron head on a long wooden shaft. **2** *Northern England* the peaked top of a hill, esp. in names of hills in the Lake District. ● *transitive verb* thrust through or kill with a pike. [Old English *pīc* point, prick: sense 2 perhaps from Old Norse]

pike³ *noun* **1** a tollgate; a toll. **2** a turnpike road. □ **come down the pike** *N Amer.* appear on the scene; come to notice. [abbreviation of TURNPIKE]

pike⁴ *noun* a jackknife position in diving or gymnastics. [20th c.: origin unknown]

pike·minnow *noun* the new official name for the SQUAWFISH.

pike-perch *noun* any of various perches of the genus *Lucioperca* or *Stizostedion*, resembling the pike, esp. the walleye.

pike pole *noun Cdn* a long pole with a sharp point and hook, used for moving floating logs.

pik·er *noun* **1** a cheap or stingy person. **2** a cautious or timid person. [origin uncertain]

pike·staff *noun* **1** the wooden shaft of a pike. **2** a walking stick with a metal point. □ **plain as a pikestaff** quite plain or obvious. [PIKE² + STAFF¹: idiom originally *plain as packstaff*, a smooth staff used by a peddler]

Pik Po·bedy /ˌpiːk pəˈbjedi/ a mountain in E Kyrgyzstan, situated close to the border with China. At 7 439 m (24,406 ft.), it is the highest peak in the Tien Shan range. [Russian, = Victory Peak]

pi·laf /ˈpiːlaf/ *noun* (also **pi·lau** /pɪˈlaʊ/) a Middle Eastern or Indian dish of spiced rice or wheat with meat, fish, vegetables, etc. [Turkish *pilâv*]

pi·las·ter /pɪˈlastər/ *noun* a rectangular column, esp. one projecting from a wall. □ **pi·las·tered** *adjective* [French *pilastre* from Italian *pilastro* from medieval Latin *pilastrum* from Latin *pila* pillar]

Pi·late /ˈpaɪlət/ **Pon·tius** (died AD *c.*36), Roman procurator of Judea *c.*26–*c.*36. He presided at the trial of Jesus Christ and sentenced him to death by crucifixion.

Pi·la·tes /pəˈlɒtiːz/ *noun* a system of exercises using specialized apparatus, designed to improve physical strength, flexibility, and posture, and enhance mental awareness and control of body movement. [named after the German physical fitness specialist Joseph Pilates d.1967]

pil·chard /ˈpɪltʃərd/ *noun* **1** a small marine fish, *Sardinia pilchardus* of the herring family which is an important food fish of European waters, the young often marketed as sardines. **2** a Pacific sardine, esp. as tinned and sold as food. [16th-c. *pilcher* etc.: origin unknown]

pile¹ ● *noun* **1** a heap of things laid or gathered upon one another (*a pile of leaves*). **2 a** a large imposing building (*a stately pile*). **b** a large group of tall buildings. **3** *informal* **a** a large quantity. **b** a large amount of money; a fortune (*made a pile by freelance editing*). **4** *Cdn* (*Nfld*) a stack of split and salted cod at any stage in the drying and curing process. **5 a** a series of plates of dissimilar metals laid one on another alternately to produce an electric current. **b** = ATOMIC PILE. **6** a funeral pyre. ● *verb* **1** *transitive* (often foll. by *up*, *on*) heap up (*piled the plates on the table*). **b** (foll. by *with*) load (*piled the bed with coats*). **2** *intransitive* (usu. foll. by *in*, *into*, *on*, *out of*, etc.) crowd hurriedly or tightly (*all piled into the car*; *piled out of the restaurant*). □ **pile it on** *informal* exaggerate. **pile up 1** accumulate; heap up. **2** *informal* run (a ship) aground or cause (a vehicle etc.) to crash. [Old French from Latin *pila* pillar, pier]

pile² ● *noun* **1** a heavy beam driven vertically into the bed of a river, soft ground, etc., to support the foundations of a superstructure. **2** *Heraldry* a wedge-shaped device. ● *transitive verb* strengthen or support a structure with piles. [Old English *pīl* from Latin *pīlum* javelin]

pile³ *noun* **1** the soft projecting surface on velvet, plush, etc., or esp. on a carpet; nap. **2** soft hair or down, or the wool of a sheep. □ **pile·less** *adjective* [prob. from Anglo-French *pyle*, *peile*, Old French *poil* from Latin *pilus* hair]

pil·eat·ed /ˈpɪliːˌeitəd/ *noun* (of a bird) having a conspicuous cap or crest. [Latin *pileatus* 'capped', from *peilus* 'felt cap']

pileated woodpecker *noun* a large N American woodpecker, *Dryocopus pileatus*, with a red-topped head.

pile·driv·er *noun* a machine for driving piles into the ground.

piles *plural noun* hemorrhoids. [Middle English prob. from Latin *pila* ball, from the globular form of external piles]

pile·up *noun informal* **1** a multiple crash of road vehicles. **2** an accumulation (of things, tasks, etc.) (*a huge pileup of papers on my desk*). **3** a confused mass of people fallen on top of one another, esp. in a sports game (*a pileup in front of the net*).

pi·leus /ˈpaɪliəs/ *noun* (*pl.* **pilei** /-liˌaɪ/) the spore-bearing circular structure surmounting the stipe in a mushroom or toadstool, which has an undersurface composed of radiating plates or gills. □ **pil·eate** /-liət/ *adjective* [Latin, = felt cap]

pil·fer *transitive & intransitive verb* steal (objects) esp. in small quantities. □ **pil·fer·age** *noun* **pil·fer·er** *noun* [Old French *pelfrer* pillage, of unknown origin: assoc. with archaic *pill* plunder: PELF]

pil·grim *noun* **1** a person who journeys to a sacred place for religious reasons. **2** a wanderer or traveller. **3** (usu. **Pilgrim**) one of a group of 102 people who pioneered British colonization of North America,

sailing in the *Mayflower* and founding a settlement at Plymouth, Mass., in 1620. The expedition was initiated by a group of English Puritans fleeing religious persecution. [Middle English *pilegrim* from Provençal *pelegrin* from Latin *peregrinus* stranger: see PEREGRINE]

pil·grim·age *noun* **1** a pilgrim's journey (*go on a pilgrimage*). **2** life viewed as a journey. **3** any journey taken for nostalgic or sentimental reasons.

Pilgrim Fathers *plural noun* the Pilgrims of Plymouth, Massachusetts.

pil·ing *noun* **1** a group or mass of piles. **2** a structure made of piles. [PILE²]

Pili·pino /ˌpɪlɪˈpiːnoː/ *noun* the national language of the Philippines. [Tagalog from Spanish *Filipino*]

pill¹ *noun* **1 a** a solid medicine formed into a ball or a flat disc for swallowing whole. **b** (usu. prec. by *the*) a contraceptive pill. **2** an unpleasant or painful necessity; a humiliation (*a bitter pill*; *must swallow the pill*). **3** *informal* an objectionable annoying person (*don't be such a pill*). **4** *informal* a ball, esp. a football. □ **sugar** (or **sweeten**) **the pill** make an unpleasant necessity acceptable. [Middle Dutch, Middle Low German *pille* prob. from Latin *pilula* diminutive of *pila* ball]

pill² *intransitive verb* (of esp. knitted fabric) form balls of fluff on the surface (*this sweater is pilling*). [Latin *pilare* deprive of hair, pillage, from *pilus* hair]

pil·lage ● *transitive & intransitive verb* plunder; sack (a place or a person). ● *noun* the act or an instance of pillaging, esp. in war. □ **pil·la·ger** *noun* [Old French from *piller* plunder]

pil·lar *noun* **1** a tall, upright column of stone, wood, metal, etc., used as a support for a building or as an ornament or monument etc. **2 a** a strong supporter or important member of something (*a pillar of society*). **b** a fundamental part or feature of a system, organization, etc. (*dismantled the pillars of the welfare state*). **3** an upright mass of air, water, rock, etc. (*pillar of salt*). **4** a solid mass of coal, ore, etc., left to support the roof of a mine. □ **from pillar to post** (driven etc.) from one place to another; to and fro. **pillar of strength** a person regarded as showing or giving great moral support, fortitude, etc. (*she has been a pillar of strength when my life was difficult*). □ **pil·lared** *adjective* **pillar·less** *adjective* [Anglo-French *piler*, Old French *pilier*, ultimately from Latin *pila* pillar]

pillar box *noun Brit.* a public mailbox shaped like a pillar.

Pillars of Hercules the two promontories known in ancient times as Calpe and Abyla and now known as the Rock of Gibraltar and Mount Acho in Ceuta. Situated opposite one another at the eastern end of the Strait of Gibraltar, they were said by the ancients to have been parted by the arm of Hercules and were regarded as marking the limit of the known world.

pill·box *noun* **1** a small shallow cylindrical box for holding pills. **2** a hat of a similar shape. **3** *Military* a small partly underground enclosed concrete fort used as an outpost.

pil·lion *noun* **1** seating for a passenger behind a motorcyclist. **2** *hist.* **a** a woman's light saddle. **b** a cushion attached to the back of a saddle for a usu. female passenger. □ **ride pillion** travel seated behind a motorcyclist etc. [Gaelic *pillean*, *pillin* diminutive of *pell* cushion, from Latin *pellis* skin]

pil·lock /ˈpɪlɒk/ *noun Brit. slang* a stupid person; a fool. [16th c., = penis (var. of *pillicock*): 20th c. in sense defined]

pil·lory /ˈpɪlɹi/ ● *noun* (*pl.* **-ies**) *hist.* a wooden framework with holes for the head and hands, enabling the public to assault or ridicule a person so imprisoned. ● *transitive verb* (**-ies, -ied**) **1** expose (a person) to ridicule or public contempt. **2** *hist.* put in the pillory. [Old French *pilori* etc.: prob. from Provençal *espilori* of uncertain origin]

pil·low ● *noun* **1** a usu. oblong support for the head, esp. in bed, with a cloth cover stuffed with feathers, flock, foam rubber, etc. **2** any pillow-shaped block or support. ● *transitive verb* **1** rest (the head etc.) on or as if on a pillow (*pillowed his head on his arms*). **2** serve as a pillow for (*moss pillowed her head*). □ **pil·lowy** *adjective* [Old English *pyle*, *pylu*, ultimately from Latin *pulvinus* cushion]

pillow·case *noun* a washable fabric cover for a pillow.

pillow fight *noun* a mock fight in which the participants try to hit one another with pillows.

pillow lace *noun* = BOBBIN LACE.

pillow lava *noun* lava forming rounded masses.

pillow sham *noun N Amer.* a decorative fabric cover for a pillow when not in use, usu. with a deep, often ruffled edging on all four sides.

pillow slip *noun* = PILLOWCASE.

pil·low talk *noun* romantic or intimate conversation in bed.

pill-popper *noun informal* **1** a person who takes pills in abundance. **2** a drug addict. □ **pill-popping** *noun & attributive adjective*

pil·ose /'paɪləʊz/ *adjective* (also **pil·ous** /'paɪləs/) covered with hair. □ **pil·os·ity** /paɪˈlɒsɪti/ *noun* [Latin *pilosus* from *pilus* hair]

pi·lot ● *noun* **1** a person who operates the flying controls of an aircraft. **2** a person qualified to take charge of a ship entering or leaving harbour, moving through dangerous waters, etc. **3 a** (usu. *attributive*) an experimental undertaking or test, esp. in advance of a larger one (*a pilot project*). **b** a test episode of a television series used to assess audience reaction etc. **4** = PILOT LIGHT 1. **5** a guide; a leader. **6** *archaic* a steersman. ● *transitive verb* (**pi·lot·ed**, **pi·lot·ing**) **1** act as a pilot on (a ship) or of (an aircraft). **2** conduct or lead; guide (*piloted the new bill through the Commons*). **3** produce a pilot or test for (an idea, scheme, etc.); try out. □ **pilot·age** *noun* **pilot·less** *adjective* [French *pilote* from medieval Latin *pilotus*, *pedot(t)a* from Greek *pēdon* oar]

pilot biscuit *noun N Amer.* = SHIP'S BISCUIT.

pilot chute *noun* a small parachute used to bring the main one into operation.

pilot fish *noun* a small fish, *Naucrates ductor*, said to act as a pilot leading a shark to food.

pilot hole *noun* a small hole drilled into something to receive a nail or screw, or act as a guide for a larger drill bit.

pilot·house *noun* = WHEELHOUSE 1.

pilot light *noun* **1** a small flame that burns continuously, e.g. on a gas stove or gas or oil furnace, and lights a larger flame when the valve controlling the gas or oil opens. **2** an electric indicator light or control light.

pilot officer *noun* (also **Pilot Officer**) (currently in the RAF or *hist.* in the RCAF) an officer of the lowest commissioned rank. Abbr.: **PO**.

pilot whale *noun* a small whale of the genus *Globicephala*, of temperate or subtropical waters.

Pil·sen /'pɪlsən/ an industrial city in the western part of the Czech Republic; pop. (2001) 166,274. It is noted for the production of lager.

Pils·ner /'pɪlznər, -snər/ *noun* (also **Pil·sen·er**) a pale lager beer with a strong flavour of hops. [PILSEN, where first brewed]

Pilt·down man *noun* a fraudulent fossil composed of a human cranium and an ape jaw that was presented in 1912 as a genuine hominid of great antiquity. It was shown to be a hoax in 1953. [*Piltdown* Common in E Sussex, where it was allegedly discovered]

pi·men·to /pɪˈmɛntəʊ/ *noun* (*pl.* **-tos**) **1** = SWEET PEPPER. **2** a small tropical tree, *Pimenta dioica*, native to Jamaica. **3** the unripe dried berries of this, usu. crushed for culinary use. *Also called* ALLSPICE. [Spanish *pimiento* (as PIMIENTO)]

pi·me·son *noun* = PION.

pi·mien·to /ˌpɪmiˈɛntəʊ, pɪmˈjɛntəʊ/ *noun* (*pl.* **-tos**) = PIMENTO. [Spanish from Latin *pigmentum* PIGMENT, in medieval Latin = spice]

pimp ● *noun* a man who lives off the earnings of a prostitute or a brothel. ● *verb* **1** *intransitive* act as a pimp. **2** *transitive* (also *reflexive*) cause to act as a prostitute. □ **pimp·ing** *noun* [17th c.: origin unknown]

pim·per·nel /'pɪmpər,nɛl/ *noun* any plant of the genus *Anagallis*, esp. = SCARLET PIMPERNEL. [Old French *pimpernelle* ultimately from Latin *piper* PEPPER]

pim·ple *noun* a small, hard, inflamed, usu. raised spot on the skin. □ **pim·pled** *adjective* **pim·ply** *adjective* [Middle English nasalized from Old English *piplian* break out in pustules]

PIN /pɪn/ *noun* (also **PIN number**) a confidential identification number issued by a bank etc. or chosen by a user to validate electronic transactions. ¶ The variant *PIN number* is common, even though the element *number* is redundant, probably because it is more readily understood than *PIN* in examples such as *I've forgotten my PIN*. [acronym from Personal Identification Number]

pin ● *noun* **1 a** a small thin pointed piece of esp. steel wire with a round or flattened head used (esp. in sewing) for holding things in place, attaching one thing to another, etc. **b** any of several types of pin (*safety pin*; *hairpin*). **c** a small brooch (*diamond pin*). **d** a badge fastened with a pin. **2** a peg or dowel used as a fastener or support. **3** a club-shaped usu. wooden peg used as a target in various types of bowling. **4** a piece of metal on a hand grenade that keeps the grenade from exploding until it is removed. **5** *Med.* a steel rod used to join the ends of fractured bones while they heal. **6** *Wrestling* a throw which keeps one's opponent on the mat for a specified period of time. **7** something of small value (*don't care a pin; for two pins I'd resign*). **8** (in *pl.*) *informal* legs (*quick on his pins*). **9** *Chess* a position in which a piece is pinned to another. **10** *Golf* a stick with a flag placed in a hole to mark its position. **11** *Music* a peg round which one string of a musical

instrument is fastened. ● *transitive verb* (**pinned**, **pin·ning**) **1 a** (often foll. by *to*, *up*, *together*) fasten with a pin or pins (*pinned up the hem; pinned the papers together*). **b** transfix with a pin, lance, etc. **2** (usu. foll. by *on*) fix (blame, responsibility, etc.) on a person etc. (*pinned the blame on her friends*). **3** (often foll. by *against*, *on*, *to*, etc.) seize and hold fast. **4** *Wrestling* capture (one's opponent) in a pin. **5** *Chess* prevent (an opposing piece) from moving except by exposing a more valuable piece to capture. □ **neat as a pin** very tidy. **pin down 1** (often foll. by *to*) bind (a person etc.) to a promise, arrangement, etc. **2** force (a person) to declare his or her intentions. **3** restrict the actions or movement of (an enemy etc.). **4** specify (a thing) precisely (*could not pin down my unease to a particular cause*). **5** hold (a person etc.) down by force. **pin one's hopes** (or **faith** etc.) **on** rely implicitly or completely on. [Old English *pinn* from Latin *pinna* point etc., assoc. with *penna* PEN[1]]

pina co·lada /ˌpiːnə kəˈlɒdə, ˈpiːnjə/ *noun* a drink made from pineapple juice, rum, and coconut. [Spanish, lit. 'strained pineapple']

pina·fore /'pɪnəˌfɔːr/ *noun* **1** a decorative apron-like garment, usu. with buttons or ties at the back, worn over a dress, esp. by small girls. **2** *Brit.* (in full **pinafore dress**) a collarless sleeveless dress worn over a blouse or sweater; a jumper. **3** *Brit.* **a** an apron, esp. with a bib. **b** a woman's sleeveless wraparound washable covering for the clothes, tied at the back. [PIN + AFORE (because originally pinned on the front of a dress)]

Pin·ang *see* PENANG.

pi·nata /pɪˈnjɒtə, piː-/ *noun* (also **pi·ñata**) an originally Mexican brightly decorated crock or papier mâché figure filled with candies or small toys etc. and suspended overhead to be broken by a blindfolded person waving a stick. [Spanish, = jug, pot]

Pina·tubo, Mount /ˌpɪnəˈtuːbəʊ/ a volcano on the island of Luzon, in the Philippines. It erupted in 1991, destroying the homes of over 200,000 people.

pin·ball ● *noun* a game in which small metal balls are shot across a board and score points by striking pins with lights etc. (also *attributive*: *pinball machine*). ● *intransitive verb informal* bounce back and forth crazily like a ball in a pinball machine.

pince-nez /'pansnei, pãsˈnei/ *noun* (*pl.* same) a pair of eyeglasses held in place by a clip on the nose instead of by arms. [French, lit. = pinch-nose]

pincer movement *noun Military* a movement by two wings of an army converging on the enemy.

pin·cers /'pɪnsərz/ *plural noun* **1** (also **pair of pincers**) a gripping tool resembling scissors but with blunt usu. concave jaws to hold a nail etc. for extraction. **2** the front claws of lobsters and some other crustaceans. [Middle English *pinsers*, *pinsours* from Anglo-French from Old French *pincier* PINCH]

pinch ● *verb* **1 a** *transitive* grip (esp. skin or flesh) tightly, e.g. between finger and thumb, two hard surfaces, etc. (*pinched my finger in the door; stop pinching me!*). **b** *transitive & intransitive* (of a shoe, garment, etc.) constrict (the flesh) painfully. **2** *transitive* (of cold, hunger, etc.) grip (a person) painfully (*she was pinched with cold*). **3** *transitive slang* **a** steal; take without permission. **b** arrest (a person) (*pinched him for loitering*). **4** *intransitive* be niggardly with money, food, etc. **5** *transitive* (usu. foll. by *out*, *back*, *down*) *Hort.* remove (leaves, buds, etc.) to encourage bushy growth. **6** *intransitive* sail very close to the wind. ● *noun* **1** the act or an instance of pinching the flesh. **2** an amount that can be taken up with fingers and thumb (*a pinch of salt*). **3** the stress or pain caused by poverty, cold, hunger, etc. **4** *Baseball* (*attributive*) (of a hit, run, etc.) made by a pinch hitter (*pinch homer*). **5** *slang* **a** an arrest. **b** a theft. □ **feel the pinch** experience the effects of poverty. **in a pinch** in an emergency; if necessary. **pinch oneself** check to make sure that one is awake and not dreaming (*when I heard the good news, I had to pinch myself*). **pinch pennies** live frugally; economize on expenditures. [Anglo-French & Old Northern French *pinchier* (unrecorded), Old French *pincier*, ultimately from Latin *pungere punct-* prick]

pinch·beck ● *noun* an alloy of copper and zinc resembling gold and used in cheap jewellery etc. ● *adjective* **1** counterfeit; sham. **2** cheap; tawdry. [C. *Pinchbeck*, English watchmaker d.1732]

pinched *adjective* (of the features) drawn, as with cold, hunger, worry, etc.

pin cherry *noun* a N American wild cherry, *Prunus pensylvanica*, with very small fruit. *Also called* BIRD CHERRY.

pinch-hitter *noun* **1** a baseball player who bats instead of another, esp. at a critical point in the game. **2** *N Amer.* a person acting as a substitute for another, esp. in an emergency. □ **pinch hit** *noun* **pinch-hit** *intransitive verb*

pinch·penny *noun* (*pl.* **-nies**) (also *attributive*) a miserly person.

Consonants: b *but*   d *dog*   f *few*   g *get*   h *her*   j *yes*   k *cat*   l *leg*   m *man*   n *no*   p *pen*   r *red*   s *sit*

pinch pleat *noun* one of a cluster of small pleats, used esp. in curtains. ☐ **pinch-pleated** *adjective*

pinch-run *intransitive verb* Baseball substitute for another runner, esp. at a critical point in the game. ☐ **pinch-runner** *noun*

Pin·court /pāˈkʊr/ a town in south central Quebec, situated on Île Perrot, southwest of Montreal; pop. (2001) 10,107. [French *pin* pine + *court* short, with reference to a nearby wooded area of short pines]

pin·curl *noun* a curl of coiled hair held in place by a hairpin while drying.

pin·cushion *noun* a small cushion for holding dressmaking pins.

Pin·dar /ˈpɪndər/ (c.518–c.438 BC), Greek lyric poet. His surviving works include four books of odes (the *Epinikia*), often in the form of choral hymns, written in an elevated style and imbued with religious significance. ☐ **Pin·dar·ic** /pɪnˈderɪk/ *adjective*

Pin·dus Mountains /ˈpɪndəs/ a range of mountains in west central Greece, stretching from the border with Albania southward to the Gulf of Corinth. The highest peak is Mount Smolikas, which rises to 2 637 m (8,136 ft.).

pine¹ *noun* **1** any evergreen tree of the genus *Pinus*, native to northern temperate regions, with needle-shaped leaves growing in clusters. **2** the soft timber of this, often used to make furniture. **3** (*attributive*) made of pine. **4** Sport informal the bench (*as third goalie on the team, he spent most of the year warming the pine*). [Old English *pin* & Old French *pin* from Latin *pinus*]

pine² *intransitive verb* **1** (often foll. by *away*) decline or waste away, esp. from grief, disease, etc. **2** (usu. foll. by *for*, *after*, or *to* + infin.) long eagerly; yearn. [Old English *pīnian*, related to obsolete English *pine* punishment, from Germanic from medieval Latin *pena*, Latin *poena*]

pin·eal /ˈpɪnɪəl, ˈpaɪ-/ *adjective* **1** shaped like a pine cone. **2** of or relating to the pineal gland. [French *pinéal* from Latin *pinea* pine cone: see PINE¹]

pineal gland *noun* (also **pineal body**) a pea-sized conical mass of tissue behind the third ventricle of the brain, secreting a hormone-like substance in some mammals.

pine·apple *noun* **1** a tropical plant, *Ananas comosus*, with a spiral of sword-shaped leaves and a thick stem bearing a large fruit developed from many flowers. **2** the fruit of this, consisting of yellow flesh surrounded by a tough segmented skin and topped with a tuft of stiff leaves. [PINE¹, from the fruit's resemblance to a pine cone]

pine beetle *noun* any of various bark beetles of the genus *Dendroctonus* which bore into the wood of pine trees.

pine cone *noun* the cone-shaped fruit of the pine tree.

pine grosbeak *noun* a large finch, *Pinicola enucleator*, of coniferous forests in N America and Eurasia, the male of which is predominantly dull red.

pine marten *noun* **1** N Amer. the most common marten of N America, *Martes americana*, with predominantly dark brown fur with a splash of orange on the chest. **2** the European marten *Martes martes*, with a dark brown coat and white throat and stomach.

pine mushroom *noun* **1** an edible mushroom, *Tricholoma matsutake*, found in pine forests of Japan and Korea and much prized as a delicacy in Japan. **2** any of several other edible fungi of the same genus, found in North American pine forests.

pine nut *noun* the edible seed of various pine trees.

Pine Pass a pass (874 m) through the Rocky Mountains of NE central BC, east of Mackenzie.

pin·ery /ˈpaɪnəri/ *noun* a grove or forest of pine trees.

pine·sap *noun* a N American saprophytic plant, *Monotropa hypopithys*, with a stem of several nodding flowers.

pine siskin *noun* a siskin, *Carduelis pinus*, of N American coniferous forests.

pine tar *noun* a sticky, brownish-black liquid obtained by distilling pinewood, used in making paints, roofing, soap, etc.

pin·etum /paɪˈniːtəm/ *noun* (*pl.* **pin·eta** /-tə/) a plantation of pine trees or other conifers for scientific or ornamental purposes. [Latin from *pinus* pine]

pine·wood *noun* **1** the timber of the pine. **2** (also **pine wood**) a forest of pines.

piney *adjective* (also **piny**) of, like, or full of pines.

pin·feather *noun* Zool. an ungrown feather.

ping ● *noun* **1** a single short high ringing sound. **2** N Amer. = KNOCK *noun* 4. ● *intransitive verb* **1** make a ping. **2** N Amer. = KNOCK *verb* 7. [imitative]

ping·er /ˈpɪŋər/ *noun* **1** a device that transmits pings at short intervals for purposes of detection or measurement etc. **2** a device to ring a bell.

pin·go /ˈpɪŋɡoː/ *noun* (*pl.* **-gos**) a dome-shaped mound found in permafrost areas, consisting of a layer of soil over a large core of ice. [Inuit *pinguq* nunatak]

Ping-Pong *noun* proprietary = TABLE TENNIS. [imitative from the sound of a bat striking a ball]

pin·guid /ˈpɪŋɡwɪd/ *adjective* formal or jocular fat, oily, or greasy. [Latin *pinguis* fat]

pin·head *noun* **1** the flattened head of a pin. **2** a very small thing. **3** informal a stupid or foolish person.

pin·head·ed *adjective* informal stupid, foolish. ☐ **pin·headed·ness** *noun*

pin-high *adjective* Golf (of a ball) at the same distance from the tee as the hole, but off to one side.

pin·hole *noun* **1** a hole made by a pin. **2** a hole into which a peg fits.

pin·ion¹ /ˈpɪnjən/ ● *noun* **1** the outer part of a bird's wing, usu. including the flight feathers. **2** literary a wing; a flight feather. ● *transitive verb* **1** cut off the pinion of (a wing or bird) to prevent flight. **2 a** bind the arms of (a person). **b** (often foll. by *to*) bind (the arms, a person, etc.) esp. to a thing. [Old French *pignon*, ultimately from Latin *pinna*: see PIN]

pin·ion² /ˈpɪnjən/ *noun* **1** a small cogwheel engaging with a larger one. **2** a cogged spindle engaging with a wheel. [French *pignon* alteration of obsolete *pignol* from Latin *pinea* pine cone (as PINE¹)]

pink¹ ● *noun* **1** a pale red colour (*decorated in pink*). **2 a** any cultivated plant of the genus *Dianthus*, with sweet-smelling white, pink, crimson, etc. flowers. **b** the flower of this plant. **3** informal often derogatory a person with socialist tendencies. **4** = PINK SALMON. **5** (prec. by *the*) the most perfect condition etc. (*the pink of elegance*). **6** (also **hunting pink**) **a** a fox hunter's red coat. **b** the cloth for this. **c** a fox hunter. ● *adjective* **1** (often in *combination*) of a pale red colour of any of various shades (*rose-pink; salmon-pink*). **2** esp. derogatory tending to socialism. **3** (of wine) rosé. **4** of or associated with gays and lesbians (*a boom in the pink economy*). ☐ **in the pink** informal in very good health. **tickled pink** see TICKLE¹. ☐ **pink·ish** *adjective* **pink·ly** *adverb* **pink·ness** *noun* **pinky** *adjective* [original sense the flower, perhaps from dial. *pink-eyed* having small eyes]

pink² *transitive verb* **1** cut a scalloped or zigzag edge on (esp. fabric). **2** pierce slightly with a sword etc. **3** (often foll. by *out*) ornament (leather etc.) with perforations. [perhaps from Low German or Dutch: compare Low German *pinken* strike, peck]

pink³ *intransitive verb* Brit. = KNOCK *verb* 7. [imitative]

pink-collar *adjective* (usu. attributive) (of a profession etc.) traditionally associated with women (*compare WHITE-COLLAR, BLUE-COLLAR*).

pink elephants *plural noun* informal hallucinations caused by alcoholism.

Pink·er·ton, Allan (1819–84), Scottish-born US detective. In 1850 he established the first US private detective agency (in Chicago), becoming famous after solving a series of train robberies.

pink eye *noun* **1** contagious ophthalmia in humans and some livestock. **2** a contagious fever in horses.

pink gin *noun* Brit. gin flavoured with angostura bitters.

pink·ie var. of PINKY.

pinking shears *plural noun* a dressmaker's serrated shears for cutting a zigzag edge.

pink lady *noun* a cocktail of gin, grenadine, cream, and an egg white shaken together.

pinko *noun* (*pl.* **-os**) esp. N Amer. slang often derogatory a socialist.

pink pepper *noun* a pink berry of either of two trees of the genus *Schinus*, *S. ariera* or *S. terebinthifolius*, of the southern hemisphere, with a pine-like peppery flavour. ☐ **pink peppercorn** *noun*

pink salmon *noun* a medium-sized pink-fleshed migratory salmon, *Oncorhynchus gorbuscha*, of the Pacific and more recently Atlantic Oceans, the male of which has a humped back at spawning time. Also called HUMPBACK SALMON.

pink slip esp. N Amer. ● *noun* a notice of dismissal from employment. ● *transitive verb* (usu. **pink-slip**) dismiss (a person) from employment (*was pink-slipped last week*).

pink triangle *noun* a pink triangle used as a symbol indicating support for gay and lesbian rights. [originally a triangle of pink cloth sewn on to clothing to identify homosexual men in Nazi concentration camps]

pinky *noun* (also **pink·ie**) (*pl.* **-ies**) esp. *N Amer. & Scot.* the little finger. [compare dial. *pink* small, half-thing (eye)]

pin·less *adjective* not having or using pins.

pin money *noun* **1** a very small sum of money, esp. for spending on inessentials (*only works for pin money*). **2** *hist.* an allowance to a woman for dress etc. from her husband.

pinna /ˈpɪnə/ *noun* (*pl.* **pin·nae** /-niː/ or **pin·nas**) **1** the auricle; the external part of the ear. **2** a primary division of a pinnate leaf. **3** a fin or fin-like structure, feather, wing, etc. [Latin, = *penna* feather, wing, fin]

pin·nace /ˈpɪnəs/ *noun* any of various kinds of small boats used by a larger ship. [French *pinnace*, *pinasse*, ultimately from Latin *pinus* PINE¹]

pin·na·cle /ˈpɪnəkəl/ ● *noun* **1** the culmination or climax (of endeavour, success, etc.). **2** a natural peak, e.g. of rock etc. **3** a small ornamental turret usu. ending in a pyramid or cone, crowning a buttress, roof, etc. ● *transitive verb* **1** set on or as if on a pinnacle. **2** provide with pinnacles. [Old French *pin(n)acle* from Late Latin *pinnaculum* from *pinna* wing, point (as PIN, -CULE)]

pin·nae *pl.* of PINNA.

pin·nate /ˈpɪneɪt/ *adjective* **1** (of a compound leaf) having leaflets arranged on either side of the stem, usu. in pairs opposite each other. **2** having branches, tentacles, etc., on each side of an axis. [Latin *pinnatus* feathered (as PINNA)]

pinni- /ˈpɪni/ *combining form* wing, fin. [Latin *pinna*]

pinni·ped /ˈpɪnɪˌped/ ● *adjective* denoting any aquatic mammal with limbs ending in fins. ● *noun* a pinniped mammal. [Latin *pinna* fin + *pes ped-* foot]

pin·nule /ˈpɪnjuːl/ *noun* **1** the secondary division of a pinnate leaf. **2** a part or organ like a small wing or fin. □ **pin·nu·lar** *adjective* [Latin *pinnula* diminutive of *pinna* fin, wing]

PIN number *var.* of PIN.

pinny *noun* (*pl.* **-nies**) *informal* **1** a pinafore. **2** *N Amer.* a simple loose sleeveless jersey worn over sports attire to identify participants as members of a team, esp. during practice. [abbreviation]

pin oak *noun* a N American oak, *Quercus palustris*, with persistent dead branches resembling pegs fixed into the trunk.

Pino·chet /ˈpiːnoʊˌʃeɪ/ **Au·gus·to** (full name Augusto Pinochet Ugarte) (b.1915), Chilean general, president 1974–90. As commander-in-chief of Chile's armed forces he masterminded the military coup which overthrew President Allende (1973); he imposed a repressive military dictatorship until forced to call elections (Dec. 1989), giving way to a democratically elected president in 1990.

pi·nochle /ˈpiːˌnʌkəl/ *noun N Amer.* **1** a card game with a double pack of 48 cards (nine to ace only). **2** the combination of queen of spades and jack of diamonds in this game. [19th c.: origin unknown]

pi·nole /pɪˈnoʊli/ *noun US* flour made from parched cornflour, esp. mixed with sweet flour made of mesquite beans, sugar, etc. [Latin American Spanish from Aztec *pinolli*]

pi·ñon /piːˈnjoːn/ *noun* (also **pin·yon**) **1** a pine, *Pinus cembra*, bearing edible seeds. **2** the seed of this, a type of pine nut. [Spanish from Latin *pinea* pine cone]

Pi·not /piːˈnoː/ *noun* **1** any of several varieties of black (esp. **Pinot Noir** /nwɑr/) or white (esp. **Pinot Blanc** /blɑ̃/ or **Pinot Bianco** /ˈbjaŋkoːɑ̃/ or greyish-blue (esp. **Pinot Gris** /griː/ or **Pinot Grigio** /ˈgriːdʒoː/) grape used in winemaking. **2** the vine on which these grapes grow. **3** a red or white wine made from these grapes. [French, *var.* of earlier *Pineau*, from *pin* pine + *-eau* diminutive suffix (from the shape of the grape cluster)]

pin·point ● *noun* **1** the point of a pin. **2** something very small or sharp. **3** (*attributive*) **a** very small. **b** precise, accurate. ● *transitive verb* locate or determine with precision or accuracy (*pinpointed the target; pinpointed the problem*).

pin·prick *noun* **1** a prick caused by a pin. **2** a trifling irritation.

pins and needles *plural noun* a tingling sensation in a limb recovering from numbness. □ **on pins and needles** in an agitated state of suspense.

Pin·sent /ˈpɪnsənt/ **Gor·don Ed·ward** (b.1930), Canadian actor and writer. He has appeared on stage, on television, and in film. His writing, mostly set in his home province of Newfoundland, includes screenplays such as *The Rowdyman* (1972, winning him a Genie Award as best actor for the title role) and *John and the Missus* (1974).

pin·spot ● *noun* a small powerful spotlight for sharp illumination of a very small area. ● *transitive verb* illuminate with a pinspot.

pin·stripe *noun* **1** a very narrow white stripe in the design of cloth, esp. of the type used for making business suits (also *attributive*: *pinstripe suit*). **2** (in *sing.* or *pl.*) a pinstripe suit (*came wearing pinstripes*). □ **pin·striped** *adjective*

pint *noun* **1** a measure of capacity for liquids etc., equal to one-eighth of a gallon (0.568 litre in Imperial measure, or 0.473 litre in US measure). **2** a dry measure, equal to a half quart or (in the US) one sixty-fourth of a bushel (0.5506 litre). **3** esp. *Brit. informal* a pint of beer. **4** *Cdn* (*Maritimes*) a mickey of liquor. [Old French *pinte*, of unknown origin]

pinta /ˈpaɪntə/ *noun Brit. informal* a pint of milk. [corruption of *pint of*]

pin·tail *noun* a duck, esp. the northern pintail, *Anas acuta*, with a pointed tail.

Pin·ten·dre /pãˈtɑ̃drə/ a former municipality in SE central Quebec, now part of Lévis; pop. (2001) 6,209. [French *pin* pine + *tendre* soft, prob. with reference to the area's abundance of soft white pines]

Pin·ter /ˈpɪntər/ **Har·old** (b.1930), English playwright, actor, and director. His plays are associated with the theatre of the absurd and are often marked by a sense of brooding menace; they include *The Birthday Party* (1958), *The Caretaker* (1960), and *Party Time* (1991).

Pin·ter·esque /ˌpɪntərˈesk/ *adjective* typical of the plays of Harold Pinter, esp. having disjointed dialogue.

pin the tail on the donkey *noun* a children's party game in which blindfolded participants attempt to attach a picture of a tail to a picture of a donkey on a wall.

pin·tle /ˈpɪntəl/ *noun* a pin or bolt, esp. one on which some other part turns. [Old English *pintel* penis, of unknown origin: compare Old Frisian etc. *pint*]

pin·to /ˈpɪntoː/ *N Amer.* ● *adjective* piebald. ● *noun* (*pl.* **-tos**) **1** a piebald horse. **2** = PINTO BEAN. [Spanish, = mottled, ultimately from Latin *pictus* past participle of *pingere* paint]

pinto bean *noun* a variety of kidney bean with mottled seeds. [PINTO]

pint pot *noun Brit.* a pot or mug holding one pint, esp. of beer.

pint-sized *adjective* (also **pint-size**) *informal* very small.

pin·tuck /ˈpɪntʌk/ *noun* a very narrow ornamental tuck. □ **pin·tucked** *adjective* **pin·tuck·ing** *noun*

pin-up *noun* **1** a photograph of a popular or sexually attractive person, affixed to a wall. **2** a person shown in such a photograph.

pin·wale *adjective* (of a fabric, esp. corduroy) having very thin wales.

pin·wheel ● *noun* **1** a hand-held toy consisting of a stick with a small vaned wheel which rotates about a fixed centre. **2** a firework which can be fixed at the centre and which rotates rapidly when lit. Also called CATHERINE WHEEL. **3** something shaped like a pinwheel (*pastry pinwheels*). ● *transitive & intransitive verb* rotate or cause to rotate like a pinwheel.

pin·worm *noun* a small parasitic nematode worm, *Enterobius vermicularis*, of which the female has a pointed tail.

piny *adjective var.* of PINEY.

Pin·yin /pɪnˈjɪn/ *noun* a system of romanized spelling for transliterating Chinese. [Chinese *pīn-yīn*, lit. 'spell sound']

pin·yon *var.* of PIÑON.

pion /ˈpaɪɒn/ *noun Physics* a meson having a mass approximately 270 times that of an electron. Also called PI MESON. □ **pi·on·ic** /paɪˈɒnɪk/ *adjective* [PI (the letter used as a symbol for the particle) + -ON]

pi·on·eer /ˌpaɪəˈniːr/ ● *noun* **1** an initiator of a new enterprise, an inventor, etc. **2** a settler in a previously unsettled land (also *attributive*: *a pioneer settlement*). **3** *Military* a member of an infantry group preparing roads, terrain, etc. for the main body of troops. ● *verb* **1 a** *transitive* initiate or originate (an enterprise etc.). **b** *intransitive* act or prepare the way as a pioneer. **2** *transitive Military* open up (a road etc.) as a pioneer. **3** *transitive* go before, lead, or conduct (another person or persons). □ **pi·on·eer·ing** *adjective* [French *pionnier* foot soldier, pioneer, Old French *paonier*, *peon(n)ier* (as PEON)]

pious /ˈpaɪəs/ *adjective* **1** devout; religious. **2** hypocritically virtuous; sanctimonious. **3** dutiful. □ **pious·ly** *adverb* **pious·ness** *noun* [Latin *pius* dutiful, pious]

Pioz·zi /ˈpjɒtsi/ **Hes·ter Lynch** (known as 'Mrs. Thrale') (1740–1821), English writer, who is best known for her celebrated friendship with Samuel Johnson; her works include *Anecdotes of the late Samuel Johnson* (1786).

PIP *abbreviation* PICTURE-IN-PICTURE.

pip¹ *noun* **1** the seed of an apple, pear, orange, grape, etc. **2** *informal* an excellent thing or person; a fine example of a thing. [abbreviation of PIPPIN]

pip² *noun Brit.* a short high-pitched sound, usu. mechanically produced, esp. as a radio time signal. [imitative]

Vowels: a *cat* ɑ *arm* e *bed* ɜr *her* ɜː *deux* ə *ago* ɪ *sit* i *cosy* iː *feed* ɒ *hot* ɔ *pore* œ *no* oː *no* ʌ *run* ʊ *put*

pip³ ● *noun* **1** any of the spots on a playing card, dice, or domino. **2** *Brit.* (also *hist.* in the Canadian army) a star (1–3 according to rank) on the shoulder of an army officer's uniform. **3** a diamond-shaped segment of the surface of a pineapple. **4** an image of an object on a radar screen. ● *verb* **1** *transitive* (of a young bird) crack (the shell of an egg) when hatching. **2** *intransitive* (of a young bird) break out from the shell. [16th c. *peep*, of unknown origin]

pip⁴ *noun* a disease of poultry etc. causing thick mucus in the throat and white scale on the tongue. □ **give a person the pip** annoy a person. [Middle Dutch *pippe*, Middle Low German *pip*, prob. ultimately from corruption of Latin *pituita* slime]

pip⁵ *transitive verb* (**pipped**, **pip·ping**) *Brit. informal* defeat. □ **pip at** (or **to**) **the post** defeat at the last moment. [PIP² or PIP¹]

pi·pal *var. of* PEEPUL.

pipe ● *noun* **1** a tube of metal, plastic, wood, etc. used to convey water, gas, exhaust, etc. **2 a** a narrow wooden or clay etc. tube with a bowl at one end containing burning tobacco, opium, etc., the smoke from which is drawn into the mouth. **b** the quantity of tobacco etc. held by this (*smoked a pipe*). **c** a pipe used as a ceremonial object in many N American Aboriginal cultures. **3** *Music* **a** a wind instrument consisting of a single tube. **b** any of the tubes by which sound is produced in an organ. **c** (in *pl.*) bagpipes. **d** (in *pl.*) a set of pipes joined together, e.g. pan pipes. **4 a** a tubal organ, vessel, etc. in an animal's body. **b** (in *pl.*) *informal* the human circulatory, respiratory, or digestive system. **5** *informal or jocular* the voice or vocal cords, esp. in reference to singing. **6** a high note or song, esp. of a bird. **7** a cylindrical vein of ore. **8 a** a boatswain's whistle. **b** the sounding of this. **9** a cask for wine, esp. as a measure of two hogsheads, usu. equivalent to 105 imperial gallons (about 477 litres). ● *verb* **1** *transitive & intransitive* play (a tune etc.) on a pipe or pipes. **2** *transitive* **a** convey (oil, water, gas, etc.) by pipes. **b** provide with pipes. **3** *transitive* (often foll. by *in*) transmit (music, a radio program, etc.) by wire or cable. **4** *transitive* (usu. foll. by *up, on, to,* etc.) *Naut.* **a** summon (a crew) to a meal, work, etc. **b** signal the arrival of (an officer etc.) on board. **5** *intransitive* utter in a shrill voice; whistle. **6** *transitive* arrange (icing, cream, etc.) in decorative lines or twists on a cake etc. **7** *transitive* trim (a dress etc.) with piping. **8** *transitive* lead or bring (a person etc.) by the sound of a pipe. □ **between the pipes** *Hockey* playing goal. **pipe down** *informal* be quiet or less insistent. **pipe up** begin to play, sing, speak, etc. **put that in your pipe and smoke it** *informal* a challenge to another to accept something frank or unwelcome. □ **pipe·ful** *noun* (*pl.* **-fuls**). [Old English *pīpe*, *pīpian* & Old French *piper* from Germanic, ultimately from Latin *pipare* peep, chirp]

pipe band *noun* a band consisting of bagpipe players, drummers, and a drum major.

pipe bomb *noun* a homemade bomb contained in a pipe.

pipe carrier *noun* a person entrusted with the keeping of a sacred pipe and the leading of pipe ceremonies amongst Aboriginal peoples.

pipe ceremony *noun* a sacred ritual of some North American Aboriginal peoples, in which tobacco or herbs are smoked in a sacred pipe, either individually or communally, with prayers addressed to the four directions, to the earth and the sky.

pipe·clay ● *noun* a fine white clay used for tobacco pipes, whitening leather, etc. ● *transitive verb* whiten (leather etc.) with this.

pipe cleaner *noun* a piece of flexible covered wire, used for cleaning a tobacco pipe and for children's crafts.

piped-in music *noun* pre-recorded background music played through loudspeakers in a public place.

pipe dream *noun* an unattainable or fanciful hope or scheme. [originally as experienced when smoking an opium pipe]

pipe·fish *noun* any of various long slender fish of the family Syngnathidae, with an elongated snout.

pipe·fit·ter *noun* a worker who installs and repairs pipe systems. □ **pipe·fit·ting** *noun*

pipe·line ● *noun* **1** a long, usu. underground, pipe for conveying oil, gas, etc. **2** a channel supplying goods, information, etc. **3** *Computing* a linear sequence of specialized modules used for pipelining. ● *transitive verb* **1** convey by a pipeline. **2** *Computing* design or execute using the technique of pipelining. □ **in the pipeline** being planned, worked on, or produced.

pipe·lin·ing *noun* a form of computer organization in which successive steps of a process are executed in turn by a sequence of modules able to operate concurrently, so that another process can be begun before the previous one is finished.

pipe major *noun* a person (in military use, a non-commissioned officer) responsible for training and leading a pipe band.

pipe organ *noun Music* an organ using pipes instead of or as well as reeds.

piper *noun* **1** a bagpiper. **2** a person who plays a pipe, esp. an itinerant musician. □ **pay the piper** *see* PAY¹.

pipe rack *noun* a rack for holding tobacco pipes.

pi·peri·dine /pɪ'perɪˌdiːn, paɪ-, -dɪn/ *noun Chem.* a peppery-smelling liquid formed by the reduction of pyridine. [Latin *piper* pepper + -IDE + -INE⁴]

pipe·stem ● *noun* the shaft of a tobacco pipe. ● *adjective* slender like a pipestem (*pipestem arms*).

pipe·stone *noun* a hard red clay of the central US, used by American Aboriginal peoples to make tobacco pipes. *Also called* CATLINITE.

pip·ette /paɪ'pet, pɪ-/ ● *noun* a slender tube for transferring or measuring small quantities of liquids esp. in chemistry. ● *transitive verb* transfer or measure (a liquid) using a pipette. [French, diminutive of *pipe* PIPE]

pipe·work *noun Brit.* pipes collectively.

pipe wrench *noun* a wrench with one fixed and one movable jaw, designed so as to grip a pipe etc. when turned in one direction only.

pip·ing ● *noun* **1** the act or an instance of piping, esp. whistling or singing. **2** lengths of pipe, or a system of pipes, esp. in domestic use. **3** a thin pipe-like fold used to edge hems or frills on clothing, seams on upholstery, etc. **4** ornamental lines of icing, cream, potato, etc. on a cake or other dish. ● *adjective* (of a noise) high; whistling.

piping hot *adjective & adverb* very or suitably hot (esp. as required of food, water, etc.). [originally so hot as to make a whistling or hissing sound]

piping plover *noun* a small buff-coloured N American bird with a whistling call, *Charadrius melodus*, which breeds along the Atlantic coast and the shores of the Great Lakes, and in the Prairies.

pipis·trelle /ˌpɪpɪ'strel/ *noun* any bat of the genus *Pipistrellus*, native to temperate regions and feeding on insects. [French from Italian *pipistrello*, *vip-*, from Latin *vespertilio* bat, from *vesper* evening]

pip·it /'pɪpɪt/ *noun* any of various birds of the family Motacillidae, esp. of the genus *Anthus*, found worldwide and having brown plumage often heavily streaked with a lighter colour. [prob. imitative]

pip·kin *noun* a small earthenware pot or pan. [16th c.: origin unknown]

pip·pin *noun* **1 a** an apple grown from seed. **b** a red and yellow dessert apple. **2** *informal* an excellent person or thing; a beauty. [Old French *pepin*, of unknown origin]

pip pip *interjection Brit. informal dated* goodbye. [imitative, prob. of the repeated short blasts on the horn of a car or bicycle]

pip·sis·sewa /pɪp'sɪsəwɒ/ *noun* an evergreen plant of the wintergreen family, *Chimaphila umbellata*, with whorls of shiny leaves and a cluster of waxy white or pink flowers. [Abenaki *kpi-pskwàhsawe* 'flower of the woods']

pip·squeak *noun informal* a contemptibly small, weak, or insignificant person or thing. [imitative]

pi·quant /piː'kɒnt, -'kant, 'piːkant/ *adjective* **1** agreeably pungent, sharp, or appetizing. **2** pleasantly exciting and stimulating to the mind (*a piquant bit of gossip*). □ **pi·quan·cy** *noun* **pi·quant·ly** *adverb* [French, pres. part. of *piquer* (as PIQUE)]

pique /piːk/ ● *transitive verb* (**piques**, **piqued**, **pi·quing**) **1** wound the pride of, irritate. **2** arouse (curiosity, interest, etc.). ● *noun* ill-feeling; enmity; resentment (*in a fit of pique*). [French *piquer* prick, irritate, from Romanic]

piqué /piː'kei/ *noun* a stiff ribbed cotton or other fabric. [French, past participle of *piquer*: see PIQUE]

pi·quet /pɪ'ket/ *noun* a game for two players with a pack of 32 cards (seven to ace only). [French, of unknown origin]

pir·acy /'paɪrəsi/ *noun* (*pl.* **-cies**) **1** the practice or an act of robbery of ships at sea. **2** a similar practice or act in other forms, esp. hijacking. **3** the infringement of copyright by unauthorized reproduction or use of a book, recording, computer program, etc. [medieval Latin *piratia* from Greek *pirateia* (as PIRATE)]

Pi·raeus /paɪ'riːəs/ the chief port of Athens, situated on the Saronic Gulf 8 km (5 miles) southwest of the city; pop. (est. 2002) 189,000.

Piran·dello /ˌpɪrən'delo/ **Luigi** (1867–1936), Italian playwright and novelist. His plays, which include *Six Characters in Search of an Author* (1921) and *Henry IV* (1922), challenged the conventions of naturalism and had a significant influence on the development of European drama; he was awarded the Nobel Prize for literature in 1934. □ **Piran·del·lian** *adjective*

Pira·nesi /ˌpɪrəˈneizi/ **Gio·van·ni Bat·tis·ta** (or **Giam·bat·tista**) (1720–78), Italian engraver and architect. In his prints of the buildings of Rome he relied on atypical viewpoints and dramatic chiaroscuro to aggrandize the power and scale of the ancient and modern city; he is also known for the series of prints *Imaginary Prisons* (1745–61). □ **Pira·nesi·an** *adjective*

pi·ranha /pɪˈrɒnə, -ˈranə/ *noun* any of various freshwater predatory fish of the genera *Pygocentrus*, *Rooseveltiella*, or *Serrasalmus*, native to S America and having sharp cutting teeth. [Portuguese from Tupi, var. of *piraya* scissors]

pir·ate /ˈpairət/ ● *noun* **1 a** a person who commits piracy. **b** a ship used by pirates. **2** a person who infringes another's copyright or other business rights. **3** (often *attributive*) a person, organization, etc., that broadcasts without official authorization (*pirate radio station*). ● *transitive verb* **1** appropriate or reproduce (the work or ideas etc. of another) without permission, for one's own benefit. **2** plunder. □ **pir·at·ed** *adjective* **pir·at·ic** /-ˈratɪk/ *adjective* **pir·at·ic·al** /-ˈratɪkəl/ *adjective* [Latin *pirata* from Greek *peiratēs* from *peiraō* attempt, assault]

piri piri /ˈpiri ˈpiri/ *noun* a sauce made with hot peppers, lemon rind and juice, and other flavourings. [Ronga, = pepper]

pi·ro·gi var. of PEROGY.

pi·rogue /pɪˈroːg/ *noun* a long narrow canoe made from a single tree trunk. [French, prob. from Galibi]

pi·roshki /pɪˈrɒʃki/ *noun* (*pl.* same or **-kis**) a small turnover of pastry filled with meat, fish, rice, etc. [Russian *pirozhki* pl. of *pirozhok*, diminutive of *pirog*, a large pie]

pirou·ette /ˌpɪruˈet/ ● *noun* a rapid turn or spin made esp. by a dancer while balanced on the point of the toe or the ball of the foot. ● *intransitive verb* perform a pirouette. [French, = spinning top]

Pisa /ˈpiːzə/ a city in N Italy, in Tuscany, on the Arno River; pop. (2001) 85,379. The city is noted for the 'Leaning Tower of Pisa', a circular bell tower which leans about 5 m (17 ft) from the perpendicular over its height of 55 m (181 ft), part of this inclination dating from its construction at the end of the 12th c. □ **Pisan** *noun & adjective*

Pisan see DE PISAN.

Pi·sano /piˈzɒnoː/ **1 An·drea** (c.1290–1348) and his son, **Nino** (died c.1368), Italian sculptors. Andrea created the earliest pair of bronze doors for the baptistery at Florence (completed 1336), and Nino was one of the first since ancient times to specialize in free-standing life-size figures. **2 Nic·ola** (c.1220–c.1278) and his son, **Gio·van·ni** (c.1250–c.1314), Italian sculptors. Nicola's works, the best-known of which are the pulpits in the baptistery at Pisa (c.1255–60) and in Siena cathedral (1265–8), signalled a revival of interest in classical sculpture; Giovanni's works carried this process further, and include a pulpit in the church of Santa Andrea in Pistoia (completed 1301), and the richly decorated facade of Siena cathedral (completed 1284).

pis·ca·tor·ial /ˌpɪskəˈtɔːriəl/ *adjective* (also **pis·ca·tory** /ˈpɪskətɔːri/) **1** of or concerning fish, fishermen or fishing. **2** *formal* enthusiastic about fishing. □ **pis·ca·tor·ial·ly** *adverb*

Pis·ces /ˈpaɪsiːz/ *noun* (*pl.* same) **1** a large constellation between Aries and Aquarius, traditionally regarded as contained in the figure of a pair of fish tied together by their tails. **2 a** the twelfth sign of the zodiac. **b** a person born when the sun is in this sign, usu. between 19 February and 20 March. □ **Pis·cean** /ˈpɔɪsiən/ *noun & adjective* [Latin, pl. of *piscis* fish]

pisci·cul·ture /ˈpɪsɪˌkʌltʃər/ *noun* the breeding and rearing of fish by artificial means. □ **pisci·cul·tur·al** *adjective* **pisci·cul·tur·ist** *noun* [Latin *piscis* fish, after *agriculture* etc.]

pis·cina /pɪˈsiːnə, -ˈsainə/ *noun* (*pl.* **pis·cinae** /-niː/ or **pis·cinas**) a stone basin for draining water used in the Mass, found chiefly in Roman Catholic and pre-Reformation churches. [Latin from *piscis* fish]

pis·cine /ˈpɪsain/ *adjective* of or concerning fish. [Latin *piscis* fish]

Piscis Aus·tri·nus /ˈpaɪsɪs ˈɒstriːnɒs/ a small southern constellation, said to represent a small fish. [Latin, lit. 'southern fish']

pisciv·or·ous /pɪˈsɪvərəs/ *adjective* fish-eating. [Latin *piscis* fish + -VOROUS]

pish *interjection* an expression of contempt, impatience, or disgust. [imitative]

Pish·pek /pɪʃˈpek/ see BISHKEK.

Pi·sidia /paɪˈsɪdiə/ an ancient region of Asia Minor, between Pamphylia and Phrygia. Traversed by the Taurus Mountains, the region maintained its independence until 25 BC, when it was incorporated into the Roman province of Galatia. □ **Pi·sid·ian** *adjective & noun*

pisi·form /ˈpɪsɪˌfɔːm/ ● *adjective* pea-shaped. ● *noun* a pea-shaped bone in the wrist in the upper row of the carpus. [modern Latin *pisiformis* from *pisum* pea]

Pi·sis·tra·tus /paɪˈsɪstrətəs/ (also **Pei·sis·tra·tus**) (c.600–527 BC), tyrant of Athens. He seized power in 561 and after twice being expelled ruled continuously from 546 until his death, reducing aristocratic power in rural Attica and promoting the financial prosperity and cultural pre-eminence of Athens.

pis·mire /ˈpɪsˌmaɪr/ *noun* dialect an ant. [Middle English from PISS (from smell of anthill) + obsolete *mire* ant]

piss *coarse slang* ● *verb* **1** *intransitive* urinate. **2** *transitive* **a** discharge (blood etc.) when urinating. **b** wet with urine. **3** *reflexive* **a** wet one's clothing with urine. **b** be very frightened, amused, or excited. ● *noun* **1** urine. **2** an act of urinating. **3** an unpalatable drink. □ **not have a pot to piss in** (or **a window to throw it out of**) be very poor. **piss around** (or *Brit.* **about**) fool or mess around. **piss away** squander; waste (*pissed away his money*). **piss down** *Cdn & Brit.* rain heavily. **piss in** (or **into, against**) **the wind** do something to no effect or against one's own interests. **piss off 1** go away. **2** (often as **pissed off** *adjective*) annoy; anger. **piss on** show utter contempt for, esp. by humiliating; defeat heavily. **go piss up a rope** go to hell. **take the piss** (often foll. by *out of*) esp. *Brit.* mock; deride. [Old French *pisser* (imitative)]

pis·sal·adi·ère /ˈpɪsaladjer/ *noun* a Provençal open tart resembling pizza, typically made with tomato sauce topped with onions, anchovies, and olives.

piss and vinegar *noun* *coarse slang* energy; aggression.

piss·ant /ˈpɪsant/ *US coarse slang* ● *noun* an insignificant or contemptible person or thing. ● *adjective* insignificant, worthless, contemptible. [from PISS *noun* + -ANT]

Pis·sarro /pɪˈsɑːroː/ **Ca·mille** (1830–1903), French painter, born in the W Indies. One of the leading Impressionist painters, he was influenced by the English landscape school and experimented with pointillism in the 1880s.

piss artist *noun* *Brit. coarse slang* **1** a drunkard. **2** a glib, unreliable person.

pissed *adjective* **1** drunk; intoxicated. **2** *N Amer.* annoyed; angry. □ **pissed as a newt** esp. *Brit.* very drunk.

piss·er *noun* *coarse slang* **1** a difficult, disappointing, or annoying thing. **2** a urinal or toilet. **3** a person who urinates.

piss·hole *noun* **1** a hole made in soluble matter by urinating. **2** a squalid place.

pissing contest *noun* *slang* an unbending and pointless contest of wills, usu. over something insignificant or petty. [from a schoolboy's game of competing to see who can urinate the furthest, highest, etc.]

piss·oir /piːˈswɑr/ *noun* a public urinal. [French]

piss-poor *adjective* *coarse slang* very bad; inferior (*a piss-poor effort*).

piss-pot *noun* a chamber pot.

piss-up *noun* *Brit. coarse slang* a drinking spree. □ **couldn't organize a piss-up in a brewery** be very disorganized or incompetent.

pissy *adjective* (**piss·i·er**, **piss·i·est**) *coarse slang* **1** disagreeable; foul (*a pissy mood*). **2** inferior; second-rate.

pis·ta·chio /pɪˈstaʃiəʊ/ ● *noun* (*pl.* **-chios**) **1** an evergreen tree, *Pistacia vera*, bearing small brownish-green flowers and ovoid reddish fruit. **2** (in full **pistachio nut**) the edible pale green seed of this. **3** (in full **pistachio green**) a pale green colour. ● *adjective* (in full **pistachio green**; hyphenated when *attributive*) pale green. [Italian *pistaccio* and Spanish *pistacho*, via Latin *pistacium* and Greek *pistakion* from Persian *pistah*]

piste /piːst/ *noun* a ski run of compacted snow. [French]

pis·til /ˈpɪstɪl/ *noun* the female organs of a flower, comprising the stigma, style, and ovary. [French *pistile* or Latin *pistillum* PESTLE]

pis·til·late /ˈpɪstɪlət/ *adjective* **1** having pistils. **2** having pistils but no stamens.

pis·tol *noun* a small firearm designed to be held in one hand. [obsolete French from German *Pistole* from Czech *pišt'al*, of which the original meaning was 'whistle', hence 'a firearm' by the resemblance in shape]

pis·tole /pɪˈstoːl/ *noun* hist. a gold coin of Spain or other European countries. [French *pistole* abbreviation of *pistolet*, of uncertain origin]

pistol-grip *noun* a handle shaped like the butt of a pistol.

pistol shot *noun* **1** a shot fired from a pistol. **2** the range of a pistol.

pistol-whip *transitive verb* (**-whipped**, **-whipping**) beat with a pistol.

pis·ton *noun* **1** a disc or short cylinder fitting closely within a tube in which it moves up and down against a liquid or gas, used in an internal combustion engine to impart motion, or in a pump to receive motion. **2** a sliding valve in a trumpet etc. [French from Italian *pistone* var. of *pestone* augmentative of *pestello* PESTLE]

piston engine *noun* an engine, esp. in an aircraft, in which motion is derived from a piston. □ **piston-engined** *adjective*

piston ring *noun* a ring on a piston sealing the gap between the piston and the cylinder wall.

piston rod *noun* a rod or crankshaft attached to a piston to drive a wheel or to impart motion.

pis·tou /ˈpiːstuː/ *noun* **1** a sauce or paste made from crushed basil, garlic, cheese, etc., used esp. in Provençal dishes. **2** a vegetable soup made with this sauce. [Provençal, = Italian PESTO]

pit¹ ● *noun* **1 a** a usu. large deep hole in the ground. **b** a hole made in digging for industrial purposes (*sand pit; gravel pit*). **c** a mine, esp. a coal mine. **d** a covered hole as a trap for esp. wild animals. **2 a** an indentation left after smallpox, acne, etc. **b** a hollow in a plant or animal body or on any surface. **3 a** = ORCHESTRA 2a. **b** *Brit. Theatre* usu. *hist.* seating at the back of the stalls. **c** the people in the pit. **4 a** (**the pit** or **bottomless pit**) hell. **b** (**the pits**) *slang* a wretched or the worst imaginable place, situation, person, etc. **5 a** an area at the side of a track where race cars are serviced and refuelled. **b** a sunken area in a garage floor for access to a car's underside. **6** esp. *N Amer.* the area of a stock market or commodity exchange in which a particular stock or commodity is traded, esp. one in which dealings in certain commodities take place by open outcry (*wheat pit*). **7** an enclosure in which animals are made to fight (compare COCKPIT 3). **8** = MOSH PIT. ● *verb* (**pit·ted**, **pit·ting**) **1** *transitive* (usu. foll. by *against*) **a** set (people or things) in opposition or rivalry. **b** match (one's wits, strengths, etc.) against an opponent. **2** *transitive* (usu. as **pit·ted** *adjective*) make pits, esp. scars, in. **3** *intransitive* (of the flesh etc.) retain the impression of a finger etc. when touched. **4** *intransitive* (of a race-car driver) make a pit stop. □ **hit the pit** esp. *Brit. slang* go to bed. [Old English *pytt*, ultimately from Latin *puteus* well]

pit² *N Amer.* ● *noun* the stone of a fruit. ● *transitive verb* (**pit·ted**, **pit·ting**) remove pits from (fruit). [perhaps Dutch, related to PITH]

pita /ˈpiːtə/ *noun N Amer.* (*Brit.* **pitta** /ˈpɪtə/) a flat hollow unleavened, usu. round bread which can be split and filled with salad etc. [modern Greek, = a cake]

pit-a-pat *var. of* PITTER-PATTER.

pit boss *noun informal* an employee in a casino in charge of gaming tables.

pit bull *noun* **1** (in full **pit bull terrier**) a dog of an American variety of bull terrier, noted for its ferocity. **2** (*attributive*) aggressive; fierce (*pit-bull personality*).

Pit·cairn Islands a British dependency comprising a group of volcanic islands in the S Pacific, east of French Polynesia. The colony's only settlement is Adamstown, on Pitcairn Island, the chief island of the group; pop. (2000) 50. Pitcairn Island was discovered in 1767, but remained uninhabited until settled in 1790 by mutineers from HMS *Bounty* and their Tahitian companions. [R. *Pitcairn*, the midshipman who first sighted the chief island]

pitch¹ ● *verb* **1** *transitive* erect and fix (a tent, camp, etc.). **2** *transitive* **a** throw; fling. **b** throw out; get rid of. **c** (in games) throw a flat object towards a mark (*pitched horseshoes*). **3** *Baseball* **a** *transitive* throw (the ball) to the batter. **b** *transitive* serve as pitcher of (a game, inning, etc.). **c** *intransitive* fill the position of pitcher. **d** *transitive* throw the ball to (a batter) in a specific way (*pitch him low and away*). **e** *intransitive* throw a pitch. **4** *transitive* fix or plant (a thing) in a definite position. **5 a** *transitive* express in a particular style or at a particular level (*pitched his argument at the most basic level*). **b** *transitive informal* promote (a product, idea, etc.); attempt to win sales or approval for (*pitched his outline to the editor*). **c** *intransitive* make a bid or offer for business. **6** *intransitive* (often foll. by *against, into*, etc.) fall heavily, esp. headlong. **7** *intransitive* (of a ship etc.) plunge in a longitudinal direction (compare ROLL *verb* 8a). **8** *transitive Music* set at a particular pitch. **9** *intransitive* (of a roof etc.) slope downwards. **10** *intransitive* move with a vigorous jogging motion, as in a train, carriage, etc.; lurch. **11** *intransitive Golf* play a pitch shot. ● *noun* **1** height, degree, intensity, etc. (*the pitch of despair; nerves were strung to a pitch*). **2 a** the steepness of a slope, esp. of a roof, stratum, etc. **b** the degree of such a pitch. **c** a downward inclination or slope, esp. a steep one. **3** *Baseball* the act or manner of pitching the ball to a batter. **4** *Music* **a** that quality of a sound which is governed by the rate of vibrations producing it; the degree of highness or lowness of a tone. **b** a standard scale of this used in performance etc. (compare CONCERT PITCH). **5** the pitching motion of a ship etc. **6 a** *Brit.* the area of play in a field game. **b** *Cricket* the area between the creases. **7** *informal* behaviour or speech intended to influence or persuade, esp. for the purpose of sales or

advertising. **8** (also **pitch shot**) *Golf* a high approach shot with a short run. **9** *Mech.* the distance between successive corresponding points or lines, e.g. between the teeth of a cogwheel etc. **10** *Typography & Computing* the density of characters on a line, usu. expressed as the number of characters per inch. **11** a measure of the angle of the blades of a screw propeller, equal to the distance forward a blade would move in one revolution if it exerted no thrust on the medium. □ **pitch in** *informal* **1** assist, co-operate. **2** set to work vigorously. **pitch into** *informal* attack forcibly with blows, words, etc. **pitch up** *informal* arrive, appear. [Middle English *pic(c)he*, perhaps from Old English *picc(e)an* (unrecorded: compare *picung* stigmata)]

pitch² ● *noun* **1** a sticky resinous black or dark brown substance obtained by distilling tar or turpentine, semi-liquid when hot, hard when cold, and used for caulking the seams of ships etc. **2** any of various bituminous substances including asphalt. **3** the resin or crude turpentine which exudes from pine and fir trees. ● *transitive verb* cover, coat, or smear with pitch. [Old English *pic* from Germanic from Latin *pix picis*]

pitch-black *adjective* (also **pitch-dark**) very or completely dark.

pitch·blende /ˈpɪtʃblɛnd/ *noun* a mineral form of uranium oxide occurring in pitch-like masses and yielding radium. [German *Pechblende* (as PITCH², BLENDE)]

pitched battle *noun* **1** a vigorous fight, argument, etc. **2** *Military* a battle planned beforehand and fought on chosen ground.

pitched roof *noun* a sloping roof.

pitch·er¹ *noun* **1** esp. *N Amer.* **a** a vessel of various sizes, usu. of glass, earthenware, or plastic, with a lip and a handle, for holding liquids. **b** the amount of liquid contained in this (*a pitcher of lemonade*). **2** the modified leaf of the pitcher plant. □ **pitcher·ful** *noun* (pl. **-fuls**). [Old French *pichier* 'pot']

pitch·er² *noun* **1** *Baseball* the player who throws the ball to the opposing batter. **2** a person or thing that pitches.

pitcher plant *noun* any of various plants, esp. *Sarracenia purpurea* of eastern N America, with pitcher leaves that can hold liquids and trap insects and a nodding dark red flower with a large flattened pistil. The floral emblem of Newfoundland and Labrador.

pitch·fork ● *noun* a long-handled fork for pitching hay etc. ● *verb* **1** *transitive & intransitive* throw with or as if with a pitchfork. **2** *transitive* (usu. foll. by *into*) thrust (a person) forcibly into a position, office, etc. [in Middle English *pickfork*, prob. from PICK² + FORK, assoc. with PITCH¹]

pitch·man *noun* (pl. **-men**) *N Amer.* a person delivering a sales pitch, esp. in a radio or television commercial.

pitch·out *noun* **1** *Football* a short lateral pass thrown behind the line of scrimmage, usu. by the quarterback to another back. **2** *Baseball* a pitch purposely thrown wide of the plate, to make it easier for the catcher to throw out a baserunner who is attempting to steal.

pitch pine *noun* any of various pine trees, esp. *Pinus rigida* or *P. palustris*, yielding much resin.

pitch pipe *noun Music* a small pipe blown to set the pitch for singing or tuning.

pitch·pole *intransitive verb* (of a boat) be overturned so that its stern pitches forward over its bow. [from PITCH¹ + *poll* head]

pitchy *adjective* (**pitch·i·er**, **pitch·i·est**) of, like, or dark as pitch.

pit·eous /ˈpɪtɪəs/ *adjective* deserving or causing pity; wretched. □ **pit·eous·ly** *adverb* **pit·eous·ness** *noun* [Anglo-French *pitous*, Old French *pitos* from Romanic (as PIETY)]

pit·fall *noun* **1** an unsuspected snare, danger, or drawback. **2** a covered pit for trapping animals etc.

pith ● *noun* **1** spongy white tissue lining the rind of an orange, lemon, etc. **2** the essential part; the quintessence (*came to the pith of his argument*). **3** *Bot.* the spongy cellular tissue in the stems and branches of dicotyledonous plants. **4 a** *archaic* physical strength; vigour. **b** force; energy, esp. of words or speech. **5** *archaic* spinal marrow. ● *transitive verb* **1** remove the pith or marrow from. **2** slaughter or immobilize (an animal) by severing the spinal cord. [Old English *pitha* from West Germanic]

pit·head *noun* **1** the top of a mine shaft. **2** the area surrounding this.

Pithecanthropus /ˌpɪθɪˈkænθrəpəs/ *noun* a genus name formerly applied to some fossil hominids of the species *Homo erectus*, named from remains found in Java in 1891. (See also JAVA MAN). [Greek *pithēkos* ape + *anthrōpos* man]

pith helmet *noun* a lightweight sun helmet made from the dried pith of the sola or a similar tropical plant.

pithos /ˈpɪθɒs/ *noun* (pl. **pithoi** /-θɔɪ/) *Archaeology* a large storage jar. [Greek]

pit house *noun* (also **pit dwelling**) a semi-subterranean dwelling consisting of a pit excavated out of the ground and then roofed over.

pithy *adjective* (**pith·i·er**, **pith·i·est**) **1** (of style, speech, etc.) condensed, terse, and forcible. **2** of, like, or containing much pith. □ **pith·i·ly** *adverb* **pith·i·ness** *noun*

piti·able *adjective* **1** deserving or causing pity. **2** contemptible. □ **piti·ably** *adverb*

piti·ful *adjective* **1** deserving of or arousing pity. **2** contemptible (*pitiful efforts*). **3** *archaic* compassionate. □ **piti·ful·ly** *adverb* **piti·ful·ness** *noun*

piti·less *adjective* **1** showing no pity; cruel (*a pitiless tyrant*). **2** very harsh or severe; unrelenting (*the pitiless heat of the desert*). □ **piti·less·ly** *adverb* **piti·less·ness** *noun*

pit-lamping *noun Cdn* (*BC*) the hunting practice of using strong portable lights to blind an animal temporarily so that it freezes in its tracks, thus allowing the hunter an easy shot; jacklighting. [the lamps originally used being those used in coal pits]

Pit·man, Sir Isaac (1813–97), English educator and inventor, who devised a phonetic shorthand system named after him (1837).

pit·man *noun* **1** (*pl.* **-men**) a miner. **2** *N Amer.* (*pl.* **-mans**) a connecting rod in machinery.

Pi·to·cin *noun proprietary* an aqueous solution of the hormone oxytocin, used to speed labour. [blend of PITUITARY + OXYTOCIN]

pit of the stomach *noun* the floor of the stomach.

piton /ˈpiːtɒn/ *noun* a peg or spike driven into a rock or crack to support a climber or a rope. [French, = eyebolt]

Pi·tons, the /ˈpiːtɒnz/ two conical mountains in St. Lucia in the W Indies. Reaching a height of 798 m (2,618 ft) and 750 m (2,461 ft), they rise up out of the Caribbean Sea just off the southwest coast of the island.

pitot tube /ˈpiːtoː/ *noun* a device consisting of an open-ended right-angled tube used to measure the speed or flow of a fluid. [H. Pitot, French physicist d.1771]

pit pony *noun Brit. & Cdn hist.* a pony kept underground for hauling in coal mines.

pit prop *noun* a balk of wood used to support the roof of a coal mine.

pit socks *plural noun Cdn* (*Cape Breton*) standard grey work socks, esp. worn by miners.

pit stop *noun* **1** *Motor Racing* a stop at a pit for servicing and refuelling. **2 a** a brief stop during a trip for a snack, rest, etc. **b** a place where one makes such a stop.

Pitt ▸ 1 Wil·liam, 1st Earl of Chat·ham (known as **Pitt the Elder**) (1708–78), English Whig politician. He became Secretary of State (effectively prime minister) in 1756 and headed coalition governments 1756–61 and 1766–8; he brought the Seven Years War to an end in 1763 and masterminded the conquest of French possessions in Canada and India. **2** his son, **Wil·liam** (known as **Pitt the Younger**) (1759–1806), English politician, prime minister 1783–1801 and 1804–6. Prime minister at the age of 24, he introduced financial reforms, reduced the national debt, and reformed the administration of India; with Britain's entry into war against France (1793), he became almost entirely occupied with the conduct of the war and with uniting European opposition to France.

pitta¹ *Brit. var. of* PITA.

pitta² /ˈpɪtə/ *noun* a brightly coloured passerine bird with a strong bill and short tail, of the Old World genus *Pitta* and family Pittidae. [Telegu *piṭṭa* '(young) bird']

pit·tance /ˈpɪtəns/ *noun* **1** a scanty or meagre allowance, remuneration, etc. (*paid him a mere pittance*). **2** a small number or amount. **3** *hist.* a pious bequest to a religious house for extra food etc. [Old French *pitance* from medieval Latin *pi(e)tantia* from Latin *pietas* PITY]

pitter-patter (also **pit-a-pat**) ● *adverb* **1** with a sound like quick light steps. **2** with a rapid beat (*heart went pitter-patter*). ● *noun* such a sound. [imitative]

Pitt Island see CHATHAM ISLANDS.

Pitt Meadows a district municipality in southwestern BC, situated at the junction of the Fraser and Pitt rivers, just east of Port Coquitlam; pop. (2001) 14,670. [prob. after W. PITT the Younger]

Pitts·burgh /ˈpɪtsbɜrg/ an industrial city in SW Pennsylvania, at the junction of the Allegheny and Monongahela rivers; pop. (2000) 334,563. □ **Pitts·burgh·er** *noun* [W. PITT (the Elder)]

pi·tu·i·tary /pɪˈtuːɪteri, -ˈtjuː-/ ● *noun* (*pl.* **-ies**) (also **pituitary gland**) a small ductless gland at the base of the brain secreting various hormones essential for growth and other bodily functions. ● *adjective* of

or relating to this gland. [Latin *pituitarius* secreting phlegm, from *pituita* phlegm]

pit viper *noun* any of various American and Asian venomous snakes of the subfamily Crotalinae, which have sensory pits on the head that can detect the heat of prey.

pity ● *noun* (*pl.* **-ies**) **1** sorrow and compassion aroused by another's condition (*felt pity for the child*). **2** something to be regretted; grounds for regret or mild annoyance (*what a pity!*). ● *transitive verb* (**-ies**, **-ied**) feel (often contemptuous) pity for (*they are to be pitied; I pity you if you think that*). □ **for pity's sake** an exclamation of urgent supplication, anger, etc. **more's the pity** so much the worse. **take** (or **have**) **pity on** feel or act compassionately towards. □ **pity·ing** *adjective* **pity·ing·ly** *adverb* [Old French *pité* from Latin *pietas* (as PIETY)]

più /pju/ *adverb Music* more (*più piano*). [Italian]

più mosso /pju ˈmɒsoː/ *adverb Music* more quickly. [Italian, PIÙ + *mosso*, past participle of *muovere*, move]

Pius II /ˈpaɪəs/ (born Enea Silvio Piccolomini) (1405–64), Italian humanist and poet, pope 1458–64. He was unsuccessful in his attempt to launch a crusade against the Turks (1458).

Pius V /ˈpaɪəs/ **St.** (born Antonio Ghislieri) (1504–72), Italian pope 1566–72. He excommunicated Elizabeth I of England (1570), and organized the Holy League, whose forces defeated the Turks at Lepanto (1571). Feast day, 30 April.

Pius VII /ˈpaɪəs/ (born Luigi Barnaba Chiaramonti) (1742–1823), Italian pope 1800–23. He negotiated a concordat with Napoleon (1801), crowned him emperor of France (1804), and after the occupation of Rome by French forces (1808), was taken prisoner by him (1809–14).

Pius IX /ˈpaɪəs/ (born Giovanni Maria Mastai-Ferretti) (1792–1878), Italian pope 1846–78. He summoned the First Vatican Council (1869–70), which proclaimed the infallibility of the Pope when speaking *ex cathedra*.

Pius X /ˈpaɪəs/ **St.** (born Giuseppe Melchiorre Sarto) (1835–1914), Italian ecclesiastic, pope 1903–14. He condemned modernism (1907) and revised and codified the canon law. Feast day, 3 Sept.

Pius XI /ˈpaɪəs/ (born Ambrogio Damiano Achille Ratti) (1857–1939), Italian pope 1922–39. He negotiated the Lateran Treaty (1929) with Mussolini, which established the Vatican City as an independent, neutral state.

Pius XII /ˈpaɪəs/ (born Eugenio Maria Giuseppe Giovanni Pacelli) (1876–1958), Italian pope 1939–58. He upheld the neutrality of the Roman Catholic Church during the Second World War, maintaining diplomatic relations with both Allied and Axis governments; after the war there was criticism of his failure to condemn Nazi atrocities and of his apparent ambivalence towards anti-Semitism.

pivot /ˈpɪvət/ ● *noun* **1** a short shaft or pin on which something turns or oscillates. **2** a crucial or essential person, point, etc., in a scheme or enterprise. **3** a pivoting movement. **4** *Basketball* **a** a movement in which the player with the ball may take one or more paces in any direction with one foot, while keeping the other foot in contact with the floor. **b** an offensive position in the frontcourt, usu. played by the centre, in which the player stands facing away from the offensive basket. **c** (also **pivot·man**) the player who plays in the pivot position. **5** *Hockey* a centreman. **6** *Military* the man or men about whom a body of troops wheels. ● *verb* (**pivot·ed**, **pivot·ing**) **1** *intransitive* turn on or as if on a pivot. **2** *intransitive* (foll. by *on*, *upon*) hinge on; depend on. **3** *transitive* provide with or attach by a pivot. □ **pivot·al** *adjective* [French, of uncertain origin]

pix¹ *plural noun informal* **1** pictures, esp. photographs. **2** movies. [abbreviation: compare PIC]

pix² *var. of* PYX.

pixel /ˈpɪksəl/ *noun Electronics* any of the minute areas of uniform illumination of which an image on a television or computer screen is composed. [abbreviation of *picture element*: compare PIX¹]

pixel·ate /ˈpɪksəleɪt/ *transitive verb Electronics* (also **pixel·late**) display as or divide into pixels. □ **pixel·a·tion** *noun*

pixie *noun* (also **pixy**) (*pl.* **pixies**) **1** a small fairy, often portrayed with pointed ears and a pointed hat. **2** a small, mischievous person. □ **pixie·ish** *adjective* [17th c.: origin unknown]

pixie cut *noun* a short, gamine haircut, esp. for a woman.

pixie dust *noun* **1** in Sir James Barrie's *Peter Pan*, magic dust taken or shaken from a pixie or fairy, enabling humans to fly. **2** unusually great success, felicity, or luck.

pix·il·at·ed /ˈpɪksəleɪtɪd/ *adjective* (also **pix·il·lated**) **1** bewildered; crazy. **2** drunk. [var. of *pixie-led* (as PIXIE, LED)]

pix·il·la·tion /ˌpɪksəˈleɪʃən/ *noun* (also **pix·il·a·tion**) a theatrical and cinematographic technique whereby human characters move or appear to move as if artificially animated. [from PIXILATED]

Pizan see DE PISAN.

Pi·zarro /pɪˈzɑːrəʊ/ **Fran·cis·co** (c.1475–1541), Spanish conquistador. In 1531 he set out from Panama to conquer the Inca Empire in Peru, executing their emperor Atahualpa (1533) and building his own capital at Lima (1535); he was assassinated in Lima by supporters of his rival Diego de Almagro (1475–1538).

piz·za noun a food consisting of a flat round base of dough baked with a topping of tomato sauce and cheese and other garnishes, e.g. meat, vegetables, etc. [Italian, = pie]

pizza face noun slang a person whose face is severely disfigured by acne.

piz·zazz /pɪˈzaz/ noun (also **piz·azz**) informal verve, energy, liveliness, sparkle. [perhaps invented by D. Vreeland, fashion editor in the 1930s of Harper's Bazaar]

piz·zelle /ˌpiːˈtseleɪ/ noun a thin, slightly sweet, waffle-like Italian wafer biscuit. [Italian, as PIZZA + elle plural diminutive ending]

piz·zeria /ˌpiːtsəˈriːə/ noun a place where pizzas are made, sold, or eaten. [Italian (as PIZZA)]

pizzi·cato /ˌpɪtsɪˈkɑːtəʊ, -ˈkatəʊ/ Music ● adverb plucking the strings of a violin etc. with the finger (compare ARCO). ● adjective (of a note, passage, etc.) performed pizzicato. ● noun (pl. **pizzi·catos** or **pizzi·cati** /-tiː/) a note, passage, etc. played pizzicato. [Italian, past participle of pizzicare twitch, from pizzare from pizza edge]

piz·zle noun the penis of an animal, esp. a bull, formerly used as a whip. [Low German pesel, diminutive of Middle Low German pēse, Middle Dutch pēze]

PJs plural noun esp. N Amer. informal PYJAMAS 1. [abbreviation]

pk. abbreviation **1** pack. **2** park. **3** peak.

PK abbreviation N Amer. slang preacher's (or pastor's) kid.

pkg. abbreviation package.

PKU abbreviation PHENYLKETONURIA.

pl. abbreviation **1** plural. **2** place. **3** plate.

plac·ard /ˈplakɑːd, -kəd/ ● noun a printed or handwritten poster used esp. as an advertisement, in protest demonstrations, picket lines, etc. ● transitive verb **1** set up placards on (a wall etc.). **2** advertise by placards. **3** display (a poster etc.) as a placard. [Old French placquart from plaquier to plaster, from Middle Dutch placken]

pla·cate /pləˈkeɪt, ˈpla-, ˈpleɪ-/ transitive verb pacify; conciliate. □ **pla·cat·ing·ly** adverb **pla·ca·tory** /pləˈkeɪtəri/ adjective [Latin placare placat- please, appease]

place ● noun **1 a** a particular portion of space. **b** a portion of space occupied by a person or thing (it has changed its place). **c** a proper or natural position (take your places). **d** situation, circumstances (put yourself in my place). **2** a city, town, village, etc. (was born in this place). **3 a** a residence; a dwelling (has a place in the country; come around to my place). **b** a particular building, room or outdoor site (looking for a place to eat; the kitchen is the sunniest room in the house). **c** (usu. with neg.) a suitable, proper, or safe area (a bus station is no place for a child to be left alone). **4 a** a group of houses in a town etc., esp. a square. **b** a country house with its surroundings. **5** a person's rank or status (know their place; a place in history). **6** role, position or function (the place of computers in modern society). **7** a seat or position, esp. one reserved for or occupied by a person or vehicle (set an extra place at the table). **8** a building or area for a specific purpose (place of worship). **9 a** a point reached in a book etc. (lost my place). **b** a passage in a book. **10** a particular spot or area on a surface, e.g. on the body (a tattoo in an embarrassing place). **11** employment or office (friends in high places). **b** the duties or entitlements of office etc. (is not my place to pass judgment). **12** a position as a member of a team, a student in a college, etc. **13 a** any of the first three or sometimes four positions in a race. **b** N Amer. the second position, esp. in a horse race. **14** the position of a figure in a series indicated in decimal or similar notation (calculated to 50 decimal places). ● verb **1** transitive put (a thing etc.) in a particular place or state; arrange. **2** transitive identify, classify, or remember correctly (cannot place him). **3** transitive assign to a particular place; locate. **4** transitive **a** appoint (a person, esp. a member of the clergy) to a post. **b** find a job, home, etc. for. **c** (usu. foll. by with) consign to a person's care etc. (placed her with her aunt). **5** transitive assign rank, importance, or worth to (I place Rebecca among the best teachers). **6** transitive **a** dispose of (goods) to a customer. **b** make (an order for goods etc.). **7** transitive esp. N Amer. order or obtain a connection for (a telephone call), esp. through an operator. **8** transitive (often foll. by in, on, etc.) have (confidence, trust, etc.). **9** transitive invest (money). **10** transitive Brit. state the position of (any of

the first three or sometimes four runners) in a race. **11** intransitive **a** N Amer. finish second in a horse race. **b** finish among the first three or sometimes four in a race. □ **all over the place** informal **1** everywhere (companies are going bankrupt all over the place). **2** in disorder; chaotic. **give place to 1** make room for. **2** yield precedence to. **3** be succeeded by. **go places** informal be successful. **in place 1** in the right position; suitable. **2** N Amer. not moving; on the spot (running in place). **in place of** in exchange for; instead of. **in places** at some places or in some parts, but not others. **keep a person in his** or **her place** suppress a person's aspirations or pretensions. **out of place 1** in the wrong position. **2** unsuitable. **put oneself in another's place** imagine oneself in another's position. **put a person in his** or **her place** deflate or humiliate a person. **take place** occur. **take one's place** go to one's correct position, be seated, etc. **take the place of** be substituted for; replace. □ **place·less** adjective **place·ment** noun [Old French via Latin platea from Greek plateia (hodos) 'broad (way)']

pla·cebo /pləˈsiːbəʊ/ noun (pl. **-cebos**) **1 a** a pill, medicine, etc. prescribed for psychological reasons but having no physiological effect. **b** a blank sample used as a control in testing new drugs etc. **2** something that is said or done to calm or humour a person but does not address the cause of his or her anxiety. [Latin, = I shall be acceptable or pleasing (first word of Ps. 116:9 in the Vulgate) from placēre 'please']

placebo effect noun a beneficial (or adverse) effect produced by a placebo that cannot be attributed to any property of the placebo itself, and must therefore be due to the patient's belief in that treatment.

place card noun a card inscribed with a person's name, marking his or her designated place at a table etc.

place·hold·er noun **1** Math. a significant zero in the decimal representation of a number. **2** a symbol or piece of text used in a mathematical expression or in an instruction in a computer program to denote a missing quantity or operator.

place in the sun noun a favourable situation, position, etc.

place kick noun Football a kick in which the ball is placed on the ground and held upright by means of a tee or by a teammate. □ **place-kick** intransitive verb **place-kicker** noun

place·man noun (pl. **-men**) Brit. a person appointed to a position chiefly to implement the political policies of a higher authority.

place·mat noun a small mat of cloth, cork, paper, etc. used to protect and keep clean a table or other surface on which dishes and eating utensils are set.

place name noun the name of a city, town, hill, lake, etc.

pla·centa /pləˈsentə/ noun (pl. **pla·cen·tas** or **pla·cen·tae** /-tiː/) **1** a flattened circular organ in the uterus of pregnant eutherian mammals, nourishing and maintaining the fetus through the umbilical cord and expelled after birth. **2** (in flowers) part of the ovary wall carrying the ovules. □ **pla·cen·tal** adjective [Latin from Greek plakous -ountos flat cake, from the root of plax plakos flat plate]

Pla·cen·tia Bay /pləˈsenʃə/ a large inlet of the N Atlantic, extending deeply into the coast of SE Newfoundland, separating the Avalon and Burin peninsulas. In 1941, while aboard warships anchored there, Churchill and Roosevelt signed the Atlantic Charter. [from French plaisance boating, perhaps after Plentzia, a seaport in the Basque region of N Spain, or Plasencia, a city in W Spain]

pla·cer /ˈplasər/ noun a deposit of sand, gravel, etc., in the bed of a stream etc., containing valuable minerals, e.g. gold, in particles (often attributive: placer mining). [Latin American Spanish, related to placel sandbank, from plaza PLACE]

place setting noun a set of plates, cutlery, etc. for one person at a meal.

pla·cid /ˈplasɪd/ adjective **1** (of a person) not easily aroused or disturbed; peaceful. **2** mild; calm; serene. □ **pla·cid·ity** /pləˈsɪdɪti/ noun **pla·cid·ly** adverb **pla·cid·ness** noun [French placide or Latin placidus from placēre please]

pla·cing noun **1** the fact or condition of being placed, esp. of being ranked in a race or of being found a situation. **2** an instance of being placed.

plack·et noun **1** an opening or slit in a garment, for fastenings or access to a pocket. **2** the flap of fabric under this. [var. of PLACARD]

plac·oid /ˈplakɔɪd/ adjective (of a fish scale) consisting of a hard base embedded in the skin and a spiny backward projection (compare CTENOID). [Greek plax plakos flat plate]

pla·gal /ˈpleɪɡəl/ adjective Music (of a church mode) containing sounds between the dominant and its octave (compare AUTHENTIC adjective 3).

[medieval Latin *plagalis* from *plaga* plagal mode, via Latin *plagius* from medieval Greek *plagios* (in classical Greek = oblique) from Greek *plagos* side]

plagal cadence *noun* (also **plagal close**) *Music* a cadence in which the chord of the subdominant immediately precedes that of the tonic.

plage /plaʒ/ *noun Astronomy* an unusually bright region on the sun. [French, = beach]

pla·giar·ism /'pleidʒə,rizəm/ *noun* **1** the act or an instance of plagiarizing. **2** something plagiarized. □ **pla·giar·ist** *noun* **pla·giar·is·tic** *adjective*

pla·giar·ize /'pleidʒə,raiz/ *transitive & intransitive verb* (also esp. *Brit.* **-ise**) **1** take and use (the thoughts, writings, inventions, etc. of another person) as one's own. **2** pass off the thoughts etc. of (another person) as one's own. □ **pla·giar·iz·er** *noun* [Latin *plagiarius* kidnapper, from *plagium* a kidnapping, from Greek *plagion*]

plagio- /'pleidʒiо:/ *combining form* oblique. [Greek *plagios* oblique, from *plagos* side]

pla·gio·clase /'pleidʒiə,kleiz/ *noun* a series of feldspar minerals forming glassy crystals. [PLAGIO- + Greek *klasis* cleavage]

plague /pleig/ ● *noun* **1 a** (prec. by *the*) a contagious bacterial disease characterized by fever and delirium, with the formation of buboes (**bubonic plague**) and sometimes infection of the lungs (**pneumonic plague**). **b** any severe or fatal contagious disease spreading rapidly over a wide area. **2** (foll. by *of*) an unusual infestation of a pest etc. (*a plague of frogs*). **3 a** great trouble. **b** an affliction, esp. as regarded as divine punishment. **4** *informal* a nuisance. **5** (in *interjection*) jocular or archaic a curse etc. (*a plague on it!*). ● *transitive verb* (**plagues**, **plagued**, **plaguing**) **1** afflict, torment (*plagued by war*). **2** *informal* pester or harass continually. [Latin *plaga* 'stroke, wound', prob. from Greek *plaga, plēgē*]

plaice /pleis/ *noun* (*pl.* same) either of two flatfishes having a brown back and a white underside, much used for food, the N Atlantic fish *Hippoglossoides platessoides* (also **Canadian plaice**, **American plaice**) or the European *Pleuronectes platessa*. [Old French *plaïz* from Late Latin *platessa* apparently from Greek *platus* broad]

plaid /plad/ *noun* **1** (often *attributive*) **a** checkered or tartan, esp. woollen, twilled cloth (*a plaid skirt*). **b** a checkered or tartan pattern. **2** a long piece of plaid worn over the shoulder as part of Highland Scottish costume. [Gaelic *plaide*, of unknown origin]

plain[1] ● *adjective* **1** clear; evident (*is plain to see*). **2 a** readily understood; simple (*in plain words*). **b** frank; straightforward (*the plain truth*). **3 a** ordinary; basic (*plain common sense*). **b** downright; utter (*plain stupidity*). **4 a** (of cooking, sewing, decoration, etc.) uncomplicated; not elaborate; unembellished; simple. **b** (of food) without added flavours, toppings, etc. (*plain yogourt*; *plain popcorn*). **c** (of a fabric, item of clothing, etc.) without a decorative pattern. **5** (esp. of a woman or girl) not beautiful or pretty. **6** (of manners, dress, etc.) unsophisticated; homely (*a plain man*). **7** (of a knitting stitch) made by putting the needle through the front of the stitch from left to right. ● *adverb* **1** clearly; unequivocally (*to speak plain, I don't approve*). **2** simply (*that is plain stupid*). ● *noun* **1** a level tract of esp. treeless and flat grassland; prairie. **2** (**the Plains**) the region of western N America originally characterized by such grassland. □ **be plain with** speak bluntly to. □ **plain·ly** *adverb* **plain·ness** *noun* [Old French *plain* (*adj. & n.*) from Latin *planus* (*adj.*), *planum* (*n.*)]

plain[2] *intransitive verb archaic* **1** mourn. **2** complain. **3** make a plaintive sound. [Old French *plaindre* (stem *plaign-*) from Latin *plangere planct-* lament]

plain brown wrapper *noun* an opaque paper cover, esp. one enclosing a pornographic magazine etc.

plain·chant *noun* = PLAINSONG.

plain clothes ● *plural noun* ordinary clothes worn esp. as a disguise by police officers etc. ● *attributive adjective* (**plain·clothes**) not wearing a uniform (*a plainclothes officer*).

plain-Jane ● *adjective* ordinary, simple, unremarkable (*a plain-Jane dress*). ● *noun* (**plain Jane**) a plain or unattractive girl or woman.

plain sailing *noun* an uncomplicated situation or course of action.

plains bison *noun* (also **plains buffalo**) a subspecies of the N American bison, distinguished by a yellow-ochre cape of hair over the shoulders.

Plains Cree *noun* **1** a member of a Cree people who moved west to the Plains in the 18th c. and now live in Manitoba, southern Saskatchewan, and central Alberta. **2** the dialect of Cree spoken by this people.

Plains Indian *noun* a member of any of a number of Aboriginal

peoples inhabiting the Plains of western N America, including the Assiniboine, Blackfoot, Gros Ventres, Peigan, Blood, and Sarcee.

plains·man *noun* (*pl.* **-men**) *hist.* a person who lives on a plain, esp. in N America.

Plains of Abraham /'eibrə,ham/ a plateau beside Quebec City. It was the scene in 1759 of a decisive battle in which the British army under General Wolfe, having scaled the heights above the city under cover of darkness, surprised and defeated the French. The battle led to British control over Canada, but both Wolfe and the French commander Montcalm died of their wounds. [*Abraham* Martin, early pioneer and property owner d.1664]

plain·song *noun* church music, usu. unaccompanied, sung in unison in medieval modes and in free rhythm corresponding to the accentuation of the words (*compare* GREGORIAN CHANT).

plain-spoken *adjective* outspoken; blunt.

plaint /pleint/ *noun* **1** *Law* an accusation; a charge. **2** *literary* or *archaic* a complaint; a lamentation. [Old French *plainte* fem. past participle of *plaindre*, and Old French *plaint* from Latin *planctus* (as PLAIN[2])]

plain text *noun* a text not in cipher or code.

plain·tiff /'pleintif/ *noun Law* a person who brings a case against another into court (*opp.* DEFENDANT). [Old French *plaintif* (*adj.*) (as PLAINTIVE)]

plain·tive /'pleintiv/ *adjective* expressing sorrow; mournful, sad. □ **plain·tive·ly** *adverb* **plain·tive·ness** *noun* [Old French (*-if, -ive*) from *plainte* (as PLAINT)]

plain-vanilla *adjective* **1** ordinary, plain, unexciting. **2** (esp. of a computer, program, or other product) having no interesting or unusual feature; safe, unadventurous. [from the popular perception of vanilla as the most ordinary, bland flavour of ice cream]

plain weave *noun* a weave made with the weft alternately over and under the warp.

plait /pleit/ ● *noun* a length of hair, straw, etc., in three or more interlaced strands; a braid. ● *transitive verb* **1** form (hair etc.) into a plait. **2** make (a belt, mat, etc.) by plaiting. [Old French *pleit* 'a fold', ultimately from Latin *plicare* 'to fold']

Pla·mon·don /plamõˈdõ/ **Luc** (b.1942), Canadian songwriter. He wrote his first song 'Dans ma Camaro' in 1970, and since that time his works have been sung by such singers as Renée Claude, Robert Charlebois, and Julien Clerc. He also composed the rock opera *Starmania* while in Paris in 1976.

plan ● *noun* **1 a** a formulated and esp. detailed method by which a thing is to be done. **b** an intention or proposed proceeding (*my plan was to distract them*). **c** an arrangement for the regular payment of contributions towards a pension, insurance policy, etc. **d** the fund thus established (*Canada Pension Plan*). **e** a scheme for economic development. **2 a** a drawing or diagram made by projection on a horizontal plane, esp. showing a building or one floor of a building (*compare* ELEVATION 4a). **b** (often in *pl.*) a detailed diagram of the parts of a machine, piece of furniture, etc. esp. with instructions for construction (*bought the plans to build a boat*). **3** a large-scale detailed map of part of a town, a group of buildings, etc. **4 a** a table etc. indicating times, places, etc. of intended proceedings. **b** a way of arranging things (*prepared the seating plan*). **5** an imaginary plane perpendicular to the line of vision and containing the objects shown in a picture. ● *verb* (**planned, plan·ning**) **1** *transitive* (often foll. by *that* + clause or *to* + infin.) arrange (a procedure etc.) beforehand; form a plan (*planned to catch the evening ferry*). **2** *transitive* **a** design (a building, urban area, etc.). **b** make a plan of (an existing building, an area, etc.). **3** *intransitive* make plans. □ **go according to plan** proceed as expected or planned. **plan on** *informal* **1** aim at doing; intend. **2** (also **plan for**) anticipate, expect; work under a specified assumption (*I was planning on both of them showing up*; *they planned for a day of rain*). [French from earlier *plant*, from Italian *pianta* plan of building]

pla·nar /'pleinər/ *adjective Math.* of, relating to, or in the form of a plane.

pla·nar·ian /plə'neriən/ *noun* any flatworm of the class Turbellaria, usu. living in fresh water. [modern Latin *Planaria* the genus name, fem. of Latin *planarius* lying flat]

Plan B *noun* a secondary plan or program of action resorted to when the original plan fails.

plan·chet /'planʃət/ *noun* a plain metal disc from which a coin is made. [diminutive of *planch* slab of metal, from Old French *planche*: see PLANK]

plan·chette /plan'ʃet/ *noun* a small usu. heart-shaped board on casters with a pencil that is supposedly caused to write spirit messages when a person's fingers rest lightly on it. [French, diminutive of *planche* PLANK]

Planck /ˈplaŋk/ **Max Karl Ernst Lud·wig** (1858–1947), German theoretical physicist, who founded the quantum theory which is one of the foundations of 20th-c. physics. In 1900 he announced his radiation law, according to which electromagnetic radiation from heated bodies was not emitted as a continuous flow but was made up of discrete units or quanta of energy, the size of which involved a fundamental physical constant (Planck's constant); he was awarded the Nobel Prize for physics in 1918.

Planck's constant *noun* (also **Planck constant**) a fundamental constant, equal to the energy of a quantum of electromagnetic radiation divided by its frequency, with a value of 6.626×10^{-34} joules. [PLANCK]

plane¹ ● *noun* **1 a** a flat surface on which a straight line joining any two points on it would wholly lie. **b** an imaginary flat surface through or joining etc. material objects. **2** a level surface. **3** *informal* = AIRPLANE. **4** a flat surface producing lift by the action of air or water over and under it (usu. in *combination*: *hydroplane*). **5** (often foll. by *of*) a level of attainment, thought, knowledge, etc. **6** a flat thin object such as a tabletop. ● *adjective* **1** (of a surface etc.) perfectly level. **2** of or relating to only two-dimensional surfaces or magnitudes (*plane geometry*). ● *intransitive verb* **1** (often foll. by *down*) travel or glide in an airplane. **2** (of a speedboat etc.) skim over water. **3** soar. [Latin *planum* flat surface, neuter of *planus* PLAIN¹ (differentiated from PLAIN¹ in 17th c.): adj. after French *plan, plane*]

plane² ● *noun* **1** a tool consisting of a wooden or metal block with a projecting steel blade, used to smooth a wooden surface by paring shavings from it. **2** a similar tool for smoothing metal. ● *transitive verb* **1** smooth (wood, metal, etc.) with a plane. **2** (often foll. by *away, down*) pare (irregularities) with a plane. [Old French var. of *plaine* from Late Latin *plana* from Latin *planus* PLAIN¹]

plane³ *noun* (in full **plane tree**) any tree of the genus *Platanus* often growing to great heights, with maple-like leaves and bark which peels in uneven patches. [Old French from Latin *platanus* from Greek *platanos* from *platus* broad]

plane·load *noun* as much or as many as can be carried in an airplane.

plane-polar·iz·a·tion *noun* a process restricting the vibrations of electromagnetic radiation, esp. light, to one direction. □ **plane-polar·ized** *adjective*

plan·er *noun* = PLANE² *noun* 1.

plan·et *noun* **1** a celestial body moving in an elliptical orbit around a star, esp.: **a** (in full **major planet**) any of the nine large rocky or gaseous bodies orbiting the sun: Mercury, Venus, Earth, Mars, Jupiter, Saturn, Uranus, Neptune, and Pluto. **b** (in full **minor planet**) an asteroid. **c** (prec. by *the*) the earth. **2** esp. *Astrology hist.* a celestial body seen from the earth, distinguished from the fixed stars by having an apparent motion of its own (including the moon and sun), esp. with reference to its supposed influence on people and events. □ **plan·et·ol·ogy** *noun* **planet·wide** *adjective* [Late Latin *planeta*, *planetes* from Greek *planētēs* wanderer, planet, from *planaomai* wander]

plan·et·ar·ium /ˌplanəˈteriəm/ *noun* (*pl.* **plan·et·ar·iums** or **plan·et·aria** /-riə/) **1** a domed building in which images of stars, planets, constellations, etc. are projected for public entertainment or education. **2** the device used for such projection. **3** = ORRERY. [modern Latin (as PLANET)]

plan·et·ary /ˈplanəˌteri/ *adjective* **1** of or like planets (*planetary influence*). **2** terrestrial; mundane. **3** wandering; erratic. **4** global, worldwide. **5** *Mech.* of, pertaining to, or involving a gear in which one wheel travels around the outside or the inside of another wheel with which it meshes.

planetary nebula *noun* a ring-shaped nebula formed by an expanding shell of gas around a star.

plan·et·es·imal /ˌplanəˈtesiməl/ *noun* **1** any of a vast number of minute planets or planetary bodies. **2** (*attributive*) designating the hypothesis that planets were formed by the accretion of planetesimals in a cold state. [PLANET, after *infinitesimal*]

plan·et·oid /ˈplanəˌtɔid/ *noun* = ASTEROID 1.

plane tree *noun* see PLANE³.

plan·form *noun* the shape or outline of something, esp. an airplane, as projected upon a horizontal plane.

plan·gent /ˈplandʒənt/ *adjective* **1** (of a sound) loud and reverberating. **2** (of a sound) plaintive; sad. □ **plan·gen·cy** *noun* **plan·gent·ly** *adverb* [Latin *plangere plangent-* lament]

plan·im·eter /pləˈnimitər/ *noun* an instrument for mechanically

measuring the area of a plane figure. □ **plani·met·ric** /-ˈmetrik/ *adjective* **plani·met·ric·al** /-ˈmetrikəl/ *adjective* **plani·met·ric·al·ly** /-ˈmetrikli/ *adverb* **plan·im·etry** *noun* [French *planimètre* from Latin *planus* level]

plan·ish /ˈplaniʃ/ *transitive verb* flatten (metal) with a smooth-faced hammer or between rollers. □ **plan·ish·er** *noun* [Old French *planir* smooth from *plain* PLANE¹ *adjective*]

plani·sphere /ˈplaniˌsfir/ *noun* a map formed by the projection of a sphere or part of a sphere on a plane, esp. to show the appearance of the heavens at a specific time or place. □ **plani·spher·ic** /-ˈsferik/ *adjective* [medieval Latin *planisphaerium* (as PLANE¹, SPHERE): influenced by French *planisphère*]

plank ● *noun* **1** a long flat piece of timber used esp. in building, flooring, etc. **2** a single item of a political or other program (*compare* PLATFORM 6). ● *verb* **1** *transitive* provide, cover, or floor, with planks. **2** *transitive & intransitive* (usu. foll. by *down*) esp. *N Amer. informal* **a** put (a thing, person, etc.) down roughly or violently. **b** pay (money) on the spot or abruptly (*planked down $20*). □ **walk the plank** *hist.* (of a pirate's captive etc.) be made to walk blindfold along a plank over the side of a ship to one's death in the sea. □ **planked** *adjective* [Old Northern French *planke*, Old French *planche* from Late Latin *planca* board, from *plancus* flat-footed]

plank house *noun* a large rectangular dwelling framed with timbers and covered with vertical or horizontal cedar or spruce planks, used esp. by the Aboriginal peoples of the Pacific coast of N America.

plank·ing *noun* planks as flooring etc.

plank road *noun* Cdn a road of planks laid across logs running end to end over rough ground.

plank·ti·vor·ous /ˌplaŋkˈtivərəs/ *adjective* eating plankton.

plank·ton *noun* the chiefly microscopic organisms drifting or floating in the sea or fresh water (*see* BENTHOS, NEKTON). □ **plank·ton·ic** /plaŋkˈtɒnik/ *adjective* [German from Greek *plagktos* wandering, from *plazomai* wander]

planned *adjective* in accordance with a plan (*his planned arrival; planned parenthood*).

planned economy *noun* an economy in which production, prices, incomes, etc. are determined centrally by government.

planned giving *noun* the process of arranging donations to be made to a charity from one's assets, usually to be realized by the charity on the donor's death, often with tax benefits to the donor's estate.

planned obsolescence *noun* the systematic policy of producing consumer goods that will become obsolete relatively quickly, thus ensuring the maintenance of consumption levels.

plan·ner *noun* **1** = URBAN PLANNER. **2** a person who makes plans. **3** a list, table, organizer, etc., with information helpful in planning.

plan·ning *noun* **1** in senses of PLAN *verb*. **2** the coordinating of land use and development.

planning permission *noun* Brit. formal permission for building development etc., esp. from a local authority.

plano- /ˈpleinɒ/ *combining form* level, flat. [Latin *planus* flat]

plano·concave /ˌpleinɒˈkɒnkeiv, -ˈkeiv/ *adjective* (of a lens etc.) with one surface plane and the other concave.

plano·convex /ˌpleinɒˈkɒnveks, -ˈveks/ *adjective* (of a lens etc.) with one surface plane and the other convex.

plant ● *noun* **1 a** any living organism of the kingdom Plantae, usu. containing chlorophyll enabling it to live wholly on inorganic substances and lacking specialized sense organs and the power of voluntary movement. **b** a small organism of this kind, as distinguished from a shrub or tree. **2 a** machinery, fixtures, etc., used in industrial processes. **b** a factory. **c** (also **physical plant**) the premises, fittings, and equipment of a business or institution. **3** *informal* **a** something, esp. incriminating or compromising, positioned or concealed so as to be discovered later. **b** a person stationed as a spy or source of information. ● *transitive verb* **1** place (a seed, bulb, or growing thing) in the ground so that it may take root and flourish. **2** (often foll. by *in, on,* etc.) **a** put or fix in position. **b** *reflexive* take up a position (*planted myself by the door*). **c** place (a bomb) in a building etc. **3** deposit (young fish, spawn, oysters, etc.) in a river or lake. **4** station (a person etc.), esp. as a spy or source of information. **5** cause (an idea etc.) to be established, esp. in another person's mind. **6** deliver (a blow, kiss, etc.) with a deliberate aim. **7** *informal* position or conceal (something incriminating or compromising) for later discovery. **8 a** settle or people (a colony etc.). **b** found or establish (a city, community, etc.). **9** bury. □ **plant out** transfer (a plant) from a pot or frame to the open ground; set out (seedlings) at intervals. □ **plant·able** *adjective* **plant·like** *adjective* [Old

English *plante* from Latin *planta* 'sprout, slip, cutting', later influenced by French *plante*]

Plan·ta·genet /plan'tadʒənət/ the English royal house which held the throne from the accession of Henry II (1154) to the deposition of Richard II (1399). In the 15th c. the line divided into two branches, the House of Lancaster and the House of York (*see* WARS OF THE ROSES).

plan·tain¹ /plan'tein, 'plan-/ *noun* any plant of the genus *Plantago*, with a rosette of leaves and seeds used as food for birds and as a mild laxative. [Old French from Latin *plantago -ginis* from *planta* sole of the foot (from its broad prostrate leaves)]

plan·tain² /plan'tein, 'plan-/ *noun* **1** a banana plant, *Musa paradisiaca*, widely grown for its fruit. **2** the starchy fruit of this containing less sugar than a standard banana and chiefly used in cooking. [earlier *platan* from Spanish *plá(n)tano* plane tree, prob. assimilated from Galibi *palatana* etc.]

plantain lily *noun* = HOSTA.

plan·tar /'plantər/ *adjective* of or relating to the sole of the foot. [Latin *plantaris* from *planta* sole]

plan·ta·tion *noun* **1** a large farm, esp. in tropical or subtropical areas, on which cotton, tobacco, sugar, etc. is cultivated, usu. by resident farm workers. **2** an area planted with trees etc., esp. as part of a reforestation program. **3** *hist.* a colony; colonization.

Plante, Jacques (1929–86), Canadian hockey player. As a goalie with the Montreal Canadiens he won five consecutive Vezina Trophies (1956–60); he won the Vezina again in 1962 (the year he also won the Hart Trophy as the league's most valuable player) and 1969. Plante was the first NHL goalie to wear a face mask regularly.

plant·er *noun* **1** a large container for growing plants, usu. outdoors. **2** the owner or manager of a coffee, cotton, tobacco, etc. plantation. **3** a person employed to plant seedlings in reforestation programs. **4** a machine for planting seeds etc. **5** *hist.* a settler in or founder of a colony; a colonist. **6** a person who cultivates the soil. **7** the founder or popularizer of a church, religion, etc.

planter's punch *noun* a cocktail consisting of rum and lime or lemon juice with water and sugar.

plant food *noun* **1** food of vegetable origin consumed by humans or animals. **2** fertilizer for plants.

planti·grade /'planti,greid/ ● *adjective* (of an animal) walking on the soles of its feet. ● *noun* a plantigrade animal, e.g. humans or bears (*compare* DIGITIGRADE). [French from modern Latin *plantigradus* from Latin *planta* sole + *-gradus* -walking]

plant·ing *noun* **1** *in senses of* PLANT *verb*. **2** an arrangement of plants in a garden or other setting.

plant·let *noun* an undeveloped or diminutive plant.

plant louse *noun* a small insect that infests plants, esp. an aphid.

plant·scape *noun* a designed arrangement of usu. indoor plants.

plants·man *noun* (*pl.* **-men**) an expert in garden plants and gardening.

plaque /plak/ *noun* **1** an ornamental usu. metal tablet, esp. affixed to a building in commemoration. **2** a sticky deposit on teeth where bacteria proliferate. **3** *Med.* **a** a patch or eruption of skin etc. as a result of damage. **b** a fibrous lesion in atherosclerosis. **4** a small badge of rank in an honorary order. [French from Dutch *plak* tablet, from *plakken* stick]

plash¹ ● *verb intransitive* (esp. of water hitting water) splash. ● *noun* **1** a plashing sound. **2 a** a marshy pool. **b** a puddle. □ **plash·ing** *adjective* **plashy** *adjective* [Old English *plæsc*, prob. imitative]

plash² *transitive verb* **1** bend down and interweave (branches, twigs, etc.) to form a hedge. **2** make or renew (a hedge) in this way. [Old French *pla(i)ssier*, ultimately from Latin *plectere* braid: compare PLEACH]

plas·ma /'plazmə/ *noun* **1 a** the colourless fluid part of blood, lymph, or milk, in which corpuscles or fat globules are suspended. **b** this taken from donated blood for administering in transfusions. **2** = PROTOPLASM. **3** a gas of positive ions and free electrons with an approximately equal positive and negative charge. **4** a green variety of quartz used in mosaic and for other decorative purposes. **5** (*attributive*) **a** designating a flat panel display screen which uses an array of cells containing an ionized inert gas such as neon (*plasma screen*). **b** the technology involved in this. **c** an item of video equipment, esp. a television, incorporating such a screen. □ **plas·mat·ic** /-'matɪk/ *adjective* **plas·mic** *adjective* [Late Latin, = mould, from Greek *plasma -atos* from *plassō* 'to shape']

plasma membrane *noun* a membrane which forms the external boundary of the cytoplasm of a cell or encloses a vacuole and regulates the passage of molecules in and out of the cytoplasm.

plas·mid /'plazmɪd/ *noun* *Biol.* a genetic structure in a cell that can replicate independently of the chromosomes, esp. a circular DNA strand in a bacterium or protozoan. [PLASMA + -ID²]

plas·min /'plazmɪn/ *noun* a proteolytic enzyme which destroys blood clots by attacking fibrin.

plas·mino·gen /plas'mɪnədʒən/ *noun* the inactive precursor, present in blood, of the enzyme plasmin.

plasmo·desma /ˌplazmə'dezmə/ *noun* (*pl.* **plasmo·desm·ata** /-mətə/) a narrow thread of cytoplasm that passes through cell walls and allows communication between plant cells. [PLASMA + Greek *desma* bond, fetter]

plas·mo·dium /plaz'moːdiəm/ *noun* (*pl.* **plas·mo·dia** /-diə/) **1** any parasitic protozoan of the genus *Plasmodium*, including those causing malaria in humans. **2** a form within the life cycle of various micro-organisms including slime moulds, usu. consisting of a mass of naked protoplasm containing many nuclei. □ **plas·mo·dial** *adjective* [modern Latin from PLASMA + -*odium*: see -ODE¹]

plas·moly·sis /plaz'mɒlɪsɪs/ *noun* contraction of the protoplast of a plant cell as a result of loss of water from the cell. [modern Latin (as PLASMA, -LYSIS)]

Plas·sey /'plasi/ a village in NE India, in West Bengal, northwest of Calcutta. In 1757, a small British army defeated the much larger forces of the nawab of Bengal there, a victory won partly because some of the Indian generals had been bribed. The victory established British supremacy in Bengal.

plas·ter ● *noun* **1** a soft pliable mixture esp. of lime or gypsum with sand and water for spreading on walls, ceilings, etc., to form a smooth hard surface when dried. **2** = PLASTER OF PARIS. **3** a curative or protective substance spread on a bandage etc. and applied to the body (*mustard plaster*). **4** *Brit.* an adhesive bandage. ● *transitive verb* **1** cover (a wall etc.) with plaster or a similar substance. **2** (often foll. by *with*) coat or cover thickly or to excess (*plastered the bread with jam; the wall was plastered with slogans*). **3 a** stick or apply (a thing) thickly like plaster (*plastered glue all over it*). **b** apply (pictures etc.) so as to cover (a wall etc.) (*pictures of him are plastered all over her office*). **c** cause to appear ubiquitously (*the scandal was plastered all over the newspapers*). **4** (often foll. by *down*) make (esp. hair) smooth with water, cream, etc.; fix flat. **5** apply a medical plaster or plaster cast to. **6** *slang* bomb or shell heavily. □ **plas·ter·er** *noun* **plas·tery** *adjective* [Old English via medieval Latin *plastrum* and Latin *emplastrum* from Greek *emplastron*, later reinforced by Old French *plastre* and French *plastrer*]

plaster·board *noun* two boards with a filling of plaster used to form or line the inner walls of houses etc.

plaster cast *noun* **1** a bandage stiffened with plaster of Paris and applied to a broken limb etc. **2** a statue or mould made of plaster.

plas·tered *adjective* *slang* drunk.

plaster of Paris *noun* fine white plaster made of gypsum and used for making plaster casts etc.

plaster saint *noun* *ironic* a person regarded as being without moral faults or human frailty.

plaster·work *noun* work done in plaster, esp. the plaster-covered surface of a wall or decorative plaster surfaces.

plas·tic ● *noun* **1** any of a number of synthetic polymeric substances that can be given any required shape. **2** *informal* = PLASTIC MONEY. **3** = PLASTIC WRAP. ● *adjective* **1 a** made of plastic (*plastic bag*). **b** artificial, insincere. **2** capable of being moulded; pliant; supple. **3** moulding or giving form to clay, wax, etc. **4** *Biol.* exhibiting an adaptability to environmental changes. **5** (esp. in philosophy) formative, creative. □ **plas·tic·ally** *adverb* **plas·ti·city** /plas'tɪsɪti/ *noun* **plas·ticky** *adjective* [French *plastique* or Latin *plasticus* from Greek *plastikos*, from *plassō* 'mould']

plastic arts *plural noun* art forms involving modelling or moulding, e.g. sculpture and ceramics, or art involving the representation of solid objects with three-dimensional effects.

plastic bullet *noun* a usu. non-lethal bullet made of PVC or another plastic material, used by security and police forces esp. for riot control.

plastic explosive *noun* a putty-like explosive capable of being moulded by hand.

Plas·ti·cine /'plasti,siːn/ *noun* *proprietary* a soft plastic material used, esp. by children, for modelling. [PLASTIC + -INE⁴]

plas·ti·cize *transitive verb* (also esp. *Brit.* **-cise**) **1** make plastic or mouldable, esp. by the addition of a plasticizer. **2** treat, coat, or make with plastic. □ **plas·ti·cized** *adjective*

plas·ti·ciz·er *noun* a substance (typically a solvent) added to a synthetic resin to produce or promote plasticity and flexibility and reduce brittleness.

plastic money *noun informal* credit cards or other types of plastic card that can be used instead of money.

plastic surgery *noun* the process of reconstructing or repairing parts of the body by the transfer of tissue, either in the treatment of injury or for cosmetic reasons. □ **plastic surgeon** *noun*

plastic wrap *noun N Amer.* a very thin clinging transparent plastic film, used as a covering esp. for food.

plas·tid /ˈplastɪd/ *noun* any small organelle in the cytoplasm of a plant cell, containing pigment or food. [German from Greek *plastos* shaped]

plas·tique /ˌplasˈtiːk/ *noun* **1** plastic explosive. **2** statuesque poses or slow graceful movements in dancing. [French, literally 'plastic']

plas·tron /ˈplastrən/ *noun* **1 a** a fencer's leather-covered breastplate. **b** a lancer's breast covering of facings material. **2 a** an ornamental front on a woman's bodice. **b** a man's starched shirt front. **3 a** the ventral part of the shell of a tortoise or turtle. **b** the corresponding part in other animals. **4** *hist.* a steel breastplate. □ **plas·tral** *adjective* [French from Italian *piastrone* augmentative of *piastra* breastplate, from Latin *emplastrum* PLASTER]

-plasty /plasti/ *combining form* forming nouns meaning the moulding, grafting, or formation of esp. a part of the body (*angioplasty*; *rhinoplasty*).

plat¹ *noun* **1** a plot of land. **2** a plan of an area of land. [16th c.: collateral form of PLOT]

plat² ● *noun* = PLAIT *noun*. ● *transitive verb* (**plat·ted**, **plat·ting**) = PLAIT *verb*.

Pla·taea, Battle of /pləˈtiːə/ a battle in 479 BC, during the Persian Wars, in which the Persian forces were defeated by the Greeks near the city of Plataea in Boeotia, central Greece.

plat du jour /ˌpla duː ˈʒur/ *noun* a dish specially featured on a day's menu. [French, = dish of the day]

plate ● *noun* **1 a** a shallow vessel, usu. circular and of earthenware or china, from which food is eaten or served. **b** the contents of this (*ate a plate of spaghetti*). **2** a similar vessel usu. of metal or wood, used esp. for taking a collection in a church etc. **3** *N Amer.* a main course of a meal, served on one plate. **4** one person's meal at a banquet etc. (*$100 per plate*). **5** (*collective*) **a** utensils of silver, gold, or other metal. **b** objects of plated metal. **6 a** a piece of metal with a name or inscription for affixing to a door, container, etc. **b** = LICENCE PLATE. **7** an illustration on special paper in a book. **8** a thin sheet of metal, glass, etc., coated with a sensitive film for photography. **9** a flat thin usu. rigid sheet of metal etc. with an even surface and uniform thickness, often as part of a mechanism or protective armour. **10 a** a smooth piece of metal etc. for engraving. **b** an impression made from this. **11 a** a silver or gold cup as a prize for a horse race etc. **b** a race with this as a prize. **12 a** a thin piece of plastic material, moulded to the shape of the mouth and gums, to which artificial teeth are attached. **b** *informal* a complete denture. **13** *Geol.* each of several rigid sheets of rock thought to form the earth's outer crust. **14** *Biol.* a thin flat organic structure or formation. **15** a light shoe for a racehorse. **16** a stereotype, electrotype, or plastic cast of a page of composed movable types, or a metal or plastic copy of filmset matter, from which sheets are printed. **17** *Baseball* a flat piece of white rubber marking the station of a batter or pitcher. **18** *N Amer.* the anode of a thermionic valve. **19** a horizontal timber laid along the top of a wall to support the ends of joists or rafters. **20** = PLATE ARMOUR. ● *transitive verb* **1** apply a thin coat esp. of silver, gold, or tin to (another metal). **2** cover (esp. a ship) with plates of metal, esp. for protection. **3** make a plate of (type etc.) for printing. □ **on a plate** = ON A PLATTER (see PLATTER). **on one's plate** for one to deal with or consider. □ **plate·ful** *noun* (*pl.* **-fuls**). **plate·less** *adjective* **plat·er** *noun* [medieval Latin *plata* 'plate armour', from *platus* (*adj.*), ultimately from Greek *platus* 'flat']

plate armour *noun* armour of metal plates, for a man, ship, etc.

pla·teau /plaˈtoː/ ● *noun* (*pl.* **pla·teaus** or **pla·teaux** /-toːz/) **1** an area of fairly level high ground. **2** a state of little variation after an increase. ● *intransitive verb* (**pla·teaus**, **pla·teaued**) (often foll. by *out*) reach a level or stable state after an increase. [French from Old French *platel* diminutive of *plat* flat surface]

plate glass *noun* fine-quality glass for windows etc., originally cast in plates.

plate·let /ˈpleɪtlət/ *noun* a small colourless disc-shaped cell fragment without a nucleus, found in large numbers in blood and involved in clotting. Also called THROMBOCYTE.

plat·en /ˈplatən/ *noun* **1** a plate in a printing press which presses the paper against the type. **2** a cylindrical roller in a typewriter against which the paper is held. [Old French *platine* a flat piece, from *plat* flat]

plate rail *noun* a narrow shelf affixed to a wall, usu. around all walls of a room, for displaying plates.

Plate River /pleɪt/ a wide estuary on the Atlantic coast of S America at the border between Argentina and Uruguay, formed by the confluence of the Paraná and Uruguay rivers. The cities of Buenos Aires and Montevideo lie on its shores.

plate tectonics *plural noun* (usu. treated as *sing.*) a theory of the earth's surface based on the interaction of rigid lithospheric plates which move slowly on the underlying mantle.

plat·form *noun* **1** a raised level surface; a natural or artificial terrace. **2 a** a raised surface from which a speaker addresses an audience. **b** an opportunity to express one's opinions; a forum. **3 a** a raised elongated structure along the side of a track in a railway or subway station. **b** *N Amer.* a slightly raised area of concrete etc. used by passengers for boarding and alighting from a bus at a bus station. **4** the floor area at the entrance to a train. **5 a** a thick sole of a shoe (often *attributive*: *platform shoes*). **b** (usu. in *pl.*) a platform shoe, boot, etc. **6** the declared policy or policies of a political party etc. **7** a computer system whose hardware and software make it sufficiently different from all other computer systems for it to require unique software versions. **8** a rigid diving board, esp. one at any of several fixed heights above the water used in diving competitions. **9** (also **drilling platform**) a structure designed to stand on the bed of the sea (or a lake) to provide a stable base above water level from which several oil or gas wells can be drilled or regulated. [French *plateforme* ground plan, from *plate* flat + *forme* FORM]

platform rocker *noun N Amer.* a rocking chair constructed with a fixed stationary base.

Plath /plaθ/ **Syl·via** (1932–63), US poet. Her work is notable for its controlled and intense treatment of alienation, and includes the verse collections *The Colossus* (1960) and *Ariel* (1965), and the novel *The Bell Jar* (1963); she married the poet Ted Hughes in 1956, and committed suicide in 1963.

plat·ing *noun* **1** a coating of gold, silver, etc. **2** armour consisting of metal plates.

plat·in·ize /ˈplatɪˌnaɪz/ *transitive verb* (also esp. *Brit.* **-ise**) coat with platinum. □ **plat·in·iz·a·tion** *noun*

plat·in·oid /ˈplatɪˌnɔɪd/ *noun* an alloy of copper, zinc, nickel, and tungsten.

plat·in·um /ˈplatɪnəm/ ● *noun* **1** *Chem.* a ductile malleable silvery-white metallic element occurring naturally in nickel and copper ores, unaffected by simple acids and fusible only at a very high temperature, used in making jewellery and laboratory apparatus. Symbol: **Pt**; at. no.: 78. **2** a greyish-white or silvery colour like that of platinum. ● *adjective* **1** (of an album or other recording) having attained the highest recognition for sales exceeding a specified high figure (which varies from country to country). **2** platinum-coloured. **3** designating a group of similar metallic elements of the transition series often associated in ores, comprising platinum, iridium, palladium, osmium, rhodium, and ruthenium. [modern Latin from earlier *platina* from Spanish, diminutive of *plata* silver]

platinum blond ● *adjective* silvery-blond. ● *noun* a person with silvery-blond hair.

platinum card *noun* a credit card with a very high or no credit limit, usu. with other benefits such as purchase insurance etc.

plati·tude /ˈplatɪtjuːd, -tʃuːd/ *noun* **1** a trite or commonplace remark, esp. one solemnly delivered. **2** the use of platitudes; dullness, insipidity. □ **plati·tud·in·ize** *intransitive verb* (also esp. *Brit.* **-ise**). **plati·tud·in·ous** *adjective* [French from *plat* flat, after *certitude*, *multitudinous*, etc.]

Plato /ˈpleɪtoː/ (*c.*429–*c.*347 BC), Greek philosopher, a disciple of Socrates and the teacher of Aristotle, whose system of thought had a profound influence on Christian theology and Western philosophy; his theory of 'ideas' or 'forms', in which abstract entities or *universals* are contrasted with their objects or *particulars* in the material world, is explored in works such as the *Symposium*, the *Phaedo*, and the *Republic*.

Pla·ton·ic /pləˈtɒnɪk/ *adjective* **1** of or associated with Plato or his ideas. **2** (**platonic**) (of love or friendship) not involving sexual relations. **3** constituting or pertaining to ideal, transcendent or eternal realities. □ **Pla·ton·ic·ally** *adverb* [Latin *Platonicus* from Greek *Platōnikos* from *Platōn* Plato]

Platonic solid *noun* (also **Platonic body**) any of the five regular solids (tetrahedron, cube, octahedron, dodecahedron, icosahedron).

Pla·ton·ism /ˈpleɪtəˌnɪzəm/ *noun* the philosophy of Plato or his followers. □ **Pla·ton·ist** *noun*

pla·toon ● *noun* **1** *Military* a subdivision of a company, a tactical unit commanded by a lieutenant and usu. divided into three sections of ten to twelve soldiers. **2** a group of persons acting together. **3** *N Amer. Sport* a pair or group of players on a team who alternate at the same position. **4** *Football* a group of offensive or defensive players sent on or off the field as a unit. ● *verb N Amer. Sport* **1** *transitive & intransitive* alternate (a player) with another at the same position on a team. **2** *intransitive* (of a player) interchange with another player at one position on a team. [French *peloton* small ball, diminutive of *pelote*: see PELLET, -OON]

Platt·deutsch /ˈplatdɔitʃ/ *noun* modern Low German. [German from Dutch *Platduitsch*, from *plat* low, flat + *Duitsch* German]

plat·ter *noun* **1** a large usu. oval dish or plate for presenting or serving food. **b** a serving of food on such a plate, usu. consisting of several different items (*vegetable platter*). **2** *slang* a phonograph record. **3** the rotating metal disc of a record player turntable. **4** *Computing* a rigid disk used to store data magnetically. □ **on a platter** *informal* available with little trouble to the recipient. [Middle English & Anglo-French *plater* from Anglo-French *plat* PLATE]

Platts·burgh /ˈplatsbərg/ a city in NE New York State, on the western shore of Lake Champlain, the site in 1814 of a naval battle in which a British fleet engaged an American flotilla. The combat resulted in the destruction of the British ships, giving the US undisputed control of the lake. The invading British army on land, lacking naval support, was defeated and forced to retreat.

platy- /ˈplati/ *combining form* broad, flat. [Greek *platu-* from *platus* broad, flat]

platy·hel·minth /ˌplatiˈhelminθ/ *noun* any invertebrate of the phylum Platyhelminthes, including flatworms, flukes, and tapeworms.

platy·pus /ˈplatipəs, -pʊs/ *noun* (*pl.* **-es**) an Australian aquatic egg-laying mammal, *Ornithorhynchus anatinus*, having a pliable duck-like bill, webbed feet, and sleek grey fur. *Also called* DUCKBILL.

platyr·rhine /ˈplatiˌrain/ ● *adjective* (of primates) having nostrils far apart and directed forwards or sideways (*compare* CATARRHINE). ● *noun* such an animal. [PLATY- + Greek *rhis rhin-* nose]

plau·dit /ˈplɔdit/ *noun* (usu. in *pl.*) **1** an emphatic expression of approval. **2** a round of applause. [shortened from Latin *plaudite* applaud, imperative pl. of *plaudere plaus-* applaud, said by Roman actors at the end of a play]

plaus·ible /ˈplɔzibəl/ *adjective* **1** (of an argument, statement, etc.) seeming reasonable, believable, or probable. **2** (of a person) persuasive. □ **plaus·ibil·ity** /-ˈbɪlɪti/ *noun* **plaus·ibly** *adverb* [Latin *plausibilis* (as PLAUDIT)]

Plau·tus /ˈplɔtəs/ **Titus Mac·cius** (*c.*250–184 BC), Roman comic dramatist. His plays, of which 21 survive, are loosely modelled on the New Comedy of Greek dramatists such as Menander, and include *Amphitryon*, *The Pot of Gold*, and *The Rope*.

play ● *verb* **1** *intransitive* (often foll. by *with*) occupy or amuse oneself pleasantly with some recreation, game, exercise, etc. **2** *intransitive* (foll. by *with*) act lightheartedly or flippantly (with feelings etc.). **3 a** *transitive* perform on or be able to perform on (a musical instrument). **b** *transitive* perform (a piece of music etc.). **c** *transitive* cause (a record, cassette player, etc.) to produce sounds, video images, etc. **d** *intransitive* (of a compact disc, cassette player, etc.) produce sounds or video images. **4 a** *intransitive* (foll. by *in*) perform a role in (a drama etc.). **b** *transitive* perform (a drama or role) on stage, or in a film or broadcast. **c** *transitive* give a dramatic performance at (a particular theatre or place). **d** *intransitive* be performed or shown in a theatre etc. (*what's playing?*). **e** *intransitive* (of a theatrical performance, a concept, political action, etc) receive acceptance by an audience, the general public, etc. (*will it play in the suburbs?; Macdonald didn't want Riel arrested because that would have played badly in Quebec*). **5** *transitive* act in real life the part of (*play the fool*). **6** *transitive* (foll. by *on*) perform (a trick or joke etc.) on (a person). **7** *transitive* (foll. by *for*) regard (a person) as (something specified) (*played me for a fool*). **8** *intransitive informal* participate, co-operate; do what is wanted (*they won't play*). **9** *transitive* gamble. **10** *transitive* gamble on. **11 a** *transitive & intransitive* take part in (a game or recreation). **b** *transitive* compete with (another player or team) in a game. **c** *transitive* occupy (a specified position) in a team for a game. **d** *transitive* (foll. by *in, on, at,* etc.) assign (a player) to a position. **12** *transitive* move (a piece) or display (a playing card) in one's turn in a game. **13** *transitive* strike (a ball etc.) or execute (a stroke) in a game. **14** *intransitive* move about in a lively or unrestrained manner. **15** *intransitive* (often foll. by *on*) **a** touch gently. **b** emit light, water, etc. (*fountains gently playing*). **16** *transitive* allow (a fish) to exhaust itself pulling against a line. **17** *intransitive* (often foll. by *at*) **a** engage in a half-hearted way (in an activity). **b** pretend to be. **18 a** *intransitive* act or behave (as specified) (*play fair*). **b** *transitive* engage in (an activity) (*play footsie*). **19** *transitive* play a concert, game, etc. at (a concert hall, stadium, etc.). ● *noun* **1** recreation, amusement, esp. as the spontaneous activity of children and young animals. **2 a** the playing of a game. **b** the action or manner of this. **c** the status of the ball etc. in a game as being available to be played according to the rules (*in play; out of play*). **d** an action or manoeuvre, esp. in or as in a game (*what a play!; practised a new play*). **3** a dramatic piece for the stage, radio, etc. **4 a** activity or operation (*brought into play*). **b** behaviour, activity (*foul play*). **5 a** freedom of movement. **b** space or scope for this. **6** brisk, light, or fitful movement. **7** gambling. **8** the button on a VCR, compact disc player, etc., which causes it to play when pushed. □ **at play** engaged in recreation. **in play** for amusement; not seriously. **make a play for** *informal* make a conspicuous attempt to acquire. **make play with** use ostentatiously. **play along 1** co-operate, comply. **2** pretend to agree or co-operate. **play around 1** behave playfully or irresponsibly. **2** (often foll. by *with*) have casual or extramarital sexual relations. **play back** play (sounds or video images recently recorded), esp. to monitor recording quality etc. **play ball** see BALL[1]. **play both ends against the middle** keep one's options open by trying to keep favour with opposing sides. **play by ear 1** perform (music) without having seen a score of it. **2** (also **play it by ear**) proceed instinctively or step by step according to results and circumstances. **play one's cards close to one's chest** see CHEST. **play one's cards right** (or **well**) make good use of opportunities; act shrewdly. **play down** minimize the importance of. **play ducks and drakes with** see DUCKS AND DRAKES. **play fast and loose** act unreliably; ignore one's obligations. **play favourites** show favouritism. **play the field** see FIELD. **play for time** seek to gain time by delaying. **play the game** see GAME[1]. **play God** see GOD. **play havoc with** see HAVOC. **play hell with** see HELL. **play hooky** see HOOKY[1]. **play host** to act as host to. **play a** (or **one's**) **hunch** make an instinctive choice. **play into a person's hands** act so as unwittingly to give a person an advantage. **play it cool** *informal* **1** affect indifference. **2** be relaxed or unemotional. **play the man** *Sport* focus one's attention on the opposing player, not the puck, stick, ball, etc. **play the market** speculate in stocks etc. **play off** (usu. foll. by *against*) **1** oppose (one person against another), esp. for one's own advantage. **2** play an extra match to decide a draw or tie. **play on 1** continue to play. **2** take advantage of (a person's feelings etc.). **play oneself in** *Brit.* become accustomed to the prevailing conditions in a game etc. **play out 1 a** exhaust, use up. **b** tire. **2** finish, bring or come to an end or resolution. **3** perform to the end. **play it safe** avoid risks. **play to the gallery** see GALLERY. **play up 1** emphasize, make the most of. **2** *Brit.* **a** behave mischievously. **b** cause trouble; be irritating (*my rheumatism is playing up again*). **c** obstruct or annoy in this way (*played the teacher up*). **3** *Brit.* put all one's energy into a game. **play up to 1** flatter, esp. to win favour. **2** perform as expected considering (one's capability, reputation, etc). **play with 1** consider (an idea etc.), but not seriously. **2** touch or fondle idly (*played with her scarf*). **play with fire** take foolish risks. **not playing with a full deck** see FULL DECK. **play with oneself** masturbate. **what is X playing at?** what is X really doing? what are X's real intentions or motives? □ **play·able** *adjective* **play·abil·ity** *noun* [Old English *plega* (n.), *pleg(i)an* (v.), originally = (to) exercise]

playa /ˈplajə/ *noun* a flat area of silt or sand at the bottom of a desert basin, dry except after rain. [Spanish, = beach, from Late Latin *plagia*]

play-act *verb* **1** *intransitive* act in a play. **2** *intransitive* behave affectedly or insincerely. **3** *transitive* act (a scene, part, etc.). □ **play-acting** *noun* **play-actor** *noun*

play-action *noun Football* an offensive play in which the quarterback fakes a hand-off to deceive the defence and then passes the ball forward (also *attributive*: *a play-action pass*).

play·back *noun* a playing back of an audio or video recording.

play·bill *noun* **1** a poster announcing a theatrical performance. **2** a slate of theatrical productions to be performed in a season etc. **3** a theatre program.

play·boat·ing *noun* a sport involving the performance of various tricks and stunts with a kayak in a stretch of whitewater.

play·book *noun N Amer.* **1** *Sport* (esp. *Football*) a book containing descriptions of a team's strategies and plays. **2** a set of strategies employed by a company, political party, etc.

play·boy *noun* **1** a sexually promiscuous man. **2** an irresponsible pleasure-seeking man, esp. a wealthy one.

play-by-play *noun N Amer.* the verbal description of a sports match etc. as it unfolds, esp. as part of a broadcast (*couldn't hear the play-by-play; also attributive: play-by-play announcer*).

play·dough *noun* a soft, malleable, coloured dough-like substance used esp. by children for modelling.

play·down *noun* (usu. in *pl.*) esp. *Cdn* & *Scot. Sport* a playoff match in a tournament etc.

Play·er, **Gary (Jim)** (b.1936), South African golfer, winner of numerous championships including the British Open (1959; 1968; 1974), the Masters (1961; 1974; 1978), the PGA (1962; 1972), and the US Open (1965).

play·er *noun* **1** a person taking part in a sport or game. **2** a person playing a musical instrument. **3** a person who plays a part on the stage; an actor. **4** a machine that plays audio or video recordings. **5** a person, company, thing, etc. playing an important or active role in an industry, activity, etc. [Old English *plegere* (as PLAY)]

player piano *noun* a piano fitted with an apparatus enabling it to play automatically.

Play·fair, **John** (1748–1819), Scottish mathematician and geologist. His *Illustrations of the Huttonian Theory of the Earth* (1802) popularized James Hutton's views on geology.

play·ful *adjective* **1** fond of or inclined to play. **2** done in fun; humorous, jocular. □ **play·ful·ly** *adverb* **play·ful·ness** *noun*

play·goer *noun* a person who goes to the theatre, esp. often.

play·ground *noun* **1** an outdoor area for children to play on. **2** any place of recreation, as a resort or tourist area.

play·group *noun* an organized group of esp. preschool children who play regularly together under supervision.

play·house *noun* **1** a theatre. **2** a toy house for children to play in.

playing card *noun* each of a set of usu. 52 oblong pieces of card or other material with an identical pattern on one side and different values represented by numbers and symbols on the other, used to play various games.

playing field *noun* **1** a field used for outdoor team games. **2** the sphere of any competition (*ensured a level playing field for the election*).

play·land *noun* a recreational area.

play·let *noun* a short play or dramatic piece.

play·list ● *noun* a list of pieces to be played, esp. of musical recordings chosen to be broadcast on a radio show. ● *transitive verb* place on a playlist.

play·maker *noun* a player in a team game who leads attacks or brings other players in the same side into a position to score. □ **play·making** *noun* & *attributive adjective*

play·mate *noun* **1** a child's companion in play. **2** a lover.

play money *noun* pieces of paper made to look like money, used in some board games etc.

play·off *noun Sport* **1** (usu. in *pl.*, except when *attributive*) a tournament played to determine a champion among competitors having advanced from preliminary competition (*advanced to the playoffs*; *playoff hero*). **2** a game or match in such a tournament. **3** a match played to decide a draw or tie.

play on words *noun* a pun.

play·pen *noun* a portable enclosure for young children to play, sleep, etc. in.

play·room *noun* a room set aside for playing in.

play·school *noun* a nursery school.

play·set *noun* a set of swings incorporating a slide, monkey bars, etc. for use by children.

play·suit *noun* a usu. one-piece outfit combining shorts and a top, worn by children and women.

play·thing *noun* **1** a toy or other thing to play with. **2** a person or thing treated as a toy.

play·time *noun* time for play or recreation.

play·wright *noun* a person who writes plays; a dramatist.

play·writing *noun* the activity or process of writing plays.

play yard *noun* = PLAYPEN.

plaza *noun* **1** *N Amer.* a shopping centre, mall. **2** an open square in an urban area. [Spanish, = place]

plc *abbreviation* (also **PLC**) *Brit.* Public Limited Company.

plea *noun* **1** an earnest appeal or entreaty. **2** *Law* a formal statement by or on behalf of a defendant, esp. in response to a charge. **3** an argument or excuse. [Middle English & Anglo-French *ple*, *plai*, Old French *plait*, *plaid* agreement, discussion, from Latin *placitum* a decree, neuter past participle of *placēre* to please]

plea bargaining *noun N Amer.* an arrangement between prosecutor and defendant whereby the defendant pleads guilty to a lesser charge in the expectation of leniency. □ **plea bargain** *noun* & *intransitive verb*

pleach *transitive verb* entwine or interlace (esp. branches to form a hedge). [Middle English *pleche* from Old French (as PLASH²)]

plead *verb* (*past* and *past participle* **plead·ed** or esp. *US* **pled**) **1 a** *intransitive* make an earnest appeal. **b** *transitive* say pleadingly. **2** *intransitive Law* address a law court as an advocate on behalf of a party. **3** *transitive* maintain (a cause) esp. in a law court. **4** *transitive Law* declare to be one's state as regards guilt in or responsibility for a crime (*plead guilty*; *plead insanity*). **5** *transitive* offer or allege as an excuse (*pleaded forgetfulness*). □ **plead·able** *adjective* **plead·er** *noun* [Anglo-French *pleder*, Old French *plaidier* (as PLEA)]

plead·ing ● *noun* (usu. in *pl.*) a formal statement of the cause of an action or defence. ● *adjective* expressing an earnest entreaty. □ **plead·ing·ly** *adverb*

pleas·ance /'plɛzəns/ *noun* a secluded enclosure or part of a garden, esp. one attached to a large house. [Old French *plaisance* (as PLEASANT)]

pleas·ant /'plɛzənt/ *adjective* **1** pleasing to the mind, feelings, or senses. **2** polite and friendly. □ **pleas·ant·ly** *adverb* **pleas·ant·ness** *noun* [Old French *plaisant* (as PLEASE)]

pleas·antry /'plɛzəntri/ *noun* (*pl.* **-ries**) **1** a pleasant or amusing remark, esp. made in casual conversation. **2** a humorous manner of speech. **3** jocularity.

please ● *verb* **1** *transitive* & *intransitive* be agreeable (to); make (a person or people) glad; give pleasure (to) (*the gift will please them*; *anxious to please*). **2** *transitive* (in *passive*) **a** (foll. by *to* + infin.) be glad or willing to (*am pleased to help*). **b** (often foll. by *about*, *at*, *with*) derive pleasure or satisfaction (from). **3** *transitive* (with *it* as subject; usu. foll. by *to* + infin.) be the inclination or wish of (*it did not please them to attend*). **4** *intransitive* think fit; have the will or desire (*take as many as you please*). ● *interjection* **1** used as a polite way of making a request or giving an order (*please come in*). **2** used to add force to a request or statement (*Children, please! I'm trying to work!*). **3** used when accepting an offer emphatically ('*Do you want some help?' 'Please!'*). **4** (also /pə'liːz/) *informal* used to express scorn ('*He said he was too busy to help.' 'Oh please!'*). □ **if you please 1** used in making a polite request (*come this way, if you please*). **2** used to express annoyance when reporting something, esp. something unexpected (*and now, if you please, I've got to rewrite the whole report!*). **pleased as punch** see PUNCH. **please God** may God let it happen; if it is pleasing to God (*please God, things will start to improve soon*). **please oneself** do as one likes. □ **pleased** *adjective* **pleas·er** *noun* **pleas·ing** *adjective* **pleas·ing·ly** *adverb* [Middle English *plaise* from Old French *plaisir* from Latin *placēre*]

pleas·ur·able /'plɛʒərəbəl/ *adjective* causing pleasure; agreeable. □ **pleas·ur·able·ness** *noun* **pleas·ur·ably** *adverb*

pleas·ure /'plɛʒər/ ● *noun* **1** a feeling of satisfaction or joy. **2** enjoyment. **3** a source of pleasure or gratification (*painting was my chief pleasure*; *it is a pleasure to talk to them*). **4** *formal* the will or desire (*is it the pleasure of the House to adopt the motion?*). **5** sensual gratification or enjoyment (*a life of pleasure*). **6** (*attributive*) done or used for pleasure (*pleasure boat*). ● *verb* **1** *transitive* give (esp. sexual) pleasure to. **2** *intransitive* (often foll. by *in*) take pleasure. □ **take pleasure in** like doing. **with pleasure** gladly. [Middle English & Old French *plesir*, *plaisir* PLEASE, used as a noun]

pleasure dome *noun* a place for pleasure, recreation, amusement, etc. [apparently coined by Samuel Coleridge in his poem 'Kubla Khan']

pleasure principle *noun Psych.* the instinctive drive to gain pleasure and avoid pain as the basic motivating force in human life.

pleat ● *noun* a fold or crease, esp. a flattened fold in cloth doubled upon itself. ● *transitive verb* (usu. as **pleat·ed** *adjective*) make a pleat or pleats in. □ **pleat·ing** *noun* [Middle English, var. of PLAIT]

pleath·er /'plɛθər/ *noun* a synthetic leather. [blend of PLASTIC + LEATHER]

pleb *noun informal* usu. *derogatory* = PLEBEIAN. [abbreviation]

plebe *noun US* a newly entered cadet at a military or naval academy; a freshman. [abbreviation of PLEBEIAN]

ple·be·ian /plɪ'biːən/ ● *noun* **1** a commoner, esp. in ancient Rome. **2** usu. *derogatory* a member of the lower social classes, esp. an uncultured one. ● *adjective* **1** of the common people. **2** uncultured; unrefined in taste. □ **ple·be·ian·ism** *noun* [Latin *plebeius* from *plebs* *plebis* 'the common people']

pleb·is·cite /'plɛbɪˌsaɪt/ *noun* **1** the direct vote of all electors on an important public question, e.g. a change in the constitution. **2** the public expression of a community's opinion, with or without binding force. **3** *Rom. Hist.* a law enacted by the plebeians' assembly.

---

t top   v voice   w we   z zoo   ʃ she   ʒ vision   θ thin   ð this   ŋ ring   x loch   tʃ chip   dʒ jar   (*see over for vowels*)

□ **pleb·is·cit·ary** /-'bɪsɪteri/ *adjective* [French *plébiscite* from Latin *plebiscitum* from *plebs plebis* the common people + *scitum* decree, from *sciscere* vote for]

plec·trum /'plektrəm/ *noun* (*pl.* **plec·trums** or **plec·tra** /-trə/) **1** a thin flat piece of plastic or horn etc. held in the hand and used to pluck a string, esp. of a guitar. **2** the corresponding mechanical part of a harpsichord etc. [Latin from Greek *plēktron* from *plēssō* strike]

pled *esp. US past of* PLEAD.

pledge ● *noun* **1** a solemn promise or undertaking. **2** a thing given as security for the fulfillment of a contract, the payment of a debt, etc., and liable to forfeiture in the event of failure. **3** a thing put in pawn. **4 a** the promise of a donation to charity, a fundraising campaign, etc. **b** such a donation. **5** a thing given as a token of love, favour, or something to come. **6** the drinking of a person's health; a toast. **7** a solemn undertaking to abstain from alcohol (*sign the pledge*). **8** the state of being pledged (*goods lying in pledge*). **9** esp. US a student who has promised to join a fraternity or sorority. ● *verb* **1** *transitive* **a** deposit as security. **b** pawn. **2** *transitive* promise solemnly by the pledge of (one's honour, word, etc.). **3** *transitive* (often *reflexive*) bind by a solemn promise. **4** *transitive* drink to the health of. **5** *transitive & intransitive* promise solemnly (*we pledged our support; they pledged to resign*). **6** *transitive* commit oneself to donate (a sum). □ **pledge one's troth** *see* TROTH.

□ **pledge·able** *adjective* **pledg·er** *noun* **pledg·or** *noun Law.* [Old French *plege* from Late Latin *plebium*, from *plebire* 'assure']

pledg·ee *noun* a person to whom a pledge is given.

Pledge of Allegiance *noun* a solemn oath of loyalty to the United States, declaimed as part of flag-saluting ceremonies.

Plei·a·des /'pleɪəˌdiːz/ *plural noun* **1** *Gk Myth* (*sing.* **Pleiad**) the seven daughters of the Titan Atlas and the Oceanid Pleione, who were pursued by the hunter Orion until Zeus changed them into a cluster of stars. **2** *Astronomy* an open cluster of stars in the constellation of Taurus, also known as 'the Seven Sisters', containing six (or more) stars visible to the naked eye; there are actually some five hundred stars. [Latin *Pleias* from Greek *Pleias -ados*]

plein-air /pleɪn'er/ *adjective* (of a painting) representing an outdoor scene and executed with a spontaneous technique, esp. representing the transient effects of atmosphere and light. [French *en plein air* 'in the open air']

plei·ot·ropy /plaɪ'ɒtrəpi/ *noun Biol.* the production by a single gene of two or more apparently unrelated effects. □ **pleio·trop·ic** /-'trɒpɪk, -'trəʊpɪk/ *adjective* **pleio·trop·ism** *noun* [Greek *pleiōn* 'more' + *tropē* 'turning']

Pleis·to·cene /'plaɪstəˌsiːn/ *Geol.* ● *adjective* of or relating to the first epoch of the Quaternary period, between the Pliocene and the Holocene, lasting from about 2,000,000 to 10,000 years BP, and notable for a succession of ice ages and the evolution of modern humankind. ● *noun* this geological epoch or system. [Greek *pleistos* most + *kainos* new]

plen·ary /'plenəri/ ● *adjective* **1** entire, unqualified, absolute (*plenary indulgence*). **2** (of an assembly, presentation, etc.) to be attended by all members or participants. ● *noun* (*pl.* **-aries**) a plenary session etc. [Late Latin *plenarius* from *plenus* full]

pleni·poten·tiary /ˌplenɪpə'tenʃieri/ ● *noun* (*pl.* **-ies**) a person (esp. a diplomat) invested with the full power of independent action. ● *adjective* **1** having this power. **2** (of power) absolute. [medieval Latin *plenipotentiarius* from *plenus* full + *potentia* power]

pleni·tude /'plenɪˌtuːd, -tjuːd/ *noun literary* **1** fullness, completeness. **2** abundance. [Late Latin *plenitudo* from *plenus* full]

plen·teous /'plentiəs/ *adjective poet.* plentiful. □ **plen·teous·ly** *adverb* **plen·teous·ness** *noun* [Old French *plentivous* from *plentif -ive* from *plenté* PLENTY: compare *bounteous*]

plen·ti·ful *adjective* abundant, copious. □ **plen·ti·ful·ly** *adverb* **plen·ti·ful·ness** *noun*

plenty ● *noun* a situation in which there is an ample supply of food, money, etc. (*poverty in the midst of plenty*). ● *pronoun* (often foll. by *of*) a great or sufficient quantity or number (*we have plenty; plenty of time*). ● *adjective informal* existing in an ample quantity. ● *adverb informal* **1** fully, entirely (*it is plenty large enough*). **2** a lot (*plenty more where that came from; it costs plenty*). [Old French *plentet* from Latin *plenitas -tatis* from *plenus* full]

plen·um /'pliːnəm/ *noun* **1** a full assembly of people or a committee etc. **2** *Physics* space filled with matter. [Latin, neuter of *plenus* full]

pleo·chro·ic /ˌpliːə'krəʊɪk/ *adjective* showing different colours when viewed in different directions. □ **pleo·chro·ism** *noun* [Greek *pleiōn* more + *-khroos* from *khrōs* colour]

pleo·morph·ism /ˌpliːə'mɔːfɪzəm/ *noun* **1** *Chem. & Mineralogy* crystallization in two or more fundamentally different forms. **2** *Biol.* the exhibiting of different forms at different stages of the life cycle. **3** the condition of a tumour containing a mixture of several cell types and different kinds of neoplastic tissue. □ **pleo·morph·ic** *adjective* [Greek *pleiōn* more + *morphē* form]

pleo·nasm /'pliːəˌnazəm/ *noun* **1** the use of more words than are needed to give the sense, e.g. *see with one's eyes*. **2** an instance of this. □ **pleo·nas·tic** /-'nastɪk/ *adjective* **pleo·nas·tic·ally** *adverb* [Late Latin *pleonasmus* from Greek *pleonasmos* from *pleonazō* be superfluous]

ple·sio·saur /'pliːsiəsɔːr/ *noun* any of a group of extinct marine reptiles with a broad flat body, short tail, long flexible neck, and large paddle-like limbs. [modern Latin from Greek *plēsios* near + *sauros* lizard]

Ples·sis·ville /'plesiːvɪl/ a town in south central Quebec, about 80 km southwest of Lévis; pop. (2001) 6,756. [Msgr. J.-O. *Plessis*, archbishop of Quebec d.1825]

ples·sor *var. of* PLEXOR.

pleth·ora /'pleθərə/ *noun* **1** an abundance. **2** an oversupply, glut, or excess. □ **pleth·or·ic** (also /plɪ'θɒrɪk/) *adjective* [Late Latin from Greek *plēthōrē* from *plēthō* be full]

pleura¹ /'plʊərə, 'plʊrə/ *noun* (*pl.* **pleurae** /-riː/) **1** each of a pair of serous membranes lining the thorax and enveloping the lungs in mammals. **2** lateral extensions of the body wall in arthropods. □ **pleur·al** *adjective* [medieval Latin from Greek, = side of the body, rib]

pleura² *pl. of* PLEURON.

pleur·isy /'plʊərisi, 'plʊrisi/ *noun* inflammation of the pleura, marked by pain in the chest or side, fever, etc. □ **pleur·it·ic** /-'rɪtɪk/ *adjective* [Old French *pleurisie* from Late Latin *pleurisis* alteration of Latin *pleuritis* from Greek (as PLEURA¹)]

pleuro- /'plʊərəʊ, 'plʊrəʊ/ *combining form* **1** denoting the pleura. **2** denoting the side.

pleur·on /'plʊərɒn, 'plʊrɒn/ *noun* (*pl.* **pleura** /-rə/) = PLEURA¹ **2**. [Greek, = side of the body, rib]

pleuro·pneu·monia /ˌplʊərəʊnjuː'məʊniə, ˌplʊr-, -nuː-/ *noun* **1** pneumonia complicated with pleurisy. **2** a contagious febrile disease of horned cattle, transmitted by a mycoplasma.

plew /pluː/ *noun N Amer. hist.* a beaver pelt. [Canadian French *pélu* = French *poilu* 'hairy', from *poil* 'hair']

-plex¹ /pleks/ *suffix* **1** forming adjectives meaning 'many' from cardinal numbers (*simplex; multiplex*). **2** forming parallel nouns, esp. in *N Amer.* with the sense of a dwelling divided into a specified number of floors, residences, etc. (*duplex*). [Latin from *plicare*, 'to fold']

-plex² *suffix* designating integrated industrial facilities or other organizations (*sportsplex*). [shortening of COMPLEX *noun*]

Plexi·glas *noun proprietary* a tough light transparent acrylic thermoplastic used instead of glass. [formed as PLEXOR + GLASS]

plex·or /'pleksɔːr/ *noun* (also **ples·sor** /'plesɔːr/) *Med.* a small hammer used to test reflexes and in percussing. [irreg. from Greek *plēxis* percussion + -OR¹]

plex·us /'pleksəs/ *noun* (*pl.* same or **plex·us·es**) **1** *Anat.* **a** a network of nerves or blood vessels in an animal body (*solar plexus*). **b** a structure consisting of a bundle of minute closely interwoven and intercommunicating fibres or tubes. **2** any network or web-like formation. □ **plexi·form** *adjective* [Latin from *plectere plex-* braid]

pli·able /'plaɪəbəl/ *adjective* **1** bending easily; supple. **2** flexible in disposition or character; yielding, compliant. □ **pli·abil·ity** *noun* **pli·able·ness** *noun* **pli·ably** *adverb* [French from *plier* bend: see PLY¹]

pli·ant /'plaɪənt/ *adjective* **1** bending, lithe, flexible; able to be bent or folded. **2** (of a person etc.) readily influenced, accommodating. □ **pli·ancy** *noun* [Old French (as PLIABLE)]

pli·cate /'plaɪkeɪt/ *adjective Biol. & Geol.* folded, crumpled, corrugated. □ **pli·cat·ed** /plɪ'keɪtɪd/ *adjective* [Latin *plicatus* past participle of *plicare* fold]

pli·ca·tion /plɪ'keɪʃən/ *noun* **1** the act of folding. **2** a fold; a folded condition. [medieval Latin *plicatio* or Latin *plicare* fold, after *complication*]

plié /'pliːeɪ/ *noun Dance* a movement in which the knees are bent outwards in line with the turned out feet. [French, past participle of *plier* bend: see PLY¹]

pliers /'plaɪərz/ *plural noun* pincers with gripping jaws usu. having parallel serrated surfaces, used for holding small objects, bending wire, etc. [(dial.) *ply* bend (as PLIABLE)]

plight¹ /plaɪt/ *noun* a condition, state, or predicament, esp. an unfortunate one. [Middle English & Anglo-French *plit* = Old French *pleit* fold: see PLAIT: *-gh-* by confusion with PLIGHT²]

plight² /plʌɪt/ *archaic* ● *transitive verb* **1** pledge or promise solemnly (one's faith, loyalty, etc.). **2** (foll. by *to*) engage, esp. in marriage. ● *noun* an engagement or act of pledging. □ **plight one's troth** see TROTH. [originally as noun, from Old English *pliht* danger, from Germanic]

plim·soll /ˈplɪmsəl/ *noun Brit.* a rubber-soled canvas leisure or sports shoe. [prob. from the resemblance of the side of the sole, usu. white with a coloured line through the middle, to a PLIMSOLL LINE]

Plimsoll line /ˈplɪmsəl/ *noun* (also **Plimsoll mark**) a marking on a ship's side showing the limit of legal submersion under various sea conditions. [S. Plimsoll, English politician d.1898, promoter of the Merchant Shipping Act of 1876]

plink ● *verb* **1** *intransitive* **a** emit a short, sharp, metallic, or ringing sound. **b** play a musical instrument in this manner. **2** *transitive* **a** shoot (a gun) at a target, esp. casually. **b** hit (something) with a shot from a gun. ● *noun* **1** the sound or action of plinking. **2** a sharp metallic noise. □ **plinky** *adjective* [imitative]

plinth *noun* **1** the lower square slab at the base of a column or pedestal. **2** a base supporting a vase or statue etc. **3** *Archit.* the projecting part of a wall immediately above the ground. [French *plinthe* or Latin *plinthus* from Greek *plinthos* tile, brick, squared stone]

Pliny /ˈplɪni/ **1** (known as Pliny the Elder; Latin name Gaius Plinius Secundus) (23–79), Roman statesman and scholar. His *Natural History* (77) is a vast encyclopedia of the natural and human worlds; he died while observing the eruption of Vesuvius in 79. **2** his nephew (known as Pliny the Younger; Latin name Gaius Plinius Caecilius Secundus) (*c*.61–*c*.112), Roman senator and writer. His books of letters deal with both public and private affairs; they include a description of the eruption of Vesuvius in 79 and correspondence with the Emperor Trajan.

Pli·o·cene /ˈplʌɪəˌsiːn/ *Geol.* ● *adjective* of or relating to the last epoch of the Tertiary period, between the Miocene and the Pleistocene, lasting from about 5.1 to 2 million years ago, during which many mammals that had flourished earlier in the Tertiary become extinct. ● *noun* this geological epoch or system. [Greek *pleiōn* more + *kainos* new]

plissé /ˈpliːseɪ/ ● *adjective* (of cloth etc.) chemically treated so as to give a wrinkled or puckered effect. ● *noun* material treated in this way. [French, past participle of *plisser* pleat]

PLO *abbreviation* Palestine Liberation Organization.

plod¹ ● *verb* (**plod·ded**, **plod·ding**) **1** *intransitive* (often foll. by *along*, *on*, etc.) walk doggedly or laboriously; trudge. **2** *intransitive* (often foll. by *at*) work slowly and steadily. **3** *transitive* tread or make (one's way) laboriously. ● *noun* the act or a period of plodding. □ **plod·der** *noun* [16th c.: prob. imitative]

plod² *noun Brit.* jocular or derogatory (also **PC Plod**) a police officer; also, the police. [the name of a police constable, Mr. *Plod*, in Enid Blyton's *Noddy* stories for children]

plod·ding *adjective* **1** slow-moving and unexciting. **2** (of a person) thorough and hard-working but lacking in imagination or intelligence. □ **plod·ding·ly** *adverb*

-ploid *combining form Biol.* forming adjectives denoting the number of sets of chromosomes in a cell (*diploid*; *polyploid*). [after HAPLOID]

ploidy *noun* the number of sets of chromosomes in a cell. [after DIPLOIDY, POLYPLOIDY (see POLYPLOID), etc.]

Ploi·eşti /plɔɪˈɛʃti/ an oil-refining city in central Romania, north of Bucharest; pop. (est. 2002) 250,600.

plonk¹ ● *transitive verb* **1** set down hurriedly or clumsily. **2** (usu. foll. by *down*) set down firmly. ● *noun* a heavy thud, as of one hard object hitting another. [imitative]

plonk² *noun informal* cheap or inferior wine. [originally Australian: prob. corruption of *blanc* in French *vin blanc* white wine]

plop ● *noun* an abrupt, hollow sound as of a smooth object dropping into water without a splash. ● *transitive & intransitive verb* (**plopped**, **plop·ping**) **1** make a plop. **2** fall or drop with a plop. □ **plop down** (also **plop oneself down**) sit down abruptly. [19th c.: imitative]

plo·sion /ˈpləʊʒ(ə)n/ *noun Phonetics* the sudden release of breath in the pronunciation of a stop consonant. [shortening of EXPLOSION]

plo·sive /ˈpləʊsɪv/ *Phonetics* ● *adjective* pronounced with a sudden release of breath. ● *noun* a stop consonant pronounced with a sudden release of air. [shortening of EXPLOSIVE]

plot ● *noun* **1 a** a defined and usu. small piece of ground, esp. one used for a special purpose. **b** a grave or area of graves, esp. as belonging to a particular family in a burial ground. **2** a plan or an outline of the main events in a play, novel, film, etc. **3** a conspiracy or secret plan,

esp. to achieve an unlawful end. ● *verb* (**plot·ted**, **plot·ting**) **1** *transitive & intransitive* plan or contrive secretly (a crime, conspiracy, etc.). **2** *transitive* make a ground plan, map, or diagram of (an existing object, a place or thing to be laid out, constructed, etc.); draw to scale. **3** *transitive* **a** mark (a point or course etc.) on a chart or diagram. **b** divide (land) for registration etc. **4** *transitive* **a** mark out or allocate (points) on a graph. **b** make (a curve etc.) by marking out a number of points on a graph. **5** *transitive* devise or plan the plot of (a play, novel, film, etc.). □ **plot·less** *adjective* **plot·less·ness** *noun* [Old English and from Old French *complot* 'secret plan': both of unknown origin]

Plo·tinus /pləˈtʌɪnəs/ (*c*.205–70), Roman philosopher, the founder and leading exponent of Neoplatonism.

plot line *noun* the main features of the plot of a play, novel, film, etc.; a summary.

plot·ter *noun* **1** a person who plots something, esp. to achieve an unlawful end; a conspirator. **2** a thing which plots something, esp. an instrument for automatically plotting a graph. **3** a device capable of drawing with a pen under the control of a computer.

plough *var. of* PLOW.

plough·man /ˈplaʊmən/ *noun* (*pl.* **-men**) (also **plow·man**) a person who uses a plough.

plough·man's lunch *noun esp. Brit.* a meal of bread and cheese with a relish or salad.

plough·share /ˈplaʊʃɛː/ *noun* (also **plow·share**) the large cutting blade of a plough. □ **beat** (or **turn**) **swords into ploughshares** devote resources to peaceful rather than warlike ends.

Plov·div /ˈplɒvdɪf/ an industrial and commercial city in central Bulgaria; pop. (2001) 340,638.

plover /ˈplʌvər, ˈpləʊvər/ *noun* any plump-breasted shorebird of the family Charadriidae, usu. having a pigeon-like bill. [Old French *plo(u)vier*, ultimately from Latin *pluvia* rain]

plow /plaʊ/ (also **plough**) ● *noun* **1** (often **plough**) a farm implement with a cutting blade fixed in a frame drawn by a tractor or by horses, for cutting furrows in the soil and turning it up. **2** an implement resembling this and having a comparable function, esp. an implement for deflecting material against which it moves or which moves against it (*snowplow*). **3** (**the Plough**) *Brit.* = BIG DIPPER. ● *verb* **1** (often **plough**) **a** *transitive* make furrows in and turn up (the earth) with a plow, esp. before sowing. **b** *intransitive* use a plow; till the ground with a plow. **2** *transitive* (often **plough**) **a** (foll. by *out*, *up*, *down*, etc.) turn or extract (roots, weeds, etc.) with a plow. **b** (foll. by *under*) bury in the soil by plowing. **3** *transitive* **a** remove (snow) from a surface with a plow. **b** clear (a surface) of snow with a plow. **4** *transitive* furrow or scratch (a surface) with or as if with a plow. **5** *transitive* produce (a furrow or line) in this way. **6** *intransitive* (foll. by *through*) advance laboriously, esp. through work, a book, etc. **7** (of a ship etc.) **a** *intransitive* (often foll. by *through*) cleave the surface of the water. **b** *transitive* cleave (the surface of the water); cut (a course) through the water. **8** *intransitive* (foll. by *through*, *into*) (esp. of a car, train, etc.) travel or be propelled clumsily or violently into or through (an obstacle). **9** *transitive* (foll. by *into*) invest (money, usu. a large amount) in (a project etc.). □ **plow back** reinvest (profits) in the business producing them. **put one's hand to the plow** undertake a task, enter on a course of life or conduct. □ **plow·able** *adjective* **plowed** *adjective* **plow·er** *noun* [Old English *plōh* from Old Norse *plógr* from Germanic]

plowing match *noun* a rural fair featuring plowing competitions, farm machinery demonstrations, and new product displays as well as various forms of entertainment.

ploy *noun informal* a stratagem; a cunning manoeuvre to gain an advantage. [originally Scots, 18th c.: origin unknown]

ploye /plɔɪ/ *noun Cdn* a buckwheat pancake in Acadian cuisine. [Acadian French, alteration of *plogue*, from English PLUG, because of the heavy nature of the dish]

pluck ● *verb* **1** *transitive* (often foll. by *out*, *off*, etc.) remove by picking or pulling out or away. **2** *transitive* **a** strip (a bird) of feathers. **b** pull off (the hair, fur, etc.) from. **c** shape or thin (the eyebrows) by removing hairs. **3** *transitive* pull at, esp. abruptly or with a jerk; twitch. **4** *intransitive* (foll. by *at*) tug or snatch at. **5** *transitive* sound (the string of a musical instrument) by doing this with the finger or plectrum etc. **6** *transitive* rescue (a person) from a difficult or unpleasant situation. **7** *transitive* remove (a person) from obscurity. **8** *transitive Geol.* (esp. of glacier ice) **a** break loose (pieces of rock) by mechanical force on projections of cavities in a rock. **b** erode (rock) by this process. ● *noun* **1** courage, spirit, boldness. **2** an act of plucking; a twitch. **3** the heart, liver, and lungs of an animal as food. □ **pluck up** summon up (one's courage, spirits, etc.). □ **pluck·er** noun [Old English *ploccian, pluccian,* from Germanic]

plucky adjective (**pluck·i·er, pluck·i·est**) brave, spirited.
□ **pluck·i·ly** adverb **pluck·i·ness** noun

plug ● noun **1 a** a piece of solid material fitting tightly into a hole, used to fill a gap or cavity, act as a wedge, etc. **b** any of various devices resembling this in form or function, esp. for temporarily stopping the pipe leading out of a sink etc. **2 a** a device of metal pins in an insulated casing fitting into holes in a socket for making an electrical connection. **b** informal an electric socket. **3** = SPARK PLUG 1. **4** informal a piece of (often free) publicity for an idea, product, etc. **5** a mass of solidified lava filling the neck of a volcano. **6 a** a cake or stick of tobacco. **b** a piece of this, esp. for chewing. **7** Angling a lure with one or more hooks attached. **8** Med. a small area of scalp with strong hair growth grafted on to a balding area in hair transplantation. **9** esp. N Amer. a small piece of turf or pre-planted soil used esp. for filling or seeding a lawn. **10** N Amer. informal a baby's pacifier. **11** N Amer. informal (in full **plug horse**) a horse, esp. an old one. **12** = FIRE PLUG.
● transitive verb (**plugged, plug·ging**) **1** (often foll. by *up*) stop, fill, or obstruct (a hole etc.) with or as if with a plug etc. **2** informal seek to popularize (an idea, product, etc.) by repeated recommendation; give free publicity to. **3 a** insert a wooden peg or block into (a wall etc.) to afford a hold for a nail or screw. **b** insert a fibre or plastic tube or cylinder for the same purpose. **4** slang shoot or hit (a person etc.).
□ **plug away** informal (often foll. by *at*) work steadily away (at); persevere doggedly. **plug a gap** remedy a deficiency. **plug in 1** connect electrically by inserting a plug in a socket. **b** be able to be connected by a plug. **2** informal incorporate, account for (*must plug in the new data*). **plug into** become connected with (a source of information, a trend, etc.). **pull the plug** see PULL. [Middle Dutch & Middle Low German *plugge,* of unknown origin]

plug and play noun Computing a standard of compatibility for peripherals, software, etc. that makes installation simpler by allowing automatic configuration of the system.

plugged adjective **1** stopped up, closed, or filled with or as if with a plug. **2** esp. N Amer. (of a coin) having a portion removed and the space filled with base material.

plugged-in adjective **1** connected by means of a plug. **2** informal aware of what is happening, in fashion, etc.

plugged nickel noun N Amer. (also **plug nickel**) a negligible amount (*not worth a plugged nickel; does anyone give a plugged nickel about it?*).

plug·ger noun **1** a person who or thing which plugs something. **2** Angling a person who fishes with a plug. **3** N Amer. informal = DIGGER 4.

plug·hole noun Brit. a hole at the lowest point of a bath, basin, sink, etc., which can be stopped with a plug; a drain.

plug-in ● adjective **1** able to be connected by means of a plug. **2** Computing (of a module or software) able to be added to a system to give extra features or functions. ● noun **1** a plug-in device or unit. **2** Cdn an electrical outlet in a garage, near a parking space, etc. for plugging in the block heater of a car etc. **3** Computing a plug-in module or software.

plug-ugly slang ● noun (pl. **-uglies**) esp. N Amer. a thug or ruffian.
● adjective very ugly. [first element by association with the verb PLUG in the informal sense 'hit with the fist' + UGLY]

plum ● noun **1 a** an oval fleshy fruit, usu. purple, reddish, or yellow when ripe, with sweet pulp and a flattish pointed stone. **b** (also **plum tree**) any of various deciduous trees of the genus *Prunus* (rose family), esp. *P. domestica,* which bears this fruit. **c** the wood of such a tree. **2 a** deep reddish-purple colour. **3** a dried grape or raisin used in cooking (*plum pudding*). **4** a highly desirable thing, a coveted prize; the pick of a collection, esp. a choice appointment etc. ● adjective **1** (also **plum-coloured**) of a reddish-purple colour. **2** choice, valuable, coveted. [Old English *plūme* via medieval Latin *pruna* from Latin *prunum*]

plum·age /ˈpluːmɪdʒ/ noun a bird's feathers. □ **plum·aged** adjective (usu. in *combination*). [Old French, from *plume* feather]

plumb¹ /plʌm/ ● noun a ball of lead or other heavy material, esp. one attached to the end of a line for finding the depth of water or determining the vertical on an upright surface. ● adverb **1** exactly (*plumb in the centre*). **2** vertically, perpendicularly, straight down. **3** N Amer. slang completely (*plumb crazy*). ● adjective **1** vertical, perpendicular. **2** downright, sheer (*plumb nonsense*). ● transitive verb **1 a** measure the depth of (water) with a plumb. **b** determine (a depth). **2 a** test (an upright surface) to determine the vertical. **b** make vertical. **3** reach, explore, or experience the esp. emotional depths of (*plumb the depths of fear*). **4** get to the bottom of, learn in detail the facts about (a

matter). □ **out of** (or **off**) **plumb** not vertical. [prob. ultimately from Latin *plumbum* lead, assimilated to Old French *plomb* lead]

plumb² /plʌm/ verb **1** transitive provide (a building or room etc.) with plumbing. **2** transitive (often foll. by *in*) fit as part of a plumbing system. **3** intransitive work as a plumber. [back-formation from PLUMBER]

plum·bago /plʌmˈbeɪɡoː/ noun (pl. **-bagos**) **1** any plant of the genus *Plumbago,* with grey or blue flowers. **2** hist. = GRAPHITE. [Latin from *plumbum* LEAD²]

plumb bob noun a usu. cone-shaped bob forming the weight of a plumb line.

plum·be·ous /ˈplʌmbɪəs/ adjective of the dull grey colour of lead. [Latin *plumbeus* from *plumbum* LEAD²]

plumb·er /ˈplʌmər/ noun a person who fits and repairs the water pipes, water tanks, etc. in a building. [Old French *plommier* from Latin *plumbarius* from *plumbum* LEAD²]

plumber's friend noun (also **plumber's helper**) a plunger for clearing blocked drains.

plumber's snake noun a long flexible wire for clearing obstacles in pipes, toilets, etc.

plum·bic /ˈplʌmbɪk/ adjective Chem. containing lead esp. in its tetravalent form. [Latin *plumbum* lead]

plumb·ing /ˈplʌmɪŋ/ noun **1** the system or apparatus of water pipes etc. in a building. **2** informal **a** the excretory system. **b** jocular the reproductive system. **3** the work of a plumber.

plum·bism /ˈplʌmbɪzəm/ noun Med. = LEAD POISONING.

plumb line noun a line with a plumb attached.

plum·bous /ˈplʌmbəs/ adjective Chem. containing lead in its divalent form.

plumb rule noun a mason's plumb line attached to a board.

plum cake noun a cake containing raisins, currants, etc.

plum duff noun Brit. a rich boiled suet pudding with raisins, currants, spices, and other ingredients.

plume ● noun **1** a feather, esp. a large one used for ornament. **2 a** a trail of vapour etc. issuing from a localized source and spreading out as the trail travels (*a plume of smoke*). **b** Geol. a column of magma rising from the lower mantle and spreading out under the lithosphere. **3** an ornament of feathers etc. attached to a helmet or hat or worn in the hair, usu. symbolizing dignity or rank. **4** a feather-like part, hair, organ, or formation. ● verb **1** transitive decorate or provide with a plume or plumes. **2** intransitive (of a trail of smoke, vapour, etc.) form a plume, move in a plume, etc. **3** transitive (of a bird) preen (itself or its feathers). **4** reflexive (foll. by *on, upon*) pride (oneself on esp. something trivial).
□ **plumed** adjective **plume·less** adjective **plume·like** adjective [Old French from Latin *pluma* down]

plum·er·ia /pluːˈmɪərɪə/ noun a fragrant flowering tropical tree of a genus that includes frangipani. [modern Latin, named after Charles *Plumier* French botanist d.1704]

Plum·mer, (Ar·thur) Chris·to·pher (Orme) (b.1929), Canadian-born actor. His numerous films include *The Sound of Music* (1965) and *Murder by Decree* (1979), for which he won a Genie Award, and his television appearances include the 1979 CBC production *Riel.* He is a Companion of the Order of Canada.

plum·met ● intransitive verb (**plum·met·ed, plum·met·ing**) drop, fall, or plunge rapidly. ● noun **1** a plumb or plumb line. **2** a sounding line. **3** a weight attached to a fishing line to keep the float upright. [Old French *plommet* diminutive (as PLUMB¹)]

plummy adjective (**plum·mi·er, plum·mi·est**) **1** resembling a plum or plums, esp. in taste or colour. **2** informal (of a voice) deep, rich, and thick-sounding, esp. as supposedly characteristic of the British upper classes. **3** Cdn & Brit. informal good, desirable.

plum·ose /ˈpluːmoːs/ adjective **1** feathered. **2** feather-like. [Latin *plumosus* (as PLUME)]

plump¹ ● adjective (esp. of a person or animal or part of the body) having a full rounded shape; fleshy; filled out. ● transitive & intransitive verb (often foll. by *up, out*) make or become plump. □ **plump·ish** adjective **plump·ly** adverb **plump·ness** noun **plumpy** adjective [Middle Dutch *plomp* blunt, Middle Low German *plump, plomp* shapeless etc.]

plump² ● verb **1** intransitive & transitive (often foll. by *down*) drop, fall, or set down abruptly, esp. heavily or with a dull thud (*plumped down on the chair; plumped it on the floor*). **2** intransitive (foll. by *for*) decide, campaign, etc. definitely in favour of (one of two or more possibilities). ● noun an abrupt plunge; a heavy fall. [Middle Low German *plumpen,* Middle Dutch *plompen:* originally imitative]

plum pudding *noun* a rich boiled or steamed suet pudding with raisins, currants, spices, etc., traditionally served at Christmas.

plum sauce *noun* a yellowish brown, slightly sweet sauce made from salted plums, vinegar, sugar, hot chili pepper and other spices, used as a condiment in Chinese cuisine, esp. as an accompaniment for egg rolls.

plum tomato *noun* a plum-shaped tomato.

plum·ule /ˈpluːmjuːl/ *noun* **1** the rudimentary shoot or stem of an embryo plant. **2** a down feather on a young bird. [French *plumule* or Latin *plumula*, diminutive (as PLUME)]

plumy /ˈpluːmi/ *adjective* (**plum·i·er**, **plum·i·est**) **1** adorned with plumes. **2** plumelike, feathery.

plun·der ● *verb* **1** *transitive & intransitive* rob (a place or person), esp. systematically or as in war. **2** *transitive & intransitive* steal or embezzle (goods). **3** *transitive* steal from (another's writings etc.). ● *noun* **1** the violent or dishonest acquisition of property. **2** property acquired by plundering. **3** *informal* profit, gain. □ **plun·der·er** *noun* [Low German *plündern* lit. 'rob of household goods' from Middle High German *plunder* clothing etc.]

plunge ● *verb* **1** (usu. foll. by *in*, *into*) **a** *transitive* thrust forcefully or abruptly. **b** *intransitive* dive; propel oneself forcibly. **c** *intransitive & transitive* enter or cause to enter a certain condition or embark on a certain course abruptly or impetuously (*they plunged into a lively discussion; the room was plunged into darkness*). **2** *transitive* immerse completely. **3** *intransitive* **a** move suddenly and dramatically downward (*the car plunged off the cliff*). **b** (foll. by *down*, *into*, etc.) move with a rush (*plunged down the stairs*). **c** diminish rapidly. **4** *intransitive* (of currency, prices, etc.) drop sharply in value or amount (*share prices have plunged*). **5** *intransitive* (of a horse) start violently forward. **6** *intransitive* (of a ship) pitch. **7** *intransitive informal* gamble heavily; run into debt. ● *noun* **1** a sudden violent movement or fall. **2** an act of jumping or diving. □ **take the plunge** *informal* **1** take a decisive first step; commit oneself irrevocably to a course of action. **2** get married. [Old French *plungier*, ultimately from Latin *plumbum* plummet]

plunge pool *noun* **1** a deep basin excavated at the foot of a waterfall by the action of the falling water. **2** a cold water pool, esp. forming part of the equipment of a sauna.

plun·ger *noun* **1** a part of a mechanism that works with a plunging or thrusting movement. **2** a rubber cup on a handle for clearing blocked pipes by a plunging and sucking action. **3** *Music slang* a plunging device resembling the type employed in plumbing, used as a mute for a trumpet or trombone, esp. in jazz. **4** *informal* a reckless gamble.

plunging neckline *noun* a low-cut neckline.

plunk ● *noun* **1** the sound made by the sharply plucked string of a stringed instrument. **2** *N Amer.* the sound of something dropping, esp. heavily. ● *verb* **1** *N Amer.* (often foll. by *down*) **a** *transitive* put or throw down heavily or abruptly. **b** *intransitive* fall or drop down heavily or abruptly. **2** *transitive* esp. *Baseball* hit abruptly, esp. with a ball. **3 a** *transitive* cause (a string) to sound with a plunk; play (a note) on a stringed instrument with a plunk. **b** *intransitive* sound with a plunk. □ **plunk down** spend (money). [imitative]

pluot /ˈpluːɒt/ *noun* a hybrid fruit that is 75% plum and 25% apricot. [blend of PLUM + APRICOT]

plu·perfect /pluːˈpɜːrfɪkt/ ● *adjective* **1** *Grammar* (of a tense) denoting an action completed prior to some past point of time specified or implied, formed in English by *had* and the past participle, as: *he had gone by then*. **2** esp. *N Amer. informal* more than perfect; complete, thorough. ● *noun* the pluperfect tense. [modern Latin *plusperfectum* from Latin *plus quam perfectum* more than perfect]

plur·al /ˈplʊrəl/ ● *adjective* **1 a** more than one in number. **b** (of a society etc.) composed of different ethnic groups or cultural traditions or in the political structure of which cultural differences are reflected. **2** *Grammar* (of a word or form) denoting more than one, or (in languages with dual number) more than two. ● *noun Grammar* **1** a plural word or form. **2** the plural number. □ **plur·al·ly** *adverb* [Old French *plurel* from Latin *pluralis* from *plus pluris* more]

plur·al·ism /ˈplʊrəˌlɪzəm/ *noun* **1 a** a form of society in which the members of minority groups maintain their independent cultural traditions. **b** the toleration or acceptance of a diversity of opinions, values, theories, etc. **2 a** a political theory or system of power-sharing among a number of political parties. **b** a theory or system of devolution and autonomy for individual bodies in preference to monolithic state control. **3** *Philos.* **a** a theory or system that recognizes more than one ultimate principle (*compare* MONISM 2). **b** the theory that the knowable world is made up of a plurality of interacting things. **4** the holding of more than one office, esp. an ecclesiastical

office or benefice, at a time. □ **plur·al·ist** *noun* **plur·al·is·tic** *adjective* **plur·al·is·tic·al·ly** *adverb*

plur·al·ity /plʊˈralɪti/ *noun* (pl. **-ities**) **1** the state or fact of being plural. **2 a** a large number or quantity; a multitude. **b** the greater number or part; more than half of the whole. **3** *N Amer. Politics* **a** the number of votes cast for a candidate who receives more than any other but does not receive an absolute majority. **b** the number by which this exceeds the number of votes cast for the candidate placing second. **4** = PLURALISM 4. [Old French *pluralité* from Late Latin *pluralitas* (as PLURAL)]

plur·al·ize *verb* (also esp. *Brit.* **-ise**) **1** *transitive & intransitive* make or become plural. **2** *transitive* express in or form the plural. □ **plur·al·iz·a·tion** *noun*

pluri- /ˈplʊri/ *combining form* several, more than one. [Latin *plus pluris* more, *plures* several]

plus ● *preposition* **1 a** *Math.* made more by, increased by (*3 plus 4 equals 7*). Symbol: +. **b** with the addition of, inclusive of (*five plus me*). **2** (of temperature) above zero (*plus 2° C*). **3** *informal* **a** with; having gained; newly possessing (*returned plus a new car*). **b** as well as (*fit five people plus all their gear in the car*). ● *adjective* **1** (after a number) at least; more than indicated (*fifteen plus*). **2 a** (after a grade etc.) rather better than (*B plus*). **b** *informal* of superior quality, excellent in its kind. **3** *Math.* positive. **4** having a positive electrical charge. **5** *N Amer.* (of a women's clothing size) designed for people larger and usu. heavier than accommodated by regular sizes. ● *noun* (pl. **-es**) **1** = PLUS SIGN. **2** *Math.* an additional or positive quantity. **3** an advantage; a positive quality (*experience is a definite plus*). ● *conjunction informal disputed* also; and furthermore (*they arrived late, plus they were hungry*). ¶ The use of *plus* as a conjunction is considered incorrect by some people. It is to be avoided in formal writing. □ **on the plus side** as an advantage. **plus or minus 1** give or take, add or subtract. **2** more or less, roughly. [Latin, = more]

Plus-15 *noun Cdn* (in Calgary) an enclosed overhead walkway between buildings. [from the original plan to connect all major buildings with walkways 15 feet above the ground]

plus ça change /plu sa ʃɑ̃ʒ/ *interjection* expressing the fundamental immutability of human nature, institutions, etc. [French, abbreviation of *plus ça change, plus c'est la même chose* 'the more it changes, the more it stays the same']

plus-fours *noun* long wide men's knickerbockers usu. worn formerly for golf etc. [20th c.: so named because the overhang at the knee requires an extra four inches]

plush ● *noun* a type of cloth with a cut pile surface like, but longer and smoother than, velvet. ● *adjective* **1** made of, of the nature of, or resembling plush. **2** stylish, luxurious. □ **plush·ly** *adverb* **plush·ness** *noun* **plushy** *adjective* (**plush·i·er**, **plush·i·est**) [obsolete French *pluche* contraction from *peluche* from Old French *peluchier* from Italian *peluzzo* diminutive of *pelo* from Latin *pilus* hair]

plus-minus *noun Hockey* (also **plus/minus**) a statistic indicating a player's effectiveness on both offence and defence, adjusted every time an even-strength goal is scored while the player is on the ice, with 1 added to the cumulative total if the player's own team scores and 1 subtracted if the opponents score (often *attributive: plus-minus leader*).

plus sign *noun* the symbol +, indicating addition or a positive value.

plus-sized *adjective N Amer.* (of a woman) large and heavy.

Plu·tarch /ˈpluːtɑːrk/ (Latin name Lucius Mestrius Plutarchus) (*c.*46–*c.*120), Greek biographer and philosopher. He is chiefly known for his *Parallel Lives*, a collection of biographies of prominent Greeks and Romans in which the moral character of his subjects is illustrated by a series of anecdotes.

Plu·ti·no *noun* any of a number of small planet-like bodies orbiting the sun in the region of the Kuiper belt. [PLUTO (because they have a similar orbit) + Italian diminutive suffix *-ino*]

Pluto /ˈpluːtoː/ **1** *Gk Myth* the god of the underworld (*compare* HADES). **2** *Astronomy* the ninth planet from the sun in the solar system, orbiting at an average distance of 5 900 million km from the sun. [Latin from Greek *Ploutōn*]

plu·toc·racy /pluːˈtɒkrəsi/ *noun* (pl. **-cies**) **1 a** a government by the wealthy. **b** a nation governed in this way. **2** a wealthy elite or ruling class. [Greek *ploutokratia* from *ploutos* wealth + -CRACY]

pluto·crat /ˈpluːtəˌkrat/ *noun* **1** *derogatory* a wealthy and influential person. **2** a member of a plutocracy or wealthy elite. □ **pluto·crat·ic** *adjective* **pluto·crat·ic·al·ly** *adverb*

pluton /ˈpluːtən/ *noun Geol.* an intrusive body of plutonic rock, esp. a large one. [back-formation from PLUTONIC]

Plu·to·nian /pluːˈtoːniən/ *adjective* **1 a** of or pertaining to the planet Pluto. **b** (**plutonian**) = PLUTONIC 1. **2 a** infernal. **b** belonging to or suggestive of the infernal regions. **c** of or pertaining to the god Pluto. [Latin *Plutonius* from Greek *Ploutōnios* (as PLUTO)]

plu·ton·ic /pluːˈtɒnɪk/ *adjective* **1** *Geol.* pertaining to or designating igneous rock formed by intense heat at great depths below the earth's surface. **2** (**Plutonic**) = PLUTONIAN 2. [formed as PLUTONIAN]

plu·to·nium /pluːˈtəʊniəm/ *noun* a dense silvery radioactive metallic transuranic element of the actinide series, used in some nuclear reactors and weapons. Symbol: **Pu**; at. no.: 94. [PLUTO (as the next planet beyond Neptune) + -IUM]

plu·vial /ˈpluːviəl/ *adjective* designating a period of relatively high average rainfall in low and intermediate latitudes during the geological past. [Latin *pluvialis* from *pluvia* rain]

ply¹ *noun* (*pl.* **plies**) **1** a thickness or layer of certain materials, esp. wood, cloth, or tissue paper (*three-ply*). **2** = PLYWOOD *noun*. **3** a strand or twist of rope, yarn, or thread. **4** a reinforcing layer of fabric in a tire. [French *pli* from *plier*, *pleier* from Latin *plicare* fold]

ply² *verb* (**plies**, **plied**) **1** *transitive* work steadily at (one's business or trade). **2 a** *intransitive* (often foll. by *between*) (of a vehicle, esp. a ship) travel regularly (to and fro between two points). **b** *transitive* work (a route) in this way. **3** *transitive* (foll. by *with*) **a** supply (a person) continuously (with food, drink, etc.). **b** approach repeatedly (with questions, demands, etc.). **4** *transitive* use or wield vigorously (a tool, weapon, etc.). **5** *intransitive* (of a taxi driver, boatman, etc.) attend regularly for custom (*ply for trade*). [Middle English *plye*, from APPLY]

Ply·mouth /ˈplɪməθ/ **1** a port and naval base in SW England, formerly in Devon; pop. (est. 2002) 249,900. It was the scene in 1620 of the departure of the *Mayflower* of the Pilgrim Fathers to N America. **2** a town in SE Massachusetts, on the Atlantic coast; pop. (2000) 51,701. The site in 1620 of the landing of the Pilgrim Fathers, it was the earliest permanent European settlement in New England. **3** the capital of the island of Montserrat in the W Indies. It was abandoned following the eruption of the Soufrière Hills volcano from 1995.

Plymouth Brethren *plural noun* a strict Calvinistic religious body formed at Plymouth in Devon *c.*1830, having no formal creed and no official order of ministers.

Plymouth Rock *noun* **1** a granite boulder at Plymouth, Massachusetts, onto which the Pilgrim Fathers are said to have stepped from the *Mayflower*. **2** a breed of medium-sized chicken, raised for meat and eggs.

Plympton-Wyoming a town in SW Ontario, just east of Sarnia; pop. (2001) 7,359. [after *Plympton*, Devon (near the childhood home of Lady Colborne) and Wyoming County in Pennsylvania, from Delaware *maughwauame* 'large meadows']

plyo·met·rics *noun* a form of exercise that involves rapid and repeated stretching and contracting of the muscles, designed to increase strength. □ **plyo·met·ric** *adjective* [Greek *plio* 'more' + METRIC]

ply·wood ● *noun* a strong thin board consisting of two or more layers of wood glued and pressed together with the directions of the grains alternating, to give increased strength and resistance to warping. ● *adjective* of, pertaining to, or made of plywood.

PM *abbreviation* **1** Prime Minister. **2** post-mortem. **3** Provost Marshal.

Pm *symbol Chem.* the element promethium.

p.m. *abbreviation* (also **P.M.**) after noon. [Latin *post meridiem*]

PMG *abbreviation* Postmaster General.

PMO *abbreviation Cdn* PRIME MINISTER'S OFFICE.

PMS *abbreviation* premenstrual syndrome.

PMU *abbreviation* pregnant mare's urine, used in the production of estrogen supplements and birth control pills.

PNE *abbreviation Cdn* Pacific National Exhibition.

pneu·mat·ic /nuːˈmatɪk, njuː-/ *adjective* **1** of or relating to air, wind, or gases. **2** containing or operated by compressed air. **3** connected with or containing air cavities esp. in the bones of birds or in fish. **4** *jocular* (of a person) having a well-rounded figure, esp. (of a woman) having a large bosom. □ **pneu·mat·ic·ally** *adverb* [Greek *pneumatikos* from *pneuma* wind, from *pneō* breathe]

pneumatic drill *noun* a heavy, mechanical drill driven by compressed air, for breaking up a hard surface.

pneu·mat·ics /nuːˈmatɪks, njuː-/ *plural noun* (treated as *sing.*) the science of the mechanical properties of gases.

pneumato- /ˈnuːmətəʊ, ˈnjuː-/ *combining form* denoting: **1** air. **2** breath. **3** spirit. [Greek from *pneuma* (as PNEUMATIC)]

pneu·mato·phore /ˈnuːmətəˌfɔːr, ˈnjuː-/ *noun* **1** the gaseous cavity of various hydrozoans, such as the Portuguese man-of-war. **2** an aerial root specialized for gaseous exchange found in various plants growing in swampy areas.

pneumo- /ˈnuːməʊ, ˈnjuːməʊ/ *combining form* denoting the lungs. [abbreviation of *pneumono-* from Greek *pneumōn* lung]

pneumo·coc·cus /nuːməˈkɒkəs, njuː-/ *noun* (*pl.* **pneumo·coc·ci** /-ˈkɒkaɪ, -ˈkɒkiː/) *Med.* a paired bacterium, *Streptococcus pneumoniae*, associated with pneumonia and sometimes meningitis. □ **pneumo·coc·cal** *adjective*

pneumo·coni·osis /ˌnuːməʊˌkɒniˈəʊsɪs, ˌnjuː-/ *noun* (*pl.* **pneumo·coni·oses** /-ˈəʊsiːs/) a lung disease caused by inhalation of dust or small particles. [PNEUMO- + Greek *konis* dust]

pneumo·cys·tis car·inii pneu·monia /nuːməˌsɪstɪs kəˈraɪniaɪ, njuː-/ *noun* = PCP 2.

pneu·monia /nəˈmoʊniə, nuː-, njuː-/ *noun* a bacterial or other infection causing inflammation of one lung (**single pneumonia**) or both lungs (**double pneumonia**) causing the air sacs to fill with pus and become solid. □ **pneu·mon·ic** /njuːˈmɒnɪk/ *adjective* [Latin from Greek from *pneumōn* lung]

pneumonic plague *noun* see PLAGUE *noun* 1a.

pneu·mon·itis /ˌnuːməˈnaɪtɪs, ˌnjuː-/ *noun* inflammation of the lungs, esp. caused by a viral or unknown agent.

pneumo·thor·ax /ˌnuːməʊˈθɔːraks, ˌnjuː-/ *noun* the presence of air or gas in the pleural cavity of the thorax, caused by the perforation of the chest wall or the lungs.

PNG *abbreviation* Papua New Guinea.

PO *abbreviation* **1** Post Office. **2** postal order. **3** purchase order. **4** PETTY OFFICER. **5** PILOT OFFICER.

Po *symbol Chem.* the element polonium.

po *noun* (*pl.* **pos**) *Brit. informal* a chamber pot.

poach¹ *transitive verb* **1** cook (an egg) without its shell in or over boiling water. **2** cook (fish, fruit, etc.) by simmering in a small amount of liquid. □ **poach·er** *noun* [Old French *pochier* from *poche* POKE²]

poach² *verb* **1** *transitive & intransitive* catch (game or fish) illegally. **2** *intransitive* (often foll. by *on*) trespass or encroach (on another's property, ideas, etc.). **3** *transitive* appropriate illicitly or unfairly (a person, thing, idea, etc.). **4** *transitive Tennis etc.* take (a shot) in one's partner's portion of the court. **5 a** *transitive* trample or cut up (turf) with hoofs. **b** *intransitive* (of land) become sodden by being trampled. □ **poach·er** *noun* [earlier *poche*, perhaps from French *pocher* put in a pocket (as POACH¹)]

pob·lano /pɒˈblanəʊ/ *noun* a large dark green chili pepper of a mild-flavoured variety. [Spanish]

po' boy *noun* (also **po' boy sandwich**) *var.* of POOR-BOY *noun*.

Poca·hon·tas /ˌpɒkəˈhɒntəs/ (*c.*1595–1617), Powhatan princess. According to the story of an English colonist in Virginia, Captain John Smith, she rescued him from death at the hands of her father, Powhatan; in 1613 she was seized as a hostage by the English, and she later married a colonist, John Rolfe.

pock ● *noun* **1** a small pus-filled spot on the skin, esp. caused by chicken pox or smallpox. **2** (also **pock·mark**) **a** a scar, mark, or pit left by a pustule, pimple, etc. **b** a disfiguring mark, hole, or pit in a surface. ● *transitive verb* mark with pocks or disfiguring spots. □ **pocked** *adjective* **pocky** *adjective* [Old English *poc* from Germanic]

pock·et ● *noun* **1** a small bag sewn into or on clothing, for carrying small articles. **2 a** a pouch-like compartment in a suitcase, car door, etc. **b** any small bag-like pouch, esp. made of pastry etc. **3** one's financial resources (*it is beyond my pocket*). **4 a** an isolated group or area contrasted with or differing from its surroundings (*a few pockets of resistance remain*). **b** a wide or deep hollow among hills or mountains, a distinct area of depth within a pond or lake, etc. **5** a cavity in a rock or stratum, usu. filled with ore (esp. gold), water, etc. **6** a pouch at the corner or on the side of a billiard table or snooker table into which balls are driven. **7 a** = AIR POCKET. **b** a local atmospheric condition. **8** (*attributive*) **a** of a suitable size and shape for carrying in a pocket. **b** smaller than the usual size. **9 a** *Sport* a position in a race etc. in which a competitor is hemmed in by others and has no chance of winning. **b** *Football* a shielded area formed by blockers, usu. just behind the line of scrimmage, from which the quarterback throws a pass. **c** *Baseball* the deep centre of a baseball mitt or glove. ● *transitive verb* (**pock·et·ed**, **pock·et·ing**) **1** put into one's pocket. **2** take possession of or appropriate, esp. dishonestly. **3** confine or enclose in a small space as in a pocket. **4** *Sport* hem in (a competitor) during a race so as to remove the chance of winning. **5** conceal or suppress (one's feelings). **6** *Billiards etc.* drive (a ball) into a pocket. □ **dig into one's pockets** spend or provide money. **in pocket 1** having gained in a transaction.

Vowels: a *cat* ɑ *arm* e *bed* ɜr *her* ɜː *deux* ə *ago* ɪ *sit* i *cosy* iː *feed* ɒ *hot* ɔ *pore* ɔː *no* ʌ *run* ʊ *put*

2 (of money) available. **in a person's pocket 1** under a person's control. **2** close to or intimate with a person. **out of pocket** having lost in a transaction. □ **pocket·able** adjective **pocket·ful** noun **pocket·less** adjective [Anglo-French *poket(e)* diminutive of *poke* POKE²]

pocket·book noun **1** N Amer. one's stock of cash or financial resources. **2** US a purse or handbag. **3** N Amer. (**pocket book**) a small book in an inexpensive edition, esp. a paperback. **4** Brit. a notebook.

pocket borough noun Brit. hist. a borough in which the election of political representatives was controlled by one person or family.

pocket change noun N Amer. **1** loose change in one's pocket. **2** a very small amount of money.

pocket coil noun a type of mattress construction in which the individual springs are tied together.

pocket door noun a sliding door which opens and closes by emerging from and disappearing into a narrow, door-sized recess contained in the adjacent wall.

pocket gopher noun = GOPHER 2.

pocket knife noun a knife with a folding blade or blades, for carrying in the pocket.

pocket money noun **1** money for minor expenses. **2** esp. Brit. an allowance of money made to a child.

pocket park noun (also **vest-pocket park**) a small area of land set aside for and developed as a park within an urban setting.

pocket protector noun **1** a plastic insert for a shirt pocket, designed to protect the garment from rips and ink stains caused by pens. **2** this viewed as typical of the attire of a computer nerd.

pocket-sized adjective (also **pocket-size**) **1** of a size suitable for carrying in the pocket. **2** petty, small-scale.

pocket veto US ● noun an indirect veto of a legislative bill by the President, a state governor, etc., by retaining the bill unsigned until it is too late for it to be dealt with in the legislative session. ● transitive verb veto (a bill) this way.

pocket watch noun a watch intended to be carried in the pocket of a waistcoat, jacket, etc.

pock·mark noun = POCK noun 2. □ **pock·marked** adjective

poco /ˈpoːkoː/ adverb Music a little; rather (*poco adagio*). [Italian]

PO'd /piːˈoːd/ adjective annoyed. [abbreviation of 'pissed off']

pod¹ ● noun **1** a long seed vessel esp. of a leguminous plant, e.g. a pea. **2 a** an elongated, streamlined compartment suspended under an aircraft for an engine, fuel tanks, equipment etc. **b** a detachable compartment in a spacecraft (*a life pod*). **3** any protruding, detachable, or more or less enclosed unit or casing on or in a tool, craft, vehicle, etc. **4** the cocoon of a silkworm. **5** the case surrounding locust eggs. ● verb (**pod·ded**, **pod·ding**) **1** intransitive bear, form, or have a pod or pods. **2** transitive remove (peas etc.) from pods. □ **pod·ded** adjective [back-formation from dial. *podware*, *podder* field crops, of unknown origin]

pod² noun a small herd or school of marine animals, esp. whales. [19th c.: origin unknown]

-pod suffix (also **-pode**) Zool. foot, footed; having feet of a specified kind or number. [Greek *pod*, *pous* 'foot']

pod·agra /pəˈdagrə/ noun Med. gout of the foot, esp. the big toe. [Latin from Greek *pous podos* foot + *agra* seizure]

Pod·bor·ski /pɒdˈbɔrski/ **Steve** (b.1957), Canadian downhill skier. Following his first World Cup win in 1979 with a bronze medal at the 1980 Olympics, he went on to win three consecutive World Cup races in 1981 and three more in 1982. He retired from skiing in 1984 as the most successful Canadian male skier to date.

Pod·gor·ica /pɒdˈɡɒriːtsə/ the capital of Montenegro; pop. (est. 2002) 137,100. Between 1946 and 1993 it was named Titograd in honour of Marshal Tito.

podgy adjective (**podgi·er**, **podgi·est**) Brit. = PUDGY. □ **podgi·ness** noun [19th c.: from *podge* a short fat person]

podi·atry /pəˈdaɪətri/ noun esp. N Amer. a medical specialty involving the care of the feet and treatment of foot disorders by surgery, manipulation of soft tissue, medication, etc. □ **podi·at·ric** /ˌpoːdiˈatrɪk/ adjective **podi·at·rist** noun [Greek *pous podos* foot + *iatros* physician]

po·dium /ˈpoːdiəm/ noun (pl. **po·diums** or **podia** /-diə/) **1 a** a raised platform or dais at the front of a hall or stage. **b** a platform from which a conductor conducts an orchestra, choir, etc. **c** a lectern. **d** the desk at which passenger agents work at a departure gate in an airport. **2** a continuous projecting base or pedestal around a room or house etc. **3** a raised platform round the arena of a Roman amphitheatre.

4 Zool. a foot or an organ acting as a foot, esp. a tubelike foot of an echinoderm. [Latin from Greek *podion* diminutive of *pous pod-* foot]

Pod·olsk /pəˈdɒlsk/ an industrial city in Russia, south of Moscow; pop. (est. 2002) 192,300.

Po·dunk /ˈpoːdʌŋk/ adjective US a hypothetical small town regarded as typically dull or insignificant. [a place name of southern New England]

pod·zol /ˈpɒdzɒl/ noun (also **pod·sol** /-sɒl/) an acidic, generally infertile soil with minerals leached from its surface layers into a lower stratum. □ **pod·zol·ic** /-ˈzɒlɪk/ adjective **pod·zol·ize** transitive & intransitive verb (also esp. Brit. **-ise**) [Russian from *pod* under, *zola* ashes]

Poe, Edgar Allan (1809–49), US short-story writer, poet, and critic. His fiction and poetry are characterized by their exploration of the macabre, the fantastic, and the grotesque, and include the short stories 'The Fall of the House of Usher' (1840) and 'The Pit and the Pendulum' (1843), and the poems 'The Raven' (1845) and 'Annabel Lee' (1849).

poem noun **1** a metrical composition of words expressing facts, thoughts, feelings, or imaginative description. **2** an esp. non-metrical composition of words having some esp. aesthetic quality or qualities in common with poetry. **3** something, other than a composition of words, with poetic qualities (*the sculpture was a poem in stone*). [ultimately from Greek *poēma* = *poiēma* from *poieō* make]

poesy /ˈpoːəzi/ noun literary **1** poetry. **2** the art or composition of poetry. [ultimately from Greek *poēsis* = *poiēsis* making, poetry (as POEM)]

poet noun **1** a writer of poems. **2** a person possessing high powers of imagination or expression etc. [ultimately from Greek *poētēs* = *poiētēs* maker, poet (as POEM)]

poet·aster /ˌpoːətˈastɜr/ noun a paltry or inferior poet. [modern Latin (as POET): see -ASTER]

poet·ess noun often offensive a female poet.

poet·ic /poːˈetɪk/ adjective (also **poet·i·cal**) **1 a** of, like, or pertaining to poetry or poets. **b** consisting of or written in verse. **2** elevated or sublime in expression. □ **poet·ic·al·ly** adverb

poeti·cize /poːˈetɪˌsaɪz/ verb (also esp. Brit. **-cise**) **1** transitive **a** give a poetic character to. **b** treat in esp. trivial or inferior poetry. **2** intransitive **a** write or speak in a poetic manner. **b** compose esp. trivial or inferior poetry.

poetic justice noun well-deserved unforeseen retribution or reward.

poetic licence noun a writer's or artist's transgression of established rules of language for effect.

poet·ics /poːˈetɪks/ noun **1** the art of writing poetry. **2** the study of poetry and its techniques.

poet·ize /ˈpoːəˌtaɪz/ verb (also esp. Brit. **-ise**) **1** intransitive write or speak in verse or in a poetic style. **2** transitive represent in poetic form.

Poet Laureate noun **1** a poet officially recognized by a nation, often one appointed to write poems for state occasions. **2** a poet considered to be both significant and representative of a region etc.

poet·ry /ˈpoːətri/ noun **1 a** the expression or embodiment of beautiful or elevated thought, imagination, or feeling, in language and a form adapted to stir the imagination and the emotions. **b** composition in verse, metrical language, or some equivalent patterned arrangement of language. **2** poems collectively. **3** a poetic or tenderly pleasing quality. **4** anything compared to poetry. [medieval Latin *poetria* from Latin *poeta* POET, prob. after *geometry*]

poetry reading noun the reading of poetry, esp. to an audience; a public performance of poetry.

poetry slam noun a competitive public event, often in a coffee house etc., where poets read their work and are judged.

Poets' Corner part of Westminster Abbey where several poets are buried or commemorated.

po-faced adjective Brit. **1** having or assuming an expressionless or impassive face; poker-faced. **2** priggish, smug. [20th c.: perhaps from PO, influenced by *poker-faced*]

pogey noun (also **pogy**) Cdn informal **1** unemployment insurance benefits. **2** welfare benefits. [origin unknown]

pogo ● noun (pl. **pogos**) **1** (in full **pogo stick**) a toy consisting of a spring-loaded stick with rests for the feet, for jumping about on. **2** (**Pogo**) Cdn proprietary (in full **Pogo stick**) a hot dog covered in cornmeal batter, deep-fried or baked, and served on a stick. **3** a dance with movements suggestive of jumping on a toy pogo stick. ● intransitive verb **1** (also **pogo-stick**) move or jump on or as on a toy pogo stick. **2** dance the pogo. [20th c.: origin uncertain]

pogo·nia /pəˈɡoːniə/ noun any of various small orchids, esp. rose

pogonia, *Pogonia ophioglossoides*, of eastern N America, with a pink flower with a crested lip. [modern Latin from Greek *pogonion* 'beard']

po·grom /poːˈɡrɒm/ *noun* **1** an organized massacre, originally and especially of Jews in Russia. **2** an organized, officially tolerated attack on any community or group. [Russian, = devastation, from *gromit'* destroy]

Po Hai see Bo Hai.

P'ohang /poːˈhaŋ/ a city on the east coast of S Korea; pop. (est. 1995) 508,899.

poi /pɔɪ/ *noun* a Hawaiian dish made from the fermented root of the taro, *Colocasia esculenta*. [Polynesian]

poign·ant /ˈpɔɪnjənt/ *adjective* **1 a** deeply moving, touching. **b** painfully sharp to the emotions or senses; distressing. **2** arousing sympathy.
□ **poign·ance** *noun* **poign·ancy** *noun* **poign·ant·ly** *adverb* [Old French, pres. part. of *poindre* prick, from Latin *pungere*]

poi·kilo·therm /ˈpɔɪkɪləˌθɜːm/ *noun* an organism that regulates its body temperature by behavioural means, such as basking or burrowing; a cold-blooded organism (compare HOMEOTHERM).
□ **poi·kilo·therm·al** *adjective* **poi·kilo·therm·ic** *adjective* [Greek *poikilos* multicoloured, changeable + *thermē* heat]

poilu /pwɒˈluː/ *noun hist.* a nickname for a French private soldier, esp. one who served in the First World War. [French, lit. 'hairy' from *poil* hair]

Poin·caré /pwãkaˈreɪ/ **Jules-Henri** (1854–1912), French mathematician and philosopher of science. He made far-reaching contributions to pure and applied mathematics, worked extensively on differential equations which allowed him to transform celestial mechanics, and was one of the pioneers of algebraic topology.

poin·ci·ana /ˌpɔɪnsiˈɑːnə/ *noun* any tropical tree of the genus *Poinciana*, with bright showy red flowers. [modern Latin from M. de *Poinci*, 17th-c. governor in the W Indies + *-ana* fem. suffix]

poin·settia /pɔɪnˈsɛtə, -sɛtiə/ *noun* a shrub, *Euphorbia pulcherrima*, with large showy scarlet or pink bracts surrounding small yellow flowers, often grown as a houseplant. [modern Latin from J. R. *Poinsett*, US diplomat d.1851]

point ● *noun* **1** the sharp or tapered end of a tool, weapon, pencil, etc. **2** a tip, apex, extreme end, or sharp projection. **3** *Math.* that which is conceived as having a position, but no extent, magnitude, or dimension, e.g. the intersection of two lines. **4 a** a specific place or position, esp. as being in a particular direction etc. (*Iqaluit and points south; point of contact*). **b** (in the Presbyterian or United churches) each of the individual congregations served by a common minister (*Rev. Bisset's two-point charge in southern Ontario*). **5 a** a precise or particular moment at which something happens (*at the point of death*). **b** the critical or decisive moment for action (*when it came to the point, he refused*). **6 a** a very small mark on a surface; a speck. **b** a tiny dot or mark of light, colour, etc. (*stars seem to be points of light in the dark sky*). **7 a** a dot or other punctuation mark, esp. a period. **b** any of various dots or small strokes used in Semitic languages to indicate vowels or distinguish consonants. **8** = DECIMAL POINT. **9** a step, stage, or degree in progress, development, increase, or decrease (*at that point we gave up*). **10** a level of temperature at which a change of state occurs (*freezing point*). **11** a separate or single item, element, detail, or particular (*it is a point of principle*). **12 a** a unit of count in scoring in a game etc. **b** a unit in appraising the qualities of a competitor or of an exhibit in a competitive show. **c** a unit of credit towards an award, benefit, etc. **d** an advantage or success in an argument, discussion, or other less quantifiable contexts (*knows how to score points with the boss*). **13 a** a recognized unit in quoting variations in price or value, as of stocks and shares etc. **b** a percentage point in quoting interest rates (*mortgages have gone up three-quarters of a point*). **c** a unit of weight (2 mg) for diamonds. **14 a** (usu. prec. by *the*) a topic or subject for discussion, esp. the essential or most important part of a discourse (*that was the point of the question*). **b** (usu. with *neg.* or *interrogative*; often foll. by *in*) sense, purpose, advantage, or value (*saw no point in staying*). **c** (usu. prec. by *the*) a salient, effective, or significant part of a story, joke, remark, etc. (*don't see the point*). **15** a distinctive or distinguishing feature, quality, or characteristic, esp. as the basis for a judgment (*it has its points; tact is not his good point*). **16** a marking woven into a Hudson's Bay blanket to indicate weight. **17 a** each of 32 directions marked at equal distances around the circumference of a compass. **b** the corresponding direction towards the horizon. **c** the angular interval between two successive points of a compass, i.e. one-eighth of a right angle (11° 15′). **18** (usu. in *pl.*) *Brit.* = SWITCH *noun* 5. **19** (usu. in *pl.*) (in an internal combustion engine) **a** either of the metal pieces on a spark plug between which the spark jumps. **b** either of the metal surfaces of a contact breaker which

touch to complete the circuit in the distributor of a motor vehicle. **20 a** *Hockey* either of two areas to the left and right of the net, just inside the blue line where it meets the boards (*a shot from the point*). **b** *Basketball* a frontcourt position, usu. manned by the guard who sets up the team's defence. **21** *Lacrosse* **a** a player stationed a short distance in front of the goalkeeper and behind the cover-point. **b** this position. **22** a tapering piece of land jutting out into a body of water. **23** the prong of a deer's antler. **24 a** the extremities of a dog, horse, etc., esp. as distinguished by contrasting colour. **b** (in *pl.*) the mane and tail of a horse. **c** (in *pl.*) the ears, face, feet, and tail tip of certain breeds of cat, esp. Siamese. **25** *Printing* a unit of measurement for type bodies (in the UK and N America 0.0138 in., in Europe 0.0148 in.). **26** *Heraldry* any of nine particular positions on a shield used for specifying the position of charges etc. **27** *Boxing* the tip of the chin, esp. as a spot for a knockout blow. **28** *Military* **a** a small patrol leading the advance of a larger body of combat troops. **b** esp. *N Amer.* the position at the head of a column or wedge of troops (*walk point*). **c** esp. *N Amer.* = POINT MAN. **29** *hist.* a tagged lace or cord for lacing a bodice, attaching a hose to a doublet, etc. **30** *Naut.* a short piece of cord at the lower edge of a sail for tying up a reef. **31** the rigid position assumed by a dog pointing game. **32** *Archaeology* a usu. worked pointed flake or blade. ● *verb* **1 a** *transitive* (usu. foll. by *to*) indicate or direct (a person, a person's attention or course, etc.). **b** *transitive* (usu. foll. by *at*) direct, level, or aim (a finger, weapon, etc.). **c** *intransitive* direct attention in a certain direction (*pointed to the house across the road*). **d** *intransitive Computing* use a device such as a mouse or a light pen to move the cursor on a computer screen until it reaches a desired item. **2** *intransitive* (foll. by *at*, *towards*) **a** lie, face, or have its point or length directed in a certain direction etc. (*the needle points north*). **b** have a motion or tendency towards, to do, etc. **3** *intransitive* (foll. by *to*) suggest, indicate, or be evidence of (*it all points to murder*). **4** *transitive* give point or force to (words or actions). **5** *transitive* fill in or repair the joints of (brickwork) with smoothly finished mortar or cement. **6** *transitive* **a** punctuate. **b** insert points indicating vowels etc. in (written Hebrew etc.). **c** insert signs to aid chanting in the text of (Psalms etc.). **7** *transitive* sharpen (a pencil, tool, etc.). **8** *transitive & intransitive* (of a dog) indicate the presence of (game) by acting as pointer. **9** *intransitive* (of an abscess etc.) come to a head. **10** *transitive* extend (the toes or feet) so as to form a point. □ **at** (or **in**) **all points** in every part or respect. **at the point of** on the verge of; about to do (the action specified). **beside the point** irrelevant or irrelevantly. **case in point** an instance that is relevant or (prec. by *the*) under consideration. **have a point 1** be correct or effective in one's contention. **2** have made a convincing or significant remark. **in point of fact** see FACT. **make** (or **prove**) **a** (or **one's**) **point** establish a proposition; prove one's contention. **make a point of** (often foll. by verbal noun) **1** insist on; treat or regard as essential. **2** make a special project of (doing). **on** (or **upon**) **the point of** (foll. by verbal noun) about to do (the action specified). **point out** (often foll. by *that* + clause) indicate, show; draw attention to. **point up** emphasize; show as important. **score points off** get the better of in an argument etc. **take a person's point 1** concede that a person has made a valid contention. **2** understand the import or significance of what a person is saying. **to the point** relevant or relevantly. **to the point of** to the stage of; to such a degree as to justify. **up to a (certain) point** to some extent, but by no means completely. **win** (or **lose** etc.) **on points** *Boxing* win (or lose etc.) by scoring (or having) more points (scored against one) in a number of rounds, not by a knockout. [Old French *point*, *pointer* from Latin *punctum* from *pungere punct-* prick]

point-and-click *noun* (*attributive*) designating computer interfaces where the user selects an action by pointing the cursor to an icon on the screen and clicks with a mouse to initiate the action.

point-and-shoot ● *attributive adjective* designating a camera which does not require any manual adjustments to advance the film or take properly exposed and focused photographs. ● *noun* a point-and-shoot camera.

point-blank ● *adjective* **1 a** (of a shooting distance or range) from or within which a gun may be fired horizontally; very close to the target. **b** (of a shot or shooting) aimed or fired from or within such a range. **2** (of a remark, question, etc.) straightforward, blunt, direct. ● *adverb* **1** at very close range. **2** directly, bluntly, straightforwardly. [prob. from POINT + BLANK = white spot in the centre of a target]

point blanket *noun* a type of Hudson's Bay blanket with distinctive markings or 'points', usu. in the form of short black lines, woven in to indicate weight.

point-counterpoint *noun* a situation in which opposing views etc. are heard in alternation.

pointe /pɔɪnt/ *noun Ballet* **1** the tip of the toe or toes, or the toe of a pointe shoe. **2** (in full **pointe work**) dance performed on the tips of the toes. [French, 'tiptoe' as POINT].

Pointe-à-Pitre /pwãta'piːtr/ the chief port and commercial capital of the French island of Guadeloupe in the W Indies; pop. (1999) 20,948.

Pointe-Claire /pwãt'kler/ a former city in south central Quebec, in the southwestern part of the Island of Montreal, now part of the city of Montreal; pop. (2001) 29,286.

point·ed adjective **1** sharpened or tapering to a point. **2** (of a remark etc.) **a** penetrating, cutting, having particular force. **b** precisely aimed, exactly directed. **3** emphasized; made evident. **4** having a point of a specified kind. □ **point·ed·ly** adverb **point·ed·ness** noun

point·elle /pɔin'tel/ noun (often attributive) **1** knitwear incorporating eyelet holes giving a lacy effect. **2** a similar pattern or stitch worked on garments other than sweaters or for trimming.

Pointe-Noire /pwãt'nwɑr/ the chief seaport of the Republic of the Congo, an oil terminal on the Atlantic coast; pop. (est. 2002) 527,700.

point·er noun **1** a thing that points, e.g. the index hand of a gauge etc. **2** a rod for pointing to features on a map, chart, etc. **3** informal a hint, clue, or indication; a suggestion. **4** Computing a numerical representation of the address in memory of a piece of data, esp. as part of a composite data type. **5 a** a dog of a breed that on scenting game stands rigid looking towards it. **b** this breed. **6** Cdn a flat-bottomed rowboat, pointed at both ends and having a shallow draft, used by loggers esp. in river drives. **7** a movable image on a computer screen, often in the shape of an arrow, used to activate a window, point to an icon, etc. **8** (usu. prec. by a numeral) **a** a thing having or earning so many points (the ball swished through the net for another three-pointer). **b** a buck having horns with so many points (an eight-pointer). **9** (in pl.) two stars in the Big Dipper in line with Polaris.

pointe shoe noun a heelless shoe worn by female ballet dancers, made of canvas and satin with a leather sole, with the toe made up of layers of fabric stiffened with glue, allowing the dancer to dance on the tip of the toes.

point form noun an abbreviated form of writing, not using full sentences or developed paragraphs.

Point Grey see GREY, POINT.

point guard noun Basketball a small fast guard with good ball-handling skills who directs the team's offence from the point and controls the tempo of the game.

poin·til·lism /'pɔintɪˌlɪzəm/ noun Art a technique of Impressionist painting in which luminous effects are produced by tiny dots of pure colours, which seem to blend when viewed. □ **poin·til·list** noun & adjective **poin·til·lis·tic** adjective [French pointillisme from pointiller mark with dots]

point·ing noun **1** in senses of POINT verb. **2 a** cement or mortar filling the joints of brickwork. **b** facing produced by this. **c** the process of producing this.

point lace noun thread lace made wholly with a needle.

point·less adjective **1** lacking force, purpose, or meaning. **2** without a sharp or tapering point; having a rounded or blunt end. **3** (in games) without a point scored. □ **point·less·ly** adverb **point·less·ness** noun

point man noun esp. N Amer. **1** the soldier at the head of a patrol. **2** a person who leads a new endeavour etc. **3** Hockey the player taking a position at the point during a power play.

point of departure noun **1** an initial assumption or the starting point of a thought, action, etc. **2** a time or place at which a journey begins.

point of honour noun an action or circumstance that affects one's reputation.

point of no return noun a point in a journey or enterprise at which it becomes essential or more practical to continue to the end.

point of order noun an objection or query in a debate etc. as to whether correct procedure is being followed.

point of presence noun a location at which telecommunications equipment is sited to support subscribers' access to a telecommunications network, esp. the Internet. Abbr.: **POP**.

point of privilege noun an objection or query in a debate etc. prompted by a violation or perceived violation of the rights of the assembly, the organization, or the members individually, e.g. the implication that a speaker has made statements that he or she did not in fact make.

point of reference noun = REFERENCE POINT.

point-of-sale noun (also **point-of-purchase**) (usu. attributive) designating, pertaining to, for use at, or associated with the place at which goods are retailed.

point of view noun **1** a position from which a thing is viewed. **2** a particular way of considering a matter. **3** (in fiction etc.) the narrator's position relative to the story being told (first-person point of view; omniscient point of view).

Point Pelee see PELEE, POINT.

Point Pelee National Park /'piːli/ a small park in SW Ontario, encompassing the peninsula of Point Pelee. Established in 1918, it is a noted birdwatcher's paradise. [see PELEE, POINT]

point source noun a source of light, sound, etc. of negligible dimensions.

point spread noun esp. N Amer. **1** the number of points constituting the margin by which a stronger team is expected to defeat a weaker one, for betting purposes. **2** a forecast of this number.

point-to-point ● noun a steeplechase over a marked course for horses used regularly in hunting. ● adjective (of a dedicated communication link etc.) joining only two nodes in a network.

pointy adjective (**point·i·er**, **point·i·est**) having a noticeably sharp end; pointed.

pointy-headed adjective informal derogatory supposedly expert or intellectual (pointy-headed bureaucrat; some pointy-headed professor). □ **pointy head** noun

poise¹ ● noun **1** composure or self-possession of manner. **2** graceful and elegant bearing in a person. ● verb (usu. in passive) transitive & intransitive be or cause to be balanced or suspended. [Old French pois, peis, peser, ultimately from Latin pensum weight, from pendere pens-weigh]

poise² noun Physics a unit of dynamic viscosity, such that a tangential force of one dyne per square centimetre causes a velocity change one centimetre per second between two parallel planes in a liquid separated by one centimetre. [J. L. M. Poiseuille, French physician d.1869]

poised adjective **1** composed, self-assured. **2** (often foll. by for, or to + infin.) ready for action.

poi·sha /'pɔiʃə/ noun (pl. same) a monetary unit of Bangladesh, equal to one-hundredth of a taka. [Bengali, alteration of PAISA]

poi·son ● noun **1** a substance that when introduced into or absorbed by a living organism causes death or injury, esp. one that kills by rapid action even in a small quantity. **2** a harmful influence or principle etc. **3** Physics & Chem. a substance that interferes with the normal progress of a nuclear reaction, chain reaction, catalytic reaction, etc. ● transitive verb **1** administer poison to (a person or animal). **2** kill or injure or infect (a person or animal) with poison. **3** infect (air, water, etc.) with poison. **4** (esp. as **poi·soned** adjective) treat (a weapon) with poison. **5** corrupt or pervert (a person or mind). **6** spoil or destroy (a person's pleasure etc.). **7** render (land etc.) unusable, e.g. by the accumulation of chemicals or toxins etc. (this landfill site has poisoned some of our best farmland). □ **what's your poison?** informal what can I get you to drink? □ **poi·son·er** noun **poi·son·ing** noun **poi·son·ous** adjective **poi·son·ous·ly** adverb [Old French poison, poisonner (as POTION)]

poisoned chalice noun an assignment, award, honour, etc. which is likely to prove a disadvantage or source of problems to the recipient.

poison gas noun = GAS noun 6.

poison ivy noun a N American climbing plant, Toxicodendron radicans, secreting an irritant oil from its leaves.

poison oak noun either of two N American shrubs, Toxicodendron diversilobum and R. diversilobia, related to poison ivy and having similar properties.

poison-pen letter noun an anonymous letter written with malicious, libellous, or abusive intent.

poison pill noun **1** a pill containing esp. fast-acting poison. **2** Business any of various ploys used by a company threatened with an unwelcome takeover bid to make itself unattractive to the bidder.

poison sumac noun a small tree or shrub with pinnate leaves, Toxicodendron vernix, of eastern N America related to poison ivy and having similar properties.

Pois·son distribution noun Statistics a discrete frequency distribution which gives the probability of events occurring in a fixed time. [S.-D. Poisson, French mathematical physicist d.1840]

Poi·tier /'pwɒtjei/ **Sid·ney** (b.1924), Bahamian-born US actor and director, whose films include Blackboard Jungle (1955), Lilies of the Field (1963), for which he won an Oscar, and In the Heat of the Night (1967).

Poi·tiers /pwɒ't͡jei/ a city in west central France, the chief town of Poitou-Charentes region and capital of the former province of Poitou; pop. (1999) 83,448. It was the site in AD 507 of the defeat of the

t top   v voice   w we   z zoo   ʃ she   ʒ vision   θ thin   ð this   ŋ ring   x loch   tʃ chip   dʒ jar   (see over for vowels)

Visigoths by Clovis and in 732 of Charles Martel's victory over the invading Muslims.

Poi·tou /pwɒˈtuː/ a former province of west central France, now united with Charente to form the region of Poitou-Charentes.

Poitou-Charentes /pwɒtuːʃaˈrɑ̃t/ a region of W France, on the Bay of Biscay, centred on Poitiers.

poke¹ ● *verb* **1** (foll. by *in*, *up*, *down*, etc.) **a** *transitive* thrust or push with the hand, point of a stick, etc. **b** *intransitive* be thrust forward. **2** *intransitive* (foll. by *at* etc.) make thrusts with a stick etc. **3** *transitive* **a** thrust the end of a finger etc. against (*poked me in the ribs*). **b** *informal* punch, hit (*would like to poke him for saying that*). **4** *transitive* (foll. by *in*) produce (a hole etc. in a thing) by poking. **5** *transitive* thrust forward, esp. obtrusively (*poked her head out of the window*). **6** *transitive* stir (a fire) with a poker. **7** *intransitive* (often foll. by *along*) move or go slowly or in an aimless manner. **8** *transitive & intransitive* (foll. by *around*, *about*) pry; search casually. **9** *transitive coarse slang* have sexual intercourse with. ● *noun* **1** the act or an instance of poking. **2** a thrust or nudge. **3** a device fastened on cattle etc. to prevent them breaking through fences. **4** *hist.* **a** a projecting brim or front of a woman's bonnet or hat. **b** (in full **poke bonnet**) a bonnet having this. □ **poke fun at** ridicule, tease. **poke holes in** *N Amer.* **1** find fault with (an idea etc.). **2** make holes in (material etc.) by plucking, poking, etc. [Middle Dutch and Middle Low German *poken*, of unknown origin]

poke² *noun* **1** *hist.* a small bag used by miners to carry gold dust or nuggets. **2** esp. *US Midlands* a bag or sack. □ **buy a pig in a poke** see PIG. [Old Northern French *poke*, *poque* = Old French *poche*: compare POUCH]

poke³ *noun* **1** = POKEWEED. **2** = INDIAN POKE.

poke check *noun* Hockey a defensive play in which a player holds his or her stick low along the ice and pokes the puck out of the puck carrier's control. □ **poke-check** *transitive verb* **poke-checking** *noun*

pok·er¹ *noun* a stiff metal rod with a handle for stirring an open fire.

pok·er² *noun* a card game in which bluff is used as players bet on the value of their hands. [19th c.: origin unknown: compare German *pochen* to brag, *Pochspiel* bragging game]

poker face *noun* the impassive countenance appropriate to a poker player. □ **poker-faced** *adjective*

poker run *noun* N Amer. (also **poker derby**) Cdn (Man., Sask., & NW Ont.) a competition in which participants race to a series of points (usu. over a large area) collecting a single playing card at each one, the winner being determined by a combination of time taken and the poker hand collected.

poke·weed *noun* a tall N American plant, *Phytolacca americana*, with spikes of cream flowers and purple berries that yield emetics and purgatives. [Algonquian *poke* + WEED]

pok·ey *noun* esp. N Amer. slang prison. [perhaps from POKY]

poky *adjective* (**pok·i·er**, **pok·i·est**) **1** (of a room etc.) small and cramped. **2** N Amer. annoyingly slow. □ **pok·i·ly** *adverb* **pok·i·ness** *noun* [POKE¹ (in informal sense 'confine') + -Y¹]

pol *noun* N Amer. informal a politician. [abbreviation]

po·lack /ˈpoʊlak/ *noun* N Amer. slang offensive a person of Polish origin. [French *Polaque* and German *Polack* from Polish *Polak*]

Po·land /ˈpoʊlənd/ a country in central Europe with a coastline on the Baltic Sea; pop. (est. 2002) 38,625,478; capital, Warsaw.

Po·lan·ski /pəˈlanski/ **Roman** (b.1933), French film director, of Polish descent, whose films include *Rosemary's Baby* (1968), *Chinatown* (1974), *Tess* (1979), and *Death and the Maiden* (1994).

Po·lanyi /pəˈlanji/ **John Charles** (b.1929), German-born Canadian chemist and professor. A professor of chemistry at the University of Toronto since 1962, he was co-recipient in 1986 of the Nobel Prize for chemistry, for his work on infrared radiation.

polar *adjective* **1 a** of or near a pole of the earth or a celestial body, or of the celestial sphere. **b** (of a species or variety) living in the north polar region. **2** having magnetic polarity. **3 a** (of a molecule) having a positive charge at one end and a negative charge at the other. **b** (of a compound) having electric charges. **4** *Math.* of or relating to a pole. **5** directly opposite in character or tendency. [French *polaire* or modern Latin *polaris* (as POLE²)]

polar bear *noun* a very large white bear, *Ursus maritimus*, of Arctic regions.

polar bear swim *noun* (also **polar bear dip**) N Amer. an organized swim in cold or partially ice-covered water, esp. on a holiday such as New Year's Day.

polar body *noun* a small cell produced from an oocyte during the formation of an ovum, which does not develop further.

polar cap *noun* a region of ice or other frozen matter surrounding a pole of a planet.

polar circle *noun* each of the circles parallel to the equator at a distance of 23° 27′ from either pole.

polar coordinates *noun* a system by which a point can be located with reference to two angles.

polar desert *noun* a type of arid region found near the poles, characterized by frost-shattered rock, small flowering plants, and few or no lichens or mosses.

polar fleece *noun* a thick and dense fleece fabric.

polari- *combining form* polar. [modern Latin *polaris* (as POLAR)]

polar ice cap *noun* = POLAR CAP.

polar·im·eter /ˌpoʊlaˈrɪmɪtər/ *noun* an instrument used to measure the polarization of light or the effect of a substance on the rotation of the plane of polarized light. □ **po·lari·met·ric** /-ˈmɛtrɪk/ *adjective* **polar·im·etry** *noun*

Po·lar·is¹ /poʊˈlɑrəs, pə-/ a variable star, the brightest in the constellation Ursa Minor, lying within one degree of the north celestial pole. Also called NORTH STAR. [medieval Latin (as POLAR)]

Po·lar·is² /poʊˈlɑrəs, pə-/ *noun* a type of submarine-launched ballistic missile. [POLARIS¹]

po·lari·scope /poʊˈlarɪˌskoʊp/ *noun* an instrument for showing the polarization of light. □ **po·lari·scop·ic** /-ˈskɒpɪk/ *adjective*

polar·ity /pəˈlarɪti/ *noun* (pl. **-ities**) **1** the tendency of a lodestone, magnetized bar, etc., to point with its extremities to the magnetic poles of the earth. **2** the condition of having two poles with contrary qualities. **3** the state of having two opposite tendencies, opinions, etc. **4** the electrical condition of a body (positive or negative). **5** (*attributive*) designating any of various treatments intended to restore a balanced distribution of the body's energy, typically involving manipulation, exercise, and dietary restrictions (*polarity therapy*).

polar·ize *verb* (also esp. *Brit.* **-ise**) **1** *transitive* restrict the vibrations of (a transverse wave, esp. light) to one direction. **2** *transitive* give magnetic or electric polarity to (a substance or body). **3** *transitive & intransitive* divide into two groups of opposing opinion etc. □ **polar·iz·able** *adjective* **polar·iz·a·tion** *noun* **polar·iz·er** *noun*

polar·og·raphy /ˌpoʊləˈrɒɡrəfi/ *noun* Chem. the analysis by measurement of current-voltage relationships in electrolysis between mercury electrodes. □ **po·laro·graph·ic** /-əˈɡrafɪk/ *adjective*

Po·lar·oid /ˈpoʊləˌrɔɪd/ *noun* proprietary **1** material in thin plastic sheets that produces a high degree of plane-polarization in light passing through it. **2 a** a type of camera with internal processing that produces a finished print rapidly after each exposure. **b** a photograph taken with such a camera. **3** (in *pl.*) sunglasses with lenses made from Polaroid. [POLARI- + -OID]

pol·der /ˈpoʊldər/ *noun* a piece of low-lying land reclaimed from the sea or a river, esp. in the Netherlands. [Dutch]

Pole¹ *noun* **1** a native or national of Poland. **2** a person of Polish descent. [German from Polish *Polanie*, lit. 'field dwellers' from *pole* field]

Pole², **Reg·in·ald** (1500–58), English clergyman. He assisted Mary I of England in her Counter-Reformation program, and was the last Roman Catholic archbishop of Canterbury (1556–8).

pole¹ ● *noun* **1** a long slender rounded piece of wood, metal, etc., esp. with the end placed in the ground as a support etc. **2** a wooden shaft fitted to the front of a wagon or carriage etc. and attached to the yokes or collars of the draft animals. **3** *Athletics* a long slender flexible rod of wood, fibreglass, etc. used by a competitor in pole vaulting. **4** esp. N Amer. = FISHING ROD. **5** *hist.* = PERCH¹ 3. ● *verb* **1** *transitive* provide with poles. **2** *transitive* push or propel (a boat etc.) with a pole. **3** *intransitive* use poles, esp. to propel a boat or oneself on skis. [Old English *pāl*, ultimately from Latin *palus* stake]

pole² *noun* **1** (in full **north pole**, **south pole**) **a** each of the two points in the celestial sphere about which the stars appear to revolve. **b** each of the extremities of the axis of rotation of the earth or another body. **c** see MAGNETIC POLE. ¶ The spelling is *North Pole* and *South Pole* when used as geographical designations. **2** each of the two opposite points on the surface of a magnet at which magnetic forces are strongest. **3** each of two terminals (positive and negative) of an electric cell or battery etc. **4** each of two opposed principles or ideas. **5** *Math.* each of two points in which the axis of a circle cuts the surface of a sphere. **6** a fixed point to which others are referred. **7** *Biol.* an extremity of the main axis of any spherical or oval organ. □ **be poles apart** differ greatly, esp. in nature or opinion. □ **pole·ward** *adjective*

pole·wards *adjective & adverb* [Latin *polus* from Greek *polos* pivot, axis, sky]

pole·axe ● *noun* a battle-axe. ● *transitive verb* **1** hit or kill with or as if with a poleaxe. **2** (usu. *passive*) affect (a person) very greatly with surprise, distress, etc. (*was poleaxed by the news of her death*). [Middle English *pol(l)ax*, *-ex* from Middle Dutch *pol(l)aex*, Middle Low German *pol(l)exe* (as POLL, AXE)]

pole barn *noun* a farm building for housing livestock etc., having relatively open walls.

pole bean *noun* any of various vine-like varieties of bean that grow upright, supported by a pole, fence, etc.

pole·cat *noun* **1** *Brit.* a small European brownish-black fetid flesh-eating mammal, *Mustela putorius*, of the weasel family. **2** *N Amer.* a skunk. [possibly from Old French *pole* chicken + CAT]

po·lem·ic /pəˈlemɪk/ ● *noun* **1** a controversial discussion. **2** *Politics* a verbal or written attack, esp. on a political opponent. **3** (in *pl.*; also treated as *sing.*) the art of controversial discussion, esp. in theology. ● *adjective* (also **po·lem·ic·al**) involving dispute; controversial. □ **po·lem·ic·al·ly** *adverb* **po·lemi·cist** /-sɪst/ *noun* **po·lemi·cize** *transitive verb* (also esp. *Brit.* **-cise**) /-saiz/. [medieval Latin *polemicus* from Greek *polemikos* from *polemos* war]

po·len·ta /pəˈlentə/ *noun* cornmeal boiled in water and often baked or fried. [Italian from Latin, = pearl barley]

pole position *noun* the most favourable position at the start of a motor race (originally next to the inside boundary fence).

pole sitter *noun* the driver who starts a motor race in pole position.

pole star *noun* **1** *Astronomy* = POLARIS[1]. **2 a** a thing or principle serving as a guide. **b** a centre of attraction.

pole vault ● *noun* the athletic sport of vaulting over a high bar with the aid of a long flexible pole held in the hands and giving extra spring. ● *intransitive verb* (**pole-vault**) take part in this sport. □ **pole vaulter** *noun*

po·lice ● *noun* (treated as *pl.*) **1** (usu. prec. by *the*) a civil force responsible for enforcing the law, maintaining public order, etc. **2** the members of a police force (*several hundred police*). **3** a force with similar functions of enforcing regulations (*military police; railway police*). **4** a group, often self-appointed, which criticizes or attempts to stop practices that it considers unacceptable (*language police; fashion police*). ● *transitive verb* **1** control (a country or area) by means of police. **2** provide with police. **3** keep order in; control. [French from medieval Latin *politia* POLICY[1]]

police action *noun* **1** the deeds or activity of the police. **2** military intervention without a formal declaration of war.

police constable *noun see* CONSTABLE 1. Abbr.: **PC**.

police dog *noun* a dog, esp. a German shepherd, used in police work.

police force *noun* the body of police of a country, district, or town.

police informer *noun* a person who gives police information about crimes and offenders.

police·man *noun* (*pl.* **-men**) **1** a member of a police force. **2** *Hockey* = ENFORCER 2. **3** a person, nation, organization, etc., regarded as maintaining or imposing order.

police officer *noun* a policeman or policewoman.

police procedural *noun* a detective novel characterized by detailed attention to police procedures in detecting crime.

police state *noun* a totalitarian state or country controlled by political police supervising the citizens' activities.

police station *noun* the office of the police in a certain district or community.

police tape *noun* tape, usu. yellow, used by police to rope off a crime scene during investigation.

police village *noun* *Cdn* (*Ont.*) a small, unincorporated village administered by a group of elected trustees. [originally governed by a *Board of Police*, from obsolete sense of *police* 'regulation and control of a community; public order']

police·woman *noun* (*pl.* **-women**) a female member of a police force.

pol·icy[1] /ˈpɒləsi/ *noun* (*pl.* **-cies**) **1** a course or principle of action adopted or proposed by a government, party, business, or individual etc. **2** prudent conduct; sagacity. [Old French *policie* from Latin *politia* from Greek *politeia* citizenship, from *politēs* citizen, from *polis* city]

pol·icy[2] /ˈpɒləsi/ *noun* (*pl.* **-cies**) **1** a contract of insurance. **2** a document containing this. [French *police* bill of lading, contract of insurance, from Provençal *poliss(i)a* prob. from medieval Latin *apodissa*, *apodixa*, from Latin *apodixis* from Greek *apodeixis* evidence, proof (as APO-, *deiknumi* show)]

policy·hold·er *noun* a person or body holding an insurance policy.

policy-maker *noun* a person who helps to determine esp. government or party policy. □ **policy-making** *noun & adjective*

policy wonk *noun* = WONK 2.

polio /ˈpəʊliəʊ/ *noun* = POLIOMYELITIS. [abbreviation]

polio·myel·itis /ˌpəʊliəʊˌmaiəˈlaitis/ *noun* *Med.* an infectious viral disease that affects the central nervous system and which can cause temporary or permanent paralysis. [modern Latin from Greek *políos* grey + *muelos* marrow + -ITIS]

polio·virus /ˈpəʊliəʊˌvairəs/ *noun* any of a group of enteroviruses, including those that cause poliomyelitis.

polis /ˈpɒlɪs/ *noun* *hist.* (*pl.* **pol·eis**) a city state, esp. in ancient Greece. [Greek, = city]

poli-sci /ˌpɒliˈsai/ *noun* *N Amer. informal* political science (also *attributive*: *a second-year poli-sci class*). [abbreviation]

Po·lish /ˈpəʊlɪʃ/ ● *adjective* **1** of or relating to Poland. **2** of the Poles or their language. ● *noun* the Slavic language of Poland. [POLE[1] + -ISH[1]]

pol·ish /ˈpɒlɪʃ/ ● *verb* **1** *transitive & intransitive* make or become smooth or glossy by rubbing. **2** *transitive* (esp. as **pol·ished** *adjective*) refine or improve; add finishing touches to. ● *noun* **1** a substance used for polishing. **2** smoothness or glossiness produced by friction. **3** the act or an instance of polishing. **4** refinement or elegance of manner, conduct, etc. □ **polish off 1** finish (esp. food) quickly. **2** get rid of (an enemy, etc.). **polish up** revise or improve (a skill etc.). □ **pol·ish·er** *noun* [Old French *polir* from Latin *polire polit-*]

Polish Corridor a former region of Poland, which extended northward to the Baltic coast and separated East Prussia from the rest of Germany. A part of Polish Pomerania in the 18th c., the area had since then been subject to German colonization, but was granted to Poland after the First World War. Its annexation by Germany in 1939 precipitated the Second World War, after which the area was restored to Poland.

Polish sausage *noun* = KIELBASA.

polit·buro /ˈpɒlɪtˌbjʊərəʊ/ *noun* (*pl.* **-buros**) the principal policy-making committee of a Communist party, esp. in the former USSR. [Russian *politbyuro* from *polítícheskoe byuró* political bureau]

po·lite *adjective* (**po·lit·er**, **po·lit·est**) **1** having good manners; courteous. **2** cultivated, cultured. **3** refined, elegant (*polite letters*). □ **po·lite·ly** *adverb* **po·lite·ness** *noun* [Latin *politus* (as POLISH)]

po·li·tesse /ˌpɒliˈtes/ *noun* formal politeness. [French]

pol·itic /ˈpɒlɪtɪk/ ● *adjective* **1** (of an action) judicious, expedient. **2** (of a person) prudent, sagacious. **3** political. ¶ Sense 3 is now used only in *body politic*. ● *intransitive verb* (**pol·it·icked**, **pol·it·ick·ing**) engage in politics. □ **pol·it·ick·ing** *noun* **pol·it·ic·ly** *adverb* [ultimately from Greek *politikos* from *politēs* citizen, from *polis* city]

pol·it·ic·al /pəˈlɪtɪkəl/ *adjective* **1 a** of or concerning the state or its government, or public affairs generally. **b** of, relating to, or engaged in politics. **c** belonging to or forming part of a civil administration. **2** having an organized form of society or government. **3** taking or belonging to a side in politics. **4** relating to or affecting interests of status or authority in an organization rather than matters of principle (*a political decision*). □ **pol·it·ic·al·ly** *adverb*

political asylum *noun* protection given by a country to a political refugee from another country.

political correctness *noun* the avoidance of forms of expression or action that exclude, marginalize, or insult certain racial or cultural groups.

political economy *noun* the study of the economic aspects of government. □ **political economist** *noun*

political football *noun* an issue, institution, etc. that is exploited by opposing political factions for their own purposes.

political geography *noun* geography dealing with boundaries and the possessions of countries, etc.

politically correct *adjective* exhibiting political correctness.

politically incorrect *adjective* failing to exhibit political correctness.

political prisoner *noun* a person imprisoned for political beliefs or actions.

political science *noun* the study of the state and systems of government. □ **political scientist** *noun*

political will *noun* support by the public for policies, esp. controversial ones.

pol·it·ician /ˌpɒlɪˈtɪʃən/ *noun* **1** a person engaged in or concerned with politics, esp. as a practitioner. **2** a person skilled in politics.

pol·iti·cize /pə'lɪtɪ,saɪz/ *verb* (also esp. *Brit.* **-cise**) **1** *transitive* **a** give a political character to. **b** make politically aware. **2** *intransitive* engage in or talk politics. □ **pol·iti·ciz·a·tion** *noun*

pol·it·ico /pə'lɪtɪ,koː/ *noun* (*pl.* **-icos**) *informal* a politician or political enthusiast. [Spanish or Italian (as POLITIC)]

politico- /pə'lɪtɪkoː/ *combining form* **1** politically. **2** political and (*politico-social*). [Greek *politikos*: see POLITIC]

pol·itics /'pɒlɪtɪks/ *plural noun* **1** (treated as *sing.* or *pl.*) **a** the art and science of government. **b** public life and affairs as involving authority and government. **2** (usu. treated as *pl.*) **a** a particular set of ideas, principles, or commitments in politics (*what are their politics?*). **b** activities concerned with the acquisition or exercise of authority or power in an organization etc. (*she's not good at playing office politics*). **c** an organizational process or principle affecting authority, status, etc. (*the politics of the decision*). **3** the assumptions or principles relating to or inherent in a sphere, theory, or thing, esp. when concerned with power and status in a society.

pol·ity /'pɒlɪti/ *noun* (*pl.* **-ities**) **1** a form or process of civil government or constitution. **2** an organized society; a state as a political entity. [Latin *politia* from Greek *politeia* from *politēs* citizen, from *polis* city]

Polk /poːk/ **James Knox** (1795–1849), US Democratic politician, 11th president of the US 1845–9. During his term of office, Texas was admitted to the Union (1845), and the successful outcome of the conflict with Mexico resulted in the annexation of California and the southwest (1847).

polka /'poːlkə, 'pɒlkə/ ● *noun* **1** a lively dance of Bohemian origin for couples in duple time. **2** the music for this. ● *intransitive verb* (**pol·kas**, **pol·kaed** or **polka'd**, **polka·ing**) dance the polka. [French and German from Czech *půlka* half-step, from *půl* half]

polka dot /'poːkə, 'pɒlkə/ *noun* a round dot as one of many forming a regular pattern on fabric etc. □ **polka-dot** *adjective* **polka-dotted** *adjective*

poll /poːl/ ● *noun* **1 a** the process of voting at an election. **b** the counting of votes at an election. **c** the result of voting. **d** the number of votes recorded (*a heavy poll*). **e** (usu. in *pl.*) a place where votes are cast. **2** = GALLUP POLL, OPINION POLL. **3 a** a human head. **b** the part of this on which hair grows. **4** a hornless animal, esp. one of a breed of hornless cattle. **5** the part of an animal's (esp. a horse's) head between the ears. ● *verb* **1** *transitive* **a** take the vote or votes of. **b** (in *passive*) have one's vote taken. **c** (of a candidate) receive (so many votes). **d** give (a vote). **2** *transitive* record the opinion of (a person or group) in an opinion poll. **3** *intransitive* give one's vote. **4** *transitive* cut off the top of (a tree or plant), esp. make a pollard of. **5** *transitive* (esp. as **polled** *adjective*) cut the horns off (cattle). **6** *transitive Computing* check the status of (a computer system) at intervals. □ **go to the polls** have an election (*the province goes to the polls next week*). [Middle English, perhaps from Low German or Dutch]

pol·lack *var. of* POLLOCK.

pol·lard /'pɒlərd/ ● *noun* **1** an animal that has lost or cast its horns; an ox, sheep, or goat of a hornless breed. **2** a tree which has been polled or cut back, so as to produce a growth of young branches at the top. ● *transitive verb* make (a tree) a pollard. [POLL + -ARD]

poll captain *noun Cdn* a person responsible for directing an election campaign for a candidate in a given area.

pol·len /'pɒlən/ *noun* the fine dust-like grains discharged from the male part of a flower containing the gamete that fertilizes the female ovule. [Latin *pollen pollinis* fine flour, dust]

pollen analysis *noun* = PALYNOLOGY.

pollen count *noun* an index of the amount of pollen in the air, published esp. for the benefit of those allergic to it.

pol·lex /'pɒleks/ *noun* (*pl.* **pol·li·ces** /-lɪ,siːz/) the innermost digit of a forelimb, usu. the thumb in primates. [Latin, = thumb or big toe]

pol·lin·ate /'pɒlɪ,neɪt/ *transitive & intransitive verb* fertilize (a plant) with pollen. □ **pol·lin·a·tion** *noun* **pol·lin·ator** *noun*

poll·ing /'poːlɪŋ/ *noun* the registering or casting of votes.

polling booth *noun* a compartment in which a voter stands or sits to mark a ballot paper.

polling day *noun* the day of a local or general election.

polling station *noun* (*N Amer.* also **polling place**) a building where voting takes place during an election, typically one that normally has another function.

pol·lin·if·er·ous /,pɒlɪ'nɪfɜrəs/ *adjective* bearing or producing pollen.

polli·wog *var. of* POLLYWOG.

Pol·lock /'pɒlək/ **(Paul) Jack·son** (1912–56), US painter. A leading figure of abstract expressionism, he developed the style known as

action painting, in which he fixed the canvas to the floor or wall, and poured, splashed, or dripped paint on it, avoiding any point of emphasis in the picture.

pol·lock /'pɒlək/ *noun* (also **pol·lack**) **1** a greenish food fish of the cod family, *Pollachius virens*, inhabiting the N Atlantic, having a characteristic protruding jaw, an important food fish. *Also called* BOSTON BLUEFISH. **2** a similar European fish, *P. pollachius*. [earlier (Scots) *podlock*: origin unknown]

poll·ster *noun* a person who conducts or analyzes opinion polls.

poll tax *noun* a tax levied on every adult, without reference to their income or resources.

pol·lute /pə'luːt/ *transitive verb* **1** contaminate or defile (the environment). **2** make foul or filthy. **3** destroy the purity or sanctity of. □ **pol·lut·ant** *adjective & noun* **pol·lut·er** *noun* [Middle English from Latin *polluere pollut-*]

pol·lut·ed /pə'luːtəd/ *adjective* **1** made unclean; contaminated. **2** *N Amer. slang* drunk.

pol·lu·tion /pə'luːʃən/ *noun* the presence in the environment, or the introduction into it, of substances, features, etc. that have harmful or unpleasant effects (*air pollution; noise pollution*).

Pol·lux /'pɒləks/ **1** *Gk Myth* the twin brother of Castor (see DIOSCURI). *Also called* POLYDEUCES. **2** *Astronomy* the brightest star in the constellation of Gemini, close to Castor.

Polly·anna /,pɒli'anə/ *noun* a cheerful optimist; an excessively cheerful person. □ **Polly·anna·ish** *adjective* **Polly·anna·ism** *noun* [unfailingly optimistic character in a novel (1913) by E. Porter]

polly·wog /'pɒli,wɒg/ *noun* (also **polli·wog**) *N Amer.* a tadpole. [earlier *polwigge, polwygle* from POLL + WIGGLE]

Polo see MARCO POLO.

polo /'poːloː/ *noun* **1** a game in which players riding on horses try to hit a ball into a goal using long wooden mallets. **2** = POLO SHIRT. [Balti, = ball]

Pol·ok·wane /pɒlɒ'kwɒni/ a town in northern South Africa, capital of Limpopo province; pop. (est. 2002) 101,600. Formerly called Pietersburg (until 2002).

polo·naise /,pɒlə'neɪz/ *noun* **1** a dance of Polish origin, consisting chiefly of an intricate march or procession in triple time. **2** the music for this. **3** *hist.* a woman's dress consisting of a bodice and a skirt open from the waist downwards to show an underskirt. [French, fem. of *polonais* 'Polish' from medieval Latin *Polonia* Poland]

polo neck *noun Brit.* = TURTLENECK 1.

polo·nium /pə'loːniəm/ *noun Chem.* a rare radioactive metallic element, occurring naturally in uranium ores. Symbol: **Po**; at. no.: 84. [French & modern Latin from medieval Latin *Polonia* Poland (the native country of Marie Curie, its discoverer) + -IUM]

polo shirt *noun* a short-sleeved casual shirt with a collar and a short buttoned vertical placket at the front neckline.

polo stick *noun* a mallet for playing polo.

Pol Pot /pɒl 'pɒt/ (*c.*1925–98), Cambodian Communist leader, prime minister 1976–9. During his regime, over two million people died from execution, forced labour, starvation, or disease; overthrown in 1979, he led the Khmer Rouge in a guerrilla war against the new Vietnamese-backed government until his official retirement from the leadership in 1985.

pol·ski ogor·ki *plural noun* Polish dill pickles with garlic. [Polish, lit. = 'Polish pickles']

Pol·tava /pəl'tɒvə/ a city in east central Ukraine; pop. (est. 2001) 318,000.

pol·ter·geist /'poːltər,gaɪst/ *noun* a noisy mischievous ghost, esp. one manifesting itself by physical damage. [German from *poltern* create a disturbance + *Geist* GHOST]

Pol·tor·atsk /,pɒltə'rɒtsk/ a former name (1919–27) of ASHGABAT.

pol·troon /pɒl'truːn/ *noun* a spiritless coward. □ **pol·troon·ery** *noun* [French *poltron* from Italian *poltrone* perhaps from *poltro* sluggard]

poly /'pɒli/ *noun* **1** polyester. **2** polyethylene. **3** (*pl.* **polys**) *Brit. informal* polytechnic. [abbreviation]

poly- /'pɒli/ *combining form* **1** denoting many or much. **2** *Chem.* denoting the presence of several or many radicals etc. of a particular kind in a molecule, esp. a polymer (*polythene; polysaccharide*). [Greek *polu-* from *polus* much, *polloi* many]

poly·acryl·amide /,pɒliə'krɪləmaɪd/ *noun* a synthetic resin made by polymerizing acrylamide, esp. a water-soluble polymer used to form or stabilize gels and as a thickening or clarifying agent.

poly·amide /,pɒli'amaɪd/ *noun Chem.* any of a class of condensation polymers produced from the interaction of an amino group of one molecule and a carboxylic acid group of another, and which includes many synthetic fibres such as nylon.

poly·amory /ˌpɒliˈaməri/ *noun* the custom or practice of engaging in multiple sexual relationships, with the full knowledge and consent of all partners concerned. □ **poly·amor·ist** *noun* **poly·amor·ous** *adjective* [POLY- + Latin *amor* love]

poly·andry /ˈpɒliˌandri/ *noun* **1** polygamy in which a woman has more than one husband. **2** *Bot.* the state of having numerous stamens. □ **poly·an·drous** /-ˈandrəs/ *adjective* [POLY- + andry from Greek *anēr andros* man]

poly·an·thus /ˌpɒliˈanθəs/ *noun* (*pl.* **poly·an·thuses**) a plant cultivated from hybridized primulas. [modern Latin, formed as POLY- + Greek *anthos* flower]

poly·bag /ˈpɒliˌbag/ ● *noun* a bag made of polyethylene, used esp. for packaging etc. ● *transitive verb* place or package (something) in a polybag. □ **poly·bagged** *adjective* **poly·bag·ging** *noun*

Po·lyb·i·us /pəˈlɪbiəs/ (*c.*200–*c.*118 BC), Greek historian. After an early political career in Greece, he was deported to Rome; his 40 books of *Histories* (only partially extant) chronicled the rise of Rome from 220 to 146 BC.

poly·carbon·ate /ˌpɒliˈkɑːbəˌneɪt/ *noun* any of a class of polymers in which the units are linked through a carbonate group, mainly used as moulding materials.

Poly·carp, St. /ˈpɒliˌkɑːp/ (*c.*69–*c.*155), Greek bishop of Smyrna in Asia Minor. Arrested during a pagan festival, he refused to recant, and was burned to death; his followers' account of his martyrdom provides the oldest authenticated account of the death of a Christian martyr. Feast day, 23 Feb.

poly·chaete /ˈpɒliˌkiːt/ *noun* any aquatic annelid worm of the class Polychaeta, including lugworms and ragworms, having numerous bristles on the fleshy lobes of each body segment. □ **poly·chaet·an** *adjective* **poly·chaet·ous** *adjective*

poly·chlor·in·ated bi·phenyl *noun* see PCB.

poly·chro·mat·ic /ˌpɒlikrəˈmatɪk/ *adjective* many-coloured. □ **poly·chro·ma·tism** /-ˈkrəʊməˌtɪzəm/ *noun*

poly·chrome /ˈpɒliˌkrəʊm/ ● *adjective* painted, printed, or decorated in many colours. ● *noun* **1** a work of art in several colours, esp. a coloured statue. **2** varied colouring. □ **poly·chromed** *adjective* **poly·chrom·ic** *adjective* **poly·chrom·ous** *adjective* [French from Greek *polukhrōmos* as POLY-, *khrōma* colour]

poly·chromy /ˈpɒliˌkrəʊmi/ *noun* the art of painting in several colours, esp. as applied to ancient pottery, architecture, etc.

Poly·cli·tus /ˌpɒliˈklaɪtəs/ (also **Poly·clei·tus**) (5th c. BC), Greek sculptor. He is known for his statues of idealized male athletes; two Roman copies of his works survive, the *Doryphoros* (spear-bearer) and the *Diadumenos* (youth fastening a band around his head).

poly·cotton /ˈpɒliˌkɒtən/ *noun* fabric made from a mixture of cotton and polyester fibre.

poly·crystal·line /ˌpɒliˈkrɪstəˌlaɪn, -ˌliːn/ *adjective* (of a solid substance) consisting of many crystalline parts at various orientations, e.g. a metal casting.

poly·cyclic /ˌpɒliˈsʌɪklɪk/ *adjective* *Chem.* having more than one ring of atoms in the molecule.

polycystic kidney disease /ˌpɒliˈsɪstɪk/ *noun* a disease in which the kidney exhibits diffuse cystic change.

polycystic ovary syndrome /ˌpɒliˈsɪstɪk/ *noun* a syndrome characterized by the presence of large ovaries with multiple follicular cysts and abnormal levels of gonadotrophin and sex hormones, often associated with menstrual disturbances, infertility, hirsutism, and obesity.

poly·dac·tyl /ˌpɒliˈdaktɪl/ *adjective* (of a person or animal) having more than five fingers or toes on one (or on each) hand or foot.

Poly·deu·ces /ˌpɒliˈdjuːsiːz/ see POLLUX 1.

poly·drug *adjective* of, relating to, or designating, (the abuse of) several drugs together.

poly·ester /ˌpɒliˈestər/ *noun* **1** any of a group of condensation polymers used to form synthetic fibres or to make resins. **2** a fabric made from such a polymer.

poly·ethene /ˈpɒliˌeθiːn/ *noun* *Chem.* = POLYETHYLENE.

poly·ethyl·ene /ˌpɒliˈeθɪˌliːn/ *noun* a tough light thermoplastic polymer of ethylene, usu. translucent and flexible or opaque and rigid, used for packaging and insulating materials.

po·lygam·ous /pəˈlɪgəməs/ *adjective* **1** having more than one wife or husband at the same time. **2** having more than one mate. **3** bearing some flowers with stamens only, some with pistils only, some with both, on the same or different plants. □ **po·lygam·ist** *noun* **po·lygam·ous·ly** *adverb* **po·lygamy** *noun* [Greek *polugamos* (as POLY-, *-gamos* marrying)]

poly·gene /ˈpɒliˌdʒiːn/ *noun* *Biol.* each of a group of independent genes that collectively affect a characteristic. □ **poly·genic** *adjective*

poly·gen·esis /ˌpɒliˈdʒɛnɪsɪs/ *noun* the (usu. postulated) origination of a race or species from several independent stocks. □ **poly·gen·etic** /-dʒɪˈnɛtɪk/ *adjective*

poly·glot /ˈpɒliˌglɒt/ ● *adjective* **1** of many languages. **2** (of a person) speaking or writing several languages. **3** (of a book, esp. the Bible) with the text translated into several languages. ● *noun* **1** a polyglot person. **2** a polyglot book, esp. a Bible. □ **poly·glot·ism** *noun* (also **poly·glot·tism**). [French *polyglotte* from Greek *poluglōttos* (as POLY-, *glōtta* tongue)]

poly·gon /ˈpɒliˌgɒn/ *noun* a plane figure with usu. four or more sides and angles. □ **po·lygon·al** /pəˈlɪgənəl/ *adjective* [Late Latin *polygonum* from Greek *polugōnon* (neuter adj.) (as POLY- + *-gōnos* angled)]

po·lygon·um /pəˈlɪgənəm/ *noun* any plant of the genus *Polygonum*, with small bell-shaped flowers. *Also called* KNOTGRASS, KNOTWEED, SMARTWEED. [modern Latin from Greek *polugonon*]

poly·graph /ˈpɒliˌgrɑːf/ *noun* **1** a machine designed to detect and record changes in physiological characteristics (e.g. rates of pulse and breathing), used esp. as a lie detector. **2** a test using a polygraph to determine whether a person is telling the truth. □ **poly·graph·er** *noun*

po·lygyny /pəˈlɪdʒɪni/ *noun* **1** polygamy in which a man has more than one wife. **2** (of male animals) the fact or state of having more than one female mate. □ **po·lygyn·ous** /pəˈlɪdʒɪnəs/ *adjective* [POLY- + gyny from Greek *gunē* woman]

poly·hed·ron /ˌpɒliˈhiːdrən, -ˈhɛdrən/ *noun* (*pl.* **-hed·rons** or **-hedra** /-drə/) a solid figure with many (usu. more than six) faces. □ **poly·hed·ral** *adjective* [Greek *poluedron* neuter of *poluedros* (as POLY-, *hedra* base)]

poly·his·tor /ˌpɒliˈhɪstər/ *noun* = POLYMATH.

Poly·hym·nia /ˌpɒliˈhɪmniə/ *Gk & Rom. Myth* the Muse of sacred dance and sacred music. [Greek, = she of the many hymns]

poly·math /ˈpɒliˌmaθ/ *noun* a person of much or varied learning; a great scholar. □ **poly·math·ic** /ˌpɒliˈmaθɪk/ *adjective* **po·lym·athy** /pəˈlɪməθi/ *noun* [Greek *polumathēs* (as POLY-, *math-* stem *manthanō* learn)]

poly·mer /ˈpɒləmər/ *noun* a compound composed of one or more large molecules that are formed from repeated units of smaller molecules. □ **poly·meric** /-ˈmɛrɪk/ *adjective* **poly·mer·ism** *noun* **poly·mer·ize** *transitive & intransitive verb* (also esp. *Brit.* **-ise**). **poly·mer·iz·a·tion** *noun* [German from Greek *polumeros* having many parts (as POLY-, *meros* share)]

poly·mer·ase /ˈpɒləmərˌeɪz/ *noun* *Biochem.* any enzyme which catalyzes the formation of a polymer, esp. of DNA or RNA.

polymerase chain reaction *noun* see PCR.

po·lymer·ous /pəˈlɪmərəs/ *adjective* *Biol.* having many parts.

poly·morph·ism /ˌpɒliˈmɔːfɪzəm/ *noun* **1 a** *Biol.* the existence of various different forms in the successive stages of the development of an organism. **b** = PLEOMORPHISM. **2** *Chem.* = ALLOTROPY. □ **poly·morph·ic** *adjective* **poly·morph·ous** *adjective*

Poly·nesia /ˌpɒləˈniːʒə/ a region of the central Pacific, lying to the east of Micronesia and Melanesia and containing the easternmost of the three great groups of Pacific islands, including Hawaii, the Marquesas Islands, Samoa, the Cook Islands, and French Polynesia. [as POLY- + Greek *nēsos* island]

Poly·nes·ian /ˌpɒliˈniːʒən/ ● *adjective* of or relating to Polynesia. ● *noun* **1 a** a native of Polynesia. **b** a person of Polynesian descent. **2** the Polynesian languages as a group, including Maori, Hawaiian, and Samoan.

Poly·nices /ˌpɒliˈnaɪsiːz/ *Gk Myth* a son of Oedipus and Jocasta. He and his brother Eteocles killed each other over the succession to the throne of Thebes.

poly·nom·ial /ˌpɒliˈnəʊmiəl/ *Math.* ● *noun* an expression of more than two algebraic terms, esp. the sum of several terms that contain different powers of the same variable(s). ● *adjective* of or being a polynomial. [POLY- after *multinomial*]

poly·nucleo·tide /ˌpɒliˈnuːkliəʊˌtaɪd, -ˈnjuː-/ *noun* a polymeric compound that is composed of many nucleotides.

po·lynya /pəˈlɪnjə/ *noun* a stretch of open water surrounded by ice, esp. in the Arctic seas. [Russian from *pole* field]

---

t *top*　v *voice*　w *we*　z *zoo*　ʃ *she*　ʒ *vision*　θ *thin*　ð *this*　ŋ *ring*　x *loch*　tʃ *chip*　dʒ *jar*　　(*see over for vowels*)

poly·ole·fin /ˌpɒliˈəʊləfɪn/ *noun* a synthetic resin that is a polymer of an olefin.

polyp /ˈpɒlɪp/ *noun* **1** *Zool.* an individual coelenterate. **2** *Med.* a small usu. benign growth protruding from a mucous membrane. [French *polype* from Latin *polypus* from Greek *pōlupos, polupous* cuttlefish, polyp (as POLY-, *pous podos* foot)]

polyp·ary /ˈpɒlɪpəri/ *noun* (pl. **-aries**) the common stem or support of a colony of polyps. [modern Latin *polyparium* as POLYP]

poly·pep·tide /ˌpɒlɪˈpɛptaɪd/ *noun Biochem.* a peptide formed by the combination of about ten or more amino acids. [German *Polypeptid* (as POLY-, PEPTONE)]

poly·phase /ˈpɒliˌfeɪz/ *adjective Electricity* (of a device or circuit) designed to supply or use simultaneously several alternating currents of the same voltage but with different phases. □ **poly·phasic** *adjective*

Poly·phe·mus /ˌpɒliˈfiːməs/ *Gk Myth* a Cyclops who trapped Odysseus and some of his companions in a cave, from which they escaped by putting out his one eye while he slept.

poly·phen·ol /ˌpɒliˈfiːnɒl/ *noun* a compound containing more than one phenolic hydroxyl group.

poly·phon·ic /ˌpɒliˈfɒnɪk/ *adjective Music* (of vocal music etc.) in two or more relatively independent parts; contrapuntal. □ **poly·phon·ic·ally** *adverb* [Greek *poluphōnos* (as POLY-, *phōnē* voice, sound)]

po·lyph·ony /pəˈlɪfəni/ *noun* (pl. **-ies**) *Music* the style of simultaneously combining a number of parts, each forming an individual melody and harmonizing with the others. □ **po·lyph·on·al** *adjective* **po·lyph·on·ous** *adjective*

poly·phos·phate /ˌpɒliˈfɒsfeɪt/ *noun* any of various complex phosphates, used esp. in detergents or as food additives.

poly·phylet·ic /ˌpɒlɪfaɪˈlɛtɪk/ *adjective Biol.* (of a group of organisms) derived from more than one common evolutionary ancestor or ancestral group.

poly·ploid /ˈpɒliˌplɔɪd/ *Biol.* ● *noun* a nucleus or organism that contains more than two sets of chromosomes. ● *adjective* of or being a polyploid. □ **poly·ploidy** *noun* [German (as POLY-, -PLOID)]

poly·pod /ˈpɒliˌpɒd/ *adjective Zool.* having many feet. [French *polypode* from Greek (as POLYP)]

poly·pody /ˈpɒliˌpəʊdi/ *noun* (pl. **-ies**) any fern of the genus *Polypodium*, usu. found in woods growing on trees, walls, and stones. [Latin *polypodium* from Greek *polupodion* (as POLYP)]

polyp·oid /ˈpɒliˌpɔɪd/ *adjective* of or like a polyp.

poly·propyl·ene /ˌpɒliˈprəʊpɪˌliːn/ *noun Chem.* any of various polymers of propylene including thermoplastic materials used for films, fibres, or moulding materials.

poly·rhythm /ˈpɒliˌrɪðəm/ *noun Music* the use of two or more different rhythms simultaneously. □ **poly·rhyth·mic** *adjective*

poly·sac·char·ide /ˌpɒliˈsakəˌraɪd/ *noun* any of a group of carbohydrates, including starch, cellulose, and glycogen, whose molecules consist of a number of sugar molecules bonded together.

poly·semy /pəˈlɪsəmi, ˌpɒliˈsiːmi, ˈpɒl-/ *noun Linguistics* the existence of many meanings (of a word etc.). □ **poly·sem·ic** /-ˈsiːmɪk/ *adjective* **poly·sem·ous** /-ˈliːsəməs, -ˈsiːməs/ *adjective* [POLY- + Greek *sēma* sign]

poly·sty·rene /ˌpɒliˈstaɪˌriːn/ *noun* a thermoplastic polymer of styrene, usu. hard and colourless or expanded with a gas to produce a lightweight rigid white substance, used for insulation and in packaging.

poly·syllab·ic /ˌpɒlɪsɪˈlabɪk/ *adjective* **1** (of a word) having many syllables. **2** characterized by the use of words of many syllables. □ **poly·syllab·ic·ally** *adverb*

poly·sylla·ble /ˈpɒliˌsɪləbəl/ *noun* a polysyllabic word.

poly·tech·nic /ˌpɒliˈtɛknɪk/ ● *noun* an institution of higher education offering courses in many (esp. vocational) subjects at degree level or below. ● *adjective* dealing with or devoted to various vocational or technical subjects. [French *polytechnique* from Greek *polutekhnos* (as POLY-, *tekhnē* art)]

poly·tetra·fluoro·ethyl·ene /ˌpɒliˌtetrəˌflɔːrəʊˈɛθɪˌliːn/ *noun Chem.* a tough translucent polymer resistant to chemicals and used to coat cooking utensils etc. Abbr.: **PTFE**. [POLY- + TETRA- + FLUORO- + ETHYLENE]

poly·theism /ˈpɒliˌθiːˌɪzəm/ *noun* the belief in or worship of more than one god. □ **poly·theist** *noun* **poly·theis·tic** /-ˈɪstɪk/ *adjective* [French *polythéisme* from Greek *polutheos* of many gods (as POLY-, *theos* god)]

poly·thene /ˈpɒliˌθiːn/ *noun Brit.* = POLYETHYLENE.

poly·tonal·ity /ˌpɒlɪtəʊˈnalɪti/ *noun Music* the simultaneous use of two or more keys in a composition. □ **poly·tonal** /-ˈtəʊnəl/ *adjective*

poly·unsat·ur·ate /ˌpɒliʌnˈsatʃʊreɪt, -ˈsatjʊreɪt/ *noun* a polyunsaturated fat or fatty acid.

poly·unsat·ur·ated /ˌpɒliʌnˈsatʃəˌreɪtəd, -tjʊˌreɪtəd/ *adjective Chem.* (of a compound, esp. a fat or oil molecule) containing several double or triple bonds and thus not encouraging the formation of cholesterol in the blood.

poly·ureth·ane /ˌpɒliˈjʊərəˌθeɪn/ *noun* any polymer containing the urethane group, used in adhesives, paints, plastics, rubbers, foams, etc.

poly·valent /ˌpɒliˈveɪlənt/ *adjective Chem.* having a valence of more than two, or several valencies. □ **poly·valence** *noun*

polyvinyl acetate /ˌpɒliˈvaɪnəl/ *noun Chem.* a soft plastic polymer used in paints and adhesives. Abbr.: **PVA**.

polyvinyl chloride /ˌpɒliˈvaɪnəl/ *noun* a tough transparent solid polymer of vinyl chloride, easily coloured and used for a wide variety of products including pipes, flooring, etc. Abbr.: **PVC**.

poly·zoan /ˌpɒliˈzəʊən/ *noun* = BRYOZOAN.

pom[1] /pɒm/ *noun* a Pomeranian dog. [abbreviation]

pom[2] /pɒm/ *noun Austral.* & *NZ slang offensive* = POMMY. [abbreviation]

Poma /ˈpəʊmə/ *noun N Amer.* proprietary a type of ski lift with detachable supports for the passengers. [J. *Pomagalski*, Polish engineer d.1969, its inventor]

pom·ace /ˈpʌmɪs/ *noun* **1** (esp. in cider making) the pulpy residue remaining after fruit has been crushed to extract its juice. **2** any crushed or pulpy substance remaining after something is pressed etc. [medieval Latin *pomacium* cider, from Latin *pomum* apple]

pom·ade /pəˈmeɪd, -ˈmɒd/ ● *noun* scented ointment for the hair and the skin of the head. ● *transitive verb* anoint with pomade. [French *pommade* from Italian *pomata* from medieval Latin from Latin *pomum* apple (from which it was originally made)]

pom·an·der /pəˈmandər/ *noun* **1** a ball of mixed aromatic substances placed in a cupboard etc. or *hist.* carried in a box, bag, etc. as a protection against infection. **2** a (usu. spherical) container for this. **3** a spiced orange etc. similarly used. [earlier *pom(e)amber* from Anglo-French from Old French *pome d'embre* from medieval Latin *pomum de ambra* apple of ambergris]

pom·ar·ine jaeger /ˈpɒməraɪn/ *noun* a large, Arctic-breeding jaeger, *Stercocarius pomarinus*, having dark brown plumage, sometimes with pale underparts. [French *pomarin* from Greek *pōma* 'lid' + *rhin-* 'nose', all jaegers having the nostrils somewhat covered by a horny plate forming the ridge of the bill]

pome /pəʊm/ *noun* a firm-fleshed fruit in which the carpels from the central core enclose the seeds, e.g. the apple, pear, and quince. [Old French, ultimately from *poma* pl. of Latin *pomum* fruit, apple]

pom·egran·ate /ˈpɒməˌgranɪt/ *noun* **1** an orange-sized fruit with a tough golden-orange outer skin containing many seeds in a red pulp. **2** the tree bearing this fruit, *Punica granatum*, native to N Africa and W Asia. [Old French *pome grenate* (as POME, Latin *granatum* having many seeds, from *granum* seed)]

pom·elo /ˈpʌmɪˌləʊ/ *noun* (pl. **-elos**) **1** the largest citrus fruit, with a thick yellow skin and bitter pulp. *Also called* SHADDOCK. **2** the tree, *Citrus maxima*, bearing these. [19th c.: origin unknown]

Pom·er·ania /ˌpɒməˈreɪniə/ a region of N Europe, extending along the south shore of the Baltic Sea between Stralsund in NE Germany and the Vistula in Poland. The region was controlled variously by Germany, Poland, the Holy Roman Empire, Prussia, and Sweden, until the larger part was restored to Poland in 1945, the western portion becoming a part of the German state of Mecklenburg-West Pomerania.

Pom·er·an·ian /ˌpɒməˈreɪniən/ *noun* a breed of small dog with long silky hair, a pointed muzzle, a tail curling over the back, and pricked ears. [POMERANIA]

pom·fret /ˈpɒmfrət/ *noun* esp. *N Amer.* a deep-bodied fish of open seas, of the family Bramidae, typically having scales on the dorsal and anal fins. [apparently from Portuguese *pampo*]

pom·mel /ˈpɒməl/ ● *noun* **1** a knob, esp. at the end of a sword hilt. **2** the upward projecting front part of a saddle. **3** either of a pair of removable curved handgrips fitted to a vaulting horse. ● *transitive verb* (**pom·melled, pom·mel·ling**; also esp. *US* **pom·meled, pom·mel·ing**) = PUMMEL. [Old French *pomel* from Romanic *pomellum* (unrecorded), diminutive of Latin *pomum* fruit, apple]

pommel horse *noun* a vaulting horse fitted with a pair of curved handgrips.

pommes frites /pɒmˈfriːt/ *plural noun* very thin french-fried potatoes. [French, = 'fried potatoes']

pommy *noun* (also **pom·mie**) (*pl.* **-mies**) *Austral. & NZ slang offensive* a British person, esp. a recent immigrant. [abbreviation of POMEGRANATE, rhyming slang for *immigrant*]

Pomo /'pɔːmoʊ/ ● *noun* (*pl.* same or **Pomos**) **1** a member of an American Indian people of northern California. **2** any of the languages spoken by this people. ● *adjective* of or pertaining to the Pomo or their languages. [Pomo = 'dweller at the red earth hole']

po·mo /'pɔːmoʊ/ ● *adjective* postmodern. ● *noun* postmodernism. [abbreviation]

pom·ol·ogy /pə'mɒlədʒi/ *noun* the science of fruit growing. □ **pomo·logic·al** *adjective* **pom·ol·o·gist** *noun* [Latin *pomum* fruit + -LOGY]

pomp *noun* **1** a splendid display; splendour. **2** *archaic* (often in *pl.*) ostentatious boastfulness or vanity (*the pomps and vanities of this wicked world*). [Old French *pompe* from Latin *pompa* from Greek *pompē* procession, pomp, from *pempō* send]

Pom·pa·dour /'pɒmpə,dɔr, -dʊr/ **Mar·quise de** (title of Jeanne Antoinette Poisson; known as Madame de Pompadour) (1721–64), French noblewoman. She became the mistress and lifelong confidante of Louis XV in 1744; a notable patron of the arts, she also founded the porcelain factory at Sèvres.

pom·pa·dour /'pɒmpə,dɔr/ *noun* **1** a woman's hairstyle with the hair in a high turned-back roll around the face. **2** a man's hairstyle with the hair combed high off the forehead. □ **pom·pa·doured** *adjective* [POMPADOUR]

pom·pano /'pɒmpənoʊ/ *noun* (*pl.* **-panos**) **1** any of various tropical fishes having a deep, laterally compressed, angular body, many of which are caught for sport. **2** any of various similar fishes, e.g. the Pacific pompano, *Peprilus simillimus*. [Spanish *pámpano*]

Pom·peii /pɒm'peɪ, -peii/ an ancient city in W Italy, southeast of Naples. The life of the city came to an abrupt end following an eruption of Mount Vesuvius in 79 AD. The city lay buried for centuries beneath several metres of volcanic ash until excavations of the site began in 1748. □ **Pom·pei·an** *adjective*

Pom·pey /'pɒmpi/ (known as Pompey the Great; Latin name Gnaeus Pompeius Magnus) (106–48 BC), Roman general and statesman. He formed the first triumvirate with Caesar and Crassus (60), but disagreement with Caesar resulted in civil war, and Pompey was defeated at the battle of Pharsalus (48); he fled to Egypt where he was murdered.

Pom·pi·dou /'pɔ̃pi,duː/ **Georges (Jean Ray·mond)** (1911–74), French politician, prime minister 1962–8 and president 1969–74. As prime minister he was instrumental in ending the conflict in Algeria between French forces and nationalist guerrillas, and he resigned after criticism of his handling of the strikes and riots of 1968; he was elected president after de Gaulle's resignation, and died in office.

pom·pom *noun* (also **pom·pon**) **1 a** a ball or bobble made of tufts of yarn etc. used for decoration. **b** a bundle of strips of fabric, paper, etc. waved or shaken by cheerleaders or spectators at a sporting event. **2** the round tuft on a soldier's cap, the front of a shako, etc. **3** (often *attributive*) a dahlia or chrysanthemum with small tightly-clustered petals. □ **pom·pommed** *adjective* [French, of unknown origin]

pom-pom *noun* an automatic quick-firing gun esp. on a ship. [imitative]

pom·pous /'pɒmpəs/ *adjective* **1** self-important, affectedly grand or solemn. **2** (of language) pretentious; unduly grand in style. □ **pom·pos·ity** /pɒm'pɒsɪti/ *noun* (*pl.* **-ities**). **pom·pous·ly** *adverb* **pom·pous·ness** *noun* [Old French *pompeux* from Late Latin *pomposus* (as POMP)]

'pon *preposition archaic* = UPON. [abbreviation]

ponce /pɒns/ *Brit. slang* ● *noun* **1** a man who lives off a prostitute's earnings; a pimp. **2** *offensive* a homosexual; an effeminate man. ● *intransitive verb* act as a ponce. □ **ponce about** move about effeminately or ineffectually. □ **pon·cey** *adjective* (also **poncy**) (in sense 2 of *noun*). [perhaps from POUNCE[1]]

Ponce de León /,pɒns də 'liːɒn, ,pɒnsei də lei'ɒn/ **Juan** (1460–1521), Spanish explorer. He accompanied Columbus on his second voyage to the New World (1493) and later became governor of Puerto Rico (1510–12); he landed on the coast of Florida in 1513, claiming the area for Spain and becoming its governor in 1514.

pon·cho *noun* (*pl.* **-chos**) **1** a S American cloak made of a blanket-like piece of cloth with a slit in the middle for the head. **2** a garment in this style, esp. a raincoat. □ **pon·choed** *adjective* [Latin American Spanish, from Araucanian]

pond ● *noun* **1** a fairly small body of still water formed naturally or by

hollowing, embanking, etc. **2** (prec. by *the*) *jocular* the sea, esp. the Atlantic Ocean. ● *intransitive verb* (of water) form a pond. [Middle English var. of POUND[3]]

pon·der *verb* **1** *transitive* weigh mentally; think over; consider. **2** *intransitive* (usu. foll. by *on, over*) think; muse. □ **pon·der·able** *adjective* [Old French *ponderer* from Latin *ponderare* from *pondus -eris* weight]

pon·der·osa /,pɒndə'roʊsə/ *noun* (also **ponderosa pine**) **1** a pine tree of western N America, *Pinus ponderosa*. **2** the red timber of this tree. [modern Latin, fem. of Latin *ponderosus*: see PONDEROUS]

pon·der·ous /'pɒndərəs/ *adjective* **1** heavy; unwieldy. **2** laborious. **3** (of style etc.) dull; tedious. □ **pon·der·ous·ly** *adverb* **pon·der·ous·ness** *noun* [Latin *ponderosus* from *pondus -eris* weight]

pond hockey *noun Cdn* **1** informal or disorganized hockey played on a frozen pond. **2** hockey played with seemingly little attention to discipline, defensive strategy, etc.

Pondi·cherry /,pɒndɪ'tʃeri/ **1** a Union Territory in SE India, on the Coromandel Coast, formed from several former French territories and incorporated into India in 1954. **2** its capital city; pop. (2001) 220,700.

pond life *noun* animals (esp. invertebrates) that live in ponds.

pond lily *noun* a water lily of the genus *Nuphar*, including bullhead lily, *N. variegatum*, and spatterdock, *N. advena*.

pond scum *noun* **1** a mass of scummy freshwater algae floating in stagnant water. **2** *N Amer. derogatory slang* a worthless or contemptible person or thing.

pond·weed *noun* any of various aquatic plants, esp. of the genus *Potamogeton*, growing in still or running water.

pone *noun US* (*South & South Midland*) **1** cornbread. **2** a cake or loaf of this. [Algonquian, = bread]

pong *esp. Brit. informal* ● *noun* an unpleasant smell. ● *intransitive verb* stink. □ **pongy** /'pɒŋi/ *adjective* [20th c.: origin unknown]

pon·gal /'pɒŋal/ *noun* **1** the Tamil New Year festival at which new rice is cooked. **2** a dish of cooked rice. [Tamil *poṇkal* boiling]

pon·gee /pɒn'dʒiː/ *noun* **1** a soft usu. unbleached type of Chinese silk fabric. **2** an imitation of this in cotton etc. [perhaps from Chinese dial. *pun-chī* own loom, i.e. homemade]

pon·gid /'pɒndʒɪd/ ● *noun* any ape of the family Pongidae, including gorillas, chimpanzees, and orangutans. ● *adjective* of or relating to this family. [modern Latin *Pongidae* from *Pongo* the genus name: see PONGO[1]]

pon·go[1] /'pɒŋgoʊ/ *noun* (*pl.* **-gos**) *slang* a member of the army. [Congolese *mpongo*, originally of African apes]

pon·go[2] /'pɒŋgoʊ/ *noun* (*pl.* **-gos**) *Austral. & NZ slang offensive* an Englishman. [20th c.: origin unknown]

poniard /'pɒnjərd/ *noun literary* a small slim dagger. [French *poignard* from Old French *poignal* from medieval Latin *pugnale* from Latin *pugnus* fist]

pönnu·kö·kur /'pœnə,kʊkʊr/ *noun* an originally Icelandic crepe made with eggs, sugar, and milk, often served sprinkled with both white and brown sugar and rolled. [Icelandic]

Pon·oka /pə'noʊkə/ a town in central Alberta, about 100 km south of Edmonton; pop. (2001) 6,330. [Blackfoot *ponokaii* elk]

pons /pɒnz/ *noun* (*pl.* **pontes** /'pɒntiːz/) *Anat.* (in full **pons Var·olii** /və'roʊli,aɪ/ the part of the brain stem that links the medulla oblongata and the thalamus. [Latin, = bridge: *Varolii* from C. *Varoli*, Italian anatomist d.1575]

pons asin·orum /,asɪ'nɔrəm/ *noun* any difficult proposition, originally a rule of geometry from Euclid. [Latin, lit. 'bridge of asses']

Ponte *see* DA PONTE.

pontes *pl.* of PONS.

Pon·tiac /'pɒnti,ak/ (c.1720–69), Odawa chief, who led an Aboriginal uprising against British forts and settlements in the Great Lakes region (1763–6).

Ponti·anak /,pɒnti'ɒnak/ a seaport in Indonesia, on the west coast of Borneo; pop. (est. 2002) 493,200. It is situated on the equator at the delta of the Kapuas river.

ponti·fex /'pɒntɪ,feks/ *noun* (*pl.* **pon·tifi·ces** /pɒn'tɪfɪ,siːz/) **1** = PONTIFF. **2** *Rom. Hist.* a member of the principal college of priests in Rome. [Latin *pontifex -ficis* from *pons pontis* bridge + *-fex* from *facere* make]

Ponti·fex Maxi·mus *noun Rom. Hist.* the head of the principal college of priests in Rome.

pon·tiff /'pɒntɪf/ *noun* the Pope. [French *pontife* (as PONTIFEX)]

pon·tif·ical /pɒn'tɪfɪkəl/ ● *adjective* **1** *Catholicism* of or befitting a pontiff; papal. **2** pompously dogmatic; with an attitude of infallibility.

● *noun* (in *pl.*) the vestments and insignia of a bishop, cardinal, or abbot. □ **pon·tif·i·cal·ly** *adverb* [French *pontifical* or Latin *pontificalis* (as PONTIFEX)]

Pontifical Mass *noun* a high Mass, usu. celebrated by a cardinal, bishop, etc.

pon·tifi·cate ● *intransitive verb* /pɒnˈtɪfɪˌkeɪt/ **1** be pompously dogmatic. **2** *Catholicism* officiate as bishop, esp. at Mass. ● *noun* /pɒnˈtɪfɪkət/ **1** the office of pontifex, bishop, or pope. **2** the period of this. □ **pon·tifi·ca·tion** *noun* [Latin *pontificatus* (as PONTIFEX)]

pon·tifi·ces *pl.* of PONTIFEX.

Pon·tine Marsh·es /ˈpɒntaɪn/ an area of reclaimed marshland in W Italy, on the Tyrrhenian coast south of Rome. An extensive plan to drain the marshes, which had been infested with malaria since ancient times, was begun in 1928.

Pon·tius Pi·late /pɒnʃəs ˈpaɪlət, pɒntɪəs-/ *see* PILATE.

pon·toon¹ /pɒnˈtuːn/ ● *noun* **1** a flat-bottomed boat. **2 a** each of several boats, hollow metal cylinders, etc., used to support a temporary bridge. **b** a hollow tube or other float for keeping a boat, float plane, etc., buoyant. **3** = CAISSON 1, 2. ● *transitive verb* cross (a river) by means of pontoons. □ **pon·tooned** *adjective* [French *ponton* from Latin *ponto -onis* from *pons pontis* bridge]

pon·toon² /pɒnˈtuːn/ *noun Brit.* = BLACKJACK¹ *noun* 1. [prob. corruption of French *vingt-un*, obsolete variant of *vingt-et-un* twenty-one]

pontoon boat *noun* a flat decked boat supported on two longitudinal pontoons.

Pon·top·pi·dan /pɒnˈtɒpɪdan/ **Hen·rik** (1857–1943), Danish novelist and short-story writer, whose novels include the trilogy *The Promised Land* (1891–95), *Lucky Peter* (1898–1904), and the quintet *The Empire of Death* (1912–6); he shared the Nobel Prize for literature in 1917.

Pont-Rouge /pɔ̃ruːʒ/ a town in SE central Quebec, west of Quebec City; pop. (2001) 7,146. [French, lit. = 'red bridge,' with reference to a red bridge over the river]

Pon·tus /ˈpɒntəs/ an ancient region of N Asia Minor, on the Black Sea coast north of Cappadocia.

pony *noun* (*pl.* **-ies**) **1** a horse of any small breed. **2** a small drinking glass. **3** (in *pl.*) *slang* **a** racehorses. **b** (*prec. by the*) horse racing. **4** *Brit. slang* £25. □ **pony up** *N Amer.* hand over (a sum of money etc.) esp. in settlement of an account. [perhaps from *poulney* (unrecorded) from French *poulenet* diminutive of *poulain* foal]

Pony Express a system of mail delivery in the US in 1860–1, over a distance of 2,900 km (1,800 miles) between St. Joseph in Missouri and Sacramento in California, by continuous relays of horse riders.

pony·tail *noun* a person's hair drawn back, tied, and hanging down like a pony's tail. □ **pony·tailed** *adjective*

Ponzi /ˈpɒnzi/ *attributive adjective N Amer.* designating a form of fraud in which belief in the success of a non-existent enterprise is fostered by payment of quick returns to the first investors from money invested by others (*Ponzi scheme*). [C. *Ponzi*, perpetrator of such a fraud in 1919–20, d.1949]

poo *esp. Cdn & Brit.* ● *noun* excrement. ● *verb* **1** *intransitive* defecate. **2** *transitive* soil; defecate in (one's pants etc.). ● *interjection var. of* POOH. [var. of POOH]

-poo *suffix* often forming a diminutive or term of endearment (*cutesy-poo*). [from CUTESY-POO]

poo·bah *var. of* POOH-BAH.

pooch *noun esp. N Amer. slang* a dog. [20th c.: origin unknown]

poo·dle *noun* **1** a breed of dog with a coat of usu. clipped tight curls. **2** *Brit.* a lackey or servile follower. [German *Pudel(hund)* from Low German *pud(d)eln* splash in water: compare PUDDLE]

poof¹ *interjection* announcing something sudden, esp. a disappearance or appearance. [imitative]

poof² /puf, puːf/ *noun* (also **pouf**) *Brit. slang derogatory* **1** an effeminate man. **2** a male homosexual. □ **poofy** /ˈpufi/ *adjective* [19th c.: compare PUFF in sense 'braggart']

poof·ter /ˈpuftər, ˈpuː-/ *noun slang derogatory* = POOF².

pooh ● *interjection* expressing impatience or contempt. ● *noun var. of* POO. [imitative]

pooh-bah *noun* **1** a person with much influence in an organization etc. **2** a pompous self-important person. [*Pooh-Bah*, a character in *The Mikado*, a light opera by W.S. GILBERT and A. SULLIVAN]

pooh-pooh *transitive verb* express contempt for; ridicule; dismiss (an idea etc.) scornfully. [reduplication of POOH]

pooja *var. of* PUJA.

pool¹ ● *noun* **1** a small body of still water, usu. of natural formation. **2** a small shallow body of any liquid. **3** a receptacle or hole filled with water for swimming, wading, etc. **4** a deep place in a river. ● *verb* **1** *transitive* form into a pool. **2** *intransitive* (of blood) become static. [Old English *pōl* from West Germanic]

pool² ● *noun* **1** *esp. N Amer.* any of various games of billiards, esp. eight ball. **2 a** a common supply of persons, commodities, resources, etc. (*gene pool*; *talent pool*). **b** *esp. Cdn* a grain farmers' co-operative for marketing etc. (*wheat pool*; *pool elevator*). **c** a group of persons sharing duties, resources, etc. (*carpool*). **3 a** the collective amount of players' stakes in gambling etc. **b** a receptacle for this. **c** a bet, esp. on the outcome of a sports match or tournament, in which players contribute to a pool, all of which is taken by one winner or divided among a few. **4 a** a joint commercial venture, esp. an arrangement between competing parties to fix prices and share business to eliminate competition. **b** the common funding for this. **5** a group of contestants who compete against each other in a tournament for the right to advance to the next round. **6** (in *pl.*; *prec. by the*) *Brit.* = FOOTBALL POOLS. ● *transitive verb* **1** put (resources etc.) into a common fund. **2** share (things) in common. [French *poule* (= hen) in same sense: assoc. with POOL¹]

Poole a port and resort town, and unitary authority on the south coast of England, just west of Bournemouth; pop. (est. 1998) 141,500.

pool hall *noun* a place for playing billiards.

pool noodle *noun see* NOODLE¹ 2.

pool·room *noun N Amer.* **1** a place for playing billiards. **2** a betting establishment.

pool shark *noun* an expert pool player.

pool·side ● *noun* the area adjoining a swimming pool (often *attributive*: *poolside bar*). ● *adverb* to, towards, or beside a swimming pool (*sat poolside*).

pool table *noun* a table on which billiards is played.

Poona /ˈpuːnə/ (also **Pune**) an industrial city in Maharashtra, W India, in the hills southeast of Bombay; pop. (2001) 2,540,100.

poon·tang /ˈpuːntaŋ/ *noun N Amer. slang* **1** sexual intercourse. **2** a woman or women regarded as a means of sexual gratification. [alteration of French *putain* prostitute]

poop¹ ● *noun* the stern of a ship; the aftermost and highest deck. ● *transitive verb* **1** (of a wave) break over the stern of (a ship). **2** (of a ship) receive (a wave) over the stern. [Old French *pupe* ultimately from Latin *puppis* stern]

poop² *transitive verb* (esp. as **pooped** *adjective* or foll. by *out*) *N Amer. informal* exhaust; tire out. [20th c.: origin unknown]

poop³ (also **poo-poo**) ● *noun* excrement. ● *verb slang* **1** *intransitive* defecate. **2** *transitive* soil; defecate in (one's pants etc.). □ **poopy** *adjective* [imitative of the sound made breaking wind]

poop⁴ *noun esp. N Amer. slang* up-to-date or inside information. [20th c.: origin unknown]

poop⁵ *noun informal* a stupid or ineffectual person. [perhaps abbreviation of NINCOMPOOP]

poop·er scoop·er *noun* an implement for clearing up (esp. dog) excrement. [POOP³]

poor *adjective* **1** lacking adequate money or means; characterized by poverty. **2** (foll. by *in*) deficient in (a possession or quality) (*oxygen-poor water*). **3 a** scanty, inadequate (*a poor crop*). **b** less good than is usual or expected (*poor visibility*; *in poor health*). **c** paltry; inferior (*poor condition*; *came a poor third*). **d** not good or skilled at (*a poor judge of character*; *a poor loser*). **4 a** deserving pity or sympathy; unfortunate (*you poor thing*). **b** with reference to a dead person (*as my poor father used to say*). **5** spiritless; despicable (*is a poor creature*). **6** often *ironic* or *jocular* humble; insignificant (*in my poor opinion*). □ **poor man's** an inferior or cheaper substitute for. **take a poor view of** regard with disfavour or pessimism. [Old French *pov(e)re*, *poure* from Latin *pauper*]

poor box *noun* a collection box, esp. in church, for the relief of the poor.

poor-boy ● *attributive adjective* designating coarse knitwear reminiscent of a kind worn by the poor in the 1920s and 1930s (*poor-boy sweater*). ● *noun* (**poor boy**) (also **poor-boy sandwich**) *US* a large sandwich filled with a range of simple but substantial ingredients, esp. a type of sandwich originating in New Orleans consisting of a hollowed-out French loaf variously filled with oysters, shrimp, meat and gravy, etc.

Poor Clare *noun* a member of an order of Franciscan nuns founded by St. Clare of Assisi *c.*1212.

poor cousin *noun* an inferior or subordinate member of a family or any other group or one treated as such.

poor·house *noun hist.* a house for poor people living on public charity.

Poor Law *noun* any of various laws relating to the support of the poor in England, which by the 19th c. proved both repressive and unable to cope with rising demand. In the early 20th c. the Poor Law was dismantled and replaced by schemes of social security.

poor·ly ● *adverb* **1** scantily; defectively. **2** with no great success. ● *predicative adjective* unwell.

poor-mouth *N Amer.* ● *noun* a person who claims to be poor, either to receive more money or to avoid giving money. ● *verb* **1** *intransitive* plead poverty. **2** *transitive* badmouth, speak disparagingly of. □ **talk** (or **cry** etc.) **poor-mouth** plead poverty.

poor·ness *noun* **1** defectiveness. **2** the lack of some good quality or constituent.

poor relation *noun* = POOR COUSIN.

poor white *noun offensive* a white person, esp. in the southern US, lacking money, education, and social status.

POP¹ *abbreviation* **1** probability of precipitation. **2** PERSISTENT ORGANIC POLLUTANT.

POP² /pɒp/ *abbreviation* **1** POINT OF PRESENCE. **2** *Computing* Post Office Protocol, an email program that stores and forwards mail when the user acts.

pop¹ ● *noun* **1** a sudden sharp explosive sound as of a cork when drawn, or of a bursting toy balloon. **2** any carbonated, sweetened, non-alcoholic beverage, e.g. cola, ginger ale, etc. **3** a single item or instance of service for which a price is set; a person paying for such an item or service (*charged us $75 a pop*). ● *verb* (**popped**, **pop·ping**) **1** *transitive & intransitive* make or cause to make a pop. **2 a** *intransitive & transitive* (foll. by *in, out, up, down*, etc.) go, move, come, or put unexpectedly or in a quick or hasty manner (*pop out to the store*; *pop in for a visit*; *pop it on your head*). **b** *transitive* engage, open, release, etc. quickly or suddenly (*pop a wheelie*; *popped the clutch*; *pop the hood*). **3 a** *intransitive & transitive* burst, making a popping sound. **b** *transitive* heat (popcorn etc.) until it pops. **4** *transitive* **a** take (a pill etc.). **b** *slang* inject (a drug etc.). **5** *intransitive* (usu. foll. by *up*) *Baseball* hit the ball high but not far, esp. for an easy out (*popped to third*; *popped up to end the inning*). **6** *intransitive* (of eyes) protrude. **7** *intransitive* (of the ears) discern a faint pop as a result of a change in altitude, pressure, etc. **8** *intransitive* (often foll. by *at*) *informal* fire a gun (at birds etc.). **9** *transitive N Amer. informal* hit, punch. **10** *transitive Brit. slang* pawn. **11** *transitive Figure Skating* substitute a jump with a single revolution for (a double or triple jump). ● *adverb* with the sound of a pop (*heard it go pop*). □ **pop off** *informal* **1** die. **2** quietly slip away (*compare sense 2a of verb*). **pop out** *Baseball* be put out by having one's pop-up caught. **pop the question** *informal* propose marriage. **pop up** appear, esp. unexpectedly. [Middle English: imitative]

pop² *informal* ● *adjective* **1** in or relating to a popular or modern style. **2** performing or relating to pop music (*pop group*; *pop star*). ● *noun* **1 a** (in full **pop music**) commercial popular music, esp. that since the 1950s. **b** a pop recording or song. **2** pop art. **3** (in *pl.*) pieces of light classical music, show tunes, etc. (*went to a pops concert*). [abbreviation]

pop³ *noun* esp. *US informal* father. [abbreviation of POPPA]

pop⁴ *noun* a snack of flavoured frozen water, yogourt, etc. with a stick embedded in it so that it can be held in the hand. [abbreviation of POPSICLE]

pop. *abbreviation* population.

pop art *noun* art based on modern popular culture and the mass media, esp. as a critical comment on traditional fine art values.

pop·corn *noun* **1** corn which bursts open when heated. **2** these kernels when popped. **3** (*attributive*) resembling popcorn in appearance (*popcorn shrimp*; *popcorn-knit sweater*). **4** *informal* (*attributive*) (of a movie, etc.) frivolous, intellectually undemanding.

pop culture *noun* commercial culture based on popular taste.

Pope ▸ **1 Alex·an·der** (1688–1744), English poet. A major figure in Augustan literature, he was known for his caustic wit and metrical skill, in particular his use of the heroic couplet; his works include the *Essay on Criticism* (1711), the mock-heroic *The Rape of the Lock* (1712; enlarged 1714), the philosophical poem *An Essay on Man* (1733–4), and his satire attacking 'Dulness', *The Dunciad* (1728). He also made notable translations of the *Iliad* (1715–20) and the *Odyssey* (1726). **2 James Col·ledge** (1826–1885), Canadian shipowner, land agent, and politician, three times premier of PEI (1865–7, 1870–72, and April–September 1873). He initiated a railway in 1871 and led PEI into Confederation in 1873. **3** his brother, **Wil·liam Henry** (1825–1879), Canadian lawyer, newspaper editor, politician, and judge, Father of

Confederation. He was one of PEI's most ardent supporters of Confederation, attending the Charlottetown conference.

pope¹ *noun* **1** (as title usu. **Pope**) the Bishop of Rome as head of the Roman Catholic Church. **2** the head of the Coptic Church, the patriarch of Alexandria. **3** = RUFF². [Old English from ecclesiastical Latin *pāpa* bishop, pope, from ecclesiastical Greek *papas* = Greek *pappas* father: compare PAPA]

pope² *noun* a parish priest of the Orthodox Church in Russia etc. [Russian *pop* from Old Slavic *popŭ* from West Germanic from ecclesiastical Greek (as POPE¹)]

Pope Joan according to a legend widely believed in the Middle Ages, a woman in male disguise who (*c.*1100) became a distinguished scholar and then pope, reigned for more than two years, and died after giving birth to a child during a procession.

Pope·mobile *noun* a bulletproof vehicle with a raised viewing area, used by the Pope on official visits.

popery /ˈpoʊpəri/ *noun derogatory* **1** the papal system. **2 a** the Roman Catholic Church. **b** the doctrines and ceremonies associated with Roman Catholicism.

pope's nose *noun* the piece of fatty flesh at the rump of a fowl.

pop-eyed *adjective informal* **1** having bulging eyes. **2** wide-eyed (with surprise etc.).

pop fly *noun* = FLY BALL.

pop·gun *noun* a child's toy gun which shoots a pellet, cork, etc. by the compression of air with a piston.

popin·jay /ˈpɒpɪnˌdʒeɪ/ *noun* **1** a fop, a conceited person, a coxcomb. **2 a** *archaic* a parrot. **b** *hist.* a figure of a parrot on a pole as a mark to shoot at. [Old French *papingay* etc. from Spanish *papagayo* from Arabic *babaġā*: assimilated to JAY]

popish /ˈpoʊpɪʃ/ *adjective derogatory* Roman Catholic.

Popish Plot a fictitious Jesuit plot concocted by an English Protestant clergyman, Titus Oates, in 1678. The plot involved a plan to kill Charles II, massacre Protestants, and put the Catholic Duke of York on the English throne. The 'discovery' of the plot led to a major panic and the execution of about thirty-five Catholics.

pop·lar *noun* **1** any tree of the genus *Populus*, with a usu. rapidly growing trunk and tremulous leaves. **2** *US* = TULIP TREE. [Anglo-French *popler* from Latin *populus*]

pop·lin *noun* a plain-woven fabric usu. of cotton, with a corded surface. [obsolete French *papeline* perhaps from Italian *papalina* (fem.) PAPAL, from the papal town Avignon where it was made]

pop·lit·eal /pɒpˈlɪtiəl, ˌpɒplɪˈtiːəl/ *adjective* of the hollow at the back of the knee. [modern Latin *popliteus* from Latin *poples -itis* this hollow]

pop music *noun see* POP² *noun* 1.

Popo·caté·petl /ˌpɒpəˈkætəˌpetəl/ an active volcano in Mexico, southeast of Mexico City, which rises to 5 452 m (17,700 ft.).

pop·out ● *noun Baseball* an instance of popping out. ● *attributive adjective* (**pop-out**) designating a part of a mechanism etc. that is easily removable for use (*pop-out panel*).

pop·over *noun N Amer.* **1** a food made from a thin batter of milk, eggs, and flour, which rises to form a hollow shell when baked. **2** a loose casual garment put on by slipping it over the head.

poppa *noun N Amer. informal* **1** father (esp. as a child's word). **2** grandfather (esp. as a child's word). [var. of PAPA]

poppa·dum *var. of* PAPPADUM.

Pop·per, Sir Karl (Rai·mund) (1902–94), Austrian-born English philosopher. In *The Logic of Scientific Discovery* (1934) he posited that scientific hypotheses can never be finally confirmed as true and are acceptable only in so far as they manage to survive frequent attempts to falsify them. □ **Pop·per·ian** *adjective*

pop·per *noun* **1** a person or thing that pops. **2** a pan or electric appliance for popping popcorn. **3** *informal* any of a number of inhalant muscle relaxants and vasodilators used as a stimulant. **4** *N Amer. Angling* a plug that makes a popping sound at the surface of the water as it moves.

pop·pet /ˈpɒpət/ *noun* **1** *Brit. informal* **a** a term of endearment. **b** a small or dainty person. **2** (in full **poppet valve**) a mushroom-shaped valve, lifted bodily from its seat rather than hinged. [Middle English *popet(te)*, ultimately from Latin *pup(p)a*: compare PUPPET]

pop-psych *attributive adjective* (in full **pop-psychology**) characterized by or relating to usu. superficial psychological concepts as popularly understood (*another pop-psych bestseller*).

pop psychology *noun* psychological concepts as popularly understood, esp. superficially.

poppy[1] *noun* (*pl.* **-pies**) **1** any plant of the genus *Papaver*, with showy often red flowers and a milky sap with narcotic properties. **2** a representation of this worn as a pin in Canada, Britain, and some other Commonwealth countries around Remembrance Day as a symbol of remembrance of the war dead. [Old English *popig*, *papæg*, etc. from medieval Latin *papauum* from Latin *papaver*]

poppy[2] *adjective* (of music, a group, etc.) having a sound characteristic of pop music (*see* POP[2]).

poppy·cock *noun slang* nonsense. [Dutch dial. *pappekak* from *pap* soft + *kak* dung]

Poppy Day *noun Brit. & Cdn* = REMEMBRANCE DAY.

poppy seed ● *noun* the small black seed of the poppy, used in fillings and toppings for bread, cakes, etc. ● *adjective* (**poppy·seed**) designating cakes, salad dressings, etc. containing poppy seeds.

pop quiz *noun N Amer.* a short test in school etc. which has not been previously announced.

Pop·sicle *noun esp. N Amer. proprietary* a piece of frozen flavoured and coloured water, juice, etc. on a stick. [fanciful name]

Popsicle stick *noun N Amer.* a thin, flat stick with rounded ends on which a Popsicle is frozen, often used in arts and crafts.

pop·ster *noun informal* a pop musician.

popsy *noun* (also **pop·sie**) (*pl.* **-sies**) *informal* (usu. as a term of endearment) a young woman. [shortening of POPPET]

pop-top *noun N Amer.* **1** a tab on pop cans etc., consisting of a ring pulled to remove a triangular seal (often *attributive*: *pop-top can*). **2** the top of something that pops up or open.

popu·lace /ˈpɒpjʊləs/ *noun* the people living in a given area. [French from Italian *popolaccio* from *popolo* people + *-accio* pejorative suffix]

popu·lar /ˈpɒpjʊlər/ *adjective* **1** liked or admired by many people or by a specified group (*popular teachers; a popular hero*). **2 a** of or carried on by the general public (*popular meetings*). **b** prevalent among the general public (*popular discontent*). **3** adapted to the understanding, taste, or means of the people (*popular science; popular psychology*). □ **popu·lar·ism** *noun* **popu·lar·ity** /-ˈlerɪti/ *noun* **popu·lar·ly** *adverb* [Latin *popularis* from *populus* people]

popular culture *noun* = POP CULTURE.

popular front *noun* a party or coalition representing the populace against an esp. totalitarian government.

popu·lar·ize *transitive verb* (also esp. *Brit.* **-ise**) **1** make popular. **2** cause (a person, principle, etc.) to be generally known or liked. **3** present (a technical subject, specialized vocabulary, etc.) in a popular or readily understandable form. □ **popu·lar·iz·a·tion** *noun* **popu·lar·iz·er** *noun*

popular music *noun* **1** songs, folk tunes, etc., appealing to popular tastes. **2** pop music.

popular vote *noun* the total number of votes cast by voters in an election (*the party won 21% of the popular vote but only two seats*).

popu·late /ˈpɒpjʊˌleɪt/ *transitive verb* **1** inhabit; form the population of (a town, country, etc.). **2** supply with inhabitants; people (*a densely populated district*). **3** *Computing* fill in data on (a computer form). [medieval Latin *populare populat-* (as PEOPLE)]

popu·la·tion /ˌpɒpjʊˈleɪʃən/ *noun* **1 a** the inhabitants of a place, country, etc. referred to collectively. **b** any specified group within this (*the Friulian population of Toronto*). **2** the total number of any of these (*a population of eight million; the seal population*). **3** the act or process of supplying with inhabitants (*the population of forest areas*). **4** *Statistics* any finite or infinite collection of items under consideration. [Late Latin *populatio* (as PEOPLE)]

population explosion *noun* a sudden large increase of population.

population pyramid *noun* a type of bar graph depicting the percentage of the total population falling within specified age groups, with bars stacked so that the bottom bar represents the youngest group and the top the oldest; in developing countries a greater proportion of the population tends to be younger so the lowest bars are longest, resulting in a pyramid shape for the graph, while in developed countries the birth rate is lower and the bulk of the population tends to be of working age, resulting in a barrel-shaped graph with a narrower top and bottom and fatter middle.

popu·list /ˈpɒpjʊlɪst/ ● *noun* **1** a member or adherent of a political party seeking support mainly from the ordinary people. **2** a person who holds, or who is concerned with, the views of ordinary people. ● *adjective* of or relating to a populist or populist ideology. □ **popu·lism** *noun* [Latin *populus* 'people']

popu·lous /ˈpɒpjʊləs/ *adjective* having many inhabitants; densely populated. □ **popu·lous·ly** *adverb* **popu·lous·ness** *noun* [Late Latin *populosus* (as PEOPLE)]

pop-under *noun* (on a website) an advertisement that appears in a separate browser window beneath the main one being viewed.

pop-up ● *attributive adjective* **1** *Computing* **a** (of a menu etc.) able to be superimposed on the screen being worked on and suppressed rapidly. **b** (of an advertisement etc.) appearing suddenly in a window in front of the main one being viewed. **2** (of a toaster etc.) operating so as to move the object (toast when ready etc.) quickly upwards. **3** (of a book, greeting card, etc.) containing three-dimensional figures, illustrations, etc., that rise up when the page is turned. ● *noun* **1** *Baseball* an instance of popping up. **2** *Computing* a pop-up menu, advertisement, window, etc.

por·beagle /ˈpɔrˌbiːɡəl/ *noun* a large shark of the N Atlantic and Mediterranean, *Lamna nasus*, having a pointed snout. [18th-c. Cornish dial., of unknown origin]

por·cel·ain /ˈpɔrsələn/ *noun* **1** a hard vitrified translucent ceramic. **2** objects made of this. □ **por·cel·ain·ize** *verb* [French *porcelaine* cowrie, porcelain, from Italian *porcellana* from *porcella* diminutive of *porca* sow, from Latin *porca* fem. of *porcus* pig]

porch *noun* **1** a covered shelter for the entrance of a building. **2** *N Amer.* a veranda. □ **porched** *adjective* **porch·less** *adjective* [Old French *porche* from Latin *porticus* (translation of Greek *stoa*) from *porta* passage]

por·cine /ˈpɔrsaɪn/ *adjective* of or like pigs. [French *porcin* or from Latin *porcinus* from *porcus* pig]

por·cini /pɔrˈtʃini/ *noun* a mushroom with a glossy brown cap and a fat stem. [Italian, lit. 'little pigs']

por·cu·pine /ˈpɔrkjʊˌpaɪn/ *noun* **1** any rodent of the family Erethizontidae native to the Americas, esp. the common porcupine *Erethizon dorsatum*, or of the family Hystricidae native to Africa, Asia, and SE Europe, having defensive spines or quills. **2** (*attributive*) denoting any of various animals or other organisms with spines. [Middle English from Old French *porc espin* from Provençal *porc espi(n)*, ultimately from Latin *porcus* pig + *spina* thorn]

porcupine fish *noun* a marine fish, *Diodon hystrix*, covered with sharp spines and often distending itself into a spherical shape.

porcupine grass *noun* a grass, *Stipa spartea* of the prairies, having long stiff awns.

Porcupine River *noun* a river in N Yukon and NE Alaska, 721 km long, rising north of Dawson and flowing first northward, then curving southwestward across the border to join the Yukon River at Fort Yukon, Alaska. [origin unknown]

pore[1] *noun* a minute opening in a surface, e.g. the skin, through which gases or fluids may pass. [Old French from Latin *porus* from Greek *poros* passage, pore]

pore[2] *intransitive verb* (foll. by *over*) **1** be absorbed in studying (a book etc.). **2** meditate on, think intently about (a subject). [perhaps from Old English *purian* (unrecorded): compare PEER[1]]

porgy /ˈpɔrɡi/ *noun* (*pl.* **-gies**) *N Amer.* any of numerous fishes found esp. in N American Atlantic coastal waters, esp. a fish of the family Sparidae, which includes several food fishes. [18th c.: origin uncertain: compare Spanish & Portuguese *pargo*]

Po River *noun* a river in N Italy. Italy's longest river, it rises in the Alps near the border with France and flows 668 km (415 miles) eastward to the Adriatic.

pork ● *noun* **1** the (esp. unsalted) flesh of a pig, used as food. **2** esp. *US slang* an instance or example of pork-barrel politics. ● *intransitive verb* stuff oneself with food; overeat. [Old French *porc* from Latin *porcus* 'pig']

pork and beans *noun N Amer.* baked beans with some salt pork or bacon.

pork barrel *noun* (hyphenated when *attributive*) *N Amer. informal* **1** a source of government funds for projects designed to win votes (*disapproved of pork-barrel funding*). **2** the funds themselves. □ **pork-barrel·ler** *noun* **pork-barrel·ling** *noun*

pork belly *noun* a side of pork, esp. as a commodity.

pork bun *noun* **1** *Cdn (Nfld)* a tea biscuit with finely chopped salt pork as an ingredient. **2** (in Chinese cuisine) a ball of dough cooked with a filling of diced pork and sauce.

pork·er *noun* **1** a pig raised for food. **2** a young fattened pig.

pork pie *noun* a pie of ground pork etc. eaten cold.

porkpie hat *noun* a hat with a flat crown and a brim turned up all around.

porky[1] ● *adjective* (**pork·i·er**, **pork·i·est**) **1** *informal* fleshy, fat. **2** of or like pork. ● *noun* (*pl.* **pork·ies**) (also **porky-pie**) *Brit. rhyming slang* a lie.

porky² noun (pl. **-ies**) N Amer. informal a porcupine. [abbreviation]

porn (also **porno**) informal ● noun pornography. ● adjective pornographic. [abbreviation]

por·nog·raphy /pɔrˈnɒɡrəfi/ noun **1** the explicit description or exhibition of sexual activity in literature, films, etc., intended to stimulate erotic rather than aesthetic or emotional feelings. **2** literature etc. characterized by this. □ **por·nog·raph·er** noun **porno·graph·ic** adjective **porno·graph·ic·ally** adverb [Greek *pornographos* writing about prostitutes, from *pornē* prostitute + *graphō* write]

por·ous /ˈpɔrəs/ adjective **1** full of pores. **2** letting through air, water, etc. **3** easily penetrated (a porous border). □ **por·os·ity** /pɔrˈɒsɪti/ noun **por·ous·ly** adverb **por·ous·ness** noun

por·phyria /pɔrˈfiːriə/ noun any of a group of genetic disorders associated with abnormal metabolism of various pigments. [modern Latin from PORPHYRIN]

por·phyr·in /ˈpɔrfɪrɪn/ noun Biochem. any of a class of pigments whose molecules contain a flat ring of four linked heterocyclic rings, occurring widely in nature esp. as derivatives containing metal atoms, e.g. heme and chlorophyll. [Greek *porphura* 'purple' + -IN]

por·phyry /ˈpɔrfɪri/ noun (pl. **-ies**) **1** a hard rock quarried in ancient Egypt, composed of crystals of white or red feldspar in a red matrix. **2** Geol. an igneous rock with large crystals scattered in a matrix of much smaller crystals. □ **por·phy·rit·ic** /-ˈrɪtɪk/ adjective [medieval Latin *porphyreum* from Greek *porphuritēs* from *porphura* purple]

por·poise /ˈpɔrpəs/ ● noun any of various small toothed whales of the family Phocaenidae, esp. of the genus *Phocaena*, with a low triangular dorsal fin and a blunt rounded snout. ● intransitive verb move through the water like a porpoise, alternately rising above it and submerging. [Old French *po(u)rpois* etc., ultimately from Latin *porcus* pig + *piscis* fish]

por·ridge /ˈpɔrɪdʒ, ˈpɒr-/ noun a dish consisting of oats or another cereal boiled in water or milk. □ **por·ridgy** adjective [16th c.: alteration of POTTAGE]

por·rin·ger /ˈpɔrɪndʒər/ noun a small bowl, often with a handle, for soup, stew, etc. [earlier *pottinger* from Old French *potager* from *potage* (see POTTAGE): -n- as in *messenger* etc.]

Porsche /ˈpɔrʃ, ˈpɔrʃə/ **Fer·di·nand** (1875–1951), Austrian car designer. In 1934 he designed the popular Volkswagen (= people's car), and his name has become famous for the high-performance sports and race cars produced by his company, originally to his designs.

port¹ noun **1** a harbour. **2** a town or place possessing a harbour where ships load or unload. □ **any port in a storm** any refuge in difficult or troubled circumstances. [Old English from Latin *portus*]

port² noun (also **port wine**) a strong, sweet, dark red (occasionally brown or white) fortified wine of Portugal. [shortened form of *Porto*, city in Portugal from which port is shipped]

port³ ● noun the left-hand side (looking forward) of a ship, boat, or aircraft (compare STARBOARD). ● transitive & intransitive verb turn (the helm) to port. ● adjective situated on or turned towards the left-hand side (looking forward) of a ship or aircraft. [prob. originally the side turned towards PORT¹]

port⁴ noun **1 a** an opening in the side of a ship for entrance, loading, etc. **b** a porthole. **2** an aperture for the passage of steam, water, etc. **3** Electricity a socket or aperture in an electronic circuit, esp. in a computer network, where connections can be made with peripheral equipment. **4** an aperture in a wall etc. for a gun to be fired through. **5** esp. Scot. a gate or gateway, esp. of a walled town. [Old French *porte* from Latin *porta*]

port⁵ ● transitive verb Military carry (a rifle, or other weapon) diagonally across and close to the body with the barrel etc. near the left shoulder (esp. *port arms!*). ● noun **1** Military this position. **2** esp. literary external deportment; carriage; bearing. [Old French *port*, ultimately from Latin *portare* carry]

port⁶ transitive verb Computing transfer (software) from one operating system etc. to another. [prob. from PORT⁵, influenced by PORT⁴ noun 3]

port·able ● adjective **1 a** easily movable or transportable, convenient for carrying (*portable TV*; *portable computer*). **b** not fixed; movable (*portable classroom*). **2** (of a right, privilege, etc.) capable of being transferred or adapted in altered circumstances (*portable pension*). **3** (of software etc.) not restricted to one machine or computer system; able to be transferred from one machine or system to another. ● noun **1** a portable object, e.g. a radio, computer, etc. (*decided to buy a portable*). **2** esp. N Amer. & Austral. a small transportable building used as a classroom. □ **port·abil·ity** noun [Old French *portable* or Late Latin *portabilis* from Latin *portare* carry]

por·tage ● noun **1** /pɔrˈtɪdʒ/ the carrying of boats or goods between two navigable waters or around an unnavigable section of a river etc. **2** /pɔrˈtɪdʒ/ **a** a place at which this is necessary. **b** the route taken during a portage. **3** /ˈpɔrtɪdʒ/ the act or an instance of carrying or transporting. ● verb /pɔrˈtɪdʒ/ **1** transitive & intransitive convey (a boat or goods) between navigable waters. **2** transitive carry a boat or goods at (a portage). **3** transitive circumvent (a stretch of unnavigable waters) by means of a portage. [Old French from *porter*: see PORT⁵]

Por·tage la Prai·rie /ˈpɔrtɪdʒ lə ˈpreri/ a city in south central Manitoba, located on the Assiniboine River, about 80 km west of Winnipeg and 25 km south of Lake Manitoba; pop. (2001) 12,976. □ **Por·tager** noun [French, lit. 'prairie portage']

portage trail noun (also **portage path**) a trail created by or cleared for people performing a portage.

por·tal¹ noun **1** a doorway or gate etc., esp. a large and elaborate one. **2** a website at which a large directory of links to other sites and usu. a search engine are available, used as a starting point for access to other sites. [medieval Latin *portale* (neuter adj.): see PORTAL²]

por·tal² adjective Anat. **1** of or relating to an aperture in an organ through which its associated vessels pass. **2** of or relating to the portal vein. [modern Latin *portalis* from Latin *porta* gate]

Port Al·ber·ni /pɔrt ælˈbɜrni/ a city located in the central part of Vancouver Island, at the northern end of Alberni Inlet; pop. (2001) 17,743. □ **Port Al·ber·nian** noun [Don Pedro *Alberni*, Spanish officer commanding the Nuu-chah-nulth garrison *c*.1791]

portal vein noun a vein conveying blood to the liver from the spleen, stomach, pancreas, and intestines.

porta·men·to /ˌpɔrtəˈmentoʊ/ noun (pl. **porta·men·ti** /-ti/) Music **1** the act or an instance of gliding from one note to another in singing, playing the violin, etc. **2** piano playing in a manner intermediate between legato and staccato. [Italian, = carrying]

porta-potty noun (pl. **-potties**) a portable building containing a toilet. [PORTABLE + POTTY²]

Port Ar·thur 1 part of the city of Thunder Bay; it was amalgamated with Fort William in 1970. **2** a former name (1898–1905) of LUSHUN. [sense 1 after Prince *Arthur*: see CONNAUGHT AND STRATHEARN]

Port au Choix /pɔrtoʊ ˈʃwɒ/ a historic site located on the northwestern coast of the island of Newfoundland, at the base of Point Riche Peninsula. It is the location of two archaeological sites: that of a Dorset Eskimo culture (AD 200–600) and that of a cemetery from an archaic maritime society (2000–1200 BC). [French alteration from Basque *portuchua* little harbour]

Port au Port Peninsula /ˌpɔrtoʊˈpɔrt/ a small, triangular peninsula of the southwestern coast of Newfoundland, extending into the Gulf of St. Lawrence. [the name of the bay it shelters, French corruption of Basque *ophorportu* port of relaxation]

Port-au-Prince /ˌpɔrtoʊˈprãs/ the capital of Haiti, a port on the west coast; pop. (est. 2002) 1,028,800. Founded by the French in 1749, it became capital of the new republic in 1806.

Port Blair a port on the southern tip of South Andaman Island in the Bay of Bengal; pop. (est. 2002) 102,100. It is the capital of the Andaman and Nicobar Islands.

Port-Cartier /pɔrkɑrˈtjei/ a town in E Quebec, on the north shore of the St. Lawrence about 70 km southwest of Sept-Îles; pop. (2001) 7,024. [with reference to Quebec Cartier Mining corporation, which used it as a transshipment site for its iron ore]

Port Col·borne /ˈkoʊlbɜrn/ a city in S Ontario, located on Lake Erie, about 30 km south of St. Catharines; pop. (2001) 18,450. □ **Port Col·born·er** noun [Sir J. COLBORNE]

Port Co·quit·lam /koʊˈkwɪtləm/ a city in southwestern BC, located on the west side of the Pitt River, about 25 km east of Vancouver; pop. (2001) 51,257. [COQUITLAM]

port·cul·lis /pɔrtˈkʌlɪs/ noun a strong heavy grating sliding up and down in vertical grooves, lowered to block a gateway in a fortress etc. □ **port·cul·lised** adjective [Old French *porte coleice* sliding door, from *porte* door, from Latin *porta* + *col(e)ice* fem. of *couleis* sliding, ultimately from Latin *colare* filter]

port de bras /ˈpɔrdəˌbrɒ/ noun Dance **1** the manner of holding the arms. **2** an exercise designed to develop graceful movement and disposition of the arms, usu. involving a bend forwards, backwards, or sideways accompanied by arm movement. [French, lit. = 'carriage of the arms']

Porte /pɔrt/ noun (in full **the Sublime Porte**) hist. the Ottoman court at Constantinople. [French (*la Sublime Porte* = the exalted gate), translation of Turkish title of the central office of the Ottoman government]

porte co·chère /ˌpɔːtkɒˈʃer/ *noun* **1** a covered gateway large enough for vehicles to pass through, usu. into a courtyard. **2** *N Amer.* a roofed structure extending from the entrance of a building over a place where vehicles stop to discharge passengers. [French from *porte* PORT⁴ + *cochère* (fem. adj.) from *coche* COACH]

Port Elgin /ˈelɡɪn/ a former town in SW Ontario, situated on Lake Huron, southwest of Owen Sound, now part of the town of Saugeen Shores; pop. (2001) 6,445. □ **Port Elgin·ite** *noun* [ELGIN, 8th Earl of]

Port Eliza·beth a port in South Africa, on the coast of the province of Eastern Cape; pop. (est. 2002) 833,900.

por·tend /pɔrˈtend/ *transitive verb* **1** foreshadow as an omen. **2** give warning of. [Latin *portendere portent-* from *por-* PRO-¹ + *tendere* stretch]

por·tent /ˈpɔrtent, -tənt/ *noun* an omen, a significant sign of something to come. [Latin *portentum* (as PORTEND)]

por·ten·tous /pɔrˈtentəs/ *adjective* **1** like or serving as a portent. **2** pompously solemn. □ **por·ten·tous·ly** *adverb* **por·ten·tous·ness** *noun*

Por·ter ▸ 1 Cole (Al·bert) (1891–1964), US songwriter. He made his name with a series of Broadway musicals during and after the 1930s, including *Anything Goes* (1934) and *Kiss me, Kate* (1948). **2 Sir George, Baron Por·ter of Lud·en·ham** (1920–2002), English physical chemist, who with Ronald Norrish (1897–1978) invented the technique of flash photolysis; they shared the Nobel Prize for chemistry in 1967. **3 Kath·er·ine Anne** (1890–1980), US short-story writer and novelist. Her short-story collections include *Pale Horse, Pale Rider* (1939) and *Collected Short Stories* (1965), for which she won a Pulitzer Prize; her novel *Ship of Fools* (1962) is an allegorical treatment of a voyage from Mexico to Germany during the rise of Nazism. **4 Rod·ney Rob·ert** (1917–85), English biochemist, who shared a Nobel Prize in 1972 for his research into the chemical structure of an antibody. **5 Wil·liam Sid·ney**, *see* O. HENRY.

por·ter¹ *noun* **1 a** a person employed to carry luggage etc., esp. a railway, airport, or hotel employee. **b** a hospital employee who moves patients, equipment, trolleys, etc. **2** a dark brown bitter beer brewed from charred or browned malt (apparently originally made esp. for porters). **3** *N Amer.* a sleeping car attendant. [Old French *port(e)our* from medieval Latin *portator -oris* from *portare* carry]

por·ter² *noun* a gatekeeper or doorkeeper, esp. of a large building. [Old French *portier* from Late Latin *portarius* from *porta* door]

porter·age *noun* **1** the work of carrying luggage etc. **2** a charge for this. [PORTER¹ + -AGE]

porter·house *noun* esp. *N Amer.* **1** *hist.* a house at which porter and other drinks were retailed, often serving steaks, chops, etc. as well. **2** (in full **porterhouse steak**) a thick steak cut from between the prime ribs and the sirloin.

port·folio /pɔrtˈfoːlioː/ *noun* (pl. **-folios**) **1** a case for keeping loose sheets of paper, drawings, etc. **2** a range of investments held by a person, a company, etc. **3** the office or responsibility of a government minister. (*compare* MINISTER WITHOUT PORTFOLIO). **4** samples of an artist's or photographer's work. [Italian *portafogli* from *portare* carry + *foglio* leaf, from Latin *folium*]

Port-Gentil /pɔrʒɑ̃ˈtiː/ the principal port of Gabon, on the Atlantic coast south of Libreville; pop. (est. 2002) 102,100.

Port Har·court /ˈhɑːrkɔrt/ a port in SE Nigeria, on the Gulf of Guinea at the eastern edge of the Niger delta; pop. (est. 2002) 1,053,900.

Port Hardy a district municipality on the northeastern coast of Vancouver Island, 238 km northwest of Campbell River; pop. (2001) 4,574. □ **Port Hardi·an** *noun* [Sir T. M. *Hardy*, first baronet and vice admiral d.1839]

port·hole *noun* **1** a usu. round window in the side of a ship or an aircraft. **2** *hist.* an aperture for pointing a cannon through.

Port Hope a town in SE Ontario, situated on Lake Ontario, just west of Cobourg; pop. (2001) 11,718. □ **Port Hoper** *noun* [Col. H. *Hope*, Lieutenant-Governor of Quebec d.1789]

por·tico /ˈpɔrtikoː/ *noun* (pl. **-coes** or **-cos**) a colonnade; a roof supported by columns at regular intervals usu. attached as a porch to a building. □ **por·ti·coed** *adjective* [Italian from Latin *porticus* PORCH]

por·ti·ère /pɔrtˈjer/ *noun* a curtain hung over a door or doorway. [French from *porte* door, from Latin *porta*]

por·tion /ˈpɔrʃən/ ● *noun* **1** a part or share. **2** the amount of food allotted to one person; a helping. **3** a specified or limited quantity. **4** one's destiny or lot. **5** a dowry. ● *transitive verb* **1** divide (a thing) into portions. **2** (foll. by *out*) distribute. **3** give a dowry to. **4** (foll. by *to*)

assign (a thing) to (a person). □ **por·tion·less** *adjective* (in sense 5 of *noun*). [Old French from Latin *portio -onis*]

Port·land /ˈpɔrtlənd/ an industrial port in NW Oregon, on the Willamette River near its confluence with the Columbia River; pop. (2000) 529,121.

Portland, Isle of a rocky limestone peninsula on the south coast of England, in Dorset. The peninsula is quarried for its fine building stone.

Portland cement /ˈpɔrtlənd/ *noun* a cement manufactured from chalk and clay. [similar in colour to limestone from the Isle of PORTLAND]

Port·laoise /pɔrtˈliːʃə/ (also **Port·laoighise**) the county town of Laois in the Republic of Ireland; pop. (est. 2002) 9,900. It is the site of a top-security prison.

Port Louis /ˈluːɪs, ˈluːi/ the capital of Mauritius, a port on the northwest coast; pop. (2000) 144,303.

port·ly *adjective* (**port·li·er**, **port·li·est**) **1** corpulent; stout. **2** *archaic* of a stately appearance. □ **port·li·ness** *noun* [PORT⁵ (in the sense 'bearing') + -LY¹]

Port Mahon *see* MAHÓN.

port·man·teau /ˌpɔrtmanˈtoː, pɔrtˈmantoː, -mɒn-/ *noun* (pl. **port·man·teaus** /-toːz/ or **port·man·teaux**) a travelling bag for clothes etc., esp. of leather and opening into two equal parts. [French *portmanteau* from *porter* carry, from Latin *portare* + *manteau* MANTLE]

portmanteau word *noun* = BLEND *noun* 2.

Port Moody a city in southwestern BC, located at the head of Burrard Inlet, about 20 km east of Vancouver; pop. (2001) 23,816. [R. C. *Moody*, commissioner of lands and works d.1887]

Port Mores·by /ˈmɔrzbi/ the capital of Papua New Guinea, situated on the south coast of the island of New Guinea, on the Coral Sea; pop. (est. 2002) 312,300.

Porto /ˈpɔrto/ the principal city and port of N Portugal, near the mouth of the Douro River, famous for port wine; pop. (2001) 262,928.

Pôrto Alegre /ˌpɔrto əˈleɡrei/ a major port and commercial city in SE Brazil; pop. (2000) 1,320,069.

porto·bello /ˌpɔrtəˈbeloː/ *noun* a brown variety of the common mushroom, *Agaricus bisporus*, harvested and eaten when mature (*compare* CREMINI).

port of call *noun* a place where a ship or a person stops on a journey.

port of entry *noun* a port etc. by which people and goods may enter a country.

Port of Spain the capital of Trinidad and Tobago, a port on the northwest coast of the island of Trinidad; pop. (est. 2002) 45,200.

por·to·lan /ˈpɔrtəˌlan/ *noun* (also **por·to·lano** /ˌpɔrtəˈlɒnoː/) (pl. **por·to·lans** or **por·to·lanos**) *hist.* a book of sailing directions with charts, descriptions of harbours, etc. [Italian *portolano* from *porto* PORT¹]

Porto Novo /ˌpɔrto ˈnoːvoː/ the capital of Benin, a port on the Gulf of Guinea close to the border with Nigeria; pop. (est. 2002) 226,700. A Portuguese settlement in the 17th c., it became a centre of the Portuguese slave trade.

Pôrto Velho /ˌpɔrto ˈveloː/ a town in W Brazil; pop. (2000) 273,496.

Port Pe·trovsk /pɪˈtrɒfsk/ a former name (until 1922) of MAKHACHKALA.

por·trait /ˈpɔrtrət, -treit/ *noun* **1** a representation of a person or animal, esp. of the face, made by drawing, painting, photography, etc. **2** a representation or impression of someone or something in language or on film. **3** (in graphic design etc.) a format in which the height of an illustration etc. is greater than the width (*compare* LANDSCAPE 3). [French, past participle of Old French *portraire* PORTRAY]

por·trait·ist /ˈpɔrtrətɪst/ *noun* a person who takes or paints portraits.

por·trait·ure /ˈpɔrtrətʃər/ *noun* **1** the art of painting or taking portraits. **2** detailed description. **3** a portrait.

por·tray /pɔrˈtrei/ *transitive verb* **1** make a likeness of. **2** describe graphically. **3** represent esp. dramatically (*portrayed the general convincingly; immigrants as portrayed in the media*). □ **por·tray·able** *adjective* **por·tray·al** *noun* **por·tray·er** *noun* [Old French *portraire* from *por-* = PRO-¹ + *traire* draw, from Latin *trahere*]

Port-Royal /pɔrtˈrɔiəl/ the former name (1605–1710) for Annapolis Royal. It is now a historic site commemorating the French colony founded by Samuel de Champlain, one of the earliest permanent European settlements in N America.

Port Said /ˈsaid/ a port in Egypt, on the Mediterranean coast at the

Consonants: b *but* d *dog* f *few* g *get* h *her* j *yes* k *cat* l *leg* m *man* n *no* p *pen* r *red* s *sit*

north end of the Suez Canal; pop. (est. 2002) 401,100. It was founded in 1859 at the start of the construction of the Suez Canal.

Port Salut /ˌpɔr səˈluː/ *noun* a pale yellow, mild, semi-soft cheese. [after the Trappist monastery in France where it was first produced]

port·side ● *adverb* to or on the port side of a ship etc. ● *adjective* designating the port side of a ship etc.

Ports·mouth /ˈpɔrtsməθ/ a port and naval base on the south coast of England, formerly in Hampshire; pop. (est. 2002) 176,300.

Port Stan·ley *see* STANLEY[1].

Port Sudan the chief port of Sudan, on the Red Sea; pop. (est. 2002) 401,000.

Por·tu·gal /ˈpɔrtʃʊgəl, ˈpɔrtjʊ-/ a country occupying the western part of the Iberian peninsula in SW Europe; pop. (est. 2002) 10,084,245; capital, Lisbon.

Portugal Cove-St. Philip's a town in SE Newfoundland, northwest of St. John's; pop. (2001) 5,866. [with reference to the numerous Portuguese fishermen who have frequented Newfoundland, and after St. Philip's Catholic Church in Portugal Cove]

Por·tu·guese /ˌpɔrtʃʊˈgiːz, ˌpɔrtjʊ-/ ● *noun* (*pl.* same) **1 a** a native or national of Portugal. **b** a person of Portuguese descent. **2** the Romance language of Portugal, also used in Brazil etc. ● *adjective* of or relating to Portugal or its people or language. [Portuguese *portuguez* from medieval Latin *portugalensis*]

Portuguese man-of-war *noun* (*pl.* **Portuguese men-of-war**) a dangerous tropical or subtropical marine hydrozoan of the genus *Physalia* with a large crest and a poisonous sting.

por·tu·laca /ˌpɔrtʃəˈlækə/ *noun* any of various succulent, bright-flowered plants, native to the tropics, of the genus *Portulaca*. [Latin, = PURSLANE]

port wine stain *noun* a kind of large red birthmark, esp. on the face.

POS *abbreviation* point-of-sale.

pose[1] ● *verb* **1** *intransitive* assume a certain attitude of body, esp. when being photographed or being painted for a portrait. **2** *intransitive* (foll. by *as*) set oneself up as or pretend to be (another person etc.) (*posing as a celebrity*). **3** *intransitive* behave affectedly in order to impress others. **4** *transitive* put forward or present (a question, threat, etc.). **5** *transitive* place (an artist's model etc.) in a certain attitude or position. ● *noun* **1** an attitude of body or mind, esp. assumed when being photographed etc. **2** an attitude or pretense, esp. one assumed for effect (*his generosity is a mere pose*). □ **pose·able** /ˈpoʊzəbəl/ *adjective* [French *poser* (v.), *pose* (n.) from Late Latin *pausare* PAUSE: some senses by confusion with Latin *ponere* place (compare COMPOSE)]

pose[2] *transitive verb* puzzle (a person) with a question or problem. [obsolete *appose* from Old French *aposer* var. of *oposer* OPPOSE]

Po·sei·don /pəˈsaɪdən/ *Gk Myth* the god of the sea, water, earthquakes, and horses, son of Cronus and Rhea and brother of Zeus, identified by the Romans with Neptune.

Posen *see* POZNAŃ.

poser *noun* **1** a person who poses (*see* POSE[1] *verb* 3). **2** a puzzling question or problem.

pos·eur /poʊˈzɜr/ *noun* a person who poses for effect or behaves affectedly. [French from *poser* POSE[1]]

posey *adjective informal* affected, pretentious. [POSE[1] + -Y[1]]

posh *informal* ● *adjective* **1** stylish; luxurious. **2** esp. *Brit.* of or associated with the upper classes (*spoke with a posh accent*). ● *adverb* esp. *Brit.* in a stylish or upper-class way (*talk posh; act posh*). □ **posh·ness** *noun* [20th c.: perhaps from slang *posh* a dandy: *port out starboard home* (referring to the more comfortable accommodation on ships to and from the East) is a later association and not the true origin]

pos·it /ˈpɒzɪt/ ● *transitive verb* (**pos·it·ed, pos·it·ing**) **1** state or assume as a fact; postulate. **2** put in place or position. ● *noun Philos.* a statement which is made on the assumption that it will prove valid. [Latin *ponere posit-* place]

pos·ition /pəˈzɪʃən/ ● *noun* **1** a place occupied by a person or thing. **2 a** the way in which a thing or its parts are placed or arranged. **b** a disposition of the parts of the body; a posture (*sitting in an uncomfortable position*). **3** the proper place (*in position*). **4** the state of being advantageously placed (*jockeying for position*). **5** an attitude or policy concerning a question or issue (*changed their position on nuclear disarmament*). **6** a person's situation in relation to others (*puts one in an awkward position*). **7** rank or status; high social standing. **8** paid employment. **9** (in team games) a set of functions considered as the responsibility of a particular player (*what position does he play?*). **10 a** place where troops etc. are posted for strategical purposes (*the position was stormed*). **11** the configuration of chessmen etc. during a game.

12 a specific disposition of the legs and feet or arms in ballet etc. (*first position*). **13** *Logic* **a** a proposition. **b** a statement of proposition. **14** the extent to which an investor, dealer, or speculator has made a commitment in the market by buying or selling securities, currencies, commodities, etc. (*long position; short position*). ● *transitive verb* **1** place in position. **2** promote (a product or service) esp. within a chosen sector of a market. □ **in a position to** enabled by circumstances, resources, information, etc. to (do, state, etc.). □ **pos·ition·al** *adjective* **pos·ition·al·ly** *adverb* **pos·ition·er** *noun* [Latin *positio -onis* (as POSIT)]

position paper *noun N Amer.* a written report of policy on a particular issue, prepared by a business, political, or interest group.

position vector *noun Math.* a vector which determines the position of a point.

pos·i·tive /ˈpɒzɪtɪv/ ● *adjective* **1** (of a person) convinced, confident, or overconfident in his or her opinion (*positive that I was not there*). **2 a** having a helpful and constructive intention or attitude towards something (*positive criticism*). **b** optimistic, hopeful (*a positive outlook*). **c** affirmative; expressing or showing assent (*a positive answer*). **3** formally or explicitly stated; definite, unquestionable (*positive proof*). **4 a** absolute; not relative. **b** *Grammar* (of an adjective or adverb) expressing a simple quality without comparison (*compare* COMPARATIVE *adjective* 3, SUPERLATIVE *adjective* 2). **5** *informal* downright; complete (*it would be a positive miracle*). **6 a** marked by the presence rather than absence of qualities or (*Med.*) symptoms (*a positive reaction to the plan; the test was positive*). **b** (of a person, blood, etc.) having a specified condition, substance, etc. (*is HIV-positive*). **7** esp. *Philos.* dealing only with matters of fact; practical (*compare* POSITIVISM 1). **8** tending in a direction naturally or arbitrarily taken as that of increase or progress (*a positive growth rate; clockwise rotation is positive*). **9** greater than zero (*positive and negative integers*) (*opp.* NEGATIVE *adjective* 8). **10 a** *Electricity* designating electric charge, potential, etc. having the same polarity as that electrode of a voltaic cell from which the current is held to flow (and towards which the actual flow of electrons occurs). **b** designating a north-seeking pole of a magnet; having the polarity of the earth's South Pole. **11** (of a photographic image) showing lights and shades or colours true to the original (*compare* NEGATIVE *adjective* 11). ● *noun* a positive adjective, photograph, quantity, result, etc. □ **pos·i·tive·ly** *adverb* **pos·i·tive·ness** *noun* **pos·i·tiv·ity** /ˌpɒzɪˈtɪvɪti/ *noun* [Latin *positivus* (as POSIT)]

positive discrimination *noun Brit. & Cdn* the practice of making distinctions in favour of groups considered to be disadvantaged or underprivileged, esp. in the allocation of resources and opportunities.

positive feedback *noun* **1** a constructive response to a presentation, experiment, questionnaire, etc. **2** *Electronics* the return of part of an output signal to the input, tending to increase the amplification etc. **3** esp. *Biol.* the enhancing or amplification of an effect by its own influence on the process which gave rise to it.

positive reinforcement *noun Psych.* reinforcement achieved by a pleasurable or satisfying stimulus provided after a desired response to increase the probability of its repetition.

positive sign *noun* = PLUS SIGN.

positive thinking *noun* the practice or result of concentrating one's mind on the good and constructive aspects of a matter so as to eliminate destructive attitudes and emotions.

posi·tiv·ism /ˈpɒzɪtɪvɪzəm/ *noun Philos.* **1 a** the philosophical system of Auguste Comte, recognizing only non-metaphysical facts and observable phenomena, and rejecting metaphysics and theism. **b** a religious system founded on this. **2** = LOGICAL POSITIVISM. □ **posi·tiv·ist** *noun & adjective* **posi·tiv·is·tic** *adjective*

posi·tron /ˈpɒzɪˌtrɒn/ *noun Physics* a subatomic particle with a positive charge equal to the negative charge of an electron and having the same mass as an electron. [POSITIVE + -TRON]

positron emission tomography *noun* a form of tomography used esp. for brain scans which employs positron-emitting isotopes introduced into the body as a source of radiation instead of applying X-rays externally. Abbr.: **PET**.

pos·se /ˈpɒsi/ *noun* **1** a body of men summoned by a sheriff etc. to find a criminal, maintain order, etc. **2** *slang* a gang, esp. a criminal gang. **3** *informal* usu. *derogatory* a band of persons acting or going about together (*a posse of photographers*). [medieval Latin, = power, from Latin *posse* 'be able']

pos·sess *transitive verb* **1** hold as property; own. **2** have a faculty, quality, etc. (*they possess a special value for us*). **3 a** (of a demon etc.) occupy; have power over (a person etc.) (*possessed by the devil*). **b** (of an emotion, infatuation, etc.) dominate, be an obsession of (*possessed by fear*). **4** *archaic* (also *reflexive*; foll. by *in*) maintain (oneself, one's soul, etc.)

t *top*   v *voice*   w *we*   z *zoo*   ʃ *she*   ʒ *vision*   θ *thin*   ð *this*   ŋ *ring*   x *loch*   tʃ *chip*   dʒ *jar*   (*see over for vowels*)

in a specified state (*possess oneself in patience*). **5** have sexual intercourse with (esp. a woman). □ **be possessed of** own, have. **what possessed you?** an expression of incredulity. □ **pos·ses·sor** *noun* **pos·ses·sory** *adjective* [Old French *possesser* from Latin *possidēre possess-* from *potis* able + *sedēre* sit]

pos·ses·sion *noun* **1** the act or state of possessing or being possessed. **2** the thing possessed. **3** the act or state of actual holding or occupancy. **4** *Law* **a** power or control over a thing, esp. land, which is similar to lawful ownership but which may exist separately from it. **b** *informal* the state of possessing an illegal drug or drugs (*charged with possession*). **5** (in *pl.*) property, wealth, subject territory, etc. **6** *Football, Hockey, etc.* **a** temporary control of the ball or puck by a particular player or team. **b** a period of such control. □ **in possession 1** (of a person) possessing. **2** (of a thing) possessed. **in possession of 1** having in one's possession. **2** maintaining control over (*in possession of one's wits*). **in the possession of** held or owned by. **take possession** (often foll. by *of*) become the owner or possessor (of a thing).

pos·ses·sive ● *adjective* **1** showing a desire to possess or retain what one already owns. **2** showing jealous and domineering tendencies towards another person. **3** *Grammar* indicating possession. ● *noun* (in full **possessive case**) *Grammar* the case of nouns and pronouns expressing possession. □ **pos·ses·sive·ly** *adverb* **pos·ses·sive·ness** *noun*

possessive adjective *noun* each of the adjectives indicating possession (*my, your, his, their*, etc. in English).

possessive pronoun *noun* each of the pronouns indicating possession (*mine, yours, his, theirs*, etc. in English).

pos·set /ˈpɒsət/ *noun hist.* a drink made of hot milk curdled with ale, wine, etc., often flavoured with spices, formerly much used as a remedy for colds etc. [Middle English *poshote*: origin unknown]

pos·si·bil·i·ty *noun* (pl. **-ies**) **1** the state or fact of being possible, or an occurrence of this (*outside the range of possibility; saw no possibility of going away*). **2 a** a thing that may exist or happen (*there are three possibilities*). **b** a possible candidate, member of a team, etc. **3** (usu. in *pl.*) the capability of being used, improved, etc.; the potential of an object or situation (esp. *have possibilities*).

pos·si·ble ● *adjective* **1** capable of existing or happening; that may be managed, achieved, etc. (*came as early as possible; did as much as possible*). **2** that is likely to happen etc. (*few thought their victory possible*). **3** acceptable; potential (*a possible way of doing it*). **4** that is perhaps true or a fact (*it's possible that he has left already*). **5** that is or perhaps will be (what is denoted by the noun) (*the police are looking for a possible serial killer*). ● *noun* **1** = POSSIBILITY *noun* 2b. **2** (prec. by *the*) whatever is likely, manageable, etc. **3** the highest possible score, esp. in shooting etc. [Latin *possibilis* from *posse* be able]

pos·si·bly *adverb* **1** perhaps. **2** in accordance with possibility (*cannot possibly refuse*).

pos·sum /ˈpɒsəm/ *noun informal* = OPOSSUM. □ **play possum** *informal* pretend to be asleep or unaware. [abbreviation]

post¹ ● *noun* **1** a long stout piece of wood or metal set upright in the ground etc.: **a** to support something, esp. in building. **b** to mark a position, boundary, etc. **c** to carry notices. **2** any of the principal upright supports of a piece of furniture, such as a chair or four-poster bed. **3 a** a pole etc. marking the start or finish of a race. **b** = GOALPOST. ● *transitive verb* **1** (often foll. by *up*) **a** attach (a paper etc.) in a prominent place; stick up (*post no bills*). **b** announce or advertise by placard, in a published text, on a computer bulletin board etc. **2** achieve (a score in a game, etc.). **3** announce or publish (something, esp. a financial result). [Old English from Latin *postis*]

post² ● *noun* **1** esp. *Brit.* the official conveyance of parcels, letters, etc. (*send it by post*). **2** esp. *Brit.* a single collection, dispatch, or delivery of these; the letters etc. dispatched (*has the post arrived yet?*). **3** *hist.* **a** one of a series of couriers who carried mail on horseback between fixed stages. **b** a letter carrier; a mail cart. ● *verb* **1** *transitive* esp. *Brit.* put (a letter etc.) in the mail. **2** *transitive* (esp. as **post·ed** *adjective*) supply a person with information (*keep me posted*). **3** *transitive* **a** enter (an item) in a ledger. **b** (often foll. by *up*) complete (a ledger) in this way. **c** carry (an entry) from an auxiliary book to a more formal one, or from one account to another. **4** *intransitive* **a** travel with haste, hurry. **b** *hist.* travel with relays of horses. **5** *intransitive* (of a rider) rise and fall in the saddle in rhythm with the horse at a trot. [French *poste* (fem.) from Italian *posta*, ultimately from Latin *ponere posit-* place]

post³ ● *noun* **1** a job; a place of paid employment. **2** a place where a soldier is stationed or which he or she patrols. **3** a place where an official is on duty (*customs post*). **4 a** a position taken up by a body of

soldiers. **b** a force occupying this. **c** a fort. **5** = TRADING POST. **6** *Basketball* the area in the vicinity of the opponent's basket (*compare* LOW POST). ● *transitive verb* **1** place or station (soldiers, an employee, etc.). **2** appoint to a post or command. □ **post up** *Basketball* position oneself in the post. [French *poste* (masc.) from Italian *posto* from Romanic *postum* (unrecorded) from Latin *ponere posit-* place]

post⁴ *transitive verb* put up, provide (esp. bail money). [apparently from Italian *posta* a stake]

post⁵ *noun informal* POST-PRODUCTION. [abbreviation]

post- *prefix* after in time or order. [from or after Latin *post* (adv. & prep.)]

post·age *noun* the amount charged for sending a letter etc. by post, usu. prepaid in the form of a stamp.

postage and handling *noun* a price charged for the mailing, packing, transport, and delivery of a package etc.

postage meter *noun* N Amer. an office machine which officially marks letters with an inked stamp in lieu of a postage stamp, and which records the cost of postage incurred.

postage stamp *noun* **1** an official stamp affixed to or imprinted on a letter etc. indicating the amount of postage paid. **2** (*attributive*) very small (*a postage-stamp lawn*).

post·al *adjective* of or relating to the post office or mail delivery. □ **go postal** *informal* become crazed or violent, esp. as the result of stress.

postal code *noun Cdn* a series of six alternating letters and numerals used as part of a postal address to expedite the processing of machine-sorted mail.

postal order *noun Brit.* a money order issued by the Post Office, payable to a specified person.

postal station *noun Cdn* one of a number of branch post offices in a community too large to be serviced by a single post office.

post-and-beam *adjective* (of a method of construction or a building) having a framework of upright and horizontal beams.

post·bag *noun Brit.* = MAILBAG.

post-boomer *noun* a person who was born after the baby boom following the Second World War.

post·box *noun esp. Brit.* a mailbox.

post·card *noun* **1** a card with a photograph or picture on one side, for sending a short message by mail without an envelope. **2** (*attributive*) such as is depicted on a postcard; picturesque, ideally pretty.

post-chaise *noun hist.* a horse-drawn usu. four-wheeled carriage used for carrying mail and passengers, esp. in the 18th and early 19th c.

post-classic·al *adjective* occurring in or characteristic of a period after one regarded as classical, esp. the classical age of Greek and Roman literature.

post·code *noun Brit.* a code of letters and numbers as part of an address.

post-coital /pəʊstˈkɔɪtəl, -ˈkɔːɪtəl/ *adjective* occurring or existing after sexual intercourse. □ **post-coital·ly** *adverb*

post-coloni·al *adjective* occurring or existing after the end of colonial rule. □ **post-coloni·al·ism** *noun* **post-coloni·al·ist** *adjective & noun*

post-Communist *adjective* of or pertaining to the time in formerly Communist countries after the fall of Communism.

post-Confed·er·a·tion *adjective Cdn* **1** of or pertaining to the period after 1867 in Canada. **2** relating to or characteristic of the period after a province or territory entered Confederation.

post-consum·er *adjective* designating waste thrown away by consumers and used in recycled products (*made from 40 per cent post-consumer material*).

post·date *transitive verb* **1** affix or assign a date later than the actual one to (a document, cheque, event, etc.). **2** follow in time; belong to a later date.

post-doc *noun informal* a post-doctoral scholar or appointment. [abbreviation]

post-doctor·al *adjective* of or relating to research undertaken after the completion of doctoral research.

post-emergence *adjective* occurring, performed, or applied after the emergence of seedlings from the soil. □ **post-emergent** *adjective*

post·er ● *noun* **1** a printed or written notice posted or displayed in a public place as an announcement or advertisement. **2** a large printed picture suitable for decorative display on a wall. **3** *Computing* a person who posts a message on a BBS etc. ● *verb* **1** *transitive* affix posters on (a wall, building, etc.). **2** *intransitive* place posters throughout a neighbourhood etc.

Vowels: a **cat** ɑ **arm** e **bed** ɜr **her** ɜː **deux** ə **ago** ɪ **sit** i **cosy** iː **feed** ɒ **hot** ɔ **pore** ɔː **no** ʌ **run** ʊ **put**

poster boy *noun esp. N Amer.* **1** a boy or man who is a poster child. **2** a male model who appears in a print advertisement.

poster child *noun esp. N Amer.* **1** a child who appears on a poster or in an advertisement for a charitable organization. **2** a person who epitomizes or represents a quality, cause, etc.

poste res·tante /ˌpoːst reˈstãt/ *noun Brit.* **1** a direction on a letter to indicate that it should be kept at a specified post office until collected by the addressee. **2** the department in a post office where such letters are kept; general delivery. [French, = letter(s) remaining]

poster girl *noun esp. N Amer.* **1** a girl or woman who is a poster child. **2** a female model who appears in a print advertisement.

pos·ter·ior /pɒˈstiːriːər/ ● *adjective* **1** situated behind or at the back (*posterior deltoid muscle*). **2** later; coming after in series, order, or time. ● *noun* the buttocks. □ **pos·ter·ior·ity** /pɒˌstiːriˈɒriti/ *noun* **pos·ter·ior·ly** *adverb* [Latin, comparative of *posterus* following, from *post* after]

pos·ter·ity /pɒˈsteriti/ *noun* **1** all succeeding generations. **2** the descendants of a person. [Latin *posteritas -tatis* from *posterus*: see POSTERIOR]

pos·tern /ˈpɒstɜrn/ *noun* **1** a back door. **2** a side way or entrance. [Old French *posterne*, *posterle*, from Late Latin *posterula* diminutive of *posterus*: see POSTERIOR]

poster paint *noun* a gummy opaque paint, such as is used on posters.

post exchange *noun US Military* a store at a military base etc.

post-feminist ● *adjective* **1** relating to or occurring in the period after the feminist movement of the 1970s. **2** of or relating to ideas, theories, etc. in feminism after the 1970s. ● *noun* a person who holds post-feminist ideas and attitudes. □ **post-feminism** *noun*

post·fix ● *transitive verb* /poːstˈfɪks/ **1** *Biol.* fix a second time; treat with a second fixative. **2** append (letters) at the end of a word. ● *noun* /ˈpoːstfɪks/ a suffix.

post·glacial ● *adjective* formed or occurring after a glacial period. ● *noun* a postglacial period or deposit.

post·grad *informal* = POSTGRADUATE. [abbreviation]

post·grad·uate ● *adjective* **1** (of a course of study) carried on after completing a bachelor's degree. **2** of or relating to students following this course of study. ● *noun* a postgraduate student.

post-haste *adverb* with great speed.

post hoc *adverb & adjective* after this; after the event; consequently. [Latin]

post·hole *noun* a hole for the insertion of a fence post.

post·hu·mous /ˈpɒstjəməs, -juːməs, ˈpɒstʃəməs/ *adjective* **1** occurring after death. **2** (of a book etc.) published after the author's death. **3** (of a child) born after the death of its father. □ **post·hu·mous·ly** *adverb* [Latin *postumus* last (superlative from *post* after): in Late Latin *posth-* by assoc. with *humus* ground]

post-hypnot·ic suggestion *noun* **1** suggestion made during hypnosis and intended to cause the subject to act in a certain way when conscious. **2** an instance of this.

post·ie *noun Brit. & Cdn informal* a postal worker, esp. a letter carrier. [abbreviation]

pos·til·ion /pɒˈstɪljən/ *noun* (also **pos·til·lion**) a person who rides the leading left-hand horse of a team or pair drawing a coach etc. when there is no coachman. [French *postillon* from Italian *postiglione* post boy from *posta* POST²]

Post-Impres·sion·ism *noun* artistic aims and methods developed from, or as a reaction against, Impressionism and intending to express the individual artist's conception of the objects represented rather than the general observer's view. □ **Post-Impres·sion·ist** *noun & adjective*

post-industri·al *adjective* relating to or characteristic of a society or economy which no longer relies on heavy industry. □ **post-industri·al·ism** *noun*

post·ing *noun* **1** an appointment to a position or post. **2** a message posted to a discussion group etc. on the Internet.

Post-it *noun* (also **Post-it Note**) *proprietary* **1** a small pad of paper with an adhesive strip on the bottom of each sheet, designed for easy positioning on and removal from smooth surfaces. **2** a sheet from such a pad.

post·lude /ˈpoːstluːd/ *noun* a piece of esp. organ music played at the conclusion of a church service. [POST-, after PRELUDE]

post·man *noun* (*pl.* **-men**) a person who is employed to deliver letters etc.

post·mark ● *noun* an official mark stamped on a letter, esp. one

giving the place, date, etc. of dispatch or arrival, and serving to cancel the stamp. ● *transitive verb* mark (an envelope etc.) with this.

post·master *noun* **1** a person in charge of a post office. **2** *hist.* a person in charge of a fur-trading post. **3** the person or persons who manage the email for a given site.

postmaster general *noun* the head of the postal service in certain countries.

post-menopaus·al *adjective* of or occurring after menopause. □ **post-menopaus·al·ly** *adverb* **post-menopause** *noun*

post-millen·nial /ˌpoːstmɪˈleniəl/ *adjective* following the millennium.

post-millen·nial·ism /ˌpoːstmɪˈleniəˌlɪzəm/ *noun* the doctrine that the Second Coming of Christ will follow the millennium. □ **post-millen·nial·ist** *noun*

post·mis·tress *noun* a woman in charge of a post office.

post·mod·ern *adjective* of or relating to postmodernism. □ **post·mod·ern·ity** *noun*

post·modern·ism *noun* a late 20th-c. style and concept in the arts, architecture, and criticism, which represents a departure from modernism and has at its heart a general distrust of grand theories and ideologies as well as a problematical relationship with any notion of 'art'. Typical features include a deliberate mixing of different artistic styles and media, the self-conscious use of earlier styles and conventions, and often the incorporation of images relating to the consumerism and mass communication of late 20th-c. post-industrial society. □ **post·modern·ist** *adjective & noun*

post-mortem /poːstˈmɔrtəm/ ● *noun* **1** (in full **post-mortem examination**) an examination made after death, esp. to determine its cause. **2** *informal* a discussion analyzing the course and result of a game, election, etc. ● *adverb & adjective* after death. [Latin]

post·natal /poːstˈneɪtəl/ *adjective* characteristic of or relating to the period after childbirth. □ **post·natal·ly** *adverb*

postnatal depression *noun* = POSTPARTUM DEPRESSION.

post-nuptial *adjective* after marriage.

post office *noun* **1** the public department or corporation responsible for postal services and (in some countries) telecommunication. **2** a building, counter in a drugstore etc. where stamps can be bought, letters can be mailed, etc. **3** *N Amer.* a children's game in which imaginary letters are delivered in exchange for kisses.

post office box *noun* a numbered locked box at a post office, in which mail for an individual or company is put and kept until called for.

post-op *informal* ● *adjective* post-operative. ● *adverb* post-operatively.

post-operative *adjective* of the period following a surgical operation. □ **post-operative·ly** *adverb*

post·paid *adjective & adverb* on which postage has been paid.

post·partum *adjective* following childbirth. [Latin *post partum* 'after childbirth']

postpartum depression *noun* (also **postnatal depression**) depression suffered by a mother following childbirth.

post-polio syndrome *noun* a variety of ailments such as fatigue, muscular atrophy, etc. affecting survivors of poliomyelitis and occurring ten to forty years after the initial infection.

post·pone *transitive verb* put off to a future time; arrange (an event etc.) to take place at a later time; defer. □ **post·pon·able** *adjective* **post·pone·ment** *noun* [Latin *postponere* (as POST-, *ponere posit-* place)]

post·pos·ition /ˌpoːstpəˈzɪʃən/ *noun* **1** a word or particle, esp. an enclitic, placed after the word it modifies, e.g. *-ward* in *homeward* and *at* in *the books we looked at*. **2** the use of a postposition. □ **post·pos·ition·al** *adjective & noun* [Late Latin *postpositio* (as POSTPONE)]

post-prandi·al *adjective formal* or *jocular* happening immediately after a meal. [POST- + Latin *prandium* a meal]

post-produc·tion *noun* work done on a film, broadcast, etc. after filming or recording has taken place.

post-punk *adjective* of or occurring after the punk music wave in the late 1970s to early 1980s.

post road *noun hist.* a road on which mail was carried.

post-rock *noun* any type of popular music composed in a style markedly different from (and often as a conscious reaction against) that of established rock music, esp. a type of experimental music combining a diverse range of influences, esp. from electronic and ambient music.

post·script *noun* **1** an additional paragraph or remark, usu. at the end of a letter after the signature and introduced by 'PS'. **2** any additional information, action, etc. [Latin *postscriptum* neuter past participle of *postscribere* (as POST-, *scribere* write)]

post·season *N Amer. Sport* ● *adjective* of or occurring after the conclusion of the regular season (*post-season play*). ● *noun* the playoffs.

post·second·ary *adjective N Amer.* of or relating to education occurring after the completion of high school.

post·structur·al·ism *noun* an extension and critique of structuralism, esp. as used in critical textual analysis. It departed from the claims to objectivity and comprehensiveness made by structuralism and emphasized instead plurality and deferral of meaning, rejecting the fixed binary oppositions of structuralism and the validity of authorial authority. □ **post·structur·al** *adjective* **post·structur·al·ist** *noun & adjective*

post-tax *attributive adjective* (of income) after the deduction of taxes.

post time *noun N Amer.* the time at which a horse race starts.

post-traumatic stress disorder *noun* (also **post-traumatic stress syndrome**) *Med.* a condition of mental and emotional stress that sometimes follows injury or severe psychological shock, characterized by withdrawal and anxiety, and a tendency to physical illness. Abbr.: **PTSD**, **PTSS**.

pos·tu·lant /ˈpɒstjʊlənt, ˈpɒstʃʊ-/ *noun* a candidate, esp. for admission into a religious order. □ **pos·tu·lancy** *noun* [French *postulant* or Latin *postulans -antis* (as POSTULATE)]

pos·tu·late ● *transitive verb* /ˈpɒstjʊleɪt, ˈpɒstʃʊ-/ **1** (often foll. by *that* + clause) assume as a necessary condition, esp. as a basis for reasoning; take for granted. **2** claim. ● *noun* /ˈpɒstjʊlət, ˈpɒstʃʊ-/ **1** a thing postulated. **2** a fundamental prerequisite or condition. **3** *Math.* an assumption used as a basis for mathematical reasoning. □ **pos·tu·la·tion** *noun* [Latin *postulare postulat-* demand]

pos·tu·la·tor /ˈpɒstjʊˌleɪtɜr, ˈpɒstʃʊ-/ *noun Catholicism* a person, usu. a priest, who presents a case for the canonization or beatification of a candidate.

pos·ture /ˈpɒstʃɜr/ ● *noun* **1** a position of a person's body when sitting or standing (*in a reclining posture; good posture will protect your spine*). **2** a particular way of dealing with or considering something; an approach or attitude. **3** a particular way of behaving that is intended to convey a false impression; a pose. ● *intransitive verb* behave in a way that is intended to impress or mislead others. □ **pos·tur·al** *adjective* **pos·tur·er** *noun* [French from Italian *postura* from Latin *positura* from *ponere posit-* place]

post·war *adjective* occurring or existing after a war (esp. the most recent major war).

post·woman *noun* (*pl.* **-women**) a woman who is employed to deliver letters etc.

posy *noun* (*pl.* **-ies**) **1** a small bunch of flowers. **2** *archaic* a short motto, line of verse, etc., inscribed within a ring. [alteration of POESY]

pot¹ ● *noun* **1 a** a vessel, usu. rounded, of ceramic ware or metal or glass for holding liquids or solids or for cooking in. **b** such a vessel designed to hold a particular substance (*coffee pot; teapot*). **2 a** = FLOWERPOT 1. **b** = CHIMNEY POT. **c** = LOBSTER POT. **d** = CHAMBER POT, POTTY² 2. **3** a drinking vessel of pewter etc. **4** the contents of a pot (*drank a whole pot of tea*). **5** the total amount of the bet in a game etc. **6** *N Amer. informal* a fund established by a group of people for a common purpose, esp. for buying food and drinks. **7** *informal* a large sum (*pots of money*). **8** = POT-BELLY. ● *verb* (**pot·ted**, **pot·ting**) **1** *transitive* place (a plant) in a flowerpot. **2** *transitive* **a** (usu. as **pot·ted** *adjective*) preserve in a sealed pot (*potted shrimps*). **b** cook (food) in a pot. **3** *transitive* **a** *Hockey* score (a goal). **b** *Brit.* pocket (a ball) in billiards etc. **4** *transitive* shoot at, hit, or kill (an animal) with a potshot. **5** *transitive* seize or secure. **6** *intransitive* make pottery. **7** *intransitive informal* take a potshot; shoot at. □ **go to pot** *informal* deteriorate; be ruined. **not have a pot to piss in** *coarse slang* be very poor. **the pot calling the kettle black** a case of accusing someone of something of which one is oneself guilty. **pot of gold** an imaginary reward; an ideal; a jackpot. □ **pot·ful** *noun* (*pl.* **-fuls**). [Old English *pott*; compare with popular Latin *potus* 'drinking cup']

pot² *noun slang* marijuana. [prob. from Latin American Spanish *potiguaya* 'cannabis leaves']

pot·able /ˈpɒtəbəl/ ● *adjective* drinkable. ● *noun* (usu. in *pl.*) a drinkable substance; a beverage. □ **pot·abil·ity** *noun* [French *potable* or Late Latin *potabilis* from Latin *potare* drink]

pot·age /pɒˈtaʒ/ *noun* thick soup. [French (as POTTAGE)]

pot·ash /ˈpɒtaʃ/ *noun* an alkaline potassium compound, usu. potassium carbonate or hydroxide. [17th-c. *pot-ashes* from Dutch

pot-asschen (as POT¹, ASH¹): originally obtained by leaching vegetable ashes and evaporating the solution in iron pots]

po·tas·sium /pəˈtasiəm/ *noun* a soft silver-white metallic element occurring naturally in sea water and various minerals, an essential element for living organisms, and forming many useful compounds used industrially. Symbol: **K**; at. no.: 19. □ **po·tas·sic** *adjective* [POTASH + -IUM]

potassium-argon dating *noun Geol.* a method of dating rocks from the relative proportions of radioactive potassium-40 and its decay produce, argon-40.

potassium carbonate *noun* a hygroscopic white crystalline solid, alkaline in solution, with many industrial applications. Chem. formula: K_2CO_3.

potassium chloride *noun* a white crystalline solid used as a fertilizer and in photographic processing.

potassium cyanide *noun* a highly toxic solid that can be hydrolyzed to give poisonous hydrogen cyanide gas. *Also called* CYANIDE.

potassium iodide *noun* a white crystalline solid used as an additive to table salt to prevent iodine deficiency.

potassium permanganate *noun* a purple crystalline solid that is used in solution as an oxidizing agent and disinfectant.

po·ta·tion /pəˈteɪʃən/ *noun formal* or *jocular* **1** a drink. **2** the act or an instance of drinking. [Old French *potation* or Latin *potatio* from *potare* drink]

po·ta·to *noun* (*pl.* **-toes**) **1** a starchy plant tuber that is cooked and used for food. **2** the plant, *Solanum tuberosum*, bearing this. [Spanish *patata* var. of Taino *batata*]

potato blight *noun* a very destructive disease of potatoes caused by a parasitic fungus, *Phytophthora infestans*.

potato cake *noun* a small patty made of potatoes, flour, eggs, etc.

potato chip *noun N Amer.* = CHIP¹ *noun* 2a.

potato crisp *noun Brit.* a potato chip.

potato famine *noun* a famine caused by failure of a potato crop, esp. the devastating one that occurred in Ireland in 1845–49 as a result of blight.

potato pancake *noun* a pancake made with grated potato.

potato sack race *noun* (also **sack race**) a race in which each competitor stands in a burlap sack and hops along the course.

potato salad *noun* cold cooked potato chopped and mixed with mayonnaise, onion, etc.

potato skins *plural noun N Amer.* wedges of baked or fried potato skin with most of the pulp removed, topped with bacon, cheese, etc. and broiled, served esp. as an appetizer in bars.

pot-au-feu /ˌpɒtoʊˈfə/ *noun* (*pl.* same) a French soup or stew of usu. beef and vegetables cooked in a large pot. [French, = pot on the fire]

Po·ta·wa·to·mi /ˌpɒtəˈwɒtəˌmiː/ ● *noun* **1** a member of an Aboriginal people living originally around Lake Michigan, now found in southwestern Ontario, Kansas, and Oklahoma. **2** the Algonquian language of these people. ● *adjective* of or relating to this people or their language.

pot barley *noun* barley with the outer hull removed, used in soups, casseroles, etc.

pot-bellied stove *noun* (also **pot-belly stove**) *N Amer.* a small bulbous stove for burning esp. wood.

pot-belly *noun* (*pl.* **-bellies**) a protruding stomach. □ **pot-bellied** *adjective*

pot·boil·er *noun* a mediocre work of literature or art done merely to make the writer or artist money.

pot-bound *adjective* (of a plant) having roots which fill the flowerpot, leaving no room to expand.

po·teen /pɒˈtiːn/ *noun Irish* alcohol made illicitly, usu. from potatoes. [Irish *poitín* diminutive of *pota* POT¹]

Po·tem·kin¹ /pɒˈtɛmkɪn/ **Grig·ori Alek·san·dro·vich** (1739–91), Russian army officer and statesman. The lover of Catherine II, he served as an administrator, and extended Russian rule in the south, carried out a series of military reforms, annexed the Crimea (1783), and built a Black Sea fleet.

Po·tem·kin² *adjective* designating things which are sham, insubstantial, or consist of little or nothing behind an impressive facade. [after 'Potemkin village', one of the sham villages said to have been built by POTEMKIN¹ in the Crimea in advance of Catherine II's visit in 1787]

Po·tem·kin /pɒˈtɛmkɪn/ Russian battleship whose crew mutinied in the Revolution of 1905, bombarding Odessa before seeking asylum in

Romania. The incident, commemorated in Eisenstein's 1925 film *The Battleship Potemkin*, persuaded the czar to agree to a measure of reform.

po·tent /ˈpəʊtənt/ *adjective* **1** powerful; strong. **2** (of a drug, alcoholic drink, poison, etc.) having strong physical or chemical properties. **3** (of a reason) cogent; forceful. **4** (of a male) capable of sexual erection or orgasm. **5** *literary* mighty. □ **po·tency** *noun* **po·tent·ly** *adverb* [Latin *potens -entis* pres. part. of *posse* be able]

po·ten·tate /ˈpəʊtənˌteɪt/ *noun* a person who possesses great power, esp. a monarch or ruler. [Old French *potentat* or Latin *potentatus* dominion (as POTENT)]

po·ten·tial /pəˈtɛnʃəl/ ● *adjective* capable of coming into being or action; latent. ● *noun* **1** the possibility of something developing or happening (*potential for error*). **2** qualities that exist and can be developed (*she has artistic potential*). **3** usable resources. **4** *Physics* the quantity determining the energy of mass in a gravitational field or of charge in an electric field. □ **po·ten·ti·al·ity** /-ʃiˈalɪti/ *noun* **po·ten·tial·ly** *adverb* [Late Latin *potentialis* from *potentia* (as POTENT)]

potential difference *noun* the difference of electric potential between two points.

potential energy *noun* a body's ability to do work by virtue of its position relative to others, stresses within itself, electric charge, etc.

po·ten·ti·ate /pəˈtɛnʃiˌeɪt/ *transitive verb* **1** make more powerful, esp. increase the effectiveness of (a drug). **2** make possible. □ **po·ten·ti·a·tion** *noun* [POTENT, on the pattern of SUBSTANTIATE]

po·ten·til·la /ˌpəʊtənˈtɪlə/ *noun* any herbaceous plant or shrub of the genus *Potentilla*; a cinquefoil. [medieval Latin, diminutive of Latin *potens* POTENT]

po·ten·ti·om·eter /pəˌtɛnʃiˈɒmɪtər/ *noun* an instrument for measuring or adjusting small electrical potentials. □ **po·ten·tio·met·ric** /-ʃiəˈmɛtrɪk/ *adjective*

Po·ten·za /pəˈtɛnzə/ a market town in S Italy, capital of Basilicata region; pop. (2001) 69,295.

pot·head¹ *noun slang* a habitual user of marijuana.

pot·head² *noun* (also **pothead whale**) the pilot whale, *Globicephala melaena*.

poth·er /ˈpɒðər/ ● *noun* a noise; commotion; fuss. ● *verb* **1** *transitive* fluster, worry. **2** *intransitive* make a fuss. [16th c.: origin unknown]

pot·herb *noun* any herb grown for culinary use.

pot holder *noun* esp. *N Amer.* a piece of quilted or thick fabric for handling hot dishes etc.

pot·hole *noun* **1** a hole in a road surface caused by wear or extremes of weather. **2** (also **pothole lake**) *N Amer.* (*West & North*) a shallow pond or lake formed by a natural hollow in the ground in which water has collected. **3** a deep hole in the ground or a riverbed. **4** a deep hole or system of caves and underground riverbeds formed by the erosion of rock esp. by the action of water. □ **pot·holed** *adjective*

pot·holing *noun* esp. *Brit.* the sport of exploring underground potholes or caves. □ **pot·holer** *noun*

pot-hook *noun* **1** a hook over a hearth for hanging a pot etc. on, or for lifting a hot pot. **2** a curved stroke in handwriting, esp. as made in learning to write.

pot·hunt·er *noun* **1** a person who hunts game for food or profit only and disregards the rules of the sport. **2** a person who finds or obtains archaeological objects, esp. by unorthodox or illicit methods, for the purpose of private collection or profit.

po·tion /ˈpəʊʃən/ *noun* a liquid medicine, poison, magic charm, etc. (*love potion*). [Old French from Latin *potio -onis* from *potus* having drunk]

pot·latch /ˈpɒtlatʃ/ *noun* (among some Aboriginal peoples of the Pacific coast of N America) a ceremonial giving away or destruction of property to enhance status. □ **pot·latch·ing** *noun* [Chinook from Nuu-chah-nulth *patlatsh* gift]

pot light *noun Cdn* an interior light encased in a cylindrical shell, mounted recessed into a ceiling. □ **pot lighting** *noun*

pot·luck *noun* **1** *N Amer.* (in full **potluck supper**, **potluck dinner**, etc.) a party to which each guest brings a dish to be shared. **2** whatever is available; whatever comes one's way.

Potok /ˈpəʊtɒk/, **Chaim** (1929-2002), US writer and editor. He was managing editor of *Conservative Judaism* from 1964 to 1975, and wrote short stories, plays, and several novels, including *The Chosen* (1967), *The Promise* (1969), and *My Name is Asher Lev* (1972), many of them drawn from his Orthodox Jewish heritage.

Po·to·mac River /pəˈtəʊmək/ a river of the eastern US, which rises in the Appalachian Mountains in West Virginia and flows about 459 km (285 miles) through Washington, DC, into Chesapeake Bay on the Atlantic coast.

pot pie *noun esp.* a pie of beef, chicken, etc. with vegetables, baked and topped with a crust.

pot plant *noun esp. Brit.* a plant grown in a flowerpot.

pot·pour·ri /pəʊˈpʊri/ *noun* **1** a mixture of dried petals and spices used to perfume a room, cupboard, etc. **2** a musical or literary medley. **3** any miscellaneous grouping (*a potpourri of regulations*). [French, = rotten pot]

pot roast ● *noun* a piece of meat, esp. beef, cooked slowly in a covered dish with a small amount of liquid. ● *transitive verb* cook (a piece of meat) in this way.

Pots·dam /ˈpɒtsdam/ a city in eastern Germany, the capital of Brandenburg, situated just southwest of Berlin on the Havel River; pop. (est. 2002) 128,000. The former summer residence of the Prussian royal family, it is the site of the rococo Sans Souci palace built for Frederick II between 1745 and 1747.

Potsdam Conference a meeting held in the summer of 1945 between US, Soviet, and British leaders, which established principles for the Allied occupation of Germany following the end of the Second World War.

pot·sherd /ˈpɒtʃɜːrd/ *noun* a broken piece of ceramic material, esp. one found on an archaeological site.

pot·shot *noun* **1** a random shot at a person or animal. **2** a shot aimed at an animal etc. within easy reach. **3** a shot taken at an animal purely to kill it for food, without regard to skill or the rules of the sport. **4** a piece of esp. random or opportunistic criticism.

pot·stick·er *noun* (in Chinese cuisine) a fried half-moon shaped dumpling filled with shredded cabbage, pork, etc.

pot·tage /ˈpɒtɪdʒ/ *noun archaic* soup, stew. [Old French *potage* (as POT¹)]

pot·ted *adjective* **1** (of a plant) planted or grown in a flowerpot, esp. indoors. **2** *N Amer. slang* intoxicated by alcohol or drugs. **3** abridged; summarized (*a potted history*).

Pot·ter, (Helen) Bea·trix (1866–1943), English writer of children's books. Her series of animal stories, illustrated with her own watercolours, began with *The Tale of Peter Rabbit* (first published privately in 1900).

pot·ter¹ *verb esp. Brit.* = PUTTER³.

pot·ter² *noun* a maker of ceramic vessels. [Old English *pottere* (as POT¹)]

Pot·ter·ies, the a district in N Staffordshire, centring on Stoke-on-Trent, where the English pottery industry is concentrated.

potter's field *noun* a burial place for paupers, strangers, etc. [with Biblical allusion to Matt. 27:7, in which it is recounted that the thirty pieces of silver given to Judas for betraying Christ are used to buy a potter's field for burying foreigners in]

potter's wheel *noun* a flat revolving disc on which wet clay is shaped by a potter.

pot·tery *noun* (pl. **-ies**) **1** vessels etc. made of fired clay. **2** a potter's work. **3** a potter's workshop.

potting shed *noun* a building in which plants are potted and tools etc. are stored.

potting soil *noun* nutrient-rich soil used esp. for potted plants.

pot·to /ˈpɒtəʊ/ *noun* (pl. **-tos**) a West African lemur-like mammal, *Perodicticus potto*. [perhaps from Guinea dialect]

potty¹ *adjective* (**pot·ti·er**, **pot·ti·est**) *slang* **1** esp. *Brit.* foolish or crazy. **2** *Brit.* insignificant, trivial (usu. foll. by *little*) (*a potty little place*). □ **pot·ti·ness** *noun* [19th c.: origin unknown]

potty² *noun* (pl. **-ties**) *informal* **1** a small seat fitting over a toilet seat, used by a young child during toilet training. **2** a child's commode.

potty train *transitive verb* train (a small child) to use a potty. □ **potty training** *noun*

pouch ● *noun* **1** a small bag. **2 a** a pocket-like receptacle in which marsupials carry their young during lactation. **b** any of several pocket-like structures in various other animals, e.g. in the cheeks of rodents. **3** a baggy area of skin underneath the eyes etc. **4** a soldier's leather ammunition bag. **5** a lockable bag for mail or dispatches. **6** *Bot.* a bag-like cavity, esp. the seed vessel, in a plant. ● *transitive verb* **1** put or make into a pouch. **2** take possession of; pocket. **3** make (part of a dress etc.) hang like a pouch. □ **pouched** *adjective* **pouchy** *adjective* [Old Northern French *pouche*: compare POKE²]

pouf¹ *var. of* POOF².

pouf² /puːf/ *noun* a soft projecting mass of material on a dress, headdress, etc. □ **poufed** *adjective* [French, ultimately imitative]

pouffe /puːf/ *noun* (also **pouf**) a large firm cushion used as a low seat or footstool. [French *pouf*; ultimately imitative]

poul·ard /puːˈlɑːd/ *noun* a domestic hen that has been spayed and fattened for eating. [French *poularde* from *poule* hen]

Pou·lenc /ˈpuːlaŋk/ **Fran·cis (Jean Mar·cel)** (1899–1963), French composer and pianist. A member of the group Les Six, he is noted for his lyrical songs and instrumental works, and his adoption of the idioms of popular music such as jazz; his works include a series of sacred choral pieces, the opera *Dialogues des Carmélites* (1957), and the ballet *Les Biches* (1923).

poult /poːlt/ *noun* a young domestic fowl, turkey, pheasant, etc. [Middle English, contraction from PULLET]

poult·er·er /ˈpoːltərər/ *noun* a dealer in poultry and usu. game. [Old French *pouletier* (as PULLET)]

poul·tice /ˈpoːltɪs/ ● *noun* a soft medicated and usu. heated mass applied to the body and kept in place with muslin etc., for relieving soreness and inflammation. ● *transitive verb* apply a poultice to. [originally *pultes* (pl.) from Latin *puls pultis* pottage, pap, etc.]

poul·try /ˈpoːltri/ *noun* domestic fowls (chickens, turkeys, ducks, geese, etc.), esp. as a source of food. [Old French *pouletrie* (as POULTERER)]

poultry seasoning *noun* a blend of herbs suitable for poultry stuffing, usu. sage, thyme, marjoram, rosemary, pepper, and nutmeg.

pounce¹ ● *intransitive verb* **1** spring or swoop, esp. as in capturing prey. **2** (often foll. by *on, upon*) **a** make a sudden attack. **b** seize eagerly upon an object, remark, etc. (*pounced on what we said*). ● *noun* **1** the act or an instance of pouncing. **2** the claw or talon of a bird of prey. □ **poun·cer** *noun* [perhaps from Old French *poinson*, ultimately from Latin *pungere* prick]

pounce² ● *noun* **1** a fine powder formerly used to prevent ink from spreading on unglazed paper. **2** powdered charcoal etc. dusted over a perforated pattern to transfer the design to the object beneath. ● *transitive verb* **1** dust with pounce. **2** transfer (a design etc.) by use of pounce. □ **poun·cer** *noun* [French *ponce, poncer* from Latin *pumex* PUMICE]

Pound, Ezra (Wes·ton Loo·mis) (1885–1972), US poet and critic. One of the founders of the imagist movement, he developed a highly eclectic poetic voice, drawing on a vast range of classical and other references, which ensured his reputation as one of the foremost modernist poets; his work from this later period includes *Hugh Selwyn Mauberley* (1920) and the long (unfinished) series of *Cantos* (1917–70). □ **Pound·ian** *noun & adjective*

pound¹ *noun* **1** a unit of weight equal to 16 oz. avoirdupois (453.6 g), or 12 oz. troy (373.2 g). **2** (in full **pound sterling**) (*pl.* same or **pounds**) the chief monetary unit of the UK and several other countries. [Old English *pund*, ultimately from Latin *pondo* Roman pound weight of 12 ounces]

pound² *verb* **1** *transitive* **a** crush or beat with repeated heavy blows. **b** thump or pummel, esp. with the fists. **c** grind to a powder or pulp. **2** *intransitive* (foll. by *at, on*) deliver heavy blows or gunfire. **3 a** *intransitive* (foll. by *along, down*, etc.) make one's way heavily or clumsily. **b** *transitive informal* walk (the streets etc.); cover on foot, esp. in search of work, business, etc. (*pounded the pavement*). **4** *intransitive* **a** (of the heart) beat heavily. **b** (of the head) throb painfully. □ **pound into** instill (an attitude, behaviour, etc.) forcefully (*religion was pounded into me*). **pound out** produce with or as if with heavy blows (*pound out a tune on the piano*). □ **pound·er** *noun* [Old English *pūnian*, related to Dutch *puin*, Low German *pün* rubbish]

pound³ ● *noun* **1** an enclosure, esp. one maintained by public authorities, where stray or homeless animals are kept. **2** a place where impounded motor vehicles are kept until redeemed. **3** a place of confinement. **4** *Cdn hist.* = BUFFALO POUND. **5** *N Amer. hist.* = BUFFALO JUMP. **6** (in full **pound net**) an enclosure of nets in the water near the shore, consisting of a long straight wall of net leading the fish into a first enclosure, and a second enclosure from which they cannot escape. ● *transitive verb* enclose (cattle etc.) in a pound. [Old English *pund-* in *pundfald*]

pound·age *noun* **1 a** a weight stated in pounds. **b** a person's weight, esp. that which is regarded as excess. **2** *Brit.* a percentage of the total earnings of a business, paid as wages. **3** *Brit.* a commission or fee of so much per pound sterling or weight.

pound·al /ˈpaundəl/ *noun Physics* a unit of force equal to the force required to give a mass of one pound an acceleration of one foot per second per second. [POUND¹ + *-al* perhaps after *quintal*]

pound cake *noun* a rich cake originally made with a pound each of butter, sugar, flour, and eggs.

pound·er *noun* (usu. in *combination*) **1** a thing or person weighing a specified number of pounds (*a five-pounder*). **2** a gun carrying a shell of a specified number of pounds.

pound·ing *noun* a resounding defeat; an onslaught resulting in heavy losses (*our team took a pounding*).

pound net *noun see* POUND³ *noun* 6.

pound of flesh *noun* a payment, penalty, etc. which is strictly due but which it is ruthless or inhuman to demand. [with allusion to Shakespeare's *Merchant of Venice*]

pound sign *noun* **1** the sign £, representing a pound sterling. **2** the sign #, esp. on a telephone keypad or computer keyboard.

pound sterling *noun see* POUND¹ 2.

pour ● *verb* **1** *intransitive & transitive* (usu. foll. by *down, out, over*, etc.) flow or cause to flow esp. downwards in a stream or shower. **2** *transitive* dispense (a drink, e.g. tea) by pouring. **3** *intransitive* (of rain, or with *it* as subject) fall heavily. **4** *intransitive* (usu. foll. by *in, out*, etc.) come or go in profusion or rapid succession (*the crowd poured out; letters poured in*). **5** *transitive* bestow or spend (money) lavishly or freely. **6** *transitive* discharge or send freely (*poured forth arrows*). **7** *transitive* (often foll. by *out*) utter at length or in a rush (*poured out their story*). **8** *transitive* (also *reflexive*) *informal* put or fit a person into a tight-fitting garment, esp. in such a way that every part of it is 'filled out' by the wearer. ● *noun* **1** the act of pouring. **2** a pouring stream. **3** a heavy fall of rain; a downpour. □ **it never rains but it pours** misfortunes rarely come singly. **pour cold water on** *see* COLD. **pour it on** proceed, work, etc. very quickly, with all one's energy. **pour oil on the waters** (or **on troubled waters**) calm a disagreement or disturbance, esp. with conciliatory words. **pour scorn on** *see* SCORN. □ **pour·able** *adjective* **pour·er** *noun* [Middle English: origin unknown]

Pous·sin /ˈpuːsã/ **Nico·las** (1594–1665), French painter. Regarded as the chief representative of French classicism in art, he developed in his painting a harmony and sense of order suffused with a rich colour sense; his subject matter included Biblical scenes (*The Adoration of the Golden Calf, c.*1635), classical mythology (*Et in Arcadia Ego, c.*1655), and historical landscapes.

pout¹ ● *verb* **1** *intransitive* **a** push the lips forward as an expression of displeasure or sulking. **b** (of the lips) be pushed forward. **2** *transitive* push (the lips) forward in pouting. ● *noun* **1** such an action or expression. **2** a fit of sulking (*in a pout*). □ **pout·ing·ly** *adverb* **pouty** *adjective* [perhaps from Old English *putian* (unrecorded) be inflated]

pout² *noun* = EELPOUT 2. [Old English *-puta* in *ælepūta* eelpout, from West Germanic]

pout·er *noun* **1** a person who pouts. **2** (also **pouter pigeon**) a kind of pigeon able to inflate its crop considerably.

pou·tine /puːˈtiːn/ *noun Cdn* **1** a dish of french fries topped with cheese curds and a sauce, usu. gravy. **2** *NB* **a** a potato dumpling. **b** a pudding or pie. [Canadian French]

POV *abbreviation* point of view.

pov·erty /ˈpɒvəti/ *noun* **1** the state of being poor; want of the necessities of life. **2** (often foll. by *of, in*) scarcity or lack. **3** inferiority, poorness, meanness. **4** *Christianity* renunciation of the right to individual ownership of property. [Old French *poverte, poverté* from Latin *paupertas -tatis* from *pauper* poor]

poverty line *noun* an income level chosen to distinguish those who are living in poverty from those who are not, representing either a level of income deemed small in comparison to those of others in the same population or a level of income that is insufficient to purchase a specified selection of goods and services deemed essential.

poverty-strick·en *adjective* extremely poor.

POW *abbreviation* prisoner of war.

pow *interjection* expressing the sound of a blow or explosion. [imitative]

pow·der ● *noun* **1** a substance in the form of fine dry particles. **2** a medicine or cosmetic in this form. **3** = GUNPOWDER. **4** loose, usu. freshly-fallen snow, esp. when considered as a type of terrain for skiing. ● *transitive verb* **1 a** sprinkle or decorate with or as with powder. **b** apply powder to. **2** (esp. as **pow·dered** *adjective*) reduce to a fine powder (*powdered ginger*). □ **keep one's powder dry** be cautious and alert. **powder one's nose 1** apply powder to one's nose. **2** *euphemism* go to a washroom. **take a powder** *slang* depart quickly. □ **pow·dery** *adjective* [Old French *poudre* from Latin *pulvis pulveris* dust]

powder blue ● *noun* pale blue. ● *adjective* (hyphenated when *attributive*) of this colour.

powder burn *noun* a burn made by the hot gases emitted by a firearm.

powder coated *adjective* covered with a polyester or epoxy powder, which is then heated to fuse into a protective layer. □ **powder coating** noun

powder keg noun **1** a barrel of gunpowder. **2** a dangerous or volatile situation.

powder·man noun (pl. **-men**) N Amer. the member of a logging crew responsible for the use of explosives.

powder monkey noun **1** N Amer. = POWDERMAN. **2** hist. a boy employed on board ship to carry powder to the guns.

powder puff noun **1** a soft pad for applying powder to the skin, esp. the face. **2** a soft or weak person (also attributive: a powder-puff performance). **3** something round and fluffy like a powder puff.

powder room noun **1** N Amer. a small room containing a toilet and sink, located off a bedroom, hallway, etc. **2** dated euphemism a women's washroom, esp. in a public building.

powdery mildew noun **1** a plant disease caused by a parasitic fungus of the family Erysiphaceae and characterized by a white floury covering of spores. **2** the fungus itself.

Pow·ell River a district municipality on the southwestern coast of BC, situated at the southern end of Powell Lake, across the Strait of Georgia from Courtenay; pop. (2001) 12,983. □ **Powell River·ite** noun [Dr. I. W. Powell, superintendent of Indian affairs d.1915]

pow·er ● noun **1** the ability to do or act (will do all in my power; has the power to change colour). **2** a particular faculty of body or mind (lost the power of speech; powers of persuasion). **3 a** government, influence, or authority. **b** political or social ascendancy or control (the party in power; people power). **4** authorization; delegated authority (power of attorney; police powers). **5** (often foll. by over) personal ascendancy. **6** an influential person, group, or organization (the press is a power in the land). **7 a** military strength. **b** a nation etc. having international influence, esp. based on military strength (the leading powers). **8** vigour, energy. **9** an active property or function (has a high heating power). **10** informal a large number or amount (has done me a power of good). **11** the capacity for exerting mechanical force or doing work (horsepower). **12** mechanical or electrical energy as distinct from hand labour. **13 a** a public supply of (esp. electrical) energy. **b** a particular source or form of energy (hydroelectric power). **14** a mechanical force applied e.g. by means of a lever. **15** Physics the rate of energy output. **16** the product obtained when a number is multiplied by itself a certain number of times (2 to the power of 3 = 8). **17** the magnifying capacity of a lens. **18 a** a deity. **b** Christianity a member of the sixth order of the nine ranks of heavenly beings (see ORDER noun 19). ● verb **1** transitive supply with mechanical or electrical energy. **2** transitive (foll. by up, down) increase or decrease the power supplied to (a device); switch on or off. **3** intransitive informal move or travel with great speed or force (they powered along the highway). ● adjective **1** of or relating to the generation or distribution of electricity (power plant; power grid). **2** driven by mechanical or electrical energy (power tools; power steering). **3** informal expressing esp. corporate power; characteristic of or involving authority or influence (power breakfast; wore a power suit). **4** Baseball of or relating to a player who displays power rather than finesse (power hitter; power pitcher). **5** designating an activity engaged in with maximum intensity (likes to have a power nap after lunch). □ **in the power of** under the control of. **power behind the throne** a person who asserts authority or influence without having formal status. **the powers that be** those in authority. □ **pow·ered** adjective (also in combination). [Anglo-French poer ultimately from Latin posse be able]

power-assist·ed adjective (esp. of steering and brakes in a motor vehicle) employing an inanimate source of power to assist manual operation.

power·band noun the range of engine speeds over which an engine is capable of delivering all or most of its power.

power bar noun N Amer. an electrical cord containing a number of outlets, an on-off switch, and often a surge suppressor, used esp. for plugging in computer equipment.

power base noun a source of authority or support.

power·boat noun a powerful motorboat.

power broker noun esp. N Amer. a person who exerts influence or affects the equilibrium of political power by intrigue. □ **power broking** noun & adjective

power centre noun **1** the centre of power in an organization, country, etc. **2** a person, organization, etc. that is at the centre of power. **3** N Amer. a shopping centre having large discount stores or superstores as its major tenants.

power chord noun a chord consisting of the root, the fifth, and an optional octave, played esp. with distortion on the low strings of a guitar.

power failure noun (also **power cut**) a temporary withdrawal or failure of an electric power supply.

power forward noun **1** Basketball **a** a large forward who plays in the low post and usu. has good shot-blocking and rebounding skills (compare SMALL FORWARD). **b** this position. **2** Hockey an effective forward known as much for strength and toughness as for skill and scoring ability.

power·ful adjective **1** having much power or strength. **2** politically or socially influential. **3** having a strong emotional effect (powerful drama). □ **power·ful·ly** adverb **power·ful·ness** noun

power grab noun informal an attempt to seize power.

power grid noun a system of electricity distribution over a wide area, consisting of a network of high-voltage power lines between major power stations.

power·house noun **1** = POWER STATION. **2** a very strong, energetic, or successful person, organization, or thing (also attributive: turned in a powerhouse performance; the country's powerhouse economy).

power·less adjective **1** without power or strength. **2** (often foll. by to + infin.) wholly unable (powerless to help). □ **power·less·ly** adverb **power·less·ness** noun

power·lift·ing noun a form of competitive weightlifting emphasizing sheer strength, consisting of three types of lift: the bench press, the squat, and the two-handed dead lift. □ **power·lift·er** noun

power line noun a conductor supplying electrical power, esp. one supported by poles etc.

power of attorney noun the authority to act for another person in legal or financial matters.

power of sale noun the authority by which a bank, trust company, etc., may seize and sell a mortgaged property on which the mortgage is in default.

power outage noun = POWER FAILURE.

power pack noun **1** a unit for supplying power. **2** the equipment for converting an alternating current to a direct current at a different (usu. lower) voltage.

power plant noun **1** an apparatus or installation which provides power for an industry, machine, etc. **2** = POWER STATION.

power play noun **1** Hockey **a** a temporary situation in which a team has a numerical advantage over the opposing team because one or more of the opposing players are serving a penalty. **b** an offensive strategy adopted by a team having such an advantage. **2** Football a running play in which a number of offensive players clear a path for the ball carrier. **3** an (often underhanded) attempt to gain or maintain power in personal relationships, business, politics, etc.

power point noun Brit. = OUTLET 2.

power politics plural noun political action based on power or influence.

power pop noun pop music that relies heavily on volume for its effect.

power-sharing noun a policy agreed between parties or within a coalition to share responsibility for decision-making and political action (also attributive: a power-sharing agreement).

power skating noun Cdn a skating technique aiming to increase a skater's power, speed, and agility by the most efficient use of the skate blades and of the muscles and alignment of the body.

power station noun a facility where electricity is generated for distribution.

power stroke noun **1** the stroke of an internal combustion engine, in which the piston is moved downward by the expansion of gases. **2** a powerful action of the arm or leg in canoeing, cycling, racquet sports, etc.

power supply noun a device that provides electrical power, esp. independently of the main electrical system or at a different voltage.

power surge noun a sudden marked increase in voltage of an electric current.

power takeoff noun a device for the transmission of mechanical power from an engine, esp. that of a tractor or similar vehicle, to another piece of equipment. Abbr.: **PTO**.

power tool noun an electrically powered tool.

power·train noun **1** the mechanism that transmits the drive from the engine of a vehicle to its axle. **2** this together with the engine and axle.

power trip noun slang something done primarily for the enjoyment of exercising power over other people (the director is on a real power trip). □ **power tripper** noun **power tripping** noun

power user noun Computing informal a knowledgeable and sophisticated user of computers.

power walking noun brisk walking for exercise, often accompanied by vigorous swinging of the arms to increase the aerobic demand. □ **power walker** noun

power washer noun = PRESSURE WASHER. □ **power washing** noun

Pow·ha·tan¹ /ˌpauəˈtan, pauˈhatən/ (d.1618), Algonquian chief, who founded the Powhatan Confederacy and negotiated a peace settlement with English colonists in Virginia following the marriage of his daughter Pocahontas to John Rolfe (1618).

Pow·ha·tan² /ˈpauətən/ ● noun 1 a member of an Algonquian Indian people of eastern Virginia. 2 = VIRGINIA ALGONQUIAN. ● adjective of, relating to, or characteristic of this people or their language. [Virginia Algonquian]

pow·wow /ˈpauwau/ ● noun 1 a cultural gathering among N American Aboriginal peoples, with dancing, music, eating, etc. 2 a conference or meeting for discussion. ● intransitive verb hold a powwow. [Algonquian powah, powwaw magician (lit. 'he dreams')]

Powys /ˈpoːɪs, ˈpauˈ/ 1 a county of east central Wales, on the border with England, formed in 1974 from the former counties of Montgomeryshire, Radnorshire, and most of Breconshire; administrative centre, Llandrindod Wells. 2 a former Welsh kingdom, most powerful in the early 12th c.

pox noun 1 any virus disease producing a rash of pimples that become pus-filled and leave pockmarks on healing. 2 informal = SYPHILIS. □ **a pox on** archaic an exclamation of anger or impatience with (a person). [alteration of spelling of pocks pl. of POCK]

poxy adjective (**poxier, poxiest**) Brit. 1 infected by pox. 2 slang of poor quality; worthless.

Poz·nań /ˈpoznanj/ (German **Posen** /ˈpoːzən/) a city in NW Poland; pop. (est. 2000) 574,896.

pp abbreviation pianissimo.

pp. abbreviation pages.

ppb abbreviation parts per billion.

PPCLI abbreviation Cdn Princess Patricia's Canadian Light Infantry regiment.

ppm abbreviation parts per million.

PPS abbreviation additional postscript.

PPV abbreviation pay-per-view.

PQ abbreviation 1 Parti Québécois. 2 Province of Quebec.

PR abbreviation 1 public relations. 2 proportional representation. 3 Puerto Rico.

Pr symbol Chem. the element praseodymium.

pr. abbreviation pair.

prac·tic·able /ˈpraktɪkəbəl/ adjective 1 that can be done or used. 2 possible in practice. □ **prac·tic·abil·ity** noun **prac·tic·able·ness** noun **prac·tic·ably** adverb [French praticable from pratiquer put into practice (as PRACTICAL)]

prac·tical /ˈpraktɪkəl/ ● adjective 1 of or concerned with practice or use rather than theory. 2 suited to use or action; designed mainly to fulfill a function (practical shoes). 3 a (of a person) inclined to action rather than speculation. b sensible as regards the conduct of everyday affairs, financial matters, etc. 4 a that is such in effect though not nominally (for all practical purposes). b virtual (in practical control). 5 feasible; concerned with what is actually possible (practical politics). ● noun Brit. a practical examination or lesson. □ **practi·cal·ity** /-ˈkalɪti/ noun (pl. **-ities**). **prac·tical·ness** noun [Late Latin practicus from Greek praktikos from prassō to act]

practical joke noun a trick played on a person which makes them look foolish and is intended to amuse others. □ **practical joker** noun

prac·tical·ly adverb 1 virtually, almost (practically nothing). 2 in a practical way.

practical nurse noun N Amer. see LICENSED PRACTICAL NURSE, REGISTERED PRACTICAL NURSE. □ **practical nursing** noun

prac·tice /ˈpraktɪs/ ● noun (also **prac·tise**) 1 the actual doing of something; action as contrasted with ideas (put a plan into practice). 2 a way of doing something that is common, habitual, or expected (it is standard practice to ask for ID). 3 a habit or custom (Gordon had a nap after lunch, as was his usual practice). 4 a repeated exercise in an activity requiring the development of skill (also attributive: dancers in practice clothes). b a session of this (time for target practice). 5 action or execution as opposed to theory. 6 the professional work or business of a doctor, lawyer, etc. (has a practice in town). 7 an established method of legal procedure. 8 procedure generally, esp. of a specified kind (bad practice). ● transitive &

intransitive verb var. of PRACTISE. □ **in practice 1** when actually applied; in reality. 2 skilful because of recent exercise in a particular pursuit. **out of practice** lacking a former skill from lack of recent practice. **put into practice** actually apply (an idea, method, etc.). [Middle English from PRACTISE, after advice, device]

prac·ti·cian /prakˈtɪʃən/ noun a worker; a practitioner. [obsolete French practicien from practique from medieval Latin practica from Greek praktikē fem. of praktikos: see PRACTICAL]

prac·ti·cum /ˈpraktɪˌkʌm/ noun N Amer. a course of practical training through experience working in a particular field. [Late Latin, neuter of practicus, from Greek praktikos, from prattein 'do']

prac·tise ● verb (also **prac·tice**) 1 transitive perform habitually; carry out in action (practise the same method). 2 transitive & intransitive do repeatedly as an exercise to improve a skill; exercise oneself in or on (an activity requiring skill) (practise your reading; you can practise on your classmates). 3 transitive pursue or be engaged in (a profession, religion, etc.). 4 intransitive archaic scheme, contrive (when first we practise to deceive). ● noun var. of PRACTICE. □ **practise what one preaches** do more or less habitually what one tells others to do. □ **prac·tis·er** noun [Old French pra(c)tiser or medieval Latin practizare alteration of practicare (as PRACTICAL)]

prac·tised adjective 1 experienced, expert (a practised liar; with a practised hand). 2 gained or perfected through practice (a practised accent).

prac·tis·ing adjective currently active or engaged in (a profession or activity) (a practising Christian; a practising lawyer).

prac·ti·tion·er /prakˈtɪʃənər/ noun 1 a person practising a profession, esp. medicine (general practitioner). 2 a person who regularly does a particular activity, esp. one requiring skill (she is an outstanding practitioner of the art of lexicography). [obsolete practitian = PRACTICIAN]

Prada /ˈprɒdə/ **Miuccia** (b.1919), Italian designer. She took over the ailing Prada company in 1978 and successfully expanded it, producing popular designs of luxury clothing, footwear, and accessories.

prae- /priː/ prefix = PRE- (esp. in words regarded as Latin or relating to Roman antiquity). [Latin: see PRE-]

prae·cipe /ˈpriːsɪpi/ noun 1 a writ demanding action or an explanation of non-action. 2 an order requesting a writ. [Latin (the first word of the writ), imperative of praecipere enjoin: see PRECEPT]

prae·nomen /priːˈnoːmen/ noun an ancient Roman's first or personal name (e.g. Marcus Tullius Cicero). [Latin from prae before + nomen name]

prae·sid·ium var. of PRESIDIUM.

prae·tor /ˈpriːtɔr, -ˈtɔr/ noun Rom. Hist. each of two magistrates ranking below consul. □ **prae·tor·ial** /-ˈtɔrɪəl/ adjective **prae·tor·ship** noun [French préteur or Latin praetor (perhaps as PRAE-, ire it- go)]

prae·tor·ian /priːˈtɔrɪən/ Rom. Hist. ● adjective of or having the powers of a praetor. [Latin praetorianus (as PRAETOR)]

praetorian guard noun 1 the bodyguard of the Roman emperor. 2 a group that uses its power and influence to support or defend a leader or central figure, or an established system, esp. in politics.

prag·mat·ic /pragˈmatɪk/ adjective 1 dealing with matters with regard to their practical requirements or consequences. 2 treating the facts of history with reference to their practical lessons. 3 hist. of or relating to the affairs of a country etc. 4 concerning pragmatism. □ **prag·mat·ic·ally** adverb [Late Latin pragmaticus from Greek pragmatikos from pragma -matos deed]

prag·mat·ics /pragˈmatɪks/ plural noun (usu. treated as sing.) the branch of linguistics dealing with language in use.

pragmatic sanction noun hist. an imperial or royal ordinance issued as a fundamental law, esp. (as **Pragmatic Sanction**) a document drafted by the Emperor Charles VI after the birth of his daughter Maria Theresa in 1717 making provision for her to succeed to all his territories should he die without a son. The opposition to its acceptance led to the War of the Austrian Succession on Charles's death in 1740.

prag·ma·tism /ˈpragməˌtɪzəm/ noun 1 a pragmatic attitude or procedure. 2 a philosophy that evaluates assertions solely by their practical consequences and bearing on human interests. □ **prag·ma·tist** noun

Prague /prɒg/ the capital of the Czech Republic, in the northeast on the Vltava River; pop. (2001) 1,178,576.

Prague Spring a brief period of liberalization in Czechoslovakia, beginning early in 1968, during which a program of political, economic, and cultural reform was initiated. On August 20,

Czechoslovakia was invaded by a Soviet-led force which re-established a more conservative communist government.

prahu /ˈprɑːuː/ *noun* (also **proa**, **prau**) a Malay boat, esp. with a large triangular sail and a canoe-like outrigger. [Malay *prāu*, *prāhū*]

Praia /ˈpraɪə/ the capital of the Cape Verde Islands, a port on the island of São Tiago; pop. (2000) 94,757.

prai·rie *noun* **1** a large area of usu. treeless and flat grassland, esp. in western Canada. **2** (also **the prairies**) the region of western N America originally characterized by such grassland. **3** (**the Prairies**) the Canadian provinces of Manitoba, Saskatchewan, and Alberta. [French from Old French *praerie*, ultimately from Latin *pratum* meadow]

prairie chicken *noun* **1** a medium-sized grouse of the N American prairies, *Tympanuchus cupido*. **2** = SHARP-TAILED GROUSE.

prairie clover *noun* any of various chiefly N American leguminous plants of the genus *Petalostemon* (*Dalea*), with dense clusters of small flowers and pinnate leaves.

prairie coneflower *noun* a usu. yellow-flowered composite plant of the genus *Ratibida*, with a thimble-shaped centre, found on prairies from Canada to Mexico.

prairie crocus *noun* Cdn a spring-flowering plant of the buttercup family, found from BC to Manitoba and the US, *Anemone* (*Pulsatilla*) *nuttalliana*, covered with silky hairs and with purple or white flowers and long plumed seeds. Floral emblem of Manitoba. *Also called* PASQUE FLOWER, PRAIRIE SMOKE.

prairie dog *noun* any N American rodent of the genus *Cynomys*, living in burrows and making a barking sound.

prairie fire *noun* N Amer. an uncontrolled fire that burns off the grasses etc. of the prairie.

prairie lily *noun* a N American lily, *Lilium philadelphicum*, with upright reddish-orange flowers with spotted petals. The floral emblem of Saskatchewan.

prairie oyster *noun* **1** a seasoned raw egg, swallowed without breaking the yolk. **2** N Amer. the testicle of a calf eaten as a delicacy.

Prairie provinces *plural noun* Alberta, Saskatchewan and Manitoba.

prairie schooner *noun* N Amer. a covered wagon used by the 19th-c. pioneers in crossing the N American prairies.

prairie skirt *noun* N Amer. a full skirt with a flounce on the bottom edge.

prairie smoke *noun* Cdn either of two plants with long-plumed seeds, purple or three-flowered avens, *Geum triflorum*, or the prairie crocus, *Anemone nuttalliana*.

prairie turnip *noun* = BREADROOT.

prairie wolf *noun* = COYOTE 1.

prairie wool *noun* Cdn the natural grassy plant cover of prairie land.

praise ● *transitive verb* **1** express warm approval or admiration of. **2** glorify (God or a deity) in words. ● *noun* the act or an instance of praising; commendation (*won high praise*; *were loud in their praises*). □ **praise be!** an exclamation of pious gratitude. **sing the praises of** commend (a person) highly. □ **praise·ful** *adjective* **prais·er** *noun* [Old French *preisier* price, prize, praise, from Late Latin *pretiare* from Latin *pretium* price: compare PRIZE¹]

praise·worthy *adjective* worthy of praise; commendable. □ **praise·worthi·ly** *adverb* **praise·worthi·ness** *noun*

Prak·rit /ˈprɒkrɪt/ *noun* any of the (esp. ancient or medieval) vernacular dialects of North and Central India existing alongside or derived from Sanskrit. [Sanskrit *prākṛta*: compare SANSKRIT]

pra·line /ˈpreɪliːn, ˈprɑː-/ *noun* **1** a confection made by browning nuts in boiling sugar, often crushed and used as a topping or in ice cream etc. **2** a fudge-like, cookie-shaped candy made of sugar, cream, nuts etc. [French from Marshal de Plessis-*Praslin*, French soldier d.1675, whose cook invented it]

pram *noun* Brit. a baby carriage. [abbreviation of PERAMBULATOR]

prana /ˈprɑːnə/ *noun* **1** (in Hinduism) breath as a life-giving force. **2** the breath; breathing. [Sanskrit]

prance ● *intransitive verb* **1** (of a horse) raise the forelegs and spring from the hind legs. **2** (often foll. by *about*) walk or behave in an elated or arrogant manner. ● *noun* **1** the act of prancing. **2** a prancing movement. □ **pran·cer** *noun* [Middle English: origin unknown]

pran·di·al /ˈprandɪəl/ *adjective* formal or jocular of dinner or lunch. [Latin *prandium* meal]

Prandtl /ˈprantəl/ **Lud·wig** (1875–1953), German physicist. He is remembered for his studies of aerodynamics and hydrodynamics,

establishing the existence of the boundary layer, and making important studies on streamlining.

prang Brit. slang ● *transitive verb* **1** crash or damage (an aircraft or vehicle). **2** bomb (a target) successfully. ● *noun* the act or an instance of pranging. [imitative]

prank *noun* a practical joke; a piece of mischief. □ **prank·ish** *adjective* **prank·ish·ly** *adverb* **prank·ish·ness** *noun* [16th c.: origin unknown]

prank·ster *noun* a person fond of playing pranks. □ **prank·ster·ism** *noun*

praseo·dym·ium /ˌpreɪzɪəˈdɪmɪəm/ *noun* Chem. a soft silvery metallic element of the lanthanide series, occurring naturally in various minerals and used in catalyst mixtures. Symbol: **Pr**; at. no.: 59. [German *Praseodym* from Greek *prasios* (adj.) leek-green, from *prason* leek (from its green salts), + German *Didym* DIDYMIUM]

prat *noun* slang **1** Brit. a silly or foolish person. **2** the buttocks. [16th-c. cant (in sense 2): origin unknown]

prate *intransitive verb* talk foolishly or at tedious length about something. □ **prat·ing** *adjective* [Middle Dutch, Middle Low German *praten*, prob. imitative]

prat·fall *noun* N Amer. informal **1** a fall on the buttocks. **2** a humiliating failure or blunder.

prat·ie /ˈpreɪti/ *noun* esp. Cdn (Nfld) & Irish a potato. [corruption]

prat·in·cole /ˈpratɪŋˌkoʊl/ *noun* any of various birds of the subfamily Glareolinae, inhabiting sandy and stony areas and feeding on insects. [modern Latin *pratincola* from Latin *pratum* meadow + *incola* inhabitant]

Prato /ˈprɑːtoʊ/ a city in west central Italy, northwest of Florence; pop. (2001) 170,388.

Pratt ▶ 1 Edwin John ('E.J.') (1882–1964), Canadian poet. He became well-known with the publication of *Newfoundland Verse* (1923). He published twelve more volumes of verse, winning three Governor General's Awards and earning a reputation as the foremost Canadian poet of the first half of the 20th c. **2 (John) Chris·to·pher** (b.1935), Canadian painter and printmaker. His work typically has an eastern Canadian focus, and is known for its realism and intensity, as well as its lack of extraneous detail. **3** his wife, **Mary** (b.1935), Canadian painter. She trained at Mount Allison under Alex Colville and Lawren Phillips Harris, and her paintings, mainly of everyday objects found in her Newfoundland kitchen, are carefully executed and intricately detailed.

prat·tle ● *transitive & intransitive verb* chatter or say in a childish way. ● *noun* **1** childish chatter. **2** inconsequential talk. □ **prat·tler** *noun* **prat·tling** *adjective* [Middle Low German *pratelen* (as PRATE)]

prau var. of PRAHU.

prawn ● *noun* **1** any of various marine crustaceans, resembling a shrimp but usu. larger. **2** esp. Brit. a large shrimp. ● *intransitive verb* fish for prawns. [Middle English *pra(y)ne*, of unknown origin]

prax·is /ˈpraksɪs/ *noun* **1** accepted practice or custom. **2** the practising of an art or skill. [medieval Latin from Greek, = doing, from *prassō* do]

Prax·it·eles /prakˈsɪtəˌliːz/ (mid-4th c. BC), Athenian sculptor. Although only one of his works, *Hermes Carrying the Infant Dionysus*, survives, he is regarded as one of the greatest Greek sculptors.

pray ● *verb* (often foll. by *for* or *to* + infin. or *that* + clause) **1** *intransitive* say prayers (to God etc.); make devout supplication. **2** *transitive* say or offer (a prayer). **3 a** *transitive* entreat, beseech. **b** *transitive & intransitive* ask earnestly (*prayed to be released*). ● *adverb* **1** *transitive* archaic & formal used as a preface to polite requests or instructions (*pray continue*). **2** (also **pray tell**) used as a way of adding ironic or sarcastic emphasis to a question (*and what, pray tell, was that supposed to mean?*). [Old French *preier* from Late Latin *precare* from Latin *precari* entreat]

pray·er¹ *noun* **1 a** a solemn request or thanksgiving to God or an object of worship (*say a prayer*). **b** a formula or form of words used in praying (*the Lord's prayer*). **c** the act of praying (*be at prayer*). **d** a religious service consisting largely of prayers (*morning prayers*). **2 a** an entreaty to a person. **b** a thing entreated or prayed for. □ **not have a prayer** N Amer. informal have no chance (of success etc.). [Old French *preiere*, ultimately from Latin *precarius* obtained by entreaty, from *prex precis* prayer]

pray·er² *noun* a person who prays.

prayer beads *noun* a rosary or other string of beads for counting prayers.

prayer book *noun* a book containing prayers for use in religious services or private devotions.

prayer breakfast *noun* N Amer. a gathering of esp. evangelical Christians for breakfast and prayer, usu. featuring a guest speaker.

---

t top   v voice   w we   z zoo   ʃ she   ʒ vision   θ thin   ð this   ŋ ring   x loch   tʃ chip   dʒ jar   (*see over for vowels*)

prayer·ful *adjective* **1** (of a person) given to praying; devout. **2** (of speech, actions, etc.) characterized by or expressive of prayer. □ **prayer·ful·ly** *adverb* **prayer·ful·ness** *noun*

prayer meeting *noun N Amer.* a gathering of esp. evangelical Christians to offer prayers.

Prayer of Manasseh /məˈnasə/ a book of the Apocrypha consisting of a penitential prayer put into the mouth of Manasseh, king of Judea; the book is not part of the Catholic canon, but is considered deuterocanonical by some Eastern Churches. Manasseh's life and reign are described at 2 Kings 21:1–18.

prayer rug *noun* (also **prayer mat**) a small carpet used by Muslims for kneeling on when praying.

prayer shawl *noun* = TALLIS.

prayer wheel *noun* a revolving cylindrical box inscribed with or containing prayers, used esp. by Tibetan Buddhists.

praying mantis *noun* a mantis, *Mantis religiosa*, that holds its forelegs in a position suggestive of hands folded in prayer, while waiting to pounce on its prey.

PRC *abbreviation* People's Republic of China.

pre- *prefix* before (in time, place, order, degree, or importance). [from or after Latin *prae-* from *prae* (adv. & prep.)]

preach *verb* **1 a** *intransitive* deliver a sermon or religious address. **b** *transitive* deliver (a sermon); proclaim or expound (the Gospel etc.). **2** *intransitive* give moral advice in an obtrusive way. **3** *transitive* advocate or inculcate (a quality or practice etc.). □ **preach to the converted** (or **choir**) commend an opinion to a person or persons already in agreement. [Old French *prechier* from Latin *praedicare* proclaim, in ecclesiastical Latin preach (as PRAE-, *dicare* declare)]

preach·er *noun* a person who preaches, esp. a minister of religion. □ **preach·er·ly** *adjective* [Old French *prech(e)or* from ecclesiastical Latin *praedicator* (as PREACH)]

preach·ment *noun* usu. *derogatory* preaching, sermonizing.

preachy *adjective* (**preachier**, **preachiest**) *informal* inclined to preach or moralize. □ **preach·i·ness** *noun*

pre·adoles·cent /ˌpriːadəˈlesənt/ ● *adjective* **1** (of a child) having nearly reached adolescence. **2** of or relating to the two or three years preceding adolescence. ● *noun* a preadolescent child. □ **pre·adoles·cence** *noun*

pre·amble /ˈpriːambəl/ *noun* **1** a preliminary statement or introduction. **2** the introductory part of a statute or deed etc. **3** a preceding fact or circumstance. [Late Latin *praeambulus* (adj.) going before (as PRE-, AMBLE)]

pre·amp /ˈpriːamp/ *noun* = PREAMPLIFIER. [abbreviation]

pre·ampli·fi·er /priːˈampliˌfaɪr/ *noun* an electronic device that amplifies a very weak signal (e.g. from a microphone or pickup) and transmits it to a main amplifier. □ **pre·ampli·fied** *adjective*

pre·arrange *transitive verb* arrange beforehand. □ **pre·arranged** *adjective* **pre·arrange·ment** *noun*

pre·atom·ic *adjective* existing or occurring before the use of atomic energy.

preb·end /ˈprebənd/ *noun* **1** = PREBENDARY 1. **2** *hist.* the stipend of a canon or member of chapter. **3** *hist.* a portion of land or tithe from which this is drawn. [Old French *prebende* from Late Latin *praebenda* pension, neuter pl. gerundive of Latin *praebēre* grant, from *prae* forth + *habēre* hold]

preb·end·al /preˈbendəl/ *adjective* of or relating to a prebend or a prebendary.

preb·end·ary /ˈprebəndəri/ *noun* (pl. **-aries**) **1** an honorary canon. **2** *hist.* the holder of a prebend. □ **preb·end·ary·ship** *noun* [medieval Latin *praebendarius* (as PREBEND)]

pre·biot·ic *adjective* existing or occurring before the emergence of life.

pre-board *transitive & intransitive verb* admit to, or go on board, an aircraft, train, etc. in advance of others (*parents with young children should be allowed to pre-board*). □ **pre-boarding** *noun*

pre-book *transitive verb* book in advance. □ **pre-bookable** *adjective*

Pre·cam·brian /priːˈkambrian/ *Geol.* ● *adjective* of or relating to the earliest geological era including the whole of the earth's history from its origin about 4,600 million years ago to the beginning of the Cambrian period about 590 million years ago. The era was once thought devoid of organic life, but it is now known that a variety of organisms did exist during that time. ● *noun* this geological era.

Precambrian Shield *noun* = CANADIAN SHIELD.

pre·cancer·ous *adjective* tending to develop into cancer.

pre·car·ious /prɪˈkeriəs/ *adjective* **1** uncertain; dependent on chance

(*makes a precarious living*). **2** not securely held or in position; dangerously likely to fall or collapse (*precarious health*). □ **pre·car·ious·ly** *adverb* **pre·car·ious·ness** *noun* [Latin *precarius*; see PRAYER[1]]

pre·cast *adjective* (of concrete) cast in its final shape before positioning.

pre·caution *noun* an action taken in advance to avoid danger, prevent problems, etc. □ **pre·caution·ary** *adjective* [French *précaution* from Late Latin *praecautio -onis* from Latin *praecavēre* (as PRAE-, *cavēre* caut-beware of)]

precautionary principle *noun* the principle that actions, substances, etc. suspected of being dangerous should be banned unless they can be proven harmless.

pre·cede *transitive verb* **1 a** come or go before in time, order, importance, etc. (*preceding generations; the preceding paragraph*). **b** walk etc. in front of (*preceded by our guide*). **2** (foll. by *by*) cause to be preceded (*must precede this measure by milder ones*). [Latin *praecedere* (as PRAE-, *cedere cess-* go)]

pre·ced·ence /ˈpresɪdəns/ *noun* **1** priority in time, order, or importance, etc. **2** the right of preceding others on formal occasions. □ **take precedence** (often foll. by *over, of*) have priority (over).

pre·ced·ent ● *noun* /ˈpresɪdənt/ **1** a previous case or legal decision etc. taken as a guide for subsequent cases or as a justification. **2** a similar event or action that occurred earlier (*there is no precedent for such a study*). ● *adjective* /prɪˈsiːdənt, ˈpresɪ-/ preceding in time, order, importance, etc.

pre·cen·tor /prɪˈsentər/ *noun* **1** a person who leads the singing or (in a synagogue) the prayers of a congregation. **2** a minor canon who administers the musical life of a cathedral. □ **pre·cen·tor·ship** *noun* [Latin *praecentor* from *praecinere* (as PRAE-, *canere* sing)]

pre·cept /ˈpriːsept/ *noun* **1** a command; a rule of conduct. **2** moral instruction (*example is better than precept*). **3** a writ or warrant. [Latin *praeceptum* neuter past participle of *praecipere praecept-* warn, instruct (as PRAE-, *capere* take)]

pre·cep·tor /prɪˈseptər/ *noun* a teacher or instructor. □ **pre·cep·tor·ship** *noun*

pre·ces·sion /prɪˈseʃən/ *noun* the slow movement of the axis of a spinning body around another axis. □ **pre·cess** *transitive verb* **pre·ces·sion·al** *adjective* [Late Latin *praecessio* (as PRECEDE)]

precession of the equinoxes *noun* **1** the slow change of direction of the earth's axis, which moves so that the pole of the equator rotates around the pole of the ecliptic once in about 25,800 years. **2** the earlier occurrence of the equinoxes in each successive sidereal year due to the precession of the earth's axis.

pre-Christian *adjective* before Christ or the advent of Christianity.

pre·cinct /ˈpriːsɪŋkt/ *noun* **1** an enclosed or clearly defined area, e.g. around a cathedral, college, etc. **2** a specially designated area in a town, esp. with the exclusion of traffic (*shopping precinct*). **3** (in *pl.*) **a** the surrounding area or environs. **b** the boundaries. **4** *N Amer.* **a** a subdivision of a county, city, etc., for police or electoral purposes. **b** *informal* the police station of such a subdivision. **c** (in *pl.*) a neighbourhood. [medieval Latin *praecinctum* neuter past participle of *praecingere* encircle (as PRAE-, *cingere* gird)]

pre·ci·os·ity /ˌpresɪˈɒsɪti/ *noun* overrefinement in art or language, esp. in the choice of words. [as PRECIOUS]

pre·cious /ˈpreʃəs/ ● *adjective* **1** of great value or worth. **2** beloved; much prized (*precious memories*). **3** affectedly refined, esp. in language or manner. **4** *informal* often *ironic* **a** considerable (*a precious lot you know about it*). **b** expressing contempt or disdain (*you can keep your precious flowers*). ● *adverb* *informal* extremely, very (*had precious little left*). □ **pre·cious·ly** *adverb* **pre·cious·ness** *noun* [Old French *precios* from Latin *pretiosus* from *pretium* price]

precious metal *noun* any of the metals gold, silver, and platinum.

precious stone *noun* a piece of mineral having great value esp. as used in jewellery.

pre·cip /prɪˈsɪp/ *noun* *N Amer. informal* precipitation. [abbreviation]

preci·pice /ˈpresɪpɪs/ *noun* **1** a vertical or steep face of a rock, cliff, mountain, etc. **2** a dangerous situation. [French *précipice* or Latin *praecipitium* falling headlong, precipice (as PRECIPITOUS)]

pre·cipi·tant /prɪˈsɪpɪtənt/ ● *adjective* = PRECIPITATE *adjective*. ● *noun* *Chem.* a substance that causes another substance to precipitate. [obsolete French *précipitant* pres. part. of *précipiter* (as PRECIPITATE)]

pre·cipi·tate ● *verb* /prɪˈsɪpɪˌteɪt/ **1** *transitive* hasten the occurrence of; cause to occur prematurely. **2** *transitive* (foll. by *into*) send rapidly into a certain state or condition (*were precipitated into war*). **3** *transitive* throw down headlong. **4** *Chem.* **a** *transitive* cause (a substance) to be deposited in solid form from a solution. **b** *intransitive* be deposited as a solid from a solution, or from suspension in a gas; settle as a precipitate. **5** *transitive Physics* **a** cause (dust etc.) to be deposited from the air on a surface. **b** condense (vapour) into drops and so deposit it. ● *adjective* /prɪˈsɪpɪtət/ **1** headlong; violently hurried (*precipitate departure*). **2** (of a person or act) hasty, rash, inconsiderate. ● *noun* /prɪˈsɪpɪtət/ **1** *Chem.* a substance precipitated from a solution. **2** *Physics* moisture condensed from vapour by cooling and depositing, e.g. rain or dew. □ **pre·cipi·tate·ly** /prɪˈsɪpɪtətli/ *adverb* **pre·cipi·tate·ness** /prɪˈsɪpɪtətnəs/ *noun* **pre·cipi·ta·tor** /prɪˈsɪpɪˌteɪtər/ *noun* [Latin *praecipitare praecipitat-* from *praeceps praecipitis* headlong (as PRAE-, *caput* head)]

pre·cipi·ta·tion /prɪˌsɪpɪˈteɪʃən/ *noun* **1 a** rain or snow etc. falling to the ground. **b** a quantity of this. **2** the act of precipitating or the process of being precipitated. [French *précipitation* or Latin *praecipitatio* (as PRECIPITATE)]

pre·cipi·tous /prɪˈsɪpɪtəs/ *adjective* **1 a** of or like a precipice. **b** dangerously steep. **2** = PRECIPITATE *adjective*. □ **pre·cipi·tous·ly** *adverb* **pre·cipi·tous·ness** *noun* [obsolete French *précipiteux* from Latin *praeceps* (as PRECIPITATE)]

pré·cis /ˈpreɪsiː/ ● *noun* (*pl.* same /ˈpreɪsiːz/) a summary or abstract, esp. of a text or speech. ● *transitive verb* (**précises** /ˈpreɪsiːz/; **précised** /ˈpreɪsiːd/; **précising** /ˈpreɪsiːɪŋ/) make a précis of. [French, = PRECISE (as n.)]

pre·cise /prɪˈsaɪs/ *adjective* **1 a** accurately expressed. **b** definite, exact. **2** punctilious; scrupulous in being exact, observing rules, etc. **3** identical, exact (*at that precise moment*). **4** (of an instrument) accurate; exact. □ **pre·cise·ness** *noun* [French *précis -ise* from Latin *praecidere praecis-* cut short (as PRAE-, *caedere* cut)]

pre·cise·ly /prɪˈsaɪsli/ *adverb* **1** in a precise manner; exactly. **2** (as a reply) quite so; as you say.

pre·ci·sion /prɪˈsɪʒən/ *noun* **1** the condition of being precise; accuracy. **2** the degree of refinement in measurement etc. **3** (*attributive*) marked by or adapted for precision (*precision instruments*; *precision timing*). [French *précision* or Latin *praecisio* (as PRECISE)]

precision bombing *noun* the practice or policy of bombing specific (usu. military or industrial) targets rather than larger areas.

precision skating *noun* the former name for SYNCHRONIZED SKATING. □ **precision skater** *noun*

pre·classic·al *adjective* before a period regarded as classical, esp. in music and literature.

pre·clinic·al *adjective* **1** (of a stage in a disease) before symptoms can be identified. **2** of or relating to the first, chiefly theoretical, stage of a medical education.

pre·clude *transitive verb* **1** (often foll. by *from*) prevent, exclude (*precluded from taking part*). **2** make impossible; remove (*so as to preclude all doubt*). □ **pre·clu·sion** *noun* [Latin *praecludere praeclus-* (as PRAE-, *claudere* shut)]

pre·co·cial /prɪˈkoʊʃəl/ *adjective* (of a bird) having young that can feed themselves as soon as they are hatched. [Latin *praecox -cocis* (as PRECOCIOUS)]

pre·co·cious /prɪˈkoʊʃəs/ *adjective* **1** often *derogatory* (of a person, esp. a child) prematurely developed in some faculty or characteristic. **2** (of an action etc.) indicating such development. **3** (of a plant) flowering or fruiting early. □ **pre·co·cious·ly** *adverb* **pre·co·cious·ness** *noun* **pre·co·city** /-ˈkɒsɪti/ *noun* [Latin *praecox -cocis* from *praecoquere* ripen fully (as PRAE-, *coquere* cook)]

pre·cog·ni·tion /ˌpriːkɒɡˈnɪʃən/ *noun* (supposed) foreknowledge, esp. of a supernatural kind. □ **pre·cog·ni·tive** /-ˈkɒɡnɪtɪv/ *adjective* [Late Latin *praecognitio* (as PRE-, COGNITION)]

pre-colonial *adjective* of or relating to the period before a region or territory became a colony (*pre-colonial history*).

pre-Columbian *adjective* of or pertaining to the period of history in the Americas before the arrival of Columbus in 1492.

pre·con·ceive *transitive verb* form (an idea or opinion etc.) beforehand.

pre·con·cep·tion *noun* **1** a preconceived idea. **2** a prejudice.

pre·con·di·tion ● *noun* a prior condition, that must be fulfilled before other things can be done. ● *transitive verb* bring into a required condition beforehand.

pre-Confeder·a·tion *adjective* *Cdn* **1** of or pertaining to the period before 1867 in Canada. **2** relating to or characteristic of the period before a province or territory entered Confederation.

pre·con·ize /ˈpriːkəˌnaɪz/ *transitive verb* (also esp. *Brit.* **-ise**) **1** proclaim or commend publicly. **2** summon by name. **3** *Catholicism* (of the Pope)

approve publicly the appointment of (a bishop). □ **pre·con·iz·a·tion** *noun* [medieval Latin *praeconizare* from Latin *praeco -onis* herald]

pre·con·scious *Psych.* ● *adjective* **1** preceding consciousness. **2** of or associated with a part of the mind below the level of immediate conscious awareness, from which memories and emotions can be recalled. ● *noun* this part of the mind. □ **pre·con·scious·ness** *noun*

pre-contact *adjective* of or relating to an Aboriginal society before contact with Europeans.

pre·cook *transitive verb* cook in advance.

pre·cool *transitive verb* cool in advance.

pre·cor·dial /priːˈkɔrdiəl/ *adjective* in front of or about the heart.

pre·cur·sor /priːˈkɜrsər/ *noun* **1 a** a forerunner. **b** a person who precedes in office etc. **2** a harbinger. **3** a substance from which another is formed by decay or chemical reaction etc. □ **pre·cur·sory** *adjective* [Latin *praecursor* from *praecurrere praecurs-* (as PRAE-, *currere* run)]

pre·cut *transitive verb* (*past* and *past participle* **-cut**) cut in advance.

pred·acious /prɪˈdeɪʃəs/ *adjective* (also **pred·aceous**) **1** (of an animal) predatory. **2** relating to such animals (*predacious instincts*). [Latin *praeda* booty: compare *audacious*]

pre·date *transitive verb* exist or occur at a date earlier than.

pred·a·tion /prɪˈdeɪʃən/ *noun* **1** (usu. in *pl.*) = DEPREDATION. **2** *Zool.* the natural preying of one animal on others. [Latin *praedatio -onis* taking of booty, from Latin *praeda* booty]

pred·a·tor /ˈpredətər/ *noun* **1** an animal naturally preying on others. **2** a predatory corporation, country, individual, etc. [Latin *praedator* plunderer, from *praedari* seize as plunder, from *praeda* booty (as PREDACIOUS)]

pred·a·tory /ˈpredətɔri/ *adjective* **1** (of an animal) preying naturally upon others. **2** (of a corporation, country, individual, etc.) plundering or exploiting others. **3** (of business or financial practices) unfairly competitive or exploitative, esp. so as to drive competitors' prices to unprofitably low levels, thus facilitating takeovers (*predatory pricing*). □ **pred·a·tor·i·ly** *adverb* **pred·a·tor·i·ness** *noun*

pre-dawn ● *noun* the period of time just before dawn. ● *adjective* relating to or occurring during this time.

pre·decease /ˌpriːdɪˈsiːs/ *transitive verb* die earlier than (another person).

pre·deces·sor /ˈpredəˌsesər, ˈpriː-/ *noun* **1** a former holder of an office or position with respect to a later holder (*my immediate predecessor*). **2** *archaic* an ancestor. **3** a thing to which another has succeeded (*the new plan will share the fate of its predecessor*). [Old French *predecesseur* from Late Latin *praedecessor* (as PRAE-, *decessor* retiring officer, as DECEASE)]

pre-decimal *adjective* of or relating to a time before the introduction of a decimal system, esp. of coinage.

pre·def·ined *adjective* defined in advance.

pre·della /prɪˈdelə/ *noun* **1** an altar step, or raised shelf at the back of an altar. **2** a painting or sculpture on this, or any picture forming an appendage to a larger one esp. beneath an altarpiece. [Italian, = stool]

pre·des·tin·ar·ian /priːˌdestɪˈneriən/ ● *noun* a person who believes in predestination. ● *adjective* of or relating to predestination.

pre·des·tin·ate ● *transitive verb* /prɪˈdestɪˌneɪt/ = PREDESTINE. ● *adjective* /prɪˈdestɪnət/ predestined. [ecclesiastical Latin *praedestinare praedestinat-* (as PRAE-, *destinare* establish)]

pre·des·tin·a·tion /priːˌdestɪˈneɪʃən/ *noun* *Theol.* (as a belief or doctrine) the divine foreordaining of all that will happen, esp. with regard to the salvation of some and not others.

pre·des·tine /priːˈdestɪn/ *transitive verb* **1** determine beforehand. **2** ordain in advance by divine will or as if by fate. [as PREDESTINATE]

pre·deter·mine /ˌpriːdɪˈtɜrmɪn/ *transitive verb* **1** determine or decree beforehand. **2** predestine. □ **pre·deter·min·a·tion** *noun*

pre·dica·ment /prɪˈdɪkəmənt/ *noun* **1** a difficult, unpleasant, or embarrassing situation. **2** *Philos.* a category in (esp. Aristotelian) logic. [in sense 2 from Late Latin *praedicamentum* thing predicated: see PREDICATE]

predi·cant /ˈpredɪkənt/ *hist.* ● *adjective* (of a religious order, esp. the Dominicans) engaged in preaching. ● *noun* a predicant person, esp. a Dominican friar. [Latin *praedicans* part. of *praedicare* (as PREDICATE)]

predi·cate ● *transitive verb* /ˈpredɪˌkeɪt/ **1** assert or affirm as true or existent. **2** (foll. by *on*) found or base (a statement etc.) on. ● *noun* /ˈpredɪkət/ **1** *Grammar* what is said about the subject of a sentence etc. (e.g. *went home* in *Earl went home*). **2** *Logic* **a** what is predicated. **b** what is affirmed or denied of the subject by means of the copula (e.g. *mortal* in *all humans are mortal*). □ **predi·ca·tion** *noun* [Latin *praedicare praedicat-* proclaim (as PRAE-, *dicare* declare)]

---

uː m**oo**d ai m**y** əi p**i**pe au br**ow**n ʌu h**ou**se ei d**ay** ɔi b**oy** ā fr**an**glais ã Ca**na**dien ɔ̄ Br**ayo**n   (*see over for consonants*)

predi·ca·tive /prɪˈdɪkətɪv/ *adjective* **1** *Grammar* (of an adjective or noun) forming or contained in the predicate, as *old* in *the dog is old* (but not in *the old dog*) and *house* in *there is a large house* (opp. ATTRIBUTIVE). **2** that predicates. □ **predi·ca·tive·ly** *adverb* [Latin *praedicativus* (as PREDICATE)]

pre·dict /prɪˈdɪkt/ *verb* **1** *transitive* (often foll. by *that* + clause) make a statement about the future; foretell, prophesy. **2** *intransitive* make a prediction; foretell the future. □ **pre·dict·ive** *adjective* **pre·dict·ive·ly** *adverb* **pre·dict·or** *noun* [Latin *praedicere praedict-* (as PRAE-, *dicere* say)]

pre·dict·able *adjective* **1** that can be predicted or is to be expected. **2** (of a person) likely to behave in a way that is easy to predict. □ **pre·dict·abil·ity** *noun* **pre·dict·ably** *adverb*

pre·dic·tion *noun* **1** the art of predicting or the process of being predicted. **2** a thing predicted; a forecast.

pre·di·gest *transitive verb* **1** render (food) easily digestible before being eaten. **2** make (reading matter, etc.) easier to read, understand, appreciate, etc. □ **pre·di·ges·tion** *noun*

pre·di·lec·tion /ˌpriːdɪˈlɛkʃən, priː-/ *noun* (often foll. by *for*) a preference or special liking. [French *prédilection*, ultimately from Latin *praediligere praedilect-* prefer (as PRAE-, *diligere* select): see DILIGENT]

pre·dis·pose *transitive verb* **1** influence favourably in advance. **2** (foll. by *to*, or *to* + infin.) render liable or inclined beforehand. □ **pre·dis·pos·ition** *noun*

pred·ni·sone /ˈprɛdnɪˌzoʊn/ *noun* a synthetic drug similar to cortisone, used to relieve rheumatic and allergic conditions and to treat leukemia. [perhaps from *pre*(gnane) (a synthetic hydrocarbon) + *diene* + *cortisone*]

pre·dom·in·ant /prɪˈdɒmɪnənt/ *adjective* **1** prevailing, exerting control. **2** being the main, most important, or most numerous or widespread element. □ **pre·dom·in·ance** *noun*

pre·dom·in·ant·ly /prɪˈdɒmɪnəntli/ *adverb* mainly; for the most part.

pre·dom·in·ate /prɪˈdɒmɪˌneɪt/ *intransitive verb* **1** (foll. by *over*) have or exert control. **2** be superior. **3** be the strongest, main, or most numerous or widespread element; preponderate (*a garden in which dahlias predominate*). [medieval Latin *praedominari* (as PRAE-, DOMINATE)]

pre·dynas·tic /ˌpriːdaɪˈnastɪk/ *adjective* of or relating to a period before the normally recognized dynasties (esp. of ancient Egypt).

pre-echo /priːˈɛkoʊ/ *noun* (*pl.* **-echoes**) **1** a faint copy heard just before an actual sound in a recording, caused by the accidental transfer of signals. **2** a foreshadowing.

pre-eclamp·sia /ˌpriːɪˈklampsiə/ *noun* a condition of pregnancy characterized by high blood pressure and other symptoms associated with eclampsia. □ **pre-eclamp·tic** *adjective* & *noun*

pre-embryo /priːˈɛmbrɪoʊ/ *noun Med.* a human embryo in the first fourteen days after fertilization. □ **pre-embryon·ic** /-ˈɒnɪk/ *adjective*

pree·mie /ˈpriːmi/ *noun* a baby born prematurely. [PREMATURE + -IE]

pre-eminent /priːˈɛmɪnənt/ *adjective* **1** excelling others. **2** outstanding; distinguished in some quality. □ **pre-eminence** *noun* **pre-eminent·ly** *adverb* [Latin *praeeminens* (as PRAE-, EMINENT)]

pre-empt /priːˈɛmpt, -ˈɛmt/ *verb* **1** *transitive* **a** forestall; act in advance to render (something) unnecessary, ineffective, etc. **b** acquire or appropriate in advance. **2** *transitive* prevent (an attack) by disabling the enemy. **3** *transitive* obtain by pre-emption. **4** *transitive N Amer.* take for oneself (esp. public land) so as to have the right of pre-emption. **5** *transitive N Amer.* (of a news bulletin etc.) interrupt and take the place of (a television or radio broadcast). **6** *intransitive Bridge* make a pre-emptive bid. □ **pre-emptor** *noun* **pre-emptory** *adjective* [back-formation from PRE-EMPTION]

pre-emption /priːˈɛmpʃən/ *noun* **1 a** the purchase or appropriation by one person or party before the opportunity is offered to others. **b** the right to purchase (esp. public land) in this way. **2** prior appropriation or acquisition. **3** *Military* the action or strategy of making a pre-emptive attack. [medieval Latin *praeemptio* (as PRAE-, *emere empt-* 'buy')]

pre-emptive /priːˈɛmptɪv/ *adjective* **1** pre-empting; serving to pre-empt. **2** (of military action) intended to prevent attack by disabling the enemy (*a pre-emptive strike*). **3** *Bridge* (of a bid) intended to be high enough to discourage further bidding. □ **pre-emptive·ly** *adverb*

preen *verb* **1** *transitive & intransitive* (of a bird) tidy (the feathers or itself) with its beak. **2** *transitive & intransitive* (also *reflexive*) (of a person) smarten or admire (oneself, one's hair, clothes, etc.). □ **preen·er** *noun* [Middle English, apparently var. of earlier *prune* (perhaps related to PRUNE[2]): assoc. with Scots & dial. *preen* pierce, pin]

preen gland *noun* a gland situated at the base of a bird's tail and producing oil used in preening.

pre-exist *intransitive verb* (esp. as **pre-existing** *adjective*) exist at an earlier time or already. □ **pre-exist·ence** *noun* **pre-exist·ent** *adjective*

pref. *abbreviation* **1** prefix. **2** preface. **3 a** preference. **b** preferred.

pre·fab /ˈpriːfab/ *informal* ● *adjective* prefabricated. ● *noun* a prefabricated building etc. [abbreviation]

pre·fabri·cate /priːˈfabrɪˌkeɪt/ *transitive verb* manufacture sections of (a building or piece of furniture) to enable quick or easy assembly on site. □ **pre·fabri·cated** *adjective* **pre·fabri·ca·tion** *noun*

pref·ace /ˈprɛfəs/ ● *noun* **1** an introduction to a book stating its subject, scope, etc. **2** the preliminary part of a speech. **3** *Christianity* the introduction to the central part of the Eucharistic service. ● *transitive verb* **1** introduce or begin (a speech or event) (*prefaced my remarks with a warning*). **2** provide (a book etc.) with a preface. **3** (of an event etc.) lead up to (another). □ **prefa·tory** /-ˌtɔri/ *adjective* [Old French from medieval Latin *praefatia* for Latin *praefatio* from *praefari* (as PRAE-, *fari* speak)]

pre·fect /ˈpriːfɛkt/ *noun* **1** a chief officer, magistrate, governor, etc. **2** the chief administrative officer of certain departments in France. **3** a senior pupil in a school etc. authorized to enforce discipline. **4** *Catholicism* a cardinal presiding over a congregation of the Curia. **5** *Rom. Hist.* a senior magistrate or military commander. [Latin *praefectus* past participle of *praeficere* set in authority over (as PRAE-, *facere* make)]

pre·fec·ture /ˈpriːfɛktʃʊr/ *noun* **1 a** a district under the government of a prefect. **b** an administrative division of a Japanese or Chinese province. **2 a** a prefect's office or tenure. **b** his or her official residence. □ **pre·fec·tur·al** /priːˈfɛktʃərəl/ *adjective*

pre·fer *transitive verb* (**pre·ferred**, **pre·fer·ring**) **1** (often foll. by *to*, or *to* + infin.) choose instead; like better (*would prefer to stay*; *prefers coffee to tea*). **2** submit (information, an accusation, etc.) for consideration. **3** give preference to as a creditor. **4** promote or advance (a person). [Old French *preferer* from Latin *praeferre* (as PRAE-, *ferre* bear, carry)]

pref·er·able /ˈprɛfərəbəl/ *adjective* **1** to be preferred. **2** more desirable. □ **pref·er·abil·ity** /-ˈbɪlɪti/ *noun* **pref·er·ably** *adverb*

pref·er·ence /ˈprɛfərəns/ *noun* **1** the act or an instance of preferring or being preferred. **2** a thing preferred. **3 a** the favouring of one person etc. before others. **b** *Commerce* the favouring of one country by admitting its products at a lower import duty. **4** *Law* a prior right, esp. to the payment of debts. □ **in preference to** as a thing preferred over (another).

preference share *noun Brit.* = PREFERRED SHARE.

pref·er·en·tial /ˌprɛfəˈrɛnʃəl/ *adjective* **1** of or involving preference (*preferential treatment*). **2** giving or receiving a favour. **3** *Commerce* (of a tariff etc.) favouring particular countries. **4** (of voting) in which the voter puts candidates in order of preference. □ **pref·er·en·tial·ly** *adverb*

pre·fer·ment *noun* promotion to office.

preferred share *noun* (also **preferred stock**) *N Amer.* a share in a company which yields a fixed rate of interest and takes preference over common stock in entitlement to dividends.

pre·fig·ure *transitive verb* **1** represent beforehand by a figure or type. **2** imagine beforehand. □ **pre·fig·ur·a·tion** *noun* **pre·figur·a·tive** *adjective* **pre·figure·ment** *noun* [ecclesiastical Latin *praefigurare* (as PRAE-, FIGURE)]

pre·fix /ˈpriːfɪks/ ● *noun* **1** a verbal element placed at the beginning of a word to adjust or qualify its meaning, e.g. *ex-*, *non-*, *re-*, or (in some languages) as an inflectional formative. **2** a title placed before a name, e.g. *Mr.* ● *transitive verb* (often foll. by *to*) **1** add as an introduction. **2** join (a word or element) as a prefix. [as PRE-, FIX]

pre-flight *attributive adjective* occurring or provided before an aircraft flight.

pre·form ● *transitive verb* form or shape beforehand. ● *noun* a moulded object which requires further processing to give it its final shape. □ **pre·form·a·tion** *noun*

pre·forma·tive /priːˈfɔrmətɪv/ ● *adjective* prefixed as the formative element of a word. ● *noun* a preformative syllable or letter.

pre·front·al *adjective* **1** in front of the frontal bone of the skull. **2** in the forepart of the frontal lobe of the brain.

pre-game *attributive adjective* occurring just before a sporting event (*pre-game jitters*; *pre-game show*).

preg·gers *adjective informal* = PREGNANT 1.

pre·glacial *adjective* before a glacial period.

preg·nancy /ˈprɛgnənsi/ *noun* (*pl.* **-cies**) the condition or an instance of being pregnant.

Consonants: b *but*   d *dog*   f *few*   g *get*   h *her*   j *yes*   k *cat*   l *leg*   m *man*   n *no*   p *pen*   r *red*   s *sit*

preg·nant /ˈpregnənt/ *adjective* **1** (of a woman or female animal) having a child or young developing in the uterus. **2** full of meaning; significant or suggestive (*a pregnant pause*). **3** (esp. of a person's mind) imaginative, inventive. **4** (foll. by *with*) plentifully provided (*pregnant with danger*). □ **preg·nant·ly** *adverb* (in sense 2). [French *prégnant* or Latin *praegnans -antis*, earlier *praegnas* (prob. as PRAE-, (*g*)*nasci* be born)]

pre-hearing *noun* a hearing preparatory to a full hearing, trial, etc.

pre·heat *transitive verb* heat beforehand.

pre·hen·sile /prɪˈhensail/ *adjective* (of a tail or limb) capable of grasping. [French *préhensile* from Latin *prehendere prehens-* (as PRE-, *hendere* grasp)]

pre·hen·sion /prɪˈhenʃən/ *noun* the action of grasping or seizing. [Latin *prehensio* (as PREHENSILE)]

pre-Hispanic *adjective* of or relating to the period in South or Central America before the arrival of the Spanish (*pre-Hispanic artifacts*).

pre·histor·ic /ˌpriːhɪˈstɔrɪk/ *adjective* **1** of or relating to the period before written records. **2** *informal* utterly out of date. □ **pre·histor·ian** /-ˈstɔriən/ *noun* **pre·histor·ic·ally** *adverb* **pre·hist·ory** /-ˈhɪstəri/ *noun*

pre·human ● *adjective* designating or pertaining to evolutionary ancestors of humankind. ● *noun* **1** a species believed to be an evolutionary ancestor of humankind. **2** an individual of such a species.

pre-ignition *noun* the premature firing of the explosive mixture in an internal combustion engine.

pre-industri·al *adjective* of or relating to the time before industrialization.

pre-install *transitive verb* = PRELOAD.

pre·judge *transitive verb* form a premature judgment on (a person, issue, etc.). □ **pre·judg·ment** *noun*

preju·dice /ˈpredʒʊdɪs/ ● *noun* **1 a** a preconceived opinion. **b** (foll. by *against, in favour of*) bias or partiality. **c** dislike or distrust of a person, group, etc. **2** harm or injury that results or may result from some action or judgment (*to the prejudice of*). ● *transitive verb* **1** impair the validity or force of (a right, claim, statement, etc.). **2** cause (a person) to have a prejudice. □ **without prejudice** (often foll. by *to*) without detriment (to any existing right or claim). [Old French *prejudice* from Latin *praejudicium* (as PRAE-, *judicium* judgment)]

preju·diced /ˈpredʒʊdɪst/ *adjective* not impartial; bigoted.

preju·di·cial /ˌpredʒʊˈdɪʃəl/ *adjective* causing or characterized by prejudice. □ **preju·di·cial·ly** *adverb*

pre-lapsar·ian /ˌpriːlapˈseriən/ *adjective* before the Fall; innocent. [from PRE- + Latin *lapsus* fall + -ARIAN]

prel·ate /ˈprelət/ *noun* **1** a high ecclesiastical dignitary, e.g. a bishop. **2** *hist.* an abbot or prior. [Old French *prelat* from medieval Latin *praelatus* 'civil dignitary', past participle (used as a noun) of Latin *praeferre* 'carry before', also 'place before in esteem']

pre-law *noun* N Amer. (often *attributive*) a program of studies taken as preparation for law school.

pre·lim /ˈpriːlɪm, prɪˈlɪm/ *noun informal* **1** (often in *pl.*) a preliminary match, contest, round, etc. **2** a preliminary examination, esp. at a university. **3** a preliminary hearing or trial. [abbreviation]

pre·lim·in·ary /prɪˈlɪmɪneri/ ● *adjective* introductory, preparatory; initial. ● *noun* (*pl.* **-aries**) (usu. in *pl.*) **1** a preliminary action or arrangement (*dispense with the preliminaries*). **2** a preliminary trial or contest. ● *adverb* (foll. by *to*) preparatory to; in advance of (*was completed preliminary to the main event*). □ **pre·lim·in·ar·i·ly** /-ˈnerɪli/ *adverb* [modern Latin *praeliminaris* or French *préliminaire* (as PRE-, Latin *limen liminis* threshold)]

preliminary hearing *noun* a hearing held before a judge to determine whether there is enough evidence to proceed to trial.

pre·lin·guis·tic *adjective* existing or occurring before the development of language or the acquisition of speech.

pre·liter·ate *adjective* of or relating to a society or culture that has not developed the use of writing.

pre·load *transitive verb* (esp. as **pre·load·ed** *adjective*) load (esp. software) beforehand.

pre·lude /ˈpreɪljuːd, ˈpreljuːd/ ● *noun* (often foll. by *to*) **1** an action, event, or situation serving as an introduction. **2 a** an introductory piece of music, often preceding a fugue or forming the first piece of a suite or beginning an act of an opera. **b** a short piece of music of a similar type, esp. for the piano. **3** the introductory part of a poem etc. ● *transitive verb* **1** serve as a prelude to. **2** introduce with a prelude. □ **pre·lud·ial** /prɪˈljuːdiəl/ *adjective* [French *prélude* or medieval Latin *praeludium* from Latin *praeludere praelus-* (as PRAE-, *ludere* play)]

Pre·marin /ˈpreˌmərɪn/ *noun* proprietary a mixture of estrogen compounds obtained from the urine of pregnant mares and used in the treatment of various conditions, esp. those caused by or involving estrogen deficiency. [pre(gnant) + mar(e) + -IN]

pre·mari·tal /priːˈmerɪtəl/ *adjective* existing or (esp. of sexual relations) occurring before marriage.

pre-match *attributive adjective* = PRE-GAME.

pre·mature /priːməˈtʃʊr, ˈprem-/ *adjective* **1 a** occurring or done before the usual or proper time; too early (*a premature decision*). **b** too hasty (*must not be premature*). **2** (of a baby) born (esp. three or more weeks) before the end of the full term of gestation. □ **pre·mature·ly** *adverb* **pre·matur·ity** *noun* [Latin *praematurus* very early (as PRAE-, MATURE)]

premature ejaculation *noun* ejaculation of semen during sexual intercourse either before penetration or immediately after it.

pre·maxil·lary /ˌpriːmakˈsɪləri/ *adjective* in front of the upper jaw.

pre-med *noun* (often *attributive*) **1** a program of studies taken in preparation for medical school. **2** a pre-med student. [abbreviation]

pre·medi·ca·tion *noun* medication to prepare for an operation or other treatment.

pre·medi·tate *transitive verb* (esp. as **pre·medi·tat·ed** *adjective*) think out or plan (an action) beforehand (*premeditated murder*). □ **pre·medi·ta·tion** *noun*

pre·meno·paus·al *adjective* preceding menopause.

pre·men·stru·al /priːˈmenstrəl, -struəl/ *adjective* of, occurring, or experienced before menstruation (*premenstrual tension*).

premenstrual syndrome *noun* any of a complex of symptoms (including tension, fluid retention, etc.) experienced by some women in the days immediately before menstruation. Abbr.: **PMS**.

pre·mier /ˈpriːmjər, ˈpriːmjɪr, ˈpriːmɪr/ ● *noun* **1** Cdn the first minister of a province or territory. **2** a prime minister or head of government in any of several other countries. ● *adjective* first in importance, order, or time. □ **premier·ship** *noun* [Old French = first, from Latin (as PRIMARY)]

pre·mier dan·seur /prəˌmjei dɑ̃ˈsɜr/ *noun* (*pl.* **pre·miers dan·seurs** *pronunc.* same) a leading male dancer in a ballet company. [French, 'first dancer']

pre·miere /prɪˈmjɪr, premˈjer/ ● *noun* the first performance or showing of a play, film, etc. ● *verb* **1** *transitive* give a premiere of. **2** *intransitive* (of a play, film, etc.) be presented for the first time. ● *adjective* = PREMIER. [French, fem. of *premier* (adj.) (as PREMIER)]

pre·mière dan·seuse /prəˌmjer dɑ̃ˈsʊz/ *noun* (*pl.* **pre·mières dan·seuses** *pronunc.* same) a leading female dancer in a ballet company. [French, 'first dancer']

pre·millen·nial /ˌpriːmɪˈleniəl/ *adjective* **1** (esp. of the prophesied Second Coming of Christ) occurring or existing before the millennium. **2** of or pertaining to premillennialism or premillennialists.

pre·millen·nial·ism /ˌpriːmɪˈleniəlɪzəm/ *noun* the doctrine or belief that the Second Coming of Christ will precede the millennium. □ **pre·millen·nial·ist** *noun*

Prem·in·ger /ˈpremɪndʒər/ **Otto (Lud·wig)** (1906–86), Austrian-born US film director, whose films include *Laura* (1944) and *Anatomy of a Murder* (1959).

prem·ise /ˈpremɪs/ ● *noun* **1** (also **prem·iss**) *Logic* a previous statement or proposition from which another is inferred or follows as a conclusion. **2** the basic plot or circumstances on which a play, film, etc., is based. **3** (in *pl.*) **a** a house or building, together with its land and outbuildings. **b** *Law* houses, lands, or tenements previously specified in a document etc. ● *transitive verb* **1 a** say or write by way of introduction. **b** assume from a premise. **2** (foll. by *on*) base on (*justice premised on fundamental equality*). □ **on the premises** in the building etc. concerned. [Old French *premisse* and medieval Latin *praemissa* (*propositio*) '(proposition) set in front' from Latin *praemittere praemiss-* (as PRAE-, *mittere* 'send')]

pre·mium /ˈpriːmiəm/ ● *noun* **1** an amount to be paid for a contract of insurance. **2 a** a sum added to interest, wages, etc.; a bonus. **b** a sum added to ordinary charges. **3** a reward or prize. ● *attributive adjective* (of a commodity) of best quality and therefore more expensive. □ **at a premium 1** highly valued; above the usual or nominal price. **2** scarce and in demand. **put a premium on 1** provide or act as an incentive to. **2** attach special value to. [Latin *praemium* booty, reward (as PRAE-, *emere* buy, take)]

pre·mix ● *transitive verb* (esp. as **pre·mixed** *adjective*) mix beforehand. ● *noun* a mixture prepared beforehand of various esp. granular or resinous materials, e.g. animal feed.

pre·molar /priːˈmoʊlər/ ● *adjective* in front of a molar tooth. ● *noun* (in an adult human) each of eight teeth situated in pairs between each of the four canine teeth and each first molar.

pre·mon·ition /ˌpreməˈnɪʃən/ *noun* a forewarning; a presentiment. □ **pre·moni·tor·i·ly** /prɪˌmɒnɪˈtɔːrɪli/ *adverb* **pre·moni·tory** /prɪˈmɒnɪˌtɔri/ *adjective* [Late Latin *praemonitio* from Latin *praemonēre praemonit-* (as PRAE-, *monēre* warn)]

pre·motor *adjective* relating to or denoting the anterior part of the motor cortex in the frontal lobe of the brain, which is concerned with coordinating voluntary movement.

pre·natal *adjective* of or concerning the period before childbirth. □ **pre·natal·ly** *adverb*

pre·nup *noun informal* a pre-nuptial agreement.

pre·nuptial /prɪˈnʌptʃʊəl, -ˈnʌpʃʊəl, -ˈnʌpʃəl/ *adjective* **1** existing or occurring before marriage. **2** (of an agreement, contract, etc.) entered into by a couple before marriage, specifying how their assets are to be split in the event of divorce.

pre·occu·pa·tion /prɪˌɒkjuˈpeɪʃən/ *noun* **1** the state of being preoccupied. **2** a thing that engrosses the mind.

pre·occu·pied /prɪˈɒkjupaɪd/ *adjective* otherwise engrossed; mentally distracted.

pre·occupy /prɪˈɒkjuˌpaɪ/ *transitive verb* (**-pies**, **-pied**) (of a thought etc.) dominate or engross the mind of (a person) to the exclusion of other thoughts. [PRE- + OCCUPY, after Latin *praeoccupare* seize beforehand]

pre-op *adjective* = PREOPERATIVE. [abbreviation]

pre·opera·tive /prɪˈɒpərətɪv/ *adjective* of or related to the period or a condition before an operation. □ **pre·opera·tive·ly** *adverb*

pre·ordain *transitive verb* (esp. as **pre·ordained** *adjective*) ordain or determine beforehand.

pre-owned *adjective* second-hand, used.

prep *informal* ● *noun* **1** = PREPARATION. **2** *N Amer.* = PREPPY. **3** *Brit.* **a** = HOMEWORK. **b** a period when this is done. **4** *N Amer.* a horse race that is a preparation for a more important event. ● *attributive adjective* **1** = PREPARATORY (*prep time*). **2** relating to a preparatory school (*prep athlete*). ● *verb* (**prepped, prep·ping**) *N Amer. informal* **1** *transitive* prepare, make ready or suitable. **2** *intransitive* prepare oneself for an event. [abbreviation]

prep. *abbreviation* preposition.

pre·pack·age *transitive verb* (also esp. *Brit.* **pre·pack**) (esp. as **pre·pack·aged, pre·packed** *adjective*) package (goods) on the site of production or before retail.

pre·paid *past and past participle of* PREPAY.

prep·ar·a·tion /ˌprepəˈreɪʃən/ *noun* **1** the act or an instance of preparing; the process of being prepared. **2** (often in *pl.*) something done to make ready. **3** a specially prepared substance, esp. a food or medicine.

pre·para·tive /prɪˈperətɪv/ ● *adjective* preparatory. ● *noun* **1** *Military & Naut.* a signal on a drum, bugle, etc., as an order to make ready. **2** a preparatory act. □ **pre·para·tive·ly** *adverb*

pre·para·tory /ˈprepərəˌtɔri, prəˈperətɔri/ ● *adjective* (often foll. by *to*) serving to prepare; introductory. ● *adverb* (often foll. by *to*) in a preparatory manner (*was packing preparatory to departure*).

preparatory school *noun* a usu. private school preparing pupils (*N Amer.*) for college or university, or (*Brit.*) for a public school.

pre·pare *verb* **1** *transitive* make or get ready for use, consideration, etc. **2** *transitive* make ready or assemble (food, a meal, etc.) for eating. **3 a** *transitive* make (a person or oneself) ready or disposed in some way (*prepares students for university*; *prepared them for a shock*). **b** *intransitive* put oneself or things in readiness, get ready (*prepare to jump*). **4** *transitive* make (a chemical product etc.) by a regular process. ● **be prepared 1** (usu. foll. by *for*) be ready or disposed (*was prepared for a legal battle*). **2** (foll. by *to*) be willing to. □ **pre·par·er** *noun* [French *préparer* or Latin *praeparare* (as PRAE-, *parare* make ready)]

pre·pared·ness *noun* a state of readiness, e.g. for war, a disaster, etc.

pre·pay *transitive verb* (*past and past participle* **pre·paid**) **1** pay (a charge) in advance. **2** pay for (goods or a service) in advance. □ **pre·pay·able** *adjective* **pre·pay·ment** *noun*

pre·pense /prɪˈpens/ *adjective* (usu. placed after noun) esp. *Law* deliberate, intentional (*malice prepense*). [alteration of earlier *purpense* from Anglo-French & Old French *purpenser* from *por-* 'beforehand' and *penser* 'think']

pre·plan *transitive verb* (**pre·planned, pre·plan·ning**) plan in advance.

pre·pon·der·ant /prɪˈpɒndərənt/ *adjective* surpassing in influence, power, number, or importance; predominant, preponderating.

□ **pre·pon·der·ance** *noun* **pre·pon·der·ant·ly** *adverb* [Latin *praeponderant-* 'weighing more']

pre·pon·der·ate /prɪˈpɒndəˌreɪt/ *intransitive verb* (often foll. by *over*) be greater in number, quantity, or importance. [Latin *praeponderare* from *pra-* 'before' and *pondere* 'consider']

pre·pose /prɪˈpoːz/ *transitive verb Linguistics* place in front; preface, prefix. [French *préposer* (as PREPOSITION)]

prep·os·ition /ˌprepəˈzɪʃən/ *noun Grammar* a word governing (and usu. preceding) a noun or pronoun and expressing a relation to another word or element, as in: 'the man *on* the platform', 'came *after* dinner', 'what did you do it *for*?'. □ **prep·os·ition·al** *adjective* **prep·os·ition·al·ly** *adverb* [Latin *praepositio* from *praeponere praeposit-* (as PRAE-, *ponere* place)]

pre·posi·tive /prɪˈpɒzɪtɪv/ *Grammar* ● *adjective* (of a word, particle, etc.) that should be placed before. ● *noun* a prepositive word or particle. [Late Latin *praepositivus* (as PREPOSITION)]

pre·pos·sess·ing *adjective* attractive, appealing.

pre·pos·ter·ous /prɪˈpɒstərəs/ *adjective* utterly absurd; outrageous; contrary to nature, reason, or common sense. □ **pre·pos·ter·ous·ly** *adverb* **pre·pos·ter·ous·ness** *noun* [Latin *praeposterus* reversed, absurd (as PRAE-, *posterus* coming after)]

pre·potent /prɪˈpoːtənt/ *adjective* **1** greater than others in power, influence, etc. **2 a** having a greater power of fertilization. **b** dominant in transmitting hereditary qualities. □ **pre·potence** *noun* **pre·potency** *noun* [Latin *praepotent-* 'having greater power', from PRAE- 'before' + *posse* be able]

preppy *N Amer.* (also **prep·pie**) *informal* ● *noun* (*pl.* **-pies**) a person attending an expensive private school or who looks like such a person (with neat and stylish hair, clothing, etc.). ● *adjective* (**prep·pi·er, prep·pi·est**) **1** of, like, or pertaining to a preppy or preppies. **2** neat and fashionable. [PREP (SCHOOL) + -Y²]

pre·prandi·al /ˌprɪˈprandɪəl/ *adjective formal* or *jocular* before dinner or lunch. [PRE- + Latin *prandium* a meal]

pre·press *adjective* of or relating to typesetting, page layout, and other work done on a publication before it is actually printed.

pre·print ● *noun* a printed document issued in advance of general publication. ● *transitive verb* (esp. as **pre·print·ed** *adjective*) print beforehand.

pre·pro·cess *transitive verb* subject to a preliminary processing.

pre·pro·ces·sor *noun* a computer program that modifies data to conform with the input requirements of another program.

pre-produc·tion *noun* work done on a film, broadcast, etc. before production begins (often *attributive: pre-production discussions*).

pre·program *transitive verb* (**pre·programmed, pre·program·ming**) (esp. as **preprogrammed** *adjective*) program (a computer etc.) beforehand.

prep school *noun* = PREPARATORY SCHOOL. [abbreviation of PREPARATORY]

pre·pubes·cent /ˌpriːpjuːˈbesənt/ ● *adjective* (also **pre·puber·tal** /-ˈpjuːbɜːtəl/) **1** occurring prior to puberty. **2** that has not yet reached puberty. ● *noun* a prepubescent boy or girl.

pre·publi·ca·tion ● *attributive adjective* produced or occurring before publication. ● *noun* publication in advance or beforehand.

pre·puce /ˈpriːpjuːs/ *noun* **1** = FORESKIN. **2** the fold of skin surrounding the clitoris. □ **pre·putial** /prɪˈpjuːʃəl/ *adjective* [Middle English from Latin *praeputium*]

pre-qualify *intransitive verb* (**-qualifies, -qualified**) qualify in advance, as for a mortgage, sporting event, etc.

pre·quel /ˈpriːkwəl/ *noun* a story, film, etc., whose events or concerns precede those of an existing work. [PRE- + SEQUEL]

Pre-Raphael·ite /priːˈrafiəˌlaɪt/ ● *noun* a member of a group of English 19th-c. artists (**Pre-Raphaelite Brotherhood**), including Holman Hunt, Millais, and D. G. Rossetti, emulating the work of Italian artists before the time of Raphael. Their early work was marked by bright colours, strong boundary lines, and meticulous detail. Later works typically depict scenes from classical mythology or medieval romance in a dreamy style. ● *adjective* **1** of or relating to the Pre-Raphaelites. **2** (**pre-Raphaelite**) (esp. of a woman) like a type painted by a Pre-Raphaelite, e.g. with long thick curly auburn hair. □ **Pre-Raphael·it·ism** *noun*

pre-record *transitive verb* (esp. as **pre-record·ed** *adjective*) record (a message, material for broadcasting, etc.) in advance.

pre-release ● *attributive adjective* of or pertaining to the period before the release of a prisoner, consumer product, etc. ● *noun* a film, record, software, etc., given restricted availability before being generally released.

pre·requi·site /pri'rekwɪzɪt/ ● *adjective* required as a precondition. ● *noun* a prerequisite thing.

pre·roga·tive /prə'rɒgətɪv/ *noun* **1** a right or privilege exclusive to an individual or class. **2** the right or privilege exercised by a monarch or head of state over all other people, which overrides the law and is in theory subject to no restriction. [Latin *praerogativa* privilege (originally to vote first) from *praerogativus* asked first (as PRAE-, *rogare* ask)]

Pres. *abbreviation* President.

pres·age ● *noun* /'presədʒ/ an omen or portent. ● *transitive verb* /prɪ'seɪdʒ/ (of an event) be a sign or warning that (something, typically something bad) will happen. [French *présage*, *présager* from Latin *praesagium* from *praesagire* forebode (as PRAE-, *sagire* perceive keenly)]

pres·by·opia /ˌprezbi'oːpiə/ *noun* far-sightedness caused by loss of elasticity of the eye lens, occurring esp. in middle and old age. □ **pres·by·opic** /-'ɒpɪk/ *adjective* [modern Latin from Greek *presbus* old man + *ōps ōpos* eye]

pres·by·ter /'presbɪtər, 'prez-/ *noun* **1** an elder in the early Christian Church. **2** (in the Presbyterian Church) an elder. **3** (in the Episcopal Church) a minister of the second order; a priest. [ecclesiastical Latin from Greek *presbuteros* elder, comparative of *presbus* old]

pres·by·ter·ial /ˌpresbɪ'tiːriəl, ˌprez-/ *noun* Cdn a women's group belonging to a presbytery in the Presbyterian or United Churches.

Pres·by·ter·ian /ˌpresbɪ'tiːriən, ˌprez-/ ● *noun* a member of any of various branches of a more or less Calvinist Protestant denomination based on the principle of ecclesiastical government by presbyteries. ● *adjective* of or relating to Presbyterians or Presbyterianism. □ **Pres·by·ter·ian·ism** *noun* [ecclesiastical Latin *presbyterium* (as PRESBYTERY)]

pres·by·tery /'presbɪtri, 'prez-/ *noun* (pl. **-ies**) **1 a** (in the Presbyterian and United Churches) an ecclesiastical body made up of all of the ministers from a specific district together with an equal number of elders, ranking next above a congregational Session. **b** a district represented by this. **2** the house of a Roman Catholic priest. **3** the eastern part of a chancel beyond the choir; the sanctuary.

pre·school ● *adjective* of or relating to the time before a child is old enough to go to school. ● *noun* = NURSERY SCHOOL. □ **pre·school·er** *noun*

pre·scient /'presiənt, 'preʃənt/ *adjective* having foresight or foreknowledge. □ **pre·science** *noun* **pre·scient·ly** *adverb* [Latin *praescire praescient-* know beforehand (as PRAE-, *scire* know)]

pre·scind /pri'sɪnd/ *verb* **1** *intransitive* (foll. by *from*) leave out of consideration. **2** *transitive* (foll. by *from*) cut off (a part from a whole), esp. prematurely or abruptly. [Latin *praescindere* (as PRAE-, *scindere* cut)]

Pres·cott[1] a town in SE Ontario, situated on the St. Lawrence, about 75 km southwest of Cornwall; pop. (2001) 4,228. [R. PRESCOTT[2]]

Pres·cott[2], **Rob·ert** (c.1726–1815), British soldier and colonial administrator. He was appointed governor-in-chief of the Canadas, New Brunswick, and Nova Scotia and commander of forces in British N America in 1796. Although he held office until 1807, he spent only three years in Canada, and was unable to solve many of the problems related to the establishment of Lower Canada.

pre-screen *transitive verb* screen beforehand; make a preliminary selection among (options, candidates, etc.).

pre·scribe /prə'skraib/ *verb* **1** *transitive* **a** advise the use of (a medicine etc.), esp. by an authorized prescription. **b** recommend, esp. as a benefit (*prescribed a change of scenery*). **2** *transitive* lay down or impose authoritatively. **3** *intransitive* (foll. by *to*, *for*) assert a prescriptive right or claim. □ **pre·scrib·er** *noun* [Latin *praescribere praescript-* direct in writing (as PRAE-, *scribere* write)]

pre·script /'priːskript/ *noun* an ordinance, law, or command. [Latin *praescriptum* neuter past participle: see PRESCRIBE]

pre·scrip·tion /prə'skrɪpʃən/ *noun* **1 a** a doctor's (usu. written) instruction for the composition and use of a medicine. **b** a medicine prescribed (also *attributive*: *prescription drugs*). **2 a** the act or an instance of prescribing. **b** a thing considered as bringing about a specified condition (*a prescription for anarchy*). **3** uninterrupted use or possession from time immemorial or for the period fixed by law as giving a title or right. **4 a** an ancient custom viewed as authoritative. **b** a claim founded on long use. [Latin *praescriptio -onis* (as PRESCRIBE)]

pre·scrip·tive /pri'skrɪptɪv/ *adjective* **1** of or relating to the imposition or enforcement of a rule or method. **2** *Linguistics* attempting to impose rules of correct usage on the users of a language. **3** (of a right, title, or institution) having become legally established or accepted by long

usage or the passage of time. □ **pre·script·ive·ly** *adverb* **pre·script·ive·ness** *noun* **pre·scrip·tiv·ism** *noun* **pre·scrip·tiv·ist** *noun & adjective* [Late Latin *praescriptivus* (as PRESCRIBE)]

pre-season *noun* the period before a season (esp. a sports season) begins (often *attributive*: *pre-season game*).

pre-select *transitive verb* select in advance. □ **pre-selection** *noun*

pre-sell *transitive verb* promote (a product) before it is available to the consumer; persuade (a consumer) in advance to buy a product.

pres·ence *noun* **1** the state or condition of being present (*your presence is requested*). **2** a place where a person is (*was admitted to their presence*). **3 a** a person's appearance or bearing, esp. when imposing (*an intimidating presence*). **b** a person's force of personality (esp. *have presence*). **4** a person, spirit, etc., that is present (*there was a presence in the room*). **5** the maintenance by a nation of political interests and influence in another country or region (*maintained a presence*). □ **in the presence of** in front of; observed by. [Old French from Latin *praesentia* (as PRESENT[1])]

presence of mind *noun* calmness and self-control in sudden difficulty etc.

pres·ent[1] /'prezənt/ ● *adjective* **1** (usu. *predicative*) **a** being in the place in question (*was present at the trial*). **b** occurring or existing (*oxygen is present in water*). **2 a** now existing, occurring, or being such (*the present premier*; *during the present season*). **b** now being considered or discussed etc. (*in the present case*). **3** *Grammar* expressing an action etc. now going on or habitually performed (*present participle*; *present tense*). ● *noun* (prec. by *the*) **1** the time now passing (*no time like the present*). **2** *Grammar* the present tense. □ **at present** now. **for the present 1** just now. **2** as far as the present is concerned. □ **pres·ent·ness** *noun* [Old French from Latin *praesens -entis* part. of *praeesse* be at hand (as PRAE-, *esse* be)]

pres·ent[2] /prə'zent/ *verb* **1** *transitive* introduce, offer, or exhibit, esp. for public attention or consideration. **2** *transitive* **a** (with a thing as object, foll. by *to*) offer or give as a gift (to a person), esp. formally or ceremonially. **b** (with a person as object, foll. by *with*) make available to; cause to have (*presented them with a new car*; *that presents us with a problem*). **3** *transitive* **a** (of a company, producer, etc.) put (a form of entertainment) before the public. **b** (of a performer, master of ceremonies, etc.) introduce or put before an audience. **4** *transitive* introduce (a person) formally (*may I present my fiancé?*; *was presented at court*). **5** *transitive* offer, give (compliments etc.) (*may I present my card*; *present my regards to your family*). **6** *transitive* **a** (of a circumstance) reveal (some quality etc.) (*this presents some difficulty*). **b** exhibit (an appearance etc.) (*presented a rough exterior*). **7** *transitive* (of an idea etc.) offer or suggest itself. **8** *transitive* deliver (a cheque, bill, etc.) for acceptance or payment. **9** *transitive* **a** (usu. foll. by *at*) aim (a weapon). **b** hold out (a weapon) in a position for aiming. **10** *intransitive & reflexive Med.* (of a patient or illness etc.) come forward for or undergo initial medical examination. **11** *intransitive Med.* (of a part of a fetus) be directed toward the cervix at the time of delivery. **12** *transitive* (foll. by *to*) *Law* bring formally before a court; submit (an offence, complaint, etc.). □ **present arms** hold a rifle etc. vertically in front of the body as a salute. **present oneself 1** appear. **2** come forward for examination etc. □ **pre·sent·er** *noun* [Old French *presenter* from Latin *praesentare* (as PRESENT[1])]

pres·ent[3] /'prezənt/ *noun* a gift; a thing given or presented. □ **make a present of** give as a gift. [Old French (as PRESENT[1]), originally in phr. *mettre une chose en présent à quelqu'un* put a thing into the presence of a person]

pre·sent·able /pri'zentəbəl/ *adjective* **1** of good appearance; fit to be presented to other people. **2** fit for presentation. □ **pre·sent·abil·ity** *noun* **pre·sent·able·ness** *noun* **pre·sent·ably** *adverb*

pres·en·ta·tion /ˌprezən'teɪʃən/ *noun* **1 a** the act or an instance of presenting; the process of being presented. **b** a thing presented. **2** the manner or quality of presenting. **3** a demonstration or display of materials, information, etc.; a lecture. **4** an exhibition or theatrical performance. **5** a formal introduction. **6** the position of the fetus in relation to the cervix at the time of delivery. **7** Cdn (Prairies) **a** a wedding at which the bride and groom receive gifts of money rather than things. **b** a gift of money at such a wedding. □ **pres·en·ta·tion·al** *adjective* **pres·en·ta·tion·al·ly** *adverb*

present company *noun* those who are here now.

present-day *attributive adjective* of this time; modern.

pre·senti·ment /pri'zentɪmənt, -'sentɪmənt/ *noun* a vague expectation; a foreboding (esp. of misfortune). [obsolete French *présentiment* (as PRE-, SENTIMENT)]

pres·ent·ism /'prezəntɪsəm/ *noun* the viewing of all cultural and social phenomena in the context of present-day attitudes, without regard for historical context. □ **pres·ent·ist** noun

pres·ent·ly adverb **1** esp. N Amer. & Scot. at the present time; now (am presently unemployed). **2** soon; after a short time (will presently appear; presently the guests arrived).

pre·sent·ment /prɪˈzentmənt/ noun the act or an instance of presenting or being presented, esp. the presentation of a statement on oath by a jury, or of a bill, note, etc., as payment.

pres·er·va·tion /ˌprezərˈveɪʃən/ noun **1** the act of preserving or process of being preserved. **2** a state of being well or badly preserved (in an excellent state of preservation).

pres·er·va·tion·ist /ˌprezərˈveɪʃənɪst/ noun a supporter or advocate of preservation, esp. of antiquities, historic buildings, natural areas, etc.

pre·serv·a·tive /prəˈzɜːrvətɪv/ ● noun a substance for preserving perishable foodstuffs, wood, etc. ● adjective tending to preserve.

pre·serve /prəˈzɜːrv/ ● transitive verb **1 a** keep safe or free from harm, decay, etc. **b** keep alive (a name, memory, etc.). **2** maintain (a thing) in its existing state. **3** retain (a quality or condition). **4 a** treat or refrigerate (food) to prevent decomposition or fermentation. **b** prepare (fruit) by boiling it with sugar, for long-term storage. **5** keep (a natural area, wildlife, etc.) undisturbed for protection or private use. ● noun **1 a** (in pl.) Cdn food that has been home-preserved in jars; jams, jellies, pickles, canned fruits and vegetables, etc. **b** (in sing. or pl.) esp. US & Brit. jam. **2** a place where game or fish etc. is preserved. **3** a sphere or area of activity regarded as a person's own. □ **pre·serv·er** noun [Old French preserver from Late Latin praeservare (as PRAE-, servare keep)]

pre·set ● transitive verb (-setting; past and past participle -set) set or fix in advance of operation or use. ● noun (**pre·set**) a setting or control, esp. on an electronic instrument, configured or adjusted beforehand to facilitate use (choose among several presets).

pre·settle·ment attributive adjective N Amer. designating the time in N America before the arrival of European settlers.

pre·shrink transitive verb (past and past participle -shrunk) treat (a fabric or garment) so that it shrinks during manufacture and not in use.

pre·side /prɪˈzaɪd/ intransitive verb **1** (often foll. by at, over) be in a position of authority, esp. as the chairperson or president of a meeting. **2** exercise control or authority. [French présider from Latin praesidēre (as PRAE-, sedēre sit)]

pres·iden·cy /ˈprezɪdənsi/ noun (pl. -cies) **1** the office of president. **2** the period of this. [Spanish & Portuguese presidencia, Italian presidenza from medieval Latin praesidentia (as PRESIDE)]

pres·ident /ˈprezɪdənt/ noun **1** the elected head of a republican state. **2** the head of an association, union, council, etc. **3** N Amer. the head of a company etc. **4** the head of a college or university. **5** a person in charge of a meeting, assembly, etc. □ **pres·iden·tial** /-ˈdenʃəl/ adjective **pres·iden·tial·ly** /-ˈdenʃəli/ adverb [Old French from Latin (as PRESIDE)]

president-elect noun (pl. **presidents-elect**) a president who has been elected but has not yet taken up office.

pre·sid·ium /prɪˈsɪdiəm, -ˈzɪdiəm/ noun (also **prae·sid·ium**) a standing executive committee in a Communist country, esp. in the former USSR. [Russian prezidium from Latin praesidium protection etc. (as PRESIDE)]

Pres·ley /ˈpresli, ˈprezli/ **Elvis (Aron)** (known as 'the King') (1935–77), US rock singer, songwriter, and film actor. The dominant personality of early rock 'n' roll, known particularly for the energy and frank sexuality of his style, he first gained fame in 1956 with the success of such songs as 'Heartbreak Hotel' and 'Blue Suede Shoes'.

pre·soak ● transitive verb soak (esp. food or laundry) prior to cooking, washing, etc. ● noun liquid in which something is presoaked.

pre·socrat·ic /ˌpriːsəˈkrætɪk/ ● adjective (of Greek philosophy) of the time before Socrates. ● noun a presocratic philosopher.

press¹ ● verb **1** transitive apply steady force to (a thing in contact) (press a switch; pressed the two surfaces together). **2** transitive **a** compress or apply pressure to a thing to flatten, shape, or smooth it, as by ironing (got my suit pressed). **b** squeeze (a fruit etc.) to extract its juice. **c** manufacture (a phonograph record etc.) by moulding under pressure. **3** transitive (foll. by out of, from, etc.) squeeze (juice etc.). **4** transitive embrace or caress by squeezing (pressed my hand). **5** intransitive **a** (foll. by on, against, etc.) exert pressure. **b** (of an athlete, team, etc.) apply offensive pressure (the Leafs were pressing, but the Canadiens held them off). **6** intransitive be urgent; demand immediate action (time was pressing). **7** intransitive (foll. by for) make an insistent demand. **8** intransitive (foll. by around, etc.) form a crowd. **9** intransitive (foll. by on, forward, etc.) hasten insistently. **10** transitive (often in passive) (of an enemy etc.) bear heavily on. **11** transitive (often foll. by for, or to + infin.) urge or entreat (pressed me to stay; pressed me for

an answer). **12** transitive (foll. by on, upon) **a** put forward or urge (an opinion, claim, or course of action). **b** insist on the acceptance of (an offer, a gift, etc.). **13** transitive insist on (did not press the point). **14** intransitive (foll. by on) produce a strong mental or moral impression; oppress; weigh heavily. **15** transitive Weightlifting raise (a specified weight) esp. by first lifting it to shoulder height, and then gradually pushing it upwards above the head. ● noun **1** the act or an instance of pressing (give it a slight press). **2 a** a device for compressing, flattening, shaping, extracting juice, etc. (cider press; garlic press). **b** a frame for preserving the shape of a racquet when not in use. **c** a machine that applies pressure to a workpiece by means of a tool, in order to punch shapes, bend it, etc. **3** = PRINTING PRESS. **4** (prec. by the) **a** the art or practice of printing. **b** newspapers, journalists, etc., generally or collectively (pursued by the press). **5** treatment given to or opinions expressed in newspapers etc. about something or someone; publicity (got good press). **6** (**Press**) **a** a printing house or establishment. **b** a publishing company (Oxford University Press). **7 a** crowding. **b** a crowd (of people etc.). **8** the pressure of affairs. **9** Weightlifting a raising of a weight up to shoulder height followed by its gradual extension above the head. **10** Basketball any of various forms of close guarding by the defending team. **11** esp. Irish & Scot. a large usu. shelved cupboard for clothes, books, etc., esp. in a recess. □ **at** (or **in**) **press** (or **the press**) being printed. **be pressed for** have barely enough (time etc.). **go** (or **send**) **to press** go or send to be printed. **press the button 1** set machinery in motion. **2** informal initiate an action or train of events, esp. nuclear war. **press** (**the**) **flesh** esp. N Amer. shake hands. □ **press·er** noun [Middle English via Old French presser, presse from Latin pressare, frequentative of premere press-]

press² ● transitive verb **1** hist. force to serve in the army or navy. **2** bring into use as a makeshift (was pressed into service). ● noun hist. compulsory enlistment esp. in the navy. [alteration of obsolete prest (v. & n.) from Old French prest loan, advance pay, from prester from Latin praestare furnish (as PRAE-, stare stand)]

press agency noun = NEWS AGENCY.

press agent noun a person employed by an organization to deal with press publicity.

press·back adjective N Amer. designating a type of antique wooden chair with a design pressed rather than carved into the chair back.

press·board noun a material made of compressed paper laminations, used as a separator or insulator in electrical equipment.

press box noun a reporters' enclosure esp. at a sports event.

press-button noun & attributive adjective esp. Brit. = PUSH BUTTON.

press clipping noun N Amer. (Brit. **press cutting**) an article, photo, etc. cut from a newspaper, magazine, etc.

press conference noun a session to which a number of journalists are invited to hear an announcement, ask questions, etc.

press corps noun a group of reporters from various publications, networks, etc. who regularly cover the same beat.

pressed glass noun glass shaped or given its pattern by being poured under pressure into a mould while still molten.

pressed steel noun steel moulded under pressure.

presser foot noun the footplate of a sewing machine which holds the material down over the feed.

press gallery noun a gallery for reporters esp. in a legislative assembly.

press gang ● noun **1** hist. a body of men employed to press men into service in the army or navy. **2** any group using similar coercive methods. ● transitive verb (**press-gang**) force into service; coerce.

press·ing ● adjective calling for immediate attention; urgent (pressing business). ● noun **1** a thing made by pressing. **2** a series of phonograph records or CDs made at one time. **3** the act or an instance of pressing a thing, esp. a record or olives etc. □ **press·ing·ly** adverb

press kit noun a portfolio, folder, etc. containing printed matter or other multimedia materials relating to a certain issue, product, etc., prepared by an organization for distribution to the media.

press·man noun (pl. **-men**) **1** a journalist. **2** an operator of a printing press.

press office noun a department, e.g. of a business firm or political party, responsible for dealings with the press. □ **press officer** noun

press release noun an official statement issued to the media by a government department, business, etc., for information and possible publication.

press room noun **1** a room containing a press, esp. the room in a printing establishment containing the presses. **2** a room reserved for the use of reporters.

press run *noun* = PRINT RUN.

press secretary *noun* a person who deals with publicity and public relations for an individual or organization.

press time *noun* the time at which a print run of a newspaper, magazine, etc. begins.

press-up *noun Brit.* = PUSH-UP.

pres·sure ● *noun* **1 a** the exertion of continuous force on or against a body by another in contact with it. **b** the force exerted. **c** the amount of this (expressed by the force on a unit area) (*atmospheric pressure*). **d** = BLOOD PRESSURE. **2** urgency; the need to meet a deadline etc. (*work under pressure*). **3** affliction or difficulty (*under financial pressure*). **4** constraining influence (*if pressure is brought to bear*). ● *transitive verb* **1** apply (esp. psychological or moral) pressure to. **2** (often foll. by *into*) persuade; coerce (*was pressured into attending*). [Middle English from Latin *pressura* (as PRESS¹)]

pressure cooker *noun* **1** an airtight pot in which food can be cooked quickly under steam pressure. **2** an environment or situation of great pressure or stress. □ **pressure-cook** *transitive verb*

pressure crack *noun* a crack in ice, rock, concrete, etc., caused by tensile stress.

pressure gauge *noun* a gauge showing the pressure of steam, air in a tire, etc.

pressure group *noun* a group or association formed to promote a particular interest or cause by influencing public policy.

pressure point *noun* **1** a small area on the skin esp. sensitive to pressure. **2** a point where an artery can be pressed against a bone to inhibit bleeding. **3** a target for political pressure or influence.

pressure ridge *noun* a ridge caused by pressure, esp. a ridge of ice in the polar sea forced up by lateral pressure.

pressure suit *noun* an inflatable suit designed to protect the wearer against low ambient pressure (as in high-altitude flight).

pressure-treated *adjective* (of wood) impregnated with a preservative fluid to reduce decay and rotting. □ **pressure-treat** *transitive verb*

pressure washer *noun* an electrical device that pumps out water under high pressure for cleaning walls, brickwork, etc.

pres·sur·ize *transitive verb* (also esp. *Brit.* **-ise**) **1** (esp. as **pres·sur·ized** *adjective*) maintain normal atmospheric pressure in (an aircraft cabin etc.) at a high altitude. **2** raise to a high pressure. **3** *Brit.* pressure (a person). □ **pres·sur·iz·a·tion** *noun*

pressurized water reactor *noun* a nuclear reactor in which the coolant is water at high pressure. Abbr.: **PWR**.

Pres·ter John a legendary medieval Christian king of Asia, said to have defeated the Muslims and to be destined to bring help to the Holy Land, whose legend spread in Europe in the mid-12th c. [Middle English from Old French *prestre Jehan*, medieval Latin *presbyter Johannes* priest John]

presti·digi·ta·tion /ˌprestɪˈdɪdʒɪˌteɪʃən/ *noun formal* the practice of conjuring or juggling; sleight of hand. □ **presti·digi·ta·tor** /-ˈteɪtər/ *noun* [French *prestidigitateur* from *preste* nimble (as PRESTO) + Latin *digitus* finger]

pres·tige /preˈstiːʒ, -ˈstiːdʒ/ *noun* **1** respect, reputation, or influence derived from achievements, power, wealth, etc. **2** (*attributive*) having or conferring prestige. □ **pres·tige·ful** *adjective* [French, = illusion, glamour, from Late Latin *praestigium* (as PRESTIGIOUS)]

pres·ti·gious /preˈstiːdʒəs, -ˈstɪdʒəs/ *adjective* having or showing prestige. □ **pres·ti·gious·ly** *adverb* **pres·ti·gious·ness** *noun* [originally = deceptive, from Latin *praestigiosus* from *praestigiae* juggler's tricks]

pres·tis·simo /preˈstɪsɪˌmoː/ *Music* ● *adverb* in a very quick tempo. ● *noun* (*pl.* **-mos**) a movement or passage played in this way. [Italian, superlative (as PRESTO)]

presto /ˈprestoː/ ● *adverb Music* in quick tempo. ● *noun* (*pl.* **-tos**) *Music* a movement to be played in a quick tempo. ● *interjection* (also **presto chango** /ˈprestoː ˈtʃeɪndʒoː/) used to announce the successful completion of a magical trick or other surprising, esp. rapid, achievement. [Italian from Latin *praestus* from *praesto* ready]

Pres·ton 1 a city in NW England, on the Ribble River; pop. (est. 2002) 183,400, the site in the 18th c. of the first English cotton mills. **2** part of the city of Cambridge, Ontario; it was amalgamated with the city of Galt and the town of Hespeler in 1973.

Pres·ton·pans, Battle of /ˌprestənˈpænz/ the first major battle of the Jacobite uprising of 1745–46, near the town of Prestonpans just east of Edinburgh, in which a small Hanoverian army was routed by an equally small Jacobite army, leaving the way clear for the Young Pretender's subsequent invasion of England.

pre-stressed *adjective* strengthened by stressing in advance, esp. of concrete by means of stretched rods or wires put in during manufacture.

Prest·wick /ˈprestwɪk/ a town to the south of Glasgow in South Ayrshire, SW Scotland, the site of an international airport; pop. (1997) 15,478.

pre·sum·ably /prɪˈzuːməbli, -ˈzjuːməbli/ *adverb* as may reasonably be presumed.

pre·sume /prɪˈzuːm, -ˈzjuːm/ *verb* **1** *transitive* **a** (often foll. by *that* + clause) suppose to be true; take for granted. **b** assume (a person) to be (*presumed dead*). **2** *transitive* (often foll. by *to* + infin.) **a** take the liberty; be impudent enough (*presumed to question their authority*). **b** dare, venture (*may I presume to ask?*). **3** *intransitive* be presumptuous; take liberties. **4** *intransitive* (foll. by *on, upon*) take advantage of or make unscrupulous use of (a person's good nature etc.). □ **pre·sum·able** *adjective* [Old French *presumer* from Latin *praesumere* anticipate, venture (as PRAE-, *sumere* take)]

pre·sump·tion /prɪˈzʌmpʃən/ *noun* **1** arrogance; presumptuous behaviour. **2 a** the act of presuming a thing to be true. **b** a thing that is or may be presumed to be true. **3** a ground for presuming (*a strong presumption against their being guilty*). **4** *Law* an inference from known facts. [Old French *presumpcion* from Latin *praesumptio* (as PRESUME)]

presumption of innocence *noun* the legal presumption that every person charged with a criminal offence is innocent until proven guilty.

pre·sump·tive /prɪˈzʌmptɪv/ *adjective* **1** giving grounds for presumption (*presumptive evidence*). **2** (of embryonic tissue) that is not yet differentiated but will develop into a specified part. □ **pre·sump·tive·ly** *adverb* [French *présomptif -ive* from Late Latin *praesumptivus* (as PRESUME)]

pre·sump·tu·ous /prɪˈzʌmptʃuːəs/ *adjective* unduly or overbearingly confident. □ **pre·sump·tu·ous·ly** *adverb* **pre·sump·tu·ous·ness** *noun* [Old French *presumptueux* from Late Latin *praesumptuosus* (as PRESUME)]

pre·sup·pose *transitive verb* (often foll. by *that* + clause) **1** assume beforehand. **2** require as a precondition; imply.

pre·sup·pos·ition /priːˌsʌpəˈzɪʃən/ *noun* **1** the act or an instance of presupposing. **2** a thing assumed beforehand as the basis of argument etc.

pre·synap·tic /ˌpriːsɪnˈaptɪk/ *adjective* existing or occurring prior to meiotic synapsis.

prêt-à-porter /ˌpretəpɔrˈtei/ ● *adjective* (of clothes) sold ready-to-wear. ● *noun* ready-to-wear clothes. [French]

pre-tax *adjective* (of income or profits) before the deduction of taxes.

pre·teen ● *adjective* of or relating to a child just under the age of thirteen. ● *noun* a preteen child.

pre·tence *var. of* PRETENSE.

pre·tend ● *verb* **1** *transitive* (usu. foll. by *to* + infin., or *that* + clause) claim or assert falsely so as to deceive (*pretended to know the answer; pretended that he was sick*). **2 a** *transitive* imagine to oneself in play (*pretended to be monsters; pretended it was a ship*). **b** *intransitive* make pretense, esp. in imagination or play; make believe (*they're just pretending*). **3** *transitive* profess, esp. falsely or extravagantly (*does not pretend to be a scholar*). **4** *intransitive* (foll. by *to*) **a** lay claim to (a right or title etc.). **b** profess to have (a quality etc.). **5** *intransitive* (foll. by *to*) aspire or presume; venture (*I cannot pretend to guess*). ● *adjective informal* pretended; in pretense (*pretend money*). [French *prétendre* from Latin (as PRAE-, *tendere tent-*, later *tens-* stretch)]

pre·tend·ed *adjective* **1** falsely claimed to be such; so-called (*a pretended friend*). **2** professed falsely or insincerely.

pre·tend·er *noun* **1** a person who claims a throne or title etc. **2** a person who pretends.

pre·tense /ˈpriːtens, prɪˈtens/ *noun* (also **pre·tence**) **1 a** a pretext or excuse (*on the slightest pretense*). **b** a false show of intentions or motives (*under the pretense of friendship; under false pretenses*). **2** (foll. by *to*) a claim, esp. a false or ambitious one (*has no pretense to any great talent*). **3** pretending, make-believe. **4 a** affectation, display. **b** pretentiousness, ostentation (*stripped of all pretense*). [Anglo-French *pretense*, ultimately from medieval Latin *pretensus* pretended (as PRETEND)]

pre·ten·sion /prɪˈtenʃən/ *noun* **1** (often foll. by *to*) an assertion of a claim. **b** a justifiable claim (*has no pretensions to the throne*). **2** (usu. in *pl.*) an unwarranted claim to some quality, merit, dignity, etc. (*literary pretensions*). **3** pretentiousness. [medieval Latin *praetensio, -tio* (as PRETEND)]

pre·ten·tious /prɪˈtenʃəs/ *adjective* **1** making an excessive claim to great merit, importance, fashionableness, etc. esp. without good cause. **2** ostentatious, showy. □ **pre·ten·tious·ly** *adverb* **pre·ten·tious·ness** *noun* [French *prétentieux* (as PRETENSION)]

preter- /ˈpriːtər/ *combining form* more than. [Latin *praeter* (adv. & prep.), = past, beyond]

pret·er·ite /ˈpretərɪt/ (*also* **pret·erit**) *Grammar* ● *adjective* expressing a past action or state. ● *noun* a preterite tense or form. [Old French *preterite* or Latin *praeteritus* past participle of *praeterire* pass (as PRETER-, *ire* it- go)]

pre·term *adjective* born or occurring prematurely.

preter·natur·al /ˌpriːtərˈnatʃərəl, -ˈnatʃrəl/ *adjective* outside the ordinary course of nature; supernatural. □ **preter·natur·al·ism** *noun* **preter·natur·al·ly** *adverb*

pre·test ● *transitive verb* test beforehand. ● *noun* a preliminary or qualifying test.

pre·text *noun* **1** an ostensible or alleged reason or intention. **2** an excuse offered. □ **on** (or **under**) **the pretext** (foll. by *of*, or *that* + clause) professing as one's object or intention. [Latin *praetextus* outward display, from *praetexere praetext-* (as PRAE-, *texere* weave)]

Pre·toria /prɪˈtɔːriə/ the administrative capital of South Africa, in Gauteng province; pop. (est. 2002) 1,228,200.

Pretoria-Witwatersrand-Vereeniging a former name for GAUTENG.

Pre·tor·ius /prɪˈtɔːriəs/ **1 An·dries (Wil·helm·us Jaco·bus)** (1798–1853), Afrikaner soldier, who was a Boer leader in the Great Trek (1835–7) away from British rule in the Cape Colony to the Transvaal. **2** his son, **Mar·thin·us Wes·sel** (1819–1901), Afrikaner soldier, who was the first president of the South African Republic (1857–71), having followed his father in the Great Trek; he was later elected president of the Orange Free State (1859–63).

pre·treat *transitive verb* treat beforehand. □ **pre·treatment** *noun*

pre·trial ● *adjective* **1** of or pertaining to the period before a trial (*pretrial publicity*). **2** of or pertaining to a preliminary hearing before a trial (*pretrial testimony*). ● *noun* a preliminary hearing before a trial.

pretti·fy /ˈprɪtɪˌfaɪ/ *transitive verb* (**-fies**, **-fied**) make (a thing or person) pretty esp. in an affected or superficial way. □ **pretti·fi·ca·tion** /-fɪˈkeɪʃən/ *noun*

pretty /ˈprɪti/ ● *adjective* (**pret·ti·er**, **pret·ti·est**) **1** (of a person, esp. a woman or girl) attractive in a delicate, dainty, or graceful way without stateliness. **2** (of a thing) pleasing to the eye, the ear, or the aesthetic sense (*a pretty dress; a pretty tune*). **3** *ironic* considerable, fine (*a pretty penny; a pretty mess you have made*). ● *adverb informal* **1** fairly, moderately (*am pretty well; find it pretty difficult*). **2** very, considerably (*you're pretty strong!*). ● *noun* (*pl.* **-ties**) **1** a pretty person (esp. as a form of address to a child). **2** a pretty thing; an ornament. ● *transitive verb* (**-ties**, **-tied**) (often foll. by *up*) make pretty or attractive. □ **pretty much** (or **nearly** or **well**) *informal* almost; very nearly. **pretty please** an emphatic form of request. **sitting pretty** *informal* in a favourable or advantageous position. □ **pret·ti·ly** *adverb* **pret·ti·ness** *noun* [Old English *prættig* from West Germanic]

pretty boy *noun slang* **1** a foppish or effeminate man. **2** a gay man.

pret·zel /ˈpretsəl/ ● *noun* a crisp salted biscuit made in the shape of a knot or a stick. ● *transitive verb* (**-zelled**, **-zel·ling**) twist, bend, or contort (an object, a part of the body, etc.). □ **pret·zelled** *adjective* [German]

pre·vail /prɪˈveɪl/ *intransitive verb* **1** (often foll. by *against*, *over*) be victorious or gain mastery. **2** be the more usual or predominant. **3** exist or occur in general use or experience; be current. **4** (foll. by *on*, *upon*) persuade. [Latin *praevalēre* (as PRAE-, *valēre* have power), influenced by AVAIL]

pre·vail·ing *adjective* **1** most usual or widespread (*prevailing opinion*). **2** (of a wind) that blows in an area most frequently. □ **pre·vail·ing·ly** *adverb*

preva·lent /ˈprevələnt/ *adjective* **1** generally existing or occurring. **2** predominant. □ **preva·lence** *noun* **preva·lent·ly** *adverb* [as PREVAIL]

pre·vari·cate /prɪˈverɪˌkeɪt/ *intransitive verb* **1** speak or act evasively or misleadingly. **2** quibble, equivocate. □ **pre·vari·ca·tion** *noun* **pre·vari·ca·tor** *noun* [Latin *praevaricari* walk crookedly, practise collusion, in ecclesiastical Latin 'transgress' (as PRAE-, *varicari* straddle, from *varus* bent, knock-kneed)]

pre·vent *transitive verb* **1** (often foll. by *from* + verbal noun) stop from happening or doing something; hinder; make impossible (*the weather prevented me from going*). **2** *archaic* go or arrive before, precede. □ **pre·vent·able** *adjective* **pre·vent·er** *noun* **pre·ven·tion** *noun*

[Middle English = anticipate, from Latin *praevenire praevent-* come before, hinder (as PRAE-, *venire* come)]

pre·venta·tive /prɪˈventətɪv/ *adjective & noun* = PREVENTIVE.

pre·vent·ive /prɪˈventɪv/ ● *adjective* serving to prevent, esp. preventing disease, breakdown, etc. (*preventive medicine; preventive maintenance*). ● *noun* a preventive agent, measure, drug, etc. □ **pre·vent·ive·ly** *adverb*

preventive detention *noun* the imprisonment of a criminal for corrective training etc.

pre·view ● *noun* **1** the act of seeing in advance. **2 a** the showing of a film, play, exhibition, etc., before the official opening. **b** a film trailer. **3** a foretaste, a preliminary glimpse. ● *transitive verb* see or show in advance.

Pre·vin /ˈprevɪn/ **André (George)** (born Andreas Ludwig Priwin) (b.1929), German-born US conductor, pianist, and composer, who was the conductor of the Royal Philharmonic Orchestra (based in London, England) (1987–91); he has also composed musicals, film scores, and orchestral and chamber works, and is a noted jazz and classical pianist.

pre·vi·ous /ˈpriːviəs/ ● *adjective* **1** (often foll. by *to*) coming before in time or order (*previous afternoon; previous attempts*). **2** overly hasty in acting or drawing a conclusion. ● *adverb* (foll. by *to*) before (*had called previous to writing*). □ **pre·vi·ous·ly** *adverb* **pre·vi·ous·ness** *noun* [Latin *praevius* (as PRAE-, *via* way)]

previous question *noun Parl.* a motion concerning the vote on a main question.

Prev·ost /ˈprevɒst/ **Sir George** (1767–1816), English soldier and colonial administrator. He was appointed Lieutenant-Governor of Nova Scotia (1808). Becoming governor-in-chief of British North America and commander of British forces in N America in 1811, he was recalled in 1815 due to his lack of success in the War of 1812.

Prévost[1] /preɪˈvoː/ a city in south central Quebec, in the Laurentians northwest of Saint Jérôme; pop. (2001) 8,280. [possibly after the *Prévost* family of politicians]

Prévost[2] /preɪˈvoː/ **André** (1934–2001), Canadian composer and teacher. After studying in Montreal and Paris, he won the Prix d'Europe for composition (1963). He was a professor at the Université de Montréal from 1964–96, and was made an Officer of the Order of Canada in 1985.

Prévost d'Exiles /preɪˈvoː degˈziːl/ **Antoine-François** (known as the Abbé Prévost) (1697–1763), French novelist. His novel *Manon Lescaut* (1731) tells the story of a mutually destructive passion between a nobleman and a courtesan.

pre-war *adjective* existing or occurring before a war (esp. the most recent major war).

pre·wash ● *noun* a preliminary wash, esp. as performed in an automatic washing machine. ● *transitive verb* give a preliminary wash to, esp. before putting on sale.

pre-wire *transitive verb* wire beforehand, esp. put in (a building or vehicle) during construction wiring for services such as alarms or communications that are normally installed afterwards.

prex *noun US slang* = PREXY. [alteration of abbreviation of PRESIDENT]

prexy *noun* (*pl.* **-ies**) *US slang* a president, esp. the president of a college. [PREX + -Y[2]]

prey ● *noun* **1** an animal that is hunted or killed by another for food. **2** (often foll. by *to*) a person or thing that is influenced by or vulnerable to (something undesirable) (*fell prey to morbid fears*). **3** *Bible* or *archaic* plunder, booty, etc. ● *intransitive verb* (foll. by *on*, *upon*) **1** seek or take as prey. **2** make a victim of. **3** (of a disease, emotion, etc.) exert a harmful influence (*fear preyed on his mind*). [Old French *preie* from Latin *praeda* booty]

Prez see JOSQUIN DES PREZ.

prez *noun esp. US slang* a president. [abbreviation]

prez·zie *noun esp. Brit. informal* a present or gift. [abbreviation]

Priam /ˈpraɪam/ *Gk Myth* the king of Troy at the time of its destruction by the Greeks under Agamemnon; the father of Paris and Hector and husband of Hecuba, he was slain by Neoptolemus, son of Achilles.

pri·ap·ic /praɪˈapɪk/ *adjective* **1** of, relating to, or resembling a phallus. **2** of or relating to male sexuality and sexual activity. **3** *Med.* (of a male) having a persistently erect penis. [as PRIAPISM + -IC]

pri·ap·ism /ˈpraɪəˌpɪzəm/ *noun Med.* persistent and painful erection of the penis. [ultimately from Greek *priapismos* from *priapizō* be lewd, from PRIAPUS]

Pria·pus /praɪˈeɪpəs/ *Gk Myth* a god of fertility, whose symbol was the phallus and whose cult spread to Greece from Turkey after Alexander's conquests; he was adopted as a god of gardens, where his statue (a misshapen little man with enormous genitals) was a sort of combined scarecrow and guardian deity.

Pri·bi·lof Islands /ˈprɪbəˌlɒf/ a group of four islands in the Bering Sea, off the coast of SW Alaska.

Price ▸ **1 (Mary) Leon·tyne** (b.1927), US opera singer. After a triumphant television performance in the title role of *Tosca* (which made her the first black to sing opera on television) in 1955, she went on to sing in the world's greatest opera houses and became one of the Metropolitan Opera's leading sopranos. **2 Vin·cent** (1911–1993), US actor. Known for his mellifluous voice, he specialized in playing debonair villains in horror films, notably in films based on stories by Edgar Allen Poe such as *The Fall of the House of Usher* (1960).

price ● *noun* **1 a** the amount of money or goods for which a thing is bought or sold. **b** value or worth (*a pearl of great price; beyond price*). **2** what is or must be given, done, sacrificed, etc., to obtain or achieve something. **3** the amount of money etc. needed to bribe a person (*everyone has a price*). **4** a sum of money offered or given as a reward, esp. for the capture or killing of a person. ● *transitive verb* **1** fix or find the price of (a thing for sale). **2** estimate the value of. □ **at any price** no matter what the cost, sacrifice, etc. (*peace at any price*). **at a price** at a high cost. **beyond** (or **without**) **price** so valuable that no price can be stated. **price on a person's head** a reward for a person's capture or death. **price oneself out of the market** lose to one's competitors by charging more than customers are willing to pay. **put a price on** value in terms of money (*can't put a price on loyalty*). **what price ...?** (often foll. by verbal noun) *informal* **1** what is the chance of ...? (*what price your finishing the course?*). **2** what is the value or use of ...? (*what price success?*). □ **priced** *adjective* (also in *combination*). **pricer** *noun* [(n.) Old French *pris* from Latin *pretium*: (v.) var. of *prise* = PRIZE¹]

price controls *plural noun* restrictions by a government on the prices of consumer goods, usu. imposed on a short-term basis as a measure to control inflation.

price discrimination *noun* the action of charging different prices to different customers for the same goods or services.

price-earnings ratio *noun* the ratio between the current market price of a company's stock and its annual per-share income.

price-fixing *noun* the maintaining of prices at a certain level by agreement between competing sellers.

price gouging *noun* N Amer. the practice of charging unjustly high prices for items, services, etc.

price index *noun* an index showing the variation in the prices of a set of goods etc. since a chosen base period.

price·less *adjective* **1** invaluable; beyond price. **2** *informal* very amusing or absurd. □ **price·less·ly** *adverb* **price·less·ness** *noun*

price list *noun* a list of current prices of items on sale.

price point *noun* a point on a scale of possible prices at which something might be marketed.

price-sensitive *adjective* **1** (of a product) whose sales are greatly influenced by its price. **2** (of information) that would affect prices if it were made public.

price support *noun* government policy of providing support for certain basic, usu. agricultural, products to stop the price falling below an agreed level.

price tag *noun* **1** the label on an item showing its price. **2** the cost of an enterprise or undertaking.

price war *noun* a period of fierce competition between two or more firms in the same industry that are seeking to increase their shares of the market by cutting the prices of their products.

pricey *adjective* (also **pricy**) (**prici·er**, **prici·est**) *informal* expensive.

prick ● *verb* **1** *transitive* pierce slightly; make a small hole in. **2** *transitive* (foll. by *off*, *out*) mark (esp. a pattern) with small holes or dots. **3** *transitive* trouble mentally (*my conscience is pricking me*). **4** *intransitive* feel a pricking sensation. **5** *transitive* (foll. by *in*, *off*, *out*) plant (seedlings etc.) in small holes pricked in the earth. **6** *transitive* spur or urge on (a horse etc.). ● *noun* **1** the act or an instance of pricking. **2** a small hole or mark made by pricking. **3** a pain caused as by pricking. **4** a mental pain (*felt the pricks of conscience*). **5** *coarse slang* **a** the penis. **b** *derogatory* (as a term of contempt) an objectionable man. □ **kick against the pricks** persist in futile resistance. **prick (up) one's ears 1** (of a dog etc.) make the ears erect when on the alert. **2** (of a person) become suddenly attentive. [Old English *prician* (v.), *pricca* (n.)]

prick·et /ˈprɪkɪt/ *noun* **1** a spike for holding a candle. **2** a male fallow

deer in its second year, having straight unbranched horns. [Anglo-Latin *prikettus -um*, diminutive of PRICK]

prickle ● *noun* **1 a** a small thorn. **b** *Bot.* a thorn-like process developed from the epidermis of a plant. **2** a prickling sensation. ● *transitive & intransitive verb* affect or be affected with a sensation as of pricking. [Old English *pricel* PRICK: the verb partly a diminutive of PRICK]

prick·ly *adjective* (**prick·li·er**, **prick·li·est**) **1** (esp. in the names of plants and animals) having prickles. **2 a** (of a person) ready to take offence; touchy. **b** (of a topic, argument, etc.) full of contentious or complicated points; thorny. **3** tingling. □ **prick·li·ness** *noun*

prickly ash *noun* a shrub or small tree of eastern N America of the genus *Xanthoxylum*, with prickly pinnate leaves.

prickly heat *noun* an itchy rash of small raised red spots caused by inflammation of the sweat glands.

prickly pear *noun* **1** any cactus of the genus *Opuntia*, native to arid regions of N and S America, bearing barbed bristles and large pear-shaped prickly fruits. **2** its fruit.

prickly poppy *noun* a tropical plant of the poppy family, *Argemone mexicana*, with prickly leaves and yellow flowers.

prickly rose *noun* a wild rose, *Rosa acicularis*, with deep pink flowers and stems thickly covered with bristles. The floral emblem of Alberta.

pricy var. of PRICEY.

Pride, Sir Thom·as (d.1658), English soldier. He fought on the Parliamentary side during the English Civil War, and was responsible for PRIDE'S PURGE.

pride ● *noun* **1 a** a feeling of elation or satisfaction at achievements or qualities or possessions etc. that do one credit. **b** (prec. by *the*; foll. by *of*) an object of this feeling (*the pride of the museum's collection*). **c** the foremost or best of a group. **2** a high or overbearing opinion of one's worth or importance. **3 a** knowledge of one's own worth or character; a sense of dignity and respect for oneself. **b** = GAY PRIDE. **4** a group or company (of animals, esp. lions). **5** esp. *literary* the best condition; the prime. ● *reflexive verb* (foll. by *on*, *upon*) be proud of. □ **my, his,** etc. **pride and joy** a thing of which one is very proud. **take pride** (or **a pride**) **in 1** be proud of. **2** maintain in good condition or appearance. □ **pride·ful** *adjective* **pride·ful·ly** *adverb* [Old English *prýtu, prýte, prýde* from *prúd* PROUD]

pride of place *noun* the most important or prominent position.

Pride's Purge the removal or arrest in December 1648 of about 140 Members of the English Parliament who were likely to vote against a trial of the captive Charles I. Those who remained, known as the Rump Parliament, voted for the trial, which resulted in Charles's execution. [Colonel PRIDE]

prie-dieu /ˈpriːdjuː/ *noun* (pl. **prie-dieux** *pronunc.* same) a piece of furniture for use during prayer, consisting of a kneeler and a wooden frame surmounted by a rest for the elbows or books. [French, = pray God]

priest /priːst/ ● *noun* **1** an ordained minister of the Roman Catholic or Orthodox Church, or of the Anglican Church (above a deacon and below a bishop), authorized to perform certain rites and administer certain sacraments. **2** an official minister of a non-Christian religion. **3** a person whose function is likened to that of a priest; a devotee or minister of a practice or thing. **4** a small mallet for killing caught fish. ● *transitive verb* make (a person) a priest; ordain. □ **priest·like** *adjective* [Old English *prēost*, ultimately from ecclesiastical Latin *presbyter*: see PRESBYTER]

priest·craft /ˈpriːstkrɑft/ *noun* usu. *derogatory* the work and influence of priests.

priest·ess /ˈpriːstes/ *noun* **1** a female priest of a non-Christian religion. **2** a woman whose function is likened to that of a priestess; a female devotee or minister of a practice or thing (*priestess of reason*).

priest·hood /ˈpriːsthud/ *noun* (usu. prec. by *the*) **1** the office or position of priest. **2** priests in general.

Priest·ley /ˈpriːstli/ **1 John Boyn·ton** (1894–1984), English novelist, playwright, and critic. His first major success came with the picaresque novel *The Good Companions* (1929); his other works include the novel *Angel Pavement* (1930) and the plays *Time and the Conways* (1937) and *An Inspector Calls* (1947). **2 Jo·seph** (1733–1804), English scientist and theologian. His most significant discovery was of 'dephlogisticated air' (oxygen) in 1774; he demonstrated that it was important to animal life, and that plants give off this gas in sunlight.

priest·ly /ˈpriːstli/ *adjective* of or associated with priests. □ **priest·li·ness** *noun*

priest's hole *noun* (also **priest hole**) *hist.* a hiding place for a Roman Catholic priest during times of religious persecution.

prig *noun* a self-righteously correct or moralistic person. □ **prig·gery** *noun* **prig·gish** *adjective* **prig·gish·ly** *adverb* **prig·gish·ness** *noun* [16th-c. cant, = tinker: origin unknown]

prim *adjective* (**prim·mer**, **prim·mest**) **1 a** (of a person or manner) stiffly formal and precise. **b** (of a thing) ordered, regular, formal (*a prim garden*). **2** (of a woman or girl) demure. **3** prudish; prissy. □ **prim·ly** *adverb* **prim·ness** *noun* [17th c.: prob. originally cant from Old French *prin* prime excellent, from Latin *primus* first]

prima ballerina /ˌpriːmə ˌbaləˈriːnə/ *noun* the chief female dancer in a ballet or ballet company. [Italian, = 'first ballerina']

pri·macy /ˈpraiməsi/ *noun* (*pl.* **-cies**) **1** the state or position of being first in order, importance, or authority; pre-eminence. **2** the office of a primate. [Old French *primatie* or medieval Latin *primatia* (as PRIMATE)]

prima donna /ˌpriːmə ˈdɒnə/ *noun* **1** the chief female singer in an opera or opera company. **2** a temperamentally self-important person. □ **prima donna-ish** *adjective* [Italian]

pri·maeval *var. of* PRIMEVAL.

prima facie /ˌpraimə ˈfeiʃi/ ● *adverb* at first sight; from a first impression (*seems prima facie to be guilty*). ● *adjective* (of evidence) based on the first impression (*can see a prima facie reason for it*). [Latin, fem. ablative of *primus* first, *facies* FACE]

pri·mal /ˈpraiməl/ *adjective* **1** primitive, primeval. **2** chief, fundamental. [medieval Latin *primalis* from Latin *primus* first]

primal scream *noun* a scream releasing emotion uncovered in primal therapy.

primal therapy *noun* therapy in which a person attempts to recover his or her earliest (esp. emotional) experiences.

pri·mary /ˈpraiməri, ˈpraiməri/ ● *adjective* **1 a** of the first importance; chief (*our primary concern*). **b** fundamental, basic. **2** earliest, original; first in a series. **3** of the first rank in a series; not derived (*the primary meaning of a word*). **4** (of education) for young children, esp. below the age of 12. **5** (of a battery or cell) generating electricity by irreversible chemical reaction. **6** *Biol.* belonging to the first stage of development. **7** (of an industry or source of production) concerned with obtaining or using raw materials. **8** *Grammar* (of a tense in Latin and Greek) present, future, perfect, or future perfect (*compare* HISTORIC 3). ● *noun* (*pl.* **-ies**) **1** a thing that is primary. **2** (in full **primary election**) (in the US) a preliminary election to appoint delegates to a party conference or to select the candidates for a principal (esp. presidential) election. **3** *Astronomy* **a** the body orbited by a satellite etc. **b** = PRIMARY PLANET. **4** = PRIMARY FEATHER. **5** = PRIMARY COIL. □ **pri·mar·i·ly** /praiˈmerili/ *adverb* [Latin *primarius*, from *primus* 'first']

primary care *noun* (also **primary health care**) health care at a basic rather than specialized level for people making an initial approach to a doctor or nurse for treatment.

primary coil *noun* a coil to which current is supplied in a transformer.

primary colour *noun* any of the colours red, green, and blue, or (for pigments) red, blue and yellow, from which all other colours can be obtained by mixing.

primary elevator *noun N Amer.* = COUNTRY ELEVATOR.

primary feather *noun* any of several large flight feathers at the end of a bird's wing.

primary market *noun Econ.* a market in which securities are sold for the first time (*opp.* SECONDARY MARKET).

primary planet *noun* a planet that directly orbits the sun (*compare* SECONDARY PLANET).

primary school *noun* **1** *N Amer.* a school for young children, esp. one covering the first three or four grades and sometimes kindergarten. **2** *Brit.* a school for children below the age of 11.

primary source *noun* first-hand historical evidence or an original account of an event, esp. used as research material.

primary tooth *noun* = BABY TOOTH.

pri·mate /ˈpraimeit/ *noun* **1** any animal of the order Primates, the highest order of mammals, including tarsiers, lemurs, apes, monkeys, and humans. **2** (also /ˈpraimət/) an archbishop or bishop ranked first amongst all the bishops of a country, region, etc. □ **pri·matial** /-ˈmeiʃəl/ *adjective* [Old French *primat* from Latin *primas -atis* (adj.) of the first rank, from *primus* first]

prima·tol·ogy /praiməˈtɒlədʒi/ *noun* the branch of zoology that deals with primates. □ **prima·to·logic·al** /-təˈlɒdʒikəl/ *adjective* **prima·tol·o·gist** *noun*

prima·vera /ˌpriːməˈverə/ ● *noun* **1** a Central American tree, *Cybistax donnell-smithii*, bearing yellow blooms. **2** the hard light-coloured timber

from this. ● *adjective N Amer.* designating a pasta dish made with lightly sautéed spring vegetables. [Spanish & Italian, = spring (the season), from Latin *primus* first + *ver* SPRING]

prime¹ ● *adjective* **1** chief, most important (*the prime agent; the prime motive*). **2** of the best or highest quality or value; first-rate, excellent (*prime real estate*). **3** primary, fundamental. **4** *Math.* **a** (of a number) divisible only by itself and unity, e.g. 2, 3, 5, 7, 11. **b** (of numbers) having no common factor but unity. ● *noun* **1** the state of the highest perfection of something (*in the prime of life*). **2** (prec. by *the*; foll. by *of*) the best part. **3** the beginning or first age of anything. **4** a prime number. **5** = PRIME RATE. **6** *Christianity* **a** the office of the second canonical hour of prayer, originally said at the first hour of the day (i.e. 6 a.m.). **b** *archaic* this time. **7** *Printing* a symbol (') added to a letter etc. as a distinguishing mark, or to a figure as a symbol for minutes or feet. □ **prime·ness** *noun* [Latin *primus* first]

prime² *transitive verb* **1** prepare (a thing) for use or action. **2** prepare (a gun) for firing or (an explosive) for detonation. **3 a** pour (a liquid) into a pump to prepare it for working. **b** inject gasoline into (the cylinder or carburetor of an internal combustion engine). **4** prepare (wood etc.) for painting by applying a substance that prevents paint from being absorbed. **5** equip (a person) with information etc. **6** ply (a person) with food or drink in preparation for something. □ **prime the pump** (esp. of a government) encourage the growth of a new or weak business or industry by investing money in it. [16th c.: origin unknown]

prime meridian *noun* **1** the meridian from which longitude is reckoned, esp. that passing through Greenwich. **2** the corresponding line on a map.

prime minister *noun* the head of the executive branch of government in most countries with a parliamentary system. □ **prime ministerial** *adjective* **prime ministership** *noun*

Prime Minister's Office *noun Cdn* the political staff of the prime minister, responsible for scheduling his or her engagements, overseeing press and public relations, advising the prime minister on candidates for appointment to various positions, etc.

prime mover *noun* **1** a person who originates or promotes an action, event, etc.; an initiator. **2** an initial natural or mechanical source of motive power.

prim·er¹ *noun* **1** a substance used to prime wood etc. **2** a cap, cylinder, etc., used to ignite the powder of a cartridge etc. **3** *Biochem.* a molecule that serves as a starting material for a polymerization. **4** a person who primes something.

prim·er² /ˈpraimər, ˈprimər/ *noun* **1** an elementary textbook for teaching children to read. **2** an introductory book. [Anglo-French from medieval Latin *primarius -arium* from Latin *primus* first]

prime rate *noun* the rate of interest at which banks lend money to their best-rated customers.

prime rib *noun N Amer.* a roast or steak cut from the seven ribs immediately before the loin.

prime time *noun* the time at which a radio or television audience is expected to be at its highest, usu. between 7 and 11 p.m. (often *attributive*: *prime-time viewing*).

pri·meval /praiˈmiːvəl/ *adjective* (also **pri·maeval**) **1** of or relating to the first age of the world. **2** ancient, primitive. □ **pri·meval·ly** *adverb* [Latin *primaevus* from *primus* first + *aevum* age]

primi·grav·ida /ˌprimiˈgravidə, ˌpraimi-/ *noun* (*pl.* **primi·grav·idae** /-ˌdiː/) a woman who is pregnant for the first time. [modern Latin fem. from Latin *primus* first + *gravidus* pregnant: see GRAVID]

prim·ing *noun* **1** a mixture used by painters for a preparatory coat. **2 a** gunpowder placed in the pan of a firearm. **b** a train of powder connecting the fuse with the charge in blasting etc.

pri·mip·ara /ˌpraiˈmipərə/ *noun* (*pl.* **pri·mip·aras** or **pri·mip·arae** /-ˌriː/) a woman who is giving birth for the first time. □ **primi·par·ity** /-ˈperiti/ *noun* **pri·mip·ar·ous** *adjective* [modern Latin fem. from *primus* first + *-parus* from *parere* bring forth]

primi·tive /ˈprimitiv/ ● *adjective* **1** early, ancient; at an early stage of civilization (*primitive man*). **2** undeveloped, crude, simple (*primitive methods*). **3** original, primary. **4** antiquated; outmoded. **5** *Grammar & Linguistics* (of words or language) radical; not derivative. **6** *Math.* (of a line, figure, etc.) from which another is derived, from which some construction begins, etc. **7** *Geol.* of the earliest period. **8** *Biol.* appearing in the earliest or a very early stage of growth or evolution. **9 a** pertaining to or designating pre-Renaissance western European art. **b** (of art etc.) simple or straightforward in style, eschewing subtlety or conventional technique; suggesting the artist's lack or rejection of

---

Consonants:　b *but*　d *dog*　f *few*　g *get*　h *her*　j *yes*　k *cat*　l *leg*　m *man*　n *no*　p *pen*　r *red*　s *sit*

formal training. ● noun **1** a primitive person or thing. **2 a** a painter of the period before the Renaissance. **b** a modern imitator of such. **c** an untutored painter with a direct naive style. **d** a picture by such a painter. **3** a primitive word, line, etc. □ **primi·tive·ly** adverb **primi·tive·ness** noun **primitivity** noun [Latin *primitivus* first of its kind, from *primitus* in the first place, from *primus* first]

primi·tiv·ism /ˈprɪmɪtɪˌvɪzəm/ noun **1** primitive behaviour. **2** belief in the superiority of what is primitive. **3** the practice of primitive art. □ **primi·tiv·ist** noun & adjective

primo /ˈpriːməʊ/ ● noun (pl. **-mos**) Music the leading or upper part in a duet etc. ● adjective slang first-class; first-rate. [Italian, = 'first']

Primo de Ri·vera /ˌpriːməʊ deɪ rɪˈveərə/ **1 Mi·guel** (1870–1930), Spanish general and leader, head of state 1923–30. He led a military coup and assumed dictatorial powers in 1923, but economic decline contributed to his forced resignation in 1930. **2** his son, **José An·tonio** (1903–36), Spanish politician, who founded the Falange in 1933 and was executed by Republicans in the Spanish Civil War.

primo·geni·tor /ˌpraɪməʊˈdʒenɪtər/ noun **1** the earliest ancestor of a people etc. **2** an ancestor. [var. of *progenitor*, after PRIMOGENITURE]

primo·geni·ture /ˌpraɪməʊˈdʒenɪtʃər/ noun **1** a fact or condition of being the first-born child. **2** (in full **right of primogeniture**) the right of succession belonging to the first-born, esp. the feudal rule by which the whole real estate of an intestate passes to the eldest son. [medieval Latin *primogenitura* from Latin *primo* first + *genitura* from *gignere genit-* beget]

pri·mor·dial /praɪˈmɔːdɪəl/ adjective **1** existing at or from the beginning, primeval. **2** original, fundamental. □ **pri·mor·di·al·ly** adverb [Late Latin *primordialis* (as PRIMORDIUM)]

primordial soup noun a solution rich in organic compounds in the primitive oceans of the earth, from which life is thought to have originated.

pri·mor·dium /praɪˈmɔːdɪəm/ noun (pl. **primor·dia** /-dɪə/) Biol. an organ or tissue in the early stages of development. [Latin, neuter of *primordius* original, from *primus* first + *ordiri* begin]

Pri·mor·sky /prɪˈmɔːskɪ/ an administrative territory in the far southeast of Siberian Russia, between the Sea of Japan and the Chinese border; capital, Vladivostok.

primp verb **1** intransitive make oneself well-groomed, esp. in a fussy or affected manner. **2** transitive make (the hair, one's clothes, etc.) tidy. [dial. var. of PRIM]

prim·rose ● noun **1** any plant of the genus *Primula*, esp. *P. vulgaris*, bearing pale yellow flowers. **2** (in full **primrose yellow**) a pale yellow colour. ● adjective (in full **primrose yellow**) pale yellow. [Old French *primerose* and medieval Latin *prima rosa*, literally 'first rose']

Primrose Lake a lake in W Saskatchewan, situated about 150 km west of Doré Lake, its southwestern tip extending across the border into Alberta.

primrose path noun the pursuit of pleasure, esp. with disastrous consequences. [with reference to Shakespeare's *Hamlet* I. iii. 50]

prim·ula /ˈprɪmjʊlə/ noun any plant of the genus *Primula*, bearing flowers in a wide variety of colours during the spring, including primroses, cowslips, and polyanthuses. [medieval Latin, fem. of *primulus* diminutive of *primus* first]

primum mobile /ˌpriːmʊm ˈməʊbɪlɪ/ noun **1** the central or most important source of motion or action. **2** Astronomy in the medieval version of the Ptolemaic system, an outer sphere supposed to move around the earth in 24 hours carrying the inner spheres with it. [medieval Latin, = first moving thing]

Pri·mus /ˈpraɪməs/ noun proprietary a brand of portable stove burning vaporized oil for cooking etc. [Latin, = first]

primus inter pares /ˌpriːmʊs ˌɪntər ˈpeəriːz/ noun a first among equals; the senior or representative member of a group. [Latin]

prince noun (as a title usu. **Prince**) **1** a male member of a royal family other than a reigning king. **2** a son or grandson of a British monarch. **3** a ruler of a small state, actually or nominally subject to a king or emperor. **4** (as an English rendering of foreign titles) a noble usu. ranking next below a duke. **5 a** (as a courtesy title in some connections) a duke, marquess, or earl. **b** Catholicism a title applied to a Cardinal (*Prince of the Church*). **6** (often foll. by *of*) the chief or greatest (*the prince of novelists*). **7** a powerful or influential man, esp. a magnate in a specified industry etc. (*merchant prince*). **8** N Amer. informal an admirable or generous man. □ **prince·dom** noun **prince·like** adjective [Old French from Latin *princeps principis* 'first, chief, sovereign', from *primus* 'first' + *capere* 'take']

Prince Al·bert a city in central Saskatchewan, located on the North

Saskatchewan River, 141 km northeast of Saskatoon; pop. (2001) 34,291. □ **Prince Al·bert·an** noun [Prince ALBERT]

Prince Albert National Park a park in central Saskatchewan, northwest of Prince Albert. Established in 1927, it is the location of Grey Owl's cabin and grave.

Prince Albert Peninsula a broad peninsula of the northwestern coast of Victoria Island, NWT. [Prince ALBERT]

Prince Charles Island an island in the northeastern quadrant of Foxe Basin, Nunavut. [CHARLES, Prince of Wales]

Prince Charming noun an idealized young hero or lover.

prince consort noun (a title conferred on) the husband of a reigning female sovereign who is himself a prince. The title was given to Prince Albert, husband of Queen Victoria, to avoid the word *king* as Albert was not reigning.

Prince Edward a city (formerly a county) in E Ontario, occupying the peninsula between the Bay of Quinte and Lake Ontario; pop. (2001) 24,901.

Prince Edward Island an island in the Gulf of St. Lawrence, E Canada, the country's smallest province; pop. (2001) 135,294; capital, Charlottetown. It became a province of Canada in 1873. [*Prince Edward* Augustus, Duke of Kent and Strathern, father of Queen Victoria d.1820]

Prince Edward Island National Park a small park reserve encompassing a narrow strip of coastline along the north central shore of PEI. Established in 1937, it preserves the site of Green Gables, the house that inspired the writings of Lucy Maud Montgomery.

Prince George a city in central BC, situated at the confluence of the Fraser and Nechako rivers, 118 km north of Quesnel; pop. (2001) 72,406. □ **Prince Georg·ian** noun [*George* Edward Alexander Edmund, fourth son of King George V and Duke of Kent d.1942]

prince·ling noun **1** a young prince. **2** the ruler of a small principality or domain.

prince·ly adjective (**prince·li·er**, **prince·li·est**) **1 a** of or worthy of a prince. **b** held by a prince (*princely state*). **2** sumptuous, generous, splendid. □ **prince·li·ness** noun

Prince of Darkness noun Satan.

Prince of Peace noun Christ.

Prince of Wales noun (a title conferred on) the nominal ruler of Wales, from 1301 the heir apparent to the English or British throne.

Prince of Wales Island 1 a large island in the central Canadian Arctic, situated between Victoria and Somerset islands. **2** an island off the SW coast of Alaska, situated north of the Queen Charlotte Islands. **3** a former name for the island of Penang (see PENANG 1). [sense 1 after Albert Edward, *Prince of Wales*: see EDWARD VII]

Prince of Wales Strait a narrow sea passage of the Canadian Arctic, situated between Banks Island and the Prince Albert Peninsula of Victoria Island. [as PRINCE OF WALES ISLAND]

Prince Patrick Island the most westerly of the Parry Islands in the Canadian High Arctic. [Arthur William *Patrick* Albert, 1st Duke of CONNAUGHT AND STRATHEARN]

Prince Regent noun a prince who acts as regent, esp. George (afterwards IV) as regent of the United Kingdom 1811–20.

prince royal noun the eldest son of the reigning monarch.

Prince Ru·pert a city and port in western BC, situated on Kaien Island, near the mouth of the Skeena River; pop. (2001) 14,643. [RUPERT, PRINCE]

Prince Rupert's Land see RUPERT'S LAND.

prince's feather noun a tall plant of the genus *Amaranthus*, with feathery spikes of red flowers.

Princes in the Tower the young sons of Edward IV, namely Edward, Prince of Wales (b.1470), and Richard, Duke of York (b.1472), supposedly murdered in the Tower of London in or shortly after 1483. Edward reigned briefly as Edward V on the death of his father in 1483 but was not crowned; he and his brother were taken to the Tower of London by their uncle (the future Richard III) and disappeared soon afterwards.

prin·cess ● noun (as a title usu. **Princess**) **1** the wife of a prince. **2** a female member of a royal family other than a reigning queen. **3** a daughter or granddaughter of a British monarch. **4** a pre-eminent woman or thing personified as a woman. **5** informal a girl or woman regarded or treated as a princess, esp. one who is pampered, egocentric, demanding, etc. ● adjective designating a style of dress, coat, etc. with a close fitted bodice and a flared skirt with a seamless waist. [Old French *princesse* (as PRINCE)]

Princess Pats *plural noun Cdn* an informal name for the Princess Patricia's Canadian Light Infantry regiment.

Princess Royal *noun* the eldest daughter of a reigning monarch, esp. as a title conferred by the British monarch.

Prince·ville /prɑsˈvɪl/ a town in south central Quebec, northeast of Victoriaville; pop. (2001) 5,703. [in honour of an early settler, Pierre *Prince*]

prin·ci·pal /ˈprɪnsɪpəl/ ● *adjective* **1** (usu. *attributive*) first in rank or importance; chief. **2** main, leading (*a principal cause of my success*). **3** (of money) constituting the original sum invested or lent. ● *noun* **1** a head, ruler, or superior. **2** the head of some schools, colleges, and universities. **3** the leading performer in a concert, play, etc. **4** a capital sum as distinguished from interest or income. **5** a person for whom another acts as agent etc. **6** *Cdn* a lawyer who supervises an articling student. **7** the person actually responsible for a crime. **8** a person for whom another is surety. **9** *hist.* each of the combatants in a duel. **10 a** a main rafter supporting purlins. **b** a main girder. **11** an organ stop sounding an octave above the diapason. **12** *Music* the leading player in each section of an orchestra (also *attributive: principal horn*). **13** = PRINCIPAL DANCER. □ **prin·ci·pal·ly** *adverb* **prin·ci·pal·ship** *noun* [Old French from Latin *principalis* first, original (as PRINCE)]

principal clause *noun Grammar* a clause to which another clause is subordinate.

principal dancer *noun* a dancer who is of the highest rank in a ballet company.

prin·ci·pal·ity /ˌprɪnsɪˈpalɪti/ *noun* (*pl.* **-ities**) **1** a state ruled by a prince. **2** the government of a prince. **3** *Christianity* a member of the fifth order of the ninefold celestial hierarchy (*see* ORDER *noun* 19). **4** (**the Principality**) *Brit.* Wales. [Old French *principalité* from Late Latin *principalitas -tatis* (as PRINCIPAL)]

principal meridian *noun Cdn* **1** a geographical meridian established by an authority as a meridian of reference for land surveying purposes. **2** (**Principal Meridian**) = FIRST MERIDIAN.

principal parts *plural noun Grammar* the parts of a verb from which all other parts can be deduced.

prin·ci·pate /ˈprɪnsɪpət/ *noun Rom. Hist.* **1** the rule of the early emperors during which some republican forms were retained. **2** this period. [Old French *principat* or Latin *principatus* 'first place' (as PRINCE)]

prin·ci·ple /ˈprɪnsɪpəl/ *noun* **1** a fundamental truth or law as the basis of reasoning or action (*arguing from first principles*). **2 a** a personal code of conduct (*a person of high principle*). **b** (in *pl.*) such rules of conduct (*has no principles*). **3** a general law in physics etc. (*the uncertainty principle*). **4** a law of nature forming the basis for the construction or working of a machine etc. **5** a fundamental source; a primary element (*held water to be the first principle of all things*). **6** *Chem.* a constituent of a substance, esp. one giving rise to some quality, etc. □ **in principle** as regards fundamentals but not necessarily in detail. **on principle** on the basis of a moral attitude (*I refuse on principle*). [Old French *principe* from Latin *principium* source, (in pl.) foundations (as PRINCE)]

prin·ci·pled /ˈprɪnsɪpəld/ *adjective* based on or having (esp. praiseworthy) principles of behaviour.

print ● *noun* **1 a** an indentation or mark on a surface left by the pressure of a thing in contact with it. **b** = FINGERPRINT. **c** = FOOTPRINT. **2 a** a printed lettering or writing (*large print*). **b** words in printed form. **c** a printed publication, esp. a newspaper (also *attributive: print reporters*). **d** the quantity of a book etc. printed at one time. **e** the state of being printed. **3** a picture or design printed from a block or plate. **4** *Photog.* a picture produced on paper from a negative. **5 a** a pattern printed on fabric. **b** a fabric printed in this way. **c** a piece of clothing made of such a fabric. **6** a positive copy of a finished motion picture, ready for release. ● *verb* **1** *transitive* **a** produce or reproduce (text, a picture, etc.) by mechanically transferring characters or designs to paper, cloth, etc., esp. from inked types, blocks, or plates. **b** (of an author, publisher, or editor) cause (a book or manuscript etc.) to be produced or reproduced in this way. **2** *transitive* express or publish in print. **3** *transitive* **a** (often foll. by *on, in*) impress or stamp (a mark or figure on a surface). **b** (often foll. by *with*) impress or stamp (a soft surface, e.g. of butter or wax, with a seal, die, etc.). **4** *intransitive & transitive* write (words or letters) without joining, in imitation of typography. **5** *transitive* (often foll. by *off, out*) *Photog.* produce (a picture) by the transmission of light through a negative. **6** *transitive* (usu. foll. by *out*) (of a computer etc.) produce output in printed form. **7** *transitive* mark (a textile fabric) with a decorative design in colours. **8** *transitive* (foll. by *on*) impress (an idea, scene, etc. on the mind or memory). **9** *transitive* transfer (a coloured or plain design) from paper etc. to the unglazed or glazed surface of ceramic ware.

● *adjective* **1** (of an article of clothing) made of a printed fabric (*often wears a print dress*). **2** of or relating to newspapers or magazines (*the print media*). □ **appear in print** have one's work published. **in print 1** (of a book etc.) available from the publisher. **2** in printed form. **out of print** no longer available from the publisher. □ **print·able** *adjective* **print·abil·ity** *noun* [Old French *priente, preinte*, fem. past participle of *preindre* press, from Latin *premere*]

printed circuit *noun* an electric circuit with thin strips of conductor on a flat insulating sheet, usu. made by a process like printing.

print·er *noun* **1** a person or company that prints books, magazines, advertising matter, etc. **2** the owner of a printing business. **3** a device that prints, esp. as part of a computer system.

printer's devil *noun hist.* an errand boy in a printing office.

print·head *noun* the component in a computer printer that prints the characters on the paper.

print·ing *noun* **1** the production of printed books etc. **2** a single impression of a book. **3** printed letters or writing imitating them.

printing press *noun* a machine for printing from types or plates etc.

print·maker *noun* **1** a person, esp. a graphic artist, who makes prints (*a noted Inuit printmaker*). **2** a person who makes print. □ **print·making** *noun*

print·out *noun* computer output in printed form.

print run *noun* the number of copies of a book etc. printed at one time.

print shop *noun* **1** a place where books etc. are printed. **2** a place where artistic prints are made or sold.

pri·on¹ /ˈpraɪən/ *noun* a small saw-billed petrel of the genus *Pachyptila*, of southern seas. [modern Latin (former genus name) from Greek *priōn* 'a saw']

pri·on² /ˈpriːɒn/ *noun Biol.* a protein particle associated with and believed to be the cause of encephalopathies such as scrapie, BSE, and Creutzfeldt–Jakob disease. [by rearrangement from 'proteinaceous infectious particle']

pri·or /ˈpraɪə/ ● *adjective* **1** earlier. **2** (often foll. by *to*) coming before in time, order, or importance. ● *adverb* (foll. by *to*) before (*decided prior to their arrival*). ● *noun* **1** the superior officer of a religious house or order. **2** (in an abbey) the officer next under the abbot. **3** *N Amer. slang* a prior criminal conviction (*the suspect has three priors*). □ **prior·ship** *noun* [Latin, = former, elder, comparative of Old Latin *pri* = Latin *prae* before]

prior·ess /ˈpraɪərəs/ *noun* **1** a female superior of a house of any of various orders of nuns. **2** (in an abbey) the officer next under the abbess.

prior·ity /praɪˈɒrɪti/ *noun* (*pl.* **-ities**) **1** something that is given prior or special attention or considered more important. **2** precedence in rank etc. **3** the fact or condition of being earlier or antecedent. □ **pri·or·itize** *transitive verb* (also esp. *Brit.* **-tise**). **pri·or·itiz·a·tion** *noun*

pri·ory /ˈpraɪəri/ *noun* (*pl.* **-ies**) a monastery governed by a prior or a convent governed by a prioress.

Pri·pyat River /ˈpriːpjət/ (also **Pri·pet** /-pət/) a river of NW Ukraine and S Belarus, which rises in Ukraine near the border with Poland and flows some 710 km (440 miles) eastward through the Pripyat Marshes to join the Dnieper River north of Kiev.

Pris·cian /ˈprɪʃiən/ (full name Priscianus Caesariensis) (6th c. AD), Byzantine grammarian. He taught Latin in Constantinople; his *Grammatical Institutions* became one of the standard Latin grammatical works in the Middle Ages.

prise esp. *Brit.* (also **prize**) ● *transitive verb* = PRY². ● *noun* leverage, purchase. [Middle English & Old French *prise* levering instrument (as PRIZE¹)]

prism /ˈprɪzəm/ *noun* **1** a solid geometric figure whose two ends are similar, equal, and parallel rectilinear figures, and whose sides are parallelograms. **2** a transparent body in this form, usu. triangular with refracting surfaces at an acute angle with each other, which separates white light into a spectrum of colours. **3** *Crystallog.* a form having three or more faces that meet in edges parallel to the vertical axis. [Late Latin *prisma* from Greek *prisma prismatos* thing sawn, from *prizō* to saw]

pris·mat·ic /prɪzˈmatɪk/ *adjective* **1** of, like, or using a prism. **2 a** (of colours) distributed by or as if by a transparent prism. **b** (of light) displayed in the form of a spectrum. **3** *Crystallog.* = ORTHORHOMBIC. □ **pris·mat·ic·ally** *adverb* [French *prismatique* from Greek *prisma* (as PRISM)]

pris·moid /ˈprɪzmɔɪd/ *noun* a body like a prism, with similar but unequal parallel polygonal ends. □ **pris·moid·al** *adjective*

pris·on ● *noun* **1** a place in which a person is kept in captivity, esp. a building to which persons are legally committed while awaiting trial or for punishment; a jail. **2** custody, confinement (*in prison*). **3** any place of real or perceived confinement. ● *transitive verb* (**pris·oned**, **pris·on·ing**) *literary* put in prison. [Old French *prisun, -on* from Latin *prensio -onis* from *prehensio* from *prehendere prehens-* lay hold of]

prison camp *noun* a camp for political prisoners or prisoners of war.

pris·on·er *noun* **1** a person kept in prison. **2** (in full **prisoner at the bar**) a person in custody on a criminal charge and on trial. **3** a person or thing confined by illness, another's grasp, etc. **4** (in full **prisoner of war**) a person who has been captured in war. □ **take no prisoners** deal very aggressively with a person or thing. **take prisoner** seize and hold as a prisoner.

prisoner of conscience *noun* a person imprisoned by a state for holding political or religious views it does not tolerate.

prisoner's base *noun* a game played by two parties of children etc., each occupying a distinct base or home.

prisoner's dilemma *noun* a situation in which two parties each have two options whose outcome depends crucially on the simultaneous choice made by the other, often formulated in terms of two prisoners separately deciding whether to confess or not.

prissy *adjective* (**pris·si·er**, **pris·si·est**) prim, prudish. □ **pris·si·ly** *adverb* **pris·si·ness** *noun* [perhaps from PRIM + SISSY]

Priš·tina /prɪˈstiːnə/ a city in S Serbia, the capital of the autonomous province of Kosovo; pop. (est. 2002) 194,300.

pris·tine /ˈprɪstiːn/ *adjective* **1** in its original condition (*a pristine copy of the first edition of her novel*). **2** fresh and clean, as if new (*a pristine bedroom*). **3** unspoiled (*pristine wilderness*). **4** *archaic* ancient, primitive. ¶ Although there is a tradition of objection to the use of *pristine* as in senses 2 and 3, they are quite common and acceptable in both spoken and written English. [Latin *pristinus* former]

Prit·chett /ˈprɪtʃət/ **Sir Vic·tor Saw·don** (1900–97), English short-story writer, novelist, and critic. His short stories combine shrewd observation and humane irony; collections include *The Spanish Virgin and Other Stories* (1930).

pri·thee /ˈprɪðiː/ *interjection archaic* please. [= *I pray thee*]

pri·vacy /ˈpraɪvəsi/ *noun* **1 a** the state of being private and undisturbed. **b** a person's right to this. **2** freedom from intrusion or public attention. **3** avoidance of publicity.

Privacy Commissioner *noun Cdn* the official responsible for investigating the collection and storage of personal information on private citizens by federal government departments.

pri·vate ● *adjective* **1** belonging to an individual; one's own; personal (*private property*). **2** confidential; not to be disclosed to others (*private talks*). **3** kept or removed from public knowledge or observation. **4 a** not open to the public. **b** for an individual's exclusive use (*private room*). **5** (of a place) secluded; affording privacy. **6** (of a person) not holding public office or an official position (*private citizens*). **7** (of a service, business, etc.) provided or owned by an individual or group of individuals rather than the government or a public body. **8** (of education) paid for directly by the student or parent rather than through taxes. **9** (of health care) paid for by an individual or insurance company rather than by the government. ● *noun* **1** (also **Private**) (in the Canadian Army and Air Force and other armies) a person holding the lowest rank. Abbr.: **Pte**. **2** (in *pl.*) *informal* the genitals. □ **in private** privately; in private company or life. □ **pri·vate·ly** *adverb* [Latin *privatus*, originally past participle of *privare* deprive]

private bill *noun* a parliamentary bill affecting an individual or corporation only.

private carrier *noun* a person or company that may carry goods or passengers but does not earn the majority of its income in this way (*compare* COMMON CARRIER 1).

private company *noun Cdn, Brit., Austral., & NZ* a company with restricted membership and no issue of shares.

private detective *noun* = PRIVATE INVESTIGATOR.

private enterprise *noun* **1** a business or businesses not under government control. **2** = FREE ENTERPRISE.

pri·va·teer *noun* **1** an armed vessel owned and officered by private individuals holding a government commission and authorized for war service. **2 a** a commander of such a vessel. **b** a crew member of such a vessel. □ **pri·va·teer·ing** *noun* [PRIVATE, after *volunteer*]

private eye *noun informal* a private investigator.

private first class *noun US* a soldier ranking above an ordinary private but below officers.

private investigator *noun* a usu. freelance detective carrying out investigations for a private employer.

private label *noun* a make of goods manufactured specially for a

retailer and bearing the retailer's name (also *attributive: private label products*).

private law *noun* a law relating to individual persons and private property.

private life *noun* life as a private person, not as an official, public performer, etc.

private member *noun Cdn, Brit., Austral., & NZ* a member of a legislative body not holding a government office.

private member's bill *noun Cdn, Brit., Austral., & NZ* a bill introduced by a private member, not part of government legislation.

private parts *plural noun* the genitals.

private patient *noun* a patient who pays for medical services directly rather than through public health insurance.

private pilot *noun* a person who is licensed to fly a plane for his or her personal use but not for hire.

private practice *noun* **1** *N Amer.* the work of a doctor, lawyer, etc. who is self-employed. **2** *Brit.* medical practice that is not part of the National Health Service.

private school *noun* a school established and supported by a private group rather than through taxes etc.

private secretary *noun* a secretary dealing with the personal and confidential concerns of a business person.

private sector *noun* the part of the economy that is free of direct governmental control.

private soldier *noun* an ordinary soldier other than the officers.

pri·va·tion /praɪˈveɪʃən/ *noun* **1** lack of the comforts or necessities of life (*suffered many privations*). **2** (often foll. by *of*) loss or absence (of a quality). [Latin *privatio* (as PRIVATE)]

priv·a·tive /ˈprɪvətɪv/ *adjective* **1** consisting in or marked by the loss or removal or absence of some quality or attribute. **2** (of a term) denoting the privation or absence of a quality etc. **3** *Grammar* (of a particle etc.) expressing privation, as Greek *a-* = 'not'. [French *privatif -ive* or Latin *privativus* (as PRIVATION)]

pri·va·tize *transitive verb* (also esp. *Brit.* **-tise**) make private, esp. assign (a business etc.) to private as distinct from governmental control or ownership. □ **pri·va·tiz·a·tion** *noun*

priv·et /ˈprɪvət/ *noun* any evergreen shrub of the genus *Ligustrum*, esp. *L. vulgare* bearing small white flowers and black berries, and used for hedges. [16th c.: origin unknown]

priv·il·ege /ˈprɪvəlɪdʒ, ˈprɪvlɪdʒ/ ● *noun* **1** a special right or advantage available only to a particular person or a group of people. **2** the rights and advantages possessed by the rich and powerful (*had led a life of luxury and privilege*). **3** (also **parliamentary privilege**) the freedom of members of a legislative assembly to speak at its meetings without risking legal action. **4** a special benefit or honour, esp. one restricted to a small group (*it is a privilege to meet you*). **5** a monopoly or patent granted to an individual, corporation, etc. ● *transitive verb* **1** invest with a privilege. **2** (foll. by *to* + infin.) allow (a person) as a privilege (to do something). **3** (often foll. by *from*) exempt (a person from a liability etc.). **4** consider or treat as more important; favour. [Old French *privilege* from Latin *privilegium* bill or law affecting an individual, from *privus* private + *lex legis* law]

priv·il·eged /ˈprɪvəlɪdʒd, ˈprɪvlɪdʒd/ *adjective* **1** having a privilege or privileges. **2** (usu. *predicative*) honoured. **3 a** legally protected from being made public (*privileged communication*). **b** (of an exchange of information) made between such people and in such circumstances that it is not actionable. **4** (of information) kept within a select group and not divulged to others.

priv·ity /ˈprɪvɪti/ *noun* (*pl.* **-ities**) **1** *Law* a relation between two parties that is recognized by law, e.g. that of blood, lease, or service. **2** (often foll. by *to*) the state of being privy (to plans etc.). [Old French *priveté* from medieval Latin *privitas -tatis* from Latin *privus* private]

privy /ˈprɪvi/ ● *adjective* **1** (foll. by *to*) sharing in the secret of (a person's plans etc.). **2** *archaic* hidden, secret. ● *noun* (*pl.* **-ies**) **1** *N Amer.* an outhouse. **2** *Law* a person having a part or interest in any action, matter, or thing. □ **priv·i·ly** *adverb* [Old French *privé* from Latin *privatus* PRIVATE]

Privy Council *noun* **1** (in Canada) a (now chiefly honorary) body of advisers appointed on the advice of the Prime Minister by the Governor General, the members of which include current and former Cabinet ministers, and may also include other distinguished persons. **2** (in the UK) a body of advisers appointed by the sovereign (now chiefly on an honorary basis and including present and former government ministers etc.). **3** usu. *hist.* a sovereign's or Governor General's private counsellors.

---

uː m**oo**d   ai m**y**   ɔi p**i**pe   au br**ow**n   ʌu h**ou**se   ei d**a**y   ɔi b**oy**   ã fr**an**glais   ã Cana**di**en   ɔ̃ Bray**on**   (*see over for consonants*)

privy coun·cil·lor *noun* (also **privy counsellor**) a member of a Privy Council.

Privy Council Office *noun* (in Canada) an administrative body which coordinates the activities of the federal Cabinet, provides advice to the prime minister, deputy prime minister, and government house leaders, and implements government objectives. Abbr.: **PCO**.

privy purse *noun Brit.* **1** an allowance from the public revenue for the monarch's private expenses. **2** the keeper of this.

privy seal *noun* (in the UK) a seal formerly affixed to documents that are afterwards to pass the Great Seal or that do not require it.

prix fixe /pri: fiks/ *noun* **1** a fixed price for a restaurant meal chosen from a usu. limited menu. **2** a meal that is served for such a price. [French, lit. 'fixed price']

prize¹ ● *noun* **1** something that can be won in a competition or lottery etc. **2** a reward given as a symbol of victory or superiority. **3** something striven for or worth striving for (*missed all the great prizes of life*). **4** a person considered highly (*he's no prize*). **5** (*attributive*) **a** to which a prize is awarded (*a prize bull; a prize poem*). **b** supremely excellent or outstanding of its kind. ● *transitive verb* value highly (*a prized possession*). □ **keep one's eyes on the prize** remain focused on the ultimate goal. **no prizes for guessing** it is obvious. [(n.) Middle English, var. of PRICE: (v.) Old French *pris*- stem of *preisier* PRAISE]

prize² ● *noun* **1** a ship or property captured in naval warfare. **2** a find or windfall. ● *transitive verb* make a prize of. [Old French *prise* taking, booty, fem. past participle of *prendre* from Latin *prehendere prehens-* seize: later identified with PRIZE¹]

prize³ *US var. of* PRISE.

prize·fight *noun* a boxing match fought for prize money. □ **prize·fight·er** *noun* **prize·fight·ing** *noun*

prize-giving *noun* an award of prizes, esp. formally at a school etc.

prize money *noun* money offered as a prize.

prize·win·ner *noun* a winner of a prize. □ **prize·win·ning** *adjective*

PRK *abbreviation* photorefractive keratectomy, a form of eye surgery which uses a laser to carve away part of the outer surface of the cornea (*compare* LASIK).

PRO *abbreviation* **1** (in the UK) PUBLIC RECORD OFFICE. **2** public relations officer.

pro¹ ● *noun* (*pl.* **pros**) a professional. ● *adjective* professional. [abbreviation]

pro² ● *adjective* (of an argument or reason) for; in favour. ● *noun* (*pl.* **pros**) a reason or argument for or in favour. ● *preposition & adverb* in favour of. □ **pros and cons** reasons or considerations for and against a proposition etc. (*Tom must examine all the pros and cons of buying a house*). [Latin, = for, on behalf of]

pro-¹ *prefix* **1** favouring or supporting (*pro-government*). **2** acting as a substitute or deputy for (*proconsul*). **3** forwards (*produce*). **4** forwards and downwards (*prostrate*). **5** onward (*proceed; progress*). **6** in front of (*protect*). [Latin *pro* in front (of), for, on behalf of, instead of, on account of]

pro-² *prefix* before in time, place, order, etc. (*problem; proboscis; prophet*). [Greek *pro* before]

proa *var. of* PRAHU.

pro·active *adjective* **1** (of a person, policy, etc.) creating or controlling a situation by taking the initiative. **2** of or relating to mental conditioning or a habit etc. which has been learned. □ **pro·active·ly** *adverb* [PRO-², after REACTIVE]

pro-am ● *adjective* (of a sports event etc.) involving professionals and amateurs. ● *noun* a pro-am event.

prob *noun informal* a problem. [abbreviation]

prob·abil·is·tic /prɒbəbə'lɪstɪk/ *adjective* relating to probability; involving chance variation.

prob·abil·ity /ˌprɒbə'bɪlɪti/ *noun* (*pl.* **-ities**) **1** the state or condition of being probable. **2** the likelihood of something happening. **3** a probable or most probable event (*the probability is that they will come*). **4** *Math.* the extent to which an event is likely to occur, measured by the ratio of the favourable cases to the whole number of cases possible. □ **in all probability** most probably.

prob·able /'prɒbəbəl/ ● *adjective* (often foll. by *that* + clause) that may be expected to happen or prove true; likely (*the probable explanation; it is probable that they forgot*). ● *noun* a probable candidate, member of a team, etc. □ **prob·ably** *adverb* [Old French from Latin *probabilis* from *probare* prove]

probable cause *noun* = REASONABLE AND PROBABLE CAUSE.

pro·band /'prɒband/ *noun* a person forming the starting point for the genetic study of a family etc. [Latin *probandus*, gerundive of *probare* test]

pro·bate /'prɒːbeɪt/ ● *noun* **1** the official proving of a will. **2** a verified copy of a will with a certificate as handed to the executors. ● *transitive verb N Amer.* establish the validity of (a will). [Latin *probatum* neuter past participle of *probare* PROVE]

probate court *noun* = SURROGATE COURT.

pro·ba·tion /prɒ'beɪʃn/ *noun* **1** *Law* a system of suspending the sentence on an offender subject to a period of good behaviour under supervision. **2** a process or period of testing the character or abilities of a person in a certain role, esp. of a new employee. □ **on probation** undergoing probation, esp. legal supervision. □ **pro·ba·tion·ary** *adjective* [Old French *probation* or Latin *probatio* (as PROVE)]

probationary constable *noun* (in the Ontario Provincial Police) the lowest ranking officer.

pro·ba·tion·er /prɒ'beɪʃənər/ *noun* **1** a person on probation, e.g. a newly appointed nurse, teacher, etc. **2** an offender on probation.

probation officer *noun* an official supervising offenders on probation.

pro·ba·tive /'prɒːbətɪv/ *adjective* affording proof; evidential. [Latin *probativus* (as PROVE)]

probe ● *noun* **1** a penetrating investigation. **2** any small device, esp. an electrode, for measuring, testing, etc. **3** a blunt-ended surgical instrument usu. of metal for exploring a wound etc. **4** (in full **space probe**) an unmanned exploratory spacecraft transmitting information about its environment. ● *verb* **1** *transitive* examine or inquire into closely. **2** *transitive* explore (a wound or part of the body) with a probe. **3** *transitive* penetrate with a sharp instrument. **4** *intransitive* pierce or explore with or as with a probe. □ **prob·er** *noun* **prob·ing·ly** *adverb* [Late Latin *proba* proof, in medieval Latin = examination, from Latin *probare* test]

pro·bity /'prɒːbɪti, 'prɒ-/ *noun* uprightness, honesty. [Latin *probitas* from *probus* good]

prob·lem *noun* **1** a doubtful or difficult matter requiring a solution (*how to prevent it is a problem; the problem of ventilation*). **2** something hard to understand or accomplish or deal with. **3** (*attributive*) **a** causing problems; difficult to deal with (*problem child*). **b** (of a play, novel, etc.) in which a social or other problem is treated. **4 a** *Physics & Math.* an inquiry starting from given conditions to investigate or demonstrate a fact, result, or law. **b** *Math.* a proposition in which something has to be constructed (*compare* THEOREM 1). **5** a puzzle or question for solution. □ **have a problem with** have an objection to or be unable to accept. **no problem** *informal* that is simple or easy. **that's your** (or **his, her,** etc.) **problem** said to disclaim responsibility or involvement. [Old French *probleme* or Latin *problema* from Greek *problēma -matos* from *proballō* (as PRO-², *ballō* throw)]

prob·lem·atic *adjective* (also **prob·lem·atic·al**) **1** attended by difficulty. **2** doubtful or questionable. **3** *Logic* enunciating or supporting what is possible but not necessarily true. □ **prob·lem·atic·al·ly** *adverb*

prob·lem·a·tize /'prɒbləmətaɪz/ *transitive verb* (also esp. *Brit.* **-tise**) make into or regard as a problem requiring a solution. □ **prob·lem·a·tiz·a·tion** *noun*

pro bono /prɒː 'bɒnɒː/ *attributive adjective N Amer. Law* **1** (of legal work) undertaken without charge. **2** (of a lawyer) undertaking such work. [Latin *pro bono publico* 'for the public good']

pro·bos·cid·ean /ˌprɒbə'sɪdɪən/ (also **pro·bos·cid·ian**) ● *adjective* of the mammalian order Proboscidea, including elephants and their extinct relatives. ● *noun* a mammal of this order. [modern Latin *Proboscidea* (as PROBOSCIS)]

pro·bos·cis /prɒ'bɒskɪs, -'bɒsɪs/ *noun* **1** the long flexible trunk or snout of some mammals, e.g. an elephant or tapir. **2** the elongated mouthparts of some insects. **3** the sucking organ in some worms. **4** *jocular* the human nose. [Latin *proboscis -cidis* from Greek *proboskis* from *proboskō* (as PRO-², *boskō* feed)]

proboscis monkey *noun* a monkey, *Nasalis larvatus*, native to Borneo, the male of which has a large pendulous nose.

pro·caine /'prɒːkeɪn/ *noun* a synthetic compound used as a local anaesthetic. [PRO-¹ + COCAINE]

pro·cary·ote *var. of* PROKARYOTE.

pro·ced·ure /prɒ'siːdʒər/ *noun* **1** a way of proceeding, esp. a mode of conducting business or a legal action. **2** a mode of performing a task. **3** a series of actions conducted in a certain order or manner. **4** a proceeding. **5** *Computing* = SUBROUTINE. □ **pro·ced·ur·al** *adjective* **pro·ced·ur·al·ly** *adverb* [French *procédure* (as PROCEED)]

pro·ceed *intransitive verb* **1** (often foll. by *to*) go forward or on further; make one's way. **2** (often foll. by *with*, or *to* + infin.) continue; go on with an activity (*proceeded with their work*; *proceeded to tell the whole story*). **3** (of an action) be carried on or continued (*the case will now proceed*). **4** adopt a course of action (*how shall we proceed*). **5** go on to say. **6** (foll. by *against*) start a lawsuit (against a person). **7** (often foll. by *from*) come forth or originate. [Old French *proceder* from Latin *procedere process-* (as PRO-[1], *cedere* go)]

pro·ceed·ing *noun* **1** an action or piece of conduct (*a high-handed proceeding*). **2** (in *pl.*) (in full **legal proceedings**) an action at law; a lawsuit. **3** (in *pl.*) a published report of discussions or a conference.

pro·ceeds *plural noun* money produced by a transaction or other undertaking. [pl. of obsolete *proceed* (n.) from PROCEED]

pro·cess[1] /'prɔːses, 'prɒ-/ ● *noun* (*pl.* **pro·cess·es** /-sesəz, -sesiːz/) **1** a course of action or proceeding, esp. a series of stages in manufacture or some other operation. **2 a** the progress or course of something (*in process of construction*). **b** the course of becoming, happening, etc. (*regeneration is in process*). **3** a natural or involuntary operation or series of changes (*the process of growing old*). **4** an action at law; a summons or writ. **5** *Anat.*, *Zool.*, & *Bot.* a natural appendage or outgrowth on an organism. ● *transitive verb* **1** put (a raw material, a food, etc.) through an industrial or manufacturing process in order to change or preserve it etc. **2** deal with (a document, request, etc.) officially (*allow two weeks for the application to be processed*). **3** *Computing* operate on (data) by means of a program. **4** mix, chop, purée, etc. (food) using a food processor. **5** treat (photographic film) chemically to make the latent image visible. □ **pro·cess·able** *adjective* [Old French *proces* from Latin *processus* (as PROCEED)]

pro·cess[2] /prɔː'ses/ *intransitive verb* walk in procession. [back-formation from PROCESSION]

processed cheese *noun* cheese made by melting, blending, and frequently emulsifying other cheeses.

pro·ces·sion /prɔː'seʃən, prə-/ *noun* **1** a number of people or vehicles etc. moving forward in orderly succession, esp. at a ceremony, demonstration, or festivity. **2** the movement of such a group (*go in procession*). **3** *Theol.* the emanation of the Holy Spirit. [Old French from Latin *processio -onis* (as PROCEED)]

pro·ces·sion·al /prɔː'seʃənəl, prə-/ ● *adjective* **1** of processions. **2** used, carried, or sung in processions. ● *noun Christianity* **1** a hymn etc. sung during a procession. **2** an office book of processional hymns etc. [medieval Latin *processionalis* (adj.), *-ale* (n.) (as PROCESSION)]

pro·ces·sor /'prɔːsesɚ, 'prɒ-/ *noun* **1** a person or company etc. that processes something, esp. food. **2** a machine that processes things. **3** = CENTRAL PROCESSING UNIT. **4** a piece of software that performs operations on data (*word processor*). **5** = FOOD PROCESSOR.

process server *noun* a person who serves writs. □ **process serving** *noun*

procès-verbal /ˌprɒseivɜːr'bɒl/ *noun* (*pl.* **procès-verbaux** /-'boː/) a written report of proceedings; minutes. [French]

pro-choice *adjective* favouring the right of a woman to choose to have an abortion.

pro·claim *transitive verb* **1** (often foll. by *that* + clause) announce or declare publicly or officially. **2** declare (a person) to be (a king, traitor, etc.). **3** reveal as being (*an accent that proclaims you a Scot*). □ **pro·claim·er** *noun* **proc·la·ma·tion** /ˌprɒklə'meiʃən/ *noun* [Latin *proclamare* cry out (as PRO-[1], CLAIM)]

pro·clit·ic /prə'klitik/ ● *adjective* (of a monosyllable) closely attached in pronunciation to a following word and having itself no accent. ● *noun* such a word, e.g. *at* in *at home*. [modern Latin *procliticus* from Greek *proklīnō* lean forward, after Late Latin *encliticus*: see ENCLITIC]

pro·cliv·ity /prə'kliviti/ *noun* (*pl.* **-ities**) a tendency or inclination. [Latin *proclivitas* from *proclivis* inclined (as PRO-[1], *clivus* slope)]

Pro·clus /'prɒkləs, 'prɒk-/ (*c.*410-85), Greek Neoplatonist philosopher, whose *Elements of Theology* provides a concise summary of Neoplatonist metaphysics.

pro·con·sul /prɔː'kɒnsəl/ *noun* **1** *Rom. Hist.* a governor of a province, in the later republic usu. an ex-consul. **2** a governor or administrator of a modern dependency or colony. □ **pro·con·sul·ar** /-sjulɚ/ *adjective* [Latin, earlier *pro consule* (one acting) for the consul]

pro·cras·tin·ate /prɔː'krasti,neit/ *intransitive verb* delay or postpone action. □ **pro·cras·tin·a·tion** *noun* **pro·cras·tin·a·tor** *noun* [Latin *procrastinare procrastinat-* (as PRO-[1], *crastinus* of tomorrow, from *cras* tomorrow)]

pro·cre·ate /'prɒkri,eit/ *transitive & intransitive verb* bring (offspring) into existence by the natural process of reproduction. □ **pro·cre·ative**

adjective **pro·cre·ation** *noun* **pro·cre·ator** *noun* [Latin *procreare procreat-* (as PRO-[1], *creare* create)]

Pro·crus·tean /prɔː'krastiən/ *adjective* seeking to enforce uniformity by forceful or ruthless methods. [PROCRUSTES]

Pro·crus·tes /prɔː'krastiːz/ *Gk Myth* a robber who forced travellers to lie on a bed and made them fit it by stretching their limbs or cutting off the appropriate length of leg; Theseus killed him in like manner. [Greek, *Prokroustēs*, lit. 'stretcher', from *prokrouō* beat out]

proc·tol·ogy /prɒk'tɒlədʒi/ *noun* the branch of medicine concerned with the anus and rectum. □ **procto·logic·al** *adjective* **proc·tol·o·gist** *noun* [Greek *prōktos* anus + -LOGY]

proc·tor ● *noun* **1** *N Amer.* a person who supervises students in an examination etc. **2** *Brit.* an officer (usu. one of two) at certain universities, appointed annually and having mainly disciplinary functions. ● *transitive & intransitive verb N Amer.* supervise an examination etc. [Middle English, syncopation of PROCURATOR]

procto·scope /'prɒktə,skoːp/ *noun* a medical instrument for inspecting the rectum. □ **procto·scop·ic** /-'skɒpik/ *adjective* **proc·tos·copy** /-'tɒskəpi/ *noun* [Greek *prōktos* anus + -SCOPE]

pro·cum·bent /prə'kambənt/ *adjective* **1** lying on the face; prostrate. **2** *Bot.* growing along the ground. [Latin *procumbere* fall forwards (as PRO-[1], *cumbere* lay oneself)]

proc·ur·a·tion /ˌprɒkju'reiʃən/ *noun* **1** *formal* the action of procuring, obtaining, or bringing about. **2** the function or an authorized action of an attorney.

proc·ur·a·tor /'prɒkju,reitɚ/ *noun* **1** an agent or proxy, esp. one who has power of attorney. **2** *Rom. Hist.* a treasury officer in an imperial province. □ **proc·ur·a·tor·ial** /-rə'tɔːriəl/ *adjective* **proc·ur·a·tor·ship** *noun* [Latin *procurator* administrator, finance-agent (as PROCURE)]

pro·cure /prə'kjur/ *verb* **1** *transitive* obtain, esp. by care or effort; acquire (*managed to procure a copy*). **2** *transitive* bring about (*procured their dismissal*). **3** *transitive & intransitive* obtain (a prostitute) for another person. □ **pro·cur·able** *adjective* [Old French *procurer* from Latin *procurare* take care of, manage (as PRO-[1], *curare* see to)]

pro·cure·ment /prə'kjurmənt/ *noun* **1** the act or an instance of procuring. **2** the act of buying or purchasing, esp. by a government (also *attributive: the federal procurement budget*).

pro·cur·er /prə'kjurɚ/ *noun* a person who obtains prostitutes for others.

pro·cur·ess /prə'kjurəs/ *noun* a woman who procures prostitutes.

Pro·cyon /prɒː'saiɒn/ a binary star, the brightest in the constellation Canis Minor, and the fifth-brightest in the sky. [Greek, lit. 'before the dog', because it rises before Sirius]

prod ● *verb* (**prod·ded**, **prod·ding**) **1** *transitive* poke with the finger or a pointed object. **2** *transitive* stimulate to action. **3** *intransitive* (foll. by *at*) make a prodding motion. ● *noun* **1** a poke or thrust. **2** a stimulus to action. **3** an implement, such as a pointed or electrified rod, used for herding cattle etc. □ **prod·der** *noun* [16th c.: perhaps imitative]

prod·i·gal /'prɒdigəl/ ● *adjective* **1** recklessly wasteful. **2** (foll. by *of*, *with*, *in*, etc.) lavish. **3** having returned after an absence. ● *noun* **1** a prodigal person. **2** a repentant wastrel etc. (Luke 15:11–32). **3** a person who returns back to a place, family, etc., after an absence. □ **prod·i·gal·ity** /-'galiti/ *noun* **prod·i·gal·ly** *adverb* [medieval Latin *prodigalis* from Latin *prodigus* lavish]

pro·di·gious /prə'didʒəs/ *adjective* **1** marvellous or amazing. **2** enormous. □ **pro·di·gious·ly** *adverb* **pro·di·gious·ness** *noun* [Latin *prodigiosus* (as PRODIGY)]

prod·i·gy /'prɒdidʒi/ *noun* (*pl.* **-gies**) **1** a person endowed with exceptional qualities or abilities, esp. a precocious child. **2** something that causes wonder or amazement. **3** (foll. by *of*) a wonderful example (of a quality). [Latin *prodigium* portent]

pro·drome /'prɒdroːm, 'prɒdrɒːm/ *noun Med.* a premonitory symptom. □ **pro·drom·al** /'prɒdroːmɒl/ *adjective* **pro·drom·ic** /prə'drɒmik/ *adjective* [French from modern Latin from Greek *prodromos* precursor (as PRO-[2], *dromos* running)]

pro·duce ● *transitive verb* **1** bring (something) into existence (*produced dinner*; *produced a masterpiece*). **2** manufacture (goods) from raw materials etc. **3** yield (fruit, a harvest, etc.) (*grain produced in the West*). **4** give birth to (a child). **5** cause or bring about (a reaction, sensation, etc.). **6** bring forward for consideration, inspection, or use (*produced the tickets*). **7 a** bring (a play, performer, book, etc.) before the public. **b** supervise the making of (a film, broadcast, etc.). **8** *Math.* extend or continue (a line). ● *noun* **1** something that has been produced. **2** agricultural and natural products collectively (*the produce of Canada's oceans*). **3** fruits and vegetables (also *attributive:* located in the produce aisle).

pro·du·ci·ble *adjective* **pro·du·ci·bil·i·ty** *noun* [Latin *producere* (as PRO-¹, *ducere* *duct-* lead)]

pro·du·cer *noun* **1** a person, company, country, etc. that produces goods or materials (*small-scale egg producers*). **2 a** a person in charge of a film, play, etc., who obtains the money to pay for it and arranges rehearsals, filming, publicity, etc. **b** the director of a theatrical event or broadcast program.

prod·uct *noun* **1** a thing that is grown or produced, usu. for sale (*dairy products*). **2** a thing or substance produced during a natural, chemical, or manufacturing process (*the products of combustion*). **3** a thing or state that is the result of something (*the product of their labours*). **4** a person who has been greatly influenced by something (*a product of her times*). **5** *Math.* a quantity obtained by multiplying quantities together. [Latin *productum*, neuter past participle of *producere* PRODUCE]

pro·duc·tion *noun* **1** the act or an instance of producing; the process of being produced. **2** the process of being manufactured, esp. in large quantities (*go into production*). **3 a** a total yield. **b** the rate at which something is produced. **4 a** the process or administrative management of making a film, play, record, etc. **b** a film, play, record, etc., produced. **5** the sets, costumes, props, lighting, etc. and other physical aspects of a theatrical entertainment. **6** *informal* an exaggeratedly or needlessly complicated situation or event (*always makes such a production out of doing the housework*). **7** (*attributive*) (of a car etc.) mass-produced; not custom-made (*a production model*).

production line *noun* = ASSEMBLY LINE.

production values *plural noun* the quality of a film, television, or theatrical production as regards the sets, costumes, props, authenticity of period detail, music, sound, etc. as distinct from the acting, direction, etc.

pro·duct·ive *adjective* **1** of or engaged in the production of goods. **2** producing much (*productive soil*; *a productive writer*). **3** *Econ.* producing commodities of exchangeable value (*productive labour*). **4** (foll. by *of*) producing or giving rise to (*productive of great annoyance*). **5** (of a word element) frequently used in forming new words. □ **pro·duct·ive·ly** *adverb* **pro·duct·ive·ness** *noun*

pro·duc·tiv·i·ty *noun* **1** the capacity to produce. **2** the quality or state of being productive. **3** the effectiveness of productive effort, esp. in industry. **4** production per unit of effort.

product placement *noun* a practice whereby manufacturers of goods or service providers gain exposure for their products by paying for them to be displayed, mentioned, or used in the media (esp. in movies and TV programs).

pro·em /ˈproːɛm/ *noun* a preface or preamble to a book or speech. [Old French *proeme* or Latin *prooemium* from Greek *prooimion* prelude (as PRO-², *oimē* song)]

Prof. *abbreviation* Professor.

prof *noun* *informal* a professor. [abbreviation]

pro-family *adjective* *N Amer.* **1** promoting or supporting traditional family life. **2** = ANTI-ABORTION.

pro·fane ● *adjective* **1** not belonging to what is sacred or Biblical; secular. **2 a** irreverent, blasphemous. **b** (of language) blasphemous or obscene. **3** (of a rite etc.) heathen. **4** not initiated into religious rites or any esoteric knowledge. ● *transitive verb* **1** treat (a sacred thing) with irreverence or disregard. **2** violate or pollute (what is entitled to respect). □ **prof·an·a·tion** /ˌprɒfəˈneɪʃən/ *noun* **pro·fane·ly** *adverb* **pro·fan·er** *noun* [Latin *profanus* before (i.e. outside) the temple, not sacred (as PRO-¹, *fanum* temple)]

pro·fan·i·ty /prəˈfanɪti/ *noun* (*pl.* **-ities**) **1** a profane act. **2 a** profane language; blasphemy. **b** an oath, a swear word. [Late Latin *profanitas* (as PROFANE)]

pro·fess *transitive verb* **1** claim openly to have (a quality or feeling). **2** (foll. by *to* + infin.) pretend. **3** declare (*profess ignorance*). **4** affirm one's faith in or allegiance to. **5** receive into a religious order under vows. **6** have as one's profession or business. [Latin *profitēri* *profess-* declare publicly (as PRO-¹, *fatēri* confess)]

pro·fessed *adjective* **1** self-acknowledged (*a professed Christian*). **2** alleged, ostensible. **3** claiming to be duly qualified. **4** (of a monk or nun) having taken the vows of a religious order. □ **pro·fess·ed·ly** *adverb* (in senses 1, 2).

pro·fes·sion *noun* **1** a vocation or calling, esp. one that involves some branch of advanced learning or science (*the medical profession*). **2** a body of people engaged in a profession. **3** a declaration or avowal. **4** a declaration of belief in a religion. **5 a** the declaration or vows made on entering a religious order. **b** the ceremony or fact of being professed in a religious order. □ **the oldest profession** *informal* or *jocular* prostitution.

pro·fes·sion·al ● *adjective* **1** of or belonging to or connected with a profession. **2 a** having or showing the skill of a professional, competent. **b** worthy of a professional (*professional conduct*). **3** engaged in a specified activity as one's main paid occupation (compare AMATEUR) (*a professional lexicographer*). **4** *derogatory* engaged in a specified activity regarded with disfavour (*a professional agitator*). ● *noun* **1** a person qualified or employed in one of the professions (*nurses and other committed health professionals*). **2** a professional player or performer. **3** a highly skilled and experienced person (*Alex is a real professional*). **4** an expert player of a game, esp. golf or tennis, who provides instruction to members of a club etc. □ **pro·fes·sion·al·ly** *adverb*

professional development *noun* development in one's profession, e.g. through seminars, courses, etc.

professional development day *noun* esp. *Cdn* a day on which classes are cancelled so that teachers may attend seminars etc. for professional development.

pro·fes·sion·al·ism *noun* **1** the skill or qualities required or expected of members of a profession. **2** great skill and ability.

pro·fes·sion·al·ize *verb* (also esp. *Brit.* **-ise**) **1** *transitive* make (an occupation, activity, etc.) professional. **2** *intransitive* become professional. □ **pro·fes·sion·al·iz·a·tion** *noun*

pro·fes·sor *noun* **1 a** *N Amer.* a university teacher. **b** (often as a title) a university teacher of the highest academic rank. **2** a person who professes a religion. □ **pro·fes·sor·ate** *noun* **pro·fes·sor·i·al** /ˌprɒfəˈsɔːrɪəl/ *adjective* **pro·fes·sor·i·al·ly** *adverb* **pro·fes·sor·i·ate** /ˌprɒfəˈsɔːrɪət/ *noun* **pro·fes·sor·ship** *noun*

prof·fer /ˈprɒfər/ ● *transitive verb* offer (a gift, services, a hand, etc.). ● *noun* an offer or proposal. [Anglo-French & Old French *proffrir* (as PRO-¹, *offrir* OFFER)]

pro·fi·cient /prəˈfɪʃənt/ *adjective* (often foll. by *in*, *at*) competent or skilled at doing or using something. □ **pro·fi·cien·cy** /-si/ *noun* **pro·fi·cient·ly** *adverb* [Latin *proficiens proficient-* (as PROFIT)]

pro·file ● *noun* **1 a** an outline (esp. of a human face) as seen from one side. **b** a representation of this. **2** a short article giving a description of a person or organization, esp. a public figure. **3** *Statistics* a representation by a graph or chart of information (esp. on certain characteristics) recorded in a quantified form. **4** the extent to which a person, company, organization, etc., attracts public notice or comment (*must try to raise our profile*). **5** a vertical cross-section of a structure etc. **6** a flat outline piece of scenery on stage. ● *transitive verb* **1** represent in profile. **2** describe (a person or organization, esp. a public figure) in a short article. □ **in profile** as seen from one side. **keep a low profile** remain inconspicuous. □ **pro·fil·er** *noun* **pro·fil·ist** *noun* [obsolete Italian *profilo*, *profilare* (as PRO-¹, *filare* spin, from Latin *filare* from *filum* thread)]

pro·fil·ing *noun* the recording and analysis of a person's psychological and behavioural characteristics, so as to assess or predict their capabilities in a certain sphere or to assist in identifying a particular subgroup of people.

prof·it ● *noun* **1** financial gain; excess of returns over outlay. **2** an advantage or benefit. ● *verb* (**prof·it·ed**, **prof·it·ing**) **1** *transitive & intransitive* be beneficial to. **2** *intransitive* obtain an advantage or benefit (*profited by the experience*). **3** *intransitive* make or earn a profit. □ **at a profit** with financial gain. □ **prof·it·less** *adjective* [Old French from Latin *profectus* progress, profit, from *proficere profect-* advance (as PRO-¹, *facere* do)]

prof·it·able *adjective* **1** yielding profit; lucrative. **2** beneficial; useful. □ **prof·it·abil·i·ty** *noun* **prof·it·able·ness** *noun* **prof·it·ably** *adverb*

profit and loss *noun* the gain and loss made in a commercial transaction or series of transactions, esp. as shown on a balance sheet (also *attributive*: *profit and loss account*).

profit centre *noun* **1** a part of a business organization with its own profits and costs and hence ascertainable profitability. **2** a profitable part of an organization.

prof·it·eer ● *intransitive verb* make or seek to make excessive profits, esp. illegally or in black market conditions. ● *noun* a person who profiteers.

prof·it·er·ole /prəˈfɪtəˌroʊl/ *noun* a small cream puff usu. filled with cream and covered with chocolate sauce. [French, diminutive of *profit* PROFIT]

profit margin *noun* the difference between the cost of buying or producing something and the price for which it is sold (*increase the profit margin to 20 per cent*).

Vowels: a cat ɑ arm e bed ɜr her ɜː deux ə ago ɪ sit i cosy iː feed ɒ hot ɔ pore ɔː no ʌ run ʊ put

profit-sharing *noun* the sharing of profits esp. between employer and employees (also *attributive*: *a profit-sharing plan*).

profit-taking *noun* the sale of shares etc. at a time when profit will accrue.

profit warning *noun* an announcement made by a publicly traded company to warn investors that it will not achieve the profits predicted by financial analysts.

prof·li·gate /ˈprɒflɪgət/ ● *adjective* **1** shamelessly immoral. **2** recklessly extravagant. ● *noun* a profligate person. □ **prof·li·gacy** /-gəsi/ *noun* **prof·li·gate·ly** *adverb* [Latin *profligatus* dissolute, past participle of *profligare* overthrow, ruin (as PRO-¹, *fligere* strike down)]

pro forma ● *adjective* **1** done or produced as a matter of form. **2** (of an invoice etc.) sent in advance of goods supplied. ● *adverb* as a matter of form. [Latin]

pro·found ● *adjective* (**pro·found·er**, **pro·found·est**) **1 a** having or showing great knowledge or insight (*a profound treatise*). **b** demanding deep study or thought (*profound doctrines*). **2** (of a state or quality) deep, intense, unqualified (*a profound sleep*; *profound indifference*). **3** at or extending to a great depth (*profound crevasses*). **4** (of a sigh) deep-drawn. ● *noun* (prec. by *the*) *literary* the vast depth (of the ocean, soul, etc.). □ **pro·found·ly** *adverb* **pro·found·ness** *noun* **pro·fund·ity** /prəˈfʌndɪti/ *noun* (*pl.* **-ities**). [Old French *profond* from Latin *profundus* deep (as PRO-¹, *fundus* bottom)]

pro·fuse /prəˈfjuːs/ *adjective* **1** (often foll. by *in*, *of*) lavish; extravagant (*was profuse in her praise of her employees*). **2** (of a thing) exuberantly plentiful; abundant (*profuse bleeding*; *a profuse variety*). □ **pro·fuse·ly** *adverb* **pro·fuse·ness** *noun* **pro·fu·sion** /prəˈfjuːʒən/ *noun* [Latin *profusus* past participle of *profundere profus-* (as PRO-¹, *fundere fus-* pour)]

prog *noun* *Cdn* (*Nfld*) food, e.g. for a meal or the winter etc. (also *attributive*: *prog bag*). [obsolete *prog* (v.) 'forage for food']

pro·geni·tive /prəˈdʒenɪtɪv/ *adjective* capable of or connected with the production of offspring.

pro·geni·tor /prəˈdʒenɪtər/ *noun* **1** the ancestor of a person, animal, or plant. **2** a political or intellectual predecessor. **3** something that serves as a model; precursor. □ **pro·geni·tor·ial** /-ˈtɔriəl/ *adjective* [Latin *progenitor* from *progignere* genit- (as PRO-¹, *gignere* beget)]

pro·geny /ˈprɒdʒəni/ *noun* **1** the offspring of a person or other organism. **2** a descendant or descendants. **3** an outcome or issue. [Old French *progenie* from Latin *progenies* from *progignere* (as PROGENITOR)]

pro·ges·ter·one /prəˈdʒestəˌroʊn/ *noun* a steroid hormone released by the corpus luteum which stimulates the preparation of the uterus for pregnancy (*see also* PROGESTIN). [*progestin* (as PRO-², GESTATION) + *luteosterone* from CORPUS LUTEUM + STEROL]

pro·ges·tin /prəˈdʒestɪn/ *noun* (also **pro·ges·to·gen** /-ˈdʒestədʒɪn/) **1** any of a group of steroid hormones (including progesterone) that maintain pregnancy and prevent further ovulation during it. **2** a similar hormone produced synthetically.

prog·nath·ous /prɒgˈneɪθəs, ˈprɒgnəθəs/ *adjective* **1** having a projecting jaw. **2** (of a jaw) projecting. □ **prog·nath·ic** /prɒgˈnæθɪk/ *adjective* [PRO-² + Greek *gnathos* jaw]

prog·no·sis /prɒgˈnoʊsɪs/ *noun* (*pl.* **prog·no·ses** /-siːz/) **1** a forecast; a prognostication. **2** a forecast of the course of a disease or other medical condition. [Greek *prognōsis* (as PRO-², *gignōskō* know)]

prog·nos·tic /prɒgˈnɒstɪk/ *adjective* serving to predict the likely outcome of a disease or ailment; of or relating to a medical prognosis. [Latin *prognosticum* from Greek *prognōstikon* neuter of *prognōstikos* (as PROGNOSIS)]

prog·nos·ti·cate /prɒgˈnɒstɪˌkeɪt/ *transitive verb* **1** (often foll. by *that* + clause) foretell; foresee; prophesy. **2** (of a thing) betoken; indicate (*future events* etc.). □ **prog·nos·ti·ca·tion** *noun* **prog·nos·ti·ca·tor** *noun* [medieval Latin *prognosticare* (as PROGNOSTIC)]

pro·gram (also **pro·gramme**) ● *noun* **1 a** a usu. printed list of a series of events, pieces of music, performers, etc. at a public function, performance etc. **b** the performance itself (*a program of pieces for violin*). **2** a radio or television broadcast. **3 a** a course of activities or actions undertaken to achieve a certain result (*started a new fitness program*; *welfare reform program*). **b** a plan of future events (*the program is dinner and an early night*). **4 a** a course of study; curriculum (*a graduate of Carleton's journalism program*). **b** a system of extracurricular, usu. athletic activities (*football program*). **5** a plan offering subscribers certain benefits (*frequent flyer program*). **6** a series of coded instructions to control the operation of a computer or other machine. ● *transitive verb* (**pro·grammed**, **pro·gram·ming** or esp. *US* **pro·gramed**, **pro·gram·ing**) **1** make a program or definite plan of. **2** provide (a computer etc.) with coded instructions for the automatic performance of a particular task. **3** train to behave in a predetermined way. **4** choose or schedule (films, plays, pieces of music, etc.) for performance. □ **get with the program** *N Amer. slang* become aware of and attuned to the realities of a situation. □ **pro·gram·mabil·ity** *noun* **pro·gram·mable** *adjective* [Greek *programma -atos*, from *prographō* 'write publicly' (as PRO-², *graphō* 'write')]

pro·gram·mat·ic *adjective* **1** of the nature of or according to a program, schedule, or method. **2** of the nature of program music. □ **pro·gram·mat·ic·ally** *adverb*

pro·gram·mer *noun* **1** a person who writes computer programs. **2** a person responsible for the programming of broadcast programs, films, etc.

pro·gram·ming *noun* **1** the writing of computer programs. **2** the choice, arrangement, or broadcasting of radio or television programs, films, etc. **3** the action of programming; planning for management or administrative purposes.

programming language *noun* a notation for the precise description of computer programs or algorithms.

program music *noun* a piece of music intended to tell a story, evoke images, etc.

program note *noun* a short description or explanation in a program about a musical work, a play, an actor's career, etc.

pro·gress ● *noun* /ˈprɒgres, ˈproʊ-/ **1** forward or onward movement towards a destination. **2** advance or development towards completion, betterment, etc.; improvement (*has made little progress this term*; *the progress of civilization*). **3** *Brit. archaic* a state journey or official tour, esp. by royalty. ● *verb* /prəˈgres/ **1** *intransitive* move or be moved forward or onward; continue (*the argument is progressing*). **2** *intransitive* advance or develop towards completion, improvement, etc. (*science progresses*). **3** *transitive* cause (a situation, condition, person etc.) to advance or improve. □ **in progress** in the course of developing; going on. [Latin *progressus* from *progredi* (as PRO-¹, *gradi* walk)]

pro·gres·sion /prəˈgreʃən/ *noun* **1** the act or an instance of progressing (*a mode of progression*). **2** a succession; a series. **3** *Math.* **a** = ARITHMETIC PROGRESSION. **b** = GEOMETRIC PROGRESSION. **c** = HARMONIC PROGRESSION. **4** *Music* passing from one note or chord to another. □ **pro·gres·sion·al** *adjective*

pro·gres·sive ● *adjective* **1** moving forward (*progressive motion*). **2** proceeding step by step; cumulative (*progressive drug use*). **3 a** (of a political party, government, etc.) favouring or implementing rapid progress or social reform. **b** holding liberal views; modern (*this is a progressive company*). **c** (of music) modern, experimental, avant-garde (*progressive jazz*). **4** (of disease, violence, etc.) increasing in severity or extent. **5** (of taxation) at rates increasing with the sum taxed. **6** *Grammar* (of an aspect) expressing an action in progress, e.g. *am writing*, *was writing*. **7** (of education) informal and without strict discipline, stressing individual needs. ● *noun* **1** an advocate of progressive political policies or social reform. **2** (**Progressive**) *hist.* (in Canada) a member or supporter of the Progressive Party. □ **pro·gres·sive·ly** *adverb* **pro·gres·sive·ness** *noun* **pro·gres·siv·ism** *noun* **pro·gres·siv·ist** *noun & adjective*

Progressive Conservative ● *noun* (in Canada) a member or supporter of the Progressive Conservative Party. ● *adjective* (in Canada) of or relating to the Progressive Conservative Party or its policies.

Progressive Conservative Party *noun* (in Canada) one of the two historically most important political parties, advocating right-of-centre policies. In 2003 the federal Progressive Conservative Party merged with the Canadian Alliance to form the Conservative Party.

Progressive Party *noun hist.* (in Canada) a political party which supported agricultural reform, nationalization of railways, and low tariffs, formed in 1920 by Ontario and prairie farmers and dissident Liberals.

progressive rock *noun* (also **prog rock**) a style of rock music popular in the 1970s which sought to expand the boundaries of popular music through the use of complex instrumentation and arrangement and non-traditional subject matter.

pro·hibit /prəˈhɪbɪt/ *transitive verb* (**pro·hibit·ed**, **pro·hibit·ing**) (often foll. by *from* + verbal noun) **1** formally forbid, esp. by authority. **2** prevent; make impossible (*his accident prohibits him from playing football*). □ **pro·hibi·tory** *adjective* [Latin *prohibēre* (as PRO-¹, *habēre* 'hold')]

prohibited degrees *plural noun* a number of degrees of consanguinity within which marriage between two related persons is forbidden.

pro·hibi·tion /ˌproʊəˈbɪʃən, -hɪˈbɪʃən/ *noun* **1** the act or an instance of forbidding; a state of being forbidden. **2** *Law* **a** an edict or order that forbids. **b** *Brit. & Cdn* a writ from a superior court forbidding an inferior court from proceeding in a suit deemed to be beyond its cognizance. **3** (usu. **Prohibition**) **a** the prevention by law of the manufacture and sale of alcoholic drink, esp. as established in the US by the 18th Amendment to the Constitution in 1920, revoked by the 21st Amendment in 1933 after the spread of bootlegging by organized crime. **b** the period during which such a prohibition is in effect. □ **pro·hibi·tion·ary** *adjective* **pro·hibi·tion·ism** *noun* **pro·hibi·tion·ist** *noun*

pro·hibi·tive /proˈhɪbɪtɪv/ *adjective* **1** prohibiting. **2** (of prices, taxes, etc.) so high as to prevent purchase, use, abuse, etc. (*published at a prohibitive price*). □ **pro·hibi·tive·ly** *adverb* **pro·hibi·tive·ness** *noun*

pro·ject ● *noun* /ˈprɒdʒekt, ˈproː-/ **1** a plan; a scheme. **2 a** an undertaking that is carefully planned and designed to achieve a particular aim. **b** any planned activity (*a do-it-yourself project*). **3** a usu. long-term exercise or study of a set topic undertaken by a student or group of students to be submitted for assessment. **4** an individual or collaborative enterprise undertaken usu. for industrial or scientific research, or having a social purpose (*Manhattan Project*). **5** *N Amer.* = HOUSING PROJECT. ● *verb* /prəˈdʒekt/ **1** *transitive* plan or contrive (a course of action, scheme, etc.). **2** *intransitive* protrude; jut out. **3** *transitive* throw; cast; impel (*projected the stone into the water*). **4** *transitive* extrapolate (results etc.) to a future time; forecast (*the unemployment rate is projected to fall*). **5** *transitive* cause (light, shadow, images, etc.) to fall on a surface, screen, etc. **6 a** *transitive* cause (a sound, esp. the voice) to be heard at a distance. **b** *intransitive* use the voice loudly enough to be heard in a large room etc. **7** *transitive & intransitive* express or convey (feelings, a particular image, etc.) forcefully or effectively, e.g. to an audience. **8** *transitive Geom.* **a** draw straight lines from a centre or parallel lines through every point of (a given figure) to produce a corresponding figure on a surface or a line by intersecting it. **b** draw (such lines). **c** produce (such a corresponding figure). **9** *Psych.* **a** *transitive & intransitive* attribute (an emotion etc.) to an external object or person, esp. unconsciously. **b** *reflexive* project (oneself) into another's feelings, the future, etc. [Latin *projectum* neuter past participle of *projicere* (as PRO-¹, *jacēre* throw)]

pro·ject·ile /prəˈdʒektaɪl/ ● *noun* **1** a missile, esp. fired by a rocket. **2** a bullet, shell, etc. fired from a gun. **3** any object thrown as a weapon. ● *adjective* **1** capable of being projected by force, esp. from a gun. **2** impelled with great force. [modern Latin *projectilis* (adj.), *-ile* (n.) (as PROJECT)]

pro·jec·tion *noun* **1** the act or an instance of projecting; the process of being projected. **2** a thing that projects or obtrudes. **3 a** the presentation of an image etc. on a surface or screen. **b** the image etc. presented. **4 a** a forecast or estimate based on present trends (*a projection of next year's profits*). **b** this process. **5** the ability to make a sound, esp. the voice, heard at a distance. **6 a** a mental image or preoccupation viewed as an objective reality. **b** the unconscious transfer of one's own impressions or feelings to external objects or persons. **7** *Math.* the act or an instance of projecting a figure. **8** the representation on a plane surface of any part of the surface of the earth or a celestial sphere (*Mercator projection*). □ **pro·jec·tion·ist** *noun* (in sense 3).

pro·ject·ive *adjective* **1** *Geom.* **a** relating to or derived by projection. **b** (of a property of a figure) unchanged by projection. **2** *Psych.* mentally projecting or projected (*a projective imagination*). □ **pro·ject·ive·ly** *adverb*

pro·ject·or *noun* **1** an apparatus containing a source of light and a system of lenses for projecting slides or film on to a screen. **2** an apparatus for projecting rays of light.

pro·kary·ote /proːˈkerioːt/ *noun* (also **pro·cary·ote**) a single-celled organism which has neither a distinct nucleus with a membrane nor other specialized organelles, e.g. a bacterium, a blue-green alga (*compare* EUKARYOTE). □ **pro·kary·ot·ic** /-ˈɒtɪk/ *adjective* [PRO-² + KARYO- + *-ote* as in ZYGOTE]

Pro·kof·iev /prəˈkɒfi͜ef/ **Ser·gei (Serge·evich)** (1891–1953), Russian composer. His works include seven symphonies, the operas *The Love for Three Oranges* (1919) and *War and Peace* (1941–3), the music for the ballets *Romeo and Juliet* (1935–6) and *Cinderella* (1944), and the symphonic fairy tale *Peter and the Wolf* (1936).

pro·lac·tin /proːˈlaktɪn/ *noun* a hormone released from the anterior pituitary gland that stimulates milk production after childbirth. [PRO-¹ + LACTATION]

pro·lapse /ˈproːlaps/ ● *noun* **1** the forward or downward displacement of a part or organ. **2** the prolapsed part or organ, esp. the uterus or rectum. ● *intransitive verb* undergo prolapse. [Latin *prolabi prolaps-* (as PRO-¹, *labi* slip)]

pro·late /ˈproːleit/ *adjective Geom.* (of a spheroid) lengthened in the direction of a polar diameter (*compare* OBLATE²). [Latin *prolatus* past participle of *proferre* prolong (as PRO-¹, *ferre* carry)]

prole /proːl/ *derogatory informal* ● *adjective* proletarian. ● *noun* a proletarian. [abbreviation]

pro·leg /ˈproːleg/ *noun* a fleshy abdominal limb of a caterpillar or other larva. [PRO-¹ + LEG]

pro·legom·en·on /ˌproːlɪˈɡɒmənən/ *noun* (*pl.* **pro·legom·ena**) (often in *pl.*) an introduction or preface to a book etc., esp. when critical or discursive. [Latin from Greek, neuter passive pres. part. of *prolegō* (as PRO-², *legō* say)]

pro·lep·sis /proːˈlepsɪs/ *noun* (*pl.* **pro·lep·ses** /-siːz/) **1** the anticipation and answering of possible objections in rhetorical speech. **2** the representation of a future act, state, etc. as already done or existing. □ **pro·lep·tic** *adjective* [Greek *prolēpsis* from *prolambanō* anticipate (as PRO-², *lambanō* take)]

pro·le·tar·ian /ˌproːlɪˈterɪən/ ● *adjective* of or concerning the proletariat. ● *noun* a member of the proletariat. □ **pro·le·tar·ian·ism** *noun* **pro·le·tar·ian·iza·tion** *noun* **pro·le·tar·ian·ize** *transitive verb* (also esp. *Brit.* **-ise**). [Latin *proletarius* from *proles* 'offspring' denoting a person having no wealth in property, who only served the state by producing offspring]

pro·le·tar·iat /ˌproːlɪˈterɪət/ *noun* **1 a** *Econ.* wage earners collectively, esp. those without capital and dependent on selling their labour. **b** esp. *derogatory* the lowest class of the community, esp. when considered as uncultured. **2** *Rom. Hist.* the lowest class of citizens. [French *prolétariat* (as PROLETARIAN)]

pro-life *adjective* in favour of preserving life, esp. in opposing abortion. □ **pro-lifer** *noun*

pro·lif·er·ate /prəˈlɪfəreit/ *verb* **1** *intransitive* **a** reproduce. **b** increase rapidly in numbers. **2** *transitive* produce (cells etc.) rapidly. □ **pro·lif·er·ation** *noun* **pro·lif·er·ative** /-rətɪv/ *adjective* **pro·lif·er·ator** *noun* [AS PROLIFEROUS]

pro·lif·er·ous /prəˈlɪfərəs/ *adjective* **1** (of a plant) producing many leaf or flower buds; growing luxuriantly. **2** growing or multiplying by budding. **3** spreading by proliferation. [Latin *proles* offspring + -FEROUS]

pro·lif·ic /prəˈlɪfɪk/ *adjective* **1** producing many offspring or much output. **2** abundantly productive. **3** (often foll. by *in*) abounding, copious. □ **pro·lif·ic·acy** *noun* **pro·lif·ic·al·ly** *adverb* [medieval Latin *prolificus* (as PROLIFEROUS)]

pro·line /ˈproːliːn, -lɪn/ *noun Biochem.* an amino acid with a cyclic molecule, present in many proteins, esp. collagen. [contraction of chemical name *pyrrolidine*-2-carboxylic acid]

pro·lix /ˈproːlɪks, prəˈlɪks/ *adjective* **1** (of speech, writing, etc.) lengthy; tedious. **2** (of a speaker, writer, etc.) verbose; long-winded. □ **pro·lix·ity** *noun* [Latin *prolixus* poured forth, extended (as PRO-¹, *liquēre* be liquid)]

pro·locu·tor /proːˈlɒkjʊtər/ *noun* a chairperson of a synod or committee in the Anglican Church. [Latin from *proloqui prolocut-* (as PRO-¹, *loqui* speak)]

PRO·LOG /ˈproːlɒg/ *noun* (also **Pro·log**) *Computing* a high-level programming language first devised for artificial intelligence applications. [*programming* (see PROGRAM) + LOGIC]

pro·logue /ˈproːlɒg/ *noun* **1 a** a preface or introduction to a literary or musical work, esp. an introductory speech or short poem addressed to the audience by one of the actors in a play (*compare* EPILOGUE 2). **b** the actor speaking the prologue. **2** a short preliminary time trial held before a cycling race to obtain a leader. **3** (usu. foll. by *to*) any act or event serving as an introduction. [Old French *prologue* from Latin *prologus* from Greek *prologos* (as PRO-², *logos* speech)]

pro·long *transitive verb* **1** extend (an action, condition, etc.) in time or space. **2** lengthen the pronunciation of (a syllable etc.). □ **pro·long·ation** *noun* /proːlɒŋˈɡeiʃən/ [Late Latin *prolongare* (as PRO-¹, *longus* long)]

pro·longed *adjective* lengthy; continuing for a long time (*a prolonged absence*).

prom *noun informal* **1** *N Amer.* a semi-formal or formal dance for high school or university students (often *attributive*: *prom dress*). **2** *Brit.* a promenade concert, esp. (**Prom**) any of those supported by the BBC. [abbreviation of PROMENADE]

prom·en·ade /ˌproməˈnad, -ˈnɒd, -ˈneid/ ● *noun* **1** a walk, or sometimes a ride or drive, taken esp. for display, leisure, etc. **2 a** esp. *Brit.* a paved public walk along the seafront at a resort. **b** any paved public walk. **3** *N Amer.* = PROM noun 1. **4** (in square dancing) a movement resembling a march made by couples in formation. ● *verb* **1** *intransitive* make a promenade. **2** *transitive* lead (a person etc.) about a place esp. for display. **3** *transitive* make a promenade through (a place). □ **prom·en·ad·er** *noun* [French from *se promener* walk, reflexive of *promener* take for a walk]

promenade concert *noun Brit.* a concert of usu. classical music at which all or part of the auditorium's floor space is without seating so that the audience stands or sits on the floor or can move about.

promenade deck *noun* an upper deck on a passenger ship where passengers may stroll.

pro·metha·zine /proʊˈmeθəˌziːn/ *noun* an antihistamine drug used to treat allergies, motion sickness, etc. [PROPYL + di*methyl*amine + *pheno*thi*azine*]

Pro·me·thean /prəˈmiːθɪən/ *adjective* **1** of or relating to Prometheus. **2** daring or inventive like Prometheus.

Pro·me·theus /prəˈmiːθɪəs/ *Gk Myth* a demigod, one of the Titans, who was worshipped by craftsmen. When Zeus hid fire away from man, Prometheus stole it by trickery and returned it to earth; as punishment, Zeus chained him to a rock where an eagle fed each day on his liver until he was rescued by Hercules.

pro·me·thium /prəˈmiːθɪəm/ *noun Chem.* a radioactive metallic element of the lanthanide series occurring in nuclear waste material. Symbol: **Pm**; at. no.: 61. [from PROMETHEUS]

prom·in·ence /ˈprɒmɪnəns/ *noun* **1** the state of being prominent. **2** a prominent thing, esp. a jutting outcrop, mountain, etc. **3** *Astronomy* a stream of incandescent gas projecting above the sun's chromosphere. [obsolete French from Latin *prominentia* jutting out (as PROMINENT)]

prom·in·ent /ˈprɒmɪnənt/ ● *adjective* **1** jutting out; projecting. **2** conspicuous. **3** distinguished; important. ● *noun* (in full **prominent moth**) a moth of the family Notodontidae, with tufted forewings and larvae with humped backs. □ **prom·in·ent·ly** *adverb* [Latin *prominēre* 'jut out': compare EMINENT]

pro·mis·cu·ous /prəˈmɪskjʊəs/ *adjective* **1 a** (of a person) having frequent and diverse sexual relationships, esp. transient ones. **b** (of sexual relationships) of this kind. **2** of mixed and indiscriminate composition or kinds; indiscriminate. □ **pro·mis·cu·ity** /-ˈskjuːɪti/ *noun* **pro·mis·cu·ous·ly** *adverb* **pro·mis·cu·ous·ness** *noun* [Latin *promiscuus* (as PRO-¹, *miscēre* mix)]

prom·ise ● *noun* **1** an assurance that one will or will not undertake a certain action, behaviour, etc. (*a promise of help; gave a promise to be generous*). **2** a sign or signs of future achievements, good results, etc. (*a writer of great promise*). ● *verb* **1** *transitive & intransitive* (usu. foll. by *to* + infin., or *that* + clause) make (a person) a promise, esp. to do, give, or procure (a thing) (*I promise you a fair hearing; they promise not to be late; promised that he would be there; cannot positively promise*). **2** *transitive* afford expectations of (*the discussions promise future problems; promises to be a good cook*). **3** *transitive informal* assure, confirm (*I promise you, it won't be easy*). **4** *transitive* (usu. in *passive*) *archaic* betroth (*she is promised to another*). □ **promise well** (or **ill** etc.) hold out good (or bad etc.) prospects. □ **prom·isee** *noun esp. Law.* **prom·iser** *noun* **prom·isor** *noun esp. Law.* [Latin *promissum* neuter past participle of *promittere* put forth, promise (as PRO-¹, *mittere* send)]

prom·ised land *noun* (prec. by *the*) **1** (**Promised Land**) *Bible* Canaan, the land promised to Abraham and his descendants by God (Gen. 12:7 etc.). **2 a** any place where happiness is expected, esp. heaven. **b** any coveted situation (*a promised land of economic freedom*).

prom·is·ing *adjective* likely to turn out well; hopeful; full of promise (*a promising start*). □ **prom·is·ing·ly** *adverb*

prom·is·sory /ˈprɒmɪsəri/ *adjective* **1** conveying or implying a promise. **2** (often foll. by *of*) full of promise. [medieval Latin *promissorius* from Latin *promissor* (as PROMISE)]

promissory note *noun esp. N Amer.* a signed document containing a written promise to pay a stated sum to a specified person or the bearer at a specified date or on demand.

promo *informal* ● *noun* (pl. **-mos**) **1** an advertising or publicity campaign for a particular product. **2 a** a trailer for a television program, theatrical production, etc. **b** *Brit.* a promotional video for a pop record. ● *adjective* of or relating to publicity for a performer, commercial product, etc.; promotional (*a short promo video*). [abbreviation]

prom·on·tory /ˈprɒmənˌtɔːri/ *noun* (pl. **-ies**) **1** a point of high land jutting out into the sea etc.; a headland. **2** *Anat.* a prominence or protuberance in the body. [medieval Latin *promontorium* alteration (influenced by *mons montis* mountain) from Latin *promunturium* (perhaps from PRO-¹, *mons*)]

pro·mote *transitive verb* **1** (often foll. by *to*) advance or raise (a person) to

a higher office, rank, etc. (*was promoted to captain*). **2** help forward; encourage; support actively (a cause, process, desired result, etc.) (*promoted women's rights; rest promotes recovery*). **3** publicize and sell (a product). **4** advance (a student) to the next grade. **5** *Chess* raise (a pawn) to the rank of queen etc. when it reaches the opponent's end of the board. □ **pro·mot·abil·ity** *noun* **pro·mot·able** *adjective*

pro·mo·tion *noun* **pro·mo·tion·al** *adjective* [Latin *promovēre promot-* (as PRO-¹, *movēre* 'move')]

pro·mot·er *noun* **1** a person who promotes. **2** a person who finances, organizes, etc. a sporting event, theatrical production, etc. **3** a person involved in setting up and funding a new company. **4** *Chem.* an additive that increases the activity of a catalyst. **5** *Genetics* a part of an operon, situated between the operator and the structural gene or genes at which transcription starts.

prompt ● *adjective* **1** (of a person) acting without delay (*we are always prompt in paying our bills*). **2** made, done, etc. readily or at once (*a prompt reply*). ● *transitive verb* **1** (usu. foll. by *to*, or *to* + infin.) incite; urge (*prompted them to action*). **2 a** supply a forgotten word, sentence, etc., to (an actor, reciter, etc.). **b** assist (a hesitating speaker) with a suggestion. **3** give rise to; inspire (a feeling, thought, action, etc.). ● *noun* **1 a** an act of prompting. **b** a thing said to help the memory of an actor etc. **2** *Computing* an indication or sign on a computer screen to show that the system is waiting for input. **3** the time limit for the payment of an account for goods purchased. □ **prompt·ing** *noun* **prompt·ly** *adverb* **prompt·ness** *noun* [Latin *promptus* past participle of *promere* prompt-produce (as PRO-¹, *emere* take)]

prompt book *noun* a copy of a play annotated with directions for a prompter's use.

prompt·er *noun* **1** *Theatre* a person seated out of sight of the audience who prompts the actors. **2** a person or thing that prompts.

prom·ul·gate /ˈprɒmʌlˌɡeɪt/ *transitive verb* **1** make known to the public; disseminate; promote (a cause etc.). **2** proclaim (a decree, news, etc.). □ **prom·ul·ga·tion** *noun* **prom·ul·ga·tor** *noun* [Latin *promulgare* (as PRO-¹, *mulgēre* milk, cause to come forth)]

pro·nate /ˈproʊneɪt/ *transitive verb* **1** put (the hand, forearm, etc.) into a prone position (with the palm etc. downwards). **2** (of a person) turn the foot outward so that the weight falls on the inner side of the foot. □ **pro·na·tion** *noun* **pro·na·tor** *noun* [back-formation from *pronation* (as PRONE)]

prone *adjective* **1 a** lying face downwards (compare SUPINE *adjective* 1). **b** lying flat; prostrate. **c** having the front part downwards, esp. the palm of the hand. **2** (usu. foll. by *to*, or *to* + infin.) disposed or liable, esp. to a bad action, condition, etc. (*is prone to depression*). **3** (usu. in *combination*) more than usually likely to suffer (*accident-prone*). **4** *archaic* with a downward slope or direction. □ **prone·ness** *noun* [Latin *pronus* from *pro* forwards]

prong ● *noun* each of two or more projecting pointed parts at the end of a fork etc. ● *transitive verb* pierce or stab with or as with a fork. [Middle English (also *prang*), perhaps related to Middle Low German *prange* pinching instrument]

pronged *adjective* **1** having a prong or prongs. **2** (in *combination*) having a specified number of points of attack, perspectives, etc. (*a three-pronged theory*).

prong·horn *noun* (also **pronghorn antelope**) a small, very swift deer-like ruminant, *Antilocapra americana*, inhabiting the plains of Western Canada and the northwestern US, the male of which has deciduous horns with forward-pointing prongs.

pro·nom·inal /proʊˈnɒmɪnəl/ *adjective* of, concerning, or being, a pronoun. [Late Latin *pronominalis* from Latin *pronomen* (as PRO-¹, *nomen*, *nominis* noun)]

pro·noun *noun* a word used instead of and to indicate a noun already mentioned or known, esp. to avoid repetition, e.g. *we, their, this, ourselves.* [PRO-¹, + NOUN, after French *pronom*, Latin *pronomen* (as PRO-¹, *nomen* name)]

pro·nounce *verb* **1** *transitive & intransitive* utter or speak (words, sounds, etc.), esp. in a certain way. **2** *transitive* **a** utter or deliver (a judgment, sentence, curse, etc.) formally or solemnly. **b** proclaim or announce officially (*I pronounce you man and wife*). **3** *transitive* state or declare, as being one's opinion (*the apples were pronounced excellent*). **4** *intransitive* (usu. foll. by *on, for, against, in favour of*) pass judgment; give one's opinion (*pronounced for the defendant*). □ **pro·nounce·abil·ity** *noun* **pro·nounce·able** *adjective* **pro·nounce·ment** *noun* [Old French *pronuncier* from Latin *pronuntiare* (as PRO-¹, *nuntiare* 'announce' from *nuntius* 'messenger')]

pro·nounced *adjective* **1** very noticeable; marked (*a pronounced limp*).

2 (of opinions etc.) strongly felt; definite (*has very pronounced views on art*). **3** (of a word, sound, etc.) uttered. □ **pro·noun·ced·ly** *adverb*

pronto *adverb informal* promptly, quickly. [Spanish from Latin (as PROMPT)]

pro·nun·cia·mento /prɔːˌnʌnsiəˈmentoː/ *noun* (*pl.* **-tos**) a pronouncement, proclamation, or manifesto, esp. a political one. [Spanish]

pro·nun·ci·a·tion /prəˌnʌnsiˈeiʃən/ *noun* **1** the way in which a word, language, etc. is pronounced, esp. with reference to a standard. **2** the act or an instance of pronouncing. **3** a person's way of pronouncing words etc. **4** a phonetic transcription of a word. [Old French *prononciation* or Latin *pronuntiatio* (as PRONOUNCE)]

pro·nuncio /proˈnʌnsio/ *noun* (*pl.* **-nuncios**) a papal ambassador to a country which does not accord the Pope's ambassador automatic precedence. [PRO-¹ + NUNCIO]

proof ● *noun* **1** facts, evidence, argument, etc. establishing or helping to establish a fact (*proof of their honesty; no proof that he was there*). **2** *Law* the spoken or written evidence in a trial. **3** a demonstration or act of proving (*not capable of proof; in proof of my assertion*). **4** a test or trial (*put them to the proof*). **5** the standard of strength of distilled alcoholic liquors, in which the strongest measure is 100%. **6** *Printing* a trial impression taken from type or film or produced electronically, used for making corrections before final printing. **7** the stages in the resolution of a mathematical or philosophical problem. **8** each of a limited number of impressions from an engraved plate before the ordinary issue is printed and usu. (in full **proof before letters**) before an inscription or signature is added. **9** a photographic print made for selection etc. **10** any of various preliminary impressions of coins struck as specimens. ● *adjective* **1** impervious to penetration, ill effects, etc. (*proof against the severest weather; his soul is proof against corruption*). **2** (in *combination*) able to withstand penetration, damage, or destruction by a specified agent (*soundproof; childproof*). **3** (of a distilled alcoholic liquor) of standard strength. **4** (of armour) of tried strength. ● *transitive verb* **1** make (something) proof, esp. make (fabric) waterproof. **2** make a proof of (a printed work, engraving, etc.). **3** proofread (printer's proofs, copy, etc.). **4** mix (yeast) with warm water or milk so that a bubbling action occurs. □ **the proof of the pudding is in the eating** (also **the proof is in the pudding**) the true value of something can be judged only from practical experience. [Old French *proeve* and Late Latin *proba* from Latin *probare* (see PROVE): the adjective and sometimes the verb formed apparently by ellipsis from the phrase *of proof* = proved to be impenetrable]

proof line *noun* Cdn (Ont.) BASELINE 5.

proof of purchase *noun* (*pl.* **proofs of purchase**) a sales receipt, label, box top, etc. associated with a product and which may be used as evidence that the product has been purchased.

proof positive *noun* absolutely certain proof.

proof·read *transitive verb* (*past* and *past participle* **-read**) read (printer's proofs, copy, etc.) and mark any errors. □ **proof·read·er** *noun* **proof·read·ing** *noun*

proof sheet *noun* a sheet of printer's proofs for examination and correction before final printing.

prop. *abbreviation* **1** proprietor. **2** proposition.

prop¹ ● *noun* **1** a rigid support, esp. one not an integral part of the thing supported. **2** a person who supplies support, assistance, comfort, etc. **3** (in full **prop forward**) *Rugby* a forward at either end of the front row of a scrum. ● *verb* (**propped, prop·ping**) **1** *transitive* (often foll. by *up*) support with or as if with a prop (*propped it up with a brick; an industry propped up by the government*). **2** *transitive* (often foll. by *against*, etc.) lean (something) against a support (*the bike was propped against the wall*). [prob. from Middle Dutch *proppe*: compare Middle Low German, Middle Dutch *proppen* (v.)]

prop² *noun* a movable object used on a theatre stage, in a film, etc. [abbreviation of PROPERTY]

prop³ *noun informal* a propeller. [abbreviation]

propa·ganda /ˌprɔpəˈɡandə/ *noun* **1 a** an organized program of publicity, selected information, etc., used to propagate a doctrine, practice, etc. **b** usu. *derogatory* the information, doctrines, etc., propagated in this way, esp. regarded as misleading or dishonest. **2** (**Propaganda**) *Catholicism* a committee of cardinals responsible for foreign missions. [Italian from modern Latin *congregatio de propaganda fide* congregation for propagation of the faith]

propa·gand·ist /prɔpəˈɡandɪst/ ● *noun* a member or agent of a propaganda organization; a person who spreads propaganda. ● *adjective* consisting of or spreading propaganda. □ **propa·gand·is·tic** *adjective*

propa·gand·is·tic·ally *adverb* **propa·gand·ize** *transitive & intransitive verb* (also esp. *Brit.* **-ise**).

propa·gate /ˈprɔpəˌɡeit/ *verb* **1 a** *transitive* breed specimens of (a plant, animal, etc.) by natural processes from the parent stock. **b** *reflexive & intransitive* (of a plant, animal, etc.) reproduce itself. **2** *transitive* disseminate; spread (a statement, belief, theory, etc.). **3** *transitive* hand down (a quality etc.) from one generation to another. **4 a** *transitive* extend the operation of; transmit (a vibration, earthquake, etc.). **b** *intransitive* be transmitted; travel. □ **propa·ga·tion** *noun*

propa·ga·tive *adjective* **propa·ga·tor** *noun* [Latin *propagare propagat-* multiply plants from layers, from *propago* (as PRO-¹, *pangere* fix, layer)]

pro·pane /ˈproːpein/ *noun* a gaseous hydrocarbon of the alkane series used as bottled fuel. Chem. formula: C_3H_8. [PROPIONIC ACID + -ANE²]

pro·pan·one /ˈproːpəˌnoːn/ *noun* Chem. = ACETONE. [PROPANE + -ONE]

pro·pel *transitive verb* (**pro·pelled, pro·pel·ling**) **1** drive or push forward. **2** urge on; encourage. [Latin *propellere* (as PRO-¹, *pellere puls-* drive)]

pro·pel·lant /prəˈpelənt/ ● *noun* **1** a thing that propels. **2** an inert compressed fluid in which the active contents of an aerosol are dispersed. **3** an explosive that fires bullets etc. from a firearm. **4** a substance used as a reagent in a rocket engine etc. to provide thrust. ● *adjective* = PROPELLENT.

pro·pel·lent /prəˈpelənt/ *adjective* propelling; capable of driving or pushing forward.

pro·pel·ler /prəˈpelər/ *noun* **1** a revolving shaft with blades, esp. for propelling a ship or aircraft. **2** a person or thing that propels.

pro·peller-head *noun slang* a computer geek; a nerd.

pro·pene /ˈproːpiːn/ *noun* Chem. = PROPYLENE. [PROPANE + ALKENE]

pro·pen·sity /prəˈpensɪti/ *noun* (*pl.* **-ties**) an inclination or tendency (*has a propensity for wandering*). [Latin *propensus* inclined, past participle of *propendēre* (as PRO-¹, *pendēre* hang)]

prop·er ● *adjective* **1 a** accurate, correct (*gave him the proper amount*). **b** fit, suitable, right (*at the proper time; do it the proper way*). **2** decent; respectable, esp. excessively so (*not quite proper*). **3** (usu. foll. by *to*) belonging or relating exclusively or distinctively (*with the respect proper to them*). **4** (usu. placed after noun) strictly so called; real; genuine (*this is the crypt, not the cathedral proper*). **5** esp. *Brit. informal* thorough; complete (*had a proper row about it*). **6** *Christianity* (of a psalm, lesson, prayer, etc.) appointed for a particular day, occasion, or season. **7** (usu. with possessive pronoun) *archaic* own (*with my proper eyes*). ● *adverb Brit. dialect or informal* **1** completely; very (*felt proper daft*). **2** (with reference to speech) in a genteel manner (*learn to talk proper*). ● *noun Christianity* the part of a service that varies with the season or feast. □ **prop·er·ness** *noun* [Old French *propre* from Latin *proprius* 'one's own, special']

proper fraction *noun* a fraction that is less than unity, with the numerator less than the denominator.

prop·er·ly *adverb* **1** fittingly; suitably (*do it properly*). **2** accurately; correctly (*properly speaking*). **3** rightly (*he very properly refused*). **4** with decency; respectably (*behave properly*). **5** esp. *Brit. informal* thoroughly (*they were properly ashamed*).

proper motion *noun Astronomy* the part of the apparent motion of a fixed star etc. that is due to its actual movement in space relative to the sun.

proper name *noun* (also **proper noun**) *Grammar* a name used for an individual person, place, animal, country, title, etc., and spelled with a capital letter, e.g. Jane, Whitehorse, Everest.

prop·er·tied *adjective* having property, esp. land.

prop·erty *noun* (*pl.* **-ties**) **1 a** something owned; a possession, either tangible, e.g. a house, land, etc., or intangible, e.g. patents, copyrights, etc. (*intellectual property*). **b** Law the right to possession, use, etc. **c** possessions collectively, esp. real estate (*has money in property*). **2** an attribute, quality, or characteristic (*medicinal properties*). **3** = PROP². **4** an artist, performer, athlete, or work regarded as a commercial asset, success, or sensation (*a hot property*). **5** *Logic* a quality common to a whole class but not necessary to distinguish it from others. □ **prop·erty·less** *adjective* [Old French *propriété* from Latin *proprietas -tatis* (as PROPER)]

property man *noun* see PROP MAN.

property manager *noun* a person whose job is to administer and oversee rental properties on behalf of a landlord.

property mistress *noun* see PROP MISTRESS.

property qualification *noun* a qualification for office, or for the exercise of a right, based on the possession of property.

property tax *noun* a tax based on the value of property owned by the taxpayer.

prop forward *noun* see PROP[1] *noun* 3.

pro·phase /'prəʊfeɪz/ *noun* Biol. the phase in cell division in which chromosomes contract and each becomes visible as two chromatids. [PRO-[2] + PHASE]

proph·ecy /'prɒfəsi/ *noun* (*pl.* **-ecies**) **1 a** a divinely inspired utterance. **b** a prediction of future events (*a prophecy of massive inflation*). **2** the faculty, function, or practice of prophesying (*the gift of prophecy*). [Old French *profecie* from Late Latin *prophetia* from Greek *prophēteia* (as PROPHET)]

proph·esy /'prɒfə,saɪ/ *verb* (**-esies**, **-esied**) **1** *transitive* (usu. foll. by *that*, *who*, etc.) foretell (an event etc.). **2** *intransitive* speak as a prophet; foretell future events. **3** *intransitive* archaic expound the Scriptures. □ **proph·esi·er** /-,saɪr/ *noun* [Old French *profecier* (as PROPHECY)]

proph·et *noun* **1 a** a teacher or interpreter of the supposed will of God. **b** one of the major or minor Hebrew prophets. **2 a** a person who foretells events. ● *noun* a person who advocates and speaks innovatively for a cause (*a prophet of the new order*). **3** (**the Prophet**) **a** Muhammad. **b** Joseph Smith, founder of the Mormons, or one of his successors. □ **prophet·ess** *noun* **prophet·hood** *noun* [Greek *prophētēs* 'spokesman' (as PRO-[2], *phētēs* 'speaker' from *phēmi* 'speak')]

proph·et·ic /prə'fetɪk/ *adjective* **1** (often foll. by *of*) containing a prediction. **2** of or concerning a prophet. □ **proph·et·ic·al** *adjective* **proph·et·ic·al·ly** *adverb*

pro·phyl·ac·tic /,prɒfə'laktɪk/ ● *adjective* **1** tending to prevent disease. **2** protective; precautionary. ● *noun* **1** a preventive medicine or course of action. **2** esp. *N Amer.* a condom. □ **pro·phyl·ac·tic·ally** *adverb* [French *prophylactique* from Greek *prophulaktikos* from *prophulassō* (as PRO-[2], *phulassō* guard)]

pro·phyl·ax·is /prɒfə'laksɪs/ *noun* preventive treatment against disease. [modern Latin, from PRO-[2] + Greek *phulaxis* 'act of guarding']

pro·pin·quity /prə'pɪŋkwɪti/ *noun* **1** nearness or place; proximity. **2** close kinship. [Latin *propinquitas* from *propinquus* near, from *prope* near to]

pro·pi·on·ic acid /prəʊpi'ɒnɪk/ *noun* a colourless sharp-smelling liquid carboxylic acid used for inhibiting the growth of mould in bread. Chem. formula: C_2H_5COOH. □ **pro·pi·on·ate** /'prəʊpiəneɪt/ *noun* [French *propionique* (as PRO-[2] + Greek *piōn* 'fat'), as being the first member of the fatty acid series to form fats]

pro·piti·ate /prə'pɪʃɪ,eɪt/ *transitive verb* appease (an offended person etc.). □ **pro·piti·ator** *noun* [Latin *propitiare* (as PROPITIOUS)]

pro·piti·a·tion /prə,pɪʃi'eɪʃən/ *noun* **1** appeasement. **2** Bible atonement, esp. Christ's.

pro·piti·a·tory /prə'pɪʃiətɔri/ *adjective* serving or intended to propitiate (*a propitiatory smile*).

pro·pi·tious /prə'pɪʃəs/ *adjective* **1** (of an omen etc.) favourable. **2** (often foll. by *for*, *to*) (of the weather, an occasion, etc.) suitable. **3** well-disposed (*the fates were propitious*). □ **pro·pi·tious·ly** *adverb* **pro·pi·tious·ness** *noun* [Latin *propitius* 'favourable']

prop-jet *noun* a turboprop.

prop man *noun* (in full **property man**) a man in charge of theatrical props.

prop mistress *noun* (in full **property mistress**) a woman in charge of theatrical props.

prop·olis /'prɒpəlɪs/ *noun* a red resinous substance collected from buds by bees, for use in constructing hives. [Latin from Greek *propolis* suburb, 'bee glue', from PRO-[2] + *polis* city]

pro·pon·ent /prə'pəʊnənt/ *noun* a person advocating a motion, theory, or proposal. [Latin *proponere* (as PROPOUND)]

Pro·pon·tis /prə'pɒntɪs/ the ancient name for the Sea of Marmara. See MARMARA, SEA OF.

pro·por·tion ● *noun* **1 a** a comparative part or share (*a large proportion of the profits*). **b** a comparative ratio (*the proportion of births to deaths*). **2** (usu. in *pl.*) a correct or ideal relationship in size, degree, etc. between one thing and another, or between the parts of a whole (*a milkshake consisting of milk and ice cream in the right proportions*). **3** (in *pl.*) dimensions; size (*large proportions*). **4** Math. **a** an equality of ratios between two pairs of quantities, e.g. 3:5 and 9:15. **b** a set of such quantities. See also DIRECT PROPORTION, INVERSE PROPORTION. ● *transitive verb* adjust or regulate in proportion to something, make (a thing) proportionate. □ **in proportion 1** by the same factor. **2** without exaggerating (importance etc.) (*must get the facts in proportion*). **out of (all) proportion 1** badly proportioned. **2** exaggerated, overemphasized. **3** (often foll. by *to*, *with*) disproportionate. □ **pro·por·tioned** *adjective* (also in *combination*). [Old French *proportion* or Latin *proportio* (as PRO-[1], PORTION)]

pro·por·tion·al *adjective* in due proportion; comparable (*a proportional increase in the expense; resentment proportional to his injuries*). □ **pro·por·tion·al·ity** *noun* **pro·por·tion·al·ly** *adverb*

proportional representation *noun* an electoral system in which all parties gain seats in proportion to the number of votes cast for them (see also FIRST PAST THE POST 2). Abbr.: **PR**.

pro·por·tion·ate *adjective* = PROPORTIONAL. □ **pro·por·tion·ate·ly** *adverb*

pro·pos·al *noun* **1 a** the act or an instance of proposing something. **b** a course of action etc. so proposed (*the proposal was never carried out*). **c** a written document outlining a proposed undertaking. **2** an offer of marriage.

pro·pose *verb* **1** *transitive & intransitive* put forward for consideration or as a plan. **2** *transitive* (usu. foll. by *to* + infin., or verbal noun) intend; purpose (*propose to open a restaurant*). **3** *transitive* make an offer of marriage, ask a person to marry one (*I proposed to Emma on one knee; she proposed last night*). **4** *transitive* nominate (a person) as a member of a society, for an office, etc. **5** *transitive* offer (a person's health, a person, etc.) as a subject for a toast. □ **pro·pos·er** *noun* [Old French *proposer* from Latin *proponere* (as PROPOUND)]

pro·posed *adjective* suggested; put forward for consideration (*the proposed site for the new arena*).

prop·os·ition /,prɒpə'zɪʃən/ ● *noun* **1** a plan proposed; a proposal. **2 a** an offer of terms for a business transaction. **b** an enterprise or undertaking esp. with regards to its financial success (*the small mining company ceased to be a profitable proposition*). **3** a statement or assertion. **4** Logic a statement consisting of subject and predicate that is subject to proof or disproof. **5** a problem, opponent, prospect, etc. that is to be dealt with (*a difficult proposition*). **6** Math. a formal statement of a theorem or problem, often including the demonstration. **7** informal a proposal to have sexual relations, esp. one made bluntly or offensively. ● *transitive verb* informal make a proposal (esp. of sexual relations) to (*he propositioned her*). □ **prop·os·ition·al** *adjective* [Old French *proposition* or Latin *propositio* (as PROPOUND)]

pro·pound *transitive verb* **1** offer for consideration; propose. **2** Cdn & Brit. Law produce (a will etc.) before the proper authority so as to establish its legality. □ **pro·pound·er** *noun* [earlier *propoune*, *propone* from Latin *proponere* (as PRO-[1], *ponere posit-* place): compare *compound*, *expound*]

pro·pran·ol·ol /prəʊ'pranəlɒl/ *noun* a beta blocker, $C_{16}H_{21}NO_2$, used mainly in the treatment of cardiac arrhythmia. [PROPYL + *propanol* (PROPANE + -OL[1]) with reduplication of -ol]

pro·pri·etary /prəʊ'praɪəteri, prə-, -təri/ *adjective* **1 a** (of a name) owned and used for a particular product only by a particular company. **b** (of goods) manufactured and sold by a particular firm (*proprietary medicines*). **2** of or relating to an owner or ownership (*proprietary rights*). **3** of, holding, or concerning property. [Late Latin *proprietarius* (as PROPERTY)]

pro·pri·etor /prə'praɪətər/ *noun* **1** the owner of a business. **2** a holder of property. □ **pro·pri·etor·ial** /-'tɔriəl/ *adjective* **pro·pri·etor·ial·ly** *adverb* **pro·pri·etor·ship** *noun*

pro·pri·etress /prə'praɪətrəs/ *noun* **1** a woman who owns a business. **2** a woman who is the holder of property.

pro·pri·ety /prə'praɪɪti/ *noun* (*pl.* **-eties**) **1** (often foll. by *of*) suitableness; rightness (*doubt the propriety of refusing them*). **2** correctness of behaviour or morals (*highest standards of propriety*). **3** (in *pl.*) the details or rules of correct conduct (*must observe the proprieties*). [Middle English, = ownership, peculiarity, from Old French *propriete* PROPERTY]

pro·prio·cep·tive /,prəʊpriə'septɪv/ *adjective* relating to stimuli produced and perceived within an organism, esp. relating to the position and movement of the body. □ **pro·prio·cep·tion** *noun* **pro·prio·cep·tor** *noun* [Latin *proprius* own + RECEPTIVE]

props *plural noun* informal expressions of praise and respect. [shortening of 'proper respect']

pro·pul·sion /prə'pʌlʃən/ *noun* **1** the act or an instance of driving or pushing forward. **2** an impelling influence. □ **pro·pul·sive** *adjective* [medieval Latin *propulsio* from Latin *propellere* (as PROPEL)]

prop wash *noun* a current of water or air created by the action of a propeller or rotor.

pro·pyl /'prəʊpəl/ *noun* Chem. either of two isomeric radicals, C_3H_7, derived from propane. [PROPIONIC (ACID) + -YL]

pro·py·laeum /,prɒpɪ'liːəm/ *noun* (also **pro·py·laea** *plural noun*) a monumental gate or entranceway to a temple, esp. (**the Propylaeum**) the entrance to the Acropolis at Athens. [Latin from Greek *propulaion* (as PRO-[2], *pulē* gate)]

pro·pyl·ene /ˈproːpəˌliːn/ *noun* *Chem.* a gaseous hydrocarbon of the alkene series used in the manufacture of chemicals. Chem. formula: C_3H_6.

propylene glycol *noun* either of two isomeric liquid alcohols, esp. one which is used as a solvent, in antifreeze, and in the food, plastics, and perfume industries.

pro·pyne /ˈproːpain/ *noun* a gaseous alkyne, methyl acetylene. [*propyl* + -YNE]

pro rata /proː ˈrɑːtə/ ● *adjective* proportional. ● *adverb* proportionally. [Latin, = according to the rate]

pro-rate *transitive verb* esp. *N Amer.* (usu. in *passive*) calculate or distribute proportionally (*pension pro-rated to years of service*). □ **pro-rated** *adjective* **pro-ration** *noun* [PRO RATA]

pro·rogue /prəˈroːg/ *verb* (**pro·rogues**, **pro·rogued**, **pro·roguing**) **1** *transitive* discontinue the meetings of (a parliament etc.) without dissolving it. **2** *intransitive* (of a parliament etc.) be prorogued. □ **pro·ro·ga·tion** /-rəˈgeiʃən/ *noun* [Old French *proroger*, *-guer* from Latin *prorogare* prolong (as PRO-[1], *rogare* ask)]

pros- /prɒs/ *prefix* **1** to, towards. **2** in addition. [Greek from *pros* (prep.)]

pro·saic /prəˈzeiːk, proː-/ *adjective* **1** like prose, lacking poetic beauty. **2** unromantic; dull; commonplace (*took a prosaic view of life*). □ **pro·saic·ally** *adverb*

pro·scen·ium /prəˈsiːniəm, proː-/ *noun* (*pl.* **pro·scen·iums** or **pro·scenia** /-niə/) **1** (also **proscenium arch**) an arch that forms a frame at the front of a stage. **2** the part of the stage in front of the drop or curtain, usu. with the enclosing arch. **3** *Gk & Rom. Hist.* the stage of an ancient theatre. [Latin from Greek *proskēnion* (as PRO-[2], *skēnē* stage)]

pro·sciut·to /prəˈʃuːtoː/ *noun* Italian cured ham, usu. served raw and thinly sliced as an hors d'oeuvre. [Italian = ham]

pro·scribe /prəˈskraib/ *transitive verb* **1** reject or denounce (a practice etc.) as dangerous etc. **2** banish, exile (*proscribed from the club*). **3** put (a person) outside the protection of the law. □ **pro·scrip·tion** *noun* **pro·scrip·tive** *adjective* [Latin *proscribere* (as PRO-[1], *scribere* script- write)]

prose ● *noun* **1** the ordinary form of the written or spoken language (*compare* POETRY 1, VERSE) (*Milton's prose works*). **2** a passage of prose, esp. for translation into a foreign language. **3 a** dull or commonplace speech, writing, etc. **b** an instance of this. **4** = SEQUENCE 8. ● *intransitive verb* (usu. foll. by *about*) talk tediously. [Old French from Latin *prosa* (*oratio*) straightforward (discourse), fem. of *prosus*, earlier *prorsus* direct]

Prosecco /proːˈsekoː/ *noun* a fizzy white wine from northeastern Italy. [Italian]

pros·ecute /ˈprɒsəˌkjuːt/ *verb* **1** *transitive & intransitive* **a** institute legal proceedings against (a person). **b** institute a prosecution with reference to (a claim, crime, etc.). **2** *transitive & intransitive* (of a lawyer) represent a person or an organization that prosecutes. **3** *transitive* follow up, pursue (an inquiry, studies, etc.). **4** *transitive* carry on (a war, pursuit, etc.). □ **pros·ecut·able** *adjective* [Latin *prosequi prosecut-* (as PRO-[1], *sequi* follow)]

pros·ecu·tion /ˌprɒsəˈkjuːʃən/ *noun* **1 a** the institution and carrying on of a criminal charge in a court. **b** the carrying on of legal proceedings against a person. **c** the prosecuting party in a court case (*the prosecution denied this*). **2** the action of carrying out or the process of being occupied with something (*the prosecution of war*).

pros·ecu·tor /ˈprɒsəˌkjuːtər/ *noun* a person who prosecutes, esp. in a criminal court. □ **pros·ecu·tor·ial** /-ˈtɔriəl/ *adjective*

pros·elyte /ˈprɒsəˌlait/ *noun* a person converted, esp. recently, from one opinion, creed, party, etc., to another. □ **pros·elyt·ism** /-ləˌtizəm/ *noun* [Late Latin *proselytus* from Greek *prosēluthos* stranger, convert (as PROS-, stem *eluth-* of *erkhomai* come)]

pros·elyt·ize /ˈprɒsələˌtaiz/ *transitive & intransitive verb* (also esp. *Brit.* **-ise**) **1** attempt to persuade others to adopt one's own belief, esp. in religion (*Islamic missionaries proselytizing in Christian countries*). **2** champion or promote a cause or opinion (*she proselytized her cause*; *he proselytizes for safe sex and committed relationships*). □ **pros·elyt·iz·a·tion** *noun* **pros·elyt·iz·er** *noun*

pros·en·chyma /prɒˈseŋkimə/ *noun* a plant tissue of elongated cells with interpenetrating tapering ends, occurring esp. in vascular tissue. □ **pros·en·chym·al** *adjective* **pros·en·chyma·tous** /-ˈkimətəs/ *adjective* [Greek *pros* toward + *egkhuma* infusion, after *parenchyma*]

prose poem *noun* a piece of imaginative poetic writing in prose.

Pros·er·pine /prəˈsɜrpini/ (also **Pros·er·pina** /prəˈsɜrpinə/) *Rom. Myth* the Roman name for Persephone.

pro shop *noun* *N Amer.* a store run by a golf or tennis club, ski resort etc. and often supervised by a resident professional or coach, where sports equipment may be bought or rented.

pros·ify /ˈproːziˌfai/ *transitive verb* (**-fies**, **-fied**) turn into prose.

pro·sim·ian /proːˈsimiən/ ● *noun* a primitive primate of the suborder *Prosimii*, which includes lemurs, lorises, galagos, and tarsiers. ● *adjective* of or relating to this suborder. [PRO-[2] + SIMIAN]

pro·sit /ˈproːzit/ *interjection* an expression used in drinking a person's health etc. [German from Latin, = may it benefit]

pros·ody /ˈprɒzədi, ˈprɒsədi/ *noun* **1** the systematic study of versification, covering the principles of metre, rhythm, rhyme, and stanza forms. **2** patterns of stress and intonation in ordinary speech. □ **pros·od·ic** /prəˈsɒdik/ *adjective* **pros·od·ic·ally** *adverb* **pros·od·ist** *noun* [Latin *prosodia* accent, from Greek *prosōidia* (as PROS-, ODE)]

proso·pog·raphy /ˌprɒsəˈpɒgrəfi, ˌprɒsoː-/ *noun* (*pl.* **-ies**) **1** a description of a person's appearance, personality, social and family connections, career, etc. **2** the study of such descriptions, esp. in Roman history. □ **proso·pog·raph·er** *noun* **proso·po·graph·ic** /-pəˈgrafik/ *adjective* **proso·po·graph·ic·al** /-pəˈgrafikəl/ *adjective* [modern Latin *prosopographia* from Greek *prosōpon* face, person]

proso·po·poeia /ˌprɒsəpəˈpiːə/ *noun* (also **proso·po·peia**) **1** a figure of speech in which an imaginary or absent person is represented as speaking or acting; the introduction of a pretended speaker. **2** a figure of speech in which an inanimate or abstract thing is personified or given human characteristics. [Latin from Greek *prosōpopoiia* from *prosōpon* person + *poieō* make]

pros·pect ● *noun* **1 a** the chance or hope that something will happen (*there is little prospect of an immediate settlement*). **b** (often in *pl.*) the chances of being successful (*her prospects for a new job were good*). **c** a vision or idea of the future (*she dreaded the prospect of her dentist's appointment*). **2 a** something viewed in terms of its profitability (*a good prospect for investment*). **b** a candidate or competitor who is likely to be successful (*the Canucks' best prospect is a defenceman drafted from Saskatoon*). **3** a possible or probable customer, subscriber, etc. **4** an extensive view of landscape. **5 a** a place likely to yield mineral deposits. **b** an excavation made in search of minerals. **c** a sample of ore for testing. **d** the resulting yield. ● *verb* **1** *transitive* (usu. foll. by *for*) explore a region for minerals. **2** *transitive* **a** explore (a region) for minerals (*Ray and Eric prospected the woods for outcroppings of calcite*). **b** work (a mine) experimentally. **c** (of a mine) promise (a specified yield). **3** *intransitive* (often foll. by *for*) search around, look out for something (*prospecting for customers*). □ **pros·pect·ing** *noun* **pros·pect·or** *noun* [Latin *prospectus*: see PROSPECTUS]

pro·spect·ive *attributive adjective* **1** expected; potential (*prospective buyer*). **2** concerned with or applying to the future (*prospective analysis*) (*compare* RETROSPECTIVE 1). □ **pro·spect·ive·ly** *adverb* [obsolete French *prospectif -ive* or Late Latin *prospectivus* (as PROSPECTUS)]

pro·spec·tus *noun* **1** a printed document advertising or describing a commercial enterprise etc., esp. to attract investors. **2** a brochure or pamphlet detailing the courses, facilities etc. of an educational institution. [Latin, = prospect, from *prospicere* (as PRO-[1], *specere* look)]

pros·per *verb* **1** *intransitive* succeed; thrive. **2** *transitive* make successful (*Heaven prosper him*). [Old French *prosperer* or Latin *prosperare*, from *prosperus* 'doing well']

pros·per·ity /prɒˈsperiti/ *noun* the state of being prosperous; wealth or success.

pros·per·ous *adjective* **1** successful; rich (*a prosperous entrepreneur*). **2** flourishing; thriving (*a prosperous enterprise*). □ **pros·per·ous·ly** *adverb*

Prost /proːst/ **Alain** (b.1955), French racing driver. He was the first French driver to win the Formula One world championship (1985), winning again in 1986, 1989, and 1993.

pros·ta·cy·clin /ˌprɒstəˈsaiklin/ *noun* a compound of the prostaglandin type that is produced in arterial walls and that functions as an anticoagulant and vasodilator. [from PROSTAGLANDIN + CYCLIC + -IN]

pros·ta·glan·din /ˌprɒstəˈglandin/ *noun* any of a group of hormone-like substances that cause muscle contraction and which may be used to induce labour. [German from PROSTATE + GLAND[1] + -IN]

pros·tate /ˈprɒsteit/ *noun* (in full **prostate gland**) a gland surrounding the neck of the bladder in male mammals and releasing a fluid forming part of the semen. □ **pros·tat·ic** /-ˈstatik/ *adjective* [French from modern Latin *prostata* from Greek *prostatēs* one that stands before (as PRO-[2], *statos* standing)]

pros·ta·tec·tomy /ˌprɒstəˈtektəmi/ *noun* surgical removal of all or part of the prostate.

Consonants: b *but* d *dog* f *few* g *get* h *her* j *yes* k *cat* l *leg* m *man* n *no* p *pen* r *red* s *sit*

pros·thesis /prɒsˈθiːsɪs/ *noun* (*pl.* **pros·theses** /-ˌsiːz/) an artificial part supplied to remedy a deficiency, e.g. a false breast, leg, tooth, etc. □ **pros·thet·ic** /-ˈθetɪk/ *adjective* [Late Latin from Greek *prosthesis* from *prostithēmi* (as PROS-, *tithēmi* place)]

pros·thet·ics /prɒsˈθetɪks/ *plural noun* (usu. treated as *sing.*) the branch of surgery that deals with the replacement of defective or missing parts of the body by artificial substitutes.

pros·tho·don·tics *noun* the branch of dentistry concerned with the design, manufacture, and fitting of artificial replacements for teeth and other parts of the mouth. □ **pros·tho·don·tist** *noun* [from PROSTHESIS, on the pattern of ORTHODONTICS]

pros·ti·tute /ˈprɒstɪˌtuːt, -ˌtjuːt/ ● *noun* **1 a** a woman or girl who engages in sexual activity for payment. **b** a man or boy who engages in sexual activity, esp. with men, for payment. **2** a person who misuses his or her talents or skills esp. for money. ● *transitive verb & reflexive* **1** use one's abilities etc. wrongly or in a way that is not worthy of them, esp. in order to earn money. **2** make a prostitute of (esp. oneself). □ **pros·ti·tu·tion** *noun* [Latin *prostituere prostitut-* offer for sale (as PRO-¹, *statuere* set up, place)]

pros·trate ● *adjective* /ˈprɒstreɪt/ **1 a** lying face downwards. **b** lying horizontally. **2** overcome, esp. by grief, exhaustion, etc. (*prostrate with self-pity*). **3** *Bot.* growing along the ground. ● *transitive verb* /prɒˈstreɪt, prə-/ **1** lay (a person etc.) flat on the ground. **2** (*reflexive*) throw (oneself) down in submission etc. **3** (of fatigue, illness, etc.) overcome; reduce to extreme physical weakness. □ **pros·tra·tion** /prɒˈstreɪʃən, prə-/ *noun* [Latin *prostratus* past participle of *prosternere* (as PRO-¹, *sternere strat-* lay flat)]

pro·style /ˈprəʊstaɪl/ ● *noun* a free-standing portico, esp. of a classical temple, with columns in the front. ● *adjective* (of a building) having such a portico. [Latin *prostylos* having pillars in front (as PRO-², STYLE)]

pro·sum·er *noun* **1** a person who buys electronic goods that are of a standard between those aimed at consumers and professionals. **2** a consumer who purchases component elements of products in order to build or administer his or her own goods and services. [PROFESSIONAL or PRODUCER + CONSUMER]

prosy *adjective* (**pros·i·er**, **pros·i·est**) **1** resembling or characteristic of prose. **2** tedious; commonplace; dull (*a prosy lecture*). □ **pros·i·ly** *adverb* **pros·i·ness** *noun*

Prot. *abbreviation* Protestant.

pro·tac·tin·ium /ˌprəʊtakˈtɪnɪəm/ *noun* a radioactive metallic element whose chief isotope yields actinium by decay. Symbol: **Pa**; at. no.: 91. [German (as PROTO-, ACTINIUM)]

pro·tag·on·ist /prəʊˈtaɡənɪst/ *noun* **1** the principal character in a work of fiction, film, drama, etc. **2** (often in *pl.*) the most prominent or most important individual in a situation or course of events. **3** a leading or respected supporter of a cause, movement, etc. (*a protagonist of women's rights*). [Greek *prōtagōnistēs* (as PROTO-, *agōnistēs* actor)]

Pro·tag·or·as /prəʊˈtaɡəˌrəs/ (*c.*485–*c.*410 BC), Greek philosopher, who was one of the earliest and most famous of the Sophists; he taught the doctrine of the relativity of all knowledge, summed up in the dictum usually rendered as 'man is the measure of all things'.

prot·amine /ˈprəʊtəˌmiːn/ *noun* any of a class of simple proteins found combined with nucleic acids (esp. in fish sperm) that may be combined with insulin to slow its absorption. [PROTO- + AMINE]

prot·asis /ˈprɒtəsɪs/ *noun* (*pl.* **prot·ases** /-ˌsiːz/) the clause expressing the condition in a conditional sentence, e.g. *If you asked my opinion* in *If you asked my opinion, I would agree.* □ **pro·tat·ic** /-ˈtatɪk/ *adjective* [Latin, from Greek *protasis* proposition (as PRO-, *teinō* stretch)]

pro·tea /ˈprəʊtɪə/ *noun* any shrub of the genus *Protea* native to southern Africa, with cone-like flower heads. [modern Latin from PROTEUS, with reference to the many species]

pro·tean /ˈprəʊtɪən, -ˈtiːən/ *adjective* **1** variable, taking many forms. **2** (of an artist, writer, etc.) versatile. [after *Proteus*: see PROTEUS]

pro·te·ase /ˈprəʊtɪˌeɪs, -ˌeɪz/ *noun* an enzyme that breaks down proteins and peptides. [PROTEIN + -ASE]

protease inhibitor *noun* a substance that breaks down protease, thereby inhibiting the replication of certain cells and viruses, including HIV.

pro·tect *verb* **1** *transitive* keep (a person or thing) safe from harm, injury, etc.; defend (*goggles protected her eyes from dust; guards protected the prime minister*). **2** *transitive* **a** attempt to preserve (a threatened plant or animal species) by legislating against hunting, collecting, etc. **b** restrict by law access to or development of (land) in order to preserve its wildlife or its undisturbed state. **3** *transitive Computing* restrict access (to a file, disk, etc.) to a specified user or users. **4** *transitive* shield (domestic industry) from competition by imposing import duties on foreign goods. **5** *intransitive* (usu. foll. by *against*) keep a person, thing, etc. safe from something (*this vaccine protects against several diseases*). □ **pro·tect·ed** *adjective* [Latin *protegere protect-* (as PRO-¹, *tegere* cover)]

pro·tect·ant *noun* a substance that provides protection, e.g. against ultraviolet radiation, rust, frost, etc.

protected area *noun* an area of land or sea especially dedicated to the protection and maintenance of biological diversity, and of natural and associated cultural resources.

protected list *noun* N Amer. a list of players whose rights are owned by a professional hockey, baseball, or football team, etc. who may not play for another team in the same league.

pro·tec·tion *noun* **1 a** the act or an instance of protecting, or the state of being protected (*provides protection against the sun*). **b** a means of protecting against something (*it is not wise to engage in sexual activity without protection; she bought a gun for protection*). **2** = PROTECTIONISM. **3 a** (in full **protection money**) money extorted by racketeers in exchange for a guarantee against threatened violence. **b** freedom from violence thus obtained. **4** insurance coverage (*she purchased health protection before she took her trip*).

pro·tec·tion·ism *noun Econ.* the theory or practice of protecting domestic industries. □ **pro·tec·tion·ist** *noun & adjective*

pro·tect·ive *adjective* **1** protecting; intended to protect (*protective equipment*). **2** (esp. of a person) having or showing the tendency to protect a person or thing (*a protective mother; protective of their culture*). **3** *Economics* of or relating to the protection of domestic industries from foreign competition (*protective tariffs*). □ **pro·tect·ive·ly** *adverb* **pro·tect·ive·ness** *noun*

protective colouring *noun* colouring disguising or camouflaging a plant or animal.

protective custody *noun* the detention of a person for his or her own protection.

pro·tect·or *noun* **1** a person who protects. **2** (often in *combination*) a thing or device that protects (*surge protector*). **3** *Brit. hist.* a regent in charge of a kingdom during the minority, absence, etc. of the sovereign. **4** (**Protector**) (in full **Lord Protector of the Commonwealth**) *Brit. hist.* the title of Oliver Cromwell 1653–58 and his son Richard Cromwell 1658–59. □ **pro·tec·tress** *noun*

pro·tect·or·ate /prəˈtektərət/ *noun* **1 a** a territory that is controlled and protected by a larger state. **b** such a relation of one state to another. **2** *hist.* **a** the office of the protector of a kingdom or country. **b** the period of this, (esp. **Protectorate**) in England under the Cromwells 1653–59. Oliver Cromwell was appointed Lord Protector in December 1653 at the behest of the army, and retained the position until his death in September 1658; his son Richard proved incapable of holding the regime together, and its subsequent collapse led to the restoration of Charles II.

pro·te·ge /ˈprəʊtəˌʒeɪ, ˈprɒt-/ *noun* (also **pro·te·gé**) a person whose welfare and career are looked after by an influential person, esp. over a long period. [French, past participle of *protéger* from Latin *protegere* PROTECT]

pro·tein *noun* **1** any of a group of organic compounds composed of one or more chains of amino acids and forming an essential part of all living organisms. **2** such substances collectively, esp. as a dietary component. [French *protéine*, German *Protein* from Greek *prōteios* primary]

pro·tein·aceous /ˌprəʊtəˈneɪʃəs/ *adjective* of the nature of or consisting of protein.

pro·tein·oid /ˈprəʊtənɔɪd/ *noun Biochem.* a polypeptide or mixture of polypeptides obtained by heating a mixture of amino acids.

pro tem *adjective & adverb* for the time being; temporarily. [abbreviation]

pro tem·pore /prəʊ ˈtempəri/ *adjective & adverb* = PRO TEM. [Latin]

pro·te·oly·sis /ˌprəʊtiˈɒlɪsɪs/ *noun* the splitting of proteins or peptides by the action of enzymes esp. during the process of digestion. □ **pro·te·o·lytic** /-ˈlɪtɪk/ *adjective* [modern Latin from PROTEIN + -LYSIS]

pro·te·om·ics /ˌprəʊtiˈɒmɪks/ *noun* the branch of molecular biology concerned with the behaviour and interaction of proteins within cells.

Pro·tero·zoic /ˌprɒtərəʊˈzəʊɪk/ *Geol.* ● *adjective* of or relating to the later part of the Precambrian era, from about 2.5 billion to 570 million years ago, characterized by the appearance of life. ● *noun* this time. [Greek *proteros* former + *zōē* life, *zōos* living]

pro·test ● *noun* **1** a statement of dissent, disapproval, or complaint; a remonstrance (*she signed the protest condemning the sale of toy guns*). **2** (often *attributive*) a usu. public demonstration of objection to

---

t *top*   v *voice*   w *we*   z *zoo*   ʃ *she*   ʒ *vision*   θ *thin*   ð *this*   ŋ *ring*   x *loch*   tʃ *chip*   dʒ *jar*   (*see over for vowels*)

government etc. policy (*marched in protest*; *protest demonstration*). **3** *Law* a written declaration that a bill has been presented and payment or acceptance refused. ● *verb* **1 a** *intransitive* (usu. foll. by *against*, *at*, *about*, etc.) make a protest against an action, proposal, etc. ¶ Although some have disputed "protest against" as redundant, this structure is long established, especially in British English, and unobjectionable. **b** *transitive* *N Amer.* object to (*he protested their decision*). **c** (usu.) *transitive & intransitive* maintain a difference of opinion, stubbornly disagree ('*I am not too tired,*' *she protested.*). **2** (usu.) *transitive* (often foll. by *that* + clause) affirm (one's innocence etc.) solemnly, esp. in reply to an accusation etc. **3** *transitive* *Law* write or obtain a protest in regard to (a bill). □ **protest too much** protest one's innocence so vociferously as to arouse suspicions of one's guilt. **under protest** unwillingly. □ **pro·test·ing·ly** *adverb* [Latin *protestari* (as PRO-¹, *testari* assert from *testis* witness)]

Prot·est·ant /ˈprɒtəstənt/ (also **protestant**) ● *noun* **1** a member or follower of any of the western Christian Churches that are separate from the Roman Catholic Church in accordance with the principles of the Reformation. **2** (**protestant**) /ˈprɒtəstənt, prəˈtestənt/ a protesting person. ● *adjective* **1** of or relating to any of the Protestant Churches or their members etc. **2** (**protestant**) (also /prəˈtestənt/) protesting. □ **Prot·est·ant·ism** *noun* [modern Latin *protestans*, part. of Latin *protestari* (see PROTEST)]

Protestant Reformation *noun see* REFORMATION 2.

Protestant work ethic *noun* (also **Protestant ethic**) hard work seen as a Christian duty and responsibility and as morally beneficial and character-building, esp. as perceived to be exemplified by Calvinists.

pro·tes·ta·tion /ˌprɒtəˈsteɪʃən, ˌprəʊ-/ *noun* **1** a strong affirmation. **2** an objection.

pro·test·er *noun* (also **protestor**) a person who participates in a protest.

protest vote *noun* a vote for a party or candidate representing a protest against the actions or policies of another party or candidate.

Pro·teus /ˈprəʊtiəs/ *Gk Myth* a minor sea god who had the power of prophecy but who would assume different shapes to avoid answering questions; his name is sometimes used to mean a changing or inconstant person or thing. **2** *Astronomy* a satellite of Neptune, the sixth closest to the planet; diameter 400 km.

pro·teus /ˈprəʊtiəs, -tjuːs/ *noun* any bacterium of the genus *Proteus*, usu. found in the intestines and feces. [PROTEUS]

pro·tha·la·mium /ˌprɒθəˈleɪmiəm/ *noun* (also **pro·tha·la·mion** /-miən/) (*pl.* **pro·tha·la·mia** /-miə/) a song or poem to celebrate a forthcoming wedding. [title of a poem by Spenser, after *epithalamium*]

pro·thal·lus /prəʊˈθaləs/ *noun* (*pl.* **pro·thalli** /-laɪ/) *Bot.* the gametophyte of certain plants, esp. a fern. [modern Latin from PRO-² + Greek *thallos* green shoot]

pro·tho·no·tary /ˌprəʊθəˈnəʊtəri, prəˈθɒnəˌtəri/ *noun* (also **pro·to·no·tary** /ˌprəʊt-, prəˈtɒnə-/) (*pl.* **-ies**) **1** a chief clerk in some law courts. **2** a member of the college of prelates who register papal acts, direct the canonization of saints, etc. [medieval Latin *protonotarius* from late Greek *protonotarios* (as PROTO-, NOTARY)]

prothonotary warbler *noun* a N American wood warbler, *Protonotarius citrea*, with a deep yellow head and breast, green back, and blue-grey wings. [from its resemblance, in colour, to the robes traditionally worn by prothonotaries]

pro·tist /ˈprəʊtɪst/ *noun* any usu. unicellular organism of the kingdom Protista regarded as intermediate between or distinct from animals and plants, including bacteria, fungi, algae, and protozoa. □ **pro·tist·ol·ogy** *noun* [modern Latin *Protista* from Greek *prōtista* neuter pl. superlative from *prōtos* first]

pro·tium /ˈprəʊtiəm/ *noun* the ordinary isotope of hydrogen (*compare* DEUTERIUM, TRITIUM). [modern Latin from PROTO- + -IUM]

proto- *combining form* **1** first in time, earliest, original; at an early or preceding stage of development (*protostar*). **2** designating or pertaining to the earliest attested or hypothetically-reconstructed form of a language or language family (*Proto-Algonquian*). **3** first in rank or importance. **4 a** (esp. in science) first in position, anterior. **b** *Biochem.* forming names of precursors or parent compounds, structures, etc. (*protochlorophyll*). [Greek *prōto-* from *prōtos* first]

pro·to·col /ˈprəʊtəˌkɒl/ *noun* **1 a** official, esp. diplomatic, formality and etiquette observed on state occasions etc. **b** the rules, formalities, etc. of any procedure, group, etc. **2** the original draft of a diplomatic document, esp. of the terms of a treaty agreed to in conference and signed by the parties. **3** a formal statement of a transaction. **4** *Computing* a set of rules governing the exchange or transmission of

data electronically between devices. [medieval Latin *protocollum* from Greek *protokollon* fly-leaf (as PROTO-, *kolla* glue)]

proto·lan·guage *noun* *Linguistics* a hypothetical parent language from which actual languages or dialects are derived.

pro·ton /ˈprəʊtɒn/ *noun* *Physics* a stable elementary particle with a positive electric charge, equal in magnitude to that of an electron, and occurring in all atomic nuclei. □ **pro·ton·ic** /prəˈtɒnɪk/ *adjective* [Greek, neuter of *prōtos* first]

pro·to·no·tary *var. of* PROTHONOTARY.

proto·planet *noun* a large diffuse body of matter in the process of accretion in a solar or stellar orbit, postulated as a preliminary stage in the evolution of a planet. □ **proto·planet·ary** *adjective*

proto·plasm *noun* the material comprising the living part of a cell, consisting of a nucleus embedded in membrane-enclosed cytoplasm. □ **proto·plas·mic** *adjective* [Greek *protoplasma* (as PROTO-, PLASMA)]

proto·plast *noun* the protoplasm of one cell. □ **proto·plas·tic** *adjective* [Greek *protoplastos* (as PROTO-, *plassō* mould)]

proto·star *noun* a contracting mass of gas representing a star in an early stage of formation.

proto·ther·ian /ˌprəʊtəʊˈθɪəriən/ ● *noun* any mammal of the subclass Prototheria, including monotremes. ● *adjective* of or relating to this subclass. [PROTO- + Greek *thēr* wild beast]

proto·type ● *noun* **1** an original thing or person of which or whom copies, imitations, improved forms, representations, etc. are made. **2** a trial model or preliminary version of a vehicle, machine, etc. ● *transitive verb* make a prototype of (a product). □ **proto·typ·al** *adjective*

proto·typ·ic·al /ˌprəʊtəˈtɪpɪkəl/ *adjective* (also **proto·typ·ic**) **1** constituting the essential type of; ideal (*her strength and build make her the prototypical figure skater*). **2** of or relating to a prototype (*it was developed from a prototypical model which looks crude by today's standards*). □ **proto·typ·ic·al·ly** *adverb*

proto·zoan /ˌprəʊtəˈzəʊən/ ● *noun* (also **proto·zoon** /-ˈzəʊɒn/) (*pl.* **proto·zoa** /-ˈzəʊə/ or **proto·zoans**) any usu. unicellular and microscopic organism of the subkingdom Protozoa, including amoebae and ciliates. ● *adjective* (also **proto·zoic** /-ˈzəʊɪk/) of or relating to this phylum. □ **proto·zoal** *adjective* [modern Latin (as PROTO-, Greek *zōion* animal)]

pro·tract /prəˈtrakt/ *transitive verb* **1** prolong or lengthen esp. in time or in space. **2** draw a plan to scale. **3** (of a muscle) extend (a limb, etc.). □ **pro·trac·tion** *noun* [Latin *protrahere* protract- (as PRO-¹, *trahere* draw)]

pro·tract·ed /prəˈtraktəd/ *adjective* of excessive length or duration (*tired of the protracted debate*). □ **pro·tract·ed·ly** *adverb* **pro·tract·ed·ness** *noun*

pro·tract·ile /prəˈtraktaɪl/ *adjective* (of a part of the body etc.) capable of being protruded or extended.

pro·tract·or /prəˈtraktər, ˈprəʊtraktər/ *noun* **1** an instrument for measuring angles, usu. in the form of a semicircle graduated by degrees. **2** a muscle that serves to extend a limb etc.

pro·trude *verb* **1** *intransitive* extend beyond or above a surface; project. **2** *transitive* thrust or cause to thrust forth. □ **pro·tru·sion** *noun* **pro·tru·sive** *adjective* [Latin *protrudere* (as PRO-¹, *trudere* trus- thrust)]

pro·tru·sible /prəˈtruːsəbəl/ *adjective* (also **pro·tru·sile** /prəˈtruːsaɪl/) (of a limb etc.) adapted or able to be protruded. [Latin *protrus-* 'extended or thrust forward' from the verb *protudere* + -IBLE or -ILE.]

pro·tuber·ant /prəˈtjuːbərənt, -ˈtjuːb-/ *adjective* bulging out; prominent (*protuberant eyes*; *a protuberant fact*). □ **pro·tuber·ance** *noun* [Late Latin *protuberare* (as PRO-¹, *tuber* bump)]

proud *adjective* **1** feeling greatly honoured or pleased (*am proud to know him*; *proud of his friendship*). **2 a** (often foll. by *of*) valuing oneself, one's possessions, etc. highly, or esp. too highly; haughty; arrogant (*she wasn't too proud to take the job*). **b** suitably satisfied with one's achievements (*proud of a job well done*). **3 a** (of an occasion etc.) justly arousing pride (*a proud day for us*; *a proud sight*). **b** (of an action etc.) showing pride (*a proud wave of the hand*). **4** (of a thing) imposing; distinguished (*the statue stands tall and proud in the main square*). **5** (esp. *Brit.*) slightly projecting from a surface etc. (*the nail stood proud of the plank*). **6** (of flesh) overgrown around a healing wound. □ **do proud** *informal* **1** be a source of pride to (someone) (*Michele's achievements did her family proud*). **2** treat (a person) with lavish generosity or honour (*they did us proud on our anniversary*). **proud as punch** very proud. □ **proud·ly** *adverb* [Old English *prūt*, *prūd* from Old French *prud*, *prod* oblique case of *pruz* etc. valiant, ultimately from Late Latin *prode* from Latin *prodesse* be of value (as PRO-¹, *esse* be)]

Prou·dhon /pruːˈdɔ̃/ **Pierre Joseph** (1809–65), French social philosopher and journalist. His writings, which exercised considerable influence on the development of anarchism and socialism in Europe, include *What is Property?* (1840), arguing that property, in the sense of the exploitation of one person's labour by another, is theft.

Proust /pruːst/ **1 Jo·seph Louis** (1754–1826), French analytical chemist. He proposed the law of constant proportions, demonstrating that any pure sample of a chemical compound (such as an oxide of a metal) always contains the same elements in fixed proportions.
2 Mar·cel (1871–1922), French novelist, essayist, and critic. His novel *À la recherche du temps perdu* (published in seven sections between 1913 and 1927) traces the life of the narrator from childhood to middle age and has as its central theme the recovery of the lost past through the stimulation of unconscious memory. □ **Proust·ian** *adjective*

Prov. *abbreviation* **1** (also **prov.**) Provincial, provincial. **2** (also. **prov.**) Province, province. **3** Proverbs (Old Testament).

prove /pruːv/ *verb* (*past participle* **prov·en** or **proved**) **1** *transitive* **a** (often foll. by *that* + clause) demonstrate the truth of by evidence or argument. **b** assert or reveal (something) (*this trial will prove my client's innocence*). **c** show (a thing or person) to be (right, wrong, etc.) (*the facts will prove me right*). **2** *transitive* **a** be found (*it proved to be untrue; the tool proved useless for the job*). **b** turn out to be, emerge as, become (*jealousy will prove his downfall*). **3** *transitive* test the accuracy of (esp. a calculation); subject to a testing process. **4** *transitive* establish the genuineness and validity of (a will). **5** *intransitive* (of dough) rise in bread making. **6** *transitive* = PROOF *verb* 2. □ **not proven** (in Scottish Law) a verdict that there is insufficient evidence to establish guilt or innocence. **prove oneself** show one's abilities, courage, etc. □ **prov·able** *adjective* **prov·ably** *adverb* [Old French *prover* from Latin *probare* test, approve, demonstrate, from *probus* good]

prov·en /ˈpruːvən/ *attributive adjective* **1** shown to be such through trial and experience (*a proven performer*). **2** (also in *combination*) demonstrated to be effective (*a time-proven technique*).

prov·en·ance /ˈprɒvənəns/ *noun* **1** the place of origin or history, esp. of a work of art, etc. **2** origin. [French from *provenir* from Latin *provenire* (as PRO-¹, *venire* come)]

Pro·ven·çal /ˌprɒvɑ̃ˈsal/, /ˌprɔːvɒnˈsal/ ● *adjective* **1** of or concerning the language, inhabitants, landscape, etc. of Provence. **2** (also **pro·ven·çale**) containing olive oil, garlic, and often tomato, and normally flavoured with mixed Provençal herbs such as tarragon, rosemary, etc. ● *noun* **1** a native of Provence. **2** the Romance language of Provence, closely related to French, Italian, and Catalan. [French; see PROVENCE]

Pro·vence /prɒˈvɒns, prɒˈvɑ̃s/ a former province of SE France, on the Mediterranean coast east of the Rhone, now part of the region of Provence-Alpes-Côte d'Azur. [Latin *provincia* province, as Latin colloquial name for S Gaul, the first Roman province to be established outside Italy]

Provence-Alpes-Côte d'Azur /prɒˈvɑ̃s alp kɔːt daˈzʊr/ a mountainous region of SE France, on the border with Italy and including the French Riviera.

Pro·ven·cher /prɒˈvɑ̃ʃei/ **Joseph-Norbert** (1787–1853), Canadian Roman Catholic priest and bishop. Ordained in 1811, he was sent to Red River in 1818 to build the settlement's first Catholic church. He attempted to strengthen the Catholic church in the North-West through education, conversion of the Indians, and encouraging Catholic immigration. He was made a bishop and apostolic vicar of the North-West two years later, and in 1835 his territory was extended to the Pacific; he became the first bishop of St. Boniface in 1847.

prov·en·der /ˈprɒvəndər/ *noun* **1** animal fodder. **2** food for human beings. [Old French *provendre*, ultimately from Latin *praebenda* (see PREBEND)]

pro·ven·ience /prəˈviːniəns/ *noun* esp. *US* = PROVENANCE. [Latin *provenire* from *venire* come]

prov·erb /ˈprɒvɜːrb/ *noun* **1** a short pithy saying in general use, held to embody a general truth. **2** (**Proverbs** or **Book of Proverbs**) *Bible* a didactic, poetic book of maxims attributed to Solomon and others. [Old French *proverbe* or Latin *proverbium* (as PRO-¹, *verbum* word)]

pro·verb·ial /prəˈvɜːrbiəl/ *adjective* **1** (esp. of a specific characteristic etc.) as well-known as a proverb; notorious (*his proverbial honesty*). **2** of or referred to in a proverb (*a proverbial phrase; the proverbial ill wind*). □ **pro·verb·ial·ly** *adverb*

pro·vide *verb* **1** *transitive* **a** supply, furnish (*provided them with food; provided food for them*). **b** offer or present (an answer, example, opportunity, etc.) (*darkness provided a chance for escape; darkness provided them the opportunity to act*). **2** (usu. foll. by *that*) ensure or specify (*this agreement provides that profits will be divided equally among the partners*). **3** *transitive* (usu. foll. by *to*) *Christianity hist.* **a** appoint (an incumbent) to a

benefice. **b** (of the Pope) appoint (a successor) to a benefice not yet vacant. □ **provide for 1** supply money and other necessities, e.g. food and clothing, for (*she worked two jobs to provide for her family*). **2** make the necessary plans to deal with something that may happen in the future (*rally organizers had not provided for rain*). **3** (of a law, etc.) make it possible for something to be done later (*freedom of speech is provided for in the constitution*). [Latin *providēre* (as PRO-¹, *vidēre* vis- see)]

pro·vid·ed *conjunction* (often foll. by *that*) on the condition or understanding (that).

Provi·dence /ˈprɒvɪdəns/ the state capital of Rhode Island, a port on the Atlantic coast; pop. (2000) 173,618.

provi·dence /ˈprɒvɪdəns/ *noun* **1** esp. *Christianity* the protective care of God or nature. **2** (**Providence**) esp. *Christianity* God as exercising prescient and beneficent power and direction. **3** timely care or preparation; foresight; thrift. [Old French *providence* or Latin *providentia* (as PROVIDE)]

provi·dent /ˈprɒvɪdənt/ *adjective* **1** having or showing foresight. **2** thrifty. □ **provi·dent·ly** *adverb* [Middle English from Latin (as PROVIDE)]

provi·den·tial /ˌprɒvɪˈdenʃəl/ *adjective* **1** of or by divine foresight or intervention. **2** opportune, lucky. □ **provi·den·tial·ly** *adverb*

pro·vid·er *noun* **1** a person or thing that provides. **2** the breadwinner of a family etc.

pro·vid·ing *conjunction* = PROVIDED.

Pro·vimi /prəˈviːmi/ *adjective proprietary* designating a type of milk-fed veal which has been raised in controlled conditions for maximum tenderness and paleness. [from protein, vitamins, and minerals, describing a particular feed mix]

prov·ince *noun* **1** a principal administrative division of a country etc., esp. (in Canada) one of the ten principal political units which, along with the Territories, constitute Canada. **2** (in *pl.*) the whole of esp. a European country outside the capital city, often regarded as uncultured, unsophisticated, etc. **3** a sphere of action, concern, or responsibility (*the Internet is no longer the province of advanced users*). **4** a branch of learning etc. (*in the province of aesthetics*). **5** an area, zone, or region containing a distinct group of animal or plant communities; a division of a biogeographical region. **6** an extensive region all parts of which have a broadly similar geology and topography, differing significantly from adjacent regions in age and degree of formation (*the Canadian Shield can be divided into nine structural provinces*). **7** in Catholic and Anglican churches, a district under an archbishop or a metropolitan, usu. consisting of adjacent dioceses. **8** a territorial division of a religious order. **9** (**the Province**) *Brit.* Northern Ireland. **10** *Rom. Hist.* a territory outside Italy under a Roman governor. [Old French from Latin *provincia* charge, province]

prov·ince·hood *noun Cdn* the quality or status of being a province (*Yukoners strive for provincehood*).

Province House *noun* the name of the legislative building in Nova Scotia and Prince Edward Island.

Province of Canada *hist.* the union (1841–67) of Canada East (formerly Lower Canada) and Canada West (formerly Upper Canada).

province-wide *adjective* esp. *Cdn* extending throughout or pertaining to a whole province.

prov·in·cial ● *adjective* **1** of, pertaining to, or under the jurisdiction of a province or provinces (*provincial demands for autonomy; provincial government; provincial highway*). **2** of or concerning the whole of esp. a European country outside the capital city (*French provincial furniture*). **3** *derogatory* having or showing a narrow or limited view of life and current affairs (*provincial attitudes*). ● *noun* **1** *Cdn* (in *pl.*) a provincial tournament or championship. **2** an inhabitant of esp. a European region outside the capital city. **3** an unsophisticated or uncultured person. **4** *Christianity* the head or chief of a province of a religious order in a province. □ **prov·in·ci·al·ity** *noun* **prov·in·cial·ly** *adverb*

provincial building *noun Cdn* a building housing provincial government offices.

provincial constable *noun* (in the Ontario Provincial Police) an officer ranking above probationary constable and below senior constable.

provincial court *noun Cdn* a court established by provincial legislation, usu. having both criminal and civil divisions, which conducts hearings by judge alone on offences of a relatively minor nature.

prov·in·cial·ism *noun* **1 a** an attitude or manners reflecting a limited or restricted view of life and current events; narrow-mindedness. **b** an unsophisticated outlook. **2** allegiance to or concern for one's province rather than one's country (*provincialism surrounding the administration of health care threatens to divide the country*). **3** a word or phrase peculiar to esp. a European region outside the capital city. □ **prov·in·cial·ist** *noun & adjective*

prov·in·cial·iz·a·tion *noun Cdn* (also **-isation**) the transfer (of responsibilities, etc.) to the provincial level (*provincialization of fisheries management*). □ **prov·in·cial·ize** *transitive verb* (also **-ise**).

provincial park *noun Cdn* an area of land owned and preserved by a provincial government for public benefit and enjoyment and for the conservation of wildlife.

provincial parliament *noun Cdn* a provincial legislative assembly.

provincial police *noun Cdn* (esp. *Ont. & Que.*) a police force under provincial authority responsible for jurisdictions without municipal police protection.

provincial right *noun Cdn* (usu. in *pl.*) the right of a province or provinces to maintain and exercise authority over specified areas under provincial jurisdiction (*control over education is a provincial right; federal government intruding upon provincial rights*).

proving ground *noun* any area or situation in which a person or thing is tested or proven (*the site is a proving ground for nuclear weapons; the musical is a proving ground for young actors*).

pro·vi·sion ● *noun* **1 a** the act or an instance of providing (*the provision of services*). **b** something provided (*a provision of bread*). **c** preparation that is made to meet future needs or eventualities (*make provision for one's old age; provision against possible disaster*). **2** (in *pl.*) food, drink, etc., esp. for an expedition. **3 a** a legal or formal statement providing for something. **b** a clause of this. **4** *Christianity hist.* an appointment to a benefice not yet vacant (compare PROVIDE 3). ● *transitive verb* supply (an expedition etc.) with provisions. □ **pro·vi·sion·er** *noun* **pro·vi·sion·ing** *noun* [Old French from Latin *provisio -onis* (as PROVIDE)]

pro·vi·sion·al ● *adjective* **1** providing for immediate needs only; temporary. **2** (**Provisional**) designating the unofficial wing of the IRA established in 1970, advocating terrorism. ● *noun* (**Provisional**) a member of the Provisional wing of the IRA. □ **pro·vi·sion·al·i·ty** /-'nalɪti/ *noun* **pro·vi·sion·al·ly** *adverb*

pro·viso /prə'vaizo:/ *noun* (*pl.* **-visos**) **1** a stipulation. **2** a clause of stipulation or limitation in a document. [Latin, neuter ablative past participle of *providēre* PROVIDE, in medieval Latin phr. *proviso quod* it being provided that]

pro·vis·ory /prə'vaizəri/ *adjective* **1** temporary, provisional. **2** conditional; having a proviso. □ **pro·vi·sor·i·ly** *adverb* [French *provisoire* or medieval Latin *provisorius* (as PROVIDE)]

pro·vita·min *noun* a substance which is converted into a vitamin within an organism (*provitamin A is carotene*).

Pro·vo /'pro:vo:/ *noun* (*pl.* **Provos**) *Brit. informal* a member of the Provisional IRA. [abbreviation]

pro·voca·teur /prɒvɒkə,tɜr, prə-/ *noun* a person who provokes a disturbance; an agitator. [French, = 'instigator, provoker']

pro·vo·ca·tion /,prɒvə'keiʃən/ *noun* **1** the act or an instance of provoking; a state of being provoked (*did it under severe provocation*). **2** a cause of annoyance. **3** *Cdn & Brit. Law* an action, insult, etc. deemed likely to provoke physical retaliation or an irrational response. [Old French *provocation*(as PROVOKE)]

pro·voca·tive /prə'vɒkətɪv/ *adjective* **1** intentionally causing anger, annoyance, controversy, etc. (*ignore him, he's just being provocative; a provocative editorial*). **2** tending to arouse sexual desire. **3** intellectually stimulating (*a provocative book*). □ **pro·voca·tive·ly** *adverb*
pro·voca·tive·ness *noun* [obsolete French *provocatif -ive* from Late Latin *provocativus* (as PROVOKE)]

pro·voke *transitive verb* **1** annoy, disturb, or harass (*don't provoke the dog, he might bite; stop provoking your sister*). **2** cause a person to do something by behaving in a certain esp. annoying way (*this last barrage of questions provoked him to end his silence; his relentless criticism finally provoked her into leaving him*). **3** cause a particular reaction in a person etc. (*her editorial provoked an angry response among readers; the goal provoked cheers from the crowd*). **4** cause, give rise to (*will provoke fermentation*). [Old French *provoquer* from Latin *provocare* (as PRO-¹, *vocare* call)]

pro·vok·ing *adjective* **1** exasperating, irritating, annoying. **2** (in *combination*) prompting (thought, anxiety, laughter, etc.) (*a thought-provoking conversation; pain-provoking contractions*).
□ **pro·vok·ing·ly** *adverb*

pro·vo·lone /,pro:vo:'lo:nei, prɒvə'lo:ni:/ *noun* a type of mellow cow's-milk cheese originally made in southern Italy, often smoked

after drying and moulded into the shape of a pear. [Italian *provola* from Latin *probula* buffalo's milk cheese]

pro·vost /'prɒvəst/ *noun* **1** *N Amer.* a high administrative officer in a university. **2** /'prɒːvo:/ *Cdn* (*hist.*) & *Brit.* a member of the military police. **3** *Christianity* a high-ranking ecclesiastical dignitary. **4** *Scot.* the head of a municipal corporation or burgh. **5** *Brit.* the head of some colleges esp. at Oxford or Cambridge. □ **provost·ship** *noun* [Old English *profost* & Anglo-French *provost*, *prevost* from medieval Latin *propositus* for *praepositus* past participle of *praeponere* set over (as PRAE-, *ponere* posit- place)]

provost marshal *noun* **1** the head of military police in camp or on active service. **2** the master-at-arms of a ship in which a court martial is to be held.

prow *noun* the forepart or bow of a ship. □ **prowed** *combining form* [French *proue* from Provençal *proa* or Italian dial. *prua* from Latin *prora* from Greek *prōira*]

prow·ess /prau'es, 'praues, -əs/ *noun* **1** skill. **2** valour; gallantry. [Old French *proesce* from *prou* valiant]

prowl ● *verb* **1 a** *intransitive* move quietly and carefully, esp. when looking or hunting for something (*dogs prowling in the night; a burglar prowling around a house*). **b** *transitive* move through or in a place in this way (*prowling the streets*). **2** *intransitive* walk or wander, e.g. because one is anxious or unable to relax (*he spent the night prowling about downstairs because he couldn't sleep*). ● *noun* the act or an instance of prowling. □ **on the prowl** moving about secretively; prowling. [Middle English *prolle*, of unknown origin]

prowl car *noun US* a police squad car.

prowl·er *noun* a person who moves stealthily about or loiters near a place with a view to committing a crime.

prox. *abbreviation* proximo.

prox·im·al /'prɒksɪməl/ *adjective* situated towards the centre of the body or point of attachment. □ **prox·im·al·ly** *adverb* [Latin *proximus* nearest]

prox·im·ate /'prɒksɪmət/ *adjective* **1** nearest or next before or after (in place, order, time, causation, thought process, etc.). **2** approximate.
□ **prox·im·ate·ly** *adverb* [Latin *proximatus* past participle of *proximare* draw near (as PROXIMAL)]

prox·im·ity /prɒk'sɪməti/ *noun* nearness in space, time, etc. (*sat in close proximity to them*). [Latin *proximitas* (as PROXIMAL)]

proximity fuse *noun* an electronic device causing a projectile to explode when near its target.

prox·imo /'prɒksɪ,mo:/ *adjective archaic* of next month (*the third proximo*). [Latin *proximo mense* in the next month]

proxy *noun* (*pl.* **-ies**) (also *attributive*) **1** the authorization given to a substitute or deputy (*a proxy vote; was married by proxy*). **2** a person authorized to act as a substitute etc. **3 a** a document giving the power to act as a proxy, esp. in voting. **b** a vote given by this. [Middle English from obsolete *procuracy* from medieval Latin *procuratia* (as PROCURE)]

proxy server *noun Computing* a server that acts as an interface between browsers and other servers on the Internet, regulating access to web pages, caching pages to improve download speed, and/or acting as a firewall to prevent the tracing of users' identities.

proxy war *noun* a war instigated by a major power that does not itself become involved.

Pro·zac /'pro:zak/ *noun proprietary* **1** the antidepressant drug fluoxetine hydrochloride. **2** a capsule etc. of this drug. [invented name]

prude *noun* a person having or affecting an attitude of extreme propriety or modesty, esp. in sexual matters. □ **prud·ery** *noun* (*pl.* **-ies**). **prud·ish** *adjective* **prud·ish·ly** *adverb* **prud·ish·ness** *noun* [French, back-formation from *prudefemme* fem. of *prud'homme* 'good man and true' from *prou* 'worthy']

pru·dent /'pru:dənt/ *adjective* **1** careful to provide for the future. **2** discreet or cautious; circumspect. **3** having or exercising good judgment. □ **pru·dence** *noun* **pru·dent·ly** *adverb* [Old French *prudent* or Latin *prudens* = *providens* PROVIDENT]

pru·den·tial /pru:'denʃəl/ *adjective* of, involving, or marked by prudence. □ **pru·den·tial·ly** *adverb* [PRUDENT + -IAL, after *evidential* etc.]

Prudhoe Bay /'pru:do:/ an inlet of the Arctic Ocean on the north coast of Alaska.

pru·in·ose /'pru:ɪ,no:s/ *adjective* esp. *Bot.* covered with white powdery granules; frosted in appearance. [Latin *pruinosus* from *pruina* hoarfrost]

prune¹ *noun* **1** a dried plum. **2** (also **prune plum**) esp. *N Amer.* a variety of plum suitable for drying. □ **prun·ey** *adjective* [Old French, ultimately from Latin *prunum* from Greek *prou(m)non* plum]

prune² *transitive verb* **1 a** (often foll. by *down*) trim (a tree etc.) by cutting away dead or overgrown branches etc. **b** (usu. foll. by *off, away*) lop (branches etc.) from a tree. **2** reduce (costs etc.) (*must try to prune expenses*). **3** reduce the extent of (something) by cutting or removing unnecessary parts etc. (*must prune down the list of people invited to the wedding*). □ **prun·er** *noun* [Middle English *prouyne* from Old French *pro(o)ignier*, ultimately from Latin *rotundus* ROUND]

pru·nel·la¹ /pruːˈnelə/ *noun* any plant of the genus *Prunella*, esp. *P. vulgaris*, bearing pink, purple, or white flower spikes, and formerly thought to cure quinsy. *Also called* SELF-HEAL. [modern Latin, = quinsy: earlier *brunella* diminutive of medieval Latin *brunus* brown]

pru·nel·la² /pruːˈnelə/ *noun* a strong silk or worsted fabric used formerly for barristers' gowns, the uppers of women's shoes, etc. [perhaps from French *prunelle*, of uncertain origin]

pruning hook *noun* a long-handled hooked cutting tool used for pruning.

pru·ri·ent /ˈpruːrɪənt/ *adjective* **1** having or showing an excessive interest in sexual matters. **2** encouraging such an excessive interest. □ **pru·ri·ence** *noun* **pru·ri·ent·ly** *adverb* [Latin *prurire* itch, be wanton]

prur·itus /pruəˈraɪtəs/ *noun* severe itching of the skin. □ **prur·it·ic** /-ˈrɪtɪk/ *adjective* [Latin, = itching]

Prus·sia /ˈprʌʃə/ *noun* a former kingdom of Germany, which grew from a small country on the southeastern shores of the Baltic to an extensive domain covering much of modern NE Germany and Poland. With Germany's defeat in the First World War, Prussia's monarchy and supremacy came to an end (*see also* EAST PRUSSIA). □ **Prus·sian** *adjective & noun*

Prussian blue *noun* **1** a deep blue pigment, ferric ferrocyanide, used in painting and dyeing. **2** a deep greenish-blue colour.

prus·sic acid *noun* hydrocyanic acid. [French *prussique* 'relating to Prussian blue']

Prut River /pruːt/ (also **Pruth**) a river of SE Europe, which rises in the Carpathian Mountains in S Ukraine and flows southeast for 850 km (530 miles), joining the Danube near Galați in Romania. For much of its course it forms the border between Ukraine and Moldova.

pry¹ *intransitive verb* (**pries, pried**) **1** (usu. foll. by *into*) inquire impertinently (into a person's private affairs etc.). **2** (usu. foll. by *into, about*, etc.) look or peer inquisitively. □ **pry·ing** *adjective* [Middle English *prie*, of unknown origin]

pry² *transitive verb* (**pries, pried**) *N Amer.* **1** (often foll. by *open, up*, etc.) move, open, raise, etc., by leverage (*pry up the lid; pried the box open*). **2** remove, obtain, or separate with difficulty (*could not pry the secret out of her*). [PRISE taken as *pries* 3rd sing. pres.]

pry bar *noun* a metal bar used for prying up nailed boards etc.

PS *abbreviation* **1** (also **ps**) postscript. **2** *N Amer.* Public School. **3** power steering.

Ps. *abbreviation* (*pl.* **Pss.**) *Bible* Psalm, Psalms.

PSA *abbreviation* **1** prostate specific antigen, a blood test used to detect prostate cancer. **2** *N Amer.* PUBLIC SERVICE ANNOUNCEMENT.

PSAC *abbreviation* Public Service Alliance of Canada.

psalm /sɑm/ *noun* **1 a** (also **Psalm**) any of the sacred songs contained in the biblical Book of Psalms. **b** a musical setting for a Psalm. **c** (**the Psalms** or **the Book of Psalms**) the book of the Old Testament and Hebrew Bible comprising a collection of religious verses, sung or recited in both Jewish and Christian worship. Many are traditionally ascribed to King David. **2** a sacred song or hymn. □ **psalm·ic** *adjective* [Greek *psalmos* song sung to a harp, from *psallō* pluck]

psalm·ist /ˈsɑmɪst/ *noun* **1** the author or composer of a psalm. **2** (**the Psalmist**) David or the author of any of the Psalms.

psalm·ody /ˈsɑmədɪ, ˈsal-/ *noun* **1** the practice or art of singing psalms, hymns, etc., esp. in public worship. **2** psalms arranged for singing. [Late Latin *psalmodia* from Greek *psalmōidia* singing to a harp (as PSALM, *ōidē* song)]

psalter /ˈsɒltər/ *noun* **1 a** (usu. **Psalter**) the Book of Psalms. **b** a version of this (*the Old English Psalter*). **2** a copy of the Psalms, esp. for liturgical use. [Late Latin *psalterium* from Greek *psaltērion* stringed instrument (*psallō* pluck)]

psal·ter·ium /sɒlˈtiːrɪəm/ *noun* = OMASUM. [Latin (see PSALTER): named from its book-like form]

psal·tery /ˈsɒltərɪ/ *noun* (*pl.* **-ies**) an ancient and medieval instrument like a dulcimer but played by plucking the strings with the fingers or a plectrum.

pseph·ol·ogy /seˈfɒlədʒɪ, pse-/ *noun* the statistical study of elections, voting, etc. □ **pseph·ol·o·gist** *noun* [Greek *psēphos* pebble, vote + -LOGY]

pseud /suːd, sjuːd/ esp. *Brit. informal* ● *adjective* intellectually or socially pretentious; not genuine. ● *noun* a person who is intellectually or socially pretentious. [abbreviation of PSEUD]

pseud- *var. of* PSEUDO-.

pseud·epig·rapha /ˌsuːdɪˈpɪɡrəfə, ˌsjuː-/ *plural noun* **1** (usu. **Pseudepigrapha**) Jewish writings ascribed to various Old Testament prophets etc. but written during or just before the early Christian period. **2** spurious writings. □ **pseud·epi·graph·ic** *adjective* [neuter pl. of Greek *pseudepigraphos* with false title (as PSEUDO-, EPIGRAPH)]

pseu·do /ˈsuːdoː, ˈsjuː-/ ● *adjective* **1** sham; spurious. **2** insincere. ● *noun* (*pl.* **-dos**) a pretentious or insincere person. [see PSEUDO-]

pseudo- /ˈsuːdoː, ˈsjuː-/ *combining form* (also **pseud-** before a vowel) **1** supposed to be but not really so; false; not genuine (*pseudo-intellectual; pseudepigrapha*). **2** resembling or imitating (often in technical applications) (*pseudo-language; pseudo-acid*). [Greek from *pseudēs* false, *pseudos* falsehood]

pseudo·carp /ˈsuːdoːˌkɑrp, ˈsjuː-/ *noun* a fruit formed from parts other than the ovary, e.g. the strawberry or fig. [PSEUDO- + Greek *karpos* fruit]

pseudo·ephed·rine /ˌsuːdoːɪˈfedrɪn/ *noun* a dextrorotatory compound commonly used as a nasal decongestant. [PSEUDO- + EPHEDRINE]

pseudo·morph /ˈsuːdəˌmɔrf, ˈsjuː-/ *noun* **1** a crystal etc. consisting of one mineral with the form proper to another. **2** a false form. □ **pseudo·morph·ic** *adjective* [PSEUDO- + Greek *morphē* form]

pseudo·nym /ˈsuːdənɪm, ˈsjuː-/ *noun* a fictitious name, esp. one assumed by an author. □ **pseudo·nym·ity** /-ˈnɪmɪtɪ/ *noun* [Greek *pseudōnymos* (as PSEUDO-, *-ōnumos* from *onoma* name)]

pseud·onym·ous /suːˈdɒnɪməs/ *adjective* **1** writing or written under a false name. **2** (of a person) bearing or taking a false name. □ **pseud·onym·ous·ly** *adverb*

pseudo·pod /ˈsuːdoːˌpɒd, ˈsjuː-/ *noun* = PSEUDOPODIUM. [modern Latin (as PSEUDOPODIUM)]

pseudo·po·dium /ˌsuːdoːˈpoːdɪəm, ˌsjuː-/ *noun* (*pl.* **pseudo·po·dia** /-dɪə/) (in amoeboid cells) a temporary protrusion of protoplasm for movement, feeding, etc. [modern Latin (as PSEUDO-, PODIUM)]

pseudo-science *noun* a pretended or spurious science. □ **pseudo-scientif·ic** *adjective*

pshaw /pʃɔ, ʃɔ/ *interjection* an expression of contempt or impatience. [imitative]

psi¹ /psai/ *noun* **1** the twenty-third letter of the Greek alphabet (Ψ, ψ). **2** supposed parapsychological faculties, phenomena, etc. regarded collectively. [Greek]

psi² *abbreviation* pounds per square inch.

psilo·cybin /ˌsɪləˈsaɪbɪn/ *noun* a hallucinogenic alkaloid found in Mexican mushrooms of the genus *Psilocybe*. [*Psilocybe* from Greek *psilos* bald + *kubē* head]

psit·ta·cine /ˈsɪtəˌsaɪn/ *adjective* of or relating to parrots; parrot-like. [Latin *psittacinus* from *psittacus* from Greek *psittakos* parrot]

psit·ta·co·sis /ˌsɪtəˈkoːsɪs/ *noun* a contagious viral disease of birds transmissible (esp. from parrots) to human beings as a form of pneumonia. [modern Latin from Latin *psittacus* (as PSITTACINE) + -OSIS]

psoas /ˈsoːəs/ *noun* either of two muscles used in flexing the hip joint. [Greek, accusative pl. of *psoa*, taken as sing.]

psor·ia·sis /səˈraɪəsɪs/ *noun* a skin disease marked by red scaly patches. □ **psori·at·ic** /ˌsɔrɪˈatɪk/ *adjective* [Greek *psōriasis* from *psōriaō* have an itch, from *psōra* itch]

psst *interjection* (also **pst**) a whispered exclamation seeking to attract a person's attention surreptitiously. [imitative]

PST *abbreviation* **1** *Cdn* provincial sales tax. **2** PACIFIC STANDARD TIME.

psych /saɪk/ *informal* ● *transitive verb* **1** (usu. foll. by *up*; often *reflexive*) prepare (oneself or another person) mentally for an ordeal etc. **2 a** (usu. foll. by *out*) analyze (a person's motivation etc.) for one's own advantage (*keeps trying to psych him out*). **b** subject to psychoanalysis. **3** (often foll. by *out*) influence a person psychologically, esp. negatively; intimidate, frighten. ● *noun N Amer.* psychology (also *attributive*: *psych textbook*). ● *adjective N Amer.* psychiatric (*psych ward*). [abbreviation]

Psy·che /ˈsaɪkɪ/ *Gk Myth* a beautiful girl who was loved by Eros (Cupid), and who overcame the superhuman tasks set by the jealous Aphrodite (Venus); she was a Hellenistic personification of the soul as female, or sometimes as a butterfly.

psy·che /ˈsaɪkɪ/ *noun* **1** the soul; the spirit. **2** the mind. [Latin from Greek *psukhē* breath, life, soul]

psyche·delia /ˌsaɪkəˈdeliə, -ˈdiːliə/ *plural noun* psychedelic articles, esp. posters, paintings, music, etc.

---

psy·che·del·ic /ˌsaɪkəˈdelɪk/ ● *adjective* **1 a** expanding the mind's awareness etc., esp. through the use of hallucinogenic drugs. **b** (of an experience) hallucinatory; bizarre. **c** (of a drug) producing hallucinations. **2** *informal* **a** producing an effect resembling that of a psychedelic drug; having vivid colours or designs etc. **b** (of colours, patterns, etc.) bright, bold and often abstract. ● *noun* a hallucinogenic drug. □ **psy·che·del·ic·ally** *adverb* [irregular from Greek (as PSYCHE, *dēlos* clear, manifest)]

psychiatric nurse *noun* a nurse dealing with mentally ill patients.

psychiatric patient *noun* = MENTAL PATIENT.

psych·iatry /saɪˈkaɪətrɪ/ *noun* the study and treatment of mental disease. □ **psychi·at·ric** /-kiˈatrɪk/ *adjective* **psychi·at·ric·al·ly** /-kiˈatrɪklɪ/ *adverb* **psych·ia·trist** *noun* [as PSYCHE + *iatreia* healing, from *iatros* healer]

psych·ic /ˈsaɪkɪk/ ● *adjective* **1 a** (of a person) considered to have occult powers, such as telepathy, clairvoyance, etc. **b** (of a faculty, phenomenon, etc.) inexplicable by natural laws. **2** of or relating to the soul or mind. ● *noun* a person considered to have psychic powers; a medium. □ **psych·ic·al** *adjective* **psych·ic·al·ly** *adverb* [Greek *psukhikos* (as PSYCHE)]

psy·cho /ˈsaɪkoː/ *informal* ● *noun* (*pl.* **-chos**) a psychopath. ● *adjective* psychopathic. [abbreviation]

psycho- /ˈsaɪkoː/ *combining form* relating to the mind or psychology. [Greek *psukho-* (as PSYCHE)]

psycho·acous·tics *noun* the branch of psychology concerned with the perception of sound and its physiological effects. □ **psycho·acous·tic** *adjective* **psycho·acous·tic·ally** *adverb*

psycho·active /ˌsaɪkoːˈaktɪv/ *adjective* (esp. of a drug) affecting the mind.

psycho·analy·sis /ˌsaɪkoːəˈnaləsəs/ *noun* a therapeutic method of treating mental disorders by investigating the interaction of conscious and unconscious elements in the mind and bringing repressed fears and conflicts into the conscious mind. □ **psycho·ana·lyze** *transitive verb* (also esp. *Brit.* **psycho·ana·lyse**). **psycho·ana·lyst** *noun* **psycho·ana·lyt·ic** *adjective* **psycho·ana·lyt·ic·al** *adjective* **psycho·ana·lyt·ic·ally** *adverb*

psycho·babble /ˈsaɪkoːˌbabəl/ *noun* *informal derogatory* writing or talk filled with psychiatric jargon, esp. concerning personality and relationships, esp. when used by lay people with little regard for accuracy.

psycho·biog·raphy /ˌsaɪkoːbaɪˈɒɡrəfɪ/ *noun* (*pl.* **-ies**) biography or a biography dealing esp. with the psychology of the subject. □ **psycho·biog·raph·er** *noun* **psycho·bio·graph·ical** *adjective*

psycho·biol·ogy /ˌsaɪkoːbaɪˈɒlədʒɪ/ *noun* the branch of science that deals with the biological basis of behaviour and mental phenomena. □ **psycho·bio·logic·al** *adjective* **psycho·biol·o·gist** *noun*

psycho·drama /ˈsaɪkoːˌdramə, -drɒmə/ *noun* **1** a form of psychotherapy in which patients act out events from their past. **2** a play or film etc. in which psychological elements are the main interest.

psycho·dynam·ics /ˌsaɪkoːdaɪˈnamɪks/ *plural noun* (treated as *sing.*) the study of the activity of and the interrelation between the various parts of an individual's personality or psyche. □ **psycho·dynam·ic** *adjective* **psycho·dynam·ic·ally** *adverb*

psycho·gen·esis /ˌsaɪkoːˈdʒenəsɪs/ *noun* the study of the origin of the mind's development.

psycho·gen·ic /ˌsaɪkoːˈdʒenɪk/ *adjective* having a psychological origin or cause rather than a physical one.

psycho·graph·ics /ˌsaɪkoːˈɡrafɪks/ *plural noun* (usu. treated as *sing.*) the study and classification of people according to their attitudes, aspirations, etc., esp. in market research. □ **psycho·graph·ic** *adjective*

psycho·hist·ory /ˌsaɪkoːˈhɪstərɪ/ *noun* **1** the interpretation of historical events with the aid of psychological theory. **2** psychobiography; the psychological history of an individual. □ **psycho·histor·ian** *noun* **psycho·histor·ic·al** *adjective*

psycho·kin·esis /ˌsaɪkoːkɪˈniːsɪs/ *noun* the movement of objects supposedly by mental effort without the action of natural forces. □ **psycho·kinet·ic** *adjective*

psycho·lin·guis·tics /ˌsaɪkoːlɪŋˈɡwɪstɪks/ *plural noun* (treated as *sing.*) the study of the psychological aspects of language and language-learning. □ **psycho·lin·guist** *noun* **psycho·lin·guis·tic** *adjective*

psych·o·logic·al /ˌsaɪkəˈlɒdʒɪkəl/ *adjective* **1** of, relating to, affecting, or arising in the mind. **2** of or relating to psychology. **3** *informal* (of an ailment etc.) having a basis in the mind; imaginary (*her cold is psychological*). □ **psych·o·logic·al·ly** *adverb*

psychological warfare *noun* a campaign, esp. involving the use of propaganda, directed at reducing an opponent's morale.

psych·ol·ogy /saɪˈkɒlədʒɪ/ *noun* (*pl.* **-gies**) **1** the scientific study of the human mind and its functions, esp. those affecting behaviour in a given context. **2 a** the mental characteristics or attitude of a person or group. **b** the mental factors governing a situation or activity (*the psychology of crime*). □ **psych·ol·o·gist** *noun* **psych·ol·o·gize** *transitive & intransitive verb* (also esp. *Brit.* **-gise**). [modern Latin *psychologia* (as PSYCHO-, -LOGY)]

psycho·metrics /ˌsaɪkoːˈmetrɪks/ *plural noun* (treated as *sing.*) the science of measuring mental capacities and processes. □ **psycho·metri·cian** *noun*

psych·om·etry /saɪˈkɒmətrɪ/ *noun* **1** the supposed divination of facts about events, people, etc., from inanimate objects associated with them. **2** the measurement of mental abilities. □ **psycho·metric** /-kəˈmetrɪk/ *adjective* **psycho·metric·ally** *adverb* **psych·om·etrist** *noun*

psycho·motor /ˈsaɪkoːˌmoːtər/ *adjective* concerning the study of movement resulting from mental activity.

psycho·neuro·immun·ol·ogy /ˌsaɪkoːˌnjuroːɪmjuːˈnɒlədʒɪ/ *noun* the study of the effect of the mind on health and resistance to disease.

psycho·neuro·sis /ˌsaɪkoːnjuːˈroːsɪs/ *noun* = NEUROSIS. □ **psycho·neurot·ic** *adjective*

psycho·path /ˈsaɪkoːˌpaθ, ˈsaɪkə-/ *noun* **1** a person suffering from chronic mental disorder esp. with abnormal or violent social behaviour. **2** a mentally or emotionally unstable person. □ **psycho·path·ic** *adjective* **psycho·path·ic·ally** *adverb*

psycho·path·ol·ogy /ˌsaɪkoːpəˈθɒlədʒɪ/ *noun* **1** the scientific study of mental disorders. **2** a mentally or behaviourally disordered state. □ **psycho·patho·logic·al** *adjective* **psycho·path·ol·o·gist** *noun*

psycho·pathy /saɪˈkɒpəθɪ/ *noun* psychopathic or psychologically abnormal behaviour.

psycho·pharma·col·ogy /ˌsaɪkoːˌfɑːrməˈkɒlədʒɪ/ *noun* the branch of science that deals with the effects of drugs on the mind and behaviour. □ **psycho·pharma·co·logic·al** *adjective* **psycho·pharma·col·o·gist** *noun*

psycho·phys·ics /ˌsaɪkoːˈfɪzɪks/ *noun* the branch of science that deals with the relations between mental states and physical events and processes. □ **psycho·physic·al** *adjective* **psycho·physi·cist** *noun*

psycho·physi·ol·ogy /ˌsaɪkoːˌfɪziˈɒlədʒɪ/ *noun* the branch of physiology dealing with mental phenomena. □ **psycho·physio·logic·al** *adjective*

psycho·pomp /ˈsaɪkoːpɒmp/ *noun* **1** a mythical conductor of souls to the place of the dead. **2** the spiritual guide of a (living) person's soul. [Greek *psukhopompos*, from *psukhē* PSYCHE + *pompos* conductor]

psycho·sex·ual /ˌsaɪkoːˈsekʃʊəl/ *adjective* of or involving the psychological aspects of the sexual impulse. □ **psycho·sex·ual·ly** *adverb*

psych·o·sis /saɪˈkoːsɪs/ *noun* (*pl.* **psych·o·ses** /-siːz/) a severe mental derangement, esp. when resulting in delusions and loss of contact with external reality. [Greek *psukhōsis* from *psukhoō* give life to (as PSYCHE)]

psycho·social /ˌsaɪkoːˈsoːʃəl/ *adjective* of or involving the influence of social factors or human interactive behaviour. □ **psycho·social·ly** *adverb*

psycho·somat·ic /ˌsaɪkoːsəˈmatɪk/ *adjective* **1** (of an illness etc.) caused or aggravated by mental conflict, stress, etc. **2** of the mind and body together. □ **psycho·somat·ic·ally** *adverb*

psycho·surgery /ˌsaɪkoːˈsɜːrdʒərɪ/ *noun* brain surgery as a means of treating mental disorder. □ **psycho·surgi·cal** *adjective*

psycho·ther·apy /ˌsaɪkoːˈθerəpɪ/ *noun* (*pl.* **-apies**) the treatment of mental disorder by psychological means. □ **psycho·thera·peut·ic** *adjective* **psycho·ther·apist** *noun*

psy·chot·ic /saɪˈkɒtɪk/ ● *adjective* of or characterized by a psychosis. ● *noun* a person suffering from a psychosis. □ **psy·chot·ic·ally** *adverb*

psycho·trop·ic /ˌsaɪkoːˈtrɒpɪk/ *noun* (of a drug) acting on the mind. [PSYCHO- + Greek *tropē* turning: see TROPIC]

psy·chrom·eter /saɪˈkrɒmətər/ *noun* a thermometer consisting of a dry bulb and a wet bulb for measuring atmospheric humidity. □ **psy·chrom·et·ric** *adjective* [Greek *psukhros* cold + -METER]

psyl·lium /ˈsɪliəm/ *noun* **1** a leafy-stemmed Mediterranean plantain, *Plantago afra*. **2** the seeds of this or several related plantains, used as a mild laxative. [Latin from Greek *psullion*, from *psulla* flea, because of the seeds' appearance]

psy-ops *plural noun* tactics intended to manipulate one's opponents or enemies, such as the dissemination of propaganda or the use of psychological warfare. [contraction of *psychological operations*]

PT *abbreviation* 1 PACIFIC TIME. 2 PHYSICAL TRAINING.

Pt *symbol Chem.* the element platinum.

pt. *abbreviation* 1 part. 2 pint. 3 point. 4 port.

PTA *abbreviation* PARENT-TEACHER ASSOCIATION.

Ptah /tɒ/ *Egyptian Myth* an ancient deity of Memphis, creator of the universe and god of artisans, who became one of the chief deities of Egypt; he was identified by the Greeks with Hephaestus.

ptar·migan /ˈtɑrmɪɡən/ *noun* (*pl.* same or **-migans**) any of various game birds of Arctic regions of the genus *Lagopus*, resembling a grouse but with feathered toes and predominantly white plumage in winter. [Gaelic *tàrmachan*: p- after Greek words in *pt-*]

Pte *abbreviation* (also **Pte.**) PRIVATE *noun* 1.

pteri·dol·ogy /ˌtɛrɪˈdɒlədʒi/ *noun* the study of ferns.
□ **pteri·do·logic·al** *adjective* **pteri·dol·o·gist** *noun* [Greek *pteris -idos* fern + -LOGY]

pteri·do·phyte /ˈtɛrɪdəˌfaɪt/ *noun* any vascular non-flowering plant of the division Pteridophyta, including ferns, clubmosses, and horsetails. [Greek *pteris -idos* fern + *phuton* plant]

ptero- /ˈtɛroː/ *combining form* wing. [Greek *pteron* wing]

ptero·dac·tyl /ˌtɛrəˈdaktɪl/ *noun* a large extinct flying birdlike reptile with a long slender head and neck. [Greek *pteron* wing + *daktulos* finger]

ptero·pod /ˈtɛrəˌpɒd/ *noun* a marine gastropod with the middle part of its foot expanded into a pair of wing-like lobes. [PTERO- + Greek *pous podos* foot]

ptero·saur /ˈtɛrəˌsɔr/ *noun* any of a group of extinct flying reptiles with large bat-like wings, including pterodactyls. [PTERO- + Greek *saura* lizard]

PTFE *abbreviation* POLYTETRAFLUOROETHYLENE.

PTH *abbreviation* parathyroid hormone (*see* PARATHYROID).

PTO *abbreviation* 1 POWER TAKEOFF. 2 please turn over.

Ptol·em·aic /ˌtɒləˈmeɪɪk/ *adjective* 1 of or relating to the astronomer Ptolemy or his theories. 2 of or relating to the Ptolemies, Macedonian rulers of Egypt from the death of Alexander the Great (323 BC) to the death of Cleopatra (30 BC).

Ptolemaic system *noun* the theory that the earth is the stationary centre of the Universe (*compare* COPERNICAN SYSTEM).

Ptol·emy /ˈtɒləmi/ (2nd c.) Greek astronomer and geographer. His *Almagest*, a textbook of astronomy based on the geocentric system of Hipparchus, influenced medieval thought enormously; his *Geography*, giving lists of places with their longitudes and latitudes, was also a standard work for centuries, despite its inaccuracies.

Ptol·emy I /ˈtɒləmi/ (known as Ptolemy Soter) (c.365–c.283 BC), Macedonian general, king of Egypt 323–285. He proclaimed himself king of Egypt after Alexander the Great's death, and founded the Ptolemaic dynasty.

pto·maine /ˈtoːmeɪn/ *noun* any of various amine compounds, some toxic, in putrefying animal and vegetable matter. [French *ptomaïne* from Italian *ptomaina* irreg. from Greek *ptōma* corpse]

ptomaine poisoning *noun* food poisoning.

ptoo·ey /pəˈtuːi/ *interjection* representing the noise of spitting, esp. in contempt, disgust, etc. [imitative]

PTSD *abbreviation* POST-TRAUMATIC STRESS DISORDER.

P2P *abbreviation* = PEER-TO-PEER.

ptya·lin /ˈtaɪəlɪn/ *noun* an enzyme which hydrolyzes certain carbohydrates and is found in the saliva of humans and some other animals. [Greek *ptualon* spittle]

Pu *symbol Chem.* the element plutonium.

pub *noun* an establishment that is licensed to sell alcoholic drinks and usu. also serves light meals etc. [abbreviation of *public house*]

pub·bing *noun* the action of going drinking in pubs.

pub-crawl ● *noun* a drinking tour of several pubs or bars. ● *intransitive verb* make such a tour.

pu·ber·ty /ˈpjuːbərti/ *noun* the period during which adolescents reach sexual maturity and become capable of reproduction. □ **pu·ber·tal** *adjective* [Latin *pubertas* from *puber* adult]

pubes¹ /ˈpjuːbiːz/ *noun* (*pl.* same) 1 the lower part of the abdomen at the front of the pelvis, covered with hair from puberty. 2 *informal* the pubic hair. [Latin]

pubes² *pl.* of PUBIS.

pu·bes·cence /pjuːˈbɛsəns/ *noun* 1 the time when puberty begins. 2 *Bot.* soft down on the leaves and stems of plants. 3 *Zool.* soft down on various parts of animals, esp. insects. □ **pu·bes·cent** *adjective* [French *pubescence* or medieval Latin *pubescentia* from Latin *pubescere* reach puberty]

pubic /ˈpjuːbɪk/ *adjective* of or relating to the pubes or pubis (*pubic hair*).

pubis /ˈpjuːbɪs/ *noun* (*pl.* **pubes** /-biːz/) either of a pair of bones forming the two sides of the pelvis. [Latin *os pubis* bone of the PUBES¹]

pub·lic ● *adjective* 1 of or concerning the people as a whole (*in the public interest*). 2 open to or shared by all the people (*public meeting*). 3 done or existing openly (*made her views public; a public protest*). 4 a (of a service, funds, etc.) provided or heavily subsidized by, or concerning a government (*public money; public expenditure; public housing; public broadcasting*). b (of a person) in government (*had a distinguished public career*). 5 devoted or directed to the promotion of the general welfare; patriotic (*public spirit*). 6 well-known; famous (*a public figure*). 7 *Cdn* of or relating to a public school or the public school system. ● *noun* 1 (as *sing.* or *pl.*) the community in general, or members of the community. 2 a section of the community having a particular interest or in some special connection (*the reading public; my public demands my loyalty*). □ **go public** 1 become a public company. 2 reveal previously unknown information etc. (*went public with her allegations*). **in public** openly, publicly. **in the public eye** at the centre of public attention; famous or notorious. □ **pub·lic·ly** *adverb* [Old French *public* or Latin *publicus* from *pubes* adult]

public access *noun* (usu. *attributive*) designating a type of television programming that is made available to community groups or members of the general public.

public accounts committee *noun Cdn & Brit.* a standing committee of a legislature, responsible for reviewing government expenditure, primarily by examining the Auditor General's report.

public address system *noun* an electronic system used to amplify sound, used at public meetings, sports events, in schools, etc.

public administration *noun* 1 the implementation of government policy, usu. by the civil service. 2 a branch of study preparing students for careers in this.

public affairs *plural noun* = CURRENT AFFAIRS.

pub·li·can /ˈpʌblɪkən/ *noun* 1 *Rom. Hist.* a tax collector, esp. one who held a contract for the collection of taxes in a specific area. 2 *Brit.* the keeper of a public house. [Latin *publicanus* from *publicum* public revenue (as PUBLIC)]

public assistance *noun N Amer.* = SOCIAL SECURITY.

pub·li·ca·tion *noun* 1 a the preparation and issuing of a book, newspaper, engraving, music, information in electronic form, etc. to the public. b a book etc. so issued. 2 the act or an instance of making something publicly known. [Latin *publicatio -onis* (as PUBLISH)]

public bill *noun* a piece of legislation affecting the public as a whole.

public company *noun* a company whose shares are traded freely on a stock exchange.

public corporation *noun* 1 a corporation that is owned and operated by a government to serve the public. 2 *N Amer.* = PUBLIC COMPANY.

Public Curator *noun Cdn* (*Que.*) a provincial government official responsible for the affairs of persons legally unfit to conduct them themselves, e.g. a minor, a mentally incompetent person, etc.

public debt *noun* debt incurred by a government.

public domain *noun* the legal status of a work on which copyright has expired, or which has never been copyrighted.

public enemy *noun* 1 a notorious wanted criminal. 2 a person or thing regarded as the greatest threat to a group or community (*he identified inflation as public enemy number one*).

public figure *noun* a famous person.

public good *noun* 1 a commodity or service that is provided without profit to all members of a society, either by the government or a private individual or organization (*library services are a public good, not a commercial commodity*). 2 the benefit or well-being of the public.

public health *noun* health services, such as immunization, preventive medicine, etc., that are provided by a government and intended to improve the general health of citizens (also *attributive*: *public health inspector; public health nurse*).

public holiday *noun Cdn & Brit.* a usu. annual holiday, often marking a historical, religious, etc. occasion, and granted to most employees.

public house *noun Brit.* = PUB.

public housing noun housing provided for low-income families and subsidized by public funds.

pub·li·cist /ˈpʌbləsɪst/ noun a person who promotes or publicizes something, esp. a person employed by a company or individual to obtain publicity for products, services, etc.

pub·li·city /pʌbˈlɪsɪti/ noun 1 the action or fact of publicizing someone or something or of being publicized. 2 a the technique or the process of promoting or advertising a product, person, company, etc. b material or information used for this. 3 public exposure; fame or notoriety. [French *publicité* (as PUBLIC)]

publicity stunt noun something done merely for the publicity that it will generate (*the lawsuit is just a publicity stunt*).

pub·li·cize /ˈpʌblɪˌsaɪz/ transitive verb (also esp. Brit. **-cise**) make publicly known; advertise, promote.

public key noun Computing a publicly available cryptographic key used to convert data into a form which cannot be read by unauthorized persons (often attributive: *public-key encryption*).

public law noun 1 the law of relations between individuals and the state. 2 a piece of legislation affecting the public as a whole.

public library noun a library, usu. funded by a municipal government, that lends books and other materials to the general public.

public mischief noun Cdn the criminal offence of making a false accusation, reporting an offence that did not occur, doing something that will cause another person to be suspected of an offence, etc.

public nuisance noun 1 an illegal act against the public generally. 2 informal an obnoxious person.

public opinion noun the prevalent view or views held by the majority of the community.

public ownership noun nationalization; ownership by the state.

public policy noun government policy relating to or affecting the general public.

public prosecutor noun a law officer conducting criminal proceedings on behalf of the state or in the public interest.

public purse noun informal the national treasury.

Public Record Office noun (in the UK) an institution keeping official archives, esp. birth, marriage, and death certificates, for public inspection.

public relations plural noun 1 the work of presenting a good image of an organization, person, etc., to the public, esp. by providing information (*she works in public relations*). 2 the state of the relationship between an organization and the public (*the company sponsors literacy groups, which is good for public relations*).

public relations officer noun a person employed by a company etc. to promote a favourable public image.

public school noun 1 a primary or secondary school that is supported by public funds. 2 Cdn (Ont.) a a school that is part of the public school system (*my high school was a public school*) (compare SEPARATE SCHOOL 1). b an elementary school that is part of the public school system (*went to Woodside Public School*). c elementary schooling in the public school system (*when I was in public school*). 3 (in England and Wales) a private fee-paying secondary school, esp. for boarders.

public school board noun Cdn 1 an elected board of trustees responsible for the public schools of a particular area. 2 the administrative unit responsible for the public schools in a given area. 3 the area within which a public school board has jurisdiction.

public school system noun Cdn a system of publicly-funded non-denominational schools (compare SEPARATE SCHOOL SYSTEM).

public sector noun that part of the economy that is under direct control by the state.

public servant noun a government employee, esp. of a federal government.

public service noun 1 public servants collectively. 2 a service provided to the public without charge by a corporation etc. (*the radio station ran the safety commercials as a public service*).

public service announcement noun N Amer. 1 free airtime donated by a radio or television station to a non-profit organization. 2 a message, e.g. a traffic safety warning, aired by a radio or television station as a service to the public. Abbr.: **PSA**.

public speaking noun an act or the skill of addressing an audience effectively.

public spirit noun a willingness to engage in community action. □ **public-spirited** adjective **public-spirited·ly** adverb **public-spirited·ness** noun

public transit noun (also **public transportation**, **public transport**) a system of buses, trains, etc., running on fixed routes, esp. when owned by a government agency (*take public transit downtown to save on parking*).

Public Trustee noun Cdn a provincial government official who administers the estates of people who die intestate, missing persons, etc.

public utility noun an organization or corporation supplying water, electricity, natural gas, etc. to the public.

public works noun building work, e.g. of roads, hospitals, schools, etc., which is paid for by the government.

pub·lish verb 1 transitive & intransitive (of an author, publisher, etc.) prepare and issue (a book, a newspaper, information in electronic form, computer software, etc.) for public consumption. 2 transitive (esp. as **pub·lished** adjective) publish the works of (a particular writer or composer) (*she was already a published poet at the age of twenty*). 3 transitive make generally known. 4 transitive announce (an edict etc.) formally; read (marriage banns). 5 transitive Law communicate (a libel etc.) to a third party. □ **publish or perish** an attitude or practice existing within academia, esp. within academic institutions, whereby researchers are under pressure to publish material in order to retain their positions or be deemed successful. □ **pub·lish·able** adjective **pub·lish·ing** noun [Middle English *puplise* etc. from Old French *puplier*, *publier* from Latin *publicare* (as PUBLIC)]

pub·lish·er noun 1 a person or esp. a company that produces and distributes copies of a book, newspaper, etc. for sale. 2 N Amer. a newspaper proprietor.

PUC abbreviation N Amer. public utilities commission, a government regulatory body for public utilities.

Puc·cini /puˈtʃiːni/ **Gia·como** (1858–1924), Italian operatic composer. His sense of the dramatic, gift for melody, and skilful use of the orchestra have ensured that his operas remain among the most popular in the repertoire; they include *Manon Lescaut* (1893), *La Bohème* (1896), *Tosca* (1900), and *Madama Butterfly* (1904).

puce /pjuːs/ ● noun a dark reddish purple. ● adjective of this colour. [French, = flea(-colour), from Latin *pulex -icis*]

Puchon /puˈtʃʌn/ a city in S Korea, just west of Seoul; pop. (est. 1995) 779,412.

Puck /pʌk/ (also **puck**) a mischievous sprite or goblin believed esp. in the 16th and 17th c. to haunt the English countryside.

puck noun 1 a hard rubber disc used in hockey. 2 Cdn something shaped like a hockey puck, esp. a disc of chlorine used in swimming pool systems or a disc of disinfectant placed in a urinal. [19th c.: perhaps from *puck* 'a stroke at the ball in hurling', from dial. *puck* (v.) 'hit, strike': compare POKE¹ verb]

pucka var. of PUKKA.

puck board noun Cdn high density polyethylene in large sheets, used esp. for the boards surrounding a hockey arena.

puck bunny noun a young female hockey fan, esp. one motivated more by a desire to watch, meet, or become esp. sexually involved with the players than by an interest in the sport itself.

puck carrier noun Hockey the player in possession of the puck.

puck·er ● transitive & intransitive verb (often foll. by up) 1 gather or cause to gather into wrinkles, folds, or bulges (*puckered her eyebrows; this seam is puckered up*). 2 contract (the lips) as when preparing to kiss (*closed her eyes and puckered*). ● noun such a wrinkle, bulge, fold, etc. □ **puck·ery** adjective [prob. frequentative, formed as POKE², POCKET (compare PURSE)]

puck-handling noun Hockey the ability to control the puck while deking, stickhandling, receiving passes, etc. □ **puck·hand·ler** noun

puck hog noun a hockey player who selfishly refuses to pass the puck to his or her teammates.

puck·ish adjective impish; mischievous (*a puckish sense of humour*). □ **puck·ish·ly** adverb **puck·ish·ness** noun [PUCK]

puck·ster noun Cdn slang a hockey player.

pud /pʊd/ noun esp. Brit. informal = PUDDING. [abbreviation]

pud·ding /ˈpʊdɪŋ/ noun 1 any of various cooked desserts that are heavier and more moist than cake, esp.: a a steamed dessert made of flour, suet, fruit, etc. (*Christmas pudding*). b a cake-like dessert with a sauce on the bottom. c a dessert incorporating bread, rice, tapioca, etc. in a sauce made of milk, eggs, etc. (*rice pudding; bread pudding*). 2 N Amer. = MILK PUDDING. 3 an unsweetened dish containing flour, suet, etc., served with the main course of a meal (*Yorkshire pudding*). 4 Brit. = DESSERT. □ **in the pudding club** Brit. slang pregnant.

Consonants: b *but*   d *dog*   f *few*   g *get*   h *her*   j *yes*   k *cat*   l *leg*   m *man*   n *no*   p *pen*   r *red*   s *sit*

□ **pud·dingy** *adjective* [Middle English *poding* from Old French *boudin* black pudding, ultimately from Latin *botellus* sausage: see BOWEL]

pudding bowl *noun* **1** a bowl in which puddings are cooked. **2** (*attributive*) a person's hair or hairstyle shaped as if cut around the edge of a pudding bowl placed on the person's head.

pud·dle ● *noun* **1** a small pool, esp. of rainwater or melted snow on a road etc. **2** clay and sand mixed with water and used as a watertight covering for embankments etc. ● *verb* **1** *intransitive* **a** dabble or wallow in mud or shallow water. **b** busy oneself in an untidy way. **2** *transitive* **a** knead (clay and sand) into puddle. **b** line (a canal etc.) with puddle. **3** *intransitive* make puddle from clay etc. **4** *transitive* stir (molten iron) to produce wrought iron by expelling carbon. **5** *transitive* make (water etc.) muddy. **6** *transitive* work (mixed water and clay) to separate gold or opal. □ **pud·dler** *noun* **pud·dly** *adjective* [Middle English *podel*, *puddel*, diminutive of Old English *pudd* ditch]

puddle jumper *noun* N Amer. informal a small, light, fast, and highly manoeuvrable airplane, esp. as used for short trips.

pu·den·dum /pjuːˈdendəm/ *noun* (*pl.* **pu·den·da** /-də/) (usu. in *pl.*) the genitals, esp. of a woman. □ **pu·den·dal** *adjective* [Latin *pudenda* (*membra*), neuter pl. of gerundive of *pudēre* be ashamed]

pudgy *adjective* (**pudgi·er**, **pudgi·est**) *informal* (esp. of a person or part of the body) plump, thickset. □ **pudge** *noun* **pudgi·ly** *adverb* **pudgi·ness** *noun* [compare PODGY]

Pueb·la /ˈpweblə/ **1** a state of south central Mexico. **2** (in full **Puebla de Zara·goza** /dei ˌsarəˈgɒsə/) its capital city; pop. (2000) 1,271,000.

pueb·lo /ˈpweblo/ ● *noun* (*pl.* **-los**) **1** a town or village in Latin America, esp. an Indian settlement. **2** (**Pueblo**) a member of a N American Indian people living esp. in New Mexico and Arizona. **3** a communal dwelling consisting of a number of multi-storey adobe or stone houses joined together, used by certain Indian peoples of the southwestern US. ● *adjective* (**Pueblo**) of or relating to the Pueblos or their culture. [Spanish, = people, from Latin *populus*]

puer·ile /ˈpjʊərail/ *adjective* **1** trivial, childish, immature. **2** of or like a child. □ **puer·ile·ly** *adverb* **puer·il·ity** /-ˈrɪlɪti/ *noun* (*pl.* **-ities**). [French *puéril* or Latin *puerilis* from *puer* boy]

puer·per·al /pjuːˈɜːpərəl/ *adjective* of or caused by childbirth. [Latin *puerperus* from *puer* child + -*parus* bearing]

puerperal fever *noun* fever following childbirth and caused by uterine infection.

Puer·to Plata /ˌpwɜːto ˈplɒtə/ a resort town in the Dominican Republic, on the north coast; pop. (est. 2002) 115,000.

Puer·to Rico /ˌpɔːto ˈriːkoː, pɔːtə-, pwerto-/ an island of the Greater Antilles in the W Indies; pop. (est. 2002) 3,957,988; capital, San Juan. One of the earliest Spanish settlements in the New World, it was ceded to the US by Spain in 1898, and in 1952 it became a Commonwealth in voluntary association with the US. □ **Puer·to Rican** *adjective & noun*

Puerto Rico Trench an ocean trench extending in an east–west direction to the north of Puerto Rico and the Leeward Islands. It reaches a depth of 9 220 m (28,397 ft.).

Puer·to Val·lar·ta /pwerto vaiˈjɑːrtə/ a resort city in W Mexico; pop. (est. 2000) 150,000.

puff ● *noun* **1 a** a short quick blast of breath or wind. **b** the sound of this; a similar sound. **c** a small quantity of vapour, smoke, etc., emitted in one blast (*went up in a puff of smoke*). **d** an inhalation or exhalation from a cigarette etc. **2** a food that is light or fluffy (*cream puff*; *potato puff*). **3** a gathered mass of material in a dress etc. **4** a roll of hair that is cylindrical in shape. **5 a** (also **puff piece**) an extravagantly, esp. uncritically enthusiastic or favourable review, article, etc., esp. in a newspaper. **b** an advertisement for goods etc., esp. in a newspaper. **6** = POWDER-PUFF. ● *verb* **1** *intransitive* emit a puff of air or breath; blow with short blasts. **2** *intransitive* (often foll. by *out*, *away*, etc.) send out or move with puffs of vapour, smoke, etc. (*a train puffed out of the station*). **3** *transitive* (usu. in *passive*; often foll. by *out*) put out of breath (*arrived somewhat inflamed*; *completely puffed him out*). **4** *intransitive* breathe hard; pant. **5** *transitive* utter pantingly ('*No more,' she puffed*). **6** *intransitive & transitive* (usu. foll. by *up*, *out*) become or cause to become inflated; swell (*my eye was inflamed and puffed up*; *puffed up the balloon*). **7** *transitive* (usu. foll. by *out*, *up*, *away*) blow or emit (dust, smoke, a light object, etc.) with a puff. **8 a** *transitive* smoke (a pipe etc.) in puffs. **b** *intransitive* (usu. foll. by *away* etc.) take puffs at a cigarette etc. (*puffing away at his cigar*). **9** *transitive* advertise or promote (goods, a book, etc.) with exaggerated or false praise. □ **puff up** = sense 9 of *verb*. [Middle English *puf*, *puffe*, perhaps from Old English, imitative of the sound of breath]

puff adder *noun* a large venomous African viper, *Bitis arietans*, which inflates the upper part of its body and hisses when excited.

puff·ball *noun* **1** any of various fungi having a ball-shaped spore case. **2** anything round and fluffy, such as a powder puff.

puffed *adjective* **1** swollen (*puffed eyelids*). **2** (of a sleeve or other part of a garment) gathered so as to have a rounded shape. **3** (of cereal grain) expanded by means of high-pressure steam. **4** made breathless by exertion.

puffed-up *adjective* **1** swollen. **2** having an exaggerated sense of importance. **3** inflated or bombastic in language or style. **4** involving or consisting of exaggerated or undue praise.

puff·er *noun* **1** a person or thing that puffs. **2** = PUFFERFISH. **3** = INHALER.

puffer·fish *noun* any tropical fish of the family Tetraodonitidae, able to inflate itself into a spherical form when threatened etc. and containing a deadly poison. Also called BLOWFISH.

puff·ery *noun* exaggerated praise or commendation. [PUFF *verb* 9 + -ERY]

puf·fin *noun* any of various seabirds of the family Alcidae native to the N Atlantic and N Pacific having a large head with a brightly coloured triangular bill, and black and white plumage, esp. the Atlantic puffin, *Fratercula arctica*. [Middle English *poffin*, *pophyn*, of unknown origin]

puff pastry *noun* a pastry prepared from alternating layers of fat and dough which expand on baking, creating large spaces between thin layers of pastry.

puffy *adjective* (**puffi·er**, **puffi·est**) **1** swollen (*her arm was all bruised and puffy*). **2** soft, rounded, and light (*puffy clouds*). □ **puff·i·ly** *adverb* **puff·i·ness** *noun*

pug[1] (in full **pug dog**) a dwarf breed of dog with a broad flat nose and deeply wrinkled face. [16th c.: perhaps from Low German or Dutch]

pug[2] *transitive verb* (**pugged**, **pug·ging**) **1** prepare (clay) for making bricks or pottery, by kneading and working into a soft and plastic condition. **2** pack (the space between floor joists) with earth, sawdust, etc., to provide sound insulation. □ **pug·ging** *noun* [19th c.: origin unknown]

pug[3] *noun* slang a boxer. [abbreviation of PUGILIST]

pug[4] ● *noun* the footprint of an animal. ● *transitive verb* (**pugged**, **pug·ging**) track by pugs. [Hindi *pag* footprint]

pug dog *noun* see PUG[1].

Puget Sound /ˈpjuːdʒɪt/ an inlet of the Pacific on the coast of Washington State. It is linked to the ocean by the Strait of Juan de Fuca and is overlooked by the city of Seattle, which is situated on its eastern shore. [P. *Puget*, aide to G. VANCOUVER[2]]

pug·gree /ˈpʌgri/ *noun* (also **pug·ree**, **pug·garee** /-ərɪ/) **1** an Indian turban. **2** a thin muslin scarf tied round a sun helmet etc. and shielding the neck. [Hindi *pagrī* turban]

pugil·ist /ˈpjuːdʒɪlɪst/ *noun* a boxer, esp. a professional. □ **pugil·ism** *noun* **pugil·is·tic** *adjective* [Latin *pugil* boxer]

Pugin /ˈpjuːdʒɪn/ **Au·gus·tus Welby North·more** (1812–52), English architect, theorist, and designer. The main champion of the Gothic revival, he designed the external detail and internal fittings for the Houses of Parliament in London.

Puglia see APULIA.

pug mill *noun* a machine for mixing and pugging clay (see PUG[2]).

pug·na·cious /pʌgˈneɪʃəs/ *adjective* quarrelsome; disposed to fight. □ **pug·na·cious·ly** *adverb* **pug·na·cious·ness** *noun* **pug·na·city** /-ˈnasɪti/ *noun* [Latin *pugnax -acis* from *pugnare* fight, from *pugnus* fist]

pug-nose *noun* a short squat or snub nose. □ **pug-nosed** *adjective*

Pug·wash /ˈpʌgwɒʃ/ a village in N Nova Scotia, situated at the mouth of the Pugwash River and the shore of the Northumberland Strait, about 50 km east of Amherst; pop. (1996) 897. It was the site of the first Pugwash conference, a meeting at which philosophers, statesmen, etc. gather to discuss issues of international concern. [Mi'kmaq *pagweak* shoal, shallow water]

puh-leeze *interjection* (also **puh-lease**) please (indicating scorn or contempt at implied gullibility). [alteration of PLEASE]

puisne /ˈpjuːni/ *adjective* Cdn & Brit. Law denoting a judge of a superior court inferior in rank to chief justices. [Old French from *puis* from Latin *postea* afterwards + *né* born, from Latin *natus*: compare PUNY]

puis·sance /ˈpjuːɪsəns, ˈpwiːs-/ *noun* **1** (also /pwiːˈsɑːs/) a test of a horse's ability to jump large obstacles in show jumping. **2** *literary* or *archaic* great power, might, or influence. [Old French (as PUISSANT)]

puis·sant /ˈpjuːɪsənt, ˈpwiːs-, -ˈpwɪs-/ *adjective* literary or archaic having great power or influence; mighty. □ **puis·sant·ly** *adverb* [Old French from Latin *posse* be able: compare POTENT]

puja /ˈpuːdʒə/ *noun* (also **pooja**) a Hindu rite of worship; a prayer. [Sanskrit]

Pukaskwa National Park /ˈpʌkəsɒ/ a park in north central Ontario, situated on the northeastern shore of Lake Superior, near Marathon. It was established in 1971. [the name of a local river, possibly from Ojibwa *pagisowinakak* bathing place]

puke *slang* ● *transitive & intransitive verb* vomit. ● *noun* vomit. □ **pukey** *adjective* [16th c.: prob. imitative]

pukka /ˈpʌkə/ *adjective* (also **puk·kah, pucka**) *Anglo-Indian* **1** genuine. **2** of good quality; perfect (*did a pukka job*). [Hindi *pakkā* cooked, ripe, substantial]

pul /puːl/ *noun* (*pl.* **puls** or **puli** /-li/) a monetary unit of Afghanistan, equal to one-hundredth of an afghani. [Pashto from Persian *pūl* copper coin]

pula /ˈpuːlə/ *noun* the basic monetary unit of Botswana, equal to 100 thebe. [Setswana, = rain]

pul·chri·tude /ˈpʌlkrɪˌtjuːd/ *noun literary* beauty. □ **pul·chri·tud·in·ous** /-ˈtjuːdɪnəs/ *adjective* [Latin *pulchritudo -dinis* from *pulcher -chri* beautiful]

pule /pjuːl/ *intransitive verb literary* cry querulously or weakly; whine, whimper. [16th c.: prob. imitative: compare French *piauler*]

Pul·itz·er /ˈpʊlɪtsər, ˈpjuː-/ **Jo·seph** (1847–1911), Hungarian-born US newspaper proprietor and editor. He owned a number of newspapers, including the *New York World*, and through his journalism he aimed to remedy abuses and reform social and economic inequalities; he made provisions in his will for the establishment of the Pulitzer Prizes.

Pul·itz·er Prize /ˈpʊlɪtsər, ˈpjuː-/ *noun* each of 13 annual awards for achievements in American journalism, literature, and music. [J. PULITZER]

pulk /pʌlk/ *noun* (also **pulka** /ˈpʌlkə/) a small toboggan-like sled, pulled esp. by a dog or a person on skis. [Finnish *pulkka*, Lappish *pulkke*]

pull ● *verb* **1** *transitive* exert force on (a thing) tending to move it towards oneself or the origin of the force (*stop pulling my hair*). **2** *transitive* cause to move in this way (*pulled it nearer; pulled me into the room*). **3** *intransitive* exert a pulling force (*the horse pulls well; the engine will not pull*). **4** *transitive* extract (a cork or tooth) by pulling. **5** *transitive* damage (a muscle etc.) by abnormal strain. **6** *intransitive* (of an engine etc.) work hard and use a lot of effort in order to operate (*the car pulled hard up the hill*). **7** *transitive* (often foll. by *on*) bring out (a weapon) for use against (a person). **8 a** *transitive* check the speed of (a horse), esp. so as to make it lose the race. **b** *intransitive* (of a horse) strain against the bit. **9** *transitive* move (a boat) by pulling on the oars. **10** *transitive* (often foll. by *in*) attract or secure (support, votes, etc.). **11** *transitive* draw (an esp. alcoholic beverage) from a barrel etc. **12** *intransitive* (foll. by *at*) tear or pluck at. **13** *intransitive* (often foll. by *on, at*) inhale deeply; draw or suck (on a pipe etc.). **14** *transitive* (often foll. by *up*) remove (a plant) by the root. **15** *transitive* a *Baseball* (of a batter) hit (the ball) away from one's opposite field, i.e. (of a right-handed batter) into left field or (of a left-handed batter) into right field. **b** *Golf* (of a right-handed player) hit (the ball) to the left or (of a left-handed player) to the right, esp. widely. **16** *transitive* print (a proof etc.). **17** *transitive informal* **a** achieve or accomplish (something illicit, cunning, etc.) (*don't pull any more stunts like that*). **b** do something characteristic of (a specified person) (*pulled a Trudeau*). **18** *intransitive* **a** (foll. by *up, in*) (of a vehicle) arrive at a place for stopping, refuelling, etc. (*pulled up to the lights; surprised to see them pull in*). **b** (foll. by *off*) (of a vehicle) exit from (a highway etc.). **19** *transitive* **a** withdraw, remove, take out of service or circulation (*pulled the goalie; the ad was pulled because of complaints*). **b** retrieve (a file). **20** *transitive* close (a curtain, blind, etc.). **21** *transitive* *N Amer.* facilitate the birth of (a calf) by reaching into the womb and pulling the animal out. ● *noun* **1** the act of pulling. **2** the force exerted by this. **3** a means of exerting influence; an advantage. **4 a** something that attracts or draws attention. **b** allure, attraction. **5** a long drink from a glass, mug, etc. **6** a handle etc. for applying a pull. **7** a session of rowing. **8** a printer's rough proof. **9** a draw or suck at a cigarette. **10** a contest involving pulling (*tractor pull; dog pull*). **11** an injury to a muscle caused by abnormal strain. □ **pull apart** (or **to pieces**) = PICK APART (see PICK[1]). **pull away 1** remove by pulling. **2** move away, depart. **3** (of a competitor) increase one's lead over others. **pull back** retreat or cause to retreat. **pull down 1** demolish (esp. a building). **2** *informal* earn (a sum of money) as wages etc. **pull even** (often foll. by *with*) reach the same level as (a leading competitor); catch up. **pull a face** assume a distinctive or specified expression (*pulled a glum face*). **pull a fast one** *see* FAST[1]. **pull for** support; desire success for. **pull in 1** (of a bus, train, etc.) arrive to take passengers. **2** (of a vehicle) arrive at a place for stopping, refuelling, etc. **3** earn or acquire. **4** *informal* arrest.

5 rein in, hold in, check. **pull one's hair out** be anxious, exasperated, frustrated, etc. **pull a person's leg** deceive a person playfully. **pull off 1** remove by pulling. **2** succeed in achieving or accomplishing. **3** remove from participation in (*we're going to pull you off the job*). **pull oneself together** recover control of oneself. **pull the other one** *Brit. informal* expressing disbelief (with reference to *pull a person's leg*). **pull out 1** take out by pulling. **2** depart. **3** withdraw from an undertaking. **4** (of a bus, train, etc.) leave with its passengers. **5** (of a vehicle) move out from the side of the road, or from its normal position to overtake. **pull out all the stops** exert extreme effort. **pull over 1** move (a vehicle) to the side of or off the road. **2** (of the police etc.) stop (a vehicle) for a traffic violation etc. **pull the plug** (often foll. by *on*) *informal* put an end to an enterprise etc.; destroy; cut off (supplies etc.). **pull punches** (usu. in *neg.*) **1** avoid using one's full force. **2** criticize less strongly than one might. **pull rank** take unfair advantage of one's seniority. **pull strings** exert (esp. clandestine) influence. **pull the strings** be the real actuator of what another does. **pull through 1** get through an illness, a dangerous situation, or a difficult undertaking. **2** enable (a person) to do this. **pull together** work in harmony. **pull up 1** stop or cause to stop moving. **2** pull out of the ground. **3** come or bring closer. **4** cause (a file etc.) to appear on a computer screen. **pull one's (own) weight** do one's fair share of work. □ **pull·er** *noun* [Old English (ā)*pullian*, perhaps related to Low German *pülen*, Middle Dutch *polen* 'to shell']

pull·back *noun* **1** an act or instance of pulling something back or retreating. **2** a withdrawal of troops. **3** a contrivance or attachment for pulling something back.

pull-down ● *attributive adjective* **1** that may be, or is designed to be, pulled down. **2** *Computing* designating a menu that need only be displayed onscreen when required. ● *noun* **1** a pull-down menu. **2** an exercise in which one pulls down a weighted bar from above the head down to the shoulders, to strengthen the latissimus dorsi muscles.

pul·let /ˈpʊlət/ *noun* a young hen, esp. one less than one year old. [Old French *poulet* diminutive of *poule*, ultimately fem. of Latin *pullus* chicken]

pul·ley /ˈpʊli/ ● *noun* (*pl.* **-leys**) **1** a grooved wheel or set of wheels for a cord etc. to pass over, set in a block and used for changing the direction of a force. **2** a wheel or drum fixed on a shaft and turned by a belt, used esp. to increase speed or power. ● *transitive verb* (**-leys, -leyed**) hoist, move, or work with a pulley. [Old French *polie* prob. ultimately from medieval Greek *polidion* (unrecorded) pivot, diminutive of *polos* POLE[2]]

pull factor *noun* a political, social, or economic consideration that influences an immigrant's decision to settle in a particular place.

pull hitter *noun* *Baseball* a hitter who tends to pull the ball (*see* PULL *verb* 15a).

Pull·man /ˈpʊlmən/ *noun* **1** a railway car affording special comfort. **2** a sleeping car. **3** a large suitcase. [G. M. *Pullman*, US designer d.1897]

pull-off ● *attributive adjective* that may be, or is designed to be, pulled off. ● *noun* **1** an act of pulling something off. **2** an area by the side of a road where vehicles may stop.

pull-on ● *attributive adjective* designating a garment without fasteners that is pulled on. ● *noun* such a garment.

pull·out ● *attributive adjective* that may be, or is designed to be, pulled out (*pullout couch*). ● *noun* **1** something that can be pulled out, esp. a section of a magazine. **2** the act of pulling out; a withdrawal, esp. from military involvement. **3** = PULL-OFF 2.

pull·over *noun* a knitted garment put on over the head and covering the top half of the body.

pull-type *adjective* (esp. *attributive*) (of farm equipment) designed to be pulled by a tractor etc.

pul·lu·late /ˈpʌljuˌleɪt/ *intransitive verb* **1** (of a seed, shoot, etc.) bud, sprout, germinate. **2** (esp. of an animal) swarm, throng; breed prolifically. **3** develop; spring up; come to life. **4** (foll. by *with*) abound. □ **pul·lu·la·tion** *noun* [Latin *pullulare* sprout, from *pullulus* diminutive of *pullus* young of an animal]

pull-up *noun* **1** an exercise involving raising oneself with one's arms by pulling up against a horizontal bar etc. fixed above one's head. **2** the act of pulling up; a sudden stop.

pul·mon·ary /ˈpʌlmənəri/ *adjective* **1** of or relating to the lungs. **2** having lungs or lung-like organs. [Latin *pulmonarius* from *pulmo -onis* lung]

pulmonary artery *noun* the artery conveying blood from the heart to the lungs.

pulmonary tuberculosis *noun* a form of tuberculosis caused by inhaling the tubercle bacillus into the lungs.

pulmonary vein *noun* the vein carrying oxygenated blood from the lungs to the heart.

pulp ● *noun* **1** the soft fleshy part of fruit etc. **2** any soft thick wet mass. **3** a soft shapeless mass made of ground wood or other vegetable fibres, etc., used in papermaking. **4 a** (often *attributive*) popular or sensational writing often regarded as of poor quality (originally printed on rough paper) (*pulp fiction*). **b** a novel, magazine, etc. containing pulp writing. **5** vascular tissue filling the interior cavity and root canals of a tooth. **6** *Mining* pulverized ore mixed with water. **7** = PULPWOOD. ● *verb* **1** *transitive* reduce to pulp. **2** *transitive* withdraw (a publication) from the market, usu. recycling the paper. **3** *transitive* remove pulp from. **4** *intransitive* become pulp. □ **beat a person to a pulp** beat a person severely. □ **pulp·er** *noun* **pulpy** *adjective* **pulp·ing** *noun* [Latin *pulpa*]

pulp cutter *noun* a logger who cuts wood into short lengths for the pulping process.

pul·pit /ˈpʊlpɪt, ˈpʊl-/ *noun* **1** a lectern or raised usu. enclosed platform in a church etc. from which the preacher delivers a sermon. **2** (prec. by *the*) preachers or preaching collectively. **3 a** a standing place on the bowsprit of a fishing vessel etc. **b** a railed-in area at the bow (or stern) of a yacht etc. [Latin *pulpitum* 'scaffold, platform']

pulp log *noun* a log suitable for making pulp.

pulp·wood *noun* timber suitable for making pulp.

pul·que /ˈpʊlkei, ˈpʊlki/ *noun* an originally Mexican fermented drink made from the sap of the maguey. [17th c.: Latin American Spanish, from Nahuatl *puliúhki* decomposed]

pul·sar /ˈpʌlsɑr/ *noun Astronomy* a celestial object, thought to be a rapidly rotating neutron star, emitting regular pulses of radio waves and other electromagnetic radiation. [*pulsating star*, after *quasar*]

pul·sate /ˈpʌlseit/ *intransitive verb* **1** expand and contract rhythmically; throb. **2** vibrate, quiver, thrill. **3** vary in magnitude, intensity, brightness, etc. (*a pulsating star*). □ **pul·sa·tion** *noun* **pul·sa·tor** *noun* [Latin *pulsare* frequentative of *pezllere puls-* drive, beat]

pul·sa·tile /ˈpʌlsəˌtail/ *adjective* of or having the property of pulsation.

pul·sa·til·la /ˌpʌlsəˈtɪlə/ *noun* any plant of the genus *Pulsatilla*, esp. the pasque flower. [modern Latin diminutive of *pulsata* fem. past participle (as PULSATE), because it quivers in the wind]

pulse¹ ● *noun* **1 a** a rhythmical throbbing of the arteries as blood is propelled through them, esp. as felt in the wrists, temples, etc. **b** each successive beat of the arteries or heart. **2** a throb or thrill of life or emotion. **3** a general feeling or opinion (*tried to read the pulse of the nation*). **4 a** a single vibration of sound, electric current, light, etc., esp. as a signal. **b** (*attributive*) designating a telephone system in which the number composed on a rotary dial or buttons is translated into electronic pulses corresponding in number to the digit dialled. **5** a musical beat. **6** any regular or recurrent rhythm, e.g. of the stroke of oars. **7 a** a feature or button on a blender etc. allowing the operator to pulse. **b** an act or instance of pulsing food in a blender etc. ● *verb* **1** *intransitive* pulsate. **2** *transitive* transmit etc. by rhythmical beats. **3** *transitive & intransitive* **a** operate (a food processor, blender, etc.) in short bursts using a button that engages the mechanism only as long as the operator keeps it depressed. **b** process (food) in a blender etc. in this way. □ **pulse·less** *adjective* [Old French *pous* from Latin *pulsus* from *pellere puls-* drive, beat]

pulse² *noun* **1** the edible seeds of various leguminous plants, e.g. chickpeas, lentils, beans, etc. **2** the plant or plants producing this. [Old French *pols* from Latin *puls pultis* porridge of meal etc.]

pulse code modulation *noun* a pulse modulation technique of representing a signal by a sequence of binary codes. Abbr.: **PCM**.

pulse modulation *noun* a type of modulation in which pulses are varied to represent a signal.

pulse point *noun* a point on the human body where the pulse is particularly noticeable, e.g. the inside of the wrist, elbow, or knee, at the ankle or on the side of the neck.

Pulu see TIGLATH-PILESER III.

pul·ver·ize /ˈpʌlvəˌraiz/ *verb* (also esp. *Brit.* **-ise**) **1** *transitive* reduce to fine particles. **2** *transitive & intransitive* crumble to dust. **3** *transitive informal* **a** demolish. **b** defeat utterly. □ **pul·ver·iz·a·tion** *noun* **pul·ver·iz·er** *noun* [Late Latin *pulverizare* from *pulvis pulveris* dust]

puma /ˈpjuːmə/ *noun* a cougar. [Spanish from Quechua]

pum·ice /ˈpʌmɪs/ ● *noun* (in full **pumice stone**) **1** a light porous volcanic rock often used as an abrasive in cleaning or polishing substances. **2** a piece of this used for removing hard skin etc. ● *transitive*

verb rub or clean with a pumice. [Old French *pomis* from Latin *pumex pumicis* (dial. *pom-*): compare POUNCE²]

pum·mel *transitive & intransitive verb* (**pum·melled**, **pum·mel·ling**; also esp. *US* **pum·meled**, **pum·mel·ing**) **1** pound or thump repeatedly. **2** beat with the fists. **3** defeat thoroughly. **4** criticize harshly. [alteration of POMMEL]

pump¹ ● *noun* **1** a device, usu. with rotary action or the reciprocal action of a piston or plunger, or functioning by suction, for raising or moving liquids or gases, inflating tires, etc. **2** an instance of pumping; a stroke of a pump. ● *verb* **1** *transitive* (often foll. by *in, out, into, up*, etc.) raise or remove (liquid, gas, etc.) with a pump. **2** *transitive* **a** (usu. foll. by *up*) fill (a tire etc.) with air. **b** increase the volume, loudness, strength, etc. of. **3** *transitive* **a** remove (water etc.) with a pump. **b** (often foll. by *out*) remove the contents of (something) with a pump (*needed to get my stomach pumped*). **4** *intransitive* work a pump. **5** *transitive* (often foll. by *out*) cause to move, pour forth, etc., in great quantities. **6** *transitive* elicit information from (a person) by persistent questioning. **7** *transitive* **a** move vigorously up and down. **b** shake (a person's hand) effusively. **8** *transitive* apply and release (brakes) quickly several times in succession, esp. to prevent skidding. **9** *transitive* (foll. by *into*) cause a major input of (money, effort, etc.). □ **pump iron** *informal* engage in bodybuilding with weights. □ **pump·able** *adjective* [Middle English *pumpe, pompe* (originally Naut.): prob. imitative]

pump² *noun* a lightweight, low-cut women's shoe, with no laces or straps. [16th c., earlier = 'light shoe for dancing': origin unknown]

pump-action *attributive adjective* designating a repeating firearm activated by a horizontally operating slide action.

pumped *adjective* (also **pumped up**) **1** in senses of PUMP¹ *verb*. **2** eager, excited, or emotionally prepared for an undertaking, event, etc.

pump·er *noun* **1** in senses of PUMP¹ *verb*. **2** (also **pumper truck**) a fire truck used to pump water or chemicals to douse a fire.

pum·per·nick·el *noun* a dense, dark, slightly sour rye bread. [German, earlier = lout, bumpkin, of uncertain origin]

pump-fake *N Amer. Sport* ● *intransitive verb* fake the intent to throw a ball by moving the arm (or arms) back etc. ● *noun* (**pump fake**) an act or instance of pump-faking.

pump·handle *intransitive verb informal* shake a person's hand effusively.

pump·house *noun* a building enclosing a pumping mechanism.

pump·jack *noun N Amer.* a pumping apparatus at an oil well.

pump·kin *noun* **1** any of various plants of the genus *Cucurbita*, esp. *C. maxima*, with large lobed leaves and tendrils. **2** the large rounded orange fruit of this with a thick rind and edible flesh. **3** *N Amer.* a term of endearment, esp. to a child, pet, etc. [alteration of earlier *pompon, pumpion* from obsolete French *po(m)pon* from Latin *pepo -onis* from Greek *pepōn* large melon]

pumpkin·seed *noun* a colourful N American sunfish, *Lepomis gibbosus*, with an orange belly, easily caught by anglers.

pump-out *noun* the action of pumping out, esp. the removal of waste, sewage, etc. from a storage tank.

pump-priming *noun* **1** the introduction of fluid etc. into a pump to prepare it for working. **2** esp. *US* the stimulation of commerce etc. by investment.

pump room *noun Brit.* **1** a room where fuel pumps etc. are stored or controlled. **2** a room at a spa etc. where medicinal water is dispensed.

pun ● *noun* the humorous use of a word to suggest different meanings, or of words of the same sound and different meanings. ● *intransitive verb* (**punned**, **pun·ning**) (foll. by *on*) make a pun or puns with (words). □ **pun·ning** *noun & adjective* **pun·ning·ly** *adverb* [17th c.: perhaps from obsolete *pundigrion*, a fanciful formation]

Punch *noun* **1** a grotesque humpbacked figure in a puppet show called *Punch and Judy*. **2** (in full **Suffolk Punch**) a short-legged thickset draft horse. □ **as pleased** (or **proud**) **as punch** showing great pleasure (or pride). [abbreviation of PUNCHINELLO]

punch¹ ● *transitive verb* **1** strike bluntly, esp. with a closed fist. **2** prod or poke with a blunt object. **3 a** pierce a hole in (metal, paper, a ticket, etc.) as or with a punch. **b** pierce (a hole) by punching. **4** *N Amer.* drive (a beast of burden) by prodding with a stick etc. **5** strike (a button on a keypad) with the fingertip. ● *noun* **1** a blow with a fist. **2** the ability to deliver this. **3** *informal* vigour; effective force. **4** any of various devices or machines for punching holes in materials, e.g. paper, leather, metal, plaster. **5** a tool or machine for impressing a design or stamping a die on a material. □ **beat someone to the punch** do something before someone else is able to; anticipate or forestall the actions of another. **punch above one's weight 1** wield influence apparently in excess of one's status. **2** perform above expectation. **punch the**

(time) clock *N Amer.* **1** record the time of one's arrival at or departure from work by inserting a card into a timed puncher. **2** be employed in a conventional, esp. nine-to-five job (*thirty years of punching the clock*). **punch in 1** punch the clock to record the time of one's arrival at work. **2** enter (data) into a computer, calculator, etc. using a keyboard or keypad. **3** dial (a number on a telephone) by hitting the keypads with the fingertip. **punch out 1** remove or detach by punching. **2** punch the clock to record the time of one's departure from work. **3** assault with punches; beat up. **punch up 1** enter or access (data) into or from a computer, cash register, etc. using a keyboard or keypad. **2** make more punchy, vigorous, effective; enliven. **3** beat up. □ **punch·er** *noun* **punch·less** *adjective* (in sense 3 of *noun*). [Middle English, var. of POUNCE¹]

punch² *noun* **1** a drink of mixed beverages, e.g. fruit juices, carbonated drinks, etc., often including wine or other alcohol, and usu. served at parties etc. with a ladle from a large bowl. **2** a drink made from the juices of several fruits, often sweetened. [apparently from Sanskrit *pañca* 'five, five kinds of' (because the drink had five ingredients)]

punch bowl *noun* a large usu. glass bowl in which punch is mixed and from which it is served with a ladle.

punch card *noun* (also **punched card**) a card perforated according to a code, for conveying instructions or data to a data processor etc.

punch-drunk *adjective* stupefied from or as though from a series of heavy blows to the head.

pun·cheon /ˈpʌntʃən/ *noun hist.* a large cask for liquids etc. holding from 150 to 545 litres. [Old French *poinson, poi(n)chon*, of unknown origin]

Pun·chin·ello /ˌpʌntʃɪˈnɛləʊ/ *noun* (*pl.* **-ellos**) **1** the chief character in a traditional Italian puppet show. **2** a short stout person of comical appearance. [Neapolitan dial. *Polecenella*, Italian *Pulcinella*, perhaps diminutive of *pollecena*, young turkeycock with a hooked beak, from *pulcino* chicken, ultimately from Latin *pullus*]

punching bag *noun N Amer.* **1** a suspended stuffed bag punched for exercise. **2** *informal* the object of repeated attack, criticism, etc.

punch·line *noun* the climactic final words or phrase of a joke or story.

punch·out *noun* a fist fight.

punch-up *noun informal* a fist fight; a brawl.

punchy *adjective* (**punch·i·er**, **punch·i·est**) **1** having punch or vigour; forceful. **2** PUNCH-DRUNK. **3** *N Amer.* in a state of nervous tension or extreme fatigue. **4 a** (of a sentence etc.) terse, short. **b** composed of punchy segments (*a punchy news program*). □ **punch·i·ly** *adverb* **punch·i·ness** *noun*

punc·tate /ˈpʌŋkteɪt/ *adjective Biol.* marked or studded with points, dots, spots, etc. □ **punc·ta·tion** *noun* [Latin *punctum* (as POINT)]

punc·tilio /pʌŋkˈtɪlɪəʊ/ *noun* (*pl.* **-os**) a fine or petty point of conduct or procedure. [Italian *puntiglio* & Spanish *puntillo* diminutive of *punto* POINT]

punc·tili·ous /pʌŋkˈtɪlɪəs/ *adjective* **1** attentive to formality or etiquette. **2** precise in behaviour. □ **punc·tili·ous·ly** *adverb* **punc·tili·ous·ness** *noun* [French *pointilleux* from *pointille* from Italian (as PUNCTILIO)]

punc·tual /ˈpʌŋktʃʊəl/ *adjective* **1** neither early nor late; precisely on time. **2** habitually occurring or arriving at the appointed time. □ **punc·tu·al·ity** *noun* **punc·tual·ly** *adverb* [medieval Latin *punctualis* from Latin *punctum* POINT]

punc·tu·ate /ˈpʌŋktʃʊeɪt/ *transitive verb* **1** insert punctuation marks in. **2** interrupt at intervals (*punctuated his tale with heavy sighs*). **3** emphasize, accentuate; give force to. [medieval Latin *punctuare punctuat-* (as PUNCTUAL)]

punctuated equilibrium *noun Biol.* a theory of evolutionary development marked by isolated episodes of rapid speciation between long periods of little or no change.

punc·tu·a·tion /ˌpʌŋktʃʊˈeɪʃən/ *noun* **1** the system or arrangement of marks used in writing to separate sentences and phrases etc. and to clarify meaning. **2** the practice or skill of punctuating.

punctuation mark *noun* any of the marks, e.g. period and comma, used in writing to separate sentences and phrases etc. and to clarify meaning.

punc·ture /ˈpʌŋktʃər/ ● *noun* **1** a small hole in a tire resulting in an escape of air. **2** a small hole in something such as the skin, caused by a sharp object (*puncture wounds*). ● *verb* **1** *transitive* make a puncture in. **2** *intransitive* undergo puncture. **3** *transitive* prick or pierce. **4** *transitive* deflate (pomposity etc.); debunk. [Latin *punctura* from *pungere punct-* prick]

pun·dit /ˈpʌndɪt/ *noun* **1** an expert in a particular subject or field who is

frequently called on to give opinions about it to the public. **2** var. of PANDIT. □ **pun·ditry** *noun* [Hindustani *paṇḍit* from Sanskrit *paṇḍita* learned]

pundit·oc·racy /ˌpʌndɪtˈɒkrəsi/ *noun* elite members of the news media, typically seen as having political power in their own right.

Pune *see* POONA.

pun·gent /ˈpʌndʒənt/ *adjective* **1** having a sharp or strong taste or smell. **2** (of remarks) penetrating, biting, caustic. □ **pun·gency** *noun* **pun·gent·ly** *adverb* [Latin *pungent-* pres. part. of *pungere* prick]

Punic /ˈpjuːnɪk/ ● *adjective* of or relating to ancient Carthage in North Africa. ● *noun* the language of Carthage, related to Phoenician. [Latin *Punicus, Poenicus* from *Poenus* from Greek *Phoinix* Phoenician]

Punic Wars three wars between Rome and Carthage, which led to the unquestioned dominance of Rome in the western Mediterranean. In the first (264–241 BC) Rome secured Sicily from Carthage; in the second (218–201 BC) the defeat of Hannibal put an end to Carthage's position as a Mediterranean power; the third (149–146 BC) ended in the total destruction of the city of Carthage.

pun·ish *verb* **1** *transitive & intransitive* cause (an offender) to suffer for an offence. **2** *transitive* inflict a penalty for (an offence). **3** *transitive informal* inflict severe blows on (an opponent). **4** *transitive & intransitive* subject (someone) to abusive, harsh, or improper treatment. □ **pun·ish·able** *adjective* **pun·ish·er** *noun* **pun·ish·ing** *adjective* **pun·ish·ing·ly** *adverb* [Old French *punir* from Latin *punire* = *poenire* from *poena* penalty]

pun·ish·ment *noun* **1** the act or an instance of punishing; the condition of being punished. **2** the loss or suffering inflicted in this. **3** *informal* severe treatment or suffering.

puni·tive /ˈpjuːnɪtɪv/ *adjective* inflicting or intended to inflict punishment. □ **puni·tive·ly** *adverb* [medieval Latin *punitivus* from *punit-* 'punished' from the verb *punire*]

punitive damages *plural noun Law* damages exceeding simple compensation and awarded to punish the defendant.

Pun·jab /ˈpʌndʒɑːb, ˈpʌn-/ **1** (also **the Punjab**) a region of NW India and Pakistan, traversed by the Indus and the five tributaries which gave the region its name, a centre of Sikhism from the 15th c. **2** a province of Pakistan; pop. (1983) 50,460,000; capital, Lahore. **3** a state of India; pop. (1991) 20,281,969; capital, Chandigarh. [Hindustani *panj* five, *āb* waters]

Pun·jabi /pʊnˈdʒɑːbi, pʌn-/ (also **Panjabi**) ● *noun* (*pl.* **-jabis**) **1** a native or inhabitant of Punjab. **2** the Indic language of Punjab. ● *adjective* of or relating to Punjab or its people or language.

punk ● *noun* **1** a young man or boy regarded as contemptible or insignificant, esp. because of rude or violent behaviour (often as a general term of abuse). **2** *N Amer.* a young hoodlum or ruffian. **3 a** (in full **punk rock**) a loud fast-moving form of angry and aggressive rock music. **b** the subculture or style associated with this, esp. that characterized by coloured spiked hair and leather clothing decorated with safety pins etc. **c** = PUNKER. **4** *N Amer.* an inexperienced person; a novice. **5** soft crumbly wood that has been attacked by fungus, used as tinder. ● *adjective* **1** worthless, rotten. **2** denoting punk rock and its associated subculture (*punk hair*). □ **punk·ish** *adjective* **punky** *adjective* [18th c.: origin unknown]

pun·kah /ˈpʌŋkə/ *noun* **1** (in India) a fan usu. made from the leaf of the palmyra. **2** a large swinging cloth fan on a frame worked by a cord or electrically. [Hindi *pankhā* fan, from Sanskrit *pakṣaka* from *pakṣa* wing]

punk·er *noun esp. N Amer.* (also **punk rocker**) a person who enjoys or plays punk music; a member of the punk subculture.

punk·ette *noun* a female punk rocker.

pun·net *noun Brit.* a small light basket or container for fruit or vegetables. [19th c.: perhaps diminutive of dial. *pun* POUND¹]

pun·ster *noun* a person who makes puns, esp. habitually.

punt¹ ● *noun* a long narrow flat-bottomed boat, square at both ends, used mainly for pleasure on rivers and propelled by a long pole. ● *verb* **1** *transitive* propel (a punt) with a pole. **2** *intransitive & transitive* travel or convey in a punt. □ **punt·er** *noun* [Middle Low German *punte, punto* & Middle Dutch *ponte* ferry boat, from Latin *ponto* Gaulish transport vessel]

punt² ● *transitive verb* kick (a ball, esp. in football or rugby) after it has dropped from the hands and before it reaches the ground. ● *noun* such a kick. □ **punt·er** *noun* [prob. from dial. *punt* push forcibly: compare BUNT¹]

punt³ ● *intransitive verb* **1** (in some card games) lay a stake against the bank. **2** esp. *Brit.* (often foll. by *on*) *informal* gamble or bet; speculate. ● *noun* **1** a bet. **2** a point in faro. [French *ponter* from *ponte* player against the bank, from Spanish *punto* POINT]

Consonants: b *but* d *dog* f *few* g *get* h *her* j *yes* k *cat* l *leg* m *man* n *no* p *pen* r *red* s *sit*

punt[4] /pʊnt/ *noun* the former chief monetary unit of the Republic of Ireland, now replaced by the euro. [Irish, = pound]

Punta Arenas /ˌpʊntə əˈreɪnəs/ a port in S Chile, on the Strait of Magellan; pop. (est. 2002) 135,000.

punt·er *noun* **1** *esp. Brit.* a person who gambles or lays a bet. **2** *Brit.* **a** *informal* a customer or client; a member of an audience. **b** *slang* a prostitute's client. **c** a participant in any activity. **3** a point in faro.

puny /ˈpjuːni/ *adjective* (**puni·er**, **puni·est**) **1** undersized. **2** weak, feeble. **3** petty. □ **puni·ly** *adverb* **puni·ness** *noun* [phonetic spelling of PUISNE]

pup ● *noun* **1** a young dog. **2** a young wolf, rat, seal, etc. **3** *Brit.* an unpleasant or arrogant young man. ● *transitive & intransitive verb* (**pupped**, **pup·ping**) (of a bitch, seal, etc.) bring forth (young). [back-formation from PUPPY as if a diminutive in -Y²]

pupa /ˈpjuːpə/ *noun* (*pl.* **pupae** /-piː/) an inactive immature form of an insect, being the resting stage between larva and adult, e.g. a chrysalis. □ **pupal** *adjective* [modern Latin from Latin *pupa* girl, doll]

pu·pate /ˈpjuːpeɪt/ *intransitive verb* become a pupa. □ **pu·pa·tion** *noun*

pu·pil[1] *noun* a person who is taught by another, esp. a schoolchild or student in relation to a teacher. □ **pupil·lage** *noun* (also **pupil·age**). **pupil·lary** *adjective* [Middle English, originally = orphan, ward, from Old French *pupille* or Latin *pupillus, -illa*, diminutive of *pupus* boy, *pupa* girl]

pu·pil[2] *noun* the dark circular opening in the centre of the iris of the eye, varying in size to regulate the passage of light to the retina. □ **pupil·lary** *adjective* [Old French *pupille* or Latin *pupilla*, diminutive of *pūpa* doll (as PUPIL¹): so called from the tiny images visible in the eye]

pup·pet *noun* **1** a small figure representing a human being or animal and moved by various means as entertainment, e.g. by pulling strings attached to its limbs or by putting one's hand inside it. **2** a person, state, etc. whose actions are controlled by another (also *attributive*: *puppet government*). □ **pup·petry** *noun* [later form of POPPET]

pup·pet·eer *noun* (also **puppet master**) **1** a person who works puppets. **2** a person who manipulates others. □ **pup·pet·eer·ing** *noun*

puppet state *noun* a country that is nominally independent but actually under the control of another power.

Pup·pis /ˈpʌpɪs/ a large southern constellation lying in the Milky Way. [Latin *puppis* stern, poop of a ship]

puppy *noun* (*pl.* **-pies**) **1** a young, esp. immature dog. **2** a conceited or arrogant young man. **3** *slang* a person having a specified character (*he's one sick puppy*). □ **puppy·hood** *noun* **puppy·ish** *adjective* [perhaps from Old French *po(u)pee* doll, plaything, toy, from Romanic (as POPPET)]

puppy dog *noun* **1** a child's word for a puppy. **2** a gentle or devotedly loyal person.

puppy fat *noun* fat on a child's body which disappears as the child grows older.

puppy love *noun* a strong, usu. temporary, feeling of love, esp. between adolescents.

puppy mill *noun* *N Amer.* a commercial concern that breeds dogs in large numbers, often with little concern for their welfare.

pup tent *noun* *N Amer.* a small triangular tent, esp. for two people, usu. without side walls or a window. [originally *dog tent*, from the tent's resemblance to a doghouse]

pup trailer *noun* *N Amer.* a second, smaller trailer hitched behind a tractor-trailer rig.

pur- *prefix* = PRO-¹ (*purchase; pursue*). [Anglo-French from Old French *por-, pur-, pour-* from Latin *por-, pro-*]

Pu·rana /pʊˈrɑːnə/ *noun* any of a class of Sanskrit sacred writings on Hindu mythology, folklore, etc. □ **Pu·ran·ic** *adjective* [Sanskrit *purāṇa* ancient legend, ancient, from *purā* formerly]

Pur·beck marble *noun* (also **Purbeck stone**) a hard usu. polished limestone from Purbeck in Dorset, used in pillars, effigies, etc.

pur·blind *adjective* **1** partly blind; having impaired or defective vision. **2** having imperfect perception or discernment; obtuse, dim-witted. □ **pur·blind·ness** *noun* [Middle English *pur(e)* blind from PURE, originally in sense 'utterly', assimilated to PUR-]

Pur·cell ▶ **1** /ˈpɜːrsel/ **Ed·ward Mills** (1912–97), US physicist, who shared the 1952 Nobel Prize for physics for his discovery of nuclear magnetic resonance (NMR) in liquids and solids (1946). **2** /ˈpɜːrsel, ˈpɜːrsəl/ **Henry** (*c.*1659–95), English composer. His works include choral odes, sacred anthems, the first English opera, *Dido and Aeneas* (1689), incidental music for plays such as *The Fairy Queen* (1692), and a series of *Fantasias* for the viol (1680). □ **Pur·cel·lian** *adjective*

Purcell Mountains /ˈpɜːrsel/ the most easterly range of the Columbia mountain system, situated in southeastern BC, between the Rocky and Selkirk mountains. [G. *Purcell*, British physician d.1876]

pur·chase /ˈpɜːrtʃəs/ ● *transitive verb* **1** acquire by payment; buy. **2** obtain or achieve at some cost. **3** *Naut.* haul up (an anchor etc.) by means of a pulley, lever, etc. ● *noun* **1** the act or an instance of buying. **2** something bought. **3** *Law* the acquisition of property by one's personal action and not by inheritance. **4 a** a firm hold on a thing to move it or to prevent it from slipping; leverage. **b** a device or tackle for moving heavy objects. □ **pur·chas·able** *adjective* **pur·chas·er** *noun* [Anglo-French *purchacer*, Old French *pourchacier* seek to obtain (as PUR-, CHASE¹)]

purchase order *noun* a form issued by an organization authorizing the purchase of a good or service, often sequentially numbered.

purchasing power *noun* **1** a person's financial ability to make purchases. **2** the amount that a sum of money etc. can purchase.

pur·dah /ˈpɜːrdə/ *noun* (also *attributive*) a system in certain Muslim and Hindu societies of screening women from strangers by means of a veil or curtain. □ **in purdah** (of a woman) screened from contact with strangers. [Urdu & Persian *pardah* veil, curtain]

Purdy, Al·fred Wel·ling·ton ('Al') (1918–2000), Canadian poet and novelist. His poetry collections include *The Enchanted Echo* (1944) and *Collected Poems 1956–86* (1986); he also wrote the novel *A Splinter in the Heart* (1990).

pure *adjective* **1 a** unmixed (*a pure white sheet; pure alcohol*). **b** clean and not mixed with any harmful substances (*the air is pure*). **2** of unmixed origin or descent (*pure-blooded*). **3** chaste. **4** morally or sexually undefiled; not corrupt. **5** guiltless. **6** sincere. **7** mere, simple, nothing but, sheer, true (*it was pure malice*). **8** (of a sound) not discordant, perfectly in tune. **9** (of a subject of study) dealing with abstract concepts and not practical application. **10 a** (of a vowel) not joined with another in a diphthong. **b** (of a consonant) not accompanied by another. **11** having no complicated or unnecessary elements (*the clean, pure lines of classical architecture*). □ **pure and simple** plainly, indisputably, certainly; and nothing else (*they were stolen, pure and simple*). □ **pure·ness** *noun* [Old French *pur* from Latin *purus*]

pure·bred ● *adjective* (of an animal) bred from parents of the same breed or variety; of unmixed ancestry. ● *noun* such an animal.

purée /pjʊrˈeɪ, ˈpjʊr-/ ● *noun* a pulp of vegetables or fruit etc. reduced to a smooth thick liquid. ● *transitive verb* (**pur·ées**, **pur·éed**) make a purée of. [French]

pure laine /pjʊr ˈlen/ *Cdn* ● *adjective* **1** designating a francophone Quebecer descended from the French settlers in New France and having exclusively French ancestry. **2** of, relating to, or consisting of pure laine Quebecers (*a pure laine company; pure laine nationalism*). ● *noun* such a person. [French, lit. = 'pure wool']

pure·ly *adverb* **1** in a pure manner. **2** merely, solely, exclusively. **3** entirely, completely.

pure play *noun* (also *attributive*) an e-commerce site that operates only online, not also having a traditional bricks-and-mortar operation.

pure science *noun* a science depending on deductions from demonstrated truths, e.g. mathematics or logic, or one studied without practical applications.

pur·fle /ˈpɜːrfəl/ ● *noun* an ornamental border, esp. on a violin etc. ● *transitive verb* decorate with a purfle. □ **purf·ling** *noun* [Old French *porfil, porfiler*, ultimately from Latin *filum* thread]

pur·ga·tion /pɜːrˈgeɪʃən/ *noun* **1** purification. **2** purging of the bowels. **3** spiritual cleansing, esp. (*Catholicism*) of a soul in purgatory. **4** *hist.* the cleansing of oneself from accusation or suspicion by an oath or ordeal. [Old French *purgation* or Latin *purgatio* (as PURGE)]

pur·ga·tive /ˈpɜːrgətɪv/ ● *adjective* **1** serving to purify. **2** strongly laxative. ● *noun* **1** a purgative thing. **2** a laxative. [Old French *purgatif -ive* or Late Latin *purgativus* (as PURGE)]

pur·ga·tory /ˈpɜːrgəˌtɔri/ ● *noun* (*pl.* **-ies**) **1** the condition or supposed place of spiritual cleansing, esp. (*Catholicism*) of those dying in the grace of God but having to expiate venial sins etc. **2** a place or state of temporary suffering or expiation. ● *adjective* purifying. □ **pur·ga·tor·ial** *adjective* [Anglo-French *purgatorie* from medieval Latin *purgatorium* (as PURGE)]

purge ● *transitive verb* **1** (often foll. by *of*) make physically or spiritually clean. **2** remove by a cleansing process. **3 a** rid (an organization, party, etc.) of persons regarded as undesirable. **b** remove (an unwanted person) from an organization. **4** rid (a person etc.) of an undesirable quality. **5 a** empty (the stomach or bowels) by inducing vomiting or evacuation. **b** empty the bowels of. **6** *Law* atone for or wipe out (an offence, esp. contempt of court). ● **noun 1** the act or an instance of purging. **2** a purgative. □ **pur·ger** *noun* [Old French *purg(i)er* from Latin *purgare* purify, from *purus* pure]

puri /ˈpuːri/ *noun* (in Indian cooking) a small round cake of unleavened wheat flour deep-fried in ghee or oil. [Hindi]

pur·ify *transitive verb* (**-fies, -fied**) **1** (often foll. by *of, from*) cleanse or make pure. **2** make ceremonially clean. **3** clear of extraneous elements. □ **puri·fi·ca·tion** *noun* **puri·fi·ca·tory** /-ˈrɪfɪkəˌtɔri/ *adjective* **puri·fi·er** *noun*

Purim /ˈpurɪm/ *noun* a Jewish spring festival commemorating the defeat of Haman's plot to massacre the Jews (Esther 9). [Hebrew, pl. of *pūr*, perhaps = LOT *noun* 2 (from the casting of lots by Haman)]

pur·ine /ˈpuriːn/ *noun* **1** *Chem.* an organic nitrogenous base forming uric acid on oxidation. **2** any of a group of compounds with a similar structure, including the nucleotide constituents adenine and guanine. [German *Purin* (from Latin *purus* pure + *uricum* uric acid + -*in* -INE⁴)]

pur·ist *noun* a stickler for or advocate of scrupulous correctness or authenticity, e.g. in language or art. □ **pur·ism** *noun* **pur·is·tic** *adjective*

puri·tan /ˈpjurɪtən, ˈpjɜr-/ ● *noun* **1** (**Puritan**) *hist.* a member of a group of English Protestants who regarded the Reformation of the Church under Elizabeth as incomplete and sought to simplify and regulate forms of worship. **2** a purist member of any party. **3** a person practising, affecting, or advocating extreme strictness in religion or morals. ● *adjective* **1** (**Puritan**) *hist.* of or relating to the Puritans. **2** scrupulous and austere in religion or morals. □ **puri·tan·ism** *noun*

puri·tan·ical /ˌpjurɪˈtanɪkəl, ˌpjɜr-/ *adjective* often *derogatory* practising, affecting, or advocating strict religious or moral behaviour, esp. one opposed to pleasure. □ **puri·tan·ical·ly** *adverb*

pur·ity *noun* pureness, cleanness; freedom from physical or moral pollution.

purl¹ ● *noun* **1** a knitting stitch made by putting the needle through the front of the previous stitch and passing the yarn around the back of the needle. **2** a cord of twisted gold or silver wire for bordering. **3** the ornamental edges of lace, ribbon, etc. ● *transitive & intransitive verb* knit with a purl stitch. [originally *pyrle, pirle* from Scots *pirl* twist: the knitting sense may be from a different word]

purl² ● *intransitive verb* **1** (of a brook etc.) flow with a swirling motion and babbling sound. **2** make a babbling sound. ● *noun* this motion or sound. [16th c.: prob. imitative: compare Norwegian *purla* bubble up]

pur·lieu /ˈpɜrljuː/ *noun* (*pl.* **pur·lieus**) **1** (in *pl.*) the outskirts; an outlying region. **2** a person's usual haunts. **3** *Brit. hist.* a tract on the border of a forest, esp. one earlier included in it and still partly subject to forest laws. **4** a person's bounds or limits. [Middle English *purlew*, prob. alteration (suggested by French *lieu* 'place') from Anglo-French *purale(e)*, Old French *pourallee* 'a going round to settle the boundaries' from *po(u)raler* traverse]

pur·lin /ˈpɜrlɪn/ *noun* a horizontal beam along the length of a roof, resting on principals and supporting the common rafters or boards. [Middle English: origin uncertain]

pur·loin /pərˈlɔɪn/ *transitive verb* *formal* or *jocular* steal, pilfer. □ **pur·loin·er** *noun* [Anglo-French *purloigner* put away, do away with (as PUR-, *loign* far, from Latin *longe*)]

pur·ple ● *noun* **1** a colour intermediate between red and blue. **2** (in full **Tyrian purple**) a crimson dye obtained from some molluscs. **3** a purple robe, esp. as the dress of royalty. **4** (prec. by *the*) a position of rank, authority, or privilege. **5 a** the scarlet official dress of a cardinal. **b** the position or office of a cardinal. ● *adjective* **1** of a purple colour. **2** (of writing, speech, etc.) excessively elaborate or ornate. ● *transitive & intransitive verb* make or become purple. □ **born to the purple 1** born into a reigning family. **2** belonging to the most privileged class. □ **purp·lish** *adjective* **purp·ly** *adjective* [Old English alteration of *purpure purpuran* from Latin *purpura* (as PURPURA)]

purple coneflower *noun* any of various composite eastern N American herbaceous plants of the genus *Echinacea* with purplish flowers, esp. *E. purpurea*, grown as an ornamental.

purple finch *noun* a finch, *Carpodacus purpureus*, of wooded parts of N America, the male of which has a red head and breast.

purple gas *noun* *Cdn* (*Prairies*) gas sold with reduced taxes to farmers for farm machinery and vehicles, dyed purple for identification.

Purple Heart *noun* (in the US) a decoration for members of the armed forces wounded in action.

purple Jesus *noun* a punch of vodka or grain alcohol and grape juice, often supplemented by whatever alcoholic beverage is at hand.

purple loosestrife *noun* a wetland plant, *Lythrum salicaria*, with a long spike of purple flowers.

purple martin *noun* a large, purplish-blue swallow, *Progne subis*, a voracious eater of insects.

purple osier *noun* a willow shrub naturalized in N America, *Salix purpurea*, used in basketry, often bearing purple twigs.

purple passage *noun* (or **purple patch**) an ornate or elaborate passage in a literary composition.

purple prose *noun* prose that is too elaborate or ornate.

purple saxifrage *noun* a saxifrage, *Saxifraga oppositifolia*, with pink or magenta flowers, the floral emblem of Nunavut.

pur·port ● *transitive verb* /pərˈpɔrt/ **1** profess; be intended to seem (*purports to be the royal seal*). **2** (of a document, speech, etc.) have as its meaning; state. ● *noun* /ˈpɜrpɔrt/ **1** the ostensible meaning of something. **2** the sense or tenor (of a document or statement). □ **pur·port·ed·ly** /pərˈpɔrtədli/ *adverb* [Old French *purport* from *purporter* from medieval Latin *proportare* (as PRO-¹, *portare* carry)]

pur·pose ● *noun* **1 a** something to be attained; a thing intended (*our purpose was to delay them*). **b** the reason for which something is done or made, or for which it exists (*for tax purposes*). **2** resolution, determination. ● *transitive verb* have as one's purpose; design, intend. □ **on purpose** intentionally. **to no purpose** with no result or effect. **to the purpose 1** relevant. **2** useful. [Old French *porpos, purpos* from Latin *proponere* (as PROPOUND)]

purpose-built *adjective* (also **purpose-made**, **purpose-designed**, etc.) built or made for a specific purpose (*purpose-built art gallery*).

pur·pose·ful *adjective* **1** having or indicating purpose. **2** intentional. **3** resolute. □ **pur·pose·ful·ly** *adverb* **pur·pose·ful·ness** *noun*

pur·pose·less *adjective* having no aim or plan. □ **pur·pose·less·ly** *adverb* **pur·pose·less·ness** *noun*

pur·pose·ly *adverb* on purpose; intentionally.

pur·pos·ive /ˈpɜrpəsɪv/ *adjective* **1** having or serving a purpose. **2** done with a purpose. **3** (of a person or conduct) having purpose or resolution; purposeful. □ **pur·pos·ive·ly** *adverb* **pur·pos·ive·ness** *noun*

pur·pura /ˈpɜrpjurə/ *noun* a rash of purple spots on the skin caused by internal bleeding from small blood vessels. [Latin from Greek *porphura* purple]

purr ● *verb* **1** *intransitive* (of a cat) make a low vibratory sound usu. expressing contentment. **2** *intransitive* (of a person, machinery, etc.) make a similar sound. **3** *intransitive* (of a person) express pleasure. **4** *transitive* utter or express (words or contentment) in this way. ● *noun* a purring sound. [imitative]

purse ● *noun* **1** *N Amer.* a small woman's bag of leather or fabric etc., for holding small personal articles, e.g. wallet, keys, makeup, etc.; a handbag or shoulder bag. **2** *Brit.* a change purse or wallet. **3** *hist.* a small pouch of leather etc. for carrying money, esp. coins. **4** a receptacle resembling a purse in form or purpose. **5** money, funds. **6** a sum collected as a present or given as a prize in a contest. ● *verb* **1** *transitive* pucker or contract (the lips). **2** *intransitive* become contracted and wrinkled. [Old English *purs* from medieval Latin *bursa, byrsa* purse, from Greek *bursa* hide, leather]

purs·er *noun* **1** an officer on a ship who keeps the accounts. **2** the head steward in a passenger vessel or airplane.

purse seine *noun* a fishing net or seine which may be drawn into the shape of a sack, used for catching shoal fish (also *attributive*: *purse seine vessels*). □ **purse seiner** *noun* **purse seining** *noun*

purse snatcher *noun* a thief who grabs women's purses. □ **purse snatching** *noun*

purse strings *plural noun* **1** control of or access to funds (*holds the purse strings; tightened the purse strings*). **2** *hist.* drawstrings used to close a money purse.

purs·lane /ˈpɜrsleɪn/ *noun* any of various plants of the genus *Portulaca*, esp. *P. oleracea*, with green or golden leaves, used as a herb and salad vegetable. [Old French *porcelaine* (compare PORCELAIN) alteration of Latin *porcil(l)aca, portulaca*]

pur·su·ance /pərˈsuːəns, -ˈsjuːəns/ *noun* (foll. by *of*) the carrying out or observance (of a plan, idea, etc.).

pur·su·ant /pərˈsuːənt, -ˈsjuːənt/ *adverb* (foll. by *to*) conforming to or in accordance with. [Middle English, = prosecuting, from Old French *po(u)rsuiant* part. of *po(u)rsu(iv)ir* (as PURSUE): assimilated to Anglo-French *pursuer* and PURSUE]

pur·sue /pərˈsuː, -ˈsjuː/ *verb* (**pur·sues, pur·sued, pur·su·ing**) **1** *transitive* follow with intent to overtake or capture or do harm to. **2** *transitive* continue or proceed along (a route or course of action).

3 *transitive* follow or engage in (study or other activity). **4** *transitive* proceed in compliance with (a plan etc.). **5** *transitive* seek after, aim at. **6** *transitive* continue to investigate or discuss (a topic). **7** *transitive* seek the attention or acquaintance of (a person) persistently. **8** *transitive* (of misfortune etc.) persistently assail. **9** *transitive* persistently attend, stick to. **10** *intransitive* **a** go in pursuit. **b** continue. □ **pur·su·er** *noun* [Anglo-French *pursuer* = Old French *porsivre* etc., ultimately from Latin *prosequi* follow after]

pur·suit /pərˈsuːt, -ˈsjuːt/ *noun* **1** the act or an instance of pursuing. **2** an occupation or activity pursued. **3** a bicycle race in which competitors start from different parts of a track and attempt to overtake one another. □ **in pursuit of** pursuing. [Old French *poursuite* (as PUR-, SUIT)]

puru·lent /ˈpjʊrʊlənt, ˈpjʊrjʊ-/ *adjective* **1** consisting of or containing pus. **2** discharging pus. □ **puru·lence** *noun* **puru·lent·ly** *adverb* [French *purulent* or Latin *purulentus* (as PUS)]

pur·vey /pərˈveɪ/ *transitive & intransitive verb* provide or supply (food, provisions, or esp. shady or dishonest information, services, etc.) esp. as one's business. □ **pur·vey·or** *noun* [Anglo-French *purveier*, Old French *porveir* from Latin *providēre* PROVIDE]

pur·view /ˈpɜrvjuː/ *noun* **1** the scope or range of a document, scheme, etc. **2** the range of physical or mental vision. [Anglo-French *purveü*, Old French *porveü* past participle of *porveir* (as PURVEY)]

pus *noun* a thick yellowish or greenish liquid produced from infected tissue, consisting of dead bacteria and white blood cells with tissue debris and serum. [Latin *pus puris*]

Pusan /ˈpuːsɒn/ an industrial city and seaport on the southeast coast of S Korea; pop. (est. 2002) 4,085,300.

Pusey /ˈpjuːzi/ **Ed·ward Bou·verie** (1800–82), English theologian. In 1833 he founded the Oxford Movement with John Henry Newman and John Keble, becoming leader of the Movement after the withdrawal of Newman (1841); his writings include a series of *Tracts for the Times* and a statement of his doctrinal position *The Doctrine of the Real Presence* (1856–57).

push ● *verb* **1** *transitive* exert a force on (a thing) to move it away from oneself or from the origin of the force. **2** *transitive* cause to move in this direction. **3** *intransitive* exert such a force (*do not push against the door*). **4** *intransitive* exert muscular pressure internally, esp. during the second stage of labour. **5** *transitive* press, depress (*push the button for service*). **6** *intransitive & transitive* **a** thrust forward or upward. **b** project or cause to project (*pushes out new roots; the cape pushes out into the sea*). **7** *intransitive* move forward by force or persistence. **8** *transitive* make (one's way) by pushing. **9** *intransitive* exert oneself, esp. to surpass others. **10** *transitive* (often foll. by *to*, *into*, or *to* + infin.) urge or impel. **11** *transitive* tax the abilities or tolerance of; press (a person) hard. **12** *transitive* pursue (an action or operation) with vigour and insistence; press (a claim etc.). **13** *transitive* promote the use or sale or adoption of, e.g. by advertising. **14** *intransitive* (foll. by *for*) demand persistently (*pushed hard for reform*). **15** *transitive informal* sell (a drug) illegally. **16** *transitive informal* approach (a certain number), esp. in years of age (*he's pushing 40*). **17** *transitive* develop (film) so as to compensate for deliberate underexposure, thus increasing the effective film speed. ● *noun* **1** the act or an instance of pushing; a shove or thrust. **2** the force exerted in this. **3** a vigorous effort. **4** a military attack in force. **5** enterprise, determination to succeed. **6** the use of influence to advance a person. **7** the pressure of affairs. □ **be pushed for** *informal* have very little of (esp. time). **get the push** *Brit. informal* be dismissed or sent away. **give a person the push** esp. *Brit. informal* dismiss or send away a person. **push around** *informal* bully. **push one's luck 1** take undue risks. **2** act presumptuously. **push off 1** push with an oar etc. to get a boat out into a river etc. **2** (often in *imperative*) *informal* go away. **push the envelope** see ENVELOPE. **push through** get (a scheme, proposal, etc.) completed or accepted quickly. **when push comes to shove** when action must be taken; when a decision, commitment, etc. must be made. [Old French *pousser*, *pou(l)ser* from Latin *pulsare* (as PULSATE)]

push broom *noun* a sturdy broom with a wide brush and long handle, used for sweeping large areas.

push button ● *noun* a button to be pushed esp. to operate an electrical device. ● *adjective* (**push-button**) **1** operated by pressing a push button. **2** easily obtainable, as at the push of a button; instant.

push·cart *noun* esp. *N Amer.* a small handcart, esp. one used by a street vendor.

push·chair *noun Brit.* = STROLLER 1.

push·er *noun* **1** *informal* a person who sells (esp. prohibited) drugs illegally. **2** a person or thing that pushes. **3** an aircraft with a propeller behind the main wings.

push factor *noun* a political, social, or economic consideration that influences a person's decision to emigrate from a particular place.

Push·kin /ˈpʊʃkɪn/ **Alek·sandr (Serge·evich)** (1799–1837), Russian poet, novelist, and dramatist. A leading figure in Russian literature, he wrote prolifically in many genres, and his works include the romantic narrative poem *Ruslan and Ludmilla* (1820), the verse novel *Eugene Onegin* (1833), and the blank-verse historical drama *Boris Godunov* (1831).

push mower *noun* a lawn mower which has no motor and is powered by manual force.

push·over *noun informal* **1** something easily done or won; an easy task or victory. **2** a person who can easily be overcome, persuaded, etc.

push-pin *noun N Amer.* a tack with a spool-shaped, usu. plastic head, used for fastening material to a bulletin board etc.

push-pull *adjective* **1** *Electronics* consisting of two valves etc. operated alternately. **2** operated by pushing and pulling.

push·rod *noun* a rod operated by cams, that opens and closes the valves in an internal combustion engine.

push-start ● *noun* the starting of a motor vehicle by pushing it to turn the engine. ● *transitive verb* start (a vehicle) in this way.

Push·tu /ˈpʌʃtuː/ *noun & adjective* = PASHTO. [Persian *puštū*]

Push·tun /ˈpʌʃtuːn/ *noun & adjective* = PASHTUN. [Persian *puštūn*]

push-up *N Amer.* ● *noun* **1** an exercise in which a person lies facing the floor and, keeping the back straight, raises the upper part of the body by pressing down on the hands to straighten the arms. **2** a muskrat's resting place, formed by pushing up vegetation through a hole in the ice. ● *adjective* designating a brassiere or similar garment which is underwired or padded to provide uplift for the breasts.

pushy *adjective* (**push·i·er, push·i·est**) *informal* excessively or unpleasantly forward or self-assertive; aggressive. □ **push·i·ly** *adverb* **push·i·ness** *noun*

pusil·lan·im·ous /ˌpjuːsəˈlanəməs/ *adjective* lacking courage; timid. □ **pusil·lan·im·ity** /-ləˈnɪmɪti/ *noun* **pusil·lan·im·ous·ly** *adverb* [ecclesiastical Latin *pusillanimis* from *pusillus* very small + *animus* mind]

puss¹ *noun informal* **1** a cat (esp. as a form of address). **2** a playful or coquettish girl. [prob. from Middle Low German *pūs*, Dutch *poes*, of unknown origin]

puss² *noun* esp. *N Amer. & Irish slang* the face or mouth. [Irish *pus*, lip, mouth]

pussy *noun* (pl. **-ies**) **1** *informal* = PUSSYCAT 1. **2** *coarse slang* **a** the female genitals. **b** sexual intercourse with a woman. **c** *offensive* women considered sexually. **3** *slang* a weak or effeminate boy or man; a male homosexual.

pussy·cat *noun informal* **1** a cat. **2** a meek, mild-tempered, or amiable person.

pussy·foot *intransitive verb* **1** move stealthily or warily. **2** act cautiously or noncommittally. □ **pussy·foot·er** *noun*

pussy·toes *noun N Amer.* any of various small woolly plants of the genus *Antennaria*, of the composite family.

pussy-whip *transitive verb coarse slang* (usu. in *passive*) (of a woman) henpeck (a man); make (a man) docile and subservient.

pussy willow *noun* any of various willows, esp. *Salix discolor*, with furry catkins.

pus·tu·late ● *transitive & intransitive verb* /ˈpʌstjʊˌleɪt/ form into pustules. ● *adjective* /-lət/ of or relating to a pustule or pustules. □ **pus·tu·la·tion** *noun* [Late Latin *pustulare* from *pustula*: see PUSTULE]

pus·tule /ˈpʌstjuːl, ˈpʌstjuːl/ *noun* a pimple containing pus. □ **pus·tu·lar** *adjective* **pus·tu·lous** *adjective* [Old French *pustule* or Latin *pustula*]

put ● *verb* (**put·ting**; *past* and *past participle* **put**) **1** *transitive* **a** move to or cause to be in a specified place or position (*put it in your pocket; put the children to bed; put your signature here*). **b** fit or fix (something) to something else (*put a new lock on the door; put a patch on these jeans*). **2** *transitive* bring into a specified condition, relation, or state (*puts me in an awkward position*). **3** *transitive* **a** (often foll. by *on*) impose or assign (*put a tax on groceries; where do you put the blame?*). **b** (foll. by *on*, *to*) impose or enforce the existence of (*put a veto on it; put a stop to it*). **4** **a** *transitive* cause (a person) to go or be, habitually or temporarily (*put them at their ease; put them on the right track*). **b** *reflexive* imagine (oneself) in a specified situation (*put yourself in my shoes*). **5** *transitive* (foll. by *for*) substitute (one thing for another). **6** *intransitive* express (a thought or idea) in a specified way (*to put it mildly*). **7** *transitive* (foll. by *at*) estimate (an amount etc.) at a specified amount (*put the cost at $50*). **8** *transitive* (foll. by *into*) express or translate in (words, or another language). **9** *transitive* set (words) to music. **10** *transitive* (foll. by *into*) invest (money) in an asset, e.g. land. **11** *transitive* (foll. by *on*) stake (money) on (a horse etc.). **12** *transitive* (foll.

by *to*) apply or devote to a use or purpose (*put it to good use*). **13** *transitive* (foll. by *to*) submit for consideration or attention (*let me put it to you another way*; *put it to a vote*). **14** *transitive* (foll. by *to*) subject (a person) to (death, suffering, etc.). **15** *transitive* throw (esp. a shot or weight) as an athletic sport or exercise. **16** *intransitive* (foll. by *back*, *off*, *out*, etc.) (of a ship etc.) proceed or follow a course in a specified direction. ● *noun* **1** a throw of the shot or weight. **2** *Stock Exch.* the option of selling stock at a fixed price at a given date. □ **put about 1** spread (information, rumour, etc.). **2** *Naut.* turn round; put (a ship) on the opposite tack. **put across 1** make acceptable or effective. **2** express in an understandable way. **put aside 1** save (esp. a sum of money), for later use. **2** reserve an item for a customer to collect later. **3** disregard; ignore or forget (*put aside our differences*). **put away 1** put (a thing) back in the place where it is normally kept. **2** lay (money etc.) aside for future use. **3 a** confine or imprison. **b** commit to a home or mental institution. **4** *informal* consume (food and drink), esp. in large quantities. **5** put (an old or sick animal) to death. **put back 1** restore to its proper or former place. **2** change (a planned event) to a later date or time. **3** move back the hands of (a clock or watch). **4** check the advance of. **put the boots to** see BOOT¹. **put by** *Brit.* lay (money etc.) aside for future use. **put down 1** suppress by force or authority. **2** *informal* snub or humiliate. **3** record or enter in writing. **4** enter the name of (a person) on a list, esp. as a member or subscriber. **5** (foll. by *as*, *for*) account or reckon. **6** (foll. by *to*) attribute (*put it down to bad planning*). **7** put (an old or sick animal) to death. **8** preserve or store (fruit, wine, etc.) for future use. **9** pay (a specified sum) as a deposit. **10** put (a baby) to bed. **11** land (an aircraft). **12** record (a musical part, song, etc.) (*put down the bass track first*). **put an end to** see END. **put one's finger on** see FINGER. **put the finger on** see FINGER. **put one's foot down** see FOOT. **put one's foot in one's mouth** see FOOT. **put forth 1** (of a plant) send out (buds or leaves). **2** *formal* submit or put into circulation. **put forward 1** suggest, propose, or nominate. **2 a** advance the hands of (a clock or watch). **b** move (an event etc.) to an earlier time or date (*put forward the date of our wedding*). **3** (often *reflexive*) put into a prominent position; draw attention to. **put one's hands on** = LAY ONE'S HANDS ON (see LAY¹). **put in 1 a** enter or submit (a claim etc.). **b** (foll. by *for*) submit a claim for (a specified thing). **2** (foll. by *for*) be a candidate for (an appointment, election, etc.). **3** spend (time) (*put in five hours of overtime*). **4** interpose (a remark, blow, etc.). **5** (of a ship) enter or call at a port, harbour, etc. **6** plant (a crop etc.). **put in an appearance** see APPEARANCE. **put a person in mind of** see MIND. **put it to a person** (often foll. by *that* + clause) present or submit a question, statement, etc. to (a person) for consideration or by way of appeal. **put one's mind to** devote all one's attention and energy to achieving something. **put off 1 a** postpone. **b** postpone an engagement with (a person). **2** (often foll. by *with*) evade (a person) with an excuse etc. **3** hinder or distract (*the sudden noise put her off her game*). **4** offend, disconcert; cause (a person) to lose interest in something. **5** (of a vehicle or its driver) stop to let a passenger get off (*asked the driver to put me off at the train station*). **put on 1** clothe oneself with. **2** apply (makeup, lotion, etc.) to the skin. **3** cause (an electrical device, light, etc.) to function. **4** stage (a play, show, etc.). **5 a** pretend to be affected by (an emotion). **b** assume, take on (a character or appearance). **c** (**put it on**) exaggerate one's feelings etc. **6** increase one's weight by (a specified amount). **7** (foll. by *to*) make aware of or put in touch with (*put us on to their new accountant*). **8** *informal* tease, play a trick on (*are you putting me on?*). **9** place (a tax etc.) on something (*put a duty on wine*). **10** bet (money) on something (*put $100 on the white horse*). **put out 1 a** (often as **put out** *adjective*) disconcert or annoy. **b** (often *reflexive*) inconvenience (*don't put yourself out*). **2** extinguish (a fire or light). **3** *Baseball* cause (a player) to be out. **4** dislocate (a joint etc.) (*put my back out*). **5** exert (strength etc.). **6** *slang* (of a woman) readily offer sexual intercourse. **7** issue, publish, or broadcast (something) (*puts out a monthly magazine*). **8** blind (a person's eyes). **put one over** (foll. by *on*) *informal* get the better of; trick. **put over 1** make acceptable or effective. **2** express in an understandable way. **3** *N Amer.* postpone. **put a sock in it** see SOCK¹. **put store by** see STORE. **put through 1** carry out or complete (a task or transaction). **2** (often foll. by *to*) connect (a person) by telephone to another user. **3** subject to an ordeal or trying experience (*put her parents through hell*). **4** arrange or pay for (someone) to attend university etc. (*put all his kids through college*). **put to flight** see FLIGHT². **put together 1** assemble (a whole) from parts. **2** combine (parts) to form a whole. **put two and two together** see TWO. **put under** render unconscious by anaesthetic etc. **put up 1** build or erect. **2 a** raise (a hand) to answer or ask a question. **b** raise (one's hands) to indicate surrender. **3** raise (a price etc.). **4** take or provide accommodation (*friends put me up for the night*). **5** engage in (a fight, struggle, etc.) as a

form of resistance. **6** present (a proposal etc.). **7 a** present oneself for election. **b** propose for election. **8** provide (money) as a backer in an enterprise. **9** display (a notice). **10** preserve or can (fruit etc.). **11** offer for sale or competition. **12** cause (game) to rise from cover. **13** put (a sword) back in its sheath. **14** arrange (long hair) in a bun or upswept hairstyle. **put upon** (usu. in *passive*; hyphenated when *attributive*) *informal* make unfair or excessive demands on; take advantage of (a person). **put up or shut up** *informal* defend or justify oneself or remain silent. **put a person up to** (usu. foll. by verbal noun) instigate a person in (*put them up to stealing the money*). **put up with** endure, tolerate; submit to. **put the wind up** see WIND¹. **put a person wise** see WISE¹. **put words into a person's mouth** see MOUTH. □ **put·ter** *noun* [Middle English from an unrecorded Old English form *putian*, of unknown origin]

pu·ta·tive /ˈpjuːtətɪv/ *adjective* reputed, supposed (*his putative father*). □ **pu·ta·tive·ly** *adverb* [Old French *putatif -ive* or Late Latin *putativus* from Latin *putare* think]

put-down *noun* *informal* a snub or humiliating remark or criticism.

Putin /ˈpuːtɪn/ **Vlad·i·mir** (b.1952), Russian statesman. Favouring economic reform and advocating a military crackdown on Chechen separatists, he was elected president in 2000.

put-in *noun* *N Amer.* a place on the banks of a river etc. from which to launch a canoe or other small craft.

put-on *noun* esp. *N Amer.* *informal* a deception or hoax.

put-out *noun* *Baseball* an instance of putting out a batter or baserunner.

put-put *var. of* PUTT-PUTT.

pu·tre·fy /ˈpjuːtrəˌfaɪ/ *verb* (**-fies**, **-fied**) **1** *intransitive & transitive* become or make putrid; go bad. **2** *intransitive* fester, suppurate. □ **pu·tre·fac·tion** *noun* **pu·tre·fac·tive** *adjective* [Latin *putrefacere* from *puter putris* rotten]

pu·tres·cent /pjuːˈtrɛs(ə)nt/ *adjective* **1** in the process of rotting. **2** of or accompanying this process. □ **pu·tres·cence** *noun* [Latin *putrescere* inceptive of *putrēre* (as PUTRID)]

pu·trid /ˈpjuːtrɪd/ *adjective* **1** decomposed, rotten. **2** foul, noxious. **3** morally corrupt. **4** *slang* of poor quality; contemptible; very unpleasant. □ **pu·trid·ity** *noun* **pu·trid·ly** *adverb* **pu·trid·ness** *noun* [Latin *putridus* from *putrēre* to rot, from *puter putris* rotten]

putsch /pʊtʃ/ *noun* an attempt at political revolution; a violent uprising. □ **putsch·ist** *noun & adjective* [Swiss German, = thrust, blow]

putt ● *transitive verb* (**putted**, **putting**) strike (a golf ball) gently to get it into or nearer to a hole on a putting green. ● *noun* a putting stroke. [differentiated from PUT]

putt·an·esca /pʊtəˈnɛskə/ *adjective* denoting a pasta sauce of tomatoes, garlic, olives, anchovies, etc. [Italian, from *puttana* prostitute (the sauce is said to have been devised by prostitutes as one which could be cooked quickly between clients' visits)]

put·tee /ˈpʌti/ *noun* **1** a long strip of cloth wound spirally round the leg from ankle to knee for protection and support. **2** *N Amer.* a leather legging. [Hindi *paṭṭī* band, bandage]

put·ter¹ *noun* **1** a golf club used in putting. **2** a golfer who putts.

put·ter² *noun & verb* = PUTT-PUTT. [imitative]

put·ter³ *intransitive verb* **1 a** (often foll. by *around*, *about*) work or occupy oneself in a desultory but pleasant manner (*likes puttering around in the garden*). **b** (often foll. by *at*, *in*) dabble in a subject or occupation. **2** go slowly, dawdle, loiter (*puttered up to the pub*). □ **put·ter·er** *noun* [frequentative of dial. *pote* push, from Old English *potian*]

putting green *noun* (in golf) the smooth area of grass around a hole.

putto /ˈpʊtoː/ *noun* (pl. **putti** /-tiː/) a representation of a naked child (esp. a cherub or a cupid) in (esp. Renaissance) art. [Italian, = boy, from Latin *putus*]

putt-putt (also **put-put**) ● *noun* **1** the rapid intermittent sound of a small gasoline engine. **2** a small boat, car, etc. fitted with such an engine. ● *intransitive verb* (**putt-putted**, **putt-putting**) make this sound. [imitative]

putty ● *noun* (pl. **-ties**) **1** a soft, malleable greyish-yellow paste made from ground chalk and raw linseed oil, used for fixing panes of glass, filling holes in woodwork, etc. **2** a fine white mortar of lime and water, used in pointing brickwork, etc. **3** a polishing powder usu. made from tin oxide, used in jewellery work. **4** a light shade of yellowish grey. ● *transitive verb* (**-ties**, **-tied**) cover, fix, join, or fill up with putty. □ **putty in a person's hands** someone who is too compliant, or easily influenced. [French *potée*, lit. potful]

putty knife *noun* a knife with a blunt flexible spatulate blade for spreading putty.

put-up *adjective* (usu. in phr. **put-up job**) fraudulently presented or devised.

Consonants: b *but* d *dog* f *few* g *get* h *her* j *yes* k *cat* l *leg* m *man* n *no* p *pen* r *red* s *sit*

putz /pʌts/ *N Amer.* ● *noun* **1** *slang* a fool; a stupid person. **2** *coarse slang* the penis. ● *intransitive verb* (usu. foll. by *around*) waste time; fool around. [Yiddish]

Puvir·ni·tuq, Rivière de /pɔːˈvɜrnətʌk/ a river in NW Quebec, flowing southwestward to empty into Hudson Bay at Puvirnituq, a village on the bay's northeastern shore. [Inuktitut, = it smells of rotting meat]

puz·zle ● *noun* **1** a difficult or confusing problem; an enigma. **2** a problem or toy designed to test knowledge or ingenuity (*crossword puzzle*; *jigsaw puzzle*). ● *verb* **1** *transitive* confound or disconcert mentally. **2** *intransitive* (usu. foll. by *over* etc.) be perplexed (about). **3** *transitive* (usu. as **puz·zling** *adjective*) require much thought to comprehend (*a puzzling situation*). **4** *transitive* (foll. by *out*) solve or understand by hard thought. □ **puz·zled** *adjective* **puzzle·ment** *noun* **puz·zling·ly** *adverb* [16th c.: origin unknown]

puz·zler *noun* **1** a difficult question or problem. **2** a person who is fond of solving puzzles.

PV *abbreviation* PHOTOVOLTAIC.

PVA *abbreviation* POLYVINYL ACETATE.

PVC *abbreviation* POLYVINYL CHLORIDE.

Pvt. *abbreviation* **1** private. **2** *US* private soldier.

PWA *abbreviation* person with AIDS.

PWC *abbreviation* PERSONAL WATERCRAFT.

PWR *abbreviation* PRESSURIZED WATER REACTOR.

PWYC *abbreviation* esp. *Cdn* pay what you can, designating theatrical etc. events where audience members pay what they can afford.

PX *abbreviation* *US* POST EXCHANGE.

pya /pjə/ *noun* a monetary unit of Burma (Myanmar), equal to one-hundredth of a kyat. [Burmese]

pye-dog /ˈpaɪdɒg/ *noun* (also **pie-dog**) a vagrant mongrel, esp. in Asia. [Anglo-Indian *pye*, *paē*, Hindi *pāhī* outsider + DOG]

pyelo- /paɪəlɔ/ *combining form* of the pelvis of the kidney. [Greek *puelos* trough, basin]

pyelo·neph·ritis /ˌpaɪələʊnəfˈraɪtɪs/ *noun* inflammation of the kidney and its pelvis, caused by a bacterial infection.

Pyg·ma·lion /pɪgˈmeɪliən/ **1** *Gk Myth* a king of Cyprus who fashioned an ivory statue of a beautiful woman and loved it so deeply that in answer to his prayer Aphrodite gave it life; the woman (at some point named Galatea) bore him a daughter, Paphos. **2** a legendary king of Tyre, brother of Elissa (Dido), whose husband he killed in the hope of obtaining his fortune.

pygmy /ˈpɪgmi/ *noun* (also **pigmy**) (*pl.* **-mies**) **1** a member of any of several small-statured peoples of equatorial Africa and parts of SE Asia. **2** a very small person, animal, or thing. **3** an insignificant person. **4** (*attributive*) **a** of or relating to pygmies. **b** (of a person, animal, etc.) dwarf. [Latin *pygmaeus* from Greek *pugmaios* dwarf, from *pugmē* the length from elbow to knuckles, fist]

pygmy chimpanzee *noun* see CHIMPANZEE.

pygmy hippopotamus *noun* see HIPPOPOTAMUS 2.

pyjama party *noun* esp. *N Amer.* = SLUMBER PARTY.

py·jamas *plural noun* (also **pa·jamas**) **1** a suit of loose trousers, shorts, or underpants and a top for sleeping in. **2** loose trousers tied around the waist, originally worn in some Asian countries. **3** (**py·jama**) (*attributive*) designating parts of a suit of pyjamas (*pyjama jacket*) or loose trousers esp. worn by women (*pyjama pants*). [Urdu *pā(ē)jāma* from Persian *pae*, *pay* leg + Hindi *jāma* clothing]

py·lon /ˈpaɪlɒn/ *noun* **1** *N Amer.* a plastic, usu. orange cone used to mark areas of roads etc. **2** *Brit.* a tall structure erected as a support (esp. for electric power cables). **3** a structure on the wing of an aircraft supporting an engine or weapon. **4** a gateway, esp. the monumental gateway to an ancient Egyptian temple, usu. formed by two truncated pyramidal towers connected by a lower architectural member containing the gate. [Greek *pulōn* from *pulē* gate]

pyl·or·us /paɪˈlɔːrəs/ *noun* (*pl.* **pylori** /-raɪ/) *Anat.* the opening from the stomach into the duodenum. □ **pyl·or·ic** *adjective* [Late Latin from Greek *pulōros*, *pulouros* gatekeeper, from *pulē* gate + *ouros* warder]

Pyn·chon /ˈpɪntʃən/ **Thom·as** (b.1937), US novelist and short-story writer, whose novels include *The Crying of Lot 49* (1966), a surreal comedy satirizing Californian life, and *Gravity's Rainbow* (1973), set in the closing years of the Second World War.

Pyong·yang /pjɒŋˈjaŋ/ the capital of N Korea; pop. (est. 2002) 2,724,700.

pyor·rhea /ˌpaɪəˈriːə/ *noun* *N Amer.* (*Brit.* **pyor·rhoea**) a disease of

periodontal tissue causing shrinkage of the gums and loosening of the teeth. [Greek *puo-* from *puon* pus + *rhoia* flux, from *rheō* flow]

pyra·can·tha /ˌpaɪrəˈkanθə/ *noun* any evergreen thorny shrub of the genus *Pyracantha*, having white flowers and bright red or yellow berries. Also called FIRETHORN. [Latin from Greek *purakantha*]

pyra·mid /ˈpɪrəmɪd/ ● *noun* **1** a monumental structure, usu. of stone, with a square base and sloping sides meeting centrally at an apex, esp. an ancient Egyptian royal tomb. **2** a polyhedron or solid figure of this type with a base of three or more sides. **3** a pyramid-shaped thing or pile of things. **4** an organization or a system seen as a structure in which the higher the level, the fewer people or things that occupy that level. **5** a system of financial growth achieved by a small initial investment, usu. in stock or in a company. ● *transitive verb* **1** arrange in the form of a pyramid; pile up. **2 a** accumulate (assets). **b** build up (stock) from the proceeds of a series of advantageous sales. □ **pyr·am·idal** *adjective* **pyra·mid·ic** *adjective* [Latin *pyramis* from Greek *puramis -idos*]

pyramid selling *noun* (also **pyramid scheme**) a system of selling goods in which the right to sell the goods is sold to an increasing number of distributors at successively lower levels, each of whom is recompensed for recruiting other distributors to the scheme.

Pyra·mus /ˈpiːrəməs/ *Rom. Myth* a Babylonian youth, lover of Thisbe. According to legend, Pyramus, supposing Thisbe to be dead, stabbed himself, and Thisbe, finding his body, threw herself upon his sword; their blood stained a mulberry tree, whose fruit has ever since been black when ripe, in sign of mourning for them.

pyre /paɪr/ *noun* a heap of combustible material esp. on which a corpse is burned. [Latin *pyra* from Greek *pura* from *pur* fire]

Pyr·en·ees /ˈpɪrəniːz/ a range of mountains extending along the border between France and Spain from the Atlantic coast to the Mediterranean. Its highest peak is the Pico de Aneto in N Spain, which rises to a height of 3 404 m (11,168 ft.). □ **Pyr·en·ean** /-ˈniːən/ *adjective*

pyr·eth·rin /paɪˈriːθrɪn/ *noun* any of a class of compounds found in pyrethrum flowers and used in the manufacture of insecticides.

pyr·eth·roid /paɪˈriːθrɔɪd/ *noun* *Chem.* any of a group of substances similar to pyrethrins in structure and properties.

pyr·eth·rum /paɪˈriːθrəm/ *noun* **1** any of several aromatic chrysanthemums of the genus *Tanacetum*, esp. *T. coccineum*. **2** an insecticide made from the dried flowers of these plants, esp. *Tanacetum cinerariifolium*. [Latin from Greek *purethron* feverfew]

py·ret·ic /paɪˈretɪk/ *adjective* of, for, or producing fever. [modern Latin *pyreticus* from Greek *puretos* fever]

Pyrex /ˈpaɪreks/ *noun* proprietary a hard heat-resistant type of glass, often used for ovenware. [invented word]

pyr·ex·ia /paɪˈreksiə/ *noun* *Med.* = FEVER 1. [modern Latin from Greek *purexis* from *puressō* be feverish, from *pur* fire]

pyr·id·ine /ˈpɪrədiːn/ *noun* *Chem.* a colourless volatile odorous liquid, formerly obtained from coal tar, used as a solvent and in chemical manufacture. Chem. formula: C_5H_5N. [Greek *pur* fire + -IDE + -INE⁴]

pyr·id·ox·ine /ˌpɪrɪˈdɒksɪn, -iːn/ *noun* a vitamin of the B complex found in yeast, and important in the body's use of unsaturated fatty acids. Also called VITAMIN B₆. [PYRIDINE + OX- + -INE⁴]

pyr·imi·dine /pɪˈrɪmɪdiːn/ *noun* **1** *Chem.* a cyclic organic nitrogenous base. Chem. formula: $C_4H_4N_2$. **2** any of a group of compounds with a similar structure, including the nucleotide constituents uracil, thymine, and cytosine. [German *Pyrimidin* from *Pyridin* (as PYRIDINE, IMIDE)]

pyr·ite /ˈpaɪraɪt/ *noun* (also **py·rit·es** /paɪˈraɪtiːz, ˈpaɪraɪts/) a yellow lustrous form of iron disulphide. □ **pyr·it·ic** /-ˈrɪtɪk/ *adjective*

pyr·it·ize /ˈpaɪrɪˌtaɪz/ *transitive verb* (also esp. *Brit.* **-ise**) [Latin from Greek *puritēs* of fire (*pur*)]

pyro- /ˈpaɪrɔ/ *combining form* **1** denoting fire. **2** *Chem.* denoting a new substance formed from another by elimination of water (*pyrophosphate*). **3** *Mineralogy* denoting a mineral etc. showing some property or change under the action of heat, or having a fiery red or yellow colour. [Greek *puro-* from *pur* fire]

pyro·clas·tic /ˌpaɪrəˈklastɪk/ ● *adjective* of or formed from fragments of rock from a volcanic eruption. ● *noun* (in *pl.*) pyroclastic rocks or rock fragments.

pyroclastic flow *noun* a dense mass of very hot ash, lava fragments, and gases ejected explosively from a volcano and often flowing at great speed.

pyro·elec·tric /ˌpaɪrəʊɪˈlektrɪk/ *adjective* having the property of becoming electrically charged when heated.

pyro·gen·ic /ˌpaɪrəˈdʒenɪk/ *adjective* **1 a** producing heat, esp. in the body. **b** producing fever. **2** produced by combustion or volcanic processes.

pyr·og·raphy /pai'rɒgrəfi/ *noun* **1** the technique of burning designs on white wood etc. with a heated metal rod. **2** a design made in this way. □ **pyr·og·raph·er** *noun*

pyr·ogy *var. of* PEROGY.

pyr·ohy *var. of* PEROGY.

pyr·ola /pai'roːlə/ *noun* a wintergreen of the genus *Pyrola*. *Also called* SHINLEAF. [medieval and modern Latin, diminutive of Latin *pyrus* 'pear']

pyr·oly·sis /pai'rɒləsɪs/ *noun* chemical decomposition brought about by heat. □ **pyro·lytic** /,pairə'lɪtɪk/ *adjective*

pyr·o·lyze /'pairə,laiz/ *transitive verb* (also **pyro·lyse**) decompose by pyrolysis. [PYROLYSIS after *analyze*]

pyro·mania /,pairo'meiniə/ *noun* an obsessive desire to set things on fire. □ **pyro·maniac** *noun* **pyro·man·iacal** /-mə'naiəkəl/ *adjective*

pyr·om·eter /pai'rɒmɪtər/ *noun* an instrument for measuring high temperatures, esp. in furnaces and kilns. □ **pyro·met·ric** /-rə'metrɪk/ *adjective* **pyro·met·ric·ally** *adverb* **pyr·om·etry** /-mɪtri/ *noun*

pyr·ope /'pairo:p/ *noun* a deep red variety of garnet. [Old French *pirope* from Latin *pyropus* from Greek *purōpos* gold-bronze, lit. fiery-eyed, from *pur* fire + *ōps* eye]

pyro·phor·ic /,pairo'fɔrɪk/ *adjective* (of a substance) liable to ignite spontaneously on exposure to air. [modern Latin *pyrophorus* from Greek *purophoros* fire-bearing, from *pur* fire + *pherō* bear]

pyr·osis /pai'roːsɪs/ *noun Med.* = HEARTBURN. [modern Latin from Greek *purōsis* from *puroō* set on fire, from *pur* fire]

pyro·tech·nic /,pairo'teknɪk/ *adjective* **1** of or relating to fireworks. **2** (of wit etc.) brilliant or sensational. □ **pyro·tech·nic·al** *adjective* **pyro·tech·ni·cian** *noun* [PYRO- + Greek *tekhnē* art]

pyro·tech·nics /,pairo'teknɪks/ *plural noun* **1** (treated as *sing.*) the art of making fireworks. **2** a display of fireworks. **3** any brilliant display.

pyr·ox·ene /pai'rɒksiːn/ *noun* any of a group of minerals commonly found as components of igneous rocks, composed of silicates of calcium, magnesium, and iron. [PYRO- + Greek *xenos* stranger (because supposed to be alien to igneous rocks)]

pyr·oxy·lin /pai'rɒksəlɪn/ *noun* a form of nitrocellulose, soluble in ether and alcohol, used as a basis for lacquers, artificial leather, etc. [French *pyroxyline* (as PYRO-, Greek *xulon* wood)]

Pyr·rha /'pirə/ *Gk Myth* the wife of Deucalion.

pyr·rhic[1] /'pirɪk/ *adjective* (of a victory) won at too great a cost to be of use to the victor. [PYRRHUS]

pyr·rhic[2] /'pirɪk/ ● *noun* a metrical foot of two short or unaccented syllables. ● *adjective* written in or based on pyrrhics. [Latin *pyrrhichius* from Greek *purrhikhios (pous)* pyrrhic (foot)]

Pyr·rho /'piro:/ (*c.*365–*c.*270 BC), Greek philosopher. Regarded as the founder of skepticism, he established the Pyrrhonic school of philosophy at Elis; he held that certainty of knowledge is impossible and that true happiness must therefore come from suspending judgment.

Pyr·rhon·ism /'pirə,nizəm/ *noun* **1** the philosophy of Pyrrho.

2 skepticism; philosophic doubt. □ **Pyr·rhon·ist** *noun & adjective* [Greek *Purrhōn* Pyrrho]

Pyr·rhus /'piːrəs/ (*c.*318–272 BC), king of Epirus *c.*307–272. After invading Italy in 280, he defeated the Romans at Asculum in 279, but sustained heavy losses; the term *pyrrhic victory* is named in allusion to this.

pyru·vate /pai'ruːveit/ *noun Biochem.* any salt or ester of pyruvic acid.

pyruvic acid /pai'ruːvɪk/ *noun* an organic acid occurring as an intermediate in many metabolic pathways. [as PYRO- + Latin *uva* grape]

pys·anka /'pisən,kʌ/ *noun* (*pl.* **pys·anky** /-,kɪ/) *Cdn* a hand-painted Ukrainian Easter egg, usu. having elaborate and intricate designs. [Ukrainian]

Py·thag·oras /pai'θagərəs, pɪ-/ (known as Pythagoras of Samos) (*c.*560–480 BC), Greek philosopher. He is said to have discovered the numerical ratios determining the intervals of the musical scale, and in astronomy analyzed the courses of the sun, moon, and stars into circular motions; he also founded a secret religious, political, and scientific sect in Italy, which held that the soul is condemned to a cycle of reincarnation, from which it may escape by attaining a state of purity.

Py·thag·or·ean /pɪ,θagə'riːən, pai-/ ● *adjective* of or relating to Pythagoras or his philosophy, esp. regarding the transmigration of souls. ● *noun* a follower of Pythagoras.

Pythagorean theorem *noun* (also **Pythagoras's theorem**) the theorem attributed to Pythagoras that the square of the hypotenuse of a right-angled triangle is equal to the sum of the squares of the other two sides.

Pyth·ia /'pɪθiə/ the priestess of Apollo at Delphi in ancient Greece (*see* DELPHI).

Pyth·ian /'pɪθiən/ *adjective* of or relating to Delphi or its ancient oracle of Apollo. [Latin *Pythius* from Greek *Puthios* from *Puthō*, an older name of Delphi]

Pythian games *plural noun* the games celebrated by the ancient Greeks every four years at Delphi.

Pyth·ias /'pɪθi,əs/ *see* DAMON.

Py·thon /'paiθɒn/ *Gk Myth* a serpent slain by Apollo at Delphi.

py·thon /'paiθɒn/ *noun* any constricting snake of the family Pythonidae, esp. of the genus *Python*, found throughout the tropics in the Old World. □ **py·thon·ic** /-'θɒnɪk/ *adjective* [Latin from Greek *Puthōn*: see PYTHON]

py·thon·ess /'paiθənəs/ *noun* **1** the Pythian priestess. **2** a witch. [Late Latin *pythonissa* fem. of *pytho* from Greek *puthōn* soothsaying demon: compare PYTHON]

pyx /pɪks/ *noun* (also **pix**) **1** *Christianity* the vessel in which the consecrated bread of the Eucharist is kept. **2** (in the UK) a box at the Royal Mint in which specimen gold and silver coins are deposited to be tested annually. [Latin (as PYXIS)]

pyx·id·ium /pɪk'sɪdiəm/ *noun* (*pl.* **pyx·idia** /-diə/) *Bot.* a seed capsule with a top that comes off like the lid of a box. [modern Latin from Greek *puxidion*, diminutive of *puxis*: see PYXIS]

pyxis /'pɪksɪs/ *noun* (*pl.* **pyx·ides** /-,diːz/) **1** a small box or casket. **2** = PYXIDIUM. [Latin from Greek *puxis* from *puxos* BOX[3]]

Q¹ *noun* (also **q**) (*pl.* **Qs** or **Q's**) the seventeenth letter of the alphabet.

Q² *abbreviation* (also **Q.**) **1** Queen, Queen's. **2** question. **3** (in Christian theology) used to denote the hypothetical source of the passages shared by the gospels of Matthew and Luke, but not found in Mark. [sense 3 prob. from German *Quelle* source]

Qad·dafi see GADHAFI.

qadi /ˈkadi, ˈkeidi/ *noun* (also **cadi, kadi**) (*pl.* **qadis**) a civil judge in a Muslim community. [Arabic *ḳāḍī* from *ḳaḍā* to judge]

qajaq *noun var. of* KAYAK.

Qal·lun·aaq /kaˈluːnak/ *noun* (*pl.* **Qal·lun·aat** /kaˈluːnat/) *Cdn* (*North*) a person who is not Inuit, esp. a white person. [Inuktitut]

qamu·tik /ˈkɒmətɪk/ *noun* = KOMATIK.

Q & A (also **Q and A**) ● *abbreviation* question and answer. ● *noun* a question-and-answer session, column, etc.

qat *noun var. of* KHAT.

Qatar /kaˈtɑr, ga-/ a sheikdom occupying a peninsula on the west coast of the Persian Gulf; pop. (est. 2002) 793,341; capital, Doha. □ **Qa·tari** *adjective & noun*

Qat·tara De·pres·sion /kəˈtɑrə/ an extensive, low-lying, and largely impassable area of desert in NE Africa, to the west of Cairo, that falls to 133 m (436 ft.) below sea level.

qaw·wali /kəˈwɒli/ *noun* a style of Muslim devotional music now associated particularly with Sufis in Pakistan. [Arabic *qawwāli*, from *qawwāl* 'loquacious', also 'singer']

QB *abbreviation* **1** quarterback. **2** Queen's Bench.

QC *abbreviation* (also **Qc**) Quebec.

Q.C. *abbreviation* **1** (also **QC**) Queen's Counsel. **2** (**QC**) quality control.

QED *abbreviation* which was to be demonstrated; loosely, as has been demonstrated. [Latin *quod erat demonstrandum*]

Q fever *noun* a mild febrile disease caused by rickettsiae. [Q = query]

qi /tʃiː/ *noun* the physical life force postulated by certain Chinese philosophers to flow through the body. [Chinese *qi* air, breath]

Qian Long /ˈtʃian ˈlɒŋ/ (also **Ch'ien-lung**) (born Hong-li) (1711–99), emperor of China 1735–95, a noted patron of the arts. During his rule China reached its greatest territorial extent.

qibla /ˈkɪblə/ *noun* **1** the direction of the Kaaba (the sacred building at Mecca), to which Muslims turn at prayer. **2** = MIHRAB. [Arabic *ḳibla* that which is opposite]

qi·gong /tʃiːˈgʊŋ/ *noun* a system of techniques to focus and strengthen qi, including breathing exercises, meditation, and hand and arm movements, used in alternative medicine and in martial-arts training. [QI + Chinese *kung* 'work']

Qin /tʃɪn/ (also **Ch'in**) a dynasty that ruled China 221–206 BC and was the first to establish rule over a united China. The construction of the Great Wall of China was begun during this period.

Qing /tʃɪŋ/ (also **Ch'ing**) the last imperial dynasty to rule China, established by the Manchus in 1644 and overthrown in 1912 by Sun Yat-sen.

Qing·dao /tʃɪŋˈdaʊ/ a port in E China, in Shandong province on the Yellow Sea coast; pop. (est. 2002) 2,510,900.

Qing·hai /tʃɪŋˈhaɪ/ (also **Tsinghai**) a mountainous province in north central China; capital, Xining.

Qiqi·har /ˌtʃitʃiˈhɑr/ a port on the Nen River, in Heilongjiang province, NE China; pop. (est. 2002) 1,628,000.

qiv·iut /ˈkɪviuːt/ *noun Cdn* (*North*) & *Alaska* fine, soft wool from the underbelly of a muskox. [Inuktitut]

Qld. *abbreviation* Queensland.

QM *abbreviation* quartermaster.

QMG *abbreviation* Quartermaster General.

Qom /kʊm/ (also **Qum, Kum**) a city in central Iran; pop. (est. 2002) 893,500. It is a holy city and a place of pilgrimage for Shiite Muslims.

QPF *abbreviation Cdn* Quebec Police Force. ¶ More commonly referred to as the Sûreté du Québec or SQ.

QPP *abbreviation Cdn* Quebec Pension Plan.

qr. *abbreviation* quarter(s).

Q rating *noun* a measurement of a celebrity's familiarity and likeability with the general public.

QSO *abbreviation* quasi-stellar object, quasar.

QST *noun Cdn* Quebec Sales Tax.

qt. *abbreviation* quart(s).

q.t. *noun informal* quiet (*on the q.t.*). [abbreviation]

Q-tip *noun N Amer. proprietary* a cotton swab on a small stick, used for cleaning ears, applying medication or makeup, etc.

qu. *abbreviation* **1** query. **2** question.

qua /kwei, kwʌ/ *conjunction* in the capacity of; as being (*Napoleon qua general*). [Latin, ablative fem. sing. of *qui* who]

Quaa·lude /ˈkweiluːd/ *noun proprietary* **1** the drug methaqualone. **2** a tablet of this. [invented word]

quack¹ ● *noun* the harsh sound made by ducks. ● *intransitive verb* **1** utter this sound. **2** *informal* talk loudly and foolishly. [imitative: compare Dutch *kwakken*, German *quacken* croak, quack]

quack² *noun* **1** an unqualified practitioner of medicine. **b** (*attributive*) of or characteristic of unskilled medical practice (*quack cure*). **2** a charlatan. **3** *Brit., Austral., & NZ slang* any doctor or medical officer. □ **quack·ery** *noun* **quack·ish** *adjective* [abbreviation of *quacksalver* from Dutch (prob. from obsolete *quacken* prattle + *salf* SALVE¹)]

quack grass *noun N Amer.* couch grass, *Agropyron repens*. [var. of *quick*, northern English variant of QUITCH]

quad /kwɒd/ *informal* ● *noun* **1** a quadrangle. **2** = QUADRUPLET 1. **3** quadraphony. **4** a quadriplegic. **5** (usu. in *pl.*) = QUADRICEPS. **6** *Figure Skating* a quadruple jump, in which a skater completes four rotations in the air. **7** (also *Brit.* **quad bike**) a small four-wheeled all-terrain vehicle. ● *adjective* **1** quadraphonic. **2** quadruple. [abbreviation]

quad chair *noun* (also **quad chairlift**) a chairlift with chairs that seat four people.

quad·ra·gen·ar·ian /ˌkwɒdrədʒəˈneriən/ ● *noun* a person from 40 to 49 years old. ● *adjective* of this age. [Late Latin *quadragenarius* from *quadrageni* distributive of *quadraginta* forty]

Quad·ra·ges·ima /ˌkwɒdrəˈdʒesɪmə/ *noun* the first Sunday in Lent. [Late Latin, fem. of Latin *quadragesimus* fortieth, from *quadraginta* forty, Lent having 40 days]

Quad·ra Island /ˈkwɒdrə/ an island in the Strait of Georgia, situated at its northern end, off the east central coast of Vancouver Island. [J. F. de la Bodega y *Quadra*, Spanish naval officer and Nuu-chah-nulth administrator d.1794]

quad·ran·gle /ˈkwɒdˌraŋgəl/ *noun* **1** a four-sided plane figure, esp. a square or rectangle. **2 a** a four-sided court, esp. enclosed by buildings, as in some colleges, schools, etc. **b** such a court with the buildings

uː m**oo**d ai m**y** əi p**i**pe au br**ow**n ʌ h**ou**se ei d**ay** ɔi b**oy** ã fr**an**glais ã C**an**adien ɔ̃ Br**ay**on (*see over for consonants*)

around it. □ **quad·ran·gu·lar** /-'raŋɡjʊlər/ adjective [Old French from Late Latin *quadrangulum* square, neuter of *quadrangulus* (as QUADRI-, ANGLE¹)]

quad·rant /'kwɒdrənt/ noun **1** a quarter of a circle's circumference. **2** a plane figure enclosed by two radii of a circle at right angles and the arc cut off by them. **3** a quarter of a sphere or spherical body. **4** any of four parts of a plane divided by two lines at right angles. **5 a** a thing, esp. a graduated strip of metal, shaped like a quarter-circle. **b** an instrument graduated (esp. through an arc of 90°) for taking angular measurements. [Latin *quadrans -antis* quarter, from *quattuor* four]

quad·ra·phon·ic /ˌkwɒdrə'fɒnɪk/ adjective (also **quad·ro·phon·ic**) (of sound reproduction) using four transmission channels.

□ **quad·ra·phon·ic·ally** adverb **quad·ra·phon·ics** plural noun **quad·raph·ony** /-'rɒfəni/ noun [QUADRI- + STEREOPHONIC]

quad·rat /'kwɒdrət/ noun Ecology a small area marked out for study. [var. of QUADRATE]

quad·rate ● adjective /'kwɒdrət/ esp. Anat. & Zool. square or rectangular (*quadrate bone*; *quadrate muscle*). ● noun /'kwɒdrət/ **1** a quadrate bone or muscle. **2** a rectangular object. [Latin *quadrare quadrat-* make square, from *quattuor* four]

quad·rat·ic /kwɒ'drætɪk/ Math. ● adjective involving the second and no higher power of an unknown quantity or variable (*quadratic equation*). ● noun **1** a quadratic equation. **2** (in pl.) the branch of algebra dealing with these. [French *quadratique* or modern Latin *quadraticus* (as QUADRATE)]

quad·ra·ture /'kwɒdrətʃər/ noun **1** Math. the process of constructing a square with an area equal to that of a figure bounded by a curve, e.g. a circle. **2** Astronomy **a** each of two points at which the moon is 90° from the sun as viewed from earth. **b** the position of a celestial body in relation to another 90° away. [French *quadrature* or Latin *quadratura* (as QUADRATE)]

quad·ren·nial /kwɒ'drenɪəl/ adjective **1** lasting four years. **2** recurring every four years. □ **quad·ren·nial·ly** adverb [as QUADRENNIUM]

quad·ren·nium /kwɒ'drenɪəm/ noun (pl. **quad·ren·niums** or **quad·ren·nia** /-nɪə/) a period of four years. [Latin *quadriennium* (as QUADRI-, *annus* year)]

quadri- /'kwɒdrɪ/ combining form denoting four. [Latin from *quattuor* four]

quad·ric /'kwɒdrɪk/ Math. ● adjective (of a surface) described by an equation of the second degree. ● noun a quadric surface. [Latin *quadra* square]

quad·ri·ceps /'kwɒdrɪˌseps/ noun a large four-headed muscle at the front of the thigh, the chief extensor of the knee. [modern Latin (as QUADRI-, BICEPS)]

quad·ri·fid /'kwɒdrɪfɪd/ adjective Bot. having four divisions or lobes. [Latin *quadrifidus* (as QUADRI-, *findere fid-* cleave)]

quad·ri·lat·eral /ˌkwɒdrə'lætərəl/ ● adjective having four sides. ● noun a four-sided figure.

quad·rille¹ /kwɒ'drɪl/ noun **1** a square dance usu. performed by four couples and containing five figures, each of which is a complete dance in itself. **2** the music for this. [French from Spanish *cuadrilla* troop, company, from *cuadra* square or Italian *quadriglia* from *quadra* square]

quad·rille² /kwɒ'drɪl/ noun a card game for four players with forty cards, fashionable in the 18th c. [French, perhaps from Spanish *cuartillo* from *cuarto* fourth, assimilated to QUADRILLE¹]

quad·ril·lion /kwɒ'drɪljən/ ● noun (pl. same or **quad·ril·lions**) **1** a thousand raised to the fifth (or formerly, esp. Brit., the eighth) power (10^{15} and 10^{24} respectively). **2** informal a very large amount. ● adjective amounting to one quadrillion in number. □ **quad·ril·lionth** noun & adjective [French (as QUADRI-, MILLION)]

quad·ri·part·ite /ˌkwɒdrə'pɑːtaɪt/ adjective **1** consisting of four parts. **2** shared by or involving four parties.

quad·ri·plegia /ˌkwɒdrə'pliːdʒə/ noun paralysis of all four limbs. □ **quad·ri·plegic** adjective & noun [modern Latin (as QUADRI-, Greek *plēgē* blow, strike)]

quad·ri·valent /ˌkwɒdrə'veɪlənt/ adjective Chem. = TETRAVALENT.

quad·riv·ium /kwɒ'drɪvɪəm/ noun hist. a medieval university course of arithmetic, geometry, astronomy, and music (compare TRIVIUM). [Latin, = the place where four roads meet (as QUADRI-, *via* road)]

quad·roon /kwɒ'druːn/ noun esp. hist. the offspring of a white person and a mulatto; a person of one quarter black ancestry. [Spanish *cuarterón* from *cuarto* fourth, assimilated to QUADRI-]

quad·ro·phon·ic var. of QUADRAPHONIC.

quad·ru·man·ous /kwɒ'druːmənəs/ adjective (of primates other than humans) four-handed, i.e. with opposable digits on all four limbs.

[modern Latin *quadrumana* neuter pl. of *quadrumanus* (as QUADRI-, Latin *manus* hand)]

quad·ru·ped /'kwɒdrʊˌped/ ● noun a four-footed animal, esp. a four-footed mammal. ● adjective four-footed. □ **quad·ru·pedal** /kwɒ'druːpɪdəl, ˌkwɒdrʊ'piːdəl/ adjective [Latin *quadrupes -pedis* from *quadru-* var. of QUADRI- + Latin *pes ped-* foot]

quad·ruple /kwɒ'druːpəl/ ● adjective **1** fourfold. **2 a** having four parts. **b** involving four participants (*quadruple alliance*). **3** being four times as many or as much. **4** (of time in music) having four beats in a bar. ● noun a fourfold number or amount. ● transitive & intransitive verb multiply by four; increase fourfold. □ **quad·ru·ply** adverb [French from Latin *quadruplus* (as QUADRI-, *-plus* as in *duplus* DUPLE)]

Quadruple Alliance the name given to various alliances involving four powers. In that of 1718, Austria joined Britain, the Netherlands, and France against Spain (which had seized Sicily and Sardinia); in that of 1813 (renewed in 1815), Britain, Russia, Austria, and Prussia united to defeat Napoleon and to maintain the international order; and in that of 1834, Britain, France, Spain, and Portugal united to support Maria Cristiana's claim to the Spanish throne and Maria de Glória's claim to the Portuguese throne.

quad·rup·let /kwɒ'druːplət/ noun **1** each of four children born at one birth. **2** a set of four things working together. **3** Music a group of four notes to be performed in the time of three. [QUADRUPLE, after *triplet*]

quad·ru·plex /'kwɒdrəˌpleks/ noun Cdn a building divided into four self-contained residences. [QUADRI- + -PLEX¹ 2, after DUPLEX noun 1]

quad·rup·li·cate /kwɒ'druːplɪkət/ adjective **1** fourfold. **2** of which four copies are made. □ **in quadruplicate** in four identical copies. □ **quad·rup·li·ca·tion** /-'keɪʃən/ noun [Latin *quadruplicare* from *quadruplex -plicis* fourfold: compare QUADRUPED, DUPLEX]

quaes·tor /'kwiːstər/ noun either of two ancient Roman magistrates with mainly financial responsibilities. [Latin from *quaerere quaesit-* seek]

quaff /kwɒf/ ● transitive & intransitive verb **1** drink deeply or in long drafts. **2** drink copiously or repeatedly. ● noun **1** a beverage quaffed. **2** an act of quaffing. □ **quaff·able** adjective **quaff·er** noun [16th c.: perhaps imitative]

quag /kwaɡ/ noun a marshy or boggy place. □ **quag·gy** adjective [related to dial. *quag* (v.) = shake: prob. imitative]

quag·ga /'kwaɡə/ noun an extinct zebra formerly native to southern Africa, with yellowish-brown stripes on the head, neck, and foreparts. [Xhosa-Kaffir *iqwara*]

quag·mire /'kwaɡˌmaɪr, kwɒɡ-/ noun **1** a soft boggy or marshy area that gives way underfoot. **2** a hazardous or awkward situation. [QUAG + MIRE]

qua·hog /'kwɒhɒɡ, 'kwa-/ noun (also **qua·haug**) the edible round clam, *Venus mercenaria*, of the Atlantic coast of N America. [Narragansett *poquauhock*]

quaich /kweik, -x/ noun Scot. a kind of drinking cup, usu. of wood and with two handles. [Gaelic *cuach* cup, prob. from Latin *caucus*]

Quai d'Orsay /keɪ dɔr'seɪ/ **1** a riverside street on the left bank of the Seine in Paris. **2** the French ministry of foreign affairs, which has its headquarters in this street.

quail¹ noun (pl. same or **quails**) **1** any small short-tailed bird of the genus *Coturnix*, related to the partridge, esp. the migratory *C. coturnix*, raised for its flesh and eggs. **2** any of various similar birds of other genera, e.g. the bobwhite. [Old French *quaille* from medieval Latin *coacula* (prob. imitative)]

quail² intransitive verb flinch; be apprehensive with fear. [Middle English, of unknown origin]

quaint adjective attractively unusual or unfamiliar in character or appearance, esp. in an old-fashioned way. □ **quaint·ly** adverb **quaint·ness** noun [earlier senses 'wise, cunning': Old French *cointe* from Latin *cognitus* past participle of *cognoscere* ascertain]

quake ● intransitive verb **1** (of the earth) shake, tremble. **2** (of a person) shake or shudder (*was quaking with fear*). ● noun **1** an earthquake. **2** an act of quaking. □ **quaky** adjective (**quaki·er**, **quaki·est**). [Old English *cwacian*]

Quak·er ● noun a member of the Society of Friends, a Christian movement devoted to peaceful principles and eschewing formal doctrine, sacraments, and ordained ministers. ● adjective of or relating to Quakers. □ **Quaker·ish** adjective **Quaker·ism** noun [QUAKE + -ER¹: originally derogatory, perhaps from its founder's direction to 'tremble at the name of the Lord', or from fits supposedly suffered when moved by the Spirit]

quaking aspen noun a N American aspen, *Populus tremuloides*.

Consonants: b *but*   d *dog*   f *few*   g *get*   h *her*   j *yes*   k *cat*   l *leg*   m *man*   n *no*   p *pen*   r *red*   s *sit*

quaking bog *noun* bogland formed over water or soft mud, which shakes underfoot.

quale /ˈkwɒli/ *noun* (*pl.* **qua·lia** /ˈkwɒliə/) a quality or property as perceived or experienced by a person. [Latin, neuter of *qualis* 'of what kind']

Qualicum Beach /ˈkwɒlɪkəm/ a town on the east coast of Vancouver Island, northwest of Nanaimo; pop. (2001) 6,921. [Sne Nay Muxw, = 'place of the chum salmon']

quali·fi·ca·tion /ˌkwɒləfɪˈkeɪʃən/ *noun* **1** the act or an instance of qualifying. **2** an accomplishment fitting a person for a position or purpose. **3 a** a circumstance, condition, etc., that modifies or limits (*the statement had many qualifications*). **b** a thing that detracts from completeness or absoluteness (*their relief had one qualification*). **4** a condition that must be fulfilled before a right can be acquired etc. □ **quali·fi·ca·tory** /ˈkwɒləfɪˌkeɪtəri/ *adjective*

qualified privilege *noun Law* the defence that a statement cannot be made the subject of an action for defamation because it was made on a privileged occasion and was not made maliciously, for an improper motive.

quali·fy /ˈkwɒləˌfaɪ/ *verb* (**-fies**, **-fied**) **1** *transitive* make competent or fit for a position or purpose. **2** *transitive* make legally entitled. **3** *intransitive* (foll. by *for*) (of a person) satisfy the conditions or requirements (for a position, award, competition, etc.). **4** *transitive* add reservations to; modify or make less absolute (a statement or assertion). **5** *transitive Grammar* (of a word, esp. an adjective) attribute a quality to (another word, esp. a noun). **6** *transitive* moderate, mitigate; make less severe or extreme. **7** *transitive* alter the strength or flavour of. **8** *transitive* (foll. by *as*) attribute a specified quality to, describe as (*the idea was qualified as absurd*). □ **quali·fi·able** *adjective* **quali·fi·er** *noun* [French *qualifier* from medieval Latin *qualificare* from Latin *qualis* such as]

quali·fy·ing /ˈkwɒləˌfaɪɪŋ/ *adjective* serving to determine those that qualify (*qualifying examination*).

quali·ta·tive /ˈkwɒlɪˌteɪtɪv/ *adjective* concerned with or depending on quality or qualities (*a qualitative difference between the two brands of soap*). □ **quali·ta·tive·ly** *adverb*

qualitative analysis *noun Chem.* identification of the constituents present in a substance (*opp.* QUANTITATIVE ANALYSIS).

qual·ity *noun* (*pl.* **-ities**) **1** the standard of something when compared to other things like it (*quality of life*; *wine of exceptional quality*). **2 a** general excellence (*we aim to provide quality at reasonable prices*). **b** (*attributive*) of high quality (*a quality product*). **3** a distinctive, usu. good, attribute or characteristic (*her sense of humour is her best quality*; *there is a particular quality of light in her paintings*). **4 a** the distinctive timbre of a voice or sound. **b** *Phonetics* the distinguishing characteristic or characteristics of a sound. **5** *archaic* high social standing (*people of quality*). **6** *Logic* the property of a proposition's being affirmative or negative. [Old French *qualité* from Latin *qualitas -tatis* from *qualis* of what kind]

quality circle *noun* a group of employees who meet to consider ways of resolving problems and improving production in their organization.

quality control *noun* a system of maintaining standards in manufactured products by testing and inspection. □ **quality controlled** *adjective*

quality time *noun* time spent devoting one's undivided attention to a favourite activity, such as a hobby, or to a person, esp. a parent or child, perceived as compensating in quality for what it lacks in duration or frequency.

qualm /kwɒm, kwɒlm/ *noun* **1** a misgiving; an uneasy doubt. **2** a scruple of conscience; a pang of doubt about one's own conduct. **3** a momentary faint or sick feeling. □ **qualm·ish** *adjective* [16th c.: origin uncertain]

quan·dary /ˈkwɒndri, ˈkwɒndəri/ *noun* (*pl.* **-ies**) **1** a state of perplexity concerning what to do in a difficult situation. **2** a difficult situation; a practical dilemma. [16th c.: origin uncertain]

quan·go /ˈkwæŋɡoʊ/ *noun esp. Brit.* (*pl.* **-gos**) a semi-public administrative body outside the civil service but with financial support from and senior members appointed by the government. □ **quan·goc·racy** *noun* **quan·go·crat** *noun* [abbreviation of *quasi* (or *quasi-autonomous*) *non-government(al)* organization]

quan·ta *pl.* of QUANTUM.

quan·tal /ˈkwɒntəl/ *adjective* of or relating to a quantum or quantum theory. □ **quan·tal·ly** *adverb* [Latin *quantus* how much]

quan·tify *transitive verb* (**-fies**, **-fied**) **1** determine the quantity of. **2** measure or express as a quantity. **3** *Logic* define the application of (a term or proposition) by the use of *all*, *some*, etc. □ **quan·ti·fi·able**

adjective **quan·ti·fi·ca·tion** *noun* **quan·ti·fi·er** *noun* [medieval Latin *quantificare* (as QUANTAL)]

quan·ti·tate *transitive verb* ascertain the quantity or extent of, measure. □ **quan·ti·tation** *noun*

quan·ti·ta·tive /ˈkwɒntɪˌteɪtɪv/ *adjective* **1 a** concerned with quantity. **b** measured or measurable by quantity. **2** pertaining to or based on vowel length. □ **quan·ti·ta·tive·ly** *adverb*

quantitative analysis *noun Chem.* measurement of the amounts and proportions of the constituents of a substance (*opp.* QUALITATIVE ANALYSIS).

quan·ti·tive /ˈkwɒntɪtɪv/ *adjective* = QUANTITATIVE. □ **quan·ti·tive·ly** *adverb*

quan·tity *noun* (*pl.* **-ties**) **1** an indefinite number or amount (*he had a considerable quantity of snow to shovel*). **2** a specified or definite number or amount that can be measured or counted (*the correct quantity of cream to add is 500 ml*). **3** a large amount or number; an abundance (*he buys in quantity*; *alcohol was available at the party in quantity*). **4** the property of things that is measurable (*quantity is easy to measure, whereas quality is not*). **5** a person or thing viewed as having a specified value (*I don't know what he'll bring to this team, he's really an unknown quantity*; *among the country's best theatre companies, theirs is a negligible quantity*). **6** the length or shortness of vowel sounds or syllables. **7** *Math.* a value, component, etc. that may be expressed in numbers. [Old French *quantité* from Latin *quantitas -tatis* from *quantus* how much]

quantity surveyor *noun* a person who calculates the quantity of materials needed for constructing buildings etc. and how much they will cost.

quan·tize /ˈkwɒntaɪz/ *transitive verb* (also esp. *Brit.* **-tise**) **1** form into quanta; restrict the number of possible values of a quantity so that certain variables can assume only certain discrete magnitudes. **2** apply quantum mechanics to. □ **quan·tiz·a·tion** *noun*

quan·tum /ˈkwɒntəm/ (*pl.* **quan·ta**) ● *noun* **1** *Physics* **a** a discrete quantity of energy proportional in magnitude to the frequency of radiation it represents. **b** an analogous discrete amount of any other physical quantity. **2 a** a required or allowed amount. **b** a share or portion. ● *attributive adjective* dramatic or significant (*a quantum advance*). [Latin, neuter of *quantus* how much]

quantum computer *noun* a (hypothetical) computer in which information is represented in terms of the possible quantum states of a set of physical systems (such as spinning particles), and in which the existence of superposed states would allow operations to be performed on all possible values of a variable simultaneously.

quantum leap *noun* (also **quantum jump**) **1** a sudden large increase or advance. **2** *Physics* an abrupt transition in an atom or molecule from one quantum state to another.

quantum mechanics *plural noun Physics* a mathematical form of quantum theory dealing with the motion and interaction of esp. subatomic particles and incorporating the concept that these particles can also be regarded as waves. □ **quantum-mechan·ic·al** *adjective*

quantum number *noun Physics* a number expressing the value of some property of a particle occurring in quanta.

quantum theory *noun Physics* a theory of matter and energy based on the concept of quanta.

Qu'Appelle River /kəˈpɛl/ a river in SE Saskatchewan, 430 km long, which rises from the southeastern arm of Lake Diefenbaker and flows generally eastward through Fort Qu'Appelle and across the border into Manitoba, where it immediately joins the Assiniboine River. [French, lit. 'who calls', prob. from Cree legend, with reference to the mournful sound of the wind in the trees]

quar·an·tine /ˈkwɒrənˌtiːn, ˌkwɒrənˈtiːn/ ● *noun* **1** isolation imposed on persons or animals that have arrived from elsewhere or been exposed to, and might spread, infectious or contagious disease. **2** the period of this isolation. **3** any comparable period, instance, or state of isolation, esp. a boycott or severance of diplomatic relations intended to isolate a nation. ● *transitive verb* impose such isolation on; put in quarantine. [Italian *quarantina* forty days, from *quaranta* forty]

quark¹ /kwɔrk, kwɑrk/ *noun Physics* any of a class of unobserved subatomic particles with a fractional electric charge, of which protons, neutrons, and other hadrons are thought to be composed. [invented word, assoc. with 'Three quarks for Muster Mark' in Joyce's *Finnegans Wake* (1939)]

quark² /kwɔrk, kwɑrk/ *noun* a type of spreadable low-fat curd cheese. [German, = 'curds']

quar·rel¹ ● *noun* **1** an angry argument or disagreement between individuals or with others. **2** an occasion of complaint against a person or thing. ● *intransitive verb* (**quar·relled**, **quar·rel·ling**; also esp. *US* **quar·reled**, **quar·rel·ing**) **1** have a dispute. **2** (often foll. by *with*) take exception; find fault. □ **quar·rel·ler** *noun* (also esp. *US* **quar·reler**). [Old French *querele* from Latin *querel(l)a* complaint, from *queri* complain]

quar·rel² *noun hist.* a short heavy square-headed arrow or bolt used in a crossbow or arbalest. [Old French *quarrel*, ultimately from Late Latin *quadrus* square]

quar·rel·some *adjective* given to or characterized by quarrelling. □ **quar·rel·some·ness** *noun*

quarry¹ ● *noun* (*pl.* **-ries**) **1** an open-air excavation from which stone for building etc. is or has been obtained by cutting, blasting, etc. **2** any place from which stone etc. may be extracted. **3** a supply or source of something (*a quarry of information*). ● *verb* (**-ries**, **-ried**) **1** *transitive* extract (stone) from a quarry. **2** *transitive* obtain or extract something by laborious methods. □ **quar·ri·er** *noun* [medieval Latin *quareria* from Old French *quarriere* from Latin *quadrum* square]

quarry² *noun* (*pl.* **-ries**) **1** the object of pursuit by a bird of prey, hounds, hunters, etc. **2** any object of chase, aim, or attack (*journalists relentlessly pursued their quarry*). [Anglo-French from Old French *cuiree*, *couree* (assimilated to *cuir* 'leather', and *curer* 'disembowel'), ultimately from Latin *cor* heart: originally = parts of deer placed on hide and given to hounds]

quarry³ *noun* (*pl.* **-ries**) **1** a diamond-shaped pane of glass as used in lattice windows. **2** (in full **quarry tile**) an unglazed floor tile. [a later form of QUARREL² in the same sense]

quarry·man *noun* (*pl.* **-men**) a worker in a quarry.

quart /'kwɔrt, kɔrt/ *noun* **1 a** a measure of capacity for liquids etc., equal to a quarter of an Imperial gallon (1.135 L or 40 fl. oz.). **b** a measure of capacity for liquids etc., equal to a quarter of a US gallon (0.946 L or 32 fl. oz.). **2** *N Amer.* a unit of dry measure, equal to one-thirty-second of a bushel (1.1 L). **3** a container holding a quart. [Old French *quarte* from Latin *quarta* fem. of *quartus* fourth, from *quattuor* four]

quar·tan /'kwɔrtən/ *adjective* (of a fever etc.) recurring every seventy-two hours. [Old French *quartaine* from Latin (*febris* fever) *quartana* from *quartus* fourth]

quar·ter /'kwɔrtər, 'kɔrtər/ ● *noun* **1 a** each of four equal parts into which a thing is or might be divided. **b** one-fourth part of something, represented by the fraction 1/4. **2 a** 25 Canadian or US cents. **b** a coin of this denomination. **3** fifteen minutes before or after any hour. **4** a period of three months, esp. for accounting purposes. **5** each of four equal periods into which a game is divided in football, basketball, etc. **6** (in *pl.*) **a** lodgings; an abode. **b** *Military* the living accommodation of members of the armed forces. **7** a part of a city or town, esp. as occupied by a particular class or group (*residential quarter*). **8** the direction, district, or source of supply etc. (*help from any quarter*; *came from all quarters*). **9** a point of the compass. **10 a** one fourth of a lunar month. **b** the moon's position between the first and second (**first quarter**) or third and fourth (**last quarter**) of these. **11** pity or mercy shown towards an enemy or an opponent who is in one's power (*his business rivals knew they could expect no quarter from him*). **12 a** each of the four parts into which an animal's or bird's carcass is divided, each including a leg or wing. **b** (in *pl.*) = HINDQUARTERS. **13** (in *pl.*) *hist.* the four parts into which a traitor etc. was cut after execution. **14** = QUARTER SECTION. **15** *Music* = QUARTER NOTE. **16** *US* a university term. **17** either side of a ship abaft the beam. **18 a** each of four divisions on a shield. **b** a charge occupying this, placed in chief. ● *verb* **1** *transitive* divide into quarters. **2** *transitive hist.* divide (the body of an executed person) in this way. **3 a** *transitive* provide with lodging. **b** *intransitive* (of a person) stay or lodge. **4** *transitive & intransitive* (esp. of a dog) range or traverse (the ground) in every direction. **5** *transitive Heraldry* **a** place or bear (charges or coats of arms) on the four quarters of a shield's surface. **b** add (another's coat) to one's hereditary arms. **c** (foll. by *with*) place in alternate quarters with. **d** divide (a shield) into four or more parts by vertical and horizontal lines. ● *attributive adjective* forming an amount equal to or roughly equal to a quarter. [Anglo-French *quarter*, Old French *quartier* from Latin *quartarius* fourth part (of a measure), from *quartus* fourth]

quar·ter·age *noun* **1** a quarterly payment. **2** a quarter's wages, allowance, pension, etc.

quarter·back *Football* ● *noun* **1** the player who directs the offence of a football team. Abbr.: **QB**. **2** this position on a football team. ● *verb* **1** *intransitive* play a game as a quarterback. **2** *transitive* lead (a team) in the role of quarterback. **3** *transitive N Amer.* lead, oversee.

quarter day *noun Brit.* one of four days on which quarterly payments are due, tenancies begin and end, etc.

quarter·deck *noun* part of a ship's upper deck near the stern, historically reserved for officers of the ship.

quarter-final *noun* a game or round of competition preceding the semifinal.

quar·ter horse *noun N Amer.* a small stocky breed of horse noted for agility and speed over short distances, often used to herd livestock.

quarter-hour *noun* **1** (also **quarter of an hour**) a period of 15 minutes. **2** = QUARTER *noun* 3.

quar·ter·ing *noun* **1** a provision of lodging. **2** the act or an instance of dividing, esp. into four equal parts. **3** (in *pl.*) the coats of arms marshalled on a shield to denote the alliances of a family with the heiresses of others.

quar·ter·ly ● *adjective* produced or occurring once every quarter of a year (*a quarterly report*). ● *adverb* **1** once every quarter of a year (*dividend rates are calculated quarterly*). **2** in the four, or in two diagonally opposite, quarters of a shield. ● *noun* (*pl.* **-lies**) a quarterly review or magazine.

quarter·master *noun* **1** a regimental officer in charge of quartering, rations, etc. **2** a naval petty officer in charge of steering, signals, etc.

quarter-miler *noun* an expert at or specialist in running a quarter-mile race.

quar·tern *noun Brit. archaic* a quarter of a pint. [Middle English, = quarter]

quarter note *noun N Amer. Music* a note having the time value of a quarter of a whole note, drawn as a large dot with a stem.

quarter rest *noun N Amer. Music* a rest having the time value of a quarter note.

quarter-round *noun* a convex moulding with an outline of a quarter circle.

quarter·saw *transitive verb* (*past participle* **quarter·sawn** or **quarter·sawed**) **1** saw (a log) radially into quarters and then into boards. **2** produce (a board) by quartersawing.

quarter section *noun N Amer.* (*West*) a quarter of a square mile of esp. agricultural land, 160 acres (approx. 64.7 hectares).

quarter sessions *plural noun hist.* (in the UK) a court of limited criminal and civil jurisdiction and of appeal, usu. held quarterly.

quarter·staff *noun hist.* a stout pole 6–8 feet long, formerly used as a weapon.

quarter-tone *noun Music* half a semitone.

quar·tet *noun* **1** *Music* **a** a composition for four voices or instruments. **b** the performers of such a piece. **2** any group of four. [French *quartette* from Italian *quartetto* from *quarto* fourth, from Latin *quartus*]

quar·tic *Math.* ● *adjective* involving the fourth and no higher power of an unknown quantity or variable. ● *noun* a quartic equation. [Latin *quartus* fourth]

quar·tier /kɑrt'jei/ *noun* in French-speaking regions, a district or area, esp. of a city. [French (compare QUARTER *noun* 7)]

quar·tile /'kwɔrtail/ *noun Statistics* one of three values of a variable dividing a population into four equal groups as regards the value of that variable. [medieval Latin *quartilis* from Latin *quartus* fourth]

quar·to /'kwɔrtoː/ *noun* (*pl.* **-tos**) *Printing* **1** the size given by folding a (usu. specified) sheet of paper twice, yielding 4 leaves or 8 pages. **2** a book consisting of sheets folded in this way. Abbr.: **4to**. [Latin (*in*) *quarto* (in) the fourth (of a sheet), ablative of *quartus* fourth]

quartz *noun* a mineral consisting of silica, crystallizing in colourless or white hexagonal prisms, often coloured by impurities (as amethyst, citrine, cairngorm), and found chiefly in igneous and metamorphic rocks. [German *Quarz* from West Slavic *kwardy*, corresponding to Czech *tvrdý* 'hard']

quartz clock *noun* a clock operated by vibrations of an electrically driven quartz crystal.

quartz·ite *noun* a hard, metamorphic rock consisting mainly of granular quartz.

quartz lamp *noun* a quartz tube containing mercury vapour and used as a source of light for automotive headlights etc.

quartz watch *noun* a watch operated by vibrations of an electrically driven quartz crystal.

qua·sar /'kweizɑr, -sɑr/ *noun Astronomy* any of a class of starlike celestial objects, apparently of great size and remoteness, often associated with a spectrum with a large red shift and intense radio emission. [*quasi-stellar*]

quash *transitive verb* **1** suppress; crush (speculation, a plan, an uprising etc.). **2** reject something and declare it no longer valid, esp. by a legal procedure. [Old French *quasser, casser* annul, from Late Latin *cassare* from *cassus* null, void, or from Latin *cassare* frequentative of *quatere* shake]

quasi *attributive adjective* **1** resembling, similar to (*a quasi marriage*). **2** being nearly or in part (*from totalitarian regime to quasi democracy*). [Latin, = as if, almost]

quasi- *combining form* **1** seemingly; apparently but not really (*quasi-scientific*). **2** being partly or almost (*quasi-independent*). [Latin *quasi* as if, almost]

Quasi·modo /ˌkwɒziːˈmoːˌdoː/ **Sal·va·tore** (1901–68), Italian poet. His early work was influenced by French symbolism, and includes *Water and Land* (1930) and *And It's Suddenly Evening* (1942), while his later work is concerned with political and social issues; he was awarded the Nobel Prize for literature in 1959.

quas·sia /ˈkwɒʃə/ *noun* **1** an evergreen tree, *Quassia amara*, native to S America. **2** the wood, bark, or root of this tree, yielding a bitter medicinal tonic and insecticide. [G. *Quassi*, 18th-c. Surinamese slave, who discovered its medicinal properties]

quater·cen·ten·ary /ˌkwɒtərsenˈtenɹi, -ˈtiːnɹi/ ● *noun* (pl. **-aries**) **1** a four-hundredth anniversary. **2** a festival marking this. ● *adjective* of this anniversary. [Latin *quater* four times + CENTENARY]

qua·ter·nary /ˈkwɒtərˌneri, kwəˈtɜrnəri/ ● *adjective* **1 a** having four parts. **b** fourth in a series. **2** (**Quaternary**) *Geol.* of or relating to the most recent period in the Cenozoic era, comprising the Pleistocene and Holocene epochs and beginning about 2 million years ago. (*compare* PLEISTOCENE, HOLOCENE). **3** *Chem.* (of an ammonium compound) containing a nitrogen atom bonded to four organic groups or atoms. ● *noun* (pl. **-ies**) **1** a set of four things. **2** (**Quaternary**) *Geol.* the Quaternary period or geological system. [Latin *quaternarius* from *quaterni* (distributive of *quattuor* four)]

qua·ter·nion /kwəˈtɜrniən/ *noun* **1** a group of four. **2** *Math.* a complex number of the form $w + xi + yj + zk$, where w, x, y, z are real numbers and i, j, k are imaginary units that satisfy certain conditions. [Late Latin *quaternio -onis* (as QUATERNARY)]

quat·rain /ˈkwɒtrein/ *noun* a stanza of four lines, usu. with alternate rhymes. [French from *quatre* four, from Latin *quattuor*]

quatre·foil /ˈkatrəˌfɔil/ *noun* a four-pointed or four-leafed figure, esp. as an ornament in architectural tracery, resembling a flower or clover leaf. [Anglo-French from *quatre* four: see FOIL²]

quattro·cento /ˌkwɒtroːˈtʃentoː/ *noun* **1** the fifteenth century in Italy. **2** the Italian style of art, literature, etc. of this period. [Italian, = 400 used with reference to the years 1400–99]

quattro formaggi /ˌkwɒtroː fɔrˈmɒdʒi/ *noun* a pasta sauce or pizza including four types of cheese. [Italian, = 'four cheeses']

qua·ver ● *verb* **1** *intransitive* **a** (esp. of a voice or musical sound) vibrate, shake, tremble. **b** use trills or shakes in singing. **2** *transitive* say or sing with a shaky or trembling voice. ● *noun* **1** a tremble in speech. **2** a trill in singing. **3** *Brit. Music* = EIGHTH NOTE. □ **qua·ver·ing·ly** *adverb* [Middle English from *quave*, perhaps from Old English *cwafian* (unrecorded: compare *cwacian* QUAKE)]

qua·very *adjective* (of a voice etc.) tremulous.

quay /kiː/ *noun* a solid stationary artificial landing place lying alongside or projecting into water for loading and unloading boats, ships, etc. [Old French *kay* from Gaulish *caio* from Old Celtic]

quay·side /ˈkiːsaid/ ● *noun* the land forming or near a quay. ● *adjective* at or by a quay.

Que. *abbreviation* Quebec.

queasy *adjective* (**queas·i·er, queas·i·est**) **1** feeling or tending to feel sick or nauseous (*the thought of another doughnut made me queasy*). **2** slightly nervous or worried about something; uneasy (*I felt queasy as I watched the neighbour's dog approach*). **3** feeling disgust or revulsion (*his pretentiousness made me queasy*). **4** causing nausea, anxiety, or disgust (*I took a queasy ride on the chairlift*). □ **queas·i·ly** *adverb* **queas·i·ness** *noun* [Middle English *queysy, coisy* perhaps related to Old French *coisir* hurt]

Que·bec /kwəˈbek, kə-, kei-/ a province in east central Canada; pop. (2001) 7,237,479; capital, Quebec City. It was settled by the French in 1608, ceded to the British in 1763, and became one of the original four provinces in the Dominion of Canada in 1867. □ **Que·bec·er** *noun* (also **Quebecker**). [see QUEBEC CITY]

Quebec Act *Cdn hist.* an act of the British parliament of 1774 which enlarged the territory of the province of Quebec to include Labrador, Anticosti Island and the Magdalen Islands and the Indian territory between the Ohio and Mississippi rivers, guaranteed religious freedom

for Catholics, established French civil law and British criminal law and provided for the continuation of the seigneurial system.

Quebec City the capital city of Quebec, a port situated on the north shore of the St. Lawrence in SE central Quebec, northeast of Trois-Rivières; pop. (2001) 507,986. Founded on the site of an Aboriginal village by the French explorer Champlain in 1608, it is Canada's oldest city, and much of it is designated a World Heritage Site. It was a centre of the struggle between the French and the British for control of colonial N America and was captured from the French by a British force in 1759 after the battle of the Plains of Abraham. It became capital of Lower Canada (later Quebec) in 1791. ¶ The official name for the city is Québec. [Algonquin and Abenaki *quebecq* where the channel (or river) narrows]

Quebec Conference a conference held in Quebec City in October 1864, at which a detailed plan for union between the Province of Canada and the three Maritime colonies was drawn up; the resulting 72 Quebec Resolutions formed the essential basis of the BNA Act.

Quebec gold *noun informal* high-potency marijuana grown in Quebec.

Quebec heater *noun Cdn* a tall, cylindrical stove using coal or wood for fuel, used esp. for heating or cooking.

Qué·bé·cois /keibekˈwɒ/ (also **Que·be·cois, Qué·be·cois**) *Cdn* ● *noun* a francophone native or inhabitant of Quebec. ● *adjective* of or relating to Quebec or the Québécois.

Qué·bé·coise /keibekˈwɒz/ (also **Que·be·coise, Qué·be·coise**) *Cdn* ● *noun* a francophone woman who is a native or inhabitant of Quebec. ● *adjective* being a Québécoise.

Que·chua /ˈketʃwə/ (also **Qui·chua** /ˈkiː-/) ● *noun* (pl. same or **Que·chuas**) **1** a member of a S American Indian people of Peru and neighbouring countries. **2** the language of this people. ● *adjective* of or relating to this people or their language. □ **Que·chu·an** *adjective* [Spanish from Quechua]

Queen, El·lery (pseudonym of Frederic Dannay, 1905–82, and Manfred Lee, 1905–71), US writers of detective fiction. Their many detective novels, featuring the detective also called Ellery Queen, include *The French Powder Mystery* (1930).

queen ● *noun* **1** (as a title usu. **Queen**) a female sovereign etc., esp. the hereditary ruler of an independent nation. **2** (in full **queen consort**) a king's wife. **3 a** a woman, country, or thing pre-eminent or supreme in a specified area or of its kind (*tennis queen*). **b** a belle or mock sovereign on some occasion (*beauty queen; queen of the fair*). **4** the fertile female among ants, bees, etc. **5 a** the most powerful piece in chess. **b** (**queen's**) designating a chess piece or pieces starting on the queen's side of the board (*queen's knight*). **6** in a deck of playing cards, any of the four cards bearing a picture of a queen. **7** *slang derogatory* **a** a male homosexual, esp. an effeminate one. **b** = DRAG QUEEN. **8** (**the Queen**) (in Canada and the UK) the anthem 'God Save the Queen'. ● *transitive verb* **1** make (a woman) queen. **2** *Chess* convert (a pawn) into a queen when it reaches the opponent's side of the board. ● *adjective* denoting a queen-size bed, mattress, sheets, etc. (see QUEEN-SIZE 1). □ **queen it** behave in an unpleasant and superior way towards other people (*she's been queening it around the office ever since her promotion*). □ **queen·dom** *noun* **queen·less** *adjective* **queen·like** *adjective* **queen·ship** *noun* [Old English *cwēn* woman, queen, from Germanic]

Queen Anne *adjective* **1** (of furniture) typical of Queen Anne's time, the early 18th c., esp. characterized by the use of walnut, cabriole legs, curving lines, and upholstery for comfort and elegance. **2** (of architecture) typical of English architecture of the early 18th c., esp. characterized by the use of red brick in simple, basically rectangular designs. **3** (also **Queen Anne Revival**) of a style of domestic architecture of the late 19th c., characterized by quaintness and old-fashionedness achieved by blending diverse elements of earlier periods, such as Queen Anne, Georgian and Gothic.

Queen Anne's lace *noun* any of several umbelliferous plants bearing lacy clusters of small white flowers, esp. cow parsley and (*N Amer.*) wild carrot, *Daucus carota*.

Queen Anne's War one of several wars fought between Great Britain and France for control of N America, 1702–13, contemporaneous with the War of the Spanish Succession in Europe (see SPANISH SUCCESSION, WAR OF THE). The French captured St. John's in 1708, while the British took Port-Royal in 1710. By the terms of the Treaty of Utrecht (1713), France conceded many of its North American claims to Britain (see UTRECHT, TREATY OF).

queen bee *noun* **1** (of bees) the fertile female in a hive. **2 a** a woman who holds a superior position in an organization etc. **b** a woman who behaves in a superior or controlling manner.

Queen Charlotte Islands (also **Queen Char·lottes**) an isolated

uː m**oo**d   ai m**y**   əi p**î**pe   au br**ow**n   ʌu h**ou**se   ei d**ay**   ɔi b**oy**   ā fr**an**glais   ã Cana**di**en   ɔ̃ Br**ay**on   (*see over for consonants*)

group of more than 150 islands off the northwest coast of BC. Noted for its timber and fishing resources, the area also contains rare forms of plant life and the 19th-c. Haida village of SGaang Gwaii, a World Heritage Site. [ultimately after *Charlotte* Sophia, queen of George III d.1818]

Queen Charlotte Sound a wide, deep inlet of the N Pacific, situated off the central coast of BC, between the Queen Charlotte Islands and Vancouver Island. It links Hecate and Queen Charlotte straits. [as QUEEN CHARLOTTE ISLANDS]

Queen Charlotte Strait a channel of the N Pacific, situated between the northeastern coast of Vancouver Island and mainland BC. It is linked to the Strait of Georgia via Johnstone Strait. [as QUEEN CHARLOTTE ISLANDS]

Queen City, the 1 a nickname for Regina. **2** a nickname for Toronto.

queen·cup *noun* (also **queen's cup**) a liliaceous plant of western N America, *Clintonia uniflora*, with a single white flower and a blue berry.

Queen Elizabeth Foreland a promontory at the tip of Hall Peninsula, Baffin Island, situated at the entrance to Frobisher Bay. [ELIZABETH I]

Queen Elizabeth Islands a group of islands in the N Arctic Archipelago, comprising those islands north of Parry Channel, including Ellesmere and Devon islands, as well as both the Parry and Sverdrup island groups. [ELIZABETH II]

queen·ly *adjective* (**queen·li·er**, **queen·li·est**) **1** fit for or appropriate to a queen. **2** majestic; queenlike. □ **queen·li·ness** *noun*

Queen Mab (in British folklore) the queen of the fairies.

Queen Mary, Mount a peak in the St. Elias Mountains of SW Yukon Territory (3 886 m). [*Mary* of Teck, queen of George V, d.1953]

Queen Maud Gulf a large inlet of the Arctic Ocean, bordered by Victoria and King William islands to the northwest and northeast respectively, and by mainland Nunavut to the south. [*Queen Maud* of Norway, third daughter of Edward VII d.1938]

Queen Maud Land a part of Antarctica bordering the Atlantic Ocean, claimed since 1939 by Norway. [as QUEEN MAUD GULF]

queen mother *noun* (as a title usu. **Queen Mother**) the dowager who is mother of the sovereign.

queen of puddings *noun* a pudding made from custard and bread crumbs, flavoured with lemon rind and vanilla, topped with jam or sliced fruit and meringue.

queen of the prairie *noun* a N American plant of the rose family, *Filipendula rubra*, with clusters of small pink flowers.

queen post *noun* one of two upright timbers between the tie beam and principal rafters of a roof truss.

Queens a borough of New York City, at the western end of Long Island; pop. (2000) 2,229,379.

Queen's Bench *noun* (in full **Court of Queen's Bench**) **1** (in Alberta, Saskatchewan, Manitoba, and New Brunswick) the superior-court trial division, which has the jurisdiction to hear the most serious indictable offences and civil cases. **2** (in the UK) a division of the High Court of Justice (formerly a court at which the monarch presided).

Queens·berry Rules *plural noun* the standard rules, esp. of boxing. [the 8th Marquess of *Queensberry*, English nobleman d.1900, who supervised the preparation of boxing laws in 1867]

Queen's Birthday *noun Cdn* in BC and Newfoundland and Labrador, a holiday falling on the Monday immediately preceding 25 May; Victoria Day.

Queen's Counsel *noun Cdn, Brit., Austral., & NZ* an appointment bestowed on a barrister by the Attorney General in recognition of excellence as an advocate and following advice from the barrister's peers.

Queen's County the former name for LAOIS.

Queen's English *noun* the English language as correctly written or spoken in Britain.

Queen's highway *noun* a public road, regarded as being under the sovereign's protection.

queen-size *adjective* (also **queen-sized**) **1** designating the second-largest standard size of mattress, usu. 153 by 208 cm (60 by 80 in.), or the bed frame, sheets, etc. designed for such a mattress. **2** of an extra-large size, esp. designating women's hosiery for heavier than average legs.

Queens·land a state comprising the northeastern part of Australia; pop. (2001) 3,635,121; capital, Brisbane. □ **Queens·land·er** *noun*

Queen's Park *noun* **1** the grounds and building in Toronto where the Ontario legislature is situated. **2** the government of Ontario.

Queen's Plate *noun* a stakes race for three-year-olds run annually at Woodbine Racetrack in Toronto. [given Royal Assent by Queen Victoria in 1859]

Queen's Printer *noun Cdn* an official printer of bills and reports, office stationery, bulletins, etc. for the federal or provincial governments.

Queen's Scout *noun Cdn & Brit.* a Scout who has reached the highest standard of proficiency.

Queen's Speech *noun Brit.* a statement including the Government's proposed measures read by the sovereign at the opening of Parliament (*compare* SPEECH FROM THE THRONE).

Queens·ton Heights a decisive battle of the War of 1812, which took place atop the escarpment at Queenston, Niagara-on-the-Lake on 13 Oct. 1812. American troops launched a surprise attack before dawn but, despite their initial advantage, were soundly defeated by defending British and Canadian forces. Though the British commander Isaac Brock was killed, the victory left the citizens of Upper Canada with the feeling that they could successfully repel American invasions.

queeny *adjective* (**-ier**, **-iest**) (of a homosexual) ostentatiously effeminate.

queer ● *adjective* **1** unnatural; odd; eccentric. **2** *slang* **a** (esp. of a man) homosexual. **b** of or pertaining to a homosexual or homosexuals. ¶ Although in recent years gay people have appropriated the word *queer* to refer to themselves, its use by others is still often *offensive*. **3** shady; suspect; of questionable character. **4** slightly ill; giddy; faint. ● *noun slang* a homosexual. ● *transitive verb slang* spoil; put out of order. □ **queer a person's pitch** *Brit.* spoil a person's chances, esp. secretly or maliciously. □ **queer·ly** *adverb* **queer·ness** *noun* [perhaps from German *quer* oblique (as THWART)]

queer bashing *noun* = GAY BASHING. □ **queer basher** *noun*

quell *transitive verb* **1 a** put an end to (something), esp. by force; suppress (*quell an uprising*). **b** cause to submit; suppress (*quell a crowd of protesters*). **2** allay or suppress (feelings, fear, anger, etc.) (*quelled the doubts of supporters*). [Old English *cwellan* kill, from Germanic]

quench *transitive verb* **1** satisfy (thirst) by drinking. **2** extinguish (a fire or light etc.). **3** esp. *Metallurgy* cool (a hot substance) in cold water, air, oil, etc. **4** stifle or suppress (desire etc.). **5** *Physics & Electronics* inhibit or prevent (oscillation, luminescence, etc.) by counteracting means. □ **quench·er** *noun* [Old English *-cwencan* extinguish]

que·nelle /kə'nel/ *noun* a small dumpling-like ball of minced or chopped seasoned fish or meat usu. cooked by poaching. [French from German *knödel* dumpling]

quercetin /'kwɜrsɪtɪn/ *noun* a yellow crystalline pigment present in plants, used as a food supplement to reduce allergic responses or boost immunity. [probably from Latin *quercetum* 'oak grove' (from *quercus* 'oak') + -IN]

Que·ré·taro /ke'retə,ro/ **1** a state of central Mexico. **2** its capital city; pop. (est. 2002) 825,500. In 1847 it was the scene of the signing of the treaty ending the US–Mexican war.

quern /kwɜrn/ *noun hist.* a hand mill for grinding grain. [Old English *cweorn(e)* from Germanic]

queru·lous /'kwerʊləs/ *adjective* of a whining, complaining, or peevish nature or disposition (*the dour man looked querulous; she spoke in a querulous voice*). □ **queru·lous·ly** *adjective* **queru·lous·ness** *noun* [Late Latin *querulosus* or Latin *querulus* from *queri* complain]

query /'kwiːri/ ● *noun* (*pl.* **-ies**) **1** a question or inquiry (*in her cooking column she responded to the queries of her readers*). **2** a question that expresses doubt or reservation (*queries about the feasibility of the project*). **3** *Computing* **a** the action of searching a string of characters in a computer database. **b** a string or set of characters searched. **4** a question mark, or the word *query* spoken or written to question accuracy or as a mark of interrogation. ● *transitive verb* (**-ies**, **-ied**) **1** express in the form of a question (*"Where am I?" he queried; she queried whether it would rain*). **2** express doubt about something (*reporters queried the coach's abilities*). **3** *N Amer.* ask a question of (*she queried him about his preference*). [anglicized form of *quaere* from Latin *quaerere* ask, after INQUIRY]

que·sa·dil·la /ˌkeɪsə'diːjə/ *noun* a dish of vegetables and grated cheese etc., stuffed between two tortillas, usu. baked or fried and served with salsa, sour cream, etc. [Spanish *quesada* cheese (ultimately from Latin *caseus*) + *illa* diminutive suffix]

Consonants: b but d dog f few g get h her j yes k cat l leg m man n no p pen r red s sit

Ques·nay /keɪˈneɪ/ **François** (1694–1774), French physician and economist. He was the leader of the physiocrats, a group of economists who opposed mercantilism and advanced laissez-faire principles; his works include *Tableau économique* (1758).

Ques·nel /kwɔˈnel/ a city in central BC, located at the confluence of the Fraser and Quesnel rivers, 407 km northwest of Kamloops; pop. (2001) 10,044. [J.-M. *Quesnel*, a North West Co. clerk d.1842]

quest ● *noun* **1** a search or the act of seeking; an expedition. **2** the thing sought. **3** (often foll. by *to* + infin.) a goal sought; an attempt or endeavour (*foiled in his quest to win twenty games*). ● *intransitive verb* (often foll. by *for*) go about in search of something; go on a quest. □ **in quest of** seeking. □ **quest·er** *noun* [Old French *queste*, *quester*, ultimately from Latin *quaerere quaest-* seek]

ques·tion ● *noun* **1** a sentence worded or expressed so as to seek information. **2 a** doubt or uncertainty about something (*there is no question about his honesty; I have serious questions about the advisability of this project*). **b** the raising of such doubt etc. (*his suitability for the position is open to question*). **3** a matter or issue that needs to be settled (*the question is how should I invest the money*). **4** (foll. by *of*) a matter or concern depending on conditions (*it's all a question of whether I can afford it*). **5** a matter to be discussed or decided or voted on (*Edmontonians will vote on the airport question*). ● *transitive verb* **1** ask questions of; interrogate (*police questioned the suspect*). **2** express or feel doubt about something (*her honesty has never been questioned; I question the wisdom of wearing shorts on such a cold day*). **3** challenge; argue against (*certain of his client's innocence, the lawyer questioned the judge's ruling*). □ **be a question of time** be certain to happen sooner or later. **beyond all question** undoubtedly. **come into question** be discussed; become of practical importance. **in question** that is being discussed or referred to (*the person in question*). **call into question** cast doubt on, dispute. **is not the question** is irrelevant. **no question of** no possibility of (*there's no question of my giving in*). **no question that** no doubt that. **out of the question** too impracticable etc. to be worth discussing; impossible. **pop the question** see POP¹. **put the question** require supporters and opponents of a proposal to record their votes. **question of fact** *Cdn & Brit. Law* an issue to be decided by the jury. **question of law** *Cdn & Brit. Law* an issue to be decided by a judge. **without question 1** undoubtedly. **2** without hesitation. □ **ques·tion·er** *noun* **ques·tion·ing·ly** *adverb* [Old French from Latin *quaestio -onis* from *quaerere quaest-* seek]

ques·tion·able *adjective* **1** doubtful as regards truth or quality (*some accurate measurements and some questionable ones*). **2** not clearly in accordance with honesty, honour, wisdom, etc. (*questionable business practices*). **3** of dubious value (*the fire-eater achieved questionable renown by once accidentally setting himself on fire*). □ **ques·tion·ably** *adverb*

ques·tion·ing ● *noun* **1** the action of posing a question or calling into question. **2** interrogation, esp. of a suspect by police officers. ● *adjective* showing that one needs information or has doubts (*a questioning look*). □ **ques·tion·ing·ly** *adverb*

question mark *noun* **1** a punctuation mark (?) indicating a question. **2** a cause for doubt or uncertainty (*we have the funds but public support remains a question mark*). **3** doubt or uncertainty (*a question mark looms over their future plans*).

ques·tion·naire *noun* a formulated series of questions, esp. for statistical study or market research. [French from *questionner* QUESTION + *-aire* -ARY¹]

question period *noun Cdn* a period of time set aside each day during parliamentary proceedings in which members may question government ministers.

question time *noun Brit., Austral. & NZ Parl.* = QUESTION PERIOD.

Quet·ta /ˈkwetə/ a city in W Pakistan, the capital of Baluchistan province; pop. (est. 1998) 560,300.

quet·zal /ˈkwetzəl, ˈketsəl/ *noun* **1** any of various brilliantly coloured birds of the family Trogonidae, esp. the Central and S. American *Pharomachrus mocinno*, the male of which has long green tail coverts. **2** the chief monetary unit of Guatemala. [Spanish from Aztec from *quetzalli* the bird's tail feather]

Quet·zal·có·atl /ˌketsəlkoːˈɒtəl/ the plumed serpent god of the Toltec and Aztec civilizations. Traditionally the god of the morning and evening star, he later became known as the patron of priests, inventor of books and of the calendar, and as the symbol of death and resurrection.

queue /kjuː/ ● *noun* **1** a line or sequence of persons, vehicles, etc., awaiting their turn to be attended to or to proceed. **2** *Computing* a list of data items, commands, etc., stored so as to be retrievable in a definite order, usu. the order of insertion. **3** a pigtail or braid of hair. ● *verb*

(**queues**, **queued**, **queuing** or **queueing**) **1** *intransitive* (often foll. by *up*) (of persons etc.) form a queue; take one's place in a queue. **2** *transitive* esp. *Computing* arrange in a queue. [French from Latin *cauda* 'tail']

queue-jump *verb* **1** *transitive & intransitive* pass (others) to the front of a line without waiting for one's turn. **2** receive attention or consideration for something before others that have waited longer. □ **queue jumper** *noun*

Que·zon City /ˈkeɪzɒn/ a city on the island of Luzon in the N Philippines; pop. (2000) 2,173,831. Forming part of a conurbation with Manila, Quezon City was established in 1940. From 1948 to 1976 it was the capital of the Philippines.

Qufu /tʃuˈfuː/ a small town in Shandong province in E China, where Confucius was born in 551 BC and lived for much of his life.

quib·ble ● *noun* a petty objection; a trivial or unimportant point of criticism, sometimes used to avoid a more important issue. ● *intransitive verb* argue about small differences or disagreements. □ **quib·bler** *noun* **quib·bling** *adjective* **quib·bling·ly** *adverb* [diminutive of obsolete *quib* prob. from Latin *quibus* dative & ablative pl. of *qui* who (familiar from use in legal documents)]

quiche /kiːʃ/ *noun* a pastry shell containing a mixture of eggs, milk, cream, cheese, etc., with vegetables, meat, fish, etc. [French from Alsatian dial. *Küchen* (German *Kuchen*) cake]

quiche lor·raine /kiːʃ ləˈreɪn/ *noun* a quiche with bacon in the filling. [French, 'quiche from Lorraine']

Qui·chua *noun* var. of QUECHUA.

quick ● *adjective* **1** capable of doing something in a short time (*a quick runner; a quick learner*). **2 a** with a short interval, rapid (*she wrote four novels in quick succession*). **b** prompt or immediate (*Earl issued a quick reply*). **3** requiring only a short time, brief (*a quick shower*). **4 a** lively, agile (*quick hands*). **b** acute, alert, perceptive (*she has a quick ear*). **5 a** (foll. by *to* + infin.) responding immediately or hastily (*she's quick to criticize, even if she doesn't know the whole story*). **b** (of a temper) easily provoked. **6** *archaic* living, alive (*the quick and the dead*). ● *adverb* **1** at a rapid rate; quickly. **2** (as *interjection*) come, go, etc., quickly (*Quick! Get your shoes and let's go!*). ● *noun* **1** the soft flesh below the nails, or the skin, or a sore. **2** the source of feeling or emotion (*hurt him to the quick*). □ **be quick** act quickly. **cut to the quick** deeply offend or upset someone, hurt a person's feelings. □ **quick·ly** *adverb* **quick·ness** *noun* [Old English *cwic(u)* alive, from Germanic]

quick and dirty *adjective* done hastily; makeshift.

quick bread *noun* a baked good, usu. less sweet and rich than a cake or cookie, leavened with baking powder or baking soda, e.g. a muffin, scone, etc.

quick-change artist *noun* a person who is adept at changing quickly from one costume, policy, etc. to another.

quick·en *verb* **1** *transitive & intransitive* make or become quicker; accelerate. **2** *transitive & intransitive* enliven, animate, rouse, or become lively, animated, or roused (*seeing her quickened his memory; his memory quickened when he saw her*). **3** *intransitive* (of a fetus) begin to show signs of life.

quick-fire *adjective* **1** (of jokes, repartee, etc.) rapid or occurring in rapid succession. **2** firing shots in quick succession.

quick fix *noun* a rapid (esp. inadequate) solution to a problem.

quick·ie *informal* ● *noun* **1** a thing done or made quickly or hastily. **2** a brief act of sexual intercourse. **3** an alcoholic drink taken quickly. ● *adjective* made or executed quickly (*quickie divorce; quickie production*).

quick·lime *noun* = LIME¹ *noun* 1.

quick march *noun Military* **1** a march in quick time. **2** the command to begin this.

quick one *noun informal* a drink taken quickly.

quick pick *noun* a method of choosing a lottery number by having a computer generate a series of digits randomly.

quick·sand *noun* **1 a** loose wet sand, easily yielding to pressure, that sucks in anything placed or falling in it. **b** a bed of this. **2** a treacherous thing or situation.

quick·silver ● *noun* mercury. ● *adjective* in constant flux; changeable, unpredictable (*a quicksilver temper*).

quick·step ● *noun* a fast foxtrot. ● *intransitive verb* (**-stepped**, **-step·ping**) dance the quickstep.

quick study *noun N Amer.* a person who adapts easily and quickly to new surroundings, a new job, etc.; a fast learner.

quick time *noun Military* marching at about 120 paces per minute.

quick trick *noun Bridge* **1** a trick in the first two rounds of a suit. **2** the card that should win this.

quick-witted *adjective* able to think quickly and issue an immediate usu. clever reply; intelligent. □ **quick-witted·ness** *noun*

quid[1] *noun* (*pl.* same) *Brit. slang* one pound sterling. [prob. from *quid* the nature of a thing, from Latin *quid* what, something]

quid[2] *noun* a lump of tobacco for chewing. [dial. var. of CUD]

quid·dity *noun* (*pl.* **-ties**) **1** *Philos.* the essence of a person or thing; what makes a thing what it is. **2** a trivial objection or distinction; a quibble. [medieval Latin *quidditas* from Latin *quid* what]

quid pro quo *noun* **1** a thing given as compensation. **2** return made (for a gift, favour, etc.). [Latin, = something for something]

qui·es·cent /kwi'esənt/ *adjective* **1** motionless, inert. **2** temporarily inactive; silent, dormant. □ **qui·es·cence** *noun* [Latin *quiescere* from *quies* QUIET]

quiet ● *adjective* (**quiet·er**, **quiet·est**) **1** making little or no sound. **2** smooth, still; not bumpy or rough (*this car offers a quiet ride; the waters were quiet*). **3** free from disturbance or activity (*a quiet time for prayer; streets were quiet because of the holiday*). **4** informal; simple (*just a quiet wedding*). **5** of gentle or peaceful disposition; shy. **6** not expressed loudly; restrained or concealed (*he kept his resentment quiet; quiet heroism*). **7** enjoyed in quiet (*a quiet bath*). ● *noun* **1** silence. **2** an undisturbed state; stillness, tranquility. **3** a state of being free from urgent tasks or agitation. ● *verb* **1** *transitive verb* soothe, make quiet. **2** *intransitive* (often foll. by *down*) become quiet or calm. □ **be quiet** (esp. in *imperative*) cease talking etc. **keep quiet 1** refrain from making a noise. **2** (often foll. by *about*) suppress or refrain from disclosing information etc. **on the quiet** unobtrusively; secretly. □ **quiet·ly** *adverb* **quiet·ness** *noun* [Old French *quiet(e)* from Latin *quietus* past participle of *quiescere* 'be quiet']

quiet·en *transitive & intransitive verb* esp. *Brit.* (often foll. by *down*) = QUIET *verb.*

quiet·ism *noun* **1** religious mysticism based on the rejection of outward forms of devotion in favour of passive contemplation and extinction of the will. **2** any philosophy emphasizing human passivity and the principle of nonresistance. □ **quiet·ist** *noun & adjective* **quiet·is·tic** *adjective* [Italian *quietismo* (as QUIET)]

Quiet Revolution *noun* *Cdn* in Quebec, the period under the Liberal provincial government of Jean Lesage from 1960 to 1966, characterized by province-wide social, economic, and educational reforms, as well as mounting separatist sentiment and the issue of a special status for Quebec within Confederation.

quiet·ude /'kwaiə,tu:d, -,tju:d/ *noun* a state of quiet.

qui·etus /kwai'i:təs/ *noun* **1** something which puts an end to or represses something. **2** discharge or release from life; death. [medieval Latin *quietus est* he is quit (see QUIT) used as a form of receipt]

quiff *noun* esp. *Brit.* **1** a man's tuft of hair, brushed upward over the forehead. **2** a curl plastered down on the forehead. □ **quiffed** *adjective* [20th c.: origin unknown]

Quil·ico /'kwɪlɪ,koː/ **Louis** (1925–2000), Canadian baritone and teacher. He made his professional debut in 1954 with the Opera Guild of Montreal and his New York debut in 1955 with the New York City Opera. A teacher at the University of Toronto from 1970, he contributed to the careers of many younger singers, including his son Gino Quilico; father and son appeared together in the 1987 Metropolitan Opera production of Massenet's *Manon*.

quill ● *noun* **1** (usu. in *pl.*) the spines of a porcupine. **2** (in full **quill feather**) a large feather in a wing or tail. **3** the hollow stem of this. **4** (in full **quill pen**) a pen made of a quill. **5** a hollow rotating sleeve of metal etc., esp. one used to transmit the drive from a motor to a concentrically mounted axle. ● *transitive verb* form into cylindrical quill-like folds; goffer. [Middle English prob. from (Middle) Low German *quiele*]

Quiller-Couch /,kwɪlər'kuːtʃ/ **Sir Ar·thur Thom·as** (known as 'Q') (1863–1944), English critic, poet, and novelist, who is best known as the editor of the *Oxford Book of English Verse* (1900).

quill·ing *noun* **1** a piece of quilled lace edging etc. **2** the art of making ornamental filigree from tightly rolled columns of paper.

quillow *noun* a quilt that can be folded over and slipped into an attached pouch to make a pillow. [blend of QUILT + PILLOW]

quill·work *noun* art using porcupine quills to decorate clothing, teepees, and utilitarian items, done by a number of Aboriginal groups, esp. the Mi'kmaq. □ **quill·worked** *adjective*

quill·wort /'kwɪlwɔrt, -wɔrt/ *noun* any grasslike plant of the genus *Isoetes.*

Quilmes /'kiːlmes/ a city in eastern Argentina, pop. (est. 1999) 550,069, near the Río de la Plata estuary, and forming part of the Buenos Aires conurbation.

quilt ● *noun* **1** a bedcover made of padding enclosed between layers of cloth etc. and kept in place by cross lines of stitching. **2** a bedspread of similar design (*patchwork quilt*). **3** a collection of diverse elements that together constitute a whole, resembling a patchwork quilt (*this multicultural city is a quilt of ethnic communities*). ● *intransitive verb* make a quilt. □ **quilt·er** *noun* [Old French *coilte, cuilte* from Latin *culcita* mattress, cushion]

quilt·ed *adjective* **1** covered or lined with padded material held together with lines of stitching (*a quilted jacket; quilted diapers*). **2** (of padding and cloth) stitched or sewn together in the manner of a quilt (*quilted goose down*).

quilt·ing *noun* **1** the practice of making quilts. **2 a** the materials, such as cloth, padding, etc., used in the production of quilts. **b** these materials having been quilted.

quina·crine /'kwɪnə,krɪn, -kriːn/ *noun* an anti-malarial drug derived from acridine. [*quinine* + *acridine*]

quin·ary /'kwainɜri/ *adjective* **1** of the number five. **2** having five parts. [Latin *quinarius* from *quini* distributive of *quinque* five]

quin·az·o·line /kwə'nazəliːn/ *noun* a yellow basic crystalline solid which has a bicyclic structure of fused benzene and pyrimidine rings; any substituted derivative of this. [Spanish from Quechua *kina* bark + -OL[1] + -INE[4] + with inserted -*az*- (see AZO-)]

quince *noun* **1** a hard acid pear-shaped fruit used as a preserve or flavouring. **2** any shrub or small tree of the genus *Cydonia*, esp. *C. oblonga*, bearing this fruit. [Middle English, originally collect. pl. of obsolete *quoyn, coyn*, from Old French *cooin* from Latin *cotoneum* var. of *cydoneum* (apple) of *Cydonia* in Crete]

quin·cen·ten·ary /,kwɪnsen'tenɜri, -'tiːnɜri/ ● *noun* (*pl.* **-aries**) **1** a five-hundredth anniversary. **2** a festival marking this. ● *adjective* of this anniversary. □ **quin·cen·ten·nial** /-'teniəl/ *adjective & noun* [irreg. from Latin *quinque* five + CENTENARY]

Quin·cey see DE QUINCEY.

quin·cunx /'kwɪnkʌŋks/ *noun* **1** five objects set so that four are at the corners of a square or rectangle and the fifth is at its centre, e.g. the five on dice or cards. **2** this arrangement, esp. in planting trees. □ **quin·cun·cial** /kwɪn'kʌnʃəl/ *adjective* [Latin, = five-twelfths from *quinque* five, *uncia* twelfth]

Quincy Adams, Mount /'kwɪnsi 'adəmz/ a peak (4 133 m) in the St. Elias Mountains of northwestern BC, situated on the border with Alaska, just east of Fairweather Mountain. [J. Quincy ADAMS]

quin·el·la /kwɪ'nelə/ *noun* a form of betting in which the better must select the first-place and second-place winners in a race, not necessarily in the correct order. [Latin American Spanish *quiniela*]

quin·ine /'kwɪnain, 'kwainain, 'kwiːniːn/ *noun* **1** an alkaloid found esp. in cinchona bark. **2** a bitter drug containing this, used as a specific remedy for malaria and as an additive to tonic water. [*quina* cinchona bark, from Spanish *quina* from Quechua *kina* bark]

quinoa /'kiːnwə/ *noun* **1** any of several annual goosefoots grown by the Indians of the Andes for their edible starchy seeds. **2** these seeds used as food. [Spanish spelling of Quechua *kinua, kinoa*]

quin·ol·ine /'kwɪnə,liːn/ *noun* *Chem.* an oily amine obtained from the distillation of coal tar or by synthesis and used in the preparation of drugs etc. [Spanish *quina* (as QUININE) + -OL + -INE[4]]

quin·ol·one /'kwɪnə,loːn/ *noun* any of several related antibiotics that inhibit the reproduction of micro-organisms, and are used to treat infections that have become resistant to other antibiotics. [QUINOLINE + -ONE]

quin·one /'kwɪnoːn, -'noːn/ *noun* *Chem.* **1** a yellow crystalline derivative of benzene with the hydrogen atoms on opposite carbon atoms replaced by two of oxygen. **2** any in a class of similar compounds. [Spanish *quina* (as QUININE) + -ONE]

quin·qua·gen·ar·ian /,kwɪŋkwədʒɪ'neriən/ ● *noun* a person from 50 to 59 years old. ● *adjective* of or relating to this age. [Latin *quinquagenarius* from *quinquageni* distributive of *quinquaginta* fifty]

Quin·qua·ges·ima /,kwɪŋkwə'dʒesimə/ *noun* (in full **Quinquagesima Sunday**) the Sunday before the beginning of Lent. [medieval Latin, fem. of Latin *quinquagesimus* fiftieth, from *quinquaginta* fifty, after QUADRAGESIMA]

quinque- /'kwɪŋkwi/ *combining form* five. [Latin from *quinque* five]

quin·quen·nial /kwɪn'keniəl/ *adjective* **1** lasting five years. **2** recurring every five years. □ **quin·quen·nial·ly** *adverb*

quin·quen·nium /kwɪn'keniəm/ *noun* (*pl.* **quin·quen·niums** or

quin·quen·nia) a period of five years. [Latin from *quinque* five + *annus* year]

quin·que·reme /ˈkwɪŋkwəˌriːm/ *noun hist.* an ancient Roman galley with five files of oarsmen on each side. [Latin *quinqueremis* (as QUINQUE-, *remus* oar)]

quin·que·valent /ˈkwɪnkwəˌveɪlənt/ *adjective* having a valence of five.

quin·sy *noun* an inflammation of the throat, esp. an abscess in the region around the tonsils. [Old French *quinencie* from medieval Latin *quinancia* from Greek *kunagkhē* from *kun-* dog + *agkhō* throttle]

quint *noun N Amer. informal* a quintuplet. [abbreviation]

quin·ta /ˈkɪntə, ˈkwɪntə/ *noun* **1** (in Spain, Portugal, and Latin America) a large house or villa in the country or on the outskirts of a town. **2** a wine-growing estate in Portugal. [Spanish & Portuguese, from *quinta parte* 'fifth part' (originally the part of a farm's produce paid as rent)]

quin·tal /ˈkwɪntəl/ *noun* **1** a hundredweight (112 lb.), used e.g. as a measure for dried salt cod. **2** a weight of about 100 lb. **3** a weight of 100 kg. [Old French *quintal*, medieval Latin *quintale* from Arabic *ḳinṭār*, based on Latin *centenarius* 'containing a hundred']

Quin·tana Roo /kiːnˌtɒnə ˈroː/ a state of SE Mexico, on the Yucatán Peninsula; capital, Chetumal.

Quinte, Bay of /ˈkwɪnti/ a long, narrow channel west of Kingston separating the north shore of Lake Ontario from the peninsula of Prince Edward. [possibly from Mohawk *kenta* 'meadow']

quin·tes·sence /kwɪnˈtesəns/ *noun* **1** the most essential part of any substance; a refined extract. **2** (usu. foll. by *of*) the purest and most perfect, or most typical, form, manifestation, or embodiment of some quality or class. **3** (in ancient philosophy) a fifth substance (beside the four elements) forming heavenly bodies and pervading all things. □ **quint·es·sen·tial** *adjective* **quint·es·sen·tial·ly** *adverb* [Middle English (in sense 3) from French from medieval Latin *quinta essentia* fifth ESSENCE]

quin·tet /kwɪnˈtet/ *noun* **1** *Music* **a** a composition for five voices or instruments. **b** a group of five musicians. **2** any group of five. [French *quintette* from Italian *quintetto* from *quinto* fifth, from Latin *quintus*]

Quinte West a city in E Ontario, just west of Belleville on the Bay of Quinte, including the former city of Trenton and surrounding townships; pop. (2001) 41,409.

quin·tile /ˈkwɪntaɪl/ *noun Statistics* **1** each of the four values of a variate which divide a frequency distribution into four groups. **2** each of the five groups so produced. [Latin *quintus* fifth]

Quin·til·ian /kwɪnˈtɪliən/ (Latin name Marcus Fabius Quintilianus) (AD c.35–c.96), Roman rhetorician. His *Education of an Orator*, a comprehensive treatment of the art of rhetoric and the training of an orator, was highly influential in the Middle Ages and the Renaissance.

quin·til·lion /kwɪnˈtɪljən/ *noun* (*pl.* same or **quin·til·lions**) a thousand raised to the sixth (or formerly, esp. *Brit.*, the tenth) power (10^{18} and 10^{30} respectively). □ **quin·til·lionth** *adjective & noun* [Latin *quintus* fifth + MILLION]

quin·tuple /kwɪnˈtʌpəl/ ● *adjective* **1** fivefold; consisting of five parts. **2** involving five parties. **3** (of time in music) having five beats in a bar. ● *noun* a fivefold number or amount. ● *transitive & intransitive verb* multiply by five; increase fivefold. [French *quintuple* from Latin *quintus* fifth, after QUADRUPLE]

quin·tup·let /kwɪnˈtʌplət/ *noun* **1** each of five children born at one birth. **2** a set of five things working together. **3** *Music* a group of five notes to be performed in the time of three or four.

quin·tup·li·cate /kwɪnˈtʌplɪkət/ *adjective* **1** fivefold. **2** of which five copies are made. □ **in quintuplicate 1** in five identical copies. **2** in groups of five.

quin·zhee /ˈkwɪnzi/ *noun* (also **quin·zie**) *N Amer.* a shelter created by piling up snow, letting it settle, and then hollowing out the interior. [Athapaskan; = 'bowl-shaped depression in snow; shelter']

quip ● *noun* a clever saying; an epigram; a sarcastic remark etc. ● *verb* (**quipped**, **quip·ping**) **1** *intransitive* make quips. **2** *transitive* say (something) as a quip. □ **quip·ster** *noun* [abbreviation of obsolete *quippy* perhaps from Latin *quippe* forsooth]

quipu /ˈkiːpuː, ˈkwɪpuː/ *noun* the ancient Peruvians' substitute for writing by variously knotting threads of various colours. [Quechua, = knot]

quire *noun* **1** four sheets of paper etc. folded to form eight leaves, as often in medieval manuscripts. **2** any collection of leaves one within another in a manuscript or book. **3** 25 (also 24) sheets of paper. □ **in quires** unbound; in sheets. [Old French *qua(i)er*, ultimately from Latin *quaterni* set of four (as QUATERNARY)]

quirk *noun* **1** a peculiarity of behaviour or character; an eccentricity.

2 a trick of fate; a freak. **3** a flourish in writing. **4** (often *attributive*) *Archit.* a hollow in a moulding. □ **quirk·ish** *adjective* **quirky** *adjective* (**quirk·i·er**, **quirk·i·est**). **quirk·i·ly** *adverb* **quirk·i·ness** *noun* [16th c.: origin unknown]

quirt ● *noun* a short-handled riding whip with a braided leather lash. ● *transitive verb* strike with this. [Spanish *cuerda* CORD]

quis·ling /ˈkwɪzlɪŋ/ *noun* **1** a person co-operating with an occupying enemy; a collaborator or fifth columnist. **2** a traitor. [V. Quisling, Norwegian army officer and diplomat d.1945, who collaborated with the German occupying force in Norway (1940–45)]

Quis·pam·sis /kwɪspamˈsɪs/ a town in S New Brunswick, northeast of Saint John; pop. (2001) 13,757. □ **Quis·pam·mer** /kwɪsˈpamɜr/ *noun* [Maliseet *quispem sis* little lake, prob. with reference to a small lake nearby]

quit ● *verb* (**quit·ting**; *past* and *past participle* **quit**) **1** *transitive & intransitive* give up; abandon (a task etc.). **2** *transitive N Amer.* cease; stop (*quit grumbling; trying to quit smoking*). **3** *transitive & intransitive* give up (one's employment); resign (*if my boss yells at me one more time I will quit!; she quit her job last summer*). **4** *transitive* (*past* and *past participle* **quit** or **quit·ted**) leave or depart from (a place, person, etc.). ● *predicative adjective* (foll. by *of*) rid (*glad to be quit of the problem*). [Old French *quitte*, *quitter* from medieval Latin *quittus* from Latin *quietus* QUIET]

quitch *noun* (in full **quitch grass**) = COUCH[2]. [Old English *cwice*, perhaps related to QUICK]

quite *adverb* **1** completely; entirely; wholly; to the utmost extent; in the fullest sense. **2** somewhat; rather; to some extent. **3** (often foll. by *so*) said to indicate agreement. □ **quite a** a remarkable or outstanding (person or thing) (*it was quite an event*). **quite another** (or **other**) very different (*that's quite another matter*). **quite a few** *informal* a fairly large number of. **quite some 1** a large amount of (*quite some time ago*). **2** *informal* = QUITE A (*that was quite some movie*). **quite something** a remarkable thing. [Middle English from obsolete *quite* (adj.) = QUIT]

Quito /ˈkiːtoː/ the capital of Ecuador, situated in the Andes just south of the equator; pop. (est. 2002) 1,648,100.

quit-rent *noun hist.* a rent, typically a small one, paid in lieu of services which might otherwise be required.

quits *predicative adjective* on even terms by retaliation or repayment (*then we'll be quits*). □ **call it quits 1** acknowledge that things are now even; agree not to proceed further in a quarrel etc. **2** cease an activity; stop working etc. (*I'm ready to call it quits for tonight*). [perhaps informal abbreviation of medieval Latin *quittus*: see QUIT]

quit·tance *noun archaic* **1** (foll. by *from*) a release. **2** an acknowledgement of payment; a receipt. [Old French *quitance* from *quiter* QUIT]

quit·ter *noun* a person who gives up easily.

quitting time *noun esp. N Amer.* the time at which work is ended for the day.

quiv·er[1] ● *intransitive verb* tremble or vibrate slightly (*she quivered with anger; leaves quivering in the breeze*). ● *noun* a quivering motion or sound. □ **quiver·ing·ly** *adverb* **quiv·ery** *adjective* [Middle English from obsolete *quiver* nimble: compare QUAVER]

quiv·er[2] *noun* a case for holding arrows. □ **quiver·ful** *noun* [Old French *quivre* from West Germanic]

qui vive /kiː ˈviːv/ *noun* □ **on the qui vive** on the alert; watching for something to happen. [French, = lit. '(long) live who?', i.e. on whose side are you?, as a sentry's challenge]

quix·ot·ic /kwɪkˈsɒtɪk/ *adjective* **1** extravagantly and romantically chivalrous; paying no heed to material interests in comparison with honour or devotion. **2** visionary; pursuing lofty but unattainable ideals. □ **quix·ot·ic·ally** *adverb* **quix·ot·ism** /ˈkwɪksəˌtɪzəm/ *noun* [Don *Quixote*, hero of Cervantes' romance, from Spanish *quixote* thigh armour]

quiz[1] ● *noun* (*pl.* **quiz·zes**) **1** *esp. N Amer.* a short test or examination. **2** a test of knowledge, esp. between individuals or teams as a form of entertainment. **3** *esp. Brit.* an interrogation or questioning. ● *transitive verb* (**quizzed**, **quiz·zing**) **1** *esp. N Amer.* test or examine (students). **2** examine by questioning. [19th-c. dial.: origin unknown]

quiz[2] *Brit. archaic* ● *transitive verb* (**quizzed**, **quiz·zing**) **1** look curiously at; observe the ways or oddities of; survey through an eyeglass. **2** make sport of; regard with a mocking air. ● *noun* (*pl.* **quiz·zes**) **1** a hoax, a thing done to burlesque or expose another's oddities. **2 a** an odd or eccentric person; a person of ridiculous appearance. **b** a person given to quizzing. □ **quiz·zer** *noun* [18th c.: origin unknown]

quiz·master *noun* a person who presides over a quiz show.

uː m**oo**d   aɪ m**y**   əi p**i**pe   au br**ow**n   ʌu h**ou**se   ei d**ay**   ɔi b**oy**   ã fr**an**glais   ã C**an**adien   ɔ̃ Br**ay**on   (*see over for consonants*)

quiz show *noun* a television or radio program in which people compete in a quiz, often for prizes.

quiz·zic·al *adjective* **1** expressing or done with mild or amused perplexity. **2** strange; comical. □ **quiz·zic·al·ity** *noun* **quiz·zic·al·ly** *adverb*

qul·liq /ˈkʌlɪk/ *noun Cdn (North)* = KUDLIK. [Inuktitut]

Qum see QOM.

Qum·ran /kʊmˈrɒn/ a region on the western shore of the Dead Sea. The Dead Sea scrolls were found (1947–56) in caves at nearby Khirbet Qumran, the site of an ancient Jewish settlement.

quod erat dem·on·stran·dum /kwɒd ˌerat ˌdemənˈstrandəm/ (esp. at the conclusion of a proof etc.) which was the thing to be proved. Abbr.: **QED**. [Latin]

quod·libet /ˈkwɒdlɪˌbet/ *noun* **1** *hist.* a topic or point for philosophical or theological discussion. **2** a lighthearted medley of well-known tunes. [Latin from *quod* what + *libet* it pleases one]

quoin /kɔɪn/ ● *noun* **1** an external angle of a building. **2** a stone or brick forming an angle; a cornerstone. **3** *hist.* a wedge for raising the level of a gun, keeping the barrel from rolling, etc. ● *transitive verb* secure or raise with quoins. □ **quoin·ing** *noun* [var. of COIN]

quoit /kɔɪt/ ● *noun* **1** (in *pl.*) a game consisting of aiming and throwing flat rings of rope or metal to encircle as near as possible to a peg. **2** a ring used in this game. ● *transitive verb* fling like a quoit. [Middle English: origin unknown]

quon·dam /ˈkwɒndam/ *predicative adjective* that once was; sometime; former. [Latin (adv.), = formerly]

Quon·set /ˈkwɒnsət/ *noun N Amer. proprietary* (in full **Quonset hut**) a prefabricated metal building with a semicylindrical corrugated roof. [*Quonset Point*, Rhode Island, where it was first made]

quor·um /ˈkwɔːrəm/ *noun* the fixed minimum number of members that must be present to make the proceedings of an assembly, society, or meeting valid. [Latin, = of whom (we wish that you be two, three, etc.), in the wording of commissions]

quota *noun* **1** the share that an individual person or company is obliged to contribute to or entitled to take from a total. **2 a** a quantity of goods etc. which under official controls a producer is obliged or entitled to produce, export, import, etc. **b** *Cdn* authorization to produce a specified quantity of an agricultural product granted to a marketing board to a farmer. **3** the number of immigrants allowed to enter a country, students allowed to enrol for a course, etc. **4** a share or portion of something that one can normally expect to receive or give (*got my quota of sleep*). [medieval Latin *quota* (*pars*) how great (a part), fem. of *quotus* from *quot* how many]

quot·able *adjective* worth, or suitable for, quoting. □ **quot·abil·ity** *noun*

quo·ta·tion *noun* **1** the act or an instance of quoting or being quoted. **2** a passage or remark quoted. **3** *Music* a short passage or tune taken from one piece of music to another. **4** *Stock Exch.* an amount stated as the current price of stocks or commodities. **5** an estimate of the cost of something.

quotation mark *noun* each of a set of punctuation marks, single (' ') or double (" "), used to mark the beginning and end of a quoted passage, a book title, etc., or words regarded as slang, jargon, or unfamiliar.

quote ● *verb* **1** *transitive* cite or appeal to (an author, book, etc.) in confirmation of some view. **2** *transitive* repeat a statement by (another person) or copy out a passage from (*don't quote me*). **3** *transitive & intransitive* **a** repeat or copy out (a passage) usu. with an indication that it is borrowed. **b** (foll. by *from*) cite (an author, book, etc.). **4** *transitive* (foll. by *as*) cite (an author etc.) as proof, evidence, etc. **5** *transitive* enclose (words) in quotation marks. **6** *transitive* **a** state (the price) of a job to a person (*they quoted $900 for the work*). **b** (often foll. by *at*) state the price of (a commodity, stock, etc.) (*the securities had not yet been quoted; gold was quoted at $700*). **c** (often foll. by *at*) name (a racehorse etc.) at specified odds (*quoted at 200 to 1*). **7** *transitive Stock Exch.* regularly list the price of. **8** (of a composer, painter, designer, etc. or their creations) reproduce or repeat a passage, style, etc. from one piece to another. ● *noun informal* **1** a passage or statement quoted. **2** a price quoted. **3** (usu. in *pl.*) quotation marks. ● *adverb* (in speech, reading aloud, etc.) indicating the presence of opening quotation marks (*he said, quote, 'We shall never surrender'*). [Middle English, earlier 'mark with numbers', from medieval Latin *quotare* from *quot* how many, or as QUOTA]

quoth /kwoʊθ/ *transitive verb* (only in 1st and 3rd person) *archaic* said. [Old English *cwæth* past of *cwethan* say, from Germanic]

quo·tid·ian /kwoʊˈtɪdɪən/ *adjective* **1** daily, of every day. **2** commonplace, trivial. [Old French *cotidien* & Latin *cotidianus* from *cotidie* daily]

quo·tient /ˈkwoʊʃənt/ *noun* **1** a result obtained by dividing one quantity by another. **2** the degree or presence of a usu. specified characteristic in a thing or person (*a magazine with a high glitz quotient*). [Latin *quotiens* how many times, from *quot* how many, by confusion with -ENT]

Quran /kərˈɑːn/ *noun* (also **Qur'an**) the Islamic sacred book, believed to be the word of God as dictated to Muhammad and written down in Arabic. □ **Quran·ic** *adjective* [Arabic *qur'ān* recitation, from *qara'a* read]

Qut·tin·ir·paaq National Park /kuˈtɪnˌɜrpak/ a large park of NE Ellesmere Island, formerly called Ellesmere Island National Park. [Inuktitut, = 'top of the world']

q.v. *abbreviation quod vide*, 'which see' (in cross-references etc.).

QWER·TY /ˈkwɜrti/ *attributive adjective* (also **qwer·ty**) denoting the standard keyboard on English-language word processors, typewriters, etc., with *q, w, e, r, t,* and *y* as the first keys on the top row of letters.

Consonants: b *but*   d *dog*   f *few*   g *get*   h *her*   j *yes*   k *cat*   l *leg*   m *man*   n *no*   p *pen*   r *red*   s *sit*

Rr

R¹ *noun* (also **r**) (*pl.* **Rs** or **R's**) the eighteenth letter of the alphabet. □ **the three Rs 1** reading, writing, and arithmetic, regarded as the fundamentals of learning. **2** reduce, reuse, recycle, as three basic principles of environmentally-friendly waste management.

R² *abbreviation* (also **R.**) **1** *N Amer.* (of films) restricted. **2** *Regina* (Elizabeth R). **3** *Rex.* **4** River. **5** (also ®) registered as a trademark. **6** (in names of societies etc.) Royal. **7** *N Amer.* R-value. **8** *Chess* rook. **9** Railway. **10** rand. **11** Regiment. **12** Réaumur. **13** radius. **14** (in a liturgy) response.

R³ *symbol* **1** roentgen. **2** electrical resistance. **3** (in chemical formulae) an organic radical or group.

r. *abbreviation* (also **r**) **1** right. **2** recto. **3** run(s). **4** radius.

R-2000 *noun Cdn* a certification designating houses built to a very high standard of energy efficiency, indoor air quality, and environmental impact.

RA *abbreviation* **1** (in the UK) Royal Academy. **2** (in the UK) Royal Artillery. **3** right ascension.

Ra¹ (also **Re**) *Egyptian Myth* the sun god, the supreme Egyptian deity, worshipped as the creator of all life, and often portrayed with a falcon's head bearing the solar disc; he appears travelling in his ship with other gods, crossing the sky by day and journeying through the underworld of the dead at night.

Ra² *symbol Chem.* the element radium.

RAAF *abbreviation* Royal Australian Air Force.

Raan·es Peninsula /ˈrɒnez/ a peninsula of the southwestern coast of Ellesmere Island. [O. *Raanes*, Norwegian Arctic explorer *c*.1900]

rab·aska /rəˈbaskə/ *noun Cdn* (Que.) (also **rabaska canoe**) a large birchbark or cedar canoe, about 8 m long with a high, usu. decorated, bow and stern, which can hold 10 to 12 people. [Canadian French, alteration of ATHABASKA, the canoes being originally used for the fur trade into the Athabaska region]

Rabat /rəˈbat/ the capital of Morocco, an industrial port on the Atlantic coast; pop. (est. 2002) 1,600,700. [from Arabic *Ribat et-Fath*, meaning 'fort of victory']

Ra·baul /rəˈbaul/ the chief town and port of the island of New Britain, Papua New Guinea; pop. (est. 2002) 16,000.

rab·bet ● *noun* a step-shaped channel etc. cut along the edge or face or projecting angle of a length of wood etc., usu. to receive the edge or tongue of another piece. ● *transitive verb* (**rab·bet·ed**, **rab·bet·ing**) **1** join or fix with a rabbet. **2** make a rabbet in. [Old French *rab(b)at* abatement, recess, from *rabattre* REBATE¹]

rab·bi /ˈrabai/ *noun* (*pl.* **rab·bis**) **1** a Jewish scholar or teacher, esp. of the law. **2** a person appointed as a Jewish religious leader. [Hebrew *rabbî* my master, from *rab* master + pronominal suffix]

rab·bin·ate /ˈrabɪnət/ *noun* **1** the position or office of a rabbi. **2** rabbis collectively.

rab·bin·ic·al /rəˈbɪnɪkəl/ *adjective* (also **rab·bin·ic**) of or relating to rabbis, or to Jewish law or teaching.

rab·bit ● *noun* **1** any of various burrowing gregarious plant-eating mammals of the hare family, with long ears and a short tail, varying in colour from brown in the wild to black and white, and kept as a pet or for meat. **2** *N Amer.* a hare. **3** the fur of the rabbit. ● *intransitive verb* (**rab·bit·ed**, **rab·bit·ing**) **1** hunt rabbits. **2** *Brit. informal* (often foll. by *on, away*) talk excessively or pointlessly; chatter (*rabbiting on about his holiday*). □ **rab·bity** *adjective* [perhaps from Old French: compare French dial. *rabotte*, Walloon *robète*, Flemish *robbe*]

rabbit·brush *noun* (also **rabbit·bush**) a shrub of the composite family, *Chrysothamnus nauseosus*, of western N America, bearing clusters of yellow flowers.

rabbit ears *plural noun N Amer.* an indoor television antenna consisting of a pair of telescoping aerials.

rabbit punch ● *noun* a short chop with the edge of the hand to the nape of the neck. ● *transitive verb* give a rabbit punch to (someone).

rabbit warren *noun* **1** an area in which rabbits have their burrows, or are kept for meat etc. **2** a building or part of a city with many narrow passages or streets.

rab·ble¹ *noun* **1** a large disorderly group of people; a mob. **2** (prec. by *the*) the lower classes. [Middle English: origin uncertain]

rab·ble² *noun* an iron bar with a bent end for stirring molten metal etc. [French *râble* from medieval Latin *rotabulum*, Latin *rutabulum* 'fire shovel' from *ruere rut-* 'rake up']

rabble-rouser *noun* a person who stirs up a crowd of people, esp. in agitation for social or political change. □ **rabble-rousing** *adjective & noun*

Rabe·lais /ˈrabəˌlei/ **Fran·çois** (*c*.1494–1553), French satirist. His allegorical works parodying medieval learning and literature, attacking asceticism, and affirming humanist values, are marked by coarse humour and an imaginative and exuberant use of language, and include *Pantagruel* (*c*.1532) and *Gargantua* (1534).

Rabe·lais·ian /ˌrabəˈleiziən/ ● *adjective* **1** of or like Rabelais or his writings. **2** marked by exuberant imagination and language, coarse humour, and satire. ● *noun* an admirer or student of Rabelais.

Rabi /ˈrɒbi/ **Isi·dor Isaac** (1898–1988), Austrian-born US physicist, who invented magnetic resonance spectroscopy; he was awarded the Nobel Prize for physics in 1944.

rabid *adjective* **1** (of a person, feelings, opinions, etc.) unreasoning; fanatical (*a rabid anarchist*). **2** of, relating to, or affected with rabies (*that dog is rabid*). □ **rabid·ly** *adverb* [Latin *rabidus* from *rabere* rave]

ra·bies /ˈreibiːz/ *noun* a contagious and fatal viral disease of dogs, cats, raccoons, and other animals, transmissible through the saliva to humans and causing madness and convulsions. [Latin from *rabere* rave]

Rabin /rəˈbin/ **Yit·zhak** (1922–1995), Israeli politician and military leader, prime minister 1974–7 and 1992–1995. As chief of staff (1964–8), he led Israel's armed forces to victory during the Six Day War of 1967. In September 1993 he and PLO leader Yasser Arafat achieved a PLO-Israeli peace accord, for which they shared a Nobel Peace Prize in 1994. In 1995 he was assassinated by a right-wing Israeli extremist in protest against his negotiations with the Palestinians.

rac·coon *noun* (also **ra·coon**) **1** any greyish-brown furry N American nocturnal flesh-eating mammal of the genus *Procyon*, with a ringed bushy tail, sharp snout, and black mask-like markings across the eyes. **2** the fur of the raccoon. [Virginia Algonquian *aroughcun*]

Race, Cape a cape on the southeastern tip of the Avalon Peninsula of Newfoundland. It is the province's most southeasterly point. [Portuguese *raso* flat, level, with reference to its cliffs; perhaps also in honour of *Cabo Raso*, a point at the mouth of the Tagus River]

race¹ ● *noun* **1** a contest of speed between athletes, horses, vehicles, ships, etc. **2** (in *pl.*) a series of these for horses, dogs, etc. at a fixed time on a regular course. **3** any contest or competition (*entered the leadership race; protested the arms race*). **4** a determined or urgent effort, esp. one involving a number of people etc. (*the race to find a cure for multiple sclerosis*). **5 a** a strong or rapid current flowing through a narrow channel in the sea or a river (*a tide race*). **b** the channel of a stream etc., esp. one built to lead water to or from a mill, mine, etc. **6** each of two grooved rings in a ball bearing or roller bearing. **7** (in weaving) the channel along which the shuttle moves. **8** *archaic* **a** the course of the sun or moon. **b** the course of life. ● *verb* **1** *intransitive* take part in a race. **2** *transitive* have a race with. **3** *transitive* try to surpass in speed. **4** *intransitive* (foll. by *with*) compete in speed with. **5** *transitive* cause (a horse, car, etc.) to race. **6** *intransitive* go at full speed (*the car raced down the highway*). **7** *intransitive* (esp. of the heart) beat very quickly. **8 a** *intransitive* (of an engine, wheel, etc.) run or revolve very swiftly, without resistance, or uncontrollably. **b** *transitive* cause (an engine, wheel, etc.) to do this. **9** *transitive* move (a person or thing) very quickly (*the victim was raced to hospital*). **10** *intransitive* (usu. as **ra·cing** *adj.*) follow or take part in horse racing (*a racing man*). [Middle English, = running, from Old Norse *rás*]

race² *noun* **1** each of the major divisions of humankind, having distinct physical characteristics. **2** a tribe, nation, etc., regarded as of a distinct ethnic stock. **3** the fact or concept of division into races (*discrimination based on race*). **4** a genus, species, breed, or variety of animals, plants, or micro-organisms. **5** a group of persons, animals, or plants connected by common descent. **6** descent; kindred (*of noble race; separate in language and race*). **7** a group of persons etc. with some common feature (*the race of poets*). [French from Italian *razza*, of unknown origin]

race car *noun* a car built for racing on a prepared track.

race card¹ *noun* a printed program giving information about races.

race card² *noun* an accusation or suggestion of racism exploited by someone for political etc. advantage.

race-car driver *noun* (also **race driver**) a driver of race cars.

race·course *noun* = RACETRACK.

race·goer *noun* a person who regularly goes to horse races.

race·horse *noun* a horse bred or kept for racing.

ra·cem·ate /ˈrasɪˌmeɪt/ *noun Chem.* a racemic mixture.

ra·ceme /rəˈsiːm/ *noun Bot.* a flower cluster with the separate flowers attached by short equal stalks at equal distances along a central stem (*compare* CYME). [Latin *racemus* cluster of grapes]

race meeting *noun Brit.* a sequence of horse races at one place.

ra·cem·ic /rəˈsiːmɪk, -ˈsemɪk/ *adjective Chem.* composed of equal numbers of dextrorotatory and levorotatory molecules of a compound. □ **racem·iz·a·tion** *noun* [RACEME + -IC, originally of tartaric acid in grape juice]

racem·ose /ˈrasəˌmoːs/ *adjective* **1** *Bot.* in the form of a raceme. **2** *Anat.* (of a gland etc.) clustered.

racer *noun* **1** a person or thing that races. **2** a horse, yacht, bicycle, etc., of a kind used for racing.

race relations *plural noun* relations between members of different races within a particular area.

race riot *noun* an outbreak of violence due to racial antagonism.

race·track *noun* **1** a ground or track for horse racing. **2** a track or course used for any race.

race walking *noun* an act or the practice or sport of walking as a contest of speed, requiring a continuous progress of steps in which one or the other of the feet is always in contact with the ground. □ **race walker** *noun*

race·way *noun* **1** esp. *N Amer.* a racetrack, esp. one used for harness racing. **2** a track or channel along which something runs, esp.: **a** a channel for water. **b** a groove in which ball bearings run. **c** a pipe or tubing enclosing electrical wires.

Rachel *Bible* the second and favourite wife of Jacob, mother of Joseph and Benjamin (Gen. 29–35).

ra·chis /ˈreɪkɪs/ *noun* (*pl.* **ra·chis·es** or **ra·chi·des** /-kɪˌdiːz/) **1** *Bot.* **a** a stem of grass etc. bearing flower stalks at short intervals. **b** the axis of a compound leaf or frond. **2** *Anat.* the vertebral column or the cord from which it develops. **3** *Zool.* a feather shaft, esp. the part bearing the barbs. [modern Latin from Greek *rhakhis*]

rach·itis /rəˈkaɪtɪs/ *noun* rickets. □ **rach·it·ic** /-ˈkɪtɪk/ *adjective* [modern Latin from Greek *rhakhitis* (as RACHIS)]

Rach·man·inov /rɒkˈmɒnɪˌnɒf, rɑːˈmɑːnɪˌnɒf/ **Ser·gei Vasil·evich** (1873–1943), Russian composer and pianist, resident in the US from 1917. His compositions for piano, in particular the Prelude in C sharp minor (1892), the Second Piano Concerto (1901), and the *Rhapsody on a Theme of Paganini* (1934) for piano and orchestra, reflect the Russian romantic tradition; he also wrote symphonies and operas.

ra·cial *adjective* **1** of or concerning race (*racial diversity; racial minority*).

2 on the grounds of or connected with difference in race (*racial discrimination; racial tension*). **3** of or relating to racism; racist (*a racial incident*). □ **racial·ly** *adverb*

racial·ism *noun* = RACISM 1. □ **racial·ist** *noun & adjective*

racial·ize *transitive verb* (also esp. *Brit.* **-ise**) **1** impose a racial interpretation on. **2** cause to become racial or racist in outlook, structure, etc. □ **racial·iz·a·tion** *noun*

racial profiling *noun* **1** selection for scrutiny by law enforcement based on racial or ethnic rather than behavioural or evidentiary criteria. **2** discrimination or stereotyping on racial or ethnic grounds.

Ra·cine /raˈsiːn/ **Jean Bap·tiste** (1639–99), French dramatist. The principal tragedian of the French classical period, he depicts the conflict of reason and passion in classically inspired works such as *Andromaque* (1667), *Iphigénie* (1674), and *Phèdre* (1677).

racing car *noun* = RACE CAR.

racing driver *noun* = RACE-CAR DRIVER.

racing stripe *noun* a thin horizontal stripe of paint along the body of a car.

ra·cism *noun* **1** a belief in the superiority of a particular race. **2** prejudice based on this. **3** antagonism towards other races, esp. as a result of this prejudice. **4** the theory that human abilities etc. are determined by race. □ **ra·cist** *noun & adjective*

rack¹ ● *noun* **1** a framework usu. with rails, bars, hooks, etc., for holding or storing things (*roof rack; coat rack*). **2** a cogged or toothed bar or rail engaging with a wheel or pinion etc., or using pegs to adjust the position of something. **3** *hist.* an instrument of torture stretching the victim's joints by the turning of rollers to which the wrists and ankles were tied. **4** *N Amer.* **a** a triangular frame in which the balls are arranged before the opening shot of a game of pool etc. **b** the balls positioned in this way. **5** *N Amer.* a set of antlers. **6** a frame for holding animal fodder. ● *transitive verb* **1** (also **wrack**) (of disease or pain) inflict suffering on. **2** *hist.* torture (a person) on the rack. **3** *N Amer.* = RACK UP 1. **4** place in or on a rack. **5** shake violently. **6** injure by straining. **7** oppress (tenants) by exacting excessive rent. □ **off the rack** *N Amer.* (of an article of clothing) available for immediate purchase; ready-made (*buys all his suits off the rack*). **on the rack** in distress or under strain. **rack one's brains** make a great mental effort (*racked my brains for something to say*). **rack up** *N Amer.* **1** place (the balls for a game of pool etc.) in the rack. **2** accumulate (points etc.) (*racked up 50 goals last season*). **3** run up (a bill, debt, etc.) (*racked up a $450 phone bill*). [Middle Dutch, Middle Low German *rak, rek*, prob. from *recken* stretch]

rack² *noun* destruction (*rack and ruin*). [var. of WRACK¹ 3, WRECK]

rack³ *noun* a roast of lamb cut from the loin. [perhaps from RACK¹]

rack⁴ *transitive verb* (often foll. by *off*) draw off (wine, beer, etc.) from the lees. [Provençal *arracar* from *raca* stems and husks of grapes, dregs]

rack⁵ ● *noun* driving clouds. ● *intransitive verb* (of clouds) be driven before the wind. [Middle English, prob. of Scandinavian origin: compare Norwegian and Swedish dial. *rak* wreckage etc., from *reka* drive]

rack⁶ ● *noun* a horse's gait between a trot and a canter. ● *intransitive verb* progress in this way. [origin unknown]

rack-and-pinion *attributive adjective* (esp. of a steering system) using a rack and pinion (*see* RACK¹ *noun* 2, PINION²).

rack·et¹ *var. of* RACQUET.

rack·et² ● *noun* **1** a loud unpleasant noise. **2** *informal* a scheme for obtaining money or attaining other ends by fraudulent and often violent means. **3** a form of organized crime. **4** *informal* an occupation or line of business (*starting up a new racket*). ● *intransitive verb* (**rack·et·ed**, **rack·et·ing**) (often foll. by *along, around*) make a racket, esp. by moving noisily. □ **rack·ety** *adjective* [16th c.: perhaps imitative]

racket·ball *var. of* RACQUETBALL.

rack·et·eer *noun* a person who makes money through dishonest or illegal activities. □ **rack·et·eer·ing** *noun*

rack railway *noun* a railway with a toothed rail between the bearing rails which engages with a cogwheel under the locomotive, for very steep slopes.

rack rate *noun* the official published rate charged for a hotel room, without special discounts etc.

rack-rent ● *noun* **1** a high rent, annually equalling the full value of the property to which it relates. **2** an extortionate rent. ● *transitive verb* exact this from (a tenant) or for (land).

ra·clette /raˈklet/ *noun* a Swiss dish of melted cheese, usu. eaten with potatoes. [French, = small scraper, from the practice of holding the cheese over the heat and scraping it on to a plate as it melts]

racon·teur /ˌrakɒnˈtɜːr/ *noun* a teller of anecdotes. [French from *raconter* relate, RECOUNT¹]

ra·coon *var. of* RACCOON.

rac·quet /ˈrakət/ *noun* (also **rack·et**) **1** a bat with a round or oval frame strung with nylon etc., used in tennis, squash, etc. **2** (in *pl.*) a ball game for two or four persons played with racquets in a plain four-walled court. **3** a snowshoe resembling a racquet. [French *racquette* from Italian *racchetta* from Arabic *rāḥa* palm of the hand]

rac·quet·ball /ˈrakətbɔːl/ *noun* esp. *N Amer.* a game played with a small hard ball and a short-handled racquet in a four-walled handball court.

racy *adjective* (**raci·er**, **raci·est**) **1** lively and vigorous in style. **2** risqué, suggestive. **3** having characteristic qualities in a high degree (*a racy flavour*). □ **raci·ly** *adverb* **raci·ness** *noun* [RACE² + -Y¹]

RAD ● *abbreviation* Royal Academy of Dance. ● *noun* the syllabus or style of ballet taught by the Royal Academy of Dance.

rad¹ *noun* (*pl.* same) radian. [abbreviation]

rad² *slang* ● *noun* a political radical. ● *adjective* excellent, fantastic. [abbreviation of RADICAL]

rad³ *noun Physics* a unit of absorbed dose of ionizing radiation, corresponding to the absorption of 0.01 joule per kilogram of absorbing material. [radiation *absorbed dose*]

rad⁴ *noun informal* radiator. [abbreviation]

RADA /ˈrɑːdə/ *abbreviation* (in the UK) Royal Academy of Dramatic Art.

radar *noun* **1** a method for detecting the position and speed of aircraft, ships, or other objects, by sending out pulses of high-frequency electromagnetic waves. **2** the apparatus used for this. **3** a person's capacity for intuitive perception or awareness; a special sensitivity to factors, trends, influences, etc. in a particular area of activity or expertise (*to be a DJ you need musical knowledge and a powerful trend radar*). **4** an ability to notice a phenomenon (*the band has fallen below the media's radar*). [radio *detection and ranging*]

RADARSAT *noun* a Canadian remote sensing satellite.

radar screen *noun* **1** the screen of a cathode-ray oscilloscope on which radar echoes are represented for observation. **2** = RADAR 4.

radar trap *noun* = SPEED TRAP.

Rad·cliffe, Ann (1764–1823), English novelist. She was a leading exponent of the Gothic novel; her works include *The Mysteries of Udolpho* (1794) and *The Italian* (1797).

rad·dle *var. of* RUDDLE.

rad·dled *adjective* untidy, unkempt.

Radha /ˈrɑːdə/ *Hinduism* the favourite mistress of the god Krishna, and an incarnation of Lakshmi. In devotional religion she represents the longing of the human soul for God. [Sanskrit, = prosperity]

ra·dial /ˈreidiəl/ ● *adjective* **1** of, concerning, or in rays. **2 a** arranged like rays or radii; having the position or direction of a radius. **b** having spokes or radiating lines. **c** acting or moving along lines diverging from a centre. **3** *Anat.* relating to the radius (*radial artery*). **4** (of a vehicle tire) having the core fabric layers arranged radially at right angles to the circumference and the tread strengthened. ● *noun* **1** a radial tire. **2** *Anat.* the radial nerve or artery. □ **ra·di·al·ly** *adverb*

radial arm saw *noun* (also **radial saw**) a type of circular saw mounted on an arm that can be adjusted to various angles.

radial engine *noun* an engine having cylinders arranged along radii.

radial keratotomy *noun see* KERATOTOMY.

radial symmetry *noun* symmetry occurring about a central axis, as in a starfish or tulip flower.

radial velocity *noun* esp. *Astronomy* the speed of motion along a radial line, esp. between a star etc. and an observer.

ra·dian /ˈreidiən/ *noun Math.* a unit of angle, equal to an angle at the centre of a circle the arc of which is equal in length to the radius; 1 radian is the same as 57.296°.

radi·ant /ˈreidiənt/ ● *adjective* **1** emitting rays of light. **2** (of a person, a look, etc.) beaming with joy or hope or love. **3** (of beauty) splendid or dazzling. **4** (of light) issuing in rays. **5** operating radially. **6** extending radially; radiating. ● *noun* **1** the point or object from which light or heat radiates, esp. in an electric or gas heater. **2** *Astronomy* a radiant point. □ **radi·ance** *noun* **radi·ant·ly** *adverb* [Latin *radiare* (as RADIUS)]

radiant energy *noun* energy in the form of radiation.

radiant heat *noun* heat transmitted by radiation, not by conduction or convection. □ **radiant heater** *noun*

radiant point *noun* **1** a point from which rays or radii proceed. **2** *Astronomy* the apparent focal point of a meteor shower.

radi·ate ● *verb* /ˈreidiˌeit/ **1** *intransitive* **a** emit rays of light, heat, or other electromagnetic waves. **b** (of light or heat) be emitted in rays.

2 *transitive* emit (light, heat, or sound) from a centre. **3** *transitive* transmit or demonstrate (an emotion, feeling, etc.) (*radiates happiness*). **4** *intransitive & transitive* diverge or cause to diverge or spread from a centre. ● *adjective* /ˈreidiət/ having divergent rays or parts radially arranged. □ **radi·a·tive** /-ətiv/ *adjective* [Latin *radiare radiat-* (as RADIUS)]

radi·a·tion /ˌreidiˈeiʃən/ *noun* **1** the act or an instance of radiating; the process of being radiated. **2** *Physics* **a** the emission of energy as electromagnetic waves or as moving particles. **b** the energy transmitted in this way, esp. invisibly.

radiation sickness *noun* sickness caused by exposure to radiation, such as X-rays or gamma rays.

radiation therapy *noun* = RADIOTHERAPY.

radi·ator /ˈreidiˌeitər, ˈrad-/ *noun* **1** a thing that radiates or emits light, heat, or sound. **2 a** a device for heating a room etc., consisting of a metal case through which hot water or steam circulates. **b** a usu. portable, esp. electric heater resembling this. **3** a device in a motor vehicle or aircraft with a large surface for cooling circulating water from the engine.

radiator grille *noun* = GRILLE 2.

rad·ical ● *adjective* **1** of the root or roots; fundamental (*a radical error*). **2** far-reaching; thorough (*a radical change in policy*). **3 a** advocating thorough reform; holding extreme political views; revolutionary. **b** (of a measure etc.) advanced by or according to principles of this kind. **4** forming the basis; primary (*the radical idea*). **5** *Math.* of the root of a number or quantity. **6** *slang* excellent, outstanding. **7** (of surgery etc.) seeking to ensure the removal of all diseased tissue. **8** of the roots of words. **9** *Music* belonging to the root of a chord. **10** *Bot.* of, or springing direct from, the root. ● *noun* **1** a person holding radical views or belonging to a radical party. **2** *Chem.* **a** a free radical. **b** an element or atom or a group of these normally forming part of a compound and remaining unaltered during the compound's ordinary chemical changes. **3** the root of a word. **4** a fundamental principle; a basis. **5** *Math.* **a** a quantity forming or expressed as the root of another. **b** a radical sign. **6** any of the basic set of approximately 214 Chinese characters from which more complex ones are mainly derived. □ **rad·ical·ism** *noun* **rad·ical·ize** *transitive & intransitive verb* (also esp. *Brit.* **-ise**). **rad·ical·iz·a·tion** *noun* **rad·ical·ly** *adverb* [Late Latin *radicalis* from Latin *radix radicis* root]

radical chic *noun* **1** the fashionable affectation of radical left-wing views. **2** the dress, lifestyle, etc., associated with this.

radical sign *noun* a symbol, $\sqrt{}$, $\sqrt[3]{}$, etc., indicating the square, cube, etc., root of the number following.

ra·dic·chio /rəˈdiːkioː/ *noun* (*pl.* **-chios**) a variety of chicory with dark red leaves, used esp. in salads. [Italian, = chicory]

rad·ices *pl. of* RADIX.

rad·icle /ˈradikəl/ *noun* **1** the part of a plant embryo that develops into the primary root; a rootlet. **2** a rootlike subdivision of a nerve or vein. □ **rad·icu·lar** /rəˈdikjuːlər/ *adjective* [Latin *radicula* (as RADIX)]

radii *pl. of* RADIUS.

radio ● *noun* (*pl.* **radios**) **1** (often *attributive*) **a** the transmission and reception of sound messages etc. by electromagnetic waves of radio frequency. **b** an apparatus for receiving, broadcasting, or transmitting radio signals. **c** a message sent or received by radio. **2** sound broadcasting in general (*prefers radio to television*). **3** a broadcasting station or network (*you're listening to CBC Radio*). ● *verb* (**-dioes**, **-dioed**) **1** *transitive* **a** send (a message) by radio. **b** send a message to (a person) by radio. **2** *intransitive* communicate or broadcast by radio. ● *adjective* **1** of, relating to, or transmitting radio signals (*a radio station*). **2** of or using radio frequencies. **3** (of a vehicle) equipped with a two-way radio for use in communication (*radio car*). [short for *radio-telegraphy* etc.]

radio- *combining form* **1** denoting radio or broadcasting. **2 a** connected with radioactivity. **b** denoting artificially prepared radioisotopes of elements (*radio-cesium*). **3** connected with rays or radiation. **4** *Anat.* belonging to the radius in conjunction with some other part (*radio-carpal*). [RADIUS + -O- or from RADIO]

radio·active *adjective* of or exhibiting radioactivity. □ **radio·active·ly** *adverb*

radio·activ·ity *noun* **1** the spontaneous disintegration of atomic nuclei, with the emission of usu. penetrating radiation or particles. **2** radioactive substances, or the radiation they emit.

radio astronomy *noun* the branch of astronomy which uses radio frequencies rather than visible light to study the universe.

radio beacon *noun* = BEACON 3.

radio·biol·ogy *noun* the biology concerned with the effects of radiation on organisms and the application in biology of radiological techniques. □ **radio·bio·log·ic·al** *adjective* **radio·biol·o·gist** *noun*

radio·carbon *noun* a radioactive isotope of carbon.

radiocarbon dating *noun* a method of estimating the age of organic archaeological specimens by determining the ratio of carbon-14 (which decays at a known rate) to another isotope which remains constant. *Also called* CARBON DATING *or* CARBON-14 DATING.

radio·chem·istry *noun* the chemistry of radioactive materials. □ **radio·chem·ical** *adjective* **radio·chem·ist** *noun*

radio collar *noun* a collar equipped with a small radio transmitter, used e.g. for tracking an animal's movement in the wild. □ **radio-collar** *transitive verb*

radio-controlled *adjective* (of a model aircraft etc.) controlled from a distance by radio.

radio·element *noun* a natural or artificial radioactive element or isotope.

radio frequency *noun* (*pl.* **-cies**) the frequency band of telecommunication, ranging from 10^4-10^{11} or 10^{12} Hz.

radio galaxy *noun* a galaxy that emits more radio waves than a typical galaxy.

radio·genic *adjective* produced by radioactivity.

radio·gram *noun* **1** a picture obtained by X-rays, gamma rays, etc. **2** a radio-telegram.

radio·graph ● *noun* = RADIOGRAM 1. ● *transitive verb* obtain a picture of by X-ray, gamma ray, etc. □ **radi·og·raph·er** *noun* **radio·graph·ic** *adjective* **radio·graph·ic·ally** *adverb* **radi·og·raphy** *noun*

radio·iso·tope *noun* a radioactive isotope. □ **radio·iso·top·ic** *adjective*

radio·lar·ian /ˌreidiəˈleriən/ *noun* any marine protozoan of the order Radiolaria, having a siliceous skeleton and radiating pseudopodia. [modern Latin *radiolaria* from Latin *radiolus* diminutive of RADIUS]

radi·ol·ogy *noun* the scientific study of X-rays and other high-energy radiation, esp. as used in medicine. □ **radio·logic** *adjective* **radio·logic·al** *adjective* **radi·ol·o·gist** *noun*

radi·om·eter /ˌreidiˈɒmɪtər/ *noun* an instrument for measuring the intensity or force of radioactivity. □ **radio·met·ric** *adjective* **radi·om·etry** *noun*

radiometric dating *noun* a method of dating geological specimens by determining the relative proportions of the isotopes of a radioactive element present in a sample.

radio·nu·clide *noun* a radioactive nuclide.

radi·opaque *adjective* (also **radio-opaque**) opaque to X-rays or similar radiation. □ **radi·opa·city** *noun*

radio phone *noun* = RADIO TELEPHONE.

radio·phon·ic *adjective* of or relating to synthetic sound, esp. music, produced electronically.

radio play *noun* **1** a play written for performance on radio. **2** broadcast time on radio (*the album received a lot of radio play*).

radi·os·copy /ˌreidiˈɒskəpi/ *noun* the examination by X-rays etc. of objects opaque to light. □ **radio·scop·ic** *adjective*

radio·sonde /ˈreidiəˌsɒnd/ *noun* a miniature radio transmitter broadcasting information about pressure, temperature, etc., from various levels of the atmosphere, carried esp. by balloon.

radio-telegram *noun* a telegram sent by radio, usu. from a ship to land.

radio-telegraphy *noun* telegraphy using radio transmission.

radio telephone *noun* a telephone that uses radio transmission. □ **radio telephony** *noun*

radio telescope *noun* a directional aerial system for collecting and analyzing radiation in the radio frequency range from stars etc.

radio·ther·apy *noun* the treatment of cancer and other diseases by X-rays or other forms of radiation. □ **radio·thera·peut·ic** *adjective* **radio·ther·apist** *noun*

rad·ish *noun* **1** a cruciferous plant, *Raphanus sativus*, with a fleshy pungent root, esp. of a variety that is small and red. **2** this root, eaten esp. raw in salads etc. [Old English *rædic* from Latin *radix radicis* root]

Radis·son /ˈradiˈsɔ, ˈradisən/ **Pierre-Esprit** (1636–1710), French-born explorer and fur trader. With his brother-in-law Des Groseilliers he explored the area around Lakes Superior and Michigan (1654–6, 1659–60). In 1668 they travelled to Hudson Bay on behalf of a group of English merchants (the nucleus of the Hudson's Bay Company).

ra·dium /ˈreidiəm/ *noun* a radioactive metallic element originally obtained from pitchblende etc., used esp. in luminous materials and in radiotherapy. Symbol: **Ra**; at. no.: 88. [Latin *radius* ray]

radium therapy *noun* the treatment of disease by the use of radium.

ra·dius /ˈreidiəs/ ● *noun* (*pl.* **radii** /-diˌai/ or **ra·dius·es**) **1** *Math.* **a** a straight line from the centre to the circumference of a circle or sphere. **b** a radial line from the focus to any point of a curve. **c** the length of the radius of a circle etc. **2** a usu. specified distance from a centre in all directions (*within a radius of 20 miles*; *has a large radius of action*). **3 a** the thicker and shorter of the two bones in the human forearm (compare ULNA). **b** the corresponding bone in a vertebrate's foreleg or a bird's wing. **4** any of the five arm-like structures of a starfish. **5 a** any of a set of lines diverging from a point like the radii of a circle. **b** an object of this kind, e.g. a spoke. **6 a** the outer rim of a composite flower head, e.g. a daisy. **b** a radiating branch of an umbel. ● *transitive verb* (as **ra·diused** *adjective*) give a rounded form to (an edge etc.). [Latin, = staff, spoke, ray]

radius vector *noun Math.* a variable line drawn from a fixed point to an orbit or other curve, or to any point as an indication of the latter's position.

radix /ˈreidiks/ *noun* (*pl.* **rad·ices** /-diˌsiːz/) *Math.* a number or symbol used as the basis of a numeration scale, e.g. ten in the decimal system. [Latin, = root]

RAdm *abbreviation Cdn* REAR ADMIRAL.

Rad·nor·shire /ˈradnərˌʃiːr/ a former county of E Wales. It became part of Powys in 1974.

Radom /ˈrɒdɒm/ an industrial city in central Poland; pop. (est. 2000) 231,341.

ra·dome /ˈreidoʊm/ *noun* a dome or other structure, transparent to radio waves, protecting radar equipment, esp. on the outer surface of an aircraft. [blend of RADAR + DOME]

radon /ˈreidɒn/ *noun Chem.* a naturally occurring gaseous radioactive inert element arising from the disintegration of radium, and used in radiotherapy. Symbol: **Rn**; at. no.: 86. [RADIUM, on the pattern of *argon* etc.]

rad·ula /ˈradjʊlə/ *noun* (*pl.* **rad·ulae** /-ˌliː/) a file-like structure in molluscs for scraping off food particles and drawing them into the mouth. □ **radu·lar** *adjective* [Latin, = scraper, from *radere* scrape]

Rae·burn, Sir Henry (1756–1823), Scottish portrait painter. He became the leading Scottish portraitist of his day, depicting the local intelligentsia and Highland chieftains in a bold and distinctive style; major works include *The Reverend Robert Walker Skating* (*c.*1784) and *The MacNab* (1803–13).

Rae-Edzo /ˈreiˈedzoʊ/ a hamlet in the south central NWT, situated at the head of the North Arm of Great Slave Lake, northwest of Yellowknife; pop. (2001) 1,552. [after Dr. J. *Rae*, who explored the area and established a Hudson's Bay Co. post here *c.*1852, and *Edzo*, Dogrib chief who negotiated a peace settlement with the Yellowknife in the early 19th c.]

RAF *abbreviation* (in the UK) Royal Air Force.

Raffi (born Raffi Cavoukian) (b.1948), Canadian singer/songwriter, best known for his children's albums, including *Baby Beluga* (1980) and *Bananaphone* (1994).

raf·fia *noun* **1** a palm tree, *Raphia ruffia*, native to Madagascar, having very long leaves. **2** the fibre from its leaves used for making hats, baskets, etc., and for tying plants etc. [Malagasy]

raff·ish *adjective* disreputable, esp. in an attractive manner; rakish. □ **raff·ish·ly** *adverb* **raff·ish·ness** *noun* [as RAFT[2] + -ISH[1]]

raf·fle ● *noun* a fundraising lottery with goods as prizes. ● *transitive verb* (often foll. by *off*) dispose of by means of a raffle. [Middle English, a kind of dice game, from Old French *raf(f)le*, of unknown origin]

Raf·fles, Sir (Thom·as) Stam·ford (1781–1826), Jamaican-born English colonial administrator. As lieutenant-general of Sumatra (1818–23), he persuaded the East India Company to purchase the undeveloped island of Singapore (1819).

Raf·san·jani /ˌrafsanˈdʒɒni/ **Ali Akbar Hash·emi** (b.1934), Iranian political and religious leader, president 1989–97. A supporter and former pupil of Ayatollah Khomeini, he emerged as Iran's leader when Khomeini died in 1989; he has sought to improve Iran's relations with the West and kept his country neutral during the Gulf War of 1991.

raft[1] ● *noun* **1** a flat floating structure of logs, barrels, etc. tied together and used as a boat or a floating platform. **2 a** a lifeboat or small (often inflatable) boat, esp. for use in emergencies. **b** an inflatable boat which can hold several people, propelled by paddles, esp. for recreational expeditions on rivers with whitewater. **3** *N Amer. Forestry* a mass of squared timber or logs fastened together for

Consonants: b *but* d *dog* f *few* g *get* h *her* j *yes* k *cat* l *leg* m *man* n *no* p *pen* r *red* s *sit*

transportation on water. **4** *N Amer.* a large floating accumulation of fallen trees, ice, etc. **5** a layer of reinforced concrete forming the foundation of a building. ● *verb* **1** *transitive* transport as or on a raft. **2** *transitive N Amer. Forestry* move (logs) by means of a raft. **3** *transitive* cross (water) on a raft. **4** *transitive* form into a raft. **5** *intransitive* use a raft; travel by raft. **6** *intransitive* engage in the sport of whitewater rafting. **7** *intransitive* (of an ice floe) be driven on top of or underneath another floe. □ **raft·ing** *noun* [Old Norse *raptr* RAFTER[1]]

raft² *noun* (foll. by *of*) *informal* a large number or amount (*a raft of new proposals*). [*raff* rubbish, perhaps of Scandinavian origin]

raft·er¹ *noun* each of the usu. sloping beams forming the framework of a roof. □ **raf·tered** *adjective* [Old English *ræfter*, related to RAFT[1]]

raft·er² *noun* **1** a person who engages in whitewater rafting. **2** *N Amer. Forestry* a person who rafts timber.

rafts·man *noun* (*pl.* **-men**) a worker on a raft.

rag¹ *noun* **1 a** a torn, frayed, or worn piece of woven material. **b** one of the irregular scraps to which cloth etc. is reduced by wear and tear. **2 a** (in *pl.*) old or worn clothes. **b** *informal* a garment of any kind. **3** (*collective*) scraps of cloth used as material for paper, stuffing, etc. **4** *derogatory* **a** a newspaper or magazine, esp. one regarded as inferior or worthless. **b** a flag, handkerchief, curtain, etc. **5** an odd scrap; an irregular piece. **6** a jagged projection, esp. on metal. □ **in rags** **1** much torn. **2** in old torn clothes. **on the rag** *N Amer. slang* **1** menstruating. **2** angry or irritable. [Middle English, prob. back-formation from RAGGED]

rag² ● *transitive verb* (**ragged, rag·ging**) **1** scold; reprove severely; criticize. **2** *Brit.* tease; torment; play rough jokes on. ● *noun Brit.* **1 a** fundraising program of stunts, parades, and entertainment organized by students. **2** *informal* a prank. □ **rag on** *N Amer. slang* nag, bother, scold (*my mother's always ragging on me!*). **rag the puck 1** *Hockey* keep possession of the puck by skilful stickhandling so as to waste time. **2** *Cdn slang* waste time intentionally. [18th c.: origin unknown]

rag³ *noun Music* a ragtime composition or tune. [perhaps from RAGGED: see RAGTIME]

raga /ˈrɑːɡə/ *noun* (in Indian music) **1** a pattern of notes used as a basis for improvisation. **2** a piece using a particular raga. [Sanskrit, = colour, musical tone]

raga·muf·fin *noun* **1** a person in ragged dirty clothes, esp. a child. **2** = RAGGAMUFFIN. [prob. based on RAG[1]: compare 14th-c. *ragamoffyn*, the name of a demon]

rag-and-bone man *noun Brit.* an itinerant dealer in old clothes, furniture, etc.

rag·bag *noun* **1** a bag in which scraps of fabric etc. are kept for use. **2** (often foll. by *of*) a miscellaneous collection. **3** *slang* a sloppily-dressed woman.

rag doll *noun* a stuffed doll made of cloth.

rage ● *noun* **1** fierce or violent anger. **2** a fit of this (*flew into a rage*). **3** the violent action of a natural force (*the rage of the storm*). **4** (foll. by *for*) **a** a vehement desire or passion. **b** a widespread temporary enthusiasm or fashion. **5** (as the second element in compounds) an outburst of esp. pent-up anger and aggression triggered by a specific incident (*road rage; air rage*). ● *intransitive verb* **1** be full of anger. **2** (often foll. by *at, against*) speak furiously or madly; rave. **3** (of wind, battle, debate, fever, etc.) be violent; be at its height; continue unchecked. **4** *Austral. & NZ informal* seek enjoyment; have a good time; revel. □ **all the rage** very popular, fashionable. □ **rage·ful** *adjective* **rager** *noun* (esp. in sense 4 of *verb*). [Old French *rager*, ultimately from Latin RABIES]

ragg ● *noun* **1** a strong wool fibre treated so as to retain its natural oils. **2** a greyish yarn made from a blend of ragg and nylon. ● *adjective* (of a garment, blanket, etc.) made from this yarn. [Norwegian, = fur, goat hair; compare Norwegian *raggesokk*, thick skiing socks made from goat hair or coarse wool]

ragga *noun* a style of popular music combining elements of reggae and hip hop. [RAGGAMUFFIN, from the style of clothing worn by its followers]

ragga·muf·fin *noun* (also **raga·muf·fin**) **1** an exponent or follower of ragga, typically dressing in ragged clothes. **2** = RAGGA. [see RAGAMUFFIN]

rag·ged /ˈraɡɪd/ *adjective* **1** (of clothes etc.) torn; frayed. **2** rough; shaggy; hanging in tufts. **3** (of a person) in ragged clothes. **4** with a broken or jagged outline or surface. **5** *Printing* (esp. of a right margin) unjustified and so uneven. **6** faulty; imperfect. **7** lacking finish, smoothness, or uniformity (*ragged rhymes*). **8** (of a sound) harsh; discordant. **9** exhausted (esp. *be run ragged*). □ **rag·ged·ly** *adverb*

rag·ged·ness *noun* **rag·gedy** *adjective* [Middle English from Old Norse *roggvathr* 'tufted']

ragged robin *noun* either of two plants with deeply lobed, pink petals: a campion of Eurasia, *Lychnis flos-cuculi*, or the western N American *Clarkia pulchella*.

Raggedy Ann *noun* proprietary a rag doll.

raggedy-ass *adjective* (also **raggedy-assed**) **1** (of a person) raw; new and inexperienced. **2** (of a thing) shabby, ragged, dilapidated.

raggedy-jacket *noun Cdn* (*Nfld*) a young harp seal whose coat is changing from pure white to brown and white.

rag·ging *noun* (also **rag rolling**) **1** the process or technique of decorating a wall etc. by applying or smudging paint with a rag or piece of material. **2** the effect or finish so produced.

raggle-taggle *adjective* constituted of an assortment of (often disreputable) people; ragtag. [apparently fanciful var. of RAGTAG]

rag·head *noun offensive slang* a person who wears a turban or cloth headdress.

raging *adjective* extreme, very painful (*raging thirst; a raging headache*).

rag·lan /ˈraɡlən/ ● *noun* an overcoat without shoulder seams, the sleeves running in a sloping line from the neck to under the arms. ● *adjective* cut in this design (*raglan sleeve*). [Lord *Raglan*, Brit. commander d.1855]

Rag·na·rök /ˈraɡnəˌrɒk/ *Scand. Myth* the final battle between the gods and the powers of evil, the Scandinavian equivalent of the *Götterdämmerung*. [translation of Icelandic *ragna rökr* (*rökr* twilight) altered, from the original *ragna rök* (= the history or judgment of the gods)]

ra·gout /raˈɡuː/ *noun* a stew. [French *ragoût* from *ragoûter* revive the taste of]

rag paper *noun* paper made from rags.

rag·pick·er *noun* esp. *hist.* a collector and seller of rags.

rag rolling *noun* = RAGGING. □ **rag-rolled** *adjective*

rag rug *noun* a small rug made from strips of rags woven together.

rags-to-riches *attributive adjective* denoting a person who starts out poor and ends up rich, or a story describing such a development.

rag·tag ● *adjective* esp. *N Amer.* **1** disorganized, ill-assorted, scraggly. **2** ragged or shabby; unkempt. ● *noun* (in full **ragtag and bobtail**) *derogatory* the rabble or riff-raff. [earlier *tag-rag, tag and rag*, from RAG[1] + TAG[1]]

rag·tail *adjective* = RAGTAG *adjective*. [RAG[1] + TAIL[1], perhaps influenced by *ragtag and bobtail*]

rag·time ● *noun* a style of popular music characterized by a syncopated melodic line and regularly accented accompaniment, evolved by American black musicians (such as Scott Joplin) in the 1890s and played esp. on the piano. ● *adjective* of or resembling ragtime. [prob. from RAG[3]]

rag·top *noun* **1** a convertible car with a top made of cloth. **2** the top of such a car.

rag trade *noun informal* the business of designing, making, and selling clothes.

Ra·gusa /raˈɡuːza/ the Italian name (until 1918) for DUBROVNIK.

rag·weed *noun* **1** *N Amer.* any plant of the genus *Ambrosia*, with allergenic pollen. **2** = RAGWORT.

rag·worm *noun* a carnivorous marine polychaete worm of the family Nereidae, esp. *Nereis diversicolor*, often used for bait.

rag·wort /ˈraɡwɔːt, -wərt/ *noun* any yellow-flowered ragged-leaved plant of the genus *Senecio*.

rah *interjection* esp. *N Amer. informal* an expression of encouragement, approval, etc. [shortening of HURRAH]

rah-rah *N Amer. slang* ● *noun* a shout of support and encouragement, as for a sports team. ● *adjective* marked by great enthusiasm or excitement.

rai /raɪ/ *noun* a style of popular music which fuses Arabic and Algerian folk elements with western styles. [perhaps from Arabic *ha er-ray* 'that's the thinking, here is the view', a phrase frequently found in the songs]

raid ● *noun* **1** a rapid surprise attack, esp.: **a** by troops, aircraft, etc. in warfare. **b** to commit a crime or do harm. **c** *N Amer. informal* as a prank or to gain food, drink, etc. (*panty raid; a raid on the kitchen*). **2** a surprise attack by police etc. to arrest suspected persons or seize illicit goods. **3** *Stock Exch.* an attempt to lower prices by the concerted selling of shares. **4** the luring away of a competitor's workers, members, etc. ● *transitive verb* **1** make a raid on (a person, place, or thing). **2** plunder, deplete. □ **raid·er** *noun* [Middle English, Scots form of Old English *rād* ROAD]

rail¹ ● *noun* **1** a level or sloping bar or series of bars: **a** forming part of a fence or barrier as protection against contact, falling over, etc. **b** used to hang things on. **c** running along the top of a set of banisters; a handrail. **2** a steel bar or continuous line of bars laid on the ground, usu. as one of a pair forming a railway track. **3** (often *attributive*) a railway (*send it by rail; rail fares*). **4** (in *pl.*) the inside boundary fence of a racetrack. **5** a horizontal piece in the frame of a panelled door etc. (*compare* STILE²). ● *transitive verb* **1** furnish with a rail or rails. **2** (usu. foll. by *in*, *off*) enclose with rails (*a small space was railed off*). □ **off the rails** deranged. [Old French *reille* iron rod, from Latin *regula* RULE]

rail² *intransitive verb* (often foll. by *at*, *against*) complain vehemently; rant. □ **rail·er** *noun* **rail·ing** *noun & adjective* [French *railler* from Provençal *ralhar* jest, ultimately from Latin *rugire* bellow]

rail³ *noun* any bird of the family Rallidae, often inhabiting marshes, including coots and moorhens. [Old Northern French *raille* from Romanic, perhaps imitative]

rail·bed *noun* the layer of broken stone, gravel, clay, etc. upon which a railway is or has been laid.

rail·bird *noun N Amer. informal* a person who watches a sports event or warm-up from the sidelines; a spectator. [from the practice of horse racing enthusiasts watching races from along the track rail]

rail·car *noun N Amer.* a railway carriage.

rail fence *noun esp. N Amer.* a fence made of wooden posts and rails.

rail gun *noun* an electromagnetic projectile launcher used esp. as an anti-missile weapon.

rail·head *noun* **1** the furthest point reached by a railway. **2** the point on a railway at which road transport of goods begins.

rail·ing *noun* **1** *esp. N Amer.* a banister; handrail. **2 a** (often in *pl.*) a fence or barrier made of rails. **b** the material for these.

rail·lery *noun* (*pl.* **-ies**) **1** good-humoured ridicule; rallying. **2** an instance of this. [French *raillerie* (as RAIL²)]

rail·man *noun* (*pl.* **-men**) = RAILWAYMAN.

rail·road ● *noun esp. N Amer.* = RAILWAY. ● *transitive verb* **1** (often foll. by *to*, *into*, *through*, etc.) rush or coerce (a person or thing) (*railroaded me into going too; railroaded the bill through the legislature*). **2** send (a person) to prison by means of false evidence. □ **rail·road·er** *noun*

rail·road·ing *noun* the act or fact of travelling, working on, or using railways.

rail-thin *adjective* extremely thin.

rail·way *noun esp. Cdn & Brit.* **1** a track or set of tracks made of steel rails upon which trains run. **2** such a system operated by a single company (*Canadian Pacific Railway*). **3** the organization and personnel required for its working. **4** a similar set of tracks for other vehicles etc.

railway hotel *noun* a hotel built and operated by a railway company, usu. close to a railway station, originally with the aim of providing accommodation for rail travellers.

rail·way·man *noun* (*pl.* **-men**) *esp. Brit. & Cdn* a railway employee.

railway yard *noun* (also **rail yard**) the area where rolling stock is kept and made up into trains.

rai·ment /ˈreɪmənt/ *noun literary & archaic* clothing. [Middle English from obsolete *arrayment* (as ARRAY)]

rain ● *noun* **1 a** the condensed moisture of the atmosphere falling visibly in separate drops. **b** the fall of such drops. **c** (*attributive*) designating garments etc. protecting against or worn in the rain (*rain jacket; rain pants*). **2** (in *pl.*) **a** (prec. by *the*) the rainy season in tropical countries. **b** rainfalls. **3 a** falling liquid or solid particles or objects. **b** the like descent of these. **c** a large or overwhelming quantity (*a rain of congratulations*). ● *verb* **1** *intransitive* (of rain) fall. **2 a** *intransitive* fall like rain (*tears rained down their cheeks; blows rained down on his head*). **b** *transitive* (prec. by *it* as subject) send in large quantities (*it rained blood; it is raining invitations*). **3** *transitive* send down like rain; lavishly bestow (*rained blows upon him; rained benefits on us*). **4** *intransitive* (of the sky, the clouds, etc.) send down rain. □ **rain cats and dogs** *see* CAT¹. **rain on someone's parade** *informal* spoil a person's good time. **rain out** (or *Brit.* **off**) (esp. in *passive*) cause (an event etc.) to be terminated or cancelled because of rain. **rain or shine** whether it rains or not. □ **rain·less** *adjective* [Old English *regn*, *rēn*, *regnian*, from Germanic]

rain barrel *noun* a barrel for collecting rainwater.

rain·bow ● *noun* **1** an arch of colours (conventionally red, orange, yellow, green, blue, indigo, violet) formed in the sky (or across a waterfall etc.) opposite the sun by reflection, twofold refraction, and dispersion of the sun's rays in rain or in spray or mist. **2** a similar effect formed by the moon's rays. **3** a wide variety of related things (*a rainbow of colours; a rainbow of political opinion*). **4** = RAINBOW TROUT.

● *adjective* many-coloured. □ **chase a rainbow** pursue an illusory goal. □ **rain·bowed** *adjective*

Rainbow Bridge a bridge of natural rock, the world's largest natural bridge, situated in S Utah, just north of the Arizona border. Its span is 86 m (278 ft.).

rainbow coalition *noun* a loose coalition or alliance of several different left-of-centre political groups, representing social, ethnic, and other minorities.

rainbow flag *noun* a flag with horizontal stripes in the colours of the rainbow as an emblem of gay pride.

rainbow lorikeet *noun* a small brightly coloured Polynesian parrot, *Trichoglossus haematodus*.

rainbow smelt *noun* a blue and silver smelt, *Osmerus mordax*, with iridescent colouring on its flanks, of inland lakes and eastern coastal waters of N America.

rainbow trout *noun* a large trout, *Oncorhynchus mykiss* (formerly *Salmo gairdneri*), originally of the Pacific coast of N America, but now widespread throughout the continent.

rain check *noun esp. N Amer.* **1** a ticket given for later use when a sports or other outdoor event is interrupted or postponed by rain. **2** a promise that an offer will be maintained though deferred. **3** a voucher given to a customer when a sale item sells out, entitling the customer to purchase the item at the sale price when more stock arrives. □ **take a rain check on** reserve the right to take up (an offer) at a later date.

rain cloud *noun* a cloud bringing rain.

rain·coat *noun* a waterproof or water-resistant coat.

rain dance *noun* a ritual dance to summon rain, as practised by some Pueblo Indians and other peoples.

rain date *noun N Amer.* an alternate date on which a sports event, garage sale, or other outdoor activity can be held if postponed because of rain.

rain·drop *noun* a single drop of rain.

rain·fall *noun* **1** a fall of rain. **2** the quantity of rain falling within a given area in a given time.

rainforest *noun* a luxuriant forest in an area of heavy rainfall with little seasonal variation.

rain gauge *noun* an instrument measuring rainfall.

rain gear *noun* waterproof outerwear.

Rai·nier III /renˈjeɪ/ (full name Rainier Louis Henri Maxence Bertrand de Grimaldi) (b.1923), prince of Monaco since 1949. He married the American actress Grace Kelly, who became Princess Grace of Monaco, in 1956.

Rai·nier, Mount /rəˈnɪːr, ˈreɪnɪːr/ a volcanic peak in the southwest of Washington State. Rising to a height of 4 395 m (14,410 ft.), it is the highest peak in the Cascade Range.

rain·maker *noun* **1** a person who seeks to cause rain to fall, either by magic or by a technique such as seeding. **2** *esp. N Amer. slang* a person who is highly successful esp. in business. □ **rain·making** *noun*

rain·out *noun* **1** *N Amer.* the cancellation or premature ending of an event because of rain. **2** radioactive debris or other atmospheric pollution carried to the earth's surface by precipitation.

rain·proof *adjective* (esp. of a building, garment, etc.) resistant to rainwater.

rain shadow *noun* an area on the leeward side of mountains or other high ground, having relatively little precipitation because clouds release their moisture on the windward side.

rain·stick *noun* a musical instrument or toy consisting of a sealed wooden cylinder filled with small seeds which, when tipped, creates a sound similar to falling rain.

rain·storm *noun* a storm with heavy rain.

rain·suit *noun* a waterproof jacket and pants.

rain-swept *adjective* exposed to the rain.

rain·water *noun* water obtained from collected rain, as distinct from a well etc.

rain·wear *noun* clothes for wearing in the rain.

rainy *adjective* (**rain·i·er**, **rain·i·est**) **1** (of weather, a climate, day, region, etc.) in or on which rain is falling or much rain usually falls. **2** (of cloud, wind, etc.) laden with or bringing rain.

rainy day *noun* a time of special need in the future.

Rainy Lake a lake situated in NW Ontario, forming part of the border between Ontario and Minnesota. [translation of French *Lac à la*

Pluie, perhaps from Ojibwa *tekamammaouen* it rains all the time, with reference to the spray from the falls at Fort Frances]

Rainy River a river in NW Ontario, flowing westward from Rainy Lake to Lake of the Woods and forming part of the border between Ontario and Minnesota. [see RAINY LAKE]

rainy season *noun* (in certain regions) an annually recurring season of relatively high rainfall.

Rai·pur /rai'pʊr/ a city in central India, capital of Chhattisgarh; pop. (2001) 605,100.

raise ● *transitive verb* **1** put or take into a higher position. **2** (often foll. by *up*) cause to rise or stand up or be vertical; set upright. **3** increase the amount or value or strength of (*raised their prices*). **4** (often foll. by *up*) construct or build up. **5** collect or bring together (*raise money*; *raise an army*). **6** cause to be heard or considered (*raise a shout*; *raise an objection*). **7** set going or bring into being; arouse (*raise a protest*; *raise hopes*). **8 a** give a higher or nobler character to (a person, style, thoughts, etc.). **b** heighten (consciousness or sensitivity). **9 a** rouse from sleep or from a lair. **b** restore to life. **10** bring up; educate. **11** breed or grow (*raise one's own vegetables*). **12** promote to a higher rank. **13** (foll. by *to*) *Math.* multiply (a quantity) to a specified power. **14** (often as **raised** *adjective*) leaven with yeast (*raised doughnuts*). **15** *Cards* **a** bet more than (another player). **b** increase (a stake). **c** *Bridge* make a bid contracting for more tricks in the same suit as (one's partner); increase (a bid) in this way. **16** abandon or force an enemy to abandon (a siege or blockade). **17** remove (a barrier or embargo). **18** cause (a ghost etc.) to appear (*opp.* LAY¹ *verb* 6b). **19** establish contact with (a person etc.) by radio or telephone. **20** *Naut.* come in sight of (land, a ship, etc.). **21** make a nap on (cloth). **22** *Curling* strike (a rock) with another rock to move it deeper on the sheet. ● *noun* **1** esp. *N Amer.* an increase in salary. **2** *Cards* an increase in a stake or bid (*compare sense* 15 *of verb*). **3** the action of raising something, esp. a part of the body as a fitness exercise. **4** *Curling* the act or an instance of striking a rock with another rock to move it deeper on the sheet. □ **raise Cain** *see* CAIN. **raise the devil** *informal* make a disturbance. **raise one's eyebrows** *see* EYEBROW. **raise one's eyes** *see* EYE. **raise from the dead** restore to life. **raise one's glass to** drink the health of. **raise one's hand to** make as if to strike (a person). **raise one's hat** (often foll. by *to*) remove it momentarily as a gesture of courtesy or respect. **raise hell** *informal* make a disturbance. **raise a laugh** cause others to laugh. **raise a person's spirits** give him or her new courage or cheerfulness. **raise a stink** create a fuss or disturbance. **raise one's voice** speak, esp. louder. □ **rais·able** *adjective* **rais·er** *noun* (also in *combination*). [Old Norse *reisa*, related to REAR²]

raised bed *noun* a flower bed enclosed by walls so that the surface of the soil is considerably higher than ground level.

raised bungalow *noun* *Cdn* a bungalow with the main floor raised to allow the basement to be partly above ground level.

rai·sin *noun* **1** a partially dried grape. **2** the dark purplish-brown colour of raisins. □ **rai·siny** *adjective* [Old French, ultimately from Latin *racemus* cluster of grapes]

rai·son d'être /ˌreizɔ̃ 'detr/ *noun* (*pl.* **rais·ons d'être** *pronunc.* same) a purpose or reason that accounts for or justifies or originally caused a thing's existence. [French, = reason for being]

raita /ra'iːtə/ *noun* an Indian side dish of chopped cucumber (or other vegetables) and spices in yogourt. [Hindustani *rāytā*]

Raj /rɒʒ, rɒdʒ/ *noun* (prec. by *the*) *hist.* the period of British rule in the Indian subcontinent before 1947. [Hindi *rāj* reign]

raja /'rɒʒə, 'rɒdʒə/ *noun* (also **rajah**) *hist.* **1** an Indian king or prince. **2** a petty dignitary or noble in India. **3** a Malay or Javanese chief. [Hindi *rājā* from Sanskrit *rājan* 'king']

Ra·jas·than /ˌrɒdʒə'stan, rɑdʒə-/ a state in W India, on the Pakistani border; capital, Jaipur. □ **Ra·jas·thani** *adjective & noun*

raja yoga *noun* a form of yoga intended to achieve control over the mind and emotions. [Sanskrit from *rājan* king + YOGA]

Raj·kot /rɒdʒ'koːt/ a city in Gujarat, W India; pop. (2001) 966,600.

Raj·put /'rɒdʒpʊt, -puːt/ *noun* a member of a Hindu soldier caste claiming Kshatriya descent. [Hindi *rājpūt* from Sanskrit *rājan* king + *putrá* son]

Raj·pu·tana /ˌrɒdʒpʊ'tɑnə/ an ancient region of India consisting of a collection of princely states ruled by dynasties, which came to power between the 9th and 16th c. Following independence from Britain in 1947, they united to form the state of Rajasthan, parts also being incorporated into Gujarat and Madhya Pradesh.

Raj·shahi /rɒdʒ'ʃɒhi/ a port on the Ganges River in W Bangladesh; pop. (est. 2002) 699,700.

rake¹ ● *noun* **1 a** an implement consisting of a pole with a crossbar toothed like a comb at the end, or with several tines held together by a crosspiece, for drawing together fallen leaves etc. or smoothing loose soil or gravel. **b** a similar larger agricultural implement mounted on wheels. **2** a similar implement used for other purposes, e.g. by a croupier drawing in money at a gaming table. ● *verb* **1** *transitive* collect or gather or remove with or as with a rake. **2** *transitive* make tidy or smooth with a rake (*raked it level*). **3** *transitive* use a rake. **4** *transitive & intransitive* search with or as with a rake; search thoroughly, ransack. **5** *transitive* **a** direct gunfire along (a line) from end to end. **b** sweep with the eyes. **6** *transitive* scratch or scrape. □ **rake in** *informal* amass (profits etc.). **rake up** (or **over**) revive the memory of (past quarrels, grievances, etc.). □ **rak·er** *noun* [Old English *raca*, *racu* from Germanic, partly from Old Norse *raka* scrape, rake]

rake² *noun* a fashionable or stylish man of dissolute or promiscuous habits. [short for archaic *rakehell* in the same sense]

rake³ ● *verb* **1** *transitive & intransitive* set or be set at a sloping angle. **2** *intransitive* (of a mast or funnel) incline from the perpendicular towards the stern. ● *noun* **1** a raking position or build. **2** the amount by which a thing rakes. **3** the slope of the stage or the auditorium in a theatre. **4** the angle of the edge or face of a cutting tool. □ **raked** *adjective* [17th c.: prob. related to German *ragen* project, of unknown origin]

rake-off *noun* *informal* a commission or share, esp. in a disreputable deal.

raki /rə'kiː, 'raki/ *noun* (*pl.* **rakis**) any of various alcoholic liquors made in E Europe and the Middle East. [Turkish *raqi*]

rak·ish¹ /'reikɪʃ/ *adjective* of or like a rake (*see* RAKE²). □ **rakish·ly** *adverb* **rakish·ness** *noun*

rak·ish² /'reikɪʃ/ *adjective* **1** (of a ship) smart and fast-looking, seemingly built for speed. **2** dashing; jaunty (*a hat worn at a rakish angle*). [RAKE³, assoc. with RAKE²]

raku /'rɑkuː/ *noun* a kind of Japanese lead-glazed earthenware, primarily for use in the tea ceremony. [Japanese, lit. 'enjoyment']

rale /rɑl/ *noun* an abnormal rattling sound heard in the auscultation of unhealthy lungs. [French from *râler* to rattle]

Ra·leigh¹ /'rɒli, 'rali/ the state capital of N Carolina; pop. (2000) 276,093.

Ra·leigh² /'rɒli, 'rali/ **Sir Wal·ter** (also **Ralegh**) (c.1552–1618), English explorer, courtier, and writer. A favourite of Elizabeth I, he attempted unsuccessfully to settle Virginia (1584–9), explored the Orinoco river in search of gold (1595), and introduced potato and tobacco plants into England; he was imprisoned by James I on a charge of conspiracy (1603–16), and eventually executed (1618).

rall. *abbreviation* rallentando.

ral·len·tando /ˌralən'tandoʊ/ *Music* ● *adverb & adjective* with a gradual decrease of speed. ● *noun* (*pl.* **-dos** or **ral·len·tandi** /-di/) a passage to be performed in this way. [Italian]

rally¹ ● *verb* (**-lies, -lied**) **1** *transitive & intransitive* (often foll. by *around, behind, to*) bring or come together as support or for concentrated action. **2** *transitive & intransitive* bring or come together again after a rout or dispersion. **3 a** *transitive* revive (courage etc.) by an effort of will. **b** *transitive* rouse (a person or animal) to fresh energy. **c** *intransitive* pull oneself together. **4** *intransitive* (of a sports team, athlete, etc.) acquire or assume fresh vigour or energy, esp. by coming from behind to tie or win a game. **5** *intransitive* recover after illness or prostration or fear; regain health or consciousness, revive. **6** *intransitive* (of share prices etc.) increase after a fall. **7** *intransitive* *Tennis etc.* engage in a rally. ● *noun* (*pl.* **-lies**) **1** an act of reassembling forces or renewing conflict; a reunion for fresh effort. **2** a recovery of energy after or in the middle of exhaustion or illness. **3** a mass meeting of supporters or persons having a common interest (*protest rally*). **4** a rapid rise in share prices etc. after a fall. **5** *Baseball* the scoring of two or more runs in one inning. **6** *Tennis etc.* an extended exchange of strokes between players. **7** a competition for motor vehicles, usu. over public roads or rough terrain. [French *rallier* (as RE-, ALLY)]

rally² *transitive verb* (**-lies, -lied**) subject to good-humoured ridicule. [French *railler* as RAIL²]

rally·ing cry *noun* a slogan.

ral·oxi·fene /'rə'lɒksəfiːn/ *noun* an anti-estrogen drug given orally as the hydrochloride for the prevention of osteoporosis in post-menopausal women. [invented name]

ralph *intransitive verb* *N Amer. slang* vomit. [imitative]

RAM *noun* *Computing* random access memory.

ram ● *noun* **1** an uncastrated male sheep. **2** (**the Ram**) the zodiacal sign or constellation Aries. **3** *hist.* **a** = BATTERING RAM. **b** a beak projecting from the bow of a battleship, for piercing the sides of other ships. **c** a battleship with such a beak. **4** the falling weight of a piledriver. **5 a** a hydraulic water-raising or lifting machine. **b** the piston of a hydraulic press. ● *transitive verb* (**rammed**, **ram·ming**) **1** force or squeeze into place by pressure. **2** (usu. foll. by *down*, *in*, *into*) beat down or drive in by heavy blows. **3** (of a ship, vehicle, etc.) strike violently, crash against. **4** (foll. by *against*, *at*, *on*, *into*) dash or violently impel. **5** (foll. by *through*) push (a bill, law, etc.) through a legislature. □ **ram home** stress forcefully (an argument, lesson, etc.). □ **ram·mer** *noun* [Old English *ram(m)*, perhaps related to Old Norse *rammr* strong]

Rama /ˈrɑːmə/ *Hinduism* the hero of the Ramayana, husband of Sita. He is the Hindu model of the ideal man, the seventh incarnation of Vishnu, and is widely venerated, by some sects as the supreme god.

-rama *combining form informal* or *jocular* (also **-ama**, **-orama**, **-arama**) forming nouns denoting abundance, a spectacle, extravaganza, etc., or the place containing it (*nostalgia-rama*; *shop-o-rama*). [after PANORAMA]

Ra·ma·dan /ˈramə,dan, ˈrɒmə,dɒn/ *noun* the ninth month of the Muslim year, during which strict fasting is observed from sunrise to sunset. [Arabic *ramaḍān* from *ramada* be hot; reason for name uncertain]

ram air *noun* air which is forced to enter a moving aperture, such as the air intake of an aircraft.

Ram·allah /rəˈmɒlə/ the acting administrative centre for the West Bank; pop. (est. 1997) 18,017.

Raman /ˈrɒmən/ **Sir Chan·dra·sekh·ara Ven·kata** (1888–1970), Indian physicist. He discovered the optical effect that is named after him, which was one of the most important proofs of the quantum theory of light, and went on to investigate the properties of crystals and minerals, and the physiology of colour vision; he was awarded the Nobel Prize for physics in 1930.

Raman effect *noun* the change of frequency in the scattering of radiation in a medium, used in spectroscopic analysis. [Sir C.V. RAMAN]

Ra·ma·nu·jan /ˌrɒməˈnuːdʒən/ **Srini·vasa (Aai·yan·gar)** (1887–1920), Indian mathematician. He produced a number of original discoveries in number theory and power series, and collaborating with G. H. Hardy (1877–1947), produced a theorem concerning the partition of numbers into a sum of smaller integers.

ram·ble ● *intransitive verb* **1** walk for pleasure, with or without a definite route. **2** (often foll. by *on*) wander in discourse; talk or write disconnectedly and usu. at length. **3** (esp. of buildings, paths, etc.) spread in various directions with no regular pattern. ● *noun* a walk taken for pleasure. [prob. from Middle Dutch *rammelen* (of an animal) wander about in sexual excitement, frequentative of *rammen* copulate with, related to RAM]

ram·bler *noun* **1** a person who rambles. **2** a straggling or climbing rose (*crimson rambler*). **3** *US* = RANCH 2b.

ramb·ling *adjective* **1** peripatetic, wandering. **2** disconnected, desultory, incoherent. **3** (of a house, street, etc.) irregularly arranged. **4** (of a plant) straggling, climbing. □ **ramb·ling·ly** *adverb*

Ram·bo *noun* (*pl.* **-bos**) a man given to displays of physical violence or aggression; a macho man. □ **Rambo·esque** *adjective* **Rambo·ism** *noun* [the hero of David Morrell's novel *First Blood* (1972), a Vietnam War veteran represented as bent on violent revenge, popularized in the films *First Blood* (1982) and *Rambo: First Blood Part II* (1985)]

ram·bunc·tious *adjective* esp. *N Amer. informal* **1** active; full of energy (*rambunctious children*). **2** boisterous; unruly; difficult to control. □ **ram·bunc·tious·ly** *adverb* **ram·bunc·tious·ness** *noun* [19th c.: origin unknown]

ram·bu·tan /ramˈbuːtən/ *noun* **1** a red plum-sized prickly fruit. **2** an E Indian tree, *Nephelium lappaceum*, that bears this. [Malay *rambūtan* from *rambut* hair, in allusion to its spines]

Ra·meau /raˈmoː/ **Jean-Philippe** (1683–1764), French composer, musical theorist, and organist. His four volumes of harpsichord pieces (1706–1741) are noted for their bold harmonies and textural diversity, and largely consist of genre pieces with descriptive titles, such as 'La Poule'; he also wrote operas, which include *Castor and Pollux* (1737).

ram·ekin /ˈramɪkɪn/ *noun* **1** a small, usu. round dish for baking and serving an individual portion of food. **2** food served in such a dish, esp. a small quantity of cheese baked with bread crumbs, eggs, etc. [French *ramequin*, of Low German or Dutch origin]

ramen /ˈrɒmən/ *plural noun* quick-cooking noodles, usu. served in a broth with meat and vegetables. [Japanese from Chinese *la* pull + *mian* noodle]

Ram·eses *see* RAMSES II, RAMSES III.

Rame·zay /ramˈzeɪ/ **Claude de** (1659–1724), French military officer and colonial administrator. Arriving in New France in 1685, he served as governor of Trois-Rivières (1690–99), commander of Canadian troops (1699–1704), and governor of Montreal (1704–24, except while serving as acting governor of New France 1714–16). Active in the fur and timber trades, he built the Château de Ramezay (1705–6) in Montreal.

ram·ie /ˈrami/ *noun* **1** a tall E Asian plant of the genus *Boehmeria nivea*, of the nettle family. **2** a strong fibre obtained from this, woven or knitted into fabric. [Malay *rāmī*]

rami·fi·ca·tion /ˌraməfɪˈkeɪʃən/ *noun* **1** the act or an instance of ramifying; the state of being ramified. **2** a subdivision of a complex structure or process comparable to a tree's branches. **3** a consequence, esp. when complex or unwelcome.

rami·fy /ˈramə,faɪ/ *verb* (**-fies**, **-fied**) **1** *intransitive* form branches or subdivisions or offshoots, branch out. **2** *transitive* (usu. in *passive*) cause to branch out; arrange in a branching manner. [French *ramifier* from medieval Latin *ramificare* from Latin *ramus* branch]

Ra·mil·lies, Battle of /ˈramiliz, ramiˈjiː/ a battle (1706) in the War of the Spanish Succession, in which the British under General Marlborough defeated the French near the village of Ramillies, north of Namur, central Belgium.

ra·min /raˈmiːn/ *noun* **1** any Malaysian tree of the genus *Gonystylus*, esp. *G. bancanus*. **2** the light-coloured hardwood obtained from this tree. [Malay]

Ram·insh /ˈrɒmɪntʃ/ **Imant** (b.1943), Canadian composer, violinist and conductor who founded the Prince George Symphony Orchestra in 1981 as well as several choirs. He is known internationally for his vocal and choral compositions, and his *Magnificat* won the 1990 National Choral Award.

ram·jet *noun* a type of jet engine in which air drawn in for combustion is compressed solely by the forward motion of the aircraft.

Ramón y Cajal /raˌmɒn iː kəˈhɒl/ **San·ti·ago** (1852–1934), Spanish physician and histologist. A founder of the science of neurology, he identified the neuron as the fundamental unit of the nervous system; he shared a Nobel Prize with Golgi in 1906.

ra·mose /ˈreɪmoːs, raˈmoːs/ *adjective* branched; branching. [Latin *ramosus* from *ramus* branch]

Ramos-Horta /ˈrɒmoːs ˈɔːrtə/ **José** (b.1949), exiled East Timorese activist who shared the Nobel Peace Prize in 1996 for his peace plan for the region.

ramp[1] ● *noun* **1** a slope or inclined plane, esp. for joining two levels of ground, floor, etc. (*a wheelchair ramp*). **2** *N Amer.* a short sloping road leading on or off a highway. **3** movable stairs for entering or leaving an aircraft. **4** the apron of an airfield. **5** part of the handrail of a stair with a concave or upward bend, as at a landing. **6** an access point to the Internet. ● *verb* **1** *transitive* (usu. as **ramped** *adjective*) furnish or build with a ramp. **2** *intransitive* **a** assume or be in a threatening posture. **b** storm, rage, rush. **c** *Heraldry* be rampant. **3** *intransitive & transitive* (often foll. by *up*) increase; gradually build. [Middle English (as verb in heraldic sense), from French *rampe* from Old French *ramper* creep, crawl]

ramp[2] *Brit. slang* ● *noun* a swindle or racket, esp. one conducted by the levying of exorbitant prices. ● *verb* **1** *intransitive* engage in a ramp. **2** *transitive* subject (a person etc.) to a ramp. [16th c.: origin unknown]

ram·page /ˈrampeɪdʒ/ ● *intransitive verb* (also /ramˈpeɪdʒ/) (often foll. by *through*, *across*, etc.) rush wildly or violently about; rage, storm. ● *noun* an instance of uncontrolled, often prolonged, unruly or violent behaviour. □ **on the rampage** rampaging. □ **ram·pa·geous** *adjective* [18th c., perhaps from RAMP[1] *verb*]

ram·pant /ˈrampənt/ *adjective* **1** unchecked, flourishing excessively (*rampant violence*). **2** violent or extravagant in action or opinion (*rampant theorists*). **3** rank, luxuriant. **4** (placed after noun) *Heraldry* (of an animal) standing on its left hind foot with its forepaws in the air (*lion rampant*). □ **ram·pant·ly** *adverb* [Old French, part. of *ramper*: see RAMP[1]]

ram·part /ˈrampɑːrt/ ● *noun* **1 a** a defensive wall with a broad top and usu. a stone parapet, built around a castle, fort, etc. **b** a walkway on top of such a wall. **2** a defence or protection. **3** (in *pl.*) *Cdn* (*BC*, *Alta.*, & *North*) steep rock walls, as found on either side of a river gorge. ● *transitive verb* fortify or protect with or as with a rampart. [French *rempart*, *rempar* from *remparer* fortify, from *emparer* take possession of, ultimately from Latin *ante* before + *parare* prepare]

ram·pion /ˈrampɪən/ *noun* **1** a bellflower, *Campanula rapunculus*, with white tuberous roots used as a salad. **2** any of various plants of the

---

Consonants: b *but*   d *dog*   f *few*   g *get*   h *her*   j *yes*   k *cat*   l *leg*   m *man*   n *no*   p *pen*   r *red*   s *sit*

genus *Phyteuma*, with clusters of hornlike buds and flowers. [ultimately from medieval Latin *rapuncium*, *rapontium*, prob. from Latin *rapum* RAPE[2]]

ramp-up *noun* an increase.

ram-raid *Brit.* ● *noun* a robbery in which a store window is rammed with a vehicle and looted. ● *transitive verb* rob (a store) in this manner. □ **ram-raider** *noun* **ram-raiding** *noun*

ram-rod ● *noun* **1** a rod for ramming down the charge of a muzzleloading firearm. **2** a thing that is very straight or rigid. **3** *N Amer. informal* a foreman or boss. ● *adjective* **1** solemn, formal. **2** very straight (*ramrod posture*). ● *adverb* like a ramrod (*ramrod straight*). ● *transitive verb* (**ram·rod·ded, ram·rod·ding**) force or drive as with a ramrod (*ramrodded the bill through the legislature*).

Ram·say ▶ 1 James An·drew Broun, see DALHOUSIE[2] **2. 2 Sir Wil·liam** (1852–1916), Scottish chemist. He discovered the five chemically inert gases argon, helium, and (with the help of M. W. Travers, 1872–1961) neon, krypton, and xenon, determined their atomic weights and places in the periodic table, and in 1910 identified the last noble gas, radon; he was awarded the Nobel Prize for chemistry in 1904.

Ram·ses II /ˈramsiːz/ (also **Ram·eses II** /ˈraməˌsiːz/) (known as Ramses the Great) (died *c.*1225 BC), king of Egypt *c.*1292–*c.*1225 BC. The third pharaoh of the 19th dynasty, he built vast monuments and statues, including the two rock temples at Abu Simbel; he launched a major offensive against the Hittites.

Ram·ses III /ˈramsiːz/ (also **Ram·eses III** /ˈraməˌsiːz/) (died *c.*1167 BC), king of Egypt *c.*1198–*c.*1167 BC. The second pharaoh of the 20th dynasty, he fought decisive battles against the Libyans and the Sea Peoples; after his death the power of Egypt declined steadily.

ram·shackle *adjective* **1** (of a house etc.) tumbledown, rickety. **2** (of an organization or system) poorly designed or organized. [earlier *ramshackled* past participle of obsolete *ransackle* RANSACK]

ram's-horn snail *noun* a herbivorous freshwater snail of the family Planorbidae, having a flat spiral shell.

ram·sons /ˈramsənz/ *plural noun* (usu. treated as *sing.*) **1** a broad-leaved garlic, *Allium ursinum*, with elongate pungent-smelling bulbous roots. **2** the root of this, eaten as a relish. [Old English *hramsan* pl. of *hramsa* wild garlic, later taken as sing.]

ran *past of* RUN.

ranch ● *noun* **1 a** a cattle-breeding farm esp. in the western US and Canada. **b** a farm where other animals are bred (*mink ranch; aquaculture ranch*). **2** (in full **ranch house, ranch home**, or **ranch bungalow**) *N Amer.* **a** a house on a cattle ranch, usu. of one storey and with a long, low design. **b** a similar type of house, usu. found in the suburbs. **3** *N Amer.* a type of thick, white salad dressing made with sour cream. ● *verb* **1** *intransitive* run or work on a ranch. **2** *transitive* breed or rear (animals) on or as on a ranch. **3** *transitive* use (land) as a ranch. □ **ranch·ing** *noun* [Spanish *rancho* group of persons eating together]

ranch·er *noun* **1** a person who owns or works on a ranch. **2** *N Amer.* = RANCH *noun* 2b.

ranch·era /ranˈtʃerə/ *noun* **1** (also **ranchera music**) a genre of Mexican popular music characterized by songs about the land, usu. accompanied by accordion, guitar, and bass. **2** one of these songs. [Mexican Spanish as RANCH, the genre having arisen in Mexican cattle-ranching country]

ranch·ero /ranˈtʃeroː/ *noun* (*pl.* **-eros**) a rancher, esp. in Mexico and the southwestern US. [Spanish (as RANCH)]

ranch·ette *noun N Amer* a small cattle ranch or piece of ranchland.

ranch hand *noun* a worker on a ranch.

Ran·chi /ˈrɒntʃi/ a city in Bihar, NE India; pop. (2001) 846,500.

ranch·land *noun* land used for or suitable for ranching.

ranch-style *adjective* (of a house) having one storey and a long, low design.

ran·cid /ˈransɪd/ *adjective* **1** (of fats, oils, or fatty meats such as bacon) smelling or tasting rank and stale as a result of oxidation. **2** nasty, disagreeable, odious. □ **ran·cid·ity** /-ˈsɪdɪti/ *noun* [Latin *rancidus* stinking]

ran·cour /ˈraŋkər/ *noun* (also esp. *US* **ran·cor**) inveterate bitterness, malignant hate, spitefulness. □ **ran·cor·ous** *adjective* **ran·cor·ous·ly** *adverb* [Old French from Late Latin *rancor -oris* (as RANCID)]

Rand, Ayn (1905–82), Russian-born US novelist, whose works present her theory of objectivism, which is anti-romantic and anti-altruistic in its appeal to a code of 'rational self-interest'; they include *The Fountainhead* (1943) and *Atlas Shrugged* (1957).

Rand, the /rand, rɒnt/ = WITWATERSRAND, THE.

rand[1] *noun* the chief monetary unit of South Africa, equal to 100 cents. [from the gold-producing district of the RAND (see WITWATERSRAND, THE)]

rand[2] *noun* a levelling strip of leather between the heel and sides of a shoe or boot. [Old English from Germanic]

R & B *abbreviation* (also **r & b**) rhythm and blues.

R & D *abbreviation* (also **R and D**) research and development.

Rand formula *noun Cdn* a stipulation in most union agreements that all employees within a bargaining unit must pay union dues, but that actual membership in the union is voluntary. [I.C. *Rand*, Canadian judge, arbitrator, and educator, d.1969]

ran·dom *adjective* **1** made, done, etc., without method or conscious choice (*random selection*). **2** *Statistics* **a** with equal chances for each item. **b** given by a random process (*random sample*). **3** (of masonry) with stones of irregular size and shape. □ **at random** without aim or purpose or principle. □ **ran·dom·ize** *transitive verb* (also esp. *Brit.* **-ise**). **ran·dom·iz·a·tion** *noun* **ran·dom·ly** *adverb* **ran·dom·ness** *noun* [Old French *randon* great speed, from *randir* gallop]

random access *noun Computing* (also *attributive*) a process that allows information in a computer to be stored or recovered quickly without reading through items stored previously.

random error *noun Statistics* an error in measurement caused by factors which vary from one measurement to another.

Random Island an island nestled in the west central shore of Trinity Bay, SE Newfoundland. [perhaps from Old English *randon* disorderly, with reference to the sea]

random walk *noun* the movements of an object or changes in a variable that follow no discernible pattern or trend.

R and R *abbreviation* (also **R & R**) **1** rest and recreation. **2** rest and relaxation. **3** rest and recuperation. **4** rescue and resuscitation.

Rand·stad /ˈrɒnstɒt/ a conurbation in the northwest of the Netherlands that stretches in a horseshoe shape from Dordrecht and Rotterdam around to Utrecht and Amersfoort via The Hague, Leiden, Haarlem, and Amsterdam. The majority of the people of the Netherlands live in this area.

randy *adjective* (**ran·di·er, ran·di·est**) **1** lustful; eager for sexual gratification. **2** bawdy, risqué. □ **ran·di·ness** *noun* [perhaps from obsolete *rand* from obsolete Dutch *randen, ranten* RANT]

ran·ee *var. of* RANI.

rang[1] *past of* RING[2].

rang[2] /rɑ̃/ *noun Cdn* (*Que.*) *hist.* Surveying a row of long lots, usu. along a road. [French, = row, range]

ran·ga·tira /ˌraŋgəˈtiːrə/ *noun NZ* a Maori chief or noble. [Maori]

range ● *noun* **1 a** the region between limits of variation, esp. as representing a scope of effective operation (*a voice of astonishing range; the whole range of politics*). **b** such limits. **c** a limited scale or series (*the range of the thermometer readings is about 10 degrees*). **d** a series representing variety or choice; a selection. **2** the area included in or concerned with something. **3 a** the distance attainable by a gun or projectile (*the enemy are out of range*). **b** the distance between a gun or projectile and its objective. **4 a** a row, series, line, or tier, esp. of mountains or buildings. **b** *Cdn* a row of prison cells. **5 a** an open or enclosed area with targets for shooting. **b** a testing ground for military equipment. **6** *N Amer.* an electric or gas stove. **7** the area over which a thing, esp. a plant or animal, is distributed (*gives the ranges of all species*). **8** the distance that can be covered by a vehicle or aircraft without refuelling. **9** the distance between a camera and the subject to be photographed. **10** the extent of time covered by a forecast etc. **11 a** a large area of open land for grazing or hunting. **b** a tract over which one wanders. **12** lie, direction (*the range of the strata is east and west*). **13** *Cdn* (*Que. & Ont.*) a row of lots forming a concession. **14** *N Amer.* (*West*) a series of townships extending north and south parallel to the principal meridian of a survey. ● *verb* **1** *intransitive* **a** vary or extend between limits (*ages ranging from twenty to sixty; prices range between $7 and $10; the discussion ranged over many different topics*). **b** run in a line (*ranges north and south*). **2** *transitive* (usu. in *passive* or *reflexive*) **a** place or arrange in a row or ranks or in a specified order (*ranged their troops; flowerpots ranged in rows on the windowsill*). **b** place or align (oneself) with a certain group, cause, etc. (*on this issue, she has ranged herself with the Opposition*). **3** *intransitive* rove, wander (*ranged through the woods; his thoughts range over past, present, and future*). **4** *transitive* traverse in all directions (*ranging the woods*). **5** *Printing* **a** *transitive* make (type) lie flush at the ends of successive lines. **b** *intransitive* (of type) lie flush. **6** *intransitive* **a** (of a gun) send a projectile over a specified distance (*ranges over a* *mile*). **b** (of a projectile) cover a specified distance. **c** obtain the range of a target by adjustment after firing past it or short of it. [Old French *range* 'row, rank', via *ranger* from *rang* RANK[1]]

range·find·er *noun* an instrument for estimating the distance of an object, esp. one to be shot at or photographed.

range·land *noun* an extensive area of open country used for grazing or hunting animals.

range of motion *noun* the ability to move bones about a joint in an arc of a circle.

ran·ger *noun* **1 a** = FOREST RANGER. **b** (in full **park ranger**) = PARK WARDEN. **c** = FIRE RANGER. **2** a member of a body of armed men, esp.: **a** a mounted soldier. **b** *US* a commando. **3** (**Ranger**) **a** *Cdn hist.* a member of the Newfoundland Rangers (1935-49), a police force which served those parts of Newfoundland and Labrador outside the jurisdiction of the St. John's police force. **b** *US* a member of the Texas state police force. **4** *Cdn* (*North*) an Indian or Inuit who serves as a military scout or observer on a voluntary basis. **5** (**Ranger**) *Brit.* & *Cdn* a member of the senior branch of the Girl Guides, aged 15 or older.

Ran·goon /raŋˈguːn/ (Burmese **Yan·gon** /janˈɡɒn/) the capital of Burma (Myanmar), a port in the Irrawaddy delta; pop. (est. 2002) 4,016,000.

rangy[1] /ˈreɪndʒi/ *adjective* (**ran·gi·er**, **ran·gi·est**) **1** (of a person) tall and slim. **2** (of an animal) having a long, slender form. **3** having a tendency or the ability to range or wander about.

rangy[2] /ˈraŋi/ *noun Cdn informal* restless, uncontrollable, and bad-tempered, esp. because of pent-up energy.

rani /ˈrɑːni/ *noun* (also **ranee**) *hist.* a raja's wife or widow; a Hindu queen. [Hindi *rānī* = Sanskrit *rājñī* fem. of *rājan* king]

Ran·jit Singh /ˌrʌndʒɪt ˈsɪŋ/ (known as the 'Lion of the Punjab') (1780–1839), Indian maharaja, founder of the Sikh state of Punjab. He proclaimed himself maharaja of Punjab in 1801 and proceeded to make the state the most powerful in India, securing the holy city of Amritsar (1802) and expanding his control northwest with the capture of Peshawar (1818) and Kashmir (1819).

rank[1] ● *noun* **1 a** a position in a hierarchy, a grade of advancement. **b** a distinct social class (*people of all ranks*). **c** a grade of dignity or achievement (*in the top rank of performers*). **d** high social position (*persons of rank*). **e** a place in a scale. **2** a row or line. **3** a single line of soldiers drawn up abreast. **4** order, array. **5** *Chess* a row of squares across the board (compare FILE[2] *noun* 2). ● *verb* **1** *intransitive* have rank or place (*ranks next to the king*). **2** *transitive* classify, give a certain grade to. **3** *transitive* arrange (esp. soldiers) in a rank or ranks. **4** *US* **a** *transitive* take precedence of (a person) in respect to rank. **b** *intransitive* have the senior position among the members of a hierarchy etc. □ **break rank** (or **ranks**) **1** fail to remain in line. **2** fail to maintain solidarity. **close ranks** maintain solidarity. **the ranks 1** the common soldiers, i.e. privates and corporals. **2** a group of people of a specified type (*joined the ranks of the unemployed*). **rise from the ranks 1** (of a private or a non-commissioned officer) receive a commission. **2** (of a self-made man or woman) advance by one's own efforts. [Old French *ranc*, *renc*, from Germanic, related to RING[1]]

rank[2] *adjective* **1** too luxuriant, coarse; choked with or apt to produce weeds or excessive foliage. **2 a** foul-smelling, offensive. **b** loathsome, indecent, corrupt. **3** complete, unmistakable, strongly marked (*rank amateur*). □ **rank·ly** *adverb* **rank·ness** *noun* [Old English *ranc* from Germanic]

rank and file *noun* (usu. treated as *pl.*) **1** the ordinary soldiers who are not officers. **2** the ordinary members of any group or society as opposed to the leaders (also *attributive*: *rank-and-file workers*). □ **rank-and-filer** *noun*

rank·er *noun Brit.* **1** a soldier in the ranks. **2** a commissioned officer who has been in the ranks.

Ran·kin Family Canadian traditional folk group consisting of the siblings **Cook·ie** (Carol Jean), **Hea·ther**, **Jimmy**, **John Mor·ris**, and **Ray·lene**. Through the 1990s the group won numerous Juno Awards and East Coast Music Awards for their music inspired by the traditions of their native Cape Breton.

rank·ing ● *noun* ordering by rank; classification. ● *adjective N Amer.* having a high rank or position.

Ran·kin Inlet 1 a small inlet of the northwestern shore of Hudson Bay, Nunavut, about 200 km (by air) northeast of Arviat. **2** a hamlet situated at its head; pop. (2001) 2,177. [J. *Rankin*, lieutenant aboard the HMS *Furnace c.*1741]

ran·kle *verb* **1** *intransitive* (of envy, disappointment, etc., or their cause) cause persistent annoyance or resentment. **2** *transitive* (of an experience,

event, etc.) cause, or continue to cause, bad, esp. bitter feelings in (a person). [Old French *rancler* from *rancle*, *draoncle* festering sore, from medieval Latin *dranculus*, *dracunculus* diminutive of *draco* serpent]

Rann of Kutch see KUTCH, RANN OF.

ran·sack *transitive verb* **1** pillage or plunder (a house, country, etc.). **2** thoroughly search (a place, a receptacle, a person's pockets, one's conscience, etc.). □ **ran·sack·er** *noun* [Old Norse *rannsaka* from *rann* house + *-saka* from *sœkja* seek]

ran·som ● *noun* **1** a sum of money or other payment demanded or paid for the release of a prisoner. **2** the liberation of a prisoner in return for this. ● *transitive verb* **1** buy the freedom or restoration of; redeem. **2** hold to ransom. **3** release for a ransom. [Old French *ransoun(er)* from Latin *redemptio -onis* REDEMPTION]

rant ● *intransitive verb* **1** (often foll. by *about*, *on*) speak vehemently or wildly, esp. at length. **2** use bombastic language. ● *noun* a piece of ranting, a tirade. □ **rant and rave** express anger noisily and forcefully. □ **rant·er** *noun* [Dutch *ranten* rave]

Rant·er *noun* a member of an antinomian Christian sect in England during the mid-17th c. which denied the authority of scripture and clergy. In the 19th c. the word was applied to members of certain Nonconformist, in particular Methodist, groups.

ra·nun·cul·aceous /rəˌnʌŋkjʊˈleɪʃəs/ *adjective* of or relating to the family Ranunculaceae of flowering plants, including clematis and delphiniums.

ra·nun·cul·us /rəˈnʌŋkjʊləs/ *noun* (*pl.* **ra·nun·cul·us·es** or **ra·nun·culi** /-ˌlaɪ/) any plant of the genus *Ranunculus*, usu. having bowl-shaped flowers with many stamens and carpels, including buttercups and crowfoots. [Latin, originally diminutive of *rana* frog]

rap[1] ● *noun* **1** a quick sharp blow or knock. **2** *slang* **a** a criticism, punishment. **b** (often foll. by *on*, *against*) a charge, accusation, or reputed fault (*would not fight the drunk driving rap*; *the usual rap against them was their stubbornness*; *pinned the rap on us*). **3** *slang* a conversation (*rap session*). **4 a** (in full **rap music**) a style of popular music characterized by the rhythmic and usu. rapid reciting of rhyming lyrics against an often sampled background with a pronounced beat. **b** the reciting of lyrics in rap music. **c** a rap song. ● *verb* (**rapped**, **rap·ping**) **1** *transitive* strike briskly. **2** *intransitive* knock; make a sharp tapping sound (*rapped on the table*). **3** *transitive informal* **a** criticize adversely. **b** accuse, charge. **4** *intransitive slang* talk. **5 a** *intransitive* perform rap music, talk in the style of rap. **b** *transitive* utter in this style. □ **beat the rap** *N Amer.* escape punishment. **rap a person's knuckles** (also **rap a person on the knuckles**) **1** strike a person's knuckles sharply. **2** criticize or reprimand a person. **rap on the knuckles** a reprimand or reproof. **rap out 1** utter (an oath, order, pun, etc.) abruptly or on the spur of the moment. **2** express or reproduce (a rhythm, signal, etc.) by raps. **take the rap** suffer the consequences. [Middle English, prob. imitative]

rap[2] *noun* a small amount, the least bit (*don't care a rap*). [Irish *ropaire* Irish counterfeit coin]

ra·pa·cious /rəˈpeɪʃəs/ *adjective* greedy, grasping, extortionate. □ **ra·pa·cious·ly** *adverb* **ra·pa·cious·ness** *noun* **ra·pa·city** /rəˈpasɪti/ *noun* [Latin *rapax -acis* from *rapere* snatch]

rape[1] ● *noun* **1** the action or an act of forcing a person, esp. a woman or girl, to have sexual intercourse unwillingly. **2** (often foll. by *of*) plunder, abuse, or violation (*the rape of our natural resources*). **3** *archaic* an instance of carrying off (esp. of a woman) by force. ● *transitive verb* **1** commit rape on (a person, usu. a woman). **2** violate, assault, pillage. **3** *literary* take by force. [Anglo-French *rap(er)* from Latin *rapere* seize]

rape[2] *noun* a plant, *Brassica napus*, the seeds of which yield oil used in cooking, as a lubricant, and in soaps etc. Also called COLZA, COLE. See also CANOLA. [Latin *rapum*, *rapa* turnip]

rape[3] *noun* the refuse of grapes after winemaking, used in making vinegar. [French *râpe*, medieval Latin *raspa*]

rape crisis centre *noun* an agency offering advice and support to victims of rape.

rape·seed *noun* **1** the seed of the rape plant. **2** the rape plant.

rapeseed oil *noun* (also **rape oil**) an oil made from rapeseed and used as a lubricant and in foodstuffs.

rape-shield *noun* (*attributive*) *N Amer. Law* designating legislation limiting the allowable questioning of the victim of an alleged sexual assault on matters of personal esp. sexual history.

Raph·ael /ˈrafaɪəl, rafaɪˈel, -feɪ-/ **1** (in the Bible) one of the seven archangels in the apocryphal Book of Enoch. He is said to have 'healed' the earth when it was defiled by the sins of the fallen angels. **2** (Italian name Raffaello Sanzio) (1483–1520), Italian painter and architect.

Vowels: a *cat*   ɑ *arm*   e *bed*   ɜr *her*   ɜ: *deux*   ə *ago*   ɪ *sit*   i *cosy*   iː *feed*   ɒ *hot*   ɔ *pore*   oː *no*   ʌ *run*   ʊ *put*

A leading figure of the High Renaissance in Italy, he is noted for his depictions of the Virgin and Child, which are distinguished by a serenity of expression, and include the *Sistine Madonna* altarpiece (c.1513); he also oversaw the planning of the longitudinal design of the new St. Peter's Basilica in Rome (1514). [Hebrew, = God has healed]

rap·id ● *adjective* **1** quick, swift. **2** acting or completed in a short time. **3** (of a slope) descending steeply. **4** *Photog.* fast. ● *noun* (usu. in *pl.*) a section of a river with a swift turbulent current. □ **rapid·ity** *noun* **rapid·ly** *adverb* [Latin *rapidus* from *rapere* seize]

rapid eye movement *noun* a type of jerky movement of the eyes during periods of dreaming. Abbr.: **REM.**

rapid-fire *attributive adjective* fired, uttered, etc., in quick succession (*a rapid-fire exchange*).

rapid prototyping *noun* the computerized construction of solid models directly from three-dimensional computer-aided designs.

rapid-reaction *adjective* designating military units which are kept in a state of readiness and can be rapidly deployed to counter hostile activity.

rapid transit *noun* high-speed urban transportation of passengers, usu. by rail.

ra·pier /ˈreɪpɪər/ ● *noun* a light slender sword used for thrusting. ● *adjective* having the sharpness or incisiveness of a rapier (*rapier wit; rapier intellect*). [prob. from Dutch *rapier* or Low German *rappir*, from French *rapière*, of unknown origin]

rap·ine /ˈrapaɪn, -pɪn/ *noun literary* plundering, robbery. [Old French or from Latin *rapina* from *rapere* seize]

ra·pini /rəˈpiːni/ *plural noun* the edible leaves of an immature white turnip. [Italian]

rap·ist *noun* a person who commits rape.

rap·pel /raˈpel/ ● *intransitive verb* (**rap·pelled, rap·pel·ling**) descend a steep rock face by using a doubled rope coiled round the body and fixed at a higher point. ● *noun* a descent made by rappelling. [French, = recall, from *rappeler* (as RE-, APPEAL)]

rap·per *noun* **1** a performer of rap music. **2** a person or thing that raps.

rap·pie pie *noun Cdn* a savoury Acadian dish of Nova Scotia and PEI consisting of grated potatoes and meat. [Acadian French *pâté râpé* from *râper* 'to grate']

rap·port /raˈpɔr/ *noun* a relationship or communication, esp. when useful and harmonious (*in rapport with; establish a rapport*). [French from *rapporter* (as RE-, AP-[1], *porter* from Latin *portare* carry)]

rap·por·teur /ˌraporˈtɜr/ *noun* a person who prepares an account of the proceedings of a committee etc. for a higher body. [French (as RAPPORT)]

rap·proche·ment /ˌraprɒʃˈmɑ̃/ *noun* the establishment or resumption of harmonious relations, esp. between nations. [French from *rapprocher* (as RE-, APPROACH)]

rap·scal·lion *noun jocular* a rascal, scamp, or rogue. [earlier *rascallion*, perhaps from RASCAL]

rap sheet *noun N Amer. slang* an official record of one's criminal activities.

rapt *adjective* **1** fully absorbed or intent, enraptured (*listen with rapt attention*). **2** carried away with feeling or lofty thought. □ **rapt·ly** *adverb* **rapt·ness** *noun* [Latin *raptus* past participle of *rapere* seize]

rap·tor *noun* **1** any bird of prey, e.g. an owl, falcon, etc. **2** *informal* = VELOCIRAPTOR. [Latin, = ravisher, plunderer, from *rapere rapt*- seize]

rap·tor·ial *adjective* (of a bird or animal) adapted for seizing prey; predatory.

rap·ture ● *noun* **1 a** ecstatic delight, mental transport. **b** (in *pl.*) great pleasure or enthusiasm or the expression of it. **2** (**Rapture**) (in some millenarian teaching) the transporting of believers to heaven at the Second Coming of Christ. ● *transitive verb* transport (believers) to heaven. □ **go into** (or **be in**) **raptures** be enthusiastic; talk enthusiastically. □ **rap·tur·ous** *adjective* **rap·tur·ous·ly** *adverb* [obsolete French *rapture* or medieval Latin *raptura* (as RAPT)]

rara avis /ˌrerə ˈeɪvɪs, ˌrɑrə ˈavɪs/ *noun* (*pl.* **rarae aves** /-ri -viːz/) = RARE BIRD. [Latin]

rare[1] *adjective* (**rarer, rarest**) **1** seldom done or found or occurring, uncommon, unusual, few and far between. **2** of less than the usual density, with only loosely packed substance (*the rare atmosphere of the mountaintops*). **3** esp. *Brit.* exceptionally good (*had a rare time*). □ **rare·ness** *noun* [Middle English from Latin *rarus*]

rare[2] *adjective* (**rarer, rarest**) (of meat) slightly cooked. □ **rare·ness** *noun* [var. of obsolete *rear* half-cooked (of eggs), from Old English *hrēr*]

rare bird *noun* a rarity; a kind of person or thing rarely encountered.

rare·bit *noun* = WELSH RABBIT. [RARE[1] + BIT[1]]

rare earth *noun* **1** a lanthanide element. **2** an oxide of such an element.

rar·efied /ˈrerɪfaɪd/ *adjective* (also **rar·ified**) **1** (of air, a gas, etc.) thinner or less dense than usual. **2 a** often *ironic* refined, subtle. **b** elevated, exalted.

rar·efy /ˈrerɪfaɪ/ *verb* (also **rar·ify**) (**-efies, -efied**) **1** *transitive & intransitive* make or become less dense or solid. **2** *transitive* purify or refine (a person's nature etc.). **3** *transitive* make (an idea etc.) subtle. □ **rar·efac·tion** *noun* [Old French *rarefier* from Latin *rarefacere*, from *rarus* 'rare' + *facere* 'make']

rare·ly *adverb* **1** seldom; not often. **2** in an unusual degree; exceptionally.

rar·ing *adjective* (foll. by *to* + infin.) *informal* enthusiastic, eager (*raring to go*). [part. of *rare*, dial. var. of ROAR or REAR[2]]

rar·ity *noun* (*pl.* **-ities**) **1** rareness. **2** an uncommon thing, esp. one valued for being rare.

Raro·tonga /ˌrerəˈtɒŋɡə/ a mountainous island in the S Pacific, the chief island of the Cook Islands. Its chief town, Avarua, is the capital of the Cook Islands.

Raro·ton·gan /ˌrerəˈtɒŋɡən/ ● *noun* **1** a native or inhabitant of Rarotonga. **2** the Polynesian language of Rarotonga. ● *adjective* of or relating to Rarotonga or its people or language.

Ras al Khai·mah /ˌrɒs al ˈkaɪmə/ **1** one of the seven member states of the United Arab Emirates; pop. (est. 2002) 188,400. **2** its capital, a port on the Persian Gulf; pop. (est. 2002) 105,000.

ras·cal *noun* often *jocular* a dishonest or mischievous person, esp. a child. □ **ras·cal·ity** *noun* **ras·cal·ly** *adjective* [Old French *rascaille* rabble, prob. ultimately from Latin *radere ras*- scrape]

rash[1] *adjective* reckless, impetuous, hasty; acting or done without due consideration. □ **rash·ly** *adverb* **rash·ness** *noun* [Middle English, prob. from Old English *ræsc* (unrecorded) from Germanic]

rash[2] *noun* **1** an eruption of the skin in spots or patches. **2** (usu. foll. by *of*) a sudden widespread phenomenon, esp. of something unwelcome (*a rash of robberies*). [18th c.: prob. related to Old French *ra(s)che* eruptive sores, = Italian *raschia* itch]

rash·er *noun* a thin slice of bacon or ham. [16th c.; origin unknown]

Ras·min·sky /razˈmɪnski/ **Louis** (1908–1998), Canadian banker. In 1944 an international conference at Bretton Woods, New Hampshire, partially adopted his plan for a postwar international monetary system. He rose through the hierarchy of the Bank of Canada, serving as governor 1961–72.

Ras·mus·sen /ˈrasmʊsən/ **Knud Johan Vic·tor** (1879–1933), Danish Arctic explorer and ethnologist, who conducted studies of Inuit culture in Greenland and N America.

rasp ● *noun* **1** a grating noise or utterance. **2** a coarse kind of file having separate teeth. ● *verb* **1** *transitive* **a** scrape with a rasp. **b** scrape roughly. **c** (foll. by *off, away*) remove by scraping. **2 a** *intransitive* make a grating sound. **b** *transitive* say gratingly or hoarsely. **3** *transitive* grate upon (a person or a person's feelings), irritate. □ **rasp·ing·ly** *adverb* **raspy** *adjective* [Old French *raspe(r)*, ultimately from West Germanic]

rasp·berry ● *noun* (*pl.* **-berries**) **1 a** a bramble of the genus *Rubus*, esp. *R. idaeus*, having usu. red berries consisting of numerous drupelets on a conical receptacle. **b** this berry. **2** the red colour of a raspberry, usu. a deep red. **3** *informal* **a** a sputtering sound made with the lips and tongue expressing dislike, derision, or disapproval. **b** a show of strong disapproval (*got a raspberry from the audience*). ● *adjective* of the colour of a raspberry; usu. deep red. [16th-c. *rasp* (now dialect) from obsolete *raspis*, of unknown origin, + BERRY, noun sense 3 from rhyming slang *raspberry tart*, = fart]

raspberry cane *noun* a raspberry plant.

raspberry vinegar *noun* a vinegar made from raspberry juice.

Ras·pu·tin /raˈspjuːtɪn/ **Grig·ori (Efimo·vich)** (c.1871–1916), Russian monk. He came to exert great influence over Czar Nicholas II and his family during the First World War by claiming miraculous powers to heal the heir to the throne, who suffered from hemophilia; he was assassinated by a group loyal to the czar.

ras·sle *transitive & intransitive verb N Amer. informal* = WRESTLE *verb*. □ **ras·sler** *noun*

Ras·ta *noun & adjective* = RASTAFARIAN. [abbreviation]

Rasta·far·ian /ˌrastəˈferiən/ ● *noun* a member of a sect of Jamaican origin regarding blacks as a chosen people and the former Emperor Haile Selassie of Ethiopia (d.1975, entitled *Ras Tafari*) as God. ● *adjective* of or relating to this sect. □ **Rasta·far·ian·ism** *noun*

---

uː mo**o**d ai m**y** əi p**i**pe au br**ow**n ʌu h**ou**se ei d**ay** ɔi b**oy** ɑ̃ fr**an**glais ã Canadi**en** ɔ̃ Br**ay**on   (*see over for consonants*)

ras·ter *noun* a pattern of horizontal lines of pixels composing an image on a cathode ray tube display or for printing etc. (also *attributive*: raster graphics). [German, = screen, from Latin *rastrum* rake, from *radere* rasscrape]

ras·ter·ize *transitive verb* (also esp. *Brit.* **-ise**) *Computing* convert (a digitized image) into a form that can be displayed on a cathode ray tube or printed. □ **ras·ter·iz·a·tion** *noun* **ras·ter·iz·er** *noun*

rat ● *noun* **1 a** any of several rodents of the genus *Rattus* usu. having a pointed snout and a long sparsely haired tail (*brown rat*). **b** = MUSKRAT. **c** any similar rodent (*water rat*). **2** a deserter from a party, cause, difficult situation, etc.; a turncoat or informant. **3** *informal* an unpleasant person. **4** a worker who refuses to join a strike; a scab. **5** *informal* a person frequently found in a specified place (*rink rat; mall rat*). ● *intransitive verb* (**rat·ted**, **rat·ting**) **1** (usu. foll. by *on*, *out*) **a** inform on; be an informant against. **b** betray; let down. **2** (of a person, dog, etc.) hunt or kill rats. **3** *informal* desert a cause, party, etc. □ **not give a rat's ass** *N Amer. slang* not care in the least. **smell a rat** *see* SMELL. [Old English *ræt* & Old French *rat*; noun sense 2 from the superstition that rats desert a sinking ship]

rat·able *var. of* RATEABLE.

rata·fia /ˌratəˈfiːə/ *noun* **1** a liqueur flavoured with almonds or kernels of peach, apricot, or cherry. **2** a kind of cookie similarly flavoured. [French, perhaps related to TAFIA]

rata·plan /ˌratəˈplan/ *noun* a drumming sound. [French: imitative]

rat-a-tat-tat (also **rat-a-tat**) *var. of* RAT-TAT-TAT.

rata·touille /ˌratəˈtuːi, -ˈtwiː/ *noun* a vegetable dish made of stewed onions, zucchini, tomatoes, eggplants, and peppers. [French dialect, from French *touiller*, 'stir', from Latin *tudiculare* 'crush, stir']

rat·bag *noun Brit. slang* an unpleasant or disgusting person.

ratch·et ● *noun* **1** a set of teeth on the edge of a bar or wheel in which a device engages to ensure motion in one direction only. **2** a wheel with a rim so toothed. ● *verb* (**ratch·et·ed**, **ratch·et·ing**) **1** *transitive* **a** provide with a ratchet. **b** make into a ratchet. **2** *transitive & intransitive* (often foll. by *up*) move as under the control of a ratchet (*ratcheted interest rates up another notch*). [French *rochet* blunt lance head, bobbin, ratchet, etc., prob. ultimately from Germanic]

rate¹ ● *noun* **1** a stated numerical proportion between two sets of things (the second usu. expressed as unity), esp. as a measure of amount or degree (*moving at a rate of 50 miles per hour*) or as the basis of calculating an amount or value (*rate of taxation*). **2** a fixed or appropriate charge or cost or value; a measure of this (*postal rates; the rate for the job*). **3** rapidity of movement or change (*travelling at a great rate; prices increasing at a dreadful rate*). **4** class or rank (*first-rate*). **5** *Brit.* (often in *pl.*) a property tax levied by local authorities. ● *verb* **1** *transitive* **a** estimate the worth or value of (*I do not rate him very highly; how do you rate your chances of winning?*). **b** assign a fixed value to (a coin or metal) in relation to a monetary standard. **c** assign a value to (work, the power of a machine, etc.). **2** *transitive* consider; regard as (*I rate them among my benefactors*). **3** *intransitive* **a** (often foll. by *as*) rank or be rated. **b** rank highly; be of importance or esteemed (*I guess I just don't rate*). **4** *transitive* be worthy of, deserve. **5** *transitive* place (a film etc.) in a category relative to its suitability for viewing. **b** *Naut.* place (a sailor) in a specified class (*compare* RATING¹ 5). □ **at any rate** in any case, whatever happens. **at this** (or **that**) **rate** if this example is typical or this assumption is true. [Old French and medieval Latin *rata* (from Latin *pro rata parte* or *portione* 'according to the proportional share') from *ratus*, past participle of *rēri* 'reckon']

rate² *transitive verb* scold angrily. [Middle English: origin unknown]

rate·able *adjective* (also **rat·able**) able to be rated or estimated.

rate of return *noun* the annual amount of income from an investment, expressed as a percentage of the original investment.

rate·pay·er *noun* **1** *Cdn & Brit.* a person paying local property taxes. **2** *US* a customer of a public utility.

rater *noun* **1** a person or thing that rates (*bond rater*). **2** a person or thing rated (*second-rater*).

rat fink *noun N Amer. slang* = FINK *noun*.

rath·er /ˈraðər/ *adverb* **1** (often foll. by *than*) by preference; for choice (*would rather not go; would rather stay than go*). **2** (usu. foll. by *than*) more truly; as a more likely alternative (*is stupid rather than honest*). **3 a** more precisely (*a book, or rather, a pamphlet*). **b** (often foll. by *than*) on the contrary, instead (of) (*it wasn't cold—rather, it was quite warm; rescheduled for Friday rather than today*). **4** slightly; to some extent; somewhat (*became rather drunk; I rather think you should do it*). **5** /-ˈðɑːr/ *Brit.* (as an emphatic response) indeed, assuredly (*Did you like it? – Rather!*). □ **had**

rather would rather. [Old English *hrathor*, comparative of *hræthe* (adv.) from *hræth* (adj.)]

rat·hole *noun N Amer.* **1** a cramped or squalid building etc. **2** a seemingly bottomless hole, esp. one down which expenditures disappear.

raths·keller /ˈrɒtsˌkelər, ˈrats-/ *noun* esp. *US* a bar or restaurant in a basement. [German, = (restaurant in) town-hall cellar]

rat·ify /ˈratɪˌfaɪ/ *transitive verb* (**-fies**, **-fied**) confirm or accept (an agreement made in one's name) by formal consent, signature, etc. □ **rati·fi·able** *adjective* **rati·fi·ca·tion** *noun* **rati·fi·er** *noun* [Old French *ratifier* from medieval Latin *ratificare* (as RATE¹)]

rat·ing¹ *noun* **1 a** the act or an instance of placing in a rank or class or assigning a value to. **b** the class, rank, or value assigned. **2** the estimated standing of a person, organization, etc. as regards credit etc. **3** the relative popularity of a broadcast program as determined by the estimated size of the audience. **4** any of the classes into which racing yachts are distributed by tonnage. **5 a** *Cdn & Brit.* a non-commissioned sailor. **b** a person's position or class on a ship's books.

rat·ing² *noun* an angry reprimand.

ratio /ˈreɪʃiːoʊ, -ʃoʊ/ *noun* (*pl.* **ratios**) **1** the quantitative relation between two similar magnitudes determined by the number of times one contains the other integrally or fractionally (*in the ratio of three to two; the ratios 1:5 and 20:100 are the same*). **2** a proportional relationship between things not precisely measurable. [Latin (as RATE¹)]

rati·ocin·ate /ˌratiˈɒsɪˌneɪt, ˌraʃi-/ *intransitive verb* *literary* go through logical processes, reason, esp. using syllogisms. □ **rati·ocin·a·tion** *noun* **rati·ocin·a·tive** /-nətɪv/ *adjective* [Latin *ratiocinari* (as RATIO)]

ra·tion /ˈraʃən/ ● *noun* **1** a fixed official allowance of food, clothing, etc., in a time of shortage. **2** (foll. by *of*) a single portion of provisions, fuel, clothing, etc. **3** (usu. in *pl.*) a fixed daily allowance of food, esp. in the armed forces. **4** (in *pl.*) provisions. ● *transitive verb* **1** limit (persons or provisions) to a fixed ration. **2** (usu. foll. by *out*) share out (food etc.) in fixed quantities. [French from Italian *razione* or Spanish *ración* from Latin *ratio -onis* reckoning, RATIO]

ration·al /ˈraʃənəl/ *adjective* **1** of or based on reasoning or reason. **2** sensible, sane, moderate; not foolish or absurd or extreme. **3** endowed with reason, reasoning. **4** rejecting what is unreasonable or cannot be tested by reason in religion or custom. **5** *Math.* (of a quantity or ratio) expressible as a ratio of whole numbers. □ **ration·al·ity** /-ˈnalɪti/ *noun* **ration·al·ly** *adverb* [orig. = 'having the ability to reason', from Latin *rationalis*, from *ratio* 'reckoning, reason']

ration·ale /ˌraʃəˈnal/ *noun* **1** (often foll. by *for*, *of*) the fundamental reason or logical basis of anything. **2** a reasoned exposition; a statement of reasons. [modern Latin, neuter of Latin *rationalis*: see RATIONAL]

ration·al·ism *noun* **1** *Philos.* the theory that reason is the foundation of certainty in knowledge (*compare* EMPIRICISM, SENSATIONALISM 2). **2** *Theol.* the practice of treating reason as the ultimate authority in religion. **3** a belief in reason rather than religion as a guiding principle in life. **4** the principle or practice of using reasoning and calculation as a basis for analysis, a course of action, etc. □ **ration·al·ist** *noun* **ration·al·is·tic** *adjective* **ration·al·is·tic·ally** *adverb*

ration·al·ize *verb* (also esp. *Brit.* **-ise**) **1 a** *transitive* offer or subconsciously adopt a rational but specious explanation of (one's behaviour or attitude). **b** *intransitive* explain one's behaviour or attitude in this way. **2** *transitive* make logical and consistent. **3** *transitive* make (a business etc.) more efficient by reorganizing it to reduce or eliminate waste of labour, time, or materials; downsize. **4** *transitive* (often foll. by *away*) explain or explain away rationally. **5** *transitive Math.* clear of irrational numbers. **6** *intransitive* be or act as a rationalist. □ **ration·al·iz·a·tion** *noun* **ration·al·iz·er** *noun*

ration book *noun* (also **ration card**) a document entitling the holder to a ration.

rat·ite /ˈratʌɪt/ ● *adjective* (of a bird) having a keelless breastbone, and unable to fly (*opp.* CARINATE). ● *noun* a flightless bird, e.g. an ostrich, emu, cassowary, etc. [Latin *ratis* raft]

rat kangaroo *noun* any of various small rat-like marsupials of the family Potoroidae, having kangaroo-like hind limbs for jumping.

rat·line *noun* (usu. in *pl.*) any of the small lines fastened across a sailing ship's shrouds like ladder rungs. [Middle English: origin unknown]

ra·toon /rəˈtuːn/ ● *noun* a new shoot springing from a root of sugar cane etc. after cropping. ● *intransitive verb* send up ratoons. [Spanish *retoño* sprout]

rat pack *noun* a group of associates, friends, etc.

rat race *noun* a fiercely competitive struggle for position, power, etc.

rat run *noun* *informal* a route on minor roads used by traffic to avoid congestion at peak periods.

rats *interjection* expressing annoyance, frustration, disappointment, etc.

rat's nest *noun* *N Amer.* *informal* a muddled or confused place or situation.

rat-tail *noun* (also **rat's tail**) a thing shaped like the tail of a rat, i.e. long, slender, and tapering (also *attributive* or as **rat-tailed** *adjective*: *rat-tail haircut; rat-tailed fir; rat-tail comb*).

rat·tan /rəˈtan/ *noun* any East Indian climbing palm of the genus *Calamus* etc. with long thin jointed pliable stems often used to make wickerwork, furniture etc. [earlier *rot(t)ang* from Malay *rōtan* prob. from *raut pare*]

rat-tat-tat *noun* (also **rat-a-tat-tat, rat-a-tat**) a knocking or rapping staccato sound (also *attributive*: *rat-tat-tat dialogue*). [imitative]

rat·ter *noun* **1** a dog or other animal that hunts rats. **2** *slang* a person who betrays a cause, party, friend, etc.

Ratti·gan, Sir Ter·ence (Mer·vyn) (1911–77), English dramatist. His plays include *The Winslow Boy* (1946), concerning a father's fight to clear the name of his accused son, *The Browning Version* (1948), about a repressed and unpopular schoolmaster, and *Ross* (1960), based on the life of T. E. Lawrence.

Rat·tle, Sir Simon (Denis), British conductor. Principal conductor with the City of Birmingham Symphony Orchestra 1980–91, he became chief conductor of the Berlin Philharmonic Orchestra in 2000, and its artistic director in 2002.

rat·tle ● *verb* **1 a** *intransitive* give out a rapid succession of short sharp hard sounds, usu. through being shaken or vibrating against something. **b** *transitive* make (a chair, window, dishes, etc.) do this. **c** *intransitive* cause such sounds by shaking something (*rattled at the door*). **2** *intransitive* move with a rattling noise. **3 a** *transitive* (usu. foll. by *off*) say or recite rapidly. **b** *intransitive* (usu. foll. by *on*) talk in a lively thoughtless way. **4** *transitive* (also in *passive*) *informal* disconcert, alarm, fluster, make nervous, frighten. ● *noun* **1** a rattling sound. **2** an instrument or plaything made to rattle esp. in order to amuse babies or to give an alarm. **3** the set of horny rings in a rattlesnake's tail. **4** a plant with seeds that rattle in their cases when ripe (*red rattle; yellow rattle*). **5** uproar, bustle, noisy gaiety, racket. **6 a** a noisy flow of words. **b** empty chatter, trivial talk. **7** *Cdn* (*Nfld & NS*) rapids or fast-flowing water. **8** *archaic* a lively or thoughtless incessant talker. □ **rattle someone's cage** *informal* make someone feel angry or annoyed. □ **rat·tly** *adjective* [Middle English, prob. from Middle Dutch & Low German *ratelen* (imitative)]

rat·tler *noun* *informal* a rattlesnake.

rattle·snake *noun* any of various poisonous snakes of the family Viperidae of the Americas, esp. of the genus *Crotalus* or *Sistrurus*, with a rattling structure of horny rings in its tail.

rattle·trap *informal* ● *noun* a rickety old vehicle etc. ● *adjective* rickety.

rat·tling ● *adjective* **1** that rattles. **2** brisk, vigorous (*a rattling pace*). ● *adverb* remarkably (*a rattling good story*). □ **rat·tling·ly** *adverb*

ratty *adjective* (**rat·ti·er, rat·ti·est**) **1** relating to or infested with rats. **2** *informal* shabby, tattered, wretched. **3** *Brit.* *informal* irritable or angry.

rau·cous *adjective* harsh-sounding, loud and hoarse. □ **rau·cous·ly** *adverb* **rau·cous·ness** *noun* [Latin *raucus*]

Rau·dot /roːˈdoː/ **1 Antoine-Denis** (1679–1737), French colonial administrator. Appointed intendant of New France jointly with his father in 1705, he devoted his energy to the depressed economy of the colony, attempting to develop agriculture, fishing, and lumbering. Handicapped both by the War of the Spanish Succession and his father's feud with Governor Vaudreuil, he requested a recall to France in 1710. **2** his father, **Jacques** (1638–1728), French colonial administrator. Appointed joint intendant with his son in 1705 after a legal career, he concentrated on the justice and social systems of New France, reforming among other things the seigneurial, judicial, educational, and agricultural systems. He held Canadians in low esteem, and spent the last few years before his departure for France in 1711 feuding with Governor Vaudreuil.

raunch *noun* *slang* **1** earthiness, bawdiness, provocative sexuality. **2** the sound of a distorted electric guitar. [20th c.: origin unknown]

raunchy *adjective* (**raunch·i·er, raunch·i·est**) *informal* **1** coarse, earthy; sexually provocative. **2 a** (of the sound of an electric guitar) distorted. **b** (of music) featuring raunchy guitars. **3** esp. *US* slovenly, grubby. □ **raunch·i·ly** *adverb* **raunch·i·ness** *noun* [20th c.: origin unknown]

Rau·schen·berg /ˈrauʃənbɜrg/ **Rob·ert** (born Milton Rauschenberg) (b.1925), US painter and experimental artist, who was a pioneer of pop art; his works include *Charlene* (1954), *Monogram* (1959), and *Soundings* (1968).

rav·age /ˈravɪdʒ/ ● *transitive & intransitive verb* devastate, plunder; damage. ● *noun* **1** the act or an instance of ravaging; devastation, damage. **2** (usu. in *pl.*; foll. by *of*) destructive effect (*survived the ravages of winter*). [French *ravage(r)* alteration of *ravine* rush of water]

rave ● *verb* **1** *intransitive* talk wildly or furiously in or as in delirium. **2** *intransitive* (usu. foll. by *about, over*) speak with rapturous admiration; go into raptures. **3** *intransitive* (of the sea, wind, etc.) howl, roar. **4** *transitive & intransitive* *Brit.* *informal* enjoy oneself freely. **5** *intransitive* *slang* attend a rave. ● *noun* **1 a** (usu. *attributive*) *informal* a highly enthusiastic review of a film, play, etc. (*a rave review*). **b** an enthusiastic reaction (*gets raves every time she makes that cake*). **2** *slang* **a** a large often illicit all-night party or event, often held in a warehouse or open field, with dancing to loud fast electronic music (also *attributive*: *rave music; rave culture*). **b** *Brit.* (also **rave-up**) a lively party. **3** the sound of the wind etc. raving. □ **ravey** *adjective* (in sense 2a of *noun*). [Middle English, prob. from Old Northern French *raver*, related to (Middle) Low German *reven* 'be senseless, rave']

Ravel /raˈvel/ **(Mau·rice) Jo·seph** (1875–1937), French composer. His works have a distinctive tone colour derived from the use of unresolved dissonances; major works include the ballet *Daphnis and Chloé* (1912), the opera *L'Enfant et les sortilèges* (1925), and the orchestral work *Boléro* (1928).

ravel /ˈravəl/ ● *verb* (**rav·elled, rav·el·ling**; also esp. *US* **rav·eled, rav·el·ing**) **1** *transitive & intransitive* entangle or become entangled or knotted. **2** *transitive* confuse or complicate (a question or problem). **3** *intransitive* fray out. **4** *transitive* (often foll. by *out*) disentangle, unravel, distinguish the separate threads or subdivisions of. ● *noun* **1** a tangle or knot. **2** a complication. **3** a frayed or loose end. [prob. from Dutch *ravelen* tangle, fray out]

rav·elin /ˈravlɪn/ *noun* *hist.* an outwork of fortifications, with two faces forming a salient angle. [French from obsolete Italian *ravellino*, of unknown origin]

rav·el·ling *noun* (also **rav·eling**) a thread from fabric which is frayed or unravelled.

raven[1] ● *noun* **1** a large glossy blue-black crow, *Corvus corax*, feeding chiefly on carrion etc., having a hoarse cry, and noted for its craftiness. **2** (**Raven**) a hero and trickster figure in the folklore of Pacific Northwest Aboriginal peoples. ● *adjective* glossy black (*raven tresses*). [Old English *hræfn* from Germanic]

raven[2] *verb* **1** *intransitive* **a** plunder. **b** prowl for prey (*ravening beast*). **2 a** *transitive* devour voraciously. **b** *intransitive* (usu. foll. by *for*) have a ravenous appetite. **c** *intransitive* (often foll. by *on*) feed voraciously. [Old French *raviner* ravage, ultimately from Latin *rapina* RAPINE]

Rav·enna /rəˈvenə/ a city near the Adriatic coast in NE central Italy; pop. (2001) 138,204. It is noted for its ancient mosaics dating from the early Christian period.

rav·en·ous /ˈravənəs/ *adjective* **1** very hungry, famished. **2** (of hunger, eagerness, etc., or of an animal) voracious. **3** rapacious. □ **rav·en·ous·ly** *adverb* [Old French *ravineus* (as RAVEN[2])]

raver *noun* **1** *slang* a person who attends raves. **2** *Brit.* *informal* an uninhibited pleasure-loving person. **3** a person who raves; a madman or madwoman.

rave-up *noun* *N Amer.* a fast, loud, or danceable piece of pop music.

ravin /ˈravɪn/ *noun* *archaic* **1** robbery, plundering. **2** the seizing and devouring of prey. **3** prey. [Old French *ravine* from Latin *rapina* RAPINE]

rav·ine /rəˈviːn/ *noun* a narrow, steep-sided valley, esp. one formed by erosion by running water. □ **rav·ined** *adjective* [French (as RAVIN)]

rav·ing ● *noun* (usu. in *pl.*) wild or delirious talk. ● *adjective* **1** delirious, frenzied. **2** *informal* as an intensifier (*a raving beauty*). ● *adverb* *informal* as an intensifier (*raving mad*).

ravi·oli /ˌraviˈoːli/ *noun* small squares of pasta stuffed with minced meat, cheese, spinach, etc. [Italian]

Ravi River /ˈrɒvi/ a river in the north of the Indian subcontinent, one of the headwaters of the Indus, which rises in the Himalayas in Himachel Pradesh, NW India, and flows for 725 km (450 miles) generally southwestward into Pakistan, where it empties into the Chenab River just north of Multan. It is one of the five rivers that gave Punjab its name.

rav·ish *transitive verb* **1** commit rape on. **2** enrapture; fill with delight. **3** *archaic* **a** carry off (a person or thing) by force. **b** (of death, circumstances, etc.) take from life or from sight. □ **rav·ish·er** *noun*

rav·ish·ment *noun* ¶ Do not confuse *ravish* with *ravage*. [Old French *ravir*, ultimately from Latin *rapere* seize]

rav·ish·ing *adjective* **1** entrancing, delightful. **2** (of a person) extraordinarily beautiful. □ **rav·ish·ing·ly** *adverb*

raw ● *adjective* **1** (of food) uncooked. **2** in the natural state; not processed (*raw sewage*). **3** (of statistics, data, etc.) not analyzed or processed. **4** (of a person) inexperienced, untrained; new to an activity (*raw recruits*). **5 a** stripped of skin; having the flesh exposed. **b** sensitive to the touch from having the flesh exposed. **c** abnormally sensitive (*touched a raw nerve*). **6** (of the atmosphere, day, etc.) chilly and damp. **7 a** crude in artistic quality; lacking finish. **b** not controlled or refined (*raw sex; raw emotion*). **8** (of the edge of cloth) without hem or selvage. **9** (of liquor) undiluted. **10** (of silk) as reeled from cocoons. **11** (of milk) not pasteurized. **12** (of leather) untanned. **13** (of film or video footage etc.) unedited. ● *noun* a raw place on a person's or horse's body. □ **in the raw 1** in its natural state without mitigation (*life in the raw*). **2** naked. □ **rawly** *adverb* **raw·ness** *noun* [Old English *hrēaw* from Germanic]

Rawal·pindi /rɒlˈpɪndi/ a city in Punjab province, N Pakistan, in the foothills of the Himalayas; pop. (1998) 1,406,200. It was the interim capital of Pakistan, 1959–67, during the construction of Islamabad.

raw-boned *adjective* gaunt and bony.

raw deal *noun* harsh or unfair treatment.

raw·hide *noun* **1** untanned hide. **2** a rope or whip of this.

raw material *noun* material from which products are manufactured.

raw sienna *noun* a brownish-yellow ferruginous earth used as a pigment.

raw umber *noun* umber in its natural state, dark yellow in colour.

Ray ▶ **1 John** (1627–1705), English naturalist. He was the first to classify flowering plants into monocotyledons and dicotyledons, and established the species as the basic taxonomic unit; his major work was the three-volume *Historia Plantarum* (1686–1704). **2 Man** (born Emmanuel Rudnitsky) (1890–1976), US photographer, painter, and filmmaker. A leading figure in the US and European Dada and surrealist movements, he pioneered the photogram or 'rayograph', placing objects on sensitized paper and exposing them to light; his photographs include *Violon d'Ingres* (1924). **3** /ˈraɪ/ **Sat·ya·jit** (1921–92), Indian film director. His films, often set in his native Bengal, include the *Apu* trilogy and *The Home and the World* (1984).

Ray, Cape the southwesternmost point of the island of Newfoundland, situated near Channel-Port aux Basques. [ultimately from Portuguese *rei* king]

ray¹ ● *noun* **1** a single line or narrow beam of light from a small or distant source. **2** a straight line in which radiation travels to a given point. **3** (in *pl.*) radiation of a specified type (*gamma rays; X-rays*). **4** a trace or beginning of an enlightening or cheering influence (*a ray of hope*). **5 a** any of a set of radiating lines or parts of things. **b** the part of a straight line extending from a point indefinitely in one direction. **6** the marginal portion of a composite flower, e.g. a daisy. **7 a** a radial division of a starfish. **b** each of a set of bones etc. supporting a fish's fin. ● *verb* **1** *intransitive* (foll. by *out, forth*) (of light, thought, emotion, etc.) issue in or as if in rays. **2** *intransitive & transitive* radiate. □ **catch** (or **get**, **bag** etc.) **some rays** *N Amer. informal* sunbathe. □ **rayed** *adjective* **ray·less** *adjective* [Old French *rai* from Latin *radius*: see RADIUS]

ray² *noun* a large cartilaginous fish of the order Batoidea, with a broad flat body, wing-like pectoral fins and a long slender tail. [Old French *raie* from Latin *raia*]

ray³ *var. of* RE².

ray gun *noun* (esp. in science fiction) a gun causing injury or damage by the emission of a ray or beam of energy.

Ray·leigh /ˈreɪli/ **John Wil·liam Strutt, 3rd Baron** (1842–1919), English physicist. He published a major work on acoustics, *The Theory of Sound*, carried out pioneering work on atmospheric airglow and blackbody radiation, and with Sir W. Ramsay measured the constituents of the atmosphere, which led to the discovery of argon and other inert gases; he received the Nobel Prize for physics in 1904.

Ray·naud's disease /reɪˈnoːz/ *noun* (also **Raynaud's phenomenon**; **Raynaud's syndrome**) an ill-defined condition characterized by spasm of arteries in the extremities, esp. the digits, leading to pallor, pain, numbness, and in severe cases gangrene. [M. *Raynaud*, French physician d.1881]

rayon *noun* any of various textile fibres or fabrics made from viscose. [arbitrary from RAY¹]

Rayside-Balfour a former town in north central Ontario, northwest of Sudbury, now part of Greater Sudbury; pop. (2001) 15,046. [J. *Rayside*

+ W. D. *Balfour*, Liberal Party members in the Ontario Legislature *c.*1882–94]

ray tracing *noun* *Computing* the creation of realistic three-dimensional graphics by calculating the path of each theoretical beam of light in the image to create precise shadows, reflections, and refractions. □ **ray-traced** *adjective*

raze *transitive verb* **1** completely destroy; tear down (*razed to the ground*). **2** erase; scratch out (esp. in abstract senses). [Middle English *rase* = wound slightly, from Old French *raser* shave close, ultimately from Latin *radere ras-* scrape]

Ra·zil·ly /raziˈjiː/ **Isaac de** (1587–1635), French naval captain and colonial administrator. In 1526, after wide-ranging naval service, he wrote a memorandum to Cardinal Richelieu calling for the expansion of French colonies in N America. In 1632 he was sent to re-establish the colony of Acadia, which had been held for three years by the British; he fulfilled this task well until his sudden death in 1635.

razor ● *noun* an instrument with a sharp blade or blades used in cutting hair or bristles esp. from the skin. ● *transitive verb* **1** use a razor on. **2 a** shave; cut down close. **b** slice.

razor·back *noun* an animal with a sharp ridged back, esp. a semi-wild hog of the southern US.

razor·bill *noun* (also **razor-billed auk**) an auk, *Alca torda*, with a sharp-edged bill, breeding along the coasts of the N Atlantic.

razor blade *noun* a blade used in a razor, esp. a flat piece of metal with a sharp edge or edges used in a safety razor.

razor clam *noun* any of various bivalve molluscs of the family Solenidae, with a shell like the handle of a straight razor.

razor cut ● *noun* a haircut made with a razor. ● *transitive verb* cut (hair) using this method.

razor's edge *noun* (also **razor edge**) **1** a sharp edge. **2** a critical situation (*found themselves on a razor's edge*). **3** a sharp line of division. □ **razor-edged** *adjective*

razor-sharp *adjective* extremely sharp.

razor-thin *adjective* extremely thin.

razor wire *noun* a type of coiled wire with extremely sharp edges or points, used as a barrier or run along the top of walls etc.

razz *N Amer. slang* ● *noun* = RASPBERRY 3. ● *transitive verb* tease, ridicule. [*razzberry*, corruption of RASPBERRY]

razzle-dazzle *noun* (also **raz·zle**) esp. *N Amer. informal* **1** glitter, showiness, pageantry; a flamboyant often insincere display, as of publicity (also *attributive*: *razzle-dazzle costumes*). **2** glamorous excitement; bustle. [reduplication of DAZZLE]

razz·ma·tazz *noun* (also *Brit.* **razza·ma·tazz**) *informal* = RAZZLE-DAZZLE. [prob. alteration of RAZZLE-DAZZLE]

Rb *symbol Chem.* the element rubidium.

RBI /ɑrbiːˈaɪ, *informal* ˈrɪbi/ *noun* (*pl.* same or **RBIs**) *Baseball* **1** run batted in (*pl.* **runs batted in**), a run scored because of a batter's hit, sacrifice fly, walk, etc., and counted among the batter's statistics (*leads the team with 57 RBIs*). **2** (*attributive*) designating a hit etc. which drives a runner home to score a run (*RBI double*). [abbreviation]

RC *abbreviation* **1** Roman Catholic. **2** Red Cross.

RCAF *abbreviation hist.* Royal Canadian Air Force.

RCL *abbreviation* Royal Canadian Legion.

RCM *abbreviation Cdn (Que.)* REGIONAL COUNTY MUNICIPALITY.

RCMP ● *abbreviation* Royal Canadian Mounted Police. ● *noun Cdn informal* an RCMP officer.

RCN *abbreviation hist.* Royal Canadian Navy.

RCNVR *abbreviation hist.* Royal Canadian Naval Volunteer Reserve.

Rd. *abbreviation* Road.

RDA *abbreviation* recommended daily allowance (for a vitamin, mineral, etc.).

RDI *abbreviation* recommended daily intake (for a vitamin, mineral, etc.).

rDNA *abbreviation* RECOMBINANT DNA.

RE *abbreviation* Royal Engineers.

Re¹ *var. of* RA¹.

Re² *symbol Chem.* the element rhenium.

re¹ /riː, reɪ/ *preposition* **1** in the matter of (as the first word in a heading). **2** *informal* about, concerning. [Latin, ablative of *res* thing]

re² /reɪ/ *noun* (also **ray**) *Music* **1** (in tonic sol-fa) the second note of a major scale. **2** the note D in the fixed-do system. [Middle English *re* from Latin *resonare*: see GAMUT]

re- *prefix* **1** attachable to almost any verb or its derivative, meaning: **a** once more; afresh, anew (*readjust; renumber*). **b** back; with return to a previous state (*reassemble*; *reverse*). ¶ A hyphen is normally used when the word begins with *e* (*re-enact*), or to distinguish the compound from a more familiar one-word form (*re-form* = form again). **2** (also **red-** before a vowel, as in *redolent*) in verbs and verbal derivatives denoting: **a** in return; mutually (*react*; *resemble*). **b** opposition (*repel*; *resist*). **c** behind or after (*relic*; *remain*). **d** retirement or secrecy (*recluse*; *reticence*). **e** off, away, down (*recede*; *relegate*; *repress*). **f** frequentative or intensive force (*redouble*; *refine*; *resplendent*). **g** negative force (*recant*; *reveal*). [Latin *re-*, *red-*, again, back, etc.]

're *abbreviation informal* (usu. after pronouns) are (*we're*; *you're*).

re·absorb *transitive verb* absorb again. □ **re·absorp·tion** *noun*

reach ● *verb* **1** *intransitive & transitive* (often foll. by *out*) stretch out; extend. **2** *intransitive* stretch out a limb, the hand, etc.; make a reaching motion or effort. **3** *intransitive* (often foll. by *for*) make a motion or effort to touch or get hold of, or to attain (*reached for his mug*). **4** *transitive* get as far as; arrive at (*reached Sudbury at lunchtime*; *your letter reached me today*). **5** *transitive* get to or attain (a specified point) on a scale (*the temperature reached 40°*; *the number of applications reached 100*). **6** *transitive & intransitive* extend as far as (*the curtains reach the floor*; *shorts that reached to his knees*). **7** *transitive* succeed in achieving; attain (*have reached agreement*). **8** *transitive* make contact with (*was out all day and could not be reached*). **9** *transitive* (of a broadcast, broadcasting station, etc.) be received by. **10** *transitive* succeed in influencing or having the required effect on (*could not manage to reach their audience*). **11** *transitive* (often foll. by *down*) hand, pass (*could you reach me down that can of cat food*). **12** *intransitive Naut.* sail with the wind abeam or abaft the beam. ● *noun* **1** the extent to which a hand etc. can be reached out, influence exerted, motion carried out, mental powers used, etc. **2** an act of reaching out. **3 a** a continuous extent, esp. a stretch of river between two bends, or an expanse of land etc. **b** (usu. in *pl.*) a level or stratum (*the higher reaches of the organization*). **4** *Naut.* a distance traversed in reaching. **5** the number of people who watch a specified television channel or listen to a specified radio station at any time during a specified period. □ **out of reach** not able to be reached or attained. □ **reach·able** *adjective* **reach·er** *noun* [Old English *ræcan*, from West Germanic]

re·acquaint *transitive verb & reflexive* (usu. foll. by *with*) make (a person or oneself) acquainted again. □ **re·acquaint·ance** *noun*

re·acquire *transitive verb* acquire anew. □ **re·acqui·si·tion** *noun*

react *verb* **1** *intransitive* (foll. by *to*) respond to a stimulus; undergo a change or show behaviour due to some influence (*how did they react to the news?*). **2** *intransitive* (often foll. by *against*) be actuated by repulsion to; tend in a reverse or contrary direction. **3** *intransitive* (often foll. by *upon*) produce a reciprocal or responsive effect; act upon the agent (*they react upon each other*). **4** *intransitive* (foll. by *with*) *Chem. & Physics* (of a substance or particle) be the cause of activity or interaction with another (*nitrous oxide reacts with the metal*). **5** *transitive* (foll. by *with*) *Chem.* cause (a substance) to react with another. [RE- + ACT or medieval Latin *reagere react-* (as RE-, Latin *agere* do, act)]

re-act *transitive verb* act (a part) again.

re·act·ance *noun Electricity* a component of impedance in an AC circuit, due to capacitance or inductance or both.

re·act·ant *noun Chem.* a substance that takes part in and undergoes change during a reaction.

re·ac·tion *noun* **1** the act or an instance of reacting; a responsive or reciprocal action. **2 a** a responsive feeling (*what was your reaction to the news?*). **b** an immediate or first impression. **3** the occurrence of a (physical or emotional) condition after a period of its opposite. **4** a bodily response to an external stimulus, e.g. a drug. **5** a tendency to oppose change or to advocate return to a former system, esp. in politics. **6** the interaction of substances undergoing chemical change. **7** *Physics* a force that is equal in magnitude but opposite in direction to some other force.

re·ac·tion·ary usu. *derogatory* ● *adjective* tending to oppose (esp. political) change and advocate return to a former system. ● *noun* (*pl.* **-aries**) a reactionary person.

re·acti·vate *transitive verb* restore to a state of activity; bring into action again. □ **re·acti·va·tion** *noun*

re·act·ive *adjective* **1** showing reaction. **2** reacting rather than taking the initiative. **3** having a tendency to react chemically. **4** of or relating to reactance. □ **re·ac·tiv·ity** *noun*

re·act·or *noun* **1** a person or thing that reacts. **2** (in full **nuclear reactor**) an apparatus or structure in which a controlled nuclear chain reaction releases energy. **3** *Electricity* a component used to provide reactance, esp. an inductor. **4** an apparatus for the chemical reaction of substances. **5** *Med.* a person who has a reaction to a drug etc.

Read, Ken·neth John ('Ken') (b.1955), US-born Canadian alpine

skier, raised in Calgary. He won five consecutive Canadian national championships (1975–80), and had five World Cup victories during the same period. Since retiring from skiing in 1983, he has been a television commentator and amateur sports administrator.

read¹ ● *verb* (*past* and *past participle* **read**) **1** *transitive & intransitive* look at and understand the meaning of written or printed words or symbols (*she has just learned to read*). **2** *transitive & intransitive* examine or peruse printed matter for recreation or personal enjoyment (*reading helps me relax*). **3** *transitive* (often foll. by *off*, *out*, *aloud*) render (written or printed matter) in speech (*the judge read off the charges*). **4** *transitive* **a** interpret (letters, words, sentences) by passing fingers over engraved or embossed characters or Braille. **b** interpret (letters, words, sentences) by examining a person's hand gestures as sign language. **c** interpret speech by observing the movements of (a speaker's lips). **5** *transitive* interpret or assess (*read a person's mood*; *the quarterback reads the defence*). **6** *transitive* interpret (a statement or action) in a certain sense (*my silence is not to be read as consent*). **7** *transitive* **a** (often foll. by *that* + clause) learn a piece of information by examining written or printed material (*I read somewhere that you are leaving*). **b** learn a piece of information by examining other signs etc. (*I knew you were leaving, I read it in your eyes*). **8** *transitive* **a** (of a meter or other recording instrument) show (a specified figure etc.) (*the thermometer reads 20°*). **b** inspect and record elsewhere the figure shown on such an instrument (*read the meter*). **9** *transitive* **a** receive and understand the words of a person by radio or telephone. **b** understand the meaning of a speaker (*don't worry, I read you loud and clear*). **10** *intransitive* give a certain impression when read (*it reads persuasively*; *it reads like a parody*). **11** *transitive Computing* sense and retrieve or interpret data from a form of storage or input medium. **12** *transitive* **a** interpret (cards, a person's palm, etc.) as a fortune teller. **b** interpret (a map, chart, graph, etc.). **c** guess (a person's mind, thoughts). **d** interpret (the sky) as an astrologer or meteorologist. **13** *transitive* check the correctness of and emend (a printed text). **14** *transitive* **a** (of a text) have at a particular place (*reads 'battery' not 'buttery'*). **b** replace (a word, etc.) with a more appropriate one (*for 'illitterate' read 'illiterate'*; *he calls himself 'financially conservative' (read 'cheap'!)*). **15** *transitive* interpret and understand (musical symbols). **16** *Brit.* **a** *transitive* study by reading (esp. a subject at university). **b** *intransitive* carry out a course of study by reading (*is reading for the Bar*). ● *noun* **1** a period or act of reading. **2** a book etc. as regards its readability (*is a really good read*). **3** (usu. foll. by *on*) an interpretation (*people often get the wrong read on things*). □ **read between the lines** look for or find hidden meaning (in a document etc.). **read a person like a book** understand a person's motives etc. **read into** find or assume meanings in the words of a speaker or writer which are not intended (*you're reading too much into her comment*). **read my lips** *N Amer. informal* listen carefully (*read my lips: I'm going home!*). **read back** read aloud (a message just received) so that the sender can check its accuracy. **read up on** make a special study of (a subject). [Old English *rædan* advise, consider, discern, from Germanic]

read² *adjective* (often in *combination*) educated or versed in a subject (esp. literature) by reading (*a well-read person*; *was widely read in law*). □ **take as read** accept without reading or discussing.

read·able *adjective* **1** able to be read; legible. **2** interesting or pleasant to read. **3** (usu. in *combination*) (of data) able to be processed (by a machine, computer, human, etc.). □ **read·abil·ity** *noun*

re-address *transitive verb* **1** change the address of (a letter or parcel). **2** address (a problem etc.) anew. **3** speak or write to anew.

read·er *noun* **1** a person who reads or is reading. **2** a device that interprets data encoded on CD-ROMs, magnetic strips, bar codes, etc., usu. in order to display it in readable form on a monitor. **3 a** a book of written passages, exercises, etc. used in learning to read. **b** a collection of writings on a subject, used esp. as a supplement to a textbook. **4** a publisher's employee who reports on submitted manuscripts. **5** a person employed by a printer to correct proofs. **6** a person appointed to read aloud, esp. parts of a service in a church. **7** a device for producing an image that can be read from microfilm etc. **8** *Brit.* **a** a university lecturer of the highest grade below professor. **b** *US* a professor's assistant at some universities.

reader-friend·ly *adjective* **1** designating written material using a format and level of language that is manageable for the reader; pleasant to read. **2** (of a setting, environment, library, etc.) comfortable to read in; conducive to reading.

read·er·ly *adjective* of or pertaining to a reader or readers.

reader-response *noun* a branch of modern literary criticism that focuses on the responses of readers to literary works rather than on the works themselves considered as self-contained entities (also *attributive: reader-response criticism*).

reader·ship *noun* **1** the readers of a newspaper etc. **2** the number or extent of these.

read·i·ly *adverb* **1** without showing reluctance; willingly. **2** easily, promptly; without difficulty.

Read·ing /ˈrediŋ/ a town in S England, formerly part of Berkshire, on the Kennet River near its junction with the Thames; pop. (est. 1993) 137,700.

read·ing *noun* **1 a** the action or an instance of reading or perusing (*I have some reading to do*). **b** matter to be read (*have plenty of good reading with me*). **2** the ability to read (*her math is good but she must work on her reading*). **3** (*attributive*) **a** used for reading (*reading glasses*). **b** of or concerning the ability to read (*reading program; reading class*). **4** an event at which a work of fiction, poetry, etc., is read aloud, often by the author (*poetry reading*). **5** the formal public recital of (a will, a sermon, etc.). **6 a** a figure etc. shown by a meter or other recording instrument (*the thermometer doesn't give an accurate reading*). **b** an instance of measuring using a recording instrument (*use your light meter to take a reading before shooting*). **7 a** an analysis or interpretation of a written or printed text, poem, etc. (*a feminist reading of a work*). **b** an analysis of a situation, facts, etc. **c** an analysis of tarot cards, a person's palm, etc. in order to predict their future. **8** literary knowledge (*a person of wide reading*). **9** the interpretation (of a dramatic role, musical composition, etc.) as reflected in its performance. **10** each of the successive occasions on which a bill must be presented to a legislature for acceptance (*see also* FIRST READING, SECOND READING, THIRD READING). **11** a passage of scripture etc. to be read aloud at a religious service. **12** the version of a text, or the particular wording, conjectured or given by an editor etc.

reading room *noun* a room in a library in which patrons may read non-circulating books and other documents.

reading week *noun Cdn* a week usu. halfway through a university term during which there are no classes, intended for students to concentrate on their reading, research, etc.

re·adjust *verb* **1** *transitive* adjust again. **2** *intransitive* adapt to a new or former situation or surroundings. □ **re·adjust·ment** *noun*

re·admit *transitive verb* (**re·admit·ted**, **re·admit·ting**) admit again. □ **re·admis·sion** *noun*

read-only memory *noun Computing* a memory read at high speed but not capable of being changed by program instructions. Abbr.: **ROM**.

re·adopt *transitive verb* adopt again. □ **re·adop·tion** *noun*

read·out *noun* **1** the display of data by an automatic device in an understandable form. **2** a record of output produced by a computer or scientific instrument.

read-through *noun* an initial rehearsal of a play at which actors read their parts from scripts.

read/write *adjective Computing* capable of reading existing data and accepting alterations or further input (*compare* READ-ONLY MEMORY).

ready ● *adjective* (**read·i·er**, **read·i·est**) (usu. *predicative*) **1** with preparations complete; prepared (*dinner is ready*). **2** having reached a certain state or maturity (*I'm ready to settle down; I'll be ready for a nap*). **3** inclined, eager, or resolved (*she is always ready to complain; she's ready for anything*). **4** within reach; easily secured (*a ready source of income*). **5** fit for immediate use (*always has a glib answer ready at hand*). **6** immediate, unqualified (*found ready acceptance*). **7** prompt, quick, facile (*is always ready with excuses; has a ready wit*). **8** (foll. by *to* + infin.) about to do something (*a building ready to collapse*). **9** (in *combination*) prepared for (*battle-ready soldiers; oven-ready chickens*). ● *adverb* (done, prepared, etc.) beforehand (*ready assembled furniture*). ● *noun* (pl. **-ies**) *slang Brit.* (prec. by *the*) = READY CASH. ● *transitive verb* (**-ies**, **-ied**) make ready; prepare. □ **at the ready** ready for action. **get** (or **make**) **ready** prepare (*go upstairs and get ready for bed*). □ **read·i·ness** *noun* [Middle English rædi(g), re(a)di, from Old English ræde from Germanic]

ready cash *noun* (also **ready money**) **1** actual coin or banknotes. **2** payment on the spot.

ready-made ● *adjective* **1** (esp. of clothes) made in a standard size, not to the measurements of a particular customer (*a ready-made suit*). **2** (esp. of food) prepared in advance (*ready-made pizza dough*). **3** ideal or very appropriate and already available (*a ready-made solution*). ● *noun* something that is ready-made.

ready-mix ● *adjective* (also **ready-mixed**) having some or all of the constituents already mixed together (*ready-mix concrete; ready-mix cookie dough*). ● *noun* concrete with some or all of the constituents mixed together.

ready-to-wear ● *noun* clothing or an article of clothing that is made in standard sizes, not tailored to a particular customer. ● *adjective* pertaining to this style of clothing; ready-made.

re·affirm *transitive verb* affirm again. □ **re·affirm·a·tion** *noun*

Rea·gan /ˈreigən/ **Ron·ald (Wil·son)** (b.1911), US Republican politician, 40th president of the US 1981–9. He was a Hollywood actor before entering politics. During his presidency, military expenditure was increased, the Strategic Defense Initiative was launched, taxes and spending on social services were reduced, and the national budget deficit rose to record levels. □ **Rea·gan·esque** *adjective* **Rea·gan·ism** *noun*

Rea·gan·ite ● *noun* (in the US) an advocate or supporter of the policies and principles of Ronald Reagan. ● *adjective* of or pertaining to Reaganites or the policies and principles of Ronald Reagan.

Rea·gan·om·ics *plural noun* (treated as *sing.*) (in the US) the economic policies advocated by Ronald Reagan.

re·agent /riːˈeidʒənt/ *noun Chem.* **1** a substance used to test for the presence of another substance by means of the reaction which it produces. **2** any substance used in chemical reactions. [RE- + AGENT: compare REACT]

real¹ ● *adjective* **1** actually existing as a thing or occurring in fact; not imaginary or fictional. **2** (*attributive*) actual or true, not just appearing so (*what's the real reason you won't go out with me?*). **3** genuine, sincere, unfeigned (*she seemed upset but I don't know if her tears were real*). **4** not artificial (*real diamonds; real cream*). **5** (*attributive*) complete, utter, serious (*that's a real shame*). **6** *Law* (usu. *attributive*) consisting of or relating to immovable property such as land or houses (*real estate*) (*compare* PERSONAL PROPERTY). **7** (usu. *attributive*) appraised by purchasing power; adjusted for changes in the wages of money (*real value; income in real terms*). **8** *Philos.* having an absolute and necessary and not merely contingent existence. **9** *Math.* (of a quantity) having no imaginary part (*see* IMAGINARY 2). **10** *Optics* (of an image etc.) such that light actually passes through it. ● *adverb N Amer. & Scot. informal* really, very. ¶ Considered non-standard by many and should not be used in writing. □ **for real** *informal* **1** in earnest (*this isn't a practice, we're playing for real*). **2** genuine (*that's just acting, it's not for real*). **get real** *N Amer. slang* get serious. **the real McCoy** *see* McCOY. **the real thing** (also **the real deal**) (of an object or emotion) genuine, not illusory or inferior (*this isn't just a crush, this is the real thing*). □ **real·ness** *noun* [Anglo-French = Old French reel, Late Latin realis from Latin res thing]

real² /reiˈal/ *noun* **1** the basic monetary unit in Brazil, introduced in 1994, equal to 100 centavos. **2** *hist.* a former coin and monetary unit of various Spanish-speaking countries. [Spanish & Portuguese, noun use of *real* (adj.) (as ROYAL)]

real ale *noun Brit.* beer regarded as brewed in a traditional way, with secondary fermentation in the cask.

real estate *noun N Amer.* **1** (also **real property**) immovable property, such as land or houses, and the proprietary rights over these. **2** the business of buying and selling land, buildings, houses, etc. (*she's in real estate*). **3** *Computing* (esp. of memory, a disk, a screen, etc.) available space.

real estate agent *noun N Amer.* a person whose business is to represent clients in the purchase, sale, or rental of houses, land, etc. □ **real estate agency** *noun*

re·algar /riˈalgər/ *noun* an orange-red monoclinic sulphide of arsenic that is an important source of that element, used as a pigment and in fireworks. [medieval Latin from Arabic rahj al-ġār dust of the cave]

re·align *transitive verb* **1** adjust or alter the direction of. **2** restructure or regroup (political parties, divisions in sports, etc.). □ **re·align·ment** *noun*

real·ism *noun* **1** an interest in regarding things in their true nature and dealing with them as they are. **2** fidelity to nature in representation; the showing of life etc. as it is in fact, esp. in literature, theatre, or the visual arts. **3** (also **Realism**) the movement in esp. French art of the 19th c. characterized by a rebellion against the traditional historical, mythological, and religious subjects in favour of unidealized scenes of modern life. **4** *Philos.* **a** the doctrine that universals or abstract concepts have an objective existence (*opp.* NOMINALISM). **b** the belief that matter as an object of perception has real existence. □ **real·ist** *noun & adjective*

real·is·tic *adjective* **1** having or showing a sensible and practical idea of what can be done, achieved, etc. (*a realistic goal; a realistic solution*). **2** true to real life; resembling the original (*the rubber snake you left on the bed was very realistic*). **3** (of art) depicting things in their true nature, free from enhancement or idealization. **4** of or pertaining to philosophical realism. □ **real·is·tic·ally** *adverb*

re·al·ity *noun* (pl. **-ities**) **1** what exists or is real; that which underlies appearances. **2** (foll. by *of*) the real nature or truth of (a thing) (*the reality of the situation is that she's not happy*). **3** one's true personal situation and the problems that exist in one's life (*he reads to escape from reality; she's lost touch with reality*). **4** a real aspect or condition of something, esp. one that cannot be avoided (*snow is one of the realities of Canadian winter*). **5** resemblance to an original (*the model was impressive in its reality*). **6** designating television programming or a television program that focuses on non-fictional subject matter with the aim of providing entertainment rather than information, e.g. recording the everyday life or work of a certain group, or placing a group of people in an unfamiliar situation and filming their behaviour (*reality TV; reality show*). □ **in reality** in fact.

reality check *noun N Amer.* an occasion on which one consciously confronts reality, esp. in contrast with one's desires, expectations, beliefs, habits, etc. (*I was planning on going to university but that D in algebra was a major reality check*).

reality principle *noun* the principle propounded by Freud that the actual conditions of living modify the pleasure-seeking activity of the libido.

real·ize *transitive verb* (also esp. *Brit.* **-ise**) **1** (often foll. by *that* + clause) become fully aware of; accept something as fact. **2** understand clearly. **3** make (plans, dreams, ideas) happen in reality; achieve (*realized a childhood dream*). **4 a** convert into money. **b** acquire (profit). **c** be sold for (a specified price). **5** present as real; make realistic; give apparent reality to (*the story was powerfully realized on stage*). **6** *reflexive* develop one's own faculties, abilities, etc. □ **real·iz·able** *adjective* **real·iz·abil·ity** *noun* **real·iz·a·tion** *noun* **real·iz·er** *noun*

real life ● *noun* life lived by actual people as distinguished from the world of fiction, television, theatre, etc. (*in real life that actor lives on a farm*). ● *attributive adjective* (usu. **real-life**) **1** not originating in fiction (*a movie based on real-life experiences*). **2** actually having occurred; not imagined or made up (*I can give you a real-life example*).

real live *attributive adjective* often *jocular* actual; not pretended or simulated (*a real live burglar*).

re·allo·cate *transitive verb* allocate again or differently. □ **re·allo·ca·tion** *noun*

real·ly *adverb* **1** in actual fact; truly. **2** thoroughly, very (*really useful*). **3** (as a strong affirmative) seriously, I assure you. **4** (also in *interrogative*) an expression of disbelief, mild protest, or surprise (*We have to go to bed? Really?*).

realm /relm/ *noun* **1** *formal* a kingdom. **2** a province of some abstract conception (*that's not out of the realm of possibility*). **3** a field of activity or interest (*the realm of public health*). [Old French *realme, reaume,* from Latin *regimen -minis* (see REGIMEN): influenced by Old French *reiel* ROYAL]

real money *noun* **1** current coin or banknotes; cash. **2** *informal* a large sum of money.

real·politik /reɪˌalpɒlɪˈtiːk/ *noun* politics based on realities and material needs, rather than on morals or ideals. □ **real·politik·er** *noun* [German]

real presence *noun* the doctrine, held by some Christian denominations, of the actual presence of Christ's body and blood in the Eucharistic elements.

real property *noun* = REAL ESTATE 1.

real tennis *noun* = COURT TENNIS.

real time ● *noun* the actual time during which a process or event occurs. ● *attributive adjective* (usu. **real-time**) *Computing* **1** (of a system) in which input data is processed within milliseconds so that it is available virtually immediately as feedback to the process from which it is coming, e.g. in an airline booking system. **2** (of information, an image, etc.) responding virtually immediately to changes in the state of affairs it reflects (*real-time weather forecasting*).

real·tor /ˈriːəltər/ *noun N Amer.* a real estate agent.

real·ty /ˈriːəlti/ *noun Law* real estate (*opp.* PERSONALTY).

real world ● *noun* (usu. prec. by *the*) **1** the world as it really exists as distinguished from any model of existence considered to be ideal, hypothetical, or fictitious (*these health reforms look good on paper, but they won't work in the real world of medicine*). **2** real life as distinguished from any lifestyle considered to be sheltered or privileged. ● *adjective* (**real-world**) **1** of or pertaining to the real world esp. consisting of harsh realities (*his real-world observations are disturbing*). **2** practical (*real-world knowledge; real-world experience*).

ream¹ *noun* **1** twenty quires or 500 (formerly 480) sheets of paper (or a larger number, to allow for waste). **2** (in *pl.*) a large quantity of paper, writing, or printed matter (*wrote reams about it*). [Old French *raime* etc., ultimately from Arabic *rizma* bundle]

ream² *transitive verb* **1** widen (a hole in metal etc.) with a borer. **2** *N Amer.*

extract the juice from (fruit) with a reamer. □ **ream a person out** *N Amer. informal* reprimand a person harshly. [19th c.: origin uncertain]

ream·er *noun* **1** a tool for enlarging or finishing drilled holes. **2** *N Amer.* a kitchen implement with a central ridged dome on which a half fruit can be pressed down and turned to extract its juice.

re·analyze *transitive verb* (also esp. *Brit.* **re·analyse**) analyze again; subject to further analysis. □ **re·analy·sis** *noun*

re·animate *transitive verb* **1** resuscitate; restore to life. **2** restore to activity, liveliness or use; revive. □ **re·anima·tion** *noun*

Rean·ey /ˈreɪni/ **James** (b.1926), Canadian poet, playwright, and literary critic, winner of the Governor General's Literary Award for *The Red Heart* (1949), *A Suit of Nettles* (1958), and *Twelve Letters to a Small Town* and *The Killdeer and Other Plays* (both cited in 1962); among his many other works is the dramatic trilogy *The Donnellys* (1974-1975).

reap *transitive verb* **1** cut (a crop, esp. grain) as a harvest. **2** gather or harvest the crop of (a field etc.). **3** receive as the consequence of one's own or others' actions (*reap the rewards of hard work*). [Old English *ripan, reopan,* of unknown origin]

reap·er *noun* **1** a person who reaps. **2** esp. *hist.* a machine for reaping. **3** (**Reaper**) (prec. by *the*) = GRIM REAPER.

re·appear *intransitive verb* appear again or as previously. □ **re·appear·ance** *noun*

re·apply *transitive & intransitive verb* (**-applies, -applied**) apply again, esp. submit a further application (for a position etc.). □ **re·appli·ca·tion** *noun*

re·appoint *transitive verb* appoint again to a position previously held. □ **re·appoint·ment** *noun*

re·appor·tion *transitive verb* apportion again or differently.

re·appor·tion·ment *noun* **1** the act or instance of changing the apportionment of something. **2** (in the US) the redistribution of members sent by their respective States to the House of Representatives (*see* APPORTIONMENT 2).

re·appraise *transitive verb* appraise or assess again. □ **re·apprais·al** *noun*

rear¹ ● *noun* **1** the back part of anything. **2** the space behind, or position at the back of, anything (*at the rear of the property was a garage*). **3** (also **rear end**) *informal* the buttocks. **4** the hindmost part of an army or fleet. ● *adjective* at the back. □ **bring up the rear** come last. **in the rear** behind; at the back. [prob. from (*in the*) REARWARD or REARGUARD]

rear² *verb* **1** *transitive* **a** bring up and educate (children). **b** breed and care for (animals). **2** *intransitive* (usu. foll. by *up*) **a** (of a horse etc.) raise itself on its hind legs. **b** get up, rise (*she reared up from the bench*). **3** *transitive* **a** set upright. **b** build. **c** hold up. **4** *intransitive* extend to a great height (*the escarpments reared over the valley*). □ **rear back** *N Amer. Baseball* (of a pitcher) lean back on one leg before lurching forward to throw a pitch. **rear** (or **raise**) **its** (**ugly**) **head** (of a situation, problem, etc.) make an (unwelcome) appearance. □ **rear·er** *noun* **rear·ing** *noun* [Old English *ræran* from Germanic]

rear admiral *noun* (also **Rear Admiral**) a naval officer ranking below a vice admiral. Abbr.: **RAdm**.

rear-end *transitive verb N Amer.* (of a car, truck, etc., or its driver) crash into the back of (another vehicle).

rear-ender *noun N Amer. informal* a collision in which one vehicle rear-ends another.

rear·guard *noun* **1** a body of troops detached to protect the rear, esp. in retreats. **2** a defensive or conservative element in an organization etc. **3** *Hockey slang* a defenceman. [Old French *rereguarde* (as RETRO-, GUARD)]

rearguard action *noun* **1** *Military* an engagement undertaken by a rearguard. **2** a defensive stand in an argument etc., esp. when losing.

rear light *noun* (also **rear lamp**) *Brit.* = TAIL LIGHT.

re·arm *transitive & intransitive verb* **1** *transitive* arm again, esp. with improved weapons. **2** *intransitive* become armed again. □ **re·arma·ment** *noun*

rear·most *adjective* furthest back; last.

re·arrange *transitive verb* arrange again in a different way. □ **re·arrange·ment** *noun* **re·arran·ging** *noun*

re·arrest ● *transitive verb* arrest again. ● *noun* an instance of rearresting or being rearrested.

rear sight *noun* the sight nearest to the stock or breech of a firearm.

rear-view mirror *noun* (also **rear-view**) a mirror fixed inside the windshield of a car, truck, etc. enabling the driver to see traffic etc. behind.

---

t top   v voice   w we   z zoo   ʃ she   ʒ vision   θ thin   ð this   ŋ ring   x loch   tʃ chip   dʒ jar   (*see over for vowels*)

rear·ward ● *adverb* (also **rear·wards**) towards the rear. ● *adjective* located at or towards the rear. [Anglo-French *rerewarde* = REARGUARD]

rear-wheel drive *noun* a drive system in a car etc. in which engine power operates through the rear wheels alone.

rea·son ● *noun* **1** a motive, cause, or justification (*has good reasons for doing this*; *there is no reason to be angry*). **2** a fact adduced or serving as this (*give me one good reason why I should let you*). ¶ The well-established idioms *the reason why* and *the reason is because* continue to be strongly criticized as redundant by many teachers of composition in spite of a long history of literary use by respected writers. To avoid such criticism, one can use *the reason* for the former and *the reason is that* for the latter. **3** the intellectual faculty by which conclusions are drawn from premises. **4** sanity (*has lost his reason*). **5** sense; sensible conduct; what is right or practical or practicable; moderation. **6** *Logic* a premise of a syllogism, esp. a minor premise when given after the conclusion. **7** a faculty transcending the understanding and providing a priori principles; intuition. ● *verb* **1** *intransitive* form or try to reach conclusions by connected thought. **2** *intransitive* (foll. by *with*) use an argument (with a person) by way of persuasion. **3** *transitive* (foll. by *that* + clause) conclude or assert in argument. **4** *transitive* (foll. by *out*) think or work out (consequences etc.). □ **by reason of** owing to. **in** (or **within**) **reason** within the bounds of sense or moderation. **it stands to reason** (often foll. by *that* + clause) it is evident or logical. **listen to reason** be persuaded to act sensibly. **see reason** acknowledge the force of an argument. **with reason** justifiably. □ **rea·soned** *adjective* **rea·son·er** *noun* **rea·son·ing** *noun* [Old French *reisun, res(o)un, raisoner*, ultimately from Latin *ratio -onis* from *reri rat-* consider]

rea·son·able *adjective* **1** having sound judgment; moderate; ready to listen to reason. **2** in accordance with reason; not absurd. **3 a** within the limits of reason; fair, moderate (*a reasonable request*). **b** inexpensive; not extortionate. **c** fairly good, average (*the food here is reasonable*). □ **rea·son·able·ness** *noun* **rea·son·ably** *adverb*

reasonable and probable cause *noun* reasonable cause or grounds (for making a search, preferring a charge, etc.).

reasonable doubt *Law noun* doubt remaining in the mind of jurors as to the facts of a case which prevents them from declaring the defendant guilty.

re·assem·ble *transitive & intransitive verb* assemble again or into a former state. □ **re·assem·bly** *noun*

re·assert *transitive verb* assert again. □ **re·asser·tion** *noun*

re·assess *transitive verb* assess again, esp. differently. □ **re·assess·ment** *noun*

re·assign *transitive verb* assign again or differently. □ **re·assign·ment** *noun*

re·assure *transitive verb* **1** restore confidence to; dispel the apprehensions of. **2** confirm; assure again. □ **re·assur·ance** *noun* **re·assur·ing** *adjective* **re·assur·ing·ly** *adverb*

re·attach *transitive verb* attach again or in a former position. □ **re·attach·ment** *noun*

re·attain *transitive verb* attain again. □ **re·attain·ment** *noun*

Réau·mur¹ /ˈreɪoˌmjuːr/ **René An·toine Fer·chault de** (1683–1757), French naturalist. His thermometer scale (the **Réaumur scale**), now obsolete, traditionally has 80 divisions between 0° (the melting point of ice) and 80° (the boiling point of water).

Réau·mur² /ˈreɪoˌmjuːr/ *adjective* expressed in or related to the Réaumur scale of temperature under standard conditions.

reave *verb* (*past* and *past participle* **reft**) *archaic* **1** *transitive* **a** (foll. by *of*) forcibly deprive of. **b** (foll. by *away, from*) take by force or carry off. **2** *intransitive* make raids; plunder; = REIVE. [Old English *reafian* from Germanic]

re·awak·en *transitive & intransitive verb* awaken again. □ **re·awak·en·ing** *noun*

REB *abbreviation* REVISED ENGLISH BIBLE.

Reb *noun* a traditional Jewish courtesy title used preceding a man's forename or surname. [Yiddish, from Hebrew *rabbi* rabbi]

re·bal·ance *transitive verb* restore the correct balance to; balance again or differently.

re·bar /ˈriːbɑːr/ *noun* a steel reinforcing rod in concrete. [from *reinforcing* + BAR¹]

re·barba·tive /riːˈbɑːrbətɪv/ *adjective literary* irritating, unattractive, objectionable. [French *rébarbatif -ive* from *barbe* beard]

re·bate¹ ● *noun* **1** a partial refund of money paid. **2** a deduction from a sum to be paid; a discount. ● *transitive verb* pay back as a rebate.

re·bat·able *adjective* [earlier = diminish: Middle English from Old French *rabattre* (as RE-, ABATE)]

re·bate² *noun & transitive verb* = RABBET. [respelling of RABBET, after REBATE¹]

reb·be /ˈrebə/ *noun* **1** a Jewish religious leader or rabbi. **2** (**Rebbe**) a title of respect used for a Hasidic religious leader. [Yiddish from Hebrew *rabbi* rabbi]

reb·betz·in /ˈrebətsɪn/ *noun* **1** the wife of a rabbi. **2** (also **Rebbetzin**) a courtesy title used preceding the name of a woman who is the wife of a rabbi. [Yiddish from Hebrew, feminine form of *rabbi* rabbi]

re·bec /ˈriːbek/ *noun* (also **re·beck**) *Music* a medieval usu. three-stringed instrument played with a bow. [French *rebec* var. of Old French *rebebe rubebe* from Arabic *rabāb*]

Reb·ecca *Bible* (also **Reb·ekah**) the wife of Isaac, mother of Esau and Jacob (Gen. 24–7).

Reb·ekah *noun* a member of a women's social and charitable society allied with the Oddfellows.

reb·el ● *noun* /ˈrebəl/ **1** a person who fights against, resists, or refuses allegiance to, the established government. **2** a person who resists authority, control, or convention. ● *adjective* /ˈrebəl/ (*attributive*) **1** rebellious. **2** of or concerning rebels. **3** in rebellion. ● *intransitive verb* /rəˈbel, rɪ-/ (**re·belled**, **re·bel·ling**) (often foll. by *against*) **1** act as a rebel; revolt. **2** feel or display repugnance. [Old French *rebelle, rebeller* from Latin *rebellis* (as RE-, *bellum* war)]

re·bel·lion *noun* **1** open resistance to authority, esp. organized armed resistance to an established government. **2** an instance of this.

Rebellions of 1837 *Cdn hist.* two nearly contemporaneous armed uprisings against British rule in Lower and Upper Canada, respectively, beginning in the late fall of 1837. The first to break out, the **Rebellion of Lower Canada**, occurred when rising tensions between French nationalists (led by Louis-Joseph Papineau) and the pro-British governing party prompted the government to attempt to arrest the leading French-Canadian reformers, who fled to the countryside. Regular troops pursued, and the subsequent battles which put down the rebellion left more than 300 dead; Papineau fled to the US. The dispatch of government troops from Upper Canada to Lower Canada occasioned the **Rebellion of Upper Canada**, as reformers and radicals led by William Lyon Mackenzie attempted to seize control of the government in Toronto. The rebels were badly disorganized, however, and were easily dispersed in two main skirmishes, one near Toronto and another a few days later near Brantford. Like Papineau, Mackenzie fled to the US.

re·bel·lious *adjective* **1** tending to rebel; insubordinate. **2** in rebellion. **3** defying lawful authority. **4** (of a thing) unmanageable, refractory. □ **re·bel·lious·ly** *adverb* **re·bel·lious·ness** *noun*

re·bind *transitive verb* (*past* and *past participle* **re·bound**) bind (esp. a book) again or differently.

re·birth *noun* **1** a new incarnation. **2** spiritual enlightenment. **3** a revival (*the rebirth of learning*).

re·birth·ing *noun* a treatment for neurosis involving controlled breathing intended to simulate the trauma of being born.

re·boot *Computing* ● *transitive & intransitive verb* boot up (a system) again. ● *noun* an act or instance of rebooting.

re·bore ● *transitive verb* make a new boring in, esp. widen the bore of (the cylinder in an internal combustion engine). ● *noun* **1** the process of doing this. **2** a rebored engine.

re·born *adjective* **1** having experienced a complete spiritual change; born-again. **2** existing or active again; brought back to life. **3** having experienced a profound transformation (*a warehouse reborn as a luxury condominium*).

re·bound¹ ● *verb* **1** *intransitive* spring back after action or impact. **2** *intransitive* make a recovery (*gold prices are beginning to rebound*; *she's trying to rebound from a bad cold*). **3** *transitive & intransitive* *Basketball* recover (a ball) that has bounced off the backboard or rim of the basket. **4** *intransitive* (foll. by *upon*) (of an action) have an adverse effect upon (the doer). ● *noun* **1** the act or an instance of rebounding; recovery. **2** *Sport* a puck, ball, etc. which has bounced back from the goal, basket, etc. or been let loose by the goaltender. ● *attributive adjective* (of a medical condition, illness, etc.) occurring again (*a rebound earache*). □ **on the rebound** **1** while still recovering from an emotional shock, esp. rejection by a lover. **2** while bouncing back (*scored on the rebound*). □ **re·bound·er** *noun* **re·bound·ing** *noun* [Old French *rebonder, rebondir* (as RE-, BOUND¹)]

re·bound² *past* and *past participle* of REBIND.

re·bo·zo /rə'bo:so:/ *noun* a long scarf covering the head and shoulders, traditionally worn by Spanish and Mexican women. [Spanish]

re·brand ● *transitive verb* **1** apply a new brand identity (as a different name, logo, livery, etc.) to (an existing product, service, or company). **2** radically change the presentation of (something or someone); reinvent. ● *noun* the act or an instance of rebranding.

re·breath·er *noun* scuba equipment in which the diver's exhaled breath is partially purified of carbon dioxide, mixed with more oxygen and then breathed again by the diver.

re·broad·cast ● *transitive verb* (*past* **re·broad·cast** or **re·broad·cast·ed**; *past participle* **re·broad·cast**) **1** broadcast (a program received from another station). **2** broadcast again. ● *noun* **1** the action or act of rebroadcasting a program. **2** a repeat broadcast.

re·buff ● *noun* **1** a rejection of one who makes advances, offers help or sympathy, shows interest or curiosity, makes a request, etc. **2** a repulse; a snub. ● *transitive verb* reject, disregard; give a rebuff to. [obsolete French *rebuffe(r)* from Italian *ribuffo* (as RE-, *buffo* puff)]

re·build ● *verb* (*past* and *past participle* **re·built**) **1** *transitive* build (a car, house, etc.) again from new or previously used parts and materials. **2** *transitive & intransitive* make or become successful, functional, etc. again. **3** *transitive* re-establish or revive (confidence, a country's economy, etc.). ● *noun* (esp. of a car or car part, such as an engine) something that has been or needs to be rebuilt.

re·buke ● *transitive verb* scold or reprimand harshly; subject to protest or censure. ● *noun* a stern reprimand or reproof. □ **re·buk·er** *noun* **re·buk·ing·ly** *adverb* [Anglo-French & Old Northern French *rebuker* (as RE-, Old French *buchier* beat, originally 'cut down wood', from *busche* log)]

re·bury *transitive verb* (**-buries**, **-buried**) bury again. □ **re·burial** *noun*

re·bus /'ri:bəs/ *noun* **1** a type of puzzle or visual pun in which a word is represented by pictures etc. suggesting its parts; for example, the letters CR followed by a picture of an eye would constitute a rebus for the word *cry*. **2** *Heraldry* a device suggesting the name of its bearer. [French *rébus* from Latin *rebus*, ablative pl. of *res* thing]

re·but *transitive verb* (**re·but·ted**, **re·but·ting**) **1** refute or disprove (evidence or a charge). **2** oppose, turn back (an opponent). □ **re·but·table** *adjective* **re·but·tal** *noun* [Anglo-French *rebuter*, Old French *rebo(u)ter* (as RE-, BUTT¹)]

re·but·ter *noun* **1** a refutation. **2** *Law* a defendant's reply to the plaintiff's surrejoinder.

rec¹ *adjective N Amer.* **1** recreation (*rec centre*). **2** recreational (*rec league*). [abbreviation]

rec² *abbreviation* record (on a button on a VCR, tape player, etc.). [abbreviation]

re·cal·ci·trant /rə'kalsɪtrent, ri-/ ● *adjective* **1** resisting discipline or authority; obstinately disobedient (*a recalcitrant child*). **2** difficult to manage or operate (*a recalcitrant lock*). ● *noun* a recalcitrant person. □ **re·cal·ci·trance** *noun* **re·cal·ci·trant·ly** *adverb* [Latin *recalcitrare* (as RE-, *calcitrare* kick out with the heels, from *calx calcis* heel)]

re·cal·cu·late *transitive verb* calculate again. □ **re·cal·cu·la·tion** *noun*

re·cal·esce /ˌrikə'les/ *intransitive verb* grow hot again (esp. of iron allowed to cool from white heat, whose temperature rises at a certain point for a short time). □ **re·cal·es·cent** *adjective* [Latin *recalescere* (as RE-, *calescere* grow hot)]

re·call ● *transitive verb* **1** recollect, remember (*the name is familiar but I can't recall the face*). **2 a** summon a person to return (*a player recalled from the minors*). **b** request the return of something, esp. a manufactured product with a defect (*the company has recalled some of its 1996 models*). **3** bring back to memory; serve as a reminder of (*that picture recalls a funny story I once heard*). **4** revoke or annul (an action or decision). ● *noun* **1** the act or an instance of recalling, esp. a summons to come back. **2** a request for the return of a faulty product. **3** the ability to remember. **4** *N Amer.* removal of an elected official from office. □ **beyond recall** that cannot be brought back to the original state or cancelled (*damaged beyond recall*). □ **re·call·able** *adjective*

re·cant *verb* **1** *transitive* withdraw and renounce (a former belief or statement) as erroneous or heretical. **2** *intransitive* disavow a former opinion, esp. with a public confession of error. □ **re·can·ta·tion** *noun* **re·cant·er** *noun* [Latin *recantare* revoke (as RE-, *cantare* sing, chant)]

re·cap *informal* ● *transitive & intransitive verb* (**re·capped**, **re·cap·ping**) recapitulate; give a summary. ● *noun* a recapitulation; a summary or review. [abbreviation]

re·cap·it·al·ize *transitive verb* (also esp. *Brit.* **-ise**) **1** capitalize (shares etc.) again. **2** reorganize the capital structure of (a corporation, etc.). □ **re·cap·it·al·iza·tion** *noun*

re·capit·u·late /ˌri:kə'pɪtʃʊˌleɪt/ *transitive verb* **1** go briefly through (the main points of a speech, argument, etc.) again; summarize. **2** repeat and reflect (an event). [Latin *recapitulare* (as RE-, *capitulum* CHAPTER)]

re·capit·u·la·tion /ˌri:kəˌpɪtʃʊ'leɪʃən/ *noun* **1** the act or an instance of recapitulating. **2** *Biol.* the repetition of an evolutionary or other process during development or growth. **3** *Music* part of a movement, esp. in sonata form, in which themes from the exposition are restated.

re·cap·ture ● *transitive verb* **1** capture again; recover or regain. **2** experience (a past emotion etc.) again. ● *noun* the act or an instance of recapturing.

re·cast ● *transitive verb* (*past* and *past participle* **re·cast**) **1** put into a new form. **2** change the cast of (a play etc.). ● *noun* **1** the act or an instance of recasting. **2** a recast form.

recce /'reki/ *Brit. informal* ● *noun* a reconnaissance. ● *transitive & intransitive verb* (**recced**, **recce·ing**) reconnoitre. [abbreviation]

recd. *abbreviation* received.

re·cede *intransitive verb* **1** withdraw or move backwards from a previous position or away from an observer, or appear to do so (*we watched the tide recede; the train station receded into the mist*). **2** fade, become remote (*hopes of a settlement are beginning to recede*). **3** slope backwards (*a receding chin*). **4** decline in force, value, or significance. **5** (foll. by *from*) withdraw or retreat from (an engagement, promise, etc.). **6** (of a person's hair) cease to grow at the front, sides, etc. (*receding hairline*). [Latin *recedere* (as RE-, *cedere cess-* go)]

re·ceipt ● *noun* **1** the act or an instance of receiving or being received into one's possession (*will pay on receipt of the goods*). **2** a printed or written acknowledgement of the acceptance of goods or payment of money. **3** a printed statement issued by a cashier to a customer detailing the items purchased and the means of payment (*a cash register receipt*). **4** (usu. in *pl.*) an amount of money etc. received (*gate receipts*). **5** *archaic* a recipe. ● *transitive verb* acknowledge the receipt of (a sum of money, etc.) by issuing a printed or written statement. □ **in receipt of** having received. □ **re·ceipt·ed** *adjective* [Anglo-French & Old Northern French *receite* from medieval Latin *recepta* fem. past participle of Latin *recipere* RECEIVE: *-p-* inserted after Latin]

re·ceiv·able ● *adjective* **1** capable of being received. **2** (of bills, accounts, etc.) for which money has not yet been received. ● *noun* (in *pl.*) debts owed to a business, esp. regarded as assets.

re·ceive *verb* **1** *transitive* acquire or accept (something offered or given) (*will receive a small fee; receive a phone call*). **2** *transitive* accept delivery of (something sent) (*receive a shipment; receive a letter*). **3** *transitive* be granted or have conferred upon one (*received many honours; received a degree; received consideration for the position*). **4** *transitive* experience (*received an injury; received treatment*). **5** *transitive* consent to hear (a confession or oath) or consider (a petition). **6** *transitive* welcome or entertain as a guest, esp. formally (*she received visitors in the afternoon*). **7** *transitive* react to, esp. in a specified manner (*the play was well received; how did they receive the news?*). **8** *transitive* allow a person to enter as a guest, member, etc. (*was received into the priesthood*). **9** *transitive* apprehend mentally (*I received the impression he was lying*). **10** *transitive* convert (broadcast signals) into sound or pictures. **11** *transitive & intransitive* *Tennis* be the player to whom the server serves (the ball). **12** *transitive & intransitive* *N Amer. Football* be the player or team to whom the offensive team kicks the ball. **13** *transitive* be able to hold (a specified amount) or bear (a specified weight). **14** *transitive* buy or accept (stolen goods) knowing that they are stolen. □ **be at** (or **on**) **the receiving end** *informal* bear the brunt of something unpleasant. [Old French *receivre, reçoivre* from Latin *recipere recept-* (as RE-, *capere* take)]

re·ceived *adjective* generally accepted as authoritative or true (*received opinion*).

Received Pronunciation *noun* the pronunciation of British English used by educated middle- and upper-class speakers in southern England. Abbr.: **RP**.

re·ceiv·er *noun* **1** a person or thing that receives. **2 a** the part of a machine or instrument that receives sound, signals, etc. **b** the apparatus contained within the earpiece of a telephone. **c** the handset of a telephone. **3** (in full **official receiver**) a person appointed by a court to manage the property of a bankrupt or insane person, or property under litigation. **4** an apparatus, such as a radio or television, etc., that receives signals transmitted as electromagnetic waves. **5** *N Amer. Football* (in full **wide receiver**) a player on the offensive team who is eligible to catch passes from the quarterback. **6** a person who receives stolen goods. **7** *Chem.* a vessel for collecting the products of distillation, chromatography, etc.

receiver general *noun* (*pl.* **receivers general**) an official appointed to receive public revenues.

---

uː m**oo**d   aɪ m**y**   əi p**i**pe   aʊ br**ow**n   ʌu h**ou**se   eɪ d**ay**   ɔi b**oy**   ɑ̃ fr**an**glais   ã C**a**nadien   ɔ̃ Br**ay**on   (*see over for consonants*)

re·ceiv·er·ship *noun* **1** the state of being dealt with by a receiver (*in receivership*). **2** the position of receiver.

re·ceiv·ing blanket *noun* N Amer. a small, soft blanket in which to wrap a baby.

re·ceiv·ing line *noun* a row of hosts greeting guests formally upon arrival at a reception, etc.

re·ceiv·ing order *noun* Cdn & Brit. an order of a court authorizing an official receiver (see RECEIVER 3) to act.

re·ceiv·ing station *noun* an apparatus, such as a satellite dish, designed for the reception of telecommunication signals.

re·cen·sion *noun* **1** the revision of a text. **2** a particular form or version of a text resulting from such revision. [Latin *recensio* from *recensēre* revise (as RE-, *censēre* review)]

re·cent ● *adjective* **1** not long past; that happened, appeared, began to exist, or existed lately. **2** not long established; lately begun; modern. **3** (**Recent**) Geol. = HOLOCENE. ● *noun* Geol. = HOLOCENE. □ **re·cent·ly** *adverb* [Latin *recens recentis* or French *récent*]

re·cep·ta·cle *noun* **1** a container or vessel in which something is stored or deposited. **2** esp. N Amer. an electrical outlet. **3** Bot. **a** the common base of floral organs. **b** the part of a leaf or thallus in some algae where the reproductive organs are situated. **4** Zool. an organ or structure which receives a secretion, eggs, sperm, etc. [Old French *receptacle* from Latin *receptaculum* (as RECEPTION)]

re·cep·tion *noun* **1** the act or an instance of receiving or the process of being received, esp. of a person into a place or group. **2** the manner in which a person or thing is received (*got a cool reception*). **3** a formal social event to which guests are invited to mark some occasion, e.g. a wedding. **4** a place where guests or clients etc. report on arrival at a hotel, office, etc. (*I'll meet you in reception*). **5 a** the receiving of broadcast signals. **b** the quality of this (*we have excellent reception*). **6** N Amer. Football a catch of a ball thrown by the quarterback. [Old French *reception* or Latin *receptio* (as RECEIVE)]

re·cep·tion·ist *noun* a person employed in an organization to welcome and direct visitors, answer the telephone, etc.

reception room *noun* **1** a room in an office or building for the reception of clients, patients, visitors, etc. **2** a large room in a restaurant, hotel, etc., where a large party or reception may be held. **3** Brit. a room in a house available or suitable for receiving company or visitors; a living room.

re·cep·tive *adjective* **1** quick or able to receive impressions or ideas. **2** (often foll. by *to*) willing or anxious to hear, acknowledge, or accept; open (*she was receptive to alternatives; a receptive audience*). **3** concerned with receiving stimuli etc. □ **re·cep·tive·ness** *noun* **re·cep·tiv·ity** *noun* [French *réceptif -ive* or medieval Latin *receptivus* (as RECEIVE)]

re·cep·tor *noun* (often *attributive*) Biol. **1** a cell or group of cells, found in the eyes, ears, nose, etc., specialized to detect a particular stimulus, such as light, heat, or a drug, and to initiate the transmission of impulses via the sensory nerves. **2** a region in a tissue or molecule in a cell (esp. in a membrane) which specifically recognizes and responds to a complimentary molecule, such as a hormone, or other substance. [Old French *receptour* or Latin *receptor* (as RECEIVE)]

re·cess ● *noun* **1** N Amer. a short break between classes, esp. in elementary school. **2** a temporary cessation from work, esp. of Parliament or of a law court. **3** a space set back in a wall; a niche. **4** (often in *pl.*) a hidden, isolated, or secret place (*the innermost recesses*). **5** Anat. a fold or indentation in an organ. ● *verb* **1** *transitive* make a recess in. **2** *transitive* place in a recess; set back. **3** *intransitive* N Amer. take a recess; adjourn. [Latin *recessus* (as RECEDE)]

re·cessed *adjective* placed in such a way as to be flush or set back from the surface in which it is set.

re·ces·sion *noun* **1** a temporary decline in economic activity or prosperity associated with lower levels of production and employment. **2** a receding or withdrawal from a place or point. **3** a receding part of an object; a recess. □ **re·ces·sion·ary** *adjective*

re·ces·sion·al ● *adjective* **1** of or pertaining to a recession or recessions. **2** (of a hymn or other piece of music) sung or played while the clergy etc. withdraw after a service. ● *noun* a recessional hymn.

re·cession-proof *adjective* (of a business, market, city, etc.) unaffected by economic recession.

re·ces·sive ● *adjective* **1** Genetics (of an inherited characteristic) appearing in offspring only when not masked by a dominant characteristic inherited from one parent. **2** tending to recede. **3** Phonetics (of an accent) falling near the beginning of a word. **4** of or relating to an economic recession. ● *noun* **1** an individual in which a particular recessive allele or gene is expressed. **2** an allele that does not function when two different alleles are present in the cells of an organism; a recessive allele. □ **re·ces·sive·ness** *noun*

re·charge ● *verb* **1** *transitive* put a fresh charge in; refill. **2** *transitive* restore an electric charge to (a battery or piece of equipment powered by batteries). **3** *intransitive* (of a battery or piece of equipment) be recharged. **4** *intransitive* (of a person) recover energy by resting or relaxing for a short time. ● *noun* a renewed charge. □ **re·charge·able** *adjective*

re·char·ger *noun* a device for recharging batteries or equipment powered by batteries.

réchauffé /ˈreɪʃɔːˌfeɪ/ *noun* **1** a warmed-up dish. **2** a rehash. [French past participle of *réchauffer* (as RE-, CHAFE)]

re·check ● *transitive & intransitive verb* check again. ● *noun* a second or further check or inspection.

re·cher·ché /rəˈʃerʃeɪ/ *adjective* **1** carefully sought out; rare or exotic. **2** far-fetched, obscure. [French, past participle of *rechercher* (as RE-, *chercher* seek)]

re·chris·ten *transitive verb* **1** give a new name to. **2** christen again.

re·cid·iv·ist /rəˈsɪdɪvɪst, rɪ-/ *noun* a person who relapses into crime. □ **re·cid·iv·ism** *noun* [French *récidiviste* from *récidiver* from medieval Latin *recidivare* from Latin *recidivus* from *recidere* (as RE-, *cadere* fall)]

Re·cife /rəˈsiːfə/ a port on the Atlantic coast of NE Brazil; pop. (2000) 1,421,947. It was formerly known as Pernambuco.

re·ci·pe /ˈresɪpi/ *noun* **1** a statement of the ingredients and procedure required for preparing a dish. **2** a means of achieving or attaining something (*a recipe for success*). [2nd sing. imperative (as used in prescriptions) of Latin *recipere* take, RECEIVE]

re·cip·i·ent /rəˈsɪpiənt, rɪ-/ ● *noun* a person who receives something. ● *adjective* **1** receiving. **2** receptive. [French *récipient* from Italian *recipiente* or Latin *recipiens* from *recipere* RECEIVE]

re·cip·ro·cal /rəˈsɪprəkəl, rɪ-/ ● *adjective* **1** in return (*offered a reciprocal greeting*). **2** mutual (*their feelings are reciprocal*). **3** Grammar (of a pronoun) expressing mutual action or relation (as in *each other*). **4** inversely correspondent; complementary (*natural kindness matched by a reciprocal severity*). ● *noun* **1** a thing corresponding in some way to another; an equivalent or counterpart. **2** Math. an expression or function so related to another that their product is unity ($\frac{1}{2}$ is the reciprocal of 2). □ **re·cip·ro·cal·ity** /-ˈkalɪti/ *noun* **re·cip·ro·cal·ly** *adverb* [Latin *reciprocus*, ultimately from *re-* back + *pro* forward]

re·cip·ro·cate /rəˈsɪprəˌkeɪt, rɪ-/ *verb* **1** *transitive* return or requite (affection etc.). **2** *intransitive* (foll. by *with*) offer or give something in return (*reciprocated with an invitation to lunch*). **3** *transitive* give and receive mutually; interchange. **4 a** *intransitive* (of a part of a machine) move backwards and forwards. **b** *transitive* cause to do this. □ **re·cip·ro·ca·tion** *noun* **re·cip·ro·ca·tor** *noun* [Latin *reciprocare reciprocat-* (as RECIPROCAL)]

reciprocating engine *noun* an engine using a piston or pistons moving up and down in cylinders.

reci·proc·i·ty /ˌresəˈprɒsɪti/ *noun* (*pl.* **-ties**) **1** the act or condition of being reciprocal. **2** give and take. **3** a mutual exchange of advantages or privileges as a basis for commercial relations between two countries. [French *réciprocité* from *réciproque* from Latin *reciprocus* (as RECIPROCAL)]

re·circu·late *transitive & intransitive verb* circulate again, esp. make available for reuse (*a fan recirculates the air*). □ **re·circu·la·tion** *noun*

re·cital *noun* **1** the act or an instance of reciting or being recited. **2** the performance of a program of instrumental music, song, or dance, by a soloist or small group. **3** (foll. by *of*) a detailed account of (connected things or facts); a narrative. **4** Cdn & Brit. Law the part of a legal document that states the facts. □ **re·cital·ist** *noun* (in sense 2).

reci·ta·tion *noun* **1** the act or an instance of reciting, esp. the act of repeating a text from memory or of reading a text aloud before an audience. **2** a thing recited.

reci·ta·tive /ˌresəˈtiːv/ *noun* **1** declamatory speech-like singing used esp. in opera or oratorio for advancing the plot (*compare* ARIA, ARIOSO). **2** a passage or part of a musical score given in this form. [Italian *recitativo* (as RECITE)]

re·cite *verb* **1** *transitive* repeat aloud or declaim (a poem or passage) from memory, esp. before an audience. **2** *intransitive* give a recitation. **3** *transitive* mention in order; enumerate (*she recited her accomplishments*). **4** *transitive* give a detailed description or account of (*he recited his adventure*). □ **re·cit·er** *noun* [Old French *reciter* or Latin *recitare* (as RE-, CITE)]

reck *verb* archaic (only in *neg.* or *interrogative*) **1** *transitive* (foll. by *of*) pay heed to; take account of; care about. **2** *transitive* pay heed to. **3** *intransitive* (usu. with *it* as subject) be of importance (*it recks little*). [Old English *reccan*, related to Old High German *ruohhen*]

reck·less *adjective* disregarding the consequences or danger etc.; lacking caution; rash. □ **reck·less·ly** *adverb* **reck·less·ness** *noun* [Old English *reccelēas* (as RECK)]

reck·on *verb* **1** *transitive* count or compute by calculation. **2** *transitive* **a** (often foll. by *that* + clause) conclude after calculation. **b** *informal* (foll. by *to* + infin.) expect (*reckons to finish by Friday*). **c** *informal* think, suppose (*reckon it'll rain today?*). **3** *intransitive* (foll. by *on*) rely on, count on, or base plans on (*didn't reckon on it being so hard*). **4** *transitive* (usu. in *passive*) consider or regard (*she is reckoned an authority on the subject*). **5** *transitive* (foll. by *in*) count in or include in computation. **6** *intransitive* (foll. by *with*) **a** take into account. **b** settle accounts with. **7** *intransitive* make calculations; add up an account or sum. □ **to be reckoned with** (also **to reckon with**) of considerable importance; not to be ignored or taken lightly (*their team is a force to be reckoned with*). □ **reck·on·able** *adjective* [Old English (*ge*)*recenian* from West Germanic]

reck·on·ing *noun* **1** the act or an instance of counting or calculating. **2** an opinion or judgment. **3 a** the settlement of an account. **b** an account. □ **day of reckoning** the time when something must be atoned for or avenged.

re·claim ● *transitive verb* **1** seek the return of (one's property, etc.). **2** make wasteland fit for cultivating, esp. by draining it. **3** recover raw material from waste products so that it can be used again. **4 a** win back or away from vice or error; reform. **b** tame, civilize. ● *noun* the act or an instance of reclaiming; the process of being reclaimed. □ **re·claim·able** *adjective* **re·claimed** *adjective* **re·claim·er** *noun* **rec·la·ma·tion** *noun* [Old French *reclamer reclaim-* from Latin *reclamare* cry out against (as RE-, *clamare* shout)]

re·clas·si·fy *transitive verb* (**-fies, -fied**) classify again or differently. □ **re·clas·si·fi·ca·tion** *noun*

re·cline *transitive & intransitive verb* lie or cause to lie backwards in a horizontal or leaning position, esp. in resting (*she reclined in the chair; he reclined the seat backwards*). □ **re·clin·ing** *adjective* [Old English *recliner* or Latin *reclinare* bend back, recline (as RE-, *clinare* bend)]

re·clin·er *noun* a comfortable chair for reclining in, usu. with adjustable back and footrest.

re·clothe *transitive verb* clothe again or differently.

re·cluse /rəˈkluːs, ˈreklus/ *noun* a person preferring or living in seclusion or isolation. □ **re·clu·sion** /rəˈkluːʒən/ *noun* **re·clu·sive** *adjective* [Old French *reclus recluse* past participle of *reclure* from Latin *recludere reclus-* (as RE-, *claudere* shut)]

re·code *transitive verb* code again or differently.

rec·og·ni·tion /ˌrekəɡˈnɪʃən/ *noun* **1** the action or an act of recognizing a person or thing; the fact of being recognized. **2** the acknowledgement or admission of a service, achievement, ability, etc.; appreciation, acclaim. **3** formal sanction or approval. **4** the mental process whereby things are identified as having been previously apprehended or as belonging to a known category. **5** (also **diplomatic recognition**) the process by which a country declares that another political entity fulfills the conditions of statehood and acknowledges its willingness to deal with it as a member of the international community. **6** the identification of printed characters through photoelectric devices (*see* OPTICAL CHARACTER RECOGNITION). □ **beyond recognition** to such a degree that it cannot be recognized (*the town has changed beyond all recognition*).

re·cog·ni·zance /rəˈkɒɡnɪzəns/ *noun* **1** a bond by which a person undertakes before a court or magistrate to observe some condition, e.g. to appear when summoned. **2** a sum pledged as surety for this. [Old French *recon(n)issance* (as RE-, COGNIZANCE)]

rec·og·nize /ˈrekəɡˌnaɪz/ *transitive verb* (also esp. *Brit.* **-nise**) **1** identify (a person or thing) as already known; know again. **2** discover the nature of, esp. by some distinctive feature (*you can recognize a cardinal by its red colour; I can always recognize a phony*). **3** (foll. by *that*) realize or admit. **4** acknowledge the existence, validity, character, or claims of. **5** show appreciation of; reward. **6** (foll. by *as, for*) treat or acknowledge. **7** (of a chairperson etc.) allow (a person) to speak in a debate etc. **8** grant diplomatic recognition to (a country). □ **rec·og·niz·able** *adjective* **rec·og·niz·abil·ity** *noun* **rec·og·niz·ably** *adverb* **rec·og·niz·er** *noun* [Old French *recon(n)iss-* stem of *reconnaistre* from Latin *recognoscere recognit-* (as RE-, *cognoscere* learn)]

re·coil ● *intransitive verb* **1** suddenly move or spring back in fear, horror, or disgust. **2** shrink mentally in this way. **3** rebound after an impact. **4** (foll. by *on, upon*) have an adverse reactive effect on (the originator). **5** (of a gun) be driven backwards by its discharge. **6** *Physics* (of an atom

etc.) move backwards by the conservation of momentum on emission of a particle. ● *noun* **1** the act or an instance of recoiling. **2** the sensation of recoiling. **3** the extent to which a gun etc. recoils when discharged. □ **re·coil·less** *adjective* (in sense 5). [Old French *reculer* (as RE-, Latin *culus* buttocks)]

re·col·lect /ˌrekəˈlekt/ *transitive verb* **1** remember. **2** succeed in remembering; call to mind. [Latin *recolligere recollect-* (as RE-, COLLECT[1])]

re·col·lec·tion *noun* **1** the act or power of recollecting. **2** a thing recollected. **3 a** a person's memory (*to the best of my recollection*). **b** the time over which memory extends (*happened within my recollection*). □ **re·col·lec·tive** *adjective*

Récol·let /ˈrekəleɪ/ *noun* a member of the reformed branch of the Franciscan Observants, founded in France in the late 16th c., and active in New France. [French *récollet*, from medieval Latin *recollectus*, past participle of *recolligere*, gather again]

re·col·on·ize *transitive verb* (also esp. *Brit.* **-ise**) colonize again. □ **re·col·on·iz·a·tion** *noun*

re·com·bin·ant /riːˈkɒmbənənt/ *Biol.* ● *adjective* (of a gene etc.) formed by recombination. ● *noun* a recombinant organism or cell.

recombinant DNA *noun* DNA that has been recombined using constituents from different sources.

re·com·bin·a·tion *noun Biol.* the rearrangement, esp. by crossing over in chromosomes, of genes to form a combination different from that of its parents.

re·com·bine *transitive & intransitive verb* combine again or differently.

re·com·mence /ˌriːkəˈmens/ *transitive & intransitive verb* begin again.

rec·om·mend /ˌrekəˈmend/ *transitive verb* **1 a** suggest as fit for some purpose or use. **b** suggest (a person) as suitable for a particular position. **2** (often foll. by *that* + clause or *to* + infin.) advise as a course of action etc. (*I recommend that you stay where you are*). **3** (of qualities, conduct, etc.) make acceptable or desirable (*a plan with little to recommend it*). **4** (foll. by *to*) *archaic* commend or entrust (to a person or a person's care). □ **rec·om·mend·able** *adjective* **rec·om·men·da·tion** *noun* **rec·om·mend·er** *noun* [Middle English (in sense 4) from medieval Latin *recommendare* (as RE-, COMMEND)]

re·com·mis·sion *transitive verb* commission again.

re·com·mit *transitive verb* (**re·com·mit·ted, re·com·mit·ting**) commit again. □ **re·com·mit·ment** *noun* **re·com·mit·tal** *noun*

re·com·pense /ˈrekəmˌpens/ ● *transitive verb* **1** make amends to (a person) or for (a loss etc.); compensate. **2** make repayment to (a person) for (a thing, action, service, etc.). ● *noun* **1** a repayment, reward, or requital. **2** retribution; satisfaction given for an injury. [Old French *recompense(r)* from Late Latin *recompensare* (as RE-, COMPENSATE)]

re·com·pile *transitive verb* compile (a computer program) again or differently. □ **re·com·pil·a·tion** *noun*

re·com·pose *transitive verb* compose again or differently. □ **re·com·pos·ition** *noun*

re·com·pute *transitive verb* compute again; recalculate. □ **re·com·pu·ta·tion** *noun*

recon /rəˈkɒn/ *noun* (often *attributive*) esp. *US slang* military reconnaissance. [abbreviation]

re·con·cep·tual·ize *transitive verb* (also esp. *Brit.* **-ise**) conceptualize again or differently. □ **re·con·cep·tual·iz·a·tion** *noun*

rec·on·cile /ˈrekənˌsaɪl/ *transitive verb* **1** make friendly again after an estrangement. **2** (usu. in *reflexive* or *passive*; foll. by *to*) make acquiescent or contentedly submissive to (something disagreeable or unwelcome) (*was reconciled to failure*). **3** settle (a quarrel etc.). **4 a** harmonize; make compatible. **b** show the compatibility of by argument or in practice (*cannot reconcile your views with the facts*). □ **rec·on·cil·able** *adjective* **rec·on·cil·er** *noun* **rec·on·cili·a·tory** /-kənˈsɪliətɔri/ *adjective* [Old French *reconcilier* or Latin *reconciliare* (as RE-, *conciliare* CONCILIATE)]

rec·on·cili·a·tion /ˌrekənˌsɪliˈeɪʃən/ *noun* **1** an act or an instance of reconciling. **2** = PENANCE 2a. **3** *Accounting* the action or practice of making one account consistent with another, esp. by allowing for transactions begun but not yet completed.

rec·on·dite /ˈrekənˌdaɪt, rɪˈkɒn-/ *adjective* **1** (of a subject or knowledge) abstruse; out of the way; little known. **2** (of an author or style) dealing in abstruse knowledge or allusions; obscure. [Latin *reconditus* (as RE-, *conditus* past participle of *condere* hide)]

re·con·di·tion *transitive verb* **1** overhaul, refit, renovate. **2** make usable again.

re·con·fig·ure *transitive verb* configure again or differently, esp. adapt (a computer system) to a new task by altering its configuration. □ **re·con·fig·ur·a·tion** *noun*

---

t *top*   v *voice*   w *we*   z *zoo*   ʃ *she*   ʒ *vision*   θ *thin*   ð *this*   ŋ *ring*   x *loch*   tʃ *chip*   dʒ *jar*   (*see over for vowels*)

re·con·firm transitive verb confirm, establish, or ratify anew. □ **re·con·firm·a·tion** noun

re·con·nais·sance /rəˈkɒnəsəns, ri-/ noun **1** a survey of a region, esp. a military examination to locate an enemy or ascertain strategic features. **2** a preliminary survey or inspection. [French (earlier -oissance) from stem of reconnaître (as RECONNOITRE)]

re·con·nect transitive verb connect again. □ **re·con·nec·tion** noun

rec·on·noitre /ˌrekəˈnɔɪtər/ (also **rec·on·noiter**) ● verb **1** transitive make a reconnaissance of (an area, enemy position, etc.). **2** intransitive make a reconnaissance. ● noun a reconnaissance. [obsolete French reconnoître from Latin recognoscere RECOGNIZE]

re·con·quer transitive verb conquer again. □ **re·con·quest** noun

re·con·se·crate transitive verb consecrate (a church etc.) again. □ **re·con·se·cra·tion** noun

re·con·sider transitive & intransitive verb consider again, esp. for a possible change of decision. □ **re·con·sid·er·a·tion** noun

re·con·sti·tute transitive verb **1** build up again from parts; reconstruct. **2** restore the previous constitution of (dried food etc.) by adding water. □ **re·con·sti·tu·tion** noun

re·con·struct transitive verb **1** build or form again. **2 a** form a mental or visual impression of (past events) by assembling the evidence for them. **b** re-enact (a crime). **3** reorganize. □ **re·con·struct·ive** adjective **re·con·struct·or** noun

re·con·struc·tion noun **1** the act or a mode of reconstructing. **2** a thing reconstructed. **3** (**Reconstruction**) US hist. the period (1865-77) following the Civil War, during which the southern states of the Confederacy were controlled by the federal government, and social legislation, including the granting of new rights to blacks, was introduced. **4** the rebuilding of, and restoration of economic stability to, an area devastated by war.

re·con·text·ual·ize transitive verb (also esp. Brit. **-ise**) contextualize again or differently. □ **re·con·text·ual·iz·a·tion** noun

re·con·vene transitive & intransitive verb convene again, esp. (of a meeting etc.) after a pause in proceedings.

re·con·vert transitive verb convert back to a former state. □ **re·con·ver·sion** noun

re·cook transitive verb cook again.

rec·ord ● noun **1 a** a piece of evidence or information constituting an (esp. official) account of something that has occurred, been said, etc. **b** a document preserving this. **2** the state of being set down or preserved in writing or some other permanent form (is a matter of record). **3 a** a thin plastic disc carrying recorded sound in grooves on each surface, for reproduction by a record player. **b** a trace made on this or some other medium, e.g. magnetic tape. **4 a** an official report of the proceedings and judgment in a court of justice. **b** a copy of the pleadings etc. constituting a case to be decided by a court (see also COURT OF RECORD). **5 a** the facts known about a person's past (has an honourable record of service). **b** a piece of evidence about the past or several such pieces cumulatively (the fossil record). **6** (in full **criminal record**) **a** a list of a person's previous criminal convictions. **b** a history of being convicted for crime (has a record). **7** the best performance (esp. in sport) or most remarkable event of its kind on record (often attributive: record low temperatures). **8** an object serving as a memorial of a person or thing; a portrait. **9** Computing a number of related items of information which are handled as a unit. ● transitive verb **1** set down in writing or some other permanent form for later reference, esp. as an official record. **2** convert (sound, a broadcast, etc.) into permanent form for later reproduction. **3** establish or constitute a historical or other record of. □ **break** (or **beat**) **the record** outdo all previous performances etc. **for the record** as an official statement etc. **go on record** state one's opinion or judgment openly or officially, so that it is recorded. **a matter of record** a thing established as a fact by being recorded. **off the record** as an unofficial or confidential statement etc. **on record** officially recorded; publicly known. **set** (or **put** or **get**) **the record straight** correct a misapprehension. □ **re·cord·abil·ity** noun **re·cord·able** adjective

record-breaking attributive adjective that breaks a record (see RECORD noun 7). □ **record-breaker** noun

re·cord·er noun **1** an apparatus for recording, esp. a tape recorder. **2 a** a keeper of records. **b** a person who makes an official record. **3** Music a reedless wind instrument of cylindrical shape, played by blowing directly into one end while covering differing combinations of holes along the cylinder. **4** (usu. **Recorder**) **a** (in England and Wales) a barrister or solicitor of at least ten years' standing, appointed to serve as a part-time judge. **b** Brit. hist. a judge in certain courts.

□ **re·corder·ship** noun (in sense 4). [Anglo-French recordour, Old French recordeur & from RECORD (in obsolete sense 'practise a tune')]

record holder noun a person who holds a record (see RECORD noun 7).

re·cord·ing noun **1** the process by which audio or video signals are recorded for later reproduction. **2** material or a program recorded. **3** the compact disc, record, or tape so produced.

Recording Angel noun an angel that supposedly registers each person's good and bad actions.

recording artist noun a musician or singer who records performances for reproduction and sale under contract to a record company.

recording secretary noun a person responsible for taking the minutes at meetings and distributing the transcripts to members of the organization, union, etc.

re·cord·ist noun a person who records sound.

record player noun an apparatus for reproducing sound from phonograph records by means of a turntable and stylus.

re·count¹ transitive verb **1** narrate. **2** tell in detail. [Anglo-French reconter (as RE-, COUNT¹)]

re·count² ● transitive verb count again. ● noun a recounting, esp. of votes in an election.

re·coup /rəˈkuːp, ri-/ transitive verb **1** recover or regain (a loss). **2** compensate or reimburse for a loss. □ **re·coup·able** adjective **re·coup·ment** noun [French recouper (as RE-, couper cut)]

re·course /ˈriːkɔːrs/ noun **1** the action or an act of turning to a possible source of help, advice, protection, etc. **2** a person or thing turned to. □ **have recourse to** turn to (a person or thing) for help. **without recourse** a formula used by the endorser of a bill etc. to disclaim responsibility for payment. [Old French recours from Latin recursus (as RE-, COURSE)]

re·cover verb **1** transitive regain possession or use or control of; reclaim. **2** intransitive return to health or consciousness or to a normal state or position (have recovered from my illness; the country never recovered from the war). **3** transitive obtain or secure (compensation etc.) by legal process. **4** transitive retrieve or make up for (a loss, setback, etc.). **5** reflexive regain composure or consciousness or control of one's limbs. **6** transitive retrieve (reusable substances) from industrial waste. **7** transitive (during psychoanalysis) discover or apparently discover (repressed memories) of childhood sexual abuse. □ **re·cover·abil·ity** noun **re·cover·able** adjective **re·cover·er** noun **re·cover·ing** adjective [Old French recovrer from Latin recuperare RECUPERATE]

re-cover transitive verb **1** cover again. **2** provide (a chair etc.) with a new cover.

re·cover·ing adjective (of an addict, victim of abuse, etc.) going through rehabilitation or treatment.

re·cov·ery noun (pl. **-eries**) **1** the act or an instance of recovering; the process of being recovered. **2** the process of overcoming an addiction to drugs, alcohol, etc. **3** Golf a stroke bringing the ball out of a bunker etc.

recovery room noun a room in a hospital where a person can recover after an operation or treatment.

re·create transitive verb create over again. □ **re·crea·tion** noun

rec·rea·tion /ˌrekriˈeɪʃən/ noun **1** the process or means of entertaining oneself. **2** an activity or pastime pursued, esp. habitually, for the pleasure or interest it gives (often attributive: recreation area; recreation centre). □ **rec·rea·tion·ist** noun [Old French from Latin recreatio -onis from recreare create again, renew]

rec·rea·tion·al adjective **1** of or pertaining to recreation. **2** used for recreation (recreational facilities). **3** designating or relating to the taking of a drug on an occasional basis for pleasure, esp. when socializing. □ **rec·rea·tion·al·ly** adverb

recreational vehicle noun a van or camper used for recreational purposes, such as touring and camping, esp. a large motorhome. Abbr.: **RV**.

recreation room noun N Amer. **1** = REC ROOM. **2** a room in a school, hospital, etc. in which people can relax, play games, etc.

re·crim·in·al·ize noun (also esp. Brit. **-ise**) make (an activity which once had been a criminal offence) into a criminal offence again. □ **re·crim·in·al·iz·a·tion** noun

re·crim·in·ate /rɪˈkrɪmɪˌneɪt, ri-/ intransitive verb make mutual or counter accusations. □ **re·crim·in·a·tion** noun **re·crim·in·a·tory** adjective [medieval Latin recriminare (as RE-, criminare accuse, from crimen CRIME)]

rec room *noun* *N Amer.* (in full **recreation room**) a room in a private house, usu. in the basement, used for relaxation and entertainment.

re·cross *transitive & intransitive verb* cross or pass over again.

re·cru·desce /ˌriːkruːˈdes, ˌrek-/ *intransitive verb* (of a disease or difficulty etc.) break out again, esp. after a dormant period. □ **re·cru·des·cence** *noun* **re·cru·des·cent** *adjective* [back-formation from *recrudescent* from Latin *recrudescere* (as RE-, *crudus* raw)]

re·cruit ● *noun* **1** a serviceman or servicewoman newly enlisted and not yet fully trained. **2** a new employee or member of a society or organization. ● *verb* **1** *transitive* **a** enlist (a person) as a recruit. **b** attempt to hire or enrol (a person) (*recruit new members*). **2** *transitive* form (an army etc.) by enlisting recruits. **3** *intransitive* get or seek recruits. **4** *transitive* *N Amer.* (attempt to) induce (an athlete) to sign on as a student at a college or university. □ **re·cruit·er** *noun* **re·cruit·ment** *noun* [earlier = reinforcement, from obsolete French dial. *recrute*, ultimately from French *recroître* increase again, from Latin *recrescere*]

re·crys·tal·lize *transitive & intransitive verb* (also esp. *Brit.* **-lise**) crystallize again. □ **re·crys·tal·liz·a·tion** *noun*

recta *pl.* of RECTUM.

rec·tal *adjective* of or relating to the rectum. □ **rec·tal·ly** *adverb*

rect·angle *noun* a plane figure with four straight sides and four right angles, esp. one with the adjacent sides unequal. [French *rectangle* or medieval Latin *rectangulum* from Late Latin *rectiangulum* from Latin *rectus* straight + *angulus* ANGLE[1]]

rect·angu·lar *adjective* **1 a** shaped like a rectangle. **b** having the base or sides or section shaped like a rectangle. **2 a** placed at right angles. **b** having parts or lines placed at right angles. □ **rect·angu·lar·ity** *noun* **rect·angu·lar·ly** *adverb*

rectangular coordinate *noun* (usu. in *pl.*) each of a set of coordinates measured along axes at right angles to one another.

rectangular hyperbola *noun* a hyperbola with rectangular asymptotes.

recti *pl.* of RECTUS.

rec·ti·fi·er *noun* **1** *Electricity* an electrical device that allows a current to flow preferentially in one direction by converting an alternating current into a direct one. **2** a person or thing that rectifies.

rec·tify *transitive verb* (**-fies, -fied**) **1** adjust or make right; correct, amend. **2** purify or refine, esp. by repeated distillation. **3** find a straight line equal in length to (a curve). **4** convert (alternating current) to direct current. □ **rec·ti·fi·able** *adjective* **rec·ti·fi·ca·tion** *noun* [Old French *rectifier* from medieval Latin *rectificare* from Latin *rectus* right]

rec·ti·linear /ˌrektɪˈlɪniər/ *adjective* (also **rec·ti·lin·eal**) **1** bounded or characterized by straight lines. **2** in or forming a straight line. □ **rec·ti·linear·ity** *noun* **rec·ti·linear·ly** *adverb* [Late Latin *rectilineus* from Latin *rectus* straight + *linea* LINE[1]]

rec·ti·tude *noun* **1** moral uprightness. **2** righteousness. **3** correctness. [Old French *rectitude* or Late Latin *rectitudo* from Latin *rectus* right]

recto *noun* (*pl.* **-tos**) **1** the right-hand page of an open book. **2** the front of a printed leaf of paper or manuscript (*opp.* VERSO 1b). [Latin *recto* (*folio*) on the right (leaf)]

rec·tor *noun* **1 a** (in the Church of England) the incumbent of a parish where all tithes formerly passed to the incumbent (*compare* VICAR 1a). **b** (in other Anglican churches) a member of the clergy who has charge of a parish. **2** *Catholicism* a priest in charge of a church or religious institution. **3** the head of some schools, universities, and colleges. □ **rec·tor·ate** *noun* **rec·tor·ial** *adjective* **rec·tor·ship** *noun* [Old French *rectour* or Latin *rector* ruler, from *regere* *rect*- rule]

rec·tory *noun* (*pl.* **-ies**) **1** a rector's house. **2** (in the Church of England) a rector's benefice.

rec·trix *noun* (*pl.* **rec·tri·ces**) a bird's strong tail feather directing flight. [Latin, fem. of *rector* ruler: see RECTOR]

rec·tum *noun* (*pl.* **rec·tums** or **recta**) the final section of the large intestine, terminating at the anus. [Latin *rectum* (*intestinum*) straight (intestine)]

rec·tus *noun* (*pl.* **recti** /ˈrektaɪ/) *Anat.* a straight muscle. [Latin, = straight]

re·cum·bent /rəˈkʌmbənt, ri-/ *adjective* lying down; reclining. □ **re·cum·bency** *noun* [Latin *recumbere* recline (as RE-, *cumbere* lie)]

re·cu·per·ate /rəˈkuːpəˌreit, ri-/ *verb* **1** *intransitive* recover from illness, exhaustion, financial loss, etc. **2** *transitive* regain (health, something lost, etc.). □ **re·cu·per·a·tion** *noun* **re·cu·per·a·tive** /-rətɪv/ *adjective* [Latin *recuperare recuperat-* recover]

recur *intransitive verb* (**re·curred, re·cur·ring**) **1** occur again; be repeated. **2** (of a thought, idea, etc.) come back to one's mind. **3** (foll. by *to*) go back in thought or speech. [Latin *recurrere recurs-* (as RE-, *currere* run)]

re·cur·rent *adjective* **1** recurring; happening repeatedly. **2** (of a nerve, vein, branch, etc.) turning back so as to reverse direction. □ **re·cur·rence** *noun* **re·cur·rent·ly** *adverb*

recurring decimal *noun* a decimal fraction in which the same figures are repeated indefinitely.

re·cur·sion *noun* *Math. & Linguistics* **1** the application or use of a recursive procedure or definition. **2** a recursive definition. [Late Latin *recursio* (as RECUR)]

re·cur·sive *adjective* **1** characterized by recurrence or repetition. **2 a** *Math. & Linguistics* relating to or involving the repeated application of a rule, definition, or procedure to successive results. **b** *Computing* relating to or involving a program or routine, a part of which requires the application of the whole. □ **re·cur·sive·ly** *adverb* [Late Latin *recurs-*, past participle stem of *recurrere* RECUR]

re·curve ● *transitive & intransitive verb* bend backwards. ● *noun* *Archery* **1** a backward-curving end of the limb of a bow. **2** a bow with this feature.

recu·sant /ˈrekjuzənt, rəˈkjuːzənt/ ● *noun* a person who refuses submission to an authority or compliance with a regulation, esp. *hist.* one who refused to attend services of the Church of England. ● *adjective* of or being a recusant. □ **recu·sancy** *noun*

re·cuse /rəˈkjuːz, ri-/ *verb* **1** *reflexive* (of a judge etc.) withdraw from hearing a case because of a possible conflict of interest or lack of impartiality. **2** *transitive* reject (a judge etc.) as prejudiced. □ **re·cus·al** *noun* [Latin *recusare* refuse]

re·cut *transitive verb* (**re·cut·ting**; *past* and *past participle* **re·cut**) cut again.

re·cycle *verb* **1 a** *transitive* return (material) to a previous stage of a cyclic process, esp. convert (waste) to reusable material. **b** *intransitive* practise recycling; participate in a recycling program (*our household recycles!*). **2** *transitive* use again with little or no alteration (*recycle a speech*). **3** *transitive* convert (an object) into something new (*recycle a wine bottle into a vase*). □ **re·cycla·bil·ity** *noun* **re·cyc·lable** *adjective & noun* **re·cyc·ler** *noun* **re·cyc·ling** *noun*

red ● *adjective* **1** of or near the colour seen at the least-refracted end of the visible spectrum, of shades ranging from that of blood to pink or deep orange. **2** flushed in the face with shame, anger, etc. **3** (of the eyes) bloodshot or red-rimmed with weeping. **4** (of the hair) reddish brown, orange. **5** involving or having to do with bloodshed, burning, violence, or revolution. **6** *informal* communist or socialist. **7** *Cdn* of or relating to the Liberal Party. **8** (**Red**) *hist.* Russian, Soviet (*the Red Army*). **9** (of wine) made from dark grapes and coloured by their skins. **10** (in the names of animals) having red or reddish colouring. **11 a** (in the names of plants, shrubs, trees, etc.) having red or reddish flowers, berries, bark, etc. **b** (in the names of vegetables) purple in colour (*red cabbage*; *red onion*). **c** (of potatoes) having a reddish skin. **d** (of wheat) designating a variety having reddish grains. **12** (of a playing card) belonging to hearts or diamonds. ● *noun* **1** a red colour or pigment. **2** red clothes or material (*dressed in red*). **3** *informal* a communist or socialist. **4** *Cdn informal* a Liberal. **5 a** a red ball, piece, etc., in a game or sport. **b** the player using such pieces. **6** *Cdn* (usu. in *pl.*) a red seat in a hockey arena etc., usu. among those closest to the playing surface. **7** the debit side of an account (*in the red*). **8** a red light. **9** red wine. **10** *slang* a red-coloured capsule of secobarbital. **11** *N Amer. informal* a sockeye salmon. □ **red·dish** *adjective* **reddy** *adjective* **redly** *adverb* **red·ness** *noun* [Old English *rēad* from Germanic]

re·dact /rəˈdakt, ri-/ *transitive verb* put into literary form; edit for publication. □ **re·dact·or** *noun* [Latin *redigere redact-* (as RE-, *agere* bring)]

re·dac·tion /rəˈdakʃən, ri-/ *noun* **1** preparation for publication. **2** revision, editing, rearrangement. **3** a new edition. □ **re·dac·tion·al** *adjective*

red admiral *noun* a Holarctic butterfly, *Vanessa atalanta*, with red bands on each pair of wings.

red alert *noun* **1** an urgent warning of imminent danger. **2** an instruction to prepare for an emergency. **3** a state of readiness for an emergency.

red alga *noun* a seaweed with red pigment found esp. in deep water of tropical seas.

redan /rɪˈdan/ *noun* a fieldwork with two faces forming a salient angle. [French from *redent* notching (as RE-, *dent* tooth)]

Red Army *noun* **1** *hist.* originally, the army of the Bolsheviks, the

Workers' and Peasants' Red Army; later, the army of the Soviet Union, formed after the Revolution of 1917. The name was officially dropped in 1946. **2** the army of China or some other (esp. Communist) countries. **3** a left-wing extremist terrorist organization in Japan.

red-backed *adjective Zool.* having a red back (*red-backed salamander*).

red-bait *transitive & intransitive verb* harass and persecute (a person) on account of known or suspected Communist sympathies. □ **red-baiter** *noun* **red-baiting** *noun*

Red Baron see RICHTHOFEN.

Red Bay 1 a small inlet of the Strait of Belle Isle, situated on the southern coast of Labrador. It was an important site for Basque whalers in the 16th c. **2** a municipal community on its eastern shore; pop. (2001) 264. [so called because of the red cliffs surrounding the bay]

red-berry *noun Cdn* (*esp. Nfld*) (*pl.* **-berries**) **1** any of various plants bearing red berries, e.g. partridgeberry, cranberry. **2** the fruit of any of these plants.

red biddy *noun informal* a mixture of cheap wine and methylated spirits.

red blood cell *noun* (also **red cell**) = ERYTHROCYTE.

red-blooded *adjective* full of life, spirited.

red book *noun* the title given to any of various publications of economic or political significance, e.g. a statement of campaign promises. [red being the conventional colour of the binding of official books]

red·breast *noun* a robin.

red-breast·ed *adjective* (of a bird) having a red breast (*red-breasted merganser*).

red-brick *adjective* **1** (of a building) made from bricks of a red-brown colour. **2** (of a UK university) founded in the late 19th or early 20th c.

Red Brigades *noun* an extreme left-wing terrorist organization based in Italy, which from the early 1970s was responsible for carrying out kidnappings, murders, and acts of sabotage. A former prime minister of Italy, Aldo Moro, was killed by the Red Brigades in 1978.

red·bud *noun* any of several early-flowering leguminous trees of the genus *Cercis* (including the Judas tree), esp. the N American *C. canadensis.*

red·cap *noun* **1** *N Amer.* a railway porter. **2** *Brit. slang* a member of the military police.

red card *noun Soccer* a card shown by the referee to indicate that a player is being sent off the field.

red carpet *noun* **1** a strip of red carpet traditionally laid down on formal occasions to greet important visitors. **2** a ceremonial welcome; a lavish reception (*rolled out the red carpet*).

red cedar *noun* **1** any of various conifers with reddish wood, esp. (in full **eastern red cedar**) a tree-sized juniper of eastern N America, *Juniperus virginiana*, or (in full **western red cedar**) an arborvitae of western N America, *Thuja plicata*. **2** the wood of a red cedar.

red cell *var. of* RED BLOOD CELL.

red cent *noun esp. N Amer.* **1** the (originally copper) coin of the lowest value. **2** a trivial sum (frequently in negative contexts) (*not one red cent of taxpayers' money was spent*).

Red Chamber *noun Cdn* **1** the Senate chamber of the Parliament Buildings in Ottawa, so called because of its red carpet and draperies. **2** the Senate itself.

red clover *noun* a Eurasian clover, *Trifolium pratense*, naturalized throughout N America and extensively cultivated for fodder.

red·coat *noun hist.* **1** *Cdn* a member of the North West Mounted Police. **2** a British soldier.

Red Crescent *noun* the name used by national branches in Muslim countries of the International Movement of the Red Cross and the Red Crescent.

Red Cross *noun* **1** the International Movement of the Red Cross and the Red Crescent, an international humanitarian organization originally established to treat the sick and wounded in war and later also aiming to help those suffering the effects of large-scale natural disasters. **2** the emblem of this organization.

red·currant *noun* **1** a widely cultivated shrub, *Ribes rubrum*. **2** the small red edible berry of this plant.

red curry paste *noun* a spicy paste used in Thai cuisine consisting of puréed red chili peppers, garlic, peppercorns, cilantro, coriander, and lime peel.

redd[1] *transitive verb* (*past and past participle* **redd**) *dialect* **1** clear up. **2** arrange, tidy, compose, settle. [Middle English: compare Middle Low German, Middle Dutch *redden*]

redd[2] *noun* a hollow in a riverbed made by a trout or salmon to spawn in. [17th c.: origin unknown]

Red Deer a city in central Alberta, located on the Red Deer River, roughly midway between Calgary and Edmonton; pop. (2001) 67,707. □ **Red Deer·ite** *noun* [see RED DEER RIVER]

red deer *noun* a large deer, *Cervus elaphus*, having a reddish-brown coat; a wapiti.

Red Deer River a river in south central Alberta, 724 km long, rising in the Rocky Mountains north of Banff and flowing northeastward to the city of Red Deer, then flowing generally southeastward to join the South Saskatchewan River just east of the border with Saskatchewan. [originally Cree *waskasioo* elk, an animal mistaken by Scottish fur traders for the red deer native to Scotland]

Red Delicious *noun see* DELICIOUS *noun.*

red·den *verb* **1** *transitive & intransitive* make or become red. **2** *intransitive* blush.

Red·ding, **Otis** (1941–67), US soul singer and songwriter, whose recordings include 'Respect' (1965), 'Try a Little Tenderness' (1966), and '(Sittin' on) The Dock of the Bay' (1968).

red·dle *noun* red ochre; ruddle. [var. of RUDDLE]

red dwarf *noun* an old relatively cool star of very small size.

rede *archaic* ● *noun* advice, counsel. ● *transitive verb* **1** advise. **2** read (a riddle or dream). [Old English *rǣd* from Germanic, related to READ[1] (of which the verb is a Middle English var. retained for archaic senses)]

re·decor·ate *transitive verb* decorate again or differently. □ **re·decor·a·tion** *noun*

re·dedi·cate *transitive verb* dedicate anew. □ **re·dedi·ca·tion** *noun*

re·deem *transitive verb* **1** buy back; recover by expenditure of effort or by a stipulated payment. **2** make a single payment to discharge (a regular charge or obligation). **3** convert (tickets, coupons, bonds etc.) into goods or cash. **4** *Theol.* deliver from sin and damnation. **5** make up for; be a compensating factor in (*has one redeeming feature*). **6** (foll. by *from*) save from (a defect). **7** *reflexive* compensate for past failings, esp. so as to regain favour. **8** save (a person's life) by ransom. **9** save or rescue or reclaim. **10** fulfill (a promise). □ **re·deem·able** *adjective* [Old French *redimer* or Latin *redimere redempt-* (as RE-, *emere* buy)]

re·deem·er *noun* **1** a person who redeems. **2** (**Redeemer**) Jesus Christ.

re·define *transitive verb* define again or differently. □ **re·defin·i·tion** *noun*

re·demp·tion *noun* **1** the act or an instance of redeeming; the process of being redeemed. **2** (in Christian theology) humankind's deliverance from sin and damnation. **3** a thing that redeems. □ **re·demp·tive** *adjective* [Old French from Latin *redemptio* (as REDEEM)]

redemption centre *noun Cdn* (*Maritimes & Nfld*) a place where consumers return beer bottles, pop cans, etc. and receive back the deposit paid at the time of purchase.

Re·demp·tor·ist /rəˈdɛmptərɪst, ri-/ *noun* a member of the Congregation of the Most Holy Redeemer, a Roman Catholic order of priests and lay brothers founded in 1732 by St. Alphonsus Liguori, devoted chiefly to preaching, esp. through parish missions and retreats.

Red Ensign *noun* any of several predominantly red flags having the Union Jack in the upper corner along the hoist, esp.: **1** *Cdn hist.* one used as Canada's national flag until 1965, with the Canadian coat of arms in the fly. **2** *Cdn* one used as the provincial flag of Ontario or Manitoba, with the provincial coat of arms in the fly. **3** *Cdn hist.* one used as the flag of the Hudson's Bay Company, having the initials HBC in the fly. **4** the ensign of the British merchant navy.

re·deploy *transitive verb* move (troops, workers, materials, etc.) from one area of activity to another; reorganize for greater effectiveness. □ **re·deploy·ment** *noun*

re·design ● *transitive verb* design again or differently. ● *noun* **1** the action of redesigning something. **2** a new design.

re·deter·mine *transitive verb* determine again or differently. □ **re·deter·min·a·tion** *noun*

re·devel·op *transitive verb* develop anew (esp. an urban area, with new buildings). □ **re·devel·op·ment** *noun*

red-eye *noun* **1** a red reflection from the blood vessels of a person's retina, seen on a colour photograph taken with a flash. **2** (in full **red-eye flight**) *informal* an overnight airline flight. **3** *Cdn* a drink made with tomato juice and beer. **4** *US slang* cheap whisky. **5** any of various fishes with red eyes, e.g. the rock bass or smallmouth bass.

Consonants: b *but*   d *dog*   f *few*   g *get*   h *her*   j *yes*   k *cat*   l *leg*   m *man*   n *no*   p *pen*   r *red*   s *sit*

red-eyed *adjective* **1** having red eyes from crying etc. **2** (of a bird) having eyes surrounded by a red ring (*red-eyed vireo*).

red-faced *adjective* embarrassed, ashamed.

Red Fife *noun* *Cdn* a high-yielding variety of wheat, with superior milling and baking qualities, developed in the 1840s near Peterborough, Ont. [D. *Fife*, Canadian farmer and wheat breeder, d.1877]

red·fish *noun* **1** any of various reddish fishes. **2** *Brit.* a male salmon in the spawning season.

red flag ● *noun* **1** a warning of danger. **2** (in auto racing etc.) a red flag waved as a signal to stop. **3** a symbol of revolution, socialism, or Communism. ● *transitive verb* **1** (of an official) wave a red flag to stop (a race, participants, etc.). **2 a** warn (a person). **b** call attention to (issues etc.) of concern.

Red·ford, (Charles) Rob·ert (b.1936), US film actor and director. He has starred in films such as *Butch Cassidy and the Sundance Kid* (1969), *The Sting* (1973), *All the President's Men* (1976), and *Out of Africa* (1986); he won an Oscar for best direction for *Ordinary People* (1980). In 1981 he founded the Sundance Institute in Utah, dedicated to the support and development of emerging screenwriters and directors, and to the national and international exhibition of new independent dramatic and documentary films.

red fox *noun* the common fox of Eurasia and N America, *Vulpes vulpes*, having a characteristic deep red or fawn coat.

red giant *noun* a very large star of high luminosity and low surface temperature.

Red·grave, 1 Lynn (b.1944), English actress, who has performed on both stage and screen, and is best known for films such as *Georgy Girl* (1966). **2** her father, **Sir Mi·chael (Scuda·more)** (1908–85), English actor and director, who played numerous Shakespearean roles as well as appearing in other plays, notably in the title role of *Uncle Vanya* (1963); he also starred in films of *The Browning Version* (1951) and *The Importance of Being Earnest* (1952). **3** his daughter, **Van·essa** (b.1937), English stage and film actress, whose films include *Mary Queen of Scots* (1972), *Julia* (1976), for which she won an Oscar, and *Howards End* (1992).

Red Guard *noun* any of various radical or socialist groups, in particular an organized detachment of workers during the Russian Revolution of 1917, or, more importantly, a militant youth movement in China (1966–76), who carried out vicious attacks on intellectuals and other disfavoured groups as part of Mao's Cultural Revolution.

red gum *noun* **1** a reddish resin. **2** any of various kinds of eucalyptus yielding this.

red-handed *adjective* in or just after the act of committing a crime, doing wrong, etc. (*was caught red-handed*).

red hat *noun* **1** a cardinal's hat. **2** the symbol of a cardinal's office.

red·head *noun* **1** a person with red hair. **2** a diving duck of N America, *Aythya americana*, with a reddish-chestnut head and grey and black body.

red-headed *adjective* **1** (of a person) having red hair. **2** (of birds etc.) having a red head (*red-headed woodpecker*).

red heat *noun* the temperature or state of something so hot as to emit red light.

red herring *noun* **1** dried smoked herring. **2** a misleading clue or distraction. [sense 2 from the practice of using the scent of red herring in training hounds]

red-hot ● *adjective* **1 a** sufficiently hot to glow red. **b** very hot (*the stove is red-hot*). **2 a** highly exciting. **b** sexy; passionate (*red-hot jazz*). **3** intensely excited. **4** (of news) sensational; completely new. **5** (of a sports team, player, etc.) on a winning streak; performing exceptionally. ● *noun* *N Amer.* (**red hot**) a hot dog.

re·dial ● *transitive & intransitive verb* (**re·dialed, re·dial·ing; re·dialled, re·dial·ling**) dial again. ● *noun* the facility on a telephone by which (in the event of a number being busy, etc.) the number just dialed may be automatically redialed by pressing a single button.

redid *past of* REDO.

Red Indian *noun* offensive a N American Indian.

Red Indian Lake a long, narrow lake in central Newfoundland, situated southeast of Grand Lake. [so called after the area's Beothuk, who painted their bodies with powdered hematite]

redin·gote /'rɛdɪŋ.gəʊt/ *noun* a woman's long coat with a cutaway front or a contrasting piece on the front. [French from English *riding-coat*]

red ink *noun* *N Amer.* fiscal deficit (*drowning in red ink*). [from the practice of using red ink to record debits and losses in ledgers]

re·direct ● *transitive verb* **1** use (resources etc.) in a different, more desirable way (*redirect funds to more immediate needs*). **2** send (an object, person, etc.) in a different direction (*redirect the ball*). **3** change the address of (a letter). ● *noun* *Cdn* **1** a situation in a hospital emergency department where ambulances with all but critically ill patients are redirected to another hospital. **2** *US Law* the re-examination of a witness after cross-examination. □ **re·direc·tion** *noun*

re·dis·cov·er *transitive verb* discover again. □ **re·dis·cov·ery** *noun* (*pl.* **-ies**).

re·dis·solve *transitive & intransitive verb* dissolve again. □ **re·dis·so·lu·tion** *noun*

re·dis·trib·ute *transitive verb* distribute again or differently. □ **re·dis·tribu·tive** /riːdɪs'trɪbjʊtɪv/ *adjective*

re·dis·tri·bu·tion *noun* **1** the action or process of redistributing something, esp. the redistribution of wealth by means of taxation. **2** *Cdn* the reapportioning, made every ten years, of the number of seats in the House of Commons to reflect changes in the size of the population. □ **re·dis·tri·bu·tion·ist** *noun & adjective*

re·dis·trict *transitive verb* *US* divide or apportion into a new set of districts.

re·div·ide *transitive verb* divide again or differently. □ **re·div·ision** *noun*

redi·vivus /ˌrɛdɪ'viːvəs/ *adjective* (placed after noun) come back to life. [Latin (as RE-, *vivus* living)]

red knot *noun* see KNOT².

Red Lake 1 a small lake in NW Ontario, situated north of Kenora, almost 600 km northwest of Thunder Bay. **2** a town on its southern shore; pop. (2001) 4,233. □ **Red Laker** (in sense 2) *noun* [translation of Ojibwa *miskwa sagaigon* blood-red lake, so called because legendary hunters are said to have killed a large beast there, thus reddening the lake with its blood]

red lead *noun* a red form of lead oxide used as a pigment.

red-letter day *noun* a day that is pleasantly noteworthy or memorable. [originally a festival marked in red on the calendar]

red light *noun* **1** a signal to stop on a road, railway, etc. **2** a warning or refusal.

red-light district *noun* a district containing many brothels, strip clubs, etc.

red line ● *noun* **1** *Hockey* the centre line on the ice surface, midway between the two blue lines. **2** a red mark on a gauge, dial, etc., indicating the maximum safe value of speed, rate of working, or other quantity. **3** a level of activity etc. considered unacceptable or dangerous. ● *transitive verb* (of a bank etc.) refuse credit to (a business, neighbourhood, etc.), esp. arbitrarily.

red man *noun* archaic & offensive a N American Indian.

red maple *noun* a maple of eastern N America, *Acer rubrum*, with red twigs, buds, and flowers.

Red Mass *noun* a votive Mass at which red vestments are worn by the priest, esp. one to mark the annual opening of the law courts.

red meat *noun* meat that is red when raw, e.g. beef or lamb.

Red·mond, John (Ed·ward) (1856–1918), Irish politician. He succeeded Parnell as leader of the Irish Nationalist Party in the House of Commons (1891–1918); the Home Rule Bill of 1912 was introduced with his support although it was never implemented because of the First World War.

red mulberry *noun* see MULBERRY.

red mullet *noun* a red or reddish-brown marine food fish, *Mullus surmuletus*, of the Mediterranean and NE Atlantic.

red·neck esp. *N Amer.* derogatory ● *noun* **1** an uneducated working-class white in the southern US, esp. one holding reactionary political views. **2** anyone holding reactionary political views. ● *adjective* reactionary; conservative.

red-necked grebe *noun* a large grebe, *Podiceps grisegena*, with a long yellowish bill and conspicuous white cheeks and throat and a chestnut-red neck.

redo ● *transitive verb* (*3rd sing. present* **redoes** ; *past* **redid**; *past participle* **redone**) **1** do again or differently. **2** redecorate or renovate. ● *noun* (*pl.* **redos**) an act or instance of redoing.

red oak *noun* **1** a N American oak, *Quercus rubra*, with leaves with bristle-tipped lobes. **2** the hard reddish wood of this tree.

red ochre *noun* a variety of ochre, esp. used for colouring or dyeing.

red·ol·ent /'rɛdələnt/ *adjective* **1** (foll. by *of*, *with*) strongly reminiscent or suggestive or mentally associated. **2** fragrant. **3** having a strong smell; odorous. □ **red·ol·ence** *noun* **red·ol·ent·ly** *adverb* [Old French *redolent* or Latin *redolēre* (as RE-, *olēre* smell)]

Redon /rə'dɔ̃/ **Odi·lon** (1840–1916), French painter and graphic artist. A leading exponent of symbolism, he was an important forerunner of the surrealists in his early charcoal drawings of fantastic, often nightmarish, subjects; from the 1890s he became known for his richly coloured pastels depicting flowers, mythological subjects, and portraits.

red osier *noun* a dogwood shrub, *Cornus stolonifera*, with red or purplish stems and white fruit.

re·double ● *verb* **1** *transitive & intransitive* make or grow greater or more intense or numerous; intensify, increase (*redoubled their efforts*). **2** *intransitive* Bridge double again a bid already doubled by an opponent. ● *noun* Bridge the redoubling of a bid.

re·doubt /rɪ'daʊt/ *noun* **1** Military an outwork or fieldwork usu. square or polygonal and without flanking defences. **2** something serving as a refuge; an entrenched standpoint. [French *redoute* from obsolete Italian *ridotta* from medieval Latin *reductus* refuge, from past participle of Latin *reducere* withdraw (see REDUCE): -b- after DOUBT (compare REDOUBTABLE)]

re·doubt·able *adjective* **1** formidable, esp. as an opponent. **2** (of a person) commanding respect. □ **re·doubt·ably** *adverb* [Old French *redoutable* from *redouter* fear (as RE-, DOUBT)]

re·dound *intransitive verb* **1** (foll. by *to*) (of an action etc.) make a great contribution to (one's credit or advantage etc.). **2** (foll. by *upon*, *on*) come as the final result to; come back or recoil upon. [Middle English, originally = overflow, from Old French *redonder* from Latin *redundare* surge (as RE-, *unda* wave)]

redox /'riːdɒks/ *noun* Chem. (often *attributive*) oxidation and reduction. [reduction + oxidation]

red pepper *noun* the ripe fruit of the sweet pepper, *Capsicum annuum*, used as a vegetable.

red pine *noun* **1** any of several coniferous trees with reddish wood, esp. a N American pine, *Pinus resinosa*, found from Newfoundland to Manitoba. **2** the wood of this tree.

red planet *noun* the planet Mars.

red·poll *noun* any of various Holarctic finches, with red crests.

re·draft ● *transitive verb* draft (a writing or document) again. ● *noun* a second or new draft.

red rag *noun* something that excites a person's rage. [so called because red is supposed to provoke bulls]

re·draw *transitive verb* (*past* **re·drew**; *past participle* **re·drawn**) draw again or differently.

re·dress ● *transitive verb* /rə'dres, rɪ-/ **1** remedy or rectify (a wrong or grievance etc.). **2** readjust; set straight again. ● *noun* /'riːdres, rə'dres/ **1** reparation for a wrong. **2** (foll. by *of*) the act or process of redressing (a grievance etc.). □ **redress the balance** restore equality. □ **re·dress·al** *noun* **re·dress·er** *noun* [Old French *redresse(r)*, *redrecier* (as RE-, DRESS)]

re-dress *transitive & intransitive verb* dress again or differently.

red ribbon ● *noun* **1 a** (in Canada) an award given for coming first place in a contest. **b** (in the US) an award given for coming second place in a contest. **2** a small loop of red ribbon worn as a symbol of AIDS awareness. ● *adjective* designating a worthy but tokenistic concern with AIDS.

Red River 1 a (also called **Red River of the North**) a river in N America, 877 km (545 miles) long, rising in N Dakota and flowing northward to Manitoba, forming for most of its length the border between N Dakota and Minnesota, before passing through Winnipeg and emptying into the southern end of Lake Winnipeg. **b** Cdn hist. = RED RIVER SETTLEMENT. **2** a river in SE Asia, which rises in S China and flows 1 175 km (730 miles) generally southeastward through northern Vietnam to the Gulf of Tonkin north of Haiphong. **3** (also called **Red River of the South**) a river in the southern US, a tributary of the Mississippi, which rises in N Texas and flows 1 966 km (1,222 miles) generally southeastward, forming part of the border between Texas and Oklahoma, and enters the Mississippi in Louisiana, north of Baton Rouge. [sense 1a originally Ojibwa *Miskwagama Sipi* red water river, prob. after the reddish-brown silt carried by its waters]

Red River cart *noun* Cdn hist. a sturdy two-wheeled wooden cart pulled by oxen or horses, used for transportation on the Prairies.

Red River Cereal *noun* Cdn proprietary a mixture of cracked wheat, cracked rye, and flax seeds, served cooked as a hot cereal.

Red River Colony see RED RIVER SETTLEMENT.

Red River jig *noun* Cdn **1** a Metis step dance originating in the Red River Colony, combining French-Canadian dance rhythms and Aboriginal powwow steps, including an element of improvisation by

dancers who compete for originality and precise footwork. **2** the music for this.

Red River Rebellion *noun* Cdn hist. an uprising in 1869–70 by the Metis of the Red River Settlement under the leadership of Louis Riel, in response to the takeover of their territory by the government of Canada.

Red River Settlement (also **Red River**, **Red River Colony**) Cdn hist. the colony founded in 1812 by Lord Selkirk in the valley of the Red River in Manitoba.

Red Rome Beauty *noun* a large red eating and cooking apple with green streaks and tiny green dots.

red·root *noun* any of various plants with red roots.

red rose *noun* the emblem of Lancashire or hist. the Lancastrians.

Red Rover *noun* a schoolyard game in which children face each other in two parallel lines with hands joined and take turns calling one person from the other team to run over and attempt to break through the human chain.

red salmon *noun* = SOCKEYE.

Red Sea a long, narrow, landlocked sea separating Africa from the Arabian peninsula. It is linked to the Indian Ocean in the south by the Gulf of Aden and to the Mediterranean in the north by the Suez Canal.

red shift *noun* the shift of spectral lines toward longer wavelengths, arising when a galaxy or celestial body and its observer are moving apart (compare BLUE SHIFT). □ **red-shifted** *adjective*

red·shirt US ● *noun* a college athlete who is kept out of varsity competition for a year in order to develop his or her skills and extend his or her period of eligibility at this level of competition (often *attributive*: *redshirt freshman*). ● *transitive verb* keep (an athlete) out of varsity competition for a year. [from the red jersey commonly worn by such an athlete in practices against the regulars]

red·skin *noun* **1** dated offensive a North American Indian. **2** a variety of peanut grown in the southeastern US with a dark red skin inside the husk, esp. when sold unblanched.

red snapper *noun* an edible marine fish of the family Lutjanidae, esp. *Lutjanus campechinus* of the W Atlantic.

red spider *noun* = SPIDER MITE.

red spruce *noun* a spruce of eastern Canada and the northeastern US, *Picea rubens*.

red squirrel *noun* **1** a small N American squirrel, *Tamiasciurus hudsonicus*, with reddish fur and white crescents around the eyes. **2** the common Eurasian squirrel, *Sciurus vulgaris*, with reddish fur.

Red Star *noun* esp. hist. the emblem of some Communist countries.

red·start *noun* **1** any of various American warblers with red markings. **2** any European red-tailed songbird of the genus *Phoenicurus*. [RED + Old English *steort* tail]

red tag sale *noun* N Amer. a sale at which items marked with a red tag are (usu. deeply) discounted.

red-tailed hawk *noun* a common North and Central American hawk, *Buteo jamaicensis*, with a russet-coloured tail.

red tape *noun* excessive bureaucracy or adherence to formalities esp. in public business. [from the red or pink tape used to secure official documents]

red-throated loon *noun* a small Holarctic loon, *Gavia stellata*, with a grey head, red throat patch, and plain, uncheckered back.

red tide *noun* a discoloration of marine waters caused by an outbreak of toxic red dinoflagellates.

Red Tory *noun* Cdn a member of a Conservative party who holds more liberal views on certain esp. social issues than his or her fellow party members. □ **Red Tory·ism** *noun*

re·duce *verb* **1** *transitive & intransitive* make or become smaller or less. **2** *transitive* (foll. by *to*) bring by force or necessity (to some undesirable state or action) (*reduced them to tears*; *were reduced to begging*). **3** *transitive* convert to another (esp. simpler) form (*reduced it to a powder*). **4** *transitive* convert (a fraction) to the form with the lowest terms. **5** *transitive* (foll. by *to*) bring or simplify or adapt by classification or analysis (*the dispute may be reduced to three issues*). **6** *transitive* make lower in status or rank. **7** *transitive* lower the price of. **8** *intransitive* lessen one's weight or size. **9** *transitive* weaken (*is in a very reduced state*). **10** *transitive* impoverish. **11** *transitive* subdue; bring back to obedience. **12** *intransitive & transitive* Chem. **a** combine or cause to combine with hydrogen. **b** undergo or cause to undergo addition of electrons (opp. OXIDIZE 3). **13** *transitive* Chem. convert (oxide etc.) to metal. **14** *transitive* **a** (in surgery) restore (a dislocated etc. part) to its proper position. **b** remedy (a dislocation etc.) in this way. **15** *transitive* Photog. make (a negative or print) less dense.

Vowels: a cat ɑ arm e bed ɜr her ɜː deux ə ago ɪ sit i cosy iː feed ɒ hot ɔ pore ɔː no ʌ run ʊ put

16 *transitive Cooking* boil so as to concentrate (a liquid, sauce, etc.).

☐ **reduce to the ranks** demote (an NCO) to the rank of private.

☐ **re·duc·er** *noun* **re·duci·bil·ity** *noun* **re·du·cible** *adjective* [Middle English in sense 'restore to original or proper position', from Latin *reducere reduct-* (as RE-, *ducere* bring)]

reduced circumstances *plural noun* poverty after relative prosperity.

reducing agent *noun Chem.* a substance that brings about reduction by becoming oxidized and losing electrons.

re·duct·ase /rɪˈdʌkteɪz, -teɪs/ *noun* an enzyme which promotes chemical reduction. [REDUCTION + -ASE]

reductio ad absurdum /rɪˌdʌktiɔː ad abˈzɜrdəm/ *noun* a method of proving the falsity of a premise by showing that the logical consequence is absurd; an instance of this. [Latin, = reduction to the absurd]

re·duc·tion *noun* **1** the act or an instance of reducing; the process of being reduced. **2** an amount by which prices etc. are reduced. **3** a reduced copy of a picture, map, etc. **4** an arrangement of an orchestral score for piano etc. **5** a thick and concentrated liquid or sauce made by boiling. [Old French *reduction* or Latin *reductio* (as REDUCE)]

re·duc·tion·ism *noun* **1** the tendency to or principle of analyzing complex things into simple constituents. **2** often *derogatory* the doctrine that a system can be fully understood in terms of its isolated parts, or an idea in terms of simple concepts (compare HOLISM 1).

☐ **re·duc·tion·ist** *noun* **re·duc·tion·is·tic** *adjective*

re·duc·tive *noun* **1** tending to present a subject or problem in a simplified form, esp. one viewed as crude. **2** (with reference to art) minimal. **3** of or relating to chemical reduction. ☐ **re·duc·tive·ly** *adverb* **re·duc·tive·ness** *noun*

re·dun·dant *adjective* **1** superfluous; not needed. **2** that can be omitted without any loss of significance. **3** (of a person) no longer needed at work and therefore unemployed. **4** *Engin. & Computing* (of a component) not needed but included in case of failure in another component. ☐ **re·dun·dancy** *noun* (pl. **-cies**). **re·dun·dant·ly** *adverb* [Latin *redundare redundant-* (as REDOUND)]

re·dupli·cate *transitive verb* **1** make double. **2** repeat. **3** repeat (a letter or syllable or word) exactly or with a slight change, e.g. hurly-burly, see-saw. ☐ **re·dupli·ca·tion** *noun* **re·dupli·ca·tive** *adjective*

redux /rɪˈdʌks/ *adjective* brought back, revived, restored (placed after noun: *romance redux*). [Latin, from *reducere* bring back]

red·water *noun* a blood disease of cattle, characterized by the passing of red or blackish urine, caused esp. by a tick-borne protozoan parasite of the genus *Babesia*.

red wiggler *noun N Amer.* = RED WORM.

red willow *noun* any of several willows with reddish twigs, esp. *Salix laevigata* of western N America.

red·wing *noun* **1** a migratory thrush, *Turdus iliacus*, of N Europe, with red underwings showing in flight. **2** any of several other red-winged birds, esp. the red-winged blackbird.

red-winged blackbird *noun* a very common North and Central American blackbird, *Agelaius phoeniceus*, the male of which has a conspicuous red patch on the wings, with a trilling note, nesting in freshwater marshes and at water edges.

red·wood *noun* **1** an exceptionally large Californian conifer, *Sequoia sempervirens*, yielding red wood. **2** any tree yielding red wood.

red worm *noun* an earthworm, *Lumbricus rubellus*, used as bait in fishing and in vermicomposting.

red zone *noun* **1** a red sector on a gauge or dial corresponding to conditions that exceed safety limits. **2** a region that is dangerous or forbidden, or in which a particular activity is prohibited. **3** *American Football* the region between the opposing team's 20-yard line and goal line, which is a major focus of their attack strategy.

ree·bok *noun* a small southern African antelope, *Pelea capreolus*, with sharp horns. [Dutch, = roebuck]

re-echo *transitive & intransitive verb* (**-echoes**, **-echoed**) **1** echo. **2** echo repeatedly; resound.

Reed ▸ **1 Lou** (born Lewis Allen Reed) (b.1942), US rock singer, guitarist, and songwriter. He led the Velvet Underground, his literate songs dealing with hitherto taboo subjects such as heroin addiction and sado-masochism. His best-known solo recordings are the song 'Walk on the Wild Side' and album *Transformer* (both 1972). **2 Wal·ter** (1851–1902), US physician. He proved that yellow fever was transmitted by the mosquito *Aedes aegypti* (1900–01), and showed that the agent responsible was a virus.

reed *noun* **1 a** any of various water or marsh plants with a firm stem,

esp. of the genus *Phragmites*. **b** a tall straight stalk of this. **2** (*collective*) reeds growing in a mass or used as material esp. for thatching. **3** a pipe of reed or straw. **4 a** the vibrating part of the mouthpiece of some wind instruments, e.g. the oboe and clarinet, made of reed or other material and producing the sound. **b** (esp. in *pl.*) a reed instrument. **5** a weaver's comb-like implement for separating the threads of the warp and correctly positioning the weft. **6** (in *pl.*) a set of semicylindrical adjacent mouldings like reeds laid together. [Old English *hrēod* from West Germanic]

reed bed *noun* a bed or growth of reeds.

reed·buck *noun* any of various African antelopes of the genus *Redunca*, characterized by their whistling calls and high bouncing jumps.

reed canary grass *noun* a tall grass, *Phalaris arundinacea*, grown for hay and fodder.

reed·ed *adjective Music* (of an instrument) having a vibrating reed.

reed·ing *noun Archit.* a small semicylindrical moulding or ornamentation (compare REED *noun* 6).

re-edit *transitive verb* (**-edited**, **-editing**) edit again or differently. ☐ **re-edition** *noun*

reed mace *noun* = BULRUSH 2.

reed·man *noun* (pl. **reed·men**) a player of a reed instrument, esp. a saxophone or a clarinet, in a jazz ensemble.

reed organ *noun* a harmonium etc. with the sound produced by metal reeds.

reed pipe *noun* **1** a wind instrument with sound produced by a reed. **2** an organ pipe with a reed.

re-educate *transitive verb* educate again, esp. to change a person's views or beliefs. ☐ **re-education** *noun*

reed warbler *noun* any bird of the genus *Acrocephalus*, esp. *A. scirpaceus*, frequenting reed beds.

reedy *adjective* (**reed·i·er**, **reed·i·est**) **1** full of reeds. **2** like a reed, esp. in weakness or slenderness. **3** (of a voice) high, thin, and harsh; not resonant. ☐ **reed·i·ness** *noun*

reef¹ *noun* **1** a ridge of rock or coral etc. at or near the surface of the sea. **2 a** a lode of ore. **b** the bedrock surrounding this. ☐ **reefy** *adjective* [earlier *riff(e)* from Middle Dutch, Middle Low German *rif*, *ref*, from Old Norse *rif* RIB]

reef² *Naut.* ● *noun* each of several strips across a sail, for taking it in or rolling it up to reduce the surface area in a high wind. ● *transitive verb* **1** take in a reef or reefs of (a sail). **2** shorten (a topmast or a bowsprit). [Dutch *reef*, *rif* from Old Norse *rif* RIB, in the same sense: compare REEF¹]

reef·er¹ *noun* **1** *slang* a marijuana cigarette. **2** a thick close-fitting double-breasted jacket. **3** a person who reefs a sail. [REEF² (in sense 1, = a thing rolled) + -ER¹]

reef·er² *noun* a refrigerated truck, railway car, or ship. [abbreviation]

reef knot *noun* a double knot made symmetrically to hold securely and cast off easily.

reef·point *noun* each of several short pieces of rope attached to a sail to secure it when reefed.

reek ● *intransitive verb* (often foll. by *of*) **1** smell strongly and unpleasantly. **2** have unpleasant or suspicious associations (*this reeks of corruption*). **3** give off smoke or fumes. ● *noun* a foul or stale smell. ☐ **reeky** *adjective* [Old English *rēocan* (v.), *rēc* (n.), from Germanic]

reel ● *noun* **1** a cylindrical device on which film, tape, etc., or *Brit.* thread, yarn, wire, etc., are wound. **2** a quantity of thread etc. wound on a reel. **3** a device for winding and unwinding a line as required, esp. in fishing. **4** a revolving part in various machines. **5 a** a lively folk or Scottish dance with two or more couples facing each other. **b** a piece of music for this. ● *verb* **1** *transitive* wind (thread, a fishing line, etc.) on a reel. **2** *transitive* (foll. by *in*, *up*) draw (fish etc.) in or up by the use of a reel. **3** *intransitive* stand or walk or run unsteadily. **4** *intransitive* be shaken mentally or physically. **5** *intransitive* rock from side to side, or swing violently. **6** *intransitive* dance a reel. ☐ **reel off** say or recite very rapidly and without apparent effort. ☐ **reel·er** *noun* [Old English *hrēol*, of unknown origin]

re-elect *transitive verb* elect again, esp. to a further term of office. ☐ **re-election** *noun*

reel mower *noun N Amer.* a push mower of a type having blades in the form of a revolving cylinder which cut the grass against a separate fixed blade.

reel-to-reel *adjective* designating a tape recorder in which the tape passes between two reels mounted separately, rather than within a cassette.

re-emerge *intransitive verb* emerge again; come back out. □ **re-emergence** *noun*

re-emphasize *transitive verb* (also esp. *Brit.* **-sise**) place renewed emphasis on. □ **re-emphasis** *noun*

re-employ *transitive verb* employ again. □ **re-employ·ment** *noun*

re-enact *transitive verb* act out (a past event). □ **re-enactment** *noun* **re-enactor** *noun*

re-energize *verb* (also esp. *Brit.* **-gise**) **1** *transitive* energize anew; revitalize; restore to an active, vigorous, or energetic state. **2** *intransitive* be energized or revitalized. **3** *transitive* supply with energy once again.

re-engineer *transitive & intransitive verb* **1** design and construct again (*a re-engineered automobile*). **2** change the structure of a business or other organization, usu. by introducing improved technology and reducing staff, to improve efficiency. □ **re-engineer·ing** *noun*

re-enlist *intransitive verb* enlist again, esp. in the armed services.

re-enter *verb* **1** *transitive & intransitive* enter (a building etc.) again; go back in. **2** *transitive* participate in (a race, politics, a contest, etc.) again. □ **re-entrance** *noun*

re-entrant ● *adjective* **1** (of an angle) pointing inwards (*opp.* SALIENT *adjective* 2). **2** *Math.* (of an interior angle in a polygon) greater than 180°. ● *noun* **1** a re-entrant angle. **2** *Geog.* an inlet, valley, etc. forming a prominent indentation in a landform. **3** a person who re-enters (esp. the workforce).

re-entry *noun* (*pl.* **-entries**) **1** the act of entering again, esp. (of a spacecraft, missile, etc.) re-entering the earth's atmosphere. **2** *Law* an act of retaking or repossession.

re-equip *transitive & intransitive verb* (**-equipped**, **-equipping**) provide or be provided with new equipment. □ **re-equipment** *noun*

re-erect *transitive verb* erect again.

re-establish *transitive verb* establish again or anew. □ **re-establish·ment** *noun*

re-evaluate *transitive verb* evaluate again or differently. □ **re-evalua·tion** *noun*

reeve¹ *noun* **1** *Cdn* (in Ontario and the Western provinces) the elected leader of the council of a town or other rural municipality. **2** *Brit. hist.* **a** the chief magistrate of a town or district. **b** an official supervising a landowner's estate. **c** any of various minor local officials. □ **reeve·ship** *noun Cdn.* [Old English (*ge*)*rēfa*, *girǣfa*]

reeve² *transitive verb* (*past* **rove** or **reeved**) *Naut.* **1** (usu. foll. by *through*) thread (a rope or rod etc.) through a ring or other aperture. **2** pass a rope through (a block etc.). **3** fasten (a rope or block) in this way. [prob. from Dutch *rēven* REEF²]

reeve³ *noun* a female ruff (*see* RUFF¹ 4). [17th c.: origin unknown]

Reeves, **Keanu** (b.1964), Canadian film actor. His first major role was in the comedy *Bill and Ted's Excellent Adventure* (1989), and among his many other films are *Speed* (1994), *The Matrix* (1999) and its sequels *The Matrix Reloaded* and *The Matrix Revolutions* (both 2003).

re-examine *transitive verb* examine again or further (esp. a witness after cross-examination). □ **re-examin·a·tion** *noun*

re-export ● *transitive verb* export again (esp. imported goods after further processing or manufacture). ● *noun* **1** the process of re-exporting. **2** something re-exported.

ref *informal* ● *noun* a referee in hockey, basketball, football, etc. ● *transitive & intransitive verb* (**reffed**, **ref'fing**) supervise (a game or match) as a referee. □ **ref'fing** *noun* [abbreviation]

ref. *abbreviation* **1** reference. **2** refer to. **3** (**Ref.**) *Cdn hist.* Reform Party.

re·face *transitive verb* repair or replace the facing on (esp. a building).

re·fash·ion *transitive verb* change the composition or appearance of (something); fashion again or differently.

re·fec·tory /rəˈfektəri, ri-/ *noun* (*pl.* **-ies**) a room used for communal meals, esp. in a monastery or college. [Late Latin *refectorium* from Latin *reficere* refresh (as RE-, *facere* make)]

refectory table *noun* a long narrow table set upon trestles joined by a stretcher, historically used in dining halls.

refer *verb* (**re·ferred**, **re·fer·ring**) (usu. foll. by *to*) **1** *intransitive* allude (to) or describe (*when I said people are stupid I wasn't referring to you*; *she refers to my mother as 'that woman'*). **2** *intransitive* represent; pertain (to) (*the word 'doe' can be used to refer to a female rabbit*; *this paragraph refers to the events of last year*). **3** *transitive* send or direct (someone) to a person or thing for help, information, advice, etc. (*my doctor referred me to a psychiatrist*; *the reader is referred to page 14 for a fuller account of the affair*). **4** *transitive* direct (questions to be answered, matters to be dealt with, issues to be resolved, etc.) to someone (*their case was referred to a judge for arbitration*; *please refer all questions to me*). **5** *intransitive* consult (notes, instructions, etc.) for information or advice (*the speaker had to refer to the written copy of his speech*). **6** *transitive* trace or attribute something to a person or thing as a cause or source (*referred their success to their popularity*). **7** *transitive Brit.* fail (a candidate in an examination). □ **re·fer·able** *adjective* [Old French *referer* from Latin *referre* carry back (as RE-, *ferre* bring)]

ref·eree /ˌrefəˈriː/ ● *noun* **1** an official who supervises a hockey, basketball, etc. game or boxing match to ensure that the competitors obey the rules. **2** a person whose opinion or judgment is sought, esp. by mutual consent of two parties in a legal dispute. **3** a person appointed to examine and assess an academic work being considered for publication. **4** *Brit.* a person willing to testify to the character of an applicant for employment etc. ● *verb* (**ref·erees**, **ref·ereed**) **1** *intransitive* act as referee. **2** *transitive* supervise (a game, match, etc.) as a referee. **3** *transitive* review (an academic publication) as a referee. □ **ref·ereed** *adjective* **ref·eree·ing** *noun*

ref·er·ence /ˈrefrəns/ ● *noun* **1** (foll. by *to*) **a** an allusion (*made no reference to our problems*). **b** a relation or correspondence (*success seems to have little reference to merit*). **2 a** a direction of attention to a book or passage of a book, esp. one used as a source of information for a research paper, article, etc. **b** a useful source of information, such as a book, article, etc. **c** such sources of information considered collectively. **d** the act of looking up a passage etc. or looking in a book for information. **3 a** a written testimonial supporting an applicant for employment etc. **b** a person giving this. **4 a** the referring of a matter for decision, settlement, or consideration to some authority. **b** a case or matter referred for consideration. ● *transitive verb* **1** cite; make mention of or a reference to. **2** provide (a book etc.) with references to authorities. □ **with** (or **in**) **reference to** regarding; as regards. **without reference to** not taking account of. □ **ref·er·en·tial** /-ˈrenʃəl/ *adjective* **ref·er·en·ti·al·ity** /-renʃiˈalɪti/ *noun*

reference book *noun* a book intended to be consulted for information on individual matters rather than read continuously.

reference group *noun* a group to which a person, perhaps subconsciously, refers as a standard in forming attitudes and behaviour.

reference library *noun* a library in which the books are for consultation, not loan. □ **reference librarian** *noun*

reference point *noun* (also **point of reference**) a basis or standard for evaluation, assessment, or comparison; a criterion.

ref·er·en·dum /ˌrefəˈrendəm/ *noun* (*pl.* **ref·er·en·dums** or **ref·er·en·da**) **1** the process of referring a political question to the electorate for a direct decision by general vote. **2** a vote taken by referendum. [Latin, gerund or neuter gerundive of *referre*: see REFER]

ref·er·ent /ˈrefərənt/ *noun* the idea or thing that a word etc. symbolizes.

re·fer·ral *noun* the referring of an individual to an expert or specialist for advice, esp. the directing of a patient by a general practitioner to a medical specialist.

referred pain *noun* pain felt in a part of the body other than its actual source.

re·fill ● *transitive & intransitive verb* fill or become filled again (*he refilled our glasses*; *the hole refilled with water*). ● *noun* **1** a replacement for something that has been used up, esp. fitting in the same container or device as the original (*a package of lead refills for a pencil*). **2** a second serving, esp. of a beverage etc., replacing one consumed, usu. served in the same cup. □ **re·fill·able** *adjective*

re·finance *verb* **1** *transitive & intransitive* finance again; arrange a new financial agreement for (*refinance a house*). **2** *transitive* repay some or all of (a loan) by obtaining fresh loans, usu. at a lower rate of interest. □ **re·finan·cing** *noun*

re·fine *transitive verb* **1** free from impurities or defects; purify, clarify. **2** make or become more polished, elegant, or cultured. **3** make or become more subtle or delicate in thought, feelings, etc. **4** fine-tune, improve or perfect (*refine a mechanism*). □ **re·fin·ing** *noun* [RE- + FINE¹ *verb*]

re·fined *adjective* **1** characterized by polish, elegance, or subtlety. **2** (esp. of sugar, oil, etc.) purified, freed from impurities or extraneous matter. **3** fine-tuned, perfected (*a refined process*).

re·fine·ment *noun* **1** the act of refining or the process of being refined. **2** polish or elegance in behaviour, manners, or taste. **3** an added development or improvement (*a car with several refinements*).

re·fin·er *noun* a person or company whose business is to refine crude oil, metal, sugar, etc.

re·fin·ery *noun* (*pl.* **-eries**) a place where oil etc. is refined.

re·finish *transitive verb* **1** apply a new finish to (a surface). **2** remove old layers of paint or varnish from (wood, furniture, etc.) and apply new stain, varnish, paint, etc. to.

refit ● *transitive & intransitive verb* (**re·fit·ted**, **re·fit·ting**) restore or be restored to a serviceable condition by renewals and repairs. ● *noun* the act or an instance of refitting; the process of being refitted.
□ **re·fit·ting** *noun*

re·flag *transitive verb* (**re·flagged**, **re·flag·ging**) change the national registration of (a ship).

re·flate *transitive verb* increase the amount of money in use in a country, usu. in order to increase demand for goods and to stimulate the economy. [RE- after *inflate*, *deflate*]

re·fla·tion *noun* the (esp. deliberate) inflation of a financial system to restore its previous condition after deflation.

re·flect *verb* **1** *transitive* (of an esp. smooth or polished surface) throw back or cause to rebound (heat, light, sound, etc.). **2** *transitive* (esp. of a mirror, water, glass) reproduce or show an image of. **3** *transitive* result from; suggest or point to something as a cause or source (*his aggressive behaviour reflects a will to win*). **4** *intransitive* (usu. foll. by *on*, *upon*) bring credit or discredit to (*this loss reflects badly on the coaching*). **5 a** *intransitive* (often foll. by *on*, *upon*) meditate on; think about. **b** *transitive* (foll. by *that*, *how*, etc. + clause) consider; remind oneself. **6** *intransitive* (of light, heat, an image, etc.) be cast back; bounce back or off (*moonlight reflected off the water*). **7** *transitive* (of an action, result, etc.) show or bring (credit, discredit, etc.). [Old French *reflecter* or Latin *reflectere* (as RE-, *flectere flex-* bend)]

re·flect·ance *noun Physics* a measure of the proportion of light or other radiation that a surface (of a particular substance) reflects or scatters.

reflecting pool *noun* an artificial pool of water incorporated into an architectural or landscape design so as to reflect images.

reflecting telescope *noun* = REFLECTOR 2a.

re·flec·tion *noun* **1** the act or an instance of a surface reflecting light, heat, sound, etc.; the process of being reflected. **2 a** reflected light, heat, or colour. **b** a reflected image. **3** long and careful consideration (*she decided, after further reflection, to accept his offer after all*). **4** (often foll. by *on*, *of*) an indication of something (*the clothes you wear are a reflection of your personality; these events are a sad reflection on the state of things*). **5** an account or representation of something; a commentary (*personal reflections on federalism*). **6** a thought (*these sad reflections came to him as he sat there*).

re·flect·ive *adjective* **1** (of a surface etc.) reflecting light, images, etc. **2** (of a person or mood etc.) given to meditation. **3** (of an account) characterized by deep thought or reflection. **4** (foll. by *of*) indicative; symptomatic. □ **re·flect·ive·ly** *adverb*

re·flec·tiv·ity *noun Physics* the property of reflecting light or radiation, esp. reflectance as measured independently of the thickness of a material.

re·flect·or *noun* **1** a piece of glass or metal etc. for reflecting light in a required direction, e.g. a red one on the back of a bicycle. **2 a** a telescope etc. using a mirror to produce images. **b** the mirror itself. **3** any surface which reflects light, heat, sound, etc., or something considered in terms of its reflective properties.

re·flex ● *noun* **1** an involuntary or automatic response of any organ or body part to a stimulus (*an irritation of the nose triggers a reflex in the form of a sneeze*). **2** an immediate or automatic reaction to something, esp. a habitual response (*hitting the snooze button is just a reflex*). **3** (in *pl.*) the ability, usu. physical, to react quickly, esp. dexterously or with coordination (*Eric's excellent reflexes made him an outstanding goalie*). **4** a word, sound unit, etc. derived from the corresponding word etc. of another language or an earlier stage of the language. **5** (in reflexology) a response in a part of the body to stimulation of a corresponding point on the feet, hands, or head (also *attributive*: *reflex points*). ● *adjective* **1** (of an action) independent of the will, as an automatic response to the stimulation of a nerve (e.g. a sneeze). **2** (of a response or reaction) automatic, immediate, unthinking. **3** (of an effect or influence) reactive; coming back upon its author or source. **4** bent backwards. □ **re·flex·ly** *adverb* [Latin *reflexus* (as REFLECT)]

reflex arc *noun Anat.* the sequence of nerves involved in a reflex action.

reflex camera *noun* a camera in which an image from the main lens is reflected onto a ground glass focusing screen and can be seen and adjusted up to the moment of exposure.

re·flexed *adjective Zool. & Bot.* bent, folded, or curved backwards (*the reflexed beak of a bird; reflexed leaves*).

re·flex·ive *adjective* **1** triggered by, or as if by, reflex. **2 a** (of a person) focused on or concerning oneself. **b** (of a thing) concerning itself; intended more for oneself than for others. **3** *Grammar* (of a word or form) referring back to the subject of a sentence (esp. of a pronoun, e.g. *myself*). **4** *Grammar* (of a verb) having a reflexive pronoun as its object (as in *to wash oneself*). □ **re·flex·ive·ly** *adverb* **re·flex·ive·ness** *noun* **re·flex·iv·ity** *noun*

re·flex·ol·ogy *noun* **1** a technique for treating tension, alleviating symptoms by massaging points on the feet, hands, and head. **2** *Psych.* **a** the theory that all behaviour consists merely of innate or conditioned responses. **b** the branch of knowledge that deals with reflex action as it affects behaviour. □ **re·flex·ol·o·gist** *noun*

re·float *transitive verb* set (a stranded ship) afloat again.

re·flux *noun* **1** a backward flow. **2** *Med.* a reverse flow, esp. of gastric fluid etc. **3** *Chem.* a method of boiling a liquid so that any vapour is liquefied and returned to the boiler.

re·focus *transitive verb* (**re·fo·cused**, **re·focus·ing** or **re·fo·cussed**, **re·focus·sing**) **1** (of a camera lens) adjust the focus of. **2** change the scope or object of (attention, a study, goals, etc.).

re·forest *transitive verb* replant with trees. □ **re·forest·a·tion** *noun*

re·forge *verb* forge again or differently.

re·form ● *verb* **1** *transitive & intransitive* make or become better by the removal of faults and errors; improve. **2** *transitive* abolish or cure (an abuse or vice). **3** *transitive N Amer.* correct (a legal document). **4** *transitive Chem.* subject (hydrocarbons) to a catalytic process in which molecules made up of atoms in straight chains are converted to branched forms for use as gasoline. ● *noun* **1** significant changes suggested or made to something; an overhaul (*Senate reform*). **2** the removal of faults or abuses, esp. of a moral or political or social kind (*we are committed to reform*). **3** (**Reform**) *Cdn hist.* = REFORM PARTY (also *attributive*: *Reform member*). **4** (**Reform**) (*attributive*) *Cdn hist.* designating those who opposed the Family Compact in Upper Canada or the Château Clique in Lower Canada in the movement for responsible government in the 19th c. **5** (usu. **Reform**) = REFORM JUDAISM (also *attributive*: *Reform synagogue*). □ **re·form·able** *adjective* **re·formed** *adjective*

re-form *transitive & intransitive verb* form again. □ **re-formation** *noun*

Reform Act any of several acts framed to amend the system of parliamentary representation in Britain. The first Reform Act (1832) disenfranchised various rotten boroughs and lowered the property qualification and so widened the electorate by about 50 per cent to include most of the male members of the upper middle class. The second (1867) doubled the electorate by again lowering the property qualification. A third Act (1884) extended the franchise to male agricultural workers.

re·format *transitive verb* (**re·format·ted**, **re·format·ting**) **1** revise or represent in another format. **2** *Computing* make adjustments to (a storage medium) to enable it to receive data.

ref·or·ma·tion /ˌrefərˈmeɪʃən/ *noun* **1** the act of reforming or process of being reformed, esp. a radical change for the better in political or religious or social affairs. **2** (**Reformation**) (also **Protestant Reformation**) (prec. by *the*) *hist.* the 16th-c. movement to reform the doctrine and practices of the Roman Catholic Church, which resulted in the establishment of the Protestant Churches. The Reformation is usually thought of as beginning in 1517 in Wittenberg when Martin Luther issued ninety-five theses criticizing the sale of indulgences, and launched an attack on papal infallibility, priestly celibacy, the doctrine of transubstantiation, and corruption within religious orders; Luther confirmed his commitment to reform at the Diet of Worms in 1521. In Switzerland a separate movement was led by Zwingli and later Calvin. □ **Ref·or·ma·tion·al** *adjective*

Reformation Sunday *noun* the last Sunday in October, observed in some Protestant churches in honour of the Reformation, commemorating Luther's attack on the sale of indulgences on October 31, 1517.

re·forma·tory /rəˈfɔrmətɔri, ri-/ ● *noun* (pl. **-ies**) *N Amer.* an institution to which young offenders are sent to be reformed. *Also called* REFORM SCHOOL. ● *adjective* tending or designed to reform.

Re·formed *adjective* **1** designating a Church that has accepted the principles of the Reformation, esp. a Calvinist Church (as distinct from Lutheran). **2** belonging to or falling under the influence of a Reformed Church.

re·form·er *noun* **1** a person who advocates or brings about (esp. political or social) reform. **2** (**Reformer**) *Cdn hist.* a supporter or member of the Reform Party. **3** (**Reformer**) *Cdn hist.* a person who participated in the movement for responsible government in Upper and Lower Canada in the 19th c.

---

t top   v voice   w we   z zoo   ʃ she   ʒ vision   θ thin   ð this   ŋ ring   x loch   tʃ chip   dʒ jar   (*see over for vowels*)

re·form·ist ● *noun* an advocate or supporter of social, political, or religious reform. ● *adjective* of or pertaining to reformists or their policies. □ **re·form·ism** *noun*

Reform Jew *noun* an adherent of Reform Judaism.

Reform Judaism *noun* a branch of Judaism which has reformed or abandoned aspects of Orthodox Jewish worship and ritual in an attempt to adapt to modern social, political, and cultural changes.

Reform Party *noun Cdn* **1** *hist.* an esp. Western Canadian right-wing political party founded in 1987 and favouring greater power for the provinces, deficit reduction, reduced power for government, and conservative social values. It joined with some members of the Progressive Conservative Party to form the Canadian Alliance in 2000. **2** *hist.* the party of Reformers that opposed the Tories in Upper Canada in the 19th c.

reform school *noun* = REFORMATORY.

re·formu·late *transitive verb* formulate again or differently. □ **re·formu·la·tion** *noun*

reformulated gasoline *noun* gasoline with oxygen added to it so as to reduce emissions.

re·found *transitive verb* found again or anew.

re·fract *transitive verb* **1** (of water, air, glass, etc.) deflect (a ray of light, sound, etc.) at a certain angle when it enters obliquely from another medium. **2** change, distort, or influence (an idea, emotion, etc.) as it is passed through an intermediary (*the realities of our lives refracted through the language of advertising*). **3** determine the refractive condition of (the eye). □ **re·fract·ed** *adjective* [Latin *refringere refract-* (as RE-, *frangere* break)]

re·frac·tion *noun* the process by which, or the extent to which, light, sound, etc., is refracted when passing obliquely through the interface between one medium and another or through a medium of varying density.

re·frac·tive *adjective* involving or capable of causing refraction. □ **re·frac·tiv·ity** *noun*

refractive index *noun* the ratio of the velocity of light in a vacuum to its velocity in a specified medium.

re·frac·tom·eter /ˌrɛfrakˈtɒmətər, ri-/ *noun* an instrument for measuring a refractive index.

re·fract·or *noun* **1** a refracting medium or lens. **2** a telescope using a lens to produce an image.

re·frac·tory ● *adjective* **1** stubborn, unmanageable, rebellious. **2 a** (of a wound, disease, etc.) not yielding to treatment. **b** (of a person etc.) resistant to infection. **3** (of a substance) hard to fuse or work. **4** temporarily unresponsive to nervous or sexual stimuli (*refractory period*). ● *noun* (*pl.* **-ies**) a substance or building material especially resistant to heat, corrosion, etc. □ **re·frac·tor·i·ness** *noun* [alteration of obsolete *refractary* from Latin *refractarius* (as REFRACT)]

re·frain¹ *intransitive verb* (usu. foll. by *from*) avoid doing (an action); abstain (*refrain from smoking*). [Old French *refrener* from Latin *refrenare* (as RE-, *frenum* bridle)]

re·frain² *noun* **1** a recurring phrase or number of lines, esp. at the ends of stanzas. **2** the music accompanying this. **3** an often repeated idea or expression. [Old French *refrain* (earlier *refrait*), ultimately from Latin *refringere* (as RE-, *frangere* break), because the refrain 'broke' the sequence]

re·frame *transitive verb* **1** reformulate the essentials of (a complex thing, idea, theory, etc.). **2** *Photography* adjust (a shot) so that it is aligned differently in the viewfinder.

re·freeze *transitive & intransitive verb* (*past* **re·froze**; *past participle* **re·frozen**) freeze again.

re·fresh ● *transitive verb* **1 a** impart strength or energy to (a person etc.); invigorate, revive (*the long nap refreshed her*). **b** (esp. *reflexive*) revive with food, rest, etc. (*I refreshed myself with a shower*). **2** revive or stimulate (the memory), esp. by consulting the source of one's information. **3** replenish. **4** *Computing* **a** replenish or recharge the data stored in a memory device. **b** update a browser's display of a website by accessing the URL again to load the latest available version. **5** *Computing* (of a monitor or screen) repeat the display of digital information on a screen or cathode ray tube at rapid intervals in order to make an image appear continuous. ● *noun Computing* **1 a** the process of renewing the data stored in a memory device. **b** the act or function of updating the display on a computer screen. **2** = REFRESH RATE. □ **re·freshed** *adjective* [Old French *refreschi(e)r* from *fres fresche* FRESH]

re·fresh·er *noun* **1** something that refreshes, esp. a drink. **2** an update or review of previous education (also *attributive*: *refresher course*). **3** *Brit. Law* an extra fee payable to counsel in a prolonged case.

re·fresh·ing *adjective* **1** serving to refresh. **2** pleasantly new or different. **3** (of food or drink) cooling or thirst-quenching. □ **re·fresh·ing·ly** *adverb*

re·fresh·ment *noun* **1** the act of refreshing or the process of being refreshed in mind or body. **2** (usu. in *pl.*) food or drink, esp. provided for or sold to people in a public place or at a public event. **3** something that refreshes or stimulates the mind.

refresh rate *noun Computing* the rate at which a screen is filled with digital information or an image, measured in hertz.

re·fried beans *plural noun* a Mexican dish of cooked beans which have been left to cool, then fried. *Also called* FRIJOLES.

re·friger·ant /rəˈfrɪdʒərənt, ri-/ ● *noun* a substance used for refrigeration. ● *adjective* cooling.

re·friger·ate /rəˈfrɪdʒəˌreit, ri-/ *verb* **1** *transitive & intransitive* make or become cool or cold. **2** *transitive* subject (food etc.) to cold in order to freeze or preserve it. □ **re·friger·at·ed** *adjective* **re·friger·a·tion** *noun* [Latin *refrigerare* (as RE-, *frigus frigoris* cold)]

re·friger·ator /rəˈfrɪdʒəˌreitər, ri-/ *noun* **1** a cabinet or room in which food etc. is kept cold. **2** (usu. *attributive*) designating a truck, railway car, etc. equipped with a refrigerator, used for transporting food that must be kept cold or frozen (*refrigerator car*).

refrigerator cookie *noun N Amer.* a cookie for which the dough is shaped into a log, chilled, and sliced before baking.

re·froze *verb past of* REFREEZE.

re·frozen *verb past participle of* REFREEZE.

reft *verb past participle of* REAVE.

re·fuel *verb* (**re·fuelled**, **re·fuel·ling**; esp. *US* **re·fueled**, **re·fuel·ing**) **1** *intransitive* replenish a fuel supply. **2** *transitive* supply with more fuel.

ref·uge /ˈrɛfjuːdʒ/ *noun* **1** a shelter from pursuit, danger, or trouble. **2** a person or place etc. offering this. **3** a thing or course used as a means of escape from difficulties, problems, etc. (*during his divorce, drugs and alcohol were his refuge*). **4** *N Amer.* a park or sanctuary in which esp. endangered animals are protected. □ **take refuge in** resort to as a means of escape or shelter (*she took refuge in reading*). [Old French from Latin *refugium* (as RE-, *fugere* flee)]

refu·gee /ˌrɛfjuˈdʒiː/ *noun* a person taking refuge, esp. in a foreign country, from war, persecution, or natural disaster (also *attributive*: *refugee status*). [French *réfugié* past participle of (*se*) *réfugier* (as REFUGE)]

refugee determination *noun* (in full **refugee determination process**) *Cdn* the process by which the validity of a claim of refugee status is assessed.

re·fu·gium /rəˈfjuːdʒiəm, ri-/ *noun* (*pl.* **re·fu·gia**) *Biol.* an area in which a population of organisms can survive through a period of unfavourable conditions, esp. glaciation. [Latin, = place of refuge]

re·ful·gent /rəˈfʌldʒənt, ri-/ *adjective literary* shining, radiant; gloriously bright. [Latin *refulgere* (as RE-, *fulgere* shine)]

re·fund¹ ● *transitive verb* **1** pay back (money or expenses). **2** reimburse (a person). ● *noun* **1** an act of refunding. **2** a sum refunded; a repayment. □ **re·fund·able** *adjective* [Middle English in sense 'pour back', from Old French *refonder* or Latin *refundere* (as RE-, *fundere* pour), later assoc. with FUND]

re·fund² *transitive verb* fund (a debt etc.) again. □ **re·fund·ing** *noun*

re·fur·bish *transitive verb* **1** brighten up, redecorate. **2** restore, repair. □ **re·fur·bished** *adjective* **re·fur·bish·ing** *noun* **re·fur·bish·ment** *noun*

re·furn·ish *transitive verb* furnish again or differently.

re·fus·al *noun* **1** the act or an instance of refusing; the state of being refused. **2** (in full **first refusal**) the right or privilege of deciding to take or leave a thing before it is offered to others.

re·fuse¹ *verb* **1** *transitive* decline to take or accept (something offered or presented); reject. **2** *transitive & intransitive* (often foll. by *to* + infin.) adamantly decline; be stubbornly unwilling (*I refuse to go; the car refuses to start; I refuse!*). **3** *transitive & intransitive* withhold permission or consent (*I refuse to let you stay up past your bedtime*). **4** *transitive* decline to give (to a person something requested); deny (*refused me a day off*). **5** *transitive* decline to admit (a person) to a particular position or place (*the restaurant refused him because he wasn't wearing a tie*). **6** *transitive & intransitive* (of a horse) be unwilling to jump (a fence etc.). [Old French *refuser*, prob. ultimately from Latin *recusare* (see RECUSE) after *refutare* REFUTE]

re·fuse² /ˈrɛfjuːs/ *noun formal* items rejected as worthless; garbage, trash. [Middle English, perhaps from Old French *refusé* past participle (as REFUSE¹)]

re·fuse·nik /rəˈfjuːznɪk, ri-/ *noun* **1** *hist.* a Jew in the former Soviet

Union who was refused permission to emigrate to Israel. **2** a person who refuses to comply with rules or regulations imposed by an establishment, esp. due to moral beliefs. [REFUSE¹ + -NIK]

re·fute /rə'fjuːt, ri-/ *transitive verb* **1** prove the falsity or error of (a statement etc. or the person proposing it). **2** rebut or repel by argument. **3** *disputed* reject, deny, or contradict (without argument or proof). ¶ Some language commentators maintain that *refute* should not be used as a simple synonym of *deny*, but that refutation must always be backed up by proof. □ **re·fut·abil·ity** *noun* **re·fut·able** *adjective* **refu·ta·tion** /ˌrefjʊ'teiʃən/ *noun* [Latin *refutare* (as RE-: compare CONFUTE)]

reg *noun* (usu. in *pl.*) regulation. [abbreviation]

Reg. *abbreviation* Regina (queen).

reg. *abbreviation* **1** registered. **2** regular price.

re·gain *transitive verb* **1** obtain possession or use of after loss. **2** get back to, reach (a place, position) again. [French *regagner* (as RE-, GAIN)]

regal *adjective* of, like, or fit for a monarch (*regal splendour; regal appearance; a regal gesture*). □ **regal·ly** *adverb* [Old French *regal* or Latin *regalis* from *rex regis* king]

re·gale ● *transitive verb* **1** (foll. by *with*) entertain or divert with (talk etc.). **2** entertain lavishly with feasting. ● *noun Cdn hist.* an extra ration of liquor, esp. one issued to employees of a fur-trading company for festive occasions, such as Christmas, New Year's Eve, or the arrival of important guests or dignitaries. [French *régaler* from Old French *gale* pleasure]

re·galia /rə'geiliə, -'geiljə/ *plural noun* **1** any distinctive or elaborate clothes or accoutrements. **2** the decorations or insignia of royalty used esp. at coronations. **3** the decorations or insignia of any order. [medieval Latin, = royal privileges, from Latin neuter pl. of *regalis* REGAL]

regal·ity /rə'galiti, ri-/ *noun* (*pl.* **-ities**) **1** the state of being or resembling a king or queen. **2** a royal privilege.

Regan /'riːgən/ **Ger·ald Aug·us·tine** (b.1928), Canadian lawyer and politician, Liberal premier of Nova Scotia 1970–78. As premier, he supported the development of offshore oil and gas and other megaprojects.

re·gard ● *transitive verb* **1** (usu. foll. by *as*) look upon or view; consider (*she is regarded as our best swimmer; she regards him as a threat; I regard them kindly*). **2** esteem, value (*we regard your work highly*). **3** (of a thing) relate to; have some connection with (*this note is regarding our conversation of last night*). **4** gaze on steadily (usu. in a specified way) (*she regarded them with apprehension*). ● *noun* **1** (foll. by *for, to*) concern (for); proper consideration or appreciation (of) (*he jumped without regard for the consequences; she lived with no regard for anyone but her children*). **2** (often foll. by *for*) esteem; opinion (*I have a warm affection and regard for her; she held his work in high regard*). **3** a respect (in this regard; *numbers have declined without regard to age or gender*). **4** (in *pl.*) an expression of friendliness in a letter etc.; compliments (*give him my regards*). **5** a gaze; a steady or significant look (*his eyes met her chilling regard*). □ **as regards** about, concerning. **with** (or **in**) **regard to** as concerns; with respect to. [Old French *regard* from *regarder* (as RE-, *garder* GUARD)]

re·gard·ing *preposition* about, concerning; with respect to.

re·gard·less ● *adjective* (usu. foll. by *of*) without regard or consideration for (*regardless of the expense*). ● *adverb* despite what might happen; anyway, nevertheless (*it's supposed to rain but we must carry on regardless*).

re·gath·er *transitive & intransitive verb* **1** gather or collect again. **2** meet again.

re·gat·ta *noun* a marine sporting event consisting of a series of races of boats, yachts, etc. [Italian (Venetian) *regata*, lit. = 'contest']

Regatta Day *noun Cdn (Nfld)* **1** a marine event held annually on usu. the first Wednesday in August on Quidi Vidi Lake in St. John's, NL, associated with a carnival that features bands, games and other attractions. **2** (in Newfoundland) a provincial statutory holiday held on this day.

regd. *abbreviation* registered.

re·gency /'riːdʒənsi/ *noun* (*pl.* **-cies**) **1 a** the office or jurisdiction of regent. **b** a commission acting as regent. **c** the period of office of a regent or regency commission. **2** (**Regency**) **a** the period (1811–20) during the reign of George III in Britain when George, Prince of Wales, was regent. **b** (usu. *attributive*) designating clothing, architecture, furniture, and other decorative arts of this period, inspired by Greco-Roman models and characterized esp. by purity and simplicity of line and detail. **3** (**Regency**) **a** (in France) the period from 1715 to 1723 during the reign of Louis XV when Philip, Duke of Orleans, was

regent. **b** (usu. *attributive*) designating architecture and furniture typical of this period, characterized esp. by delicate finishes and curved lines.

re·gener·ate ● *verb* /ri'dʒenə,reit/ **1** *transitive* reconstitute in a new and improved form; revive (*a project to regenerate the derelict neighbourhood; regenerate the economy*). **2** *transitive & intransitive* bring or come into renewed existence, esp. of a greater spiritual or moral nature. **3** *intransitive & transitive* regrow or cause (new plant or animal tissue) to regrow to replace lost or damaged tissue. **4** *transitive & intransitive Chem.* restore or be restored to an initial state of reaction or process. ● *adjective* /rɪ'dʒenərət/ **1** spiritually born again. **2** reformed. □ **re·gener·a·tive** /-rətɪv/ *adjective* **re·gener·a·tor** *noun*

re·gener·a·tion /rɪˌdʒenə'reiʃən/ *noun* **1** a revival; reconstitution in an improved form. **2** *Med. & Biol.* **a** the formation of new animal tissue. **b** the natural replacement of lost parts or organs. **3** the fact or process of being reborn, esp. spiritually. **4** the natural regrowth of a forest which has been felled or thinned. **5** *Chem.* the action or process of regenerating polymeric fibres.

re·gent /'riːdʒənt/ ● *noun* **1** a person appointed to administer a country or state because the monarch is a minor, absent, or incapacitated. **2** *N Amer.* a member of the governing body of a university or other academic institution. ● *adjective* (placed after noun) acting as regent (*Prince Regent*). [Old French *regent* or Latin *regere* rule]

reg·gae /'regei/ *noun* a W Indian style of popular music indigenous to the black culture of Jamaica, developed from an eclectic mix of African religious music, Christian black revival songs, New Orleans rhythm and blues, and Rastafarian liturgical music. [Caribbean English, possibly related to Yoruba *rege-rege* 'in a rough manner' or Hausa *rega* 'shake']

Reg·gio di Ca·lab·ria /ˌredʒioː diː kə'labriə/ a port at the southern tip of the 'toe' of Italy, on the Strait of Messina, capital of Calabria region; pop. (2001) 179,384.

regi·cide /'redʒɪ,said/ *noun* **1** the act of killing a king. **2** a person who kills or takes part in killing a king, esp. any of those involved in the trial and execution of Charles I of England, Scotland, and Ireland, or the execution of Louis XVI of France. □ **reg·icid·al** *adjective* [Latin *rex regis* king + -CIDE]

re·gie /rei'ʒiː/ *noun Cdn (Que.)* (also **Régie**) (usu. prec. by *the*) any of several Quebec government bodies regulating insurance, housing, language, etc. [French, = 'government agency']

re·gild *transitive verb* gild again, esp. to renew faded or worn gilding.

re·gime /rei'ʒiːm/ *noun* **1 a** a method of government or dominance of a country or state, esp. one that is or is considered to be oppressive (*a military regime*). **b** a period in which such a government is in power (*during the Nazi regime*). **2** a system of managing or organizing something (*a tax regime*). **3** a (medical) regimen. [French *régime* (as REGIMEN)]

regime change *noun* **1** the replacement of one governing administration by another. **2** *euphemism* the removal of a hostile government by a foreign power, esp. by means of military force.

regi·men /'redʒɪ,men/ *noun* **1** *Med.* a prescribed course of exercise, way of life, or diet. **2** a strict routine or schedule, usu. imposed or suggested. [Latin from *regere* rule]

regi·ment /'redʒɪmənt/ *noun* **1** a permanent unit of an army usu. commanded by a colonel and divided into several companies, troops, or batteries and often into two battalions. **2** (usu. foll. by *of*) a large array or number. □ **regi·ment·al** *adjective* [Old French from Late Latin *regimentum* (as REGIMEN)]

regimental colour *noun* a flag carried by a regiment.

regi·men·ta·tion /ˌredʒɪmen'teiʃən/ *noun* **1** the action of imposing order; the process by which (people etc.) are integrated in a system, institution, etc. **2** strict organization, order.

regi·ment·ed /'redʒɪment·əd/ *adjective* **1** characterized by strict discipline or order. **2** organized, usu. strictly or oppressively, in definite groups or according to an order or system. **3** belonging to a regiment.

Re·gina /rə'dʒainə/ the capital of Saskatchewan, situated in the south central part of the province; pop. (2001) 178,225. It was the administrative headquarters of the NWT until 1905. □ **Re·gin·an** *noun & adjective* [Latin, = queen, in honour of *Victoria Regina* Queen Victoria]

Regina /rə'dʒainə, re'dʒiːnə/ *noun* the reigning queen (following a name or in the titles of lawsuits, e.g. *Regina v. Jones* the Crown versus Jones). [Latin, = queen from *rex regis* king]

Regina Manifesto *noun Cdn hist.* the declaration of principles and objectives, including the goal of establishing a welfare state, adopted by the Co-operative Commonwealth Federation in 1933 at a meeting in Regina.

Regio·mon·tanus /ˌredʒio:mɒnˈtanəs/ (pseudonym of Johannes Müller) (1436–76), German astronomer and mathematician. Considered the most important astronomer of the 15th c., he completed a translation of Ptolemy's *Mathematical Syntaxis*, with revisions and comments, and wrote four monumental works on mathematics (esp. trigonometry) and astronomy.

re·gion noun **1** a (usu. specified) area of land or division of the earth's surface without fixed limits but having definable features such as climate, fauna, flora, etc. (*wine-growing region*). **2** an area of land or division of the earth's surface marked by certain boundaries (*the region between the Ottawa and St. Lawrence rivers*). **3 a** the area of land outside a principal city (*Edmonton and surrounding regions*). **b** the area of land surrounding and including a (usu. specified) place (*the Great Lakes region*). **c** (in pl.) esp. Cdn the areas of a country, province, etc. away from the political centre (*a number of civil-service jobs were shifted to the regions*). **4** a part of the body near or including a (usu. specified) organ etc. (*the lower back region*). **5** a relatively large administrative division of a country or province, esp. one uniting several large municipalities. **6** an area of the world made up of neighbouring countries which are considered socially, economically, or politically interdependent (*the Baltic region*). **7** a sphere or realm (*the region of medicine*). **8** a separate part of the world or universe. □ **in the region of** approximately. [Old French from Latin *regio -onis* direction, district, from *regere* direct]

re·gion·al ● adjective of, pertaining to, or characteristic of a region. ● noun **1** a thing, such as a stamp, newspaper, etc., produced or used in a particular region. **2** (in pl.) N Amer. a tournament or championship involving teams, athletes, etc. from a particular region. □ **re·gion·al·ly** adverb

regional county municipality noun Cdn (Que.) one of 96 regional municipalities comprising urban and rural municipalities, but excluding urban communities.

regional district noun Cdn (BC) an administrative unit that coordinates the services of municipalities and rural areas within its boundaries, similar to a regional municipality.

region·al·ism noun **1** the theory or practice of regional rather than central systems of administration of economic, cultural, or political affiliation. **2** allegiance to or concern for one's region rather than one's country. **3** a linguistic feature, custom, etc. peculiar to a particular region and not found or heard elsewhere in a country. □ **region·al·ist** noun & adjective

region·al·ize verb (also esp. Brit. **-ise**) **1** transitive bring under the control of a region for administrative purposes. **2** transitive & intransitive divide into regions; organize regionally. □ **region·al·iz·a·tion** noun

regional jet noun a small jet plane designed primarily for short-haul flights, holding between 30 and 90 passengers.

regional municipality noun Cdn (Ont. & Que.) a large municipality representing a federation of all the area municipalities within its borders. Abbr.: **RM**.

regional school noun Cdn a school located centrally within a usu. rural region or district, taking the place of several smaller schools.

re·gis·seur /ˌreiʒiˈsɜr/ noun a person who stages a theatrical production, esp. a ballet. [French *régisseur* stage manager]

regis·ter ● noun **1** an official list or record of births, deaths, marriages, guests, students in attendance at school, etc. **2** a book in which such items or names are recorded for reference. **3** a device that records information automatically; esp. = CASH REGISTER. **4** a device used to store information within a computer system for high-speed access. **5** an adjustable plate for widening or narrowing an opening and regulating the passage of air, heat, smoke, etc. (*floor register*; *heating register*). **6** a device that regulates the flow of air through an organ or woodwind instrument, thereby raising or lowering the pitch. **7 a** the range of tones of a voice or instrument. **b** a part of this range (*lower register*). **8** Linguistics each of several forms of a language (colloquial, formal, literary, etc.) usually used in particular circumstances. **9** Printing the exact correspondence of the position of printed matter on the two sides of a leaf. **10** Printing & Photog. the correspondence of the position of colour components in a printed positive. ● verb **1** transitive set down or record a name, an event, a sale, etc. in a list or register for official purposes. **2** intransitive a check into a hotel. **b** (foll. by *for*) enrol in a course etc. **3 a** intransitive (of a couple to be married etc.) have a list of gifts compiled and kept at a store for consultation by gift buyers. **b** transitive (usu. in passive) (of a gift store) compile and maintain a list of gifts for (a couple to be married etc.) (*where are you registered?*). **4** transitive a (of an instrument) record

automatically; indicate. **b** (of temperature, winds, an earthquake, etc.) be or reach a certain figure when measured. **5 a** transitive express (an emotion) facially or by gesture (*registered surprise*). **b** intransitive (of an emotion) show in a person's face or gestures. **6** intransitive make an impression; be recognized or noted mentally (*did not register at all*). **7** transitive entrust (a letter etc.) to a post office for transmission by registered mail. **8** intransitive & transitive Printing align precisely. □ **regis·ter·able** adjective **regis·trable** adjective [Old French *registre* or medieval Latin *regestrum*, *registrum*, alteration of *regestum* from Late Latin *regesta* things recorded (as RE-, Latin *gerere gest-* carry)]

regis·tered adjective **1** recorded; officially set down, esp. in a register. **2** officially licensed; certified (*registered vehicle*; *registered firearm*). **3** signed up; enrolled (*registered students should report to the auditorium*). **4** (of dogs, horses, etc.) registered as a purebred by an authorized breeder.

Registered Education Savings Plan noun Cdn = RESP.

registered mail noun (Brit. **registered post**) **1** a postal procedure with special precautions for safety and for compensation in case of loss. **2** letters or mail sent this way.

registered nurse noun esp. N Amer. a nurse who is licensed to practise and is a registered member of a nurses' association.

registered nursing assistant noun a nursing assistant who holds a certificate issued by a professional body of nurses. Abbr.: **RNA**.

registered practical nurse noun a person who is registered by a professional association of nurses as being trained to perform basic nursing tasks under the direction of a physician or registered nurse. Abbr.: **RPN**.

Registered Retirement Income Fund noun Cdn = RRIF.

Registered Retirement Savings Plan noun Cdn = RRSP.

registered trademark noun a sign, name, or logo of a manufacturer etc. which is officially recorded and protected from use by others.

register office noun Brit. a state office where civil marriages are conducted and births, marriages, and deaths are recorded with the issue of certificates.

register ton noun see TON 5b.

regis·trant noun a person who registers or has registered for something, such as a conference, course, etc.

regis·trar noun **1** an official responsible for keeping a register or official records. **2** an official at an educational institution responsible for maintaining records of students' enrolment, marks, etc. **3** Cdn & Brit. Law a judicial and administrative officer responsible for issuing and filing court documents. **4** Brit. & NZ a middle-ranking hospital doctor undergoing training as a specialist. □ **regis·trar·ship** noun [medieval Latin *registrarius* from *registrum* REGISTER]

Registrar General noun **1** a government official (in Canada, a provincial government officer) responsible for recording births, deaths, and marriages. **2** a government official responsible for keeping records of registered individuals and organizations, e.g. lobbyists.

regis·tra·tion noun **1** the act or an instance of registering; the process of being registered. **2** the form or certificate that verifies that something or someone has been registered. **3** the selection of a series of organ or harpsichord stops used in the performance of a piece. □ **regis·tra·tion·al** adjective

registration number noun **1** a number or series of numbers and letters used to identify or verify a registration. **2** (also **registration mark**) Brit.= LICENCE NUMBER.

regis·try noun (pl. **-tries**) **1** a place or office where registers or records are kept. **2** registration. **3** a list of gifts requested e.g. by a couple to be married, and of those already purchased, kept at a store for consultation by gift buyers (*bridal registry*). **4** a ship's country of origin as indicated on its registration.

registry office noun Cdn **1** a government office where private property, such as vehicles, real estate, etc., may be registered and where records of ownership are kept (*see* LAND REGISTRY OFFICE). **2** a government office where records of births, marriages, and deaths are kept.

Re·gi·us professor /ˈriːdʒiəs/ noun Brit. the holder of a university chair founded by a sovereign (esp. one at Oxford or Cambridge instituted by Henry VII) or filled by Crown appointment. [Latin, = royal, from *rex regis* king]

reg·nal /ˈregnəl/ adjective of or pertaining to a reign or monarch. [Anglo-Latin *regnalis* (as REIGN)]

reg·nant /ˈregnənt/ adjective **1** (of things, qualities, etc.) predominant, prevalent. **2** reigning (*Queen regnant*). [Latin *regnare* REIGN]

rego·lith /'rɛgəlɪθ/ noun Geol. unconsolidated solid material covering the bedrock of a planet. [erroneously from Greek *rhēgos* rug, blanket + -LITH]

re·grade transitive verb grade again or differently.

re·gress ● verb /rə'grɛs, rɪ-/ **1** intransitive **a** move backwards. **b** (esp. in abstract senses) return to a previous or less advanced state. **2** intransitive & transitive Psych. return or cause to return mentally to a former stage of life, esp. through hypnosis or mental illness. ● noun /'riːgrɛs/ **1** the act or an instance of going back. **2** reasoning from effect to cause. [Latin *regressus* from *regredi regress-* (as RE-, *gradi* step)]

re·gres·sion /rə'grɛʃən, rɪ-/ noun **1** a backward movement, esp. a return to a former state. **2** a relapse or reversion. **3** Psych. a return to an earlier stage of development, esp. through hypnosis or mental illness. **4** Statistics a measure of the relation between the mean value of one variable (e.g. output) and corresponding values of other variables (e.g. time and cost) (also attributive: *regression analysis*).

re·gres·sive /rə'grɛsɪv, rɪ-/ adjective **1** regressing; characterized by regression. **2** (of a tax) proportionally greater on lower incomes. □ **re·gres·sive·ly** adverb **re·gres·sive·ness** noun **re·gres·siv·ity** noun

re·gret ● transitive verb (**re·gret·ted**, **re·gret·ting**) (often foll. by *that* + clause) **1** feel or express sorrow or distress over (an action or loss etc.) (*we regretted your absence*). **2** express polite apologies for (an error, an inconvenience, an inability, etc.). **3 a** (often foll. by *to* + infin. or *that* + clause) acknowledge with sorrow or remorse. **b** (often foll. by *to* + infin.) be reluctant (to say something etc.) for fear of causing offence or disappointment (*certain participants, I regret to say, are not taking this seriously*). ● noun **1** a feeling of sorrow, repentance, disappointment, etc., over an action or loss etc. **2** (often in *pl.*) an (esp. polite or formal) expression of disappointment or sorrow at an occurrence, inability to comply, etc. (*refused with many regrets; heard with regret of her death*). □ **live to regret** (of an action) eventually feel the consequences of. **give** (or **send**) **one's regrets** formally decline an invitation. [Old French *regreter* bewail]

re·gret·ful adjective feeling or showing regret. □ **re·gret·ful·ly** adverb **re·gret·ful·ness** noun

re·gret·table adjective (of events or conduct) unfortunate, unwelcome; deserving censure. □ **re·gret·tably** adverb

re·group verb **1** transitive & intransitive group or arrange again or differently. **2** intransitive become organized before attempting something again. □ **re·group·ment** noun

re·grow transitive & intransitive verb (past **re·grew**; past part **re·grown**) grow again, esp. after an interval. □ **re·growth** noun

Regt. abbreviation Regiment.

reg·u·lar ● adjective **1** usual, standard, customary. **2** conforming to a rule or principle; systematic. **3** acting or done uniformly or in a calculable time or manner. **4 a** habitual (*a regular contributor*). **b** constant, steady (*a regular job*). **5** informal absolute; genuine (*a regular hero*). **6** (of coffee) containing an average amount of cream and sugar. **7** (of merchandise) of an average size, between large and small (*a regular soft drink*). **8** (of a person) defecating or menstruating at predictable times. **9** (of forces or troops etc.) relating to or constituting a permanent professional body. **10** (of a structure or arrangement) harmonious, symmetrical (*regular features*). **11** Math. **a** (of a figure) having all sides and all angles equal. **b** (of a solid) bounded by a number of equal figures. **12** Bot. (of a flower) having radial symmetry. **13** Grammar (of a noun, verb, etc.) following the normal type of inflection. **14** Christianity (placed before or after noun) **a** bound by religious rule. **b** belonging to a religious or monastic order (*canon regular*). **15** N Amer. (of gasoline) having the lowest octane rating of those sold at gas stations. **16** N Amer. of a normal or ordinary kind (*it's richer than regular yogourt*). ● noun **1** informal a regular customer, visitor, participant, etc. **2 a** a coffee containing an average amount of cream and sugar. **b** a serving of a beverage etc. of a size between a small and a large. **3** (in hockey, baseball, basketball, etc.) a player who starts every or nearly every game. **4** a regular soldier. □ **keep regular hours** do the same thing, esp. going to bed and getting up, at the same time each day. □ **reg·u·lar·ity** noun **reg·u·lar·ize** transitive verb (also esp. Brit. **-ise**). **reg·u·lar·iz·a·tion** noun [Old French *reguler* from Latin *regularis* from *regula* RULE]

regular guy noun (also **regular Joe**) N Amer. informal an ordinary, uncomplicated, sociable man.

reg·u·lar·ly adverb **1** at regular intervals or times. **2** in a balanced or regular manner.

regular season noun N Amer. Sport the schedule of games that follows the exhibition season and leads up to the playoffs (also attributive: *regular-season record*).

regu·late transitive verb **1** govern or control by law; subject to esp. legal restrictions. **2** keep (a biological function etc.) regular; maintain the health of (*doctors hope the drug will help to regulate the immune system*). **3** adapt to requirements. **4** alter the speed of (a machine or clock) so that it may work accurately. □ **regu·la·tive** adjective [Late Latin *regulare regulat-* from Latin *regula* RULE]

regu·la·tion noun **1** the act or an instance of regulating; the process of being regulated. **2 a** a prescribed rule; an authoritative direction. **b** a subordinate form of legislation that may be established without the necessity of enacting a new statute. **3** (attributive) **a** in accordance with regulations; of the correct type etc. (*the regulation speed; a regulation tie*). **b** informal usual (*the regulation soup*).

regulation time noun N Amer. Sport the time normally allotted for the completion of a game which does not result in a tie (compare OVERTIME).

regu·la·tor noun **1** a person or body that supervises a particular industry or business activity. **2** a device for controlling the rate of working of machinery or for controlling fluid flow, in particular a handle controlling the supply of steam to the cylinders of a steam engine. **3** a device for adjusting the balance of a clock or watch in order to regulate its speed.

regu·la·tory /'rɛgjʊlə,tɔri/ adjective **1** having to do with a regulation or regulations (*regulatory agency*). **2** in violation of a regulation (*speeding is a regulatory offence*).

Regu·lus /'rɛgjʊləs/ **1 Mar·cus Atil·ius** (died *c.*250 BC), Roman general, consul in 267 and 256. Captured by the Carthaginians during the First Punic War, he was allowed to return to Rome on parole to negotiate peace terms and the exchange of prisoners; he advised the senate to refuse the proposals, and returned to Carthage where he was tortured and executed. **2** the brightest star in the constellation Leo. [Latin, = 'little king']

re·gur·gi·tate /rɪ'gɜrdʒɪ,teit/ verb **1** transitive bring (swallowed food) up again to the mouth. **2** transitive cast or pour out again (*required by the exam to regurgitate facts*). **3** intransitive be brought up again; gush back. □ **re·gur·gi·ta·tion** noun [medieval Latin *regurgitare* (as RE-, Latin *gurges gurgitis* whirlpool)]

rehab noun, adjective, & verb informal ● noun rehabilitation. ● adjective rehabilitated, reconditioned. ● transitive & intransitive verb (**re·habbed**, **re·hab·bing**) N Amer. rehabilitate; undergo rehabilitation (*was rehabbing for two weeks; rehabbed homes*). [abbreviation]

re·habili·tate /,riːhə'bɪlɪteit/ transitive verb **1 a** restore (a person) to effectiveness or normal life by training etc., esp. after imprisonment, injury, addiction, or illness. **b** heal (an injury etc.). **2** recondition, overhaul. **3** restore the reputation or standing of. □ **re·habili·ta·tion** noun **re·habili·ta·tive** adjective [originally in the sense 'restore to former privileges' from medieval Latin *rehabilitare*, as RE- + *habilitare* 'make able']

re·hash ● transitive verb put (old material) into a new form without significant change or improvement. ● noun **1** material rehashed. **2** the act or an instance of rehashing.

re·hear transitive verb (past and past participle **re·heard**) hear again.

re·hears·al /rə'hɜrsəl, rɪ-/ noun **1** the act or an instance of rehearsing. **2** a trial performance or practice of a theatrical or musical performance, ceremony, etc.

rehearsal party noun a party held after a wedding rehearsal.

re·hearse /rɪ'hɜrs/ verb **1** transitive practise (a play, recital, ceremony, etc.) for later public performance. **2** intransitive hold a rehearsal. **3** transitive train (a person) by rehearsal. **4** transitive recite or say over, esp. in preparation for some subsequent event. **5** transitive give a list of; enumerate. [Anglo-French *rehearser*, Old French *reherc(i)er*, perhaps formed as RE- + *hercer* to harrow, from *herse* harrow: see HEARSE]

re·heat ● transitive verb heat again. ● noun the process of using the hot exhaust to burn extra fuel in a jet engine and produce extra power. □ **re·heat·er** noun

re·heel transitive verb fit (a shoe etc.) with a new heel.

re·hire transitive verb hire (a former employee) again.

reho·boam /,riːhə'boːm/ noun a wine bottle of about six times the standard size. [*Rehoboam* King of Israel (1 Kings 11–14)]

re·house transitive verb provide with new housing.

re·hy·drate verb **1** intransitive absorb water again after dehydration. **2** transitive cause (a person or thing) to absorb moisture or fluid. □ **re·hy·drat·able** adjective **re·hy·dra·tion** noun

Reich[1] /'raɪx/ **1 Steve** (b.1936), US minimalist composer. Drumming and the music of West Africa and Bali are major influences on his

---

t top   v voice   w we   z zoo   ʃ she   ʒ vision   θ thin   ð this   ŋ ring   x loch   tʃ chip   dʒ jar   (see over for vowels)

style, which is based on repeated short phrases within a simple harmonic field; major works include *Drumming* (1971), for percussion and two voices, and *The Desert Music* (1984), for chorus and orchestra. **2 Wil·helm** (1897–1957), Austrian psychologist, whose works include *The Function of the Orgasm* (1948). □ **Reich·ian** *adjective*

Reich² /raix, raɪk/ *noun* the former German nation or Commonwealth, esp. the Third Reich. [German, = empire]

Reichs·tag /ˈraɪxstɒg, ˈraɪkstag/ *noun* **1** the diet or parliament of the North German Confederation (1867–71), of the German Empire (1871–1918), and of post-imperial Germany until 1945. **2** the building in Berlin in which this parliament met, burnt down on the Nazi accession to power (1933). [German]

Reid /riːd/ **1 (Daphne) Kate** (1930–93), English-born Canadian actress, who appeared in a number of film, television, and stage roles. **2 George Agnew** (1860–1947), Canadian painter. He applied Parisian Academy precision to narrative paintings of country life in his native SW Ontario. He was principal of the Ontario School of Art and Design (later the Ontario College of Art) 1912–18. **3 Wil·liam Ron·ald** ('Bill') (1920–98), Canadian sculptor. The child of a Haida mother and a Scottish-American father, he discovered his Native heritage in his teens, and began exploring Haida art in 1951. Accomplished in a variety of media, his major works include *Raven and the First Humans*, a 4.5 ton cedar sculpture at UBC (1980) and a canoe commissioned for Expo 86 (1986).

reify /ˈriːɪˌfaɪ/ *transitive verb* (**-ifies**, **-ified**) convert (a concept, abstraction, etc.) into a thing; materialize. □ **reifi·ca·tion** *noun* [Latin *res* thing + -FY]

reign /reɪn/ ● *intransitive verb* **1** hold royal office; be king or queen. **2** (often in phr. **reign supreme**) prevail; hold sway (*confusion reigns*). **3** (of a winner, champion, etc.) be currently holding the title etc. ● *noun* **1** sovereignty, rule. **2** the period during which a sovereign rules. **3** a period during which a specified person, quality, etc. holds sway (*the reign of love and peace*). □ **reign·ing** *adjective* [Old French *reigne* kingdom, from Latin *regnare* from *rex regis* king]

re·ignite *transitive & intransitive verb* ignite again. □ **re·igni·tion** *noun*

reign of terror *noun* **1** a period of remorseless repression or bloodshed, during which the general population lives in constant fear of death or violence. **2** (**Reign of Terror**) *see* TERROR 4.

reiki /ˈreɪki/ *noun* a healing technique based on the principle that a therapist can channel energy into a patient by means of touch, to activate the natural healing processes of the patient's body and restore physical and emotional well-being. [Japanese, lit. 'universal life energy']

re·im·agine *transitive verb* imagine again, esp. reinterpret (an event, a work of art, etc.) imaginatively; rethink.

re·im·burse *transitive verb* **1** repay (a person who has expended money). **2** repay (a person's expenses). □ **re·im·burs·able** *adjective* **re·im·burse·ment** *noun* [RE- + obsolete *imburse* put in a purse, from medieval Latin *imbursare* (as IM-, PURSE)]

re·im·port ● *transitive verb* import (goods processed from exported materials). ● *noun* **1** the act or an instance of reimporting. **2** a reimported item. □ **re·im·port·a·tion** *noun*

re·impose *transitive verb* impose again, esp. after a lapse. □ **re·impos·ition** *noun*

Reims /riːmz, rãs/ (also **Rheims**) a city of N France, chief town of Champagne-Ardenne region and the traditional coronation place of most French kings; pop. (1999) 187,206.

rein ● *noun* (in *sing.* or *pl.*) **1** a long narrow strap with each end attached to the bit, used to guide or check a horse etc. in riding or driving. **2** a means of control (*took over the reins of government*). ● *transitive verb* **1** check or manage with reins. **2** (foll. by *up, back*) pull up or back with reins. **3** (foll. by *in*) hold in as with reins; restrain. **4** govern, restrain, control. □ **draw rein** stop one's horse. **free** (or **full**) **rein** complete freedom of action. **keep a tight rein on** allow little freedom to. [Old French *rene, reigne*, earlier *resne*, ultimately from Latin *retinēre* RETAIN]

re·incar·na·tion /ˌriːɪnkɑrˈneɪʃən/ *noun* **1** the rebirth of a soul in a new body. **2** a new embodiment or occurrence of a person, idea, etc. □ **re·incar·nate** /-ˈkɑrneɪt/ *transitive verb* **re·incar·nate** /-ˈkɑrnət/ *adjective*

re·incor·por·ate *transitive verb* incorporate afresh. □ **re·incor·por·a·tion** *noun*

rein·deer *noun* (*pl.* same) a subarctic deer, *Rangifer tarandus*, of which both sexes have large antlers, domesticated in northern Eurasia for drawing sleds and as a source of milk, flesh, and hide. [Old Norse *hreindýri* from *hreinn* reindeer + *dýr* DEER]

Reindeer Lake a large, irregularly-shaped lake in NE Saskatchewan, straddling the border with Manitoba. It occupies an area of 6 650 sq. km. [translation of Algonquian]

reindeer moss *noun* an arctic lichen, *Cladonia rangiferina*, with short branched stems growing in clumps. *Also called* CARIBOU MOSS.

re·infect *transitive verb* infect again. □ **re·infec·tion** *noun*

re·inforce *transitive verb* strengthen or support, esp. with additional personnel or material or by an increase of numbers or quantity or size etc. □ **re·infor·cer** *noun* [earlier *renforce* from French *renforcer*]

reinforced concrete *noun* concrete with metal bars or wire etc. embedded to increase its tensile strength.

re·inforce·ment *noun* **1** the act or an instance of reinforcing; the process of being reinforced. **2** a thing that reinforces. **3** (in *pl.*) reinforcing personnel or equipment etc. **4** the strengthening or establishing of a response through the repetition of a stimulus or the satisfaction of a need (*positive reinforcement*).

Rein·hardt /ˈraɪnhɑrt/ **1 Django** (born Jean Baptiste Reinhardt) (1910–53), Belgian jazz guitarist. His original improvisational style blended swing with influences from his Gypsy background; he formed the Quintette du Hot Club de France in 1934 with Stephane Grappelli. **2 Max** (born Max Goldmann) (1873–1943), Austrian director and impresario. He dominated the theatre in Berlin in the early 20th c. with his large-scale productions of such works as Sophocles' *Oedipus Rex* (1910); he also helped establish the Salzburg Festival, with Richard Strauss and Hugo von Hofmannsthal, in 1920.

re·injure *transitive verb* injure again. □ **re·injury** *noun*

re·insert *transitive verb* insert again. □ **re·inser·tion** *noun*

re·install *transitive verb* install again. □ **re·instal·la·tion** *noun*

re·instate *transitive verb* **1** replace in a former position. **2** restore to a former condition or status. □ **re·instate·ment** *noun*

re·insti·tute *transitive verb* institute or establish again.

re·insure *transitive & intransitive verb* insure again (esp. of an insurance company securing itself by transferring some or all of the risk to another insurer). □ **re·insur·ance** *noun* **re·insur·er** *noun*

re·inte·grate *verb* **1** *transitive* restore wholeness or unity to. **2** *transitive & intransitive* integrate or be reintegrated back into society. □ **re·inte·gra·tion** *noun*

re·inter *transitive verb* (**re·interred**, **re·inter·ring**) inter (a corpse) again. □ **re·inter·ment** *noun*

re·inter·pret *transitive verb* (**re·inter·pret·ed**, **re·inter·pret·ing**) interpret again or differently. □ **re·inter·pret·a·tion** *noun*

re·intro·duce *transitive verb* **1** introduce again. **2** introduce (a species) to a place it formerly inhabited. □ **re·intro·duc·tion** *noun*

re·invent *transitive verb* **1** invent again. **2** change something so much that it appears to be something completely new. □ **reinvent the wheel** waste effort by doing something that has already been done and does not need redoing. □ **re·inven·tion** *noun*

re·invest *transitive verb* invest again (esp. money made from one investment in other investments etc.). □ **re·invest·ment** *noun*

re·invig·or·ate *transitive verb* impart fresh vigour to. □ **re·invig·or·a·tion** *noun*

rei·shi *noun* a mushroom, *Ganoderma lucidum*, with a shiny cap which typically grows on dead or dying timber, found in Asia and North America. [Japanese]

re·issue ● *transitive verb* (**re·issues**, **re·issued**, **re·issu·ing**) issue again or in a different form. ● *noun* a new issue, esp. of a previously published book etc.

REIT /riːt/ *abbreviation* N Amer. real-estate investment trust.

re·iter·ate /riːˈɪtəˌreɪt/ *transitive verb* say or do again or repeatedly. □ **re·iter·a·tion** *noun* **re·iter·a·tive** /-rətɪv/ *adjective*

Reit·man /ˈraɪtmən/ **Ivan** (b.1946), Czech-born Canadian producer and director. His comedy films *National Lampoon's Animal House* (1978) and *Meatballs* (1979) led to a series of monumental successes, culminating in *Ghostbusters* (1984).

reive /riːv/ *intransitive verb* esp. *Scot.* make raids; plunder. □ **reiv·er** *noun* [var. of REAVE]

re·ject ● *transitive verb* **1** put aside or send back as not to be used or done or complied with etc. **2** refuse to accept or believe in (an idea). **3 a** fail to give (a person or an animal) due attention, care, or affection. **b** fail to accept (a person) into a group (*kept applying for jobs but kept being rejected*). **4** *Med.* show an immune response to (a transplanted organ or tissue) so that it fails to survive. ● *noun* a thing or person

Vowels: a *cat* ɑ *arm* e *bed* ɜr *her* ɜ: *deux* ə *ago* ɪ *sit* i *cosy* iː *feed* ɒ *hot* ɔ *pore* oː *no* ʌ *run* ʊ *put*

rejected as unfit or below standard. □ **re·ject·able** *adjective*

re·jec·tion *noun* **re·ject·or** *noun* [Latin *rejicere reject-* (as RE-, *jacere* throw)]

re·jec·tion·ist *noun* a person who rejects a proposed policy etc., esp. an Arab who refuses to accept a negotiated peace with Israel (often *attributive: rejectionist groups*).

rejection slip *noun* a formal notice sent by an editor or publisher to an author with a rejected manuscript.

rejig *transitive verb* (**re·jigged**, **re·jig·ging**) *Cdn & Brit.* reconfigure, rearrange; reorganize.

re·jig·ger *transitive verb US* = REJIG.

re·joice *verb* **1** *intransitive* feel great joy. **2** *intransitive* (foll. by *that* + clause or *to* + infin.) be glad. **3** *intransitive* (foll. by *in, at*) take delight. **4** *intransitive* celebrate some event. **5** *transitive archaic* cause joy to. □ **re·joi·cing** *noun* [Old French *rejoir rejoiss-* (as RE-, JOY)]

re·join[1] *verb* **1** *transitive & intransitive* join together again; reunite. **2** *transitive* join (a companion etc.) again.

re·join[2] *verb* **1** *transitive* say in answer, retort. **2** *intransitive Law* reply to a charge or pleading in a lawsuit. [Old French *rejoindre rejoign-* (as RE-, JOIN)]

re·join·der *noun* **1** what is said in reply. **2** a retort. **3** *Law* a reply by rejoining. [Anglo-French *rejoinder* (unrecorded: as REJOIN[2])]

re·juven·ate /rɪ'dʒuːvə‚neɪt, ri-/ *transitive verb* **1** make young or as if young again. **2** inject new vigour, liveliness, efficiency, etc. into (*rejuvenate the political process*). **3** make new or as if new again (*rejuvenated the old building*). □ **re·juven·a·tion** *noun* **re·juven·ator** *noun* [RE- + Latin *juvenis* young]

re·key *transitive verb* **1** esp. *Computing* re-enter (text or other data) using a keyboard. **2** change (a lock) so as to fit a different key.

re·kin·dle /ri'kɪndəl/ *transitive & intransitive verb* kindle again.

-rel *suffix* with diminutive or derogatory force (*cockerel; scoundrel*). [from or after Old French *-erel(le)*]

re·label *transitive verb* (**re·labelled**, **re·label·ling**; esp. *US* **re·labeled**, **re·label·ing**) label again or differently.

re·lapse ● *intransitive verb* (often foll. by *into*) **1** experience a return of an illness after partial or apparently complete recovery. **2** fall back or sink again into any state, practice, etc. ● *noun* the act or an instance of relapsing, esp. a deterioration in a patient's condition after a partial recovery. □ **re·laps·er** *noun* [Latin *relabi relaps-* (as RE-, *labi* slip)]

re·laps·ing fever *noun* a bacterial infectious disease with recurrent periods of fever.

re·late *verb* **1** *transitive* narrate or recount (incidents, a story, etc.). **2** *transitive* (in *passive*; often foll. by *to*) be connected by blood or marriage. **3** *transitive* (usu. foll. by *to, with*) bring into relation (with one another); establish a connection between (*cannot relate your opinion to my own experience*). **4** *intransitive* (foll. by *to*) have reference to; concern (*see only what relates to themselves*). **5** *intransitive* **a** (foll. by *to*) understand or have empathy for (*I can relate to that; relates to children well*). **b** understand, be connected to, or have empathy for a person etc. (*we just don't relate*). □ **re·lat·able** *adjective* [Latin *referre relat-* bring back: see REFER]

re·lat·ed *adjective* **1** connected by blood or marriage. **2** associated or connected (also in *combination: work-related stress*). **3** of the same type; in the same group, category, etc. (*related industries; related languages*). □ **re·lat·ed·ness** *noun*

re·la·tion *noun* **1 a** the way in which one person or thing is related to another. **b** the existence or effect of a connection, correspondence, contrast, or feeling prevailing between persons or things, esp. when qualified in some way (*bears no relation to the facts; enjoyed good relations for many years*). **2** a person connected by blood or marriage; a relative. **3** (in *pl.*) **a** (usu. foll. by *with*) dealings, rapport, interaction (with others). **b** sexual intercourse. **4** = RELATIONSHIP. **5 a** narration (*his relation of the events*). **b** a narrative. **6** *Law* the laying of an information (*see* INFORMATION 3). □ **in relation to** as regards.

re·la·tion·al *adjective* **1** of, belonging to, or characterized by relation. **2** having relation. **3** (of a word or grammar) expressing or characterized by relations between words. □ **re·la·tion·al·ly** *adverb*

relational database *noun Computing* a database structured to recognize the relation of stored items of information.

re·la·tion·ship *noun* **1** the fact or state of being related. **2 a** a connection or association (*enjoyed a good working relationship*). **b** an emotional (esp. sexual) association between two people. **3** kinship.

rela·tive ● *adjective* **1** considered or having significance in relation to something else; not absolute (*they live in relative comfort; truth is relative*). **2** (foll. by *to*) proportionate to (something else); in proportion to (*growth

is relative to input; low energy content relative to its bulk*). **3 a** comparative; compared one with another (*their relative advantages*). **b** (foll. by *to*) in relation to (*move slowly relative to each other*). **4** having mutual relations; corresponding in some way; related to each other. **5** (usu. foll. by *to*) having reference; relating, relevant (*the facts relative to the issue; need more relative proof*). **6** *Grammar* **a** (of a word, esp. a pronoun) referring to an expressed or implied antecedent and attaching a subordinate clause to it, e.g. *which, who*. **b** (of a clause) attached to an antecedent by a relative word. **7** *Music* (of major and minor keys) having the same key signature. **8** (of a service rank) corresponding in grade to another in a different service. ● *noun* **1** a person connected by blood or marriage. **2** a species related to another by common origin (*the apes, humans' closest relatives*). **3** *Grammar* a relative word, esp. a pronoun. **4** *Philos.* a relative thing or term. □ **rela·tive·ly** *adverb* [Old French *relatif -ive* or Late Latin *relativus* having reference or relation (as RELATE)]

relative atomic mass *noun* the ratio of the average mass of one atom of an element to one twelfth of the mass of an atom of carbon-12. *Also called* ATOMIC WEIGHT.

relative density *noun* = SPECIFIC GRAVITY.

relative humidity *noun* humidity expressed as the ratio of the mass of water vapour in a volume of air to the value for saturated air at the same temperature.

relative molecular mass *noun* = MOLECULAR WEIGHT.

rela·tiv·ism *noun* the doctrine or belief that knowledge, truth, morality, etc., are relative and not absolute. □ **rela·tiv·ist** *noun*

rela·tiv·is·tic *adjective* **1** of, pertaining to, or characterized by relativism. **2** *Physics* (of phenomena etc.) accurately described only by the theory of relativity. □ **rela·tiv·is·tic·al·ly** *adverb*

rela·tiv·ity *noun* **1** the fact or state of being relative. **2** *Physics* **a** (**special theory of relativity**) a theory based on the principle that all motion is relative and that light has constant velocity, regarding space-time as a four-dimensional continuum, and modifying previous conceptions of geometry. **b** (**general theory of relativity**) a theory extending this to gravitation and accelerated motion.

rela·tiv·ize *transitive verb* make relative. □ **rela·tiv·iz·a·tion** *noun*

re·launch ● *transitive verb* launch again. ● *noun* an instance of relaunching something, esp. a business or product.

relax *verb* **1 a** *transitive & intransitive* make or become less stiff or rigid or tense. **b** *intransitive* become at ease, unperturbed, etc. **2** *transitive & intransitive* make or become less formal or strict (*rules were relaxed*). **3** *transitive* reduce or abate (one's attention, efforts, etc.). **4** *intransitive* cease work or effort. **5** *transitive* make (hair) straight or less curly. □ **re·laxed** *adjective* **re·lax·ed·ly** *adverb* **re·lax·er** *noun* [Latin *relaxare* (as RE-, LAX)]

re·lax·ant ● *noun* a drug etc. that reduces tension and produces relaxation, esp. of muscles. ● *adjective* causing relaxation.

re·lax·a·tion *noun* **1** the act of relaxing or state of being relaxed. **2** recreation or rest, esp. after a period of work. **3** a partial remission or relaxing of a penalty, duty, etc. **4** a lessening of severity, precision, etc. **5** *Physics* the restoration of equilibrium following disturbance.

re·laxed-fit *adjective* (of trousers, esp. jeans) loose-fitting, esp. around the hips and thighs.

re·lax·ing *adjective* conducive to relaxation (*a relaxing atmosphere; a relaxing holiday*).

re·lay ● *noun* **1** a set of people etc. appointed to relieve others or to operate in shifts (*operated in relays*). **2** = RELAY RACE. **3** a device activating changes in an electric circuit etc. in response to other changes affecting itself. **4 a** a device, installation, satellite, etc. which receives, amplifies, and retransmits a transmission, broadcast, etc. **b** a relayed message or transmission. **5** a fresh set of people or horses substituted for tired ones. ● *transitive verb* **1** receive (a message, broadcast, etc.) and transmit it to others. **2 a** arrange in relays. **b** provide with or replace by relays. [Old French *relai* (n.), *relayer* (v.) (as RE-, *laier*, ultimately from Latin *laxare*): compare RELAX]

re-lay *transitive verb* (*past* and *past participle* **re-laid**) lay again or differently.

relay race *noun* a race between teams of which each member in turn covers part of the distance.

re·learn *transitive verb* learn again.

re·lease ● *transitive verb* **1** (often foll. by *from*) set free; liberate, unfasten. **2** allow to move from a fixed position. **3 a** make (information, a recording, etc.) publicly or generally available. **b** issue (a film etc.) for general exhibition. **4** *Law* **a** remit (a debt). **b** surrender (a right). **c** make over (property or money) to another. **d** free (a person) from the obligations of a contract. **5** give free rein to (an emotional or instinctual drive); ease (tension). ● *noun* **1** deliverance or liberation from a restriction, duty, or difficulty. **2** a handle or catch that releases part of a mechanism. **3** a document or item of information made available for publication (*press release*). **4 a** a film or CD etc. that is released. **b** the act or an instance of releasing or the process of being released in this way. **5** *Law* the act of releasing (property, money, or a right) to another. **b** a document effecting this. **6** a document freeing a person from legal responsibility or obligation. □ **re·leas·able** *adjective* **re·leas·ee** *noun* (in sense 4 of *verb*). **re·leas·er** *noun* [Old French *reles* (n.), *relesser* (v.), *relaiss(i)er* from Latin *relaxare*: see RELAX]

rel·egate /ˈrelə.geɪt/ *transitive verb* **1** consign or dismiss to an inferior or less important position, category, etc. **2** *Brit.* transfer (a sports team) to a lower division of a league etc. □ **rel·ega·tion** *noun* [Latin *relegare relegat-* (as RE-, *legare* send)]

re·lent /rəˈlent, ri-/ *intransitive verb* **1** decide to be less strict, harsh, or determined. **2** yield to compassion. **3** relax one's severity; become less stern. [medieval Latin *relentare* (unrecorded), formed as RE- + Latin *lentare* bend, from *lentus* flexible]

re·lent·less *adjective* **1** unrelenting; insistent and uncompromising. **2** continuous; oppressively constant (*the pressure was relentless*). □ **re·lent·less·ly** *adverb* **re·lent·less·ness** *noun*

rel·evant /ˈreləvənt/ *adjective* (often foll. by *to*) bearing on or having reference to the matter in hand. □ **rel·evance** *noun* **rel·evancy** *noun* **rel·evant·ly** *adverb* [medieval Latin *relevans*, part. of Latin *relevare* RELIEVE]

re·li·able *adjective* **1** that may be relied on. **2** of sound and consistent character or quality. □ **re·li·abil·ity** *noun* **re·li·ably** *adverb*

re·li·ance *noun* **1** (foll. by *on*) dependence; the act or state of relying on something (*the country's total reliance on oil imports*). **2** trust, confidence. □ **re·li·ant** *adjective*

rel·ic *noun* **1** an object interesting because of its age or association with the past. **2** a part of a deceased holy person's body or belongings etc. kept as an object of reverence. **3 a** a surviving custom, practice, belief, thing, etc. from a past age. **b** an old person, esp. one embodying old practices, customs, etc. **4** (in *pl.*) what has survived destruction or wasting or use. [Old French *relique* from Latin *reliquiae* from *reliquus* remaining, formed as RE- + *linquere liq-* leave]

rel·ict /ˈrelɪkt/ *noun* **1** *Biol. & Geol.* a species, structure, etc., surviving from a previous age or in changed circumstances after the disappearance of related species, structures, etc. **2** (foll. by *of*) *archaic* a widow. [Latin *relinquere relict-* leave behind: sense 2 from Old French *relicte* from Latin *relicta*]

re·lief *noun* **1 a** the alleviation of or deliverance from pain, distress, anxiety, etc. **b** the feeling accompanying such deliverance. **c** alleviation of some burden, esp. taxation. **d** the action of relieving pressure (also *attributive*: *relief valve*). **2** a feature etc. that diversifies monotony or relaxes tension. **3 a** assistance given to those in special need or difficulty (*disaster relief fund*). **b** financial and other assistance given to the poor from government funds. **4 a** the replacing of a person or persons on duty by another or others. **b** a person or persons replacing others in this way. **5** (foll. by *of*) the reinforcement (esp. the raising of a siege) of a place. **6 a** a method of moulding or carving or stamping in which the design stands out from the surface, with projections proportioned to and more (**high relief**) or less (**low relief**) closely approximating those of the objects depicted (compare ROUND *noun* 10). **b** a piece of sculpture etc. in relief. **c** a representation of relief given by an arrangement of line or colour or shading. **7** vividness, distinctness (*brings the facts out in sharp relief*). **8** *Baseball* the act or an instance of a pitcher entering a game already in progress to replace the current pitcher because of ineffectiveness, fatigue, etc. (*pitched three innings of relief*; also *attributive*: *relief innings*). **9** esp. *Law* the redress of a hardship or grievance. **10** (usu. *attributive*) designating a printing process using raised type (*relief printing*). **11** *Geog.* difference in height from the surrounding terrain. [Old French *relief* (in sense 6 French *relief* from Italian *rilievo*), from *relever*: see RELIEVE]

relief camp *noun Cdn hist.* one of a number of camps set up across Canada at the height of the Great Depression (1932–36) in which single, unemployed, homeless Canadian men were provided with lodging, food, medical care, work clothes, and minimal pay for work.

relief map *noun* **1** a map indicating hills and valleys, e.g. by shading or contour lines. **2** a map-model showing elevations and depressions, usu. on an exaggerated relative scale.

relief pitcher *noun Baseball* a pitcher who replaces another in mid-game.

re·lieve *transitive verb* **1** bring or provide aid or assistance to. **2** alleviate or reduce (pain, suffering, pressure, etc.). **3** mitigate the tedium or

monotony of. **4** bring military support for (a besieged place). **5** release (a person) from a duty by acting as or providing a substitute. **6** (foll. by *of*) take (a burden or responsibility) away from (a person). **7** bring into relief; cause to appear solid or detached. □ **relieve oneself** urinate or defecate. □ **re·liev·able** *adjective* [Old French *relever* from Latin *relevare* (as RE-, *levis* light)]

re·lieved *predicative adjective* freed from anxiety or distress (*am very relieved to hear it*). □ **re·liev·ed·ly** *adverb*

re·liev·er *noun* **1** in senses of RELIEVE. **2** = RELIEF PITCHER.

re·lievo /rəˈliːvoː, ri-/ *noun* (*pl.* **-lievos**) = RELIEF 6. [Italian *rilievo* RELIEF 6]

re·light *transitive verb* (*past* **relit**; *past participle* **relit** or **re·light·ed**) light (a fire etc.) again.

religio- /rɪˈlɪdʒiːoː/ *combining form* **1** religion. **2** religious.

re·li·gion /rɪˈlɪdʒən/ *noun* **1** the belief in a superhuman controlling power, esp. in a personal God or gods entitled to obedience and worship. **2** the expression of this in worship. **3** a particular system of faith and worship. **4** life under monastic vows (*the way of religion*). **5** a thing that one is strongly devoted to (*football is their religion*). □ **get religion** *informal* be converted to religious belief and practices. □ **re·li·gion·less** *adjective* [Old French from Latin *religio -onis* obligation, bond, reverence]

re·li·gion·ist /rɪˈlɪdʒənɪst/ *noun* a religious person, esp. the follower of a specified religion.

re·li·giose /rɪˈlɪdʒioːs/ *adjective* excessively religious. [Latin *religiosus* (as RELIGIOUS)]

re·li·gi·os·ity /rɪˌlɪdʒɪˈɒsɪti/ *noun* the condition of being religious or religiose.

re·li·gious /rɪˈlɪdʒəs, ri-/ ● *adjective* **1** devoted to religion; pious, devout. **2** of or concerned with religion. **3** of or belonging to a religious order, e.g. of monks. **4** scrupulous, conscientious (*a religious attention to detail*). ● *noun* (*pl.* same) a person bound by religious vows, e.g. a monk, nun, etc. □ **re·li·gious·ly** *adverb* **re·li·gious·ness** *noun*

religious right *noun* (in the US) people espousing right-wing views and esp. fundamentalist Christianity.

re·line *transitive verb* line again.

re·lin·quish /rəˈlɪŋkwɪʃ, ri-/ *transitive verb* **1** surrender or resign (a right or possession). **2** give up or cease from (a habit, plan, belief, etc.). **3** relax hold of (an object held). □ **re·lin·quish·ment** *noun* [Old French *relinquir* from Latin *relinquere* (as RE-, *linquere* leave)]

reli·quary /ˈrelɪkweri/ *noun* (*pl.* **-ies**) esp. *Christianity* a receptacle for relics. [French *reliquaire* (as RELIC)]

rel·ish ● *noun* **1** great liking, enjoyment, or satisfaction (*told the story with great relish*). **2 a** an appetizing flavour. **b** an attractive quality (*fishing loses its relish in winter*). **3** a condiment eaten with plainer food to add flavour, esp. a sauce made of pickled chopped vegetables. ● *transitive verb* **1 a** get pleasure out of; enjoy greatly. **b** look forward to, anticipate with pleasure (*did not relish what lay before her*). **2** add relish to. □ **rel·ish·able** *adjective* [alteration (with assimilation to -ISH²) of obsolete *reles* from Old French *reles*, *relais* remainder, from *relaisser*: see RELEASE]

re·live *transitive verb* live (an experience etc.) over again, esp. in the imagination.

rel·leno /reiˈjeinoː/ *noun* = CHILE RELLENO.

re·load *transitive & intransitive verb* **1** load (a gun, camera, etc.) again. **2** load (ammunition, film, etc.) into a gun, camera, etc. **3** = REFRESH *verb* 4b.

re·locate *verb* **1** *transitive* locate in a new place. **2** *transitive & intransitive* move to a new place (esp. to live or work). □ **re·locat·able** *adjective* **re·loca·tion** *noun*

re·luc·tant *adjective* **1** (often foll. by *to* + *infin.*) unwilling or disinclined (*reluctant to leave*). **2** done or produced with unwillingness or disinclination (*reluctant hospitality*). □ **re·luc·tance** *noun* **re·luc·tant·ly** *adverb* [Latin *reluctari* (as RE-, *luctari* struggle)]

rely *intransitive verb* (**relies**, **relied**) (foll. by *on, upon*) **1** depend on with confidence or assurance (*am relying on your judgment*). **2** be dependent on (*relies on her for everything*). [Middle English (earlier senses 'rally, be a vassal of') from Old French *relier* bind together, from Latin *religare* (as RE-, *ligare* bind)]

REM *abbreviation* RAPID EYE MOVEMENT.

rem *noun* (*pl.* same) a unit of effective absorbed dose of ionizing radiation in human tissue, equivalent to one roentgen of X-rays. [*r*oentgen *e*quivalent *m*an]

re·made *past and past participle of* REMAKE.

Consonants:　b *but*　d *dog*　f *few*　g *get*　h *her*　j *yes*　k *cat*　l *leg*　m *man*　n *no*　p *pen*　r *red*　s *sit*

re·mail·er *noun* (also **anonymous remailer**) an Internet service that forwards email after stripping the address and header information of the original sender and replacing it with others, so that the original sender remains anonymous. □ **re·mail·ing** *noun*

re·main *intransitive verb* **1** be left over after others or other parts have been removed or used or dealt with. **2** be in the same place or condition during further time; continue to exist or stay; be left behind (*remained at home*). **3** continue to be (*remained calm; remained friends*). □ **remain to be seen** be not yet known or certain. □ **re·main·ing** *adjective* [Old French *remain-* stressed stem of *remanoir* or from Old French *remaindre*, ultimately from Latin *remanēre* (as RE-, *manēre* stay)]

re·main·der ● *noun* **1** a part remaining or left over. **2** remaining persons or things. **3** a number left after division or subtraction. **4** a copy of a book left unsold when it is no longer in great demand, often disposed of at a reduced price. **5** *Law* an interest in an estate that becomes effective in possession only when a prior interest (devised at the same time) ends. ● *transitive verb* (esp. as **re·main·dered** *adjective*) dispose of (books for which there is little demand) at a reduced price. [Middle English (in sense 5) from Anglo-French, = Old French *remaindre*: see REMAIN]

re·mains *plural noun* **1** what remains after other parts have been removed or used etc. **2** relics of antiquity, esp. of buildings (*Roman remains*). **3** a person's body after death. **4** an author's (esp. unpublished) works left after death.

re·make ● *transitive verb* (*past* and *past participle* **re·made**) make again or differently. ● *noun* a thing that has been remade, esp. a film or recording.

re·mand ● *transitive verb* return (a prisoner) to custody, esp. to allow further inquiries to be made or while awaiting trial. ● *noun* **1** a recommittal to custody. **2** the state of having been remanded (*time served in remand*; also *attributive*: *remand centre; remand prisoners*). [Late Latin *remandare* (as RE-, *mandare* commit)]

rem·an·ent /ˈremənənt/ *adjective* **1** remaining, residual. **2** (of magnetism) remaining after the magnetizing field has been removed. □ **rem·an·ence** *noun* [Latin *remanēre* REMAIN]

re·manu·fac·ture *noun* manufacture again.

re·mark ● *verb* **1** *transitive* (often foll. by *that* + clause) **a** say by way of comment. **b** take notice of; regard with attention. **2** *intransitive* (usu. foll. by *on, upon*) make a comment. ● *noun* **1** a written or spoken comment; anything said. **2 a** the act of noticing or observing (*worthy of remark*). **b** the act of commenting (*let it pass without remark*). [French *remarque*, *remarquer* (as RE-, MARK¹)]

re·mark·able *adjective* **1** worth notice; exceptional. **2** striking, conspicuous. □ **re·mark·ably** *adverb*

Re·marque /rɪˈmɑːrk/ **Erich Maria** (1898–1970), German-born US novelist, who is best known for his first novel, *All Quiet on the Western Front* (1929), a realistic portrayal of a German soldier's experiences in the First World War.

re·marry *transitive & intransitive verb* (**-ries, -ried**) marry again. □ **re·mar·riage** *noun*

re·mas·ter *transitive verb* (often as **re·mas·tered** *adjective*) rework or adjust the master of (a recording), esp. to improve the sound quality. □ **re·master·ing** *noun*

re·match *noun* a second match or game between the same opponents.

Rem·brandt /ˈrembrant/ (full name Rembrandt Harmensz van Rijn) (1606–69), Dutch painter. His use of chiaroscuro to give his subjects a spiritual and introspective quality transformed the Dutch portrait tradition; his works include group portraits such as the *Anatomy Lesson of Dr. Tulp* (1632) and *Night Watch* (1642), a series of over 60 self-portraits (1629–69), and religious, genre, and landscape paintings.

re·meas·ure *transitive verb* measure again. □ **re·measure·ment** *noun*

re·med·ial /rɪˈmiːdɪəl/ *adjective* **1** affording or intended as a remedy (*remedial therapy; took remedial action*). **2** (of teaching etc.) for learners requiring special attention or aid. [Late Latin *remedialis* from Latin *remedium* (as REMEDY)]

re·medi·ation /rɪˌmiːdɪˈeɪʃən/ *noun* the action of remedying something, esp. the reversing or stopping of environmental damage. □ **re·medi·ate** *transitive verb* [from Latin *remediatio(n-)* from *remediare* heal, cure]

rem·edy /ˈremɪdɪ/ ● *noun* (*pl.* **-edies**) (often foll. by *for, against*) **1** a medicine or treatment (for a disease etc.). **2** a means of counteracting or removing anything undesirable. **3** redress; legal or other reparation. ● *transitive verb* (**-edies, -edied**) rectify; make good. □ **re·medi·able** /rɪˈmiːdɪəbəl/ *adjective* [Anglo-French *remedie* or Latin *remedium* (as RE-, *medēri* heal)]

re·mem·ber *verb* **1** *transitive* keep in the memory; not forget. **2 a** *transitive & intransitive* bring back into one's thoughts, call to mind (knowledge or experience etc.). **b** *transitive* (often foll. by *to* + infin. or *that* + clause) have in mind (a duty, commitment, etc.) (*will you remember to lock the door?*). **3** *transitive* think of or acknowledge (a person) in some connection, as in commemoration or in making a gift etc. **4** *transitive* (foll. by *to*) convey greetings from (one person) to (another) (*remember me to your mother*). **5** *transitive* mention (in prayer). □ **re·mem·ber·er** *noun* [Old French *remembrer* from Late Latin *rememorari* (as RE-, Latin *memor* mindful)]

re·mem·brance *noun* **1** the act of remembering or process of being remembered. **2** a memory or recollection. **3** a thing serving to remind one of another; a keepsake or souvenir. **4** a gift made in remembrance of another. **5** (in *pl.*) greetings conveyed through a third person.

Remembrance Day *noun* **1** (in Canada) 11 Nov., the anniversary of the armistice at the end of the First World War, on which the war dead are commemorated. **2** (in the UK) (also called **Remembrance Sunday**) the Sunday nearest 11 Nov., when those who were killed in the wars of 1914–18 and 1939–45 are commemorated.

re·mind *transitive verb* **1** (foll. by *of*) cause (a person) to remember or think of. **2** (foll. by *to* + infin. or *that* + clause) cause (a person) to remember (a commitment etc.) (*remind them to pay their subscriptions*).

re·mind·er *noun* **1** a thing that reminds, esp. a letter or bill. **2** (often foll. by *of*) a memento or souvenir.

re·mind·ful *adjective* (often foll. by *of*) acting as a reminder; reviving the memory.

re·min·eral·ize *transitive verb* (also esp. *Brit.* **-ise**) restore the depleted mineral content of (a part of the body, esp. the bones or teeth). □ **re·min·eral·iz·a·tion** *noun*

rem·in·isce /ˌremɪˈnɪs/ *intransitive verb* (often foll. by *about*) indulge in remembering events or experiences from one's past. [back-formation from REMINISCENCE]

rem·in·is·cence /ˌremɪˈnɪsəns/ *noun* **1** the recalling of one's past experiences or events, esp. with enjoyment. **2 a** a past fact or experience that is remembered. **b** the process of narrating this. **3** (in *pl.*) a collection in literary form of incidents and experiences that a person remembers. **4** a characteristic of one thing reminding or suggestive of another. **5** *Philos.* (esp. in Platonism) the theory of the recovery of things known to the soul in previous existences. [Late Latin *reminiscentia* from Latin *reminisci* remember]

rem·in·is·cent /ˌremɪˈnɪsənt/ *adjective* **1** (foll. by *of*) tending to remind one of or suggest. **2** concerned with reminiscence. **3** (of a person) given to reminiscing. □ **rem·in·is·cent·ly** *adverb*

re·mise /rəˈmiːz/ *transitive & intransitive verb Law* surrender or make over (a right or property). [French from *remis, remise* past participle of *remettre* put back: compare REMIT]

re·miss /rəˈmɪs, rɪ-/ *adjective* careless of duty; lax, negligent. [Latin *remissus* past participle of *remittere* slacken: see REMIT]

re·mis·sible /rɪˈmɪsəbəl/ *adjective* that may be remitted. [French *rémissible* or Late Latin *remissibilis* (as REMIT)]

re·mis·sion *noun* **1 a** a diminution of force, effect, or degree (esp. of disease or pain). **b** the period or duration of this. **2** *Cdn & Brit.* the reduction of a prison sentence on account of good behaviour etc. **3** the remitting of a debt or penalty etc. **4** (often foll. by *of*) forgiveness (of sins etc.). ● **re·mis·sive** *adjective*

re·mit ● *verb* (**re·mit·ted, re·mit·ting**) **1** *transitive* cancel or refrain from exacting or inflicting (a debt or punishment etc.). **2** *intransitive & transitive* abate or slacken; cease or cease from partly or entirely. **3** *transitive* send (money etc.) in payment. **4** *transitive* send by mail. **5** *transitive* **a** (foll. by *to*) refer (a matter for decision etc.) to some authority. **b** *Law* send back (a case) to a lower court. **6** *transitive* **a** (often foll. by *to*) postpone or defer. **b** (foll. by *in, into*) send or put back into a previous state. **7** *transitive Theol.* (usu. of God) pardon (sins etc.). ● *noun* esp. *Brit.* **1** the terms of reference of a committee etc. **2** an item remitted for consideration. □ **re·mit·table** *adjective* **re·mit·tal** *noun* [Latin *remittere remiss-* (as RE-, *mittere* send)]

re·mit·tance *noun* **1** money sent, esp. by mail, for goods or services or as an allowance. **2** the act of sending money.

remittance man *noun hist.* an emigrant who is supported or assisted by money sent from home.

re·mit·tent *adjective* that abates at intervals (*remittent fever*).

re·mix ● *transitive verb* mix (esp. a recording) again. ● *noun* a sound recording that has been remixed to produce a new version (*see* MIX *verb* 8, 9). □ **re·mix·er** *noun*

rem·nant ● *noun* **1** a small remaining quantity. **2** a piece of cloth etc.

left when the greater part has been used or sold. **3** (foll. by *of*) a surviving trace (*a remnant of empire*). ● *adjective* remaining; leftover. [Old French *remenant* from *remenoir* REMAIN]

re·mod·el *transitive verb* (**re·modelled**, **re·model·ling**; esp. *US* **re·model·ed**, **re·model·ing**) **1** model again or differently. **2** change the structure or shape of (esp. a room or building); reconstruct. □ **re·model·ler** *noun*

re·mold *var. of* REMOULD.

re·mon·strance /rəˈmɒnstrəns/ *noun* **1** the act or an instance of remonstrating. **2** an expostulation or protest. [obsolete French *remonstrance* (as REMONSTRATE)]

rem·on·strate /ˈremənˌstreɪt/ *verb* **1** *intransitive* (foll. by *with*) make a protest; argue forcibly (*remonstrated with them over the delays*). **2** *transitive* (often foll. by *that* + clause) urge protestingly. □ **rem·on·stra·tion** *noun* [medieval Latin *remonstrare* (as RE-, *monstrare* show)]

rem·ora /ˈremərə/ *noun* any of various marine fish of the family Echeneidae, which attach themselves by modified sucker-like fins to other fish and to ships. [Latin, = hindrance (as RE-, *mora* delay, from the former belief that the fish slowed ships down)]

re·morse *noun* **1** deep regret for a wrong committed. **2** a compassionate reluctance to inflict pain. [Old French *remors* from medieval Latin *remorsus* from Latin *remordēre remors-* vex (as RE-, *mordēre* bite)]

re·morse·ful *adjective* filled with repentance. □ **re·morse·fully** *adverb*

re·morse·less *adjective* **1** without compassion or compunction. **2** (of something unpleasant) never ending or improving, relentless. □ **re·morse·less·ly** *adverb* **re·morse·less·ness** *noun*

re·mort·gage /riːˈmɔːɡɪdʒ/ ● *transitive & intransitive verb* mortgage again; revise the terms of an existing mortgage on (a property). ● *noun* a different or altered mortgage.

re·mote ● *adjective* (**re·mot·er**, **re·mot·est**) **1** far away in place or time. **2** out of the way; situated away from the main centres of population, society, etc. **3** distantly related (*a remote ancestor*). **4** slight, faint (*not the remotest chance*). **5** (of a person) aloof; not friendly. **6** (foll. by *from*) widely different; separate by nature (*ideas remote from the subject*). **7** situated, occurring, operating, or performed at or from a (not necessarily great) distance (*remote computer; remote access; remote camera*). ● *noun* = REMOTE CONTROL 2. □ **re·mote·ly** *adverb* **re·mote·ness** *noun* [Latin *remotus* (as REMOVE)]

remote control *noun* **1** control of a machine or apparatus from a distance by means of signals transmitted from a radio or electronic device. **2** such a device, esp. a hand-held one controlling a television etc. □ **remote-controlled** *adjective*

remote sensing *noun* the scanning of the earth by satellite or high-flying aircraft in order to obtain information about it.

re·mou·lade /reɪmuːˈlɒd/ *noun* a cold mayonnaise-based sauce, usu. with capers, mustard, herbs, chopped pickles and hard-boiled egg yolks. [French, perhaps ultimately from Latin *armoracea* horseradish]

re·mould *transitive verb* (also **re·mold**) mould again; refashion.

re·mount ● *verb* **1 a** *transitive* mount (a horse etc.) again. **b** *intransitive* get on horseback again. **2** *transitive* get on to or ascend (a ladder, hill, etc.) again. **3** *transitive* put (a picture, object, etc.) on a new or different mount. **4** *transitive* present or perform (a play, musical, exhibition, etc.) again. ● *noun* **1** a fresh horse for a rider. **2** (also **re·mount·ing**) an instance of presenting or performing (a play, musical, exhibition, etc.) again.

re·mov·al *noun* **1** the act or an instance of removing; the process of being removed. **2** dismissal, e.g. from a job or position. **3** esp. *Brit.* the transfer of furniture and belongings on moving house.

re·move ● *verb* **1** *transitive* take off or away from the place or position occupied (*remove the top carefully*). **2** *transitive* **a** move or take to another place; change the situation of. **b** get rid of; eliminate (*will remove all doubts*). **3** *transitive* cause to be no longer present or available; take away (*all privileges were removed*). **4** *transitive* (often foll. by *from*) dismiss (a person) from office. **5** *transitive informal* kill, assassinate. **6** *transitive* (in passive; foll. by *from*) distant or remote in condition (*the country is not far removed from anarchy*). **7** *formal* **a** *intransitive* (usu. foll. by *from, to*) change one's home or place of residence. **b** *transitive* conduct the removal of. ● *noun* **1** a degree of remoteness; a distance. **2** a stage in a gradation; a degree (*is several removes from what I expected*). □ **re·mov·able** *adjective* **re·mov·abil·ity** *noun* **re·mov·er** *noun* [Old French *removeir* from Latin *removēre remot-* (as RE-, *movēre* move)]

re·moved *adjective* **1** (esp. of cousins) separated by a specified number of steps of descent (*a first cousin twice removed is a grandchild of a first cousin*). **2** (foll. by *from*) distant, remote, separated.

re·muner·ate /rɪˈmjuːnəˌreɪt/ *transitive verb* **1** reward; pay for services rendered. **2** serve as or provide recompense for (toil etc.) or to (a person). □ **re·muner·a·tion** *noun* **re·muner·a·tive** /-rətɪv/ *adjective* [Latin *remunerari* (as RE-, *munus muneris* gift)]

Remus /ˈriːməs/ *Rom. Myth* the twin brother of Romulus.

Ren·ais·sance /ˈrenəˌsɒns, -, ˌsãs, rəˈneɪ-/ *noun* **1** the period in Western European history in the 14th–16th c. of intensified classical scholarship and humanism, marked by advances in art and literature under the influence of classical models, and generally held to be the transition between the Middle Ages and the modern world. **2** the culture and style of art, architecture, etc. developed during this era. **3** (**renaissance**) a revival, esp. of culture. [French *renaissance* (as RE-, French *naissance* birth, from French *nascentia* or French *naître naiss-* be born, from Romanic: compare NASCENT]

Renaissance man *noun* a person with many talents or pursuits, esp. in the humanities.

renal /ˈriːnəl/ *adjective* of or concerning the kidneys. [French *rénal* from Late Latin *renalis* from Latin *renes* kidneys]

re·name *transitive verb* name again; give a new name to.

Renan /rəˈnɑ̃/ **Jo·seph Er·nest** (1823–92), French historian and philosopher, best known for his controversial *Vie de Jésus* (1863), which rejected the supernatural element in the life of Jesus.

re·nas·cence /rɪˈneɪsəns, rɪˈnasəns/ *noun* rebirth; renewal.

re·nas·cent /rɪˈneɪsənt, rɪˈnasənt/ *adjective* springing up anew; being reborn. [Latin *renasci* (as RE-, *nasci* be born)]

Re·nault /ˈrenoʊ/ **1** Louis (1877–1944), French engineer and car manufacturer. He established the Renault company in 1898 and produced a series of race cars, industrial and agricultural machinery, and military technology; nationalized in 1945, the company subsequently became one of France's leading car manufacturers. **2 Mary** (pseudonym of Mary Challans) (1905–83), British novelist, resident in South Africa from 1948. Her historical novels set in ancient Greece and Asia Minor include one trilogy based on the legend of Theseus (1956–62) and another based on Alexander the Great (1970–81).

rend *verb* (*past* and *past participle* **rent**) **1** *transitive & intransitive* (foll. by *off, from, away,* etc.) tear or wrench forcibly. **2** *transitive & intransitive* split or divide in pieces or into factions (*a country rent by civil war*). **3** *transitive* cause emotional pain to (the heart etc.). □ **rend the air** sound piercingly. [Old English *rendan*, related to Middle Low German *rende*]

Ren·dell /ˈrendəl/ **Ruth Bar·bara** (b.1930), English writer. She is known for her series of detective novels starting with *From Doon with Death* (1964), and psychological crime novels which include *A Judgement in Stone* (1977), and, under the pseudonym Barbara Vine, *A Dark-Adapted Eye* (1986).

ren·der *transitive verb* **1** cause to be or become; make (*rendered us helpless*). **2** give or pay (money, service, etc.), esp. in return or as a thing due (*render thanks; rendered good for evil*). **3** (often foll. by *to*) **a** give (assistance) (*rendered aid to the injured passengers*). **b** show (obedience etc.). **c** do (a service etc.). **4 a** submit; send in; present (an account, reason, etc.). **b** hand down (a verdict). **5 a** represent or portray artistically, musically, etc. **b** perform (a role); represent (a character, idea, etc.) (*the dramatist's conception was well rendered*). **c** *Music* perform; execute. **6** translate (*rendered the poem into French*). **7** (often foll. by *down*) melt down (fat etc.) esp. to clarify; extract by melting. **8** cover (stone or brick) with a coat of plaster. **9** *archaic* **a** give back; hand over; deliver, give up, surrender. **b** show (obedience). □ **ren·der·er** *noun* [Old French *rendre*, ultimately from Latin *reddere reddit-* (as RE-, *dare* give)]

ren·der·ing *noun* **1 a** the act or an instance of performing music, drama, etc.; an interpretation or performance (*an excellent rendering of the part*). **b** a translation. **2** the process of extracting, melting, or clarifying fat. **3 a** the act or an instance of plastering stone, brick, etc. **b** this coating. **4** the act or an instance of giving, yielding, or surrendering.

ren·dez·vous /ˈrɒndeɪˌvuː/ ● *noun* (*pl.* same /-, ˌvuːz/) **1** an agreed or regular meeting place. **2** a meeting by arrangement. **3** a place appointed for assembling troops, ships, etc. **4** a pre-arranged meeting between spacecraft in space. **5** *N Amer. hist.* an annual gathering of trappers etc. in a remote area. ● *intransitive verb* (**ren·dez·vouses** /-, ˌvuːz/; **ren·dez·voused** /-, ˌvuːd/; **ren·dez·vous·ing** /-, ˌvuːɪŋ/) meet at a rendezvous. [French *rendez-vous* present yourselves, from *rendre*: see RENDER]

ren·di·tion *noun* (often foll. by *of*) **1** an interpretation or rendering of a dramatic role, piece of music, etc. **2** a translation. **3** a visual

representation. 4 the act or an instance of rendering. [obsolete French from *rendre* RENDER]

ren·e·gade /ˈrenəˌgeɪd/ ● *noun* **1 a** a person who deserts a party or principles. **b** a person who changes allegiance. **2** a person living outside of or in opposition to a society; an outlaw. **3** *archaic* an apostate; a person who abandons one religion for another. ● *adjective* **1** traitorous, rebellious. **2** of changed allegiance. [Spanish *renegado* from medieval Latin *renegatus* (as RE-, Latin *negare* deny)]

re·nege /rɪˈneg, rɪ-, -ˈneɪg/ *intransitive verb* (**re·neged, re·neg·ing**) **1 a** go back on one's word; change one's mind; recant. **b** (foll. by *on*) go back on (a promise or undertaking or contract). **2** *Cards* revoke. [medieval Latin *renegare* (as RE-, Latin *negare* deny)]

re·ne·goti·ate /ˌriːnɪˈgoʊʃiˌeɪt/ *transitive & intransitive verb* negotiate again or on different terms. □ **re·negoti·able** *adjective* **re·negoti·a·tion** *noun*

re·new *verb* **1** *transitive* revive; regenerate; make new again; restore to the original state. **2** *transitive* reinforce; resupply; replace. **3** *transitive* repeat or re-establish; resume after an interruption (*renewed our acquaintance; a renewed attack*). **4** *transitive* get, begin, make, say, give, etc. anew. **5** *transitive & intransitive* **a** grant or be granted a continuation of or continued validity of (a licence, subscription, lease, etc.). **b** extend the period of loan of (a library book). **6** *transitive* recover (one's youth, strength, etc.). □ **re·new·al** *noun* **re·new·er** *noun*

re·new·able ● *adjective* **1** able to be renewed. **2** (of a source of material or energy) not depleted by utilization. ● *noun* a renewable source of material or energy. □ **re·new·abil·ity** *noun*

Ren·frew a town in E Ontario, situated on the Bonnechere River, west of Ottawa; pop. (2001) 7,942. [RENFREWSHIRE]

Ren·frew·shire a former county of west central Scotland, on the Firth of Clyde, part of Strathclyde region from 1975 to 1996, and now divided into the council areas Renfrewshire and East Renfrewshire.

Reni /ˈreɪni/ **Guido** (1575–1642), Italian baroque painter, who is noted for the graceful classicism of his frescoes of religious and mythological subjects; his works include the *Crucifixion of St. Peter* (1603) and *Aurora* (1613–4).

reni·form /ˈriːnɪˌfɔrm/ *adjective* kidney-shaped. [Latin *ren* kidney + -FORM]

renin /ˈriːnɪn/ *noun Biochem.* a proteolytic enzyme secreted by the kidneys, which helps regulate blood pressure. [as RENIFORM + -IN]

ren·min·bi /ˈrenmɪnbi/ *noun* (*pl.* same) **1** the national currency of the People's Republic of China, introduced in 1948. **2** = YUAN. [Chinese, from *rénmín* 'people' + *bì* 'currency']

Rennes /ren/ an industrial city in NW France; pop. (1999) 206,229.

ren·net /ˈrenət/ *noun* **1** curdled milk found in the stomach of an unweaned calf, used in curdling milk for cheese, junket, etc. **2** a preparation made from the stomach membrane of a calf or from certain fungi, used for the same purpose. [Middle English, prob. from an Old English form *rynet* (unrecorded), related to RUN]

ren·nin /ˈrenɪn/ *noun Biochem.* an enzyme secreted into the stomach of unweaned mammals causing the clotting of milk. [RENNET + -IN]

Reno /ˈriːnoʊ/ a city in W Nevada, a gambling resort with liberal laws enabling quick marriages and divorces; pop. (2000) 180,500.

reno /ˈrenoʊ/ *noun* (*pl.* **renos**) *Cdn informal* **1** a renovated house. **2** renovation (also *attributive: reno project*). [abbreviation]

Re·noir /ˈrenwar, rəˈnwar, renˈwar/ **1 Jean** (1894–1979), French film director. His fame is based chiefly on the films he made in France in the 1930s, including *La Grande illusion* (1937), concerning prisoners of war in the First World War, and the black comedy *La Règle du jeu* (1939). **2** his father, **(Pierre) Auguste** (1841–1919), French painter. A founding member of the Impressionists, he developed a style characterized by light colours and indistinct, subtle outlines, and in his later work concentrated on the human, esp. female, form; his best-known paintings include *Le Moulin de la galette* (1876), *Les Grandes baigneuses* (1884–7), and *The Judgement of Paris* (c.1914).

re·nomin·ate *transitive verb* nominate for a further term of office. □ **re·nomin·a·tion** *noun*

re·nounce *verb* **1** *transitive* consent formally to abandon; surrender; give up (a claim, right, possession, etc.). **2** *transitive* repudiate; refuse to recognize any longer. **3** *transitive* **a** decline further association or disclaim relationship with (*renounced my former friends*). **b** withdraw from; discontinue; forsake. **4** *intransitive Cards* follow with a card of another suit when having no card of the suit led (compare REVOKE *verb* 2). □ **renounce the world** abandon society or material affairs. □ **re·nounce·ment** *noun* **re·noun·cer** *noun* [Old French *renoncer* from Latin *renuntiare* (as RE-, *nuntiare* announce)]

reno·vate /ˈrenəˌveɪt/ *transitive verb* **1** remodel or install new fixtures etc. in (a building or part of it). **2** restore to good condition; repair. **3** refresh; reinvigorate. □ **reno·va·tion** *noun* **reno·va·tor** *noun* [Latin *renovare* (as RE-, *novus* new)]

re·nown *noun* fame; high distinction (*a dancer of great renown*). [Anglo-French *ren(o)un*, Old French *renon, renom* from *renomer* make famous (as RE-, Latin *nominare* NOMINATE)]

re·nowned *adjective* famous; celebrated.

rent¹ ● *noun* **1** a regular payment made by a tenant to an owner or landlord for the use of land or premises. **2** payment for the use of a service, equipment, etc. ● *verb* **1** *transitive* occupy or use (property, equipment, etc.) for a fixed, usu. temporary period, in return for payment (*rented a cottage at the lake; rented a car; let's rent a movie tonight*). **2** *transitive* (often foll. by *out*) allow a person to use (something) in return for rent. **3** *intransitive* occupy and use property in return for paying rent (*fed up with renting*). **4** *intransitive* be leased or hired out at a specified rate (*the apartment rents for $850 a month*). □ **for rent** *N Amer.* available to be rented. □ **rent·er** *noun* [Old French *rente* from Romanic (as RENDER)]

rent² *noun* **1** a large tear, opening. **2** a breach or split, e.g. in relations between people etc. [obsolete *rent* var. of REND]

rent³ past and past participle of REND.

rent-a- *combining form* often *jocular* denoting availability for hire (*rent-a-van; rent-a-cop*).

rent·able *adjective* **1** available or suitable for renting. **2** giving an adequate ratio of profit to capital. □ **rent·abil·ity** *noun*

rent·al ● *noun* **1** the amount paid or received as rent. **2** the act of renting. **3** *N Amer.* a rented house, car, etc. ● *adjective* **1** of or relating to rent. **2** available for rent; rented (*a rental car*).

rent boy *noun Brit.* a young male prostitute.

rent control *noun* a system of keeping rent increases within fixed limits, supervised by a government agency. □ **rent-controlled** *adjective*

rente /rãt/ *noun Cdn hist.* an annual payment made (in cash or produce) by a tenant to a landowner under the seigneurial system (compare CENS). [French (as RENT¹)]

rent-free *adjective & adverb* with exemption from rent.

ren·tier /ˈrãtiˌeɪ/ *noun* a person living on dividends from property, investments, etc. (also *attributive: the rentier class*). [French from *rente* dividend]

re·num·ber *transitive verb* change the number or numbers given or allocated to.

re·nunci·a·tion /rəˌnʌnsiˈeɪʃən/ *noun* **1** the act or an instance of renouncing or giving up. **2** self-denial. **3** a document expressing renunciation. □ **re·nunci·ant** /rəˈnʌnsiənt/ *noun & adjective* [Old French *renonciation* or Late Latin *renuntiatio* (as RENOUNCE)]

re·occupy *transitive verb* (**-pies, -pied**) occupy again. □ **re·occu·pa·tion** *noun*

re·occur *intransitive verb* (**re·occurred, re·occur·ring**) occur again or habitually. □ **re·occur·rence** *noun*

re·offend *intransitive verb* offend again; commit a further (esp. criminal) offence. □ **re·offend·er** *noun*

re-offer *intransitive verb Cdn* (*Maritimes*) stand as a candidate for re-election (*the Halifax MP has decided not to re-offer*).

re·open *transitive & intransitive verb* open again. □ **re·open·ing** *noun*

re·order ● *verb* **1** *transitive* put in order again; rearrange. **2** *transitive & intransitive* repeat an order for (a product). ● *noun* a renewed or repeated order for a product etc.

re·organ·ize *transitive verb* (also esp. *Brit.* **-ise**) **1** organize differently. **2** restructure the management of (a corporation), esp. to solve financial difficulties. □ **re·organ·iz·a·tion** *noun* **re·organ·iz·er** *noun*

re·orient /riˈɔriˌent/ *transitive verb* **1** give a new direction to (ideas etc.); redirect (a thing). **2** help (a person) find his or her bearings again. **3** change the outlook of (a person). **4** (*reflexive*) adjust oneself to or come to terms with something.

re·orien·tate /riˈɔriənˌteɪt/ *transitive verb* = REORIENT. □ **re·orien·ta·tion** *noun*

Rep. *abbreviation* **1** *US* Representative. **2** *US* Republican. **3** Republic.

rep¹ *noun informal* a representative, esp. a sales representative. [abbreviation]

rep² *noun informal* **1** repertory. **2** a repertory theatre or company. [abbreviation]

rep³ *noun* (also **repp**) a textile fabric with a corded surface, used in curtains and upholstery. [French *reps*, of unknown origin]

rep⁴ *noun N Amer. informal* reputation. [abbreviation]

rep[5] *noun informal* (usu. in *pl.*) a repetition of a fitness exercise. [abbreviation]

rep[6] *noun Cdn* = REP LEAGUE.

re·pack *transitive verb* pack again.

re·pack·age *transitive verb* **1** package again or differently. **2** present in a new form. □ **re·pack·aging** *noun*

re·paid *past and past participle of* REPAY.

re·paint *transitive verb* **1** paint again or differently. **2** restore the paint or colouring of.

re·pair[1] ● *transitive verb* **1** restore to good condition after damage or wear. **2** renovate or mend by replacing or fixing parts or by compensating for loss or exhaustion. **3** set right or make amends for (loss, wrong, error, etc.). ● *noun* **1** (usu. in *pl.*) the act or an instance of restoring to sound condition (*in need of repairs; closed during repairs*). **2** the result of this (*the repair is hardly visible*). **3** good or relative condition for working or using (*must be kept in repair; in good repair*). □ **re·pair·able** *adjective* **re·pair·er** *noun* [Old French *reparer* from Latin *reparare* (as RE-, *parare* make ready)]

re·pair[2] *intransitive verb* (foll. by *to*) go, make one's way (*repaired to the living room*). [Old French *repaire(r)* from Late Latin *repatriare* REPATRIATE]

repair·man *noun* (*pl.* **-men**) a person who repairs vehicles, machinery, appliances, etc.

re·pand /rɪˈpand/ *adjective Bot.* with an undulating margin; wavy. [Latin *repandus* (as RE-, *pandus* bent)]

re·paper *transitive verb* paper (a wall etc.) again.

rep·ar·able /ˈrɛprəbəl, ˈrɛpər-, rəˈperəbəl, rɪˈper-/ *adjective* (of a loss etc.) that can be made good. [French from Latin *reparabilis* (as REPAIR[1])]

rep·ar·a·tion /ˌrɛpəˈreɪʃən/ *noun* **1** the act or an instance of making amends. **2 a** compensation. **b** (esp. in *pl.*) compensation for war damage paid by the defeated country. **3** the act or an instance of repairing or being repaired. □ **rep·ar·a·tive** /ˈrɛpərətɪv, rɪˈperətɪv/ *adjective*

re·par·tee /ˌrɛpɑrˈteɪ, -ˈtiː/ *noun* **1** the practice or faculty of making witty retorts; sharpness or wit in quick reply. **2 a** a witty retort. **b** conversation that consists of quick clever comments and replies. [French *repartie* fem. past participle of *repartir* start again, reply promptly (as RE-, *partir* PART)]

re·par·ti·tion *transitive verb* partition again.

re·pass *transitive & intransitive verb* **1** pass again, esp. on the way back. **2** (of a legislature) pass (a bill) again.

re·past /rɪˈpast/ *noun formal* **1** a meal, esp. of a specified kind (*a light repast*). **2** food and drink supplied for or eaten at a meal. [Old French *repaistre* from Late Latin *repascere repast-* feed]

re·patri·ate /riˈpeɪtriˌeɪt/ ● *verb* **1 a** *transitive* restore (a person) to his or her native land. **b** *intransitive* return to one's own native land. **2** *transitive* bring (legislation, esp. a constitution) under the authority of the autonomous country to which it applies, used with reference to laws passed on behalf of that country by its former mother country. **3** *transitive* return (capital) from a foreign investment to investment in the country from which it originally came. ● *noun* a person who has been repatriated. □ **re·patri·a·tion** *noun* [Late Latin *repatriare* (as RE-, Latin *patria* native land)]

re·pave *transitive verb* pave (a road, driveway, etc.) again.

re·pay *verb* (*past and past participle* **re·paid**) **1** *transitive* pay back (money). **2** *transitive* return (a visit etc.). **3** *transitive* make repayment to (a person). **4** *transitive* make return for (a service, action, etc.) (*must repay their kindness; the book repays close study*). **5** *transitive* (often foll. by *for*) give in recompense. **6** *intransitive* make repayment. □ **re·pay·able** *adjective* **re·pay·ment** *noun*

rep by pop *noun Cdn hist.* = REPRESENTATION BY POPULATION. [abbreviation]

re·peal ● *transitive verb* revoke, rescind, or annul (a law, act of parliament, etc.). ● *noun* the act or an instance of repealing. □ **re·peal·able** *adjective* [Anglo-French *repeler*, Old French *rapeler* (as RE-, APPEAL)]

re·peat ● *verb* **1** *transitive* say or do over again. **2** *transitive* recite, rehearse, report, or reproduce (something from memory) (*repeated a poem*). **3** *transitive* say or report (something heard). **4** *transitive* imitate (an action etc.). **5** *intransitive* recur; appear again, perhaps several times (*a repeating pattern*). **6** *intransitive* do or say something over again. **7** *transitive & intransitive* take (an academic course) over again, esp. to obtain a passing grade (*had to repeat grade eleven math*). **8** *intransitive* (of food) be tasted intermittently for some time after being swallowed as a result of belching or indigestion. **9** *intransitive* (of a firearm) fire several shots

without reloading. **10** *intransitive US* illegally vote more than once in an election. **11** *intransitive N Amer.* repeat a particular success, achievement, etc., esp. win a particular championship etc. again, esp. for the second consecutive time. ● *noun* **1 a** the act or an instance of repeating. **b** a thing repeated (also *attributive*: *repeat prescription*). **2** a repeated broadcast. **3** *Music* **a** a passage intended to be repeated. **b** a mark indicating this. **4** a pattern repeated in wallpaper etc. **5** *Commerce* **a** a consignment similar to a previous one. **b** an order given for this; a reorder. ● *adverb* indicating emphasis (*will not, repeat not, allow this to happen*). □ **repeat itself** recur in the same form. **repeat oneself** say or do the same thing over again. □ **re·peat·able** *adjective* **re·peat·abil·ity** *noun* [Old French *repeter* from Latin *repetere* (as RE-, *petere* seek)]

re·peat·ed *adjective* frequent; done or said again and again (*ignored her repeated attempts to convince him*). □ **re·peat·ed·ly** *adverb*

re·peat·er *noun* **1** a person or thing that repeats. **2** a firearm which fires several shots without reloading. **3** a watch or clock which repeats its last strike when required. **4** a device for the automatic retransmission or amplification of an electrically transmitted message.

re·peat·ing decimal *noun* a recurring decimal.

re·pech·age /ˌrɛpəˈʃɒʒ/ *noun* (in rowing etc.) an extra contest in which the runners-up in the eliminating heats compete for a place in the final. [French *repêcher* fish out, rescue]

repel *verb* (**re·pelled**, **re·pel·ling**) **1** *transitive* drive back; ward off; repulse. **2** *transitive* refuse admission or approach or acceptance to (*repel an assailant*). **3** *transitive & intransitive* be repulsive or disgusting to. **4** *transitive* resist mixing with or admitting (*oil repels water; this surface repels moisture*). **5** *transitive & intransitive* (of a magnetic pole) push away from itself (*like poles repel*). □ **re·pel·ler** *noun* [Latin *repellere* (as RE-, *pellere puls-* drive)]

re·pel·lent ● *adjective* **1** that repels. **2** disgusting, repulsive. ● *noun* (also **re·pel·lant**) **1** a substance that repels, esp. a chemical that repels insects. **2** a substance used to treat fabric etc. so that water does not penetrate it. □ **re·pel·lency** *noun* **re·pel·lent·ly** *adverb*

re·pent[1] *verb* **1** *transitive & intransitive* wish one had not done, regret (one's wrongdoing, omission, etc.); resolve not to continue (a wrongdoing etc.). **2** *intransitive* (often foll. by *of*) feel deep sorrow about one's actions etc. □ **re·pent·ance** *noun* **re·pent·ant** *adjective* **re·pent·er** *noun* [Old French *repentir* (as RE-, *pentir*, ultimately from Latin *paenitēre*)]

re·pent[2] /ˈriːpənt/ *adjective Bot.* creeping, esp. growing along the ground or just under the surface. [Latin *repere* creep]

Re·pen·tigny /rəpɑˈtiːnjiː/ a city in south central Quebec, located on the St. Lawrence, just north of the confluence of the Rivière des Mille-Îles and Rivière l'Assomption, now including the former town of Le Gardeur; pop. (2001) 72,238. [P. Legardeur de *Repentigny*, local seigneur d.1648]

re·percus·sion /ˌriːpərˈkʌʃən, ˌrɛp-/ *noun* **1** (usu. in *pl.*; often foll. by *of*) an indirect effect or reaction following an event or action (*consider the repercussions of moving*). **2** the recoil after impact. **3** an echo or reverberation. [Old French *repercussion* or Latin *repercussio* (as RE-, PERCUSSION)]

rep·er·toire /ˈrɛpərˌtwɑr, ˈrɛpəˌtwɑr/ *noun* **1** a stock of pieces etc. that a company or a performer knows or is prepared to perform. **2** all of the works existing in a particular artistic genre (*one of the most moving ballets in the repertoire*). **3** a stock of regularly performed pieces, regularly used techniques, etc. (*went through her repertoire of excuses*). [French *répertoire* from Late Latin (as REPERTORY)]

rep·er·tory /ˈrɛpərtəri, ˈrɛpətəri/ *noun* (*pl.* **-ies**) **1** = REPERTOIRE. **2** the performance of various theatrical productions for short periods in rotation by one company. **3 a** a company performing repertory. **b** repertory theatres regarded collectively. **4** a store or collection, esp. of information, instances, etc. [Late Latin *repertorium* from Latin *reperire repert-* find]

repertory theatre *noun* **1 a** a theatre at which plays are performed for short runs in sequence by the same company. **b** such theatres collectively. **2** a movie theatre at which esp. second-run films are shown for short runs, often for one showing only.

ré·pé·ti·teur /reˌpetiˈtɜr/ *noun* **1** a tutor or coach of musicians, esp. opera singers. **2** a person who coaches dancers in their roles, esp. one who is particularly knowledgeable in one style of dance, the work of one choreographer, etc. [French]

rep·eti·tion *noun* **1 a** the act or an instance of repeating or being repeated. **b** the thing repeated. **2** a copy or replica. [French *répétition* or Latin *repetitio* (as REPEAT)]

rep·eti·tious *adjective* characterized by repetition, esp. when unnecessary or tiresome. □ **rep·eti·tious·ly** *adverb* **rep·eti·tious·ness** *noun*

re·peti·tive /rɪˈpetətɪv/ *adjective* = REPETITIOUS. □ **re·peti·tive·ly** *adverb* **re·peti·tive·ness** *noun*

repetitive strain injury *noun* injury arising from the prolonged use of particular muscles, esp. during keyboarding. Abbr.: **RSI**.

re·phrase *transitive verb* express in an alternative way.

re·pine /rɪˈpaɪn/ *intransitive verb* fret or complain; be discontented. [RE- + PINE², after *repent*]

re·place *transitive verb* **1** put back in place. **2** take the place of; succeed; be substituted for. **3** find or provide a substitute for. **4** (often foll. by *with*, *by*) fill up the place of. **5** (in *passive*, often foll. by *by*) be succeeded or have one's place filled by another; be superseded (*Jason feared that he would soon be replaced*). □ **re·place·able** *adjective* **re·placer** *noun*

re·place·ment *noun* **1** the act or an instance of replacing or being replaced. **2** a person or thing that takes the place of another.

re·plan *transitive verb* (**re·planned**, **re·plan·ning**) plan again or differently.

re·plant *transitive verb* **1** transfer (a plant etc.) to a larger pot, a new site, etc. **2** plant (ground) again; provide with new plants.

re·play ● *transitive verb* **1** play back (a piece of film, sound recording, etc.). **2** play (a game etc.) again. ● *noun* **1** the action or an instance of replaying a piece of film, sound recording, etc. (*see also* INSTANT REPLAY). **2** a replayed game or match.

rep league *noun* *Cdn* a league in children's sports for players with stronger abilities, organized on a more competitive footing than house leagues, and requiring players to pass tryouts.

re·plen·ish /rəˈplenɪʃ, rɪ-/ *transitive verb* **1** fill up again. **2** renew (a supply etc.). □ **re·plen·ish·er** *noun* **re·plen·ish·ment** *noun* [Old French *replenir* (as RE-, *plenir* from *plein* full, from Latin *plenus*)]

re·plete /rəˈpliːt, rɪ-/ *adjective* (often foll. by *with*) **1** filled or well-supplied with. **2** stuffed; gorged; sated. **3** equipped with. □ **re·pletion** *noun* [Old French *replet replete* or Latin *repletus* past participle of *replēre* (as RE-, *plēre* plet- fill)]

re·plev·in /rɪˈplevɪn/ *noun* *Law* **1** the provisional restoration or recovery of distrained goods pending the outcome of trial and judgment. **2** a writ granting this. **3** the action arising from this process. [Old French *replevir* (as REPLEVY)]

re·plevy /rɪˈplevi/ *transitive verb* (**-ies**, **-ied**) *Law* recover by replevin. [Old French *replevir* recover, from Germanic]

rep·lica /ˈreplɪkə/ *noun* **1** a facsimile, an exact copy. **2** a copy or model, esp. on a smaller scale. **3** a duplicate of a work made by the original artist. [Italian from *replicare* REPLY]

rep·li·cant /ˈreplɪkənt/ *noun* **1** (in science fiction) a genetically engineered replica of a human being. **2** an artificial or alien being in the form of a particular creature (chiefly a human being).

rep·li·cate ● *verb* /ˈreplɪˌkeɪt/ **1** *transitive* repeat (an experiment etc.). **2** *transitive* make a replica of. **3** *intransitive & reflexive* *Biol.* (of genetic material or a living organism) reproduce or give rise to a copy of (itself). ● *adjective* /ˈreplɪkət/ *Bot.* folded back on itself. □ **rep·lic·able** /ˈreplɪkəbəl/ *adjective* (in sense 1 of *verb*). **rep·lic·abil·ity** *noun* (in sense 1 of *verb*). **rep·li·ca·tion** /ˌreplɪˈkeɪʃ/ *noun* **rep·li·ca·tive** /ˈreplɪkətɪv/ *adjective* **rep·li·ca·tor** *noun* [Latin *replicare* (as RE-, *plicare* fold)]

reply ● *verb* (**-plies**, **-plied**) **1** *intransitive* (often foll. by *to*) make an answer, respond in word or action. **2** *transitive* say in answer (*he replied, 'Please yourself'*). ● *noun* (*pl.* **-plies**) **1** the act of replying (*what did they say in reply?*). **2** what is replied; a response. **3** *Law* the plaintiff's response to the defendant's plea. □ **re·pli·er** *noun* [Old French *replier* from Latin (as REPLICATE)]

repo¹ /ˈriːpoʊ/ *noun* (*pl.* **repos**) esp. *N Amer.* an instance of repossession, e.g. of a car etc. (also *attributive*: *repo man*). [abbreviation]

repo² /ˈriːpoʊ/ *noun* (*pl.* **repos**) *N Amer.* = REPURCHASE AGREEMENT. [REPURCHASE + -O]

re·point *transitive verb* point (esp. brickwork) again.

re·popu·late *transitive verb* populate again or increase the population of. □ **re·popu·la·tion** *noun*

re·port ● *verb* **1** *transitive* **a** bring back or give an account of. **b** state as fact or news, narrate or describe or repeat, esp. as an eyewitness or hearer etc. **c** relate as spoken by another. **2** *transitive* make an official or formal statement about. **3** *transitive* (often foll. by *to*) name or specify (an offender or offence) (*shall report you for insubordination*; *reported them to the police*). **4** *intransitive* (often foll. by *to*) present oneself to a person as having returned or arrived (*report to the manager on arrival*). **5** *transitive & intransitive* take down word for word or summarize or write a description of for publication. **6** *intransitive* **a** make or draw up or send in a report.

b (usu. foll. by *on*) investigate as a journalist; act as a reporter. **7** *intransitive* (often foll. by *to*) be responsible (to a superior, supervisor, etc.) (*reports directly to the vice-president*). **8** *transitive* *Parl.* (of a committee chairman) announce that the committee has dealt with (a bill). **9** *intransitive* (often foll. by *of*) give a report to convey that one is well, badly, etc. impressed (*reports well of the prospects*). ● *noun* **1** an account given or opinion formally expressed after investigation or consideration. **2** a description, summary, or reproduction of a scene or speech or law case, esp. for newspaper publication or broadcast. **3** common talk; rumour. **4** the way a person or thing is spoken of (*I hear a good report of you*). **5** = REPORT CARD 1. **6** the sound of an explosion. □ **report back** deliver a report to the person, organization, etc. for whom one acts etc. □ **re·port·able** *adjective* **re·port·ed·ly** *adverb* [Old French *reporter* from Latin *reportare* (as RE-, *portare* bring)]

re·por·tage /ˌrepɔrˈtɒʒ/ *noun* **1** the describing of events, esp. the reporting of news etc. for the press and for broadcasting. **2** the typical style of this. **3** reported news collectively (*reportage on prison life*). [REPORT, after French]

report card *noun* *N Amer.* **1** a written statement of a student's marks and behaviour at school, sent home to the parent or guardian. **2** an evaluation of performance (*a report card on Canada's health care system*).

reported speech *noun* the speaker's words with the changes of person, tense, etc. usual in reports, e.g. *she said that she would go* (opp. DIRECT SPEECH).

re·por·ter *noun* **1** a person employed to report news etc. for newspapers or broadcasts. **2** a person who reports. **3** *N Amer.* = COURT REPORTER 1.

re·por·tor·ial /ˌrɪpɔrˈtɔriəl/ *adjective* *N Amer.* of or typical of journalists. □ **re·por·tor·ial·ly** *adverb* [REPORTER, after *editorial*]

report stage *noun* *Cdn & Brit.* the debate on a bill in Parliament after it is reported.

re·pose¹ ● *noun* **1** the cessation of activity or excitement or toil. **2** sleep. **3** a peaceful or quiescent state; stillness; tranquility. ● *verb* **1** *intransitive & reflexive* lie down in rest (*reposed on a sofa*). **2** *transitive* (often foll. by *on*) lay (one's head etc.) to rest (on a pillow etc.). **3** *intransitive* (often foll. by *in*, *on*) lie; be lying or laid. **4** *transitive* give rest to; refresh with rest. **5** *intransitive* (foll. by *on*, *upon*) be supported or based on. **6** *intransitive* (foll. by *on*) dwell on. □ **re·pose·ful** *adjective* [Old French *repos(er)* from Late Latin *repausare* (as RE-, *pausare* PAUSE)]

re·pose² *verb* **1** *transitive* (foll. by *in*) place (trust etc.) in. **2** *intransitive* be kept in a place (*the manuscript reposes in the National Library*). [RE- + POSE¹ after Latin *reponere reposit-*]

re·pos·ition *verb* **1** *transitive* move or place in a different position. **2** *intransitive* adjust or alter one's position. **3** *transitive* change the image of (a company, product, etc.) to target a new or wider market.

re·pos·itory /rɪˈpɒzəˌtɔri, -ˌtri/ *noun* (*pl.* **-ies**) **1** a place where things are stored or may be found, esp. a warehouse or museum. **2** a receptacle. **3** (often foll. by *of*) **a** a book, person, etc. regarded as a store of information etc. **b** the recipient of confidences or secrets. [obsolete French *repositoire* or Latin *repositorium* (as REPOSE²)]

re·pos·sess *transitive verb* regain possession of (esp. property or goods on which repayment of a debt is in arrears). □ **re·pos·ses·sion** *noun* **re·pos·ses·sor** *noun*

repot *transitive verb* (**re·pot·ted**, **re·pot·ting**) put (a plant) in another, esp. larger, pot.

re·pous·sé /rəˈpuːseɪ/ ● *adjective* hammered into relief from the reverse side. ● *noun* ornamental metalwork fashioned in this way. [French, past participle of *repousser* (as RE-, *pousser* PUSH)]

repp *var. of* REP³.

repr. *abbreviation* **1** represent, represented, etc. **2** reprint, reprinted.

rep·re·hend /ˌreprɪˈhend/ *transitive verb* rebuke; blame; find fault with. □ **rep·re·hen·sion** *noun* [Latin *reprehendere* (as RE-, *prehendere* seize)]

rep·re·hen·sible /ˌreprɪˈhensɪbəl/ *adjective* deserving censure or rebuke; blameworthy.

rep·re·sent /ˌreprɪˈzent/ *transitive verb* **1** stand for or correspond to (*the comment does not represent all our views*). **2** (often in *passive*) be a specimen or example of; exemplify (*all types of people were represented in the audience*). **3** act as an embodiment of; symbolize (*numbers are represented by letters*). **4** call up in the mind by description or portrayal or imagination; place a likeness of before the mind or senses. **5** serve or be meant as a likeness of. **6 a** state by way of expostulation or persuasion (*represented the rashness of it*). **b** (foll. by *to*) try to bring (the facts influencing conduct) home to (*represented the risks to her client*).

---

t *top*   v *voice*   w *we*   z *zoo*   ʃ *she*   ʒ *vision*   θ *thin*   ð *this*   ŋ *ring*   x *loch*   tʃ *chip*   dʒ *jar*   (*see over for vowels*)

7 (often foll. by *as, to be*) describe or depict as; declare or make out (*represented them as martyrs; not what you represent it to be*). **8** (foll. by *that* + clause) allege. **9** show, or play the part of, on stage. **10** fill the place of; be a substitute or deputy for; be entitled to act or speak for (*the Queen was represented by the Governor General*). **11** be elected as a Member of Parliament, a legislature, etc. by (*represents a rural riding*). □ **rep·re·sent·able** *adjective*

rep·re·sen·ta·tion /ˌrɛprɪzɛnˈteɪʃən/ *noun* **1** the act or an instance of representing or being represented. **2** a thing (esp. a painting etc.) that represents another. **3** (esp. in *pl.*) a statement made by way of allegation or to convey opinion.

rep·re·sen·ta·tion·al /ˌrɛprɪzɛnˈteɪʃənəl/ *adjective* **1** (of a painting etc.) depicting an object as it actually appears to the eye (*representational art*). **2** of or relating to representation. □ **rep·re·sen·ta·tion·al·ism** *noun* **rep·re·sen·ta·tion·al·ist** *adjective & noun*

representation by population *noun Cdn* **1** the concept that legislative representation should be based proportionally on population rather than on a method giving equal representation to different regions in spite of population differences. **2** *hist.* such representation in the Province of Canada after 1851, in opposition to representation divided equally between Canada East and Canada West.

rep·re·sent·a·tive /ˌrɛprɪˈzɛntətɪv/ ● *adjective* **1** typical of a class or category. **2** containing typical specimens of all or many classes (*a representative sample*). **3 a** consisting of elected deputies etc. **b** based on the representation of a nation etc. by such deputies (*representative government*). **4** (foll. by *of*) serving as a portrayal or symbol of (*representative of their attitude to work*). **5** that presents or can present ideas to the mind (*imagination is a representative faculty*). **6** (of art) representational. ● *noun* **1** (foll. by *of*) a sample, specimen, or typical embodiment or analogue of. **2 a** the agent of a person or society. **b** a salesperson, esp. a travelling salesperson. **3** a delegate; a substitute. **4 a** a deputy in a representative assembly. **b** (**Representative**) (in the US) a member of the House of Representatives. □ **rep·re·sent·a·tive·ly** *adverb* **rep·re·sent·a·tive·ness** *noun*

re·press *transitive verb* **1 a** check; restrain; keep under; quell. **b** suppress; prevent from rioting etc. **2** *Psych.* **a** suppress or control (thoughts, desires, etc.) in oneself or another. **b** actively exclude (an unwelcome thought) from conscious awareness. □ **re·pres·sion** *noun* **re·pres·sive** *adjective* **re·pres·sive·ly** *adverb* **re·pres·sive·ness** *noun* [Middle English from Latin *reprimere* (as RE-, *premere* PRESS¹)]

re·pressed *adjective* affected or characterized by psychological repression.

re·press·or *noun Biochem.* a substance which acts on an operon to inhibit enzyme synthesis.

re·prieve /rəˈpriːv/ ● *transitive verb* **1 a** relieve or rescue from impending punishment. **b** remit, commute, or postpone the execution of (a condemned person). **2** give respite to. ● *noun* **1 a** the act or an instance of reprieving or being reprieved. **b** a warrant for this. **2 a** respite or temporary escape. [Middle English as past participle *repryed* from Old French *repris* past participle of *reprendre* (as RE-, *prendre* from Latin *prehendere* take): 16th-c. -v- unexplained]

rep·ri·mand /ˈrɛprɪˌmand/ ● *noun* (often foll. by *for*) an official or sharp rebuke (for a fault etc.). ● *transitive verb* express severe disapproval of (a person or their actions), esp. officially. [French *réprimande(r)* from Spanish *reprimenda* from Latin *reprimenda* neuter pl. gerundive of *reprimere* REPRESS]

re·print ● *transitive verb* print again. ● *noun* **1** the act or an instance of reprinting a book etc. **2** a book etc. reprinted. **3** the quantity reprinted.

re·pris·al /rɪˈpraɪzəl/ *noun* **1** retaliation against an enemy involving the infliction of equal or greater injuries. **2** any act of retaliation. **3** *hist.* the forcible seizure of a foreign subject or his or her goods as an act of retaliation. [Anglo-French *reprisaille* from medieval Latin *reprisalia* from *repraehensalia* (as REPREHEND)]

re·prise /rɪˈpraɪz, -ˈpriːz/ ● *noun* **1** a repeated passage in music. **2** a repeated item in a musical program. ● *transitive verb* repeat (a performance, song, etc.); restage, rewrite. [French, fem. past participle of *reprendre* (see REPRIEVE)]

re·pro /ˈriːproʊ/ *noun* (*pl.* **-pros**) (often *attributive*) a reproduction or copy. [abbreviation]

re·proach ● *transitive verb* **1** express disapproval to (a person) for a fault etc. **2** scold; rebuke; censure. ● *noun* **1** a rebuke or censure (*heaped reproaches on them*). **2** blame, criticism (*her behaviour was above reproach*). **3** (often foll. by *to*) a thing that brings disgrace or discredit. **4** (in *pl.*) a set of antiphons and responses for Good Friday representing the reproaches of Christ to his people. □ **above** (or **beyond**) **reproach** perfect. □ **re·proach·able** *adjective* **re·proach·er** *noun*

re·proach·ing·ly *adverb* [Old French *reproche(r)* from Romanic (as RE-, Latin *prope* near)]

re·proach·ful *adjective* full of or expressing reproach. □ **re·proach·ful·ly** *adverb* **re·proach·ful·ness** *noun*

repro·bate /ˈrɛprəˌbeɪt/ ● *noun* **1** an unprincipled person; a person of highly immoral character. **2** a person who is condemned by God. ● *adjective* **1** immoral. **2** hardened in sin. ● *transitive verb* **1** express or feel disapproval of; censure. **2** (of God) condemn; exclude from salvation. □ **repro·ba·tion** *noun* [Latin *reprobare reprobat-* disapprove (as RE-, *probare* approve)]

re·pro·cess *transitive verb* process again or differently. □ **re·pro·cess·ing** *noun*

re·pro·duce *verb* **1** *transitive* produce a copy or representation of. **2** *transitive* cause to be seen or heard etc. again (*tried to reproduce the sound exactly*). **3** *intransitive* produce further members of the same species by natural means. **4** *reflexive* produce offspring (*reproduced itself several times*). **5** *intransitive* give a specified quality or result when copied (*reproduces badly in black and white*). **6** *transitive Biol.* form afresh (a lost part etc. of the body). □ **re·pro·du·cer** *noun* **re·pro·du·cible** *adjective* **re·pro·du·ci·bil·ity** *noun* **re·pro·du·cibly** *adverb*

re·pro·duc·tion *noun* **1** the act or an instance of reproducing. **2** a copy of a work of art, esp. a print or photograph of a painting. **3** (*attributive*) (of furniture etc.) made in imitation of a certain style or of an earlier period. **4** the quality of reproduced sound. **5** the process by which a new organism is produced by or from an existing organism or organisms of the same species.

re·pro·duc·tive *adjective* **1** of, pertaining to, or effecting reproduction of an organism, esp. human reproduction (*reproductive technology; reproductive health*). **2** serving to reproduce. □ **re·pro·duct·ive·ly** *adverb*

re·pro·gram *transitive verb* (also **re·pro·gramme**) (**re·pro·grammed**, **re·pro·gram·ming** or **re·pro·gramed**, **re·pro·gram·ing**) program (esp. a computer) again or differently. □ **re·pro·gram·mable** *adjective*

rep·rog·ra·phy /rɪˈprɒɡrəfi/ *noun* the science and practice of copying documents by photography, xerography, etc. □ **repro·graph·ic** /ˌriːprəˈɡrafɪk/ *adjective* [REPRODUCE + -GRAPHY]

re·proof *noun* **1** blame (*a glance of reproof*). **2** a rebuke; words expressing blame. [Old French *reprove* from *reprover* REPROVE]

re·prove /rɪˈpruːv/ *transitive verb* rebuke (a person, a person's conduct, etc.). □ **re·prov·er** *noun* **re·prov·ing** *adjective* **re·prov·ing·ly** *adverb* [Old French *reprover* from Late Latin *reprobare* disapprove: see REPROBATE]

rept. *abbreviation* report.

rep·tile /ˈrɛptaɪl/ *noun* **1** any cold-blooded scaly animal of the class Reptilia, including snakes, lizards, crocodiles, turtles, tortoises, etc. **2** a grovelling or repulsive person. □ **rep·til·ian** /-ˈtɪliən/ *adjective & noun* [Late Latin *reptilis* from Latin *repere rept-* crawl]

re·pub·lic /rəˈpʌblɪk, ri-/ *noun* **1 a** a state in which supreme power is held by the people or their elected representatives or by an elected or nominated president, not by a monarch etc. **b** the system of government of such a state. **c** a period during which a state has such a government. **2** a society with equality between its members (*the literary republic*). [French *république* from Latin *respublica* from *res* concern + *publicus* PUBLIC]

re·pub·lic·an ● *adjective* **1** of or constituted as a republic. **2** characteristic of a republic. **3** advocating or supporting republican government. ● *noun* **1** a person advocating or supporting republican government. **2** (**Republican**) (in the US) a member or supporter of the Republican Party. **3** (also **Republican**) an advocate of a united Ireland. □ **re·pub·lic·an·ism** *noun*

Republican Party *noun* one of the two main US political parties, favouring only a moderate degree of central power (*compare* DEMOCRATIC PARTY).

re·pub·lish *transitive & intransitive verb* publish again or in a new edition etc. □ **re·pub·li·ca·tion** *noun*

re·pudi·ate /rəˈpjuːdieɪt, ri-/ *transitive verb* **1 a** disown; disavow; reject. **b** refuse dealings with. **c** deny. **2** refuse to recognize or obey (authority or a treaty). **3** refuse to discharge (an obligation or debt). □ **re·pudi·a·tion** *noun* **re·pudi·ator** *noun* [Latin *repudiare* from *repudium* 'divorce']

re·pug·nance /rəˈpʌɡnəns, ri-/ *noun* **1** (usu. foll. by *to, against*) antipathy; aversion. **2** (usu. foll. by *of, between, to, with*) inconsistency or incompatibility of ideas, statements, etc. [Latin *repugnantia* from *repugnare* oppose (as RE-, *pugnare* fight)]

Vowels: a *cat* ɑ *arm* e *bed* ɜr *her* ɜː *deux* ə *ago* ɪ *sit* i *cosy* iː *feed* ɒ *hot* ɔ *pore* oː *no* ʌ *run* ʊ *put*

re·pug·nant /rə'pʌgnənt, ri-/ *adjective* **1** (often foll. by *to*) extremely distasteful. **2** (often foll. by *to*) contradictory. **3** (often foll. by *with*) incompatible.

re·pulse ● *transitive verb* **1** drive back (an attack or attacking enemy) by force of arms. **2 a** rebuff (friendly advances or their maker). **b** refuse (a request or offer or its maker). **3** be repulsive to, repel, disgust. ● *noun* **1** the act or an instance of repulsing or being repulsed. **2** a rebuff. [Latin *repellere repuls-* drive back (as REPEL)]

re·pul·sion *noun* **1** aversion; disgust. **2** *esp. Physics* the force by which bodies tend to repel each other or increase their mutual distance (opp. ATTRACTION).

re·pul·sive *adjective* **1** causing aversion or loathing; loathsome, disgusting. **2** *Physics* exerting repulsion. □ **re·pul·sive·ly** *adverb* **re·pul·sive·ness** *noun*

re·pur·chase ● *transitive verb* purchase again. ● *noun* the act or an instance of purchasing again.

repurchase agreement *noun* a contract in which the vendor of (esp. government) securities agrees to repurchase them from the buyer.

re·pur·pose *transitive verb* to convert (something, esp. something holding electronic data) for use in a different format, or for a different purpose.

rep·ut·able /'repjʊtəbəl/ *adjective* having a good reputation; respectable. □ **rep·ut·ably** *adverb*

repu·ta·tion /ˌrepjʊ'teiʃən/ *noun* **1** what is generally said or believed about a person's or thing's character or standing (*has a reputation for honesty*). **2** the state of being well thought of; distinction; respectability (*have my reputation to think of; the artist has gained an international reputation*). **3** (foll. by *of, for* + verbal noun) fame, credit, or notoriety for doing something (*has the reputation of driving hard bargains*). **4** a reputation for promiscuity, drunkenness, etc. (*has a reputation*). □ **repu·ta·tion·al** *adjective*

re·pute /rə'pjuːt, ri-/ *noun* reputation (*a writer of great repute*). [Old French *reputer* or Latin *reputare* (as RE-, *putare* think)]

re·put·ed /rə'pjuːtəd, ri-/ *adjective* **1** (often foll. by *to* + infin.) generally considered or reckoned (*is reputed to be the best*). **2** passing as being, but probably not being (*his reputed father*). □ **re·put·ed·ly** *adverb*

re·quest ● *noun* **1** the act or an instance of asking for something; a petition (*came at his request*). **2** a thing asked for. **3 a** a letter, phone call, etc. asking for a particular recording etc. to be played on a radio program, often with a personal message. **b** the recording etc. played in response to such a letter etc. ● *transitive verb* **1** ask to be given or allowed or favoured with (*request a hearing; requests your presence*). **2** (foll. by *to* + infin.) ask a person to do something (*requested her to answer*). **3** (foll. by *that* + clause) ask that. □ **by** (or **on** or **upon**) **request** in response to an expressed wish. □ **re·quest·er** *noun* [Old French *requeste* ultimately from Latin *requaerere* (as REQUIRE)]

request program *noun* a radio etc. program composed of items requested by the audience.

requi·em /'rekwiəm, -iem/ *noun* **1** (**Requiem**) (also *attributive*) *esp. Catholicism* a Mass for the repose of the souls of the dead. **2** *Music* a musical setting for this. **3** (often foll. by *for*) a memorial (*his book was a fitting requiem*). [the accusative of Latin *requies* 'rest', the initial word of the Mass]

requiem shark *noun* a shark of the family Carcharinidae, which includes some large voracious sharks such as tiger sharks and hammerheads. [from obsolete French *requiem*, variant of *requin* 'shark', influenced by REQUIEM]

re·quire *transitive verb* **1** need; depend on for success or fulfillment (*the work requires much patience*). **2** lay down as an imperative (*did all that was required by law*). **3** command; instruct (a person etc.). **4** order; insist on (an action or measure). **5** (often foll. by *of, from*, or *that* + clause) demand (of or from a person) as a right. **6** wish to have (*is there anything else you require?*). □ **re·quire·ment** *noun* [Old French *requere*, ultimately from Latin *requirere* (as RE-, *quaerere* seek)]

requi·site /'rekwəzɪt/ ● *adjective* required by circumstances; necessary to success etc. ● *noun* (often in *pl.*; often foll. by *for*) a thing needed (for some purpose). [Latin *requisitus* past participle (as REQUIRE)]

requi·si·tion /ˌrekwə'zɪʃən/ ● *noun* **1** an official order for the use of property or materials, esp. by an army during a war. **2 a** a formal written demand that a duty etc. should be performed. **b** the form on which such a request is written (*filled out a requisition*). **3** the state or condition of being called or put into service. ● *transitive verb* demand the use or supply of, esp. by requisition order. □ **requi·si·tion·ist** *noun* [French *réquisition* or Latin *requisitio* (as REQUIRE)]

re·quite /rə'kwəit, ri-/ *transitive verb* **1** make return for (a service).

2 (often foll. by *with*) reward or avenge (a favour or injury). **3** (often foll. by *for*) make return to (a person). **4** (often foll. by *for, with*) repay with good or evil (*requite like for like; requite hate with love*). □ **re·quit·al** *noun* [RE- + *quite* var. of QUIT]

reran *past of* RERUN.

re·read *transitive verb* (*past* and *past participle* **re·read**) read again. □ **re·read·able** *adjective* **re·read·ing** *noun*

re·record *transitive verb* record again. □ **re·record·ing** *noun*

rere·dos /'riːrdɒs, 'riːrɪ-/ *noun Christianity* an ornamental screen covering the wall at the back of an altar. [Anglo-French from Old French *areredos* from *arere* behind + *dos* back: compare ARREARS]

re·release ● *transitive verb* release (a record, film, etc.) again. ● *noun* a re-released record, film, etc.

re·ride *noun* a second ride, esp. one awarded to a competitor in a rodeo.

re·roof *transitive verb* provide (a building etc.) with a new roof.

re·route /riː'ruːt, -rʌʊt/ *transitive verb* (**-rout·ing**) send or carry by a different route.

rerun ● *transitive verb* (**re·run·ning**; *past* **re·ran**; *past participle* **re·run**) **1** show a television program, film, etc. again. **2** run (a race, computer program, etc.) again. ● *noun* **1** the act or an instance of rerunning. **2** a television program etc. shown again.

res¹ /rez/ *noun informal* resolution (of a computer screen etc.). [abbreviation]

res² /rez/ *noun Cdn slang* a university or college residence. [abbreviation]

res³ *var. of* REZ. [abbreviation]

re·sale *noun* the sale of a thing previously bought (often *attributive*: *resale value*). □ **re·sale·able** *adjective* (also **re·salable**).

re·scale *transitive verb* change the scale of.

re·sched·ule *transitive verb* alter the schedule of; replan.

re·scind /rə'sɪnd, ri-/ *transitive verb* abrogate, revoke, cancel. □ **re·scis·sion** /-'sɪʒən/ *noun* [Latin *rescindere resciss-* (as RE-, *scindere* 'cut')]

re·script /riː'skrɪpt/ *noun* **1** *Rom.Hist.* an emperor's written reply to an appeal for guidance, esp. on a legal point. **2** *Catholicism* the Pope's decision on a question of doctrine or papal law. **3** an official edict or announcement. [Latin *rescriptum*, neuter past participle of *rescribere rescript-* (as RE-, *scribere* write)]

res·cue ● *transitive verb* (**res·cues, res·cued, res·cuing**) **1** (often foll. by *from*) save or set free or bring away from attack, custody, danger, harm, or an unpleasant situation. **2** *informal* keep from being lost or abandoned; retrieve (*got out of his chair to rescue his cup of coffee*). ● *noun* the act or an instance of rescuing or being rescued; deliverance. □ **res·cu·able** *adjective* **res·cu·ee** *noun* **res·cu·er** *noun* [Middle English *rescowe* from Old French *rescoure* from Romanic, formed as RE- + Latin *excutere* (as EX-¹, *quatere* shake)]

re·sculpt *transitive verb* change the shape of.

re·seal *transitive verb* seal again. □ **re·seal·able** *adjective*

re·search /'riːsɜrtʃ, rɪ'sɜrtʃ/ ● *noun* **1 a** the systematic investigation into and study of materials, sources, etc., in order to establish facts and reach new conclusions. **b** (usu. in *pl.*) an endeavour to discover new or collate old facts etc. by the scientific study of a subject or by a course of critical investigation. **2** (*attributive*) engaged in or intended for research (*research assistant*). ● *verb* **1** *transitive* do research into or for. **2** *intransitive* make researches. □ **re·search·able** *adjective* **re·search·er** *noun* [obsolete French *recerche* (as RE-, SEARCH)]

research and development *noun* (in industry etc.) work directed towards the innovation, introduction, and improvement of products and processes. Abbr.: **R & D, R and D**.

research station *noun* an establishment where scientific research and development activities in agriculture, biotechnology, etc. are conducted.

re·seat *transitive verb* **1** equip with new seats. **2** realign or repair in order to fit (a tap, nail, etc.) into its former correct position.

re·sect /rə'sekt, ri-/ *transitive verb Surgery* **1** cut out part of (a lung etc.). **2** pare down (bone, cartilage, etc.). □ **re·sec·tion** *noun* [Latin *resecare resect-* (as RE-, *secare* cut)]

re·seda /rɪ'siːdə/ *noun* any plant of the genus *Reseda*, with sweet-scented flowers, e.g. a mignonette. [Latin, perhaps from imperative of *resedare* 'assuage', with reference to its supposed curative powers]

re·seed *transitive verb* sow (land) with seed again, esp. grass seed.

re·sell *transitive verb* (*past* and *past participle* **re·sold**) sell (an object etc.) after buying it. □ **re·sell·er** *noun*

re·sem·blance *noun* (often foll. by *to*, *between*) a likeness or similarity.

re·sem·ble *transitive verb* be like; have a similarity to, or features in common with, or the same appearance as. [Old French *resembler* (as RE-, *sembler* from Latin *similare* from *similis* like)]

re·sent *transitive verb* show or feel indignation at; be aggrieved by (a circumstance, action, or person) (*we resent being patronized*). [obsolete French *resentir* (as RE-, Latin *sentire* feel)]

re·sent·ful *adjective* feeling resentment. □ **re·sent·ful·ly** *adverb*

re·sent·ment *noun* (often foll. by *at*, *of*) indignant or bitter feelings; anger.

res·erp·ine /ˈrezərpin/ *noun* an alkaloid obtained from plants of the genus *Rauwolfia*, used as a tranquilizer and in the treatment of hypertension. [German *Reserpin* from modern Latin species name *Rauwolfia serpentina* (named after L. *Rauwolf*, German botanist d.1596)]

res·er·va·tion *noun* **1** the act or an instance of reserving or being reserved. **2** a booking (of a room, seat, etc.). **3** the thing booked, e.g. a room in a hotel. **4** (often in *pl.*) an express or tacit limitation, qualification, or exception to an agreement etc.; doubt, uncertainty (*had reservations about the plan*). **5** an area of land reserved for occupation by American Indians in the US, Australian Aboriginals, etc. (*compare* RESERVE *noun* 5). **6** (in full **central reservation**) *Brit.* a strip of land along the centre of a road, dividing the traffic on either side; a median strip. **7 a** a right or interest retained in an estate being conveyed. **b** the clause reserving this. **8** *Cdn* a constitutional power residing with the Governor General or the Lieutenant-Governor of a province to withhold royal assent from a bill until it has been re-examined. **9** *Christianity* the practice of retaining for some purpose a portion of the Eucharistic elements (esp. the bread) after celebration.

re·serve ● *transitive verb* **1** postpone, put aside, keep back for a later occasion or special use. **2** order to be specially retained or allocated for a particular person or at a particular time. **3** retain or secure, esp. by formal or legal stipulation (*reserve the right to*). **4** postpone delivery of (judgment etc.) (*reserved my comments until the end*). **5** *Cdn* (of the Governor General or a Lieutenant-Governor of a province) withhold royal assent from (a bill). ● *noun* **1** a thing reserved for future use; an extra stock or amount (*a great reserve of strength*; *huge energy reserves*). **2** a limitation, qualification, or exception attached to something (*accept your offer without reserve*). **3 a** self-restraint; reticence; coolness or distance of manner (*difficult to overcome his reserve*). **b** (in artistic or literary expression) absence from exaggeration or ill-proportioned effects. **4** a place reserved for special use, esp. as a habitat for wildlife (*game reserve*; *nature reserve*). **5** (in Canada) an area of land set aside for the use of a specific group of Aboriginal people. **6** *Brit.* a company's profit added to capital. **7** (in *sing.* or *pl.*) assets kept readily available as cash or at a central bank, or as gold or foreign exchange (*reserve currency*). **8** (in *sing.* or *pl.*) **a** troops withheld from action to reinforce or protect others. **b** forces in addition to the regular army, navy, air force, etc., but available in an emergency. **9** a member of the military reserve. **10** an extra player chosen to be a possible substitute in a team. **11** the intentional suppression of the truth (*exercised a certain amount of reserve*). **12** (in the decoration of ceramics or textiles) an area which still has the original colour of the material or the colour of the background. ● *adjective* **1** of or pertaining to a reserve or reserves (*reserve land*). **2** kept in reserve; constituting a reserve (*reserve Chardonnay*; *reserve fund*). □ **in reserve** unused and available if required. □ **re·serv·er** *noun* [Old French *reserver* from Latin *reservare* (as RE-, *servare* 'keep')]

reserve bank *noun* **1** a central bank holding currency reserves. **2** *US* = FEDERAL RESERVE BANK.

re·served *adjective* **1** reticent; slow to reveal emotion or opinions; uncommunicative. **2 a** set apart, destined for some use or fate. **b** booked in advance. **c** (often foll. by *for*, *to*) left by fate for; falling first or only to. □ **re·serv·ed·ly** *adverb* **re·serv·ed·ness** *noun*

reserve price *noun* the lowest acceptable price stipulated for an item sold at an auction.

re·serv·ist *noun* a member of a country's reserve forces.

res·er·voir /ˈrezərˌvwar, ˈrezə-/ *noun* **1** a large natural or artificial lake or pool used for collecting and storing water for public and industrial use, irrigation, etc. **2 a** any natural or artificial receptacle esp. for or of fluid. **b** a place where fluid etc. collects. **3** a part of a machine etc. holding fluid. **4** a body of porous rock holding a large quantity of oil or natural gas. **5** (usu. foll. by *of*) a reserve or supply (*a reservoir of information*). [French *réservoir* from *réserver* RESERVE]

reset ● *transitive verb* (**re·set·ting**; *past* and *past participle* **reset**) **1** set (a broken bone, gems, a measuring gauge, etc.) again or differently. **2** cause (a device or appliance) to return to a former state, esp. to a condition of readiness. ● *noun* **1** the action or an act of resetting something. **2** a device for resetting an instrument, appliance, etc. □ **re·set·table** *adjective*

re·set·tle *transitive & intransitive verb* settle again. □ **re·set·tle·ment** *noun*

re·shape *transitive verb* shape or form again or differently.

re·shoot *past* and *past participle* (**re·shot**) ● *transitive & intransitive verb* shoot (a scene in a film etc.) again. ● *noun* a scene in a film etc. shot again.

re·shuffle ● *transitive verb* **1** shuffle (cards) again. **2** interchange the posts of (government ministers, employees, etc.). **3** change the position or order of; interchange (*reshuffled the deck chairs*). ● *noun* the act or an instance of reshuffling.

res·ide *intransitive verb* **1** (of a person) have one's home, dwell permanently. **2** (of power, a right, etc.) rest or be vested in. **3** (of an incumbent official) be in residence. **4** (foll. by *in*) (of a quality) be present or inherent in. [Middle English, prob. back-formation from RESIDENT influenced by French *résider* or Latin *residēre* (as RE-, *sedēre* sit)]

res·i·dence /ˈrezɪdəns/ *noun* **1** the act or an instance of residing. **2 a** the place where a person resides; an abode. **b** a house, esp. an impressive one (*returned to their Rosedale residence*). **3** *N Amer.* a building providing accommodation for students at a university or college. □ **in residence** dwelling at a specified place. **-in-residence** (in *combination*) designating a practitioner of one of the arts, working in or associated with a university, arts organization, etc., in order to share professional knowledge (*artist-in-residence*).

res·i·dency /ˈrezɪdənsi/ *noun* (*pl.* **-cies**) **1** = RESIDENCE 1. **2** *N Amer.* a period of specialized medical training; the position of a resident. **3 a** *Brit. & Cdn* a regular engagement at a club, theatre, etc. for a musician, dance company, etc. **b** the position of an artist-in-residence. **4** *hist.* **a** the official residence of the Governor General's representative or other British government agent at the court of an Indian state. **b** the territory supervised by this official.

res·i·dent /ˈrezɪdənt/ ● *noun* **1** (often foll. by *of*) **a** a permanent inhabitant (of a city, neighbourhood, building, etc.). **b** a bird belonging to a species that does not migrate. **2** *N Amer.* a medical graduate engaged in specialized practice under supervision in a hospital. **3 a** *Brit.* a guest in a hotel etc. staying overnight. **b** *US* a person who boards at a boarding school. **4** *hist.* a British government agent in any semi-independent state, esp. the Governor General's agent at the court of an Indian state. **5** an intelligence agent in a foreign country. ● *adjective* **1** residing; in residence. **2 a** having quarters on the premises of one's work etc. (*resident housekeeper*; *resident doctor*). **b** working regularly in a particular place. **c** frequenting a particular place (*the resident intellectual at our table*). **3** located; inherent (*powers of feeling are resident in the nerves*). **4** (of birds etc.) non-migratory. **5** *Computing* (of a program, file, etc.) occupying a permanent place in memory, esp. in main memory or the memory built into a particular device, and hence rapidly accessible during processing.

res·i·den·tial /ˌrezɪˈdenʃəl/ *adjective* **1** suitable for or occupied by private houses, apartment buildings, etc. (*residential area*). **2** used as a residence (*residential complex*). **3** based on or connected with residence (*the residential qualification for voters*; *a residential course of study*). □ **res·i·den·tial·ly** *adverb*

residential school *noun* *Cdn hist.* a boarding school operated or subsidized by religious orders or the federal government to accommodate Aboriginal students.

res·i·dua *pl.* of RESIDUUM.

re·sid·ual /rəˈzɪdʒuəl, rɪ-/ ● *adjective* **1** remaining; still left. **2** esp. *Chem.* left as a residue, esp. at the end of some process. **3** *Math.* resulting from subtraction. **4** (in calculation) still unaccounted for or not eliminated. ● *noun* **1** a quantity left over or *Math.* resulting from subtraction. **2** an error in calculation not accounted for or eliminated. **3** (in *pl.*) a royalty paid to an actor, musician, etc., for a repeat of a television commercial, song, etc. □ **re·sid·ual·ly** *adverb*

residual power *noun* (also **residuary power**) a power remaining with one political group after other powers have been allocated to another group, as between a federal government and a province.

re·sid·uary /rəˈzɪdʒuˌeri, rɪ-/ *adjective* **1** of the residue of an estate (*residuary bequest*). **2** residual; still remaining. **3** esp. *Chem.* of or being a residue.

res·i·due /ˈrezɪˌduː, -ˌdjuː/ *noun* **1** what is left over or remains; a remainder; the rest. **2** *Law* what remains of an estate after the payment of charges, debts, and bequests. **3** esp. *Chem.* a substance left after combustion, evaporation, etc.; a deposit, a sediment. [Old French *residu* from Latin *residuum*: see RESIDUUM]

Consonants: b *but*   d *dog*   f *few*   g *get*   h *her*   j *yes*   k *cat*   l *leg*   m *man*   n *no*   p *pen*   r *red*   s *sit*

re·sidu·um /rəˈzɪdʒʊəm, ri-/ *noun* (*pl.* **re·sidua** /-dʒʊə/) **1** *Chem.* = RESIDUE 3. **2** a remainder; that which is left. [Latin, neuter of *residuus* remaining, from *residēre*: see RESIDE]

re·sign *verb* **1** *intransitive* **a** (often foll. by *from*) give up office, one's employment, etc. (*resigned from the cabinet*). **b** (often foll. by *as*) retire (*resigned as chief executive*). **2** *transitive* **a** give up (office, one's employment, etc.). **b** surrender; hand over (a right, charge, task, etc.). **3** *reflexive* (usu. foll. by *to*) reconcile (oneself, one's mind, etc.) to the inevitable (*have resigned myself to the idea*). **4** *intransitive* Chess etc. discontinue play and admit defeat. □ **re·sign·er** *noun* [Old French *resigner* from Latin *resignare* unseal, cancel (as RE-, *signare* sign, seal)]

re-sign *verb* **1** *transitive* sign (a document, contract, etc.) again. **2** *intransitive* (of a sports player etc.) sign a contract for a further period.

re·sig·na·tion *noun* **1** the act or an instance of resigning, esp. from one's job or office. **2** the document etc. conveying this intention. **3** the state of being resigned; the uncomplaining endurance of a sorrow or difficulty.

re·signed *adjective* (often foll. by *to*) having resigned oneself; submissive, acquiescent. □ **re·sign·ed·ly** *adverb*

resile /rəˈzail, ri-/ *intransitive verb* **1** (of something stretched or compressed) recoil to resume a former size and shape; spring back. **2** (of a person) recoil from something with aversion. **3** (usu. foll. by *from*) withdraw from a course of action. [obsolete French *resilir* or Latin *resilire* (as RE-, *salire* jump)]

re·sili·ent /rəˈzɪljənt, ri-, -iənt/ *adjective* **1** (of a substance etc.) recoiling; springing back; resuming its original shape after bending, stretching, compression, etc. **2** (of a person) readily recovering from shock, depression, etc. □ **re·sili·ence** *noun* **re·sili·ency** *noun* **re·sili·ent·ly** *adverb* [Latin *resiliens* resilient- (as RESILE)]

resin /ˈrezin/ ● *noun* **1** an adhesive inflammable substance insoluble in water, secreted by some plants, and often extracted by incision, esp. from fir and pine (*compare* GUM¹ *noun* 1a). **2** (in full **synthetic resin**) a solid or liquid organic compound made by polymerization etc. and used in plastics etc. ● *transitive verb* (**re·sined, re·sin·ing**) rub or treat with resin. □ **res·in·oid** *adjective & noun* **res·in·ous** *adjective* **res·iny** *adjective* [Latin *resina* & medieval Latin *rosina, rosinum*]

re·sist /rəˈzɪst/ ● *verb* **1** *transitive* withstand the action or effect of; repel. **2** *transitive* stop the course or progress of; prevent from reaching, penetrating, etc. **3** *transitive* abstain from (pleasure, temptation, etc.). **4** *transitive* strive against; try to impede; refuse to comply with (*resist arrest*). **5** *intransitive* offer opposition; refuse to comply. ● *noun* a protective coat of a resistant substance, applied esp. to parts of calico that are not to take dye or to parts of pottery that are not to take glaze or lustre. □ **cannot** (or **could not** etc.) **resist 1** (foll. by verbal noun) feel obliged or strongly inclined to (*cannot resist teasing me about it*). **2** is tempted to be amused, attracted, etc., by (*can't resist children's clothes*). □ **resist·er** *noun* **re·sist·ible** *adjective* [Old French *resister* or Latin *resistere* (as RE-, *sistere* stop, reduplication of *stare* stand)]

re·sist·ance *noun* **1** the act or an instance of resisting; refusal to comply. **2** the power of resisting (*showed resistance to wear and tear*). **3** a *Biol.* the ability to withstand adverse conditions, esp. a person's capacity for withstanding common infections or a plant's capacity to withstand common diseases. **b** *Med. & Biol.* lack of sensitivity to a drug, insecticide, etc., esp. owing to continued exposure or genetic change. **4** the impeding, slowing, or stopping effect exerted by one material thing on another. **5** *Physics* **a** the property of hindering the conduction of electricity, heat, etc. **b** the measure of this in a body. Symbol: **R**. **6** a resistor. **7 a** (in full **resistance movement**) a secret organization resisting authority, esp. in an occupied country. **b** (**Resistance**) (prec. by *the*) the underground movement formed in France during the Second World War to fight the German occupying forces and the Vichy government. **8** *Psych.* opposition, frequently unconscious, to the emergence into consciousness of repressed memories or desires. □ **the path** (or **line**) **of least resistance** an option avoiding difficulty or unpleasantness; the easiest course of action. □ **re·sist·ant** *adjective*

resistance training *noun* = WEIGHT TRAINING.

re·sist·ive *adjective* **1** able to resist. **2** *Electricity* of or concerning resistance.

re·sis·tiv·ity *noun* *Electricity* a measure of the resisting power of a specified material to the flow of an electric current.

re·sist·less *adjective* *literary* **1** irresistible; relentless. **2** unresisting.

re·sis·tor *noun* *Electricity* a device having resistance to the passage of an electrical current.

re·size *transitive verb* alter the size of; make larger or smaller. □ **re·siz·able** *adjective*

re-skill *transitive verb* teach, or equip with, new skills.

re-sold *past and past participle of* RESELL.

re·sol·uble /rəˈzɒljʊbəl, ri-/ *adjective* **1** that can be resolved. **2** (foll. by *into*) analyzable. [French *résoluble* or Latin *resolubilis* (as RESOLVE, after *soluble*)]

re-soluble /riːˈsɒljʊbəl/ *adjective* that can be dissolved again.

Reso·lute /ˈrezəˌluːt/ a settlement on the south shore of Cornwallis Island, Nunavut; pop. (2001) 215. [HMS *Resolute*, which may have wintered there *c.*1850]

reso·lute /ˈrezəˌluːt/ *adjective* (of a person or a person's mind or action) determined; decided; firm of purpose; not vacillating. □ **reso·lute·ly** *adverb* **reso·lute·ness** *noun* [Latin *resolutus* past participle of *resolvere* (see RESOLVE)]

reso·lu·tion /rezəˈluːʃən/ *noun* **1 a** a formal expression of opinion or intention by a legislative body or meeting. **b** the formulation of this (*passed a resolution*). **2** a thing resolved on; an intention (*New Year's resolutions*). **3** a resolute temper or character; boldness and firmness of purpose. **4** (often foll. by *of*) the act or an instance of solving doubt or a problem or question (*conflict resolution; towards a resolution of the difficulty*). **5 a** esp. *Chem.* separation into components; decomposition. **b** the replacing of a single force etc. by two or more jointly equivalent to it. **6** (foll. by *into*) analysis; conversion into another form. **7** *Music* the act or an instance of causing discord to pass into concord. **8** *Physics etc.* the smallest interval measurable by a scientific (esp. optical) instrument; the resolving power. **9 a** the degree of detail visible in a photographic or television image. **b** the amount of graphical information that can be shown on a computer screen, usu. denoted by the number of lines that can be distinguished visibly, or by the number of pixels that can be displayed in the horizontal and vertical directions of a graphics screen. **10** *Med.* the disappearance of inflammation etc. [Latin *resolutio* (as RESOLVE)]

re·solve /rəˈzɒlv/ ● *verb* **1** *intransitive* make up one's mind; decide firmly (*resolve to do better*). **2** *transitive* (foll. by *that* + clause) (of an assembly or meeting) pass a resolution by vote (*the committee resolved that immediate action should be taken*). **3** *intransitive & transitive* (often foll. by *into*) separate or cause to separate into constituent parts; disintegrate; analyze; dissolve. **4** *transitive* (of optical or photographic equipment) separate or distinguish between closely adjacent objects. **5** *transitive & intransitive* (foll. by *into*) convert or be converted. **6** *transitive & intransitive* (foll. by *into*) reduce by mental analysis into. **7** *transitive* solve; explain; clear up; settle (doubt, argument, etc.). **8** *transitive & intransitive* Music convert or be converted into concord. **9** *transitive Med.* cause (a symptom or condition) to disperse, subside, or heal. ● *noun* **1** a firm mental decision or intention; a resolution (*made a resolve not to go*). **2** resoluteness; steadfastness. □ **re·solv·abil·ity** *noun* **re·solv·able** *adjective* **re·solv·er** *noun* [Latin *resolvere resolut-* (as RE-, SOLVE)]

re·solved *adjective* resolute, determined. □ **re·solv·ed·ly** *adverb* **re·solv·ed·ness** *noun*

re·solv·ing power *noun* an instrument's ability to distinguish very small or very close objects.

res·on·ance /ˈrezənəns/ *noun* **1** the reinforcement or prolongation of sound by reflection or synchronous vibration. **2** *Mech.* a condition in which an object or system is subjected to an oscillating force having a frequency close to its own natural frequency. **3** an allusion, connotation, or feature reminiscent of another person or thing; an overtone in thought, art, language, etc. **4** *Chem.* the property of a molecule having a structure best represented by two or more forms rather than a single structural formula. **5** *Physics* a short-lived subatomic particle that is an excited state of a more stable particle.

res·on·ant /ˈrezənənt/ *adjective* **1** (of sound) echoing, resounding; continuing to sound; reinforced or prolonged by reflection or synchronous vibration. **2** (of a body, room, etc.) tending to reinforce or prolong sounds esp. by synchronous vibration. **3** having the power to bring images, feelings, memories, etc. to mind (*the prints are resonant with traditions of Russian folk art and story*). **4** (often foll. by *with*) (of a place) resounding (*resonant with the sound of bees*). **5** of or relating to resonance. □ **res·on·ant·ly** *adverb* [French *résonnant* or Latin *resonare resonant-* (as RE-, *sonare* sound)]

res·on·ate /ˈrezəˌneit/ *intransitive verb* **1** produce or be filled with a deep, full, reverberating sound. **2** evoke or suggest images, memories, and emotions (*the words resonate with so many different meanings*). [Latin *resonare resonat-* (as RESONANT)]

res·on·ator /ˈrezəˌneitər/ *noun* **1** a device responding to a specific vibration frequency, and used for detecting it when it occurs in combination with other sounds. **2** a structure or device which reinforces or amplifies sound by resonance, esp. an acoustical chamber of a musical instrument, such as the hollow body of a stringed instrument. **3** a device which displays electrical resonance, esp. one used for the detection of radio waves.

re·sorb /rəˈsɔrb, ri-/ *transitive verb* absorb again. [Latin *resorbēre resorpt-* (as RE-, *sorbēre* absorb)]

re·sor·cin·ol /rəˈzɔrsəˌnɒl, ri-/ *noun Chem.* a crystalline organic compound usu. made by synthesis and used in the production of dyes, drugs, resins, glues, etc. [RESIN+ *orcin* (from Dutch *orseille* ORCHIL) + -OL]

re·sorp·tion /rəˈzɔrpʃən, ri-/ *noun* **1** the act or an instance of resorbing; the state of being resorbed. **2** *Physiol.* the breaking down and absorption of tissue within the body. □ **re·sorp·tive** *adjective* [RESORB after *absorption*]

re·sort /rəˈzɔrt, ri-/ ● *noun* **1** a place frequented esp. for holidays or for a specified purpose or quality (*ski resort; health resort*). **2 a** a person or thing to which one has recourse; an expedient or measure (*a taxi was our best resort*). **b** (foll. by *to*) recourse; use of (*without resort to violence*). ● *intransitive verb* **1** (foll. by *to*) turn to as an expedient (*resorted to threats*). **2** (foll. by *to*) go often or in large numbers to. □ **in the** (or **as a**) **last resort** when all else has failed. [Old French *resortir* (as RE-, *sortir* come or go out)]

resort village *noun Cdn* (*Sask.*) a small urban municipality having at least 50 dwellings or businesses and 100 assessed property owners who are not required to be permanent residents.

re·sound /rəˈzaund, ri-/ *intransitive verb* **1** (often foll. by *with*) (of a place) ring or echo (*the hall resounded with laughter*). **2** (of a voice, instrument, sound, etc.) produce echoes; go on sounding; fill the place with sound. **3 a** (of fame, a reputation, etc.) be much talked of. **b** (foll. by *through*) produce a sensation (*the scandal resounded through Europe*).

re·sound·ing /rəˈzaundɪŋ, ri-/ *adjective* **1** in senses of RESOUND. **2** unmistakable; emphatic (*a resounding success*). □ **re·sound·ing·ly** *adverb*

re·source /ˈriːzɔrs, rɪˈzɔrs, -sɔrs/ ● *noun* **1** (usu. in *pl.*) **a** the means available to achieve an end, fulfill a function, etc. **b** a stock or supply that can be drawn on. **c** *N Amer.* available assets. **2** (often in *pl.*) a material or condition occurring in nature and capable of economic exploitation (often *attributive: resource development*). **3** (in *pl.*) a country's collective wealth or means of defence. **4** (in *pl.*) one's personal attributes and capabilities regarded as able to help or sustain one in adverse circumstances (*we had been left very much to our own resources*). **5** (often in *pl.*) a book, videotape, or other material which supplies information on a particular topic (*excellent educational resources*). **6** an expedient or device (*escape was their only resource*). **6 a** (often in *pl.*) skill in devising expedients (*a person of great resource*). **b** practical ingenuity; quick wit (*full of resource*). ● *transitive verb* (usu. in *passive*) provide with resources. □ **re·source·ful** *adjective* **re·source·ful·ly** *adverb* **re·source·ful·ness** *noun* **re·source·less** *adjective* **re·source·less·ness** *noun* **re·sour·cing** *noun* [French *ressource, ressource,* fem. past participle of Old French dialect *resourdre* (as RE-, Latin *surgere* 'rise')]

resource centre *noun* a library or other centre which houses a collection of resources for educational purposes.

resource person *noun* a person with expertise in a certain area who may be called upon as necessary to perform a particular task.

resource teacher *noun N Amer.* **1** a teacher who provides educational resources, curriculum advice, and teaching ideas to other teachers. **2** a teacher who works with special-needs or gifted children.

RESP *abbreviation Cdn* Registered Educational Savings Plan, a tax-sheltered plan for saving money for a child's post-secondary education. [acronym]

re·spect ● *noun* **1** deferential esteem felt or shown towards a person, thing, or quality. **2 a** (foll. by *of, for*) heed or regard. **b** (foll. by *to*) attention to or consideration of (*without respect to national borders*). **3** an aspect, detail, particular, etc. (*correct except in this one respect*). **4** reference, relation (*a morality that has no respect to religion*). **5** (in *pl.*) a person's polite messages or attentions (*give my respects to your mother*). ● *transitive verb* **1** regard with deference, esteem, or honour. **2 a** avoid interfering with, harming, degrading, insulting, injuring, or interrupting. **b** treat with consideration. **c** refrain from offending, corrupting, or tempting (a person, a person's feelings, etc.). □ **with** (or **with all due**) **respect** a mollifying formula preceding an expression of disagreement with another's views. **with respect to** (or **in respect of**) as concerns; with reference to. □ **re·spect·er** *noun* [Old French *respect* from Latin *respectus* from *respicere* (as RE-, *specere* look at) or from *respectare* frequentative of *respicere*]

re·spect·able *adjective* **1** deserving respect (*an intellectually respectable hypothesis; a respectable elder statesman*). **2 a** of good social standing or

reputation (*comes from a respectable middle-class family*). **b** characteristic of or associated with people of such status or character (*a respectable neighbourhood*). **3 a** honest and decent in character or conduct. **b** characterized by (a sense of) convention or propriety; socially acceptable (*respectable behaviour; a respectable publication*). **c** *derogatory* highly conventional; prim. **4 a** commendable, meritorious (*an entirely respectable ambition*). **b** comparatively good or competent; passable, tolerable (*a respectable effort*). **5** reasonably good in condition or appearance; presentable. **6** appreciable in number, size, amount, etc. (*earns a very respectable salary*). **7** accepted or tolerated on account of prevalence (*materialism has become respectable again*). □ **re·spect·abil·ity** *noun* **re·spect·ably** *adverb*

re·spect·ful *adjective* feeling or showing respect, deferential (*stood at a respectful distance*). □ **re·spect·ful·ly** *adverb* **re·spect·ful·ness** *noun*

re·spect·ing *preposition* with reference or regard to; concerning.

re·spect·ive *adjective* concerning or appropriate to each of several individually; proper to each (*go to your respective places*). [French *respectif -ive* from medieval Latin *respectivus* (as RESPECT)]

re·spect·ive·ly *adverb* each individually or in turn, and in the order mentioned (*she and I gave $10 and $5 respectively*).

re·spell *transitive verb* (*past* and *past participle* **re·spelled** or **re·spelt**) spell again or differently, esp. phonetically.

Res·pighi /rɛˈspiːgi/ **Otto·rino** (1879–1936), Italian composer, who is best known for his suites *Fountains of Rome* (1917) and the *Pines of Rome* (1924), based on the poems of D'Annunzio and influenced by Rimsky-Korsakov.

re·spir·able /ˈrɛspərəbəl/ *adjective* (of air, gas, etc.) able or fit to be breathed.

res·pir·a·tion /ˌrɛspəˈreiʃən/ *noun* **1 a** the act or an instance of breathing. **b** a single inspiration or expiration; a breath. **2** *Biol.* in living organisms, the process involving the production of energy and release of carbon dioxide from the oxidation of complex organic substances.

res·pir·a·tor /ˈrɛspəˌreitɜr/ *noun* **1** *Med.* an apparatus for maintaining artificial respiration. **2** an apparatus worn over the face to prevent poison gas, cold air, dust particles, etc., from being inhaled.

res·pir·a·tory /ˈrɛsprəˌtɔri, ˈrɛspərə-/ *adjective* pertaining to, affecting, or serving for respiration.

respiratory tract *noun* the passage of the mouth, nose, throat, and lungs, through which air passes in respiration.

re·spire *verb* **1** *intransitive* inhale and exhale air; breathe. **2** *intransitive* (of living organisms) carry out respiration. **3** *transitive* breathe (air etc.). **4** *intransitive* breathe again; take a breath. [Old French *respirer* or from Latin *respirare* (as RE-, *spirare* breathe)]

res·pite /ˈrɛspait, -pɪt/ ● *noun* **1** an interval of rest or relief. **2** a delay permitted before the discharge of an obligation or the suffering of a penalty. ● *transitive verb* **1** grant respite to; reprieve (a condemned person). **2** postpone the execution or exaction of (a sentence, obligation, etc.). **3** give temporary relief from (pain or care) or to (a sufferer). [Old French *respit* from Latin *respectus* RESPECT]

respite care *noun* temporary institutional care of a dependent elderly, ill, or handicapped person, granting a respite to the usual caregiver.

re·splen·dent /rəˈsplɛndənt, ri-/ *adjective* brilliant, dazzlingly or gloriously bright. □ **re·splen·dence** *noun* **re·splen·dent·ly** *adverb* [Latin *resplendēre* (as RE-, *splendēre* glitter)]

re·spond *verb* **1** *intransitive* answer, give a reply. **2** *intransitive* act or behave in an answering or corresponding manner. **3** *intransitive* (usu. foll. by *to*) **a** react favourably (*the patient is not responding to treatment; animals respond to kindness*). **b** exhibit a response; react (*cells respond to stimuli*). **4** *intransitive* (of a congregation) make answers to a priest etc. **5** *intransitive Bridge* make a bid on the basis of a partner's preceding bid. **6** *transitive* say (something) in answer. □ **re·spond·er** *noun* [Old French *respondre* answer, ultimately from Latin *respondēre respons-* answer (as RE-, *spondēre* pledge)]

re·spond·ent ● *noun* **1** a person who replies to something, esp. one supplying information for a survey or questionnaire or responding to an advertisement. **2** a defendant, esp. in an appeal or divorce case. ● *adjective* **1** making answer. **2** in the position of defendant.

re·sponse *noun* **1** an answer given in word or act; a reply. **2** a feeling, movement, change, etc., caused by a stimulus or influence. **3** (often in *pl.*) *Christianity* any part of the liturgy said or sung in answer to the clergy etc. **4** *Bridge* a bid made in responding.

response time *noun* **1** *Computing* the elapsed time between the issuing of a command by a user and the receipt of some form of

Vowels: a *cat* ɑ *arm* e *bed* ɜr *her* ɜː *deux* ə *ago* ɪ *sit* i *cosy* iː *feed* ɒ *hot* ɔ *pore* oː *no* ʌ *run* ʊ *put*

response or feedback from the computer. **2** the elapsed time between the receipt of a 911 or other emergency call and the arrival of police, paramedics, etc. at the scene of the emergency.

re·spon·sibil·ity *noun* (*pl.* **-ities**) **1 a** (often foll. by *for*, *of*) the state or fact of being responsible (*accepts full responsibility for the consequences*). **b** authority; the ability to act independently and make decisions (*a job with more responsibility*). **2** a person, duty, or thing for which one is responsible (*the food is my responsibility*). □ **on one's own responsibility** without authorization.

re·spon·sible *adjective* **1** (often foll. by *to, for*) liable to be called to account (to a person or for a thing). **2** morally accountable for one's actions; capable of rational conduct. **3** of good credit, position, or repute; respectable; evidently trustworthy. **4** (often foll. by *for*) being the primary cause (*a short-circuit was responsible for the power failure*). **5** involving responsibility (*a responsible job*). □ **re·spon·sibly** *adverb* [obsolete French from Latin *respondēre*: see RESPOND]

responsible government *noun* *Cdn* a form of government in which the cabinet or executive branch is held collectively responsible and accountable to an elected legislature, and may remain in power only so long as it has the support of the legislature.

re·spon·sive *adjective* **1** (often foll. by *to*) responding readily (to some influence). **2** responding with interest or enthusiasm; receptive (*a responsive class*). □ **re·spon·sive·ly** *adverb* **re·spon·sive·ness** *noun*

re·spon·sor·ial /rəspɒnˈsɔːriəl, rɪ-/ *adjective* relating to or involving (liturgical) responses (*responsorial psalm*).

re·spon·sory /rəˈspɒnsəri, rɪ-/ *noun* (*pl.* **-ies**) *Christianity* an anthem said or sung by a soloist and choir after a reading.

re·spray ● *transitive verb* spray again (esp. to change the colour of the paint on a vehicle). ● *noun* the act or an instance of respraying.

rest¹ ● *verb* **1** *intransitive* abstain from action, exertion, or labour; be tranquil. **2** *intransitive* be still or asleep, esp. to refresh oneself or recover strength. **3** *transitive* relieve or refresh by rest (*a chair to rest my legs*). **4** *intransitive* (foll. by *on, upon, against*) lie on; be supported by; be propped against. **5** *intransitive* (foll. by *on, upon*) (of a look) fall or alight upon; remain directed on. **6** *transitive* (foll. by *on, upon*) **a** place, lay, or set for support (*she rested her elbows on the table*). **b** fix, settle, or direct (one's eyes, a look, etc.) (*she rested her eyes upon me*). **7** *intransitive* (of a problem or subject) be left without further investigation or discussion (*let the matter rest*). **8** *intransitive* (usu. foll. by *with*) be left in the hands or charge of (*the final arrangements rest with you*). **9** *intransitive* (foll. by *on, upon*) depend, be based, or rely on. **10** *intransitive* *N Amer. Law* conclude the calling of witnesses in a law case (*the prosecution rests*). **11** *intransitive* lie in death. **12** *intransitive* (of land) lie fallow. ● *noun* **1** the natural relief from daily activity obtained by repose or sleep. **2** a period of resting (*take a 15-minute rest*). **3** the cessation of, or freedom from, worry, activity, etc. (*give the subject a rest*). **4** a support or prop for holding or steadying something. **5** *Music* **a** an interval of silence of a specified duration. **b** the sign denoting this. **6** the repose of death (*eternal rest*). □ **at rest 1** not moving. **2** lying dead. **3** not agitated or troubled. **give it a rest** *N Amer.* leave (a usu. contentious or perplexing issue) for the moment. **put** (or **lay**) **to rest 1** put a decisive end to (a rumour, notion, myth, etc.). **2** bury in a grave. **rest** (or **God rest**) **his** (or **her**) **soul** may God grant his (or her) soul repose. **rest one's case** conclude one's argument etc. **rest on one's laurels** *see* LAUREL. **rest on one's oars** *see* OAR. **rest up** *N Amer.* rest oneself thoroughly. **set at rest** settle or relieve (a question, a person's mind, etc.). [Old English]

rest² ● *noun* (prec. by *the*) the remaining part or parts; the others; the remainder of some quantity or number (*finish what you can and leave the rest*). ● *intransitive verb* remain in a specified state (*you can rest assured that I'll get it done*). □ **rest easy** remain or become calm, relaxed. [Old French *reste rester* from Latin *restare* (as RE-, *stare* stand)]

re·stage *transitive verb* stage (a play etc.) again or differently.

rest area *noun* *N Amer.* a small park located off a highway, usu. having picnic tables and sometimes a public washroom, where motorists may stop to refresh themselves. *Also called* REST STOP.

re·start ● *transitive & intransitive verb* begin again. ● *noun* a new beginning.

re·state *transitive verb* express again or differently, esp. more clearly or convincingly. □ **re·state·ment** *noun*

res·tau·rant *noun* a commercial establishment where meals are prepared, served, and eaten. [French from *restaurer* RESTORE]

restaurant car *noun* esp. *Brit.* = DINING CAR.

res·tau·ra·teur /ˌrɛstərəˈtɜr/ *noun* (also **res·tau·ran·teur** /ˌrɛstərɒnˈtɜr/) a person who owns or manages a restaurant. ¶ The spelling *restauranteur* is considered incorrect by many, though accepted

by others because it is increasingly common. It is safer to avoid it, however, until it becomes more established. [French (as RESTAURANT)]

rest cure *noun* a rest usu. of some weeks as a medical treatment.

rest·ed *adjective* refreshed or reinvigorated by resting.

rest·en·osis /ˌriːstɛˈnoʊsɪs/ *noun* the recurrence of abnormal narrowing of an artery or valve after corrective surgery.

rest·ful *adjective* **1** favourable to quiet or repose; soothing. **2** free from disturbing influences. **3** relaxed or refreshed by rest.

rest home *noun* a home for old or infirm people that is run privately and offers special care for its residents.

Res·ti·gouche /ˌrɛstəˈɡuːʃ/ the former name of LISTUGUJ.

Restigouche River a river in N New Brunswick, 200 km long, rising in the northwest and flowing generally northeastward to Chaleur Bay, forming part of the border with Quebec. [Mi'kmaq *lustagooch* prob. meaning 'good river for canoeing']

Restigouche salmon *noun* a variety of Atlantic salmon associated with the Restigouche River.

resting place *noun* **1** a place provided or used for resting. **2** (esp. **final resting place**, **last resting place**) a place in which a person is buried.

resti·tu·tion *noun* **1** (often foll. by *of*) the act or an instance of restoring something lost or stolen to its proper owner. **2** compensation for an injury. **3** esp. *Theol.* the restoration of a thing to its original state. **4** the resumption of an original shape or position because of elasticity. □ **resti·tu·tive** *adjective* [Old French *restitution* or Latin *restitutio* from *restituere restitut-* restore (as RE-, *statuere* establish)]

rest·ive *adjective* **1 a** impatient, restless. **b** uneasy, nervous, anxious. **2** (of a horse) refusing to advance, stubbornly standing still or moving backwards or sideways. **3** (of a person) unmanageable; rejecting control; refractory. □ **rest·ive·ness** *noun* [Old French *restif -ive* from Romanic (as REST²)]

rest·less *adjective* **1** uneasy; agitated. **2 a** (of a person) fidgeting; unable to be still. **b** (of a thing) constantly moving (*a restless camera*). **3** affording no rest. □ **rest·less·ly** *adverb* **rest·less·ness** *noun*

restless leg syndrome *noun* aching and discomfort of the leg muscles, often characterized by an unpleasant crawling sensation, which occurs intermittently when sitting or lying down, and is relieved only by moving the legs.

re·stock *transitive & intransitive verb* stock or supply again.

res·tor·a·tion /ˌrɛstərˈeɪʃən/ *noun* **1** the return of something to a former or original state (*building restoration; ecological restoration*). **2** the act of returning something to a former owner, place, or condition; restitution. **3** a model or drawing representing the supposed original form of an extinct animal, ruined building, etc. **4** (**Restoration**) *hist.* **a** (prec. by *the*) the re-establishment of Charles II as king of England in 1660. **b** the period marked by this event. **c** (often *attributive*) the literary period following this (*Restoration comedy*).

res·tor·a·tion·ism *noun* (also **Restorationism**) **1** the doctrine that all people will ultimately be restored to a state of happiness in the future life. **2** a charismatic Christian movement seeking to restore the beliefs and practices of the early Church. **3** the doctrine and practices of this movement.

res·tor·a·tion·ist *noun* **1** a person who promotes restoration. **2** an adherent of restorationism.

re·stor·a·tive /rəˈstɔrətɪv, rɪ-/ ● *adjective* **1** tending or able to restore health or strength. **2** *Dentistry* pertaining to the use of structures provided to replace or repair dental tissue so as to restore its form and function, such as a filling, a crown, or a bridge. ● *noun* a restorative medicine, food, etc. (*needs a restorative*).

restorative justice *noun* a way of dealing with criminal offences which requires the offender to repair the harm done to the victim and to the community, and involving victims, offenders, and the community in the resolution of the problem, and seeking to restore both victims and offenders as contributing members of society.

re·store *transitive verb* **1** bring back to the original or former state by rebuilding, repairing, repainting, etc. **2** bring back to good health etc.; cure. **3** give back to the original or former owner; make restitution of. **4** bring back to dignity or right; reinstate. **5** put back; replace. **6** make a representation of the supposed original state of (a ruin, extinct animal, etc.). □ **re·stor·able** *adjective* **re·stored** *adjective* **re·stor·er** *noun* [Old French *restorer* from Latin *restaurare*]

re·strain *transitive verb* **1** (often *reflexive*) **a** (usu. foll. by *from*) prevent (someone or oneself) from doing something (*I couldn't restrain her from asking*). **b** keep (someone or oneself) under control (*I'm trying to restrain myself*). **2** impose a limit upon; repress (*high prices restrain sales*).

3 forcibly control or confine (*the owner was forced to restrain her dog*). □ **re·strain·er** *noun* [Old French *restrei(g)n-* stem of *restreindre* from Latin *restringere* restrict- (as RE-, *stringere* tie)]

re·strained *adjective* **1** repressed, confined; kept under control or within bounds. **2** not excessive or extravagant; characterized by restraint or reserve. □ **re·strain·ed·ly** *adverb*

restraining order *noun N Amer. & Austral. Law* a temporary court order issued to prevent an individual from committing a particular action, such as seeing or talking with a person.

re·straint *noun* **1** self-control; avoidance of excess or exaggeration. **2** reserve of manner. **3** a device that restrains, such as a harness, seat belt, etc. **4** restriction of liberty or freedom of action; confinement. **5** a controlling agency or influence. [Old French *restreinte* fem. past participle of *restreindre*: see RESTRAIN]

restraint of trade *noun* an action seeking to interfere with free-market conditions.

re·strict *transitive verb* **1** (foll. by *to*) **a** limit to a specific person or group of people (*parking is restricted to customers and employees*). **b** limit (a person or thing) according to specific guidelines (*he was restricted to weekly visits; restrict your speech to what is most important*). **2** control, curtail, or reduce (*trying to restrict the use of chemical weapons; restrict the flow of blood*). **3** (usu. foll. by *from*) discourage, prevent (*factors restricting men from becoming nurses*). [Latin *restringere*: see RESTRAIN]

re·strict·ed ● *adjective* **1** confined, controlled, or limited in some way. **2** (of land, access, information, etc.) available or accessible only to certain authorized individuals or to a certain group; unavailable to the general public. **3** *N Amer.* of or pertaining to a movie with the classification 'Restricted'. ● *noun* (**Restricted**) **1** *Cdn* a film classification designating movies that may contain scenes of graphic violence, sex, coarse language, etc. and which have been deemed unsuitable for people under the age of 18. **2** (usu. **R**) *US* a film classification designating movies that cannot be viewed by people under the age of 18 unless accompanied by an adult.

Restricted Adult *Cdn (Alta.) noun* a film classification designating movies that may contain scenes of graphic violence, sex, coarse language, etc., to which people under the age of 18 are not admitted.

Restricted designated *noun Cdn (BC)* a film classification designating movies containing a preponderance of graphic sexual scenes, which may be shown only in certain specifically designated theatres, to people 18 and over.

restricted weapon *noun Cdn* a firearm, esp. a handgun, of a category that is strictly licensed and may be used only by licensed operators under specific conditions.

re·stric·tion *noun* **1** the act or an instance of restricting; the state of being restricted. **2** a thing that restricts. **3** a limitation placed on action; a limiting condition or regulation.

restriction enzyme *noun Biochem.* an enzyme which divides DNA at or near a specific sequence of bases.

restriction fragment *noun Biochem.* a segment of DNA that has been cut from the strand by a restriction enzyme.

re·strict·ive *adjective* **1** tending to limit, prevent, or restrict; imposing restrictions. **2** *Grammar* (of a clause or phrase) delimiting the meaning of a reference of a modified noun phrase or element. ¶ In the phrase 'the woman that I met yesterday', 'that I met yesterday' is a restrictive clause; it is not set off by commas, and it restricts the reference of 'the woman' to the one particular woman that was met yesterday. □ **re·strict·ive·ly** *adverb* **re·strict·ive·ness** *noun*

restrictive practice *noun* (also **restrictive trade practice**) an arrangement in trade or industry aimed at restricting or controlling competition or output.

re·string *transitive verb* (*past* and *past participle* **re·strung**) **1** fit (a musical instrument) with new strings. **2** thread (beads etc.) on a new string.

rest·room *noun* esp. *US* a public washroom in a restaurant, bar, store, etc.

re·struc·ture *verb* **1** *transitive* give a new structure to; rebuild. **2** *transitive & intransitive* fundamentally reorganize (a business, corporation, etc.). □ **re·struc·tur·ing** *noun*

rest stop *noun N Amer.* = REST AREA.

re·style *transitive verb* **1** reshape; remake in a new style. **2** give a new designation to (a person or thing).

re·sub·mit *transitive verb* submit (a plan, application, etc.) again.

re·sult ● *noun* **1** a consequence or outcome of something. **2** (often in *pl.*) a satisfactory outcome; a favourable result (*she doesn't just work hard, she gets results*). **3** a quantity, formula, etc., obtained by calculation. **4** (in *pl.*) **a** a list of scores or winners etc. in an exam or sporting event.

b the findings of a research study, survey, etc. ● *intransitive verb* **1** (often foll. by *from*) arise as the actual consequence or follow as a logical consequence (from conditions, causes, etc.). **2** (often foll. by *in*) have a specified end or outcome (*resulted in a large profit*). □ **as a result** consequently, therefore. **as a result of** because of; due (to). **without result** in vain; fruitless. □ **re·sult·ing** *adjective* [medieval Latin *resultare* from Latin (as RE-, *saltare* frequentative of *salire* jump)]

re·sult·ant /rəˈzʌltənt, ri-/ ● *adjective* **1** occurring as a result; consequent (*growing economic crisis and resultant unemployment*). **2** resulting as the total outcome of more or less opposed forces. ● *noun Math.* a force etc. equivalent to two or more acting in different directions at the same point.

re·sume *verb* **1** *transitive & intransitive* begin again or continue after an interruption. **2** *transitive* recover, occupy again (*resume a lifestyle; resume a political position*). [Old French *resumer* or Latin *resumere* resumpt- (as RE-, *sumere* take)]

re·su·mé /ˈrezəˌmei, ˈrezjuˌmei/ *noun* **1** *N Amer.* a brief account of one's education, experience, previous employment, and interests, usu. submitted with a job application. *Also called* CURRICULUM VITAE. **2** a summary. [French past participle of *résumer* (as RESUME)]

re·sump·tion *noun* the act or an instance of resuming (*resumption of negotiations*). □ **re·sump·tive** *adjective* [Old French *resumption* or Late Latin *resumptio* (as RESUME)]

re·sup·ply ● *verb* (**-plies, -plied**) **1** *transitive* supply again; provide with a fresh supply. **2** *intransitive* take on or acquire a fresh supply. ● *noun* the act of resupplying something or being resupplied.

re·sur·face *verb* **1** *intransitive* rise again; turn up or appear again. **2** *transitive* lay a new surface on (a road, ice rink, etc.).

re·sur·fac·ing *noun* **1** the laying of a new surface on a road, ice rink, etc. **2** any of various cosmetic surgery procedures for improving the appearance of the skin, e.g. dermabrasion or laser peels.

re·sur·gence *noun* **1** a renewed prominence or popularity (*the resurgence of disco*). **2** a recovery; an increase after decline (*resurgence of the economy*). □ **re·sur·gent** *adjective* [Latin *resurgere* resurrect- (as RE-, *surgere* rise)]

resur·rect /ˌrezəˈrekt/ *transitive verb* **1** bring back from obscurity or disrepair; revive. **2** take from the grave; exhume. **3** raise from the dead. [back-formation from RESURRECTION]

resur·rec·tion /ˌrezəˈrekʃən/ *noun* **1** the act or an instance of rising from the dead. **2** (usu. **Resurrection**) **a** Christ's rising from the dead. **b** the rising of the dead at the Last Judgment. **3** a revival after disuse or neglect. **4** the return of something to prominence, vogue, or popularity. **5** exhumation. [Old French from Late Latin *resurrectio -onis* (as RESURGENCE)]

re-survey ● *transitive verb* survey again. ● *noun* the act or an instance of re-surveying.

re·sus·ci·tate /rəˈsʌsəˌteit, ri-/ *transitive & intransitive verb* **1** revive from unconsciousness or apparent death. **2** revive or restore (*resuscitate an ailing economy*). □ **re·sus·ci·ta·tion** *noun* **re·sus·ci·ta·tor** *noun* [Latin *resuscitare* (as RE-, *suscitare* raise)]

res·ve·ra·trol /rezˈvirəˌtrɒl/ *noun* an antioxidant naturally occurring in certain nuts and fruits, esp. grapes, present in grape products such as red wine, and supposed to reduce cholesterol levels and inhibit cancer growth. [blend of RESORCINOL + modern Latin *veratrum* 'hellebore']

ret *transitive & intransitive verb* (**ret·ted, ret·ting**) soften (flax, hemp, etc.) by soaking or by exposure to moisture. [Middle English, related to ROT]

ret. *abbreviation* **1** retired. **2** returned.

re·ta·ble /rəˈteibəl, ri-/ *noun* **1** a frame enclosing painted or decorated panels above the back of an altar. **2** a shelf or ledge for ornaments, raised above the back of an altar. [French *rétable, retable* from Spanish *retablo* (as RETABLO)]

re·tab·lo /rəˈtɑbloː, ri-/ *noun* **1** a retable, esp. in Latin America. **2** a votive picture displayed in a church. [Spanish from medieval Latin *retrotabulum* rear table (as RETRO-, TABLE)]

re·tail ● *noun* the sale of goods in relatively small quantities to the public, and usu. not for resale (*compare* WHOLESALE). ● *adjective* **1** (usu. *attributive*) of or pertaining to the retailing of goods (*retail industry*). **2** sold by retail (*retail price*). ● *adverb* by retail; at a retail price (*do you buy wholesale or retail?*). ● *verb* **1** *transitive* sell (goods) in retail trade. **2** *intransitive* (often foll. by *at, of*) (of goods) be sold in this way (esp. for a specified price) (*retails at $4.95*). **3** *transitive rare* recount; relate details of. □ **re·tail·er** *noun* **re·tail·ing** *noun* [Old French *retaille* a piece cut off, from *retaillier* (as RE-, TAIL²)]

retail price index *noun Brit.* (also **retail prices index**) an index of the variation in the prices of retail goods.

Consonants: b *but*   d *dog*   f *few*   g *get*   h *her*   j *yes*   k *cat*   l *leg*   m *man*   n *no*   p *pen*   r *red*   s *sit*

retail therapy *noun jocular* the practice of shopping in order to make oneself feel more cheerful.

re·tain *transitive verb* **1** maintain possession of; keep. **2** allow to remain or prevail; preserve (*this ball has retained its buoyancy; retains its identifiable shape*). **3** (often as **re·tain·ing**) keep in place; hold fixed (*a retaining wall*). **4** secure (a hotel room etc., or professional services, esp. of a lawyer) with a preliminary payment. **5** keep in one's memory. [Anglo-French *retei(g)n-* from stem of Old French *retenir*, ultimately from Latin *retinēre retent-* (as RE-, *tenēre* hold)]

re·tain·er *noun* **1** *Law* a fee for retaining a lawyer etc. **2 a** *hist.* a dependant or follower of a person of rank. **b** a long-standing family friend or servant. **3** a thing that holds something in place or retains (also *attributive: retainer screws*). **4** *Dentistry* **a** a device consisting of wires cemented to the teeth or a moulded plastic plate fitting over the teeth to keep teeth aligned once they have been straightened. **b** a structure cemented to a tooth to keep a bridge in place. **5** *Brit.* a reduced rent paid to retain accommodation during a period of non-occupancy. □ **on** (**a**) **retainer** with services secured by a preliminary payment (*she was available on retainer*).

retaining wall *noun* a wall supporting and confining a mass of earth or water.

re·take ● *transitive verb* (*past* **re·took**; *past participle* **re·taken**) **1** take again. **2** recapture. **3** film (a scene) or make (a recording) again. ● *noun* **1 a** the act or an instance of retaking. **b** a thing retaken, e.g. an exam. **2 a** the act or an instance of filming a scene or recording music etc. again. **b** a scene or recording obtained in this way.

re·tali·ate /rəˈtalɪˌeit, ri-/ *intransitive verb* respond to an injury, insult, assault, etc. in like manner; attack in return. □ **re·tali·a·tion** *noun* **re·talia·tory** /-ˈtaljətɔri/ *adjective* [Latin *retaliare* (as RE-, *talis* such)]

re·tard ● *transitive verb* /rəˈtɑrd, ri-/ **1** delay the progress, development, arrival, or accomplishment of. **2** make slow or late. ● *noun* /ˈriːtɑrd/ *N Amer. slang offensive* **1** a mentally retarded person. **2** a stupid or foolish person; an idiot. □ **re·tar·da·tion** /ˌriːtɑrˈdeiʃən/ *noun* **re·tard·er** *noun* [French *retarder* from Latin *retardare* (as RE-, *tardus* slow)]

re·tard·ant /rəˈtɑrdənt, ri-/ ● *adjective* (usu. in *combination*) tending to slow or resist; capable of remaining unaffected by (*fire-retardant paint*). ● *noun* **1** an agent that slows a process (*a growth retardant; a corrosion retardant*). **2** an agent that remains unaffected by or resistant to something (*flame-retardant*). □ **re·tard·ance** *noun* **re·tard·ancy** *noun*

re·tard·ate /rəˈtɑrdeit, ri-/ *noun* a mentally retarded person.

re·tard·ed /rəˈtɑrdɪd, ri-/ *adjective* **1** mentally or physically less developed than is normal for one's age. **2** slow to develop or occur; late. **3** *informal* stupid, pathetic.

retch ● *intransitive verb* make an attempt to vomit, esp. involuntarily and without effect. ● *noun* such a motion or the sound of it. □ **retch·ing** *noun* [var. of (now dial.) *reach* from Old English *hræcan* spit, Old Norse *hrækja* from Germanic, of imitative origin]

retd. *abbreviation* (also **ret'd.**) **1** retired. **2** returned.

rete /ˈriːti/ *noun* (*pl.* **retia** /-tiə, -ʃiə/) *Anat.* an elaborate network or plexus of blood vessels and nerve cells. [Latin *rete* net]

re·tell *transitive verb* (*past* and *past participle* **re·told**) tell again or in a different version. □ **re·tell·er** *noun* **re·tell·ing** *noun*

re·ten·tion *noun* **1** the act or an instance of retaining; the state of being retained. **2** the ability to retain something; the capacity for holding or keeping something. **3** the ability to retain things experienced or learned; memory. **4** *Med.* the failure to evacuate urine or another secretion. [Old French *retention* or Latin *retentio* (as RETAIN)]

re·ten·tive *adjective* **1** tending to retain (moisture etc.). **2** (of memory or a person) not forgetful. □ **re·ten·tive·ness** *noun* [Old French *retentif -ive* or medieval Latin *retentivus* (as RETAIN)]

re·think ● *transitive verb* (*past* and *past participle* **re·thought**) think about (something) again, esp. with a view to making changes. ● *noun* a reassessment; a period of rethinking.

retia *pl. of* RETE.

reti·cence /ˈretəsəns/ *noun* **1** the avoidance of saying all one knows or feels, or of saying more than is necessary. **2** reserve or restraint in speech, style, or manners. □ **reti·cent** *adjective* [Latin *reticentia* from *reticēre* (as RE-, *tacēre* be silent)]

ret·icle /ˈretɪkəl/ *noun* a network of fine threads or lines in the focal plane or eyepiece of an optical instrument to help accurate observation and measurement. [Latin *reticulum*: see RETICULUM]

re·ticu·la *pl. of* RETICULUM.

re·ticu·late ● *transitive & intransitive verb* /rɪˈtɪkjuˌleit/ **1** divide or be divided in fact or appearance into a network. **2** arrange or be arranged in small squares or with intersecting lines. ● *adjective* /rəˈtɪkjʊlət, ri-/

reticulated. □ **re·ticu·la·tion** *noun* [Latin *reticulatus* reticulated (as RETICULUM)]

reti·cule /ˈretɪˌkjuːl/ *noun* **1** a woman's small handbag, usu. with a drawstring closure, made of netting or other fabric. **2** = RETICLE. [French *réticule* from Latin (as RETICULUM)]

re·ticu·lo·cyte /rəˈtɪkjuːlɔˌsait/ *noun Physiol.* an immature red blood cell having a granular or reticulated appearance when suitably stained. [from RETICUL(ATED) + -O- + -CYTE]

re·ticu·lo·endo·thel·ial /rəˌtɪkjuːlɔˌendoˈθiːliəl/ *adjective Med.* of, pertaining to, or designating a diverse system of fixed and circulating phagocytic cells involved in the immune response, common esp. in the liver, spleen, and lymphatic system. [RETICUL(UM) + -O- + ENDOTHELIAL]

re·ticu·lum /rəˈtɪkjʊləm/ *noun* (*pl.* **re·ticu·la**) **1** a netlike structure. **2 a** a fine network of membranes etc. in living organisms. **b** a fine network within the cytoplasm of a cell (*endoplasmic reticulum*). **3** a ruminant's second stomach. □ **re·ticu·lar** *adjective* [Latin, diminutive of *rete* net]

re·tie *transitive verb* (**re·tying**) tie again.

ret·ina /ˈretɪnə/ *noun* a light-sensitive layer at the back of the eyeball that triggers nerve impulses through the optic nerve to the brain where the visual image is formed. □ **ret·in·al** *adjective* [medieval Latin from Latin *rete* net]

Retin-A /ˌretɪnˈei/ *noun proprietary* retinoic acid used as a drug.

retin·itis /ˌretɪˈnaitɪs/ *noun* inflammation of the retina.

retinitis pig·men·tosa /ˌpɪgmenˈtoːsə/ *noun* a chronic hereditary retinopathy characterized by black pigmentation and gradual degeneration of the retina. [from RETINITIS + *pigmentosa* modern Latin fem. of *pigmentosus*, from *pigmentum* pigment + *osus* (see -OSE[1])]

retino- /ˈretənoː/ *combining form* retina.

retino·blas·toma /ˌretənoːblasˈtoːmə/ *noun* a rare, malignant, familial tumour of the retina in young children. [from RETINO- + *blasto* combining form of Greek *blastos*, sprout + -OMA]

reti·noic acid /ˌretɪnˈoːɪk/ *noun* an acid chemically related to vitamin A, used esp. as a topical ointment esp. in the treatment of wrinkles and other skin disorders.

ret·in·ol /ˈretɪˌnɒl/ *noun* a vitamin found in green and yellow vegetables, egg yolk, and fish-liver oil, essential for growth and vision in dim light. *Also called* VITAMIN A. [from Greek *rhetine* resin + -OL[1]]

retin·op·athy /ˌretənˈɒpəθiː/ *noun* any (esp. non-inflammatory) disease of the retina.

reti·nue /ˈretəˌnjuː, ˈretəˌnuː/ *noun* a body of attendants accompanying an important person. [Old French *retenue* fem. past participle of *retenir* RETAIN]

re·tire *verb* **1 a** *intransitive* leave office or employment, esp. because of age. **b** *transitive* cause (a person) to retire from work. **c** *transitive* cease to employ or use (something) or remove it from service (*the company has retired their earlier model; the player had his sweater number retired*). **2** *intransitive* withdraw or retreat, esp. to another room or location. **3** *intransitive* go to bed. **4 a** *transitive Baseball* put out (a batter); cause (a side) to end a turn at bat. **b** *intransitive & transitive Cricket* (of a batsman) end one's innings, esp. due to injury. **5** *transitive Econ.* withdraw (a bill or note) from circulation or currency. **6** *transitive & intransitive* retreat; withdraw (troops). [French *retirer* (as RE-, *tirer* draw)]

re·tired *adjective* **1** having retired from employment (*a retired teacher*). **2** withdrawn from society or public life; secluded (*lives a retired life*).

re·tir·ee *noun* esp. *N Amer.* a person who has retired from work.

re·tire·ment *noun* **1 a** the act or an instance of retiring. **b** the condition of having retired, esp. from office or employment. **2** seclusion or privacy.

retirement age *noun* the age at which most people retire from work.

retirement community *noun N Amer.* **1** a community of homes with recreational facilities designed for people who are retired but still active. **2** a retirement home.

retirement home *noun* **1** a house, apartment, etc. to which a person moves in old age. **2** an institution for elderly people needing care.

re·tir·ing *adjective* shy; fond of seclusion.

re·title *transitive verb* give a different title to.

re·told *past* and *past participle of* RETELL.

re·took *past of* RETAKE.

re·tool *verb* **1** *transitive* equip (a factory etc.) with new tools. **2** *intransitive N Amer.* equip or prepare oneself again or for a new challenge or task. **3** *transitive N Amer.* change the essential components or qualities of (*they retooled the stories for younger children*).

re·tort[1] ● *noun* **1** an incisive, witty, or angry reply. **2** the turning of a

charge or argument against its originator. **3** an act of retaliation.
● *verb* **1** *transitive* reply angrily or wittily; say by way of a retort.
2 *intransitive* make a retort. [Latin *retorquēre retort-* (as RE-, *torquēre* twist)]

re·tort² *noun* **1** a vessel usu. of glass with a long recurved neck used in distilling liquids. **2** a vessel for heating mercury for purification, coal to generate gas, or iron and carbon to make steel. [French *retorte* from medieval Latin *retorta* fem. past participle of *retorquēre*: see RETORT¹]

re·touch ● *transitive verb* **1** improve or repair (a painting, makeup, etc.) by fresh touches or alterations; touch up. **2** alter or restore a photograph, print, negative, etc. by making minor changes after development. **3** *Archaeology* apply secondary trimming or shaping to (a stone implement) at some period after initial manufacture. ● *noun* **1** the act or an instance of retouching. **2** *Archaeology* secondary trimming or shaping applied to a stone implement at some period after initial manufacture. □ **re·touch·er** *noun* **re·touch·ing** *noun*

re·trace *transitive verb* **1** go back over (one's steps etc.). **2** go back over (the course of an event etc.) in one's memory. **3** trace back to a source or beginning.

re·tract *transitive & intransitive verb* **1** withdraw or revoke (a statement, accusation, proposal, etc.). **2** (of a part of the body) draw or be drawn back or in. **3 a** (of a part of a device or mechanism) draw or be drawn back. **b** draw (an undercarriage etc.) into the body of an aircraft. □ **re·tract·able** *adjective* **re·trac·tion** *noun* **re·tract·ive** *adjective* [Latin *retrahere* or (in sense 1) *retractare* (as RE-, *trahere tract-* draw)]

re·tract·ile /rəˈtraktaɪl, rɪ-/ *adjective* capable of being retracted.

re·tract·or *noun* **1** a muscle used for retracting. **2** a device for retracting. **3** *Med.* an instrument or appliance used in surgical operations to hold back skin, tissues, etc. from the area of the operation.

re·train *transitive & intransitive verb* train again or further, esp. for new work. □ **re·train·ing** *noun*

re·trans·mit *transitive verb* (**re·trans·mit·ted**, **re·trans·mit·ting**) transmit (esp. radio signals or broadcast programs) back again or to a further distance. □ **re·trans·mis·sion** *noun*

re·tread ● *transitive verb* **1** put a fresh tread on (a tire). **2** alter (a person or thing) so that it is superficially different but essentially the same as its predecessor. ● *noun* **1** a retreaded tire. **2** a superficial reworking or revival of a well-known song, story, idea, etc. **3** a person recalled to service or retrained for new work.

re·treat ● *intransitive verb* **1** (esp. of military forces) retire or draw back from a superior force during or following defeat; turn away from difficulty or opposition. **2** relinquish or abandon a position, stance, or view; back down. **3** become smaller in size or extent; decline, recede. **4** withdraw into privacy or security, one's own thoughts, etc.; take refuge. **5** move backwards. ● *noun* **1 a** the act or an instance of retiring or withdrawing in the face of opposition, difficulty, or danger. **b** *Military* a signal for this (*sound the retreat*). **2** a place of seclusion. **3 a** a period of seclusion for prayer and religious meditation. **b** a period during which co-workers or people sharing a common interest meet away from their home or workplace to exchange ideas (*corporate retreat*). **4** *Military* **a** a bugle call at sunset. **b** a flag-lowering ceremony including this. [Old French *retret* (n.), *retraiter* (v.) from Latin *retrahere*: see RETRACT]

re·treat·ant *noun* a person participating in a religious or corporate etc. retreat.

re·trench *verb* **1 a** *transitive* reduce or eliminate (costs, employees, etc.). **b** *intransitive* cut down expenses; introduce economies. **2** *transitive* shorten or abridge. □ **re·trench·ment** *noun* [obsolete French *retrencher* (as RE-, TRENCH)]

re·trial *noun* a second or further (judicial) trial.

ret·ri·bu·tion /ˌretrɪˈbjuːʃən/ *noun* **1** punishment for a crime, injury, etc.; vengeance. **2** requital or recompense in another life for one's good or bad deeds in this world. □ **re·trib·u·tive** /rəˈtrɪbjʊtɪv, rɪ-/ *adjective* [Late Latin *retributio* (as RE-, *tribuere tribut-* assign)]

re·triev·al *noun* **1** the action of retrieving, recovering, or recalling something; an instance of this. **2** the obtaining or consulting of material stored in a computer system, in books, on tape, etc. (*retrieval system*).

re·trieve ● *verb* **1** *transitive* regain possession of; recover and bring back. **2** *transitive & intransitive* (of a dog) find and bring back (game, a ball, a stick, etc.); fetch. **3** *transitive* *Computing* find or extract (information stored in a computer). **4** *transitive & intransitive* *Angling* reel in (a line). **5** *transitive* repair or set right (a loss or error etc.) (*managed to retrieve the situation*). ● *noun* **1** the act or an instance of recovering and returning something (*the Labrador completed his retrieve*). **2** *Fishing* the action or an act of reeling or drawing in a line. □ **re·triev·able** *adjective* [Old French *retroeve-* stressed stem of *retrover* (as RE-, *trover* find)]

re·triev·er *noun* **1** a breed of dog used for retrieving game. **2** a person or thing that retrieves something.

ret·ro /ˈretrəʊ/ ● *noun* (*pl.* **-ros**) style or fashion imitating the past, esp. in dress, music, etc. ● *adjective* **1** imitative of a style or fashion from the past (also in *combination*: *retro-chic*). **2** nostalgic for a previous time (*a retro mood*). [French *rétro*, abbreviation of *rétrograde*]

retro- /ˈretrəʊ/ *combining form* **1** denoting action back, backwards, or in return (*retroactive*). **2** *Anat. & Med.* denoting location behind (*retrosternal*). [Latin *retro* backwards]

retro·ac·tive *adjective* **1** (esp. of legislation) applying to the past as well as to the present or future; retrospective. **2** (often foll. by *to*) taking effect from a past date (*we were given pay raises retroactive to January 1*). □ **retro·ac·tive·ly** *adverb* **retro·ac·tiv·ity** *noun*

retro·fit ● *transitive verb* (**retro·fit·ted**, **retro·fit·ting**) **1** modify (machinery, vehicles, etc.) to incorporate changes and developments introduced after manufacture. **2** provide (an older building etc.) with new fixtures, equipment, etc. that did not exist at the time of construction. ● *noun* **1** a modification made to a product to incorporate changes made in later products of the same type or model. **2** a retrofitted product. [RETRO(ACTIVE) + (RE)FIT]

retro·flex *adjective* (also **retro·flexed**) **1** *Phonetics* pronounced with the tip of the tongue curled up towards the hard palate. **2** *Anat., Med., & Bot.* turned backwards. □ **retro·flex·ion** *noun* [Latin *retroflectere retroflex-* (as RETRO-, *flectere* bend)]

retro-futurist *adjective* (also **retro-futuristic**) denoting a style of music, art, etc. imitative of early- to mid-20th century conceptions of the future.

retro·grade ● *adjective* **1** directed backwards; retreating. **2** reverting to a less developed or inferior state; reactionary. **3** *Astronomy* in retrograde or showing retrograde. ● *noun* **1** *Astronomy* the apparent backward motion of a planet in the zodiac. **2** *Astronomy* the apparent motion of a celestial body from east to west. **3** a degenerate person. ● *adverb* *Astronomy* in a retrograde manner. ● *intransitive verb* **1** move backwards; recede, retire. **2** decline, revert. **3** *Astronomy* show retrograde. [Latin *retrogradus* (as RETRO-, *gradus* step, *gradi* walk)]

retro·gress *intransitive verb* **1** go back; move backwards. **2** deteriorate. [RETRO-, after PROGRESS *verb*]

retro·gres·sion *noun* **1** backward or reversed movement. **2** a reversal of development or return to a less advanced state. □ **retro·gres·sive** *adjective*

retro·rocket *noun* an auxiliary rocket for slowing down a spacecraft etc., e.g. when re-entering the earth's atmosphere.

re·trorse /rəˈtrɔːs, rɪ-/ *adjective* *Biol.* turned back or down. [Latin *retrorsus = retroversus* (as RETRO-, *versus* past participle of *vertere* turn)]

retro·spect *noun* a survey of past time or events. □ **in retrospect** **1** when looked back on. **2** when looking back; with hindsight. [RETRO-, after PROSPECT *noun*]

retro·spec·tion *noun* the action or an instance of looking back on or surveying past time or events.

retro·spec·tive ● *adjective* **1** looking back on or dealing with the past. **2** (of a film series, exhibition, recital, etc.) showing an artist's development over his or her lifetime. **3** (of a statute etc.) applying to the past as well as the future; retroactive. ● *noun* a retrospective film series, concert, exhibition, etc. □ **retro·spec·tive·ly** *adverb*

retro·vert·ed *adjective* *Med.* (of the womb) having a backward inclination. □ **retro·ver·sion** *noun*

retro·virus *noun* any of a group of RNA viruses which insert a DNA copy of their genome into the host cell in order to replicate, e.g. HIV. □ **retro·viral** *adjective* **retro·virol·ogist** *noun* **retro·virol·ogy** *noun* [modern Latin from initial letters of *reverse transcriptase* + VIRUS]

retry *verb* (**-tries**, **-tried**) **1** *transitive* *Law* try (a defendant or lawsuit) a second or further time. **2** *transitive & intransitive* *Computing* endeavour to complete (a function) or run (a program) after a failed attempt.

ret·sina /retˈsiːnə/ *noun* a Greek white wine flavoured with resin. [modern Greek *retsini* from *retine* pine resin]

re·tune *verb* **1** *transitive & intransitive* tune (a musical instrument) again or differently. **2** *transitive* tune (a radio etc.) to a different frequency. **3** *transitive* alter the tuning of (an engine etc.) to improve smoothness and efficiency.

re·turn ● *verb* **1** *intransitive* come or go back (to or from a place etc.). **2** *intransitive* go back (to a particular state or condition) (*things will return to normal*). **3** *transitive* bring, put, or send (something) back to the person or place etc. that it came from (*returned the fish to the river; have you returned my scissors?*). **4** *transitive* feel, say, or do the same in response; reciprocate (*return a favour; did not return her love; doesn't return phone* calls). **5** *transitive* yield (a profit). **6** *transitive* (esp. of a jury) render or give (a verdict, decision, etc.). **7** *transitive* (of an electorate) elect as an MP, government, etc. **8** *transitive* (in tennis etc.) hit or send (the ball) back after receiving it. **9** *transitive & intransitive* *N Amer.* *Football* catch a ball that has been kicked by the opposing team and carry it back downfield. **10** *transitive* say in reply; retort. ● *noun* **1** the act or an instance of coming or going back. **2** an act of coming or going back to an earlier state or position (*a return to prominence*). **3 a** the act or an instance of giving, sending, or putting back. **b** a thing given or sent back. **4** (in *sing.* or *pl.*) **a** the proceeds or profit of an investment or undertaking. **b** the acquisition of these. **5** a formal report or statement compiled or submitted by order (*an income tax return*). **6** (in *pl.*) decision; results (*election returns*). **7 a** (in full **carriage return key**) a key pressed to return the carriage of an electric typewriter to a fixed position. **b** (in full **return key**) a key pressed on a computer keyboard to simulate this. **8** (in tennis etc.) the act of hitting a ball back in the direction of the server. **9** *N Amer.* *Football* the act of receiving a kicked ball and bringing it back downfield. **10** an air vent allowing fresh, cool air to return to a gas furnace. **11** (in full **return ticket**) esp. *Brit.* a ticket for a journey to a place and back to the point of origin. **12** esp. *Brit.* a person's election as an MP etc. **13** a report made by a court official, e.g. a sheriff, on the carrying out of a court order. ● *adjective* **1** characterized by return or returning (*return fire*). **2** *Cdn & Brit.* providing for transportation to a destination and back (*return airfare to Regina*). **3** designating part of a journey etc. during which one returns to one's place of departure (*the return leg of our trip*). **4** occurring for a second or subsequent time (*a return engagement*). **5** facilitating the delivery of mail, a package, etc. (*return envelope; return address*). ● *adverb* *Cdn & Brit.* (of travel) to a particular destination and back (*I'm flying return to Edmonton*). □ **by return** (**mail**) by the next available mail delivery in the return direction. **in return** as an exchange or reciprocal action. **many happy returns** a greeting on a birthday. □ **re·turn·er** *noun* [Old French *returner* (as RE-, TURN)]

re·turn·able ● *adjective* **1** able or intended to be returned. **2** (esp. of bottles etc.) that may be returned for money, esp. a deposit paid at the time of purchase. ● *noun* a bottle, can, etc. that may be returned, esp. for money.

re·turned *adjective* **1** that has come or been brought back. **2** *Cdn, Austral., & NZ* (of a member of the armed forces) discharged after active service, esp. abroad (*returned man; returned soldier*).

re·turn·ee *noun* **1** a person who returns to or from a place or position. **2** a person who has returned home after war or service abroad.

returning office *noun* *Cdn* an office where the returning officer and other administrative staff for an election etc. work.

returning officer *noun* *Cdn, Brit., Austral., & NZ* an official organizing and overseeing the conduct of an election, referendum, etc. in a constituency and announcing the results.

re·tuse /rə'tjuːs, ri-/ *adjective* esp. *Bot.* having a broad end with a central depression. [Latin *retundere retus-* (as RE-, *tundere* beat)]

re·tying *pres. part. of* RETIE.

re·type *transitive verb* type again, esp. to correct errors.

Reu·ben[1] /'ruːbən/ *Bible* **1** a Hebrew patriarch, eldest son of Jacob and Leah. **2** the tribe of Israel traditionally descended from him.

Reu·ben[2] /'ruːbən/ *noun* *N Amer.* (in full **Reuben sandwich**) a sandwich containing corned beef, sauerkraut, and usu. Swiss cheese, made with rye bread and served hot. [20th c.: origin unknown]

Reuch·lin /'rɔɪklɪn/ **Jo·hann** (1455–1522), German humanist and scholar, who is known for his defence of Jewish literature and philosophy *De Verbo Mirifico* (1494) and his Hebrew grammar and lexicon *De Rudimentis Hebraicis* (1506).

re·unify *transitive verb* (**-fies**, **-fied**) restore (esp. separated territories) to a political unity. □ **re·unifi·ca·tion** *noun*

Ré·union /riːˈjuːnjən, reiuˈnjɔ̃/ a volcanically active, subtropical island in the Indian Ocean east of Madagascar, one of the Mascarene Islands; pop. (est. 2002) 743,981; capital, Saint-Denis. A French possession since 1638, the island became an overseas department of France in 1946 and an administrative region in 1974.

re·union *noun* **1 a** the act or an instance of reuniting. **b** the condition of being reunited. **2** a social gathering esp. of relatives, friends, or former classmates after a long period of separation.

re·unite *transitive & intransitive verb* bring or come back together.

re·up *intransitive verb* *US informal* **1** re-enlist in the army etc. **2** renew a contract or sign to a new contract with a previous employer.

re·uphol·ster *transitive verb* repair or replace the stuffing, springs, covering, etc. of (a piece of furniture). □ **re·uphol·stery** *noun*

re·uptake *noun* the absorption by a presynaptic nerve ending of a neurotransmitter that it has secreted.

reuse ● *transitive verb* use again or more than once. ● *noun* a second or further use. □ **re·usabil·ity** *noun* **re·usable** *adjective* **re·used** *adjective*

Reu·ter /'rɔɪtər/ **Paul Jul·ius, Baron von** (born Israel Beer Josaphat) (1816–99), German pioneer of telegraphy and news reporting. After establishing a service for sending commercial telegrams in Aachen (1849), he moved his headquarters to London, where he founded the news agency Reuters.

Rev. *abbreviation* **1** Reverend. **2** Review. **3** Revelation (New Testament).

rev *informal* ● *noun* (in *pl.*) the number of revolutions of an engine per minute (*running at 3,000 revs*). ● *verb* (**revved**, **rev·ving**) (often foll. by *up*) **1** *intransitive* **a** (of an internal combustion engine) revolve with increasing speed; turn over. **b** (of a vehicle) operate with increasing revolution of the engine, esp. with the clutch disengaged. **2** *transitive & intransitive* **a** increase the speed of revolution of (an internal combustion engine). **b** increase the speed of revolution of the engine of (a vehicle), with the clutch disengaged. **3** *transitive* *N Amer.* stimulate, activate, or accelerate (*it's time to rev up your love life*). **4** *intransitive* *N Amer.* **a** (of a person) become enthusiastic or excited (*revving up for the game*). **b** (of a thing) increase in activity or pace (*the fashion industry is revving up for spring*). [abbreviation]

re·vaccin·ate *transitive verb* vaccinate again. □ **re·vaccin·a·tion** *noun*

re·value *transitive verb* (**re·values**, **re·valued**, **re·valuing**) *Econ.* **1** assess the value of something again. **2** give a different or esp. higher value to (a currency) in relation to other currencies or gold (*opp.* DEVALUE 2). □ **re·valu·a·tion** *noun*

re·vamp ● *transitive verb* **1** repair, restore (*revamp a damaged reputation*). **2** renovate, overhaul (*completely revamp the education system*). ● *noun* **1** a revamped version; a renovation, overhaul, or revision. **2** an act of revamping something. [RE- + VAMP[1]]

re·vanch·ism /rə'vantʃɪzəm, ri-/ *noun* *Politics* a policy of seeking to retaliate, esp. to recover lost territory. □ **re·vanch·ist** *noun & adjective* [French *revanche* (as REVENGE)]

RevCan *noun* *Cdn slang* Revenue Canada (the former name of the Canada Revenue Agency). [abbreviation]

Revd *abbreviation* Reverend.

re·veal[1] *transitive verb* **1** display, show, or expose; allow to appear. **2** disclose, divulge, betray (*revealed her plans; he revealed that he was cheating*). **3** (esp. of God) make known by inspiration or supernatural means. **4** *transitive* (in *reflexive* or *passive*) appear or become apparent; come into view (*as night falls the stars reveal themselves; months of frustration were revealed in her outburst*). □ **re·veal·er** *noun* [Old French *reveler* or Latin *revelare* (as RE-, *velum* veil)]

re·veal[2] *noun* an internal side surface of an opening or recess, esp. of a doorway or window frame. [obsolete *revale* (v.) lower, from Old French *revaler* from *avaler* (as RE-, VAIL)]

revealed religion *noun* a religion based on revelation (*opp.* NATURAL RELIGION).

re·veal·ing *adjective* **1 a** providing insight esp. into something obscure or private (*her autobiography is quite revealing*). **b** striking, shocking. **2** (of an article of dress etc.) allowing more of the body to be seen than is usual or conventional (*a revealing blouse*). □ **re·veal·ing·ly** *adverb*

re·veget·ate *transitive verb* produce a new growth of vegetation on (disturbed or barren ground). □ **re·vegeta·tion** *noun*

rev·eil·le /'revəli/ *noun* a signal given in the morning, usu. on a drum or bugle, to waken soldiers and indicate that it is time to rise. [French *réveillez* imperative pl. of *réveiller* awaken (as RE-, *veiller* from Latin *vigilare* keep watch)]

ré·veill·on /'revei,ɔ̃/ *noun* (among francophones) a festive meal on Christmas morning after midnight Mass or on New Year's Eve. [French]

revel /'revəl/ ● *intransitive verb* (**re·velled**, **re·vel·ling**) esp. *US* **re·veled**, **rev·el·ing**) **1** (foll. by *in*) take great delight in (*she revelled in her new-found freedom*). **2** engage in riotous or noisy festivities. ● *noun* (in *sing.* or *pl.*) the act or an instance of revelling. □ **rev·el·ler** *noun* (*US* **re·vel·er**). [Old French *reveler* riot, from Latin *rebellare* REBEL *verb*]

rev·el·a·tion /,revə'leiʃən/ *noun* **1** the act or an instance of making something known (*the revelation of truth*). **2** something dramatic and striking disclosure (*revelations about her private life*). **3 a** the disclosure of knowledge to humankind by a divine or supernatural agency. **b** an instance of this. **c** a thing disclosed or made known by supernatural or divine means. **4** (**Revelation**) the last book of the New Testament, describing visions of heaven and the Last Judgment.

---

uː m**oo**d ai m**y** əi p**i**pe au br**ow**n ʌu h**ou**se ei d**ay** ɔi b**oy** ã fr**an**glais ã Ca**na**dien ɔ̃ Br**ay**on   (*see over for consonants*)

rev·el·a·tory /ˈrɛvələˌtɔri/ *adjective* serving to reveal, esp. something significant.

rev·elry /ˈrɛvəlri/ *noun* (*pl.* **-ries**) the action of revelling or merrymaking; boisterous gaiety or mirth.

Revel·stoke /ˈrɛvəlstoːk/ a city in SE central BC, located on the Columbia River, 210 km east of Kamloops; pop. (2001) 7,500. □ **Revel·stok·ian** *noun* [E. C. Baring, 1st Lord *Revelstoke* d.1897]

rev·en·ant /ˈrɛvənənt/ *noun* a person who has returned, esp. supposedly from the dead. [French, pres. part. of *revenir*: see REVENUE]

re·venge ● *noun* **1** retaliation for an offence or injury. **2 a** an act of retaliation. **b** the opportunity to retaliate or avenge a loss etc. **3** the desire for this; a vindictive feeling. ● *verb* **1** *transitive* take revenge for (an offence). **2** *transitive & reflexive* retaliate on behalf of (a person). □ **re·veng·er** *noun* [Old French *revenger, revencher* from Late Latin *revindicare* (as RE-, *vindicare* lay claim to)]

re·venge·ful *adjective* eager for revenge.

revenge of the cradle *noun Cdn* (prec. by *the*) the extremely high birth rate of French Canadians from the 19th to the mid-20th c., perceived as a means of retaliation against the English.

rev·enue /ˈrɛvəˌnjuː, -ˌnuː/ *noun* **1 a** income, esp. of a large amount, from any source. **b** (in *pl.*) items constituting this. **2** a government's annual income from which public expenses are met. **3** the department of the civil service collecting this. [Old French *revenu(e)* past participle of *revenir* from Latin *revenire* return (as RE-, *venire* come)]

rev·enu·er *noun N Amer.* a person who collects taxes or customs duties etc.

revenue stream *noun* one of a number of sources generating revenue for a company etc.

re·verb /rɪˈvɜrb, ˈriːvɜrb/ *noun Music informal* **1** reverberation. **2** a device to produce this.

re·ver·ber·ate /rɪˈvɜrbəˌreit/ *verb* **1 a** *intransitive* (of sound, light, or heat) be returned or echoed or reflected repeatedly. **b** *transitive* return (a sound etc.) in this way. **2** *intransitive* **a** (of a story, rumour, etc.) be heard much or repeatedly. **b** (of an event) have continuing effects. □ **re·ver·ber·ant** *adjective* **re·ver·ber·a·tion** *noun* **re·ver·ber·a·tive** /-rətɪv/ *adjective* **re·ver·ber·ator** *noun* [Latin *reverberare* (as RE-, *verberare* lash, from *verbera* (pl.) scourge)]

Re·vere /rəˈviːr/ **Paul** (1735–1818), US silversmith, who rode from Boston to Lexington to warn fellow American revolutionaries of the approach of British troops (1775).

re·vere /rəˈviːr/ *transitive verb* hold in deep and usu. affectionate or religious respect; venerate. [French *révérer* or Latin *reverēri* (as RE-, *verēri* fear)]

rev·er·ence /ˈrɛvərəns/ ● *noun* **1 a** the act of revering or the state of being revered (*hold in reverence; feel reverence for*). **b** the capacity for revering (*lacks reverence*). **2** (**Reverence**) a title used of or to some members of the clergy. ● *transitive verb* regard or treat with reverence.

Reverend /ˈrɛvrənd, ˈrɛvərənd/ ● *adjective* (as the title of a member of the clergy). Abbr.: **Rev.** ¶ Some clergy prefer *The Reverend* (or *The Rev.*) to *Reverend* (or *Rev.*) on the grounds that since *Reverend* is an adjective, it needs to be preceded by an article. ● *noun informal* (also **reverend**) a clergyman. [Old French *reverend* or Latin *reverendus* gerundive of *reverēri*: see REVERE]

Reverend Mother *noun* the title of the Mother Superior of a convent.

rev·er·ent /ˈrɛvərənt/ *adjective* feeling or showing great respect or admiration. □ **rev·er·ent·ly** *adverb*

rev·er·en·tial /ˌrɛvəˈrɛnʃəl/ *adjective* of the nature of, due to, or characterized by reverence. □ **rev·er·en·tial·ly** *adverb*

rev·erie /ˈrɛvri/ *noun* **1** a state of absent-minded meditation or musing; a daydream (*was lost in a reverie*). **2** *Music* an instrumental piece suggesting a dreamy or musing state. [Old French *reverie* rejoicing, revelry, from *rever* be delirious, of unknown origin]

re·vers /rɪˈviːr/ *noun* (*pl.* same /-ˈviːrz/) **1** the turned-back edge of a garment revealing the undersurface. **2** the material on this surface. [French, = REVERSE]

re·verse ● *verb* **1** *transitive* turn the other way around or up or inside out. **2** *transitive* change to the opposite character or effect (*reversed the decision; reversing the trend; they reversed roles*). **3** *intransitive & transitive* move backwards or in the opposite direction. **4** *transitive* make (an engine etc.) work in a contrary direction. **5** *transitive* revoke or annul (a verdict, decree, act, etc.). ● *adjective* **1** placed or turned in an opposite direction or position. **2** opposite or contrary in character or order; inverted. ● *noun* **1** the opposite or contrary (*the reverse is the case; is the reverse of the truth*). **2** the contrary of the usual manner. **3** an occurrence of

misfortune; a disaster, esp. a defeat in battle (*suffered a reverse*). **4** reverse gear or motion. **5** the reverse side of something. **6** *Football* a play in which one offensive player hands the ball off to a player running in the opposite direction. **7 a** the side of a coin or medal etc. bearing the secondary design. **b** this design (*compare* OBVERSE 1). **8** the verso of a leaf. **9** a device, as on a tape player, that turns something over or backwards. □ **reverse the charges** make the recipient of a telephone call responsible for payment. □ **re·ver·sal** *noun* **re·verse·ly** *adverb* **re·vers·er** *noun* **re·vers·ibil·ity** *noun* **re·vers·ible** *adjective* **re·vers·ibly** *adverb* [Old French *revers* (n.), *reverser* (v.), from Latin *revertere revers-* (as RE-, *vertere* turn)]

reverse discrimination *noun* discrimination against men or white people that results from policies intended to end discrimination against women or racial minorities.

reverse engineering *noun* the reproduction of another manufacturer's product following detailed examination of its construction or composition. □ **reverse-engineer** *transitive verb*

reverse fault *noun Geol.* a fault in which the overlying side of a mass of rock is displaced upward in relation to the underlying side.

reverse gear *noun* a gear used to make a vehicle etc. travel backwards.

reverse mortgage *noun N Amer.* a mortgage taken out esp. by a senior citizen against the capital investment in a home; the principal plus accrued interest is paid off only when the house is sold.

reverse osmosis *noun* the process by which a solvent passes through a porous membrane in the direction opposite to that for natural osmosis when subjected to a hydrostatic pressure greater than the osmotic pressure.

reverse psychology *noun* the principle or practice of suggesting (implicitly or explicitly) to a person that he or she do the opposite of what one really wants him or her to do.

reverse takeover *noun* the takeover of a public company by a smaller esp. private one.

reverse transcriptase *noun see* TRANSCRIPTASE.

reverse video *noun* a mode on a computer monitor in which the colours normally used for the background and characters are reversed.

reversing falls *noun Cdn* a set of rapids on a tidal river, the flow of which reverses regularly due to the pressure of the incoming tide.

re·ver·sion *noun* **1** a return to a previous state, habit, etc. **2** *Biol.* a return to ancestral type. **3 a** the legal right (esp. of the original owner, or his or her heirs) to possess or succeed to property on the death of the present possessor. **b** property to which a person has such a right. **4** a sum payable on a person's death, esp. by way of life insurance. □ **re·ver·sion·ary** *adjective*

re·vert *intransitive verb* **1** (foll. by *to*) **a** return to a former state or condition. **b** return to a former practice or habit. **c** return to an earlier topic of conversation or thought. **2** (of property, an office, etc.) return by reversion. **3** fall back into a wild state. [Old French *revertir* or Latin *revertere* (as REVERSE)]

re·vert·ible *adjective* (of property) subject to reversion.

revet /rəˈvɛt, rɪ-/ *transitive verb* (**re·vet·ted, re·vet·ting**) face (a rampart, wall, etc.) with masonry, esp. in fortification. [French *revêtir* from Late Latin *revestire* (as RE-, *vestire* clothe, from *vestis*)]

revet·ment /rəˈvɛtmənt, rɪ-/ *noun* a retaining wall or facing, esp. supporting an embankment etc.

re·view ● *noun* **1** a general survey or assessment of a subject or thing. **2** a retrospect or survey of the past. **3** a reconsideration or examination, with the possibility or intention of change if desirable or necessary (*is under review; rent review*). **4** *N Amer.* an act or instance of reviewing a subject or material already learned. **5** *Law* consideration of a judgment, sentence, etc., by some higher court or authority. **6** a display and formal inspection of troops etc. **7** an account or criticism of a book, performance, etc., esp. when published or broadcast. **8** a periodical publication with critical articles on current events, the arts, etc. **9** a second view. ● *verb* **1** *transitive* survey or look back on. **2** *transitive* reconsider or revise. **3** *N Amer.* **a** *transitive* go over (a lesson, or series of lessons) to reinforce a subject already learned. **b** *intransitive* present or study material again, e.g. to prepare for a test. **4** *transitive* hold a review of (troops etc.). **5** *transitive* **a** publish or broadcast a review of (a book, performance, etc.). **b** write a review of (a scholarly article) to assess its suitability for publication. **6** *transitive Law* submit (a sentence, decision, etc.) to review. **7** *transitive* view again. □ **re·view·able** *adjective* [obsolete French *reveue* from *revoir* (as RE-, *voir* see)]

re·view·er *noun* a person who writes or broadcasts reviews of books, performances, etc.; a critic.

Consonants: b *but* d *dog* f *few* g *get* h *her* j *yes* k *cat* l *leg* m *man* n *no* p *pen* r *red* s *sit*

re·vile *verb* **1** *transitive* abuse; criticize abusively. **2** *intransitive* talk abusively; rail. □ **re·vil·er** *noun* **re·vil·ing** *noun* [Old French *reviler* (as RE-, VILE)]

re·vise *verb* **1** *transitive* examine or re-examine and improve or amend (esp. written or printed matter). **2** *transitive* consider and alter (an opinion etc.). **3** *transitive & intransitive Brit.* = REVIEW *verb* 3. □ **re·vis·able** *adjective* **re·vis·er** *noun* [French *réviser* look at, or Latin *revisere* (as RE-, *visere* intensive of *vidēre vis-* see)]

Revised English Bible *noun* a translation of the Bible published in 1989 and intended for use by both Roman Catholic and Protestant churches. Abbr.: **REB**.

Revised Standard Version *noun* a revision in 1946–52 of the Authorized Version of the Bible. Abbr.: **RSV**.

Revised Version *noun* a revision in 1881–5 of the Authorized Version of the Bible. Abbr.: **RV**.

re·vision *noun* **1** the act or an instance of revising; the process of being revised. **2** a revised edition or form. □ **re·vision·ary** *adjective*

re·vision·ism *noun often derogatory* **1** a policy of revision or modification, esp. of Marxism on evolutionary socialist (rather than revolutionary) or pluralist principles. **2** the theory or practice of revising a previously accepted situation or point of view. □ **re·vision·ist** *noun & adjective*

re·visit *transitive verb* (**re·visit·ed**, **re·visit·ing**) **1** visit again. **2** take up (a subject etc.) again; reconsider or re-examine.

re·vital·ize *transitive verb* (also esp. *Brit.* **-ise**) imbue with new life and vitality. □ **re·vital·iz·a·tion** *noun*

re·vival *noun* **1** an improvement in the condition or strength of something; a recovery. **2** the process of bringing something back into existence, use, fashion, etc. **3 a** a reawakening of religious fervour. **b** a series of evangelistic meetings to promote this. **4** a new production of an old play etc. **5** restoration to bodily or mental vigour or to life or consciousness.

re·vival·ism *noun* **1** belief in or the promotion of a revival, esp. of religious fervour. **2** a tendency or desire to revive a former custom or practice. □ **re·vival·ist** *noun & adjective* **re·vival·is·tic** *adjective*

re·vive *verb* **1** *transitive & intransitive* come or bring back to consciousness or life or strength. **2** *transitive & intransitive* come or bring back to existence, use, notice, etc. **3** *transitive* produce (a play etc.) that has not been performed for some time. □ **re·viv·able** *adjective* [Late Latin *revivere* (as RE-, Latin *vivere* live)]

re·viv·ify /ri'vivi,fai/ *transitive verb* (**-fies**, **-fied**) restore to animation, activity, vigour, or life. □ **re·vivi·fi·ca·tion** *noun*

re·voke ● *verb* **1** *transitive* rescind, withdraw, or cancel (a licence, decision, promise, etc.). **2** *intransitive Cards* fail to follow suit when able to do so. ● *noun Cards* the act of revoking. □ **re·voc·able** /rə'voːkəbəl, 'revək-/ *adjective* **revo·ca·tion** /,revə'keiʃən/ *noun* [Latin *revocare* (as RE-, *vocare* call)]

re·volt ● *verb* **1** *intransitive* rise in rebellion against authority. **2** *transitive* (often in *passive*) affect with strong disgust; nauseate (*was revolted by the thought of it*). ● *noun* **1** an act of rebelling. **2** a state of insurrection (*in revolt*). **3** a sense of loathing. **4** a mood of protest or defiance. [French *révolter* from Italian *rivoltare* ultimately from Latin *revolvere* (as REVOLVE)]

re·volt·ing *adjective* disgusting, horrible. □ **re·volt·ing·ly** *adverb*

revo·lute /'revə,luːt/ *adjective Bot. etc.* having a rolled-back edge. [Latin *revolutus* past participle of *revolvere*: see REVOLVE]

revo·lu·tion /,revə'luːʃən/ *noun* **1 a** the forcible overthrow of a government or social order, in favour of a new system. **b** (in Marxism) the replacement of one ruling class by another; the class struggle which is expected to lead to political change and the triumph of communism. **2** any fundamental change or reversal of conditions (*the Industrial Revolution*). **3** the act or an instance of revolving. **4 a** motion in orbit or a circular course or around an axis or centre; rotation. **b** the single completion of an orbit or rotation. **c** the time taken for this. **5** a cyclic recurrence. □ **revo·lu·tion·ist** *noun*

revo·lu·tion·ary ● *adjective* **1** involving a complete or dramatic change. **2** of or causing political revolution. **3** (**Revolutionary**) of or relating to a particular revolution, esp. the American Revolution. ● *noun* (*pl.* **-aries**) an instigator or supporter of esp. political revolution.

Revolutionary War see AMERICAN REVOLUTION.

revo·lu·tion·ize *transitive verb* (also esp. *Brit.* **-ise**) introduce fundamental change to.

Revolutions of 1848 a series of revolts against autocratic rule in France, Austria, and the German and Italian states during 1848,

springing from lack of representation for the middle classes, economic grievances, and growing nationalism. All of the revolutions ended in failure and repression, but some of the liberal reforms gained (such as universal suffrage in France) survived, and nationalist aims in Germany and Italy were soon achieved (see RISORGIMENTO).

Ré·vo·lu·tion tran·quille /reivɒluːˈsjɔ̃ trɑ̃ˈkiːl/ *noun Cdn* = QUIET REVOLUTION.

re·volve *verb* **1** *intransitive & transitive* turn or cause to turn around, esp. on an axis; rotate. **2** *intransitive* move in a circular orbit. **3** *transitive* ponder (a problem etc.) in the mind. **4** *intransitive* (foll. by *around*) have as its chief concern; be centred upon (*my life revolves around my job*). [Latin *revolvere* (as RE-, *volvere* roll)]

re·volv·er *noun* a pistol with revolving chambers enabling several shots to be fired without reloading.

revolving credit *noun* credit that is automatically renewed as debts are paid off.

revolving door *noun* **1** a door with usu. four partitions turning around a central axis. **2 a** a situation, organization, etc. in which new arrivals depart again almost immediately, usu. without due care or attention given them, and often return again very soon (*the revolving door of psychiatric care*). **b** (*attributive*) (usu. **revolving-door**) designating or describing an institution etc. where people are processed quickly or through which people pass constantly (*it's a revolving-door workplace, with constant staff turnover*).

re·vue /ri'vjuː, ri-/ *noun* a theatrical entertainment of a series of short usu. satirical sketches and songs. [French, = REVIEW *noun*]

re·vul·sion *noun* abhorrence; a sense of loathing. [French *revulsion* or Latin *revulsio* (as RE-, *vellere vuls-* pull)]

re·ward ● *noun* **1 a** a return or recompense for service or merit. **b** requital for good or evil; retribution. **2** a sum offered for the detection of a criminal, the restoration of lost property, etc. **3** a benefit provided in return for frequent use of a commercial service, as in a frequent-flyer program. ● *transitive verb* **1** give a reward to (a person) or for (a service etc.). **2** make return for (an action) (*the book rewards a close reading*). □ **go to one's reward** die. [Anglo-French *reward* = Old French *reguard* REGARD]

re·ward·ing *adjective* (of an activity etc.) well worth doing; providing satisfaction. □ **re·ward·ing·ly** *adverb*

re·wash *transitive verb* wash again.

re·weigh *transitive verb* weigh again.

re·wind (*past and past participle* **re·wound**) ● *verb* **1** *transitive* wind (a film or tape etc.) back to the beginning. **2** *intransitive* go back to an earlier point in time. ● *noun* **1** a mechanism for rewinding film, tape, etc. **2** the action or process of rewinding film, tape, etc. □ **re·wind·er** *noun*

re·wire *transitive verb* **1** provide (a building etc.) with new wiring. **2** cause a fundamental change in (the brain, neurological function, one's outlook, etc.). □ **re·wir·able** *adjective*

re·word *transitive verb* change the wording of.

re·work *transitive verb* revise; refashion, remake. □ **re·work·ing** *noun*

re·wound *past and past participle* of REWIND.

re·wrap *transitive verb* (**re·wrapped**, **re·wrap·ping**) wrap again or differently.

re·writ·able *adjective* (of a data storage device or medium) capable of being overwritten with new data, esp. designating a type of optical storage medium on which data can be written, and subsequently erased and rewritten, by the user.

re·write ● *transitive verb* (*past* **re·wrote**; *past participle* **re·writ·ten**) **1** write again or differently. **2** present or depict (history or a historical event) in a new or different light, esp. to further one's own interests. ● *noun* **1** the act or an instance of rewriting. **2** a thing rewritten.

Rex *noun* the reigning king (following a name or in the titles of lawsuits, e.g. *Rex v. Jones* the Crown versus Jones). [Latin]

Reye's syndrome /raiz, reiz/ *noun* a frequently fatal metabolic disorder in young children, of uncertain cause but sometimes precipitated by acetylsalicylic acid, involving encephalitis and degeneration of the liver. [R. D. K. *Reye*, Australian pediatrician d.1978]

Rey·kja·vik /'reikjə,vik/ the capital of Iceland, a port on the west coast; pop. (1999) 109,152.

Rey·nolds, Sir Joshua (1723–92), English portrait painter. He sought to raise portraiture to the status of historical painting by adapting poses and settings from classical statues and Renaissance paintings.

Reynolds number *noun Physics* a quantity indicating the degree of turbulence of flow past an obstacle etc. [O. *Reynolds*, English physicist d.1912]

rez *noun* (also **res**) *N Amer. informal* an Indian reserve or reservation.

re·zone *transitive verb* classify (a property, area, etc.) as belonging to a different zone or subject to a different set of zoning regulations.

Rf *symbol* the element rutherfordium.

r.f. *abbreviation* (also **RF**) radio frequency.

RFC *abbreviation hist.* Royal Flying Corps.

RFP *noun esp. N Amer.* request for proposal, a detailed specification of goods or services required by an organization, sent to potential contractors or suppliers.

RGB *abbreviation* red-green-blue.

Rh¹ *symbol* the element rhodium.

Rh² *abbreviation* **1** rhesus. **2** rhesus factor.

r.h. *abbreviation* right hand.

Rhada·man·thus /ˌradəˈmanθəs/ *Gk Myth* the son of Zeus and Europa, and brother of Minos, who, as a ruler and judge in the underworld, was renowned for his justice. □ **Rhada·man·thine** /-θɪn, -θaɪn/ *adjective*

Rhaeto-Romance /ˌriːtɔːrɔːˈmans/ (also **Rhaeto-Romanic** /-ˈmanɪk/) ● *noun* a group of Romance dialects spoken in SE Switzerland, the Tyrol, and Friuli-Venezia Giulia, including Friulian, Romansh, and Ladin. ● *adjective* of or relating to this group of dialects. [Latin *Rhaetus* of Rhaetia in the Alps + ROMANCE]

rhap·sode /ˈrapsɔːd/ *noun* a reciter of epic poems, esp. of Homer in ancient Greece. [Greek *rhapsōidos* from *rhaptō* stitch + *ōidē* song, ODE]

rhap·sod·ist /ˈrapsədɪst/ *noun* **1** a person who rhapsodizes. **2** = RHAPSODE.

rhap·sod·ize /ˈrapsəˌdaɪz/ *intransitive verb* (also esp. *Brit.* **-ise**) **1** talk or write about a person or thing with great enthusiasm. **2** write a rhapsody or rhapsodies.

rhap·sody /ˈrapsədi/ *noun* (*pl.* **-ies**) **1** an exaggeratedly enthusiastic or ecstatic expression of feeling. **2** *Music* a piece of music in one extended movement, usu. emotional in character. **3** *Gk Hist.* an epic poem, or part of it, of a length for one recitation. □ **rhap·sod·ic** /rapˈsɒdɪk/ *adjective* **rhap·sod·ical** /rapˈsɒdɪkəl/ *adjective* (in senses 1, 2). **rhap·sod·ical·ly** *adverb* [Latin *rhapsodia* from Greek *rhapsōidia* (as RHAPSODE)]

rhat·any /ˈratəni/ *noun* (*pl.* **-ies**) **1** either of two American shrubs, *Krameria trianda* and *K. argentea*, having an astringent root when dried. **2** the root of either of these. [modern Latin *rhatania* from Portuguese *ratanha*, Spanish *ratania*, from Quechua *rataña*]

Rhea /ˈriːə/ **1** *Gk Myth* one of the Titans, wife of Cronus and mother of Zeus, Demeter, Poseidon, Hera, and Hades. Frightened of betrayal by their children, Cronus ate them; Rhea rescued Zeus from this fate by hiding him and giving Cronus a stone wrapped in blankets instead. **2** *Astronomy* satellite V of Saturn, the fourteenth closest to the planet, discovered by Cassini in 1672 (diameter 1 530 km).

rhea /ˈriːə/ *noun* any of several S American flightless birds of the family Rheidae, like but smaller than an ostrich. [modern Latin genus name from Latin from Greek *Rhea*]

Rheims see REIMS.

Rhen·ish /ˈriːnɪʃ, ˈren-/ ● *adjective* of the Rhine and the regions adjoining it. ● *noun* wine from this area. [Anglo-French *reneis* from Latin *Rhenanus* from *Rhenus* Rhine]

rhe·nium /ˈriːniəm/ *noun Chem.* a rare metallic element of the manganese group, occurring naturally in molybdenum ores and used in the manufacture of superconducting alloys. Symbol: **Re**; at. no.: 75. [modern Latin from Latin *Rhenus* Rhine]

rhe·ol·ogy /riːˈɒlədʒi/ *noun* the science dealing with the flow and deformation of matter. □ **rheo·logic·al** *adjective* **rhe·ol·o·gist** *noun* [Greek *rheos* stream + -LOGY]

rheo·stat /ˈriːəˌstat/ *noun Electricity* an instrument used to control a current by varying the resistance. □ **rheo·stat·ic** *adjective* [Greek *rheos* stream + -STAT]

rhe·sus /ˈriːsəs/ *noun* (in full **rhesus monkey**) a small catarrhine monkey, *Macaca mulatta*, common in N India. [modern Latin, arbitrary use of Latin *Rhesus* from Greek *Rhēsos*, mythical King of Thrace]

rhesus factor *noun* an antigen occurring on the red blood cells of most humans and some other primates. [RHESUS, because first observed in the rhesus monkey]

rhesus negative *adjective* lacking the rhesus factor.

rhesus positive *adjective* having the rhesus factor.

rhe·tor /ˈriːtɔr, ˈret-/ *noun* **1** an ancient Greek or Roman teacher or professor of rhetoric. **2** usu. *derogatory* an orator. [Greek *rhētōr*]

rhet·or·ic /ˈretərɪk/ *noun* **1** the art of effective or persuasive speaking or writing. **2** language designed to persuade or impress (often with an implication of insincerity or exaggeration etc.). [Greek *rhētorikē* (*tekhnē*) (art) of rhetoric (as RHETOR)]

rhet·or·ic·al /rɪˈtɒrɪkəl/ *adjective* **1** expressed with a view to persuasive or impressive effect; artificial or extravagant in language. **2** of the nature of rhetoric. **3 a** of or relating to the art of rhetoric. **b** given to rhetoric; oratorical. □ **rhet·or·ic·al·ly** *adverb*

rhetorical question *noun* a question asked not for information but to produce an effect, e.g. *who cares?* for *nobody cares*.

rhet·or·ician /ˌretəˈrɪʃən/ *noun* **1** an orator. **2** a teacher of rhetoric. **3** a rhetorical speaker or writer.

rheum /ruːm/ *noun* a watery discharge from a mucous membrane, esp. of the eyes or nose. □ **rheumy** *adjective* [Old French *reume* ultimately from Greek *rheuma -atos* stream, from *rheō* flow]

rheum·at·ic /ruːˈmatɪk/ ● *adjective* **1** of, relating to, or suffering from rheumatism. **2** producing or produced by rheumatism. ● *noun* a person suffering from rheumatism. □ **rheum·at·icky** *adjective informal*. [as RHEUM]

rheumatic fever *noun* a non-infectious fever with inflammation and pain in the joints.

rheuma·tism /ˈruːməˌtɪzəm/ *noun* any disease marked by inflammation and pain in the joints, muscles, or fibrous tissue, esp. rheumatoid arthritis. [ultimately from Greek *rheumatismos* from *rheumatizō* from *rheuma* stream; the disease was originally supposed to be caused by the internal flow of 'watery' humours]

rheuma·toid /ˈruːməˌtɔɪd/ *adjective* having the character of rheumatism.

rheumatoid arthritis *noun* a chronic progressive disease causing inflammation and stiffening of the joints.

rheuma·tol·ogy /ˌruːməˈtɒlədʒi/ *noun* the study of rheumatic diseases. □ **rheum·ato·logic·al** *adjective* **rheuma·tol·o·gist** *noun*

Rh factor *noun* = RHESUS FACTOR.

rhinal /ˈraɪnəl/ *adjective Anat.* of a nostril or the nose. [Greek *rhis rhin-*: see RHINO-]

Rhine·land the region of western Germany through which the Rhine flows, esp. the part to the west of the river.

Rhineland-Palatin·ate /ˌraɪnlandpəˈlatɪnət/ a state of western Germany; capital, Mainz.

Rhine River a river in W Europe which rises in the Swiss Alps and flows for 1 320 km (820 miles), first westward through Lake Constance, forming the German–Swiss border, then turning northward through Germany, forming the southern part of the German–French border, before flowing westward again through the Netherlands to empty into the North Sea near Rotterdam.

rhine·stone *noun* an imitation diamond. [translation of French *caillou du Rhin*, lit. 'pebble of the Rhine']

rhin·itis /raɪˈnaɪtɪs/ *noun* inflammation of the mucous membrane of the nose. [Greek *rhis rhinos* nose + -ITIS]

rhino *noun* (*pl.* same or **rhinos**) **1** *informal* a rhinoceros. **2** (**Rhino**) *Cdn slang* a member of the Rhinoceros Party. [abbreviation]

rhino- *combining form* the nose. [Greek *rhis rhinos* nostril, nose]

rhin·ocer·os /raɪˈnɒsərəs/ *noun* (*pl.* same or **rhin·ocer·oses**) **1** any of various large thick-skinned plant-eating ungulates of the family Rhinocerotidae of Africa and S Asia, with one horn or in some cases two horns on the nose and plated or folded skin. **2** (**Rhinoceros**) *Cdn* a member of the Rhinoceros Party. [Latin from Greek *rhinokerōs* (as RHINO-, *keras* horn)]

rhinoceros auklet *noun* a mainly blackish-brown auk, *Cerorhinca monocerata*, of northern Pacific coasts, having a yellowish horn at the base of the bill.

Rhinoceros Party *noun Cdn* a spoof political party which first ran candidates in the 1960s; the party's goal is to demonstrate the supposed shortcomings of the traditional Canadian political parties.

rhino·plasty /ˈraɪnɔːˌplasti/ *noun* plastic surgery of the nose. □ **rhino·plas·tic** *adjective*

rhin·ovirus /ˈraɪnɔːˌvaɪrəs/ *noun* any of a group of very small RNA viruses including those which cause some forms of the common cold.

rhizo- /ˈraɪzɔ/ *combining form Bot.* a root. [Greek *rhiza* root]

rhi·zo·bium /raɪˈzɔːbiəm/ *noun* (*pl.* **-bia**) a nitrogen-fixing soil bacterium of the genus *Rhizobium*, found esp. in the root nodules of leguminous plants. [modern Latin genus name, from RHIZO- + Greek *bios* 'life' + -IUM]

rhi·zoid /ˈraizɔid/ *Bot.* ● *adjective* rootlike. ● *noun* a root hair or filament in mosses, ferns, etc. □ **rhi·zoid·al** *adjective*

rhi·zome /ˈraizəʊm/ *noun* an underground rootlike stem bearing both roots and shoots. □ **rhi·zoma·tous** *adjective* [Greek *rhizōma* from *rhizoō* take root (as RHIZO-)]

rhizo·pod /ˈraizəˌpɒd/ *noun* any protozoan of the superclass Rhizopoda, forming rootlike pseudopodia, e.g. an amoeba.

Rh-negative *adjective* = RHESUS NEGATIVE.

rho *noun* the seventeenth letter of the Greek alphabet (P, ρ). [Greek]

rhoda·mine /ˈrəʊdəmɪn/ *noun Chem.* any of various red synthetic dyes used to colour textiles. [RHODO- + AMINE]

Rhode Island a state in the northeastern US, on the Atlantic coast; pop. (2000) 1,048,319; capital, Providence. □ **Rhode Island·er** *noun* [after an island in Narragansett Bay, one of the original settlements]

Rhode Island Green·ing *noun* a variety of green-skinned apple.

Rhode Island Red *noun* a reddish-black domestic fowl raised for meat and eggs.

Rhodes¹ 1 a Greek island in the SE Aegean, off the Turkish coast, the largest of the Dodecanese and the most easterly island in the Aegean; pop. (est. 2001) 100,000. **2** its capital, a port on the northernmost tip; pop. (est. 2002) 49,300.

Rhodes² ▸ 1 Cecil John (1853–1902), English-born South African politician, prime minister of Cape Colony 1890–96. He amassed a fortune from diamond production, and entering politics in 1881, expanded British territory in southern Africa, annexing Bechuanaland (now Botswana) in 1884 and developing Rhodesia from 1889 onward with his British South Africa Company; in his will, he established the Rhodes Scholarships. **2 Edgar Nel·son** (1877–1942), Canadian lawyer and politician, Conservative premier and provincial secretary of Nova Scotia 1925–30.

Rho·desia /rɒˈdiːʒə/ **1** the former name of a large territory in central southern Africa, divided into Northern Rhodesia (now Zambia) and Southern Rhodesia (now Zimbabwe). From 1953 to 1963 Northern and Southern Rhodesia were united with Nyasaland (now Malawi) to form the Federation of Rhodesia and Nyasaland. **2** the name adopted by Southern Rhodesia when Northern Rhodesia left the Federation in 1963 to become the independent republic of Zambia, until 1979 when the country became independent as Zimbabwe. □ **Rho·desian** *adjective & noun*

Rhodes Scholarship /rɒːdz/ *noun* any of several scholarships awarded annually and tenable at Oxford University by students from certain Commonwealth countries, South Africa, the United States, and Germany. □ **Rhodes Scholar** *noun* [C. RHODES]

rho·dium /ˈrəʊdiəm/ *noun* a hard white metallic element of the platinum group, occurring naturally in platinum ores and used in making alloys and plating jewellery. Symbol: **Rh**; at. no.: 45. [Greek *rhodon* rose (from the colour of the solution of its salts)]

rhodo- *combining form* esp. Mineralogy & Chem. rose-coloured. [Greek *rhodon* rose]

rhodo·chros·ite /ˌrəʊdəʊˈkrɒsʌit/ *noun* a mineral form of manganese carbonate occurring in pink, brown, or grey crystals. [Greek *rhodokhrous* rose-coloured]

rhodo·den·dron /ˌrəʊdəˈdendrən/ *noun* any evergreen shrub or small tree of the genus *Rhododendron*, with usu. large clusters of trumpet-shaped flowers. [Latin, = oleander, from Greek (as RHODO-, *dendron* tree)]

Rho·dope Mountains /ˈrɒdəpi/ a mountain system in the Balkans, SE Europe, on the frontier between Bulgaria and Greece, rising to a height of over 2 000 m (6,600 ft.) and including the Rila Mountains in the northwest.

rho·dop·sin /rəʊˈdɒpsɪn/ *noun* a light-sensitive pigment in the retina. [Greek *rhodon* rose + *opsis* sight]

rho·dora /rəˈdɔrə/ *noun* a N American pink-flowered shrub, *Rhodora canadense*. [modern Latin from Latin plant name from Greek *rhodon* rose]

rhomb /rɒm/ *noun* = RHOMBUS. □ **rhom·bic** /ˈrɒmbɪk/ *adjective* [French *rhombe* or Latin *rhombus*]

rhombi *pl.* of RHOMBUS.

rhombo·hed·ron /ˌrɒmbəˈhiːdrən/ *noun* (pl. **-hed·rons** or **-hed·ra**) a solid bounded by six equal rhombuses. □ **rhombo·hed·ral** *adjective* [RHOMBUS, after *polyhedron* etc.]

rhom·boid /ˈrɒmbɔid/ ● *adjective* (also **rhom·boid·al**) having or nearly having the shape of a rhombus. ● *noun* a quadrilateral of which only the opposite sides and angles are equal. [French *rhomboïde* or Late Latin *rhomboides* from Greek *rhomboeidēs* (as RHOMB)]

rhom·boid·eus /rɒmˈbɔidiəs/ *noun* (pl. **rhom·boidei** /-di̯ai/) *Anat.* a muscle connecting the shoulder blade to the vertebrae. [modern Latin *rhomboideus* RHOMBOID]

rhom·bus /ˈrɒmbəs/ *noun* (pl. **rhom·bus·es** or **rhombi** /-bai/) *Math.* a parallelogram with oblique angles and equal sides. [Latin from Greek *rhombos*]

Rhône-Alpes /rɒnˈalp/ a region of SE France, extending from the Rhone valley to the borders with Switzerland and Italy and including much of the former duchy of Savoy.

Rhone River a river in SW Europe which rises in the Swiss Alps and flows 812 km (505 miles), at first westward through Lake Geneva into France, then to Lyons, where it turns southward, passing Avignon, to the Mediterranean west of Marseilles, where it forms a wide delta that includes the Camargue.

rhotic /ˈrəʊtɪk/ *adjective* of or relating to a dialect or variety of English in which r is pronounced before a consonant (as in *hard*) and at the ends of words (as in *far*). [Greek *rhot-*, stem of RHO + -IC]

Rh-positive *adjective* = RHESUS POSITIVE.

RHR *abbreviation* (in Canada) Royal Highland Regiment.

rhu·barb *noun* **1 a** any of various plants of the genus *Rheum*, esp. *R. rhaponticum*, producing long fleshy dark red leaf stalks used cooked as food. **b** the leaf stalks of this. **2 a** a root of a Chinese and Tibetan plant of the genus *Rheum*. **b** a purgative made from this. **3** *Brit.* **a** informal a murmurous conversation or noise, esp. the repetition of the word 'rhubarb' by crowd actors. **b** *slang* nonsense; worthless stuff. **4** *N Amer. slang* a heated dispute. [Old French *r(e)ubarbe*, shortening of medieval Latin *r(h)eubarbarum*, alteration (by assoc. with Greek *rhēon* rhubarb) of *rhabarbarum* foreign 'rha', ultimately from Greek *rha* + *barbaros* foreign]

rhumb /rʌm/ *noun Naut.* **1** any of the 32 points of the compass. **2** (in full **rhumb line**) **a** a line cutting all meridians at the same angle. **b** the line followed by a ship sailing in a fixed direction. [French *rumb* prob. from Dutch *ruim* room, assoc. with Latin *rhombus*: see RHOMBUS]

rhum·ba *var.* of RUMBA.

rhyme ● *noun* **1** the quality shared by words or syllables that have or end with the same sound as each other, esp. when such words etc. are used at the ends of lines of poetry. **2** (in *sing.* or *pl.*) verse having rhymes. **3** a poem having rhymes. **4** a word that has the same sound as another. ● *verb* **1** *intransitive* **a** (of words or lines) produce a rhyme. **b** (foll. by *with*) act as a rhyme (with another). **2** *intransitive* make or write rhymes; versify. **3** *transitive* put or make (a story etc.) into rhyme. **4** *transitive* (foll. by *with*) treat (a word) as rhyming with another. □ **rhyme off** *Cdn* recite rapidly and spontaneously (a list of items). **rhyme or reason** (usu. in negative expressions) sense or logic (*there's no rhyme or reason to it*). □ **rhym·er** *noun* [Old French *rime* from medieval Latin *rithmus, rythmus* from Latin from Greek *rhuthmos* RHYTHM]

rhyme·ster *noun* derogatory a writer of (esp. simple) rhymes.

rhyming slang *noun* a form of slang that replaces words by rhyming words or phrases, e.g. *stairs* by *apples and pears*, often with the rhyming element omitted.

rhyo·lite /ˈraiəˌlait/ *noun* a fine-grained volcanic rock of granitic composition. □ **rhyo·lit·ic** /raiəˈlitik/ *adjective* [German *Rhyolit* from Greek *rhuax* lava stream + *lithos* stone]

rhythm /ˈrɪðəm/ *noun* **1** a measured flow of words and phrases in verse or prose determined by various relations of long and short or accented and unaccented syllables. **2 a** the aspect of musical composition concerned with periodical accent and the duration of notes. **b** a particular type of pattern formed by this (*samba rhythm*). **3** movement with a regular succession of strong and weak elements. **4** a regularly recurring sequence of events. **5** a sense of rhythm. **6** *Art* a harmonious correlation of parts. □ **rhythm·less** *adjective* [French *rhythme* or Latin *rhythmus* from Greek *rhuthmos*, related to *rheō* flow]

rhythm and blues *noun* popular music with a blues theme and a strong rhythm.

rhyth·mic *adjective* (also **rhyth·mic·al**) **1** relating to or characterized by rhythm. **2** regularly occurring. □ **rhyth·mic·al·ly** *adverb*

rhythmic gymnastics *noun* a form of gymnastics emphasizing dance-like rhythmic routines, typically accentuated by the use of ribbons or hoops. □ **rhythmic gymnast** *noun*

rhyth·mi·city *noun* **1** rhythmical quality or character. **2** the capacity for maintaining a rhythm.

rhythm method *noun* birth control by avoiding sexual intercourse when ovulation is likely to occur.

---

rhythm section *noun* the part of a band etc. mainly supplying rhythm, usu. consisting of drums, bass, etc.

RI *abbreviation* **1** Rhode Island (also in official postal use). **2** King and Emperor. **3** Queen and Empress. [sense 2 from Latin *rex et imperator*: sense 3 from Latin *regina et imperatrix*]

rial /ˈriːɒl, ˈraɪəl/ *noun* the chief monetary unit of Iran and Oman, equal to 1,000 baizas in Oman. [Persian from Arabic *riyal* from Spanish *real* ROYAL]

Ri·alto /riˈɒltɔː, riˈaltɔ/ an island in Venice, containing the old mercantile quarter of medieval Venice.

rib ● *noun* **1** each of the curved bones articulated in pairs to the spine and protecting the thoracic cavity and its organs. **2 a** a roast of meat from this part of an animal. **b** (usu. in *pl.*) = SPARERIBS. **3** a ridge or long raised piece often of stronger or thicker material across a surface or through a structure serving to support or strengthen it. **4** any of a ship's transverse curved timbers forming the framework of the hull. **5** *Knitting* a combination of plain and purl stitches producing a ribbed, somewhat elastic fabric. **6** each of the hinged rods supporting the fabric of an umbrella. **7** a vein of a leaf or an insect's wing. **8** a structural member in an airfoil. ● *transitive verb* (**ribbed**, **rib·bing**) **1** provide with ribs; act as the ribs of. **2** *informal* make fun of; tease. **3** mark with ridges. [Old English *rib*, *ribb* from Germanic]

rib·ald /ˈraɪbəld, ˈrɪb-/ *adjective* (of language or its user) referring to sexual matters in a rude but humorous way. [Old French *ribau(l)d* from *riber* pursue licentious pleasures, from Germanic]

rib·ald·ry *noun* ribald talk or behaviour.

rib·and /ˈrɪbənd/ *noun* a ribbon. [Old French *riban*, prob. from a Germanic compound of BAND¹]

rib·a·virin /ˌraɪbəˈvaɪrɪn/ *noun* a drug which interferes with the synthesis of viral nucleic acids and is used to treat some viral infections. [RIBOSE + VIRUS + -IN]

ribbed *adjective* **1** having ribs or rib-like markings. **2** *Knitting* having ribbing.

Rib·ben·trop /ˈrɪbən,trɒp/ **Jo·a·chim von** (1893–1946), German Nazi politician. A close associate of Hitler, he served as Foreign Minister from 1938 to 1945; he was convicted as a war criminal in the Nuremberg trials and hanged.

rib·bing *noun* **1** ribs or a rib-like structure. **2** a pattern in knitting of alternate ridges and depressions. **3** *informal* the act or an instance of teasing.

rib·bit *noun* N Amer. the characteristic sound made by a frog. [imitative]

rib·bon *noun* **1 a** a narrow strip or band of fabric, used esp. for trimming or decoration. **b** material in this form. **2** a ribbon of a special colour etc. worn to indicate some honour or membership of a sports team etc. **3** a long narrow strip of anything, e.g. impregnated material forming the inking agent in a typewriter or printer. **4** (in *pl.*) ragged strips (*torn to ribbons*). □ **rib·boned** *adjective* [var. of RIBAND]

ribbon cutting *noun* the formal cutting of a ribbon across the entrance to somewhere, as an opening ceremony.

ribbon·fish *noun* any of various long slender flat fishes of the family Trachipteridae.

ribbon grass *noun* a cultivated variety of reed canary grass with green and white striped leaves.

ribbon worm *noun* a chiefly aquatic worm with an elongated, unsegmented, flattened body that is typically brightly coloured and tangled in knots, and a long proboscis for catching food.

rib cage *noun* the wall of bones formed by the ribs around the chest.

Ri·bei·rão Preto /rɪbeˈrau ˌpreɪtɔ/ a city in S Brazil, northeast of Rio de Janeiro; pop. (est. 2000) 502,333.

Ri·bera /rɪˈbera/ **José** (or **Ju·sepe**) **de** (known as 'Lo Spagnoletto' = the little Spaniard) (*c.*1591–1652), Spanish painter and etcher. His paintings of religious subjects and genre scenes are noted for their dramatic chiaroscuro effects and for their realistic depiction of torture and martyrdom, and include the *Martyrdom of St. Bartholomew* (*c.*1630).

rib-eye *noun* (in full **rib-eye steak**) a roundish steak cut from the rib.

Ribier /ˈrɪbjɜr/ *noun* a variety of large, round, purple-black grape, orig. French but much grown in the US as a table grape.

rib-knit *noun* a knitted garment or fabric having a ribbed pattern.

rib·lets *plural noun* N Amer. spareribs cut from the end of the rib furthest from the backbone.

ribo·flavin /ˈraɪbəˌfleɪvɪn/ *noun* a vitamin of the B complex, found in liver, milk, and eggs, essential for energy production. Also called VITAMIN B₂. [RIBOSE + Latin *flavus* yellow]

ribo·nucleic acid /ˌraɪbənuːˈkleɪɪk, -njuː-, -ˌkliːɪk/ *noun* a nucleic acid yielding ribose on hydrolysis, present in living cells, esp. in ribosomes where it is involved in protein synthesis. Abbr.: **RNA**. [RIBOSE + NUCLEIC ACID]

rib·ose /ˈraɪbɔːs/ *noun* a sugar found in many nucleosides and in several vitamins and enzymes. [German, alteration of *Arabinose*, a related sugar]

ribo·some /ˈraɪbəˌsɔm/ *noun Biochem.* each of the minute particles consisting of RNA and associated proteins found in the cytoplasm of living cells, concerned with the synthesis of proteins. □ **ribo·som·al** *adjective* [RIBONUCLEIC (ACID) + -SOME³]

rib-tickler *noun* something amusing; a joke. □ **rib-tickling** *adjective*

Ri·car·do /rɪˈkɑːdɔː/ **David** (1772–1823), English economist, whose best-known work is *On the Principles of Political Economy and Taxation* (1817), in which he sets forward his views on prices, wages, and profits, and his theory of rent.

Ricci /ˈriːtʃi/ **Nino** (b.1959), Canadian novelist. He recounted the experiences of an Italian immigrant family in his trilogy *Lives of the Saints* (1990, winner of the Governor General's Award), *In a Glass House* (1993), and *Where She Has Gone* (1997).

Rice, Sir Tim·othy Miles Bin·don ('Tim') (b.1944), English lyricist and entertainer. Together with Andrew Lloyd Webber he co-wrote a number of hit musicals, including *Joseph and the Amazing Technicolor Dreamcoat* (1968), *Jesus Christ Superstar* (1971), and *Evita* (1978).

rice ● *noun* **1** the grain of the grass *Oryza sativa*, a major world cereal. **2** the plant producing this grain, grown in warmer parts of the world, usu. in standing water. ● *transitive verb* N Amer. pass (cooked potatoes etc.) through a coarse sieve to produce long strands. □ **ricer** *noun* [Old French *ris* from Italian *riso*, ultimately from Greek *oruza*, of oriental origin]

rice cake *noun* a round, crisp biscuit made of puffed rice.

rice paper *noun* **1** edible paper made from the pith of an oriental tree and used for painting and in cookery. **2** paper made wholly or partly from the straw of rice.

ri·cer·car /ˌriːʃerˈkɑr/ *noun* (also **ric·er·care** /-ˈkɑre/) an elaborate contrapuntal instrumental composition in fugal or canonic style, esp. of the 16th–18th c. [Italian = seek out]

rice root *noun* = CHOCOLATE LILY.

rice wine *noun* an alcoholic drink made by fermenting cooked rice.

Rich ▸ 1 Ad·ri·enne Ce·cile (b.1929), US poet, essayist, and feminist theorist. Her work addresses issues of language, sexuality, oppression, and power, and includes the essay collection *On Lies, Secrets, and Silence* (1979), and poetry collections such as *Diving into the Wreck* (1973) and *An Atlas of the Difficult World* (1991). **2 Buddy** (born Bernard Rich) (1917–87), US jazz drummer and bandleader. In 1933 he joined the band of clarinetist Joe Marsala, and subsequently played for bandleaders such as Artie Shaw and Tommy Dorsey. He first formed his own band in 1946 and toured extensively until his death.

rich *adjective* **1** having much wealth. **2** (often foll. by *in, with*) splendid, costly, elaborate (*rich tapestries*; *rich with lace*). **3** valuable (*rich offerings*). **4** copious, abundant, ample (*a rich harvest*; *a rich supply of ideas*). **5** (often foll. by *in, with*) abundantly supplied with (*rich in nutrients*; *the area is rich with Arctic wildlife*; also in *combination*: *iron-rich foods*). **6** (of food or diet) containing a large amount of fat, butter, eggs, sugar, etc. **7** (of the mixture in an internal combustion engine) containing a high proportion of fuel (compare LEAN² 6). **8** (of colour or sound or smell) mellow and deep, strong and full. **9 a** (of an incident or assertion etc.) highly ludicrous; outrageous. **b** (of humour) earthy. **10** (of soil) very fertile; abounding in nutrients. **11** (of a country, region, etc.) abounding in natural resources or means of production. □ **rich·en** *transitive & intransitive verb* **rich·ness** *noun* [Old English *rice* from Germanic from Celtic, related to Latin *rex* king: reinforced in Middle English from Old French *riche* rich, powerful, of Germanic origin]

-rich *combining form* having or containing much; abundant in (*oil-rich*; *vitamin-rich*).

Ri·chard /riˈʃɑr/ **(Jo·seph-Henri-)Mau·rice 'Rocket'** (1921–2000), Canadian hockey player. Playing as a forward for the Montreal Canadiens, he became the first player ever to score 50 goals in 50 games. His suspension in 1955 for attacking an opposing player and a linesman provoked the worst sports riot in Canadian history on March 17 of that year.

Rich·ard I (known as **Rich·ard Coeur de Lion** or **Rich·ard the Lion-Heart**) (1157–99), son of Henry II, king of England 1189–99. Soon after becoming king, he left to lead the Third Crusade; he was taken prisoner in 1192 by Duke Leopold of Austria and subsequently held hostage by the Holy Roman emperor Henry VI, only being released in 1194 after the payment of a huge ransom; he was fatally wounded during a campaign against Philip II of France.

Richard II (1367–1400), son of the Black Prince, king of England 1377–99. During his minority, the government was in the hands of selected nobles, dominated by his uncle John of Gaunt. In 1389 he asserted his right to rule independently of his protectors and later executed or banished most of his former opponents; his confiscation of John of Gaunt's estate on the latter's death provoked Henry Bolingbroke's return from exile to overthrow him.

Richard III (1452–85), brother of Edward IV, king of England 1483–5. After his brother's death, he served as Protector to his nephew Edward V, who, two months later, was declared illegitimate on dubious grounds and subsequently disappeared (see PRINCES IN THE TOWER). As king, he ruled with some success for a brief period, before being defeated and killed at Bosworth Field (1485) by Henry Tudor (later Henry VII).

Rich·ards, Ivor Arm·strong (1893–1979), English critic and educator. He is best known for his influential study *Practical Criticism: A Study of Literary Judgement* (1929), which revolutionized the teaching and study of English and helped to found New Criticism.

Rich·ard·son ▶ 1 John (1796–1852), Canadian soldier and writer. He fought in the War of 1812, but left the military to pursue a career in writing and journalism. His most enduring work, *Wacousta; or, The Prophecy* (1832), set during the time of Pontiac's rebellion, tells a story of betrayal, disguise, and slaughter. **2 Sir Ralph David** (1902–83), English actor, whose notable stage roles included Shakespeare's Falstaff and the title role in *Peer Gynt*; his films include *Richard III* (1955), *Doctor Zhivago* (1965), and *Greystoke* (1984). **3 Sam·uel** (1689–1761), English novelist. His first novel *Pamela* (1740–1) was responsible for popularizing the epistolary novel, while *Clarissa* (1747–8) explored moral issues in a detailed social context with psychological intensity.

Richardson's ground squirrel *noun* a ground squirrel, *Spermophilus richardsonii*, of western N America, commonly called a gopher. [Sir John *Richardson*, Scottish naturalist and explorer d.1865]

Richelieu, Ri·vière /rɪʃəˈljə, ˈrɪʃəluː/ a river in S Quebec, about 130 km long, which issues from Lake Champlain in the US and flows northward into Quebec to empty into the St. Lawrence at Sorel. [RICHELIEU]

Riche·lieu /rɪʃəˈljə, ˈrɪʃəluː/ **Ar·mand Jean du Ples·sis** (1585–1642), French cardinal and statesman. As chief minister to Louis XIII (1624–42) he destroyed the power base of the Huguenots in the late 1620s and set out to undermine the Hapsburg Empire by supporting the Swedish king Gustavus Adolphus in the Thirty Years War, involving France from 1635; he also established the Académie française (1635).

rich·es *plural noun* wealth; money and valuable possessions. [Old French *richeise* from *riche* RICH, taken as pl.]

Rich·ler /ˈrɪtʃlər/ **Mor·de·cai** (1931–2001), Canadian novelist, whose works include *The Apprenticeship of Duddy Kravitz* (1959), *St. Urbain's Horseman* (1971), and *Solomon Gursky Was Here* (1989).

rich·ly *adverb* **1** in a rich way. **2** fully, thoroughly.

Rich·mond 1 the state capital of Virginia, a port on the James River; pop. (2000) 197,790. **2** a city in southwestern BC, on Lulu Island just south of Vancouver; pop. (2001) 164,345. **3** (in full **Richmond-upon-Thames**) a residential borough of Greater London, situated on the Thames. □ **Rich·mond·ite** *noun* (in sense 2) [sense 2 after a farm called *Richmond View*, possibly after *Richmond*, a town in SE Australia]

Rich·mond Hill a town in S Ontario, just north of Toronto; pop. (2001) 132,030. □ **Rich·mond Hill·er** *noun* [prob. after *Richmond Hill* in Surrey, England]

Rich·ter ▶ 1 /ˈrɪktər/ **Bur·ton** (b.1931), US physicist, who shared the 1976 Nobel Prize for physics with Samuel Ting (b.1936) for their independent discoveries of the subatomic particle known as the psi-particle or J-particle. **2** /ˈrɪxtər/ **Jo·hann Paul Frie·drich**, see JEAN PAUL.

Rich·ter scale /ˈrɪktər/ *noun* **1** a scale for representing the strength of an earthquake, beginning at near 0 for the smallest earthquakes and increasing exponentially; the largest earthquakes recorded have not exceeded 9, but the scale is, in theory, open-ended. **2** a notional scale measuring the intensity of something. [C. F. *Richter*, US seismologist d.1985]

rich text format *noun* see RTF.

Richt·hof·en /ˈrɪxtˌhoːfən/ **Baron Man·fred von** (known as 'the Red Baron') (1892–1918), German aviator. He was the top German fighter

pilot of the First World War, downing 80 Allied aircraft between 1916 and 1918 before being shot down.

ricin /ˈraɪsɪn/ *noun* a toxic substance obtained from castor oil beans and causing gastroenteritis, jaundice, and heart failure. [modern Latin *ricinus communis* castor oil]

rick ● *noun* a stack of hay, straw, etc., built into a regular shape and usu. covered or thatched. ● *transitive verb* form into a rick or ricks. [Old English *hrēac*, of unknown origin]

rick·ets *noun* a disease of children characterized by softening of the bones (esp. the spine) and bow legs, caused by a deficiency of vitamin D. [17th c.: origin uncertain, but associated by medical writers with Greek *rhakhitis* RACHITIS]

rick·ett·sia /rɪˈketsiə/ *noun* (pl. **-siae** or **-sias**) a parasitic micro-organism of the genus *Rickettsia* causing typhus and other febrile diseases. □ **rick·ett·sial** *adjective* [modern Latin from H. T. *Ricketts*, US pathologist d.1910]

rick·ety *adjective* **1 a** insecure or shaky in construction; likely to collapse. **b** feeble. **2 a** suffering from rickets. **b** resembling or of the nature of rickets. □ **rick·et·i·ness** *noun* [RICKETS + -Y¹]

rick·ey *noun* (pl. **-eys**) a drink of lime juice, soda water, and usu. gin. [20th c.: prob. from the surname *Rickey*]

rick·rack *noun* (also **ric·rac**) a zigzag braided trimming for garments. [reduplication of RACK¹]

rick·shaw *noun* (also **rick·sha**) a light, two-wheeled, usu. hooded vehicle drawn by one or more persons. [abbreviation of *jinricksha, jinrikshaw* from Japanese *jinrikisha* from *jin* person + *riki* power + *sha* vehicle]

RICO /ˈriːkoʊ/ *abbreviation* (in the US) Racketeer Influenced and Corrupt Organizations Act.

rico·chet /ˈrɪkəˌʃeɪ/ ● *noun* the action of a projectile, esp. a shell or bullet, in rebounding off a surface. ● *intransitive verb* (**rico·cheted** /-ˌʃeɪd/; **rico·cheting** /-ˌʃeɪɪŋ/) rebound one or more times from a surface. [French, of unknown origin]

ri·cotta /rɪˈkɒtə/ *noun* a soft Italian cheese with a texture resembling that of fine cottage cheese, used esp. in pasta dishes and desserts. [Italian, = re-cooked, from Latin *recoquere* (as RE-, *coquere* cook)]

ric·rac *var. of* RICKRACK.

ric·tus *noun* **1** *Anat. & Zool.* the expanse or gape of a mouth or beak. **2** a fixed grimace or grin. □ **ric·tal** *adjective* [Latin, = open mouth, from *ringi rict-* to gape]

rid *transitive verb* (**rid·ding**; past and past participle **rid**) (foll. by *of*) make (a person or place) free of something unwanted. □ **be** (or **get**) **rid of** be freed or relieved of (something unwanted); dispose of. [Middle English, earlier = 'clear (land etc.)' from Old Norse *rythja*]

rid·dance *noun* the act of getting rid of something. *See also* GOOD RIDDANCE.

rid·den ● *verb* past participle of RIDE. ● *adjective* (in *combination*) infested or afflicted (*a rat-ridden cellar*).

rid·dle¹ ● *noun* **1** a question or statement testing ingenuity in divining its answer or meaning. **2** a puzzling fact, thing, or person. ● *verb* **1** *intransitive* speak in or propound riddles. **2** *transitive* solve or explain (a riddle). □ **rid·dler** *noun* [Old English *rǣdels, rǣdelse* opinion, riddle, related to READ¹]

rid·dle² ● *transitive verb* (usu. foll. by *with*) **1** make many holes in, esp. with gunshot. **2** (in *passive*) fill; spread through; permeate (*was riddled with errors*). **3** pass through a riddle. ● *noun* a coarse sieve. [Old English *hriddel*, earlier *hrīder*: compare *hrīdrian* sift]

rid·dle³ *noun* Cdn (Nfld) a short pliable wooden rod woven between horizontal rails in making fences (also *attributive*: *riddle fence*). [var. of earlier *raddle*, from Anglo-French *reidele* 'stout stick or pole', of obscure origin]

rid·dling *adjective* expressed in riddles; puzzling.

RIDE *noun* Cdn (Ont.) a program to reduce impaired driving, in which police stop vehicles randomly and check drivers for signs of intoxication, esp. during the holiday season (*got stopped by RIDE*; also *attributive: a RIDE checkpoint*). [acronym from Reduce Impaired Driving Everywhere]

ride ● *verb* (past **rode**; past participle **rid·den**) **1 a** *transitive* travel or be carried on (a bicycle, motorcycle, etc.) or esp. *N Amer.* in or on (a vehicle, bus, etc.). **b** *intransitive* (often foll. by *on, in*) travel or be conveyed (on or in a vehicle). **2 a** *transitive* sit on and control or be carried by (a horse etc.). **b** *intransitive* (often foll. by *on*) be carried (on a horse etc.). **3** *transitive* **a** traverse on horseback etc.; ride over or through or along (*ride 50 miles*; *rode the prairie*; *riding the rails*). **b** compete or take part in on horseback etc. (*rode a good race*). **4** *transitive* (of a rider) cause (a horse etc.)

---

t **top**   v **voice**   w **we**   z **zoo**   ʃ **she**   ʒ **vision**   θ **thin**   ð **this**   ŋ **ring**   x **loch**   tʃ **chip**   dʒ **jar**   (*see over for vowels*)

to move forward (*rode their horses at the fence*). **5 a** *intransitive* lie at anchor; float or appear to float buoyantly. **b** *transitive* be carried or supported by (*the ship rides the waves*). **c** *transitive* be animated, stimulated, or spurred on by circumstance etc. (*riding a boom; riding a wave of popularity*). **6** *transitive* give a ride to; cause to ride (*rode the child on his back*). **7** *transitive* yield to (a blow) so as to reduce its impact. **8** *transitive* (in *passive*; foll. by *by*, *with*) be oppressed or dominated by; be infested with (*was ridden with guilt*). **9** *intransitive* (of a thing normally level or even) project or overlap. **10** *transitive coarse slang* have sexual intercourse with. **11** *transitive N Amer.* annoy or seek to annoy. ● *noun* **1 a** an act or period of travel in a vehicle. **b** a period of riding on a horse, bicycle, person's back, etc. **c** a demonstration of (esp. horse) riding as entertainment (*musical ride*). **2** the quality of sensations when riding (*gives a bumpy ride*). **3** a roller coaster, merry-go-round, etc., ridden at an amusement park or fairground. **4** a means of transportation esp. at no cost (*do you need a ride?; still waiting for my ride*). **5** a path (esp. through woods) for riding on. □ **come** (or **go** etc.) **along for the ride** participate disinterestedly or just for fun. **let a thing ride** leave it alone; let it take its natural course. **ride again** reappear, esp. unexpectedly and reinvigorated. **ride down** overtake or trample on horseback. **ride for a fall** act recklessly risking defeat or failure. **ride herd on** *see* HERD. **ride high** be elated or successful. **ride on** be dependent on or conditioned by (*so much is riding on the outcome*). **ride out** come safely through; endure, bear (a storm etc. or a danger or difficulty). **ride roughshod over** *see* ROUGHSHOD. **ride shotgun** esp. *N Amer.* **1** travel as a guard in the seat next to the driver of a vehicle. **2** ride in the passenger seat of a vehicle. **3** act as a protector. **ride the pine** (or **bench**) *N Amer. Sport* (of an athlete) not participate, esp. because of poor performance; be benched. **ride the rods** *see* ROD. **ride to hounds** *see* HOUND. **ride up** (of a garment) work or move upwards out of its proper position (*the shirt rides up at the back when I bend over*). **take for a ride** *informal* hoax or deceive. □ **ride·able** *adjective* (also **rid·able**). [Old English *ridan*]

Ri·deau Canal /ˈriːdoː/ a canal in SE central Ontario, originally conceived in the 19th c. as a military supply route from Kingston to Ottawa. Completed in 1832, the canal is approximately 200 km in length and consists of a series of 47 locks. [see RIDEAU FALLS]

Ri·deau Falls a waterfall in E Ontario, 12 m high, situated at the junction of the Rideau and Ottawa rivers. [French, lit. 'curtain', with reference to their appearance]

Ri·deau Hall the official residence in Ottawa of the Governor General of Canada.

Ri·deau River a river in SE central Ontario, rising (originally) in Rideau Lake northeast of Kingston, and flowing northeastward to join the Ottawa River at Ottawa. It is now linked via a series of lakes to Lake Ontario (at Kingston). *See* RIDEAU CANAL. [see RIDEAU FALLS]

ride-off *noun* (in a riding competition) a round held to resolve a tie or determine qualifiers for a later stage.

ride-on *attributive adjective* (esp. of a lawn mower) on which one rides while operating it.

rider *noun* **1** a person who rides (a horse, bus, bicycle, etc.). **2 a** an additional clause amending or supplementing a document. **b** an addition or amendment to a bill before it is passed. **c** a condition, proviso, qualification, etc. **3** a piece in a machine etc. that surmounts or bridges or works on or over others. □ **rider·less** *adjective*

rider·ship *noun* esp. *N Amer.* the number of passengers using a particular form of mass transportation.

ridge ● *noun* **1** the line of the junction of two surfaces sloping upwards towards each other (*the ridge of a roof*). **2** a long narrow hilltop, mountain range, or watershed. **3** any narrow elevation across a surface. **4** *Meteorol.* an elongated region of high barometric pressure. **5** *Agriculture* a raised strip of arable land, usu. one of a set separated by furrows. ● *verb* **1** *transitive* mark with ridges. **2** *transitive & intransitive* gather into ridges. [Old English *hrycg* from Germanic]

ridged *adjective* with a surface marked by ridges.

ridge·line *noun* the line formed by the highest point of a ridge.

ridge·pole *noun* esp. *N Amer.* **1** the horizontal pole of a long tent. **2** a beam along the ridge of a roof.

ridge·top *noun N Amer.* the top or crest of a ridge.

Ridge·way part of the town of Fort Erie in S Ontario, the scene of a battle (2 June 1866) between invading Fenian Civil War veterans from the US and a group of Canadian volunteers. [because of its location along *Ridge Road*, marking the division of the flow of drainage water to the Niagara River and Lake Erie]

ridge·way *noun* esp. *Brit.* a road or track along a ridge.

ridi·cule ● *noun* derision or mockery. ● *transitive verb* make fun of; subject to ridicule; laugh at. [French from Latin *ridiculus* laughable, from *ridēre* laugh]

ri·dicu·lous /rɪˈdɪkjʊləs/ *adjective* **1** unreasonable, absurd. **2** deserving or inviting ridicule. **3** outrageous, astounding. □ **ri·dicu·lous·ly** *adverb* **ri·dicu·lous·ness** *noun*

rid·ing¹ *noun* **1** *in senses of* RIDE *verb*. **2** the practice or skill of riders or horses. **3** = RIDE *noun* 5.

rid·ing² *noun* **1** (in Canada) a district whose voters elect a representative member to a legislative body; a constituency or electoral district. **2** (in the UK) each of three former administrative divisions (**East Riding**, **North Riding**, **West Riding**) of Yorkshire. [Old English *thriding* (unrecorded) from Old Norse *thrithjungr* third part, from *thrithi* THIRD: *th*- was lost owing to the preceding -*t* or -*th* of *east* etc.]

riding association *noun Cdn* a unit of organization of a political party at the level of the riding, responsible for nominating a candidate for election and conducting the election campaign in the riding.

riding habit *noun see* HABIT 6b.

Riding Mountain (also **Manitoba Escarpment**) an escarpment in SW Manitoba, northwest of Winnipeg. It is part of a ridge that extends from N Dakota, through Manitoba and into Saskatchewan. [with reference to Aboriginal riding trails]

Riding Mountain National Park a park in SW Manitoba, northwest of Winnipeg. Established in 1929 to preserve the Manitoba Escarpment, it is an oasis of evergreen forests and rolling parklands in the midst of prairie farmland.

riding mower *noun N Amer.* a lawn mower on which one rides while operating it.

riding school *noun* an establishment teaching skills in horsemanship.

Rid·ley, Nicho·las (*c.*1500–55), English Protestant bishop and martyr. As bishop of Rochester (1547) and then of London (1550) he emerged as one of the leaders of the Reformation, opposing the Catholic policies of Mary I, for which he was eventually imprisoned (1553) and burned at the stake.

Rief·en·stahl /ˈriːfənˌʃtɒl/ **Leni** (full name Bertha Helene Amalie Riefenstahl) (1902–2003), German filmmaker and photographer. Her *Triumph of the Will* (1934) is a powerful depiction of the 1934 Nuremberg Nazi Party rallies, and *Olympia* (1938) is a two-part documentary of the 1936 Berlin Olympic Games.

Riel /riˈel/ **Louis** (1844–85), Canadian political leader. He headed the rebellion of the Metis at Red River Settlement (now in Manitoba) in 1869 to protest against the planned transfer of the territorial holdings of the Hudson's Bay Company to Canadian jurisdiction; forming a provisional government with himself at its head, he oversaw negotiations for acceptable terms for union with Canada, including the establishment of the province of Manitoba, and was executed for treason after leading the Northwest Rebellion (1884–5).

riel /ˈriəl/*noun* the basic monetary unit of Cambodia, equal to one hundred sen. [Khmer]

Riel Rebellion *noun Cdn* **1** = RED RIVER REBELLION. **2** = NORTHWEST REBELLION. **3** these rebellions collectively.

Rie·mann /ˈriːmən/ **(Georg Frie·drich) Bern·hard** (1826–66), German mathematician. He founded Riemannian geometry, which is of fundamental importance to both mathematics and physics; the *Riemann hypothesis*, about the complex numbers which are roots of a certain transcendental equation, remains one of the unsolved problems of mathematics. □ **Rie·mann·ian** *adjective*

Ries·ling /ˈriːzlɪŋ, -slɪŋ/ *noun* **1** a kind of dry white wine produced in Germany, Austria, and elsewhere. **2** the variety of grape from which this is produced. [German]

ri·fam·pin /rɪˈfampɪn/ *noun* (also esp. *Brit.* **ri·fam·pi·cin** /-ˈfampɪsɪn/) a reddish-brown crystalline antibiotic given orally to treat a range of diseases, esp. tuberculosis. [prob. ultimately from Italian *riformare* reform]

rife *predicative adjective* **1** of common occurrence; widespread (esp. of something undesirable). **2** (foll. by *with*) abounding in; teeming with (esp. something undesirable). □ **rife·ness** *noun* [Old English *rȳfe* prob. from Old Norse *rífr* acceptable, from *reifa* enrich, *reifr* cheerful]

riff ● *noun* **1** a short repeated phrase in rock, jazz, etc., often played over changing chords or harmonies or used as a background to a solo (*a guitar riff*). **2** *informal* any commentary, improvisation, etc. on a theme (*launched into a riff on old movies*). ● *intransitive verb* **1** play riffs. **2** *informal* (foll. by *on*) comment or expound. □ **riff·age** *noun* [20th c.: abbreviation of RIFFLE *noun*]

rif·fle ● *verb* **1** *transitive* **a** turn (pages) in quick succession. **b** shuffle (playing cards) esp. by flicking up and releasing the corners or sides of two piles of cards so that they intermingle and may be slid together to form a single pile. **2** *intransitive* (often foll. by *through*) leaf quickly (through pages etc.). **3** *transitive* (esp. of wind) disturb the smoothness of or cause ripples in or on; ruffle (*wind-riffled hair*). ● *noun* **1** the act or an instance of riffling. **2** *N Amer.* **a** a shallow part of a stream where the water flows brokenly. **b** a patch of waves or ripples on water. **3** a groove or slat set in a trough or sluice to catch gold particles. [perhaps var. of RUFFLE]

riff-raff *noun* (often prec. by *the*) rabble; disreputable or undesirable persons. [Middle English *riff and raff* from Old French *rif et raf*]

rifle[1] ● *noun* **1** a gun with a long rifled barrel, esp. one fired from shoulder level. **2** (in *pl.*) infantry armed with rifles. ● *transitive verb* **1** (esp. as **rifled** *adjective*) make spiral grooves in (a gun or its barrel or bore) to make a bullet spin. **2** shoot, throw, launch, etc. forcefully in a straight line. [Old French *rifler* graze, scratch, from Germanic]

rifle[2] *verb* **1** *intransitive* (foll. by *through*) search through. **2** *transitive* search and rob, esp. of all that can be found; ransack. **3** *transitive* carry off as booty. [Old French *rifler* 'graze, scratch, plunder' from Old Dutch *riffelen*]

rifle·man *noun* (*pl.* **-men**) a soldier armed with a rifle.

rifle range *noun* a place for rifle practice.

rif·ling *noun* the arrangement of grooves on the inside of a gun's barrel.

Rif Mountains (also **Er Rif**) a mountain range of N Morocco, running parallel to the Mediterranean for about 290 km (180 miles) eastward from Tangier. Rising to over 2 250 m (7,000 ft.), it forms a westward extension of the Atlas Mountains.

rift ● *noun* **1 a** a crack or split in an object. **b** an opening in a cloud etc. **2** a cleft or fissure in earth or rock. **3 a** a large fault bounding a rift valley. **b** = RIFT VALLEY. **4** a disagreement; a breach in friendly relations. ● *verb* **1** *transitive* tear or burst apart. **2** *intransitive* form fissures or clefts; split or move apart. [Middle English, of Scandinavian origin]

Rift Valley see GREAT RIFT VALLEY.

rift valley *noun* a steep-sided valley formed by subsidence of the earth's crust between nearly parallel faults.

rig ● *transitive verb* (**rigged**, **rig·ging**) **1 a** provide (a ship) with sails, rigging, etc. **b** prepare (a sailing ship) for sailing. **2** (often foll. by *out*, *up*) fit with clothes or other equipment. **3** (foll. by *up*) set up hastily, esp. by making do with what is available. **4** (often foll. by *to*) connect with ropes, wires, etc. **5** assemble and adjust the parts of (an aircraft etc.). **6** *Forestry* prepare (a spar tree) by attaching guy lines, skylines, and the mainline. **7** manage or conduct fraudulently; fix (*they rigged the election*). ● *noun* **1** the arrangement of masts, sails, rigging, etc. of a sailing ship. **2** equipment for a special purpose, e.g. a radio transmitter or fishing tackle; gear. **3** = OIL RIG, DRILLING RIG. **4** esp. *N Amer. & Austral.* a large vehicle, esp. a transport truck or tractor-trailer. **5** an outfit, uniform, or style of dress. □ **rigged** *adjective* (also in *combination*). [Middle English, perhaps of Scandinavian origin: compare Norwegian *rigga* 'bind or wrap up']

Riga /ˈriːɡə/ a port on the Baltic Sea, capital of Latvia; pop. (2000) 764,328.

riga·ma·role /ˈrɪɡəməˌroːl/ *N Amer.* var. of RIGMAROLE.

riga·toni /rɪɡəˈtoːni/ *noun* pasta in the form of short broad hollow fluted tubes. [Italian, from *rigato* past participle of *rigare* draw a line, make fluting, from *riga* a line]

Rigel /ˈraɪdʒəl/ a supergiant star, the brightest in the constellation Orion. [Arabic, lit. 'leg of the giant']

rig·ger *noun* **1** a person who rigs or who arranges rigging. **2** *Forestry* = HIGH RIGGER. **3** *Rowing* = OUTRIGGER 5a. **4** a ship rigged in a specified way. **5** a worker on an oil rig. **6** a person who manages an election etc. fraudulently.

rig·ging *noun* **1** a ship's spars, ropes, etc., supporting and controlling the sails. **2** an arrangement of ropes, wires, etc. in any structure or system, e.g. on an airship. **3** the lines, blocks, hooks, and other equipment used in yarding logs by means of cables.

rigging crew *noun* *Forestry* the work crew in charge of rigging trees.

rigging slinger *noun* a person supervising a rigging crew, responsible for choosing the logs to be yarded, disentangling rigging, etc.

right ● *adjective* **1** (of conduct etc.) just, morally or socially correct (*it is only right to tell you*; *I want to do the right thing*). **2** true, correct; not mistaken (*the right time*; *you were right about the weather*). **3** more or most

suitable, preferable, or helpful (*the right person for the job*; *along the right lines*; *doesn't know the right people*). **4** in a sound or normal condition; physically or mentally healthy; satisfactory (*the engine doesn't sound right*). **5 a** on or towards the side of the human body which corresponds to the position of east if one faces north. **b** on or towards that part of an object which is analogous to a person's right side or (with opposite sense) which is nearer to a spectator's right hand. **6** (of a side of a piece of paper, fabric, etc.) meant for display or use (*turn it right side up*). **7 a** formed by or with reference to a straight line or plane perpendicular to another straight line or plane. **b** (of a solid figure) having the ends or base at right angles with the axis. *See* RIGHT ANGLE. **8** of or relating to the political right. **9** esp. *Brit. dialect* real; properly so called (*made a right mess of it*; *a right royal welcome*). ● *noun* **1 a** that which is morally or socially correct or just; justice. **b** the just, good, equitable, or correct points or aspects of something (often in *pl.*: *the rights and wrongs of the case*). **2** (often foll. by *to*, or *to* + infin.) a justification or fair claim (*has no right to speak like that*). **3 a** a thing one may legally or morally claim; the state of being entitled to a privilege or immunity or authority to act (*a right of reply*; *human rights*). **b** (in *pl.*) a title or authority to perform, publish, film, or televise a particular work, event, etc. **c** (in *pl.*) a legal claim to possession or exploitation (*owns the mineral rights*). **4** the right-hand part or region or direction. **5 a** a street etc. on the right (*take the next right*). **b** a right turn (*make a right at the lights*). **6** *Boxing* **a** the right hand. **b** a blow with this. **7** (often **Right**) **a** a political group or section favouring conservatism (originally the more conservative section of a continental legislature, seated on the president's right). **b** such conservatives collectively. **8** = STAGE RIGHT. ● *transitive verb* **1** (often *reflexive*) restore to a proper or straight or vertical position. **2 a** correct (mistakes etc.); set in order. **b** avenge (a wrong or a wronged person); make reparation for or to. **c** vindicate, justify, rehabilitate. ● *adverb* **1** straight (*go right on in*). **2** immediately; without delay (*I'll be right back*; *do it right now*). **3 a** (foll. by *to*, *around*, *through*, etc.) all the way (*sank right to the bottom*; *ran right around the block*). **b** (foll. by *off*, *out*, etc.) completely (*came right off its hinges*; *am right out of butter*). **4** exactly, quite (*right in the middle*). **5** justly, properly, correctly, truly, satisfactorily (*did not act right*; *not holding it right*; *if I remember right*). **6** on or to the right side. **7** *archaic* very; to the full (*am right glad to hear it*; *dined right royally*). ● *interjection informal* **1** expressing agreement or assent. **2** *ironic* expressing scorn. □ **as right as rain** perfectly sound and healthy. **by right** (or **rights**) justly, in fairness, properly. **do right by** act dutifully towards (a person). **in one's own right** on account of one's own status, effort, etc.; independently of one's relationship with others. **in the right** having justice or truth on one's side. **in one's right mind** sane; competent to think and act. **of** (or **as of**) **right** having legal or moral etc. entitlement. **on the right side of 1** not violating (a law etc.). **2** in the favour of (a person etc.). **put** (or **set**) **right 1** restore to order, health, etc. **2** correct the mistaken impression etc. of (a person or thing). **put** (or **set**) **to rights** make correct or well ordered. **right and left** (or **right, left, and centre**) on all sides. **right away** (also **right off**) immediately. **right enough** *Cdn & Brit. informal* certainly, indeed, undeniably, sure enough. **right oh!** (or **ho!**) = RIGHTO. **right on** *informal* **1** an expression of strong approval or encouragement. **2** absolutely to the point (*the speech was right on*). **right you are!** *informal* an exclamation of assent. **too right** *informal* an expression of agreement. **within one's rights** not exceeding one's authority or entitlement. □ **right·able** *adjective* **right·er** *noun* **right·ish** *adjective* **right·ness** *noun* [Old English *riht* (adj.), *rihtan* (v.), *rihte* (adv.)]

right angle *noun* an angle of 90°, as formed by dividing a circle into equal quarters. □ **at right angles** (**to**) placed to form a right angle (with). □ **right-angled** *adjective*

right arm *noun* one's most reliable helper.

right ascension *noun* *Astronomy* longitude measured eastwards along the celestial equator from the point of its intersection with the ecliptic.

right bank *noun* the bank of a river on one's right when one is facing downstream.

right bower *noun* see BOWER[3].

right brain *noun* the right half of the cerebrum, controlling the left side of the body, in humans often associated with spatial perception and intuition.

right-centre *noun* (in full **right-centre field**) *Baseball* the part of the outfield between centre field and right field (*a fly to deep right-centre*).

right-click *intransitive verb* click the right-hand button of a computer mouse.

right·eous /ˈraɪtʃəs/ *adjective* (of a person or conduct) morally right; virtuous. □ **right·eous·ly** *adverb* **right·eous·ness** *noun* [Old English *rihtwīs* (as RIGHT *noun* + -WISE[1] or RIGHT *adjective* + WISE[2]), assimilated to *bounteous* etc.]

right field *noun Baseball* **1** the part of the outfield to the right of the batter as he or she faces the pitcher. **2** the position of the player who covers this area. □ **right fielder** *noun*

right-footed *adjective* **1** using the right foot by preference as more serviceable than the left. **2** (of a kick etc.) done or made with the right foot.

right·ful *adjective* **1 a** (of a person) having status etc. legitimately or justly (*the rightful owner*). **b** (of status, position, property, etc.) that one is entitled to (*has assumed its rightful place*). **2** (of an action etc.) equitable, fair. □ **right·ful·ly** *adverb* **right·ful·ness** *noun*

right hand *noun* **1** = RIGHT-HAND MAN. **2** the most important position next to a person (*stand at God's right hand*).

right-hand *adjective* **1** on or towards the right side of a person or thing (*right-hand corner*). **2** done with the right hand (*right-hand blow*). **3** (of a screw) = RIGHT-HANDED 4b.

right-handed ● *adjective* **1 a** using the right hand by preference as more serviceable than the left. **b** using a tool etc. by preference on one's right side (*right-handed batter*). **2** (of a tool, instrument, etc.) made to be used by right-handed people (*right-handed guitar*). **3** (of a blow) struck with the right hand. **4 a** turning to the right; towards the right. **b** (of a screw) advanced by turning to the right (clockwise). ● *adverb* with the right hand or to the right side (*plays right-handed; bats right-handed*). □ **right-handed·ly** *adverb* **right-handed·ness** *noun*

right-hander *noun* **1** a right-handed person. **2** a right-handed blow etc.

right-hand man *noun* an indispensable or chief assistant.

Right Honourable *adjective* **1** (in Canada) a title given for life to the Governor General, the prime minister, and the chief justice. Abbr.: **Rt. Hon. 2** (in the UK) a title given to certain high officials, e.g. privy councillors. Abbr.: **Rt. Hon.**

right·ist ● *adjective* professing or supporting the principles or policies of the right. ● *noun* a person or thing supporting or professing such principles or policies. □ **right·ism** *noun*

right·ly *adverb* justly, properly, correctly, justifiably.

right-minded *adjective* having sound views and principles.

right·most *adjective* furthest to the right.

righto *interjection* esp. *Brit. informal* expressing agreement or assent.

right-of-centre *adjective* (of political parties, voters, etc.) having somewhat rightist views, policies, etc.

right-of-way *noun* (*pl.* **rights-of-way**) **1** a right established by usage to pass over another's ground. **2** a path subject to such a right. **3** the right of one vehicle to proceed before another. **4** *N Amer.* a strip of land reserved for a road, railway, hydro lines, etc.

Right Reverend *noun* the title of an Anglican bishop.

right·sizing *noun* **1** the reducing of something in size or scope, esp. of a company (by firing workers, eliminating positions, etc.); downsizing. **2** the replacing of a larger computer with a smaller one or a network of smaller ones. □ **right·size** *transitive & intransitive verb*

right stuff *noun* (prec. by *the*) esp. *N Amer.* requisite talent, disposition, character, etc.

right-thinking *adjective* **1** = RIGHT-MINDED. **2** having views in accord with what might be expected.

right-to-life *adjective* = PRO-LIFE. □ **right-to-lifer** *noun*

right·ward ● *adverb* (also **right·wards**) towards the right. ● *adjective* going towards or facing the right.

right whale *noun* each of three baleen whales of the family Balaenidae, of Arctic and temperate waters, having long baleen plates and a deeply curved jaw, esp. the widespread *Balaena glacialis*.

right wing ● *noun* **1** the conservative or reactionary section of a political party or system. **2** *Hockey* **a** the forward position to the right of centre. **b** the player at this position. **3** the right side of an army. ● *adjective* (usu. **right-wing**) conservative or reactionary. □ **right winger** *noun*

righty (*pl.* **-ies**) ● *noun* **1** a right-handed person. **2** *Polit.* a right winger. ● *adjective* **1** right-handed. **2** rightist. ● *adverb* esp. *Baseball* with the right hand or to the right side (*bats righty*).

rigid *adjective* **1** not flexible; that cannot be bent (*a rigid frame*). **2** (of a person, conduct, etc.) inflexible, unbending, strict, harsh (*a rigid disciplinarian; rigid economy*). □ **rigid·ity** *noun* **rigid·ly** *adverb* [French *rigide* or Latin *rigidus* from *rigēre* be stiff]

rigid·ify *transitive & intransitive verb* (**-ifies**, **-ified**) make or become rigid.

rig·ma·role *noun* (also esp. *N Amer.* **riga·ma·role**) **1** a lengthy and

complicated procedure. **2 a** a rambling or meaningless account or tale. **b** such talk. [originally *ragman roll* = a catalogue, of unknown origin]

rig·or¹ *noun Med.* **1** a sudden feeling of cold with shivering accompanied by a rise in temperature, preceding a fever etc. **2** = RIGOR MORTIS. [Latin from *rigēre* be stiff]

rig·or² *var.* of RIGOUR.

rigor mor·tis *noun* stiffening of the body after death. [Latin, = stiffness of death]

rigor·ous *adjective* **1** characterized by or showing rigour; strict, severe. **2** strictly exact or accurate. **3** (of the weather) cold, severe. □ **rigor·ous·ly** *adverb*

rig·our *noun* (also **rigor**) **1 a** severity, strictness, harshness. **b** (in *pl.*) harsh measures or conditions. **c** (often in *pl.*) severity of weather or climate; extremity of cold. **2** logical exactitude. **3** strict enforcement of rules etc. (*the utmost rigour of the law*). **4** austerity of life; puritanical discipline. [Old French *rigour* from Latin *rigor* (as RIGOR¹)]

rig-out *informal* ● *noun* an outfit of clothes. ● *transitive verb* (**rig out**) (esp. as **rigged out** *adjective*) dress in an outfit etc. (*all rigged out*).

Rig-Veda /rɪgˈveɪdə, -ˈviːdə/ *noun* the oldest and principal of the Hindu Vedas (see VEDA). [Sanskrit *ṛigvēda* from *ṛic* praise + *vēda* VEDA]

Ri·je·ka /riːˈekə/ (called in Italian **Fiume**) a port on the Adriatic coast of Croatia; pop. (2001) 143,800.

rijst·tafel /ˈraɪstɒfəl/ *noun* an originally SE Asian meal consisting of a selection of different foods (such as eggs, meat, fish, fruit, curry, etc.) mixed with rice and served in separate dishes. [Dutch, from *rijst* rice + *tafel* table]

Rila Mountains /ˈriːlə/ a range of mountains in W Bulgaria, forming the westernmost extent of the Rhodope Mountains. It is the highest range in Bulgaria, rising to a height of 2 925 m (9,596 ft.) at Mount Musala.

rile *transitive verb* **1** *informal* (often foll. by *up*) anger, irritate. **2** *N Amer.* make (water) turbulent or muddy. [var. of ROIL]

Rilke /ˈrɪlkə/ **Rai·ner Maria** (pseudonym of René Karl Wilhelm Josef Maria Rilke) (1875–1926), Austrian poet, born in Bohemia. He is best known for the hymnic lyrics, the *Duino Elegies* and *Sonnets to Orpheus* (both 1923); in these he sought to define a poet's spiritual role in the face of transience and death.

rill *noun* **1** a small stream. **2** a shallow channel cut in the surface of soil or rocks by running water. **3** *var.* of RILLE. [Low German *ril*, *rille*]

rille /rɪl/ *noun* (also **rill**) *Astronomy* a cleft or narrow valley on the moon's surface. [German (as RILL)]

ril·lettes /riːˈjet/ *plural noun* a soft pâté of small pieces of shredded pork, poultry, etc., cooked for a long time in fat. [French]

rim ● *noun* **1 a** a raised edge or border. **b** a margin or verge, esp. of something circular. **2** the part of a pair of eyeglasses surrounding the lenses. **3** the outer edge of a wheel, on which the tire is fitted. **4** a boundary line (*the rim of the horizon*). ● *transitive verb* (**rimmed**, **rim·ming**) **1 a** provide with a rim. **b** be a rim for or to. **2** edge, border. □ **rim·less** *adjective* **rimmed** *adjective* (also in *combination*). [Old English *rima* edge: compare Old Norse *rimi* ridge (the only known cognate)]

Rim·baud /rãˈboː/ **(Jean Nicho·las) Ar·thur** (1854–91), French poet. In his collection of symbolist prose poems *Une Saison en enfer* (1873) and *Les Illuminations* (*c.*1872; published 1884), he explored the visionary possibilities of systematically 'disorienting the senses'; he stopped writing at about the age of 20 and spent the rest of his life travelling. (See also VERLAINE.)

rime¹ ● *noun* **1** frost, esp. formed from cloud or fog. **2** *literary* hoarfrost. ● *transitive verb* cover with rime. [Old English *hrīm*]

rime² *archaic var.* of RHYME.

rim·fire *attributive adjective* **1** designating ammunition having the primer around the edge of the base. **2** designating a rifle or gun designed to fire such ammunition.

Rim·ini /ˈrɪməni/ a port and resort on the Adriatic coast of NE Italy; pop. (2001) 128,301.

Rim·mon /ˈrɪmən/ *Bible* a deity worshipped in ancient Damascus.

Ri·mou·ski /riːˈmuːskiː, rɪˈmuːski/ a city in E Quebec, located on the south shore of the St. Lawrence, about 100 km northeast of Rivière-du-Loup; pop. (2001) 41,549. [ultimately from Mi'kmaq *animouski* place of the dog]

rim·rock *noun* esp. *N Amer.* an outcrop of resistant rock, esp. one forming a cliff at the edge of a plateau.

rim shot *noun* a drum stroke in which the stick strikes the rim and the head of the drum simultaneously.

Rimsky-Korsakov /ˌrɪmskiˈkɔːrsəˌkɒf/ **Niko·lai (Andre·evich)**

(1844–1908), Russian composer. He achieved fame with his orchestral suite *Scheherazade* (1888) and his many operas drawing on Russian and Slavic folk tales, notably *The Golden Cockerel* (1906–7).

rimy *adjective* (**rimi·er**, **rimi·est**) frosty; covered with frost.

rind ● *noun* **1** the tough outer layer or covering of fruit and vegetables, cheese, bacon, etc. **2** the bark of a tree or plant. ● *transitive verb* strip the bark from. □ **rind·ed** *adjective* (also in *combination*). **rind·less** *adjective* [Old English rind(e)]

rin·der·pest /ˈrɪndər‚pest/ *noun* a virulent infectious disease of ruminants (esp. cattle). [German from *Rinder* cattle + *Pest* PEST]

ring¹ ● *noun* **1** a circular band, usu. of precious metal, worn on a finger as an ornament or a token of marriage or betrothal. **2** a circular band of any material. **3** the rim of a cylindrical or circular object, or a line or band around it. **4** a mark or part having the form of a circular band (*had rings around his eyes*; *smoke rings*). **5** = GROWTH RING. **6 a** an enclosure for a circus performance, bullfighting, the showing of cattle, etc. **b** a roped enclosure for boxing or wrestling. **7 a** a group of people or things arranged in a circle. **b** such an arrangement. **8 a** a combination of traders, bookmakers, spies, politicians, etc. acting together usu. illicitly for the control of operations or profit. **b** a group of people engaged in a criminal activity (*drug trafficking ring*). **9** a circular or spiral course. **10** = GAS RING. **11** *Astronomy* **a** a thin band or disc of particles etc. around a planet. **b** a halo around the moon. **12** *Archaeology* a circular prehistoric earthwork usu. of a bank and ditch. **13** *Chem.* a group of atoms each bonded to two others in a closed sequence. **14** *Math.* a set of elements with two binary operations, addition and multiplication, the second being distributive over the first and associative. **15** (in *pl.*) a gymnastics event in which the gymnast holds on to two suspended rings. **16** a small ring, stud, or other ornament worn on the flesh, usu. by piercing (*nose ring*). ● *transitive verb* **1** make or draw a circle around. **2** (often foll. by *around*, *about*, *in*) encircle or hem in. **3** put a ring on (a bird etc.) or through the nose of (a pig, bull, etc.). **4** cut (fruit, vegetables, etc.) into rings. □ **run** (or **make**) **rings around** *informal* outclass or outwit (another person). □ **ringed** *adjective* (also in *combination*). **ring·less** *adjective* [Old English *hring* from Germanic]

ring² ● *verb* (past **rang**; past participle **rung**) **1** *intransitive* (often foll. by *out* etc.) give a clear resonant or vibrating sound of or as of a bell (*a shot rang out*; *the doorbell rang*). **2 a** *transitive* make (esp. a bell) ring. **b** *intransitive* call for service or attention by ringing a bell (*you rang, madam?*). **3 a** *intransitive* (of a telephone) emit a ring, buzz, beep, or other sound indicating an incoming call. **b** *transitive & intransitive* (often foll. by *up*) esp. *Brit.* call by telephone (*will ring you on Monday*; *did you ring?*). **4** *intransitive* (usu. foll. by *with*, *to*) (of a place) resound or be permeated with a sound (*the theatre rang with applause*). **5** *intransitive* (of the ears) be filled with a sensation of ringing. **6** *transitive* **a** sound (a peal etc.) on bells. **b** (of a bell) sound (the hour etc.). **7** *transitive* (foll. by *in*, *out*) usher in or out with bell-ringing (*ring in the May*; *rang out the old year*). **8** *intransitive* (of sentiments etc.) convey a specified impression (*words rang hollow*). ● *noun* **1** a ringing sound or tone. **2 a** the act of ringing a bell. **b** the sound caused by this. **3** *informal* a telephone call (*give me a ring*). **4** a specified feeling conveyed by an utterance (*had a melancholy ring*). **5** a set of esp. church bells. □ **ring back** *Brit.* make a return telephone call to (a person who has telephoned earlier). **ring a bell** *see* BELL¹. **ring the changes (on)** *see* CHANGE. **ring down** (or **up**) **the curtain 1** cause the curtain to be lowered (or raised). **2** (foll. by *on*) mark the end (or the beginning) of (an enterprise etc.). **ring in one's ears** (or **heart** etc.) linger in the memory. **ring off** end a telephone call by replacing the receiver; hang up. **ring off the hook** (of a telephone) ring incessantly. **ring true** (or **false**) convey an impression of truth (or falsehood). **ring up 1** record (an amount spent or earned) on or as on a cash register. **2** accomplish; record (a victory etc.). **3** *Brit.* call by telephone. □ **ringed** *adjective* (also in *combination*). **ring·er** *noun* **ring·ing** *adjective* **ring·ing·ly** *adverb* [Old English *hringan*]

ring·bark *transitive verb* cut a ring in the bark of (a tree) to kill it or retard its growth and thereby improve fruit production.

ring bearer *noun N Amer.* the person, usu. a young boy, who ceremoniously bears the rings at a wedding.

ring-billed gull *noun* a small grey N American gull, *Larus delawarensis*, with black wing tips and a black band across a yellow bill, commonly found scavenging in garbage dumps and fields.

ring binder *noun* a loose-leaf binder with ring-shaped clasps that can be opened to pass through holes in the paper.

ring·bolt *noun* a bolt with a ring attached for fitting a rope to etc.

ringed plover *noun* either of two small plovers, *Charadrius hiaticula* and *C. dubius*.

ringed seal *noun* an Arctic seal, *Phoca hispida*, with irregular ring-shaped markings.

ring·er *noun slang* **1 a** esp. *N Amer.* a fraudulent substitute, esp. in sports. **b** a person resembling another, esp. an imposter. **c** *N Amer.* a person who is highly proficient at a particular skill or sport and is brought in to supplement a team or group of people. **2** a person or thing that rings. □ **be a ringer** (or **dead ringer**) **for** resemble (a person) exactly. [RING² + -ER¹]

Ringer's solution *noun* a physiological saline solution, usu. containing, in addition to sodium chloride, salts of potassium and calcium. [S. *Ringer*, English physician (d.1910) who introduced it]

ring·ette *noun Cdn* a game resembling hockey, played (esp. by women and girls) on ice with a straight stick and a rubber ring.

ring fence ● *noun* **1** a fence completely enclosing a piece of land. **2** an effective barrier. ● (**ring-fence**) *transitive verb Brit.* **1** enclose with a ring fence. **2 a** guard securely. **b** *Business* guarantee that funds allocated for a particular purpose will not be spent on anything else.

ring finger *noun* the finger next to the little finger, esp. of the left hand, on which the wedding ring is usu. worn.

ring·git /ˈrɪŋɡɪt/ *noun* (*pl.* same or **ring·gits**) the basic monetary unit of Malaysia, equivalent to 100 cents.

ring·lead·er *noun* a leading instigator in an esp. illicit or illegal activity.

ring·let *noun* **1** a curly lock of hair, esp. a long one. **2** any of various butterflies of the genus *Coenonympha* with spots on the wings. □ **ring·let·ed** *adjective*

ring·master *noun* **1** the person directing a circus performance. **2** *informal* a leader or director.

ring mould *noun* a tube pan with smooth sides and a rounded bottom.

ring·neck *noun* any of various ring-necked birds, esp. the ring-necked pheasant, *Phasianus colchicus*, with a white ring around the neck.

ring-necked *adjective Zool.* having a band or bands of colour around the neck.

Ring of Fire *noun* a zone of high seismic and volcanic activity surrounding the Pacific Ocean.

ring pull *noun* a ring on a door, lid, etc. for pulling it open.

ring road *noun* a bypass encircling a town.

ring·side *noun* the area immediately beside a boxing ring, circus ring, or other centre of attention (often *attributive*: *a ringside seat*; *a ringside view*). □ **ring·sider** *noun*

ring·tail *noun* **1** a ring-tailed opossum, lemur, or phalanger. **2** a golden eagle up to its third year.

ring-tailed *adjective* **1** (of monkeys, lemurs, raccoons, etc.) having a tail ringed in alternate colours. **2** with the tail curled at the end.

ring tone *noun* a sound made by a cellphone when a call is received.

ring toss *noun N Amer.* a game in which rings are tossed onto an upright peg.

ring·worm *noun* any of various fungous infections of the skin causing circular inflamed patches.

rink *noun* **1** an area of natural or artificial ice for skating, playing hockey, curling, etc. **2** an area for roller skating. **3** a building containing either of these. **4** a team in curling. [Middle English (originally Scots), = jousting ground: perhaps originally from Old French *renc* RANK¹]

rink rat *noun see* RAT *noun* 5.

rink·side *N Amer.* ● *noun* the area adjacent to the ice at a rink (often *attributive*: *rinkside seats*). ● *adverb* along the edge of the ice at a rink (*sat rinkside*).

rinky-dink *adjective* esp. *N Amer. informal* second-rate, small-time, inferior, amateurish (*a rinky-dink production*). [origin unknown]

rinse ● *verb* **1** (often foll. by *out*) *transitive* wash with clean water, esp. to remove soap or detergent. **2** *transitive* apply liquid to. **3** *transitive* wash lightly. **4** (also foll. by *away*) **a** *transitive* remove (soap, impurities, etc.) by rinsing. **b** *intransitive* be removed by rinsing (*soap that rinses out easily*). ● *noun* **1** the act or an instance of rinsing (*give it a rinse*). **2** a dye for the temporary tinting of hair (*a blue rinse*). □ **rins·able** *adjective* **rins·er** *noun* [Old French *rincer*, *raincier*, of unknown origin]

rinse agent *noun* a liquid used in a dishwasher to increase the sheeting action of the rinse water, thus preventing spotting.

Rio de Ja·neiro /‚riːoʊ diː ʒəˈneroʊ/ **1** a state of E Brazil, on the Atlantic coast. **2** (also **Rio**) its capital; pop. (2000) 5,850,544. The chief port of Brazil, it was the country's capital from 1763 until 1960, when it was replaced by Brasilia.

---

t top　v voice　w we　z zoo　ʃ she　ʒ vision　θ thin　ð this　ŋ ring　x loch　tʃ chip　dʒ jar　　(*see over for vowels*)

Río de Oro /ˌriːoː dei ˈɔːroː/ an arid region on the Atlantic coast of NW Africa, forming the southern part of Western Sahara.

Rio Gran·de /ˌriːoː ˈgrand, ˈgrandi/ a river of N America which rises in the Rocky Mountains of SW Colorado and flows 3 030 km (1,880 miles) generally southeastward to the Gulf of Mexico, forming the US–Mexico frontier from El Paso to the sea.

Ri·oja /rɪˈoːhə/ noun wine produced in Rioja, a district in N Spain.

Rio Muni /ˌriːoː ˈmuːni/ the part of Equatorial Guinea that lies on the mainland of West Africa. Its chief town is Bata.

Rio Negro /ˌriːoː ˈneigroː, ˈneg-/ a river of S America, which rises as the Guainia in E Colombia and flows for about 2 255 km (1,400 miles) through NW Brazil before joining the Amazon near Manaus.

Rio·pelle /riːɒˈpel/ **Jean-Paul** (1923–2002), Canadian painter and sculptor, resident in Paris from 1948. One of the most internationally acclaimed painters of the 20th c., he was one of the founding members of the Automatistes, and participated in the 1946 Montreal exhibition that marked the first show in Canada by a group of Canadian abstract painters. His style is marked by his use of the palette knife to create mosaic-like surfaces of paint.

riot ● noun **1 a** an esp. violent disturbance of the peace by a crowd; an occurrence of serious public disorder. **b** (attributive) involved in suppressing riots (riot police; riot shield). **2** uncontrolled revelry; noisy behaviour. **3** (foll. by of) a lavish display or enjoyment (a riot of emotion; a riot of colour and sound). **4** informal a very amusing thing or person. ● intransitive verb make or engage in a riot. □ **run riot 1** throw off all restraint. **2** (of plants) grow or spread uncontrolled. □ **riot·er** noun [Old French riote, rioter, rihoter, of unknown origin]

Riot Act noun **1** an act passed by the British legislature in 1715 (repealed in 1967) making it a felony for an assembly of twelve or more people to refuse to disperse after having been ordered to do so and having been read a specified portion of the Act by lawful authority. **2** a proclamation in the Criminal Code of Canada which is read to order rioters to disperse. □ **read the riot act** put a firm stop to insubordination etc.; give a severe warning.

riot gear noun protective clothing, helmets, etc., worn by police or prison officers in situations of violence or potential violence.

riot·ous adjective **1** marked by or involving rioting. **2** characterized by wanton conduct. **3** uproarious, characterized by boisterous revelry. **4** wildly profuse. □ **riot·ous·ly** adverb **riot·ous·ness** noun

RIP abbreviation may he or she or they rest in peace. [Latin requiescat (pl. requiescant) in pace]

rip[1] ● verb (**ripped**, **rip·ping**) **1** transitive tear (a thing) quickly or forcibly away or apart (ripped out the lining; ripped the book up). **2** transitive **a** make (a hole etc.) by ripping. **b** make a long tear or cut in. **c** cut (wood) along the grain. **3** intransitive come violently apart; split. **4** intransitive rush along. **5** transitive informal criticize or castigate. **6** Computing use a program to copy (a sound sequence) on to a computer's hard drive. ● noun **1** a long tear or cut. **2** an act of ripping. **3** the sound of something being ripped. **4** informal an instance of fraud; a swindle, a rip-off (what a rip!). □ **let rip** informal **1** act or proceed without restraint. **2** speak violently. **3** not check the speed of or interfere with (a person or thing). **rip into** attack verbally. **rip off** informal **1 a** defraud (a person etc.). **b** steal (a thing). **2** rob (a store). [Middle English: origin unknown]

rip[2] noun a stretch of rough water in the sea or in a river, caused by the meeting of currents. [18th c.: perhaps related to RIP[1]]

ri·par·ian /rɪˈperiən/ adjective of or on a riverbank (riparian rights). [Latin riparius from ripa bank]

rip cord noun a cord for releasing a parachute from its pack.

rip current noun a strong surface current from the shore.

ripe adjective **1** (of grain, fruit, cheese, etc.) ready to be reaped or picked or eaten. **2** mature; fully developed (ripe in judgment; a ripe beauty). **3** (of a person's age) advanced. **4** (often foll. by for) fit or ready (when the time is ripe; land ripe for development). **5** (of the complexion etc.) red and full like ripe fruit. □ **ripe·ly** adverb **ripe·ness** noun [Old English rīpe from West Germanic]

rip·en transitive & intransitive verb make or become ripe.

rip-off noun informal **1** a fraud or swindle. **2** an act or instance of financial exploitation. **3** part of a song etc. seemingly copied from another.

ri·poste /rɪˈpɒst/ ● noun **1** a quick sharp reply or retort. **2** a quick return thrust in fencing. ● intransitive verb deliver a riposte. [French ri(s)poste, ri(s)poster from Italian risposta response]

ripped adjective **1** in senses of RIP[1]. **2** informal drunk, intoxicated; high.

rip·per noun **1** a person or thing that rips. **2** a murderer who rips the victims' bodies.

rip·ping adjective Brit. dated informal very enjoyable (a ripping good yarn). □ **rip·ping·ly** adverb

rip·ple ● noun **1** a ruffling of the water's surface; a small wave or series of waves. **2** a gentle lively sound that rises and falls, e.g. of laughter or applause. **3** a wavy appearance in hair, material, etc. **4** Electricity a slight variation in the strength of a current etc. **5** ice cream with added syrup giving a coloured rippled effect (raspberry ripple). **6** N Amer. a riffle in a stream. **7** (usu. attributive) designating potato chips having a corrugated appearance. ● verb **1 a** intransitive form ripples; flow in ripples. **b** transitive cause to do this. **2** intransitive show or sound like ripples. □ **rip·plet** noun **rip·ply** adjective [17th c.: origin unknown]

ripple effect noun the continuous and spreading results or consequences of an event or action.

ripple mark noun a ridge or ridged surface left on sand, mud, or rock by the action of water or wind.

rip-rap esp. N Amer. ● noun a collection of loose stone as a foundation for a breakwater, embankment, etc. ● transitive verb (**-rapped**, **-rapping**) fortify (the bank of a river etc.) with loose stone. [reduplication of RAP[1]]

rip-roaring adjective **1** wildly noisy or boisterous. **2** excellent, first-rate. □ **rip-roaring·ly** adverb

rip·saw noun a coarse saw for sawing wood along the grain.

rip·snort·er noun informal a person or thing of exceptionally remarkable strength, energy, quality, etc., e.g. a storm. □ **rip·snort·ing** adjective **rip·snort·ing·ly** adverb

rip·stop ● attributive adjective (of fabric, clothing, etc.) woven so that a tear will not spread. ● noun ripstop fabric.

rip·tide noun **1** = RIP CURRENT. **2** = RIP[2].

Rip Van Winkle noun **1** a person who has been asleep or unperceptive for a long time. **2** a person who has remained oblivious to fundamental social and political changes over an extended period. [hero of a story in Washington Irving's Sketch Book (1819–20), who fell asleep and awoke after 20 years to find the world completely changed]

RISC /rɪsk/ noun **1** a computer designed to perform a limited set of operations at high speed. **2** computing using this kind of computer. [acronym, from reduced instruction set computer (or computing)]

rise ● intransitive verb (past **rose**; past participle **risen**) **1** move from a lower position to a higher one; come or go up. **2** grow, project, expand, or incline upwards; become higher. **3** (of the sun, moon, or stars) appear above the horizon. **4 a** get up from lying or sitting or kneeling (rose to their feet). **b** formal get out of bed, esp. in the morning (she rose early). **5** recover a standing or vertical position; become erect (rose to my full height). **6** (of a meeting etc.) cease to sit for business; adjourn (Parliament rises next week; the court will rise). **7** reach a higher position or level or amount (the flood has risen; prices are rising). **8** develop greater intensity, strength, volume, or pitch (the colour rose in her cheeks; the wind is rising; their voices rose with excitement). **9** make progress; reach a higher social position (rose from the ranks). **10 a** come to the surface of liquid (bubbles rose from the bottom; waited for the fish to rise). **b** (of a person) react to provocation (rise to the bait). **11** become or be visible above the surroundings etc., stand prominently (mountains rose to our right). **12 a** (of buildings etc.) undergo construction from the foundations (office blocks were rising all around). **b** (of a tree etc.) grow to a (usu. specified) height. **13** come to life again (rise from the ashes; risen from the dead). **14** (of dough) swell by the action of yeast etc. **15** (often foll. by up) cease to be quiet or submissive; rebel (rise in arms). **16** originate; have as its source (the river rises in the mountains). **17** (of wind) start to blow. **18** (of a person's spirits) become cheerful or more optimistic. **19** (of a barometer) show a higher atmospheric pressure. **20** (of a horse) rear (rose on its hind legs). **21** (of a bump, blister, etc.) form. ● noun **1** an act or manner or amount of rising. **2** an upward slope or hill or movement (a rise in the road; the house stood on a rise; the rise and fall of the waves). **3** an increase in sound or pitch. **4 a** an increase in amount, extent, etc. (a rise in unemployment). **b** Brit. an increase in salary, wages, etc. **5** an increase in status or power. **6** social, commercial, or political advancement; upward progress. **7** the movement of fish to the surface. **8** origin. **9 a** the vertical height of a step, arch, incline, etc. **b** = RISER 2. □ **get a rise out of** informal provoke an emotional reaction from (a person), esp. by teasing. **on the rise** on the increase. **rise above 1** be superior to (petty feelings etc.). **2** show dignity or strength in the face of (difficulty, poor conditions, etc.). **rise and shine** (usu. as imperative) informal get out of bed; wake up. **rise in the world** attain a higher position in a hierarchy. **rise**

to develop powers equal to (an occasion). **rise with the sun** get up early in the morning. [Old English *rīsan* from Germanic]

ris·er *noun* **1** a person who rises esp. from bed (*an early riser*). **2 a** vertical section between the treads of a staircase. **3** a vertical pipe for the flow of liquid or gas. **4 a** a low platform on a stage, in a studio, etc. **b** one of a series of these arranged in step-like fashion, usu. for seating.

rishi /ˈrɪʃi/ *noun* (pl. **rishis**) a Hindu sage or saint. [Sanskrit *r̥ṣi*]

ris·ible /ˈrɪzɪbəl/ *adjective* **1** laughable, ludicrous. **2** inclined to laugh; capable of laughter. □ **risi·bil·ity** *noun* **ris·ibly** *adverb* [Late Latin *risibilis* from Latin *rīdēre ris-* laugh]

ris·ing ● *adjective* **1** going up; getting higher. **2** increasing (*rising costs*). **3** advancing to maturity or high standing (*the rising generation; a rising young lawyer*). **4** (of ground) sloping upwards. **●** *noun* **1** a revolt or insurrection. **2** a piece of rising ground; a hill, a mound.

risk ● *noun* **1** a chance or possibility of danger, loss, injury, or other adverse consequences (*a health risk; a risk of fire*). **2** a person or thing causing a risk or regarded in relation to risk (*is a poor risk*). **●** *transitive verb* **1** expose to risk. **2** accept the chance of (*could not risk getting wet*). **3** venture on. □ **at risk** exposed to danger. **at one's (own) risk** accepting responsibility, agreeing to make no claims. **at the risk of** with the possibility of (an adverse consequence). **put at risk** expose to danger. **risk one's neck** put one's own life in danger. **run a (or the) risk** (often foll. by *of*) expose oneself to danger or loss etc. **take (or run) a risk** chance the possibility of danger etc. [French *risque, risquer* from Italian *risco* danger, *riscare* run into danger]

risk-averse *adjective* averse to taking risks, esp. with investments.

risk capital *noun* = VENTURE CAPITAL.

risk factor *noun* a circumstance or condition increasing a specified risk.

risky *adjective* (**risk·i·er, risk·i·est**) **1** involving risk. **2** = RISQUÉ. □ **risk·i·ly** *adverb* **risk·i·ness** *noun*

Ri·sor·gi·mento /rɪˌsɔrdʒɪˈmɛntoː/ the movement for the unification and independence of Italy in the 19th c., inspired by Mazzini and led in the south by Garibaldi and in the north by Cavour, who secured the aid of France in expelling the Austrians from most of northern Italy by 1859. Subsequent voting resulted in the acceptance of Victor Emmanuel II as the first king of a united Italy in 1861. [Italian, = renewal, renaissance, resurrection]

ris·otto /rɪˈzɒtoː/ *noun* (pl. **-tos**) an Italian dish of esp. arborio rice cooked in broth with various other ingredients, as meat, onions, etc. [Italian, from *riso* rice]

ris·qué /rɪsˈkeɪ/ *adjective* slightly indecent or liable to shock slightly. [French, past participle of *risquer* RISK]

ris·sole /ˈrɪsoːl/ *noun* Brit. a compressed mixture of meat and spices, coated in bread crumbs and fried. [French from Old French *ruissole, roussole*, ultimately from Late Latin *russeolus* reddish, from Latin *russus* red]

rit. *abbreviation* Music ritardando.

Rit·alin /ˈrɪtəlɪn/ *noun* proprietary a drug which stimulates the central nervous system, used esp. to treat attention deficit disorder.

ri·tard /rɪˈtɑrd/ *noun* Music a ritardando passage in a musical composition. [abbreviation]

rit·ar·dando /ˌrɪtɑrˈdɒndoː/ *adverb, adjective & noun* Music (pl. **-dos** or **rit·ar·dandi** /-di/) = RALLENTANDO. [Italian]

Ritch·ie, John W. (1808–90), Canadian lawyer and politician, Father of Confederation. Appointed to the Nova Scotia legislative council as Solicitor General in 1864, he was a delegate to the London Conference. Appointed to the Senate in 1867, he was a judge of the Supreme Court of Nova Scotia 1873–82.

rite *noun* **1** a religious or solemn observance or act (*burial rites*). **2** an action or procedure required or usual in this. **3** a body of customary observances characteristic of a Church or a part of it (*the Latin rite*). [Old French *rit, rite* or Latin *ritus* (esp. religious) usage]

rite of passage *noun* (often in *pl.*) a ritual or event marking a stage of a person's advance through life, e.g. marriage.

rit·or·nello /ˌrɪtɔrˈnɛloː/ *noun* Music (pl. **-los** or **rit·or·nelli** /-li/) a short instrumental refrain, interlude, etc., in a vocal work. [Italian, diminutive of *ritorno* return]

rit·ual /ˈrɪtʃʊəl/ **●** *noun* **1** a prescribed order of performing rites. **2** a procedure regularly followed. **●** *adjective* of or done as a ritual or rites (*ritual dance*). □ **rit·ual·ize** *transitive & intransitive verb* (also esp. Brit. **-ise**). **rit·ual·iz·a·tion** *noun* (also esp. Brit. **-isation**). **rit·ual·ly** *adverb* [Latin *ritualis* as RITE]

rit·ual·ism *noun* the regular or excessive practice of ritual. □ **rit·ual·ist** *noun* **rit·ual·is·tic** *adjective* **rit·ual·is·tic·ally** *adverb*

ritz *noun* esp. ostentatious luxury. □ **put on the ritz** behave ostentatiously. [back-formation from RITZY]

ritzy *adjective* (**ritz·i·er, ritz·i·est**) *informal* **1** high-class, luxurious. **2** ostentatiously fashionable. □ **ritz·i·ness** *noun* [*Ritz*, the name of luxury hotels, from C. Ritz, Swiss hotel owner d.1918]

rival ● *noun* **1** a person, team, organization, etc. competing with another for the same objective. **2** a person or thing that equals another in quality etc. **3** (*attributive*) being a rival or rivals (*a rival firm*). **●** *transitive verb* (**ri·valled, ri·val·ling**; esp. US **ri·valed, ri·val·ing**) **1** be the rival of or comparable to. **2** seem or claim to be as good as. [Latin *rivalis*, originally = using the same stream, from *rivus* stream]

ri·valry *noun* (pl. **-ries**) the state or an instance of being rivals; competition. □ **ri·val·rous** *adjective*

rive /raiv/ *verb* (past **rived**; past participle **riven** /ˈrɪvən/) *archaic* or *literary* (usu. in *passive*) **1** *transitive* split or tear apart violently. **2 a** *transitive* split (wood or stone). **b** *intransitive* be split. [Old Norse *rífa*]

riv·er *noun* **1** a natural stream of water flowing in a channel to the ocean or a lake etc. (often *attributive: river basin; river valley*). **2** a copious flow (*a river of lava; rivers of blood*). **3** (*attributive*) (in the names of animals, plants, etc.) living in or associated with rivers. □ **sell down the river** *informal* betray or let down. **up the river** *informal* to or in prison. □ **riv·er·less** *adjective* [Anglo-French *river* river or riverbank, ultimately from Latin *riparius* from *ripa* bank]

Ri·vera /rɪˈvɛrɑ/ **Diego** (1886–1957), Mexican painter. His monumental frescoes of the 1920s and 1930s gave rise to a revival of fresco painting in Latin America and the US; his largest and most ambitious mural was a history of Mexico for the National Palace in Mexico City (1929–57).

river·bank *noun* the raised or sloping edge or border of a river.

river beauty *noun* a willow herb found along riverbanks, *Epilobium latifolium*, with pink to purple flowers.

river·bed *noun* the bed or channel in which a river flows.

river birch *noun* any of several N American birches found on riverbanks.

river blindness *noun* a tropical skin disease transmitted by the bite of blackflies and caused by the parasitic threadworm *Onchocerca volvulus*, the larvae of which can migrate into the eye and cause blindness.

river·boat *noun* a boat designed for use on rivers.

river bottom *noun* **1** the bottom of a river. **2** N Amer. low-lying alluvial land along the banks of a river.

river drive *noun* Cdn a log drive down a river. □ **river-drive** *transitive verb* **river driver** *noun*

river·front ● *noun* land adjacent to a river. **●** *adjective* situated or occurring beside a river.

river·ine /ˈrɪvəraɪn/ *adjective* of or on a river or riverbank; riparian.

river lot *noun* Cdn hist. a long narrow farm lot extending back from a river, esp. one along the St. Lawrence River or in the Red River Settlement.

river·man *noun* **1** a person who has worked on a river for many years and possesses a great deal of knowledge about its currents, fluctuations in level, etc. **2** hist. (in Canada) a voyageur.

river otter *noun* an otter of N America, *Lutra canadensis*, noted for its agile swimming and playful behaviour.

river rat *noun* N Amer. *informal* a person who spends much time on a river; a boatman.

river runner *noun* N Amer. a whitewater rafter. □ **river running** *noun*

River·side a city in S California, east of Los Angeles; pop. (2000) 255,166.

river·side *noun* the ground along a riverbank (often *attributive: riverside path*).

River·view a town in E New Brunswick, situated on the Petitcodiac River opposite Moncton; pop. (2001) 17,010.

river walk *noun* a walkway along a riverbank.

riv·et /ˈrɪvət/ **●** *noun* a nail or bolt for holding together metal plates etc., its headless end being beaten out or pressed down when in place. **●** *transitive verb* (**riv·et·ed, riv·et·ing**) **1 a** join or fasten with rivets. **b** beat out or press down the end of (a nail or bolt). **c** fix; make immovable. **2 a** (foll. by *on, upon*) direct intently (one's eyes or attention etc.). **b** (esp. as **riv·et·ing** *adjective*) engross (a person or the attention). □ **riv·et·er** *noun* [Old French from *river* clench, of unknown origin]

Ri·vi·era, the /ˌrɪviˈɛrə/ **1** part of the Mediterranean coastal region of S France and N Italy, extending from Cannes to La Spezia, famous for its scenic beauty, fertility, mild climate, and many fashionable and expensive resorts. **2** a similar coastal region elsewhere (*the Mexican Riviera*). [Italian, = seashore]

Ri·vière des Mille-Îles /riː,vjɛrdeimiːl'iːl/ a river in S Quebec, along the north shore of Île-Jésus. [French, lit. = 'river of the thousand islands']

Ri·vière des Prairies /riː,vjɛrdeipreˈriː/ a river in S Quebec, between Île-Jésus and the Island of Montreal. [apparently named after an early settler called *des Prairies*]

Ri·vière-du-Loup /riː,vjɛrduˈluː/ a town in E Quebec, on the south shore of the St. Lawrence, about 200 km northeast of Quebec City; pop. (2001) 17,772. [origin uncertain: possibly with reference to French *loups marins* harbour seals]

Ri·vière-Rouge /riː,vjɛrˈruːʒ/ a town in SW central Quebec, merging L'Annonciation, La Macaza, Marchand, and Sainte-Véronique; pop. (2001) 5,469.

rivu·let /ˈrɪvjʊlət/ *noun* **1** a small stream or brook. **2** a thin stream of liquid (*rivulets of sweat poured down her face*). [obsolete *riveret* from French, diminutive of *rivière* RIVER, perhaps after Italian *rivoletto* diminutive of *rivolo* diminutive of *rivo* from Latin *rivus* stream]

Riy·adh /riːˈɒd/ the capital of Saudi Arabia; pop. (est. 2002) 3,627,700.

riyal /ˈriːɒl, ˈraiɑl/ *noun* the chief monetary unit of Saudi Arabia, Qatar, and Yemen, equal to 100 halalah in Saudi Arabia, 100 dirhams in Qatar, and 100 fils in Yemen. [Persian from Arabic *riyal* from Spanish *real* ROYAL]

RK *noun* = RADIAL KERATOTOMY.

RM *abbreviation Cdn* **1** RURAL MUNICIPALITY. **2** REGIONAL MUNICIPALITY.

rm. *abbreviation* room.

r.m.s. *abbreviation Math.* root-mean-square.

RMT *abbreviation* Registered Massage Therapist.

RN *abbreviation* **1** Registered Nurse. **2** (in the UK) Royal Navy.

Rn *symbol Chem.* the element radon.

RNA *abbreviation* **1** ribonucleic acid. **2** = REGISTERED NURSING ASSISTANT.

RNWMP *abbreviation Cdn hist.* Royal North West Mounted Police (see NORTH WEST MOUNTED POLICE).

roach[1] *noun* (*pl.* same) **1** a small freshwater fish of Europe, esp. *Rutilus rutilus*, allied to the carp. **2** any of various freshwater fishes of N America. [Old French *roc(h)e*, of unknown origin]

roach[2] *noun* **1** *informal* a cockroach. **2** *slang* the butt of a marijuana cigarette. [abbreviation]

roach[3] *noun Naut.* **1 a** a curved part of a fore-and-aft sail extending beyond a straight line between its corners, esp. on the leech side. **b** the breadth of this. **2** an upward curve in the foot of a square sail. [18th c.: origin unknown]

roach clip *noun slang* a tweezer-like clip for holding the butt of a marijuana cigarette.

road ● *noun* **1** a path or way with a specially prepared surface, used by motor vehicles, cyclists, etc.; a street. **2 a** one's way or route (*our road took us through unexplored territory*). **b** a method or means of accomplishing something. **3** an underground passage in a mine. **4** *N Amer.* a railway. **5** (usu. in *pl.*) a partly sheltered piece of water near the shore in which ships can ride at anchor. ● *adjective N Amer. Sport* of or relating to a game or games played at an opponent's venue (*a poor road record*). □ **by road** using transport along roads. **get out of the** (or **my** etc.) **road** *informal* cease to obstruct a person. **go down the road** *Cdn* leave one's hometown in search of employment, adventure, etc., esp. leave the Maritimes for central or western Canada. **in the** (or **my** etc.) **road** *informal* obstructing a person or thing. **one for the road** *informal* a final (esp. alcoholic) drink before departure. **on the road 1** travelling, esp. as a sales representative or a performer (*the band has been on the road for two months*). **2** (of a car etc.) in working condition; able to be driven. **the road to** the way of getting to or achieving (*the road to Owen Sound; the road to ruin*). **take to the road** set out. □ **road·less** *adjective* [Old English *rād* from *ridan* RIDE]

road allowance *noun Cdn* **1** a strip of land retained by government authorities for the construction of a road. **2** an area at either side of a road which remains a public right-of-way.

road apple *noun slang* (usu. in *pl.*) **1** *N Amer.* a piece of horse manure. **2** *Cdn hist.* a frozen piece of horse manure used as a hockey puck, esp. on the Prairies.

road·bed *noun* **1** the foundation structure of a railway. **2** the material laid down to form a road. **3** *N Amer.* the part of a road on which vehicles travel.

road·block *noun* **1** a barrier or barricade on a road, esp. one set up by police or military personnel to stop and check vehicles. **2** any

obstruction (*roadblocks to the peace process*). **3** the action of blocking a road as a protest (*a roadblock in BC that lasted a week*).

road cut *noun* = ROCK CUT 1.

road·eo *noun* (*pl.* **-eos**) *N Amer.* a display or competition exhibiting the driving skills of esp. bus drivers or bicyclists. [from ROAD *noun* after RODEO]

road gang *noun N Amer.* **1** a construction crew building or repairing a road. **2** = CHAIN GANG.

road grader *noun* a vehicle with a heavy blade, used in road construction for levelling the ground.

road hockey *noun Cdn* (esp. *S Ont.*) = STREET HOCKEY.

road hog *noun informal* an inconsiderate (usu. obstructive) driver or cyclist.

road·hold·ing *noun* the capacity of a moving vehicle to remain stable when cornering at high speeds etc.

road·house *noun* **1** a restaurant, bar, or nightclub located on a major road usu. on the outskirts of a town or city. **2** a theatre designed for touring companies.

road·ie *noun informal* a person employed by a touring pop group etc. to set up and maintain equipment.

road·kill *noun* esp. *N Amer.* **1** the killing of an animal by a vehicle on a road. **2** an animal killed in this way. □ **road-killed** *adjective*

road manager *noun* the organizer and supervisor of a musicians' tour.

road map *noun* **1** a folding map showing the roads of a country or area, used esp. by motorists. **2** any plan or guide (*our road map to the future*).

road movie *noun* **1** a genre of dramatic film whose central motif is a motorcycle or car journey undertaken by the main characters to elude capture by authorities, for adventure, etc. **2** a film of this type.

road racing *noun* a competitive event of racing on foot or in cars, motorcycles, or bicycles over public roads, as distinct from racing on a closed track or drag strip. □ **road race** *noun* **road racer** *noun*

road rage *noun* anger caused by the stress and frustration of driving, esp. resulting in violent action.

road rash *noun N Amer. slang* skin abrasions and cuts caused by falling off a bicycle, motorcycle, etc.

road·run·ner *noun* a bird of Mexican and US deserts, *Geococcyx californianus*, related to the cuckoo, which flies poorly but runs fast.

road salt *noun* coarse salt used to melt ice on roads.

road show *noun* **1 a** a performance given by a group of touring entertainers, esp. a theatre company. **b** a company giving such performances. **2** a radio or television program done on location, esp. a series of programs each from a different venue. **3** a touring political or advertising campaign.

road·side *noun* the strip of land beside a road (often *attributive*: *a roadside stand*).

road sign *noun* a sign giving information or instructions to road users.

road·stead *noun* = ROAD 5. [ROAD + *stead* in obsolete sense 'place']

road·ster *noun* **1** an open two-seater car. **2** a horse or motorcycle for use on roads.

road test ● *noun* **1 a** a test of the performance of a vehicle on the road. **b** a test of any new product. **2** = DRIVING TEST. ● *transitive verb* (**road-test**) **1** test (a vehicle) on the road. **2** test (any new product). **3** perform a preliminary version of (a new song, play, etc.) before an audience to gauge reaction to it.

road to Damascus *noun* an experience of radical conversion (often *attributive*: *a road to Damascus moment*).

Road Town the capital of the British Virgin Islands, situated on the island of Tortola; pop. (est. 2002) 8,800.

road trip ● *noun* **1** *N Amer. Sport* a series of games played away from home. **2** any journey made by car, bicycle, bus, etc. ● *intransitive verb* (**road-trip**) go on a road trip.

road warrior *noun N Amer. informal* a person who travels a great deal on business.

road·way *noun* **1** a road. **2** the main or central portion of a road, esp. that part used by vehicles. **3** the part of a bridge or railway used for traffic.

road·weary *adjective* exhausted from travelling (*road-weary tourists*).

road·work *noun* **1** the construction or repair of roads, or other work involving digging up a road surface. **2** athletic exercise or training involving running on roads.

Consonants: b *but* d *dog* f *few* g *get* h *her* j *yes* k *cat* l *leg* m *man* n *no* p *pen* r *red* s *sit*

road·worthy *adjective* fit to be used on the road.
  □ **road·worthi·ness** *noun*

roam ● *verb* **1** *intransitive* ramble, wander. **2** *transitive* travel unsystematically over, through, or about. **3** *transitive* move from site to site on (the Internet); browse. **4** *intransitive* (of a cellphone user) move from one geographic area to another without losing phone service. ● *noun* an act of roaming; a ramble. □ **roam·er** *noun* [Middle English: origin unknown]

roan[1] ● *adjective* (of an animal, esp. a horse or cow) having a coat of which the prevailing colour is thickly interspersed with hairs of another colour, esp. bay or sorrel or chestnut mixed with white or grey. ● *noun* a roan animal. [Old French, of unknown origin]

roan[2] *noun* soft sheepskin leather used in bookbinding as a substitute for morocco. [perhaps from *Roan*, old name of ROUEN]

roar ● *noun* **1** a loud deep hoarse sound, as made by a lion, a loud engine, thunder, a person in pain or rage or excitement, etc. **2** a loud laugh. ● *verb* **1** *intransitive* **a** utter or make a roar. **b** utter loud laughter. **c** (of a horse) make a loud noise in breathing as a symptom of disease. **2** *intransitive* travel in a vehicle at high speed, esp. with the engine roaring. **3** *transitive* (often foll. by *out*) say, sing, or utter (words, an oath, etc.) in a loud tone. □ **roar·er** *noun* [Old English *rārian*, of imitative origin]

roar·ing *adjective* in senses of ROAR *verb*. □ **roaring drunk** *informal* very drunk and noisy. **roaring success** *informal* a great success. **roaring trade** (or **business**) *informal* very brisk trade or business.
  □ **roar·ing·ly** *adverb*

Roaring Forties *plural noun* stormy ocean tracts between latitudes 40° and 50° S.

roaring game *noun* the sport of curling. [from the sound the rocks make as they move along the ice]

Roaring Twenties *plural noun informal* the decade of the 1920s (with reference to its postwar buoyancy).

roast ● *verb* **1** *transitive* **a** cook (food, esp. meat) in an oven or by exposure to open heat. **b** heat (coffee beans) before grinding. **2** *transitive* heat (the ore of metal) in a furnace. **3** *transitive* criticize severely, denounce. **4** *transitive N Amer.* honour (a person) with a roast. **5** *intransitive* undergo roasting. ● *attributive adjective* (of meat or a potato, chestnut, etc.) roasted. ● *noun* **1 a** roast meat. **b** a dish of this. **c** a piece of meat for roasting. **2** the process of roasting. **3** *N Amer.* a party where roasted food is eaten (*invited to the pig roast*). **4** *N Amer.* a mock-serious ceremonial tribute at which friends of the guest of honour offer short speeches of praise and good-natured insult. □ **roast alive** subject to intense heat. **roast in hell** suffer damnation. [Old French *rost, rostir*, from Germanic]

roast·er *noun* **1** a person or thing that roasts. **2 a** an oven or dish for roasting food in. **b** an ore-roasting furnace. **c** a coffee-roasting apparatus. **3** something fit for roasting, e.g. a fowl, a potato, etc.

roast·ing ● *adjective* **1** very hot. **2** used for or fit for roasting (*roasting pan; roasting chicken*). ● *noun* **1** in senses of ROAST *verb*. **2** a severe criticism or denunciation.

rob *verb* (**robbed, rob·bing**) (often foll. by *of*) **1** *transitive* take unlawfully from, esp. by force or threat of force (*robbed the safe; robbed her of her jewels*). **2** *transitive* deprive of what is due or normal (*was robbed of my sleep*). **3** *intransitive* commit robbery. **4** *transitive informal* overcharge (a customer). □ **rob Peter to pay Paul** take away from one to give to another, discharge one debt by incurring another. [Old French *rob(b)er* from Germanic]

Ro·barts /ˈroːbɑrts/ **John Par·men·ter** (1917–82), Canadian politician, Conservative premier of Ontario 1961–71. As premier, he defended provincial rights and Canadian unity.

ro·ba·ta /roːˈbɑtɑ/ *noun* a type of charcoal grill used in Japanese cooking. [Japanese, lit. = 'open fireplace']

Robbe-Grillet /rɒbɡriːˈjei/ **Alain** (b.1922), French novelist, who established himself as a leading exponent of the *nouveau roman* in the 1950s; his works include the novels *The Erasers* (1953), *The Voyeur* (1955), and *Jealousy* (1957), and the collection of essays *Towards a New Novel* (1963).

rob·ber *noun* a person who commits robbery.

robber baron *noun* **1** *hist.* a plundering feudal lord. **2** a financial or industrial magnate who behaves with ruthless and irresponsible acquisitiveness.

rob·bery *noun* (*pl.* **-ies**) **1 a** the act or process of robbing, esp. with force or threat of force. **b** an instance of this. **2** excessive financial demand or cost (*set us back $50—it was sheer robbery*).

Rob·bia see DELLA ROBBIA.

Rob·bins, Jer·ome (born Jerome Rabinowitz) (1918–98), US dancer and choreographer, who choreographed a long series of successful musicals, including *The King and I* (1951), *West Side Story* (1957), and *Fiddler on the Roof* (1964), and, over the course of a long association with the New York City Ballet, a number of ballets, notably *Fancy Free* (1944), *Afternoon of a Faun* (1953), and *Dances at a Gathering* (1969).

robe ● *noun* **1** a long loose outer garment. **2** esp. *N Amer.* a dressing gown or bathrobe. **3** (often in *pl.*) a long outer garment worn as an indication of the wearer's rank, office, profession, etc.; a gown or vestment. **4** *N Amer.* a blanket or wrap of fur. ● *verb* **1** *transitive* clothe (a person) in a robe; dress. **2** *intransitive* put on one's robes or vestments. [Old French from Germanic (as ROB, original sense 'booty')]

Rob·ert I (known as Robert the Bruce) (1274–1329), king of Scotland 1306–29. He led the successful Scottish campaign against Edward II of England at Bannockburn (1314), and went on to re-establish Scotland as a separate kingdom.

Rob·ert II (1316–90), grandson of Robert the Bruce, king of Scotland 1371–90. He was steward of Scotland from 1326 to 1371, and the first of the Stuart line.

Rob·erts ▶ 1 Sir Charles George Doug·las (1860–1943), Canadian poet and writer. He is known esp. for his animal stories; he also published several volumes of poetry, including *Songs of the Common Day* (1893) and *The Iceberg and Other Poems* (1934). **2 Julia** (b.1967), US film actress. She received Oscar nominations for her work in *Steel Magnolias* (1989) and *Pretty Woman* (1990) before performing her Oscar-winning role in *Erin Brockovich* (2000), for which she was paid the highest sum ever commanded by an actress.

Rob·ert·son *noun Cdn proprietary* **1** a type of screw with a square notch on the head. **2** a type of screwdriver with a square tip designed to fit into a Robertson screw. [P. L. *Robertson*, Canadian businessman, d.1950]

Rob·ert the Bruce see ROBERT I.

Rober·val[1] /rɒbɛrˈval/ a town in NE central Quebec, situated on the west shore of Lac Saint-Jean; pop. (2001) 10,906. [ROBERVAL[2]]

Rober·val[2] /rɒbɛrˈval/ **Jean-François de La Rocque, Sieur de** (c.1500–1560), French colonial explorer. Appointed lieutenant general of Canada in 1541, he was put in charge of Jacques Cartier. Arriving in Canada in 1542, he and his 200 colonists occupied a settlement just abandoned by Cartier. The ensuing winter was too much for them, and the survivors returned to France the next spring, resulting in financial ruin for Roberval and a postponement of French attempts to colonize that part of N America.

Robe·son /ˈroːbsən/ **Paul (Bus·till)** (1898–1976), US singer, actor, and black activist. He was noted for his rich and resonant bass voice, and his singing of 'Ol' Man River' in Jerome Kern's musical *Show Boat* (1927) established his international reputation; as an actor, he was particularly identified with the title role of *Othello*.

Robes·pierre /ˈroːbzpjer/ **Maxi·mi·lien Fran·çois Marie Isi·dore de** (1758–94), French revolutionary. As leader of the radical Jacobins in the National Convention, he backed the execution of Louis XVI and implemented a successful purge of the moderate Girondins (both 1793); elected to the Committee of Public Safety and appointed president of the National Convention, he was later guillotined for his role in the Terror.

Robi·chaud /rɒbiˈʃoː/ **Louis Jo·seph** (b.1925), Canadian lawyer and politician, Liberal premier of New Brunswick 1960–70. The first Acadian premier of New Brunswick, he introduced a wide range of social reforms and passed an Official Languages Act.

rob·in *noun* **1** *N Amer.* a red-breasted thrush, *Turdus migratorius.* **2** (also **robin redbreast**) a small brown European bird, *Erithacus rubecula*, the adult of which has a red throat and breast. **3** a bird similar in appearance etc. to either of these. [Old French, familiar var. of the name *Robert*]

Robin Hood 1 a semi-legendary English medieval outlaw, associated with Sherwood Forest in Nottinghamshire, and reputed to have robbed the rich and helped the poor. **2** a person who acts illegally or unfavourably towards the rich for the benefit of the poor.

rob·inia /rəˈbɪniə/ *noun* any N American tree or shrub of the genus *Robinia*, e.g. a locust tree or false acacia. [modern Latin, from J. *Robin*, 17th-c. French gardener]

robin's egg blue ● *noun* a pale greenish-blue colour. ● *adjective* of this colour.

Rob·in·son ▶ 1 Ed·ward G. (born Emanuel Goldenberg) (1893–1973), Romanian-born US actor. He specialized in gangster films after playing Rico Bandello in *Little Caesar* (1930); his later film roles include the father in Arthur Miller's *All My Sons* (1948). **2 Jackie** (full name Jack Roosevelt Robinson) (1919–72), US baseball player, who was the first black player in the major leagues, playing as an infielder and outfielder for the Brooklyn Dodgers (1947–56). **3 Smokey** (born William Robinson) (b.1940), US singer and songwriter, who recorded with the Motown group The Miracles, and whose songs include 'The Tracks of my Tears' (1965) and 'The Tears of a Clown' (1970). **4 Sugar Ray** (born Walker Smith) (1920–89), US boxer. He was world welterweight champion (1946–51) and seven times middleweight champion (1951, twice; 1955; 1957; 1958–60).

Rob·lin ▶ 1 Duf·fer·in ('Duff') (b.1917), Canadian businessman and politician, Conservative premier of Manitoba 1958–67. His government upgraded highways, created parks, and built the floodway (nicknamed 'Duff's Ditch') around Winnipeg. **2** his grandfather, **Sir Rod·mond Palen** (1853–1937), Canadian businessman and politician, premier of Manitoba 1900–1915. His greatest achievement as premier was an agreement with the Canadian Northern railway to build a line to the Lakehead and leave rate controls in the hands of the province.

robo- *combining form* relating to robots or robotics. [see ROBOT]

ro·bot *noun* **1** a machine with a human appearance or functioning like a human. **2** a machine capable of carrying out a complex series of actions automatically. **3** a person who works mechanically and efficiently but insensitively. □ **ro·bot·ic** *adjective* **ro·bot·ic·ally** *adverb* **ro·bot·ize** *transitive verb* (also esp. *Brit.* **-ise**). **ro·bot·iz·a·tion** *noun* (also esp. *Brit.* **-isation**). [Czech (used in K. Čapek's play *R.U.R.* (*Rossum's Universal Robots*), 1920), from *robota* 'forced labour']

ro·bot·ics *plural noun* (usu. treated as *sing.*) the study of robots; the art or science of their design and operation. □ **ro·bot·icist** *noun*

Rob Roy (born Robert MacGregor) (1671–1734), Scottish outlaw. His adventures as a highland cattle thief and opponent of the government's agents on the eve of the Jacobite uprising of 1715 were popularized in Sir Walter Scott's novel *Rob Roy* (1817).

Robson, Mount a peak in the Rocky Mountains of eastern BC, situated near the border with Alberta, northwest of Jasper. Rising to a height of 3 954 m, it is the highest point in the Canadian Rockies. [prob. an alteration after C. *Robertson*, Hudson's Bay Co. officer d.1842]

ro·bust *adjective* (**ro·bust·er**, **ro·bust·est**) **1 a** (of a person, animal, or thing) strong and sturdy, esp. in physique or construction. **b** healthy, vigorous; not readily damaged or weakened (*a robust industry*). **2** (of exercise, discipline, etc.) vigorous, requiring strength. **3** (of intellect or mental attitude) straightforward, not given to nor confused by subtleties. **4** (of a statement, reply, etc.) bold, firm, unyielding. **5** (of wine etc.) rich and full-bodied. **6** (of a computer system) resistant to malfunctioning. □ **ro·bust·ly** *adverb* **ro·bust·ness** *noun* [French *robuste* or Latin *robustus* firm and hard, from *robus*, *robur* oak, strength]

ro·busta *noun* **1** coffee or coffee beans from a widely grown African species of coffee plant, *Coffea canephora* (formerly *robusta*). **2** the plant itself (*compare* ARABICA). [modern Latin, from Latin *robustus* 'robust']

ROC /rɒk/ *abbreviation Cdn* the parts of Canada outside the province of Quebec. [rest of Canada]

roc /rɒk/ *noun* a gigantic bird of Eastern legend. [Spanish *rocho*, ultimately from Arabic *ruk*]

ro·caille /rɒˈkaɪ/ *noun* **1** an 18th-c. style of ornamentation characterized by ornate rock and shell motifs. **2** a rococo style. [French from *roc* (as ROCK¹)]

roc·am·bole /ˈrɒkəmˌbəʊl/ *noun* an alliaceous plant with a garlic-like bulb that is sometimes used for seasoning. [French from German *Rockenbolle*]

Roch·dale /ˈrɒtʃdeɪl/ a town in N England, just northeast of Manchester; pop. (est. 1999) 202,164.

roche mou·ton·née /ˌrɒʃ muːtəˈneɪ/ *noun Geol.* (*pl.* **roches mou·ton·nées**) a small bare outcrop of rock shaped by glacial erosion. [French, = fleecy rock]

Ro·ches·ter¹ 1 a city in NW New York State, on Lake Ontario; pop. (2000) 219,773. **2** a town on the Medway estuary southeast of London, England; pop. (est. 2002) 24,100.

Ro·ches·ter², 2nd Earl of (title of John Wilmot) (1647–80), English poet and courtier. Notorious for his dissolute life at the court of Charles II, he wrote many sexually explicit love poems and, with his social and literary verse satires, is regarded as one of the first Augustans; his works include the *Satire against Mankind* (1675).

roch·et /ˈrɒtʃət/ *noun* a vestment resembling a surplice, used chiefly by bishops and abbots. [Old French, diminutive of a Germanic word related to Old High German *roch* 'coat']

rock¹ *noun* **1 a** the hard material of the earth's crust, exposed on the surface or underlying the soil. **b** a similar material on other planets.

2 *Geol.* any natural material, hard or soft, e.g. clay, consisting of one or more minerals. **3** a mass of rock projecting and forming a hill, cliff, reef, etc. **4** (**the Rock**) **a** *Cdn* the island of Newfoundland. **b** Gibraltar. **5** a large detached stone. **6** *N Amer.* a stone of any size. **7** a large polished circular stone with a handle on top, used in the game of curling. **8** a firm and dependable support or protection. **9** (usu. in *pl.*) a source of danger or destruction. **10** *Brit.* = ROCK CANDY. **11** *slang* a precious stone, esp. a diamond. **12** *slang* a solid form of cocaine. **13** (in *pl.*) *coarse slang* the testicles. □ **between a rock and a hard place** *N Amer.* in a dilemma. **get one's rocks off** *coarse slang* **1** achieve sexual satisfaction. **2** obtain enjoyment. **on the rocks** *informal* **1** (esp. of a marriage) in danger of breaking up. **2** (of a drink) served undiluted with ice cubes. □ **rock·like** *adjective* [Old French *ro(c)que*, *roche*, medieval Latin *rocca*, of unknown origin]

rock² ● *verb* **1** *transitive* move gently to and fro in or as if in a cradle; set or maintain such motion (*rock her to sleep*; *the ship was rocked by the waves*). **2** *intransitive* be or continue in such motion (*sat rocking in his chair*; *the ship was rocking on the waves*). **3 a** *intransitive* sway from side to side under some impact or stress; shake, oscillate, reel (*the house rocks*). **b** *transitive* cause to do this (*an earthquake rocked the house*). **4** *transitive* distress, perturb. **5** *intransitive* (often foll. by *out*) dance to or play rock music. **6** *intransitive* (of popular music) possess a strong beat, esp. in 2/4 or 4/4 time; exhibit the characteristics of rock music. **7** *intransitive slang* be cool or impressive (*the latest version really rocks*). ● *noun* **1** a rocking movement (*gave the chair a rock*). **2** a period of rocking (*had a rock in his chair*). **3** (often *attributive*) **a** = ROCK 'N' ROLL. **b** a form of popular music which evolved from rock 'n' roll and pop music, usu. characterized by a harsher sound. □ **rock the boat** *informal* disturb the equilibrium of a situation. [Old English *roccian*, prob. from Germanic]

rock·a·billy *noun* a type of popular music combining elements of rock 'n' roll and hillbilly music. [blend of *rock 'n' roll* and *hillbilly*]

rock and roll *var. of* ROCK 'N' ROLL.

rock bass *noun* a N American freshwater fish, *Ambloplites rupestris*, frequenting rocky shallows in weedy lakes and streams.

rock bed *noun* a base of rock or a rocky bottom.

rock-bottom ● *adjective* the very lowest (*rock-bottom prices*). ● *noun* (**rock bottom**) the very lowest level.

rock-bound *adjective* (of a coast) rocky and inaccessible.

rock·burst *noun* a sudden rupture or collapse of highly stressed rock in a mine.

rock cake *noun* esp. *Brit.* a small currant cake with a hard rough surface.

rock candy *noun N Amer.* a kind of hard candy usu. made in cylindrical peppermint-flavoured sticks.

Rock·cliffe (also **Rockcliffe Park**) a former village within the city of Ottawa, a wealthy enclave where the residences of ambassadors, etc. are located; pop. (2001) 2,028. [after *Rockcliff House*, a home purchased by T. C. Keefer, the village's engineer, in 1864]

rock climbing *noun* the sport of climbing rock faces, esp. with the aid of ropes etc. □ **rock climb** *noun & intransitive verb* **rock climber** *noun*

Rock Cornish *noun* (also **Rock Cornish hen**, **Rock Cornish game hen**) a compact, meaty chicken, a hybrid of Cornish and White Rock chickens, slaughtered at six weeks to provide a single-serving sized bird, usu. roasted.

rock cress *noun* = ARABIS.

rock crystal *noun* transparent colourless quartz usu. in hexagonal prisms.

rock cut *noun* **1** a sheer rock face along a highway or road, the result of blasting through a mountain or hill to create the highway or road. **2** a tunnel for cars, trains, etc. cut through a mountain or hill.

rock dove *noun* a wild dove, *Columba livia*, known when in captivity as the domestic pigeon.

Rocke·fel·ler /ˈrɒkəˌfelər/ **John Davi·son** (1839–1937), US industrialist and philanthropist. He established the Standard Oil Company (1870) and by the end of the decade exercised a virtual monopoly over oil refining in the US; after handing over his business interests to his son, John D(avison) Rockefeller Jr. (1874–1960), he devoted his private fortune to numerous philanthropic projects, such as the establishment of the Rockefeller Foundation (1913).

rock elm *noun* an elm of eastern N America, *Ulmus thomasii*, with extremely hard wood, formerly used to make piano frames.

rock·er *noun* **1** a person or thing that rocks. **2** a curved bar or similar support, on which something can rock. **3** a rocking chair. **4 a** (in the UK) a member of a group of young people, esp. in the 1960s, who liked to wear leather jackets, ride motorcycles, and listen to rock music. **b** a person who performs, dances to, or enjoys rock music. **c** a popular song that rocks; a rock song. **5** a skate with a highly curved blade. **6** = CRADLE *noun* 3. **7** a switch constructed on a pivot mechanism operating between the 'on' and 'off' positions. **8** any rocking device forming part of a mechanism. □ **off one's rocker** *slang* crazy.

rocker panel *noun* (in a motor vehicle) a panel forming part of the bodywork below the level of the doors.

rock·ery *noun* (*pl.* **-eries**) = ROCK GARDEN.

rock·et¹ ● *noun* **1** a cylindrical projectile that can be propelled to a great height or distance by combustion of its contents, used esp. as a firework or signal. **2** (in full **rocket engine** or **rocket motor**) an engine using a similar principle but not dependent on air intake for its operation. **3** a rocket-propelled spacecraft. **4** a weapon propelled by combustion, differing from a missile in not having a guidance system. **5** anything that moves very quickly, e.g. a train, ball, etc. (*hit a rocket to left field*). ● *verb* (**rock·et·ed, rock·et·ing**) **1** *transitive* bombard with rockets. **2** *intransitive* **a** move rapidly upwards or away. **b** increase rapidly (*prices rocketed*). **3** *transitive* propel (someone or something) at speed; send by or as by rocket. **4** *intransitive* (of a game bird) fly up almost vertically when flushed; fly fast and high overhead. [French *roquette* from Italian *rochetto* diminutive of *rocca* distaff, with reference to its cylindrical shape]

rock·et² *noun* **1** (also **sweet rocket**) any of various fast-growing plants of the mustard family. **2** = ARUGULA. [French *roquette* from Italian *rochetta, ruchetta* diminutive of *ruca* from Latin *eruca* downy-stemmed plant]

rocket·eer *noun* **1** a person who discharges rocket-propelled missiles. **2** a person who works with space rockets; a rocket enthusiast.

rocket launcher *noun* a device for launching a rocket-propelled weapon, esp. a tube set on the shoulder to launch rocket-propelled grenades against tanks etc.

rock·et·ry *noun* the science or practice of rocket propulsion.

rocket science *noun* **1** *jocular* something requiring a high level of skill or intellectual capability. **2** the science of rockets.

rocket scientist *noun* **1** a scientific expert in the field of rocketry. **2** *jocular* a person who is highly intelligent, esp. in scientific and mathematical matters.

rocket ship *noun* a spaceship powered by rockets.

rock face *noun* a vertical surface of natural rock.

rock·fall *noun* **1** a descent of loose rocks. **2** a mass of fallen rock.

rock·fish *noun* any of various fishes frequenting rocks or rocky bottoms, e.g. the striped bass.

rock flour *noun* finely powdered rock, esp. that formed as a result of glacial erosion.

Rock Forest a former town in S Quebec, now part of Sherbrooke; pop. (2001) 18,667. [the name of a residence in Ireland *c.*1870]

rock garden *noun* **1** a garden composed of large stones with plants growing between them. **2** an area in a river, on a ski slope, etc., covered with many rocks.

rock-hard *adjective* extremely hard, strong, or tough.

rock·hop·per *noun* a small penguin, *Eudyptes crestatus*, of the Antarctic and New Zealand, with a crest of feathers on the forehead.

rock·hound *noun* esp. *N Amer. informal* **1** a geologist. **2** an amateur collector or student of rocks and minerals. □ **rock·hound·ing** *noun*

Rockies, the = ROCKY MOUNTAINS.

rocking chair *noun* a chair mounted on rockers or springs for gently rocking in.

Rock·ing·ham /ˈrɒkɪŋəm/ **2nd Marquess of** (title of Charles Watson-Wentworth) (1730–82), English Whig politician, prime minister 1765–6 and 1782. He led the political faction known as the Rockingham Whigs, who opposed Britain's war against its American colonists and argued for financial reforms.

rocking horse *noun* a wooden or plastic horse mounted on rockers or springs for a child to rock on.

Rock·land a former town in E Ontario, situated on the Ottawa River, northeast of Ottawa, now part of the city of Clarence-Rockland; pop. (2001) 8,517.

rock·ling *noun* any of various small marine fish of the cod family, esp. of the genera *Ciliata* and *Rhinonemus*, found in pools among rocks.

rock lobster *noun* = SPINY LOBSTER.

rock maple *noun* **1** the sugar maple, *Acer saccharum*. **2** the wood of this tree.

Rock·ne /ˈrɒkni/ **Knute (Ken·neth)** (1888–1931), Norwegian-born US

football coach. He came to national prominence as the football coach at the University of Notre Dame, Indiana (1918–31), and introduced the forward pass and other innovations.

rock 'n' roll (also **rock and roll**; **rock & roll**) ● *noun* a type of popular music originating in the 1950s, characterized by a heavy beat and simple melodies, often with a blues element. ● *adjective informal* exciting, energetic (*a rock 'n' roll performance*). ● *intransitive verb informal* get down to business; make progress. □ **rock 'n' roll·er** *noun*

rock plant *noun* any plant growing on or among rocks.

rock pool *noun* a pool of water among rocks.

rock ptarmigan *noun* a ptarmigan, *Lagopus mutus*, found in extreme northern regions, distinguished by its black tail feathers in winter.

rock python *noun* any large snake of the family Boidae, esp. the African python *Python sebae*.

rock rabbit *noun* *N Amer.* = PIKA.

rock-ribbed *adjective* **1** having ribs of rock. **2** resolute; uncompromising, esp. in political allegiance.

rock rose *noun* any plant of the genus *Cistus, Helianthemum*, etc., with roselike flowers.

rock salt *noun* common salt as a solid mineral.

rock slide *noun* **1** the sliding down of a mass of rock from a mountain, cliff, etc. **2** the mass of rock fragments which has so fallen.

rock-solid *adjective* very solid or firm.

rock-steady ● *adjective* unlikely to collapse, be changed, etc.; rock-solid. ● *noun* (**rock steady**) a style of popular music originating in Jamaica, characterized by a slow tempo and accentuated offbeat.

rocku·men·tary /rɒkjuˈmentəri/ *noun* (*pl.* **-ies**) a documentary about rock music and musicians. [ROCK² + DOCUMENTARY]

rock·weed *noun* any of various seaweeds growing on tide-washed rocks.

Rock·well, Nor·man (1894–1978), US illustrator, best known for his cover illustrations for *The Saturday Evening Post* magazine; these portrayed a sentimentalized, nostalgic view of US life. □ **Rock·well·ian** *adjective*

rock·wool *noun* a wool-like substance made from inorganic material, used esp. for insulation etc.

rocky¹ *adjective* (**rock·i·er, rock·i·est**) **1** of or like rock. **2** full of or abounding in rock or rocks (*a rocky shore*). □ **rock·i·ness** *noun*

rocky² *adjective* (**rock·i·er, rock·i·est**) *informal* **1** fraught with difficulties, disagreements, etc. (*the marriage got off to a rocky start*). **2** unsteady, tottering. **3** relating to or characteristic of rock music. □ **rock·i·ly** *adverb* **rock·i·ness** *noun*

Rocky Mountain goat *noun* see MOUNTAIN GOAT 1.

Rocky Mountain House a town in central Alberta, situated on the North Saskatchewan River, west of Red Deer; pop. (2001) 6,208. Nearby is a historic site by the same name, commemorating several trading posts built by the North West and the Hudson's Bay companies. The area was also home to map-maker and explorer David Thompson.

Rocky Mountains (also **the Rockies**) a major mountain system of N America, the easternmost range of the Western Cordillera, extending from the US–Mexico border to the Yukon Territory of N Canada. The highest peak is Mount Elbert in central Colorado, at 4 399 m (14,431 ft.).

Rocky Mountain spotted fever *noun* see SPOTTED FEVER 3.

rocky road *noun* **1** (*attributive*) *N Amer.* designating a mixture of chocolate chips, marshmallow, and nuts used in ice cream or as a topping for brownies etc. **2** a course of action filled with difficulties, obstacles, etc.

ro·coco /rəˈkoːkoː/ ● *adjective* **1** of a late baroque style of decoration prevalent in 18th-c. continental Europe, with asymmetrical patterns involving scroll-work, shell motifs, etc. **2** (of literature, music, architecture, and the decorative arts) highly ornamented, florid. ● *noun* the rococo style. [French, jocular alteration of ROCAILLE]

rod *noun* **1** a slender straight bar esp. of wood or metal. **2** a symbol of office. **3 a** a stick or bundle of twigs used in caning or flogging. **b** (prec. by *the*) the use of this. **4 a** = FISHING ROD. **b** an angler using a rod. **5 a** a slender straight round stick growing as a shoot on a tree. **b** this when cut. **6** (as a measure) a perch or square perch (see PERCH¹ 3). **7** *N Amer. slang* = HOT ROD *noun*. **8** *US slang* a pistol or revolver. **9** = CURTAIN ROD. **10** *Anat.* any of numerous rod-shaped structures in the eye, detecting dim light. **11** *N Amer.* the metal rod connecting the drawbars of a railway car or truck. **12** a metal shaft in an internal combustion engine etc. (*piston rod*). **13** a long slender piece of fuel for a nuclear reactor. □ **ride the rods** *N Amer. hist. informal* ride surreptitiously and without paying on a freight train. □ **rod·less** *adjective* **rod-like** *adjective* [Old English *rodd*, prob. related to Old Norse *rudda* club]

Rod·den·berry, Gene (full name Eugene Wesley Roddenberry) (1921–91), US television producer and scriptwriter, who created the TV science fiction drama series *Star Trek*, first broadcast 1966–9; he later worked on feature films and launched a successful follow-up series, *Star Trek: The Next Generation*, in 1987.

rode[1] *past of* RIDE.

rode[2] *noun N Amer.* a rope securing an anchor or net. [origin unknown]

ro·dent ● *noun* any mammal of the order Rodentia with strong incisors and no canine teeth, e.g. rat, mouse, squirrel, beaver, porcupine. ● *adjective* **1** of the order Rodentia. **2** gnawing (esp. *Med.* of slow-growing ulcers). □ **ro·den·tial** *adjective* **rodent-like** *adjective* [Latin *rodere ros-* gnaw]

ro·den·ti·cide *noun* a poison used to kill rodents.

rodeo /ˈroːdioː/ ● *noun* (*pl.* **rodeos**) **1** a display or competition exhibiting the skills of riding broncos, roping cattle, wrestling steers, etc. **2** a similar (usu. competitive) exhibition of other skills, e.g. motorcycle riding, cycling, etc. **3** a roundup of cattle on a ranch for branding etc. ● *intransitive verb* (**rodeoed, rodeo·ing**) compete in a rodeo. [Spanish from *rodear* go round, ultimately from Latin *rotare* ROTATE] ¶ Agnes de Mille's ballet *Rodeo* and the music for it by Aaron Copland are pronounced /roːˈdeioː/.

Rodg·ers, Rich·ard (Charles) (1902–79), US composer. He collaborated with librettist Lorenz Hart on musicals such as *On Your Toes* (1936), and with Oscar Hammerstein II on a further succession of popular musicals, including *Oklahoma!* (1943), *Carousel* (1945), *South Pacific* (1949), and *The Sound of Music* (1959).

Rodin /roˈdã/ **(René Fran·çois) Au·guste** (1840–1917), French sculptor. His naturalistic depiction of the human form made him controversial; his works include *The Age of Bronze* (1875–6) and *The Gate of Hell* (unfinished), which inspired such independent statues as *The Thinker* (1880) and *The Kiss* (1886).

rod·man *noun* (*pl.* **-men**) *N Amer.* a surveyor's assistant who holds the levelling rod.

rod·ney *noun Cdn* (*Nfld*) a small fishing boat or punt. [origin unknown]

rodo·mon·tade /ˌrɒdəmənˈteid, -tad/ ● *noun* **1** boastful or bragging talk or behaviour. **2** an instance of this. ● *adjective* boastful or bragging. [French from obsolete Italian *rodomontada* from French *rodomont* & Italian *rodomonte* from the name of a boastful character in the *Orlando* epics]

Rod·rigo /ˌrɒdˈriːgoː/ **Joa·quín** (1901–99), Spanish composer, most noted for his works for guitar *Concierto de Aranjuez* (1939) and *Fantasía para un Gentilhombre* (1954).

Roe, Sir (Edwin) Al·liott Ver·don (1877–1958), English engineer and aircraft designer. He founded two aircraft companies, the A.V. Roe Company (Avro) (founded 1910) and the Saunders-Roe Company (1928). The former went on to build some of the world's most successful aircraft, particularly the Lancaster bomber used in the Second World War and the delta-winged Vulcan bomber in use during the Cold War period. A Canadian branch founded in 1945 built the Avro Arrow, an advanced supersonic interceptor cancelled by the Canadian government with much controversy in 1959.

ROE *abbreviation* return on equity.

roe[1] *noun* **1** (also **hard roe**) the mass of eggs in a female fish's ovary. **2** (also **soft roe**) the milt of a male fish. [Middle English *row(e)*, *rough*, from Middle Low German, Middle Dutch *roge(n)*, Old High German *rogo, rogan*, Old Norse *hrogn*]

roe[2] *noun* (*pl.* same or **roes**) (also **roe-deer**) a small European and Asian deer, *Capreolus capreolus*. [Old English *rā(ha)*]

roe·buck *noun* a male roe.

Roent·gen /ˈrentɡən, ˈrʌnt-, -jən/ **Wil·helm Kon·rad** (also **Rönt·gen**) (1845–1923), German physicist, who was awarded the 1901 Nobel Prize for physics for his discovery of X-rays.

roent·gen /ˈrɒntɡən, ˈrʌnt-/ *noun* (also **rönt·gen**) a unit of ionizing radiation, the amount producing one electrostatic unit of positive or negative ionic charge in one cubic centimetre of air under standard conditions. Symbol: **R**. [ROENTGEN]

roent·gen·og·raphy /ˌrʌntɡəˈnɒɡrəfi/ *noun* photography using X-rays. □ **roent·geno·graph·ic** /-ˈɡrafɪk/ *adjective*

roentgen rays *plural noun hist.* X-rays.

Roeth·ke /ˈretkə/ **Theo·dore** (1908–63), US poet, whose lyrics are collected in volumes such as *Words for the Wind* (1958), *I Am! Says the Lamb* (1961), and *The Far Field* (1964).

rogan josh /ˌroːɡən ˈdʒoːʃ/ *noun* an Indian dish of curried meat, typically lamb, in a rich tomato-based sauce.

ro·ga·tion /roˈɡeiʃən/ *noun* (usu. in *pl.*) *Christianity* a solemn supplication consisting of the litany of the saints chanted on the three days before Ascension Day. [Latin *rogatio* from *rogare* ask]

roger ● *interjection* **1** your message has been received and understood (used in radio communication etc.). **2** *slang* all right; okay. ● *verb* esp. *Brit. coarse slang* **1** *intransitive* have sexual intercourse. **2** *transitive* have sexual intercourse with (a woman). [the name *Roger*, code for *R*; the verb is from an obsolete sense, 'penis', of the noun]

Rogers ▸ 1 Al·bert Bow·man (1829–89), American-born engineer and railway surveyor. Hired by the CPR in 1881 to locate a route through the western mountains, he explored the Kicking Horse Pass and discovered the Rogers Pass, laying out the railway's route through both passes. **2 Gin·ger** (born Virginia Katherine McMath) (1911–95), US actress and dancer, best known for her dancing partnership with Fred Astaire in film musicals such as *Top Hat* (1935), *Swing Time* (1936), and *Shall We Dance?* (1937); her solo acting career included the film *Kitty Foyle* (1940), for which she won an Oscar. **3 Sir Rich·ard (George)** (b.1933), Italian-born English architect. A leading exponent of high-tech architecture, he gained international recognition for the Pompidou Centre in Paris (1971–7), which he co-designed with the Italian architect Renzo Piano (b.1937), featuring ducts and pipes on the outside of the steel and glass building. **4 Stan** (1949–83), Canadian singer and songwriter. His work, mostly folk songs with a distinctive Canadian style, includes *Fogarty's Cove* and *Between the Breaks*. **5 Will** (full name William Penn Adair Rogers) (1879–1935), US humorist, actor, and journalist, who was noted as a homespun philosopher and incisive commentator on society and politics.

Rogers Pass a pass (1 327 m) through the Selkirk Mountains of SE central BC, situated northeast of Revelstoke. [A. B. ROGERS].

Roget /ˈroːʒei/ **Peter Mark** (1779–1869), English scholar. His *Roget's Thesaurus of English Words and Phrases* (1852) offered an innovative classification of words according to underlying concept or meaning.

rogue /roːɡ/ ● *noun* **1** a dishonest or unprincipled person. **2** *jocular* a mischievous person, esp. a child. **3** (usu. *attributive*) **a** a wild animal driven away or living apart from the herd and of fierce temper (*rogue elephant*). **b** a stray, irresponsible, or undisciplined person or thing (*rogue trader*). **4** an inferior or defective specimen among many acceptable ones. ● *transitive verb* remove inferior or defective plants or seedlings from (a crop). [16th-c. cant word: origin unknown]

roguery /ˈroːɡəri/ *noun* (*pl.* **-ies**) conduct or an action characteristic of rogues.

rogues' gallery *noun* **1** a collection of photographs of known criminals etc., used for identification of suspects. **2** any collection of people notable for a certain shared quality or characteristic, esp. a disreputable one.

rogue state *noun* (also **rogue nation, rogue regime**) a national government that refuses to accept the norms of the international community as expressed in international treaties, esp. by refusing to accept international controls over the control, development, and proliferation of nuclear weapons, or by supporting international terrorism from their territory.

roguish /ˈroːɡɪʃ/ *adjective* **1** playfully mischievous. **2** characteristic of rogues. □ **roguish·ly** *adverb* **roguish·ness** *noun*

Ro·hyp·nol /roːˈhɪpnɒl/ *noun proprietary* a powerful sedative drug of the benzodiazepine class, notorious for its use as a date-rape drug until reformulated to turn blue when dissolved in a drink. [origin uncertain; prob. from *ro-* (perhaps from the name of the manufacturer, Hoffman-La *Roche*) + HYPNO- + -OL]

ROI *abbreviation* return on investment.

'roid *noun slang* an anabolic steroid, when taken for its muscle-building properties by an athlete. [abbreviation of STEROID]

'roid rage *noun slang* an outburst of heightened aggression manifested as a side effect of anabolic steroid use.

roil *verb* **1** *transitive* make (a liquid) turbid by agitating it. **2** *transitive US* = RILE 1. **3** *intransitive* move in a confused or turbulent manner. □ **roily** *adjective* [perhaps from Old French *ruiler* mix mortar, from Late Latin *regulare* regulate]

rois·ter *intransitive verb* (esp. as **rois·ter·ing** *adjective*) revel noisily; be uproarious. □ **rois·ter·er** *noun* **rois·ter·ing** *noun* **rois·ter·ous** *adjective* [obsolete *roister* roisterer, from French *rustre* ruffian, var. of *ruste* from Latin *rusticus* RUSTIC]

Ro·land the most famous of Charlemagne's paladins, hero of the *Chanson de Roland* (12th c.) and other (esp. French and Italian) medieval romances; he is said to have become a friend of Oliver, another paladin, after engaging him in single combat in which neither won. Roland was killed at the Battle of Roncesvalles.

role *noun* **1** an actor's part in a play, film, etc. **2** a person's or thing's characteristic or expected function (*the role of the tape recorder in language learning*). **3** the part played or assumed by a person in society, life, etc., influenced by his or her conception of what is appropriate. [French *rôle* and obsolete French *roule, rolle*, = ROLL *noun*]

role model *noun* a person looked to by others as an example in a particular role or situation.

role-playing *noun* (also **role play**) an exercise in which participants act the part of another character, used in psychotherapy, language teaching, etc. □ **role-play** *transitive & intransitive verb* **role player** *noun*

role-playing game *noun* a game in which players take on the roles of imaginary characters, usu. in a setting created by a referee, and vicariously experience the imaginary adventures of these characters.

role reversal *noun* the assumption of a role which is the reverse of that normally performed.

Rolf see ROLLO.

Rolf·ing *noun* proprietary a technique of deep massage aimed at releasing muscular tension at skeletal level, claimed to relieve long-standing tension and neuroses. □ **Rolf** *transitive verb* **Rolf·er** *noun* [Ida P. Rolf, US physiotherapist d.1979]

roll ● *verb* **1 a** *intransitive* move or go in some direction by turning over and over on an axis (*the ball rolled under the table*). **b** *transitive* cause to do this (*rolled the barrel across the yard*). **2** *transitive* make revolve between two surfaces (*rolled the clay between her palms*). **3 a** *intransitive* (foll. by *along, by*, etc.) move or advance on or (of time etc.) as if on wheels etc. (*the bus rolled past; the baby carriage rolled down the driveway; the years rolled by*). **b** *transitive* cause to do this (*rolled the cart into the classroom*). **c** *intransitive* (of a person) be conveyed in a vehicle (*the farmer rolled by on his tractor*). **4 a** *transitive* turn over and over on itself to form a more or less cylindrical or spherical shape, or to make shorter (*rolled a newspaper; rolled up his sleeves*). **b** *transitive* make by forming material into a cylinder or ball (*rolled a cigarette; rolled a huge snowball*). **c** *transitive* accumulate into a mass (*rolled the dough into a ball*). **d** *intransitive* (foll. by *into*) make a specified shape of itself (*the cat rolled into a ball*). **5** *transitive* flatten or form by passing a roller etc. over or by passing between rollers (*roll pastry; roll thin foil*). **6** *intransitive & transitive* change or cause to change direction by rotatory movement (*his eyes rolled; he rolled his eyes*). **7** *intransitive* **a** wallow, turn about in a fluid or a loose medium (*the dog rolled in the dust*). **b** (of a horse etc.) lie on its back and kick about, esp. so as to dislodge its rider. **8** *intransitive* **a** (of a moving ship, aircraft, or vehicle) sway to and fro on an axis parallel to the direction of motion. **b** walk with an unsteady swaying gait (*they rolled out of the pub*). **9 a** *intransitive* undulate, show or go with an undulating surface or motion (*rolling hills; rolling mist; the waves roll in*). **b** *transitive* carry or propel with such motion (*the river rolls its waters to the sea*). **10 a** *intransitive* (of machinery) start functioning or moving (*the cameras rolled; the train began to roll*). **b** *transitive* cause (machinery) to do this. **c** *intransitive* set out; start moving, working, etc. (*it's 11 o'clock — let's roll!*). **d** *intransitive* (often foll. by *along*) progress satisfactorily or speedily (*the rewriting is rolling right along*). **11 a** *transitive* display (credits for a film or television program) moving as if on a roller up the screen. **b** *intransitive* (of credits) be displayed in this way. **12** *intransitive & transitive* sound or utter with a vibratory or trilling effect (*words rolled off her tongue; thunder rolled in the distance; they roll their r's*). **13** *N Amer. slang* **a** *transitive* overturn (a car etc.). **b** *intransitive* (of a car etc.) overturn. **14** *transitive N Amer.* throw (dice). **15** *transitive slang* rob (esp. a helpless victim). **16** *intransitive Cdn (Nfld)* (of capelin) be swept ashore to spawn. ● *noun* **1 a** a cylinder formed by turning flexible material over and over on itself without folding (*a roll of carpet; a roll of wallpaper*). **b** a filled item of food of similar form (*jelly roll; sausage roll; cabbage roll*). **2 a** a small portion of bread individually baked; a bun. **b** this with a specified filling (*lobster roll*). **3** a more or less cylindrical or semicylindrical straight or curved mass of something (*rolls of fat; a roll of hair*). **4 a** an official list or register (*the electoral roll*). **b** the total numbers on this (*the schools' rolls have fallen*). **c** a document, esp. an official record, in scroll form. **5** a rolling motion or gait; undulation (*the roll of the hills*). **6 a** a period of rolling (*a roll in the mud*). **b** a gymnastic exercise in which the body is rolled into a tucked position and turned in a forward or backward circle. **c** (esp. **a roll in the hay**) *informal* an act of sexual intercourse or erotic fondling. **7** the continuous rhythmic sound of thunder or a drum. **8** a complete revolution of an aircraft about its longitudinal axis. **9** a cylinder or roller, esp. to shape metal in a rolling mill. **10** *Archit.* a moulding of convex section. **b** a spiral scroll of an Ionic capital. **11** *N Amer. & Austral.* money, esp. as banknotes rolled

together. **12** a throw of dice. **13** *slang* a bout of success or progress. □ **be rolling** *informal* be very rich. **be rolling in** *informal* have plenty of (esp. money). **on a roll** *slang* experiencing a bout of success or progress; engaged in a period of intense activity. **roll back 1** *N Amer.* cause (esp. prices or wages) to decrease; reduce. **2** turn or force back or further away (*roll back Communism*). **3** cancel; annul (*roll back a decision*). **rolled into one** combined in one person or thing. **roll in** arrive in great numbers or quantity. **roll in the aisles** *informal* laugh uproariously. **roll on** put on or apply by rolling. **roll out 1 a** unveil (a new aircraft or spacecraft). **b** launch (a new product, campaign, etc.). **2** *N Amer. slang* get out of bed. **roll over 1** send (a person) sprawling or rolling. **2** *Econ.* reinvest (stocks, bonds, mutual funds, etc.) **roll up 1** *informal* arrive in a vehicle; appear on the scene. **2** make into or form a roll. **roll up one's sleeves** *see* SLEEVE. **roll with the punches** *informal* adapt oneself to difficult circumstances. □ **roll·able** *adjective* [Old French *rol(l)er, rouler, ro(u)lle* from Latin *rotulus*, diminutive of *rota* 'wheel']

Rol·land /rɒˈlɑ̃/ **Ro·main** (1866–1944), French novelist, dramatist, and essayist, best known for *Jean-Christophe* (1904–12), a cycle of ten novels about a German composer which epitomize the literary form known as the *roman-fleuve*. He received the Nobel Prize for literature in 1915.

roll·away ● *adjective* (of a bed etc.) that can be removed on wheels or casters. ● *noun* a rollaway bed etc.

roll·back *noun* **1** a reduction or decrease in prices, wages, taxes, etc. **2** the action or an act of rolling backwards.

roll bar *noun* an overhead metal bar strengthening the frame of a vehicle (esp. in racing) and protecting the occupants if the vehicle overturns.

roll cage *noun* a centre box section in a motor vehicle for protecting the occupants if the vehicle overturns.

roll call *noun* **1** a process of calling out a list of names to establish who is present. **2** a distinguished list of persons, things, etc. (*a roll call of former champions*).

rolled gold *noun* gold in the form of a thin coating applied to a baser metal by rolling.

rolled oats *plural noun* oats that have been husked and crushed.

roll·er *noun* **1 a** a hard revolving cylinder for smoothing the ground, spreading ink or paint, crushing or stamping, rolling up cloth on, hanging a towel on, etc., used alone or as a rotating part of a machine. **b** a cylinder for diminishing friction when moving a heavy object. **2** a small cylinder on which hair is rolled for setting. **3** a long swelling wave. **4** *Baseball* a weakly-hit ground ball which simply rolls rather than bouncing. **5 a** any brilliantly plumaged bird of the family Coraciidae, with characteristic tumbling display flight. **b** a breed of canary with a trilling song.

roller·ball *noun* a ballpoint pen using thinner ink than other ballpoints.

roller bearing *noun* a bearing like a ball bearing but with small cylinders instead of balls.

Roller·blade ● *noun* proprietary an in-line skate. ● *intransitive verb* (**rollerblade**) skate using in-line skates. □ **roller·blad·er** *noun*

roller blind *noun* (*N Amer.* also **roller shade**) a blind over a window etc., fitted on a roller.

roller coaster ● *noun* **1** a ride at an amusement park etc., having small open railway cars which travel in a linked line on an elevated, winding track up and down steep hills and around sharp corners. **2** any experience, time, etc. marked by sudden ups and downs or changes (*an emotional roller coaster*). ● *attributive adjective* (**roller-coaster**) that goes up and down, or changes, suddenly and repeatedly (*a roller-coaster economy*). ● *intransitive verb* (**roller-coaster**) (also **roller·coast**) go up and down or change in this way.

roller derby *noun* a type of speed skating competition on roller skates.

roller hockey *noun N Amer.* hockey played on in-line skates.

roller rink *noun* **1** a rink used for roller skating. **2** a building containing such a rink.

roller shade *N Amer. var. of* ROLLER BLIND.

roller skate ● *noun* each of a pair of boots with wheels attached (or metal or plastic frames with small wheels, fitted to shoes) for riding on paved surfaces etc. ● *intransitive verb* move on roller skates. □ **roller skater** *noun*

roller ski *noun* a kind of ski, approx. 90 cm (3 ft) in length, fitted with small wheels like those on a roller skate, and used for skiing on roads etc.

roller towel *noun* a towel with the ends joined, hung on a roller.

rol·lick·ing *adjective* exuberantly lively and amusing. [19th-c., prob. dial.; perhaps from ROMP + FROLIC]

roll·ie *noun* Cdn & Brit. informal a hand-rolled cigarette.

roll·ing *adjective* **1** that turns over and over, esp. so as to move forward on a surface or down a slope. **2** that moves or runs upon wheels. **3** (esp. of strikes, power cuts, etc.) taking place in different places in succession; staggered, rotating. **4** (of a landscape) gently undulating.

rolling boil *noun* Cooking a continuous rapid boil that cannot be stirred down.

rolling mill *noun* a machine or factory for rolling metal into shape.

rolling pin *noun* a cylinder made of wood, plastic, marble, etc. for rolling out pastry, dough, etc.

rolling stock *noun* the locomotives, cars, or other vehicles used on a railway.

rolling stone *noun* a person who is unwilling to settle for long in one place.

roll·mop /ˈroːlmɒp/ *noun* a rolled uncooked pickled herring fillet. [German *Rollmops*]

roll-neck ● *noun* **1** a high loosely turned-over neck of a sweater etc. **2** a sweater etc. having this. ● *attributive adjective* having a roll-neck.

Rollo /ˈrɒloː/ (also **Rolf**) (c.860–c.930), Norse chieftain, who led a band of Vikings which invaded NW France; in 912 as Duke Robert he accepted Normandy as a duchy from the French king Charles II.

roll-on ● *attributive adjective* (of deodorant etc.) applied by means of a rotating ball in the neck of the container. ● *noun* a roll-on deodorant, cosmetic, etc.

roll-on roll-off *adjective* esp. Brit. (usu. *attributive*) (of a ship, a method of transport, etc.) in which vehicles are driven directly on at the start of the voyage and off at the end of it.

roll·out *noun* **1 a** the official wheeling out of a new aircraft or spacecraft. **b** the official launch of a new product. **2** the part of a landing during which an aircraft travels along the runway losing speed.

roll·over *noun* **1** Econ. the extension or transfer of a debt or other financial relationship, esp. the reinvestment of stocks, bonds, mutual funds, etc. **2** informal the overturning of a vehicle etc.

Rolls, Charles Stew·art (1877–1910), English automobile manufacturer and aviation pioneer. In 1906 he and Henry Royce formed the automobile company Rolls-Royce Ltd.; he was the first Englishman to fly across the English Channel, and made the first double crossing in 1910 shortly before he was killed in an air crash, the first English casualty of aviation.

roll·top desk *noun* a desk with a flexible cover sliding in curved grooves.

roll-up *adjective* that can be rolled up; made by rolling up (*roll-up awnings*).

roll-your-own *noun* (also Brit. **roll-up**) a hand-rolled cigarette.

Ro·lo·dex /ˈroːlədeks/ *noun* proprietary a desktop card index mounted on a rotating axis, used for storing names, addresses, and telephone numbers. [ROLL + INDEX]

roly-poly /ˈroːlipoːli/ ● *adjective* pudgy, plump. ● *noun* (pl. **-polies**) (also **roly-poly pudding**) esp. Brit. a pudding made of a strip of suet pastry covered with jam etc., formed into a roll, and steamed or baked. [prob. formed on ROLL]

ROM /rɒm/ *noun* Computing read-only memory. [abbreviation]

Rom /rɒm/ *noun* (pl. **Roma** /ˈrɒmə/) a gypsy, esp. a man. [Romany, = man]

Rom. *abbreviation* Romans (New Testament).

rom. *abbreviation* roman (type).

Roma /ˈroːmə/ *noun* a variety of tomato with pear-shaped fruit, thick flesh, and few seeds, used esp. for making tomato sauce. [*Roma*, Italian for ROME]

ro·maine /roːˈmein/ *noun* N Amer. a variety of lettuce with crisp narrow leaves forming a long upright head. [French, fem. of *romain* 'Roman']

Ro·mains /roːˈmã/ **Jules** (pseudonym of Louis Henri Jean Farigoule) (1885–1972), French novelist, dramatist, and poet. His epic novel cycle in 27 volumes, *Men of Good Will* (1933–46), examines the evolution of French society between 1908 and 1933.

romaji /ˈroːmədʒi/ *noun* a system of Romanized spelling used to transliterate Japanese. [Japanese]

Rom·an ● *adjective* **1 a** of ancient Rome or its territory or people. **b** archaic of its language. **2** of medieval or modern Rome. **3** of papal Rome, esp. = ROMAN CATHOLIC. **4** of a kind ascribed to the early Romans (*Roman honesty*; *Roman virtue*). **5** surviving from a period of

Roman rule (*Roman road*). **6** (**roman**) (of type) of a plain upright kind used in ordinary print. **7** (of the alphabet etc.) based on the ancient Roman system with letters A–Z. ● *noun* **1 a** a citizen of the ancient Roman Republic or Empire. **b** a soldier of the Roman Empire. **2** a citizen of modern Rome. **3** = ROMAN CATHOLIC. **4** (**roman**) roman type.

roman à clef /roːˌmãaˈklei/ *noun* (pl. **romans à clef** pronunc. same) a novel in which real persons or events appear with invented names. [French, = novel with a key]

Roman arch *noun* a semicircular arch.

Roman baths *plural noun* Roman hist. a building containing a complex of rooms designed for bathing, relaxing, and socializing, consisting of a hot room (*caldarium*), which was warmed by underfloor heating, a hot air or steam room (*sudatorium*), where the bather's body was scraped of sweat and dirt with a strigil, a warm room (*tepidarium*), and finally the cold room (*frigidarium*).

Roman blind *noun* (also **Roman shade**) a window blind which gathers into a series of horizontal folds when it is raised.

Roman Britain Britain during the period AD 43–410, when the territory south of Hadrian's Wall was part of the Roman Empire. The Romans established or developed roads and the towns of London (Londinium), York (Eboracum), Lincoln (Lindum Colonia), St. Albans (Verulamium), and Colchester (Camulodunum).

Roman candle *noun* a firework discharging a series of flaming coloured balls and sparks.

Roman Catholic ● *adjective* of or relating to the part of the Christian Church acknowledging the Pope as its head. ● *noun* a member of this Church. □ **Roman Catholicism** *noun* [17th-c. translation of Latin (*Ecclesia*) *Romana Catholica* (*et Apostolica*), apparently originally as a conciliatory term in place of the earlier *Roman*, *Romanist*, or *Romish*, which had acquired derogatory overtones: see ROMAN, CATHOLIC]

ro·mance /ˈroːmans, roːˈmans/ ● *noun* **1 a** a love affair. **b** sentimental or idealized love. **c** a prevailing sense of wonder or mystery surrounding the mutual attraction in a love affair. **2** a feeling of excitement and adventure (*the romance of travel*). **3 a** a literary genre with romantic love or highly imaginative unrealistic episodes forming the central theme. **b** a work of this genre. **4** a medieval tale, usu. in verse, of some hero of chivalry, of the kind common in the Romance languages. **5 a** exaggeration or picturesque falsehood. **b** an instance of this. **6** (**Romance**) the languages descended from Latin regarded collectively. **7** Music a short informal piece. ● *adjective* (**Romance**) of any of the languages descended from Latin (French, Italian, Spanish, etc.). ● *verb* **1** *intransitive* exaggerate or distort the truth, esp. fantastically. **2** *transitive* **a** court, woo. **b** seek the attention or custom of, esp. by flattery. [Old French *romanz*, *-ans*, *-ance*, ultimately from Latin *Romanicus* ROMANIC]

ro·man·cer /roːˈmansər/ *noun* **1** a writer of romances, esp. in the medieval period. **2** a liar who resorts to fantasy.

Roman Empire the territories under Roman rule from 27 BC, when Augustus became the first emperor, to the deposition of Romulus Augustus in AD 476 in the West, or the fall of Constantinople in 1453 in the East (the empire having been divided in AD 395 into the Western Empire and the Eastern or Byzantine Empire). At its greatest extent Roman rule or influence extended from Armenia and Mesopotamia in the east to the Iberian peninsula in the west, and from the Rhine and Danube in the north to Egypt and provinces on the Mediterranean coast of North Africa. (See BYZANTINE EMPIRE).

Roman·esque /ˌroːməˈnesk/ ● *noun* a style of architecture prevalent in Europe c. 900–1200, with massive vaulting and round arches (*compare* NORMAN[1] *noun* 4). ● *adjective* of the Romanesque style of architecture. [French from *roman* ROMANCE]

roman-fleuve /ˌroːmãˈfluv/ *noun* (pl. **romans-fleuves** pronunc. same) **1** a novel featuring the leisurely description of the lives of members of a family etc. **2** a sequence of self-contained novels. [French, = river novel]

Roman holiday *noun* enjoyment derived from others' discomfiture. [originally with reference to a holiday given for gladiatorial combat]

Ro·ma·nia /roːˈmeiniə/ (also **Ru·ma·nia** /ruːˈmei-/) a country in SE Europe with a coastline on the Black Sea; pop. (est. 2002) 22,317,730; capital, Bucharest. □ **Ro·ma·nian** *noun & adjective* (also **Ru·ma·nian**).

Ro·man·ic /roːˈmanik/ ● *noun* = ROMANCE *noun* 6. ● *adjective* **1 a** of or relating to Romance. **b** Romance-speaking. **2** descended from the ancient Romans or inheriting aspects of their social or political life.

Roman·ism /ˈroːməˌnizəm/ *noun* derogatory Roman Catholicism.

Roman·ist /ˈroːmənist/ *noun* **1** a student of Roman history or law or of

the Romance languages. **2 a** a supporter of Roman Catholicism.
b *derogatory* a Roman Catholic.

roman·ize *transitive verb* (also esp. *Brit.* **-ise**) **1** make Roman or Roman Catholic in character. **2** put into the Roman alphabet or into roman type. **3** *hist.* bring (something, esp. a region or people) under Roman influence or authority. □ **roman·iz·a·tion** *noun*

Roman law *noun* the law code developed by the ancient Romans and forming the basis of many modern codes.

Roman nose *noun* a nose with a high bridge; an aquiline nose.

Roman numeral *noun* any of the Roman letters representing numbers: I = 1, V = 5, X = 10, L = 50, C = 100, D = 500, M = 1000.

Ro·mano /rɔːˈmɑːnoʊ/ *noun* a strong-tasting hard cheese, originally made in Italy. [Italian, = 'Roman']

Romano- /rɔːˈmɑːnoʊ/ *combining form* Roman; Roman and (*Romano-British*).

romano bean *noun* a variety of green or yellow snap bean, with a strong flavour and a meaty texture. [Italian, = 'Roman']

Roma·nov /ˈroʊmənɒf/ a dynasty that ruled in Russia from the accession of Michael Romanov in 1613 until the overthrow of the last czar, Nicholas II, in 1917.

Roma·now /ˈroʊmənoʊ/ **Roy John** (b.1939), Canadian lawyer and politician, premier of Saskatchewan 1991–2001. He played a major role in the conferences leading up to the patriation of the Constitution. In 2001–2002 he was commissioner for the commission on the future of health care in Canada.

Roman Republic the ancient Roman state from the expulsion of the Etruscan monarchs (see TARQUIN 2) in 510 BC until the assumption of power by Augustus (Octavian) in 27 BC. The republic of Rome, dominated by a landed aristocracy ruling through an advisory Senate, came to dominate the rest of Italy and began to acquire extensive dominions in the Mediterranean and Asia Minor before the ambitions of several military leaders (Marius, Sulla, Pompey, Julius Caesar, Mark Antony) resulted in civil wars which culminated in Caesar's brief dictatorship. After Caesar's assassination another round of civil war ended with Octavian's assumption of authority (see ROMAN EMPIRE).

Romans *noun* a book of the New Testament, an epistle of St. Paul to the Church at Rome.

Ro·mansh /roʊˈmænʃ/ ● *noun* the Rhaeto-Romance language spoken in the Swiss canton of Grisons; it is an official language of Switzerland. ● *adjective* of this language. [Romansh *Ruman(t)sch, Roman(t)sch* from medieval Latin *romanice* (adv.) (as ROMANCE)]

Roman shade *var. of* ROMAN BLIND.

ro·man·tic ● *adjective* **1** inclined towards or suggestive of romance in love (*a romantic woman; a romantic evening; romantic words*). **2** of, characterized by, or suggestive of an idealized, sentimental, or fantastic view of reality (*a romantic picture; a romantic setting*). **3** (of a person) imaginative, visionary, idealistic. **4 a** (of style in art, music, etc.) concerned more with feeling and emotion than with form and aesthetic qualities; preferring grandeur or picturesqueness to finish and proportion. **b** (also **Romantic**) of or relating to the Romanticism of the 18th & 19th c. **5** (of a project etc.) unpractical, fantastic. ● *noun* **1** a romantic person. **2** a romanticist. □ **ro·man·tic·ally** *adverb* [*romant* tale of chivalry etc., from Old French from *romanz* ROMANCE]

ro·man·ti·cism *noun* **1** (also **Romanticism**) adherence to a romantic style in art, music, etc. **2** a tendency towards romance or romantic views. **3** (**Romanticism**) a movement in the arts and literature, originating in the late 18th c., characterized by a rejection of rationalism and the order and restraint of classicism and neoclassicism, favouring instead inspiration, irrationality, subjectivity, and the primacy of the individual.

ro·man·ti·cist *noun* (also **Romanticist**) a writer or artist of the romantic school.

ro·man·ti·cize *verb* (also esp. *Brit.* **-cise**) **1** *transitive* **a** make or render romantic or unreal (*a romanticized account of war*). **b** describe or portray in a romantic fashion. **2** *intransitive* indulge in romantic thoughts or actions. □ **ro·man·ti·ciz·a·tion** *noun*

Rom·any /ˈrɒməni, ˈroʊ-/ ● *noun* (pl. **-ies**) **1** a gypsy. **2** the Indo-European language of the gypsies. ● *adjective* of or relating to gypsies or their language. [Romany *Romani*, fem. and pl. of *Romano* (adj.), from ROM]

Rome 1 the capital of Italy and of Lazio region, situated on the Tiber River about 25 km (16 miles) inland; pop. (2001) 2,459,776. **2** the Roman Republic. **3** the Roman Empire. **4** the Roman Catholic Church.

Rome, Treaty of a treaty setting up and defining the aims of the European Economic Community. It was signed at Rome on 25 March

1957 by France, West Germany, Italy, Belgium, the Netherlands, and Luxembourg.

Rome Beauty *noun see* RED ROME BEAUTY.

Romeo /ˈroʊmioʊ/ *noun* (pl. **Romeos**) a passionate male lover or seducer. [the hero of Shakespeare's play *Romeo and Juliet*]

Rom·ish *adjective derogatory* Roman Catholic.

Rom·mel /ˈrɒməl/ **Erwin** (1891–1944), German Field Marshal; known as the **Desert Fox**. As commander of the Afrika Korps in the Second World War, he deployed a series of surprise manoeuvres and succeeded in capturing Tobruk in Libya (1942), but was defeated by Montgomery at El Alamein later that year. He was forced to commit suicide after being implicated in the officers' conspiracy against Hitler in 1944.

romp ● *intransitive verb* **1** play about roughly and energetically. **2** *informal* proceed easily or rapidly. **3** win a race, contest, etc. with ease. **4** engage in sexual activity, esp. illicitly. ● *noun* **1** a period of romping or boisterous play. **2** a song, play, etc. that is lively, energetic, and lighthearted. **3** a playful and lighthearted journey or excursion. **4** *Sport* an easy victory. **5** a sexual encounter that is usu. spontaneous, playful, lighthearted, and carefree. [perhaps var. of RAMP¹]

romp·er *noun* **1** (also **romper suit**, **romp·ers** *plural noun*) a young child's one-piece garment covering the legs and trunk. **2 a** a loose-fitting woman's garment combining esp. a short-sleeved or sleeveless top and wide-legged shorts. **b** a similar garment worn in bed.

Rom·ulus /ˈrɒmjʊlɨs/ *Rom. Myth* the traditional founder of Rome, one of the twin sons of Mars by the Vestal Virgin Rhea Silvia. He and his brother Remus were abandoned at birth in a basket on the Tiber River but were found and suckled by a she-wolf and later brought up by a shepherd family; Remus was killed before the founding of the city, which was named after Romulus.

Ron·ces·valles, Battle of /ˈrɒnsəˌvæl/ (French **Ron·ce·vaux** /-ˌvɔː/) a battle which took place in 778 at a mountain pass in the Pyrenees, near the Spanish village of Roncesvalles, in which the rearguard of Charlemagne's army was attacked by the Basques and massacred; the death of one of the nobles, Roland, was much celebrated in medieval literature, notably in the *Chanson de Roland* (in which the attackers are wrongly identified as the Moors).

ron·deau /ˈrɒndoʊ/ *noun* (pl. **ron·deaux** *pronunc.* same or /-oːz/) a poem of ten or thirteen lines with only two rhymes throughout and with the opening words used twice as a refrain. [French, earlier *rondel* from Old French *rond* ROUND]

ron·del /ˈrɒndəl/ *noun* a rondeau, esp. one of special form. [Old French from *rond* ROUND compare ROUNDEL]

rondo *noun* (pl. **-dos**) *Music* a form of composition with a recurring theme, often found in the final movement of a sonata or concerto etc. [Italian from French *rondeau*: see RONDEAU]

Ronga ● *noun* **1** a member of a Bantu-speaking people of southern Mozambique. **2** the Bantu language of this people. ● *adjective* of or pertaining to the Ronga or their language. [Ronga]

ronin /ˈroʊnɪn/ *noun* (pl. same) *hist.* (in feudal Japan) a lordless wandering samurai; an outlaw. [Japanese]

Ron·sard /rɔ̃ˈsɑr/ **Pierre de** (1524–85), French poet. He was one of the leading poets of the group known as the Pléiade, and is noted for his lyric sequences, including *Sonnets pour Hélène* (1578).

Rönt·gen *see* ROENTGEN.

rönt·gen etc. *var. of* ROENTGEN etc.

roo *noun* (also **'roo**) *Austral. informal* a kangaroo. [abbreviation]

rood *noun* a crucifix, esp. one raised on a screen or beam at the entrance to the chancel. [Old English *rōd*]

rood screen *noun* a wooden or stone carved screen, often topped with a crucifix, separating nave and chancel in a church.

roof ● *noun* (pl. **roofs**) **1 a** the upper outside covering of a building, esp. a house, usu. supported by its walls. **b** any external covering forming a shelter or top (*I left my coffee mug on the roof of the car*). **2 a** the overhead inner surface of a room, cavity, etc. (*the roof of a cave*). **b** the top inner surface of a compartment or opening (*the roof of the oven; the roof of the mouth*). **3** (of prices etc.) the upper limit or highest point. **4** *literary* the area overhead, such as the sky, heaven, etc. ● *transitive verb* **1** (usu. in *passive*) (often foll. by *over*) cover with or as with a roof. **2** put (something) on top of a roof, accidentally or intentionally (*I roofed a tennis ball at school*). □ **go through the roof** *informal* (of prices etc.) reach extreme or unexpected heights. **hit** (or **go through**) **the roof** *informal* become very angry. **raise the roof** make a lot of noise inside a building, esp. by cheering or shouting. **a roof over one's head** somewhere to live. **under one roof** in the same building. **under a**

person's roof in a person's home. □ **roof·less** *adjective* [Old English *hrōf*]

roofed *adjective* **1** having or covered with a roof. **2** (usu. in *combination*) having a roof of a specified kind or nature (*thatch-roofed cottage*; *red-roofed house*).

roof·er *noun* a person who constructs or repairs roofs.

roof garden *noun* an area, usu. with plants etc., built on the flat roof of a building for outdoor eating or entertainment.

roof·ie *noun slang* a tablet of Rohypnol.

roof·ing *noun* **1 a** material for constructing a roof. **b** (*attributive*) designating materials or equipment used for constructing a roof (*roofing felt; roofing nails*). **2** the process of constructing a roof or roofs.

roof·line *noun* the outline or silhouette of a roof or roofs.

roof of the mouth *noun* the palate.

roof prism *noun* **1** a triangular prism in which the reflecting surface is in two parts that are angled like two parts of a pitched roof. **2** (*attributive*) designating esp. binoculars etc. using such prisms.

roof rack *noun* a frame that can be mounted on the roof of a car, truck, etc. for carrying luggage, skis, bicycles, etc.

roof·top *noun* the outer surface of a roof, esp. the roof of a house.

roof·tree *noun* = RIDGEPOLE 2.

rooi·bos /ˈrɔɪbɒs/*noun* **1** an evergreen South African shrub of the genus *Aspalathus* belonging to the family Leguminosae, and cultivated for its leaves which are used to make a kind of tea. **2** this tea. [Afrikaans, from *rooi* 'red' + *bos* 'bush']

rook[1] /rʊk/ ● *noun* a black European and Asiatic bird, *Corvus frugilegus*, of the crow family, nesting in colonies in treetops. ● *transitive verb* **1** charge (a customer) extortionately. **2** win money from (a person) at cards etc. esp. by swindling. [Old English *hrōc*]

rook[2] /rʊk/ *noun* in chess, each of the four pieces set in the corner squares at the beginning of a game, moving in a straight line forwards, backwards, or laterally over any number of unoccupied squares. *Also called* CASTLE. [Old French *roc(k)*, ultimately from Arabic *rukk*, original sense uncertain]

rook[3] /rʊk/ *noun informal* = ROOKIE. [abbreviation]

rook·ery *noun* (*pl.* **-eries**) **1 a** a colony of seabirds (esp. penguins) or seals. **b** a place where seabirds, sea lions, seals, etc. breed. **2 a** a colony of rooks. **b** a clump of trees having rooks' nests.

rook·ie *noun informal* **1** *N Amer.* an athlete who is playing his or her first full season in a particular league (also *attributive: rookie season*). **2** a new recruit, esp. in the army or police force. **3** (usu. *attributive*) a novice (*a rookie politician*). [corruption of *recruit*, after ROOK[1]]

room ● *noun* **1 a** a space that is or might be occupied by something. **b** the ability to accommodate contents; available or required space (*I can't have a dog, I don't have room*). **c** available space in or on (*houseroom; shelf room*). **d** space required or available for something specified (*this car has lots of headroom*). **2 a** a part of a building enclosed by walls or partitions, floor, and ceiling. **b** (in *pl.*) a set of these occupied by a person or family; apartments or lodgings. **c** a bedroom (*finish your dinner or you'll be sent to your room*). **3** (in *combination*) a room or area for a specified purpose (*lunchroom*). **4** (foll. by *for* or *to* + infin.) capacity to allow a particular action; opportunity (*room to improve things; no room for dispute*). **5** people present in a room (*the room fell silent*). **6** *Cdn* (*Nfld*) *hist.* the harbourfront on which a fishery is located, including wharves, lodges, and other buildings or facilities used by the fishery. ● *intransitive verb N Amer.* rent a room or rooms; lodge; board. □ **make room** (often foll. by *for*) clear a space (for a person or thing) by removal of others. **not enough** (or **no**) **room to swing a cat** not enough space to live or work in. □ **-roomed** *adjective* (in *combination*). **room·ful** *noun* (*pl.* **-fuls**). [Old English *rūm* from Germanic]

room and board *noun N Amer.* **1** accommodation and meals (*she paid $120 a week for room and board*). **2** the cost of accommodation and meals (*room and board was deducted from their wages*).

room·er *noun N Amer.* **1** a lodger occupying a room or rooms without meals. **2** a house or apartment having a specified number of rooms (*a one-roomer*).

room·ette *noun N Amer.* **1** a private single compartment in the sleeping car of a train. **2** a small bedroom that is rented out.

room·ie *noun N Amer. informal* a roommate.

room·ing house *noun esp. N Amer.* a house or building divided into furnished rooms or apartments for rent.

room·mate *noun* a person who lives in the same apartment, room, etc. as another.

room service *noun* **1** (in a hotel etc.) drinks or a meal served in a guest's room. **2** the department that provides this service.

room temperature *noun* a temperature that would be considered comfortable for a normal room in a house, usu. approx. 20° C or 68° F.

roomy *adjective* (**room·ier, room·iest**) having plenty of room to contain people or things; spacious. □ **room·i·ness** *noun*

Roon·ey, Mick·ey (born Joseph Yule Jr.) (b.1920), US actor. He first appeared in *Not to Be Trusted* (1926) before playing Andy Hardy in sixteen comedy drama films over twenty years about the Hardy family. He received Oscar nominations for his roles in *Babes in Arms* (1939) and *The Human Comedy* (1943).

Roos·evelt /ˈrəʊzəˌvɛlt/ **1 (Anna) Elea·nor** (1884–1962), US humanitarian and diplomat, niece of Theodore Roosevelt and wife of Franklin Roosevelt. Involved in a wide range of liberal causes, including civil and women's rights, she became a delegate to the United Nations after her husband's death in 1945, and, as chair of the UN Commission on Human Rights, played a major role in drafting the Declaration of Human Rights (1948). **2** her husband, **Frank·lin Del·ano** (known as 'FDR') (1882–1945), US Democratic politician, 32nd president of the US 1933–45. His New Deal of 1933 helped to lift the US out of the Depression, and after the US entry into the Second World War he played an important part in the coordination of the Allied war effort. **3 Theo·dore** ('**Teddy**') (1858–1919), US Republican politician, 26th president of the US 1901–9. He succeeded McKinley in 1901 following the latter's assassination, and was noted for his antitrust laws and for successfully engineering the US bid to build the Panama Canal (1904–14); he won the Nobel Peace Prize in 1906 for negotiating the end of the Russo-Japanese War. □ **Roos·evelt·ian** *adjective & noun*

roost ● *noun* **1 a** a branch, perch, etc. where birds or bats regularly settle, esp. to sleep. **b** a place where domestic fowl perch at night, esp. in a henhouse. **2** a place offering temporary rest or accommodation. ● *intransitive verb* **1** (of a bird) settle for rest or sleep. **2** (of a person) stay for the night. □ **come home to roost** (of a scheme etc.) recoil unfavourably upon the originator. [Old English *hrōst*]

roost·er *noun esp. N Amer.* a male chicken.

rooster tail *noun* **1** the spray of water thrown up behind a speedboat or surfboard. **2** the spray of dust, sand, or gravel thrown up behind a truck, car, etc.

Root, Mount a peak (3 901 m) in the St. Elias Mountains of northwestern BC, situated on the border with Alaska, northeast of Fairweather Mountain. [E. *Root*, US lawyer d.1937]

root[1] ● *noun* **1 a** the part of a plant normally below the ground, attaching it to the earth and conveying nourishment to it from the soil. **b** (in *pl.*) such a part divided into branches or fibres. **c** the permanent underground stock of a plant. **2** a plant that is grown for its edible underground part to be used as food, spice, or medicine, e.g. a turnip, ginger, or ginseng. **3 a** the embedded part of a bodily organ or structure, such as a hair, tooth, nail, etc. **b** the part of a thing attaching it to a greater or more fundamental whole. **4** (in *pl.*) social, cultural, or ethnic origins, esp. as the reasons for one's long-standing emotional attachment to a place, community, etc. **5 a** the basic cause, source, origin, or ancestor (*love of money is the root of all evil; has its roots in the distant past*). **b** (*attributive*) designating a problem, idea, etc. from which something has ensued (*the root cause of the situation*). **6** the essential substance or nature of something (*get to the root of things*). **7** *Math.* **a** a number or quantity that when multiplied by itself a usu. specified number of times gives a specified number or quantity (*the cube root of eight is two*). **b** a square root. **c** a value of an unknown quantity satisfying a given equation. **8** *Linguistics* any ultimate unanalyzable element of language, not necessarily surviving as a word in itself, from which words are made by affixation or other modification. **9** *Music* the fundamental note of a chord. **10** *Bible* a descendant. ● *verb* **1** *intransitive* develop roots and become firmly established. **2** *transitive* **a** fix firmly with roots or as if with roots (*fear rooted him to the spot*). **b** be based in (*fear is rooted in ignorance*). **3** *transitive* (usu. foll. by *out*, *up*) dig up by the roots. □ **pull up by the roots 1** uproot. **2** eradicate, destroy. **put down roots 1** begin to draw nourishment from the soil. **2** become settled or established. **root and branch** thorough(ly), radical(ly). **strike at the root** (or **roots**) **of** set about destroying. **take root 1** begin to grow and draw nourishment from the soil. **2** become fixed or established. **root out** find and get rid of. □ **root·less** *adjective* **root·less·ness** *noun* **root·like** *adjective* **rooty** *adjective* [Old English *rōt* from Old Norse *rót*, related to WORT & Latin *radix*: see RADIX]

root[2] *verb* **1** *intransitive* (of an animal, esp. a pig) turn up (the ground) with the snout, beak, etc., in search of food. **2 a** *intransitive* (foll. by *around, in*, etc.) rummage around or look for something. **b** *transitive* (foll.

by *out* or *up*) find or extract by rummaging. **3** *intransitive* (foll. by *for*) *N Amer. informal* **a** *Sports* encourage with cheering, applause, etc. **b** offer support to. □ **root·er** *noun* (in sense 3). [earlier *wroot* from Old English *wrōtan* & Old Norse *róta*: related to Old English *wrōt* snout]

root ball *noun* the mass formed by the roots of a plant and the soil surrounding them.

root beer *noun N Amer.* a carbonated drink made from an extract of roots.

root canal *noun Dentistry* **1** the pulp-filled cavity in the root of a tooth. **2** (in full **root canal surgery** or **therapy**) *N Amer.* a procedure to replace the infected pulp of a tooth with an inert material.

root cellar *noun N Amer.* an underground room in a house for storing esp. vegetables and fruit.

root·ed *adjective* **1** firmly established (*her affection was deeply rooted; rooted objection to*). **2 a** having a root or roots. **b** (in *combination*) having roots of a specified type, number, or quality (*tuberous-rooted*). □ **root·ed·ness** *noun*

rootin' tootin' *adjective N Amer. informal* **1** resembling or characteristic of the Wild West or an inhabitant of the Wild West. **2** boisterous, noisy, rip-roaring (*a rootin' tootin' good time*).

roo·tle *transitive & intransitive verb Brit.* = ROOT² 2. [ROOT²]

root·let *noun* **1** a slender root or division of a root. **2** a thin strand of something.

root-mean-square *noun Math.* the square root of the arithmetic mean of the squares of a set of values.

root rot *noun* a plant disease that attacks the roots.

root sign *noun Math.* = RADICAL SIGN.

roots music *noun* music expressive of a distinctive (sometimes specified, esp. black or W Indian) ethnic origin or cultural identity.

root·stock *noun* **1** a stock onto which another variety has been grafted or budded. **2** a rhizome, esp. one from which new leaves and shoots are reproduced annually. **3** a primary form from which offshoots have arisen.

root·sy *adjective* (**root·si·er**, **root·si·est**) *informal* (esp. of music) showing traditional origins. □ **root·si·ness** *noun*

rope ● *noun* **1 a** strong thick cord made by twisting together strands of hemp, sisal, flax, cotton, nylon, wire, or similar material. **b** a piece of this. **2** (foll. by *of*) **a** a quantity of similar things held together by or as if by a string passed through the middle of each (*a rope of pearls*). **b** a strand of a semi-liquid substance (*rope of saliva*). **3** (in *pl.*, prec. by *the*) **a** the rules and procedures of a business, operation, etc. (*it'll be a while before she learns the ropes; we'll show you the ropes*). **b** the ropes enclosing a boxing or wrestling ring etc. **4** (prec. by *the*) **a** a halter for hanging a person. **b** execution by hanging. **5** *N Amer.* a lasso. ● *transitive verb* **1** fasten, secure, or catch with rope. **2** (usu. foll. by *off*) enclose (a space) with rope. **3** (usu. foll. by *in, into*) persuade or entice someone to join or participate in an activity (*I got roped into doing the dishes*). **4** *Mountaineering* connect (a party) with a rope; attach (a person) to a rope. □ **give a person plenty of rope** (or **enough rope to hang himself**) give a person enough freedom of action to bring about his or her own downfall. **on the ropes 1** *Boxing* forced against the ropes by the opponent's attack. **2** near defeat. **rope up** (or **down**) *Mountaineering* climb up (or down) using a rope. □ **rop·ing** *noun* **rope·like** *adjective* [Old English *rāp* from Germanic]

rope-a-dope *noun N Amer. Boxing* a tactic whereby a boxer rests against the ropes and protects himself with his arms and gloves, goading an opponent to throw tiring and ineffective punches.

rope burn *noun* a burn caused by the friction of rope esp. on the hands.

rope dancer *noun* = TIGHTROPE WALKER.

rope ladder *noun* two long ropes connected by short crosspieces, used as a ladder.

roper *noun N Amer.* a person who uses a lasso to rope cattle etc.

rope tow *noun* a type of ski lift consisting of an endless moving rope driven by a motor, used esp. on bunny hills and smaller runs.

ropy *adjective* (also **ropey**) (**ropi·er**, **ropi·est**) **1** like a rope. **2** (of wine, bread, etc.) forming viscous or gelatinous threads. **3** *Brit. informal* **a** poor in quality. **b** unwell.

roque·fort /ˈroːkfərt, ˈrɒkfərt, ˈrɒkfɔr/ *noun* **1** a soft blue cheese made from ewes' milk. **2** a salad dressing made of this. [*Roquefort* in S. France]

ro·quet /ˈroːkei, -ki/ *Croquet* ● *verb* (**ro·queted**, **ro·quet·ing**) **1** *transitive* **a** cause one's ball to strike (another ball). **b** (of a ball) strike (another). **2** *intransitive* strike another ball thus. ● *noun* an instance of roqueting.

[apparently arbitrary alteration of CROQUET *verb*, originally used in the same sense]

Ror·ai·ma, Mount /rɒˈraimə/ a mountain in the Guiana Highlands of S America, situated at the junction of the borders of Venezuela, Brazil, and Guyana. Rising to 2 774 m (9,094 ft.), it is the highest peak in the range.

ro-ro *noun* a roll-on, roll-off ferry. [abbreviation]

ror·qual /ˈrɔːkwəl/ *noun* any of various baleen whales of the family Balaenopteridae characterized by a pleated throat and small dorsal fin, esp. the finback or the minke whale. [French from Norwegian *røyrkval* from Old Icelandic *reythr* the specific name + *hvalr* WHALE¹]

Ror·schach /ˈrɔːʃak, -ʃɒk/ *adjective Psych.* designating or pertaining to a type of personality test in which a standard set of ink blots is presented one by one to the subject, who is asked to describe what they suggest or resemble. [H. *Rorschach*, Swiss psychiatrist d.1922]

ros·acea /rɒˈzeiʃə/ *noun* a condition in which certain blood vessels enlarge, giving the cheeks and nose a flushed appearance. [Latin, fem. of *rosaceus* in the sense 'rose-coloured']

ros·aceous /rɒˈzeiʃəs/ *adjective* relating or belonging to the large plant family Rosaceae, which includes the rose. [Latin *rosaceus* from *rosa* rose]

Ros·ario /rɒˈsɑːriəʊ/ an inland port on the Paraná river in E central Argentina; pop. (est. 2002) 1,261,400.

ros·ary /ˈroːzəri/ *noun* (*pl.* **-aries**) **1** *Catholicism* a form of devotion accompanying the contemplation of fifteen mysteries (now usu. in groups of five) in which fifteen decades (sets of ten) of Hail Marys are repeated, each decade preceded by an Our Father and followed by a Glory Be. **2** *Catholicism* a string of beads divided into sets used for keeping count in the recital of this. **3** a similar string of beads or knotted cord used for counting prayers in other religions. [Latin *rosarium* rose garden, neuter of *rosarius* (as ROSE¹)]

Ros·com·mon /rɒsˈkɒmən/ **1** a county in the north central part of the Republic of Ireland, in the province of Connacht; pop. (2002) 54,100. **2** its county town; pop. (2002) 18,492.

rose¹ ● *noun* **1** a prickly, erect or climbing shrub of the genus *Rosa*. **2** the flower of this bush or shrub, generally fragrant and of a red, pink, yellow, or white colour. **3** any flowering plant resembling this (*Christmas rose; rock rose*). **4 a** a light crimson colour; pink. **b** (usu. in *pl.*) a rosy complexion (*roses in her cheeks*). **5 a** (*attributive*) representing or designating something resembling a rose in form or appearance (*rose diamond*). **b** a rose-shaped design, e.g. on a compass. **c** a representation of a rose in heraldry or decoration (esp. as the national emblem of England). **6** a thing of beauty, perfection, or superior standing. **7** a perforated cap attached to the spout of a watering can or hose. **8** a rose window. ● *adjective* pink or pale red. □ **come up roses** develop in a very favourable way. **come up smelling of roses** emerge in a very favourable light, esp. from a difficult situation. □ **rose·like** *adjective* [Old English *rōse* from Latin *rosa*]

rose² *past of* RISE.

rosé /ˈroːzei/ *noun* **1** any pale red or pink wine, coloured by only brief contact with the skins of red grapes. **2** designating a pasta sauce made by combining tomato sauce and cream sauce. [French, lit. 'pink']

ros·eate /ˈroːziət/ *adjective* **1** having a partly pink plumage (*roseate spoonbill; roseate tern*). **2** = ROSE-COLOURED. [Latin *roseus* rosy (as ROSE¹)]

Ros·eau /rɒˈzoː/ the capital of Dominica in the W Indies; pop. (est. 2002) 19,700.

rose·bay *noun* an oleander, rhododendron, or willow herb.

rose·bowl *noun* a bowl for displaying cut roses.

rose-breasted grosbeak *noun* a grosbeak, *Pheucticus ludovicianus*, which breeds across most of N America east of the Rockies, the male of which is black and white with a red patch on its breast.

rose·bud *noun* **1** a bud of a rose. **2** (often *attributive*) representing or designating something resembling a rosebud in nature or appearance (*rosebud mouth*).

rose bush *noun* a rose plant.

rose campion *noun* an ornamental garden campion, *Lychnis coronaria*, with woolly leaves and magenta flowers.

rose chafer *noun* a green or copper-coloured beetle, *Cetonia aurata*, frequently found on roses.

rose-coloured *adjective* **1** of the colour of a pale red rose; rose-pink. **2** optimistic, sanguine, cheerful (*a rose-coloured view of things*). □ **see through rose-coloured glasses** regard (circumstances etc.) with unfounded optimism or naïveté.

Rose·dale a wealthy residential area of Toronto.

rose·fish *noun* a bright red food fish of the genus *Sebastes*, of the N Atlantic.

rose geranium *noun* a pink-flowered sweet-scented pelargonium, *Pelargonium graveolens*.

rose·hip *noun* = HIP².

rose madder *noun* a pale pink pigment.

rose·maling /ˈrɔːzəˌmalɪŋ/ *noun* the art of painting wooden furniture etc. with flower motifs. [Norwegian, = rose painting]

rose mallow *noun* = HIBISCUS.

rose·mary *noun* **1** a fragrant shrub of the mint family, *Rosmarinus officinalis*, native to southern Europe, cultivated esp. for its use as a spice and in perfume. **2** the leaves of this plant as used as a flavouring. [Middle English, earlier *rosmarine*, ultimately from Latin *ros marinus* from *ros* dew + *marinus* MARINE, assimilated to ROSE¹ and *Mary* name of the Virgin]

Rose·mère /rozˈmeɪ/ (also **Rose·mere** /ˈrozmɪːr/) a town in south central Quebec, situated on the Rivière des Mille Îles, northwest of Montreal; pop. (2001) 13,391. [French form of *Rosemere*, with reference to the area's abundance of wild roses + MERE²]

Rosen·berg ▸ 1 Al·fred (1893–1946), German Nazi politician and editor, who helped to formulate Nazi racial ideology; he was executed as a war criminal. **2 Jul·ius** (1918–53), US army engineer, who was executed, with his wife Ethel (1915–53), for passing military secrets to Soviet intelligence agents.

rose of Jericho *noun* a plant of the genus *Anastatica hierochuntica*, which will unfold when moistened after being dried.

rose of Sharon *noun* **1** a hardy hibiscus shrub, *Hibiscus syriacus*, with late-blooming rose, white, or blue flowers. **2** a species of hypericum, *Hypericum calycinum*, with dense foliage and golden-yellow flowers. **3** *Bible* a flowering plant of unknown identity.

ros·eola /rɔːˈziːələ/ *noun* **1** a rosy rash in measles and similar diseases. **2** a mild febrile disease of infants. [modern var. of RUBEOLA from Latin *roseus* rose-coloured]

rose pink ● *noun* the colour of a pale red rose, warm pink. ● *adjective* (usu. **rose-pink**) of this colour.

rose pogonia *noun* see POGONIA.

rose quartz *noun* a pink translucent variety of quartz.

rose red ● *noun* the colour of a red rose; dark red, crimson. ● *adjective* (usu. **rose-red**) of this colour.

rose·root *noun* a yellow-flowered plant, *Rhodiola rosea* (*Sedum roseum*).

Roses, Wars of the see WARS OF THE ROSES.

rose-tinted *adjective* = ROSE-COLOURED.

Ros·etta stone /rɔːˈzetə/ *noun* **1** a stone found near Rosetta in Egypt bearing a 2nd c. BC trilingual inscription in Egyptian hieroglyphs, demotic, and Greek, important in deciphering hieroglyphs. **2 a** a key to previously unattainable understanding. **b** a person or thing that is difficult to interpret or understand.

ros·ette /rɔːˈzet/ *noun* **1** an ornament or other object carved, moulded, shaped, or arranged to resemble or represent a rose (*a rosette of butter*). **2 a** a naturally occurring circular arrangement of horizontally spreading leaves, esp. about the base of a stem. **b** a similar but abnormal cluster of leaves on the stem resulting from a shortening of the internodes, a symptom of disease. **3** a rose-shaped arrangement of ribbon worn esp. as a badge of membership or support, or as a symbol of a prize won in a competition. **4** markings resembling a rose, esp. on the skin of a leopard. [French diminutive of *rose* ROSE¹]

rose·water *noun* water distilled from roses, or scented with the essence of roses, used as a perfume and as a flavouring in cooking.

rose window *noun* a circular window, usu. of stained glass, with roselike or spoke-like tracery.

rose·wood *noun* any of several fragrant close-grained woods derived esp. from tropical leguminous trees of the genus *Dalbergia* used in making furniture.

Rosh Cho·desh /rɒʃ ˈxoːdeʃ/ *noun* a Jewish half-holiday observed at the appearance of the new moon, the beginning of the Jewish month. [Hebrew = beginning (lit. 'head') of the month]

Rosh Hash·anah /rɒʃ həˈʃɒnə/ *noun* the festival celebrating the Jewish New Year marked by penitence, self-reflection, and an examination of one's relationship with and responsibilities to God. [Hebrew, = beginning (lit. 'head') of the year]

roshi /ˈroːʃi/ *noun* (*pl.* **rosh·is**) the spiritual leader of a community of Zen Buddhist monks. [Japanese]

Rosi·cru·cian /ˌrɔːzɪˈkruːʃən/ ● *noun* **1** *hist.* a member of a 17th–18th-c. society, said to have been founded by Christian Rosenkreuz in

1484, devoted to metaphysical and mystical lore, such as that concerning the prolongation of life and power over the elements and elemental spirits. **2** a member of any of various modern organizations deriving from this. ● *adjective* belonging to, associated with, or characteristic of this society. □ **Rosi·cru·cianism** *noun* [modern Latin *rosa crucis* (or *crux*), as Latinization of German *Rosenkreuz*]

ros·in /ˈrɒzɪn/ ● *noun* the solid amber residue obtained after the distillation of crude turpentine oleoresin, or of naphtha extract from pine stumps, used in adhesives, varnishes, inks, etc. It is also used, esp. powdered, to prevent slipping when applied to the bows of stringed instruments, the hands of baseball players etc., and dancers' shoes. ● *transitive verb* (**ros·ined, ros·in·ing**) treat with rosin. □ **ros·iny** *adjective* [Middle English, alteration of RESIN]

Ros·kilde /ˈrɒskɪlə/ a port in Denmark, on the island of Zealand; pop. (1998) 42,462. It was the seat of Danish kings from *c.*1020 and the capital of Denmark until 1443.

Ross ▸ 1 Diana (b.1944), US pop and soul singer. She made her name as the lead singer of the Supremes, and after leaving the group in 1969 became a successful solo artist with songs such as 'Touch Me in the Morning' (1973); she has also appeared in several films, including *Lady Sings the Blues* (1973), for which she received an Oscar for her role as the jazz singer Billie Holiday. **2 Sir George Wil·liam** (1841–1914), Canadian politician, Liberal premier of Ontario 1899–1905. **3 (James) Sin·clair** (1908–96), Canadian writer. After leaving school at 16 to begin a banking career, he published his first short story in 1934. He became well known in 1941 when his first novel *As For Me and My House* was published; his short stories, including 'The Painted Door' and 'The Lamp at Noon' are frequently anthologized. Most of his writing is set on the prairies. **4 Sir John** (1777–1856) and **Sir James Clark** (1800–62), English explorers. Sir John led an expedition to Baffin Bay in 1818 and another in search of the Northwest Passage between 1829 and 1833, during which he surveyed King William Land, the Boothia Peninsula, and the Gulf of Boothia; his nephew Sir James Clark Ross located the north magnetic pole in 1831, and headed an expedition to the Antarctic from 1839 to 1843. Ross Island, Ross Dependency, and the Ross Sea are all named after him. **5 Sir Ron·ald** (1857–1932), English physician. He confirmed that the *Anopheles* mosquito was the vector of malaria, and went on to elucidate the stages in the malarial parasite's life cycle; he was awarded a Nobel Prize in 1902.

Ross and Crom·arty /ˈkrɒmərti/ a former county of N Scotland, stretching from the Moray Firth to the North Minch. Since 1975 it has been part of Highland Region.

Ross Dependency part of Antarctica consisting of everything lying to the south of latitude 60° S between longitudes 150° and 160° W. It is administered by New Zealand.

Ros·seau, Lake /ˈrɒsoː/ a small lake in south central Ontario, immediately east of Lake Joseph, off the eastern shore of Georgian Bay. [J. B. *Rousseau*, fur trader and interpreter d.1812]

Ros·sel·lini /ˌrɒsəˈliːni/ **Ro·ber·to** (1906–77), Italian film director. He is known for his neo-realist films, particularly his quasi-documentary trilogy about the Second World War, filmed using a mainly non-professional cast; this comprises *Open City* (1945), *Paisà* (1946), and *Germany, Year Zero* (1947).

Ros·setti /rəˈzeti/ **1 Chris·tina (Geor·gina)** (1830–94), English poet. Her work is marked by technical virtuosity, deep religious feeling, a sense of melancholy, and recurrent themes of frustrated love and premature resignation. Her best-known poem is probably 'Mid-winter' (1875) in its musical setting as a Christmas carol 'In the bleak mid-winter'. **2** her brother, **Dante Gab·riel** (full name Gabriel Charles Dante Rossetti) (1828–82), English painter and poet. A founding member of the Pre-Raphaelites (1848), he encouraged the movement to make links between painting and literature, and based many of his paintings on the work of Dante; he is best known for his dreamy and idealized images of women including *Beata Beatrix* (*c.*1863) and *The Blessed Damozel* (1871–9).

Ros·si·gnol, Lake /ˌrɒzɪˈnɒl/ a lake in SW Nova Scotia, situated north of Shelburne. [J. *Rossignol*, fur trader *c.*1604]

Ros·sini /rɒˈsiːni/ **Gioac·chino (An·tonio)** (1792–1868), Italian composer. He wrote over 30 operas, of which the best-known are the comic opera *The Barber of Seville* (1816) and the grand opera *William Tell* (1829). □ **Ros·sin·ian** *adjective*

Ross rifle *noun* *Cdn hist.* a type of .303 rifle developed in the 1890s and used by the Canadian Army, esp. in the First World War. [Sir Charles A. F. L. *Ross*, Scottish-born engineer and soldier d.1930]

Ross Sea a large arm of the Pacific forming a deep indentation in the coast of Antarctica. At its head is the Ross Ice Shelf, the world's largest body of floating ice, approximately the size of France. On the eastern shores of the Ross Sea lies Ross Island, which is the site of Mount Erebus and of Scott Base, an Antarctic station established by New Zealand in 1957.

Ross's gull *noun* an Arctic gull, *Rhodostethia rosea*, with pinkish-white plumage on the breast and belly. [Sir J. C. Ross]

Ros·tand /rɒˈstɑ̃/ **Ed·mond** (1868–1918), French dramatist and poet, best known for the poetic drama *Cyrano de Bergerac* (1897).

ros·ter ● *noun* **1** *N Amer. Sport* a list of players belonging or available to a team. **2** (often foll. by *of*) **a** any list of people or things belonging to a specified group (*a roster of experts*). **b** a group of people or things considered as being on a roster (*the whole roster will be performing tonight*). **3** a list or plan showing turns of duty or leave for individuals or groups in any organization, originally a military force. ● *transitive verb* place on a roster. [Dutch *rooster* list, originally gridiron, from *roosten* ROAST, with reference to its parallel lines]

rösti /ˈrɜsti/ *plural noun* a dish of grated potatoes, sometimes flavoured with onion or bacon, compacted into a large cake and fried. [Swiss German from German *rösten*, 'roast, grill']

Ros·tock an industrial port on the Baltic coast of Germany; pop. (est. 2002) 193,300.

Rostov-on-Don (also **Ros·tov**) a port and industrial city in SW Russia, on the Don River near its point of entry into the Sea of Azov; pop. (est. 2002) 1,012,500.

ros·tra *pl. of* ROSTRUM.

ros·tral /ˈrɒstrəl/ *adjective* **1** *Anat.* **a** near the region of the nose and mouth. **b** nearer the hypophyseal area in the early embryo. **2** *Zool. & Bot.* of or on the rostrum. □ **ros·tral·ly** *adverb*

Ros·tro·povich /ˌrɒstrəˈpoʊvɪtʃ/ **Msti·slav (Leo·pold·ovich)** (b.1927), US cellist, pianist, and conductor, born in the Soviet Union, who is particularly known as a conductor of opera; he left the Soviet Union in 1975.

ros·trum *noun* (*pl.* **ros·tra** or **ros·trums**) **1** a platform or pulpit for public speaking. **2** *Zool. & Bot.* a beak, stiff snout, or beaklike part. **3** *Rom. Hist.* the beak of a war galley. [Latin, = beak from *rodere* ros-gnaw: originally *rostra* (pl., in sense 1a) in the Roman forum adorned with beaks of captured galleys]

rosy *adjective* (**ros·i·er**, **ros·i·est**) **1 a** coloured like a pink or red rose. **b** (esp. of the complexion) pink as an indication of health or youth (*rosy cheeks*). **2 a** promising (*a rosy future*). **b** optimistic, esp. unjustifiably so (*painted a rosy picture of the situation*). □ **ros·i·ly** *adverb* **ros·i·ness** *noun*

rosy periwinkle *noun* = MADAGASCAR PERIWINKLE.

rot ● *verb* (**rot·ted**, **rot·ting**) **1** *intransitive* **a** (of animal or vegetable matter) lose its original form by the chemical action of bacteria, fungi, etc.; decay. **b** (foll. by *away*) decay to the point of falling apart (*the old barn was rotting away*). **c** (foll. by *off*) separate from the main body because of decay (*dead branches rotted off*). **d** (of ice on lakes etc.) disintegrate into a honeycombed structure due to thawing. **2** *intransitive* (of society, institutions, etc.) deteriorate; become corrupt or degenerate due to neglect or abuse. **3** *intransitive* (of a person) languish, waste away (*he was left to rot in prison*). **4** *transitive* cause to rot, make rotten (*too much candy will rot your teeth*). **5** *transitive* = RET. ● *noun* **1 a** the process or state of rotting. **b** rotten or decayed matter. **2** *Bot.* any of various diseases in plants characterized by the weakening or decay of tissue. **3** a decline or breakdown in standards or behaviour (*the rot has set in and it will be hard to stop*). **4** *slang* nonsense (*her political ideas were nothing but rot*). **5** (often prec. by *the*) a virulent liver disease of sheep. ● *interjection* esp. *Brit.* expressing incredulity or ridicule. [Old English *rotian* (v.): (n.) Middle English, perhaps from Scandinavian: compare Icelandic, Norwegian *rot*]

rota /ˈroʊtə/ *noun* **1** (**Rota**) *Catholicism* the supreme ecclesiastical and secular court. **2** esp. *Brit.* a rotational order of people, duties to be done, etc. [Latin, = wheel]

Ro·tar·ian /roʊˈtɛriən/ ● *noun* a member of a Rotary Club. ● *adjective* of a Rotary Club or its members.

ro·tary /ˈroʊtəri/ ● *adjective* **1** acting by rotation (*a rotary blade*). **2** operating through the rotation of some part (*a rotary mower*). ● *noun* (*pl.* **-ies**) **1** *US & Cdn* (*NS, Nfld, & BC*) a traffic circle or roundabout. **2** (**Rotary**) **a** (in full **Rotary International**) a worldwide organization of charitable societies for businesspeople and professionals, founded in Chicago in 1905 to promote international goodwill. **b** a Rotary Club. [medieval Latin *rotarius* (as ROTA)]

Rotary Club *noun* a local branch of Rotary International.

rotary phone *noun* (in full **rotary-dial phone**) a telephone with a

numbered dial which is rotated for each digit of a number being called (*compare* TOUCH-TONE).

ro·tate *verb* **1** *intransitive & transitive* move around an axis or centre; spin, revolve. **2 a** *transitive* change the position, responsibility, etc. of a person or thing in a regularly recurring order (*you should rotate your tires every six months*). **b** *intransitive* act or occur in turns or in a particular order (*you wash, I'll dry, and tomorrow we'll rotate*). □ **ro·tat·able** *adjective* **ro·ta·tory** *adjective* [Latin *rotare* from *rota* wheel]

ro·ta·tion *noun* **1** the act or an instance of rotating or being rotated. **2** a regular organized sequence of things or events. **3 a** a regular succession of members of a group through positions or duties etc. **b** (in full **starting rotation**) *Baseball* the group of usu. four or five pitchers on a team that start games in succession. **4** *Astronomy* the movement of a celestial body on its axis. **5** a system of growing different crops in regular order to maintain soil fertility and reduce insect and disease problems. **6** *N Amer.* a tour of duty. □ **ro·ta·tion·al** *adjective* **ro·ta·tion·al·ly** *adverb*

ro·ta·tor *noun* **1** *Anat.* a muscle that rotates a limb etc. **2** a machine or device for causing something to rotate. **3** a revolving apparatus or part.

rotator cuff *noun Anat.* the muscles associated with a capsule with fused tendons that supports the arm at the shoulder joint.

rota·virus /ˈroʊtəˌvaɪrəs/ *noun Biol.* any of a class of wheel-shaped double-stranded RNA viruses, some of which cause acute enteritis in humans. □ **rota·viral** *adjective* [modern Latin, from Latin *rota* wheel + VIRUS]

ROTC *abbreviation US* Reserve Officers Training Corps, a military division with units at civilian educational centres to qualify students for appointment as reserve officers.

rote *noun* (usu. *attributive*) a mechanical practice, routine, performance, etc. (*she was bored by his rote lectures every time she came home late*). □ **by rote 1** in a mechanical or repetitious manner. **2** acquired through memorization without proper understanding or reflection. [Middle English: origin unknown]

rote·none /ˈroʊtəˌnoʊn/ *noun* a toxic crystalline substance, $C_{23}H_{22}O_6$, obtained from the roots of derris and other plants, used as an insecticide. [Japanese *rotenon* from *roten* derris]

rot·gut *noun slang* cheap adulterated usu. inferior alcoholic liquor (also *attributive: rotgut whisky*).

Roth, Phil·ip (Mil·ton) (b.1933), US novelist and short-story writer. Many of his works address the complexity and diversity of contemporary US Jewish life with irony and humour; his best-known novel, *Portnoy's Complaint* (1969), records the intimate confessions of a teenager, Alexander Portnoy, to his psychiatrist.

Rothe·say a town in S New Brunswick, just northeast of Saint John; pop. (2001) 11,505. [after the future Edward VII, one of whose titles was Duke of Rothesay]

Roth·ko, Mark (born Marcus Rothkovich) (1903–70), Latvian-born US painter, whose abstract expressionist canvases consisting of hazy and apparently floating rectangles of colour, usually arranged vertically and in parallel, are meant to absorb the viewer in an act of contemplation; famous works include his series of nine paintings for the Seagram Building in New York, notably *Black on Maroon* (1958).

Roths·child /ˈrɒstʃaɪld, ˈrɒθtʃaɪld/ **Meyer Am·schel** (1743–1812), German financier. He was the founder of the Rothschild banking house in Frankfurt; his five sons all entered banking, setting up branches of the organization across W Europe; notable among them were Nathan Meyer, Baron de Rothschild (1777–1836), who founded a bank in London (1804), and his son, Lionel Nathan, Baron de Rothschild (1808–79), who became Britain's first Jewish MP.

roti /ˈroʊti/ *noun* a dish of Indian origin, common in the Caribbean, consisting of a flat pancake or unleavened bread folded over usu. a spicy meat filling with chickpeas. [Hindi *roti* bread]

roti·fer /ˈroʊtəfər/ *noun* any minute aquatic animal of the phylum Rotifera, with rotatory organs used in swimming and feeding. [modern Latin *rotiferus* from *rota* wheel + *-fer* bearing]

ro·tini /roʊˈtiːni/ *noun N Amer.* a variety of pasta in small spirals. [Italian, = 'little wheels']

ro·tis·serie /roʊˈtɪsəri/ ● *noun* **1** a usu. motor-driven rotating spit for roasting meat esp. over a barbecue or in an oven. **2** (in full **rotisserie league baseball**) a game in which fans draft imaginary baseball teams of usu. 23 players by bidding on actual players with a set amount of money, and collect points for each home run, RBI, stolen base, etc. their players compile. **3** (*attributive*) designating things pertaining to rotisserie or to any similar esp. baseball fantasy league (*rotisserie player*). ● *transitive verb* barbecue or roast meat with a rotisserie.

[French *rôtisserie* (as ROAST); in sports senses after a *Rotisserie* restaurant in Manhattan, where first devised]

roto·grav·ure /ˌroːtəgrəˈvjʊr/ *noun* **1** a printing system using a rotary press with intaglio cylinders, usu. running at high speed for long print runs of magazines, stamps, etc. **2** a section of a newspaper or magazine consisting of pages printed by rotogravure. **3** a sheet etc. printed with this system. [German *Rotogravur* (name of a company) assimilated to PHOTOGRAVURE]

rotor *noun* **1** a rotary part of a machine, esp. in the distributor of an internal combustion engine. **2** a hub with a set of radiating airfoils on a helicopter etc. that provides lift when rotated in an approximately horizontal plane. [irreg. for ROTATOR]

Roto-Rooter *noun* N Amer. *proprietary* a long motor-driven cable or snake which spins through a drain and is used to remove blockages, tree roots, etc. [ROT(ARY) + -O + ROOT[1] + -ER[1]]

Roto·rua /ˌroːtəˈruːə/ a city and health resort on North Island, New Zealand, on the southwest shore of Lake Rotorua, at the centre of a region of thermal springs and geysers; pop. (2001) 56,301.

roto·scope ● *noun* **1** a device which projects and enlarges individual frames of filmed live action to permit them to be used to create cartoon animation and composite film sequences. **2** a computer application which combines live action and other images in a film. ● *transitive verb* transfer (an image from live action film) into another film sequence using a rotoscope. [origin obscure: perhaps the same word as 19th-c. *rotascope*, denoting a kind of gyroscope]

Roto·till·er *noun* N Amer. a machine with rotating blades and prongs used for breaking up or tilling the soil. □ **roto·till** *transitive & intransitive verb*

rot·ten *adjective* (**rot·ten·er**, **rot·ten·est**) **1 a** in a state of decomposition or decay. **b** falling to pieces or liable to break from age or use. **2** miserable, wretched, unfortunate (*I feel rotten today; rotten luck*). **3** despicable, vile, loathsome (*dirty rotten scoundrel; what a rotten thing to do!*). **4** Cdn designating ice or snow which, in the course of melting, has become granular and weak; disintegrating. **5** morally, socially, or politically corrupt. □ **spoil someone rotten** spoil or indulge a person excessively. □ **rot·ten·ness** *noun* [Old Norse *rotinn*, related to ROT, RET]

rotten borough *noun* Brit. hist. (before the Reform Act of 1832) an English borough able to elect an MP though having very few voters.

rot·ten·stone *noun* decomposed siliceous limestone used as a powder for polishing metals.

rot·ter *noun* esp. Brit. slang an objectionable, unpleasant, or reprehensible person.

Rot·ter·dam a city in the Netherlands, one of the world's busiest ports, in the deltas of the Rhine and Meuse rivers, 25 km (15 miles) inland from the North Sea; pop. (est. 2002) 598,100.

rot·ting *adjective* (of snow and ice) = ROTTEN 4.

Rott·weil·er /ˈrɒtˌwaɪlər/ *noun* **1** a breed of large, stocky, powerful dog having short coarse hair with black and tan markings, a broad head with pendent ears, and usu. a docked tail. **2** a very tenacious person. [German from *Rottweil* in SW Germany]

ro·tund /roːˈtʌnd/ *adjective* **1** round, circular, spherical. **2** (of a person) large and plump; fat. □ **ro·tund·ity** *noun* [Latin *rotundus* from *rotare* ROTATE]

ro·tun·da /roːˈtʌndə/ *noun* **1 a** a circular hall or room. **b** the main hall of a public building; a concourse. **2** a building with a circular ground plan, esp. one with a dome. [earlier *rotonda* from Italian *rotonda* (*camera*) round (chamber), fem. of *rotondo* round (as ROTUND)]

Rou·ault /ˈruːoː/ **Georges (Henri)** (1871–1958), French painter and engraver. His best-known expressionist paintings, including *Christ Mocked by Soldiers* (1932), use vivid colours and simplified forms enclosed in thick black outlines.

rou·ble /ˈruːbəl/ Brit. var. of RUBLE.

roué /ˈruːeɪ/ *noun* a debauched man, esp. an elderly one. [French, past participle of *rouer* break (a person) on the wheel (the punishment said to be deserved by such a womanizer)]

Rouen /ruːˈɑ̃, rwɑ̃/ a port on the Seine River in NW France, chief city of Haute-Normandie; pop. (1999) 106,592. It was the medieval capital of Normandy; in 1431 Joan of Arc's trial and execution took place there.

rouge /ruːʒ/ ● *noun* **1** a red powder or cream used for colouring the cheeks. **2** (*rouge*) Cdn esp. hist. a Quebec supporter of a Liberal party. **3** Cdn Football a single point scored when the receiving team fails to run a kick out of the end zone, such as on a punt, kickoff, or missed field goal. **4** powdered ferric oxide etc. as a polishing agent esp. for metal.

● *verb* **1** *transitive* colour with rouge. **2** *intransitive* apply rouge to one's cheeks. [French, = red, from Latin *rubeus*, related to RED]

rouge-et-noir /ˌruːʒeɪˈnwɑr/ *noun* a gambling game using cards, played at a table with red and black marks on which the bettors place their stakes. [French, = 'red and black']

Rou·get de Lisle /ruːˈʒeɪ də ˈliːl/ **Claude Jo·seph** (1760–1836), French army officer, who composed the words and music of the French national anthem, 'La Marseillaise' (1792).

rough ● *adjective* **1** having an uneven or irregular surface, not smooth or level or polished. **2** (of ground, country, etc.) uneven, uncultivated, rugged, wild. **3 a** (of a person) aggressive, rugged, hard; not mild or quiet or gentle. **b** disorderly, riotous, violent (*a rough neighbourhood; a rough sport*). **c** (usu. foll. by *on*) harsh, unreasonable, or unfair (*the teacher is quite rough on them; rough justice*). **4 a** difficult, rigorous, arduous. **b** unfortunate, unreasonable, undeserved (*had rough luck*). **5** harsh, insensitive, indelicate, inconsiderate (*rough words*). **6 a** (of the sea, weather, etc.) violent, stormy, turbulent. **b** (of a flight, landing, trip, etc.) turbulent, bumpy. **7 a** lacking finish, elaboration, comfort, etc. (*rough lodgings*). **b** incomplete, rudimentary (*a rough copy*). **8 a** inexact, approximate, preliminary (*a rough estimate; a rough sketch*). **b** (of paper etc.) for use in writing rough notes etc. **9 a** (of hair, a beard, etc.) shaggy, unkempt, coarse. **b** (of hands, skin, cloth, etc.) coarse in texture or feel; not soft. **10** *informal* **a** sick, unwell (*I'm feeling rough*). **b** depressed, dejected. **11 a** (of food or drink) sharp or harsh in taste (*rough wine*). **b** (of a voice, music, etc.) harsh, grating. ● *adverb* **1** in a rough manner (*he likes to play rough*). **2** (live or sleep etc.) outdoors, without a proper bed or accommodation; on the street. ● *noun* **1** (usu. prec. by *the*) a hard part or aspect of life; hardship (*take the rough with the smooth*). **2** rough or uncultivated ground. **3** Golf rough ground off the fairway between tee and green. **4** an unfinished, provisional, or natural state (*I've written it in rough; she drew up a rough*). **5** Brit. a rough or violent person (*met a bunch of roughs*). ● *transitive verb* (foll. by *out*) **1** shape or plan roughly. **2** make course or heavy cuts in a workpiece of stone, metal, wood, etc. to produce a rough form to be detailed, finished, etc. later. □ **rough and ready** simple or crude but effective; not elaborate but adequate. **rough around the edges 1** (of a person) irritable. **2** (of a thing) having a few imperfections, unpolished. **rough in 1** install (wiring, plumbing, ductwork, etc.) for a room that is planned but is not yet built. **2** lay the groundwork or make preliminary arrangements for (a room) (*rough in a bedroom*). **rough it** live in rough accommodation without basic comforts or conveniences. **rough up** *slang* treat (a person) with violence or abuse. □ **rough·ness** *noun* [Old English *rūh* from West Germanic]

rough·age *noun* **1** = DIETARY FIBRE. **2** coarse fodder.

rough-and-tumble ● *adjective* disregarding rules or convention; riotous, disorderly. ● *noun* **1** a scuffle or fight. **2** rough and aggressive but often enjoyable activity, competition, etc.

rough breathing *noun* see BREATHING 2.

rough·cast Brit. ● *noun* plaster of lime and gravel, used on outside walls. ● *adjective* (of a wall etc.) coated with roughcast.

rough collie *noun* a breed of collie with a long black and white (or black, tan, and white) coat.

rough cut ● *noun* Film the first version of a film after preliminary editing. ● *adjective* N Amer. (usu. **rough-cut**) (of a log, lumber, etc.) having been cut with a coarse blade to an approximate size before a more precise, finished cut is made.

rough diamond *noun* = DIAMOND IN THE ROUGH.

rough·en *transitive & intransitive verb* make or become rough.

rough-hew *transitive verb* (past participle **-hewed** or **-hewn**) shape out roughly; give crude form to.

rough-hewn *adjective* **1** uncouth, unrefined. **2** (of timber, stone, etc.) cut or shaped out roughly.

rough·house esp. N Amer. ● *noun* boisterous or rambunctious play or wrestling, esp. indoors. ● *intransitive verb* engage in rambunctious behaviour or roughhouse. □ **rough·hous·ing** *noun*

rough ice *noun* Cdn a large bank of ice that has accumulated on the shore of a river from the freezing of successive tides.

rough-in *noun* N Amer. **1** (in a building) a preliminary installation of wiring, plumbing, ductwork, etc. for a room that will be added later. **2** the foundation or groundwork for a room that will be added later.

rough·ing *noun* Hockey an unnecessary or excessive use of force for which a player is given a penalty.

rough-legged hawk *noun* a hawk of boreal regions, *Buteo lagopus*, having legs covered with feathers to the base of the toes.

rough·ly *adverb* **1** approximately (*roughly 20 people attended*). **2** in a

---

Consonants: b **but** d **dog** f **few** g **get** h **her** j **yes** k **cat** l **leg** m **man** n **no** p **pen** r **red** s **sit**

coarse or uneven manner (*roughly cut timbers*). **3** in a harsh manner (*she spoke to us roughly*). □ **roughly speaking** in an approximate sense (*it is, roughly speaking, a square*).

rough·neck *informal* ● *noun* **1** a rough or rowdy person. **2** a worker on an oil rig. ● *intransitive verb* work as a roughneck on an oil-drilling operation.

rough·out ● *adjective N Amer.* designating informal outdoor clothing, or materials used for making outdoor clothing, accessories, etc. (*roughout boots*; *chaps finished with roughout suede*). ● *noun Archaeology* an artifact left or abandoned at a preparatory stage of manufacture, the intended final form being clear.

rough ride *noun* a difficult time or experience.

rough·rider *noun* a person who breaks in or can ride unbroken horses.

rough·shod *adjective* (of a horse) having shoes with nailheads projecting to prevent slipping. □ **ride roughshod over** domineer over; treat with disrespect or disregard.

rough stuff *noun informal* boisterous or violent behaviour.

rough trade *noun slang* a tough or sadistic usu. lower-class element among male homosexuals.

roughy *noun* (*pl.* **-ies**) any of several rough-skinned fish of the family Trachichthyidae, esp. the orange roughy. [perhaps from ROUGH]

rou·ille /ˈruːi/ *noun* a Provençal sauce made from pounded red peppers, garlic, olive oil, and bread crumbs or potatoes, blended with stock and served with bouillabaisse or other fish dishes. [French, lit. 'rust', the colour of this sauce]

rou·lade /ruːˈlɑːd/ *noun* **1** any of various dishes cooked or served in the shape of a roll, esp. a slice of meat or a piece of sponge cake spread with a filling and rolled up. **2** a florid passage of runs etc. in solo vocal music, usu. sung to one syllable. [French from *rouler* to roll]

rou·lette /ruːˈlet/ *noun* **1** a gambling game in which a ball is dropped onto a revolving wheel with numbered compartments in the centre of a table, players betting on the number at which the ball will come to rest. **2 a** a revolving toothed wheel used in engraving. **b** a similar wheel for making perforations between postage stamps in a sheet. □ **rou·let·ted** *adjective* (in sense 2b). [French, diminutive of *rouelle* from Late Latin *rotella* diminutive of Latin *rota* wheel]

Rou·melia see RUMELIA.

round ● *adjective* **1 a** shaped like or approximately like a circle, sphere, or cylinder; having a convex or circular outline or surface; curved, not angular. **b** (esp. of a part of the body) full and curved; plump (*round cheeks*; *small, round hands*). **2** done with or involving circular motion. **3 a** entire, continuous, complete (*a round dozen*); fully expressed or developed; all together, not broken or defective or scanty. **b** (of a sum of money) considerable. **4** genuine, candid, outspoken; (of a statement etc.) categorical, unmistakable. **5** (usu. *attributive*) (of a number) expressed for convenience or as an estimate in fewer significant numerals or with a fraction removed (*spent $297.32, or in round numbers $300*). **6 a** (of a style) flowing. **b** (of a voice) full and mellow; not harsh. **7** (of a wine or spirit) having a good balance between taste, smell, and alcoholic strength. **8** *Phonetics* (of a vowel) pronounced with rounded lips. **9** (of a fish) not gutted; whole. ● *noun* **1** a round object or form. **2 a** a revolving motion, a circular or recurring course (*the earth in its yearly round*). **b** a regular recurring series of activities or functions (*one's daily round*; *her life is one long round of parties*). **c** a recurring succession or series of meetings for discussion etc. (*a new round of talks on disarmament*). **3 a** esp. *Brit.* a fixed route on which things are regularly delivered (*milk round*). **b** (often in *pl.*) a route or sequence by which people or things are regularly supervised or inspected (*a doctor's rounds*). **4** an allowance of something distributed or measured out, esp.: **a** a single provision of drinks etc. to each member of a group. **b** ammunition to fire one shot; the act of firing this. **5** each of a set or series, a sequence of actions by each member of a group in turn, esp.: **a** one spell of play in a game etc. **b** one stage in a competition. **c** a cut of beef taken from the thigh, below the rump and above the shank. **7** *Golf* the playing of all the holes in a course once. **8** *Archery* a fixed number of arrows shot from a fixed distance. **9** *Boxing* one of a number of three-minute periods that make up a match. **10** (**the round**) a form of sculpture in which the figure stands clear of any ground (*compare* RELIEF 6a). **11** *Music* a canon for three or more unaccompanied voices singing at the same pitch or in octaves. **12** a single distinct outburst of applause. **13** (in *pl.*) *Military* **a** a watch that goes round inspecting sentries. **b** a circuit made by this. **14** a rung of a ladder. **15** (foll. by *of*) the circumference, bounds, or extent of (*in all the round of Nature*). ● *adverb* & *preposition* esp. *Brit.* = AROUND. ● *verb* **1 a** *transitive* give a round shape to. **b** *intransitive* assume a round shape. **2** *transitive* double or pass around (a corner, cape, etc.). **3** *transitive* (usu. foll. by *off*)

express (a number) in a less exact but more convenient form (also foll. by *down* when the number is decreased and *up* when it is increased). **4** *transitive Phonetics* pronounce (a vowel) with rounded lips. □ **go the rounds** (of news etc.) be passed on from person to person. **in the round 1** with all features shown; all things considered. **2** *Theatre* with the audience around at least three sides of the stage. **3** (of sculpture) with all sides shown; not in relief. **4** (of undressed timber or logs) trimmed on only two sides. **5** (of a fish) not gutted; whole. **make** (or **do**) **the rounds of** go around from place to place. **make one's rounds** take a customary route for inspection etc. **round about 1** in a ring (about); all round; on all sides (of). **2** with a change to an opposite position. **3** approximately (*cost round about $50*). **round and round** several times round. **round the bend** see BEND¹. **round down** see sense 3 of *verb*. **round off 1** bring to a complete or symmetrical or well-ordered state. **2** smooth out; blunt the corners or angles of. **3** = ROUND *verb* 3. **round on a person** make a sudden verbal attack on or unexpected retort to a person. **round out 1** = ROUND OFF 1. **2** provide more detail about. **round peg in a square hole** = SQUARE PEG IN A ROUND HOLE (see PEG). **round the twist** = ROUND THE BEND (see BEND¹). **round up** collect or bring together (members of a group, suspects, cattle, etc.) (see also sense 3 of *verb*). □ **round·ish** *adjective* **round·ness** *noun* [Old French *ro(u)nd-*, stem of *ro(o)nt*, *reont*, from Latin *rotundus* ROTUND]

round·about ● *noun* **1** esp. *Brit.* = TRAFFIC CIRCLE. **2** esp. *Brit.* = CAROUSEL 1. ● *adjective* circuitous, circumlocutory, indirect.

round·ball *noun US* basketball.

round brackets *plural noun* brackets of the form ().

round dance *noun* **1** a dance in which couples move in circles around the ballroom. **2** a dance in which the dancers form one large circle. □ **round dancing** *noun*

round·ed *adjective* **1** that has been rounded. **2** having a circular, spherical, or curving shape. **3** possessing a pleasing depth or wide range of characteristics etc. (*wine with a smooth rounded flavour*; *the book provides a rounded picture of his early life*). **4** (of the voice etc.) sonorous; mellow, full. **5** *Phonetics* (of a vowel etc.) enunciated by contracting the lips to form a circular shape. □ **round·ed·ness** *noun*

round·el /ˈraʊndəl/ *noun* **1 a** a small circular object, esp. a decorative medallion. **b** *Heraldry* any of various circular charges. **2** a circular identifying mark, usu. incorporating the colours of the national flag, painted on military aircraft. **3** a poem of eleven lines in three stanzas. [Old French *rondel(le)* (as ROUND)]

round·elay /ˈraʊndəˌleɪ/ *noun* a short simple song with a refrain. [French *rondelet*, assimilated to LAY³ or *virelay*, a medieval song or lyric poem]

round·er *noun* **1** *N Amer. slang* a person who makes the rounds of prisons or bars; a habitual criminal or drunkard. **2** (in *combination*) a boxing match of a specified number of rounds. **3** (in *pl.*; treated as *sing.*) an English field game resembling baseball. **4** *Cdn* (*Nfld*) a small cod that is gutted, salted and dried without being split.

Round·head *noun* (also called **Parliamentarian**) a member or supporter of the party opposing Charles I in the English Civil War (1642–9), so called because of the short-cropped hairstyle of the Puritans, who were an important element in the forces.

round·house *noun* **1** a circular repair shed for railway locomotives, built around a turntable. **2** *slang* a punch given with a wide sweep of the arm. **3** *hist.* a prison; a place of detention. **4** *Naut.* a cabin or set of cabins on the after part of the quarterdeck, esp. on a sailing ship.

roundhouse kick *noun* (esp. in karate) a kick made with a wide sweep of the leg and rotation of the body.

round·ly *adverb* **1** bluntly, in plain language, severely (*was roundly criticized*). **2** vigorously; energetically (*was roundly applauded*). **3** in a circular way (*swells out roundly*).

round roast *noun* a roast cut from the round of beef.

round robin *noun* **1** *N Amer.* a tournament in which each competitor plays in turn against every other. **2** a petition esp. with signatures written in a circle to conceal the order of writing. **3** any letter or petition which is passed from person to person in a group, often with written contributions added by each. **4** a sequence; a series.

round-shouldered *adjective* with shoulders bent forward so that the back is rounded.

rounds·man *noun* (*pl.* **-men**) a person who makes rounds of inspection, esp. *US* a police officer in charge of a patrol.

round steak *noun N Amer.* a steak cut from a round of beef.

round table *noun* an assembly for discussion, esp. at a conference (often *attributive*: *round-table talks*). [alluding to the one at which King Arthur and his knights sat so that none should have precedence]

round-the-clock *attributive adjective* lasting or covering all day and usu. all night (*round-the-clock care*).

round trip *noun* a trip to a place and back to the point of origin (often *attributive*: *round-trip airfare*).

round-tripper *noun* **1** a person who makes a round trip. **2** *Baseball informal* a home run.

round·up *noun* **1** a systematic rounding up of people or things, esp.: **a** the arrest of people suspected of a particular crime or crimes. **b** the rounding up of cattle etc. usu. for the purpose of registering ownership, counting, etc. **2** the people and horses engaged in the rounding up of cattle etc. **3** a summary; a resumé of facts or events.

round·wood *noun* timber used in the round without being squared by sawing or hewing, such as logs, posts, and pilings.

round·worm *noun* a nematode worm, esp. a parasitic one infesting the gut of a mammal or bird, as *Ascaris lumbricoides* (which infests humans).

roup /ruːp/ *noun* an infectious respiratory disease of poultry. □ **roupy** *adjective* [16th c.: origin unknown]

rouse *verb* **1** *transitive* (often foll. by *from*, *out of*) bring out of sleep; wake. **b** *intransitive* (often foll. by *up*) cease to sleep, wake up. **2** (often foll. by *up*) **a** *transitive* stir up, make active or excited, startle out of inactivity or confidence or carelessness (*roused them from their complacency*; *was roused to protest*). **b** *intransitive* become active. **3** *transitive* provoke to anger (*is terrible when roused*). **4** *transitive* evoke (feelings). **5** *transitive* startle (game) from a lair or cover. □ **rouse oneself** overcome one's indolence; become active. □ **rous·able** *adjective* **rous·er** *noun* [originally as a hawking and hunting term, so prob. from Anglo-French: origin unknown]

rous·ing *adjective* exciting, stirring (*a rousing cheer*; *a rousing game of tennis*). □ **rous·ing·ly** *adverb*

Rousse see RUSE.

Rous·seau /ruː'soː/ **1 Henri (Julien)** (known as 'le Douanier' = customs officer) (1844–1910), French painter. He retired as a customs official in 1885, and became a prominent naive artist; fantastic dreams and exotic jungle landscapes often form the subjects of his bold and colourful paintings, which include *Sleeping Gypsy* (1897) and *Tropical Storm with Tiger* (1891). **2 Jean-Jacques** (1712–78), French philosopher and writer, born in Switzerland. His philosophy is underpinned by a belief in the superiority of the 'noble savage'. His works, highly critical of the existing social order, include the novel *Émile* (1762), the *Social Contract* (1762), which anticipated much of the thinking of the French Revolution, and the *Confessions* (1782), considered one of the earliest autobiographies. **3 (Pierre Étienne) Théo·dore** (1812–67), French landscape painter. A leading figure of the Barbizon school, he championed painting directly from nature; important works include *Under the Birches, Evening* (1842–4). □ **Rous·seau·esque** *adjective* **Rous·seau·ian** *adjective* **Rous·seau·ist** *noun & adjective*

Rous·sil·lon /ruːsiˈjɔ̃/ a former province of S France, on the border with Spain in the E Pyrenees, now part of Languedoc-Roussillon. It was acquired from Spain for France by Louis XIV in 1659, and retains many Spanish characteristics and traditions; Catalan is widely spoken.

roust *transitive verb* **1** (often foll. by *up*, *out*) **a** rouse, stir up. **b** root out. **2** *N Amer. slang* jostle, harass, rough up. [perhaps alteration of ROUSE]

roust·about *noun* **1** a labourer on an oil rig. **2** an unskilled or casual labourer. **3** *esp. N Amer.* **a** a dock labourer or deckhand. **b** a circus labourer.

rout¹ ● *noun* **1 a** a disorderly retreat of defeated troops. **b** a decisive defeat. **2** *Brit. archaic* a large evening party or reception. ● *transitive verb* **1** cause to retreat in disorder. **2** defeat decisively. □ **put to rout** put to flight, defeat utterly. [Old French *route*, ultimately from Latin *ruptus* broken]

rout² *verb* **1** *intransitive & transitive* = ROOT² 1, 2. **2** *transitive* cut a groove, or any pattern not extending to the edges, in (a wooden or metal surface). □ **rout out** force or fetch out of bed or from a house or hiding place. [var. of ROOT²]

route /ruːt, rʌut/ ● *noun* **1 a** a way or course taken (esp. regularly) in getting from a starting point to a destination (*drove home by the quickest route*). **b** a series of steps taken to achieve something (*the route to success*). **c** (esp. in the US) (with following numeral) a specific highway (*Route 66*). **2** *N Amer.* a round of stops regularly travelled in delivering, selling, or collecting goods (*paper route*). ● *transitive verb* (**rout·ing**) send or forward or direct to be sent by a particular route. [Old French *r(o)ute* road, ultimately from Latin *ruptus* broken]

route march ● *noun* **1** a training march for troops. **2** *informal* any long gruelling walk. ● *intransitive verb* go on a route march.

rout·er¹ /ˈrʌutər/ *noun* a tool used for routing, cutting grooves, etc.

rout·er² /ˈrʌutər/ *noun* a device which forwards data packets to the appropriate parts of a computer network.

rou·tine /ruːˈtiːn/ ● *noun* **1** a regular course or procedure, an unvarying performance of certain acts. **2** a set sequence in a performance, esp. a dance, comedy act, etc. **3** *informal* a hackneyed, predictable response or formula of speech (*went into her overprotective mother routine*). **4** *Computing* a sequence of instructions for performing a task. ● *adjective* **1** performed as part of a routine (*routine duties*). **2** of a customary or standard kind (*a routine tooth extraction*). □ **rou·tine·ly** *adverb* [French (as ROUTE)]

rou·tin·ize *transitive verb* (also esp. *Brit.* **-ise**) subject to a routine; make into a matter of routine. □ **rou·tin·iz·a·tion** *noun*

roux /ruː/ *noun* (*pl.* same) a mixture of fat (esp. butter) and flour used to thicken sauces etc. [French, = browned (butter): see RUSSET]

Rouyn-Noranda /ruːˌɑnɔrˈɑndə/ a city in NW central Quebec, about 40 km east of the border with Ontario and 100 km west of Val-d'Or; pop. (2001) 39,621. [after J.-B. *Rouyn*, captain with the Royal-Roussillon Regiment *c.*1759 + *Noranda*, blend of *north* + *Canada*]

ROV *abbreviation* remotely operated vehicle.

Ro·van·iemi /ˈroːvəˌniəmi/ the principal town of Finnish Lapland; pop. (est. 1999) 35,700.

rove¹ *verb* **1** *intransitive* wander without a settled destination, roam, ramble. **2** *intransitive* (of eyes) look in changing directions. **3** *transitive* wander over or through. [Middle English, originally an archery term = shoot at a casual mark with the range not determined, perhaps from dial. *rave* stray, prob. of Scandinavian origin]

rove² ● *noun* (also **roving**) a sliver of cotton, wool, etc., drawn out and slightly twisted. ● *transitive verb* form into roves. [18th c.: origin unknown]

rove³ *noun* a small metal plate or ring for a rivet to pass through and be clenched over, esp. in boat building. [Old Norse *ró*, with excrescent *v*]

rove beetle *noun* any long-bodied beetle of the family Staphylinidae, usu. found in decaying animal and vegetable matter.

rov·er¹ *noun* **1** a roving person; a wanderer. **2** *Football* a defensive linebacker assigned to move around in anticipation of opponents' play. **3** a remote-controlled surface vehicle for extraterrestrial exploration. **4** (**Rover**) *Cdn* a member of the senior level (ages 18-26) in Scouting. **5** (**Rover**) a pet dog.

rov·er² *noun* a sea robber, a pirate. [Middle Low German, Middle Dutch *rōver* from *rōven* rob, related to REAVE]

rov·ing *adjective* **1** wandering, roaming. **2** (of a journalist etc.) required to travel to locations to deal with events as they occur. **3** characterized by roving; inclined to wander (*a roving life*).

roving commission *noun* *Cdn & Brit.* authority given to a person or persons conducting an inquiry to travel as may be necessary.

roving eye *noun* (esp. in a man) a tendency to flirt or to be fickle sexually.

row¹ /roː/ *noun* **1** a number of persons or things in a more or less straight line. **2** a line of seats across a theatre etc. (*in the front row*). **3** a street with a continuous line of houses along one or each side. **4** a line of plants in a field or garden. **5** a horizontal line of entries in a table etc. **6** a complete line of stitches in knitting or crochet. **7** a rank on a chessboard or checkerboard. □ **a hard** (or **long etc.**) **row to hoe** a difficult task. **in a row 1** forming a row. **2** in succession (*two Sundays in a row*). [Middle English *raw*, *row*, from Old English from Germanic]

row² /roː/ ● *verb* **1** *transitive* propel (a boat) with oars. **2** *transitive* convey (a passenger) in a boat in this way. **3** *transitive* propel a boat in this way. **4** *transitive* make (a stroke) or achieve (a rate of striking) in rowing. **5** *transitive* compete in (a race) by rowing. **6** *transitive* row a race with. ● *noun* **1** a period of rowing. **2** an excursion in a rowboat. □ **row·er** *noun* [Old English *rōwan* from Germanic, related to RUDDER, Latin *remus* oar]

row³ /rʌu/ *informal* ● *noun* **1** a fierce quarrel or dispute. **2** *esp. Brit.* a loud noise or commotion. **3** *Brit.* **a** a severe reprimand. **b** the condition of being reprimanded (*shall get into a row*). ● *verb* **1** *intransitive* make or engage in a row. **2** *transitive Brit.* reprimand. □ **make** (or **kick up**) **a row 1** *esp. Brit.* raise a noise. **2** make a vigorous protest. [18th-c. slang: origin unknown]

rowan /ˈroːən, ˈrʌu-/ *noun* **1** (in full **rowan tree**) = MOUNTAIN ASH. **2** (in full **rowanberry**) the scarlet berry of this tree. [Scandinavian, corresponding to Norwegian *rogn*, *raun*, Icelandic *reynir*]

row·boat *noun* *N Amer.* a small boat propelled by oars.

Vowels: a *cat* ɑ *arm* e *bed* ɜr *her* ɜ: *deux* ə *ago* ɪ *sit* i *cosy* iː *feed* ɒ *hot* ɔ *pore* oː *no* ʌ *run* ʊ *put*

row crop *noun* crops, e.g. corn or beans, grown in rows with enough space between them to allow cultivation through the growing season.

rowdy ● *adjective* (**row·di·er**, **row·di·est**) noisy and disorderly. ● *noun* (*pl.* **-dies**) a rowdy person. □ **row·di·ly** *adverb* **row·di·ness** *noun* **row·dy·ism** *noun* [19th-c. US, originally = lawless backwoodsman: origin unknown]

rowel /'rauəl/ ● *noun* a spiked revolving disc at the end of a spur. ● *transitive verb* (**row·elled**, **row·el·ling**; **row·eled**, **row·el·ing**) urge with a rowel. [Old French *roel(e)* from Late Latin *rotella* diminutive of Latin *rota* wheel]

row house *noun* N Amer. any of a row of usu. similar houses joined by party walls.

rowing boat *noun* esp. *Brit.* = ROWBOAT.

rowing machine *noun* an exercise machine for simulating the action of rowing.

Row·land·son /'rɔːləndsən/ **Thom·as** (1756–1827), English painter and caricaturist. In many watercolours and drawings he satirized the manners, morals, and occupations of Georgian England; his best-known ones appear in a series of books known as *The Tours of Dr. Syntax* (1812–21).

Row·ling /'rɔːlɪŋ/ **Joanne Kath·leen** (b.1965), British novelist, author of the highly successful *Harry Potter* series of children's books, the first volume of which, *Harry Potter and the Philosopher's Stone*, was published in 1997.

row·lock /'rɒlək, 'rʌlək/ *noun Brit.* = OARLOCK. [alteration of earlier OARLOCK, after ROW²]

Rown·tree a family of English business entrepreneurs and philanthropists: **Jo·seph** (1801–59) was a grocer, who established several Quaker schools. **Henry Isaac** (1838–83), Joseph's son, founded the family cocoa and chocolate manufacturing firm in York, England. **Jo·seph** (1836–1925), Henry's brother, became Henry's business partner in 1869 and founded three Rowntree trusts (1904) to support research into social welfare and policy. **Ben·jam·in See·bohm** (1871–1954) was Joseph (Jr.)'s son and chairman of the firm from 1925 to 1941. He conducted surveys of poverty in York (1897–98; 1936).

Rox·boro /'rɒksbərə/ a former town in south central Quebec, on the Rivière des Prairies toward the southwest end of the Island of Montreal, now part of the city of Montreal; pop. (2001) 5,642. [origin uncertain]

Rox·burgh·shire /'rɒksbərə,ʃɪr/ a former county of S Scotland. Since 1975 it has been part of Borders region (now Scottish Borders).

Roy ▶ **1** /rɔɪ/ **Arun·dhati** (b.1961), Indian novelist. She won the Booker Prize in 1997 for *The God of Small Things*. **2** /rwɒ/ **Gab·ri·elle** (1909–83), Canadian writer. Her first novel, *Bonheur d'occasion* (translated as *The Tin Flute*) appeared in 1945. Her later novels, almost all of which were translated into English, include *Rue Deschambault* (1955) and *Ces enfants de ma vie* (1977) and often evoke her Franco-Manitoban childhood. The first woman to be elected to the Royal Society of Canada, she won the Governor General's Award three times. **3** /rwɒ/ **Pat·rick** (b.1965), Canadian hockey player. A goalie known for his butterfly style, he led the Montreal Canadiens to the Stanley Cup as a rookie in 1986 and again in 1993 before being traded to the Colorado Avalanche, with whom he won two more Stanley Cups (1996, 2001). He retired in 2003 holding numerous records, including that for most career regular-season wins (551).

Royal, Mount see MOUNT ROYAL.

roy·al ● *adjective* **1** of or suited to or worthy of a king or queen. **2** in the service or under the patronage of a king or queen (*Royal Winnipeg Ballet*). **3** belonging to the king or queen (*the royal hands; the royal anger*). **4** of the family of a king or queen. **5** kingly, majestic, stately, splendid. **6** on a great scale, of exceptional size or quality, first-rate (*gave us a royal send-off*). **7** *informal* extreme; of the highest degree (*a royal pain*). ● *noun* **1** *informal* a member of the royal family. **2** a royal sail or mast. **3** a size of paper, about 620 × 500 mm (25 × 20 in.). □ **royal road to** way of attaining without trouble. □ **royal·ly** *adverb* [Old French *roial* from Latin *regalis* REGAL]

Royal Air Force *noun* the British air force. Abbr.: RAF.

royal assent *noun* (in Canada, the UK, and other Commonwealth countries) the formal consent of the sovereign or his or her representative to a bill passed by a legislature.

royal blue ● *noun* a deep vivid blue. ● *adjective* of this colour.

Royal Canadian Air Force *noun hist.* Canada's permanent air force between 1924 and unification of the armed forces in 1968. Abbr.: RCAF.

Royal Canadian Legion *noun* see LEGION 2.

Royal Canadian Mounted Police *noun* Canada's national police force, which enforces federal statutes and provides policing for jurisdictions without municipal police protection in all provinces and territories except Ontario and Quebec. Abbr.: RCMP.

Royal Canadian Navy *noun hist.* Canada's permanent naval force between 1910 and unification of the armed forces in 1968. Abbr.: RCN.

Royal Commission *noun* (in Canada, the UK, and other Commonwealth countries) **1** a commission of inquiry appointed by the Crown at the request of the government to investigate and report on a particular matter. **2** a committee so appointed.

Roy·ale, Île /rwa'jal/ the former French name (until 1758) for Cape Breton Island.

royal family *noun* the family to which a sovereign belongs.

royal fern *noun* a fern, *Osmunda regalis*, with large spreading fronds.

royal flush *noun* a poker hand consisting of the five highest cards in one suit.

Royal Flying Corps *noun hist.* the name of the British air force from 1912 to 1918, when it was amalgamated with the Royal Naval Air Service to form the Royal Air Force.

royal gala *noun* a variety of gala apple with higher colour.

royal icing *noun* a hard white icing made from icing sugar and egg whites, used typically on wedding cakes.

royal·ist ● *noun* **1 a** a supporter of monarchy. **b** *hist.* a supporter of the King against Parliament in the English Civil War. **2** *informal* a member of a conservative or reactionary right-wing group; one who believes in the superiority of a minority over the majority (*an economic royalist*). ● *adjective* of or pertaining to royalists or royalism. □ **royal·ism** *noun*

royal jelly *noun* a substance secreted by honeybee workers and fed by them to future queen bees.

Royal Marine *noun* a British marine (see MARINE *noun* 2a).

royal mast *noun* a mast above a topgallant mast.

Royal Navy *noun* the British navy. Abbr.: RN.

royal prerogative *noun* see PREROGATIVE 2.

Royal Purple *noun* (in full **Royal Purple of Canada**) a women's social organization affiliated with the Elks.

royal sail *noun* a sail above a topgallant sail.

royal tennis *noun* = COURT TENNIS.

roy·al·ty *noun* (*pl.* **-ties**) **1** the office or dignity or power of a king or queen, sovereignty. **2 a** royal persons. **b** a member of a royal family. **3** a sum paid to a patentee for the use of a patent or to an author etc. for each copy of a book etc. sold or for each public performance of a work. **4 a** a royal right (now esp. over minerals) granted by the sovereign to an individual or corporation. **b** a payment made by a producer of minerals, oil, or natural gas to the owner of the site or of the mineral rights over it.

Royal Victorian Order *noun* (in the UK) an order founded by Queen Victoria in 1896 and conferred usu. for great service rendered to the sovereign.

royal warrant *noun* a warrant authorizing a manufacturer etc. to supply goods to a specified royal person.

royal 'we' *noun* the use of 'we' instead of 'I' by a single person (as traditionally by a sovereign).

Royce ▶ **1 Sir (Fred·erick) Henry** (1863–1933), English engine designer. He founded the company of Rolls-Royce Ltd. with C. S. Rolls in 1906, and became famous for designing the Rolls-Royce Silver Ghost automobile and aircraft engines. **2 Jo·siah** (1855–1916), US idealist philosopher, whose thought was important in the development of formal logic in the US; his works include *The Religious Aspect of Philosophy* (1885), *The Conception of God* (1897), and *The Problem of Christianity* (1913).

roz·zer *noun Brit. slang* a police officer. [19th c.: origin unknown]

RP *abbreviation* RECEIVED PRONUNCIATION.

RPG *abbreviation* **1** *Computing* report program generator, a high-level commercial programming language. **2** rocket-propelled grenade. **3** role-playing game.

RPI *abbreviation* (in the UK) retail price index.

rpm *abbreviation* revolutions per minute.

RPN *abbreviation* **1** REGISTERED PRACTICAL NURSE. **2** registered psychiatric nurse.

RR *abbreviation* N Amer. **1** railroad. **2** RURAL ROUTE.

RRIF /rɪf/ *abbreviation* Cdn Registered Retirement Income Fund, a tax-sheltered savings plan which provides retirement income.

RRSP *abbreviation Cdn* Registered Retirement Savings Plan, a tax-sheltered plan for saving for retirement.

Rs. *abbreviation* rupee(s).

RSA *abbreviation* designating the Rivest Shamir Adelman key encryption algorithm used for encrypting most networks. [named after three computer scientists who proposed it]

R.S.C. *abbreviation Cdn* Revised Statutes of Canada.

RSFSR *abbreviation hist.* Russian Soviet Federative Socialist Republic.

RSI *abbreviation* REPETITIVE STRAIN INJURY.

RSM *abbreviation* Regimental Sergeant Major.

RSP *abbreviation Cdn* Retirement Savings Plan.

RSV *abbreviation* REVISED STANDARD VERSION.

RSVP ● *noun* a reply to an invitation. ● *intransitive verb* (**RSVP'd, RSVPd; RSVP'ing, RSVP·ing**) reply to an invitation (*have you RSVP'd yet?*). [French, abbreviation of *répondez s'il vous plaît*, please answer]

rt. *abbreviation* right.

Rte. *abbreviation* route.

RTF *abbreviation* rich text format, a file format which permits easy transfer of graphics and formatted text between different applications and operating systems.

Rt. Hon. *abbreviation* Right Honourable.

Rt. Rev. *abbreviation* (also **Rt. Revd.**) Right Reverend.

RU-486 *noun* a commonly-used name for the drug mifepristone, which can be used to induce abortion in early pregnancy. [the initials of *Roussel-Uclaf*, the French manufacturer of the drug + 486, the drug's laboratory serial number]

Ru *symbol Chem.* the element ruthenium.

rub ● *verb* (**rubbed, rub·bing**) **1** *transitive* move one's hand or another object with firm pressure over the surface of. **2** *transitive* (usu. foll. by *against, in, on, over*) apply (one's hand etc.) in this way. **3** *transitive* clean or polish or make dry or bare by rubbing. **4** *transitive* (often foll. by *over*) apply (polish, ointment, etc.) by rubbing. **5** *transitive* (foll. by *in, into, through*) use rubbing to make (a substance) go into or through something. **6** *transitive* (often foll. by *together*) move or slide (objects) against each other. **7** *intransitive* (foll. by *against, on*) move with contact or friction. **8** *transitive* chafe or make sore by rubbing. **9** *intransitive* (of cloth, skin, etc.) become frayed or worn or sore or bare with friction. **10** *transitive* reproduce the design of (a sepulchral brass or a stone) by rubbing paper laid on it with coloured chalk etc. **11** *transitive* (foll. by *to*) reduce to powder etc. by rubbing. ● *noun* **1** a period or an instance of rubbing (*give it a rub*). **2** an impediment or difficulty (*there's the rub*). **3** a substance applied by rubbing. **4** a massage. □ **not have two coins to rub together** have no money. **rub along** *Brit. informal* cope or manage without undue difficulty. **rub down 1** dry or smooth or clean by rubbing. **2** massage. **rub elbows with** *N Amer.* associate or come into contact with (another person or thing). **rub one's hands** rub one's hands together usu. in sign of keen satisfaction, or for warmth. **rub it in** (or **rub a person's nose in it**) emphasize or repeat an embarrassing fact etc. **rub noses** (of two people) touch noses in greeting, as a sign of friendship in some societies. **rub off 1** (usu. foll. by *on*) be transferred by contact, be transmitted (*some of his attitudes have rubbed off on me*). **2** remove by rubbing. **rub out 1** erase. **2** esp. *N Amer. slang* kill, eliminate. **rub salt into** (or **in**) **the wound** (or **wounds**) behave or speak so as to aggravate a hurt already inflicted. **rub shoulders with** = RUB ELBOWS WITH. **rub** (or *Brit.* rub up) **the wrong way** irritate or repel as by stroking a cat against the lie of its fur. [Middle English *rubben*, perhaps from Low German *rubben*, of unknown origin]

Rub' al Khali /ˌrub al ˈkɒli/ a vast desert in the Arabian peninsula, extending from central Saudi Arabia southward to Yemen and eastward to the United Arab Emirates and Oman. It is also known as the Great Sandy Desert and the Empty Quarter.

ru·bato /ruːˈbɑːtoː/ *Music* ● *noun* (*pl.* **-tos** or **ru·bati** /-tiː/) the temporary disregarding of strict tempo. ● *adjective* performed with a flexible tempo. [Italian, = robbed]

rub·ber¹ *noun* **1** a tough elastic polymeric substance made from the latex of plants or synthetically (often *attributive*: *rubber ball; rubber boots*). **2** a piece of this or another substance for erasing pencil or ink marks. **3** *informal* a condom. **4** (in *pl.*) **a** *N Amer.* galoshes. **b** *Cdn* (*Nfld*) long, waterproof boots worn esp. by fishermen and sealers. **5** a person who rubs; a masseur or masseuse. **6** an implement used for rubbing. **7** (*prec. by the*) *Hockey slang* the puck. **8** *Baseball* an oblong piece of rubber embedded in the pitcher's mound on which the pitcher stands to deliver the ball. □ **burn** (or **lay**) **rubber** esp. *N Amer.* **1** travel very quickly in a car; speed. **2** leave tire tracks on a surface, usu. by

accelerating or braking rapidly. □ **rub·bery** *adjective* **rubber·i·ness** *noun* [RUB + -ER¹, from its early use to rub out pencil marks]

rub·ber² *noun* **1** a match of three or five successive games between the same sides or persons at bridge, whist, cricket, lawn tennis, etc. **2** (*prec. by the*) **a** the act of winning a majority of games in a rubber. **b** a deciding game when scores are even (*rubber match*). [origin unknown: used as a term in bowls from *c.* 1600]

rubber band *noun* a loop of rubber for holding papers etc. together.

rubber cement *noun* an adhesive containing rubber in a solvent.

rubber cheque *noun slang* a cheque that bounces.

rubber-chicken *adjective N Amer. slang* of or relating to the round of dinner and luncheon appearances made by a speaker, politician, etc. (*rubber-chicken circuit*). [so called because of the stereotypically mediocre food served at these functions]

rubber dam *noun* = DAM¹ *noun* 4a.

rubber-faced *adjective* having a face that is able to assume easily many esp. grotesque expressions (*a rubber-faced comedian*).

rubber·ize *transitive verb* (also esp. *Brit.* **-ise**) treat or coat with rubber.

rubber·neck *informal* ● *noun* a person who stares inquisitively or stupidly. ● *intransitive verb* act in this way. □ **rubber·neck·er** *noun*

rubber plant *noun* **1** an evergreen plant, *Ficus elastica*, with dark green shiny leaves, often cultivated as a houseplant. **2** (also **rubber tree**) any of various tropical trees yielding latex, esp. *Hevea brasiliensis*.

rubber stamp ● *noun* **1** a device for inking and imprinting on a surface. **2 a** a person who mechanically copies or agrees to others' actions. **b** an indication of such agreement. ● *transitive verb* (**rubber-stamp**) approve automatically without proper consideration.

rub·bing *noun* **1** in senses of RUB *verb*. **2** an impression or copy made by rubbing (see RUB *verb* 10).

rubbing alcohol *noun* denatured alcohol used in massaging, as an antiseptic, etc.

rub·bish ● *noun* **1** esp. *Brit.* waste material; debris, refuse, litter. **2** worthless material or articles. **3** absurd ideas or suggestions; nonsense. ● *transitive verb Brit. informal* **1** criticize severely. **2** reject as worthless. □ **rub·bishy** *adjective* [Anglo-French *rubbous* etc., perhaps from RUBBLE]

rub·ble *noun* **1** rough fragments of stone or brick etc., esp. from demolished or decaying buildings. **2** pieces of undressed stone used esp. as a filling for walls. **3** *Geol.* loose angular stones etc. forming a mantle over some rocks, and found beneath alluvium or soil. **4** water-worn stones. □ **rub·bly** *adjective* [Middle English *robyl, rubel*, of uncertain origin: compare Old French *robe* spoils]

rubby *noun* (*pl.* **-bies**) (also **rubby·dub**) *Cdn slang* a person who drinks rubbing alcohol, aftershave, etc. mixed with cheap wine etc.; a derelict alcoholic. [abbreviation of RUBBING ALCOHOL]

rub·down *noun* an act of drying, smoothing down, or cleaning something by rubbing.

rube *noun N Amer. informal* a country bumpkin. [abbreviation of the name *Reuben*]

Rube Gold·berg *adjective N Amer.* designating a device that is unnecessarily complicated, impractical, or ingenious. [R. *Goldberg* US humorist and artist d.1970, whose illustrations often depicted such devices]

rubel /ˈruːbel/ *noun* (*pl.* **rubli**) a monetary unit of Belarus. [Belarussian, as RUBLE]

ru·bella /ruːˈbelə/ *noun Med.* an acute infectious viral disease with a red rash; German measles. [modern Latin, neuter pl. of Latin *rubellus* reddish]

ru·bel·lite /ˈruːbəˌlaɪt/ *noun* a red variety of tourmaline. [Latin *rubellus* reddish]

Ru·ben·esque /ˌruːbənˈesk/ *adjective* (esp. of a woman's body) plump and voluptuous.

Ru·bens /ˈruːbənz/ **Sir Peter Paul** (1577–1640), Flemish painter. The foremost exponent of northern Baroque, he was appointed court portraitist in Antwerp (1609); his works include altarpieces such as *Descent from the Cross* (1611–14), and mythological paintings featuring voluptuous female nudes, as in *Venus and Adonis* (*c.*1635).

ru·beo·la /ruːˈbiːələ, ˌruːbiˈoːlə/ *noun Med.* measles. [medieval Latin from Latin *rubeus* red]

Ru·bi·con /ˈruːbɪˌkɒn/ a stream in NE Italy which marked the ancient boundary between Italy and Cisalpine Gaul. By taking his army across it into Italy in 49 BC, Julius Caesar broke the law forbidding a general to lead an army out of his province, and so committed himself to war

Consonants: b *but*   d *dog*   f *few*   g *get*   h *her*   j *yes*   k *cat*   l *leg*   m *man*   n *no*   p *pen*   r *red*   s *sit*

against the Senate. Thus to 'cross the Rubicon' is to commit oneself irrevocably to a course of action.

ru·bi·cund /ˈruːbɪˌkʌnd/ *adjective* (of a face, complexion, or person in these respects) ruddy, high-coloured. □ **ru·bi·cund·ity** /-ˈkʌndɪti/ *noun* [French *rubicond* or Latin *rubicundus* from *rubēre* be red]

ru·bid·ium /ruːˈbɪdɪəm/ *noun Chem.* a soft silvery element occurring naturally in various minerals and as the radioactive isotope rubidium-87. Symbol **Rb**; at. no.: 37. [Latin *rubidus* 'red' (with reference to its spectral lines)]

Rubik's cube /ˈruːbɪks/ *noun proprietary* a puzzle in which the aim is to restore the faces of a composite cube to single colours by rotating layers of constituent smaller cubes. [E. *Rubik*, Hungarian inventor, b.1944]

Rub·in·stein /ˈruːbɪnˌstaɪn/ **1 Anton (Grigor·evich)** (1829–94), Russian composer and pianist, who founded the St. Petersburg Conservatory (1862) and was its director (1862–7 and 1887–91), composing symphonies, operas, songs, and piano music, including *Melody in F* (1852); his brother Nikolai (1835–81) was also a pianist and composer. **2 Artur** (1888–1982), Polish-born US pianist. At the age of 12 he made his public debut in Berlin, and thereafter toured extensively in Europe and the US; his recordings include the complete works of Chopin.

ru·ble /ˈruːbəl/ *noun* (also *Brit.* **rou·ble**) the chief monetary unit of Russia and some other former republics of the USSR, equal to 100 kopecks. [French from Russian *rubl*′]

ru·bric /ˈruːbrɪk/ *noun* **1** a heading or passage in red or special lettering. **2** a direction for the conduct of divine service inserted in a liturgical book. **3** a category or designation. **4** explanatory words. **5** an established custom. [Old French *rubrique*, *rubrice* or Latin *rubrica* (*terra*) red (earth or ochre) as writing material, related to *rubeus* red]

rubri·cate /ˈruːbrɪˌkeɪt/ *transitive verb* **1** mark with red; print or write in red. **2** provide with rubrics. □ **rubri·ca·tion** *noun* **rubri·ca·tor** *noun* [Latin *rubricare* from *rubrica*: see RUBRIC]

ruby ● *noun* (*pl.* **-bies**) **1** a rare precious stone consisting of corundum with a colour varying from deep crimson or purple to pale rose. **2** a glowing purplish-red colour. ● *adjective* of this colour. ● *transitive verb* (**-bies, -bied**) dye or tinge with a ruby colour. [Old French *rubi* from medieval Latin *rubinus* (*lapis*) red (stone), related to Latin *rubeus* red]

ruby red *noun* (also **ruby red grapefruit**) a sweet variety of grapefruit with dark red flesh.

ruby-throated hummingbird *noun* a hummingbird, *Archilochus colubris*, that has a metallic green back (the male having a bright red throat) and is the commonest hummingbird in much of N America.

ruby wedding *noun* the fortieth anniversary of a wedding.

ruche /ruːʃ/ *noun* a frill or gathering of lace etc. as a trimming. □ **ruched** *adjective* **ruch·ing** *noun* [French from medieval Latin *rusca* tree bark, of Celtic origin]

ruck[1] *noun* **1** (prec. by *the*) **a** an undistinguished crowd of persons or things. **b** (in racing) the main body of competitors not likely to overtake the leaders. **2** *Rugby* a loose scrum with the ball on the ground. [Middle English, = stack of fuel, heap, rick: apparently Scandinavian, = Norwegian *ruka* in the same senses]

ruck[2] ● *transitive & intransitive verb* (often foll. by *up*) make or become creased or wrinkled. ● *noun* a crease or wrinkle. [Old Norse *hrukka*]

ruckle *verb & noun esp. Brit.* = RUCK[2].

ruck·sack *noun* a backpack. [German from *rucken* dial. var. of *Rücken* back + *Sack* SACK[1]]

ruck·us *noun esp. N Amer.* a noisy disturbance; an uproar or commotion. [compare RUCTION, RUMPUS]

ruc·tion *noun informal* **1** a disturbance or tumult. **2** (in *pl.*) unpleasant arguments or reactions. [19th c.: origin unknown]

rud·beck·ia /rʌdˈbekɪə/ *noun* any of various tall plants constituting the genus *Rudbeckia* of the composite family, native to N America, bearing yellow or orange flowers with a prominent conical dark-coloured disc, and including black-eyed Susan and various coneflowers. [modern Latin from O. *Rudbeck*, Swedish botanist d.1740]

rudd *noun* (*pl.* same) a European freshwater fish of the carp family, *Scardinius erythrophthalmus*, with red fins. [apparently related to *rud* red colour, from Old English *rudu*, related to RED]

rud·der *noun* **1 a** a flat piece hinged vertically to the stern of a vessel for steering. **b** a vertical airfoil pivoted from the tailplane of an aircraft, for controlling its horizontal movement. **2** a guiding principle etc. □ **rud·der·less** *adjective* [Old English *rōther* from West Germanic *rōthra-* from the stem of ROW[2]]

rud·dle ● *noun* a red ochre, esp. of a kind used for marking sheep. ● *transitive verb* mark or colour with or as with ruddle. [related to obsolete *rud*: see RUDD]

ruddy *adjective* (**rud·di·er**, **rud·di·est**) **1** (of a person or complexion) freshly or healthily red. **2** reddish. **3** *Brit. informal* bloody, damnable. □ **rud·di·ly** *adverb* **rud·di·ness** *noun* [Old English *rudig* (as RUDD)]

ruddy duck *noun* a duck, *Oxyura jamaicensis*, the male of which has deep red-brown plumage.

rude *adjective* **1** (of a person, remark, etc.) impolite or offensive. **2** roughly made or done; lacking subtlety or accuracy (*a rude plow*). **3 a** primitive or unsophisticated (*rude simplicity*). **b** *archaic* uneducated. **4** abrupt, sudden, startling, violent (*a rude reminder*). **5** *informal* indecent, lewd (*a rude joke*). **6** esp. *Brit.* vigorous or hearty (*rude health*). □ **rude·ly** *adverb* **rude·ness** *noun* [Old French from Latin *rudis* 'unwrought']

rude awakening *noun* a severe disillusionment or arousal from complacency.

ruder·al /ˈruːdərəl/ ● *adjective* (of a plant) growing on or in rubbish or rubble. ● *noun* a ruderal plant. [modern Latin *ruderalis* from Latin *rudera* pl. of *rudus* rubble]

rudi·ment /ˈruːdɪmənt/ *noun* **1** (in *pl.*) the elements or first principles of a subject. **2** (in *pl.*) an imperfect beginning of something undeveloped or yet to develop. **3** *Biol.* an undeveloped or immature part or organ, esp. a structure in an embryo or larva which will develop into a limb etc. [French *rudiment* or Latin *rudimentum* (as RUDE, after *elementum* ELEMENT)]

rudi·ment·ary /ˌruːdɪˈmentri, -təri/ *adjective* **1** involving basic principles; fundamental. **2** incompletely developed; vestigial. □ **rudi·men·tar·i·ly** *adverb* **rudi·men·tar·i·ness** *noun*

Ru·dolf (1858–89), archduke and crown prince of Austria, son of Franz Josef I; he committed suicide with his mistress at his hunting lodge at Mayerling, Austria.

Rudolf I (1218–91), king of Germany 1273–91 and founder of the Hapsburg dynasty.

Rudolf, Lake the former name (until 1979) for Lake Turkana. (See TURKANA, LAKE.)

Rudra /ˈrʊdrə/ **1** (in the Rig-Veda) a Vedic minor god, associated with the storm, father of the Maruts. **2** *Hinduism* one of the names of Shiva. [Sanskrit, = howler (*rud* howl, roar)]

rue[1] ● *transitive verb* (**rues, rued, rue·ing** or **ruing**) repent of; bitterly feel the consequences of; wish to be undone or non-existent (esp. *rue the day*). ● *noun* **1** repentance; dejection at some occurrence. **2** compassion or pity. [Old English *hrēow*, *hrēowan*]

rue[2] *noun* a perennial evergreen shrub, *Ruta graveolens*, with bitter strong-scented leaves formerly used in medicine. [Old French from Latin *ruta* from Greek *rhutē*]

rue·ful *adjective* expressing sorrow or regret in a genuine or humorous way. □ **rue·ful·ly** *adverb* **rue·ful·ness** *noun* [Middle English, from RUE[1]]

ruff[1] *noun* **1** a projecting starched frill worn round the neck esp. in the 16th c. **2** a projecting or conspicuously coloured ring of feathers or hair round a bird's or animal's neck. **3** *N Amer.* a fringe of fur around the hood or along the edges of a jacket or parka. **4** (*fem.* **reeve**) a wading bird, *Philomachus pugnax*, of which the male has a ruff and ear tufts in the breeding season. [perhaps from *ruff* = ROUGH]

ruff[2] *noun* (also **ruffe**) a small olive-brown Eurasian freshwater fish with dark spots and rough prickly scales, *Gymnocephalus cernua*, of the perch family. [Middle English, prob. from ROUGH]

ruff[3] ● *transitive & intransitive verb* trump at cards. ● *noun* an act of ruffing. [originally the name of a card game: from Old French *roffle*, *rouffle* = Italian *ronfa* (perhaps alteration of *trionfo* TRUMP[1])]

ruff[4] *noun* a representation of a dog's bark. [imitative]

ruffed grouse *noun* a N American woodland grouse, *Bonasa umbellus*, which has a black or reddish ruff on the sides of the neck, much prized as a game bird.

ruf·fian *noun* a violent lawless person. □ **ruf·fian·ism** *noun* **ruf·fian·ly** *adverb* [French *ru(f)fian* from Italian *ruffiano*, perhaps from dial. *rofia* scurf]

ruf·fle ● *verb* **1** *transitive* disturb the smoothness or tranquility of. **2** *transitive* upset the calmness of (a person). **3** *transitive* gather (fabric) into a ruffle. **4** *transitive* **a** (of a bird) erect (its feathers) in anger, display, etc. **b** disorder or disarrange (hair); cause to stick up or out irregularly. **5** *intransitive* undergo ruffling. **6** *intransitive* lose smoothness or calmness. ● *noun* **1** an ornamental frill of fabric, lace, etc. used to decorate the edge of a garment, pillowcase, etc. **2** perturbation, bustle. **3** a rippling effect on water. **4** the ruff of a bird etc. (see RUFF[1] 2). **5** *Military* a vibrating drumbeat. □ **ruffle feathers** (or **a person's feathers**) *informal* upset or annoy (a person). □ **ruf·fly** *adjective* [Middle English: origin unknown]

rufi·yaa /ˈruːfiːˌjə/ *noun* (*pl.* same) the basic monetary unit of the Maldives, equal to 100 laari. [Maldivian]

ruf·ous /ˈruːfəs/ *adjective* (esp. of animals) reddish brown. [Latin *rufus* red, reddish]

rug *noun* **1** a piece of thick material, usu. with a deep or shaggy pile or woven in a pattern of colours, or a piece of dressed animal skin, placed as a covering or decoration on part of a floor. **2** esp. *Brit.* a thick woollen coverlet or wrap. **3** esp. *N Amer. slang* a toupée, a wig. □ **pull the rug (out) from under** deprive of support; weaken, unsettle. [prob. from Scandinavian: compare Norwegian dial. *rugga* coverlet, Swedish *rugg* ruffled hair: related to RAG[1]]

Rugby a town in central England, on the Avon River in Warwickshire; pop. (est. 2002) 62,400, site of a famous boys' private school founded in 1567.

rugby *noun* (in full **rugby football**) **1** (also **Rugby**) a team game played with an oval ball that may be kicked, carried, and passed from hand to hand. **2** *hist.* = CANADIAN FOOTBALL. [*Rugby* School in central England, where it was first played]

Rugby League *noun* a professional form of rugby with teams of 13.

rugby pants *plural noun* men's casual pants, usu. made of cotton, with pockets, an elastic waistband, and no fly.

rugby shirt *noun* a men's usu. cotton casual shirt with a collar and a few buttons at the neck, usu. worn not tucked in.

Rugby Union *noun* a non-professional form of rugby with teams of 15.

rugel·ach /ˈruːɡələx/ *noun* (in Jewish cuisine) a type of small cookie consisting of pastry rolled up to form a crescent shape over a filling of cinnamon sugar, nuts, etc. [Yiddish]

rug·ged *adjective* **1** (of ground or terrain) having a rough uneven surface. **2** (of features) strongly marked; irregular in outline. **3 a** unpolished; lacking gentleness or refinement (*rugged grandeur*). **b** austere, unbending (*rugged honesty*). **c** involving hardship (*a rugged life*). **4** (esp. of a machine) robust, sturdy. □ **rug·ged·ly** *adverb* **rug·ged·ness** *noun* [Middle English, prob. from Scandinavian: compare RUG, and Swedish *rugga*, roughen]

rug·ged·ized *adjective* (also esp. *Brit.* **-ised**) (of a piece of computer equipment etc.) made hard-wearing or shock-resistant. □ **rug·ged·iz·a·tion** *noun*

rug·ger *noun Brit. informal* rugby.

ru·gosa /ruːˈɡoːsə/ *noun* a Japanese rose, *Rosa rugosa*, which has dark green wrinkled leaves and deep pink flowers. [Latin, fem. of *rugosus* (see RUGOSE) used as specific epithet]

ru·gose /ˈruːɡoːs, ruːˈɡoːs/ *adjective esp. Biol.* wrinkled, corrugated. □ **ru·gos·ity** /-ˈɡɒsɪti/ *noun* [Latin *rugosus* from *ruga* wrinkle]

rug rat *noun* esp. *N Amer. slang* a small child.

Ruhr /rʊr/ a region of coal mining and heavy industry in North Rhine-Westphalia, western Germany. [after the *Ruhr* River, which flows through it]

ruin ● *noun* **1** a destroyed or wrecked state (*after centuries of neglect, the palace fell to ruin*). **2** a person's or thing's downfall or elimination (*the ruin of my hopes*). **3** the complete loss of one's property or position (*bring to ruin*). **4** (in *sing.* or *pl.*) the remains of a building etc. that has suffered ruin (*an old ruin; ancient ruins*). **5** a cause of ruin; a destructive thing or influence (*will be the ruin of us*). ● *transitive verb* **1 a** bring to ruin (*your extravagance has ruined me*). **b** utterly impair or wreck (*the rain ruined my hat*). **2** (esp. as **ruined** *adjective*) reduce to ruins. □ **in ruins 1** in a state of ruin. **2** completely wrecked (*their hopes were in ruins*). [Old French *ruine* from Latin *ruina* from *ruere* fall]

ruin·a·tion *noun* **1** the act of bringing to ruin. **2** the act of ruining or the state of being ruined.

ruin·ous *adjective* **1** bringing ruin; disastrous (*at ruinous expense*). **2** in ruins; dilapidated. □ **ruin·ous·ly** *adverb* **ruin·ous·ness** *noun*

Ruis·dael /ˈriːzdɒl, ˈrɔiz-, -deil/ **Jacob van** (also **Ruys·dael**) (*c.*1628–82), Dutch landscape painter. His forest scenes, seascapes, and cloudscapes demonstrated the possibilities of investing landscape with subtle intimations of mood.

Rule, Jane Vance (b.1931), American-born Canadian writer. Most of her novels, essays, and short stories, e.g. *Desert of the Heart* (1964) and *Contract with the World* (1980), deal with social and emotional relationships, both homosexual and heterosexual.

rule ● *noun* **1** a principle to which an action, procedure, etc. conforms or is required to conform. **2** a prevailing custom or standard; the

normal state of things (*his lateness was the rule rather than an exception*). **3** government or dominion (*under British rule; the rule of law*). **4** the period of time during which a government or monarch holds power. **5** = RULER 2. **6** *Printing* **a** a thin strip of metal for separating headings, columns, etc. **b** a thin line or dash. **7** a code of discipline of a religious order. **8** *Law* an order made by a judge or court with reference to a particular case only. ● *verb* **1** *transitive* exercise decisive influence over; keep under control. **2** *transitive & intransitive* have sovereign control of (*rules over a vast kingdom*). **3** *transitive* (often foll. by *that* + clause) pronounce authoritatively (*was ruled out of order*). **4** *transitive* **a** make parallel lines across (paper). **b** make (a straight line) with a ruler etc. **5** *intransitive* be customary or prevalent (*apathy rules in this organization*). **6** *intransitive slang* be superior or pre-eminent (*hockey rules!*). **7** *transitive* (in passive; foll. by *by*) consent to follow (advice etc.); be guided by. **8** *intransitive* (of a court etc.) make a formal decision or ruling (*waiting for the Supreme Court to rule*). □ **as a rule** usually; more often than not. **by rule** in a regulation manner; mechanically. **rule out 1** exclude; pronounce irrelevant or ineligible. **2** prevent; make impossible. **rule the roost** be in control. □ **rule·less** *adjective* [Old French *reule, reuler* from Late Latin *regulare* from Latin *regula* straight stick]

rule book *noun* a book containing the rules governing a particular activity, organization, etc.

rule of law *noun* the restriction of the arbitrary exercise of power by subordinating it to well-defined and established laws.

rule of the road *noun* a custom or law regulating the direction in which two vehicles (or riders or ships) should move to pass one another on meeting, or which should give way to the other to avoid collision.

rule of three *noun* a method of finding a number in the same ratio to one given as exists between two others given.

rule of thumb *noun* a rule for general guidance, based on experience or practice rather than theory. [prob. derived from the practice of using the thumb as a rough measuring guide, e.g. by tailors]

rul·er *noun* **1** a person exercising government or dominion. **2** a straight usu. graduated strip or cylinder of plastic, wood, metal, etc., used to draw lines or measure distance. □ **ruler·ship** *noun*

rules of engagement *noun* directives issued by military or political authority setting out the circumstances and limitations under which a military force operates in a potentially hostile environment, particularly regarding when force may be used.

rul·ing ● *noun* an authoritative decision or announcement. ● *adjective* prevailing; currently in force (*ruling prices*).

ruling passion *noun* a motive that habitually directs one's actions.

rum[1] *noun* a spirit distilled from sugar cane residues or molasses. [17th c.: perhaps abbreviation of contemporary forms *rumbullion, rumbustion*, of unknown origin]

rum[2] *adjective Brit. informal* **1** odd, strange, queer. **2** difficult, dangerous. □ **rum go** (or **start**) *informal* a surprising occurrence or unforeseen turn of affairs. □ **rum·ness** *noun* [16th-c. cant, originally = 'fine, spirited', perhaps var. of ROM[1]]

Ru·ma·nia see ROMANIA.

rumba (also **rhum·ba**) ● *noun* **1** an Afro-Cuban dance. **2 a** a ballroom dance imitative of this, danced on the spot with a pronounced movement of the hips. **b** the music for it. ● *transitive verb* (**rum·bas**, **rum·baed** or **rumba'd**, **rumba·ing**) dance the rumba. [Latin American Spanish]

rum baba *noun see* BABA[1].

rum ball *noun* a confection of cake or cookie crumbs, chocolate, and rum, formed into a ball.

rum·ble ● *verb* **1** *intransitive* make a continuous deep resonant sound as of distant thunder. **2** *intransitive* (foll. by *along, by, past*, etc.) (of a person or vehicle) move with a rumbling noise. **3** *transitive* (often foll. by *out*) utter or say with a rumbling sound. **4** *intransitive N Amer. slang* engage in a street fight. **5** *transitive Brit. slang* find out about (esp. something illicit). ● *noun* **1** a rumbling sound. **2** *N Amer. slang* a street fight between gangs. □ **rum·bler** *noun* [Middle English *romble*, prob. from Middle Dutch *rommelen, rummelen* (imitative)]

rumble seat *noun N Amer. hist.* an uncovered folding seat in the rear of a car.

rumble strip *noun* a series of raised strips across a road or along its edge to make vehicles vibrate, warning drivers of an intersection or of the edge of the road.

rum·blings *plural noun* early indications of some state of things or incipient change (*rumblings of discontent*).

rum·bus·tious /rʌmˈbʌstʃəs/ *adjective* esp. *Brit. informal* boisterous, noisy, uproarious. [prob. var. of *robustious* boisterous, ROBUST]

Vowels: a cat ɑ arm e bed ɜr her ɜː deux ə ago ɪ sit i cosy iː feed ɒ hot ɔ pore ɔː no ʌ run ʊ put

Ru·melia /ru:ˈmiːlɪə/ (also **Rou·melia**) the territories in Europe which formerly belonged to the Ottoman Empire, including Macedonia, Thrace, and Albania. [Turkish *Rumeli* 'land of the Romans']

rumen /ˈruːmen/ *noun* (*pl.* **rumens** or **ru·mina** /-mɪnə/) the first stomach of a ruminant, in which food, esp. cellulose, is partly digested by bacteria. [Latin *rumen ruminis* throat]

ru·min·ant /ˈruːmənənt/ ● *noun* an animal that chews the cud regurgitated from its rumen. ● *adjective* **1** of or belonging to ruminants. **2** contemplative; given to or engaged in meditation. [Latin *ruminari ruminant-* (as RUMEN)]

ru·min·ate /ˈruːmɪˌneɪt/ *verb* **1** *transitive & intransitive* meditate, ponder. **2** *intransitive* (of ruminants) chew the cud. □ **ru·min·a·tion** *noun* **ru·mina·tive** /-nətɪv/ *adjective* **ru·mina·tive·ly** /-nətɪvli/ *adverb*

rum·mage ● *verb* **1** *transitive & intransitive* search, esp. untidily and unsystematically. **2** *transitive* (foll. by *around*) disarrange; make untidy in searching. **3** *transitive* (foll. by *out, up*) find among other things. ● *noun* **1** an instance of rummaging. **2** things found by rummaging; a miscellaneous accumulation. □ **rum·ma·ger** *noun* [earlier as noun in obsolete sense 'arranging of casks etc. in a hold': Old French *arrumage* from *arrumer* stow (as AD-, *run* ship's hold, from Middle Dutch *ruim* ROOM)]

rummage sale *noun* esp. *N Amer.* a sale of miscellaneous usu. second-hand articles, esp. for charity.

rummy[1] *noun* a card game in which the players try to form sets and sequences of cards. [20th c.: origin unknown]

rummy[2] *noun* *N Amer. slang* an alcoholic or drunkard. [RUM[1]]

rummy[3] *adjective* *Brit. informal* = RUM[2].

ru·mour (also **ru·mor**) ● *noun* **1** general talk or hearsay of doubtful accuracy. **2** (often foll. by *of*, or *that* + clause) a current but unverified statement or assertion (*heard a rumour that you are leaving*). ● *transitive verb* (usu. in *passive*) report by way of rumour (*it is rumoured that you are leaving; you are rumoured to be leaving*). □ **rumour has it** it is rumoured (*rumour has it that she is resigning*). [Old French *rumor* from Latin *rumor -oris* noise]

rumour monger *noun* a person who spreads rumours. □ **rumour monger·ing** *noun*

rump *noun* **1** the hind part of a mammal, esp. the buttocks. **2 a** a small remnant of a parliament or similar body. **b** (**the Rump**; in full **Rump Parliament**) *hist.* that part of the Long Parliament which continued to sit after Pride's Purge in 1648, voting for the trial which resulted in the execution of Charles II. It voted its own dissolution early in 1660. □ **rump·less** *adjective* [prob. from Scandinavian]

rum·ple *transitive & intransitive verb* make or become creased or ruffled. □ **rum·pled** *adjective* **rum·ply** *adjective* [obsolete *rumple* (n.) from Middle Dutch *rompel* from *rompe* wrinkle]

rump steak *noun* a cut of beef from the rump.

rum·pus *noun informal* a disturbance, brawl, row, or uproar. [18th c.: prob. fanciful]

rumpus room *noun* *N Amer., Austral., & NZ* a room, usu. in the basement of a house, for games and play.

rum-runner *noun* *N Amer.* a person or ship engaged in smuggling alcohol, esp. during Prohibition. □ **rum-running** *noun*

run ● *verb* (**run·ning**; *past* **ran**; *past participle* **run**) **1** *intransitive* go with quick steps on alternate feet, never having both or all feet on the ground at the same time. **2** *intransitive* **a** flee, abscond. **b** (often foll. by *to*) have recourse for support, comfort, help, etc. (*she's always running to her father*). **3 a** *intransitive* go or travel hurriedly, briefly, etc. **b** *transitive* pass or cause to pass quickly (*ran the vacuum over the living room; run a comb through your hair*). **4** *intransitive* advance by or as by rolling or on wheels, or smoothly or easily. **b** be in action or operation (*left the engine running*). **5** *intransitive* be current or operative; have duration (*the lease runs for 99 years; the movie ran for three hours*). **6 a** *intransitive* (of a bus, train, airplane, etc.) travel or be travelling on its route (*this train runs between Toronto and London*). **b** *transitive* cause (a bus, train, airplane, etc.) to travel a specified route (*the company runs buses from Fredericton to Saint John*). **7** *intransitive* (of a play, exhibition, etc.) be staged or presented (*the musical is now running in Vancouver*). **8** *intransitive* **a** extend (*the road runs by the lakeshore*). **b** have a course or order or tendency (*prices are running high; this writer runs to hyperbole*). **c** proceed in a specified manner (*I was running late this morning*). **9 a** *intransitive* compete in a race. **b** *transitive* finish a race in a specified position. **c** *intransitive* compete in (a race). **10 a** *intransitive* (often foll. by *for*) seek election (*ran for president*). **b** *transitive* (esp. of a political party) sponsor (a candidate) in an election (*ran a candidate in almost every riding*). **11 a** *intransitive* (of a liquid etc.) flow, drip profusely. **b** *transitive* flow with. **c** *intransitive* (foll. by *with*) flow

or be wet; drip (*his face ran with sweat*). **12** *transitive* **a** cause (water etc.) to flow. **b** fill (a bathtub etc.) with water. **c** cause water to flow over (a thing) held under a tap etc. (*run the vegetables under cold water to cool them quickly*). **13** *intransitive* spread or pass rapidly (*a shiver ran down my spine*). **14** *transitive* esp. *N Amer. informal* drive past or fail to stop at (a red traffic light, stop sign, etc.). **15** *transitive* traverse or make one's way through or over (a course, race, or distance). **16** *transitive* perform (an errand). **17 a** *transitive* publish (an article etc.) in a newspaper or magazine. **b** *intransitive* (of an article etc.) appear in print (*the story ran in all the major newspapers*). **18 a** *transitive* cause (a machine or vehicle etc.) to operate. **b** *intransitive* (of a mechanism or component etc.) move or work freely. **19** *transitive* direct or manage (a business etc.). **20** *transitive* own and drive (a vehicle) regularly. **21** *transitive* take (a person) for a journey in a vehicle (*I'll run you to the bank*). **22** *transitive* cause to run or go in a specified way (*ran the car into a tree*). **23** *transitive* enter (a horse etc.) in a race. **24** *transitive* smuggle (guns etc.). **25** *transitive* chase or hunt. **26** *transitive* be suffering from (a fever or high temperature). **27** *intransitive Naut.* (of a ship etc.) go straight and fast. **28** *intransitive* (of salmon) go upriver from the sea. **29** *intransitive* (of a colour in a fabric) spread from the dyed parts. **30 a** *intransitive* (of a thought, the eye, the memory, etc.) pass in a transitory or cursory way (*ideas ran through my mind*). **b** *transitive* cause (one's eye) to look cursorily (*ran my eye down the page*). **31** *intransitive* (of a stocking etc.) develop a run. **32** *intransitive* (of a rumour etc.) spread quickly (*the story ran all over town*). **33** *intransitive* (esp. of the eyes or nose) exude liquid matter. **34** *N Amer.* **a** *transitive* (of something purchased etc.) cost (a person) a certain amount (*the repairs will run you $500*). **b** *intransitive* amount or total (*the final bill will run to over ten million dollars*). **35** *transitive* perform (a test, experiment, etc.) using a particular procedure. **36** *Computing* **a** *transitive* cause (a computer) to execute a program or series of commands. **b** *intransitive* (often foll. by *under*) (of a computer program or system) operate within a specified environment. **c** *intransitive* operate a computer system under a specified environment. **d** *intransitive* (of a computer) execute a program or series of commands. **37** *transitive & intransitive* Football = RUSH[1] *verb* 8a, b, c. **38** *transitive* graze or pasture (cattle etc.) on a piece of land. **39** *transitive N Amer.* navigate (rapids, a waterfall, etc.) in a boat. **40** *transitive* sew (fabric) loosely or hastily with running stitches. **41** *intransitive* (of a candle) gutter. ● *noun* **1 a** an act, instance, or period of running. **b** a running race (*the 5 km run*). **2** a short trip or excursion, esp. for pleasure. **3** a distance travelled. **4** a general tendency of development or movement. **5** a rapid motion. **6** a regular route. **7** a continuous or long stretch or period or course (*a metre's run of wiring; had a run of bad luck*). **8** (often foll. by *on*) **a** a high general demand (for a commodity, currency, etc.) (*a run on the dollar*). **b** a sudden demand for repayment by a large number of customers (of a bank). **9** a quantity produced in one period of production (*a print run*). **10** a general or average type or class (*not typical of the general run*). **11** *Baseball* a point scored usu. by the batter returning to the plate after touching the other bases. **12** (foll. by *of*) free use of or access to (*had the run of the house*). **13 a** an animal's regular track. **b** an enclosure for fowls, rabbits, etc. **c** a range of pasture. **14** a vertical strip of unravelled fabric in hosiery. **15** *Music* a rapid scale passage. **16** a class or line of goods. **17** a batch or drove of animals born or reared together. **18** a shoal of fish in motion. **19** a trough for water to run in. **20 a** a single journey, esp. by an aircraft. **b** (of an aircraft) a flight on a straight and even course at a constant speed before or while dropping bombs. **c** an offensive military operation. **21** (in *pl.*) (prec. by *the*) *informal* diarrhea. **22** a continuous series of performances (*the show had a long run in Montreal*). **23** a sequence of cards in the same suit. **24** a snow-covered slope used for skiing, tobogganing, etc. **25** *N Amer.* = BUFFALO RUN. **26** *Cdn* (*Nfld & Maritimes*) a narrow passage of water. □ **at a run** running. **on the run 1** escaping, running away. **2** hurrying about from place to place. **run across 1** happen to meet. **2** (foll. by *to*) make a brief journey or a flying visit (to a place). **run after 1** pursue with attentions; seek the society of. **2** give much time to (a pursuit etc.). **3** pursue at a run. **run along** *informal* depart. **run around 1** bustle; hurry from one place to another (*spent the whole morning running around to get things for the party*). **2** deceive or evade repeatedly. **3** (often foll. by *with*) *informal* engage in sexual relations (esp. casually or illicitly). **4** *Brit.* take from place to place by car etc. **run at** attack by charging or rushing. **run away 1** get away by running; flee, abscond. **2** elope. **3** (of a horse) bolt. **4** (of a child) leave the parental home. **run away with 1** carry off (a person, stolen property, etc.). **2** win (a prize) easily. **3** (of a horse) bolt with (a rider, carriage, etc.). **4** leave home to have a relationship with. **5** deprive of self-control or common sense (*lets her ideas run away with her*). **run a blockade** see BLOCKADE. **run down 1** knock down or collide with. **2** reduce the strength or numbers of (resources). **3** (of an unwound clock etc.) stop. **4** (of a person or a person's health) become feeble from overwork or undernourishment. **5** discover after a search. **6** disparage. **run dry** cease to flow, be exhausted. **run for it** seek safety by fleeing. **a run** (or **a good run**) **for one's money 1** vigorous competition. **2** pleasure derived from an activity. **3** return for outlay or effort. **run afoul** (or **foul**) **of 1** act contrary to; go against (*ran afoul of their code of practice*). **2** *Naut.* collide or become entangled with (another vessel etc.). **run the gauntlet** see GAUNTLET². **run herd on** *N Amer.* = RIDE HERD ON (see HERD). **run high 1** (of feelings) be strong. **2** (of the sea) have a strong current with a high tide. **run in 1** *Brit.* run (a new engine or vehicle) carefully in the early stages. **2** *informal* arrest. **3** (of a combatant) rush to close quarters. **4** incur (a debt). **run in the family** (of a trait) be common in the members of a family. **run into 1** collide with. **2** encounter. **3** reach as many as (a specified figure). **4** be continuous or coalesce with. **run into the ground** *informal* bring (a person) to exhaustion etc. **run its course** follow its natural progress; be left to itself. **run low** (or **short**) become depleted, have too little (*our supplies ran low; we ran short of sugar*). **run off 1** flee. **2** produce (copies etc.) on a machine. **3** decide (a race or other contest) after a series of heats or in the event of a tie. **4** flow or cause to flow away. **5** write or recite fluently. **6** digress suddenly. **run off at the mouth** *esp. N Amer. informal* talk indiscreetly or incessantly. **run off one's feet** very busy. **run on 1** (of written characters) be joined together. **2** continue in operation. **3** elapse. **4** speak volubly. **5** talk incessantly. **6** *Printing* continue on the same line as the preceding matter. **run out 1** come to an end; become used up. **2** (foll. by *of*) exhaust one's stock of. **3** escape from a container. **4** (of rope) pass out; be paid out. **5** jut out. **6** complete (a race). **7** advance (a gun etc.) so as to project. **8** exhaust oneself by running. **run out on** *informal* desert (a person). **run over 1** overflow. **2** study or repeat quickly. **3** (of a vehicle or its driver) pass over; knock down or crush. **4** touch (the keys of a piano etc.) in quick succession. **5** (often foll. by *to*) go quickly by a brief journey or for a flying visit. **run ragged** exhaust (a person). **run rings around** See RING¹. **run riot** see RIOT. **run a** (or **the**) **risk** See RISK. **run the show** *informal* dominate in an undertaking etc. **run through 1** examine or rehearse briefly. **2** peruse. **3** deal successively with. **4** consume (an estate etc.) by reckless or quick spending. **5** pass through by running. **6** pervade. **7** pierce with a sword etc. **8** draw a line through (written words). **run to 1** have the money or ability for. **2** reach (an amount or number). **3** (of a person) show a tendency to (*runs to fat*). **4 a** be enough for (some expense or undertaking). **b** have the resources or capacity for. **5** fall into (ruin). **run to earth** (or **to ground**) **1** *Hunting* chase to its lair. **2** discover after a long search. **run to meet** anticipate (one's troubles etc.). **run to seed** see SEED. **run up 1** accumulate (a debt etc.) quickly. **2** build or make hurriedly. **3** raise (a flag). **4** grow quickly. **5** rise in price. **6** (foll. by *to*) amount to. **7** force (a rival bidder) to bid higher. **8** add up (a column of figures). **9** (foll. by *to*) go quickly by a brief journey or for a flying visit. **run up against** meet with (a difficulty or difficulties). **run wild 1** grow unchecked or untrained. **2** act or behave without any control or restraint. **run with 1** proceed with (*if she agrees to the idea we'll run with it*). **2** associate with (*runs with a rough crowd*). □ **run·nable** *adjective* [Old English *rinnan*]

run·about *noun* **1** a light car. **2** a small pleasure boat.

run-and-shoot *noun* (in full **run-and-shoot offence**) *N Amer. Football* a style of offence featuring a speedy mobile quarterback throwing quick short passes while scrambling.

run·around *noun* (esp. in phr. **give a person the runaround**) deceit or evasion.

run·away ● *adjective* **1** (of a person) having run away (*a shelter for runaway children*). **2** (of an animal or vehicle) no longer under the control of its rider or owner (*a runaway freight train*). **3** happening very rapidly; out of control (*runaway inflation*). **4** happening very easily (*a runaway victory*). ● *noun* **1** a person who has run away (*the city's streets are filled with teenage runaways*). **2** an animal or vehicle that is running out of control. **3** an easy victory. **4** a fugitive.

run·cible spoon /ˈrʌnsɪbəl/ *noun* a fork curved like a spoon, with three broad prongs, one edged. [nonsense word used by E. LEAR, perhaps after *rouncival* large pea]

run·cin·ate /ˈrʌnsɪnət/ *adjective Bot.* (of a leaf) sawtoothed, with lobes pointing towards the base. [modern Latin *runcinatus* from Latin *runcina* PLANE² (formerly taken to mean saw)]

Run·dle, Mount a mountain in SW Alberta, in Banff National Park (2 949 m). [R. T. *Rundle*, Methodist missionary d.1896]

run·down ● *noun* **1** a reduction in numbers. **2** a detailed analysis. **3** *Baseball* a play in which usu. two fielders try to tag out a runner caught between bases. ● *adjective* **1** decayed after prosperity. **2** enfeebled through overwork etc. **3** dilapidated.

rune *noun* **1** any of the letters of the earliest Germanic alphabet used by Scandinavians and Anglo-Saxons from about the 3rd c. and formed by modifying Roman or Greek characters to suit carving. **2** something mysterious or secret. **3** a Finnish poem or a division of it. □ **runic** *adjective* [Old Norse *rún* (only in pl. *rúnar*) magic sign, related to Old English *rún*]

rung¹ *noun* **1** each of the horizontal supports of a ladder. **2** a strengthening crosspiece in the structure of a chair etc. **3** a level or rank in society, an organization, one's career, etc. □ **runged** *adjective* **rung·less** *adjective* [Old English *hrung*]

rung² *past participle of* RING².

run-in *noun* a quarrel.

run·nel /ˈrʌnəl/ *noun* **1** a brook or small stream. **2** a gutter. [later form (assimilated to RUN) of *rinel* from Old English *rynel* (as RUN)]

run·ner *noun* **1** a person, horse, etc., that runs, esp. in a race or for fitness. **2 a** *Baseball* = BASERUNNER. **b** *Football* the ball carrier. **3** *Cdn & Irish* = RUNNING SHOE. **4 a** a creeping plant stem that can take root. **b** a twining plant. **5** each of the long pieces on the underside of a sleigh etc. that forms the contact in sliding. **6** a rod or groove or blade on which a thing slides. **7** a long narrow ornamental cloth or rug. **8 a** a messenger, collector, or agent for a bank, stockbroker, etc. **b** a messenger or agent for a bookmaker, drug dealer, etc. **9 a** a smuggler. **b** a ship used in smuggling. **c** = BLOCKADE-RUNNER. **10** (in full **runner bean**) any of several cultivated climbing varieties of bean or their edible pods, esp. the scarlet runner bean *Phaseolus coccineus*, with red flowers and long green pods. **11** a sliding ring on a rod etc. **12** *hist.* a police officer. **13** a running bird. **14** a revolving millstone. **15** *Naut.* a rope in a single block with one end round a tackle block and the other having a hook. **16** a roller for moving a heavy article. **17** *N Amer.* = BUFFALO RUNNER. □ **do a runner** *Brit. slang* leave hastily; flee.

runner's high *noun* a feeling of euphoria and well-being directly associated with vigorous exercise, thought to be related to the release of endorphins in the brain.

runner-up *noun* (pl. **runners-up**) **1** the competitor or team taking second place. **2** a competitor or team that comes close to winning.

run·ning ● *noun* **1** the action of runners in a race etc. **2** the way a race etc. proceeds. **3** management or operation (*takes care of the running of the company*). **4** an act or an instance of racing (*this year's running of the Queen's Plate*). ● *adjective* **1** continuing on an essentially continuous basis though changing in detail (*a running battle; a running joke*). **2** consecutive; one after another (*three days running*). **3** done with a run (*a running jump*). □ **in** (or **out of**) **the running** (of a competitor) with a good (or poor) chance of winning. **make** (or **take up**) **the running** take the lead; set the pace. **take a running jump** (esp. as *interjection*) *slang* go away. **up and running** in operation (*how soon can we get the system up and running again?*).

running back *noun Football* a back whose main task is to run carrying the ball.

running board *noun* a footboard on either side of a motor vehicle, used as a step etc.

running commentary *noun* an oral description of events as they occur.

running dog *noun derogatory* a servile political follower. [translation of Chinese *zǒugǒu*]

running gear *noun* the moving or running parts of a machine, esp. the wheels and suspension of a vehicle.

running head *noun* a heading printed at the top of a number of consecutive pages of a book etc.

running ice *noun Cdn* (*Nfld & Maritimes*) ice that is moving, carried by currents or the wind.

running knot *noun* a knot that slips along the rope etc. and changes the size of a noose.

running light *noun* **1** = NAVIGATION LIGHT. **2** each of a small set of lights on a motor vehicle that remain illuminated while the vehicle is running.

running mate *noun* **1** *US* a candidate for a supporting position in an election, esp. for the vice presidency. **2** a horse entered in a race in order to set the pace for another horse from the same stable which is intended to win.

running shoe *noun* any of various shoes having an upper made of nylon, canvas, etc. and a rubber or synthetic sole.

running stitch *noun* **1** a line of small non-overlapping stitches for gathering etc. **2** one of these stitches.

running water *noun* **1** water flowing in a stream etc. **2** indoor plumbing (*our cottage has no running water*).

Consonants: b *but*   d *dog*   f *few*   g *get*   h *her*   j *yes*   k *cat*   l *leg*   m *man*   n *no*   p *pen*   r *red*   s *sit*

runny *adjective* (**run·ni·er**, **run·ni·est**) **1** tending to run or flow. **2** excessively fluid.

Runny·mede a meadow on the south bank of the Thames at Egham near Windsor, England. The Magna Carta was signed there in 1215.

run·off *noun* **1** an amount of rainfall or melted snow that is carried off an area by streams and rivers. **2** *N Amer.* the spring thaw. **3** an amount of water coming off a roof etc. **4** an additional competition, election, race, etc., after a tie.

run-of-the-mill *adjective* ordinary, undistinguished.

run-on sentence *noun* an undesirably long sentence, esp. one composed of many independent clauses linked by conjunctions.

runt *noun* **1** a small pig, esp. the smallest in a litter. **2** a weakling; an undersized person. □ **runt·ish** *adjective* **runty** *adjective* [16th c.: origin unknown]

run-through *noun* **1** a rehearsal, usu. of a whole production, complete act, etc., with as few stops as possible. **2** a brief survey.

run-up *noun* **1** (often foll. by *to*) the period preceding an important event. **2** *Golf* a low approach shot.

run·way *noun* **1** a specially prepared surface along which aircraft take off and land. **2** a trail to an animals' watering place. **3** an incline down which logs are slid. **4** a long raised platform in a theatre, fashion display, etc. **5** a large enclosure for domestic animals; a run.

Run·yon /ˈrʌnjən/ **Al·fred Damon** (1884–1946), US author and journalist, best known for his short stories about New York's Broadway and underworld characters, including the collection *Guys and Dolls* (1932), on which the musical of the same name was based (1950). □ **Runyon·esque** *adjective*

ru·pee /ruːˈpiː/ *noun* the basic monetary unit of India, Pakistan, Sri Lanka, Nepal, Mauritius, and the Seychelles, equal to 100 paisa in India, Pakistan, and Nepal, and 100 cents in Sri Lanka, Mauritius, and the Seychelles. [Hindustani *rūpiyah* from Sanskrit *rūpya* wrought silver]

Ru·pert, Prince (1619–82), English Royalist general, son of Frederick V, elector of the Palatinate, and nephew of Charles I. A leading Royalist general during the English Civil War, he was defeated by Parliamentarian forces at Marston Moor (1644) and Naseby (1645); following the Restoration (1660) he commanded naval operations against the Dutch (1665–7 and 1672–4) and in 1670 became the first governor of the Hudson's Bay Company.

Rupert·ite *noun* a native or resident of Prince Rupert.

Ru·pert River a river in W Quebec, flowing 483 km from Lac Mistassini generally southward to the southeastern shore of James Bay. [after Prince Rupert: *see* RUPERT, PRINCE]

Ru·pert's Land (also **Prince Rupert's Land**) a historic region of northern and western Canada, originally granted in 1670 by Charles II to the Hudson's Bay Company. It comprised the drainage basin of Hudson Bay, territory corresponding to all of Manitoba and parts of Alberta, Saskatchewan, Ontario, Quebec, the NWT, and Nunavut. It ceased to exist in 1870, when the land was purchased by Canada, although the name is still used for an Anglican diocese of Western Canada. [RUPERT, PRINCE]

ru·piah /ruːˈpiːə/ *noun* the basic monetary unit of Indonesia. [as RUPEE]

rup·ture ● *noun* **1** the act or an instance of breaking; a breach. **2** a breach of harmonious relations; a disagreement and parting. **3** *Med.* an abdominal hernia. ● *verb* **1** *transitive* break or burst (a cell or membrane etc.). **2** *transitive* sever (a connection). **3** *intransitive* undergo a rupture. **4** *transitive & intransitive* affect with or suffer a hernia. [Old French *rupture* or Latin *ruptura* from *rumpere rupt-* break]

rural *adjective* **1** of, relating to, or suggesting the country (*opp.* URBAN). **2** living in the country. **3** of or concerning agriculture. □ **rur·al·ism** *noun* **rur·al·ist** *noun* **rur·al·ity** *noun* **rur·al·ize** *transitive verb* (also esp. *Brit.* **-ise**). **rur·al·iz·a·tion** *noun* **rur·al·ly** *adverb* [Old French *rural* or Late Latin *ruralis* from *rus ruris* the country]

rural dean *noun Brit. see* DEAN 2b.

rural municipality *noun* **1** *Cdn* (*Prairies & Que.*) a usu. sparsely populated municipality outside of urban municipalities that is administered by an elected council or the provincial government. Abbr.: **RM**. **2** *Cdn* (*NS*) one of the 24 districts that contain incorporated cities and towns.

rural route *noun N Amer.* a mail delivery route in an area outside of a town or city. Abbr.: **RR**.

Rurik /ˈrʊrɪk/ *noun* (also **Ryur·ik**) a member of a dynasty that ruled in Russia from the 9th c. until 1598, reputedly founded by a Varangian chief who settled in Novgorod in 862.

Ruri·tan·ian /ˌrʊrɪˈteɪnɪən/ *adjective* relating to or characteristic of courtly intrigue and romantic adventure or its setting. [*Ruritania*, an imaginary setting in SE Europe in the novels of A. HOPE, esp. *The Prisoner of Zenda*]

Ruse /ˈruːseɪ/ (also **Rousse**) an industrial city and the principal port of Bulgaria, on the Danube; pop. (2001) 162,128.

ruse /ruːz, ruːs/ *noun* a stratagem or trick. [Old French from *ruser* drive back, perhaps ultimately from Latin *rursus* backwards: compare RUSH[1]]

rush[1] ● *verb* **1** *intransitive* go, move, or act precipitately or with great speed. **2** *transitive* move or transport with great haste (*was rushed to hospital; rush the parcel to me tomorrow*). **3** *intransitive* (foll. by *at*) **a** move suddenly and quickly towards. **b** begin impetuously. **4** *transitive* perform or deal with hurriedly (*don't rush your dinner; the bill was rushed through Parliament*). **5** *transitive* force (a person) to act hastily. **6** *transitive* attack or capture by sudden assault. **7** *intransitive Hockey* bring the puck up the ice, esp. into the opposing team's zone. **8** *Football* **a** *transitive* move (the ball) forward by carrying it rather than by passing etc. **b** *intransitive* move the ball forward by carrying it. **c** *transitive* move the ball forward (a distance) by carrying it. **d** *transitive* attempt to force a way into the backfield in pursuit of (the back with the ball). **9** *transitive US* pay attentions to (a person) with a view to securing acceptance of a proposal. **10** *intransitive* flow, fall, spread, or roll impetuously or fast (*felt the blood rush to my face; the river rushes past*). ● *noun* **1** an act of rushing; a violent advance or attack. **2 a** a period of great activity (*shop early to beat the Christmas rush*). **b** = RUSH HOUR. **3** (*attributive*) done with great haste or speed (*a rush job*). **4** *informal* a thrill or feeling of excitement; a high (*gets a rush out of performing*). **5** (foll. by *on, for*) a sudden strong demand for a commodity. **6** (in *pl.*) *informal* the first prints of a film after a period of shooting. **7** *N Amer.* (*attributive*) designating a seat at a performance purchased at a reduced price on the day of the performance, or a ticket purchased for such a seat (*bought a rush ticket for the evening concert*). **8** *Hockey* an instance of bringing the puck up the ice. **9** *Football N Amer.* an instance of rushing the football (*scored a touchdown on an 8-yard rush*). **10** a sudden migration of large numbers. □ **rush·er** *noun* [Anglo-French *russher*, = Old French *ruser, russer*: see RUSE]

rush[2] *noun* **1** any marsh or waterside plant of the family Juncaceae, with slender stems and inconspicuous greenish or brownish flowers formerly used for strewing floors and still used for making chair seats, baskets, etc. **2** a stem of this. **3** (*collective*) rushes as a material. □ **rush·like** *adverb* **rushy** *adjective* [Old English *rysc, rysce*, corresponding to Middle Low German, Middle High German *rusch*]

Rush·die /ˈrʌʃdi/ **(Ahmed) Sal·man** (b.1947), Indian-born English novelist. His work is chiefly associated with magic realism, and includes the novels *Midnight's Children* (1981), which won the Booker Prize, and *The Satanic Verses* (1988), regarded by many Muslims as blasphemous for its portrayal of a figure identified with Muhammad; Rushdie was forced to live in hiding when the Ayatollah Khomeini issued a fatwa in 1989 condemning him to death (the fatwa was rescinded in 1998).

rush hour *noun* a time of day when traffic is at its heaviest.

rush·light *noun* a candle made by dipping the pith of a rush in tallow.

Rush·more, Mount a mountain in the Black Hills of S Dakota, noted for its giant busts of four US Presidents (Washington, Jefferson, Lincoln, and Theodore Roosevelt) carved (1927–41) under the direction of the sculptor Gutzon Borglum.

rusk *noun* a slice of bread baked a second time, usu. as a light biscuit. [Spanish or Portuguese *rosca* twist, coil, roll of bread]

Rus·kin, John (1819–1900), English art and social critic. His prolific writings profoundly influenced 19th-c. opinion and the development of the Labour movement, and he was a champion of the painter Turner, the Pre-Raphaelite Brotherhood, and of Gothic architecture, which he saw as a religious expression of medieval piety; his works include *The Stones of Venice* (1851–3), *Unto This Last* (1860), and *Fors Clavigera* (1871–84). □ **Rus·kinian** *adjective*

Rus·sell ▶ **1 Ber·trand (Ar·thur Wil·liam), 3rd Earl Russell** (1872–1970), English philosopher, mathematician, and social reformer. His *Principia Mathematica* (1910–13), written with A. N. Whitehead, had a great influence on symbolic logic and on set theory in mathematics; he wrote several books in the empiricist tradition (e.g. *Our Knowledge of the External World*, 1914), was a leading advocate of nuclear disarmament, and was awarded the Nobel Prize for literature in 1950. **2 George Wil·liam** (1867–1935), Irish poet. After the performance of his poetic drama *Deirdre* (1902) he became a leading figure in the Irish literary revival. **3 Henry Nor·ris** (1877–1957), US astronomer. Working mainly in astrophysics and spectroscopy, he is best known for his independent discovery of the relationship between stellar magnitude and spectral type. **4 John, 1st Earl Russell** (1792–

1878), English Whig politician, prime minister 1846–52 and 1865–6. As a member of Lord Grey's government (1830–4), he was responsible for introducing the Reform Bill of 1832 into Parliament; his second premiership ended with his resignation when his attempt to extend the franchise again in a further Reform Bill was unsuccessful. **5 Ken** (born Henry Kenneth Alfred Russell) (b.1927), English film director. His films, with their extravagant and extreme imagery, have often been controversial for their depiction of sex and violence. His prolific output includes three adaptations of D. H. Lawrence: *Women in Love* (1969), *The Rainbow* (1989), and the television film *Lady Chatterley* (1993).

rus·set ● *adjective* reddish brown. ● *noun* **1** a reddish-brown colour. **2** a kind of rough-skinned russet-coloured apple. **3** a variety of potato with a reddish skin. **4** *hist.* a coarse homespun reddish-brown or grey cloth used for simple clothing. ☐ **rus·sety** *adjective* [Old French *rosset*, *rousset*, diminutive of *roux* red, from Provençal *ros*, Italian *rosso* from Latin *russus* red]

Russet Burbank *noun* a large, elongated variety of potato suitable for baking, making french fries, etc. [L. *Burbank*, US plant breeder d.1926]

Rus·sia (official name **Russian Federation**) a country in N Asia and E Europe; pop. (est. 2002) 144,978,573; capital, Moscow.

Russia leather *noun* a durable bookbinding leather from skins impregnated with birchbark oil. [RUSSIA, where first made]

Rus·sian ● *noun* **1 a** a native or national of Russia or the Russian Federation. **b** a person of Russian descent. **2** *hist.* a native or national of the former Soviet Union. ¶ The use of *Russian* to mean *Soviet* can be misleading and is best avoided. **3** the language of Russia and the official language of the former Soviet Union. ● *adjective* **1** of or relating to Russia. **2** of or in Russian. ☐ **Rus·sian·ize** *transitive verb* (also esp. *Brit.* **-ise**). **Rus·sian·iz·a·tion** *noun* **Rus·sian·ness** *noun*

Russian Civil War a conflict fought in Russia (1918–21) after the Revolution, between the Bolshevik Red Army and the counter-revolutionary White Russians. Although the White Russians were aided by international forces, the Bolsheviks were ultimately victorious, and the Union of Soviet Socialist Republics was established.

Russian doll *noun* a set of hollow and usu. decorated wooden doll figures of differing sizes, each one made so as to nest inside the next largest. *Also called* MATRYOSHKA.

Russian dressing *noun* a mayonnaise-based salad dressing containing chili sauce, chopped pickles, etc.

Russian Federation the official name of RUSSIA.

Russian Mafia *noun* organized crime groups in Russia since the fall of the Soviet Union.

Russian olive *noun* = OLEASTER.

Russian Orthodox Church *noun* the national Church of Russia (*see also* ORTHODOX CHURCH). ☐ **Russian Orthodox** *adjective*

Russian Revolution the revolution in the Russian Empire in 1917, in which the czarist regime was overthrown and replaced by Bolshevik rule. In March (Old Style, February, whence *February Revolution*), food and fuel shortages in Petrograd (St. Petersburg) sparked off strikes and riots supported by the liberal Mensheviks, forcing the czar to abdicate; a provisional government was set up. The following November (Old Style, October, whence *October Revolution*), the Bolsheviks seized power in a coup led by Lenin; after workers' councils or *soviets* took power in major cities, the new Soviet constitution was declared in 1918.

Russian Revolution of 1905 the uprising in Russia in 1905. Popular discontent, fuelled by heavy taxation and the country's defeat in the Russo-Japanese War, led to a peaceful demonstration in St. Petersburg, which was fired on by troops. The crew of the battleship *Potemkin* mutinied and a soviet (or workers' council) was formed in St. Petersburg, prompting Czar Nicholas II to make a number of short-lived concessions including the formation of an elected legislative body or Duma.

Russian roulette *noun* **1** an act of daring in which one (usu. with others in turn) squeezes the trigger of a revolver held to one's head with one chamber loaded, having first spun the chamber. **2** a potentially dangerous enterprise.

Russian thistle *noun* *N Amer.* a European prickly tumbleweed, *Salsola kali*, which has become an agricultural weed in N America.

Rus·sify *transitive verb* (**-fies**, **-fied**) make Russian in character. ☐ **Rus·si·fi·ca·tion** *noun*

Rus·ski *noun* (also **Rus·sky**) (*pl.* **Rus·skis** or **-skies**) *slang derogatory* a Russian or Soviet. [RUSSIAN after Russian surnames ending in *-ski*]

Russo- *combining form* Russian; Russian and.

Russo-Japanese War a war (1904–5) between the Russian Empire and Japan over territory in Manchuria and Korea. Russia's humiliating defeat contributed to the Revolution of 1905, while the peace settlement gave Japan the ascendancy in the disputed region.

Russo·phile *noun* a person who is fond of Russia or the Russians.

Russo·phobe *noun* a person who fears or hates Russia or the Russians. ☐ **Russo·phobia** *noun*

Russo-Turkish Wars a series of wars between Russia and the Ottoman Empire, fought largely in the Balkans, the Crimea, and the Caucasus in the 19th c. The wars accelerated the decline of the Ottoman Empire, leading eventually to the freeing of Romania, Serbia, and Bulgaria from Turkish rule.

rust ● *noun* **1 a** a reddish-brown or yellowish-brown coating formed on iron or steel by oxidation, esp. as a result of moisture. **b** a similar coating on other metals. **2 a** any of various plant diseases with rust-coloured spots caused by fungi of the order Uredinales. **b** the fungus causing this. **3** an impaired state due to disuse or inactivity. **4** a reddish-brown or brownish-red colour. ● *adjective* of a reddish-brown or brownish-red colour. ● *verb* **1** *transitive & intransitive* affect or be affected with rust; undergo oxidation. **2** *intransitive* lose quality or efficiency by disuse or inactivity. ☐ **rust·less** *adjective* [Old English *rūst* from Germanic]

rust belt *noun* *informal* an area of once profitable heavy industry, esp. (**Rust Belt**) in the US Midwest and northeastern states.

rust·bucket *noun* *informal* an old and rusty car or ship etc.

rus·tic ● *adjective* **1** having a simplicity and charm that is typical of the countryside. **2** lacking the sophistication of the city. **3** constructed or made in a plain and simple fashion. **4** *Archit.* with rough-hewn or roughened surface or with sunk joints. ● *noun* a person from or living in the country, esp. a simple unsophisticated one. ☐ **rus·tic·ally** *adverb* **rus·ti·city** *noun* [Latin *rusticus* from *rus* the country]

rus·ti·cate *verb* **1** *intransitive* retire to or live in the country. **2** *transitive* mark (masonry) with sunk joints or a roughened surface. ☐ **rus·ti·ca·tion** *noun*

rus·tle ● *verb* **1** *intransitive & transitive* make or cause to make a gentle sound as of dry leaves blown in a breeze. **2** *intransitive* (often foll. by *along* etc.) move with a rustling sound. **3** *transitive & intransitive* steal (cattle or horses). **4** *intransitive* *N Amer. informal* move or act quickly or energetically. ● *noun* a rustling sound or movement. ☐ **rustle up** *informal* produce quickly when needed. ☐ **rust·ler** *noun* (esp. in sense 3 of *verb*). [Middle English *rustel* etc. (imitative): compare obsolete Flemish *ruysselen*, Dutch *ritselen*]

rust·proof ● *adjective* (of a metal) not susceptible to corrosion by rust. ● *transitive verb* make rustproof.

rusty *adjective* (**rust·i·er**, **rust·i·est**) **1** rusted or affected by rust. **2** stiff with age or disuse. **3** (of knowledge etc.) faded or impaired by neglect (*my French is a bit rusty*). **4** rust-coloured. **5** (of clothes) discoloured by age. **6 a** of antiquated appearance. **b** antiquated or behind the times. **7** (of a voice) croaking or creaking. ☐ **rust·i·ly** *adverb* **rust·i·ness** *noun*

rusty nail *noun* a mixed drink of scotch whisky and Drambuie.

rut¹ ● *noun* **1** a deep track made by the passage of wheels. **2** any groove, furrow, etc. **3** an established (esp. tedious) mode of practice or procedure. ● *transitive verb* (**rutted**, **rut·ting**) mark with ruts. ☐ **in a rut** following a fixed (esp. tedious or dreary) pattern of behaviour that is difficult to change. ☐ **rutty** *adjective* [prob. from Old French *rote* (as ROUTE)]

rut² ● *noun* **1** the periodic sexual excitement or activity of a male deer, goat, ram, etc. **2** the period during which this happens. ● *intransitive verb* (**rut·ted**, **rut·ting**) be affected with rut. ☐ **rut·tish** *adjective* [Old French *rut*, *ruit* from Latin *rugitus* from *rugire* roar]

ruta·baga /ˈruːtəˌbeigə, -bagə/ *noun* esp. *N Amer.* **1** a cruciferous plant, *Brassica napus*, with a large yellow-fleshed root, originally from Sweden. *Also called* TURNIP. **2** this root as a vegetable. [Swedish dial. *rotabagge*]

Ruth ▸ **1** *Bible* a book of the Bible telling the story of Ruth, a Moabite woman, who married her deceased husband's kinsman Boaz. David is descended from her. **2 'Babe'** (born George Herman Ruth) (1895–1948), US baseball player, who pitched for the Boston Red Sox (1914–19) and was an outfielder with the New York Yankees (1919–35); during his career he set the record for the most home runs (714), which remained unbroken until 1974. ☐ **Ruth·ian** *adjective* (in sense 2).

Ru·the·nia /ruːˈθiːniə/ a region of central Europe on the southern slopes of the Carpathian Mountains, now forming part of W Ukraine. ☐ **Ru·the·nian** *adjective & noun*

ru·the·nium /ruːˈθiːniəm/ *noun* *Chem.* a rare hard white metallic transition element, occurring naturally in platinum ores, and used as a chemical catalyst and in certain alloys. Symbol: **Ru**; at. no.: 44. [medieval Latin *Ruthenia* Russia (from its discovery in ores from the Urals)]

Ruth·er·ford /ˈrʌðərfərd/ **1 Alex·an·der Cam·eron** (1857–1941), Canadian lawyer and politician. He became the first premier, treasurer, and minister of education of the new province of Alberta in 1905. His administration promoted public education and expanded the railway and telephone networks; he resigned in 1910 amid charges of corruption, but was later found innocent. In 1913 he returned to his law practice, and was chancellor of the University of Alberta 1927–41. **2 Sir Er·nest, 1st Baron Rutherford of Nelson** (1871–1937), New Zealand-born English physicist. Regarded as the founder of nuclear physics, he established the nature of alpha and beta particles, proposed the laws of radioactive decay (with Frederick Soddy), and later concluded that the positive charge in an atom, and virtually all its mass, is concentrated in a central nucleus, with negatively charged electrons in orbit around it. From 1898–1907 he taught at McGill University; he was awarded the Nobel Prize for chemistry in 1908 for research done in Montreal.

ruth·er·ford·ium /ˌrʌðərˈfɔrdiəm/ *noun Chem.* a very unstable chemical element made by high-energy atomic collisions. Symbol: **Rf**; at. no. 104. [E. RUTHERFORD]

ruth·less *adjective* having no pity or compassion. □ **ruth·less·ly** *adverb* **ruth·less·ness** *noun* [Middle English, from *ruth* compassion, from RUE¹]

ru·tile /ˈruːtail/ *noun* a mineral form of titanium dioxide. [French *rutile* or German *Rutil* from Latin *rutilus* reddish]

Rut·ter /ˈrutər/ **John** (b.1945), British composer and conductor. His abundant church music includes a *Requiem* (1985) and *Magnificat* (1990) and many hymns and carols.

Ruwen·zori /ˌruːenˈzɔri/ a mountain range in central Africa, on the Ugandan–Congo (formerly Zaire) border between Lake Edward and Lake Albert, rising to 5 110 m (16,765 ft.) at Margherita Peak on Mount Stanley.

Ruys·dael *var. of* RUISDAEL.

RV *abbreviation* **1** *N Amer.* RECREATIONAL VEHICLE. **2** REVISED VERSION. □ **RVer** *noun* (in sense 1).

R-value *noun N Amer.* a measure of the insulating capability of a wall, building material, etc., with greater numbers indicating greater resistance to heat loss. [*resistance* value]

Rwan·da /ruːˈɒndə/ a landlocked country in central Africa, to the north of Burundi and the south of Uganda; pop. (est. 2002) 7,398,074; capital, Kigali. In 1994 ongoing tension between the majority Hutus and minority Tutsis flared into a bloody civil war, in which at least 800,000 people, mostly Tutsis, were slaughtered. □ **Rwan·dan** *adjective & noun*

Rx *abbreviation* **1** prescription. **2** (in prescriptions) take. [Latin abbreviation of *recipe* take (see RECIPE)]

Ry. *abbreviation* Railway.

-ry *suffix* = -ERY (*infantry*; *rivalry*). [shortened from -ERY, or by analogy]

Ryan /ˈraiən/ **Claude** (1925-2004), Canadian journalist and politician. He ran *Le Devoir* (1964–78), and in 1978 was chosen as leader of the Quebec provincial Liberals. He resigned as leader in 1982, but remained in the National Assembly and was a member of Robert Bourassa's cabinet.

Rya·zan /riəˈzɒn/ an industrial city in European Russia, situated to the southeast of Moscow; pop. (est. 2002) 526,000.

Ryb·insk /ˈrɪbɪnsk/ a city in NW Russia, a port on the Volga River; pop. (est. 2002) 236,100. It was formerly known as Shcherbakov (1946-57) and, in honour of the former President of the Soviet Union, Yuri Andropov, as Andropov (1984–9).

rye *noun* **1 a** a cereal plant, *Secale cereale*, with spikes bearing florets which yield wheat-like grains. **b** the grain of this used for bread and fodder. **2** (in full **rye whisky**) **a** *Cdn* whisky blended from rye and other grains. **b** whisky distilled from fermented rye. **3** rye bread. [Old English *ryge* from Germanic]

rye·grass *noun* any forage or lawn grass of the genus *Lolium*, esp. *L. perenne*. [obsolete *ray-grass*, of unknown origin]

Ryer·son, Adol·phus Eg·er·ton (1803–82), Canadian Methodist clergyman and educator. An opponent of the established position of the Church of England, he founded Upper Canada Academy (1836), was the first principal of Victoria College (1841), and was education superintendent for Canada West 1844–76; his belief in universal compulsory education culminated in the Education Act (1871).

Ryga /ˈriːgə/ **George** (1932–87), Canadian playwright and novelist. He won great acclaim with the publication of *The Ecstasy of Rita Joe and Other Plays* (1970), which depicted the plight of Canada's Aboriginal peoples as they relate to contemporary society. His other works, all very critical of modern society, include numerous plays, such as *Seven Hours to Sundown* (1977), and three novels.

Ryle ▸ 1 Gil·bert (1900–76), English philosopher. His most famous work, *The Concept of Mind* (1949), is a strong attack on the mind-and-body dualism of Descartes. **2** his cousin, **Sir Mar·tin** (1918–84), English astronomer. His demonstration that remote objects appeared to be different from closer ones helped to establish the big bang as opposed to the steady-state theory of the universe; he was Astronomer Royal 1972-82 and was awarded the Nobel Prize for physics in 1974.

ryo·kan /riˈoːkan/ *noun* a traditional Japanese inn. [Japanese]

ryot /ˈraiət/ *noun* an Indian peasant. [Urdu *raʿīyat* from Arabic *raʿiya* flock, subjects, from *raʿā* to pasture]

Rysy /ˈrɪsi/ a peak in the Tatra Mountains rising to a height of 2 499 m (8,197 ft.).

Ryu·kyu Islands /riˈuːkjuː/ a chain of islands in the W Pacific, stretching for about 960 km (600 miles) from the southern tip of the island of Kyushu, Japan, to Taiwan. The largest island is Okinawa.

Ryur·ik *var. of* RURIK.

Ss

S¹ *noun* (also **s**) (*pl.* **Ss** or **S's**) **1** the nineteenth letter of the alphabet. **2** an S-shaped object or curve.

S² *abbreviation* (also **S.**) **1** small. **2 a** Saturday. **b** Sunday. **3** soprano. **4** South, Southern. **5** *Cdn* Senate. **6** Saint. **7** Society.

S³ *symbol Chem.* **1** the element sulphur. **2** siemens.

s *abbreviation* (also **s.**) **1** second(s). **2** shilling(s). **3** singular. **4** son. **5** succeeded. **6** section. [sense 2 originally from Latin *solidus*: see SOLIDUS]

's- *prefix archaic* (esp. in oaths) God's ('*sblood*; '*struth*). [abbreviation]

's *abbreviation* **1** is, has (*he's*; *it's*; *Mary's*; *Charles's*). **2** us (*let's*). **3** *informal* does (*what's he say?*).

-s¹ *suffix* denoting the plurals of nouns (*compare* -ES¹). [Old English *-as* pl. ending]

-s² *suffix* forming the 3rd person singular present of verbs (*compare* -ES²). [Old English dial., prob. from Old English 2nd person singular present ending *-es*, *-as*]

-s³ *suffix* **1** forming adverbs (*afterwards*; *besides*). **2** forming possessive pronouns (*hers*; *ours*). [formed as -'s¹]

-s⁴ *suffix* forming nicknames or pet names (*Fats*). [after -s¹]

-'s¹ *suffix* denoting the possessive case of singular nouns and of plural nouns not ending in *-s* (*John's book*; *the book's cover*; *the children's shoes*). [Old English genitive singular ending]

-'s² *suffix* denoting the plural of a letter or symbol (*S's*; *8's*). [as -s¹]

SA *abbreviation* **1** Salvation Army. **2** sex appeal. **3 a** South Africa. **b** South America. **c** South Australia. **4** *hist.* Sturmabteilung (*see* BROWNSHIRT 1).

Saale River /ˈsɒlə/ a river of east central Germany. Rising in N Bavaria near the border with the Czech Republic, it flows 425 km (265 miles) north to join the Elbe near Magdeburg.

Saan·ich¹ /ˈsanɪtʃ/ a district municipality situated on the Saanich Peninsula of Vancouver Island, just northwest of Victoria; pop. (2001) 103,654. [SAANICH²]

Saan·ich² /ˈsanɪtʃ/ *noun* **1** a member of a division of Straits people living on the Saanich Peninsula. **2** the dialect of Straits spoken by the Saanich. [Straits, lit. 'elevated', with reference to the likeness of nearby Mount Newton's profile to a raised rump]

Saanich Peninsula a peninsula of the southeastern coast of Vancouver Island. Stretching from Sidney to Victoria, it is formed by Saanich Inlet, a bay of the Strait of Georgia extending 23 km inland. [as SAANICH¹]

Saar /sɑr/ the Saarland.

Saar·brück·en /sɑrˈbrʊkən/ an industrial city in western Germany, the capital of Saarland, on the Saar River close to the border with France; pop. (est. 2002) 380,000.

Saar·in·en /ˈsɑrɪnən/ **Eero** (1910–61), Finnish-born US architect, designer of the US Embassy in London (1955–60), the law school at the University of Chicago (1956–60), and the Trans World Airlines (TWA) terminal at Kennedy Airport, New York (1956–62).

Saar·land /ˈsɑrland/ a state of western Germany, on the border with France; capital, Saarbrücken. It is traversed by the Saar River and has rich deposits of coal and iron ore.

Saar River /sɑr/ a river of W Europe. Rising in the Vosges mountains in E France, it flows 240 km (150 miles) northward to join the Mosel River in Germany, just east of the border with Luxembourg.

Saba /ˈsɒbə/ the smallest island in the Netherlands Antilles, situated in the Caribbean to the northwest of St. Kitts.

Saba·dell /sabəˈdel/ a city in NE Spain, near Barcelona; pop. (est. 1998) 184,859.

saba·dil·la /ˌsabəˈdɪlə/ *noun* **1** a Mexican plant, *Schoenocaulon officinale*. **2** a preparation of its seeds, used in medicine and agriculture. [Spanish *cebadilla* diminutive of *cebada* barley]

Sabah /ˈsɒbɒ/ a state of Malaysia, comprising the northern part of Borneo and some offshore islands; capital, Kota Kinabalu.

Saba·tier /sabaˈtjei/ **Paul** (1854–1941), French chemist, who shared the 1912 Nobel Prize for chemistry for discovering a method for hydrogenating organic compounds.

sab·ayon /ˈsabaijɒn/ *noun* = ZABAGLIONE. [French from Italian *sabaione*, var. of ZABAGLIONE]

Sab·ba·tar·ian /ˌsabəˈteriən/ ● *noun* **1** a Christian who favours observing Sunday strictly as the Sabbath. **2** a Christian who observes Saturday as the Sabbath. ● *adjective* relating to or holding the tenets of Sabbatarians. □ **Sab·ba·tar·ian·ism** *noun* [Late Latin *sabbatarius* from Latin *sabbatum*: see SABBATH]

Sab·bath /ˈsabəθ/ *noun* **1** a day of rest and religious observance kept by Jews and some Christians on Saturday. **2** a day of religious observance celebrated by most Christians on Sunday, in commemoration of Christ's resurrection. **3** a period of rest. **4** (in full **witches' Sabbath**) a supposed general midnight meeting of witches with the Devil. [ultimately from Hebrew *šabbāt* from *šābat* to rest]

sab·bat·ical /səˈbatɪkəl/ ● *adjective* **1** (of leave) granted at intervals to a professor or teacher for study or travel, originally every seventh year. **2** of or appropriate to the Sabbath. ● *noun* a period of sabbatical leave. [Late Latin *sabbaticus* from Greek *sabbatikos* of the Sabbath]

sabbatical year *noun* **1** a year's sabbatical leave. **2** *Bible* every seventh year, prescribed by the Mosaic law to be observed as a 'Sabbath', during which the land was allowed to rest.

saber esp. *US var. of* SABRE.

sab·icu /ˈsabɪˌkuː/ *noun* **1** a Caribbean tree, *Lysiloma latisiliqua*, grown for timber. **2** the mahogany-like wood of this tree. [Cuban Spanish *sabicú*]

Sabin /ˈseibɪn/ **Al·bert Bruce** (1906–1993), Polish-born US microbiologist, who developed the oral vaccine against poliomyelitis that is named after him.

Sab·ine /ˈsabain/ ● *adjective* of or relating to a people of the central Apennines in ancient Italy. ● *noun* a member of this people. [Latin *Sabinus*]

Sabine Peninsula /səˈbain/ a peninsula of the northeastern coast of Melville Island, Nunavut. [Sir E. *Sabine*, British general and explorer d.1883]

Sabine's gull /ˈsabainz/ *noun* an Arctic gull, *Xema sabini*, with a forked tail, dark grey head, and black and yellow bill. [as SABINE PENINSULA]

Sabin vaccine /ˈseibɪn/ *noun* an oral vaccine giving immunity against poliomyelitis. [A.B. SABIN]

Sable, Cape the southwesternmost point of Nova Scotia, situated at the southern tip of Cape Sable Island. [French *sable* sand]

sable¹ *noun* **1** a small brown-furred flesh-eating mammal, *Martes zibellina*, of N Europe and parts of N Asia, related to the marten. **2** its skin or fur. [Old French from medieval Latin *sabelum* from Slavic]

sable² ● *noun* **1** esp. *literary* black. **2** (in *pl.*) mourning garments. **3** (in full **sable antelope**) a large African antelope with long curved horns, *Hippotragus niger*, the males of which are mostly black in old

---

Consonants: b *but*   d *dog*   f *few*   g *get*   h *her*   j *yes*   k *cat*   l *leg*   m *man*   n *no*   p *pen*   r *red*   s *sit*

age. ● *adjective* **1** (usu. placed after noun) *Heraldry* black. **2** esp. *literary* dark, gloomy. [Old French (in Heraldry): generally taken to be identical with SABLE[1], although sable fur is dark brown]

sable·fish *noun* = BLACK COD.

Sable Island a small island located some 300 km off the east central coast of Nova Scotia. [French *sable*, translation of a designation on an Italian map, *rena* sand]

sabot /sa'boː, 'saboʊ/ *noun* **1** a kind of simple shoe hollowed out from a block of wood. **2** a wooden-soled shoe. **3** a metal cup or ring fixed to a conical projectile to make it conform to the grooves of the rifling. □ **saboted** /'saboʊd/ *adjective* [French, blend of *savate* shoe + *botte* boot]

sabo·tage /'sabəˌtɔʒ, -taʒ/ ● *noun* deliberate damage to or destruction of property, esp. in order to disrupt the production of goods or as a political or military act. ● *transitive verb* **1** commit sabotage on. **2** destroy, spoil; make useless (*sabotaged my plans*). [French from *saboter* make a noise with sabots, bungle, wilfully destroy: see SABOT]

sabo·teur /ˌsabə'tɜr/ *noun* a person who commits sabotage. [French]

sab·ra /'sabrə/ *noun* a Jew born in Israel. [modern Hebrew *sābrāh* opuntia fruit]

Sab·ra·tha /'sabrəθə/ (also **Sab·ra·ta** /-brətə/) an ancient city on the coast of N Africa, near present-day Tripoli. It was one of three Phoenician colonies established in the region in the 7th c. BC (see TRIPOLITANIA).

sabre (also esp. *US* **saber**) ● *noun* **1** a cavalry sword with a curved blade. **2** a cavalry soldier and horse. **3** a light fencing sword with a tapering blade. ● *transitive verb* cut down or wound with a sabre. [French, earlier *sable* from German *Sabel*, *Säbel*, *Schabel* from Polish *szabla* or Magyar *szablya*]

sabre-rattling *noun* a display or threat of military force.

sabre saw *noun* a portable electric jigsaw.

sabre-toothed *adjective* designating any of various extinct mammals having long sabre-shaped upper canines.

SAC *abbreviation* (in the UK) Senior Aircraftman.

Sac *var. of* SAUK.

sac *noun* **1** a bag-like cavity, enclosed by a membrane, in an animal or plant. **2** the distended membrane surrounding a hernia, cyst, tumour, etc. [French *sac* or Latin *saccus* SACK[1]]

sac·cade /sa'kɒd/ *noun* a brief rapid movement of the eye between fixation points. □ **sac·cad·ic** /sə'kadɪk/ *adjective* [French, = violent pull, from Old French *saquer*, *sachier* pull]

sac·char·ide /'sakəˌraɪd/ *noun Chem.* = SUGAR 2. [modern Latin *saccharum* sugar + -IDE]

sac·char·in /'sakərɪn, 'sakrɪn/ *noun* a very sweet substance, C₇H₅NO₃S, used as a substitute for sugar. [German (as SACCHARIDE) + -IN]

sac·char·ine /'sakəˌrɪn, 'sakrɪn/ ● *adjective* **1** sweet; sugary. **2** of, containing, or like sugar. **3** unpleasantly over-polite, sentimental, etc. ● *noun* something that is excessively sweet, sentimental, etc.

saccharo- /'sakərɔː/ *combining form* sugar; sugar and. [Greek *sakkharon* sugar]

sac·char·ose /'sakəˌrɔːs, -ˌrɔːz/ *noun* sucrose. [modern Latin *saccharum* sugar + -OSE[2]]

sac·cule /'sakjuːl/ *noun* a small sac or cyst. □ **sac·cu·lar** *adjective* [Latin *sacculus* (as SAC)]

SACD *abbreviation* SUPER AUDIO COMPACT DISC.

sacer·dot·al /ˌsasɜr'dɔːtəl, ˌsak-/ *adjective* of priests or the priestly office; priestly. [Latin *sacerdotalis* from *sacerdos -dotis* priest]

sa·chem /'seitʃəm/ *noun* **1** the supreme chief of some N American Aboriginal peoples. **2** *US informal* a chief or leader in some field, e.g. business, politics, etc. [Narragansett, = SAGAMORE]

Sacher·torte /'sakɜrtɔrt/ *noun* a Viennese chocolate cake with apricot jam filling and chocolate icing. [German, from Franz *Sacher* Austrian pastry chef, its inventor + *Torte* cake]

sa·chet /sa'ʃei/ *noun* **1** a small perfumed bag. **2** a packet of potpourri or dry perfume for laying among clothes etc. **3** esp. *Brit.* a small usu. sealed and airtight bag or packet. [French, diminutive of *sac* from Latin *saccus*]

Sachs /'saks, zaks/ **1 Hans** (1494–1576), German poet and dramatist. A shoemaker, he was a renowned member of the Guild of Meistersinger as well as the prolific author of verse and some 200 plays; forgotten after his death, he was restored to fame in a poem by Goethe, and Wagner made him the hero of his opera *Die Meistersinger von Nürnberg* (1868). **2 Nelly (Leonie)** (1891–1970), German poet and dramatist, whose works include the poem 'O the Chimneys', about the Nazi concentration camps, and the play *Eli: A Mystery Play of the*

Sufferings of Israel (1951); she shared the Nobel Prize for literature in 1966.

sack[1] ● *noun* **1 a** a large strong bag, esp. one made of heavy fabric, for storing or conveying goods. **b** (usu. foll. by *of*) this with its contents (*a sack of potatoes*). **c** a quantity contained in a sack. **2** (prec. by *the*) *informal* dismissal, esp. from employment. **3** (prec. by *the*) *N Amer. slang* bed. **4** *Baseball* a base. **5** *Football* an act or instance of sacking. **6 a** a woman's short loose dress with a sacklike appearance. **b** *archaic* or *hist.* a woman's loose gown, or a silk train attached to the shoulders of this. **7** a man's or woman's loose-hanging coat not shaped to the back. ● *transitive verb* **1** put into a sack or sacks. **2** *informal* dismiss esp. from employment. **3** *Football* tackle (the quarterback) behind the line of scrimmage before he is able to throw the ball. □ **hit the sack** *informal* go to bed. **sack out** esp. *N Amer. informal* go to bed; go to sleep. □ **sack·ful** *noun* (pl. **-fuls**). **sack·like** *adjective* [Old English *sacc* via Latin *saccus* from Greek *sakkos*, of Semitic origin]

sack[2] ● *transitive verb* **1** plunder and destroy (a captured town etc.). **2** steal valuables from (a place). ● *noun* the sacking of a captured place. [originally as noun, from French *sac* in phr. *mettre à sac* put to sack, from Italian *sacco* SACK[1]]

sack[3] *noun hist.* a white wine formerly imported into Britain from Spain and the Canaries. [16th-c. *wyne seck*, from French *vin sec* dry wine]

sack·but *noun* an early form of trombone, of the Renaissance period. [French *saquebute*, earlier *saqueboute* hook for pulling a man off a horse, from *saquer* pull, *boute* (as BUTT[1])]

sack·cloth *noun* **1** a coarse fabric, as of flax or hemp. **2** clothing made of this, formerly worn as a penance or in mourning (esp. *sackcloth and ashes*).

sack·ing *noun* material for making sacks; sackcloth.

sack race *noun* = POTATO SACK RACE.

Sack·ville a town in E New Brunswick, just west of the border with Nova Scotia; pop. (2001) 5,361. □ **Sack·vill·ian** *noun* [G. *Sackville-Germain*, British soldier and statesman d.1785]

Sackville-West, Vic·toria Mary ('Vita') (1892–1962), English novelist and poet. Her works include the long poem *The Land* (1927), notable for its evocation of the English countryside, and the novel *All Passion Spent* (1931); she is also known for the garden which she created at Sissinghurst in Kent and for her friendship with Virginia Woolf.

sacra pl. *of* SACRUM.

sac·ral /'seikrəl/ *adjective* **1** *Anat.* of or relating to the sacrum. **2** *Anthropology* of or for sacred rites.

sac·ral·ize /ˌseikrə'laiz/ *transitive verb* (also esp. *Brit.* **-ise**) endow with sacred significance. □ **sac·ral·iz·a·tion** *noun*

sac·ra·ment /'sakrəmənt/ *noun* **1** a religious ceremony or act of the Christian Churches regarded as an outward and visible sign of inward and spiritual grace: applied by the Eastern, pre-Reformation Western, and Roman Catholic Churches to the seven rites of baptism, confirmation, the Eucharist, penance, anointing of the sick, ordination, and matrimony, but restricted by most Protestants to baptism and the Eucharist. **2** a thing of mysterious and sacred significance; a sacred influence, symbol, etc. **3** (also **Blessed** or **Holy Sacrament**) (prec. by *the*) **a** the Eucharist. **b** the consecrated elements, esp. the bread or Host. [Old French *sacrement* from Latin *sacramentum* solemn oath etc., from *sacrare* hallow, from *sacer* SACRED, used in Christian Latin as translation of Greek *mustērion* MYSTERY[1]]

sac·ra·men·tal /ˌsakrə'mentəl/ ● *adjective* **1** of or of the nature of a sacrament or the sacrament. **2** (of a doctrine etc.) attaching great importance to the sacraments. ● *noun* an observance analogous to but not reckoned among the sacraments, e.g. the use of holy water or the sign of the cross. □ **sac·ra·men·tal·ism** *noun* **sac·ra·men·tal·ist** *noun* **sac·ra·men·tal·ize** *transitive verb* **sac·ra·men·tal·ly** *adverb*

Sac·ra·mento /ˌsakrə'mentɔː/ the state capital of California, situated on the Sacramento River northeast of San Francisco; pop. (2000) 407,018.

Sacramento River a river of N California, which rises near the border with Oregon and flows some 611 km (380 miles) southward to San Francisco Bay.

sac·rar·ium /sə'kreriəm/ *noun* (pl. **sac·rar·ia**) **1** the sanctuary of a church. **2** *Catholicism* a piscina. **3** *Rom. Hist.* a shrine; the room (in a house) containing the penates. [Latin from *sacer sacri* holy]

sacred *adjective* **1 a** (often foll. by *to*) exclusively dedicated or appropriated (to a god or to some religious purpose). **b** made holy by religious association. **c** connected with religion; used for a religious purpose (*sacred music*). **2 a** safeguarded or required by religion, reverence, or tradition. **b** sacrosanct. **3** (of writings etc.) embodying the laws or doctrines of a religion. **4** treated with utmost respect; inviolable. □ **sacred·ly** *adverb* **sacred·ness** *noun* [Middle English, past participle of obsolete *sacre* from Old French *sacrer* from Latin *sacrare* from *sacer sacri* holy]

sacred cow *noun informal* an idea or institution unreasonably held to be above criticism. [with reference to Hindus' respect for the cow as a holy animal]

Sacred Heart *noun Catholicism* **1** the heart of Christ as an object of devotion. **2** an image representing this.

sacred number *noun* a number associated with religious symbolism, e.g. 7.

sac·ri·fice /ˈsakrɪˌfəɪs/ ● *noun* **1 a** the act of giving up something valued for the sake of something else more important or worthy. **b** a thing given up in this way. **c** the loss entailed in this. **2 a** the slaughter of an animal or person or the surrender of a possession as an offering to a deity. **b** an animal, person, or thing offered in this way. **3** an act of prayer, thanksgiving, or penitence as propitiation. **4** *Christianity* **a** Christ's offering of himself in the Crucifixion. **b** the Eucharist as either a propitiatory offering of the body and blood of Christ or an act of thanksgiving. **5** *Baseball* a play in which a batter deliberately hits the ball solely to advance a baserunner and is himself put out (usu. *attributive: sacrifice bunt; sacrifice fly*). **6** (in games) a loss incurred deliberately to avoid a greater loss or to obtain a compensating advantage. ● *verb* **1** *transitive & intransitive* give up or offer (a thing) as a sacrifice. **2** *transitive* (foll. by *to*) devote or give over to. **3** *transitive Baseball* advance (a baserunner) by hitting a sacrifice fly, bunt, etc. □ **sac·ri·fi·cial** /-ˈfɪʃəl/ *adjective* **sac·ri·fi·cial·ly** *adverb* [Old French from Latin *sacrificium* from *sacrificus* (as SACRED)]

sacrificial lamb *noun* **1** a lamb offered as a religious sacrifice. **2** a person, principle, etc. sacrificed to achieve an end.

sac·ri·lege /ˈsakrɪlɪdʒ/ *noun* **1** the violation or misuse of what is regarded as sacred. **2** an act or instance of this. □ **sac·ri·le·gious** /-ˈlɪdʒəs/ *adjective* **sac·ri·le·gious·ly** *adverb* [Old French from Latin *sacrilegium* from *sacrilegus* stealer of sacred things, from *sacer sacri* sacred + *legere* take possession of]

sac·ris·tan /ˈsakrɪstən/ *noun* a person in charge of a sacristy and its contents. [medieval Latin *sacristanus* (as SACRED)]

sac·ris·ty /ˈsakrɪsti/ *noun* (*pl.* **-ties**) a room in a church or chapel, where the vestments, sacred vessels, etc., are kept and the celebrant can prepare for a service. [medieval Latin *sacristia* (as SACRED)]

sacro- /ˈseɪkrɔː, ˈsakrɔː/ *combining form* denoting the sacrum (*sacroiliac*).

sac·ro·iliac /sakrɔːˈɪliak, seɪk-/ *adjective Anat.* relating to the sacrum and the ilium, esp. designating the rigid joint between them at the back of the pelvis.

sacro·sanct /ˈsakrɔːˌsaŋkt/ *adjective* (of a person, place, law, etc.) most sacred; inviolable; exempt from charge or criticism etc. □ **sacro·sanct·ity** /-ˈsaŋktɪti/ *noun* [Latin *sacrosanctus* from *sacro* ablative of *sacrum* sacred rite (see SACRED) + *sanctus* (as SAINT)]

sac·rum /ˈsakrəm, ˈseɪkrəm/ *noun* (*pl.* **sacra**) *Anat.* a triangular bone formed from fused vertebrae and situated between the two hip bones of the pelvis. [Latin *os sacrum* translation of Greek *hieron osteon* sacred bone (from its sacrificial use)]

SAD *abbreviation* SEASONAL AFFECTIVE DISORDER.

sad *adjective* (**sad·der**, **sad·dest**) **1** unhappy; feeling sorrow or regret. **2** causing or suggesting sorrow (*a sad story*). **3** regrettable. **4** shameful, deplorable (*is in a sad state*). **5** (of a colour) dull, neutral-tinted. **6** *slang* contemptible, pathetic, unfashionable. □ **sadly** *adverb* **sad·ness** *noun* [Old English *sæd* from Germanic: related to Latin *satis*]

sad-ass *adjective informal* contemptible, pathetic.

Sadat /səˈdat/ **(Muham·mad) Anwar al-** (1918–81), Egyptian leader, president 1970–81. He decentralized Egypt's political structure and diversified the economy, and later worked to achieve peace in the Middle East, visiting Israel (1977), and attending talks with President Begin at Camp David in 1978, the year they shared the Nobel Peace Prize; he was assassinated following opposition from Muslim hard-liners.

Sad·dam Hus·sein /səˈdam/ see HUSSEIN 3.

sad·den *transitive & intransitive verb* make or become sad.

sad·dhu *var. of* SADHU.

saddle ● *noun* **1** a seat of leather etc., usu. raised at the front and rear, fastened on a horse etc. for riding. **2** a seat for the rider of a bicycle etc. **3** a cut of meat consisting of the two loins. **4** a ridge rising to a summit at each end. **5** the part of a draft horse's harness to which the shafts are attached. **6** a part of an animal's back resembling a saddle in shape or marking. **7** the rear part of a male fowl's back. **8** a support for a cable or wire on top of a suspension bridge, pier, etc. **9** a fireclay bar for supporting ceramic ware in a kiln. ● *transitive verb* **1** put a saddle on (a horse etc.). **2 a** (foll. by *with*) burden (a person) with a task, responsibility, debt, etc. **b** (foll. by *on, upon*) impose (a burden) on a person. **3** (of a trainer) enter (a horse) for a race. □ **in the saddle 1** mounted. **2** in office or control. **saddle up** put a saddle on (a horse) in preparation for riding. [Old English *sadol, sadul* from Germanic]

saddle·back *noun* **1** a thing, esp. a hill or ridge, with a concave upper outline. **2** any of various animals or birds with saddle-like markings on the back. **3** *Archit.* a roof of a tower with two opposite gables. □ **saddle·backed** *adjective*

saddle·bag *noun* **1** each of a pair of bags laid across a horse etc. behind the saddle. **2** a bag attached behind the saddle of a bicycle, motorcycle, snowmobile, etc. **3** (*attributive*) *Cdn hist.* designating a preacher, doctor, etc., who travelled from place to place to work; itinerant. **4** *N Amer. informal* excess fat around the hips and thighs.

saddle-bow *noun* the arched front or rear of a saddle.

saddle bronc *noun N Amer.* **1** a saddled horse ridden in rodeo competition. **2** a rodeo event in which a rider attempts to stay on a saddled bucking horse (often *attributive: saddle bronc event; saddle bronc champion*).

saddle cloth *noun* a cloth laid on a horse's back under the saddle.

saddle horn *noun* a pommel on a saddle.

saddle horse *noun* a horse for riding.

sad·dler *noun* a maker of or dealer in saddles and other equipment for horses.

sad·dlery *noun* (*pl.* **-ies**) **1** the saddles and other equipment of a saddler. **2** a saddler's business or premises.

saddle shoe *noun* esp. *N Amer.* a two-toned oxford shoe with a band of leather in the second colour across the instep, originally popular in the 1950s.

saddle soap *noun* a mild soap for cleaning and preserving leather.

saddle sore ● *noun* a sore caused by the chafing of a saddle. ● *adjective* (**saddle-sore**) **1** (of a horse or rider) chafed by the saddle. **2** stiff and sore from riding a bicycle.

saddle stitch ● *noun* **1** a stitch of thread or a wire staple passed through the centre of a magazine or booklet. **2** a stitch made with long stitches on the upper side alternated with short stitches on the underside. ● *transitive verb* (**saddle-stitch**) **1** sew with a saddle stitch. **2** bind (a booklet etc.) with a saddle stitch or saddle stitches. □ **saddle-stitched** *adjective* **saddle-stitch·ing** *noun*

saddle tree *noun* the frame of a saddle.

Sad·du·cee /ˈsadjuˌsiː/ *noun* a member of a Jewish sect or party of the time of Christ that denied the resurrection of the dead, the existence of spirits, and the obligation of the traditional oral law (*compare* PHARISEE 1, ESSENE). □ **Sad·du·cean** /-ˈsiːən/ *adjective* [Old English *sadducēas* from Late Latin *Sadducaeus* from Greek *Saddoukaios* from Hebrew *ṣᵉdūḳī*, prob. = descendant of Zadok (2 Sam. 8:17)]

Sade /sɑd/ **Dona·tien Al·phonse Fran·çois, Comte de** (known as the Marquis de Sade) (1740–1814), French writer and soldier, who wrote a number of sexually explicit works, including *Les 120 Journées de Sodome* (1784), *Justine* (1791), and *La Philosophie dans le boudoir* (1795); the word *sadism* owes its origin to his name, referring to the cruel sexual practices which he described. □ **Sade·ian** *adjective*

sadhu /ˈsɒduː/ *noun* (also **saddhu**) (in India) a holy man, sage, or ascetic. [Sanskrit, = holy man]

sad·ism /ˈseɪdɪzəm/ *noun* **1** a form of sexual perversion characterized by the enjoyment of inflicting pain or suffering on others (*compare* MASOCHISM 1). **2** *informal* the enjoyment of cruelty to others. □ **sad·ist** *noun* **sad·is·tic** /səˈdɪstɪk/ *adjective* **sad·is·tic·ally** *adverb* [French *sadisme* from SADE]

Sad·ler·miut /sadˈlɜrmiːʊt/ *noun* a member of an extinct Aboriginal people formerly living on Southampton Island, Hudson Bay. [variant of SALLIRMIUT]

sado- /ˌseɪdoː/ *combining form* of, relating to, or involving sadism.

sado-masochism /ˌseɪdoːˈmasəˌkɪzəm/ *noun* sexual gratification achieved through inflicting and receiving pain. □ **sado-masochist** *noun* **sado-masochis·tic** *adjective*

sad sack *noun* esp. *N Amer. informal* a very inept person (also *attributive: a sad-sack character*).

S.A.E. *abbreviation* **1** self-addressed envelope. **2** stamped addressed envelope.

Safa·qis see SFAX.

sa·fari /səˈfɑri/ *noun* (*pl.* **sa·faris**) **1** a hunting or scientific expedition, esp. in East Africa (*go on safari*). **2** a sightseeing trip esp. to see African animals in their natural habitat. [Swahili from Arabic *safara* to travel]

safari jacket *noun* a light cotton jacket, usu. having a belt and four patch pockets.

safari park *noun* an enclosed area where lions etc. are kept in relatively open spaces for public viewing from vehicles driven through.

safari suit *noun* a lightweight suit usu. with short sleeves and four pleated pockets in the jacket.

Safa·vid /ˈsafəˌvɪd/ *noun* a member of a dynasty which ruled Persia (Iran) AD 1502–1736, installing Shia rather than Sunni Islam as the state religion.

Saf·die /ˈsafdiː/ **Moshe** (b.1938), Israeli-born Canadian architect. Educated at McGill University, he built his university thesis as Habitat for Expo 67 in Montreal; his designs tend to be prefabricated, cellular multi-unit housing complexes or large public buildings such as the National Gallery of Canada in Ottawa.

safe ● *adjective* **1 a** free of danger or injury. **b** (often foll. by *from*) out of or not exposed to danger (*safe from their enemies*). **2** affording security or not involving danger or risk (*put it in a safe place*). **3 a** reliable, certain; that can be reckoned on (*a safe investment; a safe method*). **b** *Cdn & Brit.* (of a riding, seat in Parliament, etc.) usually won easily by a particular party. **4** prevented from escaping or doing harm (*have got him safe*). **5** (also **safe and sound**) uninjured; with no harm done. **6 a** cautious and unenterprising; consistently moderate. **b** (of an action etc.) moderate, cautious, conservative (*a safe estimate*). **7** *Baseball* having reached a base without being put out (*safe at second*). **8** (in combination) **a** resistant to damage etc. by the specified object or condition (*the dishes are microwave-safe*). **b** not harmful to something specified (*child-safe*). ● *noun* **1** a strong lockable cabinet etc. for valuables. **2** a cupboard etc. for storing food (*pie safe*). **3** *N Amer.* (esp. *Cdn*) *slang* a condom. ● *adverb informal* in a safe manner (*play safe*). □ **on the safe side** with a margin of security against risks. □ **safe·ly** *adverb* **safe·ness** *noun* [Anglo-French *saf*, Old French *sauf* from Latin *salvus* uninjured: (n.) originally *save* from SAVE[1]]

safe bet *noun* a bet that is certain to succeed.

safe conduct *noun* **1** a privilege of immunity from arrest or harm, esp. on a particular occasion. **2** a document securing this.

safe·cracker *noun* a person who breaks open and robs safes.

safe deposit *noun* = SAFETY DEPOSIT.

safe·guard ● *noun* **1** a proviso, stipulation, quality, or circumstance, that tends to prevent something undesirable. **2** a safe conduct. ● *transitive verb* guard or protect (rights etc.) by a precaution or stipulation.

safe harbour *noun* **1** a harbour affording protection to ships. **2** any place or circumstance affording protection.

safe house *noun* **1** a place of refuge or rendezvous for spies, criminals, police informants, etc. **2** a place providing free temporary emergency accommodation for those fleeing abuse.

safe·keep·ing *noun* preservation in a safe place.

safe·light *noun Photog.* a filtered light for use in a darkroom.

safe sex *noun* (also **safer sex**) sexual activity in which precautions are taken to reduce the risk of spreading sexually transmitted diseases, esp. AIDS.

safe·ty *noun* (pl. **-ties**) **1** the condition of being safe; freedom from danger or risks. **2 a** any of various devices for preventing injury from machinery (also *attributive: safety bar; safety lock; safety feature*). **b** (*attributive*) designating items of protective clothing (*safety helmet*). **3** *Football* **a** a defensive back who plays in a deep position. **b** (also *Cdn* **safety touch**) a play in which the offensive team moves the ball into its own end zone and either downs the ball or is tackled there or moves it out of bounds, resulting in two points being awarded to the defensive team. **c** the two points so awarded. **4** *Baseball* = BASE HIT. □ **safety first** a motto advising caution.

safety belt *noun* **1** = SEAT BELT. **2** a belt or strap securing a person to prevent injury.

safety cage *noun* the reinforced protective frame structure of the passenger compartment of some cars.

safety catch *noun* a contrivance for locking a gun trigger or preventing the accidental operation of machinery.

safety curtain *noun* a fireproof curtain that can be lowered to cut off the auditorium in a theatre from the stage.

safety deposit *noun* (also **safe deposit**) a place in which valuables are stored (also *attributive: safety deposit box*).

safety factor *noun* **1** a margin of security against risks. **2** the ratio of a material's strength to an expected strain.

safety glass *noun* glass that will not splinter when broken.

safety glasses *plural noun* eyeglasses with reinforced lenses to protect the eyes.

safety harness *noun* a system of belts or restraints to hold a person to prevent falling or injury.

safety match *noun* a match igniting only on a specially prepared surface.

safety net *noun* **1** a net placed to catch an acrobat etc. in case of a fall. **2** any means of protection against difficulty or loss (*the social safety net*).

safety pin ● *noun* a pin with a point that is bent back to the head and is held in a guard when closed. ● *transitive verb* (**safety-pin**) fasten with a safety pin.

safety razor *noun* a razor with a guard to reduce the risk of cutting the skin.

safety touch *noun Cdn Football* = SAFETY 3b.

safety valve *noun* **1** (in a steam boiler) a valve opening automatically to relieve excessive pressure. **2** a means of giving harmless vent to excitement, energy, etc.

saf·flower /ˈsaflaʊr/ *noun* **1** an orange-flowered thistle-like plant, *Carthamus tinctorius*, whose seeds yield an edible oil. **2 a** its dried petals. **b** a red dye made from these, used in lipstick. [Dutch *saffloer* or German *Safflor* via Old French *saffleur* from obsolete Italian *saffiore* from Arabic *asfar*]

saf·fron ● *noun* **1** an orange-yellow flavouring and food colouring made from the dried stigmas of the crocus, *Crocus sativus*. **2** the orange-yellow colour of this. **3** = MEADOW SAFFRON. ● *adjective* of an orange-yellow colour. □ **saf·froned** *adjective* **saf·frony** *adjective* [Old French *safran* from Arabic *za'farān*]

saf·ra·nine /ˈsafrəˌniːn/ *noun* (also **saf·ra·nin** /-nɪn/) any of a large group of mainly red dyes used in biological staining etc. [French *safranine* (as SAFFRON): originally of dye from saffron]

sag ● *intransitive verb* (**sagged**, **sag·ging**) **1 a** sink or subside under weight or pressure, esp. unevenly. **b** droop, hang down loosely. **2** have a downward bulge or curve in the middle. **3** decline, weaken, diminish. **4** fall in price. ● *noun* **1 a** the amount that a rope etc. sags. **b** the distance from the middle of its curve to a straight line between its supports. **2** a sinking condition; subsidence. **3** a fall in price. □ **saggy** *adjective* [Middle Low German *sacken*, Dutch *zakken* subside]

saga /ˈsɑːgə, ˈsɒgə/ *noun* **1** a long story of heroic achievement, esp. a medieval Icelandic or Norwegian prose narrative. **2** a series of connected books giving the history of a family etc. **3** a long involved story. [Old Norse = narrative, related to SAW[3]]

sag·acious /səˈgeɪʃəs/ *adjective* **1** mentally penetrating; gifted with discernment; having practical wisdom. **2** acute-minded, shrewd. **3** (of a saying, plan, etc.) showing wisdom. **4** (of an animal) exceptionally intelligent; seeming to reason or deliberate. □ **sag·acious·ly** *adverb* **sag·acity** /səˈgasɪti/ *noun* [Latin *sagax sagacis*]

Sa·ga·mi·hara /səˌgɒmiˈhɑːrə/ a city in south central Japan, just west of Tokyo; pop. (est. 1995) 570,597.

saga·more /ˈsagəˌmɔːr/ *noun* = SACHEM 1. [Penobscot *sagamo*]

Sagan ▸ **1** /ˈseɪgən/ **Carl (Ed·ward)** (1934–96), US astronomer. He showed that amino acids can be synthesized in an artificial primordial soup irradiated by ultraviolet light – a possible origin of life on earth. In 1983 he and several other scientists put forward the concept of a nuclear winter as a consequence of global nuclear war; he wrote several popular science books, and was co-producer and narrator of the television series *Cosmos* (1980). **2** /saˈgɑ̃/ **Fran·çoise** (pseudonym of Françoise Quoirez) (b.1935), French novelist, dramatist, and short-story writer. Her novels examine the transitory nature of love as experienced in brief liaisons, and include *Bonjour Tristesse* (1954), *Un Certain sourire* (1956), and *Aimez-vous Brahms?* (1959).

sage[1] *noun* **1** an aromatic herb, *Salvia officinalis*, with dull greyish-green leaves. **2** its leaves used in cooking. [Old French *sauge* from Latin *salvia* healing plant, from *salvus* safe]

sage[2] ● *noun* **1** often *ironic* a profoundly wise person. **2** any of the ancients traditionally regarded as the wisest of their time. ● *adjective* **1** profoundly wise, esp. from experience. **2** of or indicating profound wisdom. **3** often *ironic* wise-looking; solemn-faced. □ **sage·hood** *noun* **sage·ly** *adverb* [Old French, ultimately from Latin *sapere* be wise]

sage·brush *noun* **1** a growth of shrubby aromatic plants of the genus *Artemisia*, esp. *A. tridentata*, found in some semi-arid regions of western N America. **2** this plant.

sage green ● *noun* the dull greyish-green colour of sage leaves. ● *adjective* (hyphenated when *attributive*) of this colour.

sage grouse *noun* a large grouse, *Centrocercus urophasianus*, of western N America, noted for the male's courtship display.

sage tea *noun* a medicinal infusion of sage leaves.

sag·gar /ˈsagər/ *noun* (also **sag·ger**) a protective fireclay box enclosing ceramic ware while it is being fired. [prob. contraction of SAFEGUARD]

sagit·tal /ˈsadʒɪtəl/ *adjective Anat.* **1** of or relating to the suture between the parietal bones of the skull. **2** in the same plane as this, or in a parallel plane. [French from medieval Latin *sagittalis* from *sagitta* arrow]

Sagit·tar·ius /sadʒɪˈterɪəs/ *noun* a large constellation between Scorpio and Capricorn, said to represent a centaur carrying a bow and arrow, and in which the centre of the Milky Way is situated. **2 a** the ninth sign of the zodiac. **b** a person born when the sun is in this sign, usu. between 22 November and 21 December. □ **Sagit·tar·ian** *adjective & noun* [Latin, = archer, from *sagitta* 'arrow']

sagit·tate /ˈsadʒɪˌteɪt/ *adjective Bot. & Zool.* shaped like an arrowhead.

sago /ˈseɪɡoʊ/ *noun* (*pl.* **sagos**) **1** a kind of starch, made from the powdered pith of the sago palm and used in puddings etc. **2** (in full **sago palm**) any of several tropical palms and cycads, esp. *Cycas circinalis* and *Metroxylon sagu*, from which sago is made. [Malay *sāgū* (originally through Portuguese)]

sa·guaro /səˈɡwɑːroʊ/ *noun* (also **sa·huaro** /saˈwɑːroʊ/) (*pl.* **-os**) a giant cactus, *Carnegiea gigantea*, of the SW United States and Mexico. [Latin American Spanish]

Sa·gue·nay /ˈsaɡənei/ a city in NE Quebec, formed by the merging of Chicoutimi, Jonquière, La Baie, Laterrière and some other communities; pop. (2001) 144,471.

Saguenay River a river in east central Quebec, 698 km long (to the head of the Rivière Péribonka), which flows southeastward 160 km from Lac Saint-Jean into the St. Lawrence at Tadoussac. [prob. from Montagnais or Algonquin, = place where the water flows out, with reference to the territory, not the river]

Saguenay-St. Lawrence Marine Park a marine park in Quebec, situated where the Saguenay Fjord meets the St. Lawrence estuary. It was established in 1988.

Sa·guia el Hamra /səˌɡiːə el ˈhamrə/ **1** an intermittent river in the north of Western Sahara. It flows into the Atlantic west of La'youn. **2** the region through which it flows. A territory of Spain from 1934, it united with Rio de Oro in 1958 to become a part of the former province of Spanish Sahara.

sag wagon *noun informal* a motorized vehicle accompanying a group of long-distance cyclists to provide transport to those who are tired etc.

Saha /səˈhɑː/ **Megh·nad** (1894–1956), Indian theoretical physicist. He worked on thermal ionization in stars, showing that the ionization of metal atoms increases with temperature, leading to a reduction in the absorption lines visible in stellar spectra, and devised an equation, now named after him, expressing the relationship between ionization and temperature.

Sahara Desert /səˈherə, -ˈhɑːrə/ (also **Sahara**) a vast desert in N Africa, extending from the Atlantic in the west to the Red Sea in the east, and from the Mediterranean and the Atlas Mountains in the north to the Sahel in the south. The largest desert in the world, it covers an area of about 9 065 000 sq. km (3,500,000 sq. miles). □ **Sa·haran** *adjective* [Arabic, = desert]

Sahel /səˈhel/ a vast semi-arid region of North Africa, to the south of the Sahara. An area of dry savannah, it forms a transitional zone at the southern limits of the desert and comprises the northern part of the region known as Sudan. □ **Sahel·ian** /-ˈhiːliən/ *adjective*

sahib /ˈsɑːhɪb, ˈsɑːɪb/ *noun* **1** (in India) a polite form of address, often placed after a person's name or title. **2** a gentleman (*pukka sahib*). [Urdu from Arabic *ṣāḥib* 'friend, lord']

SAHM *noun* a stay-at-home mother.

Sahtu Dene /ˌsɒtuːˈdeneɪ/ ● *noun* **1** a member of a Dene people living near Great Bear Lake, NWT. **2** the Athapaskan language of this people. ● *adjective* of or relating to this people or their culture or language. [Dene = 'people of Great Bear Lake']

Said /saˈiːd/ **Ed·ward W.** (1935–2003), US critic, born in Palestine. In *The Question of Palestine* (1985), he defended the Palestinian struggle for political autonomy and has since played an active role in moves to form a Palestinian state; other works include *Orientalism* (1978) and *Culture and Imperialism* (1993).

said ● *verb* past and past participle of SAY. ● *adjective* (prec. by *the*) previously mentioned (*the said witness*).

saiga /ˈsaɪɡə, ˈseɪ-/ *noun* a gazelle, *Saiga tatarica*, of the Asian steppes, distinguished by an inflated snout. [Russian]

Sai·gon /saɪˈɡɒn/ a city and port on the south coast of Vietnam; pop. (est. 2002) 3,378,500. Officially renamed Ho Chi Minh City after the reunification of Vietnam in 1975, it is now the largest city and chief industrial centre of Vietnam.

sail ● *noun* **1** a piece of material (originally canvas, now usu. nylon etc.) extended on rigging to catch the wind and propel a boat or ship. **2** a ship's sails collectively. **3 a** a voyage or excursion in a sailing ship. **b** a voyage of specified duration. **4** a ship, esp. as discerned from its sails. **5** (*collective*) ships in a squadron or company (*a fleet of twenty sail*). **6** a wind-catching apparatus, usu. a set of boards, attached to the arm of a windmill. **7 a** the dorsal fin of a sailfish. **b** the tentacle of a nautilus. **c** the float of a Portuguese man-of-war. ● *verb* **1** *intransitive* travel on water by the use of sails or engine power. **2** *transitive* a navigate (a ship etc.). **b** travel on (a sea). **3** *transitive* set (a toy boat) afloat. **4** *intransitive* glide or move smoothly or in a stately manner. **5** *intransitive* (often foll. by *through*) *informal* move or succeed easily (*sailed through the exams*). □ **make sail** *Naut.* **1** spread a sail or sails. **2** start a voyage. **sail close to the wind 1** sail as nearly against the wind as possible. **2** come close to indecency or dishonesty; risk overstepping the mark. **sail into** *informal* attack physically or verbally with force. **under sail** with sails set; sailing. □ **sail·able** *adjective* **sailed** *adjective* (also in *combination*). **sail·less** *adjective* [Old English *segel* from Germanic]

sail·board *noun* a board with a mast and sail, used in windsurfing. □ **sail·board·er** *noun* **sail·board·ing** *noun*

sail·boat *noun N Amer.* a boat driven by sails.

sail·cloth *noun* **1** canvas for sails. **2** a canvas-like dress material.

sail·er *noun* a sailing vessel, esp. one that sails in a specified way.

sail·fish *noun* **1** any fish of the genus *Istiophorus*, with a large dorsal fin. **2** a basking shark.

sailing boat *noun esp. Brit.* = SAILBOAT.

sailing master *noun* an officer navigating a ship, esp. *Brit.* a yacht.

sailing ship *noun* (also **sailing craft**, **sailing vessel**, etc.) a vessel driven by sails.

sail·maker *noun* a person who makes, repairs, or alters sails. □ **sail·making** *noun*

sail·or *noun* **1** a member of a ship's crew, esp. one below the rank of officer. **2** a person who sails for recreation. **3** a person considered as liable or not liable to seasickness (*a good sailor*). □ **sail·or·ly** *adjective*

sailor collar *noun* a collar consisting of a large square flap hanging down at the back, tapering to a V at the front, usu. outlined in contrasting piping along the edges.

sailor hat *noun* **1** a straw hat with a straight narrow brim and flat top. **2** a hat with a turned-up brim.

sailor suit *noun* a boy's or girl's outfit, usu. navy and white, the top having a sailor collar.

sail·past *noun* a ceremonial sailing of ships etc. past a person or place.

sail·plane *noun* a glider designed for sustained flight.

sain·foin /ˈseɪnfɔɪn, ˈsan-/ *noun* a leguminous plant, *Onobrychis viciifolia*, grown for fodder and having pink flowers. [obsolete French *saintfoin* from modern Latin *sanum foenum* wholesome hay (because of its medicinal properties)]

saint ● *noun* (*abbr.* **St.** or **S.**; *pl.* **Sts.** or **SS.**) **1** a holy or (in some Churches) a canonized person regarded as having a place in heaven. **2** (**Saint** or **St.**) the title of a saint or archangel, hence the name of a church etc. (*St. Michael's*) or (often with the loss of the apostrophe) the name of a town etc. (*St. Catharines*; *St. Andrews*). **3 a** a very virtuous person; a person of great real or affected holiness (*would try the patience of a saint*). **b** a person regarded as worthy of high esteem by the followers of a movement or cause. **4** a member of the company of heaven (*with all the angels and saints*). **5** (*Bible, archaic*, and used by Puritans, Mormons, etc.) one of God's chosen people; a member of the Christian Church or one's own branch of it. ● *transitive verb* **1** canonize; admit to the calendar of saints. **2** call or regard as a saint. □ **saint·hood** *noun* **saint·like** *adjective* [Old French from Latin *sanctus* holy, past participle of *sancire* consecrate]

St. Al·bert a city in central Alberta, immediately northwest of Edmonton; pop. (2001) 53,081. [patron saint of Fr. A. LACOMBE]

St. An·drews 1 a town in east Scotland, in Fife, on the North Sea; pop. (est. 2001) 16,000. The ecclesiastical capital of Scotland until the Reformation, it is noted today for its university, founded in 1412, and its golf courses. **2** a town in SW New Brunswick, situated at the mouth of the St. Croix River, 96 km (60 miles) west of Saint John; pop. (2001) 1,869. [sense 2 perhaps after a priest called *St. André*, or perhaps in honour of a mass celebrated there on St. Andrew's Day]

Consonants: **b** *but* **d** *dog* **f** *few* **g** *get* **h** *her* **j** *yes* **k** *cat* **l** *leg* **m** *man* **n** *no* **p** *pen* **r** *red* **s** *sit*

St. An·drew's cross *noun* an X-shaped cross, esp. white on a blue background as the flag of Scotland.

St. An·drew's Day *noun* November 30, the feast of St. Andrew, esp. as a celebration of Scottish heritage or patriotism.

St. An·thony cross *noun* (also **St. Anthony's cross**) a T-shaped cross.

St. An·thony's fire *noun* erysipelas or ergotism.

Saint-Antoine /sãtɑ̃'twɒn/ a former town in south central Quebec, now part of Saint-Jérôme; pop. (2001) 11,488. [in honour of Fr. *Antoine* Labelle, parish priest of Saint-Jérôme d.1891]

Saint-Athanase /sãtatɑ'nnz/ a former parish in south central Quebec, now part of Saint-Jean-sur-Richelieu; pop. (2001) 6,691. [St. ATHANASIUS]

Saint-Augustin-de-Desmaures /sãto:gu:stãdədeimɔr/ a former municipality in SE central Quebec, now part of the city of Québec; pop. (2001) 15,727. [in honour of Augustin de MÉZY and Jean Juchereau de Maure, grantee of the seigneury]

St. Bartholomew's Day Massacre the massacre of Huguenots throughout France ordered by Charles IX at the instigation of his mother, Catherine de' Medici, and begun without warning on 24 Aug. (the feast of St. Bartholomew) 1572.

Saint-Basile-le-Grand /sãba,zi:llɔ'grɑ̃/ a town in south central Quebec, situated on the Richelieu, east of Montreal; pop. (2001) 12,385. [*Basile* Daigneault, a local farmer whose name recalled St. Basil the Great: see BASIL]

St. Bernard *noun* a breed of very large dog originally kept to rescue travellers by the monks of the Hospice on the Great St. Bernard Pass in the Alps.

St. Bernard Pass either of two passes across the Alps in S Europe. The **Great St. Bernard Pass**, on the border between SW Switzerland and Italy, rises to 2 469 m (8,100 ft.). The **Little St. Bernard Pass**, on the French–Italian border southeast of Mont Blanc, rises to 2 188 m (7,178 ft.). [after the hospices founded on their summits in the 11th c. by St. BERNARD]

Saint-Bruno-de-Montarville /sãbru:noːdəmɔ̃tɑr'vil/ a former city in south central Quebec, located on the south side of Mount St. Bruno, east of Montreal, now part of Longueuil; pop. (2001) 23,843. [in honour of F.-P. *Bruneau*, seigneur of *Montarville* (blend of French *montagne* mountain + *Boucherville*, after P. Boucher de *Boucherville* the Younger, original seigneur d.1740)]

St. Cath·ar·ines a city in S Ontario, located on the southwestern shore of Lake Ontario, about 50 km east of Hamilton; pop. (2001) 129,170. [in honour of *Catharine* A. Robertson, wife of Queenston merchant R. Hamilton c.1796]

Saint-Charles /sã'ʃɑrl/ a former village, at the site of present-day Saint-Charles-sur-Richelieu, in south central Quebec, east of Montreal. It was the scene on 25 Nov. 1837 of a decisive battle during the Lower Canada Rebellion; the Patriote forces were soundly defeated.

St. Christopher and Nevis, Federation of the official name for ST. KITTS AND NEVIS.

St. Clair, Lake a lake in SW Ontario and SE Michigan, forming part of the US–Canadian border. It is connected to Lake Huron in the north by the St. Clair River and to Lake Erie to the south by the Detroit River. The cities of Detroit and Windsor lie on its shores. [originally French *Ste.-Claire*, after *St. Clare*: see CLARE OF ASSISI, ST.]

St. Clair River a river in SW Ontario and SE Michigan, 64 km long, which flows southward from Lake Huron to Lake St. Clair, forming part of the border between Ontario and Michigan. [see ST. CLAIR, LAKE]

Saint-Constant /sãkɔ̃'stã/ a town in S Quebec, south of Montreal; pop. (2001) 22,577. [origin uncertain: possibly in honour of *Constant* Le Marchand de Lignery d.1731, father of J. Le Marchand de Lignery who served for a time at the mission there]

St. Croix /krɔi/ an island in the West Indies, the largest of the US Virgin Islands; chief town, Christiansted. Purchased by Denmark in 1753, it was sold to the US in 1917.

St. Croix River /san 'krwʌ/ a river in SW New Brunswick and SE Maine, 121 km long, rising in the Chiputneticook Lakes southeast of Fredericton and flowing generally southeastward to Passamaquoddy Bay. [French *croix* cross, because the water branches at the mouth of the river to form such a shape]

St. David's Day *noun* March 1, the feast of St. David, esp. as a celebration of Welsh heritage or patriotism.

Saint-Denis /ˌsãdə'niː/ **1** a city in France, now a northern suburb of Paris; pop. (1982) 91,275. Its magnificent abbey church, significant for marking a transition between Romanesque and Gothic architecture, is the burial place of the kings of France. **2** the capital of the French island of Réunion in the Indian Ocean, a port on the north coast; pop. (1999) 85,832. **3** a village in south central Quebec, situated on the Richelieu, east of Montreal; pop. (2001) 1,050. It was the scene on 23 Nov. 1837 of the first battle fought during the Lower Canada Rebellion, the sole battle won by the Patriotes. Several days later, however, the British returned, following their decisive victory at Saint-Charles, and set the village ablaze. [sense 3 ultimately in honour of B. *Denis*, wife of seigneur L. de Gannes c.1694]

Sainte-Adèle /sãta'del/ an all-season resort town in south central Quebec, situated north of Saint-Jérôme; pop. (2001) 9,215. [in honour of *Adèle* Raymond, whose husband donated land for the church c.1852]

Sainte-Agathe-des-Monts /sãta,gatdei'mɔ̃/ a town in south central Quebec, situated in the mountains northwest of Saint-Jérôme; pop. (2001) 9,088. [St. *Agatha*, 3rd-c. Sicilian virgin and martyr]

Sainte-Anne, Mont /mɔ̃sãt'an/ a mountain (820 m) in SE central Quebec, situated northeast of Quebec City. It is a popular destination for skiers. [ultimately after St. ANNE]

Sainte-Anne-de-Beaupré /sãtandəbɔː'prei/ a town in SE central Quebec, situated on the St. Lawrence, about 30 km northeast of Quebec City; pop. (2001) 2,752. The town is the site of the Sainte-Anne-de-Beaupré Basilica, a major place of pilgrimage since 1658, although the present Romanesque basilica was constructed c.1926. [St. ANNE + French *beau pré* pretty meadow]

Sainte-Anne-de-Bellevue /sãtandəbel'vju:/ a former city in south central Quebec, at the southwestern tip of the Island of Montreal, now part of the city of Montreal; pop. (2001) 5,062. [*Bellevue* with reference to the beautiful views over Lac des Deux Montagnes and Lac Saint-Louis]

Sainte-Anne-de-Bellevue Canal a historic canal in south central Quebec, situated at the southwestern corner of Île de Montréal. Built in 1816, the canal links Lac des Deux Montagnes and Lac Saint-Louis.

Sainte-Anne-des-Monts-Tourelle /sãtandei'mɔ̃tuː'rel/ a town in E Quebec, situated on the south shore of the St. Lawrence beneath the Monts Chic-Chocs, about 75 km northeast of Matane; pop. (2001) 6,835. [possibly after *Sainte-Anne-de-la-Pocatière* in France, birthplace of Fr. Jean-Baptiste, who established a parish there c.1815]

Sainte-Anne-des-Plaines /sãtandei'plen/ a town in south central Quebec, northeast of Blainville; pop. (2001) 12,908. [originally *Sainte-Anne-de-Mascouche*, from Algonquin *mascouche* level plain]

Sainte-Beuve /sãtbɜːv/ **Charles Au·gus·tin** (1804–69), French critic and writer. His literary criticism concentrated on the influence of social and other factors in the development of authors' characters; his works include the collections of critical essays, *Causeries du lundi* (1851–62) and *Nouvelles lundis* (1863–70), and a study of Jansenism, *Port-Royal* (1840–59).

Sainte-Catherine /sãtkat'riːn/ a town in south central Quebec, situated on the south shore of the St. Lawrence, directly south of Montreal; pop. (2001) 15,953. [CATHERINE OF ALEXANDRIA]

saint·ed *adjective* sacred; of a saintly life; worthy to be regarded as a saint. □ **my sainted aunt** see AUNT.

Sainte-Élie-d'Orford /sãtei'liːdɔrfɔrd/ a former municipality in S Quebec, now part of Sherbrooke; pop. (2001) 7,947. [in honour of Fr. Alfred-Élie Dufresne d.1891, who opened a mission there]

Sainte-Foy /sãt'fwɒ/ a former city in SE central Quebec, now part of the city of Québec; pop. (2001) 72,547. It was the scene in April 1760 of a battle fought during the Seven Years War. Although the French proved victorious and were subsequently able to lay siege to Quebec City, they soon chose to retreat when British supply ships arrived ahead of their own. [possibly after a village in France]

Sainte-Hélène, Île /iːl sãtei'len/ a small island park in the St. Lawrence River, linked to the city of Montreal by bridge. [prob. in honour of *Hélène* Boullé, wife of Samuel de Champlain, d.1654]

Sainte-Julie /sãtʒuː'liː/ a city in south central Quebec, located east of Montreal between the Richelieu and St. Lawrence rivers; pop. (2001) 26,580. [in honour of both *St. Julia*, a 5th-c. martyr, and *Julie* Gauthier *dit* Saint-Germain, whose husband donated land for the parish's chapel c.1849]

St. Elias, Mount /ɪ'laiəs/ a peak in the St. Elias Mountains, situated on the Yukon–Alaska border, southwest of Mount Logan. Rising to a height of 5 489 m, it is the second highest mountain in Canada. [*St. Elias*, an alternative name for ELIJAH]

St. Elias Mountains a mountain range extending southeastward some 500 km from Alaska, through Yukon Territory, into the northwestern corner of BC. Its highest peak is Mount Logan (5 959 m). [see ST. ELIAS, MOUNT]

St. Elmo's fire *noun* a luminous electrical discharge sometimes seen on a ship or aircraft during a storm. [Italian corruption of *St. Erasmus*, patron saint of Mediterranean sailors, who interpreted this as a sign of his guardianship]

Sainte-Marie¹ /sãtma'ri:/ a town in SE central Quebec, situated on the Chaudière river, about 50 km southeast of Quebec City; pop. (2001) 11,320. [in honour of *Marie-Claire de Fleury de La Gorgendière* d.1797, stepdaughter of the seigneur T.-J. Taschereau]

Sainte-Marie² /ˌseint mə'ri:/ **Buffy** (b.1941), Canadian Cree singer and songwriter, raised in the US. She became an important folksinger in New York in the 1960s. Some of her music centres on the Aboriginal people of N America; other songs include 'The Universal Soldier' and 'Until It's Time for You To Go'.

Sainte-Marie-Among-the-Hurons /seint mə'ri:/ a former Roman Catholic missionary centre (est. *c.*1639) in Huronia, east of present-day Midland, Ontario. The first European community in Ontario, it was removed to Quebec in 1650. It has been recreated in its original location as a historic site. [the Virgin MARY]

Sainte-Marthe-du-Cap /sãtmɑrtdu:kap/ a town in SE central Quebec, situated on the north shore of the St. Lawrence just east of the Saint-Maurice, now the eastern part of Trois-Rivières; pop. (2001) 6,162. [in honour of MARTHA]

Sainte-Marthe-sur-le-Lac /sãtmɑrtsurlǝlak/ a town in SE central Quebec, situated on the north shore of Lac des Deux Montagnes; pop. (2001) 6,162. [in honour of MARTHA]

Saint-Émile /sãtei'mil/ a former town in SE central Quebec, , now part of the city of Québec; pop. (2001) 10,940. [in honour of Fr. J.-N.-*Émile* Bédard, local pastor *c.*1925–40]

Saint-Émilion /ˌsãt ei'mi:ljɔ̃/ a small town situated to the north of the Dordogne in SW France. It gives its name to a group of Bordeaux wines.

Sainte-Thérèse /sãttei'rez/ a city in south central Quebec, located between Blainville and Laval; pop. (2001) 24,269. [in honour of Marie-*Thérèse*, daughter of M.-S. Dugué de Boisbriand, seigneur of Mille-Îles and Blainville *c.*1683]

Saint-Étienne /ˌsãtei'tjen/ an industrial city in SE central France, southwest of Lyons; pop. (1999) 180,210.

Saint-Étienne-de-Lauzon /sãtei'tjendǝlɔ:'zɔ̃/ a former municipality in SE central Quebec, now part of Lévis; pop. (2001) 8,897. [in honour of St. Stephen and with reference to the seigneury of Lauzon, named for Jean de Lauson (d.1666)]

Saint-Eustache /sãtɜ'staʃ/ a city in south central Quebec, located on the Rivière des Mille Îles, west of Montreal; pop. (2001) 40,378. It was the scene on 14 Dec. 1837 of a brutal battle during the Lower Canada Rebellion, at which some 70 Patriotes were killed. [in honour of *Eustache* L. Dumont, local seigneur and miller *c.*1749]

Saint-Exupéry /sãteks,u:peir'i:/ **An·toine (Marie Roger) de** (1900–44), French novelist and aviator. Most of his novels are based on his experiences as a pilot, including *Night Flight* (1931) and *Wind, Sand, and Stars* (1939); his best-known work is the fable *The Little Prince* (1943).

Saint-Félicien /sãfeili'sjã/ a town in NE central Quebec, near the northwestern end of Lac Saint-Jean; pop. (2001) 10,622. [*St. Felician*, Roman martyr d. *c.*297]

St. Francis, Lake (also **Lac Saint-François**) a lake forming part of the border between E Ontario and S Quebec, a widening of the St. Lawrence, situated just northeast of Cornwall. [XAVIER, ST. FRANCIS]

Saint-François, Ri·vière /sãfrã'swɒ/ a river in south central Quebec, 280 km long, which rises near Thetford Mines and flows southwestward to Sherbrooke, then bends northwestward to flow through Drummondville into Lac Saint-Pierre. [in honour of *François* de Lauson, son of the governor of New France *c.*1650]

Saint-Georges /sã'ʒɔrʒ/ a city in SE Quebec, located about 90 km southeast of Quebec City and 40 km from the border with Maine; pop. (2001) 28,127. [in honour of J. *Georg* Pfozer, seigneur and recruiter of German settlers to the area d.1848]

St. George's the capital of Grenada in the W Indies, a port in the southwest of the island; pop. (est. 1999) 35,000.

St. George's Channel a channel between Wales and Ireland, linking the Irish Sea with the Celtic Sea.

St. George's cross *noun* a +-shaped cross, red on a white background.

St. George's Day *noun* April 23, the feast day of St. George, esp. as a celebration of English heritage or patriotism.

St. Got·thard Pass /'gɒtard/ a mountain pass in the Alps in S Switzerland, situated at an altitude of 2 108 m (6,916 ft.).

St. Hel·ena /'helǝnǝ/ a solitary island in the S Atlantic, a British dependency; pop. (est. 2002) 7,317; capital, Jamestown. St. Helena is famous as the place of Napoleon's exile and death. □ **St. Helen·ian** *adjective & noun*

St. Hel·ens, Mount an active volcano in SW Washington, in the Cascade Range, rising to 2 560 m (8,312 ft.).

St. Hel·ier /'heli:ǝr/ a market town and resort on the south coast of Jersey; pop. (2001) 28,300. It is the capital of the island. [after a 6th-c. Christian hermit]

Saint-Hubert /sãtu:'ber/ a former city in south central Quebec, now part of Longueuil; pop. (2001) 75,912. [*St. Hubert*, bishop of Maastricht and Liège d.727]

Saint-Hyacinthe /sãtiǝ'sãt/ a city in south central Quebec, located on the Rivière Yamaska, about 50 km east of Montreal; pop. (2001) 50,394. [in honour of J.-*Hyacinthe*-Simon Delorme *dit* Lapointe, local seigneur d.1778]

St. James Street *noun Cdn* **1** a street in Montreal where the offices of many financial institutions are located. **2** the moneyed interests of Montreal, esp. as opposed to other regions of Canada (*the latest polls worry St. James Street*).

Saint-Jean, Île /i:l sã'ʒã/ the former French name (*c.*1604–1759) for Prince Edward Island.

Saint-Jean, Lac /lak sã'ʒã/ a lake in NE central Quebec, situated at the head of the Saguenay River, about 200 km north of Quebec City. [after the patron saint of Fr. Jean de Quen, Jesuit missionary *c.*1650]

Saint-Jean-Baptiste Day /sã ,ʒã ba'ti:st/ *noun Cdn* (in Quebec) the former official name (still commonly in use) for the Fête nationale, June 24. [French, lit. 'St. John the Baptist' (whose feast is celebrated on this day), patron saint of French Canadians]

Saint-Jean-Baptiste Society *noun Cdn* a Quebec-based organization promoting French culture in Canada, founded in 1834.

Saint-Jean-Chrysos·tome /sãʒãkri:zɒ'stoːm/ a former town in SE central Quebec, on the south side of the St. Lawrence, south of Quebec City, now part of Lévis; pop. (2001) 17,089. [St. John CHRYSOSTOM]

Saint-Jean-Port-Joli /sãʒãpɔrʒɔ'li:/ a municipality in SE central Quebec, situated on the south shore of the St. Lawrence, about 30 km northeast of Montmagny; pop. (2001) 3,372. [JOHN THE BAPTIST + French *port joli* pretty harbour]

Saint-Jean-sur-Richelieu /sãʒãsurriʃǝ'ljǝ/ a city in south central Quebec, situated on the Richelieu, about 40 km southeast of Montreal; pop. (2001) 79,600. [in honour of *Jean*-Frédéric Phélypeaux, who established a fort there in 1665, + RICHELIEU]

Saint-Jérôme /sãʒei'roːm/ a city in south central Quebec, situated about 40 km northwest of Montreal; pop. (2001) 59,614. [JEROME, ST.]

Saint John a city and port in S New Brunswick, situated on the Bay of Fundy at the mouth of the Saint John River; pop. (2001) 69,661. It became a Loyalist refuge after the American Revolution. □ **Saint John·er** *noun* [as SAINT JOHN RIVER]

St. John an island in the West Indies, one of the three principal islands of the US Virgin Islands.

St. John Ambulance *noun* an organization providing services and training in first aid, nursing, etc., founded by English Knights Hospitallers in 1878.

Saint John River a river in W New Brunswick, rising in N Maine and flowing 673 km first northeastward, then generally southward through Edmundston, Grand Falls, and Fredericton, to empty into the Bay of Fundy at Saint John. [in honour of JOHN THE BAPTIST]

St. John's 1 the capital of Newfoundland, a port situated on the southeastern coast of the island; pop. (2001) 99,182. One of the oldest European settlements in N America, it was colonized by the British in 1583. **2** the capital of Antigua and Barbuda, situated on the northwest coast of Antigua; pop. (est. 2002) 23,400. [sense 1 possibly from the harbour's early name of *Rio de Sam Johan*, as it appeared on a Portuguese map (1519–20), or possibly in honour of the feast day of *St. John the Baptist* (24 June), because it is said that the harbour was first entered by Cabot on this day in 1497]

St. John's Island the former name (1759–98) for Prince Edward Island. [translation of French *Île Saint-Jean*: see SAINT-JEAN, ÎLE]

St. John's wort *noun* **1** any yellow-flowered plant of the genus *Hypericum*, often cultivated for ornament. **2** an extract from this flower used esp. as an antidepressant.

St. Joseph Island an island in north central Ontario, situated in

---

Vowels: a *cat* ɑ *arm* e *bed* ɜr *her* ɜː *deux* ə *ago* ɪ *sit* i *cosy* iː *feed* ɒ *hot* ɔ *pore* ɔː *no* ʌ *run* ʊ *put*

the west end of the North Channel of Lake Huron, southeast of Sault Ste. Marie. [St. JOSEPH]

Saint-Just /sã'ju:st/ **Louis An·toine Léon de** (1767–94), French Revolutionary leader. A member of the Committee of Public Safety (1793–4), he organized the Reign of Terror, and carried out many missions to enforce discipline in the revolutionary armies; he was executed with Robespierre.

St. Kitts /kɪts/ a nickname for St. Catharines. [alteration and shortening]

St. Kitts and Nevis (official name **Federation of St. Christopher and Nevis**) a country in the West Indies consisting of two adjoining islands (St. Kitts and Nevis) of the Leeward Islands; pop. (est. 2002) 38,736; capital, Basseterre (on St. Kitts). □ **Kit·ti·tian** /kɪ'tɪʃən/ *adjective & noun*

Saint-Lambert /sãlã'ber/ a former city in south central Quebec, on the south shore of the St. Lawrence, opposite Montreal, now part of Longueuil; pop. (2001) 21,051. [origin uncertain: possibly after the name of the shoreline *Côte-Saint-Lambert* (as it was known in the 17th c.), prob. in honour of R.-*Lambert* Closse, commander of Ville-Marie (Montreal) d.1662, or possibly after the area's Protestant parish, perhaps in honour of the reformer F. *Lambert* d.1530]

Saint-Laurent /sãlɒ'rã/ a former city in south central Quebec, in the centre of the Island of Montreal, now part of the city of Montreal; pop. (2001) 77,391. [French, after St. LAWRENCE]

Saint Lau·rent /sãlɒ'rã/ **Yves (Ma·thieu)** (b.1936), French fashion designer. He opened his own fashion house in 1962 and four years later launched the first of a worldwide chain of Rive Gauche boutiques to sell ready-to-wear garments; from the 1970s he expanded the business to include perfumes and household fabrics.

St. Lau·rent /sãlɒ'rã/ **Louis Ste·phen** (1882–1973), Canadian lawyer and politician, Liberal prime minister 1948–57. A prominent lawyer and (after 1914) law professor at McGill University, he was asked to become Minister of Justice in the King government in 1941; he agreed and was elected in 1942. The only cabinet minister from Quebec to support King's stand on conscription in 1944, he became minister of external affairs in 1946 and followed King as Liberal leader and prime minister in 1948. The party won overwhelming majorities in 1949 and 1953, but was defeated in 1957.

St. Lawrence, Gulf of a large inland sea of the N Atlantic, situated in SE Canada at the mouth of the St. Lawrence River. Bordering Quebec and each of the four Maritime provinces, it is connected to the Atlantic via the Strait of Belle Isle and Cabot Strait. [St. LAWRENCE]

St. Lawrence Islands National Park a tiny park in SE Ontario, comprising a series of islands and islets in the St. Lawrence, between Kingston and Brockville. It is Canada's smallest national park.

St. Lawrence Lowlands see GREAT LAKES–ST. LAWRENCE LOWLANDS.

St. Lawrence River a river of N America, which flows for some 1 200 km (750 miles) from Lake Ontario along the border between Canada and the US to the Gulf of St. Lawrence on the Atlantic coast. [St. LAWRENCE]

St. Lawrence Seaway a waterway in N America, which flows for 3 768 km (2,342 miles) through the Great Lakes and along the course of the St. Lawrence River to the Atlantic. Consisting of the navigable parts of the lakes and the rivers connecting them and the St. Lawrence, supplemented by canals to bypass rapids and Niagara Falls, it can be navigated along its entire length by ocean-going vessels. It was inaugurated in 1959.

Saint-Lazare /sãla'zɑr/ a parish municipality in S Quebec, southwest of Montreal; pop. (2001) 12,895. [LAZARUS 1]

Saint-Léonard /sãleio:'nɑr/ a former city in south central Quebec, in the northeastern part of the Island of Montreal, now part of the city of Montreal; pop. (2001) 69,604. [origin uncertain: perhaps after *St. Leonard of Port Maurice*, Franciscan priest d.1751, or *Léonard* Chaigneau, Sulpician missionary who recruited settlers to the area d.1711]

Saint-Lin-Laurentides /sãlãlɒrɑ̃ti:d/ a town in SE central Quebec, northeast of Saint-Jérôme; pop. (2001) 12,384. [in honour of St. *Linus*, successor to St. Peter as Pope, and French *Laurentides* = LAURENTIAN MOUNTAINS]

St. Louis /'lu:ɪs/ a city and port in E Missouri, on the Mississippi just south of its confluence with the Missouri; pop. (2000) 348,189.

Saint-Louis, Lac /laksãlu:'i:/ a widening of the St. Lawrence River where the Ottawa River joins it, off the south shore of the Island of Montreal. [in honour of a young man called Louis who drowned in the Lachine Rapids]

Saint-Louis-de-France /sãlwidə'frãs/ a former town in south central Quebec, now forming the northeast of Trois-Rivières; pop. (2001) 7,246. [ultimately in honour of LOUIS IX]

Saint-Luc /sã'lu:k/ a former town in south central Quebec, now part of Saint-Jean-sur-Richelieu; pop. (2001) 20,573. [St. LUKE]

St. Lucia /'lu:ʃə/ a country in the West Indies, one of the Windward Islands; pop. (est. 2002) 160,145; capital, Castries. □ **St. Lu·cian** *adjective & noun*

saint·ly *adjective* (**saint·li·er**, **saint·li·est**) very holy or virtuous; befitting a saint. □ **saint·li·ness** *noun*

Saint Malo /sã ma'lo:/ a walled town and port on the north coast of Brittany, in NW France; pop. (1999) 50,675. Jacques Cartier sailed from here on his first voyage of exploration to Canada.

St. Mar·garets Bay an inlet of the N Atlantic, situated on the east central coast of Nova Scotia, between Halifax and Mahone Bay.

St. Martin /ˌsã mɑr'tã/ (Dutch **Sint Maar·ten** /sɪnt 'mɑrtə/) a small island in the Caribbean, one of the Leeward Islands; pop. (est. 2002) 47,400. The southern section of the island is administered by the Dutch, forming part of the Netherlands Antilles; chief town and seat of the island's administration, Philipsburg. The larger northern part of the island is part of the French overseas department of Guadeloupe; chief town, Marigot.

St. Martin's summer *noun Brit.* a period of fine weather expected about 11 Nov.

St. Marys a town in SW Ontario, southwest of Stratford; pop. (2001) 6,293. [in honour of E. *Mary* Jones, wife of the commissioner of the Canada Company, who donated the sum of ten pounds toward the construction of the area's school *c.*1844]

St. Mary's Bay an inlet of the N Atlantic, indenting the southern coast of the Avalon Peninsula, SE Newfoundland. [prob. after *Cape St. Mary's*, a point located to the west, at the mouth of Placentia Bay]

St. Marys River a river in E Nova Scotia, rising east of Truro and flowing generally southeastward to empty into the Atlantic Ocean west of Tor Bay. [the Virgin MARY]

St. Mary's River a river in north central Ontario and N Michigan, flowing some 100 km from Lake Superior at Sault Ste. Marie to Lake Huron and forming part of the border between Canada and the US. [the Virgin MARY]

Saint-Maurice, Ri·vière /sãmɒ'ri:s/ a river in south central Quebec, 563 km long, which rises in Réservoir Gouin and flows southeastward to empty into the St. Lawrence at Trois-Rivières. [in honour of *Maurice* Poulin de La Fontaine, seigneur and king's attorney of Trois-Rivières d. *c.*1676]

St. Mor·itz /sã mə'rɪts/ a resort and winter-sports centre in SE Switzerland.

Saint-Nicéphore /sãni:sei'fɔr/ a town in SE central Quebec, southeast of Drummondville; pop. (2001) 9,966. [in honour of St. *Nicephorus*, a patriarch of Constantinople]

Saint-Nicolas /sãni:kə'lɒ/ a former city in SE central Quebec, on the south shore of the St. Lawrence west of Quebec City, now part of Lévis; pop. (2001) 16,645. [in honour of *Saint-Nicolas-de-la-Ferté*, a parish in the diocese of Chartres in France, ultimately after NICHOLAS, ST.]

Saint-Ours Canal /sã'u:rs/ a historic canal in south central Quebec, situated on the Richelieu, roughly midway between Chambly and Sorel. Opened in 1849, the canal removed the final obstruction for boats en route from Lake Champlain to the St. Lawrence. [ultimately after P. de *Saint-Ours*, military officer and local seigneur d.1724]

St. Patrick's Day *noun* March 17, the feast day of St. Patrick, on which Irish heritage is celebrated.

St. Paul 1 the state capital of Minnesota, situated on the Mississippi adjacent to Minneapolis, with which it forms the Twin Cities metropolitan area; pop. (2000) 287,151. **2** a town in east central Alberta, about 200 km northeast of Edmonton; pop. (2001) 5,061. [sense 2 after the name of a mission]

saint·paul·ia /sənt'pɒliə/ *noun* any plant of the genus *Saintpaulia*, esp. the African violet. [Baron W. von *Saint Paul*, German soldier d.1910, its discoverer]

St. Peter Port the capital of Guernsey; pop. (est. 1996) 16,194.

St. Peters·burg 1 a city and seaport in NW Russia, situated on the delta of the Neva River, on the eastern shores of the Gulf of Finland; pop. (est. 2002) 4,619,800. A city of waterways and bridges, it is a major industrial and cultural centre. It was formerly called Petrograd (1914–

24) and Leningrad (1924–91). **2** a resort city in W Florida, on the Gulf of Mexico; pop. (2000) 248,232.

Saint-Pierre, Lac a lake in south central Quebec, a widening of the St. Lawrence, situated between Sorel and Trois-Rivières. [French, St. PETER]

Saint-Pierre and Mi·que·lon /sã 'pjer, 'miːklɔ̃/ a group of eight small islands in the N Atlantic, off the south coast of Newfoundland; pop. (est. 2002) 6,954. The islands form the last remaining French possession in N America. The chief settlement is Saint Pierre.

Saint-Rédemp·teur /sãreidũp'tɜr/ a former town in SE central Quebec, situated on the south side of the St. Lawrence, south of Quebec City, now part of Lévis; pop. (2001) 6,349. [originally *Très-Saint-Rédempteur* (French, lit. 'The Most Holy Redeemer'), a title given to Christ]

Saint-Rémi /sãrei'miː/ a town in south central Quebec, located south of Montreal; pop. (2001) 5,736. [D. de *Rémy* de Courcelle, governor of New France and devotee of *St. Remi* d.1698]

Saint-Romuald /sãromu'ald/ a former town in SE central Quebec, situated on the south shore of the St. Lawrence, just southwest of Quebec City, now part of Lévis; pop. (2001) 10,825. [*St. Romuald of Ravenna*, Benedictine abbot d.1027]

Saint-Saëns /sã'sãs/ **(Charles) Ca·mille** (1835–1921), French composer, pianist, and organist. His works include operas (notably *Samson et Dalila*, 1877) and oratorios, but he is probably now best known for his Third Symphony (1886), the tone poem *Danse macabre* (1874), and the *Carnival of the Animals* (1886).

Saint-Sauveur /sãsoː'vɜr/ a town in SW central Quebec, a popular resort in the Laurentians; pop. (2001) 8,122. [French, lit. = 'Blessed Saviour']

saint's day *noun* (*pl.* **saints' days**) a Church festival in memory of a saint.

Saint-Simon /sãsi'mɔ̃/ **1 Claude-Henri de Rouv·roy, Comte de** (1760–1825), French social reformer and philosopher. His central theory was that society should be organized in an industrial order, controlled by leaders of industry, and given spiritual direction by scientists; his influential works include *Du système industriel* (1821) and *Nouveau Christianisme* (1825). **2 Louis de Rouv·roy, Duc de** (1675–1755), French writer. He is best known for his *Mémoires*, a detailed record of court life between 1694 and 1723, in the reigns of Louis XIV and XV. □ **Saint-Simonian** /sãsi'moːniən/ *adjective & noun*

St. So·phia /sə'fiːə/ (also called **Hagia Sophia, Santa Sophia**) the key monument of Byzantine architecture, built as a church (537) in Constantinople (now Istanbul), converted to a mosque in 1453 with the addition of minarets, and declared a museum in 1935.

St. Stephen a town in SW New Brunswick, situated on the St. Croix River, 29 km (18 miles) northwest of St. Andrews; pop. (2001) 4,667. □ **St. Ste·phen·er** *noun* [in honour of *Stephen* Pendleton, local surveyor *c.*1786]

St. Thomas 1 an island in the Caribbean, the second largest of the US Virgin Islands, situated to the east of Puerto Rico; pop. (est. 2002) 72,600; chief town, Charlotte Amalie. **2** a city in SW Ontario, about 30 km south of London; pop. (2001) 33,236. [sense 2 in honour of *Thomas* Talbot, founder of a local settlement d.1853]

Saint-Timothée /sãtimoː'tei/ a former municipality in S Quebec, situated east of Salaberry-de-Valleyfield, now merged with Salaberry-de-Valleyfield; pop. (2001) 8,299. [St. TIMOTHY]

Saint-Tropez /ˌsãtroː'pei/ a fishing port and fashionable resort on the Mediterranean coast of S France, southwest of Cannes; pop. (1999) 5,754.

St. Valentine's Day Massacre the shooting on 14th Feb. 1929 of seven members of 'Bugsy' Moran's gang by some of Al Capone's men disguised as policemen.

St. Vincent, Cape a headland in SW Portugal, which forms the southwesternmost tip of the country.

St. Vincent and the Grenadines /'vɪnsənt, 'grenə,diːnz/ an island state in the Windward Islands in the West Indies, consisting of the mountainous island of St. Vincent and some of the Grenadines; pop. (est. 2002) 116,394; capital, Kingstown.

St. Vitus's dance /'vəitəsɪz/ *noun* = SYDENHAM'S CHOREA. [VITUS, ST.]

Sai·pan /sai'pan/ the largest of the Northern Marianas islands in the W Pacific.

saith /seθ, 'seiɪθ/ *archaic 3rd sing. present of* SAY.

Sakai /sɒ'kai/ an industrial city in Japan, on Osaka Bay just south of the city of Osaka; pop. (est. 2002) 790,500.

sake¹ *noun* (esp. **for the sake of** or **for one's sake**) **1** out of consideration for; in the interest of; because of; owing to (*for my own sake as well as yours; art for art's sake*). **2** in order to please, honour, get, or keep (*for the sake of uniformity*). □ **for Christ's** (or **God's** or **goodness'** or **Heaven's** or **Pete's** etc.) **sake** an expression of urgency, impatience, supplication, anger, etc. **for old times' sake** in memory of former times. [Old English *sacu* contention, charge, fault, sake, from Germanic]

sake² /'saki, 'sɒki, -ei/ *noun* (also **saki**) a Japanese alcoholic drink made from fermented rice. [Japanese]

saker /'seikər/ *noun* a large falcon, *Falco cherrug*, used in hawking, esp. the larger female bird. [Old French *sacre* from Arabic *ṣaḳr*]

Sakha, Republic of /'sɒkə/ the official name for YAKUTIA.

Sakh·alin /ˌsakə'liːn/ a large island in the Sea of Okhotsk, situated off the coast of E Russia and separated from it by the Tatar Strait; capital, Yuzhno-Sakhalinsk.

Sakh·arov /'sakə,rɒf/ **An·drei (Dmitri·evich)** (1921–89), Russian nuclear physicist. Having helped to develop the Soviet hydrogen bomb, he campaigned against nuclear proliferation, called for Soviet–US co-operation, and was awarded the 1975 Nobel Peace Prize for his advocacy of reform and human rights in the USSR; between 1980 and 1986 he was banished to Gorky (Nizhni Novgorod) and kept under police surveillance.

Saki /'saki/ (pseudonym of Hector Hugh Munro) (1870–1916), Burmese-born Scottish short-story writer. His stories include the satiric, comic, macabre, and supernatural, and frequently depict animals as agents seeking revenge upon humankind; collections include *Reginald* (1904).

saki¹ /'sɒki/ *noun* (*pl.* **sakis**) any monkey of the genus *Pithecia* or *Chiropotes*, native to S America, having coarse fur and a long non-prehensile tail. [French from Tupi *çahy*]

saki² *var. of* SAKE².

Sakta /'ʃɒktə/ *noun* a member of a Hindu sect worshipping the Sakti. [Sanskrit *śākta* relating to power or to the SAKTI]

Sakti /'ʃakti/ *noun* (also **sakti; Shakti**) *Hinduism* **1** the female principle, esp. when personified as the wife of a god. For example, Durga is the Sakti of Shiva. **2** the goddess as supreme deity (Devi). □ **Sakt·ism** *noun* [Sanskrit *śakti* power, divine energy]

sa·laam /sə'lɒm/ ● *noun* **1** (in Muslim countries and India) the salutation 'Peace'. **2** an Indian obeisance, with or without the salutation, consisting of a low bow of the head and body with the right palm on the forehead. **3** (in *pl.*) respectful compliments. ● *verb* **1** *transitive* make a salaam to (a person). **2** *intransitive* make a salaam. [Arabic *salām*]

Sala·berry /salabe'riː/ **Charles-Michel d'Irum·berry de** (1778–1829), Canadian soldier. Commissioned in the British army in 1794, he served in Ireland, the West Indies, and the Low Countries (during the Napoleonic Wars). He returned to Lower Canada in 1810, and commanded a French-Canadian militia in the War of 1812. He retired in 1815 and was appointed to the legislative council of Lower Canada in 1818.

Salaberry-de-Valley·field /salabe,riːdə'valiːfiːld/ a city in S Quebec, situated at the eastern end of Lake St. Francis, about 50 km southwest of Montreal; pop. (2001) 39,028. [in honour of SALABERRY + *Valleyfield* Paper Mills, a local company]

salable esp. US *var. of* SALEABLE.

sal·acious /sə'leiʃəs/ *adjective* **1** lustful; lecherous. **2** (of writings, pictures, talk, etc.) tending to cause sexual desire. □ **sal·acious·ly** *adverb* **sal·acious·ness** *noun* [Latin *salax salacis* from *salire* leap]

salad *noun* **1** a cold dish of various mixtures of raw or cooked vegetables, esp. lettuce, tomatoes, cucumbers, etc., or pasta, sometimes combined with meat or cheese, and usu. seasoned with oil and vinegar or other dressing. **2** *N Amer.* a mixture of fish, meat, etc. with mayonnaise and other seasonings, often as a sandwich filling (*tuna salad; egg salad*). **3** a vegetable or herb suitable for eating raw, e.g. lettuce. [Old French *salade* from Provençal *salada*, ultimately from Latin *sal* salt]

salad bar *noun* a self-serve stand in a restaurant offering patrons various ingredients for creating salads.

salad bowl *noun* a large bowl suitable for serving a salad.

salad burnet *noun* a herb, *Sanguisorba minor*, with a flavour of cucumber, used as a seasoning.

salad days *plural noun* a period of youthful inexperience.

salad dressing *noun* a seasoned mixture or sauce for pouring on a salad, usu. based on oil and vinegar or mayonnaise.

Sala·din /'salədɪn/ (Arabic name Salah-ad-Din Yusuf ibn-Ayyub) (1137–93), sultan of Egypt and Syria 1174–93. He invaded the Holy Land and reconquered Jerusalem from the Christians (1187) before holding out against the Third Crusade; defeated by Richard I of England at Arsuf (1191), he withdrew to Damascus, where he died.

salad oil *noun* = COOKING OIL.

salad servers *plural noun* a set of utensils, usu. a very large spoon and fork, for serving salad.

salal /sə'lal/ *noun* a shrub of western N America, *Gaultheria shallon*, with racemes of pink or white flowers and edible purple-black berries. [Chinook Jargon *sallal*]

Salam /sə'lɒm/ **Abdus** (1926–96), Pakistani theoretical physicist. He worked on the interaction of subatomic particles, and independently developed a unified theory to explain electromagnetic interactions and the weak nuclear force; he shared the Nobel Prize for physics in 1979.

Sala·man·ca /ˌsalə'maŋkə/ a city in W Spain, in Castilla-León; pop. (est. 2001) 158,523.

sala·man·der /'salə,mandər/ *noun* **1** any tailed scaleless newt-like amphibian of the order Caudata. **2** a mythical lizard-like creature thought able to endure fire. **3** an elemental spirit living in fire. **4** a portable stove. **5** *Brit.* a metal plate heated and placed over food to brown it. □ **sala·man·drine** /-'mandrɪn/ *adjective* [ultimately from Greek *salamandra*]

sa·lami /sə'lɒmi/ *noun* (*pl.* **sa·lamis**) a highly-seasoned dried sausage often flavoured with garlic. [Italian, pl. of *salame*, from Late Latin *salare* (unrecorded) to salt]

Sala·mis /'saləmɪs/ an island in the Saronic Gulf in Greece, to the west of Athens.

sal am·mo·niac /ˌsal ə'məʊnɪˌak/ *noun* an old-fashioned name for AMMONIUM CHLORIDE. [Latin *sal ammoniacus* 'salt of Ammon', associated with the Roman temple of Ammon in North Africa]

Sal·ang Pass /'sɒlaŋ/ a high-altitude route across the Hindu Kush mountain range in Afghanistan. The Salang Pass and tunnel were built by the Soviet Union during the 1960s in an attempt to improve the supply route from the Soviet frontier to Kabul.

sal·ary ● *noun* (*pl.* **-ies**) a fixed regular payment made by an employer to an employee, esp. payment made for professional or non-manual work, usu. expressed as an annual sum (*a $35,000 salary*) (compare WAGE *noun* 1). ● *transitive verb* (**-ies, -ied**) (usu. as **sal·ar·ied** *adjective*) pay a salary to. [Anglo-French *salarie*, Old French *salaire* from Latin *salarium* originally soldier's salt-money, from *sal* salt]

salary·man *noun* (*pl.* **salary·men**) (in Japan) a white-collar worker.

Sala·zar /ˌsalə'zɑr/ **An·tonio de Oli·veira** (1889–1970), Portuguese political leader, prime minister 1932–68. He ruled the country as a virtual dictator, firmly suppressing opposition, enacting a new authoritarian constitution along Fascist lines, and maintaining Portugal's neutrality throughout the Spanish Civil War and the Second World War.

sal·buta·mol /sal'bjuːtəmɒl/ *noun Pharm.* a drug used esp. as a bronchodilator to treat asthma. Compare VENTOLIN. [from SALICYLIC ACID + BUTYL + AMINE + -OL[1]]

Sal·chow /'saʊkaʊ/ *noun Figure Skating* a jump from the backward inside edge of one skate to the backward outside edge of the other, with a full turn in the air. [U. *Salchow*, Swedish skater d.1949]

sale *noun* **1** the exchange of a commodity for money etc.; an act or instance of selling. **2** the amount sold (*the sales were enormous*). **3** (in *pl.*) the branch of a company etc. concerned with the selling of goods (*spent eight years in sales*; also *attributive*: *sales staff*). **4** an offering of goods or services at reduced prices for a period, e.g. at the end of a season etc. **5 a** an event at which goods are sold. **b** a public auction. □ **for sale** offered for purchase. **on sale** for sale, esp. at a reduced price. [Old English *sala* from Old Norse]

Salé /sal'ei/ a city on the coast of Morocco, close to Rabat; pop. (est. 1994) 504,420.

sale·able *adjective* (also esp. *US* **sal·able**) fit to be sold; finding purchasers. □ **sale·abil·ity** *noun*

Salem /'seiləm/ **1** an industrial city in Tamil Nadu in S India; pop. (2001) 693,200. It is a centre for the production of textiles. **2** the state capital of Oregon, situated on the Willamette River southwest of Portland; pop. (2000) 136,900. **3** a city and port in NE Massachusetts, on the Atlantic coast north of Boston; pop. (2000) 40,400. It was the scene in 1692 of a notorious series of witchcraft trials.

salep /'saləp/ *noun* a starchy preparation of the dried tubers of various orchids, used in cookery and formerly medicinally. [French from Turkish *sâlep* from Arabic (kuṣa-'l-) *ta'lab* fox, fox's testicles]

Sal·erno /sə'lernɔ/ a port on the west coast of Italy, on the Gulf of Salerno southeast of Naples; pop. (2001) 144,078.

sale·room *noun* esp. *Brit.* = SALESROOM.

sales clerk *noun N Amer.* a salesperson in a store.

Sal·esian /sə'liːʒən/ ● *noun* a member of an educational religious society within the Roman Catholic Church, founded in Italy by St. John Bosco in 1859. ● *adjective* of or relating to this order. [St. François de Sales, French bishop d.1622]

sales·lady *noun* (*pl.* **-ladies**) a saleswoman.

sales·man *noun* (*pl.* **-men**) a man employed to sell goods or services in a store etc. or as an agent between the producer and retailer; a sales representative.

sales·man·ship *noun* **1** skill in selling. **2** the techniques used in selling.

sales·person *noun* (*pl.* **-people** or **-persons**) a salesman or saleswoman.

sales pitch *noun* an argument used to persuade someone, esp. to buy something.

sales representative *noun* (also *informal* **sales rep**) a person who represents a business to prospective customers and solicits orders.

sales·room *noun* **1** a room in which merchandise is displayed for sale. **2** a room in which items are sold at auction.

sales talk *noun* persuasive talk to promote the sale of goods or the acceptance of an idea etc.

sales tax *noun* a tax on sales or on the receipts from sales, added to the cost of a purchase.

sales·woman *noun* (*pl.* **-women**) a woman employed to sell goods or services in a store etc. or as an agent between the producer and retailer; a sales representative.

Sal·ford /'sɒlfərd/ an industrial city in NW England, near Manchester; pop. (est. 1999) 220,463.

Salian /'seiliən/ ● *adjective* of or relating to the Salii, a 4th-c. Frankish people living near the Ijssel River, from which the Merovingians were descended. ● *noun* a member of this people. [Late Latin *Salii*]

Salic /'salɪk, 'sei-/ *adjective* = SALIAN. [French *Salique* or medieval Latin *Salicus* from *Salii* (as SALIAN)]

sal·icin /'salɪsɪn/ *noun* a bitter crystalline glucoside with analgesic properties, found in willow bark. [French *salicine* from Latin *salix -icis* willow]

sa·li·cion·al /sə'lɪʃənəl/ *noun* an organ stop with a soft reedy tone like that of a willow pipe. [German from Latin *salix* willow]

Salic law *noun hist.* a law excluding females from dynastic succession esp. in the French monarchy. Used in the 14th c. by the French to deny Edward III's claim to the French throne, it was a direct cause of the Hundred Years War.

sa·li·cyl·ate /sə'lɪsɪˌleit/ *noun* a salt or ester of salicylic acid.

sali·cyl·ic acid /ˌsalɪ'sɪlɪk/ *noun* a bitter chemical used as a fungicide and in the production of acetylsalicylic acid and dyestuffs. [*salicyl* its radical, from French *salicyle* (as SALICIN)]

sali·ent /'seiliənt/ ● *adjective* **1** most important or notable. **2** (of an angle etc.) pointing outwards (opp. RE-ENTRANT *adjective* 1). **3** *Heraldry* (of a lion etc.) standing on its hind legs with the forepaws raised. ● *noun* **1** a salient angle or part of a work in fortification. **2** an outward bulge in a line of military attack or defence. □ **sali·ence** *noun* **sali·ency** *noun* **sali·ent·ly** *adverb* [Latin *salire* 'leap']

Sali·eri /ˌsali'eri/ **An·tonio** (1750–1825), Italian composer. His output includes over 40 operas, four oratorios, and church music; he was hostile to Mozart, but the legend that he poisoned him is apparently without foundation.

sal·ifer·ous /sə'lɪfərəs/ *adjective Geol.* (of rock etc.) containing much salt. [Latin *sal* salt + -FEROUS]

sal·ina /sə'lainə/ *noun* a salt lake. [Spanish from medieval Latin, = salt pit (as SALINE)]

sa·line /'seilɪn/ ● *adjective* **1** (of natural waters, springs, etc.) impregnated with or containing salt or salts. **2** (of food or drink etc.) tasting of salt. **3** of chemical salts. **4** of the nature of a salt. **5** (of medicine) containing a salt or salts of alkaline metals or magnesium, esp. sodium chloride. ● *noun* **1** (in full **saline solution**) a solution of salt in water. **2** a saline substance, esp. a medicine. □ **sal·in·ity** /sə'lɪnɪti/ *noun* (*pl.* **-ities**) **sal·in·iz·ation** /ˌsalɪnɒmɪtər/ *noun* **salin·om·eter** /ˌsalɪ'nɒmɪtər/ *noun* [Middle English from Latin *sal* salt]

Sal·in·ger /'salɪndʒər/ **Jer·ome David** (b.1919), US novelist and short-story writer. He is best known for his colloquial novel of adolescence *The Catcher in the Rye* (1951); other works include *Franny and Zooey* (1961).

Salis·bury[1] /ˈsɔlzbəri/ **1** a city in S England, in Wiltshire; pop. (est. 2002) 40,500. It is noted for its 13th-c. cathedral, whose spire, at 123 m (404 ft.), is the highest in England. **2** the former name (until 1982) for HARARE.

Salis·bury[2] /ˈsɔlzbəri/ **Rob·ert Ar·thur Tal·bot Gascoigne-Cecil, 3rd Marquess of** (1830–1903), English Conservative politician, prime minister 1885–6, 1886–92, and 1895–1902. His main area of concern was foreign affairs; he was a firm defender of British imperial interests and supported the policies which resulted in the Second Boer War (1899–1902).

Salisbury steak *noun N Amer.* a patty of minced beef mixed with milk, bread crumbs, and seasoning, and cooked. [J. H. *Salisbury* (d.1905) US physician specializing in the chemistry of foods]

Sal·ish /ˈsalɪʃ/ *noun* = SNE NAY MUXW. [Sne Nay Muxw *séʔliš* 'Flatheads']

Sal·ish·an /ˈsalɪʃən/ ● *noun* an Aboriginal language group of the west coast of N America, including Comox, Halkomelem, Lillooet, Nuxalk, Okanagan, Sechelt, Shuswap, Squamish, Straits, and Nlaka'pamux. ● *adjective* of or relating to this language group.

sal·iva /səˈlaɪvə/ *noun* liquid secreted into the mouth by glands to provide moisture and facilitate chewing and swallowing; spittle. □ **sali·vary** /ˈsalɪveri/ *adjective* [Middle English from Latin]

sali·vate /ˈsalɪveɪt/ *intransitive verb* secrete or discharge saliva esp. in excess or in greedy anticipation. □ **sali·va·tion** *noun*

saliva test *noun* a scientific test requiring a saliva sample.

Salk /sɔlk/ **Jonas Ed·ward** (1914–95), US microbiologist, who developed the first effective vaccine (the **Salk vaccine**) against poliomyelitis, using killed viruses (1954).

sal·let /ˈsalət/ *noun hist.* a light helmet with an outward-curving rear part, worn as part of medieval armour. [French *salade*, ultimately from Latin *caelare* engrave, from *caelum* chisel]

Sal·lir·miut *noun var. of* SADLERMIUT. [Inuktitut from *Salliq* 'large flat island' (designating Southampton Island) + -MIUT]

sal·low[1] /ˈsaloʊ/ ● *adjective* (**sal·low·er, sal·low·est**) (of the skin or complexion, or of a person) of a sickly yellow or pale brown. ● *transitive & intransitive verb* make or become sallow. □ **sal·low·ness** *noun* [Old English *salo* dusky, from Germanic]

sal·low[2] /ˈsaloʊ/ *noun Brit.* **1** a willow tree, esp. one of a low-growing or shrubby kind. **2** the wood or a shoot of this. [Old English *salh salg-* from Germanic, related to Old High German *salaha*, Old Norse *selja*, Latin *salix*]

Sal·lust /ˈsaləst/ (Latin name Gaius Sallustius Crispus) (*c.*86–*c.*35 BC), Roman historian and politician. He viewed the political decline of Rome after the fall of Carthage in 146 BC as being accompanied by a moral decline.

Sally *noun informal* (usu. prec. by *the*) the Salvation Army. [abbreviation]

sally (*pl.* **-lies**) ● *noun* **1** a sudden charge from a fortification upon its besiegers; a sortie. **2** a going forth; an excursion. **3** a witticism; a piece of banter; a lively remark esp. by way of attack upon a person or thing or of a diversion in argument. **4** a sudden start into activity; an outburst. ● *intransitive verb* (**-lies, -lied**) **1** (usu. foll. by *out, forth*) go for a walk, set out on a journey, etc. **2** (usu. foll. by *out*) make a military sally. **3** *archaic* issue or come out suddenly. [French *saillie* fem. past participle of *saillir* issue, from Old French *salir* from Latin *salire* leap]

Sally Ann *noun Cdn & Brit. informal* (usu. prec. by *the*) the Salvation Army.

Sally Lunn *noun* a sweet light bread. [perhaps from the name of a woman selling them at Bath *c.*1800]

sally port *noun* **1** an opening in a fortification for making a sally from. **2** a prison gate.

sal·ma·gundi /ˌsalməˈɡʌndi/ *noun* (*pl.* **sal·ma·gundis**) **1** a dish of chopped meat, anchovies, eggs, onions, etc., and seasoning. **2** a general mixture; a miscellaneous collection of articles, subjects, qualities, etc. [French *salmigondis* 'game stew', from *sel* 'salt' + *condir* 'seasoning']

sal·ma·nazar /ˌsalməˈneɪzər/ *noun* a wine bottle of about 12 times the standard size. [Shalmaneser king of Assyria (2 Kings 17-18)]

sal·mi /ˈsɔlmi/ *noun* (*pl.* **sal·mis**) a ragout or casserole made esp. of partly roasted game birds stewed in a rich sauce made with wine and the cooking juices. [French, abbreviation formed as SALMAGUNDI]

sal·mon /ˈsamən/ ● *noun* (*pl.* same or (esp. of types) **sal·mons**) **1** a migratory fish of the family Salmonidae, esp. of the genus *Salmo*, much prized for its pink flesh. *See also* ATLANTIC SALMON, PACIFIC SALMON. **2** any of various similar but unrelated fishes, including the Australian salmon, *Arripis trutta*, a large green and silver marine fish. **3** salmon

pink. ● *adjective* salmon-pink. [Old French *saumon* from Latin *salmo -onis*]

Salmon Arm a district municipality in south central BC, situated on Shuswap Lake, 108 km east of Kamloops; pop. (2001) 15,210. [the name of the southwestern arm of Shuswap Lake]

salmon·berry *noun* (*pl.* **-berries**) *N Amer.* **1** any of several pink- or orange-fruited N American brambles, esp. the pink-flowered *Rubus spectabilis* of the west coast. **2** the fruit of such a shrub.

salmon-coloured *adjective* = SALMON PINK *adjective*.

sal·mon·ella /ˌsalməˈnelə/ *noun* (*pl.* **sal·mon·ellae** /-liː/ or **sal·mon·ellas**) **1** a bacterium of the genus *Salmonella* comprising pathogenic rod-shaped forms, some of which cause food poisoning, typhoid, and paratyphoid in people and various diseases in animals. **2** food poisoning caused by infection with salmonellae. [modern Latin from D. E. *Salmon*, US veterinary surgeon d.1914]

sal·mon·el·lo·sis /ˌsalmənəˈloʊsɪs/ *noun* infection with, or a disease caused by, salmonellae. [from SALMONELL(A) + -OSIS]

sal·mon·id /ˈsalmənɪd, salˈmɒnɪd/ ● *adjective* of or relating to the family Salmonidae, which includes salmon and trout. ● *noun* a fish of this family.

salmon ladder *noun* a series of steps or other arrangement incorporated in a dam to allow salmon to pass upstream.

salmon loaf *noun* a dish of mashed cooked salmon mixed with onion, bread crumbs, egg, etc. and baked.

sal·mon·oid /ˈsamənˌɔɪd/ ● *noun* a fish of the family Salmonidae or the superfamily Salmonoidea. ● *adjective* **1** of or belonging to this family or superfamily. **2** of or resembling salmon.

salmon pink ● *noun* the colour of salmon flesh, usu. pink with a tinge of orange. ● *adjective* (usu. **salmon-pink**) of this colour.

salmon roe *noun* the red or orange eggs of pregnant salmon on their way to spawn, eaten as food and considered a delicacy.

salmon run *noun* a migration of salmon up a river from the sea.

salmon trout *noun* a lake trout or Dolly Varden trout.

Sal·ome /səˈloʊmi, ˈsaləmei/ *New Testament* the daughter of Herodias, who danced before her stepfather Herod Antipas; given a choice of reward for her dancing, she asked for the head of St. John the Baptist and thus caused him to be beheaded.

sal·on /səˈlɒn/ *noun* **1** a boutique or parlour specializing in fashionable products such as clothes, or services such as hairdressing. **2** a large room for receiving guests in a mansion or large house. **3 a** an exhibition of painting, sculpture, books, etc. **b** (**Salon**) an annual exhibition in Paris of the work of living artists. **4** (usu. *attributive*) sometimes *derogatory* designating a style or piece of music that is light and soft, such as might be played in a drawing-room or salon. **5** a gathering of intellectuals etc. hosted by a celebrity or socialite. [French: see SALOON]

Sal·on·ika see THESSALONÍKI.

sal·oon *noun* **1** *N Amer.* **a** *hist.* a bar found esp. in mining, logging, and ranching communities of the Old West, often associated with heavy drinking, gambling, prostitution, and fighting. **b** a bar or tavern, esp. one modelled after a saloon of the Old West. **2** esp. *Brit.* a public room or lounge on a ship or train. **3** *Brit.* (in full **saloon car**) a luxury car for four or more people; a sedan. **4** (in full **saloon bar**) *Brit.* a more comfortable bar in a pub; a lounge. [French *salon* from Italian *salone* augmentative of *sala* hall]

saloon keeper *noun N Amer.* **1** an owner or manager of a saloon. **2** a bartender.

salop·ettes /ˌsaləˈpets/ *plural noun* weather-resistant pants with a high waist and shoulder straps, worn esp. for skiing. [French *salopette*, = 'bib overalls' + -*s* by analogy with *trousers* etc.]

Sal·op·ian /səˈloʊpiən/ ● *noun* a native or inhabitant of Shropshire. ● *adjective* of or relating to Shropshire. [Anglo-French *Salopesberia* from Middle English from Old English *Scrobbesbyrig* Shrewsbury]

sal·pi·con /ˈsalpɪkɒn/ *noun* a mixture of finely chopped meat, fish, vegetables, or eggs bound together in a thick sauce and used for fillings and stuffings. [French, from Spanish *salpicar* sprinkle (with salt)]

sal·pi·glos·sis /ˌsalpɪˈɡlɒsɪs/ *noun* any solanaceous plant of the genus *Salpiglossis*, cultivated for its funnel-shaped flowers. [modern Latin, irreg. from Greek *salpigx* trumpet + *glōssa* tongue]

salping- /ˈsalpɪŋ/ *combining form Med.* denoting the Fallopian tubes. [Greek *salpigx salpiggos*, lit. 'trumpet']

sal·pin·gec·tomy /ˌsalpɪŋˈdʒektəmi/ *noun* (*pl.* **-mies**) *Med.* the surgical removal of the Fallopian tube or tubes, esp. to remove a cyst or tumour or to sterilize.

sal·pin·gitis /ˌsalpən'dʒəitɪs/ *noun Med.* inflammation of the Fallopian tube or tubes caused by bacterial infection.

sal·sa /'sɒlsə, sal-/ *noun* **1** a Latin American spicy sauce made with tomatoes or fruit and chilies etc. and used usu. as a dip or garnish. **2 a** a kind of dance music of Latin American origin, incorporating jazz and rock elements. **b** a dance performed to this music. [Spanish (as SAUCE)]

salsa verde *noun* **1** an Italian sauce made with olive oil, garlic, capers, anchovies, vinegar or lemon juice, and a large quantity of chopped parsley, usu. served with fish. **2** a Mexican sauce of finely chopped onion, garlic, coriander, parsley, and hot peppers. [Italian or Spanish = 'green sauce']

sal·sify /'salsə,fi/ *noun* (pl. **-fies**) **1** a plant of the genus *Tragopogon*, esp. *T. porrifolius*, with long, thin, white-fleshed cylindrical roots. **2** the edible root of this plant. *Also called* OYSTER PLANT. [French *salsifis* from obsolete Italian *salsefica*, of unknown origin]

SALT /sɒlt/ *abbreviation* Strategic Arms Limitation Talks (or Treaty).

salt ● *noun* **1** (also **common salt**) **a** a substance, sodium chloride, found esp. in water or as a reddish brown mineral. **b** this substance, esp. in a white, granular form, obtained by evaporation of sea water or mining, used esp. for seasoning and preserving food. **c** a coarse form of this used to melt ice on driveways, sidewalks, roads, etc. (*compare* ROAD SALT). **2** a chemical compound formed from the reaction of an acid with a base, with all or part of the hydrogen of the acid replaced by a metal or metal-like radical. **3** (often in *pl.*) a substance resembling common salt in appearance, form, taste, etc., used esp. as a medicine or cosmetic (*smelling salts*; *bath salts*). **4** salt mixed with a usu. specified flavouring used as a seasoning (*garlic salt*; *celery salt*). **5** (also **old salt**) an experienced sailor. **6** liveliness, wit; pungency, sting (*added salt to the conversation*). **7** (*attributive*) *Cdn* (*Nfld*) pertaining to the use of salt as a preservative for fish, esp. cod (*salt room*). ● *adjective* **1** containing or tasting of salt; salty (*she could taste the salt air*). **2** (of beef, fish, etc.) treated, cured, or preserved with salt (*salt cod*; *salt herring*). **3** (of a plant) growing in the sea or in salt marshes. ● *transitive verb* **1** cure or preserve (meat or fish etc.) with salt or brine. **2** season with salt. **3** sprinkle (the ground etc.) with salt esp. in order to melt snow or ice. **4** add wit, piquancy, or controversy to (a conversation, story, etc.). **5 a** make (a geological sample, a mine, site, etc.) appear to be more valuable a source than it is by depositing extraneous ore etc. in it. **b** fraudulently increase the figures represented in (the books, accounts, etc.). □ **below the salt** among the less honoured guests; of a lower social standing. **in salt** sprinkled with salt or immersed in brine as a preservative. **salt away** *informal* save or stash (money, information, etc.) for the future. **the salt of the earth 1** a person or people of great worthiness, reliability, honesty, etc. **2** those people whose qualities are a model for the rest (Matt. 5:13). **take with a grain** (or **pinch**) **of salt** be justifiably skeptical of; believe only in part. **worth one's salt** deserving what one earns; capable. □ **salt·ness** *noun* [Old English *s(e)alt s(e)altan*, Old Saxon, Old Norse, Gothic *salt*, Old High German *salz* from Germanic]

salt and pepper *adjective* **1** (of hair) of a dark colour streaked with a lighter one, esp. grey (*salt and pepper beard*). **2** (of materials) consisting of light and dark colours stitched together (*salt and pepper scarf*). **3** designating a mixture of two ethnic races, cultures, etc. (*salt and pepper couple*).

salt·box *N Amer.* (*Maritimes, Nfld, & New England*) ● *adjective* designating a house etc. with two storeys at the front and one at the back, having a steep pitched roof sloping towards the back. ● *noun* a saltbox house. [from its resemblance to a box with a sloping lid used for storing salt]

salt·bush *noun* = ORACHE.

salt cedar *noun N Amer.* an introduced European tamarisk, *Tamarix gallica*.

salt·cellar *noun* **1** a small container for holding salt. **2** *informal* an unusually deep hollow above the collarbone, esp. found in women. [SALT + obsolete *saler* from Anglo-French from Old French *salier* salt box, from Latin (as SALARY), assimilated to CELLAR]

salt·chuck *noun N Amer.* (*BC, Alaska, & US Northwest*) *informal* the ocean, or an inlet, canal, or bay, etc. of salt water. [Chinook Jargon, from English SALT *noun* + Nuu-chah-nulth *ch'a'ak* water]

salt dome *noun* **1** a mass of salt forced up into the overlying strata of sedimentary rock, sometimes forming a trap for gas and oil etc. **2** a large building in the shape of a pointed dome used for storing road salt.

Sal·teaux *var. of* SAULTEAUX.

salt·ed *adjective* seasoned, treated, or preserved with salt.

salt·er *noun* **1** esp. *Cdn* a truck which dispenses salt on roads to melt snow and ice. **2** *Cdn* (*Nfld*) a member of a pickling crew who washes fish etc. and treats it with salt. [Old English *sealtere* (as SALT)]

salt·ery *noun* (pl. **-ies**) *N Amer.* a factory where fish is prepared for storage by salting.

salt fish *noun N Amer. & Caribbean* preserved cod that has been split, salted, and dried.

salt-glaze *noun* a hard stoneware glaze produced by throwing salt into a hot kiln in which articles of pottery are being fired. □ **salt-glazed** *adjective*

salt hay *noun N Amer.* hay made from grasses that have grown in salt meadows.

salt·ie *noun N Amer. informal* an ocean-going ship.

sal·ti·grade /'salti,greid/ *Fauna* ● *adjective* (of arthropods) moving by leaping or jumping. ● *noun* a saltigrade arthropod, e.g. a spider, sand hopper, etc. [modern Latin *Saltigradae* from Latin *saltus* leap, from *salire* salt- + -*gradus* walking]

Sal·tillo /sal'tiːjo/ a city in N Mexico, capital of the state of Coahuila, situated in the Sierra Madre southwest of Monterrey; pop. (est. 2002) 657,800.

sal·tim·boc·ca /ˌsaltɪm'bɒkə/ *noun* an Italian dish consisting of thin pieces of veal, each individually wrapped around a slice of prosciutto and a sage leaf and braised in wine. [Italian, from *saltare* to leap + *in* into + *bocca* mouth]

salt·ine /sɒl'tiːn/ *noun esp. N Amer.* a salted cracker. [from SALT *noun* + -INE⁴]

salt·ing *noun* **1 a** the action of applying salt as a seasoning. **b** the process of covering meat, fish, etc. in salt or soaking it in brine in order to preserve it. **2** (esp. in *pl.*) a salt marsh.

sal·tire /'sɒl,tair/ *noun Heraldry* an ordinary formed by a bend and a bend sinister crossing like a St. Andrew's cross. [Old French *sau(l)toir* etc. stirrup cord, stile, saltire, from medieval Latin *saltatorium* from *saltare* frequentative of *salire* salt- leap]

salt lake *noun* a lake of salt water.

Salt Lake City the capital of Utah, situated near the southeastern shores of the Great Salt Lake; pop. (2000) 181,743. Founded in 1847 by Brigham Young for the Mormon community, the city is the world headquarters of the Church of Latter-day Saints (Mormons).

salt lick *noun* **1** a place where animals go to lick naturally occurring salt from the ground. **2** a block of salt or a preparation of salt given to domestic horses and cattle etc. to lick.

salt marsh *noun* (also **saltwater marsh**) a marsh that has been flooded by the tide, sometimes used as a pasture or for collecting water for making salt.

salt meadow *noun N Amer.* a meadow subject to flooding with salt water.

salt mine *noun* **1** a mine yielding rock salt. **2** *jocular* a place of gruelling labour, esp. one's workplace.

salt pan *noun* a shallow depression in the ground in which salt water evaporates to leave a deposit of salt.

salt·petre /ˌsɒlt'piːtər/ *noun* (US **salt·peter**) potassium nitrate, a white crystalline salty substance used esp. in the manufacture of gunpowder and wrongly believed to curb sexual desire. [Old French *salpetre* from medieval Latin *salpetra* prob. for *sal petrae* (unrecorded) salt of rock (i.e. found as an encrustation): assimilated to SALT]

salt pond *noun* (also **saltwater pond**) *N Amer.* an inlet or small pool of sea water barely joined to the ocean.

salt pork *noun N Amer.* cured pork fat, highly salted.

salt shaker *noun N Amer.* a container for salt with tiny holes on the top allowing salt to be sprinkled lightly over food.

Salt·spring Island the largest of the Gulf Islands in the Strait of Georgia, BC, situated north of the Saanich Peninsula. [so called with reference to its interior salt pools]

salt water ● *noun* **1** water having a high concentration of salt, esp. sea water; brine. **2** the ocean or sea or any body of water from the ocean or sea. ● *adjective* (usu. **salt·water**) **1** of, pertaining to, or consisting of salt water. **2** living in or by a body of salt water (*saltwater fish*).

saltwater marsh *noun N Amer.* = SALT MARSH.

saltwater pond *noun N Amer.* = SALT POND.

saltwater taffy *noun N Amer.* a candy made by boiling sugar or molasses and butter in sea water or salted fresh water.

uː mood ai my əi pipe au brown ʌu house ei day ɔi boy ã franglais â Canadien ɔ̃ Brayon (*see over for consonants*)

salt well *noun* a spring of salt water, esp. a bored well from which brine is obtained for making salt.

salt·wort /ˈsɒltwɜrt, -wɔrt/ *noun* any of various plants which tolerate saline conditions, esp. of the genus *Salsola*.

salty *adjective* (**salt·i·er**, **salt·i·est**) **1** tasting of, containing, or preserved with salt. **2 a** (of humour etc.) racy, risqué. **b** (of language) coarse, vulgar. **3** relating to or characteristic of a sailor or life at sea. □ **salt·i·ness** *noun*

sa·lu·bri·ous /səˈluːbrɪəs/ *adjective* **1** conducive or favourable to good health; healthy. **2** pleasant; agreeable. □ **sa·lu·bri·ous·ly** *adverb* **sa·lu·bri·ous·ness** *noun* **sa·lu·brity** *noun* [Latin *salubris* from *salus* health]

Sa·luki /səˈluːki/ *noun* (*pl.* **Sa·luk·is**) a breed of tall swift slender dog having a fringed tail and feet, large ears, and a silky coat. [Arabic *salūkī*, from *Salūk* a town in Arabia]

salu·tary /ˈsaljʊˌteri/ *adjective* producing good effects; beneficial. [French *salutaire* or Latin *salutaris* from *salus -utis* health]

salu·ta·tion /ˌsaljuˈteɪʃən/ *noun* **1** a sign or expression of greeting or recognition of another's arrival or departure. **2** the initial words of a letter used to address the person being written to. **3** the act or an instance of saluting; a gesture of respect (*she raised her hands in salutation*).

sa·lu·ta·tory /səˈluːtəˌtɔri/ *adjective* of salutation.

sa·lute ● *noun* **1** a gesture of respect, courteous recognition, or solidarity, esp. made to or by a person when arriving or departing. **2** *Military & Naut.* a prescribed or specified movement of the hand, weapons, or flags as a sign of respect or recognition. **3** the discharge of a gun or guns as a formal or ceremonial sign of respect or celebration. **4** a tribute or testimonial (to). **5** *ironic* a usu. obscene hand gesture issued in anger as a threat or curse. ● *verb* **1 a** *transitive* make a salute to. **b** *intransitive* (often foll. by *to*) perform a salute. **2** *transitive* (foll. by *with*) receive or greet with (a smile, handshake, etc.). □ **in salute** as a form of salute (*we raised our glass in salute*). **take the salute** receive and return ceremonial salutes by members of a procession. [Latin *salutare* from *salus -utis* health]

Sa·lu·tin /səˈluːtɪn/ **Rick** (b.1942), Canadian playwright, social activist, and journalist. After writing his first play, *Fanshen*, he began to collaborate with Toronto's Theatre Passe Muraille, esp. on collective creations; he also wrote *Les Canadiens* (1977), dealing with hockey and nationalism in Quebec, and has been the scriptwriter for a number of TV docudramas.

Sal·va·dor /ˈsalvəˌdɔr/ a port on the Atlantic coast of E Brazil; pop. (2000) 2,439,881. It was formerly known as Bahia.

Sal·va·dor·an /salvəˈdɔrən/ (also **Sal·va·dor·ean** /salvəˈdɔriən/) ● *adjective* of or relating to El Salvador. ● *noun* a native or national of El Salvador.

sal·vage /ˈsalvɪdʒ/ ● *transitive verb* **1** save or recover (materials) from a shipwreck, fire, etc. **2** recover, save, or preserve (something) from the brink of loss or ruin (*tried to salvage some dignity; they tried to salvage their marriage*). ● *noun* **1** the rescue of a ship, its cargo, or other property from loss at sea, destruction by fire, etc. **2** the retrieval or saving of waste materials for recycling. **3** property or materials that have been salvaged. □ **sal·vage·able** *adjective* **sal·va·ger** *noun* [French from medieval Latin *salvagium* from *salvare* SAVE¹]

sal·va·tion *noun* **1** the act of saving or being saved. **2** preservation from destruction, ruin, loss, or harm. **3** the saving of the soul through deliverance from sin and its consequences. **4** a person or thing that saves (*her policies were the salvation of the country's economy*). [Old French *sauvacion, salvacion*, from ecclesiastical Latin *salvatio -onis* from *salvare* SAVE¹, translation of Greek *sōtēria*]

Salvation Army *noun* an international evangelical organization with a military structure founded by William Booth in 1865 for the revival of Christianity and assistance to the poor and homeless.

sal·va·tion·ism *noun* **1** (**Salvationism**) the principles or methods of the Salvation Army. **2** a religious teaching which lays particular stress on individual salvation. □ **sal·va·tion·ist** *noun & adjective* (also **Sal·va·tion·ist**).

salve¹ /salv, sav/ ● *noun* **1** a healing ointment. **2** a thing that soothes, consoles, or assuages (guilt, hurt feelings, an uneasy conscience, etc.) (*her flattery was the perfect salve for his wounded ego*). ● *transitive verb* **1** soothe or calm (pride, self-love, conscience, etc.). **2** *archaic* apply ointment to (a wound etc.). [Old English *s(e)alf(e), s(e)alfian* from Germanic; v. senses partly from Latin *salvare* SAVE¹]

salve² /salv/ *transitive verb* save (a ship or its cargo) from loss at sea; salvage. □ **salv·able** *adjective* [back-formation from SALVAGE]

sal·ver /ˈsalvər/ *noun* a tray usu. of silver or other metal, on which drinks, letters, etc. are presented. [French *salve* tray for presenting food to the king, from Spanish *salva* testing of food, from *salvar* SAVE¹: assoc. with *platter*]

Salve Regina /ˌsalvei reˈdʒiːnə/ *noun* **1** a Roman Catholic prayer that begins with the words 'Hail Holy Queen'. **2** a musical setting of this. [Latin]

sal·via /ˈsalviə/ *noun* any plant of the genus *Salvia* of the mint family, esp. *S. splendens* with red or blue flowers. [Latin, = SAGE¹]

salv·ific /salˈvɪfɪk/ *adjective* causing or able to cause salvation. [Latin *salvificus* saving]

salvo /ˈsalvoː/ *noun* (*pl.* **-voes** or **-vos**) **1** the simultaneous or concentrated discharge of artillery or other weapons in battle or as a salute. **2** a sudden vigorous or aggressive act or series of acts (*she fired the first salvo of the election campaign; he wasn't prepared for the verbal salvo his comment would provoke*). [earlier *salve* from French from Italian *salva* salutation (as SAVE¹)]

sal volatile /ˌsal vɒˈlatɪli/ *noun* ammonium carbonate, esp. in the form of an aromatic solution in alcohol to be used as smelling salts. [modern Latin, = volatile salt]

sal·vor /ˈsalvər/ *noun* a person engaged in, assisting in, or attempting salvage. [SALVE²]

sal·war /sʌlˈwɑr/ *noun var.* of SHALWAR.

Sal·ween River /ˈsalwiːn/ a river of SE Asia, which rises in Tibet and flows for 2 400 km (1,500 miles) southeast and south through Burma to the Gulf of Martaban, an inlet of the Andaman Sea.

Salz·burg /ˈsɒltsbɜrg/ a city in W Austria, near the border with Germany, the capital of a state of the same name; pop. (2001) 144,800. It is noted for its annual music festivals, one of which is dedicated to Mozart, who was born in the city in 1756.

Salz·kam·mer·gut /ˈzɒltskamərˌɡʊt/ a resort area of lakes and mountains in the state of Salzburg in W Austria.

SAM *abbreviation* surface-to-air missile.

Sam. *abbreviation Bible* Samuel.

sam·adhi /səˈmadi/ *noun Buddhism & Hinduism* **1** a state of concentration induced by meditation. **2** a state into which a perfected holy man is said to pass at his apparent death. [Sanskrit *samādhi* contemplation]

Samar /ˈsɒmər/ an island in the Philippines, situated to the southeast of Luzon. It is the third largest island of the group.

Sam·ara /səˈmarə/ a city and river port in SW central Russia, situated on the Volga at its confluence with the Samara River; pop. (est. 2002) 1,150,000. It was known as Kuibyshev from 1935 to 1991.

sam·ara /ˈsamərə, səˈmɑrə/ *noun Bot.* a dry fruit in which the pericarp is extended to form a wing, as in the elm, ash, maple, sycamore, etc. [modern Latin from Latin, = elm seed]

Sam·aria /səˈmeriə/ **1** an ancient city of central Palestine, founded in the 9th c. BC as the capital of the northern Hebrew kingdom of Israel. The ancient site is situated in the modern West Bank, northwest of Nablus. **2** the region of ancient Palestine around this city, bounded by Galilee in the north and Judea in the south.

Sam·arin·da /ˌsaməˈrɪndə/ a city of Indonesia, in E Borneo; pop. (est. 2002) 585,900.

Sam·ar·itan /səˈmerɪtən/ ● *noun* **1** (in full **good Samaritan**) a charitable or helpful person (with reference to Luke 10:33 etc.). **2** a member of an organization which counsels people in distress by telephone or face to face. **3** a native of Samaria in W Jordan. **4** the language of this people. ● *adjective* of Samaria or the Samaritans. □ **Sam·ar·itan·ism** *noun* [Late Latin *Samaritanus* from Greek *Samareitēs* from *Samareia* Samaria]

sam·ar·ium /səˈmeriəm/ *noun Chem.* a soft silvery metallic element of the lanthanide series, occurring naturally in monazite etc. and used in making ferromagnetic alloys. Symbol: **Sm**; at. no.: 62. [*samarskite* the mineral in which its spectrum was first observed, from *Samarski* name of a 19th-c. Russian official]

Sam·ar·kand /ˌsamərˈkand, ˈsamərˌkand/ (also **Sam·ar·qand**) a city in E Uzbekistan; pop. (est. 2002) 373,400. One of the oldest cities of Asia, it was founded in the 3rd or 4th millennium BC and was a prosperous centre of the silk trade in the Middle Ages.

Sam·arra /səˈmarə/ a city in Iraq, on the Tigris River north of Baghdad; pop. (est. 2002) 201,700. Its 17th-c. mosque is a place of Shiite pilgrimage.

Sama-Veda /ˌsaməˈveidə, -ˌviːdə/ *noun* an ancient collection of sacred Hindu hymns and incantations, traditionally called the third Veda but originating outside Vedic society. [Sanskrit *sāman* chant + *vēda* knowledge]

Consonants: b *but*   d *dog*   f *few*   g *get*   h *her*   j *yes*   k *cat*   l *leg*   m *man*   n *no*   p *pen*   r *red*   s *sit*

samba ● *noun* **1** (in full **rural samba**) a rhythmically complex Brazilian dance of African origin. **2** (in full **urban samba**) a related ballroom dance of moderate tempo developed in the dance halls of Rio de Janeiro. **3** the music for this. ● *intransitive verb* (**sam·bas**, **sam·baed** or **samba'd**, **samba·ing**) dance the samba. [Portuguese, of African origin]

sam·bal /ˈsambəl/ *noun* (in Malayan and Indonesian cooking) a hot mixture of chilies, onions, and spices, used as a relish with other foods. [Malay]

Sam Browne *noun* (in full **Sam Browne belt**) a wide belt with a supporting strap passing from the left hip over the right shoulder, esp. worn by army and police officers. [Sir *Samuel J. Browne*, Brit. military commander d.1901]

sam·buca /samˈbuːkə/ *noun* an Italian aniseed-flavoured liqueur traditionally served aflame with a coffee bean floating on top. [Latin *sambucus* elder tree]

same ● *adjective* **1** (often prec. by *the*) **a** identical in form, appearance, or number (*how embarrassing, we're wearing the same dress*; *they are the same age*). **b** not different (*we go to the same doctor*). **2** unchanged, unvarying, uniform (*they've been giving the same service for over fifty years*). **3** (usu. prec. by *this*, *these*, *that*, *those*) (of a person or thing) previously alluded to; just mentioned (*this same medical student went on to become a doctor*). **4** (in combination) identical, not different (*same-age partners*). ● *pronoun* (prec. by *the*) **1** the same person or thing (*I ordered ice cream and she asked for the same*). **2** *Law* or *archaic* the person or thing just mentioned (*detected the youth trespassing and apprehended the same*). ● *adverb* (usu. prec. by *the*) similarly; in the same way (*I really like you and I hope you feel the same*; *you look the same as you did twenty years ago*). □ **all** (or **just**) **the same** nevertheless; anyway (*I don't need a ride, but thanks for offering all the same*). **at the same time 1** simultaneously. **2** notwithstanding; in spite of circumstances etc. **be all** (or **just**) **the same to** be a matter of indifference, or of little importance or interest (*if it's all the same to you, I'd rather go out tomorrow night*). **by the same token** see TOKEN. **same difference** *informal* no difference, the same thing. **same here** *informal* the same applies to me. **same old same old** *informal* something predictably unchanging. **the same to you!** may you do, have, find, etc., the same thing; likewise. **the very same** emphatically the same. □ **same·ness** *noun* [Old Norse *sami*, *sama*, with Germanic cognates]

same-day *adjective* **1** designating a service that is provided on the same day that it is purchased or requested (*the store offers same-day delivery*). **2** occurring on the same day as another related event (*on Tuesday the Minister resigned and held a same-day news conference*).

same-sex *adjective* designating or pertaining to a sexual relationship in which both partners are of the same sex (*same-sex couple*).

samey *adjective* *informal* lacking in variety; monotonous.

sam·fu /ˈsamfuː/ *noun* a casual outfit consisting of a jacket and pants, worn by Chinese women and sometimes men. [Cantonese]

Samhain /saun, ˈsauɪn/ *noun* (in Britain) a Celtic festival marking the beginning of winter, celebrated on 1 Nov. [Irish *Samhain*]

Sam Hill *noun* *N Amer. slang* euphemism (usu. prec. by *in* or *the*) (usu. in exclamatory phrases) = HELL *interjection* (*what in the Sam Hill are we going to do now?*). [19th c.: origin unknown]

Sami /ˈsɒmi/ ● *noun* the Lapps collectively. ● *adjective* of or relating to the Lapps. ¶ The preferred native and scholarly term. [Lappish (earlier *Sabme*, *Samek*), ultimate origin unknown]

Sami·an /ˈseimiən/ ● *noun* a native or inhabitant of Samos. ● *adjective* **1** of Samos. **2** designating a type of fine red pottery from various parts of the Roman Empire, esp. Gaulish pottery often found on Roman sites in Britain (*Samian ware*). [Latin *Samius* from Greek *Samios* Samos]

Sam·iel /ˈsamiəl/ *noun* = SIMOOM. [Turkish *samyeli* hot wind, from Arabic *samm* poison + Turkish *yel* wind]

sami·sen /ˈsamisən/ *var.* OF SHAMISEN.

sam·ite /ˈsamʌit, ˈsei-/ *noun* *hist.* a rich medieval dress fabric of silk occasionally interwoven with gold. [Old French *samit* from medieval Latin *examitum* from medieval Greek *hexamiton* from Greek *hexa-* six + *mitos* thread]

sam·iz·dat /ˈsamizˌdat, -ˈdat/ *noun* *hist.* **1** a system of clandestine publication of banned literature in the USSR. **2** literature so produced. [Russian, = self-publishing house]

Sam·nite /ˈsamnʌit/ ● *noun* **1** a member of a people of ancient Italy often at war with republican Rome. **2** the language of this people. ● *adjective* of this people or their language. [Latin *Samnites* (pl.), related to *Sabinus* SABINE]

Samoa /səˈmoʊə/ a group of islands in Polynesia. The group was divided administratively in 1899 into American Samoa in the east and German Samoa in the west. The latter, mandated to New Zealand in 1919, gained independence in 1962 as Western Samoa. In 1997 this country became known as Samoa; pop. (est. 2002) 178,631; capital, Apia. See also AMERICAN SAMOA. □ **Samo·an** *noun & adjective*

Samos /ˈseimɒs/ a Greek island in the Aegean, situated close to the coast of W Turkey.

sam·osa /səˈmoʊsə/ *noun* an Indian snack consisting of a triangular pastry stuffed with a spicy mixture of diced vegetables or meat, fried in ghee or oil. [Persian and Urdu]

samo·var /ˈsaməˌvɑr/ *noun* a metal, usu. ornate, Russian urn for making tea, with an internal heating tube to keep water at boiling point. [Russian, from *samo-* self + *varit* boil]

Samo·yed /ˈsaməˌjed/ *noun* **1** a breed of white dog, once used for working in the Arctic, having a thick shaggy coat, stocky build, pricked ears, and a tail curling over the back. **2** a member of any of several peoples inhabiting N Siberia. **3** any of the Uralic group of languages of these people. □ **Samo·yed·ic** *adjective* [Russian *samoed*]

samp *noun* *esp. US* **1** coarsely ground corn. **2** porridge made of this. [Algonquian (Massachusetts) *nasamp* softened by water]

sam·pan /ˈsamˌpan/ *noun* a small boat or skiff with a flat bottom usu. propelled by a scull or oars set in the stern, used along the coasts and rivers of the Far East. [Chinese *san-ban* from *san* three + *ban* board]

sam·phire *noun* **1** an umbelliferous maritime rock plant, *Crithmum maritimum*, with aromatic fleshy leaves used as a salad vegetable. **2** (in full **marsh samphire**) the succulent glasswort of seacoasts, *Salicornia europaea*. [earlier *samp(i)ere* from French (*herbe de*) *Saint Pierre* St. Peter('s herb)]

sam·pla·del·ic *adjective* denoting a type of dance music that is psychedelic or disorienting in nature and created using samples or other digital technology.

sam·ple ● *noun* **1** a small part or quantity intended to show what the whole is like. **2** a small amount of a product given usu. free of charge to prospective customers. **3** a specimen, esp. one taken for scientific testing or analysis (*a blood sample*). **4** *Statistics* a portion selected from a population, the study of which is intended to provide statistical estimates relating to the whole. **5** a unit of sound or piece of music that has been digitalized. **6** an illustrative or typical example (*please provide a writing sample*). **7** a prototype created by a garment manufacturer so that buyers know what a garment looks like before ordering a whole line. ● *transitive verb* **1** try or examine (something) by experiencing it or taking a sample (*sample our down-home cooking*). **2 a** ascertain the momentary value of (an analog signal) many times a second so that these values may be represented digitally; convert (an analog signal) to a digital one. **b** record or extract a small piece of music or sound digitally for reuse as part of a composition or song. [Anglo-French *assample*, Old French *essample* EXAMPLE]

sam·pler¹ *noun* a piece of embroidery sewn in various stitches as a demonstration of skill, usu. containing the alphabet or mottos and often displayed on a wall. [Old French *essamplaire* (as EXEMPLAR)]

sam·pler² *noun* **1** an electronic device used to digitalize analog sound or music. **2** *esp. N Amer.* a collection of representative items etc. **3** a device for obtaining samples for scientific study.

sam·pling *noun* **1** the action or process of testing the quality of something from a sample or samples. **2** (often foll. by *of*) *esp. N Amer.* a representative selection of items (*a sampling of Italian dishes*). **3** *Music* the technique or process of digitally encoding analog sound and reusing it as part of a composition or recording.

Sam·pras /ˈsamprəs/ **Pete** (b.1971), US tennis player. He won a record number of major championship titles, including seven victories at Wimbledon and five at the US Open.

sam·sara /samˈsɑrə/ *noun* *Ind. Philos.* the endless cycle of death and rebirth to which life in the material world is bound. [Sanskrit *saṃsāra* a wandering through]

sam·skara /samˈskɑrə/ *noun* *Ind. Philos.* **1** a purificatory ceremony or rite marking an event in one's life. **2** a mental impression, instinct, or memory. [Sanskrit *saṃskāra* a making perfect, preparation]

Sam·son *Bible* an Israelite leader (prob. 11th c. BC) famous for his strength (Judges 13–16). He confided to his lover Delilah that his strength lay in his hair, and she betrayed him to the Philistines, who cut off his hair while he slept and captured and blinded him; when his hair grew again his strength returned and he pulled down the pillars of a house, destroying himself and a large gathering of Philistines.

Sam·sun /samˈsuːn/ a city on the north coast of Turkey; pop. (est. 1997) 338,387.

Sam·uel ▶ 1 a Hebrew prophet who rallied the Israelites after their defeat by the Philistines and became their ruler. **2** *Bible* either of two books of the Bible covering the history of ancient Israel from Samuel's birth to the end of the reign of David.

samu·rai /ˈsaməˌraɪ/ *noun* (*pl.* same) **1** *hist.* in feudal Japan, a member of a military caste, esp. a member of the class of military retainers of the daimyos. **2** a Japanese army officer. [Japanese]

SAN *abbreviation* storage area network.

San /sɒn/ ● *noun* (*pl.* same) **1** a member of the aboriginal Bushmen of southern Africa. **2** the group of Khoisan languages spoken by the San; any of these languages. ● *adjective* of or relating to the San or their languages. [Nama]

san *noun* = SANATORIUM. [abbreviation]

San'a /saˈnɑː, ˈsɒnə/ (also **Sanaa**) the capital of Yemen; pop. (est. 2002) 1,653,300. It is noted for its medina, one of the largest completely preserved walled city centres in the Arab world.

San An·dreas fault /ˌsan anˈdreɪəs/ *noun* a fault line or fracture of the earth's crust extending for some 965 km (600 miles) through the length of California. Seismic activity is common along its course and caused the earthquake of 1906, and a further convulsion in 1989, which devastated the area including the city of San Francisco, located close to the fault.

San An·tonio /ˌsan anˈtoːniˌoʊ/ an industrial city in S central Texas; pop. (2000) 1,144,646. It is the site of the Alamo mission (see ALAMO). □ **San An·ton·ian** *noun & adjective*

sana·tor·ium /ˌsanəˈtɔːriəm/ *noun* (*pl.* **sana·tor·iums** or **sana·tor·ia** /-riə/) an establishment for the medical treatment and recuperation of convalescents and those suffering chronic mental or physical disorders, tuberculosis, etc. [modern Latin from Latin *sanare* cure]

San Car·los de Bari·loche /san ˌkarlos deɪ ˌbarɪˈloːtʃi/ a ski resort in the Andes of Argentina, on the shores of Lake Nahuel Huapi; pop. (est. 1999) 105,093.

San·cerre /sɑ̃ˈser/ *noun* a light white (occasionally red) wine, produced in the area around Sancerre, in central France.

sanc·ti·fy *transitive verb* (**-fies, -fied**) **1** consecrate; make holy. **2** purify or free from sin. **3** make legitimate or binding by religious sanction. **4** make productive of or conducive to holiness. □ **sanc·ti·fi·ca·tion** *noun* [Old French *saintifier* from ecclesiastical Latin *sanctificare* from Latin *sanctus* holy]

sanc·ti·moni·ous /ˌsaŋktɪˈmoːniəs/ *adjective* **1** affecting or pretending piety, sanctity, or holiness. **2** *archaic* holy in character, sacred. □ **sanc·ti·moni·ous·ly** *adverb* **sanc·ti·moni·ous·ness** *noun* **sanc·ti·mony** /ˈsaŋktɪˌmoːni/ *noun* [Latin *sanctimonia* sanctity (as SAINT)]

sanc·tion ● *noun* **1** approval, permission, or encouragement granted for a particular action (*the book was translated without the sanction of the author*). **2** the action of making something legally binding; official ratification (of a law etc.). **3** (esp. in *pl.*) military or esp. economic action by a country to coerce another to conform to an international agreement or norms of conduct. **4** a penalty or reward enacted to enforce obedience to a law or rule. **5** an ethical consideration operating to enforce obedience to any standard or rule of moral conduct. ● *transitive verb* **1** authorize, ratify, or agree to (an action etc.). **2** enforce (conduct, a legal obligation, etc.) esp. by attaching a penalty to the transgression. [French from Latin *sanctio -onis* from *sancire sanct-* make sacred]

sanc·tity *noun* (*pl.* **-ties**) **1** holiness of life; saintliness. **2** sacredness; the state of being hallowed. **3** inviolability. [Old French *sain(c)tité* or Latin *sanctitas* (as SAINT)]

sanc·tu·ary *noun* (*pl.* **-ies**) **1** a holy place such as a church or temple etc. **2 a** esp. *Jewish Hist.* the inmost recess or holiest part of a temple etc.; the holy of holies. **b** the part of a church containing the altar. **3** a place where birds, wild animals, etc., are bred and protected. **4** a place of refuge, esp. a church or sacred building. **5** immunity from arrest; asylum. □ **take sanctuary** resort to a place of refuge. [Anglo-French *sanctuarie* from Latin *sanctuarium* (as SAINT)]

sanc·tum /ˈsaŋktəm/ *noun* (*pl.* **sanc·tums, sanc·ta**) **1** a holy place. **2** *informal* a person's private room, study, or den. [Latin, neuter of *sanctus* holy, past participle of *sancire* consecrate: *sanctorum* genitive pl. in translation of Hebrew *ḳōḏeš haḳḳoḏāšîm* holy of holies]

sanc·tum sanc·tor·um /saŋkˈtɔːrəm/ **1** the holy of holies in the Jewish temple. **2** a private room or inner retreat.

Sanc·tus /ˈsaŋktəs ˈsɒŋktəs/ *noun* **1** the prayer beginning 'Holy, holy, holy' said or sung at the end of the Eucharistic preface in some Christian liturgies. **2** a musical setting of this. [Latin, = holy]

Sand /sɑ̃/ **George** (pseudonym of Amandine-Aurore Lucille Dupin, Baronne Dudevant) (1804–76), French novelist. Her early romantic novels, including *Lélia* (1833), portray women's struggles against conventional morals; other works include *Elle et lui* (1859), a fictionalized account of her affair with the poet Alfred de Musset, and *Un Hiver à Majorque* (1841), describing an episode during her ten-year relationship with Chopin.

sand ● *noun* **1** a loose granular substance resulting from the weathering of esp. siliceous rocks and found on the seashore, riverbeds, deserts, etc. **2** (in *pl.*) an expanse or region composed mainly of sand. **3** a light yellow-brown colour like that of sand. **4** *N Amer. informal* courage, determination, grit. ● *transitive verb* **1** smooth or grind (a surface) by rubbing it with sandpaper. **2** sprinkle or cover with, or bury under, sand. **3** adulterate (sugar etc.) with sand. □ **sand down** sand (a usu. painted surface) down to the bare wood etc. **sands of time** the moments or passage of time. **the sands are running out** the allotted time is nearly at an end. [Old English *sand* from Germanic]

san·dal *noun* **1** a light open shoe consisting of a sole attaching to the foot with light straps, worn esp. in warm weather. **2** a strap for fastening a low shoe, passing over the instep or around the ankle. [Latin *sandalium* from Greek *sandalion* diminutive of *sandalon* wooden shoe, prob. of Asiatic origin]

san·dal·foot *noun* *N Amer.* (usu. *attributive*) designating pantyhose etc. that do not have visibly reinforced toes or heels and which are suitable for wearing with sandals and open-toed shoes.

san·dalled *adjective* (also esp. *US* **san·daled**) wearing sandals.

sandal·wood *noun* the scented wood of any of several trees of the genus *Santalum*, esp. the white sandalwood, *Santalum album*, of India, used esp. in carving and incense.

Sandalwood Island an alternative name for SUMBA.

sandalwood oil *noun* a yellow aromatic oil distilled from sandalwood, used in perfumes and cosmetics and formerly as an antiseptic.

san·da·rac /ˈsandəˌrak/ *noun* (also **san·da·rach**) the gummy resin of a North African conifer, *Tetraclinis articulata*, used in making varnish. [Latin *sandaraca* from Greek *sandarakē*, of Asiatic origin]

sand·bag ● *noun* **1 a** a bag filled with sand and stacked with others to make temporary fortifications for the defence of a military camp against enemy fire. **b** a similar bag used to protect buildings etc. against flood waters, heavy winds, etc. **2** a bag filled with sand used as a weapon to inflict a heavy blow without leaving a mark. **3** a similar bag used as ballast esp. for a boat or balloon. ● *transitive verb* (**-bagged, -bag·ging**) **1 a** *transitive* place sandbags around or against (a building, river, etc.) in order to fortify it. **b** *intransitive* build protective dikes with sandbags. **2** *transitive* knock down with a blow from a sandbag. **3** *transitive N Amer.* coerce by harsh means; bully. **4** *transitive & intransitive* hinder or obstruct (a business transaction, the passage of legislation, etc.), esp. with prolonged talks or debate. **5** *transitive & intransitive Sport* lull (an opponent) into overconfidence by downplaying one's chances or abilities. □ **sand·bag·ger** *noun*

sand·bank *noun* a deposit of sand formed in a shallow place in the sea or a river by the action of tides and currents.

sand·bar *noun* a large bank of sand forming in a river or sea, often exposed at low tide.

sandbar willow *noun* a willow shrub, *Salix interior*, which often colonizes sandbars and beaches. *Also called* COYOTE WILLOW.

sand·blast ● *transitive verb* roughen, treat, or clean (glass, stone, wood, or metal) with a jet of sand driven by compressed air or steam. ● *noun* such a jet or stream of sand. □ **sand·blast·er** *noun*

sand·box *noun* *N Amer.* **1** a shallow pile of sand enclosed on four sides for children to play in. **2** (*attributive*) *jocular* designating juvenile behaviour or an attitude characteristic of a child at play (*the leaders approached the issue with sandbox diplomacy*).

Sand·burg, Carl (1878–1967), US poet, novelist, and historian. His poetry is marked by the use of colloquialism and free verse, and is collected in works such as *Chicago Poems* (1916), *Good Morning, America* (1928), and *Wind Song* (1960).

sand·castle *noun* a shape like a castle made in sand, usu. by a child on a beach.

sand·cherry *noun* (*pl.* **-ries**) *N Amer.* any of several shrubby wild cherries of N America, purple-leaved varieties of which are often cultivated in gardens.

sand dab *noun* any of various flatfish of sandy coasts, e.g. the plaice or flounder.

sand dollar *noun* esp. *N Amer.* any of various round flat sea urchins, esp. of the order Clypeasteroida.

sand dune *noun* a shifting mound or ridge of sand formed by the wind.

sand eel *noun* = SAND LANCE.

sand·er *noun* **1** a power tool that uses sandpaper to smooth surfaces, remove layers of paint, etc. **2 a** a vehicle that sprinkles sand on icy streets and highways etc. **b** a person operating such a vehicle.

sand·er·ling *noun* a small wading bird, *Calidris alba*, of the sandpiper family. [perhaps from an Old English form *sandyrthling* (unrecorded, as SAND + *yrthling* ploughman, also the name of a bird)]

sand flea *noun N Amer.* any of various small jumping crustaceans of the order Amphipoda, burrowing on the seashore.

sand·fly *noun* (*pl.* **-flies**) **1** any midge of the genus *Simulium*; a blackfly. **2** any biting fly of the genus *Phlebotomus* transmitting the viral disease leishmaniasis.

sandfly fever *noun* a mild viral disease resembling the flu and transmitted by sandflies of the genus *Phlebotomus*.

sand·glass *noun* = HOURGLASS.

sand·grouse *noun* a seed-eating ground bird of the family Pteroclididae, related to pigeons and found in arid regions of the Old World.

S&H *abbreviation* shipping and handling.

san·dhi /ˈsandi/ *noun Grammar* the process whereby the form or sound of a word changes as a result of its position in a phrase, e.g. the change from *a* to *an* before a vowel. [Sanskrit *saṃdhi* putting together]

sand·hill *noun* a hill or bank of sand, e.g. a dune on the seashore.

sandhill crane *noun* a slate-coloured N American crane, *Grus canadensis*, with a bare reddish patch on the forehead.

sand·hog *noun N Amer.* a person who works underwater or underground laying foundations, constructing tunnels, etc.

sand hopper *noun* = SAND FLEA.

San Diego /ˌsan diˈeɪɡoː/ an industrial city and naval port on the Pacific coast of S California, just north of the border with Mexico; pop. (2000) 1,223,400.

San·di·nis·ta /ˌsandəˈniːstə, -ˈnɪstə/ *noun* **1** *hist.* a member of a revolutionary Nicaraguan guerrilla organization founded by Sandíno. **2** a left-wing revolutionary movement founded in his name, which overthrew the Nicaraguan president in 1979 and formed a government (compare CONTRA). [Augusto César *Sandíno*, Nicaraguan revolutionary leader d.1934]

S&L *abbreviation US* = SAVINGS AND LOAN.

sand lance *noun* (also **sand launce**) *N Amer.* any eel-like fish of the family Ammodytidae or Hypotychidae.

sand·lot *noun N Amer.* a small plot of unoccupied land used by children for games and sports (also *attributive*: *sandlot baseball*). □ **sand·lot·ter** *noun*

S&M *abbreviation* sexual gratification achieved through inflicting and receiving pain; sadism and masochism or sado-masochism.

sand·man *noun* a make-believe figure that is supposed to make children sleep by sprinkling sand or sleep in their eyes; a personification of tiredness.

S&P *abbreviation* STANDARD AND POOR.

sand painting *noun* **1** a technique of painting with coloured sands, used esp. by Navajo Indians. **2** a piece of artwork produced with this technique. □ **sand painted** *adjective* **sand painter** *noun*

sand·paper ● *noun* strong paper coated with sand or another abrasive ranging in grit from very fine to coarse, used either for smoothing or roughening up a surface. ● *transitive verb* = SAND *verb* 1. □ **sand·papery** *adjective*

sand·piper *noun* any of various wading birds of the family Scolopacidae.

sand·pit *noun* **1** a pit from which sand is or has been excavated. **2** *Brit.* = SANDBOX.

sand·spit *noun* a spit of land created by sand dunes.

sand·stone *noun* **1** any of various sedimentary rocks of consolidated grains of sand, esp. of quartz, red, yellow, brown, grey, or white in colour. **2** any clastic rock containing particles visible to the naked eye.

sand·storm *noun* a storm, esp. in a desert, of wind with clouds of sand.

sand table *noun* a sand-covered surface on which models etc. can be placed and removed, esp. a relief model in sand used to demonstrate military tactics.

sand trap *noun N Amer.* a shallow pit filled with fine sand serving as an obstacle or hazard on a golf course. *Also called* BUNKER.

sand-wash ● *noun N Amer.* a sloping surface of sand spread out along an intermittent stream. ● *transitive verb* (esp. as **sand-washed** *adjective*) designating esp. silk that has been washed with sand in the water, giving it a slightly roughened texture.

sand wedge *noun Golf* an iron adapted for lifting the ball out of a sand trap or bunker.

sand·wich /ˈsandwɪʃ, ˌsanwɪʃ, ˈsam-/ ● *noun* **1** two or more slices of usu. buttered bread with a filling of meat, cheese, etc. between them. **2** anything resembling a sandwich in composition or appearance (*an ice cream sandwich*). **3** *Brit.* = LAYER CAKE. ● *verb* **1** *transitive* place or insert (a thing) between two dissimilar ones (*his wife's picture sandwiched between portraits of his two dogs*). **2** *transitive & intransitive* squeeze in between others (*he sandwiched between us on the couch*). **3** *transitive* (in football, hockey, etc.) trap or crush (an opposing player) between oneself and a teammate, the boards, etc. [4th Earl of *Sandwich*, English nobleman d.1792, said to have eaten food in this form so as not to leave the gaming table]

sandwich board *noun* **1** a pair of signs, usu. bearing advertisements, joined at the top by straps and suspended from the shoulders so that one sign is displayed over the front of the wearer, the other over the back. **2** a similar pair of signs joined at the top and forming a tent so that they may be free-standing.

sandwich generation *noun N Amer.* the generation of adults in their late 20s or early 30s trying to raise children while having to care for aged parents at the same time.

Sandwich Islands a former name for HAWAII.

sandwich man *noun* a man who walks the streets wearing a sandwich board.

sand·wort /ˈsandwɜrt, -wɔrt/ *noun* any low-growing plant of the genus *Arenaria*, usu. bearing small white flowers.

sandy *adjective* (**sand·i·er**, **sand·i·est**) **1** composed of or containing a large proportion of sand. **2** having the texture of sand. **3 a** (of hair) light reddish-blond. **b** (of a person) having sandy hair. □ **sand·i·ness** *noun* [Old English *sandig* (as SAND)]

sane *adjective* **1** of sound mind; not mad. **2** (of views etc.) sensible, reasonable; moderate. □ **sane·ly** *adverb* **sane·ness** *noun* [Latin *sanus* healthy]

San·for·ized /ˈsanfəraɪzd/ *adjective* (also esp. *Brit.* **-ised**) *proprietary* (of cotton or other fabrics) pre-shrunk by a special process. [L. Cluett *Sandford*, US inventor of the process d.1968 + -IZE]

San Fran·cis·co /ˌsan frənˈsɪskoː/ a city and seaport on the coast of California, situated on a peninsula between the Pacific and San Francisco Bay; pop. (2000) 776,733. □ **San Fran·cis·can** *noun & adjective*

sang *past of* SING.

san·gar /ˈsaŋɡər/ *noun* a stone breastwork or parapet around a hollow; a fortified lookout. [Persian & Pashto, prob. from Persian *sang* stone]

Sang·er /ˈsaŋɡər/ **1 Fred·erick** (b.1918), English biochemist, who has been awarded two Nobel Prizes for chemistry (1958 and 1980) for his work on the structure of complex biological molecules. **2 Mar·garet (Hig·gins)** (1883–1966), US nurse and birth control campaigner. She founded the first US birth control clinic in Brooklyn (1916), set up the first World Population Conference in Geneva (1927), and became the first president of the International Planned Parenthood Federation (1953).

sang-froid /saŋˈfrwɒ, sã-, -fwɒ/ *noun* composure, self-possession; coolness of mind or action, esp. in the face of danger or adversity. [French, = cold blood]

sangha /ˈsɒŋɡə/ *noun* the Buddhist monastic order, including monks, nuns, and novices. [Hindi *saṅgha* from Sanskrit *saṃgha* community, from *sam* together + *han* come in contact]

san·giov·ese /ˌsandʒoːˈveːzi/ *noun* **1** a vine yielding a black grape used in making Chianti and other Italian red wines. **2** wine made from these grapes. [Italian]

Sango /ˈsaŋɡoː/ ● *noun* **1** a dialect of Ngbandi. **2** a lingua franca developed from this and other dialects of Ngbandi, one of the official languages of the Central African Republic. ● *adjective* of or relating to Sango or its speakers. [Ngbandi]

san·gria /saŋˈɡriːə/ *noun* a drink of red wine with water, sugar, fruit juice, sliced citrus fruit, and usu. soda water. [Spanish, = bleeding]

san·guin·ary /ˈsaŋwɪnˌeri/ *adjective* **1** characterized or accompanied by bloodshed; bloody. **2** delighting in bloodshed; bloodthirsty. [Latin *sanguinarius* from *sanguis -inis* blood]

san·guine /ˈsaŋgwɪn/ ● *adjective* **1** optimistic; confident. **2** *hist.* relating to the predominance of blood over the bodily humours, characterized by a ruddy complexion and a courageous, amorous disposition. **3** *literary* blood-red. **4** *archaic* bloody; bloodthirsty. ● *noun* a blood-red or flesh-coloured pigment. □ **san·guine·ly** *adverb* [Old French *sanguin -ine* blood-red, from Latin *sanguineus* (as SANGUINARY)]

San·hed·rin /sanˈhedrɪn/ *noun Jewish Hist.* the highest court of justice and the supreme council in ancient Jerusalem with 71 members. [late Hebrew *sanhedrîn* from Greek *sunedrion* (as SYN-, *hedra* seat)]

sani·tar·ian /ˌsanɪˈteriən/ *noun* a person who studies sanitation or is in favour of sanitary reform.

sani·tar·ium /ˌsanɪˈteriəm/ *noun* (*pl.* **sani·tar·iums** or **sani·tar·ia** /-riə/) *N Amer.* = SANATORIUM. [pseudo-Latin from Latin *sanitas* health]

sani·tary /ˈsanɪˌteri/ *adjective* **1** of or pertaining to the conditions affecting health, the promotion of good health, or protection against infection. **2** hygienic; free from or designed to kill or protect against germs, infection, etc. □ **sani·tar·i·ly** *adverb* [French *sanitaire* from Latin *sanitas*: see SANE]

sanitary engineer *noun* a person who works on the design, construction, or maintenance of systems needed to maintain public health, such as sewerage. □ **sanitary engineering** *noun*

sanitary landfill *noun* an area of garbage disposed of under layers of earth.

sanitary pad *noun* (also **sanitary napkin**) *N Amer.* a pad worn during menstruation to absorb menstrual flow.

sanitary towel *noun Brit.* a sanitary pad.

sani·ta·tion *noun* **1** systems designed to protect or promote health. **2** the maintenance or improving of these. **3** the disposal of sewage and garbage from houses etc. [irreg. from SANITARY]

sani·tize *transitive verb* (also esp. *Brit.* **-tise**) **1** make (something) hygienic or thoroughly free from germs; sterilize, disinfect. **2** render (information etc.) more acceptable by removing indecent or disturbing material. □ **sani·tiz·a·tion** *noun* **sani·tiz·er** *noun*

sani·tor·ium /ˌsanəˈtoriəm/ *noun* (*pl.* **sani·tor·iums** or **sani·tor·ia** /-riə/) *N Amer.* = SANATORIUM. [pseudo-Latin from Latin *sanitas* health]

san·ity /ˈsanɪti/ *noun* **1 a** the state of being sane. **b** mental health. **2** reasonableness, moderation.

San Jose /ˌsan hoˈzeɪ/ a city in W California, situated south of San Francisco Bay; pop. (2000) 894,893.

San José /ˌsan hoˈzeɪ/ the capital of Costa Rica; pop. (est. 2002) 374,700.

San Juan /san ˈhwɒn/ the capital and chief port of Puerto Rico, on the north coast of the island; pop. (2000) 421,958.

sank *past of* SINK.

San Luis Pot·osí /ˌsan luˌis pɒtoˈsiː/ **1** a state of central Mexico. **2** its capital; pop. (2000) 628,134. It is an industrial city and a centre for the surrounding silver mines.

San Mar·ino /ˌsan məˈriːnoʊ/ **1** a republic forming a small enclave in Italy, near Rimini; pop. (est. 2002) 27,730. **2** its capital, the town of San Marino; pop. (est. 1997) 2,294.

San Mar·tín /ˌsan marˈtiːn/ **José de** (1778–1850), Argentinian leader. Having assisted in the liberation of his country from Spanish rule (1812–13) he went on to aid Bernardo O'Higgins in the liberation of Chile (1817–18); he was also involved in gaining Peruvian independence, becoming Protector of Peru (1821).

San Mi·guel de Tu·cu·mán /san mɪˌgel də tuːkəˈman/ a city in northwestern Argentina, capital of the province of Tucumán; pop. (est. 1999) 519,252.

san·nyasi /sʌnˈjasi/ *noun* (also **san·nyas·in**, **san·yasi**) (*pl.* same) a wandering Hindu fakir; a religious mendicant. [Hindi & Urdu *sannyāsī* from Sanskrit *saṃnyāsin* laying aside, from *saṃ* together, *ni* down, *as* throw]

San Pedro Sula /san ˌpedroː ˈsuːlə/ a city in N Honduras, near the Caribbean coast; pop. (est. 2002) 486,800.

sans /sɒnz, sɑ̃/ *preposition jocular* without (*he had the gall to show up at my party sans gift*). [Old French *san(z)*, *sen(s)*, ultimately from Latin *sine*, influenced by Latin *absentia* in the absence of]

San Sal·va·dor /san ˈsalvəˌdɔr/ the capital of El Salvador; pop. (est. 2002) 1,719,700.

sans-culotte /ˌsãkjuːˈlɒt/ *noun* **1** *hist.* a lower-class Parisian republican in the French Revolution. **2** an extreme republican or revolutionary. □ **sans-culott·ism** *noun* [French, lit. 'without knee breeches', knee breeches being the attire of the aristocrats, and the wearing of long trousers instead being a marked political statement of republicanism]

San Sebas·tián /ˌsan səˈbastiən/ a port and resort in N Spain, situated on the Bay of Biscay close to the border with France; pop. (est. 2001) 180,300.

San·sei /ˈsansei/ *noun* (*pl.* same) a N American whose grandparents were immigrants from Japan (*compare* ISSEI, NISEI). [Japanese, from *san* three + *sei* generation]

san·sev·eria /ˌsansəˈveriə/ *noun* (also **san·se·vi·eria**) any of various tropical African and Asian plants constituting the genus *Sansevieria*, of the agave family, having stiff erect leaves yielding a tough fibre and which include the houseplant mother-in-law's tongue, *S. trifasciata*. [modern Latin, from Raimondo di Sangro, Prince of *Sanseviero* in Italy d.1771]

San·skrit /ˈsanskrɪt/ ● *noun* the ancient Indo-Aryan language of the Indian subcontinent, the principal language of religious writings and scholarship, the source of some of the modern languages of the area (such as Hindi, Bengali, etc.), and now also one of the languages recognized for official use in India. ● *adjective* of or in this language. □ **San·skrit·ic** /-ˈskrɪtɪk/ *adjective* **San·skrit·ist** *noun* [Sanskrit *saṃskṛta* composed, elaborated, from *saṃ* together, *kṛ* make, *-ta* past participle ending]

San·so·vino /ˌsansəˈviːnoː/ **Jac·opo** (born Jacopo Tatti) (1486–1570), Italian sculptor and architect. As city architect of Venice from 1529, he designed buildings such as the Palazzo Corner (1533) and St. Mark's Library (begun 1536), which show the development of classical architectural style for contemporary use; his sculpture includes the colossal statues *Mars* and *Neptune* (1554–6) for the staircase of the Doges' Palace.

sans ser·if /ˌsanˈserɪf/ *Printing* ● *noun* a form of type without serifs. ● *adjective* without serifs.

Santa = SANTA CLAUS.

Santa Ana 1 a city in S California, southeast of Los Angeles; pop. (2000) 337,977. Lying to the east of the city are the Santa Ana Mountains. The region gives its name to the hot dry winds which blow from the mountains across the coastal plain of S California. **2** a city in El Salvador, situated close to the border with Guatemala; pop. (est. 2002) 164,500.

Santa Ana Volcano a volcano in El Salvador, southwest of the city of Santa Ana; elevation: 2 381 m (7,730 ft.).

Santa Anna, **An·tonio López de** (1794–1876), Mexican general, president 1833–36, 1841–45, 1847–48, and 1853–55. He led the attack on the Alamo (1836), and served as the commanding general of Mexican forces during the Mexican War (1846–48).

Santa Bar·bara a resort city in California, on the Pacific coast northwest of Los Angeles; pop. (2000) 92,325.

Santa Claus (also **Santa**) a folk figure, usu. represented as a rotund, white-bearded old man in a red suit, said to bring children presents on Christmas Eve. [Dutch dial. *Sante Klaas* St. Nicholas]

Santa Claus melon *noun* a large variety of melon with a striped green and yellow skin and yellowish-green flesh similar to a honeydew. [with reference to its peak season being in December]

Santa Cruz /ˌsantə ˈkruːz/ **1** a city in the central region of Bolivia; pop. (2001) 1,116,059. **2** (in full **Santa Cruz de Tenerife**) a port and the chief city of the island of Tenerife, in the Canary Islands; pop. (est. 2001) 214,153.

Santa Fe /ˌsantə ˈfeɪ/ (also **Santa Fé**) **1** a city in N Argentina, on the Salado river near its confluence with the Paraná; pop. (est. 2002) 502,200. **2** the state capital of New Mexico; pop. (2000) 62,203. □ **Santa Fean** *noun & adjective* (in sense 2).

Santa Mon·ica a resort city on the coast of SW California, situated to the west of Los Angeles; pop. (2000) 84,100. □ **Santa Mon·ican** *noun*

San·tan·der /ˌsantanˈder/ a port in N Spain, on the Bay of Biscay, capital of Cantabria; pop. (est. 2001) 185,231.

Santa Rosa *noun* a large round plum with red skin and yellow flesh. [*Santa Rosa*, California]

Santa So·phia = ST. SOPHIA.

Santa·yana /ˌsantiˈanə/ **George** (1863–1952), Spanish-born US philosopher and poet, whose philosophical works include *The Life of Reason* (1905–6) and *The Realms of Being* (1927–40), which stresses the role of faith but asserts that scientific analysis should be the method of reasoning.

San·tee /sanˈtiː/ *noun* **1** a member of a Dakota group originally inhabiting Minnesota, now also living in Manitoba and Saskatchewan. **2** the Siouan language of this people. [Dakota *Is(y)ati*, said to refer to a former residence at Knife Lake, Minnesota]

Consonants: b *but*   d *dog*   f *few*   g *get*   h *her*   j *yes*   k *cat*   l *leg*   m *man*   n *no*   p *pen*   r *red*   s *sit*

San·te·ria /ˌsantəˈriːə/ *noun* (also **Sante·ría**) an Afro-Cuban religion that combines elements of Catholicism with the worship of Yoruba deities. [Spanish, lit. 'holiness, sanctity']

san·tero /sanˈterɒ/ *noun* (*pl.* **-teros**) **1** a priest of Santeria. **2** (esp. in Mexico and Spanish-speaking areas of the US) a maker of religious images. [Spanish]

San·ti·ago /ˌsantiˈngɒ/ the capital of Chile, situated to the west of the Andes in the central part of the country; pop. (est. 2002) 5,034,500.

Santiago de Com·po·stela /dei ˌkɒmpɒˈstelə/ a city of NW Spain, capital of Galicia; pop. (est. 2001) 93,381. From the 9th c., the city became the centre of a national and Christian movement against the Moors and an important place of pilgrimage. [after St. James the Great (Spanish *Sant Iago*), whose remains, according to Spanish tradition, were brought there after his death in AD 44]

Santiago de Cuba /dei ˈkjuːbə/ a port on the coast of SE Cuba, the second largest city on the island; pop. (est. 2002) 544,400.

sant·im /ˈsantiːm/ *noun* (*pl.* **sant·imi**) a monetary unit of Latvia, equal to one-hundredth of a lat. [Latvian *santims*, from French *centime* + Latvian masculine ending *-s*]

Santo Do·min·go the capital of the Dominican Republic, a port on the south coast; pop. (est. 2002) 2,061,200. Founded in 1496 by the brother of Christopher Columbus, it is the oldest European settlement in the Americas. From 1936 to 1961 it was called Ciudad Trujillo.

san·to·lina /ˌsantɒˈliːnə/ *noun* any aromatic shrub of the genus *Santolina*, with finely divided leaves and small usu. yellow flowers. [modern Latin, var. of SANTONICA]

san·ton·ica /sanˈtɒnɪkə/ *noun* **1** a shrubby wormwood plant, *Artemisia cina*, yielding santonin. **2** the dried flower heads of this used as an anti-parasitic agent. [Latin from *Santones* a tribe living in SW Gaul]

san·tonin /ˈsantənɪn/ *noun* a toxic drug extracted from santonica and other plants of the genus *Artemisia*, used as an anti-parasitic agent. [SANTONICA + -IN]

San·tor·ini /ˌsantɒˈriːni/ see THERA.

San·tos /ˈsantɒs/ a port on the coast of Brazil, situated just southeast of São Paulo; pop. (2000) 415,543.

san·yasi *var. of* SANNYASI.

São Fran·cis·co /ˌsau franˈsɪskɒ/ a river of E Brazil. It rises in Minas Gerais and flows for 3 200 km (1,990 miles) northward then eastward, meeting the Atlantic to the north of Aracajú.

São Jose dos Campos /ˌsau hɒˈzei dɒs ˌkampɒs/ a city in SE Brazil, northeast of São Paulo; pop. (est. 2000) 532,403.

São Luís /ˌsau luːˈiːs/ a port in NE Brazil, on the Atlantic coast; pop. (2000) 834,968.

Saône /soːn/ a river of E France, which rises in the Vosges mountains and flows 480 km (298 miles) southwest to join the Rhone at Lyons.

São Paulo /sau ˈpaulɒ/ **1** a state of S Brazil, on the Atlantic coast. **2** its capital city; pop. (2000) 9,785,640.

São Tomé and Prin·cipe /ˌsau tɒˈmei, ˈprɪnsɪpi/ **1** a country consisting of two main islands and several smaller ones in the Gulf of Guinea; pop. (est. 2002) 170,372. **2** its capital, São Tomé; pop. (est. 1991) 43,420.

sap¹ ● *noun* **1** the fluid, chiefly water with dissolved sugars and mineral salts, that circulates in the vascular system of a plant and is essential to its growth. **2** the sap of the sugar maple, used for making maple syrup and maple sugar (also *attributive*: *sap bucket*). **3** vigour; vitality. **4** = SAPWOOD. ● *transitive verb* (**sapped**, **sap·ping**) drain or dry (wood) of sap. □ **sap·less** *adjective* [Old English *sæp* prob. from Germanic]

sap² ● *noun* a tunnel or trench to conceal assailants' approach to a fortified place. ● *verb* (**sapped**, **sap·ping**) **1** *intransitive* **a** dig a sap or saps. **b** approach by a sap. **2** *transitive* undermine; make insecure by removing the foundations. **3** *transitive* weaken or destroy insidiously (*his confidence has been sapped*; *my energy had been sapped by disappointment*). [ultimately from Italian *zappa* spade, spadework, in part through French *sappe* sap(p)er, prob. of Arabic origin]

sap³ *noun slang* a foolish person. [abbreviation of *sapskull* from SAP¹ = sapwood + SKULL]

sa·pele /səˈpiːli/ *noun* **1** any of several large West African hardwood trees of the genus *Entandrophragma*. **2** the reddish-brown mahogany-like timber of these trees. [West African name]

sapid /ˈsapɪd/ *adjective literary* **1** having (esp. an agreeable) flavour; savoury; palatable; not insipid. **2** *literary* (of talk, writing, etc.) not vapid or uninteresting. [Latin *sapidus* from *sapere* taste]

sapi·ent /ˈseipiənt/ *adjective literary* **1** wise, or attempting to appear wise.

2 of or relating to the human species. □ **sapi·ence** *noun* [Old French *sapient* or Latin part. stem of *sapere* be wise]

Sapir /səˈpiːr/ **Ed·ward** (1884–1939), German-born US linguistics scholar and anthropologist. One of the founders of American structural linguistics, he carried out important work on N American Aboriginal languages and linguistic theory and was chief of anthropology for the National Museum in Ottawa 1910–25.

sap·ling *noun* **1** a young tree. **2** a youth.

sapo·dilla /ˌsapəˈdɪlə/ *noun* **1** a large tropical American evergreen tree, *Manilkara zapota*, with edible fruit and durable wood, and sap from which chicle is obtained. **2** (also **sapodilla plum**) the fruit of this tree. [Spanish *zapotillo* diminutive of *zapote* from Aztec *tzápotl*]

sap·on·ify /səˈpɒnɪˌfai/ *verb* (**-fies**, **-fied**) **1** *transitive* convert (fat or oil) into soap by reaction with an alkali. **2** *transitive* convert (an ester) to an acid and alcohol. **3** *intransitive* become saponified. □ **sap·oni·fi·ca·tion** *noun* [French *saponifier* from Latin *sapo -onis* soap]

sap·onin /ˈsapənɪn/ *noun* any of a group of plant glycosides, esp. those derived from the bark of the tree *Quillaja saponaria*, that foam when shaken with water and are used in detergents and fire extinguishers. [French *saponine* from Latin *sapo -onis* soap]

sap·pan·wood /ˈsapənˌwʊd/ *noun* the heartwood of an E Indian tree, *Caesalpinia sappan*, formerly used as a source of red dye. [Dutch *sapan* from Malay *sapang*, of S Indian origin]

sap·per *noun* **1** a person who digs saps. **2** *N Amer.* a military engineer who lays or detects and disarms mines. **3** (also **Sapper**) *Cdn & Brit.* a soldier having the rank of private in regiments of engineers.

Sap·phic /ˈsafɪk/ ● *adjective* **1** of or relating to Sappho or her poetry. **2** lesbian. ● *noun* (in *pl.*) (**sapphics**) verse in a metre associated with Sappho.

sap·phire /ˈsafair/ ● *noun* **1** a transparent blue precious stone consisting of corundum. **2** precious transparent corundum of any colour. **3** the bright blue of a sapphire. ● *adjective* **1** of sapphire blue (*his sapphire eyes*). **2** set with a sapphire or sapphires (*a sapphire ring*). □ **sap·phir·ine** /ˈsafɪˌrain/ *adjective* [Old French *safir* from Latin *sapphirus* from Greek *sappheiros* prob. = lapis lazuli]

sapphire blue ● *noun* a bright blue colour. ● *adjective* (hyphenated when *attributive*) of this colour.

sapphire wedding *noun* a 45th wedding anniversary.

Sap·pho /ˈsafɒ/ (early 7th c. BC) Greek lyric poet. She became the centre of a circle of women and young girls on the island of Lesbos; many of her poems express her affection and love for women, and have given rise to her association with lesbianism.

Sap·poro /səˈpɒrɒ/ a city in N Japan, capital of the island of Hokkaido; pop. (est. 2002) 1,842,100.

sappy *adjective* (**sap·pier**, **sap·piest**) **1** *N Amer. informal* overly sentimental. **2** full of sap. □ **sap·pi·ly** *adverb* **sap·pi·ness** *noun*

sapro- *combining form Biol.* rotten, putrefying. [Greek *sapros* putrid]

sapro·genic /ˌsaprəˈdʒenɪk/ *adjective* causing or produced by putrefaction.

sap·roph·a·gous /saˈprɒfəgəs/ *adjective* feeding on decaying matter.

sapro·phyte /ˈsaprəˌfait/ *noun* any plant or micro-organism living on dead or decayed organic matter. □ **sapro·phyt·ic** /-ˈfɪtɪk/ *adjective*

sap·suck·er *noun* a small woodpecker of the genus *Sphyrapicus*, which pecks holes in trees and visits them for sap and insects.

sap·wood *noun* the soft outer layers of recently formed wood between the heartwood and the bark.

SAR /sɑr/ *abbreviation* **1** SEARCH AND RESCUE. **2** SPECIAL ADMINISTRATIVE REGION.

sara·band /ˈserəˌband/ *noun* (also **sara·bande**) **1** a stately Spanish dance of the 17th and 18th c. **2** music for this or in its rhythm, usu. in triple time with a long note on the second beat of the bar. [French *sarabande* from Spanish & Italian *zarabanda*]

Sara·cen /ˈserəsən/ *hist.* ● *noun* **1** an Arab or Muslim at the time of the Crusades. **2** a nomad of the Syrian and Arabian desert. ● *adjective* of the Saracens. □ **Sara·cen·ic** /ˌserəˈsenɪk/ *adjective* [Old French *sarrazin*, *sarracin* from Late Latin *Saracenus* from late Greek *Sarakēnos* perhaps from Arabic *šarḳī* eastern]

Sara·gossa /ˌserəˈgɒsə/ a city of N Spain, capital of Aragon, situated on the Ebro River; pop. (est. 2002) 607,000.

Sarah *Bible* the wife of Abraham and mother of Isaac (Gen. 17:15 ff.).

Sara·jevo /ˌserəˈjeivɒ/ the capital of Bosnia and Herzegovina; pop. (est. 2002) 434,000. Archduke Franz Ferdinand, the heir to the Austrian throne, was assassinated there in June 1914, an event which triggered the outbreak of the First World War. The city also suffered severely

t top   v voice   w we   z zoo   ʃ she   ʒ vision   θ thin   ð this   ŋ ring   x loch   tʃ chip   dʒ jar   (*see over for vowels*)

from the ethnic conflicts that followed the breakup of Yugoslavia in 1991. □ **Sar·a·jevan** *noun*

Sara·mago /ˌsarəˈmaɡoː/ **José** (b.1922), Portuguese writer, winner of the Nobel Prize for literature in 1998. English translations of his works include *Baltasar and Blimunda*, *The History of the Seige of Lisbon*, *Blindness*, and *The Cave*.

saran /səˈran/ *noun* (also **saran wrap**) clear thin film made of polyvinyl chloride, used to wrap foods.

sar·angi /səˈraŋɡi/ *noun* (*pl.* **sar·angis**) an Indian stringed instrument played with a bow. [Hindi *sāraṅgī*]

Sar·ansk /səˈransk/ a city in European Russia, capital of the autonomous republic of Mordvinia, situated to the south of Nizhni Novgorod; pop. (est. 2002) 311,800.

sar·ape *var. of* SERAPE.

Sara·toga, Battle of /ˌserəˈtoːɡə/ either of two battles fought in 1777 during the American Revolution near the modern city of Saratoga Springs in New York State. The Americans were victorious in both, thus winning French support for their cause.

Sara·tov /səˈrɒtəf/ a city in SW central Russia, situated on the Volga River north of Volgograd; pop. (est. 2002) 867,900.

Sara·wak /səˈrɒwək/ a state of Malaysia, comprising the northwestern part of Borneo; capital, Kuching.

sar·casm /ˈsɑrˌkazəm/ *noun* **1** the use of bitter or wounding, esp. ironic, remarks; language consisting of such remarks (*suffered from constant sarcasm about his work*). **2** such a remark. □ **sar·cas·tic** /sɑrˈkastɪk/ *adjective* **sar·cas·tic·ally** *adverb* [French *sarcasme* or Late Latin *sarcasmus* from late Greek *sarkasmos*, from Greek *sarkazō* 'tear flesh', in late Greek 'gnash the teeth, speak bitterly', from *sarx sarkos* 'flesh']

Sar·cee /ˈsɑrsiː, -ˈsiː/ ● *noun* **1** a member of a small Aboriginal group living on the Bow River near Calgary, the only Athapaskan people living within the Plains area. **2** the Athapaskan language of this people. ● *adjective* of or relating to this people or their culture or language. ¶ Also called TSUU TʼINA. [Blackfoot *saaxsiiwa*]

sar·coma /sɑrˈkoːmə/ *noun* (*pl.* **sar·co·mas** or **sar·co·mata** /-mətə/) a malignant tumour of connective or other non-epithelial tissue. □ **sar·coma·to·sis** /-ˈtoːsɪs/ *noun* **sar·coma·tous** *adjective* [modern Latin from Greek *sarkōma* from *sarkoō* become fleshy, from *sarx sarkos* flesh]

sar·coph·agus /sɑrˈkɒfəɡəs/ *noun* (*pl.* **sar·coph·agi** /-ˌɡaɪ, -ˌdʒaɪ/) a stone coffin, esp. one adorned with a sculpture or inscription. [Latin from Greek *sarkophagos* flesh-consuming (as SARCOMA, *-phagos* -eating)]

sar·co·plasm /ˈsɑrkəˌplazəm/ *noun* Anat. the cytoplasm in which muscle fibrils are embedded. [Greek *sarx sarkos* flesh + PLASMA]

sard *noun* a yellow or orange-red carnelian. [French *sarde* or Latin *sarda* = Late Latin *sardius* from Greek *sardios* prob. from *Sardō* Sardinia]

Sar·da·napa·lus /ˌsɑrdəˈnapələs/ the name given by ancient Greek historians to the last king of Assyria (died *c*.626 BC), portrayed as being notorious for his wealth and sensuality.

sar·dine /sɑrˈdiːn/ ● *noun* **1** any of various fish of the herring family. **2** a young Atlantic or Pacific herring preserved in oil or brine and canned. **3** a young European pilchard likewise preserved. ● *transitive verb* informal pack closely together. □ **like sardines** crowded close together (as sardines are in cans). [Old French *sardine* = Italian *sardina* from Latin from *sarda* from Greek, perhaps from *Sardō* Sardinia]

Sar·dinia /sɑrˈdɪniə/ a large Italian island in the Mediterranean Sea to the west of Italy; pop. (est. 2002) 1,669,000; capital, Cagliari. The island is separated from the French island of Corsica to the north by the Strait of Bonifacio.

Sardinia, Kingdom of a kingdom consisting of Piedmont and Savoy and the island of Sardinia, in existence from 1720 until the creation of a united Italy in 1861, when Victor Emmanuel II of Sardinia became the first king of Italy.

Sar·din·ian ● *noun* **1** a native or inhabitant of Sardinia. **2** the Romance language of Sardinia. ● *adjective* of or relating to Sardinia or its people or language.

Sar·dis /ˈsɑrdɪs/ an ancient city of Asia Minor, the capital of Lydia, whose ruins lie near the west coast of modern Turkey, to the northeast of Izmir. It was destroyed by Tamerlane in the 14th c.

sar·don·ic /sɑrˈdɒnɪk/ *adjective* (of laughter, a person's character, etc.) bitterly mocking or cynical. □ **sar·don·ic·ally** *adverb* **sar·doni·cism** /-ˌsɪzəm/ *noun* [French *sardonique* from Latin *sardonius* from Greek *sardonios* of Sardinia, alteration of *sardanios* Homeric epithet of bitter or scornful laughter]

sard·onyx /ˈsɑrdənɪks/ *noun* onyx in which white layers alternate with sard. [Latin from Greek *sardonux* (prob. as SARD, ONYX)]

saree *var. of* SARI.

sar·gasso /sɑrˈɡasoː/ *noun* (also **sar·gas·sum**) (*pl.* **-sos** or **-soes** or **sar·gassa**) any seaweed of the genus *Sargassum*, with berry-like air vessels, found floating in island-like masses, esp. in the Sargasso Sea. Also called GULFWEED. [Portuguese *sargaço*, of unknown origin]

Sargasso Sea a region of the W Atlantic Ocean between the Azores and the W Indies, around latitude 35°N. It is the breeding place of eels from the rivers of Europe and eastern N America, and is known for its usu. calm conditions.

sarge *noun slang* sergeant. [abbreviation]

Sar·gent ▶ **1 Sir (Henry) Mal·colm (Watts)** (1895–1967), English conductor and composer. In 1921 he made an acclaimed debut at a promenade concert conducting his own *Impressions of a Windy Day*. He conducted a number of ensembles, including the BBC Symphony Orchestra (1950–7) and was responsible for the BBC Promenade Concerts from 1948. **2 John Sing·er** (1856–1925), Italian-born US painter. In the 1870s he painted some Impressionist landscapes, but it was in portraiture that he developed the bold brushwork typical of his style; his works include *Madame Gautreau* (1884).

Sar·godha /sɑrˈɡoːdə/ a city in north central Pakistan; pop. (1998) 455,400. Situated near the Jhelum River, it is an agricultural centre and railway junction.

Sar·gon /ˈsɑrɡɒn/ (2334–2279 BC), the semi-legendary founder of the ancient kingdom of Akkad.

Sargon II (d.705 BC), king of Assyria 721–705. He was probably a son of Tiglath-pileser III, and is famous for his conquest of a number of cities in Syria and Palestine; he also took ten of the tribes of Israel into captivity.

sari /ˈsɑriː/ *noun* (also **saree**) (*pl.* **saris** or **sarees**) a length of cotton or silk draped around the body, traditionally worn as a main garment by Indian women. [Hindi *sāṛ(h)ī*]

sarin /ˈsɑrɪn/ *noun* an organic phosphorus compound used as a nerve gas. [German]

Sark one of the Channel Islands, a small island lying to the east of Guernsey. It is divided by an isthmus into **Great Sark** and **Little Sark**.

sarky *adjective* (**sark·i·er**, **sark·i·est**) Brit. slang sarcastic. □ **sark·i·ly** *adverb* [abbreviation]

Sar·ma·tia /sɑrˈmeɪʃə/ an ancient region situated to the north of the Black Sea. Extending originally from the Urals to the Don, by Roman times the region consisted of the area between the Volga and the Vistula, corresponding to modern Poland and SW Russia. It was inhabited by Slavic peoples from ancient times. □ **Sar·ma·tian** *adjective & noun*

sar·men·tose /ˈsɑrmənˌtoːs/ *adjective* (also **sar·men·tous** /-ˈmentəs/) *Bot.* having long thin trailing shoots. [Latin *sarmentosus* from *sarmenta* (pl.) twigs, brushwood, from *sarpere* to prune]

Sar·nia /ˈsɑrniə/ a city in SW Ontario, situated on the St. Clair River at the southern end of Lake Huron, about 100 km due west of London; pop. (2001) 70,876. □ **Sar·nian** *noun* [the Roman name for GUERNSEY¹]

sar·nie *noun Brit. informal* a sandwich. [prob. representing a slang or dial. pronunciation of the first element of SANDWICH]

sarod /səˈroːd/ *noun* a stringed musical instrument of India, played with a bow. [Urdu, from Persian *surod* song, melody]

sar·ong /səˈrɒŋ/ *noun* **1** a Malay and Javanese garment, worn by both sexes, consisting of a long strip of (often striped) cloth worn tucked around the waist or under the armpits. **2** a woman's garment resembling this. [Malay, lit. 'sheath']

Sar·on·ic Gulf /səˈrɒnɪk/ an inlet of the Aegean Sea on the coast of SE Greece. Athens and the port of Piraeus lie on its northern shores.

saros /ˈsɑrɒs/ *noun* Astronomy a period of about 18 years between repetitions of eclipses. [Greek from Babylonian *šār(u)* 3,600 (years)]

Sar·pedon /sɑrˈpiːdən/ Gk Myth son of Zeus and Laodamia, king of Lycia, who was killed by Patroclus during the Trojan War.

SARS /sɑrz/ *abbreviation* SEVERE ACUTE RESPIRATORY SYNDROME.

sarsa·pa·rilla /ˌsɑspəˈrɪlə/ *noun* **1** a preparation of the dried roots of various plants of the genus *Smilax*, used to flavour some drinks and medicines and formerly as a tonic. **2** any of the plants yielding this. **3** a soft drink flavoured with sarsaparilla. **4** a plant of the genus *Aralia*, esp. bristly sarsaparilla *A. hispida* and wild sarsaparilla *A. nudicaulis*, used as a substitute for sarsaparilla. [Spanish *zarzaparilla* from *zarza* bramble, prob. + diminutive of *parra* vine]

Vowels: a *cat* ɑ *arm* e *bed* ɜr *her* ɜː *deux* ə *ago* ɪ *sit* i *cosy* iː *feed* ɒ *hot* ɔ *pore* ɔː *no* ʌ *run* ʊ *put*

sar·sen /ˈsɑːsən/ *noun Geol.* a sandstone boulder carried by ice during a glacial period. [prob. var. of SARACEN]

SAR Tech *noun Cdn* a search and rescue technician, a non-commissioned member of the Canadian Forces specialized in performing rescue operations at crash and emergency sites, and highly trained in such related skills as parachuting, mountain climbing, first aid, etc. [abbreviation]

Sarto see ANDREA DEL SARTO.

sar·tor·ial /sɑːˈtɔːriəl/ *adjective* **1** of or relating to clothes or clothing. **2** of a tailor or tailoring. □ **sar·tor·ial·ly** *adverb* [Latin *sartor* tailor, from *sarcire sart-* patch]

sar·tor·ius /sɑːˈtɔːriəs/ *noun* the long narrow muscle running across the front of each thigh. [modern Latin from Latin *sartor* tailor (the muscle being used in adopting a tailor's cross-legged posture)]

Sartre /ˈsɑːtrə/ **Jean-Paul** (1905–80), French philosopher, novelist, dramatist, and critic. He was a leading exponent of existentialism, and his later philosophy deals with the social responsibility of freedom, attempting to synthesize existentialism with Marxist sociology; his works include the treatise *Being and Nothingness* (1943), the novel *Nausée* (1938) and the trilogy *Les Chemins de la liberté* (1945–9), and the plays *Les Mouches* (1943) and *Huis clos* (1944). □ **Sar·trean** *adjective & noun* (also **Sar·trian**).

Sarum use /ˈserəm/ *noun Christianity* the order of divine service used in the diocese of Salisbury before the Reformation. [medieval Latin *Sarum* Salisbury, perhaps from Latin *Sarisburia*]

SAS *abbreviation* (in the UK) Special Air Service.

SASE *abbreviation* (also **S.A.S.E.**) *N Amer.* self-addressed stamped envelope.

sash[1] *noun* a long strip of cloth worn tied around the waist or over one shoulder, e.g. as part of a uniform or as decoration. □ **sashed** *adjective* [earlier *shash* from Arabic *šāš* muslin, turban]

sash[2] *noun* **1** a frame holding the glass in a sash window and usu. made to slide up and down in the grooves of a window aperture. **2** the glazed sliding light of a greenhouse or garden frame. □ **sashed** *adjective* [*sashes* corruption of CHASSIS, mistaken for pl.]

sa·shay *intransitive verb esp. N Amer. informal* **1** walk or move casually or nonchalantly; saunter (*sashay over to the hotel for lunch*). **2** walk or move so as to attract attention (*sashayed into the room*). [corruption of CHASSÉ]

sa·shi·mi /saˈʃiːmi/ *noun* a Japanese dish of garnished raw fish in thin slices. [Japanese, from *sashi* pierce + *mi* flesh]

sash window *noun* a window with one or two sashes of which one or each can be slid vertically over the other to make an opening.

Sask. *abbreviation* Saskatchewan.

Sas·ka·bush a nickname for Saskatoon.

Sas·katch·ewan /səˈskætʃəwən, -wən/ a province of west central Canada; pop. (2001) 978,933; capital, Regina. It was administered by the Hudson's Bay Company until 1870, when it was acquired by Canada as part of the North-West Territories. It became a separate province in 1905. □ **Sas·katch·ewan·ian** *adjective & noun* [see SASKATCHEWAN RIVER]

Saskatchewan, District of a provisional district (1882–1905) of the North-West Territories, corresponding roughly to what is now central Saskatchewan. [see SASKATCHEWAN RIVER]

Saskatchewan Day *noun Cdn* (*Sask.*) a statutory holiday occurring on the first Monday in August.

Saskatchewan Party *noun* a political party of Saskatchewan formed in 1997 by the Conservatives and some Liberals.

Saskatchewan River a river of east central Saskatchewan and west central Manitoba, formed by the confluence of its two headstreams, the **North Saskatchewan** and the **South Saskatchewan**; it flows generally eastward to Lake Winnipeg. [Cree *kisiskatchewan* swift current]

Sas·ka·toon an industrial city in central Saskatchewan, located on the South Saskatchewan River, 259 km northwest of Regina; pop. (2001) 196,811. □ **Sas·ka·ton·ian** /ˌsaskəˈtoːniən/ *noun* (also **Sas·ka·toon·ian**). [SASKATOON]

sas·ka·toon /ˌsaskəˈtuːn/ *noun Cdn* (*Prairies*) **1** a shrub, *Amelanchier alnifolia*, of western N America. **2** (also **saskatoon berry**) the sweet purple berry of this shrub. [Cree *misa:skwato:min*, from *misa:skwat* saskatoon + *min* berry]

sas·quatch /ˈsaskwɒtʃ/ *noun* a supposed yeti-like animal of northwestern N America. [Halkomelem]

sass *N Amer. informal* ● *noun* impudence, cheek. ● *transitive verb* be impudent to. [var. of SAUCE]

sas·saby /ˈsasəbi/ *noun* (*pl.* **-bies**) a southern African antelope, *Damaliscus lunatus*, similar to the hartebeest. [Setswana *tsessébe*, *-ábi*]

sas·sa·fras /ˈsasəˌfras/ *noun* **1** a small tree, *Sassafras albidum*, native to N America, with aromatic leaves and bark. **2** a preparation of oil extracted from the leaves, or from its bark, used medicinally or in perfumery. [Spanish *sasafrás* or Portuguese *sassafraz*, of unknown origin]

Sas·san·ian /saˈseiniən/ (also **Sas·san·id** /ˈsasənid/) ● *adjective* of, relating to, or denoting the dynasty ruling the Persian Empire from AD 224 until driven from Mesopotamia by the Arabs (637–51). ● *noun* a member of this dynasty. [*Sasan* the grandfather of the first Sassanian, Ardashir]

Sas·sen·ach /ˈsasəˌnax, -ˌnak/ *Scot. & Irish* usu. *derogatory* ● *noun* an English person. ● *adjective* English. [Gaelic *Sasunnoch*, Irish *Sasanach* from Latin *Saxones* Saxons]

Sas·soon /səˈsuːn/ **Sieg·fried Lor·raine** (1886–1967), English poet and writer. He is known for his starkly realistic poems written while serving in the First World War, expressing his contempt for war leaders and patriotic cant as well as compassion for his comrades.

sassy *adjective* (**sas·si·er**, **sas·si·est**) esp. *N Amer. informal* lively, bold, and full of spirit. □ **sas·si·ly** *adverb* **sas·si·ness** *noun* [var. of SAUCY]

sas·trugi /saˈstruːgi/ *plural noun* wavelike irregularities on the surface of hard polar snow, caused by winds. [Russian *zastrugi* small ridges]

SAT *abbreviation proprietary* SCHOLASTIC APTITUDE TEST.

Sat. *abbreviation* Saturday.

sat *past and past participle of* SIT.

Satan /ˈseitən/ the Devil; Lucifer. [Hebrew *śāṭān* lit. 'adversary' from *śaṭan* oppose, plot against]

sat·ang /ˈsataŋ/ *noun* (*pl.* **sat·angs** or same) a monetary unit of Thailand, equal to one-hundredth of a baht. [Thai from Pali *sata* hundred]

satan·ic /səˈtanɪk/ *adjective* **1** of, like, or befitting Satan or Satanism. **2** diabolical, hellish. □ **satan·ic·ally** *adverb*

Satan·ism /ˈseitəˌnɪzəm/ *noun* **1** the worship of Satan. **2** a travesty of Christian forms, used in worship of Satan. **3** deliberate evil or wickedness. □ **Satan·ist** *noun*

satay /saˈtei, ˈsatei/ *noun* (also **saté**) an Indonesian and Malaysian dish consisting of small pieces of meat grilled on a skewer and usu. served with spicy peanut sauce. [Malayan *satai sate*, Indonesian *sate*]

SATB *abbreviation Music* soprano, alto, tenor, and bass (as a combination of voices).

satch·el *noun* a small bag usu. of leather and hung from the shoulder with a strap, for carrying books etc. esp. to and from school. [Old French *sachel* from Latin *saccellus* (as SACK[1])]

sate *transitive verb* **1** gratify (desire, or a desirous person) to the full. **2** cloy, surfeit, weary with overabundance (*sated with pleasure*). [prob. from dial. *sade*, Old English *sadian* (as SAD), assimilated to SATIATE]

sateen /saˈtiːn/ *noun* cotton fabric woven like satin with a glossy surface. [*satin* after *velveteen*]

sat·el·lite /ˈsatəˌlaɪt/ *noun* **1** a celestial body orbiting the earth or another planet. **2** an artificial body placed in orbit round the earth or another planet, esp. for observation or remote sensing of the earth's surface, for astronomical observation, or as a relay for telecommunication. **3** a follower; a hanger-on. **4** something that is subordinate to or reliant on another place or thing (*lives in a satellite of Toronto*). ● *adjective* **1** transmitted by satellite (*satellite communications*; *satellite television*). **2** (of a region etc.) subordinate to another body etc. [French *satellite* or Latin *satelles satellitis* attendant]

satellite dish *noun* a concave dish-shaped antenna for receiving broadcasting signals transmitted by satellite.

sat fat *noun informal* saturated fat.

Sati /ˈsʌti/ *Hinduism* the wife of Shiva, reborn as Parvati. According to some accounts, she died by throwing herself into the sacred fire, hence the custom of suttee. [Sanskrit, as SUTTEE]

sati *var. of* SUTTEE.

sati·ate /ˈseiʃiˌeit/ *transitive verb* = SATE. □ **sati·ation** *noun* [Latin *satiatus* past participle of *satiare* from *satis* enough]

Satie /saˈtiː/ **Erik Al·fred Les·lie** (1866–1925), French composer. His piano piece *Gymnopédies* (1888) is typical of his deceptively simple, almost naive, style; he was associated with Cocteau, Picasso, Dada, and surrealism, as well as influencing composers such as Poulenc.

sa·ti·ety /səˈtaɪɪti/ *noun* the state of being or feeling satiated. [obsolete French *sacieté* from Latin *satietas -tatis* from *satis* enough]

sat·in ● *noun* **1** a fabric of silk or various synthetic fibres, with a glossy surface on one side produced by a twill weave with the weft threads almost hidden. **2** a low-lustre paint. ● *adjective* **1** smooth as satin. **2** made of satin. ● *transitive verb* (**sat·ined**, **sat·in·ing**) give a glossy surface to (paper). □ **sat·iny** *adjective* [Old French from Arabic *zaytūnī* of *Tsinkiang* in China]

satin flower *noun* any of various plants whose flowers or seed capsules have a satiny sheen, esp. of the genus *Clarkia*, with pink or lavender flowers.

satin stitch *noun* a long straight embroidery stitch, giving the appearance of satin.

satin·wood *noun* **1 a** (in full **Ceylon satinwood**) a tree, *Chloroxylon swietenia*, native to central and southern India and Ceylon. **b** (in full **Jamaican satinwood** or **West Indian satinwood**) a tree, *Zanthoxylum flavum*, native to the Caribbean and southern Florida. **2** the yellow glossy timber of either of these trees.

sat·ire *noun* **1** the use of ridicule, irony, sarcasm, etc., to expose folly or vice or to lampoon an individual. **2** a work or composition in prose or verse using satire. **3** this genre of literature. [French *satire* or Latin *satira* later form of *satura* medley]

sa·tir·ic /sə'tɪrɪk/ *adjective* (also **sa·tir·ic·al**) **1** of satire or satires. **2** containing satire (*wrote a satiric review*). **3** writing satire (*a satiric poet*). **4** given to the use of satire in speech or writing or to cynical observation of others; sarcastic; humorously critical. □ **sa·tir·ic·al·ly** *adverb*

sat·ir·ist /'satɪrɪst/ *noun* **1** a writer of satires. **2** a satirical person.

sat·ir·ize /'satɪraɪz/ *transitive verb* (also esp. *Brit.* **-ise**) **1** assail or ridicule with satire. **2** write a satire upon. **3** describe satirically. □ **sat·ir·iz·a·tion** *noun*

satis·fac·tion *noun* **1** the act or an instance of satisfying; the state of being satisfied (*heard this with great satisfaction*). **2** a thing that satisfies desire or gratifies feeling (*is a great satisfaction to me*). **3** a thing that settles an obligation or pays a debt. **4 a** (foll. by *for*) atonement; compensation (*demanded satisfaction*). **b** *Theol.* Christ's atonement for the sins of mankind. □ **to one's satisfaction** so that one is satisfied.

satis·fac·tory *adjective* **1** adequate; causing or giving satisfaction (*was a satisfactory pupil*). **2** satisfying expectations or needs; leaving no room for complaint (*a satisfactory result*). □ **satis·fac·tor·i·ly** *adverb* **satis·fac·tor·i·ness** *noun* [medieval Latin *satisfactorius* (as SATISFY)]

satis·fy *verb* (**-fies**, **-fied**) **1** *transitive* **a** meet the expectations or desires of; comply with (a demand). **b** be accepted by (a person, a person's taste) as adequate; be equal to (a preconception etc.). **2** *transitive* put an end to (an appetite or want) by supplying what was required. **3** *transitive* rid (a person) of an appetite or want in a similar way. **4** *intransitive* give satisfaction; leave nothing to be desired. **5** *transitive* pay (a debt or creditor). **6** *transitive* adequately meet, fulfill, or comply with (conditions, obligations, etc.) (*has satisfied all the legal conditions*). **7** *transitive* (often foll. by *of*, *that*) provide with adequate information or proof, convince (*satisfied the others that they were right*; *satisfy the court of their innocence*). **8** *transitive Math.* (of a quantity) make (an equation) true. **9** *transitive* (in *passive*) **a** (foll. by *with*) contented or pleased with. **b** (foll. by *to*) demand no more than or consider it enough to do. □ **satisfy oneself** (often foll. by *that* + clause) be certain in one's own mind. □ **satis·fi·able** *adjective* **satis·fy·ing** *adjective* **satis·fy·ing·ly** *adverb* [Old French *satisfier* from Latin *satisfacere satisfact-* from *satis* enough]

Sato Eisaku /'sato: aizaku:/ (1901–75), Japanese prime minister 1964–72, who presided over the postwar economic growth of Japan; he shared the Nobel Peace Prize in 1974 for his opposition to nuclear weapons.

sa·tori /sə'tɔːri/ *noun Buddhism* sudden enlightenment. [Japanese]

sat·rap /'satrap/ *noun* **1** a provincial governor in the ancient Persian Empire. **2** a subordinate ruler, colonial governor, etc. [Old French *satrape* or Latin *satrapa* from Greek *satrapēs* from Old Persian *xšathra-pāvan* country protector]

sat·rapy /'satrəpi/ *noun* (*pl.* **-ies**) a province ruled over by a satrap.

sat·sang /'satsaŋ, 'sʌtsʌŋ/ *noun Hinduism* a spiritual discourse or sacred gathering. [Sanskrit *satsaṇga* 'association with good men']

Sat·suma /'satsumə/ a former province of SW Japan. It comprised the major part of the southwestern peninsula of Kyushu island, also known as the Satsuma Peninsula. It was noted for the pottery made there from the end of the 16th c.

sat·suma /'satsumə, sat'suːmə/ *noun* a variety of tangerine originally grown in Japan. [SATSUMA]

sat·ur·ate /'satʃə,reɪt/ *transitive verb* **1** fill with moisture; soak thoroughly. **2** (often foll. by *with*) fill to capacity. **3** cause (a substance, solution, vapour, metal, or air) to absorb, hold, or combine with the greatest possible amount of another substance, or of moisture, magnetism, electricity, etc. **4** supply (a market) beyond the point at which the demand for a product is satisfied. **5** (foll. by *with*, *in*) imbue with or steep in (learning, tradition, prejudice, etc.). **6** overwhelm (enemy defences, a target area, etc.) by concentrated bombing. □ **sat·ur·able** *adjective* [Latin *saturare* from *satur* full]

sat·ur·at·ed *adjective* **1** completely wet. **2** (of a solution) containing the greatest amount of solute that it can for the temperature it is at. **3** (of fat molecules) containing the greatest number of hydrogen atoms. **4** (of colour) full; rich; free from an admixture of white.

sat·ur·a·tion *noun* **1** the act or an instance of saturating. **2** the state of being saturated.

saturation bombing *noun* intensive aerial bombing.

saturation point *noun* the stage beyond which no more can be absorbed or accepted.

Sat·ur·day ● *noun* the seventh day of the week, following Friday. ● *adverb* **1** on Saturday. **2** (**Saturdays**) on Saturdays; each Saturday. [Old English *Sætern(es) dæg* translation of Latin *Saturni dies* day of Saturn]

Saturday night special *noun N Amer. informal* a cheap low-calibre pistol, easily obtained and concealed.

Sat·urn ▶ **1** *Rom. Myth* an ancient god identified with the Greek Cronus, often regarded as a god of agriculture. **2** *noun Astronomy* the sixth planet from the sun in the solar system, orbiting between Jupiter and Uranus at an average distance of 1 427 million km from the sun.

Saturna Island /sə'tɜːrnə/ the southeasternmost of the Gulf Islands in the Strait of Georgia, situated roughly midway between Vancouver Island and the BC mainland. [*Saturnina*, the name of a Spanish ship c.1791]

sat·ur·na·lia /,satər'neɪliə/ *noun* (*pl.* same or **sat·ur·na·lias**) **1** (usu. **Saturnalia**) *Rom. Hist.* the festival of Saturn in December, characterized by unrestrained merrymaking for all, the predecessor of Christmas. **2** (as *sing.* or *pl.*) a scene of wild revelry or tumult; an orgy. [Latin, neuter pl. of *Saturnalis* (as SATURN)]

Sat·urn·ian /sə'tɜːrniən/ *adjective* **1** of or relating to the planet Saturn. **2** = SATURNINE 1.

sat·urn·i·id /sə'tɜːrniɪd/ *noun* any large moth of the family Saturniidae of silk moths. [modern Latin]

sat·ur·nine /'satər,naɪn/ *adjective* **1** a sluggish gloomy temperament. **2** (of looks etc.) dark and brooding. [Old French *saturnin* from medieval Latin *Saturninus* 'of Saturn' (identified with lead by the alchemists and associated with slowness and gloom by the astrologers]

sat·ya·graha /sʌt'jɒɡrə,hə/ *noun Ind.* **1** *hist.* a policy of passive resistance to British rule advocated by Gandhi. **2** passive resistance as a policy. [Sanskrit from *satya* truth + *āgraha* obstinacy]

satyr /'satər, 'seɪtər/ *noun* **1** (in Greek mythology) one of a class of Greek woodland gods with a horse's ears and tail, or (in Roman representations) with a goat's ears, tail, legs, and budding horns. **2** a lustful or sensual man. **3** = SATYRID. □ **sa·tyr·ic** *adjective* [Old French *satyre* or Latin *satyrus* from Greek *saturos*]

satyr·ia·sis /,satɪ'raɪəsɪs/ *noun Med.* excessive sexual desire in men.

sa·tyrid /sə'tɪrɪd/ *noun* any butterfly of the family Satyridae, with distinctive eyelike markings on the wings.

sauce ● *noun* **1** any of various liquid or semi-liquid preparations eaten with food (*tomato sauce*; *chicken in a mushroom sauce*). **2** *N Amer.* stewed fruit, e.g. apples or cranberries, eaten as dessert or used as a garnish. **3** something adding piquancy or excitement. **4** *informal* impudence, impertinence, cheek. **5** esp. *N Amer. informal* alcohol. ● *transitive verb informal* be impudent to; cheek. □ **(what is) sauce for the goose (is sauce for the gander)** see GOOSE. □ **sauce·less** *adjective* [Old French ultimately from Latin *salsus* from *salere sals-* to salt, from *sal* salt]

sauce·boat *noun* = GRAVY BOAT.

sauced *adjective* **1** (of food) served with a sauce. **2** *N Amer. slang* drunk.

sauce·pan *noun* a usu. metal pot, usu. round and often with a lid and a long handle, used for cooking things over heat.

sau·cer *noun* **1** a shallow circular dish used for standing a teacup on. **2** any similar dish. **3** something shaped like a saucer (*a flying saucer*). [Middle English, = condiment dish, from Old French *saussier(e)* sauceboat, prob. from Late Latin *salsarium* (as SAUCE)]

saucer magnolia *noun* a hybrid magnolia with large saucer-shaped flowers.

sau·ci·er /'sɔːsieɪ/ *noun* a chef who prepares sauces. [French]

saucy *adjective* (**sau·ci·er**, **sau·ci·est**) **1** impudent, cheeky. **2** (of a person) perky. **3** *N Amer.* (of food) covered with sauce. **4** *Brit. informal* sexually suggestive. **5** (of clothing) dashing (*a saucy hat*). □ **sau·ci·ly** *adverb* **sau·ci·ness** *noun* [earlier sense 'savoury', from SAUCE]

Saud /saud/ **1** (full name Saud ibn Abdul-Aziz) (1902–69), king of Saudi Arabia 1953–64. The son of ibn-Saud, he was deposed in favour of his brother Faisal. **2** *see* IBN-SAUD.

Saudi /ˈsaudi, sɒdi/ ● *noun* (*pl.* **Saudis**) **1 a** a native or national of Saudi Arabia. **b** a person of Saudi descent. **2** a member of the dynasty founded by King Saud. ● *adjective* of or relating to Saudi Arabia or the Saudi dynasty. [IBN-SAUD]

Saudi Arabia a country in SW Asia occupying most of the Arabian peninsula; pop. (est. 2002) 23,513,330; capital, Riyadh. □ **Saudi Arabian** *adjective & noun*

sauer·braten /ˈsauər,brɒtən/ *noun* a roast of beef marinated in vinegar with peppercorns, onions, and other seasonings before cooking. [German, from *sauer* SOUR + *Braten* roast meat]

sauer·kraut /ˈsauər,kraut/ *noun* finely chopped pickled cabbage. [German from *sauer* SOUR + *Kraut* vegetable]

Sau·geen Shores /ˈsɒgiːn/ a town in SW Ontario, on Lake Huron just south of the Bruce Peninsula, including the former town of Port Elgin; pop. (2001) 11,388. [after the *Saugeen* River, from Ojibwa, = 'river mouth']

sau·ger /ˈsɒgɜr/ *noun* a N American fish of the perch family, *Stizoostedion canadense*, with a large mouth. [19th c.: origin unknown]

Sauk /sɒk/ (also **Sac** /sak/) (*pl.* same or **Sauks**) ● *noun* **1** a member of an Algonquian people inhabiting parts of the central US, formerly in Wisconsin, Illinois, and Iowa, now in Oklahoma and Kansas. **2** the language of this people. ● *adjective* of or relating to this people or their language. [Canadian French *Saki* from Ojibwa *osāki* (compare Sauk *asākiwa* person of the outlet)]

Saul ▶ **1** *Bible* the first king of Israel (11th c. BC). **2** (also **Saul of Tarsus**) the original name of St. Paul. **3 John Ral·ston** (b.1947), Canadian novelist and social critic. His novels include *The Birds of Prey* (1977) and *The Paradise Eater* (1988); his analyses of Western culture and politics include *Voltaire's Bastards* (1992), *The Doubter's Companion* (1994), and *Reflections of a Siamese Twin: Canada at the End of the Twentieth Century* (1998).

Saul·teaux /ˈsɔːtoː/ *noun* (also **Sal·teaux**) (*pl.* same) **1** a member of an Aboriginal people formerly living on the shore of Lake Superior north of Sault Ste. Marie, and now living esp. in Manitoba. **2** the Ojibwa dialect spoken by this people. [French, = 'people of the rapids' from *sault* 'rapids']

Sault Ste. Marie /ˌsuː seint məˈriː/ each of two river ports which face each other across the falls of the St. Mary's River, between Lakes Superior and Huron. The northern city and port is in north central Ontario; pop. (2001) 74,566. The southern port is in Michigan; pop. (2000) 16,542. A system of canals serves to bypass the falls on either side of the river. □ **Sault·ite** /ˈsuːait/ *noun* [French, = the falls of St. Mary, in honour of the Virgin MARY]

sauna /ˈsɒnə/ *noun* **1** a special room heated to a high temperature to clean and refresh the body. **2** a period spent in such a room. [Finnish]

Saun·ders, Sir Charles Ed·ward (1867–1937), Canadian civil servant and plant breeder. Working from Red Fife wheat, he eventually hybridized Marquis wheat, which matured ten days earlier than Red Fife. By 1920 ninety per cent of all wheat grown in western Canada and a large amount of that grown in the US was Marquis.

saun·ter ● *intransitive verb* walk or go slowly; amble, stroll. ● *noun* **1** a leisurely ramble. **2** a slow gait. □ **saun·ter·er** *noun* [Middle English, = muse: origin unknown]

saur·ian /ˈsɔriən/ *adjective* of or like a lizard. [modern Latin *Sauria* from Greek *saura* lizard]

saur·is·chian /sɔrˈiskiən, -ˈrɪʃiən/ ● *adjective* of or relating to the order Saurischia of dinosaurs with a pelvic structure like that of lizards. ● *noun* a dinosaur of this order. [modern Latin *Saurischia*, from Greek *sauros* 'lizard' + *iskhion* 'hip joint']

sauro·pod /ˈsɔrɔ,pɒd/ *noun* any of a group of plant-eating dinosaurs with a long neck and tail, and four thick limbs. [Greek *saura* lizard + *pous pod-* foot]

saury /ˈsɔri/ *noun* (*pl.* **-ies**) any of various elongated marine fishes of the family Scomberescocidae, having narrow beaklike jaws, esp. *Scomberesox saurus* of the N Atlantic and southern hemisphere or *Cololabis saira* of the N Pacific. [perhaps from Late Latin from Greek *sauros* horse mackerel]

saus·age *noun* **1 a** minced pork, beef, or other meat seasoned and often mixed with other ingredients, usu. encased in cylindrical form

in a skin. **b** a length of this. **2** a sausage-shaped object. □ **not a sausage** *Brit. informal* nothing at all. [Old Northern French *saussiche* from medieval Latin *salsicia* from Latin *salsus*: see SAUCE]

sausage meat *noun* minced pork used in sausages or as a stuffing etc.

sausage roll *noun* sausage meat enclosed in a pastry roll and baked.

Saus·sure /sɔːˈsʊr/ **Fer·di·nand de** (1857–1913), Swiss linguist. One of the founders of modern linguistics, he treated language as a structural system; his most influential work, *Cours de linguistique générale* (1916), was compiled from lecture notes and published posthumously. □ **Saus·sur·ean** *noun & adjective*

sauté /ˈsɒtei, -ˈtei, sɔː-/ ● *transitive verb* (**sau·téed**) fry (food) quickly in a little hot fat. ● *noun* food cooked in this way. ● *adjective* cooked in this way. [French, past participle of *sauter* jump]

Sau·ternes /sɔːˈtɜrn/ *noun* a sweet white wine from Sauternes in the Bordeaux region of France.

Sauvé /sɔːˈvei/ **Jeanne(-Mathilde)** (born Jeanne-Mathilde Benoît) (1922–93), Canadian journalist and politician, Governor General 1984–90. She was elected to the House of Commons 1972 and served as the first female French-Canadian Cabinet minister. The first female Speaker of the House of Commons (1980–83), she completely reformed the administration of the House. She was Canada's first female Governor General.

Sau·vi·gnon /ˈsɒviːnjɔ̃/ *noun* (also **Sauvignon Blanc**) **1** a variety of white grape used in winemaking. **2** a dry white wine made from these grapes. [French]

sav·age ● *adjective* **1** fierce; cruel (*savage persecution; a savage blow*). **2** wild (*a savage animal*). **3** *archaic offensive* uncivilized; primitive. **4** *informal* angry; bad-tempered (*in a savage mood*). **5** *archaic* (of scenery etc.) uncultivated (*a savage scene*). **6** *Heraldry* (of the human figure) naked. ● *noun* **1** *archaic offensive* a member of a primitive tribe. **2** a cruel or barbarous person. ● *transitive verb* **1** (esp. of a dog, wolf, etc.) attack and bite or maul etc. **2** (of a critic etc.) attack fiercely. □ **sav·age·ly** *adverb* **sav·age·ness** *noun* **sav·agery** *noun* (*pl.* **-ries**). [Old French *sauvage* wild, from Latin *silvaticus* from *silva* 'woods']

Savai'i /sɒˈvaiʔi/ (also **Savaii**) a mountainous volcanic island in the SW Pacific, in Western Samoa. It is the largest of the Samoan islands.

Sa·van·nah /səˈvanə/ a port in Georgia, on the Savannah River close to its outlet on the Atlantic; pop. (2000) 131,510.

sa·van·nah /səˈvanə/ *noun* (also **sa·van·na**) a grassy plain in tropical and subtropical regions, with few or no trees. [Spanish *zavana* perhaps of Carib origin]

savannah sparrow *noun* a small sparrow, *Passerculus sandwichensis*, of the family Emberizidae, common throughout most of N America, found esp. in moist grasslands such as hayfields and meadows.

sav·ant /saˈvɑ̃, -ˈvɑ̃t/ *noun* a learned person, esp. a distinguished scientist etc. [French, part. of *savoir* know (as SAPIENT)]

Sav·ard /səˈvɑr/ **Félix-Antoine** (1896–1982), Canadian Catholic priest, writer, and educator. He researched folklore and wrote plays, poetry, short stories, and non-fiction, his best-known work being the novel *Menaud, maître-draveur* (1937).

sa·vate /səˈvat/ *noun* a form of boxing in which feet and fists are used. [French, originally a kind of shoe: compare SABOT]

save¹ ● *verb* **1** *transitive* (often foll. by *from*) rescue, preserve, protect, or deliver from danger, harm, discredit, etc. (*saved your life; saved me from drowning*). **2** *transitive* (often foll. by *up*) keep for future use; reserve; refrain from spending or using (*saved up $450 for a new bike; trying to save fuel*). **3** *transitive* (often *reflexive*) **a** relieve (another person or oneself) from spending (money, time, trouble, etc.); prevent exposure to (annoyance etc.) (*saved myself $50; a word processor saves time*). **b** obviate the need or likelihood of (*soaking saves scrubbing*). **4** *transitive* preserve from damnation; convert (*saved her soul*). **5** *transitive & reflexive* husband or preserve (one's strength, health, etc.) (*saving herself for the last lap; save your energy*). **6** *intransitive* (often foll. by *up*) save money for future use. **7** *transitive & intransitive Computing* store (data) on a hard drive, disk, tape, etc. **8** *transitive* **a** avoid losing (a game, match, etc.). **b** prevent an opponent from scoring (a goal etc.). **c** stop (a ball etc.) from entering the goal. ● *noun* **1** *Hockey etc.* an act of preventing an opponent from scoring, esp. as performed by a goaltender. **2** *Baseball* **a** a statistical credit given to a relief pitcher for maintaining a team's winning lead. **b** the action of maintaining such a lead. □ **save one's breath** (**to cool one's porridge**) not waste time speaking to no effect. **saved by the bell** *see* BELL¹. **save the day** (or **situation**) find or provide a solution to difficulty or disaster. **save face** preserve esteem; avoid humiliation. **save it** *N Amer. slang* shut up. **save one's neck** (or **skin** or **ass** or **bacon**) avoid loss, injury, or death; escape from danger. **save the tide** get in or out (of port etc.) while it lasts. **save the trouble** avoid useless or pointless effort. □ **sav·able** adjective (also **save·able**). **saver** noun [Old French salver, sauver from Late Latin salvare from Latin salvus SAFE]

save² archaic or literary ● preposition except; but (all save him). ● conjunction (often foll. by for) unless; but; except (happy save for one want; is well save that she has a cold). [Old French sauf sauve from Latin salvo, salva, ablative sing. of salvus SAFE]

sav·eloy /'savə,lɔɪ/ noun Brit. a seasoned red pork sausage, dried and smoked, and sold ready to eat. [corruption of French cervelas, -at, from Italian cervellata (cervello brain)]

Sav·ery /'seɪvəri/ **Thom·as** (known as 'Captain Savery') (c.1650–1715), English engineer, who devised the first steam engine (1698).

savin /'savɪn/ noun (also **sav·ine**) a bushy juniper, Juniperus sabina, usu. spreading horizontally, and yielding oil formerly used in the treatment of amenorrhea. [Old English from Old French savine from Latin sabina (herba) Sabine (herb)]

sav·ing ● adjective (often in combination) making economical use of (labour-saving). ● noun **1** anything that is saved. **2** an economy (a saving in expenses). **3** (usu. in pl.) money saved. ● preposition **1** with the exception of; except (all saving that one). **2** without offence to (saving your presence).

saving clause noun Law a clause containing a stipulation of exemption etc.

saving grace noun a redeeming quality or characteristic.

savings account noun a bank account that pays interest and on which cheques may not usually be drawn.

savings and loan noun (in the US) a co-operative association which accepts savings at interest and lends money to savers for houses or other purchases. Abbr.: **S&L**.

savings bank noun a bank receiving small deposits at interest and returning the profits to the depositors.

savings bond noun = BOND noun 4.

saving voyage noun Cdn (Nfld) a moderately successful or profitable sealing or fishing trip.

sav·iour noun (also **sav·ior**) **1** a person who saves or delivers from danger, destruction, etc. (the saviour of the nation). **2** (**Saviour**) (prec. by the, our) Christ. [Old French sauveour from ecclesiastical Latin salvator -oris (translation of Greek sōtēr) from Late Latin salvare SAVE¹]

savoir faire /,savwar 'fer/ noun the ability to act suitably in any situation. [French, = know how to do]

Sav·ona·rola /,savənə'roːlə/ **Gi·ro·la·mo** (1452–98), Italian preacher and reformer. A Dominican monk and strict ascetic, he denounced immorality, vanity, and Church corruption in his sermons, and became virtual ruler of Florence (1494–5); in 1497 he was excommunicated, and later hanged and burned as a schismatic and heretic.

Sav·on·linna /'sɒvɒn,lɪnə/ a town in SE Finland; pop. (1999) 28,102. Founded in 1639, it became a lakeside resort of the Russian czars.

savor var. of SAVOUR.

savory¹ noun (pl. **-ies**) any herb of the genus Satureja, esp. summer savory, S. hortensis, and winter savory, S. montana, used esp. in cookery. [Middle English saverey, perhaps from Old English sætherie from Latin satureia]

savory² var. of SAVOURY.

sav·our (also **savor**) ● verb **1** transitive **a** appreciate and enjoy the taste of (food). **b** enjoy or appreciate (an experience etc.). **2** intransitive (foll. by of) **a** suggest by taste, smell, etc. (savours of mushrooms). **b** imply or suggest a specified quality (savours of impertinence). ● noun **1** a characteristic taste, flavour, etc. **2** a quality suggestive of or containing a small amount of another. □ **sav·our·less** adjective [Old French from Latin sapor -oris from sapere to taste]

sav·oury (also **savory**) ● adjective **1** having an appetizing taste or smell. **2** (of food) salty or piquant, not sweet (a savoury omelette). **3** pleasant; acceptable. ● noun (pl. **-ies**) Brit. a savoury dish served as an appetizer or at the end of dinner. □ **sav·our·i·ly** adverb **sav·our·i·ness** noun

Savoy¹ /sə'vɔɪ/ an area of SE France bordering on NW Italy, ruled by the counts of Savoy from the 11th c., and joined with Sardinia and Piedmont in 1720 to form the Kingdom of Sardinia. At the time of Italian unification (1860) Savoy was ceded to France.

Savoy² /'savɔɪ, sə'vɔɪ/ noun (also **Savoy cabbage**) a hardy variety of cabbage with wrinkled leaves. [SAVOY¹]

Savoy·ard /sə'vɔɪɑrd, ,savɔɪ'ɑrd/ ● noun a native of Savoy. ● adjective of or relating to Savoy or its people etc. [French from Savoie Savoy]

Savu Sea /'sɒvuː/ a part of the Indian Ocean which is encircled by the islands of Sumba, Flores, and Timor.

savvy slang ● noun knowingness; shrewdness; understanding. ● adjective (**sav·vi·er**, **sav·vi·est**) N Amer. knowing; shrewd. [originally black & Pidgin English after Spanish sabe usted you know]

saw¹ ● noun **1 a** a hand tool having a toothed blade used to cut esp. wood with a to-and-fro movement. **b** any of several mechanical power-driven devices with a toothed rotating disc or moving band, for cutting. **2** Zool. etc. a serrated organ or part. ● verb (past participle **sawn** or **sawed**) **1** transitive **a** cut (wood etc.) with a saw. **b** make (boards etc.) with a saw. **c** cut (a hole) in something with a saw. **2** intransitive use a saw. **3 a** intransitive move to and fro with a motion as of a saw or person sawing (sawing away on his violin). **b** transitive divide (the air etc.) with gesticulations. □ **saw logs** N Amer. slang snore. **saw off** Cdn compromise by trading concessions (they sawed off over wages and security and concluded the deal). See also SAW-OFF. **saw up** saw into pieces. □ **saw·like** adjective [Old English saga from Germanic]

saw² past of SEE¹.

saw³ noun a proverb; a maxim (that's just an old saw). [Old English sagu from Germanic, related to SAY: compare SAGA]

saw·bill noun a merganser.

saw blade noun the blade of a saw.

saw·bones noun slang a doctor or surgeon.

saw·buck noun N Amer. **1** a sawhorse. **2** slang a $10 bill. **3** (also **sawbuck saddle**) a packsaddle shaped like a sawhorse. [sense 2 with allusion to the X-shaped ends of a sawhorse]

Saw·chuk, Ter·rence Gor·don ('Terry') (1929–70), Canadian hockey player. He joined the NHL Detroit Red Wings in 1951, winning the Calder Trophy as best rookie. He moved to the Toronto Maple Leafs in 1965. During his 20 seasons in the NHL he had 103 shutouts, a league record.

saw·dust noun powdery particles of wood produced in sawing.

sawed-off adjective **1** (of a gun) having part of the barrel sawn off to make it easier to handle and give a wider field of fire (sawed-off shotgun). **2** informal (of a person) short.

saw·fish noun any large marine fish of the family Pristidae, with a toothed flat snout used as a weapon.

saw·fly noun (pl. **-flies**) any of various hymenopteran insects mainly of the superfamily Tenthredinoidea, members of which have a serrated ovipositor, lack a constriction between the thorax and abdomen, and include many kinds whose larvae are injurious to plants.

saw·grass noun esp. N Amer. a sedge of the genus Cladium, with sharp-edged leaves.

saw·horse noun a rack or frame supporting wood for sawing.

saw·log noun a felled tree trunk suitable for cutting up into timber.

saw·mill noun a factory in which wood is sawn mechanically into planks, boards, etc. □ **saw·mill·er** noun **saw·mill·ing** attributive adjective

sawn past participle of SAW¹.

sawn-off adjective esp. Brit. = SAWED-OFF.

saw-off noun Cdn **1** an arrangement between political rivals in which each agrees not to contest a seat etc. held by the other. **2** any compromise involving mutual concessions. **3** a tie, deadlock, stalemate, etc.

saw palmetto noun **1** a small palm, Serenoa repens, with fan-shaped leaves that have sharply toothed stalks, native to the southeastern US. **2** the fruit of this, used to treat symptoms of benign prostatic hyperplasia such as difficulty urinating.

saw pit noun a pit over which large logs are sawn by two loggers with one saw, one above the log, the other in the pit below.

saw·tooth adjective **1** (also **saw·toothed**) (esp. of a roof, wave, etc.) shaped like the teeth of a saw, esp. with one steep and one slanting side. **2** (of a waveform) showing a slow linear rise and rapid linear fall, or the reverse.

saw-whet owl noun a small brown N American owl of the genus Aegolius esp. A. acadicus, frequenting coniferous and deciduous woodlands. [from one of its calls, which sounds like a saw being sharpened]

saw·yer /'sɔɪər, 'sɔjər/ noun **1** a person who saws timber professionally. **2** any of various longhorn beetles esp. of the genus Monochamus, the larvae of which bore in the wood of conifers. [Middle English, earlier sawer, from SAW¹]

sax noun informal **1** a saxophone. **2** a saxophone player. □ **sax·ist** noun [abbreviation]

Vowels:　a cat　ɑ arm　e bed　ɜr her　ɜː deux　ə ago　ɪ sit　i cosy　iː feed　ɒ hot　ɔ pore　ɔː no　ʌ run　ʊ put

saxa·tile /'saksə,tail, -tɪl/ *adjective* living or growing on or among rocks. [French *saxatile* or Latin *saxatilis* from *saxum* rock]

Saxe-Coburg-Gotha /saks,koːbɜrg'goːtə, -'goːθə/ the name of the British royal house 1901–17. The name dates from the accession of Edward VII, whose father Prince Albert, consort of Queen Victoria, was a prince of the German duchy of Saxe-Coburg and Gotha; during the First World War, with anti-German feeling running high, George V changed the family name to Windsor.

sax·horn *noun* any of a series of different-sized brass wind instruments with valves and a funnel-shaped mouthpiece, used mainly in military and brass bands. [*Sax*, name of its Belgian inventors, + HORN]

saxi·frage /'saksɪfreidʒ, -frədʒ/ *noun* any plant of the genus *Saxifraga*, growing on rocky or stony ground and usu. bearing small white, yellow, or red flowers. [Old French *saxifrage* or Late Latin *saxifraga* (*herba*) from Latin *saxum* rock + *frangere* break]

sax·man *noun* (pl. **-men**) a saxophone player.

Sax·on ● *noun* **1** *hist.* **a** a member of a Germanic people originally of N Germany, of which a portion conquered and occupied parts of England in the 5th–6th c. **b** (usu. **Old Saxon**) the language of the Saxons. **2** = ANGLO-SAXON *noun.* **3** a native of modern Saxony in Germany. **●** *adjective* **1** *hist.* of or concerning the Saxons. **2** belonging to or originating from the Saxon language or Old English. **3** of or concerning modern Saxony or Saxons. **4** designating the form of Romanesque architecture preceding the Norman in England. □ **Saxon·ism** *noun* [Old French from Late Latin *Saxo -onis* from Greek *Saxones* (pl.) from West Germanic: compare Old English *Seaxan*, *Seaxe* (pl.)]

Sax·ony 1 a state of eastern Germany, on the upper reaches of the Elbe River; capital, Dresden. **2** a large region of Germany, including the modern states of Saxony, Saxony-Anhalt, and Lower Saxony.

sax·ony *noun* **1** a fine kind of wool. **2** cloth made from this. [SAXONY]

Saxony-Anhalt /,saksəni'anhalt/ a state of Germany, on the plains of the Elbe and the Saale rivers; capital, Magdeburg. It corresponds to the former duchy of Anhalt and the central part of the former kingdom of Saxony.

saxo·phone *noun* **1** a metal woodwind reed instrument in several sizes and registers, the most recognizable form of which has an upturned bell, used esp. in jazz and popular music. **2** a saxophone player. □ **saxo·phon·ist** *noun* [*Sax* (as SAXHORN) + -PHONE]

say ● *verb* (3rd sing. present **says**; past and past participle **said**) **1** *transitive* (often foll. by *that* + clause) **a** utter (specified words) in a speaking voice; remark (*said 'Hello!'; said that she was satisfied*). **b** put into words; express (*that was well said; cannot say what I feel*). **2** *transitive* (often foll. by *that* + clause) a state; promise or prophesy; maintain, allege (*says that there will be war; says he saw you do it*). **b** have specified wording; indicate (*says here that he was killed; the clock says ten to six*). **3** *transitive* (in passive; usu. foll. by *to* + infin.) be asserted or described (*is said to be 93 years old*). **4** *transitive* (foll. by *to* + infin.) *informal* tell a person to do something (*he said to bring the car*). **5** *transitive* convey (information) (*spoke for an hour but said little*). **6** *transitive* put forward as an argument or excuse (*much to be said in favour of it; what have you to say for yourself?*). **7 a** *transitive & intransitive* form and give an opinion or decision as to (*who did it I cannot say; do say which you prefer*). **b** *transitive* present as an opinion (*I say we wait a little longer*). **8** *transitive* select, assume, or take as an example or (a specified number etc.) as near enough (*shall we say this one?*). **9** *transitive* **a** speak the words of (prayers, Mass, a grace, etc.). **b** repeat (a lesson etc.); recite (*can't say his times tables*). **10** *transitive* convey (inner meaning or intention) (*what is the director saying in this film?*). **●** *interjection* esp. *US* an exclamation of surprise, to attract attention, etc. **●** *noun* **1 a** an opportunity for stating one's opinion etc. (*let him have his say*). **b** a stated opinion. **2** a share in a decision (*had no say in the matter*). **●** *adverb* selecting, assuming, or taking as an example or (a specified number etc.) as near enough (*paid, say, $20*). □ **have to say for oneself** have to say by way of conversation or in explanation of one's actions etc. **I** etc. **cannot** (or **could not**) **say** I etc. do not know. **I'll say** *informal* yes indeed. **I say!** *Brit.* an exclamation expressing surprise, drawing attention, etc. **it is said** the rumour is that. **not to say** and indeed; or possibly even (*his language was rude not to say offensive*). **say again?** please repeat. **say much** (or **something**) **for** indicate the high quality of. **say no** refuse or disagree. **says you!** *informal* I disagree. **say what?** *slang* an expression of astonishment. **say when** *informal* indicate when enough drink or food has been given. **say the word 1** indicate that you agree or give permission. **2** give the order etc. **say yes** agree. **that is to say 1** in other words, more explicitly. **2** or at least. **they say** it is rumoured. **to say nothing of** = NOT TO MENTION (see MENTION). **what do** (or **would**) **you say to?** would

you like? **when all is said and done** after all, in the long run. **you can say that again!** (or **you said it!**) *informal* I agree emphatically. **you don't say** *informal* an expression of amazement or disbelief. □ **say·able** *adjective* **say·er** *noun* [Old English *secgan* from Germanic]

Say·ers, Dor·othy Leigh (1893–1957), English novelist and dramatist, whose detective fiction features the amateur detective Lord Peter Wimsey; titles include *Murder Must Advertise* (1933) and *The Nine Tailors* (1934).

say·ing *noun* **1** the act or an instance of saying. **2** a maxim, proverb, adage, etc. □ **as the saying goes** (or **is**) an expression used in introducing a proverb, cliché, etc. **go without saying** be too well known or obvious to need mention. **there is no saying** it is impossible to know.

sayo·nara /saiə'nɑrə/ *interjection* goodbye. [Japanese, lit. 'if it be so']

say-so *noun* **1** the power of decision. **2** mere assertion (*cannot proceed merely on his say-so*).

say·yid /'seiid/ *noun* **1** a Muslim claiming descent from Muhammad through Husain, the prophet's elder grandson. **2** a title of respect in some Muslim countries. [Arabic, lit. 'lord, prince']

Sb *symbol Chem.* the element antimony. [Latin *stibium*]

SC *abbreviation* **1** South Carolina (also in official postal use). **2** *Cdn* STAR OF COURAGE. **3** *Cdn & Brit.* SPECIAL CONSTABLE.

Sc *symbol Chem.* the element scandium.

Sc. *abbreviation* science.

sc. *abbreviation* scilicet.

s.c. *abbreviation* small capitals.

scab ● *noun* **1** a dry rough crust formed over a cut, sore, etc. in healing. **2** (often *attributive*) *informal derogatory* a person who refuses to strike or join a trade union, or who tries to break a strike by working. **3** mange or a similar skin disease esp. in animals. **4** a fungous plant disease causing scablike roughness. **5** an unlikeable person. **●** *intransitive verb* (**scabbed**, **scab·bing**) **1** act as a scab. **2** (of a wound etc.) form a scab; heal over. □ **scabbed** *adjective* **scab·by** *adjective* (**scab·bi·er, scab·bi·est**). **scab·like** *adjective* [Old Norse *skabbr* (unrecorded), corresponding to Old English *sceabb*]

scab·bard /'skabərd/ *noun* **1** *hist.* a sheath for a sword, bayonet, etc. **2** esp. *US* a sheath for a revolver etc. [Middle English *sca(u)berc* etc. from Anglo-French prob. from Frankish]

sca·bies /'skeibiːz/ *noun* a contagious skin disease causing severe itching. [Latin from *scabere* scratch]

sca·bi·ous /'skeibiəs/ **●** *noun* any of various plants with pink, white or esp. blue pincushion-shaped flowers, esp. of the genus *Scabiosa* or *Knautia*. **●** *adjective* affected with mange or scabies; scabby. [medieval Latin *scabiosa* (*herba*) formerly regarded as a cure for skin disease: see SCABIES]

scab·rous /'skabrəs/ *adjective* **1** having a rough surface; bearing short stiff hairs, scales, etc. **2** (of a subject, situation, etc.) requiring tactful treatment; hard to handle with decency. **3 a** indecent, salacious; scandalous. **b** behaving licentiously. □ **scab·rous·ly** *adverb* **scab·rous·ness** *noun* [French *scabreux* or Late Latin *scabrosus* from Latin *scaber* rough]

scad *noun* any of numerous fish of the family Carangidae, usu. having an elongated body and very large spiky scales. [17th c.: origin unknown]

scads *plural noun* N Amer. *informal* large quantities. [19th c.: origin unknown]

scaf·fold /'skafoːld, -fəld/ **●** *noun* **1 a** *hist.* a raised wooden platform used for the execution of criminals. **b** any similar raised platform. **2** = SCAFFOLDING. **3** (prec. by *the*) death by execution. **●** *transitive verb* attach scaffolding to (a building). □ **scaf·fold·er** *noun* [Anglo-French from Old French (*e*)*schaffaut*, earlier *escadafaut*]

scaf·fold·ing *noun* **1** a temporary structure formed of poles, planks, etc., erected by workers and used by them while building or repairing a house etc. **2** materials used for this. **3** any supporting framework.

scag *var. of* SKAG.

sca·glio·la /ska'ljoːlə/ *noun* imitation stone or plaster mixed with glue. [Italian *scagliuola* diminutive of *scaglia* SCALE[1]]

scal·able *adjective* **1** capable of being scaled or climbed. **2** *Computing* able to be used or produced at different ranges of size, capability, etc. □ **scal·abil·ity** *noun*

scalar /'skeilər/ *Math. & Physics* **●** *adjective* (of a quantity) having only magnitude, not direction. **●** *noun* a scalar quantity (compare VECTOR). [Latin *scalaris* from *scala* ladder; see SCALE[3]]

scala·wag /ˈskaləˌwag/ *noun* (also **scal·la·wag**, **scal·ly·wag**) a scamp; a rascal. [19th-c. US slang: origin unknown]

scald¹ ● *transitive verb* **1** burn (the skin etc.) with hot liquid or steam. **2** heat (esp. milk) to near boiling point. **3** (usu. foll. by *out*) clean (a pan etc.) by rinsing with boiling water. **4 a** treat (poultry etc.) with boiling water to remove feathers etc. **b** treat (food) with boiling water in preparation for cooking etc. ● *noun* **1** a burn etc. caused by scalding. **2** a disease of fruit marked by browning etc., caused esp. by air pollution etc. [Old Northern French *escalder* from Late Latin *excaldare* (as EX-¹, Latin *calidus* 'hot')]

scald² *var. of* SKALD.

scald·ing *adjective* **1** extremely hot (*scalding cups of tea*). **2** producing an effect or sensation like that of scalding (*scalding tears*; *scalding truths*).

scale¹ ● *noun* **1** each of the small thin bony or horny overlapping plates protecting the skin of fish and reptiles. **2** something resembling a fish scale, esp.: **a** a pod or husk. **b** a flake of skin; a scab. **c** a rudimentary leaf, feather, or bract. **d** each of the structures covering the wings of butterflies and moths. **e** *Bot.* a layer of a bulb. **3 a** a flake formed on the surface of rusty iron. **b** a thick white deposit formed in a kettle, boiler, etc. by the action of heat on water. **4** plaque formed on teeth. **5 a** = SCALE INSECT. **b** the diseased condition of plants infested with scale insects. ● *verb* **1** *transitive* remove scale or scales from (fish, nuts, iron, etc.). **2** *transitive* remove plaque from (teeth) by scraping. **3** *intransitive* **a** (of skin, metal, etc.) form, come off in, or drop, scales. **b** (usu. foll. by *off*) (of scales) come off. □ **scales fall from a person's eyes** a person is no longer deceived (compare Acts 9:18). □ **scaled** *adjective* (also in *combination*). **scale·less** *adjective* **scaler** *noun* [Old French *escale* from Germanic, related to SCALE²]

scale² ● *noun* **1 a** (also in *pl.*) a weighing machine or device (*bathroom scale*). **b** each of the dishes or pans on a simple scale balance. **2** (**the Scales**) the zodiacal sign or constellation Libra. ● *transitive verb* (of something weighed) show (a specified weight) in the scales. □ **tip the scales 1** (usu. foll. by *at*) outweigh the opposite scale pan (at a specified weight); weigh (*tips the scale at 200 pounds*). **2** (of a motive, circumstance, etc.) be decisive. [Old Norse *skál* bowl, from Germanic]

scale³ ● *noun* **1** a series of degrees; a graded classification system (*pay fees according to a prescribed scale; high on the social scale; seven points on the Richter scale*). **2 a** (often *attributive*) Geog. & Archit. a relation between the actual size of something and a map, diagram, etc. which represents it (*on a scale of one centimetre to the kilometre; a scale model*). **b** relative dimensions or degree (*generosity on a grand scale*). **3 a** a set of marks on a line used in measuring, reducing, enlarging, etc. **b** a rule determining the distances between these. **c** a piece of metal, apparatus, etc. on which these are marked. **4** *Music* an arrangement of all the notes in any system of music in ascending or descending order (*chromatic scale; major scale*). **5** *Math.* the ratio between units in a numerical system (*decimal scale*). **6** (also **union scale**) the minimum pay rate for a particular job, as determined by a union contract. ● *verb* **1 a** *transitive & intransitive* climb (a wall, height, etc.). **b** *transitive* climb (the social scale, heights of ambition, etc.). **2** *transitive* represent in proportional dimensions; reduce to a common scale. **3** *intransitive* (of quantities etc.) have a common scale; be commensurable. **4** *transitive* Forestry **a** estimate the amount of (standing timber). **b** measure (a log) to estimate how much cut timber it will yield. □ **in scale** (of drawing etc.) in proportion to the surroundings etc. **play** (or **sing** etc.) **scales** *Music* perform the notes of a scale as an exercise for the fingers or voice. **scale back** reduce the scale, scope, or size of. **scale down** make smaller in proportion; reduce in size. **scale up** make larger in proportion; increase in size. **to scale** with a uniform reduction or enlargement. [(n.) Middle English (= ladder): (v.) Middle English from Old French *escaler* or medieval Latin *scalare* from Latin *scala* from *scandere* climb]

scale insect *noun* any of various insects which cling to plants and secrete a shield-like scale as covering.

scale leaf *noun* a modified leaf resembling a scale.

sca·lene /ˈskeiliːn, skeiˈliːn/ ● *adjective* **1** (of a triangle) having three unequal sides. **2** (of a cone or cylinder) with the axis not perpendicular to the base. ● *noun* a scalene triangle. [Late Latin *scalenus* from Greek *skalēnos* unequal, related to *skolios* bent]

scaler *noun* a person who scales timber or logs.

scal·la·wag *var. of* SCALAWAG.

scal·lion *noun* a shallot or green onion; any long-necked onion with a small bulb. [Anglo-French *scal(o)un* = Old French *escalo(i)gne*, ultimately from Latin *Ascalonia* (*caepa*) (onion) of *Ascalon* (see ASHQELON) in ancient Palestine]

scal·lop /ˈskaləp, ˈskɒləp/ ● *noun* **1** any of various bivalve molluscs of the family Pectinidae, used as food. **2** (in full **scallop shell**) **a** a single valve from the shell of a scallop, with grooves and ridges radiating from the middle of the hinge and edged with small rounded lobes. **b** *hist.* a representation of this shell worn as a pilgrim's badge. **3** (in *pl.*) an ornamental edging cut in material in imitation of the edge of a scallop shell. **4** a small pan or dish shaped like a scallop shell and used for baking or serving food. **5** = ESCALOPE. ● *transitive verb* (**scal·loped**, **scal·lop·ing**) **1 a** ornament (an edge or material) with scallops or scalloping. **b** cut or shape in the form of a scallop. **2** (esp. as **scal·loped** *adjective*) N Amer. bake (food, esp. potatoes) in a cream sauce, usu. with bread crumbs or cheese on top. **3** cook in a scallop. □ **scal·lop·ing** *noun* (in sense 3 of *noun*). [Old French *escalope*, prob. from Germanic]

scal·lop·er /ˈskaləpər, ˈskɒləpər/ *noun* (also **scallop dragger**) a boat for fishing for scallops.

scallop squash *noun* a squash shaped somewhat like a scallop. *Also* called PATTYPAN SQUASH.

scal·ly·wag *var. of* SCALAWAG.

scal·op·pine /ˌskaləˈpiːni/ *noun* (also **scal·lo·pini**) thin, boneless slices of meat, esp. veal, sautéed or fried. [Italian, plural of *scaloppina*, diminutive of *scaloppa* escalope]

scalp ● *noun* **1** the skin covering the top of the head, with the hair etc. attached. **2 a** *hist.* the scalp of an enemy cut or torn away as a trophy. **b** a trophy or symbol of triumph, conquest, etc. ● *transitive verb* **1** *hist.* take the scalp of (an enemy). **2** N Amer. *informal* resell (esp. tickets) at inflated prices. □ **scalp·er** *noun* (in sense 2 of *noun*). **scalp·less** *adjective* [Middle English, prob. of Scandinavian origin]

scal·pel /ˈskalpəl/ *noun* a surgeon's small sharp knife shaped for holding like a pen. [French *scalpel* or Latin *scalpellum* diminutive of *scalprum* chisel, from *scalpere* scratch]

scaly *adjective* (**scali·er**, **scali·est**) **1** covered in or having many scales or flakes. **2** of or like a deposit of scale. □ **scali·ness** *noun*

scam ● *noun* N Amer. *slang* a trick or swindle; a fraud. ● *transitive verb* (**scammed**, **scam·ming**) **1** swindle. **2** obtain in a manner not considered ethical or proper (*scammed four tickets to the game*). □ **scam·mer** *noun* **scam·ster** *noun* [20th c.: origin unknown]

scam artist *noun* a perpetrator of scams.

scamp¹ *noun* *informal* a rascal; a rogue. □ **scamp·ish** *adjective* [*scamp* rob on highway, prob. from Middle Dutch *schampen* decamp, from Old French *esc(h)amper* (as EX-¹, Latin *campus* field)]

scamp² *transitive verb* do (work etc.) in a perfunctory or inadequate way. [perhaps formed as SCAMP¹: compare SKIMP]

scam·per ● *intransitive verb* (usu. foll. by *about*, *through*) **1** run and skip impulsively or playfully. **2** move quickly, go hastily. ● *noun* the act or an instance of scampering. [prob. formed as SCAMP¹]

scam·pi /ˈskampi/ *plural noun* **1** large prawns. **2** (often treated as *sing.*) a dish of these, usu. fried. [Italian]

scan ● *verb* (**scanned**, **scan·ning**) **1** *transitive* look at intently or quickly (*scanned the horizon; rapidly scanned the speech for errors*). **2** *transitive* **a** cause (a particular region) to be traversed or swept by a radar etc. beam. **b** examine all parts of (a surface etc.) to detect radioactivity etc. **3** *transitive* **a** resolve (a picture) into its elements of light and shade in a pre-arranged pattern esp. for the purposes of television transmission. **b** (often foll. by *in*, *into*) use a beam or detector to convert (an image, text, etc.) into a sequence of signals for processing, transmission, etc. (*a book scanned into the computer*). **4** *transitive* **a** make a scan of (the body or part of it). **b** examine (a patient etc.) with a scanner. **5** *transitive* test the metre of (a line of verse etc.) by reading with the emphasis on its rhythm, or by examining the number of feet etc. **6** *intransitive* (of a verse etc.) be metrically correct; be capable of being recited etc. metrically (*this line doesn't scan*). ● *noun* **1** the act or an instance of scanning. **2** an image obtained by scanning or with a scanner. □ **scan·nable** *adjective* [Latin *scandere* climb: in Late Latin = scan verses (from the raising of one's foot in marking rhythm)]

scan·dal *noun* **1 a** a person, thing, event, or circumstance causing general public outrage or indignation. **b** the outrage etc. so caused, esp. as a subject of common talk. **c** malicious gossip or backbiting. **2** *Law* a public affront, esp. an irrelevant abusive statement in court. □ **scan·dal·ous** *adjective* **scan·dal·ous·ly** *adverb* **scan·dal·ous·ness** *noun* [Old French *scandale* from ecclesiastical Latin *scandalum* from Greek *skandalon* snare, stumbling block]

scan·dal·ize *transitive verb* (also esp. *Brit.* **-ise**) offend the moral feelings, sensibilities, etc. of; shock.

scandal·monger /ˈskandəlˌmɒŋgər, -ˌmʌŋgər/ *noun* a person who spreads malicious scandal.

scandal sheet *noun derogatory* a newspaper etc. giving prominence to esp. malicious gossip.

Scan·di·na·via 1 a large peninsula in NW Europe, occupied by Norway and Sweden. It is bounded by the Arctic Ocean in the north, the Atlantic in the west, and the Baltic Sea in the south and east. **2** a cultural region consisting of the countries of Norway, Sweden and Denmark, and sometimes also of Iceland, Finland, and the Faeroe Islands.

Scan·di·nav·ian ● *noun* **1 a** a native or inhabitant of Scandinavia. **b** a person of Scandinavian descent. **2** the family of languages of Scandinavia. **●** *adjective* of or relating to Scandinavia or its people or languages.

scan·dium *noun Chem.* a rare soft silver-white metallic element occurring naturally in lanthanide ores. Symbol: **Sc**; at. no.: 21. [modern Latin from *Scandia* Scandinavia (source of the minerals containing it)]

scan·nable *adjective* that can be scanned.

scan·ner *noun* **1** a device for scanning, systematically examining, reading, or monitoring something. **2** a device for converting text, an image, etc. into a sequence of signals for processing, transmission, etc. **3** a machine for measuring the intensity of radiation, ultrasound reflections, etc., from the body as a diagnostic aid. **4** a radio that can scan hundreds of frequencies.

scanning electron microscope *noun* an electron microscope in which the surface of a specimen is scanned by a beam of electrons which are reflected to form an image. Abbr.: **SEM**.

scan·sion *noun* **1** the metrical scanning of verse. **2** the way a verse etc. scans. [Latin *scansio* (Late Latin of metre) from *scandere scans-* climb]

scant *adjective* **1** barely sufficient; deficient (*with scant regard for the truth*; *scant of breath*). **2** barely amounting to, hardly reaching (a specified quantity) (*a scant 150 kilograms*). □ **scant·ly** *adverb* [Old Norse *skamt* neuter of *skammr* short]

scant·ling *noun* **1 a** a timber beam of small cross-section. **b** a size to which a stone or timber is to be cut. **2** a set of standard dimensions for parts of a structure, esp. in shipbuilding. **3** (usu. foll. by *of*) *archaic* **a** a specimen or sample. **b** one's necessary supply; a modicum or small amount. [alteration suggested by -LING¹ from obsolete *scantlon*, from Old French *escantillon* sample]

scanty *adjective* (**scant·i·er**, **scant·i·est**) **1** of small extent or amount. **2** barely sufficient. □ **scant·i·ly** *adverb* **scant·i·ness** *noun*

Scapa Flow /ˌskapə ˈfloː/ a strait in the Orkney Islands, Scotland. It was an important British naval base in the First World War.

scape *noun* a long flower stalk coming directly from the root. [Latin *scapus* from Greek *skapos*, related to SCEPTRE]

-scape *combining form* forming nouns denoting a view or a representation of a view (*moonscape*; *seascape*). [after LANDSCAPE]

scape·goat ● *noun* **1** a person bearing the blame for the sins, shortcomings, etc. of others, esp. as an expedient. **2** *Bible* a goat sent into the wilderness after the Jewish chief priest had symbolically laid the sins of the people upon it (Lev. 16). **●** *transitive verb* make a scapegoat of. □ **scape·goat·er** *noun* **scape·goat·ing** *noun* [*scape* (archaic, = escape) + GOAT, = the goat that escapes]

scape·grace *noun* a rascal; a scamp, esp. a young person or child. [*scape* (as SCAPEGOAT) + GRACE = one who escapes the grace of God]

scaph·oid /ˈskafɔɪd/ *adjective* & *noun Anat.* = NAVICULAR. [modern Latin *scaphoides* from Greek *skaphoeidēs* from *skaphos* boat]

scap·u·la /ˈskapjʊlə/ *noun* (*pl.* **scap·u·lae** /-ˌliː/ or **scap·u·las**) the shoulder blade. [Late Latin, sing. of Latin *scapulae*]

scapu·lar /ˈskapjʊlər/ **●** *adjective* of or relating to the shoulder or shoulder blade. **●** *noun* **1** *Christianity* **a** a monastic cloak consisting of a piece of cloth covering the shoulders and extending in front and behind almost to the feet. **b** two small rectangles of woollen cloth joined by tapes or strings passing over the shoulders, worn under one's clothing as a symbol of affiliation to a religious order or as a form of devotion. **2** a feather growing near the insertion of a bird's wing.

scar¹ ● *noun* **1** a usu. permanent mark on the skin left after the healing of a wound, burn, or sore. **2** the lasting effect of grief, suffering, etc. on a person's character or disposition. **3** a mark left by damage etc. (*the table bore many scars*). **4** a mark left on the stem etc. of a plant by the fall of a leaf etc. **●** *verb* (**scarred**, **scar·ring**) **1** *transitive* (esp. as **scarred** *adjective*) mark with a scar or scars (*was scarred for life*). **2** *intransitive* heal over; form a scar. **3** *transitive* form a scar on. □ **scar·less** *adjective* [Old French *escharre* from Late Latin *eschara* from Greek *eskhara* scab]

scar² *noun* a steep craggy outcrop of a mountain or cliff. [Old Norse *sker* low reef in the sea]

scar·ab /ˈskerəb, ˈska-/ *noun* **1 a** the sacred dung beetle of ancient Egypt. **b** = SCARABAEID. **2** an ancient Egyptian gem cut in the form of a beetle and engraved with symbols on its flat side, used as a signet etc. [Latin *scarabaeus* from Greek *skarabeios*]

scara·bae·id /ˌskerəˈbiːɪd/ *noun* any beetle of the family Scarabaeidae, typically having strong spiky forelegs for burrowing.

scara·bae·oid /ˌskerəˈbiːɔɪd/ *noun* a beetle of a large group, superfamily Scarabaeoidea, having plate-like terminal segments in the antennae, including the largest-known beetles, such as the stag beetle, cockchafer, dung beetle, etc.

Scar·ber·ia /skarˈbiːriə/ *noun Cdn* a nickname for Scarborough, Ontario. □ **Scar·ber·ian** *noun* [blend of SCARBOROUGH + SIBERIA]

Scar·bor·ough /ˈskarbərɔː, -bərə/ a former city in S Ontario, now part of the city of Toronto; pop. (2001) 593,297. [*Scarborough* in North Yorkshire, England]

scarce /skers/ **●** *adjective* **1** (usu. *predicative*) (esp. of food, money, etc.) insufficient for the demand; scanty. **2** hard to find; rare. **●** *adverb archaic* or *literary* scarcely. □ **make oneself scarce** *informal* keep out of the way; surreptitiously disappear. [Old French *eschars* from Latin *excerpere*: see EXCERPT]

scarce·ly /ˈskersli/ *adverb* **1** hardly; barely; only just (*I scarcely know him*). **2** surely not (*he can scarcely have said so*). **3** a mild or apologetic or ironical substitute for 'not' (*I scarcely expected to be insulted*).

scar·city /ˈskersɪti/ *noun* (*pl.* **-ties**) (often foll. by *of*) a lack or inadequacy.

scare ● *verb* **1** *transitive* frighten, esp. suddenly (*her expression scared us*). **2** *transitive* (usu. foll. by *away*, *off*, *up*, etc.) drive away by frightening. **3** *intransitive* become scared (*they don't scare easily*). **●** *noun* **1** a sudden attack of fright or worry (*gave me a scare*). **2** a general, esp. baseless, fear of war, invasion, epidemic, etc. (*a measles scare*). **3** (*attributive*) denoting an effort to influence others by highlighting or exaggerating a perceived threat (*scare tactics*; *a scare campaign*). **4** a financial panic causing share selling etc. □ **scare up** (or **out**) esp. *N Amer.* **1** frighten (game etc.) out of cover. **2** *informal* manage to find; discover (*see if we can scare up a meal*). □ **scarer** *noun* [Middle English *skerre* from Old Norse *skirra* frighten, from *skjarr* timid]

scare·crow *noun* **1** an object, esp. a human figure dressed in old clothes, set up in a field to scare birds away. **2** *informal* a badly dressed, grotesque-looking, or very thin person.

scared *adjective* (usu. foll. by *of*, or *to* + infin.) frightened; terrified (*scared of his own shadow*).

scaredy-cat *noun informal* a timid or easily frightened person.

scare·monger /ˈskerˌmɒŋɡər, -ˌmʌŋɡər/ *noun* a person who spreads frightening reports or rumours. □ **scare·monger·ing** *noun*

scarf¹ *noun* (*pl.* **scarves** or **scarfs**) **1** a square, triangular, or esp. oblong strip of material worn around the neck, over the shoulders, or tied around the head, for warmth or ornament. **2** *N Amer.* a cloth or other covering for a table, dresser, etc. □ **scarfed** *adjective* [prob. alteration of *scarp* (influenced by SCARF²) from Old Northern French *escarpe* = Old French *escherpe* sash]

scarf² ● *transitive verb* join the ends of (pieces of esp. timber, metal, or leather) by bevelling or notching them to fit and then bolting, brazing, or sewing them together. **●** *noun* a joint made by scarfing. [Middle English (earlier as noun), prob. via Old French from Old Norse]

scarf³ *transitive verb* (often foll. by *down*) *N Amer. informal* eat or drink greedily. [variant of SCOFF²]

scari·fier /ˈskerɪfaɪr, ˈska-/ *noun* **1** a machine for loosening soil, esp. in reforestation. **2 a** a spiked road-breaking machine. **b** a machine or implement for roughening up the iced surface of a road. **3** an implement for cutting and removing debris from the turf of a lawn. [SCARIFY¹]

scari·fy¹ /ˈskerɪfaɪ, ˈska-/ *transitive verb* (**-fies**, **-fied**) **1** make superficial incisions in. **2** loosen (esp. soil) with a scarifier. **3** nick or make an incision in (a hard seed) to facilitate its germination. **4** hurt by severe criticism etc. □ **scari·fi·ca·tion** *noun* [French *scarifier* from Late Latin *scarificare* from Latin *scarifare* from Greek *skariphaomai* from *skariphos* stylus]

scari·fy² /ˈskerɪfaɪ/ *transitive & intransitive verb* (**-fies**, **-fied**) *informal* scare; terrify. [blend of SCARE + TERRIFY]

scar·lat·ina /ˌskɑrləˈtiːnə/ *noun* = SCARLET FEVER. [modern Latin from Italian *scarlattina* (*febbre* fever) diminutive of *scarlatto* SCARLET]

Scar·latti /skɑrˈlati/ **1 (Giu·seppe) Domen·ico** (1685–1757), Italian composer. He wrote more than 550 sonatas for the harpsichord; his work made an important contribution to the development of the sonata form and did much to expand the range of the instrument. **2** his father, **(Pietro) Ales·san·dro (Gas·pare)** (1660–1725), Italian composer. A prolific composer of operas and choral music, he established the three-part form of the opera overture which was a precursor of the classical symphony.

scar·let ● *noun* **1** a brilliant red colour tinged with orange. **2** clothes or material of this colour (*dressed in scarlet*). ● *adjective* **1** of a scarlet colour. **2** sinful, immoral; promiscuous, unchaste. [Old French *escarlate*: ultimate origin unknown]

scarlet fever *noun* an infectious bacterial fever, affecting esp. children, with a scarlet rash.

scarlet oak *noun* an oak of eastern N America, *Quercus coccinea*, having bright red leaves in the fall and wood used for timber.

scarlet pimpernel *noun* a small annual wild plant, *Anagallis arvensis*, with small esp. scarlet flowers closing in rainy or cloudy weather.

scarlet runner *noun* see RUNNER 10.

scarlet tanager *noun* a tanager, *Piranga olivacea*, which breeds in eastern N America, the breeding male of which is bright red with black wings and tail.

scarlet woman *noun derogatory* a notoriously promiscuous woman.

scarp ● *noun* **1** the inner wall or slope of a ditch in a fortification. **2** a steep slope, esp. an escarpment. ● *transitive verb* **1** make (a slope) perpendicular or steep. **2** provide (a ditch) with a steep scarp and counterscarp. [Italian *scarpa*]

scar·per *intransitive verb* esp. *Brit. slang* run away; escape. [prob. from Italian *scappare* escape, influenced by rhyming slang *Scapa Flow* = go]

scar tissue *noun* fibrous and dense connective tissue on the skin or in the body formed by healing.

scarves *pl.* of SCARF[1].

scary *adjective* (**scari·er, scari·est**) scaring, frightening. □ **scari·ly** *adverb* **scari·ness** *noun*

scat[1] *informal* ● *intransitive verb* (**scat·ted, scat·ting**) depart quickly. ● *interjection* go! [perhaps abbreviation of SCATTER]

scat[2] ● *noun* (also **scat singing**) improvised jazz singing using sounds imitating instruments, instead of words. ● *intransitive verb* (**scat·ted, scat·ting**) sing scat. [prob. imitative]

scat[3] *noun* excrement; the droppings of an animal, esp. a carnivore. [Greek *skōr skatos* 'dung']

scat·back *noun* *Football* a fast-running backfield player, esp. a running back. [SCAT[1] + BACK *noun* 4]

scathe /skeɪð/ *transitive verb* **1** *literary* injure esp. by blasting, scorching, or withering. **2** (with *neg.*) do the least harm to (*shall not be scathed*) (*compare* UNSCATHED). [Old Norse *skatha* = Old English *sceathian*]

scath·ing /ˈskeɪðɪŋ/ *adjective* witheringly scornful; showing contempt; severe, harsh (*scathing sarcasm*). □ **scath·ing·ly** *adverb*

scat·ol·ogy /skəˈtɒlədʒi/ *noun* **1 a** a morbid interest in excrement. **b** a preoccupation with obscene literature, esp. that concerned with the excretory functions. **2** the medical or zoological study or analysis of excrement. □ **scato·logic·al** /ˌskatəˈlɒdʒɪkəl/ *adjective* [Greek *skōr skatos* dung + -LOGY]

scat·ter ● *verb* **1** *transitive* **a** throw here and there; strew (*scattered gravel on the road*). **b** cover by scattering (*scattered the road with gravel*). **2** *transitive & intransitive* **a** move or cause to move in flight etc.; disperse (*scattered to safety at the sound*). **b** disperse or cause (hopes, clouds, etc.) to disperse. **3** *transitive Physics* deflect or diffuse (light, particles, etc.). **4 a** *intransitive* (of esp. a shotgun) fire a charge of shot diffusely. **b** *transitive* fire (a charge) in this way. ● *noun* **1** the act or an instance of scattering. **2** an esp. small amount scattered. **3** the extent of distribution of esp. shot. □ **scat·ter·er** *noun* [Middle English, prob. var. of SHATTER]

scatter·brain *noun* a person given to silly or disorganized thought with lack of concentration. □ **scatter·brained** *adjective*

scatter cushion *noun* (also **scatter pillow**) = THROW CUSHION.

scat·tered *adjective* **1** not clustered together; wide apart; sporadic (*scattered villages*). **2** scatterbrained.

scatter·gun esp. *N Amer.* ● *noun* a shotgun. ● *adjective* = SCATTERSHOT.

scat·ter·ing *noun* **1** a quantity or amount scattered. **2** a small number or amount. **3** the process in which electromagnetic radiation or particles are deflected or diffused.

scatter plot *noun Statistics* (also called **scatter·gram, scatter graph**) a graph in which the values of two variables are plotted along two axes, the pattern of the resulting points revealing any correlation present.

scatter rug *noun* a small decorative rug designed to be placed with a casual effect and moved as required.

scatter·shot *adjective* esp. *N Amer.* random, haphazard; indiscriminate.

scatty *adjective* (**scat·ti·er, scat·ti·est**) *informal* scatterbrained; disorganized. □ **scat·ti·ly** *adverb* **scat·ti·ness** *noun* [abbreviation]

scaup *noun* either of two diving ducks of the genus *Aythya*, the males having a dark head and breast and a white-sided body, the greater scaup, *A. marila* of Canada and Eurasia, or the lesser scaup, *A. affinis* of N America. [*scaup* Scots var. of *scalp* mussel bed, which it frequents]

scav·enge ● *verb* **1** *transitive & intransitive* (usu. foll. by *for*) search for and collect (useful items) from among usu. discarded material. **2** *intransitive* (often foll. by *on*) (of an animal or bird) feed on (carrion) or search for food in (garbage etc.) (*scavenging back road dumps*). **3** *transitive* combine with or remove (free radicals, electrons, etc.). **4** *transitive* remove unwanted products from (an internal combustion engine cylinder etc.). ● *noun* the action or process of scavenging. □ **scav·en·ger** *noun* [back-formation from *scavenger*, Middle English *scavager* from Anglo-French *scawager* from *scawage* from Old Northern French *escauwer* inspect, from Flemish *scauwen*, related to SHOW: for *-n-* compare MESSENGER]

scavenger hunt *noun N Amer.* a game in which people try to collect certain miscellaneous objects, usu. outdoors over a wide area.

SCC *abbreviation* Supreme Court of Canada.

scena /ˈʃeɪnə/ *noun Music* **1** a scene or part of an opera. **2** an elaborate dramatic solo usu. including recitative. [Italian from Latin: see SCENE]

scen·ar·io /səˈnɛːriːoʊ, -ɑːrioʊ/ *noun* (*pl.* **-ios**) **1** an outline of the plot of a play, film, opera, etc., with details of the scenes, situations, etc. **2** a postulated sequence of future events; a hypothetical sequence of events. **3** *informal* a situation or scene. [Italian (as SCENA)]

scen·ar·ist /səˈnɛːrɪst/ *noun* a writer of film or television scenarios.

scend /send/ *Naut.* ● *noun* **1** the impulse given by a wave or waves. **2** a plunge of a vessel. ● *intransitive verb* (of a vessel) plunge or pitch owing to the impulse of a wave. [alteration of SEND or DESCEND]

scene *noun* **1** a place in which events in real life, drama, or fiction occur; the locality of an event etc. (*the scene was set in India*; *the scene of the disaster*). **2 a** an incident in real life, fiction, etc. (*distressing scenes occurred*). **b** a description or representation of an incident etc. (*scenes of clerical life*). **3** a public incident displaying emotion, temper, etc., esp. when embarrassing to others (*made a scene in the restaurant*). **4 a** a continuous portion of a theatrical production in a fixed setting and usu. without a change of performers; a subdivision of an act. **b** a similar section of a film, book, etc. **5 a** any of the pieces of scenery used in a play etc. **b** these collectively. **6** a landscape or a view (*a desolate scene*). **7** *informal* **a** an area of action or interest (*not my scene*). **b** a way of life; a milieu (*well-known on the jazz scene*). **8** *archaic* the stage of a theatre. □ **behind the scenes 1** *Theatre* among the actors, scenery, etc. offstage. **2** not known to the public; secret. **behind-the-scenes** (*attributive*) secret, using secret information (*a behind-the-scenes investigation*). **change of scene** a move to different surroundings esp. through travel. **come on the scene** arrive. **quit the scene** depart. **set the scene 1** describe the location of events. **2** give preliminary information. [Latin *scena* from Greek *skēnē* tent, stage]

scen·ery *noun* **1** the general appearance of the natural features of a landscape, esp. when picturesque. **2** *Theatre* the painted representations of landscape, rooms, etc., used as the background in a play etc. □ **change of scenery** = CHANGE OF SCENE (see SCENE). **chew the scenery** *N Amer. informal* (of an actor etc.) overact. [earlier *scenary* from Italian SCENARIO: assimilated to -ERY]

scene-stealer *noun* a person or thing which takes more than their fair share of attention.

scen·ster *noun slang* a person associated with or immersed in a specific cultural scene (*downtown scensters*).

scen·ic ● *adjective* **1 a** (esp. of natural scenery) picturesque; impressive or beautiful (*took the scenic route*). **b** of or concerning natural scenery (*flatness is the main scenic feature*). **2** (of a picture etc.) representing an incident. **3** *Theatre* of or on the stage (*the scenic art*). ● *noun* a scenic photograph, film, etc. □ **scen·ic·ally** *adverb*

scen·og·raphy /siːˈnɒɡrəfi/ *noun* **1** the painting or design of theatrical scenery. **2** *Art* the representation of objects in perspective. □ **sceno·graph·ic** *adjective* **scen·og·raph·er** *noun*

scent /sent/ ● *noun* **1** a distinctive, esp. pleasant, smell (*the scent of spring flowers*). **2 a** a scent trail left by an animal perceptible to hounds etc. **b** clues etc. that can be followed like a scent trail (*lost the scent in Niagara Falls*). **c** the power of detecting or distinguishing smells etc. or of discovering things (*some dogs have little scent*; *the scent for talent*). **3** esp.

Brit. = PERFUME 2. ● *transitive verb* **1 a** discern by scent (*the dog scented game*). **b** sense the presence of; detect (*scent treachery*). **2** make fragrant or foul-smelling. **3** apply the sense of smell to (*scented the air*). □ **on the scent** in possession of a useful clue in an investigation. **put** (or **throw**) **off the scent** deceive by false clues etc. □ **scent·less** *adjective* [Middle English *sent* via Old French *sentir* 'perceive, smell' from Latin *sentire*; the *-c-* (added in 17th c.) is unexplained]

scent·ed *adjective* having esp. a pleasant smell (*scented soap*).

scent gland *noun* (also **scent organ**) a gland in some animals secreting musk, civet, etc.

scent marking *noun* the deposition by a mammal of a secreted pheromone, esp. on prominent objects in the area. □ **scent mark** *noun & verb*

scent strip *noun* a folded paper strip saturated with perfume, usu. part of a magazine advertisement, which, when opened, releases the scent.

scep·tic etc. *var. of* SKEPTIC etc.

scep·tre /ˈsɛptər/ *noun* (*US* **scep·ter**) **1** a staff borne esp. at a coronation as a symbol of sovereignty. **2** royal or imperial authority. □ **scep·tred** *adjective* [Old French (*s*)*ceptre* from Latin *sceptrum* from Greek *skēptron* from *skēptō* lean on]

schaden·freude /ˈʃɑːdənˌfrɔɪdə/ *noun* the malicious enjoyment of another's misfortunes. [German from *Schaden* harm + *Freude* joy]

Schafer /ˈʃeɪfər/ **(Ray·mond) Mur·ray** (b.1933), Canadian composer, writer, and educator. Artist-in-residence at Memorial University (1963–64) and Simon Fraser University (1965–75), he earned an international reputation for his experiments in early music education. His compositions reveal a concern with alienation, political oppression, and the search for a Canadian identity.

sched·ule /ˈskɛdʒuəl, ˈskɛdʒuːl, ˈʃɛdjuːl, ˈʃɛdʒuːl/ ● *noun* **1 a** a list or plan of intended events, times, etc.; a timetable. **b** a plan of work (*not on my schedule for next week*). **2** any list, form, classification, or tabular statement, e.g. a list of rates or prices, a tabulated inventory, etc. **3** any of a number of forms (named 'A', 'B', etc.) attached to a tax return, which are completed if necessary to provide details of information summarized on the return. ● *transitive verb* **1** include in a schedule; arrange (an event etc.) for a certain time. **2** make a schedule of. □ **according to** (or **on**) **schedule** as planned; on time. **behind schedule** behind time. □ **sched·ul·er** *noun* **sched·ul·ing** *noun* [Old French *cedule* from Late Latin *schedula* 'slip of paper', diminutive of *scheda* from Greek *skhedē* 'papyrus leaf']

scheduled caste *noun* (in India) a caste officially regarded as socially disadvantaged.

scheduled flight *noun* (also **scheduled service**) a public flight, service, etc., according to a regular timetable.

Scheele /ˈʃiːlə/ **Carl Wil·helm** (1742–86), Swedish chemist, who discovered a forerunner of pasteurization and a number of substances, including oxygen (1773), chlorine, and glycerol.

scheel·ite /ˈʃiːlaɪt/ *noun* calcium tungstate in its mineral crystalline form, CaWO₄, an important ore of tungsten. [C.W. SCHEELE]

schef·flera /ˈʃɛflərə/ *noun* any of various tropical and subtropical plants of the genus *Schefflera*, esp. the umbrella tree, *S. actinophylla*, with glossy leaves, often grown as a houseplant. [modern Latin, from J.C. *Scheffler*, 18th-c. botanist of Danzig]

Sche·hera·zade /ʃəˌhɛrəˈzɑːd/ the female narrator of the *Arabian Nights*, who keeps her husband intrigued with new tales for 1001 nights, so that he spares her life.

Scheldt River /skɛlt, ʃɛlt/ a river of N Europe, flowing 432 km (270 miles) from N France through Belgium and the Netherlands to the North Sea.

Schel·ling /ˈʃɛlɪŋ/ **Frie·drich Wil·helm Jo·seph von** (1775–1854), German philosopher. He departed from the doctrine of Fichte, considering the universe rather than the ego as the element of reality and asserting that nature is a single living organism working towards self-consciousness; his works include *Ideas towards a Philosophy of Nature* (1797) and *System of Transcendental Idealism* (1800).

schema /ˈskiːmə/ *noun* (*pl.* **schem·ata** /-mətə/ or **schem·as**) **1** a synopsis, outline, or diagram. **2** a proposed arrangement. **3** *Logic* a syllogistic figure. **4** (in Kantian philosophy) a conception of what is common to all members of a class; a general type or essential form. [Greek *skhēma -atos* form, figure]

schem·at·ic /skiːˈmatɪk, skɪ-/ ● *adjective* **1** of or concerning a scheme or schema. **2** representing objects by symbols etc. ● *noun* a schematic diagram, esp. of an electronic circuit. □ **schem·at·ic·ally** *adverb*

schema·tism /ˈskiːməˌtɪzəm/ *noun* a schematic arrangement or presentation.

schema·tize /ˈskiːməˌtaɪz/ *transitive verb* (also esp. *Brit.* **-tise**) **1** put in a schematic form; arrange. **2** represent by a scheme or schema. □ **schema·tiz·a·tion** *noun*

scheme /skiːm/ ● *noun* **1 a** a systematic plan or arrangement for work, action, etc. **b** a proposed or operational systematic arrangement (*a colour scheme*). **2** an artful or deceitful plot. **3** a timetable, outline, syllabus, etc. ● *verb* **1** *intransitive* (often foll. by *for*, or *to* + infin.) plan esp. to secure or deceitfully; intrigue. **2** *transitive* plan to bring about, esp. artfully or deceitfully (*schemed their downfall*). □ **scheme of things** the way things are or are planned (*has little influence in the overall scheme of things*). □ **schem·er** *noun* [Latin *schema* from Greek (as SCHEMA)]

schem·ing /ˈskiːmɪŋ/ ● *adjective* artful, cunning, or deceitful. ● *noun* plots; intrigues.

sche·mozzle *var. of* SHEMOZZLE.

Scheng·en /ˈʃɛŋən/ *noun* **1** (in full **Schengen agreement**) an intergovernmental agreement on the relaxation of border controls between participating European countries, the first version of which was signed in Schengen, Luxembourg in June 1985 by France, West Germany, Belgium, the Netherlands, and Luxembourg, and ratified (in revised form) in 1995. **2** (*attributive*) of, relating to, or designating the Schengen agreement, the countries which signed or implemented it, or the area that these countries form.

scherz·ando /skɛrtˈsandoː/ *Music* ● *adverb & adjective* in a playful manner. ● *noun* (*pl.* **scherz·andos** or **scherz·andi**) a passage played in this way. [Italian, gerund of *scherzare* to jest (as SCHERZO)]

scherzo /ˈskɛrtsoː/ *noun* (*pl.* **-os**) *Music* a vigorous, light, or playful composition, usu. as a movement in a symphony, sonata, etc. [Italian, lit. 'jest']

Schia·pa·relli /ˌskjapəˈrɛli/ **1 Elsa** (1896–1973), Italian-born French fashion designer, who was noted for her innovative use of synthetic fabrics and bold colours; she later expanded her interests into ready-to-wear fashions, perfume, and cosmetics. **2 Gio·van·ni Vir·ginio** (1835–1910), Italian astronomer. He studied the nature of cometary tails, showed that many meteors are derived from comets and follow similar orbits, and observed Mars closely from 1877, identifying the southern polar ice cap and features which he termed 'seas', 'continents', and 'channels' (*canali*).

Schil·ler /ˈʃɪlər/ **(Jo·hann Chris·toph) Frie·drich von** (1759–1805), German dramatist, poet, historian, and critic. His works, often concerned with freedom and responsibility, whether political, personal, or moral, include the plays *Don Carlos* (1787), *Mary Stuart* (1800), and *William Tell* (1804). His 'Ode to Joy' (*c.*1787) was set to music by Beethoven in his Ninth Symphony.

schil·ling /ˈʃɪlɪŋ/ *noun* **1** the former chief monetary unit of Austria, now replaced by the euro. **2** a coin of this value. [German (as SHILLING)]

schip·perke /ˈskɪpərki, ˈʃɪp-, -kə/ *noun* a breed of small black tailless dog with a ruff of fur around its neck. [Dutch dial., = little boatman, from its use as a watchdog on barges]

schism /ˈskɪzəm/ *noun* **1 a** the division of a group into opposing sections or parties. **b** any of the sections so formed. **2 a** the separation of a Church into two Churches or the secession of a group owing to doctrinal, disciplinary, etc., differences. **b** the offence of causing or promoting such a separation. [ecclesiastical Latin *schisma* from Greek *skhisma -atos* cleft, from *skhizō* to split]

schis·mat·ic /skɪzˈmatɪk/ ● *adjective* **1** of, concerning, or inclining to, schism. **2** *Christianity* guilty of the offence of schism. ● *noun* **1** a holder of schismatic opinions. **2** a member of a schismatic faction or a seceded branch of a Church. □ **schis·mat·ic·al·ly** *adverb*

schist /ʃɪst/ *noun* a foliated metamorphic rock composed of layers of different minerals and splitting into thin irregular plates. □ **schis·tose** *adjective* **schis·tos·ity** /ʃɪˈstɒsɪti/ *noun* [French *schiste* from Latin *schistos* from Greek *skhistos* split (as SCHISM)]

schis·to·some /ˈʃɪstəˌsoːm/ *noun* = BILHARZIA 1. [Greek *skhistos* divided (as SCHISM) + *sōma* body]

schis·to·som·ia·sis /ˌʃɪstəsoːˈmaɪəsɪs/ *noun* = BILHARZIA 2.

schiz·an·thus /skɪtˈsanθəs/ *noun* any plant of the genus *Schizanthus*, with showy flowers in various colours, and finely-divided leaves. *Also called* BUTTERFLY FLOWER. [modern Latin from Greek *skhizō* to split + *anthos* flower]

schizo /ˈskɪtsoː/ *informal offensive* ● *adjective* schizophrenic. ● *noun* (*pl.* **schizos**) a schizophrenic. [abbreviation]

schizo·carp /ˈskɪtsəˌkɑːrp/ *noun Bot.* any of a group of dry fruits that split into single-seeded parts when ripe. [Greek *skhizō* to split + *karpos* fruit]

schiz·oid /ˈskɪtsɔɪd/ ● *adjective* **1** (of a person or personality etc.) tending to or resembling schizophrenia or a schizophrenic, but usu. without delusions. **2** having inconsistent or contradictory elements (*a schizoid musical arrangement*). ● *noun* a schizoid person.

schizo·phre·nia /skɪtsəˈfriːnɪə, -ˈfrɪnjə/ *noun* **1** a mental disease marked by a breakdown in the relation between thoughts, feelings, and actions, frequently accompanied by delusions and retreat from social life. **2** *informal* a mentality or approach characterized by inconsistent or contradictory elements (*political schizophrenia*). ¶ Some people feel that using *schizophrenia* and *schizophrenic* in reference to mere contradiction or inconsistency makes light of what is a serious disease. □ **schizo·phren·ic** /-ˈfrenɪk/ *adjective & noun* [modern Latin, from Greek *skhizō* 'to split' + *phrēn* 'mind']

schizo·type /ˈskɪtsətaɪp/ *noun* a personality type in which mild symptoms of schizophrenia are present. □ **schizo·typ·al** *adjective*

Schle·gel /ˈʃleɪɡəl/ **1 Aug·ust Wil·helm von** (1767–1845), German romanticist, critic, and philologist, who is chiefly known for his German translations of Shakespeare's plays. **2** his brother, **Frie·drich von** (1772–1829), German romanticist, philosopher and historian, who was an important influence on the German romantic movement, and is noted for his studies of the history of literature.

schle·miel /ʃləˈmiːl/ *noun* (also **shle·miel**) *N Amer. informal* an awkward or unlucky person. [Yiddish *shlumiel*]

schlep /ʃlep/ (also **schlepp, shlep**) *informal* ● *verb* (**schlepped, schlep·ping**) **1** *transitive* carry (esp. something burdensome); drag. **2** *intransitive* go or work tediously or effortfully. ● *noun* *N Amer.* **1** a tedious journey; a trek. **2** an inept or stupid person. □ **schlep·per** *noun* **schlep·py** *adjective* (**schlep·pi·er, schlep·pi·est**). [Yiddish *shlepn* from German *schleppen* 'drag']

Schles·wig /ˈʃlesvɪɡ/ a former Danish duchy, situated in the southern part of the Jutland peninsula. The southern part belongs to the German state of Schleswig-Holstein, while the northern part belongs to Denmark.

Schleswig-Holstein /ˌʃlesvɪɡˈhɔːlʃtaɪn/ a state of NW Germany, occupying the southern part of the Jutland peninsula; capital, Kiel. It comprises the former duchies of Schleswig and Holstein.

Schlick /ʃlɪk/ **Mor·itz** (1882–1936), German philosopher and physicist. Professor of inductive sciences at Vienna, in the late 1920s he formed the Vienna Circle, a group of young empiricist thinkers who laid the foundations of logical positivism. His major works include *General Theory of Knowledge* (1918).

Schlie·mann /ˈʃliːmɒn/ **Hein·rich** (1822–90), German archaeologist. A former businessman with an amateur interest in archaeology, he excavated a succession of nine cities on the site of ancient Troy (1871–90), and subsequently undertook significant excavations at Mycenae (1876).

schlier·en /ˈʃliːrən/ *noun* **1** a visually discernible area or stratum of different density in a transparent medium. **2** *Geol.* an irregular streak of mineral in igneous rock. [German, pl. of *Schliere* streak]

schlock /ʃlɒk/ *noun* (also **shlock**) esp. *N Amer. informal* **1** cheap, shoddy or defective goods. **2** junk (esp. applied to inferior art or entertainment). □ **schlocky** *adjective* (**schlock·i·er, schlock·i·est**). [Yiddish *shlak* an apoplectic stroke, *schlog* wretch, untidy person, apoplectic stroke]

schlock·ey /ˈʃlɒki/ *noun* *Cdn* a children's game played on a four-foot by eight-foot framed plywood sheet stationed between two players, in which each player, using a cut-off hockey stick, attempts to score by shooting a puck past a centre barrier and through a hole in the framing board at the opposing end. [punningly after HOCKEY + SCHLOCKY]

schlock·meist·er /ˈʃlɒkmaɪstər/ *noun* (also **shlock·meist·er**) a person who produces trashy films, music, etc.

schlong *noun* (also **shlong**) *slang* the penis. [Yiddish *shlang* from Middle High German *slange* (German *Schlange*) 'serpent']

schlub /ʃlʌb/ *noun* (also **shlub**) *N Amer. slang* a clumsy, stupid, or untidy person. [Yiddish, perhaps from Polish *żłób*, blockhead]

schlump /ʃlʌmp/ *noun* (also **shlump**) esp. *N Amer. slang* a slow or slovenly person; a slob, a fool. [apparently related to Yiddish *shlumperdik* 'dowdy' and German *Schlumpe* 'slattern']

schm- /ʃm/ *prefix* (also **shm-**) *N Amer. slang* used in the second element of a reduplication to express contemptuous dismissal (*fancy-schmancy; sensitive schmensitive!*). [common initial element in Yiddish words]

schmaltz /ʃmɒlts/ *noun* (also **shmaltz**) esp. *N Amer. informal*

1 sentimentality, esp. in music, drama, etc. **2** melted chicken fat. □ **schmaltzy** *adjective* (**schmaltz·i·er, schmaltz·i·est**). [Yiddish from German *Schmalz* dripping, lard]

schmatte *var. of* SHMATTE.

schmear /ʃmɪr, ʃəˈmɪr/ *noun* *N Amer. informal* (also **schmeer**) □ **the whole schmear** everything (possible or available); every aspect of the situation. [Yiddish *schmirn*, flatter, grease; compare German *shmieren*, smear]

Schmidt /ʃmɪt/ **Hel·mut (Hein·rich Wal·de·mar)** (b.1918), German politician and chancellor of the Federal Republic of Germany 1974–82.

schmo /ʃmoː/ *noun* *N Amer. slang* (also **shmoe**) (*pl.* **schmoes, schmos**) an ordinary, unremarkable person. [alteration of SCHMUCK¹]

schmooze /ʃmuːz/ (also **shmooze**) *informal* ● *verb* **1** *intransitive* talk, chat, esp. at a social function; network. **2** *transitive* talk to (a person, esp. an important or influential one) (*he's upstairs schmoozing the director*). ● *noun* conversation, esp. at a social function. □ **schmooze·fest** *noun* **schmooz·er** *noun* **schmoozy** *adjective* (**schmooz·i·er, schmooz·i·est**). [Yiddish *schmuesn* talk, converse, chat, *schmues* (noun) from Hebrew *shĕmū'ah* rumour]

schmuck¹ /ʃmʌk/ *noun* (also **shmuck**) esp. *N Amer. slang* an objectionable or contemptible person; idiot. □ **schmucky** *adjective* (**schmuck·i·er, schmuck·i·est**). [Yiddish *shmok* penis]

schmuck² /ʃmʌk/ *transitive verb* *Cdn slang* hit, flatten (*got schmucked on the road*). [origin unknown]

Schna·bel /ˈʃnɒbəl/ **Artur** (1882–1951), Austrian-born US pianist, who is known particularly for his interpretations of Beethoven and Schubert.

schnapps /ʃnaps, ʃnɒps/ *noun* any of various strong usu. colourless spirits made from grain, with added flavourings such as peppermint, peach, etc. [German, = dram of liquor, from Low German & Dutch *snaps* mouthful (as SNAP)]

schnau·zer /ˈʃnauzər, ˈʃnʌutsər/ *noun* a German breed of dog with a close wiry coat and heavy whiskers round the muzzle. [German from *Schnauze* muzzle, SNOUT]

schnit·zel /ˈʃnɪtzəl/ *noun* a thin cutlet, esp. of veal or pork, breaded and fried. [German, = slice]

Schnitz·ler /ˈʃnɪtslər/ **Ar·thur** (1862–1931), Austrian dramatist and novelist, whose works include *Anatol* (1893), a series of seven one-act plays, and the novel *None but the Brave* (1926).

schnook *noun* *N Amer. slang* a foolish or contemptible person. [perhaps from German *Schnucke* 'small sheep' or from Yiddish *shnuk* 'snout']

schnor·rer /ˈʃnɔrər/ *noun* (also **shnor·rer**) esp. *N Amer. slang* a beggar or scrounger; a layabout. [Yiddish from German *Schnurrer*]

schnozz /ʃnɒz/ *noun* (also **schnoz, schnoz·zle, schnozz·ola** /ʃnɒˈzoːlə/) *N Amer. slang* the nose. [Yiddish *shnoytz* from German *Schnauze* snout]

Schoen·berg /ˈʃənbɜrɡ/ **Ar·nold (Franz Wal·ter)** (1874–1951), Austrian-born US composer and music theorist. His major contribution to modernism is his development of the concepts of atonality and serialism; his works include *Three Piano Pieces* (1909) and the *Serenade* (1923) for seven instruments and bass voice. □ **Schoen·berg·ian** *adjective*

schol·ar /ˈskɒlər/ *noun* **1** a learned person, esp. in language, literature, etc.; an academic. **2** the holder of a scholarship (*Rhodes scholar*). **3 a** a person with specified academic ability (*is a poor scholar*). **b** a person who learns (*am a scholar of life*). **4** *archaic informal* a person able to read and write. **5** *archaic* a schoolboy or schoolgirl. □ **schol·ar·ly** *adjective* [Old English *scol(i)er* & Old French *escol(i)er* from Late Latin *scholaris* from Latin *schola* SCHOOL¹]

schol·ar·ship /ˈskɒlərʃɪp/ *noun* **1 a** academic achievement; learning of a high level. **b** the methods and standards characteristic of a good scholar (*shows great scholarship*). **2** payment from the funds of a school, university, government, etc., to maintain a student in full-time education, awarded on the basis of scholarly achievement.

scho·las·tic /skəˈlastɪk/ ● *adjective* **1** of or concerning universities, schools, education, teachers, etc. **2 a** academic. **b** pedantic; formal (*shows scholastic precision*). **3** *Philos.* of, resembling, or concerning scholasticism, esp. in dealing with logical subtleties. ● *noun* **1** an adherent of scholasticism. **2** *Catholicism* a member of any of several religious orders, who is between the novitiate and the priesthood. □ **scho·las·tic·ally** *adverb* [Latin *scholasticus* from Greek *skholastikos* 'studious', via *skholazō* 'be at leisure, devote one's leisure to study' from *skholē*: see SCHOOL¹]

scholastic aptitude test *noun* a standardized test of a student's

---

Consonants: b but   d dog   f few   g get   h her   j yes   k cat   l leg   m man   n no   p pen   r red   s sit

verbal and mathematical skills, used for admission to American colleges. Abbr.: **SAT**.

scho·las·ti·cism /skəˈlastəˌsɪzəm/ noun **1** the educational tradition of medieval universities, characterized esp. by a method of philosophical and theological speculation which aimed at a better understanding of Christianity by defining, systematizing, and reasoning. **2** narrow or unenlightened insistence on traditional doctrines and forms of exposition; pedantry.

Scholes /ʃoːlz/ **Myr·on Sam·uel** (b.1941), Canadian-born US economist, co-winner (with Robert C. Merton) of the 1997 Nobel Prize for economics for determining how to calculate the value of stock options.

scho·li·ast /ˈskoːliˌast/ noun hist. an ancient or medieval scholar, esp. a grammarian, who annotated ancient literary texts. □ **scho·li·as·tic** adjective [medieval Greek skholiastēs from skholiazō write scholia: see SCHOLIUM]

scho·li·um /ˈskoːliəm/ noun (pl. **scho·lia**) a marginal note or explanatory comment, esp. by an ancient grammarian on a classical text. [modern Latin from Greek skholion from skholē disputation: see SCHOOL¹]

school¹ ● noun **1 a** an institution for educating or giving instruction, esp. one for students under 19 years. **b** N Amer. a college or university. **c** an institution for teaching a particular subject (art school; dance school). **d** (attributive) associated with or for use in school (a school bag; school books). **2 a** the buildings used by such institutions. **b** the pupils, staff, etc. of a school. **c** the time during which teaching is done, or the teaching itself (no school today). **3** a department or faculty of a university concerned with a particular area of study (law school). **4** a structured program of studies (summer school). **5 a** the disciples, imitators, or followers of a philosopher, artist, etc. (the school of Epicurus). **b** a group of artists etc. whose works share distinctive characteristics. **c** a group of people sharing a cause, principle, method, etc. (school of thought). **6** informal instructive or disciplinary circumstances, occupation, etc. (the school of adversity). ● transitive verb **1** send to school; provide for the education of. **2** (often foll. by to) discipline; train; control. **3** (esp. as **schooled** adjective) (foll. by in) educate or train (schooled in humility). □ **at** (or **in**) **school** attending lessons etc. **go to school 1** begin one's education. **2** attend lessons. **leave school** finish one's education. **of the old school** according to former and esp. better tradition (a gentleman of the old school). **school of hard knocks** experience gained from adversity. [Old English scōl, scolu, ultimately via Latin schola 'school' from Greek skholē 'leisure, disputation, philosophy, lecture place', reinforced in Middle English by Old French escole]

school² ● noun (often foll. by of) a large number of fish, porpoises, whales, etc. swimming together. ● intransitive verb form schools. [Middle Low German, Middle Dutch schōle from West Germanic]

school age noun the age range in which children normally attend school (often attributive: school-age children). □ **school-aged** adjective

school board noun N Amer. **1** an elected board responsible for decisions and policy concerning the schools in a given area. **2** the administrative unit responsible for the schools in a given area. **3** the area under the jurisdiction of a school board.

school·boy noun a boy attending school.

school bus noun a bus used for the transportation of school students.

school·child noun (pl. **school·children**) a child attending school.

school commission noun Cdn (Que.) = SCHOOL BOARD 1.

school days noun the time of being at school, esp. in retrospect.

school district noun N Amer. **1** an administrative unit responsible for the schools in a given area. **2** the area under the jurisdiction of a school district.

school division noun Cdn (Man. & Sask.) **1** an administrative unit responsible for the schools in a given area. **2** the area under the jurisdiction of a school division.

school·er noun (usu. in combination) a person attending a school (high-schooler).

school·girl noun a girl attending school.

school·house noun a building used as a school, esp. a small one in a village or rural area.

school·ing noun **1** education, esp. at school. **2** training or discipline, esp. of an animal.

school inspector noun (in the UK and Canada) an official appointed to inspect and report on the efficiency, teaching standards, etc. of schools.

school leaver noun esp. Brit. a teenager who is about to leave or has just left school. □ **school-leaving** adjective

school·man noun (pl. **-men**) **1** hist. a teacher in a medieval European university. **2** Catholicism hist. a theologian seeking to deal with religious doctrines by the rules of Aristotelian logic.

school·marm noun **1** a female schoolteacher, esp. one who is prim and fussy. **2** N Amer. slang a tree which has forked to form two trunks. □ **school·marm·ish** adjective (in sense 1). **school·marm·ism** noun (in sense 1). [from SCHOOL¹ noun 1a + marm, a respelling of MA'AM]

school·master noun a male teacher in an esp. private school. □ **school·master·ing** noun **school·master·ly** adjective

school·mate noun a companion at school; a fellow student.

school·mis·tress noun a female teacher in an esp. private school.

school night noun an evening from Sunday to Thursday, preceding a day on which one has to attend school (not allowed to go to the movies on a school night).

school patrol noun a student who is appointed to help fellow students cross at a busy intersection or crosswalk on their way to and from school.

school·room noun a room where students are taught; a classroom.

school section noun Cdn (Ont.) esp. hist. a subdivision of a school district.

school·teacher noun a person who teaches in a school. □ **school teaching** noun

school unit noun Cdn (PEI) = SCHOOL DISTRICT.

school work noun educational exercises done during school hours and at home as homework.

school·yard noun a playing area beside a school.

school year noun = ACADEMIC YEAR.

schoon·er /ˈskuːnər/ noun **1** a fore-and-aft rigged ship with two or more masts, the foremast being smaller than the other masts. **2 a** esp. Brit. a measure or glass for esp. sherry. **b** N Amer. & Austral. a tall beer glass. **3** N Amer. hist. = PRAIRIE SCHOONER. [18th c.: origin uncertain]

Schop·en·hauer /ˈʃoːpənˌhauər, ˈʃɒp-/ **Ar·thur** (1788–1860), German philosopher. His pessimistic philosophy is based on studies of Kant, Plato, and the Hindu Vedas, and is embodied in his principal work The World as Will and Idea (1819); according to this, the will (self-consciousness in humans and the unconscious forces of nature) is the only reality, and the material world is an illusion created by the will. □ **Schop·en·hauer·ian** adjective

schot·tische /ʃɒˈtiːʃ/ noun **1** a kind of slow polka. **2** the music for this. [German der schottische Tanz the Scottish dance]

Schrey·er /ˈʃraiər/ **Ed·ward Rich·ard** (b.1935), Canadian politician, NDP premier of Manitoba 1969–77 and Governor General 1979–84. As premier he advocated bilingualism and a strong federal government. As Governor General he made that position more accessible to ordinary Canadians and took an active role in the patriation of the constitution; he was High Commissioner to Australia 1984–88.

Schrö·der /ˈʃroːdər/ **Ger·hard** (b.1944), German politician, Social Democratic chancellor of the Federal Republic of Germany since 1998. As Chancellor he has led a coalition with the Green Party, and supported German military participation in Kosovo and Afghanistan but opposed war on Iraq.

Schröd·inger /ˈʃroːdɪŋər/ **Erwin** (1887–1961), Austrian theoretical physicist. He founded the study of wave mechanics, deriving the equation whose roots define the energy levels of atoms, and shared the Nobel Prize for physics in 1933.

Schrödinger equation /ˈʃroːdɪŋər/ noun Physics a differential equation used in quantum mechanics for the wave function of a particle.

schtick var. of SHTICK.

schtum /ʃtʊm/ adjective (also **shtum**) Brit. informal silent, non-communicative (keep schtum about it). [Yiddish, from German stumm 'quiet']

Schu·bert /ˈʃuːbərt/ **Franz (Peter)** (1797–1828), Austrian Romantic composer. He is considered the foremost composer of German lieder with song cycles such as Die Schöne Müllerin (1823) and Winterreise (1827); among his other significant works are the 'Trout' piano quintet (1819), and ten symphonies including the Eighth in B Minor (the 'Unfinished', 1822) and the Ninth (the 'Great C Major', 1825). □ **Schu·bert·ian** adjective

Schulz /ʃʊlts/ **Charles** (1922–2000), US cartoonist. He created the 'Peanuts' comic strip (originally entitled 'Li'l Folks') featuring a range of characters including Charlie Brown and his dog Snoopy.

---

t top   v voice   w we   z zoo   ʃ she   ʒ vision   θ thin   ð this   ŋ ring   x loch   tʃ chip   dʒ jar   (see over for vowels)

Schu·mach·er /ˈʃuːmakɜr/ **Mi·chael** (b.1969), German race car driver. He won his sixth Formula One world championship in 2003 and holds the world record for number of Grand Prix wins.

Schu·mann /ˈʃuːmɒn/ **1 Clara (Jo·seph·ine)** (née Wieck) (1819–96) German pianist and composer. As Robert Schumann's wife, she was his foremost interpreter, and after his death championed Brahms. She composed numerous piano pieces. **2 Rob·ert (Alex·an·der)** (1810–56), German composer. A leading figure in Romanticism, he is particularly noted for his songs and piano music; he also wrote four symphonies and much chamber music.

schuss /ʃʊs/ ● *noun* a straight downhill run on skis. ● *intransitive verb* **1** make a schuss. **2** move rapidly downwards. [German, lit. 'shot']

schvitz *var. of* SHVITZ.

schwa /ʃwɒ/ *noun Phonetics* **1** the indistinct unstressed vowel sound as in *a* moment *ago*. **2** the symbol /ə/ representing this in the International Phonetic Alphabet. [German from Hebrew šᵉwā, apparently from šaw' emptiness]

Schwann /ʃwɒn, ˈʃvan/ **Theo·dor (Am·brose Hu·bert)** (1810–82), German physiologist. He showed that animals (as well as plants) are made up of individual cells, isolated the first animal enzyme, pepsin, recognized that fermentation is caused by processes in the yeast cells, and discovered the cells forming the myelin sheaths of nerve fibres (**Schwann cells**).

Schwarz·eneg·ger /ˈʃwɔrtsə,negɜr/ **Ar·nold** (b.1947), Austrian-born US actor. He won the bodybuilding title Mr Olympia seven times (1970–75; 1980) before retiring to concentrate on acting. After playing a number of action roles, for instance in *Conan The Barbarian* (1982) and *The Terminator* (1984), he diversified in films such as the comedy *Kindergarten Cop* (1990) and the spy thriller *True Lies* (1994). He was elected Republican Governor of California in 2003.

Schwarz·kopf /ˈʃwɔrtskɒpf/ **Nor·man** (known as 'Stormin' Norman') (b.1935), US general, who became internationally known as the overall commander of the US-led UN alliance against Iraq in the Gulf War (1990).

Schweit·zer /ˈʃwaitsɜr, ˈʃvai-/ **Al·bert** (1875–1965), Alsatian-born German medical missionary, theologian, and musician. In 1913 he qualified as a doctor and went as a missionary to Lambaréné in French Equatorial Africa (now Gabon), where he established a hospital and lived for most of the rest of his life, exemplifying his ethical principle of 'reverence for life'; he was awarded the Nobel Peace Prize in 1952.

sci·at·ic /saiˈatɪk/ *adjective* **1** of the hip. **2** of or affecting the sciatic nerve. [French *sciatique* from Late Latin *sciaticus* from Latin *ischiadicus* from Greek *iskhiadikos* subject to sciatica, from *iskhion* hip joint]

sci·at·ica /saiˈatɪkə/ *noun* neuralgia of the hip and thigh; a pain in the sciatic nerve.

sciatic nerve *noun* the largest nerve in the human body, running from the pelvis to the thigh.

SCID *abbreviation* SEVERE COMBINED IMMUNODEFICIENCY.

sci·ence *noun* **1** the intellectual and practical activity encompassing the systematic study of the structure and behaviour of the physical and natural world through observation and experiment (*see also* NATURAL SCIENCE). **2 a** systematic and formulated knowledge, esp. of a specified type or on a specified subject (*political science*). **b** the pursuit or principles of this. **3** an organized body of knowledge on a subject (*the science of philology*). **4** skilful technique (*has nothing cleaning down to a science*). **5** *archaic* knowledge of any kind. [Old French from Latin *scientia* from *scire* know]

science centre *noun* an institution which aims to inform and educate the non-specialist public about the principles of science and technology; a science museum.

science fair *noun N Amer.* an esp. competitive fair in which elementary school or high school students design and exhibit science projects.

science fiction *noun* fiction based on imagined future scientific or technological advances, major social or environmental changes, etc., frequently portraying space or time travel, life on other planets, etc.

science park *noun* an area devoted to scientific research or the development of science-based or technological industries.

sci·en·tif·ic *adjective* **1 a** (of an investigation etc.) according to rules laid down in exact science for performing observations and testing the soundness of conclusions. **b** systematic, accurate. **2** used in, engaged in, or relating to (esp. natural) science (*scientific discoveries; scientific terminology*). **3** constituted of scientists (*the scientific community*). □ **sci·en·tif·ic·ally** *adverb*

scientific method *noun* a method of procedure that has

characterized natural science since the 17th c., consisting of systematic observation, measurement, and experiment, and the formulation, testing, and modification of hypotheses.

sci·en·tism *noun* **1 a** a method or doctrine regarded as characteristic of scientists. **b** the use or practice of this. **2** often *derogatory* an excessive belief in or application of scientific method. □ **sci·en·tis·tic** *adjective*

sci·en·tist *noun* **1** a person with expert knowledge of a (usu. physical or natural) science. **2** a person using scientific methods.

Sci·en·tol·ogy *noun proprietary* a religious system whose adherents seek self-knowledge and spiritual fulfillment through graded courses of study and training. □ **Sci·en·tol·o·gist** *noun* [Latin *scientia* knowledge + -LOGY]

sci-fi /ˈsaifai, saiˈfai/ *noun* (often *attributive*) *informal* science fiction. [abbreviation: compare HI-FI]

scili·cet /ˈsɪlə,set/ *adverb* to wit; that is to say; namely (introducing a word to be supplied or an explanation of an ambiguity). [Middle English from Latin, = *scire licet* one is permitted to know]

scilla /ˈsɪlə/ *noun* any liliaceous plant of the genus *Scilla*, related to the bluebell, usu. bearing small blue star-shaped or bell-shaped flowers and having long glossy strap-like leaves. [Latin from Greek *skilla*]

Scilly Isles /ˈsɪli/ (also **Scil·lies**) a group of about 140 small islands (of which five are inhabited) off the southwestern tip of England; pop. (2001) 2,153; capital, Hugh Town (on St. Mary's). □ **Scil·lo·nian** /sɪˈloːniən/ *adjective & noun*

scim·itar /ˈsɪmɪtɜr/ *noun* an oriental curved sword usu. broadening towards the point. [French *cimeterre*, Italian *scimitarra*, etc., of unknown origin]

scin·tig·raphy /sɪnˈtɪgrəfi/ *noun* the use of a radioisotope and a scintillation counter to get an image or record of a bodily organ etc. [SCINTILLATION + -GRAPHY]

scin·til·la /sɪnˈtɪlə/ *noun* **1** a trace, a tiny amount. **2** a spark. [Latin]

scin·til·late /ˈsɪntɪ,leit/ *intransitive verb* **1** (esp. as **scin·til·lat·ing** *adjective*) talk cleverly or wittily; be brilliant. **2** sparkle; twinkle; emit sparks. **3** *Physics* fluoresce momentarily when struck by a charged particle etc. □ **scin·til·lant** *adjective* **scin·til·lat·ing·ly** *adverb* [Latin *scintillare* (as SCINTILLA)]

scin·til·la·tion /,sɪntɪˈleiʃən/ *noun* **1** the process or state of scintillating. **2** the twinkling of a star. **3** a flash produced in a material by an ionizing particle etc.

scintillation counter *noun* a device for detecting and recording scintillation.

scion /ˈsaiən/ *noun* **1** a shoot of a plant etc., esp. one cut for grafting or planting. **2** a descendant; a younger member of a (esp. distinguished) family. [Old French *cion, sion* shoot, twig, of unknown origin]

Scipio Aemil·i·an·us /,skɪpiːɔ iː,mɪliˈanəs, ,sɪp-/ (full name Publius Cornelius Scipio Aemilianus Africanus Minor) (c.185–129 BC), Roman general and politician. He achieved distinction in the third Punic War, and blockaded and destroyed Carthage in 146; following his return to Rome he initiated moves against the reforms introduced by his brother-in-law Tiberius Gracchus.

Scipio Af·ri·canus /,skɪpiːɔ ,afrɪˈkanəs, ,sɪp-/ (full name Publius Cornelius Scipio Africanus Major) (236–c.184 BC), Roman general and politician. He defeated the Carthaginians in Spain in 206 and Hannibal in Africa in 202, thus bringing the Second Punic War to an end; his son was the adoptive father of Scipio Aemilianus.

sci·rocco *var. of* SIROCCO.

scir·rhus /ˈsɪrəs, ˈskɪ-/ *noun* (*pl.* **scir·rhi** /-rai/) a carcinoma which is hard to the touch. □ **scir·rhous** *adjective* [modern Latin from Greek *skirros* from *skiros* hard]

scis·sile /ˈsɪsail/ *adjective* able to be cut or divided. [Latin *scissilis* from *scindere sciss-* cut]

scis·sion /ˈsɪʃən/ *noun* **1** the act or an instance of cutting; the state of being cut. **2** a division or split. [Old French *scission* or Late Latin *scissio* (as SCISSILE)]

scis·sor *verb* **1** *transitive* (usu. foll. by *off, up, into*, etc.) cut with or as with scissors. **2** *transitive* (usu. foll. by *out*) clip out (a newspaper cutting etc.). **3** *intransitive & transitive* move or cause to move like scissors.

scissor kick *noun Swimming* a movement, esp. in the side stroke, in which the legs are parted slowly and brought together forcefully. □ **scissor-kick** *intransitive verb*

scissor lift *noun* a surface raised or lowered by the closing or opening of crossed supports pivoted like the two halves of a pair of scissors.

scis·sors *plural noun* **1** (also **pair of scissors** *singular*) an instrument for cutting fabric, paper, hair, etc., having two pivoted blades with finger and thumb holes in the handles, operating by closing on the material to be cut. **2** (treated as *sing.*) **a** a method of high jump with a forward and backward movement of the legs. **b** a hold in wrestling in which the opponent's body or esp. head is gripped between the legs. [Middle English *sisoures* from Old French *cisoires* from Late Latin *cisoria* pl. of *cisorium* cutting instrument (as CHISEL): assoc. with Latin *scindere sciss-* cut]

sclera /ˈsklɪːrə/ *noun* the white of the eye; a white membrane coating the eyeball. □ **scler·al** *adjective* [modern Latin from fem. of Greek *sklēros* hard]

scler·en·chyma /sklɪˈrɛŋkɪmə/ *noun* the woody tissue found in a plant, formed from lignified cells and usu. providing support. [modern Latin from Greek *sklēros* hard + *egkhuma* infusion, after *parenchyma*]

scler·ite /ˈsklɪːraɪt, ˈsklɛr-/ *noun* Zool. a component section of an exoskeleton, esp. each of the plates forming the skeleton of an arthropod. [Greek *sklēros* 'hard']

sclero·derma /sklɪːrəˈdɜːmə, sklɛr-/ *noun* Med. a chronic hardening of the skin and connective tissue. [Greek *sklēros* 'hard' + *derma* 'skin']

sclero·phyll /ˈsklɪːrəfɪl, ˈsklɛr-/ *noun* any woody plant with leathery leaves retaining water. □ **scler·ophyl·lous** /-ˈrɒfɪləs/ *adjective* [Greek *sklēros* hard + *phullon* leaf]

sclero·pro·tein /ˌsklɪːrəʊˈprəʊtiːn, ˌsklɛrəʊ-/ *noun* Biochem. any insoluble structural protein. [Greek *sklēros* hard + PROTEIN]

scler·osed /ˈsklɪːrɒst, -ˌrɒzd/ *adjective* affected by sclerosis.

scler·o·sis /sklɪˈrəʊsɪs/ *noun* **1** an abnormal hardening of body tissue (*see also* ARTERIOSCLEROSIS, ATHEROSCLEROSIS, MULTIPLE SCLEROSIS). **2** Bot. the hardening of a cell wall with lignified matter. **3** rigidity; excessive resistance to change. □ **scler·os·ing** *adjective* [Greek *sklērōsis* from *sklēroō* harden]

sclero·ther·apy /ˌsklɪːrəˈθɛrəpi, ˌsklɛr-/ *noun* the treatment of varicose veins etc. by the injection of a hardening agent. [Greek *sklēros* hard + THERAPY]

scler·otic /sklɪˈrɒtɪk/ ● *adjective* **1** of or having sclerosis. **2** of or relating to the sclera. **3** rigid; unchanging. ● *noun* = SCLERA. [medieval Latin *sclerotica* (as SCLEROSIS)]

scler·ous /ˈsklɪːrəs, ˈsklɛr-/ *adjective* Physiol. hardened; bony. [Greek *sklēros* hard]

Sco·bie /ˈskəʊbi/ **Ste·phen** (b.1943), Scottish-born Canadian poet, critic, and professor. His poetry, mostly using open verse forms, contains a wide range of historical and literary allusions. His many collections include *The Birkin Tree* (1973) and *Ghosts: A Glossary of the Intertext* (1990).

scoff¹ ● *intransitive verb* (usu. foll. by *at*) speak derisively, esp. of serious subjects; mock; be scornful. ● *noun* **1** mocking words; a taunt. **2** an object of ridicule. □ **scoff·er** *noun* [perhaps from Scandinavian: compare early modern Danish *skuf, skof* jest, mockery]

scoff² *informal* ● *transitive & intransitive verb* eat greedily. ● *noun* **1** food; a meal. **2** Cdn (Maritimes & Nfld) a big meal, esp. of seafood, served in conjunction with a party. [the noun from Afrikaans *schoff* representing Dutch *schoft* quarter of a day (hence, a meal): the verb originally a variant of dialect *scaff*, associated with the noun]

scoff·law *noun* N Amer. informal a person who flouts the law, esp. a person not complying with various laws which are difficult to enforce effectively. [from SCOFF¹ *verb* + LAW *noun*]

scold ● *verb* **1** *transitive* rebuke or chide (esp. a child). **2** *intransitive* find fault noisily; complain; rail. ● *noun* a nagging or grumbling person, esp. a woman. □ **scold·ing** *noun* **scold·ing·ly** *adverb* [prob. from Old Norse *skáld* SKALD]

sco·lex /ˈskəʊlɛks/ *noun* (*pl.* **sco·le·ces** /-ˈliːsiːz/ or **sco·li·ces** /-ləˌsiːz/) the head of a larval or adult tapeworm. [modern Latin from Greek *skōlēx* worm]

scoli·o·sis /ˌskɒliˈəʊsɪs/ *noun* an abnormal lateral curvature of the spine. □ **scoli·otic** /-ˈɒtɪk/ *adjective* [modern Latin from Greek from *skolios* bent]

scom·broid /ˈskɒmbrɔɪd/ ● *noun* any marine fish of the family Scombridae, including mackerels, tunas, and bonitos, or of the superfamily Scombroidea. ● *adjective* of or relating to this family or superfamily. □ **scom·brid** *noun* [Latin from Greek *skombros*]

sconce¹ /skɒns/ *noun* **1** a semicircular or triangular lighting fixture attached to a wall. **2** a bracket to support a candle, attached to a wall. [Old French *esconse* lantern or medieval Latin *sconsa* from Latin *absconsa* fem. past participle of *abscondere* hide: see ABSCOND]

sconce² /skɒns/ *noun* a small fort or earthwork usu. defending a ford, pass, etc. [Dutch *schans* brushwood, from Middle High German *schanze*]

Scone /skuːn/ an ancient Scottish settlement, believed to be on the site of the capital of the Picts, where the kings of medieval Scotland were crowned. It lay near the modern villages of Old Scone and New Scone in Tayside to the north of Perth.

scone /skɒn, skəʊn/ *noun* a small quick bread often containing raisins or currants, usu. served with butter and jam. [originally Scots, perhaps from Middle Dutch *schoon(broot)*, Middle Low German *schon(brot)* fine (bread)]

scooch *intransitive verb* N Amer. informal move quickly. [orig. unknown]

S cookie *noun* N Amer. a plain Italian cookie baked in the shape of an S.

scoop ● *noun* **1** any of various objects resembling a spoon, esp.: **a** a short-handled deep shovel used for transferring grain, sugar, coal, etc. **b** a short-handled implement with a roughly rectangular bowl, used for measuring or transferring dry foodstuffs. **c** an instrument with a rounded bowl used for serving portions of ice cream, mashed potato, etc. **d** a large long-handled ladle used for transferring liquids. **e** the excavating part of a digging machine etc. **2** a quantity taken up by a scoop. **3** a movement of or resembling scooping. **4 a** a piece of news published by a newspaper etc. in advance of its rivals. **b** *informal* the latest information; news (*what's the scoop on why she quit?*). **5** a large profit made quickly or by anticipating one's competitors. **6** *Music* a singer's attack which slides on a lower note before reaching the correct note. **7** a scooped-out hollow etc. ● *transitive verb* **1** (usu. foll. by *out*) hollow out with or as if with a scoop. **2** (usu. foll. by *up*) **a** lift with a scoop. **b** pick up rapidly in the hands or arms. **3** forestall (a rival newspaper, reporter, etc.) with a scoop. **4** (usu. foll. by *up*) secure (something of monetary value) esp. suddenly. □ **scoop·able** *adjective* **scoop·er** *noun*. [Middle Dutch, Middle Low German *schōpe* bucket etc., related to SHAPE]

scoop neck *noun* a rounded low-cut neckline on a garment. □ **scoop-necked** *adjective*

scoot *informal* ● *verb* **1** *intransitive* move quickly. **2** *transitive* move or convey suddenly or swiftly. ● *noun* the act or an instance of scooting. [19th-c. US (earlier *scout*): origin unknown]

scoot·er *noun* **1** (in full **motor scooter**) a light motorcycle with a low seat and a curved metal shield protecting the driver's legs. **2** a motorized cart used by a disabled or elderly person. **3** a child's toy consisting of a footboard mounted on two wheels and a steering column with handles, propelled by resting one foot on the footboard and pushing the other against the ground. **4** Cdn a snowmobile.

scope¹ ● *noun* **1 a** the extent to which it is possible to range (*this is beyond the scope of our research*). **b** the sweep or reach of mental activity, observation, or outlook (*an intellect limited in its scope*). **c** space or freedom to act (*doesn't leave us much scope*). **2** Naut. the length of cable extended when a ship rides at anchor. **3** archaic a purpose, end, or intention. ● *transitive verb* (often foll. by *out*) *slang* investigate or assess (a person, situation, etc.); check out, examine. [Italian *scopo* 'aim' from Greek *skopos* 'target', from *skeptomai* 'look at']

scope² *noun* informal a telescope, microscope, or other device designated by a word ending in *-scope*. □ **scoped** *adjective* [abbreviation]

-scope *combining form* forming nouns denoting: **1** a device looked at or through (*kaleidoscope; telescope*). **2** an instrument for observing or showing (*gyroscope; oscilloscope*). □ **-scopic** *combining form*. [from or after modern Latin *-scopium* from Greek *skopeō* look at]

Scopes Trial a famous trial in Tennessee (July 10–21, 1925), in which a high school teacher, John Thomas Scopes (d.1970), was tried for teaching the Darwinian theory of evolution in defiance of a state law making illegal the teaching of any doctrine denying the Biblical account of creation.

sco·pola·mine /skəˈpɒləˌmiːn/ *noun* a poisonous alkaloid found in plants of the nightshade family, esp. of the genus *Scopolia*, and used to prevent vomiting in motion sickness and as a preoperative medication for examination of the eye. *Also called* HYOSCINE. [*Scopolia* genus name of the plants yielding it, from G. A. *Scopoli*, Italian naturalist d.1788 + AMINE]

scop·ula /ˈskɒpjʊlə/ *noun* (*pl.* **scop·ulae** /-ˌliː/) any of various small brushlike structures, esp. on the legs of spiders. [Late Latin, diminutive of Latin *scopa*, twig, broom]

-scopy /skəpi/ *combining form* indicating viewing or observation, usu. with an instrument ending in *-scope* (*microscopy*).

scor·bu·tic /skɔːˈbjuːtɪk/ *adjective* relating to, resembling, or affected with scurvy. [modern Latin *scorbuticus* from medieval Latin *scorbutus* scurvy, perhaps from Middle Low German *schorbūk* from *schoren* break + *būk* belly]

scorch ● *verb* **1** *transitive* **a** burn the surface of with flame or heat so as to discolour, parch, injure, or hurt. **b** affect with the sensation of burning. **2** *intransitive* become discoloured etc. with heat. **3** *intransitive informal* (of a motorist etc.) go at excessive speed. ● *noun* **1** a mark made by scorching. **2** a scorching effect. **3** *Bot.* a form of necrosis, esp. of fungal origin, marked by browning of leaf margins. [Middle English, perhaps related to *skorkle* in the same sense]

scorched earth policy *noun* a military strategy of burning or destroying an area's crops and other resources that would otherwise sustain an invading enemy force.

scorch·er *noun informal* **1** a very hot day. **2** *Sport* an extremely fast shot or hit. **3** a scathing or harsh rebuke, attack, glance, etc. **4** a thing, esp. a book or play, that is licentious or risqué.

scorch·ing *adjective* **1** *informal* very hot (*a scorching July day*). **2** (of criticism etc.) stringent; harsh. □ **scorch·ing·ly** *adverb*

score ● *noun* **1 a** the number of points, goals, runs, etc., made by a player, side, etc., in some games. **b** the total number of points etc. at the end of a game (*the score was 5–0*). **c** a number of marks gained on a test, examination, etc. (*a score of 120 on the IQ test*). **2** (*pl.* same or **scores**) twenty or a set of twenty. **3** (in *pl.*) a great many (*scores of people arrived*). **4 a** a reason or motive (*rejected on the score of absurdity*). **b** topic, subject (*no worries on that score*). **5** *Music* **a** a usu. printed copy of a composition showing all the vocal and instrumental parts arranged one below the other. **b** the music composed for a film or play, esp. for a musical. **6** *Dance* notation indicating the sequence of steps and movements to be performed. **7** *informal* **a** a piece of good fortune. **b** the act or an instance of scoring off another person. **8** *informal* the state of affairs; the present situation (*asked what the score was*). **9** a notch, line, etc. cut or scratched into a surface. **10** an amount due for payment. **11** *Naut.* a groove in a block or deadeye to hold a rope. **12** *slang* **a** the money or goods obtained by a successful crime. **b** the victim of a robbery or swindle. **13** *slang* the act or process of obtaining or consuming illegal drugs. ● *verb* **1** *transitive* **a** win or gain (a goal, run, points, success, etc.). **b** count for a score of (points in a game etc.) (*a bull's eye scores the most points*). **c** allot a score to (a competitor etc.). **d** make a record of (a point etc.). **2** *intransitive* **a** make a score in a game (*failed to score*). **b** keep the tally of points, runs, etc. in a game. **3** *transitive & intransitive* gain marks on a test or an examination. **4** *transitive* **a** mark with notches, incisions, lines, etc.; slash (*scored his name on the desk*). **b** cut shallow grooves across (meat) to prevent curling when heated. **c** make a shallow cut in (cardboard etc.) without cutting right through. **5 a** *transitive* secure (an advantage etc.) by luck, cunning, etc. (*scored a great apartment*). **b** *intransitive* succeed (*scored again with her latest hit single*). **6** *transitive Music* **a** orchestrate (a piece of music). **b** (usu. foll. by *for*) arrange for an instrument or instruments. **c** write the music for (a film, musical, etc.). **d** write out in a score. **7** *transitive* **a** (usu. foll. by *up*) mark (a total owed etc.) in a score (*see* sense 10 of *noun*). **b** (usu. foll. by *against, to*) enter (an item of debt to a customer). **8** *slang* **a** *transitive & intransitive* obtain (drugs) illegally. **b** *transitive & intransitive* steal (goods). **c** *intransitive* make a sexual conquest. **9** *transitive N Amer.* criticize (a person) severely. □ **keep score** register the score as it is made. **know the score** *informal* be aware of the essential facts. **on the score of** *Brit.* for the reason that; because of. **on that score** so far as that is concerned. **settle** (or **pay off**) a (or **the**) **score 1** requite an obligation. **2** avenge an injury. **score off** (or **score points off**) *Brit. & Cdn informal* humiliate, esp. verbally in repartee etc. **score points** outdo another person; make a more favourable impression. □ **score·less** *adjective* **scor·er** *noun* **scor·ing** *noun Music*. [the noun from Old English (sense 5 from the line or bar drawn through all staffs): the verb partly from Old Norse *skora* from *skor* 'notch, tally, twenty', from Germanic: related to SHEAR]

score·board *noun* a large board in an arena, stadium, etc., for publicly displaying the score in a game, contest, etc.

score·card *noun* (also **score·sheet**) a printed card on which esp. sports scores are recorded.

score·keep·er *noun N Amer.* an official who records the score at a game, contest, etc. □ **score·keep·ing** *noun*

scoria /ˈskɔːrɪə/ *noun* (*pl.* **scor·iae** /-rɪˌiː/) **1** cellular lava, or fragments of it. **2** the slag or dross of metals. □ **scori·aceous** /-ˈeɪʃəs/ *adjective* [Latin from Greek *skōria* refuse, from *skōr* dung]

scorn ● *noun* **1** disdain, contempt, derision. **2** an object of contempt etc. (*the scorn of all onlookers*). ● *transitive verb* **1** hold in contempt or disdain. **2** (often foll. by *to* + infin.) abstain from or refuse to do as unworthy (*scorns lying; scorns to lie*). □ **pour scorn on** express contempt or disdain for. □ **scorn·er** *noun* [Old French *esc(h)arn(ir)*, ultimately from Germanic: compare Old Saxon *skern* MOCKERY]

scorn·ful *adjective* (often foll. by *of*) full of scorn; contemptuous. □ **scorn·ful·ly** *adverb* **scorn·ful·ness** *noun*

Scor·pio *noun* (*pl.* **-pios**) **1** (usu. **Scor·pius** /-pɪəs/) a large constellation between Sagittarius and Libra, traditionally regarded as contained in the figure of a scorpion. **2 a** the eighth sign of the zodiac. **b** a person born when the sun is in this sign, usu. between 23 October and 21 November. □ **Scor·pian** *adjective & noun* [Latin (as SCORPION)]

scor·pi·oid /ˈskɔːrpɪˌɔɪd/ ● *adjective* **1** *Zool.* of, relating to, or resembling a scorpion; of the scorpion order. **2** *Bot.* (of an inflorescence) curled up at the end, and uncurling as the flowers develop. ● *noun* this type of inflorescence.

scor·pion /ˈskɔːrpɪən/ *noun* **1** an arachnid of the order Scorpionida, with lobster-like pincers and a jointed tail that can be bent over to inflict a poisoned sting on prey held in its pincers. **2** (in full **false scorpion**) a similar arachnid of the order Pseudoscorpionida, smaller and without a tail. **3** (**the Scorpion**) the zodiacal sign or constellation Scorpio. [Old French from Latin *scorpio -onis* from *scorpius* from Greek *skorpios*]

scorpion fish *noun* any of various marine fish of the family Scorpaenidae, many of which have venomous spines on the head and gills.

scorpion fly *noun* any insect of the order Mecoptera, esp. of the family Panorpidae, the males of which have a swollen abdomen curved upwards like a scorpion's sting.

Scor·sese /skɔːrˈseɪzi/ **Mar·tin** (b.1942), US film director, whose works are often concerned with the themes of brutality and conflict; his films include *Taxi Driver* (1976), *Raging Bull* (1980), *The Last Temptation of Christ* (1988), and *The Age of Innocence* (1993).

scor·zon·era /ˌskɔːrzəˈnɪːrə/ *noun* **1** a composite plant, *Scorzonera hispanica*, with long tapering purple-brown roots. **2** the root used as a vegetable. [Italian from *scorzone* venomous snake, ultimately from medieval Latin *curtio*]

Scot *noun* **1 a** a native of Scotland. **b** a person of Scottish descent. **2** *hist.* a member of a Gaelic people that migrated from Ireland to Scotland around the 6th c. [Old English *Scottas* (pl.) from Late Latin *Scottus*]

scot *noun hist.* a payment corresponding to a modern tax. [Old Norse *skot* & from Old French *escot*, of Germanic origin: compare SHOT[1]]

Scotch ● *adjective var.* of SCOTTISH or SCOTS. ● *noun var.* of SCOTTISH or SCOTS. ¶ The use of *Scotch* as an alternative to *Scottish* or *Scots* is generally regarded as offensive or old-fashioned by Scottish people. It should be avoided except to mean 'Scotch whisky' and in the special compounds (*Scotch broth* etc.) listed below. **2** Scotch whisky. [contraction of SCOTTISH]

scotch[1] ● *transitive verb* **1** put an end to; frustrate (*injury scotched his attempt*). **2** *archaic* **a** wound without killing; slightly disable. **b** make incisions in; score. ● *noun* **1** *archaic* a slash. **2** a line on the ground for hopscotch. [Middle English: origin unknown]

scotch[2] ● *noun* a wedge or block placed against a wheel etc. to prevent its slipping. ● *transitive verb* hold back (a wheel, barrel, etc.) with a scotch. [17th c.: perhaps = *scatch* stilt, from Old French *escache*]

Scotch bonnet *noun* a variety of small, round, red, hot pepper.

Scotch broom *noun* a leguminous plant, *Cytisus scoparius*, bearing bright yellow flowers and naturalized in N America.

Scotch broth *noun* a soup made from beef or mutton with pearl barley and vegetables etc.

Scotch egg *noun* a hard-boiled egg enclosed in sausage meat and fried.

Scotch·gard *noun proprietary* a chemical added to upholstery, a carpet, etc. to make it waterproof and resistant to stains. □ **Scotch·gard·ed** *adjective*

Scotch-Irish ● *adjective* of or pertaining to the 17th c. Scottish settlers of Ulster or their descendants. ● *noun* (treated as *pl.*) these people collectively.

Scotch·man *noun* (*pl.* **-men**) = SCOTSMAN. ¶ Like *Scotch* and *Scotchwoman*, *Scotchman* is old-fashioned and may be regarded as offensive by Scottish people. *Scot, Scotsman,* or *Scotswoman* should be used instead.

Scotch mist *noun* a thick drizzly mist.

Scotch pie *noun* a small, round meat pie with a filling of seasoned ground meat enclosed in pastry.

Scotch pine *noun* esp. *N Amer.* a pine tree, *Pinus sylvestris*, native to Eurasia and much planted for timber and other products.

Scotch snap *noun Music* a short note on the beat followed by a long one.

Consonants: b *but*   d *dog*   f *few*   g *get*   h *her*   j *yes*   k *cat*   l *leg*   m *man*   n *no*   p *pen*   r *red*   s *sit*

Scotch tape esp. *N Amer. proprietary* ● *noun* transparent adhesive tape. ● *transitive verb* (**Scotch-tape**) fasten with Scotch tape.

Scotch terrier *noun* = SCOTTISH TERRIER.

Scotch thistle *noun* any of various thistles of the genus *Cirsium* or *Onopordum*, esp. *O. acanthium*, naturalized in N America.

Scotch whisky *noun* whisky distilled in Scotland, esp. from malted barley.

Scotch·woman *noun* (*pl.* **-women**) a woman of Scotland or of Scottish descent. ¶ Like *Scotch* and *Scotchman*, *Scotchwoman* is old-fashioned and may be regarded as offensive by Scottish people. *Scot*, *Scotsman*, or *Scotswoman* should be used instead.

sco·ter /ˈskoːtər/ *noun* (*pl.* same or **scoters**) each of three northern diving ducks of the genus *Melanitta*, which breed in the Arctic and Subarctic and overwinter off coasts further south, esp. the surf scoter or the white-winged scoter. [17th c.: origin unknown]

scot-free *adverb* without being punished or harmed; safely. [SCOT]

sco·tia /ˈskoːʃə/ *noun* a concave moulding, esp. at the base of a column. [Latin from Greek *skotia* from *skotos* darkness, with reference to the shadow produced]

Scot·land a country forming the northernmost part of Great Britain and the UK; pop. (2001) 5,062,011; capital, Edinburgh.

Scotland Yard *noun* 1 the headquarters of the London Metropolitan Police. 2 its Criminal Investigation Department. [Great and New *Scotland Yard*, streets where it was successively situated until 1967]

scot·oma /skɒˈtoːmə/ *noun* (*pl.* **scot·o·mata** /-mətə/) a partial loss of vision or blind spot in an otherwise normal visual field. [Late Latin from Greek *skotōma* from *skotoō* darken, from *skotos* darkness]

Scots ● *adjective* 1 = SCOTTISH *adjective*. 2 in the dialect, accent, etc., of (esp. Lowlands) Scotland. ● *noun* 1 = SCOTTISH *noun*. 2 the form of English spoken in (esp. Lowlands) Scotland. [Middle English originally *Scottis*, northern var. of SCOTTISH]

Scots·man *noun* (*pl.* **-men**) 1 a native of Scotland. 2 a person of Scottish descent.

Scots·woman *noun* (*pl.* **-women**) 1 a Scottish woman. 2 a woman of Scottish descent.

Scott ▶ 1 **Bar·bara Ann** (b.1928), Canadian figure skater. The Canadian senior women's champion 1944–48, N American champion 1945–48, and world champion 1947–48, her competitive career culminated in an Olympic gold medal in 1948; she toured with a professional ice show 1949–54. 2 **Dun·can Camp·bell** (1862–1947), Canadian poet, writer, and civil servant. Joining the federal Department of Indian Affairs in 1879, he was deputy superintendent 1913–1932. A lifelong friend of Archibald Lampman, he published four collections of short stories and seven volumes of poetry as well as many essays. 3 **Fran·cis Reg·in·ald** 'F.R.' (1899–1985), Canadian poet and professor. With Frank Underhill, he founded the League for Social Reconstruction (1931–2); he also helped write the Regina Manifesto of the CCF. 4 **Rid·ley** (b.1939), English film director. He is one of modern cinema's foremost visual stylists, with films including *Alien* (1979), *Blade Runner* (1982), and *Thelma and Louise* (1991). 5 **Rob·ert Fal·con** (1868–1912), English explorer and naval officer. On the second of his two expeditions to the Antarctic (1900–4 and 1910–12) he and four companions journeyed to the South Pole by sled, arriving there in Jan. 1912 to discover that the Norwegian explorer Amundsen had beaten them to their goal by a month; Scott and his companions died on the journey back to base. 6 **Thom·as** (*c*.1842–70), Irish-born Canadian settler. After opposing Louis Riel, he was tried and executed by him; his death increased Ontario's opposition to the Metis. 7 **Sir Wal·ter** (1771–1832), Scottish novelist and poet. He established the form of the historical novel in Britain, and among his novels are *Waverley* (1814), *Rob Roy* (1817), *Ivanhoe* (1819), and *Kenilworth* (1821); his poetry includes the romantic narrative poems *The Lay of the Last Minstrel* (1805) and *The Lady of the Lake* (1810).

Scott, Cape the northwesternmost point of Vancouver Island. [D. *Scott*, Bombay financier of trade expeditions *c*.1786]

Scot·ti·cism *noun* a Scottish phrase, word, or idiom.

Scot·tie *noun informal* (also **Scottie dog**) a Scottish terrier.

Scot·tish ● *adjective* of or relating to Scotland or its inhabitants or their descendants. ● *noun* (*prec.* by *the*; treated as *pl.*) the people of Scotland or their descendants (*see also* SCOTS). □ **Scot·tish·ness** *noun*

Scottish Borders an administrative region of SE Scotland; administrative centre, Melrose.

Scottish terrier *noun* a breed of small terrier with a rough coat and short legs.

scoun·drel *noun* a person who shows no moral principles or

conscience. □ **scoun·drel·ism** *noun* **scoun·drel·ly** *adjective* [16th c.: origin unknown]

scour¹ /skaʊr/ ● *transitive verb* 1 a cleanse or brighten (esp. metal) by rubbing, esp. with soap, chemicals, or an abrasive substance. b (usu. foll. by *away*, *off*, etc.) clear (rust, stains, etc.) by rubbing. 2 (of water, or a person with water) clear out (a pipe, channel, etc.) by flushing through. 3 wear away, erode. ● *noun* 1 the act or an instance of scouring; the state of being scoured. 2 (also in *pl.*, treated as *sing.*) diarrhea in livestock. 3 a substance used for scouring. □ **scour·er** *noun* [Middle Dutch, Middle Low German *schüren* from Old French *escurer* from Late Latin *excurare* 'clean (off)', from *ex-* 'away' + *curare* 'to clean']

scour² /skaʊr/ *verb* 1 *transitive* hasten over (an area etc.) searching thoroughly (*scoured the streets for him; scoured the pages of the newspaper*). 2 *intransitive* range hastily esp. in search or pursuit. [Middle English: related to obsolete *scour* 'moving hastily', of unknown origin]

scourge /skɜːdʒ/ ● *noun* 1 a whip used for punishment, esp. of people. 2 a person or thing that causes trouble or suffering (*the scourge of acid rain; the scourge of cynical politicians*). ● *transitive verb* 1 whip. 2 punish; afflict; oppress. [Old French *escorge* (n.), *escorgier* (v.) (ultimately as EX-¹, Latin *corrigia* thong, whip)]

scouring pad *noun* a pad of abrasive material, e.g. steel wool, for cleaning kitchenware etc.

scouring powder *noun* an abrasive powder for cleaning surfaces.

scouring rush *noun* any of several horsetails having stems rough with silica, used for scouring and polishing.

Scouse /skaʊs/ *informal* ● *noun* 1 the dialect of Liverpool. 2 (also **Scous·er** /ˈskaʊsər/) a native of Liverpool. 3 (**scouse**) = LOBSCOUSE. ● *adjective* of or relating to Liverpool. [abbreviation of LOBSCOUSE]

scout¹ ● *noun* 1 a person, esp. a soldier, sent out to get information about the enemy's position, strength, etc. 2 a = TALENT SCOUT. b = ADVANCE SCOUT. c a person employed by a mining company to find new mining opportunities or report on the activities of competitors. 3 a car, ship, aircraft, etc. designed or sent out for reconnoitring. 4 (**Scout**) a boy (usu. aged 11–14) who is a member of a Scouting organization (*see also* GIRL SCOUT). 5 the act of seeking (esp. military) information (*on the scout*). ● *verb* 1 *intransitive* act as a scout. 2 *intransitive* (often foll. by *about*, *around*) make a search. 3 *transitive* (often foll. by *out*) *informal* explore to get information about (territory, an organization, etc.). 4 *transitive* a look for (new talent etc.). b discover or examine (a prospective recruit). □ **scout·er** *noun* **scout·ing** *noun* [Old French *escouter* listen, earlier *ascolter*, ultimately from Latin *auscultare*]

scout² *transitive verb* reject (an idea etc.) with scorn. [Scandinavian: compare Old Norse *skúta*, *skúti* taunt]

Scout·er *noun* an adult member of a Scouting organization.

Scout·ing *noun* an international movement, founded in England in 1908 by Robert Baden-Powell, intending to develop character and promote responsible behaviour in young people, usu. through outdoor activities.

scouting report *noun N Amer.* esp. *Sport* a list of characteristics or attributes of an opponent etc., as determined by the scrutiny of scouts.

scout·master *noun* a person in charge of a group of Scouts.

scout's honour *interjection* professing honesty or genuineness.

Sco·ville unit *noun* a measure of the relative pungency of a hot pepper, esp. of the quantity of capsaicin. [W.L. *Scoville*, US pharmacologist]

scow /skaʊ/ *noun* esp. *N Amer.* a flat-bottomed boat used as a barge, lighter, etc. [Dutch *schouw* ferry boat]

scowl ● *noun* a severe frown producing a sullen, bad-tempered, or threatening look on a person's face. ● *intransitive verb* make a scowl. □ **scowl·er** *noun* [Middle English, prob. from Scandinavian: compare Danish *skule* look down or sidelong]

scrab·ble ● *intransitive verb* 1 (often foll. by *around*, *about*, *at*) scratch or grope to find or collect or hold on to something. 2 scramble on hands and feet; stumble or struggle along. ● *noun* 1 an act of scrabbling. 2 (**Scrabble**) *proprietary* a game in which players use lettered tiles to form words on a special board. [Middle Dutch *schrabbelen* frequentative of *schrabben* SCRAPE]

scrag ● *noun* 1 (also **scrag end**) the inferior, lean end of a neck of mutton or lamb. 2 *informal* a skinny person or animal. 3 *informal* a person's neck. ● *transitive verb* (**scragged**, **scrag·ging**) *slang* 1 strangle, hang. 2 seize roughly by the neck. 3 handle roughly; beat up. [perhaps alteration of dial. *crag* neck, related to Middle Dutch *crāghe*, Middle Low German *krage*]

scrag·gly *adjective* sparse and irregular; ragged.

scraggy *adjective* (**scrag·gi·er, scrag·gi·est**) **1** thin and bony. **2** = SCRAGGLY. □ **scrag·gi·ly** *adverb* **scrag·gi·ness** *noun*

scram *intransitive verb* (**scrammed, scram·ming**) (esp. in *imperative*) *informal* go away. [20th c.: perhaps from SCRAMBLE]

scram·ble ● *verb* **1** *intransitive* make one's way over rough ground, rocks, etc., by clambering, crawling, etc. **2** *intransitive* (foll. by *for, at*) struggle with competitors (for a thing or share of it). **3** *intransitive* **a** move or act with difficulty or anxiously. **b** move hastily. **4** *transitive* **a** mix together indiscriminately. **b** jumble or muddle. **5** *transitive* cook (eggs) by breaking them into a pan, often with milk etc., and stirring the mixture over heat. **6** *transitive* make (a broadcast transmission, telephone conversation, etc.) unintelligible to those without a corresponding decoding device. **7** *transitive* *informal* execute (an action etc.) awkwardly and inefficiently. **8** *intransitive* (of fighter aircraft or their pilots) take off quickly in an emergency or for action. **9** *intransitive Football* (of a quarterback) move quickly to dodge or evade tacklers while waiting for an opportunity to throw the ball. **10** *transitive* distribute by scattering randomly to a crowd (*scrambling hockey cards in the schoolyard*). ● *noun* **1** an act of scrambling. **2** a difficult climb or walk. **3** (foll. by *for*) an eager or disorganized struggle or competition. **4** an emergency takeoff by fighter aircraft. [16th c. (imitative): compare dial. synonyms *scamble, cramble*]

scrambled eggs *plural noun* **1** a dish of eggs cooked by scrambling. **2** *informal* or *jocular* gold braid on a military officer's cap.

scram·bler *noun* **1** a person or thing that scrambles. **2** a device used to make television signals, telephone conversations, etc. unintelligible without a corresponding decoding device. **3** a motorcycle for racing on rough ground.

scram·jet *noun* a ramjet in which combustion takes place in a stream of gas moving at supersonic speed. [*s(upersonic)* + *c(ombustion)* RAMJET]

scran *noun Brit. slang* food, eatables. [18th c.: origin unknown]

scrap¹ ● *noun* **1** a fragment or remnant; a small detached piece. **2** rubbish or waste, usu. of some value for the material it contains. **3** an extract or cutting from something written or printed. **4** discarded metal for reprocessing (often *attributive*: *scrap metal*). **5** (with *neg.*) the smallest piece or amount (*not a scrap of food left*). **6** (in *pl.*) **a** odds and ends. **b** bits of uneaten food. ● *transitive verb* (**scrapped, scrap·ping**) **1** discard, esp. as useless. **2** get rid of; cancel. **3** make scrap of. [Old Norse *skrap*, related to *skrapa* SCRAPE]

scrap² *informal* ● *noun* a fight or rough quarrel, esp. a spontaneous one. ● *transitive verb* (**scrapped, scrap·ping**) (often foll. by *with*) have a scrap. [perhaps from SCRAPE]

scrap·book *noun* a book of blank pages for sticking cuttings, drawings, photographs, etc. in.

scrape ● *verb* **1** *transitive* **a** move a hard or sharp edge across (a surface), as to make something smooth or clean. **b** apply (a hard or sharp edge) in this way. **2** *transitive* (foll. by *away, off, up,* etc.) remove (a stain, projection, mass, etc.) by scraping. **3** *transitive* **a** rub (a surface) harshly against or with another. **b** scratch or damage by scraping. **4** *transitive* (often foll. by *out*) make (a hollow) by scraping. **5 a** *transitive* draw or move with a sound of, or resembling, scraping. **b** *intransitive* emit or produce such a sound. **6** *intransitive* (often foll. by *along, by, through,* etc.) move or pass along while almost touching close or surrounding features, obstacles, etc. (*the car scraped through the narrow lane*). **7** *transitive* just manage to achieve (a living etc.). **8** *intransitive* (often foll. by *by, through*) **a** barely manage. **b** pass (an examination etc.) with difficulty. **9** *transitive* (foll. by *together, up*) contrive to bring or provide; amass with difficulty. **10** *intransitive* be economical. **11** *intransitive* draw back a foot in making a bow (chiefly in **bow and scrape**, see BOW²). ● *noun* **1** the act or sound of scraping. **2** a scraped place (on the skin etc.). **3** a scrap; a fight or quarrel. **4** *informal* an awkward predicament, esp. resulting from an escapade. **5** *Cdn (Nfld)* a steep slope or bank worn bare esp. by landslide or the sliding of timber to the shore (esp. in place names). □ **scrape (the bottom of) the barrel** *informal* be obliged to use one's last resources. [Old Norse *skrapa* or Middle Dutch *schrapen*]

scrap·er *noun* a tool, device, or machine used for scraping, esp. for removing ice, paint, dirt, etc. from a surface.

scrap heap *noun* a collection of discarded or cancelled things.

scrap·ie /ˈskreɪpi/ *noun* a disease of sheep involving the central nervous system and characterized by lack of coordination and itching causing affected animals to rub against trees etc., and thought to be caused by a virus-like agent such as a prion.

scrap·ing *noun* **1** in senses of SCRAPE *verb & noun.* **2** (esp. in *pl.*) a fragment produced by this.

scrap paper *noun* loose pieces of paper, often partly used, for writing notes, rough drafts, etc. on.

scrap·per *noun* **1** a person who fights; a pugnacious person. **2** a competitive or tenacious person; one who puts up a strong resistance.

scrap·ple *noun US* scraps of pork etc. stewed with cornmeal and shaped into large cakes. [SCRAP¹ + -LE²]

scrap·py¹ *adjective* (**scrap·pi·er, scrap·pi·est**) **1** consisting of scraps. **2** incomplete; carelessly arranged or put together. □ **scrap·pi·ly** *adverb* **scrap·pi·ness** *noun*

scrap·py² *adjective* (**scrap·pi·er, scrap·pi·est**) pugnacious or tenacious. □ **scrap·pi·ly** *adverb* **scrap·pi·ness** *noun*

scrap·yard *noun* = JUNKYARD.

scratch ● *verb* **1** *transitive* score or mark the surface of with a sharp or pointed object. **2** *transitive* **a** make a long narrow superficial wound in (the skin). **b** cause (a person or part of the body) to be scratched (*scratched himself on the table*). **3** *transitive & intransitive* scrape (something) without marking, esp. with the hand to relieve itching (*stood there scratching*). **4** *transitive* make or form by scratching. **5** *transitive* scribble; write hurriedly or awkwardly (*scratched a quick reply; scratched a large A*). **6** *transitive* (often foll. by *together, up,* etc.) obtain or achieve (a thing, a living, etc.) by scratching or with difficulty. **7** *transitive* (often foll. by *out, off, through*) cancel or strike (out) with or as with a pencil etc. **8 a** *transitive* withdraw (a competitor, candidate, etc.) from a race or competition. **b** *intransitive* (of a competitor) withdraw from a race or competition. **9** *intransitive* (often foll. by *about, around,* etc.) **a** scratch the ground etc. in search. **b** look around haphazardly (*they were scratching around for evidence*). **10** *intransitive Billiards* make a stroke that incurs a penalty, e.g. hitting the cue ball into a pocket. **11** *intransitive* produce a rhythmic scratching sound by stopping a record by hand and moving it back and forth. ● *noun* **1** a mark or wound made by scratching. **2** a sound of scratching. **3** an act of scratching oneself. **4** *informal* a superficial wound. **5** a line from which competitors in a race (esp. those not receiving a handicap) start. **6** (in *pl.*) a disease of horses in which the pastern appears scratched. **7** *slang* money. **8** a technique, used esp. in rap music, of stopping a record by hand and moving it back and forth to make a scratching sound. **9** an athlete or competitor withdrawn from a competition etc. (*was a last-minute scratch*). **10** *Billiards* an act or instance of scratching. ● *attributive adjective* **1** collected by chance. **2 a** collected or made from whatever is available; heterogeneous (*a scratch crew*). **b** made from basic or rudimentary ingredients, not from prefabricated components (*scratch cake*). **3** with no handicap given (*a scratch race*). □ **from scratch 1** from the beginning. **2** (of food) prepared from the basic ingredients, without the use of prepared mixes etc. **3** without help or advantage. **scratch along** make a living etc. with difficulty. **scratch one's head** be perplexed. **scratch my back and I will scratch yours 1** do me a favour and I will return it. **2** used in reference to mutual aid or flattery. **scratch the surface 1** understand or deal with a matter only superficially. **2** investigate further (*scratch the surface and you'll find corruption*). **up to scratch** up to the required standard. □ **scratch·er** *noun* [Middle English, prob. from synonymous Middle English *scrat* and *cratch*, both of uncertain origin: compare Middle Low German *kratsen*, Old High German *krazzōn*]

scratch-and-dent sale *noun N Amer.* a sale of items that have been somewhat damaged.

scratch-and-sniff *noun* (*attributive*) designating a perfumed card etc. whose perfume is released when the card is scratched.

scratch-and-win *noun N Amer.* a lottery ticket coated with an opaque substance which is scratched away to reveal whether the ticket holder wins a prize (usu. *attributive*: *scratch-and-win tickets*).

scratch·board *noun* a white board with a blackened surface which can be scraped off to make white line drawings.

scratch card *noun* a card with a section or sections coated in an opaque waxy substance which may be scraped away to reveal a symbol indicating whether a prize has been won.

scratching post *noun* **1** a stake or post against which an animal rubs itself to relieve itching. **2** a stake or post which a cat stretches itself against and scratches with its claws.

scratch pad *noun* **1** esp. *N Amer.* a pad of paper for scribbling. **2** *Computing* a small fast memory for the temporary storage of data.

scratch·proof *adjective* that cannot be marred with scratches.

scratchy *adjective* (**scratch·i·er, scratch·i·est**) **1** tending to make scratches or a scratching noise. **2** (esp. of a garment) tending to cause itchiness (*a scratchy sweater*). **3** demanding relief by or as if by scratching; itchy (*I have a scratchy throat*). **4** (of a drawing etc.) done in scratches or carelessly. **5** (of a record) making a crackling or rough sound because of scratches on the surface. □ **scratch·i·ly** *adverb* **scratch·i·ness** *noun*

scrav·el /ˈskravəl/ *verb Cdn (Nfld)* **1** *intransitive* move quickly, scramble. **2** *transitive & intransitive* grab, claw or scratch (at). [perhaps alteration of SCRABBLE]

scrawb *var. of* SCROB.

scrawl ● *transitive & intransitive verb* write in a hurried untidy way. ● *noun* **1** a piece of hurried writing. **2** a scrawled note. **3** a careless, illegible style of handwriting. □ **scrawly** *adjective* [perhaps from obsolete *scrawl* sprawl, alteration of CRAWL]

scrawny *adjective* (**scrawn·i·er**, **scrawn·i·est**) lean, scraggy. □ **scrawn·i·ness** *noun* [var. of dial. *scranny*: compare archaic *scrannel* (of sound) weak, feeble]

scream ● *noun* **1** a loud high-pitched piercing cry expressing fear, pain, etc. **2** a similar sound, e.g. of sirens. **3** *informal* an irresistibly funny thing, person, event, etc. ● *verb* **1** *intransitive* emit a scream. **2** *transitive* speak or sing (words etc.) in a screaming tone. **3** *intransitive* make or move with a shrill sound like a scream. **4** *intransitive* laugh uncontrollably. **5** *intransitive N Amer. informal* move very quickly. **6** *intransitive* be blatantly obvious or conspicuous. [Old English or Middle Dutch]

scream·er *noun* **1** a person or thing that screams. **2** *informal* a person or thing that raises screams of laughter, excitement, fear, etc. **3** *N Amer. Sport* something moving very fast, esp. a powerful base hit, slapshot, etc. **4** any S American goose-like bird of the family Anhimidae, frequenting marshland and having a characteristic shrill cry. **5** esp. *US informal* a sensational headline. **6** *slang* a male homosexual who is extremely effeminate, flamboyant, etc.

scream·ing·ly *adverb* **1** extremely (*screamingly funny*). **2** blatantly (*screamingly obvious*).

scream·ing meem·ies *plural noun* (prec. by *the*) anxious hysteria (*a case of the screaming meemies*). [origin unknown]

scree *noun* (in *sing.* or *pl.*) **1** small loose stones. **2** a mountain slope covered with these. [prob. back-formation from *screes* (pl.), ultimately from Old Norse *skritha* landslide, related to *skrítha* glide]

screech[1] ● *noun* a harsh high-pitched scream etc. ● *transitive & intransitive verb* utter with or make a screech. □ **screech·er** *noun* **screechy** *adjective* (**screech·i·er**, **screech·i·est**). [16th-c. var. of Middle English *scritch* (imitative)]

screech[2] *noun* **1** (in Canada) a potent dark rum of Newfoundland. **2** any cheap liquor. □ **screech in** *Cdn (Nfld)* (usu. in *passive*) initiate (a visitor) by means of a screech-in. [ultimately from Scottish dialect *screigh* whisky]

screech-in *noun Cdn (Nfld)* a jocular ritual by which visitors to Newfoundland are 'initiated', involving the drinking of screech and performing acts such as dipping a foot in the ocean, kissing a cod, etc.

screech owl *noun* **1** any of various small N American eared owls of the genus *Otus*. **2** any owl that screeches instead of hooting, esp. a barn owl.

screed *noun* **1** a long usu. tiresome piece of writing or speech. **2 a** a strip of plaster or other material placed on a surface as a guide to thickness. **b** a levelled layer of material, e.g. cement, applied to a floor or other surface. [Middle English, prob. var. of SHRED]

screen ● *noun* **1** a fixed or movable upright partition for separating, concealing, or sheltering from light, wind, excessive heat, etc. **2 a** thing used as a shelter, esp. from observation. **3 a** a measure adopted for concealment. **b** the protection afforded by this (*under the screen of night*). **4 a** a blank usu. white or silver surface on which a photographic image is projected. **b** (prec. by *the*) the film industry. **5 a** the surface of a cathode ray tube or similar electronic device, esp. of a television, computer, etc., on which images appear. **b** the collection of images etc. displayed on a computer screen at one time (*move to the next screen*). **6 a** frame with fine wire netting to keep out flies, mosquitoes, etc. **7** *Physics* a body intercepting light, heat, electric or magnetic induction, etc., in a physical apparatus. **8** *Photog.* a piece of ground glass in a camera for focusing. **9** a large sieve or riddle, esp. for sorting grain, coal, etc., into sizes. **10** a system of checking for the presence or absence of a disease, ability, attribute, etc. **11** *Printing* a transparent finely ruled plate or film used in halftone reproduction. **12** *Military* a body of troops, ships, etc., detached to warn of the presence of an enemy force. ● *transitive verb* **1** (often foll. by *from*) **a** afford shelter to; hide partly or completely. **b** protect from detection, censure, etc. **2** (foll. by *off*) shut off or hide behind a screen. **3** *Hockey* obstruct the vision of (a goalie) by being positioned in front of him or her. **4 a** show (a film etc.) on a screen. **b** broadcast (a television program). **5** prevent from causing, or protect from, electrical interference. **6 a** test (a

person or group) for the presence or absence of a disease. **b** check on (a person) for the presence or absence of a quality, esp. reliability, suitability, etc. **c** find out details about (an incoming telephone call) to determine whether it should be answered. **d** check (a person, luggage, etc.) for possible security risks before boarding an aircraft etc. **7** pass (grain, coal, etc.) through a screen. □ **screen·able** *adjective*

screen·er *noun* [Old Northern French *escren*, *escran*: compare Old High German *skrank* barrier]

screen door *noun N Amer.* a light outer door of a house etc., with a screen for keeping out insects while allowing ventilation.

screened *adjective* (also **screened-in**) (of a porch etc.) having the window openings covered with screens.

screened shot *noun* (also **screen shot**) *Hockey* a shot taken while the goalie's vision is obstructed.

screen·ing *noun* **1** the showing of a film (also *attributive*: *screening room*). **2** the testing of a group of people for a disease etc. **3** material used for making mesh screens. **4** (in *pl.*) refuse separated by sifting.

screen·play *noun* the script of a film, with acting instructions, scene directions, etc.

screen printing *noun* a process like stencilling with ink forced through a prepared sheet of fine material (originally silk). □ **screen print** *noun* **screen-print** *transitive verb* (usu. as **screen-printed** *adjective*).

screen saver *noun Computing* a program which, after a set time, replaces an unchanging screen display with a moving image to prevent damage to the phosphor.

screen·shot *noun* a photograph of the display on a computer screen to demonstrate the operation of a program.

screen test *noun* a filmed audition of a prospective film or television actor.

screen·writ·er *noun* a person who writes a screenplay. □ **screen·writ·ing** *noun*

screw ● *noun* **1** a thin cylinder or cone with a spiral ridge or thread running around the outside, used esp. for fastening. **2** (in full **wood screw**) a metal screw with a slotted or notched head and a sharp point for fastening things, esp. in carpentry, by being rotated to form a thread in wood etc. **3** a metal screw with a blunt end on which a nut is threaded to bolt things together. Also called BOLT[1] 2. **4** a wooden or metal straight screw used to exert pressure. **5** (in *sing.* or *pl.*) an instrument of torture acting in this way. **6** (in full **screw propeller**) a form of propeller with twisted blades acting like a screw on the water or air. **7** one turn of a screw. **8** (in full **female screw**) a shaft with a spiral ridge or thread running around the inside wall. **9** *coarse slang* **a** an act of sexual intercourse. **b** a partner in this. **10** *slang* a prison guard. **11** (foll. by *of*) *Brit.* a small twisted-up paper (of tobacco etc.). **12** *Brit.* (in billiards etc.) an oblique curling motion of the ball. **13** *Brit. slang* an amount of salary or wages. **14** *Brit. slang* a mean or miserly person. **15** *Brit. slang* a worn-out horse. ● *verb* **1** *transitive* fasten or tighten with a screw or screws. **2** *transitive* turn (a screw). **3** *intransitive* twist or turn around like or as a screw (*screws in easily*). **4** *transitive* **a** *slang* (often in *passive*) cheat or take advantage of; treat unfairly (*got screwed by them again*). **b** (often foll. by *up*) put psychological etc. pressure on to achieve an end. **c** oppress. **5** *transitive* (foll. by *out of*) extort (consent, money, etc.) from (a person). **6** *coarse slang* **a** *transitive & intransitive* have sexual intercourse (with). **b** *transitive* (as an exclamation) used to express frustration, anger, dismissive contempt, etc. (*well screw you then!*; *screw the rules, let's go*). **7** *intransitive* (of a rolling ball, or of a person etc.) take a curling course; swerve. **8** *transitive* = SCREW UP. □ **have one's head screwed on (straight)** *informal* have common sense. **have a screw loose** *informal* be slightly crazy. **put the screws on** *informal* exert pressure, esp. to extort or intimidate. **screw around** *esp. N Amer.* **1** be promiscuous. **2** fool around, waste time. **3** (foll. by *with*) toy with someone psychologically. **screw up 1** *slang* **a** bungle or mismanage; handle something badly, make a mistake. **b** spoil or ruin (an event, opportunity, etc.). **2** *slang* (usu. as **screwed-up** *adjective*) disturb mentally. **3** summon up (one's courage etc.). **4** contract or contort (one's face etc.). **5** contract and crush into a tight mass (a piece of paper etc.). □ **screw·able** *adjective* **screw·er** *noun* [Old French *escroue* female screw, nut, from Latin *scrofa* sow]

screw·ball *N Amer.* ● *noun* **1** *Baseball* a ball pitched so that it curves towards the side from which it was thrown. **2** *slang* a crazy or eccentric person. ● *adjective* **1** *slang* crazy, eccentric. **2** designating a style of zany fast-moving comedy film involving eccentric characters or ridiculous situations. □ **screw·ball·er** *noun* (in sense 1 of *noun*)

screw cap *noun* = SCREW-TOP.

screw·driv·er *noun* **1** a tool with a shaped tip to fit into the head of a screw to turn it. **2** a cocktail made from vodka and orange juice. **3** (*attributive*) designating a factory, plant, etc., which merely assembles products from components designed and manufactured elsewhere (*another screwdriver plant*).

screwed *adjective* **1** *slang* ruined; rendered ineffective; in a hopeless state (*now we're screwed!*). **2** twisted.

screw eye *noun* a screw with a loop for passing cord etc. through instead of a slotted head.

screw pine *noun* any plant of the genus *Pandanus*, with its leaves arranged spirally and resembling those of a pineapple.

screw plate *noun* a steel plate with threaded holes for making screws.

screw propeller *noun see* SCREW *noun* 6.

screw-top *noun* (also *attributive*) a cap or lid that can be screwed on to a bottle, jar, etc.

screw-up *noun* esp. *N Amer. slang* a bungle, muddle, mess, or mistake.

screwy *adjective* (**screw·i·er**, **screw·i·est**) esp. *N Amer. slang* **1** crazy or eccentric. **2** absurd. **3** messed up, confused. □ **screw·i·ness** *noun*

Scri·abin /skriːˈɒbɪn/ **Alek·sandr (Nikola·evich)** (1872–1915), Russian composer and pianist. He wrote symphonies, tone poems, and numerous pieces for the piano, including sonatas and preludes; much of his later music reflects his interest in mysticism and theosophy, esp. his third symphony *The Divine Poem* (1903) and the tone poem *Prometheus; The Poem of Fire* (1909–10).

scrib·ble ● *verb* **1** *transitive & intransitive* write carelessly or hurriedly. **2** *intransitive* often *derogatory* be an author or writer. **3** *intransitive & transitive* draw carelessly or meaninglessly. ● *noun* **1** a scrawl. **2** a note etc. written in haste. **3** careless handwriting. □ **scrib·bly** *adjective* [medieval Latin *scribillare* diminutive of Latin *scribere* write]

scrib·bler *noun* **1** *informal* a person or thing that scribbles, esp. a professional writer. **2** *Cdn* a small, soft-covered booklet for writing in; a student's notebook.

scrib·blings *plural noun* scribbled writing.

Scribe /skriːb/ **(Au·gus·tin) Eu·gène** (1791–1861), French dramatist, who wrote more than 300 plays, consisting mainly of vaudevilles and comedies of manners such as *Le Mariage de raison* (1826) and *Le Mariage d'argent* (1828).

scribe ● *noun* **1** a person who writes out documents, esp. an ancient or medieval copyist of manuscripts. **2** *Jewish Hist.* an ancient Jewish record-keeper or, later, professional theologian and jurist. **3** (also **scrib·er**) a pointed instrument for making marks on wood, bricks, etc., to guide a saw, or in sign writing. **4** *N Amer. informal* a writer, esp. a journalist. ● *transitive verb* **1 a** mark (wood etc.) with a scribe. **b** make (a mark etc.) on wood with a scribe (*see* sense 3 of *noun*). **2** *transitive informal* write. □ **scribal** *adjective* [(n.) from Latin *scriba* from *scribere* write: (v.) perhaps from DESCRIBE]

scrim *noun* **1 a** a theatrical drop made of an open-weave fabric that looks opaque when lit from in front but becomes transparent when lit from behind. **b** the fabric of which such drops are made. **2** open-weave fabric for lining or upholstery etc. **3** something that conceals what is happening; a veil, a screen (*a scrim of fog*). [18th c.: origin unknown]

scrim·mage /ˈskrɪmɪdʒ/ ● *noun* **1** a rough or confused struggle; a brawl. **2** *Football* **a** a sequence of play beginning with a backward pass from the centre to put the ball in play and continuing until the ball is declared dead. **b** = LINE OF SCRIMMAGE. **3** *N Amer. Sport* a session or informal game in which a team's various squads practise plays against each other. ● *intransitive verb* engage in a scrimmage. □ **scrim·ma·ger** *noun* [var. of SKIRMISH]

scrimmage line *noun* = LINE OF SCRIMMAGE.

scrimp *verb* **1** *intransitive* (often foll. by *on*) be sparing or parsimonious. **2** *transitive* use sparingly. □ **scrimp and save** practise thrift to save money or in order to pay for something else. □ **scrimp·er** *noun* [18th c., originally Scots: perhaps related to SHRIMP]

scrim·shan·der /ˈskrɪmʃændər/ *noun* a person who scrimshaws.

scrim·shaw ● *transitive & intransitive verb* adorn (whalebone, ivory, shells, etc.) with carved or coloured designs. ● *noun* work or a piece of work of this kind. [19th c.: perhaps from a surname]

scrip¹ *noun* **1** a provisional certificate of money subscribed to a bank or company etc. entitling the holder to a formal certificate and dividends. **2** (*collective*) such certificates. **3** an extra share or shares instead of a dividend. **4** temporary paper currency. [abbreviation of *subscription receipt*]

scrip² *noun* (in full **land scrip**) *N Amer.* **1** a certificate entitling the holder to acquire possession of certain portions of public land. **2** *Cdn hist.* a certificate issued to Metis entitling the bearer to 240 acres or

money for the purchase of land, issued in compensation for lands lost by the Metis after the Northwest Rebellion. [perhaps alteration of SCRIPT by association with SCRAP¹, prob. influenced by SCRIP¹]

scrip³ *noun* *slang* a pharmaceutical prescription. [abbreviation]

script ● *noun* **1** handwriting as distinct from print; written characters. **2** type imitating handwriting. **3** an alphabet or system of writing (*the Russian script*). **4 a** the text of a play, film, or broadcast. **b** a predictable or planned series of statements, actions, etc. (*she refused to stick to the script her campaign manager favoured*). **5** *Law* an original document as distinct from a copy. **6** *Computing* a file containing commands or other actions that could have been entered from the keyboard, used to replay often-used sequences of actions. **7** *Psych.* the social role or behaviour appropriate to particular situations that an individual absorbs through cultural influences and association with others. ● *transitive verb* **1 a** write a script for (a film etc.). **b** write (a script, dialogue, etc.). **2** (esp. as **script·ed** *adjective*) provide with or have follow a script (*a scripted debate*). [Middle English, = thing written, from Old French *escri(p)t* from Latin *scriptum*, neuter past participle of *scribere* write]

script doctor *noun* a person who edits a script for a movie or television show to improve it. □ **script-doctoring** *noun*

scripting language *noun* any programming language that can be used to write programs to control an application or class of applications.

scrip·tor·ium /ˌskrɪpˈtɔːriəm/ *noun* (*pl.* **scrip·toria** or **scrip·tor·iums**) a room set apart for writing, esp. in a monastery. □ **scrip·tor·ial** *adjective* [medieval Latin (as SCRIPT)]

scrip·tur·al *adjective* **1** of or relating to a scripture, esp. the Bible. **2** having the authority of a scripture. □ **scrip·tur·al·ly** *adverb*

scrip·ture *noun* writings sacred to a religion or group, esp. (as **Scripture** or **the Scriptures**) the Bible. [Latin *scriptura* (as SCRIPT)]

script·writer *noun* a person who writes a script for a film, broadcast, etc. □ **script·writing** *noun*

scritch *noun* a quiet scraping or scratching sound. □ **scritch·ing** *noun & adjective* [imitative]

scriv·ener /ˈskrɪvənər/ *noun hist.* **1** a copyist or drafter of documents. **2** a notary. [Middle English from obsolete *scrivein* from Old French *escrivein*, ultimately from Latin (as SCRIBE)]

scrob *transitive & intransitive verb* (also **scrawb**) *Cdn* (*Nfld*) & *Irish* scratch or scrape with or as with claws; claw. [origin uncertain; compare Irish *scrábaim, scrabhaim* scrape]

scrod *noun N Amer.* a young cod or haddock, esp. as food. [19th c.: perhaps related to SHRED]

scrof·ula /ˈskrɒfjʊlə/ *noun archaic* a disease with glandular swellings, prob. a form of tuberculosis. *Also called* KING'S EVIL. [Late Latin *scrofulae* (pl.) scrofulous swelling, diminutive of Latin *scrofa* a sow]

scrofu·lous /ˈskrɒfjʊləs/ *adjective* **1** caused by, resembling, of the nature of, or affected with scrofula. **2** morally corrupt.

scroll ● *noun* **1** a roll of parchment or paper esp. with writing on it. **2** a book in the ancient roll form. **3** an ornamental design or carving imitating a roll of parchment. ● *verb* **1** *transitive* (often foll. by *down*, etc.) *Computing* move (displayed text etc.) up, down, or across on a screen or in a window in order to display different parts of it. **2** *transitive* inscribe in or like a scroll. **3** *intransitive* curl up like paper. □ **scroll·able** *adjective* (in sense 1 of *verb*). [Middle English *scrowle* alteration of *rowle* ROLL, perhaps after *scrow* (in the same sense), formed as ESCROW]

scroll bar *noun* a long thin section at the edge of a computer display by which material can be scrolled using a mouse.

scrolled *adjective* having a scroll ornament.

scroll saw *noun* a narrow-bladed saw for cutting along curved lines in ornamental work.

scroll·work *noun* decoration of spiral lines, esp. as cut by a scroll saw.

Scrooge *noun* a mean or miserly person. [a character in Dickens's *Christmas Carol*]

scro·tum /ˈskrəʊtəm/ *noun* (*pl.* **scrota** or **scro·tums**) a pouch of skin containing the testicles. □ **scro·tal** *adjective* [Latin]

scrounge *informal* ● *verb* **1 a** *transitive* (often foll. by *up*) *N Amer.* search or forage for; obtain by or as by foraging. **b** *intransitive* forage. **2** *intransitive* search about to find something at no cost. **3** *transitive & intransitive* obtain (things) illicitly or by cadging. ● *noun* an act of scrounging. □ **on the scrounge** esp. *Brit.* engaged in scrounging. □ **scroun·ger** *noun* [var. of dial. *scrunge* steal]

scrub¹ ● *verb* (**scrubbed**, **scrub·bing**) **1** *transitive* **a** rub (a surface) hard so as to clean, esp. with a hard brush. **b** remove (dirt etc.) in this way. **2** *intransitive* use a brush in this way. **3** *intransitive* (often foll. by *up*) (of

Consonants: b *but* d *dog* f *few* g *get* h *her* j *yes* k *cat* l *leg* m *man* n *no* p *pen* r *red* s *sit*

a surgeon etc.) thoroughly clean the hands and arms by scrubbing, before operating. **4** *transitive informal* scrap or cancel (a plan, order, etc.). **5** *transitive* use water to remove impurities from (gas etc.). ● *noun* **1** the act or an instance of scrubbing; the process of being scrubbed. **2** a substance, implement, etc., used in scrubbing (*apricot facial scrub*). **3** (in *pl.*) special hygienic clothing worn by surgeons and nurses during operations. □ **scrub·ble** *adjective* [Middle English prob. from Middle Low German, Middle Dutch *schrobben, schrubben*]

scrub² *noun* **1 a** vegetation consisting mainly of brushwood or stunted forest growth. **b** an area of land covered with this. **2** *N Amer.* an animal of inferior breed or physique (often *attributive: scrub horse*). **3** a small or dwarf variety (often *attributive: scrub oak*). **4** *Sport* **a** *N Amer. informal* a team or player not of the first class. **b** *Cdn* an informal match played by children, amateurs, etc.; a pickup game (also *attributive: playing scrub baseball*). **5** a worthless, insignificant, or contemptible person. □ **scrub·by** *adjective* [Middle English, var. of SHRUB¹]

scrub·ber *noun* **1** a person or thing that scrubs, esp. apparatus for purifying gases, removing excess pollutants from exhaust, etc. **2** *Brit. slang offensive* a sexually promiscuous woman.

scrub brush¹ *noun* a hard brush for scrubbing floors etc.

scrub brush² *noun* = SCRUB² 1.

scrub·land *noun* land consisting of scrub vegetation.

scrub nurse *noun* an operating room nurse who handles sterile instruments etc. and assists the surgeon.

scrub typhus *noun* a rickettsial disease of the W Pacific transmitted by mites.

scrub·woman *noun* (*pl.* **-women**) a woman employed as a cleaner.

scruff¹ *noun* the back of the neck as used to grasp and lift or drag an animal or person by (esp. *scruff of the neck*). [alteration of *scuff*, perhaps from Old Norse *skoft* hair]

scruff² *informal* ● *noun* esp. *Brit.* an untidy or scruffy person. ● *transitive verb* make scruffy. [originally = SCURF, later 'worthless thing', or back-formation from SCRUFFY]

scruffy *adjective* (**scruff·i·er, scruff·i·est**) *informal* shabby, slovenly, untidy; ragged. □ **scruff·i·ly** *adverb* **scruff·i·ness** *noun* [*scruff* var. of SCURF + -Y¹]

scrum ● *noun* **1** *Rugby* an arrangement of the forwards of each team in two opposing groups, each with arms interlocked and heads down, with the ball thrown in between them to restart play. **2** *Brit. & Cdn informal* a disorderly crowd. **3** *Cdn* **a** a situation where a crowd of reporters surround and interrogate a politician in an impromptu, informal, or disorderly manner. **b** the crowd of reporters in such a situation. ● *verb* **1** *intransitive* (often foll. by *down*) *Rugby* form a scrum. **2** *Cdn* **a** *intransitive* (of a politician or reporter) engage in a scrum. **b** *transitive* (of reporters) surround and interrogate (a politician) in a scrum. [abbreviation of SCRUMMAGE]

scrum half *noun Rugby* a halfback who puts the ball into the scrum.

scrum·mage *Rugby* ● *noun* = SCRUM *noun* 1. ● *intransitive verb* = SCRUM *verb* 1. □ **scrum·ma·ger** *noun* [as SCRIMMAGE]

scrum·my *adjective Brit. informal* (esp. of food) excellent; delicious. [blend of SCRUMPTIOUS + -Y¹]

scrum·ple *transitive verb* crumple, wrinkle. [var. of CRUMPLE]

scrump·tious *adjective informal* **1** delicious. **2** pleasing, delightful. □ **scrump·tious·ly** *adverb* **scrump·tious·ness** *noun* [19th c.: origin unknown]

scrumpy *noun Brit. informal* rough cider, esp. as made in the West Country of England. [dial. *scrump* small apple]

scrunch ● *verb* **1 a** *transitive & intransitive* (usu. foll. by *up*) make or become crushed or crumpled. **b** *intransitive* (often foll. by *up, down*) *N Amer.* squeeze oneself into a compact shape; crouch. **2** *intransitive & transitive* make or cause to make a crunching sound. **3** *transitive* style (hair) by squeezing or crushing in the hands to give a tousled look. ● *noun* the act or an instance of scrunching. [variant of CRUNCH]

scrunch-dry *transitive verb* dry (hair) while scrunching it.

scrun·cheon /ˈskrʌnʃən/ *noun* (also **scrun·chion, scrun·chin**) *Cdn* (*Nfld*) (in *pl.*) small pieces of pork fat or fatback fried to a crisp and usu. eaten with fish and brewis. [origin uncertain; perhaps related to English dial. *scrunchings* table scraps]

scrunchy *noun* (*pl.* **-ies**) (also **scrunch·ie**) a circular band of elastic covered in loose fabric, used for fastening the hair in a ponytail etc.

scru·ple /ˈskruːpəl/ ● *noun* **1** (in *sing.* or *pl.*) **a** regard to the morality or propriety of an action. **b** a feeling of doubt or hesitation caused by this. **2** *hist.* an apothecaries' weight of 20 grains. **3** *archaic* a very small quantity. ● *intransitive verb* **1** (foll. by *to* + infin.; usu. with *neg.*) be reluctant because of scruples (*did not scruple to stop their allowance*).

2 feel or be influenced by scruples. [French *scrupule* or Latin *scrupulus* from *scrupus* rough pebble, anxiety]

scru·pu·lous /ˈskruːpjʊləs/ *adjective* **1** conscientious or thorough even in small matters. **2** careful to avoid doing wrong. **3** punctilious; over-attentive to details. □ **scru·pu·los·i·ty** /-ˈlɒsɪti/ *noun* **scru·pu·lous·ly** *adverb* **scru·pu·lous·ness** *noun* [French *scrupuleux* or Latin *scrupulosus* (as SCRUPLE)]

scru·tin·eer /skruːtɪˈnɪːr/ *noun* esp. *Cdn & Brit.* a person who scrutinizes or examines something, esp. the conduct and result of a ballot.

scru·tin·ize /ˈskruːtɪˌnaɪz/ *transitive verb* (also esp. *Brit.* **-ise**) look closely at; examine with close scrutiny. □ **scru·tin·iz·er** *noun*

scru·tiny /ˈskruːtɪni/ *noun* (*pl.* **-ies**) **1** a critical gaze. **2** a close investigation or examination of details. **3** an official examination of ballot papers to check their validity or accuracy of counting. [Latin *scrutinium* from *scrutari* search, from *scruta* rubbish: originally of rag collectors]

scry *intransitive verb* (**scries, scried**) divine, esp. by crystal gazing or looking in a mirror or water. □ **scry·er** *noun* [shortening from DESCRY]

SCSI /ˈskʌzi/ *noun Computing* a standard interface connecting peripheral devices, such as disk storage units, to small and medium-sized computers. [acronym from Small Computer Systems Interface]

scu·ba /ˈskuːbə/ *noun* (*pl.* **scu·bas**) **1** a portable breathing apparatus for divers, consisting of cylinders of compressed air strapped on the back, feeding air automatically through a mask or mouthpiece. **2** scuba diving (often *attributive: scuba gear*). [acronym from self-contained underwater breathing apparatus]

scuba diving *noun* swimming underwater using a scuba, esp. as a sport. □ **scuba dive** *intransitive verb* **scuba diver** *noun*

scud ● *intransitive verb* (**scud·ded, scud·ding**) **1** fly or run straight, fast, and lightly; skim along. **2** (of a sailboat) run before the wind. **3** (of a cloud, foam, etc.) be driven by the wind. ● *noun* **1** a period of scudding. **2** a scudding motion. **3** vapoury driving clouds. **4** a driving shower; a gust. **5** windblown spray. **6** (usu. **Scud**) a type of long-range surface-to-surface guided missile originally developed in the former USSR. [perhaps alteration of SCUT, as if to race like a hare]

scuff ● *verb* **1** *transitive* graze or brush against. **2** *transitive* mark or wear the surface off (leather, esp. of shoe uppers, a floor, etc.) by scratching or grazing with or against something. **3** *transitive Baseball* (often foll. by *up*) scratch or roughen up the surface of (the ball) illicitly to increase its movement when pitched (see MOVEMENT 11). **4** *intransitive* **a** a walk with dragging feet; shuffle. **b** drag (one's feet) across a surface. ● *noun* a mark of scuffing. □ **scuffed** *adjective* [imitative]

scuf·fle¹ ● *noun* **1** a confused struggle or disorderly fight at close quarters; a tussle. **2** the shuffling of feet. ● *intransitive verb* **1** engage in a scuffle. **2** move with a shuffling gait. [prob. from Scandinavian: compare Swedish *skuffa* to push, related to SHOVE]

scuf·fle² *transitive verb* scarify or stir the surface of the ground, esp. between rows of crops. □ **scuf·fler** *noun* [Dutch *schoffel*, weeding hoe]

scull¹ ● *noun* **1** either of a pair of small oars used by a single rower. **2** an oar placed over the stern of a boat to propel it, usu. by a twisting motion. **3** a small boat propelled with a scull, or a pair or pairs of sculls. **4** (in *pl.*) a race between boats with two oars per rower. ● **1** *transitive verb* propel (a boat) with sculls. **2** *Swimming* stay afloat or propel oneself through water by making a waving motion in the water with the hands. □ **scull·er** *noun* [Middle English: origin unknown]

scull² *noun Cdn* (*Nfld*) the seasonal migration of capelin from the sea to inshore waters to spawn. [obsolete variant of SCHOOL²]

scul·lery *noun* (*pl.* **-ies**) a small kitchen or room at the back of a house for washing dishes etc. [Anglo-French *squillerie*, Old French *escuelerie* from *escuele* dish, from Latin *scutella* salver, diminutive of *scutra* wooden platter]

scull·ing oar *noun Cdn* (*Nfld*) = SCULL¹ 2.

scul·lion *noun archaic* a servant employed to wash dishes and perform other menial kitchen tasks. [Middle English: origin unknown]

scul·pin *noun* any of numerous fish of the family Cottidae, native to non-tropical regions, having large spiny heads. [perhaps from obsolete *scorpene* from Latin *scorpaena* from Greek *skorpaina* a fish]

sculpt *transitive & intransitive verb* (usu. in *passive*) **1** create a sculpture. **2** carve. **3** provide with a highly contoured relief. □ **sculpt·ing** *noun* [French *sculpter* from *sculpteur* SCULPTOR: now regarded as an abbreviation]

sculp·tor *noun* an artist who makes sculptures. □ **sculp·tress** *noun* [Latin (as SCULPTURE)]

sculp·ture ● *noun* **1** the art of making forms, often representational, in the round or in relief by chiselling stone, carving wood, modelling clay, casting metal, etc. **2** a work or works of sculpture. **3** *Zool. & Bot.* raised or sunken markings on a shell etc. ● *verb* **1** *transitive* represent in or adorn with sculpture. **2** *transitive* make a sculpture in or using (a medium). **3** *intransitive* practise sculpture. **4** *transitive* (esp. as **sculp·tured** *adjective*) give a markedly contoured form to. □ **sculp·tur·al** *adjective* **sculp·tur·al·ly** *adverb* [Latin *sculptura* from *sculpere* sculpt- carve]

scum ● *noun* **1** a layer of dirt, froth, or impurities, etc. forming at the top of liquid, esp. in boiling or fermentation or on stagnant water. **2** (foll. by *of*) the most worthless part of something. **3** *informal* a worthless, despicable person or group. ● *verb* (**scummed**, **scum·ming**) **1** *transitive* remove scum from; skim. **2** *transitive* be or form a scum on. **3** *intransitive* (of a liquid) develop scum. □ **scum·my** *adjective* (**scum·mi·er**, **scum·mi·est**). [Middle Low German, Middle Dutch *schūm*, Old High German *scūm* from Germanic]

scum·bag *noun* (also **scum·ball**) *slang* a contemptible, despicable, or disgusting person.

scum·ble ● *transitive verb* **1** modify (a painting) by applying a thin opaque coat of paint to give a softer or duller effect. **2** modify (a drawing) similarly with light pencilling etc. ● *noun* **1** material used in scumbling. **2** the effect produced by scumbling. [perhaps frequentative of SCUM *transitive verb*]

scum-bucket *noun* *N Amer.* = SCUMBAG.

scum of the earth *noun* *informal* an extremely contemptible or despicable person or group.

scun·cheon /ˈskʌnʃən/ *noun* the inside face of a door jamb, window frame, etc. [Old French *escoinson* (as EX-[1], COIN)]

scun·ner[1] *esp. Scot.* ● *intransitive verb* feel disgust or nausea. ● *noun* **1** a strong dislike (usu. *take a scunner against* or *to*). **2** an object of loathing. [14th c.: origin uncertain]

scun·ner[2] *noun* *Cdn* (*Nfld*) a lookout in a crow's nest who directs a ship, esp. through ice floes. [from *scun*, perhaps alteration of CON[4]]

scup *noun* a kind of porgy, *Stenostomus chrysops*, of the Atlantic coast of N America. [Narragansett *mishcup* thick-scaled, from *mishe* large + *cuppi* scale]

scup·per[1] *noun* (often in *pl.*) a hole in a ship's side to carry off water from the deck. [Old French *escopir* from Romanic *skuppire* (unrecorded) to spit: originally imitative]

scup·per[2] *transitive verb* *slang* **1** sink (a ship or its crew). **2** defeat or ruin (a plan etc.). [19th c.: origin unknown]

scup·per·nong *noun* a variety of the muscadine grape native to the basin of the Scuppernong River in N Carolina.

scurf *noun* **1** flakes on the surface of the skin, cast off as fresh skin develops below, esp. those of the head; dandruff. **2** any scaly matter on a surface. □ **scurfy** *adjective* [Old English, prob. from Old Norse & earlier Old English *sceorf*, related to *sceorfan* gnaw, *sceorfian* cut to shreds]

scur·ri·lous /ˈskʌrɪləs/ *adjective* **1** (of a person or language) grossly or indecently abusive. **2** given to or expressed with coarse humour. □ **scur·ril·i·ty** /-ˈrɪlɪti/ *noun* **scur·ri·lous·ly** *adverb* **scur·ri·lous·ness** *noun* [French *scurrile* or Latin *scurrilus* from *scurra* buffoon]

scurry ● *intransitive verb* (**-ries**, **-ried**) run or move hurriedly, esp. with short quick steps; scamper. ● *noun* (*pl.* **-ries**) **1** the act or sound of scurrying. **2** bustle, haste. **3** a flurry of rain or snow. [abbreviation of *hurry-scurry*; reduplication of HURRY]

S-curve *noun* two curves in a road etc., one following the other in the opposite direction.

scur·vy ● *noun* a disease caused by a deficiency of vitamin C, characterized by swollen bleeding gums and the opening of previously healed wounds. ● *adjective* (**scur·vi·er**, **scur·vi·est**) despicable, rotten, dishonourable, contemptible. □ **scur·vi·ly** *adverb* [SCURF + -Y[1]: noun sense by assoc. with French *scorbut* (compare SCORBUTIC)]

scut *noun* **1** a short tail, esp. of a hare, rabbit, or deer. **2** *slang* a term of contempt for a fool or a disgusting or detestable person. [Middle English: origin unknown: compare obsolete *scut* short, shorten]

scuta *pl.* of SCUTUM.

scut·age /ˈskjuːtɪdʒ/ *noun* *hist.* money paid to a feudal lord by a landowner or vassal instead of military service. [medieval Latin *scutagium* from Latin *scutum* shield]

Scu·tari /skuːˈtɑri/ a former name for Üsküdar near Istanbul, site of a British army hospital in which Florence Nightingale worked during the Crimean War.

scutch *transitive verb* dress (fibrous material, esp. retted flax) by beating.

[Old French *escouche*, *escoucher* (dial.), *escousser*, ultimately from Latin *excutere excuss-* (as EX-[1], *quatere* shake)]

scutch·eon *noun* = ESCUTCHEON. [Middle English from ESCUTCHEON]

scute /skjuːt/ *noun* each of the shield-like plates or scales forming the bony covering of a crocodile, sturgeon, turtle, armadillo, etc. [Latin (as SCUTUM)]

scu·tel·lum /skuˈteləm/ *noun* (*pl.* **scu·tel·la**) *Bot. & Zool.* a scale, plate, or any shield-like formation on a plant, insect, bird, etc., esp. one of the horny scales on a bird's foot. [modern Latin diminutive of Latin *scutum* shield]

scut·ter ● *intransitive verb* *informal* scurry. ● *noun* the act or an instance of scuttering. [perhaps alteration of SCUTTLE[2]]

scut·tle[1] *noun* a bucket, usu. with a sloping lip for pouring, carrying, and holding a small supply of coal. [Old Norse *skutill*, Old High German *scuzzila* from Latin *scutella* dish]

scut·tle[2] ● *intransitive verb* run or move hurriedly with short quick steps, esp. furtively or busily; scurry, scamper, hurry along. ● *noun* a hurried pace. [compare dial. *scuddle* frequentative of SCUD]

scut·tle[3] ● *noun* **1** a hole with a lid in a ship's deck or side. **2** *N Amer.* an opening in the ceiling, floor, or wall of a building; a trap door. ● *transitive verb* **1** let water into (a ship) to sink it, esp. by opening the seacocks. **2** esp. *N Amer.* abandon, thwart, or dismiss (a plan, rumour, etc.). [Middle English, perhaps from obsolete French *escoutille* from Spanish *escotilla* hatchway, diminutive of *escota* cutting out cloth]

scuttle·butt *noun* **1** esp. *N Amer. informal* rumour, gossip. **2** a barrel of water kept on the deck of a ship for drinking from.

scu·tum /ˈskjuːtəm/ *noun* (*pl.* **scuta**) = SCUTE. [Latin, = oblong shield]

scut·work *noun* esp. *US informal* tedious menial work.

scuzz·ball *noun* (also **scuzz·bag**) esp. *N Amer. slang* a filthy, sleazy, or shady person.

scuz·zy *adjective* (**scuz·zi·er**, **scuz·zi·est**) *slang* squalid, sleazy, abhorrent, or disgusting. □ **scuzz** *noun* **scuz·zi·ness** *noun* [prob. an abbreviation of DISGUSTING]

Scylla /ˈsɪlə/ *Gk Myth* a female sea monster who devoured sailors when they tried to navigate the narrow channel between her cave and the whirlpool Charybdis; later legend substituted a dangerous rock for the monster and located it on the Italian side of the Strait of Messina. □ **Scylla and Charybdis** either of two dangers such that to avoid one increases the risk from the other.

scy·pho·zoan /ˌsaɪfəˈzoʊən/ ● *noun* any marine jellyfish of the class Scyphozoa, with tentacles bearing stinging cells. ● *adjective* of or relating to this class. [modern Latin *scyphus* from Greek *skuphos* a drinking cup with two handles below the level of the rim + Greek *zōion* animal]

scythe /saɪð/ ● *noun* an agricultural tool consisting of a pole with two short handles projecting from it and a long thin curving blade at the bottom, which is swung over the ground to cut grass, grain, etc. ● *transitive verb* cut with, or as if with, a scythe. [Old English *sīthe* from Germanic]

Scythia /ˈsɪðɪə/ an ancient region of SE Europe and Asia. The Scythian Empire, which existed between the 8th and 2nd c. BC, was centred on the northern shores of the Black Sea and extended from S Russia to the northern borders of Persia.

Scyth·ian /ˈsɪðɪən/ ● *adjective* of or relating to ancient Scythia. ● *noun* **1** an inhabitant of Scythia. **2** the language of this region.

SD *abbreviation* **1** South Dakota (in official postal use). **2** *Statistics* standard deviation.

SDI *abbreviation* STRATEGIC DEFENCE INITIATIVE.

SDR *abbreviation* special drawing right (from the International Monetary Fund).

SE *abbreviation* **1** southeast. **2** southeastern.

Se *symbol Chem.* the element selenium.

se- *prefix* apart, without (*seclude*; *secure*). [Latin from Old Latin *se* (prep. & adv.)]

sea /siː/ *noun* **1** the expanse of salt water that covers most of the earth's surface and surrounds its land masses. **2** any part of this as opposed to land or fresh water. **3** a particular (usu. named) tract of salt water partly or wholly enclosed by land (*the Beaufort Sea*; *the Dead Sea*). **4** a large inland lake (*the Sea of Galilee*). **5** (esp. in *pl.*) the state of the sea with regard to the roughness or smoothness of the waves, the presence or absence of swell, etc. (*choppy seas*). **6** (foll. by *of*) a vast quantity or expanse (*a sea of troubles*; *a sea of faces*). **7** (*attributive*) **a** of, related to, or designed for the sea. **b** (often prefixed to the name of an animal or plant having a superficial resemblance to what it is named after) living in or near the sea (*sea lettuce*). □ **at sea 1** in a ship on the sea. **2** (also **all at sea**) perplexed, confused. **by sea** in a ship or ships. **go to sea** become a sailor. **on the sea 1** in a ship at sea. **2** situated on the coast. **put** (or **put out**) **to sea** leave land or port. [Old English *sæ* from Germanic]

sea anchor *noun* a device such as a weighted bag dragged in the water to prevent a ship from drifting.

sea anemone *noun* any of various coelenterates of the order Actiniaria having a polypoid body bearing a ring of tentacles around the mouth.

sea·bag *noun* N Amer. a sailor's duffle bag.

sea bass *noun* any of various marine fishes of the family Serranidae, like the bass, esp. *Centropristis striatus*.

sea·bed *noun* = SEA FLOOR.

sea·bird *noun* any bird that lives on or near the sea.

sea biscuit *noun* a hard biscuit kept as a ration on board a ship. *Also called* SHIP'S BISCUIT, HARDTACK.

sea·board *noun* the coastal region or land bordering the sea.

sea·boot *noun* (usu. in *pl.*) a knee-high usu. leather waterproof boot worn esp. by fishermen and sealers.

Sea·borg, Glenn Theo·dore (1912–99), US chemist, who won the 1951 Nobel Prize for chemistry for discovering a large number of transuranic elements, including plutonium (1940) and americium (1944).

sea·borg·ium *noun* a very unstable chemical element made by high-energy atomic collisions. Symbol: **Sg**; at. no. 106. [modern Latin, from SEABORG]

sea·borne *adjective* carried over or supported by the sea.

sea bottom *noun* esp. N Amer. the sea floor.

sea bream *noun* = PORGY.

sea breeze *noun* a cool gentle breeze blowing landward from the sea, esp. during the late afternoon when the temperature of the sea is cooler than coastal temperatures.

sea buckthorn *noun* a maritime shrub, *Hippophae rhamnoides*, with orange berries.

sea cadet *noun* a volunteer youth receiving training and education in naval affairs.

sea captain *noun* the captain or commander of esp. a merchant ship.

sea change *noun* a notable or unexpected transformation; a radical change. [with reference to Shakespeare's *Tempest* I. ii. 403.]

sea-chest *noun* a sailor's box for storing clothes etc.

sea·coast *noun* the border of land near the sea; the seashore.

sea·cock *noun* a valve below a ship's waterline for letting water in or out.

sea cow *noun* **1** a sirenian. **2** *archaic* a walrus.

sea cucumber *noun* any of several hundred species of holothurian. *See also* BÊCHE-DE-MER.

sea dog *noun* **1** an old or experienced sailor. **2** N Amer. *informal* a harbour seal.

Sea-Doo *noun* *proprietary* = PERSONAL WATERCRAFT.

sea eagle *noun* any fish-eating eagle esp. of the genus *Haliaeetus*.

sea elephant *noun* = ELEPHANT SEAL.

sea fan *noun* any colonial coral of the order Gorgonacea supported by a fan-like horny skeleton.

sea·farer *noun* **1** a sailor. **2** a traveller by sea.

sea·faring ● *adjective* **1** travelling by sea. **2 a** of or related to the occupation or business of a sailor. **b** involved in or dependent upon the life, business, or occupation of a sailor (*a seafaring nation*). ● *noun* **1** travel by sea. **2** the business or occupation of a sailor.

sea floor *noun* the ground under the sea; the bottom of the sea.

sea·foam ● *noun* **1** foam formed on the sea. **2** (also **seafoam green**) a pastel bluish-green. ● *adjective* of the colour of seafoam green.

sea·food *noun* any edible animal obtained from the sea, including fish, crustaceans, and molluscs.

sea·front *noun* an area or esp. the part of a coastal town directly facing the sea.

sea·girt *adjective* *literary* surrounded by sea.

sea·going *adjective* **1** (of ships) fit for crossing the sea. **2** (of a person) **a** travelling by sea. **b** involved in the occupation of a sailor. **3** of or related to the occupation or lifestyle of a sailor.

Sea·gram /'siːgrəm/ **Jo·seph Emm** (1841–1919), Canadian distiller and politician. In 1883 he became the sole owner of a distillery in Waterloo, Ontario and created what was to become one of Canada's most popular whiskies. The company later became the world's largest producer of distilled spirits and wines.

sea grape *noun* **1 a** a salt-resistant shrub of the knotgrass family, *Coccoloba uvifera*, bearing edible purple fruit in clusters like bunches of grapes, native to coastal regions of tropical America. **b** the fruit of this shrub. **2** = SARGASSO.

sea·grass *noun* any of various grasslike plants growing in or by the sea, esp. eelgrass, *Zostera marina*.

sea green ● *noun* the colour of the sea, a pale bluish green. ● *adjective* (usu. **sea-green**) of this colour.

sea·gull *noun* a gull, esp. a herring gull.

sea hare *noun* any of various marine molluscs of the order Anaspidea, having an internal shell and long extensions from its foot.

sea holly *noun* a European evergreen umbelliferous plant, *Eryngium maritimum*, with spiny leaves and blue flowers, naturalized in N America.

sea horse *noun* **1** any of various small upright marine fish of the family Syngnathidae, esp. of the genus *Hippocampus*, having a body suggestive of the head and neck of a horse. **2** a mythical creature with a horse's head and fish's tail.

sea ice *noun* a large expanse of ice formed from frozen salt water, esp. occurring in the sea.

Sea Island cotton *noun* a fine variety of cotton, *Gossypium barbadense*, distinguished by long silky fibres, originally grown on islands off the coast of Georgia and S Carolina.

sea·kale *noun* a cruciferous maritime plant, *Crambe maritima*, with white flowers and wavy coarsely-toothed leaves, the shoots of which are cultivated and eaten as a vegetable.

sea kayak ● *noun* a usu. fibreglass kayak with a rudder. ● *intransitive verb* travel by sea kayak, esp. for sport or recreation. □ **sea kayaker** *noun* **sea kayaking** *noun*

sea·kind·ly *adjective* (of a ship) easy to handle. □ **sea·kind·li·ness** *noun*

SEAL /siːl/ *noun* a member of an elite force within the US Navy specializing in guerrilla warfare and counter-insurgency. [abbreviation of *(se)al (a)ir (l)and* (team)]

seal¹ ● *noun* **1 a** a design, crest, motto, etc. impressed esp. on a piece of wax or paper adhering or affixed to a document as a guarantee of authenticity. **b** an engraved stamp of metal, gemstone, or other hard material used to make an impression on wax or paper. **c** a piece of wax etc. bearing such an impression, often used on a folded letter so that it cannot be opened unless the seal is broken. **2** a plastic wrapper etc. that must be broken before a box or container can be opened, used esp. in packaging to ensure that a product is not tampered with before it is bought. **3 a** a material or substance used to fill a gap or crack so that air, liquid, etc. cannot enter or escape (*a strip of sponge rubber seal around the door; a rubber seal on a jar*). **b** protection given by this (*caulking gives a good seal around the window*). **4** an act, gesture, or event regarded as a confirmation or guarantee, esp. of a vow or promise. **5** a significant or prophetic mark (*has the seal of death in his face*). **6** a decorative label or stamp usu. sold for charity and placed on an envelope (*Christmas seals*). **7** an amount of water standing in the trap of a drain to prevent foul air from rising. ● *transitive verb* **1 a** (often foll. by *up*) fasten or close securely. **b** close (an envelope) by sticking the flap down. **2 a** close (a jar or container etc.) so that it is airtight and watertight. **b** insulate or set a seal around (a window, pipe joint, etc.) so that it is airtight or watertight. **3** certify as correct, authentic, or approved by marking (a document etc.) with a seal or stamp. **4** determine irrevocably (*their fate is sealed*). **5** complete and place (a victory, defeat, etc.) beyond dispute or reversal. **6** (foll. by *off*) put barriers around (an area) to prevent entry and exit, esp. as a security measure. **7** apply a heavy non-porous coating to (new wood, a wall, etc.) to make it impervious, esp. to facilitate the application of a second, finishing coat. □ **one's lips are sealed** one promises to keep a secret. **set one's seal to** (or **on**) authorize, endorse, or confirm. □ **seal·able** *adjective* **seal·ing** *noun* [Anglo-French *seal*, Old French *seel* from Latin *sigillum* diminutive of *signum* SIGN]

seal² ● *noun* **1** any fish-eating amphibious sea mammal of the family Phocidae or Otariidae, with flippers and webbed feet. **2** sealskin. ● *intransitive verb* hunt for seals. [Old English *seolh seol-* from Germanic]

sea lane *noun* a route at sea designated for use or regularly used by ships.

seal·ant *noun* **1** any of various substances used to prevent air or water from passing through cracks, seams, joints, etc. **2** any of various substances applied to a surface to make it impervious or resistant to water, dirt, stains, etc.

sea lavender *noun* any maritime plant of the genus *Limonium*, with small brightly coloured funnel-shaped flowers, used in dried flower arrangements.

sealed-beam *noun* (*attributive*) designating a car headlight with a sealed unit consisting of the light source, reflector, and lens.

sea legs *noun* the ability to keep one's balance and avoid becoming sick while at sea.

seal·er[1] *noun* **1** (in full **sealer jar**) *Cdn* (esp. *Prairies & BC*) **a** a glass jar used for preserves etc., having a glass or metal lid secured by a metal band screwed onto the mouth of the jar. **b** the contents of a sealer. **2** an undercoating of paint etc. used to give porous building materials, such as new wood or drywall, a surface more receptive to finishing coats. **3** a device or substance used to make something airtight or impervious to water, oil, etc. (*a bag sealer; driveway sealer*).

seal·er[2] *noun* **1** a person who hunts seals. **2** a ship used for hunting seals.

sealer ring *noun* *Cdn* (esp. *Prairies & BC*) a rubber ring inserted between the lid and the rim of a sealer jar to ensure an airtight seal.

sea lettuce *noun* a seaweed, *Ulva lactuca*, with green fronds resembling lettuce leaves.

sea level *noun* the average level of the sea's surface, used as an international standard in calculating the height of mountains etc. and as a barometric standard.

seal flipper pie *noun* *Cdn* (*Nfld*) a pie with a filling of seal flippers.

sea lice *plural noun* **1** any of various parasitic copepods of the genus *Lepeophtheirus* or *Caligus*, which cause disease esp. amongst salmonids. **2** (esp. in Florida) the microscopic larvae of jellyfish, which cause eruptions of itchy blisters on swimmers' skin.

sea·lift *noun* esp. *N Amer.* a large-scale transportation of supplies, troops, etc. by sea.

sea lily *noun* any of various sessile echinoderms, esp. of the class Crinoidea, with long jointed stalks and feather-like arms for trapping food.

seal·ing *noun* the hunting of seals.

sealing wax *noun* a mixture of shellac and rosin with turpentine and pigment, softened by heating and used to make seals.

sea lion *noun* any of several large-eared seals having broader muzzles and sparser under-fur than the fur seals, esp. the California sea lion or the Steller's sea lion.

seal of approval *noun* (also **stamp of approval**) **1** a seal or stamp on a product etc. indicating that it has been approved by an authority. **2** an expression of endorsement, support, etc.

seal oil *noun* oil obtained from the fat of seals.

seal-oil lamp *noun* = KUDLIK.

Sea Lord *noun* (in the UK) a naval member of the Admiralty Board.

seal·point *noun* **1** a dark brown marking on the fur of one type of Siamese cat. **2** such a cat. [SEAL[2]]

seal·skin *noun* **1** the skin or prepared fur of a seal. **2** (often *attributive*) a garment made from this.

Sealy·ham /ˈsiːlɪhəm/ *noun* (in full **Sealyham terrier**) a breed of small stocky wire-haired terrier, having a medium-length usu. white coat, drooping ears, a small erect tail, and a square bearded muzzle. [*Sealyham* in S Wales]

sea lyme grass *noun* = LYME GRASS.

seam ● *noun* **1** a line along which two pieces of cloth etc. are stitched together. **2** a line or ridge where two parallel edges join or meet, e.g. of floorboards fitted edge to edge. **3** a stratum of coal etc. **4** a wrinkle or scar. ● *transitive verb* **1** join with a seam. **2** (esp. as **seamed** *adjective*) mark or score (a surface) with lines or indentations. □ **come** (or **fall**) **apart at the seams** have a breakdown; collapse emotionally. □ **seam·er** *noun* [Old English *séam* from Germanic]

seam allowance *noun* the amount of material along each edge of the pieces of a garment which is taken in by a seam.

sea·man *noun* (*pl.* **-men**) **1** a person whose occupation or business is on the sea; a sailor. **2** an enlisted member of the navy below the rank of petty officer.

sea·man·ship *noun* the art and skill of managing, handling, and maintaining a ship or boat.

sea·mark *noun* a conspicuous object distinguishable at sea serving to guide or warn sailors in navigation (*compare* LANDMARK).

sea mile *noun* a unit of length varying between approx. 1 842 metres (2,014 yards) at the equator and 1 861 metres (2,035 yards) at the pole.

seam·less *adjective* **1** without a seam or seams. **2** uninterrupted, smooth; not disjointed. □ **seam·less·ly** *adverb* **seam·less·ness** *noun*

sea monkey *noun* **1** a brine shrimp, *Artemia salina*, often used as food for fish in aquariums. **2** the eggs of these, which hatch when deposited in water, packaged and sold esp. to children.

sea·mount *noun* a mountain submerged entirely beneath the surface of the sea.

sea mouse *noun* any iridescent marine annelid of the genus *Aphrodite*.

seam·stress *noun* a woman who makes and mends clothing, esp. professionally. [Old English *séamestre* fem. from *séamere* tailor, formed as SEAM + -STER + -ESS[1]]

seamy *adjective* (**seam·i·er**, **seam·i·est**) **1** marked with or showing seams. **2** disreputable, degenerate, sordid, base (*the seamy side of their romance*).

Seanad /ˈʃanəð/ *noun* the upper House of Parliament in the Republic of Ireland. [Irish, = senate]

se·ance /ˈseɪɒns, -ɑ̃s/ *noun* a meeting at which spiritualists attempt to make contact with the dead. [French *séance* from Old French *seoir* from Latin *sedēre* sit]

sea otter *noun* a Pacific otter, *Enhydra lutris*, having thick dark fur.

sea pen *noun* a colonial hydroid of the order Pennatulacea, resembling a quill pen.

Sea Peoples (also **Peoples of the Sea**) groups of invaders who encroached on Egypt and the eastern Mediterranean by land and sea in the late 13th c. BC, some of whom, including the Philistines, settling in Palestine.

sea pie *noun* *Cdn* a dish of esp. leftover meat and vegetables stewed and baked in a crust. [perhaps a misspelling of CIPAILLE]

sea pigeon *noun* any of various marine birds resembling or likened to pigeons, esp. a rock dove, kittiwake, or black guillemot.

sea pink *noun* a maritime plant, *Armeria maritima*, with bright pink flowers. *Also called* THRIFT.

sea·plane *noun* an aircraft designed to take off from and land and float on water.

sea·port *noun* **1** a harbour or port for seagoing ships. **2** a town or city having such a harbour or port.

sea·quake *noun* a convulsion or sudden agitation of the sea from a submarine eruption or earthquake.

sear[1] ● *verb* **1** *transitive* burn or scorch the surface of. **2** *transitive & intransitive* cause great pain or anguish (to). **3** *transitive* brown (meat) quickly at a high temperature so that it will retain its juices in cooking. **4** *transitive* **a** leave an esp. disturbing impression etc. on (a person, mind, etc.) (*the image seared her memory*). **b** impress (esp. a disturbing image etc.) in a person's mind, memory, etc. (*the image was seared in her memory*). ● *adjective* = SERE[2]. [Old English *séar* (adj.), *séarian* (v.), from Germanic]

sear[2] *noun* (also **sere**) a catch of a gunlock holding the hammer at half or full cock. [prob. from Old French *serre* lock, bolt, from *serrer* (see SERRIED)]

sea raven *noun* a large Atlantic sculpin, *Hemitripterus americanus*, found off the shores of N America.

search ● *verb* **1** *transitive* look through or go over thoroughly to find something (*he searched the drawer for his keys; she searched the text for errors*). **2** *transitive* examine (a person, their pockets, clothes, etc.) to find anything concealed. **3** *intransitive* (often foll. by *for*) make a search or investigation. **4** *transitive & intransitive* *Computing* locate a specified piece of information or text in a table, file, document, etc. **5** *transitive* examine or question (one's mind, conscience, etc.) thoroughly; probe (*search your heart for the truth*). **6** *transitive* (foll. by *out*) look probingly for; seek out. ● *noun* **1** an act of searching; an investigation. **2** *Computing* the locating of a specified piece of information or text. □ **in search of** trying to find. **search me!** *informal* I don't know. □ **search·able** *adjective* **search·er** *noun* [Anglo-French *sercher*, Old French *cerchier* from Late Latin *circare* go round (as CIRCUS)]

search and destroy *noun* (*attributive*) designating an uncompromising military strategy effected by the advance of troops through a given territory.

search and replace *noun* a computer function which allows a user to find a specified string of characters in a text and replace it automatically or interactively with another string.

search and rescue *noun* **1** an operation designed to find the survivors of a disaster, people who are lost or in danger, etc. and bring them to safety. **2** (*attributive*) **a** designating an operation, situation,

---

Consonants: b *but*   d *dog*   f *few*   g *get*   h *her*   j *yes*   k *cat*   l *leg*   m *man*   n *no*   p *pen*   r *red*   s *sit*

mission, etc. in which search and rescue is required or employed. **b** designating facilities, equipment, personnel, etc. used in search and rescue.

search engine *noun Computing* a program for the retrieval of data, files, etc. from a database or network.

Search for Extraterrestrial Life *noun* = SETI.

search·ing *adjective* (of an examination etc.) thorough, penetrating. □ **search·ing·ly** *adverb*

search·light *noun* **1** a powerful outdoor electric light with a concentrated beam that can be turned in any direction. **2** the light or beam from this.

search·master *noun Cdn* an air force officer in charge of coordinating a search and rescue operation, usu. from the airfield nearest the missing person or vehicle etc.

search party *noun* a group of people organized to look for a lost person or thing.

search warrant *noun* an order issued by a judge authorizing a person to enter and search a building and to seize evidence.

sear·ing *adjective* **1** very hot; scorching (*searing heat of the sun*). **2** very painful; agonizing (*a searing headache*). **3 a** upsetting, disturbing. **b** vicious, caustic; fuelled by anger (*searing criticism*). □ **sear·ing·ly** *adverb*

Searle /sɜːl/ **Ron·ald (Wil·liam Ford·ham)** (b.1920), English artist and cartoonist. His most famous creations are the schoolgirls of St. Trinian's, who became the subjects of four films (starting with *The Belles of St. Trinians*, 1954) and a number of books.

sea robin *noun N Amer.* any marine fish of the family Triglidae, having a large spiny head with mailed sides, and three finger-like pectoral rays used for walking on the seabed etc. *Also called* GURNARD.

sea rocket *noun* a European cruciferous plant, *Cakile maritima*, of sandy coasts, with purple flowers and fleshy leaves.

sea salt *noun* salt produced by evaporating sea water.

sea scallop *noun* **1** a large scallop, *Placopecten magellanicus*, of the N Atlantic. **2** the edible muscle of this scallop.

sea·scape *noun* **1** a picturesque view or prospect of the sea. **2** a representation of such a view, esp. a painting.

Sea Scout *noun* a member of the maritime branch of the Scouts.

sea serpent *noun* **1** (also **sea snake**) a snake of the family Hydrophidae, living in the sea. **2** an enormous legendary serpent-like sea monster.

sea·shell *noun* the shell of a marine mollusc.

sea·shore *noun* **1** land close to or bordering on the sea. **2** *Law* the area between high and low water marks.

sea·sick *adjective* suffering from dizziness or nausea from the motion of a ship at sea. □ **sea·sick·ness** *noun*

sea·side ● *noun* the seacoast, esp. resorted to for a holiday or pleasure. ● *attributive adjective* situated at the seaside (*seaside resort*).

sea slug *noun* a shell-less marine gastropod mollusc, esp. of the order Nudibranchia, with external gills.

sea smoke *noun* fog caused by cold air flowing over relatively warmer sea water, rising in columns giving the appearance of smoke.

sea snail *noun* **1** a small slimy fish of the family Liparididae, with a ventral sucker. **2** any spiral-shelled mollusc, e.g. a whelk.

sea snake *noun* = SEA SERPENT 1.

sea·son ● *noun* **1** each of the four periods (spring, summer, fall, and winter) into which the year is divided by the passage of the sun from equinox to solstice and from solstice to equinox, associated with a type of weather and a stage of vegetation. **2** a time of year characterized by climatic features (*the dry season*). **3** a time when something is plentiful or in vogue (*berry season*; *tourist season*). **4** the time of year regularly devoted to a usu. specified activity (*ski season*). **5 a** *Sport* the period of competition for a league or a team measured in games (*they struggled through the first ten games of the season*). **b** a schedule of shows or performances for theatrical performance, broadcast, etc. (*the fall television season*). **6** (also **Season**) the time of year surrounding a particular holiday (*Season's greetings*). **7** the time of year when a usu. specified animal breeds or is hunted or fished (*salmon season*). **8** a period of indefinite or varying length (*the season of her youth*). **9** *hist.* the time of year devoted to social events in fashionable society (*the first ball of the season*). ● *verb* **1** *transitive* flavour (food) with salt, herbs, spices, etc. **2** *transitive & intransitive* **a** make or become suitable or conditioned, esp. by exposure to the air or weather; mature (*seasoned hardwood*). **b** make or become mature or experienced (*a seasoned pro*). **c** condition (cast iron cookware) by coating with oil and heating, esp. to prevent sticking.

3 *transitive* enhance with wit, excitement, etc. **4** *transitive archaic* temper or moderate. □ **for all seasons 1** ready for any situation or emergency. **2** welcome or appropriate at any time under any conditions (*shoes for all seasons*). **in season 1** (of food) available in quantity and in good condition; ripe. **2** (of an animal) in heat. □ **sea·son·less** *adjective* [Old French *seson* from Latin *satio -onis* (in Romanic sense 'seed time') from *serere sat-* sow]

sea·son·able *adjective* **1** (of weather) usual or appropriate for the time of year (*seasonable spring temperatures*). **2** meeting the needs of the occasion; opportune (*seasonable advice*). □ **sea·son·ably** *adverb*

sea·son·al *adjective* **1** of, depending on, or characteristic of the seasons of the year or a particular season. **2** varying with the season (*seasonal temperature shifts*). **3** (of a person) employed only during a particular season. □ **sea·son·al·ity** *noun* **sea·son·al·ly** *adverb*

seasonal affective disorder *noun* a depressive state associated with late fall and winter and thought to be caused by a lack of light. Abbr.: **SAD**.

sea·son·ing *noun* **1** an ingredient, such as salt, a spice, a herb, etc., added to food to enhance its flavour. **2** the flavouring of a dish achieved by adding such ingredients (*adjust the seasoning*).

season opener *noun* the first game of a sports season or episode of a television season.

season ticket *noun* (usu. in *pl.*) (also esp. *Cdn* **season's ticket**) tickets or a pass for esp. a schedule of sporting or cultural events during a specified period, usu. bought at a reduced rate (*I have season tickets for the ballet*).

sea squirt *noun* any marine tunicate of the class Ascidiacea, consisting of a bag-like structure with apertures for the flow of water.

sea stack *noun* a column of rock detached from the mainland by erosion and rising precipitously out of the sea.

sea star *noun N Amer.* = STARFISH.

sea swallow *noun* any of various marine birds resembling swallows, esp. a tern.

seat ● *noun* **1 a** a thing made or used for sitting on, such as a chair, stool, bench, etc. **b** the part of a chair etc. on which one actually sits (*the chair had a wooden seat and a leather back*). **2 a** a place for one person to sit in a theatre, vehicle, etc. (*he gave me his seat on the bus*). **b** entitlement to a place to sit in a theatre etc.; a ticket (*I've got an extra seat for the game tonight*). **3 a** the right to sit as a member of a deliberative or administrative body. **b** *Cdn & Brit.* a Member of Parliament's constituency. **c** *N Amer.* = COUNTY SEAT. **4** the buttocks. **5** the part of the pants etc. covering the buttocks. **6** the part of a thing on which it rests or appears to rest; the base. **7** the manner of sitting on a horse etc. **8** a place in the membership of a stock exchange. **9** a site or location of something specified (*a seat of learning; the seat of the emotions*). **10** *Brit.* a country mansion, esp. with large grounds. ● *transitive verb* **1** find, and guide a person or oneself to, an available seat (*the waiter seated us near the window*). **2** provide sitting accommodation for (*the cinema seats 500*). **3** place or fit in position. □ **be seated** sit down. **by the seat of one's pants** *informal* by instinct rather than logic or knowledge. **take a** (or **one's**) **seat** sit down. □ **seat·less** *adjective* [Old Norse *sæti* (= Old English *gesete* from Germanic)]

seat·back *noun* the back support of a seat in a motor vehicle, airplane, etc.

seat belt *noun* a strap or set of straps designed to secure a person in a seat of a vehicle, aircraft, etc.

seat·ed *adjective* **1** sitting. **2** positioned.

-seater *noun* (in *combination*) a car, aircraft, piece of furniture, auditorium, etc. having a specified seating capacity (*that bus is a 16-seater*).

seat·ing *noun* **1** seats collectively (*seating area*). **2** sitting accommodation (*seating capacity*).

seat·mate *noun N Amer.* a person sitting in a neighbouring or adjoining seat.

SEATO /ˈsiːtoː/ *abbreviation* Southeast Asia Treaty Organization.

seat-of-the-pants *adjective* based on instinct or intuition rather than logic or knowledge.

sea trout *noun* **1** any of various migratory trout, esp. a large silvery race of the trout *Salmo trutta*. **2** any of various marine fishes that resemble trout, esp. a sciaenid of the genus *Cynoscion* and the Australian salmon *Arripis trutta*. *Also called* SALMON TROUT.

seat sale *noun Cdn & Brit.* a sale of esp. airline tickets at a reduced price.

Se·attle /siˈatəl/ a port and industrial city in the state of Washington,

on the eastern shores of Puget Sound; pop. (2000) 563,374.
□ **Seattle·ite** noun

sea urchin noun a small marine echinoderm of the class Echinoidea, with a spherical or flattened spiny shell.

sea·wall noun a wall or embankment erected as a breakwater to prevent encroachment by the sea.

sea·ward ● adverb (also **seawards**) towards the sea. ● adjective **1** going out to sea. **2** directed or facing towards the sea; situated on the side nearest the sea. ● noun the direction or position in which the sea lies.

sea·way noun **1** an inland waterway open to seagoing ships. **2** a ship's progress. **3** a ship's path across the sea.

sea·weed noun any of various algae growing in the sea or on the rocks on a shore. □ **sea·weedy** adjective

sea·worthy adjective (esp. of a ship) in a suitable condition to undergo a sea voyage. □ **sea·worth·i·ness** noun

sea-wrack noun seaweed, esp. coarse seaweed cast ashore.

seb·aceous /sɪˈbeɪʃəs/ adjective fatty; of or relating to tallow or fat. [Latin *sebaceus* from *sebum* tallow]

sebaceous gland noun a small gland found in the skin of mammals, esp. associated with hair follicles, which secretes oily matter or sebum to lubricate the skin and hair.

Sebastian, St. /sɪˈbastʃən, -tjən/ (late 3rd c.), Roman martyr. According to legend he was a soldier who was shot by archers on the orders of Diocletian, but who recovered, confronted the emperor, and was then clubbed to death. Feast day, 20 Jan.

Se·bas·to·pol /sɪˈbastəpɒl/ a fortress and naval base in Ukraine, near the southern tip of the Crimea; pop. (est. 2001) 341,000. It was the focal point of military operations during the Crimean War, falling eventually to Anglo-French forces in Sept. 1855 after a year-long siege.

seb·or·rhea /ˌsebəˈriə/ noun (*Brit.* **seb·or·rhoea**) excessive discharge of sebum from the sebaceous glands. □ **seb·or·rhe·ic** adjective (*Brit.* **seb·or·rhoe·ic**). [SEBUM after *gonorrhea* etc.]

sebum /ˈsiːbəm/ noun the oily secretion of the sebaceous glands which lubricates and protects the hair and skin. [modern Latin from Latin *sebum* grease]

SEC abbreviation Securities and Exchange Commission.

Sec. abbreviation secretary.

sec¹ abbreviation secant.

sec² noun informal an instant or moment; a second (*wait there, I'll be with you in a sec*). [abbreviation]

sec³ adjective (of wine) dry. [French from Latin *siccus*]

sec. abbreviation second(s).

se·cant /ˈsiːkənt/ *Math.* ● noun **1** a line cutting a curve at one or more points. **2** the ratio of the hypotenuse to the shorter side adjacent to an acute angle (in a right-angled triangle). Abbr.: **sec.** ● adjective cutting (*secant line*). [French *sécant(e)* from Latin *secare secant-* cut]

seca·teurs /ˌsekəˈtɜrz/ *plural noun Cdn & Brit.* a pair of pruning shears that can be used with one hand to clip usu. thin branches and flowers etc. [French *sécateur* cutter, irreg. from Latin *secare* cut]

secco ● noun **1** the process or technique of painting on dry plaster with colours mixed in water. **2** *Music* a secco recitative. ● adjective **1** *Music* (of recitative) having only occasional instrumental accompaniment. **2** var. of SEC³. [Italian, = dry, from Latin *siccus*]

se·cede /sɪˈsiːd/ intransitive verb (usu. foll. by *from*) withdraw formally from an alliance, an association, a federal union, or a political or religious organization. □ **se·ced·er** noun [Latin *secedere secess-* (as SE-, *cedere* go)]

se·ces·sion /sɪˈseʃən/ noun **1** the act or an instance of seceding. **2** (**Secession**) *hist.* the withdrawal of eleven southern States from the US Union in 1860, leading to the Civil War. □ **se·ces·sion·al** adjective [French *sécession* or Latin *secessio* (as SECEDE)]

se·ces·sion·ism /sɪˈseʃənˌɪzm/ noun **1** the principles of those in favour of secession. **2** *hist.* **a** the principles and beliefs of those favouring the secession of the Southern States from the US Union. **b** the principles and beliefs of those favouring the secession of certain ministers from the established Church of Scotland to form a separate church, the Secession Church, in 1733. □ **se·ces·sion·ist** noun & adjective

Se·chelt¹ /ˈsiːʃelt/ a district municipality on the southwestern coast of BC, situated on Sechelt Peninsula, between Powell River and Vancouver; pop. (2001) 7,775. [SECHELT²]

Se·chelt² /ˈsiːʃelt/ noun (pl. same) **1** a member of an Aboriginal people

living on the coast of BC, north of Vancouver. **2** the Sne Nay Muxw language of this people. [Sechelt, = 'land between two waters']

Sechelt Peninsula a peninsula of the southwestern coast of BC, situated east of Texada Island.

Seckel pear noun a pear of a small sweet juicy brownish-red variety. [from the surname of an early grower]

se·clude transitive verb (also *reflexive*) keep (a person) sequestered or shut up in order to prevent access or influence from outside (*the girls are secluded from the boys; after a long day she secludes herself in the library*). [Latin *secludere seclus-* (as SE-, *claudere* shut)]

se·clud·ed adjective **1** remote; hidden from view (*a secluded park bench*). **2** isolated or withdrawn from human contact; sequestered (*the monks live secluded from the outside world*).

se·clu·sion noun **1** a secluded state; confinement, isolation, privacy. **2** a secluded place.

seco·barbi·tal /ˌsekoˈbɑrbɪtɒl/ noun a sedative and hypnotic derivative of barbituric acid, $C_{12}H_{17}N_2O_3Na$, used esp. for preoperative sedation. [SECO(NDARY) + BARBITAL]

Seco·nal /ˈsekənɒl/ noun proprietary = SECOBARBITAL. [SECON(DARY) + AL(LYL)]

second¹ ● adjective **1** coming next after the first in time, order, or succession. **2** coming next in rank, quality, or importance to a person or thing regarded as first; subordinate, inferior. **3** another; in addition to one previously mentioned or considered (*I'd like a second helping of pie*). **4** alternate (*garbage collection is every second Monday*). **5** of the same quality or standard as a previous one; closely reminiscent of (*sociologists are calling it the second Industrial Revolution*). **6** *Music* performing a lower or different part (*I play second trumpet*). ● noun **1** a person or thing that is second; another person or thing in addition to one previously mentioned or considered. **2** a second-place finish in a race or competition (*our team placed two firsts and two seconds*). **3** (in *pl.*) *informal* a second helping of food at a meal. **4** (in *pl.*) goods that are slightly flawed or of an inferior quality. **5** = SECOND GEAR. **6** an assistant or attendant, esp. in a boxing match or duel. **7** *Baseball* **a** the second inning. **b** = SECOND BASE. **8** *N Amer.* Football = SECOND DOWN. **9** *Curling* the second player on a curling rink. **10** *Cdn & Brit.* (in Scouts, Girl Guides, etc.) a boy or girl chosen by their pack to assist the Sixer and replace him or her if absent. **11** *Music* **a** an interval or chord spanning two consecutive notes in the diatonic scale e.g. C to D. **b** a note separated from another by this interval. ● adverb in the second place; secondly. ● transitive verb **1** support, assist; offer backing to. **2** formally support or endorse (a nomination, resolution, motion, etc., or its proposer). □ **in the second place** as a second consideration etc. **second to none** superior; better than the rest. □ **sec·ond·er** noun [Old French from Latin *secundus* from *sequi* follow]

sec·ond² noun **1 a** a sixtieth part of a minute of time. **b** a sixtieth part of a minute of angular measurement. Symbol: ″. **2** *informal* a brief moment or instant (*I'll be there in a second*). **3** the SI unit of time, based on the natural periodicity of the radiation of a cesium-133 atom. Abbr.: **s** or ″. [French from medieval Latin *secunda (minuta)* secondary (minute)]

sec·ond³ /sɪˈkɒnd/ transitive verb **1** *Military* remove (an officer) temporarily from a regiment or corps for employment on the staff or in some other extra-regimental appointment. **2** transfer (a worker) temporarily to another position or employment. □ **se·cond·ee** noun *Brit.* **se·cond·ment** noun [French *en second* in the second rank (of officers)]

Second Advent noun = SECOND COMING 1.

sec·ond·ary ● adjective **1** second in rank, sequence, importance, etc. to what is primary. **2** derived from, based on, or supplementing something else that is primary; not original (*she used several secondary sources for her research*). **3** designating, relating to, or involved in education above primary or elementary education, below college or university, usu. for students in their mid to late teens. **4** *Med.* arising after or in consequence of an earlier symptom, infection, etc.; arising by metastasis. **5** *Electricity* (of a cell or battery) generating electricity by a reversible chemical reaction and therefore able to store applied energy. **6** *Electricity* (of a current) induced, not supplied directly from a source; of, pertaining to, or carrying the output of electrical power in a transformer etc. **7** *Chem.* (of an organic compound) having the characteristic functional group located on a saturated carbon atom which is bonded to two other carbon atoms. ● noun (pl. **-ies**) **1** a secondary person or thing. **2** = SECONDARY SCHOOL. **3** *Med.* a secondary tumour, infection, etc. **4** *N Amer.* Football **a** the defensive backs collectively. **b** the area of the field they cover; the defensive backfield.

5 *Electricity* a secondary coil, current, etc. □ **sec·ond·ar·i·ly** *adverb* **sec·ond·ar·i·ness** *noun*

secondary colour *noun* a colour derived from the mixing of two primary colours (*purple is a secondary colour obtained by blending red and blue*).

secondary feather *noun* any of the smaller flight feathers growing from the second joint or ulna of a bird's wing.

secondary market *noun* *Econ.* a financial market in which existing securities are traded (*opp.* PRIMARY MARKET).

secondary picketing *noun* **1** the picketing of a firm's premises by union members not employed there. **2** the picketing of premises of a firm doing business with an employer engaged in a labour dispute but not otherwise involved.

secondary planet *noun* a satellite of a planet (*compare* PRIMARY PLANET).

secondary rainbow *noun* an additional arch with the colours in reverse order formed inside or outside a rainbow by twofold reflection and twofold refraction.

secondary school *noun* a school offering secondary education.

secondary sexual characteristics *plural noun* the physical characteristics that are distinctive to each sex but are not essential to reproduction, and which typically develop, in humans, during puberty.

second ballot *noun* a deciding ballot taken between a candidate who has won a previous ballot without securing an absolute majority and the candidate with the next highest number of votes.

second banana *noun* *esp.* *N Amer.* *informal* **1** a supporting comedian in a show or vaudeville skit etc. **2** a person who plays a subordinate or secondary role (*compare* TOP BANANA).

second base *noun* *Baseball* **1** the second of three bases that must be touched to score a run, located directly beyond the pitcher's mound from home plate. **2** the position of the player covering this base and the area of the infield between it and first base. □ **second baseman** *noun*

second-best ● *adjective* next in quality to the best or first. ● *noun* **1** a second-best person or thing. **2** a less adequate or desirable alternative.

second chamber *noun* the upper house of a bicameral legislature, usu. having the function of revising measures prepared and passed by the lower.

second childhood *noun* a state of childishness that sometimes accompanies old age; senility, dotage.

second class ● *noun* **1** a set of persons or things grouped together as second-best. **2** the second-best accommodation in a train, ship, etc., usu. available at a lower rate. **3 a** *Cdn hist.* & *US* a class of mail for the handling of newspapers, flyers, and periodicals. **b** *Brit.* a class of mail costing less than first-class mail but not given priority in handling. **4** *Brit.* **a** the second highest division in a list of examination results. **b** a place in this. ● *adjective* (usu. **second-class**) **1** belonging to or travelling by the second class. **2** inferior in quality, standard, status, etc. ● *adverb* (usu. **second-class**) by second class.

second-class citizen *noun* **1** a person deprived of normal civic and legal rights. **2** a person treated as socially inferior.

second coming *noun* **1** (usu. **Second Coming**) the prophesied return of Christ to earth on Judgment Day. **2** (often foll. by *of*) the return of a person or thing, esp. in a new incarnation (*he writes so well they're calling him the second coming of Shakespeare*).

second cousin *noun* a child of one's parent's first cousin.

second-degree *adjective* **1** *N Amer.* **a** designating the second-most serious category of crime. **b** (of murder) next in culpability to first-degree murder, committed with intent but without premeditation and with certain mitigating circumstances. **2** denoting burns that are sufficiently severe to cause blistering but not permanent scarring.

second down *noun* *Football* the second of three attempts (four in American football) to advance the ball ten yards, thereby achieving a new first down.

Second Empire ● *noun* *hist.* **1** the French imperial government of Napoleon III, 1852–70, followed by the Third Republic. **2** this period in France. ● *adjective* designating a style of architecture prominent in the third quarter of the 19th c., influenced by French Renaissance architecture and characterized esp. by use of the mansard roof.

second fiddle *see* FIDDLE.

second floor *noun* **1** *N Amer.* the floor above the ground floor. **2** *Brit.* the floor two levels above the ground floor.

second gear *noun* the second (and next to lowest) in a sequence of gears of a car, bicycle, etc.

second generation ● *noun* **1** the grandchildren of immigrants who have settled in a particular country; the offspring of the first generation born in a country. **2** (of technology) an advanced or refined stage of development. ● *adjective* (usu. **second-generation**) **1** designating the offspring of a first generation. **2** designating something in an improved stage of development.

second-growth ● *noun* a growth of trees or other vegetation replacing one that has been destroyed by fire, removed by logging, etc. ● *adjective* **1** designating a forest, trees, etc. replacing vegetation that has been destroyed. **2** designating timber etc. that has been removed from a second-growth.

second-guess *transitive verb* **1** anticipate or predict by guesswork. **2** question, judge, or criticize with hindsight.

second hand *noun* the hand on an analog clock or watch that indicates the passing of seconds.

second-hand ● *adjective* **1 a** (of goods) previously owned or used; not new. **b** (of a store etc.) selling goods that have been previously owned or used. **2 a** (of information etc.) not heard or obtained directly from the original source, but accepted on another's authority. **b** (of an experience etc.) not undergone or felt personally, but vicariously through another. ● *adverb* **1** through an intermediary; not from the original source (*she heard the news second-hand*). **2** after being previously owned or used; not new (*she buys second-hand*).

second-hand smoke *noun* the smoke from a smoker's cigarette, cigar, etc. that is inhaled unwillingly by others.

second honeymoon *noun* a holiday like a honeymoon, taken by a couple after several years of marriage.

second-in-command *noun* **1** the officer next in rank to the commanding or chief officer. **2** a person next in authority to the person in charge.

Second International *noun* *see* INTERNATIONAL 1a.

second language *noun* a language spoken or used in addition to one's native language.

second-last ● *adjective* immediately preceding the final or most recent. ● *adverb* occurring or finishing immediately before the person or thing that is last or most recent. ● *noun* the penultimate person or thing.

second lieutenant *noun* (also **Second Lieutenant**) **1** (in the Canadian Army and Air Force) an officer holding a rank below lieutenant and above officer cadet, the lowest ranking commissioned officer. Abbr.: **2Lt**. **2** (in the US Army, Air Force, or Marines) a commissioned officer of the lowest rank, below first lieutenant. **3** *Brit.* an army officer ranking below lieutenant.

sec·ond·ly *adverb* **1** furthermore; in the second place. **2** as a second item.

second messenger *noun* *Physiol.* a substance whose release within a cell is promoted by a hormone and which brings about a response in the cell.

second mortgage *noun* a mortgage obtained on an already mortgaged property, usu. at a higher rate of interest than that given for first mortgages, and having a secondary priority in case of default etc.

second nature *noun* an acquired ability or habit etc. that has become instinctive (*skiing is second nature to him*).

se·con·do /səˈkɒndoʊ/ *noun* (pl. **se·con·di** /-diː/) *Music* the second or lower part in a duet etc. (*compare* PRIMO *noun*). [Italian]

second officer *noun* an assistant to the mate or pilot of a ship, airplane, etc.

second opinion *noun* *Med.* a diagnosis etc. performed by another person who has been consulted because there is doubt or argument surrounding the initial diagnosis.

second person *noun* *Grammar see* PERSON 4.

second position *noun* **1** *Ballet* **a** a position of the feet in which the legs are turned outwards with the backs of the heels a short distance apart so that the feet form a straight line. **b** a position of the arms in which they are curved and held extended to the sides of the body at waist height. **2** *Music* the second lowest position of the left hand on the fingerboard of a stringed instrument.

second-rate *adjective* of mediocre quality; inferior. □ **second-rateness** *noun* **second rater** *noun*

second reading *noun* the second of three successive occasions on which a bill must be presented to a legislature before it becomes law.

Second Reich *noun* the German Empire 1871–1918.

Second Republic *hist.* **1** the republican regime in France from the deposition of Louis Philippe in 1848 to the beginning of the Second Empire (1852). **2** this period in France.

second-run *noun* (*attributive*) designating a movie theatre showing films after their first release.

second sight *noun* the ability to perceive future or distant events; clairvoyance.

second storey *noun* = SECOND FLOOR.

second-storey man *noun* N Amer. a person who robs a house by breaking in through an upstairs window; a cat burglar.

second-strike *noun* a retaliatory attack conducted with weapons designed to withstand an initial nuclear attack or first strike.

second string ● *noun* **1** *Sport* **a** a roster of backup players available to replace players from the starting lineup if they become unable to play, esp. due to injury. **b** a backup player or substitute on this roster. **2** *Brit.* an alternative course of action, means of livelihood, etc., invoked if the main one is unsuccessful. ● *adjective* (**second-string**) **1** *Sport* designating a player etc. who is a backup or substitute (*second-string defenceman*). **2** designating a person or thing not of the first class or rank (*a second-string composer*). □ **second stringer** *noun*

second team *N Amer. Sport* ● *noun* a lineup of second-string players. ● *adjective* (usu. **second-team**) belonging or relating to the second team.

second thoughts *plural noun* **1** a new opinion or resolution reached after further consideration. **2** apprehension or doubt about a decision, action, etc. that has already been made.

second tooth *noun* a tooth that replaces a milk tooth in a mammal.

Second Vatican Council *see* VATICAN II.

second wind *noun* **1** recovery of the power of normal breathing during exercise after initial breathlessness. **2** a renewed energy or vigour needed to continue an effort.

Second World War (also **World War II**) (1939–45), a war in which the Axis Powers (Germany, Italy, and Japan) were defeated by an alliance eventually including the United Kingdom, Canada, Australia, New Zealand, the Soviet Union, and the United States. Beginning with the German invasion of Poland in September 1939, the war spread throughout Europe, North Africa, SE Asia and the western Pacific, ending after the exploding of nuclear weapons over Japan in August 1945. A high proportion of civilian casualties were among the estimated 55 million killed, including at least 6 million Jews and other persecuted minorities murdered in the Holocaust.

Se·cord /ˈsiːkərd/ **Laura** (born Laura Ingersoll) (1775–1868), Canadian heroine. In June of 1813 she walked 30 km from Queenston to Beaver Dams to warn the British that she had overheard American officers discussing a plan to attack; two days later the British ambushed and defeated the American forces as a result of her warning.

se·crecy *noun* **1** the ability or tendency to withhold information or keep things secret. **2** a state or condition in which disclosure of facts and events is strictly limited (*the deal was done in great secrecy*). □ **sworn to secrecy** having been made to promise to keep a secret.

se·cret ● *adjective* **1** kept or meant to be kept private, unknown, or hidden from others (*no one knew about her secret life*). **2** intended to be concealed from all but a few (*they communicate using a secret code*). **3** (of a person) **a** having a role or position unknown to others (*secret agent*). **b** fond of, prone to, or able to preserve secrecy. **4** (of a place) hidden, completely secluded (*secret hideaway*). ● *noun* **1** a fact, matter, or action that is kept private or is shared only with those concerned. **2** a thing known only to a few, though not intentionally concealed (*this cozy restaurant is one of the city's best kept secrets*). **3** a mystery (*the secrets of the universe*). **4** a valid but not commonly known or recognized method of achieving or maintaining something (*what's their secret?; being concise is the secret of good writing*). **5** *Catholicism* a prayer concluding the offertory of the Mass. □ **in secret** without others knowing. **in on the secret** among the number of those who know it. **keep a secret** not reveal it. **make no secret of** make perfectly clear. □ **se·cret·ly** *adverb* [Old French from Latin *secretus* (adj.) separate, set apart, from *secernere secret-* (as SE-, *cernere* sift)]

secret agent *noun* a person operating covertly or engaged on secret service; a spy.

se·cret·a·gogue /səˈkriːtəgɒg/ *noun Physiol.* a substance which promotes secretion. [from SECRETE¹ + Greek *agōgos* leading, eliciting]

sec·re·taire /ˌsekrəˈter/ *noun* a writing desk with drawers and pigeonholes, and usu. a bookcase above. [French (as SECRETARY)]

sec·re·tar·iat /ˌsekrəˈterɪət/ *noun* **1** a permanent administrative and executive department of a government or similar organization. **2** the staff of such a department, or its premises. **3** the position or office of secretary. [French *secrétariat* from medieval Latin *secretariatus* (as SECRETARY)]

sec·re·tary *noun* (*pl.* **-ies**) **1** a person employed by an individual or a company to manage or assist with files, records, and correspondence, make appointments, etc. **2** an official appointed by an organization, society, company board, etc. to conduct its correspondence, keep its records, etc. **3 a** *Cdn & Brit.* = PARLIAMENTARY SECRETARY. **b** *US* a member of the president's cabinet in charge of a particular department of state. **4** a civil servant employed as the principal assistant to an ambassador. **5** esp. *US* = SECRETAIRE. □ **sec·re·tar·ial** *adjective* **sec·re·tary·ship** *noun* [Late Latin *secretarius* (as SECRET)]

secretary bird *noun* a long-legged snake-eating African bird, *Sagittarius serpentarius*, with a crest likened to a quill pen stuck over a writer's ear.

Secretary-General *noun* the principal administrator of an organization, such as the United Nations.

Secretary of State *noun* **1** *Cdn* **a** *hist.* a department established in 1867 as a link between the Dominion of Canada and the imperial government, subsequently responsible for a variety of matters, esp. those falling outside of existing jurisdictions but not considered important enough for the creation of a new department; these have included citizenship, multiculturalism, translation, etc.; the department was eliminated in 1993. **b** (usu. **secretary of state** when not used as a title) a government minister responsible for a specific area within a department, such as scientific research, the status of women, etc. **2** *Brit.* a government minister in charge of a particular department of state. **3** *US* the chief government official responsible for foreign affairs.

secret ballot *noun* a ballot in which votes are cast in secret.

se·crete¹ /səˈkriːt/ *transitive verb Biol.* (of a cell, organ, etc.) produce (a substance) by means of secretion. □ **se·cre·tory** *adjective* [back-formation from SECRETION]

se·crete² /səˈkriːt/ *transitive verb* conceal; put into hiding. [obsolete *secret* (v.) from SECRET]

se·cre·tin /səˈkriːtən/ *noun* a hormone released into the bloodstream by the duodenum, esp. in response to acidity, to stimulate secretion by the liver and pancreas.

se·cre·tion /səˈkriːʃən/ *noun Biol.* **1** the production and release of a specific substance by a cell, gland, or organ into a cavity or vessel or into the surrounding medium either for a function in the organism or for excretion. **2** the secreted substance. [French *sécrétion* or Latin *secretio* separation (as SECRET)]

se·cret·ive /ˈsiːkrətɪv/ *adjective* inclined to make or keep secrets; reticent. □ **se·cret·ive·ly** *adverb* **se·cret·ive·ness** *noun*

secret police *noun* a police force operating in secret for political purposes.

secret service *noun* **1** a government department concerned with espionage and national security. **2** (**Secret Service**) (in the US) a branch of the Treasury Department dealing with counterfeiting and providing protection for the President etc.

secret society *noun* an organization formed to promote some cause by covert methods and whose members are sworn to secrecy about its existence and proceedings.

secs. *abbreviation* seconds.

Sec·State *noun* N Amer. slang = SECRETARY OF STATE.

sect *noun* **1 a** a body of people subscribing to religious doctrines usu. different from those of an established church from which they have separated. **b** a separately organized group, existing within a larger religious body, but with its own places of worship; a denomination. **2** usu. *derogatory* a religious faction or group regarded as heretical or as deviating from orthodox tradition. **3** the system or body of adherents of a particular philosopher or philosophy, or school of thought in politics etc. [Old French *secte* or Latin *secta* from the stem of *sequi secut-* follow]

sect. *abbreviation* section.

sect·ar·ian ● *adjective* **1** of or concerning a sect. **2** pertaining to or created by differences of religion or denomination (*sectarian violence*). **3** bigoted or narrow-minded esp. in following the doctrines of one's sect. ● *noun* **1** a member of a sect. **2** a bigot. □ **sect·ar·ian·ism** *noun*

sect·ary /ˈsektəri/ *noun* (*pl.* **-aries**) a member of a religious or political sect.

sec·tion ● *noun* **1** a part cut off or separated from something. **2 a** each of the parts into which a thing is or may be divided (actually or conceptually). **b** each of the parts out of which a structure can be fitted together. **3** a group of musicians playing similar instruments forming part of a band or orchestra or singing the same part in a choir (*the trumpet section*; *the rhythm section*). **4** a subdivision of a newspaper, book, document, statute, etc. (*I've finished reading the sports section*). **5** *N Amer.* **a** (*West*) one square mile of esp. agricultural land, 640 acres (approx. 260 hectares). **b** a particular district or community of a town (*residential section*). **6** a department of a store, library, etc. in which similar items may be found together (*produce section*; *children's section*). **7** one of the naturally divided segments of a citrus fruit, such as an orange. **8** *Cdn* = SCHOOL SECTION. **9** *N Amer.* the smallest administrative subdivision of a railway, usu. a mile or two in length. **10** a subdivision of an army platoon. **11 a** a thin slice of tissue, rock, etc., cut off for microscopic examination. **b** *Surgery* a cut or incision. **12 a** the cutting of a solid along a plane. **b** the resulting figure or the area of this. **13** a representation of the internal structure of something as it would appear if cut across a vertical or horizontal plane. ● *transitive verb* **1** arrange in or divide into sections. **2** cut into thin slices for microscopic examination. **3** *Brit.* commit (a person) to a psychiatric hospital. [French *section* or Latin *sectio* from *secare sect-* cut]

sec·tion·al ● *adjective* **1** of or relating to a section. **2 a** relating to a section or sections of a country, society, community, etc. **b** concerned with local or regional matters as opposed to general ones. **3** assembled or made from several sections (*sectional table*). ● *noun* a piece of furniture, such as a couch, composed of sections which can be used separately. □ **sec·tion·al·ism** *noun* **sec·tion·al·ist** *noun & adjective* **sec·tion·al·ize** *transitive verb* (also esp. *Brit.* **-ise**). **sec·tion·al·ly** *adverb*

section gang *noun N Amer.* a crew of workers in charge of maintaining a section of a railway.

section hand *noun* (also **section man**) *N Amer.* a member of a section gang.

section house *noun N Amer.* a house occupied by people responsible for maintaining a section of the railway.

section mark *noun* the sign (§) used as a reference mark to indicate the start of a section of a book etc.

section road *noun N Amer.* (*West*) a road bordering a section of land.

sec·tor *noun* **1 a** a distinct part or branch of an economy (*the tourism sector*). **b** an area of industry or of economic activity (*the private sector*). **2** the plane figure enclosed by two radii of a circle, ellipse, etc., and the arc between them. **3** a mathematical instrument consisting of two flat rulers hinged together at one end, sometimes attached to a graduated arc, and marked with various kinds of scales, used for making diagrams etc. **4** *Military* a subdivision of an area for military operations, controlled by one commander or headquarters. □ **sec·tor·al** *adjective* **sec·tor·ial** /sekˈtɔriəl/ *adjective* [Late Latin, techn. use of Latin *sector* cutter (as SECTION)]

secu·lar ● *adjective* **1** concerned with or belonging to the material world and the affairs of this world as opposed to the eternal or spiritual world. **2 a** (of literature, music, an artist, etc.) not concerned with religious subjects. **b** (of education etc.) excluding religious instruction; not promoting religious belief. **3** (of clergy) not bound by a religious or monastic rule. **4** occurring once in an age or century (*the secular games*). **5** lasting for or occurring over an indefinitely long time. ● *noun* a secular priest. □ **secu·lar·ism** *noun* **secu·lar·ist** *noun* **secu·lar·ity** /-ˈlerəti/ *noun* **secu·lar·ly** *adverb* [Latin *saecularis* from *saeculum* generation, age]

secular humanism *noun N Amer.* liberalism, esp. with regard to the belief that religion should not be taught or practised within a publicly funded education system. □ **secular humanist** *noun & adjective*

secu·lar·ize *transitive verb* (also esp. *Brit.* **-ise**) **1** dissociate from religious or spiritual concerns; convert to material and temporal purposes. **2** turn (a person) from a religious or spiritual state to worldliness. □ **secu·lar·iz·a·tion** *noun*

se·cund /səˈkʌnd/ *adjective Bot.* arranged on one side only. □ **se·cund·ly** *adverb* [Latin *secundus* (as SECOND[1])]

se·cure ● *adjective* **1** free from apprehension or anxiety; assured, confident (*I feel secure about our relationship*). **2** free from risk, reliable, certain not to fail (*secure investment*). **3** fixed or fastened so as not to give way or yield under strain (*made the door secure*). **4** not likely to be lost or stolen etc. **5** (of a place) **a** affording protection or safety. **b** difficult to escape from. **6** protected against attack, theft, or other criminal activity (*no airport could be totally secure*; *our secure server software encrypts all of your personal information*). ● *transitive verb* **1** make secure or safe; fortify. **2** fasten or close securely. **3** obtain or achieve. **4** ensure (a situation, outcome, result, etc.) (*the final goal secured the victory*). **5** guarantee against loss (*a loan secured by property*; *a secured line of credit*).

6 seize and hold (a person) in custody; confine. □ **secur·able** *adjective* **secure·ly** *adverb* [Latin *securus* (as SE-, *cura* care)]

secure custody *noun Cdn* custody in a correctional facility designed and designated for the detention of young offenders.

Se·curi·tate /səˌkjuriˈtotei/ the internal security force of Romania, set up in 1948 and officially disbanded during the revolution of December 1989. [Romanian, = security]

securities commission *noun* an agency established to supervise and regulate the selling and trading of securities.

se·curi·tize *transitive verb* (also esp. *Brit.* **-tise**) (often in *passive*) convert (an asset, esp. a loan) into securities, usu. in order to raise capital. □ **se·curi·tiz·a·tion** *noun*

se·cur·ity *noun* (*pl.* **-ies**) **1 a** the condition of being protected from or not exposed to danger; safety. **b** freedom from care, anxiety, worry, doubt, etc. **2** something that provides protection or safety (*we bought a lock for security*). **3 a** measures taken to ensure safety and prevent crime or other danger in a building, office, country, etc. **b** the department or members responsible for ensuring safety (*I'll call building security to have him removed*). **4** measures taken to ensure confinement of a prisoner etc. (*maximum-security prison*). **5** the guarantee or assurance of something (*job security*). **6** (often in *pl.*) **a** a certificate attesting the ownership of, or interest in, the capital, assets, property, profits, earnings, or royalties of any person or company. **b** a document, such as a bond, debenture, or note, acknowledging a debt. **7 a** an investment contract. **b** an agreement in which a person acquires a proportionate interest in a group of assets, such as an investment in a mutual fund. **8** property etc. deposited or pledged as a guarantee of the fulfillment of an obligation, such as an appearance in court or the payment of a debt, and liable to forfeit in the event of a default.

security blanket *noun* **1** a blanket or other object given to a child to provide comfort or reassurance by its familiarity. **2** *informal* something that offers comfort or reassurance (*he won't throw away that old shirt, it's his security blanket*).

security clearance *noun* an authorization to have access to sensitive or classified material, sites etc.

Security Council *noun* a permanent body of the United Nations seeking to maintain peace and security.

security deposit *noun* money etc. given by a tenant to a landlord as a guarantee of rent payments.

security guard *noun* a person employed to ensure the security of a person, building, vehicles, etc.

security risk *noun* a person whose presence may threaten security.

Sec·wep·emc /ˈsəxwepməx/ *noun* (*pl.* same) = SHUSWAP. [Secwepemc, self-designation]

sedan /sɪˈdan/ *noun* **1** *N Amer.* a luxury car for four or more people. **2** (in full **sedan chair**) an enclosed chair for conveying one person, carried between horizontal poles by two porters, common in the 17th–18th c. [perhaps alteration of Italian dial., ultimately from Latin *sella* saddle, from *sedēre* sit]

Sedan, Battle of /səˈdan, səˈdɑ̃/ a decisive battle of the Franco-Prussian War fought in 1870 near the town of Sedan in NE France, in which the Prussians succeeded in surrounding the French army and forcing it to surrender, opening the way for a Prussian advance on Paris and marking the end of the French Second Empire.

sed·ate[1] /səˈdeit/ *adjective* **1** calm, dignified, and unhurried (*walk at a sedate pace*). **2** quiet and rather dull (*sedate suburban domesticity*). □ **sed·ate·ly** *adverb* **sed·ate·ness** *noun* [Latin *sedatus* past participle of *sedare* settle, from *sedēre* sit]

sed·ate[2] /səˈdeit/ *transitive verb* make sleepy or quiet by means of drugs; administer a sedative to. [back-formation from SEDATION]

sed·ation /səˈdeiʃən/ *noun* **1** the action of sedating a person or thing. **2** a state of rest or sleep esp. produced by a sedative drug. [French *sédation* or Latin *sedatio* (as SEDATE[1])]

seda·tive /ˈsedətɪv/ ● *noun* a drug, influence, etc., that tends to calm or soothe. ● *adjective* calming, soothing; inducing sleep.

sed·en·tary /ˈsedənˌteri/ *adjective* **1** (of work etc.) characterized by much sitting and little physical exercise. **2** (of a person) spending much time seated; not getting much exercise. **3** *Zool.* **a** (esp. of a bird) not migratory. **b** confined to one spot; sessile. □ **sed·en·tar·i·ness** *noun* [French *sédentaire* or Latin *sedentarius* from *sedēre* sit]

Seder /ˈseidər/ *noun* a Jewish ritual service and ceremonial dinner for the first night or first two nights of the Passover. [Hebrew *sēder* order]

sed·er·unt /səˈderənt/ *noun* (in some Presbyterian Churches) a single sitting of a church court. [Latin, = (the following persons) sat, from *sedēre* sit]

sedge *noun* **1** any of various grasslike plants of the family Cyperaceae, esp. of the genus *Carex* with triangular stems, usu. growing in wet areas. **2** an expanse of this plant. □ **sedgy** *adjective* [Old English *secg* from Germanic]

Sedge·moor, Battle of a battle fought in 1685 on the plain of Sedgemoor in Somerset, in which the troops of James II decisively defeated the forces of the rebel Duke of Monmouth, who had landed in Dorset as champion of the Protestant cause and pretender to the throne.

Sedg·wick, Adam (1785–1873), English geologist, who specialized in the fossil record of rocks from N Wales, assigning the oldest of these to a period that he named the Cambrian.

sed·ile /sə'daɪlɪ/ *noun* (*pl.* **sed·ilia** /-'dɪlɪə/) (usu. in *pl.*) *Christianity* each of usu. three stone seats for priests in the south wall of a chancel, often canopied and decorated. [Latin, = seat, from *sedēre* sit]

sed·i·ment /'sedəmənt/ *noun* **1** matter that settles to the bottom of a liquid; dregs. **2** *Geol.* matter that is carried by water or wind and deposited on the surface of the land. [French *sédiment* or Latin *sedimentum* (as SEDILE)]

sed·i·ment·ary /ˌsedə'mentəri/ *adjective* **1** of or like sediment. **2** (esp. of rocks) formed from sediment, characteristically laid down in strata which are initially horizontal or nearly so.

sed·i·ment·a·tion /ˌsedəmən'teɪʃən/ *noun* deposition of material in the form of a sediment, as a geological process, or in a liquid in a tank, centrifuge, etc.

sed·i·ment·ol·ogy /ˌsedəmən'tɒlədʒi/ *noun* the branch of geology that deals with the nature and properties of sediments and sedimentary rocks. □ **sed·i·ment·o·logic·al** *adjective* **sed·i·ment·olo·gist** *noun*

se·di·tion /sə'dɪʃən/ *noun* **1** conduct or speech inciting to rebellion or a breach of public order. **2** agitation against the authority of a government. □ **se·di·tious** *adjective* **se·di·tious·ly** *adverb* [Old French *sedition* or Latin *seditio* from *sed-* = SE- + *ire* it- go]

Sedna (in Inuit mythology) the spirit that rules the underwater world.

se·duce *transitive verb* **1** tempt or entice into sexual activity. **2 a** tempt, lure (*seduced by the smell of coffee*). **b** (often foll. by *into*) lead astray (*seduced into a life of crime*). **c** (often as **se·duced** *adjective*) beguiled (*seduced by outward appearances*). □ **se·du·cible** *adjective* [Latin *seducere seduct-* (as SE-, *ducere* lead)]

se·du·cer *noun* a person, esp. a man, who sexually seduces, esp. habitually.

se·duc·tion *noun* **1** the act or an instance of seducing; the process of being seduced. **2** something that tempts or allures. [French *séduction* or Latin *seductio* (as SEDUCE)]

se·duc·tive *adjective* tending to seduce; alluring, enticing. □ **se·duc·tive·ly** *adverb* **se·duc·tive·ness** *noun*

se·duc·tress *noun* a female seducer. [obsolete *seductor* male seducer (as SEDUCE)]

sedu·lous /'sedjuləs/ *adjective* **1** persevering, diligent, assiduous. **2** (of an action etc.) deliberately and consciously continued; painstaking. □ **sedu·lous·ly** *adverb* [Latin *sedulus* zealous]

se·dum /'siːdəm, 'sed-/ *noun* any plant of the genus *Sedum*, with fleshy leaves and star-shaped yellow, pink, or white flowers, e.g. stonecrop. [Latin, = houseleek]

see¹ *verb* (*past* **saw**; *past participle* **seen**) **1** *transitive* discern by use of the eyes; observe; look at (*did you see that?*; *saw her fall over*). **2** *intransitive* have or use the power of discerning objects with the eyes (*sees best at night*). **3** *transitive* discern mentally; understand (*I see what you mean*; *could not see the point*). **4** *transitive* watch; be a spectator of (a film, game, etc.). **5** *transitive* ascertain or establish by inquiry or research or reflection (*I will see if the door is open*). **6** *transitive* consider; deduce from observation (*I see that you are a brave person*). **7** *transitive* contemplate; foresee mentally (*we saw that no good would come of it*; *can see myself doing this job indefinitely*). **8** *transitive* look at for information (usu. in *imperative* as a direction in or to printed material: *see page 15*). **9** *transitive* meet or be near and recognize (*I saw Eunice yesterday*). **10** *transitive* **a** meet socially (*sees her sister most weekends*). **b** meet regularly as a boyfriend or girlfriend; date (*is not seeing anyone*). **11** *transitive* give an interview, examination, etc. to (*the dentist will see you now*). **12** *transitive* visit to consult (*went to see the doctor*). **13** *transitive* find out or learn, esp. from a visual source (*I see the game has been cancelled*). **14** *intransitive* reflect; consider further; wait until one knows more (*we'll have to see*). **15** *transitive* interpret or have an opinion of (*I see things differently now*). **16** *transitive* experience; have presented to one's attention (*I never thought I would see this day*). **17** *transitive* recognize as acceptable; foresee (*do you see your daughter marrying this man?*). **18** *transitive* observe without interfering (*stood by and saw them squander my money*). **19** *transitive* find attractive (*can't think what she sees in him*). **20** *intransitive* (usu. foll. by *to*, or *that* + infin.) make provision for; ensure; attend to (*shall see to your request immediately*; *see that they get home safely*) (*compare* SEE TO IT). **21** *transitive* escort or conduct (to a place etc.) (*saw them home*). **22** *transitive* be a witness of (an event etc.) (*see the New Year in*; *the last decade has seen extraordinary expansion*). **23** *transitive* supervise (an action etc.) (*will stay and see the doors locked*). **24** *transitive* **a** (in gambling, esp. poker) equal (a bet). **b** equal the bet of (a player), esp. to see the player's cards. ● *interjection* **1** ascertaining the comprehension, continued interest, agreement, etc. of the person or persons addressed (*was driving along, see, when all of a sudden this guy ran in front of my car*). **2** expressing triumph (*see, I told you she'd be here!*). □ **as far as I can see** to the best of my understanding or belief. **as I see it** in my opinion. **do you see?** do you understand? **has seen better days** has declined from former prosperity, good condition, etc. **I'll be seeing you** *informal* an expression on parting. **I see** I understand (referring to an explanation etc.). **let me see** an appeal for time to think before speaking etc. **see about** attend to. **see after 1** take care of. **2** = SEE ABOUT. **see the back of** *Brit. informal* be rid of (an unwanted person or thing). **see a man about a dog** (or **horse**) *N Amer. informal* go to the bathroom (*excuse me, I have to see a man about a dog*). **see fit** see FIT¹. **see here!** = LOOK HERE! (*see* LOOK *interjection*). **see into** investigate. **see life** gain experience of the world, often by enjoying oneself. **see the light 1** realize one's mistakes etc. **2** suddenly see the way to proceed. **3** undergo religious conversion. **see off 1** be present at the departure of (a person) (*saw them off at the airport*). **2** *Brit. informal* ward off, get the better of (*managed to see off an investigation into their working methods*). **see out 1** accompany out of a building etc. **2** finish (a project etc.) completely. **3** remain awake, alive, etc., until the end of (a period). **4** last longer than; outlive. **see over** inspect; tour and examine. **see reason** see REASON. **see red** become suddenly enraged. **see a person right** make sure that a person is rewarded, safe, etc. **see stars** *informal* see lights before one's eyes as a result of a blow to the head. **see things** have hallucinations or false imaginings. **see through 1** not be deceived by; detect the true nature of. **2** penetrate visually. **see a person through** support a person during a difficult time. **see a thing through** persist with it until it is completed. **see to it** (foll. by *that* + clause) ensure (*see to it that I am not disturbed*) (*compare* sense 20 of *verb*). **see one's way clear to** feel able or entitled to. **see the world** see WORLD. **see you** (or **see you later**) *informal* an expression on parting. **we shall see** let us await the outcome. **2** a formula for declining to act at once. **will see about it** a formula for declining to act at once. **you see 1** you understand. **2** you will understand when I explain. □ **see·able** *adjective* [Old English *sēon* from Germanic]

see² *noun* **1** the area under the authority of a bishop or archbishop; a diocese. **2** the office or jurisdiction of a bishop or archbishop. [Anglo-French *se(d)* ultimately from Latin *sedes* seat, from *sedēre* sit]

seed ● *noun* **1 a** a flowering plant's unit of reproduction (esp. in the form of grain) capable of developing into another such plant. **b** seeds collectively, esp. for sowing (*must buy seed*). **c** (*attributive*) suitable or kept for seed (*seed potatoes*). **2** (foll. by *of*) a prime cause or beginning (*seeds of doubt*). **3** *archaic* semen or sperm. **4** *archaic* offspring, progeny, descendants (*the seed of Abraham*). **5** *Sport* a seeded player. **6** a small seed-like container for the application of radium etc. **7** a seed crystal. ● *verb* **1** *transitive* **a** place seeds in. **b** sprinkle with or as with seed. **2** *intransitive* sow seeds. **3** *intransitive* produce or drop seed. **4** *transitive* remove seeds from (fruit etc.). **5** *transitive* place a crystal or crystalline substance in (a solution etc.) to cause crystallization or condensation (esp. in a cloud to produce rain). **6** *transitive Sport* assign to (a strong competitor in a competition) a position in an ordered list so that strong competitors do not meet each other in early rounds (*is seeded seventh*). **b** arrange (the order of play) in this way. **7** *intransitive* go to seed. ● *attributive adjective* (of funding etc.) intended to initiate a project etc. (*seed grant*; *seed capital*). □ **go** (or **run**) **to seed 1** cease flowering as seed develops. **2** become degenerate, unkempt, ineffective, etc. □ **seed·less** *adjective* [Old English *sǣd* from Germanic, related to SOW¹]

seed·bed *noun* **1** a bed of fine soil in which to sow seeds. **2** a place of development.

seed·cake *noun* cake containing whole seeds esp. of caraway as flavouring.

seed coat *noun* the outer integument of a seed.

seed corn *noun* **1** corn kept for seed. **2** *Brit.* assets reused for future profit or benefit.

seed crystal *noun* a crystal used to initiate crystallization.

seed drill noun = DRILL² noun 1.

seed-eater noun a bird (esp. a finch) living mainly on seeds.
□ **seed-eating** adjective

seed·er noun 1 a person or thing that seeds. 2 a machine for sowing seed, esp. a drill. 3 an apparatus for seeding grapes etc.

seed head noun a flower head in seed.

seed house noun N Amer. a company that sells seeds.

seed leaf noun a cotyledon.

seed·ling noun a young plant, esp. one raised from seed and not from a cutting etc.

seed money noun money allocated to initiate a project.

seed pearl noun a very small pearl.

seed pod noun a long seed vessel that splits when it is ripe.

seed potato noun a potato kept for seed.

seeds·man noun (pl. **-men**) a dealer in seeds.

seed·time noun the sowing season.

seed vessel noun a pericarp.

seedy adjective (**seed·i·er**, **seed·i·est**) 1 full of seed. 2 going to seed. 3 rundown; dilapidated. 4 shabby-looking; in worn clothes. 5 disreputable. 6 informal unwell. □ **seed·i·ly** adverb **seed·i·ness** noun

See·ger /'siːɡər/ **Pete** (b.1919), US folk musician and songwriter. In 1949 he formed the folk group the Weavers, with whom he recorded a series of bestselling protest songs, including 'Where Have All the Flowers Gone?' (1956).

see·ing ● conjunction (usu. foll. by that + clause) considering that, inasmuch as, because (seeing that you do not know it yourself). ● noun 1 the sense or faculty of sight; vision. 2 Astronomy the quality of observed images as determined by atmospheric conditions.

Seeing Eye dog noun proprietary a dog that is specially trained to guide a blind person.

seek verb (past and past participle **sought**) 1 a transitive make a search or inquiry for. b intransitive (foll. by for, after) make a search or inquiry. 2 transitive a try or want to find or get. b ask for; request (sought help from him; seeks my aid). 3 transitive (foll. by to + infin.) endeavour or try. 4 transitive make for or resort to (a place or person, for advice, health, etc.) (sought her bed; sought a fortune teller). □ **seek out** 1 search for and find. 2 single out for companionship or attention. **far to seek** difficult to find (the reason is not far to seek). □ **seek·er** noun (also in combination). [Old English sēcan from Germanic]

seekh kebab /'siːk kəbɒb, -bab/ noun a kebab made of ground meat (esp. lamb) mixed with spices and moulded into the shape of a small sausage. [Arabic sīk spit, skewer + KEBAB]

seem intransitive verb 1 give the impression or sensation of being (seems ridiculous; seems certain to win). 2 (foll. by to + infin.) appear or be perceived or ascertained (he seems to be breathing; they seem to have left). □ **can't seem to** informal seem unable to. **it seems** (or **would seem**) (often foll. by that + clause) it appears to be true or the fact (in a hesitant, guarded, or ironical statement). [Old Norse sœma honour, from sœmr fitting]

seem·ing ● adjective apparent but not genuine (with seeming sincerity). ● noun 1 appearance, aspect. 2 deceptive appearance. □ **seem·ing·ly** adverb

seem·ly adjective (**seem·li·er**, **seem·li·est**) conforming to propriety or good taste; decorous, suitable. □ **seem·li·ness** noun

seen past participle of SEE¹.

See of Rome noun the papacy, the Holy See.

seep ● intransitive verb 1 ooze, filter, or percolate slowly. 2 permeate. 3 pass gradually (her anger seeped away). ● noun N Amer. a place where water, petroleum, etc. oozes slowly out of the ground. [perhaps dial. form of Old English sipian to soak]

seep·age noun 1 the act of seeping. 2 the quantity that seeps out.

seer noun 1 a person who sees. 2 a prophet; a person who sees visions; a person of supposed supernatural insight esp. as regards the future.

seer·sucker noun material of linen, cotton, etc., with a puckered surface. [Persian šīr o šakar, lit. 'milk and sugar']

see-saw ● noun 1 a a device consisting of a long plank balanced on a central support for children to sit on at each end and move up and down by pushing the ground with their feet. b a game played on this. 2 an up-and-down or to-and-fro motion. 3 a contest or situation with each of the opposing forces repeatedly gaining the advantage. ● intransitive verb 1 play on a see-saw. 2 move up and down as on a see-saw. 3 vacillate in policy, emotion, etc. ● adjective 1 with up-and-down or backward-and-forward motion (see-saw motion).

2 characterized by vacillation or progress alternating in two opposite directions (the law has a see-saw effect). [reduplication of SAW¹]

seethe verb 1 intransitive boil, bubble over. 2 intransitive be very agitated, esp. with anger (seething with discontent; I was seething inwardly). □ **seeth·ing·ly** adverb [Old English sēothan from Germanic]

see-through adjective (esp. of clothing) translucent.

Se·fer·is /sə'ferɪs/ **George** (pseudonym of Giorgios Stylianou Seferiades) (1900–71), Greek poet, critic, and diplomat. His poetry, in collections such as Strophe (1931) and Mythistorema (1935), combines traditional elements, everyday diction, and demotic and folk-poetry materials; he was awarded the Nobel Prize for literature in 1963.

seg·ment ● noun 1 each of several parts into which a thing is or can be divided or marked off. 2 Math. a part of a figure cut off by a line or plane intersecting it, esp.: a the part of a circle enclosed between an arc and a chord. b the part of a line included between two points. c the part of a sphere cut off by any plane not passing through the centre. 3 Broadcasting a a division of a day's broadcasting time; a time slot. b a separate item, esp. within a program. 4 Zool. each of the longitudinal sections of the body of certain animals (e.g. worms). ● verb 1 intransitive & transitive divide into segments. 2 intransitive Biol. (of a cell) undergo cleavage or divide into many cells. □ **seg·ment·al** adjective **seg·ment·al·ly** adverb **seg·ment·ary** adjective **seg·ment·a·tion** noun [Latin segmentum from secare cut]

Se·go·via¹ /sə'ɡoʊviə/ a city in north central Spain, northeast of Madrid; pop. (est. 2001) 54,0390. It is the site of an aqueduct built by the Romans in the 2nd c. AD.

Se·go·via² /sə'ɡoʊviə/ **An·drés** (1893–1987), Spanish guitarist and composer, who was largely responsible for the revival of interest in the guitar as a classical instrument; he transcribed many classical works, including Bach, and commissioned works from contemporary composers such as Manuel de Falla.

seg·re·gate /'seɡrəˌɡeɪt/ verb 1 transitive put apart from the rest; isolate. 2 transitive enforce racial segregation on (persons) or in (a community etc.). 3 intransitive Biol. (of alleles) separate into dominant and recessive groups. □ **seg·re·ga·tive** adjective [Latin segregare (as SE-, grex gregis flock)]

seg·re·ga·tion /ˌseɡrə'ɡeɪʃən/ noun 1 enforced separation of racial groups in a community etc. 2 the act or an instance of segregating; the state of being segregated. 3 an area of a prison where inmates are isolated from others, usu. because they represent a risk to others or because they are at risk from other inmates (also attributive: segregation unit). □ **seg·re·ga·tion·al** adjective **seg·re·ga·tion·ist** noun & adjective

segue /'seɡweɪ/ ● intransitive verb (**segues**, **segued**, **segue·ing**) 1 Music (usu. foll. by into) go on without a pause into the next section. 2 move smoothly from one thing or topic to another. ● noun an uninterrupted transition from one musical section or melody to another. [Italian, = follows]

sei /seɪ/ noun a small rorqual, Balaenoptera borealis. [Norwegian sejhval sei whale]

sei·cento /seɪ'tʃentoʊ/ noun the style of Italian art and literature of the 17th c. [Italian, = 600, used with reference to the years 1600–99]

seiche /seɪʃ/ noun a fluctuation in the water level of a lake etc., usu. caused by changes in barometric pressure. [Swiss French, perhaps from German Seiche 'sinking (of water)']

Sei·fert /'saɪfərt/ **Jaro·slav** (1901–86), Czech poet and journalist, whose works include City in Tears (1920), Clothed in Light (1940), and The Helmet of Clay (1945); he was awarded the Nobel Prize for literature in 1984.

sei·gneur /siː'njɜr/ noun 1 Cdn hist. a holder of land under the seigneurial system. 2 a feudal lord; the lord of a manor. □ **sei·gneur·ial** adjective [French from Latin SENIOR]

seigneurial system noun Cdn hist. a system of land tenure established in New France, based on the feudal system, under which land was owned by seigneurs who rented it to tenant farmers and provided mills, a court system, and other services. The system was left in place after the Conquest, and was officially abolished in 1854.

sei·gneury /'siːnjəri/ noun (pl. **-ies**) 1 Cdn hist. a a tract of land held by a seigneur under the seigneurial system. b a grant of land in the interior, esp. for the harvesting of furs, fish, etc. 2 lordship, sovereign authority. 3 a seigneur's domain.

sei·gnior·age /'siːnjərɪdʒ/ noun (also **sei·gnor·age**) 1 a a profit made by issuing currency, esp. by issuing coins rated above their intrinsic value. b hist. the Crown's right to a percentage on bullion brought to a mint for coining. 2 hist. something claimed by a sovereign or feudal superior as a prerogative.

seine /seɪn/ ● *noun* (also **seine net**) a fishing net for encircling fish, with floats at the top and weights at the bottom edge, and usu. hauled ashore (also *attributive*: *seine boat*). ● *transitive & intransitive verb* fish or catch with a seine. □ **sein·er** *noun* **sein·ing** *noun* [Old French *saine*, & Old English *segne* from West Germanic from Latin *sagena* from Greek *sagēnē*]

Seine River /seɪn/ a river of N France. Rising north of Dijon, it flows northwestward for 761 km (473 miles), through the cities of Troyes, Paris, and Rouen, to the English Channel near Le Havre.

seisin /ˈsiːzɪn/ *noun* (also **seizin**) *Law* **1** possession of land by freehold. **2** the act of taking such possession. **3** what is so held. [Old French *seisine* (as SEIZE)]

seis·mic /ˈsaɪzmɪk/ *adjective* **1** of or relating to an earthquake or earthquakes or other vibrations of the earth and its crust. **2** relating to or involving vibrations of the earth produced artificially by explosions. **3** of enormous proportions or effect (*seismic shifts in the global economy*). □ **seis·mic·al·ly** *adverb* [Greek *seismos* earthquake, from *seiō* shake]

seis·mi·city /saɪzˈmɪsɪti/ *noun* seismic activity; esp. the frequency of earthquakes per unit area in a region.

seismic survey *noun* a survey for oil and gas, employing seismic methods.

seismo- /ˈsaɪzmɔː/ *combining form* earthquake. [Greek *seismos*]

seis·mo·gram /ˈsaɪzmə,ɡram/ *noun* a record given by a seismograph.

seis·mo·graph /ˈsaɪzmə,ɡraf/ *noun* an instrument that records the force, direction, etc. of earthquakes. □ **seis·mo·graph·ic** *adjective*

seis·mol·ogy /saɪzˈmɒlədʒi/ *noun* the scientific study and recording of earthquakes and related phenomena. □ **seis·mo·log·ic·al** *adjective* **seis·mo·log·ic·al·ly** *adverb* **seis·mo·log·ist** *noun*

seize *verb* **1** *transitive* take hold of forcibly or suddenly. **2** *transitive* take possession of forcibly (*seized the fortress; seized power*). **3** *transitive* take possession of (contraband goods, documents, etc.) by warrant or legal right; confiscate, impound. **4** *transitive* affect suddenly (*panic seized us; was seized by apoplexy; was seized with remorse*). **5** *transitive* take advantage of (an opportunity). **6** *transitive* comprehend quickly or clearly. **7** *intransitive* (usu. foll. by *on, upon*) **a** take hold forcibly or suddenly. **b** take advantage eagerly (*seized on a pretext*). **8** *intransitive* (usu. foll. by *up*) **a** (of a moving part in a machine) become stuck or jammed from undue heat, friction, etc. **b** (of part of the body etc.) become stiff. **9** *intransitive* (of melted chocolate) become solid and grainy after coming into contact with a liquid. **10** *transitive* (usu. foll. by *of*) *Law* put in possession of. **11** *transitive Naut.* fasten or attach by binding with turns of yarn etc. □ **seized of 1** possessing legally. **2** aware or informed of. □ **seiz·er** *noun* [Old French *seizir, saisir* give seisin, from Frankish from Latin *sacire* from Germanic]

seizin *var. of* SEISIN.

seiz·ing *noun Naut.* a cord or cords used for seizing (*see* SEIZE 11).

seiz·ure /ˈsiːʒər/ *noun* **1** the act or an instance of seizing; the state of being seized. **2** a sudden attack of epilepsy etc.

se·jant /ˈsiːdʒənt/ *adjective* (placed after noun) *Heraldry* (of an animal) sitting upright on its haunches. [properly *seiant* from Old French var. of *seant* sitting, from *seoir* from Latin *sedēre* sit]

Sejm /seɪm/ *noun* (also **Seim**) the lower house of parliament in Poland. [Polish]

Sek·ani /səˈkɑːni/ *noun* (*pl.* same or **Sek·anis**) **1** a member of an Aboriginal group living on the western slope of the Rocky Mountains in north central BC. **2** the Athapaskan language of this people. [Sekani, = 'people of the rocks, people of the mountains']

Sekh·met /ˈsɛkmɛt/ *Egyptian Myth* a ferocious lioness goddess, counterpart of the gentle cat goddess Bastet and wife of Ptah at Memphis; her messengers could inflict disease and other scourges upon humankind.

sekt /zɛkt/ *noun* a German sparkling white wine. [German]

selach·ian /sɪˈleɪkiən/ ● *noun* any fish of the subclass Selachii, including sharks and dogfish. ● *adjective* of or relating to this subclass. [modern Latin *Selachii* from Greek *selakhos* shark]

selah /ˈsiːlə/ *interjection Bible* often used at the end of a verse in Psalms and Habakkuk, supposed to be a musical direction. [Hebrew *selāh*]

Se·lang·or /səˈlaŋər/ a state of Malaysia, on the west coast of the Malay Peninsula; capital, Shah Alam.

Sel·craig /ˈselkreiɡ/ *see* SELKIRK[2].

sel·dom *adverb* rarely, not often. [Old English *seldan* from Germanic]

se·lect ● *verb* **1** *transitive* choose, esp. as the best or most suitable. **2** *intransitive* choose or pick out something from a number; make a selection. ● *adjective* **1** chosen for excellence or suitability; choice. **2** (of a society etc.) exclusive, cautious in admitting members. □ **se·lect·able** *adjective* **se·lect·ed** *adjective* **se·lect·ness** *noun* **se·lect·or** *noun* [Latin *seligere select-* (as SE-, *legere* choose)]

select committee *noun* a small parliamentary committee appointed for a special purpose.

se·lec·tion *noun* **1** the act or an instance of selecting; the state of being selected. **2** a selected person or thing. **3** things from which a choice may be made. **4** *Biol.* the process in which environmental and genetic influences determine which types of organism thrive better than others, regarded as a factor in evolution. □ **se·lec·tion·al** *adjective* **se·lec·tion·al·ly** *adverb*

selection committee *noun* a committee that chooses a person or thing, esp. one that chooses a person for a job.

se·lect·ive *adjective* **1** using or characterized by selection. **2** able to select, esp. (of a radio receiver) able to respond to a chosen frequency without interference from others. **3** (of one's memory, hearing, etc.) selecting what is convenient. **4** (of a herbicide etc.) affecting only a particular species. □ **se·lect·ive·ly** *adverb* **se·lect·ive·ness** *noun* **se·lec·tiv·ity** *noun*

selective serotonin reuptake inhibitor *noun* any of a group of antidepressant drugs that increase the levels of serotonin in the brain by blocking its reabsorption by nerve endings. Abbr.: **SSRI**.

selective service *noun N Amer.* service in the armed forces under conscription.

Sel·ene /səˈliːni/ *Gk Myth* the goddess of the moon, identified with Artemis. According to one story, she fell in love with Endymion and asked Zeus to grant him a wish; Endymion chose immortality and eternal youth, which Zeus granted, but only on condition that Endymion remain forever asleep. [Greek *selēnē* moon]

selen·ite /ˈsɛlə,naɪt/ *noun* a form of gypsum occurring as transparent crystals or thin plates. [Latin *selenites* from Greek *selēnitēs lithos* moonstone, from *selēnē* moon]

sel·en·ium /səˈliːniəm/ *noun* a non-metallic element occurring naturally in various metallic sulphide ores and characterized by the variation of its electrical resistivity with intensity of illumination. Symbol: **Se**; at. no.: 34. [modern Latin from Greek *selēnē* moon + -IUM]

selenium cell *noun* a photovoltaic cell containing selenium.

seleno- /səˈliːnɔː/ *combining form* moon. [Greek *selēnē* moon]

selen·og·raphy /,sɛlɪˈnɒɡrəfi/ *noun* the study or mapping of the moon. □ **selen·og·raph·er** *noun* **sel·eno·graph·ic** *adjective*

selen·ol·ogy /,sɛlɪˈnɒlədʒi/ *noun* the scientific study of the moon. □ **selen·olo·gist** *noun*

Seles /ˈsɛlez/ **Mon·ica** (b.1973), American tennis player, born in Yugoslavia. She became the youngest woman to win a grand slam singles title with her victory in the French Open in 1990. She was stabbed on court by a fan of Steffi Graf in 1993, but she returned to play in 1995 and won the Australian Open in 1996.

Seleu·cid /səˈluːsɪd/ a dynasty founded by Seleucus Nicator, one of the generals of Alexander the Great, ruling over Syria and a great part of W Asia 311–65 BC. Its capital was at Antioch.

self ● *noun* (*pl.* **selves**) **1** a person's or thing's own individuality or essence (*showed his true self*). **2** a person or thing as the object of introspection or reflexive action (*the consciousness of self*). **3 a** one's own interests or pleasure (*cares for nothing but self*). **b** concentration on these (*self is a bad guide to happiness*). **4** used in phrases equivalent to *myself, yourself, himself*, etc. (*his very self; your good selves*). **5** (*pl.* **selfs**) a flower of uniform colour, or of the natural wild colour. ● *adjective* **1** of the same colour as the rest or throughout. **2** (of a flower) of the natural wild colour. **3** (of colour) uniform, the same throughout. ● *pronoun informal* myself, yourself, himself, herself, etc. (*ticket admitting self and friend*). □ **one's better self** one's nobler impulses. **one's former** (or **old**) **self** oneself as one formerly was. [Old English from Germanic]

self- *combining form* expressing reflexive action: **1** of or directed towards oneself or itself (*self-respect; self-cleaning*). **2** by oneself or itself, esp. without external agency (*self-evident*). **3** on, in, for, or relating to oneself or itself (*self-absorbed; self-confident*).

self-abasement *noun* the abasement of oneself; self-humiliation. □ **self-abasing** *adjective*

self-abnega·tion *noun* the abnegation of oneself, one's interests, needs, etc.; self-sacrifice.

self-absorp·tion *noun* **1** absorption in oneself. **2** *Physics* the absorption, by a body, of radiation emitted within it. □ **self-absorbed** *adjective*

self-abuse *noun* **1** behaviour which causes damage or harm to oneself. **2** *archaic* masturbation.

self-accusa·tion *noun* the accusing of oneself.
□ **self-accusa·tory** *adjective*

self-acting *adjective* acting without external influence or control; automatic.

self-actual·iz·a·tion *noun Psych.* the realization of one's talents and potentialities, esp. considered as a drive or need present in everyone.
□ **self-actual·ize** *intransitive verb*

self-addressed *adjective* (of an envelope etc.) having one's own address on for return communication.

self-adhesive *adjective* (of a label, stamp, etc.) adhesive, esp. without being moistened.

self-adjust·ing *adjective* (of machinery etc.) adjusting itself.

self-admira·tion *noun* the admiration of oneself; pride; conceit.
□ **self-admiring** *adjective*

self-advance·ment *noun* the advancement of oneself.

self-advertise·ment *noun* the advertising or promotion of oneself.
□ **self-advertis·ing** *adjective*

self-affirm·a·tion *noun Psych.* the recognition and assertion of the existence of the conscious self.

self-aggrand·ize·ment *noun* the act or process of promoting oneself as being powerful or important. □ **self-aggrand·iz·ing** *adjective*

self-analysis *noun Psych.* the analysis of oneself, one's motives, character, etc. □ **self-analyz·ing** *adjective*

self-appoint·ed *adjective* designated so by oneself, not authorized by another (*a self-appointed expert*).

self-approv·al *noun* a good opinion of oneself; conceit.

self-assertion *noun* the aggressive promotion of oneself, one's views, etc. □ **self-assert·ing** *adjective* **self-assert·ive** *adjective* **self-assert·ive·ness** *noun*

self-assess·ment *noun* **1 a** assessment or evaluation of oneself, or one's actions, attitudes, or performance. **b** an instance of this. **2** calculation of one's own taxable liability.

self-assurance *noun* confidence in one's own abilities etc.
□ **self-assured** *adjective* **self-assured·ly** *adverb*

self-aware *adjective* conscious of one's character, feelings, motives, etc. □ **self-awareness** *noun*

self-basting *adjective* (esp. of a turkey) injected with butter or oil before cooking to make the cooked meat more moist.

self-belief *noun* belief in one's abilities or worth.

self-betray·al *noun* **1** the betrayal of oneself. **2** the inadvertent revelation of one's true thoughts etc.

self-care *noun Medicine* the practice of activities that are necessary to sustain life and health, carried out by individuals for themselves.

self-catering *adjective* (esp. of a holiday or holiday premises) providing rented accommodation with cooking facilities but without food.

self-censor·ship *noun* the censoring of oneself.

self-centred *adjective* (also **self-centered**) preoccupied with one's own personality or affairs. □ **self-centred·ly** *adverb* **self-centred·ness** *noun*

self-cleaning *adjective* (esp. of an oven) equipped with a mechanism that allows heating of the oven to sufficiently high temperatures to burn off grease, dirt, etc.

self-closing *adjective* (of a door etc.) closing automatically.

self-collect·ed *adjective* composed, serene, self-assured.

self-conceit *noun* a high or exaggerated opinion of oneself, one's talents, one's achievements, etc. □ **self-conceit·ed** *adjective*

self-confessed *adjective* openly admitting oneself to be (*a self-confessed fanatic*).

self-confidence *noun* = SELF-ASSURANCE. □ **self-confident** *adjective* **self-confident·ly** *adverb*

self-congratu·la·tion *noun* = SELF-SATISFACTION.
□ **self-congratu·la·tory** *adjective*

self-conscious *adjective* **1** nervous or awkward because one is shy or worried about what other people think of one. **2** strongly aware of who one is or what one is doing. □ **self-conscious·ly** *adverb* **self-conscious·ness** *noun*

self-consist·ent *adjective* (of parts of the same whole etc.) consistent; not conflicting. □ **self-consist·ency** *noun*

self-consti·tut·ed *adjective* (of a person, group, etc.) assuming a function without authorization or right; self-appointed.

self-contained *adjective* **1** independent. **2** (esp. of living accommodation) complete in itself. **3** (of a person) uncommunicative.
□ **self-contain·ment** *noun*

self-contempt *noun* contempt for oneself.

self-content *noun* satisfaction with oneself, one's life, achievements, etc. □ **self-content·ed** *adjective*

self-contra·dic·tion *noun* internal inconsistency.
□ **self-contra·dict·ing** *adjective* **self-contra·dict·ory** *adjective*

self-control *noun* the power of controlling one's external reactions, emotions, etc. □ **self-controlled** *adjective*

self-correct·ing *adjective* correcting itself without external help.

self-created *adjective* created by oneself or itself. □ **self-creation** *noun*

self-critical *adjective* critical of oneself, one's abilities, etc.
□ **self-criticism** *noun*

self-deception *noun* deceiving oneself esp. concerning one's true feelings etc. □ **self-deceit** *noun* **self-deceiv·er** *noun* **self-deceiv·ing** *adjective* **self-decep·tive** *adjective*

self-defeat·ing *adjective* (of an attempt, action, etc.) doomed to failure because of internal inconsistencies etc.

self-defence *noun* **1** a defence of oneself, one's rights or position (*hit him in self-defence*). **2** an instance of aggression in such defence (*it was self-defence*). □ **self-defensive** *adjective*

self-delusion *noun* the act or an instance of deluding oneself.
□ **self-deluded** *adjective*

self-denial *noun* = SELF-ABNEGATION. □ **self-denying** *adjective*

self-depreca·tion *noun* the act of disparaging or belittling oneself.
¶ See Usage Note at DEPRECATE. □ **self-deprecat·ing** *adjective* **self-deprecat·ing·ly** *adverb* **self-depreca·tory** *adjective*

self-depreci·a·tion *noun* = SELF-DEPRECATION. ¶ See Usage Note at DEPRECATE.

self-destroy·ing *adjective* destroying oneself or itself.

self-destruct *esp. N Amer.* ● *intransitive verb* **1** (of a spacecraft, bomb, etc.) explode or disintegrate automatically, esp. when pre-set to do so. **2** destroy oneself. ● *attributive adjective* enabling a thing to self-destruct (*a self-destruct device*).

self-destruc·tion *noun* **1** the process or an act of destroying oneself or itself. **2** esp. *N Amer.* the process or an act of self-destructing. **3** *N Amer. informal* suicide. □ **self-destruct·ive** *adjective* **self-destruct·ive·ly** *adverb*

self-determin·a·tion *noun* **1** the freedom of a people to decide their own allegiance or form of government. **2** the freedom to live or act as one chooses, without needing to consult others. □ **self-determined** *adjective* **self-determin·ing** *adjective*

self-develop·ment *noun* the development of oneself, one's abilities, etc.

self-direct·ed *adjective* **1** designating an investment trust, such as an RSP, in which the investment instruments are selected by the trust holder. **2** (of a person) exercising personal control over one's own life, career, etc. **3** (of criticism, a joke, etc.) directed towards oneself.

self-disci·pline *noun* the act of or ability to apply oneself, control one's feelings, etc.; self-control. □ **self-disci·plined** *adjective*

self-discov·ery *noun* the process of acquiring insight into oneself, one's character, desires, etc.

self-disgust *noun* disgust with oneself.

self-doubt *noun* lack of confidence in oneself, one's abilities, etc.
□ **self-doubting** *adjective*

self-educat·ed *adjective* educated by oneself by reading etc., without formal instruction. □ **self-education** *noun*

self-effacing *adjective* retiring; modest; timid. □ **self-efface·ment** *noun* **self-effacing·ly** *adverb*

self-elected *adjective* = SELF-APPOINTED.

self-employed *adjective* working for oneself, as a freelancer or owner of a business etc.; not employed by an employer.
□ **self-employ·ment** *noun*

self-empower·ment *noun* the act or an instance of empowering oneself. □ **self-empower·ing** *adjective*

self-esteem *noun* a good opinion of one's own character and abilities.

self-evident *adjective* obvious; without the need of evidence or further explanation. □ **self-evidence** *noun* **self-evident·ly** *adverb*

self-examin·a·tion *noun* **1** the study of one's own conduct, reasons, etc. **2** the examining of one's body or a part of one's body for signs of illness etc.

self-exile *noun* a state of voluntary exile imposed upon oneself. □ **self-exiled** *adjective*

self-explan·a·tory *adjective* easily understood; not needing explanation.

self-expres·sion *noun* the expression of one's feelings, thoughts, etc., esp. in writing, painting, music, etc. □ **self-expres·sive** *adjective*

self-feeder *noun* **1** a device for supplying food to farm animals automatically. **2** a furnace, machine, etc., that renews its own fuel or material automatically. □ **self-feeding** *adjective*

self-fertile *adjective* (of a plant etc.) self-fertilizing.

self-fertil·iz·a·tion *noun* the fertilization of plants by their own pollen, not from others. □ **self-fertil·ized** *adjective* **self-fertil·iz·ing** *adjective*

self-financing *adjective* that finances itself, esp. (of a project or undertaking) that pays for its own implementation or continuation. □ **self-finance** *transitive verb*

self-flagel·la·tion *noun* **1** the flagellation of oneself, esp. as a form of religious discipline. **2** excessive self-criticism.

self-forget·ful *adjective* unselfish. □ **self-forget·ful·ness** *noun*

self-fulfill·ing *adjective* **1** (of a prophecy, forecast, etc.) bound to come true as a result of actions brought about by its being made. **2** causing or bringing about self-fulfillment.

self-fulfill·ment *noun* (also **-fulfilment**) the fulfillment of one's own hopes and ambitions.

self-generat·ing *adjective* generated by itself or oneself, not externally. □ **self-generat·ed** *adjective*

self-glorifi·ca·tion *noun* exaltation of oneself, one's abilities, etc. □ **self-glorify·ing** *adjective*

self-govern·ment *noun* **1** (esp. of a former colony etc.) government by its own people. **2** = SELF-CONTROL. □ **self-governed** *adjective* **self-govern·ing** *adjective*

self-guided *adjective* **1** (of a hike, visit to a tourist attraction, etc.) performed without the supervision of a tour guide. **2** (of a hiking trail, scenic route, etc.) equipped with informative signs, plaques, etc., so as to be suitable for a self-guided tour.

self-hate *noun* = SELF-HATRED. □ **self-hater** *noun*

self-hatred *noun* hatred of oneself, esp. of one's actual self when contrasted with one's imagined self.

self-heal *noun* any of several plants, esp. *Prunella vulgaris*, believed to have healing properties.

self-healing ● *adjective* denoting a type of equipment, computer software, or mechanical or electrical system that identifies errors in its operation and either corrects them or suggests solutions to the user. ● *noun* (in alternative medicine) the process of using the body's ability to improve its own physical or emotional health without the aid of conventional drugs.

self-help *noun* **1** the theory that individuals should provide for their own support and improvement in society. **2** the act or faculty of providing for or improving oneself (also *attributive*: *self-help book*).

self·hood *noun* personality; separate and conscious existence.

self-image *noun* one's own idea or picture of oneself, esp. in relation to others.

self-immola·tion *noun* the offering of oneself as a sacrifice.

self-importance *noun* a high opinion of oneself; pompousness. □ **self-important** *adjective* **self-important·ly** *adverb*

self-imposed *adjective* (of a task or condition etc.) imposed on and by oneself, not externally (*self-imposed exile*).

self-improve·ment *noun* the improvement of one's own position or disposition by one's own efforts (also *attributive*: *self-improvement course*). □ **self-improv·ing** *adjective*

self-incrimin·a·tion *noun* the act or an instance of incriminating oneself. □ **self-incrimin·a·ting** *adjective*

self-induced *adjective* **1** induced by oneself or itself. **2** *Electricity* produced by self-induction.

self-inductance *noun* *Electricity* the property of an electric circuit that causes an electromotive force to be generated in it by a change in the current flowing through it (*compare* MUTUAL INDUCTANCE).

self-induction *noun* *Electricity* the production of an electromotive force in a circuit when the current in that circuit is varied.

self-indulgent *adjective* indulging or tending to indulge oneself in pleasure, idleness, etc. □ **self-indulgence** *noun* **self-indulgent·ly** *adverb*

self-inflicted *adjective* (of a wound, damage, etc.) inflicted on oneself, esp. deliberately.

self-insurance *noun* insurance of oneself or one's interests by maintaining a fund to cover possible losses. □ **self-insure** *intransitive verb*

self-interest *noun* **1** one's personal interest or advantage. **2** concern for one's own interest or advantage. □ **self-interest·ed** *adjective*

self-involved *adjective* wrapped up in oneself or one's own thoughts. □ **self-involve·ment** *noun*

self·ish *adjective* **1** deficient in consideration for others; concerned chiefly with one's own personal profit or pleasure; actuated by self-interest. **2** (of a motive etc.) appealing to self-interest. □ **self·ish·ly** *adverb* **self·ish·ness** *noun*

self-justifi·ca·tion *noun* the justification or excusing of oneself, one's actions, etc. □ **self-justify·ing** *adjective*

self-knowledge *noun* the understanding of oneself, one's motives, etc.

self·less *adjective* disregarding oneself or one's own interests; unselfish. □ **self·less·ly** *adverb* **self·less·ness** *noun*

self-loading *adjective* (esp. of a gun) loading itself. □ **self-loader** *noun*

self-loathing *noun* = SELF-HATRED.

self-locking *adjective* locking itself.

self-love *noun* **1** selfishness; self-indulgence. **2** regard for one's own well-being and happiness.

self-made *adjective* **1** successful or rich by one's own effort. **2** made by oneself.

self-mastery *noun* = SELF-CONTROL.

self-medica·tion *noun* the use of medication to treat oneself without seeking any medical supervision. □ **self-medicate** *intransitive verb*

self-mocking *adjective* mocking oneself or itself. □ **self-mockery** *noun*

self-motivat·ed *adjective* acting on one's own initiative without external pressure. □ **self-motiva·tion** *noun*

self-murder *noun* = SUICIDE. □ **self-murder·er** *noun*

self-mutila·tion *noun* the mutilation of oneself. □ **self-mutila·tor** *noun*

self-neglect *noun* neglect of oneself.

self·ness *noun* **1** individuality, personality, essence. **2** selfishness or self-regard.

self-parody *noun* the act or an instance of parodying oneself. □ **self-parodic** *adjective* **self-parody·ing** *adjective*

self-perpetu·at·ing *adjective* perpetuating itself or oneself without external agency. □ **self-perpetu·a·tion** *noun*

self-pity *noun* extreme sorrow for one's own troubles etc. □ **self-pitying** *adjective* **self-pitying·ly** *adverb*

self-policing ● *noun* the process of keeping order or maintaining control within a community without accountability or reference to an external authority. ● *adjective* (of a community) independently responsible for keeping and maintaining order.

self-pollin·a·tion *noun* the pollination of a flower by pollen from the same plant. □ **self-pollin·at·ed** *adjective* **self-pollin·at·ing** *adjective*

self-portrait *noun* a portrait or description of an artist, writer, etc., by himself or herself.

self-possessed *adjective* calm and confident, esp. at times of stress or difficulty. □ **self-posses·sion** *noun*

self-praise *noun* boasting; self-glorification.

self-preser·va·tion *noun* the preservation of one's own life, safety, best interests, etc., esp. as a basic instinct. □ **self-preserv·ing** *adjective*

self-proclaimed *adjective* proclaimed by oneself or itself to be such.

self-promotion *noun* the promotion or publicizing of oneself, esp. when done aggressively. □ **self-promoter** *noun* **self-promoting** *adjective*

self-propagating *adjective* (esp. of a plant) able to propagate itself. □ **self-propaga·tion** *noun*

self-propelled *adjective* (esp. of a motor vehicle etc.) moving or able to move without external propulsion. □ **self-propel·ling** *adjective*

self-protec·tion *noun* the act of protecting oneself or itself. □ **self-protect·ive** *adjective*

self-publish *transitive verb* publish (a book etc.) oneself rather than through a publishing house. □ **self-published** *adjective* **self-publish·ing** *noun*

self-raising *adjective Cdn & Brit.* (of flour) having leavening (usu. baking powder) already added.

self-realiz·a·tion *noun* **1** the development of one's faculties, abilities, etc. **2** this as an ethical principle.

self-referen·tial *adjective* characterized by or making reference to oneself or itself. □ **self-referen·tial·ity** *noun*

self-reflexive *adjective* containing a reflection or image of itself; self-referential (*sociology's self-reflexive critique*). □ **self-reflexive·ly** *adverb* **self-reflexiv·ity** *noun*

self-regard *noun* **1** a proper regard for oneself. **2 a** selfishness. **b** conceit. □ **self-regard·ing** *adjective*

self-regulat·ing *adjective* regulating oneself or itself without intervention. □ **self-regula·tion** *noun* **self-regula·tory** *adjective*

self-reliance *noun* reliance on one's own resources etc.; independence. □ **self-reliant** *adjective* **self-reliant·ly** *adverb*

self-renewal *noun* the act or process of renewing oneself or itself.

self-report ● *noun Psych.* a report about oneself or aspects of one's behaviour made by oneself. ● *transitive & intransitive verb* make such a report. □ **self-reported** *adjective*

self-reproach *noun* reproach or blame directed at oneself. □ **self-reproach·ful** *adjective*

self-respect *noun* respect for oneself; a feeling that one is behaving with honour, dignity, etc.

self-respect·ing *adjective* **1** having self-respect. **2** meriting a particular role or name (*no self-respecting editor would run such an article*).

self-restraint *noun* = SELF-CONTROL. □ **self-restrained** *adjective*

self-reveal·ing *adjective* revealing one's character, motives, etc., esp. inadvertently. □ **self-revela·tion** *noun*

self-righteous *adjective* excessively confident of one's own righteousness or virtuousness, esp. in comparison to others. □ **self-righteous·ly** *adverb* **self-righteous·ness** *noun*

self-righting *adjective* (of a boat) righting itself when capsized.

self-rising *adjective N Amer.* = SELF-RAISING.

self-rule *noun* = SELF-GOVERNMENT 1.

self-sacri·fice *noun* the negation of one's own interests, wishes, etc., in favour of those of others. □ **self-sacri·fi·cing** *adjective*

self·same *attributive adjective* (prec. by *the*) the very same (*the selfsame thing*).

self-satisfac·tion *noun* excessive and unwarranted satisfaction with oneself, one's achievements, etc.; complacency. □ **self-satisfied** *adjective* **self-satisfy·ing** *adjective*

self-sealing *adjective* **1** (of a pneumatic tire, fuel tank, etc.) automatically able to seal small punctures. **2** (of an envelope) self-adhesive.

self-seed *intransitive verb* (of a plant) propagate itself by seed. □ **self-seeder** *noun* **self-seeding** *adjective*

self-seeking *adjective & noun* seeking one's own welfare before that of others. □ **self-seeker** *noun*

self-selection *noun* the act of selecting oneself or itself. □ **self-select·ed** *adjective* **self-select·ing** *adjective*

self-serve (also **self-service**) ● *adjective* (often *attributive*) **1** (esp. of a gas station) where customers serve themselves and pay at a checkout counter etc. **2** (of a machine) serving goods after the insertion of coins. ● *noun informal* a self-serve gas station etc.

self-serving *adjective & noun* = SELF-SEEKING.

self-sown *adjective* grown from seed scattered naturally. □ **self-sow** *intransitive verb*

self-starter *noun* **1** an ambitious person who needs no external motivation. **2** = STARTER 2.

self-sterile *adjective Biol.* not being self-fertile. □ **self-steril·ity** *noun*

self-styled *adjective* called so by oneself; would-be; pretended (*a self-styled artist*).

self-sufficient *adjective* **1 a** needing nothing; independent. **b** (of a person, nation, etc.) able to supply one's needs for a commodity, esp. food, from one's own resources. **2** content with one's own opinion; arrogant. □ **self-sufficien·cy** *noun* **self-sufficient·ly** *adverb*

self-sugges·tion *noun* = AUTOSUGGESTION.

self-support·ing *adjective* **1** capable of maintaining oneself or itself financially. **2** staying up or standing without external aid. □ **self-support** *noun*

self-surren·der *noun* the surrender of oneself or one's will etc. to an influence, emotion, or other person.

self-sustain·ing *adjective* sustaining oneself or itself. □ **self-sustained** *adjective*

self-tanner *noun* a cream or lotion that contains ingredients that react with the skin to produce a tan-like tint. □ **self-tanning** *adjective & noun*

self-tapping *adjective* (of a screw) able to cut its own thread.

self-taught *adjective* educated or trained by oneself.

self-torture *noun* the inflicting of pain, esp. mental pain, on oneself.

self-understand·ing *noun* **1** the act or an instance of comprehending one's actions and reactions. **2** sympathetic tolerance or awareness of oneself.

self-willed *adjective* obstinately pursuing one's own wishes. □ **self-will** *noun*

self-winding *adjective* (of a watch etc.) having an automatic winding apparatus.

self-worth *noun* = SELF-ESTEEM.

Sel·juk /ˈsɛldʒʊk, selˈdʒuːk/ of, relating to, or denoting the Turkish dynasty which ruled Asia Minor in the 11th–13th centuries, successfully invading the Byzantine Empire and defending the Holy Land against the Crusaders. □ **Sel·juk·ian** /selˈdʒuːkiən/ *adjective & noun* [Turkish *seljûq* (name of their reputed ancestor)]

Sel·kirk[1] a town in SE central Manitoba, situated on the Red River, northeast of Winnipeg; pop. (2001) 9,752. □ **Sel·kirk·ian** *noun* [Thomas Douglas, Lord SELKIRK]

Sel·kirk[2], **1 Alex·an·der** (also called Selcraig) (1676–1721), Scottish sailor. While on a privateering expedition in 1704, he quarrelled with his captain and was put ashore, at his own request, on one of the uninhabited Juan Fernandez Islands in the Pacific, where he remained until he was rescued in 1709; his experiences later formed the basis of Defoe's novel *Robinson Crusoe* (1719). **2 Thom·as Doug·las, 5th Earl of** (1771–1820), Scottish-born Canadian colonizer and humanitarian. In 1803 he settled 800 displaced Highlanders on land he purchased in PEI, and the following year he established a settlement at Baldoon, Upper Canada. In 1811 he received a large land grant from the Hudson's Bay Company in what is now Manitoba, and here he established the Red River Colony in 1812, arriving to supervise it himself in 1815. He returned to Europe three years later.

Selkirk Mountains a mountain range in SE central BC, part of the Columbia mountain system. It lies between the Purcell and Monashee mountains. [Thomas Douglas, Lord SELKIRK]

Selkirk settler *noun Cdn hist.* an early settler at the Red River Settlement founded by the Earl of Selkirk. □ **Selkirk settlement** *noun*

Sel·kirk·shire a former county of SE Scotland, made a part of Borders region (now Scottish Borders) in 1975.

sell ● *verb* (past and past participle **sold**) **1** *transitive* exchange (goods, services, etc.) for money. **2** *transitive* keep a stock of for sale or be a dealer in (*do you sell stamps?*). **3 a** *intransitive* (of goods) be purchased (*will never sell; these are selling well*). **b** *transitive* (of a publication or recording) attain sales of (a specified number of copies) (*the book has sold 10,000 copies*). **4** *intransitive* (foll. by *for*) have a specified price (*sells for $5*). **5** *transitive* betray for money or other reward (*sell one's country*). **6** *transitive* offer dishonourably for money or other consideration; make a matter of corrupt bargaining (*sell oneself; sell one's honour*). **7** *transitive* **a** advertise or publish the merits of. **b** give (a person) information on the value of something, inspire with a desire to buy or acquire or agree to something. **8** *transitive* cause to be sold (*her name alone will sell many copies*). **9** *transitive esp. slang* disappoint by not keeping an engagement etc., by failing in some way, or by trickery. ● *noun* **1** a manner of selling (*soft sell*). **2** *informal* a deception or disappointment. □ **sell a person a bill of goods** *N Amer. see* BILL OF GOODS. **sell down the river** *see* RIVER. **sell off** sell the remainder of (goods) at reduced prices. **sell one's body** work as a prostitute. **sell oneself 1** promote one's own abilities. **2 a** offer one's services dishonourably for money or other reward. **b** be a prostitute. **sell out 1 a** (often foll. by *of*) sell all one's stock of a commodity (*the store sold out of bread; wanted to buy some milk but the store had sold out*). **b** (of a commodity) be completely or all sold (*tickets are quickly selling out*). **c** (of a performance etc.) sell all its tickets (*the concert was sold out weeks ago*). **d** dispose of the whole of (one's property, shares, etc.) by sale. **2 a** (often foll. by *to*) abandon one's principles, honourable aims, etc. for personal gain. **b** betray (a person etc.). **sell short** disparage, underestimate. **sell up** *Brit.* **1** sell one's business, house, etc. **2** sell the goods of (a debtor). □ **sell·able** *adjective* [Old English *sellan* from Germanic]

Sella·field the site of a nuclear power station and reprocessing plant on the coast of Cumbria in NW England. It was the scene in 1957 of a fire which caused a serious escape of radioactive material. The site was known as Windscale between 1947 and 1981.

sell-by date *noun Brit.* **1** the latest recommended date of sale marked on the packaging of esp. perishable food. **2** (often in phr. **past his, her, its**, etc. **sell-by date**) the time after which a commodity is not saleable, or a person or thing is no longer attractive or fit for an activity (*the bus was well past its sell-by date*).

sell·er *noun* **1** a person who sells. **2** a commodity that sells well or badly.

Sel·lers, **Peter** (1925–80), English comic actor. He made his name with Spike Milligan and Harry Secombe (1921–2001), appearing in *The Goon Show*, a British radio series of the 1950s; he then turned to films, starring in many comedies such as *I'm All Right Jack* (1959), *Dr. Strangelove* (1964), the 'Pink Panther' films of the 1960s and 1970s, and *Being There* (1979).

seller's market *noun* (also **sellers' market**) an economic position in which goods are scarce and expensive and sellers have the advantage over buyers.

selling point *noun* a feature of something that makes it attractive, esp. to buyers or customers.

sell-off *noun* **1** the privatization of a state company by a sale of shares. **2** *Stock Exch.* a sale or disposal of bonds, shares, etc., usu. causing a fall in price. **3** a sale, esp. to dispose of property.

Sel·lo·tape *Brit.* ● *noun* proprietary adhesive usu. transparent cellulose or plastic tape; Scotch tape. ● *transitive verb* (**sellotape**) fix with Sellotape. [CELLULOSE + TAPE]

sell-out *noun* **1** a commercial success, esp. the selling of all tickets for a show (also *attributive: a sellout crowd*). **2** a betrayal.

sell-through *noun* the ratio of the quantity of goods sold by a retail outlet to the quantity distributed to it wholesale.

selt·zer *noun* (in full **seltzer water**) **1** natural effervescent mineral water. **2** an artificial substitute for this; soda water. [German *Selterser* (adj.) from *(Nieder)selters* in Germany, site of a mineral spring]

sel·vage /'sɛlvɪdʒ/ *noun* (also **sel·vedge**) **1 a** an edging that prevents cloth from unravelling (either an edge along the warp or a specially woven edging). **b** a border of different material or finish intended to be removed or hidden. **2** *Geol.* an alteration zone at the edge of a rock mass. **3** the edge plate of a lock with an opening for the bolt. [Middle English from SELF + EDGE, after Dutch *selfegghe*]

selves *pl. of* SELF.

Sel·wyn Mountains a mountain range extending over 600 km along the eastern boundary of Yukon Territory, part of the Mackenzie Mountains. [A. R. C. *Selwyn*, British geologist d.1902]

Selye /'sɛljei/ **Hans Hugo Bruno** (1907–82), Austrian-born Canadian physician. He showed that environmental stress and anxiety could result in the release of hormones that, over a long period, could produce biochemical and physiological disorders.

Selz·nick, **David Oli·ver** (1902–65), US film producer, who produced such films as *King Kong* (1933) and *Anna Karenina* (1935), *Gone with the Wind* (1939) and *Rebecca* (1940).

SEM *abbreviation* scanning electron microscope.

seman·tic /sə'mantɪk/ *adjective* **1** relating to meaning in language; relating to the denotations and connotations of words. **2** of or relating to semantics. □ **seman·tic·ally** *adverb* [French *sémantique* from Greek *sēmantikos* significant, from *sēmainō* signify, from *sēma* sign]

seman·tics /sə'mantɪks/ *plural noun* (usu. treated as *sing.*) **1** the branch of linguistics concerned with meaning. **2** the interpretation or meaning of a sentence, word, etc. (*let's not fight over semantics*). □ **seman·ti·cist** /-tɪsɪst/ *noun*

sema·phore /'sɛmə,fɔr/ ● *noun* **1** a system of sending messages by holding the arms or two flags in certain positions according to an alphabetic code. **2** a signalling apparatus consisting of a post with a movable arm or arms esp. for use on railways. ● *transitive & intransitive verb* signal or send by semaphore. □ **sema·phor·ic** *adjective* **sema·phor·ic·ally** *adverb* [French *sémaphore*, irreg. from Greek *sēma* sign + -*phoros* -PHORE]

Se·mar·ang /sə'mɑraŋ/ a port in Indonesia, on the north coast of Java; pop. (est. 2002) 1,134,700.

sem·blance /'sɛmbləns/ *noun* **1** the outward or superficial appearance of something (*put on a semblance of anger*). **2** resemblance. [Old French from *sembler* from Latin *similare, simulare* SIMULATE]

semé /'sɛmi, 'sɛmei/ *adjective* (also **semée**) *Heraldry* covered with small bearings of indefinite number (e.g. stars, fleurs-de-lys) arranged all over the field. [French, past participle of *semer* to sow]

Semei /sə'mei/ (also **Semey**) an industrial city and river port in

E Kazakhstan, on the Irtysh River close to the border with Russia; pop. (1999) 269,600. It was known as Semipalatinsk until 1991.

Sem·ele /'sɛmɪli/ *Gk Myth* the mother, by Zeus, of Dionysus. She entreated Zeus to come to her in his full majesty and the fire of his thunderbolts killed her but made her child immortal.

sem·eme /'sɛmiːm, 'siːm-/ *noun Linguistics* the unit of meaning carried by a morpheme. [as SEMANTIC]

semen /'siːmən/ *noun* the reproductive fluid of male animals, containing spermatozoa in suspension. [Latin *semen seminis* seed, from *serere* to sow]

se·mes·ter /sɛ'mɛstər/ *noun* **1** esp. *N Amer.* an academic session occupying half of the academic year, lasting usu. for 15 to 18 weeks. **2** (in German universities) a six-month term. [German from Latin *semestris* six-monthly, from *sex* six + *mensis* month]

se·mes·ter·ing /sɛ'mɛstərɪŋ/ *noun Cdn* an educational system in which the school year is divided into two terms having school days with a reduced number of longer periods, with the whole year's course material in any given subject concentrated into one or the other term. □ **se·mes·tered** *adjective*

Semey see SEMEI.

semi /'sɛmi/ *noun* (*pl.* **semis**) *informal* **1** *Cdn & Brit.* a semi-detached house. **2** a semifinal. **3** *N Amer. & Austral.* a semi-trailer. [abbreviation]

semi- /'sɛmi, -mai/ *prefix* **1** half (*semicircle*). **2** partly; in some degree or particular (*semi-official; semi-detached*). **3** almost. **4** occurring or appearing twice in a specified period (*semi-annual*). [French, Italian, etc. or Latin, corresponding to Greek HEMI-, Sanskrit *sāmi*]

semi-annual *adjective* occurring, published, etc., twice a year. □ **semi-annual·ly** *adverb*

semi-aquatic *adjective* **1** (of an animal) living partly on land and partly in water. **2** (of a plant) growing in very wet ground.

semi-arid *adjective* having slightly more precipitation than an arid climate, and characterized by coarse grasses and scrub.

semi-auto *slang* ● *adjective* (of a firearm) semi-automatic. ● *noun* a semi-automatic firearm.

semi-autobio·graph·ic·al *adjective* (of a novel etc.) based in part on the author's life.

semi-automat·ic ● *adjective* **1** partially automatic. **2** (of a firearm) having a mechanism for continuous loading but not for continuous firing. ● *noun* a semi-automatic firearm.

semi-autono·mous *adjective* **1** partly self-governing. **2** acting to some degree independently or having the partial freedom to do so.

semi-basement *noun* a storey partly below ground level.

semi·breve /'sɛmi,briːv/ *noun Brit. Music* = WHOLE NOTE.

semi·circle *noun* **1** half of a circle or of its circumference. **2** a set of objects ranged in, or an object forming, a semicircle. □ **semi·circu·lar** *adjective*

semicircular canal *noun* one of three fluid-filled channels in the ear giving information to the brain to help maintain balance.

semi·colon *noun* a punctuation mark (;) of intermediate value between a comma and a period.

semi·conduct·or *noun* a solid substance that is a non-conductor when pure or at a low temperature but has a conductivity between that of insulators and that of most metals when containing a suitable impurity or at a higher temperature and is used in integrated circuits, transistors, diodes, etc. (also *attributive: semiconductor chip*). □ **semi·conduct·ing** *adjective*

semi·conscious *adjective* partly or imperfectly conscious. □ **semi·conscious·ly** *adverb* **semi·conscious·ness** *noun*

semi·cylin·der *noun* half of a cylinder cut longitudinally. □ **semi·cylin·drical** *adjective*

semi·desert *noun* a semi-arid area intermediate between grassland and desert (also *attributive: semi-desert region*).

semi·detached ● *adjective* (of a house) joined to another by a shared wall on one side only. ● *noun* a semi-detached house.

semi·diameter *noun* half of a diameter.

semi·documen·tary ● *adjective* (of a film) having a factual background and a fictitious story. ● *noun* (*pl.* **-taries**) a semi-documentary film.

semi·double *adjective* (of a flower) intermediate between single and double in having only the outer stamens converted to petals.

semi·final *noun* a match or round immediately preceding the final. □ **semi·final·ist** *noun*

semi·finished *adjective* prepared for the final stage of manufacture.

Consonants: b *but*   d *dog*   f *few*   g *get*   h *her*   j *yes*   k *cat*   l *leg*   m *man*   n *no*   p *pen*   r *red*   s *sit*

semi-fitted *adjective* (of a garment) shaped to the body but not closely fitted.

semi-fluid = SEMI-LIQUID.

semi-formal ● *adjective* (esp. of clothing) having some formal elements. ● *noun* a dance or other social occasion to which semi-formal dress is worn.

semi-freddo *noun* an Italian ice-cream-like dessert, often with cookies, nuts, cake, chocolate, etc. incorporated, served chilled or slightly frozen. [Italian, from *semi* 'half' and *freddo* 'cold']

semi-gloss ● *adjective* (of a paint or painted surface) having or producing a moderately satiny finish. ● *noun* a paint that has or produces a moderately satiny finish.

semi-independent *adjective* **1 a** partially independent of control or authority. **b** partially self-governing. **2** partially independent of financial support from public funds.

semi-invalid *noun* a person somewhat enfeebled or partially disabled.

semi-liquid ● *adjective* of a consistency between solid and liquid. ● *noun* a semi-liquid substance.

semi-literate *adjective* **1** unable to read or write with ease or fluency; poorly educated. **2** (of a text) poorly written. □ **semi-literacy** *noun*

Sémillon /ˈsemɪjɔ̃/ *noun* **1** a white grape grown esp. in France. **2** a white wine made from these grapes. [French dial., ultimately from Latin *semen* seed]

semi-lunar *adjective* shaped like a half moon or crescent.

semi-lunar valve *noun* a valve with half-moon shaped cusps, e.g. the aortic valve.

semi-monthly ● *adjective* occurring, published, etc., twice a month. ● *adverb* twice a month.

seminal /ˈsemənəl/ *adjective* **1 a** of or relating to semen. **b** of or relating to the seeds of plants. **2 a** (of ideas etc.) providing the basis for future development. **b** (of a person, literary work, etc.) central to the understanding of a subject; influential. □ **seminally** *adverb* [Old French *seminal* or Latin *seminalis* (as SEMEN)]

seminal fluid *noun* semen.

seminar *noun* **1** a small group of students, esp. at a university, meeting to discuss or study a particular topic with a teacher. **2** any meeting or class for discussion or training. [German (as SEMINARY)]

seminary /ˈseməˌneri/ *noun* (*pl.* **-ies**) **1** a training college for priests, rabbis, etc. **2** a place of education or development. □ **seminarian** /-ˈneriən/ *noun* **seminarist** *noun* [Latin *seminarium* seedbed, neuter of *seminarius* (adj.) (as SEMEN)]

seminiferous /ˌsemiˈnɪfərəs/ *adjective* **1** bearing seed. **2** conveying semen. [Latin *semin-* from SEMEN + -FEROUS]

Seminole /ˈsemənoʊl/ ● *noun* **1** a member of any of several groupings of N American Aboriginal peoples comprising Creek Confederacy emigrants to Florida or their descendants in Florida and Oklahoma. **2** the Muskogean language of the Seminoles. ● *adjective* of or relating to this people or their language. [Creek *simanó:ni* from Latin American Spanish *cimarrón* wild, untamed; runaway slave]

semi-nomadic *adjective* (of a people, way of life, etc.) partially nomadic and partially settled, esp. because dependent largely on seasonal pasturing.

semi-official *adjective* partly official. □ **semi-officially** *adverb*

semiology /ˌsemiˈɒlədʒi, ˌsiːm-/ *noun* = SEMIOTICS. □ **semiological** *adjective* **semiologist** *noun* [Greek *sēmeion* sign, from *sēma* mark]

semi-opaque *adjective* partially transparent.

semiotics /ˌsemiˈɒtɪks, ˌsiːm-/ *noun* the study of signs and symbols in various fields, esp. language. □ **semiotic** *adjective* **semiotically** *adverb* **semiotician** /-ˈtɪʃən/ *noun* [Greek *sēmeiōtikos* of signs (as SEMIOLOGY)]

Semipalatinsk /ˌsemipəˈlɒtɪnsk/ the former name (until 1991) for SEMEI.

semi-palmated *adjective* Zool. having toes etc. webbed for part of their length. [SEMI- + Latin *palmatus* PALMATE]

semi-permanent *adjective* rather less than permanent. □ **semi-permanently** *adverb*

semi-permeable *adjective* (of a membrane etc.) allowing small molecules, but not large ones, to pass through. □ **semi-permeability** *noun*

semi-precious *adjective* (of a gem) less valuable than a precious stone.

semi-private *adjective* **1** partially or somewhat private. **2** N Amer. (of a hospital room) shared by two patients.

semi-pro *adjective* & *noun* (*pl.* **-pros**) N Amer. informal = SEMI-PROFESSIONAL.

semi-professional ● *adjective* **1** receiving payment for an activity but not relying on it for a living. **2** involving semi-professionals. ● *noun* a semi-professional musician, sportsman, etc. □ **semi-professionally** *adverb*

semiquaver *noun* Brit. Music = SIXTEENTH NOTE.

Semiramis /sɪˈmɪrəmɪs/ Gk Myth the daughter of a Syrian goddess, who later married a king of Assyria and after his death ruled for many years, becoming one of the founders of Babylon. Semiramis is thought to have been based on a historical Sammuramat, who ruled 810–805 BC.

semi-retired *adjective* (of a person) partially but not completely retired. □ **semi-retirement** *noun*

semi-rigid *adjective* **1** somewhat rigid; having a certain amount of rigidity. **2** (of an airship) having a stiffened keel attached to a flexible gas container.

semi-skilled *adjective* (of work or a worker) having or needing some training but less than for a skilled worker.

semi-soft *noun* (of cheese) having a consistency between firm and soft.

semi-solid *adjective* viscous, semi-liquid.

semi-submersible ● *adjective* (of an offshore drilling platform) equipped with submerged hollow pontoons that may be flooded with water when the vessel is anchored on site in order to provide stability. ● *noun* a semi-submersible drilling platform.

semi-sweet *adjective* (esp. of chocolate) slightly sweetened.

semi-synthetic *adjective* Chem. (of a substance) that is prepared synthetically but derives from a naturally occurring material.

Semite /ˈsemaɪt, ˈsiːm-/ *noun* a member of any of the peoples supposed to be descended from Shem, son of Noah, including esp. the Jews, Arabs, Assyrians, and Phoenicians. [modern Latin *Semita* from Late Latin from Greek *Sēm* Shem]

Semitic /səˈmɪtɪk/ ● *adjective* **1** of or relating to the Semites, esp. the Jews. **2** of or relating to the languages of the family including Hebrew and Arabic. ● *noun* the Semitic language family.

semitone *noun* Music the smallest interval used in classical European music; half a tone. □ **semitonal** *adjective*

semi-trailer *noun* a trailer having wheels at the back but supported at the front by a towing vehicle.

semi-transparent *adjective* partially or imperfectly transparent.

semi-tropics *plural noun* = SUBTROPICS. □ **semi-tropical** *adjective*

semi-vowel *noun* **1** a sound intermediate between a vowel and a consonant (e.g. *w*, *y*). **2** a letter representing this.

semi-weekly ● *adjective* occurring, published, etc., twice a week. ● *adverb* twice a week.

Semliki River /semˈliki/ a river in SW Uganda and E Democratic Republic of the Congo, flowing from Lake Edward to Lake Albert.

Semmelweis /ˈseməlˌvaɪs/ **Ignaz Philipp** (1818–65), Austro-Hungarian obstetrician, who discovered the infectious character of puerperal fever, then a major cause of maternal mortality; he demonstrated that the infection was transmitted by the hands of doctors who examined patients after working in the dissecting room, and advocated rigorous cleanliness and the use of antiseptics.

semolina /ˌseməˈliːnə/ *noun* the hard grains left after the milling of flour, used esp. in making pasta. [Italian *semolino* diminutive of *semola* bran, from Latin *simila* flour]

sempervivum /sempərˈvaɪvəm/ *noun* a succulent plant of the genus Sempervivum, esp. the houseleek. [modern Latin genus name, from Latin *semper* 'always' + *vivus* 'living']

sempiternal /ˌsempɪˈtɜːnəl/ *adjective* literary eternal, everlasting. [Old French *sempiternel* from Late Latin *sempiternalis* from Latin *sempiternus* from *semper* always + *aeternus* eternal]

semplice /ˈsemplɪˌtʃeɪ, -tʃi/ *adverb* Music in a simple style of performance. [Italian, = SIMPLE]

sempre /ˈsempreɪ, -ri/ *adverb* Music throughout, always (*sempre forte*). [Italian]

Semtex *noun* a very pliable, odourless plastic explosive. [prob. from Semtín, a village in the Czech Republic near the place of production + explosive]

Sen. *abbreviation* **1** Senior. **2** N Amer. **a** Senator. **b** Senate.

sen *noun* (*pl.* same) a monetary unit of Cambodia and Indonesia, equal to one-hundredth of a riel in Cambodia, and one-hundredth of a rupiah in Indonesia. [a representation of CENT]

sen·ary /'siːnɘri, 'sen-/ *adjective* of six, by sixes. [Latin *senarius* from *seni* distributive of *sex* six]

sen·ate *noun* **1** (**Senate**) **a** (in Canada) the upper chamber of Parliament, consisting of senators appointed to represent the regions of Canada. **b** (in the US) the upper, elected, house of Congress or of a state legislature. **c** a similar legislative body in other countries, e.g. France. **2** the governing body of a university or college. **3** *Rom. Hist.* the state council of the republic and empire sharing legislative power with the popular assemblies, administration with the magistrates, and judicial power with the knights. [Old French *senat* from Latin *senatus* from *senex* old man]

sen·ator *noun* a member of a senate. □ **sen·ator·ial** *adjective* **sen·ator·ship** *noun*

send *verb* (*past* and *past participle* **sent**) **1** *transitive* **a** order or cause to go or be conveyed (*send a message to head office*; *sent me a book*). **b** propel; cause to move (*sent him flying*). **c** cause to go or become (*his dancing sends her into raptures*). **d** dismiss with or without force (*sent her away*; *sent him about his business*). **2** *intransitive* send a message or letter (*she sent to warn me*). **3** *transitive* (of God, providence, etc.) grant or bestow or inflict; bring about; cause to be (*send rain*; *send a judgment*). **4** *transitive slang* affect emotionally, put into ecstasy. □ **send away for** send an order to a dealer for (goods). **send down** *Brit.* **1** expel from a university. **2** sentence to imprisonment. **send for 1** summon. **2** order by mail. **send in 1** cause to go in. **2** submit (an entry etc.) for a competition etc. **send off 1** get (a letter, parcel, etc.) dispatched. **2** attend the departure of (a person) as a sign of respect etc. **3** *Sport* (of a referee) order (a player) to leave the field and take no further part in the game. **send off for** = SEND AWAY FOR. **send on** transmit to a further destination or in advance of one's own arrival. **send out for** order delivery of (food) (*let's send out for pizza tonight*). **send up 1** cause to go up. **2** transmit to a higher authority. **3** *informal* satirize or ridicule, esp. by mimicking. **4** *US* sentence to imprisonment. **send word** send a message. □ **send·er** *noun* [Old English *sendan* from Germanic]

Sen·dai /sen'daɪ/ a city in Japan, situated near the northeast coast of the island of Honshu; pop. (est. 2002) 1,022,400. It is the capital of the region of Tohoku.

Sen·dak /'sendak/ **Mau·rice (Ber·nard)** (b.1928), US artist, illustrator, stage designer, and writer, who is best known for his trilogy of children's books *Where the Wild Things Are* (1963), *In the Night Kitchen* (1970), and *Outside Over There* (1981).

sen·dal /'sendɘl/ *noun hist.* **1** a thin rich silk material. **2** a garment of this. [Old French *cendal*, ultimately from Greek *sindōn*]

Sen·dero Lumin·oso /sen,dero: luːmɪ'noːsoː/ *noun* = SHINING PATH. [Spanish, lit. 'shining path']

send-off *noun* a demonstration of goodwill etc. at a person's departure, the start of a project, etc.

send-up *noun informal* a satire or parody.

sene /'seni/ *noun* (*pl.* same or **senes**) a monetary unit of Samoa, equal to one-hundredth of a tala. [Samoan]

Sen·eca¹ /'senɘkɘ/ **1 Lu·cius An·naeus** (known as Seneca the Younger) (*c.*4 BC–AD 65), Roman statesman, philosopher, and dramatist. He expounded the ethics of Stoicism in such works as *Epistulae morales*, and the lurid violence and rhetoric of his nine plays later influenced Elizabethan and Jacobean tragedy. **2** his father, **Mar·cus** (or **Lu·cius**) **An·naeus** (known as Seneca the Elder) (*c.*55 BC–*c.* AD 39), Roman rhetorician. He is best known for his works on rhetoric, only parts of which survive.

Sen·eca² /'senɘkɘ/ ● *noun* **1** a member of one of the founding members of the Iroquois Five Nations confederacy, now living in Ontario and New York. **2** the Iroquoian language of this people. ● *adjective* of or relating to this people or their culture or language. [Dutch *Sennec(a)s* the upper Iroquois people collectively, ultimately from Algonquian]

Seneca snakeroot *noun* a plant of eastern N America, *Polygala senega*, with a cluster of white flowers.

Sen·egal /'senɘgɒl/ a country on the coast of West Africa; pop. (est. 2002) 10,589,571; capital, Dakar. □ **Sen·egal·ese** /-gɘ'liːz/ *adjective & noun*

Sene·gam·bia /senɘ'gambiɘ/ a region of West Africa consisting of the Senegal and Gambia rivers and the area between them. It lies mostly in Senegal and W Mali. □ **Sene·gam·bian** *adjective*

sen·esce /sɘ'nes/ *intransitive verb* grow old. □ **sen·es·cence** *noun* **sen·es·cent** *adjective* [Latin *senescere* from *senex* old]

sene·schal /'senɘʃɘl/ *noun* the steward or major-domo of a medieval great house. [Old French from medieval Latin *seniscalus* from Germanic, = old servant]

se·nile /'siːnaɪl, 'sen-/ ● *adjective* **1** of or characteristic of old age (*senile apathy*; *senile decay*). **2** having the weaknesses or diseases of old age, esp. a loss of mental faculties. ● *noun* a senile person. □ **sen·il·ity** /sɘ'nɪlɪti/ *noun* [French *sénile* or Latin *senilis* from *senex* old man]

senile dementia *noun* a severe form of mental deterioration in old age, characterized by loss of memory and control of bodily functions.

sen·ior ● *adjective* **1** (often foll. by *to*) more or most advanced in age, standing, rank, etc. **2** of high or highest position. **3** (placed after a person's name) senior to another of the same name. **4** (of a school) having students in an older age range (esp. over 11). **5** esp. *US* of the final year at a university, high school, etc. ● *noun* **1 a** = SENIOR CITIZEN. **b** a person of comparatively long service etc. **2** one's elder, or one's superior in length of service, membership, etc. (*is my senior*). **3** esp. *US* a student in the final year at a university, high school, etc. □ **sen·ior·ity** *noun* [Latin, = older, older man, comparative of *senex senis* old man, old]

senior citizen *noun* an elderly person, esp. a person over 65.

senior common room *noun Cdn & Brit.* (in certain universities) a room for use by senior members of a college.

senior constable *noun* (in the Ontario Provincial Police) an officer ranking above provincial constable and below sergeant.

senior government *noun Cdn* the federal or a provincial government, or both, as opposed to a municipal government.

senior high school *noun N Amer.* a secondary school comprising usu. the three highest grades.

senior kindergarten *noun Cdn (Ont.)* a class for young children, usu. five-year-olds, in preparation for grade one. Abbr.: **SK**.

senior management *noun* **1** the highest level of management in an organization, immediately below the board of directors. **2** the managers at this level (*compare* MIDDLE MANAGEMENT, JUNIOR MANAGEMENT).

senior matriculation *noun* (also *informal* **senior matric**) *Cdn hist.* (in certain provinces) completion of secondary education to a level required for admission to university (*compare* JUNIOR MATRICULATION).

senior moment *noun* an instance of temporary forgetfulness in an older person, esp. the inability to recall a word.

sen·iti /'senɪti/ *noun* a monetary unit of Tonga, equal to one-hundredth of a pa'anga. [Tongan, from CENT]

Senna, Ayr·ton (1960–94), Brazilian racing driver. He won the Formula One world championship in 1988, 1990, and 1991. He died from injuries sustained in a crash during the San Marino Grand Prix in 1994.

senna *noun* **1** a cassia tree. **2** a laxative prepared from the dried pods of this. [medieval Latin *sena* from Arabic *sanā*]

Sen·nach·erib /sɪ'nakɘrɪb/ (d.681 BC) king of Assyria 704–681. The son of Sargon II, he sacked Babylon in 689, put down a Jewish rebellion in 701 (laying siege to Jerusalem but sparing it from destruction), and rebuilt and extended the city of Nineveh, making it his capital.

sen·net /'senɘt/ *noun hist.* a signal call on a trumpet or cornet (in the stage directions of Elizabethan plays). [perhaps var. of SIGNET]

Sen·nett /'senɘt/ **Mack** (1884–1960) (born Michael Sinnott), Canadian-born US film director, producer, and actor, whose Keystone studio produced many celebrated silent comedies featuring the Keystone Kops and Charlie Chaplin among others.

sen·night *noun archaic* a week. [Old English *seofon nihta* seven nights]

se·ñor /sen'jɔr/ *noun* (*pl.* **se·ñores** /-rez/) a title used of or to a Spanish-speaking man. [Spanish from Latin *senior*: see SENIOR]

se·ñora /sen'jɔrɘ/ *noun* a title used of or to a Spanish-speaking married woman. [Spanish, fem. of SEÑOR]

señor·ita /,senjɘ'riːtɘ/ *noun* a title used of or to a Spanish-speaking unmarried woman. [Spanish, diminutive of SEÑORA]

sens·ate *adjective* perceived by the senses. [Late Latin *sensatus* having senses (as SENSE)]

sen·sa·tion *noun* **1** the consciousness of perceiving or seeming to perceive some state or condition of one's body or its parts or of the senses; an instance of such consciousness (*lost all sensation in my left arm*; *the sensation of falling*; *a burning sensation in her leg*). **2** an awareness or impression (*created the sensation of time passing*; *a sensation of being watched*). **3 a** a stirring of emotions or intense interest, esp. among a large group of people (*the news caused a sensation*). **b** a person, event, etc., causing such interest. **c** the sensational use of printed material. [medieval Latin *sensatio* from Latin *sensus* SENSE]

sen·sa·tion·al *adjective* **1 a** causing a sensation (*a sensational crime*). **b** deliberately trying to provoke interest by including material that is exciting, shocking, salacious, etc. (*sensational journalism*). **2** very good (*a sensational singer*). **3** of or causing sensation. □ **sen·sa·tion·al·ize** *transitive verb* (also esp. *Brit.* **-ise**). **sen·sa·tion·al·ly** *adverb*

sen·sa·tion·al·ism *noun* **1** the use of or interest in sensational material in journalism, political agitation, etc. **2** *Philos.* the theory that ideas are derived solely from sensation (*opp.* RATIONALISM 1). □ **sen·sa·tion·al·ist** *noun & adjective* **sen·sa·tion·al·is·tic** *adjective*

sense ● *noun* **1 a** any of the special bodily faculties by which sensation is roused (*has keen senses; has a dull sense of smell*). **b** sensitiveness of all or any of these. **2** the ability to perceive or feel or to be conscious of the presence or properties of things. **3** (foll. by *of*) consciousness (*sense of having done well; sense of one's own importance*). **4** (often foll. by *of*) **a** an appreciation, understanding, or instinct regarding a specified matter (*sense of the ridiculous; the moral sense; my sense is that they won't come*). **b** the habit of basing one's conduct on such instinct. **5** the instinctive or acquired capacity to comprehend or appreciate a specified quality, subject, etc. (*has no fashion sense*). **6** practical wisdom or judgment, common sense; conformity to these (*has plenty of sense; what is the sense of talking like that?; has more sense than to do that*). **7 a** a meaning; the way in which a word etc. is to be understood (*the sense of the word is clear; I mean that in the literal sense*). **b** intelligibility or coherence or possession of a meaning. **8** the prevailing opinion among a number of people. **9** (in *pl.*) a person's sanity or normal state of mind. **10** *Math. etc.* **a** a direction of movement. **b** that which distinguishes a pair of entities which differ only in that each is the reverse of the other. ● *transitive verb* **1** perceive by a sense or senses. **2** be vaguely aware of. **3** realize. **4** (of a machine etc.) detect. □ **bring a person to his** or **her senses 1** cure a person of folly. **2** restore a person to consciousness. **come to one's senses 1** regain consciousness. **2** become sensible after acting foolishly. **in a** (or **one**) **sense** if the statement is understood in a particular way (*what you say is true in a sense*). **make sense** be intelligible, reasonable, or practicable. **make sense of** show or find the meaning of. **out of one's senses** in or into a state of madness (*is out of her senses; frightened him out of his senses*). **take leave of one's senses** go mad. [Latin *sensus* faculty of feeling, thought, meaning, from *sentire sens-* feel]

sense datum *noun* (*pl.* **sense data**) *Philos.* an element of experience received through the senses.

sen·sei /sen'sei/ *noun* (*pl.* same) (in martial arts) a teacher. [Japanese, from *sen* 'previous' + *sei* 'birth']

sense·less *adjective* **1** unconscious. **2** wildly foolish. **3** without meaning or purpose. **4** incapable of sensation. □ **sense·less·ly** *adverb* **sense·less·ness** *noun*

sense of humour *noun* see HUMOUR 2.

sense organ *noun* a bodily organ conveying external stimuli to the sensory system.

sens·ibil·ity *noun* (*pl.* **-ities**) **1 a** openness to emotional impressions, susceptibility, sensitiveness (*sensibility to kindness*). **b** *archaic* an exceptional or excessive degree of this. **2 a** (in *pl.*) emotional capacities or feelings (*was limited in his sensibilities*). **b** (in *sing.* or *pl.*) a person's moral, emotional, or aesthetic ideas or standards (*offended the sensibilities of believers*). **3** sensitivity to sensory stimuli (*sensibility in the retina*).

sens·ible *adjective* **1** having or showing wisdom or common sense; reasonable, judicious (*a sensible person; a sensible compromise*). **2 a** perceptible by the senses (*sensible phenomena*). **b** great enough to be perceived; appreciable (*a sensible difference*). **3** (of clothing etc.) practical and functional. **4** (foll. by *of*) aware; not unmindful (*was sensible of her peril*). □ **sens·ible·ness** *noun* **sens·ibly** *adverb*

sensible horizon *noun* see HORIZON 1b.

sensi·tive ● *adjective* **1** (often foll. by *to*) very open to or acutely affected by external stimuli or mental impressions; having sensibility. **2** (of a person) **a** easily offended or emotionally hurt. **b** attuned to others' emotions. **c** deeply and easily affected by emotion, beauty, etc. **3** (often foll. by *to*) (of an instrument etc.) responsive to or recording slight changes. **4** (often foll. by *to*) **a** (of photographic materials) prepared so as to respond (esp. rapidly) to the action of light. **b** readily affected by or responsive to external influences (*an environmentally sensitive area*). **5 a** (of a topic etc.) needing careful handling to avoid causing offence, embarrassment, etc. **b** involved with or likely to affect (esp. national) security. **6** (of a market) liable to quick changes of price. ● *noun* a person who is sensitive (esp. to supposed occult influences). □ **sensi·tive·ly** *adverb* **sensi·tive·ness** *noun* [Middle English, =

sensory, from Old French *sensitif -ive* or medieval Latin *sensitivus*, irreg. from Latin *sentire sens-* feel]

sensitive plant *noun* a plant whose leaves curve downwards and leaflets fold together when touched, esp. mimosa.

sensi·tiv·ity *noun* (*pl.* **-ities**) the quality or degree of being sensitive.

sensitivity training *noun N Amer.* a form of therapy intended to foster a greater understanding of oneself and others through open, unstructured discussion.

sensi·tize *transitive verb* (also esp. *Brit.* **-tise**) **1** make sensitive. **2** *Photog.* make sensitive to light. **3** make (an organism etc.) abnormally sensitive to a foreign substance. □ **sensi·tiz·a·tion** *noun* **sensi·tiz·er** *noun*

sensi·tom·eter /ˌsensə'tɒmɪtər/ *noun Photog.* a device for measuring sensitivity to light.

sensor /'sensər/ *noun* a device giving a signal for the detection or measurement of a physical property to which it responds. [SENSORY, after MOTOR]

sen·sor·ium /sen'sɔriəm/ *noun* (*pl.* **sen·sor·ia** or **sen·sor·iums**) **1** the seat of sensation, the brain, brain and spinal cord, or grey matter of these. **2** *Biol.* the whole sensory apparatus including the nerve system. □ **sen·sor·ial** *adjective* **sen·sor·ial·ly** *adverb* [Late Latin from Latin *sentire sens-* feel]

sen·sory /'sensəri/ *adjective* of sensation or the senses. □ **sen·sor·ily** *adverb* [as SENSORIUM]

sensory overload *noun* the bombardment of the senses with excessive stimuli.

sen·su·al /'senʃuəl/ *adjective* **1 a** of or depending on the senses only and not on the intellect or spirit; carnal, fleshly (*sensual pleasures*). **b** given to the pursuit of sensual pleasures or the gratification of the appetites; self-indulgent sexually or in regard to food and drink; voluptuous, licentious. **c** indicative of a sensual nature (*sensual lips*). ¶ *Sensual* is sometimes confused with *sensuous*. While *sensual* is used to describe things that are gratifying to the body, and has sexual overtones, *sensuous* is used to mean 'affecting or appealing to the senses' in an aesthetic sense, without the pejorative implications of *sensual*. **2** of sense or sensation, sensory. □ **sen·su·al·ism** *noun* **sen·su·al·ist** *noun* **sen·su·al·ize** *transitive verb* (also esp. *Brit.* **-ise**). **sen·su·al·ly** *adverb*

sen·su·al·ity /ˌsenʃu'alɪti/ *noun* **1** the state or quality of being sensual. **2** gratification of the senses, self-indulgence.

sen·su·ous /'senʃuəs/ *adjective* of or derived from or affecting the senses, esp. aesthetically rather than sensually. ¶ See Usage Note at SENSUAL. □ **sen·su·ous·ly** *adverb* **sen·su·ous·ness** *noun*

sent¹ *noun* a monetary unit of Estonia, equal to one-hundredth of a kroon. [Estonian = cent]

sent² past and past participle of SEND.

sente /'senti/ *noun* (*pl.* **li·sente** /lɪ'senti/) a monetary unit of Lesotho, equal to one-hundredth of a loti. [Sesotho]

sen·tence ● *noun* **1 a** a set of words complete in itself as the expression of a thought, containing or implying a subject and predicate, and conveying a statement, question, exclamation, or command. **b** a piece of writing or speech between two periods or equivalent pauses, often including several grammatical sentences, e.g. *I went; he came*. **2 a** a decision of a law court, esp. the punishment allotted to a person convicted in a criminal trial. **b** the declaration of this. **3** *Logic* a series of signs or symbols expressing a proposition in an artificial or logical language. ● *transitive verb* **1** declare the sentence of (a convicted criminal etc.). **2** (foll. by *to*) declare (such a person) to be condemned to a specified punishment. □ **under sentence of** having been condemned to (*under sentence of death*). □ **sen·ten·cing** *noun* [Old French from Latin *sententia* opinion, from *sentire* be of opinion]

sentencing circle *noun* (esp. among Aboriginal peoples) a group convened to determine, through discussion, an appropriate penalty for a crime, constituted of the offender, the victim, members of the community, and other affected parties.

sen·ten·tial /sen'tenʃəl/ *adjective Grammar & Logic* of a sentence.

sen·ten·tious /sen'tenʃəs/ *adjective* **1** (of a person) fond of pompous moralizing. **2** (of a style) affectedly formal. **3** aphoristic, pithy, given to the use of maxims, affecting a concise impressive style. □ **sen·ten·tious·ly** *adverb* **sen·ten·tious·ness** *noun*

sen·tient /'senʃənt/ *adjective* having the power of perception by the senses. □ **sen·tience** *noun* **sen·tiency** *noun* **sen·tient·ly** *adverb* [Latin *sentire* feel]

senti·ment *noun* **1** a view of or attitude towards a situation or event; an opinion or point of view. **2** an opinion or feeling as distinguished from the words meant to convey it; an emotional feeling conveyed in literature, art, etc. (*the sentiment is good though the words are injudicious*). **3 a** emotional or tender feelings collectively, esp. mawkish tenderness. **b** the display of this. **4** a mental feeling (*the sentiment of pity*). [medieval Latin *sentimentum* from Latin *sentire* 'feel']

sen·ti·ment·al *adjective* **1** of or prompted by feelings of tenderness, sadness, or nostalgia (*a sentimental attachment*). **2** dealing with feelings of tenderness, sadness, or nostalgia in an exaggerated and self-indulgent way (*a sentimental ballad*). **3** excessively prone to feelings of tenderness, sadness, or nostalgia (*a sentimental old fool*). □ **sen·ti·ment·al·ism** *noun* **sen·ti·ment·al·ist** *noun* **sen·ti·men·tal·ity** *noun* **sen·ti·ment·al·ize** *transitive & intransitive verb* (also esp. *Brit.* **-ise**). **sen·ti·ment·al·iz·a·tion** *noun* **sen·ti·ment·al·ly** *adverb*

sentimental value *noun* the value of a thing to a particular person because of its associations.

sen·ti·nel ● *noun* a sentry or lookout; a guard. ● *transitive verb* (**sen·ti·nelled**, **sen·ti·nel·ling**; *US* **sen·ti·neled**, **sen·ti·nel·ing**) **1** station sentinels at or in. **2** *literary* keep guard over or in. [French *sentinelle* from Italian *sentinella*, of unknown origin]

sen·try *noun* (*pl.* **-tries**) a soldier etc. stationed to keep guard. [perhaps from obsolete *centrinel*, var. of SENTINEL]

sentry box *noun* a wooden cabin intended to shelter a standing sentry.

Seoul /soːl/ the capital of S Korea, situated in the northwest on the Han River; pop. (est. 2002) 11,153,200. It was the capital of the Korean Yi dynasty from the late 14th c. until 1910.

sepal /ˈsiːpəl, ˈsep-/ *noun Bot.* each of the divisions or leaves of the calyx. [French *sépale*, modern Latin *sepalum*, perhaps formed as SEPARATE + PETAL]

sep·ar·able *adjective* **1** able to be separated. **2** *Grammar* (of a prefix, or a verb with respect to a prefix) written as a separate word in some collocations. □ **sep·ar·abil·ity** *noun* **sep·ar·ably** *adverb*

sep·ar·ate ● *adjective* **1** (often foll. by *from*) forming a unit that is or may be regarded as apart or by itself; physically disconnected, distinct, or individual (*living in separate rooms; the two questions are essentially separate*). **2** *Cdn* of or relating to a separate school or the separate school system. ● *noun* (in *pl.*) separate articles of clothing suitable for wearing together in various combinations. ● *verb* **1** *transitive* make separate, sever. **2** *transitive* a prevent union or contact of. **b** part by occupying an intervening space (*a river separates the two counties*). **3** *intransitive* go different ways, disperse. **4** *intransitive* cease to live together as a married couple. **5** *intransitive* (often foll. by *from*) secede. **6** *transitive* distinguish between; consider individually (*we can't separate his thinking from his activity*). **7** *transitive* = DISLOCATE 1. **8** *transitive* a divide or sort (milk, ore, fruit, light, etc.) into constituent parts or sizes. **b** (often foll. by *out*) extract or remove (an ingredient, waste product, etc.) by such a process for use or rejection. **9** *intransitive* (of a substance) stop being combined; divide into constituent parts (*yogurt will separate when heated*). **10** *transitive US* discharge, dismiss. □ **sep·ar·ate·ly** *adverb* **sep·ar·ate·ness** *noun* [Latin *separare separat-* (as SE-, *parare* make ready)]

separate school *noun Cdn* **1** (in Ontario) a publicly funded school for Catholic students (*compare* PUBLIC SCHOOL 2a). **2** (in Alberta and Saskatchewan) a publicly funded school for children belonging to the religious minority (usu. Catholics) in a given district.

separate school board *noun Cdn* **1** an elected board of trustees responsible for the separate schools of a particular area. **2** the administrative unit responsible for the separate schools in a given area. **3** the area within which a separate school board has jurisdiction.

separate school district *noun Cdn* (in Alberta and Saskatchewan) the area within which a separate school board has jurisdiction.

separate school system *noun Cdn* a system of publicly funded denominational (usu. Catholic) schools operated alongside a public school system.

sep·ar·a·tion *noun* **1** the act or an instance of separating; the state of being separated. **2** the place or point where two or more objects are divided from one another. **3** (in full **legal separation**) an arrangement by which spouses remain married but live apart. **4** any of three or more monochrome reproductions of a coloured picture which can combine to reproduce the full colour of the original. **5** *Physics & Aviation* the generation of a turbulent boundary layer between the surface of a body and a moving fluid, or between two fluids moving at different speeds. **6 a** distinction or difference between the signals carried by the two channels of a stereophonic system. **b** a measure of this.

separation anxiety *noun Psych.* anxiety provoked in a child by the threat of separation from its parents or familiar surroundings.

separation of powers *noun* the vesting of the legislative, executive, and judiciary powers of government in separate bodies.

sep·ara·tist ● *noun* a person who favours separation, esp. for political or ecclesiastical independence; (in Canada) a person who favours the secession of Quebec or the Western provinces from Canada. ● *adjective* of, pertaining to, or characteristic of separatists or their views. □ **sep·ara·tism** *noun*

sep·ar·ator *noun* a machine or device for separating, e.g. cream from milk or egg yolk from egg white.

Seph·ar·di /səˈfɑrdi/ *noun* (*pl.* **Seph·ar·dim** /-dɪm/) (often *attributive*) a Jew of Spanish or Portuguese descent (*compare* ASHKENAZI). □ **Seph·ar·dic** *adjective* [Late Hebrew, from *sᵉpārad*, a country mentioned in Obad. 20 and taken to be Spain]

sep·ia /ˈsiːpiə/ ● *noun* **1** a dark reddish-brown colour associated particularly with monochrome photographs of the 19th and early 20th centuries. **2** a brown pigment prepared from a black fluid secreted by cuttlefish, used in monochrome drawing and in watercolours. **3** a drawing done in sepia. **4** the fluid secreted by cuttlefish. ● *adjective* of a dark reddish-brown colour. [Latin from Greek *sēpia* 'cuttlefish']

se·poy /ˈsiːpɔɪ/ *noun hist.* (in India) a native soldier serving under British or other European orders. [Urdu & Persian *sipāhī* soldier, from *sipāh* army]

sep·puku /səˈpuːkuː/ *noun* hara-kiri. [Japanese]

sep·sis *noun* **1** the state of being septic. **2** blood poisoning. [modern Latin from Greek *sēpsis* from *sēpō* make rotten]

Sept. *abbreviation* **1** September. **2** Septuagint.

sept *noun* a clan, esp. in Ireland. [prob. alteration of SECT]

sept- *var. of* SEPTI-.

septa *pl. of* SEPTUM.

sep·tal *adjective* **1** of a septum or septa. **2** *Archaeology* (of a stone or slab) separating compartments in a burial chamber.

sep·tate *adjective Bot., Zool., & Anat.* having a septum or septa; partitioned. □ **sep·ta·tion** *noun*

Sep·tem·ber *noun* the ninth month of the year. [Latin *September* from *septem* seven: originally the seventh month of the Roman year]

September 11 (also **9/11**) the terrorist attacks of September 11, 2001, in which hijackers with links to the al Qaeda terrorist network crashed airliners into the twin towers of the World Trade Center in New York and into the Pentagon; a fourth hijacked plane crashed into a field in Pennsylvania. In all, almost 3000 people were killed.

sep·ten·arius /ˌseptəˈneriəs/ *noun* (*pl.* **sep·ten·arii** /-riˌaɪ/) *Prosody* a verse of seven feet, esp. a trochaic or iambic tetrameter lacking a syllable in the last foot. [Latin from *septeni* distributive of *septem* seven]

sep·ten·ary /ˈseptəˌneri, sepˈtiːnəri/ ● *adjective* of seven, by sevens, on the basis of seven. ● *noun* (*pl.* **-ies**) **1** a group or set of seven (esp. years). **2** a septenarius. [Latin *septenarius* (as SEPTENARIUS)]

sep·ten·nial *adjective* **1** lasting for seven years. **2** recurring every seven years. [Late Latin *septennis* from Latin *septem* seven + *annus* year]

sep·tet *noun* **1** *Music* **a** a composition for seven performers. **b** the performers of such a composition. **2** any group of seven.

septi- *combining form* (also **sept-** before a vowel) seven. [Latin from *septem* seven]

sep·tic ● *adjective* **1** contaminated with bacteria from a festering wound etc.; putrefying. **2** of or relating to a septic system. ● *noun* = SEPTIC SYSTEM. □ **sep·tic·ally** *adverb* [Latin *septicus* from Greek *sēptikos* from *sēpō* make rotten]

septi·cemia /ˌseptəˈsiːmiə/ *noun* (*Brit.* **septi·caemia**) blood poisoning. □ **septi·cemic** *adjective* [modern Latin from Greek *sēptikos* + *haima* blood]

septic field *noun* (also **septic bed**) a bed of gravel and tile laid underneath the ground to serve as a drainage area for the effluent from a septic tank. *Also called* TILE BED, WEEPING BED.

septic system *noun* a sewage disposal system consisting of a septic tank and septic field.

septic tank *noun* a usu. underground tank in which the organic matter in sewage is decomposed through bacterial activity.

Sept-Îles /setˈiːl/ a city in E Quebec, situated on the north shore of the St. Lawrence, about 175 km northeast of Baie-Comeau; pop. (2001) 25,392. [French, lit. 'Seven Islands', so called because seven islands lie at the entrance to its harbour]

sep·til·lion /sepˈtɪljən/ *noun* (*pl.* same) a thousand raised to the eighth (or formerly, esp. *Brit.*, the fourteenth) power (10²⁴ and 10⁴² respectively). [French from *sept* seven, after *billion* etc.]

sep·to·ria /sepˈtɔːrɪə/ *noun* any of numerous parasitic fungi constituting the genus *Septoria*. [modern Latin *Septoria* from Latin SEPTUM]

sep·tu·a·gen·ar·ian /ˌseptuːədʒəˈnerɪən, ˌseptəgəˈnerɪən, ˌseptʃuːə-/ ● *noun* a person from 70 to 79 years old. ● *adjective* of this age. [Latin *septuagenarius* from *septuageni* distributive of *septuaginta* seventy]

Sep·tu·a·ges·i·ma /ˌseptjuːəˈdʒesɪmə/ *noun* (in full **Septuagesima Sunday**) the Sunday before Sexagesima. [Latin, = seventieth (day), formed as SEPTUAGINT, perhaps after QUINQUAGESIMA or with reference to the period of 70 days from Septuagesima to the Saturday after Easter]

Sep·tu·a·gint /ˈseptuːəˌdʒɪnt, ˌsepˈtuːədʒɪnt, ˈseptʃuː-/ *noun* a Greek version of the Hebrew Scriptures including the Apocrypha, said to have been made about 270 BC by about 70 translators. [Latin *septuaginta* seventy]

sep·tum *noun* (*pl.* **septa**) *Anat.*, *Bot.*, & *Zool.* a partition, such as that between the nostrils or the chambers of a shell. [Latin *s(a)eptum* from *saepire saept-* enclose, from *saepes* hedge]

se·pul·chral /sɪˈpʌlkrəl/ *adjective* **1** of a tomb or interment (*sepulchral mound*; *sepulchral customs*). **2** suggestive of the tomb, funereal, gloomy, dismal (*sepulchral look*). □ **se·pul·chral·ly** *adverb*

sep·ul·chre /ˈsepəlkər/ (*US* **sep·ul·cher**) ● *noun* a tomb esp. cut in rock or built of stone or brick, a burial vault or cave. ● *transitive verb* lay in a sepulchre. [Old French from Latin *sepulc(h)rum* from *sepelire sepult-* bury]

seq. *abbreviation* (*pl.* **seqq.**) the following. [Latin *sequens* etc.]

se·quel /ˈsiːkwəl/ *noun* **1** what follows after or as a result of an earlier event (*famine is often the sequel to war*). **2** a novel, film, etc., that continues the story of an earlier one. [Old French *sequelle* or Latin *sequel(l)a* from *sequi* follow]

se·quela /sɪˈkwiːlə/ *noun* (*pl.* **se·quelae** /-liː/) *Med.* (esp. in *pl.*) a condition or symptom following a disease. [Latin from *sequi* follow]

se·quence /ˈsiːkwəns/ ● *noun* **1** succession, coming after or next. **2** order of succession (*shall follow the sequence of events*; *give the facts in historical sequence*). **3** a set of things belonging next to one another on some principle of order; a series without gaps. **4** a part of a film dealing with one scene or topic. **5** a set of poems on one theme (*sonnet sequence*). **6** a set of three or more playing cards next to one another in value. **7** *Music* repetition of a phrase or melody at a higher or lower pitch. **8** *Christianity* a hymn said or sung after the Gradual or Alleluia that precedes the Gospel. **9** succession without implication of causality (*opp.* CONSEQUENCE 1). **10** *Biochem.* the unique order of monomers in esp. a polypeptide or nucleic acid. ● *transitive verb* **1** arrange in a definite order. **2** *Biochem.* ascertain the sequence of monomers in (esp. a polypeptide or nucleic acid). [Late Latin *sequentia* from Latin *sequens* pres. part. of *sequi* follow]

sequence of tenses *noun Grammar* the dependence of the tense of a subordinate verb on the tense of the principal verb, according to certain rules, e.g. *I think you* are, *thought you* were, *wrong*.

se·quen·cer /ˈsiːkwənsər/ *noun* **1** *Music* a programmable electronic device for storing sequences of musical notes, chords, rhythms, etc. and transmitting them when required to an electronic musical instrument. **2** an apparatus for performing or initiating operations in the correct sequence, esp. one forming part of the control system of a computer. **3** *Biochem.* an apparatus for determining the sequence of monomers in a biological polymer.

se·quen·tial /sɪˈkwenʃəl/ *adjective* **1** forming a sequence, consequence, or sequela. **2** esp. *Computing* occurring or performed in a particular order. □ **se·quen·tial·ity** /-ʃiˈalɪti/ *noun* **se·quen·tial·ly** *adverb*

se·ques·ter /sɪˈkwestər/ *transitive verb* **1** seclude, isolate, set apart (*sequester oneself from the world*; *sequester a jury*; *a sequestered cottage*). **2** = SEQUESTRATE. **3** *Chem.* bind (a metal ion) so that it cannot react. [Old French *sequestrer* or Late Latin *sequestrare* commit for safekeeping, from Latin *sequester* trustee]

se·ques·trate /sɪˈkwestreɪt/ *transitive verb* **1** confiscate, appropriate. **2** *Law* take temporary possession of (a debtor's estate etc.). □ **se·ques·tra·tion** /ˌsiːkwɪˈstreɪʃən/ *noun* **se·ques·tra·tor** /ˈsiːkwɪˌstreɪtər/

se·ques·trum /sɪˈkwestrəm/ *noun* (*pl.* **se·ques·tra**) a piece of dead bone or other tissue detached from the surrounding parts. [modern Latin, neuter of Latin *sequester* standing apart]

se·quin /ˈsiːkwɪn/ *noun* **1** a circular spangle for attaching to clothing as an ornament. **2** *hist.* a Venetian gold coin. □ **se·quined** *adjective* (also

se·quinned). [French from Italian *zecchino* from *zecca* a mint, from Arabic *sikka* a die]

se·quoia /səˈkwɔɪə/ *noun* a Californian evergreen coniferous tree, *Sequoia sempervirens*, of very great height and breadth. [modern Latin genus name, from *Sequoiah*, the name of a Cherokee]

Sequoia National Park a US national park in the Sierra Nevada of California, east of Fresno. It was established in 1890 to protect groves of giant sequoia trees, of which the largest, the General Sherman Tree, is thought to be between 3,000 and 4,000 years old.

sera *pl.* of SERUM.

serac /seˈrak/ *noun* a pinnacle or ridge of ice on the surface of a glacier where crevasses intersect. [Swiss French *sérac*, originally the name of a compact white cheese]

se·ra·glio /səˈraliːoʊ/ *noun* (*pl.* **-glios**) **1** a harem. **2** *hist.* a Turkish palace, esp. that of the Sultan with government offices etc. at Constantinople. [Italian *serraglio* from Turkish from Persian *sarāy* palace: compare SERAI]

serai /səˈraɪ/ *noun* a caravanserai. [Turkish from Persian (as SERAGLIO)]

Seram Sea see CERAM SEA.

ser·ape /səˈrapi/ *noun* (also **sar·ape**) a shawl or blanket worn as a cloak esp. in Mexico. [Latin American Spanish]

ser·aph /ˈserəf/ *noun* (*pl.* **ser·aph·im** or **ser·aphs**) **1** *Bible* a supernatural being with three pairs of wings (Isaiah 6:2). **2** *Christianity* a member of the highest order of the nine ranks of heavenly beings (see ORDER *noun* 19), gifted esp. with love and associated with light, ardour, and purity. [back-formation from *seraphim* (compare CHERUB) (pl.) from Late Latin from Greek *seraphim* from Hebrew *śᵉrāpîm*]

ser·aph·ic /səˈrafɪk/ *adjective* **1** of or like the seraphim. **2** ecstatically adoring, fervent, or serene. □ **ser·aph·ic·ally** *adverb*

Sera·pis /ˈserəpɪs/ *Egyptian Myth* a god whose cult was developed by Ptolemy I at Memphis as a combination of Apis and Osiris, to unite Greeks and Egyptians in a common worship.

Serb ● *noun* **1** a native of Serbia. **2** a person of Serbian descent. ● *adjective* = SERBIAN *adjective*. [Serbian *Srb*]

Serbia a republic in the Balkans, formerly part of Yugoslavia; pop. (est. 2003) 9,817,800; official language, Serbian; capital, Belgrade. After the secession of four out of the six Yugoslav republics in 1991–2, Serbia struggled to retain the viability of Yugoslavia, and was involved in armed conflict with neighbouring Croatia, the civil war in Bosnia, and the suppression of Albanian nationalism in Kosovo. Serbia and Montenegro now make up the Union of Serbia and Montenegro.

Serb·ian ● *noun* **1** the dialect of the Serbs (*compare* SERBO-CROAT). **2** = SERB. ● *adjective* of or relating to the Serbs or their dialect.

Serbo- *combining form* Serbian.

Serbo-Croat /ˌsɔːbəʊˈkroʊat/ (also **Serbo-Croatian** /-kroʊˈeɪʃən/) ● *noun* the Slavic language of the Serbs and Croats, written in the Cyrillic alphabet by Serbs and the Roman alphabet by Croats. ● *adjective* of or relating to this language.

sere¹ *var.* of SEAR².

sere² /sɪər/ *adjective literary* (esp. of a plant, landscape, etc.) withered, dried.

sere³ /sɪər/ *noun Ecology* a natural succession of plant (or animal) communities, esp. a full series from uncolonized habitat to the appropriate climax vegetation (*compare* SUCCESSION 3). [Latin *serere* join in a SERIES]

Ser·em·ban /səˈrembən/ the capital of the state of Negri Sembilan in Malaysia, situated in the southwest of the Malay Peninsula; pop. (2000) 290,999.

ser·en·ade /ˌserəˈneɪd/ ● *noun* **1** a piece of music sung or played in the open air, esp. by a lover at night under the window of his beloved. **2** a suite of diverse pieces for an instrumental ensemble, esp. a string orchestra or wind ensemble. ● *transitive verb* sing or play a serenade to. □ **ser·en·ad·er** *noun* [French *sérénade* from Italian *serenata* from *sereno* SERENE]

ser·en·ata /ˌserəˈnɑːtə/ *noun Music* a cantata with a pastoral subject. [Italian (as SERENADE)]

ser·en·dip·ity /ˌserənˈdɪpɪti/ *noun* **1** the faculty of making happy and unexpected discoveries by accident. **2** good luck; good fortune. □ **ser·en·dip·it·ous** *adjective* **ser·en·dip·it·ous·ly** *adverb* [coined by Horace Walpole (1754) after *The Three Princes of Serendip* (now Sri Lanka), a fairy tale]

se·rene *adjective* (**se·ren·er**, **se·ren·est**) **1** placid, tranquil, unperturbed. **2 a** (of the sky, the air, etc.) clear and calm. **b** (of the sea etc.) unruffled. □ **se·rene·ly** *adverb* [Latin *serenus*]

Serene Highness *noun* a title used in addressing and referring to members of some European royal families (*His Serene Highness*).

Ser·en·geti /ˌserənˈgeti/ a vast plain in Tanzania, lying to the west of the Great Rift Valley. In 1951 the Serengeti National Park was created to protect the area's large numbers of wildebeest, zebra, and Thomson's gazelle.

se·ren·ity /səˈreniti/ *noun* the state or quality of being serene; tranquility.

serf *noun* **1** *hist.* (under the feudal system) a labourer who was not free to move from the land on which he worked. Serfs were allowed to farm part of their lord's estate for their own benefit, but had to work the lord's land without pay for a certain number of days, and give the lord a share of their produce. Serfdom in England lasted until the 14th or 15th century, in France until 1789, and in Russia and parts of eastern Europe until the 19th century. **2** an oppressed person, a drudge. □ **serf·dom** *noun* [Old French from Latin *servus* slave]

serge /sɜrdʒ/ *noun* a durable twilled woollen or worsted fabric used mainly for clothing. [Old French, ultimately from Latin *serica (lana)*: see SILK]

ser·geant /ˈsɑrdʒənt/ *noun* **1** (in the Canadian Army and Air Force and other armies) a non-commissioned officer ranking above master corporal and below warrant officer. Abbr.: **Sgt. 2** (in some Canadian police forces) = STAFF SERGEANT. **3** (in the Sûreté du Québec) an officer ranking above corporal and below lieutenant. **4** (in Quebec municipal police forces) an officer ranking above constable and below lieutenant. **5** (in the Royal Newfoundland Constabulary) an officer ranking above constable and below staff sergeant. **6** a police officer ranking below inspector (in the UK), or below lieutenant (in the US). [Old French *sergent* from Latin *servien -entis* servant, from *servire* SERVE]

sergeant-at-arms *noun* (*pl.* **sergeants-at-arms**) an official of a court or city or parliament, with ceremonial duties.

sergeant fish *noun* a marine fish, *Rachycentron canadum*, with lateral stripes suggesting a chevron.

sergeant major *noun* **1** (in the RCMP) an officer ranking above staff sergeant major and below corps sergeant major. **2** (in the Ontario Provincial Police) an officer ranking above staff sergeant, detective staff sergeant, or traffic staff sergeant, and below inspector. **3** (in full **regimental sergeant major**) (in the UK) a warrant officer assisting the adjutant of a regiment or battalion. **4** (in the US) the highest-ranking non-commissioned officer.

ser·ger /ˈsɜrdʒər/ *noun* a machine used for close-stitching or overcasting to prevent material from fraying at the edge.

Sergt. *abbreviation* Sergeant.

ser·ial ● *noun* **1** a story, play, or film which is published, broadcast, or shown in regular instalments. **2** a periodical. ● *adjective* **1** of or in or forming a series. **2** (of a story etc.) in the form of a serial. **3** *Music* using transformations of a fixed series of notes (see SERIES 8). **4** (of a publication) appearing in successive parts published usu. at regular intervals, periodical. **5** *Computing* **a** performed or used in sequence, sequential. **b** (of a device) involving the transfer of data as a single sequence of bits (*serial port*). **6** (of a person, action, etc.) habitual, inveterate, given to or characterized by the repetition of certain behaviour in a sequential pattern (*serial monogamy*; *serial rapist*). □ **seri·al·ity** *noun* **seri·al·ly** *adverb*

seri·al·ism *noun* a compositional technique in which a fixed series of notes, esp. the twelve notes of the chromatic scale, are used to generate the harmonic and melodic basis of a piece and are subject to change only in specific ways. □ **seri·al·ist** *noun*

seri·al·ize *transitive verb* (also esp. *Brit.* **-ise**) **1** publish or produce in instalments. **2** arrange in a series. □ **seri·al·iz·a·tion** *noun*

serial killer *noun* a person who murders repeatedly, often with no apparent motive and usually following a characteristic, predictable pattern of behaviour. □ **serial killing** *noun*

serial number *noun* a number showing the position of an item in a series, esp. one printed on a banknote or manufactured article by which it can be individually identified.

seri·ate ● *adjective* /ˈsɪəriət/ in the form of a series; in orderly sequence. ● *transitive & intransitive verb* /ˈsɪriˌeit/ arrange in a seriate manner. □ **seri·a·tion** *noun*

seri·cul·ture /ˈserɪˌkʌltʃər/ *noun* **1** silkworm breeding. **2** the production of raw silk. [French *sériciculture* from Late Latin *sericum*: see SILK, CULTURE]

seri·ema /ˌseriˈiːmə/ *noun* any S American bird of the family Cariamidae, having a long neck and legs and a crest above the bill. [modern Latin from Tupi *siriema* etc. crested]

ser·ies *noun* (*pl.* same) **1** a number of things of which each is similar to the preceding or in which each successive pair are similarly related; a sequence, succession, order, row, or set. **2** a set of successive games between the same teams. **3 a** a set of programs with the same actors etc. or on related subjects but each complete in itself. **b** a set of performances offered for purchase by subscription. **4** a set of lectures by the same speaker or on the same subject. **5 a** a set of successive issues of a periodical, of articles on one subject or by one writer, etc., esp. when numbered separately from a preceding or following set (*second series*). **b** a set of independent books in a common format or under a common title or supervised by a common general editor. **6 a** a set of stamps, coins, etc., of different denominations but issued at one time, in one reign, etc. **b** a set or class of aircraft, vehicles, machines, etc., developed over a period of time and sharing many features of design or assembly. **7** *Geol.* **a** a set of strata with a common characteristic. **b** the rocks deposited during a specific epoch. **8** *Music* an arrangement of the twelve notes of the chromatic scale as a basis for serial music. **9** *Electricity* **a** a set of circuits or components arranged so that the current passes through each successively. **b** a set of batteries etc. having the positive electrode of each connected with the negative electrode of the next. **10** *Chem.* a set of elements with common properties or of compounds related in composition or structure. **11** *Math.* a set of quantities constituting a progression or having the several values determined by a common relation. □ **in series 1** in ordered succession. **2** *Electricity* (of a set of circuits or components) arranged so that the current passes through each successively. [Latin, = row, chain, from *serere* join, connect]

ser·if /ˈserɪf/ *noun* **1** a slight projection finishing off a stroke of a letter as in T contrasted with T (*compare* SANS SERIF). **2** a form of type with serifs. □ **ser·ifed** *adjective* [perhaps from Dutch *schreef* 'dash, line', from Germanic]

seri·graph /ˈserɪgraf/ *noun* a print made by silkscreen printing. [formed irregularly from Latin *sericum* SILK]

ser·ine /ˈseriːn, ˈsɪr-, -ɪn/ *noun* *Biochem.* a hydrophilic amino acid present in proteins. [Latin *sericum* 'silk' + -INE⁴]

ser·inga /səˈrɪŋgə/ *noun* **1** = SYRINGA. **2** any of various rubber trees of the genus *Hevea*, native to Brazil. [French (as SYRINGA)]

serio·comic /ˌsɪəriːoˈkɒmɪk/ *adjective* combining the serious and the comic; jocular in intention but simulating seriousness or vice versa. □ **serio·com·edy** *noun* (*pl.* **-ies**).

ser·ious *adjective* **1** thoughtful, earnest, sober, sedate, responsible, not reckless or given to trifling (*has a serious air; a serious young person*). **2** important, demanding consideration (*this is a serious matter*). **3** not slight or negligible (*a serious injury; a serious offence*). **4** sincere, in earnest, not ironic or joking (*are you serious?*). **5** (of music and literature) not merely for amusement (*opp.* LIGHT² 5a). **6** not perfunctory (*serious thought*). **7** not to be trifled with (*a serious opponent*). **8** (of a relationship or the people involved in it) involving profound love, the intention to marry, etc. **9** *informal* large in size or amount (*serious money*). **10** *informal* remarkable; impressive. □ **ser·ious·ness** *noun* [Old French *serieux* or Late Latin *seriosus* from Latin *serius*]

ser·ious·ly *adverb* **1** in a serious manner (esp. introducing a sentence, implying that irony etc. is now to cease). **2** to a serious extent. **3** *informal* very, really (*seriously rich*).

ser·mon *noun* **1** a spoken or written discourse on a religious or moral subject, esp. a discourse based on a text or passage of Scripture and delivered in a service by way of religious instruction or exhortation. **2** a piece of admonition or reproof; a lecture. □ **ser·mon·ic** /sɜrˈmɒnɪk/ *adjective* [Old French from Latin *sermo -onis* discourse, talk]

ser·mon·ette *noun* a short sermon.

ser·mon·ize *verb* (also esp. *Brit.* **-ise**) **1** *transitive* deliver a moral lecture to. **2** *intransitive* deliver a moral lecture. □ **ser·mon·iz·er** *noun*

Sermon on the Mount *noun* the discourse of Christ recorded in Matt. 5-7, an important collection of Christian ethical teachings that contains the Beatitudes and the Lord's Prayer.

sero- /ˈsɪəroʊ/ *combining form* of or pertaining to serum.

sero·con·ver·sion *noun* a change from a seronegative to a seropositive state. □ **sero·con·vert** *intransitive verb*

ser·ol·ogy /sɪˈrɒlədʒi/ *noun* the scientific study of blood sera and their effects. □ **sero·logic** *adjective* **sero·logic·al** *adjective* **sero·logic·al·ly** *adverb* **ser·olo·gist** *noun*

sero·nega·tive *adjective* giving a negative result in a test of blood serum, e.g. for presence of a virus. □ **sero·nega·tiv·ity** *noun*

sero·posi·tive *adjective* giving a positive result in a test of blood serum, e.g. for presence of a virus. □ **sero·posi·tiv·ity** *noun*

Vowels: a *cat* ɑ *arm* e *bed* ɜr *her* ɜː *deux* ə *ago* ɪ *sit* i *cosy* iː *feed* ɒ *hot* ɔ *pore* ɔː *no* ʌ *run* ʊ *put*

ser·osa /sɪˈroːsə/ *noun* a serous membrane. □ **ser·os·al** *adjective* [modern Latin, fem. of medieval Latin *serosus* SEROUS]

sero·tin·ous /səˈrɒtɪnəs/ *adjective Botany* (of a pine etc. cone) remaining long unopened, slow to release seed. [Latin *serotinus* 'late']

sero·tonin /ˌserəˈtoːnɪn/ *noun Biol.* a compound present in blood platelets and serum, which constricts the blood vessels and acts as a neurotransmitter. [SERUM + TONIC + -IN]

sero·type /ˈsiːroˌtəɪp/ *noun* a serologically distinguishable strain of a micro-organism.

ser·ous /ˈsiːrəs/ *adjective* of or like or producing serum; watery.

serous membrane *noun* (also **serous gland**) a membrane or gland with a serous secretion.

Ser·pens /ˈsɜrpenz/ a constellation near the celestial equator, traditionally seen as a serpent in the hands of the constellation Ophiuchus, the serpent bearer. [Latin *serpens* snake (as SERPENT)]

ser·pent *noun* **1** usu. *literary* a snake, esp. of a large kind. **2** a sly or treacherous person, esp. one who exploits a position of trust to betray it. **3** (**the Serpent**) *Bible* Satan (see Gen. 3, Rev. 20). **4** *Music* an obsolete bass wind instrument made from leather-covered wood, roughly in the form of an S. [Old French from Latin *serpens -entis* part. of *serpere* creep]

ser·pen·tine /ˈsɜrpənˌtaɪn, -tiːn/ ● *adjective* **1** of or like a serpent. **2** coiling, tortuous, sinuous, meandering, writhing (*the serpentine windings of the stream*). **3** cunning, subtle, treacherous. ● *noun* usu. /-tiːn/ a soft rock mainly of hydrated magnesium silicate, usu. dark green and sometimes mottled or spotted like a serpent's skin, taking a high polish and used as a decorative material.

ser·ran·id /səˈranɪd, ˈserə-/ ● *noun* any marine fish of the family Serranidae, comprising heavy predatory fishes such as sea basses and groupers. ● *adjective* of or relating to this family. [modern Latin *Serranus* (genus name) from Latin *serra* 'saw']

ser·rano /səˈrɒnɔɪ/ *noun* (*pl.* **-nos**) a hot chili pepper with green, red, or yellow skin, used in salsas etc. [Spanish, = from the mountain]

Serra Peaks /ˈserə/ a series of peaks in the Coast Mountains of western BC, situated northeast of Mount Waddington. [with reference to their crest having a serrated edge]

ser·rate ● *transitive verb* /seˈreɪt/ (usu. as **ser·rat·ed** *adjective*) provide with a sawlike edge (*a serrated knife*). ● *adjective* /ˈsereɪt/ *Anat., Bot., & Zool.* notched like a saw. □ **ser·ra·tion** *noun* [Late Latin *serrare serrat-* from Latin *serra* saw]

ser·ried *adjective* (of ranks of soldiers, rows of trees, etc.) pressed together; without gaps; close. [prob. from French *serré* past participle of *serrer* close, ultimately from Latin *sera* lock]

ser·ru·late /ˈseruˌleɪt, -ˌlət/ *adjective* esp. *Anat., Bot., & Zool.* finely serrate; with a series of small notches. □ **ser·ru·la·tion** *noun* [modern Latin *serrulatus* from Latin *serrula* diminutive of *serra* saw]

serum /ˈsiːrəm/ *noun* (*pl.* **sera** /-rə/ or **serums**) **1** the amber-coloured protein-rich liquid in which blood cells are suspended and which separates out when blood coagulates. **2** *Med.* the blood serum of an animal used esp. to provide immunity to a pathogen or toxin by inoculation or as a diagnostic agent. **3** a watery fluid in animal bodies. **4** whey. [Latin, = whey]

serum albumin *noun* the soluble protein present in blood serum.

serum hepatitis *noun* = HEPATITIS B.

serum sickness *noun* a reaction to an injection of serum, characterized by skin eruption, fever, etc.

ser·val /ˈsɜrvəl/ *noun* a tawny black-spotted long-legged African cat, *Felis serval.* [French from Portuguese *cerval* deer-like, from *cervo* deer, from Latin *cervus*]

ser·vant *noun* **1** a person hired to carry out the orders of an individual or corporate employer, esp. a person employed in a house on domestic duties or as a personal attendant. **2** a devoted follower, a person willing to serve another (*a servant of Jesus Christ*). **3** a person employed by a government (*civil servant; public servant*). **4** *Cdn hist.* an employee of the Hudson's Bay Company. □ **servant·hood** *noun* **servant·less** *adjective*

serve ● *verb* **1** *transitive* do a service for (a person, community, etc.). **2 a** *transitive* be a servant to. **b** *intransitive* act as a servant. **3** *intransitive* carry out duties (*served on six committees*). **4** *intransitive* **a** (foll. by *in*) be employed in (an organization, esp. the armed forces, or a place, esp. a foreign country) (*served in the air force*). **b** be a member of the armed forces. **5 a** *transitive* be useful or serviceable for; meet the needs of; do what is required for (*serve a purpose; this program has served us well*). **b** *intransitive* meet requirements; perform a function (*a sofa serving as a bed*). **c** *intransitive* (foll. by *to* + infin.) avail, suffice (*his attempt served only to postpone the inevitable; it serves to show the folly of such action*). **6** *transitive*

a go through a due period of (office, apprenticeship, a prison sentence, etc.). **b** go through (a due period) of imprisonment etc. **7** *transitive* set out or present (food) for those about to eat it (*asparagus served with butter; dinner is served*). **8** *intransitive* act as a waiter. **9** *transitive* **a** attend to (a customer in a store). **b** (foll. by *with*) supply with (goods) (*was serving a customer with apples; served the town with gas*). **10** *transitive* treat or act towards (a person) in a specified way (*has served me well*). **11** *transitive* **a** (often foll. by *on*) deliver (a writ etc.) to the person concerned in a legally formal manner (*served a warrant on him*). **b** (foll. by *with*) deliver a writ etc. to (a person) in this way (*served her with a summons*). **12** *transitive & intransitive Tennis etc.* **a** deliver (a ball etc.) to begin or resume play. **b** make (a fault etc.) in doing this. **13** *transitive Military* keep (a gun, battery, etc.) firing. **14** *transitive* (of an animal, esp. a stallion etc. hired for the purpose) copulate with (a female). **15** *transitive Brit.* distribute (*served the ammunition out; served the rations round*). **16** *transitive* render obedience to (a deity, monarch, etc.). **17** *Christianity* **a** *intransitive* act as a server. **b** *transitive* act as a server at (a service). **18** *intransitive* (of a tide) be suitable for a ship to leave harbour etc. **19** *transitive Naut.* bind (a rope etc.) with thin cord to strengthen it. ● *noun Tennis etc.* **1** the act or an instance of serving. **2** a manner of serving. **3** a person's turn to serve. □ **serve one's needs** be adequate. **serve the purpose of** take the place of, be used as. **serve a person right** be a person's deserved punishment or misfortune. **serve** (or esp. *N Amer.* **serve out**) **one's time 1** hold office for the normal period. **2** (also **serve time**) undergo imprisonment, apprenticeship, etc. **serve one's** (or **the**) **turn** be adequate. **serve up** offer for acceptance. [Old French *servir* from Latin *servire*, from *servus* 'slave']

serve-and-volley *adjective Tennis* denoting a style of play in which the server moves close to the net after serving, ready to play an attacking volley off the service return. □ **serve-and-volleyer** *noun*

serv·er *noun* **1** a person who serves or attends to the requirements of another, esp. a waiter. **2** (in tennis etc.) the player who serves the ball. **3** *Christianity* a person assisting the celebrant at a service, esp. the Eucharist. **4** *Computing* **a** a program which manages shared access to a centralized resource or service in a network. **b** a device on which such a program is run. **5** a utensil for serving food (*salad servers*).

serv·ery *noun* (*pl.* **-ies**) esp. *Brit.* a counter or room from which meals are served in a cafeteria etc.

serve·ware *noun* items on or from which food etc. is served, e.g. bowls, butter dishes, shakers, creamers, etc.

Ser·vice, Rob·ert Wil·liam (1874–1958), British-born Canadian poet and novelist. Poems such as 'The Shooting of Dan McGrew' and 'The Cremation of Sam McGee' earned him lasting fame and the nickname 'the Poet of the Yukon'.

ser·vice¹ ● *noun* (often *attributive*) **1** the act of helping or doing work for another or for a community etc. **2** work done in this way. **3** assistance or benefit given to someone. **4** the provision or system of supplying a public need, e.g. transport, or (often in *pl.*) the supply of water, gas, electricity, telephone, etc. **5 a** the fact or status of being a servant. **b** employment or a position as a servant. **6** a state or period of employment doing work for an individual or organization (*resigned after 15 years' service*). **7 a** a public department or organization employing officials working for the government (*civil service; secret service; the provincial forest service*). **b** employment in this. **8** (in *sing.* or *pl.*) the armed forces. **9** (*attributive*) of the kind issued to the armed forces (*a service revolver*). **10 a** (in *pl.*) the sector of the economy that supplies the needs of the consumer but produces no tangible goods, as banking or tourism. **b** a business which provides a specified service to the public (*runs a water taxi service*). **11 a** a ceremony of worship according to prescribed forms. **b** a form of liturgy for this. **12 a** the provision of what is necessary for the installation and maintenance of a machine etc. or operation. **b** the maintenance and repair of a vehicle, machine etc. at regular intervals. **13 a** the act or process of serving customers in a store. **b** assistance or advice given to customers after the sale of goods. **14 a** the act or process of serving food, drinks, etc. **b** an extra charge nominally made for this. **15** a set of dishes, plates, etc., used for serving meals (*a dinner service*). **16** *Tennis etc.* **a** the act or an instance of serving. **b** a person's turn to serve. **c** the manner or quality of serving. **d** (in full **service game**) a game in which a particular player serves. **17** *Law* the formal delivery of a writ, summons, etc. ● *transitive verb* **1** provide service or services for, esp. maintain. **2** maintain or repair (a car, machine, etc.). **3** pay interest on (a debt). **4** supply with a service. **5 a** (of a male animal) copulate with (a female animal). **b** *coarse slang* perform sexual favours for (a person). □ **at a person's service** ready to serve or assist a person. **be of service** be available to assist. **in service 1** employed as a servant. **2** available for use. **on active service** serving in the armed forces in wartime. **out of service** not available for use. **see service 1** have experience of service, esp. in the armed forces. **2** (of a thing) be much used. [Old French from Latin *servitium* from *servus* 'slave']

ser·vice[2] *noun* **1** (in full **service tree**) a southern European tree of the rose family, *Sorbus domestica*, with cream-coloured flowers, and small round or pear-shaped fruit eaten when overripe. **2** (in full **wild service tree**) a related small Eurasian tree, *Sorbus torminalis*, with bitter fruit. [earlier *serves*, pl. of obsolete *serve*, via Old English *syrfe* from Germanic, ultimately from Latin *sorbus*]

ser·vice·able *adjective* **1** useful or usable. **2** able to render service. **3** durable; capable of withstanding difficult conditions. **4** suited for ordinary use rather than ornament. □ **ser·vice·abil·ity** *noun* **ser·vice·ably** *adverb*

service area *noun* **1** the area served by a broadcasting station, public utility, etc. **2** the area in a store, garage, etc. set aside for the maintenance and repair of machines, cars, etc. **3** *Brit.* an area beside a major road for the supply of gasoline, refreshments, etc.

service bay *noun N Amer.* a space in an auto repair shop designed to accommodate one car at a time for servicing, repairs, etc.

service·berry *noun* (*pl.* **-berries**) **1 a** any N American shrub or small tree of the genus *Amelanchier*. **b** the edible fruit of this. **2** the fruit of the service tree.

service book *noun* a book of authorized forms of worship of a Church.

service break *noun Tennis* an instance of winning a game when one's opponent is serving.

service centre *noun* **1** a registered commercial operation where cars, appliances, etc. can be taken for maintenance and repair. **2** *Cdn* a town or city which serves as a shopping and distribution centre for a surrounding sparsely populated area.

service charge *noun* (also **service fee**) a fee charged for a service, e.g. by a bank, ticket agent, or restaurant.

service club *noun N Amer.* an association of business or professional people having the aims of promoting community welfare and goodwill.

service contract *noun* **1** a contract of employment. **2** a business agreement between contractor and customer, usu. guaranteeing the maintenance and servicing of equipment over a specified period.

ser·viced *adjective Cdn & Brit.* hooked up to utilities such as gas, water, and hydro (*a serviced campsite*).

service game *noun see* SERVICE[1] *noun* 16d.

service industry *noun* an industry engaged in the provision of services rather than the manufacture of goods.

service line *noun* (in tennis etc.) a line marking the limit of the area into which the ball must be served.

service·man *noun* (*pl.* **-men**) **1** a man serving in the armed forces. **2** a man providing service or maintenance.

service provider *noun* a company, organization, etc. which provides a service to customers, esp. one which provides access to the Internet.

service road *noun* a road parallel to a main road, giving access to houses, stores, etc.

service station *noun* = GAS STATION.

service tree *noun see* SERVICE[2].

service·woman *noun* (*pl.* **-women**) a woman serving in the armed forces.

ser·vi·ette *noun Cdn & Brit.* a napkin for use at table, esp. a paper one. [Old French from *servir* SERVE]

ser·vile /ˈsɜrvaɪl/ *adjective* **1** slavish, fawning; completely dependent. **2** of or being or like a slave or slaves. □ **ser·vile·ly** *adverb* **ser·vil·ity** /-ˈvɪlɪti/ *noun* [Latin *servilis* from *servus* slave]

serv·ing *noun* **1** the action of SERVE[1] *verb*. **2** a quantity of food served to one person. **3** (*attributive*) used for serving food (*serving spoons; serving tray*).

ser·vi·tor /ˈsɜrvɪtər/ *noun* **1** a servant. **2** an attendant.

ser·vi·tude /ˈsɜrvɪˌtuːd, -ˌtjuːd/ *noun* **1** slavery. **2** subjection (esp. involuntary); bondage. **3** *Law* the subjection of property to an easement. [Old French from Latin *servitudo -inis* from *servus* slave]

ser·vo *noun* (*pl.* **-vos**) **1** (in full **servo·mech·an·ism**) a powered mechanism producing motion or forces at a higher level of energy than the input level, e.g. in the brakes and steering of large motor vehicles, esp. where feedback is employed to make the control automatic. **2** (in full **servo·motor**) the motive element in a servomechanism. **3** (in *combination*) of or involving a servomechanism (*servo-assisted*). [Latin *servus* slave]

sesa·me /ˈsɛsəmi/ *noun* **1** an E Indian herbaceous plant, *Sesamum indicum*, with seeds used as food and yielding an edible oil. **2** its seeds. □ **open sesame** a means of acquiring or achieving what is normally unattainable. [Latin *sesamum* from Greek *sēsamon*, *sēsamē*; 'open sesame' with reference to the magic words used in the *Arabian Nights' Entertainments*]

sesa·moid /ˈsɛsəˌmɔɪd/ ● *adjective* shaped like a sesame seed; nodular (esp. of small independent bones developed in tendons passing over an angular structure such as the kneecap and the navicular bone). ● *noun* a sesamoid bone.

sesh *noun informal esp. Brit.* a session.

Se·sotho /sɛˈsuːtuː/ ● *noun* the South Eastern Bantu language of the Sotho. ● *adjective* of or relating to this language. [Sesotho, from *se-* prefix + SOTHO]

sesqui- /ˈsɛskwi, -kwə/ *combining form* **1** denoting one and a half. **2** *Chem.* (of a compound) in which there are three equivalents of a named element or radical to two others. [Latin (as SEMI-, *-que* and)]

ses·qui·cen·ten·ary /ˌsɛskwɪsɛnˈtɛnəri, -ˈtiːnəri, ˌsɛskwə-/ *noun* (*pl.* **-aries**) a one-hundred-and-fiftieth anniversary.

ses·qui·cen·ten·nial /ˌsɛskwɪsɛnˈtɛniəl, ˌsɛskwə-/ ● *noun* a one-hundred-and-fiftieth anniversary. ● *adjective* of or relating to a sesquicentennial.

ses·qui·ped·al·ian /ˌsɛskwɪpəˈdeɪliən/ *adjective* **1** (of a word) long, polysyllabic. **2** (of prose etc.) using such words. [from Latin *sesquipedalis* 'a foot and a half long']

ses·sile /ˈsɛsaɪl/ *adjective* **1** *Bot. & Zool.* (of a flower, leaf, eye, etc.) attached directly by its base without a stalk or peduncle. **2** fixed in one position; immobile. [Latin *sessilis* from *sedēre sess-* sit]

ses·sion *noun* **1** the process of assembly of a deliberative or judicial body to conduct its business. **2** a single meeting for this purpose. **3** a period during which such meetings are regularly held. **4 a** an academic year or term. **b** the period during which a school etc. has classes. **5 a** a period devoted to an activity (*poker session; recording session*). **b** (*attributive*) designating a freelance musician hired to play in a recording session (*a session guitarist*). **6** the governing body of a Presbyterian or United Church congregation, composed of the minister and the elders. □ **in session** assembled for business; not on vacation. □ **ses·sion·al** *adjective* [Old French *session* or Latin *sessio -onis* from *sedēre sess-* sit]

sessional indemnity *noun Cdn* = INDEMNITY 4.

ses·terce /ˈsɛstɜrs/ *noun* (also **ses·ter·tius** /sɛˈstɜrʃəs, -ˈstɜrtiəs/) (*pl.* **ses·terces** /ˈsɛstɜrˌsiːz/ or **ses·ter·tii** /sɛˈstɜrʃiː, -ˈstɜrtiː/) an ancient Roman coin and monetary unit equal to one quarter of a denarius. [Latin *sestertius* (*nummus* coin) = $2\frac{1}{2}$ from *semis* half + *tertius* third]

ses·tet *noun* **1** the last six lines of a sonnet. **2** a sextet. [Italian *sestetto* from *sesto* from Latin *sextus* a sixth]

ses·tina /sɛsˈtiːnə/ *noun* a form of rhymed or unrhymed poem with six stanzas of six lines and a final triplet, all stanzas having the same six words at the line endings in six different sequences. [Italian (as SESTET)]

Set *var. of* SETH[1].

set[1] *verb* (**set·ting**; *past* and *past participle* **set**) **1** *transitive* put, lay, or stand (a thing) in a certain position or location (*set it on the table; set it upright*). **2** *transitive* (foll. by *to*) apply (one thing) to (another) (*set pen to paper*). **3** *transitive* **a** fix ready or in position. **b** dispose suitably for use, action, or display. **4** *transitive* **a** adjust the hands of (a clock or watch) to show the right time. **b** adjust (an alarm clock) to sound at the required time. **c** adjust (a dial etc.) to a certain point (*set the thermostat at 21°C*). **5** *transitive* **a** fix, arrange, or mount. **b** insert (a jewel) in a ring, framework, etc. **6** *transitive* make (a device) ready to operate. **7** *transitive* arrange knives, forks, glasses, etc. on (a table) for a meal (*set the table for five people*). **8** *transitive* arrange (the hair) while damp so that it dries in the required style. **9** *transitive* (foll. by *with*) ornament or provide (a surface, esp. a precious item) (*gold set with gems*). **10** *transitive* bring by placing or arranging or other means into a specified state; cause to be (*set things in motion; set it on fire*). **11** *intransitive & transitive* **a** harden or solidify (*the jelly is set; the concrete has set*). **b** (of a stain or dye etc.) make or become permanent (*better rinse out your shirt before that stain sets*). **12** *intransitive* (of the sun, moon, etc.) appear to move towards and below the earth's horizon (as the earth rotates). **13** *transitive* represent (a story, play, scene, etc.) as happening in a certain time or place. **14** *transitive* **a** (foll. by *to* + infin.) cause or instruct (a person) to perform a specified activity (*set them to work*). **b** (foll. by pres. part.) start (a person or thing) doing something (*set him chatting; set the ball rolling*). **15** *transitive* present or impose as work to be done or a matter to be dealt with (*set them an essay*). **16** *transitive* exhibit as a type or model (*set a good example*).

17 *transitive* initiate; take the lead in (*set the fashion*; *set the pace*). **18** *transitive* establish (a record etc.). **19** *transitive* determine or decide (*the itinerary is set*). **20** *transitive* appoint or establish (*set them in authority*). **21** *transitive* join, attach, or fasten. **22** *transitive* **a** put parts of (a broken or dislocated bone, limb, etc.) into the correct position for healing. **b** deal with (a fracture or dislocation) in this way. **23** *transitive* (in full **set to music**) provide (words etc.) with music for singing. **24** *transitive* (often foll. by *up*) *Printing* **a** arrange or produce (type or film etc.) as required. **b** arrange the type or film etc. for (a book etc.). **25** *intransitive* (of a tide, current, etc.) have a certain motion or direction. **26** *intransitive* (of a face) assume a hard expression. **27 a** *intransitive* (of a hen) sit on eggs. **b** *transitive* cause (a hen) to sit on eggs. **c** *transitive* place (eggs) for a hen to sit on. **28** *transitive* put (a seed, plant, etc.) in the ground to grow. **29** *transitive* give the teeth of (a saw) an alternate outward inclination. **30** *transitive* esp. *N Amer.* start (a fire). **31** *transitive* fix or put (the price of something) at a certain amount. **32** *intransitive* (of eyes etc.) become motionless. **33** *intransitive* feel or show a certain tendency (*opinion is setting against it*). **34** *intransitive* **a** (of blossom) form into fruit. **b** (of fruit) develop from blossom. **c** (of a tree) develop fruit. **35** *transitive* incite (esp. a dog or other animal) to make an attack. **36** *intransitive* (of a hunting dog) take a rigid position indicating the presence of game. **37 a** *transitive* rig (a sail) so as to catch the wind. **b** *intransitive* (of a sail) be rigged so as to catch the wind. **38** *transitive* drive (the head of a nail) below the surface using a set. **39** *transitive* put aside (dough containing yeast) to rise. **40** *transitive* fix (a fish hook) firmly into the jaws of a fish by jerking the line sharply after the fish has taken the bait. **41** *transitive* (in volleyball) hit (the ball) above the net to permit a teammate to spike it. **42** *intransitive* (in full **set to partner**) (of a dancer) take a position facing one's partner. **43** *intransitive* dialect or slang sit. □ **set about 1** begin or take steps towards. **2** *informal* attack. **set (a person or thing) against (another) 1** consider or reckon (a thing) as a counterpoise or compensation for. **2** cause to oppose. **set apart** separate, reserve, differentiate. **set aside** see ASIDE. **set back 1** place further back in place or time. **2** impede or reverse the progress of. **3** *informal* cost (a person) a specified amount. **set by** *archaic* save for future use. **set down 1** record in writing. **2** allow to alight from a vehicle. **3** (foll. by *to*) attribute to. **4** (foll. by *as*) explain or describe to oneself as. **set eyes on** see EYE. **set one's face against** see FACE. **set foot in** (or **on**) see FOOT. **set forth 1** begin a journey. **2** make known; expound. **set forward** begin to advance. **set free** release. **set one's hand to** see HAND. **set one's heart** (or **hopes**) **on** want or hope for eagerly. **set in 1** (of weather, a condition, etc.) begin (and seem likely to continue), become established. **2** insert (esp. a sleeve etc. into a garment). **set little by** consider to be of little value. **set a person's mind at rest** see MIND. **set much by** consider to be of much value. **set off 1** begin a journey. **2** detonate (a bomb etc.). **3** initiate, stimulate. **4** cause (a person) to start laughing, talking, etc. **5** serve as an adornment or foil to; enhance. **6** (foll. by *against*) use as a compensating item. **set on** (or **upon**) **1** attack violently. **2** cause or urge to attack. **set out 1** begin a journey. **2** (foll. by *to* + infin.) aim or intend. **3** demonstrate, arrange, or exhibit. **4** mark out. **5** declare. **set sail 1** hoist the sails. **2** begin a voyage. **set the scene** see SCENE. **set store by** (or **on**) see STORE. **set one's teeth 1** clench them. **2** summon one's resolve. **set to** begin doing something vigorously, esp. fighting, arguing, or eating. **set up 1** place in position or view. **2** organize or start (a business etc.). **3** establish in some capacity. **4** supply the needs of. **5** begin making (a loud sound). **6** cause or make arrangements for (a condition or situation). **7** prepare (a task etc.) for another. **8** restore or enhance the health of (a person). **9** establish (a record). **10** propound (a theory). **11** *informal* put (a person) in a dangerous or vulnerable position. **set oneself up as** make pretensions to being. [Old English *settan* from Germanic]

set² *noun* **1** a number of things or persons that belong together or resemble one another or are usually found together. **2** a collection or group. **3** a section of society consorting together or having similar interests etc. **4** a collection of implements, vessels, etc., regarded collectively and needed for a specified purpose. **5** a piece of electric or electronic apparatus, esp. a radio or television receiver. **6 a** (in tennis etc.) a group of games counting as a unit towards a match for the player or side that wins a defined number or proportion of the games. **b** (in volleyball) the act or an instance of setting the ball. **7** *Math. & Logic* a collection of distinct entities, individually specified or satisfying specified conditions, forming a unit. **8** a group of pupils or students having the same average ability. **9 a** a slip, shoot, bulb, etc., for planting. **b** a young fruit just set. **10 a** a habitual posture or conformation; the way the head etc. is carried or a dress etc. flows. **b** a setter's pointing in the presence of game. **11** the way, drift, or tendency (of a current, public opinion, state of mind, etc.) (*the set of*

public feeling is against it). **12** the way in which a machine, device, etc. is set or adjusted. **13** = NAIL SET. **14 a** the alternate outward deflection of the teeth of a saw. **b** the amount of this. **c** a tool for setting saw teeth. **15** a condition of firmness or hardness, e.g. of glue. **16** *Printing* **a** the amount of spacing in type controlling the distance between letters. **b** the width of a piece of type. **17** a warp or bend or displacement caused by continued pressure or a continued position. **18** a setting, including stage furniture etc., for a theatrical production or film etc. **19 a** a sequence of songs or pieces performed by a musical ensemble, e.g. a dance band, before or after an intermission. **b** the period during which such a sequence is played. **20** the setting of the hair when damp. **21** (also **sett**) a badger's burrow. **22** (also **sett**) a granite paving stone. **23** a predisposition or expectation influencing a response. **24** a number of people making up a square dance. **25** the last coat of plaster on a wall. [sense 1 (and related senses) from Old French *sette* from Latin *secta* SECT: other senses from SET¹]

set³ *adjective* **1** *in senses of* SET¹. **2** prescribed or determined in advance. **3** fixed, unchanging, unmoving. **4** (of a phrase or speech etc.) having invariable or predetermined wording; not extempore. **5** prepared for action. **6** (foll. by *on*, *upon*) determined to acquire or achieve etc. **7** (of a book etc.) specified for reading in preparation for an examination. [past participle of SET¹]

seta /ˈsiːtə/ *noun* (*pl.* **setae** /-tiː/) *Bot. & Zool.* stiff hair; bristle. □ **se·ta·ceous** /-ˈteɪʃəs/ *adjective* [Latin, = bristle]

set-aside *noun* **1** the action of setting something aside for a special purpose. **2** the policy of taking land out of production to reduce crop surpluses (often *attributive*: *set-aside land*).

set·back *noun* **1** a reversal or arrest of progress. **2** a relapse. **3** *N Amer.* the distance by which a building or a part of a building is set back from the property line.

Seth¹ (also **Set**) *Egyptian Myth* an evil god who murdered his brother Osiris and wounded Osiris's son Horus; Seth is represented as having the head of a beast with a long pointed snout.

Seth², **Vik·ram** (b.1952), Indian novelist and poet. He is known for his verse novel, *The Golden Gate*, and his novels *A Suitable Boy* and *An Equal Music*.

SETI *abbreviation* Search for Extraterrestrial Intelligence, a program initiated by NASA to search extraterrestrial microwave radio waves for signals deriving from intelligent life forms.

set menu *noun* a limited menu of a set number of courses.

set-off *noun* **1** a thing set off against another. **2** a thing of which the amount or effect may be deducted from that of another or opposite tendency. **3** a counterpoise. **4** a counterclaim. **5** a thing that embellishes; an adornment to something. **6** *Printing* = OFFSET 4.

Seton /ˈsiːtən/ **Er·nest Thomp·son** (1860–1946), British-born N American naturalist and author. His collection of realistic animal stories *Wild Animals I Have Known* (1898) established him as creator and master of the genre. He was also an accomplished wildlife painter and in 1910 helped to found the Boy Scouts of America.

se·tose /ˈsiːtoʊz/ *adjective* *Biol.* bristly. [Latin *seta* bristle]

set phrase *noun* an invariable or usual arrangement of words.

set piece *noun* **1** a formal or elaborate arrangement, esp. in art or literature. **2** a sequence of rehearsed movements etc., as in sports or military operations. **3** *Theatre* a piece of scenery representing a single feature, such as a tree, a gate, etc. **4** an arrangement of fireworks composing a picture or design.

set point *noun* *Tennis etc.* **1** the state of a game when one side needs only one more point to win the set. **2** this point.

set screw *noun* a screw, usu. threaded the full length of the shank, that enables two contiguous parts in a machine etc. to be brought into and held in their correct relative position.

set shot *noun* *Basketball* a two-handed shot made from a standing position.

Se·tswa·na /setˈswɒnə/ *noun* the Bantu language of the Tswana. [Setswana *se-* language prefix + TSWANA]

sett *var. of* SET² 21, 22.

set·tee *noun* a seat (usu. upholstered), with a back and usu. arms, for more than one person. [18th c.: perhaps a fanciful var. of SETTLE²]

set·ter *noun* **1** a breed of large, long-haired dog trained to stand rigid when scenting game (see SET¹ 36). **2** a person or thing that sets.

set theory *noun* the branch of mathematics concerned with the manipulation of sets.

set·ting *noun* **1** the position or manner in which a thing is set. **2** the immediate surroundings (of a house etc.). **3** the surroundings of any object regarded as its framework; the environment of a thing. **4 a** the place and time, in which a story, drama, etc. is set. **b** the scenery and stage properties etc. used in a play, film, etc. **5** a frame in which a jewel is set. **6** the music to which words of a poem, song, etc., are set. **7** a set of cutlery, dishes, etc. for one person. **8** the way in which or level at which a machine is set to operate.

setting lotion *noun* lotion used to prepare the hair for being set.

set·tle¹ *verb* **1** *transitive & intransitive* (often foll. by *down*) establish or become established in a more or less permanent abode or way of life. **2** *intransitive & transitive* (often foll. by *down*) **a** cease or cause to cease from disturbance, movement, etc. **b** adopt a regular or secure style of life. **c** (foll. by *to*) apply oneself (to work, an activity, a way of life, etc.) (*settled down to writing her memoirs*). **3 a** *intransitive* sit or come down to stay for some time. **b** *transitive* cause to do this. **4** *transitive & intransitive* bring to or attain fixity, certainty, composure, or quietness. **5** *transitive* determine or decide or agree upon (*shall we settle a date?*). **6** *transitive* **a** resolve (a dispute etc.). **b** deal with (a matter) finally. **7** *transitive & intransitive* terminate (a lawsuit) by mutual agreement. **8** *intransitive* **a** (foll. by *for*) accept or agree to (esp. an alternative not one's first choice). **b** (foll. by *on*) decide on. **9** *transitive & intransitive* pay (a debt, an account, etc.). **10** *transitive* **a** aid the digestion of (food). **b** remedy the disordered state of (nerves, the stomach, etc.). **11 a** *transitive* people (a place) with inhabitants. **b** *intransitive* take up residence in a new place (*our family settled here in 1827*). **12** *intransitive* fall to the bottom or on to a surface (*wait till the sediment settles; dust had settled everywhere*). **13** *intransitive* sink down gradually, as by its own weight (*the foundations are settling*). **14** *intransitive* (of the ground etc.) become firm or compact. **15** *intransitive* (of a ship) begin to sink. **16** *transitive* dispose of or arrange for the disposal of (an estate, etc.). **17** *transitive* get rid of the obstruction of (a person) by argument or conflict or killing. □ **settle a person's hash** see HASH¹. **settle in 1** become established in a new home etc. **2** become accustomed to a new home, new surroundings, etc. (*I don't really feel as though I've settled in yet*). **3** dispose oneself comfortably for remaining indoors (*settled in and waited until the blizzard ended*). **settle up 1** pay (an account, debt, etc.). **2** finally arrange (a matter). **settle with 1** pay all or part of an amount due to (a creditor). **2** get revenge on. □ **settle·able** *adjective* [Old English *setlan* (as SETTLE²) from Germanic]

set·tle² *noun* a bench with a high back and arms and often with a box fitted below the seat. [Old English *setl* place to sit, from Germanic]

set·tled *adjective* **1** that has settled or been settled; fixed, unchanging, established. **2** (of a person's expression or bearing) indicating a settled mind, character, or disposition. **3** (of weather) calm and fair.

settle·ment *noun* **1** the act or an instance of settling; the process of being settled. **2 a** the colonization of a region. **b** a place or area occupied by settlers. **c** a small village. **3 a** a political or financial etc. agreement. **b** an arrangement ending a dispute. **4 a** the terms on which property is given to a person. **b** a deed stating these. **c** the amount of property given. **d** = MARRIAGE SETTLEMENT. **5** the process of settling an account. **6** subsidence of a wall, house, soil, etc.

set·tler *noun* a person who goes to settle in a new country or place.

settler's effects *plural noun* *Cdn* items which a new immigrant is allowed to bring into Canada duty free.

set·tlor *noun* *Law* a person who makes a settlement esp. of a property.

set-to *noun* (*pl.* **-tos**) *informal* a fight or argument.

set-top box *noun* a digital decoding device used to connect a television set to a source of signals.

set-up *noun* **1** an arrangement or organization. **2** the act or an instance of setting up. **3** *informal* a conspiracy or trick whereby a person is caused to incriminate himself or herself or to look foolish, or a criminal is caught red-handed. **4** *Sport* a pass or play intended to provide an opportunity for another player to score. **5** a plan or course of action. **6** a set or collection of the equipment etc. needed for a particular activity or purpose. **7** *N Amer. informal* an event or activity with a pre-arranged conclusion.

set-up man *noun* *Baseball* a relief pitcher whose job is not to finish a game but to preserve a team's lead so that the closer can enter the game in a position to earn a save.

set-up role *noun* *Baseball* **1** the job or position of a set-up man. **2** a situation in a particular game in which a set-up man is required.

Seul, Lac see LAC SEUL.

Seurat /sɜ'rɑ/ **Georges Pierre** (1859–91), French painter. The founder of neo-Impressionism, he is chiefly associated with pointillism, which he developed during the 1880s; among his major paintings using this technique is *Sunday Afternoon on the Island of La Grande Jatte* (1884–6).

Seuss /'suːs/ **Dr.** (pseudonym of Theodore Seuss Geisel) (1904–91), US

writer and illustrator, whose highly popular children's books include *How the Grinch Stole Christmas* (1957), *The Cat in the Hat* (1957), and *Green Eggs and Ham* (1960). □ **Seuss·ian** *adjective*

sev·en ● *noun* **1** one more than six, or three less than ten; the sum of four units and three units. **2** a symbol for this (7, vii, VII). **3** a size etc. denoted by seven. **4** a set or team of seven individuals. **5** seven o'clock. **6** a card with seven pips. ● *adjective* that amount to seven. [Old English *seofon* from Germanic]

Seven against Thebes *Gk Myth* seven heroes who joined Polynices in an expedition against his brother, Eteocles, who had usurped the throne of Thebes.

seven deadly sins *plural noun* (in Christian tradition) pride, covetousness, lust, envy, gluttony, anger, and sloth, regarded as the basic human vices.

seven·fold *adjective & adverb* **1** seven times as much or as many. **2** consisting of seven parts.

Seven Hills of Rome *plural noun* the seven hills on which ancient Rome was built: the Aventine, Caelian, Capitoline, Esquiline, Palatine, Quirinal, and Viminal.

seven-minute icing *noun* (also **seven-minute frosting**) *N Amer.* a fluffy icing made of egg whites and sugar etc. beaten together over low heat.

Seven Oaks a site near the Red River Settlement's Fort Douglas in SE central Manitoba (now in north Winnipeg), at which a fierce battle took place on 19 June 1816 between the Red River colonists and a group of Metis led by Cuthbert Grant. Regarded as the worst incident during the rivalry between the Hudson's Bay Co. and the North West Co., the skirmish resulted in the deaths of 21 HBC men.

seven seas *plural noun* the oceans of the world: the Arctic, Antarctic, North Pacific, South Pacific, North Atlantic, South Atlantic, and Indian Oceans.

Seven Sisters *plural noun* (prec. by *the*) = PLEIADES 2.

seven·teen ● *noun* **1** one more than sixteen, or seven more than ten. **2** a symbol for this (17, xvii, XVII). **3** a size etc. denoted by seventeen. ● *adjective* that amount to seventeen. □ **seven·teenth** *adjective, adverb, & noun*

sev·enth ● *noun* **1** the position in a sequence corresponding to the number 7 in the sequence 1–7. **2** something occupying this position. **3** one of seven equal parts of a thing. **4** *Music* **a** an interval or chord spanning seven consecutive notes in the diatonic scale (e.g. C to B). **b** a note separated from another by this interval. **5** *Baseball* the seventh inning. ● *adjective* that is the seventh. ● *adverb* in the seventh place; seventhly. □ **in seventh heaven** see HEAVEN. □ **seventh·ly** *adverb*

Seventh-day Adventist ● *noun* a member of a staunchly Protestant branch of the Adventists with beliefs based rigidly on faith and the Scriptures and the imminent return of Christ to earth, and observing the Sabbath on Saturday. ● *adjective* of or relating to the Seventh-day Adventists.

seventh-inning stretch *noun* a pause during a baseball game, usu. between the top and bottom of the seventh inning, when fans are invited to stand and stretch their legs.

seven·ty ● *noun* (*pl.* **-ties**) **1** the product of seven and ten. **2** a symbol for this (70, lxx, LXX). **3** (in *pl.*) the numbers from 70 to 79, esp. the years of a century or of a person's life. ● *adjective* that amount to seventy. □ **seventy-first, -second**, etc. the ordinal numbers between seventieth and eightieth. **seventy-one, -two**, etc. the cardinal numbers between seventy and eighty. □ **seven·ti·eth** *adjective, adverb, & noun* **seventy·fold** *adjective & adverb*

seventy-eight *noun* *hist.* a gramophone record played at 78 rpm.

seven wonders of the world *plural noun* seven buildings and monuments regarded in antiquity as specially remarkable: the Egyptian pyramids, the Mausoleum at Halicarnassus, the Temple of Artemis at Ephesus, the Hanging Gardens of Babylon, the Colossus of Rhodes, the statue of Zeus at Olympia, and the lighthouse at Alexandria.

seven year itch *noun* a supposed tendency to infidelity after seven years of marriage.

Seven Years War a war (1756–63) which ranged Britain, Prussia, and Hanover against Austria, France, Russia, Saxony, Sweden, and Spain. By the war's end Britain had become the supreme European colonial power, having captured French Canada and having reduced French influence in India. The N American phase of this war was called the FRENCH AND INDIAN WAR.

sev·er /'sɛvər/ *verb* **1** *transitive & intransitive* (often foll. by *from*) divide, break, or make separate, esp. by cutting. **2** *transitive & intransitive* end (a relationship or connection); break off something (*sever ties*). **3** *transitive* separate (a piece of land) from a larger lot. **4** *transitive* end the employment contract of (a person). □ **sev·er·able** *adjective* [Old French *severer* ultimately from Latin *separare* SEPARATE *verb*]

sev·er·al *adjective* **1** more than two but not many. **2** separate or respective; distinct (*all went their several ways*). **3** *Law* applied or regarded separately (*opp.* JOINT). [Anglo-French from Anglo-Latin *separalis* from Latin *separ* SEPARATE *adjective*]

sev·er·ally *adverb* **1** separately; individually. **2** respectively. **3** *Law* pertaining to or involving several persons individually, not jointly.

sev·er·al·ty *noun* **1** separateness. **2** the individual or unshared tenure of an estate etc.

sev·er·ance /ˈsevərəns/ *noun* **1** the act or an instance of severing. **2** (also **severance pay**) an amount paid to an employee who is dismissed (also *attributive*: *got a good severance package*). **3** the act or an instance of severing a piece of land from a larger lot (*applied for severance of a building lot*). **4** a severed state.

se·vere *adjective* **1** rigorous, strict, and harsh in attitude or treatment (*a severe critic; severe discipline*). **2** serious, critical (*a severe shortage*). **3** vehement or forceful (*a severe storm*). **4** extreme (in an unpleasant quality) (*a severe winter; severe cold*). **5** arduous or exacting; making great demands on energy, skill, etc. (*severe competition*). **6** unadorned; plain in style (*severe dress*). □ **se·vere·ly** *adverb* **se·ver·i·ty** *noun* [French *sévère* or Latin *severus*]

severe acute respiratory syndrome *noun* a highly contagious viral ailment causing severe pneumonia-like and flu-like symptoms. Abbr.: **SARS**.

severe combined immunodeficiency *noun* a usu. fatal disorder due to reduced numbers of white blood cells. Abbr.: **SCID**.

Se·ver·naya Zem·lya /ˌsevərˌnaiə zɪmˈljɒ/ a group of uninhabited islands in the Arctic Ocean off the north coast of Russia, to the north of the Taimyr Peninsula.

Sev·ern River /ˈsevərn/ **1** a river in NW Ontario, 982 km long (to the head of Black Birch River), which rises over 300 km north of Kenora and flows northeastward to Hudson Bay. **2** a river of SW Britain. Rising in central Wales, it flows northeast then south in a broad curve for some 290 km (180 miles) to its mouth on the Bristol Channel.

Sev·ero·dvinsk /ˌsevərəˈdvinsk/ a port in NW Russia, on the White Sea coast west of Archangel; pop. (est. 2002) 223,500.

Se·verus /sɪˈviːrəs/ **Sep·tim·ius** (full name Lucius Septimius Severus Pertinax) (146–211), Roman emperor 193–211. He was active in reforms of the imperial administration and of the army, and in 208 led an army to Britain to suppress a rebellion in the north of the country.

se·viche *var. of* CEVICHE.

Sévi·gné /seiviːnˈjei/ **Mar·quise de** (title of Marie de Rabutin-Chantal) (1626–96), French letter writer. Her reputation rests on her lifelong correspondence with her daughter (published 1725 and 1735–54), which gives a vivid portrait of Paris under Louis XIV.

Se·ville /səˈvɪl/ a city in S Spain, the capital of Andalusia, situated on the Guadalquivir River; pop. (est. 2001) 702,520. Once a leading cultural centre of Moorish Spain, it was reclaimed by the Spanish under Ferdinand III and rapidly grew to prominence as a centre of trade with the colonies of the New World.

Seville orange /səˈvɪl/ *noun* a bitter orange used for marmalade. [SEVILLE]

Sèvres /sevr/ *noun* fine porcelain, often with elaborate decoration, made at Sèvres in the suburbs of Paris.

sev·ruga /sevˈruːɡə/ *noun* **1** a migratory sturgeon, *Acipenser stellatus*, of the Caspian and Black Sea basins. **2** caviar obtained from it. [Russian *sevryuga*]

sew *verb* (*past participle* **sewn** or **sewed**) **1** *transitive & intransitive* fasten, join, etc., by making stitches with a needle and thread or a sewing machine. **2** *transitive* make (a garment etc.) by sewing. **3** *transitive* (often foll. by *on, in*, etc.) attach by sewing (*shall I sew on your buttons?*). □ **sew up 1** join or enclose by sewing. **2** *informal* (esp. in *passive*) bring to a desired conclusion or condition; complete satisfactorily; ensure the favourable outcome of (a thing). **3** close (a hole, wound, etc.) using stitches. **4** gain complete control of (*we've sewn up the Canadian market*). □ **sew·er** *noun* [Old English *si(o)wan*]

sew·age *noun* waste matter, esp. excremental, conveyed in sewers. [formed after SEWER by substitution of suffix -AGE for -*er*]

sew·er *noun* a conduit, usu. underground, for carrying off drainage water and sewage. [Old Northern French *se(u)wiere* channel to carry off the overflow from a fish pond, ultimately from Latin *ex-* out of + *aqua* water]

sewer·age *noun* a system of or drainage by sewers.

sewer rat *noun* the common brown rat.

sew·ing *noun* **1** a piece of material or work to be sewn. **2** the act or an instance of sewing.

sewing machine *noun* a machine for sewing or stitching.

sewn *past participle of* SEW.

sex ● *noun* **1** either of the main divisions (male and female) into which living things are placed on the basis of their reproductive functions. **2** the fact of belonging to one of these. **3** males or females collectively. **4** sexual intercourse. **5** sexual instincts, desires, etc., or their manifestation (*all you ever think about is sex!*). ● *adjective* **1** of or relating to sex (*sex education*). **2** arising from a difference of consciousness of sex (*sex discrimination*). ● *transitive verb* **1** determine the sex of. **2** *slang* have sex with. □ **sex up** *informal* make more attractive or sexy. □ **sex·er** *noun* [Old French *sexe* or Latin *sexus*]

sex act *noun* (usu. prec. by *the*) the (or an) act of sexual intercourse.

sexa·gen·ar·ian /ˌseksədʒɪˈneriən/ ● *noun* a person from 60 to 69 years old. ● *adjective* of this age. [Latin *sexagenarius* from *sexageni* distributive of *sexaginta* sixty]

Sexa·ges·ima /ˌseksəˈdʒesɪmə/ *noun* the second Sunday before Lent. [ecclesiastical Latin, = sixtieth (day), prob. named loosely as preceding QUINQUAGESIMA]

sexa·ges·imal /ˌseksəˈdʒesɪməl/ ● *adjective* **1** of sixtieths. **2** of sixty. **3** reckoning or reckoned by sixtieths. ● *noun* (in full **sexagesimal fraction**) a fraction with a denominator equal to a power of 60 as in the divisions of the degree and hour. [Latin *sexagesimus* (as SEXAGESIMA)]

sex appeal *noun* sexual attractiveness.

sex bomb *noun* *informal* a very sexually attractive person, esp. a woman.

sex·cap·ade *noun* *informal* a sexual escapade; an illicit affair.

sex·cen·ten·ary /ˌseksenˈtenəri, -ˈtiːnəri/ ● *noun* (*pl.* **-aries**) **1** a six-hundredth anniversary. **2** a celebration of this. ● *adjective* **1** of or relating to a sexcentenary. **2** occurring every six hundred years.

sex change *noun* an apparent change of sex by surgical means and hormone treatment.

sex chromosome *noun* a chromosome concerned in determining the sex of an organism, which in most animals are of two kinds, the X chromosome and the Y chromosome.

sexed *adjective* **1** having a sexual appetite (*highly sexed*). **2** having sexual characteristics.

sexed-up *adjective* *informal* sexually aroused.

sex·en·nial /sekˈseniəl/ *adjective* **1** lasting six years. **2** recurring every six years. [SEXI- + Latin *annus* year]

sex hormone *noun* a hormone affecting sexual development or behaviour.

sexi- *combining form* (also **sex-** before a vowel) six. [Latin *sex* six]

sex·ism *noun* **1** prejudice or discrimination, esp. against women, on the grounds of sex. **2** behaviour or attitudes derived from a traditional stereotype of sexual roles. □ **sex·ist** *adjective & noun*

sex kitten *noun* *informal* a flirtatious, sexy young woman.

sex·less *adjective* **1** *Biol.* neither male nor female. **2** lacking in sexual desire or attractiveness. □ **sex·less·ness** *noun*

sex life *noun* a person's sexual activities viewed collectively (*has an active sex life*).

sex-linked *adjective* *Genetics* carried on or by a sex chromosome.

sex maniac *noun* *informal* a person needing or seeking excessive gratification of the sexual instincts.

sex object *noun* a person regarded mainly in terms of sexual attractiveness.

sex offender *noun* a person who commits a sexual crime.

sex·ol·ogy *noun* the study of sexual life or relationships, esp. in human beings. □ **sex·olog·ic·al** *adjective* **sex·ol·o·gist** *noun*

sex·part·ite *adjective* divided into six parts.

sex·pert *noun* *slang* an expert on sexual matters.

sex·ploit·a·tion *noun* *informal* the exploitation of sex, esp. commercially.

sex·pot *noun* *informal* a sexy person (esp. a woman).

sex-starved *adjective* lacking sexual gratification.

sex symbol *noun* a person widely noted for sex appeal.

sext *noun* *Christianity* the office of the fourth canonical hour of prayer, originally said at the sixth hour of the day (i.e. noon). [Latin *sexta hora* sixth hour]

uː mood   ai my   ɔi pipe   au brown   ʌu house   ei day   ɔi boy   ɑ̃ franglais   ã Canadien   ɔ̃ Brayon   *(see over for consonants)*

sex·tant *noun* an instrument with a graduated arc of 60° used in navigation and surveying for measuring the angular distance of objects by means of mirrors. [Latin *sextans -ntis* sixth part]

sex·tet *noun* **1** a musical composition for six voices or instruments. **2** the performers of such a piece. **3** any group of six. [alteration of SESTET after Latin *sex* six]

sex·til·lion *noun* (*pl.* same or **sex·til·lions**) a thousand raised to the seventh (or formerly, esp. *Brit.*, the twelfth) power (10^{21} and 10^{36} respectively) (*compare* BILLION). [French from Latin *sex* six, after *septillion* etc.]

sex·ton *noun* a person who looks after a church and churchyard, often acting as bell-ringer and gravedigger. [Anglo-French, Old French *segerstein, secrestein* from medieval Latin *sacristanus* SACRISTAN]

sex tourism *noun* travel undertaken with the intent of taking advantage of another country's more permissive laws regarding sexual activity or prostitution. □ **sex tourist** *noun*

sex trade *noun* = SEX WORK.

sex·tuple /ˈseks,tʌpəl/ ● *adjective* **1** sixfold. **2** having six parts. **3** being six times as many or much. ● *noun* a sixfold number or amount. ● *transitive & intransitive verb* multiply by six; increase sixfold. [medieval Latin *sextuplus*, irreg. from Latin *sex* six]

sex·tup·let /ˈseks,tʌplət/ *noun* **1** each of six children born at one birth. **2** *Music* a group of six notes to be played in the time of four.

sex·ual *adjective* **1** of or relating to sex or the desire for sex (*sexual fantasies; sexual activity*). **2** of or relating to the sexes or the relations between them (*sexual discrimination*). **3** *Bot.* (of classification) based on the distinction of sexes in plants. **4** *Biol.* having a sex. □ **sex·ual·ly** *adverb*

sexual abuse *noun* the forcing of a person, esp. a child, to engage in sexual activity or relations; the making of unwanted sexual advances etc.

sexual assault *noun* threatened or actual sexual contact with another person without consent.

sexual harassment *noun* harassment (esp. of a woman) in a workplace etc. involving the making of unwanted sexual advances, obscene remarks, demands for sexual favours in return for advancement, etc.

sexual intercourse *noun* genital contact between individuals, esp. involving the insertion of a man's penis into a woman's vagina.

sexual interference *noun Law* the act or an instance of touching directly or indirectly any part of the body of a person under 14 years of age for sexual purposes.

sex·u·al·ity *noun* **1** possession of sexual powers; capacity for sexual feelings. **2** sexual feelings, desires, etc. collectively. **3** = SEXUAL ORIENTATION.

sex·ual·ize *transitive verb* (also esp. *Brit.* **-ise**) **1** make sexual. **2** attribute sex or a sexual role to. □ **sex·ual·iz·a·tion** *noun*

sexually transmitted disease *noun* a disease transmitted by sexual contact, e.g. AIDS, gonorrhea, syphilis, or chlamydia. Abbr.: **STD**.

sexual orientation *noun* (also **sexual preference**) the fact of being attracted to people of the opposite sex, of one's own sex, or both sexes.

sex work *noun* prostitution. □ **sex worker** *noun*

sexy *adjective* (**sex·i·er, sex·i·est**) **1** sexually attractive or stimulating. **2** sexually aroused. **3** concerned with or engrossed in sex. **4** *informal* (of a project etc.) exciting, appealing, trendy. □ **sex·i·ly** *adverb* **sex·i·ness** *noun*

Sey·chelles, the /seiˈʃelz, -ˈʃel/ (also **Seychelles**) a country consisting of a group of about ninety islands in the Indian Ocean, about 1 000 km (600 miles) northeast of Madagascar; pop. (est. 2002) 80,098; capital, Victoria. □ **Sey·chel·lois** /ˌseiʃelˈwɒ/ *adjective & noun*

Sey·fert galaxy /ˈseifərt/ *noun Astron.* a galaxy of a type characterized by a bright compact core that shows strong infrared emission. [Carl K. *Seyfert*, US astronomer d.1960]

Sey·mour /ˈsiːmɔr/ **1 Fred·erick** (1829–1869), Irish-born British colonial administrator, he was appointed governor of mainland BC in 1864. In 1866 he became the first governor of the unified colony of British Columbia under an Act of union that incorporated many of his own suggestions. **2 Jane** (*c.*1509–37), third wife of Henry VIII of England and mother of Edward VI. **3 Lynn** (née Springbett) (b.1939), Canadian-born ballet dancer, noted esp. for her dramatic talent in ballets by Sir Kenneth MacMillan and Sir Frederick Ashton; her most acclaimed role was Natalia in Ashton's *A Month in the Country* (1976).

sez *verb slang* says (*sez you*). [phonetic representation]

SF *abbreviation* **1** science fiction. **2** San Francisco.

sf *abbreviation Music* sforzando.

Sfax /sfaks/ (also **Safa·qis** /səˈfɒkɪs/) a port on the east coast of Tunisia; pop. (2000) 257,800.

Sfor·za /ˈsfɔrtsə/ **1 Carlo, Count** (1873–1952), Italian politician and diplomat. After serving as minister of foreign affairs (1920–21) and ambassador to France (1922), he resigned, refusing to serve under Mussolini, and spent nearly 20 years in Belgium and the US. Returning to Italy in 1943, he held several cabinet posts, and helped obtain Italian ratification of the treaty that ended World War II. **2 Fran·cesco** (1401–66), Italian condottiere, who led his armies in wars against the Milanese republic and Venice, and proclaimed himself duke of Milan (1450). **3** his son, **Lodo·vico** (known as 'The Moor') (1451–1508), Italian condottiere, duke of Milan 1481–99, who was noted as the patron of Bramante and Leonardo da Vinci.

sfor·zan·do /sfɔrˈtsando/ (also **sfor·za·to** /-ˈtsɒtɒ/) *Music* ● *adjective & adverb* with sudden emphasis. ● *noun* (*pl.* **-tos** or **sfor·zan·di** /-di/) **1** a note or group of notes especially emphasized. **2** an increase in emphasis and loudness. [Italian, verbal noun and past participle of *sforzare* use force]

sfu·mato /sfuˈmɒtɒ/ *Art* ● *adjective* with indistinct outlines. ● *noun* the technique of allowing tones and colours to shade gradually into one another. [Italian, past participle of *sfumare* shade off, from *s-* = EX-[1] + *fumare* smoke]

SFX *abbreviation* special effects. [*FX* representing a pronunciation of *effects*]

sfz *abbreviation Music* sforzando.

SG *abbreviation* **1** *US* senior grade. **2** *Law* Solicitor General. **3** specific gravity.

SGaang Gwaii /sɡɒŋ ˈɡwai/ a UNESCO World Heritage Site on an island at the southern tip of the Queen Charlotte Islands, incorporating the remains of a 19th-c. Haida village, including the ruins of 10 houses and 32 mortuary poles.

sgd. *abbreviation* signed.

SGML *abbreviation Computing* Standard Generalized Mark-up Language, a form of generic coding used for producing printed material in electronic form.

sgraf·fito /sɡrɒˈfiːtɒ/ *noun* (*pl.* **sgraf·fiti**) a form of decoration made by scratching through wet plaster on a wall or through slip on ceramic ware, showing a different-coloured undersurface. [Italian, past participle of *sgraffire* scratch, from *s-* = EX-[1] + *graffio* scratch]

Sgt *abbreviation* (also **Sgt.**) SERGEANT.

sh *interjection* calling for silence. [var. of HUSH]

sh. *abbreviation Brit. hist.* shilling(s).

Shaan·xi /ʃɒnˈʃiː/ (also **Shen·si** /ʃenˈsiː/) a mountainous province of central China; capital, Xian. It is the site of the earliest settlements of the ancient Chinese civilizations.

Shaba /ˈʃɒbə/ a copper-mining region of SE Congo (formerly Zaire); capital, Lubumbashi. It was known as Katanga until 1972.

Shab·bat /ʃɒˈbɒt/ *noun* the Jewish Sabbath. [Hebrew *šabbāt* Sabbath]

Shab·bos /ˈʃɒbəs/ *noun* (also **Shab·bes**) the Jewish Sabbath. [Yiddish from Hebrew *šabbāt* Sabbath]

shabby *adjective* (**shab·bi·er, shab·bi·est**) **1** in bad repair or condition; faded and worn, dingy, dilapidated. **2** dressed in old or worn clothes. **3** of poor quality. **4** contemptible, dishonourable (*a shabby trick*). □ **shab·bi·ly** *adverb* **shab·bi·ness** *noun* [*shab* scab, from Old English *sceabb* from Old Norse, related to SCAB]

shabu-shabu /ˈʃɒbuː ˌʃɒbuː/ *noun* a Japanese dish of pieces of thinly sliced beef or pork cooked quickly with vegetables in boiling water. [Japanese]

shack *noun* **1** a roughly built hut or cabin. **2** *Cdn* (*Maritimes & Nfld*) = COTTAGE 1. □ **shack up 1** *slang* live together in a sexual relationship without being married. **2** (foll. by *in*) dwell, lodge, be housed. □ **shacky** *adjective* [perhaps from Mexican Spanish *jacal*, Aztec *xacatli* wooden hut]

shackle ● *noun* **1** a fetter enclosing the ankle or wrist. **2** (usu. in *pl.*) a restraint or impediment. **3** a metal loop or link, closed by a bolt, to connect chains etc. **4** the U-shaped part of a padlock. ● *transitive verb* **1** fetter, impede, restrain. **2** (often foll. by *to*) fasten with a shackle. [Old English *sc(e)acul* fetter]

shack locker *noun Cdn* (*Nfld*) a locker or compartment on a ship used for holding snacks etc.

shack·town *noun Cdn* a community or section of a community composed of shacks or other temporary housing.

Consonants: b *but* d *dog* f *few* ɡ *get* h *her* j *yes* k *cat* l *leg* m *man* n *no* p *pen* r *red* s *sit*

shad noun (pl. same or **shads**) a deep-bodied edible fish of the herring family, esp. the marine fish *Alosa sapidissima*, spawning in fresh water, or the freshwater fish *Dorosoma cepedianum*, found in tributaries and distributaries of the Great Lakes. [Old English *sceadd*, of unknown origin]

shad·berry noun (pl. **-berries**) the fruit of the shadbush.

Shad·bolt, **Jack Leon·ard** (1909–98), English-born Canadian artist and teacher. A prolific artist, he incorporated his experience of nature and British Columbia Native culture into his works, which include murals and set and costume designs.

shad·bush noun N Amer. (also **shad·blow**) a Juneberry, esp. *Amelanchier canadensis*. [so called because it flowers when shad appear in the rivers]

shad·dock /ˈʃadək/ noun = POMELO. [Capt. *Shaddock*, who introduced it to the W Indies in the 17th c.]

shade ● noun **1** comparative darkness (and usu. coolness) caused by shelter from direct light and heat. **2** a place or area sheltered from the sun. **3** a darker part of a picture etc. **4** a colour, esp. with regard to its depth or as distinguished from one nearly like it. **5** a slight amount (*am a shade better today*). **6 a** = LAMPSHADE. **b** = WINDOW SHADE. **7** something that excludes or moderates light. **8** (in *pl.*) esp. N Amer. *informal* sunglasses. **9** a slightly differing variety (*many shades of opinion*). **10** *literary* **a** a ghost. **b** (in *pl.*) the underworld. **11** (in *pl.*; foll. by *of*) suggesting reminiscence or unfavourable comparison (*shades of fascism*). ● verb **1** *transitive* screen from light. **2** *transitive* cover, moderate, or exclude the light of. **3** *transitive* darken, esp. with parallel pencil lines to represent shadow etc. **4** *intransitive & transitive* (often foll. by *away, off, into*) pass or change by degrees. □ **put in the shade** appear or be very superior to (a person or thing). □ **shad·er** noun **shade·less** adjective [Old English *sc(e)adu* from Germanic]

shad·fly noun = MAYFLY 1. [so-called because hatching at the time of the shad run]

shad·ing noun **1** the representation of light and shade, e.g. by pencilled lines, on a map or drawing. **2** the graduation of tones from light to dark to create a sense of depth.

sha·doof /ʃəˈduːf/ noun a pole with a bucket and counterweight used esp. in Egypt for raising water. [Egyptian Arabic *šādūf*]

shad·ow ● noun **1** shade or a patch of shade. **2** a dark figure projected by a body intercepting rays of light. **3** an inseparable attendant or companion. **4** a person secretly following another. **5** the slightest trace (*not the shadow of a doubt*). **6** a weak or insubstantial remnant or thing (*a shadow of my former self*). **7** (*attributive*) Cdn & Brit. denoting members of a political party in opposition holding responsibilities parallel to those of the government (*shadow cabinet*). **8** the shaded part of a picture. **9** = EYESHADOW. **10** gloom or sadness. ● *transitive verb* **1** cast a shadow over. **2** secretly follow and watch the movements of. **3** accompany (a person) at work either as training or to obtain insight into a profession. □ **in the shadow of 1** close to; very near. **2** under the influence or power of. **3** dominated or eclipsed by the personality of. □ **shadow·er** noun **shadow·less** adjective [representing Old English *scead(u)we*, oblique case of *sceadu* SHADE]

shadow box noun a case with a protective transparent front for the display of a painting, jewel, etc.

shadow·box·ing noun boxing against an imaginary opponent as a form of training. □ **shadow·box** intransitive verb

shadow cabinet noun Cdn & Brit. see SHADOW 7.

shadow·graph noun **1** = RADIOGRAM 1. **2** a picture formed by a shadow cast on a lighted surface.

shadow·land noun (usu. in *pl.*) a place in shadow, esp. an indeterminate borderland between places or states.

shadow puppet noun a flat jointed puppet for use in shadow theatre.

shadow theatre noun (also **shadow play**) a display in which the shadows of puppets are cast on a screen which is viewed by the audience from the other side.

shad·owy adjective **1** like or having a shadow. **2** full of shadows. **3** vague, indistinct. □ **shadow·i·ness** noun

Shad·rach /ˈʃadrak/ Bible one of Daniel's companions. With Meshach and Abednego he was miraculously saved from the fiery furnace of Nebuchadnezzar (Daniel 3:12–30).

shady adjective (**shad·i·er**, **shad·i·est**) **1** giving shade. **2** situated in shade. **3** (of a person or behaviour) disreputable; of doubtful honesty. □ **shad·i·ness** noun

shaft ● noun **1** the stem or handle of a tool, implement, etc. **2** a column, esp. between the base and capital. **3** a long narrow space, usu. vertical, for access to a mine, an elevator in a building, for ventilation, etc. **4** a long and narrow part supporting or connecting or driving a part or parts of greater thickness etc. **5** each of the pair of poles between which an animal is harnessed to a vehicle. **6 a** an arrow or spear. **b** the long slender stem of these. **7** a remark intended to hurt or provoke (*a shaft of malice; shafts of wit*). **8** (foll. by *of*) **a** a ray (of light). **b** a bolt (of lightning). **9** the central stem of a feather. **10** *Mech.* a large axle or revolving bar transferring force by belts or cogs. **11** *slang* the penis. **12** N Amer. *informal* (prec. by *the*) harsh or unfair treatment. ● *transitive verb informal* treat unfairly. [Old English *scæft, sceaft* from Germanic]

Shaftes·bury /ˈʃaftsbəri/ **7th Earl of** (title of Anthony Ashley Cooper) (1801–85), English philanthropist and social reformer. A dominant figure of the 19th-c. social reform movement, he inspired much of the legislation designed to improve conditions for the large working class created as a result of the Industrial Revolution.

shaft·ing noun *Mech.* **1** a system of connected shafts for transmitting motion. **2** material from which shafts are cut.

shag¹ noun **1** a rough growth or mass of hair. **2** a hairstyle in which the hair is cut in layers from the top. **3 a** (*attributive*) (of a carpet, rug, etc.) having a long rough pile. **b** a shag carpet. **c** (*attributive*) (of a pile) long and rough. **4** a coarse kind of cut tobacco. **5** a cormorant, esp. the crested cormorant, *Phalacrocorax aristotelis*. [Old English *sceacga*, related to Old Norse *skegg* beard, Old English *sceaga* coppice]

shag² coarse slang ● *transitive verb* (**shagged**, **shag·ging**) **1** have sexual intercourse with. **2** (usu. in *passive*; often foll. by *out*) exhaust; tire out. ● noun an act of sexual intercourse. □ **shag·ger** noun (in sense 1 of verb; often as a term of abuse). [18th c.: origin unknown]

shag³ *transitive verb* (**shagged**, **shag·ging**) **1** retrieve; go after and bring back. **2** *Baseball* retrieve and throw back (fly balls), esp. in batting practice. **3** chase or follow after. [19th c.: origin unknown]

shag⁴ noun Cdn (NW Ont.) a stag and doe party. [blend of SHOWER noun 4 and STAG noun 2]

shaga·nap·pi /ˌʃagəˈnapi/ esp. Cdn (West) ● noun **1** thread, cord, or thong made of rawhide. **2** a rough pony. ● adjective of inferior quality. [Swampy Cree *pi-ša-kana-piy* (compare Cree *pi-ša-kan* leather, *-a-piy* string)]

shag·bark hickory noun a hickory of eastern N America, *Carya ovata*, with bark that splits into long loose strips.

shaggy adjective (**shag·gi·er**, **shag·gi·est**) **1** hairy, rough-haired. **2** unkempt. **3** (of the hair) coarse and abundant. **4** (of cloth) having a long and coarse nap; rough in texture. **5** *Biol.* having a hairlike covering. □ **shag·gi·ness** noun

shaggy-dog story noun a long rambling story, more amusing to the teller than the audience or amusing only by its inconsequentiality or pointlessness.

shaggy·mane noun a mushroom of the genus *Coprinus*, with a cap that peels in shaggy strips. Also called INK CAP.

shag·reen /ʃaˈɡriːn/ noun **1** a kind of untanned leather with a rough granulated surface. **2** a sharkskin rough with natural papillae, used for rasping and polishing. [var. of CHAGRIN in the sense 'rough skin']

Shah Karim Al-Hussain, (b.1937), the current AGA KHAN.

shah noun a title of the former monarch of Iran. The last shah, Muhammad Reza Pahlavi (see PAHLAVI¹), was overthrown in 1979 by Ayatollah Khomeini's Islamic revolution. □ **shah·dom** noun [Persian *šāh* from Old Persian *kšāyṯiya* king]

sha·hid /ʃəˈhiːd/ noun (also **sha·heed**) a Muslim martyr. [Arabic *šhīd* 'witness, martyr']

Shah Jahan /ˈʃɒ ˌdʒəˈhɒn/ (1592–1666), Mogul emperor of India 1628–58. He extended Mogul power and rebuilt the capital at Delhi; his buildings there and in Agra, notably the Taj Mahal, mark the high point of Indo-Muslim architecture.

Shahn /ʃɒn/ **Ben** (1898–1969), Lithuanian-born US painter, whose work often addresses social and political issues, as in his series of paintings from the early 1930s depicting the Dreyfus affair.

shah·toosh /ʃəˈtuːʃ/ noun (also **sha·toosh**) **1** high-quality fabric made from the wool of the chiru. **2** a shawl or scarf made from this fabric. [via Punjabi from Persian *šāh* 'king' + Kashmiri *toša* 'fine shawl material']

shake ● verb (past **shook**; past participle **shaken**) **1** *transitive & intransitive* move or quickly up and down or to and fro. **2 a** *intransitive* tremble or vibrate markedly. **b** *transitive* cause to do this. **3** *transitive* **a** agitate or shock. **b** upset the composure of. **4** *transitive* weaken or impair; make less convincing or firm or courageous (*shook their confidence*). **5** *intransitive* (of a voice, note, etc.) make tremulous or rapidly alternating sounds (*his voice shook with emotion*). **6** *transitive* brandish;

make a threatening gesture with (one's fist, a stick, etc.). **7** *intransitive* shake hands (*they shook on the deal*). **8** *transitive* esp. *N Amer. informal* = SHAKE OFF. ● *noun* **1** the act or an instance of shaking; the process of being shaken. **2** a jerk or shock. **3** (in *pl.*; prec. by *the*) a fit of or tendency to trembling or shivering, esp. caused by fear or withdrawal from drugs or alcohol. **4** = MILKSHAKE. **5** = CEDAR SHAKE. **6** *Music* a trill. □ **fair shake** see FAIR[1]. **in two shakes (of a lamb's tail)** very quickly. **more than you can shake a stick at** esp. *N Amer.* more than one can count, a considerable amount or number. **no great shakes** *informal* not very good or significant. **shake a person by the hand** = SHAKE HANDS. **shake down 1** settle or cause to fall by shaking. **2** settle down. **3** become established; get into harmony with circumstances, surroundings, etc. **4** *N Amer. slang* extort money from. **shake the dust off one's feet** depart indignantly or disdainfully. **shake hands** (often foll. by *with*) clasp right hands at meeting or parting, in reconciliation or congratulation, or over a concluded bargain. **shake one's head** move one's head from side to side in refusal, denial, disapproval, incredulity, or concern. **shake in one's shoes** tremble with apprehension. **shake a leg** *informal* **1** hurry. **2** begin dancing. **shake off 1** get rid of (something unwanted). **2** manage to evade (a person who is following or pestering one). **shake out 1** empty by shaking. **2** spread or open (a sail, flag, etc.) by shaking. **3** *informal* (of an action etc.) turn out well or in a specified way. **shake up 1** mix (ingredients) by shaking. **2** restore to shape by shaking. **3** disturb or make uncomfortable. **4** rouse from lethargy, apathy, conventionality, etc. [Old English *sc(e)acan* from Germanic]

shake·down *noun* **1** a period or process of adjustment or change. **2** esp. *N Amer. slang* a swindle; a piece of extortion. **3** *N Amer.* a search. **4** a makeshift bed. **5** (*attributive*) denoting a voyage, flight, etc., to test a new ship or aircraft and its crew.

shak·en *past participle of* SHAKE.

shaken baby syndrome *noun* a condition characterized by cranial injury, retinal hemorrhage, etc. observed in infants who have been violently jolted.

shake·out *noun* an upheaval or reorganization, esp. in a business and involving streamlining, closures, redundancies, etc.

shak·er *noun* **1** a person or thing that shakes. **2** esp. *N Amer.* a container, usu. with a perforated top, from which something is shaken (*pepper shaker*). **3** a container for shaking together the ingredients of cocktails etc. **4** (**Shaker**) **a** a member of an American religious sect living simply, in celibate mixed communities. **b** (*attributive*) (of furniture etc.) produced by or of a type produced by Shakers, characterized by simplicity and lack of ornamentation. **5** (*attributive*) (also **shaker knit**) designating a style of knitting, used esp. in sweaters, having parallel rows of ribbing. □ **mover and shaker** see MOVER 4. □ **Shaker·ism** *noun* (in sense 4).

Shake·speare, Wil·liam (known as 'the Bard (of Avon)') (1564–1616), English poet and dramatist, considered one of the greatest in English literature. His plays are written mostly in blank verse and include comedies (e.g. *A Midsummer Night's Dream* and *As You Like It*), histories (e.g. *Richard III*), and tragedies (e.g. *Hamlet* and *Macbeth*). He also wrote more than 150 sonnets.

Shake·spear·ean (also **Shake·spear·ian**) ● *adjective* **1** of or relating to Shakespeare. **2** in the style of Shakespeare. ● *noun* a student of Shakespeare's works etc. □ **Shake·spear·ean·ism** *noun*

shake·up *noun* an upheaval or drastic reorganization.

Shakhty /ˈʃɒkti/ a coal-mining city in SW Russia, situated in the Donets Basin northeast of Rostov; pop. (est. 2002) 220,200.

shaking tent *noun* (among some Algonquian peoples) a tent or lodge in which a shaman consulted the spirits for advice or assistance (also *attributive*: *shaking tent ceremony*).

shako /ˈʃeɪkəʊ/ *noun* (*pl.* **shakos**) a cylindrical peaked military hat with a plume. [French *schako* from Magyar *csákó* (*süveg*) peaked (cap), from *csák* peak, from German *Zacken* spike]

Shak·ti /ˈʃʌkti/ *var. of* SAKTI.

shaku·hachi /ˌʃækuˈhætʃi/ *noun* (*pl.* **shaku·hachis**) a Japanese bamboo flute. [Japanese from *shaku* a measure of length + *hachi* eight (tenths)]

shaky *adjective* (**shak·i·er**, **shak·i·est**) **1** unsteady; apt to shake; trembling. **2** unsound, infirm. **3** unreliable, wavering (*a shaky promise*; *got off to a shaky start*). □ **shak·i·ly** *adverb* **shak·i·ness** *noun*

shale *noun* soft finely stratified rock that splits easily, consisting of consolidated mud or clay. □ **shaley** *adjective* **shaly** *adjective* [prob. from German *Schale* from Old English *sc(e)alu* related to Old Norse *skál* (see SCALE[2])]

shall *auxiliary verb* (*3rd sing. present* **shall**; *archaic 2nd sing. present* **shalt**;

past **should**) **1** indicating future predictions. **2** indicating will or determination. **3** indicating or offering suggestions. **4** indicating orders or instructions. ¶ Despite traditional attempts to distinguish clearly between *shall* and *will*, in practice *will* is most commonly used today in all persons, both to form the future tense and to express a strong assertion or command; *shall* is used less commonly, but is often found in all persons in sentences expressing determination, a command, or a suggestion. [Old English *sceal* from Germanic]

shal·lop /ˈʃaləp/ *noun* a boat for use in shallow waters. [French *chaloupe* from Dutch *sloep* sloop]

shal·lot /ʃəˈlɒt, ˈʃalət/ *noun* **1** a variety of onion which forms clumps of small bulbs. **2** the bulb of this, esp. as used in cooking. [French *eschalotte* alteration of Old French *eschaloigne*: see SCALLION]

shal·low ● *adjective* **1** of little depth. **2** superficial, trivial (*a shallow mind*). ● *noun* (often in *pl.*) shallow waters. ● *transitive & intransitive verb* become or make shallow. □ **shal·low·ly** *adverb* **shal·low·ness** *noun* [Middle English, prob. related to *schald*, Old English *sceald* SHOAL[2]]

sha·lom /ʃəˈlɒm/ *noun & interjection* a Jewish salutation at meeting or parting. [Hebrew *šālôm* peace]

shalt *archaic 2nd person sing. of* SHALL.

shal·war /ʃʌlˈwɑr/ *noun* (also **sal·war**) a pair of light, loose, pleated trousers tapering to a tight fit around the ankles, worn by women from the Indian subcontinent, typically (as **shalwar kameez**) with a matching kameez. [Persian and Urdu *šalwār*]

sham ● *noun* **1 a** a person or thing pretending or pretended to be what he or she or it is not. **b** imposture, pretense. **2** *N Amer.* a decorative cover for a bed pillow when not in use. ● *adjective* pretended, counterfeit. ● *verb* (**shammed**, **sham·ming**) **1** *intransitive* feign, pretend. **2** *transitive* a pretend to be. **b** simulate (*is shamming sleep*). □ **sham·mer** *noun* [perhaps northern English dialect var. of SHAME]

sha·mal /ʃəˈmɒl/ *noun* a hot, dry northwesterly wind blowing across the Persian Gulf in summer, typically causing sandstorms. [Arabic *šamāl* 'north (wind)']

sha·man /ˈʃeɪmən/ *noun* a person regarded as having access to the world of good and evil spirits, esp. among some peoples of northern Asia and N America. □ **sha·man·ic** /ʃəˈmanɪk/ *adjective* **sha·man·ic·ally** *adverb* **sha·man·ism** *noun* **sha·man·is·tic** /-ˈnɪstɪk/ *adjective* **sha·man·is·tic·ally** *adverb* [German *Schamane* & Russian *shaman* from Tungus *samán*]

shama·teur /ˈʃaməˌtʃər, -tər/ *noun* derogatory a sports player who makes money from sporting activities though classed as an amateur. □ **shama·teur·ism** *noun*

shamba *noun* (in East Africa) a cultivated plot of ground; a farm or plantation. [Kiswahili]

sham·ble ● *intransitive verb* walk or run with a shuffling or awkward gait. ● *noun* a shambling gait. [prob. from dial. *shamble* (adj.) ungainly, perhaps from *shamble legs* with reference to straddling trestles: see SHAMBLES]

sham·bles *plural noun* (usu. treated as *sing.*) **1** *informal* a scene or situation of complete disorder; a mess (*the room was a shambles*; *the economy was a shambles*). **2** a butcher's slaughterhouse. [pl. of *shamble* stool, stall, from Old English *sc(e)amul* from West Germanic from Latin *scamellum* diminutive of *scamnum* bench]

sham·bol·ic /ʃamˈbɒlɪk/ *adjective* esp. *Brit. informal* chaotic, unorganized. [SHAMBLES, prob. after SYMBOLIC]

shame ● *noun* **1** a feeling of distress or humiliation caused by consciousness of the guilt or foolishness of oneself or an associate. **2** a capacity for experiencing this feeling, esp. as imposing a restraint on behaviour (*has no sense of shame*). **3** a state of disgrace, discredit, or intense regret. **4 a** a person or thing that brings disgrace etc. **b** a thing or action that is wrong or regrettable. ● *transitive verb* **1** bring shame on; make ashamed; put to shame. **2** (foll. by *into*, *out of*) force by shame (*was shamed into confessing*). □ **for shame!** a reproof to a person for not showing shame. **put to shame** disgrace or humiliate by revealing superior qualities etc. **shame on you!** you should be ashamed. **what a shame!** how unfortunate! [Old English *sc(e)amu*]

shame·faced *adjective* **1** showing shame. **2** bashful, diffident. □ **shame·faced·ly** *adverb* **shame·faced·ness** *noun* [16th-c. alteration of *shamefast*, assimilated to FACE]

shame·ful *adjective* **1** that causes or is worthy of shame. **2** disgraceful, scandalous. □ **shame·ful·ly** *adverb* **shame·ful·ness** *noun*

shame·less *adjective* **1** having or showing no sense of shame. **2** impudent, brazen. □ **shame·less·ly** *adverb* **shame·less·ness** *noun*

shami·ana /ˌʃamiˈɑːnə/ *noun* (in India) a large tent. [Persian *shāmiyāna*]

Sha·mir /ʃa'miːr/ **Yit·zhak** (Polish name Yitzhak Jazernicki) (b.1915), Polish-born Israeli politician, prime minister 1983–4 and 1986–92. On Begin's retirement in 1983, Shamir became premier, but his Likud party was narrowly defeated in elections a year later; as prime minister of a coalition government with Labour, he dismissed Peres in 1990 and formed a new government with a policy of conceding no land to a Palestinian state.

shami·sen /'ʃamɪsən/ noun a Japanese guitar with a long neck, no frets, and three strings of waxed silk, played with a plectrum. [Japanese from Chinese *san-hsien* from *san* three + *hsien* string]

shammy noun (pl. **-mies**) (in full **shammy leather**) informal = CHAMOIS 2. [representing pronunciation]

sham·poo ● noun 1 liquid or cream used to lather and wash the hair. 2 a similar substance for washing a car or carpet etc. 3 an act or instance of cleaning with shampoo. ● transitive verb (**sham·poos**, **sham·pooed**) wash with shampoo. [Hindustani *chhampo*, imperative of *chhāmpnā* to press]

sham·poo·er noun a machine for shampooing rugs, carpets, etc.

sham·rock noun any of various plants with trifoliate leaves, esp. *Trifolium repens* or *Medicago lupulina*, used as the national emblem of Ireland or the Irish. [Irish *seamróg* trefoil, diminutive of *seamar* clover + *og* young]

shamus /'ʃeɪməs/ noun N Amer. slang a detective. [20th c.: origin uncertain]

Shan /ʃɒn, ʃan/ ● noun (pl. same or **Shans**) 1 a member of a group of Thai peoples, inhabiting parts of Burma (Myanmar), S China, and Indochina. 2 the Sino-Tibetan language of these peoples. ● adjective of or pertaining to the Shan or their language. [Burmese]

Shan·dong /ʃan'dʊŋ/ (also **Shan·tung** /-'tʊŋ/) a coastal province of E China; capital, Jinan. It occupies the Shandong Peninsula, separating southern Bo Hai from the Yellow Sea.

shan·dy noun (pl. **-dies**) a drink of beer mixed with a lemon-lime soft drink or ginger ale. [19th c.: origin unknown]

Shang a dynasty which ruled China during part of the 2nd millennium BC, probably 16th–11th centuries, during which Chinese ideographic script was invented and methods of bronze casting were developed.

Shang·hai /ʃaŋ'haɪ/ a city on the east coast of China, a port on the estuary of the Yangtze; pop. (est. 2002) 11,900,000.
□ **Shang·hai·nese** adjective & noun

shang·hai /'ʃaŋhaɪ, -'haɪ/ transitive verb (**shang·hais**, **shang·haied**, **shang·hai·ing**) 1 trick or force (a person) into doing something or going somewhere. 2 hist. force (a person) to be a sailor on a ship by using drugs or other trickery. [SHANGHAI]

Shanghai noodles plural noun N Amer. a Chinese dish similar to lo mein, consisting of thick spaghetti-like noodles stir-fried with meat and vegetables.

Shan·go /'ʃaŋgoː/ noun 1 a religious cult originating in W Nigeria and now chiefly practised in parts of the Caribbean. 2 a spirit dance associated with this cult. [Yoruba]

Shangri-La /ˌʃaŋɡrɪ'lɑ/ noun an imaginary paradise on earth. [the name of a hidden Tibetan valley in J. Hilton's *Lost Horizon* (1933)]

shank ● noun 1 a the leg. b the lower part of the leg; the leg from knee to ankle. c the shin bone. 2 a the lower part of an animal's foreleg, esp. that of a horse. b the upper part of the foreleg or hind leg of an animal as a cut of meat. 3 a shaft or stem. 4 a the long narrow part of a tool etc. joining the handle to the working end. b the stem of a key, spoon, anchor, etc. c the straight part of a nail or fish hook. 5 the narrow middle of the sole of a shoe. 6 N Amer. slang an improvised knife, esp. as made by a prison inmate. ● transitive verb 1 Golf mis-hit (the ball) with the heel of the club. 2 N Amer. slash with a knife.
□ **shanked** adjective (also in combination). [Old English *sceanca* from West Germanic]

Shan·kar /'ʃaŋkɑr/ 1 **Ravi** (b.1920), Indian sitar player and composer. Already an established musician in his own country, from the mid-1950s he embarked on tours of Europe and the US giving sitar recitals, doing much to stimulate contemporary Western interest in Indian music. 2 his brother **Uday** (1900–77), Indian dancer. He introduced Anna Pavlova to Indian dance and performed with her in his ballet *Radha Krishna*. He later toured the world with his own company, introducing Indian dance to European audiences.

shank's mare noun (also Brit. **shank's pony**) one's own legs as a means of conveyance (on shank's mare for four miles).

Shan·non 1 the chief river of Ireland. It rises in County Leitrim near Lough Allen and flows 390 km (240 miles) south and west to its estuary

on the Atlantic. 2 an international airport in the Republic of Ireland, situated on the Shannon River west of Limerick.

Shan·si see SHANXI.

shan't contraction shall not.

Shan·tou /ʃan'taʊ/ (formerly called **Swa·tow**) a port in the province of Guangdong in SE China, situated on the South China Sea at the mouth of the Han River; pop. (est. 2002) 1,763,400.

Shan·tung see SHANDONG.

shan·tung /ʃan'tʌŋ/ noun a fabric of silk or artificial fibres, with slubs in the yarn producing a slightly rough surface. [SHANTUNG]

shanty[1] noun (pl. **-ties**) 1 a crudely built shack or cabin. 2 a hut or cabin. 3 esp. Cdn hist. a lumberjack's log cabin or shack. 4 esp. Cdn hist. a logging camp. [19th c., originally N American: perhaps from Canadian French *chantier* a lumberjack's cabin or logging camp]

shanty[2] noun (also **chanty**) (pl. **-ties**) (in full **sea shanty**) a song with alternating solo and chorus, of a kind originally sung by sailors while hauling ropes etc. [prob. French *chantez*, imperative pl. of *chanter* sing: see CHANT]

shanty·man noun (pl. **-men**) Cdn hist. a lumberjack; a worker at a lumber camp.

shanty·town noun a poor or depressed area of a city or town, consisting of shanties.

Shan·xi /ʃan'ʃiː/ (also **Shan·si** /-'siː/) a province of N central China, to the south of Inner Mongolia; capital, Taiyuan.

Shao·lin /ʃaʊ'lɪn/ noun a martial art which developed in NE central China. [the Buddhist monastery of *Shaolin* (founded AD 495), where it originated]

SHAPE /ʃeɪp/ abbreviation Supreme Headquarters Allied Powers Europe.

shape ● noun 1 the total effect produced by the outlines of a thing. 2 the external form or appearance of a person or thing. 3 a specific form or guise. 4 a description or sort or way (not tolerated in any way, shape, or form). 5 a definite or proper arrangement (must get our ideas into shape). 6 a condition, as qualified in some way (in good shape; in poor shape). b (when unqualified) good condition (back in shape). c the nature, qualities, or characteristics of something (the shape of things to come). 7 a person or thing as seen, esp. indistinctly or in the imagination (a shape emerged from the mist). 8 a mould or pattern. 9 a piece of material, paper, etc., made or cut in a particular form. ● verb 1 transitive give a certain shape or form to; fashion, create. 2 transitive (foll. by to) adapt or make conform. 3 intransitive give signs of a future shape or development. 4 transitive frame mentally; imagine. 5 intransitive assume or develop into a shape. 6 transitive direct (one's life, course, etc.). □ **give shape to** form, mould; provide with a distinct outline or form; express clearly. **in shape** physically fit. **lick into shape** make presentable or efficient. **out of shape** physically unfit. **shape up 1** take a (specified) form or suggest that such a form will be taken (shaping up to be a cold winter). 2 show promise; make good progress; improve (were told to shape up). **shape up or ship out** achieve a satisfactory performance or be dismissed. **take shape** assume a distinct form; develop into something definite. **whip into shape** make presentable or efficient, esp. severely. □ **shaped** adjective (also in combination). **shap·er** noun [Old English *gesceap* creation, from Germanic]

shape·less adjective lacking definite or attractive shape.
□ **shape·less·ly** adverb **shape·less·ness** noun

shape·ly adjective (**shape·li·er**, **shape·li·est**) 1 well formed or proportioned. 2 of elegant or pleasing shape or appearance.
□ **shape·li·ness** noun

shape memory noun a property exhibited by certain alloys of recovering their initial shape when they are heated after having been plastically deformed.

shape-shifter noun (also **shape-changer**) (in folklore, science fiction, etc.) any creature capable of changing its form, e.g. a werewolf.
□ **shape-shift** verb **shape-shifting** noun

Shap·ley, Har·low (1885–1972), US astronomer. He studied globular star clusters, using Cepheid variables within them to determine their distance; he then used their distribution to locate the likely centre of the Milky Way, and went on to suggest its structure and dimensions.

shard noun 1 a broken piece of pottery or glass etc. 2 = POTSHERD. 3 a remnant or fragment of something shattered, split, broken, etc. 4 the wing-case of a beetle. [Old English *sceard*: sense 4 perhaps from *shard-borne* (Shakespeare) = born in a shard (dial., = cow dung) (rather than 'borne on shards')]

share[1] ● noun 1 a portion that a person receives from or gives to a common amount. 2 a a part that is or ought to be contributed by an individual to an enterprise or commitment. **b** a part that is or ought to be received by an individual from this (*got a large share of the credit; didn't get their share*). **3** part-proprietorship of property held by joint owners, esp. any of the equal parts into which a company's capital is divided entitling its owner to a proportion of the profits. ● *verb* **1** *transitive* get or have or give a share of. **2** *transitive* use or benefit from jointly with others. **3** *transitive* have in common (*I share your opinion*). **4** *intransitive* have a share; be a sharer (*children must learn to share*). **5** *intransitive* (foll. by *in*) participate. **6** *transitive* (often foll. by *out*) **a** divide and distribute. **b** give away part of. **7 a** *transitive* tell, recount (a story, joke, one's feelings, etc.). **b** *intransitive* tell others an esp. personal story, one's feelings, etc. □ **share and share alike** make an equal division. □ **share·able** *adjective* (also **shar·able**). **sharer** *noun* [Old English *scearu* 'division' from Germanic: related to SHEAR]

share² *noun* = PLOUGHSHARE. [Old English *scear, scær* from Germanic]

share·crop·per *noun* a tenant farmer who gives a part of each crop as rent. □ **share·crop** *transitive & intransitive verb* (**-cropped, -crop·ping**). **share·crop·ping** *noun*

shared-cost *adjective* (of a government program) financed by two or more levels of government.

share·hold·er *noun* an owner of shares in a company. □ **share·hold·ing** *noun*

share·ware *noun* *Computing* software that is available free of charge and often distributed informally for evaluation, after which a fee is requested for continued use.

sha·ria /ʃəˈriːə/ *noun* (also **sha·riah** or **sha·riat**) Islamic canonical law based on the teachings of the Quran and the traditions of the Prophet. [Arabic *šarīʿa*]

sha·rif /ʃəˈriːf/ *noun* (also **she·rif**) **1** a descendant of Muhammad through his daughter Fatima, entitled to wear a green turban or veil. **2** a Muslim leader. [Arabic *šarīf* noble, from *šarafa* be exalted]

Shar·jah /ˈʃɑrdʒə/ (Arabic **Ash Shari·qah** /ˌaʃ ʃɒˈriːkə/) **1** one of the seven member states of the United Arab Emirates; pop. (est. 2002) 522,100. **2** its capital city, situated on the Persian Gulf; pop. (est. 1989) 125,123.

shark¹ *noun* any of various large usu. voracious marine fish with a long body and prominent dorsal fin. [16th c.: origin unknown]

shark² *noun informal* a person who unscrupulously exploits or swindles others (*loan shark*). □ **shark·ish** *adjective* [16th c.: originally perhaps from German *Schurke* worthless rogue: influenced by SHARK¹]

shark·skin *noun* **1** the rough scaly skin of a shark. **2** a smooth slightly lustrous fabric.

Shar·on¹ /ˈʃɛrən/ a fertile coastal plain in Israel, lying between the Mediterranean Sea and the hills of Samaria.

Shar·on² /ʃəˈrɒn/ Ariel (b.1928), Israeli general and politician who became prime minister of Israel in 2001.

sharp ● *adjective* **1** having an edge or point able to cut or pierce. **2** tapering to a point or edge. **3** abrupt, steep, angular (*a sharp fall; a sharp turn*). **4** well defined, clean-cut (*a sharp edge; in sharp contrast*). **5 a** severe or intense (*a sharp pain*). **b** (of food or its flavour) pungent, acid. **c** keen (*a sharp appetite; has a sharp ear*). **d** (of a frost) severe, hard. **6** (of a voice or sound) shrill and piercing. **7** (of sand etc.) composed of angular grains. **8** (of words, temper, a person, etc.) harsh or acrimonious (*had a sharp tongue*). **9** (of a person) acute; quick to perceive or comprehend. **10** *derogatory* quick to take advantage; artful, unscrupulous, dishonest. **11** vigorous or brisk. **12** *Music* **a** above the desired or true pitch. **b** (of a key) having a sharp or sharps in the signature. **c** (as **C sharp, F sharp**, etc.) a semitone higher than C, F, etc. **13** *informal* stylish or flashy with regard to dress. ● *noun* **1** *Music* **a** a note above a semitone above natural pitch. **b** the sign (♯) indicating this. **2** *informal* a swindler or cheat. **3 a** a fine sewing needle. **b** (usu. in *pl.*) a thing with a sharp edge or point, e.g. a blade, piece of glass, or syringe. ● *adverb* **1** punctually (*at nine o'clock sharp*). **2** suddenly, abruptly, promptly (*pulled up sharp*). **3** at a sharp angle. **4** *Music* above the true pitch (*sings sharp*). **5** *informal* stylishly (*was dressed sharp*). ● *transitive verb US Music* make sharp. □ **keep a sharp eye on** (or **out for**) watch carefully (for). **look sharp** see LOOK. **sharp as a tack** *N Amer.* extremely quick, clever, astute, alert, etc. □ **sharp·ly** *adverb* **sharp·ness** *noun* [Old English *sc(e)arp*, from Germanic]

sharp-edged *adjective* **1** having a sharp edge. **2** biting, caustic; sharp-tongued.

Shar-Pei /ˌʃɑr ˈpeɪ/ *noun* a compact squarely built breed of dog of Chinese origin, with a characteristic wrinkly skin and short bristly coat of a fawn, cream, black, or red colour. [Chinese *shā pí*, lit. 'sand skin']

sharp·en *transitive & intransitive verb* make or become sharp. □ **sharp·en·er** *noun*

sharp end *noun informal* **1** the bow of a ship. **2** the scene of direct action or decision; the front line.

sharp·en·ing stone *noun* = WHETSTONE.

sharp·er *noun* a swindler, esp. at cards.

Sharpe·ville massacre the killing of 67 anti-apartheid demonstrators by security forces at the South African black township of Sharpeville in southern Transvaal on 21 Mar. 1960.

sharp-featured *adjective* (of a person) having well-defined facial features.

sharp·ie *noun* = SHARPER.

sharp·ish *informal* ● *adjective* fairly sharp. ● *adverb* **1** fairly sharply. **2** quite quickly.

sharp practice *noun* dishonest or barely honest dealings.

sharp-shinned hawk *noun* (also **sharp-shin**) a small hawk, *Accipiter striatus*, of N America.

sharp·shoot·er *noun* a skilled shooter or marksman. □ **sharp·shoot·ing** *noun & adjective*

sharp-tailed grouse *noun* (also **sharp·tail**) a medium-sized grouse of grasslands in western N America, *Tympanuchus phasianellus*, with a short pointed tail and V-shaped markings on the underparts.

sharp-tongued *adjective* harsh or cutting in speech; abrasive.

sharp-witted *adjective* keenly perceptive or intelligent.

shash·lik /ˈʃaʃlɪk/ *noun* (in Asia and E Europe) a kebab of mutton and garnishes. [Russian *shashlyk*, ultimately from Turkish *šiš* spit, skewer: compare SHISH KEBAB]

shas·ta *noun* (in full **shasta daisy**) a plant, *Chrysanthemum maximum*, with large daisy-like flowers. [*Mt. Shasta* in California]

Shas·tra /ˈʃɒstrə/ *noun* Hindu sacred writings. [Hindi *śāstr*, Sanskrit *śāstra*]

shat *past and past participle of* SHIT.

Shat·ner, Wil·liam (b.1931), Canadian actor. While he has performed other roles in his long acting career, that of Captain James T. Kirk in the *Star Trek* TV series (1966–69) and follow-up movies is by far his most internationally famous.

sha·toosh *var. of* SHAHTOOSH.

Shatt al-Arab River /ˌʃat al ˈarəb/ a river of SW Asia, formed by the confluence of the Tigris and Euphrates rivers and flowing some 195 km (120 miles) through SE Iraq to the Persian Gulf. Its lower course forms the border between Iraq and Iran.

shat·ter *verb* **1** *transitive & intransitive* break suddenly in pieces. **2** *transitive* severely damage or utterly destroy (*shattered hopes; shattered the myth*). **3** *transitive* greatly upset or discompose; dumbfound. □ **shat·ter·er** *noun* **shat·ter·ing** *adjective* **shat·ter·ing·ly** *adverb* [Middle English, related to SCATTER]

shatter·proof *adjective* (of glass etc.) designed to resist shattering.

Shaula /ˈʃɔlə/ the second-brightest star in the constellation Scorpius, marking the scorpion's sting. [Arabic *shaulah* 'sting']

shave ● *verb* (*past participle* **shaved** or (as *adj.*) **shav·en**) **1** *transitive & intransitive* remove (bristles or hair) from the face etc. with a razor. **2** *transitive & intransitive* remove bristles or hair with a razor from the face etc. of (a person) or from (a part of the body). **3** *transitive* reduce by a small amount. **b** take (a small amount) away from. **4** *transitive* cut thin slices from the surface of (wood etc.). **5** *transitive* pass close to without touching; miss narrowly. **6** *transitive* cut (hair, grass, etc.) very short. ● *noun* **1** an act of shaving or the process of being shaved. **2** a close approach without contact. **3** a narrow miss or escape; = CLOSE SHAVE. **4** a tool for shaving wood etc. [Old English *sc(e)afan* (sense 4 of noun from Old English *sceafa*) from Germanic]

shav·en *see* SHAVE.

shav·er *noun* **1** a person or thing that shaves. **2** an electric razor. **3** *informal* a young boy.

Sha·vian /ˈʃeɪviən/ ● *adjective* of or in the manner of G. B. Shaw or his ideas. ● *noun* an admirer of Shaw. [*Shavius*, Latinized form of SHAW]

shav·ing *noun* **1** a thin, curled strip cut off the surface of wood, chocolate, etc. **2** (*attributive*) used in shaving the face (*shaving cream*).

shaving kit *noun* a small bag or case for holding shaving supplies and other toiletries.

Sha·vuot /ʃəˈvuːəs, ˌʃɒvʊˈɒt/ *noun* (also **Sha·vuoth**) *Judaism* = PENTECOST 2. [Hebrew *šābūʿōt*, = weeks, with reference to the weeks between Passover and Pentecost]

Shaw ▶ 1 Artie (born Arthur Jacob Arshawsky) (b.1910), US jazz clarinetist, bandleader, and composer, whose bands were among the most popular of the late 1930s and 1940s. **2 George Ber·nard** (1856–1950), Irish dramatist and writer. His best-known plays combine comedy with intellectual debate in challenging conventional morality and thought; they include *Man and Superman* (1903), *Pygmalion* (1913), and *St. Joan* (1923); a socialist, he was an active member of the Fabian Society during its early period, championing many progressive causes, including feminism. He was awarded the Nobel Prize for literature in 1925. **3 Wal·ter Rus·sell** (1887–1981), Canadian politician, Conservative premier of PEI 1959–66. He remained Leader of the Opposition until 1970.

sha·war·ma /ʃəˈwɑrmə/ *noun* (in the cuisine of certain Arabic countries) meat cooked on a spit and served in thin slices, often rolled in pita bread. [Syrian Arabic *shāwirma* from Turkish *çevirme* piece of meat roasted on a spit, from *çevirme* turn, rotate]

Sha·wini·gan /ʃəˈwɪnɪɡən/ a city in south central Quebec, situated on the Rivière Saint-Maurice, 30 km northwest of Trois-Rivières; pop. (2001) 52,040. [Abenaki, = portage (or portage over a pointed crest)]

Shawinigan-Sud /ʃawɪniɡənˈsud/ a former town in south central Quebec, situated on the Rivière Saint-Maurice, now the southern part of Shawinigan; pop. (1996) 11,804. [French, lit. 'Shawinigan South']

shawl *noun* a piece of fabric, usu. rectangular and often folded into a triangle, worn over the shoulders or head or wrapped around a baby. □ **shawled** *adjective* [Urdu etc. from Persian *šāl*, prob. from *Shāliāt* in India]

shawl collar *noun* a collar extended down the front of a garment without lapel notches.

shawm *noun Music* a medieval double-reed wind instrument with a sharp penetrating tone. [Old French *chalemie*, ultimately from Latin *calamus* from Greek *kalamos* reed]

Shaw·nee /ʃɔˈniː/ ● *noun* **1** a member of an Algonquian people formerly resident in the eastern US and now chiefly in Oklahoma. **2** the language of this people. ● *adjective* of or pertaining to the Shawnee or their language. [Delaware *ša:wano:w*]

shaykh *var. of* SHEIK.

sha·zam /ʃəˈzam/ *interjection* used to introduce a sudden esp. extraordinary event, transformation, etc. [invented word]

she ● *pronoun* (*obj.* **her**; *poss.* **her**; *pl.* **they**) **1** the woman or girl or female animal previously named or in question. **2** a thing regarded as female, e.g. a vehicle or ship. **3** a person etc. of unspecified sex, esp. referring to one already named or identified (*ask any doctor and she will tell you*). **4** *Austral. & NZ informal* it; the state of affairs (*she'll be right*). ● *noun* **1** a female; a woman. **2** (*in combination*) female (*she-goat*). [Middle English *scæ, sche*, etc., prob. a phonetic development of Old English fem. personal pronoun *heō*, accusative *hīe* (other suggested etymologies include derivation from Old English fem. demonstrative pron. & adj. *sīo, sēo*, accusative *sīe*)]

s/he *pronoun* a written representation of 'he or she' used to indicate both sexes.

shea /ʃiː, ˈʃiːə/ *noun* a W African tree, *Vitellaria paradoxa*, bearing nuts containing a large amount of fat. [from a W African name]

shea butter *noun* a butter made from the fat of shea nuts.

sheaf ● *noun* (*pl.* **sheaves**) **1** a pile or bundle of things, esp. paper. **2** a bundle of stalks and ears of grain tied after reaping. ● *transitive verb* make into sheaves. [Old English *scéaf* from Germanic (as SHOVE)]

shear ● *verb* (*past* **sheared**, *archaic except Austral. & NZ* **shore**; *past participle* **shorn** or **sheared**) **1** *transitive* clip the wool off (a sheep etc.). **2** *transitive* remove or take off by cutting. **3** *transitive* **a** cut with scissors or shears etc. **b** cut down (a tree). **4** *transitive* (foll. by *of*) strip bare. **b** deprive. **5** *transitive & intransitive* (often foll. by *off*) distort or be distorted, or break, from a structural strain. ● *noun* **1** *Mech. & Geol.* a strain produced by pressure in the structure of a substance, when its layers are laterally shifted in relation to each other. **2** (in *pl.*) (also **pair of shears** *singular*) a large clipping or cutting instrument shaped like scissors for use in gardens etc. **3** a hydraulically powered cutter used in logging to fell trees. **4** = WIND SHEAR. □ **shear·er** *noun* [Old English *sceran* from Germanic]

shear·ling *noun* **1** a sheep that has been shorn once. **2** a fleece or wool from a shearling, esp. the tanned fleece used to make garments, with the wool to the inside.

shear·water *noun* **1** any of a number of seabirds of the family Procellariidae, related to petrels, which habitually skim low over the open sea with wings outstretched. **2** = SKIMMER 4.

sheath *noun* (*pl.* **sheaths**) **1** a close-fitting cover, esp. for the blade of a knife or sword. **2** a condom. **3** *Bot., Anat., & Zool.* an enclosing case or

tissue. **4** the protective covering round an electric cable. **5** a woman's close-fitting dress. □ **sheath·less** *adjective* [Old English *scǣth, scéath*]

sheathe *transitive verb* **1** put into a sheath. **2** encase; protect with a sheath or sheathing.

sheath·ing *noun* **1** a protective casing or covering. **2** a layer of plywood etc. covering the framing etc. of a house.

sheath knife *noun* a dagger-like knife carried in a sheath.

sheave¹ *transitive verb* make (grain) into sheaves.

sheave² *noun* a grooved wheel in a pulley block etc., for a rope to run on. [Old English *scife* (unrecorded) from Germanic]

sheaves *pl. of* SHEAF.

Sheba /ˈʃiːbə/ the biblical name of Saba, an ancient country in SW Arabia famous for its trade in gold and spices. The queen of Sheba visited King Solomon in Jerusalem.

she·bang /ʃəˈbaŋ/ *noun N Amer. slang* □ **the whole shebang** the whole situation, thing, etc. [19th c.: origin unknown]

she·been /ʃəˈbiːn/ *noun* (esp. in Ireland, Scotland, Newfoundland, and South Africa) an unlicensed house selling alcoholic liquor. [Anglo-Irish *síbín* from *séibe* mugful]

She·bib /ʃəˈbɪb/ **Don·ald** (b.1938), Canadian filmmaker. After directing several documentaries for the CBC, he made *Goin' Down the Road* (1970), which followed the lives of two Maritimers in Toronto, and which became one of the most important English-Canadian films. His later films include *Second Wind* (1976) and *Running Brave* (1983).

shed¹ *noun* **1 a** a one-storey structure usu. of wood for storage or shelter for animals etc., or as a workshop etc. **b** (in full **storage shed**) *N Amer.* a small structure, often of aluminum, for storing backyard tools etc. **2** a large roofed structure often with one side or more sides open, for storing or maintaining machinery, vehicles, etc. (*machine shed; drive shed*). **3** *Austral. & NZ* an open-sided building for shearing sheep or milking cattle. [apparently a variant of SHADE]

shed² *verb* (**shed·ding**; *past and past participle* **shed**) **1 a** *transitive* let or cause to fall off (*trees shed their leaves*). **b** *intransitive* (of an animal) lose hair, feathers, etc. **2** *transitive* take off (clothes). **3** *transitive* reduce (an electrical power load) by disconnection etc. **4** *transitive* cause to fall or flow (*shed blood; shed tears*). **5** *transitive* disperse, diffuse, radiate (*shed light*). **6** *transitive* remove or get rid of (*has shed 25 pounds in the last few months; corporations are shedding jobs at an unprecedented rate*). □ **shed light on** *see* LIGHT¹. □ **shed·der** *noun* [Old English *sc(e)adan*, from Germanic]

she'd *contraction* **1** she had. **2** she would.

she-devil *noun* a malicious or spiteful woman.

sheen ● *noun* **1** a gloss or lustre on a surface. **2** radiance, brightness. ● *transitive & intransitive verb* shine or cause to shine. [obsolete *sheen* beautiful, resplendent, from Old English *scéne*: sense assimilated to SHINE]

sheeny¹ *adjective* having a sheen; glossy, lustrous.

sheeny² *noun* (*pl.* **-ies**) *offensive* a Jew. [origin unknown]

sheep *noun* (*pl.* same) **1** any ruminant mammal of the genus *Ovis* with a thick woolly coat, of which domesticated varieties are kept in flocks for wool or meat. **2** a bashful, defenceless, or esp. easily-led person. □ **count sheep** *see* COUNT¹. **might as well be hanged for a sheep as a lamb** might as well attempt the bolder of two strategies if the consequences of failure are the same. **separate the sheep from the goats** divide into desirable and undesirable groups (compare Matt. 25:33). □ **sheep·like** *adjective* [Old English *scép, scǽp, scéap*]

sheep dip *noun* **1** a preparation for cleansing sheep of vermin or preserving their wool. **2** the place where sheep are dipped in this.

sheep·dog *noun* **1** a dog trained to guard and herd sheep. **2** a dog of various breeds suitable for this.

sheep·fold *noun* an enclosure for penning sheep.

sheep·herder *noun* a person who herds sheep; a shepherd.

sheep·ish *adjective* **1** embarrassed through shame or foolishness. **2** bashful, shy, reticent. □ **sheep·ish·ly** *adverb* **sheep·ish·ness** *noun*

sheep laurel *noun* a N American evergreen shrub, *Kalmia angustifolia*, of the heath family, reputedly very poisonous to stock. *Also called* LAMBKILL.

sheep·man *noun* (*pl.* **-men**) a breeder or owner of sheep.

sheep's eyes *plural noun* an amorous or longing glance.

sheep's fescue *noun* a small wiry fescue, *Festuca ovina*, characteristic of hill grassland.

sheep·shank *noun* a knot used to shorten a rope temporarily.

---

t *top*   v *voice*   w *we*   z *zoo*   ʃ *she*   ʒ *vision*   θ *thin*   ð *this*   ŋ *ring*   x *loch*   tʃ *chip*   dʒ *jar*   (*see over for vowels*)

sheep·skin *noun* **1** a garment or rug of sheep's skin with the wool on. **2** leather from a sheep's skin used in bookbinding.

sheep sorrel *noun* a small reddish sorrel, *Rumex acetosella*, of heaths and acid sandy soils.

sheep·walk *noun* (in the UK) a tract of land on which sheep are pastured.

sheer[1] ● *adjective* **1** complete; nothing more than (*sheer luck; sheer determination*). **2** (of a cliff or ascent etc.) perpendicular; very steep. **3** (of a textile) very thin; diaphanous. ● *adverb* **1** directly, outright. **2** perpendicularly. ● *noun* **1** sheer fabric. **2** (in *pl.*) **a** curtains made of sheer fabric. **b** sheer nylon hosiery. □ **sheer·ly** *adverb* **sheer·ness** *noun* [Middle English *schere* prob. from dial. *shire* pure, clear, from Old English *scīr* from Germanic]

sheer[2] ● *intransitive verb* **1** esp. *Naut.* swerve or change course. **2** (foll. by *away, off*) go away, esp. from a person or topic one dislikes or fears. ● *noun Naut.* a deviation from a course. [perhaps from Middle Low German *scheren* = SHEAR *verb*]

sheer[3] *noun* the upward slope of a ship's lines towards the bow and stern. [prob. from SHEAR *noun*]

sheesh *interjection N Amer.* expressing mild frustration, exasperation, surprise, embarrassment, etc. [perhaps alteration of JEEZ]

sheet[1] ● *noun* **1** a large rectangular piece of cotton or other fabric, used esp. in pairs as inner bedclothes. **2 a** a broad usu. thin flat piece of material, e.g. paper or metal. **b** (*attributive*) made in sheets (*sheet iron*). **3** the long rectangular ice surface on which curling is played. **4** a wide continuous surface or expanse of water, ice, flame, falling rain, etc. **5** a set of unseparated postage stamps. **6** *derogatory* a newspaper, esp. a disreputable one. **7** a complete piece of paper of the size in which it was made, for printing and folding as part of a book. **8** = BAKING SHEET. ● *verb* **1** *transitive* provide or cover with sheets. **2** *transitive* form into sheets. **3** *intransitive* (of rain etc.) fall in sheets. □ **between the sheets** in bed, esp. engaged in sexual activity. [Old English *scēte, scīete* from Germanic]

sheet[2] ● *noun* a rope or chain attached to the lower corner of a sail for securing or controlling it. ● *verb* (foll. by *in, out*) make a sail more or less taut. □ **three sheets to the wind** *slang* drunk. [Old English *scēata*, Old Norse *skaut*]

sheet anchor *noun* a second anchor for use in emergencies.

sheet bend *noun* a method of temporarily fastening one rope through the loop of another.

sheet feeder *noun* a device for feeding paper into a printer etc. one sheet at a time.

sheet ice *noun* ice formed in a thin, smooth layer.

sheet·ing *noun* **1** an act or instance of making or covering with sheets. **2** material for making bed linen. **3** material covering another in sheets.

sheet lightning *noun* a lightning flash whose bolt is unseen, observed as a sudden flash of brightness illuminating a wide area.

sheet metal *noun* metal formed into thin sheets by rolling, hammering, etc.

sheet music *noun* **1** printed music, as opposed to performed or recorded music about music. **2** music published in single or interleaved sheets, not bound.

Sheet·rock *noun proprietary* = DRYWALL.

Shef·field an industrial city in northern England, formerly in South Yorkshire; pop. (est. 2002) 421,800. It is noted for the production of cutlery, silverware, and steel.

she/he *pronoun* a written representation of 'he or she' used to indicate both sexes.

sheh·nai /ʃeˈnaɪ/ *noun* (also **she·nai**) a double-reed wind instrument of northern India, similar to the oboe. [Hindi and Urdu *śahnāī*, from Persian *śāhnāy*]

sheik /ʃiːk, ʃeɪk/ *noun* (also **sheikh, shaykh**) **1** a chief or head of an Arab tribe, family, or village. **2** a Muslim leader. □ **sheik·dom** *noun* (also **sheikh·dom**). [ultimately from Arabic *šayḵ* old man, sheikh, from *šāka* be or grow old]

sheila *noun Austral.* & *NZ slang* a girl or young woman. [originally *shaler* (of unknown origin): assimilated to the name *Sheila*]

shek·el /ˈʃekəl/ *noun* **1** the chief monetary unit of modern Israel. **2** *hist.* a silver coin and unit of weight used in ancient Israel and the Middle East. **3** (in *pl.*) *informal* money; riches. [Hebrew *šeḳel* from *šāḳal* weigh]

Shek·in·ah /ʃəˈkaɪnə/ *noun* (also **Shekh·in·ah**) *Judaism* the glory of the divine presence, conventionally represented as light or interpreted (in kabbalism) as a divine feminine aspect. [late Hebrew *šāḵan* dwell, rest]

Shel·burne a town in SW Nova Scotia, situated at the head of Shelburne Harbour, about 200 km southwest of Halifax; pop. (2001) 2,013. [Sir W. Petty, 2nd Earl of *Shelburne* and prime minister of Great Britain d.1805]

shel·duck *noun* (*pl.* same or **shel·ducks**; *masc.* **shel·drake**, *pl.* same or **shel·drakes**) any bright-plumaged large goose-like wild duck of the genus *Tadorna*, esp. *T. tadorna* of shores and brackish inland waters in Eurasia and N Africa. [Middle English prob. from dial. *sheld* pied, related to Middle Dutch *schillede* variegated, + DUCK[1], DRAKE]

shelf *noun* (*pl.* **shelves**) **1** a thin flat piece of wood or metal etc. projecting from a wall, or as part of a unit, used to support books etc. **b** a flat-topped recess in a wall etc. used for supporting objects. **c** an object or objects placed on a shelf (*three shelves of books*). **2 a** a projecting horizontal ledge in a cliff face etc. **b** a reef or sandbank under water. **c** = CONTINENTAL SHELF. □ **off the shelf** (of goods) available immediately from a retailer's stock, as opposed to custom-made. **on the shelf 1** put away indefinitely; set aside. **2** no longer active or of use. **3** *informal derogatory* (of a woman) past the age when she might expect to be married. □ **shelved** *adjective* **shelf·ful** *noun* (*pl.* **-fuls**). **shelf-like** *adjective* [(Middle) Low German *schelf*, related to Old English *scylfe* partition, *scylf* crag]

shelf ice *noun* floating ice permanently attached to a land mass.

shelf life *noun* **1** the amount of time for which a stored item of food etc. remains usable. **2** the length of time during which an idea, practice, etc. is fashionable or practicable.

shell ● *noun* **1 a** the hard outer case of many marine molluscs, snails, etc. (*seashell*). **b** the esp. hard but fragile outer covering of a bird's, reptile's, etc. egg. **c** the usu. hard outer case of a nut kernel, seed, etc. **d** the carapace of a tortoise, turtle, etc. **e** the wing-case or pupa case of many insects etc. **2 a** an explosive projectile or bomb for use in a big gun or mortar. **b** a hollow metal or paper case used as a container for fireworks, explosives, cartridges, etc. **c** *N Amer.* a cartridge. **3** a mere semblance or outer form without substance. **4** any of several things resembling a shell in being an outer case, esp.: **a** a light racing boat. **b** a hollow pastry case. **c** the metal framework of a vehicle body etc. **d** the walls of an unfinished or gutted building, ship, etc. **5** a group of electrons in an atom with almost equal energy. **6** *N Amer.* a very light all-weather jacket, often with a removable lining. **7** (in full **shell program**) *Computing* a program which provides an interface between the user and the operating system. **8** something resembling a seashell (*pasta shells*). ● *verb* **1** *transitive* remove the shell or pod from. **2** *transitive* **a** bombard (a town, troops, etc.) with shells. **b** *informal* (usu. in *passive*) score repeatedly against an opposing goaltender, pitcher, etc. **3** *transitive* provide or cover with a shell or shells. **4** *intransitive* (of a seed etc.) be released from a shell. **5** *transitive* separate (grain, a seed, etc.) from its shell, husk, ear, etc. **6** *intransitive* collect seashells. □ **come out of one's shell** cease to be shy; become communicative. **shell out** *informal* **1** pay (money). **2** hand over (a required sum). □ **shell-less** *adjective* **shell-like** *adjective* **shelly** *adjective* [Old English *sc(i)ell* from Germanic: related to SCALE[1]]

she'll *contraction* she will; she shall.

shel·lac /ʃəˈlak/ ● *noun* **1** lac resin melted into thin flakes and used for making varnish (compare LAC[1]). **2** varnish made from this. ● *transitive verb* (**shel·lacked, shel·lack·ing**) **1** varnish with shellac. **2** *N Amer. slang* defeat or thrash soundly. [SHELL + LAC[1], translation of French *laque en écailles* lac in thin plates]

shel·lack·ing *noun N Amer. slang* a severe defeat or beating.

shell·back *noun slang* an experienced sailor, esp. one who has crossed the equator.

shell company *noun* (also **shell corporation**) **1** a non-trading company used as a vehicle for various company manoeuvres or kept dormant for future use in some other capacity. **2** a company that has ceased to trade and is sold to new owners for a small fee to minimize the cost and trouble of setting up a new company.

shelled *adjective* **1** (of an animal, fruit, etc.) having a shell or shells, esp. of a specific kind (*hard-shelled nuts*). **2** (of an edible animal, fruit, etc.) that has had its shell removed (*shelled shrimp*).

Shel·ley, 1 Mary (Woll·stone·craft) (1797–1851), English novelist. The daughter of William Godwin and Mary Wollstonecraft, she eloped with the poet Shelley in 1814, and is chiefly remembered as the author of the Gothic novel *Frankenstein, or the Modern Prometheus* (1818). **2** her husband, **Percy Bysshe** (1792–1822), English poet. He was a leading figure of the romantic movement with radical political views. Notable works include *Ozymandias* (sonnet, 1818), *The Mask of Anarchy* (political poem, 1819), *Prometheus Unbound* (lyrical drama, 1820), *To a Skylark* (lyric poem, 1820), and *The Defence of Poetry* (essay, 1821). □ **Shel·ley·an** *adjective & noun*

shell·fire *noun* the firing of shells, esp. repeatedly.

shell·fish *noun* (*pl.* same) **1** an aquatic shelled mollusc, e.g. an oyster, scallop, etc. **2** a crustacean, e.g. a crab, shrimp, etc.

shell game *noun N Amer.* **1** a sleight-of-hand game or trick in which a small object is concealed under a walnut shell etc., with bystanders encouraged to place bets or to guess as to which shell the object is under. **2** *informal* a confidence trick; a deception.

shell hole *noun* a crater left in the earth by an exploding shell.

shell midden *noun hist.* (also **shell mound**) a kitchen midden.

shell pink ● *noun* a delicate pale pink. ● *adjective* (hyphenated when attributive) of this colour.

shell shock *noun* a nervous breakdown or other psychological disturbance resulting from exposure to battle.

shell-shocked *adjective* **1** suffering from shell shock. **2** *informal* having received stunning news etc., or having been overwhelmingly defeated.

shell suit *noun Brit.* a track suit with a soft lining and a weatherproof nylon outer shell, used for leisure wear.

shell·work *noun* ornamentation consisting of shells cemented onto wood etc.

Shel·ta *noun* an ancient hybrid secret language used by Irish tinkers, gypsies, etc. [19th c.: origin unknown]

shel·ter ● *noun* **1** a structure built to give protection, esp. from the weather or from attack (*bus shelter*; *bomb shelter*). **2 a** a place of refuge provided for the homeless, abused women, etc. **b** *N Amer.* an animal sanctuary. **3** a shielded condition; protection (*took shelter under a tree*). **4** = TAX SHELTER. ● *verb* **1** *transitive* **a** provide (a person or thing) with protection from the weather, danger, etc. (*sheltered them from the storm*). **b** protect (a person or thing) from unpleasantness or difficulty (*he is trying to shelter his boss from criticism*; *is our country's industry sheltered from foreign competition?*). **2** *intransitive & reflexive* find refuge; take cover (*sheltered under a tree*; *sheltered themselves from the icy wind*). **3** *transitive* protect (invested income) from taxation; invest (money) with this purpose. □ **shel·ter·er** *noun* **shelter·less** *adjective* [16th c.: perhaps from obsolete *sheltron* phalanx, from Old English *scieldtruma* (as SHIELD, *truma* troop)]

shel·ter·belt *noun* a line of trees etc. serving to break the force of the wind.

shel·tered *adjective* **1** (of a place) not greatly exposed to bad weather, sun, etc. (*find a sheltered spot for a picnic*). **2** kept away from or not exposed to unpleasant circumstances, harmful influences, or the normal difficulties of life (*had a sheltered upbringing*). **3** (of a course of study, activity, etc.) provided for people with some sort of disability (*sheltered workshop*).

shelter·wood *noun* mature trees left standing to provide shelter in which saplings can grow.

shel·tie *noun* (also **shelty**) (*pl.* **-ties**) a Shetland pony or sheepdog. [prob. representing Old Norse *Hjalti* Shetlander (as pronounced in Orkney)]

shelve[1] *transitive verb* **1** put (books etc.) on a shelf. **2 a** abandon or defer (a plan etc.). **b** remove (a person) from active work etc. **3** fit (a cupboard etc.) with shelves. □ **shelv·er** *noun* [*shelves* pl. of SHELF]

shelve[2] *intransitive verb* (of ground etc.) slope in a specified direction (*land shelved away to the horizon*). [perhaps from *shelvy* (adj.) having underwater reefs, from *shelve* (n.) ledge, from SHELVE[1]]

shelves *pl.* of SHELF.

shelv·ing *noun* **1** in senses of SHELVE[1]. **2** a set of shelves; shelves collectively.

Shem *Bible* a son of Noah (Gen. 10:21), traditional ancestor of the Semites.

Shema /ʃeˈmɒ/ a Hebrew text forming an important part of Jewish evening and morning prayer and used as a Jewish confession of faith, beginning 'Hear, O Israel, the Lord our God is one Lord'. [Hebrew, = hear]

she-male *noun informal* a man displaying female characteristics, e.g. through cross-dressing and/or hormone treatment.

she·moz·zle /ʃəˈmɒzəl/ *noun* (also **sche·moz·zle**) *slang* **1** a brawl or commotion. **2** a muddle. [Yiddish after Late Hebrew *šel-lō'-mazzāl* of no luck]

shen /ʃen/ *noun* (*pl.* same) (in Chinese thought) the spiritual element of a person's psyche. [Chinese *shén*]

Shen·an·doah River /ˌʃenənˈdoːə/ a river of Virginia. Rising in two headstreams, one on each side of the Blue Ridge Mountains, it flows

some 240 km (150 miles) northward to join the Potomac at Harpers Ferry.

she·nani·gan /ʃəˈnanɪɡən/ *noun* (esp. in *pl.*) *informal* **1** high-spirited behaviour; nonsense. **2** trickery; dubious manoeuvres. [19th c.: origin unknown]

Shen·si see SHAANXI.

Shen·yang /ʃenˈjan/ a city in NE China, the capital of the province of Liaoning; pop. (est. 2002) 6,394,500.

Shen·zhen /ʃenˈʒen/ an industrial city in S China, just north of Hong Kong; pop. (est. 2002) 1,113,500.

Sheol /ˈʃiːɒl, ˈʃiːɒl/ (in the Old Testament and Hebrew Bible) the underworld, the abode of the dead. [Hebrew *š'ōl*]

Shep·ard, Alan Bart·lett, Jr. (1923–98), US naval officer, who was the first US astronaut in space (1961).

shep·herd ● *noun* **1** a person employed to tend sheep, esp. at pasture. **2** a person, esp. a member of the clergy etc., who guides, cares for, or watches over a group of people. **3** = GERMAN SHEPHERD. ● *transitive verb* **1 a** tend (sheep etc.) as a shepherd. **b** guide (followers etc.). **2** marshal, drive, or direct the movement of. [Old English *scēaphierde* (as SHEEP, HERD)]

shep·herd·ess *noun* a woman who tends and rears sheep.

shepherd's crook *noun* a staff with a hook at one end used by shepherds.

shepherd's pie *noun* a dish of ground meat under a layer of mashed potato.

shepherd's purse *noun* a white-flowered plant of the mustard family, *Capsella bursa-pastoris*, with triangular or cordate pods.

Shera·ton[1]**, Thom·as** (1751–1806), English cabinetmaker and furniture designer, who is known for works such as *The Cabinet-Maker and Upholsterer's Drawing Book* (1791–4).

Shera·ton[2] *noun* (often *attributive*) the style of furniture introduced in England *c*.1790 by Sheraton, known for its delicate and graceful forms.

sher·bet /ˈʃɜːbət/ *noun* **1** /ˈʃɜːbət, -bɜːt/ *N Amer.* a frozen dessert, similar to ice cream, made from water, milk, and sugar, and usu. fruit-flavoured. **2** a flavoured sweet powder containing bicarbonate of soda, tartaric acid, etc., eaten as a candy or used to make an effervescing drink. **3** a cooling drink of sweet diluted fruit juices, esp. in Arab countries. [Turkish *şerbet*, Persian *šerbet* from Arabic *šarba* drink, from *šariba* to drink: compare SHRUB[2], SYRUP]

Sher·brooke[1] a city in S Quebec, about 150 km east of Montreal; pop. (2001) 139,388. □ **Sher·brook·er** *noun* [Sir J. C. SHERBROOKE]

Sher·brooke[2]**, Sir John Coape** (1764–1830), British soldier and colonial administrator. He was appointed Lieutenant-Governor of Nova Scotia in 1811. His active defence of the colony during the War of 1812 led to his appointment as governor-in-chief of British North America in 1816; ill health forced him to resign two years later.

sherd *noun* = POTSHERD. [var. of SHARD]

Sheri·dan, Rich·ard Brins·ley (1751–1816), Irish dramatist and Whig politician. Comedies of manners include *The Rivals* (1775)—whose character Mrs. Malaprop gave her name to the word *malapropism*—and *The School for Scandal* (1777).

sher·iff *noun* **1** *Cdn* an appointed official responsible for court administration and trial preparation, the selection of jury panels, the serving of legal documents, and the seizure and sale of property to settle damage claims. **2** *US* an officer in a county, usu. elected, responsible for keeping the peace, administering justice, etc. **3** *Brit.* **a** (also **High Sheriff**) the chief executive officer of the Crown in a county, administering justice etc. **b** an honorary officer elected annually in some towns. □ **sheriff·dom** *noun* [Old English *scīr-gerēfa* (as SHIRE, REEVE)]

Sher·lock Holmes *noun* (also **Sher·lock**) an investigator of mysteries, esp. a remarkably astute one. □ **Sher·lock·ian** *adjective & noun* [the amateur detective hero of the stories of A.C. DOYLE]

Sher·man, Wil·liam Tecum·seh (1820–91), US general. Chief Union commander in the west from March 1864 onward, he set out with 60,000 men on a march through Georgia, during which he crushed Confederate forces and broke civilian morale through his policy of deliberate destruction of the South's sources of supply. He was later appointed commander of the US army (1869–84).

Sher·pa *noun* **1** (*pl.* same or **Sher·pas**) a member of a Himalayan people living on the border of Nepal and Tibet renowned for their skill in mountaineering. **2** (**sherpa**) a civil servant or diplomat who undertakes preparatory political work prior to a summit conference. [Tibetan *sharpa* inhabitant of an eastern country]

sher·ried *adjective* marinated in, or cooked or flavoured with sherry.

Sher·ring·ton, **Sir Charles Scott** (1857–1952), English physiologist, who studied the mechanisms of integration in the nervous system, and introduced the concepts of reflex actions and the reflex arc; he shared a Nobel Prize in 1932.

sherry ● *noun* (*pl.* **-ries**) **1 a** a fortified wine originally from S Spain. **b** a glass of this. **2** the amber colour of common varieties of this. ● *adjective* of this colour. [earlier *sherris* from Spanish (*vino de*) *Xeres* (now Jerez de la Frontera) in Andalusia]

sher·wani /ʃɜrˈwʊni/ *noun* a knee-length coat buttoning to the neck, worn by men from the Indian subcontinent. [Urdu and Persian *šïrwānī* 'from Shirvan' (referring to a town in NE Persia)]

she's *contraction* **1** she is. **2** she has.

Shet·land ● *attributive adjective* of or pertaining to the Shetland Islands. ● *noun* (in full **Shetland wool**) a fine loosely twisted wool from Shetland sheep.

Shetland Islands (also **Shet·land**, **Shet·lands**) a group of about 100 islands off the north coast of Scotland, northeast of the Orkneys, constituting the administrative region of Shetland; pop. (2001) 21,988; chief town, Lerwick. Noted for the production of knitwear, they have provided in the late 20th c. a base for the North Sea oil and gas industries. □ **Shet·land·er** *noun* **Shet·land·ic** *adjective*

Shetland pony *noun* a small hardy rough-coated breed of pony.

Shetland sheepdog *noun* a small collie-like breed of dog.

Shev·ard·nadze /ˌʃevardˈnɒdzi/ **Ed·uard (Am·vrosi·evich)** (b.1928), Soviet leader and head of state of Georgia 1992–2003. As Minister of Foreign Affairs (1985–90) under Gorbachev, he played a key role in arms control negotiations with the West; he was elected head of state of his native Georgia in 1992, following the toppling of President Zviad Gamsakhurdia (1939–94), but resigned in the face of mass demonstrations in late 2003.

Shev·chenko, **Taras Hryhor·ovych** (1814–1861) Ukrainian poet and nationalist. His poetry portrayed Ukrainian history in a sombre light; while in exile because of his nationalist activity, he wrote satirical poetry about Russian oppression of Ukraine and prophesied a revolution.

shew *archaic var. of* SHOW.

shew·bread /ˈʃoʊbred/ *noun Judaism hist.* twelve loaves that were displayed in the Temple and renewed each Sabbath.

shh *var. of* SH.

Shia /ˈʃiə/ (also **Shiah**; **Shi'a**) ● *noun* (*pl.* same or **Shias**) **1** one of the two main branches of Islam, esp. in Iran, that rejects the first three Sunni caliphs and regards Ali, the fourth caliph, as Muhammad's first successor (*compare* SUNNI). **2** a Shiite. ● *adjective* of or relating to Shia. [Arabic *šī'a* 'party' (of Ali, Muhammad's cousin and son-in-law)]

shi·atsu /ʃiˈatsuː/ *noun* a kind of therapy of Japanese origin, in which pressure is applied with the fingers or palms to certain points of the body. [Japanese, = finger pressure]

shib·bo·leth /ˈʃɪbəˌleθ/ *noun* **1** a long-standing formula, doctrine, or phrase, etc., held to be true (esp. unreflectingly) by a party or group (*must abandon outdated shibboleths*). **2** a word, phrase, pronunciation, usage, etc. distinguishing a particular class or group of people. [Hebrew *šibbōleṯ* ear of wheat, used as a test of nationality for its difficult pronunciation (Judg. 12:6)]

shied *past and past participle of* SHY[1], SHY[2].

shield ● *noun* **1 a** a piece of metal, wooden, acrylic, etc. armour, carried on the arm or in the hand to deflect blows from the head or body. **b** a thing serving to protect (*insurance is a shield against disaster*). **2** a thing resembling a shield, esp.: **a** a trophy in the form of a shield. **b** a protective plate or screen in machinery etc. **c** a shield-like part of an animal, esp. a shell. **d** a similar part of a plant. **e** *US* a police officer's shield-shaped badge. **3** a piece of fabric etc. worn as a liner to protect part of a garment from staining (*dress shield*). **4** *Geol.* **a** a large rigid area of the earth's crust, usu. of Precambrian rock, which has been unaffected by later orogenic episodes. **b** (**Shield**) (in Canada) = CANADIAN SHIELD. **5** *Heraldry* a stylized representation of a shield, characteristically of a flat-topped heart shape, used for displaying a coat of arms etc. ● *transitive verb* protect, shelter, or screen with or as with a shield from attack, danger, exposure, etc., or from blame or lawful punishment; cover or hide with a shield. [Old English *sc(i)eld* from Germanic: prob. originally = board, related to SCALE[1]]

Shield country *noun Cdn* the area covered by the Canadian Shield, characterized by thin soil, rock outcrops, countless lakes and rivers, and, in the southern areas, vast coniferous forests.

Shields, **Carol** (1935–2003), US-born Canadian poet and novelist. Her novel *The Stone Diaries* (1993) won a Governor General's Award and a Pulitzer Prize. She also published several poetry collections and a volume of short stories.

shield volcano *noun Geol.* a broad domed volcano with gently sloping sides.

shiel·ing /ˈʃiːlɪŋ/ *noun Scot.* **1** a roughly constructed hut originally esp. for pastoral use. **2** pasture for cattle. [Scots *shiel* hut: Middle English, of unknown origin]

shift ● *verb* **1 a** *intransitive & transitive* change or move or cause to change or move from one position or state to another. **b** *intransitive* (of cargo) get shaken out of place. **2** *N Amer.* **a** *transitive* change (gear) in a vehicle. **b** *intransitive* change gear. **3** *intransitive* contrive or manage as best one can. **4** *transitive Brit.* remove, esp. with effort (*washing won't shift the stains*). **5** *Brit. slang* **a** *intransitive* hurry (*we'll have to shift!*). **b** *transitive* consume (food or drink) hastily or in bulk. **c** *transitive* sell (esp. dubious goods). ● *noun* **1 a** the act or an instance of shifting. **b** the substitution of one thing for another; a rotation. **2 a** a relay of workers, players on a hockey team, etc. (*the night shift*; *sent the next shift out on the ice*). **b** the time for which they work, play, etc. (*an eight-hour shift*; *scored on his last shift*). **3 a** a device, stratagem, or expedient. **b** a dodge, trick, or evasion. **4 a** a woman's straight unwaisted dress. **b** a woman's loose-fitting undergarment; a slip. **5** a displacement of spectral lines (*see also* BLUE SHIFT, RED SHIFT). **6** (also **sound shift**) a systematic change in pronunciation as a language evolves. **7** a key on a keyboard used to switch between lower and upper case, conduct special operations, etc. **8** *Bridge* **a** a change of suit in bidding. **b** *US* a change of suit in play. **9** the positioning of successive rows of bricks so that their ends do not coincide. **10** *N Amer.* **a** a gear lever in a motor vehicle. **b** a mechanism for this. □ **make shift** manage or contrive; get along somehow (*made shift without it*). **shift for oneself** rely on one's own efforts. **shift gears** esp. *N Amer.* change one's course of action, strategy, intensity, etc. **shift (one's) ground** take up a new position in an argument etc. □ **shift·able** *adjective* **shift·ing** *noun* [Old English *sciftan* arrange, divide, etc., from Germanic]

shift·er *noun* **1** a person or thing that shifts. **2** = GEARSHIFT.

shifting sand *noun* (also **shifting sands**; **shifting ground**) a changing or unstable state of affairs, condition, etc.

shift·less *adjective* lacking resourcefulness; lazy; inefficient. □ **shift·less·ness** *noun*

shift-on-the-fly *attributive adjective N Amer.* designating the capability of a vehicle to be switched between two-wheel drive and four-wheel drive while running.

shift work *noun* work conducted in often variable periods independent of a standard workday, usu. at night (*tired after a month of shift work*). □ **shift worker** *noun*

shifty *adjective* (**shift·i·er**, **shift·i·est**) *informal* not straightforward; evasive; deceitful; furtive. □ **shift·i·ly** *adverb* **shift·i·ness** *noun*

shi·gel·la /ʃɪˈɡelə/ *noun* (*pl.* **shi·gel·lae** /-liː/ or **shi·gel·las**) any airborne bacterium of the genus *Shigella*, some of which cause dysentery. [modern Latin from K. *Shiga*, Japanese bacteriologist d.1957 + diminutive suffix]

shig·el·lo·sis /ˌʃɪɡəˈloʊsəs/ *noun* (*pl.* **shig·el·lo·ses** /-siːz/) infection with, or a disease caused by, shigella bacteria.

Shih Tzu /ˈʃiːˈtsuː/ *noun* a breed of small short-legged dog originating in China, with long silky erect hair, long ears, and a tail curling over the back. [Chinese *shizi* lion + *gou* dog]

shii·ta·ke /ʃɪˈtɒki, -ˈtak-, -kei/ *noun* (also **shiitake mushroom**) an edible mushroom, *Lentinus edodes*, cultivated on oak logs etc. [Japanese, from *shii* a kind of oak + *take* 'mushroom']

Shi·ite /ˈʃiːaɪt/ (also **Shi'ite**) ● *noun* an adherent of the Shia branch of Islam. ● *adjective* of or relating to Shia. □ **Shi·ism** *noun*

Shi·jia·zhuang /ˌʃiːdʒiɑˈʒwɑŋ/ a city in NE central China, capital of Hebei province; pop. (est. 2002) 1,693,600.

Shi·ko·ku /ʃɪˈkoːkuː/ the smallest of the four main islands of Japan, constituting an administrative region; pop. (2000) 4,154,000; capital, Matsuyama. It is divided from Kyushu to the west and S Honshu to the north by the Inland Sea.

shik·sa (also **shik·se**) often *offensive* ● *noun* **1** a Gentile girl or woman. **2** a Jewish girl or woman not observing traditional Jewish behaviour. ● *adjective* (of a girl or woman) Gentile. [Yiddish *shikse* from Hebrew *šiqṣâ* from *sheqeṣ* detested thing + *-â fem. suffix*]

shill *N Amer.* ● *noun* **1** an accomplice, esp. one posing as an enthusiastic or successful customer to encourage or entice potential buyers, gamblers, etc. **2** an adherent of a party or point of view etc. posing as a disinterested advocate. ● *verb* **1** *transitive & intransitive* (often foll. by *for*) promote a cause, esp. with feigned disinterest (*he shilled for the* *candidate, who happened to be his uncle; he's shilling a new book*]. **2** *intransitive* act as an accomplice or shill in a scam. [prob. from earlier *shillaber*, of unknown origin]

shil·le·lagh /ʃɪˈleɪli, -lə/ *noun* a thick stick or club of blackthorn or oak used in Ireland esp. as a weapon. [*Shillelagh* in Co. Wicklow, Ireland]

shil·ling *noun* **1** *hist.* a former British coin and monetary unit equal to one-twentieth of a pound or twelve pence. **2** *hist.* any of various coins of equal or similar value used in countries of the British Empire. **3** a monetary unit currently used in Kenya, Tanzania, Uganda, and Somalia. ◻ **the King's** (or **Queen's**) **shilling** *hist.* the shilling formerly given to a recruit when enlisting in the army (*take the King's shilling*). [Old English *scilling*, from Germanic]

shilly-shally *intransitive verb* (**-shallies, -shallied**) act with indecision or hesitation about a choice or decision; vacillate.
◻ **shilly-shally·ing** *noun* [originally *shill I, shall I*, reduplication of *shall I?*]

shim ● *noun* a thin strip, wedge, or washer of metal, wood, rubber, etc. inserted in a space in machinery etc. to make parts fit or align.
● *transitive verb* (**shimmed, shim·ming**) wedge, raise, or fill up with a shim. [18th c.: origin unknown]

shim·mer ● *intransitive verb* **1** shine with a tremulous or faint diffused light. **2** quiver or tremble, or appear to do so, esp. when distorted by heat waves (*the hot asphalt shimmered*). ● *noun* a faint tremulous light or image. ◻ **shim·mer·ing** *adjective* **shim·mer·ing·ly** *adverb* **shim·mery** *adjective* [Old English *scymrian* from Germanic: compare SHINE]

shim·my ● *noun* (*pl.* **-mies**) **1** *hist.* any of a number of black American ragtime dances, usu. of a sexually suggestive nature involving esp. a rolling of the hips and a shaking of the shoulders and breasts, precursors to several jazz and popular dances including the Charleston. **2** an abnormal vibration of esp. the front wheels of a car or truck etc. ● *intransitive verb* (**-mies, -mied**) **1 a** *hist.* dance a shimmy. **b** shake or sway the body, esp. in a manner suggestive of a shimmy. **2** (esp. of a car etc.) shake or vibrate abnormally. [20th c.: origin uncertain]

shin ● *noun* **1** the front of the leg below the knee. **2** the front or sharp edge of the tibia. **3** a cut of beef from the lower part of an animal's foreleg. ● *transitive & intransitive verb* (**shinned, shin·ning**) *Brit.* = SHINNY[1]. [Old English *sinu*]

shin bone *noun* = TIBIA 1.

shin·dig *noun informal* **1** a lively or festive gathering; a party. **2** a brawl, commotion, or noisy disturbance. [perhaps from SHIN *noun* + DIG *noun*]

shine ● *verb* (*past* and *past participle* **shone** /ʃɒn/) **1** *intransitive* **a** emit or give off light (*the lamp was shining*). **b** (of the sun, a star, etc.) not be obscured by clouds etc.; be visible (*the sun is shining today*). **2** *intransitive* **a** glow or be bright, esp. with reflected light (*the water shone*). **b** (of a person's eyes or face) be unusually bright, vibrant, or animated, esp. with excitement, joy, etc. (*her face shone with gratitude*). **3** *transitive* direct (light or a source of light) in a particular direction (*he shone the flashlight in my eyes*). **4** *transitive* (*past* and *past participle* **shined**) make bright; polish (*shined his shoes*). **5** *intransitive* be brilliant in some respect; excel (*the company shines in this production*). ● *noun* **1** brightness or radiance emanating from a light or source of light. **2** a lustre or glow of light reflecting off a surface, esp. the result of cleaning or polishing; gloss (*the shine of chrome; the shine of her hair*). **3** *N Amer.* the act or an instance of shining esp. shoes (*how much for a shine?*). **4** *slang* = MOONSHINE 1. ◻ **rain or shine** see RAIN. **shine through** be clearly evident. **take the shine off** spoil the brilliance or newness of. **take a shine to** *informal* take a fancy to; like. ◻ **shin·ing** *adjective* **shin·ing·ly** *adverb* [Old English *scīnan* from Germanic]

shin·er *noun* **1** *informal* a black eye. **2** any of various silvery fishes, esp. any of the N American minnows of the genus *Notropis*, or the common shiner *Luxilus cornutus*.

shin·gle[1] *noun* (in *sing.* or *pl.*) **1** small rounded pebbles, esp. on a seashore. **2** a beach or other stretch of land covered with loose rounded pebbles. ◻ **shin·gly** *adjective* [16th c.: origin uncertain]

shin·gle[2] ● *noun* **1** a thin rectangular tile, usu. made of asphalt or wood, used to cover esp. walls or roofs. **2** *N Amer.* a small sign or nameplate hanging outside a store or esp. the office of a doctor or lawyer etc. ● *transitive verb* **1** install shingles on (a roof or wall etc). **2** cut (hair) very short, so as to create an effect of overlapping or tapering. ◻ **hang out one's shingle** set up a practice or profession.
◻ **shin·gled** *adjective* [Middle English apparently from Latin *scindula*, earlier *scandula*]

shin·gles *plural noun* (usu. treated as *sing.*) a disease caused by a herpesvirus and characterized by a rash of minute blisters on the skin,

often in a band across the body above affected nerve ganglia, and accompanied by localized pain. *Also called* HERPES ZOSTER. [medieval Latin *cingulus* from Latin *cingulum* girdle, from *cingere* gird]

Shining Path *noun* a neo-Maoist Peruvian revolutionary movement and terrorist group. *Also called* SENDERO LUMINOSO.

shin·kan·sen /ʃiːnˈkɒnˌsen/ *noun* (in Japan) a high-speed passenger train; a bullet train. [Japanese, from *shin* 'new' + *kansen* 'main line']

shin·leaf *noun* = PYROLA.

shin·ny[1] *intransitive verb* (**-nies, -nied**) (usu. foll. by *up* or *down*) *N Amer. informal* climb up or down a tree etc. by clasping it with the arms and legs and hauling oneself up without the help of steps etc. [from SHIN *noun* + -Y[2]]

shin·ny[2] *noun Cdn* **1** (in full **shinny hockey**) informal pickup hockey played usu. without nets, referees, or equipment except for skates, sticks, and a ball or puck or an object serving as a puck. **2** = STREET HOCKEY. **3** *informal* hockey. [var. of SHINTY]

shin·ola /ʃaɪˈnoːlə/ *noun* ◻ **not tell** (or **know**) **shit from shinola** *coarse slang* used to indicate that someone is ignorant or innocent. [SHINE + -OLA, orig. a US brand of shoe polish]

shin pad *noun* (also **shin guard**) a piece of protective equipment used to cover the shin when playing esp. hockey, football, etc.

shin·plaster *noun hist. slang.* **1** *Cdn* a banknote worth twenty-five cents. **2** *US & Austral.* a banknote of a denomination less than a dollar. [from its resemblance to a square piece of paper soaked in vinegar and used as a bandage for the shin, known as a shinplaster]

shin splints *plural noun* (usu. treated as *sing.*) acute pain in the shin and lower leg caused esp. by prolonged running on hard surfaces.

Shin·to *noun* a religious system incorporating the worship of ancestors, nature spirits and other divinities, and prior to 1945 the state religion of Japan, founded on a belief in the divinity of the Japanese emperor. ◻ **Shin·to·ism** *noun* **Shin·to·ist** *noun* [Japanese from Chinese *shen dao* way of the gods]

shin·ty *noun* (*pl.* **-ties**) *Brit.* **1** a game originating in Scotland and similar to field hockey, played with a light wooden ball and narrow sticks curved at one end, but with taller goalposts. **2** a stick or ball used in shinty. [earlier *shinny*, apparently from the cry used in the game *shin ye, shin you, shin t' ye*, of unknown origin]

shiny *adjective* (**shin·i·er, shin·i·est**) **1** full of brightness; having a polished or gleaming surface. **2** conspicuously or apparently new (*they've just installed a shiny new phone system*). **3** (of clothing, esp. the seat of the pants etc.) having the nap worn off. ◻ **shin·i·ly** *adverb* **shin·i·ness** *noun*

ship ● *noun* **1 a** a large seagoing vessel propelled by engine or sail (*compare* BOAT). **b** a sailing vessel with a bowsprit and three, four, or five square-rigged masts. **2** an aircraft. **3** a spacecraft. **4** the crew or passengers of a ship. ● *verb* (**shipped, ship·ping**) **1** *transitive* transport, deliver, or convey (goods, passengers, sailors, etc.) by or on a ship. **2** *transitive* (also foll. by *off, out*) esp. *N Amer.* **a** transport (goods) by truck, rail, or other means. **b** *informal* send (a person) away; dispatch (*we shipped the kids off to school*). **3** *intransitive* (often foll. by *out*) **a** (of a sailor) become employed on a ship. **b** (of a ship or passenger etc.) set out on a journey, esp. by sea. **4** *transitive* **a** take in (water or waves) over the side of a ship. **b** take or draw (an anchor, oars, etc.) into the ship or boat to which it belongs. **c** put (an oar etc.) in its correct position in readiness to function. ◻ **jump ship** see JUMP. **run a tight ship** *N Amer.* manage a company or organization etc. with strict authority. **ship of the line** *hist.* a large battleship fighting in the front line of battle. **when a person's ship comes in** (or **home**) when a person's fortune is made. ◻ **ship·pable** *adjective* [Old English *scip, scipian* from Germanic]

-ship *suffix* forming nouns denoting: **1** a quality or condition (*friendship; hardship*). **2** status, title, or office (*authorship; lordship*). **3** a skill in a certain capacity (*workmanship*). **4** the collective individuals of a group (*membership*). [Old English *-scipe* etc. from Germanic]

ship·board *adjective* occurring or used on board a ship (*a shipboard romance*).

ship·build·er *noun* a person or company whose occupation or business is the design and construction of ships. ◻ **ship·build·ing** *noun*

ship chandler *noun* a dealer specializing in the supply of provisions, equipment, etc. for ships and boats. ◻ **ship chandlery** *noun*

ship·lap *noun* a type of wooden siding consisting of horizontal boards rabbeted in such a way that each overlaps the one below it.

ship·load *noun* as large a cargo as a ship is capable of holding.

ship·master *noun* a ship's captain.

ship·mate *noun* a fellow member of a ship's crew.

ship·ment *noun* **1** an amount of goods transported, delivered, or received. **2** the action or an instance of shipping goods.

ship-money *noun* *hist.* a medieval wartime tax which in 1634 Charles I attempted to levy in peacetime and without parliamentary consent, causing public discontent which contributed to the outbreak of the English Civil War.

ship of state *noun* *N Amer.* the volatile economic and political affairs of a country characterized as a ship sailing at sea.

ship·own·er *noun* a person owning a ship or ships or shares in ships.

ship·per *noun* a person or company that transports or receives goods by land, sea, or air.

ship·ping *noun* **1** the act or an instance of shipping or transporting goods by sea, land, or air. **2** ships collectively, esp. the ships of a particular country, frequenting a particular port, or used for a particular purpose.

shipping agent *noun* a licensed agent conducting a ship's affairs, such as insurance, documentation, etc., for the ship's owner.

shipping and handling *noun* **1** the transportation of goods and the processing involved in transporting goods, including packaging, delivery, and carrying goods through customs etc. **2** the cost of transporting and processing goods (*it costs $20 plus shipping and handling*) (*compare* POSTAGE AND HANDLING).

shipping fever *noun* *esp. N Amer.* any of several diseases typically contracted by cattle while being shipped from place to place, esp. one caused by bacteria of the genus *Pasteurella*.

shipping lane *noun* a route at sea designated for the passage of large ships; a sea lane.

ship's biscuit *noun* *hist.* a hard coarse kind of biscuit kept and eaten on board ship. *Also called* SEA BISCUIT, HARDTACK.

ship's boat *noun* a small boat carried on board a ship.

ship's company *noun* the crew of a ship.

ship·shape *adjective* in good order; tidy and neat.

ship's master *noun* an official superintending the signing of ship's articles, paying off of sailors, etc.

ship's papers *noun* documents establishing the ownership and nationality of a ship, the nature of its cargo, etc.

ship·time *noun* *Cdn.* (*North*) *hist.* the annual arrival of a supply ship after the ice breaks up.

ship-to-shore ● *adjective* **1** from a ship to land. **2** (of radio telephones etc.) capable of transmitting communication from a point at sea to a point on land. ● *noun* a ship-to-shore radio telephone.

ship·worm *noun* any bivalve mollusc of the genus *Teredo*, esp. *Teredo navalis*, that bores into wooden ships, piers, and other submerged wood. *Also called* TEREDO.

ship·wreck ● *noun* **1 a** the destruction of a ship by a storm, sinking, etc. **b** the remains of a ship so destroyed. **2** (often foll. by *of*) the destruction of hopes, dreams, etc.; total loss or ruin. ● *verb* **1** *transitive* cause (a person or ship etc.) to suffer shipwreck. **2** *transitive* destroy or cause the loss of (a person's hopes, fortunes, etc.). **3** *intransitive* suffer shipwreck.

ship·wright *noun* a carpenter employed in the manufacture or repair of ships.

ship·yard *noun* a large enclosed area adjoining the sea or a major river in which ships are built or repaired.

Shi·raz /ʃəˈraz, ʃɪ-/ a city in SW central Iran; pop. (est. 2002) 1,258,500. The city is noted for the school of miniature painting based there between the 14th and 16th c., and for the manufacture of carpets.

shi·raz /ʃəˈraz, ʃɪ-/ *noun* the variety of Syrah produced in Australia and South Africa. [alteration of French *syrah* influenced by the belief that the vine was brought from Iran by the Crusaders]

Shire /ʃair/ *noun* (also **Shire horse**) a heavy powerful type of draft horse, originally bred in the midland counties of England, usu. bay, brown, black, grey, or chestnut, with feathering on the legs.

shire /ʃair/ *noun* **1** *Brit.* a county. **2** (**the Shires**) *Brit.* **a** the midland counties of England extending northeast from Hampshire and Devon. **b** the fox hunting district of mainly Leicestershire and Northamptonshire. **3** *Austral.* a rural area with its own elected council. [Old English *scīr*, Old High German *scīra* care, official charge: origin unknown]

-shire /ʃər, ʃɪr/ *suffix* forming the names of counties (*Derbyshire*; *Hampshire*).

shire·town *noun* (in Nova Scotia, New Brunswick, and Maine) a county seat.

shirk *verb* **1** *transitive* shrink from; avoid, evade, or attempt to get out of (duty, work, responsibility, fighting, etc.). **2** *intransitive* make a habit or practice of avoiding work or responsibility etc. □ **shirk·er** *noun* [obsolete *shirk* (n.) sponger, perhaps from German *Schurke* scoundrel]

Shir·ley Tem·ple *noun* a non-alcoholic drink usu. consisting of ginger ale and grenadine, served so as to resemble a cocktail. [S. TEMPLE]

shiro plum *noun* a medium-sized yellow plum. [origin unknown: perhaps from Japanese *shiro* white]

shirred /ʃɪrd, ʃərd/ *adjective* **1** (of material, curtains, a dress etc.) gathered with several parallel rows of stitches in order to provide decoration and (of an article of clothing) a better or more comfortable fit. **2** *N Amer.* (of eggs) baked in a muffin cup, ramekin, etc. [19th c.: origin unknown]

shir·ring /ʃɪrɪŋ, ʃərɪŋ/ *noun* multiple rows of stitching in the material of a garment etc. forming a decorative gathering or smocking. [19th c.: origin unknown]

shirt *noun* **1** an article of clothing of a light woven fabric, designed to cover the upper body and arms, having short or long sleeves, a collar, and buttons down the front. **2** any of a number of articles of clothing designed to cover the upper body, having short or long sleeves, and which may or may not have buttons or a collar, including a T-SHIRT, GOLF SHIRT, MUSCLE SHIRT, UNDERSHIRT, etc. □ **get one's shirt in a knot** *see* KNICKERS. **keep one's shirt on** *informal* refrain from becoming excited, anxious, or impatient. **lose one's shirt** *informal* lose all one's money, esp. in a bet, investment, etc. **the shirt off one's back** *informal* one's last remaining possessions. □ **shirt·less** *adjective* [Old English *scyrte*, corresponding to Old Norse *skyrta* (compare SKIRT) from Germanic: compare SHORT]

shirt-dress *noun* a woman's dress similar in cut to a man's shirt, with the bodice buttoning at the front.

shirt·ed *adjective* **1** wearing a shirt. **2** (in *combination*) wearing a shirt of a specified kind or colour (*red-shirted youth*).

shirt front *noun* the breast of a shirt, esp. of a stiffened dress shirt.

shirt·ing *noun* a material for making shirts, especially a fine cotton in plain colours or incorporating a traditional woven stripe.

shirt jacket *noun* a loose-fitting linen jacket or a shirt worn as a jacket.

shirt·maker *noun* a manufacturer of shirts.

shirt sleeve *noun* (usu. in *pl.*) **1** the sleeve of a shirt. **2** (*attributive*, usu. **shirt-sleeve**) **a** designating weather that is warm enough that a jacket is not required (*shirt-sleeve October days*). **b** designating an environment etc. that is casual, informal, or relaxed (*a shirt-sleeve working environment*). **c** designating a person etc. that is hard-working or working-class (*a shirt-sleeve crowd*). □ **in shirt sleeves** wearing a shirt with no jacket etc. over it. □ **shirt-sleeved** *adjective*

shirt·tail ● *noun* (also in *pl.*) the lower curved part of a shirt below the waist. ● *adjective* *N Amer.* designating something small and insignificant or of remote relationship (*shirttail cousin*; *her theory was pretty shirttail*).

shirt·waist *noun* *esp. N Amer.* (also **shirtwaist dress**, **shirt·waist·er**) a dress having a bodice like a shirt or blouse.

shirty *adjective* (**shirt·i·er**, **shirt·i·est**) *informal* angry; annoyed.

shish ke·bab /ˌʃɪʃ kəˈbɒb, -bab/ *noun* = KEBAB. [Turkish *şiş kebabı* from *şiş* skewer, KEBAB roast meat]

shit *coarse slang* ● *transitive & intransitive verb* (**shit·ting**; *past and past participle* **shat**, **shit**, **shit·ted**) **1** *transitive & intransitive* defecate; expel (feces etc.) from the body. **2** *reflexive* **a** defecate in one's own clothing. **b** be scared or worried. **3** *transitive* lie or exaggerate to; deceive. ● *noun* **1** feces. **2** an act of defecating. **3** a despicable or hateful person or thing. **4** nonsense, garbage. **5** serious trouble or difficulty; a hassle or grief. **6** possessions, belongings; stuff. **7** a narcotic drug or substance. **8** (in *pl.*, prec. by *the*) **a** diarrhea. **b** a bad or unfavourable situation etc. **9 a** nothing (*you know shit*). **b** (with *neg.*) anything (*he doesn't know shit*). ● *interjection* an exclamation of anger, disgust, etc. □ **beat** (or **scare** or **annoy** etc.) **the shit out of someone** beat, scare, or annoy etc. a person excessively. **get one's shit together** *N Amer.* organize oneself. **give a shit** = GIVE A CRAP (*see* CRAP[1]). **shit bricks** be anxious, scared, or worried. **shit hits the fan** a serious screw-up or mistake is revealed. **shit out of luck** completely out of luck. **up shit creek** in an unpleasant situation, in an awkward predicament. □ **shit·ter** *noun* [Old English *scítte*, related to Modern Low German *shite* dung, Middle Dutch *schitte* excrement]

shit·can *verb* *N Amer.* coarse slang var. of CAN[2] *verb* 2.

shit disturber *noun* *Cdn* coarse slang a person who enjoys causing trouble or discord. □ **shit disturbing** *noun & adjective*

shite *noun* (esp. *Irish & Brit.*) *var. of* SHIT.

shit-eating *adjective coarse slang* smug, self-satisfied (*a shit-eating grin*).

shit-faced *adjective coarse slang* extremely drunk.

shit for brains *noun coarse slang* a stupid person. □ **have shit for brains** be foolish or stupid.

shit·head *noun* (also **shit·bag**) *coarse slang* a contemptible or worthless person. □ **shit·head·ed** *adjective*

shit·heel *noun coarse slang* a contemptible person.

shit·hole *noun coarse slang* an extremely dirty, shabby, or otherwise unpleasant place.

shit·house *noun coarse slang* **1** an outhouse, washroom, or stall in a washroom. **2** a disgusting, filthy, or messy place. □ **built like a brick shithouse** very sturdily built. **crazy as a shithouse rat** extremely crazy.

shit·kicker *noun N Amer. coarse slang* an unsophisticated or oafish person, esp. from a rural area. □ **shit-kicking** *adjective*

shit·less *predicative adjective coarse slang* □ **scared shitless** extremely frightened, worried, or nervous.

shit list *esp. N Amer. coarse slang* a list of those who have angered or fallen out of favour with someone. [*var.* OF HIT LIST]

shit·load *noun esp. N Amer. coarse slang* a considerable quantity or amount.

shit-scared *adjective coarse slang* extremely frightened.

shit·storm *noun coarse slang* a dispute or uproar.

shit·ter *noun coarse slang* an outhouse, washroom, or toilet.

shit·ty *adjective* (**shit·ti·er**, **shit·ti·est**) *coarse slang* **1 a** ill. **b** bad-tempered. **c** awful, horrible. **2** disgusting, contemptible. **3** covered with excrement. □ **shit·ti·ness** *noun*

shit·work *noun coarse slang* work considered to be menial or routine.

shiur /ˈʃiʊr/ *noun* (*pl.* **shiur·im** /-ɪm/) *Judaism* a Talmudic study session, usu. led by a rabbi. [Hebrew šiˈūr measure, portion]

shiv *noun esp. N Amer. slang* a knife, switchblade, or razor. [prob. from Romany *chiv* 'blade']

Shiva /ˈʃiːvə/ (also **Siva** /ˈsiːvə, ˈʃiːvə/) *Hinduism* one of the major gods, who forms a triad with Brahma and Vishnu. He is worshipped as a fierce destroyer, naked ascetic, lord of the cosmic dance, lord of beasts, and, most commonly, in the form of the phallus (*linga*); he is typically depicted with a third eye in the middle of his forehead. □ **Shiva·ism** *noun* **Shiva·ite** *noun & adjective* [Sanskrit *Śiva*, lit. 'the auspicious one']

shiva /ˈʃɪvə/ (also **shivah**) *noun Judaism* a period of seven days' mourning for the dead beginning immediately after the funeral. □ **sit shiva** mourn. [Hebrew *šibˈāh* seven]

shiv·a·ree /ˈʃɪvəri/ *noun N Amer.* **1** a noisy celebration or gathering. **2** (also **charivari**) a serenade of banging saucepans etc. to a newly married couple. [corruption of CHARIVARI]

shiv·er[1] *intransitive verb* **1** tremble with cold, fear, etc. **2** suffer a quick trembling movement of the body; shudder. ● *noun* **1** a momentary quivering or trembling of the body. **2** (in *pl.*) **a** an attack of shivering, esp. from fear or awe (*sent shivers down my spine*). **b** excitement, fear, or disquiet (*his appearance sent shivers through the room*). □ **shiv·er·ing·ly** *adverb* **shiv·ery** *adjective* [Middle English *chivere*, perhaps from *chavele* chatter (as JOWL[1])]

shiv·er[2] ● *noun* (esp. in *pl.*) each of the small pieces into which esp. glass is shattered when broken; a splinter. ● *transitive & intransitive verb* break into shivers. □ **shiver my timbers** a curse thought to be used by pirates. [Middle English *scifre*, related to Old High German *scivaro* splinter, from Germanic]

Shizu·oka /ˌʃɪzuˈoːkə/ a port on the south coast of the island of Honshu in Japan; pop. (est. 2002) 490,000.

shle·miel *var. of* SCHLEMIEL.

shlep *var. of* SCHLEP.

shlock *var. of* SCHLOCK.

shlock·meister *var. of* SCHLOCKMEISTER.

shlong *var. of* SCHLONG.

shlub *var. of* SCHLUB.

shlump *var. of* SCHLUMP.

shm- *var. of* SCHM-.

shmaltz *var. of* SCHMALTZ.

shmat·te /ˈʃmatə/ *noun* (also **schmat·te**) *N Amer. informal* **1** a rag. **2** a garment (often *attributive*: *the shmatte district*). [Yiddish *schmatte*, from Polish *szmata* rag]

shmoe *noun var. of* SCHMO.

shmooze *var. of* SCHMOOZE.

shmuck *var. of* SCHMUCK[1].

shnor·rer *var. of* SCHNORRER.

Shoah /ˈʃoːə/ *noun* = HOLOCAUST 2.

shoal[1] ● *noun* **1** a school of fish, porpoises, etc. **2** a large number; a multitude. ● *intransitive verb* (of fish) gather in schools. [prob. readoption of Middle Dutch *schōle* SCHOOL[2]]

shoal[2] ● *noun* **1** an area of shallow water. **2** a submerged sandbank visible at low tide. **3** (esp. in *pl.*) hidden danger or difficulty (*steering through the shoals of constitutional reform*). ● *intransitive verb* **1** (of water) become increasingly shallow. **2** (of a ship etc.) move into shallower waters. ● *adjective* (of water) shallow. [Old English *sceald* from Germanic, related to SHALLOW]

sho·chet /ˈʃoːkət/ *noun* (*pl.* **sho·chet·im**) a person officially certified as competent to kill cattle and poultry in the manner prescribed by Jewish law. [Hebrew *šōḥēṭ* slaughtering]

shock[1] ● *noun* **1 a** a sudden and usu. disturbing effect on the mind, feelings, or emotions, resulting in surprise, distress, depression, etc. **b** something causing such an effect (*the news of her pregnancy was a huge shock*). **2** the condition associated with circulatory failure and a sudden drop in blood pressure, characterized esp. by pallor, sweating, a fast but weak pulse, and occasionally fainting, usu. caused by pain, fright, disease, or an injury resulting in severe blood loss. **3** a sudden and violent collision, impact, tremor, etc. **4** = ELECTRIC SHOCK 1. **5** esp. *N Amer.* = SHOCK ABSORBER. ● *verb* **1** *transitive & intransitive* **a** arouse surprise or bewilderment etc. (in a person) (*she shocked us with the news*). **b** arouse outrage, disgust, anger, etc. (in a person) (*I'm shocked to hear you say such a thing*). **2** *intransitive* experience shock (*I don't shock easily*). **3** *transitive* (esp. in *passive*) affect with an electric or physical shock. □ **shock·able** *adjective* **shocked** *adjective* [French *choc*, *choquer*, of unknown origin]

shock[2] *noun* = STOOK[1]. [Middle English, perhaps representing Old English *sc(e)oc* (unrecorded)]

shock[3] *noun* an unkempt or shaggy mass of hair. [compare obsolete *shock(-dog)*, earlier *shough*, shaggy-haired poodle]

shock absorber *noun* **1** a device used on a car etc. to compensate for the roughness of a road by absorbing mechanical shock and vibrations. **2** anything that absorbs shocks. □ **shock absorbency** *noun* **shock absorbent** *adjective* **shock-absorb·ing** *adjective*

shock cord *noun* **1** a heavy elasticized cord designed to fasten or bind something or secure it in place. **2** a similar cord used to absorb shock. □ **shock-corded** *adjective*

shock·er *noun informal* **1** a revelation, rumour, news item, result, etc. that causes surprise or outrage etc. **2** *hist.* a sensational novel, movie, etc.

shock·ing *adjective* causing indignation, scandal, or disgust. □ **shock·ing·ly** *adverb* **shock·ing·ness** *noun*

shocking pink ● *noun* a vibrant or garish shade of pink. ● *adjective* (usu. **shocking-pink**) of this colour.

shock jock *noun N Amer. slang* a radio personality who expresses outrageous or controversial views.

Shock·ley, **Wil·liam Brad·ford** (1910–89), English-born US physicist, who co-developed the transistor in 1948, and shared the Nobel Prize for physics in 1958; he later became controversial because of his views on a supposed connection between race and intelligence.

shock·proof *adjective* able to sustain esp. intense abuse without cracking or breaking etc.

shock resistant *adjective* able to withstand light abuse without cracking or breaking etc. □ **shock resistance** *noun*

shock tactics *plural noun* a method of drawing attention to a subject by being controversial, outrageous, or obnoxious; devices in art, advertising, etc. that are intended to shock rather than inform.

shock treatment *noun Psych.* (also **shock therapy**; in full **electric shock treatment** or **electric shock therapy**) **1** a method of treating depressive patients by artificially inducing convulsions using anaphylactic or electric shock or by drugs. **2** sudden and harsh or drastic measures taken to improve a situation (*shock treatment economics*).

shock troops *plural noun* a group of people likened to troops specially trained for carrying out a sudden assault.

shock wave *noun* **1** a sharp change of pressure in a narrow region travelling through air etc. caused by explosion or by a body moving faster than sound. **2** a series of reactions to or repercussions of a significant event.

shod ● *verb* past and past participle of SHOE. ● *adjective* **1** having or wearing shoes or other footwear. **2** (in combination) having or wearing shoes etc. of a specified kind (*dry-shod*; *roughshod*).

shoddy ● *adjective* (**shod·di·er**, **shod·di·est**) of a poor or inferior quality; shabby, worthless. ● *noun* (pl. **-dies**) **1** an inferior cloth made partly from the shredded fibre of old woollen cloth. **2** this fibre. □ **shod·di·ly** *adverb* **shod·di·ness** *noun* [19th c.: originally dial.]

shoe ● *noun* **1** one of a matching pair of protective coverings for the foot having a sturdy sole and made esp. of leather ending below, at, or just above the ankle. **2** a band of iron shaped to the hard part of the hoof of an animal, esp. a horse, and secured by nails to the underside to prevent wear or injury; a horseshoe. **3** anything resembling a shoe in shape or use. **4** = BRAKE SHOE. **5** a metal rim or casing, esp. one used on the runner of a sleigh. **6** a block, plate, or cap serving as a socket or support for, or to prevent slippage or sinking of, the foot of a pole, ladder, mast, etc. **7** *Photog.* = HOT SHOE. **8** a box from which cards are dealt in blackjack, baccarat, etc., esp. found in casinos. **9** a block attached to an electric vehicle, such as a streetcar, which slides along the conductor wire or rail and collects the current for propulsion. ● *transitive verb* (**shoes**, **shoe·ing**; past and past participle **shod** or **shoed**) **1** fit (esp. a horse etc.) with a shoe or shoes. **2** cover or protect with a shoe or shoes. □ **be in a person's shoes** be in his or her situation, predicament, etc. **dead men's shoes** a position or property etc. coveted by a prospective successor, but available only upon the owner's departure or death. **fill** (or **step into**) **a person's shoes** adequately fill a person's position or role. **if the shoe fits** *N Amer.* if a criticism or description seems applicable, one should be guided by it. **the shoe is on the other foot** the situation is reversed. **wait for the other** (or **second**) **shoe to drop** *N Amer.* be prepared for a further or consequential event or complication to occur. □ **-shoed** *combining form* **shoe·less** *adjective* [Old English *scōh*, *scōg(e)an* from Germanic]

shoe·bill *noun* an African stork-like bird, *Balaeniceps rex*, with a large flattened bill for catching aquatic prey.

shoe·box *noun* **1** the oblong box in which a new pair of shoes is packaged. **2** a small or cramped room, apartment, etc.

shoe·horn ● *noun* a curved piece of metal, plastic, horn, etc., used to ease the heel into a shoe. ● *transitive verb* force into a tight, inadequate, or unsuitable space or position (*he shoehorned himself into his old university football jersey*).

shoe·lace *noun* a short length of string used for tying shoes and boots etc.

shoe leather *noun* **1** leather used to manufacture or repair shoes, esp. when worn through by walking. **2** (*attributive*) designating investigation undertaken by visiting places and people, as opposed to research conducted in a library, laboratory, etc. (*shoe-leather journalism*).

Shoe·maker, Wil·lie (full name William Lee Shoemaker) (1931–2003), the most successful US jockey of the second half of the 20th c. Between 1949 and 1990 he rode in 24 Kentucky Derbies, winning four.

shoe·maker *noun* a person who makes and repairs shoes and boots. □ **shoe·making** *noun*

shoe·pack *noun* (also **shoe·pac**) *N Amer.* **1** a moccasin with an extra sole. **2** a commercially manufactured oiled leather boot, esp. with a rubber sole. [Delaware *seppock*, *sippack* shoes, from *čipahko* moccasins, with later assimilation to SHOE noun, PACK[1] noun]

shoer *noun* a person who shoes horses.

shoe·shine *noun* esp. *N Amer.* an act or instance of cleaning and polishing shoes.

shoe·string *noun* **1** a shoelace. **2** *informal* a small esp. inadequate amount of money (*living on a shoestring*). **3** (*attributive*) designating a business, project, plan, etc. based on or conducted with a limited amount of money (*a shoestring budget*).

shoestring catch *noun* *Baseball* a play in which a charging fielder catches a quickly sinking ball just above the level of the playing field or above the top of his or her shoe.

shoestring potatoes *plural noun* potatoes cut into long thin strips and deep-fried.

shoe·tree *noun* a device made of a block of wood or a piece of moulded metal shaped to fit the inside of a shoe, used to preserve its shape when not being worn.

sho·far /ˈʃoːfɜr/ *noun* (pl. **-fars** or **sho·froth** /ˈʃoːfroːt/) a trumpet made of a ram's horn used by Jews in religious ceremonies and, in Biblical times, as a war trumpet. [Hebrew *šōp̄ār*, pl. *šōp̄ārôt*]

sho·gun /ˈʃoːɡʌn/ *noun* any of a succession of hereditary commanders-in-chief in feudal Japan who were generally the real rulers of the country until the last shogunate (the Tokugawa dynasty) was replaced by a restoration of imperial power in 1867. [Japanese, = general, from Chinese *jiang jun*]

sho·gun·ate /ˈʃoːɡʊnət/ *noun* **1** the title or position of shogun. **2** the period of a shogun's rule.

shoji /ˈʃoːʒi/ *noun* (pl. same) (in full **shoji screen**) (in Japan) a sliding outer or inner door made of a latticed screen covered usu. with white translucent paper. [Japanese]

Sho·la·pur /ˈʃoːlə,pʊr/ a city of W India, on the Deccan plateau in the state of Maharashtra; pop. (2001) 873,000.

Sholo·khov /ˈʃɒləkɒf/ **Mik·hail Alek·san·dro·vich** (1905–84), Soviet novelist, whose major work is the epic novel of the Russian Revolution, *And Quiet Flows the Don* (1928–40); he was awarded the Nobel Prize for literature in 1965.

Sho·na /ˈʃoːnə/ ● *noun* **1** a member of any of several related Bantu-speaking peoples inhabiting Mashonaland in Zimbabwe and parts of Zambia and Mozambique. **2** the group of closely related languages of these peoples. ● *adjective* of or pertaining to the Shona or their languages.

shone past and past participle of SHINE.

shoo ● *interjection* an exclamation used to frighten or drive away. ● *transitive verb* (**shoos**, **shooed**) **1** utter the word 'shoo!' in order to drive away. **2** drive or urge (a person, animal, etc.) in a desired direction. [imitative]

shoo·fly pie *noun* *N Amer.* an open-faced pie with a molasses or brown sugar filling, topped with streusel. [referring to the need to wave flies away from the sweet filling]

shoo-in *noun* *N Amer. informal* something sure to succeed or win; a certainty. [originally 'the winner of a horse race for which the result has been fraudulently arranged,' from obsolete *shoo* (v.) allow (a horse) to win easily]

shook[1] ● *verb* past of SHAKE. ● *predicative adjective* *informal* (foll. by *up*) emotionally or physically disturbed; upset.

shook[2] *noun* *N Amer.* a set of staves and headings for a cask, ready for fitting together. [18th c.: origin unknown]

shoosh ● *verb* **1** *transitive & intransitive* move or cause to move with a rushing sound. **2** *transitive* SHUSH 1. ● *interjection* calling for silence. [imitative]

shoot ● *verb* (past and past participle **shot**) **1** *transitive* **a** cause (a gun, bow, etc.) to discharge a bullet, arrow, etc. **b** discharge (a bullet, arrow, etc.) from a gun, bow, etc. **c** kill or wound (a person, animal, etc.) with a bullet, arrow, etc. from a gun, bow, etc. **2** *intransitive* discharge a gun etc. esp. in a specified way (*shoots well*). **3 a** *transitive & intransitive* discharge, propel, emit, etc., esp. violently or swiftly (*the iron shoots steam onto the clothes*; *blood shot from the wound*). **b** *transitive* cast, issue (a smile, glance, etc.). **4** *intransitive* come or go quickly or vigorously (*the car came shooting around the corner*). **5** *transitive* **a** (of a plant etc.) put forth buds etc. **b** (of a bud etc.) appear, germinate. **6** *transitive* a film or photograph (a scene, subject, etc.). **b** use up or fill (a roll of film) in photographing or filming a scene etc. **7 a** *transitive & intransitive* (in hockey, basketball, etc.) direct (a puck or ball) toward the net, basket, etc. **b** *transitive* *Basketball* successfully make or score (a basket, three-pointer, etc.). **c** *transitive* *Basketball* practise taking shots at (a basket) (*went out to shoot hoops*). **8** *transitive* *N Amer.* **a** play a game or round of (pool, golf, craps, etc.). **b** *Golf* make (a specified score) for a round or hole. **c** throw (a die or dice). **9** *slang* **a** *intransitive* (foll. by *up*) take a drug, esp. intravenously. **b** *transitive* (often foll. by *up*) inject (esp. oneself) with a drug. **c** *transitive* take or inject (a particular drug). **10 a** *intransitive* hunt game, esp. with a gun. **b** *transitive* go hunting for (duck, deer, etc.). **c** *transitive* esp. *Brit.* cross (land, an estate, etc.) while hunting game. **11** *transitive* navigate or swiftly pass over (rapids, falls, etc.). **12** *intransitive* (usu. foll. by *through*, *up*) (of a pain) pass suddenly and sharply with a stabbing sensation. **13** (often foll. by *out*) **a** *intransitive* project abruptly (*the mountain seems to shoot out of the water*). **b** *transitive* extend or project (*he shot out his glove to make the catch*). **14** *transitive* slide (a bolt) into position to lock or unlock a door etc. **15** *transitive* (usu. foll. by *for*) plan, aim (*we'll shoot for a Halloween launch date*). ● *noun* **1** a competition in shooting. **2** a film or photography session. **3** a young branch or new growth of a plant. **4** *Brit.* **a** a hunting party, expedition, etc. **b** land shot over for game. **5** = CHUTE[1]. ● *interjection* *informal* **1** an invitation for a comment, question, etc. **2** *N Amer.* an exclamation of disappointment, anger, frustration, etc. □ **shoot back** retort. **shoot one's bolt** see BOLT[1]. **shoot down 1** kill (a person) by shooting. **2** cause (an aircraft, its pilot, etc.) to crash by shooting. **3** reject (a person, argument, proposal, etc.). **shoot from the hip** *informal* speak or act spontaneously or hastily, usu. without proper consideration. **shoot it out** *slang* engage in a decisive confrontation. **shoot a line** *slang* speak misleadingly. **shoot one's cuffs** pull the cuffs of one's shirt out to project beyond the cuffs of one's jacket or coat. **shoot oneself in the foot** *informal* inadvertently make a situation worse, esp. while trying to make it better. **shoot one's mouth off** *slang* talk too much or indiscreetly. **shoot the breeze** (or **bull** or **shit**) *slang* chat idly. **shoot up 1** grow rapidly, esp. (of a person) grow taller. **2** rise suddenly. **3** terrorize (a district) by indiscriminate shooting. □ **shoot·abil·ity** *noun* **shoot·able** *adjective* **shoot·ist** *noun* [Old English *scēotan* from Germanic: compare SHEET[1], SHOT[1], SHUT]

shoot·around *noun* *Basketball* a practice or pre-game warm-up in which players take turns shooting baskets.

shoot-'em-up *noun* *slang* **1** a fast-moving show or movie, esp. a Western, which features extensive shooting and gunplay. **2** (*attributive*) designating movies, games, etc. based on or featuring abundant use of weapons and violence.

shoot·er *noun* **1** a person who discharges a firearm. **2 a** (in *combination*) a gun or other device for shooting (*peashooter*; *six-shooter*). **b** *slang* a firearm. **3** a player who takes a shot or is in position to take a shot in hockey, basketball, etc. **4** a small drink of alcohol, esp. liquor. **5** *slang* a person who takes drugs intravenously. **6** a playing marble used to knock other marbles out of the circle (*compare* ALLEY[2]).

shoot·ing ● *noun* **1 a** the wounding or killing of esp. a person by gunfire. **b** the discharge of a firearm (*they ducked when they heard shooting*). **2 a** the hobby or sport of hunting game. **b** the hobby or sport of firing at targets (*skeet shooting*). **3** (in hockey and basketball etc.) the ability to shoot accurately. ● *adjective* (of a pain etc.) sharp and spreading quickly. □ **the whole shooting match** *informal* everything.

shooting gallery *noun* **1** a long room or fairground booth used for recreational shooting at usu. moving targets with real or simulated guns. **2** *N Amer. slang* a place where addictive drugs may be illicitly obtained and injected.

shooting guard *noun* *Basketball* **1** the second guard on a team, usu. having strong ball-handling skills and good three-point shooting. **2** the position played by this guard (*compare* POINT GUARD).

shooting range *noun* esp. *N Amer.* a field equipped with targets for practising one's accuracy in rifle shooting.

shooting script *noun* the final draft of a movie or television script, providing an outline of the scenes and detailing the order in which they are to be shot.

shooting star *noun* **1** a small meteor moving rapidly and burning up upon entering the earth's atmosphere. **2** *N Amer.* a plant of the primrose family *Dodecatheon meadia* and related species, with pink, swept-back petals. *Also called* AMERICAN COWSLIP.

shooting stick *noun* a walking stick with a makeshift seat that folds down from the top.

shooting war *noun* a war in which there is actual fighting and physical combat (*opp.* COLD WAR, WAR OF NERVES).

shoot·out *noun* **1** a decisive gunfight. **2** (in full **penalty shootout**) (in soccer, hockey, etc.) a method of deciding games ending in a tie in which each team takes a specified number of penalty shots, the team scoring the most being declared the winner. **3** esp. *Hockey* a close high-scoring game.

shop ● *noun* **1** a building, room, or other establishment used for the retail sale of esp. specialty goods or services (*souvenir shop*; *barber shop*; *coffee shop*). **2 a** a building or room equipped to carry out repairs or a specific type of manufacture. **b** = BODY SHOP. **3** *N Amer.* **a** a room in a school equipped for teaching woodworking or mechanical skills etc. for use in a workshop. **b** (in full **shop class**) the study of these skills as a course. **4** one's trade, profession, or business, esp. as a subject of conversation (*talk shop*). **5** esp. *Brit. informal* an act of going shopping (*we have to do a big shop this week*). ● *verb* (**shopped**, **shop·ping**) **1** *intransitive* **a** go to one or several stores or shops to buy goods. **b** visit shops to look at merchandise without the express intention of making a purchase; window shop. **2** *intransitive* order and buy merchandise by mail, phone, etc. **3** *transitive* shop at (a particular store), esp. regularly. **4** *transitive* (often foll. by *around*) sell or propose (an idea, information, etc.) to several prospective buyers. □ **all over the shop** *Brit. informal* **1** in disorder (*the weather's been all over the shop lately*). **2** in every place (*looked for it all over the shop*). **3** wildly (*hitting out all over the shop*) (*compare* ALL OVER THE MAP (*see* MAP)). □ **set up shop** establish oneself in business etc. **shop around** visit several stores, service providers, etc. in search of the best price or service. **shop till one drops** *N Amer. informal* shop excessively, esp. to the point of exhaustion. □ **shop·less**

adjective **shop·py** *adjective* [Old French *eschoppe* booth, from Middle Low German *schoppe*, Old High German *scopf* porch]

shop·ahol·ic *noun* *jocular* an avid or compulsive shopper. [blend of SHOP + ALCOHOLIC]

shop assistant *noun* *Brit.* a sales clerk.

shop floor *noun* *Brit. & Cdn* **1** the working environment in a factory, esp. as distinct from a management environment. **2** the workers in a factory etc. **3** (*attributive*) (usu. **shop-floor**) working or occurring in or pertaining to a factory, workshop, etc. (*shop-floor productivity*).

shop·front *noun* *Brit.* = STOREFRONT 1.

shop·girl *noun* *dated* a female sales clerk.

shop·house *noun* (in SE Asia) a shop opening on to the pavement and also used as the owner's residence.

shop·keep·er *noun* a person who owns or manages a shop or store. □ **shop·keep·ing** *noun*

shop·lift·er *noun* a person who poses as a customer to steal merchandise from a store. □ **shop·lift** *transitive & intransitive verb* **shop·lift·ing** *noun*

shoppe *noun* a shop or small store having a usu. spurious old-fashioned charm or quaintness. [alteration of SHOP]

shop·per *noun* **1** (often *attributive*) the purchase of merchandise etc. (*shopping expedition*). **2** goods purchased (*put the shopping on the table*).

shopping bag *noun* a bag made of paper, plastic, nylon, or cotton, used for carrying groceries or other items bought in a store.

shopping cart *noun* *N Amer.* **1** a large and sturdy rectangular usu. steel cart with four wheels used by customers in a supermarket etc. to carry groceries while shopping. **2** = BUNDLE BUGGY. **3** a list of items which one has selected for purchase while shopping online.

shopping centre *noun* a shopping mall (*see* MALL 1).

shopping channel *noun* (in full **home shopping channel**) a television station whose programming features items for sale that may be ordered by telephone.

shopping list *noun* **1** a list of purchases to be made. **2** a list of items to be considered or acted on (*a whole shopping list of potential projects*).

shopping mall *noun* = MALL 1.

shopping plaza *noun* *N Amer.* = PLAZA 1.

shopping trolley *noun* *Brit.* = SHOPPING CART 1.

shop-soiled *adjective* *Brit.* = SHOPWORN.

shop steward *noun* a person elected by workers in a factory etc. to represent them in dealings with management.

shop·talk *noun* conversation about one's job or business.

shop window *noun* **1** esp. *Brit.* = STORE WINDOW. **2** an opportunity for displaying skills, talents, etc.

shop worker *noun* a person who works in a factory or workshop.

shop·worn *adjective* **1** (of an item for sale) faded or dirty from being on display in a store. **2** (of a person, idea, etc.) no longer fresh or new; hackneyed or stale from overuse.

shore[1] *noun* **1** the land at the edge of the sea or a large body of water; a coast. **2** land, as opposed to sea (*ship-to-shore*). **3** (usu. in *pl.*) a country, esp. one bounded by a coast (*the news has travelled to foreign shores*). **4** *Law* = SEASHORE 2. □ **shore·less** *adjective* **shore·ward** *adjective & adverb* **shore·wards** *adverb* [Middle Dutch, Middle Low German *schōre*, perhaps related to SHEAR]

shore[2] ● *transitive verb* (often foll. by *up*) **1** reinforce; strengthen or fortify (*a new plan to shore up their ailing economy*). **2** support with a shore or shores. ● *noun* a beam of timber or iron set obliquely against an unsafe wall, tree, ship, etc., as a support. □ **shor·ing** *noun* [Middle Dutch, Middle Low German *schōre* prop, of unknown origin]

shore[3] *see* SHEAR.

shore·bird *noun* a bird which frequents the shore, e.g a plover or a sandpiper.

shore dinner *noun* *N Amer.* **1** a dinner served by a restaurant, community group, etc., including usu. copious quantities of shellfish. **2** = SHORE LUNCH.

shore·fast *attributive adjective* LANDFAST.

shore·front *noun* = SHORESIDE.

shore ice *noun* (also **shorefast ice**) *N Amer.* a flat expanse of sea ice that has become anchored to the shore.

shore lead *noun* a band of open water between an ice pack and the shore.

shore leave *noun* **1** permission granted to a sailor etc. to go on shore. **2** a period of time on shore by a sailor on leave.

shore·line *noun* the line along which a stretch of water, esp. a sea or lake, meets the shore.

shore lunch *noun Cdn* a meal cooked on a lakeshore or riverbank etc. as part of a fishing trip or other boating excursion, featuring freshly caught fish, pan-fried.

shore·side *noun* the strip of land adjoining a shore (also *attributive: shoreside golf course*).

shorn ● *verb past participle of* SHEAR. ● *adjective* **1 a** (of a person or animal) having had all or most of the hair of the head, wool, etc. removed; bald. **b** (of hair, wool, etc.) having been cut. **2** (usu. foll. by *of*) deprived.

short ● *adjective* **1 a** measuring little; not long from end to end (*a short distance*). **b** not long in duration; brief (*a short time ago; had a short life*). **c** seeming less than the stated amount (*this week has seemed short*). **2** of little height; not tall (*a short tower; was shorter than average*). **3 a** (usu. foll. by *of, on*) having a partial or total lack; deficient (*short of spoons; is rather short on sense*). **b** not having the amount expected, stated, or required (*I seem to be short a dollar*). **c** not reaching a great distance or the distance expected or required; not far or far enough (*within short range; the throw was short*). **4 a** concise; brief (*kept his speech short*). **b** curt, abrupt; uncivil (*was short with her*). **5** (of memory) of limited range; unable to remember distant events. **6** *Phonetics & Prosody* **a** (of a vowel or syllable) having the lesser of two recognized durations; unstressed. **b** (of a vowel) categorized as short with regard to quality and length, such as the short vowel *i* in the word *bit* as opposed to *bite* (compare LONG[1] *adjective* 8c). **7 a** (of pastry) having a high fat content and crumbling into small flakes when broken. **b** (of clay or metal etc.) brittle, fragile. **8** esp. *Stock Exch.* **a** (of stocks and other commodities) sold in advance of being acquired, in the hope that the price will fall and a profit can be made. **b** (of a broker, position in the market, etc.) buying or based on such stocks or commodities. **c** (of a bill of exchange) maturing at an early date. **9** *Baseball* (of a position in the field) near, close; shallow (*he was playing in short centre field*). **10** (of betting odds) offering nearly equal stakes for a winning wager. **11** *Brit.* (of an alcoholic drink or liquor) undiluted. ● *adverb* **1** before the natural or expected time or place; abruptly (*pulled up short; cut short the celebrations*). **2** (sell or trade etc.) without sufficient quantities of a particular commodity. ● *noun* **1** a short-circuit. **2** a short film. **3** *Baseball* **a** = SHORTSTOP 2. **b** the area of the field covered by the shortstop. **4** *Stock Exch.* **a** a person who sells short. **b** (in *pl.*) stocks due for early payment or redemption. **5** *Brit. informal* a drink of liquor. ● *verb* **1** *transitive & intransitive* short-circuit. **2** *transitive* esp. *N Amer. informal* cheat (a person) out of something; shortchange (*he shorted me a dollar when he gave me my change*). **3** *transitive & intransitive Stock Exch.* acquire short stocks or commodities. □ **be caught** (or **taken**) **short 1** be put at a disadvantage, esp. by being without something one badly needs. **2** *informal* urgently need to urinate or defecate. **fall** (or **come**) **short of** fail to reach or amount to. **for short** as an abbreviation (*I'm Thomas, but you can call me Tom for short*). **go short** (often foll. by *of*) not have enough. **have** (or **get**) **by the short and curlies** (or **short hairs**) *informal* have under one's complete control. **in short** to use few words; briefly. **in short supply** scarce. **in the short term** (or **run**) over a short period of time. **make short work of** accomplish, dispose of, consume, etc. quickly. **pull up** (or **bring up**) **short** stop or pause abruptly or before the expected destination. **short and curlies** (also **short hairs**) *slang* pubic hair. **short and sweet** esp. *ironic* brief and enjoyable. **short end of the stick** the less favourable part of a deal. **short for** an abbreviation for (*'Bob' is short for 'Robert'*). **short of 1** see sense 3a of *adjective*. **2** without going so far as; except (*did everything short of destroying it; nothing short of a miracle*). **3** distant from (*two miles short of home*). **short of breath** panting, out of breath. □ **short·ish** *adjective* **short·ness** *noun* [Old English *sceort* from Germanic: compare SHIRT, SKIRT]

short-acting *adjective* (of a drug or medication etc.) effective soon after being taken or administered but lasting only a brief time so that repeated doses are required for extended treatment.

short·age *noun* (often foll. by *of*) a deficiency or lack of something needed (*a shortage of funds; an oil shortage*).

short·bread *noun* a crisp rich crumbly type of cookie made with butter, flour, and sugar.

short·cake *noun* a cake with a filling of fruit and whipped cream (*strawberry shortcake*).

short chain *noun Chem.* a relatively small number of esp. carbon atoms linked together in a line (also *attributive: short-chain protein*).

short·change *transitive verb* **1** cheat (a customer), accidentally or intentionally, by giving insufficient change. **2** cheat or treat unfairly.

short-circuit ● *noun* a faulty electrical connection resulting in a condition of low resistance between two points in a circuit, often causing a flow of excess current which could damage an appliance or cause a fuse to blow. ● *verb* **1** *intransitive* (of an electrical appliance or apparatus) fail or cease working as a result of a short-circuit. **2** *intransitive* collapse or self-destruct. **3** *transitive* bypass or avoid (a task etc.) by taking a more direct route or course of action.

short·com·ing *noun* a fault, e.g. in a person's character, a plan, or system.

short·cover·ing *noun* the buying of stock or goods to cover a short sale.

short·cut ● *noun* **1** a route between two places that shortens the distance travelled or the time required to make a journey. **2** a quick or easy way of accomplishing something. ● *transitive verb* (**-cut·ting**; past and past participle **-cut**) reduce the amount of time or effort required to complete (a journey, job, etc.).

short division *noun Math.* division in which the quotient is written directly without being worked out in writing.

short-eared owl *noun* a medium-sized whitish owl with brown streaks, *Asio flammeus*, with very short ear tufts, frequenting open country and hunting at dawn or dusk.

short·en *verb* **1** *transitive & intransitive* become or make shorter or short; curtail. **2** *transitive Naut.* reduce the amount of (sail spread).

short·en·ing *noun* **1** a soft fat that produces a crisp flaky effect in baked products, such as pastry, esp. a solid white fat made from hydrogenated vegetable oils, sometimes combined with lard. **2** an act or instance of making something short or shorter. **3** an act or instance of abbreviating a word, such as *ad* is a shortening of *advertisement*.

short·fall *noun* **1** a failure to reach esp. a financial goal or expectations; a failure to meet budget. **2** an esp. financial loss or deficit below what was expected (*a $250 million shortfall*).

short fuse *noun informal* a quick temper. □ **short-fused** *adjective*

short game *noun Golf* the part of the game concerned with approaching and putting.

short·grass *noun N Amer.* any of a number of short grasses especially resistant to drought (also *attributive: shortgrass prairie*).

short·hair *noun* a short-haired domestic cat or dog.

short-haired *adjective* having short hair.

short·hand *noun* **1** a method of writing or typing in abbreviations and symbols esp. for taking dictation quickly (also *attributive: shorthand typist*). **2** (often foll. by *for*) any abbreviated or symbolic mode of expression; code (*'lunch-pail' became shorthand for anything characteristic of the working class*).

short-handed ● *adjective* **1** not having the usual number of workers etc; understaffed. **2** *Hockey* (of a team) playing with fewer than six players on the ice, esp. because one or more players is serving a penalty. **3** *Hockey* **a** (of a goal) scored by a team playing with fewer players on the ice than their opponent, esp. while killing a penalty. **b** (of an opportunity or situation etc.) occurring while or because a team has fewer than six players on the ice. ● *adverb* with fewer players, workers, etc. than usual (*they were forced to play short-handed for the rest of the game*).

short-haul *noun* the transport of goods over a short distance (also *attributive: short-haul route*).

short hop *Baseball* ● *noun* **1** the action of a ball that bounces directly in front of a fielder and is therefore usu. difficult to catch. **2** a ball that bounces this way. ● *transitive verb* (usu. **short-hop**) catch (a ball) on a short hop.

Short·horn *noun* a breed of beef or dairy cattle with short horns.

short hundredweight *noun see* HUNDREDWEIGHT 3.

shortie *noun* (also **shorty**) an article of clothing that is short in length, such as a nightdress or raincoat (also *attributive: shortie pyjamas*).

short list ● *noun* a list of selected candidates for a position from which a final choice is made. ● *transitive verb* (usu. **short·list**) add (a person) to a list of candidates for a position.

short-lived *adjective* lasting only for a short time; ephemeral.

short loin *noun* a cut of beef from the hindquarters starting behind the ribs, from which porterhouse and T-bone steaks are cut.

short·ly *adverb* **1** in a short time; before long; soon (*we will be arriving shortly*). **2** (foll. by *before* or *after*) a short time (before or after); not long (*they arrived shortly before noon; she arrived shortly after him*). **3** in a few words; briefly or curtly.

short notice *noun* an announcement or warning of an event etc. made only briefly before its occurrence (*she gave him such short notice* *before leaving*). □ **on** (or **at**) **short notice** with little advance warning.

short order *noun N Amer.* restaurant food that can be prepared and served quickly; fast food (also *attributive*: *short-order cook*). □ **in short order** quickly, immediately.

Short Parliament the first of two parliaments summoned by Charles I in 1640, which he dismissed after only three weeks because it insisted on seeking a general redress of grievances against him before granting the money he required (*compare* LONG PARLIAMENT).

short-range *adjective* **1** operating or capable of operating within a small or limited area (*short-range missile*). **2** relating to a fairly immediate future time (*short-range forecast*).

short rib *noun* **1** any of the lower ribs which are not attached to the breastbone. *Also called* FLOATING RIB. **2** *N Amer.* a piece of meat containing one or more of these ribs.

short-run *adjective* **1** taken or considered on a short time scale; short-term. **2** *Printing* produced in or relating to a print run of relatively few copies.

shorts *plural noun* **1** a pair of pants extending only as far as the knees or higher. **2** *N Amer.* men's underpants.

short-sheet *transitive verb* (as a trick or joke) fold the top sheet of (a bed) in half before tucking it in such a way that it appears to be the top and bottom sheets, so that the person getting into the bed will only be able to enter halfway.

short shrift *noun* **1** brusque or dismissive treatment. **2** *archaic* little time given to a prisoner between condemnation and execution or punishment.

short side *noun Hockey* the area between a goalie and the goalpost closest to the shooter (*he scored high on the short side*).

short-sighted *adjective* **1** unable to focus except on comparatively near objects. **2** lacking imagination, foresight, or proper consideration (*a short-sighted plan*). □ **short sight** *noun* **short-sighted·ly** *adverb* **short-sighted·ness** *noun*

short-sleeved *adjective* (of a shirt etc.) with sleeves not reaching below the elbow.

short-staffed *adjective* having insufficient staff.

short·stop *noun Baseball* **1** the player that covers the part of the infield between second and third base. **2** this position.

short story *noun* a prose narrative shorter than a novel usu. involving only a few characters and concentrating on a single event or theme.

short straw *noun* the shortest straw drawn randomly from a bunch, usu. committing the person choosing it to an onerous or undesirable task.

short stuff *noun N Amer. informal* (as a term of address) a small or short person, esp. a child.

short-tempered *adjective* quick to lose one's temper; easily irritable; irascible. □ **short temper** *noun*

short-term *adjective* **1** lasting for, occurring in, or pertaining to a relatively short period of time (*short-term solution*). **2** maturing or becoming effective after a short period (*short-term deposit*). □ **in the short term** for the near or immediate future.

short-termism *noun Brit.* concentration on short-term projects etc. for immediate profit at the expense of long-term security.

short time *noun* the condition of working fewer than the regular hours per day or days per week (also *attributive*: *short-time worker*).

short title *noun* an abbreviated form of a title of a book etc.

short ton *noun see* TON 1.

short-track speed skating *noun* a form of speed skating competition performed on a standard-size hockey rink rather than on a speed skating oval.

short waist *noun* a high or shallow waist of a dress.

short-waisted *adjective* (of a person's body or article of clothing) having a shorter than average distance between the shoulders and waist.

short·wave *noun* **1** a radio wave with a wavelength of less than about 100 metres, a frequency of three to 30 MHz. **2** (*attributive*) designating radio communication or broadcasting systems employing such waves.

short-winded *adjective* **1** liable to become out of breath with minimal exertion. **2** incapable of sustained effort.

shorty *noun* (pl. **-ies**) *informal* or *derogatory* **1** a person shorter than average. **2** *var. of* SHORTIE.

Sho·sho·ne /ʃəˈʃoːni/ (also **Sho·sho·ni**) ● *noun* **1** a member of a N American Aboriginal people of Wyoming, Idaho, Nevada, and

neighbouring states. **2** the Uto-Aztecan language of these people. ● *adjective* of or pertaining to the Shoshone or their language. [19th c.: origin unknown]

Shosta·ko·vich /ˌʃɒstəˈkoːvitʃ/ **Dmitri (Dmitrie·vich)** (1906–75), Russian composer. One of the most important figures in 20th-c. music, he experimented with atonality and 12-note techniques; his works include 15 symphonies, operas, and many chamber pieces.

shot[1] *noun* **1** the act or an instance of firing a gun, cannon, etc. (*several shots were heard*). **2** an attempt to hit by shooting or throwing etc. (*took a shot at him*). **3 a** a single non-explosive missile for a cannon, gun, etc. **b** (*pl.* same or **shots**) a small lead pellet used in quantity in a single charge or cartridge in a shotgun. **c** (treated as *pl.*) these collectively. **4** *informal* a person having a specified skill with a gun etc. (*is not a good shot*). **5 a** *Sport* a stroke, kick, throw, etc., esp. one made with the aim of scoring. **b** *informal* an attempt to guess or do something (*gave it my best shot*). **6 a** a photograph. **b** a film sequence photographed continuously by one camera. **7** a heavy ball thrown by a shot putter. **8** the launch of a space rocket (*a moon shot*). **9** the range, reach, or distance to or at which a thing will carry or act. **10** a remark aimed at a person. **11** *informal* **a** a drink of esp. hard liquor. **b** an injection of a drug, vaccine, etc. (*has had his shots*). **12** *informal* a thing with a chance of success (frequently with specified odds). □ **have** (or **take**) **a shot at** *informal* make an attempt at; try. **give something a shot** try something. **like a shot** *informal* without hesitation; willingly. **shot across the bow(s)** *see* BOW[3]. **shot in the arm** *informal* stimulus or encouragement. **shot in the dark** a mere guess. [Old English *sc(e)ot*, *gesc(e)ot*, from Germanic]

shot[2] ● *verb* past and past participle of SHOOT. ● *adjective* **1** (of coloured material) woven so as to show different colours at different angles (*shot silk*). **2** *informal* **a** ruined; worn out (*the transmission's shot*). **b** exhausted. **3** (of a board edge) accurately planed. □ **be** (or **get**) **shot of** *Brit. slang* be (or get) rid of. **shot through** permeated or suffused. **shot to pieces 1** killed, destroyed, heavily damaged etc. by gunfire. **2** in a state of ruin or collapse. [past participle of SHOOT]

shot[3] *noun informal* a sum of money owed or due (*paid the whole shot*). [Middle English, = SHOT[1]: compare Old English *scēotan* shoot, pay, contribute, and SCOT]

shot-blasting *noun* the cleaning of metal etc. by the impact of a stream of shot. □ **shot-blast** *transitive verb*

shot clock *noun Basketball* a clock which indicates how much time a team has to take a shot.

shot·crete *noun* a mixture of cement, sand, and water applied through a hose. [SHOT[2] + (CON)CRETE *adjective & noun*]

shot glass *noun N Amer.* a small, often graduated, glass for measuring or serving small amounts of liquor.

shot·gun ● *noun* a smoothbore gun for firing small shot at short range, used esp. for hunting. ● *adjective* **1** of, pertaining to, or resembling a shotgun. **2** *US* designating a house or other building with rooms on either side of a long central hallway. **3** made or done hastily or under pressure of necessity. **4** wide-ranging, but random. ● *transitive verb* **1** shoot with a shotgun. **2** force as if with a shotgun; bring about forcibly. □ **ride shotgun** *see* RIDE. □ **shot·gun·ner** *noun* **shot·gun·ning** *noun*

shotgun formation *noun Football* an offensive formation to facilitate passing in which the quarterback is positioned several yards behind the line of scrimmage.

shotgun marriage *noun* (also **shotgun wedding**) *informal* **1** an enforced or hurried wedding, esp. because of the bride's pregnancy. **2** any enforced alliance, partnership, etc.

shotgun mike *noun* (also **shotgun microphone**) a highly directional microphone with a long barrel to be directed towards a distant source of sound.

shot·making *noun* the playing of (esp. successful or attacking) strokes in golf, tennis, etc. □ **shot·maker** *noun*

Sho·to·kan /ʃoːˈtoːkan/ *noun* one of the five main styles of karate. [Japanese, from *shō* 'right, true' + *to* 'way' + *kan* 'mansion']

shot put *noun* an athletic contest in which a shot is thrown a great distance. □ **shot put·ter** *noun*

shot rock *noun Curling* the rock lying nearest to the centre of the rings.

should *auxiliary verb* (3rd sing. **should**) past of SHALL, used esp.: **1** esp. *Brit.* in reported speech, esp. with the reported element in the 1st person (*I said I should be home by evening*). **2 a** to express a duty, obligation, or likelihood; = OUGHT[1] (*I should tell you; you should have been more careful; they should have arrived by now*). **b** (in the 1st person) to express a tentative suggestion (*I should like to say something*). **3 a** esp. *Brit.*

u: m**oo**d   ai m**y**   əi p**i**pe   au br**ow**n   ʌu h**ou**se   ei d**ay**   ɔi b**oy**   ā fr**an**glais   ã Ca**n**adien   ɔ̃ Br**ay**on   (*see over for consonants*) expressing the conditional mood in the 1st person (*compare* WOULD) (*I should have been killed if I had gone*). **b** forming a conditional protasis or indefinite clause (*if you should see him; should they arrive, tell them where to go*). **4** expressing purpose = MAY, MIGHT¹ (*in order that we should not worry*).

shoul·der • *noun* **1 a** the part of the body at which the arm, foreleg, or wing is attached. **b** (in full **shoulder joint**) the end of the upper arm joining with the collarbone and shoulder blade. **c** either of the two projections below the neck from which the arms hang. **2** the upper foreleg and shoulder blade of a pig, lamb, etc. when butchered. **3** (often in *pl.*) **a** the upper part of the back and arms. **b** this part of the body regarded as capable of bearing a burden or blame, providing comfort, etc. (*needs a shoulder to cry on*). **4** a strip of ground bordering a road, where vehicles may stop in an emergency (*pulled over on to the shoulder*). **5** a part of a garment covering the shoulder. **6** a part of anything resembling a shoulder in form or function, as in a bottle, mountain, tool, etc. • *verb* **1 a** *transitive* push with the shoulder; jostle. **b** *intransitive* make one's way by jostling (*shouldered through the crowd*). **2** *transitive* take (a burden etc.) on one's shoulders (*shouldered the family's problems*). □ **put one's shoulder to the wheel** make an effort. **shoulder arms** hold a rifle with the barrel against the shoulder and the butt in the hand. **shoulder to shoulder 1** side by side. **2** with closed ranks or united effort. □ **shoul·dered** *adjective* (also in *combination*). [Old English *sculdor* from West Germanic]

shoulder bag *noun* a woman's handbag that can be hung from the shoulder.

shoulder belt *noun* a seat belt or other strap passing over one shoulder and under the opposite arm.

shoulder blade *noun* either of the large flat bones of the upper back; the scapula.

shoulder butt *noun see* BUTT³ *noun* 2.

shoulder check *noun* a quick glance backwards over the shoulder made by the driver of a vehicle when changing lanes etc.

shoulder-high *adjective & adverb* up to or as high as the shoulders.

shoulder holster *noun* a gun holster worn in the armpit.

shoulder joint *noun see* SHOULDER *noun* 1b.

shoulder-length *adjective* (of hair etc.) reaching to the shoulders.

shoulder pad *noun* **1** a pad sewn into a garment to bulk out the shoulder. **2** a protective pad for the shoulders, worn when playing hockey etc.

shoulder season *noun* a travel period between peak and off-peak seasons.

shoulder strap *noun* **1** a strip of cloth going over the shoulder from front to back of a garment. **2** a strap suspending a bag etc. from the shoulder.

shoulder surfing *noun* the practice of looking over the shoulder of a person to obtain a confidential code or password, esp. spying on the user of a bank machine, in order to obtain their PIN. □ **shoulder surf** *intransitive verb* **shoulder surfer** *noun*

shouldn't *contraction* should not.

shout • *verb* **1** *intransitive* make a loud cry or vocal sound; speak loudly (*shouted for attention*). **2** *transitive* say or express loudly; call out (*shouted that the coast was clear*). **3** *transitive & intransitive* Austral. & NZ *informal* treat (another person) to drinks etc. • *noun* **1** a loud cry expressing joy etc. or calling attention. **2** *Brit. informal* one's turn to order a round of drinks etc. (*your shout I think*). □ **give someone a shout 1** call for someone's attention. **2** call on or get in touch with someone. **shout at** speak loudly to etc. **shout down** reduce to silence by shouting. **shout for** call for by shouting. **shout it from the rooftops** make a thing embarrassingly public. □ **shout·er** *noun* **shouty** *adjective* [Middle English, perhaps related to SHOOT: compare Old Norse *skúta* SCOUT²]

shout·ing match *noun* a loud altercation.

shout-out *noun* a mention, acknowledgement, or greeting, esp. one made over the radio or during a live performance.

shove • *verb* **1** *transitive & intransitive* push vigorously; move by hard or rough pushing (*shoved him out of the way*). **2** *intransitive* (usu. foll. by *along, past, through*, etc.) make one's way by pushing (*shoved through the crowd*). **3** *transitive informal* put somewhere (*shoved it in the drawer*). • *noun* an act of shoving or of prompting a person into action. □ **shove it** *coarse slang* used for expressing contemptuous rejection or dismissal. **shove off 1** start from the shore in a boat. **2** *slang* depart; go away (*told him to shove off*). **shove over** (usu. in *imperative*) *informal* move over. [Old English *scúfan* from Germanic]

shov·el • *noun* **1 a** a spade-like tool for shifting quantities of snow,

coal, earth, etc., esp. having the sides curved upwards. **b** the amount contained in a shovel; a shovelful. **2** a machine or part of a machine having a similar form or function. **3** *Cdn* the wide flat part of a moose's antler. • *verb* (**shov·elled, shov·el·ling**; esp. *US* **shov·eled, shov·el·ing**) **1** *transitive* shift or clear (snow etc.) with or as if with a shovel. **2** *transitive* clear (an area) of snow etc. using a shovel (*shovelled the driveway*). **3** *intransitive* use a shovel. **4** *transitive informal* move (esp. food) in large quantities or roughly (*shovelled peas into his mouth*). □ **shovel·ful** *noun* (*pl.* **-fuls**). [Old English *scofl* from Germanic (see SHOVE)]

shovel hat *noun* a black felt hat with a low round crown and a broad brim turned up at the sides, formerly worn esp. by some clergymen.

shovel·head *noun* a hammerhead shark.

shov·el·ler *noun* (also **shov·el·er**) **1** a person or thing that shovels. **2** a duck, *Anas clypeata*, with a broad shovel-like beak. [SHOVEL: sense 2 earlier *shovelard* from -ARD, perhaps after *mallard*]

show • *verb* (*past participle* **shown** or **showed**) **1** *intransitive & transitive* be, or allow or cause to be, visible; manifest; appear (*the buds are beginning to show; white shows the dirt*). **2** *transitive* (often foll. by *to*) offer, exhibit, or produce (a thing) for scrutiny etc. (*show your tickets please; showed him my poems*). **3** *transitive* (often foll. by *to, towards*) demonstrate (kindness, rudeness, etc.) to a person (*showed respect towards him; showed him no mercy*). **4** *intransitive* (of feelings etc.) be manifest (*his dislike shows*). **5** *transitive* **a** point out; prove (*has shown it to be false; showed that he knew the answer*). **b** (usu. foll. by *how to* + infin.) cause (a person) to understand or be capable of doing (*showed them how to knit*). **6** *transitive* (reflexive) **a** exhibit oneself as being (*showed herself a generous host*). **b** (foll. by *to be*) exhibit oneself to be (*showed herself to be fair*). **7** *transitive & intransitive* (with reference to a film) be presented or cause to be presented. **8** *transitive* exhibit (a picture, animal, flower, etc.) in a show. **9** *intransitive* (of a house etc.) make a good, bad, etc. impression on prospective buyers or renters (*this condo shows well*). **10** *intransitive* (of an artist, designer, etc.) hold an exhibition of one's work. **11** *transitive* (often foll. by *in, out, up*, etc.) conduct or lead (*showed them to their rooms*). **12** *intransitive* appear (*waited but he didn't show*). **13** *intransitive N Amer.* finish third, esp. in a horse race. **14** *transitive* indicate (a time, measurement, etc.) (*the town hall clock showed midnight*). **15** *intransitive* (of a woman) manifest visible signs of pregnancy (*she's beginning to show*). • *noun* **1** the act or an instance of showing; the state of being shown. **2 a** a spectacle, display, exhibition, etc. (*a fine show of blossom*). **b** a collection of things etc. shown for public entertainment or in competition (*dog show; flower show*) (also *attributive*: *show horse*). **c** a display of new products (*car show*). **3 a** a play etc., esp. a musical. **b** a radio or television program. **c** a movie. **d** any public entertainment or performance. **4 a** an outward appearance, semblance, or display (*made a show of agreeing; a show of strength*). **b** empty appearance; mere display (*did it for show; that's all show*). **5** *informal* an undertaking, business, etc. (*sold the whole show*). **6** esp. *Brit. informal* an opportunity of acting, defending oneself, etc. (*gave him a fair show; made a good show of it*). **7** *Med.* a discharge of blood etc. from the vagina at the onset of childbirth. **8** *N Amer.* the third position, esp. in a horse race. **9** *Cdn* a logging operation. □ **get this show on the road** *informal* get moving; make a start. **give the show** (or **whole show**) **away** demonstrate the inadequacies or reveal the truth. **good** (or **bad** or **poor**) **show!** esp. *Brit. informal* **1** that was well (or badly) done. **2** that was lucky (or unlucky). **nothing to show for** no visible result of (effort etc.). **on show** being exhibited. **show around** (esp. *Brit.* **round**) take (a person) to places of interest; act as guide for (a person) in a building etc. **show one's cards** = SHOW ONE'S HAND. **show cause** *Law* allege with justification. **show a person** etc. **a clean pair of heels** *informal* retreat speedily from a person etc.; run away. **show one's colours** make one's opinion clear. **show a person the door** dismiss or eject a person. **show one's face** make an appearance; let oneself be seen. **show the flag** *see* FLAG¹. **show forth** *archaic* exhibit; expound. **show one's hand 1** disclose one's plans. **2** reveal one's cards. **show in** *see* sense 11 of *verb*. **show off 1** display to advantage. **2** act pretentiously; ostentatiously display one's knowledge, talent, etc. **show oneself 1** be seen in public. **2** *see* sense 6 of *verb*. **show out** *see* sense 11 of *verb*. **show one's teeth** reveal one's strength; be aggressive. **show through 1** be visible through a covering. **2** (of real feelings etc.) be revealed inadvertently. **show up 1** make or be conspicuous or clearly visible. **2** expose (a fraud, imposter, inferiority, etc.). **3** *informal* appear; be present; arrive. **4** *informal* embarrass or humiliate (*she showed him up by beating him at tennis*). **show the way 1** indicate what has to be done etc. by attempting it first. **2** show others which way to go etc. **show willing** *Cdn & Brit.* display a willingness to help or to do something. [Old English *scéawian*, from West Germanic]

show and tell *noun* esp. *N Amer.* **1** a classroom activity for young children in which each student brings an object from home and describes it to his or her classmates. **2** any informative display and discussion of assembled objects.

show band *noun* a marching band, brass band, etc., which performs in parades and festivals.

show·biz *noun informal* = SHOW BUSINESS. □ **show·bizzy** *adjective*

show·boat ● *noun* **1** a river steamer on which theatrical performances are given. **2** *informal* a show-off. ● *intransitive verb* show off. □ **show·boat·er** *noun* **show·boat·ing** *noun*

show business *noun informal* the entertainment industry, esp. theatre, movies, and television.

show·case ● *noun* **1** a glass case used for exhibiting goods etc. **2** a place or medium for presenting (esp. attractively) to general attention. ● *transitive verb* exhibit or display.

show-cause hearing *noun* a judicial hearing where a party involved in litigation must show cause why something must be done or must not be done, esp. a hearing at which the prosecution shows cause why an accused should be kept in custody rather than granted bail.

show·down *noun* **1** a final test or confrontation; a decisive situation. **2** the laying down face up of the players' cards in poker.

shower ● *noun* **1** a brief fall of esp. rain, hail, sleet, or snow. **2** (often *attributive*) **a** a cubicle, bath, etc. in which one stands under a spray of water. **b** the apparatus etc. used for this. **c** the act of washing oneself in a shower. **3 a** a brisk flurry of bullets, dust, stones, sparks, etc. **b** a similar flurry of gifts, letters, honours, praise, etc. **4** *N Amer.* a party for giving presents to a prospective bride, pregnant woman, etc. **5** a group of particles initiated by a cosmic-ray particle in the earth's atmosphere. ● *verb* **1** *transitive* discharge (water, missiles, etc.) in a shower. **2** *intransitive* use a shower. **3** *transitive* (usu. foll. by *on, upon*) lavishly bestow (gifts, praise, etc.). **4** *intransitive* descend or come in a shower (*it showered on and off all day*). □ **shower·less** *adjective* **showery** *adjective* [Old English *scūr* from Germanic]

shower cap *noun* a plastic cap worn to keep the hair dry when having a shower or bath.

shower curtain *noun* a waterproof curtain hung in a shower stall or bathtub.

shower head *noun* a nozzle from which the water sprays out in a shower.

shower·proof *adjective* resistant to light rain.

show·girl *noun* an actress who sings and dances in musicals, variety shows, etc.

show·goer *noun* a person who attends a show, esp. a trade show or an entertainment spectacle.

show·ground *noun* an area of land on which a fair, race, etc. takes place.

show home *noun* (also **show house**) = MODEL HOME.

show·ing *noun* **1** the act or an instance of showing. **2** a usu. specified quality of performance (*made a poor showing*). **3** a presentation or broadcasting of a film or a television program. **4** the presentation of a case; evidence (*on present showing it must be true*). **5** a visit by a prospective buyer to a property that is for sale.

show jumping *noun* the sport of riding horses over a course of fences and other obstacles, with penalty points for errors. □ **show jumper** *noun*

show·man *noun* (*pl.* **-men**) **1** a person who presents or produces an esp. theatrical show; an impresario. **2** an entertainer who performs with panache and style. **3** a person skilled in self-advertisement or publicity. □ **show·man·ship** *noun*

shown *past participle of* SHOW.

show-off *informal* ● *noun* a person who shows off. ● *adjective* ostentatious, showy. □ **show-offish** *adjective* **show-offish·ly** *adverb* **show-offy** *adjective*

show of force *noun* a demonstration of one's readiness to use force.

show of hands *noun* raised hands as a means of voting, showing interest, etc.

show·piece *noun* **1** an item of work presented for exhibition or display. **2** an outstanding example or specimen.

show·place *noun* a place serving to display something to its best advantage.

show ring *noun* an enclosed, usu. circular area where animals, plants, etc. are exhibited in competition.

show·room *noun* a room in a factory, office building, etc. used to display goods for sale.

show·stop·per *noun informal* **1** a performance receiving prolonged applause. **2** anything which draws great attention and admiration. □ **show-stopping** *adjective*

show·time *noun* *N Amer.* the time at which a movie, concert, etc. is scheduled to begin.

show trial *noun* esp. *hist.* a judicial trial designed by the state to terrorize or impress the public, esp. (as in the Soviet Union under Stalin) a prejudged trial of a political dissident.

show tune *noun* a popular tune from a musical.

showy *adjective* (**show·i·er**, **show·i·est**) **1** gaudy, ostentatious, esp. excessively so. **2** (of a person, quality, etc.) brilliant, striking, effective. □ **show·i·ly** *adverb* **show·i·ness** *noun*

shoyu /ˈʃoːjuː/ *noun* a type of Japanese soy sauce. [Japanese, = SOY]

shrank *past of* SHRINK.

shrap·nel *noun* **1** fragments of a bomb etc. thrown out by an explosion. **2** a shell containing bullets or pieces of metal timed to burst short of impact. [Gen. H. *Shrapnel*, British soldier d.1842, inventor of the shell]

shred ● *noun* **1** a scrap, fragment, or strip of esp. cloth, paper, etc. **2** the least amount, remnant (*not a shred of evidence*). ● *transitive verb* (**shred·ded**, **shred·ding**) tear or cut into shreds. □ **tear to shreds** completely refute (an argument etc.). [Old English *scrēad* (unrecorded) piece cut off, *scrēadian* from West Germanic: see SHROUD]

shred·der *noun* **1** a machine used to reduce documents to shreds. **2** any device used for shredding. **3** *N Amer. slang* a snowboarder.

Shreve·port an industrial city in NW Louisiana, on the Red River near the border with Texas; pop. (2000) 200,145.

shrew *noun* **1** any small usu. insect-eating mouselike mammal of the family Soricidae, with a long pointed snout. **2** a bad-tempered or scolding woman. □ **shrew·ish** *adjective* (in sense 2). **shrew·ish·ly** *adverb* **shrew·ish·ness** *noun* [Old English *scrēawa*, *scrǣwa* shrew mouse: compare Old High German *scrawaz* dwarf, Middle High German *schrawaz* etc. devil]

shrewd *adjective* **1** showing astute powers of judgment; clever and judicious (*a shrewd observer*; *made a shrewd guess*). **2** (of a face etc.) shrewd-looking. □ **shrewd·ly** *adverb* **shrewd·ness** *noun* [Middle English, = malignant, from SHREW in sense 'evil person or thing', or past participle of obsolete *shrew* to curse, from SHREW]

Shrews·bury /ˈʃroːzbəri, ˈʃruːz-/ a town in W England, the county town of Shropshire, situated on the Severn River near the border with Wales; pop. (est. 2002) 67,200.

shriek ● *verb* **1** *intransitive* utter a shrill screeching sound or words esp. in pain or terror. **2** *transitive* **a** utter (sounds or words) by shrieking (*shrieked his name*). **b** indicate clearly or blatantly. ● *noun* a high-pitched piercing cry or sound; a scream. □ **shriek with laughter** laugh uncontrollably. □ **shriek·er** *noun* [imitative: compare dial. *screak*, Old Norse *skrækja*, and SCREECH¹]

shrift *noun archaic* **1** confession to a priest. **2** confession and absolution. [Old English *scrift* (verbal noun) from SHRIVE]

shrike *noun* any bird of the family Laniidae, with a strong hooked and toothed bill, that impales its prey of small birds and insects on thorns. [perhaps related to Old English *scric* thrush, Middle Low German *schrīk* corncrake (imitative): compare SHRIEK]

shrill ● *adjective* **1** piercing and high-pitched in sound. **2** (of a person, argument, etc.) sharp, unrestrained, unreasoning. ● *verb* **1** *intransitive* (of a cry etc.) sound shrilly. **2** *transitive* (of a person etc.) utter or send out (a song, complaint, etc.) shrilly. □ **shrilly** *adverb* **shrill·ness** *noun* [Middle English, related to Low German *schrell* sharp in tone or taste, from Germanic]

shrimp ● *noun* **1** (*pl.* same or **shrimps**) any of various small (esp. marine) edible crustaceans, with ten legs, grey-green when alive and pink when cooked. **2** *informal* a very small slight person. ● *intransitive verb* go catching shrimps. □ **shrimp-like** *adjective* [Middle English, prob. related to Middle Low German *schrempen* wrinkle, Middle High German *schrimpfen* contract, and SCRIMP]

shrimp·er *noun* **1** a person who fishes for shrimp. **2** a boat used for shrimping.

shrimp plant *noun* an evergreen shrub, *Justicia brandegeeana*, bearing small white flowers in clusters of pinkish-brown bracts, grown as a houseplant.

shrine *noun* **1** esp. *Catholicism* **a** a chapel, church, altar, etc., sacred to a saint, holy person, relic, etc. **b** the tomb of a saint etc. **c** a casket esp. containing sacred relics; a reliquary. **d** a niche containing a holy statue etc. **2** a place associated with or containing memorabilia of a particular person, event, etc. **3** a Shinto place of worship. [Old English *scrin* from Germanic from Latin *scrinium* case for books etc.]

Shrin·er *noun* a member of the Order of Nobles of the Mystic Shrine, a charitable society founded in the US in 1872.

shrink ● *verb* (*past* **shrank** or **shrunk**; *past participle* **shrunk**) **1** *transitive & intransitive* **a** make or become smaller, esp. by the action of moisture, heat, or cold. **b** make or become reduced in size or number (*the workforce has shrunk considerably*). **2** *intransitive* (usu. foll. by *from, back*) recoil (*shrank from her touch*). **3** *intransitive* be averse from doing (*shrinks from meeting them*). ● *noun* **1** the act or an instance of shrinking; shrinkage. **2** *informal* a psychiatrist. □ **shrink·able** *adjective* **shrink·er** *noun* [Old English *scrincan*: compare *skrynka* to wrinkle; sense 2 of *noun* from 'head-shrinker']

shrink·age *noun* **1 a** the process or fact of shrinking. **b** the degree or amount of shrinking. **2** a reduction in a company's budget or profits due to wastage, theft, etc.

shrink·ing violet *noun informal* an exaggeratedly shy person.

shrink wrap ● *noun* thin transparent plastic film wrapped around and then shrunk tightly on to an article as packaging, protection, etc. ● *transitive verb* (**shrink-wrap**) (**-wrapped**, **-wrapping**) enclose (an article) in shrink wrap.

shrink-wrapped *adjective* **1** packaged in shrink wrap. **2** (of software) readily available commercially, and usu. standardized for a mass market.

shrive *transitive verb* (*past* **shrove**; *past participle* **shriv·en** /ˈʃrɪvən/) *Catholicism archaic* **1** (of a priest) hear the confession of, assign penance to, and absolve. **2** (*reflexive*) (of a penitent) submit oneself to a priest for confession etc. [Old English *scrifan* impose as penance, West Germanic from Latin *scribere* write]

shriv·el *transitive & intransitive verb* (**shriv·elled**, **shriv·el·ling** or esp. *US* **shriv·eled**, **shriv·el·ing**) contract or wither into a wrinkled, folded, rolled-up, contorted, or dried-up state. [perhaps from Old Norse: compare Swedish dial. *skryvla* to wrinkle]

shriv·en *past participle* of SHRIVE.

shroom (also **'shroom**) *noun slang* = MAGIC MUSHROOM. [abbreviation]

Shrop·shire /ˈʃrɒpʃɪr/ (also called **Salop**) a county of England, situated on the border with Wales; county town, Shrewsbury.

shroud ● *noun* **1** a sheet-like garment for wrapping a corpse for burial. **2** anything that conceals like a shroud (*wrapped in a shroud of mystery*). **3** (in *pl.*) *Naut.* a set of ropes forming part of the standing rigging and supporting the mast or topmast. ● *transitive verb* **1** clothe (a body) for burial. **2** cover, conceal, or disguise (*hills shrouded in mist*). [Old English *scrūd* from Germanic: see SHRED]

Shroud of Turin a relic, preserved at Turin since 1578, venerated as the sheet in which Christ's body was wrapped for burial. It bears the mysterious imprint of the front and back of a human body as well as markings that correspond to the traditional stigmata. Scientific tests carried out in 1988 dated the shroud to the 13th–14th centuries.

shrove *past* of SHRIVE.

Shrove·tide *noun* Shrove Tuesday and the two days preceding it when it was formerly customary to be shriven.

Shrove Tuesday *noun* the day before Ash Wednesday.

shrub[1] *noun* a woody plant smaller than a tree and having a very short stem with branches near the ground. □ **shrub·by** *adjective* [Old English *scrubb, scrybb* shrubbery: compare North Frisian *skrobb* brushwood, West Flemish *schrobbe* vetch, Norwegian *skrubba* dwarf cornel, and SCRUB[2]]

shrub[2] *noun* a cordial made of sweetened fruit juice and spirits, esp. rum. [Arabic *šurb, šarāb* from *šariba* to drink: compare SHERBET, SYRUP]

shrub·bery *noun* (*pl.* **-ies**) **1** an area planted with shrubs. **2** shrubs collectively.

shrubby cinquefoil *noun* see BUCKBRUSH.

shrub rose *noun* a rose, esp. a species or variety long in cultivation, allowed to follow its natural pattern of growth.

shrug ● *verb* (**shrugged**, **shrug·ging**) **1** *intransitive* slightly and momentarily raise the shoulders to express indifference, helplessness, contempt, etc. **2** *transitive* **a** raise (the shoulders) in this way. **b** shrug the shoulders to express (indifference etc.) (*shrugged his consent*). ● *noun* the act or an instance of shrugging. □ **shrug off** dismiss as unimportant etc. by or as if by shrugging. [Middle English: origin unknown]

shrunk *past participle* of SHRINK.

shrunk·en *adjective* (esp. of a face, person, etc.) having grown smaller esp. because of age, illness, etc.

shtetl /ˈʃtetəl, ˈʃteɪtəl/ *noun* (*pl.* **shtetls, shtet·lach** /-lax/) *hist.* a small Jewish town or village in E Europe. [Yiddish, = little town]

shtick *noun* (also **schtick**) *slang* **1** a theatrical routine, gimmick, etc. **2** a particular area of activity or interest; a sphere or scene. [Yiddish from German *Stück* piece]

shtreim·el /ˈʃtreiməl/ *noun* a round, broad-brimmed hat edged with fur worn by some Hasidic Jews. [Yiddish, from Middle High German *streimel* 'stripe, strip']

shtum *adjective* var. of SCHTUM.

shtup *transitive verb coarse slang* have sexual intercourse with. [Yiddish, compare German dial. *stupfen* 'nudge']

Shu·ben·aca·die River /ˈʃuːbeˈnakədi/ a river in central Nova Scotia, which rises north of Dartmouth and flows generally northeastward to empty into Cobequid Bay, a head of the Bay of Fundy (extending to Truro). [Mi'kmaq *segubunakade* place where groundnuts grow]

Shubrā al-Khaymah /ˈʃuːbrə alˈkeimɒ/ a city in N Egypt, part of the conurbation of Cairo; pop. (est. 1996) 870,716.

shuck *N Amer.* ● *noun* **1** a husk or pod, esp. the husk of an ear of corn. **2** the shell of an oyster or clam. ● *transitive verb* **1** remove the shucks of. **2** (often foll. by *off*) **a** remove, throw or strip off (clothes etc.). **b** get rid of, abandon. □ **shuck·er** *noun* [17th c.: origin unknown]

shucks *interjection informal* an expression of contempt or regret or self-deprecation in response to praise.

shud·der ● *intransitive verb* **1** shiver esp. convulsively from fear, cold, repugnance, etc. **2** feel strong repugnance etc. (*shudder to think what might happen*). **3** (of a machine etc.) vibrate or quiver. ● *noun* **1** the act or an instance of shuddering. **2** (in *pl.*; prec. by *the*) *informal* a state of shuddering. □ **shud·der·ing·ly** *adverb* **shud·dery** *adjective* [Middle Dutch *schūderen*, Middle Low German *schōderen* from Germanic]

shuf·fle ● *verb* **1** *transitive & intransitive* move with a scraping, sliding, or dragging motion (*shuffles along*; *shuffling his feet*). **2 a** *transitive & intransitive* rearrange (a pack of cards) by sliding them over each other quickly. **b** *transitive* rearrange; intermingle; confuse (*shuffled the documents*). **c** *transitive* redistribute posts within a (cabinet, organization, etc.). **3** *transitive* (usu. foll. by *on, off, into*) assume or remove (clothes, a burden, etc.) esp. clumsily or evasively (*shuffled on his clothes*; *shuffled off responsibility*). **4** *intransitive* **a** act in a shifting or evasive manner; equivocate; prevaricate. **b** continually shift one's position; fidget. **5** *intransitive* (foll. by *out of*) escape evasively (*shuffled out of the blame*). ● *noun* **1** a shuffling movement. **2** the act or an instance of shuffling cards. **3** a general change of relative positions. **4** a rearrangement of ministerial posts within a government or cabinet. **5** a piece of equivocation; an evasive trick. **6 a** a quick brushing movement of the feet in dancing. **b** a dance performed with such a step. **c** a piece of music for such a dance. □ **lost in the shuffle** overlooked in a crowd, confusion, etc. □ **shuf·fler** *noun* [perhaps from Low German *schuffeln* walk clumsily, from Germanic: compare SHOVE]

shuffle·board *noun* a game played esp. on a ship's deck in which competitors use a long-handled implement to push discs into numbered scoring sections.

shul /ʃuːl/ *noun* **1** a synagogue. **2** a service at a synagogue. [Yiddish from German *Schule* 'school']

shun *transitive verb* (**shunned, shun·ning**) avoid; keep clear of (*shuns human company*). [Old English *scunian*, of unknown origin]

shunt ● *verb* **1** *intransitive & transitive* diverge or cause (a train) to be diverted esp. on to a siding. **2** *transitive* Electricity provide (a current) with a shunt. **3** *transitive* a push aside or out of the way. **b** move (a person) to a different place, often a less important one (*she was shunted off to a regional office*). **4** *transitive* pass (blood, fluid, etc.) through a shunt. ● *noun* **1** the act or an instance of shunting on to a siding. **2** Electricity a conductor joining two points of a circuit, through which more or less of a current may be diverted. **3** Surgery **a** an alternative path for the circulation of blood or other fluid. **b** the construction of such a route. □ **shunt·er** *noun* [Middle English, perhaps from SHUN]

shush ● *interjection* = HUSH *interjection*. ● *verb* **1** *transitive* make or attempt to make silent (*shushed the baby*). **2** *intransitive* be silent (*they shushed at once*). **3** *intransitive* make a soft, shushing sound; move with the sound of a rush of air. ● *noun* an utterance of 'shush'. [imitative]

Shus·ter /ˈʃuːstər/ **1 Frank** see WAYNE AND SHUSTER. **2 Joe** (1914–92), Canadian-born cartoonist. Working with writer Jerome Siegel in Cleveland, he created the character Superman in 1931.

Shus·wap /ˈʃuːswɒp/ *noun* (*pl.* same or **Shus·waps**) **1** a member of an Aboriginal people living in the Thompson River area of BC. **2** the Salishan language of this people. ¶ Also called Secwepemc. [corruption of Shuswap *Secwepemc*, self-designation]

Vowels: a *cat* ɑ *arm* e *bed* ɜr *her* ɜː *deux* ə *ago* ɪ *sit* i *cosy* iː *feed* ɒ *hot* ɔ *pore* ɔː *no* ʌ *run* ʊ *put*

Shuswap Lake /ˈʃʊswɒp/ a four-armed lake in south central BC, situated just west of the Monashee Mountains.

shut *verb* (**shut·ting**; *past* and *past participle* **shut**) **1** *transitive* **a** move (a door, window, lid, etc.) into position so as to block an aperture. **b** close or seal (a box, eye, mouth, etc.). **2** *intransitive* become or be capable of being closed or sealed (*the door shut with a bang; the lid shuts automatically*). **3** *intransitive & transitive* esp. *Brit.* become or make (a shop, business, etc.) closed for trade (*the shops shut at five; shuts his shop at five*). **4** *transitive* bring (a book, hand, telescope, etc.) into a folded-up or contracted state. **5** *transitive* (usu. foll. by *in*, *out*) keep (a person, sound, etc.) in or out of a room etc. by shutting a door etc. (*shut out the noise; shut them in*). **6** *transitive* (usu. foll. by *in*) catch (a finger, dress, etc.) by shutting something on it (*shut her finger in the door*). **7** *transitive* bar access to (a place etc.) (*this entrance is shut*). □ **be** (or **get**) **shut of** *slang* be (or get) rid of (*were glad to get shut of him*). **shut the door on** refuse to consider; make impossible. **shut down 1** stop (a factory, nuclear reactor, etc.) from operating. **2** (of a factory etc.) stop operating. **3** turn off (an engine, machine, etc.). **4** *N Amer. Sport informal* render an opponent's offence ineffective (*shut down the Jays*). **shut one's eyes** (or **ears** or **heart** or **mind**) **to** pretend not, or refuse, to see (or hear or feel sympathy for or think about). **shut in** (of hills, houses, etc.) encircle, prevent access etc. to or escape from (*were shut in by the sea on three sides*) (*see also* sense 5). **shut off 1 a** stop the flow of (water, gas, etc.) by shutting a valve. **b** switch off (a machine, light, etc.). **2** separate from society etc. **shut out 1** exclude (a person, light, etc.) from a place, situation, etc. **2** screen (landscape etc.) from view. **3** prevent (a possibility etc.). **4** block (a painful memory etc.) from the mind. **5** *N Amer.* prevent (the opposing team) from scoring (*see also* sense 5). **shut up 1** close all doors and windows of (a house etc.); bolt and bar. **2** imprison (a person). **3** close (a box etc.) securely. **4** *informal* reduce to silence by rebuke etc. **5** put (a thing) away in a box etc. **6** (esp. in *imperative*) *informal* stop talking. **shut up shop 1** close a business, shop, etc. **2** cease business etc. permanently. **shut your face** (or **mouth** or **trap**)! *slang* an impolite request to stop talking. [Old English *scyttan* from West Germanic: related to SHOOT]

shut·down *noun* **1** the closure of a factory etc. **2** the turning off of a machine, computer, etc.

Shute, Nevil (pseudonym of Nevil Shute Norway) (1899–1960), English novelist. After the Second World War he settled in Australia, which provides the setting for his later novels; among the best-known are *A Town Like Alice* (1950) and *On the Beach* (1957).

shut-eye *noun informal* sleep.

shut-in *noun N Amer.* (also *attributive*) a person who is confined indoors because of ill health.

shut-off *noun* **1** something used for stopping an operation. **2** a cessation of flow, supply, or activity.

shut-off valve *noun* a valve used to cut off the flow of water esp. to a sink, toilet, etc. when doing repairs etc.

shut·out *noun N Amer.* **1** the act of preventing an opposing team from scoring. **2** any game in which one side does not score.

shut·ter ● *noun* **1 a** each of a pair or set of hinged panels fixed inside or outside a window for security or privacy or to keep the light in or out. **b** a structure of slats on rollers used for the same purpose. **2** a device on a camera that opens to allow light to pass through the lens. **3** a person or thing that shuts. ● *transitive verb* **1** put up the shutters of. **2** close (a business, factory, etc.) permanently. **3** provide with shutters. □ **shutter·less** *adjective*

shutter·bug *noun* an enthusiastic photographer.

shutter release *noun* the button on a camera that is pressed to cause the shutter to open.

shutter speed *noun* the nominal time for which a shutter on a camera is open at a given setting.

shut·tle ● *noun* **1 a** a bobbin with two pointed ends used for carrying the weft thread across between the warp threads in weaving. **b** a bobbin carrying the lower thread in a sewing machine. **2** a plane, bus, etc., going to and fro over a short route continuously (also *attributive*: *shuttle flight; shuttle bus*). **3** = SHUTTLECOCK. **4** = SPACE SHUTTLE. **5** a journey made in the course of shuttle diplomacy. ● *verb* **1** *transitive* transport (a person) in a shuttle. **2** *intransitive* (of a person, train, etc.) travel backwards and forwards between places. **3** *intransitive & transitive* move or cause to move to and fro like a shuttle. [Old English *scytel* dart, from Germanic: compare SHOOT]

shuttle·cock *noun* **1** a small piece of cork, rubber, etc. fitted with a ring of feathers, or a similar device of plastic, used instead of a ball in badminton. **2** a thing passed repeatedly back and forth. [SHUTTLE + COCK¹, prob. from the flying motion]

shuttle diplomacy *noun* diplomatic negotiations conducted by a mediator travelling between disputing parties.

shvitz (also **schvitz**) ● *intransitive verb* sweat. ● *noun* a steam bath. [Yiddish 'sweat']

shy¹ ● *adjective* (**shyer, shy·est**) **1 a** diffident or uneasy in company; timid. **b** (of a thing, action, etc.) characterized by or done with reserve or timidity (*a shy smile*). **c** (of an animal, bird, etc.) easily startled; timid. **2** (foll. by *of*) avoiding; chary of (*shy of going to meetings*). **3** (in *combination*) showing fear of or distaste for (*gun-shy; work-shy*). **4** (often foll. by *of*) *informal* short of (a stated amount, measurement, etc.) (*two months shy of his fifteenth birthday; three points shy of a world record*). ● *intransitive verb* (**shies, shied**) **1** (usu. foll. by *at*) (esp. of a horse) start suddenly aside (at an object, noise, etc.) in fright. **2** (usu. foll. by *away from, at*) avoid accepting or becoming involved in (a proposal etc.) in alarm. ● *noun* a sudden startled movement. □ **shyer** *noun* **shyly** *adverb* **shy·ness** *noun* [Old English *sceoh* from Germanic]

shy² ● *transitive verb* (**shies, shied**) fling or throw (a stone etc.). ● *noun* (*pl.* **shies**) the act or an instance of shying. □ **shyer** *noun* [18th c.: origin unknown]

Shy·lock *noun derogatory* a hard-hearted moneylender; a miser. [character in Shakespeare's *Merchant of Venice*]

shy·ster *noun esp. N Amer. informal* a person, esp. a lawyer, who uses unscrupulous methods. [19th c.: origin uncertain]

SI *abbreviation* INTERNATIONAL SYSTEM OF UNITS. [from French *Système International*]

Si *symbol Chem.* the element silicon.

si /siː/ *noun Music* = TI². [French from Italian, perhaps from the initials of *Sancte Iohannes*: see GAMUT]

Si·achen Glacier /siˈɒtʃən/ a glacier in the Karakoram Mountains in NW India, situated at an altitude of some 5 500 m (17,800 ft.). Extending over 70 km (44 miles), it is one of the world's longest glaciers.

Sial·kot /siˈɒlkɒt/ an industrial city in the province of Punjab, in Pakistan; pop. (1998) 417,600.

Siam /saiˈam/ the former name (until 1939) for THAILAND.

Siam, Gulf of a former name for the Gulf of Thailand (see THAILAND, GULF OF).

sia·mang /ˈsaiəˌmaŋ, ˈsiːəˌmaŋ/ *noun* a large black gibbon, *Hylobates syndactylus*, native to Sumatra and the Malay peninsula. [Malay]

Siam·ese /saiˈmiːz, ˌsaiəˈmiːz/ ● *noun* (*pl.* same) **1 a** a native of Siam (now Thailand) in SE Asia. **b** the language of Siam. **2** (in full **Siamese cat**) **a** a cat of a cream-coloured short-haired breed with blue eyes and brown ears, face, paws, and tail. **b** this breed. ● *adjective* of or concerning Siam, its people, or language.

Siamese fighting fish *noun see* FIGHTING FISH.

Siamese twins *plural noun* **1** = CONJOINED TWINS. **2** any closely associated pair. [after Chang and Eng (d.1874), conjoined twins born in Siam]

Sian see XIAN.

sib ● *noun* **1** esp. *Genetics* a brother or sister; a sibling. **2** a blood relative. **3** a group of people recognized by an individual as his or her kindred. ● *adjective* (usu. foll. by *to*) esp. *Scot.* related; akin. [Old English *sib(b)*]

Sibel·ius /sɪˈbeiliəs/ **Jean** (born Johan Julius Christian Sibelius) (1865–1957), Finnish composer. He is best known for his seven symphonies, and his tone poems evoking his country's landscape and legends, including *The Swan of Tuonela* (1893), *Finlandia* (1899).

Si·ber·ia /saiˈbiːriə/ a vast region of Russia, extending from the Urals to the Pacific and from the Arctic coast to the northern borders of Kazakhstan, Mongolia, and China. Noted for the severity of its winters, it was traditionally used as a place of exile. □ **Si·ber·ian** *noun & adjective*

Siberian elm *noun* an elm of northeastern Asia, *Ulmus pumila*, frequently planted as a hedge.

Siberian husky *noun* a hardy breed of husky, originally from Siberia, with stocky body and blue eyes.

Siberian iris *noun* a beardless iris of the species *Iris sibirica* or a hybrid of *I. sibirica* and *I. sanguinia*, native to Central Europe and Asia but widely cultivated for its delicate blooms and spiky stems.

Siberian pea *noun* a leguminous shrub or small tree, *Caragana arborescens*, native to eastern Asia and widely planted in N America as hedging.

Siberian tiger *noun* a very large tiger of an endangered race occurring in SE Siberia and NE China, having a long thick coat.

uː mo**od**   ai my   əi p**i**pe   au br**ow**n   ʌu h**ou**se   ei day   ɔi b**oy**   ã franglais   ã Canadien   ɔ̃ Brayon   (*see over for consonants*)

sibi·lant /ˈsɪbɪlənt/ ● *adjective* **1** (of a letter or set of letters, as *s*, *sh*) articulated with a hissing sound. **2** hissing (*a sibilant whisper*). ● *noun* a sibilant letter or letters. □ **sibi·lance** *noun* **sibi·lancy** *noun* [Latin *sibilare sibilant- hiss*]

Sibiu /siˈbjuː/ an industrial city in central Romania; pop. (est. 2002) 167,000.

Sib·ley, Dame An·toin·ette (b.1939), English dancer. A principal dancer with the Royal Ballet 1960–1981 known for her musicality, she created roles in MacMillan's *Manon* (1974) and Ashton's *The Dream* (1964), among many others. Her partnership with Anthony Dowell was legendary. Since 1992 she has been President of the Royal Academy of Dance.

Sibley Peninsula a peninsula of the northern shore of Lake Superior in NW Ontario, sheltering the city of Thunder Bay. [A. *Sibley*, US military officer who purchased a nearby silver mine *c.*1873]

sib·ling *noun* each of two or more children having one or both parents in common. [SIB + -LING¹]

sibling rivalry *noun* competition arising from jealousy between siblings.

sib·ship *noun* **1** the state of belonging to a sib or the same sib. **2** a group of children having the same two parents.

sibyl /ˈsɪbəl/ *noun* **1** any of the women in ancient times supposed to utter the oracles and prophecies of a god. **2** a prophetess, fortune teller, or witch. [Latin *Sibylla* from Greek *Sibulla*]

sibyl·line /ˈsɪbɪˌlaɪn/ *adjective* **1** of or from a sibyl. **2** oracular; prophetic.

sic¹ *adverb* (usu. in brackets) used, spelled, etc., as written (confirming, or calling attention to, the form of quoted or copied words). ¶ The word *sic* is placed in brackets after a word that appears odd or erroneous to show that the word is quoted exactly as it stands in the original, e.g. *They say they will take measures to insure* [sic] *compliance.* [Latin, = so, thus]

sic² *transitive verb* (**sicced, sic·cing**) (also **sick**) **1** (usu. in *imperative*) (esp. to a dog) attack (a person or animal) (*sic 'em!*). **2** (usu. foll. by *on*) **a** set (an animal) on another animal or person. **b** set (a person) to follow, harass, etc. another person (*sicced his lawyers on me*). [19th c., dial. var. of SEEK]

sic bo *noun* a gambling game based on an ancient Chinese game of chance, in which the player rolls three dice or balls along the table into a wheel resembling a roulette wheel. [Chinese, = dice of fortune]

sice *var. of* SYCE.

Si·chuan /sɪˈtʃwɒn/ (also **Sze·chuan**, **Sze·chwan** /seˈtʃwɒn/) a province of west central China; capital, Chengdu.

Sicilian Vespers a massacre of French inhabitants of Sicily, which began near Palermo at the time of vespers on Easter Tuesday in 1282. The ensuing war resulted in the replacement of the French Angevin dynasty by the Spanish House of Aragon.

Sicily /ˈsɪsɪli/ a large Italian island in the Mediterranean, off the southwestern tip of Italy; capital, Palermo. The island's highest point is the volcano Mount Etna. □ **Sicil·ian** /sɪˈsɪliən/ *adjective & noun*

sick¹ ● *adjective* **1** ill; affected by illness (*has been sick for a week; a sick man; sick with measles*). **2** (often in *combination*) vomiting or tending to vomit (*feels sick; has been sick; seasick*). **3** mentally disturbed or perverted (*the product of a sick mind*). **4** *informal* (of humour etc.) jeering at misfortune, illness, death, etc.; morbid (*sick joke*). **5 a** (often foll. by *for*, or in *combination*) pining; longing (*sick for a sight of home; lovesick*). **b** deeply affected by disappointment, fear, sorrow, grief, etc. (*sick at heart; worried sick*). **6** (often foll. by *of*) *informal* **a** disgusted by too much exposure (*sick of chocolates*). **b** angry, esp. because of surfeit (*am sick of being teased*). **7** of a sickly colour; pale, wan. ● *noun Brit. informal* vomit. ● *transitive verb* (usu. foll. by *up*) esp. *Brit. informal* vomit (*sicked up his dinner*). □ **be** (or **get**) **sick** vomit; throw up. **get** (or **fall** or **take**) **sick** be taken ill. **make a person sick** disgust a person (*his hypocrisy makes me sick*). **sick and tired** fed up with; wearied of. **sick as a dog** extremely ill. **sick to one's stomach** *N Amer.* vomiting or nauseous. □ **sick·ish** *adjective* **sick·ish·ly** *adverb* [Old English *sēoc* from Germanic]

sick² *var. of* SIC².

sick bay *noun* **1** part of a ship used as a hospital. **2** any room etc. for sick people.

sick·bed *noun* **1** an invalid's bed. **2** the state of being an invalid.

sick benefit *noun* = SICKNESS BENEFIT.

sick building syndrome *noun* a high incidence of illness in office workers, attributed to pollutants etc. in the immediate working surroundings.

sick call *noun* **1** a visit by a doctor to a sick person etc. **2** *Military* a summons for those reporting sick to assemble for treatment.

sick day *noun* a paid day off for a worker because of illness.

sick·en *verb* **1** *transitive* affect with loathing or disgust. **2** *intransitive* (often foll. by *at*, or *to* + *infin.*) feel nausea or disgust (*he sickened at the sight*). **3** *intransitive* fall ill. **4** *transitive* afflict with an illness.

sick·en·er *noun* **1** something causing nausea, disgust, or severe disappointment. **2** a red toadstool of the genus *Russula*, esp. the poisonous *R. emetica*.

sick·en·ing *adjective* **1** causing or liable to cause sickness or nausea. **2** loathsome, disgusting. □ **sick·en·ing·ly** *adverb*

sick headache *noun* a severe headache accompanied by nausea or vomiting.

sick·ie *noun N Amer. informal* (also **sicky**) (*pl.* **-ies**) **1** a psychotic or perverted person. **2** a person who is unwell.

sickle *noun* **1** a short-handled farm tool with a semicircular blade, used esp. for cutting grass, grain, etc. **2** (in full **sickle bar**) the cutting mechanism of a combine, mower, etc., consisting of a heavy bar with several blades. **3** anything sickle-shaped, esp. the crescent moon. [Old English *sicol, sicel* from Latin *secula* from *secare* cut]

sick leave *noun* leave of absence granted because of illness.

sickle cell *noun* a sickle-shaped blood cell, found in the blood of people with sickle-cell anemia.

sickle-cell anemia *noun* a severe hereditary form of anemia, affecting mainly blacks, in which a mutated form of hemoglobin distorts the red blood cells into a crescent shape at low oxygen levels.

sickle feather *noun* each of the long middle feathers of a rooster's tail.

sick·ly *adjective* (**sick·li·er, sick·li·est**) **1 a** of weak health; apt to be ill. **b** (of a person's complexion, look, etc.) languid, faint, or pale, suggesting sickness (*a sickly smile*). **c** (of light or colour) faint, pale, feeble. **2** causing ill health (*a sickly climate*). **3** (of a book etc.) sentimental or mawkish. **4** inducing or connected with nausea (*a sickly taste*). **5** (of a colour etc.) of an unpleasant shade inducing nausea (*a sickly green*). □ **sick·li·ness** *noun*

sick·ness *noun* **1** the state of being ill; disease. **2** a specified disease (*sleeping sickness*). **3** vomiting or a tendency to vomit.

sickness benefit *noun* an allowance paid by a government for sickness interrupting paid employment.

sicko *noun* (*pl.* **-os**) esp. *N Amer. slang* a mentally ill or perverted person.

sick pay *noun* pay given to an employee on sick leave.

sick·room *noun* **1** a room occupied by a sick person. **2** a room adapted for sick people.

Sid·dhar·tha Gau·tama /sɪˌdɑːtə ˈgautəmə/ see BUDDHA.

Sid·dons, Sarah (née Kemble) (1755–1831), English tragic actress, noted particularly for her role as Lady Macbeth.

side ● *noun* **1 a** each of the more or less flat surfaces bounding an object (*a cube has six sides*). **b** a vertical lateral surface or plane as distinct from the top or bottom, front or back, or ends (*the side of the box*). **2** the more or less vertical slope of a hill or bank (*the side of the mountain*). **3** either surface of a thing regarded as having two surfaces. **4 a** a specified direction or position relating to a person or thing (*on the north side of; came from all sides*). **b** (often in *combination*) a position next to a person or thing (*graveside; stand by my side*). **5** a position nearer or farther than, or right or left of, a dividing line (*on this side of the Alps; on the other side of the road*). **6 a** a specified part or region in relation to a central point (*the east side of town*). **b** (*attributive*) a subordinate, peripheral, or detached part (*a side bet; a side dish*). **7 a** either of two parts of a person's body between the left or right shoulder and the corresponding hip (*has a pain in his right side*). **b** the analogous part of an animal's body. **c** either of the lateral halves of the body of a butchered animal (*a side of bacon*). **8 a** each of two sets of opponents in a dispute, political debate, game, etc. (*whose side are you on?; cheer for the home side*). **b** a cause or philosophical position etc. regarded as being in conflict with another. **c** *Baseball* a team's batters in one inning (*he struck out the side in the fifth*). **9** any of several aspects of a question, character, etc. (*try to avoid his moody side; look on the bright side*). **10** either side of a phonograph record or audio cassette tape. **11** a line of hereditary descent through the father or the mother. **12** *N Amer.* = SIDE ORDER. **13** *Geom.* each of the bounding lines of a plane rectilinear figure (*a hexagon has six sides*). ● *intransitive verb* (usu. foll. by *with*) share an opinion, view, stance, etc. with (a person), esp. in a particular argument or dispute (*she sided with her father*). □ **from side to side 1** across the whole width. **2** alternately each way from a central line (*the drunk staggered from side to side*). **let the side down** fail one's colleagues, esp. by frustrating their efforts or embarrassing them. **on the ... side** fairly, somewhat (*he's a little on the chubby side*). **on the side 1** in addition to one's regular work etc. **2** secretly or illicitly. **3** *N Amer.* as a side dish. **side by side 1** close together. **2** in collaboration or solidarity. **take sides** favour or support one party in a dispute. **to one side** aside (*she took me to one side after class*). □ **side·less** *adjective* [Old English *sīde* from Germanic]

side arm *noun* (often in *pl.*) a weapon worn on one's belt or at one's side, such as a sword, dagger, or pistol.

side·arm *Baseball* ● *adjective* **1** (of a pitch or throw) performed or delivered with the arm swung or extended out to the side, parallel to the ground (*compare* OVERHAND 1). **2** (of a pitcher) that throws such a pitch. ● *adverb* with the arm swung or extended out to the side (*he throws sidearm*). ● *transitive verb* throw (a pitch) sidearm. □ **side·arm·er** *noun*

side bacon *noun Cdn* bacon from the belly of a pig, having alternate strips of fat and lean.

side·band *noun* a range of frequencies above or below a carrier frequency of a radio wave, within which lie the frequencies produced by modulation of the carrier.

side·bar *noun esp. N Amer.* **1** a short, usu. boxed, article in a newspaper, magazine, etc. placed alongside a main article and containing additional or explanatory material, data, etc. **2** a secondary, additional, or incidental issue etc.

side bet *noun* a bet between opponents, esp. in card games, over and above the ordinary stakes.

side·board *noun* **1** a piece of dining room furniture used to store dishes, cutlery, table linen, etc., esp. one with a flat top, cupboards, and drawers; a buffet. **2** (**side·boards**) *Brit.* sideburns.

side·burns *plural noun esp. N Amer.* hair grown by a man down the sides of his face beginning at the top of the ear and sometimes extending down as far as the cheek. [*burnsides* pl. of *burnside* from General Burnside d.1881 who affected this style]

side·car *noun* **1** a small usu. open car with one wheel for one or more passengers attached to the side of a motorcycle. **2** a cocktail of orange liqueur, lemon juice, and brandy.

side chain *noun Chem.* a group of atoms attached to the main part of a molecule.

side·chair *noun N Amer.* an upright wooden chair without arms.

side channel *noun Cdn* a shallow and narrow tributary running into a river.

side cutters *plural noun* (in full **side-cutting pliers**) a pair of pliers resembling scissors, having blades set at an angle, used for cutting esp. small pieces of metal, such as nails or wire.

sided *adjective* (usu. in *combination*) having a specified number or kind of sides (*double-sided tape; cedar-sided home; one-sided game*). □ **sided·ly** *adverb* **sided·ness** *noun*

side dish *noun* an extra dish accompanying the main course but usu. served on a separate plate.

side door *noun* **1** a door in or at the side of a building, vehicle, etc. **2** *informal* an indirect means of escape or method of resolving a problem etc. (also *attributive*: *side-door deal*).

side-dress *transitive verb* apply fertilizer to the soil alongside (a plant).

side drum *noun Brit.* = SNARE 4b. [originally hung at the drummer's side]

side effect *noun* **1** *Med.* a usu. adverse reaction caused by a drug in addition to the effect for which it is administered. **2** an additional consequence of an action, occurrence, or state of affairs; an unintended secondary result.

side·hill *noun US & Cdn* (esp. *BC*) a hillside.

side impact *noun* **1** a collision against the side of a car or truck etc. **2** (*attributive*) (usu. **side-impact**) relating to, or esp. designed to protect in case of, a collision against the side of a vehicle (*side-impact beams*).

side issue *noun* a point that distracts attention from what is important.

side·kick *noun informal* **1** a close companion or partner, esp. in adventure. **2** the second member of a duo, subordinate and loyal to the first.

side·light *noun* **1** a light coming from the side, esp. used in photography. **2** a piece of incidental information on a subject; an anecdote or item serving as a companion to the full account of an event etc. (*compare* HIGHLIGHT 2). **3** a window by the side of a door or other window. **4 a** the red port or green starboard light on a ship.

b *Brit.* a light at the side of the front of a car etc. to warn of its presence. □ **side·light·ing** *noun*

side·line ● *noun* **1 a** a part-time job or business taken up in addition to one's main employment, esp. as a secondary source of income. **b** any activity pursued as a secondary interest, hobby, etc. **2 a** (in football, basketball, soccer, etc.) one of two lines running the length of a field or court to separate the part of the playing surface that is in bounds from that which is out of bounds. **b** (usu. in *pl.*) the part of the playing surface out of bounds where coaches, players, and occasionally spectators sit. ● *transitive verb* **1** remove (a player) from participation in a game or games, esp. through injury or a suspension (*she's been sidelined for three games with a sore elbow*). **2** remove from action or consideration etc. (*they've sidelined their plans to build the airport*). □ **on** (or **from**) **the sidelines** in (or from) a position removed from the main action.

side·lock *noun* a long curly lock of hair falling from the side of the head down along the cheek, worn esp. by Orthodox Jews as a distinguishing mark.

side·long ● *adjective* directed to one side; oblique (*a sidelong glance*). ● *adverb* towards the side; obliquely (*moved sidelong*). [*sideling* (as SIDE, -LING²): see -LONG]

side·man *noun* a supporting musician in a jazz or dance band.

side·meat *noun N Amer.* salt pork or bacon, usu. cut from the side of the pig.

side order *noun N Amer.* a separate serving of food supplementing a meal ordered from a menu in a restaurant etc.

side plate *noun* a plate of approximately 15–20 cm in diameter, used for bread etc.

side rail *noun* a rail placed or fixed at the side of something.

si·dereal /saɪˈdiːriəl/ *adjective* **1** of or concerning the constellations or fixed stars. **2** (of a period of time) determined or measured with reference to the apparent motion of the stars. [Latin *sidereus* from *sidus sideris* star]

sidereal clock *noun* a clock showing sidereal time.

sidereal day *noun* the period of time required for a star, usu. the first star in the constellation Aries, to make successive passages across the meridian, about four minutes shorter than the solar day.

sidereal time *noun* time measured by the apparent diurnal motion of the stars.

sidereal year *noun* the time taken for the earth to travel once around the sun, measured relative to fixed stars, a period longer than the solar year by 20 minutes 23 seconds.

side ribs *plural noun Cdn* a cut of pork from the belly including the ribs and adhering meat.

sid·er·ite /ˈsɪdəˌraɪt/ *noun* **1** a mineral form of ferrous carbonate that is a source of iron and occurs in sedimentary rocks and ore veins as translucent usu. brown or yellow crystals. **2** a meteorite consisting mainly of nickel and iron. □ **sid·er·itic** /ˌsɪdəˈrɪtɪk/ *adjective* [Greek *sidēros* iron]

sidero- /ˈsɪdrəʊ, ˈsaɪ-/ *combining form* **1** of or relating to iron. **2** of or relating to the stars. [sense 1 from Greek *sidēros* 'iron'; sense 2 from Latin *sider- sidus* 'star']

side road *noun* **1** a minor road, esp. joining or diverging from a main road; a back road. **2** (**side·road**) *Cdn* (esp. *Ont.*) a rural road running perpendicular to a concession road (*compare* CONCESSION 4b).

sid·ero·phore /ˈsɪdərəˌfɔːr/ *noun Biol. & Med.* an agent which binds and transports iron in micro-organisms.

side·saddle ● *noun* a saddle originally designed to allow a woman wearing a skirt to sit with both feet on one side of the horse, now usu. made with supports for the knees of the rider, who sits facing forward with the right knee raised. ● *adverb* sitting in this position on a horse.

side salad *noun* a salad served as a side dish.

side-scan sonar *noun* a sonar that sends a beam sideways (from a ship) or downwards and sideways (from an aircraft).

side seat *noun* a seat in a vehicle etc. in which the occupant has his or her back to the side of the vehicle.

side·show *noun* **1** a minor show or attraction in an exhibition, circus, etc. **2** a minor attraction, incident, or issue.

side·slip ● *noun* **1** (esp. of a bicycle, car, etc.) the action or instance of slipping sideways; a skid. **2** a sideways movement of an aircraft in flight, esp. downwards towards the centre of curvature of a turn. **3** *Skiing* the action of travelling at an angle down a slope or run. ● *intransitive verb* **1** skid or slip sideways. **2** (of an aircraft) move sideways, esp. while turning. **3** *Skiing* travel downwards at an angle. **4** move elusively or adroitly.

sides·man noun (pl. **-men**) (also **sides·person**) (in the Anglican Church) an assistant churchwarden, who shows worshippers to their seats, takes the collection, etc.

side·split noun Cdn a split-level house having floors raised half a level on one side thus having an upper and lower basement and an upper and lower main floor (compare BACKSPLIT).

side-splitting adjective uproariously funny, causing violent laughter. □ **side-splitter** noun **side-splitting·ly** noun

side·step ● verb (**-stepped, -step·ping**) **1** transitive evade or dodge (an issue etc.) by refusing to address or confront it. **2** transitive Sport avoid (another player, a tackle, etc.) by stepping sideways. **3** intransitive move laterally by stepping to the side. ● noun a step taken sideways. □ **side·step·per** noun

side street noun a minor street usu. leading away from a main street or busy thoroughfare.

side stroke noun a swimming stroke in which the swimmer lies on his or her side, drawing the arms through the water in opposite directions from the chest, one stretching forward beyond the head, the other pulled towards the feet, while using a scissor kick.

side-swipe ● noun **1** a passing jibe or verbal attack; an indirect rebuke or criticism. **2** a glancing blow along the side of esp. a car or truck etc. ● transitive verb **1** strike a glancing blow on the side of (esp. a car or truck etc.) in passing. **2** affect or attack indirectly (tactics directed at her detractors have side-swiped some of her allies).

side table noun a table placed next to the wall of a room or at the side of a larger table.

side·track ● transitive verb **1 a** distract (a person) from an objective, issue, topic, etc. **b** divert (a plan etc.) from its intended purpose or aim. **2** run or shunt (a train) into a siding. ● noun a railway siding.

side trip noun a minor excursion during a voyage or trip; a detour.

side-valve noun a valve in a vehicle engine, operated from the side of the cylinder.

side view noun **1** a view obtained by looking sideways. **2** a view of something or someone from its side; a profile.

side-view mirror noun (also **side mirror**) a mirror fixed on one or both sides of a car or truck etc. to give the driver a view behind and to the side of the vehicle.

side·walk noun N Amer. **1** a paved pedestrian path or walkway on either side of a street. **2** (attributive) designating things appearing or occurring on a sidewalk, esp. on the sidewalk in front of stores and other commercial buildings (sidewalk vendor; sidewalk sale). □ **side·walk·less** adjective

sidewalk café noun N Amer. a small restaurant or coffee shop that opens onto a sidewalk and has tables set up so that customers may eat outdoors.

side wall noun **1 a** a wall forming the side of a structure, room, or enclosure. **b** a wall forming the side of a squash or racquetball court. **2 a** the side of a tire, usu. untreaded and distinctively marked or coloured. **b** (in full **side wall tire**) a tire with distinctive side walls.

side·ways (also esp. US **side·wise, side·ward**) ● adverb (also **side·wards**) **1** to or from a side (moved sideways). **2** with one side facing forward (sat sideways on the bus). **3** in an odd or unconventional manner. ● adjective **1** to or from a side (a sideways movement). **2** odd or unconventional.

side·wheel·er noun N Amer. a steamboat etc. propelled by paddlewheels mounted on its sides.

side·whis·ker noun (usu. in pl.) hair growing on the side of a man's face and cheeks; sideburns.

side wind noun a wind blowing from the side, or on the side, of a vehicle etc.; a crosswind (compare HEADWIND).

side·wind·er /ˈsaɪdˌwaɪndər/ noun **1** a desert rattlesnake, Crotalus cerastes, native to N America, moving with a side-to-side slithering motion. **2** a punch delivered with a winding swing of the fist across the body. **3** (**Sidewinder**) a heat-seeking air-to-air missile.

Sidi bel Abbès /ˌsɪdɪ bel əˈbes/ a town in N Algeria, situated to the south of Oran; pop. (est. 2002) 201,200. Established as a French military outpost in 1843, it was the headquarters of the French Foreign Legion until Algeria's independence in 1962.

siding noun **1** N Amer. material used to cover the outside of a building, usu. made of wood, aluminum, or vinyl. **2** a short length of railway track connected to an adjacent line for storing and shunting trains and for enabling trains on the same line to pass each other.

sidle /ˈsaɪdəl/ intransitive verb **1** (often foll. by up) move in a sly, guileful, or devious manner. **2** move in a cautious, timid, or furtive manner. [back-formation from sideling, SIDELONG]

Sid·ney[1] a town situated at the northeastern tip of the Saanich Peninsula of Vancouver Island, about 30 km north of Victoria; pop. (2001) 10,929. [prob. after F. W. Sidney, British naval surveyor c.1859]

Sid·ney[2] ▸ **Sir Phil·ip** (1554–86), English poet, courtier, and soldier. A leading Elizabethan poet, he is best known for the Arcadia (1590), a prose romance including poems and pastoral eclogues in a wide variety of verse forms, his sonnet sequence Astrophel and Stella (1591), and The Defence of Poesie (1595).

Sidon /ˈsaɪdən/ a city in Lebanon, on the Mediterranean coast south of Beirut; pop. (est. 2002) 146,100. Founded in the third millennium BC, it was a Phoenician seaport and city state. □ **Si·don·ian** adjective

Sidra, Gulf of /ˈsɪdrə/ (also **Gulf of Sirte** /ˈsɜːrti/) a broad inlet of the Mediterranean on the coast of Libya, between the towns of Benghazi and Misratah.

SIDS /sɪdz/ noun = SUDDEN INFANT DEATH SYNDROME.

Sie·ben·ge·birge /ˈziːbəngəˌbiːrgə/ a range of hills in western Germany, on the right bank of the Rhine southeast of Bonn.

siege /siːdʒ/ noun **1 a** a military operation in which an attacking army attempts to force the surrender of a fortified place by surrounding it and cutting off supplies and communication etc. **b** a similar operation by police etc. to force the surrender of an armed person. **2** a prolonged and determined attack. **3** N Amer. a long period of illness or difficulty. □ **lay siege to** esp. Military conduct the siege of. **under siege** the object of a fierce attack or criticism. [Old French sege seat, from assegier BESIEGE]

siege mentality noun a defensive or paranoid attitude based on an assumption of hostility in others.

Sieg·fried /ˈsiːɡfriːd/ Germanic Myth the hero of the first part of the Nibelungenlied. A prince of the Netherlands, Siegfried obtains a treasure by killing the dragon Fafner; he marries Kriemhild, and helps Gunther to win Brunhild before being treacherously slain by Hagen.

Siegfried Line 1 see HINDENBURG LINE. **2** the line of defence constructed by the Germans along the western frontier of Germany before the Second World War.

Sie·mens /ˈsiːmənz/ **1** (Ernst) **Wer·ner von** (1816–92), German electrical engineer. He developed electroplating and an electric generator which used an electromagnet, and set up a factory which manufactured telegraph systems and electric cables and pioneered electrical traction. **2** his brother, **Karl Wil·helm** (Sir Charles William, 1823–83), German-born English engineer, who developed the open-hearth steel furnace and designed the cable-laying steamship Faraday.

sie·mens /ˈsiːmənz/ noun Electricity the SI unit of conductance, equal to one reciprocal ohm. Abbr.: **S**. [W. von SIEMENS]

Siena /siˈenə/ a city in W central Italy, in Tuscany; pop. (2001) 48,884. It is noted for the school of art which flourished there in the 13th and 14th c. □ **Sien·ese** /siəˈniːz/ adjective & noun

Sien·kie·wicz /ʃeŋˈkjeɪvɪtʃ/ **Hen·ryk** (Adam Alex·an·der Pius) (1846–1916), Polish novelist and short-story writer. His novels combine carefully researched detail with romantic intrigue, and include Quo Vadis (1896), and the trilogy With Fire and Sword (1884), The Deluge (1886), and Pan Michael (1887–8); he was awarded the Nobel Prize for literature in 1905.

si·en·na /siˈenə/ noun **1** a kind of iron-rich earth used as a pigment in oil and watercolour painting. **2 a** (in full **raw sienna**) the natural colour of this earth, a yellowish brown. **b** (in full **burnt sienna**) the colour of this earth when roasted, a reddish brown. [Italian (terra di) Sienna (earth of) Siena]

si·er·ra /siˈerə/ noun a long jagged mountain chain, esp. in Spain, the US, or Latin America. [Spanish from Latin serra saw]

Sierra Leone /siˌerə liˈoːn/ a country on the coast of West Africa; pop. (est. 2002) 5,614,743; capital, Freetown. □ **Si·er·ra Leon·ean** adjective & noun

Sierra Madre /siˌerə ˈmɒdreɪ/ a mountain system in Mexico, extending from the border with the US in the north to the southern border with Guatemala. It is divided into the **Sierra Madre Occidental** in the west, the **Sierra Madre Oriental** in the east, and the **Sierra Madre del Sur** in the south. The highest peak is Citlaltépetl, in the Sierra Madre Oriental southeast of Mexico City, which rises to a height of 5 699 m (18,697 ft.).

Sierra Nevada /siˌerə nəˈvɒdə/ **1** a mountain range in S Spain, in Andalusia, southeast of Granada. Its highest peak is Mulhacén, which rises to 3 482 m (11,424 ft.). **2** (also **Sierras**) a mountain range in E California. Rising sharply from the Great Basin in the east, it descends more gently to California's Central Valley in the west. Its highest peak is Mount Whitney in Sequoia National Park, which rises to 4 418 m (14,495 ft.).

si·esta *noun* an afternoon nap or rest, esp. one taken during the hottest hours of the day in a country with an especially warm climate. [Spanish from Latin *sexta* (*hora*) sixth hour]

sieur /sjɜr/ *noun hist.* a title for a member of the minor nobility, e.g. a seigneur, in France or New France. [Old French, = lord]

sieve /sɪv/ ● *noun* **1** a device consisting of a meshed or perforated surface enclosed in a frame, used to separate coarse particles from finer ones or from a liquid. **2** a similar kitchen utensil consisting of a fine rounded metal or plastic mesh and a circular frame with a handle, used to strain liquids or to reduce soft solids to a pulp or purée; a strainer. **3** *slang Hockey* a goalie who lets in a large number of (esp. easily stopped) goals. ● *transitive verb* esp. *Brit.* **1** put through or sift with a sieve. **2** sort through or examine (evidence etc.) for specific details. **3** (often foll. by *out*) remove or separate by or as if by screening through a sieve. □ **memory** (or **head**) **like a sieve** *informal* a memory that retains little. [Old English *sife* from W Germanic]

sie·vert /ˈsiːvɜrt/ *noun* an SI unit of dosage of ionizing radiation, defined as that which delivers a joule of energy per kilogram of recipient mass. Symbol: **Sv**. [R. M. *Sievert*, Swedish radiologist b.1896]

sift *verb* **1** *transitive* pass through a sieve or sifter, esp. in order to separate coarser from finer particles or to combine and aerate (*sift together flour, salt, and baking powder; I sifted the icing sugar onto the cake*). **2** *transitive* (usu. foll. by *out, from*) remove selectively (*read through these articles and sift out the better ones*). **3** *transitive* subject (evidence, facts, etc.) to a close or thorough examination, esp. as part of a selection process; scrutinize. **4** *intransitive* (of snow, rain, sunlight, etc.) fall as if from a sieve. □ **sift through** sort through or examine (evidence etc.) for specific details. [Old English *siftan* from W Germanic]

sift·er *noun Cooking* **1** *N Amer.* a metal or plastic cylinder, open at the top and having a meshed or perforated bottom through which dry ingredients are forced by means of a manual rotary blade in order to combine and aerate them. **2** a container with a perforated top used to sprinkle dry ingredients onto a surface.

sift·ings *plural noun* a light dusting of a material passed or as if passed through a sifter or sieve.

Sif·ton ► **1 Ar·thur Lewis** (1858–1921), Canadian lawyer, judge, and politician, Liberal premier of Alberta 1910–1917. In 1903 he was appointed chief justice of the North-West Territories, and in 1907 he became the first chief justice of Alberta. He resigned as premier to join Robert Borden's Union Government as minister of customs. **2** his brother, **Sir Clif·ford** (1861–1929), Canadian lawyer, politician, and businessman. In 1896 he became federal minister of the interior and superintendent general of Indian affairs, and in this capacity promoted immigration to the Canadian prairies, esp. from central Europe. He resigned in 1905 but was instrumental in the formation of the Union Government of 1917.

SIG *abbreviation* SPECIAL INTEREST GROUP 2.

sig *abbreviation* signature.

Sig. *abbreviation* Signor.

sigh ● *verb* **1** *intransitive* emit a long deep audible breath as an expression of sadness, weariness, longing, relief, etc. **2** *transitive* utter or express with sighs (*'I give up!' he sighed*). **3** *intransitive* (of the wind etc.) make a sound that resembles sighing. **4** *intransitive* (foll. by *for*) yearn for (a lost person or thing). ● *noun* a long and audible exhalation expressing sadness, weariness, etc. □ **breathe a sigh of relief** become free of the anxiety or distress esp. caused by a particular situation. [Middle English *sihen* etc., prob. back-formation from *sihte* past of *sihen* from Old English *sican*]

sight ● *noun* **1** the faculty of seeing with the eyes. **2** the act or an instance of seeing (*the sight of him makes me ill*). **3 a** a thing seen, esp. one that is striking or remarkable; a spectacle (*that evening's sunset was a beautiful sight*). **b** *informal* a person or thing having a ridiculous, repulsive, or dishevelled appearance (*after the party this house was quite a sight*). **4** (usu. in *pl.*) the noteworthy features or attractions of a city, area, etc. (*went to see the sights*). **5** a range of space within which a person etc. can see or be seen (*they are just coming into sight*). **6** a view of something; a look or glimpse (*I caught sight of her in the crowd*). **7** (also in *pl.*) a device on a gun or surveying instrument used to make one's aim or observation more precise. **8** *informal* a great quantity (*will cost a sight of money; she's a sight better than she was*). **9** = SECOND SIGHT. **10** (attributive) designating a text previously unseen by students presented to them for commentary, translation, etc. (*we often had sight passages in high school*). ● *verb* **1** *transitive* note the presence of; observe, notice, or glimpse (*we have sighted the suspect fleeing north*). **2** *transitive* watch or locate (an object,

target, etc.), esp. by viewing it through a sight. **3 a** *transitive & intransitive* aim or adjust the sight of (a gun etc.). **b** *transitive* provide (a gun etc.) with sights. □ **at first sight** on first glimpse or impression. **at** (or **on**) **sight** as soon as a person or a thing has been seen (*the bill must be paid at sight; liked him on sight*). **catch sight of** manage to see or notice; glimpse. **in** (or **within**) **sight 1** visible. **2** within reach, attainable (*the end is in sight*). **in one's sight** in one's opinion. **in** (or **within**) **sight of** visible by (a person) or from (a location). **lose sight of 1** no longer see or know the whereabouts of. **2** cease to be aware of. **lower one's sights** become less ambitious. **out of my sight!** go at once! **out of sight out of mind** it is easy to forget what is absent. **set one's sights on** strive for (*set her sights on a directorship*). **sight for sore eyes** a welcome person or thing, esp. a visitor. □ **sight·er** *noun* [Old English (*ge*)*sihth*]

sight·ed *adjective* **1** capable of seeing; not blind. **2** (in *combination*) having a specified kind of sight (*far-sighted*). □ **sight·ed·ness** *noun* (in sense 2).

sight gag *noun* a humorous effect produced by a visual action or gesture as opposed to something spoken or written.

sight·ing *noun* **1** an act or instance of seeing something, esp. an observation reported or recorded formally (*there have been two confirmed sightings of the fugitive*). **2** the act or procedure of adjusting the aim or sights of a gun, bow, etc.

sight·less *adjective* unable to see; blind. □ **sight·less·ly** *adverb* **sight·less·ness** *noun*

sight·line *noun* a line of vision extending from a person's eye to what is seen, esp. one extending from the eye of a spectator in a theatre or sports venue to the stage or playing surface etc.

sight-read *transitive & intransitive verb* (*past* and *past participle* **-read**) play or sing a piece of music that one has not seen or practised prior to performing. □ **sight-reader** *noun* **sight-reading** *noun*

sight·seer *noun* a person who visits places of interest, esp. in a foreign city or country etc.; a tourist. □ **sight·see** *intransitive verb* **sight·see·ing** *noun*

sight-sing *transitive & intransitive verb* sing a piece of music that one has not seen or practised prior to performing. □ **sight-singing** *noun*

sight unseen *adverb* without a chance to look at or inspect a purchase etc. beforehand (*they bought the car sight unseen*).

sigil /ˈsɪdʒəl/ *noun* **1** a mark or seal; a signet. **2** an occult symbol. [from Latin *sigillum* seal, diminutive of *signum*, sign]

SIGINT /ˈsɪdʒɪnt/ *abbreviation* signals intelligence.

Sig·is·mund /ˈsɪɡɪsmənd/ (1368–1437), king of Hungary 1387–1437 and Bohemia 1419–37; Holy Roman emperor 1411–37. He helped to convene the Council of Constance (1414–18), which brought an end to the Great Schism in the Western Church (1378–1417).

sig·lum /ˈsɪɡləm/ *noun* (*pl.* **sigla**) a letter (esp. an initial) or other symbol used to denote a word in a book, esp. to refer to a particular text. [Late Latin *sigla* (pl.), perhaps from *singula* neuter pl. of *singulus* single]

sig·ma *noun* the eighteenth letter of the Greek alphabet (Σ, σ, or, when final, ς), represented in English by S, s, its uncial form having the shape of English C. [Latin from Greek]

sig·moid ● *adjective* (also **sig·moid·al**) **1** curved like the uncial sigma (C); crescent-shaped. **2** S-shaped. ● *noun* (in full **sigmoid colon, sigmoid flexure**) *Anat.* the terminal portion of the descending colon, leading to the rectum. [Greek *sigmoeidēs* (see SIGMA)]

sig·moid·os·copy /sɪɡmɔɪˈdɒskəpi/ *noun* (*pl.* **-ies**) an examination of the lower intestine by means of a flexible tube inserted through the anus. □ **sig·moid·o·scope** /sɪɡˈmɔɪdəskoːp/ *noun*

sign ● *noun* **1 a** an indication or suggestion of a quality or state (*trembling is a sign of fear*). **b** an act or gesture intended to prove a quality or state (*I give you this rose as a sign of my love*). **2 a** evidence of the existence or occurrence of something; a trace or vestige (*no signs of forced entry; there's no sign of him anywhere*). **b** a miracle or event serving as evidence of a supernatural or divine authority. **3** an indication or suggestion of a future state or occurrence; a portent (*first signs of spring; a sign that things will improve*). **4** a publicly displayed board or placard etc. used to give information or warning, or to identify or advertise a store, etc. (*street sign*). **5** a gesture or action used to convey an idea, order, request, etc. (*gave him a sign to leave; she flashed a peace sign*). **6 a** a gesture used in a system of sign language. **b** = SIGN LANGUAGE. **7 a** mark or symbol used to represent a word, phrase, idea, etc. (*a dollar sign*). **8 a** a technical mark or symbol used in mathematics, algebra, etc. to indicate an operation (*plus and minus signs*). **b** the positiveness or negativeness of a quantity. **9** *Music* a technical symbol used in music to indicate key, sharps and flats, tempo, etc. (*a repeat sign*). **10** each of the twelve divisions of the zodiac, named from the constellations formerly situated in them (*the sign of Cancer; what's your sign?*). **11** an objective indication of a disease, usu. specified (*Babinski's sign*) (*compare* SYMPTOM 1). **12** *N Amer.* the trace or evidence of a wild animal, such as its path or tracks. **13** *Linguistics* a basic element of communication, either linguistic (such as a letter or word) or non-linguistic (such as an image, article of dress, etc.); anything that can be construed as having a meaning. ● *verb* **1** *transitive & intransitive* **a** write (one's name or initials etc.) on a document etc. to authorize or authenticate it. **b** mark (a document etc.) with one's name or autograph etc. to authorize or authenticate it. **2** *transitive & intransitive* hire or be hired by signing a contract etc. (*see also* SIGN ON, SIGN UP). **3** *transitive & intransitive* **a** communicate with gestures and body language (*they signed their assent*). **b** communicate in a sign language. **4** *transitive* mark (a person) with the sign of the cross, esp. in baptism. □ **make no sign** not react or protest. **signed, sealed, and delivered** properly settled or taken care of with all the necessary formalities having been completed. **sign for** acknowledge receipt of by signing. **sign in 1** sign a register upon arrival in a hotel etc. **2** authorize the admittance of (a person) by signing a register. **sign off 1** say or write one's name to mark the end of a letter, television or radio broadcast, etc. **2** *Bridge* indicate by a conventional bid that one is seeking to end the bidding. **sign off on** *N Amer.* approve; give one's approval to. **sign on 1** agree to a contract, employment, etc. **2** begin work, broadcasting, etc., esp. by writing or announcing one's name. **sign over** (or **away**) surrender (one's right, property, etc.) by signing a document etc. **sign out 1** sign a register upon leaving a hotel etc. **2** authorize or record the release or departure of (a person or thing). **3** borrow (a book from a library). **sign up 1** engage or employ (a person). **2** enlist in the armed forces. **3 a** commit (a person) to a class or activity by signing the participant's name to a list (*signed my daughter up for swimming lessons*). **b** enrol (*signed up for evening classes*). [Old French *signe, signer* from Latin *signum, signare*]

Signac /siːˈnjak/ (1863–1935), French neo-Impressionist painter, an ardent disciple of Seurat. His technique was characterized by the use of small dashes and patches of pure colour rather than dots; his subject matter includes landscapes, seascapes, and city scenes.

sign·age *noun* signs collectively, esp. those used commercially for identifying or advertising a store or business etc.

sig·nal¹ ● *noun* **1** any sound or gesture used to convey warning, direction, or information (*we heard a distress signal; cyclists should use hand signals*). **2** a usu. pre-arranged sound or gesture acting as the prompt for a particular action (*she gave us the signal to start*). **3** *Electricity* **a** a modulation of an electric current, electromagnetic wave, etc., by means of which information is conveyed from one place to another. **b** the current or wave itself, esp. regarded as conveying information. **4 a** a device, such as a light or semaphore, used to give instructions or warnings to drivers of cars and trains at railway crossings, intersections, etc. (*traffic signal; railway signal*). **b** *N Amer.* = TURN SIGNAL. **5** an immediate occasion or cause of movement, action, etc. (*her entrance on stage was the signal for cheering and applause*). **6** *N Amer. Football* a series of letters and numbers called out by a player on offence or defence to indicate to teammates which play will be run on the next down. **7** *Bridge* a pre-arranged mode of bidding or play to convey information to one's partner. ● *verb* (**signalled, sig·nal·ling**; esp. *US* **sig·naled, sig·nal·ing**) **1** *intransitive* make a sound or gesture as a signal (*just signal if you need anything*). **2** *transitive* **a** (often foll. by *to* + infin.) make signals to (a person); direct (*she signalled me to approach*). **b** transmit (an order, information, etc.) by signal; announce (*with a nod, she signalled her assent*). **3** *transitive* be a sign or indication of; mark (*their surrender signalled the end of the war*). **4** *transitive & intransitive* (of a cyclist or driver) indicate (one's intention to turn) by means of a hand signal or turn signal (*he signalled a left turn; I forgot to signal at the intersection*). [Old French from Romanic & medieval Latin *signale* neuter of Late Latin *signalis* from Latin *signum* SIGN]

sig·nal² *adjective* remarkably good or bad; noteworthy (*a signal victory*). □ **sig·nal·ly** *adverb* [French *signalé* from Italian past participle *segnalato* distinguished, from *segnale* SIGNAL¹]

signal box *noun Brit.* a building beside a railway track from which signals are controlled.

signal fire *noun Cdn* a small fire or the remnant smoke of an extinguished fire serving to inform others of one's presence at a campsite etc.

Signal Hill a historic site in SE Newfoundland, a hill of some 150 m overlooking St. John's Harbour. Used for centuries as a lookout to warn

approaching ships of hazards and bad weather, it was here that the first transatlantic radio signal was received.

sig·nal·man *noun* (*pl.* **-men**) **1** a railway employee responsible for operating signals and switches. **2** (also **sig·nal·ler**) a person employed to make or transmit signals, esp. in the army or navy.

signals intelligence *noun* information derived from the monitoring, interception, and interpretation of radio signals.

signals officer *noun hist.* the officer in charge of transmitting and receiving signals.

signal-to-noise ratio *noun* the ratio of the strength of an electrical or other signal carrying information to that of unwanted interference, usu. expressed in decibels.

sig·na·tory /ˈsɪɡnəˌtɔri/ ● *noun* (*pl.* **-ies**) a person, party, or country that has signed a particular document, such as a treaty. ● *adjective* (of a party or country etc.) that has signed a treaty or similar document. [Latin *signatorius* of sealing, from *signare signat-* mark]

sig·na·ture /ˈsɪɡnətʃər/ *noun* **1 a** a person's name, initials, or distinctive mark used in signing a letter, document, etc. **b** the written name of a celebrity; autograph. **c** the act of signing a document etc. (*this bill is ready for signature*). **2 a** a distinctive or identifying feature or characteristic. **b** (*attributive*) designating a characteristic or skill etc. that distinguishes or typifies a person, their work, etc. (*this is the chef's signature dish*). **3** *Music* **a** = KEY SIGNATURE. **b** = TIME SIGNATURE. **4** *Printing* **a** a letter or figure placed at the foot of one or more pages of each sheet of a book as a guide for binding. **b** such a sheet after folding. **5** directions given to a patient as part of a medical prescription. Abbr.: **sig.** [medieval Latin *signatura* (Late Latin = marking of sheep), as SIGNATORY]

signature tune *noun Brit.* = THEME SONG 1.

sign·board *noun* **1** a board displaying the name or logo of a store, hotel, or other business. **2** *N Amer.* a board mounted on a signpost to direct travellers in a particular direction.

sign·ee /saɪˈniː/ *noun* a person who has signed a contract, register, etc.

sig·net /ˈsɪɡnət/ *noun* **1** a small seal, usu. set in a ring, used with or instead of a signature to authenticate a document. **2** the stamp or impression of a seal. [Old French *signet* or medieval Latin *signetum* (as SIGN)]

signet ring *noun* a ring worn on the finger usu. bearing the wearer's initials or an emblem etc.

sig·nifi·cance /sɪɡˈnɪfɪkəns/ *noun* **1** consequence, importance (*his opinion is of no significance*). **2** a concealed or real meaning (*what is the significance of his statement?*). **3** *Statistics* the extent to which a result deviates from a hypothesis such that the difference is due to more than errors in sampling. **4** the state of being significant.

sig·nifi·cant /sɪɡˈnɪfɪkənt/ *adjective* **1** of great importance or consequence (*a significant medical breakthrough*). **2** having or conveying an unstated meaning; having information that may be gathered (*I find it significant that he cannot talk to her; she shot me a significant glare*). **3** noteworthy, noticeable (*a significant drop in temperature*). **4** *Statistics* of or relating to the significance in the difference between an observed and calculated result. □ **sig·nifi·cant·ly** *adverb* [Latin *significare*: see SIGNIFY]

significant digit *noun* (also **significant figure**) *Math.* a digit which has its precise numerical meaning in the number containing it, and is not a zero used simply to fill a vacant place at the beginning or end.

significant other *noun N Amer.* often *jocular* a spouse, partner, or lover.

sig·nifi·ca·tion /ˌsɪɡnɪfɪˈkeɪʃən/ *noun* **1** the act of signifying. **2** (often foll. by *of*) that which is signified; the implication, sense, or meaning, esp. of a word or phrase.

sig·ni·fied *noun Linguistics* the idea or meaning conventionally indicated by the signifier, as distinct from the external object to which it refers.

sig·ni·fier *noun* **1** *Linguistics* a physical medium (such as a sound, symbol, image, etc.) expressing meaning, as distinct from the meaning expressed. **2** a thing that signifies or conveys meaning.

sig·ni·fy /ˈsɪɡnɪˌfaɪ/ *verb* (**-fies, -fied**) **1** *transitive* **a** be a sign or symbol of; represent, denote (*a white flag signifies surrender; this badge signifies authority*). **b** offer a suggestion or hint of; portend (*his shortness of breath signifies that he may have a heart condition; those clouds signify a storm*). **2** *transitive* mean; have as its meaning (*'anorexia' signifies a type of eating disorder*). **3** *transitive* communicate; announce, declare (*she signified her disappointment to me*). **4** *intransitive* be of importance; matter (*it signifies little*). [Old French *signifier* from Latin *significare* (as SIGN)]

sign·ing *noun* **1 a** an act or instance of signing a contract or signing a

Consonants: b *but* d *dog* f *few* g *get* h *her* j *yes* k *cat* l *leg* m *man* n *no* p *pen* r *red* s *sit*

person to a contract. **b** a person who has signed a contract, esp. to join a professional sports team. **2** an instance of using, or the ability to use, sign language. **3** a session or period of time devoted to signing autographs (*a book-signing*).

signing bonus *noun* esp. *Sport* a single lump payment paid to a signee upon signing a contract.

sign language *noun* a system of communication by visual gestures, used esp. by the hearing impaired.

sign law *noun Cdn informal* a Quebec provincial law regulating the use of languages other than French on signs.

sign-off *noun* an act or instance of terminating a letter or broadcast etc.

sign of the cross *noun* a Christian sign made in blessing or prayer, by tracing a cross from the forehead to the chest and to each shoulder, or in the air.

sign of the times *noun* an incident, event, person, etc. that typifies or foreshadows a trend developing or likely to develop in society.

sign of the zodiac *noun* = SIGN *noun* 10.

sign-on *noun* an act or instance of beginning a broadcast etc.

si·gnor /siːˈnjɔr/ *noun* (also **si·gnore** /-ˈnjore/) (*pl.* **si·gnori** /-ˈnjɔri/) **1** used as a title (preceding the surname or other designation) of, or as a respectful form of address to, an Italian or Italian-speaking man, corresponding to English Mr. or sir. **2** an Italian man of distinction, rank, or authority; a nobleman. [Italian from Latin *senior*: see SENIOR]

si·gnora /siːˈnjɔrə/ *noun* **1** used as a title (preceding the surname or other designation) of, or as a respectful form of address to, an Italian or Italian-speaking married woman, corresponding to English Mrs. or madam. **2** a married Italian woman. [Italian, fem. of SIGNOR]

si·gnor·ina /ˌsiːnjɔˈriːnə/ *noun* **1** used as a title (preceding the surname or other designation) of, or as a respectful form of address to, an Italian or Italian-speaking unmarried woman. **2** an Italian unmarried woman. [Italian, diminutive of SIGNORA]

sign painter *noun* (also **sign writer**) a person who paints esp. commercial signs.

sign·post ● *noun* **1** a post with a sign giving directions or information. **2** a means of guidance; an indication or clue. ● *transitive verb* (usu. in *passive*) **1 a** provide with a signpost or signposts. **b** convey (information) by means of a signpost. **2** indicate (a course of action, direction, etc.).

Sig·urd /ˈsɪɡərd/ (in Norse legend) the Norse equivalent of Siegfried, husband of Gudrun.

Siha·nouk /ˈsiənʊk/ **Prince Noro·dom** (b.1922), Cambodian king 1941–55, prime minister 1955–60, and head of state 1960–70, 1975–6, and since 1993. He proclaimed himself head of state in 1960, a position he retained until a US-backed military coup ten years later; he was reinstated by the Khmer Rouge (1975–6), and, after serving as president of the government-in-exile (1982–9), he was appointed Cambodian head of state by the provisional government (1993).

sika /ˈsiːkə/ *noun* (in full **sika deer**) a small forest-dwelling deer, *Cervus nippon*, native to Japan and widely naturalized elsewhere. [Japanese *shika*]

Sikh /siːk/ ● *noun* a member of a monotheistic religion founded in Punjab by Guru Nanak in the 16th c., combining Hindu and Islamic elements. ● *adjective* of or relating to Sikhs or Sikhism. [Punjabi, Hindi, from Sanskrit *śiṣya* 'disciple']

Sikh·ism *noun* the beliefs and principles of the Sikhs.

Sikh Wars a series of wars between the Sikhs and the British in 1845 and 1848–9, culminating in the British annexation of Punjab.

Siking /ʃiːˈkɪŋ/ a former name for XIAN.

Sik·kim /ˈsɪkɪm/ a state of NE India, in the E Himalayas between Bhutan and Nepal, on the border with Tibet; capital, Gangtok. □ **Sik·kim·ese** *adjective & noun*

Si·kor·sky /sɪˈkɔrski/ **Igor (Ivan·ovich)** (1889–1972), Russian-born US aircraft designer. He established the Sikorsky Aero Engineering Co. and produced many famous amphibious aircraft and flying boats; in the 1930s he turned his attention to helicopters, personally flying the prototype of the first mass-produced helicopter in 1939, and was closely associated with their subsequent development.

sik·sik /ˈsiːksiːk/ *noun N Amer. (North)* = ARCTIC GROUND SQUIRREL. [Inuktitut, imitative of its call]

Sik·sika /sɪkˈsɪkə/ *noun* **1** a member of an Aboriginal people, part of the Blackfoot, living in central Alberta. **2** the Algonquian language of this people. [Blackfoot, from *siksi-* black + *-ka* foot]

silage /ˈsailədʒ/ *noun* green crops preserved by pressure esp. in a silo or occasionally in a stack. [alteration of ENSILAGE 2 after *silo*]

si·lence ● *noun* **1 a** absence of sound or noise. **b** the state or a period of this (*we sat in silence; there was an awkward silence before she spoke*). **2** abstinence from, or renunciation of, speech, esp. as a religious vow or payment of respect to a deceased person or group. **3** the avoidance of mentioning or discussing a particular topic or thing; reticence (*silence is golden*). **4** the inability to speak, esp. as a result of shock, surprise, fear, etc. (*she watched in stunned silence*). **5** death, oblivion. ● *transitive verb* **1** make quiet or silent (*she silenced the ringing alarm clock*). **2** defy (critics, detractors, arguments) by successfully defending one's position. **3** quell or disable (an esp. military opponent, their artillery, etc.). **4** prohibit or prevent (a person) from speaking, esp. to prevent the free expression of opinion. □ **reduce** (or **put**) **to silence** overwhelm with superior argument.

si·lenced *adjective* (of a gun) fitted with a silencer.

si·len·cer *noun* **1** a device used to reduce the sound of a gun as it is fired. **2** anything used to reduce the noise or sound of something. **3** *Brit.* = MUFFLER 1.

si·lent ● *adjective* **1** characterized by an absence of sound or noise. **2** characterized by an absence of speech; not talking (*she offered a silent greeting; silent reading*). **3** (of a person) taciturn; speaking little. **4** (of a speaker, writer, book, etc.) omitting mention or discussion of a particular subject; offering no account or record. **5** (of a movie or film etc.) not having a recorded soundtrack or audible dialogue, but usu. having dialogue represented in printed form onscreen (*stars of the silent screen*). **6** *Med.* producing no detectable signs or symptoms (*silent coronary*). **7** (of a letter) written but not pronounced, e.g. *b* in doubt. **8** inactive, quiescent (*their guns were silent that night*). ● *noun* a silent movie or film. □ **si·lent·ly** *adverb* [Latin *silēre silent-* be silent]

silent auction *noun N Amer.* an auction in which bids for displayed items are written down during a specified period at the end of which each item goes to its highest bidder.

silent majority *noun* the presumed majority of people having moderate opinions but being too passive to assert them.

silent partner *noun N Amer.* a person who has capital in a partnership but takes no part in its commercial activities.

silent treatment *noun* the stubborn refusal to talk to a person, esp. a person with whom one has had a recent argument or disagreement (*after I forgot her birthday, she gave me the silent treatment for a week*).

Si·len·us /saiˈliːnəs/ *Gk Myth* an aged woodland deity, who was entrusted with the education of Dionysus; he is depicted either as dignified, inspired and musical, or as an old drunkard.

si·len·us /saiˈliːnəs/ *noun* (*pl.* **si·leni** /-nai/) *Gk Myth* a bearded old man like a satyr, sometimes with the tail and legs of a horse. [Latin from Greek *seilēnos*]

Si·lesia /saiˈliːziə, -ˈliːʒə/ a region of central Europe, centred on the upper Oder valley, now largely in SW Poland. It was partitioned at various times between the states of Prussia, Austria-Hungary, Poland, and Czechoslovakia. □ **Si·lesian** *adjective & noun*

sil·hou·ette /ˌsɪluˈet/ ● *noun* **1** a portrait or representation of a thing showing the outline only, usu. done in solid black and placed on a white or contrasting background. **2** the dark shadow or outline of a person or thing against a lighter background. **3** the contour or outline of a garment or person's body. ● *transitive verb* (usu. in *passive*) show or represent in silhouette. □ **in silhouette** seen or placed in outline. [Étienne de *Silhouette*, French author and politician d.1767]

sili·ca /ˈsɪləkə/ *noun* a hard mineral substance, silicon dioxide, occurring in many rocks, soils, and sands as flint, opal, or crystals of quartz, etc., used esp. in the manufacture of glass and ceramics. □ **si·li·ceous** /-ˈlɪʃəs/ *adjective* (also **si·li·cious**). [Latin *silex -icis* 'flint', on the pattern of *alumina* etc.]

silica gel *noun* hydrated silica in a hard granular form used as a desiccant.

sili·cate /ˈsɪləˌkət/ *noun* any of the many insoluble compounds of a metal combined with silicon and oxygen, which include many rock-forming minerals such as mica, feldspar, garnet, tourmaline, etc.

si·li·cic /səˈlɪsɪk/ *adjective Chem.* pertaining to, consisting of, or formed from silicon or silica.

si·li·ci·fy /sɪˈlɪsɪfai/ *transitive verb* (**-fies, -fied**) convert into or impregnate with silica. □ **si·li·ci·fi·ca·tion** *noun*

sili·con /ˈsɪlɪkən/ *noun Chem.* **1** a non-metallic element occurring abundantly in the earth's crust in oxides and silicates, used in electronic components for its semiconducting properties, as well as in the manufacture of glass. Symbol: **Si**; at. no.: 14. **2** (**Silicon**) prefixed to nouns denoting geographical features, to designate an area with a high density of industry devoted to information technology (*Silicon Alley*; *Silicon Glen*). [Latin *silex -icis* flint (after *carbon*, *boron*), alteration of earlier *silicium*]

silicon carbide *noun* = CARBORUNDUM.

silicon chip *noun* a silicon microchip.

sili·cone /ˈsɪləˌkoːn/ *noun* any of the many polymeric organic compounds of silicon and oxygen used as electrical insulators, waterproofing agents, adhesives, and rubbers.

silicone implant *noun* = BREAST IMPLANT.

Silicon Valley *noun* an area with a high concentration of electronics industries, esp. the Santa Clara valley southeast of San Francisco.

Silicon Valley North Ottawa and its suburbs, esp. Kanata, as a centre of computer-related industries.

silicon wafer *noun* *Electronics* a wafer of silicon bearing an integrated circuit.

sili·co·sis /ˌsɪləˈkoːsɪs/ *noun* lung fibrosis caused by the inhalation of dust containing silica. □ **sili·cot·ic** /-ˈkɒtɪk/ *adjective & noun*

sili·qua /ˈsɪlɪkwə/ *noun* (also **si·lique** /sɪˈliːk/) (*pl.* **sili·quae** /-kwiː/ or **si·liques** /sɪˈliːks/) the long narrow seed pod of a cruciferous plant. □ **sili·quose** /-ˌkwoːs/ *adjective* **sili·quous** /-kwəs/ *adjective* [Latin, = pod]

silk ● *noun* 1 a fine lustrous soft strong fibre produced by silkworms in making cocoons. 2 a similar fibre spun by some spiders. 3 a thread or cloth made from silk fibre. b a thread or fabric resembling silk. c (*attributive*) denoting articles of clothing made of silk (*silk blouse*). 4 (in *pl.*) garments made of silk, esp. a jockey's cap and jacket bearing the colours of the horse's owner. 5 the long silky threadlike styles of an ear of corn. 6 *Brit. informal* the silk gown worn by a Queen's (or King's) Counsel. ● *transitive verb* *N Amer.* (of corn) produce silk; be in the stage of growth in which the silk is produced. □ **take silk** *Brit.* become a Queen's (or King's) Counsel. **you can't make a silk purse out of a sow's ear** you can't create a superior product from inferior materials. □ **silk-like** *adjective* [Old English *sioloc*, *seolec* (compare Old Norse *silki*) from Late Latin *sericum* neuter of Latin *sericus* from *seres* from Greek *Sēres* an oriental people]

silk-cotton tree *noun* any of several trees producing seeds surrounded by a silky fibre, used esp. as a packing or stuffing material, such as the *Ceiba pentandra* or *Bombax ceiba*.

silk·en *adjective* 1 made of silk. 2 resembling silk, esp. in texture, softness, or lustre. 3 dressed in or adorned with silk. 4 (of a person, their manner, etc.) elegant, suave, ingratiating.

silk gland *noun* a gland secreting the substance produced as silk.

silk hat *noun* a top hat covered with silk plush.

silk moth *noun* (in full **silkworm moth**) any of various large moths whose larvae spin silk cocoons, esp. of the families Saturniidae and Bombycidae, esp. *Bombyx mori*.

Silk Road (also **Silk Route**) an ancient caravan route linking Xian in central China with the E Mediterranean. Skirting the northern edge of the Taklimakan Desert and passing through Turkestan, it covered a distance of some 6 400 km (4,000 miles). Established during the period of Roman rule in Europe, it took its name from the silk which was brought to the west from China. It was also the route by which Christianity spread to the East. A railway (completed in 1963) follows the Chinese part of the route, from Xian to Urumqi.

silk·screen ● *noun* 1 a screen of fine mesh used in screen printing. 2 the process of screen printing. 3 a print made by this process. ● *transitive verb* print, decorate, or reproduce using a silkscreen.

silk stocking *noun* 1 (often in *pl.*) a stocking made of silk. 2 (usu. *attributive*, **silk-stocking**) maintaining or suggesting a wealthy lifestyle (*silk-stocking crowd*; *silk-stocking attire*).

silk·worm *noun* the caterpillar of the moth *Bombyx mori*, which spins its cocoon of silk.

silkworm moth *noun* = SILK MOTH.

silky *adjective* (**silk·i·er**, **silk·i·est**) 1 like silk in smoothness, softness, fineness, or lustre. 2 (of a person's manner, voice, etc.) suave, smooth. 3 *Bot.* (of leaves) covered with fine close-set hairs having a gloss and lustre like that of silk. □ **silk·i·ly** *adverb* **silk·i·ness** *noun*

sill *noun* 1 a strong horizontal beam forming the base or foundation of esp. a house. 2 (in full **window·sill**) a horizontal shelf of wood, stone, or metal forming the bottom part of a window opening. 3 the bottom timber or lowest part of a door frame; a threshold. 4 any of the lower horizontal pieces forming the frame of a car or truck etc. 5 *Geol.* a tabular sheet of igneous rock intruded between other rocks and parallel with their planar structure. [Old English *syll*, *sylle*]

Sil·lan·pää /ˈsɪlənpa/ **Frans Eemil** (1888–1964), Finnish novelist and short-story writer, whose novels include *Meek Heritage* (1919), *The Maid Silja* (1931), and *People in the Summer Night* (1934); he was awarded the Nobel Prize for literature in 1939.

Sil·lery /siːjəˈriː/ a former town in SE central Quebec, now part of the city of Québec; pop. (2001) 11,909. [N. Brulart de *Sillery*, French nobleman d.1640 who financially supported a mission in the area]

sil·li·man·ite /ˈsɪləmənˌnait/ *noun* an aluminum silicate occurring in orthorhombic crystals or fibrous masses. [B. *Silliman*, US chemist d.1864]

Sills, Bev·er·ley (born Belle Silverman) (b.1929), US operatic soprano. A highly popular singer, she joined the New York City Opera in 1975 and served as its director from 1979 to 1989.

silly ● *adjective* (**sil·li·er**, **sil·li·est**) 1 displaying a lack of judgment or common sense; stupid, foolish. 2 absurd, ridiculous, laughable (*she looked silly in that hat*). 3 senseless, stupefied, dazed (*we drank ourselves silly; was bored silly*). 4 *archaic* innocent, simple, helpless. ● *noun* (*pl.* **-lies**) *informal* a foolish person. □ **sil·li·ness** *noun* [later form of Middle English *sely* (dial. *seely*) happy, representing Old English *sælig* (recorded in *unsælig* unhappy) from Germanic]

silly-billy *noun* (*pl.* **-billies**) *informal* a foolish person.

Silly Putty *noun* *proprietary* a mouldable silicone-based substance with remarkable properties of stretching and bouncing, sold chiefly as a toy.

silly season *noun* the time of year, usu. during summer, when newspapers often publish trivial material for lack of important news.

silo /ˈsailoː/ *noun* (*pl.* **silos**) 1 a tall cylinder or pit in which green corn or hay etc. is pressed and kept for fodder, undergoing fermentation. 2 a pit or tower for the storage of grain, cement, etc. 3 an underground chamber in which a guided missile is kept ready for firing. [Spanish from Latin *sirus* from Greek *siros* grain pit]

silt ● *noun* fine sand, clay, or other soil carried by moving or running water and deposited as sediment on the bottom or on the shore of a lake or stream etc. ● *verb* 1 *transitive & intransitive* (often foll. by *up*) fill or block, or be filled or blocked, with silt. 2 *intransitive* flow, drift, or settle like silt; pass gradually (*affluence has silted into this neighbourhood*). □ **silt·a·tion** *noun* **silty** *adjective* [Middle English, perhaps related to Danish, Norwegian *sylt*, Old Low German *sulta*, Old High German *sulza* salt marsh, formed as SALT]

silt·stone *noun* a fine-grained sandstone consisting of consolidated silt.

Si·lur·ian /səˈlʊriən/ *Geol.* ● *adjective* of or relating to the third period of the Paleozoic era, lasting from about 438 to 408 million years BP, between the Ordovician and Devonian periods. The first land plants and the first true fish appeared during this period. ● *noun* this geological period or system. [Latin *Silures*, a people of ancient SE Wales]

silva *var. of* SYLVA.

sil·van *var. of* SYLVAN.

Sil·van·us /sɪlˈveinəs, sɪlˈvɒnəs/ *Rom. Myth* an Italian woodland deity later identified with Pan.

sil·ver ● *noun* *Chem.* 1 a greyish-white lustrous malleable ductile precious metallic element, occurring naturally as the element and in mineral form, and used chiefly with an admixture of harder metals for coin, plate, and ornaments, as a subordinate monetary medium, and in compounds for photography etc. Symbol: **Ag**; at. no.: 47. 2 the colour of silver. 3 silver or cupro-nickel coins collectively; change. 4 utensils and vessels made of or plated with silver collectively, esp. cutlery. 5 household cutlery of any material. 6 = SILVER MEDAL. 7 = SILVER SALMON. ● *adjective* 1 made wholly or chiefly of silver. 2 coloured like silver. 3 designating the twenty-fifth event of an esp. annual series (*silver wedding anniversary*). ● *transitive verb* 1 coat or plate with silver. 2 provide (mirror glass) with a backing of tin amalgam etc. 3 (of the moon or a white light) give a silvery appearance to. 4 turn (the hair) grey or white. [Old English *seolfor* from Germanic]

silver age *noun* a period regarded as inferior to a golden age, e.g. that of post-classical Latin literature in the early period of the Roman Empire.

silver·back *noun* a mature male mountain gorilla, distinguished by an area of white or silvery hair across the back.

silver band *noun* a brass band playing silver-plated instruments.

silver·berry *noun* (*pl.* **-berries**) a silvery-leaved N American oleaster, *Elaeagnus commutata*. Also called SILVER WILLOW, WOLF WILLOW.

silver birch *noun* a European birch, *Betula pendula*, with silver-coloured bark peeling in long strips.

Silver Broom *noun hist.* the trophy awarded annually to the winner of the men's World Curling Championships from 1968–1987.

silver buffalo berry *noun see* BUFFALO BERRY.

silver bullet *noun informal* a cure-all or universal remedy, esp. any usu. undiscovered highly specific and highly successful drug.

silver dollar *noun* **1** = HONESTY 3. **2** a dollar coin.

silver dollar pancakes *plural noun N Amer.* small pancakes roughly the size of a dollar coin.

silver fir *noun* any fir of the genus *Abies*, with the undersides of its leaves coloured silver.

silver·fish *noun* (*pl.* same or **-fishes**) **1** any small silvery wingless insect of the order Thysanura, esp. *Lepisma saccharina* often found living in houses and other buildings. **2** a silver-coloured fish, esp. a colourless variety of goldfish.

silver foil *noun* thin metal foil, esp. of aluminum, used for wrapping candy etc.

silver fox *noun* **1** a N American red fox at a time when its fur is black with white tips. **2** its fur or pelt.

silver-gilt *noun* **1** gilded silver (also *attributive*: *silver-gilt goblet*). **2** an imitation gilding of yellow lacquer over silver leaf.

silver-grey ● *noun* a pale or lustrous grey. ● *adjective* of this colour.

Sil·ver·heels, Jay (born Harold Jay Smith) (1919–80), Canadian-born film actor. A leading athlete during his youth on the Six Nations Reserve, he travelled to Hollywood with a lacrosse team in 1938 and went on to play roles in over 30 films. His most remembered role is that of Tonto in the *Lone Ranger* films (1956, 1958). He founded the Indian Actors Workshop in Hollywood in 1963.

sil·ver·ing *noun* **1** the act of plating or coating something with silver or an amalgam of tin etc. **2** silver plating.

silver jubilee *noun* **1** the 25th anniversary of a sovereign's accession. **2** any other 25th anniversary.

silver lining *noun* a consolation or hopeful prospect in misfortune.

silver maple *noun* a maple of eastern N America, *Acer saccharinum*, with leaves that are silvery underneath.

silver medal *noun* a medal of silver, usu. awarded as second prize. □ **silver medallist** *noun*

silver mound *noun* a type of artemisia with silvery green leaves forming a round mound-like shape.

silver nitrate *noun* a colourless solid that is soluble in water, used in photographic emulsions, as an antiseptic, and as an astringent, etc.

silver plate *noun* **1** vessels or utensils made of or plated with silver or an alloy of silver. **2** the material of which these are made. □ **silver-plated** *adjective*

silver·point *noun* **1** the art of drawing with a silver-pointed stylus on specially prepared paper. **2** a drawing made in this way.

silver poplar *noun* the European white poplar, *Populus alba*, bearing leaves with white woolly hairs underneath.

silver salmon *noun* a coho.

silver screen *noun* (usu. prec. by *the*) the movie industry; motion pictures collectively.

silver·side *noun* **1** (also **silver·sides**) any of various fish with silvery sides, e.g. a common shiner. **2** *Brit.* the upper side of a round of beef from the outside of the leg.

silver·smith *noun* a person who works with silver; a manufacturer of silver articles. □ **silver·smith·ing** *noun*

silver spoon *noun* **1** a spoon made of silver. **2** a sign of wealth or future prosperity (*she was born with a silver spoon in her mouth*).

silver standard *noun* a system by which the value of a currency is defined in terms of silver, for which the currency may be exchanged.

silver thaw *noun Cdn* (*Maritimes & Nfld*) a slick glassy coating of ice formed on the ground or an exposed surface, caused by freezing rain or a sudden light frost.

silver·tip *noun* (in full **silvertip grizzly**) *Cdn* (*West*) a mature grizzly bear with white-tipped hairs esp. native to the Rocky Mountains.

silver-tongued *adjective* eloquent, persuasive. □ **silver-tongue** *noun*

silver·ware *noun* tableware, esp. utensils used for eating and serving, made of silver or an alloy of silver, or of a metal coated with silver, stainless steel, etc.

silver·weed *noun* a plant with silvery leaves, *Potentilla anserina*, with red stolons.

silver willow *noun* **1** a variety of willow with silvery leaves, planted as an ornamental. **2** = SILVERBERRY.

sil·very *adjective* **1** like silver in colour or appearance. **2** having a clear gentle ringing sound. **3** (of the hair) white and lustrous. □ **sil·ver·i·ness** *noun*

silvi·cul·ture /ˈsɪlvəˌkʌltʃər/ *noun* the branch of forestry concerned with the growing and cultivation of trees. □ **silvi·cul·tur·al** *adjective* **silvi·cul·tur·ist** *noun* [French from Latin *silva* a wood + French *culture* CULTURE]

sim *noun* simulation. [abbreviation]

Sim·birsk /sɪmˈbiːrsk/ a city in European Russia, a port on the Volga River southeast of Nizhni Novgorod; pop. (est. 2002) 664,800. Between 1924 and 1992 it was called Ulyanovsk, in honour of Lenin (Vladimir Ilich Ulyanov), who was born there in 1870.

SIM card *noun* a card containing a microprocessor, which is slotted into a mobile phone (and may be transferred between compatible sets) and holds details of the user's network registration, payments, messages, calls, etc. [acronym from *subscriber identification module*]

sim·cha /ˈsɪmtʃə, -xə/ *noun* a Jewish private party or celebration. [Hebrew *śimḥāh* rejoicing]

Sim·chas Torah /ˌsɪmtʃəs ˈtɔrə, -xəs/ *noun* (also **Sim·hath Torah** /-xə/, **Sim·chat Torah** /-xət/) the final day of the festival of Sukkot, on which the annual cycle of the reading of the Torah is completed and begun anew. [Hebrew *śimḥat tōrā* from SIMCHA + TORAH]

Sim·coe¹ a former town in SW Ontario, about 65 km southwest of Hamilton, now part of the city of Norfolk County; pop. (2001) 14,941. □ **Sim·con·ian** *noun* [J.G. SIMCOE²]

Sim·coe², John Graves (1752–1806), British army officer and colonial administrator. Commander of the Queen's Rangers during the American Revolution, he was appointed the first Lieutenant-Governor of Upper Canada in 1791, and began the policy of granting lands to the Loyalists. He founded the city of York (now Toronto), organized a road system, and abolished slavery. After leaving British North America in 1796, he served in Santo Domingo and in England until his death.

Simcoe, Lake a lake in south central Ontario, situated off the southeastern shore of Georgian Bay, over 60 km north of Toronto. [J. Simcoe, father of J.G. SIMCOE², d.1759]

Simcoe Day *noun Cdn* (*S Ont.*) (esp. in Toronto) a civic holiday celebrated on the first Monday in August.

Sime·non /ˈsiːməˌnɔ̃/ **Georges (Jo·seph Chris·tian)** (1903–89), Belgian-born French novelist. Of his many works of fiction he is best known for his series of detective novels featuring Commissaire Maigret, introduced in 1931.

Sim·eon /ˈsɪmiən/ **1** Hebrew patriarch, son of Jacob and Leah (Gen. 29:33). **2** the tribe of Israel that was traditionally descended from him.

Sim·eon Styl·ites, St. /staɪˈlaɪtiːz/ (*c.*390–459) Syrian monk. After living in a monastic community he became the first to practise an extreme form of asceticism which involved living on top of a pillar; this became a site of pilgrimage.

sim·eth·i·cone /sɪˈmeθɪkoːn/ *noun* the active ingredient in many preparations to relieve intestinal gas, which causes mucus-trapped gas bubbles to form larger bubbles which are more easily eliminated. [SILICA + METHYL + SILICONE]

Sim·fer·o·pol /ˌsɪmfəˈrɒpəl/ a city in S Ukraine, on the Crimean peninsula, northeast of Sevastopol; pop. (est. 2001) 343,000.

sim·ian /ˈsɪmiən/ ● *adjective* **1** of or concerning the anthropod apes. **2** characteristic of an ape or monkey (*a simian walk*). ● *noun* an ape or monkey. [Latin *simia* ape, perhaps from Latin *simus* from Greek *simos* flat-nosed]

sim·i·lar *adjective* **1** of the same nature or kind; alike. **2** (often foll. by *to*) having a resemblance. **3** *Math.* (of two geometrical figures etc.) shaped alike; containing the same angles, having the same shape or proportions. □ **sim·i·lar·ly** *adverb* [French *similaire* or medieval Latin *similaris* from Latin *similis* like]

sim·i·lar·ity *noun* (*pl.* **-ities**) **1** the state or fact of being similar; resemblance. **2** a point of resemblance; a particular aspect resembling another.

sim·ile /ˈsɪmili/ *noun* **1** a figure of speech involving the explicit comparison of two different things, often using the words 'like' or 'as', e.g. *as brave as a lion*. **2** the use of such comparison. [Middle English from Latin, neuter of *similis* like]

sim·ili·tude /sɪˈmɪləˌtuːd, -tjuːd/ *noun* the quality or state of being similar; similarity. [Old French *similitude* or Latin *similitudo* (as SIMILE)]

Simil·ka·meen River /ˌsɪmɪlkəˈmiːn, səˌmɪlkə-/ a river in southern BC, which rises east of Chilliwack and flows first northward, then southeastward, to join the Okanagan River just south of the Washington border. [from Nicola-Similkameen (an extinct Athapaskan language), a designation of several Okanagan bands: meaning unknown]

Simla a city in NE India, capital of the state of Himachal Pradesh; pop. (2001) 142,200. Situated in the foothills of the Himalayas, it served from 1865 to 1939 as the summer capital of British India. It is a popular hill resort.

SIMM *abbreviation* single in-line memory module, containing RAM chips.

Sim·men·tal /ˈsɪməntəl/ *noun* a breed of large red and white cattle farmed for both milk and meat. [a valley in central Switzerland]

sim·mer ● *verb* **1 a** *intransitive* (of a liquid) be at a heat at or just below the boiling point; boil or bubble gently. **b** *transitive* cook (a liquid or foods immersed in liquid) at a temperature at or just below the boiling point. **2** *intransitive* be in a state of suppressed anger or excitement. ● *noun* a simmering condition. □ **simmer down** become calm or less agitated. [alteration of Middle English (now dial.) *simper*, perhaps imitative]

sim·nel cake *noun* esp. *Brit.* a rich fruitcake, usu. with a marzipan layer and decoration, eaten esp. at Easter or during Lent. [Old French *simenel*, ultimately from Latin *simila* or Greek *semidalis* fine flour]

sim·oleon /sɪmˈoːliən/ *noun US slang* a dollar. [perhaps after NAPOLEON 2]

Simon ▸ **1 (Mar·vin) Neil** (b.1927), US dramatist. Most of his plays are wry comedies portraying aspects of middle-class life; they include *Barefoot in the Park* (1963), *The Odd Couple* (1965), and *Brighton Beach Memoirs* (1983); among his musicals are *Sweet Charity* (1966) and *They're Playing Our Song* (1979). **2 Paul** (b.1942), US pop singer and songwriter. With Art Garfunkel (b.1941) he recorded a number of popular albums, including *Sounds of Silence* (1966), the soundtrack music to the film *The Graduate* (1968), and *Bridge Over Troubled Water* (1970); the duo split up in 1970 and Simon went on to pursue a successful solo career, recording albums such as *Graceland* (1986) and *The Rhythm of the Saints* (1990). **3 St.** (known as Simon the Zealot), an Apostle. According to one tradition he preached and was martyred in Persia along with St. Jude. Feast day (with St. Jude), 28 Oct.

Sim·oni·des /saɪˈmɒnɪˌdiːz/ (*c*.556–468 BC), Greek lyric poet. Much of his poetry, which includes elegies, odes, and epigrams, celebrates the heroes of Greece's war with Persia, and includes verse commemorating those killed at Marathon and Thermopylae.

simon-pure *adjective* real, genuine. [*Simon Pure*, a character in Centlivre's *Bold Stroke for a Wife* (1717), who is impersonated by another character during part of the play]

Simon Says *noun* a children's game in which players must obey the leader's instructions if (and only if) they are prefaced with the words 'Simon says'.

si·mony /ˈsaɪməni, ˈsɪm-/ *noun* the buying or selling of ecclesiastical privileges, e.g. pardons or benefices. □ **sim·oni·ac** /-ˈmoːniˌak/ *adjective & noun* [Old French *simonie* from Late Latin *simonia* from *Simon* Magus (Acts 8:18)]

sim·oom /səˈmuːm/ *noun* (also **sim·oon** /-ˈmuːn/) a hot dry dust-laden wind blowing at intervals esp. in the Arabian desert. [Arabic *samūm* from *samma* to poison]

simp *noun N Amer. informal* a simpleton. [abbreviation]

sim·pat·ico /sɪmˈpatɪˌkoː/ *adjective* (also **sym·pat·ico**) congenial, likeable. [Italian & Spanish (as SYMPATHY)]

sim·per ● *verb* **1** *intransitive* smile in a silly or affected way. **2** *transitive* express by or with simpering. ● *noun* such a smile. □ **sim·per·ing·ly** *adverb* [16th c.: compare Dutch and Scandinavian *semper*, *simper*, German *zimp(f)er* elegant, delicate]

sim·ple ● *adjective* **1** easily understood or done; presenting no difficulty (*a simple explanation*; *a simple task*). **2** not complicated or elaborate; without luxury or sophistication. **3 a** not compound; consisting of or involving only one element or operation etc. **b** *Grammar* (of a tense) formed without an auxiliary verb. **4** absolute, unqualified, straightforward (*the simple truth*; *a simple majority*). **5** foolish or ignorant; gullible, feeble-minded (*am not so simple as to agree to that*). **6** plain in appearance or manner; unsophisticated, ingenuous, artless. **7** not of high social standing; ordinary (*simple people*). **8** *Bot.* **a** consisting of one part. **b** (of fruit) formed from one pistil. ● *noun archaic* **1** a herb used medicinally. **2** a medicine made from it. □ **simple·ness** *noun* [Old French from Latin *simplus*]

simple eye *noun* an eye of an insect, having only one lens. *Also called* OCELLUS; compare COMPOUND EYE.

simple fracture *noun* a fracture of the bone only, without a skin wound.

simple harmonic motion *noun* = HARMONIC MOTION.

simple interest *noun* interest payable on a capital sum only (*compare* COMPOUND INTEREST).

simple machine *noun* any of the basic mechanical devices for applying a force, e.g. an inclined plane, wedge, or lever.

simple-minded *adjective* **1** feeble-minded, stupid, foolish. **2** ingenuous, unsophisticated. □ **simple-minded·ness** *noun*

simple sentence *noun* a sentence with a single subject and predicate.

Simple Simon *noun* a foolish person (from the nursery-rhyme character).

simple syrup *noun* a syrup of sugar dissolved in water, used in cooking, mixing drinks, etc.

simple time *noun Music* a time with two, three, or four beats in a bar.

simple·ton *noun* a foolish, gullible, or halfwitted person. [SIMPLE, after surnames derived from place names in -*ton*]

sim·plex ● *adjective* **1** simple; not compounded. **2** *Computing* (of a circuit) allowing transmission of signals in one direction only. ● *noun* a simple or uncompounded thing, esp. a word. [Latin, = single, var. of *simplus* simple]

sim·pli·city *noun* the fact or condition of being simple. □ **be simplicity itself** be extremely easy. [Old French *simplicité* or Latin *simplicitas* (as SIMPLEX)]

sim·pli·fy *transitive verb* (-**fies**, -**fied**) make simple; make easy or easier to do or understand. □ **sim·pli·fi·ca·tion** *noun*

sim·plis·tic *adjective* **1** excessively or affectedly simple. **2** oversimplified so as to conceal or distort difficulties. □ **sim·plis·tic·ally** *adverb*

Sim·plon /ˈsɪmplon/ a pass in the Alps in S Switzerland, consisting of a road built by Napoleon in 1801–5 at an altitude of 2 028 m (6,591 ft.) and a railway tunnel (completed in 1922) which links Switzerland and Italy.

sim·ply *adverb* **1** in a simple manner. **2** absolutely; without doubt (*simply astonishing*). **3** merely (*was simply trying to please*).

Simp·son ▸ **1 Sir George** (*c*.1787–1860), Scottish-born Canadian businessman and traveller. Sent to N America by the Hudson's Bay Company in 1820, he became governor of the Northern Department in 1821, and governor of the company's trading territories five years later, holding this position until his death. He also held positions in railways and banking. **2 Sir James Young** (1811–70), Scottish surgeon and obstetrician. He discovered the usefulness of chloroform as an anaesthetic, and was active in the debate over whether it or ether was better for use in surgery; he made a famous attack on Lister and antisepsis. **3 Wal·lis** (née Wallis Warfield) (1896–1986), wife of Edward VIII of England. An American divorcee, she caused a scandal by her relationship with the king in 1936 which forced the king's abdication the following year; the couple were married shortly after and she became the Duchess of Windsor.

Simpson Desert a desert in central Australia, situated between Alice Springs and the Channel Country to the east.

Simpson Peninsula a peninsula of the northeastern coast of mainland Nunavut, situated between Boothia and Melville peninsulas.

simu·la·crum /ˌsɪmjʊˈleikrəm/ *noun* (*pl.* **simu·la·cra** /-krə/) **1** an image of something. **2 a** a shadowy likeness; a deceptive substitute. **b** mere pretense. [Latin (as SIMULATE)]

simu·late /ˈsɪmjʊleit/ *transitive verb* **1 a** pretend to have or feel (an attribute or feeling). **b** pretend to be. **2** imitate or counterfeit. **3 a** imitate the conditions of (a situation etc.), e.g. for training or amusement. **b** produce a computer model of (a process etc.). [Latin *simulare* from *similis* like]

simu·lat·ed *adjective* made to resemble the real thing but not genuinely such (*simulated fur*).

simu·la·tion *noun* **1** an act or instance of simulating something. **2** a model or set of circumstances imitating real or hypothetical conditions etc. (*a realistic computer simulation*).

simu·la·tor *noun* **1** a person or thing that simulates. **2** a device designed to simulate the operations of a complex system, used in training etc.

simul·cast /ˈsaiməlˌkast, ˈsɪm-/ ● *noun* **1** a simultaneous transmission of the same program on radio and television, or on two or more channels, in two or more languages, etc. **2** *N Amer.* a live transmission of a sports event, esp. a horse race, for usu. off-track betting purposes. ● *transitive verb* broadcast (a program) in such a way. □ **simul·cast·ing** *noun* [SIMULTANEOUS + BROADCAST]

simul·tan·eous /ˌsaiməl'teiniəs, ˌsɪm-/ *adjective* (often foll. by *with*) occurring or operating at the same time. □ **simul·tan·eity** /-tə'neiɪti/ *noun* **simul·tan·eous·ly** *adverb* [medieval Latin *simultaneus* from Latin *simul* at the same time, prob. after *instantaneous* etc.]

simultaneous equations *plural noun* equations involving two or more unknowns that are to have the same values in each equation.

simultaneous translation *noun* (also **simultaneous interpretation**) oral translation from one language to another performed with a minimal time lapse between the original speech and the translation.

SIN /sɪn/ *abbreviation Cdn* SOCIAL INSURANCE NUMBER.

sin¹ ● *noun* **1 a** the breaking of divine or moral law, esp. by a conscious act. **b** such an act. **2** the condition or state resulting from such transgression. **3** an action regarded as a serious offence or fault (*it's a sin to stay inside on a nice day like this*). ● *intransitive verb* (**sinned, sin·ning**) **1** commit a sin. **2** (foll. by *against*) offend. □ **as sin** *informal* extremely (*ugly as sin*). **cover** (or **hide** etc.) **a multitude of sins** conceal the real, usu. unpleasant, facts or situation. **do** (or **be**) **something for one's sins** *jocular* do (or be) something as a supposed punishment for something (*Alex had to judge the spelling bee for his sins*). **live in sin** *jocular* live together in a sexual relationship without being married. □ **sin·less** *adjective* **sin·less·ly** *adverb* **sin·less·ness** *noun* [Old English *syn(n)*]

sin² /sain/ *abbreviation* sine.

Sinai /'sainai/ an arid, mountainous peninsula in NE Egypt, extending into the Red Sea between the Gulf of Suez and the Gulf of Aqaba. In the south is Mount Sinai where, according to the Bible, Moses received the Ten Commandments and the Tables of the Law (Exod. 19–34).

Sina·itic /ˌsainei'ɪtɪk/ *adjective* of or relating to Mount Sinai or of the Sinai peninsula. [var. of *Sinaic* from *Sinai* from Hebrew *sīnay*, with *t* added for euphony]

Sina·loa /ˌsi:nə'lo:ə/ a state on the Pacific coast of Mexico; capital, Culiacán Rosales.

Sin·atra /sɪ'nɒtrə/ **Fran·cis Al·bert ('Frank')** (1915–98), US singer and actor. He began his long career as a singer in 1938 performing with big bands on the radio, becoming a solo star in the 1940s with a large teenage following; his many hits include 'Night and Day' and 'My Way'. Among his numerous films are *From Here to Eternity* (1953), for which he won an Oscar.

sin bin *noun informal* **1** *Hockey* the penalty box. **2** a place set aside for offenders of various kinds.

since ● *preposition* throughout, or at a point in, the period between (a specified time, event, etc.) and the time present or being considered (*must have happened since yesterday; has been going on since June; the greatest composer since Beethoven*). ● *conjunction* **1** during or in the time after (*what have you been doing since we met?; has not spoken since the dog died*). **2** for the reason that, because; inasmuch as (*since you are drunk I will drive you home*). **3** (*elliptical*) as being (*a more useful, since better designed, tool*). ● *adverb* **1** from that time or event until now or the time being considered (*have not seen them since; had been healthy ever since; has since been cut down*). **2** ago, before now (*happened many years since; long since forgotten*). □ **since when?** used as an inquiry into the duration of a state of affairs mentioned in a previous statement (often expressing doubt or incredulity). [Middle English, reduced form of obsolete *sithence* or from dial. *sin* (from *sithen*) from Old English *siththon*]

sin·cere *adjective* (**sin·cer·er, sin·cer·est**) **1** free from pretense or deceit; the same in reality as in appearance. **2** genuine, honest, frank. □ **sin·cer·ity** /sɪn'serɪti/ *noun* [Latin *sincerus* clean, pure]

sin·cere·ly *adverb* in a sincere manner. □ (**yours**) **sincerely** (also **sincerely yours**) a formula for ending a letter.

sin·ci·put /'sɪnsɪˌpʊt/ *noun Anat.* the front of the skull from the forehead to the crown. [Latin from *semi-* half + *caput* head]

Sin·clair /sɪŋ'klɛr/ **Upton (Beall)** (1878–1968), US novelist, whose political fiction helped to bring about social reform in the US; his works include *The Jungle* (1906), which exposed the appalling conditions in a meat-packing house in Chicago, and *King Coal* (1917).

Sind a province of SE Pakistan, traversed by the lower reaches of the Indus; capital, Karachi. □ **Sindhi** *noun & adjective*

sine *noun Math.* **1** the trigonometric function that is equal to the ratio of the side opposite a given angle (in a right-angled triangle) to the hypotenuse. **2** a function of the line drawn from one end of an arc perpendicular to the radius through the other. [Latin *sinus* curve, fold of a toga, used in medieval Latin as translation of Arabic *jayb* bosom, sine]

sine·cure /'sɪnəˌkjʊr/ *noun* a position that requires little or no work

but usu. yields profit or honour. □ **sine·cur·ist** *noun* [Latin *sine cura* without care]

sine curve *noun* = SINE WAVE.

sine die /ˌsainɪ 'daii, ˌsinɪ 'di:ei/ *adverb* (of business adjourned indefinitely) with no appointed date. [Latin, = without day]

sine qua non /ˌsinei kwɒ 'nɒn, -no:n/ *noun* an indispensable condition or qualification. [Latin, = without which not]

sinew /'sɪnju:/ ● *noun* **1** tough fibrous tissue uniting muscle to bone; a tendon. **2** (in *pl.*) muscles; bodily strength; wiriness. **3** (in *pl.*) something providing strength to an organization etc. ● *transitive verb literary* serve as the sinews of; sustain; hold together. □ **sinewy** *adjective* [Old English *sin(e)we* from Germanic]

sine wave *noun* a curve representing periodic oscillations of constant amplitude as given by a sine function. *Also called* SINUSOID.

sin·fonia /ˌsɪnfə'ni:ə, sɪn'fo:niə/ *noun Music* **1** a symphony. **2** (in Baroque music) an orchestral piece used as an introduction to an opera, cantata, or suite. **3** (**Sinfonia**; usu. in names) a small symphony orchestra. [Italian, = SYMPHONY]

sin·foni·etta /ˌsɪnfə'njetə/ *noun Music* **1** a short or simple symphony. **2** (**Sinfonietta**; usu. in names) a small symphony orchestra. [Italian, diminutive of *sinfonia*: see SINFONIA]

sin·ful *adjective* **1** (of a person) committing sin, esp. habitually. **2 a** (of an act) involving or characterized by sin. **b** *informal* reprehensible. **3** *informal* self-indulgently delicious (*a sinful chocolate torte*). □ **sin·ful·ly** *adverb* **sin·ful·ness** *noun*

sing ● *verb* (*past* **sang**; *past participle* **sung**) **1** *intransitive* utter musical sounds with the voice, esp. words with a set tune. **2** *transitive* **a** utter or produce by singing (*sing another song*). **b** perform (a role in an opera etc.). **3** *intransitive* (of the wind, a kettle, etc.) make melodious, humming, buzzing, or whistling sounds. **4** *intransitive* (of the ears) be affected as with a buzzing sound. **5** *transitive* bring to a specified state by singing (*sang the child to sleep*). **6** *intransitive slang* turn informer; confess. **7** *transitive & intransitive* celebrate in verse. ● *noun* an act or instance of singing (*our annual carol sing*). □ **sing for one's supper** see SUPPER. **sing out** call out loudly; shout. **sing the praises of** see PRAISE. □ **sing·able** *adjective* **sing·ing** *noun & adjective* [Old English *singan*, from Germanic] ¶ The use of *sung* instead of *sang* for the past tense as in *She sung three songs* is non-standard.

sing. *abbreviation* singular.

sing·along *noun* an informal occasion when a group of people sing songs together (also *attributive*: *a singalong evening*).

Singa·pore /'sɪŋəpɔr/ a country in SE Asia consisting of the island of Singapore and about 54 smaller islands, off the southern tip of the Malay Peninsula; pop. (est. 2002) 4,452,732. It is a world trade and financial centre. □ **Singa·por·ean** /-'pɔriən/ *adjective & noun*

Singapore sling *noun* a cocktail with a base of gin and cherry brandy.

singe ● *verb* (**singe·ing**) **1** *transitive & intransitive* burn superficially or lightly. **2** *transitive* burn the bristles or down off (the carcass of a pig or fowl) to prepare it for cooking. ● *noun* a superficial burn. [Old English *sencgan* from West Germanic]

Sing·er ▶ **1 Isaac Bash·evis** (1904–91), Polish-born US novelist and short-story writer. His work, written in Yiddish but chiefly known from English translations, blends realistic detail and elements of fantasy, mysticism, and magic to portray the lives of Polish Jews from many periods; notable titles include the novels *The Magician of Lublin* (1955) and *The Slave* (1962), and the short-story collection *The Spinoza of Market Street* (1961). He was awarded the Nobel Prize for literature in 1978. **2 Isaac Mer·rit** (1811–75), US inventor. In 1851 he designed and built the first commercially successful sewing machine, and later became the world's largest sewing machine manufacturer.

sing·er *noun* a person who sings.

singer-songwriter *noun* a person who sings and writes songs, esp. professionally.

Singh /sɪŋ/ *noun* **1** a surname adopted by male Sikhs initiated into the Khalsa. **2** a title adopted by the warrior castes of N India. [Hindustani *siṅgh* from Sanskrit *sinhá* lion]

Sing·hal·ese *var. of* SINHALESE.

singing sands *plural noun* beach or desert sand that emits a singing or squeaking sound when stepped on because of its silica content.

singing saw *noun* = MUSICAL SAW.

singing telegram *noun* a telegram or other message delivered by someone who sings its contents to the recipient.

sin·gle ● *adjective* **1** one only, not double or multiple. **2** united or undivided. **3 a** designed or suitable for one person (*single room; single* *bed*). **b** used or done by one person etc. or one set or pair. **4** one by itself; not one of several (*a single tree*). **5** regarded separately (*every single thing*). **6** not married; not involved in a romantic or sexual relationship. **7** *Brit.* (of a ticket) valid for an outward journey only, not for the return; one-way. **8** (with *neg.* or *interrogative*) even one; not to speak of more (*did not see a single person*). **9** (of a flower) having only one circle of petals. **10** lonely, unaided. ● *noun* **1** a single thing, or item in a series. **2 a** a record, compact disc, etc., containing only one or two songs or other short pieces of music. **b** one of these pieces of music. **3 a** *Baseball* a one-base hit. **b** *Cricket* a hit for one run. **4** (usu. *in pl.*) a game with one player on each side. **5** an unmarried person (*young singles*). **6** *US informal* a one-dollar bill. **7** *Brit.* a one-way ticket. ● *verb* **1** *transitive* (foll. by *out* and often by *for, as*) select from a group as worthy of special attention, praise, etc. (*singled out for praise; singled out as the finest*). **2** *Baseball* **a** *intransitive* hit a single. **b** *transitive* cause (a baserunner) to advance by hitting a single. **c** *transitive* (usu. foll. by *in*) cause (a run) to score by hitting a single. □ **single·hood** *noun* (in sense 6 of *adjective*).

single·ness *noun* **sin·gly** *adverb* [Old French from Latin *singulus*, related to *simplus* SIMPLE]

single-blind *adjective* designating a test etc. in which information that may lead to biased results is concealed from either the tester or the subject (*compare* DOUBLE-BLIND).

single-breasted *adjective* (of a coat etc.) having only one set of buttons and buttonholes, not overlapping.

single combat *noun* a fight between two people.

single cut *adjective* (of a file) with grooves cut in one direction only, not crossing.

single-digit *adjective* esp. *N Amer.* (of a quantity, numerical value, or percentage) less than ten (*single-digit interest rates*).

single entry *noun* a system of bookkeeping in which each transaction is entered in one account only.

single file ● *noun* a line of people or things arranged one behind another. ● *adverb* one behind another.

single·foot *N Amer.* ● *noun* a horse's fast walking pace with one foot on the ground at a time. ● *intransitive verb* (of a horse) go at this pace.

single-handed ● *adverb* **1** without help from another. **2** with one hand. ● *adjective* **1** done etc. single-handed. **2** for one hand. □ **single-handed·ly** *adverb*

single-issue *noun* (*attributive*) designating a group, political platform, etc., characterized by an exclusive concern with one issue (*single-issue voters*).

single-lens reflex *noun* denoting a reflex camera in which a single lens serves the film and the viewfinder.

single malt *noun* (often *attributive*) a malt whisky from one distillery, not blended with any other malt.

single market *noun* an association of countries trading without restrictions, esp. in the European Community.

single-minded *adjective* having or intent on only one purpose. □ **single-minded·ly** *adverb* **single-minded·ness** *noun*

single parent *noun* a person bringing up a child or children without a partner (also *attributive: single-parent families*). □ **single parenthood** *noun*

single point *noun* *Cdn Football* = ROUGE *noun* 3.

singles bar *noun* a bar frequented by esp. single people seeking a sexual partner, potential spouse, etc.

single-seater *noun* a vehicle, aircraft, etc. with one seat.

single-sex *noun* (*attributive*) of, for, or pertaining to males only or females only (*single-sex schools*).

single space *transitive & intransitive verb* lay out or print (text) on consecutive lines, leaving no empty lines between lines of text. □ **single-spaced** *adjective*

sing·let *noun* **1** esp. *Brit.* a usu. sleeveless undershirt, often worn instead of a shirt. **2** (usu. *attributive*) a molecular state in which all electron spins are paired. **3** a single unresolvable line in a spectrum. [SINGLE + -ET¹, after *doublet*, the garment being unlined]

single·ton *noun* **1** the only card of a suit in a hand. **2 a** a single person or thing. **b** an only child. **3** a single child or animal born, not a twin etc. [SINGLE, after *simpleton*]

single tree *noun* *N Amer.* = SWINGLETREE.

single-use *noun* (*attributive*) designating something designed to be used only once (*a single-use camera*).

single-user *noun* (*attributive*) **1** having one user. **2** (of a computer system, software, etc.) designed to be used by one person at a time.

Sing Sing a state prison in Ossining, New York.

sing·song ● *adjective* characterized by or uttered with a monotonous or rising and falling rhythm, cadence, or intonation. ● *noun* **1** a singsong manner. **2** *Cdn & Brit.* an informal gathering for singing; a singalong. □ **sing·songy** *adjective*

sin·gu·lar ● *adjective* **1** unique; much beyond the average; extraordinary. **2** eccentric or strange. **3** *Grammar* (of a word or form) denoting or referring to a single person or thing. **4** *Math.* possessing unique properties. **5** single, individual. ● *noun* *Grammar* **1** a singular word or form. **2** the singular number. □ **sin·gu·lar·ly** *adverb* [Old French *singuler* from Latin *singularis* (as SINGLE)]

sin·gu·lar·ity *noun* (*pl.* **-ities**) **1** the state or condition of being singular. **2** an odd trait or peculiarity. **3** *Physics & Math.* a point at which a function takes an infinite value, esp. in space-time when matter is infinitely dense.

sin·gu·lar·ize *transitive verb* (also esp. *Brit.* **-ise**) **1** make singular. **2** distinguish, individualize. □ **sin·gu·lar·iz·a·tion** *noun*

sinh /ʃain, sintʃ, sai'neitʃ/ *abbreviation Math.* hyperbolic sine. [*sine* + *hyperbolic*]

Sin·hal·ese /ˌsinhəˈliːz, ˌsinəˈliːz/ ● *noun* (*pl.* same) **1** a member of a people originally from N India and now forming the majority of the population of Sri Lanka. **2** (also **Sin·hala** /ˌsinˈhalə/) an Indic language spoken by this people. ● *adjective* (also **Sinhala**) of or relating to this people or language. [Sanskrit *sinhalam* Sri Lanka (Ceylon) + -ESE]

Sining see XINING.

sin·is·ter /ˈsinistər/ *adjective* **1** suggestive of evil; looking malignant or villainous. **2** wicked or criminal (*a sinister motive*). **3** of evil omen. **4** *Heraldry* of or on the left-hand side of a shield etc. (i.e. to the observer's right). **5** *archaic* left-hand. □ **sin·is·ter·ly** *adverb* **sin·is·ter·ness** *noun* [Old French *sinistre* or Latin *sinister* left]

sin·is·tral /ˈsinistrəl/ *adjective* **1** left-handed. **2** of or on the left. **3** (of a spiral shell) with whorls rising to the left and not (as usually) to the right. □ **sin·is·tral·ity** *noun*

sink ● *verb* (*past* **sank** or **sunk**; *past participle* **sunk**. ¶ Although both *sank* and *sunk* are used as the simple past of *sink*, *sunk* is more informal and is best avoided in written text.) **1** *intransitive* fall or come slowly downwards; drop. **2** *intransitive* **a** go or penetrate below the surface esp. of a liquid. **b** (of a ship) go to the bottom of the sea etc. **3** *transitive* send (a ship) to the bottom of the sea etc. **4** *intransitive* disappear below the horizon (*the sun is sinking*). **5** *intransitive* settle down comfortably (*sank into a chair*). **6** *intransitive* **a** gradually lose strength or value or quality etc.; decline (*my heart sank*). **b** (of the voice) descend in pitch or volume. **c** (of a sick person) approach death. **d** gradually fall into a specified condition (*sank into sleep; sinking into poverty*). **7** *transitive* cause or allow to sink or penetrate (*sank its teeth into my leg*). **8** *transitive* cause the failure of (a plan etc.) or the discomfiture of (a person). **9** *transitive* dig (a well) or bore (a shaft). **10** *transitive* engrave (a die) or inlay (a design). **11** *transitive* **a** invest (money) (*sank a large sum into the business*). **b** lose (money) by investment. **12** *transitive* **a** cause (a ball) to enter a pocket in billiards, a hole at golf, a basket in basketball, etc. **b** achieve this by (a stroke, shot, etc.). **13** *transitive* overlook or forget; keep in the background (*sank their differences*). **14** *intransitive* (of a price etc.) become lower. **15** *intransitive* (of a storm or river) subside. **16** *intransitive* (of ground) slope down, or reach a lower level by subsidence. **17** *transitive* lower the level of. **18** *transitive* (usu. in *passive*; foll. by *in*) absorb; hold the attention of (*be sunk in thought*). ● *noun* **1** a fixed basin with a water supply and outflow pipe. **2** a place where foul liquid collects. **3** a place of vice or corruption. **4** a pool or marsh in which a river's water disappears by evaporation or percolation. **5** a body or process which acts to absorb or remove energy or a particular component from a system (*a heat sink; a carbon sink*). **6** = SINKHOLE 1. □ **sink in 1** penetrate or make its way in; be absorbed. **2** become gradually comprehended (*paused to let the words sink in*). **sink one's teeth into** take up (a challenge, cause, etc.) fervently or energetically. **sink or swim** fail totally or survive by one's own efforts. □ **sink·able** *adjective* **sink·age** *noun* **sink·ful** *noun* [Old English *sincan* from Germanic]

sink·er *noun* **1** a person or thing which sinks. **2** a weight used to sink a fishing line or sounding line. **3** *Baseball* **a** = SINKERBALL. **b** a hit in which the ball drops markedly. **4** *US* a doughnut.

sinker·ball *noun* *Baseball* (also **sink·er**) a pitch in which the ball drops markedly. □ **sinker·ball·er** *noun*

sink·hole *noun* esp. *N Amer.* **1** (also **sink**) **a** a large circular depression in the ground, occurring e.g. as a result of the collapse of a subterranean cave. **b** a cavity in limestone etc. into which a stream etc. disappears. **2** *informal* a place of vice or corruption. **3** *informal* an enterprise etc. which seems to swallow all invested money to no effect.

Sin·kiang see XINJIANG.

Vowels: a *cat* ɑ *arm* e *bed* ɜr *her* ɜː *deux* ə *ago* ɪ *sit* i *cosy* iː *feed* ɒ *hot* ɔ *pore* ɔː *no* ʌ *run* ʊ *put*

sinking feeling *noun* a bodily sensation, esp. in the abdomen, caused by apprehension.

sinking fund *noun* money set aside for the gradual repayment of a debt.

sin·ner *noun* a person who sins, esp. habitually.

Sinn Fein /ʃɪn ˈfeɪn/ *noun* an Irish movement founded in 1905, originally aiming at the independence of Ireland and a revival of Irish culture and language, now dedicated, as the political wing of the IRA, to the political unification of Northern Ireland and the Republic of Ireland. □ **Sinn Fein·er** *noun* [Irish *sinn féin* we ourselves]

Sino- /ˈsaɪnoʊ/ *combining form* Chinese; Chinese and (*Sino-American*). [Greek *Sinai* the Chinese]

sino-atrial /saɪnoʊˈeɪtriəl/ *adjective* of, pertaining to, or designating a small node or body of tissue in the wall of the right atrium of the heart that acts as a pacemaker by producing a contractile signal at regular intervals. [as SINUS + *atrial*: see ATRIUM]

sin of omission *noun* (*pl.* **sins of omission**) **1** a sinful failure to perform a good action, esp. one commanded by Christian teaching. **2** a failure to do something one ought to have done.

Sino-Japanese Wars two wars fought between China and Japan. The first, in 1894–5, caused by rivalry over Korea, ended in Japan's favour. Japanese expansionism in Manchuria in the early 1930s led to the second war (1937–45), in which two years of dramatic Japanese successes were followed by stalemate and then the gradual erosion of the Japanese position by Communist guerrillas.

sino·logue /ˈsaɪnəˌlɒɡ, ˈsɪ-/ *noun* an expert in sinology. [French, formed as SINO- + Greek *-logos* speaking]

sin·ol·ogy /saɪˈnɒlədʒi, sɪ-/ *noun* the study of Chinese language, history, customs, etc. □ **sino·logic·al** *adjective* **sin·ol·o·gist** *noun*

Sino-Tibetan *noun* a language family comprising Chinese, Burmese, Tibetan, and (according to some scholars) Thai.

sin·se·milla /sɪnsəˈmɪlə/ *noun* **1** a seedless form of the cannabis plant, having a particularly high narcotic content. **2** the drug obtained from this plant. □ **sin·se·mil·lan** *adjective* [Latin American Spanish, lit. 'without seed']

sin tax *noun N Amer. informal* a tax levied on cigarettes, liquor, etc.

sin·ter ● *noun* **1** a siliceous or calcareous rock formed by deposition from springs. **2** a substance formed by sintering. ● *transitive & intransitive verb* coalesce or cause to coalesce from powder into solid by heating. □ **sin·tered** *adjective* [German, = English *sinder* CINDER]

Sint Maar·ten see ST. MARTIN.

Sin·tra (also **Cin·tra**) a small town in W Portugal, situated in a mountainous area to the northwest of Lisbon; pop. (2001) 24,730. It was formerly a summer residence of the Portuguese royal family.

sinu·ate /ˈsɪnjʊət/ *adjective esp. Bot.* wavy-edged; with distinct inward and outward bends along the edge. [Latin *sinuatus* past participle of *sinuare* bend]

Sin·ui·ju /ʃɪnwiːˈdʒuː/ a city and port in N Korea, situated on the Yalu River near its mouth on the Yellow Sea; pop. (est. 2002) 377,200. It lies across the river from the Chinese city of Dandong.

sinu·os·ity /ˌsɪnjʊˈɒsɪti/ *noun* (*pl.* **-ities**) **1** the state of being sinuous. **2** a bend, esp. in a stream or road.

sinu·ous /ˈsɪnjʊəs/ *adjective* **1** with many curves. **2** moving in a smooth, flowing way. □ **sinu·ous·ly** *adverb* [French *sinueux* or Latin *sinuosus* (as SINUS)]

sinus /ˈsaɪnəs/ *noun* **1** a cavity of bone or tissue, esp. in the skull connecting with the nostrils. **2** *Med.* a fistula esp. to a deep abscess. **3** *Bot.* the curve between the lobes of a leaf. **4** (*attributive*) relating to or denoting the sino-atrial node of the heart or its function as a pacemaker (*sinus tachycardia*). [Latin, = bosom, recess]

sinus·itis /ˌsaɪnəˈsaɪtɪs/ *noun* inflammation of a nasal sinus.

sinus·oid /ˈsaɪnəsɔɪd/ *noun* **1** a curve having the form of a sine wave. **2** a small irregularly-shaped blood vessel, esp. found in the liver. □ **sinus·oid·al** *adjective* **sinus·oid·al·ly** *adverb* [French *sinusoïde* from Latin *sinus*: see SINUS]

Sion *var. of* ZION.

-sion *suffix* forming nouns (see -ION) from Latin participial stems in *-s-* (*mansion*; *mission*; *persuasion*).

Siou·an /ˈsuːən/ ● *noun* an Aboriginal language family including Dakota and Assiniboine (the only Siouan languages spoken in Canada), Lakota, Sioux, and Omaha. ● *adjective* pertaining to or designating this language family.

Sioux /suː/ ● *noun* (*pl.* same) **1** a member of a group of N American Aboriginal peoples chiefly inhabiting the upper Mississippi and Missouri river basins. **2** the language of this group. ● *adjective* of or relating to these people or their language. [N American French from *Nadouessioux* from Ojibwa (Odawa dialect) *nātowĕssiwak*: French pl. ending *-x* replaced Ojibwa pl. ending *-ak*]

Sioux Lookout a town in NW Ontario, NE of Dryden; pop. (2001) 5,336. □ **Sioux Look·out·er** *noun* [in memory of a defeat of the Sioux by the Ojibwa in the 1700s or 1800s]

sip ● *transitive & intransitive verb* (**sipped**, **sip·ping**) drink in one or more small amounts. ● *noun* **1** a small mouthful of liquid (*a sip of brandy*). **2** the act of taking this. □ **sip·pable** *adjective* [Middle English: perhaps a modification of SUP¹]

si·phon /ˈsaɪfən/ (also esp. *Brit.* **sy·phon**) ● *noun* **1** a pipe or tube used for conveying liquid from one level to a lower level, using the liquid pressure differential to force a column of the liquid up to a higher level before it falls to the outlet. **2** a bottle from which carbonated water is dispensed by allowing the gas pressure to force it out. **3** *Zool.* a tubular organ in an aquatic animal, esp. a mollusc, through which water is drawn in or expelled. ● *transitive & intransitive verb* (often foll. by *off*) **1** conduct or flow through a siphon. **2** divert or set aside (funds etc.). □ **si·phon·age** *noun* **si·phon·al** *adjective* **si·phon·ic** /-ˈfɒnɪk/ *adjective* [ultimately from Greek *siphōn* pipe]

si·phono·phore /saɪˈfɒnəˌfɔːr/ *noun* any usu. translucent marine hydrozoan of the order Siphonophora, e.g. the Portuguese man-of-war.

sip·per *noun* **1** a person who sips. **2** *N Amer.* a drink suitable for sipping. **3** a device, cup, etc., used for sipping.

sippy cup *noun N Amer.* a cup for a baby, with a lid incorporating a perforated spout so as to discourage spilling.

sir *noun* **1** a polite, respectful, or formal form of address or mode of reference to a man. **2** (**Sir**) a titular prefix to the first name of a knight or baronet. [Middle English, reduced form of SIRE]

Sir·ach /ˈsiːrak, ˈsaɪ-/ = ECCLESIASTICUS.

sir·dar /ˈsɜːrdɑːr/ *noun* **1** (esp. in the Indian subcontinent) a person of high political or military rank. **2** a Sikh. [Urdu *sardār* from Persian *sar* head + *dār* possessor]

Sir·dar·yo River /ˌsiːrdɑːrˈjɔː/ a river of central Asia. Rising in two headstreams in the Tien Shan mountains in E Uzbekistan, it flows for some 2 220 km (1,380 miles) west and northwest through S Kazakhstan to the Aral Sea.

sire ● *noun* **1** the male parent of an animal, esp. of a domestic quadruped. **2** *archaic* a respectful form of address, esp. to a king. **3** *archaic literary* a father or male ancestor. ● *transitive verb* (of a male domestic quadruped) beget. [Old French, ultimately from Latin *senior*: see SENIOR]

siree /sɜːˈriː/ *interjection* (also **sir·ree**) *N Amer. informal* as an emphatic, esp. after *yes* or *no*. [SIR + emphatic suffix]

siren /ˈsaɪrən/ ● *noun* **1 a** a device for making a loud prolonged signal or warning sound, esp. by revolving a perforated disc over a jet of compressed air or steam. **b** the sound made by this. **2** (in Greek mythology) each of a number of women or winged creatures whose singing lured unwary sailors on to rocks. **3** a sweet singer. **4 a** a dangerously fascinating woman; a temptress. **b** a tempting pursuit etc. **5** any of three eel-like aquatic N American amphibians of the family Sirenidae, with external gills, no hind limbs, and tiny forelimbs, found in the southeastern US. ● *adjective* irresistibly tempting (*lured by the siren call of power*). [Old French *sirene* from Late Latin *Sirena* fem. from Latin from Greek *Seirēn*]

siren·ian /saɪˈriːniən/ ● *adjective* of the order Sirenia of large aquatic plant-eating mammals, with stocky streamlined bodies, forelimbs modified as flippers, and no hind limbs, e.g. the manatee and dugong. ● *noun* any mammal of this order. [modern Latin *Sirenia* (as SIREN)]

Sir·ius /ˈsiːriəs/ a binary star, the brightest in the constellation Canis Major and the brightest in the sky. *Also called* DOG STAR. [Greek, = scorching, with reference to its brilliance]

sir·loin *noun* the choicer part of a loin of beef, from in front of the rump. [Old French (as SUR-¹, LOIN)]

sirloin tip *noun* a cut of beef taken from the hip along the underside of the leg bone.

Sir·mi·lik National Park /ˈsɜːrməlɪk/ a park on the northern edge of Baffin Island, including the Borden Peninsula and Bylot Island. It is noted for its birds and its glaciers. [Inuktitut, = 'place of glaciers']

si·rocco /sɪˈrɒkoʊ/ *noun* (also **sci·rocco**) (*pl.* **-roccos**) a hot, oppressive, often dusty or rainy wind blowing from N Africa across the Mediterranean to southern Europe. [French from Italian *scirocco*, ultimately from Arabic *šaruḳ* east wind]

sir·rah /ˈsɪrə/ *noun archaic* a form of address to a man or boy, expressing

uː mood   aɪ my   əi pipe   au brown   ʌu house   ei day   ɔi boy   ā franglais   ã Canadien   ɔ̃ Brayon   (*see over for consonants*)

contempt, reprimand, or authoritativeness. [prob. from Middle English *sire* SIR]

sir·ree *var. of* SIREE.

Sirte, Gulf of see SIDRA, GULF OF.

sirup *US var. of* SYRUP.

sis *noun informal* a sister. [abbreviation]

sisal /ˈsaɪsəl/ *noun* **1** a Mexican plant, *Agave sisalana*, with large fleshy leaves. **2** the fibre made from this plant, used for cordage, ropes, flooring, etc. [*Sisal*, the port of Yucatan, Mexico]

sis-boom-bah *N Amer.* ● *interjection* expressing support or encouragement esp. to a sports team. ● *noun* enthusiastic or partisan support esp. of spectator sports (*the sis-boom-bah of their university years*). [imitative, representing the sound of a skyrocket hissing in flight then exploding, and the exclamation of delight from spectators]

sis·kin *noun* any of various small streaked yellowish-green finches of the genus *Carduelis*, esp. the N American pine siskin *C. pinus* or the Eurasian common siskin, *C. spinus*, allied to the goldfinch. [Middle Dutch *siseken* diminutive, related to Middle Low German *sīsek*, Middle High German *zīse*, *zīsec*, of Slavic origin]

Sis·ley, Al·fred (1839–99), French Impressionist painter, of English descent. His paintings of the countryside around Paris in the 1870s are noted for their concentration on reflecting surfaces and fluid brushwork.

sissy *informal* ● *noun* (*pl.* **-sies**) an effeminate or cowardly person. ● *adjective* (**sis·si·er**, **sis·si·est**) effeminate; cowardly. □ **sis·si·fied** *adjective* **sis·si·ness** *noun* **sissy·ish** *adjective* [SIS + -Y²]

sis·ter *noun* **1** a woman or girl in relation to sons and other daughters of her parents. **2 a** (often as a form of address) a close female friend or associate. **b** a female fellow member of a trade union, class, sect, or the human race. **3** *Brit.* a senior female nurse. **4** (often as a form of address) a member of a female religious order. **5** (often *attributive*) of the same type or design or origin etc. (*sister ship*). **6** *N Amer.* used as a form of address to another woman (*listen, sister, you're not as smart as you think you are*). □ **sister·ly** *adjective* **sister·li·ness** *noun* [Middle English *sister* (from Old Norse), *suster* etc. (representing Old English *sweoster* from Germanic)]

sister city *noun* **1** a city that is twinned with another. **2** a city linked to another by proximity, common interests, etc. (*Dartmouth, Halifax's sister city*).

sister german *noun see* GERMAN.

sister·hood *noun* **1** the relationship between sisters. **2 a** a society or association of women, esp. when bound by monastic vows or devoting themselves to religious or charitable work or the feminist cause. **b** its members collectively. **3** community of feeling and mutual support between women.

sister-in-law *noun* (*pl.* **sisters-in-law**) **1** the sister of one's spouse. **2** the wife of one's brother. **3** the wife of one's brother-in-law.

Sister of Charity *noun* = GREY NUN.

Sister of Mercy *noun* a member of a Roman Catholic educational or charitable religious order of women, esp. that founded in Dublin in 1827.

Sister of Providence *noun* a member of a Roman Catholic congregation of women religious founded in Montreal in 1844 as the Daughters of Charity, Servants of the Poor, and working esp. in education and social services.

Sister of St. Anne *noun* a member of a Roman Catholic congregation of women religious founded in Vaudreuil, Quebec, in 1850 and devoted esp. to the education of young girls.

Sister of St. Joseph *noun* a member of a Roman Catholic congregation of women religious tracing its roots to a congregation founded in France in 1648, devoted to health care and education.

Sister of the Holy Names of Jesus and Mary *noun* a member of a Roman Catholic congregation of women religious founded in Longueuil, Quebec, in 1843 to educate young girls.

sister uterine *noun see* UTERINE.

Sis·tine /ˈsɪstiːn, ˈsɪstaɪn/ *adjective* **1** of any of the Popes called Sixtus, esp. Sixtus IV. **2** of or relating to the Sistine Chapel. [Italian *Sistino* from *Sisto* Sixtus]

Sistine Chapel *noun* a chapel in the Vatican, with frescoes by Michelangelo and other painters.

sis·trum *noun* (*pl.* **sis·tra**) a jingling metal instrument used by the ancient Egyptians esp. in the worship of Isis. [Latin from Greek *seistron* from *seiō* shake]

Sisy·phean /ˌsɪsɪˈfiːən/ *adjective* (of toil) endless and fruitless like that of Sisyphus.

Sisy·phus /ˈsɪsɪfəs/ *Gk Myth* the son of Aeolus, punished in Hades for his misdeeds in life by being condemned to the eternal task of rolling a large stone to the top of a hill, from which it always rolled down again.

sit *verb* (**sit·ting**; *past* and *past participle* **sat**) **1** *intransitive* adopt or be in a position in which the body is supported more or less upright by the buttocks resting on the ground or a raised seat etc., with the thighs usu. horizontal. **2** *transitive* cause to sit; place in a sitting position. **3** *intransitive* **a** (of a bird) perch. **b** (of an animal) rest with the hind legs bent and the body close to the ground. **4** *intransitive* (of a bird) remain on its nest to hatch its eggs. **5** *intransitive* **a** be engaged in an occupation in which the sitting position is usual. **b** (of a committee, legislative body, etc.) be engaged in business. **c** (of an individual) be entitled to hold some office or position (*sat as a magistrate*). **6** *intransitive* be positioned, placed, or situated (*sits just outside the city; sitting in fourth place*). **7** *intransitive* (usu. foll. by *for*) pose in a sitting position (for a portrait). **8** *intransitive* (foll. by *for*) be a Member of Parliament (for a constituency). **9** *transitive & intransitive* *Brit.* be a candidate for (an examination). **10** *intransitive* be in a more or less permanent position or condition (esp. of inactivity or being out of use or out of place). **11** *intransitive* (of clothes etc.) fit or hang in a certain way. **12** *transitive* keep or have one's seat on (a horse etc.). **13** *intransitive & transitive* (esp. in *combination*) take care of a baby, house, etc. while the parents, owners, etc. are away (*babysit; house-sit*). **14** *intransitive* (often foll. by *before*) (of an army) take a position outside a city etc. to besiege it. **15** *transitive* (esp. of a table) be large enough for (a designated number of seated people) (*sits six*). **16** esp. *N Amer. Sport* **a** *intransitive* (often foll. by *out*) not participate in a game or games because of poor play, a suspension, etc. (*sat for six games*) (*see also* SIT OUT). **b** *transitive* (of a player) not participate in (a game) or for (a specified period); not play for the duration of (a suspension) (*currently sitting out a four-game suspension; sat out half the season*). **c** *transitive* (often foll. by *out*) (of a coach etc.) keep (a player) from participating because of poor play etc. (*sat out the rookie*). **17** *intransitive* (usu. in *neg.*) (of food) be settled in the stomach (*the chicken didn't sit right*). □ **be sitting pretty** be comfortably or advantageously placed. **make a person sit up** *informal* surprise or interest a person. **sit around** sit doing nothing, esp. while waiting. **sit at a person's feet** be a person's pupil. **sit at home** be inactive. **sit back** relax one's efforts. **sit by** look on without interfering. **sit down 1** sit after standing. **2** cause to sit. **3** (foll. by *under*) *Brit.* submit tamely to (an insult etc.). **sit heavy on the stomach** take a long time to be digested. **sit in 1** occupy a place as a protest. **2** (foll. by *for*) take the place of. **3** (foll. by *on*) be present as a guest or observer at (a meeting etc.). **sit in judgment** assume the right of judging others; be censorious. **sit on 1** be a member of (a committee etc.). **2** hold a session or inquiry concerning. **3** *informal* delay action about (*the government has been sitting on the report*). **4** *informal* repress or rebuke or snub (*felt rather sat on*). **sit on the fence** see FENCE. **sit on one's hands** take no action. **sit out 1** take no part in (a dance etc.). **2** stay till the end of (esp. an ordeal). **sit tight** *informal* **1** remain firmly in one's place. **2** not be shaken off or move away or yield to distractions. **sit up 1** rise from a lying to a sitting position. **2** sit firmly upright. **3** stay awake and later than usual, esp. while waiting for someone (*sat up watching TV*). **4** *informal* become interested or aroused etc. **sit up and take notice** *informal* have one's interest aroused, esp. suddenly. **sit well** (often foll. by *with*; usu. in *neg.*) be acceptable or undisturbing to (*their decision did not sit well with her*). **sit well on** suit or fit. [Old English *sittan* from Germanic]

Sita /ˈsiːtɒ/ *Hinduism* (in the Ramayama) the wife of Rama. She is the Hindu model of the ideal woman, an incarnation of Lakshmi. [Sanskrit, = furrow]

sitar /sɪˈtɑr, ˈsɪtɑr/ *noun* a long-necked Indian lute with movable frets. □ **sitar·ist** *noun* [Hindi *sitār*]

sit·com *noun informal* a situation comedy. [abbreviation]

sit-down ● *adjective* **1** (of a meal) eaten sitting at a table. **2** (of a protest etc.) in which demonstrators occupy their workplace or sit down on the ground in a public place. ● *noun* **1** a period of sitting. **2** a sit-down protest etc.

site ● *noun* **1** the ground chosen or used for a town or building. **2** a place where some activity is or has been conducted (*camping site; launching site; heritage site*). **3** *Computing* a single source for files, services, etc. on the Internet (*downloaded the file directly from the company's site*). ● *transitive verb* **1** locate or place. **2** provide with a site. [Anglo-French *site* or Latin *situs* local position]

site licence *noun* a licence granted by a software company to a business etc. to make and use a number of copies of a software program at a specified site.

Consonants: b *but* d *dog* f *few* g *get* h *her* j *yes* k *cat* l *leg* m *man* n *no* p *pen* r *red* s *sit*

site-specif·ic *adjective* designed for or pertaining to a specific site (*site-specific installation artwork*; *a site-specific solution*).

sit-in *noun* a protest, strike, demonstration, etc. in which people occupy a workplace, public building, etc.

Sitka *noun* (in full **Sitka spruce**) a fast-growing spruce, *Picea sitchensis*, native to western N America and yielding timber. [*Sitka* in Alaska]

sit·rep *noun* a report on the current military situation in an area. [*situation report*]

sit spin *noun Figure Skating* a spin performed on the foot of one deeply bent leg, with the other extended forward.

Sit·tang River /ˈsɪtaŋ/ a river of S Burma. Rising in the Pegu mountains, it flows some 560 km (350 miles) south into the Bay of Bengal at the Gulf of Martaban.

Sit·ter, Wil·lem de (1872–1934), Dutch mathematician and astronomer, who showed that the theory of general relativity favoured the idea of an expanding universe.

sit·ter *noun* **1** a person who sits, esp. for a portrait. **2 a** = BABYSITTER (*see* BABYSIT). **b** (esp. in *combination*) a person who takes care of a house, pet, etc. while the owners are away (*house-sitter*). **3** a sitting hen.

sit·ting ● *noun* **1** a continuous period of being seated, esp. engaged in an activity (*finished the book in one sitting*). **2** a time during which an assembly is engaged in business. **3** a session in which a meal is served (*dinner will be served in two sittings*). **4** a period during which a law court, legislature, etc. holds sessions. **●** *adjective* **1** having sat down. **2** (of a legislator, Member of Parliament, etc.) currently holding office. **3** (of an animal or bird) not running or flying. **4** (of a hen) engaged in hatching. □ **sitting pretty** *see* PRETTY.

Sitting Bull (Sioux name Tatanka Iyotake) (c.1831–90), Sioux chief. As the main chief of the Sioux from about 1867, he resisted the US government order of 1875 forcibly resetting the Sioux on reservations; when the US Army opened hostilities in 1876, he led the Sioux in the fight to retain their lands, which resulted in the massacre of General Custer and his men at Little Bighorn. He surrendered in 1881, and was later killed.

sitting duck *noun* (also **sitting target**) *informal* a person or thing that is very easy to attack.

sitting room *noun* a living room in a house.

sitting tenant *noun Brit.* a tenant already in occupation of premises, esp. when there is a change of owner.

situ *see* IN SITU.

situ·ate /ˈsɪtʃʊeɪt/ **●** *transitive verb* (usu. in *passive*) **1** put in a certain position or circumstances (*is situated at the top of a hill*). **2** establish or indicate the place of; put in a context. **●** *adjective* (also /ˈsɪtʃʊət/) *Law* or *archaic* situated. [medieval Latin *situare situat-* from Latin *situs* site]

situ·a·tion *noun* **1** a place and its surroundings (*the house stands in a fine situation*). **2** a set of circumstances; a position in which one finds oneself; a state of affairs (*came out of a difficult situation with credit*). **3** an employee's position or job. **4** a critical point or complication in a drama. □ **situ·a·tion·al** *adjective* **situ·a·tion·al·ly** *adverb*

situation comedy *noun* a comedy, esp. on television, in which the humour derives from the situations the characters are placed in.

situation ethics *plural noun* (treated as *sing.*) (also **situational ethics**) the belief in flexibility in the application of moral laws according to individual circumstances.

situ·a·tion·ism *noun* the theory that human behaviour is determined by surrounding circumstances rather than by personal qualities. □ **situ·a·tion·ist** *noun & adjective*

sit-up *noun* an exercise to strengthen the stomach muscles, in which a person lies with the back flat on the ground and lifts the torso into a sitting position.

sit-upon *noun informal* the buttocks.

Sit·well, Dame Edith (Lou·isa) (1887–1964), English poet and critic. Lighthearted and experimental, her early verse, like that of her brothers Osbert (1892–1969) and Sacheverell (1897–1988), marked a revolt against the prevailing Georgian style of the day; in 1923 she attracted attention with *Façade*, a group of poems in notated rhythm recited to music by William Walton.

sitz bath *noun* a therapeutic bath taken sitting up in the bathtub, often with salts or herbs added to the water. [partial translation of German *Sitzbad* from *sitzen* sit + *Bad* bath]

SIU *abbreviation* SPECIAL INVESTIGATIONS UNIT.

Siva *var. of* SHIVA.

Si·walik Hills /sɪˈwɒlɪk/ a range of foothills in the S Himalayas, extending from NE India across Nepal to Sikkim.

Si·wash /ˈsaiwɒʃ/ *noun* **1** *Cdn* (*West*) (in full **Siwash sweater**) a thick woollen sweater decorated with symbols or animals from Aboriginal mythology. **2** *N Amer.* (esp. *West*) *dated offensive* an Aboriginal person. [Chinook Jargon, from Canadian French *sauvage*]

six ● *noun* **1** one more than five, or four less than ten; the product of two units and three units. **2** a symbol for this (6, vi, VI). **3** a size etc. denoted by six. **4** a set or team of six individuals. **5** six o'clock. **6** a card etc. with six pips. **7** *Cdn & Brit.* a group of six Brownies, Cubs, etc. **8** *informal* = SIX-PACK. **●** *adjective* that amount to six. □ **at sixes and sevens** in confusion or disagreement. **knock for six** *Brit. informal* utterly surprise or overcome (a person). **six of one and half a dozen of the other** a situation of little real difference between the alternatives. **six ways to** (or **from**) **Sunday** in every conceivable manner. [Old English *siex* etc. from Germanic]

Six Counties the Ulster counties of Antrim, Down, Armagh, Londonderry, Tyrone, and Fermanagh, which since 1920 have comprised the province of Northern Ireland.

Six Day War an Arab–Israeli war, 5–10 June 1967 (known to the Arabs as the **June War**), in which Israel occupied Sinai, the Old City of Jerusalem, the West Bank, and the Golan Heights and defeated an Egyptian, Jordanian, and Syrian alliance.

six·er *noun Cdn & Brit.* the leader of a group of six Brownies, Cubs, etc.

six-figure *attributive adjective* indicating a sum of hundreds of thousands of dollars, pounds, etc. (*dreams of a six-figure salary*).

six·fold *adjective & adverb* **1** six times as much or as many. **2** consisting of six parts.

six-gun *noun* = SIX-SHOOTER.

Six Nations *noun* the Iroquois confederacy after the Tuscarora joined in 1722.

six-pack *noun* **1** a pack of six identical items, esp. cans or bottles of beer. **2** a set of well-developed and well-defined abdominal muscles.

six·pence /ˈsɪkspəns/ *noun Brit.* **1** the sum of six pence, esp. before decimalization. **2** *hist.* a coin worth six old pence (2¹/₂p).

six·penny /ˈsɪkspəni/ *adjective Brit.* costing or worth six pence, esp. before decimalization.

six-shooter *noun* a revolver with six chambers.

six-string *noun informal* a guitar (also *attributive*: *six-string versatility*).

six·teen ● *noun* **1** one more than fifteen, or six more than ten. **2** a symbol for this (16, xvi, XVI). **3** a set of sixteen people or things. **4** a size etc. denoted by sixteen. **●** *adjective* that amount to sixteen. □ **six·teenth** *adjective, adverb, & noun*

sixteenth note *noun* esp. *N Amer. Music* a note having the time value of half an eighth note and represented by a large dot with a two-hooked stem.

sixteenth rest *noun N Amer. Music* a rest having the time value of a sixteenth note.

sixth ● *noun* **1** the position in a sequence corresponding to that of the number 6 in the sequence 1-6. **2** something occupying this position. **3** any of six equal parts of a thing. **4** *Music* **a** an interval or chord spanning six consecutive notes in the diatonic scale, e.g. C to A. **b** a note separated from another by this interval. **5** *Baseball* the sixth inning. **●** *adjective* that is the sixth. **●** *adverb* in the sixth place; sixthly. □ **sixth·ly** *adverb*

sixth form *noun Brit.* a level of education in a secondary school for students over 16. □ **sixth-former** *noun*

sixth sense *noun* **1** a supposed faculty giving intuitive or extrasensory knowledge. **2** such knowledge.

sixty ● *noun* (pl. **sixties**) **1** the product of six and ten. **2** a symbol for this (60, lx, LX). **3** (in pl.) the numbers from 60 to 69, esp. the years of a century or of a person's life. **4** a set of sixty persons or things. **5** (**Sixty**) *Cdn* the parallel of latitude 60° north of the equator as forming the boundary between the western provinces to the south and the territories to the north (*living North of Sixty*). **●** *adjective* that amount to sixty. □ **sixty-first, -second**, etc. the ordinal numbers between sixtieth and seventieth. **sixty-one, -two**, etc. the cardinal numbers between sixty and seventy. □ **six·ti·eth** *adjective, adverb, & noun*

sixty·fold *adjective & adverb*

sixty-fourth note *noun N Amer. Music* a note having the time value of half a thirty-second note and represented by a large dot with a four-hooked stem.

sixty-four thousand dollar question *noun* (also **sixty-four dollar question**) a difficult and crucial question. [from the top prize in a broadcast quiz show]

sixty-fourth rest *noun N Amer. Music* a rest having the time value of a sixty-fourth note.

sixty-nine *noun slang* sexual activity between two people involving mutual oral stimulation of the genitals. [from the position of the couple]

60% whole wheat *noun Cdn* designating bread, crackers, etc. made with a proportion of 60% whole wheat flour and 40% white flour.

siz·able *adjective* (also **size·able**) large or fairly large. □ **siz·ably** *adverb*

sizar /ˈsaɪzər/ *noun* an undergraduate at Cambridge University or at Trinity College, Dublin, receiving financial help from the college and formerly having certain menial duties. □ **sizar·ship** *noun* [SIZE[1] = ration]

size[1] ● *noun* **1** the relative bigness or extent of a thing; dimensions; magnitude (*is of vast size; size matters less than quality*). **2** each of the classes, usu. numbered, into which things otherwise similar, esp. garments, are divided according to size (*is made in several sizes; takes size 7 in shoes; is three sizes too big*). ● *transitive verb* sort or group in sizes or according to size. □ **of a size** having the same size. **of some size** fairly large. **the size of** as big as. **the size of it** *informal* a true account of the matter (*that is the size of it*). **size up 1** estimate the size of. **2** *informal* form a judgment of. □ **sized** *adjective* (also in *combination*). **sizer** *noun* [Old French *sise* from *assise* ASSIZE, or from ASSIZE]

size[2] ● *noun* a gelatinous solution used in glazing paper, stiffening textiles, preparing plastered walls for decoration, etc. ● *transitive verb* glaze or stiffen or treat with size. [Middle English, perhaps = SIZE[1]]

size·able *var. of* SIZABLE.

siz·zle ● *verb* **1 a** *intransitive* make a sputtering or hissing sound when or as if frying. **b** *transitive* fry or burn. **2** *intransitive informal* **a** be in a state of great heat or excitement (*Toronto sizzled in the heat wave; the hotline sizzled with calls*). **b** be salacious or risqué. ● *noun* **1** a sizzling sound. **2** *informal* intense heat or excitement. □ **more sizzle than steak** *N Amer. slang* more flash than substance. □ **siz·zler** *noun* **siz·zling** *adjective & adverb* [imitative]

SJ *abbreviation* Society of Jesus.

sjam·bok /ˈʃambɒk/ ● *noun* (in South Africa) a long stiff whip, originally made of rhinoceros hide. ● *transitive verb* flog with a sjambok. [Afrikaans from Malay *samboq*, *chambok* from Urdu *chābuk*]

SK *abbreviation* **1** Saskatchewan (in official postal use). **2** SENIOR KINDERGARTEN.

ska *noun* a style of popular music of Jamaican origin, with a fast tempo and strongly accentuated offbeat. [20th c.: origin unknown]

skag *noun* (also **scag**) *slang* heroin. [20th c.: origin unknown]

Skag·er·rak /ˈskagəˌrak/ a strait separating S Norway from the northwest coast of Denmark.

skald /skɒld, skald/ *noun* (also **scald**) (in ancient Scandinavia) a composer and reciter of poems honouring heroes and their deeds. □ **skald·ic** *adjective* [Old Norse *skáld*, of unknown origin]

Skan·da /ˈskandə/ *Hinduism* the Hindu war god, first son of Shiva and Parvati and brother of Ganesha; he is depicted as a boy or youth, sometimes with six heads and often with his mount, a peacock.

skank[1] ● *noun* **1** a steady-paced dance performed to reggae music, characterized by rhythmically bending forward, raising the knees, and extending the hands palms-downwards. **2** a piece of reggae music suitable for such dancing. ● *intransitive verb* play reggae music or dance in this style. [origin unknown]

skank[2] *noun slang* a person, esp. a woman, regarded as unattractive, sleazy, sexually promiscuous, or immoral. [origin unknown]

skanky *adjective slang* unattractive or disgusting, esp. because dirty.

skat *noun* a three-handed card game with bidding. [German from Italian *scarto* a discard, from *scartare* discard]

skate[1] ● *noun* **1** each of a pair of boots with steel blades fixed to the bottom for gliding on ice. **2** = ROLLER SKATE. **3** = IN-LINE SKATE. **4** an act or period of skating. **5** a device on which a heavy object moves. ● *verb* **1 a** *intransitive* move on or as if on skates. **b** *transitive* perform (a specified figure, a routine, etc.) on skates. **2** *intransitive* (foll. by *around*, *over*) refer fleetingly to, disregard. **3** *intransitive* skateboard. □ **get one's skates on** *Brit. slang* make haste. **hang up one's skates** *Cdn informal* retire from professional life. **skate on thin ice** *informal* behave rashly, risk danger, esp. by dealing with a subject needing tactful treatment. □ **skat·ing** *noun* [originally *scates* (pl.) from Dutch *schaats* (sing.) from Old Northern French *escace*, Old French *eschasse* stilt]

skate[2] *noun* (*pl.* same or **skates**) any cartilaginous marine fish of the family Rajidae, with a roughly diamond-shaped body and a long thin tail. [Old Norse *skata*]

skate[3] *noun slang* a contemptible, mean, or dishonest person (esp. *cheapskate*). [19th c.: origin uncertain]

skate-a-thon *noun esp. Cdn* a prolonged period of skating, organized to raise money for a charity or cause.

skate·board ● *noun* a short narrow board mounted on roller skate wheels, used for riding on while standing, and propelled by one foot pushing occasionally against the ground. ● *intransitive verb* ride on a skateboard. □ **skate·board·er** *noun* **skate·board·ing** *noun*

skate guard *noun* a hard plastic protective device fitted over the blade of a skate.

skate lace *noun* a length of string used for lacing up a skate.

skate park *noun* an area designated and equipped for skateboarding.

skate·punk *noun* a participant in skateboarding subculture.

skat·er *noun* **1** a person who skates. **2** *Hockey* a player other than the goalie. **3** a skateboarder.

skating rink *noun* **1** an area of ice for skating. **2** a building containing a rink for skating.

skean /skiːn, ˈskiːən/ *noun hist.* a Gaelic dagger formerly used in Ireland and Scotland. [Gaelic *sgian* knife]

skean-dhu /skiːn ˈduː, ˌskiːən-/ *noun* a dagger worn in the stocking as part of Highland costume. [SKEAN + Gaelic *dubh* 'black']

sked *esp. N Amer. informal* ● *noun* **1** = SCHEDULE. **2** *Cdn (North)* a scheduled flight. ● *transitive verb* (**sked·ded**, **sked·ding**) = SCHEDULE. [abbreviation]

ske·dad·dle *informal* ● *intransitive verb* run away, depart quickly, flee. ● *noun* a hurried departure or flight. [19th c.: origin unknown]

Skeena Mountains a mountain range in NW central BC, lying to the east of the Coast Mountains. [see SKEENA RIVER]

Skeena River a river in northwestern BC, 579 km long, rising in the Skeena Mountains and flowing first southeastward, then generally southwestward through Terrace to empty into the Pacific Ocean at Chatham Sound, just south of Prince Rupert. [Tsimshian, = water out of the clouds]

skeet *noun* (also **skeet shooting**) a shooting sport in which a clay target is thrown from a trap to simulate the flight of a bird. [Old Norse *skjóta* SHOOT]

skeet·er *noun esp. N Amer. & Austral. slang* a mosquito. [abbreviation]

skeg *noun* **1** the after part of a vessel's keel or a projection from it. **2** a fin underneath the rear of a surfboard. [Old Norse *skeg* beard, perhaps via Dutch *scheg(ge)*]

skein /skeɪn/ *noun* **1** a loosely coiled bundle of yarn or thread. **2** a cluster or arrangement resembling a skein. **3** a flock of wild geese etc. in flight. **4** a tangle or confusion. [Old French *escaigne*, of unknown origin]

skel·etal *adjective* **1** of, forming, or resembling a skeleton. **2** very thin, emaciated. **3** consisting of only a bare outline or minimum. □ **skel·etal·ly** *adverb*

skeletal muscle *noun* muscle with the contractile fibrils in the cells aligned to form stripes visible in a microscope, attached to bones by tendons and under voluntary control. *Also called* STRIATED MUSCLE.

skel·eton *noun* **1 a** a hard internal or external framework of bones, cartilage, shell, woody fibre, etc., supporting or containing the body of an animal or plant. **b** the dried bones of a human being or other animal fastened together in the same relative positions as in life. **2** the supporting framework or structure or essential part of a thing. **3** a very thin or emaciated person or animal. **4** the remaining part of anything after its life or usefulness is gone. **5** (*attributive*) having only the essential or minimum number of persons, parts, etc. (*skeleton plan; skeleton staff*). **6** a sport in which participants slide down a bobsled track at high speed lying face-down and headfirst on a small sled consisting of a fibreglass plate with handles on top of bobsled runners. □ **skel·eton·ic** /ˌskeləˈtɒnɪk/ *adjective* **skel·eton·ize** *transitive verb* (also esp. *Brit.* **-ise**). [modern Latin from Greek, neuter of *skeletos* 'dried-up' from *skellō* 'dry up']

Skeleton Coast an arid coastal area in Namibia. Comprising the northern part of the Namib desert, it extends from Walvis Bay in the south to the border with Angola. A part of the area was designated a national park in 1971.

skeleton in the closet *noun* (also *Brit.* **skeleton in the cupboard**) a discreditable or embarrassing fact kept secret.

skeleton key *noun* a key designed to fit many locks by having the interior of the bit hollowed.

skep *noun* **1** a straw or wicker beehive. **2** a wooden or wicker basket of any of various forms. [Old Norse *skeppa*]

Vowels: a *cat* ɑ *arm* e *bed* ɜr *her* ɜː *deux* ə *ago* ɪ *sit* i *cosy* iː *feed* ɒ *hot* ɔ *pore* ɔː *no* ʌ *run* ʊ *put*

skep·tic (also **scep·tic**) ● *noun* **1** a person who doubts the validity of accepted beliefs in a particular subject. **2** a person who doubts the truth of Christianity and other religions. **3** a person who accepts the philosophy of skepticism. ● *adjective* = SKEPTICAL. [via French and Latin from Greek *skeptikos*, from *scepsis* inquiry; doubt]

skep·tic·al *adjective* (also **scep·tic·al**) **1** inclined to question the truth or soundness of accepted ideas, facts, etc.; critical; incredulous. **2** *Philos.* of or accepting skepticism; denying the possibility of knowledge. □ **skep·tic·al·ly** *adverb*

skep·ti·cism *noun* (also **scep·ti·cism**) **1** a skeptical attitude in relation to accepted ideas, facts, etc.; doubting or critical disposition. **2** *Philos.* the doctrine of the skeptics; the opinion that real knowledge is unattainable.

skerry *noun* (*pl.* **-ries**) esp. *Scot. & Cdn* (*Nfld*) a reef or rocky island. [Orkney dial. from Old Norse *sker*: compare SCAR²]

sketch ● *noun* **1** a rough, slight, merely outlined, or unfinished drawing or painting, often made to assist in making a more finished picture. **2** a brief account without many details conveying a general idea of something; a rough draft or general outline. **3 a** a very short play, usu. humorous and limited to one scene. **b** an item or scene in a comedy program. **4** a short descriptive piece of writing. **5** a musical composition of a single movement. ● *verb* **1** *transitive* make or give a sketch of. **2** *intransitive* draw sketches esp. of landscape (*went out sketching*). **3** *transitive* (often foll. by *in*, *out*) indicate briefly or in outline. □ **sketch·er** *noun* [Dutch *schets* or German *Skizze* from Italian *schizzo* from *schizzare* make a sketch, ultimately from Greek *skhēdios* extempore]

sketch·book *noun* **1** (also **sketch pad**) a book or pad of drawing paper for doing sketches on. **2** a notebook containing preliminary pictorial, verbal, or musical sketches or studies. **3** (usu. as a title) a book containing narrative or descriptive essays.

sketch map *noun* a roughly-drawn map with few details.

sketchy *adjective* (**sketch·i·er**, **sketch·i·est**) **1** giving only a slight or rough outline, like a sketch. **2** unsubstantial or imperfect. □ **sketch·i·ly** *adverb* **sketch·i·ness** *noun*

skew ● *adjective* **1** oblique, slanting, set askew. **2** *Math.* **a** lying in three dimensions (*skew curve*). **b** (of lines) not coplanar. **c** (of a statistical distribution) not symmetrical. ● *noun* **1** a slant. **2** *Statistics* the condition of being skewed; skewness. ● *verb* **1** *transitive* make skew. **2** *transitive* depict or represent unfairly; distort. **3** *intransitive* move obliquely; twist. □ **skew·ness** *noun* [Old Northern French *eskiu(w)er* (v.) = Old French *eschuer*: see ESCHEW]

skew arch *noun* (also **skew bridge**) an arch (or bridge) with the line of the arch not at right angles to the abutment.

skew·back *noun* the sloping face of the abutment on which an extremity of an arch rests.

skew·bald ● *adjective* (of an animal) with irregular patches of white and another colour (properly not black) (*compare* PIEBALD). ● *noun* a skewbald animal, esp. a horse. [Middle English *skued* (origin uncertain), after PIEBALD]

skew chisel *noun* a chisel with an oblique edge.

skew·er ● *noun* **1 a** a long metal or wooden pin for holding meat, vegetables, etc. compactly together while cooking. **b** the pieces of meat, vegetables, etc. of a kebab secured on such a pin. **2** any similar pin for fastening or securing something in place. ● *transitive verb* **1** fasten together or pierce with or as with a skewer. **2** esp. *N Amer.* criticize sharply. [Middle English: origin unknown]

skew-whiff *adjective Brit. informal* askew.

ski ● *noun* (*pl.* **skis**) **1** each of a pair of long narrow pieces of wood etc., usu. pointed and turned up at the front, fastened under the feet for travelling over snow. **2** a similar device under a vehicle or aircraft. **3** = WATER SKI. **4** (*attributive*) **a** of or pertaining to skis or skiing (*ski instructor*). **b** for wear when skiing (*ski boots*). ● *verb* (**skis**, **skied**, **ski·ing**) **1** *intransitive* travel on skis. **2** *transitive* ski at (a place). □ **ski·able** *adjective* [Norwegian from Old Norse *skíth* billet, snowshoe]

Ski·athos /ski'aθɒs/ a Greek island in the Aegean Sea, the most westerly of the Northern Sporades group.

ski-bob ● *noun* a machine like a bicycle with skis instead of wheels. ● *intransitive verb* (**-bobbed**, **-bobbing**) ride a ski-bob. □ **ski-bobber** *noun*

ski bum *noun slang* an avid skier, esp. one who spends a great deal of time skiing.

skid ● *verb* (**skid·ded**, **skid·ding**) **1** *intransitive* (of a vehicle, wheel, or driver) slide on slippery ground, esp. sideways or obliquely. **2** *transitive* cause (a vehicle etc.) to skid. **3** *intransitive* slip, slide. **4** *intransitive informal*

fail or decline or err. **5** *transitive* support or move or protect or check with a skid. **6** *N Amer. transitive & intransitive* slide or haul (logs) down a prepared slide or along a skid trail or skid road. ● *noun* **1** the act or an instance of skidding. **2** a plank or roller on which a heavy object may be placed to facilitate moving. **3** a piece of wood etc. serving as a support, ship's fender, inclined plane, etc. **4** *N Amer.* **a** each of a number of peeled and partially sunk logs or timbers forming a skid road. **b** = SKID ROAD 1. **5** a braking device, esp. a wooden or metal shoe preventing a wheel from revolving or used as a drag. **6** a runner beneath an aircraft for use when landing. **7** *N Amer. Sport informal* a losing streak. □ **grease the skids** *N Amer. informal* help make things run smoothly. **hit the skids** *informal* enter a rapid decline or deterioration. **on the skids** *informal* in a steadily worsening state. [17th c.: origin unknown]

skid·der *noun N Amer.* **1** a type of powerful four-wheel tractor used to haul logs from a cutting area. **2** a teamster who hauls logs from a cutting area.

skid·ding *noun N Amer.* the process of hauling logs from a cutting area.

skid mark *noun* (usu. in *pl.*) **1** a mark made on the road by the tire of a skidding vehicle. **2** *slang* something resembling such a mark, esp. a stain left on underwear by feces.

Ski-Doo ● *noun proprietary* a snowmobile (also *attributive*: Ski-Doo suit). ● *intransitive verb* (**ski·doo**) ride on a snowmobile. □ **ski·doo·er** *noun* **ski·doo·ing** *noun* [from SKI + SKIDOO]

ski·doo *intransitive verb* (also **skid·doo**) (**-doos**, **-dooed**) *N Amer. slang* go away; depart. [perhaps from SKEDADDLE]

Ski-doo suit *noun* = SNOWMOBILE SUIT.

skid road *noun N Amer.* **1** *hist.* a road formed of skids along which logs were hauled. **2** *hist.* a part of a town or city frequented by loggers. **3** = SKID ROW. □ **skid road·er** *noun*

skid row *noun N Amer.* a part of a town or city frequented by vagrants, alcoholics, etc. □ **on skid row** down and out; destitute.

skid-steer loader *noun* a farm vehicle with a large bucket or fork at the front end.

skid trail *noun N Amer.* a trail cut through the bush for hauling logs from a cutting area.

skid·way *N Amer. noun* **1** a platform (usu. inclined) for piling logs before transportation or sawing. **2** = SKID ROAD 1. **3** an inclined ramp of planks or logs used for sliding boats etc. from a higher to a lower position or vice versa.

ski·er *noun* a person who skis.

skiff¹ *noun* any of various types of small light boat, esp. one adapted for rowing and sailing. [French *esquif* from Italian *schifo*, related to SHIP]

skiff² *noun N Amer.* a light dusting of snow. [possibly from Old Norse *skipta*, = Old English *sciftan* shift (verb)]

skif·fle *noun* **1** *Brit.* a kind of folk music with a blues or jazz flavour, popular in the 1950s and played by a small group, mainly with a rhythmic accompaniment to a singing guitarist or banjoist, often incorporating improvised instruments such as washboard, jug, etc. **2** *US* a style of 1920s and 30s jazz deriving from blues, ragtime, and folk music, and using improvised as well as conventional instruments. [perhaps imitative]

ski·ing *noun* the activity or sport of moving on skis.

ski·jor·ing /ˈskiːˌdʒɔrɪŋ, ʃiːˈjɔrɪŋ/ *noun* a winter sport in which a skier is towed by a horse or vehicle. □ **ski·jor·er** *noun* [Norwegian *skikjøring* (as SKI, *kjøre* drive)]

ski jump *noun* **1** an artificial structure consisting of a steep ramp levelling off at the end to allow a skier to leap through the air. **2** a jump executed from this. **3** a competition in which such jumps are made. □ **ski jumper** *noun* **ski jumping** *noun*

skil·ful *adjective* (also **skill·ful**) (often foll. by *at*, *in*) having or showing skill; practised, expert, adroit, ingenious. □ **skil·ful·ly** *adverb* **skil·ful·ness** *noun*

ski lift *noun* a device for carrying skiers up a slope, usu. on seats hung from an overhead cable.

skill *noun* **1** (often foll. by *in*) expertness, practised ability, facility in an action; dexterity or tact. **2** (usu. in *pl.*) a specific aptitude, esp. of a particular type (*good management skills*). [Old Norse *skil* distinction]

skilled *adjective* **1** (often foll. by *in*) having or showing skill; skilful. **2** (of a person) highly trained or experienced. **3** (of work) requiring skill or special training.

skil·let *noun* **1** *N Amer.* a frying pan. **2** *Brit.* a small metal cooking pot with a long handle and usu. legs. [Middle English, perhaps from Old French *escuelete* diminutive of *escuele* platter, from Late Latin *scutella*]

skill·ful *var. of* SKILFUL.

skill set *noun* a person's skills.

skim ● *verb* (**skimmed**, **skim·ming**) **1** *transitive* **a** take scum or cream or a floating layer from the surface of (a liquid). **b** take (cream etc.) from the surface of a liquid. **2 a** *transitive* keep touching lightly or nearly touching (a surface) in passing over. **b** *transitive* (or *intransitive* foll. by *over*) deal with or treat (a subject) superficially. **3** *intransitive* (often foll. by *over*, *along*) go lightly over a surface, glide along in the air. **4** *transitive* throw (a flat stone) low over water so that it bounces on the surface several times. **5 a** *transitive* read superficially, look over cursorily, gather the salient facts contained in. **b** *intransitive* (usu. foll. by *through*) read or look over cursorily. **6** *transitive* N Amer. (often foll. by *off*) *slang* conceal or divert (earnings or takings, esp. from gambling) to avoid paying tax. ● *noun* **1** the act or an instance of skimming. **2** a thin covering on the surface of something, esp. a liquid (*skim of ice*). **3** = SKIM MILK. □ **skim the cream off** take the best part of. [Middle English, back-formation from SKIMMER]

ski mask *noun* a protective, usu. knitted covering for the head and face, with holes for the eyes, mouth, and sometimes the nose, originally worn by skiers.

skim·board *noun* a type of surfboard used for riding shallow water.

skim·mer *noun* **1** a device for skimming liquids. **2** a person who skims. **3** a flat hat, esp. a broad-brimmed straw hat. **4** any long-winged marine bird of the genus *Rynchops* that feeds by skimming over water with its knifelike lower mandible immersed. **5** a hydroplane, hydrofoil, hovercraft, or other vessel that has little or no displacement at speed. **6** N Amer. a sheath-like dress. **7** a device that records credit card or debit card numbers for fraudulent use. [Middle English from Old French *escumoir* from *escumer* from *escume* SCUM]

skim·mia *noun* any evergreen shrub of the genus *Skimmia*, native to E Asia, with red berries. [modern Latin from Japanese]

skim milk *noun* milk from which the cream has been skimmed.

skim·ming *noun* the fraudulent copying of credit or debit card details with a card swipe or other device.

skimp *verb* **1** *transitive* (often foll. by *on*) use or provide a meagre or insufficient amount of, stint (material, expenses, etc.). **2** *transitive* supply (a person etc.) meagrely with food, money, etc. **3** *transitive* do hastily or carelessly. **4** *intransitive* be parsimonious. [18th c.: origin unknown: compare SCAMP², SCRIMP]

skimpy *adjective* (**skimp·i·er**, **skimp·i·est**) **1** meagre; not ample or sufficient (*a skimpy budget*). **2** (of clothing) very short or revealing; made of too little material (*a skimpy bathing suit*). □ **skimp·i·ly** *adverb* **skimp·i·ness** *noun*

skin ● *noun* **1** the flexible continuous covering of a human or other animal body. **2 a** the skin of a flayed animal with or without the hair etc. **b** esp. *hist.* this used as a unit of value (*cost seven beaver skins*). **c** a material prepared from skins esp. of smaller animals (*opp.* HIDE² *noun* 1). **3** a person's skin with reference to its colour or complexion (*has a fair skin*). **4** an outer layer or covering, esp. the coating of a plant, fruit, or sausage. **5** a film like skin on the surface of a liquid etc. **6** a container for liquid, made of an animal's whole skin. **7 a** the planking or plating of a ship or boat, inside or outside the ribs. **b** the outer covering of any craft or vehicle, esp. an aircraft or spacecraft. **8** *slang* a skinhead. **9** (usu. in *pl.*) a strip of sealskin or other material attached to the bottom of a ski to give traction when climbing slopes. **10** (usu. in *pl.*) *slang* a drum. **11** *see* SKINS GAME. **12** *Computing* a program which allows a user to change the appearance and functionality of an existing graphical user interface. ● *transitive verb* (**skinned**, **skin·ning**) **1 a** remove the skin from. **b** graze (a part of the body). **2** (often foll. by *over*) cover (a sore etc.) with or as with skin. **3** *slang* fleece or swindle. ● *adjective* of, depicting, or presenting pornographic material. □ **be skin and bone** be very thin. **by the skin of one's teeth** by a very narrow margin. **get under a person's skin** *informal* interest or annoy a person intensely. **have a thick** (or **thin**) **skin** be insensitive (or sensitive) to criticism etc. **no skin off one's nose** (or **ass**) *informal* a matter of indifference or even benefit to one. **skin a person alive** used when threatening to punish someone severely. **to the skin** through all one's clothing (*soaked to the skin*). □ **skin·less** *adjective* **skin-like** *adjective* **skinned** *adjective* (also in *combination*). [Old English *scin(n)* from Old Norse *skinn*]

skin care *noun* care of the skin by use of cleansers, moisturizers etc.

skin deep *adjective* (of an emotion, an impression, a quality, etc.) superficial, not deep or lasting.

skin diver *noun* a person who swims underwater without a diving suit, usu. in deep water with scuba equipment and flippers. □ **skin diving** *noun*

skin flick *noun* *slang* a pornographic film.

skin·flint *noun* a miserly person.

skin·ful *noun* (*pl.* **-fuls**) *informal* enough alcoholic liquor to make one drunk.

skin game *noun* *slang* a rigged gambling game; a swindle.

skin graft *noun* **1** the surgical transplanting of skin. **2** a piece of skin transferred in this way.

skin·head *noun* a person, esp. a youth, with shaven or close-cropped hair worn as a symbol of anarchy, racism, or nonconformity.

skink *noun* any of numerous lizards of the family Scincidae, which have smooth elongated bodies, small heads, and limbs that are small or entirely absent. [French *scinc* or Latin *scincus* from Greek *skigkos*]

skin magazine *noun* (also **skin mag**) *slang* a pornographic magazine.

Skin·ner, Bur·rhus Fred·eric (1904–90), US psychologist. He promoted the view that the proper aim of psychology should be to predict, and hence be able to control, behaviour, and demonstrated that arbitrary responses in animals could be obtained by using reinforcements (i.e. rewards and punishments). □ **Skin·ner·ian** *adjective*

skin·ner *noun* **1** a person who skins animals or prepares skins. **2** a dealer in skins, a furrier. **3** N Amer. = CATSKINNER.

skin·ny ● *adjective* (**skin·ni·er**, **skin·ni·est**) **1 a** (of a person) thin or emaciated. **b** (of an object) narrow, slim (*a skinny tie*). **2** (of clothing) tight-fitting. **3** made of or like skin. ● *noun* N Amer. *slang* gossip; inside information. □ **skin·ni·ness** *noun*

skinny-dipping *noun* esp. N Amer. *informal* swimming in the nude. □ **skinny-dip** *intransitive verb* **skinny dip** *noun* **skinny dipper** *noun*

skins game *noun* *Sport* a form of golf, curling, bowling, etc., in which the winner of each hole, end, or frame is awarded a financial prize, or 'skin', with the value of the skin increasing as the game goes on.

skint *adjective* Brit. *slang* having no money left. [= *skinned*, past participle of SKIN]

skin test *noun* a test to determine whether an immune reaction is elicited when a substance is applied to or injected into the skin.

skin-tight *adjective* (of a garment) very close-fitting.

skip¹ ● *verb* (**skipped**, **skip·ping**) **1** *intransitive* **a** move along lightly, esp. by taking two steps with each foot in turn. **b** jump lightly from the ground, esp. so as to clear a skipping rope. **c** jump about, gambol, caper, frisk. **2** *intransitive* (often foll. by *from*, *off*, *to*) move quickly from one point, subject, or occupation to another. **3** *transitive* omit in dealing with a series or in reading; miss (*skip every tenth row*; *always skips the small print*; *my heart skipped a beat*). **4** *transitive* *informal* **a** not attend or participate in (*skipped class*). **b** forgo; not have (*skipped breakfast*). **5** *transitive informal* depart quickly from; leave hurriedly (*skipped town*). **6** *intransitive* (often foll. by *out*, *off*) *informal* make off, disappear. **7** *transitive* make (a stone) ricochet on the surface of water. **8** *intransitive* (of a record or compact disc) play erratically because of a defect in the playing surface. **9** *transitive* **a** advance (a student) two or more grades. **b** (of a student) advance (two or more grades). ● *noun* **1** a skipping movement or action. **2** a defect in the playing surface of a record or compact disc which causes the needle or laser to jump forwards or backwards or to remain stuck, resulting in erratic playback. **3** *Computing* the action of passing over part of a sequence of data or instructions. **4** N Amer. *informal* a person who defaults or absconds. □ **skip a beat** pause temporarily. **skip it** *slang* abandon a topic etc. **skip off** *Cdn* (*S Ont*) play truant from school. **skip out** *Cdn* (*West*) = SKIP OFF. **skip rope** N Amer. play or exercise with a skipping rope. [Middle English, prob. from Scandinavian]

skip² *noun* **1** Brit. a large container for builders' refuse etc. **2** a cage, bucket, etc., in which workers or materials are lowered and raised in mines and quarries. [var. of SKEP]

skip³ ● *noun* the captain of a curling or bowling team. ● *transitive verb* (**skipped**, **skip·ping**) be the skip of. [abbreviation of SKIPPER¹]

ski patrol *noun* a person or persons patrolling a ski area to check on the safety of skiers, monitor snow conditions, perform first aid, etc. □ **ski patroller** *noun*

skip·jack *noun* **1** (in full **skipjack tuna**) a small striped Pacific tuna, *Katsuwonus pelamis*, used as food. **2** a click beetle. **3** a kind of sailing boat used off the east coast of the US. [SKIP¹ + JACK¹]

ski plane *noun* an airplane having its undercarriage fitted with skis for landing on snow or ice.

ski pole *noun* either of two poles held by a skier to assist with balance, propulsion, and braking.

Consonants: b *but*   d *dog*   f *few*   g *get*   h *her*   j *yes*   k *cat*   l *leg*   m *man*   n *no*   p *pen*   r *red*   s *sit*

skip·per¹ ● *noun* **1** the captain of a ship, esp. of a small trading or fishing vessel. **2** the captain of an aircraft. **3** the captain of a side in a game or sport. ● *transitive verb* act as captain of. [Middle Dutch, Middle Low German *schipper* from *schip* SHIP]

skip·per² *noun* **1** a person who skips. **2** any brown thick-bodied butterfly of the family Hesperiidae, with a rapid, skipping flight.

skipping rope *noun Cdn & Brit.* a length of rope or rubber cord, usu. with handles at each end, revolved over the head and under the feet while jumping as a game or exercise.

skip rock *noun Curling* one of a rink's last two rocks of an end, usu. delivered by the skip.

skip tracer *noun N Amer.* a person or business that locates persons who are in default on payments. □ **skip tracing** *noun*

skirl ● *noun* the shrill sound characteristic of bagpipes. ● *intransitive verb* make a skirl. [prob. Scandinavian: ultimately imitative]

skir·mish ● *noun* **1** a piece of irregular or unpremeditated fighting esp. between small or outlying parts of armies or fleets; a slight engagement. **2** a short argument or contest of wit etc. ● *intransitive verb* engage in a skirmish. □ **skir·mish·er** *noun* [Old French *eskirmir, escrimir* from Frankish]

skirr *intransitive verb* move rapidly esp. with a whirring sound. [perhaps related to SCOUR¹ or SCOUR²]

skirt ● *noun* **1** a woman's outer garment hanging from the waist. **2** the part of a dress, coat, etc. that hangs below the waist. **3** a piece of material fitting around the sides of a bed, chair, table, etc. to conceal the legs. **4** (in *sing.* or *pl.*) an edge, border, or extreme part. **5** (also *Brit.* **bit of skirt**) *slang offensive* a woman regarded as an object of sexual desire. **6** (in full **skirt of beef** etc.) **a** the diaphragm and other membranes as food. **b** *Brit.* a cut of meat from the lower flank. **7** a flap of a saddle. **8** a surface that conceals or protects the wheels or underside of a vehicle or aircraft. **9** a hanging part around the base of a hovercraft. ● *verb* **1** *transitive* go along or around or past the edge of. **2** *transitive* be situated along. **3** *transitive* avoid dealing with (an issue etc.). **4** *intransitive* (foll. by *along*) go along the coast, a wall, etc. □ **skirt·ed** *adjective* (also in *combination*). [Old Norse *skyrta* shirt, corresponding to Old English *scyrte*: see SHIRT]

skirt chaser *noun slang derogatory* a man who obsessively pursues women.

skirt·ing *noun* (in full **skirting board**) *Brit.* = BASEBOARD.

ski run *noun* a slope, trail, etc. prepared for skiing.

skit *noun* a light, usu. short, piece of satire or comedy. [related to *skit* move lightly and rapidly, perhaps from Old Norse (compare *skjóta* SHOOT)]

skit·ter *intransitive verb* **1 a** (usu. foll. by *along, across*) move lightly or hastily. **b** (usu. foll. by *about, off*) hurry about, dart off. **2** fish by drawing bait jerkily across the surface of the water. [apparently frequentative of dial. *skite*, perhaps formed as SKIT]

skit·tery *adjective* skittish, restless.

skit·tish *adjective* **1** lively, playful. **2** (of a horse etc.) nervous, inclined to shy, fidgety. **3** fickle, changeable. □ **skit·tish·ly** *adverb* **skit·tish·ness** *noun* [Middle English, perhaps formed as SKIT]

skit·tle *noun* **1** a pin used in the game of skittles. **2** (in *pl.*; usu. treated as *sing.*) a game played with usu. nine wooden pins set up at the end of an alley to be bowled down usu. with wooden balls or a wooden disc. [17th c. (also *kittle-pins*): origin unknown]

skive *verb* **1** *transitive* split or pare (hides, leather, etc.). **2** *intransitive Brit. slang* **a** evade a duty, shirk. **b** (often foll. by *off*) avoid work by absenting oneself, play truant. □ **skiv·er** *noun* [Old Norse *skífa*, related to Middle English *schíve* slice]

skivvy ● *noun* (pl. **-vies**) **1 a** esp. *Brit. informal derogatory* a female domestic servant. **b** a person doing work considered menial or poorly paid. **2 a** (in *pl.*) *N Amer.* underwear, esp. men's underwear. **b** (in full **skivvy shirt**) *US & Austral.* a thin high-necked long-sleeved garment. ● *intransitive verb* (**-vies, -vied**) *informal* work as a skivvy. [20th c.: origin unknown]

skol /skɒl, skɔːl/ *noun* used as a toast in drinking. [Danish *skaal*, Swedish *skål*, from Old Norse *skál* bowl]

skoo·kum esp. *Cdn (West)* ● *adjective* excellent, impressive, good. ● *noun* (esp. among Aboriginal peoples of the Northwest coast) an evil spirit. [Chinook Jargon]

Skopje /ˈskɒpjeɪ/ the capital of the republic of Macedonia, situated in the north on the Vardar River; pop. (est. 2002) 448,600.

skor·dalia /skɔrˈdaliə/ *noun* a Greek dip of cold whipped potatoes and garlic served with pita bread. [modern Greek, = garlic sauce, from Greek *skordo* garlic]

skort *noun N Amer.* a pair of women's shorts for casual or semi-casual wear, with a flap of material draping the front, giving the appearance of a wraparound skirt. [blend of SKIRT *noun* 1 + SHORTS 1]

SKU /ˈskjuː/ *abbreviation* stock-keeping unit, designating a number used in retail stock control.

skua /ˈskjuːə/ *noun* any of various large predatory seabirds of the family Stercorariinae, typically having brown or brown and white plumage and a strongly hooked bill, breeding in polar or cold regions, and with a habit of robbing other seabirds of food by forcing them to disgorge the fish they have caught. [modern Latin from Faroese *skúgvur*, Old Norse *skúfr*]

skul·dug·gery *noun* (also **skull·dug·gery**) trickery; unscrupulous behaviour. [earlier *sculduddery*, originally Scots = unchastity (18th c.: origin unknown)]

skulk ● *intransitive verb* **1** move stealthily, lurk, or keep oneself concealed, esp. in a cowardly or sinister way. **2** stay or sneak away in time of danger. **3** *Brit.* shirk duty. ● *noun* **1** a person who skulks. **2** a pack of foxes or other animals characterized by skulking. □ **skulk·er** *noun* [Middle English from Scandinavian: compare Norwegian *skulka* lurk, Danish *skulke*, Swedish *skolka* shirk]

skull *noun* **1** the bony case of the brain of a vertebrate. **2 a** the part of the skeleton corresponding to the head. **b** this with the skin and soft internal parts removed. **c** a representation of this. **3** the head as the centre of thought or intelligence. □ **out of one's skull** *slang* **1** out of one's mind, crazy. **2** very drunk. □ **skulled** *adjective* (also in *combination*). [Middle English *scolle*: origin unknown]

skull and crossbones *plural noun* a representation of a skull with two thigh bones crossed below, used formerly on the flags of pirate ships and now to warn of danger, e.g. on bottles of poison.

skull·cap *noun* **1** a small close-fitting peakless cap. **2** the top part of the skull. **3** any plant of the genus *Scutellaria*, having a helmet-shaped calyx after flowering.

skull session *noun US slang* a discussion or conference.

skunk ● *noun* **1 a** any of various cat-sized flesh-eating mammals of the family Mustelidae, esp. *Mephitis mephitis* having a distinctive black and white striped fur and able to emit a powerful stench from a liquid secreted by its anal glands as a defence. **b** its fur. **2** *informal* a thoroughly contemptible person. ● *transitive verb N Amer.* **1** *slang* defeat soundly. **2** (in cribbage) defeat (one's opponent) by a margin of at least 31 points. [cognate of Western Abenaki *segongw*]

skunk cabbage *noun N Amer.* either of two plants of the arum family, *Lysichiton americanum* of western N America or *Symplocarpus foetidus* of eastern N America, with an offensive-smelling spathe.

skunk·weed *noun informal* cannabis of a variety which has a high concentration of narcotic.

skunky *adjective N Amer. informal* (of beer) foul-tasting, esp. as a result of exposure to light.

sky ● *noun* (pl. **skies**) (in *sing.* or *pl.*) **1** the region of the atmosphere and outer space seen from the earth. **2** the weather or climate evidenced by this. ● *transitive verb* (**skies, skied**) **1** *Baseball etc.* hit (a ball) high into the air. **2** hang (a picture) high on a wall. □ **the sky is the limit** there is practically no limit. **to the skies** very highly; without reserve (*praised to the skies*). **under the open sky** out of doors. □ **skyey** *adjective* **sky·less** *adjective* [Middle English *ski(es)* cloud(s), from Old Norse *skÿ*]

sky blue ● *noun* a bright clear blue. ● *adjective* (**sky-blue**) of this colour.

sky·box *noun* esp. *N Amer.* a private box situated near the top of a sports stadium or arena, from where the game or event may be viewed.

sky-clad *adjective slang* naked (esp. in connection with modern pagan ritual). [prob. translation of Sanskrit *Digāmbara*, denoting a Jain sect]

sky·div·ing *noun* the sport of jumping from an aircraft and falling for as long as one safely can before opening one's parachute. □ **sky·dive** *intransitive verb* **sky·div·er** *noun*

Skye a mountainous island of the Inner Hebrides, lying just off the west coast of Scotland; chief town, Portree. It is the largest island of the group.

Skye terrier *noun* a small long-haired slate-coloured or fawn-coloured variety of Scottish terrier.

sky-high *adverb & adjective* very high (*sky-high interest rates*).

sky·hook *noun* **1** *Basketball* a high-arcing throw, a lob. **2** a launching device for aircraft, satellites, etc. **3** *Mountaineering* a small flattened hook with an eye for attaching a rope etc. fixed temporarily into a rock face. **4** an imaginary or fanciful device for suspension in or attachment to the sky.

sky·jack *transitive verb* hijack (an aircraft). □ **sky·jack·er** *noun* [SKY + HIJACK]

sky·lark ● *noun* a lark, *Alauda arvensis* of Eurasia and North Africa, that sings while hovering in flight. ● *intransitive verb* play tricks or practical jokes, indulge in horseplay, frolic. [SKY + LARK: (v.) with pun on LARK²]

sky·light *noun* an opening in a roof or ceiling, covered with glass, Plexiglas, etc., for letting in daylight. □ **sky·light·ed** *adjective* **sky·lit** *adjective*

sky·line *noun* **1** the outline of hills, buildings, etc., defined against the sky. **2** *N Amer. Forestry* an overhead cable for transporting logs.

sky marshal *noun* a plainclothes armed guard on an airplane, employed to counter hijacking.

sky pilot *noun slang* a clergyman.

sky·rock·et ● *intransitive verb* (**sky·rock·et·ed, sky·rock·et·ing**) (esp. of prices etc.) rise very steeply or rapidly. ● *noun* a rocket firework exploding high in the air.

sky·sail *noun* a light sail above the royal in a square-rigged ship.

sky·scape *noun* **1** a picture chiefly representing the sky. **2** a view of the sky.

sky·scrap·er *noun* a very tall building with many storeys.

sky·surf·ing *noun* the sport of jumping from an aircraft and surfing through the air on a board before landing by parachute.

sky·walk *noun* = SKYWAY 3.

sky·ward ● *adverb* (also **sky·wards**) towards the sky. ● *adjective* moving skyward.

sky·watch·er *noun* a person who watches the sky for aircraft, astronomical phenomena, etc.

sky·way *noun* esp. *N Amer.* **1** a route used by aircraft. **2** the sky as a medium of transport. **3** a covered overhead walkway between buildings. **4** a long highly elevated section of highway, esp. one spanning water (*Burlington Skyway*).

sky·writ·ing *noun* legible smoke trails made by an airplane esp. for advertising. □ **sky·writ·er** *noun*

slab ● *noun* **1** a flat broad fairly thick usu. square or rectangular piece of solid material, e.g. concrete or stone. **2** a large flat piece of cake, chocolate, etc. **3** an outer piece of wood sawn from a log. **4** a mortuary table. ● *transitive verb* (**slabbed, slab·bing**) remove slabs from (a log or tree) to prepare it for sawing into planks. [Middle English: origin unknown]

slack¹ ● *adjective* **1** not taut; not held tensely (*slack rope; slack muscles*; also in *combination*: *slack-jawed*). **2** inactive or sluggish. **3** negligent or remiss. **4** (of tide etc.) neither ebbing nor flowing. **5** (of trade or business or a market) with little happening. **6** *Phonetics* = LAX 2. **7** relaxed, languid. ● *noun* **1** the slack part of a rope etc. (*haul in the slack*). **2** a slack time in trade etc. **3** *informal* a period of inactivity or laziness. ● *verb* **1 a** *transitive & intransitive* slacken. **b** *transitive* loosen (rope etc.). **2** *intransitive informal* be lazy; shirk. ● *adverb* slackly. □ **cut a person some slack** *N Amer. see* CUT. **slack off 1** loosen. **2** reduce activity, effort, speed, etc. **slack up** reduce the speed of a train etc. before stopping. **take** (or **pick**) **up the slack** use up a surplus or make up a deficiency; avoid an undesirable lull. □ **slack·ly** *adverb* **slack·ness** *noun* [Old English *slæc*, from Germanic]

slack² *noun* coal dust or small pieces of coal. [Middle English prob. from Low German or Dutch]

slack·en *transitive & intransitive verb* make or become slack. □ **slacken off** = SLACK OFF (see SLACK¹).

slack·er *noun* **1** a shirker; an indolent person. **2** such a person regarded as one of a large group or generation of (esp. young) people who find themselves without direction in life.

slacks *plural noun* trousers, esp. for informal wear.

slack suit *noun N Amer.* casual clothes of slacks and a jacket or shirt.

slack water *noun* a time near the turn of the tide, esp. at low tide.

slag ● *noun* **1** vitreous refuse left after ore has been smelted; dross separated in a fused state in the reduction of ore. **2** volcanic scoria. **3** *esp. Brit. slang derogatory* a prostitute or promiscuous woman. ● *verb* (**slagged, slag·ging**) **1** *intransitive* **a** form slag. **b** cohere into a mass like slag. **2** *transitive* (*Brit.* often foll. by *off*) *slang* criticize, insult. □ **slag·gy** *adjective* (**slag·gi·er, slag·gi·est**). [Middle Low German *slagge*, perhaps from *slagen* strike, with reference to fragments formed by hammering]

Slag·gard, Mount a peak in SW Yukon Territory, in the St. Elias mountain range (4 663 m). [J. R. *Slaggard*, local prospector *c.*1958]

slag heap *noun* a hill of refuse from a mine etc.

slain *past participle of* SLAY.

slainte /ˈslantʃə/ *interjection* a Gaelic toast: good health! [Gaelic *sláinte*, lit. 'health']

slake *transitive verb* **1** assuage or satisfy (thirst, revenge, etc.). **2** disintegrate (quicklime) by chemical combination with water. [Old English *slacian* from *slæc* SLACK¹]

slaked lime *noun see* LIME¹ *noun* 2.

slal·om /ˈslɒləm/ ● *noun* **1** a downhill ski race on a zigzag course marked by artificial obstacles, usu. flags, and descended singly by each competitor in turn. **2** a similar obstacle race for canoeists, water skiers, skateboarders, etc. ● *intransitive verb* (**slal·omed, slal·om·ing**) **1** perform or compete in a slalom. **2** make frequent sharp turns in or as in a slalom. □ **slalom·er** *noun* [Norwegian, lit. 'sloping track']

slam¹ ● *verb* (**slammed, slam·ming**) **1** *transitive & intransitive* shut forcefully and loudly. **2** *transitive* put down (an object) with a similar sound. **3** *intransitive* move violently (*he slammed out of the room*). **4** *transitive & intransitive* put or come into sudden action (*slam the brakes on*). **5** *transitive slang* criticize severely. **6** *transitive slang* hit. **7** *transitive slang* gain an easy victory over. ● *noun* **1** a sound of or as of a slammed door. **2** the shutting of a door etc. with a loud bang. **3** (usu. prec. by *the*) *N Amer. slang* prison. **4** a criticism or insult. **5** *Basketball* = SLAM DUNK 1. [prob. from Scandinavian: compare Old Norse *slam(b)ra*]

slam² *noun Cards* the winning of every trick in a game. [originally name of a card game: perhaps from obsolete *slampant* trickery]

slam-bang ● *adverb* with the sound of a slam. ● *adjective informal* **1** impressive, exciting, or energetic. **2** noisy, violent.

slam-dancing *noun N Amer.* a form of dancing to rock music (originally at punk rock concerts) in which participants deliberately collide violently with one another. □ **slam-dance** *noun & intransitive verb* **slam-dancer** *noun*

slam dunk ● *noun* **1** *Basketball* a forceful and often dramatic dunk shot. **2** a sure thing; an easy victory. ● *verb* (**slam-dunk**) **1** *Basketball* **a** *transitive* dunk (the ball) in a forceful, often dramatic manner. **b** *intransitive* make a forceful, often dramatic dunk shot or shots. **2** *transitive* easily defeat (a person or thing). **3** *transitive* achieve (something) in a forceful, often dramatic way (*slam-dunked a deal*).

slam·mer *noun esp. N Amer. slang* **1** (usu. prec. by *the*) prison. **2** a slam-dancer.

slan·der ● *noun* **1** a malicious, false, and injurious statement spoken about a person. **2** the uttering of such statements; calumny. **3** *Law* false oral defamation (*compare* LIBEL *noun* 1). ● *transitive verb* utter slander about; defame falsely. □ **slan·der·er** *noun* **slan·der·ous** *adjective* **slan·der·ous·ly** *adverb* [Middle English *sclaundre* from Anglo-French *esclaundre*, Old French *esclandre* alteration of *escandle* from Late Latin *scandalum*: see SCANDAL]

slang ● *noun* words, phrases, and uses that are regarded as very informal and are often restricted to special contexts or are peculiar to a specified profession, class, geographic area, etc. (*military slang; street slang*). ● *verb* **1** *transitive* use abusive language to. **2** *intransitive* use such language. [18th-c. cant: origin unknown]

slanging match *noun esp. Brit.* a prolonged exchange of insults.

slangy *adjective* (**slang·i·er, slang·i·est**) **1** of the character of slang. **2** fond of using slang. □ **slang·i·ly** *adverb* **slang·i·ness** *noun*

slant ● *verb* **1** *intransitive* slope; diverge from a line; lie or go obliquely to a vertical or horizontal line. **2** *transitive* cause to do this. **3** *transitive* (often as **slant·ed** *adjective*) present (information) from a particular angle esp. in a biased or unfair way. ● *noun* **1** a slope; an oblique position. **2** a way of regarding a thing; a point of view, esp. a biased one. ● *adjective* sloping, oblique. □ **on a slant** aslant. □ **slanty** *adjective* [apheetic form of ASLANT: (v.) related to Middle English *slent* from Old Norse *sletta* dash, throw]

slant-eyed *adjective* often *derogatory* having slanting eyes.

slant·wise *adverb* aslant.

slap ● *verb* (**slapped, slap·ping**) **1** *transitive & intransitive* strike with the palm of the hand or a flat object, or so as to make a similar noise. **2** *transitive* lay forcefully (*slapped the money on the table; slapped a writ on the offender*). **3** *transitive* put hastily or carelessly (*slap some paint on the walls*). **4** *transitive* (often foll. by *down*) *informal* reprimand or snub. **5** *transitive N Amer.* strike (the ball, puck, etc.) with a sharp slap. **6** *transitive N Amer.* punish with a fine, sentence, etc. (*slapped him with a three-game suspension*). ● *noun* **1** a blow with the palm of the hand or a flat object. **2** a slapping sound. ● *adverb* **1** with the suddenness or effectiveness or true aim of a blow; suddenly, fully, directly (*ran slap into him; hit me slap in the eye*). **2** = SLAP BANG. □ **slap on the back** *see* BACK. **slap a**

person on the back see BACK. **slap someone around** beat someone. [Low German *slapp* (imitative)]

slap bang *adverb Brit.* **1** exactly, precisely (*slap bang in the middle of the town*). **2** violently, noisily, headlong. **3** conspicuously, prominently.

slap·dash ● *adjective* hasty and careless. ● *adverb* in a slapdash manner.

slap-happy *adjective informal* **1** cheerfully casual or flippant. **2** punch-drunk.

slap in the face *noun* a rebuff or affront.

slap on the wrist *noun* a mild rebuke or reprimand.

slap·shot *noun Hockey* a hard shot taken by raising the stick just above or below waist height before striking the puck or ball.

slap·stick *noun* **1** boisterous physical comedy, characterized by pratfalls etc. **2** a device consisting of two flexible pieces of wood joined together at one end, designed to produce a loud slapping noise, used esp. by a clown etc. to simulate the dealing of a hard blow.

slap-up *adjective Brit. informal* excellent, lavish; done regardless of expense (*slap-up meal*).

slash ● *verb* **1** *intransitive* make a sweeping or random cut or cuts with a knife, sword, whip, etc. **2** *transitive* make such a cut or cuts at. **3** *transitive* make a long narrow gash or gashes in. **4** *transitive* reduce (prices etc.) drastically. **5** *transitive Hockey* strike or swing at (an opponent) with the stick. **6** *transitive* censure vigorously. **7** *transitive* make (one's way) by slashing. **8** *transitive* **a** lash (a person etc.) with a whip. **b** crack (a whip). **9** *transitive N Amer.* clear (land) of vegetation; cut down (trees or undergrowth). ● *noun* **1 a** a slashing cut or stroke. **b** a wound or slit made by this. **2** an oblique stroke; a solidus. **3** *N Amer. Forestry* **a** debris resulting from the felling or destruction of trees. **b** an area in a forest strewn with such debris. **4** a severe or drastic reduction. **5** *Hockey* an act or instance of slashing. **6** *Brit. slang* an act of urinating. [Middle English perhaps from Old French *esclachier* break in pieces]

slash-and-burn *adjective* **1** (of cultivation) in which vegetation is cut down, allowed to dry, and then burned off before seeds are planted. **2** (of a person, action, etc.) outstandingly aggressive or ruthless.

slash·er *noun* **1** a person or thing that slashes. **2** (in full **slasher film, slasher movie**) a film depicting violent assault with a knife etc. **3** *Cdn* a form of circular saw with several blades, used to cut logs into predetermined lengths.

slash·ing ● *noun* **1** *Hockey* the infraction of striking or swinging at an opponent with the stick. **2** = SLASH *noun* 3. ● *adjective* vigorously incisive or effective.

slash pine *noun* a pine growing in a swamp or low-lying coastal region, esp. *Pinus caribaea* of Central America and the Caribbean.

slash pocket *noun* a pocket set in a garment with a slit for the opening.

slat *noun* **1** any thin narrow piece of wood, plastic, or metal, such as one of those found on a fence or Venetian blind. **2** (in *pl.*) *N Amer. informal* the buttocks. **3** (in *pl.*) *informal* skis. [Old French *esclat* splinter, from *esclater* split, from Romanic]

slate ● *noun* **1** a fine-grained metamorphic sedimentary rock, typically dark grey, green, or bluish-purple in colour, characterized by splitting readily into flat smooth plates. **2** a piece of such a plate used as a tile esp. to cover a roof or pave a walkway. **3** a piece of such a plate, usu. framed in wood, formerly used for writing on. **4** a bluish-grey or bluish-purple colour. **5** *N Amer.* a list of nominees for election or appointment to an official post. **6** *Film* a board giving information about a shot, held in front of the camera so that the film can be identified later. **7** *informal* an agenda, schedule, or list (*what's on the slate for tonight?*). ● *transitive verb* **1** *N Amer.* (usu. foll. by *for*, *to*) make arrangements for (an event etc.); plan, schedule (*this house has been slated for demolition*). **2** *N Amer.* propose or nominate (a candidate or candidates) for a position, political office etc. **3** cover (a roof etc.) with slates. **4** *Brit. informal* criticize severely. ● *adjective* **1** made of slate. **2** of the colour of slate. □ **wipe the slate clean** forgive or cancel the record of past offences. □ **slat·ing** *noun* [Old French *esclate*, fem. form of *esclat* SLAT]

slate blue ● *noun* a shade of blue occurring in slate, usu. a greyish or purplish blue. ● *adjective* (usu. **slate-blue**) of this colour.

slate-coloured *adjective* of a dark bluish, purplish, or greenish grey.

slate grey ● *noun* a shade of grey occurring in slate, usu. a bluish, purplish, or greenish grey. ● *adjective* (usu. **slate-grey**) of this colour.

slater *noun* a person who slates roofs etc.

slath·er *esp. N Amer. informal* ● *transitive verb* **1** (often foll. by *with*) cover (a surface) with a large or excessive portion of a substance. **2** spread or smear (a substance) lavishly or excessively. ● *noun* (often in *pl.*) a large amount. [19th c.: origin unknown]

slat·ted *adjective* consisting of or having slats (*a chair with a slatted back*).

slat·tern *noun* **1** a promiscuous woman; a slut. **2** an untidy and slovenly woman. □ **slat·tern·ly** *adjective* **slat·tern·li·ness** *noun* [17th c.: related to *slattering* slovenly, from dial. *slatter* to spill, slop, waste, frequentative of *slat* strike]

slaty *adjective* **1** resembling slate in colour, texture, or appearance. **2** characteristic of slate.

slaugh·ter /ˈslɒtɜr/ ● *noun* **1 a** the killing of an animal or animals for food. **b** (*attributive*) designating animals that are intended or set aside to be killed for food (*slaughter cattle*). **2** the killing of a person or animal in a brutal or ruthless manner. **3** the killing of many people or animals at once or over a period of time, as in a war; massacre. ● *transitive verb* **1** kill (an animal) for food; butcher. **2** kill or murder (a person) in a ruthless or brutal manner. **3** kill large numbers of people or animals at once or over a period of time. **4** *informal* defeat easily or by a wide margin. □ **slaugh·ter·er** *noun* **slaugh·ter·ous** *adjective* [Middle English *slahter*, ultimately from Old Norse *slátr* butcher's meat, related to SLAY]

slaugh·ter·house *noun* a place where animals are butchered for food.

Slav ● *noun* a member of a group of peoples in Central and Eastern Europe speaking Slavic languages. ● *adjective* of or relating to the Slavs or the Slavic languages. [Middle English *Sclave* from medieval Latin *Sclavus*, late Greek *Sklabos*, & from medieval Latin *Slavus*]

slave ● *noun* **1** a person who is the legal property of another or others and is bound to absolute obedience; a human chattel. **2** a person working very hard, esp. without appropriate reward or appreciation; a drudge. **3** a person completely under the domination of or subject to a specified influence (*he's a slave to his passions*). **4** a willing devotee to a particular activity, cause, person, etc. (*a slave to fashion*). **5** a subsidiary part, esp. a device which is controlled by, or which follows the movements of, another. **6** = LOVE SLAVE. ● *verb* **1** *intransitive* (often foll. by *at*, *away*, *over*) toil or work very hard. **2** *transitive* (foll. by *to*) subject (a device) to control by another. [Old French *esclave* from medieval Latin *sclavus*, *sclava*, a captive, identical to *Sclavus* SLAV, the Slavic peoples having been reduced to a servile state by conquest during the 9th c.]

Slave Coast *noun hist.* a section of the coast of W Africa extending approximately from the Volta River to the Bight of Benin from which slaves were exported from the 16th–19th c.

slave-driver *noun* **1** a person who works others hard; a demanding and unyielding supervisor, employer, teacher, etc. **2** an overseer of slaves at work.

slave·hold·er *noun* a person who owns slaves. □ **slave·hold·ing** *noun & adjective*

slave labour *noun* **1** arduous work assigned to slaves; forced labour. **2** slaves collectively. **3** gruelling or forced labour for which one receives little remuneration.

Slave Lake a town in north central Alberta, situated at the eastern end of Lesser Slave Lake, about 210 km northwest of Edmonton; pop. (2001) 6,600.

slav·er¹ *noun hist.* **1** a ship used in the slave trade. **2** a person dealing in or owning slaves.

slav·er² /ˈslavɜr/ ● *noun* **1** saliva running from the mouth. **2** drivel, nonsense. ● *intransitive verb* **1** let saliva run from the mouth; drool. **2** show excessive desire, eagerness, or obsequiousness. [Middle English prob. from Low German or Dutch: compare SLOBBER]

Slave River a river in NE Alberta and the southern NWT, 415 km long, which flows northward from Lake Athabasca to Great Slave Lake. It is part of the Mackenzie River system. [SLAVEY]

slav·ery *noun* **1** the practice or institution of keeping slaves. **2** the condition or fact of being a slave; servitude, bondage, subjugation. **3** any condition or practice similar to slavery, esp. involving rigorous service or labour with little reward.

slave ship *noun hist.* a ship used to transport slaves, esp. from Africa.

Slave State *noun hist.* any of the 15 southern States of the US in which slavery was legal before the Civil War.

slave trade *noun hist.* the business of procuring, transporting, and selling humans as slaves, esp. the transporting of African blacks to the US to be sold into slavery. □ **slave trader** *noun*

Slav·ey /ˈsleɪvɪ/ *noun* **1** a member of a number of Dene Aboriginal groups (subdivided into the **North Slavey** and **South Slavey**) living in the Mackenzie River basin in western NWT. **2** any of the Athapaskan languages spoken by the Slavey. [translation of Cree *awahkān* 'captive, slave']

Slav·ic /ˈslavɪk/ ● *adjective* **1** of, pertaining to, or designating the branch of Indo-European languages including Russian, Polish, Ukrainian, and Czech, spoken throughout most of Central and Eastern Europe. **2** pertaining to, characteristic of, or designating the Slavs. ● *noun* one of the Slavic languages or the Slavic languages collectively.

slav·ish /ˈsleɪvɪʃ/ *adjective* **1** befitting or characteristic of a slave; servile. **2** showing no attempt at originality or development (*a slavish reproduction of their work*). **3** abject, base. □ **slav·ish·ly** *adverb*

Slav·ist /ˈslavɪst/ *noun* an expert on Slavic languages and literature.

Slav·onic /sləˈvɒnɪk/ *adjective & noun* = SLAVIC. [medieval Latin *S(c)lavonicus* from *S(c)lavonia* country of Slavs, from *Sclavus* SLAV]

Slavo·phile /ˈslavəˌfaɪl/ *noun* **1** an admirer or champion of Slavic languages, culture, history, etc. **2** esp. *hist.* one of a group of mid-19th-c. Russian intellectuals favouring traditional Slavic ways over Western cultural and political innovations.

slaw noun coleslaw. [Dutch *sla*, shortened from *salade* SALAD]

slay *transitive verb* (*past* **slew**; *past participle* **slain**) **1** *literary* or *jocular* kill; fell; strike down (*slay a dragon*). **2** (in *passive*) esp. *N Amer.* murder; kill (a person) in a ruthless or violent manner (*the victim was slain in the parking lot*). **3** *slang* overwhelm with amusement (*this joke will slay you*). **4** *jocular* defeat or overthrow (esp. a person or institution characterized as evil). [Old English *slēan* from Germanic]

slay·er noun (usu. in *combination*) **1** *literary* a person who kills or has killed mythological creatures, monsters, dragons, etc. **2** *jocular* a nemesis or conqueror, esp. of a person, institution, or thing portrayed as being evil.

slay·ing noun esp. *N Amer.* an act or instance of killing; a murder.

SLBM *abbreviation* submarine-launched ballistic missile.

SLCM *abbreviation* sea-launched cruise missile.

SLE *abbreviation* systemic lupus erythematosus (*see* LUPUS ERYTHEMATOSUS).

sleaze *informal* ● *noun* **1** sleazy material, conditions, or behaviour (*the city's growing reputation for sleaze*). **2** a person who behaves in a sleazy way. ● *intransitive verb* move or prowl in a sleazy fashion, esp. with shady or indecent intentions. [back-formation from SLEAZY]

sleaze·bag noun (also **sleaze·ball**) *slang* a sordid, despicable, or shady person.

sleaz·oid *N Amer. slang* ● *noun* a corrupt or vulgar person; a sleaze. ● *adjective* of a disreputable quality or nature; typical of a sleazoid.

sleazy *adjective* (**sleaz·i·er**, **sleaz·i·est**) **1** disreputable or corrupt. **2** sexually immoral or promiscuous. **3** filthy, grimy; dilapidated. **4 a** (of clothes, materials, etc.) thin or flimsy. **b** (of clothing) sexually revealing. □ **sleaz·i·ly** *adverb* **sleaz·i·ness** noun [17th c.: origin unknown]

sled *N Amer.* ● *noun* **1** a low vehicle mounted on runners for conveying heavy loads or passengers over snow or ice, usu. drawn by horses, dogs, or people. **2** a similar but usu. smaller vehicle, or any of various devices made of moulded plastic, used by children to coast down hills for amusement. **3** a snowmobile. **4** *Cdn (North)* a covered vehicle mounted on runners used to carry freight or crew as part of a cat train. ● *verb* (**sled·ded**, **sled·ding**) **1** *intransitive* ride or race on a sled. **2** *transitive* convey or carry by sled. [Middle Low German *sledde*, related to SLIDE]

sled·der noun *N Amer.* a person who races or rides a sled or snowmobile.

sled·ding noun *N Amer.* **1** the activity or action of racing or riding a sled or snowmobile. **2** progress in any sphere of action (*tough sledding*).

sled dog noun *N Amer.* a dog trained to pull a sled, esp. as part of a team.

sled dog race noun *N Amer.* a race of sleds pulled by dogs. □ **sled dog racing** noun

sledge¹ ● *noun* a sled. ● *transitive & intransitive verb* travel or convey by sledge. [Middle Dutch *sleedse*, related to SLED]

sledge² noun a sledgehammer.

sledge·ham·mer ● *noun* **1** a large heavy hammer with a long handle used to break stone etc. **2** (*attributive*) heavy-handed, unwieldy, excessive (*a sledgehammer approach*). ● *transitive verb* hit or break with or as if with a sledgehammer. [Old English *slecg*, related to SLAY]

sledge hockey noun (also **sled hockey**) a type of hockey played esp. by people with physical disabilities in which players, sitting on boards mounted on long skate blades or runners, propel themselves across the ice with shortened hockey sticks equipped with steel picks on one end.

sled train noun *Cdn (North)* = CAT TRAIN.

sleek *adjective* **1 a** (of hair, fur, or skin) having a smooth and shiny appearance. **b** (of a person or animal) having a shiny coat or hair. **c** having a well-groomed and healthy appearance. **2** smooth and polished in manners and behaviour; suave. **3 a** streamlined, smooth, aerodynamic (*a sleek sports car*). **b** contemporary, stylish (*a sleek interior*). □ **sleek·ly** *adverb* **sleek·ness** noun [later var. of SLICK]

sleep ● *noun* **1** the naturally recurring condition of rest and inactivity assumed by people and most higher animals, in which consciousness, response to external stimuli, and voluntary muscular action are largely suspended. **2** a period of sleep (*I need to have a sleep*). **3** *euphemism* a state resembling sleep, esp. death. **4** the prolonged inert condition of hibernating animals. **5** a condition assumed by many plants, esp. at night, marked by the closing of petals or folding of leaves. **6** a gummy secretion found in the corners of the eyes after sleep. **7** a function of some radios, televisions, etc. that allows them to remain on for a specified period of time before shutting off automatically. ● *verb* (*past* and *past participle* **slept**) **1** *intransitive* **a** be in a state of sleep. **b** achieve a state of sleep; fall asleep. **2** *intransitive* (foll. by *with*, *together*) **a** have or share a sexual encounter. **b** have or share a sexual relationship. **3** *intransitive* (foll. by *on*) postpone a decision on (a matter or question) until the next day. **4** *transitive* provide sleeping accommodation for (*the camper sleeps six*). **5** *transitive* **a** (foll. by *off*) cure by sleeping (*slept off her hangover*). **b** (foll. by *away*) lose, waste, or spend in sleeping (*sleep the hours away*). **6** *intransitive* be inactive or dormant (*trouble never sleeps*). **7** *intransitive* (of a plant) have its flowers or leaves folded over in sleep. **8** *intransitive* *euphemism* be at peace in death; lie buried. **9** *intransitive* (of a top or yo-yo) spin so steadily as to seem motionless. □ **get to sleep** manage to fall asleep. **go to sleep 1** achieve a state of sleep. **2** (of a limb) become numb as a result of prolonged pressure. **in one's sleep** while asleep. **let sleeping dogs lie** avoid stirring up trouble. **lose sleep over something** lie awake worrying about something. **put to sleep 1** kill (an animal) in a humane manner. **2** anaesthetize. **sleep around** *informal* be sexually promiscuous. **sleep in 1** remain asleep later than usual in the morning. **2** (esp. of domestic help) sleep on the premises where one is employed. **sleep like a log** (or **a baby** or **the dead**) sleep soundly. **the sleep of the just** sound sleep. **sleep out 1** sleep out of doors. **2** sleep away from the premises where one is employed. **sleep over** *N Amer.* spend the night at another's house. **sleep through 1** (esp. of a baby) sleep uninterruptedly through a period of time, usu. the night. **2** fail to be woken by (*slept through my alarm this morning*). **sleep tight!** sleep well. [Old English *slēp*, *slæp* (n.), *slēpan*, *slæpan* (v.) from Germanic]

sleep apnea noun an interruption or cessation of breathing during sleep.

sleep·er noun **1** a person that sleeps, esp. in a specified way (*a sound sleeper*). **2** a thing that is produced or introduced with little attention, fanfare, or promotion, but which turns out to be successful or popular (also *attributive*: *the sleeper hit of the summer*). **3** a sleeping car. **4** a berth in the cab of a truck or the sleeping car of a train etc. **5** (usu. in *pl.*) one-piece pyjamas for infants or children. **6** a strong usu. horizontal beam or timber used to support a wall or floorboards. **7** esp. *Brit.* a railway tie. **8** *N Amer.* a couch or chair that turns into a bed. **9** a spy or saboteur etc. who remains inactive while establishing a secure position. **10** *Brit.* = KEEPER 7a.

sleeper seat noun a first-class seat on an airplane capable of reclining further than other seats and having extra legroom so that a passenger may sleep comfortably on an overnight flight.

sleeping bag noun a warm lined or padded body-length bag, usu. having a zipper down one side and the bottom, designed for sleeping in esp. outdoors or when camping etc.

sleeping car noun a railway car provided with beds or berths for passengers to sleep in on overnight trips.

Sleeping Giant part of the Sibley Peninsula in NW Ontario, a mountainous landform which, when viewed from the city of Thunder Bay, resembles a huge man, lying on his back with arms folded over his chest.

sleeping giant noun *informal* a dormant power or force that could become active at any moment.

sleeping partner noun *Brit.* = SILENT PARTNER.

sleeping pill noun a pill containing a sedative, taken to induce sleep.

sleeping platform noun *Cdn (North)* the bench or ledge for sleeping left around the inside of an igloo at snow level after digging out the central space for other activities such as cooking.

sleeping policeman noun *Brit.* a speed bump.

sleeping sickness noun **1** a tropical African disease caused by the protozoans *Trypanosoma gambiense* and *T. rhodesiense*, which are transmitted by tsetse flies and proliferate in the blood vessels, ultimately affecting the central nervous system and leading to lethargy and death. *Also called* TRYPANOSOMIASIS. **2** (also **sleepy sickness**) = ENCEPHALITIS LETHARGICA.

sleep·less *adjective* **1** without sleep (*many sleepless nights*). **2** unable to sleep. **3** continually active or moving. □ **sleep·less·ly** *adverb* **sleep·less·ness** *noun*

sleep mode *noun* a power-saving mode of operation in which electronic devices or parts of devices are kept in a state of reduced power demand until needed.

sleep·over *noun* esp. *N Amer.* an occasion of spending the night away from home, esp. (of children) at a friend's house or party.

sleep set *noun* a mattress and box spring sold together as a set.

sleep·shirt *noun* a long T-shirt worn for sleeping.

sleep·walk *intransitive verb* walk or perform other actions in one's sleep, as if one were awake. □ **sleep·walk·er** *noun*

sleep·wear *noun* clothing worn to bed.

sleepy *adjective* (**sleep·i·er, sleep·i·est**) **1** drowsy; ready for sleep; about to fall asleep. **2** given to sleep; lazy, indolent. **3** lacking activity or bustle; quiet, tranquil (*a sleepy little town*). **4** suggestive of or conducive to sleep (*her soft sleepy voice*). □ **sleep·i·ly** *adverb* **sleep·i·ness** *noun*

sleepy·head *noun* (esp. as a form of address) a sleepy or inattentive person.

sleepy sickness *noun* = ENCEPHALITIS LETHARGICA.

sleet *noun* precipitation in the form of melting snow, freezing rain, or a mixture of these. □ **sleety** *adjective* [Middle English prob. from Old English: related to Middle Low German *slōten* (pl.) hail, Middle High German *slōz(e)* from Germanic]

sleeve *noun* **1** the part of a shirt or jacket etc. that wholly or partly covers the arm. **2** the paper or cardboard envelope used to protect a record. **3** any tubular piece of plastic or metal etc. resembling a sleeve, used esp. to cover or protect a rod or shaft etc. of a similar shape and size. **4** *Electronics* a metal cylinder fitted around the full length of the core of an electromagnetic relay to modify the speeds of opening and closing. □ **roll up one's sleeves** prepare to fight or work. **up one's sleeve** concealed but ready for use; in reserve. □ **sleeved** *adjective* (also in *combination*). **sleeve·less** *adjective* [Old English *slēfe, slīefe, slȳf*]

slee·veen /slə'viːn, sliː-/ *noun Cdn (Nfld)* & *Irish derogatory* an untrustworthy or mischievous person; a rascal. [Irish *slighbhín, slíbhín* a sly person]

sleeve notes *plural noun* = LINER NOTES.

sleeve nut *noun* a long nut with right-hand and left-hand screw threads for drawing together pipes or shafts conversely threaded.

sleev·ing *noun* tubular insulation for electric cable etc.

sleigh /sleɪ/ esp. *N Amer.* ● *noun* a sled, now a large one drawn by horses and used to convey passengers over snow and ice. ● *intransitive verb* travel on a sleigh. □ **sleigh·ing** *noun* [Dutch *slee*, related to SLED]

sleigh bed *noun N Amer.* a bed of a design common in the early 19th c. resembling a sleigh, with a headboard and footboard curling outwards at the top.

sleigh bell *noun* any of a number of small bells attached to a sleigh or to the harness of a horse drawing a sleigh.

sleight /slaɪt/ *noun archaic* **1** a deceptive trick or movement. **2** dexterity. **3** cunning. [Middle English *sleghth* from Old Norse *slœgth* from *slœgr* SLY]

sleight of hand *noun* **1** manual dexterity, esp. in performing a trick or magic. **2** a particular display of this, esp. a magic trick. **3** a cunning manoeuvre, scheme, or deception.

slen·der *adjective* (**slen·der·er, slen·der·est**) **1** (of a person, a person's body, etc.) gracefully thin (*a slender waist*). **2** of small girth or width in proportion to length or height (*a slender post*). **3** relatively small; slight, meagre, inadequate (*slender hopes; slender resources*). □ **slen·der·ly** *adverb* **slen·der·ness** *noun* [Middle English: origin unknown]

slen·der·ize *verb* (also esp. *Brit.* **-ise**) **1** *transitive* make (a person or thing) slender or appear slender. **2** *intransitive* become slender in fact or appearance.

slender loris *noun see* LORIS.

slept *past and past participle of* SLEEP.

sleuth *informal* ● *noun* a detective or investigator. ● *verb* **1** *intransitive* act as a detective. **2** *transitive* investigate, research. [originally in *sleuth-hound* bloodhound: Old Norse *slóth* track, trail (compare SLOT²)]

slew¹ *verb* (also **slue**) **1** *intransitive* (often foll. by *around*) turn or swing around, esp. without moving from a position. **2** *intransitive* (esp. of a car or truck etc.) skid or slide uncontrollably. **3** *transitive* turn or swing (a thing) around; send toppling or spinning. [18th-c. Naut.: origin unknown]

slew² *past of* SLAY.

slew³ *noun* esp. *N Amer. informal* (usu. foll. by *of*) a large number or quantity. [Irish *sluagh*]

slew⁴ *N Amer. var. of* SLOUGH¹.

slew-footing *noun* the action of tripping a hockey player by knocking their skates out from under them with a kicking motion.

Sli·ammon /slaɪˈʔʊmʊn/ *noun* **1** a dialect of mainland Comox spoken in the area surrounding Powell River. **2** the people speaking this dialect.

slice ● *noun* **1** a thin broad piece or wedge cut off or out of an item of food. **2** a share; a part taken, allotted, or gained (*a slice of the profits*). **3** *Baseball, Golf, & Tennis* **a** the flight of a ball that has been struck from underneath producing a spin that causes it to drift or curve forward and away from the person hitting it. **b** a swing or stroke producing such an effect. **c** a ball hit in this way. **4** a dessert that is cut into small squares for serving. **5** a cut or incision (*the blade left a deep slice in my hand*). **6** *Brit.* a kitchen utensil with a broad flat often perforated blade for serving fish, cake, etc. ● *verb* **1** *transitive* (often foll. by *up*) cut into slices. **2** *transitive* (foll. by *off*) cut (a piece) off. **3** *intransitive* (foll. by *into, through*) **a** make a cut or incision with a knife or other sharp object. **b** penetrate or cut through as if with something sharp; move quickly and effortlessly through (*the boat sliced through the water*). **4** *transitive Baseball, Golf, & Tennis* **a** strike (the ball) so that it deviates away from the person hitting it or (in baseball) into the opposite field. **b** *intransitive* (of a ball) drift or deviate away from the hitter. □ **slice·able** *adjective* **slicer** *noun* (also in *combination*). [Old French *esclice* splinter, from Frankish *slītjan*, related to SLIT]

sliced *adjective* **1** cut cleanly into slices. **2** (of food) sold already cut into slices. □ **the best** (or **greatest**) **thing since sliced bread** *informal* the most wonderful thing to happen, be discovered, etc., in a long time.

slice of life ● *noun* a movie, play, incident, etc. that offers a realistic representation of everyday life. ● *adjective* (usu. **slice-of-life**) characteristic of real life; realistic, unembellished.

slick ● *adjective* **1 a** (of a person) clever, artful, skilful, crafty. **b** (of an action) deftly or skilfully executed (*a slick performance*). **2 a** (of a person) superficially smooth or suave; flattering and insincere. **b** shallow in spite of its appearance; plausible but insincere. **3 a** smooth and glossy; sleek (*slick photo*). **b** (often foll. by *with*) slippery (*the road was slick with ice*). ● *noun* **1 a** a patch or stretch of oil or ice etc., esp. floating on a body of water. **b** a smooth patch on the surface of a fast-moving body of water. **2** a smooth tire having little or no tread, used for racing. **3** *N Amer.* a magazine with a glossy finish. **4** *N Amer. slang* a slick person, esp. a cheat or swindler. ● *transitive verb informal* **1** (often foll. by *up*) smarten or tidy up; make sleek. **2** (usu. foll. by *back, down*) flatten (one's hair etc.). □ **slick·ly** *adverb* **slick·ness** *noun* [Middle English *slike(n)*, prob. from Old English: compare SLEEK]

slick·er *noun* esp. *N Amer.* **1** a raincoat of oilskin, rubber, plastic, etc., usu. in a bright colour. **2** *informal* = CITY SLICKER.

slick·ster *noun* a slick person.

slide ● *verb* (*past and past participle* **slid**) **1** *intransitive* move along a smooth surface while in continuous contact with it through the same part. **2** *transitive* cause (a person or thing) to move across or down a surface while maintaining continuous contact with it. **3** *intransitive* move or pass smoothly, quietly, easily, or imperceptibly (*she slid into the room*). **4** *transitive* (often foll. by *into*) slip or move (a thing) dexterously, quietly, or unobtrusively (*he slid his hand into mine*). **5** *intransitive Baseball* dive headfirst or throw one's body feet first across the field, esp. in order to reach a base or make a catch. **6** *intransitive* decline or decrease (*my marks were starting to slide; the dollar slid half a cent today*). **7** *intransitive* pass or fall gradually into a particular state (*began to slide into depression*). **8** *intransitive informal* take its own course (*let it slide*). ● *noun* **1** an act or instance of sliding. **2** a structure with a smooth sloping surface down which people, esp. children, may slide for amusement, e.g. at a playground, swimming pool, etc. **3** a rapid decline or deterioration. **4** a photographic negative or transparency mounted on a thin plastic or cardboard frame, usu. placed in a projector to be shown on a screen. **5** *Baseball* an instance of sliding to reach a base or make a catch. **6** esp. *N Amer.* **a** the falling of mud, snow, ice, etc. down the side of a slope or mountain; a landslide or avalanche. **b** the material that has fallen in this way. **7 a** a steel or glass tube worn by a guitarist and placed across the frets of a guitar in order to achieve a bluesy effect (*compare* BOTTLENECK 3). **b** = SLIDE GUITAR. **8** *Cdn* a track or slope prepared with snow or ice for tobogganing. **9** a slip of glass on which an object is mounted or placed for examination under a microscope. **10** (in full **timber slide**) *Cdn* an artificial sluice way made to assist the passage of logs downstream past obstructions such as rapids or falls. **11** a part of a machine or mechanism that slides, esp. on a firearm. **12** a bed, track, or groove etc. on or in which something may slide. **13** *Music* a curved sliding part on a brass wind instrument used to alter the length of the air column and thus change the pitch. **14** *Brit.* = BARRETTE. □ **let things slide** be negligent; allow deterioration. [Old English *slīdan*]

slide guitar *noun* a style of blues guitar playing in which a slide or bottleneck is moved across the strings, producing a glissando effect.

slide projector *noun* a projector used to display photographic slides on a screen.

slid·er *noun* **1** a part or device that slides. **2** *Baseball* a fast pitch that breaks sharply over the plate in front of the batter, curving away from the direction in which it was thrown. **3** (in full **slider bar**) *Computing* a long thin rectangle usu. appearing on the side of a screen or window, used to indicate what portion of a document is being shown and to allow the user to advance to the next screen etc.

slide rule *noun* a device consisting of two rulers, one of which slides along the length of the other, both graduated logarithmically and used to make fast calculations, esp. multiplication and division.

slide show *noun* a presentation supplemented by or based on a series of photographic slides.

slide valve *noun* a sliding piece that opens and closes an aperture by sliding across it.

sliding door *noun* a door that is drawn on a track across an opening instead of swinging on hinges.

sliding scale *noun* a scale of fees, taxes, wages, etc., that varies in accordance with variation of some standard.

slight ● *adjective* **1** small in quantity or degree; barely perceptible (*a slight increase in temperature; speaks with a slight accent*). **2** of little significance, importance, or value (*a slight acquaintance*). **3** slender (*slight of build*). **4** insubstantial, weak (*made of a slight fabric*). **5** (in superlative, with *neg.* or *interrogative*) any whatever (*wasn't the slightest bit interested*). ● *transitive verb* **1** treat or speak of (a person etc.) with disrespect or a lack of courtesy; snub. **2** *hist.* raze or level (a fortification etc.). ● *noun* a marked display of disregard or disrespect. □ **slight·ing·ly** *adverb* **slight·ly** *adverb* **slight·ness** *noun* [Middle English *slyght, sleght* from Old Norse *sléttr* level, smooth, from Germanic]

Sligo /ˈslaɪɡoʊ/ **1** a county of the Republic of Ireland, in the west in the province of Connacht. **2** its county town, a seaport on Sligo Bay, an inlet of the Atlantic; pop. (est. 2002) 19,300.

slim ● *adjective* (**slim·mer, slim·mest**) **1** of small girth or thickness; of long narrow shape. **2** (of a person) of thin or slender build; not fat. **3** poor, meagre (*a slim chance of success; slim pickings*). **4** (of clothing) cut on slender lines (*a slim skirt*). **5** reduced to an economical or efficient size, level, etc. (*a slim budget*). ● *verb* (**slimmed, slim·ming**) **1** *transitive & intransitive* (often foll. by *down*) make or become slim or slimmer; reduce in size or extent. **2** *intransitive esp. Brit.* try to reduce one's weight by dieting, exercise, etc. ● *noun* (in full **slim disease**) (esp. in African use) AIDS. □ **slim·ly** *adverb* **slim·mer** *noun* (in sense 2 of verb). **slim·ming** *noun* (esp. in sense 2 of verb). **slim·ness** *noun* [Low German or Dutch from Germanic]

slime ● *noun* **1** thick slippery mud or any soft substance of a similar consistency, esp. when considered noxious or unpleasant. **2** a viscous mucous secretion exuded by fish, snails, slugs, etc. **3** *N Amer. slang* = SLIMEBALL. ● *transitive verb* cover with or as if with slime. [Old English *slīm* from Germanic, related to Latin *limus* mud, Greek *limnē* marsh]

slime·ball *noun slang* a filthy, corrupt, morally degenerate, or despicable person; a sleaze.

slime mould *noun* a slime-like aggregate of small simple organisms that reproduce by means of spores, found esp. in damp habitats on land. *Also called* MYXOMYCETE.

slim jim *noun* a long flat bar with a hooked end used to unlock a car door without using a key.

slim·line *adjective* of sleek and slender design.

slimy *adjective* (**slim·i·er, slim·i·est**) **1** of the consistency of slime. **2** covered, smeared with, or full of slime. **3** disgustingly or offensively foul or dishonest. **4** slippery; hard to hold. □ **slim·i·ly** *adverb* **slim·i·ness** *noun*

sling[1] ● *noun* **1** a strap, rope, belt, etc., in the form of a loop, in which

an object may be raised, lowered, or suspended. **2** a bandage looped around the neck to support an injured arm. **3** a simple weapon for throwing stones etc. consisting of a loop of leather or other material in which a projectile is whirled and then released. **4** a rope or net used to raise and lower cargo, esp. to or from a ship. **5** a pouch or frame supported by a strap around the neck or shoulders for carrying a young child. **6** a strap attached to a rifle etc. enabling it to be slung over the shoulder. ● *transitive verb* (*past* and *past participle* **slung**) **1** hurl or cast from, or as if from, a sling. **2** *informal* speak or utter (insults, criticism, etc.). **3** hang or allow to hang, esp. loosely or sloppily; carry (*had a bag slung over her shoulder*). **4** hoist or transfer (cargo etc.) with a sling. □ **have one's ass in a sling** *N Amer.* be in trouble. **sling beer** *slang* work as a bartender. **sling hash** (or **plates**) *N Amer. slang* work as a chef or server in a restaurant. **sling one's hook** *see* HOOK. [Middle English, probably from Old Norse verb *slyngva*]

sling[2] *noun* a drink consisting usu. of gin diluted with water or soda and lemon juice and usu. sweetened. [18th c.: origin unknown]

sling·back *noun* a woman's shoe with an open back held in place by a strap above the heel.

sling·er *noun* **1** *N Amer. informal* a person who serves food or drinks in a bar or restaurant. **2** a person who operates a sling to hoist cargo. **3** (usu. in *combination*) a person who uses or carries etc. a specified thing (*gunslinger*).

slings and arrows *plural noun informal* or *jocular* (usu. foll. by *of*) **1** criticisms. **2** hardships. [with reference to Shakespeare's *Hamlet* III. i. 56.]

sling·shot *noun* **1** *N Amer.* a Y-shaped frame supporting an elastic which can be used to launch a small rock or projectile. **2** the use of the gravitational pull of a celestial body to accelerate and change the course of a spacecraft.

slink[1] *intransitive verb* (*past* and *past participle* **slunk**) (often foll. by *off, away, by*) **1** move or sneak away inconspicuously as if ashamed, embarrassed, timid, or guilty. **2** walk or move in a provocative, seductive, or alluring manner. [Old English *slincan* crawl]

slink[2] ● *transitive verb* (of an animal) produce (young) prematurely. ● *noun* an abortive or premature animal, esp. a calf. [apparently from SLINK[1]]

slinky *adjective* (**slink·i·er, slink·i·est**) **1** attempting to be inconspicuous, esp. in a sly or cowardly manner. **2** moving in an alluring or seductive manner. **3** (of clothes) close-fitting; provocative. □ **slink·i·ly** *adverb* **slink·i·ness** *noun*

slip[1] ● *verb* (**slipped, slip·ping**) **1** *intransitive* **a** slide unintentionally (*her finger slipped on the trigger*). **b** lose one's footing or balance by sliding inadvertently (*he slipped on the ice*). **2** *intransitive* go or move easily with a sliding motion (*as the door closes the catch slips into place*). **3** *intransitive* **a** fall from one's hand or through one's fingers by being slippery or hard to hold. **b** escape restraint or capture by sneaking or running away. **c** pass or elapse quickly, fleetingly, or without notice (*the years slip by*). **4** *intransitive* (often foll. by *out*) **a** make a brief or unnoticed exit (*I have to slip out for a few minutes*). **b** be expressed or revealed inadvertently (*the truth slipped out*). **5 a** *intransitive* (usu. foll. by *up*) make a careless or casual mistake. **b** *intransitive* fall below the normal standard, deteriorate, lapse (*her marks are slipping*). **c** *transitive* lose or fall behind by (a number of points, positions, etc.) in a standing or total (*the stock market slipped 26 points today*). **6** *transitive* insert or transfer stealthily or casually (*she slipped him a note*). **7** *transitive* **a** detach, release from restraint (*slipped the greyhounds from the leash*). **b** release (the clutch of a car or truck etc.) for a moment. **8 a** *transitive* (foll. by *on, off*) pull (an article of clothing) on or off quickly. **b** *intransitive* (foll. by *into*) change into (an article of clothing). **9** *transitive* escape from; give the slip to (*the dog slipped its collar; it slipped my mind*). **10** *transitive Med.* suffer the dislocation of (a joint) or the herniation of (an intervertebral disc). **11** *transitive* move (a stitch) to the other needle without knitting it. ● *noun* **1** the act or an instance of slipping. **2** an accidental or slight error. **3 a** an article of lingerie usu. made of a slippery material, suspended by straps over the shoulder and extending to the hemline of a dress or skirt. **b** = HALF-SLIP. **4 a** an artificial slope of stone etc. on which boats are landed. **b** *N Amer.* a space at a dock or between two piers where a boat may be kept. **c** an inclined structure on which ships are built or repaired. **5** a pillowcase. **6** a leash to slip dogs. **7 a** a reduction in the movement of a pulley etc. due to slipping of the belt. **b** a reduction in the distance travelled by a ship or aircraft arising from the nature of the medium in which its propeller revolves. □ **give a person the slip** escape from or evade a person. **let slip 1** accidentally utter or reveal or disclose (information, a secret, the truth, etc.). **2** allow (an opportunity) to pass without taking advantage of it. **let slip through one's fingers 1** drop; lose hold of. **2** miss the opportunity of having. **slip away** (or **off**) depart without leave-taking etc. **slip of the tongue** (or **pen**) a small mistake in which something is said (or written) unintentionally. **there's many a slip 'twixt cup and lip** nothing is certain until it has happened. [Middle English prob. from Middle Low German *slippen*: compare SLIPPERY]

slip² ● *noun* **1 a** a small piece of paper esp. for writing on. **b** a small piece of paper with information printed on it; a receipt (*a sales slip; a withdrawal slip*). **2** a long and narrow piece; a strip (*a slip of land*). **3** an esp. young person of a small or slender build (*a slip of a girl*). **4** a cutting taken from a plant for grafting or planting. **5** a printer's proof on a long piece of paper; a galley proof. ● *transitive verb* take (a cutting or slip) from a plant. [Middle English, prob. from Middle Dutch, Middle Low German *slippe* cut, strip, etc.]

slip³ *noun* a creamy mixture of clay and water used to attach decorations, handles, etc. to articles of pottery or to coat ceramics. [Old English *slipa*, *slyppe* slime: compare COWSLIP]

slip·case *noun* a close-fitting case for a book or set of books that allows the spine or spines to remain visible. □ **slip·cased** *adjective*

slip·cover *N Amer.* ● *noun* a removable cover for a chair, couch, etc. or for a furniture cushion. ● *transitive verb* cover (furniture) with a slipcover.

slip dress *noun* a short, loose-fitting dress resembling a slip.

slip·form ● *noun* an open-ended mould in which a long uniform structure can be cast by filling the mould with concrete and continually moving and refilling it as the concrete sets. ● *transitive verb* cast using this technique.

slip-joint pliers *plural noun* a type of pliers with a sliding joint that allows the maximum width to which the jaws may open to be adjusted.

slip knot *noun* **1** a knot that can be undone by pulling one end. **2** a running knot.

slip-on ● *adjective* (of shoes or clothes) that can be easily slipped on and off. ● *noun* a shoe without laces or straps etc.

slip·page *noun* **1 a** the act or an instance of slipping. **b** the amount or extent of this. **2** a falling away from a standard; a decline. **3** the difference between expected and actual output of a mechanical system.

slipped disc *noun* = HERNIATED DISC.

slip·per *noun* **1** a light loose comfortable shoe meant to be worn indoors. **2** a light, slip-on, heelless shoe for dancing etc. □ **slip·pered** *adjective*

slipper sock *noun* a thick sock, usu. with a leather sole, for use as a slipper.

slipper·wort /ˈslɪpərˌwɜrt, -wɔrt/ *noun* = CALCEOLARIA.

slip·pery *adjective* **1** difficult to hold firmly because of smoothness, wetness, sliminess, or elusive motion. **2** (of a horizontal surface) difficult to stand on or move on without slipping due to its smoothness, wetness, muddiness, etc. **3** (of a subject) requiring tactful handling. **4** (of a concept etc.) uncertain; difficult to grasp or comprehend due to its complexity. **5** unreliable, unscrupulous, shifty. □ **slip·per·i·ness** *noun* [prob. coined by Coverdale (1535) after Luther's *schlipfferig*, Middle High German *slipferig* from *slipfern*, *slipfen* from Germanic: partly from *slipper* slippery (now dial.) from Old English *slipor* from Germanic]

slippery elm *noun* **1** the N American red elm, *Ulmus rubra*. **2** (also **slippery elm bark**) the inner bark of this, formerly used as a demulcent.

slippery slope *noun* an irreversible course leading to disaster.

slip·py *adjective* (**slip·pi·er**, **slip·pi·est**) *informal* slippery. □ **slip·pi·ness** *noun*

slip ring *noun* a ring of conducting material which is attached to and rotates with a shaft so that electric current may be transferred to a stationary circuit through a fixed brush pressing against the ring.

slip-road *noun* Brit. = RAMP¹ *noun* 2.

slip·shod *adjective* **1** careless, unsystematic, esp. in working or in handling ideas or words. **2** shabby, untidy. [originally 'wearing loose or shabby shoes', from SLIP¹ + SHOD]

slip-slide *intransitive verb* slip and slide.

slip·stitch ● *noun* **1** a loose stitch joining layers of fabric and not visible externally. **2** a stitch moved to the other needle without being knitted. ● *transitive verb* sew with slipstitch.

slip·stream *noun* **1** a current of air or water driven back by a revolving propeller or a moving vehicle. **2** an assisting force regarded as drawing something along with or behind something else.

slip-up *noun informal* a mistake or blunder.

slip·way *noun* a slip for building ships or landing boats.

slit ● *noun* **1** a long straight narrow incision. **2** a long narrow opening comparable to a cut. ● *transitive verb* (**slit·ting**; *past* and *past participle* **slit**) **1** make a slit in. **2** cut into strips. □ **slit one's eyes** squint. □ **slit-like** *adjective* **slit·ted** *adjective* **slit·ter** *noun* [Middle English *slitte*, related to Old English *slitan*, from Germanic]

slit-eyed *adjective* **1** squinting. **2** having long narrow eyes.

slither ● *intransitive verb* **1** slide or slip with an unsteady movement, esp. from side to side or in different directions. **2** move along in a way similar to this, esp. with the body close to the ground. **3** move or go stealthily; sneak (*they slithered out of the country*). ● *noun* a slithering movement. □ **slith·ery** *adjective* [Middle English var. of *slidder* (now dial.) from Old English *slid(e)rian* frequentative from *slid-*, weak grade of *slidan* SLIDE]

slit pocket *noun* a pocket with a vertical opening giving access to the pocket or to a garment beneath.

slit skirt *noun* a tight skirt slit upward from the hem for ease of movement or to reveal the legs.

slit trench *noun* a narrow trench in which a soldier may remain hidden or protected from enemy fire.

slitty *adjective* (**slit·ti·er**, **slit·ti·est**) (of the eyes) narrow or squinting.

sliver ● *noun* **1** a usu. long thin piece that has been split, broken, or sliced off a larger one. **2** a sharp fragment of wood, glass, metal, etc.; a splinter. **3** (foll. by *of*) a small amount (*a sliver of reality*). **4** a continuous strip of loose untwisted textile fibres after carding. ● *transitive & intransitive verb* **1** break off as a sliver. **2** break up into slivers. □ **sliv·ered** *adjective* [Middle English, related to *slive* cleave (now dial.) from Old English]

slivo·vitz /ˈslɪvəvɪts/ *noun* a dry slightly bitter colourless plum brandy made esp. in Romania and Serbia. [Serbo-Croat *šljivovica* from *šljiva* plum]

Sloane *noun* (in full **Sloane Ranger**) Brit. *slang* a fashionable and conventional upper-class young person, esp. living in London. □ **Sloany** *adjective* (also **Sloaney**). [*Sloane Square*, London + *Lone Ranger*, a cowboy hero]

slob *noun* **1** *informal* an untidy, lazy, or fat person. **2** (in full **slob ice**) *Cdn* sludgy masses of densely packed sea ice. □ **slob·bish** *adjective* **slobby** *adjective* [Irish *slab* mud, from English *slab* ooze, sludge, prob. from Scandinavian]

slob·ber ● *intransitive verb* **1** let saliva or food run from the mouth, esp. while eating; drool. **2** (foll. by *over*) **a** be too attentive or excessively affectionate towards a person. **b** be excessively sentimental or enthusiastic about a thing. ● *noun* saliva running from the mouth. □ **slob·bery** *adjective* [Middle English, = Dutch *slobbern*, of imitative origin]

sloe *noun* **1** the fruit of the blackthorn, a small blue-black drupe with a sharp sour taste. **2** the blackthorn, *Prunus spinosa*. [Old English *slā(h)* from Germanic]

sloe-eyed *adjective* **1** having dark eyes the colour of a sloe. **2** having slanted eyes.

sloe gin *noun* a liqueur of sloes steeped in gin.

slog ● *verb* (**slogged**, **slog·ging**) **1** *intransitive* (often foll. by *away*, *on*) work hard or steadily at something. **2** *intransitive* walk or move steadily with great effort or toil. **3** *transitive & intransitive* hit hard. ● *noun* **1 a** a hard, steady work or effort. **b** a period of this. **2** a long, tiring walk or march. **3** a vigorous blow. □ **slog it out** fight or struggle until a conclusion is reached. □ **slog·ger** *noun* [19th c.: origin unknown: compare SLUG²]

slo·gan *noun* **1** a word or phrase that is easy to remember, used by a political party or in advertising etc. to attract people's attention or suggest an idea quickly. **2** *hist.* a Scottish Highland war cry. □ **slo·ganed** *adjective* [Gaelic *sluagh-ghairm* from *sluagh* army + *gairm* shout]

slogan·eer ● *intransitive verb* devise or use slogans. ● *noun* a person who devises or uses slogans. □ **slogan·eer·ing** *noun*

slogan·ize *intransitive verb* (also esp. Brit. **-ise**) = SLOGANEER *verb*.

slo-mo *noun informal* = SLOW MOTION. [abbreviation]

sloop *noun* **1** a small, one-masted, fore-and-aft-rigged vessel with mainsail and jib. **2** (in full **sloop of war**) Brit. *hist.* a small warship with guns on the upper deck only. [Dutch *sloep(e)*, of unknown origin]

sloop-rigged *adjective* rigged like a sloop.

slop¹ ● *verb* (**slopped**, **slop·ping**) **1** (often foll. by *over*) **a** *intransitive* (of a liquid) run, flow, or spill over the edge of a container, vessel, etc. **b** *transitive* splash or spill (a liquid etc.). **2** *transitive* spill or splash liquid on (clothes, the floor, etc.). **3** *intransitive* walk or wander through a wet or muddy place. **4** *transitive* N Amer. feed (pigs etc.) with slop. **5** *intransitive* (usu. foll. by *over*) gush; be effusive. ● *noun* **1** a puddle or mess of spilled or splashed liquid. **2** unappetizing or poorly cooked food. **3** (in *sing.* or *pl.*) semi-liquid food for pigs, esp. the remains of food intended for people. **4** (in *pl.*) liquid household waste matter, such as the contents of a chamber pot or dirty dishwater. **5** *informal* weakly sentimental language. □ **slop about** move about in a slovenly manner. **slop out** carry waste matter out of a house, prison, etc. [earlier sense 'slush', prob. related to *slyppe*: compare COWSLIP]

slop² *noun* **1** loose clothing worn esp. by a sailor or worker. **2** (in *pl.*) cheap ready-made clothing. **3** (in *pl.*) clothes and bedding issued to sailors in the navy. [Middle English: compare Old English *oferslop* surplice, from Germanic]

slop bucket *noun* a bucket for removing waste from a kitchen etc.

slope ● *noun* **1** a piece of rising or falling ground. **2** a place for skiing on the side of a hill or mountain. **3** an upward or downward inclination; an inclined position or direction. **4 a** a difference in level between the two ends or sides of a thing (*a slope of 5 metres*). **b** the rate at which this increases with distance etc. **5** *Math.* **a** the tangent of the angle between a line and the horizontal. **b** the gradient of a graph at any point. **c** the value of the first differential of a quantity, esp. with respect to distance. **d** (prec. by *the*) the position in which a rifle is held against the shoulder. ● *verb* **1** *intransitive* lie obliquely, esp. downwards; have or follow a slope; slant. **2** *transitive* place or arrange or make in a sloping position. □ **hit the slopes** go skiing. **slope arms** place one's rifle in a sloping position against one's shoulder. **slope off** *Brit. slang* go away, esp. to evade work etc. □ **sloped** *adjective* [Middle English, originally 'aslope', ultimate origin uncertain]

slope·side *noun* **1** the side of a slope, esp. a ski slope. **2** (*attributive*) designating an establishment or fixture found on the side of a slope, esp. of a ski slope (*slopeside condominiums*).

slo-pitch *noun* N Amer. a modified form of baseball in which the batter has three chances to hit a softball that is lobbed by the pitcher and must land within a circle encompassing the plate.

slop pail *noun* = SLOP BUCKET.

sloppy *adjective* (**slop·pi·er**, **slop·pi·est**) **1** careless, slipshod. **2** splashed with liquid. **3** untidy. **4** (of the ground, sidewalk, etc.) wet with rain or slush. **5** (of clothes) loose; baggy. **6** (of a substance) in a semi-liquid state, having a muddy consistency. **7** (of a thought or comment etc.) overly sentimental or emotional. □ **slop·pi·ly** *adverb* **slop·pi·ness** *noun*

sloppy joe *noun* **1** N Amer. a sandwich consisting of a thick filling made with ground beef and tomato or barbecue sauce served on a bun. **2** Brit. a long loose-fitting sweater.

slosh ● *verb* **1** *intransitive* (often foll. by *around*, *about*, etc.) move with a splashing sound. **2** *transitive informal* **a** pour (liquid) clumsily. **b** pour or spill liquid on. **3** *transitive* splash (liquid) onto or over a surface. **4** *transitive* esp. Brit. slang hit (a person), esp. hard. ● *noun* **1 a** an instance of splashing or sloshing. **b** the sound of this. **2** slush, sludge. **3** esp. Brit. slang a heavy blow. □ **sloshy** *adjective* [var. of SLUSH]

sloshed *adjective* slang drunk.

slot¹ ● *noun* **1** a slit, groove, channel, or long opening into which something fits. **2** a slit or other opening in a machine for a coin or credit card etc. to be inserted. **3 a** a position to be filled in a schedule, order, or timetable. **b** (in full **time slot**) an allotted place in a broadcasting schedule. **4** *Hockey* an unmarked area in front of the net considered an excellent shooting position for an offensive player. **5** (often *attributive*) designating a screwdriver with a straight flat blade used for inserting and removing slotted screws. **6** *informal* = SLOT MACHINE. **7** *Computing* = EXPANSION SLOT. ● *verb* (**slot·ted**, **slot·ting**) **1** *transitive & intransitive* place or be placed into or as if into a slot. **2** *transitive* provide with a slot or slots. [Middle English, = hollow of the breast, from Old French *esclot*, of unknown origin]

slot² *noun* **1** the track of a deer etc. esp. as shown by footprints. **2** a deer's foot. [Old French *esclot* hoof print of a horse, prob. from Old Norse *slóth* trail: compare SLEUTH]

slot·back *noun* N Amer. Football **1** either of two offensive players lining up in the backfield between the offensive linemen and wide receivers, usu. to catch short passes. **2** this position.

sloth /slōθ/ *noun* **1** laziness or indolence; reluctance to make an effort. **2** any slow-moving nocturnal mammal of the family Bradypodidae or Megalonychidae of S America, having long limbs and hooked claws for

hanging upside down from branches of trees. **3** *informal* a lazy or indolent person. [Middle English from SLOW + -TH²]

sloth bear *noun* a small to medium-sized bear, *Melursus ursinus*, found in the lowland forests of Sri Lanka and eastern India, with a shaggy blackish coat and long curved claws.

sloth·ful *adjective* lazy, inactive; sluggish. □ **sloth·ful·ly** *adverb* **sloth·ful·ness** *noun*

slot machine *noun* a coin-operated gambling machine, activated by a lever, that produces random combinations of symbols which must match for the player to win.

slot·ted *adjective* **1** having a slot or slots. **2** (of a screw) having a narrow slot on the head so that it may be turned with a slot screwdriver.

slotted spoon *noun* a large serving spoon with holes or slots in its bowl, used for draining liquid from food.

slouch ● *verb* **1** *intransitive* stand or sit with the back, shoulders, and neck bent or drooping forwards. **2** *intransitive* walk or move with a shuffling gait and slouching posture. **3** *transitive* bend one side of the brim of (a hat) downwards (opp. COCK¹ *verb* 3). **4** *intransitive* droop or hang down loosely. ● *noun* **1** (usu. with *neg.*) *informal* a useless or incompetent person or performer esp. of a particular task or pursuit (*she's no slouch at golf*). **2** a slouching posture or movement; a stoop. **3** a downward bend of a hat brim. □ **slouchy** *adjective* (**slouch·i·er**, **slouch·i·est**). [16th c.: origin unknown]

slouch hat *noun* a soft hat with a wide brim that may be turned or pulled down.

slough¹ /sluː, slau/ *noun* (also **slew**) **1** an area of soft miry ground; a swamp or quagmire. **2** /sluː/ Cdn (West) & US Northwest a small marshy pool or lake produced by rain or melting snow flooding a depression in the soil. **3** Cdn (BC) a shallow inlet or estuary lined with grass. □ **sloughy** *adjective* [Old English *slōh*, *slō(g)*]

slough² /slʌf/ (also **sluff**) ● *noun* **1** a part that an animal sheds, esp. a snake's skin. **2** a layer of dead tissue, such as a scab, that will fall away from the skin. **3** a thing that is cast off, abandoned, or discarded. ● *verb* **1** *transitive* (often foll. by *off*) shed, remove, or cast off (skin, tissue, etc.). **2** *intransitive* (often foll. by *off*) (of skin, tissue, etc.) come away; drop or fall off. **3** *intransitive* (of a snake etc.) cast off or shed the skin. **4** *transitive* (foll. by *off*) get rid of or abandon something (*sloughed off his complaints*). □ **sloughy** *adjective* [Middle English, perhaps related to Low German *slu(we)* husk]

slough grass *noun* N Amer. any of various grasses of sloughs or watery depressions.

slough of despond *noun* a state of hopeless depression. [with reference to Bunyan's *Pilgrim's Progress*]

Slo·vak /ˈsloːvak/ ● *noun* **1** an inhabitant of Slovakia. **2** the official language of Slovakia. ● *adjective* of or relating to the country, people, or language of Slovakia. [Slovak etc. *Slovák*, related to SLOVENIAN]

Slo·va·kia /sləˈvakiə, -ˈvɒkiə/ a country in central Europe, formerly a constituent republic of Czechoslovakia; pop. (est. 2002) 5,422,366; capital, Bratislava. □ **Slo·vak·ian** *noun & adjective*

slov·en /ˈslʌvən, ˈslɒv-/ *noun* **1** a person who is habitually untidy or careless. **2** Cdn (Maritimes & Nfld) a long low wagon esp. drawn by horses. [Middle English perhaps from Flemish *sloef* dirty or Dutch *slof* careless]

Slo·ve·nia /sləˈviːniə/ a country in SE Europe, formerly a constituent republic of Yugoslavia; pop. (est. 2002) 1,932,917; capital, Ljubljana.

Slo·ven·ian /ˌsləˈviːniən/ (also **Slo·vene** /ˈsloːviːn/) ● *noun* **1** an inhabitant of Slovenia. **2** the official language of Slovenia. ● *adjective* of or relating to Slovenia, its language or people. [German *Slowene* from Styrian etc. *Slovenec* from Old Slavic *Slov-*, perhaps related to *slovo* word]

slov·en·ly /ˈslʌvənli, ˈslɒv-/ *adjective* **1** (of a person, the appearance, habits, etc.) careless, untidy, negligent. **2** (of an action etc.) characterized by a lack of care or precision. □ **slov·en·li·ness** *noun*

slow ● *adjective* **1 a** taking a relatively long time to do a thing or cover a distance (also foll. by *of*: *slow of speech*). **b** not quick; acting or moving or done without speed. **2** gradual; obtained over a length of time (*slow growth*). **3** not producing, allowing, or conducive to speed (*in the slow lane*). **4** (of a clock etc.) showing a time earlier than is the case. **5** (of a person) not understanding readily; not learning easily. **6** dull; uninteresting; tedious. **7** slack or sluggish (*business is slow*). **8** (of oven temperature) between 300°–325° F. **9** Photog. **a** (of a film) needing long exposure. **b** (of a lens) having a small aperture. **10 a** reluctant; tardy (*not slow to defend himself*). **b** not hasty or easily moved (*slow to take offence*). **11** (of a sports field, racetrack, ice surface, tennis court, etc.) not allowing quick movement of players, the ball, puck, etc. (*the field was slow after the rain*). ● *adverb* **1** at a slow pace; slowly. **2** (in combination) (*slow-moving traffic*). ¶ The use of *slow* as an adverb is standard in compounds such as *slow-acting, slow-burning, slow-moving*. It is also established in short imperative expressions such as *go slow*, but in sentences such as *he drives too slow* and *go as slow as you can*, *slowly* is preferable in formal contexts. Compare *fast* which is fully acceptable as an adverb in standard English. ● *verb* (usu. foll. by *down, up*) **1** *intransitive & transitive* reduce one's speed or the speed of (a vehicle etc.). **2** *intransitive* reduce one's pace of life; live or work less intensely. **3** *intransitive & transitive* become or cause to be slow (*business is slowing down*). □ **slow but** (or **and**) **sure** (or **steady**) achieving the required result eventually. **slow off the mark** *see* MARK[1]. □ **slow·ish** *adjective* **slow·ly** *adverb* **slow·ness** *noun* [Old English *slāw* from Germanic]

slow burn *noun* (often hyphenated when *attributive*) slowly mounting intensity, esp. of anger or annoyance. □ **slow-burning** *adjective*

slow·coach *noun Brit.* = SLOWPOKE.

slow cooker *noun* a large electric pot used for cooking stews etc. very slowly.

slow dance *intransitive verb N Amer.* dance to soft music in the embrace of a partner.

slow·down *noun* **1** the action of slowing down. **2** a form of job action in which employees deliberately work slowly.

slow-footed *adjective* esp. *N Amer.* that walks, runs, etc. slowly.

slow loris *noun see* LORIS.

slow march *noun* the marching time adopted by troops in a funeral procession etc.

slow match *noun* a slow-burning match or fuse for lighting explosives etc.

slow motion *noun* (often hyphenated when *attributive*) **1** the technique of making or playing a film or video recording so that actions and movements appear to be slower than in real life. **2** the simulation of this in real action; motion of slower speed than normal.

slow neutron *noun* a neutron with low kinetic energy esp. after moderation (*compare* FAST NEUTRON).

slow-pitch *noun N Amer.* = SLO-PITCH.

slow·poke *noun N Amer.* a slow or lazy person, driver, etc.

slow-release *attributive adjective* designating a drug, fertilizer, etc. that releases a substance slowly or intermittently so as to maintain a steady concentration.

slow track *noun* a route, course, method, etc., which results in slow progress (*at school he was assigned to the slow track*).

slow-twitch *adjective* (of a muscle fibre) that contracts slowly, providing endurance rather than strength (*compare* FAST-TWITCH).

slow virus *noun* a virus or virus-like organism that multiplies slowly in the host organism and has a long incubation period.

slow-wave sleep *noun* sleep characterized by waves of low frequency and high amplitude on an electroencephalogram, in contrast to REM sleep (*see* RAPID EYE MOVEMENT).

slow-witted *adjective* slow to understand, learn, etc.; unintelligent. □ **slow-witted·ness** *noun*

slow-worm *noun* a small European legless lizard, *Anguis fragilis*, giving birth to live young. *Also called* BLINDWORM. [Old English *slā-wyrm*: first element of uncertain origin, assimilated to SLOW]

SLR *abbreviation* **1** *Photog.* SINGLE-LENS REFLEX. **2** a single-lens reflex camera.

SLt *abbreviation Cdn* SUB-LIEUTENANT.

slub[1] ● *noun* **1** a lump or thick place in yarn or thread. **2** fabric woven from thread etc. with slubs. ● *adjective* (of material etc.) with an irregular appearance caused by uneven thickness of the warp. [19th c.: origin unknown]

slub[2] ● *noun* wool slightly twisted in preparation for spinning. ● *transitive verb* (**slubbed, slub·bing**) twist (wool) in this way. [18th c.: origin unknown]

slub[3] *noun Cdn* (*Nfld*) **1** the slimy or gelatinous substance coating fish. **2** a slimy or gelatinous substance adhering to and clogging fishnets, formed of minute marine organisms. [perhaps from Middle Dutch *slubbe* slimy mud, ooze]

sludge *noun* **1** thick greasy mud, mire, ooze, etc. **2** muddy or slimy sediment, as in the bed of a river etc. **3** a precipitate in a sewage tank. **4** *Mech.* an accumulation of dirty oil, esp. formed as waste in any of various industrial and mechanical processes. **5** *Geol.* sea ice newly formed in small pieces. **6** (usu. *attributive*) a muddy colour (*sludge green*). □ **sludgy** *adjective* [17th c., origin uncertain; compare SLUSH]

slue *var. of* SLEW[1].

sluff *N Amer. var. of* SLOUGH[2].

slug[1] ● *noun* **1 a** a small shell-less mollusc of the class Gastropoda often destructive to plants. **b** *informal* a slow or lazy person or thing. **2 a** a bullet esp. of irregular shape. **b** a projectile for an air gun. **3** *Printing* a metal bar used in spacing. **4** a drink esp. of liquor; a swig. **5** a unit of mass, given an acceleration of 1 foot per second per second by a force of 1 lb. **6** a roundish lump of metal. **7** a thick piece or lump of something; a (large) portion. **8** *N Amer.* a small circular piece of metal used as a counterfeit coin, esp. in machines. ● *verb* (**slugged, slug·ging**) **1** *intransitive* (usu. foll. by *around*) move slowly or sluggishly; trudge. **2** *transitive* drink (esp. alcohol) quickly. [Middle English *slugg(e)* sluggard, prob. from Scandinavian]

slug[2] *N Amer.* ● *transitive verb* (**slugged, slug·ging**) **1** strike with a hard blow. **2** *Baseball* hit (esp. a home run). ● *noun* a hard blow. □ **slug it out 1** fight it out. **2** endure; stick it out. [19th c.: origin unknown]

slug·a·bed *noun* a lazy person who sleeps in.

slug·fest *noun* esp. *N Amer. informal* **1** a violent or intense fight or quarrel. **2 a** a boxing match in which the boxers throw many punches. **b** a baseball game in which many runs are scored, esp. with many home runs.

slug·gard *noun* a lazy sluggish person. □ **slug·gard·ly** *adverb* **slug·gard·li·ness** *noun* [Middle English from *slug* (v.) be slothful, (prob. from Scandinavian: compare SLUG[1]) + -ARD]

slug·ger *noun* **1** a person who delivers heavy blows, esp. a boxer. **2** a baseball player noted for hitting powerful home runs.

slugging percentage *noun* (also **slugging average**) *Baseball* a statistic indicating a batter's proficiency at hitting extra-base hits, calculated by dividing the total number of bases reached by the number of at-bats.

slug·gish *adjective* inert; inactive; slow-moving; torpid; indolent (*a sluggish circulation; a sluggish stream*). □ **slug·gish·ly** *adverb* **slug·gish·ness** *noun*

sluice ● *noun* **1** (also **sluice gate**) a sliding gate or other contrivance for controlling the volume or flow of water. **2** (also **sluice·way**) a channel or waterway controlled by means of a sluice or sluices. **3** (also **sluice box**) *N Amer. & Austral.* an artificial water channel fitted with grooves esp. for washing ore. **4** the act or an instance of rinsing. **5** the water above or below or issuing through a floodgate. ● *verb* **1** *transitive* provide or wash with a sluice or sluices. **2** *transitive* rinse, pour or throw water freely upon. **3** *transitive* (usu. foll. by *out, away*) wash out or away with a flow of water. **4** *transitive* flood with water from a sluice. **5** *intransitive* (of water) rush out from a sluice, or as if from a sluice. [Middle English from Old French *escluse*, ultimately from Latin *excludere* EXCLUDE]

slum ● *noun* **1** an overcrowded and squalid district etc., usu. in a city and inhabited by very poor people. **2** a house or building unfit for human habitation. ● *intransitive verb* (**slummed, slum·ming**) **1** (often as **slum it**) put up with less comfortable conditions, associate with persons of a lower social class, or frequent venues of a lower status etc. than one is used to. **2** live in slum-like conditions. **3** go about the slums through curiosity, to examine or experience the condition of the inhabitants. □ **slummy** *adjective* (**slum·mi·er, slum·mi·est**). **slum·mi·ness** *noun* [19th c.: originally slang]

slum·ber ● *intransitive verb* **1** sleep, esp. in a specified manner. **2** be idle, drowsy, or inactive. ● *noun* a sleep, esp. of a specified kind (*fell into a fitful slumber*). □ **slum·ber·er** *noun* **slum·ber·ous** *adjective* **slum·brous** *adjective* [Middle English *slūmere* etc. from *slūmen* (v.) or *slūme* (n.) from Old English *slūma*: -*b*- as in *number*]

slumber party *noun N Amer.* a party for youngsters (esp. girls) who stay and sleep overnight.

slum clearance *noun* the demolition of slums and rehousing of their inhabitants.

slum·gul·lion *noun US slang* sludge, esp. watery stew.

slum·lord *noun N Amer.* a landlord who rents slum property to tenants.

slump ● *noun* **1** a sudden severe or prolonged fall in prices or values of commodities or securities. **2** a sharp or sudden decline in trade or business usu. bringing widespread unemployment. **3** a reduction in performance; a state of lessened productivity etc. (*the team has been in a slump for weeks*). ● *intransitive verb* **1** undergo a slump; fail; fall in price. **2** (often foll. by *back, down*) sit or fall heavily or limply (*slumps into a chair*). **3** lean or subside. [17th c., originally 'sink in a bog': imitative]

slumped *adjective* limp, hunched, or slouched (*was slumped in the chair*).

slung *past and past participle of* SLING[1].

slunk *past and past participle of* SLINK[1].

slur ● *verb* (**slurred, slur·ring**) **1** *transitive & intransitive* pronounce or write indistinctly so that the sounds or letters run into one another. **2** *transitive Music* **a** perform (a group of two or more notes) legato.

t top   v voice   w we   z zoo   ʃ she   ʒ vision   θ thin   ð this   ŋ ring   x loch   tʃ chip   dʒ jar   (*see over for vowels*)

b mark (notes) with a slur. **3** *transitive archaic* put a slur on (a person or a person's character); make insinuations against. **4** *transitive* (usu. foll. by *over*) pass over (a fact, fault, etc.) lightly; conceal or minimize. ● *noun* **1** an insult, aspersion, or disparaging remark; an imputation of wrongdoing (*a slur on my reputation*). **2** the act or an instance of slurring in pronunciation, singing, or writing. **3** *Music* a curved line to show that two or more notes are to be sung to one syllable or played or sung legato. [17th c.: origin unknown]

slurp ● *transitive & intransitive verb* drink or eat noisily, esp. producing a sucking or lapping noise. ● *noun* **1** the sound of this. **2** a slurping gulp. □ **slurpy** *adjective* [Dutch *slurpen, slorpen*]

slurry *noun* (*pl.* **-ries**) **1** a semi-liquid mixture of fine particles and water; thin mud. **2** thin liquid cement. **3** a fluid form of manure. **4** a residue of water and particles of coal left at pithead washing plants. [Middle English, related to dial. *slur* thin mud]

slush ● *noun* **1** partially melted snow or ice. **2** watery mud. **3** silly sentiment. **4** *N Amer.* a confection consisting of flavoured slushy ice. **5** *slang* unsolicited manuscripts received by a publisher. ● *intransitive verb* squelch, splash; make a squelching or splashing sound. [17th c., also *sludge* and *slutch*: origin unknown]

slush fund *noun* reserve funding esp. as used for political bribery.

slush pile *noun* the collection of unsolicited manuscripts received by a publisher.

slushy ● *adjective* (**slush·i·er, slush·i·est**) **1** like slush; watery. **2** *informal* sentimental; mawkish. ● *noun* (*pl.* **-ies**) *N Amer.* = SLUSH 4. □ **slush·i·ness** *noun*

slut *noun derogatory* **1** a promiscuous woman; a hussy. **2** esp. *Brit.* a slovenly woman; a slattern. □ **slut·tish** *adjective* **slut·tish·ness** *noun* **slut·ty** *adjective* [Middle English: origin unknown]

sly *adjective* (**slyer, sly·est**) **1** cunning; crafty; wily. **2 a** (of a person) practising secrecy or stealth. **b** (of an action etc.) done etc. in secret. **3** hypocritical; ironical. **4** playfully mischievous; roguish. **5** knowing; arch; bantering; insinuating. □ **on the sly** privately; covertly (*smuggled some through on the sly*). □ **slyly** *adverb* **sly·ness** *noun* [Middle English *sleh* etc. from Old Norse *slœgr* cunning, originally 'able to strike' from *slóg*- past stem of *slá* strike: compare SLEIGHT]

sly·boots *noun informal* a sly person.

slype /slaɪp/ *noun* a covered way or passage, esp. between a cathedral etc. transept and the chapter house or deanery. [perhaps = *slipe* a long narrow piece of ground, = SLIP² 2]

SM *abbreviation* Sergeant Major.

Sm *symbol Chem.* the element samarium.

S/M *abbreviation* = S&M.

smack¹ ● *noun* **1** a sharp slap or blow esp. with the palm of the hand or a flat object. **2** a hard hit in baseball etc. **3** a loud kiss (*gave her a hearty smack*). **4** a loud sharp sound (*heard the smack as it hit the floor*). **5** a noisy parting of the lips in eager anticipation or enjoyment. ● *verb* **1** *transitive* strike sharply, as with an open hand, a bat, etc. **2** *transitive* part (one's lips) noisily in eager anticipation or enjoyment of food or another delight. **3** *transitive & intransitive* hit, move, propel, etc., with a smack. ● *adverb informal* **1** with a smack. **2** suddenly; directly; violently (*landed smack on my desk*). **3** exactly (*hit it smack in the centre*). [Middle Dutch *smack(en)* of imitative origin]

smack² (foll. by *of*) ● *intransitive verb* **1** have a flavour of; taste of (*smacked of garlic*). **2** suggest the presence or effects of (usu. something undesirable) (*it smacks of nepotism*). ● *noun* **1** a flavour; a taste that suggests the presence of something. **2** (in a person's character etc.) a barely discernible quality (*just a smack of superciliousness*). **3** (in food etc.) a very small amount (*add a smack of ginger*). [Old English *smæc*]

smack³ *noun* a single-masted sailboat for coasting or fishing. [Dutch *smak* from earlier *smacke*; origin unknown]

smack⁴ *noun slang* a hard drug, esp. heroin, sold or used illegally. [prob. alteration of Yiddish *schmeck* sniff]

smack dab *see* DAB¹.

smack·er *noun* (also **smack·eroo**) *slang* **1** a loud kiss. **2 a** *N Amer.* a dollar. **b** *Brit.* a pound sterling.

small ● *adjective* **1 a** not large or big. **b** not large in comparison with others of the same kind (*a small city*). **2** slender; thin. **3** not great in importance, amount, number, strength, or power. **4** not much; trifling (*a small token; paid small attention*). **5** insignificant; unimportant (*a small matter; from small beginnings*). **6** consisting of small particles (*small gravel; small shot*). **7** doing something on a small scale (*a small farmer; small businesses*). **8** socially undistinguished; poor or humble. **9** petty; mean; ungenerous; paltry (*a small spiteful nature*). **10** young; not fully grown or developed (*a small child*). **11** lower case. ● *noun* **1** the

slenderest part of something. **2 a** a garment etc. of a size suited for people smaller than average. **b** a small serving of a beverage or food that is sold in more than one size. **3** (in *pl.*) *Brit. informal* small items of laundry, esp. underwear. ● *adverb* into small pieces (*chop it small*). □ **be small potatoes** be insignificant. **feel** (or **look**) **small** be humiliated; appear mean or humiliated. **in a small way** unambitiously; on a small scale. **no small** considerable; a good deal of (*no small excitement about it*). **small-a** (or **b, c,** etc.) designating a common noun or general term rather than a proper name (*small-l liberal*). **small wonder** *see* WONDER. □ **small·ish** *adjective* **small·ness** *noun* [Old English *smæl* from Germanic]

small arms *plural noun* portable firearms, esp. rifles, pistols, light machine guns, submachine guns, etc.

small beer *noun* **1** a trifling matter; something unimportant. **2** weak beer.

small-bore *adjective* (esp. *attributive*) **1** (of a firearm) with a narrow bore, in international and Olympic shooting usu. .22 inch calibre (5.6 millimetre bore). **2** *informal* petty, insignificant, small-time.

small calorie *noun see* CALORIE 2.

small cap¹ *noun* (in full **small capital**) (esp. in *pl.*) a capital letter which is of the same dimensions as the lower case letters in the same typeface minus ascenders and descenders, as THIS.

small cap² *noun* a company with a relatively small market capitalization (usu., with hyphen, *attributive: small-cap stocks*). [abbreviation]

small change *noun* **1** money in the form of coins as opposed to bills. **2** a relatively insignificant amount of money. **3** a trivial thing.

small claims court *noun* a general name given to a court with jurisdiction over civil claims involving relatively small amounts of money, with trials conducted by judges alone and legal representation unnecessary and often prohibited.

small forward *noun Basketball* **1** a versatile forward who is effective outside the key as well as near the net. **2** the position played by such a forward (*compare* POWER FORWARD 1).

small fry *plural noun* **1** young children or the young of various species. **2** small or insignificant things or people.

small game *noun* small animals hunted for sport (also *attributive: small-game hunter*).

small·hold·er *noun* esp. *Brit.* a person who farms a small holding.

small holding *noun Brit.* an agricultural holding smaller than a farm.

small hours *plural noun* the early hours of the morning after midnight.

small intestine *noun* the duodenum, jejunum, and ileum collectively.

small letter *noun* (in printed material) a lower case letter.

small mercy *noun* a minor concession, benefit, etc. (*be grateful for small mercies*).

small-minded *adjective* petty; of rigid opinions or narrow outlook. □ **small-minded·ly** *adverb* **small-minded·ness** *noun*

small·mouth *noun* (*pl.* same or **small·mouths**) (in full **smallmouth bass**) a N American freshwater bass with a small mouth, *Micropterus dolomieu*, widely introduced throughout the world as a game fish.

small of the back *noun* the lower part of the back.

small·pox *noun* an acute contagious viral disease, with fever and pustules usu. leaving permanent scars, effectively eradicated through vaccination by 1979. *Also called* VARIOLA.

small press *noun* (esp. *attributive*) an independent, relatively small publisher (*small press publishing*).

small print *noun* **1** printed matter in small type. **2** = FINE PRINT.

small-scale *adjective* made or occurring in small amounts, to a lesser degree, on a small scale, etc.

small screen *noun* (prec. by *the*) *informal* television (*a star of the small screen; watched the small screen all night*).

small slam *noun Bridge* the winning of 12 tricks.

small-sword *noun* a light tapering thrusting sword, esp. *hist.* for duelling.

small talk *noun* light social conversation. □ **small-talk** *intransitive verb*

small-time *attributive adjective informal* unimportant or petty. □ **small-timer** *noun*

small-town *attributive adjective* esp. *N Amer.* relating to or characteristic of a small town; unsophisticated. □ **small-towner** *noun*

Small·wood, Jo·seph Rob·erts ('Joey') (1900–91), Canadian journalist and politician, Newfoundland's first premier 1949–70. An advocate for Confederation with Canada, he was elected in 1946 to a Convention on Newfoundland's political future and led the pro-Confederation side to victory. As premier he encouraged industrialization and resettlement away from the outports.

Smallwood Reservoir a large reservoir in W Labrador, created in 1965 by the damming of the Churchill River. With an area of 6 527 sq. km, it is the third-largest artificial lake in the world. [J. R. SMALLWOOD]

smalt /smolt/ *noun* **1** glass coloured blue with cobalt. **2** a pigment made by pulverizing this. [French from Italian *smalto* from Germanic, related to SMELT¹]

smarm *informal* ● *verb* **1** *intransitive* behave in a fulsomely flattering or toadying manner; be ingratiating. **2** *transitive* Brit. (often foll. by *down*) smooth, plaster down (hair etc.) usu. with cream or oil. ● *noun* obsequiousness. [originally dialect (also *smalm*), of uncertain origin]

smarmy *adjective* (**smarm·i·er**, **smarm·i·est**) *informal* ingratiating; flattering; obsequious. □ **smarm·i·ly** *adverb* **smarm·i·ness** *noun*

Smart, Eliza·beth (1913–86), Canadian novelist and poet. Her first novel, *By Grand Central Station I Sat Down and Wept* (1945) was followed by poetry, including *A Bonus* (1977).

smart ● *adjective* **1 a** esp. N Amer. intelligent, keen, bright (*the smartest kid in the class*). **b** clever, witty; impudent (*gave a smart answer; don't be smart*). **c** keen in bargaining; quick to take advantage; shrewd. **2** well-groomed; neat; bright and fresh in appearance (*a smart suit*). **3** in good repair; showing bright colours, new paint, etc. (*a smart red bicycle*). **4** stylish; fashionable; prominent in society (*in all the smart restaurants; the smart set*). **5** quick; brisk (*set a smart pace*). **6** painfully severe; sharp; vigorous (*a smart blow*). **7 a** (of a device) capable of independent and seemingly intelligent action. **b** (of a powered missile, bomb, etc.) guided to a target by an optical system. **8** (of a drug, drink, etc.) that supposedly improves memory or mental acuteness (*smart drinks*). ● *intransitive verb* **1** (of a person or a part of the body) feel or give acute pain or distress (*my eye smarts; smarting from the insult*). **2** (of an insult, grievance, etc.) rankle; cause bad or bitter feelings. **3** (foll. by *for*) suffer the consequences of (*you will smart for this*). ● *noun* **1** a bodily or mental sharp pain; a stinging sensation. **2** (in *pl.*) esp. N Amer. intelligence, esp. of a specified kind; savvy (*lacking street smarts*). ● *adverb* smartly; in a smart manner. □ **look smart** see LOOK. **smart as a whip** very smart. □ **smart·ish** *adjective & adverb* **smart·ly** *adverb* **smart·ness** *noun* [Old English *smeart, smeortan*]

smart al·eck *noun* (also **smart alec**) (also, with hyphen, *attributive*) *informal* a person displaying impudent or smug cleverness. □ **smart-alecky** *adjective* [SMART + *Aleck*, diminutive of the name *Alexander*]

smart·ass *noun slang* = SMART ALECK. □ **smart·ass** *attributive adjective* **smart·assed** *adjective*

smart card *noun* a plastic card with a built-in microprocessor, esp. as a credit or other bank card for the instant transfer of funds etc.

smart cookie *noun* N Amer. informal a smart or shrewd person.

smart drug *noun* a drug which supposedly improves memory and mental acuteness.

smart·en *transitive & intransitive verb* (usu. foll. by *up*) make or become smart or smarter.

smart money *noun* **1 a** money invested by persons with expert knowledge. **b** people, esp. investors or bettors, with expert knowledge (*the smart money says it won't last*; also *attributive: the smart-money favourite*). **2** money paid or exacted as a penalty or compensation.

smart-mouth *transitive & intransitive verb* esp. N Amer. informal give a cheeky retort to someone. □ **smart-mouthed** *adjective*

smart phone *noun* a mobile phone with computer-like capabilities, e.g. transmitting email, taking and transmitting video images, storing data, browsing the web, etc.

smart·weed *noun* any of various plants of the genus *Polygonum* with swollen, sheathed leaf joints and long clusters of small pink or white flowers.

smarty *noun* (*pl.* **-ies**) (also **smarty-pants**) *informal* a know-it-all; a smart aleck.

smash ● *verb* **1** *transitive & intransitive* (often foll. by *up*) **a** break into pieces; shatter. **b** bring or come to sudden or complete destruction, defeat, or disaster. **2** *transitive* (foll. by *into, through*) (of a vehicle etc.) move with great force and impact. **3** *transitive & intransitive* (foll. by *in*) break in with a crushing blow (*smashed in the window*). **4** *transitive* **a** (in tennis, squash, etc.) hit (a ball etc.) with great force, esp. downwards (*smashed it back over the net*). **b** (in baseball, golf, etc.) hit (the ball) powerfully.

● *noun* **1** the act or an instance of smashing; a violent fall, collision, or disaster. **2** the sound of this. **3** (also **smash hit**) a very successful movie, song, performer, etc. **4 a** a stroke in tennis, squash, etc., in which the ball is hit esp. downwards with great force. **b** *Baseball* a powerful hit. **5** a violent blow with a fist etc. **6** bankruptcy; a series of commercial failures. [18th c., prob. imitative after *smack, smite* and *bash, mash,* etc.]

smash-and-grab *noun* (usu. *attributive*) a robbery in which the thief smashes a store window and seizes goods quickly.

smashed *adjective* **1** broken into pieces; shattered. **2** *slang* intoxicated.

smash·er *noun* **1** a person or thing that smashes. **2** *informal* a very beautiful or pleasing person or thing.

smash·ing *adjective informal* superlative; excellent; wonderful; beautiful. □ **smash·ing·ly** *adverb*

smash-mouth *noun* (often *attributive*) N Amer. Sport (esp. *Football*) a style of play characterized by aggression, direct confrontation, an in-your-face attitude, etc. (*smash-mouth football; play smash-mouth*).

smash-up *noun* a violent collision; a complete smash.

smat·ter·ing *noun* **1** a slight superficial knowledge of a language or subject. **2** a small amount, esp. sparsely distributed (*a smattering of applause*). □ **smat·ter·er** *noun* [Middle English *smatter* talk ignorantly, prate: origin unknown]

SME *abbreviation* small to medium-sized enterprise, a company with no more than 500 employees.

smear ● *transitive verb* **1 a** daub or mark with a greasy or sticky substance or with something that stains. **b** spread a layer of (a greasy, sticky, or staining substance) on something. **2** blot; smudge; obscure the outline of (writing, artwork, etc.). **3** defame the character of; slander; attempt to or succeed in discrediting (a person or his or her name) publicly. ● *noun* **1** the act or an instance of smearing. **2** *Med.* **a** material smeared on a microscopic slide etc. for examination. **b** a specimen of this. **c** a procedure involving the removal of material to be examined in this way. **3** a substance smeared on another; a smeared stain. □ **smeary** *adjective* [Old English *smierwan* from Germanic]

smear campaign *noun* a planned effort to slander and so discredit a public figure.

smec·tic *adjective* designating or involving a state of a liquid crystal in which the molecules are oriented in parallel and arranged in well-defined planes (compare NEMATIC). [Latin *smecticus*, Greek *smēktikos* 'cleansing' (from the soap-like consistency)]

smeg·ma *noun* a sebaceous secretion in the folds of the skin, esp. of the foreskin. [Latin from Greek *smēgma -atos* detergent, from *smēkhō* cleanse]

smell ● *noun* **1** the faculty of perceiving odours or scents (*has a fine sense of smell*). **2** the quality in substances that is perceived by this (*the smell of oranges; this rose has no smell*). **3** an unpleasant odour. **4** the act of inhaling to ascertain smell. **5** a trace or suggestion of something; the special character of something (*the smell of success; the smell of money*). ● *verb* (*past* and *past participle* esp. N Amer. **smelled** or esp. *Brit., Austral.,* etc. **smelt**) **1** *transitive* perceive the smell of; examine by smell (*thought I could smell gas*). **2** *intransitive* emit odour. **3** *intransitive* seem by smell to be (*this milk smells sour*). **4** *intransitive* (foll. by *of*) **a** be redolent of (*smells of fish*). **b** be suggestive of (*smells of dishonesty*). **5** *intransitive* stink; be rank. **6** *transitive* perceive as if by smell; detect, discern, suspect (*smell a bargain*). **7** *intransitive* have or use a sense of smell. **8** *intransitive* (foll. by *around, about*) sniff or search about. **9** *transitive* (foll. by *up*) fill or affect with an esp. offensive odour. □ **smell blood** (of an attacker or aggressor) be encouraged by the discernment of another's vulnerability. **smell a rat** begin to suspect trickery etc. **smell the roses** enjoy or appreciate what is often ignored. □ **smell·er** *noun* [Middle English *smel(le)*, prob. from Old English]

smelling salts *plural noun* ammonium carbonate mixed with scent to be sniffed as a restorative in faintness etc.

smelly *adjective* (**smell·i·er**, **smell·i·est**) having a strong or unpleasant smell. □ **smell·i·ness** *noun*

smelt¹ *transitive verb* **1** extract metal from (ore) by melting. **2** extract (metal) from ore by melting. □ **smelt·ing** *noun* [Middle Dutch, Middle Low German *smelten*, related to MELT]

smelt² esp. *Brit., Austral.,* etc. *past and past participle of* SMELL.

smelt³ *noun* (*pl.* same or **smelts**) any of various small silvery carnivorous fish of the family Osmeridae, of coastal sea waters and fresh waters near the coasts of the northern hemisphere, including the capelin, eulachon, and rainbow smelt. [Old English, of uncertain origin: compare SMOLT]

smelt·er noun **1** a person engaged in smelting. **2** a place where ores are smelted. □ **smelt·ery** noun (pl. **-eries**).

Smet·ana /'smetənə/ **Bed·řich** (1824–84), Czech composer. A patriot and nationalist, he often used folk tunes, esp. in his most famous works, which include the opera *The Bartered Bride* (1866) and the cycle of tone poems *My Country* (1874–9), which includes *The Moldau*.

smew noun a small merganser, *Mergus albellus*. [17th c., related to *smeath*, *smee* = smew, widgeon, etc.]

smidg·en noun (also **smidg·eon, smidg·in**; also **smidge**) *informal* a small bit or amount. [perhaps from *smitch* in the same sense: compare dialect *smitch* woodsmoke]

smi·lax /'smailaks/ noun **1** any climbing shrub of the genus *Smilax*, the roots of some species of which yield sarsaparilla. **2** a related climbing plant, *Myrsiphyllum asparagoides*, used decoratively by florists. [Latin from Greek, = bindweed]

smile ● verb **1** *intransitive* form one's features into a pleased or kind or amused expression or a forced imitation of these, usu. with the corners of the mouth turned up. **2** *transitive* express by smiling (*smiled their consent*). **3** *transitive* give (a smile) of a specified kind (*smiled a sardonic smile*). **4** *intransitive* (foll. by *on, upon*) adopt a favourable attitude towards; encourage (*fortune smiled on me*). **5** *intransitive* have a bright or favourable aspect (*the smiling countryside*). **6** *intransitive* (foll. by *at*) **a** ridicule or show indifference to (*smiled at my feeble attempts*). **b** favour; smile on. ● noun **1** the act or an instance of smiling. **2** a smiling expression or aspect. □ **be all smiles** look very cheerful and pleased, esp. in contrast to a previous mood. □ **smile·less** adjective **smil·er** noun **smil·ing** adjective **smil·ing·ly** adverb [Middle English perhaps from Scandinavian, related to SMIRK: compare Old High German *smīlenter*]

smil·ey ● adjective displaying a smile or characterized by smiling. ● noun = EMOTICON.

smiley face noun a schematic drawing of a face with two dots for eyes and an upturned curve for a mouth, usu. enclosed in a circle.

smirch ● *transitive verb* mark, soil, or smear (a thing, a person's reputation, etc.). ● noun **1** a spot or stain. **2** a blot (on one's character etc.). [Middle English: origin unknown]

smirk ● noun a conceited, smug, scornful, or silly smile. ● *intransitive verb* put on or wear a smirk. □ **smirk·er** noun **smirk·ing·ly** adverb **smirky** adjective [Old English *sme(a)rcian*]

smite *transitive verb* (past **smote**; past participle **smit·ten**) **1** strike or hit forcefully. **2** chastise; defeat. **3** (in *passive*) **a** have a sudden strong effect on (*was smitten by his conscience*). **b** infatuate, fascinate (*was smitten by her beauty*). □ **smit·er** noun [Old English *smītan* smear, from Germanic]

Smith ▶ **1 Adam** (1723–90), Scottish economist and philosopher. His *Inquiry into the Nature and Causes of the Wealth of Nations* (1776), regarded as founding the modern study of economics, established theories of labour, distribution, wages, prices, and money, and advocated free trade and minimal state interference in economic matters. **2 Arthur James Mar·shall** (1902–80), Canadian poet and critic. In 1925, he founded the *McGill Fortnightly Review* with F.R. Scott; he later edited several anthologies. He also published his own poetry, including *News of the Phoenix* (1943, Governor General's Award), and *Towards a View of Canadian Letters* (1973), a volume of critical essays. **3 Bes·sie** (known as 'the Empress of the Blues') (1894–1937), US blues singer. She became a leading artist in the 1920s and made over 150 recordings, including some with Benny Goodman and Louis Armstrong; she died as a result of a car accident, reportedly after being refused admission to a 'whites only' hospital. **4 David (Ro·land)** (1906–65), US sculptor. His early work, including *Pillars of Sunday* (1945), is marked by recurring motifs of human violence and greed. These later give way to a calmer, more monumental style, as in the *Cubi* series. **5 Don·ald Alex·an·der, 1st Baron Strath·cona and Mount Royal** (1820–1914), Scottish-born Canadian fur trader and railroad financier. Joining the Hudson's Bay Company as an apprentice clerk in 1838, by 1883 he was the company's largest shareholder and was its governor from 1889. In 1887 he became president of the Bank of Montreal; he was also an enthusiastic supporter of the CPR, which would not have been built without his financial backing. **6 Gold·win** (1823–1910), English-born Canadian historian and journalist. He is remembered as the most prominent advocate of Canadian union with the US in the late 19th c. **7 Ian (Doug·las)** (b.1919), Rhodesian politician, prime minister 1964–79. In 1965 he unilaterally declared independence from Britain, maintaining white minority rule until 1979. **8 John** (1580–1631), English explorer. He founded Virginia and promoted colonization in America, and his works include *A Description of New England* (1616); he claimed that he was taken prisoner by Indians and rescued by

Pocahontas. **9 Jo·seph** (1805–44), US religious leader, founder of the Church of Jesus Christ of Latter-day Saints (the Mormon Church) (1830). He based his faith on sacred texts which he claimed to have discovered in 1827 through divine revelation and which he published as the Book of Mormon. **10 Lois** (b.1929), Canadian ballet dancer. Regarded as Canada's first prima ballerina, she was a dancer with the National Ballet of Canada 1951–69. **11 Dame Maggie** (born Margaret Natalie Smith) (b.1934), English stage and film actress, whose films include *The Prime of Miss Jean Brodie* (1969), for which she won an Oscar, *A Room with a View* (1986), and *The Lonely Passion of Judith Hearne* (1988). **12 Mi·chael** (1932–2000), British-born Canadian biochemist, co-winner (with Kary Mullis) of the 1993 Nobel Prize for chemistry. **13 Syd·ney** (1771–1845), English Anglican churchman and essayist, who is notable as the author of the *Letters of Peter Plymley* (1807), in defence of Catholic Emancipation. **14 Wil·liam** (1769–1839), English land surveyor and geologist, who discovered that rock strata could be identified by their characteristic assemblages of fossils; he produced the first geological map of England and Wales.

smith noun **1** (esp. in *combination*) a worker in metal (*goldsmith*; *tinsmith*). **2** a person who forges iron; a blacksmith. □ **smith·ing** noun [Old English from Germanic]

smith·er·eens plural noun small fragments (*smashed to smithereens*). [probably from Irish *smidirín*]

Smith·ers /'smɪðərz/ a town in west central BC, situated on the Bulkley River, northeast of Prince Rupert; pop. (2001) 5,414. □ **Smith·er·een** noun [Sir A. W. *Smithers*, chairman of the board for the Grand Trunk Pacific Railway d.1924]

smith·ery noun (pl. **-eries**) **1** a smith's work. **2** (esp. in naval dockyards) a smithy.

Smiths Falls /smɪθ 'fɒlz, smɪθs/ a town in SE central Ontario, situated on the Rideau River east of Perth; pop. (2001) 9,140. [alteration of its original name *Smyth's Falls*, after T. *Smyth*, Loyalist and landowner d.1832]

Smith·son, James (born James Lewes Macie) (1765–1829), English chemist and mineralogist, who left his inherited fortune for the foundation of the Smithsonian Institution in Washington, DC.

smithy /'smɪθi, 'smɪði/ noun (pl. **-ies**) a blacksmith's workshop; a forge.

smit·ten ● verb past participle of SMITE. ● adjective **1** struck, hit. **2** (often foll. by *with*) affected with or by something specified. **3** in love; infatuated.

smock ● noun **1** a loose garment, esp. as worn by artists etc. to protect their clothes, or *hist.* by labourers in fields. **2** a loose shirt-like garment for women and girls, with the upper part closely gathered in smocking. ● *transitive verb* (usu. as **smocked**) adorn with smocking. [Old English *smoc*, prob. related to Old English *smūgan* creep, Old Norse *smjúga* put on a garment]

smock·ing noun an ornamental effect on cloth made by gathering the material tightly into pleats, often with stitches in a honeycomb pattern.

smog noun fog intensified by atmospheric pollutants esp. smoke. □ **smog·less** adjective **smoggy** adjective (**smog·gi·er, smog·gi·est**). [blend of SMOKE + FOG]

smoke ● noun **1 a** a visible suspension of carbon etc. in air, emitted from a burning substance. **b** vapour etc. resembling smoke. **2** an act or period of smoking tobacco (*had a quiet smoke*). **3** *informal* a cigarette or cigar (*got a smoke?*). **4** *Baseball informal* a very effective fastball; a pitcher's arsenal of unhittable fastballs (*throws smoke*). **5** a clouding or obscuring medium or influence; esp. false information intended as a distraction. **6** (**the Smoke**) *Brit. informal* a big city, esp. London. **7** a colour like that of smoke, esp. a bluish or brownish grey. ● verb **1** *intransitive* **a** emit smoke or visible vapour (*the ruins continued to smoke*). **b** (of an oil lamp etc.) burn badly with the emission of smoke. **c** (of a chimney or fire) discharge smoke into the room. **2 a** *intransitive* inhale and exhale the smoke of a cigarette, cigar, etc. **b** *intransitive* do this habitually. **c** *transitive* use (a cigarette etc.) in this way. **3** *transitive* cure or darken by the action of smoke (*smoked salmon*). **4** *transitive* **a** rid of insects etc. by the action of smoke. **b** subdue (insects, esp. bees) in this way. **5** *transitive* N Amer. *informal* **a** shoot with a firearm; snuff out. **b** defeat overwhelmingly. **6** *transitive* N Amer. esp. *Sport* hit and propel (a ball etc.) with great speed and force; make (a powerful shot, stroke, hit, etc.). **7** *transitive* bring (oneself) into a specified state by smoking. □ **go up in smoke** *informal* **1** be destroyed by fire. **2** (of a plan etc.) come to nothing. **where there's smoke there's fire** rumours are not entirely baseless. **smoke out 1** drive out by means of smoke. **2** drive out of hiding or secrecy etc. **smoke up** *Cdn* smoke a drug, esp. marijuana. □ **smok·able** adjective (also **smoke·able**). **smok·ing** noun & adjective

[Old English *smoca* from weak grade of the stem of *smēocan* emit smoke]

smoke and mirrors *plural noun N Amer.* a thing or things intended to deceive or confuse; deceit (also, with hyphens, *attributive*: *smoke-and-mirrors campaign*).

smoke bomb *noun* **1** a bomb or other projectile that emits dense smoke on exploding. **2** a similar device used as a special effect in concerts etc.

smoke bush *noun* = SMOKE PLANT.

smoke detector *noun* (also **smoke alarm**) a device which warns of the presence of smoke.

smoked glass *noun* glass darkened with smoke (also, with hyphen, *attributive*: *smoked-glass door*).

smoked meat *noun* **1** meat that has been cured by smoking. **2** *Cdn* (esp. *Que. & Ont.*) cured beef similar to pastrami but more heavily smoked.

smoke-dry *transitive verb* dry or cure (meat, fish, etc.) in smoke. □ **smoke-dried** *adjective*

smoke-free *adjective* **1** free from smoke. **2** where smoking is not permitted.

smoke·house *noun* esp. *N Amer.* a house or room for curing meat, fish, etc. by exposure to smoke.

smoke jumper *noun N Amer.* a firefighter who arrives by parachute to extinguish a forest fire. □ **smoke jump** *intransitive verb*

smoke·less *adjective* having or producing little or no smoke.

smoke plant *noun* (also **smoke bush**, **smoke tree**) any shrub or small tree of the genus *Cotinus*, with feathery smoke-like fruit stalks, frequently planted as an ornamental.

smok·er *noun* **1** a person or thing that smokes, esp. a person who habitually smokes tobacco. **2** a compartment on a train, in which smoking is allowed. **3** esp. *N Amer.* an informal social gathering of men. **4** esp. *N Amer.* a small box used for smoking fish or other meat. **5** a device for stupefying bees.

smoke ring *noun* smoke from a cigarette etc. exhaled in the shape of a ring.

smoke room *noun* = SMOKING ROOM.

smoker's cough *noun* a persistent cough caused by excessive smoking.

smoke·screen *noun* **1** a cloud of smoke diffused to conceal (esp. military) operations. **2** a device or ruse for disguising one's activities.

smoke shop *noun N Amer.* **1** a store selling tobacco products. **2** a convenience store.

smoke signal *noun* a column of smoke used as a signal.

smoke·stack *noun* **1** a tall chimney, esp. of a factory. **2** a chimney or funnel for discharging the smoke of a locomotive or steamer. **3** (*attributive*) designating heavy manufacturing industry, typically associated with high pollution levels and outmoded technology (*smokestack economy*).

smok·ey ● *adjective var. of* SMOKY. ● *noun* (*pl.* **smok·eys**, **smok·ies**) esp. *N Amer.* a police officer or car, esp. patrolling a highway. [noun sense from *Smokey the Bear*, cartoon mascot of the US Forest Service, whose uniform resembles that of US highway patrol officers]

smok·ie *noun Cdn* a sausage or hot dog.

smok·ing gun *noun* (also **smoking pistol**) a piece of incontrovertible incriminating evidence.

smok·ing jacket *noun* an ornamental jacket formerly worn by men while smoking.

smok·ing room *noun* a room in a hotel or house, kept for smoking in.

smoky *adjective* (also **smokey**) (**smok·i·er**, **smok·i·est**) **1** emitting, veiled or filled with, or obscured by, smoke (*smoky fire*; *smoky room*). **2 a** stained with smoke (*smoky glass*). **b** (of a colour etc.) resembling smoke; of a bluish-grey tinge (*smoky grey*). **3** having the taste or flavour of smoked food (*smoky bacon*). **4** (of a voice) having the slightly hoarse overtones characteristic of a heavy smoker. □ **smok·i·ly** *adverb* **smok·i·ness** *noun*

smol·der *var. of* SMOULDER.

Smo·lensk /sməˈljensk/ a city in W European Russia, on the Dnieper River close to the border with Belarus; pop. (est. 2002) 351,900.

Smol·lett /ˈsmɒlət/ **To·bias (George)** (1721–71), Scottish novelist. His novels are picaresque tales characterized by fast-moving narrative and humorous caricature.

smolt /smoːlt/ *noun* a young salmon migrating to the sea for the first time. [Middle English (originally Scots & Northern English): origin unknown]

smooch *informal* ● *intransitive verb* **1** kiss. **2** cuddle and caress. ● *noun* **1** a kiss. **2** *Brit.* a period of slow dancing close together. □ **smooch·er** *noun* **smoochy** *adjective* (**smooch·i·er**, **smooch·i·est**). [dial. *smouch* imitative]

smoosh *transitive verb N Amer. informal* flatten, squash. [origin unknown]

smooth ● *adjective* **1** having a relatively even and regular surface; free from perceptible projections, lumps, indentations, and roughness. **2** (of the skin, a complexion, etc.) not wrinkled, pitted, scored, or hairy. **3** that can be traversed without check. **4** (of liquids) of even consistency; without lumps (*mix to a smooth paste*). **5** (of the sea etc.) without waves or undulations. **6** (of a journey, passage, progress, etc.) untroubled by difficulties or adverse conditions. **7** having an easy flow or correct rhythm (*a smooth metre*). **8 a** not harsh in sound or taste. **b** (of wine etc.) not astringent. **9** often *derogatory* (of a person, his or her manner, etc.) suave, conciliatory, flattering, unruffled, or polite (*a smooth talker*; *he's very smooth*). **10** (of movement etc.) not suddenly varying; not jerky. ● *verb* (also **smoothe**) **1** *transitive & intransitive* (often foll. by *out*, *down*) make or become smooth. **2** (often foll. by *out*, *down*, *over*, *away*) **a** *transitive* reduce or get rid of (differences, faults, difficulties, etc.) in fact or appearance. **b** *intransitive* (of difficulties etc.) diminish, become less obtrusive (*it will all smooth over*). **3** *transitive* modify (a graph, curve, etc.) so as to lessen irregularities. **4** *transitive* free from impediments or discomfort (*smooth the way*; *smooth the declining years*). ● *noun* **1** a smoothing touch or stroke (*gave his hair a smooth*). **2** the easy part of life (*take the rough with the smooth*). ● *adverb* smoothly (*goes down smooth*; *the course of true love never did run smooth*). □ **smooth·able** *adjective* **smooth·er** *noun* **smooth·ish** *adjective* **smooth·ly** *adverb* **smooth·ness** *noun* [Old English *smōth*]

smooth·bore *noun* a gun with an unrifled barrel (also *attributive*: *smoothbore gun*).

smooth·en *verb informal* = SMOOTH.

smooth-faced *adjective* **1** with a smooth face or skin. **2** hypocritically friendly.

smooth·ie *noun informal* **1** a person who is smooth (*see* SMOOTH *adjective* 9). **2** (also **smoothy**) esp. *N Amer., Austral., & NZ* a thick smooth drink of fresh fruit puréed with milk, yogourt, or ice cream.

smooth muscle *noun* a muscle without striations, usu. occurring in hollow organs and performing involuntary functions.

smooth sailing *noun* easy progress.

smooth talk *informal* ● *noun* bland specious language. ● *transitive & intransitive verb* (**smooth-talk**) address or persuade with this. □ **smooth talker** *noun* **smooth-talking** *adjective*

smooth-tongued *adjective* insincerely flattering.

smoothy *var. of* SMOOTHIE 2.

s'more /smɔr/ *noun N Amer.* a dessert made of a graham cracker topped with melted chocolate and a marshmallow. [contraction of *some more*]

smorg *noun Cdn* = SMORGASBORD 2, 3.

smor·gas·bord *noun* **1** a buffet offering a wide variety of dishes. **2** open sandwiches served with delicacies as hors d'oeuvres or a buffet. **3** a medley; a miscellany; a variety. [Swedish, from *smörgas* 'slice of' bread and butter' (from *smör* 'butter' + *gås* 'goose, lump of butter') + *bord* 'table']

smote *past of* SMITE.

smoth·er ● *verb* **1** *transitive* suffocate; stifle; kill by stopping the breath of or excluding air from. **2** *transitive* (foll. by *with*) overwhelm with (kisses, gifts, kindness, etc.) (*smothered with affection*). **3** *transitive* (foll. by *in*, *with*) cover entirely in or with (*chicken smothered in mayonnaise*). **4** *transitive* extinguish or deaden (a fire or flame) by covering it or heaping it with ashes etc. **5** *intransitive* **a** die of suffocation. **b** have difficulty breathing. **6** *transitive* **a** suppress or conceal; prevent from developing. **b** repress or refrain from displaying (feeling etc.) by self-control. **c** make (words etc.) indistinct or inaudible. **7** *transitive US* defeat rapidly or utterly. **8** *transitive* cook in a covered vessel. **9** *transitive Hockey* immobilize (the puck) on the ice by falling on top of it, covering it with a glove, etc. ● *noun* **1** a cloud of dust or smoke. **2** obscurity caused by this. [Middle English *smorther* from the stem of Old English *smorian* 'suffocate']

smoul·der (also **smol·der**) ● *intransitive verb* **1** burn slowly with smoke but without a flame; slowly burn internally or invisibly. **2** (of emotions etc.) exist in a suppressed or concealed state. **3** (of a person) show silent or suppressed anger, hatred, passion, etc. ● *noun* a smouldering or slow-burning fire. □ **smoul·der·ing** *adjective* [Middle English, related to Low German *smöln*, Middle Dutch *smölen*]

SMPTE /ˈsɪmpti/ *abbreviation* used to denote a time coding system for synchronizing video and audio tapes. [Society of Television and Motion Picture Engineers]

SMS *abbreviation* Short Message (or Messaging) Service, a system that enables mobile phone users to send and receive text messages.

smudge¹ ● *noun* a blurred or smeared line or mark; a blot; a smear of dirt. ● *verb* **1** *transitive* make a smudge on. **2** *intransitive* become smeared or blurred (*smudges easily*). **3** *transitive* smear or blur the lines of (writing, drawing, etc.) (*smudge the outline*). **4** *transitive* defile, sully, stain, or disgrace. [Middle English: origin unknown]

smudge² *N Amer.* ● *noun* **1** (in full **smudge fire**) an outdoor fire with dense smoke made to keep off insects, protect plants against frost, etc. **2** dense smoke as produced by such a fire. **3** a burning bundle of sage, sweetgrass, cedar, etc., used in ritually purifying a house, room, person, etc. (usu. *attributive: smudge stick*). ● *transitive & intransitive verb* burn sage, sweetgrass, cedar, etc., with the intention of ritually purifying (a house, room, person, etc.). □ **smudg·ing** *noun* [*smudge* cure (herring) by smoking (16th c.: origin unknown)]

smudge pot *noun* a container holding burning material that produces smudge.

smudgy *adjective* (**smudg·i·er, smudg·i·est**) **1** smudged. **2** likely to produce smudges. □ **smudg·i·ly** *adverb* **smudg·i·ness** *noun*

smug *adjective* (**smug·ger, smug·gest**) self-satisfied; complacent. □ **smug·ly** *adverb* **smug·ness** *noun* [16th c., originally 'neat' from Low German *smuk* pretty]

smug·gle *verb* **1** *transitive & intransitive* convey (goods) in contravention of legal prohibition or without payment of customs duties; import or export illegally. **2** *transitive* (foll. by *in, out*) convey secretly. **3** *transitive* (foll. by *away*) put into concealment. □ **smug·gler** *noun* **smug·gling** *noun* [17th c. (also *smuckle*) from Low German *smukkeln smuggelen*]

smush /smʌʃ/ *transitive verb* esp. *N Amer. informal* mash, crush, smash. [imitative after SMASH, MUSH¹, etc.]

smut ● *noun* **1** obscene or lascivious talk, pictures, or stories. **2 a** a fungous disease of cereals in which parts of the ear change to black powder. **b** any fungus of the order Ustilaginales causing this. **3** a small flake of soot etc. **4** a spot or smudge made by this. ● *verb* (**smut·ted, smut·ting**) **1** *transitive* mark with smuts. **2** *transitive* infect (a plant) with smut. **3** *intransitive* (of a plant) contract smut. □ **smutty** *adjective* (**smut·ti·er, smut·ti·est**) (esp. in sense 1 of *noun*). **smut·ti·ly** *adverb* **smut·ti·ness** *noun* [related to Low German *smutt*, Middle High German *smutz(en)* etc.: compare Old English *smitt(ian)* smear, and SMUDGE¹]

Smuts /smʌts/ **Jan (Chris·tiaan)** (1870–1950), South African politician and soldier, prime minister 1919–24 and 1939–48. He led Boer forces during the Second Boer War, and during the First World War led Allied troops against the Germans in East Africa (1916); he helped to found the League of Nations and the United Nations.

Smyr·na /ˈsmɜːnə/ an ancient city on the west coast of Asia Minor, on the site of modern Izmir in Turkey.

Smythe /smaɪθ/ **Con·stan·tine Falk·land Cary** ('Conn') (1895–1980), Canadian businessman and sports entrepreneur. After assembling the original New York Rangers team (1926), he and his associates purchased the Toronto St. Pats in 1927, and changed their name to the Toronto Maple Leafs. Maple Leaf Gardens in Toronto was built largely because of his efforts.

Sn *symbol Chem.* the element tin.

snack ● *noun* **1** a light, casual, or hurried meal. **2** a small amount or item of food eaten between meals. ● *intransitive verb* (often foll. by *on*) eat a snack. □ **snack·er** *noun* **snacky** *adjective* [Middle English, originally a snap or bite, from Middle Dutch *snac(k)* from *snacken* (v.), var. of *snappen*]

snack bar *noun* a usu. small store, kiosk, counter, etc. where snacks are sold.

snaf·fle ● *noun* (in full **snaffle bit**) (on a bridle) a simple bit without a curb and usu. with a single rein. ● *transitive verb* **1** put a snaffle on. **2** *informal* steal; seize; appropriate. [prob. from Low German or Dutch: compare Middle Low German, Middle Dutch *snavel* beak, mouth]

snafu /snaˈfuː, ˈsnafuː/ *slang* ● *noun* (pl. **-fus**) **1** a confused, muddled, or messed-up condition or state. **2** a mistake or blunder. ● *adjective* in utter confusion or chaos; messed up. ● *verb* (**-fued, -ing**) **1** *transitive* mess up, bungle, play havoc with. **2** *intransitive* go wrong; mess up. [acronym from 'situation normal: all fucked (or fouled) up']

snag ● *noun* **1** an unexpected or hidden obstacle, drawback, or problem. **2 a** a jagged or projecting point. **b** a standing dead tree; a broken stump or branch. **c** a tree trunk or branch embedded under water, forming an obstruction to navigation. **3** a tear in material etc. **4** an act or instance of snagging. ● *verb* (**snagged, snag·ging**) **1 a** *transitive* catch or tear on a snag (*snagged my sleeve on the branch*). **b** *transitive* (of a projecting point) catch or tear (something) (*something snagged my sleeve*). **c** *transitive* catch onto (a projecting point) (*the fishing line snagged a branch*). **d** *intransitive* catch onto a projecting point (*the line snagged*). **2** *transitive N Amer.* catch, seize, or obtain, esp. by quick action (*snagged the fly ball; snagged a passing waiter*). **3** *transitive* clear (land, a waterway, a tree trunk, etc.) of snags. □ **snagged** *adjective* **snag·gy** *adjective* [prob. from Scandinavian: compare Norwegian dial. *snag(e)* sharp point]

snag·ger *noun N Amer.* a person using illegal angling or fishing methods.

snaggle-toothed *adjective* having irregular or projecting teeth. □ **snag·gle·tooth** *noun* (pl. **snag·gle·teeth**). [SNAG + -LE²]

snail *noun* any slow-moving gastropod mollusc with a spiral shell able to enclose the whole body. □ **snail-like** *adjective* [Old English *snæg(e)l* from Germanic]

snail mail *noun slang* **1** the ordinary postal system as opposed to the electronic mail system. **2** correspondence sent using this.

snail's pace *noun* a very slow movement.

snake ● *noun* **1 a** any long limbless reptile of the suborder Ophidia, including boas, pythons, and poisonous forms such as cobras and vipers. **b** a limbless lizard or amphibian. **2** (also **snake in the grass**) a treacherous person or secret enemy. **3** (in full **plumber's snake**) a long flexible wire for clearing obstacles in piping. ● *verb* **1** *transitive & intransitive* move or twist or cause to move or twist like a snake. **2** *transitive* make (one's way) by snaking. □ **snake·like** *adjective* **snak·ish** *adjective* [Old English *snaca*]

snakebark maple *noun* any of several maples, esp. *Acer pennsylvanicum* of eastern N America, with bark streaked with whitish stripes.

snake·bite *noun* a wound or condition resulting from being bitten by an esp. poisonous snake.

snake-bitten *adjective* (also **snake·bit**) **1** bitten by a snake. **2** *N Amer. informal* unlucky, doomed to misfortune (*has been snake-bitten from the start*).

snake charmer *noun* a person appearing to make snakes move by music etc.

snake dance *noun* a dance or parade in which participants form a line which moves in zigzag fashion.

snake eyes *noun N Amer.* **1** *slang* a throw of two ones with one pair of dice. **2** *informal* an unlucky result; bad luck. □ **come up snake eyes** prove unsuccessful. [from the resemblance of two dice, each showing a single dot, to a pair of eyes]

snake fence *noun* (also **snake-rail fence**) esp. *Cdn* a fence of stacked roughly-split logs laid in a zigzag pattern with ends overlapping at an angle.

snake·head *noun* a member of a Chinese criminal network chiefly engaged in smuggling emigrants illegally out of China. [translation of Chinese *shetou*]

snake oil *noun informal* **1** a quack medicine. **2** a fraudulent product. **3** nonsense.

snake oil salesman *noun* a person promoting spurious solutions for problems, cures for ailments, etc.

snake·pit *noun* **1** a pit containing snakes. **2** a scene of vicious behaviour.

Snake River a river of the northwestern US. Rising in Yellowstone National Park in Wyoming, it flows for 1 670 km (1,038 miles) through Idaho into the state of Washington, where it joins the Columbia River.

snake·root *noun* any of various N American plants, e.g. *Cimicifuga racemosa*, with roots reputed to contain an antidote to snake's poison. See also SENECA SNAKEROOT.

Snakes and Ladders *noun Cdn & Brit.* a game in which counters are moved by dice throws along a board on which snakes and ladders are depicted, a counter that lands on the head of a snake being moved back to the tail, while one that lands at the foot of a ladder advances to the top.

snake's head *noun* a bulbous plant, *Fritillaria meleagris*, with bell-shaped pendent flowers.

snake·skin ● *noun* the skin of a snake. ● *adjective* made of or resembling snakeskin.

snaky *adjective* (also **snakey**) (**snak·i·er, snak·i·est**) **1** of or like a snake. **2** winding; sinuous. **3** showing coldness, ingratitude, venom, or guile. **4** infested with or composed of snakes. **5** *Austral. slang* angry;

irritable. □ **go** (or **drive someone**) **snaky** *Cdn* lose (or cause someone to lose) self-control. □ **snak·i·ly** *adverb* **snak·i·ness** *noun*

snap ● *verb* (**snapped**, **snap·ping**) **1** *intransitive & transitive* break suddenly or with a snap. **2** *intransitive & transitive* emit or cause to emit a sudden sharp sound or crack. **3** *intransitive & transitive* open or close, turn off or on, etc. with a snapping sound (*the bag snapped shut*). **4 a** *intransitive* (often foll. by *at*) speak irritably or spitefully (to a person) (*did not mean to snap at you*). **b** *transitive* say irritably or spitefully. **5** *intransitive* (often foll. by *at*) (esp. of a dog etc.) make a sudden audible bite. **6** *transitive & intransitive* move quickly (*snapped into action*; *snap to it*). **7** *transitive* take a snapshot of. **8** *transitive Football* put (the ball) into play on the ground by a quick backward movement. **9** *transitive* bring an end to (an esp. undecided condition, state of affairs, etc.) (*snapped a 2–2 tie*; *snapped their losing streak*). **10** *intransitive* lose one's composure suddenly after having resisted increasing tension or pressure (*I finally snapped*). ● *noun* **1** an act or sound of snapping. **2** *N Amer. slang* an easy task (*it was a snap*). **3** a crisp biscuit or cake (*brandy snap*; *gingersnap*). **4** a snapshot. **5** (in full **cold snap**) a sudden brief spell of cold weather. **6** a card game in which players call 'snap' when two similar cards are exposed. **7** crispness of style; fresh vigour or liveliness in action; zest; dash; spring. **8** *Football* an act or instance of snapping the ball. **9** *N Amer.* = DOME FASTENER. ● *attributive adjective* done or taken on the spur of the moment, unexpectedly, or without notice (*snap decision*). □ **in a snap** with no hesitation or difficulty. **snap at** accept (bait, a chance, etc.) eagerly (*see also* senses 4a and 5 of *verb*). **snap off** break off or bite off. **snap one's fingers** suddenly release a finger which has been bent and checked by another finger or thumb, producing an audible snap as the finger strikes the hand, esp. in rhythm to music. **snap out** utter forcefully. **snap out of** *informal* get rid of (a mood, habit, etc.) by a sudden effort. **snap up 1** accept (an offer, a bargain) quickly or eagerly. **2** pick up or catch hastily. □ **snap·pable** *adjective* **snap·ping·ly** *adverb* [probably from Middle Dutch or Middle Low German *snappen* 'seize': partly imitative]

snap bean *noun N Amer.* a bean with edible pods.

snap-brim *noun* a hat brim, as on a fedora, that can be turned up and down, worn usu. with the front turned down and the back up (usu. *attributive: snap-brim hat*). □ **snap-brimmed** *adjective*

snap·dragon *noun* any of several plants of the genus *Antirrhinum* and of related genera, with a bag-shaped flower like a dragon's mouth, esp. *A. majus*, cultivated in gardens.

snap fastener *noun* = DOME FASTENER.

snap-on *attributive adjective* denoting a cover or attachment that is attached or secured with a snap.

snap·per *noun* **1** a person or thing that snaps. **2** any of several fish of the family Lutjanidae, used as food. **3** = BLUEFISH. **4** a snapping turtle.

snapping turtle *noun* either of two large aggressive Central and N American freshwater turtles of the family Chelydridae, having large heads and long tails, and seizing prey with a snap of the jaws, *Chelydra serpentina* (also **common** or **Florida snapping turtle**), and *Macroclemys temminckii* (also **alligator snapping turtle**).

snap·pish *adjective* **1** (of a person's manner or a remark) curt; ill-tempered; sharp. **2** (of a dog etc.) inclined to snap. □ **snap·pish·ly** *adverb* **snap·pish·ness** *noun*

snappy *adjective* (**snap·pi·er**, **snap·pi·est**) *informal* **1** brisk, full of zest. **2** fashionable, up-to-date (*a snappy dresser*; *drives a snappy red convertible*). **3** snappish. □ **make it snappy** be quick about it. □ **snap·pi·ly** *adverb* **snap·pi·ness** *noun*

snap·shot *noun* **1** a casual photograph taken quickly with a small camera. **2** a description or profile of a thing or of one stage of a process etc. **3** (**snap shot**) *Sport* a quick shot at a goal, esp. (*Hockey*) a shot taken by lifting the stick a short distance off the ice before striking the puck quickly with a hard flicking motion (*compare* SLAPSHOT).

snare ● *noun* **1** a trap for catching birds or animals, esp. with a noose of wire or cord. **2** a thing that acts as a temptation. **3** a device for tempting an enemy etc. to expose himself or herself to danger, failure, loss, capture, defeat, etc. **4** *Music* **a** (in *sing.* or *pl.*) twisted strings of gut, hide, or wire stretched across the lower head of a drum to produce a rattling sound. **b** (in full **snare drum**) a drum fitted with snares. ● *transitive verb* **1** catch (a bird etc.) in a snare. **2** ensnare; lure or trap (a person) with a snare. **3** grab; catch (*snared a seat*; *snared the ball*). □ **snar·er** *noun* (also in *combination*). [Old English *snearе* from Old Norse *snara*: sense 4 prob. from Middle Low German or Middle Dutch]

snarf *transitive & intransitive verb* (also **snarf·le**) esp. *N Amer. slang* eat or drink greedily. [origin obscure]

snarky *adjective informal* (**snark·i·er**, **snark·i·est**) sharply critical, cutting; irritable. [19th c. dial *snark* (v.), 'find fault with, nag' + -Y¹]

snarl¹ ● *verb* **1** *intransitive* (of a dog) make an angry growl with bared teeth. **2** *intransitive* (of a person) make bad-tempered complaints or criticisms. **3** *transitive* (often foll. by *out*) **a** utter in a snarling tone. **b** express (discontent etc.) by snarling. ● *noun* the act or sound of snarling. □ **snarl·er** *noun* **snarl·ing·ly** *adverb* **snarly** *adjective* (**snarl·i·er**, **snarl·i·est**). [earlier *snar* from (Middle) Low German, Middle High German *snarren*]

snarl² ● *verb* **1** *transitive* (often foll. by *up*) twist; entangle; confuse and hamper the movement of (traffic etc.). **2** *intransitive* (often foll. by *up*) become entangled, congested, or confused. ● *noun* a knot or tangle. [Middle English from *snare* (n. & v.)]

snarl-up *noun Cdn & Brit. informal* **1** a traffic jam. **2** a muddle or mistake.

snatch ● *verb* **1** take or seize something quickly or roughly (*snatched the book away from me*). **2 a** steal (a wallet, purse, etc.). **b** kidnap (esp. a child). **3** take or get something quickly, esp. when a chance to do so occurs (*snatch an hour's rest*; *snatched a bite to eat*). **4** (foll. by *away*, *from*) take away or from esp. suddenly (*snatched away my hand*). **5** (foll. by *from*) rescue narrowly (*snatched from the jaws of death*). **6** (foll. by *at*) **a** try to take something with the hands. **b** take (an offer, opportunity, etc.) eagerly. ● *noun* **1** an act of snatching (*made a snatch at it*). **2** a fragment of a song or talk etc. (*caught a snatch of their conversation*). **3** *esp. N Amer. slang* a kidnapping. **4** (in weightlifting) a movement in which a barbell is raised rapidly from the floor to above the head, followed by a straightening of the knees. **5** a short period of doing something (*slept in snatches*). **6** *coarse slang* the female genitals. □ **snatch·er** *noun* (esp. in sense 2b of *verb*). **snatchy** *adjective* [Middle English *snecchen*, *sna(c)che*, perhaps related to SNACK]

snaz·zy *adjective* (**snaz·zi·er**, **snaz·zi·est**) *slang* smart or fashionable. □ **snaz·zi·ly** *adverb* **snaz·zi·ness** *noun* [20th c.: origin unknown]

Snead /ˈsniːd/ **Sam** (full name Samuel Jackson Snead) (1912–2002), US golfer. He won numerous championships, including the Canadian Open (1938; 1940; 1941), the Masters (1949; 1952; 1954), the British Open (1946), and the PGA (1942; 1949; 1951).

sneak ● *verb* (*past* and *past participle* **snuck** or **sneaked**) **1** *intransitive & transitive* (foll. by *in*, *out*, *past*, *away*, etc.) go quietly and secretly in the direction specified. **2** *transitive informal* take or do something secretly, often without permission (*snuck a chocolate from the box*). ¶ There is a long tradition of objection to *snuck*, though it is in fact more common than *sneaked* in spoken English, fiction, and journalism, and is for many people the only form used. It may, however, be safer to use *sneaked* in formal writing. ● *noun* **1** a cowardly deceitful person, esp. one who informs on others. **2** (in *pl.*) *informal* sneakers. ● *adjective* acting or done without warning; secret (*a sneak attack*). □ **sneak up** approach a person or thing quietly and stealthily (*he's always sneaking up on me to eavesdrop*). □ **sneak·ing·ly** *adverb* [16th c., prob. dial.: perhaps related to Middle English *snike*, Old English *snican* creep]

sneak·er *noun* = RUNNING SHOE. □ **sneak·ered** *adjective*

sneaker·net *noun informal* the transmission of files between computers through the use of disks or other physically-transported storage devices.

sneak·ing *adjective* **1** furtive; undisclosed (*have a sneaking affection for her*). **2** = SNEAKY 2.

sneak preview *noun* a special showing of a new film, exhibition, etc. to certain people before it is shown to the general public.

sneak thief *noun* a thief who steals without breaking in; a pickpocket.

sneaky *adjective* (**sneak·i·er**, **sneak·i·est**) **1** given to or characterized by sneaking; furtive. **2** persistent in one's mind; nagging (*a sneaky feeling that it is not right*). □ **sneak·i·ly** *adverb* **sneak·i·ness** *noun*

sneer ● *noun* a derisive smile or remark. ● *verb* **1** *intransitive* (often foll. by *at*) smile derisively. **2** *transitive* say sneeringly. **3** *intransitive* (often foll. by *at*) speak derisively esp. covertly or ironically (*sneered at her attempts*). □ **sneer·er** *noun* **sneer·ing** *adjective* **sneer·ing·ly** *adverb* [16th c.: origin unknown]

sneeze ● *noun* **1** a sudden involuntary expulsion of air from the nose and mouth caused by irritation of the nostrils. **2** the sound of this. ● *intransitive verb* make a sneeze. □ **sneeze at** (usu. with *neg.*) regard as of little value, note, or importance; despise, disregard, underrate. □ **sneez·er** *noun* **sneezy** *adjective* [Middle English *snese*, apparently alteration of obsolete *fnese* from Old English *-fnēsan*, Old Norse *fnȳsa* & replacing earlier and less expressive *nese*]

sneeze guard *noun* a plexiglass barrier shielding food in public places, e.g. over a salad bar.

sneeze·wort /ˈsniːzwɜrt, -wɔrt/ *noun* (also **sneeze·weed**) a kind of yarrow, *Achillea ptarmica*, whose dried leaves are used to induce sneezing.

snell *N Amer.* ● *noun* a short line of nylon, gut, etc. by which a fish hook is attached to a longer line. ● *transitive verb* tie or fasten (a hook) to a line. [origin unknown]

Sne Nay Muxw /snəˈneimuk/ *noun* (also **Xwe Nal Mewx**) **1** a member of an Aboriginal people inhabiting lower Vancouver Island and the mainland north of Vancouver and around the Fraser River delta. **2** the Salishan language of this people. *Also called* COAST SALISH. [Salishan = 'the great and mighty people']

snick¹ ● *transitive verb* cut a small notch or incision in. ● *noun* a small notch or cut. [18th c.: prob. from *snick-a-snee* fight with knives]

snick² ● *noun* a slight, sharp sound; a click. ● *verb* **1** *intransitive* make a sharp clicking noise. **2** *transitive* snap or click (a trigger, gun, etc.). [imitative]

snick·er ● *noun* **1** a half-suppressed secretive laugh. **2** a whinny, a neigh. ● *intransitive verb* **1** make such a laugh. **2** whinny, neigh. □ **snick·er·ing·ly** *adverb* [imitative]

snide *adjective* (of a person, remark, etc.) sneering; slyly derogatory; insinuating. □ **snide·ly** *adverb* **snide·ness** *noun* [19th-c. informal: origin unknown]

sniff ● *verb* **1** *intransitive* draw up air audibly through the nose. **2** *intransitive* clear one's nose by sniffing. **3** *intransitive* express disdain, contempt, etc. by sniffing. **4** *intransitive* smell by sniffing. **5** *transitive* draw in the scent of (food, drink, flowers, etc.) through the nose. **6** *transitive & intransitive informal* take (a drug etc.) by breathing it in through the nose. **7** *transitive* (often foll. by *up*) draw in (a scent etc.) through the nose. **8** *transitive* perceive as if by smell; discover, suspect. **9** *transitive* **a** say (something) in a complaining way. **b** say (something) in a proud or disdainful way. ● *noun* **1** an act or sound of sniffing. **2** the amount of air etc. sniffed up. **3** a hint or intimation (*left at the first sniff of danger*). □ **sniff around** search around, esp. in an underhanded way. **sniff at 1** try the smell of; show interest in. **2** show contempt for or discontent with. **sniff out** detect; discover by investigation. □ **sniff·able** *adjective* [Middle English, imitative]

sniff·er *noun* **1** a person who sniffs, esp. one who sniffs a drug or toxic substance (*glue sniffer*). **2** *informal* the nose. **3** *informal* any device for detecting gas, radiation, etc. **4** (in full **sniffer program**) a computer program that detects and records a variety of restricted information, esp. the secret passwords needed to gain access to files or networks.

sniffer dog *noun informal* a dog trained to sniff out drugs or explosives.

snif·fle ● *intransitive verb* sniff slightly or repeatedly, esp. as a result of weeping. ● *noun* **1** the act of sniffling. **2** (in *sing.* or *pl.*) a cold in the head causing a running nose and sniffling. □ **snif·fler** *noun* **snif·fly** *adjective* [imitative: compare SNIVEL]

sniffy *adjective* (**sniff·i·er**, **sniff·i·est**) *informal* **1** disdainful; contemptuous. **2** inclined to sniff. □ **sniff·i·ly** *adverb* **sniff·i·ness** *noun*

snif·ter *noun* **1** esp. *N Amer.* a short-stemmed glass with a large bowl tapering towards the top, used for drinking brandy. **2** *slang* a small drink of alcohol. [dial. *snift* sniff, perhaps from Scandinavian: imitative]

snig·ger ● *noun* = SNICKER *noun* 1. ● *intransitive verb* = SNICKER *verb* 1. □ **snig·ger·er** *noun* **snig·ger·ing·ly** *adverb* [var. of SNICKER]

snip ● *verb* (**snipped**, **snip·ping**) **1** *transitive & intransitive* cut (cloth, a hole, etc.) with scissors or shears, esp. in small quick strokes. **2** *transitive* cut off or remove (something) in this way (*snip small bunches of grapes*). ● *noun* **1** an act of snipping. **2** a piece of material etc. snipped off. **3** (in *pl.*) hand shears for metal cutting. **4** *N Amer. informal* **a** an insignificant person. **b** an irritating or impertinent person. **5** *Brit. informal* **a** something easily achieved. **b** a bargain; something cheaply acquired. □ **snip at** make snipping strokes at. □ **snip·per** *noun* **snip·ping** *noun* [Low German & Dutch *snippen* imitative]

snipe ● *noun* **1** (*pl.* same or **snipes**) any of various wading birds, esp. of the genus *Gallinago*, with a long straight bill and frequenting marshes. **2** (*pl.* **snipes**) the act or an instance of sniping. ● *intransitive verb* **1** fire shots from hiding usu. at long range. **2** (foll. by *at*) make a sly critical attack. **3** hunt for or shoot snipe. □ **sniping** *noun* [Middle English, prob. from Scandinavian: compare Icelandic *mȳrisnípa*, & Middle Dutch, Middle Low German *snippe*, Old High German *snepfa*]

sniper *noun* **1** a person, e.g. a soldier, who shoots others from hiding, usu. at long range. **2** *Hockey informal* a proficient shooter.

snip·pet *noun* a small fragment or bit (*snippets of cloth*; *a snippet of information*). □ **snip·pety** *adjective*

snip·py *adjective* (**snip·pi·er**, **snip·pi·est**) *informal* impertinently brusque. □ **snip·pi·ly** *adverb* **snip·pi·ness** *noun*

snit *noun N Amer.* a state of agitation, irritation, pique, etc. (*she's always in a snit*). [20th c.: origin unknown]

snitch ● *verb slang* **1** *transitive* steal. **2** *intransitive* (often foll. by *on*) inform on a person. ● *noun* an informer. [17th c.: origin unknown]

snitch line *noun esp. Cdn* a telephone number which a person can call anonymously in order to report another's non-compliance with particular laws, regulations, etc.

snivel /ˈsnɪvəl/ ● *intransitive verb* (**sniv·elled**, **sniv·el·ling**; esp. *US* **sniv·eled**, **sniv·el·ing**) **1** cry and sniff in a miserable way. **2** complain, esp. in a miserable, crying voice. **3 a** have a runny nose. **b** make a repeated sniffing sound. ● *noun* **1** running mucus. **2** hypocritical talk; cant. □ **sniv·el·ler** *noun* **sniv·el·ling** *adjective* **sniv·el·ling·ly** *adverb* **sniv·el·ly** *adjective* [Old English *snyflan* (unrecorded) from *snofl* mucus: compare SNUFFLE]

snob *noun* **1 a** a person with an exaggerated respect for social position or wealth. **b** a person who seeks to cultivate people considered socially superior. **c** (*attributive*) related to or characteristic of these attitudes. **2** a person who is condescending to others whose (usu. specified) tastes or attainments are considered inferior (*an intellectual snob*; *a wine snob*). □ **snob·bery** *noun* (*pl.* **-ies**). **snob·bish** *adjective* **snob·bish·ly** *adverb* **snob·bish·ness** *noun* **snob·bism** *noun* **snob·by** *adjective* (**snob·bi·er**, **snob·bi·est**). [18th c. (now dial.) 'cobbler': origin unknown]

snob appeal *noun* an item's attractiveness to those with an exaggerated opinion of their own tastes.

sno-cone *N Amer.* var. of SNOW CONE.

snog *Brit. slang* ● *transitive & intransitive verb* (**snogged**, **snog·ging**) engage in kissing and caressing. ● *noun* a period of snogging. □ **snog·ger** *noun* [20th c.: origin unknown]

snood *noun* **1** an ornamental hairnet usu. worn at the back of the head. **2** a ring of woollen etc. material worn as a hood. **3** *hist.* a ribbon or band worn by unmarried women in Scotland to confine their hair. [Old English *snōd*]

snook¹ /snuːk/ *noun slang* a contemptuous gesture with the thumb to the nose and the fingers spread out. □ **cock a snook** (often foll. by *at*) **1** make this gesture. **2** register one's contempt (for a person, establishment, etc.). [19th c.: origin unknown]

snook² /snuːk/ *noun* any of various fishes, esp. Caribbean food fishes of the family Centropomidae, inferior *Centropomus undecimalis*. [Dutch *snoek* PIKE¹, from Middle Low German *snōk*, prob. related to SNACK]

snook·er /ˈsnʊkər, ˈsnuːk-/ ● *noun* **1** a game played with cues on a rectangular baize-covered table in which the players use a (white) cue ball to pocket the other balls (15 red and 6 variously coloured) in a set order. **2** a position in this game in which a direct shot at a permitted ball is impossible. ● *transitive verb* **1** (also *reflexive*) subject (oneself or another player) to a snooker. **2** *slang* (usu. in *passive*) **a** defeat; thwart. **b** trick; dupe. [19th c.: origin unknown]

snoop *informal* ● *intransitive verb* look around a place secretly in order to find something, obtain information, etc. ● *noun* **1** an act of snooping. **2 a** a person who snoops. **b** a detective. □ **snoop·er** *noun* **snoopy** *adjective* [Dutch *snœpen* eat on the sly]

snoose /snuːs/ *noun N Amer. informal* chewing tobacco. [Danish, Norwegian, Swedish *snus* snuff]

snoot *noun informal* **1** the nose. **2** a person who shows contempt for those considered to be of a lower social class (also *attributive*: *a snoot girls' school*). [var. of SNOUT]

snoot·ful *noun informal* a quantity of alcohol, esp. one sufficient to cause drunkenness (*you've already had a snootful*).

snooty *adjective* (**snoot·i·er**, **snoot·i·est**) *informal* snobbish; conceited; contemptuous. □ **snoot·i·ly** *adverb* **snoot·i·ness** *noun* [20th c.: origin unknown]

snooze *informal* ● *noun* **1** a short sleep, esp. in the daytime. **2** *N Amer. informal* something boring or tedious (*that meeting was a real snooze!*). **3** (*attributive*) designating a function, button, etc. on an alarm clock or clock radio which turns off the alarm or radio for a short, fixed period of time, and then reactivates it. ● *intransitive verb* take a snooze. □ **snoozy** *adjective* (**snooz·i·er**, **snooz·i·est**). [18th-c. slang: origin unknown]

snooz·er *noun* **1** a person who snoozes. **2** *N Amer. informal* something boring or tedious.

sno-pitch *noun* (also **snow pitch**) esp. *Cdn* a game similar to slo-pitch, played on snow.

snore ● *noun* a snorting or grunting sound in breathing during sleep.

● *intransitive verb* make this sound. □ **snor·er** *noun* [Middle English, prob. imitative: compare SNORT]

snor·kel ● *noun* **1** a breathing tube for an underwater swimmer. **2** a device for supplying air to a submerged submarine. ● *intransitive verb* (**snor·kelled, snor·kel·ling** or **snor·keled, snor·kel·ing**) use a snorkel. □ **snor·kel·ler** *noun* [German *Schnorchel*]

snort ● *noun* **1** an explosive sound made by the sudden forcing of breath through the nose, esp. expressing indignation or incredulity. **2** a similar sound made by an engine etc. **3** *informal* a small drink of liquor. **4** *slang* an inhaled dose of a (usu. illegal) powdered drug. ● *verb* **1** *intransitive* make a snort. **2** *intransitive* (of an engine etc.) make a sound resembling this. **3** *transitive & intransitive slang* inhale (a usu. illegal narcotic drug, esp. cocaine or heroin). **4** *transitive* utter (words) or express (defiance etc.) by snorting. [Middle English, prob. imitative: compare SNORE]

snort·er *noun* **1** a person or animal that snorts. **2** *Brit. informal* **a** something very impressive or difficult. **b** something vigorous or violent.

snot *noun slang* **1** nasal mucus. **2** a contemptible person. [prob. from Middle Dutch, Middle Low German *snotte*, Middle High German *snuz*, related to SNOUT]

snot-nosed *adjective* (also **snotty-nosed**) **1** = SNOTTY. **2** *informal* childish or inexperienced (*some impudent snot-nosed kid*).

snot rag *noun slang* a facial tissue or handkerchief.

snot·ty *adjective* (**snot·ti·er, snot·ti·est**) *slang* **1** producing or covered with snot. **2** showing a superior attitude towards others; conceited. **3** contemptible. □ **snot·ti·ly** *adverb* **snot·ti·ness** *noun*

snout *noun* **1** the projecting nose and mouth of an animal. **2** *derogatory* a person's nose. **3** the pointed front of a thing; a nozzle. **4** *Brit. slang* tobacco or a cigarette. □ **snout·ed** *adjective* (also in *combination*). **snouty** *adjective* [Middle Dutch, Middle Low German *snūt*]

snout beetle *noun* a weevil.

Snow ▶ 1 Charles Percy, 1st Baron Snow of Leicester (1905–80), English novelist and scientist. The title novel of his sequence of 11 novels *Strangers and Brothers* appeared in 1940; the series, which also includes *The Masters* (1951) and *The Corridors of Power* (1964), deals with moral dilemmas and power struggles in the academic world. **2 Clar·ence Eu·gene** ('Hank') (1914–1999), Canadian singer and songwriter. Singing professionally by 1929, he signed his first record contract in 1936. In 1950 he released 'I'm Movin' On', which established his career in the US; he became one of the top country artists of the 1950s. **3 Mi·chael James Aleck** (b.1929), Canadian painter, photographer, and filmmaker. He is perhaps best known for his series of works in various media based on a woman's silhouette, *Walking Woman Works* (1961–7). He has also made films, including *Presents* (1981).

snow ● *noun* **1** atmospheric vapour frozen into ice crystals and falling to earth in light white flakes. **2** a fall of this, or a layer of it on the ground. **3** a thing resembling snow in whiteness or texture etc. **4** a mass of flickering white spots on a television or radar screen, caused by interference or a poor signal. **5** *slang* cocaine. **6** a dessert or other dish resembling snow. **7** frozen carbon dioxide. ● *verb* **1** *intransitive* (of snow) fall (*it is snowing; if it snows*). **2** *transitive* (foll. by *in, over, up*, etc.) confine or block with large quantities of snow. **3** *transitive & intransitive* sprinkle or scatter or fall as or like snow. **4** *transitive N Amer. slang* deceive or charm with plausible words. □ **be snowed under** be overwhelmed, esp. with work. □ **snow·less** *adjective* **snow·like** *adjective* [Old English *snāw* from Germanic]

snow angel *noun N Amer.* the outline of an angel made by lying on one's back in the snow and sweeping one's arms and legs back and forth.

Snow Apple *noun* a variety of apple grown esp. in Quebec from the 17th to the 19th c. [from the whiteness of its flesh]

snow·ball ● *noun* **1** snow packed together or rolled into a ball, esp. for throwing. **2** any of various plants, esp. of the honeysuckle family, bearing rounded clusters of white flowers. ● *intransitive verb* grow or increase rapidly (*the idea just snowballed from there*). □ **not a snowball's chance in hell** *informal* no chance at all (*he hasn't got a snowball's chance in hell of winning this race*).

snowball effect *noun* the tendency of an event, action, idea, etc. to grow or increase, as a snowball does in rolling down a hill.

snowball tree *noun* = GUELDER ROSE.

snow·bank *noun* a heap or mound of snow, esp. one caused by plowing or drifting.

snow bear *noun* a white kermode bear.

snow·belt *noun N Amer.* a region subject to heavy snowfalls.

snow·berry *noun* (*pl.* **-berries**) **1** any shrub of the genus *Symphoricarpos*, with white berries. **2** (in full **creeping snowberry**) a wintergreen, *Gaultheria hispidula*, with an edible white berry.

snow·bird *noun* **1** *N Amer. informal* a person from Canada or the northern US who moves to a southern state in the winter. **2** any of various small birds resembling the finch, esp. the snow bunting or junco.

snow-blind *adjective* temporarily blinded by the glare of light reflected by large expanses of snow. □ **snow-blinded** *adjective* **snow blindness** *noun*

snow blower *noun* a machine that clears snow by blowing it to one side.

snow·board *noun* a wide board like a ski, ridden in a standing position, used for sliding downhill on snow. □ **snow·board·er** *noun* **snow·board·ing** *noun*

snow boot *noun* a usu. insulated boot for wearing in the winter.

snow·bound *adjective* prevented by snow from going out or travelling.

snow bunting *noun* a mainly white finch, *Plectrophenax nivalis*, which breeds in the Arctic and migrates further south in autumn, often seen in flocks on snow-covered fields.

snow·cap *noun* the tip of a mountain when covered with snow. □ **snow-capped** *adjective*

snow·cat *noun* a vehicle with caterpillar tracks for travelling through snow, esp. an enclosed one used for grooming ski trails, transporting skiers, etc.

snow·coach *noun* (also **sno·coach**) an enclosed bus-like vehicle with large tires or caterpillar tracks used esp. to take sightseeing tourists through snowy terrain.

snow cone *noun* (also **sno-cone**) *N Amer.* a paper cone filled with crushed ice flavoured with fruit syrup.

snow crab *noun* an edible spider crab, *Chionoecetes opilio*, found off the eastern coast of Canada.

snow devil *noun N Amer.* a whirling column of snow sucked up by the wind.

Snowdon, Mount a mountain in NW Wales. Rising to 1 085 m (3,560 ft.), it is the highest mountain in Wales.

Snow·donia /snoʊˈdoʊniə/ a massif region in Gwynedd, NW Wales. Its highest peak is Mount Snowdon.

snow·drift *noun* a bank of snow heaped up by the action of the wind.

snow·drop *noun* a bulbous plant, *Galanthus nivalis*, with white drooping flowers in the early spring.

snow·fall *noun* **1** a fall of snow. **2** the amount of snow that falls on one occasion or on a given area within a given time.

snow fence *noun* a usu. portable fence erected on the windward side of a road, building, etc., serving as a barrier to drifting snow. □ **snow fencing** *noun*

snow·field *noun* a permanent wide expanse of snow in mountainous or polar regions.

snow·flake *noun* **1** each of the small collections of crystals in which snow falls. **2 a** any bulbous plant of the genus *Leucojum*, with flowers similar to those of the snowdrop. **b** the white flower of this plant.

snow·flea *noun* a small, dark blue, cylindrical springtail, *Achorutes nivicola*, living in leaf litter, and appearing in swarms on the surface of snow in the spring.

snow flurry *noun* = FLURRY *noun* 1a.

snow globe *noun* (also **snow dome**) a trinket consisting of a figurine etc. encased in a clear water-filled sphere with small white particles that swirl about like snow when the sphere is shaken.

snow goggles *plural noun* (also **snow glasses**) *N Amer.* slotted goggles of wood, bone, etc., worn as a protection against snow blindness.

snow golf *noun* a form of golf played on packed snow, using a coloured golf ball.

snow goose *noun* an Arctic goose, *Chen* (or *Anser*) *caerulescens*, usu. white with black-tipped wings (see also BLUE GOOSE).

snow house *noun N Amer.* a structure made of blocks of snow, e.g. an igloo.

snow-in-summer *noun* a low-growing plant, *Cerastium tomentosum*, with masses of white flowers, often cultivated in rock gardens.

snow job *noun* esp. *N Amer.* an attempt to deceive or persuade (a person), esp. through flattery.

snow knife *noun Cdn* a knife with a long, broad blade, used for cutting blocks of snow in building an igloo.

snow leopard *noun* an Asian wild cat, *Panthera uncia*, with leopard-like markings on a cream-coloured coat. Also called OUNCE².

snow lily *noun* = AVALANCHE LILY.

snow line *noun* the level, e.g. on a mountain, above which snow never melts entirely.

snow machine *noun N Amer.* a motor vehicle designed to travel over snow.

snow-making *noun* the production of artificial snow (often *attributive*: *snow-making machine*).

snow·man *noun (pl. -men)* a figure resembling a person, made of packed snow.

snow·melt *noun* **1** the melting of fallen snow, esp. in the spring. **2** the water that results from this.

snow·mobile *noun* a motor vehicle equipped with runners and Caterpillar tracks for travelling over snow. □ **snow·mobil·er** *noun* **snow·mobil·ing** *noun*

snowmobile boot *noun Cdn* a high, heavy snow boot worn esp. when snowmobiling.

snowmobile suit *noun N Amer.* a one-piece outer garment combining both coat and pants, worn outdoors in winter.

snow owl *noun* = SNOWY OWL.

snow·pack *noun N Amer.* the accumulation of winter snow, compressed and hardened by its own weight.

snow-packed *adjective N Amer.* (of a road, etc.) covered with a layer of hard packed snow.

snow pants *plural noun* a pair of pants worn over regular leggings in wintery conditions, usu. of padded nylon.

snow partridge *noun* a mainly white partridge, *Lerwa lerwa*.

snow pea *noun* esp. *N Amer.* a variety of pea with an edible pod, eaten esp. when the pod is young and flat.

snow pitch *var. of* SNO-PITCH.

snow·plow (also **snow·plough**) ● *noun* **1** a device, or a vehicle equipped with one, for clearing roads etc. of snow. **2** *Skiing* a technique for slowing down or stopping in which the points of the skis are turned inwards. ● *verb* **1** *transitive & intransitive* clear (a road etc.) of snow using a snowplow. **2** *intransitive Skiing* execute a snowplow.

snow route *noun N Amer.* a major arterial road in a city which is designated for priority snow clearing after heavy snowfalls.

snow·scape *noun* **1** a snowy landscape. **2** a picture of this.

snow·shed *noun* a structure built over a railway, highway, etc. to provide protection from avalanches.

snow·shoe ● *noun* a flat device like a racquet attached to a boot for walking on snow without sinking in. ● *intransitive verb* (**snow·shoed**, **snow·shoe·ing**) travel on snowshoes. □ **snow·shoer** *noun*

snowshoe hare *noun* (also **snowshoe rabbit**) a N American hare, *Lepus americanus*, with large hind feet and a white coat in winter.

snow shovel *noun* a shovel used to clear snow from a sidewalk, driveway, etc.

snow·slide *noun* = AVALANCHE.

snow·snake *noun N Amer.* **1** an Indian game in which a straight wooden rod having a weighted head like that of a snake is slid over a smooth field of snow or down specially constructed runways. **2** the rod used in this game.

snow·storm *noun* a heavy fall of snow, esp. with a high wind.

snow·suit *noun N Amer.* a one- or two-piece outer garment combining both coat and pants, worn outdoors in winter esp. by children.

snow·throw·er *noun N Amer.* = SNOW BLOWER.

snow tire *noun* a tire equipped with deep treads etc. to give increased traction on snow or ice.

snow-white *adjective* pure white.

snowy *adjective* (**snow·i·er**, **snow·i·est**) **1 a** of or like snow. **b** pure white. **2** (of the weather etc.) with much snow. **3** covered with snow (*snowy fields*). □ **snow·i·ness** *noun*

snowy owl *noun* a large white owl, *Nyctea scandiaca*, native to the Arctic.

snub ● *transitive verb* (**snubbed**, **snub·bing**) **1** rebuff or humiliate with sharp words or a marked lack of cordiality. **2** check the movement of (a boat, horse, etc.) esp. by a rope wound around a post etc. ● *noun* an act of snubbing; a rebuff. ● *adjective* short and blunt in shape. □ **snub·ber** *noun* **snub·bing·ly** *adverb* [Old Norse *snubba* chide, check the growth of]

snub nose *noun* a short turned-up nose. □ **snub-nosed** *adjective*

snuck *past and past participle of* SNEAK.

snuff¹ ● *noun* the charred part of a candle wick. ● *transitive verb* **1** smother the flame of (a candle). **2** trim the snuff from (a candle). **3** *slang* kill (a person). □ **snuff it** *esp. Brit. slang* die. **snuff out** **1** extinguish by snuffing. **2** kill; put an end to. [Middle English *snoffe*, *snuffe*: origin unknown]

snuff² ● *noun* powdered tobacco taken by sniffing it up the nostrils. ● *intransitive verb* take snuff. □ **up to snuff** *informal* **1** up to standard. **2** *Brit.* knowing; not easily deceived. [Dutch *snuf* (*tabak* tobacco) from Middle Dutch *snuffen* snuffle]

snuff box *noun* a small usu. ornamental box for holding snuff.

snuf·fer *noun* **1** a small hollow cone with a handle used to extinguish a candle. **2** (in *pl.*) an implement like scissors used to extinguish a candle or trim its wick.

snuff film *noun* (also **snuff video**, **snuff movie**, etc.) *slang* a pornographic film depicting an actual murder.

snuf·fle ● *verb* **1** *intransitive* make sniffing sounds. **2 a** *intransitive* speak nasally, whiningly, or like one with a cold. **b** *transitive* say in this way. **3** *intransitive* breathe noisily as through a partially blocked nose. **4** *intransitive* sniff. ● *noun* **1** a snuffling sound or tone. **2** (in *pl.*) a partial blockage of the nose causing snuffling. **3** a sniff. □ **snuf·fler** *noun* **snuf·fly** *adjective* [prob. from Low German & Dutch *snuffelen* (as SNUFF²): compare SNIVEL]

snug ● *adjective* (**snug·ger**, **snug·gest**) **1** comfortably warm and cozy. **2** secure and sheltered (*a snug harbour*). **3** compact and well-organized. **4** (of clothing etc.) close-fitting. **5** fitting exactly (*make sure that the nuts are snug but not too tight*). **6** (of an income etc.) allowing comfort and comparative ease. ● *transitive verb* make snug. ● *noun Brit.* a small room in a pub or inn. □ **snug·ly** *adverb* **snug·ness** *noun* [16th c. (originally Naut.): prob. of Low German or Dutch origin]

snug·gery *noun* (*pl.* -ies) **1** a snug place, esp. a person's private room or den. **2** = SNUG *noun*.

snug·gle *transitive & intransitive verb* **1** (often foll. by *up*, *down*, etc.) lie or get close to a person or thing for warmth, comfort, or affection. **2** place something into a warm comfortable position. [SNUG + -LE⁴]

snug·gly *adjective* comfortably warm, cosy (*a snuggly blanket*).

Snug·li *noun N Amer.* *proprietary* a pouch used for carrying a baby. [SNUGGLE]

snye /snaɪ/ *noun Cdn* **1** (*E Ont.*) a side channel, esp. one that bypasses a falls or rapids and rejoins the main river downstream, creating an island. **2 a** a narrow or meandering side channel, esp. one that comes to a dead end. **b** such a channel used by bush pilots for landing aircraft. [Canadian French *chenail*, French *chenal* channel]

SO *abbreviation N Amer.* SIGNIFICANT OTHER.

So. *abbreviation* South.

so¹ ● *adverb* **1** (often foll. by *that* + clause) to such an extent, or to the extent implied (*why are you so angry?*; *do stop complaining so*; *they were so pleased that they gave us a bonus*). **2** (with *neg.*; often foll. by *as* + clause) to the extent to which ... is or does etc., or to the extent implied (*was not so late as I expected*; *am not so eager as you*). ¶ In positive constructions *as ... as ... is* used: see AS¹. **3** (foll. by *that* or *as* + clause) to the degree or in the manner implied (*so expensive that few can afford it*; *so small as to be invisible*; *am not so foolish as to agree to that*). **4** (adding emphasis) to that extent; in that or a similar manner (*I want to leave and so does she*; *you said it was good, and so it is*). **5** to a great or notable degree (*I am so glad*; *it's so expensive*). **6** in the way described (*am not very fond of it but may become so*). **7** (with verb of saying or thinking etc.) as previously mentioned or described (*I think so*; *so they said*; *so I should hope*). **8** *informal* used to emphatically contradict a negative statement (*it is so!*). **9** *slang* (as an intensifier modifying a word or phrase that would not normally allow for comparison) extremely (*that's so not my problem*; *they're so 1990s*; *it so could have been a disaster*). ¶ Not used in formal speech or writing. ● *conjunction* (often foll. by *that* + clause) **1** with the result that (*there was none left, so we had to go without*). **2** in order that (*came home early so that I could see you*). **3** and then; as the next step (*so then the car broke down*; *and so to bed*). **4 a** (introducing a question) then; after that (*so what did you tell them?*). **b** = SO WHAT? ● *adjective* in conformity with reality; true as reported (*please say it isn't so*; *can it be so?*). ● *pronoun* **1** something that is near or approximate to the number in question (*only six or so remained*). **2** used as a substitute for a clause of sentence (*you'll do it because I said so*). ● *interjection* expressing shock, surprise, indifference, inquiry, etc. □ **and so on** (also **and so forth**) **1** and others of the same kind. **2** and in other similar ways. **so as** (foll. by *to* + infin.) in order to (*did it so as to get it finished*). **so be it** an expression of acceptance or resignation. **so far** *see* FAR. **so far as** *see* FAR. **so far**

so good *see* FAR. **so long!** *informal* goodbye till we meet again. **so long as** *see* LONG[1]. **so much 1** a certain amount (of). **2** a great deal of (*is so much nonsense*). **3** (with *neg.*) **a** less than; to a lesser extent (*not so much forgotten as ignored*). **b** not even (*didn't give me so much as a penny*). **so much for** that is all that need be done or said about. **so to speak** (or **say**) an expression of reserve or apology for an exaggeration or neologism etc. **so what?** *informal* why should that be considered significant? [Old English *swā* etc.]

so² *noun* (also **soh, sol** /sɒl/) *Music* **1** (in tonic sol-fa) the fifth note of a major scale. **2** the note G in the fixed-do system. [*sol* from Middle English *sol* from Latin *solve*: see GAMUT]

-so *combining form* = -SOEVER.

soak ● *verb* **1** *transitive & intransitive* make or become thoroughly wet through saturation with or in liquid. **2** *transitive* (of rain etc.) drench. **3** *reflexive* (often foll. by *in*) immerse (oneself) in a subject of study etc. **4** *intransitive* (foll. by *in, into, through*) **a** (of liquid) make its way or penetrate by saturation. **b** (of sunlight) penetrate thoroughly. **5** *transitive* (foll. by *up*) **a** absorb (liquid). **b** acquire (knowledge, experiences, etc.) copiously. **c** expose oneself to (the sun, heat, etc.) so as to absorb the maximum possible. **6** *transitive* (foll. by *out, out of, off*, etc.) remove by soaking in water etc. (*trying to soak the stain out of the shirt; soaked the label off the jar*). **7** *transitive informal* extract money from by an extortionate charge, taxation, etc. (*soak the rich*). **8** *intransitive informal* drink persistently, booze. ● *noun* **1** the act of soaking or the state of being soaked. **2** *informal* a hard drinker. □ **soak·age** *noun* **soak·er** *noun* [Old English *socian* related to *soc* sucking at the breast, *sūcan* SUCK]

soaked *adjective* **1** thoroughly wet; drenched. **2** very drunk.

soaker hose *noun* a hose for watering gardens with perforations along its length allowing water to trickle out.

soak·ing ● *adjective* (in full **soaking wet**) very wet; wet through. ● *noun* the act of soaking; an instance of being soaked.

soaking tub *noun* N Amer. a large, deep bathtub.

so-and-so *noun* (pl. **so-and-sos**) **1** a particular person or thing not needing to be specified (*told me to do so-and-so*). **2** *informal* a person disliked or regarded with disfavour (*the so-and-so left me behind*).

soap ● *noun* **1** a cleansing agent that is a compound of fatty acid with soda or potash which, when rubbed in water, yields a lather used in washing. **2** *informal* = SOAP OPERA (also *attributive*: *soap fan*). ● *transitive verb* **1** apply soap to. **2** scrub or rub with soap. □ **soap·less** *adjective* [Old English *sāpe* from West Germanic]

soap·bark *noun* a S American tree, *Quillaja saponaria*, with bark yielding saponin.

soap·berry *noun* (pl. **-berries**) **1** = BUFFALO BERRY. **2** any of various tropical American shrubs, esp. of the genus *Sapindus*, with fruits yielding saponin.

soap·box *noun* **1** a makeshift stand for a public speaker. **2** something that provides an outlet for a person's opinions etc. (*her column is nothing but a soapbox*). **3** a child's homemade cart consisting of a wooden box mounted on wheels, and steerable at the front. **4** *hist.* an esp. wooden box for holding soap.

soapbox derby *noun* a race or competition between children in soapboxes.

soap flakes *plural noun* soap in the form of thin flakes, for washing clothes etc.

soap opera *noun* **1** a television or radio drama with continuous episodes about the events and problems in the daily lives of the same group of characters. **2** *informal* a series of sensational, unexpected, or melodramatic events (*I'm glad the whole soap opera's over*). □ **soap operatic** *adjective* [so called because originally sponsored in the US by soap manufacturers]

soap powder *noun* powdered soap esp. with additives.

soap·stone *noun* a soft metamorphic rock with a smooth greasy feel, composed of talc with micas etc., and readily sawn into slabs or carved. *Also called* STEATITE.

soap·suds *plural noun* = SUDS 1.

soap·wort /ˈsoːpwɜrt, -wɔrt/ *noun* a European plant, *Saponaria officinalis*, naturalized in N America, with pink or white flowers and leaves yielding a soapy substance. *Also called* BOUNCING BET.

soapy *adjective* (**soap·i·er, soap·i·est**) **1** of or like soap. **2** containing or smeared with soap. **3** of or like a soap opera. **4** (of a person or manner) unctuous or flattering.

soar *intransitive verb* **1** fly or rise high. **2** reach a high level or standard (*prices soared*). **3** maintain height in the air without flapping the wings or using power. **4** sing or play esp. in the higher ranges in a particularly impressive or moving manner. □ **soar·er** *noun* **soar·ing**

adjective **soar·ing·ly** *adverb* [Old French *essorer* ultimately from Latin (as EX-[1], *aura* breeze)]

Soave /ˈswɒvei/ *noun* a dry white wine produced in the region around Soave. [*Soave*, a town in N Italy]

SOB *abbreviation* esp. N Amer. *slang* SON OF A BITCH.

sob ● *verb* (**sobbed, sob·bing**) **1** *intransitive* **a** draw breath in convulsive gasps usu. with weeping under mental distress or physical exhaustion. **b** weep in this way. **2** *transitive* (usu. foll. by *out*) utter with sobs. **3** *reflexive* bring (oneself) to a specified state by sobbing (*sobbed themselves to sleep*). ● *noun* a convulsive drawing of breath, esp. in weeping. □ **sob·bing·ly** *adverb* [Middle English *sobbe* (prob. imitative)]

soba /ˈsoːbə/ *noun* (treated as *sing.* or *pl.*) Japanese noodles made from buckwheat flour. [Japanese]

so·ber ● *adjective* (**so·ber·er, so·ber·est**) **1** not affected by alcohol. **2** not given to excessive drinking of alcohol. **3** moderate, well-balanced, tranquil, sedate. **4** not fanciful or exaggerated (*the sober truth*). **5** (of a colour etc.) quiet and inconspicuous. **b** (of a meeting etc.) quiet and sedate. ● *transitive & intransitive verb* (often foll. by *down, up*) make or become sober or less wild, reckless, enthusiastic, visionary, etc. (*a sobering thought*). □ **sober as a judge** completely sober. □ **sober·ing·ly** *adverb* **sober·ly** *adverb* [Old French *sobre* from Latin *sobrius*]

sober sides *noun* a sedate, serious person. □ **sober-sided** *adjective*

So·bies·ki /sɒˈbjeski/ **John,** *see* JOHN III.

so·bri·ety /səˈbraiəti/ *noun* **1** the state of being sober. **2** moderation, esp. in the use of alcohol. **3** seriousness or sedateness. [Old French *sobrieté* (as SOBER)]

so·bri·quet /ˈsoːbriˌkei, ˌsoːbriˈkei, -ket/ *noun* (also **sou·bri·quet**) **1** a nickname. **2** an assumed name. [French, originally = 'tap under the chin']

sob sister *noun informal* a female journalist writing sentimental reports or answering readers' problems.

sob story *noun informal* a story or explanation intended to make the listener or reader feel sympathy or sadness, esp. one that fails to do so.

Soc. *abbreviation* **1** Socialist. **2** Society.

soc /soːʃ/ *noun* N Amer. *informal* sociology (also *attributive*: *soc prof*). [abbreviation]

soca /ˈsoːkə/ *noun* a kind of calypso music with elements of soul, originally from Trinidad. [SOUL + CALYPSO]

soc·age /ˈsɒkɪdʒ/ *noun* (also **soc·cage**) a feudal tenure of land involving payment of rent or other non-military service to a superior. [Anglo-French *socage* from *soc* from Old English *sōcn* SOKE]

SoCal *noun* Southern California (esp. *attributive*: *SoCal suburbs*).

so-called *adjective* commonly designated or known as, often incorrectly.

SOCAN /ˈsoːkan/ *abbreviation* (in Canada) Society of Composers, Authors and Music Publishers of Canada.

soc·cer *noun* a form of football played by two teams of 11 persons each, in which a round ball may be kicked or bounced off any part of the body except the arms and hands; only the goalkeeper is allowed to touch the ball with the hands. [Assoc. (as in ASSOCIATION FOOTBALL) + -ER[3]]

soccer mom *noun* esp. *US* a usu. middle-class suburban housewife committed to driving her children to their soccer games and practices, viewed esp. as a member of a particular class of voter or consumer.

Sochi /ˈsɒtʃi/ a port in SW Russia, situated in the western foothills of the Caucasus, on the Black Sea coast close to the border with Georgia; pop. (est. 2002) 366,100.

so·cia·ble /ˈsoːʃəbəl/ *adjective* **1** fitted for or liking the society of other people; ready and willing to talk and act with others. **2** (of a person's manner or behaviour etc.) friendly. **3** (of a meeting etc.) marked by friendliness, not stiff or formal. □ **so·cia·bil·i·ty** *noun* **so·cia·ble·ness** *noun* **so·cia·bly** *adverb* [French *sociable* or Latin *sociabilis* from *sociare* to unite, from *socius* companion]

so·cial ● *adjective* **1** of or relating to society or its organization. **2** concerned with the mutual relations of human beings or of classes of human beings. **3** living in organized communities; unfitted for a solitary life (*humans are social animals*). **4 a** needing companionship; gregarious, interdependent. **b** co-operative; practising the division of labour. **5** of or relating to activities in which people meet each other for pleasure (*social gatherings; a full social life*). **6** existing only as a member of a compound organism. **7 a** (of insects) living together in organized communities. **b** (of birds) nesting near each other in communities. **8** (of plants) growing thickly together and monopolizing the ground they grow on. ● *noun* **1** a social gathering, esp. one organized by a club, congregation, etc. **2** *Cdn* (*Prairies*) a public social gathering held before a wedding to raise money for the couple that is to be married. □ **so·cial·ity** /ˌsoːʃiˈaliti/ *noun* **so·cial·ly** *adverb* [French *social* or Latin *socialis* allied, from *socius* friend]

social anthropology *noun* = CULTURAL ANTHROPOLOGY.

social assistance *noun Cdn* = SOCIAL SECURITY.

social butterfly *noun* **1** a socialite; a person who is or claims to be prominent in fashionable society. **2** a person who attends a large number of social events.

social charter *noun* a document dealing with social policy, esp. outlining commitments to employment, housing, health care, etc.

social climber *noun derogatory* a person anxious to gain a higher social status. □ **social climbing** *noun* **social-climbing** *adjective*

social conscience *noun* a sense of responsibility or concern for the problems and injustices of society.

social contract *noun* (also **social compact**) a notional agreement between individuals and the state to co-operate for social benefits, e.g. by sacrificing some individual freedom for state protection.

social credit ● *noun* **1** the economic theory that the purchasing power of consumers should be increased either by subsidizing producers so that they can reduce prices or by distributing the profits of industry to the general public. **2** (**Social Credit**) *Cdn* the Social Credit party, its supporters, etc. **●** *adjective* (**Social Credit**) *Cdn* of or relating to the Social Credit Party.

Social Cred·it·er *noun Cdn* a member of the Social Credit Party.

Social Credit Party *noun Cdn* a political party formed in the 1930s espousing the economic theories of social credit, but soon evolving into a mainstream party with conservative financial and social policies.

social Darwinism *noun* a theory, advanced in the late 19th c., that individuals, groups, and peoples are subject to the same Darwinian laws of natural selection as plants and animals, and that superior individuals or groups survived and succeeded while the weaker disappeared, to the benefit of society. □ **social Darwinist** *noun*

social democracy *noun* a socialist system achieved by democratic means. □ **social democrat** *noun*

social drinker *noun* a person who drinks alcohol only at social gatherings etc.

social engineering *noun* the use of sociological principles in approaching social problems.

social exclusion *noun* exclusion from the prevailing social system and its rights and privileges, typically as a result of poverty or the fact of belonging to a minority social group.

social gospel *noun* the gospel interpreted as having a social application, esp. as used to advocate social reform. □ **social gospeller** *noun*

social housing *noun Cdn & Brit.* = PUBLIC HOUSING.

social insurance number *noun Cdn* a nine-digit number by which the federal government identifies individuals for the purposes of taxation, employment insurance, pensions, etc. Abbr.: **SIN**.

so·cial·ism *noun* **1** a political and economic theory of social organization which advocates that the community as a whole should own and control the means of production, distribution, and exchange. **2** policy or practice based on this theory. **3** (in Marxist theory) a transitional social state between the overthrow of capitalism and the realization of communism. □ **so·cial·ist** *noun & adjective* **so·cial·is·tic** *adjective* **so·cial·is·tic·ally** *adverb* [French *socialisme* (as SOCIAL)]

so·cial·ite *noun* a person who is well-known in fashionable society and goes to a lot of fashionable parties.

so·cial·ize *verb* (also esp. *Brit.* **-ise**) **1** *intransitive* act in a sociable manner. **2** *transitive* prepare for life in society. **3** *transitive* organize on socialistic principles. □ **so·cial·iz·a·tion** *noun*

socialized medicine *noun* esp. *US* often *derogatory* the provision of medical services for all from public funds.

social justice *noun* the notion that society should be organized in a way that allows equal opportunity for all its members (also *attributive*: *social justice issues*).

social life *noun* leisure activities in which one associates with one's friends and acquaintances.

social order *noun* the network of human relationships in society.

social realism *noun* the realistic depiction of social conditions or political views in art and literature. □ **social realist** *noun*

social science *noun* **1** the scientific study of human society and

social relationships. **2** a branch of this (e.g. politics or economics). □ **social scientist** *noun*

social secretary *noun* a person who makes arrangements for the social activities of a person or organization.

social security *noun* state assistance to those lacking in economic security and welfare, e.g. the aged and the unemployed.

social service *noun* (usu. in *pl.*) a service provided by the state or a charitable organization for the community, esp. education, health, and housing (also *attributive*: *social service agency*).

social studies *plural noun* (treated as *sing.*) a school course encompassing such subjects as geography, history, anthropology, sociology, etc. (*Joey always does well in social studies*).

social work *noun* work done to help people in the community with special needs. □ **social worker** *noun*

so·ci·e·ty *noun* (pl. **-eties**) **1** the sum of human conditions and activity regarded as a whole functioning interdependently. **2** a social community (*all societies must have firm laws*). **3 a** a social mode of life. **b** the customs and organization of an ordered community. **4** *Ecology* a plant community. **5 a** the socially advantaged or prominent members of a community (*society would not approve*). **b** this, or a part of it, qualified in some way (*is not done in polite society*). **6** participation in hospitality; other people's homes or company (*avoids society*). **7** companionship, company (*avoids the society of such people*). **8** an association of persons united by a common aim or interest or principle (*formed a music society*). □ **so·ciet·al** *adjective* (esp. in sense 1). **so·ciet·al·ly** *adverb* [French *société* from Latin *societas -tatis* from *socius* companion]

Society Islands a group of islands in the S Pacific, forming part of French Polynesia. [in honour of the Royal *Society*]

Society of Friends *noun see* QUAKER.

Society of Jesus *noun see* JESUIT.

socio- *combining form* **1** of society (and). **2** of or relating to sociology (and). [Latin *socius* companion]

socio·biol·ogy *noun* the scientific study of the biological aspects of social behaviour. □ **socio·bio·logic·al** *adjective* **socio·bio·logic·ally** *adverb* **socio·biol·o·gist** *noun*

socio-cultur·al *adjective* combining social and cultural factors or elements. □ **socio-cultur·ally** *adverb*

socio-econom·ic *adjective* relating to or concerned with the interaction of social and economic factors. □ **socio-econom·ic·ally** *adverb*

socio·linguis·tic *adjective* relating to or concerned with language in its social aspects. □ **socio·linguist** *noun* **socio·linguis·tic·ally** *adverb*

socio·linguis·tics *noun* the study of language in relation to social factors.

soci·ol·ogy *noun* **1** the study of the development, structure, and functioning of human society. **2** the study of social problems. □ **socio·logic·al** *adjective* **socio·logic·ally** *adverb* **soci·ol·o·gist** *noun*

soci·om·etry /ˌsoːsiˈɒmɪtri, ˌsoːʃi-/ *noun* the study of relationships within a group of people. □ **socio·metric** /-ɔˈmetrik/ *adjective*

socio·path *noun* a person with a personality disorder manifesting itself in extreme anti-social attitudes and behaviour, particularly a lack of moral responsibility or social conscience. □ **socio·path·ic** *adjective* **soci·op·athy** *noun* [SOCIO-, after PSYCHOPATH]

socio-political *adjective* combining social and political factors.

sock¹ ● *noun* (pl. **socks** or *informal* **sox**) **1** a short knitted covering for the foot, usu. not reaching the knee. **2** a removable inner sole put into a shoe for warmth etc. **3** an ancient Greek or Roman comic actor's light shoe. **4** = WINDSOCK. **●** *transitive verb* (usu. foll. by *away*) put money aside as savings (*they had millions socked away*). □ **in one's sock feet** *N Amer.* = IN ONE'S STOCKING FEET (see STOCKING). **knock** (or **blow**) **one's socks off** astound, amaze. **pull up one's socks** *informal* make an effort to improve. **put a sock in it** *informal* be quiet. **sock in** (of weather, esp. fog or snow) arrive and put a stop to all travel. [Old English *socc* from Latin *soccus* comic actor's shoe, light low-heeled slipper, from Greek *sukkhos*]

sock² *informal* **●** *transitive verb* hit (esp. a person) forcefully. **●** *noun* **1** a hard blow. **2** *N Amer.* the power to deliver a blow. □ **sock it to** attack or address (a person) vigorously. [c.1700 (cant): origin unknown]

socked in *adjective N Amer.* **1** (of an airport) closed because of snow, fog, etc. **2** (of an aircraft) grounded by adverse weather conditions. [SOCK¹, the airport windsock indicating adverse conditions]

Consonants: b *but* d *dog* f *few* g *get* h *her* j *yes* k *cat* l *leg* m *man* n *no* p *pen* r *red* s *sit*

socket ● *noun* **1** a natural or artificial hollow for something to fit into or stand firm or revolve in. **2** *Electricity* a device receiving a plug, light bulb, etc., to make a connection. ● *transitive verb* (**sock·et·ed**, **sock·et·ing**) place in or fit with a socket. [Anglo-French, diminutive of Old French *soc* ploughshare, prob. of Celtic origin]

sock·ette *noun* a very short sock.

sock·et wrench *noun* a wrench having a socket which fits over the nut.

sock·eye *noun* a blue-backed salmon of the N American Pacific coast, *Oncorhynchus nerka*. *Also called* RED SALMON. [Sne Nay Muxw *sukai* fish of fishes]

sock hop *noun* N Amer. a social dance at which participants dance in their stocking feet.

socko *adjective slang* stunningly effective or successful. [SOCK² + -O]

socle /ˈsoːkəl/ *noun Archit.* a plain low block or plinth serving as a support for a column, urn, statue, etc., or as the foundation of a wall. [French from Italian *zoccolo* originally 'wooden shoe' from Latin *socculus* from *soccus* SOCK¹]

SOCO /ˈsokoː/ *noun Cdn & Brit.* a police officer trained to examine scenes of crime for forensic evidence or clues. [acronym from *scene of crime officer*]

Soc·ra·tes /ˈsɒkrəˌtiːz/ (469–399 BC), Greek philosopher. His method of inquiry (the *Socratic method*) by careful questioning was designed to reveal truth and expose error; his disciple Plato recorded his dialogues and teachings in, for example, the *Symposium* and the *Phaedo*. Charged with introducing strange gods and corrupting the young, Socrates was sentenced to death and forced to take hemlock.

So·crat·ic /səˈkratɪk/ ● *adjective* of or relating to Socrates or his philosophy, esp. the method associated with him of seeking the truth by a series of questions and answers. ● *noun* a follower of Socrates. □ **So·crat·ic·ally** *adverb*

Socratic irony *noun* a pose of ignorance assumed in order to entice others into making statements that can then be challenged.

So·cred /ˈsoːkred/ *Cdn* ● *adjective* = SOCIAL CREDIT *adjective.* ● *noun* = SOCIAL CREDITER. [abbreviation]

sod¹ ● *noun* **1** turf or a piece of turf. **2** the surface of the ground. ● *transitive verb* (**sod·ded**, **sod·ding**) cover (the ground) with sod. [Middle Dutch, Middle Low German *sode*, of unknown origin]

sod² *esp. Brit. slang* ● *noun* **1** an unpleasant or awkward person or thing. **2** a person of a specified kind; a fellow (*the lucky sod*). ● *interjection* an exclamation of annoyance (*sod them, I don't care!*). □ **sod off** go away. □ **sod·ding** *adjective* [abbreviation of SODOMITE]

soda *noun* **1** any of various compounds of sodium in common use (*washing soda; baking soda*). **2** (in full **soda water**) water made effervescent by impregnation with carbon dioxide under pressure (originally made with sodium bicarbonate), and used alone or with an alcoholic beverage etc. as a drink. **3** *esp. US* = POP¹ *noun* 2. **4** *N Amer.* a sweet fizzy drink made with soda water, fruit juice and sometimes ice cream. [late Middle English, from medieval Latin, from Arabic *suwwad* 'saltwort']

soda biscuit *noun* **1** N Amer. = SODA CRACKER. **2** a biscuit leavened with baking soda.

soda bread *noun* bread leavened with baking soda.

soda cracker *noun* N Amer. a thin crisp cracker leavened with baking soda.

soda fountain *noun* esp. N Amer. **1** a shop or counter serving soft drinks, ice cream, etc. **2** a device dispensing soda water or soft drinks.

soda jerk *noun* (also **soda jerker**) N Amer. informal a person who mixes and sells soft drinks etc. at a soda fountain.

soda lime *noun* a mixture of calcium oxide and sodium hydroxide.

so·dal·ity /soˈdalɪti/ *noun* (pl. **-ities**) a confraternity or association, esp. a Catholic religious guild or brotherhood. [French *sodalité* or Latin *sodalitas* from *sodalis* comrade]

soda pop *noun* esp. US = POP¹ *noun* 2.

soda water *noun* see SODA 2.

sod·bust·er *noun* N Amer. informal a farmer who raises crops rather than livestock, esp. one of the early homesteaders on the Prairies.

sod·den *adjective* **1** saturated with liquid; soaked through. **2** having drunk an excessive amount of a particular alcoholic drink (*a whisky-sodden criminal*). □ **sod·den·ly** *adverb* **sod·den·ness** *noun* [archaic past participle of SEETHE]

sod·die *noun* (also **soddy**) N Amer. a sod house.

Soddy, Fred·erick (1877–1956), English physicist. He worked with Rutherford in Montreal on radioactive decay and formulated a theory of isotopes, the word *isotope* being coined by him in 1913; he also assisted Ramsay in London in the discovery of helium, and was awarded the Nobel Prize for chemistry in 1921.

sod house *noun* (also **sod hut**, **sod shack**) N Amer. a house with walls of sod and a canvas or sod roof supported by wooden rafters, built esp. by settlers on the Prairies.

so·dium *noun Chem.* a soft silver-white reactive metallic element, occurring naturally in soda, salt, etc., that is important in industry and is an essential element in living organisms. Symbol: **Na**; at. no.: 11. □ **sodic** *adjective* [SODA + -IUM]

sodium bicarbonate *noun* a soluble white powder used in fire extinguishers and effervescent drinks and as a raising agent in baking. *Also called* BAKING SODA. Chem. formula: $NaHCO_3$.

sodium carbonate *noun* a white powder with many commercial applications including the manufacture of soap and glass. *Also called* WASHING SODA. Chem. formula: Na_2CO_3.

sodium chloride *noun* a colourless crystalline compound occurring naturally in sea water and halite; common salt. Chem. formula: $NaCl$.

sodium hydroxide *noun* a deliquescent compound which is strongly alkaline and used in the manufacture of soap and paper. *Also called* CAUSTIC SODA. Chem. formula: $NaOH$.

sodium light *noun* (also **sodium vapour light**, **sodium lamp**) a street light using an electrical discharge in sodium vapour and giving a yellow light.

sodium nitrate *noun* a white powdery compound used mainly in the manufacture of fertilizers. Chem. formula: $NaNO_3$.

sodium pentothal *noun* = THIOPENTAL SODIUM.

Sodom /ˈsɒdəm/ *noun* a depraved or corrupt place. [*Sodom* in ancient Palestine, destroyed for its wickedness (Gen. 18–19)]

sod·om·ite /ˈsɒdəˌmaɪt/ *noun* a person who engages in sodomy.

sod·omy /ˈsɒdəmi/ *noun* anal intercourse. □ **sod·om·ize** *transitive verb* (also esp. *Brit.* **-ise**). [medieval Latin *sodomia* from Late Latin *peccatum Sodomiticum* sin of Sodom: see SODOM]

sod shack *var. of* SOD HOUSE.

Sod's Law *noun Brit.* = MURPHY'S LAW.

sod-turning *noun* esp. Cdn = GROUNDBREAKING *noun*.

Soeurs, Île des /iːl dei ˈsɜr/ (also **Nuns' Island**) a small island in the St. Lawrence, part of the city of Verdun in south central Quebec.

so·ever *adverb literary* of any kind; to any extent (*how great soever it may be*).

-soever *combining form* (added to relative pronouns, adverbs, and adjectives) of any kind; to any extent (*whatsoever; howsoever*).

sofa *noun* a long upholstered seat with a back and arms, for two or more people. [French, ultimately from Arabic *ṣuffa*]

sofa bed *noun* a sofa that can be folded out to form a bed.

sofa table *noun* a high, long table usu. placed behind a sofa.

sof·fit *noun* the undersurface of an arch, a balcony, overhanging eaves, etc. [French *soffite* or Italian *soffitta*, *-itto*, ultimately from Latin *suffixus* (as SUFFIX)]

Sofia /ˈsəfiːə/ (also **So·phia**) the capital of Bulgaria; pop. (est. 2001) 1,096,389.

soft ● *adjective* **1** (of a substance, material, etc.) lacking hardness or firmness; yielding to pressure; easily cut, moulded or compressed. **2** (of cloth, skin, etc.) having a smooth surface or texture; not rough or coarse. **3** (of a light or colour etc.) not brilliant or glaring. **4** (of a voice or sounds) gentle and pleasing; not loud. **5** (of air etc.) mellow, mild, balmy; not noticeably cold or hot. **6** (of water) free from mineral salts and therefore good for lathering. **7** *Phonetics* **a** (of a consonant) sibilant or palatal (as *c* in *ice*, *g* in *age*). **b** voiced or unaspirated. **8** (of an outline etc.) not sharply defined. **9** (of an action or manner etc.) gentle, conciliatory, complimentary, amorous. **10** (of the heart or feelings etc.) compassionate, sympathetic, esp. to too great an extent. **11 a** lacking in determination, courage, etc.; weak or sentimental. **b** foolish, silly (*soft in the head*). **12** *informal* (of a job etc.) easy, undemanding. **13** (of drugs) mild; not likely to cause addiction. **14** (also **soft-core**) (of pornography) suggestive or erotic but not explicit. **15** (of radiation) having little penetrating power. **16 a** (of currency) likely to fall in value; not readily exchangeable into other currencies. **b** (of a market, prices, etc.) declining; weak. **17** (of a statistic, fact, etc.) insubstantial, imprecise. **18** (of support for a political candidate, platform, etc.) not solid; liable to shift. **19** *Politics* moderate; willing to compromise (*the soft left*). **20** (of wheat) having a soft kernel rich in starch, used to make pastry flour (*compare* HARD *adjective* 16). **21 a** *Sport* (of a ball, puck, etc.) weakly or lightly hit. **b** *Hockey* (of a goal) not outstanding; that the goalie should have been able to stop. **22** peaceful (*soft slumbers*). **23** *Brit.* (of the weather etc.) rainy or moist or thawing. ● *adverb* softly (*play soft*). ● *noun* a soft or yielding thing; the soft part of something. □ **be soft on** *informal* **1** be lenient towards. **2** be infatuated with. **have a soft spot for** be fond of or affectionate towards (a person). □ **soft·ish** *adjective* **soft·ness** *noun* [Old English *sōfte* agreeable, earlier *sēfte* from West Germanic]

soft·ball *noun* **1** a modified form of baseball played on a smaller diamond using a larger and softer ball that is pitched underarm. **2** the ball used in this sport.

soft-boiled *adjective* **1** (of an egg) lightly boiled leaving the yolk semi-liquid. **2** *informal* (of a person) mild, easygoing.

soft-centred *adjective* **1** (of a chocolate, pastry, etc.) having a soft filling or centre. **2** (of a literary or artistic work) having a weak or sentimental core.

soft coal *noun* bituminous coal.

soft-core *adjective see* SOFT *adjective* 14.

soft·cover *adjective & noun* = PAPERBACK *adjective & noun*.

soft drink *noun* a flavoured, carbonated, non-alcoholic drink.

soft·en *verb* **1** *transitive & intransitive* make or become soft or softer. **2** *transitive & intransitive* make or become less severe (*his face softened and he almost smiled*). **3** *transitive* modify, tone down; make less pronounced or prominent. **4** *transitive* reduce the force of something (*soften the blow*). **5** *transitive* (often foll. by *up*) **a** reduce the strength of (defences) by bombing or some other preliminary attack. **b** reduce the resistance of (a person). □ **soft·en·er** *noun*

soft-focus ● *adjective* **1** characterized by or producing a deliberate slight blurring or lack of definition in a photograph (*soft-focus filter*). **2** deliberately diffuse, unclear, or imprecise. ● *noun* (**soft focus**) **1** a deliberate slight blurring or lack of definition in a photograph. **2** deliberate diffuseness or imprecision.

soft fruit *noun esp. Brit.* small stoneless fruit, e.g. strawberries, raspberries, etc.

soft furnishings *plural noun Brit.* curtains, rugs, etc.

soft goods *plural noun* textiles.

soft-headed *adjective* foolish, feeble-minded.

soft-hearted *adjective* tender, compassionate; easily moved.

soft hyphen *noun* a hyphen introduced into a word, formula, etc. not otherwise hyphenated, for reasons of page or column layout or onscreen formatting, as at the end of a line of text.

soft·ie *noun* (also **softy**) (*pl.* **-ies**) *informal* **1** a kind, sympathetic, or sentimental person. **2** a weak or silly person. **3** *Hockey slang* a goal scored on a weak shot.

soft landing *noun* **1** a landing by a spacecraft during which no serious damage is incurred. **2** a slowing down of economic growth at an acceptable degree relative to inflation and unemployment. □ **soft-land** *transitive & intransitive verb*

soft·ly *adverb* in a soft, gentle, or quiet manner.

softly-softly *attributive adjective Brit.* (of an approach or strategy) cautious; discreet and cunning.

soft maple *noun* any of several maples with less durable wood, esp. red maple, *Acer rubrum*, and silver maple, *Acer saccharinum*.

soft money *noun US* donations to a political candidate or party which circumvent federal campaign finance laws.

soft news *noun* news that focuses on personalities, provides background for hard news, or is not immediately topical, e.g. entertainment and lifestyle reporting.

soft option *noun* the easier alternative.

soft palate *noun* the rear part of the palate.

soft-paste *adjective* denoting an 'artificial' porcelain containing glassy materials and fired at a comparatively low temperature.

soft pedal ● *noun* a pedal on a piano that makes the tone softer. ● *transitive & intransitive verb* (**soft-pedal**) (**-pedalled**, **-pedalling**; esp. *US* **-pedaled**, **-pedaling**) **1** refrain from emphasizing; be restrained (about). **2** play with the soft pedal down.

soft porn *noun informal* soft-core pornography (often *attributive*: *soft-porn movie*).

soft return *noun* a carriage return inserted automatically by a word processor at the end of a line of text.

soft rock *noun* a type of rock music originating in the 1970s characterized by a pleasant, melodic sound and usu. romantic lyrics.

soft roe *noun see* ROE[1] 2.

soft sculpture *noun* sculpture using pliable materials, as cloth, foam, rubber, etc.

soft sell ● *noun* restrained or subtly persuasive salesmanship. ● *transitive verb* (**soft-sell**) (*past* and *past participle* **-sold**) sell by this method.

soft-shell crab *noun* a crab, esp. a blue crab, that has recently moulted and has a new shell that is still soft and edible.

soft-shoe ● *noun* a kind of tap dance performed in soft-soled shoes. ● *intransitive verb* **1** perform this dance. **2** move quietly or lightly.

soft-side *adjective* designating a suitcase, cooler, etc. made of leather, vinyl, nylon etc. rather than a hard, inflexible material such as plastic.

soft-skinned *adjective* **1** having soft skin. **2** *Military* (of a vehicle) unprotected, unarmoured.

soft soap ● *noun* **1** a semi-liquid soap, esp. one made with potassium not sodium salts. **2** *informal* persuasive flattery. ● *transitive verb* (**soft-soap**) *informal* persuade (a person) with flattery.

soft-spoken *adjective* speaking with a gentle quiet voice.

soft target *noun* a relatively vulnerable or unprotected target, esp. for military or terrorist attack.

soft tissue *noun* body tissue other than bone or cartilage.

soft-top *noun* **1** a convertible car with a soft roof that can be folded back. **2** such a roof.

soft touch *noun slang* a person easily manipulated, esp. one easily induced to part with money.

soft·ware *noun* **1** the programs and other operating information used by a computer (*compare* HARDWARE 3). **2** storage media such as videocassettes, audiotapes, etc. requiring playback on electronic equipment.

software agent *noun* = INTELLIGENT AGENT.

software engineering *noun* the professional development, production, and management of system software. □ **software engineer** *noun*

software house *noun* a company that specializes in producing and testing software.

software package *noun* a set of computer programs directed at some application in general, e.g. computer graphics, word processing, computer-aided design, etc.

soft·wood ● *noun* **1** the wood of pine, spruce, or other conifers, easily sawn. **2** a tree producing such wood. ● *adjective* **1** made of softwood (*softwood lumber*). **2** containing softwoods (*softwood forest*).

softy var. of SOFTIE.

soggy *adjective* (**sog·gi·er**, **sog·gi·est**) **1** sodden, saturated. **2** (of weather) rainy, dank. **3** dull, boring, lifeless. □ **sog·gi·ly** *adverb* **sog·gi·ness** *noun* [dial. *sog* a swamp]

soh var. of SO[2].

SOHC *abbreviation* single overhead camshaft.

SOHO *adjective* relating to a market for inexpensive electronics suitable for individuals and small companies. [acronym from *small office, home office*]

soi-disant /ˌswɒdiːˈzɑ̃/ *adjective* self-styled or pretended. [French from *soi* oneself + *disant* saying]

soi·gné /ˈswɒnjei/ *adjective* (*fem.* **soi·gnée** pronunc. same) carefully finished or arranged; well-groomed. [past participle of French *soigner* take care, from *soin* care]

soil[1] *noun* **1** the upper layer of earth in which plants grow, consisting of disintegrated rock usu. with an admixture of organic remains (*alluvial soil*; *rich soil*). **2** the ground, the earth (*a tiller of the soil*). **3** ground belonging to a nation; territory (*on Canadian soil*). **4** any environment encouraging growth. □ **soil·less** *adjective* [Anglo-French, perhaps from Latin *solium* seat, taken in sense of Latin *solum* ground]

soil[2] ● *transitive verb* **1** make dirty; smear or stain with dirt. **2** dirty (diapers, clothes etc.) by involuntary defecation. **3** tarnish, defile; bring discredit to (*would not soil my hands with it*). ● *noun* **1** a dirty mark; a stain, smear, or defilement. **2** filth; refuse matter. [Old French *suiller*, *soiller*, etc., ultimately from Latin *sucula* diminutive of *sus* pig]

soil amendment *noun* a substance added to the soil to improve its physical properties.

soil conditioner *noun* = SOIL AMENDMENT.

soil conservation *noun* protection of soil against erosion, loss of fertility, and damage.

soil science *noun* the branch of science concerned with the formation, nature, ecology, and classification of soil; pedology.

soiree /ˈswɑːreɪ, ˈswɑːr-/ *noun* **1** a party in the evening. **2** *Cdn* (*Nfld*)

/swɑrˈiː/ **a** a social gathering held by an organization or service club. **b** a large party or community social with singing, dancing, and eating. [French from *soir* evening]

soixante-neuf /ˌswʌsɑ̃tˈnɜf/ *noun slang* = SIXTY-NINE. [French]

so·journ /ˈsoːdʒɜrn/ ● *noun* a temporary stay. ● *intransitive verb* (also /soˈdʒɜrn/) stay temporarily. □ **so·journ·er** *noun* [Old French *sojorn* etc. from Late Latin SUB- + *diurnum* day]

soke /soːk/ *noun Brit. hist.* **1** a right of local jurisdiction. **2** a district under a particular jurisdiction and administration. [Anglo-Latin *sōca* from Old English *sōcn* prosecution, from Germanic]

S.O.L. *adjective slang* SHIT OUT OF LUCK (see SHIT).

Sol *Rom. Myth* the sun, esp. as a personification. [Latin]

sol[1] *var. of* SO[2].

sol[2] *noun Chem.* a liquid suspension of a colloid. [abbreviation of SOLUTION]

sol[3] *noun (pl.* **soles** /ˈsoːles/) (also **nuevo sol**) a monetary unit of Peru that is equal to 100 centimos and which replaced the inti in 1991. [Spanish, = sun, from Latin]

sol[4] *noun hist.* a former coin and monetary unit of France and New France and some other countries, notionally equivalent to one-twentieth of a livre but varying in actual value. [French from Latin SOLIDUS]

sola[1] /ˈsoːlə/ *noun* a pithy-stemmed E Indian swamp plant of the genus *Aeschynomene*, the pith being used to make sun hats. [Urdu & Bengali *solā*, Hindi *sholā*]

sola[2] *fem. of* SOLUS.

sol·ace /ˈsoːləs, ˈsɒləs/ ● *noun* comfort in distress, disappointment, or tedium. ● *transitive verb* give solace to. [Old French *solas* from Latin *solatium* from *solari* CONSOLE[1]]

so·la·na·ceous /ˌsɒləˈneiʃəs/ *adjective* of or relating to the plant family Solanaceae, including potatoes, nightshades, and tobacco. [modern Latin *solanaceae* from Latin *sōlānum* nightshade]

so·la·nine /ˈsɒləniːn/ *noun* a poisonous compound present in green potatoes and in related plants. [from French, from the genus name *Solanum* + -INE[4]]

sol·ar ● *adjective* of, relating to, or reckoned by the sun (*solar eclipse*; *solar time*). ● *noun* **1** a solarium. **2** an upper chamber in a medieval house. [Latin *solaris* from *sol* sun]

solar cell *noun* a photoelectric device converting solar radiation into electricity.

solar collector *noun* = SOLAR PANEL.

solar constant *noun* the rate at which energy reaches the earth's surface from the sun, usu. taken to be 1,388 watts per square metre.

solar day *noun* the interval between successive meridian transits of the sun at a place.

solar eclipse *noun* an eclipse in which the sun is obscured by the moon.

solar energy *noun* **1** radiant energy emitted by the sun. **2** = SOLAR POWER.

solar flare *noun* a short-lived, cataclysmic outburst of solar material, driven by magnetic forces, from a relatively small area of the solar surface.

sol·ar·i·um /səˈleriəm/ *noun (pl.* **sol·ar·iums** or **sol·aria** /-riə/) **1** a room, balcony, etc. fitted with extensive areas of glass to provide exposure to the sun. **2** *Brit.* a room at a health club etc. equipped with sun lamps. [Latin, = sundial, sunning place (as SOLAR)]

sol·ar·ize *transitive & intransitive verb* (also esp. *Brit.* **-ise**) *Photog.* undergo or cause to undergo change in the relative darkness of parts of an image by long exposure. □ **sol·ar·iz·a·tion** *noun*

solar month *noun* one-twelfth of the solar year.

solar panel *noun* a panel that harnesses the energy in the sun's radiation, either to generate electricity using solar cells or to heat water.

solar plexus *noun* **1** a complex of radiating nerves at the pit of the stomach. **2** the region of the torso in front of this, esp. as regarded as vulnerable to a blow.

solar power *noun* power obtained by harnessing the energy of the sun's rays. □ **solar-powered** *adjective*

solar radiation *noun* electromagnetic radiated energy from the sun.

solar sail *noun* a surface designed to harness the pressure of solar radiation to propel a spaceship. □ **solar sailing** *noun*

solar system *noun* the collection of nine planets and their moons in orbit around the sun, together with smaller bodies in the form of asteroids, meteoroids, and comets.

solar wind *noun* the continuous flow of charged particles from the sun into surrounding space.

solar year *noun* the time taken for the earth to travel once around the sun, measured from equinox to equinox, equal to 365 days, 5 hours, 48 minutes, and 46 seconds.

sold *past and past participle of* SELL. □ **sold on** *informal* enthusiastic about.

solder /ˈsɒdɜr/ ● *noun* a fusible alloy used to join less fusible metals or wires etc. ● *transitive verb* join with solder. □ **solder·able** *noun* **solder·er** *noun* **solder·less** *adjective* [Old French *soudure* from *souder* from Latin *solidare* fasten, from *solidus* SOLID]

solder·ing iron *noun* a tool used for applying solder.

sol·dier ● *noun* **1** a person serving in or having served in an army. **2** (in full **common soldier**) a private or NCO in an army. **3** a military commander of specified ability (*a great soldier*). **4** a person who fights for a cause. **5** a rank-and-file member of the Mafia. **6** (in full **soldier ant**) a wingless ant or termite with a large head and jaws for fighting in defence of its colony. **7** (in full **soldier beetle**) a carnivorous beetle of the family Cantharidae, with soft reddish wing-cases. **8** *Brit. & Cdn* a finger of toast for dipping in a soft-boiled egg. **9** each of an orderly series of upright bricks, timbers, etc., suggestive of a line of soldiers on parade. ● *intransitive verb* serve as a soldier (*was off soldiering*). □ **soldier on** *informal* persevere doggedly. □ **sol·dier·ly** *adjective* [via Old French *soldier* from *soulde* '(soldier's) pay', from Latin *solidus*: see SOLIDUS]

soldier of fortune *noun* an adventurous person ready to take service under any state or person; a mercenary.

sol·diery *noun (pl.* **-ies**) **1** soldiers, esp. of a specified character. **2** a group of soldiers. **3** the profession of being a soldier.

sold-out *attributive adjective* having all tickets sold (*a sold-out show*).

sole[1] ● *noun* **1** the undersurface of the foot. **2** the part of a shoe, sock, etc., corresponding to this (esp. excluding the heel). **3** the lower surface or base of an implement, e.g. a plow, golf club head, etc. **4** the floor of a ship's cabin. ● *transitive verb* provide (a shoe etc.) with a sole; replace the sole of. □ **-soled** *adjective* (in *combination*). [Old French, ultimately from Latin *solea* sandal, sill]

sole[2] *noun* **1** any of various flatfish of the family Pleuronectidae or Soleidae, used as food. **2** the flesh of any flatfish prepared as food. [Old French from Provençal *sola*, ultimately from Latin *solea* (as SOLE[1], named from its shape)]

sole[3] *adjective* **1** (*attributive*) one and only; single, exclusive (*the sole reason*; *has the sole right*). **2** *archaic* or *Law* (esp. of a woman) unmarried. **3** *archaic* alone, unaccompanied. □ **sole·ly** *adverb* [Old French *soule* from Latin *sola* fem. of *solus* alone]

sol·ecism /ˈsɒləˌsɪzəm/ *noun* **1** a mistake of grammar or idiom; a blunder in the manner of speaking or writing. **2** a piece of bad manners or incorrect behaviour. [French *solécisme* or Latin *soloecismus* from Greek *soloikismos* from *soloikos* speaking incorrectly]

sol·emn /ˈsɒləm/ *adjective* **1** serious and dignified (*a solemn occasion*). **2** formal; accompanied by ceremony, esp. for religious purposes. **3** (of a person) serious or cheerless in manner (*looks rather solemn*). **4** mysteriously impressive. **5** full of importance; weighty (*a solemn warning*). **6** grave, sober, deliberate; slow in movement or action (*a solemn promise*; *solemn music*). □ **sol·emn·ly** *adverb* **sol·emn·ness** *noun* [Old French *solemne* from Latin *sol(l)emnis* customary, celebrated at a fixed date, from *sollus* entire]

so·lem·nity /səˈlemnɪti/ *noun (pl.* **-ties**) **1** the state of being solemn; a solemn character or feeling; solemn behaviour. **2** a rite or celebration; a piece of ceremony.

sol·em·nize /ˈsɒləmˌnaiz/ *transitive verb* (also esp. *Brit.* **-nise**) **1** duly perform (a ceremony esp. of marriage). **2** celebrate or commemorate (an occasion etc.) by special observances or with special formality. **3** make solemn. □ **sol·em·niz·a·tion** *noun*

Solemn Mass *noun* = HIGH MASS.

sol·en·oid /ˈsoːləˌnɔid, ˈsɒl-/ *noun* a cylindrical coil of wire acting as a magnet when carrying electric current. □ **sol·en·oidal** *adjective* [French *solénoïde* from Greek *sōlēn* 'channel, pipe' + -OID]

So·lent, the /ˈsoːlənt/ a channel between the northwest coast of the Isle of Wight and the mainland of S England.

sole plate *noun* a metal plate forming the working surface of an iron.

sole practitioner *noun Cdn* a lawyer, accountant, or other professional who is the sole member of a firm, rather than one who works in partnership with others.

---

uː m**oo**d   ai m**y**   əi p**i**pe   au br**o**wn   ʌu h**ou**se   ei d**ay**   ɔi b**oy**   ɑ̃ fr**an**glais   ã C**an**adien   ɔ̃ Br**ay**on   (*see over for consonants*)

sol-fa /ˌsɒlˈfɑː/ ● *noun* = SOLMIZATION (*compare* TONIC SOL-FA). ● *transitive verb* (**-fas, -faed**) sing (a tune) with sol-fa syllables.

soli *pl. of* SOLO 1.

so·lic·it /səˈlɪsɪt/ *verb* (**so·lic·it·ed, so·lic·it·ing**) **1** *transitive & intransitive* ask repeatedly or earnestly for or seek or invite (business etc.). **2** *transitive* (often foll. by *for*) make a request or petition to (a person). **3** *transitive & intransitive* accost (a person) and offer one's services as a prostitute. □ **so·lic·it·a·tion** *noun* [Old French *solliciter* from Latin *sollicitare* agitate, from *sollicitus* anxious, from *sollus* entire + *citus* past participle, = set in motion]

so·lic·i·tor /səˈlɪsɪtər/ *noun* **1** *Cdn* a lawyer. **2** *Brit.* a member of the legal profession qualified to deal with conveyancing, draw up wills, etc., advise clients and instruct barristers, and represent clients in the lower courts. **3** a person who solicits. **4** *N Amer.* a canvasser. **5** *N Amer.* the chief law officer of a city etc.

solicitor-client privilege *noun* the right of a lawyer and client to keep their professional communications confidential.

Solicitor General *noun* (*pl.* **Solicitors General**) **1** (in Canada) a federal or provincial cabinet member who is responsible for correctional services, law enforcement, and some forms of licensing. **2** (in the UK) the Crown law officer below the Attorney General or (in Scotland) below the Lord Advocate. **3** (in the US) the law officer below the Attorney General.

so·lic·i·tous /səˈlɪsɪtəs/ *adjective* **1** (often foll. by *of*, *about*, etc.) showing interest or concern. **2** eager, anxious. □ **so·lic·i·tous·ly** *adverb* **so·lic·i·tous·ness** *noun* [Latin *sollicitus* (as SOLICIT)]

so·lic·i·tude /səˈlɪsɪˌtuːd, -ˌtjuːd/ *noun* **1** the state of being solicitous; solicitous behaviour. **2** anxiety or concern.

sol·id ● *adjective* **1** firm and stable in shape; not liquid or fluid (*solid food; water becomes solid at 0°C*). **2 a** of such material throughout, not hollow or containing cavities (*a solid sphere*). **b** (of a wall etc.) having no opening or window. **c** (of a line, row, etc.) continuous, unbroken. **3** of the same substance or colour throughout (*solid silver; a solid green sweater*). **4** of strong material or construction or build, not flimsy or slender etc. **5** (of a cloud etc.) having the appearance of an unbroken mass; dense, thick, compact. **6 a** having three dimensions. **b** concerned with solids (*solid geometry*). **7 a** sound and reliable; genuine (*solid arguments*). **b** staunch and dependable (*a solid Tory; a solid worker*). **8** sound but without any special flair etc. (*a solid piece of work*). **9** financially sound. **10** (of time) uninterrupted, continuous (*spend four solid hours on it*). **11** unanimous, undivided (*support has been pretty solid so far*). **12** (of printing) without spaces between the lines etc. **13** (foll. by *with*) *US informal* on good terms. ● *noun* **1** a solid substance or body. **2** (in *pl.*) solid food. **3** a solidly coloured garment or fabric (*mix stripes with solids*). **4** *Math.* a body or magnitude having three dimensions. ● *adverb* so as to become solid; solidly (*booked solid; frozen solid*). □ **sol·id·ly** *adverb* **sol·id·ness** *noun* [Old French *solide* from Latin *solidus*, related to *salvus* 'safe', *sollus* 'entire']

solid angle *noun* an angle formed by planes etc. meeting at a point.

soli·dar·ity /ˌsɒlɪˈdɛrɪti/ *noun* **1** unity or agreement of feeling or action, esp. among individuals with a common interest. **2** mutual support or cohesiveness within a group. **3** (**Solidarity**) an independent trade union movement formed in Poland in 1980 which developed into a mass campaign for political change and inspired popular opposition to Communist regimes in other eastern European countries. [French *solidarité* from *solidaire* from *solide* SOLID]

solid colour *noun* colour covering the whole of an object, without a pattern etc. □ **solid-coloured** *adjective*

sol·idi *pl. of* SOLIDUS.

so·lid·ify *verb* (**-ifies, -ified**) **1** *transitive & intransitive* make or become solid (*the magma slowly solidifies*). **2** *transitive* secure or strengthen (a position, reputation, etc.) (*the victory solidified her claim to supremacy*). □ **so·lid·ifi·ca·tion** *noun* **so·lid·ifi·er** *noun*

so·lid·ity *noun* the state of being solid; firmness.

solid solution *noun* solid material containing one substance uniformly distributed in another.

solid state ● *noun* the state of matter that retains its boundaries without support. ● *adjective* using the electronic properties of solids, e.g. a semiconductor, to replace those of valves.

sol·idus /ˈsɒlɪdəs/ *noun* (*pl.* **sol·idi** /-ˌdaɪ/) **1** an oblique stroke (/) used in writing fractions (³/₄), to separate other figures and letters, or to denote alternatives (*and/or*) and ratios (*miles/day*). **2** (in full **solidus curve**) a curve in a graph of the temperature and composition of a mixture, below which the substance is entirely solid. **3** *hist.* a gold coin of the later Roman Empire. [Middle English (in sense 3) from Latin: see SOLID]

soli·fluc·tion /ˌsɒlɪˈflʌkʃən, ˌsɒl-/ *noun* the gradual movement of wet soil etc. down a slope. [Latin *solum* soil + Latin *fluctio* flowing, from *fluere fluct-* flow]

so·lilo·quy /səˈlɪləkwi/ *noun* (*pl.* **-quies**) **1** the act of talking when alone or regardless of any hearers, esp. in drama. **2** part of a play involving this. □ **so·lilo·quist** *noun* **so·lilo·quize** *intransitive verb* (also esp. *Brit.* **-quise**). [Late Latin *soliloquium* from Latin *solus* alone + *loqui* speak]

Soli·man see SULEIMAN I.

Sol·ing·en /ˈzɒlɪŋən/ a city in western Germany, north of Bonn; pop. (est. 1999) 165,400.

sol·ip·sism /ˈsɒlɪpˌsɪzm/ *noun* **1** *Philos.* the view that the self is all that exists, or is all that can be known. **2** self-centredness, selfishness. □ **sol·ip·sist** *noun* **sol·ip·sis·tic** *adjective* **sol·ip·sis·tic·ally** *adverb* [Latin *solus* alone + *ipse* self]

soli·taire /ˈsɒlɪˌter/ *noun* **1** *N Amer.* a game for one player in which cards taken in random order have to be arranged in certain groups or sequences. **2** a game for one player played by removing pegs etc. one at a time from a board by jumping others over them until only one is left. **3** a diamond or other gem set by itself. **4** a ring having a single gem. **5** any of various New World thrushes of the genera *Myadestes* and *Entomodestes*, some of which are noted for their beautiful songs. **6** either of two extinct flightless birds related to the dodo and formerly found in the Mascarene Islands. [French from Latin *solitarius* (as SOLITARY)]

soli·tary /ˈsɒlɪteri/ ● *adjective* **1** living alone; not gregarious; without companions; lonely (*a solitary existence*). **2** performed alone (*a solitary expedition*). **3** (of a place) secluded or unfrequented. **4** single or sole (*a solitary instance*). **5** (of an insect) not living in communities. **6** *Bot.* growing singly, not in a cluster. ● *noun* (*pl.* **-ies**) **1** a recluse or hermit. **2** *informal* = SOLITARY CONFINEMENT. □ **soli·tar·i·ly** *adverb* **soli·tar·i·ness** *noun* [Latin *solitarius* from *solus* alone]

solitary confinement *noun* isolation of a prisoner in a separate cell as a punishment.

soli·tude /ˈsɒlɪˌtuːd, -ˌtjuːd/ *noun* **1** the state of being or living alone; solitariness. **2** a lonely or unfrequented place. **3** one of any number of communities seen as having little in common with and living completely independently from others in the larger society (*Canada's two solitudes*). [Old French *solitude* or Latin *solitudo* from *solus* alone]

sol·miz·a·tion /ˌsɒlməˈzeɪʃən/ *noun* (also esp. *Brit.* **-isation**) *Music* a system of associating each note of a scale with a particular syllable, now usu. *do re mi fa so la ti*, with do as C in the fixed-do system and as the keynote in the movable-do or tonic sol-fa system. [French *solmisation* (as SOL¹, MI)]

solo ● *noun* (*pl.* **solos**) **1** (*pl.* **solos** or *Music* **soli**) **a** a vocal or instrumental piece or passage, or a dance, performed by one person with or without accompaniment. **b** (*attributive*) performed or performing as a solo (*solo passage; solo violin*). **2 a** an unaccompanied flight by a pilot in an aircraft. **b** anything done by one person unaccompanied. **c** (*attributive*) unaccompanied, alone. **3** (*attributive*) *Baseball* designating a home run hit with no one on base. **4** (in full **solo whist**) **a** a card game like whist in which one player may oppose the others. **b** a declaration or the act of playing to win five tricks at this. ● *verb* (**soloes, soloed**) **1** *intransitive* perform a solo, esp. a musical solo or a solo flight. **2** *transitive* climb (a mountain etc.) without a partner. ● *adverb* unaccompanied, alone (*flew solo for the first time*). [Italian from Latin *solus* alone]

solo·ist *noun* **1** a performer of a solo, esp. in music or dance. **2** a dancer of a rank between corps de ballet and principal dancer, who performs some solo roles.

Solo·mon¹ son of David, king of Israel *c.*970–*c.*930 BC. During his reign he extended the kingdom of Israel to the border with Egypt and the Euphrates and he became famous both for his wisdom and for the magnificence of his palaces. In the Bible, he is traditionally associated with the Song of Solomon, Ecclesiastes, and Proverbs; the Wisdom of Solomon in the Apocrypha is also ascribed to him. □ **Solo·monic** /ˌsɒləˈmɒnɪk/ *adjective*

Solo·mon² *noun* a very wise person.

Solomon Gundy *noun* (also **Solomon Grundy**) *Cdn* (*NS*) a dish of salted herring marinated in vinegar, pickling spices, sugar, and onions. [corruption of SALMAGUNDI]

Solomon Islands (also **So·lo·mons**) a country consisting of a group of islands in the SW Pacific, to the east of New Guinea; pop. (est. 2002) 494,786; capital, Honiara. The islands were the scene of heavy fighting between Allied and Japanese forces in 1942–3. **2** an

---

Consonants: b *but*   d *dog*   f *few*   g *get*   h *her*   j *yes*   k *cat*   l *leg*   m *man*   n *no*   p *pen*   r *red*   s *sit*

archipelago including these and Bougainville Island to the north.
□ **Solomon Islander** *noun*

Solomon's seal *noun* **1** a figure like the Star of David. **2** any liliaceous plant of the genus *Polygonatum*, with arching stems and drooping green and white flowers.

So·lon[1] /'soːlon/ (c.630–c.560 BC), Athenian statesman and poet. His economic, constitutional, and legal reforms, making the existing code of laws established by Draco less severe, and dividing Athenians into four classes based on wealth rather than birth, laid the foundations of Athenian democracy.

So·lon[2] /'soːlon/ *noun* a wise lawmaker.

solo whist *noun see* SOLO *noun* 4.

sol·stice /'soːlstɪs, 'sɒl-/ *noun* **1** either of the two times in the year when the sun reaches its highest or lowest point in the sky at noon, marked by the longest and shortest days (*compare* SUMMER SOLSTICE, WINTER SOLSTICE). **2** the point in the ecliptic reached by the sun at a solstice. □ **sol·sti·tial** /sɒl'stɪʃəl/ *adjective* [Old French from Latin *solstitium* from *sol* sun + *sistere stit-* make stand]

Solti /'ʃɒlti/ **Sir Georg** (1912–97), Hungarian-born British conductor. He revivified Covent Garden as musical director (1961–71) and was conductor of the Chicago Symphony Orchestra (1969–91) and the London Philharmonic Orchestra (1979–83). He became artistic director of the Salzburg Easter Festival in 1992.

solu·bil·ize /'sɒljʊbə,laɪz/ *transitive verb* (also esp. *Brit.* **-ise**) make soluble or more soluble. □ **solu·bil·iz·a·tion** *noun*

sol·uble /'sɒljʊbəl/ *adjective* **1** that can be dissolved, esp. in water. **2** that can be solved. □ **solu·bil·ity** *noun* [Old French from Late Latin *solubilis* (as SOLVE)]

solus /'soːləs/ *predicative adjective* (*fem.* **sola**) (esp. in a stage direction) alone, unaccompanied. [Latin]

sol·ute /'sɒljuːt/ *noun* a dissolved substance. [Latin *solutum*, neuter of *solutus*: see SOLVE]

solu·tion /sə'luːʃən/ *noun* **1 a** the act or a means of solving a problem or difficulty. **b** an explanation, answer, or decision. **c** *Math.* the value of an unknown or variable that satisfies an equation or set of equations. **d** (esp. in *pl.*) a product peddled by a high-tech company or consultant. **2 a** the conversion of a solid or gas into a liquid by mixture with a liquid solvent. **b** the state resulting from this (*held in solution*). **c** a homogeneous liquid, semi-liquid, or solid mixture produced by this process. **3** the act of dissolving or the state of being dissolved. **4** the act of separating or breaking. [Old French from Latin *solutio -onis* (as SOLVE)]

Solu·trean /sə'luːtrɪən/ ● *adjective* of or relating to an upper paleolithic culture in W Europe, following the Aurignacian and dated to c.21,000-18,000 years ago. ● *noun* this culture. [*Solutré* in E France, where remains of it were found]

sol·vate *transitive & intransitive verb* enter or cause to enter combination with a solvent. □ **sol·va·tion** *noun*

solve *transitive verb* find an answer to, or an action or course that removes or effectively deals with (a problem or difficulty).
□ **solv·abil·ity** *noun* **solv·able** *adjective* **solv·er** *noun* [Middle English, = loosen, from Latin *solvere solut-* unfasten, release]

sol·vent /'sɒlvənt/ ● *adjective* **1** having enough money to meet one's liabilities. **2** able to dissolve or form a solution with something. ● *noun* **1** a solvent liquid etc. **2** a dissolving or weakening agent.
□ **sol·vency** *noun* (in sense 1 of *adjective*).

solvent abuse *noun* the use of volatile organic solvents as intoxicants by inhalation, e.g. glue sniffing.

Sol·way Firth /'sɒlweɪ/ an inlet of the Irish Sea, separating Cumbria (England) from Dumfries and Galloway (Scotland).

Soly·man *see* SULEIMAN I.

Sol·zhe·nit·syn /ˌsɒlʒə'niːtsɪn/ **Alek·sandr (Isa·evich)** (b.1918), Russian novelist. He spent eight years in a labour camp for criticizing Stalin, and another three in internal exile; in 1974 he was exiled from the Soviet Union. In novels such as *One Day in the Life of Ivan Denisovich* (1962), describing conditions in a labour camp, and *The Gulag Archipelago* (1973–5), he examines the theme of people in extreme situations facing basic moral choices; he was awarded the Nobel Prize for literature in 1970.

som /soːm/ *noun* (*pl.* same) a monetary unit of Kyrgyzstan and Uzbekistan, equal to 100 tiyin. [Kyrgyz and Uzbek, 'rouble']

soma[1] /'soːmə/ *noun* **1** the body as distinct from the soul. **2** the body of an organism as distinct from its reproductive cells. [Greek *sōma -atos* body]

soma[2] /'soːmə/ *noun* **1** an intoxicating drink used in Vedic ritual. **2** a

plant yielding this. **3** a narcotic drug which produces euphoria and hallucination, esp. one distributed by an authority to promote social harmony. [Sanskrit *sōma*; sense 3 after a drug in A. Huxley's novel *Brave New World*]

So·mali /sə'mɒli, -'mɑli/ ● *noun* **1** (*pl.* same or **So·malis**) **a** a member of a Hamitic Muslim people of Somalia. **b** a native or national of Somalia. **2** the language of this people, which belongs to the Cushitic branch of the Afro-Asiatic family of languages and is the official language of Somalia. ● *adjective* of or relating to Somalia, the Somalis, or their language. □ **So·mal·ian** *adjective & noun* [African name]

So·mal·ia /sə'mɒliə, -'mɑliə/ a country in the Horn of Africa; pop. (est. 2002) 7,753,310; capital, Mogadishu. The modern republic (which became independent in 1960) is a result of the unification of the former British Somaliland and Italian Somalia.

Somali Peninsula an alternative name for the HORN OF AFRICA, THE.

som·at·ic /sə'matɪk/ *adjective* of or relating to the body, esp. as distinct from the mind. □ **som·at·ic·ally** *adverb* [Greek *sōmatikos* (as SOMA[1])]

somatic cell *noun* any cell of a living organism except the reproductive cells.

som·at·iz·a·tion *noun* the production of recurrent and multiple medical symptoms with no discernible organic cause (also *attributive*: *somatization disorder*).

somato- /'soːmətoː/ *combining form* the human body. [Greek *sōma -atos* body]

som·ato·sen·sory *adjective* relating to or denoting a sensation (such as pressure, pain, or warmth) which can occur anywhere in the body, in contrast to one localized at a sense organ (e.g. sight, hearing, or taste).

som·ato·stat·in *noun* a hormone secreted in the pancreas and pituitary gland which inhibits gastric secretion and somatotrophin release.

som·ato·trop·in /ˌsoːmətoː'troːpɪn/ *noun* (also **som·ato·troph·in** /-fɪn/) a growth hormone secreted by the pituitary gland. [as SOMATO-, TROPIC]

som·ato·type /'soːmətoː,taɪp/ *noun* physique expressed in relation to various extreme types.

sombre /'sɒmbər/ *adjective* (also esp. *US* **som·ber**) **1** gloomy, shadowy (*a sombre sky*). **2** dark in colour (*sombre clothes*). **3** oppressively solemn or sober. **4** dismal, foreboding (*a sombre prospect*). □ **sombre·ly** *adverb* **sombre·ness** *noun* [French *sombre* from Old French *sombre* (n.), ultimately from Latin SUB- + *umbra* shade]

som·brero /sɒm'breːroː/ *noun* (*pl.* **-os**) a broad-brimmed felt or straw hat worn esp. in Mexico. [Spanish from *sombra* shade (as SOMBRE)]

some ● *adjective* **1** an unspecified amount or number of (*some water*; *some apples*; *some of them*). **2** that is unknown or unnamed (*will return some day*; *some fool has locked the door*; *to some extent*). **3** denoting an approximate number (*waited some twenty minutes*). **4** a considerable amount or number of (*went to some trouble*). **5** (*usu.* stressed) **a** at least a small amount of (*do have some consideration*). **b** such to a certain extent (*that is some help*). **c** *informal* notably such (*that was some hockey game*). **d** (used at the beginning of a sentence for expressing negative opinions) no; no kind of (*some help you are!*). ● *pronoun* some people or things, some number or amount (*I have some already*; *some feel that we have already done too much*). ● *adverb informal* **1** to some extent (*we talked some*). **2** *N Amer.* very; to a high degree (*we were some proud*). □ **and then some** *informal* and plenty more than that. **some few** *see* FEW. [Old English *sum* from Germanic]

-some[1] *suffix* forming adjectives meaning: **1** adapted to; productive of (*cuddlesome*; *fearsome*). **2** characterized by being (*fulsome*). **3** apt to (*tiresome*; *meddlesome*). [Old English *-sum*]

-some[2] *suffix* forming nouns from numerals, meaning 'a group of (so many)' (*foursome*). [Old English *sum* SOME, used after numerals in genitive pl.]

-some[3] *combining form* denoting a portion of a body, esp. of a cell (*chromosome*; *ribosome*). [Greek *sōma* body]

some·body ● *pronoun* some person. ● *noun* (*pl.* **-bodies**) a person of importance (*she wants to be a somebody*).

some·day *adverb* at some time in the future.

some·how *adverb* **1** in some way; by some means (*must get it finished somehow*). **2** for some reason or other (*somehow I never liked them*). **3** in some unspecified or unknown way (*he somehow dropped behind*).

some·one *noun & pronoun* = SOMEBODY.

some·place *adverb N Amer.* = SOMEWHERE.

Som·ers /'sʌmərz/ **Harry Stew·art** (1925–99), Canadian composer.

---

t *top*   v *voice*   w *we*   z *zoo*   ʃ *she*   ʒ *vision*   θ *thin*   ð *this*   ŋ *ring*   x *loch*   tʃ *chip*   dʒ *jar*   (*see over for vowels*)

One of Canada's most original composers, he was also an enthusiastic supporter of Canadian music; his opera *Louis Riel* was commissioned for Canada's centennial celebrations.

som·er·sault /ˈsʌmərˌsɒlt/ ● *noun* **1** an acrobatic movement in which a person turns head over heels in the air or on the ground, making a complete revolution. **2 a** a complete overturn or upset. **b** a reversal of opinion, policy, etc. ● *intransitive verb* perform a somersault. [Old French *sombresault* alteration of *sobresault*, ultimately from Latin *supra* above + *saltus* leap, from *salire* to leap]

Som·er·set /ˈsʌmərˌset/ a county of SW England, on the Bristol Channel; county town, Taunton.

Somerset Island /ˈsʌmərˌset/ a large island in the central Canadian Arctic, situated between Prince of Wales Island and the Brodeur Peninsula of Baffin Island. [SOMERSET]

some·thing ● *noun & pronoun* **1 a** some unspecified or unknown thing (*have something to tell you; something has happened*). **b** (in full **something or other**) as a substitute for an unknown or forgotten description (*she's a professor of something or other*). **2** a known or understood but unexpressed quantity, quality, or extent (*there is something about it I do not like; there's something in what she says*). **3** *informal* an important or notable person or thing (*the party was quite something*). **4** (in *combination*) used to denote a person's approximate age, esp. as being suggestive of the characteristic tastes and outlook of a particular generation (*twentysomething; thirtysomething*). ● *adverb* **1** somewhat; in some degree. **2** *informal* to a high degree (*my foot hurts something terrible*). □ **or something** or some unspecified alternative possibility (*must have run away or something*). **see something of** encounter (a person) briefly or occasionally. **something like 1** an amount in the region of (*left something like a million dollars*). **2** somewhat like (*shaped something like a cigar*). **3** *informal* impressive; a fine specimen of. **something of** to some extent; in some sense (*is something of an expert*).

something else *noun* **1** something different. **2** *informal* something exceptional.

some·time ● *adverb* at some unspecified time. ● *adjective* **1** former (*the sometime mayor*). **2** occasional (*a sometime contributor*).

some·times *adverb* at some times; occasionally.

some·way *adverb* (also **some·ways**) in some way or manner; by some means; somehow.

some·what ● *adverb* to some extent (*behaviour that was somewhat strange; answered somewhat hastily*). ● *noun & pronoun* something (*loses somewhat of its force*).

some·when *adverb informal* at some time.

some·where ● *adverb* in or to some place. ● *pronoun* some unspecified place. □ **get somewhere** *informal* achieve success. **somewhere around** approximately.

some·wheres *adverb* N Amer. dialect = SOMEWHERE.

som·ite /ˈsoːmaɪt/ *noun* = METAMERE. □ **som·itic** /soːˈmɪtɪk/ *adjective* [Greek *sōma* body + -ITE¹]

Somme, Battle of the /sɒm/ a battle of the First World War between British-led forces (including Canadians) and the Germans, on the Western Front in northern France July–Nov. 1916, in which the Germans were forced to retreat a few kilometres at a cost of more than a million casualties on both sides.

som·me·lier /ˌsɒməlˈjeɪ/ *noun* a wine waiter. [French, = butler, from *somme* pack (as SUMPTER)]

Somme River /sɒm/ a river of N France. Rising east of Saint-Quentin, it flows 245 km (153 miles) through Amiens to the English Channel northeast of Dieppe.

som·nam·bu·lism /sɒmˈnambjuˌlɪzəm/ *noun* **1** sleepwalking. **2** a condition of the brain inducing this. □ **som·nam·bu·lant** *adjective* **som·nam·bu·lantly** *adverb* **som·nam·bu·late** *intransitive verb* **som·nam·bu·list** *noun* **som·nam·bu·lis·tic** *adjective* [Latin *somnus* sleep + *ambulare* walk]

som·no·lent /ˈsɒmnələnt/ *adjective* **1** sleepy, drowsy. **2** inducing drowsiness. □ **som·no·lence** *noun* [Old French *sompnolent* or Latin *somnolentus* from *somnus* sleep]

som·oni /sɒˈmoːniː/ *noun* (pl. same or **som·onis**) the basic monetary unit of Tajikistan, equal to one hundred dirams. [Tajik, from the name of Ismail *Samani*, the 9th-c. founder of the Tajik nation]

Som·oza /səˈmoːzə/ **1 Ana·sta·sio** (full surname Somoza García) (1896–1956), Nicaraguan military and political leader, president 1937–47 and 1951–6. As commander-in-chief of the Nicaraguan army he organized a military coup in 1936 and subsequently ruled Nicaragua as a virtual dictator; he was assassinated in 1956. **2** his son **Ana·sta·sio** (full surname Somoza Debayle) (1925–80), Nicaraguan

leader, president 1967–72 and 1974–79. His dictatorial regime was overthrown by the Sandinistas in 1979, and he was assassinated while in exile in Paraguay. **3 Luis** (full surname Somoza Debayle) (1922–67), Nicaraguan leader, eldest son of Anastasio Somoza García, who succeeded his father as president, serving from 1957 to 1963.

son *noun* **1** a boy or man in relation to either or both of his parents. **2 a** a male descendant. **b** (foll. by *of*) a male member of a family, nation, etc. **3** a person regarded as inheriting an occupation, quality, etc., or associated with a particular attribute (*sons of freedom; sons of the soil*). **4** (also **my son**) a form of address esp. to a boy. **5** (**the Son**) (in Christian belief) the second person of the Trinity; Jesus Christ. □ **son·less** *adjective* **son·ship** *noun* [Old English *sunu* from Germanic]

son·ant /ˈsoːnənt/ *Phonetics* ● *adjective* (of a sound) voiced and syllabic. ● *noun* a voiced sound forming a syllable, a vowel, or any of the consonants *l*, *m*, *n* pronounced as a syllable. [Latin *sonare sonant-* sound]

so·nar /ˈsoːnɑr/ *noun* **1** a system for the underwater detection of objects by reflected or emitted sound. **2** an apparatus for this. **3** the method of echolocation used in air or water by animals such as whales and bats. [*sound navigation and ranging*, after *radar*]

so·nata /səˈnɒtə, -ˈnɑtə/ *noun* a composition for one instrument or two (one usu. being a piano accompaniment), usu. in several movements with one (esp. the first) or more in sonata form. [Italian, = sounded (originally as distinct from sung): fem. past participle of *sonare* sound]

sonata form *noun* a type of composition in three sections (exposition, development, and recapitulation) in which two themes (or subjects) are explored according to set key relationships.

sona·tina /ˌsɒnəˈtiːnə/ *noun* a simple or short sonata. [Italian, diminutive of SONATA]

sonde /sɒnd/ *noun* a device sent up to obtain information about atmospheric conditions, esp. = RADIOSONDE. [French, = line for sounding]

Sond·heim /ˈsɒndhaɪm/ **Ste·phen (Joshua)** (b.1930), US composer and lyricist. He became famous with his lyrics for Bernstein's *West Side Story* (1957), and later wrote both words and music for a number of musicals including *A Funny Thing Happened on the Way to the Forum* (1962), *A Little Night Music* (1973), and *Sweeney Todd* (1979).

sone /soːn/ *noun* a unit of subjective loudness. [Latin *sonus* sound]

son et lu·mière /ˌsɒneɪˈluːmjer/ *noun* = SOUND-AND-LIGHT. [French]

Song see SUNG¹.

song *noun* **1** a musical composition comprising a short poem or other set of words set to music; a set of words meant to be sung. **2** singing or vocal music (*burst into song*). **3** a musical composition suggestive of a song. **4** a sound suggestive of singing. **5** the usu. repeated musical call of some birds. **6** a short poem in rhymed stanzas. □ **for a song** *informal* very cheaply. □ **song·ful** *adjective* **song-like** *adjective* [Old English *sang* from Germanic (as SING)]

song and dance *noun informal* a fuss or commotion.

song·bird *noun* **1** a bird with a musical call. **2** a perching bird of the group Oscines, possessing a syrinx. **3** *informal* a superb female singer.

song·book *noun* a collection of songs with music.

song·craft *noun* skill in composing songs.

song cycle *noun* a series of related songs, often on a romantic theme, intended to form one musical entity.

song·fest *noun* a gathering or celebration with much singing.

Song Hong the Vietnamese name for the Red River in SE Asia (see RED RIVER 2).

Song·nam /sɒŋˈnam/ a city in S Korea, just east of Seoul; pop. (est. 1995) 869,094.

Song of Solomon (also called the **Song of Songs** or **the Canticles**) a book of the Bible, an anthology of love poems ascribed to Solomon but dating from a much later period. From an early date Jewish and Christian writers interpreted the book allegorically, in the Talmud as God's dealings with the congregation of Israel and in Christian exegesis as God's relations with the Church or the individual soul.

Song of the Three (Holy Children) a book of the Apocrypha, telling of three Hebrew exiles thrown into a fiery furnace by Nebuchadnezzar; in Catholic and Orthodox Bibles the story is included in the Book of Daniel.

song·smith *noun* a writer of songs.

song sparrow *noun* a N American sparrow, *Melospiza melodia*, with a characteristic musical song.

song·ster *noun informal* **1** a singer, esp. a fluent and skilful one. **2** a songbird.

song·stress *noun* a female singer, esp. a fluent and skilful one.

song thrush *noun* a thrush, *Turdus philomelos*, of Europe and W Asia, with a song partly mimicked from other birds.

song·writ·er *noun* a writer of songs or the music for them. □ **song·writ·ing** *noun*

son·ic /ˈsɒnɪk/ *adjective* of or relating to or using sound or sound waves. □ **son·ic·ally** *adverb* [Latin *sonus* sound]

sonic barrier *noun* = SOUND BARRIER 1.

sonic boom *noun* a loud explosive noise caused by the shock wave from an aircraft when it passes the speed of sound.

son-in-law *noun* (*pl.* **sons-in-law**) the husband of one's daughter.

son·net *noun* a poem of fourteen lines using any of a number of formal rhyme schemes, in English typically in iambic pentameter. [French *sonnet* or Italian *sonetto* diminutive of *suono* SOUND¹]

son·net·eer *noun* a writer of sonnets. □ **son·net·eer·ing** *noun*

sonny *noun informal* often *derogatory* a familiar form of address to a young boy or man who is one's junior.

sono·buoy /ˈsɒnəˌbɔɪ/ *noun* a buoy for detecting underwater sounds and transmitting them by radio. [Latin *sonus* sound + BUOY]

son of a bitch *coarse slang* ● *noun* (*pl.* **sons of bitches**) **1** a general term of contempt or abuse. **2** a despicable or pathetic person. ● *interjection* an exclamation of anger.

son·of·a·bitching *attributive adjective coarse slang* used as an intensifier, esp. expressing hatred or disgust.

son of a gun *informal* ● *noun* **1** a jocular or affectionate form of address or reference. **2** a rascal or rogue. ● *interjection* an exclamation of shock or amazement.

son of God *noun* **1** (**Son of God**) Jesus Christ. **2** a person spiritually attached to God.

son of man *noun* **1** (**Son of Man**) Jesus Christ. **2** a member of the human race; a mortal.

sono·gram /ˈsɒnəˌgram/ *noun* **1** *Med.* the visual image produced by reflected sound waves in a diagnostic ultrasound examination. **2** a graphical representation produced by a sonograph of the distributions of sound energy at different frequencies.

sono·graph /ˈsɒnəˌgraf/ *noun* an instrument which analyzes sound into its component frequencies and produces a graphical record of the results. □ **sono·graph·er** *noun* **sono·graph·ic** *adjective* **sono·graph·ic·ally** *adverb* **sono·graphy** /səˈnɒgrəfi/ *noun*

So·nora /səˈnɔrə/ a state of NW Mexico, on the Gulf of California; capital, Hermosillo. □ **So·nor·an** *adjective*

Sonoran Desert an arid region of N America, comprising SE California and SW Arizona in the US and, in Mexico, much of Baja California Norte and the western part of Sonora.

so·nor·ous /ˈsɒnərəs, ˈsɒn-, səˈnɔrəs/ *adjective* **1** having a loud, full, or deep sound; resonant. **2** (of speech, style, etc.) imposing, grand. □ **so·nor·ity** /səˈnɒrɪti/ *noun* (*pl.* **-ities**). **so·nor·ous·ly** *adverb* **so·nor·ous·ness** *noun* [Latin *sonorus* from *sonor* sound]

Sons of Freedom *Cdn hist.* an extremist splinter group of Doukhobors that became notorious for its violent acts of terrorism and protest which included arson, bombings, and nude protest parades, waged against the government esp. in BC throughout the first half of the 20th c.

Sons of Liberty *Cdn hist.* an organization active in 1837 in Montreal to pursue the republican ideals of the American Revolution and fight for the right of a colony to become independent. [French *Fils de la Liberté*]

Son·tag /ˈsɒntag/ **Susan** (b.1933), US critic, essayist, and novelist. She established her reputation as a 'new intellectual' with a series of essays on culture, which were collected in *Against Interpretation* (1966); her other works include the essay collection *Illness as Metaphor* (1979) and the novel *The Volcano Lover* (1992).

Soo, the an informal name for SAULT STE. MARIE, Ontario. [phonetic spelling]

Soo·chow see SUZHOU.

sook /suk/ *noun Austral., NZ, & Cdn* (*Maritimes & Nfld*) *derogatory* a person acting childishly; a wimp, coward, or sissy. [English dial. *suck*, used to call a calf]

sooky baby *noun Cdn* (*Maritimes & Nfld*) = SOOK.

soon *adverb* **1** within a short period of time (*we shall soon know the result*). **2** relatively early (*must you go so soon?*). **3** readily or willingly (in expressing choice or preference: *which would you sooner do?; I would as soon stay behind*). □ **as** (or **so**) **soon as** at the moment that; not later than (*I came as soon as I heard about it*). **how soon?** in what period of time; how early (*how soon will it be ready?*). **no sooner ... than** at the very moment that (*no sooner had we arrived than the rain stopped*). **sooner or later** at some time in the future; eventually. □ **soon·ish** *adverb* [Old English *sōna* from West Germanic]

soo·pol·lalie /ˈsoːpəˌlali/ (also **sopal·lil·lie** /ˈsoːpəlɪli/) *Cdn* (*BC*) **1** = BUFFALO BERRY. **2** a thick drink made from crushed buffalo berries. [from *soop*, var. of SOAP + Chinook Jargon *olallie* berry]

soot /sut/ ● *noun* a black carbonaceous substance rising in fine flakes in the smoke of wood, coal, oil, etc., and deposited on the sides of a chimney etc. ● *transitive verb* cover with soot. [Old English *sōt* from Germanic]

sooth /suːθ/ *noun archaic* truth, fact. □ **in sooth** really, truly. [Old English *sōth* (originally adj., = true) from Germanic]

soothe *verb* **1** *transitive* bring or restore (a person or feelings etc.) to a peaceful or tranquil state; calm. **2** *transitive* reduce the intensity of; soften, allay, or relieve (pain, an emotion, etc.). **3** *intransitive* provide relief or tranquility. □ **sooth·ing** *adjective* **sooth·ing·ly** *adverb* [Old English *sōthian* verify, from *sōth* true: see SOOTH]

sooth·er *noun* **1** *Cdn & Brit.* a ring or nipple made of rubber or plastic given to a baby to suck. **2** a thing that calms or comforts.

sooth·say·er *noun* a person who predicts future events; a prophet. □ **sooth·say·ing** *noun* [Middle English, = one who says the truth: see SOOTH]

sooty *adjective* (**soot·i·er**, **soot·i·est**) **1** covered with or full of soot. **2** (esp. of an animal or bird) of a dusky black or brownish black colour. □ **soot·i·ness** *noun*

sooty shearwater *noun* a southern shearwater, *Puffinus griseus*, which has mainly dark plumage and breeds from New Zealand to Chile and the Falklands, and spends its summer on the west and east coasts of N America.

SOP *abbreviation* Standard Operating Procedure.

sop ● *noun* **1** a thing given or done to pacify or appease a person; a concession or bribe. **2** a piece of bread etc. dipped in gravy or wine etc. ● *transitive verb* (**sopped**, **sop·ping**) **1** (foll. by *up*) absorb (liquid) in a sponge or towel etc. **2** soak or drench with liquid; make thoroughly wet. [Old English *sopp*, related to Old High German *sopfa* bread and milk, and SUP¹]

sopal·lil·lie *var.* of SOOPOLLALIE.

So·phia see SOFIA.

soph·ism /ˈsɒfɪzəm/ *noun* a plausible but false argument, esp. one intended to deceive or display ingenuity in reasoning. [Old French *sophime* from Latin from Greek *sophisma* clever device, from *sophos* wise]

soph·ist /ˈsɒfɪst/ *noun* **1** a person who reasons with clever but fallacious arguments. **2** (usu. **Sophist**) *Gk Hist.* a paid teacher of philosophy and rhetoric, esp. one associated with moral skepticism and specious reasoning. □ **so·phis·tic** *adjective* **so·phis·tical** *adjective* **so·phis·tic·ally** *adverb*

so·phis·ti·cate ● *transitive verb* /səˈfɪstəˌkeit/ **1** deprive (a person) of natural simplicity or innocence, esp. through education or experience. **2** make (a theory, piece of equipment, etc.) highly developed or complex; refine. **3** falsify or corrupt (a text, argument, etc.). ● *noun* /səˈfɪstəkət/ a sophisticated person. □ **so·phis·ti·ca·tion** *noun* [medieval Latin *sophisticate* tamper with, from *sophisticus* (as SOPHISM)]

so·phis·ti·cat·ed *adjective* **1 a** (of a person) worldly, cultured, and refined; discriminating in taste and judgment. **b** showing awareness of the complexities of a subject; knowledgeable, experienced. **2** appealing to sophisticated people or sophisticated tastes. **3 a** (of a theory or idea etc.) based on or involving advanced concepts; complex, not plain or straightforward. **b** (of a piece of equipment etc.) highly developed; technologically advanced. □ **so·phis·ti·cat·ed·ly** *adverb*

soph·istry /ˈsɒfəstri/ *noun* (*pl.* **-tries**) **1** the use of intentionally deceptive or specious arguments or reasoning, esp. as a dialectic exercise. **2** an instance of this.

Soph·o·cles /ˈsɒfəˌkliːz/ (c.496–406 BC), Greek dramatist. His seven surviving plays are notable for their addition of a third actor to the previous two plus chorus, as well as for their examination of the relationship between mortals and the divine order; they include *Antigone, Electra*, and *Oedipus Tyrannus* (also called *Oedipus Rex*).

soph·o·more /ˈsɒfmɔr, ˈsɒfəˌmɔr/ *noun N Amer.* **1** (esp. in the US) a student in his or her second year of high school, college, or university (also *attributive*: *sophomore year*). **2** *Sport* an athlete in his or her second year at a particular level or in a particular league (also *attributive*: *sophomore season*). **3** (*attributive*) designating the second work, production, etc. of an artist or performer (*sophomore album*). [earlier *sophumer* from *sophum*, obsolete var. of SOPHISM]

soph·o·moric /sɒfˈmɔːrɪk/ *adjective* esp. *N Amer.* **1** of, relating to, or befitting a sophomore. **2** maintaining a pretentious demeanour of intellectual sophistication and maturity while immature, juvenile, or shallow.

sopo·rific /ˌsɒpəˈrɪfɪk/ ● *adjective* **1 a** tending to induce or produce sleep. **b** tedious, boring. **2** (of a person) sleepy, drowsy. ● *noun* a soporific drug or influence. □ **sopo·rific·ally** *adverb* [Latin *sopor* sleep + -FIC]

sop·ping *adjective* (also **sopping wet**) soaked with liquid; thoroughly drenched.

sop·pres·sata /ˌsɒprɛˈsɑːtə/ *noun* a kind of dense unsmoked Italian salami (*Ezio makes the best soppressata in Toronto*). [Italian, lit. = 'compressed']

soppy *adjective* (**sop·pi·er**, **sop·pi·est**) **1** *informal* **a** mawkishly sentimental; sappy, mushy. **b** *Brit.* (foll. by *on*) foolishly infatuated with. **2** soaked with water. □ **sop·pi·ly** *adverb* **sop·pi·ness** *noun*

sop·ra·nino /ˌsɒprəˈniːnoʊ/ *noun* (*pl.* **-nos**) *Music* an instrument of a pitch higher than that of a soprano, esp. a recorder or saxophone. [Italian, diminutive of SOPRANO]

sop·rano /səˈprɑːnoʊ/ *noun* (*pl.* **-ranos** or **sop·rani** /-niː/) **1 a** the highest singing voice. **b** a female or boy singer with this voice. **c** a part written for it. **2 a** an instrument of a high or the highest pitch in its family. **b** its player. [Italian from *sopra* above, from Latin *supra*]

soprano recorder *noun* *N Amer.* the most common size of recorder, about 12 inches long, with a range of two octaves starting at C above middle C.

sora /ˈsɔːrə/ *noun* (*pl.* same or **soras**) (also **sora rail**) a small N American rail, *Porzana carolina*. [origin uncertain]

sor·bet /sɔrˈbeɪ, ˈsɔrbeɪ, ˈsɔrbət/ *noun* a soft water ice made with fruit juice or fruit purée served esp. between main courses to cleanse the palate and reinvigorate the appetite, or as a dessert. [French from Italian *sorbetto* from Turkish *şerbet* from Arabic *šarba* to drink: compare SHERBET]

sorb·itol /ˈsɔrbɪtɒl/ *noun* a sweet crystalline alcohol found in some fruit, used commercially as a substitute for sugar. [*sorb* (from French *sorbe* or Latin *sorbus* 'service tree', *sorbum* 'serviceberry') + -ITE[1] + -OL[1]]

sor·cer·er *noun* a person who claims to use magic powers; a wizard or magician. □ **sor·cer·ous** *adjective* **sor·cery** *noun* (*pl.* **-ies**). [obsolete *sorcer* from Old French *sorcier*, ultimately from Latin *sors sortis* lot]

sor·cer·ess *noun* a woman who claims to use magic powers.

sor·did *adjective* **1** immoral, base, degenerate. **2** characterized by or proceeding from self-interest; mercenary. **3** dirty, filthy, squalid. □ **sor·did·ly** *adverb* **sor·did·ness** *noun* [French *sordide* or Latin *sordidus* from *sordēre* be dirty]

sor·dino /sɔrˈdiːnoʊ/ *noun* (*pl.* **sor·dini** /-niː/) *Music* a mute for a bowed or wind instrument. [Italian from *sordo* mute, from Latin *surdus*]

sore ● *adjective* **1** (of a part of the body) painful from injury or disease. **2** (of a person) suffering bodily pain. **3** esp. *N Amer.* angry, irritated, or vexed. **4** *archaic* grievous or severe (*in sore need*). ● *noun* **1** a raw or tender place on the body, such as a cut or wound. **2** a source of distress or annoyance (*reopen old sores*). ● *adverb* *archaic* grievously, severely. □ **sore·ness** *noun* [Old English *sār* (n. & adj.), *sāre* (adv.), from Germanic]

sore·head *noun* esp. *N Amer.* an irritable, grumpy, or disgruntled person.

Sorel /sɔˈrɛl, sə-/ a former city in south central Quebec, located at the confluence of the Richelieu and St. Lawrence rivers, just south of Lac Saint-Pierre, now joined with Tracy as the city of Sorel-Tracy; pop. (2001) 21,804. [alteration of P. de *Saurel*, an officer with the Carignan-Salières Regiment d.1682]

sore loser *noun* a person who cannot accept losing a game etc. graciously.

Sorel-Tracy /sɔˈrɛl, sə-/ a city in south central Quebec, located at the confluence of the Richelieu and St. Lawrence rivers, just south of Lac Saint-Pierre; pop. (2001) 34,194.

sore·ly *adverb* extremely, greatly, desperately (*Michael will be sorely missed*).

sore point *noun* (also **sore spot**) a subject causing distress or annoyance; a contentious issue.

sore throat *noun* an inflammation of the mucous membrane lining the back of the mouth, or of the tonsils.

sor·ghum /ˈsɔrgəm/ *noun* any tropical cereal grass of the genus

Sorghum, e.g. durra. [modern Latin from Italian *sorgo*, perhaps from unrecorded Romanic *syricum* (*gramen*) Syrian (grass)]

sori *pl.* of SORUS.

Sor·opti·mist /səˈrɒptɪmɪst/ *noun* a member of an international association of clubs for professional and business women. [Latin *soror* sister + OPTIMIST]

soror·al /səˈrɔːrəl/ *adjective* of, pertaining to, or characteristic of a sister or sisterhood. [Latin *soror* sister + -AL]

soror·ity /səˈrɒrɪti/ *noun* (*pl.* **-ities**) *N Amer.* a society for female students in a university or college. [Latin *soror* sister, after *fraternity*]

so·ro·sis /səˈroʊsɪs/ *noun* (*pl.* **so·ro·ses** /-siːz/) *Bot.* a fleshy compound fruit, e.g. a pineapple or mulberry, derived from the ovaries of several flowers. [modern Latin from Greek *sōros* heap]

sorp·tion *noun* absorption or adsorption occurring jointly or separately. [back-formation from *absorption, adsorption*]

sor·rel[1] /ˈsɒrəl/ *noun* any of several plants of the genus *Rumex* having acid leaves, esp. *R. acetosa*, a plant of meadows with hastate leaves sometimes used in salads and for flavouring. *See also* WOOD SORREL. [Old French *surele, sorele* from Germanic]

sor·rel[2] /ˈsɒrəl/ ● *adjective* of a light reddish-brown or chestnut colour. ● *noun* **1** this colour. **2** an animal of this colour, esp. a horse. [Old French *sorel* from *sor* yellowish, from Frankish]

sor·row ● *noun* **1** mental distress caused by bereavement, suffering, or disappointment; grief. **2** a cause of grief or sadness. **3** the outward expression of grief; lamentation, mourning. ● *intransitive verb* feel or express sorrow or sadness; grieve, mourn. □ **sor·row·ing** *adjective* [Old English *sorh, sorg*]

sor·row·ful *adjective* **1** feeling sorrow or grief; unhappy, sad. **2** characterized by or causing sorrow; distressing, lamentable. **3** expressing sorrow (*a sorrowful expression*). □ **sor·row·fully** *adverb* **sor·row·ful·ness** *noun*

sorry (**sor·ri·er**, **sor·ri·est**) ● *adjective* **1** (*predicative*) feeling sadness or regret (*we were sorry to hear of your mother's illness*). **2** (*predicative*) full of shame, guilt, and remorse, esp. about a past action (*I'm sorry I spilled coffee on the rug*). **3** used to express mild regret, disagreement, or refusal, and for making apologies and excuses (*I'm sorry we won't be able to come*). **4** wretched, pitiful, pathetic (*the sorry state of our finances*). ● *interjection* **1** used to express apology or regret (*did I kick you? Sorry.*). **2** (in *interrogative*) (as a request for something to be repeated) I beg your pardon; what did you say? □ **feel** (or **be**) **sorry for someone** feel sympathy or pity for. **feel** (or **be**) **sorry for oneself** bewail one's problems or plight; be self-indulgently depressed. □ **sor·ri·ness** *noun* [Old English *sārig* from West Germanic origin, from the base of the noun SORE]

sort ● *noun* **1** a group of things or people determined on the basis of common attributes; a type or kind. **2** (foll. by *of*) an unusual or uncertain example of a specified thing (*she is some sort of writer*). **3** *informal* a person of a specified character or kind (*a good sort*). **4** *Computing* the arrangement of data in a prescribed sequence. **5** *Printing* a letter in a particular font of type. **6** *archaic* a manner or way. ● *transitive verb* (often foll. by *out, through*) arrange systematically or according to type, class, etc.; separate and put into a different order or different groups. □ **in some sort** to a certain extent. **of sorts** (or **of a sort**) *informal* of an unusual kind; not fully deserving the name (*a holiday of sorts*). **out of sorts 1** slightly irritable or grumpy. **2** slightly unwell. **sort of** *informal* to some extent; somewhat (*I sort of expected it*). **sort out 1** separate and arrange into groups according to kind or type. **2** separate (things of one type) from a miscellaneous group. **3** resolve (a problem or difficulty). **4** *informal* deal with or reprimand (a person). □ **sort·able** *adjective* **sort·er** *noun* **sort·ing** *noun* [Old French *sorte*, ultimately from Latin *sors sortis* lot, condition]

sorta *adverb* *informal* = SORT OF (see SORT). [corruption]

sor·tie /ˈsɔrti/ ● *noun* **1** a sudden emergence, dash, or attack made by troops from a besieged garrison. **2** an operational flight by a single military aircraft. **3** *informal* a jaunt or excursion. ● *intransitive verb* (**sor·ties**, **sor·tied**, **sor·tie·ing**) make or go on a sortie. [French, fem. past participle of *sortir* go out]

sorus /ˈsɔrəs/ *noun* (*pl.* **sori** /-raɪ/) *Bot.* a heap or cluster, esp. of spore cases on the underside of a fern leaf, or in a fungus or lichen. [modern Latin from Greek *sōros* heap]

SOS *noun* (*pl.* **SOS's**) **1** an international code signal of extreme distress, used esp. by ships at sea. **2** an urgent appeal for help. [the letters *s*, *o*, and *s*, chosen as being easily transmitted and recognized in Morse code; by folk etymology an abbreviation of *save our souls*]

Consonants: b *but* d *dog* f *few* g *get* h *her* j *yes* k *cat* l *leg* m *man* n *no* p *pen* r *red* s *sit*

Sos·now·iec /sɒsˈnɒvjets/ an industrial mining town in SW Poland, west of Cracow; pop. (est. 2000) 241,102.

so-so ● *adjective* (usu. *predicative*) indifferent; mediocre; neither very good nor very bad. ● *adverb* indifferently; only moderately well.

SOS pad /ˌesoːˈes/ *noun proprietary* a scouring pad of steel wool impregnated with soap.

sos·tenu·to /ˌsɒstəˈnuːtoː/ *Music* ● *adverb & adjective* in a sustained or prolonged manner. ● *noun* (*pl.* **-tos**) a passage to be played in this way. [Italian, past participle of *sostenere* SUSTAIN]

sot *noun* a habitual drunk. □ **sot·tish** *adjective* [Old English *sott* & Old French *sot* foolish, from medieval Latin *sottus*]

so·teri·ol·ogy /soːˌtiːriːˈɒlədʒi, sɒ-/ *noun Theol.* the doctrine of salvation. □ **so·teri·o·logic·al** /-riˈɒlɒdʒɪkəl/ *adjective* [Greek *sōtēria* 'salvation' + -LOGY]

Sothic /ˈsoːθɪk/ *adjective* of or relating to Sirius, the Dog Star, esp. with reference to the ancient Egyptian year fixed by its heliacal rising. [Greek *Sōthis*, an Egyptian name for Sirius, the Dog Star]

Sotho /ˈsuːtuː/ ● *noun* **1** a member of a Bantu-speaking people chiefly inhabiting Lesotho, Botswana, and the Transvaal. **2** = SESOTHO. ● *adjective* of or relating to the Sotho or their language. [Bantu]

sotto voce /ˌsɒtoː ˈvoːtʃei/ ● *adverb* in a low voice so as not to be heard. ● *adjective* (of a remark, comment, etc.) uttered or spoken etc. in a soft voice or undertone. [Italian *sotto* under + *voce* voice]

sou /su/ *noun* **1** *hist.* a former French coin of low value. **2** (usu. with *neg.*) *informal* a very small amount of money (*hasn't a sou*). [French, originally pl. *sous* from Old French *sout* from Latin SOLIDUS]

sou·brette /suːˈbret/ *noun* **1** a pert maidservant or similar female character in a play, ballet, or musical comedy. **2** an actress taking this part. [French from Provençal *soubreto* fem. of *soubret* coy, from *sobrar* from Latin *superare* be above]

sou·bri·quet *var. of* SOBRIQUET.

sou·chong /ˈsuːʃɒŋ/ *noun* a fine black kind of China tea. [Chinese *xiao* small + *zhong* sort]

souf·fle /ˈsuːfəl/ *noun Med.* a low murmur audible in a stethoscope, caused chiefly by the flow of blood through an organ. [French from *souffler* blow, from Latin *sufflare*]

souf·flé /suːˈflei/ ● *noun* a light spongy dish usu. made by adding egg yolks and a sweet or savoury filling to stiffly beaten egg whites then baked until puffy (*cheese soufflé*). ● *adjective* (of ceramics) decorated with small spots of colour applied by blowing. □ **souf·fléd** *adjective* [French past participle (as SOUFFLE)]

Sou·frière /ˌsuːfriˈer/ **1** a dormant volcano on the French island of Guadeloupe in the W Indies. Rising to 1 468 m (4,813 ft.), it is the highest peak in the Lesser Antilles. **2** an active volcanic peak on the island of St. Vincent in the W Indies. It rises to a height of 1 234 m (4,006 ft.). [French, from *soufre* SULPHUR]

sough /sau, sʌf/ ● *intransitive verb* make a moaning, whistling, or rushing sound as of the wind in trees etc. ● *noun* a gentle rushing or murmuring sound. [Old English *swōgan* resound]

sought past and past participle of SEEK.

sought-after *adjective* in high demand; generally desired or coveted.

souk /suːk/ *noun* (also **suk, sukh, suq**) an open marketplace or bazaar in Muslim countries. [Arabic *sūk*]

sou·kous /ˈsuːkuːs/ *noun* a style of African popular music characterized by syncopated rhythms and intricate contrasting guitar melodies, originating in Congo (formerly Zaire). [Congolese alteration of French *secouer* to shake]

soul *noun* **1** the spiritual or immaterial component or nature of a human being or animal, regarded as the seat of the emotions or intellect. **2 a** the spiritual part of a human being considered in its moral aspect or in relation to God, esp. regarded as immortal and being capable of redemption or damnation in a future state. **b** the disembodied spirit of a dead person, regarded as invested with some degree of personality and form. **3 a** (usu. foll. by *of*) a person regarded as the personification of a certain quality (*the very soul of discretion*). **b** a person regarded as embodying moral or intellectual qualities (*left that to meaner souls*). **4** (usu. with *neg.*) an individual (*not a soul in sight*). **5** a person regarded with familiarity, affection, pity, etc. (*the poor soul was utterly confused*). **6** (usu. foll. by *of*) **a** a person regarded as the inspirer or animating spirit of an activity or cause etc. (*she is the life and soul of the party*). **b** the essential quality or animating element of something (*honesty is the soul of this relationship*). **7** emotional or intellectual energy or intensity, esp. as revealed in a work of art. **8** (also *attributive*) the emotional or spiritual quality of black American life and culture, manifested in art, music, etc. **9** = SOUL MUSIC. □ **upon my soul!** an

exclamation of surprise. □ **-souled** *adjective* (in *combination*). [Old English *sāwol, sāwel, sāwl,* from Germanic]

soul brother *noun informal* **1** a black man or boy, esp. as regarded by other blacks. **2** a spiritual brother.

soul-destroy·ing *adjective* **1** (of an activity etc.) stultifyingly monotonous. **2** capable of suppressing a person's emotional or intellectual spirit or faculties (*a soul-destroying drug*).

soul food *noun* food traditionally eaten by American blacks, esp. those dishes originating in the rural southern US.

soul·ful *adjective* **1** full of soul or feeling; of a highly emotional or spiritual nature. **2** *ironic* excessively or artificially sentimental or emotional. □ **soul·ful·ly** *adverb* **soul·ful·ness** *noun*

soul·less *adjective* **1** lacking sensitivity; cruel, ruthless. **2** having no soul (*the soulless machine*). **3** (of a person) lacking ambition or passion; dull, uninteresting. **4** (of a thing) made or done without imagination; lacking humanizing or distinguishing characteristics (*a soulless stretch of identical houses*). □ **soul·less·ly** *adverb* **soul·less·ness** *noun*

soul·mate *noun* a person with whom one shares an interest, passion, understanding, or bond, esp. a friend, lover, or spouse.

soul music *noun* a type of black American pop music which combines rhythm and blues with the emotional intensity and expressiveness of gospel, characterized by its emphasis on vocals and an impassioned improvisatory delivery.

soul-search·ing ● *noun* a penetrating or critical examination of one's actions, beliefs, motives, or emotions. ● *adjective* characterized by such analysis or scrutiny.

soul sister *noun informal* **1** a black woman or girl, esp. as regarded by other blacks. **2** a spiritual sister.

soul·ster *noun* a singer of soul music.

soul-stirring *adjective* moving, touching (*a soul-stirring performance*).

Sound, the the English name for the ØRESUND.

sound¹ ● *noun* **1** a sensation caused in the ear by vibrations of longitudinal waves of pressure passing through the surrounding air or other medium. **2 a** vibrations causing this sensation. **b** similar vibrations whether audible or not. **3** anything that can be heard; a noise (*I heard a sound at the door*). **4** a pleasant or harmonious effect produced by a continuous and regular series of audible vibrations (*opp.* NOISE *noun* 3a). **5** a particular sound or series of sounds associated with a specific source (*the sound of a drum*). **6** an idea or impression conveyed by words (*don't like the sound of that*). **7** a distinctive or readily identifiable style of esp. pop music (*this band developed their own sound*). **8** speech or music etc. accompanying a movie, TV show, computer multimedia package, or other visual presentation (*he was watching TV with the sound off*). **9 a** (in full **sound crew**) the department of engineers responsible for producing or recording sound for a movie or concert etc. **b** = SOUND SYSTEM. **10** (in full **speech sound**) any of a series of articulate utterances (*vowel and consonant sounds*). **11** (often *attributive*) broadcasting by radio as distinct from television. ● *verb* **1** *intransitive* convey a specific impression when heard (*you sound like you know what you're doing*). **2** *transitive* cause (an instrument etc.) to make a sound. **3** *transitive* give an audible signal for (an alarm etc.) (*sound the retreat*). **4** *transitive* utter, pronounce, or declare; make known (*they sound her praises*). **5** *intransitive* produce or emit sound (*the alarm clock sounded and I woke up*). **6** *transitive* (often foll. by *out*) pronounce or articulate (words) sound by sound. □ **sound and fury 1** talk or words without substance. **2** a noisy disturbance, activity, excitement, etc. **sound off** talk loudly or express one's opinions vehemently; complain. □ **sound·less** *adjective* **sound·lessly** *adverb* **sound·less·ness** *noun* [Anglo-French *soun*, Old French *son* from Latin *sonus*]

sound² ● *adjective* **1** healthy, well; free from disease or injury. **2** (of a building, structure, etc.) free from any decay or defect; undamaged, unbroken, in good condition. **3** (of advice, judgment, a policy, etc.) in full accordance with fact or reason, based on well-grounded principles; sensible, fair, correct. **4 a** financially secure (*a sound investment*). **b** (of currency) having a fixed or stable value, esp. based on gold (*sound money*). **5 a** (of sleep) deep, unbroken, undisturbed. **b** (of a person sleeping) tending to sleep deeply without being easily woken. **6** severe, hard, thorough (*a sound thrashing*). **7** (of theology) orthodox. **8** (of a person, character, etc.) honourable, honest, trustworthy. ● *adverb* in a sound manner; soundly (*sound asleep*). □ **sound·ly** *adverb* **sound·ness** *noun* [Middle English *sund, isund* from Old English *gesund* from West Germanic]

sound³ *verb* **1** *transitive* **a** test the depth or quality of the bottom of (the sea or a river etc.). **b** measure (depth). **2** *transitive* **a** (often foll. by *out*) inquire (esp. cautiously or discreetly) into the opinions or feelings of (a person). **b** investigate, attempt to ascertain (a matter, a person's opinions, etc.). **3** *intransitive* (of a whale or fish) dive to the bottom. **4** *transitive* get records of temperature, humidity, pressure, etc. from (the upper atmosphere). □ **sound·er** *noun* [Old French *sonder*, ultimately from Latin SUB- + *unda* wave]

sound⁴ *noun* **1 a** a narrow channel or stretch of water, esp. one between the mainland and an island or connecting two large bodies of water. **b** an arm of the sea. **2** the swim bladder of certain fish, esp. cod, which may be salted and eaten and is considered a delicacy. [Old English *sund*, = Old Norse *sund* swimming, strait]

sound-alike *noun* a person or thing closely resembling another in sound (*this band is a Beatles sound-alike*).

sound-and-light *noun* (*attributive*) designating a nighttime show or spectacle in which a building, historic site, etc. is illuminated while its historical significance is explained through narration and sound effects.

sound barrier *noun* **1** the increased drag, reduced controllability, etc. which occurs when an aircraft approaches the speed of sound. **2** a wall erected or insulated to prevent the passage of sound, as from one room to another. □ **break the sound barrier** travel faster than or accelerate past the speed of sound.

sound bite *noun* a short extract from a recorded interview, speech, etc., chosen for its pungency or appropriateness and edited into a news broadcast.

sound·board *noun* **1** a thin resonating sheet of wood in a piano or sound box of a stringed instrument, such as a violin or cello, over which the strings pass to increase the sound produced. **2** *Computing* a sound card.

sound box *noun* the hollow chamber providing resonance and forming the body of a stringed musical instrument.

sound card *noun* a device capable of converting digitized audio signals into an analog audio signal, inserted in a computer to allow the use of audio components for multimedia applications.

sound check *noun* a test of sound equipment before a concert or recording session to ensure that the desired sound is being produced.

sound effect *noun* a sound other than speech or music made artificially to evoke a particular atmosphere or produce a realistic effect in a movie or play etc.

sound engineer *noun* = SOUNDMAN.

sound hole *noun* any of a number of variously shaped apertures in the belly or soundboard of some stringed instruments.

sound·ing¹ *noun* (usu. in *pl.*) **1 a** the action or process of measuring the depth of water, now usu. by means of echo. **b** (in *pl.*) the determination of any physical property at a depth in the sea or at a height in the atmosphere. **c** an instance of this. **2** cautious investigation. **3** *Naut.* measurements taken by sounding. **4** a region close to the shore that is a depth suitable for sounding.

sound·ing² *adjective* **1** (in *combination*) **a** having a specified sound (*she had a youthful-sounding voice*). **b** giving a mental impression of a specified kind (*it was a funny-sounding idea*). **2** producing or capable of producing esp. loud or resonant sound (*sounding brass*). **3** having a resonant or imposing sound with little substance; boastful (*sounding promises*).

sounding board *noun* **1** a canopy, screen, or board placed above or behind a stage or pulpit to direct sound towards the audience or congregation. **2** a means of making one's opinions, beliefs, etc. more widely known (*the magazine became a sounding board for its editor's beliefs*). **3** a person whose feedback will serve as an accurate assessment of how well a plan, idea, theory, etc. will succeed or be received. **4** = SOUNDBOARD 1.

sounding line *noun* a graduated line weighted at one end with a lead plumb used to sound the depth of water.

sound·man *noun* (*pl.* **-men**) *N Amer.* an engineer responsible for producing sound for a concert, movie, etc.

sound poetry *noun* a type of poetry that is most effective when read or performed, attempting to convey meaning through the sound of words when grouped rather than through their semantic meaning.

sound post *noun* a small peg of wood fixed as a support beneath the bridge of a violin or similar stringed instrument, connecting the belly and the back.

sound·proof ● *adjective* impervious to sound. ● *transitive verb* make soundproof. □ **sound·proof·ing** *noun*

sound·scape *noun* **1** a musical composition consisting of a texture of sounds. **2** the sounds which form an auditory environment.

sound stage *noun* an enclosed soundproof stage or large studio with excellent acoustic properties, suitable for filming and recording concerts, movies, etc.

sound system *noun* a set of equipment used for the reproduction and amplification of sound, such as a stereo or public address system.

sound·track ● *noun* **1 a** the sound element of a film recorded optically, digitally, or magnetically. **b** a narrow band on the edge of a strip of film containing this recording. **2** such a recording, or selected excerpts from it, made available for sale. **3** any constituent single track in a multi-track recording. ● *transitive verb* **1** provide with a soundtrack. **2** serve as a soundtrack for.

sound wave *noun* a longitudinal pressure wave in an elastic medium, such as air, esp. one that propagates audible sound.

soup ● *noun* **1** a usu. savoury liquid dish made by boiling meat, fish, or vegetables etc. with seasoning in stock or water, and often served as a first course. **2** *informal* anything jumbled, blended, or mixed, or having a consistency resembling that of soup, esp. a dense fog. ● *transitive verb* (usu. foll. by *up*) *informal* **1** modify (an engine, car, etc.) so as to increase its power or efficiency. **2** revise (writing, music, etc.) so as to increase its power or impact; enhance. □ **from soup to nuts** *N Amer. informal* from beginning to end, completely. **in the soup** *informal* in trouble. □ **soup·like** *adjective* [French *soupe* sop, broth, from Late Latin *suppa* from Germanic: compare SOP, SUP¹]

soup·çon /ˈsuːpsɔ̃/ *noun* a very small amount; a dash, or hint (*a soupçon of garlic*). [French from Old French *sou(s)peçon* from medieval Latin *suspectio -onis*: see SUSPICION]

soup du jour *noun* the soup featured by a restaurant on a particular day. [French *soupe du jour*, lit. 'soup of the day']

souped-up *adjective* modified so as to increase efficiency, power, appeal, etc. (*a souped-up computer*).

soup kitchen *noun* a place where warm meals, usu. soup, are served to the needy for little or no charge.

soup line *noun* *N Amer.* a lineup for food at a soup kitchen.

soup plate *noun* a shallow, flat-bottomed, wide-rimmed bowl in which soup is served.

soup spoon *noun* a large spoon with a round bowl for eating soup.

soupy *adjective* (**soup·i·er**, **soup·i·est**) **1** of the consistency of soup. **2** *N Amer. informal* sentimental; mawkish. **3 a** (of fog, mist, etc.) thick, dense. **b** (of the weather) foggy. □ **soup·i·ness** *noun*

sour ● *adjective* **1** having a tart or acid taste like that of lemon, vinegar, or unripe fruit (*sour apples*). **2 a** (of food, esp. milk or cream) having gone bad because of fermentation. **b** smelling or tasting rancid or unpleasant. **3 a** (of a person, temper, etc.) angry, resentful, bitter, cranky. **b** (of a comment, facial expression, etc.) expressing discontent or irritation. **4** (of a thing) unpleasant; disagreeable (*a sour experience*). **5** (of a musical note) out of tune. **6** (of oil or gas etc.) containing a relatively high proportion of sulphur. **7** (of the soil) highly acidic. ● *noun* **1** *N Amer.* an alcoholic drink with lemon or lime juice and ice (*whisky sour*). **2** an acid solution used in bleaching, tanning, etc. ● *transitive & intransitive verb* **1** make or become sour. **2** make or become unpleasant or strained. □ **go** (or **turn**) **sour 1** (of food etc.) become bad because of fermentation. **2** turn out badly. **sour on** stop liking or supporting (*they soon began to sour on federalism*). □ **sour·ish** *adjective* **sour·ly** *adverb* **sour·ness** *noun* [Old English *sūr* from Germanic]

source ● *noun* **1 a** a place, person, or thing from which something originates or may be obtained. **b** (foll. by *of*) a cause of or reason for (*her grades were a source of concern for her parents*). **2 a** a document from which original information or evidence in support of some fact or event may be obtained (also *attributive: source material*). **b** a person who supplies information or gives esp. unattributable statements to the media (*sources close to the politician say she will not run in the next election*). **3** the beginning or origin of a river or stream. **4** *Computing* (*attributive*) denoting files, programs, software, etc. written using a source code rather than machine code. **5 a** a body emitting radiation etc. **b** *Physics* a place from which a fluid or current flows. **c** *Electronics* a part of a transistor from which carriers flow into the channel between electrodes. ● *transitive verb* **1** contract a particular manufacturer or company to supply (a product, part, or materials). **2** have, cite, or identify (a book etc.) as a source of information. □ **at source** at the point of origin or issue. □ **source·less** *adjective* **sourcing** *noun* [Old French *sors, sourse*, past participle of *sourdre* rise, from Latin *surgere*]

source·book *noun* **1** a collection of writings, articles, etc. on a particular subject used as a basic introduction to that subject. **2** a comprehensive directory or catalogue of a particular subject.

source code *noun* *Computing* the complex series of instructions supplied to a computer by a programmer using a compiler or interpreter which translates it into machine code.

Vowels: a *cat*   ɑ *arm*   e *bed*   ɜr *her*   ɜː *deux*   ə *ago*   ɪ *sit*   i *cosy*   iː *feed*   ɒ *hot*   ɔ *pore*   ɔː *no*   ʌ *run*   ʊ *put*

source language noun **1** the language from which a translation is made. **2** *Computing* a language in which a program or procedure is originally written before being translated into a form that can be read by a computer, such as machine code.

sour cherry noun **1** the acid fruit of the cherry *Prunus cerasus*, used in cooking. **2** the small bushy tree which bears this fruit.

sour cream noun cream soured by lactic acid bacteria, used esp. in dips, salads, and as a garnish.

sour·dough noun *N Amer.* **1** a leaven for making bread etc. consisting of fermenting dough, originally the dough left over from a previous baking. **2** bread made from sourdough (also *attributive: sourdough rolls*). **3** *N Amer.* (*Yukon & Alaska*) **a** *hist.* an experienced prospector or miner. **b** an old-timer. [sense 3a with allusion to the use of sourdough to raise bread baked during the winter when supplies of yeast were hard to come by in remote areas]

sour grapes plural noun (treated as *sing.*) resentful disparagement of something one envies or covets but cannot achieve or acquire personally. [with allusion to Aesop's fable *The Fox and the Grapes*]

sour gum noun *N Amer.* a deciduous tree of eastern N America, *Nyssa sylvatica*, with soft wood and purple fruits. *Also called* BLACK GUM.

Souris River /'sɜrɪs/ a river, some 720 km long, which rises in south central Saskatchewan and flows generally southeastward into N Dakota where it loops around, flowing northward into Manitoba to join the Assiniboine River southeast of Brandon. [French, lit. 'mouse']

sour mash noun esp. *US* a grain mash that has been acidified, used to promote fermentation in the distilling of whisky.

sour note noun *informal* a disturbing aspect or incident marring an otherwise enjoyable event, occasion, etc.

sour·puss noun *informal* an irritable or sullen person; a grouch. [SOUR + PUSS²]

sour·sop noun **1** an evergreen tree of tropical America, *Annona muricata*. **2** the large succulent fruit of this tree.

sour·wood noun a tree of eastern US of the heath family, *Oxydendrum arboreum*, with sour tasting leaves.

Sousa /'suːzə, 'suːsə/ **John Phil·ip** (1854–1932), US composer and bandmaster. His works include more than 100 marches, for example *Semper Fidelis* (1888), *The Liberty Bell* (1893), and *The Stars and Stripes Forever* (1897).

sousa·phone /'suːzəˌfoːn, 'suːsə-/ noun a large brass wind instrument, similar to a tuba, which encircles the player's body with the bell above the player's head. [J.P. SOUSA, after *saxophone*]

sous-chef /'suːʃef/ noun the person ranking next below the head chef in a restaurant kitchen. [French]

souse /saʊs/ ● *transitive verb* **1** soak, immerse, or drench (a thing) in liquid. **2** preserve (gherkins, fish, etc.) in pickle, esp. vinegar. ● *noun* **1 a** a liquid, esp. made with salt, used in pickling. **b** *N Amer.* pickled meat, esp. a pig's feet and ears. **2** a dip, plunge, or drenching in water. **3** *informal* **a** a drinking bout. **b** (also **sous·er**) a drunkard. [Old French *sous*, of Germanic origin]

soused adjective *informal* drunk.

sou·tache /suː'taʃ/ noun a narrow flat ornamental braid used to trim clothing. [French from Magyar *sujtás*]

sou·tane /suː'tan/ noun *Catholicism* a cassock worn by a priest. [French from Italian *sottana* from *sotto* under, from Latin *subtus*]

south ● *noun* **1** the point of the horizon 90° clockwise from east. **2** the compass point corresponding to this. **3** the direction in which this lies. **4** (usu. **the South**) **a** the part of the world or a country or a town lying to the south. **b** *Cdn* the ten provinces south of the Yukon, Northwest Territories, and Nunavut. **c** the Southern States of the US, bounded on the north by Maryland, the Ohio River, and Missouri. **d** *hist.* the Confederate slaveholding States of the US south of the Mason-Dixon line. **5** (**South**) *Bridge* a player occupying the position designated 'south'. ● *adjective* **1** towards, at, near, or facing the south (*a south wall; south country*). **2** coming from the south (*south wind*). ● *adverb* **1** towards, at, or near the south (*they travelled south*). **2** (foll. by *of*) further south than. **3** *informal* into a sharp decline (*house prices went south this month*). □ **south by east** (or **west**) between south and south-southeast (or south-southwest). **to the south** (often foll. by *of*) in a southerly direction. [Old English *sūth*]

South Africa a country occupying the southernmost part of the continent of Africa; pop. (est. 2002) 43,647,658; administrative capital, Pretoria; seat of legislature, Cape Town. □ **South African** *adjective & noun*

South African War noun = BOER WAR.

South America a continent comprising the southern half of the

American land mass, connected to North America by the Isthmus of Panama. See also AMERICA 2. □ **South American** *adjective & noun*

South·amp·ton¹ an industrial city and seaport on the south coast of England, formerly in Hampshire; pop. (est. 2002) 211,500. It lies on an inlet of the English Channel opposite the Isle of Wight.

Southampton², 3rd Earl of (title of Henry Wriothesley) (1573–1624), English nobleman, who was the patron of Shakespeare.

Southampton Island a large island at the entrance to Hudson Bay, off the northeastern coast of mainland Nunavut. [3rd Earl of SOUTHAMPTON²]

South Asian ● *noun* **1** a native or inhabitant of the Indian subcontinent including India, Pakistan, Bangladesh, and Sri Lanka. **2** a South Asian emigrant or a descendant of a South Asian living outside of the Indian subcontinent. ● *adjective* of or relating to the Indian subcontinent, South Asians, or their culture.

South Atlantic Ocean see ATLANTIC OCEAN.

South Australia a state comprising the central southern part of Australia; pop. (est. 2000) 1,514,854; capital, Adelaide.

south·bound adjective & adverb travelling or leading in a southward direction.

South Bruce Peninsula a town in SW Ontario, on the SW side of the Bruce Peninsula, including the former town of Wiarton; pop. (2001) 8,090.

South Carolina a state of the US on the Atlantic coast; pop. (est. 2000) 4,012,012; capital, Columbia. Separated from North Carolina in 1729, South Carolina became one of the original thirteen states of the Union (1788). □ **South Carolinian** *noun & adjective*

South China Sea see CHINA SEA.

South Dakota a state in the north central US; pop. (est. 2000) 754,844; capital, Pierre. □ **South Dakotan** *noun & adjective*

South·down noun a breed of sheep with short fine wool raised esp. for mutton, originally on the South Downs of Hampshire and Sussex in England.

south·east ● *noun* **1** the point of the horizon midway between south and east. **2** the point on a compass corresponding to this. **3** the direction in which this lies. **4** (**Southeast**) the part of a country or city lying to the southeast. ● *adjective* of, towards, or coming from the southeast. ● *adverb* towards, at, or near the southeast. □ **south·east·ern** *adjective* **south·east·ern·er** *noun* **south·east·ern·most** *adjective*

Southeast Asia noun a region bounded roughly by China in the north, India in the west, and the Pacific Ocean in the east, including Brunei, Burma, Cambodia, Indonesia, Laos, Malaysia, the Philippines, Singapore, Thailand, and Vietnam. □ **Southeast Asian** *noun & adjective*

south·easter·ly ● *adjective & adverb* = SOUTHEAST. ● *noun* (*pl.* **-lies**) (also **south·easter**) a southeast wind or storm.

south·east·ward adjective & adverb (also **south·east·wards**) towards the southeast.

Southend-on-Sea a resort town on the Thames estuary east of London, England; pop. (est. 2002) 160,000.

south·erly /'sʌðərli/ ● *adjective & adverb* **1** in a southern position or direction. **2** (of a wind) blowing from the south. ● *noun* (*pl.* **-lies**) a southerly wind.

south·ern /'sʌðərn/ ● *adjective* **1 a** of or in the south; inhabiting the south. **b** (also **Southern**) of, relating to, or inhabiting the States of the American South. **2** lying or directed towards the south (*at the southern end*). **3** (of a wind) blowing from the south. ● *noun* the dialect of English spoken in the southern US. □ **south·ern·most** *adjective*

Southern Alps a mountain range in South Island, New Zealand. Mount Cook, its highest peak, rises to 3 764 m (12,349 ft.).

Southern Baptist noun **1** (in full **Southern Baptist Convention**) a body of Baptist churches in the US, established in 1845. **2** a member of any of these churches.

Southern blot noun (also **Southern hybridization**) *Biochem.* a procedure for identifying specific sequences of DNA, in which fragments separated on a gel are transferred directly to a second medium on which assay by hybridization etc. may be carried out (*compare* WESTERN BLOT). □ **Southern blotting** noun [E.M. *Southern*, Brit. biochemist b.1938]

Southern Cone the region of S America comprising the countries of Brazil, Paraguay, Uruguay, and Argentina.

Southern Cross noun a southern constellation in the shape of a cross.

south·ern·er *noun* **1** a native or inhabitant of the south. **2** (also **Southerner**) **a** *Cdn* an inhabitant of any of the ten provinces, as opposed to an inhabitant of the Yukon, Northwest Territories, or Nunavut. **b** an inhabitant of the southern US.

southern-fried *adjective* **1** denoting a dish of esp. chicken dipped in a coating of bread crumbs and deep-fried. **2** *informal* characteristic of or originating in the southern US (*a southern-fried figure of speech*).

southern hemisphere *noun* **1** the half of the earth below the equator. **2** the half of the celestial sphere south of the celestial equator.

Southern Indian Lake an irregularly-shaped lake in north central Manitoba, an enlargement of the Churchill River, situated about 150 km northwest of Thompson. [prob. after the *southern Indians*, i.e. the Cree]

southern lights *plural noun* the aurora australis.

Southern Ocean see ANTARCTIC OCEAN.

Southern Rhodesia see ZIMBABWE.

southern rock *noun* a style of guitar-driven popular music blending elements of rock, blues, and country, originating in the southern US and popular esp. through the 1970s.

Southey /ˈsaʊði/ **Rob·ert** (1774–1843), English poet. Associated with the Lake Poets, he is best known for his shorter poems such as the anti-militarist ballad the 'Battle of Blenheim' (1798), and his biography the *Life of Nelson* (1813); he was made Poet Laureate in 1813.

South Georgia a barren island in the S Atlantic, situated 1 120 km (700 miles) east of the Falkland Islands, of which it is a dependency.

South Glamorgan a former county of S Wales, on the Bristol Channel, dissolved in 1996.

South Huron a town in SW Ontario, formed by the amalgamation of three townships, between Bluewater and Lambton Shores; pop. (2001) 10,019.

south·ing /ˈsaʊθɪŋ/ *noun* **1** a southern movement. **2** *Naut.* the distance travelled or measured southward. **3** *Astronomy* the angular distance of a star etc. south of the celestial equator.

South Island the southernmost and largest of the two main islands of New Zealand, separated from North Island by Cook Strait.

South Korea (official name **Republic of Korea**) a country in the Far East, occupying the southern part of the peninsula of Korea; pop. (est. 2002) 48,324,000; capital, Seoul. South Korea was formed in 1948, when Korea was partitioned along the 38th parallel. □ **South Korean** *adjective & noun*

South Nahanni River /nəˈhani/ a river in the southwestern NWT, 563 km long, flowing southeastward from the Selwyn Mountains to join the Liard River, 150 km southwest of Fort Simpson. [ultimately after *Nahani*, an Athapaskan name applied in the 19th c. to various Dene peoples]

south of 60 *noun* (also **south of sixty**) *Cdn* the areas of Canada south of 60 degrees latitude, esp. the ten provinces south of the Yukon, Northwest Territories, and Nunavut.

South Orkney Islands a group of uninhabited islands in the S Atlantic, lying to the northeast of the Antarctic Peninsula. The islands are now administered as part of the British Antarctic Territory.

South Ossetia an autonomous region of Georgia, situated in the Caucasus on the border with Russia; capital, Tskhinvali. □ **South Ossetian** *noun & adjective*

south·paw *noun informal* **1** *Baseball* a pitcher who throws with his or her left hand. **2** *Boxing* a fighter who punches or leads with the left hand. **3** a left-handed person. [SOUTH *adjective* + PAW, perhaps because the left hand of a pitcher, traditionally facing west towards home plate, is on the south side of his body]

South Pender Island one of the Gulf Islands in the Strait of Georgia, BC, lying to the southeast of North Pender Island. [as NORTH PENDER ISLAND]

South Pole *noun* see POLE² 1.

South Sandwich Islands a group of uninhabited volcanic islands in the S Atlantic, lying 480 km (300 miles) southeast of South Georgia. It is administered from the Falkland Islands.

South Saskatchewan River a river in south central Saskatchewan, 1 392 km long, formed in SE Alberta by the junction of the Bow and Oldman rivers and flowing generally northeastward through Saskatoon to join the North Saskatchewan east of Prince Albert. [see SASKATCHEWAN RIVER]

South Sea Bubble *noun hist.* a scheme for trading in the southern hemisphere to repay the British national debt, which started and collapsed in 1720.

South Seas (also **South Sea**) *hist.* the S Pacific Ocean.

South Shetland Islands a group of uninhabited islands in the S Atlantic, lying north of the Antarctic Peninsula. The islands are now administered as part of the British Antarctic Territory.

South Slavey *noun* **1** a Dene people living in the area southwest of Great Slave Lake. **2** the language of this people.

south-southeast ● *noun* the point or direction midway between south and southeast. ● *adjective & adverb* from, towards, in, or facing this direction.

south-southwest ● *noun* the point or direction midway between south and southwest. ● *adjective & adverb* from, towards, in, or facing this direction.

South Vietnam see VIETNAM.

south·ward ● *adjective & adverb* (also **south·wards**) towards the south. ● *noun* a southward direction or region.

south·west ● *noun* **1** the point of the horizon midway between south and west. **2** the point on a compass corresponding to this. **3** the direction in which this lies. **4** (**Southwest**) the part of a country or city lying to the southwest. ● *adjective* of, towards, or coming from the southwest. ● *adverb* towards, at, or near the southwest. □ **south·west·ern** *adjective* **south·west·ern·er** *noun* **south·west·ern·most** *adjective*

South West Africa the former name for NAMIBIA.

south·wester·ly ● *adjective & adverb* = SOUTHWEST. ● *noun* (also **south·wester**) a southwest wind or storm.

Southwest Miramichi River a major branch of the Miramichi River, rising in west central New Brunswick and flowing generally northeastward to join the Miramichi River at the city of Miramichi. [see MIRAMICHI]

south·west·ward *adjective & adverb* (also **south·west·wards**) towards the southwest.

South Yorkshire a former metropolitan county of N England.

Sou·tine /suːˈtiːn/ **Chaim** (c.1893–1943), Lithuanian-born French expressionist painter. His style is characterized by thick, convulsive brushwork, through which he often depicts turbulent psychological states; his work includes landscapes, portraits, studies of choirboys and cooks, and pictures of animal carcasses.

sou·ven·ir /ˌsuːvəˈniːr/ *noun* a usu. inexpensive article given or purchased as a reminder of a place visited or an event witnessed etc.; a memento or keepsake (also *attributive: souvenir postcard*). [French from *souvenir* remember, from Latin *subvenire* occur to the mind (as SUB-, *venire* come)]

souv·laki /suːˈvlaki/ *noun* a Greek dish of pieces of marinated meat, esp. lamb or pork, grilled on a skewer. [modern Greek *soublaki* from *soubla* skewer]

sou'west·er *noun* **1** a waterproof hat, usu. made of oilskin, with a broad flap covering the neck and flaps tied under the chin, worn esp. at sea. **2** = SOUTHWESTERLY *noun*.

sover·eign /ˈsɒvrən/ ● *noun* **1** the recognized supreme ruler of a people or country under monarchical government; a monarch. **2** a person or body of people that has supremacy or authority over another or others. **3** *Brit. hist.* a gold coin nominally worth £1. ● *adjective* **1 a** (of a thing, quality, power, etc.) supreme, greatest. **b** unmitigated (*sovereign contempt*). **2 a** characterized by independence or autonomy, esp. having the rights and responsibilities of self-government (*a sovereign state*). **b** concerned with or pertaining to independence or autonomy (*sovereign ambitions*). **3 a** (of a person) having superior or supreme rank or power, esp. holding the position of ruler or monarch. **b** of or related to a monarch; royal. **4** excellent; effective (*a sovereign remedy*). □ **sover·eign·ly** *adverb* [Old French *so(u)verain* from Latin: -g- by assoc. with *reign*]

sover·eign·ist (also **sover·eign·tist**) *Cdn* ● *noun* a supporter of Quebec's right to self-government; an adherent to the principle of sovereignty-association or full independence. ● *adjective* concerned with or relating to the movement for Quebec independence.

sover·eign·ty *noun* (*pl.* **-ties**) **1** the absolute and independent authority of a community, nation, etc.; the right to autonomy or self-government. **2** (often foll. by *over*) supremacy with respect to power and rank; supreme authority. **3** a territory or community existing as a self-governing or independent state.

sover·eignty-associ·a·tion *noun Cdn* a proposed arrangement introduced in 1967 which would grant Quebec political independence while maintaining a formal esp. economic association with the rest of Canada, including a shared currency. [first used as the slogan of the

Consonants: **b** but   **d** dog   **f** few   **g** get   **h** her   **j** yes   **k** cat   **l** leg   **m** man   **n** no   **p** pen   **r** red   **s** sit

Mouvement Souveraineté-Association, forerunners to the Parti Québécois]

Soviet /ˈsoːvɪət/ *hist.* ● *noun* **1** a citizen of the former Soviet Union. **2** (**soviet**) an elected local, district, or national council in the former Soviet Union with legislative and executive functions. **3** (**soviet**) a revolutionary council of workers, peasants, etc. before 1917. ● *adjective* of or concerning the former Soviet Union or its people. □ **Soviet·ism** *noun* **Soviet·ize** *transitive verb* (also esp. *Brit.* **-ise**). **Soviet·iz·a·tion** *noun* [Russian *sovet* council]

Soviet·ol·o·gist *noun* a person who studies the former Soviet Union.

Soviet Union (called in full **Union of Soviet Socialist Republics**) a former federation of Communist republics occupying N Asia and part of E Europe; capital, Moscow. Created as a Communist state after the 1917 Russian Revolution and the Russian Civil War, the Soviet Union comprised fifteen republics. It was formally dissolved in 1991, some of its constituents joining a looser confederation, the Commonwealth of Independent States.

sow¹ /soʊ/ *verb* (*past* **sowed**; *past participle* **sown** or **sowed**) **1** *transitive & intransitive* **a** scatter, sprinkle, or deposit (seed) on or in the earth. **b** (often foll. by *with*) plant (a field etc.) with seed. **2** *transitive* initiate; arouse or spread (*sowed doubt in her mind*). **3** *transitive* (foll. by *with*) cover thickly with. □ **sow one's wild oats** *informal* see OAT. **sow the seed** (or **seeds**) **of** instigate, introduce; implant (an idea etc.). □ **sower** *noun* **sow·ing** *noun* [Old English *sāwan* from Germanic]

sow² /saʊ/ *noun* **1 a** a female adult pig, esp. a domestic one after farrowing. **b** the full-grown female of certain other animals, e.g. the bear and guinea pig. **2 a** a large bar or block of metal, esp. iron. **b** any of the larger channels in a smelting furnace serving as a feeder to the smaller channels. [Old English *sugu*]

sow·belly /ˈsaʊbeli/ *noun* N Amer. informal salt pork, esp. from the belly.

sow·bug /ˈsaʊbʌg/ *noun* N Amer. a small terrestrial isopod crustacean of the genus *Oniscus* feeding on rotten wood in esp. damp and shady habitats, often able to roll into a ball.

So·weto /səˈweɪtoʊ/ a large urban area, consisting of several townships, in South Africa southwest of Johannesburg. □ **So·wetan** *noun & adjective* [acronym from South Western Townships]

sown *past participle of* SOW¹.

sow thistle /saʊ/ *noun* any plant of the genus *Sonchus* with thistle-like leaves and milky juice.

sox *informal pl. of* SOCK¹.

soy *noun* (also **soya**) **1** *see* SOY SAUCE. **2** *see* SOYBEAN. [Japanese *shō-yu* from *shi* salted beans + *you* oil]

soya burger *noun* (also **soy·burger**) a vegetarian hamburger made with tofu instead of ground beef. *Also called* TOFU BURGER.

soy·bean *noun* (also esp. *Brit.* **soya bean**) **1** a leguminous plant, *Glycine max*, originally of SE Asia, cultivated for the edible oil and flour it yields, and used as a replacement for animal protein in certain foods. **2** the seed of this. [Dutch *soja* from Malay *soi* (as SOY)]

soybean meal *noun* (also **soy·meal**) the residue of soybean seeds after the extraction of the oil, used as animal feed.

soybean milk *noun* (also **soy milk**, *Brit.* **soya milk**) a substitute for milk made by suspending soybean flour in water.

Soy·inka, Wole (b.1934), Nigerian dramatist, novelist, and critic. His writing often uses satire and humour to explore the contrast between traditional and modern society in Africa, and includes the novel *The Interpreters* (1965), the play *Kongi's Harvest* (1964), and the collection of poems and other writings *The Man Died* (1972); he was awarded the Nobel Prize for literature in 1986.

soy sauce *noun* (also **soya sauce**) a dark brown salty sauce made originally in Japan and China from pickled soybeans.

soz·zled *adjective informal* very drunk. [past participle of dial. *sozzle* mix sloppily (prob. imitative)]

SP *abbreviation* **1** standard play, a setting on a VCR allowing two hours of material to be recorded on a standard tape (*compare* EP 2). **2** *Racing* starting price.

Sp. *abbreviation* **1** Spanish. **2** Spain.

sp. *abbreviation* **1** *Biol.* species. **2** speed. **3 a** spelled. **b** spelling.

spa *noun* **1** a curative or medicinal mineral spring. **2** a commercial establishment or resort offering health and beauty treatment through steam baths, exercise equipment, massage, etc. **3** (in full **spa bath**) = HOT TUB. [Spa, in Belgium, celebrated since medieval times for the curative properties of its mineral springs]

space ● *noun* **1 a** a continuous unlimited area or expanse which may or may not contain objects. **b** an interval between one, two, or three-dimensional points or objects (*a space of 10 metres*). **c** an empty area; room (*clear a space in the corner*). **2 a** area sufficient, required, or available for some purpose or thing (*parking space; cargo space*). **b** any of a number of places or positions for a person or thing (*spaces are limited so sign up now!*). **3 a** (also **outer space**, **deep space**) the immense expanse of the physical universe beyond the earth's atmosphere. **b** the near vacuum occupying the regions between the planets and stars, containing small amounts of gas and dust. **4** an interval of time (*in the space of an hour*). **5 a** time spent alone and used to think, reflect, or relax (*she seems upset, you should just give her some space*). **b** = PERSONAL SPACE. **6** a usu. designated place in a book, letter, form, etc. available for or occupied by written or printed matter (*sign your name in the space below*). **7 a** an interval or blank space between printed or written words or lines. **b** the width occupied by a single typed character. **c** *Printing* any of certain small pieces of cast metal shorter than a type, used to separate words or letters in a word and to justify the line. **8 a** a place in a newspaper or magazine, or between television or radio programs, used for advertising. **b** (in full **commercial space**) an area rented or sold as business premises. **9** *Math.* an instance of any of various mathematical concepts, usu. regarded as a set of points having some specified structure. **10** *Music* each of the blanks between the lines of a staff. ● *transitive verb* **1** set, place, or arrange at determinate intervals. **2 a** separate (words, letters, or lines) by means of a space or spaces. **b** make or insert more or wider spaces between (esp. words, letters, lines, etc. in printing, typing, or writing). □ **space out 1** spread out with more or wider spaces or intervals between. **2** experience an esp. drug-induced stupor or daze. □ **spacer** *noun* [Old French *espace* from Latin *spatium*]

space age ● *noun* (also **Space Age**) the present period, in which human exploration of space takes place. ● *attributive adjective* (**space-age**) **1** characteristic of the space age. **2** designed with the most sophisticated or advanced technology; extremely modern.

space bar *noun* **1** a long horizontal key on a typewriter used to make a space between characters or words etc. **2** a similar key on a computer keyboard which also moves the cursor and advances the text.

space blanket *noun* a light plastic sheet coated on both sides with metal that retains warmth by reflecting the heat radiating from the person or thing wrapped in it.

space cadet *noun* **1** *slang* a drug addict. **2** *informal* a person who seems out of touch with reality. **3** a trainee astronaut.

space capsule *noun see* CAPSULE 2.

space·craft *noun* any of various manned or unmanned vehicles designed to travel in outer space, esp. for research or exploration.

spaced *adjective slang* (also **spaced out**) in a dazed, disoriented, or confused state, esp. from taking drugs.

space·faring *noun* (often *attributive*) the action or activity of travelling in space. □ **space·farer** *noun*

space flight *noun* **1** a journey through outer space. **2** = SPACE TRAVEL.

space·frame *noun* a three-dimensional structural framework which is designed to behave as an integral unit and to withstand loads applied at any point.

space heater *noun* a small portable esp. electrical appliance used to heat a contained space or room. □ **space heating** *noun*

space junk *noun* spacecraft debris in orbit around the earth.

space·lab *noun* a spacecraft equipped with a laboratory where research and experiments may be conducted.

space·man *noun* (pl. **-men**) *dated* **1** = ASTRONAUT 1. **2** a visitor from outer space.

space opera *noun* a work of science fiction, esp. a TV show or movie, set in outer space.

space·plane *noun* an aircraft that takes off and lands conventionally but is capable of entry into orbit or travel through space.

space·port *noun* a base where spacecraft are serviced, launched, etc.

space probe *noun* = PROBE *noun* 4.

space program *noun* a program designed for the exploration of outer space and development of space technology.

space race *noun* the competition between countries in developments and achievements in space exploration (*compare* ARMS RACE).

space rocket *noun* a rocket used to launch a spacecraft.

space-saving *adjective* **1** designed to occupy little space. **2** that saves space.

space·ship *noun* a manned spacecraft.

space shuttle *noun* a spacecraft that is designed and built for repeated use carrying equipment and astronauts into orbit or to a space station.

space station *noun* a manned artificial satellite used as a long-term base for operations in space.

space·suit *noun* a sealed and pressurized protective suit that allows an astronaut to survive in space.

space-time *noun* (in full **space-time continuum**) **1** time and three-dimensional space regarded as fused in a four-dimensional continuum containing all events. **2** (*attributive*) pertaining to or situated in both space and time (*space-time model*).

space tourist *noun* a person who pays to be taken up in a spaceship. □ **space tourism** *noun*

space travel *noun* travel through outer space. □ **space traveller** *noun*

space vehicle *noun* = SPACECRAFT.

space·walk *noun* any operation or activity performed by an astronaut in space outside of a spacecraft. □ **space·walk·er** *noun* **space·walk·ing** *noun*

spacey *adjective* (also **spacy**) (**spaci·er, spaci·est**) **1** esp. *N Amer. slang* absent-minded or out of touch with reality. **2** (esp. of music) relating to or characteristic of supposed conditions in outer space. □ **spaci·ness** *noun*

spa·cial *var. of* SPATIAL.

spa·cing *noun* **1** the arrangement of typed or written text, esp. the precise amount of space inserted between each character, word, or line, used to make text legible. **2** the arrangement of objects at particular intervals.

spa·cious *adjective* **1** having ample space; roomy (*a spacious living room*). **2** (of land etc.) of vast or indefinite extent; covering a wide area, extensive (*spacious gardens*). □ **spa·cious·ly** *adverb* **spa·cious·ness** *noun*

Spackle *N Amer.* ● *noun* proprietary (in full **spackling compound**) a compound used to fill cracks in plaster and produce a smooth surface before painting. ● *transitive verb* (**spackle**) **1** cover or fill (a wall, crack, etc.) with Spackle. **2** cover with a substance of a consistency similar to that of Spackle (*her face was spackled with makeup*). [20th c.: origin uncertain; perhaps a blend of SPARKLE *verb* and German *Spachtel* putty knife]

spa cuisine *noun* a variety of cuisine that emphasizes foods low in calories, sodium, fat, and cholesterol, e.g. whole grains and fish.

spacy *var. of* SPACEY.

spade¹ ● *noun* **1** a tool resembling a shovel used for digging or cutting the ground, consisting of a long handle with a grip or crossbar at the top attached to a sharp-edged square metal blade that may be driven into the ground with the foot. **2** any tool resembling this in shape or function, esp. a knife with an oblong blade used to remove the blubber from a whale. ● *transitive verb* dig up, work, or remove with or as if with a spade. □ **call a spade a spade** speak plainly or bluntly. □ **spade·ful** *noun* (*pl.* **-fuls**). [Old English *spadu, spada*]

spade² *noun* **1 a** a black inverted heart-shaped figure with a small stalk used to denote a playing card of a particular suit. **b** (in *pl.*) the suit denoted by this figure. **c** a playing card of this suit. **2** *slang offensive* a black person. □ **in spades** *informal* with great or excessive force or persistence. [Italian *spade* pl. of *spada* sword, from Latin *spatha* from Greek *spathē*, related to SPADE¹: assoc. with the shape of a pointed spade]

spade beard *noun* a rounded oblong-shaped beard.

spade bit *noun* a drill bit with a broad flat pointed tip used for boring esp. large holes in wood.

spade·fish *noun* a fish having a spade-like body or organ, esp. any of various very deep-bodied fishes of warm seas, of the small family Ephippidae, esp. the large grey or black *Chaetodipterus faber* of the W Atlantic.

spade·foot *noun* a square spade-like enlargement at the end of a chair leg.

spadefoot toad *noun* any of several plump, short-legged burrowing toads of the family Pelobatidae, with a prominent sharp-edged tubercle on the hind feet, native to North America and Europe.

spade·work *noun* preparatory work that is necessary for a project to be successful.

spadix /ˈspeɪdɪks/ *noun* (*pl.* **spadi·ces** /-ˌsiːz/) *Bot.* a spike of flowers closely arranged around a fleshy axis and usu. enclosed in a spathe. [Latin from Greek, = palm branch]

spaetzle /ˈʃpetslə, ˈʃpetsəl/ *plural noun* very small egg noodles made by forcing dough through a colander directly into boiling water. [German dial., lit. 'little sparrows']

spa·ghetti *noun* **1** pasta made in solid thin strings, thicker than vermicelli. **2** a dish of this with a sauce. **3** a tangled or confusing mass or system (*a spaghetti of traffic lanes; spaghetti code*). □ **spa·ghetti-like** *adjective* [Italian, pl. of diminutive of *spago* string]

spa·ghet·tini *plural noun* very thin spaghetti. [Italian, diminutive of SPAGHETTI]

spaghetti squash *noun* a squash with stringy flesh.

spaghetti strap *noun* a thin stringlike shoulder strap on a dress etc.

spaghetti western *noun* a western film made cheaply in Italy.

Spain a country in SW Europe, occupying the greater part of the Iberian peninsula; pop. (est. 2002) 40,077,100; capital, Madrid.

spake *archaic past of* SPEAK.

spall ● *noun* a splinter or chip, esp. of rock. ● *transitive & intransitive verb* **1** (of concrete, brick, etc.) flake away. **2** break up or cause (ore) to break up in preparation for sorting. □ **spall·ing** *noun* [Middle English (also *spale*): origin unknown]

Spal·lan·zani /ˌspalənˈsɒni/ **Laz·zaro** (1729–99), Italian physiologist and biologist. He explained the circulation of the blood and the digestive system of animals, showed that fertilization can only result from contact between egg and seminal fluid, demonstrated that protozoa do not appear as a result of spontaneous generation, and studied regeneration in invertebrates.

Spal·lum·cheen /ˈspalʌmˌtʃiːn/ a district municipality in south central BC, just north of Vernon; pop. (2001) 5,134. □ **Spal·lum·cheen·ite** *noun* **Spal·lum·nite** *noun* [Okanagan *spalmtsin* flat area along the edge]

Spam ● *noun* **1** proprietary a tinned meat product made mainly from ham. **2** (**spam**) *Computing slang* **a** an esp. advertising message sent indiscriminately to a large number of newsgroups, mailing lists, etc. **b** such messages collectively. ● *verb* (**spam**) *Computing slang* **1** *intransitive* send spam. **2** *transitive* send spam to (a person, newsgroup, etc.). □ **spam·mer** *noun* **spam·ming** *noun* [spiced ham; computing senses prob. from a sketch by the British comedy troupe *Monty Python*, in which Spam appears in every item on a diner's menu]

spam·bot *noun* a piece of software that seeks email addresses on the Internet for spamming purposes.

span¹ ● *noun* **1** the full extent from end to end in space or time (*the span of a bridge; the whole span of history*). **2** the length of time for which attention, concentration, etc. can be maintained. **3** each arch or part of a bridge between piers or supports. **4** the maximum lateral extent of an airplane, its wing, a bird's wing, etc. **5 a** the maximum distance between the tips of the thumb and little finger. **b** this as a measurement, equal to 23 cm (9 inches). **6** a short distance or time (*our life is but a span*). ● *transitive verb* (**spanned, span·ning**) **1 a** (of a bridge, arch, etc.) stretch from side to side of; extend across (*the bridge spanned the river*). **b** (of a builder etc.) bridge (a river etc.). **2** extend across (space or a period of time etc.). **3** measure or cover the extent of (a thing) with one's hand with the fingers stretched (*spanned a tenth on the piano*). [Old English *span(n)* or Old French *espan*]

span² *noun* **1** *Naut.* a rope with both ends fastened to take purchase in a loop. **2** a matched pair of horses, mules, oxen, etc. [Low German & Dutch *span* from *spannen* unite]

span³ *see* SPIC AND SPAN.

span⁴ *archaic past of* SPIN.

spana·ko·pita /ˌspanəˈkɒpɪtə/ *noun* an originally Greek phyllo pastry stuffed with spinach, feta cheese, etc. [modern Greek, from *spanaki* spinach + *pita* cake, pie]

span·dex *noun* an elastic polyurethane fabric used in foundation garments, tights, bathing suits, and other tight-fitting stretchy garments. □ **span·dexed** *adjective* [arbitrary formation from EXPAND]

span·drel /ˈspandrəl/ *noun* *Archit.* **1** the almost triangular space between one side of the outer curve of an arch, a wall, and the ceiling or framework. **2** the space between the shoulders of adjoining arches and the ceiling or moulding above. [perhaps from Anglo-French *spaund(e)re*, or from *espaundre* EXPAND]

spang *adverb* *US informal* exactly; completely (*spang in the middle*). [20th c.: origin unknown]

span·gle ● *noun* **1** a small thin piece of glittering material esp. used in quantity to ornament a dress etc.; a sequin. **2** a small sparkling object. ● *transitive verb* (esp. as **span·gled** *adjective*) cover with or as with spangles (*star-spangled; spangled costume*). □ **span·gly** *adjective* [Middle English from *spang* from Middle Dutch *spange* 'buckle']

Spang·lish *noun* a version of Latin American Spanish marked by the use of English words and phrases. [blend of SPANISH + ENGLISH]

Span·iard /ˈspanjɜrd/ *noun* a native or national of Spain. [Old French *Espaignart* from *Espaigne* Spain]

Spaniard's Bay 1 a small inlet on the southwestern shore of Conception Bay, SE Newfoundland. **2** a town situated at its head; pop. (2001) 2,694. [perhaps after early Portuguese and Basque fishermen]

span·iel *noun* a dog of any of various breeds with a long silky coat and drooping ears. [Old French *espaigneul* Spanish (dog), from Romanic *Hispaniolus* (unrecorded) from *Hispania* Spain]

Span·ish ● *adjective* of or relating to Spain or its people or language. ● *noun* **1** the principal language of Spain and Spanish America. **2** (prec. by *the*; treated as *pl.*) the people of Spain. □ **Span·ish·ness** *noun*

Spanish America the parts of the Americas colonized in the 16th c. by the Spanish, including Central and S America (except for Brazil) and parts of the W Indies.

Spanish-American War a war between Spain and the US in 1898. In response to Spanish atrocities in Cuba and the destruction of the US warship *Maine* in Santiago harbour, the United States successfully invaded Cuba, Puerto Rico, and the Philippines, all of which Spain gave up by the Treaty of Paris.

Spanish Armada a Spanish naval invasion force sent against England in 1588 by Philip II of Spain. The Armada of 129 ships and almost 20,000 soldiers was defeated in the English Channel before it could rendezvous with an army waiting to be ferried across to England.

Spanish Civil War (1936–9) the bitter conflict in Spain in which the Nationalists (including monarchists and members of the Falange Party, led by General Franco and supported by Fascist Germany and Italy) defeated the Republicans (including socialists, Communists, and Catalan and Basque separatists, supported by the Soviet Union and an International Brigade of volunteers). Franco established a Fascist dictatorship that lasted until his death in 1975.

Spanish coffee *noun* coffee with brandy and coffee liqueur, served topped with whipped cream.

Spanish flu *noun* (also **Spanish influenza**) a severe form of influenza which killed 20 million people worldwide in 1918.

Spanish fly *noun* **1** a bright green European beetle, *Lytta vesicatoria*. **2** a toxic preparation of the dried bodies of these beetles, formerly used to raise blisters, and supposedly an aphrodisiac. *Also called* CANTHARIDES.

Spanish guitar *noun* = CLASSICAL GUITAR.

Spanish Inquisition *noun see* INQUISITION 3b.

Spanish mackerel *noun* any of various large mackerels.

Spanish Main *hist.* the northern coast and coastal waters of S America, between the Orinoco river and Panama.

Spanish moss *noun* a tropical American plant, *Tillandsia usneoides*, an epiphytic bromeliad which grows as silvery festoons on trees.

Spanish onion *noun* a large mild-flavoured variety of onion.

Spanish rice *noun* rice cooked with onion, tomato, green or red peppers, and spices.

Spanish River a river in north central Ontario, which rises northwest of Sudbury and flows southward through Espanola to Lake Huron's North Channel.

Spanish Sahara the former name (1958–75) for WESTERN SAHARA.

Spanish Succession, War of the (1701–14), a European war in which the Grand Alliance of Britain, the Netherlands, and the Holy Roman emperor frustrated Louis XIV's attempts to establish French dominance over Europe. The Peace of Utrecht (1713–14) prevented Spain and France from being united under one crown. The N American phase of this war was QUEEN ANNE'S WAR.

Spanish Town a town in Jamaica, west of Kingston, the second largest town and a former capital of Jamaica; pop. (2002) 130,300.

spank ● *verb* **1** *transitive* slap esp. on the buttocks with the open hand, a slipper, etc. **2** *intransitive* (of a horse etc.) move briskly, esp. between a trot and a gallop. ● *noun* a slap esp. with the open hand on the buttocks. [perhaps imitative]

spank·er *noun* **1** a person or thing that spanks. **2** *Naut.* a fore-and-aft sail set on the after side of the mizzen-mast. **3** a fast horse.

spank·ing ● *adverb informal* very, exceedingly (*spanking new*). ● *noun* the act or an instance of slapping, esp. on the buttocks as a punishment for children. ● *adjective* **1** *informal* striking; excellent. **2** (esp. of a horse) moving quickly; lively; brisk (*at a spanking trot*).

span·ner *noun* esp. *Brit.* an instrument for turning or gripping a nut on a screw etc.; a wrench. [German *spannen* draw tight: see SPAN[2]]

spanner in the works *noun informal* a problem or impediment.

spar[1] *noun* **1** a stout pole esp. used for the mast, yard, etc. of a ship. **2** the main longitudinal beam of an airplane wing. [Old French *esparre* or Old Norse *sperra* or direct from Germanic]

spar[2] ● *intransitive verb* (**sparred**, **spar·ring**) **1** (often foll. by *at*) make the motions of boxing without landing heavy blows. **2** engage in argument (*they are always sparring*). **3** (of a gamecock) fight with the feet or spurs. ● *noun* **1 a** a sparring motion. **b** a boxing match. **2** a cockfight. **3** an argument or dispute. [Old English *sperran*, *spyrran*, of unknown origin: compare Old Norse *sperrask* kick out]

spar[3] *noun* any crystalline, easily cleavable and non-lustrous mineral, e.g. calcite or fluorspar. □ **spar·ry** *adjective* [Middle Low German, related to Old English *spæren* of plaster, *spærstān* gypsum]

spare ● *adjective* **1 a** not required for ordinary use; extra, available (*have no spare cash*; *spare time*). **b** reserved for emergency or occasional use (*slept in the spare room*). **2** lean; thin. **3** scanty; frugal; not copious (*a spare diet*; *a spare prose style*). **4** *informal* not wanted or used by others (*a spare seat in the front row*). ● *noun* **1** a spare part, esp. a spare tire; a duplicate. **2** *Bowling* the knocking down of all the pins with the first two balls. **3** *Cdn* a period in one's school day schedule in which one is not required to be in class. **4** *Curling* a substitute player; an alternate. ● *verb* **1** *transitive* afford to give or do without; dispense with (*cannot spare him just now*; *can spare you a couple*). **2** *transitive* **a** abstain from killing, hurting, wounding, etc. (*spared his feelings*; *spared her life*). **b** abstain from inflicting or causing; relieve from; refrain from troubling with (*spare me the details*; *would spare me the trouble*). **3** *transitive* be frugal or grudging of (*no expense spared*). **4** *intransitive archaic* be frugal. □ **go spare** *informal Brit.* become extremely angry or distraught. **not spare oneself** exert one's utmost efforts. **to spare** left over; additional, more than necessary (*an hour to spare*). □ **spare·ly** *adverb* **spare·ness** *noun* [Old English *spær*, *sparian* from Germanic]

spare·ribs *plural noun* a cut of meat, esp. pork, consisting of closely-trimmed ribs. [prob. from Middle Low German *ribbesper*, by transposition and assoc. with SPARE]

spare tire *noun* **1** an extra tire carried in a motor vehicle for emergencies. **2** *informal* a roll of fat around the waist.

sparge *transitive verb* moisten by sprinkling, esp. in brewing. □ **spar·ger** *noun* [apparently from Latin *spargere* sprinkle]

spar·ing *adjective* **1** inclined to save; economical. **2** restrained; limited. □ **spar·ing·ly** *adverb*

Spark, Dame Mur·iel (Sarah) (b.1918), Scottish novelist. Her novels include *Memento Mori* (1959), *The Prime of Miss Jean Brodie* (1961), a sardonic portrait of an Edinburgh schoolmistress and her favourite pupils, and *A Far Cry from Kensington* (1988).

spark ● *noun* **1** a fiery particle thrown off from a fire, or alight in ashes, or produced by a flint, match, etc. **2** (often foll. by *of*) a particle of a quality etc. (*not a spark of life*; *a spark of interest*). **3** *Electricity* **a** a light produced by a sudden disruptive discharge through the air etc. **b** such a discharge serving to ignite the explosive mixture in an internal combustion engine. **4 a** anything acting as an incitement or inspiration to action, or which excites emotions; a catalyst. **b** energy or enthusiasm. **5** a small bright object or point, e.g. in a gem. **6** (**Spark**) *Cdn* a member of the branch of Girl Guides for 5- or 6-year-olds. **7** (**Sparks**) a nickname for a radio operator or an electrician. **8** a lively young fellow. ● *verb* **1** *intransitive* emit sparks of fire or electricity. **2** *transitive* (often foll. by *off*) stir into activity; initiate (a process) suddenly. **3** *intransitive Electricity* produce sparks at the point where a circuit is interrupted. □ **sparks flew** (or **will fly** etc.) there was (or will be etc.) a heated confrontation, friction, etc. □ **spark·less** *adjective* **sparky** *adjective* [Old English *spærca*, *spearca*]

spark chamber *noun* an apparatus designed to show ionizing particles.

spark-gap *noun* the space between electric terminals where sparks occur.

sparking plug *noun Brit.* = SPARK PLUG 1.

spar·kle ● *intransitive verb* **1 a** emit or seem to emit sparks; glitter; glisten (*her eyes sparkled*). **b** be witty; scintillate (*sparkling repartee*). **c** perform conspicuously well. **2** (of wine etc.) effervesce (compare STILL[1] *adjective* 4). ● *noun* **1** a flash of light; a gleam, spark. **2** a glittering particle. **3 a** a glittering or flashing appearance or quality. **b** vivacity, liveliness of spirit; effervescence. □ **spark·ling** *adjective* **spark·ling·ly** *adverb* **spark·ly** *adjective*

spark·ler *noun* **1** a person or thing that sparkles. **2** a hand-held firework that produces showers of sparks when lit. **3** *informal* a diamond or other gem. **4** a sparkling wine, mineral water, etc.

spark plug *noun* **1** a device fitted to the cylinder head of an internal combustion engine, used to ignite the explosive mixture by the discharge of a spark between two electrodes at its end. **2** (usu. **spark·plug**) *esp. N Amer. informal* a person or thing which initiates, inspires, or encourages an activity or undertaking; a catalyst.

sparring partner *noun* **1** a boxer employed to engage in sparring with another as training. **2** a person with whom one enjoys arguing.

spar·row *noun* **1** any small brownish-grey bird of the genus *Passer*, esp. the house sparrow or tree sparrow. **2** any of various small New World birds of the family Emberezidae of similar appearance, such as the chipping sparrow. [Old English *spearwa* from Germanic]

sparrow hawk *noun* **1** the American kestrel, *Falco sparverius*. **2** any of various small Old World hawks, esp. *Accipiter nisus*, preying on small birds.

sparse *adjective* **1** thinly dispersed or scattered; not dense (*sparse population; sparse greying hair*). **2** scanty, meagre. □ **sparse·ly** *adverb* **sparse·ness** *noun* **spars·ity** *noun* [Latin *sparsus* past participle of *spargere* scatter]

Spar·ta a city in the S Peloponnese in Greece, capital of the department of Laconia; pop. (2002) 15,700. It was a powerful city state in the 5th c. BC, defeating its rival Athens in the Peloponnesian War. The ancient Spartans were renowned for the military organization of their state and for their rigorous discipline, courage, and austerity.

Spar·ta·cist /'spɑːtəsɪst, -təkɪst/ *noun* a member of the Spartacus League, a German revolutionary socialist group founded in 1916 by Rosa Luxemburg and Karl Liebknecht (1871–1919) with the aims of overthrowing the government and ending the First World War. In 1918 the group helped organize an uprising in Berlin that was brutally crushed. [German *Spartakist* from SPARTACUS, adopted as a pseudonym by Liebknecht]

Spar·ta·cus /'spɑːtəkəs/ (died *c.*71 BC), Thracian slave and gladiator. He led a revolt against Rome in 73 but was eventually defeated by Crassus and crucified.

Spar·tan ● *adjective* **1** of or relating to Sparta in ancient Greece. **2 a** possessing the qualities of courage, endurance, stern frugality, etc., associated with Sparta. **b** (**spartan**) (of a regime, conditions, etc.) lacking comfort; austere. ● *noun* **1** a citizen of Sparta. **2** esp. *Cdn* a medium- or large-sized red eating or cooking apple with tiny white dots, bred to withstand relatively cold winters.

spar·tina /spɑːˈtiːnə/ *noun* any grass of the genus *Spartina*, with rhizomatous roots and growing in wet or marshy ground. *Also called* CORDGRASS. [Greek *spartinē* rope]

spar tree *noun* esp. *Cdn* a tree or other tall structure to which cables are attached for hauling logs.

spasm ● *noun* **1** a sudden involuntary muscular contraction. **2 a** a sudden convulsive movement or emotion etc. (*a spasm of coughing*). **b** a condition or state characterized by a spasm or spasms. **3** (usu. foll. by *of*) *informal* a brief or sudden spell of an activity, condition, etc. ● *intransitive verb* twitch convulsively; suffer a spasm. [Old French *spasme* or Latin *spasmus* from Greek *spasmos, spasma* from *spaō* pull]

spas·mod·ic /spazˈmɒdɪk/ *adjective* **1** of, caused by, or subject to, a spasm or spasms (*a spasmodic jerk; spasmodic asthma*). **2** occurring or done by fits and starts (*spasmodic efforts*). □ **spas·mod·ic·al·ly** *adverb* [modern Latin *spasmodicus* from Greek *spasmōdēs* (as SPASM)]

Spas·sky, Boris (Vasily·evich) (b.1937), Russian chess player. In 1969 he won the world championship, losing his title to the American Bobby Fischer in 1972. In a rematch with Fischer in 1992 he was again defeated.

spas·tic ● *adjective* **1** *Med.* affected by or pertaining to a spasm or sudden involuntary movements. **2** esp. *Brit.* suffering from cerebral palsy with spasm of the muscles. **3** *offensive* uncoordinated, incompetent, stupid. ● *noun* offensive a spastic person. □ **spas·tic·al·ly** *adverb* **spas·tic·ity** *noun* [Latin *spasticus* from Greek *spastikos* pulling, from *spaō* pull]

spat¹ *past and past participle of* SPIT¹.

spat² *noun* **1** (usu. in *pl.*) *hist.* a short cloth gaiter protecting the shoe from mud etc. **2** a cover for an aircraft wheel. [abbreviation of SPATTERDASH]

spat³ *N Amer. informal* ● *noun* a petty quarrel. ● *intransitive verb* (**spat·ted, spat·ting**) quarrel pettily. [prob. imitative]

spat⁴ *noun* the spawn of shellfish, esp. the oyster. [Anglo-French, of unknown origin]

spatch·cock ● *noun* a chicken or esp. game bird split open and

grilled. ● *transitive verb* **1** treat (poultry) in this way. **2** *informal* insert or interpolate (a phrase, sentence, story, etc.) esp. incongruously. [perhaps var. of SPITCHCOCK]

spate *noun* **1** a situation in which the volume of water flowing through a river is much higher than normal, usu. temporarily as a result of heavy rains or melting snow. **2** a sudden outburst; a large or excessive amount (*a spate of inquiries*). □ **in** (**full**) **spate 1** (of a river) flowing strongly at a much higher level than normal. **2** completely involved in something and likely to continue for some time. [Middle English, Scots & Northern English: origin unknown]

spathe /speɪð/ *noun Bot.* a large bract or pair of bracts enveloping a spadix or flower cluster. [Latin from Greek *spathē* broad blade etc.]

spa·tial *adjective* (also **spa·cial**) **1** of or concerning space (*spatial extent*). **2** having extension in space; occupying space. □ **spa·tial·ity** *noun* **spa·tial·ize** *transitive verb* (also esp. *Brit.* **-ise**) **spa·tial·ly** *adverb* [Latin *spatium* space]

spatio·temp·oral /ˌspeɪʃɪəˈtɛmpərəl/ *adjective Physics & Philos.* belonging to both space and time or to space-time.
□ **spatio·temp·or·ally** *adverb*

Spät·lese /'ʃpɛtleɪzə/ *noun* (pl. **-leses** or **-lesen** /'ʃpɛtleɪzən/) a white, esp. German, wine made from grapes harvested late in the season. [German, from *spät*, 'late' + *Lese* 'picking, vintage']

spat·ter ● *verb* **1** *transitive* **a** (often foll. by *with*) splash or stain (a person etc.) with spots of liquid etc. (*spattered him with mud*). **b** scatter or splash (liquid, mud, etc.), esp. in drops or small particles. **2** *intransitive* (of rain etc.) fall here and there (*glass spattered down*). ● *noun* **1** (usu. foll. by *of*) a splash (*a spatter of mud*). **2** a quick pattering sound. [frequentative from base found in Dutch, Low German *spatten* burst, spout]

spat·ter·dash *noun* (usu. in *pl.*) *hist.* a long gaiter or other legging to protect the stockings etc. from mud etc., esp. when riding.

spat·ter·dock *noun* a pond lily, *Nuphar advena*, with floating leaves and yellow flowers.

spat·ula /'spatʃʊlə/ *noun* **1** any of various cooking utensils, esp.: **a** an implement with a broad flexible rubber blade, used to scrape the sides of a bowl etc. **b** a knifelike implement with a blunt blade, used to spread icing etc. **c** an implement with a rigid usu. square blade set at an angle, used to lift or flip pancakes, hamburgers, eggs, etc. **2** any of various broad-bladed implements for stirring, spreading, or technical uses. [Latin, var. of *spathula*, diminutive of *spatha* SPATHE]

spatu·late /'spatjʊlət/ *adjective* **1** having a broad rounded end. **2** (of a leaf) broad at the apex and tapering towards the base.

spav·in /'spavɪn/ *noun* enlargement of a horse's hock caused by distension of the vein (**blood spavin**), swelling of the joint due to excess fluid (**bog spavin**), or an outgrowth of the bone (**bone spavin**), often leading to lameness. [Old French *espavin*, var. of *esparvain* from Germanic]

spav·ined /'spavɪnd/ *adjective* **1** (of a horse) affected with spavin. **2** lame, maimed; decrepit, decaying.

spawn ● *verb* **1 a** *transitive & intransitive* (of a fish, frog, mollusc, or crustacean) produce or fertilize (eggs). **b** *intransitive* be produced as eggs or young. **2** *transitive & intransitive derogatory* (of people) produce (offspring). **3** *transitive* produce or generate, esp. in large numbers. ● *noun* **1** the eggs of fish, frogs, etc. **2** *derogatory* human offspring. **3** a product, result, or effect of something. **4** a white fibrous matter from which fungi are produced; mycelium. □ **spawn·er** *noun* [Anglo-French *espaundre* shed roe, Old French *espandre* EXPAND]

spay *transitive verb* sterilize (a female animal) by removing the ovaries. □ **spayed** *adjective* [Anglo-French *espeier*, Old French *espeer* cut with a sword, from *espee* sword, from Latin *spatha*: see SPATHE]

spaz *noun* (pl. **spaz·zes**) *N Amer. slang* an uncoordinated, awkward, or disturbed person. □ **spaz out** (**spazzed, spaz·zing**) lose control; become frenetic, overly excited, emotional, etc.; freak out. **take a spaz** (also **have a spaz**) = SPAZ OUT. [abbreviation of SPASTIC]

SPCA *abbreviation N Amer.* Society for the Prevention of Cruelty to Animals.

speak *verb* (*past* **spoke**; *past participle* **spok·en**) **1** *intransitive* make articulate verbal utterances in an ordinary (not singing) voice. **2** *transitive* **a** utter (words). **b** make known or communicate (one's opinion, the truth, etc.) in this way (*never speaks sense*). **3** *intransitive* **a** (foll. by *to, with*) hold a conversation (*spoke to him for an hour; spoke with them about their work*). **b** (foll. by *of*) mention in writing etc. (*speaks of it in his novel*). **c** (foll. by *for*) articulate the feelings of (another person etc.) in speech or writing (*speaks for our generation*). **4** *intransitive* (foll. by *to*) **a** address; converse with (a person etc.). **b** speak in confirmation of or with reference to (*spoke to the resolution; can speak to his innocence*).

Consonants: b *but*   d *dog*   f *few*   g *get*   h *her*   j *yes*   k *cat*   l *leg*   m *man*   n *no*   p *pen*   r *red*   s *sit*

c *informal* reprove (*spoke to them about their lateness*). **d** attest; give an indication of. **5** *intransitive* make a speech before an audience etc. (*spoke for an hour on the topic; has a good speaking voice*). **6** *transitive* use or be able to use (a specified language) (*cannot speak French*). **7** *intransitive* (of a gun, a musical instrument, etc.) make a sound. **8** *intransitive* (usu. foll. by *to*) *literary* communicate feeling etc., affect, touch (*the sunset spoke to her*). **9** *intransitive* (of a hound) bark. **10** *transitive* hail and hold communication with (a ship). □ **nothing to speak of** nothing worth mentioning; practically nothing. **not to speak of** = NOT TO MENTION (*see* MENTION). **so to speak** *see* SO¹. **speak for itself** need no supporting evidence. **speak for oneself 1** give one's own opinions. **2** not presume to speak for others. **speaking of** used to introduce a statement etc. on a topic recently alluded to. **speak in tongues** *Christianity* speak or be able to speak in a language one does not know, identified as a gift of the Holy Spirit (Acts 2; 1 Cor. 14). **speak one's mind** speak bluntly or frankly. **speak out** speak loudly or freely, give one's opinion. **speak up** = SPEAK OUT. **speak volumes** (of a fact etc.) be very significant. **speak volumes** (or **well** etc.) **about** (or **for**) **1** be abundant evidence of. **2** place in a favourable light. □ **speak·able** *adjective* [Old English *sprecan*, later *specan*]

-speak *combining form* forming nouns denoting a particular variety of language or characteristic mode of speaking (*football-speak; doublespeak*). [after NEWSPEAK]

speak·easy *noun* (*pl.* **-easies**) *N Amer. esp. hist. slang* a bar etc. selling liquor illicitly.

speak·er *noun* **1** a person who speaks, esp. in public. **2** a person who speaks a specified language (esp. in *combination: a French-speaker*). **3** (**Speaker**) the presiding officer in a legislative assembly. **4** = LOUDSPEAKER. □ **speak·er·ship** *noun*

speak·er·phone *noun* esp. *N Amer.* a telephone with a loudspeaker and microphone, which does not need to be held in the hand.

speak·ing ● *noun* the act or an instance of uttering words etc. ● *adjective* **1** that speaks; capable of articulate speech. **2** (in *combination*) speaking or capable of speaking a specified language (*French-speaking*). **3** with a reference or from a point of view specified (*roughly speaking; professionally speaking*). **4** (of a portrait) lifelike; true to its subject (*a speaking likeness*). □ **on speaking terms** (foll. by *with*) **1** slightly acquainted. **2** on friendly terms.

speaking acquaintance *noun* **1** a person one knows slightly. **2** this degree of familiarity.

speaking tube *noun* a tube for conveying the voice from one room, building, etc., to another.

Spear, Cape the easternmost point of N America, situated 11 km southeast of St. John's, Newfoundland. It is a designated historic site, having the oldest lighthouse in Newfoundland. [ultimately from Portuguese *spera* waiting]

spear ● *noun* **1** a thrusting or throwing weapon with a pointed tip and a long shaft. **2** a similar barbed instrument used for catching fish etc. **3** *archaic* a spearman. **4** a pointed stem of asparagus etc. ● *transitive verb* **1** pierce or strike with or as if with a spear (*speared an olive*). **2** *Hockey* jab or poke (a player) with the blade of the stick. [Old English *spere*]

spear carrier *noun* **1** a soldier etc. wielding a spear. **2 a** an actor etc. with a walk-on part. **b** a person with an insignificant role; an unimportant person. **3** *N Amer.* a person spearheading an initiative; a standard-bearer.

spear·fish·ing *noun* fishing esp. underwater using a spear.

spear grass *noun* any of several grasses, e.g. *Poa pratensis*.

spear·gun *noun* a gun used to propel a spear in underwater fishing.

spear·head ● *noun* **1** the point of a spear; a piece of stone or metal forming this. **2** an individual or group leading a campaign, attack, initiative, etc. ● *transitive verb* act as the spearhead of (an attack etc.).

spear·ing *noun* **1** *in senses of* SPEAR *verb*. **2** *Hockey* the illegal jabbing or poking of an opponent with the blade of one's stick.

spear·man *noun* (*pl.* **-men**) *hist.* a person, esp. a soldier, who uses a spear.

spear·mint *noun* a common garden mint, *Mentha spicata*, used in cooking and to flavour chewing gum etc.

spear point *noun* = SPEARHEAD 1.

spear side *noun* the male side of a family. *Compare* DISTAFF SIDE.

spear thrower *noun* esp. *hist.* a long bone, wood, or antler tool with an upturned end fitted into a notch in the base of a spear, used to increase the force and distance of a spear throw.

spear·wort /ˈspiːrwɜrt, -wɔrt/ *noun* an aquatic plant, *Ranunculus lingua*, with thick hollow stems, long narrow spear-shaped leaves, and yellow flowers.

spec¹ *noun informal* **1** a commercial speculation or venture. **2** (*attributive*) designating something produced without the assurance that it will be bought etc. (*a spec script; spec homes*). □ **on spec** without the assurance of success or reward; as a gamble. [abbreviation of SPECULATION]

spec² *informal* ● *noun* (usu. in *pl.*) a detailed working description; a specification or specifications. ● *transitive verb* (**spec'd, spec'ing**) (esp. as **spec'd** *adjective*) build to certain specifications; provide with specifications (*the military-spec'd version*). [abbreviation of SPECIFICATION]

spe·cial ● *adjective* **1 a** particularly good; exceptional; out of the ordinary (*bought them a special present; took special trouble*). **b** peculiar; specific; not general (*lacks the special qualities required; the word has a special sense*). **2** for a particular purpose (*sent on a special assignment*). **3** in which a person specializes (*statistics is her special field*). **4** denoting education for children with particular needs, e.g. the handicapped. ● *noun* **1** a special person or thing, e.g. a special train, constable, dish on a menu, etc. **2** *N Amer.* the offering of a product or service at a temporarily reduced price (*this week's specials*). **3** esp. *N Amer. Broadcasting* a program scheduled and aired in place of regular programming, usu. to mark an occasion, season, holiday, etc. (*another Christmas special*). **4** a newspaper article by a writer who is not a regular member of the newspaper's staff. □ **on special** *N Amer.* available for purchase at a temporarily reduced price. □ **spe·cial·ly** *adverb* **spe·cial·ness** *noun* [Old French *especial* ESPECIAL or Latin *specialis* (as SPECIES)]

Special Administrative Region *noun* either of two regions in China, the former British colony of Hong Kong and the former Portuguese colony of Macau, where a capitalist economy and internal autonomy are permitted.

special area *noun* *Cdn* (*Alta.*) a large, sparsely populated area administered by the Alberta provincial government.

special branch *noun* a police department or unit dealing with political security.

special case *noun* **1** a written statement of fact presented by litigants to a court, raising a matter to be tried separately from the main action. **2** an exceptional or unusual case.

special committee *noun* a committee, e.g. of a legislature, formed to examine one particular issue or piece of proposed legislation.

special constable *noun* *Cdn & Brit.* a police officer sworn in to assist in times of emergency etc. or having a limited range of responsibilities.

special delivery *noun* **1** *N Amer.* mail delivery in advance of the regular delivery. **2** (in the UK) guaranteed delivery of a letter within the UK the day after posting.

special drawing rights *plural noun* the right to purchase extra foreign currency from the International Monetary Fund, treated as a currency in international loans.

special edition *noun* **1** an extra edition of a newspaper etc. including later news than the ordinary edition. **2** (often *attributive*) a specially-modified version of a product, esp. available in limited quantities (*special edition coupe*).

special education *noun* (also *N Amer. informal* **special ed**) **1** the education of children with special needs arising from physical or mental disabilities. **2** a program providing such education.

special effects *plural noun* scenic or optical illusions for films, television, or the stage, created by computers, props, camerawork, etc.

special intention *noun* *Catholicism* a special aim or purpose for which a Mass is celebrated, prayers are said, etc.

special interest *noun* (in full **special interest group**) a group of people or a corporation with a common political, social, environmental, etc. interest, concern, or purpose.

special interest group *noun* **1** *see* SPECIAL INTEREST. **2** a computerized discussion group on a specific topic, interest, etc. Abbr.: **SIG**.

special investigations unit *noun* an independent police unit responsible for investigating the conduct of police officers of other forces. Abbr.: **SIU**.

spe·cial·ist *noun* **1** a person who is trained in a particular branch of a profession, esp. medicine (*a specialist in dermatology*). **2** a person who especially or exclusively studies a subject or a particular branch of a subject. □ **spe·cial·ism** *noun* esp. *Brit.*

spe·cial·ity (*pl.* **-ities**) *var. of* SPECIALTY 1, 2.

spe·cial·ize *verb* (also esp. *Brit.* **-ise**) **1** *intransitive* (often foll. by *in*) **a** be or become a specialist (*specializes in optics*). **b** devote oneself to an area of interest, skill, etc. (*specializes in insulting people*). **2** *Biol.* **a** *transitive* (esp. in *passive*) adapt or set apart (an organ etc.) for a particular purpose. **b** *intransitive* (of an organ etc.) become adapted etc. in this way. **3** *transitive* make specific or individual. **4** *transitive* modify or limit (an idea, statement, etc.). □ **spe·cial·iz·a·tion** *noun*

specialized municipality *noun Cdn (Alta.)* a municipality with a unique form of local government established to encourage its development into a village, town, or city.

Special K *noun slang* = KETAMINE. [punningly after a brand of breakfast cereal]

special needs *plural noun* **1** the special esp. educational requirements of people with disabilities. **2** (*attributive*) designating such people or their education (*special-needs children*).

Special Olympics an international multi-event sporting competition for people with mental disabilities, similar to the Olympic Games.

special-operations *plural noun* (also **special-ops**) (*attributive*) designating military forces specially trained to conduct difficult, clandestine, or unusual operations (*special-ops forces*).

special pleading *noun* **1** *Law* pleading with reference to new facts in a case. **2** (in general use) a specious or unfair argument favouring the speaker's point of view. □ **special pleader** *noun*

special prosecutor *noun* a lawyer not otherwise in the employ of an Attorney General's department or Ministry of Justice hired to prosecute a special case or series of cases.

special relativity *noun see* RELATIVITY 2a.

special school *noun* (in the UK) a school catering for children with special educational needs resulting from a disability or learning difficulty.

special team *noun* (also **specialty team**) *N Amer. Sport* a group of players on a team used especially or exclusively in certain well-defined circumstances, e.g. when killing penalties in hockey or when receiving punts in football.

spe·cialty *noun* (*pl.* **-ties**) **1** esp. *N Amer.* a special pursuit, product, operation, etc., to which a company or a person gives special attention. **2** esp. *N Amer.* a special feature, characteristic, or skill. **3** *N Amer.* (*attributive*) designating a product, store, etc. pertaining or devoted to a very specific interest (*a specialty bookstore for science fiction readers; specialty products*). **4** *Law* an instrument under seal; a sealed contract.

speci·a·tion /spiːʃiˈeɪʃən, spiːs-/ *noun Biol.* the formation of new species in the course of evolution. □ **speci·ate** /ˈspiː-/ *intransitive verb*

spe·cie /ˈspiːʃi/ *noun* coin money as opposed to paper money. [Latin, ablative of SPECIES in phrase *in specie*]

spe·cies /ˈspiːsiːz, ˈspiːʃ-/ *noun* (*pl.* same) **1** a class of things having some common characteristics. **2** *Biol.* a group of living organisms consisting of related similar individuals capable of exchanging genes or interbreeding, classified as a taxonomic rank below a genus and denoted by a Latin binomial. **3** a kind or sort. **4** *Logic* a group subordinate to a genus and containing individuals agreeing in some common attribute(s) and called by a common name. **5** *Law* a form or shape given to materials. **6** esp. *Catholicism* the visible form of each of the elements of consecrated bread and wine in the Eucharist. [Latin, = appearance, kind, beauty, from *specere* look]

species·ism /ˈspiːsiːzɪzəm, ˈspiːʃ-/ *noun* an assumption of human superiority leading to the exploitation of animals. □ **species·ist** *adjective & noun*

spe·cif·ic /spəˈsɪfɪk/ ● *adjective* **1** clearly defined; definite, precise (*has no specific name; told me so in specific terms*). **2** relating to one particular subject or thing; peculiar, particular (*music specific to the region; often in combination: culture-specific*). **3 a** of or concerning a species (*the specific name for a plant*). **b** possessing, or concerned with, the properties that characterize a species (*the specific forms of animals*). **4** (of a duty or a tax) assessed by quantity or amount, not by the value of goods. ● *noun* **1** (esp. in *pl.*) a specific aspect or factor (*shall we discuss specifics?*). **2** *archaic* a medicine or remedy specifically effective for a disease or part of the body. □ **spe·cif·ic·ally** *adverb* **spe·cif·i·city** /ˌspesɪˈfɪsɪti/ *noun* [Late Latin *specificus* (as SPECIES)]

speci·fi·ca·tion /ˌspesɪfɪˈkeɪʃən/ *noun* **1** the act or an instance of specifying; the state of being specified. **2 a** (esp. in *pl.*) a detailed description of the construction, workmanship, materials, etc., of work done or to be done, prepared by an architect, engineer, etc. **b** (in *pl.*) a detailed description of the components of an electronic system, e.g. a computer. **c** a specified standard of workmanship, materials, etc., to be achieved (*built to a high specification*). **3** a description by an applicant for a patent of the construction and use of his invention. **4** *Law* the conversion of materials into a new product not held to be the property of the owner of the materials.

specific cause *noun* the cause of a particular form of a disease.

specific difference *noun* a factor that differentiates a species.

specific gravity *noun Chem.* the ratio of the density of a substance to the density of a standard, usu. water for a liquid or solid, and air for a gas. *Also called* RELATIVE DENSITY.

specific heat *noun* (in full **specific heat capacity**) the heat required to raise the temperature of the unit mass of a given substance by a given amount (usu. one degree).

specific land claim *noun Cdn* a land claim made against the federal government when specific treaty terms have not been met.

specific performance *noun Law* the performance of a contractual duty, as ordered in cases where damages would not be adequate remedy.

speci·fy /ˈspesɪˌfaɪ/ *verb* (**-fies, -fied**) **1** *transitive & intransitive* name or mention expressly (*specified the type he needed*). **2** *transitive* (usu. foll. by *that* + clause) name as a condition (*specified that he must be paid at once*). **3** *transitive* include in specifications (*a French door was not specified*). □ **speci·fi·able** *adjective* **speci·fi·er** *noun* [Old French *specifier* or Late Latin *specificare* (as SPECIFIC)]

speci·men /ˈspesɪmən/ *noun* **1** an individual or part taken as an example of a class or whole, esp. when used for investigation or scientific examination (*specimens of copper ore; a specimen of your handwriting*). **2** *Med.* a sample of urine, blood, tissue, etc. for testing. **3** *informal* usu. *derogatory* a person of a specified sort. [Latin from *specere*]

spe·cious /ˈspiːʃəs/ *adjective* **1** superficially plausible or genuine but actually wrong or false (*a specious argument*). **2** misleadingly attractive in appearance. □ **spe·cious·ly** *adverb* **spe·cious·ness** *noun* [Middle English, = beautiful, from Latin *speciosus* (as SPECIES)]

speck ● *noun* **1** a small spot, dot, or stain. **2** (foll. by *of*) a particle (*speck of dirt*). **3** a rotten spot in fruit. ● *transitive verb* (esp. as **specked** *adjective*) marked with specks. □ **specky** *adjective* [Old English *specca*: compare SPECKLE]

speckle ● *noun* a small spot, mark, or stain, esp. in quantity on the skin, a bird's egg, etc. ● *transitive verb* (esp. as **speckled** *adjective*) mark with speckles or patches. [Middle Dutch *spekkel*]

speckled alder *noun* a shrub or small tree, *Alnus rugosa*, the common alder found in wet places across Canada.

speckled trout *noun* = BROOK TROUT.

specs *plural noun informal* a pair of eyeglasses. [abbreviation of SPECTACLES]

spec sheet *noun* a list of an item's specifications.

spec·tacle *noun* **1** a public show, ceremony, etc. **2** anything attracting public attention (*a charming spectacle; a disgusting spectacle*). **3** a ridiculous person or thing. □ **make a spectacle of oneself** make oneself an object of ridicule. [Old French from Latin *spectaculum* from *spectare* frequentative of *specere* look]

spec·tacled *adjective* **1** wearing eyeglasses. **2** (of an animal) having facial markings resembling eyeglasses.

spec·tacles *plural noun* (also **pair of spectacles** *singular*) a pair of eyeglasses.

spec·tacu·lar /spekˈtakjʊlər/ ● *adjective* **1** beautiful in a dramatic and eye-catching way (*spectacular mountain scenery*). **2** strikingly large or obvious (*a spectacular increase in output*). ● *noun* a spectacular thing or event, esp. a musical film or play. □ **spec·tacu·lar·ly** *adverb* [SPECTACLE, after *oracular* etc.]

spec·tate *intransitive verb* be a spectator, esp. at a sporting event. [back-formation from SPECTATOR]

spec·ta·tor *noun* a person who looks on at a show, game, incident, etc. □ **spec·ta·tor·ial** *adjective* **spec·ta·tor·ship** *noun* [French *spectateur* or Latin *spectator* from *spectare*: see SPECTACLE]

spectator pump *noun N Amer.* a woman's dress shoe, usu. with a white body and contrasting darker toe and heel, often with decorative perforations in the leather.

spectator sport *noun* **1** a sport providing popular entertainment for spectators. **2** *informal* an event or activity that attracts much interest (*in this town a mayoralty race is a spectator sport*).

spec·ter *US var. of* SPECTRE.

spec·tra *pl. of* SPECTRUM.

spec·tral *adjective* **1 a** of or relating to spectres or ghosts. **b** ghostlike. **2** of or concerning spectra or the spectrum (*spectral colours; spectral analysis*). □ **spec·tral·ly** *adverb*

spectral analysis *noun* **1** chemical analysis using a spectroscope. **2** analysis of light, sound, etc. into a spectrum.

spectral line *noun* a line in a spectrum due to the emission or absorption of radiation, occurring at discrete wavelengths characteristic of the material producing them.

spectral type *noun* (also **spectral class**) *Astronomy* the group in which a star is classified according to its spectrum, esp. using the Harvard classification.

spectre *noun* (*US* **spec·ter**) **1** a ghost. **2** a haunting presentiment or preoccupation (*the spectre of war*). **3** (esp. in *combination*) used in the names of some animals because of their thinness, transparency, etc. [French *spectre* or Latin *spectrum*: see SPECTRUM]

spectro- *combining form* a spectrum.

spec·tro·gram *noun* a record obtained with a spectrograph.

spec·tro·graph *noun* an apparatus for photographing or otherwise recording spectra. □ **spec·tro·graph·ic** *adjective* **spec·tro·graph·ic·ally** *adverb* **spec·trog·raphy** *noun*

spec·tro·helio·graph /ˌspektroʊˈhiːliəˌgraf/ *noun* an instrument for taking photographs of the sun in the light of one wavelength only.

spec·trom·eter /spekˈtrɒmətər/ *noun* an instrument used for the measurement of observed spectra. □ **spec·tro·met·ric** /ˌspektrəˈmetrɪk/ *adjective* **spec·trom·etry** *noun*

spec·tro·pho·tom·eter /ˌspektroʊfoʊˈtɒmətər/ *noun* an instrument for measuring the intensity of light in various parts of the spectrum, esp. as transmitted or emitted by a substance or solution at a particular wavelength. □ **spec·tro·photo·met·ric** /-təˈmetrɪk/ *adjective* **spec·tro·pho·tom·etry** *noun*

spec·tro·scope *noun* an instrument for producing and recording spectra for examination. □ **spec·tro·scop·ic** *adjective* **spec·tros·cop·ist** *noun* **spec·tros·copy** *noun*

spec·trum *noun* (*pl.* **spec·tra**, **spec·trums**) **1** a band of colours, as seen in a rainbow etc., produced by separation of the components of light by their different degrees of refraction according to wavelength. **2** the entire range of wavelengths of electromagnetic radiation. **3 a** an image or distribution of components of any electromagnetic radiation arranged in a progressive series according to wavelength. **b** this as characteristic of a body or substance when emitting or absorbing radiation. **4** a similar image or distribution of components of sound, particles, etc., arranged according to frequency, charge, energy, etc. **5** the entire range or a wide range of anything arranged by degree or quality etc. (*political spectrum*). **6** an afterimage. [Latin, = image, apparition, from *specere* 'to look']

spectrum analysis *noun* = SPECTRAL ANALYSIS.

spectrum analyzer *noun* a device for analyzing oscillation, esp. sound, into its separate components.

specu·la *pl.* of SPECULUM.

specu·lar /ˈspekjʊlər/ *adjective* of or having the properties of a mirror. [Latin *specularis* (as SPECULUM)]

specu·late /ˈspekjʊˌleɪt/ *verb* **1** *intransitive* (usu. foll. by *on, upon, about*) form a theory or conjecture, esp. without a firm factual basis; meditate (*speculated on their prospects*). **2** *transitive* (foll. by *that, how*, etc. + clause) conjecture, consider (*speculated how he might achieve it*). **3** *intransitive* **a** invest in stocks etc. in the hope of gain but with the possibility of loss. **b** gamble recklessly. □ **specu·la·tor** *noun* [Latin *speculari* spy out, observe, from *specula* watchtower, from *specere* look]

specu·la·tion *noun* **1** the act or an instance of speculating; a theory or conjecture (*made no speculation as to her age; is given to speculation*). **2 a** a speculative investment or enterprise (*bought it as a speculation*). **b** the practice of business speculating.

specu·la·tive /ˈspekjʊlətɪv/ *adjective* **1** of, based on, engaged in, or inclined to speculation. **2** (of a business investment) involving the risk of loss (*a speculative builder*). □ **specu·la·tive·ly** *adverb* **specu·la·tive·ness** *noun*

speculative fiction *noun* literature, as science fiction or fantasy writing, dealing with imaginary or hypothetical worlds or environments.

specu·lum /ˈspekjʊləm/ *noun* (*pl.* **specu·la** /-lə/) **1** an instrument to hold open or dilate a part of the body, esp. the vagina, for examination. **2** a mirror, usu. of polished metal, esp. in a reflecting telescope. **3** *Ornithol.* a lustrous coloured area on the wing of some birds, esp. ducks. [Latin, = mirror, from *specere* look]

sped *past and past participle of* SPEED.

speech *noun* **1** the faculty or act of speaking. **2** a usu. formal address or discourse delivered to an audience or assembly. **3** a manner of speaking (*a man of blunt speech*). **4** a remark (*after this speech he was silent*). **5** the language of a nation, region, group, etc. **6** = SOUND¹ *noun* 10. [Old English *sprǣc*, later *spēc* from West Germanic, related to SPEAK]

speech act *noun* an utterance regarded as an act performed with a

particular purpose and effect, e.g. the statement 'It's cold in here' made with the intended effect that the interlocutor will close a window, turn up the heat, etc.

Speech from the Throne *noun* *Cdn* a statement summarizing the government's proposed measures, read by the sovereign, Governor General, or Lieutenant-Governor at the opening of a session of Parliament or a legislature.

speech·ify *intransitive verb* (**-fies**, **-fied**) *jocular* or *derogatory* make esp. boring or long speeches. □ **speech·ifi·ca·tion** *noun* **speech·ifi·er** *noun*

speech-language pathology *noun* *N Amer., Austral., NZ, & South Africa* (also **speech pathology**) the treatment of disorders of speech and communication. □ **speech-language pathologist** *noun*

speech·less *adjective* **1** temporarily unable to speak because of emotion etc. (*speechless with rage*). **2** dumb. **3** (of an emotion etc.) tending to deprive one temporarily of speech. □ **speech·less·ly** *adverb* **speech·less·ness** *noun*

speech recognition *noun* the identification and interpretation or response by a computer to the sounds produced in human speech.

speech therapy *noun* esp. *Brit.* = SPEECH-LANGUAGE PATHOLOGY. □ **speech therapist** *noun*

speech writ·er *noun* a person employed to write speeches for a politician etc. to deliver. □ **speech writing** *noun*

speed ● *noun* **1** rapidity of movement (*with all speed; at full speed*). **2 a** a rate of progress or motion over a distance in time (*attains a high speed*). **b** (*attributive*) designating a sport or activity undertaken at an increased speed (*speed climbing, speed chess*). **3** a gear ratio in a motor vehicle, bicycle, etc. **4** *Photog.* **a** the sensitivity of film to light. **b** the light gathering power of a lens. **c** the duration of an exposure. **5** *slang* an amphetamine drug, esp. methamphetamine. **6** esp. *N Amer. informal* a person, activity, etc. that suits one's abilities or personality (*robbing banks is hardly his speed*). **7** *archaic* success, prosperity. ● *verb* (*past and past participle* **sped** or **speed·ed**) **1** *intransitive* go fast (*sped down the street*). **2 a** *intransitive* (of a motorist etc.) travel at an illegal or dangerous speed. **b** *transitive* regulate the speed of (an engine etc.). **c** *transitive* cause (an engine etc.) to go at a fixed speed. **3** *transitive* send fast or on its way (*speed an arrow from the bow*). □ **at speed** moving quickly. **speed up** move or work at greater speed. **up to speed 1** operating at full speed. **2** operating or functioning at an anticipated level (*trying to get the company up to speed*). **3** (of a person) fully informed or up to date. [Old English *spēd, spēdan* from Germanic]

speed bag *noun* *N Amer.* a small punching bag for practising quick punches.

speed·ball *noun* *slang* a mixture of cocaine with heroin or morphine.

speed·boat *noun* a motorboat designed for high speed. □ **speed·boat·er** *noun* **speed·boat·ing** *noun*

speed bump *noun* **1** a transverse ridge in a roadway requiring drivers to slow down to pass over it. **2** any sort of minor impediment to a course of action.

speed demon *noun* *N Amer. informal* a person or thing that moves or goes very quickly, esp. a driver who routinely breaks the speed limit.

speed-dial ● *noun* a function on some telephones which allows frequently-called numbers to be entered into a memory for faster dialing. ● *transitive verb* use this function to telephone (someone). □ **speed-dialing** *noun*

speed·er *noun* **1** in senses of SPEED *verb*. **2** *N Amer.* = JIGGER¹ *noun* 5.

speed freak *noun* *slang* a habitual user of an amphetamine drug.

speed·ing *noun* the traffic offence of driving at an illegal or dangerous speed.

speed limit *noun* the maximum speed at which a road vehicle may legally be driven in a particular area etc.

speed merchant *noun* *informal* a motorist who enjoys driving fast.

speed metal *noun* a variety of heavy metal music with a very fast tempo.

speedo *noun* (*pl.* **-os**) *informal* **1** = SPEEDOMETER. **2** (**Speedo**) *proprietary* a men's brief, tight-fitting bathing suit. [abbreviation]

speed·om·eter *noun* an instrument displaying the speed of motor vehicle etc.

speed-read *transitive & intransitive verb* read rapidly, e.g. by assimilating several phrases or sentences at once. □ **speed-reader** *noun*

speed skat·ing *noun* racing performed on skates around a usu. oval track against other skaters or the clock. □ **speed skater** *noun* **speed·skates** *plural noun*

---

uː m**oo**d   a**i** m**y**   ə**i** p**i**pe   a**u** br**ow**n   ʌ**u** h**ou**se   e**i** d**ay**   ɔ**i** b**oy**   ã fr**an**glais   ã C**an**adien   ɔ̃ Br**ay**on   (*see over for consonants*)

speed·ster *noun* **1** a fast motor vehicle, esp. a sports car. **2** a person or animal that runs etc. quickly. **3** a person who drives too quickly.

speed trap *noun* a part of a highway etc. where police, usu. concealed, check the speed of passing vehicles.

speed-up *noun* an increase in the speed or rate of working.

speed·way *noun* **1** N Amer. a road or track used for motor car racing. **2** US a highway for fast motor traffic. **3 a** a motorcycle racing. **b** a stadium or track used for this.

speed·well *noun* any small herb of the genus *Veronica*, with a creeping or ascending stem and tiny blue or pink flowers.

speedy *adjective* (**speed·i·er**, **speed·i·est**) **1** moving quickly; rapid. **2** done without delay; prompt (*a speedy answer*). □ **speed·i·ly** *adverb* **speed·i·ness** *noun*

Speedy Gon·za·les *noun* = SPEEDSTER 2. [after a cartoon character mouse in Bugs Bunny cartoons]

Speer /spiːr, ʃper/ **Albert** (1905–81), German architect and Nazi leader. He was Hitler's chief architect (1933–45), designing the stadium at Nuremberg (1934), and as minister of armaments (1942–45) was mainly responsible for the planning of Germany's war economy. The only Nazi leader to admit responsibility at the Nuremberg trials for the regime's actions, he served twenty years in Spandau prison (1946–66).

speiss /spʌis/ *noun* a compound of arsenic, iron, etc., formed in smelting certain lead ores. [German *Speise* food, amalgam]

spele·ol·ogy /ˌspiːlɪˈɒlədʒi, ˌspe-/ *noun* **1** the scientific study of caves. **2** the exploration of caves. □ **spele·o·logic·al** *adjective* **spele·ol·o·gist** *noun* [French *spéléologie* from Latin *spelaeum* from Greek *spēlaion* cave]

spell¹ *verb* (*past* and *past participle* **spelled** or **spelt**) **1** *transitive & intransitive* write or name the letters that form (a word etc.) in correct sequence. **2** *transitive* (of letters) make up or form (a word etc.). **3** *transitive* (of circumstances, a scheme, etc.) result in; involve (*this decision spells ruin for the project*). □ **spell out 1** make out (words, writing, etc.) letter by letter. **2** explain in detail (*spelled out what the change would mean*). [Old French *espel(l)er*, from Frankish (as SPELL²)]

spell² *noun* **1 a** a words which when spoken are thought to have magical power (*the wizard recited a spell*). **b** a state or condition caused by a person speaking such words (*put a spell on her*). **2** a fascinating or very attractive influence that a person or thing has. □ **under a spell** mastered by or as if by a spell. [Old English *spel(l)* 'narration' from Germanic]

spell³ ● *noun* **1** a period of time during which something lasts. **2** a period of a specified type of weather (*a hot spell*). **3** a bout or fit of something (*had a dizzy spell*). **4** a period of activity or duty, esp. one which two or more people share (*take a spell at the wheel of the car*). ● *transitive verb* (often foll. by *off*) **1** relieve or take the place of (a person) in work etc. **2** allow to rest briefly. [earlier as verb: later form of dial. *spele* take place of, from Old English *spelian*, of unknown origin]

spell·bind *transitive verb* (*past* and *past participle* **spell·bound**) bind with or as if with a spell; entrance. □ **spell·bind·er** *noun* **spell·bind·ing** *adjective* **spell·bind·ing·ly** *adverb*

spell·bound *adjective* entranced, fascinated, esp. by a speaker, activity, quality, etc.

spell-check *Computing* ● *noun* a check of the spelling in a file of text using a spell-checker. ● *transitive verb* check the spelling in (a text) using a spell-checker.

spell-checker *noun* a computer program which checks the spelling of words in files of text, usually by comparison with a stored list of words.

spell·er *noun* **1** a person who spells esp. in a specified way (*is a poor speller*). **2** a book for teaching spelling. **3** N Amer. = SPELL-CHECKER.

spell·ing *noun* **1** the process or activity of writing or naming the letters of a word etc. **2** the way a word is spelled. **3** the ability to spell (*her spelling was very poor*).

spelling bee *noun* a spelling competition in which competitors spell words orally and are eliminated for misspellings, until the competitor who spells the most words correctly is named the winner.

spelling checker *noun* = SPELL-CHECKER.

spelt¹ *past* and *past participle* of SPELL¹.

spelt² *noun* a species of wheat, *Triticum aestivum*. [Old English from Old Saxon *spelta* (Old High German *spelza*), Middle English from Middle Low German, Middle Dutch *spelte*]

spe·lunk·er /spɪˈlʌŋkər/ *noun* N Amer. a person who explores caves, esp. as a hobby. □ **spe·lunk·ing** *noun* [obsolete *spelunk* cave, from Latin *spelunca*]

Spen·cer, Her·bert (1820–1903), English philosopher and sociologist. He embraced Darwin's theory of natural selection, coining the phrase the 'survival of the fittest' (1864), and advocating social and economic laissez-faire.

spen·cer *noun* a short close-fitting jacket. [prob. from the 2nd Earl *Spencer*, English politician d.1834]

spend *verb* (*past* and *past participle* **spent**) **1** (usu. foll. by *on*) **a** *transitive & intransitive* pay out (money) in making a purchase etc. (*spent $50 on a new sweater*). **b** *transitive* pay out (money) for a particular person's benefit or for the improvement of a thing (*had to spend $200 on the car*). **2** *transitive* **a** use or consume (time or energy) (*shall spend no more effort; spent three hours fixing it*). **b** (also *reflexive*) use up; exhaust; wear out (*their ammunition was all spent; his anger was soon spent; spent herself campaigning for justice*). **3** *transitive* pass (time, one's life, etc.) (*spent all our summers in Goderich*). □ **spend a penny** *Brit. informal* urinate or defecate. □ **spend·able** *adjective* **spend·er** *noun* [Old English *spendan* from Latin *expendere* (see EXPEND): in Middle English perhaps also from obsolete *dispend* from Old French *despendre* expend, from Latin *dispendere*: see DISPENSE; idiom 'spend a penny' from the coin-operated locks of public washrooms]

spending money *noun* pocket money.

spend·thrift ● *noun* a person who spends money too freely or wastes money. ● *adjective* extravagant; prodigal.

Spen·gler, Os·wald (1880–1936), German philosopher. In his book *The Decline of the West* (1918–22), he argued that civilizations undergo a seasonal cycle of about a thousand years and are subject to growth, flowering, and decay analogous to biological species.

Spen·ser, Ed·mund (*c*.1552–99), English poet. He is best known for his allegorical romance celebrating Queen Elizabeth I, the *Faerie Queene* (1590; 1596), which is written in the stanza invented by Spenser with eight iambic pentameters and an alexandrine, rhyming *ababbcbcc* (the **Spenserian stanza**). □ **Spen·ser·ian** /spenˈsiːrɪən/ *adjective*

spent ● *verb* past and past participle of SPEND. ● *adjective* having lost its original force or strength; exhausted (*the storm is spent; spent bullets*).

sperm *noun* (*pl.* same or **sperms**) **1** = SPERMATOZOON. **2** the male reproductive fluid containing spermatozoa; semen. **3** = SPERM WHALE. **4** = SPERMACETI. [Late Latin *sperma* from Greek *sperma -atos* seed, from *speirō* sow; in *sperm whale* an abbreviation of SPERMACETI]

sperm·a·ceti /ˌspɜːrməˈsetɪ/ *noun* a white waxy substance produced by the sperm whale to aid buoyancy, and used in the manufacture of candles, ointments, etc. [medieval Latin from Late Latin *sperma* sperm + *ceti* genitive of *cetus* from Greek *kētos* whale, from the belief that it was whale spawn]

sperm·ary /ˈspɜːrmɛri/ *noun* (*pl.* **-aries**) an organ in which human or animal sperms are generated.

sperm·at·ic /spɜːrˈmatɪk/ *adjective* of or relating to a sperm or spermary.

spermatic cord *noun* a bundle of nerves, ducts, and blood vessels passing to the testicles.

sperm·a·tid /ˈspɜːrmətɪd/ *noun* Biol. an immature male sex cell formed from a spermatocyte, which may develop into a spermatozoon.

spermato- /spɜːrˈmatəʊ/ *combining form* Biol. a sperm or seed.

sperm·at·o·cyte /spɜːrˈmatəʊˌsʌɪt/ *noun* a cell produced from a spermatogonium and which may divide by meiosis into spermatids.

sperm·at·o·gen·esis /spɜːrˌmatəʊˈdʒenɪsɪs/ *noun* the production or development of mature spermatozoa.

sperm·at·o·gon·ium /spɜːrˌmatəʊˈɡoʊnɪəm/ *noun* (*pl.* **sperm·at·o·gon·ia** /spɜːrˌmatəʊˈɡoʊnɪə/) a cell produced at an early stage in the formation of spermatozoa, from which spermatocytes develop. □ **sperm·at·o·gon·ic·al** *adjective* [SPERM + modern Latin *gonium* from Greek *gonos* offspring, seed]

sperm·at·o·phore /spɜːrˈmatəʊˌfɔːr/ *noun* an albuminous capsule containing spermatozoa found in various invertebrates.

sperm·at·o·phyte /spɜːrˈmatəʊˌfʌɪt/ *noun* any seed-bearing plant.

sperm·at·o·zoid /spɜːrˌmatəʊˈzɔːɪd/ *noun* the mature motile male sex cell of some plants.

sperm·at·o·zoon /spɜːrˌmatəʊˈzəʊɒn/ *noun* (*pl.* **sperm·at·o·zoa** /spɜːrˌmatəʊˈzəʊə/) the mature motile male sex cell of an animal, by which the ovum is fertilized. □ **sperm·at·o·zoal** *adjective* **sperm·at·o·zoan** *adjective* [SPERM + Greek *zōion* animal]

sperm bank *noun* a place where semen is stored for use in artificial insemination.

sperm count *noun* the number of spermatozoa in one ejaculation or a measured amount of semen.

sperm·i·cide *noun* a substance able to kill spermatozoa.
□ **sperm·i·cid·al** *adjective* **sperm·i·cid·ally** *adverb*

spermo- *combining form* = SPERMATO-.

sperm oil *noun* an oil obtained from the head of a sperm whale, and used as a lubricant.

sperm whale *noun* a large whale, *Physeter macrocephalus*, hunted for the spermaceti and sperm oil contained in its bulbous head, and for the ambergris found in its intestines. *Also called* CACHALOT.

spew ● *verb* **1** *transitive & intransitive* vomit. **2** (often foll. by *out*) **a** *transitive* expel (contents) rapidly and forcibly. **b** *intransitive* (of contents) be expelled in this way. **3** *transitive* (often foll. by *out, forth*) utter (language, esp. abusive or objectionable language) (*was always spewing lies about us*). ● *noun* **1** vomited food etc. **2** something spewed out. □ **spew·er** *noun* [Old English *spīwan, spēowan* from Germanic]

SPF *abbreviation* sun protection factor (indicating the effectiveness of sunscreens etc.).

sp. gr. *abbreviation* specific gravity.

sphag·num /ˈsfagnəm, ˈspag-/ *noun* (in full **sphagnum moss**) any moss of the genus *Sphagnum*, growing in bogs, with spongy, absorbent leaves and stems, and used as packing esp. for plants, as a soil conditioner or fertilizer, etc. [modern Latin from Greek *sphagnos* a moss]

sphal·er·ite /ˈsfaləˌraɪt/ *noun* = BLENDE. [Greek *sphaleros* deceptive: compare BLENDE]

sphen·oid /ˈsfiːnɔɪd/ ● *adjective* **1** wedge-shaped. **2** of or relating to the sphenoid bone. ● *noun* (in full **sphenoid bone**) a large compound bone forming the base of the cranium behind the eyes.
□ **sphen·oid·al** /-ˈnɔɪdəl/ *adjective* [modern Latin *sphenoides* from Greek *sphēnoeidēs* from *sphēn* wedge]

sphere /sfɪər/ *noun* **1** a solid figure, or its surface, with every point on its surface equidistant from its centre. **2** an object having this shape; a ball or globe. **3 a** any celestial body. **b** a globe representing the earth. **c** *literary* the heavens; the sky. **d** the sky perceived as a vault upon or in which celestial bodies are represented as lying. **e** *hist.* each of a series of revolving concentrically arranged spherical shells in which celestial bodies were formerly thought to be set in a fixed relationship. **4 a** a field of action, influence, or existence (*have done much within their own sphere*). **b** a (usu. specified) stratum of society or social class (*moves in quite another sphere*). □ **music** (or **harmony**) **of the spheres** the natural harmonic tones supposedly produced by the movement of the celestial spheres (*see* sense 3e of *noun*) or the bodies fixed in them. **sphere of influence** the claimed or recognized area of a state's interests, an individual's control, etc. [Old French *espere* from Late Latin *sphera*, Latin from Greek *sphaira* ball]

-sphere /sfɪər/ *combining form* **1** having the form of a sphere (*bathysphere*). **2** a region around the earth (*atmosphere*).

spher·ic /ˈsfɪərɪk/ *adjective* = SPHERICAL. □ **spher·icity** /-ˈrɪsɪti/ *noun*

spher·ical /ˈsfɪərɪkəl, ˈsfer-/ *adjective* **1** shaped like a sphere; globular. **2 a** of or relating to the properties of spheres (*spherical geometry*). **b** formed inside or on the surface of a sphere (*spherical triangle*).
□ **spher·ical·ly** *adverb*

spherical aberration *noun* a loss of definition in the image produced by a spherically curved mirror or lens.

spherical angle *noun* an angle formed by the intersection of two great circles of a sphere.

spher·oid /ˈsfɪərɔɪd/ *noun* a body resembling or approximating to a sphere in shape, esp. one formed by the revolution of an ellipse about one of its axes. □ **spher·oid·al** *adjective*

spher·ule /ˈsferuːl/ *noun* a small sphere.

spher·u·lite /ˈsferəˌlaɪt/ *noun* a vitreous globule as a constituent of volcanic rocks. □ **spher·u·litic** /-ˈlɪtɪk/ *adjective*

sphinc·ter /ˈsfɪŋktər/ *noun Anat.* a ring of muscle surrounding and serving to guard or close an opening or tube, esp. the anus. [Latin from Greek *sphigktēr* from *sphiggō* bind tight]

sphin·gid /ˈsfɪŋɡɪd/ *noun* any hawk moth of the family Sphingidae. [as SPHINX + -ID³]

sphinx *noun* **1** (**Sphinx**) (in Greek mythology) the winged monster of Thebes, having a woman's head and a lion's body, whose riddle Oedipus guessed and who consequently killed herself. **2 a** any of several ancient Egyptian stone figures having a lion's body and a human or animal head. **b** (**the Sphinx**) the huge sphinx near the Pyramids at Giza. **3** a mysterious or inscrutable person. **4** (in full **sphinx moth**) a hawk moth. [Latin from Greek *Sphigx*, apparently from *sphiggō* draw tight]

sphyg·mo·ma·nom·eter /ˌsfɪɡmoʊməˈnɒmətər/ *noun* an instrument for measuring blood pressure. □ **sphyg·mo·mano·metric** /-nəˈmetrɪk/ *adjective* [Greek *sphugmo-* from *sphugmos* pulse, from *sphuzō* to throb + MANOMETER]

spic *noun US slang offensive* a Spanish-speaking person from Central or S America or the Caribbean, esp. a Mexican. [abbreviation of *spiggoty*, of uncertain origin: perhaps alteration of *speak the* in 'no speak the English']

Spica /ˈspaɪkə/ a binary star, the brightest in the constellation Virgo. [as SPICA]

spica /ˈspaɪkə/ *noun* **1** *Surgery* a spiral bandage shaped like a figure eight, often applied to parts such as the thumb. **2** *Bot.* a spike or spike-like form. [Latin, = spike, ear of corn, related to *spina* SPINE: in sense 2 after Greek *stakhus*]

spic and span *adjective* (also **spick and span**) **1** smart and new. **2** neat and clean. [16th-c. *spick and span new*, emphatic extension of Middle English *span new* from Old Norse *spán-nýr* from *spánn* chip + *nýr* new]

spic·cato /spɪˈkɑːtoʊ, -ˈkɒtoː/ *Music* ● *noun* a style of staccato playing on stringed instruments involving bouncing the bow on the strings. ● *adjective* performed or to be performed in this style. ● *adverb* in this style. [Italian, = detailed, distinct]

spice ● *noun* **1** an aromatic or pungent vegetable substance used to flavour food, e.g. ginger, pepper, or cinnamon. **2** spices collectively. **3 a** an interesting or piquant quality. **b** (foll. by *of*) a slight flavour or suggestion (*a spice of malice*). ● *transitive verb* **1** flavour with spice. **2** (often foll. by *up*) add an interesting or piquant quality to, make more interesting (*she tried to spice up the story*). [Old French *espice(r)* from Latin *species* specific kind: in Late Latin pl. = merchandise]

spice·bush *noun* any aromatic shrub of the genus *Lindera* or *Calycanthus*, native to America.

spice cake *noun* a cake flavoured with a combination of spices, esp. cinnamon, nutmeg, cloves, and allspice.

Spice Islands a former name for the MOLUCCA ISLANDS.

spick and span *var. of* SPIC AND SPAN.

spic·ule /ˈspɪkjuːl/ *noun* **1** any small sharp-pointed body. **2** *Zool.* a small hard calcareous or siliceous body, esp. in the framework of a sponge. **3** *Bot.* a small or secondary spike. **4** *Astronomy* a spike-like prominence, esp. one appearing as a jet of gas in the sun's corona. □ **spicu·lar** *adjective* **spicu·late** /-lət/ *adjective* [modern Latin *spicula, spiculum*, diminutives of SPICA]

spicy *adjective* (**spic·i·er, spic·i·est**) **1** of, flavoured with, or fragrant with spice. **2** piquant, pungent; sensational or improper (*a spicy story*). □ **spi·ci·ly** *adverb* **spi·ci·ness** *noun*

spi·der ● *noun* **1 a** any eight-legged arthropod of the order Araneae with a round unsegmented body, many of which spin webs for the capture of insects as food. **b** any of various similar or related arachnids, e.g. a red spider. **2** any object comparable to a spider, esp. as having numerous or prominent legs or radiating spokes. **3** *Computing* a program which automatically explores the World Wide Web by retrieving a document and then retrieving other documents that are linked to it. ● *intransitive verb* **1** move in a scuttling manner suggestive of a spider (*fingers spidered across the map*). **2** cause to move or appear in this way. □ **spider·ish** *adjective* [Old English *spithra* (as SPIN)]

spider crab *noun* any of various crabs of the family Majidae with a pear-shaped body and long thin legs.

spider flower *noun* a plant of the genus *Cleome*, with long protruding stamens, frequently grown in gardens.

spider mite *noun* (in full **red spider mite**) a plant-feeding mite of the family Tetranychidae, esp. *Tetranychus urticae*, a serious garden and hothouse pest (also called RED SPIDER).

spider monkey *noun* any of several monkeys of central and S America, esp. of the genera *Ateles* and *Brachyteles*, having long slender limbs and a prehensile tail.

spider plant *noun* a southern African plant, *Chlorophytum comosum*, which spreads by producing plantlets and is grown as a houseplant.

spider vein *noun* a very slender vein, esp. one on the face that is visible through the skin.

spider·web *noun* **1** a web spun by a spider. **2** something resembling this.

spider·wort *noun* any plant of the genus *Tradescantia*, esp. *T. virginiana*, having flowers with long hairy stamens.

spi·dery *adjective* elongated and thin (*spidery handwriting*).

spiel¹ /ʃpiːl, spiːl/ *slang* ● *noun* a long or prepared speech or story, esp. a sales pitch. ● *verb* **1** *intransitive* speak in this style; hold forth. **2** *transitive* reel off (a sales pitch etc.). □ **spiel·er** *noun* [German, = play, game]

---

t *top*   v *voice*   w *we*   z *zoo*   ʃ *she*   ʒ *vision*   θ *thin*   ð *this*   ŋ *ring*   x *loch*   tʃ *chip*   dʒ *jar*   (*see over for vowels*)

spiel² /spiːl/ *noun informal* a bonspiel. [shortening]

Spiel·berg /ˈspiːlbɜrg/ **Ste·ven** (b.1947), US film director and producer. He established a wide popular appeal with films concentrating on sensational and fantastic themes, such as *Jaws* (1975), *Close Encounters of the Third Kind* (1977), *ET* (1982), and the adventure films *Raiders of the Lost Ark* (1981) and *Indiana Jones and the Temple of Doom* (1984); other films include *Jurassic Park* (1992) and *Schindler's List* (1993), which won seven Oscars. □ **Spiel·berg·ian** *adjective*

spiff *transitive verb* (foll. by *up*) *N Amer. informal* make attractive or smart. [perhaps from dialect *spiff* 'well-dressed']

spif·fing *adjective Brit. dated slang* = SPIFFY. [19th c.: origin unknown]

spif·fy *adjective* (**spif·fi·er**, **spif·fi·est**) *esp. N Amer. informal* **1** excellent. **2** well-dressed. **3** elegant, fashionable. □ **spif·fi·ly** *adverb* [19th c.: origin unknown]

spig·ot /ˈspɪgət/ *noun* **1** a small peg or plug, esp. for insertion into the vent of a cask. **2 a** *US* a tap. **b** a device for controlling the flow of liquid in a tap. [Middle English, perhaps from Provençal *espigou(n)* from Latin *spiculum* diminutive of *spicum* = SPICA]

spike¹ ● *noun* **1 a** a sharp point. **b** a pointed piece of metal, esp. the top of an iron railing etc. **c** an upstanding pointed object. **2** a large nail, e.g. one used for railways or in eavestroughing. **3 a** any of several metal points set into the sole of a running shoe to prevent slipping. **b** (in *pl.*) a pair of running shoes with spikes. **c** (in *pl.*) spike heels. **4 a** a sharp increase. **b** *Electronics* a pulse of very short duration in which a rapid increase in voltage is followed by a rapid decrease. **5** (in volleyball) the act or an instance of spiking the ball. **6 a** a pointed metal rod standing on a base and used for filing news items etc. esp. when rejected for publication. **b** a similar spike used for bills, messages, etc. **7** *slang* a hypodermic needle. ● *verb* **1** *transitive* **a** fasten or provide with spikes. **b** fix on or pierce with spikes. **c** form into spikes. **2** *transitive informal* **a** lace (a drink) with alcohol, a drug, etc. **b** contaminate (a substance) with something added. **c** flavour (a dish) with a strong herb, spice, condiment, etc. **3** *transitive* (in volleyball) hit (the ball) forcefully from a position near the net so that it moves downward into the opposite court. **4** *transitive Football* fling (the ball) forcefully to the ground, esp. in celebration of a touchdown or victory. **5** *transitive* (of a newspaper editor etc.) reject (a story) by filing it on a spike. **6** *transitive* make useless, put an end to, thwart (an idea etc.). **7** *transitive hist.* plug up the vent of (a gun) with a spike. **8** *transitive* drive a long nail into (a tree) so as to make it dangerous to cut down the tree with a chainsaw. **9 a** *transitive* experience (a rapidly rising fever). **b** *intransitive* (of a fever) rapidly rise to a high level. □ **spike a person's guns** spoil his or her plans. [Middle English perhaps from Middle Low German, Middle Dutch *spiker*, related to SPOKE¹]

spike² *noun* **1** a flower cluster formed of many flower heads attached closely on a long stem. **2** a separate sprig of any plant in which flowers form a spike-like cluster. □ **spike·let** *noun* [Middle English, = ear of corn, from Latin SPICA]

spike heel *noun* **1** a high tapering heel of a shoe. **2** a shoe having this type of heel.

spike·nard /ˈspaɪknɑrd/ *noun* **1** a Himalayan plant of the valerian family, *Nardostachys grandiflora*. **2** *hist.* a costly perfumed ointment made from this. **3** (in full **American spikenard**) a plant of the ginseng family, *Aralia racemosa*, of eastern N America, with aromatic roots and dark purple berries. [Middle English, ultimately from medieval Latin *spica nardi* (as SPIKE², NARD) after Greek *nardostakhus*]

spiky *adjective* (**spik·i·er**, **spik·i·est**) **1** resembling a spike. **2** having a spike or spikes. **3** *informal* easily offended; prickly. □ **spik·i·ly** *adverb* **spik·i·ness** *noun*

spile *noun* **1** *N Amer.* a small spout for tapping sap from a sugar maple. **2** a wooden peg or spigot. **3** a large timber or pile for driving into the ground. [Middle Dutch, Middle Low German, = wooden peg etc.: in sense 'pile' apparently alteration of PILE²]

spill¹ ● *verb* (*past and past participle* **spilled** or **spilt**) **1** *intransitive & transitive* **a** fall or run or cause (a liquid, powder, etc.) to fall or run out of a container, esp. unintentionally. **b** cast (light) or (of light) be cast into a darker area. **2** *intransitive* (esp. of a crowd) move out quickly from a place etc., esp. in great numbers (*the fans spilled into the street*). **3** *transitive slang* disclose (information etc.). **4** *transitive & intransitive* throw (a person etc.) from a vehicle, saddle, etc. **5** *transitive Naut.* **a** empty (a sail) of wind. **b** lose (wind) from a sail. ● *noun* **1 a** the act or an instance of spilling or being spilled. **b** a quantity spilled. **2** a tumble or fall, esp. from a horse etc. (*had a nasty spill*). □ **spill the beans** *informal* divulge information etc., esp. unintentionally or indiscreetly. **spill blood** be guilty of bloodshed. **spill one's guts** *informal* reveal one's thoughts or feelings without restraint; confess. **spill over 1** overflow. **2** (of a

surplus population) encroach upon an area (*compare* OVERSPILL 2). □ **spill·age** *noun* **spill·er** *noun* [Old English *spillan* kill, related to Old English *spildan* destroy: origin unknown]

spill² *noun* a thin strip of wood, folded or twisted paper, etc., used for lighting a fire, candles, a pipe, etc. [Middle English, related to SPILE]

Spil·lane /spɪˈleɪn/ **Mick·ey** (pseudonym of Frank Morrison Spillane) (b.1918), US writer of detective stories, whose works include *I, the Jury* (1947), *My Gun is Quick* (1950), and *The Big Kill* (1951).

spil·li·kin *noun* = JACKSTRAW. [SPILL² + -KIN]

spill·over *noun* **1 a** the process or an instance of spilling over. **b** a thing that spills over. **2** a consequence, repercussion, or by-product.

spill·way *noun* a passage for surplus water from a dam, reservoir, etc.

spilt *past and past participle* of SPILL¹.

spin ● *verb* (**spin·ning**; *past and past participle* **spun**) **1** *intransitive & transitive* turn or cause (a person or thing) to turn or whirl round quickly. **2** *transitive & intransitive* **a** draw out and twist (wool, cotton, etc.) into threads. **b** make (yarn) in this way. **c** make a similar type of thread from (a synthetic substance etc.). **3** *transitive* (of a spider, silkworm, etc.) make (a web, gossamer, a cocoon, etc.) by extruding a fine viscous thread. **4** *transitive* tell or write (a story etc.) (*spins a good tale*). **5** *transitive* impart spin to (a ball). **6** *intransitive* (of a person's head etc.) be dizzy through sickness, excitement, astonishment, etc. **7** *transitive* shape (metal) on a mould in a lathe etc. **8** *intransitive* (of a wheel or wheels) revolve rapidly without providing traction (*my tires kept spinning on the slippery road*). **9** *intransitive* (of a ball) move through the air with spin. **10** *transitive* fish in (a stream, pool, etc.) with a spinner. **11** *transitive & intransitive informal* play (records); act as a disc jockey (*she spins at a local dance club*). **12** *intransitive* (of a washing machine) rotate wet clothing rapidly to remove excess water. ● *noun* **1** a spinning motion; a whirl. **2** = TAILSPIN *noun* 3. **3** a revolving motion through the air, esp. in a rifle bullet or ball. **4** *informal* **a** a brief excursion in a motor vehicle, airplane, etc., esp. for pleasure. **b** a rapid perusal (*a quick spin through her memoirs*). **5** *Physics* the intrinsic angular momentum of an elementary particle. **6** a bias in information to give a favourable impression. **7** the cycle on a washing machine during which the clothing is spun (also *attributive*: *spin cycle*). **8** *Figure Skating* any of a number of movements involving rotating rapidly in one spot. □ **spin off 1** *N Amer.* produce as a spinoff. **2 a** distribute (stock of a new company) to shareholders of a parent company. **b** create (a company) in this way. **3** throw off by centrifugal force in spinning. **spin out 1** prolong (a discussion etc.). **2** make (a story, money, etc.) last as long as possible. **3** spend or consume (time, one's life, etc., by discussion or in an occupation etc.). **4** *N Amer.* (esp. of a driver or car) lose or go out of control, esp. in a skid. **spin one's wheels** *N Amer.* waste one's time or efforts. □ **spin·ning** *noun* [Old English *spinnan*]

spina bif·ida /ˌspaɪnə ˈbɪfɪdə/ *noun* a congenital defect of the spine, in which part of the spinal cord and its meninges are exposed through a gap in the backbone. [modern Latin (as SPINE, BIFID)]

spin·ach *noun* **1** a green garden vegetable, *Spinacia oleracea*, with succulent leaves. **2** the leaves of this plant used as food. □ **spin·achy** *adjective* [prob. Middle Dutch *spinaetse*, *spinag(i)e*, from Old French *espinage*, *espinache* from medieval Latin *spinac(h)ia* etc. from Arabic *'isfānāk* from Persian *ispānāk*: perhaps assimilated to Latin *spina* SPINE, with reference to its prickly seeds]

spin·al /ˈspaɪnəl/ ● *adjective* of or relating to the spine (*spinal curvature*; *spinal disease*). ● *noun N Amer. informal* = EPIDURAL *noun*. □ **spin·al·ly** *adverb*

spinal canal *noun* a cavity through the vertebrae containing the spinal cord.

spinal column *noun* the spine.

spinal cord *noun* a cylindrical structure of the central nervous system enclosed in the spine, connecting all parts of the body with the brain.

spinal fluid *noun* = CEREBROSPINAL FLUID.

spinal tap *noun* the insertion of a needle into the spine, usu. in the lumbar region, so that cerebrospinal fluid may be withdrawn or something (such as an anesthetic) may be introduced.

spin·arama *noun Cdn* an evasive move, esp. in hockey, consisting of an abrupt 360-degree turn.

spin·cast·er *noun esp. N Amer.* a fishing reel mounted on top of the rod, with an enclosed spool and thumb trigger (*compare* SPINNING REEL, BAITCASTER). □ **spin casting** *noun*

spin control *noun N Amer. slang* an attempt to give a particular slant or bias to esp. political news coverage.

spin·dle ● *noun* **1 a** a pin in a spinning wheel used for twisting and winding the thread. **b** a small bar with tapered ends used for the same purpose in hand spinning. **c** a pin bearing the bobbin of a spinning machine. **2** a pin or axis that revolves or on which something revolves. **3** a turned piece of wood used as a banister, chair leg, etc. **4** *Biol.* a spindle-shaped mass of microtubules formed when a cell divides. **5** a pointed metal rod standing on a base and used for holding bills, order forms, memos, etc. **6** a varying measure of length for yarn. ● *verb* **1** *transitive & intransitive* impale (a piece of paper) on a spindle (*do not fold, spindle, or mutilate this card*). **2** *intransitive* have, or grow into, a long slender form. [Old English *spinel* (as SPIN)]

spindle-shanks *plural noun* **1** long thin legs. **2** (treated as *sing.*) a person with such legs. □ **spindle-shanked** *adjective*

spindle-shaped *adjective* having a circular cross-section and tapering towards each end.

spindle tree *noun* any shrub or small tree of the genus *Euonymus*, esp. *E. europaeus* with greenish-white flowers, pink or red berries, and hard wood formerly used for spindles.

spind·ly *adjective* (**spind·li·er**, **spind·li·est**) long or tall and thin; thin and weak.

spin doctor *noun* informal a political or corporate spokesperson employed to give a favourable interpretation of events to the media. □ **spin-doctor** *transitive verb* **spin-doctoring** *noun*

spin·drift *noun* spray blown along the surface of the sea. [Scots var. of *spoondrift* from *spoon* run before wind or sea + DRIFT]

spine *noun* **1** a series of vertebrae extending from the skull to the tailbone, enclosing the spinal cord and providing support for the thorax and abdomen; the backbone. **2** *Zool. & Bot.* any hard, pointed process or structure, e.g. a porcupine's quill or a sharp-pointed ray on the fin of a fish. **3** a sharp ridge or projection, esp. of a mountain range or slope. **4** resolution, firmness of character (*he has no spine whatsoever*). **5** the part of a book's jacket or cover that encloses the part where the pages are stitched or glued and usu. faces outwards on a shelf. **6** a central feature, main support, or source of strength. □ **spined** *adjective* (also in *combination*). [Old French *espine* or Latin *spina* thorn, backbone]

spine-chiller *noun* a frightening story, film, etc. □ **spine-chilling** *adjective*

spi·nel /spɪˈnel/ *noun* **1** any of a group of hard crystalline minerals of various colours, consisting chiefly of oxides of magnesium and aluminum. **2** any substance of similar composition or properties. [French *spinelle* from Italian *spinella*, diminutive of *spina*: see SPINE]

spine·less *adjective* **1** (of a person or action etc.) lacking energy or resolution; weak and purposeless. **2 a** having no spine; invertebrate. **b** (of a fish) having fins without spines. □ **spine·less·ly** *adverb* **spine·less·ness** *noun*

spin·et /ˈspɪnət, spɪˈnet/ *noun Music hist.* **1** a small harpsichord with oblique strings. **2** *US* a type of small upright piano. [obsolete French *espinette* from Italian *spinetta* virginal, spinet, diminutive of *spina* thorn etc. (as SPINE), with reference to the plucked strings]

spine-tingling *adjective* thrilling or pleasurably frightening. □ **spine-tingler** *noun*

spini·fex /ˈspɪnɪˌfeks/ *noun* any Australian grass of the genus *Spinifex*, with coarse, spiny leaves. [modern Latin from Latin *spina* SPINE + *-fex* maker, from *facere* make]

spin·na·ker /ˈspɪnəkər/ *noun* a large triangular sail carried opposite the mainsail of a racing yacht running before the wind. [fanciful from *Sphinx*, name of yacht first using it, perhaps after *spanker*]

spin·ner *noun* **1** a person or thing that spins. **2** a fishing bait or lure fixed so as to revolve when pulled through the water.

spin·ner·bait *noun* = SPINNER 2.

spin·ner·et /ˈspɪnəˌret/ *noun* **1** any of various organs through which the silk, gossamer, or thread of spiders, silkworms, and certain other insects is produced. **2** a device for forming filaments of synthetic fibre.

spin·ney *noun* (pl. **-neys**) *Brit.* a small wood; a thicket. [Old French *espinei* from Latin *spinetum* thicket, from *spina* thorn]

spin·ning *noun* **1** in senses of SPIN verb. **2** a form of physical exercise in which participants ride stationary bicycles in a group session accompanied by music.

spinning jenny *noun* hist. a machine for spinning with more than one spindle at a time.

spinning machine *noun* a machine that spins fibres continuously.

spinning reel *noun* esp. *N Amer.* a fishing reel mounted under the rod, with a fixed open spool (*compare* BAITCASTER, SPINCASTER).

spinning top *noun* = TOP².

spinning wheel *noun* a device formerly used for spinning yarn or thread with a spindle driven by a wheel attached to a crank or treadle.

spinny *adjective Cdn* crazy, foolish.

spin·off *noun* **1** an incidental result or results. **2** something, e.g. a television program, book, magazine, etc., derived from another product of a similar type. **3** an incidental benefit arising from industrial or military technology. **4** a distribution of stock in a new company to shareholders of the parent company.

spin·ose /ˈspaɪnoːs/ *adjective* (also **spin·ous** /-nəs/) esp. *Bot. & Zool.* having spines, spiny.

Spi·noza /spɪˈnoːzə/ **Bar·uch** (or **Bene·dict**) **de** (1632–77), Dutch philosopher. He rejected the Cartesian dualism of spirit and matter in favour of a pantheistic system, seeing God as the immanent cause of the universe and not a ruler outside it; his *Ethics* (1677) sought to deduce a metaphysical system from theorems and hypotheses. □ **Spi·noz·ism** *noun* **Spi·noz·ist** *noun* **Spi·noz·is·tic** /-ˈzɪstɪk/ *adjective*

spin·ster *noun* **1** a woman, esp. an older one, thought unlikely to marry. **2** *Law* an unmarried woman. □ **spin·ster·hood** *noun* [Middle English, originally = woman who spins]

spin·ster·ish *adjective* having qualities thought characteristic of a spinster, e.g. prudishness, unattractiveness, primness.

spin the bottle *noun* a party game in which a bottle is spun and the person towards whom it points upon ceasing to spin kisses the spinner.

spin·to ● *noun* (pl. **-tos**) **1** a lyric soprano or tenor voice of powerful dramatic quality. **2** a singer with such a voice. ● *adjective* of or relating to such a voice or singer. [Italian, past participle of *springere* push]

spin·ule /ˈspɪnjuːl/ *noun Bot. & Zool.* a small spine. [Latin *spinula* diminutive of *spina* SPINE]

spiny *adjective* (**spin·i·er**, **spin·i·est**) **1** full of spines; prickly. **2** perplexing, troublesome, thorny. **3** having the form of a spine; sharp-pointed. □ **spin·i·ness** *noun*

spiny anteater *noun* = ECHIDNA.

spiny lobster *noun* any of various large edible crustaceans of the family Palinuridae, with a spiny shell and no large anterior claws.

spir·acle /ˈspaɪrəkəl/ *noun* an external respiratory opening in insects, whales, and some fish. □ **spir·acu·lar** /-ˈrakjʊlər/ *adjective* [Latin *spiraculum* from *spirare* breathe]

spi·raea var. of SPIREA.

spir·al ● *adjective* **1** winding about a centre in an enlarging or decreasing continuous circular motion, either on a flat plane or rising in a cone; coiled. **2** winding continuously along or as if along a cylinder, like the thread of a screw. **3** spiral-bound (*a spiral workbook*). ● *noun* **1** a plane or three-dimensional spiral curve. **2** a spiral spring. **3** a spiral formation in a shell etc. **4** a progressive increase or deterioration, esp. one seen as being out of control (*a spiral of rising prices and wages*). **5** a continuous banking turn accompanying a descent or (rarely) ascent. **6** a spiral galaxy. ● *verb* (**spir·alled**, **spiral·ling**; also **spir·aled**, **spiral·ing**) **1** *intransitive* move in a spiral course, esp. upwards or downwards. **2** *transitive* make spiral. **3** *intransitive* increase rapidly. □ **spiral·ling** *adjective* **spiral·ly** *adverb* [French *spiral* or medieval Latin *spiralis* (as SPIRE²)]

spiral binding *noun* a type of binding used esp. for notebooks in which the pages are held together by a spiral of wire or plastic that coils through holes punched into the side of each page.

spiral-bound *adjective* (of a notebook etc.) having a spiral binding.

spiral galaxy *noun* a galaxy in which the matter is concentrated mainly in one or more spiral arms.

spiral staircase *noun* a staircase rising in a spiral around a central axis.

spir·ant /ˈspaɪrənt/ *Phonetics* = FRICATIVE *adjective & noun.* [Latin *spirare spirant-* breathe]

spire¹ ● *noun* **1** a tapering cone- or pyramid-shaped structure built esp. on a church tower (*compare* STEEPLE). **2** any conical, pointed, or tapering thing, e.g. the spike of a flower. **3** the highest point of something. ● *transitive verb* provide with a spire. [Old English *spir*]

spire² *noun* **1 a** a spiral; a coil. **b** a single twist of this. **2** the upper part of a spiral shell. [French from Latin *spira* from Greek *speira* coil]

spi·rea /ˌspaɪˈriːə/ *noun* (also **spi·raea**) any rosaceous shrub of the genus *Spiraea*, with clusters of small white or pink flowers. [Latin from Greek *speiraia* from *speira* coil]

spir·il·lum /ˌspaɪˈrɪləm/ *noun* (pl. **spir·il·la**) **1** any bacterium of the genus *Spirillum*, characterized by a rigid spiral structure. **2** any bacterium with a similar shape. [modern Latin, irreg. diminutive of Latin *spira* SPIRE²]

spir·it • *noun* **1 a** the vital animating essence of a person or animal (*was sadly broken in spirit*). **b** the intelligent non-physical part of a person; the soul. **2 a** a rational or intelligent being without a material body. **b** a supernatural being such as a ghost, fairy, etc. (*haunted by spirits*). **c** (**the Spirit**) = HOLY SPIRIT. **3** a prevailing mental or moral condition or attitude; a mood; a tendency (*the spirit of the pre-Confederation era; getting into the Christmas spirit*). **4 a** (usu. in *pl.*) strong distilled liquor, e.g. brandy, whisky, gin, rum. **b** a distilled volatile liquid (*wood spirit*). **c** purified alcohol (*methylated spirits*). **d** a solution in alcohol of a specified substance (*spirit of ammonia*). **5 a** a person's mental or moral nature or qualities, usu. specified (*has an unbending spirit*). **b** a person viewed as possessing these (*is an ardent spirit*). **c** energy, vivacity, dash (*played with spirit*). **d** courage; assertiveness, determination (*argued her case with spirit*). **6** the general intent or true meaning of a statement etc. as opposed to its strict verbal interpretation (*opp.* LETTER 3) (*the spirit of the law*). **7** feelings of loyalty to a team, group, organization, etc. (*team spirit*). **8** (in *pl.*) a person's feelings or state of mind (*my spirits have been very low lately*). **9** *archaic* an immaterial principle thought to govern vital phenomena (*animal spirits*). • *transitive verb* (**spirit·ed, spirit·ing**) (usu. foll. by *away, off*, etc.) convey rapidly and secretly by or as if by spirits. • *adjective* **1** of or relating to supernatural spirits (*the spirit world*). **2** (of a fuel-burning appliance) powered by alcoholic spirits (*spirit lamp*). □ **in spirit** in one's thoughts (*shall be with you in spirit*). **keep a person's spirits up** cheer a person up. **the spirit moves a person** he or she feels inclined (to do something). **the spirit is willing (but the flesh is weak)** one's intentions and wishes are good but weakness, love of pleasure, etc. prevent one from acting according to them. [Anglo-French (*e*)*spirit*, Old French *esp*(*e*)*rit*, from Latin *spiritus* breath, spirit, from *spirare* breathe]

spirit bear *noun Cdn* a white kermode bear.

spirit·ed *adjective* **1** full of spirit; animated, lively, brisk, or courageous (*a spirited attack; a spirited translation*). **2** having a spirit or spirits of a specified kind (*high-spirited; mean-spirited*). □ **spirit·ed·ly** *adverb* **spirit·ed·ness** *noun*

spirit guide *noun* a supernatural being believed to provide protection and advice to a person.

spirit gum *noun* a type of quick-drying glue used esp. for attaching false hair.

spirit·less *adjective* lacking courage, vigour, or vivacity. □ **spirit·less·ly** *adverb* **spirit·less·ness** *noun*

spirit level *noun* a device containing a bent glass tube nearly filled with alcohol, used to test horizontality by the position of an air bubble.

spirit·ual • *adjective* **1** of or relating to the human spirit or soul; not of physical things. **2** concerned with sacred or religious things; holy; divine; inspired (*the spiritual life*). **3** of or relating to the Church. **4** (of the mind etc.) refined, sensitive; not concerned with the material. **5** (of a relationship etc.) concerned with the soul or spirit etc., not with external reality (*his spiritual home*). • *noun* an emotional Christian song derived from the musical traditions of Blacks in the southern US. □ **spirit·u·al·ity** *noun* **spirit·u·al·ly** *adverb*

spirit·ual·ism *noun* **1 a** a belief that the spirits of the dead can communicate with the living, esp. through mediums. **b** the practices associated with this belief. **2** *Philos.* the doctrine that the spirit exists as distinct from matter, or that spirit is the only reality (compare MATERIALISM 2a). □ **spirit·ual·ist** *noun & adjective* **spirit·ual·is·tic** *adjective*

spirit·ual·ize *transitive verb* (also esp. *Brit.* **-ise**) **1** make (a person or a person's character, thoughts, etc.) spiritual; elevate. **2** attach a spiritual as opposed to a literal meaning to. □ **spirit·u·al·iz·a·tion** *noun*

spirit·u·ous *adjective* **1** containing much alcohol. **2** distilled, as whisky, rum, etc. (*spirituous liquor*).

spiro-¹ /ˈspaɪroʊ/ *combining form* a coil. [Latin *spira*, Greek *speira* coil]

spiro-² /ˈspaɪroʊ/ *combining form* breath. [irreg. from Latin *spirare* breathe]

spiro·chete /ˈspaɪroʊˌkiːt/ *noun* (also esp. *Brit.* **spiro·chaete**) any of various flexible spirally twisted bacteria of the order Spirochaetales, esp. one that causes syphilis. [SPIRO-¹ + Greek *khaitē* long hair]

spiro·gyra /ˌspaɪroʊˈdʒaɪrə/ *noun* any freshwater alga of the genus *Spirogyra*, with cells containing spiral bands of chlorophyll. [modern Latin from SPIRO-¹ + Greek *guros gura* round]

spi·rom·eter /spaɪˈrɒmətər/ *noun* an instrument for measuring the air capacity of the lungs. □ **spi·rom·etry** *noun*

spiru·lina /ˌspaɪrəˈliːnə/ *noun* **1** any alga of the genus *Spirulina*, found growing in dense tangled masses in warm alkaline lakes in Africa and Central and S America. **2** the substance of these growths, which when dried may be prepared in various ways as a food or food additive. [from modern Latin genus name *Spirulina*]

spit¹ • *verb* (**spit·ting**; *past* and *past participle* **spat** or **spit**) **1** *intransitive* **a** eject saliva from the mouth. **b** do this as a sign of hatred or contempt (*spat at him*). **2** *transitive* (usu. foll. by *out*) **a** eject (saliva, blood, food, etc.) from the mouth (*spat the meat out*). **b** emit or throw forcefully in a manner resembling spitting. **c** utter (oaths, threats, etc.) vehemently ('*Damn you!' he spat*). **3** *intransitive* (of a fire, pen, pan, etc.) send out sparks, ink, hot fat, etc. **4** *intransitive* (of rain) fall lightly (*it's only spitting*). **5** *intransitive* (esp. of a cat) make a spitting or hissing noise in anger or hostility. • *noun* **1** spittle. **2** the act or an instance of spitting. **3** the foamy liquid secretion of some insects used to protect their young. **4** (usu. in *pl.*) *Cdn* (*West*) *informal* a sunflower seed. □ **the spit of** esp. *Brit. informal* the exact double of (compare SPITTING IMAGE). **spit it out** *informal* say what is on one's mind. **spit up** *N Amer.* (esp. of a baby) vomit. □ **spit·ter** *noun* **spit·ty** *adjective* [Old English *spittan*, of imitative origin; sense 4 of *noun* with reference to the habit of spitting out the shells]

spit² • *noun* **1** a slender rod on which meat is skewered before being roasted on a fire etc. **2 a** a small point of land projecting into the water. **b** a long narrow underwater bank. • *transitive verb* (**spit·ted, spit·ting**) **1** thrust a spit through (meat etc.). **2** pierce or transfix with a sword etc. [Old English *spitu* from West Germanic]

spit and polish *noun* **1** thorough cleaning and polishing of equipment, esp. by a soldier etc. **2** exaggerated neatness and cleanliness.

spit·ball • *noun N Amer.* **1** a ball of chewed paper etc. usu. blown through a straw at a person as a prank. **2** *Baseball* an illegal swerving pitch made with a ball moistened with saliva or sweat. • *intransitive verb informal* throw out suggestions for discussion. □ **spit·ball·er** *noun*

spitch·cock /ˈspɪtʃkɒk/ • *noun* an eel split and grilled or fried. • *transitive verb* prepare (an eel, fish, bird, etc.) in this way. [16th c.: origin unknown: compare SPATCHCOCK]

spit curl *noun N Amer.* a curl of hair pressed flat against the forehead or cheek.

spite • *noun* **1** ill will, malice towards a person (*did it from spite*). **2** a grudge. • *transitive verb* thwart, mortify, annoy (*does it to spite me*). □ **in spite of** notwithstanding. **in spite of oneself** etc. though one would rather have done otherwise (*found himself smiling in spite of himself*). [Middle English from Old French *despit* DESPITE]

spite·ful *adjective* motivated by spite; malevolent. □ **spite·ful·ly** *adverb* **spite·ful·ness** *noun*

spit·fire *noun* a person of fiery temper.

spit-roast *transitive verb* cook on a spit.

Spits·berg·en /ˈspɪtsˌbɜrɡən/ a Norwegian island in the Svalbard archipelago, in the Arctic Ocean north of Norway; principal settlement, Longyearbyen.

spit-shined *adjective N Amer.* extremely neat and clean.

spitting cobra *noun* the African black-necked cobra, *Naja nigricollis*, that ejects venom by spitting, not striking.

spitting distance *noun* a very short distance.

spitting image *noun* (foll. by *of*) *informal* the exact likeness of (another person or thing).

spit·tle *noun* **1** saliva, esp. as ejected from the mouth. **2** = SPIT¹ *noun* 3. [alteration of Middle English (now dial.) *spattle* = Old English *spātl* from *spǣtan* to spit, after SPIT¹]

spit·toon /spɪˈtuːn/ *noun* a metal or earthenware pot with esp. a funnel-shaped top, used for spitting into.

Spitz, Mark (An·drew) (b.1950), US swimmer. He won seven gold medals in the 1972 Olympic Games at Munich and set 27 world records for freestyle and butterfly (1967–72).

spitz *noun* a small breed of dog with a pointed muzzle, esp. a Pomeranian. [German *Spitz(hund)* from *spitz* pointed + *Hund* dog]

spiv *noun Brit. informal* a man, often characterized by flashy dress, who makes a living by illicit or unscrupulous dealings. □ **spiv·vish** *adjective* **spiv·vy** *adjective* [20th c.: origin unknown]

splake *noun* a hybrid trout produced by crossing the N American lake trout and the brook trout. [*speckled* (trout) + *lake* (trout)]

splanch·nic /ˈsplæŋknɪk/ *adjective* of or relating to the viscera;

intestinal. [modern Latin *splanchnicus* from Greek *splagkhnikos* from *splagkhna* entrails]

splash ● *verb* **1 a** *transitive* dash (liquid) against (deliberately or inadvertently) in an irregular or spasmodic way. **b** *transitive* make (something) wet or dirty by this action (*splashed her face*). **2 a** *transitive & intransitive* cause (liquid) to spill, scatter, or fly about, esp. by sudden movement or agitation. **b** *intransitive* (of a liquid) scatter or fly about in some quantity, esp. because of sudden movement or agitation. **3 a** *intransitive* (usu. foll. by *across, along,* etc.) progress while scattering liquid etc. (*splashed across the river*). **b** *transitive & intransitive* step, fall, or plunge etc. into a liquid etc. so as to cause a splash (*splashed into the lake; splashed their oars*). **4** *transitive* display (news) prominently. **5** *transitive* decorate with scattered colour. **6** *transitive* *Brit.* spend (money) ostentatiously. ● *noun* **1** the act or an instance of splashing. **2 a** a quantity of liquid splashed. **b** the resulting noise (*heard a splash*). **3** a spot of dirt etc. splashed on to a thing. **4** a striking or ostentatious display or effect. **5** a prominent news feature etc. **6** a daub or patch of colour, sunlight, etc. **7** *informal* a small quantity of liquid, esp. of soda water etc. to dilute liquor. □ **make a splash** attract much attention, esp. by extravagance. **splash down** (esp. of a spacecraft) land on water. **splash out** *Brit. informal* spend money freely. [alteration of PLASH¹]

splash·back *noun Brit.* = BACKSPLASH.

splash·board *noun* a screen protecting the driver of a horse-drawn vehicle from splashes.

splash·down *noun* the landing of a spacecraft in a body of water, esp. the ocean.

splash guard *noun* **1** = MUD FLAP. **2** any protective guard against splashes, e.g. on a nozzle of a gas pump.

splash page *noun* a web page that introduces a website, often by presenting an animation along with various options for viewing the site.

splash pants *plural noun N Amer.* light nylon water-resistant pants worn by children over other garments to protect them from water and mud.

splash pool *noun* (also **splash pad**) **1** a paved area in a park, playground etc. equipped with a large sprinkler for children to run through. **2** a wading pool.

splashy *adjective* **1** attracting attention; ostentatious, sensational. **2** involving splashing.

splat¹ *noun* a flat piece of thin wood in the centre of a chair back. [*splat* split up, related to SPLIT]

splat² *informal* ● *noun* a slapping sound, as of something wet hitting a surface (*the tomato hit the wall with a splat*). ● *adverb* with a splat (*the omelette fell splat on the floor*). ● *transitive & intransitive verb* (**splat·ted, splat·ting**) fall or hit with a splat. [abbreviation of SPLATTER]

splat·ter ● *verb* **1** *transitive* (often foll. by *with*) make wet or dirty by splashing, esp. in droplets. **2** *transitive & intransitive* splash, esp. with a continuous noisy action. **3** *transitive* (often foll. by *over*) publicize or spread (news etc.) (*the story was splattered over the front page*). ● *noun* **1** a noisy splashing sound. **2** a quantity splattered. **3** a rough patch of colour etc., esp. splashed on a surface. **4** (*attributive*) *slang* designating or relating to films involving the depiction of many violent deaths. [imitative]

splat·ter·punk *noun* a sub-genre of horror writing characterized by a strong emphasis on the graphic description of numerous acts of violence and sexual perversion. [SPLATTER *noun* 4 + PUNK *noun* 3]

splay ● *verb* **1** *transitive* (usu. foll. by *out*) spread (the fingers, legs, etc.) apart. **2** *intransitive* (of an opening or its sides) diverge in shape or position. **3** *transitive* construct (a window, doorway, opening, etc.) so that it diverges or is wider at one side of the wall than the other. ● *noun* a surface making an oblique angle with another, e.g. the splayed side of a window or embrasure. ● *adjective* **1** wide and flat. **2** turned outward. [Middle English from DISPLAY]

splay foot *noun* a broad flat foot turned outward. □ **splay-footed** *adjective*

spleen *noun* **1** an abdominal organ involved in the production and removal of red blood cells in most vertebrates, forming part of the immune system. **2** lowness of spirits; moroseness, ill temper, spite (*a fit of spleen; vented their spleen*). [Old French *esplen* from Latin *splen* from Greek *splēn*; sense 2 from the earlier belief that the spleen was the seat of such feelings]

spleen·wort /ˈspliːnwɜːt, -wɔːt/ *noun* any fern of the genus *Asplenium*, formerly used as a remedy for disorders of the spleen.

splen- /spliːn/ *combining form Anat.* the spleen. [Greek (as SPLEEN)]

splen·did *adjective* **1** magnificent, gorgeous, brilliant, sumptuous (*a splendid palace; a splendid achievement*). **2** dignified; impressive (*splendid isolation*). **3** excellent; fine (*a splendid chance*). □ **splen·did·ly** *adverb* **splen·did·ness** *noun* [Latin *splendidus* from *splendēre* to shine]

splen·dif·er·ous /splenˈdɪfərəs/ *adjective informal* or *jocular* splendid. □ **splen·dif·er·ous·ly** *adverb* **splen·dif·er·ous·ness** *noun* [irreg. from SPLENDOUR]

splen·dour *noun* (also **splen·dor**) **1** magnificence; grandeur. **2** great or dazzling brightness. [Anglo-French *splendeur* or Latin *splendor* (as SPLENDID)]

splen·ec·tomy /splɪˈnektəmi/ *noun* (*pl.* **-mies**) the surgical excision of the spleen.

splen·etic /splɪˈnetɪk/ ● *adjective* **1** ill-tempered; peevish. **2** of or concerning the spleen. ● *noun* a splenetic person. □ **splen·etic·ally** *adverb* [Late Latin *spleneticus* (as SPLEEN)]

splen·ic /ˈsplɪnɪk, ˈsplenɪk/ *adjective* of or in the spleen. [French *splénique* or Latin *splenicus* from Greek *splēnikos* (as SPLEEN)]

splen·ius /ˈspliːniəs/ *noun* (*pl.* **splenii** /-niˌaɪ/) *Anat.* either section of muscle on each side of the neck and back serving to draw back the head. □ **splen·ial** *adjective* [modern Latin from Greek *splēnion* bandage]

spleno·meg·a·ly /ˌspliːnəʊˈmegəli/ *noun* a pathological enlargement of the spleen. [SPLEN- + *megaly* (as MEGALO-)]

splice ● *transitive verb* **1** join the ends (of ropes) by interweaving strands. **2** join (pieces of film, magnetic tape, etc.) by sticking together the ends. **3** join (girders, beams, etc.) by partly overlapping the ends and fastening them together. **4** unite, join. **5** (esp. as **spliced** *adjective*) *informal* join in marriage. ● *noun* a place in a film, tape, rope, etc. where it has been joined. □ **spli·cer** *noun* [prob. from Middle Dutch *splissen*, of uncertain origin]

spliff *noun slang* a marijuana cigarette. [20th c.: origin unknown]

spline ● *noun* **1** a rectangular key fitting into grooves in the hub and shaft of a wheel and allowing longitudinal play. **2** a slat. **3** a flexible wood or rubber strip, esp. one used in drawing large curves. ● *transitive verb* fit with a spline (sense 1). [originally E Anglian dial., perhaps related to SPLINTER]

splint ● *noun* **1 a** a strip of rigid material used for holding a broken bone etc. when set. **b** a rigid device for maintaining a part of the body, e.g. the teeth, in a fixed position. **c** a rigid or flexible strip of esp. wood used in basketwork etc. **2** a tumour or bony excrescence on the inside of a horse's leg. **3** a thin strip of wood etc. used to light a fire, pipe, etc. ● *transitive verb* secure (a broken limb etc.) with a splint or splints. [Middle Dutch *splinte* or Middle Low German *splinte, splente* metal plate or pin, related to SPLINTER]

splint bone *noun* either of two small bones in a horse's foreleg lying behind and close to the cannon bone.

splin·ter ● *noun* **1** a small thin sharp piece broken off from wood, glass, stone, etc. **2** = SPLINTER GROUP. ● *transitive & intransitive verb* break into fragments or factions. □ **splin·tery** *adjective* [Middle Dutch (= Low German) *splinter, splenter*, related to SPLINT]

splinter group *noun* (also **splinter party**) a group or party that has broken away from a larger one.

Split a seaport on the coast of S Croatia; pop. (2001) 188,694. Founded as a Roman colony in 78 BC, it contains the ruins of the palace of the emperor Diocletian, built in about AD 300.

Split, Cape a point at the end of Cape Blomidon Peninsula, a hooked peninsula on the west central coast of Nova Scotia. Cape Split extends westward into the Minas Channel thereby separating it from Minas Basin. [translation of French *cap fendu* split cape: compare FUNDY, BAY OF]

split ● *verb* (**split·ting**; *past* and *past participle* **split**) **1 a** *intransitive & transitive* break or cause to break forcibly into parts, esp. into halves or (of a log) along the grain. **b** *intransitive & transitive* (often foll. by *up*) divide into parts (*split into groups*). **c** *transitive* share between two or more people (*split the cost of a meal; split a bottle of wine*). **2** *transitive & intransitive* (often foll. by *off, away*) remove or be removed by breaking, separating, or dividing (*split the top off the bottle; split away from the main group*). **3** *intransitive & transitive* **a** (usu. foll. by *up*) *informal* separate, esp. through discord (*split up after ten years*). **b** (foll. by *with*) *informal* quarrel or cease association with (another person etc.). **c** (often as **split** *adjective*) (usu. foll. by *on, over*) separate or divide as a result of opposing views (*the government is split over cuts to education*). **4** *transitive* cause the fission of (an atom). **5** *intransitive & transitive slang* leave, esp. suddenly. **6** *transitive N Amer.* (of a team) win half of the games in (a match or series) (*split a doubleheader*). **7** *transitive* (often foll. by *up*) divide (a stock) into two or more stocks of the same total value. ● *noun* **1** the act or an instance of splitting; the state of being split. **2** a fissure, vent, crack, cleft, etc. **3 a** a separation into parties; a schism. **b** an incompatibility. **4** (in *pl.*) the feat of leaping in the air or sitting down with the legs at right angles to the body in front and behind, or at the sides with the trunk facing forwards. **5** a formation of bowling pins left standing after the first bowl in which there is a large gap between two pins or two groups of pins, making a spare difficult. **6** the time taken to complete a portion of a race, esp. recorded by a split-second watch and used as a comparative measure of performance. **7** *N Amer.* a match or series that ends with both teams having won an equal number of games. **8** *Cdn* (*Nfld*) (in *pl.*) a small piece of wood used esp. for kindling. **9** a single thickness of split hide. **10** the turning up of two cards of equal value in faro, so that the stakes are divided. **11** a half-bottle of wine. ● *adjective* **1** that has split or been split (*split logs*; *split fish*). **2** divided in opinion etc.; disunited. □ **split the difference** take the average of two proposed amounts. **split a gut** *N Amer. informal* be convulsed with laughter. **split hairs** make small and insignificant distinctions. **split one's sides** be convulsed with laughter. **split the ticket** *US* vote for candidates of more than one party. **split the vote** *Cdn & Brit.* (of a candidate or minority party) attract votes from another so that both are defeated by a third. [originally nautical, from Middle Dutch *splitten*, related to *spletten*, *spliten*, Middle High German *splizen*]

split decision *noun* **1** a decision in a boxing match in which the judges and referee are not unanimous in their choice of a winner. **2** a court ruling etc. which is not unanimous.

split end *noun* **1** (usu. in *pl.*) a hair which has split at the end from dryness etc. **2** *Football* a player at the end of and some distance from a line of players in formation.

split-finger *adjective* (also **split-fingered**) *Baseball* designating a pitch thrown with the motion of a fastball, but with the index and middle fingers spread wide apart along the seams, so that it has little backspin and dips sharply and deceptively as it approaches the plate.

split infinitive *noun* a phrase consisting of an infinitive with an adverb etc. inserted between *to* and the verb, e.g. *seems to really like it.* ¶ It is often said that an infinitive should never be split. However, this is an artificial rule and can produce clumsy or ambiguous sentences. In many cases a split infinitive sounds more natural than its avoidance, e.g. *What is it like to actually live in France?* On other occasions, it is better to place the adverb after the infinitive, e.g. *He wanted to completely give up his business* is better as *He wanted to give up his business completely*, which more effectively places the emphasis on *completely*.

split-level ● *adjective* (of a room or a building, esp. a house) having the floor level of one part about half a storey above or below the floor level of an adjacent part. ● *noun* a split-level building.

split pea *noun* a pea dried and split in half for cooking.

split personality *noun* **1** the coexistence within one person, institution, etc. of seemingly contradictory or conflicting characteristics. **2** *informal* schizophrenia or multiple personality disorder. ¶ Not in technical use.

split pin *noun* a metal cotter pin passed through a hole and held in place by its gaping split end.

split-rail *adjective* designating a type of fence, corral, etc. made from split logs.

split ring *noun* a small steel ring with two spiral turns, such as a key ring.

split-run *noun* a press run of a newspaper, magazine, etc., in which some portions contain certain copy, advertisements, etc., not carried by other portions, e.g. a Canadian edition of a foreign magazine with advertising directed at the Canadian market but little or no Canadian editorial content.

split-screen *noun* a screen on a computer, television, etc. on which two or more separate images are displayed.

split second ● *noun* a very brief moment of time. ● *attributive adjective* (**split-second**) **1** very rapid. **2** (of timing) very precise.

split shift *noun* a shift comprising two or more separate periods of duty separated by an interval or intervals of several hours.

split shot *noun* broken lead shot attached to a fishing line to add casting weight.

splits·ville ● *noun informal* the termination of an (esp. romantic) relationship. ● *adjective* (of a couple) separated.

split·ter *noun* **1** a person who splits, esp. someone employed in splitting fish. **2** a person (esp. a taxonomist) who attaches importance to differences rather than similarities in classification or analysis (*compare* LUMPER 2). **3** any of various devices that send electrical

current, a received or transmitted signal, etc. along two or more routes. **4** *Brit. informal* a severe headache.

split time *noun* the time taken to complete a portion of a race, esp. recorded by a split-second watch and used as a comparative measure of performance.

split·ting *adjective* **1** (esp. of a headache) very painful; acute. **2** (of the head) suffering great pain from a headache, noise, etc.

split-up *noun* **1** the act of splitting or dividing. **2** the termination of a relationship. **3** the division of a stock into two or more stocks of the same total value.

splodge *noun & verb* esp. *Brit. informal* = SPLOTCH. □ **splodgy** *adjective* [imitative, or alteration of SPLOTCH]

splosh *informal* ● *transitive & intransitive verb* move with a splashing sound. ● *noun* **1** a splashing sound. **2** a splash of water etc. [imitative]

splotch esp. *N Amer.* ● *noun* a daub, blot, or smear. ● *transitive verb* make a large, esp. irregular, spot or patch on. □ **splotchy** *adjective* [perhaps from SPOT + obsolete *plotch* BLOTCH]

splurge *informal* ● *noun* **1** an ostentatious display or effort. **2** an instance of sudden great extravagance. ● *verb* **1** *intransitive* (usu. foll. by *on*) spend effort or esp. large sums of money (*splurged on new furniture*). **2** *transitive* spend (money etc.) extravagantly. [19th-c. US: prob. imitative]

splut·ter ● *verb* **1** *intransitive* **a** speak in a hurried, vehement, or choking manner. **b** make a series of spitting or choking sounds (*the engine spluttered into life*; *jumped in the pool and came up coughing and spluttering*). **2** *transitive* **a** speak or utter (words, threats, a language, etc.) rapidly or incoherently. **b** emit (food, sparks, hot oil, etc.) with a spitting sound. ● *noun* spluttering speech or sound. □ **splut·ter·er** *noun* [SPUTTER by assoc. with *splash*]

Spock, Ben·ja·min (Mc·Lane) (known as Dr. Spock) (1903–98), US pediatrician and writer. His manual *The Common Sense Book of Baby and Child Care* (1946) challenged traditional ideas of discipline and rigid routine in child rearing in favour of a psychological approach and influenced a generation of parents after the Second World War.

Spohr, Ar·nold Theo·dore (b.1927), Canadian dancer and ballet director, who was artistic director of the Royal Winnipeg Ballet 1958–88, leading it to international acclaim with an eclectic repertoire.

spoil ● *verb* (*past* and *past participle* **spoiled** or esp. *Brit.* **spoilt**) **1** *transitive* **a** damage, ruin; diminish the value of (*was spoiled by the rain*; *will spoil all the fun*). **b** reduce a person's enjoyment etc. of (*the news spoiled his dinner*). **2** *transitive* **a** harm the character of (esp. a child, pet, etc.) by excessive indulgence. **b** (also *reflexive*) pamper; pay attention to the comfort and wishes of (a person). **c** accustom (a person etc.) to ease, favourable conditions, etc. so as to be unsuited to adversity (*we have been spoiled by five weeks of fine weather*). **3** *intransitive* (of food) go bad, decay; become unfit for eating. **4** *transitive* render (a ballot) invalid by improper marking. **5** *transitive* (foll. by *of*) *archaic* or *literary* plunder or deprive (a person of a thing) by force or stealth (*spoiled him of all his possessions*). ● *noun* **1** (usu. in *pl.*) **a** plunder taken from an enemy in war, or seized by force. **b** esp. *jocular* profit or advantages gained by succeeding to public office, high position, etc. **2** earth etc. thrown up in excavating, dredging, etc. □ **be spoiling for** aggressively seek (a fight etc.). **spoiled for choice** *Brit.* having so many choices that it is difficult to choose. [Old French *espoillier*, *espoille* from Latin *spoliare* from *spolium* spoil, plunder, or from DESPOIL]

spoil·age *noun* **1** the deterioration or decay of food etc. **2** the amount of material that is spoiled.

spoil·er *noun* **1 a** a person or thing that spoils something. **b** a person who obstructs or prevents an opponent's success while not being a potential winner. **2 a** a flap able to be projected from the upper surface of an aircraft wing to break up a smooth airflow and so reduce speed. **b** a similar device on a vehicle intended to reduce lift and so improve traction at high speed.

spoil·sport *noun* a person who spoils others' pleasure or enjoyment.

spoils system *noun US* the practice of a successful political party replacing existing holders of government or public positions with its own supporters.

spoilt esp. *Brit. past* and *past participle* of SPOIL.

Spo·kane /spoˈkan/ a city in E Washington, situated on the falls of the Spokane River, near the border with Idaho; pop. (est. 2000) 195,629.

spoke¹ ● *noun* **1** each of the wire rods or bars running from the hub to the rim of a wheel. **2** a rung of a ladder. **3** each radial handle of the wheel of a ship etc. ● *transitive verb* provide with spokes. □ **spoked** *adjective* [Old English *spāca*, from West Germanic]

spoke² *past* of SPEAK.

spok·en ● *verb* past participle of SPEAK. ● *adjective* **1** (in *combination*) speaking in a specified way (*soft-spoken*; *well-spoken*). **2** (of language, words, etc.) uttered in speech; oral as opposed to written. □ **spoken for** claimed, requisitioned (*this seat is spoken for*).

spoken word *noun* **1** speech (as opposed to written language), esp. in the context of radio broadcasting. **2** a type of performance poetry, often combining elements of storytelling, stand-up comedy, and music.

spokes- *combining form* informal or jocular forming nouns denoting a person or animal appearing in advertising for a particular product (*spokesdog*). [back-formation from SPOKESMAN]

spoke·shave *noun* a blade set between two handles, used for shaping spokes and other esp. curved work where an ordinary plane is not suitable.

spokes·man *noun* (*pl.* **-men**) **1** a person who speaks on behalf of others, esp. in the course of public relations. **2** a person deputed to express the views of a group etc. [irreg. from SPOKE² after *craftsman* etc.]

spokes·model *noun* an attractive person appearing prominently in advertising for a particular product.

spokes·person *noun* (*pl.* **-persons** or **-people**) a spokesman or spokeswoman.

spokes·woman *noun* (*pl.* **-women**) **1** a woman who speaks on behalf of others, esp. in the course of public relations. **2** a woman deputed to express the views of a group etc.

spoli·a·tion /ˌspoʊliˈeɪʃən/ *noun* **1 a** plunder or pillage, esp. of neutral vessels in war. **b** extortion. **2** *Law* the destruction, mutilation, or alteration of a document to prevent its being used as evidence. □ **spoli·ator** /ˈspoʊ-/ *noun* [Latin *spoliatio* (as SPOIL)]

spon·daic /spɒnˈdeɪɪk/ *adjective* **1** of or concerning spondees. **2** (of a hexameter) having a spondee as a fifth foot. [French *spondaïque* or Late Latin *spondaicus* = Late Latin *spondiacus* from Greek *spondeiakos* (as SPONDEE)]

spon·dee /ˈspɒndiː/ *noun Prosody* a foot consisting of two long (or stressed) syllables. [ultimately from Greek *spondeios* (*pous* foot) from *spondē* libation, as being characteristic of music accompanying libations]

spon·dyl·itis /ˌspɒndɪˈlaɪtɪs/ *noun* inflammation of the vertebrae. □ **spon·dyl·itic** *adjective* [Latin *spondylus* vertebra, from Greek *spondulos* + -ITIS]

sponge ● *noun* **1** any sessile aquatic animal of the phylum Porifera, with a porous bag-like body structure and a rigid or elastic internal skeleton. **2 a** the skeleton of a sponge, the soft light elastic absorbent kind used in bathing, cleansing surfaces, etc. **b** a piece of porous rubber or plastic etc. used similarly. **c** a piece of sponge or similar material (esp. one impregnated with spermicide) inserted in the vagina as a contraceptive. **3 a** a thing of spongelike absorbency or consistency, e.g. a sponge pudding, sponge cake, porous metal, etc. (*lemon sponge*). **b** soft fermenting bread dough. **c** *Brit.* any kind of cake. **4** = SPONGER. **5** informal a person who drinks heavily. **6** cleansing with or as with a sponge (*had a quick sponge this morning*). ● *verb* (**spon·ging** or **sponge·ing**) **1** *transitive* wipe or cleanse with a sponge. **2** *transitive* (often foll. by *down*, *over*) sluice water over (the body, a car, etc.). **3** *transitive* (often foll. by *out*, *away*, etc.) wipe off or efface (writing, a memory, etc.) with or as with a sponge. **4** *transitive* (often foll. by *up*) absorb with or as with a sponge. **5** *intransitive* (often foll. by *on*, *off*) live at the expense of (another person) with no intention of reimbursement etc. **6** *transitive* obtain (drink etc.) by sponging. **7** *transitive* **a** apply paint with a sponge to (walls, furniture, pottery, etc.) to achieve a mottled effect. **b** apply (paint) in this manner. □ **sponge·able** *adjective* **sponge·like** *adjective* [Old English via Latin *spongia* from Greek *spoggia*, *spoggos*]

sponge bag *noun Brit.* a waterproof bag for toilet articles.

sponge bath *noun N Amer.* a cleaning of the body using a wet sponge or washcloth, without immersion in a tub of water.

sponge cake *noun* a very light cake with a spongelike consistency, made from beaten eggs, sugar, and flour, with little or no fat.

sponge hockey *noun Cdn* a form of hockey played on ice with rubber-soled boots and a sponge puck.

sponge puck *noun Cdn* a hockey puck made of hard sponge, used in recreational play or with young children.

sponge pudding *noun Brit.* a steamed or baked pudding of fat, flour, and eggs with a usu. specified flavour.

spon·ger *noun* a person who contrives to live at another's expense.

sponge rubber *noun* liquid rubber latex processed into a spongelike substance.

sponge toffee *noun Cdn & Brit.* a type of light, crispy, aerated toffee.

sponge tree *noun* a spiny acacia native to tropical America, *Acacia farnesiana*, with globose heads of fragrant yellow flowers yielding a perfume. *Also called* OPOPANAX.

spon·gi·form /ˈspʌndʒɪˌfɔrm/ *adjective* spongelike; spongy.

spongiform encephalopathy *noun* any of various degenerative diseases of the central nervous system characterized by histological change in brain tissue, which assumes a spongelike appearance due to the degeneration and loss of neurons, and the appearance of vacuoles.

spongy *adjective* (**spon·gi·er**, **spon·gi·est**) like a sponge, esp. in being porous, compressible, elastic, or absorbent. □ **spon·gi·ly** *adverb* **spon·gi·ness** *noun*

spon·son /ˈspɒnsən/ *noun* **1** a projection from the side of a warship or tank to enable a gun to be trained forward and aft. **2 a** short subsidiary wing to stabilize a seaplane. **3** an air-filled buoyancy chamber in a canoe, intended to reduce the risk of capsizing. **4** a triangular platform supporting the wheel on a paddle steamer. [19th c.: origin unknown]

spon·sor ● *noun* **1** a person who supports an activity done for charity by pledging money in advance. **2 a** person or organization that promotes or supports an artistic or sporting activity etc. **b** esp. *N Amer.* a business organization that buys advertising time on a broadcast program. **3** an organization lending support to an election candidate. **4** a person who introduces a proposal for legislation. **5 a** a godparent at baptism. **b** esp. *Catholicism* a person who presents a candidate for confirmation. **6** a person who makes himself or herself responsible for another. ● *transitive verb* be a sponsor for. □ **spon·sor·ial** /spɒnˈsɔriəl/ *adjective* **spon·sor·ship** *noun* [Latin *spondēre spons-* promise solemnly]

spon·tan·eous /spɒnˈteɪniəs/ *adjective* **1** acting or done or occurring because of a sudden impulse from within; not planned or caused or suggested by external forces (*spontaneous applause*). **2** voluntary, without external incitement (*made a spontaneous offer of his services*). **3** *Biol.* (of structural changes in plants and muscular activity esp. in young animals) instinctive, automatic, prompted by no motive. **4** (of bodily movement, literary style, etc.) gracefully natural and unconstrained. **5** (of sudden movement etc.) involuntary, not due to conscious volition. **6** growing naturally without cultivation. □ **spon·tan·eity** /ˌspɒntəˈneɪɪti/ *noun* **spon·tan·eous·ly** *adverb* [Late Latin *spontaneus* from *sponte* of one's own accord]

spontaneous abortion *noun* = MISCARRIAGE 1.

spontaneous combustion *noun* the ignition of a mineral or vegetable substance, e.g. a heap of rags soaked with oil, a mass of wet coal, etc., from heat engendered within itself, usu. by rapid oxidation.

spontaneous generation *noun hist.* the supposed production of living from non-living matter as inferred from the appearance of life (due in fact to bacteria etc.) in some infusions; abiogenesis.

spoof *informal* ● *noun* **1** a parody. **2** a hoax or swindle. ● *transitive verb* **1** parody. **2 a** hoax, swindle. **b** *Computing* deceive (a server) by assuming another user's identity. □ **spoof·er** *noun* **spoof·ery** *noun* [invented by A. Roberts, English comedian d.1933]

spook ● *noun* **1** informal a ghost. **2** esp. *N Amer. slang* a spy. ● *verb* esp. *N Amer. slang* **1** *transitive* frighten, unnerve, alarm. **2** *intransitive* take fright, become alarmed. [Dutch, = Middle Low German *spōk*, of unknown origin]

spooky *adjective* (**spook·i·er**, **spook·i·est**) **1** informal ghostly, eerie. **2** *N Amer. slang* (of a person or animal) nervous; easily frightened. **3** *US slang* of spies or espionage. □ **spook·i·ly** *adverb* **spook·i·ness** *noun*

spool¹ ● *noun* **1 a** a reel for winding thread, yarn, or wire on. **b** a reel for winding magnetic tape, photographic film, etc., on. **c** a quantity of thread, tape, etc., wound on a spool. **2** the revolving cylinder of an angler's reel. ● *transitive verb* wind on a spool. [Old French *espole* or Middle Low German *spōle*, Middle Dutch *spoele*, Old High German *spuolo*, of unknown origin]

spool² *transitive verb Computing* print out, read in, or otherwise process (data) on a peripheral device at the same time that an operating system is carrying out other processes. □ **spool·er** *noun* **spool·ing** *noun* [acronym from the initial letters of simultaneous peripheral operation on line]

spool bed *noun N Amer.* a design of bed with spool-shaped turnings in the headboard and footboard, produced esp. in the 19th c.

spoon ● *noun* **1 a** a utensil consisting of an oval or round bowl and a handle for conveying food (esp. liquid) to the mouth, for stirring, mixing, etc. **b** a spoonful, esp. of sugar. **c** (in *pl.*) *Music* a pair of spoons held in the hand and beaten together rhythmically as a percussion instrument. **2** a spoon-shaped thing, esp.: **a** (in full **spoon bait**) a bright revolving piece of metal used as a lure in fishing. **b** an oar with a broad curved blade. ● *verb* **1** *transitive* (often foll. by *up, out*) lift and move (food, liquid etc.) with a spoon. **2** *transitive* hit (a ball) feebly upwards. **3** *informal intransitive* behave in an amorous way, esp. foolishly. **4** *intransitive* fish with a spoon bait. **5** *intransitive* lie close together or fit into each other in the manner of spoons. □ **born with a silver spoon in one's mouth** born in affluence. □ **spoon·er** (in sense 3 of *verb*). **spoon·ful** *noun* (*pl.* **-fuls**). [Old English *spōn* 'chip of wood', from Germanic]

spoon·bill *noun* any of various wading birds which with ibises constitute the family Threskiornithidae, and have a long spatulate or spoon-shaped bill specialized for feeding in water.

spoon bread *noun US* a baked dish of cornmeal, milk, eggs, and shortening.

spoon·er·ism *noun* a transposition, usu. accidental, of the initial letters etc. of two or more words, e.g. *you have hissed the mystery lectures*. [Rev. W A. Spooner, English scholar d.1930, reputed to make such errors in speaking]

spoon-feed *transitive verb* (*past* and *past participle* **-fed**) **1** feed (a baby etc.) with a spoon. **2** provide help, information, etc., to (a person etc.) without requiring any effort on the recipient's part.

spoor ● *noun* the track or scent of a person or animal, esp. the footprints of a wild animal hunted as game. ● *transitive & intransitive verb* follow by the spoor. [Afrikaans from Middle Dutch *spo(o)r* from Germanic]

Spora·des /'spɒrə,diːz/ two groups of Greek islands in the Aegean Sea. The **Northern Sporades**, which lie close to the east coast of mainland Greece, include the islands of Euboea, Skiros, Skiathos, and Skopelos. The **Southern Sporades**, situated off the west coast of Turkey, include Rhodes and the islands of the Dodecanese.

spor·adic /spə'radɪk/ *adjective* occurring only here and there or occasionally, separate, scattered. □ **spor·adic·ally** *adverb* [medieval Latin *sporadicus* from Greek *sporadikos* from *sporas -ados* scattered: compare *speirō* to sow]

spor·an·gium /spə'randʒɪəm/ *noun* (*pl.* **spor·an·gia** /-dʒɪə/) *Bot.* a receptacle in which spores are found. □ **spor·an·gial** *adjective* [modern Latin from Greek *spora* SPORE + *aggeion* vessel]

spore *noun* **1** a specialized reproductive cell of many plants and micro-organisms. **2** these collectively. [modern Latin *spora* from Greek *spora* sowing, seed, from *speirō* sow]

sporo- *combining form Biol.* a spore. [Greek *spora* (as SPORE)]

sporo·cyst /'spɒrəsɪst/ *noun* an intermediate stage in the life cycle of various parasites.

sporo·gen·esis /,spɒrə'dʒenəsɪs/ *noun* the process of spore formation.

sporo·phore /'spɒrəfɔː/ *noun* a spore-bearing structure esp. in a fungus.

sporo·phyte /'spɒrə,faɪt/ *noun* the asexual form of a plant that has alternation of generations between this and the gamete-producing form (gametophyte). □ **sporo·phyt·ic** /-'fɪtɪk/ *adjective*

sporo·zo·ite /spɒrə'zəʊaɪt/ *noun Biol.* a small motile stage in the life cycle of some protozoans, e.g. the malaria parasite, usually produced inside a host. [SPORO- + Greek *zoion* 'animal' + -ITE[1]]

spor·ran /'spɒrən/ *noun* a pouch, usu. of leather or sealskin covered with fur etc., worn in front of the kilt as part of Highland costume. [Gaelic *sporan* from medieval Latin *bursa* PURSE]

sport ● *noun* **1 a** a game or competitive activity, esp. one involving physical exertion, e.g. hockey, football, tennis, etc. **b** (usu. in *pl.*) such activities collectively (often *attributive*: *sports stadium*; *sports equipment*). **2** (often *attributive*) recreation, amusement, diversion, fun (*sport hunting*). **3** *informal* **a** a fair, cheerful, or generous person (*be a sport and lend me your bike*). **b** a person behaving in a specified way, esp. regarding games, rules, etc. (*a bad sport*). **c** *Austral.* a form of address, esp. between males. **d** *US* a playboy. **4** *Biol.* an animal or plant deviating suddenly or strikingly from the normal type. **5** a plaything (*was the sport of Fortune*). **6** (*attributive*) a sports car; a sports model of a car (*sport coupe*). ● *verb* **1** *transitive* wear, exhibit, or produce, esp. ostentatiously (*sported a gold tie pin*). **2** *intransitive* frolic, gambol. **3** *intransitive* divert oneself, take part in a pastime. **4** *intransitive Biol.* become or produce a sport. □ **make sport of** make fun of, ridicule. □ **sport·er** *noun* [Middle English from DISPORT]

sport·bike *noun* a type of high-powered, fast motorcycle driven by leaning low over the gas tank.

sport·coat *noun* = SPORTS JACKET.

sport fish *noun* a kind of fish caught for sport. □ **sport fisherman** *noun* **sport fishery** *noun*

sport fishing *noun* fishing with a rod and line for sport or recreation.

sport·ing *adjective* **1** connected with or interested in sports (*sporting event*; *a sporting man*). **2** fair, generous (*a sporting offer*). **3** used for sports (*sporting goods*). □ **sport·ing·ly** *adverb*

sporting chance *noun* a reasonable chance of success.

sport·ive *adjective* **1** playful. **2** taking part in or interested in athletic sports. □ **sport·ive·ly** *adverb* **sport·ive·ness** *noun*

sport of kings *noun* (prec. by *the*) horse racing (less often war, hunting, or surfing).

sports bar *noun N Amer.* a bar where televised sports events are shown continuously.

sports book *noun US* a gambling establishment where customers bet on the outcome of various sporting events.

sports car *noun* a low, fast car designed for superior acceleration and performance at high speed.

sports card *noun* a card with a photograph of a sports figure on one side and statistics etc. on the reverse, collected as part of a set.

sports·cast *noun N Amer.* a broadcast of a sports event or information about sport. □ **sports·cast·er** *noun*

sports coat *noun* = SPORTS JACKET.

sports day *noun Cdn & Brit.* a day on which schoolchildren participate in games, races, and other sports activities.

sport seat *noun* an articulated, adjustable front seat in a car.

sports grounds *plural noun* a piece of land used for sports.

sports jacket *noun* (also **sport jacket**) a man's jacket for informal wear, not part of a suit.

sports·man *noun* (*pl.* **-men**) **1** a person who takes part in sports, esp. professionally. **2** a person who behaves fairly and generously. **3** (esp. *N Amer.*) a person who hunts or fishes recreationally. □ **sports·man·like** *adjective* **sports·man·ly** *adjective* **sports·man·ship** *noun*

sports medicine *noun* the branch of medicine that deals with injuries etc. sustained in athletic activities.

sports page *noun* (also **sports section**) a page or section of a newspaper devoted to coverage of sports.

sports·person *noun* (*pl.* **-persons** or **-people**) a sportsman or sportswoman.

sports·plex *noun N Amer.* a building offering different sports facilities under one roof, e.g. a rink, pool, etc.

sports shirt *noun* (also **sport shirt**) a men's casual shirt with a squared-off shirttail.

sports·wear *noun* **1** clothes worn for playing sports. **2** clothing of a somewhat informal type, e.g. ladies' separates etc.

sports·woman *noun* (*pl.* **-women**) **1** a woman who takes part in sports, esp. professionally. **2** a woman who behaves fairly and generously.

sports·writ·er *noun* a journalist who writes on sports.

sport-utility *noun* (in full **sport-utility vehicle**) (also *informal* **sport-ute**) *N Amer.* a rugged, sporty vehicle which is a hybrid between a Jeep and a minivan, used for everyday driving as well as driving over rough terrain.

sporty *adjective* (**sport·i·er**, **sport·i·est**) *informal* **1 a** fond of sports. **b** (esp. of clothes) suitable for informal wear; designed in a casual style. **2** rakish, showy. **3** (of a car) resembling a sports car in appearance or performance. □ **sport·i·ly** *adverb* **sport·i·ness** *noun*

spor·u·late /'spɒrjuleɪt/ *intransitive verb* form spores or sporules. □ **spor·u·la·tion** *noun*

spor·ule /'spɒruːl/ *noun* a small spore or a single spore. [French *sporule* or modern Latin *sporula* (as SPORE)]

spot ● *noun* **1 a** a small part of the surface of a thing distinguished by colour, texture, etc., usu. round or less elongated than a streak or stripe (*a blue tie with pink spots*). **b** a small mark or stain. **c** a pimple or other mark on the skin. **d** a small circle or other shape used in various numbers to distinguish faces of dice, playing cards in a suit, etc. **e** a moral blemish or stain (*a spot on his reputation*). **f** any of various plant diseases producing small round areas of discoloration on the leaves or fruit. **2 a** a particular place; a definite locality (*dropped it on this precise spot*). **b** a place used for a particular activity (often in *combination*: *nightspot*). **c** a place in a class, group, etc. (*phone early to reserve a spot*). **3** a particular part of one's body or aspect of one's character (*bald spot*; *soft spot*). **4 a** *informal* one's (esp. regular) position in an organization, program of events, etc. **b** a place or position in a performance or show (*a ten-minute guest spot*). **5** an awkward or difficult situation (*in a tight spot*). **6** esp. *Brit.* **a** *informal* a small quantity of anything (*a spot of lunch*; *a spot of trouble*). **b** a drop (*a spot of rain*). **c** *informal* a drink. **7** = SPOTLIGHT *noun* 1, 2. **8** (usu. *attributive*) money paid or goods delivered immediately after a sale (*spot cash*; *spot silver*). **9** *Billiards* etc. **a** a small round black patch to mark the position where a ball is placed at certain times. **b** (in full **spot-ball**) the white ball distinguished from the other by two black spots. ● *verb* (**spot·ted, spot·ting**) **1 a** *transitive & intransitive* mark or become marked with spots. **b** *transitive* stain, soil (a person's character etc.). **2** *transitive* **a** catch sight of; notice, perceive. **b** *informal* single out beforehand (the winner of a race etc.). **c** watch for and take note of (trains, talent, etc.). **d** *Military* locate (an enemy's position), esp. from the air. **3** *intransitive Brit.* rain slightly. **4** *transitive Billiards* place (a ball) on a spot. **5** *transitive N Amer. informal* loan (*can you spot me ten bucks?*). **6** *transitive* provide safety assistance to (a gymnast etc.). □ **hit the spot** *informal* be exactly what is required. **on the spot 1** at the scene of an action or event. **2** *informal* in a position such that response or action is required. **3** without delay or change of place, then and there. **4** (of a person) wide awake, equal to the situation, in good form at a game etc. **put on the spot** *informal* force to make a difficult decision, answer an awkward question, etc. **running on the spot** *Cdn & Brit.* raising the feet alternately as in running but without moving forwards or backwards. [perhaps from Middle Dutch *spotte*, Low German *spot*, Old Norse *spotti* 'small piece']

spot check ● *noun* a test made on the spot or on a randomly selected subject. ● *transitive verb* (**spot-check**) subject to a spot check.

spot·less *adjective* immaculate; absolutely clean or pure. □ **spot·less·ly** *adverb* **spot·less·ness** *noun*

spot·light ● *noun* **1** a beam of light directed on a small area, esp. on a particular part of a theatre stage. **2** a lamp projecting this. **3** full attention or publicity. ● *transitive verb* (*past and past participle* **spot·light·ed** or **spot·lit**) **1** direct a spotlight on. **2** make conspicuous, draw attention to.

spot market *noun* a market in which currencies, commodities, etc. are traded for delivery within two days.

spot meter *noun Photography* a photometer that measures the intensity of light received within a cone of small angle, usually 2° or less. □ **spot metering** *noun*

spot-on *Brit. informal* ● *adjective* precise; on target. ● *adverb* precisely.

spot price *noun* a price charged for goods that are available for immediate delivery.

spot·ted *adjective* marked or decorated with spots.

spotted dick *noun Brit.* a suet pudding containing currants.

spotted fever *noun* **1** cerebrospinal meningitis. **2** typhus. **3** (in full **Rocky Mountain spotted fever**) a rickettsial disease transmitted by ticks.

spotted hyena *noun* a hyena, *Crocuta crocuta*, of sub-Saharan Africa.

spotted owl *noun* a large, dark brown hornless owl with black eyes, *Strix occidentalis*, of the west coast of N America.

spot·ter *noun* **1** (often in *combination*) a person who spots people or things (*trend spotter*; *trainspotter*). **2** an aviator or aircraft employed in locating enemy positions etc. **3** (in gymnastics etc.) a person stationed to prevent possible accident or otherwise to provide safety assistance to the performer.

spot·ting *noun* **1** in senses of SPOT *verb*. **2 a** a slight discharge of blood from the vagina. **b** light staining due to this.

spotting scope *noun* a small telescope.

spot·ty *adjective* (**spot·ti·er, spot·ti·est**) **1** marked with spots. **2** patchy, irregular. **3** *Brit.* having pimples, esp. on the face. □ **spot·ti·ly** *adverb* **spot·ti·ness** *noun*

spot weld *transitive verb* join (two metal surfaces) by welding at discrete points. □ **spot weld** *noun* **spot welder** *noun* **spot welding** *noun*

spous·al /ˈspaʊzəl/ *adjective* of or relating to marriage or to a spouse.

spouse *noun* a person who is part of a married couple. [Old French *sp(o)us* (masc.), *sp(o)use* (fem.), vars. of *espous(e)* from Latin *sponsus sponsa* past participle of *spondēre* betroth]

Spouse's Allowance *noun Cdn* a federal benefit paid to low-income 60–64-year-old spouses of Old Age Security pensioners.

spout ● *noun* **1 a** a projecting tube or lip through which a liquid etc. is poured from a teapot, kettle, jug, etc., or issues from a fountain, pump, etc. **b** a sloping trough down which a thing may be shot into a receptacle. **2** a jet or column of liquid, grain, etc. **3** a whale's blowhole. ● *transitive & intransitive verb* **1** discharge or issue forcibly in a

jet. **2** utter (verses etc.) or speak in a declamatory manner, speechify. □ **up the spout** *Brit. slang* **1** useless, ruined, hopeless. **2** pregnant. **3** (of a bullet or cartridge) in the barrel and ready to be fired. □ **spout·er** *noun* [Middle Dutch *spouten*, originally imitative]

spp. *abbreviation* species (plural).

SPQR *abbreviation hist.* the Senate and people of Rome. [from Latin *Senatus Populusque Romanus*]

sprad·dle *transitive & intransitive verb N Amer.* straddle, splay. [prob. a dialect form related to SPREAD]

sprain ● *transitive verb* wrench (an ankle, wrist, etc.) violently so as to cause pain and swelling but not dislocation. ● *noun* **1** such a wrench. **2** the resulting inflammation and swelling. [17th c.: origin unknown]

sprang *past of* SPRING.

sprat *noun* **1** a small European herring-like fish, *Sprattus sprattus*, much used as food. **2** a similar fish, e.g. a sand eel or a young herring. [Old English *sprot*]

Sprat·ly Islands a group of small islands and coral reefs in the South China Sea, between Vietnam and Borneo. Dispersed over a distance of some 965 km (600 miles), the islands are variously claimed by China, Taiwan, Vietnam, the Philippines, and Malaysia.

sprawl ● *verb* **1 a** *intransitive* sit or lie or fall with limbs flung out or in an ungainly way. **b** *transitive* spread (one's limbs) in this way. **2** *intransitive* **a** (of a building complex, a town, etc.) spread out irregularly to cover a large area. **b** (of a plant) be of irregular or straggling form. ● *noun* **1** a sprawling movement or attitude. **2** a straggling group or mass. **3** the straggling expansion of an urban or industrial area. □ **sprawl·ing** *adjective* [Old English *spreawlian*]

spray¹ ● *noun* **1 a** water or other liquid flying in small drops from the force of the wind, the dashing of waves, or the action of an atomizer etc. **b** a quantity of small objects flying or propelled through the air (*a spray of bullets*). **2** a liquid preparation to be applied in this form with an atomizer etc., e.g. for cosmetic or medical purposes (*hairspray*; *nasal spray*). **3** an instrument or apparatus for such application. ● *verb* **1** *transitive & intransitive* throw (liquid) in the form of spray. **2** *transitive & intransitive* sprinkle (an object) with small drops or particles, esp. (a plant) with an insecticide. **3** *intransitive* (of a male animal, esp. a cat) mark its environment with the smell of its urine, as an attraction to females. □ **spray·er** *noun* [earlier *spry*, perhaps related to Middle Dutch *spra(e)yen*, Middle High German *sprӕjen* sprinkle]

spray² *noun* **1** a sprig of flowers or leaves, or a branch of a tree with branchlets or flowers, esp. a slender or graceful one. **2** a bunch of flowers decoratively arranged. **3** an ornament in a similar form (*a spray of diamonds*). [Old English *(e)sprei*, recorded in personal and place names]

spray can *noun* an aerosol can for applying paint etc. as a fine spray.

spray-dry *transitive verb* (**-dries, -dried**) dry (milk, ceramic material, etc.) by spraying as a fine powder into a current of hot air etc., the water in the particles being rapidly evaporated. □ **spray dryer** *noun* **spray drying** *noun*

spray gun *noun* a device resembling a gun for applying paint etc. onto a surface.

spray-on *adjective* (of a product, esp. a liquid) applied in the form of a spray.

spray paint ● *noun* paint packaged in an aerosol can for spraying upon a surface. ● *transitive verb* (**spray-paint**) paint (a surface) using spray paint.

spray skirt *noun* a cover of waterproof material which fits snugly around a paddler sitting in the cockpit of a kayak or canoe.

spread ● *verb* (*past and past participle* **spread**) **1** *transitive* (often foll. by *out*) **a** open up or unfold (a map, blanket, etc.) so that it is laid out flat and to its fullest width, esp. so that it may be properly read or seen. **b** lay (a collection of items, such as cards) out on a flat surface, esp. so that they may be properly displayed or viewed. **c** display fully to the eye or the mind (*the landscape was spread out before us*). **2 a** *transitive* apply (a substance, etc.) to a surface and distribute it in an even layer (*spread butter on her toast*). **b** *transitive* cover the surface of (*spread the cake with icing*). **c** *intransitive* be capable of being spread (*butter spreads more easily when it's warm*). **3** *intransitive* become distributed over a wider space or area; grow or increase in extent (*put out the fire before it spreads*). **4 a** *transitive* make (information, rumours, joy, etc.) better known or felt etc.; disseminate, diffuse. **b** *intransitive* (of an immaterial thing such as information or an emotion) become known or felt (*rumours are spreading*). **5** *transitive* separate, open, or stretch out (legs, wings, etc.) so that they are divergent or set a greater distance apart. **6** *transitive* (often foll. by *out*) distribute over a period of time (*I'd like to spread the payments* out over 5 months). **7** *transitive* scatter, distribute, or disperse over a certain area (*spread the seed over the lawn*). **8 a** *intransitive & reflexive* (often foll. by *out*) (of a group of people etc.) separate or disperse in order to cover a wider area. **b** *reflexive* (often foll. by *around*) make (oneself) available to others. **9** *transitive* **a** lay (a meal) on a table. **b** set (a table) by laying food upon it. ● *noun* **1** the act or an instance of spreading. **2 a** the degree or extent of spreading; breadth, width. **b** the wingspan of an aircraft or bird. **3** diffusion or expansion (*the spread of knowledge*). **4** the distance between two points in space or time. **5** *Stock Exch.* **a** the difference between the buying and selling price of a commodity. **b** a contract combining the option of buying shares within a specified time at a specified price above that prevailing when the contract is signed, with the option of selling shares of the same stock within the same time at a specified price below that prevailing when the contract is signed. **6** a garnish or topping, such as jam, peanut butter, or margarine, that is put on bread or toast etc. **7** an article or advertisement displayed prominently in a newspaper or magazine, esp. on two facing pages or across more than one column. **8** *informal* an elaborate meal. **9** = POINT SPREAD. **10** *N Amer.* a farm or ranch with extensive land. **11** a cover, such as a bedspread or tablecloth. **12** = MIDDLE-AGE SPREAD. □ **spread oneself too thin** attempt to undertake too many projects at once so that none can be done properly. **spread one's wings** *see* WING. □ **spread·abil·ity** *noun* **spread·able** *adjective* [Old English *-sprædan* from West Germanic]

spread betting *noun Brit.* a form of gambling in which the amount of money won or lost depends upon the degree to which a score or result in an (esp. sporting) event exceeds or falls short of the gambler's prediction.

spread-eagle ● *noun* **1** a representation of an eagle with legs and wings extended, used as an emblem. **2** *Figure Skating* a straight glide made with the feet a short distance apart and turned outwards in a straight line and the arms held out to either side. ● *verb* **1 a** *transitive & reflexive* place (a person or oneself) in a position with arms and legs spread out. **b** *intransitive* assume the position of a spread-eagle. **2** *transitive* defeat thoroughly or by a wide margin. **3** *intransitive Figure Skating* perform a spread-eagle. ● *adjective* **1** *US* bombastic; boisterously boastful or patriotic. **2** in the position of a spread-eagle. ● *adverb* in the position of a spread-eagle. □ **spread-eagled** *adjective*

spread·er *noun* **1** a person or thing that spreads. **2** an implement used to spread manure, fertilizer, seed, etc. over a field or lawn. **3** *Naut.* a bar attached to the mast of a yacht in order to spread the angle of the upper shrouds. **4** *Fishing* a type of lure consisting of a weight with three baited hooks radiating from it. **5** a bar for stretching something out or keeping things apart.

spread·sheet *noun* a computer program allowing manipulation and flexible retrieval of esp. tabulated numerical data.

spread spectrum *noun* (often *attributive*) a technique of broadcasting using multiple and varying frequencies in order to reduce signal interference.

Sprech·ge·sang /ˈʃprexɡəˌzaŋ/ *noun Music* a style of dramatic vocalization between speech and song. [German, lit. 'speech song']

spree *noun* **1** a period or bout of extravagant indulgence; a frenzy (*a shopping spree; a drinking spree*). **2** a lively outing or revelry; a romp. **3** a period or outburst of a (usu. specified) activity (*a shooting spree*). [19th c.: origin unknown]

sprig¹ ● *noun* **1 a** a small branch or shoot. **b** a representation of this used in a design or ornament decorating esp. fabric. **2** usu. *derogatory* a youth or young man, esp. a representative of a class or institution etc. (*a sprig of the nobility*). ● *transitive verb* (**sprigged, sprig·ging**) adorn or decorate (esp. fabric) with sprigs or similar designs. [Middle English from or related to Low German *sprick*]

sprig² *noun* a small thin tapering headless tack used esp. to hold glass in a window frame until the putty dries. [Middle English: origin unknown]

spright·ly *adjective* (**spright·li·er, spright·li·est**) characterized by animation or cheerful vitality; brisk, lively, spirited. □ **spright·li·ness** *noun* [*spright* var. of SPRITE + -LY¹]

spring ● *verb* (*past* **sprang** or *N Amer.* **sprung**; *past participle* **sprung**) **1** *intransitive* jump suddenly or quickly in a single movement; move suddenly upwards or forwards. **2** *intransitive* move rapidly as from a constrained position or by the action of a spring; recoil (*the branch sprang back and hit me in the face*). **3** *intransitive* (usu. foll. by *from*) **a** originate or arise (*their actions sprang from a false conviction*). **b** originate through birth or descent; be descended. **4** *intransitive* (usu. foll. by *up*) come into being; appear, develop, esp. suddenly (*new houses are springing up all over*). **5** *transitive* operate or cause (a device etc.) to

operate suddenly, esp. by means of a mechanism (*spring a trap*). **6** *transitive* (often foll. by *on*) reveal, introduce, or make known suddenly or unexpectedly (*she loves to spring surprises on him*). **7** *transitive slang* contrive or effect the escape or release of (a prisoner etc.). **8** *N Amer. & Austral. informal* **a** *intransitive* (usu. foll. by *for*) pay or offer to pay for something; indulge in a purchase (*I'll spring for dinner*). **b** *transitive* spend (money). **9 a** *intransitive* become warped or split. **b** *transitive* split or crack (wood or a wooden implement). **10** *transitive* (usu. as **sprung** *adjective*) fit (a car or truck etc.) with springs. **11** *transitive* rouse (game) from a thicket or bush. ● *noun* **1 a** (also **Spring**) the first season of the year, in which vegetation begins to appear, lasting in the northern hemisphere from March or April to May and in the southern hemisphere from September to November. **b** the period from the vernal equinox to the summer solstice. **c** (often foll. by *of*) an early period or the initial stage. **d** = SPRING TIDE. **2** an act of springing; a bound, jump, or leap. **3** a resilient device usu. of bent or coiled metal having the ability to return to its original shape with the removal of force or pressure, used esp. to drive clockwork or for cushioning in furniture, automobiles, etc. **4** a recoil, rebound, or backward movement of something bent or forced out of its normal position or form. **5** elasticity; ability to bounce back strongly (*a mattress with plenty of spring*). **6** liveliness in a person or of a person's mind, faculties, etc. (*a spring in her step*). **7 a** a flow of water etc. rising or welling naturally from the earth. **b** such a flow of water having special esp. medicinal or curative properties. **c** (usu. in *pl.*) a community or locality having such springs. **8** the motive, source, or origin of an action, custom, etc. **9** *slang* an escape or release from prison. **10** the upward curve of a beam etc. from a horizontal line. **11** the splitting or yielding of a plank etc. under strain. □ **hope springs eternal** even in the worst situations, one tends to hope for improvement. **spring a leak** develop a leak (originally *Naut.*, from timbers springing out of position). □ **spring·like** *adjective* [Old English *springan* from Germanic]

spring beauty *noun* any of several esp. N American succulent plants that bear pink or white flowers in the spring, belonging to the genera *Claytonia* and *Montia* of the purslane family.

spring·board *noun* **1** (often foll. by *for, to*) a starting point or impetus for an activity, discussion, etc. **2 a** a springy board used in gymnastics to gain height or momentum in vaulting or mounting an apparatus etc. **b** esp. *Brit.* a diving board. **3** *Cdn & Austral.* a platform inserted into a notch cut in the side of a tree on which a lumberjack stands to chop at some height from the ground.

spring·bok *noun* **1** a southern African gazelle, *Antidorcas marsupialis*, with the ability to run with high springing jumps. **2** (**Springbok**) a South African, esp. one who has played for South Africa in international sporting competitions. [Afrikaans from Dutch *springen* SPRING + *bok* antelope]

spring break *noun N Amer.* an esp. college or university holiday of one or two weeks occurring usu. in February or March.

spring breakup *noun Cdn* = BREAKUP 4.

spring chicken *noun* **1** a young chicken for eating. **2** (usu. with *neg.*) a young person (*she's no spring chicken*). [sense 1 because orig. available only in spring]

spring cleaning *noun* a thorough cleaning of a house or room, esp. in spring. □ **spring clean** *transitive & intransitive verb*

spring equinox *noun* the date on which the sun crosses the celestial equator in a southerly direction (approx. 21 March) or, in the southern hemisphere, in a northerly direction (approx. 22 September) (*compare* AUTUMNAL EQUINOX). *Also called* VERNAL EQUINOX.

spring·er *noun* **1** = SPRINGER SPANIEL. **2** a cow about to calve. **3** *Archit.* **a** the part of an arch where the curve begins. **b** the lowest stone of this. **c** the bottom stone of the coping of a gable.

springer spaniel *noun* either of two breeds of sturdy dog of medium height used esp. in hunting to spring game, including the English springer spaniel, having a wavy coat with black or brown and white markings, and the Welsh springer spaniel, having a straighter coat with red and white markings.

spring-fed *adjective N Amer.* (of a river, pond, etc.) having a spring as its source.

spring fever *noun* a restless or lethargic feeling sometimes associated with spring.

Spring·field 1 a city in SW Missouri, on the northern edge of the Ozark Mountains; pop. (est. 2000) 151,580. **2** a city in SW Massachusetts, on the Connecticut River; pop. (est. 2000) 152,082. **3** the state capital of Illinois; pop. (est. 2000) 111,454. It was the home and burial place of Abraham Lincoln. **4** a rural municipality in SE central Manitoba, just east of Winnipeg; pop. (2001) 12,602.

Vowels:　a cat　ɑ arm　e bed　ɜr her　ɜː deux　ə ago　ɪ sit　i cosy　iː feed　ɒ hot　ɔ pore　oː no　ʌ run　ʊ put

spring·form pan *noun* N Amer. a round metal cake pan with sides that may be released from the bottom, allowing the cake to be easily removed when done.

spring·house *noun* N Amer. hist. a shed built over a spring or stream and used to cool milk, food, etc.

spring-loaded *adjective* (of a machine or device etc.) containing a spring that presses one part against another.

spring onion *noun* esp. Brit. = GREEN ONION.

spring peeper *noun* a small brown tree frog, *Hyla crucifer*, that occurs throughout much of eastern N America and has a high-pitched piping call.

spring roll *noun* an appetizer or snack, of Oriental origin, consisting of a very thin wrapper made with flour and water rolled around a mixture of chopped vegetables, usu. including bean sprouts, and sometimes meat, and deep-fried.

spring salmon *noun* Cdn = CHINOOK 2.

Spring·steen, Bruce (b.1949), US rock singer, songwriter, and guitarist. He is noted for his songs about working-class life in the US and for his energetic stage performances; major albums include *Born to Run* (1975), *The River* (1981), and *Born in the USA* (1984).

spring sunflower *noun* = BALSAMROOT.

spring·tail *noun* any wingless insect of the order Collembola, leaping by means of a springlike caudal part.

spring tide *noun* a tide occurring just after the new and full moon, in which there is the greatest difference between high and low water.

spring·time *noun* 1 the season of spring. 2 (often foll. by *of*) the earliest and usu. most pleasant stage or period of something (*the springtime of their youth*).

spring training *noun* Baseball a period before the regular season during which players practise and participate in pre-season games while managers decide on the roster.

spring water *noun* water from a spring, often bottled and sold.

spring wheat *noun* wheat that is planted in the spring (compare WINTER WHEAT).

springy *adjective* (**spring·i·er, spring·i·est**) 1 springing back when compressed, squeezed, or stretched; elastic, resilient. 2 (of movement, music, etc.) buoyant and vigorous; bouncing. □ **spring·i·ly** *adverb* **spring·i·ness** *noun*

sprin·kle ● *verb* 1 *transitive* scatter (liquid, powder, etc.) in small drops or particles; strew thinly or lightly. 2 *transitive* (often foll. by *with*) cover (a surface) with scattered drops or grains; powder or dust lightly. 3 *transitive* (usu. in *pass.*) distribute in small amounts. 4 *intransitive* (of precipitation, esp. rain) fall in a fine mist. ● *noun* (usu. foll. by *of*) 1 the action or an act of sprinkling. 2 a dusting or light shower. 3 a small thinly distributed number or amount. 4 N Amer. (usu. in *pl.*) each of an assortment of tiny usu. multicoloured bits of candy used to decorate cookies, cupcakes, etc. [Middle English, perhaps from Middle Dutch *sprenkelen*]

sprink·ler *noun* 1 a device, machine, vehicle, etc. used to sprinkle esp. water. 2 an attachment for a garden hose used for watering flowers, a lawn, etc. 3 a plumbing fixture or system of fixtures installed overhead to extinguish fires.

sprink·ling *noun* (usu. foll. by *of*) 1 a thinly distributed amount of a liquid or powder. 2 a relatively small number of things scattered over a broad area (*a sprinkling of sunbathers on the beach*).

sprint ● *verb* 1 *intransitive* run a short distance at full speed. 2 *intransitive* cycle, ride, paddle, or drive at full speed over a short distance, esp. while participating in a race. 3 *transitive* cover or traverse (a certain distance) by sprinting. ● *noun* 1 **a** Sport a fast race in which the participants run, cycle, ride, etc. at full speed over a short distance. **b** a short burst of speed used to finish a longer race. 2 an instance or short period of running etc. at maximum speed. □ **sprint·er** *noun* [Old Norse *sprinta* (unrecorded), of unknown origin]

sprit *noun* a small pole or spar reaching diagonally from the mast to the upper outer corner of the sail. [Old English *sprēot* pole, related to SPROUT]

sprite *noun* 1 an elf or fairy, esp. a small mischievous or playful one. 2 a dainty or lively person. 3 Computing a user-defined graphical figure consisting of a pattern of pixels that can be moved about onscreen as a single entity. [Middle English from *sprit* var. of SPIRIT]

sprit·sail /ˈsprɪtsəl, -seil/ *noun* 1 a sail extended by a sprit. 2 hist. a sail attached to a yard set under the bowsprit.

spritz esp. N Amer. ● *transitive verb* 1 sprinkle, squirt, or spray (something) with a liquid (*spritzed her neck with perfume*). 2 apply (a liquid) by spraying (*spritzed some cleaner on the window*). ● *noun* 1 a small spray; a splash or squirt (*gin with a spritz of lemon*). 2 a type of hairspray. □ **spritzy** *adjective* [German *spritzen* to squirt]

spritz·er *noun* a mixture of wine and soda water. [German *Spritzer* a splash]

sprock·et *noun* 1 each of several teeth on a wheel engaging with links of a chain on a bicycle or with holes in film etc. 2 a wheel with sprockets, esp. one that engages with a bicycle chain or that propels film through a projector or camera. [16th c.: origin unknown]

sprog *noun* esp. Brit. slang (also **sprog·let**) a youngster; a child or baby. [originally military slang, = new recruit: perhaps from obsolete *sprag* lively young man]

sprout ● *verb* 1 *transitive* put forth, produce, or develop (shoots, hair, etc.) (*he's sprouted a moustache*). 2 *intransitive* begin to grow, put forth shoots. 3 *intransitive* spring up or emerge, esp. suddenly (*new houses are sprouting up all over town*). 4 *transitive* cause, produce, or seem to cause or produce; give rise to. ● *noun* 1 a new growth developing from a bud, seed, or other part of a plant; a shoot. 2 (usu. in *pl.*) a young tender shoot of a plant, esp. a bean or alfalfa, eaten as a vegetable. 3 (usu. in *pl.*) = BRUSSELS SPROUTS. 4 N Amer. a young person or child. [Old English *sprūtan* (unrecorded) from West Germanic]

spruce¹ ● *adjective* neat in dress and appearance; trim, smart. ● *transitive, intransitive, & reflexive verb* (usu. foll. by *up*) make or become trim, neat, or smart. □ **spruce·ly** *adverb* **spruce·ness** *noun* [perhaps from SPRUCE² in obsolete sense 'Prussian', in the collocation *spruce* (leather) *jerkin*]

spruce² *noun* 1 any of various pyramidal evergreen coniferous trees constituting the genus *Picea*, of the pine family, with pendulous cones and with needles inserted in peg-like projections. 2 the wood of this tree used as timber. [alteration of obsolete *Pruce* PRUSSIA]

spruce beer *noun* N Amer. 1 a drink made by adding sugar or molasses to the water of boiled spruce twigs and needles, which is then fermented with yeast. 2 a similar non-alcoholic carbonated drink flavoured, usu. artificially, with spruce.

spruce budworm *noun* the brown larva of a N American moth of the large family Tortricidae, *Choristoneura fumiferana*, which is a serious pest of spruce and other conifers.

spruce grouse *noun* a grouse, *Dendragapus canadensis*, of N American coniferous forests.

Spruce Grove a city in central Alberta, 25 km west of Edmonton; pop. (2001) 15,983. □ **Spruce Grover** *noun* [so called because of a nearby grove of spruce trees]

sprue¹ *noun* 1 a channel through which molten metal or plastic is poured into a mould. 2 a piece of metal or plastic attached to a casting, having solidified in the mould channel. [19th c.: origin unknown]

sprue² *noun* a condition caused by deficient absorption of food by a diseased small intestine, characterized by ulceration of the mucous membrane of the mouth, anemia, and diarrhea, afflicting esp. visitors to tropical countries. [Dutch *spruw* THRUSH²; compare Flemish *spruwen* sprinkle]

sprung ● *verb* past and past participle of SPRING. ● *adjective* 1 provided or fitted with springs. 2 (esp. of a dance floor) suspended above a subfloor in order to be resilient, flexible, or springy. 3 that has been sprung.

sprung rhythm *noun* a poetic metre approximating to speech, each foot having one stressed syllable followed by a varying number of unstressed syllables.

spry *adjective* (**spry·er, spry·est**) nimble, active, lively. □ **spry·ly** *adverb* [18th c.: origin unknown]

spud ● *noun* 1 slang a potato. 2 a tool resembling a small spade with a narrow chisel-shaped blade, sometimes used for cutting the roots of weeds. 3 derogatory **a** a person with a stout or stocky build. **b** a lazy or dull-witted person. 4 a short length of pipe used to connect two plumbing fixtures. ● *transitive verb* (**spud·ded, spud·ding**) 1 make the initial drilling for (an oil well). 2 cut or remove (weeds etc.) with a spud. [Middle English: origin unknown]

spudg·el *noun* Cdn (Nfld) a metal or wooden bucket attached to a long pole used esp. to bail water from a boat or to draw water from a well. [18th c.: origin unknown]

Spud Island Cdn informal Prince Edward Island. □ **Spud Islander** *noun* [with reference to the province's reputation as a producer of potatoes]

spu·mante /spuːˈmanti, -ˈmɒnteɪ/ *noun* any of a number of Italian sparkling white wines, the most important of which is Asti. [Italian, = 'sparkling']

spume /spjuːm/ ● *noun* foam or froth on or from a liquid. ● *intransitive verb* froth, foam. □ **spumy** *adjective* (**spum·i·er**, **spum·i·est**). [Old French (e)spume or Latin *spuma*]

spu·moni /spəˈmoːni/ *noun N Amer.* a kind of rich layered ice cream with candied fruit and nuts. [Italian *spumone* from *spuma* SPUME]

spun ● *verb* past and past participle of SPIN. ● *adjective* converted into threads (*spun glass*; *spun gold*).

spunk *noun* **1** *informal* spirit, energy, courage, mettle. **2** *esp. Brit. coarse slang* semen. [16th c.: origin uncertain]

spunky *adjective* (**spunk·i·er**, **spunk·i·est**) *informal* full of energy, grit, or courage; spirited. □ **spunk·i·ly** *adverb* **spunk·i·ness** *noun*

spun silk *noun* a material made of short-fibred and waste silk.

spun sugar *noun* hardened sugar syrup drawn out into filaments, used as a confection as in candy floss, or as a decoration.

spur ● *noun* **1** a device with a small spike or a spiked wheel worn on a rider's heel for urging a horse forward. **2** a stimulus, incentive, or encouragement. **3** (in full **spur line**) a short stretch of track branching off a railway line, esp. one making a connection to another line. **4** a mountain or hill etc., or a ridge that projects from a mountain or hill. **5** an abnormal growth or calcareous deposit occurring esp. in the heel or elbow. **6** a sharp hard claw on the back foot or lower hind leg of a bird or animal, esp. a rooster. **7** *Bot.* **a** a slender hollow projection from part of a flower. **b** a short lateral branch or shoot, esp. one bearing fruit. **8** a pair of spikes that may be attached to a boot to facilitate climbing mountains, telephone poles, etc. ● *verb* (**spurred**, **spur·ring**) **1** *transitive* prick (a horse) with spurs. **2** *transitive* **a** (often foll. by *on*) encourage or incite (a person) (*the crowd spurred her on*). **b** be the cause of; stimulate (interest etc.) (*recent reforms have spurred economic growth*). □ **earn** (or **win**) **one's spurs 1** gain knighthood by an act of valour. **2** attain distinction, earn a high honour. **on the spur of the moment** on a sudden whim or impulse; without prior consideration or planning. [Old English *spora*, *spura* from Germanic, related to SPURN]

spurge *noun* any plant of the genus *Euphorbia*, exuding an acrid milky juice once used medicinally as a purgative. [Old French *espurge* from *espurgier* from Latin *expurgare* (as EX-¹, PURGE)]

spur gear *noun* a wheel which has cogs or teeth arranged radially around its edge.

spurge laurel *noun* any shrub of the genus *Daphne*, esp. *D. laureola*, with small yellow flowers.

spur·i·ous /ˈspɜriəs, ˈspjʊr-/ *adjective* **1** not proceeding from the reputed origin, source, or author; not genuine or authentic. **2** based on false reasoning; not true or accurate (*a spurious argument*). **3** superficially resembling or simulating something, but lacking its genuine character or qualities (*spurious charm*). □ **spur·i·ous·ly** *adverb* **spur·i·ous·ness** *noun* [Latin *spurius* false]

spurn *transitive verb* reject or refuse (a person or thing) in a way that indicates contempt. [Old English *spurnan*, *spornan*, related to SPUR]

spur-of-the-moment *adjective* impromptu, sudden; unplanned or unpremeditated.

spurred *adjective* (of a person, boots, etc.) fitted or provided with spurs.

spurt ● *verb* **1 a** *intransitive* gush out in a jet or stream. **b** *transitive* send out or expel (liquid, smoke, dust, etc.) in a jet or rapid stream; squirt. **2** *intransitive* move or act with a greater speed or exertion for a short time. **3** *intransitive* (of a stock, price, etc.) rise suddenly in price or value. ● *noun* **1** a short stream of liquid etc. ejected or thrown up with some force and suddenness. **2** a marked or sudden increase of speed or exertion. **3** a sudden unsustained period of activity, growth, effort, or exertion. **4** a marked increase or improvement, esp. in business, prices, etc. **5** *Cdn* (*Nfld*) a short period of time or activity (*a spurt of fishing*). [16th c.: origin unknown]

Sput·nik /ˈspʌtnɪk, ˈspʊt-/ *noun* (also **sputnik**) an unmanned Russian earth satellite, esp. each of a series of such satellites launched by the Soviet Union between 1957 and 1961. [Russian, = fellow-traveller]

sput·ter ● *verb* **1** *intransitive* **a** (esp. of a machine) emit a spitting, sizzling, or slight explosive sound or series of such sounds, often suggesting a struggling operation (*the boat sputtered as it finally neared the shore*; *he heard the radio sputter with static*). **b** proceed with difficulty, struggle; show signs of fatigue or failure (*the team has sputtered lately*). **2** *transitive & intransitive* say or speak in a hurried, confused, or incoherent manner, esp. from anger or excitement. **3** *transitive & intransitive* emit (liquid, food, smoke, sparks, etc.) in small particles or puffs with a spitting sound. **4** *transitive & intransitive* *Physics* **a** remove atoms of (a metal)

from a cathode by bombarding it with fast positive ions. **b** deposit (metal removed in this way) on another surface. **c** cover (a surface) with metal by sputtering. ● *noun* **1** the action or an act of stammering or producing a slight explosive sound or series of sounds, esp. with the emission of small particles. **2** such a sound, esp. while speaking. □ **sput·ter·er** *noun* **sput·tery** *adjective* [Dutch *sputteren* (imitative)]

spu·tum /ˈspjuːtəm/ *noun* (*pl.* **sputa**) **1** saliva, spittle. **2** a mixture of saliva and mucus coughed up from the respiratory tract, usu. a sign of certain diseases of the lungs, chest, or throat. [Latin, neuter past participle of *spuere* spit]

spy ● *noun* (*pl.* **spies**) **1** a person employed by a country or organization to collect and report secret information on esp. the military activities of an enemy or hostile foreign state, or on the activities of a rival organization. **2** a person who keeps watch on others, esp. furtively. **3** (**Spy**) = NORTHERN SPY. ● *verb* (**spies**, **spied**) **1** *transitive* catch sight of, discern, or make out, esp. by careful observation (*spied a house in the distance*). **2** *intransitive* work as a spy; be on the watch or lookout. □ **spy on** maintain a close and secret investigation or observation of a person or group. **spy out** find out or discover by observation or scrutiny. [Old French *espie* espying, *espier* espy, from Germanic]

spy·glass *noun* a small telescope.

spy hole *noun* esp. *Brit.* a peephole, especially one in a door for observing callers before opening.

spy·master *noun* *informal* the head of an organization of spies.

spy·ware *noun* *Computing* software that secretly gathers information from the user, e.g. that tracks the user's internet browsing for the purpose of targeting advertising (compare ADWARE).

SQ *abbreviation Cdn* (in Quebec) Sûreté du Québec (see SÛRETÉ).

sq. *abbreviation* square.

SQL *abbreviation Computing* structured query language.

Sqn *abbreviation* Squadron.

Sqn. Ldr. *abbreviation* SQUADRON LEADER.

squab /skwɒb/ *noun* **1** a newly hatched or very young bird, esp. an unfledged pigeon. **2** a stuffed cushion. [17th c.: origin unknown: compare obsolete *quab* shapeless thing, Swedish dial. *sqvabba* fat woman]

squab·ble ● *noun* a petty or noisy quarrel; a dispute. ● *intransitive verb* engage in a petty quarrel or argument. □ **squab·bler** *noun* [prob. imitative: compare Swedish dial. *sqvabbel* a dispute]

squad *noun* **1** a small group of people sharing a task etc. **2** *Military* a small number of soldiers assembled for drill or assigned to some special task. **3** *Sport informal* a group of players forming a team. **4 a** (often in *combination*) a specialized unit or division within a police force (*drug squad*). **b** = FLYING SQUAD. **5** a group or class of people of a specified kind. [French *escouade* var. of *escadre* from Italian *squadra* SQUARE]

squad car *noun* a police car having a radio link with headquarters.

squad·die *noun* (also **squad·dy**) (*pl.* **-dies**) *Brit. Military slang* **1** a recruit. **2** a private.

squad·ron *noun* **1** a principal division of an armoured or cavalry regiment consisting of two or more troops. **2** the basic administrative unit of an air force, usu. consisting of two or more flights. **3** a formal unit in a navy consisting of a number of ships. **4** often *jocular* an organized body of people or things. [Italian *squadrone* (as SQUAD)]

squadron leader *noun* (also **Squadron Leader**) (currently in the RAF or *hist.* in the RCAF) the commander of a squadron, an officer of a commissioned rank below wing commander and above flight lieutenant.

squal·ene /ˈskweiliːn/ *noun Biochem.* an oily liquid hydrocarbon which occurs in shark liver oil and human sebum, and is a metabolic precursor of sterols. [Latin *squalus* a kind of marine fish]

squal·id /ˈskwɒlɪd/ *adjective* **1** rundown, degenerate, unsanitary, esp. through neglect or poverty. **2** covered with filth or grime; repulsively dirty. **3** morally degraded (*a squalid lifestyle*). [Latin *squalidus* from *squalēre* be rough or dirty]

squall ● *noun* **1** a sudden and short-lived violent storm or gust of wind, esp. with rain, snow, or sleet. **2** a shrill cry or scream, as of a baby. **3** a disturbance or commotion; a quarrel. ● *intransitive verb* scream, cry out violently as in fear or pain. □ **squally** *adjective* [prob. from SQUEAL after BAWL]

squall line *noun Metereol.* a cold front along which squalls take place.

squal·or /ˈskwɒlɚ/ *noun* the state of being filthy or squalid. [Latin, as SQUALID]

squa·ma /ˈskweimə/ *noun* (*pl.* **squa·mae** /-miː/) **1** a scale on an animal or plant. **2** a thin scale-like plate of bone. □ **squa·mate** /-meit/ *adjective* [Latin *squama*]

Squa·mish¹ /ˈskwɒmɪʃ/ a district municipality in southwestern BC, situated at the mouth of the Squamish River and the head of Howe Sound, about 60 km north of Vancouver; pop. (2001) 14,247. [SQUAMISH²]

Squa·mish² /ˈskwɒmɪʃ/ ● *noun* **1** a member of an Aboriginal people living in southwestern BC. **2** the Salishan language of the Squamish. ● *adjective* of or relating to this people or their culture or language. [alteration of Squamish name for themselves]

squa·mous /ˈskweiməs/ *adjective* (also **squa·mose** /-moːs/) *Med. & Anat.* **1** (of a substance) covered with or composed of scales. **2 a** (of the skin) characterized by the development of scales. **b** (of a disease) accompanied by skin of this kind (*squamous carcinoma*).

squan·der *transitive verb* **1** spend (time, money, etc.) recklessly or lavishly; use or consume in a wasteful manner (*we have squandered many of our greatest natural resources*). **2** allow (an opportunity) to pass or be lost; miss (*he squandered the chance to redeem himself*). □ **squan·der·er** *noun* [16th c.: origin unknown]

square ● *noun* **1 a** a plane figure with four right angles and four equal straight sides. **b** any object of this shape or approximately this shape. **2 a** an open usu. four-sided area enclosed by buildings in a town or city, esp. one containing a small park or laid out with trees. **b** an open space resembling this, esp. an area within army barracks used for a drill. **3** an L-shaped or T-shaped instrument used esp. by a carpenter or architect to draw, obtain, or verify right angles. **4** the product of a number multiplied by itself (*81 is the square of 9*). **5** *slang* a conventional or old-fashioned person, esp. one ignorant of or opposed to current trends. **6** esp. *US* **a** a block of buildings bounded by four streets. **b** an open area at the meeting of streets. **7** *N Amer. slang* a square meal (*three squares a day*). **8** *N Amer.* **a** a dessert served cut into square pieces. **b** one of these pieces. **9** a small square area on a game board. **10** a body of infantry drawn up in rectangular form. ● *adjective* **1 a** having the shape of a square; bounded by four equal straight sides at right angles to each other. **b** having a cross-section in the form of a square. **2** having or in the form of a right angle (*table with square corners*). **3 a** (of a person, animal, or body) having a width more nearly equal to the height or length than is usual; solid, stocky. **b** (of a feature, such as the shoulders or nose) having a square outline; not round (*a square jaw*). **4 a** (*attributive*) designating a unit of measure equal to the area of a square whose side is one of the unit specified (*one square metre*). **b** (*predicative*) (of an area) being a square having four sides of the same specified length (*5 metres square*). **5 a** (often foll. by *with*) even, straight, level. **b** (usu. foll. by *to*) perpendicular; at right angles (*the wall is perfectly square to the floor*). **6** (also **all square**) **a** with all accounts settled, with no money owed; not in debt. **b** (of teams or scores) equal, tied. **7** fair and honest (*a square deal*). **8** uncompromising, direct, thorough (*was met with a square refusal*). **9** *slang* out of touch with the ideas and conventions of a current trend; conservative, old-fashioned. **10** properly arranged; in good order, settled (*got the books square*). **11** *Music* (of rhythm) simple, straightforward. ● *adverb* **1** *N Amer. informal* exactly, directly (*the ball hit him square on the nose*). **2** in a rectangular form or position; upright, straight (*sat square on his seat*). **3** in a straightforward manner; fairly, honestly (*won fair and square*). ● *verb* **1** *transitive* **a** make square or rectangular. **b** give a rectangular cross-section to (timber etc.). **2** *transitive* multiply (a number) by itself (*3 squared is 9*). **3** (usu. foll. by *to*, *with*) **a** *intransitive* correspond, harmonize, be consistent (*her conclusion doesn't square with her observations*). **b** *transitive* make consistent, harmonize, reconcile (*how do we square these solutions to our problem?*). **4** *transitive & intransitive* (usu. foll. by *up*) settle (an account, debt, etc.) by means of payment. **5 a** *transitive* place (one's shoulders) squarely facing forwards, esp. in a defensive position. **b** *intransitive* (often foll. by *up*, *around*) *Baseball* (of a batter) turn and set one's body in a crouch facing the pitcher with the bat held parallel to the ground while preparing to bunt. **6** *transitive* (usu. in *passive*) mark out in squares (*she drew a graph on squared paper*). **7** *transitive informal* satisfy or secure the compliance of (a person), esp. by bribery. **8** *transitive* tie (a game or series); make scores square. **9** *transitive Naut.* set or lay (yards, deadeyes, ratlines, etc.) horizontal. □ **back to square one** *informal* back to the starting point with no progress made. **on the square** *informal* ● *adjective* honest, fair. ● *adverb* honestly, fairly. **out of square** not at right angles. **square accounts with** see ACCOUNT. **square away** sail away with the yards squared. **squared away** *N Amer.* taken care of, dealt with, put in proper order. **square the circle 1** construct a square equal in area to a given circle (a problem incapable of a purely geometrical solution). **2** do what is impossible. **square off 1** *N Amer.*

assume the stance or crouch of a boxer. **2** *N Amer.* meet in competition or opposition. **3** mark out in squares. **square peg in a round hole** see PEG. **square up to 1** move towards (a person) in a fighting attitude. **2** face or tackle (a difficulty etc.) resolutely. □ **square·ly** *adverb* **square·ness** *noun* **squar·ish** *adjective* [Old French *esquare*, ultimately from EX-¹ + Latin *quadra* square]

square bashing *noun Military slang* drill on a parade ground or barrack square.

square brackets *plural noun* brackets of the form [ ].

square-built *adjective* having a broad or sturdy build or construction.

square dance esp. *N Amer.* ● *noun* a type of dance which starts with four couples facing one another in a square, with steps and movements shouted out by a caller. ● *intransitive verb* participate in a square dance. □ **square dancer** *noun*

square-eyed *adjective jocular* affected by or given to excessive viewing of television.

square-flipper seal *noun Cdn (Nfld)* = BEARDED SEAL.

square knot *noun* = REEF KNOT.

square meal *noun* a substantial and satisfying meal.

square number *noun* the square of an integer, e.g. 1, 4, 9, 16.

square-rigged *adjective Naut.* with the principal sails at right angles to the length of the ship and extended by horizontal yards slung to the mast by the middle (opp. FORE-AND-AFT RIGGED).

square root *noun* a number which produces a specified quantity when multiplied by itself (*3 is the square root of 9*).

square sail *noun* a four-cornered sail extended on a yard slung to the mast by the middle.

square shooter *noun* esp. *N Amer.* an honest dependable person. □ **square shooting** *adjective*

square-shouldered *adjective* with broad shoulders that do not slope.

square timber *noun Cdn hist.* logs cut into lengths with the round sides cut flat, leaving a timber with a cross-section usu. no more than ten inches square, ready to be rafted or shipped.

square-toed *adjective* **1** (of shoes or boots) having square toes. **2** old-fashioned, formal, prim.

square wave *noun Physics* a voltage represented by a periodic wave that varies abruptly in amplitude between two fixed values, spending equal time at each.

squash¹ ● *verb* **1** *transitive* crush or squeeze into a pulp, flat mass, or distorted shape. **2** *transitive* pack tightly, crowd together. **3** *transitive* reject, dismiss, silence, or suppress (*the assembly squashed his proposal*; *he was squashed by her criticism*). **4** *intransitive* (often foll. by *into*) make one's way by squeezing (*he squashed into the crowded subway car*). **5** *intransitive* flatten or be crushed under pressure. ● *noun* **1** a game for two or four players with racquets and a small fairly soft ball that is struck against the walls of a closed court. **2** *Brit.* a concentrated drink made of crushed fruit, such as oranges or lemons, diluted with water. **3 a** a substance, mass, or crowd, etc. that is or has been squashed. **b** a sound of or as of something being squashed. □ **squashy** *adjective* (**squash·i·er**, **squash·i·est**). **squash·i·ly** *adverb* **squash·i·ness** *noun* [alteration of QUASH]

squash² *noun* (*pl.* same or **squash·es**) **1** the fruit of any of several kinds of gourd, cooked and eaten as a vegetable esp. in N America, esp. that of *Cucurbita melo* (in full **summer squash**), eaten before the seeds and rinds have hardened, and that of *C. maxima* or *C. moschata* (in full **winter squash**), stored and eaten when matured. **2** any of the various trailing plants producing this fruit. [obsolete (*i*)*squoutersquash* from Narragansett *asquutasquash* from *asq* uncooked + *squash* green]

squash·berry *noun* (*pl.* **-berries**) *Cdn* the edible fruit of several N American shrubs, that of *Viburnum edule*, used to make jam. Also called LOWBUSH CRANBERRY (see LOWBUSH 2).

squash bug *noun* a N American hemipterous bug, *Anasa tristis*, which is a pest of squash, pumpkins, and melons.

squat ● *verb* (**squat·ted**, **squat·ting**) **1** *intransitive* **a** crouch on the balls of one's feet with the hams resting on the backs of the heels. **b** sit on the ground etc. with the knees drawn up and the heels close to or touching the buttocks. **2 a** *intransitive* settle on new, uncultivated, or unoccupied land without any legal title and without the payment of rent. **b** *intransitive* live without legal right on land or in premises otherwise unoccupied. **c** *transitive* occupy (a property or building) as a squatter. **3** *Weightlifting* **a** *intransitive* perform a squat. **b** *transitive* lift (a certain weight) while performing a squat. **4** *intransitive* (of an animal) crouch close to the ground. ● *adjective* (**squat·ter**, **squat·test**) **1** disproportionately broad or wide; short and fat. **2** in a squatting posture. ● *noun* **1** *N Amer. slang* = DIDDLY-SQUAT. **2** a property occupied by a squatter or squatters. **3** *Weightlifting* an exercise or lift in which a person squats down and rises again while carrying a barbell behind the neck. **4** a squatting posture. [Old French *esquatir* 'flatten', from *es-* EX-¹ + *quatir* 'press down, crouch', ultimately from Latin *coactus*, past participle of *cogere* 'compel': see COGENT]

squat·ter *noun* **1** an unauthorized or illegal occupant of otherwise unoccupied land or premises. **2** *hist.* **a** a settler with no legal title to the land occupied, esp. one on land not yet allocated by a government. **b** a person who has obtained a tract of land from the government on easy terms (also *attributive: squatter settlement*).

squat thrust *noun* an exercise in which the legs are thrust backwards starting from a squatting position with the hands on the floor.

squat·ty *adjective* *N Amer.* rather squat; somewhat short and broad or fat.

squaw *noun offensive* **1** a N American Indian woman or wife. **2** *slang* any woman or girl, esp. one who is a wife. [Narragansett *squaws* woman]

squaw·fish *noun* either of two large freshwater fish-eating fishes, *Ptychocheilus oregonensis* and *P. lucius* of NW Canada and the US, formerly important food fishes for N American Indians. Now officially called PIKEMINNOW.

squawk ● *noun* **1** a loud harsh cry esp. of a bird. **2** a loud complaint or protest. ● *verb* **1** *intransitive* utter a squawk. **2** *transitive* utter with a squawk. **3** *intransitive* complain or protest loudly or vehemently. **4** *transitive* (of an aircraft) transmit (a signal) as identification. □ **squawk·er** *noun* [imitative]

squawk box *noun informal* **1** an intercom. **2** the loudspeaker of a public address system.

squaw root *noun* any of various N American plants, e.g. cohosh or the broomrape, *Conopholis americana*, parasitic on roots of trees. [from the former practice amongst Native peoples of using cohosh to treat female disorders]

squeak ● *noun* **1** a sharp, shrill, high-pitched sound or cry. **2** = NARROW SQUEAK. ● *verb* **1** *intransitive* make or emit a thin high-pitched cry or squeak. **2** *transitive* utter or sing in a shrill voice. **3** *intransitive* (usu. foll. by *by, through*) *informal* manage, succeed, or pass by only a narrow margin. **4** *intransitive slang* turn informer. [Middle English, imitative: compare SQUEAL, SHRIEK, and Swedish *skväka* croak]

squeak·er *noun* **1** esp. *N Amer.* a game, election, etc. won by a narrow margin. **2** a person or thing that squeaks.

squeaky *adjective* (**squeak·i·er, squeak·i·est**) tending to squeak. □ **squeak·i·ly** *adverb* **squeak·i·ness** *noun*

squeaky clean *adjective* **1** above reproach; respectable, upstanding. **2** completely clean.

squeaky toy *noun* (also **squeeze toy**) a plush or plastic toy containing a device that emits a squeak when squeezed.

squeaky wheel *noun* a person who complains greatly. [with reference to the proverb 'the squeaky wheel gets the grease']

squeal ● *noun* a long shrill sound, such as the cry of a pig or an exclamation of delight. ● *verb* **1** *intransitive* make a squeal. **2** *transitive* utter (words) with a squeal. **3** *intransitive* (often foll. by *on*) *slang* reveal confidential information about a person; turn informer against. **4** *intransitive slang* protest loudly or excitedly. □ **squeal·er** *noun* [Middle English, imitative]

squeam·ish *adjective* **1** easily turned sick, disgusted, or faint. **2** fastidious or over-scrupulous in questions of propriety, honesty, etc. □ **squeam·ish·ly** *adverb* **squeam·ish·ness** *noun* [Middle English var. of *squeamous* (now dial.), from Anglo-French *escoymos*, of unknown origin]

squee·gee /ˈskwiːdʒiː/ ● *noun* **1** an implement with a handle attached to a wide rubber blade used to remove the excess liquid from glass when cleaning windows. **2** a rubber strip, pad, or roller used for squeezing or wiping moisture from a print, pressing a film closer to its mount, etc. ● *transitive verb* (**squee·gees, squee·geed**) clean or treat (glass, photographic film, etc.) with a squeegee. [*squeege*, strengthened form of SQUEEZE]

squeegee kid *noun N Amer. informal* a youth who offers to clean the windows of cars stopped at a traffic light, esp. for money.

squeeze ● *verb* **1** *transitive* **a** exert pressure on from opposite or all sides, esp. in order to extract moisture or reduce size. **b** compress with one's hand or between two bodies. **c** reduce the size of or alter the shape of by squeezing. **2** *transitive* (usu. foll. by *out*) **a** extract (moisture) by squeezing. **b** produce with effort (*squeezed a tear out*). **3 a** *transitive* force or cram (a person or thing) into or through a small or narrow space. **b** *transitive* (often foll. by *in*) fit (a person or activity) into a busy

schedule, day, etc. (*she's awfully busy, but she might squeeze you in*). **c** *transitive & intransitive* make (one's way) by squeezing. **4** *transitive* **a** exert financial pressure on; impose financial hardship on. **b** put pressure on (a person); harass, constrain. **c** obtain or extort (money etc.) from a person by force, pressure, entreaty, etc. **5** *transitive* **a** press (a person's arm, elbow, hand, etc.) with one's hand as a sign of sympathy, affection, etc. **b** hug or embrace (a person) firmly. **6** *transitive* **a** (often foll. by *off*) *informal* fire (a shot, round, etc.) from a gun. **b** pull or depress (the trigger of a gun). **7** *Bridge* subject (a player) to a squeeze. ● *noun* **1** an instance of squeezing; the state of being squeezed. **2** a state of being forced into a small, restricted, or crowded space (*you can sit with the others in the back seat but it will be a tight squeeze*). **3 a** *Econ.* a strong financial demand or pressure, esp. a restriction on borrowing, investment, etc., in a financial crisis. **b** mental or emotional pressure, a constraining influence; coercion. **4 a** a hug or close embrace. **b** strong or firm pressure of the hand on the arm etc. of another as a sign of friendship or affection. **5** *N Amer. slang* = MAIN SQUEEZE. **6 a** a small quantity squeezed out of something (*a squeeze of lemon*). **b** a sum of money extorted or exacted, esp. an illicit commission. **7** *Baseball* **a** (in full **squeeze play**) a play in which the batter attempts to bring a player home from third on a sacrifice bunt. **b** (in full **suicide squeeze**) a similar play in which the baserunner breaks towards the plate just as the pitch has left the pitcher's hand, before a successful bunt has been made. **8** a difficult situation; a bind. **9** (in full **squeeze play**) *Bridge* a tactic used to force an opponent to discard or unguard a potentially winning card. □ **put the squeeze on** *informal* coerce or pressure (a person). □ **squeez·able** *adjective* **squeez·er** *noun* [earlier *squise*, intensive of obsolete *queise*, of unknown origin]

squeeze bottle *noun* a bottle made of flexible plastic from which contents, esp. condiments, may be dispensed by squeezing.

squeeze·box *noun informal* an accordion or concertina.

squeeze bunt *noun Baseball* a sacrifice bunt attempted while executing a squeeze play.

squeeze toy *noun* = SQUEAKY TOY.

squelch ● *verb* **1** *intransitive* **a** walk or tread heavily in mud, on wet ground, or with water in the shoes, so as to make a sucking sound. **b** make or emit a sucking sound. **2** *transitive* crush, silence, suppress, extinguish; put an end to (an idea, plan, rally, etc.). ● *noun* **1** a sucking sound as made by falling or walking on wet muddy ground. **2** (in full **squelch circuit**) *Radio* a circuit that suppresses the output of a receiver if the signal strength falls below a certain level. □ **squelchy** *adjective* [imitative]

squib ● *noun* **1** a small firework burning with a hissing sound and usu. a final slight explosion. **2 a** a short piece of writing or written information, esp. a brief news item used as a filler in a newspaper. **b** a short satirical composition, a lampoon. **3** (also **squib·ber**) (esp. in baseball and football) a weakly hit or kicked ball. **4** *derogatory* a meek or cowardly person, esp. a child. ● *verb* (**squibbed, squib·bing**) **1** *transitive* (esp. in baseball or football) hit or kick (the ball) weakly so that it travels only a short distance. **2** *intransitive* (of a ball) travel a short distance after being hit or kicked weakly. [16th c.: origin unknown: perhaps imitative]

SQUID /skwɪd/ *noun* a device capable of detecting small changes in a magnetic field used esp. to record or detect neural activity in the brain. [acronym from superconducting *quantum interference device*]

squid *noun* any of various fast-swimming marine cephalopods of the order Teuthoidea, having an elongated body with two stabilizing fins at the back, eight arms in a ring around two longer tentacles at the front, and a reduced internal horny shell, esp. any of the common edible squid of the genera *Loligo* and *Illex*. [17th c.: origin unknown]

squidgy *adjective* (**squidg·i·er, squidg·i·est**) *informal* soft, squashy, soggy, or moist. [imitative]

squid jigger *noun Cdn (Nfld)* a weighted line with several tiny esp. unbaited hooks, used to catch small squid for bait. □ **squid jigging** *noun*

squiffed *adjective slang* slightly drunk. [19th c.: origin unknown]

squif·fy *adjective* (**squif·fi·er, squif·fi·est**) esp. *Brit. slang* = SQUIFFED. [19th c.: origin unknown]

squig·gle ● *noun* a short curly or wavy line, esp. in handwriting or doodling. ● *verb* **1** *transitive* write in squiggles; scrawl. **2** *intransitive* wriggle, squirm. □ **squig·gly** *adjective* [imitative]

squill *noun* **1 a** a scilla, typically with star-shaped blue flowers. **b** (in full **striped squill**) the related plant *Puschkinia scilloides*. **2** a white-flowered Mediterranean plant, *Drimia maritima*, of the lily family. **3** a crustacean of the genus *Squilla* with spiny front legs like a mantis. [Middle English via Latin *squilla, scilla* from Greek *skilla*]

Vowels: a *cat* ɑ *arm* e *bed* ɜr *her* ɜ: *deux* ə *ago* ɪ *sit* i *cosy* iː *feed* ɒ *hot* ɔ *pore* ɔː *no* ʌ *run* ʊ *put*

squil·lion *noun Brit.* an indefinite very large number.

squinch[1] *noun* a straight or arched structure across an interior angle of a square tower to carry a superstructure, e.g. a dome. [var. of obsolete *scunch*, abbreviation of SCUNCHEON]

squinch[2] *verb* esp. *N Amer.* **1** (usu. foll. by *up*) **a** *transitive* screw up one's eyes, face, etc. **b** *intransitive* (of the eyes etc.) screw up, squint. **2** *transitive & intransitive* (often foll. by *up, down*) squeeze or squash compactly. [perhaps a blend of SQUEEZE *verb* + PINCH *verb*]

squint ● *verb* **1** *intransitive* (often foll. by *at*) look obliquely or with the eyes partly closed, esp. in order to see something better or because of very bright light. **2** *transitive* close (one's eyes) quickly; hold (one's eyes) half-shut. **3** *intransitive* suffer from a disorder of the eye muscles which causes each eye to look in a different direction. ● *noun* **1** a permanent deviation or defective alignment of one or both eyes; strabismus. **2** a stealthy or sidelong glance through half-closed eyes. **3** *informal* a glance or look (*have a squint at this*). **4** a leaning or inclination towards a particular object or aim. **5** an oblique opening through the wall of a church affording a view of the altar. □ **squinty** *adjective* [ASQUINT: (adj.) perhaps from *squint-eyed* from obsolete *squint* (adv.) from ASQUINT]

squinty-eyed *adjective* (also **squint-eyed**) cross-eyed, squinting.

squire ● *noun* **1** (in Britain) a country gentleman, esp. the chief landowner in a country district. **2** *hist.* a young nobleman serving as a knight's attendant. **3** *Brit. informal* a jocular form of address to a man. ● *transitive verb* (of a man) attend upon or escort (a woman). □ **squire·ly** *adjective* [Old French *esquier* ESQUIRE]

squire·arch /ˈskwair‚ark/ *noun* (also **squir·arch**) (in Britain) a member of the class of landowners, esp. having political or social influence. □ **squire·arch·ical** *adjective* **squire·archy** *noun* (*pl.* **-ies**).

squirm *intransitive verb* **1** wriggle, writhe. **2** show or feel embarrassment or discomfiture. □ **squirmy** *adjective* (**squirm·i·er, squirm·i·est**). [imitative, prob. assoc. with WORM]

squir·rel ● *noun* **1 a** any of various slender agile arboreal rodents having a long bushy tail, a furry coat, and pointy ears, esp. of the genus *Sciurus* and related genera, noted for hoarding nuts for food in winter. **b** any of various arboreal or ground-dwelling rodents, esp. of the family Sciuridae. **2** *N Amer.* the meat of the squirrel. **3** the fur of the squirrel. **4** a person who hoards objects, food, etc. ● *verb* (**squir·relled, squir·rel·ling;** also **squir·reled, squir·rel·ing**) **1** *transitive* (usu. foll. by *away*) store or save; hoard (objects, food, time, etc.) (*squirrelled it away in the cupboard*). **2** *intransitive* (often foll. by *around*) move about in an active or industrious manner; bustle, scurry. [Old French *esquireul*, ultimately from Latin *sciurus* from Greek *skiouros* from *skia* shade + *oura* tail]

squirrel cage *noun* **1** a small cage for a squirrel, esp. one containing a stationary revolving wheel like a treadmill on which the captive squirrel may exercise. **2** (*attributive*) (usu. **squirrel-cage**) designating an electric appliance containing a small electric rotor or other device having a series of bars, rods, etc., arranged parallel to the axis of a cylinder (*squirrel-cage fan*). **3** a monotonous or repetitive task, assignment, etc.

squirrel fish *noun* any of various brightly coloured tropical fish with large eyes of the family Holocentridae.

squir·rel·ly *adjective* **1** restless, fidgety, anxious. **2** eccentric, crazy.

squirrel monkey *noun* a small yellow-haired monkey, *Saimiri sciureus*, native to S America.

squirt ● *verb* **1** *transitive* eject or propel (a liquid or semi-liquid substance) in a jet-like stream, esp. from a small opening. **2** *intransitive* (of liquid or a semi-liquid substance) be discharged in this way. **3** *transitive* splash with liquid ejected by squirting. **4 a** *intransitive* (often foll. by *free* or *loose*) be lost or dropped; slip or fall, esp. from one's hand. **b** *intransitive* move suddenly and unpredictably. ● *noun* **1 a** a jet or stream of liquid. **b** a small quantity produced by squirting. **2** *informal* **a** a young person, esp. a meddlesome child. **b** an insignificant but presumptuous person. **3 a** an initiation level of sports competition for young children. **b** a player at this level. □ **squirt·er** *noun* [Middle English, imitative]

squirt gun *noun N Amer.* a water pistol.

squish esp. *N Amer.* ● *verb* **1** *intransitive* yield easily to pressure when walked upon, squeezed, or squashed, esp. making a gushing or squelching sound. **2** *transitive* crush, squash, or squeeze. **3** *transitive & intransitive* force or be forced into a small space; pack or be packed tightly (*there were eight of us in the car and we were squished!*). **4** *intransitive* move with a squishing sound. ● *noun* **1** the sound of something as it is crushed or squashed; a slight squelching sound. **2** the feel of

something as it is squished (*the squish of sand beneath his toes*). [imitative]

squishy (**squish·i·er, squish·i·est**) *adjective* **1** of a soft wet texture that yields easily to pressure. **2 a** lacking strength or substance (*a squishy philosophy*). **b** feebly sentimental; mushy.

squit·ters *plural noun informal* diarrhea. [perhaps from dialect *squit* 'to squirt']

squoosh *transitive & intransitive verb N Amer. informal* squash, squish. □ **squooshy** *adjective* [alteration of SQUASH[1]]

SR *abbreviation* **1** side road. **2** speech rate. **3** *Psych.* stimulus-response.

Sr *symbol* the element strontium.

Sr. *abbreviation* **1** Senior. **2** Señor. **3** Signor. **4** Sir. **5** *Christianity* Sister.

sr *abbreviation* steradian(s).

Sra. *abbreviation* Señora.

SRAM /ˈesram/ *abbreviation Computing* static random access memory.

Sreb·re·nica /‚srebreˈnitsə/ a town in eastern Bosnia-Herzegovina; pop. (est. 2002) 7,000. The town was the scene of a massacre of thousands of Muslim men by Serb forces in 1995. It was included in Serb-held territory in the 1995 partition of Bosnia-Herzegovina.

Sri /ʃri, sri/ *noun* (also **Shri**) (in the Indian subcontinent) a title of respect preceding the name of a deity or distinguished person, or the title of a sacred book. [Sanskrit 'beauty']

Sri Lanka /ʃri ˈlaŋkə, sri-/ (formerly called **Ceylon**) an island country off the southeast coast of India; pop. (est. 2002) 19,576,783; capital, Colombo. □ **Sri Lan·kan** *adjective & noun* [lit., 'resplendent island']

Sri·nagar /ʃriˈnʌgər, sri-/ a city in NW India, the summer capital of the state of Jammu and Kashmir, situated on the Jhelum River in the foothills of the Himalayas; pop. (2001) 894,900.

SRO *abbreviation* **1** standing room only. **2** single-room occupancy.

SRP *abbreviation* suggested retail price.

SRS *abbreviation* supplemental restraint system.

SS[1] *abbreviation* **1** Saints. **2** steamship. **3** secondary school. **4** *Cdn* SCHOOL SECTION. **5** shortstop. **6** Sunday School.

SS[2] *hist.* a ruthless Nazi special police force which included the Gestapo, founded in 1925 by Hitler as a personal bodyguard, and headed by Himmler from 1929 until 1945. It was responsible for security and for administering the concentration camps, and also provided combat units independent of the armed forces. [German *Schutzstaffel* defence squadron]

SSC *abbreviation* Superconducting Super Collider.

SSE *abbreviation* south-southeast.

S/Sgt. *abbreviation* STAFF SERGEANT.

SSHRC /ʃɜrk/ *abbreviation* Social Sciences and Humanities Research Council (of Canada).

ssp. *abbreviation Biol.* subspecies.

SSR *abbreviation hist.* Soviet Socialist Republic.

SSRI *abbreviation* SELECTIVE SEROTONIN REUPTAKE INHIBITOR.

SSW *abbreviation* south-southwest.

St. *abbreviation* **1** Street. **2** Saint.

st. *abbreviation* stone (in weight).

-st *var. of* -EST[2].

Sta. *abbreviation* Station.

stab ● *verb* (**stabbed, stab·bing**) **1** *transitive* pierce or wound with a (usu. short) pointed tool or weapon, e.g. a knife or dagger. **2** *intransitive* (often foll. by *at*) aim a blow with such a weapon. **3** *intransitive* cause a sensation like being stabbed (*stabbing pain*). **4** *transitive* hurt or distress (a person, feelings, conscience, etc.). **5** *transitive* pierce (a hole) in something. **6** *transitive* thrust (a pointed object) into or through something. **7 a** *transitive* direct (the hand, finger, etc.) in a jabbing lunge or gesture. **b** *intransitive* (of the hand, finger, etc.) make such a gesture. ● *noun* **1 a** an instance of stabbing. **b** a blow or thrust with a knife etc. **2** a wound made in this way. **3** a sharply painful physical or mental sensation. **4** *informal* (usu. foll. by *at*) an attempt, a try (*took a stab at it*). **5** a vigorous thrust; a jabbing lunge or gesture. □ **stab in the back 1** a treacherous or slanderous attack. **2** slander or betray. **stab in the dark** a blind attempt; an effort made without adequate information. □ **stab·ber** *noun* **stab·bing** *noun* [Middle English: origin unknown]

Sta·bat Mat·er /‚stabət ˈmater/ *noun* **1** a Latin hymn on the suffering of the Virgin Mary at the Crucifixion. **2** a musical setting for this. [the opening words, Latin *Stabat mater dolorosa* 'Stood the mother, full of grief']

sta·bil·ity /stəˈbɪlɪti/ *noun* the quality or state of being stable.

sta·bil·iz·a·tion *noun* an act or instance of making or becoming stable.

stabilization payment *noun Cdn* a payment made esp. by the federal government to a region or sector in order to stabilize a faltering economy.

sta·bil·ize /ˈsteɪbɪˌlaɪz/ *transitive & intransitive verb* (also esp. *Brit.* **-ise**) make or become stable.

sta·bil·iz·er *noun* (also esp. *Brit.* **-iser**) a device or substance used to keep something stable, esp.: **1** *N Amer.* the horizontal tailplane of an aircraft. **2** a gyroscopic device to prevent rolling of a ship. **3** a substance which prevents the breakdown of emulsions, esp. as a food additive maintaining texture. **4** (in *pl.*) *Brit.* = TRAINING WHEEL.

stabilizer bar *noun* esp. *N Amer.* a bar attached to the suspension of a motor vehicle, designed to reduce rolling when cornering.

stable¹ *adjective* (**sta·bler**, **sta·blest**) **1** firmly fixed or established; not easily adjusted, destroyed, disturbed or altered (*a stable structure*; *a stable government*). **2 a** firm, resolute; not wavering or fickle (*a stable and steadfast friend*). **b** mentally and emotionally sound; sane and sensible. **3** *Chem.* (of a compound) not readily decomposing. **4** *Physics* (of an isotope) not subject to radioactive decay. **5** in a stable medical condition after an injury, operation, etc. □ **stably** *adverb* [Old French *estable* from Latin *stabilis* from *stare* stand]

stable² ● *noun* **1** a building or part of one adapted for keeping horses. **2** an establishment where racehorses are kept and trained. **3** the racehorses of a particular stable. **4 a** persons, products, etc., having a common origin or affiliation. **b** such an origin or affiliation. ● *transitive verb* put or keep (a horse) in a stable. [Old French *estable* from Latin *stabulum* from *stare* stand]

stable·boy *noun* a boy employed in a stable.

stable cleaner *noun Cdn.* a machine that removes manure from a barn or stable.

stable fly *noun* a biting fly of the species *Stomoxys calcitrans*, breeding in decaying vegetation and often feeding on the blood of domestic livestock.

stable·man *noun* (*pl.* **-men**) a person employed in a stable.

stable·mate *noun* **1** a horse of the same stable. **2** a person, product, etc. from the same source; a member of the same organization etc.

sta·bling *noun* accommodation for horses.

stac·ca·to /stəˈkɑːtoʊ, -ˈkɒtoʊ/ ● *adverb & adjective* **1** *Music* with each note sharply detached or separated from the others (*compare* LEGATO, TENUTO). **2** with short and sharp sounds (*a staccato burst of gunfire*). ● *noun* (*pl.* **-tos**) **1** a staccato passage in music etc. **2** staccato delivery or presentation. [Italian, past participle of *staccare* = *distaccare* DETACH]

stack ● *noun* **1** a pile or heap, esp. in orderly arrangement. **2** a circular or rectangular pile of hay, straw, etc. **3** *informal* a large quantity (*a stack of work*; *has stacks of money*). **4 a** = CHIMNEY STACK. **b** = SMOKESTACK. **5** a stacked group of aircraft. **6** (in *pl.*) a part of a library where most of the books are stored on shelving, often one to which the public does not have direct access. **7** *Computing* a set of storage locations which store data in such a way that the most recently stored item is the first to be retrieved. **8** a vertical arrangement of stereo components, speakers, public address equipment, etc. **9** a pyramidal pile of rifles. **10** *Brit.* a measure for a pile of wood of 108 cu. ft. (3.06 cubic metres). **11** a vertical vent pipe or waste pipe. ● *transitive verb* **1** pile in a stack or stacks. **2** arrange (cards) secretly for cheating. **3** cause (aircraft) to fly around the same point at different levels while waiting to land at an airport. **4** create a disproportion in the representation on (a committee etc.) so that it will act in one's interests. □ **blow one's stack** *see* BLOW¹. **stack the deck** (or **cards**) cause (circumstances etc.) to favour one person, group, etc. over another. **stack up** *N Amer. informal* present oneself, measure up. □ **stack·able** *adjective* **stack·er** *noun* [Old Norse *stakkr* 'haystack', from Germanic]

stacked *adjective* **1 a** put into a stack or stacks. **b** piled with goods etc. **2 a** (of odds) biased, esp. unfavourably. **b** (of circumstances etc.) (foll. by *against*) unfavourable to. **3** (of a woman) having large breasts. **4** (of an aircraft) being one of a number of aircraft flying around the same point at different levels while waiting to land.

stacking chair *noun* a chair designed so that it can be stacked with others like it for efficient storage.

stack·yard *noun* an enclosure for stacks of hay, straw, etc.

stacte /ˈstaktiː/ *noun* a sweet spice used by the ancient Jews in making incense. [Latin from Greek *staktē* from *stazō* drip]

Stad·a·cona /ˌstadəˈkoʊnə/ a former Iroquoian village located at the present-day site of Quebec City.

sta·dium /ˈsteɪdiəm/ *noun* (*pl.* **-diums** or **sta·dia**) **1** an athletic or sports ground with tiers of seats for spectators. **2** *hist.* **a** (in ancient Greece and Rome) a course for a foot race or chariot race. **b** (in ancient Rome) a measure of length, about 185 metres. **3** a stage or period of development etc. [Latin from Greek *stadion*]

stadium seating *noun* an arrangement of seats, esp. in a movie theatre, in which each row of seats is on a tier one step higher than the one in front of it.

stadt·hold·er /ˈstɒdˌhoʊldər, ˈstɒt-, ˈstɑː-/ *noun* (also **stad·hold·er**) *hist.* **1** the chief magistrate of the United Provinces of the Netherlands. **2** the viceroy or governor of a province or town in the Netherlands. [Dutch *stadhouder* deputy, from *stad* STEAD + *houder* HOLDER, after medieval Latin LOCUM TENENS (*see* LOCUM)]

Staël /stɒl/ **Madame de** (born Anne Louise Germaine Necker) (1766–1817), French novelist and critic. A precursor of French Romanticism, she is best known for the novels *Delphine* (1802) and *Corinne* (1807), and the critical work *De l'Allemagne* (1810).

staff¹ ● *noun* (*pl.* **staffs**) **1** (*pl.* also **staves**) **a** a stick or pole for use in walking or climbing or as a weapon. **b** a stick or pole as a sign of office or authority. **c** a person or thing that supports or sustains. **d** a flagpole. **e** *Surveying* a rod for measuring distances, heights, etc. **2 a** a body of persons employed in a business etc. (*editorial staff of a newspaper*; often *attributive*: *staff writer*; *staff lawyers*). **b** those in authority within an organization, esp. the teachers in a school. **c** *Mil. etc.* a body of officers assisting an officer in high command and concerned with an army, regiment, fleet, or air force as a whole (*general staff*). **d** (in full **pitching staff**) *Baseball* all of a team's pitchers. **3** (*pl.* also **staves**) *Music* a set of usu. five parallel lines in relation to which a note is placed to indicate its pitch. ● *transitive verb* **1** provide (an institution etc.) with staff. **2** work as a member of staff in (an institution etc.). □ **on staff** serving as a member of an organization's staff. □ **staffed** *adjective* (also in *combination*). **staff·ing** *noun* [Old English *stæf* from Germanic]

staff² *noun* a mixture of plaster of Paris, cement, etc., as a temporary building material. [19th c.: origin unknown]

staff college *noun* a college at which military officers are trained for staff duties.

staff·er *noun* esp. *N Amer.* a member of a staff, esp. of a newspaper.

staff inspector *noun* (in some Canadian municipal police forces) an officer ranking above inspector and below superintendent.

staff nurse *noun Brit.* a nurse ranking just below a sister.

staff officer *noun Military* an officer serving on the staff of an army etc.

Staf·ford an industrial town in central England, to the south of Stoke-on-Trent; pop. (est. 2002) 62,800.

Staf·ford·shire /ˈstafərdˌʃɪr/ a county of central England; county town, Stafford.

Staffordshire bull terrier *noun* a dog of a small stocky breed of terrier, with a short broad head and dropped ears.

staff room *noun* esp. *Cdn & Brit.* **1** a common room for staff, esp. in a school. **2** the staff themselves.

staff sergeant *noun* **1** (in some Canadian police forces) an officer ranking above sergeant and below inspector. **2** (in the Ontario Provincial Police) an officer ranking above sergeant and below sergeant major. **3** (in the Royal Newfoundland Constabulary) an officer ranking above sergeant and below lieutenant. **4** (in the RCMP) an officer ranking above sergeant and below staff sergeant major. **5** (in the US) a non-commissioned officer ranking just above sergeant. **6** (in the UK) the senior sergeant of a non-infantry company. **7** *hist.* (in the Canadian Army before unification) a non-commissioned officer of a rank above sergeant.

staff sergeant major *noun* (in the RCMP) an officer ranking above staff sergeant and below sergeant major.

staff superintendent *noun* (in some Canadian municipal police forces) an officer ranking above superintendent and below deputy chief.

stag ● *noun* **1** an adult male deer, esp. one with a set of antlers. **2** *N Amer.* = STAG PARTY. **3** a man who attends a social gathering unaccompanied by a woman. ● *attributive adjective* **1** of, for, or composed of men only (*a stag gathering*). **2** pornographic (*a stag film*). ● *adverb* without a date, unaccompanied (*went stag*). [Middle English, related to Old Norse *steggr* male bird, Icelandic *steggi* tomcat.]

stag and doe *noun* (in full **stag and doe party**) *Cdn* (*Ont.*) a dance held in honour of an engaged couple, to whom the money raised from ticket sales is given.

stag beetle *noun* any beetle of the family Lucanidae, the male of which has large branched mandibles resembling a stag's antlers.

stage ● *noun* **1** a point or period in a process or development (*reached a critical stage; is in the larval stage*). **2 a** a raised floor or platform, esp. one on which plays etc. are performed before an audience. **b** (prec. by *the*) the acting or theatrical profession, esp. live theatre as opposed to film or television. **c** the art of writing or presenting plays. **d** the scene of action (*the stage of politics*). **e** = LANDING STAGE. **3** *Cdn* (*Nfld*) = FISHING STAGE. **4 a** a regular stopping place on a route. **b** the distance between two stopping places. **5** a section of a rocket with a separate engine, jettisoned when its propellant is exhausted. **6** *Geol.* a range of strata forming a subdivision of a series. **7** *Electronics* a single amplifying transistor or valve with the associated equipment. **8** a raised plate on which an object is placed for inspection through a microscope. **9** = STAGECOACH. ● *verb* **1** *transitive* present (a theatrical production) on stage. **2** *transitive* arrange the occurrence of (*staged a demonstration; staged a comeback*). **3** *transitive* (esp. as **staged** *adjective*) present or arrange a contrived, spurious, or mock version of (an event) (*it had all been staged*). **4** *intransitive* (esp. of migrating animals) stop at a regular place on a route. □ **by easy stages** gradually; without sudden or disproportionate changes. **go on the stage** become an actor. **hold the stage** dominate a conversation etc. **on** (**the**) **stage** performing as an actor, dancer, singer, etc. (*back on the stage after an injury*). **set the stage** (usu. foll. by *for*) prepare the way or conditions for (an event etc.). □ **stage·able** *adjective* [Old French *estage* 'dwelling', ultimately from Latin *stare* 'stand']

stage band *noun* a usu. small musical ensemble consisting esp. of saxophones, trumpets, trombones, and drums, often also accompanied by guitars, performing esp. swing and jazz (compare CONCERT BAND, MARCHING BAND).

stage business *noun* action on stage (as opposed to dialogue).

stage·coach *noun hist.* a large closed horse-drawn coach running regularly by stages between two places.

stage·craft *noun* skill in mounting theatrical performances and creating theatrical effect.

stage direction *noun* an instruction in the text of a play as to the movement, position, tone, etc., of an actor, or sound effects etc.

stage-dive *intransitive verb* (of a performer or audience member) leap from a stage so as to land on top of the crowd at a music concert.

stage door *noun* an entrance from the street to a theatre behind the stage, usu. reserved for performers and stage crew etc.

stage door Johnny *noun N Amer. slang* a man who frequents the stage door or backstage areas of theatres in the hope of meeting (esp. female) performers.

stage effect *noun* **1** an effect produced in acting or on the stage. **2** an artificial or theatrical effect produced in real life.

stage fright *noun* nervousness on facing an audience.

stage·hand *noun* a person handling scenery etc. during a performance on stage.

stage·head *noun Cdn* (*Nfld*) the part of a fishing stage which extends over the water.

stage left *noun* the part of a stage which is to the left of a person facing the audience.

stage-manage *transitive verb* **1** be the stage manager of. **2** arrange and control for effect.

stage manager *noun* the person responsible for overseeing the details of a performance, giving cues to performers, stage hands, lighting crew, etc. □ **stage management** *noun*

stage mother *noun* a mother involved to a great or excessive extent in the performance career of her child.

stage name *noun* a name assumed for professional purposes by a theatrical performer.

stage play *noun* a play performed on stage rather than broadcast etc.

stage presence *noun* a performer's ability to rivet the audience's attention while on stage.

sta·ger *noun* **1** in senses of STAGE *verb*. **2** see OLD STAGER.

stage right *noun* the part of a stage which is to the right of a person facing the audience.

stage-struck *adjective* **1** filled with a passionate desire to become an actor. **2** passionately interested in the theatre and everything associated with it.

stag·ette *noun* an all-female celebration in honour of a woman about to marry.

stage whisper ● *noun* **1** a loud whisper addressed by one actor to another, meant to be heard by the audience; an aside. **2** any loud whisper meant to be heard by people other than the person addressed. ● *transitive verb* (**stage-whisper**) utter in a loud whisper.

stage-worthy *adjective* (of a play etc.) worthy of presentation on the stage. □ **stage·worthi·ness** *noun*

sta·gey *var. of* STAGY.

stag·fla·tion *noun Econ.* a state of inflation without a corresponding increase of demand and employment. [STAGNATION (as STAGNATE) + INFLATION]

stag·ger ● *verb* **1** *intransitive* walk unsteadily, totter. **b** *transitive* cause to totter (*was staggered by the blow*). **2 a** *transitive* shock, confuse; cause to hesitate or waver (*the question staggered them; they were staggered at the suggestion*). **b** *intransitive* hesitate; waver in purpose. **3** *transitive* arrange (events, hours of work, etc.) so that they do not coincide. **4** *transitive* arrange (objects, people, etc.) so that they are not in line. ● *noun* **1** a tottering movement. **2** (*in pl.*) **a** any of various parasitic or deficiency diseases of farm animals marked by staggering or loss of balance. **b** giddiness. **3** an overhanging or slantwise or zigzag arrangement of like parts in a structure etc. [alteration of Middle English *stacker* (now dial.) from Old Norse *stakra* frequentative of *staka* push, stagger]

stag·ger·ing *adjective* **1** astonishing, bewildering. **2** that staggers. □ **stag·ger·ing·ly** *adverb*

stag·horn *noun* (also **stag's horn**) **1** the horn of a stag, used to make knife handles etc. **2** any of various ferns, esp. of the genus *Platycerium*, having fronds like antlers. **3** (in full **staghorn sumac**) a sumac of eastern N America with twigs covered with velvety hairs.

stag·hound *noun* a dog of any large breed used for hunting deer by sight or scent.

sta·ging *noun* **1** the presentation of a play etc. **2** a platform or support or scaffolding, esp. temporary. **3** (*attributive*) of or referring to a stop or assembly en route to an esp. military or migratory destination (*staging area; staging ground; staging period*).

stag·nant *adjective* **1** (of liquid) motionless, having no current. **2** (of life, action, the mind, business, a person) showing no activity, dull, sluggish. **3** stale or foul due to lack of motion or activity. □ **stag·nancy** *noun* **stag·nant·ly** *adverb* [Latin *stagnare stagnant-* from *stagnum* pool]

stag·nate *intransitive verb* be or become stagnant. □ **stag·na·tion** *noun*

stag party *noun* (also *Brit.* **stag night**) an all-male celebration in honour of a man about to marry.

stagy *adjective* (also **stagey**) (**stagi·er**, **stagi·est**) theatrical; artificial, exaggerated. □ **stagi·ly** *adverb* **stagi·ness** *noun*

staid *adjective* usu. *derogatory* **1** serious and dull; sedate. **2** fixed, permanent, unchanging. □ **staid·ly** *adverb* **staid·ness** *noun* [= *stayed*, past participle of STAY[1]]

stain ● *verb* **1** *transitive & intransitive* discolour or be discoloured by the action of liquid sinking in. **2** *transitive* sully, blemish, spoil, damage (a reputation, character, etc.). **3** *transitive* colour (wood, glass, etc.) by a process other than painting or covering the surface. **4** *transitive* impregnate (a specimen) for microscopic examination with colouring matter that makes the structure visible by being deposited in some parts more than in others. ● *noun* **1** a discoloration, a spot or mark caused esp. by contact with foreign matter and not easily removed (*socks covered with grass stains*). **2 a** a blot or blemish. **b** damage to a reputation etc. (*a stain on one's character*). **3** a substance used in staining. □ **stain·able** *adjective* **stain·er** *noun* [Middle English from *distain* from Old French *desteindre desteign-* (as DIS-, TINGE)]

stained glass *noun* dyed or coloured glass, esp. in a lead framework in a window (also *attributive*: **stained glass window**).

stain·less *adjective* **1** (esp. of a reputation) without stains. **2** not liable to stain.

stainless steel *noun* an iron alloy containing chromium and resistant to tarnishing and rust, esp. steel containing 11 to 14 per cent chromium, used for cutlery etc.

stair *noun* **1** each of a set of fixed steps, esp. in a building (*on the top stair but one*). **2** (esp. in *pl.*) a set of such steps (*passed him on the stairs; down a winding stair*). [Old English *stæger*, from Germanic]

stair·case *noun* a flight or flights of stairs and the supporting structure.

stair·climber *noun* an exercise machine for simulating the action of climbing stairs.

stair·lift *noun* a lift in the form of a chair built into a domestic staircase for carrying an esp. disabled person up and down stairs.

Stair·master *noun proprietary* = STAIRCLIMBER

stair·way *noun* a flight of stairs, a staircase; a passageway with stairs.

stair·well *noun* the shaft in which a staircase is built.

staithe /steɪð/ *noun Brit.* a wharf, esp. a waterside coal depot equipped for loading vessels. [Old Norse *stöth* landing stage, from Germanic, related to STAND]

stake¹ ● *noun* **1** a stout stick or post sharpened at one end and driven into the ground as a support, boundary mark, etc. **2** *hist.* **a** the post to which a person was tied to be burned alive. **b** (prec. by *the*) death by burning as a punishment (*was condemned to the stake*). **3** a territorial division or jurisdiction in the Mormon church. ● *verb* **1** *transitive* fasten, secure, or support with a stake or stakes. **2** *transitive & intransitive* (usu. foll. by *out*) mark off (an area) with stakes, esp. to claim a site for prospecting. **3** *transitive* state or establish (a claim). □ **pull** (or **pull up**) **stakes** depart; go to live elsewhere. **stake a** (or **one's**) **claim to** declare a special interest in; claim a right to. **stake out** *informal* **1** place under surveillance. **2** place (a person) to maintain surveillance. **3** declare a special interest in or right to e.g. a place or an area of study. [Old English *staca* from West Germanic, related to STICK²]

stake² ● *noun* **1** a sum of money etc. wagered on an event, esp. deposited with a stakeholder. **2 a** (often foll. by *in*) an interest or concern, esp. financial. **b** (in *pl.*) what is being risked; potential losses or consequences (*the stakes were high*). **3** (in *pl.*) **a** money offered as a prize esp. in a horse race. **b** a horse race in which all the owners of the horses contribute to the prize money (*stakes race*). ● *transitive verb* **1 a** wager (*staked $10 on the next race*). **b** risk (*staked everything on convincing him*). **2** *N Amer. informal* give financial or other support to. □ **at stake 1** risked, to be won or lost (*life itself is at stake*). **2** at issue, in question. [Middle English: perhaps from STAKE¹, from placing an object as a wager on a post or stake]

stake·hold·er *noun* **1** an independent party with whom each of those who make a wager deposits the money etc. wagered. **2** a person with an interest or concern in something.

stake·out *noun* esp. *N Amer. informal* a continuous secret watch by the police.

stak·er *noun* a person who stakes a mining claim etc.

stake truck *noun* a truck with a flat open platform with usu. removable posts along the sides to which a load can be secured.

Sta·kha·no·vite /stəˈkɒnəˌvaɪt/ *noun* a worker (esp. in the former USSR) who increases his output to an exceptional extent, and so gains special awards. ● **Sta·kha·nov·ism** /-ˌvɪzəm/ *noun* [A. G. *Stakhanov*, Russian coal miner d.1977]

staking rush *noun Cdn* a rush of people staking mining claims; a stampede (*see* STAMPEDE 4).

sta·lac·tite /stəˈlakˌtaɪt, ˈstalək-/ *noun* a tapering deposit of calcite hanging down like an icicle from the roof of a cave, cliff overhang, etc., formed by dripping water. [modern Latin *stalactites* from Greek *stalaktos* dripping, from *stalassō* drip]

Stalag /ˈstalag/ *noun hist.* a German prison camp, esp. for non-commissioned officers and privates. [German from *Stamm* base, main stock, *Lager* camp]

sta·lag·mite /stəˈlagˌmaɪt, ˈsta-/ *noun* a mound or tapering column of calcite rising from the floor of a cave etc., deposited by dripping water and often uniting with a stalactite. [modern Latin *stalagmites* from Greek *stalagma* a drop, from *stalassō* (as STALACTITE)]

stale¹ ● *adjective* (**stal·er**, **stal·est**) **1 a** not fresh, not quite new (*stale bread*). **b** musty, insipid, or otherwise the worse for age or use. **2** lacking novelty or interest; trite or unoriginal (*a stale joke*; *stale news*). **3** (of an athlete or other performer) having ability impaired by excessive exertion or practice. **4** *Law* (esp. of a claim) having been left dormant for an unreasonably long time. ● *transitive & intransitive verb* make or become stale. □ **stale·ness** *noun* [prob. from Old French from *estaler* halt: compare STALL¹]

stale² ● *noun* the urine of horses and cattle. ● *intransitive verb* (esp. of horses and cattle) urinate. [Middle English, perhaps from Old French *estaler* adopt a position]

stale-dated *adjective* **1** (of food etc.) that has remained unconsumed beyond its best-before date or a period of reasonable freshness. **2** (of a cheque) no longer negotiable because of its age. **3** out of date, stale.

stale·mate ● *noun* **1** *Chess* a position counting as a draw, in which a player is not in check but cannot move except into check. **2** a deadlock or drawn contest. ● *transitive verb* **1** *Chess* bring (a player) to a stalemate. **2** bring to a standstill. [obsolete *stale* (from Anglo-French *estale* from *estaler* be placed: compare STALE¹) + MATE²]

Stal·in /ˈstalɪn, ˈstɒlɪn/ **Jo·seph** (born Iosif Vissarionovich Dzhugashvili) (1879–1953), Soviet leader, general secretary of the Communist Party of the USSR 1922–53. He was the successor of Lenin and went on to become the virtual dictator of the USSR. His rule is now regarded as a reign of terror, marked by the persecution of all political opposition, arbitrary purges, the disastrous reorganization of Soviet agriculture, and the subjection of E Europe.

Stal·in·grad /ˈstalɪnˌgrad, ˈstɒlɪn-/ a former name (1925–61) for VOLGOGRAD.

Stalingrad, Battle of a long and bitterly fought battle of the Second World War, in which the German advance into the Soviet Union was turned back at Stalingrad in 1942–3. Grim house-to-house fighting took place until Jan. 1943, when the Germans surrendered after suffering more than 300,000 casualties.

Stal·in·ism *noun* **1** the policies followed by Stalin, esp. centralization, totalitarianism, and the pursuit of Communism. **2** any rigid centralized authoritarian form of socialism. □ **Stal·in·ist** *noun*

stalk¹ *noun* **1** the main stem of a herbaceous plant. **2** the slender attachment or support of a leaf, flower, fruit, etc. **3** a similar support for an organ etc. in an animal. **4** a slender support or linking shaft in a machine, object, etc., e.g. the stem of a wineglass. **5** the tall chimney of a factory etc. □ **stalked** *adjective* (also in *combination*). **stalk·less** *adjective* **stalk·like** *adjective* **stalky** *adjective* [Middle English *stalke*, prob. diminutive of (now dial.) *stale* rung of a ladder, long handle, from Old English *stalu*]

stalk² ● *verb* **1 a** *transitive* pursue or approach (game, prey, an enemy, etc.) stealthily. **b** *intransitive* steal up to game under cover. **2** *intransitive* stride, walk in a stately or haughty manner. **3** *transitive formal* or *literary* move silently or threateningly through (a place) (*fear stalked the streets*). **4** *transitive* harass or persecute (a person) with unwanted and obsessive attention. ● *noun* **1** the stalking of game. **2** an imposing gait. □ **stalk·ing** *noun* [Old English from Germanic: related to STEAL]

stalk·er *noun* a person who stalks, hounds, or follows a particular person, esp. stealthily or obsessively. **2** a person who stalks game.

stalk-eyed *adjective* (of crabs, snails, etc.) having the eyes mounted on stalks.

stalking horse *noun* **1** a horse or screen behind which a hunter is concealed. **2** a pretext concealing one's real intentions or actions. **3** a weak political candidate who forces an election in the hope of a more serious contender coming forward.

stall¹ ● *noun* **1 a** a trader's stand or booth in a market etc., or out of doors. **b** a compartment in a building for the sale of goods. **c** a table in this on which goods are displayed. **2 a** a stable. **b** a compartment for one animal in this. **c** a compartment for one horse at the start of a race. **3** a compartment or cubicle with a single shower or toilet, esp. in a public washroom. **4** a fixed seat in the choir or chancel of a church, more or less enclosed at the back and sides. **5** *N Amer.* (*West*) an area marked off for a single vehicle in a parking lot etc.; a parking space. **6** (usu. in *pl.*) *Brit.* each of a set of seats in a theatre, usu. on the ground floor. **7 a** the stalling of an engine or aircraft. **b** the condition resulting from this. **8** a receptacle for one object. ● *verb* **1 a** *intransitive* (of a motor vehicle or its engine) stop because of an overload on the engine or an inadequate supply of fuel to it. **b** *intransitive* (of an aircraft or its pilot) reach a condition where the speed is too low to allow effective operation of the controls. **c** *transitive* cause (an engine or vehicle or aircraft) to stall. **2** *intransitive* **a** (of a vehicle) stick fast as in mud or snow. **b** (of a process etc.) stop moving or progressing. **3** *transitive* **a** put or keep (cattle etc.) in a stall or stalls esp. for fattening. **b** furnish (a stable etc.) with stalls. [Old English *steall* from Germanic, related to STAND: partly from Old French *estal* from Frankish]

stall² ● *verb* **1** *intransitive* play for time when being questioned etc. **2** *transitive* delay, obstruct, block. ● *noun* an instance of stalling. [*stall* pickpocket's confederate, originally 'decoy' from Anglo-French *estal(e)*, prob. related to STALL¹]

stall-feed *transitive verb* fatten (cattle) in a stall.

stall·hold·er *noun Cdn & Brit.* a person in charge of a stall at a market etc.

stalling speed *noun* (also **stall speed**) the minimum airspeed at which an aircraft can maintain straight and level flight.

stal·lion *noun* an uncastrated adult male horse, esp. one kept for breeding. [Old French *estalon*, ultimately from a Germanic root related to STALL¹]

stal·wart /ˈstɔlwərt/ ● *adjective* **1** strongly built, sturdy. **2** courageous, resolute, determined (*stalwart supporters*). ● *noun* a loyal, reliable, and hard-working supporter of or participant in an organization or team.

☐ **stal·wart·ly** adverb [Scots var. of obsolete stalworth from Old English stælwierthe from stæl place, WORTH]

Stam·boul /stam'buːl/ an obsolete name for ISTANBUL.

sta·men /'steimən/ noun the male fertilizing organ of a flowering plant, including the anther containing pollen. [Latin stamen warp in an upright loom, thread]

stam·ina /'staminə/ noun the ability to endure prolonged physical or mental strain; staying power, power of endurance. [Latin, pl. of STAMEN in sense 'warp, threads spun by the Fates']

stam·in·ate /'staminət, -neit/ adjective (of a plant) having stamens, esp. stamens but not pistils.

stam·mer ● verb 1 intransitive speak (habitually, or on occasion from embarrassment etc.) with halting articulation, esp. with pauses or rapid repetitions of the same syllable. 2 transitive (often foll. by out) utter (words) in this way (stammered out an excuse). ● noun 1 a tendency to stammer. 2 an instance of stammering. ☐ **stam·mer·er** noun [Old English stamerian from West Germanic]

stamp ● verb 1 a transitive bring down (one's foot) heavily on the ground etc. b transitive crush, flatten, or bring into a specified state in this way (stamped down the earth around the plant). c intransitive bring down one's foot heavily; walk with heavy steps; strike the feet against the ground to ward off cold. 2 transitive a impress (a pattern, mark, etc.) on metal, paper, etc., with a die or similar instrument of metal, wood, rubber, etc. b impress (a surface) with a pattern etc. in this way. 3 transitive affix a postage or other stamp to (an envelope or document). 4 transitive a assign a specific character to; characterize; mark out (this latest novel stamps her as a genius). b (usu. in passive) mark or affect with a particular feeling or attitude (reluctance was stamped all over their faces). 5 transitive crush or pulverize (ore etc.). ● noun 1 an instrument for stamping a pattern or mark. 2 a a mark or pattern made by this. b the impression of an official mark required to be made for revenue purposes on deeds, bills of exchange, etc., as evidence of payment of tax. 3 a = POSTAGE STAMP 1. b a small adhesive piece of paper indicating that a price, fee, or tax has been paid. 4 Cdn (Maritimes & Nfld) a hist. an adhesive piece of paper affixed by an employer to an employee's record of employment, collected by the employee to prove eligibility for employment insurance. b (in pl.) slang employment insurance benefits. 5 a mark impressed on or label etc. affixed to a commodity as evidence of quality etc. 6 a a heavy downward blow with the foot. b the sound of this. 7 a a characteristic mark or impress (bears the stamp of genius; left her stamp on the organization). b character, kind (avoid people of that stamp). c a mark of authoritative approval. 8 an audio or digital mark made on a recorded message, data file, etc., e.g. to indicate the time the information was recorded. 9 the block that crushes ore in a stamp mill. ☐ **stamp one's foot** (or **feet**) bring one's foot heavily down on the ground, to keep warm, to keep time to music, or to express petulance. **stamp out 1** produce by cutting out with a die etc. 2 put an end to, crush, destroy. ☐ **stamp·er** noun [prob. from Old English stampian (v.) (unrecorded) from Germanic]

Stamp Act noun an act of the British Parliament in 1765 imposing a duty on certain kinds of documents in the American colonies, repealed in 1766.

stamp collecting noun the collecting of postage stamps as objects of interest or value. ☐ **stamp collector** noun

stamp duty noun Brit. a duty imposed on certain kinds of legal document.

stam·pede ● noun 1 a sudden flight and scattering of a number of horses, cattle, etc. 2 a sudden flight or hurried movement of people due to interest or panic. 3 N Amer. the spontaneous and simultaneous response of many persons to a common impulse. 4 N Amer. hist. a rush of prospectors to a newly-discovered deposit of esp. gold. 5 Cdn & US West an exhibition or fair involving rodeo events and other contests and entertainment. ● verb 1 intransitive take part in a stampede. 2 transitive cause to do this. 3 transitive cause to act hurriedly or unreasonably. ☐ **stam·ped·er** noun [Spanish estampida crash, uproar, ultimately from Germanic, related to STAMP]

stamping ground esp. Brit. var. of STOMPING GROUND.

stamp mill noun a mill for crushing ore etc.

stamp of approval noun = SEAL OF APPROVAL.

stamp pad noun an ink-soaked pad, usu. in a box, used for inking a rubber stamp etc.

stance noun 1 an attitude or position of the body, esp. in sports. 2 a moral or intellectual attitude to something, esp. one that is expressed publicly. [French from Italian stanza: see STANZA]

stanch /stantʃ/ var. of STAUNCH[2].

stan·chion /'stanʃən/ ● noun 1 a post or pillar, an upright support, a vertical strut. 2 an upright bar, pair of bars, or frame, for confining cattle in a stall. ● transitive verb 1 supply with a stanchion. 2 fasten (cattle) to a stanchion. [Anglo-French stanchon, prob. ultimately from Latin stare stand]

stand ● verb (past and past participle **stood**) 1 intransitive have or take or maintain an upright position, esp. on the feet or a base. 2 intransitive be situated or located (here a village once stood). 3 intransitive be of a specified height (stands six foot three). 4 intransitive be in a specified condition (stands accused; the thermometer stood at 40°; the matter stands as follows; stood in awe of her). 5 transitive place or set in an upright or specified position (stood it against the wall). 6 intransitive a move to and remain in a specified position (stand aside). b take a specified attitude (stand aloof). 7 intransitive maintain a position; avoid falling or moving or being moved (the house will stand for another century; stood for hours arguing). 8 intransitive assume a stationary position; cease to move (now stand still). 9 intransitive remain valid or unaltered; hold good (the former conditions must stand). 10 intransitive Naut. hold a specified course (stand in for the shore; you are standing into danger). 11 transitive endure without yielding or complaining; tolerate (cannot stand the pain; how can you stand him?). 12 transitive provide for another or others at one's own expense (let me stand you a drink). 13 intransitive (often foll. by for) be a candidate (for an office, legislature, or constituency) (stood for Parliament). 14 intransitive act in a specified capacity (stood proxy). 15 transitive undergo (trial). 16 intransitive (of a dog) point, set. 17 intransitive (of a stallion) be available for breeding. ● noun 1 a cessation from motion or progress, a stoppage (was brought to a stand). 2 a a halt made, or a stationary condition assumed, for the purpose of resistance. b resistance to attack or compulsion (make a stand). 3 a a position taken up (took his stand near the door). b an attitude adopted. 4 a declared opinion or view; a stance (what is your stand?). 5 a rack, set of shelves, table, etc., on or in which things may be placed (music stand; hat stand). 6 a a small open-fronted structure for a vendor outdoors or in a market etc. b a structure occupied by a participating organization at an exhibition. 7 a standing place for vehicles (taxi stand). 8 a (esp. in pl.) a raised structure for spectators to sit or stand on at a performance, sports event, etc. b a raised structure for performers etc. 9 N Amer. a witness box (take the stand). 10 each halt made on a tour to give one or more performances, play one or more games, etc. (concluded their home stand with a win). 11 a group of tall growing plants (stand of trees). ☐ **as it stands 1** in its present condition, unaltered. 2 (also **as things stand**) in the present circumstances. **it stands to reason** see REASON. **stand alone** be unequalled; be without peers. **stand and deliver!** hist. a highwayman's order to hand over valuables etc. **stand at bay** see BAY[5]. **stand back 1** withdraw; take up a position further from the front. 2 withdraw emotionally in order to take an objective view. **stand behind** support, remain loyal to (someone). **stand by 1** stand nearby; look on without interfering (will not stand by and see a cat ill-treated). 2 uphold, support, side with (a person). 3 adhere to, abide by (terms or promises). 4 a Naut. stand ready to take hold of or operate (an anchor etc.). b be ready to act or assist. **stand a chance** see CHANCE. **stand corrected** accept correction. **stand down 1** withdraw from a team, election, etc. 2 leave the witness box. 3 Military go off duty; relax after a state of alert. **stand easy!** see EASY. **stand firm** (or **fast**) be steadfast or unfaltering. **stand for 1** represent, signify, imply ('BC' stands for 'British Columbia'; democracy stands for a great deal more than that). 2 (often with neg.) informal endure, tolerate, acquiesce in. 3 espouse the cause of. **stand one's ground** maintain one's position, not yield. **stand high** be high in status, price, etc. **stand in** (usu. foll. by for) act in place of another. **stand a person in good stead** see STEAD. **stand off** move or keep away, keep one's distance. **stand on 1** insist on, observe scrupulously (stand on ceremony; stand on one's dignity). 2 Naut. continue on the same course. **stand on one's own** not depend on an associated or related thing or person for legitimacy; be recognized for one's own merits (the second movement stands on its own). **stand on one's own two feet** (or **own feet**) be self-reliant or independent. **stand out 1** be prominent or conspicuous or outstanding. 2 (usu. foll. by against, for) hold out; persist in opposition or support or endurance. **stand over 1** stand close to (a person) to watch, control, threaten, etc. 2 be postponed, be left for later settlement etc. **stand pat** see PAT[2]. **stand to 1** Military stand ready for an attack (esp. before dawn or after dark). 2 abide by, adhere to (terms or promises). 3 be likely or certain to (stands to lose everything). **stand up 1 a** rise to one's feet from a sitting or other position. **b** come to or remain in or place in a standing position. 2 (of an argument etc.) be valid. 3 informal fail to keep an appointment with. **stand up for 1** support, side with, maintain, defend (a person or cause). **2** N Amer. (also **stand up with**) act as best man or maid or matron of honour for (a bride or groom or both). **stand up to 1** meet or face (an opponent) courageously. **2** be resistant to the harmful effects of (wear, use, etc.). **take a** (or **one's**) **stand** commit to or declare a position in a debate etc. **where one stands 1** where one positions oneself in a debate, controversy, etc. (*where do you stand?*). **2** what one's situation, status, or condition is in a relationship etc. (*I wish they'd tell us where we stand*). □ **stand·er** *noun* [Old English *standan*, from Germanic]

stand-alone *attributive adjective* **1** (of a computer) operating independently of a network or other system. **2** designed or intended not to rely on an external structure or system (*stand-alone copiers; a stand-alone business*).

stan·dard ● *noun* **1** an object or quality or measure serving as a basis or example or principle to which others conform or should conform or by which the accuracy or quality of others is judged (*by present-day standards*). **2 a** the degree of excellence etc. required for a particular purpose (*not up to standard*). **b** average quality (*of a low standard*). **3** the ordinary procedure, or quality or design of a product, without added or novel features. **4 a** a ceremonial or distinctive flag, esp. one associated with a particular person or group of people (*the Governor General's standard*). **b** the flag of a cavalry regiment. **5** an upright support. **6 a** a tree or shrub that grows on an erect stem of full height and stands alone without support. **b** a shrub grafted on an upright stem and trained in tree form (*standard rose*). **7** a document specifying nationally or internationally agreed properties for manufactured goods etc. **8** a thing recognized as a model for imitation etc. **9** a tune or song of established popularity. **10 a** a system by which the value of a currency is defined in terms of gold or silver or both. **b** the prescribed proportion of the weight of fine metal in gold or silver coins. **11** a measure for timber, equivalent to 4.67 cubic metres (165 cu. ft.). ● *adjective* **1** serving or used as a standard (*a standard size*). **2** of a normal or prescribed quality or size etc. **3** having recognized and permanent value; authoritative (*the standard book on the subject*). **4** (of language) conforming to established educated usage (*standard English*). ● *adverb* N Amer. in its standard or normal state, form, etc. (*comes standard with racing stripes*). □ **set the standard** reach a level of excellence which others must try to match. [Anglo-French *estaundart*, Old French *estendart* from *estendre*, as EXTEND: in senses 5 and 6 of *n.* affected by association with STAND]

Standard and Poor *noun* a large US credit-rating agency, which produces the S&P 500 stock price index, which covers about 80 percent of the total value of stocks traded on the New York Stock Exchange.

standard-bearer *noun* **1** a soldier who carries a standard. **2** a prominent leader in a cause.

stan·dard·bred *noun* N Amer. a horse of a breed able to attain a specified speed, developed esp. for harness racing.

standard deviation *noun Statistics* a quantity calculated to indicate the extent of deviation for a group as a whole.

standard issue *noun* **1** that which is issued or supplied as a matter of course, esp. to military personnel. **2** (*attributive*) ordinary, undistinguished (*some standard-issue rhythm and blues*).

stan·dard·ize *verb* (also esp. Brit. **-ise**) **1** *transitive* cause to conform to a standard. **2** *transitive* determine the properties of by comparison with a standard. **3** *intransitive* (foll. by *on*) adopt as one's standard or model. □ **stan·dard·iz·a·tion** *noun*

standard lamp *noun Brit., Austral., & NZ* = FLOOR LAMP.

standard model *noun* a mathematical description of the elementary particles of matter and the forces by which they interact.

standard of living *noun* the degree of material comfort available to a person or class or community.

standard operating procedure *noun* an established routine.

standard time *noun* a uniform time officially adopted for a country or region.

standby ● *noun* (pl. **-bys**) **1** a person or thing ready if needed in an emergency etc. **2** esp. N Amer. a thing which has proven to be reliable; a trusted or long-used resource etc. (*that old standby*). **3** (in full **standby time**) the maximum length of time the battery of a cellphone will remain charged while awaiting incoming calls (*compare* TALK TIME). ● *attributive adjective* **1** ready for immediate use, as in an emergency etc. **2** designating or pertaining to a system of air travel whereby seats are not booked in advance but allocated on the basis of availability just before departure (*standby fares*). **3** Cdn & Brit. designating theatre tickets sold on the basis of availability on the day of performance, often at a reduced price. ● *adverb* without having booked seats in advance (*fly*

standby). □ **on standby** prepared for immediate use or activity and awaiting instructions etc.

standee *noun* informal a person who stands, esp. when all seats are occupied.

stand-in *noun* a substitute, esp. for an actor when the latter's acting ability is not needed.

stand·ing ● *noun* **1** esteem or repute, esp. high; status, position (*people of high standing; is of no standing*). **2** duration (*a dispute of long standing*). **3** length of service, membership, etc. **4** *Law* the right to prosecute a claim or seek legal redress. **5** (in pl.) esp. N Amer. **a** a ranking of teams or competitors in a league etc. esp. according to total points (*moving up in the standings*). **b** a table etc. indicating this (*check the standings*). **6** one's position in a classification or ranking. ● *adjective* **1** that stands, upright. **2** remaining in force or use, permanent (*a standing rule, a standing army*). **3** (of a jump, start, race, etc.) performed from rest or from a standing position. **4** (of water) stagnant. **5** (of wheat etc.) not reaped. □ **in good standing 1** fully paid-up as a member etc. **2** in favour. **leave a person standing** make far more rapid progress than he or she.

standing committee *noun* a committee that is permanent during the existence of the appointing body.

standing eight-count *noun Boxing* an eight-second stoppage of a boxing match counted by a referee when a boxer is being beaten severely but is still on his feet.

standing joke *noun* = RUNNING JOKE (*see* RUNNING *adjective* 1).

standing order *noun* **1** (in pl.) the rules governing the manner in which all business shall be conducted in a parliament, council, society, etc. **2** an esp. military order that remains valid and does not have to be repeated. **3** an order with a supplier to supply a product whenever it is available.

standing ovation *noun* prolonged applause during which the crowd or audience rises to its feet.

standing rigging *noun* rigging which is fixed in position.

standing room *noun* **1** space to stand in. **2** accommodation in a theatre, arena, etc. where people must stand. **3** (**standing-room**; also **standing-room-only**) (*attributive*) designating an audience etc. filling all available seats and overflowing into standing room (*another standing-room-only crowd*).

standing start *noun* **1** a start of a race in which the runners are positioned standing. **2** a beginning or launch of an enterprise etc. without prior experience or preparation (*from a standing start last year, production has reached 30,000 units a month*).

standing wave *noun Physics* the vibration of a system in which some particular points remain fixed while others between them vibrate with the maximum amplitude (*compare* TRAVELLING WAVE).

Stan·dish, Myles (also **Miles**) (c.1584–1656), English colonist, who served as the military leader of the colony at Plymouth, Massachusetts.

stand·off *noun* **1** N Amer. **a** a deadlock. **b** a confrontation in which each side is entrenched and threatening. **2** (**stand-off**; in full **stand-off half**) *Rugby* a halfback who forms a link between the scrum half and the three-quarters.

stand·off·ish *adjective* cold or distant in manner. □ **stand·off·ish·ness** *noun*

stand·out *noun* informal ● *noun* a remarkable, notable, or outstanding person or thing. ● *attributive adjective* remarkable, notable, outstanding.

stand·pipe *noun* a vertical pipe extending from a water supply, esp. one connecting a temporary tap to the water mains.

stand·point *noun* **1** the position from which a thing is viewed. **2** a mental attitude.

stand·still *noun* a stoppage; an inability to proceed.

stand-to *noun Military* the action or state of standing to; readiness for action or attack.

stand-up ● *attributive adjective* **1** denoting a brand of comedy performed by standing before an audience and telling jokes (*a stand-up comic*). **2** that stands or is used upright, not turned down or on its side (*playing stand-up bass; a stand-up collar*). **3** designating a bar, reception, meal, etc., at which people stand rather than sit. **4** *Baseball* designating a double or triple in which the batter reaches base standing up, i.e. easily, not needing to slide (*a stand-up double*). **5** *Hockey* designating a goaltender who makes most of his or her saves from a standing position instead of dropping to a butterfly position. **6** (of a fight) violent, thorough, or fair and square. **7** (of a person) honest, trustworthy. ● *noun* **1** a stand-up comedian. **2** stand-up comedy (*nine years in stand-up*).

Consonants:　**b** *but*　**d** *dog*　**f** *few*　**g** *get*　**h** *her*　**j** *yes*　**k** *cat*　**l** *leg*　**m** *man*　**n** *no*　**p** *pen*　**r** *red*　**s** *sit*

Stan·fields *plural noun Cdn proprietary* men's underwear, esp. long underwear. [*Stanfield's* Ltd., an underwear manufacturer in Truro, NS]

Stan·ford, (Amasa) Le·land (1824–93), US financier and politician, who served as governor of California (1861–3), helped to finance the first US transcontinental railway, and founded Stanford University (1885).

stang /staŋ/ *noun* a monetary unit of Thailand, equal to one-hundredth of a baht. [Thai]

stan·hope /'stanhoːp/ *noun* a light open horse-drawn carriage for one, with two or four wheels. [Fitzroy *Stanhope*, English clergyman d.1864, for whom the first one was made]

Stan·is·laus, St. /'stanɪs,lɒs/ (known as St. Stanislaus of Cracow) (1030–79), patron saint of Poland, bishop of Cracow (1072–79). According to tradition, he was murdered by King Boleslaus II (1039–81), whom he had excommunicated. Feast day, 11 April (formerly 7 May).

Stan·is·lav·sky /ˌstanɪsˈlavski/ **Kon·stan·tin (Serge·evich)** (born Konstantin Sergeevich Alekseev) (1863–1938), Russian theatre director and actor. He co-founded the Moscow Art Theatre (1898) and his theories later formed a basis for the development of method acting. □ **Stan·is·lav·skian** *adjective*

stank *past of* STINK.

Stan·ley¹ (also **Port Stanley**) the chief port and town of the Falkland Islands, situated on the island of East Falkland; pop. (2002) 1,800.

Stan·ley² ▸ **1 Fred·erick Ar·thur, Baron Stan·ley of Pres·ton, 16th Earl of Derby** (1841–1908), English politician, Governor General of Canada 1888–93; during his term he promoted closer ties between Canada and Britain. In 1893 he donated the hockey trophy that bears his name. **2 Sir Henry Mor·ton** (born John Rowlands) (1841–1904), Welsh explorer and journalist. He became famous by discovering the lost missionary David Livingstone in 1871. He continued exploring Africa, tracing the course of the Congo (1874–77; he helped establish the Congo Free State (subsequently Zaire, now Congo), with Belgian support, from 1879 to 1885.

Stanley, Mount (known in Congo as **Mount Ngaliema**) a mountain in the Ruwenzori range in central Africa, on the border between Congo (formerly Zaire) and Uganda. It has several peaks, of which the highest, Margherita Peak, rises to 5 110 m (16,765 ft.). [Sir H. M. STANLEY², the first European to reach it]

Stanley Cup *noun* a trophy awarded annually to the hockey team that wins the NHL championships. [STANLEY² 1]

Stanley·ville the former name (1882–1966) for KISANGANI.

stan·nous *adjective Chem.* of or relating to bivalent tin (*stannous salts*; *stannous chloride*). [Late Latin *stannum* tin]

Stan·ton, Eliza·beth Cady (1815–1902), US feminist and leader of the women's rights movement. She worked for women's suffrage with Susan B. Anthony, publishing the journal *Revolution* (1868–9) and compiling the three volume *History of Woman Suffrage* (1881–6).

stan·za *noun* the basic metrical unit in a poem or verse, consisting of a recurring group of lines (often four lines and usu. not more than twelve) which may or may not rhyme. □ **stan·zaic** /stanˈzeiɪk/ *adjective* [Italian, = standing place, chamber, stanza, ultimately from Latin *stare* stand]

sta·pelia /stəˈpiːliə/ *noun* any southern African plant of the genus *Stapelia*, with flowers having an unpleasant smell. [modern Latin from J. B. von *Stapel*, Dutch botanist d.1636]

sta·pes /'steipiːz/ *noun* (*pl.* same) a small stirrup-shaped bone in the ears of mammals. [modern Latin from medieval Latin *stapes* stirrup]

staph *noun informal* = STAPHYLOCOCCUS. [abbreviation]

staphyl·o·coc·cus /ˌstafɪlə'kɒkəs/ *noun* (*pl.* **staphyl·o·cocci** /-kaɪ/) any bacterium of the genus *Staphylococcus*, occurring in grape-like clusters, and sometimes causing pus formation usu. in the skin and mucous membranes of animals. □ **staphyl·o·coc·cal** *adjective* [Greek *staphulē* bunch of grapes + COCCUS]

staple¹ ● *noun* **1** a small thin piece of bent wire that is forced by a stapler into sheets of paper etc. to hold them together or to fasten them to something. **2** a piece of metal in the shape of a U with pointed ends that is hammered into wood etc. ● *transitive verb* fasten with a staple or staples. [Old English *stapol* from Germanic]

staple² ● *noun* **1** the principal or an important article of commerce. **2** the chief element or a main component, e.g. of a diet. **3** a raw material. **4** the fibre of cotton or wool etc. as determining its quality (*long-staple cotton*). ● *adjective* **1** main or principal (*staple commodities*). **2** important as a product or an export. ● *transitive verb* sort or classify (wool etc.) according to fibre. [Old French *estaple* market, from Middle Low German, Middle Dutch *stapel* market]

staple gun *noun* a hand-held device for driving in staples.

stap·ler *noun* a small device for forcing staples into paper etc. or for stapling papers etc. together.

star ● *noun* **1** a celestial body appearing as a luminous point in the night sky. **2** (in full **fixed star**) such a body so far from the earth as to appear motionless (*compare* PLANET, COMET). **3** a large naturally luminous gaseous body, e.g. the sun. **4** a celestial body regarded as influencing a person's fortunes etc. (*born under a lucky star*). **5** a thing resembling a star in shape or appearance. **6** a small white mark between a horse's eyes. **7** a figure or object with radiating points esp. as the insignia of an order, as a decoration or mark of rank, or showing a category of excellence (*a five-star hotel; was awarded a gold star*). **8 a** a famous person; a celebrity. **b** the principal or most prominent performer in a play, film, etc. (*the star of the show*). **c** an outstanding or particularly brilliant person (*you're a star!; our star pupil*). **d** one of three players judged to have made the most valuable contribution to a hockey game. ● *verb* (**starred, star·ring**) **1** *transitive* (of a film etc.) feature as a principal performer. **b** *intransitive* (of a performer) be featured in a film etc. **2** (esp. as **starred** *adjective*) **a** mark, set, or adorn with a star or stars. **b** put an asterisk or star beside (a name, an item in a list, etc.). □ **my stars!** *informal* an expression of surprise. □ **star·dom** *noun* **star·less** *adjective* **star·like** *adjective* [Old English *steorra* from Germanic]

star anise *noun see* ANISE 2.

star apple *noun* an edible purple apple-like fruit (with a starlike cross-section) of a tropical evergreen tree, *Chrysophyllum cainito*.

Stara Za·gora /ˌstɑrə zəˈgɒrə/ a city in east central Bulgaria; pop. (est. 2001) 143,989.

star·board /'stɑrbərd, -bɔrd/ ● *noun* the right-hand side (looking forward) of a ship, boat, or aircraft (*compare* PORT³). ● *adjective* situated on or turned towards the starboard side. ● *transitive & intransitive verb* turn (the helm) to starboard. [Old English *stēorbord* = rudder side (see STEER¹, BOARD), early Teutonic ships being steered with a paddle over the right side]

star·burst *noun* **1 a** a pattern of radiating lines or rays around a central object, light source, etc. **b** an explosion or *Photog.* a lens attachment producing this effect (*starburst filter*). **2** *Astronomy* a period of intense activity, apparently star formation, in certain galaxies.

starch ● *noun* **1** an odourless tasteless polysaccharide occurring widely in plants and obtained chiefly from cereals and potatoes, forming an important constituent of the human diet. **2** a preparation of this for stiffening fabric before ironing. **3** (in *pl.*) foods containing much starch, e.g. potatoes, rice, pasta, etc. **4** stiffness of manner; formality. **5** strength, backbone; vigour. ● *transitive verb* stiffen (clothing) with starch. □ **starch·er** *noun* [earlier as verb: Middle English *sterche* from Old English *stercan* (unrecorded) stiffen, from Germanic: compare STARK]

Star Chamber *noun* **1** *Brit. Law hist.* a court of civil and criminal jurisdiction noted for its arbitrary procedure, and abolished in 1641. **2** (also **star chamber**) any arbitrary or oppressive tribunal.

starchy *adjective* (**starch·i·er, starch·i·est**) **1 a** of or like starch. **b** containing much starch. **2** stiffened with starch. **3** (of a person) stiff in manner, bearing, or character. □ **starch·i·ly** *adverb* **starch·i·ness** *noun*

star cluster *noun Astronomy* a group of stars forming a relatively close association.

star-crossed *adjective* ill-fated.

star·dust *noun* **1** a romantic mystical look or sensation. **2** a multitude of stars looking like dust.

stare ● *intransitive verb* **1** (usu. foll. by *at*) look fixedly with eyes open, esp. as the result of curiosity, surprise, bewilderment, admiration, horror, etc. (*sat staring at the poster on the wall; stared in amazement*). **2** (of eyes) be wide open and fixed. **3** be unpleasantly prominent or striking. ● *noun* a staring gaze. □ **stare down** look fixedly at someone until they feel forced to lower their eyes or turn away. **stare one in the face** be evident or imminent. □ **star·er** *noun* [Old English *starian* from Germanic]

stare de·ci·sis /'steriː dɪˈsəisɪs/ *noun Law* the legal principle of determining points in litigation according to precedent. [Latin, = 'to stand by things decided']

star field *noun* a range of stars as visible through a telescope, in a photograph, computer image, etc.

star·fish *noun* an echinoderm of the class Asteroidea with five or more radiating arms.

star·flower *noun* a woodland plant of eastern N America, *Trientalis borealis*, bearing two star-shaped white flowers above a whorl of leaves.

star·fruit *noun* = CARAMBOLA.

star·fuck·er *noun* *coarse slang* a sycophant who fawns on celebrities in order to establish social bonds and/or sexual relations with them.

star·gazer *noun* *informal* **1** an astronomer or astrologer. **2** a daydreamer. □ **star·gaze** *intransitive verb*

stark ● *adjective* **1** desolate, bare (*a stark landscape*). **2** sharply evident (*in stark contrast*). **3** downright, sheer (*stark madness*). **4** devoid of any elaboration or adornment; brutally simple. **5** completely naked.
● *adverb* completely, wholly (*stark mad*; *stark naked*). □ **stark·ly** *adverb* **stark·ness** *noun* [Old English *stearc* from Germanic: stark naked, from earlier *start-naked* from obsolete *start* tail: compare REDSTART]

stark·ers *adjective* esp. *Brit. slang* stark naked.

star·let *noun* **1** a promising young performer, esp. a woman. **2** a little star.

star·light *noun* **1** the light of the stars (*walked home by starlight*). **2** (*attributive*) = STARLIT (*a starlight night*).

Star·ling, Er·nest Henry (1866–1927), English physiologist. He founded the science of endocrinology.

star·ling *noun* **1** a small gregarious partly migratory bird, *Sturnus vulgaris*, with blackish-brown speckled lustrous plumage, chiefly inhabiting cultivated areas. **2** any similar bird of the family Sturnidae. [Old English *stærlinc* from *stær* starling, from Germanic: compare -LING¹]

star·lit *adjective* **1** lighted by stars. **2** with stars visible.

star magnolia *noun* a magnolia, *Magnolia stellata*, with starry flowers.

Star of Bethlehem *noun* **1** *New Testament* the star that guided the Magi to Bethlehem after Jesus' birth. **2** (also **star of Bethlehem**) any of various plants with starlike flowers esp. *Ornithogalum umbellatum* with white star-shaped flowers striped with green on the outside.

Star of Courage *noun* Canada's second-highest award for bravery, given to civilians and military personnel who perform acts of courage involving personal risk. Abbr.: **SC**. *See also* CROSS OF VALOUR, MEDAL OF BRAVERY.

Star of David *noun* a figure consisting of two interlaced equilateral triangles, used as a Jewish and Israeli symbol.

Starr, Ringo (born Richard Starkey) (b.1940), English rock drummer and singer, who was the drummer with the Beatles (1962–70).

star·ry *adjective* (**star·ri·er, star·ri·est**) **1** covered with stars. **2** resembling a star. □ **star·ri·ly** *adverb* **star·ri·ness** *noun*

starry-eyed *adjective* *informal* **1** visionary; enthusiastic but impractical. **2** euphoric.

Stars and Bars *hist.* the popular name of the flag of the Confederate states of the US.

Stars and Stripes *noun* the national flag of the US.

star sapphire *noun* a cabochon sapphire reflecting a starlike image due to its regular internal structure.

star shell *noun* an explosive projectile designed to burst in the air and light up the enemy's position.

star·shine *noun* the light of the stars.

star·ship *noun* (in science fiction) a large usu. manned spacecraft for interstellar space travel.

star sign *noun* a sign of the zodiac.

star-spangled *adjective* **1** covered or glittering with stars. **2** = STAR-STUDDED.

Star-Spangled Banner *noun* (prec. by *the*) **1** the US national anthem. **2** = STARS AND STRIPES.

star-struck *adjective* fascinated or greatly impressed by celebrities or stardom.

star-studded *noun* **1** containing or covered with many stars. **2** featuring many famous performers.

star system *noun* **1** a structured collection of stars; a galaxy. **2** the way in which certain sports teams, movie productions etc. are managed, with priority given to the promotion and needs of a few celebrity performers.

START /stɑːt/ *abbreviation* Strategic Arms Reduction Treaty (or Talks).

start ● *verb* **1** *transitive & intransitive* begin; commence (*started work*; *started crying*; *started to shout*; *the play starts at eight*). **2** *transitive* set (proceedings, an event, etc.) in motion (*start the meeting*; *started a fire*). **3** *intransitive* (often foll. by *on*) make a beginning (*started on a new project*). **4** *intransitive* (often foll. by *after, for*) set oneself in motion or action (*'wait!' he shouted, and started after her*). **5** *intransitive* set out; begin a journey etc. (*we start at 6 a.m.*). **6** (often foll. by *up*) **a** *intransitive* (of a machine) begin operating (*the car wouldn't start*). **b** *transitive* cause (a machine etc.) to begin operating (*tried to start the engine*). **7** *transitive* **a** cause or enable (a person) to make a beginning (with something) (*started me in business with $50,000*). **b** (foll. by pres. part.) cause (a person) to begin (doing something) (*the smoke started me coughing*). **8** *transitive* (often foll. by *up*) found or establish; originate. **9** *intransitive* (foll. by *at, with*) be the first of a series of items, e.g. in a meal (*we started with soup*). **10** *transitive* give a signal to (competitors) to start in a race. **11** *intransitive* (often foll. by *up, from*, etc.) make a sudden movement from surprise, pain, etc. (*started at the sound of her voice*). **12** *intransitive* (foll. by *out, up, from*, etc.) spring out, up, etc. (*started up from the chair*). **13** *transitive & intransitive* **a** *Sport* be one of the players chosen to play at the outset of (a game). **b** *Baseball* be the starting pitcher of (a game). **14** *transitive* rouse (game etc.) from its lair. **15 a** *intransitive* be displaced by pressure or shrinkage; come loose. **b** *transitive* cause to do this. **16** *intransitive* (foll. by *out, to*, etc.) (of a thing) move or appear suddenly (*tears started to his eyes*). **17** *intransitive* (foll. by *from*) (of eyes, usu. with exaggeration) burst forward (from their sockets etc.). **18** *transitive* pour out (liquor) from a cask. **19** *transitive* conceive (a baby). ● *noun* **1** a beginning of an event, action, journey, etc. (*missed the start*; *an early start tomorrow*; *housing starts are up again this month*; *made a fresh start*). **2** the place from which a race etc. begins. **3** an advantage given at the beginning of a race etc. (*a 15-second start*). **4** an advantageous initial position in life, business, etc. (*a good start in life*). **5** a sudden movement of surprise, pain, etc. (*you gave me a start*). **6** an intermittent or spasmodic effort or movement (*by fits and starts*). □ **don't you start!** *informal* don't criticize or grumble. **for a start** *informal* as a beginning; in the first place. **start in** *informal* **1** begin. **2** (foll. by *on*) *N Amer.* make a beginning on. **start off 1** begin; commence (*started off on a lengthy monologue*). **2** begin to move (*it's time we started off*). **start out 1** begin a journey. **2** *informal* (foll. by *to* + infin.) proceed as intending (to do something). **start over** *N Amer.* begin again. **start something** *informal* cause trouble. **start up** arise; occur. **to start with 1** in the first place; before anything else is considered (*should never have been there to start with*). **2** at the beginning (*had six members to start with*). [Old English (originally in sense 11) from Germanic]

start·er ● *noun* **1** a person or thing that starts. **2** an esp. automatic device for starting the engine of a motor vehicle etc. **3 a** *N Amer.* a player who plays at the beginning of a game. **b** *Baseball* = STARTING PITCHER. **4** a person giving the signal for the start of a race. **5** a horse or competitor starting in a race (*a list of probable starters*). **6** the first course of a meal. **7** a culture used to initiate souring or fermentation in making yogourt, cheese, dough, etc. **8** the initial action etc. ● *adjective* relating to or suitable for a start or beginning (*a starter home*). □ **for starters** *informal* to start with.

starter's pistol (also *Brit.* **starting pistol**) *noun* a pistol used to give the signal for the start of a race.

starting block *noun* a shaped rigid block for bracing the feet of a runner at the start of a race.

starting gate *noun* a movable barrier for securing a fair start in horse races.

starting lineup *noun* *Sport* a list of players chosen from a team's roster to start a game.

starting pitcher *noun* *Baseball* a pitcher who pitches the initial innings of a game but does not necessarily complete it.

starting point *noun* the point from which a journey, process, argument, etc. begins.

starting price *noun* the odds ruling at the start of a horse race.

starting rotation *noun* *Baseball* = ROTATION 3b.

starting stall *noun* a compartment for one horse at the start of a race.

star·tle ● *transitive verb* give a shock or surprise to; cause (a person etc.) to start with surprise or sudden alarm. ● *noun* a sudden start or shock of surprise, alarm, etc. □ **star·tled** *adjective* **star·tle·ment** *noun* [Old English *steartlian* (as START, -LE⁴)]

start·ling *adjective* **1** surprising. **2** alarming (*startling news*). □ **start·ling·ly** *adverb*

start-up *noun* **1** the action or an instance of starting up, esp. the starting up of a business, machine, or series of operations (often *attributive*: *start-up costs*). **2** a newly established business.

star turn *noun* the principal item in an entertainment or performance.

Vowels: a cat ɑ arm e bed ɜr her ɜː deux ə ago ɪ sit i cosy iː feed ɒ hot ɔ pore ɔː no ʌ run ʊ put

star·va·tion ● *noun* **1** the action of starving or depriving a person or animal of food. **2** the condition of being starved or having too little food to sustain life or health. ● *adjective* **1** liable to cause starvation (*a starvation diet*). **2** seeming to cause starvation (*starvation wages*).

starve *verb* **1** *intransitive* die of hunger; suffer from malnourishment. **2** *transitive* cause to die of hunger or suffer from lack of food. **3** *intransitive* suffer from extreme poverty. **4** *intransitive* feel very hungry (*I'm starving*). **5** *intransitive* **a** suffer from mental or spiritual want. **b** (foll. by *for*) feel a strong craving for (sympathy, amusement, knowledge, etc.). **6** *transitive* **a** (foll. by *of*) deprive of; keep scantily supplied with (*starved of affection*). **b** cause to suffer from mental or spiritual want. **7** *transitive* **a** (foll. by *into*) compel by starving (*starved into submission*). **b** (foll. by *out*) compel to surrender etc. by starving (*starved them out*). □ **-starved** *combining form* [Old English *steorfan* die]

starve·ling /ˈstɑrvlɪŋ/ ● *noun* a starving or poorly-fed person or animal. ● *adjective* starving.

Star Wars *noun informal* = STRATEGIC DEFENCE INITIATIVE. [from the title of a science fiction film (1977)]

star·wort /ˈstɑrwɜrt, -wɔrt/ *noun* a plant of the genus *Stellaria* with starlike flowers.

stash *informal* ● *transitive verb* (often foll. by *away*) **1** conceal; put in a safe or hidden place. **2** hoard, stow, store. ● *noun* **1** a hiding place or hideout. **2** a thing hidden; a cache. **3** a cache or quantity of an illegal drug. [18th c.: origin unknown]

Stasi /ˈʃtɑzi/ *noun hist.* the internal security force of the former German Democratic Republic, abolished in 1989. [German, from *Staatssicherheit*(sdienst) 'state security (service)']

sta·sis /ˈsteɪsɪs, ˈstasɪs/ *noun* (*pl.* **sta·ses** /-siːz/) **1** a state of inactivity or equilibrium. **2** a stoppage of circulation of any of the body fluids. [modern Latin from Greek *sta-* STAND]

-stasis /ˈstasɪs, ˈsteɪsɪs/ *combining form* (*pl.* **-stases** /-siːz/) *Physiol.* forming nouns denoting a slowing or stopping (*hemostasis*). □ **-static** *combining form.*

stat[1] *noun informal esp. N Amer.* a statistic (also *attributive: stat book*). [shortening]

stat[2] *adverb esp. Med.* immediately. [abbreviation of Latin *statim*]

stat[3] *noun Cdn informal* a statutory holiday. [abbreviation]

-stat *combining form* forming nouns with reference to keeping fixed or stationary (*rheostat*). [Greek *statos* stationary]

state ● *noun* **1** the existing condition or position of a person or thing (*in a bad state of repair*; *in a precarious state of health*). **2** *informal* **a** an excited, anxious, or agitated mental condition (*was in a state all morning*). **b** an untidy condition. **3 a** an organized political community under one government; a nation. **b** a political unit forming part of a federation, as in the United States of America. **c** (**the States**) the US. **4** (*attributive*) **a** of, for, or concerned with the state (*state documents*). **b** reserved for or done on occasions of ceremony (*state apartments*; *state visit*). **c** involving ceremony (*state opening of Parliament*). **5** (usu. **State**) civil government (*Church and State*). **6** pomp, rank, dignity. ● *transitive verb* **1** express, esp. fully or clearly, in speech or writing (*have stated my opinion*). **2** fix, specify (*at stated intervals*). **3** *Law* specify the facts of (a case) for consideration. **4** *Music* play (a theme etc.) so as to make it known to the listener. □ **lie in state** *see* LIE[1]. **of state** concerning politics or government. □ **state·hood** *noun* [Middle English: partly from ESTATE, partly from Latin STATUS]

state capitalism *noun* a political system in which the state has control of production and the use of capital.

state·craft *noun* the art of diplomacy and government.

stated *adjective* **1** fixed, established; regular. **2** explicitly set forth.

State Department *noun* (in the US) the department of foreign affairs.

state·house *noun US* the building where a state legislature meets.

state·less *adjective* **1** (of a person) having no nationality or citizenship. **2** without a state or states. □ **state·less·ness** *noun*

state·let *noun* a small state.

state line *noun* (in the US) the boundary between two states.

state·ly *adjective* (**state·li·er**, **state·li·est**) dignified; imposing; grand. □ **state·li·ness** *noun*

stately home *noun Brit.* a large magnificent house, esp. one open to the public.

state·ment *noun* **1** the act or an instance of stating or being stated; expression in words. **2** a thing stated; a declaration (*that statement is unfounded*). **3** a formal account of facts, esp. to the police or in a court of law (*make a statement*). **4** a record of transactions in a bank account

etc. **5** an account containing a list of bills, invoices, or payments, and showing the total amount due or the balance owing. **6** the communication of a mood, idea, etc., through something other than words (*wears that sort of clothing as a statement*).

statement of claim *noun Cdn Law* a legal document served in a civil suit which sets out the relief applied for by the plaintiff and the reasons for such relief.

Stat·en Island /ˈstatən/ an island borough of New York City; pop. (2000) 443,728. Situated in the southwestern part of the city, it is separated from New Jersey by a narrow channel.

state of affairs *noun* circumstances; the current situation.

state of emergency *noun* a condition of danger or disaster affecting a region or country, esp. with normal constitutional procedures suspended.

state of grace *noun* the condition of being free from grave sin.

state of the art *noun* **1** the current stage of development of a practical or technological subject. **2** (usu. **state-of-the-art**) (*attributive*) using the latest techniques or equipment (*state-of-the-art computer technology*).

state of things *noun* = STATE OF AFFAIRS.

state of war *noun* the situation when war has been declared or is in progress.

stater /ˈsteɪtər/ *noun* an ancient Greek gold or silver coin. [Late Latin from Greek *statēr*]

state·room *noun* **1** a private compartment in a passenger ship, train, etc. **2** esp. *Brit.* a state apartment in a palace, hotel, etc.

state school *noun* (in the UK) a school managed and funded by the public authorities.

state's evidence *noun US Law* evidence given on behalf of the prosecution by an accused person who has confessed his or her own guilt and who then acts as a witness against his or her accomplices (*turned state's evidence*).

States General *noun hist.* **1** the legislative body in the Netherlands from the 15th to the 18th c. **2** = ESTATES GENERAL. [Dutch *staten generaal*]

state·side esp. *US informal* ● *adjective* of, in, or relating to the US. ● *adverb* in or towards the continental US.

states·man *noun* (*pl.* **-men**) **1** a person skilled in affairs of state, esp. one taking an active part in politics. **2** a distinguished and capable politician. *See also* ELDER STATESMAN. □ **states·man·like** *adjective* **states·man·ly** *adjective* **states·man·ship** *noun*

state socialism *noun* socialism achieved by state ownership of public utilities and industry. □ **state socialist** *noun & adjective*

states' rights *plural noun US* the rights and powers not assumed by the United States federal government but reserved to its individual states.

states·woman *noun* (*pl.* **-women**) **1** a woman skilled in affairs of state, esp. one taking an active part in politics. **2** a distinguished and capable female politician.

state trooper *noun US* a member of a state police force.

state university *noun US* a university managed by the public authorities of a state.

state·wide *US* ● *adjective* extending over or affecting an entire state. ● *adverb* so as to extend over or affect an entire state.

stat·ic ● *adjective* **1** stationary; not acting or changing; passive. **2** of or relating to static electricity. **3** *Physics* **a** concerned with bodies at rest or forces in equilibrium (*opp.* DYNAMIC 2a). **b** acting as weight but not moving (*static pressure*). **c** of statics. **4** *Computing* (of memory) not needing to be periodically refreshed by an applied voltage. ● *noun* **1** static electricity. **2** electrical disturbances producing interference with the reception of telecommunications and broadcasts. **3** esp. *N Amer.* = STATIC CLING. **4** *slang* aggravation; interference; criticism. □ **staticky** *adjective* (in senses 2 & 3 of *noun*). **stat·ic·ally** *adverb* [modern Latin *staticus* from Greek *statikos* from *sta-* stand]

static cling *noun esp. N Amer.* the adhering of a piece of clothing to a person's body or to other clothing etc., caused by a buildup of static electricity.

stat·ice /ˈstatɪs/ *noun* **1** = SEA LAVENDER. **2** = SEA PINK. [Latin from Greek, fem. of *statikos* STATIC (with reference to staunching of blood)]

static electricity *noun* a stationary electric charge, usu. produced by friction, which causes sparks or cracking, or the attraction of dust, hair, fabric, etc.

static line *noun* a length of cord attached to an aircraft etc. which releases a parachute without the use of a rip cord.

stat·ics *plural noun* (usu. treated as *sing.*) the science of bodies at rest or of forces in equilibrium (*opp.* DYNAMICS 1). [STATIC *noun* in the same senses + -ICS]

sta·tion ● *noun* **1 a** a regular stopping place on a railway or subway line, with a platform and usu. administrative buildings or offices. **b** = BUS STATION. **c** these buildings (*go into the station and buy a ticket*). **2** a place or building etc. where a person or thing stands or is placed, esp. habitually or for a definite purpose. **3 a** a designated point or establishment where a particular service or activity is based or organized (*police station; polling station*). **b** *N Amer.* a subsidiary post office. **4 a** a studio or building used in making television or radio broadcasts. **b** an organization or establishment involved in radio or television broadcasting. **c** a specific frequency or band of frequencies assigned to a broadcaster. **5** a plant for generating electricity, esp. of a specified kind (*built a new hydro station on the river*). **6 a** a small military base. **b** the inhabitants of this. **7** position in life; rank or status (*one's station in life*). **8** *Cdn* (*Nfld*) a cove or harbour with space on the foreshore for the erection of facilities to support the fishery in nearby waters. **9** *Austral. & NZ* a large sheep or cattle farm. **10** *Bot.* a particular place where an unusual species etc. grows. ● *transitive verb* **1** assign a station to. **2** put in position. [Middle English, = standing, from Old French from Latin *statio -onis* from *stare* stand]

sta·tion·ary *adjective* **1** remaining in one place, not moving (*hit a stationary car*). **2** not meant to be moved; not portable (*stationary troops; stationary engine*). **3** not changing in magnitude, number, quality, efficiency, etc. (*stationary temperature*).

stationary bicycle *noun* a fixed exercise machine resembling a bicycle.

stationary engineer *noun* a person in charge of the operation of a boiler or steam plant etc.

stationary wave *noun* = STANDING WAVE.

station break *noun N Amer.* a pause between broadcast programs for an announcement of the identity of the station transmitting them.

sta·tion·er *noun* **1** a person who sells writing materials etc. **2** *Cdn* (*Nfld*) a migratory fisherman who conducts the summer fishery from a cove or harbour. [Middle English, = bookseller (as STATIONARY in medieval Latin sense 'shopkeeper', esp. bookseller, as opposed to peddler)]

sta·tion·ery *noun* **1** writing paper. **2** writing materials, such as paper, envelopes, pens, pencils, etc.

station hand *noun Austral.* a worker on a large sheep or cattle farm.

station house *noun N Amer.* a police station.

station-keeping *noun* the maintenance of one's proper relative position in a moving body of ships etc.

station master *noun* the official in charge of a railway station.

station of the cross *noun Catholicism* **1** each of a series of usu. 14 images or pictures representing the events in Christ's passion, before which devotions are performed in some churches. **2** (**Stations of the Cross**) the act of performing such a series of devotions.

station wagon *noun N Amer., Austral., & NZ* a car with the passenger area extended and combined with space for luggage, usu. with an extra door at the rear.

stat·ism /ˈsteɪtɪzəm/ *noun* centralized state administration and control of social and economic affairs.

stat·ist /ˈsteɪtɪst/ ● *noun* **1** a supporter of statism. **2** a statistician. ● *adjective* of or relating to statism.

sta·tis·tic ● *noun* a statistical fact or item. ● *adjective* = STATISTICAL. [German *Statistik* 'of the State']

sta·tis·tical *adjective* of or relating to statistics. □ **sta·tis·tic·ally** *adverb*

statistical significance *noun* = SIGNIFICANCE 3.

sta·tis·tics *plural noun* **1** (usu. treated as *sing.*) the science of collecting and analyzing numerical data, esp. in or for large quantities, and usu. inferring proportions in a whole from proportions in a representative sample. **2** any systematic collection or presentation of such facts. □ **stat·is·ti·cian** /ˌstatɪˈstɪʃən/ *noun*

sta·tor /ˈsteɪtər/ *noun Electricity* the stationary part of a machine, esp. of an electric motor or generator. [STATIONARY, after ROTOR]

Stats·Can *noun Cdn informal* Statistics Canada. [abbreviation]

stat·u·ary /ˈstatʃuˌeri/ ● *adjective* of or for statues (*statuary art*). ● *noun* (*pl.* **-ies**) **1** statues collectively. **2** the art of making statues.

stat·ue *noun* a sculptured, cast, carved, or moulded figure of a person or animal, esp. life-size or larger (*compare* STATUETTE). □ **stat·ued** *adjective* [Old French from Latin *statua* from *stare* stand]

statu·esque *adjective* **1** like a statue in size, dignity, or lack of movement. **2** (esp. of a woman) tall and graceful (*her statuesque figure*). □ **statu·esque·ly** *adverb* **statu·esque·ness** *noun*

statu·ette *noun* a small statue; a statue less than life-size.

stat·ure *noun* **1** a person's natural height (*small in stature*). **2** importance and reputation gained by ability or achievement (*her growing political stature*). **3** the height of a tree. □ **stat·ured** *adjective* (also in *combination*). [Old French from Latin *statura* from *stare* stand]

stat·us /ˈstatəs, ˈsteɪt-/ *noun* **1** the social or professional position of a person or thing in relation to others; relative importance (*be given equal status with other members of the staff*). **2** high rank or social position (*seeking status and security*). **3** *Law* a person's legal standing which determines his or her rights and duties, e.g. citizen, civilian, refugee, etc. (*see also* MARITAL STATUS). **4** *Cdn* (*attributive*) (of an Aboriginal person) registered as an Indian under the Indian Act. **5** the position of affairs (*let me know if the status changes*). [Latin, = standing, from *stare* stand]

status bar *noun Computing* a horizontal bar, usually at the bottom of the screen or window, showing information about a document being edited or a program running.

status quo /ˌstatəs ˈkwoː, ˌsteɪt-/ *noun* the existing state of affairs. [Latin, = the state in which]

status quo ante /ˌstatəs kwoː ˈanti, ˌsteɪt-/ *noun* the previously existing state of affairs. [Latin, = 'the state in which before']

status symbol *noun* a possession that is thought to show a person's high social rank, wealth, etc.

stat·ute /ˈstatʃuːt/ *noun* **1 a** a decree or enactment passed by a legislative body, and expressed in a formal document. **b** the document containing such an enactment. **2** any of the rules of an organization or institution (*against the University statutes*). **3** divine law (*kept thy statutes*). [Old French *statut* from Late Latin *statutum* neuter past participle of Latin *statuere* set up, from *status*: see STATUS]

statute-barred *adjective* (of a case etc.) no longer legally enforceable by reason of the lapse of time.

statute book *noun* **1** a book or books containing the statute law. **2** the body of a country's statutes.

statute law *noun* **1** (*collective*) the body of principles and rules of law laid down in statutes as distinct from rules formulated in practical application (*compare* COMMON LAW 1, CASE LAW). **2** a statute.

statute mile *noun see* MILE 1.

statute of limitations *noun* (*pl.* **statutes of limitations**) a law that fixes the time within which criminal charges must be laid or legal action taken.

statu·tory /ˈstatʃətəri, ˈstatʃʊtri/ *adjective* **1** required, permitted, or enacted by statute. **2** (of an offence) punishable under a statute. **3** of, relating to, or of the nature of a statute. □ **statu·tor·i·ly** *adverb*

statutory holiday *noun Cdn* a public holiday established by federal or provincial statute.

statutory rape *noun N Amer.* the act of sexual intercourse with a minor. ¶ In Canada, this term has been replaced in legal usage by *sexual interference*.

statutory release *noun Cdn Law* parole as required by statute, esp. after two-thirds of a sentence has been served.

staunch[1] *adjective* **1** trustworthy, loyal (*my staunch friend and supporter*). **2** (of a ship, joint, etc.) strong, watertight, airtight, etc. □ **staunch·ly** *adverb* **staunch·ness** *noun* [Old French *estanche* fem. of *estanc* from Romanic]

staunch[2] *transitive verb* (also **stanch** /stantʃ/) **1** restrain the flow of (esp. blood). **2** restrain the flow from (esp. a wound). [Old French *estanchier* from Romanic]

stave ● *noun* **1** each of the curved pieces of wood forming the sides of a cask, pail, etc. **2** = STAFF[1] *noun* 3. **3** a stanza or verse. **4** the rung of a ladder. ● *transitive verb* (*past* and *past participle* **stove** or **staved**) **1** break a hole in. **2** crush or knock out of shape. **3** fit or furnish (a cask etc.) with staves. □ **stave in** crush by forcing inwards. **stave off** (*past* and *past participle* **staved**) avert or defer (esp. danger or misfortune). [Middle English, back-formation from *staves*, pl. of STAFF[1]]

staves *pl.* of STAFF[1] *noun* 3.

Stav·ro·pol /ˈstavrəˌpɒl, stavˈrɒpəl/ **1** a krai in S Russia, in the N Caucasus; pop. (est. 1995) 2,650,000. **2** its capital city; pop. (est. 2002) 346,800.

stay[1] ● *verb* **1** *intransitive* continue to be in the same place or condition;

not depart or change (*stay here until I come back*). **2** *intransitive* **a** (often foll. by *at*, *in*, *with*) have temporary residence as a visitor etc. (*stayed with them for Christmas*). **b** *Scot. & South Africa* dwell permanently. **3** *archaic or literary* **a** *transitive* stop or check (progress, the inroads of a disease, etc.). **b** *intransitive* (esp. in *imperative*) pause in movement, action, speech, etc. (*Stay! You forget one thing*). **4** *transitive* postpone (judgment, decision, etc.). **5** *transitive* assuage (hunger etc.) esp. for a short time. **6 a** *intransitive* show endurance. **b** *transitive* show endurance to the end of (a race etc.). **7** *transitive* (often foll. by *up*) *literary* support, prop up (as or with a buttress etc.). **8** *intransitive* (foll. by *for*, *to*) wait long enough to share or join in an activity etc. (*stay to supper; stay for the film*). **9** *intransitive* (often foll. by *with*) (of an image etc.) remain in the mind or memory (*the sound of Dad's voice will stay with me forever*). **10** *N Amer. intransitive* (foll. by *with*) (of food) give lasting satisfaction to hunger (*need a breakfast that will stay with you till lunch*). **11** *intransitive* (in poker) raise one's ante sufficiently to remain in a round. **12** *intransitive* (foll. by *with*) **a** keep up with (a competitor etc.). **b** apply oneself to, continue with (*said she was committed to staying with this project*). ● *noun* **1 a** the act or an instance of staying or dwelling in one place. **b** the duration of this (*just a ten-minute stay; a long stay in Montreal*). **2** a suspension or postponement of a sentence, judgment, etc. (*was granted a stay of execution*). **3** *archaic or literary* a check or restraint. **4** endurance, staying power. **5** a prop or support. **6** a stiff material used in collars, waistlines, etc. to prevent them from curling. **7** (in *pl.*) *hist.* a corset esp. with whalebone etc. stiffening, and laced. □ **has come** (or **is here**) **to stay** *informal* must be regarded as permanent. **stay the course** pursue a course of action or endure a struggle etc. to the end. **stay one's hand** *see* HAND. **stay in** remain indoors, esp. at home or in school after hours as a punishment. **stay the night** remain until the next day. **stay on** remain in a place or position. **stay put** remain where it is placed or where one is. **stay up** not go to bed (until late at night). □ **stay·er** *noun* [Anglo-French *estai-* stem of Old French *ester* from Latin *stare* stand: sense 5 from Old French *estaye(r)* prop, formed as STAY²]

stay² ● *noun* **1** *Naut.* a large rope, wire, or rod used to support a ship's mast or spar or down to another part of the ship. **2** a guy wire or rope supporting a flagstaff or other upright pole. **3** a supporting wire or cable on an aircraft. ● *transitive verb* support (a mast etc.) by stays. □ **be in stays** (of a sailing ship) be head to the wind while tacking. [Old English *stæg* be firm, from Germanic]

stay-at-home ● *adjective* **1** remaining habitually at home. **2** (esp. of a parent) choosing to remain at home, esp. to care for children, rather than seeking outside employment (*a stay-at-home mom*). **3** *Hockey* (of a defenceman) conservative; unlikely to take risks or be caught out of position. ● *noun* a person who does this.

staying power *noun* endurance, stamina.

stay·sail /ˈsteiseil, ˈsteisəl/ *noun* a triangular fore-and-aft sail extended on a stay.

stay·stitch·ing *noun* stitching placed along a bias or curved seam to prevent the fabric of a garment from stretching while the garment is being made. □ **stay·stitch** *transitive verb*

stay-up ● *attributive adjective* (of stockings) having elasticized tops and not needing garters to stay up. ● *noun* such a stocking.

STD SEXUALLY TRANSMITTED DISEASE.

stead /sted/ *noun* □ **in a person's** (or **thing's**) **stead** as a substitute; instead of him or her or it. **stand a person in good stead** be advantageous or serviceable to him or her. [Old English *stede* from Germanic]

stead·fast /ˈstedfast, ˈstedfəst/ *adjective* **1** constant, firm, unwavering. **2** (of a person's gaze etc.) fixed in intensity; steadily directed. □ **stead·fastly** *adverb* **stead·fast·ness** *noun* [Old English *stedefæst* (as STEAD, FAST¹)]

Stead·i·cam *noun* proprietary **1** a lightweight mounting for a film camera that allows a single operator to make smooth shots while moving. **2** a camera mounted on this.

stead·ing /ˈstediŋ/ *noun Brit.* a farmstead.

steady ● *adjective* (**stead·i·er**, **stead·i·est**) **1** firmly fixed or supported or standing or balanced; not tottering, rocking, or wavering. **2** done or operating or happening in a uniform and regular manner (*a steady pace; a steady increase*). **3 a** constant in mind or conduct; not changeable. **b** persistent. **4** (of a person) serious and dependable in behaviour; of industrious and temperate habits; safe; cautious. **5** not changing (*a steady girlfriend; get a steady job*). **6** accurately directed; not faltering (*a steady hand; a steady eye*). **7** (of a ship) on course and upright. ● *transitive & intransitive verb* (**-ies**, **-ied**) make or become steady (*steady the boat*). ● *adverb* steadily (*hold it steady*). ● *interjection* as a command or warning to take care. ● *noun* (pl. **-ies**) **1** *informal* a regular boyfriend or

girlfriend. **2** *Cdn* (*Nfld*) **a** a stretch of still water in a river or pond; a pool. **b** a small freshwater pond. □ **go steady** (often foll. by *with*) *informal* have as a regular boyfriend or girlfriend. **steady on!** *Brit.* calm down, be reasonable. □ **stead·i·ly** *adverb* **stead·i·ness** *noun* [STEAD = place, + -Y¹]

steady state *noun* an unvarying condition, esp. in a physical process, e.g. of the universe theoretically having no beginning and no end.

steak *noun* **1** a thick slice of meat (esp. beef) or fish, often cut for broiling, frying, barbecuing, etc. **2** beef cut for stewing or braising. [Old Norse *steik* related to *steikja* roast on spit, *stikna* be roasted]

steak Diane *noun* a dish containing thin slices of beefsteak fried with seasonings, esp. Worcestershire sauce.

steak·ette *noun Cdn* a thin patty of ground beef, meant to be cooked quickly.

steak house *noun* a restaurant specializing in serving beefsteaks.

steak knife *noun* a table knife with a serrated steel blade, used esp. when eating steak.

steak tar·tare *noun* (also **steak tar·tar**) a dish consisting of raw chopped beefsteak mixed with raw egg, onion, and seasonings and shaped into small cakes or patties. [*French*, = tartar (see TARTAR)]

steal ● *verb* (past **stole**; past participle **stolen**) **1** *transitive & intransitive* **a** take (another person's property) illegally. **b** take (property etc.) without right or permission, esp. in secret with the intention of not returning it. **2** *transitive* obtain surreptitiously or by surprise (*stole a kiss*). **3** *transitive* gain insidiously or artfully. **b** (often foll. by *away*) win or get possession of (a person's affections etc.), esp. insidiously (*stole her heart away*). **4** *intransitive* (foll. by *in*, *out*, *away*, *up*, etc.) **a** move, esp. silently or stealthily (*stole out of the room*). **b** (of a sound etc.) become gradually perceptible. **5** *transitive* **a** (in various sports) gain (a run, the ball, etc.) surreptitiously or by luck. **b** *Baseball* reach (a base) by running to it while the ball is being pitched to the batter. ● *noun* **1** *informal* an unexpectedly easy task or good bargain. **2** *Baseball* the act of advancing a base by stealing. **3** *US informal* the act or an instance of stealing or theft. □ **steal a march on** get an advantage over by surreptitious means; anticipate. **steal the show** outshine other performers, esp. unexpectedly. **steal a person's thunder 1** use another person's idea, policy, etc., and spoil the effect the originator hoped to achieve by expressing it or acting upon it first. **2** take the limelight or attention from another person. □ **steal·er** *noun* (also in *combination*). [Old English *stelan* from Germanic]

stealth /stelθ/ *noun* **1** secrecy; a secret procedure. **2** (*attributive*) designed in accordance with or designating the technology which makes detection by radar or sonar difficult (*stealth bomber*). □ **by stealth** surreptitiously. [Middle English from Old English (as STEAL, -TH²)]

stealthy /ˈstelθi/ *adjective* (**stealth·i·er**, **stealth·i·est**) **1** (of an action) done with stealth; proceeding imperceptibly. **2** (of a person or thing) moving with stealth. □ **stealth·i·ly** *adverb* **stealth·i·ness** *noun*

steam ● *noun* **1 a** the gas into which water is changed by boiling, often used as a source of power by virtue of its expansion of volume. **b** a mist of liquid particles of water produced by the condensation of this gas. **2** any similar vapour. **3 a** energy or power provided by a steam engine or other machine. **b** *informal* power or energy generally. ● *verb* **1** *transitive* **a** cook (food) in steam. **b** soften or make pliable (timber etc.) or otherwise treat with steam, e.g. to remove wrinkles from garments. **2** *intransitive* give off steam or other vapour, esp. visibly. **3** *intransitive* **a** move under steam power (*the ship steamed down the river*). **b** (foll. by *along*, *ahead*, etc.) *informal* proceed or travel fast or with vigour. **4** *transitive & intransitive* cover or become covered with condensed water vapour. **5** *transitive & intransitive informal* be or cause to be angry or upset. **6** *transitive* (foll. by *open* etc.) apply steam to the gum of (a sealed envelope) to get it open. □ **blow** (or **let**) **off steam** relieve one's pent up feelings or energy. **full steam** full speed; as quickly as possible. **full steam ahead** with as much speed and vigour as possible. **get up steam 1** generate enough power to work a steam engine. **2** work oneself into an energetic or angry state. **lose steam** slow down (*the economy is starting to lose steam*). **pick up steam** speed up (*the project is really picking up steam!*). **run out of steam** = RUN OUT OF GAS (see GAS). **under one's own steam** without assistance; unaided. [Old English *stēam* from Germanic]

steam bath *noun* **1** a room etc. filled with steam for cleaning or refreshing oneself by sweating. **2** a bath taken in such a room.

steam·boat *noun* a boat propelled by a steam engine.

steam boiler *noun* a vessel (in a steam engine etc.) in which water is boiled to generate steam.

---

t top   v voice   w we   z zoo   ʃ she   ʒ vision   θ thin   ð this   ŋ ring   x loch   tʃ chip   dʒ jar   (*see over for vowels*)

steam cleaning *noun* a method of cleaning (esp. carpets) using a machine that sprays a mixture of hot water and detergent then vacuums it back up. □ **steam-clean** *transitive verb*

steamed *adjective* **1** *informal* angry; upset. **2** (of food) cooked or heated by steaming.

steamed up *adjective* **1** (of a surface) covered with condensed vapour. **2** *informal* agitated or upset; angry.

steam engine *noun* **1** an engine which uses the expansion or rapid condensation of steam to generate power. **2** a locomotive powered by such an engine.

steam·er *noun* **1** a person or thing that steams. **2** a vessel propelled by steam, esp. a ship. **3** a usu. perforated container in which things are steamed, esp. cooked by steam. **4** (also **steamer clam**) an edible clam, *Mya arenaria*, with a long siphon.

steamer trunk *noun* a rectangular travelling trunk made so as to slide under a ship's bunk.

steam gauge *noun* a pressure gauge attached to a steam boiler.

steam hammer *noun* a forging hammer powered by steam.

steam·ie *noun Cdn* (*Que.*) a steamed hot dog.

steam iron *noun* an electric iron that emits steam from its flat surface, to improve its pressing ability.

steam power *noun* the force of steam applied to machinery etc. □ **steam-powered** *adjective*

steam·punk *noun* a sub-genre of science fiction, usually set in the industrial 19th century. [jocular, alteration of CYBERPUNK]

steam·roll *transitive verb* esp. *N Amer.* = STEAMROLLER *verb*.

steam·roll·er ● *noun* **1** a heavy slow-moving vehicle with a roller, used for levelling roads. **2** a crushing power or force. ● *transitive verb* **1** crush forcibly or indiscriminately. **2 a** (foll. by *through*) force (a measure etc.) through a legislature by overriding opposition. **b** force (someone) into accepting or doing something.

steam room *noun* a room that may be filled with steam for taking steam baths.

steam·ship *noun* a ship propelled by a steam engine.

steam shovel *noun* an excavator powered by steam.

steam table *noun* a table or counter in a cafeteria etc., with openings in the top into which containers of food are placed to be kept warm by hot water or steam in the compartment beneath them.

steam turbine *noun* a turbine in which a high-velocity jet of steam rotates a bladed disc or drum.

steamy *adjective* (**steam·i·er**, **steam·i·est**) **1** like or full of steam. **2** *informal* erotic, passionate. **3** hot and humid (*a steamy July night*). □ **steam·i·ly** *adverb* **steam·i·ness** *noun*

stear·ic /ˈstɪːrɪk, stiːˈærɪk/ *adjective* derived from stearin. □ **stear·ate** /ˈstiːreɪt, ˈstiːəˌreɪt/ *noun* [French *stéarique* from Greek *stear steatos* tallow]

stearic acid *noun* a solid saturated fatty acid obtained from animal or vegetable fats.

stear·in /ˈstiːrɪn/ *noun* **1** a white crystalline substance which is the main constituent of tallow and suet. **2** a mixture of fatty acids used in candle making. [French *stéarine*, as STEARIC]

stea·tite /ˈstiːətaɪt/ *noun* a soapstone or other impure form of talc. [Latin *steatitis* from Greek *steatitēs* from *stear steatos* tallow]

steato·pygous /ˌstiːətəˈpaɪɡəs, -ˈtɒpɪɡəs/ *adjective* having an excess of fat on the buttocks. □ **steato·pygia** /-ˈpɪdʒɪə/ *noun* **steato·pygic** /-ˈpɪdʒɪk/ *adjective* [modern Latin (as STEATITE + Greek *pugē* rump)]

steed *noun archaic* or *literary* a horse, esp. a fast powerful one. [Old English *stēda* stallion, related to STUD[2]]

steel ● *noun* **1** a hard strong usu. grey or greyish-blue alloy of iron with carbon and usu. other elements, much used as a structural and fabricating material (*carbon steel*; *stainless steel*). **2** hardness of character; strength, firmness (*nerves of steel*). **3 a** a rod of steel, usu. roughened and tapering, on which knives are sharpened. **b** a piece of steel used with a flint to produce sparks. **c** a strip of steel for expanding a skirt or stiffening a corset. **4** (not in *pl.*) *literary* a sword, lance, etc. (*warriors worthy of their steel*). **5** *Cdn* **a** a railway track or length of railway track. **b** a railway line. ● *adjective* **1** made of steel. **2** like or having the characteristics of steel. ● *verb* **1** *transitive* & *reflexive* harden or make resolute (*steeled myself for a shock*). **2** *transitive* sharpen (a knife) with a steel. [Old English *stȳle*, *stēli* from Germanic, related to STAY[2]]

steel band *noun* a group of musicians who play (chiefly calypso-style) music on steel drums.

steel blue ● *noun* a dark bluish-grey colour. ● *adjective* (**steel-blue**) of this colour.

Steel City 1 a nickname for Hamilton, Ontario. **2** a nickname for Sydney, Nova Scotia.

steel-clad *adjective* plated with steel.

steel drum *noun* a percussion instrument originating in the W Indies, made out of an oil drum with one end beaten down and divided into grooved sections to give different notes.

Steele ▸ **1** Sir **Rich·ard** (1672–1729), Irish essayist and dramatist. He founded and wrote for the periodicals the *Tatler* (1709–11) and the *Spectator* (1711–12), the latter in collaboration with Addison; both had an important influence on the manners, morals, and literature of the time. **2** Sir **Sam·uel Ben·field** ('**Sam**') (1849–1919), English-born Canadian mounted policeman and soldier. Having served during the Fenian crisis and the Red River Expedition (1870), he joined the new NWMP in 1873. In 1879 he was placed in command of all detachments supervising the building of the CPR; in 1898 he helped police the Klondike gold rush.

Steele, Mount a peak in SW Yukon Territory, in the St. Elias mountain range. Rising to a height of 5 067 m, it is the fifth highest mountain in Canada. [Sir S. B. STEELE]

steel engraving *noun* the process of engraving on or an impression taken from a steel-coated copper plate.

steel grey ● *noun* a dark metallic grey colour. ● *adjective* (**steel-grey**) of this colour.

steel guitar *noun* **1** a type of hand-held acoustic guitar with steel resonating discs inside the body under the bridge. **2** = PEDAL STEEL. **3** = HAWAIIAN GUITAR.

steel·head *noun* a large silvery N American rainbow trout, esp. after returning from the sea or when found in the Great Lakes and tributaries.

steel·head·er *noun N Amer.* a person who fishes for steelhead. □ **steel·head·ing** *noun*

steel·ie *noun informal* **1** a steel ball bearing used as a marble. **2** *N Amer.* a steelhead.

steel·maker *noun* a business that manufactures steel. □ **steel·making** *noun & adjective*

steel mill *noun* a steelworks.

steel pan *noun* = STEEL DRUM.

Steel·town a nickname for Hamilton. [because of the city's steel production]

steel trap *noun* a trap with jaws and springs of steel. □ **steel-trap mind** (also **mind like a steel trap**) a mind which retains everything to which it is exposed.

steel wool *noun* an abrasive substance consisting of a mass of fine steel threads, used for cleaning metal, making a surface smooth, etc.

steel·work *noun* articles of steel.

steel·works *plural noun* (usu. treated as *sing.*) a plant where steel is manufactured. □ **steel·work·er** *noun*

steely *adjective* (**steel·i·er**, **steel·i·est**) **1** of, or hard as, steel. **2** inflexibly severe; cold; ruthless (*steely composure*; *steely-eyed glance*). □ **steel·i·ness** *noun*

steel·yard *noun* a kind of balance with a short arm to take the item to be weighed and a long graduated arm along which a weight is moved until it balances.

steen·bok *noun* an African dwarf antelope, *Raphicerus campestris*. [Dutch from *steen* STONE + *bok* BUCK[1]]

steep[1] ● *adjective* **1** sloping sharply; almost perpendicular (*a steep hill*; *steep stairs*). **2** (of a rise or fall in an amount) very large or rapid (*a steep drop in share prices*). **3** (*predicative*) *informal* (of a demand, price, etc.) exorbitant; unreasonable (esp. *a bit steep*). ● *noun* a steep slope; a precipice. □ **steep·en** *transitive* & *intransitive verb* **steep·ish** *adjective* **steep·ly** *adverb* **steep·ness** *noun* [Old English *stēap* from West Germanic, related to STOOP[1]]

steep[2] ● *verb* **1** *transitive* (often foll. by *in*) soak or bathe in liquid. **2** *intransitive* undergo the process of soaking (*the tea is steeping*). **3** *transitive* (foll. by *in*; usu. in *passive*) **a** pervade or imbue with (*steeped in misery*). **b** make deeply acquainted with (a subject) (*steeped in the classics*). ● *noun* **1** the act or process of steeping. **2** the liquid for steeping. [Old English from Germanic (as STOUP)]

stee·ple ● *noun* **1** a tall tower, esp. one surmounted by a spire, above the roof of a church. **2** a steeple-shaped formation of two hands, with the palms facing and the extended fingers meeting at the tips. ● *transitive verb* place (the fingers or hands) together in the shape of a steeple. □ **stee·pled** *adjective* [Old English *stēpel stȳpel* from Germanic (as STEEP[1])]

steeple·chase noun **1** a horse race (originally with a steeple as the goal) across the countryside or on a racecourse with ditches, hedges, etc., to jump. **2** a running race in which runners must clear hurdles and water jumps. □ **steeple·chas·er** noun **steeple·chas·ing** noun

steeple·jack noun a person who climbs tall chimneys, steeples, etc., to do repairs etc.

steer¹ ● verb **1** transitive **a** guide (a vehicle, aircraft, etc.) by a wheel etc. **b** guide (a vessel) by a rudder or helm. **2** intransitive direct or control the movement of a vehicle or vessel (you steer and I'll push). **3** intransitive (of a vehicle or vessel) move in a particular direction as a result of being steered (the boat steered around the rocks). **4** transitive direct (one's course). **5** intransitive direct one's course in a specified direction (steered for shore). **6** transitive guide (a person, action, etc.) by admonition, advice, or instruction. **7** transitive guide the movement or trend of (steered them into the garden; steered the conversation away from that subject). ● noun esp. N Amer. a piece of advice or information; guidance. □ **steer clear of** take care to avoid. □ **steer·able** adjective **steer·er** noun **steer·ing** noun (esp. in senses 1, 2 of verb). [Old English stieran from Germanic]

steer² noun a castrated male of domestic cattle, esp. one raised for beef. [Old English stéor from Germanic]

steer·age noun **1** esp. hist. the part of a ship allotted to passengers travelling at the cheapest rate. **2** the act of steering. **3** the effect of the helm on a ship.

steerage-way noun the amount of headway required by a vessel to enable it to be controlled by the helm.

steering column noun the shaft or column which connects the steering wheel, handlebars, etc. of a vehicle to the rest of the steering gear.

steering committee noun (also **steering group**) a committee that decides the order of certain business activities and guides their general course.

steering wheel noun a wheel by which a vehicle etc. is steered.

steer riding noun N Amer. a rodeo event in which contestants, often bull riders in training, attempt to remain on a bucking steer. □ **steer rider** noun

steer roping noun N Amer. a rodeo event in which a contestant on a horse chases a steer, lassos it, throws it to the ground, and ties three of its feet together. □ **steer roper** noun

steers·man noun (pl. **-men**) a person who steers a vessel.

steer wrestling noun N Amer. a rodeo event in which a contestant on a horse chases a steer, dismounts, and wrestles the steer to the ground. □ **steer wrestler** noun

Stef·ans·son /ˈstefənsən/ **Vilhjal·mur** (1879–1962), Canadian explorer and ethnologist, who explored the Canadian Arctic and studied Inuit culture; his works include My Life with the Eskimo (1913) and Unsolved Mysteries of the Arctic (1939).

Stefansson Island /ˈstefənsən/ an island in the central Canadian Arctic, situated off the northeast coast of Victoria Island, from which it is separated by the narrow Goldsmith Channel. [STEFANSSON]

stego·saur·us /ˌstegəˈsɔrəs/ noun (also **stego·saur** /ˈstegəsɔr/) a small-headed plant-eating dinosaur of the suborder Stegosauria, with a double row of large bony plates (or spines) along the back. [modern Latin from Greek stegē covering + sauros lizard]

Stein /ʃtaɪn/ **Ger·trude** (1874–1946), US writer. A member of the Paris avant-garde during the 1920s and 1930s, she developed an esoteric stream-of-consciousness writing style whose hallmarks include use of repetition and lack of punctuation; her best-known work is The Autobiography of Alice B. Toklas (1933).

stein /staɪn/ noun **1** a large (usu. earthenware) mug, esp. for beer. **2** the quantity contained in such a mug. [German, lit. 'stone']

Stein·bach /ˈstaɪnbak/ a city in SE central Manitoba, about 50 km southeast of Winnipeg; pop. (2001) 9,227. □ **Stein·bach·er** noun [Steinbach, Ukraine]

Stein·beck /ˈstaɪnbek/ **John (Ernst)** (1902–68), US novelist. In novels such as Of Mice and Men (1937) and The Grapes of Wrath (1939), he portrays the migrant agricultural workers of California with sympathy and realism; his later novels include East of Eden (1952). He was awarded the Nobel Prize for literature in 1962. □ **Stein·beck·ian** noun & adjective

stein·bock /ˈstaɪnbɒk/ noun **1** an ibex native to the Alps. **2** = STEENBOK. [German from Stein STONE + Bock BUCK¹]

Stein·em /ˈstaɪnəm/ **Gloria** (b.1934), US feminist, activist, and editor. A leading figure in the US women's movement, she founded Ms.

magazine in 1971; her works include Outrageous Acts and Everyday Rebellions (1983) and Revolution from Within (1991).

Stein·er /ˈstaɪnər/ **Ru·dolf** (1861–1925), Austrian philosopher, founder of anthroposophy. He believed that nurturing the faculty of cognition would counteract the negative effects on the human spirit of over-attention to the material world. He developed a child-centred pedagogy with a strong emphasis on the arts.

Stein·way /ˈstaɪnweɪ/ **Henry (Engel·hard)** (born Heinrich Engelhardt Steinweg) (1797–1871), German-born US piano maker, whose name is used to designate pianos manufactured by the firm which he founded in New York in 1853.

stela /ˈstiːlə/ noun (pl. **stelae** /-liː/) an upright slab or pillar usu. with an inscription and sculpture, used in ancient times esp. as a tombstone. [Latin from Greek (as STELE)]

stele /stiːl, ˈstiːli/ noun **1** Bot. the axial cylinder of vascular tissue in the stem and roots of most plants. **2** = STELA. □ **ste·lar** adjective [Greek stēlē standing block]

stel·lar adjective **1** of or relating to a star or stars. **2** esp. N Amer. **a** having star performers (stellar cast). **b** informal outstanding (stellar performance by the team). [Late Latin stellaris from Latin stella 'star']

Stel·lar·ton a town in north central Nova Scotia, immediately south of New Glasgow, formerly a coal-mining centre; pop. (2001) 4,809. [after the Stellar coal mined there]

stellar wind noun a continuous flow of charged particles from a star.

stel·late /ˈsteleɪt, -lət/ adjective (also **stel·lat·ed** /steˈleɪtɪd/) **1** arranged like a star; radiating. **2** Bot. (of leaves) surrounding the stem in a whorl. [Latin stellatus from stella star]

Stel·ler's jay noun a blue jay with a dark crest, Cyanocitta stelleri, found in central and western N America. [G. Steller, German naturalist and explorer d.1746]

Stel·ler's sea lion noun a large red-brown sea lion, Eumetopias jubatus, of the northern Pacific. [as STELLER'S JAY]

stem¹ ● noun **1 a** the main body or stalk of a plant or shrub, usu. rising into light, but occasionally subterranean. **b** this with the flowers attached to it (pinks are $3 a stem). **2 a** the stalk supporting a fruit, flower, or leaf, and attaching it to a larger branch, twig, or stalk. **b** a stalk supporting or forming part of an organ or structure (brain stem). **3** a stem-shaped part of an object: **a** the slender part of a wineglass between the body and the base. **b** the tube of a tobacco pipe. **c** a vertical stroke in a letter or musical note. **d** the winding shaft of a watch. **4** Grammar the root or main part of a noun, verb, etc., to which inflections are added; the part that appears unchanged throughout the cases and derivatives of a noun, persons of a tense, etc. **5** Naut. the main upright timber or metal piece at the bow of a ship to which the ship's sides are joined at the fore end (from stem to stern). **6** a line of ancestry, branch of a family, etc. (descended from an ancient stem). ● verb (**stemmed**, **stem·ming**) **1** intransitive (foll. by from) spring or originate from (stems from a desire to win). **2** transitive remove the stem or stems from (fruit, tobacco, etc.). **3** transitive (of a vessel etc.) hold its own or make headway against (the tide etc.). □ **stem·less** adjective **stem·like** adjective **stemmed** adjective (also in combination). **stem·mer** noun **stem·my** adjective □ **stem the tide** work against a difficult trend. [Old English stemn, stefn from Germanic, related to STAND]

stem² ● verb (**stemmed**, **stem·ming**) **1** transitive check or stop. **2** transitive dam up (a stream etc.). **3** intransitive slide the tail of one ski or both skis outwards usu. in order to turn or slow down. ● noun an act of stemming on skis. [Old Norse stemma from Germanic]

stem cell noun Biol. an undifferentiated cell from which specialized cells develop.

stem·ma noun (pl. **stem·mata** /ˈstemətə/) **1** a family tree; a pedigree. **2** the line of descent e.g. of variant texts of a work. **3** Zool. a simple eye; a facet of a compound eye. [Latin from Greek stemma wreath, from stephō wreathe]

stem turn noun a turn on skis made by stemming with one ski.

stem·ware noun esp. N Amer. crystal or glass vessels with rounded bowls on stems, used esp. for wine.

stem·wind·er noun N Amer. **1** a watch wound by turning a head on the end of a stem. **2 a** a forceful, energetic person, esp. one who makes inspiring, dynamic speeches. **b** such a speech.

stench noun an offensive or foul smell. [Old English stenc smell, from Germanic, related to STINK]

sten·cil ● noun **1** a thin sheet of plastic, metal, cardboard, etc., in which a pattern or lettering is cut, used to produce a corresponding pattern on the surface beneath it by applying ink, paint, etc. to the cut-out areas. **2** the pattern, lettering, etc., produced by a stencil. ● *transitive verb* (**sten·cilled, sten·cil·ling**; esp. *US* **sten·ciled, sten·cil·ing**) **1** (often foll. by *on*) produce (a pattern) with a stencil. **2** decorate or mark (a surface) in this way. [Old French *estanceler* sparkle, cover with stars, from *estencele* spark, ultimately from Latin *scintilla*]

Sten·dhal /'stɛndɒl/ (pseudonym of Marie-Henri Beyle) (1783–1842), French novelist. His two best-known novels, *Le Rouge et le noir* (1830) and *La Chartreuse de Parme* (1839), are notable for their psychological realism and political analysis.

Sten gun *noun* a type of lightweight submachine gun. [*S* and *T* (the initials of the inventors' surnames, Shepherd and Turpin) + *-en* after BREN]

Steno /'sti:noː/ **Nico·laus** (Danish name Niels Steensen) (1638–86), Danish anatomist and geologist. He proposed several ideas now regarded as fundamental to geology — that fossils are the petrified remains of living organisms, that many rocks arise from consolidation of sediments, and that such rocks occur in layers in the order in which they were laid down, thereby constituting a record of the geological history of the earth.

steno *noun* (pl. **stenos**) *N Amer. informal* a stenographer (often *attributive*: *steno pool*). [abbreviation]

sten·og·ra·phy /stə'nɒɡrəfi/ *noun* shorthand or the art of writing shorthand. □ **sten·og·raph·er** *noun* **steno·graph·ic** *adjective* [Greek *stenos* narrow + -GRAPHY]

steno pad *noun* a lined notepad with a spiral binding along the top and rigid covers, used for taking dictation etc.

sten·o·sis /stɪ'noːsɪs/ *noun Med.* the abnormal narrowing of a passage in the body. □ **sten·ot·ic** /-'nɒtɪk/ *adjective* [modern Latin from Greek *stenōsis* narrowing, from *stenoō* make narrow, from *stenos* narrow]

steno·type /'stɛnə,tʌɪp/ *noun* **1** a machine like a typewriter for recording speech in phonetic shorthand. **2** a symbol or the symbols used in this process. [STENOGRAPHY + TYPE]

stent *noun* a splint placed temporarily inside a duct, canal, or blood vessel to aid healing or relieve an obstruction. [Charles T. *Stent*, English dentist d.1885.]

sten·tor·ian /stɛn'tɔːrɪən/ *adjective* (of a voice, sound, etc.) very loud and powerful. [Greek *Stentōr*, herald in the Trojan War]

step ● *noun* **1 a** the complete movement of one leg in walking or running (*took a step forward*). **b** the distance covered by this. **c** (in *pl.*) the course followed by a person in walking etc. (*retraced her steps*). **2** a unit of movement in dancing. **3** a measure taken, esp. one of several in a course of action (*took steps to prevent it; a step in the right direction*). **4 a** a flat-topped structure used singly or as one of a series, for passing from one level to another. **b** the rung of a ladder. **c** a notch cut for a foot in ice climbing. **5** a short distance (*only a step from my door*). **6** the sound or mark made by a foot in walking etc. (*heard a step on the stairs*). **7** the manner of walking etc. as seen or heard (*know her by her step*). **8 a** a degree in the scale of promotion, advancement, or precedence. **b** one of a series of fixed points on a pay scale etc. **9** (in *pl.*) *Brit.* = STEPLADDER. **10** esp. *US Music* a melodic interval of one degree of the scale, i.e. a tone or semitone. **11** *Naut.* a block, socket, or platform supporting a mast. **12** (often *attributive*) = STEP AEROBICS (*step class*). ● *verb* (**stepped, step·ping**) **1** *intransitive* lift and set down one's foot or alternate feet in walking. **2** *intransitive* come or go in a specified direction by stepping. **3** *intransitive* make progress in a specified way (*stepped into a new job*). **4** *intransitive* (foll. by *off, out*) measure (distance) by stepping. **5** *transitive* perform (a dance). **6** *transitive Naut.* set up (a mast) in a step. □ **in step** (often foll. by *with*) **1** stepping in time with music or other marchers. **2** conforming with others. **in a person's steps** following a person's example. **keep step** remain in step. **out of step** (often foll. by *with*) not in step. **step aside** = STEP DOWN 1. **step back** mentally withdraw from a situation in order to consider it objectively. **step by step** gradually; cautiously; by stages or degrees. **step down 1** resign from a position etc. **2** *Electricity* decrease (voltage) by using a transformer. **step forward** offer one's help, services, etc. **step in 1** enter a room, house, etc. **2 a** intervene to help or hinder. **b** act as a substitute for an indisposed colleague etc. **step into a person's shoes** take control of a task or job from another person. **step on it** (or **on the gas**) *informal* **1** accelerate a motor vehicle. **2** hurry up. **step on a person's toes** see TOE. **step out 1** leave a room, house, etc. **2 a** be active socially. **b** *N Amer. dialect & informal* (often foll. by *with*) = DATE[1] *verb* 3b. **3** take large steps. **step out of line** behave inappropriately or disobediently. **step outside** agree to settle a matter by fighting. **step this way** a deferential formula meaning 'follow me'. **step up 1 a** increase, intensify (*must step up production*).

b *Electricity* increase (voltage) using a transformer. **2** come forward for some purpose. **watch one's step** be careful. □ **step·less** *adjective* **step-like** *adjective* **stepped** *adjective* **step·wise** *adverb & adjective* [Old English *stæpe, stepe* (n.), *stæppan, steppan* (v.), from Germanic]

step- *combining form* denoting a relationship like the one specified but resulting from a parent's remarriage. [Old English *stēop-* orphan-]

step aerobics *plural noun* a type of aerobics involving stepping up on to and down from a portable block.

Step·ana·kert /,stəpanə'kert/ the Russian name for XANKÄNDI.

step·broth·er *noun* a son of one's stepmother or stepfather by an earlier marriage.

step-by-step *attributive adjective* (of an approach, guide, etc.) that proceeds through or involves a series of distinct stages or operations.

step·child *noun* a child of one's husband or wife by a previous marriage. **2** *informal* a neglected or scorned member of a group.

step·dad *noun informal* = STEPFATHER.

step dance ● *noun* a dance intended to display special steps by an individual performer, esp. popular in Celtic cultures. ● *intransitive verb* (**step-dance**) perform a step dance. □ **step dancer** *noun* **step-dancing** *noun*

step·daughter *noun* a female stepchild.

step·fam·ily *noun* (pl. **-ies**) a family unit in which either or both of the parents has children from a previous relationship or marriage.

step·father *noun* a male step-parent.

Step·ford *noun* (*attributive*) denoting someone who is regarded as robotically conformist or obedient. [allusion to *The Stepford Wives*, a 1972 novel by Ira Levin (b.1929) in which *Stepford* is a fictional idyllic suburb where the men have replaced their wives with robots]

steph·an·otis /,stefə'noːtɪs/ *noun* any climbing tropical plant of the genus *Stephanotis*, cultivated for its fragrant waxy usu. white flowers. [modern Latin from Greek, = fit for a wreath, from *stephanos* wreath]

Ste·phen ▶ **1 St.** (died *c*.35), the first Christian martyr. One of the original seven deacons in Jerusalem appointed by the Apostles, he incurred the hostility of the Jews and was charged with blasphemy before the Sanhedrin and stoned to death. Feast day (in the Western Church) 26 Dec.; (in the Eastern Church) 27 Dec. **2 St.** (*c*.977–1038), king and patron saint of Hungary, reigned 1000–38. The first king of Hungary, he united Pannonia and Dacia as one kingdom, and took steps to Christianize the country. Feast day, 2 Sept. or (in Hungary) 20 Aug.

Ste·phen·son ▶ **1 George** (1781–1848), English engineer. Considered the founder of railways, he designed the first steam locomotive (1814) and constructed the first passenger-carrying railway line in the 1820s. **2** his son, **Rob·ert** (1803–59), English engineer, who assisted his father in the building of the Liverpool to Manchester railway, for which they built the famous *Rocket* (1829) steam locomotive; Robert also became famous as a designer of bridges, notably one at Menai Strait in Wales and the Victoria Bridge across the St. Lawrence at Montreal.

Ste·phen·ville a town in SW Newfoundland, situated on St. George's Bay, about 65 km southwest of Corner Brook; pop. (2001) 7,109. [St. *Stephen's* Catholic Church, after *Stephen* Le Blanc, first child baptized there]

step-in ● *noun* **1** a garment or shoe put on by stepping into it. **2** esp. *N Amer. dated* loose underwear for women. ● *attributive adjective* (of a garment or shoe) put on by being stepped into without unfastening.

step·lad·der *noun* a short folding ladder with flat steps and a small platform at the top.

step·mom *noun informal* = STEPMOTHER.

step·mother *noun* a female step-parent.

step-parent *noun* a mother's or father's later husband or wife.

steppe *noun* a level grassy unforested plain, esp. in SE Europe and Siberia. [Russian *step'*]

stepped-up *attributive adjective* raised by degrees to a higher level; increased, intensified.

step·per *noun* **1** an exercise machine in which the exerciser stands upright, places each foot on a slightly angled bar, and pushes it down by walking in place. **2** *informal* a person who steps, esp. a dancer.

stepping stone *noun* **1** a raised stone, usu. one of a series, placed in the bed of a stream, on muddy ground, etc., to facilitate crossing on foot. **2** something used as a means of advancement in a career etc.

step·sister *noun* a daughter of one's stepmother or stepfather by an earlier marriage.

Consonants: b *but*   d *dog*   f *few*   g *get*   h *her*   j *yes*   k *cat*   l *leg*   m *man*   n *no*   p *pen*   r *red*   s *sit*

step·son *noun* a male stepchild.

step·stool *noun* **1** a small stool for stepping on. **2** a short folding stepladder of two or three steps.

step·wise *adjective & adverb* in a series of distinct stages.

-ster *suffix* denoting a person engaged in or associated with a particular activity or thing (*gangster*; *youngster*). [Old English *-estre* etc. from Germanic]

ste·radi·an /stəˈreɪdɪən/ *noun* the SI unit of solid angle, equal to the angle at the centre of a sphere subtended by a part of the surface equal in area to the square of the radius. Abbr.: **sr**. [Greek *stereos* solid + RADIAN]

stere /stɪːr/ *noun* a unit of volume equal to one cubic metre. [French *stère* from Greek *stereos* solid]

stereo ● *noun* (*pl.* **stereos**) **1 a** a stereophonic CD player, tape deck, etc. **b** stereophony (*broadcast in stereo*). **2** = STEREOSCOPE. ● *adjective* **1** = STEREOPHONIC. **2** stereoscopic. [abbreviation]

stereo- *combining form* solid; having three dimensions. [Greek *stereos* solid]

stereo·chem·istry /ˌsteriːəˈkemɪstri/ *noun* the branch of chemistry dealing with the three-dimensional arrangement of atoms in molecules. □ **stereo·chem·ical** *adjective*

stereo·gram *noun* a diagram or computer-generated image giving a three-dimensional representation of a solid object or surface.

ster·eog·raphy /ˌsteriˈɒɡrəfi/ *noun* the depiction or representation of three-dimensional things by projection onto a two-dimensional surface, e.g. in cartography. □ **stereo·graph** *noun* **stereo·graph·ic** *adjective*

stereo·iso·mer /ˌsteriːˈaɪsəmər/ *noun Chem.* any of two or more compounds differing only in their spatial arrangement of atoms.

stereo·lith·og·raphy *noun* a technique or process for creating three-dimensional objects, in which a computer-controlled moving laser beam is used to build up the required structure, layer by layer, from a liquid polymer that hardens on contact with laser light.

stereo·phon·ic /ˌsteriːəˈfɒnɪk/ *adjective* (of sound reproduction) using two or more channels so that the sound has the effect of being distributed and of coming from more than one source.
□ **stereo·phon·ic·ally** *adverb* **ster·eoph·ony** /-ˈɒfəni/ *noun*

ster·eop·sis /steriˈɒpsɪs/ *noun* the perception of depth produced by combining the visual images from both eyes; binocular vision.
□ **ster·eop·tic** *adjective* [STEREO- + Greek *opsis* 'sight']

ster·eop·ti·con /steriˈɒptɪkən, -kɒn/ *noun* a projector which combines two images to give a three-dimensional effect, or makes one image dissolve into another. [STEREO- + Greek *optikon*, neuter of *optikos* OPTIC]

stereo·scope /ˈsteriəˌskoʊp/ *noun* a device by which two photographs of the same object taken at slightly different angles are viewed together, giving an impression of depth and solidity as in ordinary human vision. □ **stereo·scop·ic** *adjective* **stereo·scopic·ally** *adverb* **ster·eos·copy** /-ˈɒskəpi/ *noun*

stereo·specif·ic /ˌsteriːspəˈsɪfɪk/ *adjective Chem.* of or relating to a particular stereoisomer of a substance. □ **stereo·specif·ic·ally** *adverb* **stereo·speci·fi·city** /-ˈfɪsɪti/ *noun*

stereo·taxis /ˌsteriːˈtaksɪs/ *noun Biol. & Med.* surgery involving the accurate positioning of probes etc. inside the brain. □ **stereo·tac·tic** *adjective* **stereo·taxic** *adjective* [STEREO- + Greek *taxis* 'orientation']

stereo·type /ˈsteriːˌtaɪp/ ● *noun* **1 a** a preconceived, standardized, and oversimplified impression of the characteristics which typify a person, situation, etc. **b** a person or thing appearing to conform closely to such a standardized impression. **2** a printing plate cast from a mould of composed type. ● *transitive verb* (esp. as **stereo·typed** *adjective*) view or represent as a stereotype. □ **stereo·typ·ic** /-ˈtɪpɪk/ *adjective* **stereo·typ·ical** /-ˈtɪpɪkəl/ *adjective* **stereo·typ·ical·ly** /-ˈtɪpɪkli/ *adverb* **stereo·typy** *noun* [French *stéréotype* (adj.) (as STEREO-, TYPE)]

ster·ic /ˈstɪːrɪk/ *adjective* (also **steric·al**) *Chem.* relating to the spatial arrangement of atoms in a molecule. □ **steric·ally** *adverb* [irreg. from Greek *stereos* solid]

steric hindrance *noun* the inhibiting of a chemical reaction by the obstruction of reacting atoms.

ster·ile *adjective* **1** (of humans or animals) not able to produce children or young; infertile. **2** free from bacteria etc. (*sterile bandages*). **3** unfruitful, unproductive (*sterile discussions*). **4** lacking originality or emotive force (*the room felt cold and sterile*). **5** (of plants) not producing fruit or seeds. □ **ster·ile·ly** *adverb* **ster·il·ity** *noun* [French *stérile* or Latin *sterilis*]

ster·il·ize *transitive verb* (also esp. *Brit.* **-ise**) **1** make sterile. **2** deprive of

the ability to produce offspring, esp. by removing or blocking the sex organs. □ **ster·il·iz·able** *adjective* **ster·il·iza·tion** *noun* **ster·il·iz·er** *noun*

ster·let *noun* a small sturgeon, *Acipenser ruthenus*, found in the Caspian Sea area and yielding fine caviar. [Russian *sterlyad'*]

ster·ling ● *adjective* **1** of or in British money (*pound sterling*). **2** (of a coin or precious metal) genuine; of standard value or purity. **3** made of sterling silver (*sterling jewellery*). **4** (of a person or qualities etc.) of solid worth; genuine, reliable (*sterling work*). ● *noun* **1** British money (*paid in sterling*). **2** = STERLING SILVER. **3** manufactured articles of sterling silver, esp. tableware. [prob. from late Old English *steorling* (unrecorded) from *steorra* star + -LING[1] (because some early Norman pennies bore a small star): recorded earlier in Old French *esterlin*]

sterling silver *noun* silver of $92\frac{1}{4}$% purity.

Ster·lita·mak /ˌsterlɪtəˈmɒk/ an industrial city in S Russia, situated on the Belaya River to the north of Orenburg; pop. (est. 2002) 267,000.

Stern, Isaac (1920–2001), Russian-born US violinist. He made his public debut with the San Francisco Symphony Orchestra in 1936, and went on to become an internationally acclaimed virtuoso.

stern[1] *adjective* severe, grim, strict; enforcing discipline or submission (*a stern expression*; *stern treatment*). □ **be made of sterner stuff** be more resolute; be less inclined to yield, esp. to self-indulgence, weakness, emotion, etc. □ **stern·ly** *adverb* **stern·ness** *noun* [Old English *styrne*, prob. from a Germanic root = be rigid]

stern[2] *noun* **1** the rear part of a ship or boat. **2** any rear part. □ **sterned** *adjective* (also in *combination*). **stern·most** *adjective* **stern·ward** *adjective & adverb* **stern·wards** *adverb* [prob. from Old Norse *stjórn* steering, from *stýra* STEER[1]]

ster·nal *adjective* of or relating to the sternum.

stern drive *noun* **1** an inboard engine connected to an outboard drive unit at the rear of a powerboat. **2** a boat equipped with such an engine.

Sterne, Lau·rence (1713–68), Irish novelist and clergyman. His *The Life and Opinions of Tristram Shandy* (1759–67) parodied the developing conventions of the novel form and anticipated modern stream-of-consciousness techniques.

Stern Gang the British name for a militant Zionist group that campaigned in Palestine during the 1940s for the creation of a Jewish state, assassinating several government officials, notably the British Minister for the Middle East and the UN mediator for Palestine. [Avraham *Stern* (d.1942) its founder]

stern·post *noun* the central upright support at the stern of a boat, usu. bearing the rudder.

stern trawler *noun* a trawler whose nets are operated from the stern of the vessel.

ster·num *noun* (*pl.* **ster·nums** or **sterna**) the breastbone. [modern Latin from Greek *sternon* chest]

stern·way *noun Naut.* a backward motion or impetus of a ship.

stern·wheel·er *noun* a steamer propelled by a paddlewheel positioned at the stern.

ster·oid /ˈsterɔɪd, ˈstɪːrɔɪd/ *noun Biochem.* any of a group of organic compounds with a characteristic structure of four rings of carbon atoms, including many hormones, alkaloids, and vitamins, used to treat various diseases and to increase muscle size. □ **on steroids** *informal* being likened to a larger, more potent, or more aggressive version of (*a Swiss army knife on steroids*). □ **ster·oid·al** *adjective* [STEROL + -OID]

ster·ol /ˈsterɒl/ *noun Chem.* any of a group of naturally occurring steroid alcohols. [CHOLESTEROL, ERGOSTEROL, etc.]

ster·tor·ous /ˈstɜrtərəs/ *adjective* (of breathing etc.) laboured and noisy; sounding like snoring. □ **ster·tor·ous·ly** *adverb* [*stertor*, modern Latin from Latin *stertere* snore]

stet *verb* (**stet·ted, stet·ting**) **1** *intransitive* (usu. as an instruction written on a proof sheet etc.) ignore or cancel the correction or alteration; let the original form stand. **2** *transitive* write 'stet' against; cancel the correction of. [Latin, = let it stand, from *stare* stand]

stetho·scope /ˈsteθəˌskoʊp/ *noun* an instrument used in listening to the action of the heart, lungs, etc., usu. consisting of a circular piece placed against the chest or back, with flexible tubes leading to earpieces. □ **stetho·scop·ic** /-ˈskɒpɪk/ *adjective* **steth·os·copy** /-ˈɒskəpi/ *noun* [French *stéthoscope* from Greek *stēthos* breast: see -SCOPE]

stet·son *noun* a slouch hat with a very wide brim and a high crown, associated with cowboys of the western US and Canada. [J. B. *Stetson*, US hat maker d.1906]

Stet·tler a town in central Alberta, east of Red Deer; pop. (2001) 5,215. ◻ **Stet·tler·ite** *noun* [C. *Stettler*, Swiss immigrant and homesteader d.1919]

steve·dore /ˈstiːvəˌdɔr/ ● *noun* a person employed in loading and unloading ships. ● *transitive verb* load or unload the cargo of (a ship). ◻ **steve·dor·ing** *noun & adjective* [Spanish *estivador* from *estivar* stow a cargo, from Latin *stipare* pack tight]

Ste·vens, **Wal·lace** (1879–1955), US poet. He spent most of his working life as a lawyer for an insurance firm, writing poetry privately and developing an original and colourful style; collections of his work include *Harmonium* (1923), *Man with the Blue Guitar and Other Poems* (1937), and *Collected Poems* (1954), which won a Pulitzer Prize.

Ste·ven·son ▶ 1 Adlai Ewing (1900–65), US politician, who twice stood unsuccessfully as Democratic presidential candidate, and served as US ambassador to the United Nations under John F. Kennedy. **2 Rob·ert Louis (Bal·four)** (1850–94), Scottish novelist. Besides his famous adventure stories such as *Treasure Island* (1883) and *Kidnapped* (1886) and his poetry for children, he wrote more serious psychological works like *The Strange Case of Dr. Jekyll and Mr. Hyde* (1886).

stew ● *verb* **1** *transitive & intransitive* cook slowly in simmering liquid in a pot, slow cooker, etc. **2** *intransitive informal* be oppressed by heat or humidity, esp. in a confined space. **3** *intransitive informal* **a** suffer prolonged embarrassment, anxiety, etc. **b** (foll. by *about*, *over*) fret or be anxious. **4** *transitive Brit.* make (tea) bitter or strong with prolonged brewing. ● *noun* **1** a dish of stewed meat, fish, vegetables, etc. **2** *informal* an agitated or angry state (*be in a stew*). **3** a mixture, an assortment (*a stew of different sounds and rhythms*). **4** *archaic* (in *pl.*) a brothel. ◻ **stew in one's own juice** (or **juices**) be left to suffer the consequences of one's own actions. [Old French *estuve*, *estuver*, prob. ultimately from EX-¹ + Greek *tuphos* smoke, steam]

stew·ard ● *noun* **1** a passengers' attendant on an aircraft, ship, or train. **2** an official appointed to keep order or supervise arrangements at a meeting or show or demonstration etc. **3** = SHOP STEWARD. **4** a person responsible for supplies of food etc. for a college or club etc. **5** a person whose responsibility it is to take care of something (*they see themselves as stewards of the countryside*). **6** a person employed to manage another's property, esp. a large house or land. **7** (esp. in the United Church) a layperson appointed to manage the financial affairs of a congregation or circuit. **8** *Brit.* the title of several officers of state or the royal household (*Lord High Steward*). **9** *hist.* the principal officer of the Scottish sovereign in early times, in charge of administering Crown revenues, supervising the royal household, and having the privilege of standing in the army in battle second only to the sovereign. ● *transitive verb* act as a steward of (*will steward the meeting*). ◻ **stew·ard·ship** *noun* [Old English *stiweard* from *stig* prob. = house, hall + *weard* WARD]

stew·ard·ess *noun* a female flight attendant. ¶ *Flight attendant* is now usu. preferred.

Stew·art ▶ 1 Jack·ie (born John Young Stewart) (b.1939), Scottish racing driver, who was three times world champion (1969; 1971; 1973) and won 27 Grand Prix races. **2 James (Mait·land)** (1908–97), US actor, who typically portrayed slow-speaking honest heroes; his films include *The Philadelphia Story* (1940), which earned him an Oscar, Hitchcock's *Rear Window* (1954) and *Vertigo* (1958), and *It's a Wonderful Life* (1946). **3 Rod** (full name Roderick David Stewart) (b.1945), English rock singer and songwriter. His albums include *Gasoline Alley* (1970), *Every Picture Tells a Story* (1971), and *Vagabond Heart* (1991). **4** *var.* of STUART 1.

Stewart Island an island of New Zealand, situated off the south coast of South Island, from which it is separated by the Foveaux Strait; chief settlement, Oban.

Stewart River a river in central Yukon Territory, 644 km long, which rises in the Selwyn Mountains and flows westward to join the Yukon River about 80 km south of Dawson. [J. G. *Stewart*, assistant to a Hudson's Bay Co. trader *c.*1849]

stewed *adjective* **1** (of meat, fish, fruit, etc.) cooked by stewing. **2** *Brit.* (of tea) strong or bitter due to prolonged brewing. **3** *informal* drunk.

stew·ing beef *noun* beef cut up into chunks suitable for making stew.

stew·pot *noun* **1** a pot for cooking stew. **2** a mixture (*ethnic stewpot*).

stg. *abbreviation* sterling.

Stheno /ˈsθiːnoʊ/ *Gk Myth* one of the three Gorgons.

sticho·mythia /ˌstɪkoʊˈmɪθiə/ *noun* dialogue in alternate lines of verse, used in disputation in Greek drama, and characterized by antithesis and repetition. [modern Latin from Greek *stikhomuthia*, from *stikhos* 'row, line of verse' + *muthos* 'speech, talk']

stick¹ *noun* **1 a** a short slender branch or length of wood broken or cut from a tree. **b** this trimmed for use as a support or weapon. **2** a thin rod or spike of wood etc. for a particular purpose (*Popsicle stick*). **3** a slender thing resembling a stick in shape (*celery stick*; *stick of gum*). **4** a long thin implement used to propel a puck or ball in hockey, lacrosse, etc. **5 a** = STICK SHIFT. **b** = JOYSTICK. **6** a conductor's baton. **7** a number of bombs or paratroops released rapidly from aircraft. **8** (often prec. by *the*) punishment, esp. by beating (also used with allusion to the traditional use of a stick to try and force a donkey to move; *see* CARROT-AND-STICK). **9** esp. *Brit. informal* adverse criticism; censure, reproof (*took a lot of stick*). **10** *informal* a piece of wood as part of a house or furniture (*a few sticks of furniture*). **11** *informal* a person, esp. one who is dull or unsociable (*a funny old stick*). **12** (in *pl.*; prec. by *the*) *informal* remote rural areas. ◻ **sticks and stones may break my bones but names** (or **words**) **will never hurt me** a proverb used to express indifference to an insult or abuse. **up sticks** *Brit. informal* go to live elsewhere. ◻ **stick-like** *adjective* [Old English *sticca* from West Germanic]

stick² *verb* (*past* and *past participle* **stuck**) **1** *transitive* (foll. by *in*, *into*, *through*) insert or thrust (a thing or its point) (*stuck a finger in my eye*; *stick a pin through it*). **2** *transitive* insert a pointed thing into; stab. **3** *transitive & intransitive* (foll. by *in*, *into*, *on*, etc.) **a** fix or be fixed on a pointed thing. **b** fix or be fixed by or as by a pointed end. **4** *transitive & intransitive* fix or become or remain fixed by or as by adhesive etc. (*stick a label on it*; *the label won't stick*). **5** *intransitive* make a continued impression (*the scene stuck in my mind*; *the name stuck*). **6** *intransitive* lose or be deprived of the power of motion or action through adhesion or jamming or other impediment. **7** *informal* **a** *transitive* put in a specified position or place, esp. quickly or haphazardly (*stick it in your pocket*). **b** *intransitive* remain in a place (*stuck indoors*). **8** *informal* **a** *intransitive* (of an accusation etc.) be convincing or regarded as valid (*could not make the charges stick*). **b** *transitive* (foll. by *on*) place the blame for (a thing) on (a person). **9** *transitive Brit.* endure, tolerate (*could not stick it any longer*). **10** *transitive* (foll. by *at*) *informal* persevere with. ◻ **stick around** *informal* linger; remain at the same place. **stick at it** *informal* persevere. **stick by** (or **with** or **to**) stay loyal or close to. **stick 'em up!** *informal* hands up! **stick fast** adhere or become firmly fixed or trapped in a position or place. **stick in one's throat** be against one's principles. **stick it out** *informal* put up with or persevere with a burden etc. to the end. **stick it to (a person)** *N Amer. informal* **1** treat unfairly; cheat or take advantage of (*cut taxes for the rich while sticking it to the poor*). **2** get even with; achieve revenge. **stick one's chin up** show firmness or fortitude. **stick one's neck out** expose oneself to censure etc. by acting or speaking boldly. **stick out** protrude or cause to protrude or project (*stuck his tongue out*; *stick out your chest*). **stick out like a sore thumb** *informal* be very obvious or incongruous. **stick to 1** remain close to or fixed on or to. **2** remain faithful to. **3** keep to (a subject etc.) (*stick to the point*). **stick together** *informal* remain united or mutually loyal. **stick to one's guns** *see* GUN. **stick to it** persevere. **stick to the ribs** (of food) be hearty and filling. **stick up 1** be or make erect or protruding upwards. **2** fasten to an upright surface. **3** *informal* rob or threaten with a gun. **stick up for** support or defend or champion (a person or cause). **stick up to** be assertive in the face of; offer resistance to. **stick with** *informal* remain in touch with or faithful to; persevere with. [Old English *stician*, from Germanic]

stick·ball *noun* a form of baseball using a rubber ball and a broomstick etc., usu. played by children.

stick boy *noun Hockey* the person responsible for preparing, organizing, and supplying the hockey sticks for each player during a game.

stick·er *noun* **1** an adhesive label, price tag, notice etc. **2** a person or thing that sticks. **3** *Brit.* a persistent person. **4** a thin strip of wood placed between stacked logs or pieces of timber to separate them and allow for ventilation. ● *transitive verb N Amer.* **1** affix a sticker to. **2** attach a sticker to (a CD, tape, etc.) warning that the lyrics may be offensive to some listeners.

sticker price *noun* the full asking price for an item, esp. a motor vehicle, from which a discount may be given.

sticker shock *noun N Amer. informal* shock experienced on discovering the high, or increased, price of a product, esp. a big-ticket item such as a car.

stick figure *noun* a figure drawn in thin simple lines.

stick·handle *verb* **1** *intransitive Hockey* skilfully control the puck with the stick. **2** *intransitive & transitive Cdn* manoeuvre (a project etc.) skilfully through obstacles. ◻ **stick·hand·ler** *noun* **stick·hand·ling** *noun*

stick·ing plaster *noun Brit.* an adhesive bandage for wounds etc.

stick·ing point *noun* the limit of progress, agreement, etc.

stick insect *noun* any usu. wingless female insect of the family Phasmidae with a twig-like body.

stick-in-the-mud *noun informal* an unprogressive or old-fashioned person.

stickle·back *noun* any small fish of the family Gasterosteidae, esp. *Gasterosteus aculeatus*, with sharp spines along the back. [Middle English from Old English *sticel* thorn, sting + *bæc* BACK]

stick·ler *noun* (usu. foll. by *for*) **1** a person who insists on something (*a stickler for detail*). **2** a difficult problem or puzzle. [obsolete *stickle* be umpire, Middle English *stightle* control, frequentative of *stight* from Old English *stiht(i)an* set in order]

stick-on *adjective* that can be stuck on; adhesive (*stick-on address labels*).

stick pen *noun* a ballpoint pen with a narrow, usu. opaque barrel.

stick pin *noun* esp. *N Amer.* a straight pin with an ornamented head, worn on a tie, scarf, lapel, etc.

stick shift *noun N Amer.* **1** a manual transmission for a motor vehicle. **2** a motor vehicle having a manual transmission. **3** = GEARSHIFT.

stick-to-it-iveness *noun informal* dogged perseverance.

stick·um *noun N Amer.* a sticky or adhesive substance.

stick·up *noun informal* a robbery using a gun.

stick·weed *noun US* = RAGWEED 2.

stick·work *noun Hockey* interference with the stick, e.g. butt-ending, slashing, etc.

sticky (**stick·i·er, stick·i·est**) ● *adjective* **1** tending or intended to stick or adhere. **2** glutinous, viscous. **3 a** (of the weather) humid. **b** damp with sweat. **4** *informal* awkward or uncooperative; intransigent (*was very sticky about giving me a day off*). **5** *informal* difficult, awkward (*a sticky problem*). **6** (of a website) attracting long visits or repeat visits from users. ● *noun* (*pl.* **-ies**) (also **sticky note**) *informal* = POST-IT. □ **come to a sticky end** die or come to grief in an unpleasant or painful way. **have sticky fingers** be in the habit of stealing. □ **stick·i·ly** *adverb* **stick·i·ness** *noun*

sticky bun *noun* a sweet bread roll covered with a sticky glaze or icing or with a syrup-coated bottom.

sticky rice *noun* any type of rice which cooks to a glutinous consistency, used esp. in the cuisine of eastern and southeastern Asia.

sticky tape *noun* clear adhesive tape; Scotch tape.

sticky wicket *noun* **1** *Cricket* a field that is damp from rain, causing the ball to bounce awkwardly. **2** *informal* difficult or awkward circumstances.

Stieg·litz /ˈstiːɡlɪts/ **Al·fred** (1864–1946), US photographer, who established photography as a fine art in the US and, through his galleries and publications, introduced Americans to the modern art of Picasso, Matisse, and Georgia O'Keeffe, whom he married in 1924.

stiff ● *adjective* **1** rigid; not flexible. **2** hard to bend or move or turn etc.; not working freely. **3** thick, viscous; capable of retaining a definite shape (*beat the egg whites until stiff*). **4** hard to cope with; needing strength or effort (*a stiff climb*). **5** severe or strong (*a stiff breeze; a stiff penalty; stiff opposition*). **6** (of a person or manner) formal, constrained; lacking spontaneity. **7** (of a muscle or limb etc., or a person affected by these) aching when used, owing to previous exertion, injury, etc. **8** (of an alcoholic or medicinal drink) strong. **9** (of a price, demand, etc.) unusually high, severe, or excessive. **10** (foll. by *with*) *informal* abounding in (*a place stiff with tourists*). ● *adverb informal* to an extreme degree (*bored stiff; scared stiff*). ● *noun slang* **1** a corpse. **2 a** a foolish or useless person (*you big stiff*). **b** an ordinary person (*a working stiff*). **3** a commercial venture (esp. in the entertainment business) which merits or meets with public indifference; a flop. ● *verb* esp. *N Amer. slang* **1** *transitive* cheat; refuse to pay or tip. **2** *transitive* kill, murder. **3** *intransitive* fail to sell well or be popular (*his last album stiffed*). □ **stiff·ish** *adjective* **stiff·ly** *adverb* **stiff·ness** *noun* [Old English *stif* from Germanic]

stiff-arm ● *transitive verb* tackle, fend off, or push with a rigid arm. ● *noun* the action or an act of stiff-arming someone.

stiff·en *transitive & intransitive verb* make or become stiff. □ **stiff·en·er** *noun* **stiff·en·ing** *noun*

stiff-necked *adjective* obstinate or haughty.

stiff upper lip *noun* fortitude; stoicism in adversity.

stiffy *noun* (also **stiff·ie**) (*pl.* **-ies**) *coarse slang* an erection.

stifle[1] /ˈstaɪfəl/ *verb* **1** *transitive* prevent or constrain (an activity or idea) (*high taxes were stifling small businesses*). **2** *transitive* smother, suppress (*stifled a yawn*). **3** *intransitive & transitive* suffocate; stop or cause to stop

breathing. □ **stif·ler** *noun* [perhaps alteration of Middle English *stuffe*, *stuffle* from Old French *estouffer*]

stifle[2] /ˈstaɪfəl/ *noun* (in full **stifle joint**) a joint in the legs of horses, dogs, etc., equivalent to the knee in humans. [Middle English: origin unknown]

stif·ling *adjective* **1** unbearably hot. **2** oppressive. □ **stif·ling·ly** *adverb*

stig·ma *noun* (*pl.* **stig·mas** or esp. in sense 4 **stig·mata** /stɪɡˈmɑːtə/) **1 a** a mark or sign of disgrace or discredit. **b** an unfavourable reputation. **2** (foll. by *of*) a distinguishing mark or characteristic. **3** the part of a pistil that receives the pollen in pollination. **4** (in *pl.*) (in Christian belief) marks corresponding to those left on Christ's body by the Crucifixion, said to have been impressed by divine favour on the bodies of St. Francis of Assisi and others. **5** a mark or spot on the skin or on a butterfly's wing. **6** *Med.* a visible sign or characteristic of a disease. **7** an insect's spiracle. [Latin from Greek *stigma -atos* a mark made by a pointed instrument, a brand, a dot: related to STICK[1]]

stig·mat·ic /stɪɡˈmatɪk/ ● *adjective* **1** of or relating to a stigma or stigmas. **2** = ANASTIGMATIC. ● *noun Christianity* a person bearing stigmata.

stig·ma·tist /ˈstɪɡmətɪst/ *noun Christianity* = STIGMATIC *noun*.

stig·ma·tize /ˈstɪɡməˌtaɪz/ *transitive verb* (also esp. *Brit.* **-tise**) **1** (often foll. by *as*) describe as discreditable or undesirable. **2** *Christianity* produce stigmata on. □ **stig·ma·tiz·a·tion** *noun*

Sti·kine River /stɪˈkiːn/ a river in northwestern BC, 539 km long, which rises in the north central part of the province and flows generally westward, then southwestward, crossing the Alaska border and emptying into an inlet of the Pacific Ocean northeast of Prince of Wales Island. [Tlingit, = the (big) river]

Sti·kine Territory /stɪˈkiːn/ (also **Stick·een Territory**) *hist.* a British territory (1862–63) of NW Canada, encompassing what is now the southern region of Yukon Territory. Established to ensure British authority in an area potentially rich in gold, it was administered by the colony of British Columbia. [see STIKINE RIVER]

stil·bene *noun Chem.* an aromatic hydrocarbon forming phosphorescent crystals. [French from Greek *stilbō* glitter + -ENE]

stil·bes·trol /stɪlˈbestrɒl/ *noun* (*Brit.* **stil·boes·trol**) a powerful synthetic estrogen derived from stilbene. [STILBENE + ESTRUS]

stile[1] *noun* an arrangement of steps allowing people but not cattle to climb over a fence or wall. [Old English *stigel* from a Germanic root *stig-* (unrecorded) climb]

stile[2] *noun* a vertical piece in the frame of a panelled door, wainscot, etc. (*compare* RAIL[1] *noun* 5). [prob. from Dutch *stijl* pillar, doorpost]

stil·etto /stɪˈletoː/ *noun* (*pl.* **-tos**) **1** a short dagger with a thick blade. **2** (in full **stiletto heel**) **a** a high tapering heel on a women's shoe. **b** a shoe with such a heel. **3** a small pointed instrument for making eyelets etc. [Italian, diminutive of *stilo* dagger (as STYLUS)]

still[1] ● *adjective* **1** not or hardly moving. **2** with little or no sound; calm and tranquil (*a still evening*). **3** (of sounds) hushed, stilled. **4** (of a drink) not effervescing. ● *noun* **1** deep silence (*in the still of the night*). **2** an ordinary static photograph (as opposed to a motion picture), esp. a single shot from a movie. ● *adverb* **1** without moving (*stand still*). **2** even now or at a particular time (*they still did not understand; why are you still here?*). **3** nevertheless; all the same. **4** (with comparative etc.) even, yet, increasingly (*still greater efforts; still another explanation*). ● *transitive & intransitive verb* make or become still; quieten. □ **still and all** *informal* nevertheless. **still waters run deep** a quiet manner conceals depths of feeling or knowledge or cunning. □ **still·ness** *noun* [Old English *stille* (adj. & adv.), *stillan* (v.), from West Germanic]

still[2] *noun* an apparatus for distilling alcoholic drinks etc. [obsolete *still* (v.), Middle English from DISTILL]

stil·lage /ˈstɪlɪdʒ/ *noun* a bench, frame, etc., for keeping articles off the floor while draining, drying, waiting to be packed, etc. [apparently from Dutch *stellagie* scaffold, from *stellen* to place + French *-age*]

still·birth *noun* the birth of a dead child.

still·born *adjective* **1** (of a child) born dead. **2** (of an idea, plan, etc.) abortive; not able to succeed.

still-hunt *intransitive verb N Amer.* hunt stealthily or covertly; stalk. □ **still-hunter** *noun* **still-hunting** *noun*

still life *noun* (*pl.* **still lifes**) **1** a painting, drawing, or photograph of inanimate objects such as fruit or flowers. **2** this genre of painting, drawing, or photography.

still·son *noun* (in full **stillson wrench**) a large wrench with jaws that tighten as pressure is increased. [D. C. *Stillson*, its inventor d.1899]

stilly ● *adverb* in a still manner. ● *adjective literary* still, quiet.

stilt *noun* **1** either of a pair of poles with supports for the feet enabling the user to walk at a distance above the ground. **2** each of a set of piles or posts supporting a building etc. **3** any wading bird of the genus *Himantopus*, with long slender legs. [Middle English & Low German *stilte*]

stilt·ed *adjective* **1** (of a literary style etc.) stiff and unnatural. **2** standing on stilts. **3** *Archit.* (of an arch) with pieces of upright masonry between the imposts and the springers. □ **stilt·ed·ly** *adverb* **stilt·ed·ness** *noun*

Stil·ton *noun proprietary* a kind of strong rich cheese, often with blue veins, originally made at various places in Leicestershire in S England and formerly sold to travellers at an inn in Stilton (now in Cambridgeshire).

Stil·well, Jo·seph War·ren (known as 'Vinegar Joe') (1883–1946), US general, who commanded US and Chinese forces in S China and Burma during the Second World War.

stimu·lant /'stɪmjʊlənt/ ● *noun* **1** an agent that stimulates, esp. a drug or alcoholic drink. **2** a stimulating influence. ● *adjective* that stimulates, esp. bodily or mental activity. [Latin *stimulare stimulant-* urge, goad]

stimu·late /'stɪmjʊleɪt/ *transitive verb* **1** apply or act as a stimulus to. **2** animate, excite, arouse. **3** be a stimulant to. □ **stimu·lat·ing** *adjective* **stimu·lat·ing·ly** *adverb* **stimu·la·tion** *noun* **stimu·la·tive** *adjective* **stimu·la·tor** *noun* **stimu·la·tory** *adjective*

stimu·lus /'stɪmjʊləs/ *noun* (*pl.* **stimu·li** /-ˌlaɪ/) **1** a thing that rouses to activity or energy. **2** a stimulating or rousing effect. **3** a thing that evokes a specific functional reaction in an organ or tissue. [Latin, = goad, spur, incentive]

Sting (born Gordon Matthew Sumner) (b.1951), English rock singer, songwriter, and bassist, a founder of the reggae-influenced rock group the Police (1977–83); his solo recordings, often influenced by jazz, include . . . *Nothing Like the Sun* (1987) and *The Soul Cages* (1991).

sting ● *noun* **1 a** a sharp painful wound inflicted by any of a number of insects, animals, and plants possessing a stinger. **b** an act or instance of inflicting such a wound. **2** a sharp physical pain, such as one caused by the sting of a wasp or bee etc. **3** (often foll. by *of*) the painful quality or effect of something that causes emotional or social distress or anguish (*the sting of poverty*). **4** pungency, sharpness, vigour (*her satire has lost its sting*). **5** (in full **sting operation**) esp. *N Amer.* a police undercover operation in which police officers pose as buyers or sellers in an ostensibly illegal transaction in an attempt to implicate a presumed criminal. **6** *slang* a swindle or robbery. **7** = STINGER[1] 1a. ● *verb* (*past* and *past participle* **stung**) **1 a** *transitive & intransitive* (of an insect or animal) prick or pierce with a sting. **b** *intransitive* be capable of stinging. **2** *transitive & intransitive* cause or be capable of causing a sharp physical pain or irritation, or emotional pain (in a person). **3** *intransitive* feel sharp emotional or physical pain (*my fingers are stinging from the cold*). **4** *transitive informal* **a** cause (a person, business, etc.) to suffer a financial loss or hardship (*small businesses were stung by the recession*). **b** cheat, swindle. **5** *transitive* (foll. by *into*) incite by a strong or painful mental effect (*their jeers stung him into a reply*). □ **sting in the tail** unexpected pain or difficulty at the end. □ **sting·ing** *adjective* **sting·ing·ly** *adverb* **sting·less** *adjective* [Old English *sting* (n.), *stingan* (v.), from Germanic]

sting·er[1] *noun* *N Amer.* **a** a sharp organ in various insects and other animals, such as bees, wasps, and scorpions, capable of inflicting a dangerous and painful wound, esp. by injecting poison. **b** (also **stinging hair**) (in plants) a stiff sharp tubular hair which emits an irritating fluid when touched. **c** a stinging insect, snake, nettle, etc. **2** a sharp painful blow or comment.

sting·er[2] *noun* **1** *N Amer.* a drink made with brandy and crème de menthe. **2** *Brit.* a drink consisting of equal quantities of whisky and soda or water with crushed ice. [corruption of Malaysian *satēngah* one half]

stinging nettle *noun* a nettle, *Urtica dioica*, with stinging hairs, small green flowers, and strongly toothed ovate leaves.

sting·ray *noun* any of various broad flatfish esp. of the family Dasyatidae, having a flattened, roughly diamond-shaped body tapering to a tail with a long poisonous serrated spine at its base.

stingy /'stɪndʒi/ *adjective* (**stin·gi·er, stin·gi·est**) **1** (of a person) having or displaying an unwillingness to give, spend, or use anything up. **2** (of food, a portion, supply, etc.) given sparingly or grudgingly; scanty, meagre. **3** *Sport* (of a team, goaltender, etc.) being strong defensively; giving up few goals, points, or scoring opportunities. □ **stin·gi·ly** *adverb* **stin·gi·ness** *noun* [perhaps from dial. *stinge* STING]

stink ● *verb* (*past* **stank** or **stunk**; *past participle* **stunk**) **1** *intransitive* emit a strong offensive smell. **2** *intransitive informal* **a** be or seem appallingly or offensively bad, inept, or incompetent (*this team stinks*).

b be or seem unbearably unpleasant (*she said her job stinks*). **3** *transitive & intransitive* (foll. by *up*) fill (a place) with an offensive odour (*your perfume stinks the whole room up*). **4** *intransitive* (foll. by *of*) *informal* have or be surrounded by an offensive amount or degree of something (*the whole affair just stinks of scandal*). ● *noun* **1** a strong or offensive smell; a stench. **2** *informal* a fuss. **3** *informal* a scandal. □ **like stink** *informal* intensely; extremely hard or fast etc. (*working like stink*). [Old English *stincan*, ultimately from W Germanic: compare STENCH]

stink bomb *noun* a small bomb that releases a foul smell upon exploding.

stink·bug *noun* any insect which emits an unpleasant smell when attacked, esp. a bug of the family Pentatomidae with a broad flat shield-shaped scutellum.

stink·er *noun* **1** *slang* a despicable person. **2** a difficult or unpleasant thing. **3** something of inferior quality. **4** any person or thing that gives off a foul or offensive odour.

stink·horn *noun* any foul-smelling fungus of the order Phallales.

stink·ing ● *adjective* **1** that gives off a foul or offensive odour. **2** *slang* very objectionable or despicable (*you're a stinking liar!*). ● *adverb slang* extremely and usu. to an objectionable degree (*stinking rich*). □ **stink·ing·ly** *adverb*

stinking willie *noun* any of various ragworts.

stinko *adjective slang* drunk.

stink·pot *noun* esp. *US slang* a term of contempt for a person.

stink·weed *noun* any of various plants emitting a foul smell when crushed.

stink·wood *noun* **1** any of various trees having wood which gives off a disagreeable smell, esp. *Ocotea bullata*, of the laurel family, *Zieria arborescens*, of the rue family, and *Coprosma foetisissima*, of the madder family. **2** the strong wood of such a tree.

stinky *adjective* (**stink·i·er, stink·i·est**) *informal* having a strong or unpleasant smell.

stint ● *verb* **1** *transitive* use, spend, offer, or distribute (something) grudgingly or in small amounts (*she never stinted her praise for him*). **2** *intransitive* (often foll. by *on*) be sparing or cheap; economize. ● *noun* **1** a short period of time spent on a particular job or in a particular place. **2** a limitation of supply or effort (*without stint*). **3** a small sandpiper. [Old English *styntan* to blunt, dull, from Germanic, related to STUNT[1]]

stipe *noun Bot.* & *Zool.* **1** a stalk or stem, such as that which supports the pileus or cap of a mushroom or toadstool. **2** the petiole of a fern blade. **3** (in certain algae) the part that joins the lamina to the holdfast. **4** (in certain crustaceans) an eye-stalk. □ **stiped** *adjective* **stipi·tate** /'stɪpɪˌteɪt/ *adjective* [French from Latin *stipes*: see STIPES]

sti·pend /'staɪpend/ *noun* **1** a salary or fixed regular sum paid for the services of a teacher, public official, or clergyman. **2** any fixed regular payment, such as an allowance or scholarship. [Old French *stipend(i)e* or Latin *stipendium* from *stips* wages + *pendere* to pay]

sti·pend·i·ary /stɪ'pendjəri, -iːeri, staɪ-/ ● *adjective* receiving a stipend; working for pay, not voluntarily. ● *noun* (*pl.* **-ies**) a person receiving a stipend, esp. a salaried magistrate or minister.

stipes /'staɪpiːz/ *noun* (*pl.* **stipi·tes** /'stɪpəˌtiːz/) = STIPE. [Latin, = log, tree trunk]

stip·ple ● *verb* **1** *transitive & intransitive* draw, paint, or engrave (a surface, illustration, etc.) with dots, small spots, or flecks instead of lines. **2** *transitive* produce a roughened or gritty texture on (paint or cement etc.). ● *noun* **1** (also **stip·pling**) the process or technique of providing a surface etc. with a dotted or textured appearance. **2** work that has been produced using this technique. □ **stip·pler** *noun* [Dutch *stippelen* frequentative of *stippen* to prick, from *stip* point]

stipu·late[1] /'stɪpjuˌleɪt/ *transitive verb* **1** demand or specify as an essential part or condition of an agreement or contract etc. **2** promise or guarantee. □ **stipu·la·tion** *noun* [Latin *stipulari*]

stipu·late[2] /'stɪpjʊlət/ *adjective Bot.* having stipules.

stipu·lated /'stɪpjuˌleɪtɪd/ *adjective* specified or set out in the terms of a contract or agreement.

stip·ule /'stɪpjuːl/ *noun* a small leaflike appendage of a leaf, usu. occurring in pairs at the base of a petiole where the leaf joins the stem. [French *stipule* or Latin *stipula* straw]

stir[1] ● *verb* (**stirred, stir·ring**) **1** *transitive & intransitive* move a spoon or other utensil or tool around and around in (a liquid or soft mass) in order to mix the ingredients or constituents. **2** *transitive* cause to move or be disturbed, esp. slightly (*a breeze stirred the lake*). **b** *reflexive* rouse (oneself), esp. from a lethargic state. **3** *intransitive* **a** be or begin to be in motion (*not a creature was stirring*). **b** rise from sleep (*is still not* *stirring*). **4** *intransitive* (foll. by *from* or *out of*) move from a particular place or position. **5 a** *transitive* arouse, inspire, or provoke (the emotions etc., or a person as regards these) (*was stirred to anger*). **b** *intransitive* (of the emotions etc.) become active or excited (*anger stirred within my breast*). • *noun* **1** commotion or excitement; public attention or reaction (*caused quite a stir*). **2** an act of stirring (*give it a stir*). **3** the slightest movement (*not a stir*). □ **not stir a finger** make no effort to help. **stir the blood** inspire enthusiasm etc. **stir in** add (an ingredient) to a substance or mixture while stirring. **stir the pot** do something provocative to draw someone out of a state of inertia. **stir one's stumps** *Brit. informal* begin to move or become active. **stir up 1** cause, start, or instigate (trouble etc.) (*loved stirring things up*). **2** provoke, excite, arouse (a person or emotion etc.) (*stirred up their curiosity*). [Old English *styrian* from Germanic]

stir² *noun slang* prison (*in stir*). [19th c.: origin unknown]

stir-crazy *adjective* **1** restless, antsy, or fidgety, esp. from prolonged confinement indoors. **2** deranged from long imprisonment.

stir-fry • *noun* (*pl.* **-fries**) a dish consisting of an assortment of vegetables, such as peppers, bean sprouts, mushrooms, onions, etc., and sometimes meat fried rapidly at a high temperature, esp. in a wok. • *transitive verb* (**-fries**, **-fried**) fry (vegetables and meat etc.) rapidly at high heat while stirring and tossing, esp. in a wok.

Stir·ling¹ a town in central Scotland, on the Forth River, chief town of an administrative region of the same name; pop. (2002) 26,600. Its 12th-c. castle was a residence of the Stuart kings.

Stir·ling² ▶ **1 James** (1692–1770), Scottish mathematician. His main work, *Methodus Differentialis* (1730), was concerned with summation and interpolation; a formula named after him, giving the approximate value of the factorial of a large number, was actually first worked out by the French-born mathematician Abraham De Moivre (1667–1754). **2 Sir James Frazer** (1926–92), English architect. His grand and imposing designs include the Neuestaatsgalerie in Stuttgart (1977), which is regarded as his most accomplished and sophisticated work. **3 Rob·ert** (1796–1878), Scottish engineer and Presbyterian minister. In 1816–17 he was co-inventor (with his brother James) of a type of external-combustion engine using heated air, and both the engine and the heat cycle that it uses are named after him.

stir·rer *noun* **1** an object or device used for stirring something. **2** *informal* a person who deliberately causes trouble.

stir·ring • *adjective* **1** inspiring, exciting, rousing. **2** *archaic* actively occupied; busy. • *noun* (usu. in *pl.*) **1** initial stages or indications of a particular activity (*stirrings of a reform movement*). **2** initial feelings (*stirrings of sympathy*). □ **stir·ring·ly** *adverb*

stir·rup *noun* **1** either of a pair of supports for the foot of a person riding a horse, consisting of a metal loop with a flat base and a leather strap which attaches this loop to each side of a saddle. **2** a thing shaped like a stirrup, esp. a U-shaped clamp or support. **3** either of a pair of stirrup-shaped supports protruding from the end of a medical examination table, on which female patients place their heels during a gynecological exam. **4 a** a loop attached to the bottom of a pant leg meant to pass beneath the foot in order to keep the pants from rising above the ankle. **b** (*attributive*) designating an article of clothing having such straps (*stirrup pants*). **5** (in full **stirrup bone**) = STAPES. [Old English *stigrāp* from *stigan* climb (as STILE¹) + ROPE]

stirrup cup *noun* **1** a vessel originally used to serve an offering of wine etc. to a person about to depart on horseback. **2** a drink of esp. wine offered to a person about to depart.

stirrup leather *noun* the strap attaching a stirrup to a saddle.

stir stick *noun* a small disposable plastic stick used for stirring coffee etc.

stitch • *noun* **1 a** a single pass of a threaded needle in and out of a fabric which is being sewn. **b** the thread or loop left in the fabric between two successive needle holes as a result of this action. **c** (usu. with *neg.*) the least bit of fabric of an article of clothing (*hadn't a stitch on*). **2 a** a single complete movement of the needle or other implement used in knitting, crochet, embroidery, etc. **b** a particular method of knitting or crochet etc. (*I'm learning a new stitch*). **3** (usu. in *pl.*) *Surgery* each of the loops of material used in sewing up a wound. **4** an acutely painful cramp in the side of the body often resulting from running or vigorous exercise. • *transitive verb* **1 a** join (one or more pieces of fabric) with a stitch or usu. a continuous line or series of stitches. **b** make or mend (an article of clothing etc.) with a stitch or series of stitches. **2** (usu. foll. by *on*) fasten or attach (something) by sewing. **3** decorate with stitches; embroider. □ **in stitches** *informal* laughing uncontrollably. **stitch in time** a timely or preventative remedy. **stitch up 1** join, mend, or make by sewing or stitching. **2** *Brit. slang*

betray or cheat. □ **stitch·er** *noun* **stitch·ing** *noun* **stitch·less** *adjective* [Old English *stice* from Germanic, related to STICK²]

stitch·ery *noun* needlework or embroidery.

stitch·wort /ˈstɪtʃwɜrt, -wɔrt/ *noun* any plant of the genus *Stellaria*, esp. *S. media*, naturalized in N America, with an erect stem and white starry flowers, once thought to cure a stitch in the side.

Stl'atl'imx /ˈstatliːəm/ *noun* **1** a member of an Aboriginal people living in southwestern BC, northeast of Vancouver. **2** the Salishan language of this people. ¶ Formerly called LILLOOET.

STM *abbreviation* **1** scanning tunnelling microscope. **2** Master of Sacred Theology.

stn. *abbreviation* **1** station. **2** (**Stn.**) *Cdn* Postal Station.

stoa /ˈstoːə/ *noun* (*pl.* **stoas**) a portico or roofed colonnade in ancient Greek architecture. [Greek: compare STOIC]

stoat /stoːt/ *noun* esp. *Brit.* = ERMINE 1. [Middle English: origin unknown]

sto·chas·tic /stəˈkastɪk/ *adjective* **1** determined by a random distribution or pattern of probabilities, so that its behaviour may be analyzed statistically but not predicted precisely. **2** (of a process) characterized by a sequence of random variables. **3** governed by the laws of probability. □ **sto·chas·tic·ally** *adverb* [Greek *stokhastikos* from *stokhazomai* aim at, guess, from *stokhos* aim]

stock • *noun* **1** (esp. in a store or warehouse) a supply of merchandise etc. available for sale or distribution etc. **2** a supply or quantity of anything, esp. acquired or allowed to accumulate for future use (*a great stock of information; declining cod stocks*). **3** the raw materials or equipment used in the manufacture or trade of a particular product. **4** = LIVESTOCK. **5 a** capital raised by a business, company, corporation, etc. through the issue and subscription of shares. **b** a quantity of shares represented by a certificate, the holder of which is considered a part owner of the company, entitled to receive dividends of its profits. **c** a quantity of shares in a commodity or industry etc. (*gold stock*). **d** a security issued by the government or a company in fixed units with a fixed rate of interest. **6** one's reputation or popularity (*his stock is rising*). **7** liquid made by stewing bones, meat, vegetables, or fish, kept for use as a basis for soup, gravy, sauce, etc. **8 a** the source or progenitor of a line of descendants; family origins (*she is of Prairie stock*). **b** a family (of human beings, animals, plants, or languages). **9 a** a roll of film that has not been exposed or processed. **b** a selection of esp. outdoor scenes and cityscapes used to lend verisimilitude to a production shot on a set (also *attributive*: *stock footage*). **10 a** the trunk or woody stem of a living tree or shrub, esp. one into which a graft is inserted. **b** a plant from which cuttings are taken. **11** any plant of the cruciferous genus *Matthiola* or related genera, esp. Virginia stock, *Malcolmia maritima*, with flowers in racemes. **12** (in *pl.*) *hist.* a device for punishment, usu. consisting of an adjustable framework mounted between posts, with holes for securing the ankles and wrists, in which an offender was locked and exposed to public assault and ridicule. **13 a** = STOCK COMPANY 2. **b** the repertory of a stock company. **14 a** the handle, support, or base of a tool or machine. **b** the crossbar of an anchor. **15** a band of usu. stiff close-fitting material worn around the neck, esp. below a clerical collar or as part of a horseback riding outfit. **16 a** the usu. wooden part of a rifle to which the barrel is attached, usu. held against the shooter's shoulder. **b** an analogous part of an automatic or semi-automatic weapon and various other firearms. **17** hard solid brick pressed in a mould. **18** = ROLLING STOCK. **19 a** = HEADSTOCK. **b** = TAILSTOCK. • *adjective* **1** kept regularly in stock for sale, loan, distribution, or use. **2 a** constantly appearing or recurring; common or conventional (*the stock scenarios of television sitcoms*). **b** (of a theme, phrase, response) automatic and superficial; hackneyed, trite. • *transitive verb* **1** have or keep (merchandise) available for sale or use. **2 a** furnish (a store or farm etc.) with goods, equipment, or livestock. **b** fill (a shelf or shelves) with goods or merchandise. **c** fill (a pond or river etc.) with fish. **3** fit (a gun etc.) with a stock. □ **in stock** on the premises of a store or warehouse etc. and available for immediate sale. **out of stock** not available for immediate sale. **stock up 1** obtain or purchase stocks or supplies. **2** (foll. by *on* or *with*) obtain or purchase a supply of (food, fuel, etc.). **take stock 1** make an inventory of one's stock. **2** (often foll. by *of*) assess or review (a situation etc.). **3** (foll. by *in*) concern oneself with; attach importance to. □ **stocked** *adjective* **stock·less** *adjective* [Old English *stoc, stocc* from Germanic; sense 11 originally *stock-gillyflower*, so-called because it had a stronger stem than the clove gillyflower)]

stock·ade • *noun* **1** a line or enclosure of upright stakes or posts, erected for defensive purposes. **2** esp. *N Amer.* a prison, esp. a military one. • *transitive verb* fortify with a stockade. [obsolete French *estocade*, alteration of *estacade* from Spanish *estacada*, ultimately from Germanic: related to STAKE[1]]

stock boy *noun N Amer.* = STOCKER 2.

stock·breed·er *noun* a farmer who raises livestock. ☐ **stock·breed·ing** *noun*

stock·brok·er *noun* = BROKER 2. ☐ **stock·broker·age** *noun* **stock·brok·ing** *noun*

stock car *noun* **1** a car with the basic chassis of a commercially produced vehicle, extensively modified and strengthened for a form of racing in which collisions often occur. **2** *N Amer.* a boxcar used to transport livestock.

stock certificate *noun* a certificate attesting ownership of a share or shares.

stock character *noun* a stereotyped fictional character easily recognized from recurrent appearances in literary or folk traditions, usu. within a specific genre such as comedy or fairy tale, e.g. the wicked stepmother or damsel in distress.

stock company *noun N Amer.* **1** a company the capital of which is divided into shares represented by stock. **2** a repertory company performing mainly at a particular theatre.

stock·er *noun esp. N Amer.* **1** an animal, esp. a young steer or heifer, destined for butchering but kept until matured or fattened (also *attributive: stocker cattle*). **2** a person responsible for stocking shelves in a store. **3** = STOCK CAR.

stock exchange *noun* **1** (also **Stock Exchange**) a building where stocks and shares are traded publicly. *Also called* STOCK MARKET. **2** the body of dealers working there. **3** the composite index of share prices or trading activity at a particular stock exchange (*the Vancouver Stock Exchange fell 30 points today*).

stock·fish *noun* cod or a similar fish split and dried in the open air without salt.

stock·hold·er *noun* an owner of stocks or shares. ☐ **stock·hold·ing** *noun*

Stock·holm /ˈstɒkhoːm/ the capital of Sweden, a seaport on the east coast, situated on the mainland and on numerous adjacent islands; pop. (est. 2000) 750,348.

Stockholm Syndrome *noun* a sense of trust or affection felt by a hostage or victim towards a captor. [originally with reference to a bank robbery in Stockholm in which the hostages developed a fondness for their abductors]

stock index *noun* = COMPOSITE INDEX.

stock·i·nette *noun* (also **stock·i·net**) an elastic knitted material used esp. to make clothes, such as underwear. [prob. from *stocking-net*]

stock·ing *noun* **1 a** either of a pair of separate, close-fitting knitted or woven coverings for the feet and part or all of the leg worn by women or girls, esp. one of diaphanous silk or nylon reaching the thigh and held up by a garter. **b** (in *pl.*) = PANTYHOSE. **c** *esp. N Amer.* = SOCK[1] 1. **2** any close-fitting article of clothing resembling a stocking (*body stocking*). **3** = CHRISTMAS STOCKING. **4** a cylindrical bandage for the leg, esp. one worn as a remedial support, such as for a leg affected with varicose veins. **5** a differently-coloured, usu. white, marking on the leg of a horse above the hoof no higher than the knee. ☐ **in one's stocking** (or **stockinged**) **feet** wearing socks but no shoes. ☐ **stock·inged** *adjective* (also in *combination*). [STOCK in (now dial.) sense 'stocking' + -ING[1]]

stocking cap *noun* a knitted toque with a long tapered end which hangs down.

stocking stitch *noun Knitting* a stitch of alternate rows of plain and purl, making an even pattern.

stocking stuffer *noun N Amer.* (also *Brit.* **stocking filler**) a small usu. inexpensive present suitable for putting in a Christmas stocking.

stock-in-trade *noun* **1 a** the everyday requisites or equipment required for a particular business or profession. **b** goods and merchandise, esp. kept in sufficient supply by a dealer or shopkeeper to maintain business. **2** a collection of attitudes, phrases, tendencies, etc. characteristic of a person or group (*flippant remarks are part of his stock-in-trade*).

stock·ist *noun Brit.* a dealer who stocks goods of a particular type for sale.

stock·job·ber *noun* a dealer in stocks and shares, esp. an unscrupulous one. ☐ **stock·job·bing** *noun*

stock·man *noun* (pl. **-men**) **1** a person employed to look after livestock on a farm. **2** an owner of livestock. ☐ **stock·man·ship** *noun*

stock market *noun* **1** a stock exchange. **2** the level of transactions or prices in the national or international market for stocks.

stock option *noun N Amer. see* OPTION *noun* 3a.

stock·pile ● *noun* an accumulated stock of goods, materials, weapons, etc., held in reserve and available for use esp. during a shortage or emergency. ● *transitive verb* accumulate a stockpile of. ☐ **stock·piler** *noun*

Stock·port an industrial town in NW England, near Manchester; pop. (est. 2002) 132,000.

stock·pot *noun* a usu. large pot with two handles used for making soup, stews, or sauces, etc., esp. in large quantities.

stock·room *noun* a room in a store or factory etc. where surplus merchandise and overstock is kept.

stock split *noun N Amer.* the division of a stock into an increased number of shares.

stock-still *adverb* completely motionless.

stock-taking *noun* **1** the process of making an inventory of goods or merchandise in a store or factory etc. **2** an evaluation, assessment, or review of one's situation, prospects, and resources.

stocky *adjective* (**stock·i·er**, **stock·i·est**) (of a person, plant, or animal) short and strongly built; thickset. ☐ **stock·i·ly** *adverb* **stock·i·ness** *noun*

stock·yard *noun* an enclosure with pens and sheds where livestock are temporarily confined and sorted, esp. prior to being sold, shipped, or slaughtered.

stodge *noun informal* food, esp. of a thick or heavy kind. [earlier as verb: imitative, after *stuff* and *podge*]

stodgy *adjective* (**stodg·i·er**, **stodg·i·est**) **1** (of food) heavy and filling. **2** tediously slow; dull and uninteresting. **3** stuffy and excessively conventional or traditional. **4** (of a person) clumsy or awkward, esp. due to obesity. ☐ **stodg·i·ly** *adverb* **stodg·i·ness** *noun*

sto·gie /ˈstoːgi/ *noun* (also **stogy**) (pl. **-gies**) **1** *N Amer. informal* a cigar. **2** *US* a rough heavy boot. [originally *stoga*, short for *Conestoga* in Pennsylvania]

Stoic /ˈstoːɪk/ ● *noun* **1** a member of the ancient Greek school of philosophy founded at Athens by Zeno *c.*308 BC, which taught control of one's feelings and passions and advocated indifference to the vicissitudes of fortune and pleasure and pain. **2** (**stoic**) a person who practises repression of emotion, indifference to pleasure and pain, and patient endurance in adversity. ● *adjective* **1** (**stoic**) (also **stoic·al** /ˈstoːɪkəl/) (of a person, behaviour, or an action) characterized by an austere impassivity or resignation characteristic of a Stoic. **2** of or belonging to the school of the Stoics or its system of philosophy. ☐ **stoic·ally** *adverb* [Latin *stoicus* from Greek *stōïkos* from STOA (with reference to Zeno's teaching in the *Stoa Poïkilē* or Painted Porch at Athens)]

Sto·icism /ˈstoːəˌsɪzəm/ *noun* **1** the philosophy of the Stoics. **2** (**stoicism**) a stoic attitude.

Stoj·ko /ˈstɔɪkoː/ **Elvis** (b.1972), Canadian figure skater noted for his technical excellence and athletic style. Four times Canadian champion (1994, 1996, 1997, 1998) and three times world champion (1994, 1995, 1997), he has also won two Olympic silver medals (1994, 1998).

stoke *verb* (often foll. by *up*) **1** *transitive* feed or tend (a fire, furnace, boiler, etc.) to maintain or increase the heat produced. **2** *transitive* encourage, fuel (*her laughter stoked his anger*). **3** *informal* **a** *intransitive* fill oneself up with food and drink consumed esp. steadily and in large quantities. **b** *transitive* feed (oneself or another). [back-formation from STOKER]

stoked *adjective* (often foll. by *up*) **1** exhilarated, ecstatic. **2** completely full with food or drink.

stoke·hold *noun* a compartment in a steamship, containing its boilers and furnace.

stoke·hole *noun* an opening in a furnace through which a fire is stoked.

Stoke-on-Trent a city on the Trent River in central England, formerly in Staffordshire, a major centre of the ceramics industry; pop. (est. 2001) 240,643.

Stok·er, Abra·ham ('Bram') (1847–1912), Irish novelist, chiefly remembered as the author of the vampire story *Dracula* (1897).

stok·er *noun* **1** a person who tends the furnace on a steamship. **2** a tool or esp. mechanical device used to feed or tend a fire. [Dutch from *stoken* stoke, from Middle Dutch *stoken* push, related to STICK[1]]

stokes *noun* (pl. same) the cgs unit of kinematic viscosity, corresponding to a dynamic viscosity of 1 poise and a density of

1 gram per cubic centimetre, equivalent to 10^{-4} square metres per second. [Sir G. G. *Stokes*, Brit. physicist d.1903]

Sto·kow·ski /stɒˈkɒfski/ **Leo·pold An·toni Stan·is·law Bole·slawa·wicz** (1882–1977), English-born US conductor. He is best known for arranging and conducting the music for Walt Disney's animated film *Fantasia* (1940).

STOL /stɒl/ *noun* (usu. *attributive*) **1** designating aircraft designed to take off and land on a short runway. **2** designating an airport or runway etc. designed to accommodate such aircraft. [acronym from Short Takeoff and Landing.]

stole¹ *noun* **1** a woman's long scarf or shawl made esp. of fur or wool and worn loosely over the shoulders. **2** an ecclesiastical vestment consisting of a narrow strip of silk or linen, worn over one or both shoulders and hanging down to the knee or lower. [Old English *stol*, *stole* (originally a long robe), from Latin *stola* from Greek *stolē* equipment, clothing]

stole² *past of* STEAL.

stolen ● *verb past participle of* STEAL. ● *adjective* **1** obtained by theft (*sells stolen cars*). **2** accomplished or enjoyed by stealth or in secret (*they made the most of their stolen hours together*).

stolen base *noun Baseball* an instance of advancing to the next base while the pitcher is in the process of delivering a pitch (*has thirteen stolen bases already this season*).

stolen generation *noun Austral.* the Aboriginal people forcibly removed from their families as children between the 1900s and the 1960s, to be brought up by white foster families or in institutions.

stol·id *adjective* **1** failing or unlikely to feel or express emotion. **2** failing or unlikely to excite emotion; dull, uninspired. □ **sto·lid·ity** *noun* **stol·id·ly** *adverb* **stol·id·ness** *noun* [obsolete French *stolide* or Latin *stolidus*]

stol·len /ˈstɒlən/ *noun* a rich bread with dried fruit and nuts, eaten esp. at Christmas. [German]

Sto:lo /ˈstɒlɔː, ˈstɒlɔ/ *noun* **1** a member of an Aboriginal people living along the lower Fraser River, BC. **2** the Halkomelem language of this people. [Sto:lo, = 'people of the river']

stol·on /ˈstoːlɒn/ *noun* **1** *Bot.* a horizontal stem or branch that takes root at points along its length, forming new plants. **2** *Zool.* a branched structure connecting parts of a compound organism such as coral. □ **sto·lon·if·er·ous** /-ˈnɪfərəs/ *adjective* [Latin *stolo -onis*]

stoma /ˈstoːmə/ *noun* (pl. **sto·mata** /ˈstɒmatə, ˈstoːmətə/ or **stomas**) **1** *Bot.* any of the minute pores in the epidermis of a leaf or stem of a plant which allow movement of gases in and out of the plant. **2** *Surgery* an artificial opening made in a hollow organ, esp. one on the surface of the body leading to the gut or trachea. **3** *Zool.* a small mouth-like opening in some lower animals. □ **stomal** *adjective* [modern Latin from Greek *stoma -atos* mouth]

stom·ach ● *noun* **1 a** the internal organ in which the first part of digestion occurs, in humans a pear-shaped enlargement of the alimentary canal linking the esophagus to the small intestine. **b** any of several such organs in animals, esp. ruminants, in which there are four (*compare* RUMEN, RETICULUM 3, OMASUM, ABOMASUM). **2 a** the belly, abdomen, or lower front of the body (*she punched me in the stomach*). **b** a protuberant belly (*you're getting quite a stomach!*). **3 a** (usu. foll. by *for*) an appetite (for food). **b** the ability to digest food without becoming sick (*has a weak stomach*). **4 a** courage, inclination (*you haven't got the stomach to fight*). **b** tolerance, appreciation (*I have no stomach for bickering politicians*). ● *transitive verb* **1** (usu. with *neg.*) tolerate, endure; bear (*I can't stomach this sort of behaviour any longer*). **2 a** find sufficiently palatable to swallow or keep down (*I can't stomach seafood*). **b** have sufficient appetite remaining for (*I couldn't stomach another bite*). □ **on an empty stomach** not having eaten recently. **on a full stomach** soon after a large meal. □ **stom·ach·ful** *noun* (pl. **-fuls**). [Old French *stomaque*, *estomac* from Latin *stomachus* from Greek *stomakhos* gullet, from *stoma* mouth]

stomach ache *noun* a pain in the belly or abdominal region, esp. from indigestion.

stomach-churning *adjective* causing or tending to cause nausea (*a stomach-churning ride*).

stomach crunch *noun N Amer.* = CRUNCH *noun* 5.

stom·ach·er /ˈstʌməkər/ *noun hist.* an ornamental triangular panel, often jewelled or embroidered, filling the open front of a woman's dress, covering the breast and part of the stomach.

stomach flu *noun informal* a bout of gastrointestinal trouble characterized by diarrhea and/or vomiting. ¶ Strictly speaking, such an illness is not the flu.

stomach pump *noun* a device for removing the contents of the stomach, as in the case of poisoning.

stomach upset *noun* an instance of indigestion or nausea.

sto·mata *pl.* of STOMA.

sto·ma·tal /stoːˈmatəl, ˈstoːmətəl/ *adjective Bot. & Zool.* of or relating to a stoma or stomata.

sto·ma·titis /ˌstoːməˈtaɪtəs/ *noun Med.* inflammation of the mucous membrane of the mouth.

stomato- /stoːˈmatə/ *combining form Zool. & Med.* forming nouns and adjectives in the sense 'of or relating to the mouth, a stoma, or a structure resembling the mouth'. [modern Latin or Greek *stomat-*, *stoma* mouth]

sto·ma·tol·ogy /ˌstoːməˈtɒlədʒi/ *noun* the scientific study of the mouth or its diseases. □ **sto·mato·logic·al** *adjective* **sto·ma·tol·o·gist** *noun*

stomp ● *verb* **1** *intransitive* walk with loud, heavy, deliberate steps, often as a sign of anger; tread heavily. **2** *transitive N Amer.* stamp or trample on (a person or thing). **3** *intransitive* dance or play a stomp. ● *noun* **1** any lively dance involving a heavy stamping step. **2** (also **stomper**) a tune or song with a percussive rhythm and upbeat tempo suitable for such a dance. **3** a heavy stamping step to the beat of such a dance. □ **stomp one's foot** beat out a rhythm with one's foot. □ **stomp·er** *noun* [US dialect variant of STAMP]

stomp·ing ground *noun* (also **stamping ground**) (usu. in *pl.*) a favourite or familiar haunt or place of action.

Stone, Oli·ver (b.1946), US film director, screenwriter, and producer. He has won Oscars for his adaptation of the novel *Midnight Express* (1978) and his direction of *Platoon* (1986) and *Born on the Fourth of July* (1989), which indict American involvement in the Vietnam War. Other notable films: *JFK* (1991) and *Natural Born Killers* (1994).

stone ● *noun* **1 a** solid non-metallic mineral matter, of which rock is made. **b** a piece of this, esp. a small piece. **2 a** (often in *combination*) a piece of stone of a definite form and size, usu. artificially shaped, used for some special purpose, such as building, paving, or in the form of a slab or block set up as a memorial or boundary marker etc. **b** = TOMBSTONE. **3** *Archit.* **a** = FIELDSTONE. **b** = LIMESTONE. **c** = SANDSTONE 2. **4** *Mineralogy* a precious or semi-precious mineral or gemstone. **5** *Med.* (often in *pl.*) a hard abnormal concretion in the body, esp. in the kidney, the urinary bladder, or the gallbladder. **6** a stony endocarp enclosing the seed or kernel of certain pulpy or fleshy fruits, such as a peach, plum, or olive; a pit. **7** a shaped piece of stone used for grinding or sharpening something. **8** (pl. same) *Brit.* a unit of weight equal to 14 lb (6.35 kg), used esp. in expressing the weight of a person or large animal. **9** a brownish-grey colour. **10** (in full **curling stone**) = ROCK¹ 7. **11** a meteorite, esp. one containing a high proportion of silicates or other non-metals. ● *adjective* **1** made of stone. **2** of a brownish-grey colour. ● *adverb* completely, totally (*stone dead*; *stone deaf*). ● *transitive verb* **1 a** pelt with stones. **b** put to death by pelting with stones. **2** remove the stones from (fruit). **3** pave, line, or build up with stone or stones. **4** *Hockey informal* (esp. of a goaltender) thwart (an opponent attempting to score). □ **throw** (or **cast**) **stones** cast aspersions on a person's character etc. **throw** (or **cast**) **the first stone** be the first to make an accusation, esp. though guilty oneself. **leave no stone unturned** explore every possibility, try by every possible means. **a stone's throw** a short distance. □ **stone·less** *adjective* [Old English *stān*, from Germanic]

Stone Age *noun* **1** a prehistoric period characterized by the use of weapons and tools made of stone. **2** (*attributive*) (also **stone-age**) primitive, outmoded, obsolete.

stone·boat *noun N Amer.* a flat-bottomed sled consisting of a wooden deck on runners used esp. for removing stones from fields.

stone·chat *noun* any small brown bird of the thrush family with black and white markings, esp. *Saxicola torquata* of Eurasia and N Africa, with a call like stones being knocked together.

stone circle *noun Archaeology* = CIRCLE *noun* 6.

stone cold ● *adjective* **1** completely cold. **2** heartless, unfeeling (*stone cold killers*). ● *adverb* completely (*stone cold sober*).

stone crab *noun* any of various crabs, esp. the edible *Menippe mercenaria* inhabiting the rocky shores of the southern US, Mexico, and parts of the Caribbean.

stone·crop *noun* any succulent plant of the genus *Sedum*, usu. having yellow or white flowers and growing amongst rocks or in walls.

stone·cut *noun* **1** a printing technique in which an image engraved on the flat face of a stone that has been cut in half is impressed on paper

u: m**oo**d　ai m**y**　əi p**i**pe　au br**ow**n　ʌu h**ou**se　ei d**ay**　ɔi b**oy**　ã fr**an**glais　ã Cana**di**en　ɔ̃ Bra**yon**　(*see over for consonants*)

with coloured inks, used esp. in Inuit art. **2** a print made using this technique (also *attributive*: *stonecut print*).

stone·cut·ter *noun* a person or machine that cuts, shapes, or carves stone for building or for ornamental purposes.

stoned *adjective slang* under the influence of drugs or alcohol.

stone-faced *adjective* expressionless.

stone·fish *noun* (*pl.* same) a venomous tropical fish, *Synanceia verrucosa*, with poison glands underlying its erect dorsal spines.

stone·fly *noun* (*pl.* **-flies**) **1** any insect of the order Plecoptera whose larvae are typically found under stones in streams. **2** *Angling* a lure tied to resemble this.

stone fruit *noun* a fruit with flesh or pulp enclosing a stone.

stone-ground *adjective* **1** (of flour) ground using millstones rather than metal rollers. **2** (esp. of bread) made with stone-ground flour.

stone hands *plural noun N Amer. Sport slang* a lack of skill or finesse, e.g. in stickhandling, fielding, or catching.

Stone·henge a large megalithic monument on Salisbury Plain in Wiltshire, England, consisting of a concentric bank and ditch around a circle of bluestones, which in turn surrounds a circle of sarsen stones, all originally surmounted by stone lintels, often associated with the Druids and believed to have been used as a temple or for astronomical purposes. [from STONE + 2nd element prob. derived from HANG *noun*]

stone·mason *noun* a person who cuts, prepares, and builds with stone. □ **stone·mason·ry** *noun*

Stone of Scone the stone on which medieval Scottish kings were crowned. It was brought to England by Edward I and since then kings and queens of England have been crowned with it in the coronation chair in Westminster Abbey. It was returned to Scotland in 1996 to be kept in Edinburgh castle between coronations.

stone pine *noun* a S European pine tree, *Pinus pinea*, with branches at the top spreading like an umbrella.

ston·er *noun* **1** *slang* a person, esp. a youth, who is or is perceived to be a habitual user of drugs. **2** a device for removing stones from fruit (*cherry stoner*).

Stone sheep *noun* (also **Stone's sheep**) a thinhorn sheep, *Ovis dalli stonei*, of the south central Yukon and northern Rockies of British Columbia, with a blackish coat and white underparts. [Andrew Jackson *Stone*, US naturalist and explorer d.1918]

stone·wall *verb* **1** *transitive & intransitive* avoid or prevent the progress of a discussion or interrogation etc. by making lengthy speeches and vague or evasive answers; stall. **2** *transitive* hinder, block, or prevent (a thing) from occurring or (a person) from doing something (*she stonewalled their attempt to pass the legislation*). **3** *transitive Sport* thwart (an opponent) with strong defensive play. □ **stone·waller** *noun* **stone·wall·ing** *noun*

stone·ware *noun* a kind of dense, impermeable, usu. opaque pottery made from clay containing a high proportion of silica and partly vitrified during firing (also *attributive*: *stoneware jug*).

stone·wash ● *noun* **1** a worn or faded appearance given to denim by washing it with abrasives. **2** (*attributive*) designating denim or clothing made of denim that has been washed with abrasives to produce such an appearance (*stonewash jeans*). ● *transitive verb* wash (denim etc.) with abrasives. □ **stone·washed** *adjective*

stone·work *noun* **1** masonry. **2** the parts of a building made of stone. **3** the art, craft, or process of working with stone. □ **stone·work·er** *noun*

stone·wort /ˈstoːnwɜrt, -wort/ *noun* any of several chiefly freshwater algae of the family Characeae, with whorls of short branches, often partly encrusted with calcium carbonate.

Stoney *noun* **1** a member of an Aboriginal people now living in southern Alberta, and formerly living in southern Manitoba and southern Saskatchewan. **2** any of the languages spoken by this people. [so called because of their traditional use of hot stones for boiling water]

Stoney Creek a former city in S Ontario, located on Lake Ontario at the east end of Hamilton, now part of the city of Hamilton; pop. (2001) 57,327. It was the scene (6 June 1813) of a decisive battle during the War of 1812, in which British troops launched a surprise attack on the camp of an American invasion force. [origin uncertain: prob. after the name of a creek flowing north into Lake Ontario]

stonk·er *noun* esp. *Brit. informal* something which is very large or impressive of its kind (*a real stonker of a plan*). [from *stonk* 'bombard', 'bombardment', said to be formed from the artillery term *Standard Regimental Concentration*]

stonk·ing *adjective* esp. *Brit. informal* used to emphasize something remarkable or exciting (*a stonking good plan*).

stony *adjective* (also **stoney**) (**ston·i·er**, **ston·i·est**) **1** full of or covered with stones (*stony soil*). **2** lacking sensitivity or feeling; hardened, obdurate. **3** (also **stony-faced**) cold, expressionless; unable or refusing to express any emotion (*a stony gaze; a stony-faced stare*). **4** (of silence, grief, fear, etc.) cold and harsh, grim, unrelenting. **5** *Brit.* (in full **stony broke**) *informal* entirely without money. **6** having the hardness of stone; rigid. □ **ston·i·ly** *adverb* **ston·i·ness** *noun*

Stony Mountain a community in SE central Manitoba, part of the rural municipality of Rockwood and the site of a penitentiary, situated 25 km north of Winnipeg.

Stony Plain a town in central Alberta, 30 km west of Edmonton; pop. (2001) 9,589. [so called because of the surrounding rocky plain]

stood *past and past participle of* STAND.

stooge *informal* ● *noun* **1** an unquestioningly loyal or obsequious assistant; a puppet. **2** a person of subordinate or inferior rank who performs esp. routine or unpleasant labour. **3** an entertainer who feeds lines to another comedian and serves as a butt of the other's jokes. ● *intransitive verb* (usu. foll. by *about, around*, etc.) move about aimlessly. [20th c.: origin unknown]

stook¹ /stʊk, stuːk/ *Cdn & Brit.* ● *noun* a small stack of bales of hay or straw, or sheaves of grain, collected in a field, esp. to hasten drying. ● *transitive verb* arrange (bales or sheaves) in stooks. □ **stook·er** *noun* **stook·ing** *noun* [Middle English *stouk*, from or related to Middle Low German *stūke*]

stook² /stʊk, stuːk/ *noun Cdn* (*West*) a card game similar to blackjack but which may be played by several players. [origin unknown]

stool *noun* **1** a seat without a back or arms, usu. for one person and consisting of a usu. flat seat set on three or four legs or on a central pedestal. **2** a short low bench on which to step or kneel, or for resting the foot; a footstool. **3** (often in *pl.*) = FECES. **4** the root or stump of a tree or plant from which the shoots spring. **5** *US* a decoy used in hunting birds. □ **fall between two stools** fail because of vacillation between two courses of action etc. [Old English *stōl* from Germanic, related to STAND]

stool pigeon *noun* **1** (*N Amer.* also **stool·ie**) a police informer. **2** a person acting as a decoy. [originally a decoy of a pigeon fixed to a stool]

stoop¹ ● *verb* **1** *transitive & intransitive* lower one's body by bending (the head and shoulders or trunk) forwards and downwards. **2** *intransitive* carry one's head and shoulders habitually bowed forward. **3** *intransitive* (foll. by *to* + infin.) deign or condescend to adopt a position, course of action, etc. regarded as beneath oneself. **4** *intransitive* (foll. by *to*) descend or lower oneself to some conduct, esp. of an unworthy or morally reprehensible nature. **5** *intransitive* (of a hawk etc.) swoop on its prey. ● *noun* **1** a stooping posture. **2** the downward swoop of a hawk etc. □ **stoop and scoop** *Cdn* ● *noun* (often *attributive*) designating a law requiring owners to pick up the excrement of their pets in parks and on streets and lawns. ● *intransitive verb* pick up after one's pet. [Old English *stūpian* from Germanic, related to STEEP¹]

stoop² *noun N Amer.* a small raised platform or set of steps at the entrance of a house; a porch. [Dutch *stoep*, related to STEP]

stoop·ball *noun* esp. *US* a form of baseball played esp. in a schoolyard in which a ball is thrown against a wall or set of stairs, with bases and runs being awarded to the thrower according to the number of times the ball bounces before being caught by an opponent.

stooped *adjective* **1** (of a person) afflicted with a habitual stoop. **2** (of the head, shoulders, posture, etc.) bent forward, esp. as a habitual trait.

stop ● *verb* (**stopped**, **stop·ping**) **1** *transitive* **a** check or impede the operation or onward movement of (a person or thing); bring to a state of rest (*tried to escape but she stopped him; stop the car*). **b** (often foll. by *from*) cause (a person or thing) to desist from or pause in a course of action; prevent (*stopped them from fighting*). **c** interrupt or prevent (an activity or process etc.) or cause it to cease (*stop the spread of disease*). **2** *transitive* **a** discontinue, suspend (an action or sequence of actions) (*it stopped raining*). **b** desist from (a thing or activity etc. one is accustomed to) (*stopped smoking*). **3** *intransitive* **a** leave off or pause momentarily in an activity (*she stopped in mid sentence*). **b** (of a thing, process, etc.) cease from motion, action, or operation (*my watch has stopped*). **4 a** *transitive* not permit or supply as usual; discontinue or withhold (*shall stop their wages*). **b** *intransitive* come to an end; cease to occur or arrive etc. as usual (*her weekly sessions have stopped*). **5** *intransitive* cease from forward movement; come to a standstill or state of rest. **6** *transitive Sport* **a** defeat (an opposing player or team). **b** block, save, or thwart (a puck or ball, shot, opponent, punch, etc.). **c** *Boxing* defeat (an opponent) by a knockout or technical knockout. **7** *transitive* (often foll. by *up*) **a** fill or close up (a hole, leak, cavity in a tooth, etc.). **b** plug or clog (a drain etc.); block. **8** *transitive* (in full **stop payment on** or **of**) instruct a bank to withhold payment on (a cheque). **9** *transitive Music* **a** obtain the required pitch from (the string of a guitar or violin etc.) by pressing it at the appropriate point with the finger. **b** close (a finger hole or aperture of a wind instrument) in order to alter the pitch. **c** produce (sound or a note) by these means. **10** *transitive* plug the upper end of (an organ pipe), giving a note an octave lower. **11** *transitive* provide (a line, page, etc.) with punctuation. **12** *transitive Bridge* be able to prevent opponents from taking all the tricks in (a suit). ● *noun* **1** the act or an instance of stopping; the state of being stopped (*put a stop to this nonsense*; *the vehicle came to a stop*). **2 a** a place designated for a bus or subway etc. to stop for passengers to get on and off. **b** a stay of considerable duration at a place, esp. during the course of a journey. **3** (in full **stop-payment**) an order stopping payment, esp. of a cheque. **4** a part of a mechanism, such as a pin, bolt, or block of wood, used to check the motion or thrust of something, keep another part in place, or determine the position of something. **5** *Sport* a save or tackle made on an opponent or attempt to score. **6 a** the effective diameter of a lens as indicated by an f-number. **b** a plate or diaphragm with a central hole used to reduce this. **c** a unit of change of relative aperture (or exposure or film speed), a reduction of one stop being equivalent to a halving of the value. **d** = DIAPHRAGM 3. **7** a change of pitch effected by stopping a string of a violin etc. or by blocking the finger hole or aperture of a wind instrument. **8 a** (in an organ) a graduated row of pipes producing tones of the same character. **b** the handle or knob by which air is admitted to or excluded from a set of organ pipes. **9** any of a class of consonants the formation of which is effected by first closing the vocal tract and then releasing the breath abruptly, such as /p/, /b/, /d/, /t/. **10** *esp. Brit.* a punctuation mark, esp. = FULL STOP 1. **11** *Bridge* a card or cards stopping a suit. **12** *Naut.* a small line used as a lashing. **13** (in telegrams etc.) a period. □ **pull out all the stops** *see* PULL. **put a stop to** cause to end, esp. abruptly. **stop at nothing** do everything required to complete a task without being deterred by setbacks; be ruthless. **stop by** *N Amer.* **1** visit (a place). **2** pay a brief visit. **stop dead** cease abruptly. **stop down** *Photog.* reduce the aperture of (a lens) with a diaphragm. **stop a gap** meet a temporary need or serve as a temporary solution. **stop in** *N Amer.* = *stop by*. **stop over** rest or make a break in one's journey. **stop short** cease abruptly. **stop short of** come very close to (doing something) (*they stopped short of demanding her resignation*). □ **stop·pable** *adjective* [Old English (*for*)*stoppian* from W Germanic, from Late Latin *stuppare* STUFF: see ESTOP]

stop-action *noun* = STOP-MOTION.

stop-and-go ● *noun* **1** alternate stopping and restarting of progress. **2** *Econ.* a policy of alternately restricting demand to contain inflation and expanding credit to stimulate demand and reduce unemployment. ● *adjective* alternately stopping and going (*traffic this morning is stop-and-go*).

stop·cock *noun* an externally operated valve regulating the flow of a liquid or gas through a pipe etc.

stope *noun* an excavation forming steps or notches made in a mine or quarry in order to facilitate the extraction of ore etc. [apparently related to STEP *noun*]

Stopes, Marie (Char·lotte Car·mi·chael) (1880–1958), Scottish birth control campaigner. In 1921 she established the first birth control clinic in Britain; her study *Contraception: Its Theory, History, and Practice* (1923) was one of the first comprehensive works on the subject.

stop·gap *noun* a thing that temporarily supplies a need; a temporary substitute or solution (also *attributive*: *stopgap measures*).

stop-go *noun* = STOP-AND-GO *noun*.

stop·light *noun* **1 a** *N Amer.* a traffic light. **b** a red traffic light. **2** = BRAKE LIGHT.

stop-loss *adjective Stock Market* denoting or relating to an order to sell a security or commodity at a specified price in order to limit a loss.

stop-motion *noun* **1** a method of animation in which a model is filmed one frame at a time with its position changed slightly between shots so that running film will give it the appearance of motion (also *attributive*: *stop-motion photography*). **2** a function on some VCRs that enables a single frame of film to be displayed on a television screen for an extended period of time.

stop·over *noun* (also **stop·off**) **1** a break or brief stop in a journey. **2** such a break or stop made with the ability to proceed on the original ticket at a later time. **3** a city, resort, hotel, etc. where one stops during a journey.

stop·page *noun* **1** an interruption of service, labour, a game, etc. (*a work stoppage*). **2** the condition of being blocked or plugged up.

stoppage time *noun* = INJURY TIME.

Stop·pard /ˈstɒpɑːd/ **Sir Tom** (born Tomas Straussler) (b.1937), Czech-born English dramatist. His best-known plays are comedies, which often deal with metaphysical and ethical questions and are characterized by verbal wit and the use of pastiche; his plays include *Rosencrantz and Guildenstern are Dead* (1966), based on the characters in *Hamlet*, *Jumpers* (1972), and *Hapgood* (1988).

stop-payment *noun see* STOP *noun* 3.

stop·per ● *noun* **1** a plug for closing a bottle. **2** a plug used to close the drain of a bathtub or sink. **3** *Baseball* **a** a relief pitcher who enters the game in esp. the last inning to preserve a team's lead. **b** a starting pitcher depended upon to win a game or reverse a losing streak. **4** a thing which attracts and holds attention. ● *transitive verb* close or plug (a bottle etc.) with a stopper.

stopping house *noun Cdn hist.* a modest house or inn offering accommodation to travellers; a boarding house.

stopping place *noun Cdn hist.* **a** a settlement where groups of travellers customarily stop for food and lodging. **b** a stopping house. **2** a place at which a person, animal, or thing may stop.

stop sign *noun* a red octagonal sign at an intersection indicating that traffic should stop before proceeding.

stop-start *adjective* alternately stopping and starting; progressing with interruptions (*stop-start driving*).

stop valve *noun* = SHUT-OFF VALVE.

stop·watch *noun* a watch with a mechanism for recording elapsed time, used to time races etc.

stor·age *noun* **1 a** the action of storing or keeping a thing or things in reserve; the condition of being stored. **b** a place or amount of space available or used for storing (also *attributive*: *storage box*). **2** the cost of storing something. **3** *Computing* **a** the electronic retention of data and instructions in a device from which they can be retrieved. **b** (in full **storage device**) = MEMORY 4b.

storage battery *noun* a rechargeable cell for storing electricity in the form of chemical energy, usu. consisting of one or more secondary cells.

storage heater *noun Brit.* an electric heater accumulating heat outside peak hours for later release.

storage shed *noun see* SHED¹ 1b.

stor·ax /ˈstɔːraks/ *noun* **1 a** a fragrant resin, obtained from the tree *Styrax officinalis* and formerly used in perfume. **b** this tree. **2** (in full **liquid storax**) a balsam obtained from the tree *Liquidambar orientalis*. [Latin from Greek, var. of STYRAX]

store ● *noun* **1 a** *N Amer.* a building or establishment where merchandise and services are available for sale at retail prices. **b** a chain of retail outlets operating under one name. **2** a quantity of something available for future use; a stock or supply (*a store of wine*; *a store of wit*). **3** (in *pl.*) articles such as food, clothing, weapons, etc., accumulated for a particular purpose, esp. to supply and maintain an army or ship etc. **4** *Brit.* a warehouse. **5** *Cdn (Nfld & Maritimes)* = FISH STORE 2. ● *transitive verb* **1 a** (often foll. by *up*, *away*) accumulate or collect a stock or supply of (goods etc.); keep in reserve, esp. for future use. **b** place or keep (possessions, merchandise, etc.) in a storage facility or warehouse. **2** retain (data or instructions) in some physical form that enables subsequent retrieval; transfer into a memory or storage device. **3** (of a receptacle) hold, keep, contain (*these wooden casks are used to store wine*). **4** stock or provide with something useful (*a mind stored with facts*). □ **in store** **1** kept in readiness. **2** coming in the future; about to happen. **3** (foll. by *for*) destined or awaiting to befall or be encountered by (a person). **set** (or **lay** or **put**) **store by** (or **on**) consider to be of importance, worth, or value. □ **stor·able** *adjective* **stor·er** *noun* [Old French *estore*, *estorer* from Latin *instaurare* renew: compare RESTORE]

store-bought *adjective N Amer.* commercially manufactured and purchased in a store; not homemade.

store·front *noun esp. N Amer.* **1** the side of a store that faces onto the street. **2** a commercial property, such as a store, that has a store window or that faces onto the street. **3 a** a room or rooms at the front of a commercial property or store, esp. as used for some other purpose, such as a small business, a centre for religious worship, etc. **b** (*attributive*) designating a business operating out of such an establishment, or the proprietor of such (*a storefront café*; *a storefront lawyer*).

store·house *noun* **1** a place where things are stored; a warehouse. **2** (often foll. by *of*) a person or thing considered to be a treasury or repository of something (*he is a storehouse of useful information*).

store·keep·er *noun* **1** *N Amer.* a store manager. **2** a store owner. **3** a storeman.

store·man *noun* (*pl.* **-men**) a person responsible for looking after stored goods, esp. in the army.

store manager *noun* esp. *N Amer.* a person responsible for operating a retail establishment, managing staff, etc.

store owner *noun* esp. *N Amer.* the proprietor of a retail establishment.

store·room *noun* a room in a house or office etc. in which supplies and other items may be kept.

store·wide *adjective* applying to all merchandise in every department of a store (*a storewide sale*).

store window *noun N Amer.* **1** a large window in a storefront. **2** a space inside a store in front of a window in which merchandise is displayed to passing pedestrians.

stor·ey *noun* (also **story**) (*pl.* **-eys** or **-ies**) **1 a** a single level of a house or building including rooms or offices located on it; a floor. **b** (*attributive*; in *combination*) designating a house or building consisting of a specified number of levels (*a ten-storey apartment building*). **2** each of a number of tiers or rows of windows, columns, panels, etc. arranged horizontally on the facade of a building and dividing it into levels. **3** a rough estimate of height based on the approximate height of one storey of a building. □ **-stor·eyed** *adjective* (in *combination*) (also **-storied**). [Anglo-Latin *historia* HISTORY (perhaps originally meaning a tier of painted windows or sculpture)]

storied *adjective* celebrated in or associated with stories or legend; legendary.

stork *noun* **1** any of various large wading or terrestrial birds chiefly of the family Ciconiidae, having long legs and a long stout bill, esp. the Eurasian white stork, *Ciconia ciconia*, which stands over three feet high, has brilliant white plumage with black wing tips and red legs and bill, and nests on tall trees, buildings, etc. **2** this bird as a symbol of childbirth, a fabled deliverer of newborn infants to fortunate parents. [Old English *storc*, prob. related to STARK (from its rigid posture)]

storm ● *noun* **1** a violent weather disturbance with high winds and usu. heavy precipitation, thunder and lightning, etc. **2** *Meteorol.* a wind classed as force 10 or 11 on the Beaufort scale (between a gale and a hurricane), having an average velocity of 48–63 knots (55–72 mph). **3** (foll. by *of*) **a** a violent outburst (of protest, controversy, ridicule, etc.). **b** a violent shower of projectiles or blows. **4** (in *pl.*) *N Amer. informal* storm windows. **5** a violent disturbance of affairs, whether political, social, or domestic; controversy. **6** a direct assault by troops on a stronghold. ● *verb* **1 a** *intransitive* (usu. foll. by *in, out of,* etc.) move violently or angrily (*stormed out of the meeting*). **b** *transitive* say or shout in an angry or violent manner ('*Get out of my house!*' *she stormed*). **2** *transitive* rush, attack, or assault; attempt to overwhelm or enter by force. **3** *intransitive* (of wind, rain, etc.) be violent or tempestuous; rage. □ **cook, dance, etc. up a storm** *N Amer.* cook, dance, etc. with great enthusiasm and energy. **storm in a teacup** *Brit.* = *tempest in a teapot* (see TEMPEST). **take by storm 1** capture by direct assault. **2** achieve sudden or overwhelming success with (an audience, city, etc.). □ **storm·proof** *adjective* [Old English from Germanic]

storm·bound *adjective* confined or isolated by a storm or storms.

storm centre *noun* the comparatively calm area of low pressure in the centre of a cyclonic storm point to which the wind blows spirally inward in a cyclonic storm.

storm cloud *noun* **1** a dark heavy cloud. **2** a threatening state of affairs.

storm coat *noun N Amer.* a waterproof coat or heavy overcoat for use in stormy weather.

storm collar *noun* a high coat collar that can be turned up and fastened.

storm cuff *noun* a tight-fitting elastic cuff inside the end of the sleeve of a coat which prevents rain or wind from getting in.

storm door *noun* esp. *N Amer.* an additional outer door to keep out cold and bad weather and protect the inner door.

storm drain *noun* = STORM SEWER.

storm flap *noun* a piece of material that can be fastened to protect an opening from the effects of rain, such as on a tent or coat etc.

storm lantern *noun* a hurricane lamp.

storm petrel *noun* any of various small ocean birds of the family Hydrobatidae, which fly close to the surface of the ocean, often appearing to walk on the waves.

storm sewer *noun N Amer.* a drain built to carry away excess water in times of heavy rain.

storm-stayed *adjective Cdn* (*Maritimes & Ont.*) stranded due to severe or inclement weather conditions; snowbound.

storm surge *noun* a rising of the sea in a region as a result of the wind and atmospheric pressure changes associated with a storm.

storm trooper *noun* **1** *hist.* a member of the Nazi political militia. **2** a militant activist or member of any group of vigilantes or shock troops.

storm·water *noun* surface water in abnormal quantity resulting from heavy rainfall.

storm window *noun N Amer.* a detachable outer window put up in winter as insulation and to protect an inner window from the effects of storms.

stormy *adjective* (**storm·i·er**, **storm·i·est**) **1** (of the weather, sky, sea, etc.) disturbed or affected by a storm; wild, rough, tempestuous. **2** (of a place or region) subject to or affected by storms. **3 a** (of an event, period, etc.) turbulent, tempestuous; full of anger or angry outbursts (*a stormy meeting; a stormy relationship*). **b** (of a person or their looks) angry or suggestive of anger. □ **storm·i·ly** *adverb* **storm·i·ness** *noun*

stormy petrel *noun* = STORM PETREL.

Storn·o·way /ˈstɔːnəˌweɪ/ **1** a house in Rockcliffe (an enclave within Ottawa), the official residence of the Leader of the Official Opposition of Canada. **2** a port on the east coast of Lewis, in the Outer Hebrides; pop. (1981) 8,640. The administrative centre for the Western Isles, it is noted for the manufacture of Harris tweed.

story[1] *noun* (*pl.* **-ies**) **1 a** an account of imaginary or past events; a narrative, tale, or anecdote. **b** = SHORT STORY. **2** the past course of the life of a person or institution etc. (*my story is a strange one*). **3** = STORYLINE. **4** facts or experiences that deserve narration. **5** *informal* a fib or lie. **6 a** a narrative or descriptive item of news. **b** material or a subject which is or can be made suitable for such an article; a piece of news (*the media picked up on the story right away*). □ **another story** a different thing altogether; a matter requiring or meriting separate treatment. **end of story** *informal* used to emphasize that there is nothing to add on a matter just mentioned (*Men don't cry in public. End of story.*) **the same old story** the familiar or predictable course of events. **the story goes** it is said. **to make a long story short** a formula excusing the omission of details. **the story of my** (or **your, his, her** etc.) **life** an event, statement, or situation that supposedly epitomizes a person's life or experience (*of course she didn't show up—that's the story of my life*). □ **story·less** *adjective* [Anglo-French *estorie* (Old French *estoire*) from Latin *historia* (as HISTORY)]

story[2] *var. of* STOREY.

story arc *noun* a background plot or ongoing storyline in a television series etc., within which self-contained episodes are set.

story ballet *noun* a ballet recounting a story, as opposed to an abstract dance piece.

story·board ● *noun* a displayed sequence of pictures etc. outlining the plan of a film, television advertisement, etc. ● *transitive verb* (esp. in *passive*) produce a storyboard of (a film etc.). □ **story·board·ing** *noun*

story·book ● *noun* a book of stories for children. ● *attributive adjective* denoting something that as is idyllically perfect as things typically are in storybooks (*a storybook ending*).

story·line *noun* the narrative or plot of a novel or play etc.

story·tell·er *noun* **1** a person who tells stories. **2** *informal* a liar. □ **story·tell·ing** *noun & adjective*

story·time *noun* a time for reading stories to children.

sto·tin /ˈstɔtiːn/ *noun* (*pl.* same) a monetary unit of Slovenia, equal to one-hundredth of a tolar. [Slovene]

sto·tin·ka /stɒˈtɪŋkə/ *noun* (*pl.* **sto·tin·ki** /-ki/) a monetary unit of Bulgaria, equal to one-hundredth of a lev. [Bulgarian, = hundredth]

stoup /stuːp/ *noun* **1** a basin for holy water, as at the entrance of a church etc. **2** *archaic* a flagon, beaker, or drinking vessel. [Old Norse *staup* (= Old English *stēap*) from Germanic, related to STEEP[2]]

stout ● *adjective* **1** rather fat; corpulent; bulky. **2** of considerable thickness or strength (*a stout stick*). **3** brave, resolute, vigorous (*a stout fellow; put up stout resistance*). ● *noun* a strong dark beer brewed with roasted malt or barley. □ **stout·ish** *adjective* **stout·ly** *adverb* **stout·ness** *noun* [Anglo-French from West Germanic, perhaps related to STILT]

stout-hearted *adjective* courageous. □ **stout-hearted·ly** *adverb* **stout-hearted·ness** *noun*

stove[1] *noun* an apparatus burning fuel or using electricity for heating or cooking. [Middle English = sweating room, from Middle Dutch, Middle Low German *stove*, from Germanic, perhaps related to STEW]

stove² *past and past participle of* STAVE *verb*.

stove·pipe *noun* a pipe conducting smoke and gases from a stove to a chimney.

stovepipe hat *noun informal* a tall silk top hat.

stove·top ● *noun* the top surface of a stove, esp. the cooking elements. ● *adjective* located on or cooked on a stovetop (*unsuitable for stovetop use; stovetop pork roast*).

stove·wood *noun N Amer.* wood split for burning in a stove.

stow *transitive verb* **1** pack (goods etc.) tidily and compactly. **2** place (a cargo or provisions) in its proper place and order. **3** fill (a receptacle) with articles compactly arranged. **4** (usu. in *imperative*) *slang* abstain or cease from (*stow the noise!*). □ **stow away 1** place (a thing) where it will not cause an obstruction. **2** be a stowaway on a ship etc. [Middle English, from BESTOW: in Naut. use perhaps influenced by Dutch *stouwen*]

stow·age *noun* **1** the act or an instance of stowing. **2** a place for this.

stow·away *noun* a person who hides on board a ship or aircraft etc. to get free passage.

Stowe, Har·riet Eliza·beth Bee·cher (1811–96), US novelist. Her anti-slavery novel *Uncle Tom's Cabin* (1852) strengthened the abolitionist cause with its descriptions of the sufferings endured by slaves.

STP *abbreviation* standard temperature and pressure.

stra·bis·mus /strə'bɪzməs/ *noun Med.* the abnormal condition of one or both eyes not correctly aligned in direction; a squint. □ **stra·bis·mic** *adjective* [modern Latin from Greek *strabismos* from *strabizō* squint, from *strabos* squinting]

Strabo /'streɪbəʊ/ (c.63 BC–AD c.23), Greek historian and geographer. His only extant work, *Geographica*, in 17 volumes, provides a detailed physical and historical geography of the ancient world during the reign of Augustus.

strac·cia·tel·la /,stratʃə'telə/ *noun* an Italian soup made by adding beaten eggs and Parmesan cheese to broth. [Italian, from *stracciare* 'tear up']

Stra·chey /'streɪtʃi/ **(Giles) Lyt·ton** (1880–1932), English biographer. He was a prominent member of the Bloomsbury Group, and his best-known work, *Eminent Victorians* (1918), attacked the literary establishment through satirical biographies of Florence Nightingale, Thomas Arnold, and others.

Strad *noun informal* a Stradivarius.

strad·dle ● *verb* **1** *transitive* **a** sit or stand with the legs one on either side of (a thing, person, horse, etc.). **b** be situated across or on both sides of (*the town straddles the border*). **2** *intransitive* **a** sit or stand in this way. **b** (of the legs) be wide apart. **3** *transitive* part (one's legs) widely. **4** *transitive* drop shots or bombs short of and beyond (a target). **5** *transitive* vacillate between two policies etc. regarding (an issue). **6** *transitive* participate in (two opposing or vastly different cultures, genres, etc.). ● *noun* **1** the act or an instance of straddling. **2** *Stock Exch.* an option giving the holder the right of either calling for or delivering stock at a fixed price. □ **strad·dler** *noun* [alteration of *striddle*, back-formation from *striddlings* astride, from *strid-* = STRIDE]

Stradi·vari /,strɑdə'vɑri/ **An·tonio** (Latin name Antonius Stradivarius) (c.1644–1737), Italian maker of violins, violas, and cellos. He devised the proportions of the modern violin, producing a more powerful and rounded sound than earlier instruments. About 650 of his celebrated instruments are still in existence.

Stradi·var·ius /,strɑdə'verɪəs/ *noun* a violin or other stringed instrument made by Antonio Stradivari or his family.

strafe ● *transitive verb* attack repeatedly with bullets or bombs from aircraft flying low over their target. ● *noun* an act of strafing. [jocular adaptation of German catchword (1914) *Gott strafe England* may God punish England]

strag·gle ● *intransitive verb* **1** lack or lose compactness or tidiness. **2** be or become dispersed or sporadic. **3** trail behind others in a march or race etc. **4** (of a plant, beard, etc.) grow long and loose. ● *noun* a body or group of straggling or scattered persons or things. □ **strag·gler** *noun* **strag·gly** *adjective* (**strag·gli·er, strag·gli·est**). [Middle English, perhaps related to dial. *strake* go, related to STRETCH]

straight ● *adjective* **1 a** extending uniformly in the same direction; without a curve or bend etc. **b** *Math.* (of a line) lying on the shortest path between any two of its points. **2** successive, uninterrupted (*three straight wins*). **3** in proper order or place or condition; duly arranged; level, symmetrical (*is the picture straight?*; *put things straight*). **4** honest,

candid; not evasive (*a straight answer*; *straight talk*). **5** (of thinking etc.) logical, unemotional. **6** (of drama etc.) serious as opposed to popular or comic; employing the conventional techniques of its art form. **7 a** unmodified. **b** (of a drink) undiluted. **8** *informal* **a** heterosexual. **b** (of a person etc.) conventional or respectable. **9** (of an arch) flat-topped. **10** (of a person's back) not bowed. **11** (of the hair) not curly or wavy. **12** (of a knee) not bent. **13** (of the legs) not bandy or knock-kneed. **14** (of a garment) not flared. **15** coming direct from its source. **16** (of an aim, look, blow, or course) going direct to the mark. ● *noun* **1** the straight part of something, esp. the concluding stretch of a racecourse. **2** a straight condition. **3** a sequence of five cards in poker. **4** *informal* **a** a heterosexual. **b** a conventional person. ● *adverb* **1** in a straight line; directly; without deviation or hesitation or circumlocution (*came straight from work*). **2** in the right direction, with a good aim (*shoot straight*). **3** continuously, without a break (*have been working for 16 hours straight*). **4** correctly (*can't see straight*). **5** honestly and directly; in a straightforward manner. **6** upright; in an erect posture (*stand straight!*). **7** clearly and logically (*you're not thinking straight*). **8** completely (*a scene straight out of Dickens*). **9** *archaic* at once or immediately. □ **go straight** live an honest life after being a criminal. **set** (or **put**) **a person straight** correct a person's mistake; make sure that someone knows the correct facts etc. when they have the wrong idea or impression. **the straight and narrow** morally correct behaviour. **straight away** at once; immediately. **straight from the shoulder 1** (of a blow) well delivered. **2** (of a verbal attack) frank or direct. **straight off** *informal* without hesitation, deliberation, etc. (*cannot tell you straight off*). **straight up** *informal* **1** esp. *N Amer.* unmixed, undiluted. **2** truthfully, honestly. □ **straight·ish** *adjective* **straight·ly** *adverb* **straight·ness** *noun* [Middle English, past participle of STRETCH]

straight-ahead *adjective* **1** simple, straightforward. **2** (esp. of music or a musical style) unembellished; unadorned.

straight angle *noun* an angle of 180°.

straight-arm ● *transitive verb* push away or deflect (an opponent or obstacle) with the arm outstretched. ● *noun* an act of straight-arming an opponent or obstacle.

straight arrow *noun N Amer. informal* a person who lives an honest, sober life. □ **straight-arrow** *adjective*

straight·away ● *adverb* = straight away (see STRAIGHT). ● *adjective* esp. US (of a course etc.) straight, direct. ● *noun* esp. *N Amer.* a straight course or section.

straight-backed *adjective* **1** (of a chair) having a straight rather than a sloping back. **2** (of a person) not bowed or stooping.

straight·edge *noun* a bar with one edge accurately straight, used for testing.

straight-eight *noun* **1** an internal combustion engine with eight cylinders in line. **2** a vehicle having such an engine.

straight·en *verb* **1** *transitive & intransitive* (often foll. by *out*) make or become straight. **2** *transitive* (often foll. by *up*) make (something) neat, tidy, or orderly. □ **straighten out 1** clarify or unravel (something that is confused or in disorder) (*Liz says we must straighten out our finances*). **2** settle or resolve (a dispute or argument etc.). **3** (of a person) improve in character or conduct. **straighten up 1** stand erect after bending. **2** *N Amer.* reform or become reformed in character or conduct. □ **straight·en·er** *noun*

straight face *noun* an intentionally expressionless face, esp. one that conceals an impulse to laugh or smile (*she couldn't keep a straight face*). □ **straight-faced** *adjective* **straight-facedly** *adverb*

straight flush *noun Cards* a flush that is a numerical sequence (see FLUSH³).

straight·forward *adjective* **1** honest or frank. **2** (of a task etc.) uncomplicated. □ **straight·forward·ly** *adverb* **straight·forward·ness** *noun*

straight goods *plural noun* (prec. by *the*) the unadorned truth.

straight·jacket *var. of* STRAITJACKET.

straight·laced *var. of* STRAITLACED.

straight-line *adjective* **1** containing, characterized by, or relating to straight lines or motion in a straight line (*a straight-line graph*). **2** *Finance* of or relating to a method of depreciation allocating a given percentage of the cost of an asset each year for a fixed period.

straight man *noun* a member of a comedy team who makes remarks or creates situations for the main performer to make jokes about.

straight-on *adverb & adjective* from directly in front (*they wouldn't face him straight-on*; *a straight-on attack*).

straight-out *adjective N Amer.* **1** uncompromising. **2** straightforward, genuine.

straight pin *noun* = PIN *noun* 1a.

straight razor *noun* esp. *N Amer.* a razor having a long blade set in a handle and usu. folding like a penknife.

straight shooter *noun* esp. *N Amer. slang* a person who states bluntly what they think. □ **straight-shooting** *adjective*

straight-six *noun* **1** an internal combustion engine with six cylinders in line. **2** a vehicle having such an engine.

straight-up *adjective informal* **1** true; trustworthy. **2** esp. *N Amer.* unmixed, undiluted, unmodified.

straight·way *adverb archaic* = straight away (see STRAIGHT).

strain¹ ● *verb* **1** *transitive & intransitive* stretch tightly; make or become taut or tense. **2** *transitive* exercise (oneself, one's senses, a thing, etc.) intensely or excessively, press to extremes. **3** *intransitive* **a** make an intensive effort. **b** (foll. by *after*) strive intensely for (*straining after perfection*). **4** *intransitive* (foll. by *at*) tug, pull (*the dog strained at the leash*). **5** *intransitive* hold out with difficulty under pressure (*straining under the load*). **6** *transitive* **a** distort from the true intention or meaning. **b** apply (authority, laws, etc.) beyond their province or in violation of their true intention. **7** *transitive* overtask or injure by overuse or excessive demands (*strain a muscle*; *strained their loyalty*). **8 a** *transitive* clear (a liquid) of solid matter by passing it through a sieve etc. **b** *transitive* (foll. by *out*) filter (solids) out from a liquid. **c** *intransitive* (of a liquid) percolate. **9** *transitive* hug or squeeze tightly. **10** *transitive* use (one's ears, eyes, voice, etc.) to the best of one's power. ● *noun* **1 a** the act or an instance of straining. **b** the force exerted in this. **2** an injury caused by straining a muscle etc. **3 a** a severe demand on physical or mental strength or resources. **b** the exertion needed to meet this (*is suffering from strain*). **4** (in *sing.* or *pl.*) a snatch or spell of music or poetry. **5** a tone or tendency in speech or writing (*more in the same strain*). **6** *Physics* **a** the condition of a body subjected to stress; molecular displacement. **b** a quantity measuring this, equal to the amount of deformation usu. divided by the original dimension. □ **strain oneself 1** injure oneself by effort. **2** make undue efforts. □ **strain·able** *adjective* [Old French *estreindre estreign-* from Latin *stringere strict-* draw tight]

strain² *noun* **1** a breed or stock of animals, plants, etc. **2** a tendency, quality, or feature of a person's character (*a strain of aggression*). **3** a distinct (natural or cultured) variety of a micro-organism. [Middle English, = progeny, from Old English *strēon*, related to Latin *struere* build]

strained *adjective* **1** constrained, forced, artificial. **2** (of a relationship) mutually distrustful or tense. **3** (of an interpretation) involving an unreasonable assumption; far-fetched, laboured. **4** (of a liquid or semi-liquid, esp. a food) that has been passed through a strainer.

strain·er *noun* a device for straining liquids, vegetables, etc.

strain gauge *noun Engin.* a device for indicating the strain of a material or structure at the point of attachment.

strait ● *noun* **1** (in *sing.* or *pl.*) a narrow passage of water connecting two seas or large bodies of water. **2** (usu. in *pl.*) difficulty, trouble, or distress (*in dire straits*; *desperate straits*). ● *adjective archaic* **1** narrow, limited; confined or confining. **2** strict or rigorous. □ **strait·ly** *adverb* **strait·ness** *noun* [Old French *estreit* tight, narrow, from Latin *strictus* STRICT]

strait·en *verb* **1** *transitive* restrict in range or scope. **2** *transitive & intransitive archaic* make or become narrow.

strait·ened *adjective* of or marked by poverty.

strait·jacket (also **straight·jacket**) ● *noun* **1** a strong garment with long sleeves which are tied in the back to prevent the person wearing it from acting violently. **2** restrictive measures. ● *transitive verb* (**strait·jacket·ed**, **strait·jacket·ing**) **1** restrain with a straitjacket. **2** severely restrict.

strait·laced *adjective* (also **straight·laced**) severely virtuous; morally scrupulous; puritanical.

Straits *noun* a N American Aboriginal language of British Columbia, part of the Salishan language group, spoken along the straits off the southern tip of Vancouver Island.

Straits Settlements a former British Crown Colony in SE Asia, centred on the Strait of Malacca. Established in 1867, it comprised Singapore, Penang, and Malacca, and later included Labuan, Christmas Island, and the Cocos Islands. It was disbanded in 1946.

strake *noun* a continuous line of planking or plates from the stem to the stern of a ship. [Middle English: prob. related to Old English *streccan* STRETCH]

stra·mo·nium /strəˈmoːniəm/ *noun* **1** datura. **2** the dried leaves of this plant used in the treatment of asthma. [modern Latin, perhaps from Tartar *turman* horse medicine]

strand¹ ● *verb* **1** *transitive* (esp. as **strand·ed** *adjective*) leave (a person) in a place where they are helpless or in a difficult situation, e.g. without money or transport. **2** *transitive Baseball* fail to score (a baserunner). **3** *transitive & intransitive* run aground. ● *noun literary* the margin of a sea, lake, or river, esp. the foreshore. [Old English]

strand² ● *noun* **1** each of the threads or wires twisted round each other to make a rope or cable. **2 a** a single thread or strip of fibre. **b** a constituent filament. **c** a single linear polymer of a long-chain molecule, esp. DNA. **3** a lock of hair. **4** an element or strain in any composite whole. ● *transitive verb* **1** break a strand in (a rope). **2** arrange in strands. [Middle English: origin unknown]

strange *adjective* **1** unusual, surprising; difficult to understand. **2** (often foll. by *to*) not previously visited, seen, or met; not familiar. **3** having unpleasant feelings; not well (*was feeling strange, so went to lie down*). **4** not at ease or comfortable in a situation; feeling that one does not fit in (*felt strange in such company*). **5** (foll. by *to*) unaccustomed. □ **make strange** *Cdn & Irish* (of a baby or child) fuss or be shy in company. **strange to say** it is surprising or unusual (that). □ **strange·ly** *adverb* [Old French *estrange* from Latin *extraneus* EXTRANEOUS]

strange attractor *noun Math.* an equation or fractal set representing a complex pattern of behaviour in a chaotic system.

strange·ness *noun* **1** the state or fact of being strange or unfamiliar etc. **2** *Physics* a property of certain elementary particles that is conserved in strong interactions.

strange particle *noun Physics* a subatomic particle classified as having a non-zero value for strangeness.

stran·ger *noun* **1** a person who does not know or is not known in a particular place or company. **2** (often foll. by *to*) a person one does not know (*was a complete stranger to me*). **3** (foll. by *to*) a person entirely unaccustomed to (a feeling, experience, etc.) (*no stranger to controversy*). **4** *Parl.* a person who is not a member or official of the House of Commons.

stran·gle *transitive verb* **1** kill (a person or animal) by squeezing or gripping their throat tightly. **2** restrict or prevent the proper growth, operation, or development of. **3** suppress (an utterance) (*strangled a scream*). □ **stran·gler** *noun* [Old French *estrangler* from Latin *strangulare* from Greek *straggalaō* from *straggalē* halter: compare *straggos* twisted]

strangle·hold *noun* **1** a wrestling hold that throttles an opponent. **2** a deadly grip. **3** complete and exclusive control.

stran·gles *plural noun* (usu. treated as *sing.*) an infectious streptococcal fever, esp. affecting the respiratory tract, in a horse, etc.

stran·gu·late /ˈstraŋɡjuˌleɪt/ *transitive verb* **1** *Med.* constrict or compress (an organ, duct, hernia, etc.) so as to prevent circulation or the passage of a fluid. **2** strangle. □ **stran·gu·la·tion** *noun* [Latin *strangulare* *strangulat-* (as STRANGLE)]

stran·gu·lat·ed hernia *noun Med.* a hernia in which the protruding part is constricted, preventing circulation.

strap ● *noun* **1** a strip of cloth, leather, or other flexible material, often with a buckle or other fastening, used for keeping something in place or for fastening, carrying, or holding onto something. **2** a loop for grasping to steady oneself while standing in a moving vehicle. **3** (prec. by *the*) punishment by beating with a leather strap. **4 a** a strip of metal used to secure or connect. **b** a leaf of a hinge. ● *transitive verb* (**strapped**, **strap·ping**) **1** (often foll. by *down*, *on*, etc.) secure or bind with a strap. **2** beat with a strap. □ **strap·per** *noun* [dial. form of STROP]

strap·hang·er *noun slang* **1** a standing passenger in a bus or train. **2** a person who commutes to work by public transport. □ **strap·hang** *intransitive verb*

strap·less *adjective* (of a garment) without straps, esp. shoulder straps.

strap-on *adjective* able to be attached by a strap or straps.

strap·pado /strəˈpɒdoː/ *noun* (pl. **-dos**) *hist.* a form of torture in which the victim is secured to a rope and made to fall from a height almost to the ground then stopped with a jerk. [French *(e)strapade* from Italian *strappata* from *strappare* snatch]

strapped *adjective* subject to a shortage (esp. of money) (*I'm a bit strapped for cash this week*).

strap·ping ● *adjective* (esp. of a person) large and sturdy. ● *noun* **1** material for making straps. **2** a punishment by beating with a strap.

Consonants: b *but* d *dog* f *few* g *get* h *her* j *yes* k *cat* l *leg* m *man* n *no* p *pen* r *red* s *sit*

strap·py *adjective* (of esp. footwear or clothes) having especially prominent or numerous straps (*wore strappy sandals*).

Stras·bourg /ˈstrazbɜːrg/ a city in NE France, in Alsace, close to the border with Germany; pop. (1999) 264,115. It is the headquarters of the Council of Europe and of the European Parliament.

strata /ˈstratə/ *noun* **1** *pl. of* STRATUM. **2** a dish made of alternating layers of foods, esp. of layers of bread with cheese etc., soaked in eggs and milk and baked. **3** (*attributive*) esp. *BC & Austral.* **a** denoting a building or piece of land shared between various owners, esp. in the form of separate condominiums. **b** denoting a company or collective managing the property.

strata·gem /ˈstratədʒəm/ *noun* a cunning plan or scheme, esp. for deceiving an enemy. [ultimately from Greek *stratēgēma* from *stratēgeō* be a general (*stratēgos*) from *stratos* army + *agō* lead]

Stra·tas /ˈstratəs/ **Ter·esa** (b.1938), Canadian operatic soprano. Her international career included the singing of 40 major roles at the Metropolitan Opera in New York and a lead performance opposite Placido Domingo in Franco Zeffirelli's film production of *La Traviata* (1983).

stra·tegic /strəˈtiːdʒɪk/ *adjective* **1** of or serving the ends of strategy (*strategic considerations*). **2** (of materials) essential in fighting a war. **3** (of bombing or weapons) done or for use against an enemy's home territory as a longer-term military objective (*opp.* TACTICAL 2). □ **stra·tegic·ally** *adverb*

Strategic Defence Initiative *noun* a projected US system of defence against nuclear weapons using satellites.

strat·egize /ˈstratədʒaiz/ *intransitive verb* (also **-egise**) *N Amer.* formulate a strategy or strategies; plan a course of action.

strat·egy /ˈstratədʒi/ *noun* (*pl.* **-egies**) **1** an esp. long-range policy designed for a particular purpose (*economic strategy*). **2** the process of planning something or carrying out a plan in a skilful way. **3** a plan or stratagem. **4 a** the art of planning and directing military activity in a battle or war (*compare* TACTICS 1). **b** an instance of this. □ **strat·egist** *noun* [French *stratégie* from Greek *stratēgia* generalship, from *stratēgos*: see STRATAGEM]

Strat·ford 1 a city in SW Ontario, northeast of London; pop. (2001) 29,676. It is the site of an internationally known and acclaimed annual drama festival, with a program that includes Shakespearean, classical, and modern theatre. **2** a town in PEI, south of Charlottetown; pop. (2001) 6,314. □ **Strat·ford·ian** *noun* [STRATFORD-UPON-AVON]

Stratford-upon-Avon a town in Warwickshire, in central England, on the Avon River; pop. (est. 2002) 23,900. Famous as the birth and burial place of William Shakespeare, it is the site of the Royal Shakespeare Theatre.

strath *noun Scot.* a broad mountain valley. [Gaelic *srath*]

Strath·clyde a former local government region in west central Scotland, dissolved in 1996.

Strath·more a town in S Alberta, east of Calgary; pop. (2001) 7,621. [after the 13th earl of *Strathmore* (1824–1904)]

Strath·roy a former town in SW Ontario, situated on the Sydenham River west of London, now part of Strathroy-Caradoc township; pop. (2001) 12,978. [*Straughroy* (also called *Strathroy*), Ireland]

strath·spey /straθˈspei/ *noun* **1** a slow Scottish dance with gliding steps in quadruple metre. **2** the music for this. [*Strathspey*, valley of the Spey River]

strat·ify /ˈstratɪˌfai/ *verb* (**-fies**, **-fied**) **1 a** *transitive* (esp. as **strat·i·fied** *adjective*) arrange in strata. **b** *intransitive* become arranged in strata. **2** *transitive* **a** construct or devise in layers. **b** arrange in a hierarchical way. □ **strat·i·fi·ca·tion** *noun* [French *stratifier* (as STRATUM)]

stra·tig·raphy /strəˈtɪgrəfi/ *noun Geol. & Archaeology* **1** the order and relative position of strata. **2** the study of this as a means of historical interpretation. □ **stra·tig·raph·er** *noun* **strati·graph·ic** *adjective* **strati·graph·ical** *adjective* **strati·graph·ic·ally** *adverb* [STRATUM + -GRAPHY]

strato- /ˈstratoː/ *combining form* denoting cloud formed in horizontal sheets or layers. [combining form of STRATUS]

strato·cumu·lus /ˌstratoːˈkjuːmjʊləs/ *noun* cloud formed as a low layer of clumped or broken grey masses.

strato·sphere /ˈstratəˌsfiːr/ *noun* **1** a layer of atmospheric air above the troposphere extending to about 50 km above the earth's surface, in which the lower part changes little in temperature and the upper part increases in temperature with height (*compare* IONOSPHERE). **2** a very high or the highest level on or as if on a stratified scale (*costs have hit the stratosphere*). □ **strato·spher·ic** /-ˈsfiːrɪk, -ˈsferɪk/ *adjective* **strato·spher·ic·al·ly** *adverb* [STRATUM + SPHERE after *atmosphere*]

strato·vol·cano *noun* (*pl.* **-noes**) a volcano built up of alternate layers of lava and ash.

strat·um /ˈstratəm/ *noun* (*pl.* **strata**) **1** esp. *Geol.* a layer or set of successive layers of any deposited substance. **2** an atmospheric layer. **3** a layer of tissue etc. **4 a** a social grade, class, etc. (*the various strata of society*). **b** *Statistics* each of the groups into which a population is divided in stratified sampling. [Latin, = something spread or laid down, neuter past participle of *sternere* strew]

strat·us /ˈstratəs/ *noun* cloud forming a continuous horizontal sheet. [Latin, past participle of *sternere*: see STRATUM]

Strauss /straus/ **1 Jo·hann** (known as Strauss the Elder) (1804–49), Austrian composer. He was a leading composer of waltzes from the 1830s, although his best-known work is probably the *Radetzky March* (1838). **2** his son, **Jo·hann** (known as Strauss the Younger) (1825–99), Austrian composer. He became known as 'the waltz king', composing many well-known waltzes such as *The Blue Danube* (1867) and *Tales from the Vienna Woods* (1868); he also composed the operetta *Die Fledermaus* (1874). **3 Levi** (c.1829–1902), US clothing manufacturer who developed heavy denim jeans and overalls. **4 Rich·ard Georg** (1864–1949), German composer. Often regarded as the last of the 19th-c. romantic composers, he is known for his tone poems such as *Also Sprach Zarathustra* (1896), and operas such as *Salome* (1905) and *Der Rosenkavalier* (1911). □ **Strauss·ian** *adjective*

Stra·vin·sky /strəˈvɪnski/ **Igor Fyodor·ovich** (1882–1971), Russian-born US composer. He made his name as a composer for Diaghilev's Ballets Russes with *The Firebird* (1910) and *The Rite of Spring* (1913), and later developed a neoclassical style, typified by the ballet *Pulcinella* (1920) and, ultimately, the opera *The Rake's Progress* (1948–51). □ **Stra·vin·skian** *adjective*

straw ● *noun* **1** dry cut stalks of grain, used esp. as bedding for animals. **2** a single stalk or piece of straw. **3** material made from straw and used for weaving hats, baskets, etc. **4** a hollow plastic or paper tube for sucking drink from a glass etc. **5** an insignificant thing (*not worth a straw*). **6** the pale yellow colour of straw. ● *adjective* **1** made of straw. **2** pale yellow. □ **draw the short straw** be chosen by lot, esp. for some disagreeable task. **grasp** (or **clutch**) **at straws** resort to an utterly inadequate expedient in desperation. **the last** (or **final**) **straw** a slight addition to a burden or difficulty that makes it finally unbearable. **straw in the wind** a slight hint of future developments. □ **strawy** *adjective* [Old English *strēaw* from Germanic, related to STREW]

straw·berry ● *noun* (*pl.* **-berries**) **1 a** any plant of the genus *Fragaria*, esp. any of various cultivated varieties, with white flowers, trifoliate leaves, and runners. **b** the pulpy red edible fruit of this, having a seed-studded surface. **2** a deep pinkish-red colour. ● *adjective* of a deep pinkish-red colour. [Old English *strēa(w)berige*, *strēowberige* (as STRAW, BERRY): reason for the name unknown]

strawberry blite *noun* a goosefoot of eastern Canada and the northern US, *Chenopodium capitatum*, with red berry-like fruits. [Latin *blitum* 'orache' from Greek *bliton*]

strawberry blond ● *noun* **1** reddish-blond hair. **2** a woman with such hair. ● *adjective* (hyphenated when *attributive*) of a reddish-blond colour.

strawberry bush *noun* a shrub of the genus *Euonymus* of eastern N America, with rough crimson fruit, either *E. americanus*, an upright shrub, or (in full **running strawberry bush**) *E. obovatus*, a trailing shrub.

strawberry mark *noun* a soft reddish birthmark.

strawberry pear *noun* **1** a widely cultivated cactus, *Hylocereus undatus*. **2** the fruit of this.

strawberry roan ● *adjective* chestnut mixed with white or grey. ● *noun* a strawberry roan horse.

strawberry social *noun* (also **strawberry tea**) *N Amer.* a public event sponsored by a church or community group as a fundraiser, where desserts featuring strawberries are served.

strawberry tree *noun* an evergreen tree, *Arbutus unedo*, bearing strawberry-like fruit.

straw·board *noun* a coarse cardboard made of straw pulp.

straw boss *noun N Amer.* an assistant foreman.

straw-colour *noun* pale yellow. □ **straw-coloured** *adjective*

straw·flower *noun* any of various kinds of everlasting, esp. a helichrysum.

straw man *noun* a person or issue etc. set up as the object of an argument in order to be defeated.

straw poll *noun* (also **straw vote**) an unofficial ballot as a test of opinion.

stray ● *intransitive verb* **1** wander from the right place; become separated from one's companions etc.; go astray. **2** leave the subject one is supposed to be thinking about or discussing (*we seem to have strayed from the point*). **3** deviate morally, esp. be sexually unfaithful. **4** wander or roam around aimlessly. ● *noun* **1** a domestic animal that has strayed or wandered away from its home, owner, etc. **2** a homeless or friendless person or animal. ● *adjective* **1** strayed or lost. **2** isolated; found or occurring occasionally (*a stray customer or two; hit by a stray bullet*). **3** that is not in the normal or right place (*tucked in a few stray hairs*). □ **stray·er** *noun* [Old French *estrayer* (as ASTRAY)]

streak ● *noun* **1** a long thin usu. irregular line or band, esp. distinguished by colour (*black with red streaks; has streaks on her glasses; a streak of light above the horizon*). **2** a strain or element in a person's character (*has a streak of mischief*). **3 a** a run or spell (*that was a streak of good luck*). **b** a continuous or uninterrupted series (*a 12-game losing streak*). **4** a flash of lightning. **5** a line of bacteria etc. placed on a culture medium. ● *verb* **1** *transitive* mark with streaks. **2** *intransitive* move very rapidly, esp. in a straight line. **3** *intransitive* form streaks. **4** *intransitive informal* run naked in a public place as a stunt. **5** *transitive* tint (the hair) with streaks. □ **streak·er** *noun* (esp. in sense 4 of *verb*). **streak·ing** *noun* [Old English *strica* 'pen stroke' from Germanic: related to STRIKE]

streaky *adjective* (**streak·i·er**, **streak·i·est**) **1** full of streaks. **2** *N Amer. Sport* (of a player or team) prone to extended spells of performing well or badly. □ **streak·i·ly** *adverb* **streak·i·ness** *noun*

stream ● *noun* **1** a flowing body of water, esp. a small river. **2 a** the flow of a fluid (*a stream of lava*). **b** (in *sing.* or *pl.*) a large quantity of something that flows or moves along. **c** an unbroken mass of people or things moving constantly in the same direction. **d** a continuous flow or series of words, time, events, etc. (*a stream of obscenities*). **e** *Computing* a continuous flow of data or instructions, esp. one having a constant or predictable rate. **3** a current or direction in which things are moving or tending (*against the stream*). **4** *Cdn & Brit.* a group of schoolchildren taught together as being of similar ability for a given age. ● *verb* **1** *intransitive* flow or move as a stream. **2** *intransitive* run with liquid (*my eyes were streaming*). **3** *intransitive* (of a banner or hair etc.) float or wave in the wind. **4** *transitive* emit a stream of (blood etc.). **5** *intransitive* (foll. by *in, out, down*, etc.) (of people or animals) move together continuously in an unbroken mass. **6** *intransitive* extend in rays or beams (*sunlight was streaming through the windows*). **7** *transitive Brit. & Cdn* arrange (schoolchildren) in streams. **8** *transitive Computing* (often as **streamed** *adjective*) transmit (esp. video and audio data) over a computer network in a steady stream. □ **stream·let** *noun* [Old English *strēam* from Germanic]

stream bank *noun* the raised or sloping edge or border of a stream.

stream bed *noun* a channel in which a stream flows or once flowed.

stream·er *noun* **1** a long narrow flag. **2** a long narrow strip of ribbon or paper, esp. in a coil that unrolls when thrown. **3** *esp. N Amer.* a fishing fly with feathers attached, resembling a small fish. **4** a banner headline. **5** (in *pl.*) the aurora borealis or australis. **6** *Cdn* an elongated band of clouds, ranging from 10 to 20 km in width and from 50 to 100 km in length, formed by convection around the Great Lakes, and generating large amounts of localized snow.

stream·ing *adjective* **1** (of a cold) accompanied by copious running of the nose and eyes. **2** *Computing* designating a method of relaying data (esp. video and audio material) over a computer network as a steady continuous stream (*streaming video*).

stream·line ● *transitive verb* **1** give (a vehicle etc.) the form which presents the least resistance to motion. **2** make (an organization, process, etc.) simple or more efficient or better organized. ● *noun* **1** the natural course of water or air currents. **2** (often *attributive*) the shape of an aircraft, car, etc., calculated to cause the least air resistance. □ **stream·lined** *adjective*

stream of consciousness *noun* **1** *Psych.* a person's thoughts and conscious reactions to events perceived as a continuous flow. **2** a literary style depicting events in such a flow in the mind of a character. □ **stream-of-consciousness** *adjective*

stream·side *noun* the ground along a stream bank (often *attributive*: *streamside trail*).

Streep, Meryl (born Mary Louise Streep) (b.1949), US actress. She became a leading star in the 1980s, winning an Oscar for *Kramer vs. Kramer* (1980); her other films include *The French Lieutenant's Woman*

(1981), *Sophie's Choice* (1982), for which she won a second Oscar, and *The Bridges of Madison County* (1995).

street ● *noun* **1 a** a public road in a city, town, or village. **b** this including sidewalks. **c** this with the houses or other buildings on each side. **d** (in many N American grid-layout cities) a road running perpendicular to an avenue, esp. north-south (*compare* AVENUE 1b). **2** the persons who live or work on a particular street. **3** (**the Street**) **a** *Cdn* = BAY STREET. **b** *US* = WALL STREET. ● *attributive adjective* **1** of or adjoining the street (*use the street door*). **2** (of clothes etc.) suitable for everyday wear or use in public (*street clothes*). **3** occurring on a street (*a street party*). **4** appearing or performing on a street (*street performers*). **5** *esp. N Amer.* (of a person) homeless (*street people*). **6** (also *predicative*) of or relating to the outlook, values, or lifestyle of the young urban subculture. □ **on the street** (also **on the streets**) **1** homeless. **2** through everyday urban life (*learned it on the streets*). **3** *N Amer.* out of prison; released from custody. **streets ahead** (often foll. by *of*) *Brit. informal* much superior (to). **take to the streets** (of people) gather outdoors in a town or city in order to protest, celebrate, etc. **up** (or **right up**) **one's street** *Brit. informal* = UP ONE'S ALLEY (see ALLEY¹). □ **street·ed** *adjective* (also in *combination*). [Old English *strǣt* from Late Latin *strāta* (*via*) paved (way), fem. past participle of *sternere* lay down]

street address *noun* the address designating the location of a residence, office, etc. on a street in a city or town, esp. if different from the mailing address.

street·car *noun N Amer.* an electrically-powered passenger vehicle running on rails laid in an urban street.

street credibility *noun* (also **street cred**) *slang* popularity with or acceptability to people involved in fashionable street culture.

street culture *noun* the outlook, values, lifestyle, etc., of esp. young people living in an urban environment, regarded as a fashionable subculture.

street drug *noun* an illegal drug sold on the streets.

street furniture *noun* mailboxes, road signs, garbage cans, and other objects placed in the street for public use.

street hockey *noun Cdn* a version of hockey played on a street usu. by children using hockey sticks and a ball in place of a puck.

street lamp *noun* = STREET LIGHT.

street legal *adjective* **1** (of a vehicle) legally roadworthy. **2** *informal* legitimate; above board.

street light *noun* a light or lamp esp. on a lamppost, serving to illuminate a road etc. □ **street lighting** *noun*

street luge *noun* an activity in which participants race down paved roads lying on wheeled luge-like sleds. □ **street luging** *noun*

street name *noun* the nickname of a person or colloquial name for a thing as used on the streets.

street price *noun* the retail price, esp. of a piece of computer equipment.

street·proof *transitive verb N Amer.* train (children) to be wary of dangers outside the home or school, esp. from child molesters, drug dealers, etc.

street racing *noun* the illegal racing of automobiles on public roads, esp. late at night. □ **street racer** *noun*

street railway *noun hist. Cdn* an urban transportation system run on rails along city streets.

street sale *noun esp. Cdn* a sale of used household goods, clothes, books, etc. held by several residents on the same street.

street·scape *noun* a view or prospect provided by the design of a city street or streets.

street·side *noun* the strip of property along a street (often *attributive*: *a streetside café*).

street smarts *plural noun N Amer. informal* **1** shrewd or cunning awareness of how to survive in an urban society or environment. **2** common sense. □ **street-smart** *adjective*

street trader *noun* a person who trades in the street, either from a market stall or often from an improvised pitch.

street value *noun* the price for which something illegal or illegally obtained can be sold (*the seized drugs have a street value of over $5 million*).

street·walk·er *noun* a prostitute seeking customers in the street. □ **street·walk·ing** *noun & adjective*

street·wear *noun* casual clothing inspired by urban fashions and worn esp. by youth.

street·wise *adjective* esp. *N Amer.* familiar with the ways of modern urban life.

Vowels: a cat ɑ arm e bed ɜr her ɜː deux ə ago ɪ sit i cosy iː feed ɒ hot ɔ pore ɔː no ʌ run ʊ put

Strei·sand /'straizand/ **Bar·bra** (born Barbara Joan Streisand) (b.1942), US actress, movie director, and singer. She became a star in 1964 in the Broadway musical *Funny Girl*, winning an Oscar in 1968 for her performance in the film of the same name; her other films include *A Star is Born* (1976), *Yentl* (1983) (which she also directed), and *The Prince of Tides* (1991).

strength *noun* **1** the state of being strong; the degree to which or respect in which a person or thing is strong. **2** the ability to resist force or support heavy objects without breaking or being damaged. **3 a** a person or thing affording strength or support. **b** an attribute making for strength of character (*patience is your great strength*). **4** a positive quality or attribute (*identified my strengths and weaknesses*). **5** the extent to which a feeling or opinion is strong (*underestimated the strength of public opinion against the plan*). **6** the potency or intensity of a drug, drink, active ingredient, etc. **7** *Commerce* firmness of prices. **8** the number of persons present or available. **9** a full complement (*below strength*). □ **from strength** from a strong position. **from strength to strength** with ever-increasing success. **in strength** in large numbers. **on the strength of** on the basis of. **the strength of** the essence or main features of. □ **strength·less** *adjective* [Old English *strengthu* from Germanic (as STRONG)]

strength·en *transitive & intransitive verb* make or become stronger. □ **strengthen a person's hand** enable a person to act with greater effect or vigour. □ **strength·en·er** *noun*

strenu·ous /'strenjʊəs/ *adjective* **1** requiring or using great effort. **2** energetic; vigorously active. □ **strenu·ous·ly** *adverb* **strenu·ous·ness** *noun* [Latin *strenuus* brisk]

strep *informal* ● *noun* **1** = STREPTOCOCCUS. **2** *N Amer.* = STREP THROAT. ● *adjective* streptococcal.

strep throat *noun N Amer.* an acute sore throat with fever caused by streptococcal infection.

strep·to·car·pus /streptɔː'kɑrpəs/ *noun* a southern African plant of the genus *Streptocarpus*, with funnel-shaped flowers, often violet or pink, and spirally twisted fruits. [Greek *streptos* 'twisted' + *karpos* 'fruit']

strep·to·coc·cus /ˌstreptɔː'kɒkəs/ *noun* (*pl.* **strep·to·cocci** /-'kɒkai/) any bacterium of the genus *Streptococcus*, usu. occurring in chains, some of which cause infectious diseases. □ **strep·to·coc·cal** *adjective* [Greek *streptos* twisted, from *strephō* turn + COCCUS]

strep·to·kin·ase /streptɔː'kaineiz/ *noun Med. & Pharm.* an enzyme produced by some streptococci and used to treat inflammation and blood clots. [STREPTOCOCCUS + Greek *kinein* 'move' + -ASE]

strep·to·mycin /ˌstreptɔː'maisin/ *noun* an antibiotic produced by the bacterium *Streptomyces griseus*, effective against many disease-producing bacteria. [Greek *streptos* (as STREPTOCOCCUS) + *mukēs* fungus]

Strese·mann /'streizəman/ **Gus·tav** (1878–1929), German politician, chancellor (1923) and foreign minister (1923; 1924–9) of the Weimar Republic. He negotiated the Dawes Plan (1924) to reduce German reparations following the First World War, and gained Germany membership in the League of Nations (1926); he shared the Nobel Peace Prize in 1926.

stress ● *noun* **1 a** pressure or tension exerted on a material object. **b** a quantity measuring this. **2 a** a demand on physical or mental energy. **b** a condition or adverse circumstance that disturbs, or is likely to disturb, the normal physiological or psychological functioning of an individual. **c** distress caused by this (*suffering from stress*). **3 a** emphasis (*the stress was on the need for success*). **b** accentuation; emphasis laid on a syllable or word. **c** an accent, esp. the principal one in a word (*the stress is on the first syllable*). **4** *Mech.* force per unit area exerted between contiguous bodies or parts of a body. ● *verb* **1** *transitive* lay stress on; emphasize. **2** *transitive* subject to mechanical or physical or mental stress. **3** *transitive* give extra force to (a word or syllable) when pronouncing it (*do you stress the first syllable or the last syllable?*). **4** *transitive* (usu. in *passive*) cause stress to. **5** *intransitive informal* be tense or anxious (*stop stressing*). □ **lay stress on** indicate as important. **stress out** cause (a person) mental or physical stress. □ **stressed** *adjective* **stress·less** *adjective* [Middle English from DISTRESS, or partly from Old French *estresse* narrowness, oppression, ultimately from Latin *strictus* STRICT]

stressed out *adjective informal* debilitated or exhausted as a result of stress.

stress fracture *noun* a fracture of a bone caused by the repeated application of a high load.

stress·ful *adjective* causing stress; mentally tiring (*Patti's had another stressful day*). □ **stress·ful·ly** *adverb* **stress·ful·ness** *noun*

stres·sor /'stresɔr, -ɔr/ *noun* a situation, experience, event, or other stimulus that causes stress.

stress test *noun* a test of cardiovascular fitness made by monitoring the heart rate and electrocardiogram during exercise.

stretch ● *verb* **1** *transitive & intransitive* draw or be drawn or admit of being drawn out into greater length or size. **2** *transitive & intransitive* make or become taut. **3** *transitive & intransitive* place or lie at full length or spread out (*with a canopy stretched over them*). **4 a** *transitive* extend (an arm, leg, etc.). **b** *intransitive & reflexive* thrust out one's limbs and tighten one's muscles after being relaxed. **c** *transitive & intransitive* perform exercises to lengthen the muscles and improve flexibility, esp. before vigorous exercise. **5** *intransitive* have a specified length or extension; extend (*farmland stretches for many miles*). **6** *transitive* strain or exert extremely or excessively; exaggerate (*stretch the truth*). **7** *transitive* increase the quantity or amount of (food, a beverage, paint, etc.) by dilution or the addition of something else (*stretch the leftover casserole by serving it with a vegetable*). ● *noun* **1** a continuous extent or expanse or period (*a stretch of open road*). **2 a** the act or an instance of stretching; the state of being stretched. **b** a stretching exercise. **3** (*attributive*) able to stretch; elastic (*stretch fabric*). **4** *informal* a period of imprisonment. **b** a period of time or service. **5** *N Amer.* the straight side of a racetrack. **6** (usu. *attributive*) *informal* an aircraft or motor vehicle modified so as to have extra seating or storage capacity (*stretch limousine*). **7 a** the act or an instance of extending oneself or one's abilities or resources beyond normal limits (*it'll be a stretch to come up with that much money*). **b** *informal* an exaggeration or distortion (*well, that's a bit of a stretch*). **8** *Naut.* the distance covered on one tack. □ **at full stretch** working to capacity. **at a stretch 1** in one continuous period (*slept for two hours at a stretch*). **2** with much effort. **not by any stretch (of the imagination)** used to emphasize that something is definitely not the case (*it can't by any stretch of the imagination be called wholesome*). **stretch one's legs** exercise oneself by walking, esp. after prolonged sitting. **stretch out 1** extend (a hand or foot etc.). **2** last for a longer period; prolong. **3** make (money etc.) last for a sufficient time. **4** relax by lying at full length. **stretch a point** agree to something not normally allowed. **stretch one's wings** see WING. □ **stretch·able** *adjective* **stretch·abil·ity** *noun* **stretch·i·ness** *noun* [Old English *streccan* from West Germanic: compare STRAIGHT]

stretch·er ● *noun* **1** a framework of two poles with canvas etc. between, for carrying a sick, injured, or dead person in a lying position. **2** a brick or stone laid with its long side along the face of a wall (compare HEADER 4). **3** a board in a boat against which a rower presses the feet. **4** a rod or bar as a tie between chair legs etc. **5** a wooden frame over which a canvas is stretched ready for painting. ● *transitive verb* (often foll. by *off*) convey (a sick or injured person) on a stretcher.

stretcher-bearer *noun* a person who helps to carry a stretcher, esp. in war or at a major accident.

stretch marks *plural noun* marks on the skin resulting from a gain of weight, or esp. on the abdomen after pregnancy.

streu·sel /'struːzəl, 'struːsəl/ *noun esp. N Amer.* a crumbly mixture of flour, butter, sugar, and usu. cinnamon, used as a topping or filling for cakes etc. (also *attributive*: *a cherry streusel cake*). [German, from *streuen* to sprinkle]

strew *transitive verb* (*past participle* **strewn** or **strewed**) **1** scatter or spread or be scattered or spread over a surface. **2** (usu. foll. by *with*) spread (a surface) with scattered things. □ **strew·er** *noun* [Old English *stre(o)wian*]

stria /'straiə/ *noun* (*pl.* **striae** /-iː/) **1** *Anat., Zool., Bot., & Geol.* **a** a linear mark on a surface. **b** a slight ridge, furrow, or score. **2** *Archit.* a fillet between the flutes of a column. [Latin]

stri·ate ● *adjective* /'straiət/ (also **stri·at·ed** /-eitəd/) *Anat., Zool., Bot., & Geol.* marked with striae. ● *transitive verb* /'straieit/ mark with striae. □ **stri·a·tion** *noun*

striated muscle *noun Anat.* = SKELETAL MUSCLE.

strick·en *adjective* **1** affected or overcome with illness or misfortune etc. (*stricken with measles*; *grief-stricken*). **2** (often foll. by *from* etc.) *US Law* deleted. □ **stricken in years** *archaic* enfeebled by age. [archaic past participle of STRIKE]

Strick·land, Mount a peak in the St. Elias Mountains of SW Yukon Territory (4 212 m). [D'Arcy *Strickland*, North West Mounted Police inspector d.1908]

strict *adjective* **1** (of a person) demanding that rules, esp. those concerning behaviour, are obeyed or observed (*a strict teacher*; *her parents were very strict*). **2** following rules or beliefs exactly (*a strict Catholic*). **3** precisely limited or defined. **4** without exception or deviation (*lives in strict seclusion*). **5** requiring complete compliance or exact performance; enforced rigidly (*gave strict orders*). **6** complete or absolute (*was told this in strict confidence*). □ **strict·ly** *adverb* **strict·ness** *noun* [Latin *strictus* past participle of *stringere* tighten]

strict liability *noun Law* liability which does not depend on actual negligence or intent to harm.

stric·ture *noun* **1** (usu. in *pl.*) a critical or censorious remark. **2** (usu. in *pl.*) rules that restrict behaviour or action. **3** *Med.* an abnormal narrowing of a canal or duct in the body. □ **stric·tured** *adjective* [Latin *strictura* (as STRICT)]

stride ● *verb* (*past* **strode**; *past participle* **strid·den**) **1** *intransitive & transitive* walk with long firm steps. **2** *transitive* cross with one step. **3** *transitive* bestride; straddle. ● *noun* **1 a** a single long step. **b** the length of this. **2** a person's gait as determined by the length of stride. **3** (usu. in *pl.*) progress (*has made great strides*). **4** the distance between the feet parted either laterally or as in walking. □ **break stride 1** change one's gait. **2** slow down. **hit** (or **get into**) **one's stride** reach a settled or steady rate of progress or level of performance. **take in** (**one's**) **stride 1** manage without difficulty. **2** clear (an obstacle) without changing one's gait to jump. □ **strid·er** *noun* [Old English *strīdan*]

stri·dent /ˈstraɪdənt/ *adjective* **1** loud and harsh. **2** urgent and aggressive (*strident demands*). □ **stri·dency** *noun* **strid·ent·ly** *adverb* [Latin *stridere strident-* creak]

stridu·late /ˈstrɪdjʊˌleɪt/ *intransitive verb* (of insects, esp. the cicada and grasshopper) make a shrill sound by rubbing esp. the legs or wing-cases together. □ **stridu·la·tion** *noun* [French *striduler* from Latin *stridulus* creaking (as STRIDENT)]

strife *noun* **1** conflict or struggle. **2** enmity or rivalry, esp. of a bitter kind. [Old French *estrif*: compare Old French *estriver* STRIVE]

stri·gil /ˈstrɪdʒɪl/ *noun* **1** *Gk & Rom. Hist.* an instrument with a curved blade, used to scrape sweat and dirt from the skin after exercise. **2** a structure on the leg of an insect used to clean its antennae etc. [Latin *strigilis* from *stringere* graze]

strike ● *verb* (*past* **struck**; *past participle* **struck** or *archaic* **strick·en**) **1** *transitive* **a** subject to an impact. **b** deliver (a blow) or inflict a blow on. **2** *transitive* come or bring sharply into contact with (*the car struck a tree*). **3** *transitive* propel or divert with a blow (*struck the ball into the pond*). **4** *intransitive* (foll. by *at*) try to hit. **5** *transitive* penetrate or cause to penetrate (*struck terror into her*). **6** *transitive* ignite (a match) or produce (sparks etc.) by rubbing. **7** *transitive* make (a coin) by stamping. **8** *transitive* produce (a musical note) by striking. **9 a** *transitive & intransitive* (of a clock) indicate (the time) by the sounding of a chime etc. **b** *intransitive* (of time) be indicated in this way. **10** *transitive* **a** attack suddenly (*was struck with sudden terror*). **b** (of a disease) afflict. **11** *transitive* cause to become suddenly (*was struck dumb*). **12** *transitive* reach or achieve (*strike a balance*). **13** *transitive* agree on (a bargain). **14** *transitive* assume (an attitude) suddenly and dramatically (*strike a pose*). **15** *transitive* **a** discover or come across. **b** find (oil etc.) by drilling. **c** encounter (an unusual thing etc.). **16** *transitive* come to the attention of or appear to (*it strikes me as silly; an idea suddenly struck me*). **17 a** *intransitive* (of employees) engage in a strike; cease work as a protest. **b** *transitive N Amer.* act in this way against (an employer). **18 a** *transitive* lower or take down (a flag or tent etc.). **b** *intransitive* signify surrender by striking a flag; surrender. **c** *transitive* take down or dismantle (a theatre set etc.). **19** *intransitive* take a specified direction (*struck east*). **20** *transitive & intransitive* **a** secure a hook in the mouth of (a fish) by jerking the tackle. **b** (of a fish) attack prey or bait. **21** *transitive* (of a snake) wound with its fangs. **22** *intransitive* (of oysters) attach themselves to a bed. **23 a** *transitive* insert (the cutting of a plant) in soil to take root. **b** *transitive & intransitive* (of a plant or cutting etc.) put forth (roots). **24** *transitive* **a** ascertain (a balance) by deducting credit or debit from the other. **b** arrive at (an average, state of balance) by equalizing all items. **25** *transitive* compose (a jury) esp. by allowing both sides to reject the same number. **26** *transitive Cdn* create (a committee). ● *noun* **1** the act or an instance of striking. **2 a** the organized refusal by employees to work until some grievance is remedied. **b** a similar refusal to participate in some other expected activity. **3 a** a discovery of oil, ore, etc. by drilling, mining, etc. **b** a sudden find or success (*a lucky strike*). **4** an attack, esp. from the air. **5** *Baseball* a batter's unsuccessful attempt to hit a pitched ball, or another event counting equivalently against a batter. **6** the act of knocking down all the pins with the first ball in bowling. **7 a** a jerk by which an angler secures a hooked fish. **b** a pull on a fishing line indicating that a fish has taken the bait. **8** horizontal direction in a geological structure. **9** *N Amer.* a thing to one's discredit (*several strikes against him*). □ **on strike** taking part in an industrial etc. strike. **strike at the root** (or **roots**) **of** *see* ROOT[1]. **strike down 1** knock

down. **2** bring low; afflict (*struck down by a virus*). **strike home 1** deal an effective blow. **2** have an intended effect (*my words struck home*). **strike in 1** intervene in a conversation etc. **2** (of a disease) attack the interior of the body from the surface. **strike it rich** *informal* find a source of abundance or success. **strike a light** produce a light by striking a match. **strike it lucky** have a lucky success. **strike off 1** remove with a stroke. **2** delete (a name etc.) from a list. **3** produce (copies of a document). **strike oil 1** find petroleum by sinking a shaft. **2** attain prosperity or success. **strike out 1** hit out. **2** act vigorously. **3** delete (an item or name etc.). **4** set off or begin (*struck out eastwards*). **5** use the arms and legs in swimming. **6** forge or devise (a plan etc.). **7** *Baseball* **a** dismiss (a batter) by means of three strikes. **b** be dismissed in this way. **8** be unsuccessful. **strike through** delete (a word etc.) with a stroke of one's pen. **strike up 1** start (an acquaintance, conversation, etc.) esp. casually. **2** begin playing (a tune etc.). **strike upon 1** have (an idea etc.) luckily occur to one. **2** (of light) illuminate. **strike while the iron is hot** act promptly at a good opportunity. **struck on** *informal* infatuated with. □ **strik·able** *adjective* [Old English *strican* go, stroke, from West Germanic]

strike·bound *adjective* immobilized or closed by a strike.

strike·break·er *noun* a person working or employed in place of others who are on strike. □ **strike·break·ing** *noun & adjective*

strike force *noun* **1** a military or police force ready for rapid effective action. **2** a similar group, e.g. of activists etc., that is organized to act quickly in a specific way.

strike·out *noun Baseball* an out called when a batter has had three strikes.

strike pay *noun* an allowance paid to strikers by their labour union.

strik·er *noun* **1** a person or thing that strikes. **2** an employee on strike. **3** *Soccer* an attacking player positioned well forward in order to score goals. **4** a device striking the primer in a gun.

strike-slip *noun* (*attributive*) *Geol.* designating a fault or motion in which rock strata are displaced mainly in a horizontal direction, parallel to the line of the fault.

strike zone *noun* **1** *Baseball* an imaginary rectangle above home plate extending from the armpits to the knees of a batter. **2** the area surrounding a fish within which it will strike at prey.

strik·ing *adjective* **1** impressive; attracting attention. **2** conspicuous (*a striking lack of effort on her part*). **3** (of a person) on strike (*striking workers*). **4** (of a clock) making a chime to indicate the hours etc. ● *noun* the act or an instance of striking. □ **within striking distance** near enough to hit or achieve. □ **strik·ing·ly** *adverb*

Strind·berg /ˈstrɪndbɜːrɡ/ **Johan Aug·ust** (1849–1912), Swedish dramatist and novelist. His earlier plays depict a bitter power struggle between the sexes, notably in *The Father* (1887) and *Miss Julie* (1888), while his later plays are typically tense, symbolic, psychic dramas, as in the *Dance of Death* (1901). □ **Strind·berg·ian** *adjective*

Strine *noun* **1** a comic transliteration of Australian speech, e.g. *Emma Chissitt* = 'How much is it?'. **2** (esp. uneducated) Australian English. [= *Australian* in Strine]

string ● *noun* **1** twine or narrow cord. **2** a piece of this or of similar material used for tying or holding together, pulling, etc. **3** a length of wire or catgut etc. on a musical instrument, producing a note by vibration. **4 a** (in *pl.*) stringed instruments (i.e. violin, viola, cello, double bass) forming a section of an orchestra, group, etc. **b** (*attributive*) relating to or consisting of stringed instruments (*string section*). **5** (in *pl.*) an awkward associated or consequent condition or complication (*the offer has no strings attached*). **6 a** a set of things strung together; a series or line of persons or things (*a string of beads; a string of oaths; a string of boyfriends*). **b** *Sport* a roster of players in order of selection or skill (*second string; third string.*) **7** a group of racehorses trained at one stable. **8** a tough piece connecting the two halves of a bean pod etc. **9** a piece of nylon etc. interwoven with others to form the head of a tennis etc. racquet. **10** = STRINGER 4. **11 a** a hypothetical one-dimensional subatomic particle having the dynamical properties of a flexible loop. **b** (in full **cosmic string**) in some cosmological theories, a threadlike concentration of energy hypothesized to exist within the structure of space-time. **12** *Computing* a linear sequence of characters, records, or data. **13** esp. *N Amer.* a continuous series of successes or failures; a continuous sequence of games, turns at play, etc. ● *adjective* **1** made of or consisting of string (*a string bag*). **2** of the usual natural colour of string, light greyish brown. ● *verb* (*past* and *past participle* **strung**) **1** *transitive* supply with a string or strings. **2** *transitive* **a** arrange in or as a string (*strung lights on the Christmas tree*). **b** put (esp. words, ideas, etc.) together in a connected sequence. **3** *transitive* provide, equip, or adorn with something suspended or slung (*the backyard was strung with* lanterns). **4** *transitive* thread (beads etc.) on a string. **5** *transitive* tie with string. **6** *transitive* remove the strings from (a bean). **7** *transitive* place a string ready for use on (a musical instrument, racquet, bow, etc.). **8** *transitive* esp. *N Amer. slang* deceive. **9** *intransitive* (of glue etc.) become stringy. **10** *intransitive Billiards* make the preliminary strokes that decide which player begins. **11** *intransitive* (often foll. by *out*) extend, stretch out. **12** *intransitive* work as a stringer in journalism. **13** *transitive informal* kill by hanging. □ **play out the string** continue to the end of a series of games, tasks, etc., esp. without much exertion or application. **string a person a line** purposely mislead a person. **string along** *informal* deceive, mislead (a person) about one's own intentions or beliefs. **string out** extend; prolong (esp. unduly). **string up 1** hang up on strings etc. **2** *informal* kill by hanging. **3** (usu. as **strung up** *adjective*) esp. *Brit.* make tense. □ **string·less** *adjective* **string·like** *adjective* [Old English *streng* from Germanic: related to STRONG]

string bag *noun* a bag of netted string, taking up little space when empty but expanding to carry a load.

string band *noun* an esp. jazz or bluegrass music ensemble of string instruments, typically banjo or guitar, violin, and double bass.

string bass *noun Music* a double bass.

string bean *noun* **1** any of various beans eaten in their fibrous pods, esp. runner beans or French beans. **2** *informal* a tall thin person.

string bikini *noun* a very scanty bikini.

string·course *noun* a raised horizontal band or course of bricks etc. on a building.

stringed *adjective* (of musical instruments) having strings (also in *combination: twelve-stringed guitar*).

strin·gendo /strɪnˈdʒendoː/ *adjective & adverb Music* with increasing speed. [Italian from *stringere* press: see STRINGENT]

strin·gent /ˈstrɪndʒənt/ *adjective* **1** (of rules etc.) strict, precise; requiring exact performance; leaving no loophole or discretion. **2** (of a money market etc.) tight; hampered by scarcity; unaccommodating; hard to operate in. □ **strin·gency** *noun* **strin·gent·ly** *adverb* [Latin *stringere* draw tight]

string·er *noun* **1** a horizontal member connecting uprights in a framework, supporting a floor, supporting or tying together a bridge, etc. **2** a longitudinal structural member in a framework, esp. of a ship or aircraft. **3** *informal* a newspaper correspondent not on the regular staff, esp. one retained on a freelance basis to report on events in a particular place. **4** a supporting timber or skirting in which the ends of a staircase steps are set. **5** *N Amer.* a chain with hooks on which caught fish are strung. **6** a narrow mineral vein traversing a mass of different material. **7** (usu. in *combination*) an athlete, performer, etc. ranked according to ability (*first-stringer*).

string game *noun* (also **string-figure game**) a game in which figures are made by passing string around the fingers of both hands, e.g. cat's cradle.

string·halt *noun* spasmodic movement of a horse's hind leg.

string quartet *noun* **1** a chamber music ensemble consisting of first and second violins, viola, and cello. **2** a piece of music for such an ensemble.

string theory *noun* a cosmological theory based on the hypothetical existence of cosmic strings.

string tie *noun* a very narrow necktie.

stringy *adjective* (**string·i·er**, **string·i·est**) **1** (of food etc.) fibrous, tough. **2** of or like string. **3** (of a person) tall, wiry, and thin. **4** (of a liquid) viscous; forming strings. □ **string·i·ness** *noun*

strip¹ ● *verb* (**stripped**, **strip·ping**) **1** *transitive* **a** (often foll. by *of*) remove the clothes or covering from (a person or thing). **b** (often foll. by *from, away*) pull off or remove (a covering or property etc.) (*stripped the masks from their faces; strip away the pretense*). **2** *intransitive* (often foll. by *off, down*) undress oneself. **3** *transitive* (often foll. by *of*) deprive (a person) of property, titles, etc. **4** *transitive* leave bare of accessories or fittings. **5** *transitive* remove bark and branches from (a tree). **6** *transitive* (often foll. by *down*) remove the accessory fittings of or take apart (a machine etc.) to inspect or adjust it. **7** *transitive* sell off (the assets of a company) for profit. **8** *transitive* remove (paint, wax, etc.) or remove paint, wax, etc. from (a surface) (*strip a floor*). **9** *transitive* remove the stems from (tobacco). **10 a** *transitive* tear the thread from (a screw). **b** *intransitive* (of a screw) lose its thread. **11** *transitive* tear the teeth from (a gearwheel). **12** *transitive* milk (a cow) to the last drop. **13** *intransitive* (of a bullet) issue from a rifled gun without spin owing to a loss of surface. **14** *transitive* (often foll. by *in*) draw in (a line or fish) with the hand. ● *noun* **1** an act of stripping, esp. of performing a striptease. **2** *Brit.* the identifying

outfit worn by the members of a sports team while playing. [Old English *bestrīepan* 'plunder', from Germanic]

strip² *noun* **1** a long narrow piece (*a strip of land*). **2** a narrow flat bar of iron or steel. **3** (in full **strip cartoon**) = COMIC STRIP. **4** *N Amer.* **a** an area of commercial development along a road in a town or city. **b** a part of a city street frequented by prostitutes, drug addicts, etc. **5** = AIRSTRIP. **6** = DRAG STRIP. □ **tear a strip off a person** *informal* angrily rebuke a person. [Middle English, from or related to Middle Low German *strippe* strap, thong, prob. related to STRIPE]

strip bond *noun* (also **stripped bond**) *N Amer.* a fixed-interest bond of which the principal and interest coupons are sold separately to investors.

strip club *noun* (also **strip joint**) a club at which striptease performances are given.

stripe ● *noun* **1** a long narrow band or strip differing in colour or texture from the surface on either side of it (*black with a red stripe*). **2** *Military* a chevron etc. denoting military rank. **3** esp. *N Amer.* a category of character, opinion, etc. (*politicians of all stripes*). **4** (usu. in *pl.*) *archaic* a blow with a scourge or lash. ● *transitive verb* mark with stripes. [perhaps back-formation from *striped*: compare Middle Dutch, Middle Low German *stripe*, Middle High German *strife*]

striped *adjective* marked with stripes (also in *combination: red-striped*).

striped bass *noun* a large bass of N American coastal waters, *Morone saxatilis*, with dark horizontal stripes along the upper sides.

striped maple *noun* a maple, *Acer pensylvanicum*, of eastern N America, having green bark striped with white. *Also called* MOOSEWOOD.

striped squill *noun see* SQUILL 1b.

striper *noun* **1** *N Amer.* = STRIPED BASS. **2** (with specifying numeral) a member of the navy, army, etc. whose uniform carries a number of stripes denoting rank (*four-striper*). **3** a person or thing that paints stripes on something.

stripey *adjective* (also **stripy**) striped, having many stripes.

strip light *noun* a tubular fluorescent lamp.

strip·ling *noun* a youth not yet fully grown. [Middle English, prob. from STRIP² + -LING¹, in the sense of having a figure not yet filled out]

strip loin *noun N Amer.* a long strip of beef cut from the loin.

strip mall *noun* a shopping mall on an esp. suburban street, with the stores arranged in a row and accessed only from outside.

strip mine *N Amer.* ● *noun* a mine worked by removing surface material in successive parallel strips to expose the ore etc. ● *transitive verb* (**strip-mine**) obtain or work by strip mining. □ **strip mining** *noun*

strip-o-gram *noun* a novelty telegram or greetings message delivered by a person who performs a striptease for the recipient.

stripped bond *noun N Amer.* = STRIP BOND.

stripped-down *adjective* **1** (of a car, machine, etc.) that has had all superfluous or extraneous parts removed. **2** reduced to essentials; bare, lean (*a stripped-down musical style*).

strip·per *noun* **1** a person who performs striptease. **2** a device or solvent for removing paint etc. **3** a person or thing that strips something.

strip poker *noun* a form of poker in which the losing players in a hand each shed a garment.

strip search ● *noun* a body search for hidden weapons, concealed drugs, etc., in which the person being searched is stripped naked. ● *transitive verb* (**strip-search**) search in this way.

strip·tease *noun* a form of erotic entertainment in which a performer removes his or her clothes in front of an audience, usu. to musical accompaniment. □ **strip·teas·er** *noun*

stripy *adjective var. of* STRIPEY.

strive *intransitive verb* (*past* **strove** *or* **strived**; *past participle* **striv·en** /ˈstrɪvən/) **1** (often foll. by *for, or to* + infin.) try hard, make efforts (*strive to succeed*). **2** (often foll. by *with, against*) struggle or contend. □ **striv·er** *noun* [Old French *estriver*, related to *estrif* STRIFE]

strobe ● *noun* (in full **strobe light**) **1** a bright light that flashes on and off, e.g. in a discotheque. **2** a stroboscopic lamp. **3** an electronic flash for a camera. ● *verb* **1** *transitive* light as if with a strobe. **2** *intransitive* flash intermittently. [abbreviation]

stro·bila /stroːˈbaɪlə/ *noun* (*pl.* **stro·bilae** /-liː/) **1** a chain of proglottids in a tapeworm. **2** a sessile polyp-like form which divides horizontally to produce jellyfish larvae. [modern Latin from Greek *strobilē* twisted lint plug, from *strephō* twist]

stro·bile /ˈstrəʊbaɪl/ *noun* **1** the cone of a pine etc. **2** a cone-like structure, e.g. the flower of the hop. [French *strobile* or Late Latin *strobilus* from Greek *strobilos* from *strephō* twist]

stro·bilus /ˈstrəʊbɪləs/ *noun* (pl. **stro·bili** /-ˌlaɪ/) *Bot.* = STROBILE. [Late Latin (as STROBILE)]

strob·o·scope /ˈstrəʊbəˌskəʊp/ *noun* **1** *Physics* an instrument for determining speeds of rotation etc. by shining a bright light at intervals so that a rotating object appears stationary. **2** = STROBE *noun* 1. □ **strob·o·scop·ic** /-ˈskɒpɪk/ *adjective* **strob·o·scop·ic·ally** *adverb* [Greek *strobos* whirling + -SCOPE]

strode *past of* STRIDE.

stro·gan·off /ˈstrəʊgəˌnɒf/ *noun* (in full **beef stroganoff**) a dish of strips of beef cooked in a sauce containing mushrooms and sour cream. [P. *Stroganoff*, Russian diplomat, d.1817]

Stro·heim /ˈstrəʊˌhaɪm/ **Erich von** (full name Hans Erich Maria Stroheim von Nordenwall) (1885–1957), Austrian-born US film director and actor, whose films include *Foolish Wives* (1922), *Greed* (1924), and *Queen Kelly* (1928).

stroke ● *noun* **1** the act or an instance of striking; a blow or hit (*with a single stroke*; *a stroke of lightning*). **2** a sudden disabling attack or loss of consciousness caused by an interruption in the flow of blood to the brain, esp. through thrombosis; apoplexy. **3 a** an action or movement esp. as one of a series. **b** the time or way in which such movements are done. **c** the slightest such action (*has not done a stroke of work*). **4** the whole of the motion (of a wing, oar, etc.) until the starting position is regained. **5** (in rowing) the mode or action of moving the oar (*row a fast stroke*). **6** the whole motion (of a piston) in either direction. **7** *Golf* the action of hitting (or hitting at) a ball with a club, as a unit of scoring. **8 a** a mode of moving the arms and legs in swimming. **b** a single movement of the legs in walking or running. **c** a pushing off movement of the legs in skating. **9** a method of striking with the bat etc. in games etc. **10 a** a specially successful or effective action or event (*a stroke of diplomacy*). **b** a feat, an achievement (*a stroke of genius*). **c** an unexpected piece of luck or misfortune. **11 a** a mark made by the movement in one direction of a pen or pencil or paintbrush. **b** a similar mark printed. **12** a detail contributing to the general effect in a description. **13** the sound made by a striking clock. **14** (in full **stroke oar**) the oar or oarsman nearest the stern, setting the time of the stroke. **15** the act or a period of stroking. ● *verb* **1** *transitive* pass one's hand gently along the surface of (hair or fur etc.); caress lightly. **2** *transitive N Amer. informal* manipulate (a person) by means of flattery, persuasion, etc. **3** *transitive* **a** (foll. by *on*) apply (a cosmetic, paint, etc.) to a surface (*stroked on blue eyeshadow*). **b** brush (a thing) gently over a surface (*stroked the cloth across the table*). **4** *transitive* act as the stroke of (a boat or crew). **5** *intransitive* execute swimming, skating, or rowing strokes (*stroked to victory*). **6** *transitive* hit (a ball) with a smooth, controlled movement. □ **at a stroke** by a single action. **off one's stroke** not performing as well as usual. **on** (or **at**) **the stroke of nine** etc. with the clock about to strike nine etc. □ **strok·er** *noun* (also in *combination*). [Old English *strācian* from Germanic, related to STRIKE]

stroke play *noun Golf* play in which the score is reckoned by counting the number of strokes taken for the round (*compare* MATCH PLAY).

stroll ● *verb* **1** *intransitive* saunter or walk in a leisurely way. **2** *transitive* walk in a leisurely fashion along (a street etc.). **3** *intransitive* achieve something easily, without effort. ● *noun* **1** a short leisurely walk (*go for a stroll*). **2** something easily achieved; a walkover. **3** *slang* a usu. downtown area in a city where prostitutes loiter for the purposes of solicitation. □ **on the stroll** *N Amer. slang* working as a prostitute. [originally of a vagrant, probably via German *strollen*, *strolchen* from *Strolch* 'vagabond', of unknown origin]

stroll·er *noun* **1** esp. *N Amer.* a folding chair on wheels in which a baby or small child can be pushed along from place to place. **2** a person who strolls.

stroll·ing *adjective* (of a performer) wandering, itinerant (*strolling players*).

stro·ma /ˈstrəʊmə/ *noun* (pl. **stro·mata** /-mətə/) *Biol.* **1** the framework of an organ or cell. **2** a fungous tissue containing spore-producing bodies. □ **stro·matic** /-ˈmatɪk/ *adjective* [modern Latin from Late Latin from Greek *strōma* coverlet]

stro·mato·lite /strəʊˈmatəlaɪt/ *noun Biol.* a mound built up of layers of blue-green algae and trapped sediment, found in lagoons in Australasia and fossilized in Precambrian rocks elsewhere. □ **stro·mato·litic** /-lɪtɪk/ *adjective* [STROMA + -LITE]

Strom·boli /ˈstrɒmbəli, strɒmˈbəʊli/ a volcanic island in the Mediterranean, the most northeasterly of the Lipari Islands northeast

of Sicily. Its volcano has been in a state of continual mild eruption throughout history.

strong ● *adjective* (**strong·er**; **strong·est**) **1** having the power of resistance; able to withstand great force or opposition; not easily damaged or overcome (*strong material*; *strong faith*; *a strong character*). **2** capable of exerting great physical force or of doing much. **3** forceful or powerful in effect (*a strong wind*; *a strong protest*). **4** (of a person's constitution) able to overcome, or not liable to, disease. **5** (of a person's nerves) resistant to fright, irritation, etc. **6** (of a patient) restored to health. **7** (of an economy) stable and prosperous; (of a market) having steadily high or rising prices. **8** decided or firmly held (*a strong suspicion*; *strong views*). **9** (of an argument etc.) convincing or striking. **10** powerfully affecting the senses or emotions (*a strong light*; *strong acting*). **11** (of a person) effective; skilful; competent in a certain sphere (*she's strong in physics but weak in English*). **12** powerful in terms of size or numbers or quality (*a strong army*). **13** capable of doing much when united (*a strong combination*). **14 a** formidable; likely to succeed (*a strong candidate*). **b** tending to assert or dominate (*a strong personality*). **15** (of a solution or drink etc.) concentrated; containing a large proportion of a substance in water or another solvent (*strong tea*). **16** *Chem.* (of an acid or base) fully ionized into cations and anions in aqueous solution. **17** (of a group) having a specified number (*200 strong*). **18** (of a voice) loud or penetrating. **19** (of food or its flavour) pungent. **20** (of a colour) bright, intense (*strong colours suit you*). **21** (of a measure) drastic. **22** *Grammar* in Germanic languages: **a** (of a verb) forming inflections by change of vowel within the stem rather than by the addition of a suffix, e.g. *swim*, *swam*. **b** (of a noun or adjective) belonging to a declension in which the stem originally ended otherwise than in -*n* (opp. WEAK 9b). **23** *Cdn* (of a measurement) slightly more than the stated measurement (*a strong quarter of an inch*). ● *adverb* strongly (*the tide is running strong*). □ **come it strong** *Brit. informal* go to great lengths; use exaggeration. **come on strong** behave aggressively or assertively. **going strong** *informal* continuing action vigorously; continuing to flourish; in good health or trim. □ **strong·ish** *adjective* **strong·ly** *adverb* [Old English from Germanic: related to STRING]

strong-arm ● *adjective* using threats or force (*strong-arm tactics*). ● *transitive verb* threaten, intimidate; treat violently or aggressively.

strong·box *noun* a strongly made, usu. metal chest for safeguarding valuables.

strong drink *noun* alcohol, esp. hard liquor.

strong force *noun Physics* the force which mediates the strong interaction between subatomic particles.

strong·hold *noun* **1** a fortified place. **2** a secure refuge. **3** a centre of support for a cause etc.

strong interaction *noun Physics* an interaction between certain subatomic particles that is very strong but is effective only at short distances.

strong language *noun* **1** forceful language. **2** swearing.

strong·man *noun* (pl. **-men**) **1** *Politics* a forceful leader who exercises firm control over a state, group, etc. **2** a performer (at a fair, circus, etc.) of feats of strength.

strong medicine *noun* a remedy which is effective but difficult to accept.

strong-minded *adjective* having a strong will; determined. □ **strong-minded·ness** *noun*

strong point *noun* **1 a** a thing at which one excels; one's forte. **b** a feature of something that makes it attractive. **2** (**strong·point**) a specially fortified defensive position.

strong·room *noun* a room designed to protect valuables against fire and theft.

strong silent type *noun* a person, esp. a man, who controls or conceals emotion.

strong stomach *noun* a stomach not easily affected by nausea.

strong suit *noun* **1** a suit at cards in which one can take tricks. **2** a thing at which one excels.

strong-willed *adjective* **1** determined, resolute. **2** stubborn, headstrong.

stron·tia /ˈstrɒnʃə/ *noun Chem.* strontium oxide. [*strontian* native strontium carbonate, from Strontian in the Highland Region of Scotland, where it was discovered]

stron·tium /ˈstrɒnʃɪəm, -ʃəm, -tɪəm/ *noun Chem.* a soft silver-white metallic element occurring naturally in various minerals. Symbol: **Sr**; at. no.: 38. [STRONTIA + -IUM]

Vowels: a *cat* ɑ *arm* e *bed* ɜr *her* ɜː *deux* ə *ago* ɪ *sit* i *cosy* iː *feed* ɒ *hot* ɔ *pore* oː *no* ʌ *run* ʊ *put*

strontium-90 *noun* a radioactive isotope of strontium concentrated selectively in bones and teeth when taken into the body.

strontium oxide *noun* a white compound used in the manufacture of fireworks and flares to give a brilliant red light.

strop ● *noun* 1 a device, esp. a strip of leather, for sharpening razors. 2 *Naut.* a collar of leather or spliced rope or iron used for handling cargo. ● *transitive verb* (**stropped, strop·ping**) sharpen on or with a strop. [Middle Dutch, Middle Low German *strop*, Old High German *strupf*, West Germanic from Latin *stroppus*]

stro·phe /'strəʊfi/ *noun* 1 a a turn in dancing made by an ancient Greek chorus. b lines recited during this. c the first section of an ancient Greek choral ode or of one division of it. 2 a group of lines forming a section of a lyric poem. □ **stro·phic** *adjective* [Greek *strophē*, lit. turning, from *strephō* turn]

stroppy *adjective* (**strop·pi·er, strop·pi·est**) *Brit. informal* bad-tempered; awkward to deal with. □ **strop·pi·ly** *adverb* **strop·pi·ness** *noun* [20th c.: perhaps abbreviation of OBSTREPEROUS]

stroud *noun Cdn* a coarse woollen cloth used esp. in the North to make blankets, leggings, etc. [perhaps from *Stroud*, a town in Gloucestershire, UK]

strove *past of* STRIVE.

struck ● *verb past and past participle of* STRIKE. ● *adjective N Amer.* pertaining to or affected by an industrial strike (*a struck factory*).

struc·tur·al *adjective* of, concerning, or having a structure. □ **struc·tur·al·ly** *adverb*

structural analysis *noun* analysis of a system in terms of its components and their relationship to one another.

structural engineering *noun* the branch of civil engineering concerned with large modern buildings etc.

structural formula *noun Chem.* a formula showing the arrangement of atoms in the molecule of a compound.

struc·tur·al·ism *noun* a method of analyzing and organizing concepts in anthropology, linguistics, psychology, and other cognitive and social sciences in terms of contrasting relations (esp. binary oppositions) among sets of items within conceptual systems. □ **struc·tur·al·ist** *noun & adjective*

structural linguistics *noun* the study of language as a system of interrelated elements, without reference to their historical development.

structural steel *noun* strong mild steel in shapes suited to construction work.

structural unemployment *noun* unemployment resulting from industrial reorganization due to technological change etc. rather than from fluctuations in supply and demand.

struc·ture ● *noun* 1 a a whole constructed unit, esp. a building. b the way in which a building etc. is constructed (*has a flimsy structure*). c the state of being well planned or organized (*your essay lacks structure*). 2 a set of interconnecting parts of any complex thing; a framework (*the structure of a sentence; a new wages structure*). ● *transitive verb* give structure to; organize; frame. □ **struc·tured** *adjective* (also in *combination*). **struc·ture·less** *adjective* [Old French *structure* or Latin *structura* from *struere struct-* build]

stru·del /'struːdəl/ *noun* a dessert of thin pastry rolled up around a usu. fruit filling and baked (*apple strudel*). [German *Strudel*, lit. = 'whirlpool']

strug·gle ● *intransitive verb* 1 make forceful or violent efforts to get free of restraint or constriction. 2 (often foll. by *for*, or *to* + infin.) make violent or determined efforts under difficulties; strive hard (*struggled for supremacy; struggled to get the words out*). 3 (foll. by *with*, *against*) contend; fight strenuously (*struggled with the disease; struggled against superior numbers*). 4 (foll. by *along, up*, etc.) make one's way with difficulty (*struggled to my feet*). 5 (esp. as **strug·gling** *adjective*) have difficulty in gaining recognition or maintaining financial viability (*a struggling artist; the struggling airline*). ● *noun* 1 the act or a period of struggling. 2 a hard or confused contest. 3 a determined effort under difficulties. □ **the struggle for existence** (or **life**) the competition between organisms esp. as an element in natural selection, or between persons seeking a livelihood. □ **strug·gler** *noun* [Middle English *strugle* frequentative of uncertain origin (perhaps imitative)]

strum ● *verb* (**strummed, strum·ming**) 1 *transitive & intransitive* play (a stringed musical instrument, esp. a guitar or banjo) by sweeping the thumb or a plectrum up or down the strings. 2 *transitive* play (a tune etc.) in this way. ● *noun* 1 the sound made by strumming. 2 an instance or period of strumming. □ **strum·mer** *noun* [imitative: compare THRUM[1]]

stru·ma /'struːmə/ *noun* (*pl.* **stru·mae** /-miː/) 1 *Med.* a = SCROFULA. b = GOITRE. 2 *Bot.* a cushion-like swelling of an organ. □ **stru·mous** *adjective* [Latin, = scrofulous tumour]

strum·pet *noun archaic* or *jocular* a prostitute or promiscuous woman. [Middle English: origin unknown]

strung *past and past participle of* STRING.

strung out *adjective* 1 addicted to, using, or high on drugs. 2 (of a person) in a state of extreme nervous tension.

strut ● *noun* 1 a bar forming part of a framework and designed to resist compression. 2 a strutting gait. ● *verb* (**strut·ted, strut·ting**) 1 *intransitive* walk in a proud upright way. 2 *transitive* brace with a strut or struts. □ **strut one's stuff** *informal* display one's ability. □ **strut·ter** *noun* **strut·ting·ly** *adverb* [Middle English 'bulge, swell, strive', earlier *stroute* from Old English *strūtian* protrude stiffly]

Struve /'struːvə/ Otto (1897–1963), Russian-born US astronomer. He belonged to the fourth generation of a line of distinguished astronomers that began with the German-born F. G. W. Struve (1793–1864); his most important contribution was his discovery of the presence of ionized hydrogen in interstellar space (1938).

strych·nine /'strɪknaɪn, -niːn, -nɪn/ *noun* a bitter and highly poisonous vegetable alkaloid obtained from plants of the genus *Strychnos* (esp. nux vomica). [French from Latin *strychnos* from Greek *strukhnos* a kind of nightshade]

Sts. *abbreviation* 1 Saints. 2 Streets.

sts *abbreviation* (in knitting etc.) stitches.

Stu·art ▸ 1 (also **Stew·art**) the name of the royal house of Scotland from the accession (1371) of Robert II, one of the hereditary stewards of Scotland, and of Britain from the accession of James VI of Scotland to the English throne as James I (1603) to the death of Queen Anne (1714), though for the period between 1650 and 1659 England was a republic. 2 **Charles Ed·ward** (known as 'the Young Pretender' or 'Bonnie Prince Charlie') (1720–88), grandson of James II of England and pretender to the British throne. He led the Jacobite uprising of 1745–46 and invaded England, but was driven back to Scotland and defeated at the Battle of Culloden (1746). 3 his father, **James (Fran·cis Ed·ward)** (known as 'the Old Pretender') (1688–1766), son of James II (James VII of Scotland), pretender to the British throne. He arrived in Scotland too late to alter the outcome of the 1715 Jacobite uprising and left the leadership of the 1745–46 uprising to his son Charles Edward Stuart. 4 **Mary**, see MARY, QUEEN OF SCOTS.

Stuart Lake a lake in central BC, situated in the Nechako Plateau, northwest of Prince George. [J. Stuart, chief factor of the Hudson's Bay Co. d.1847]

stub ● *noun* 1 the remnant of a pencil or cigarette etc. after use. 2 the small part of a cheque, receipt, ticket etc. that remains, to be kept as a record, after the main part has been detached and given to someone. 3 a stunted tail etc. 4 the stump of a tree, plant, tooth, etc. ● *transitive verb* (**stubbed, stub·bing**) 1 strike (one's toe) against something. 2 (usu. foll. by *out*) extinguish (a lighted cigarette) by pressing the lighted end against something. [Old English *stub, stubb* from Germanic]

stub·ble *noun* 1 the cut stalks of cereal plants left sticking up after the harvest. 2 a short bristly growth of unshaven hair, esp. on a man's face. □ **stub·bled** *adjective* **stub·bly** *adjective* [Old French *estuble* from Latin *stupla, stupula* var. of *stipula* straw]

stubble field *noun* a reaped field that has not been plowed.

stubble-jumper *noun Cdn slang* a prairie farmer.

stub·born *adjective* 1 unreasonably obstinate. 2 unyielding, obdurate, inflexible (*stubborn resistance*). 3 that will not respond to treatment (*a stubborn cough*). □ **stub·born·ly** *adjective* **stub·born·ness** *noun* [Middle English *stiborn, stoburn*, etc., of unknown origin]

stub·by ● *adjective* (**stub·bi·er, stub·bi·est**) short and thick. ● *noun* (*pl.* **-bies**) *Cdn hist.* & *Austral. informal* a small squat bottle of beer. □ **stub·bi·ly** *adverb* **stub·bi·ness** *noun*

stuc·co ● *noun* (*pl.* **-coes**) plaster or cement used for coating wall surfaces or moulding into architectural decorations. ● *transitive verb* (**-coes, -coed**) coat with stucco. □ **stuc·coed** *adjective* [Italian, of Germanic origin]

stuck ● *verb past and past participle of* STICK[2]. ● *adjective* 1 unable to progress. 2 confined in a place (*was stuck in the house*). 3 (of an animal, esp. a pig) stabbed by a spear, knife, etc; butchered by having its throat cut (*screaming like a stuck pig*). □ **be stuck for** be at a loss for or in need of. **be stuck on** *informal* be infatuated with. **be stuck with** *informal* be unable to get rid of or escape from; be permanently involved with. **get stuck in** (or **into**) *informal* begin in earnest.

stuck-up *adjective informal* affectedly superior and aloof, snobbish.

stud¹ ● *noun* **1** a large-headed nail, boss, or knob, projecting from a surface esp. for ornament. **2** a small piece of jewellery for wearing in pierced ears or nostrils. **3** a small object like a button with two heads, used esp. formerly to fasten a collar or the front of a shirt. **4** a small object projecting slightly from a road surface as a marker etc. **5** a rivet or crosspiece in each link of a chain cable. **6** a two-by-four to which drywall etc. is nailed. **7** *N Amer.* any of a number of metal pieces set into the tire of a motor vehicle to improve roadholding in slippery conditions. ● *transitive verb* (**stud·ded**, **stud·ding**) **1** set with or as with studs. **2** be scattered over or about (a surface). [Old English *studu*, *stuthu* 'post, prop': related to German *stützen* 'to prop']

stud² *noun* **1 a** a number of horses kept for breeding etc. **b** a place where these are kept. **2** (in full **stud horse**) a stallion. **3** *informal* a man thought to be very active sexually or regarded as a good sexual partner. **4** (in full **stud poker**) a form of poker with betting after the dealing of successive rounds of cards face up. □ **at stud** (of a male horse or dog) publicly available for breeding on payment of a fee. [Old English *stōd* from Germanic: related to STAND]

stud book *noun* a book containing the pedigrees of thoroughbred horses or other animals, esp. dogs.

studded *adjective* (often in *combination*) thickly set or strewn (*diamond-studded*).

studding *noun* the wood framing of a wall in a house or other building.

studding sail *noun* a sail set on a small extra yard and boom beyond the leech of a square sail in light winds. [16th c.: origin uncertain: perhaps from Middle Low German, Middle Dutch *stōtinge* a thrusting]

stu·dent *noun* **1 a** a person who is studying, esp. at university or another place of higher education. **b** *N Amer.* a school pupil. **2** (*attributive*) studying in order to become (*a student nurse*). **3** a person who observes or has a particular interest in something (*a student of current affairs*). □ **stu·dent·ish** *adjective* **stu·dent·ship** *noun* esp. *Brit.* [Middle English from Latin *studēre*, from *studium* STUDY]

student-at-law *noun Cdn* an articling student.

student council *noun* an elected body of students representing students in a school, college, etc.

student loan *noun* a usu. government loan available to university and college students to help pay for education costs.

student teacher *noun* a person who teaches under supervision at a school as part of the qualification for a teaching certificate.

stud farm *noun* a place where horses are bred.

stud horse *noun see* STUD² 2.

stud·ied *adjective* deliberate, intentional, affected (*with studied politeness*). □ **stud·ied·ly** *adverb* **stud·ied·ness** *noun*

stu·dio *noun* (*pl.* **-dios**) **1** a place where films or recordings are made or where television or radio programs are made or produced. **2** a company which produces films (*works for a major studio*). **3** the workroom of a painter or photographer etc. **4** a large room where dancers rehearse (*a dance studio*). **5** = STUDIO APARTMENT. [Italian from Latin (as STUDY)]

studio apartment *noun* (also *Brit.* **studio flat**) an apartment containing only one main room.

studio couch *noun* a couch that can be converted into a bed.

stu·di·ous *adjective* **1** devoted to or assiduous in study or reading. **2** studied, deliberate, painstaking (*with studious care*). **3** (foll. by *to* + infin. or *in* + verbal noun) showing care or attention. □ **stu·di·ous·ly** *adverb* **stu·di·ous·ness** *noun*

stud·ly *adjective informal* masculine; macho, esp. in an alluring or sexual way, and often with the implication of brawn over brain.

stud·muffin *noun N Amer. informal* a man perceived as sexually attractive, typically one with well-developed muscles.

stud poker *noun see* STUD² 4.

stud wall *noun* a wall built of studs.

study ● *noun* (*pl.* **-ies**) **1 a** the devotion of time and attention to acquiring information or knowledge, esp. of a specified subject. **b** consideration, examination (*the proposals deserve special study*). **2** (in *pl.*) the pursuit of academic knowledge (*continued their studies abroad; a Native Studies program*). **3** a detailed consideration or investigation into a specified subject, phenomenon, etc. (*a study of child poverty in Canada*). **4** a report, essay, book, etc., devoted to such an investigation. **5** a room used for reading, writing, etc. **6** a piece of work, esp. a drawing, done for practice or as an experiment (*a study of a head*). **7** the portrayal in literature or another art form of an aspect of behaviour or character

etc. **8** a musical composition designed to develop a player's skill. **9** a thing worth observing closely (*his face was a study in concentration*). **10** *Theatre* **a** the act of memorizing a role. **b** a person who memorizes a role (*a quick study*). **11** *archaic* a thing to be secured by pains or attention. ● *verb* (**-ies**, **-ied**) **1** *transitive* make a study of; investigate or examine (a subject) (*study law*). **2** *intransitive* (often foll. by *for*) apply oneself to study. **3** *transitive* scrutinize or earnestly contemplate (a visible object) (*studied their faces*). **4** *transitive* try to learn (the words of one's role etc.). **5** *transitive* take pains to achieve (a result) or pay regard to (a subject or principle etc.). **6** *transitive* read (a book) attentively. **7** *transitive* (foll. by *to* + infin.) *archaic* **a** be on the watch. **b** try constantly to manage. □ **in a brown study** in a reverie; absorbed in one's thoughts. **make a study of** investigate carefully. [Old French *estudie* from Latin *studium* zeal, study]

study group *noun* a group of people meeting from time to time to study a particular subject or topic.

study hall *noun N Amer.* a period of time in a school day designated for study and the preparation of homework.

stuff ● *noun* **1** the material that a thing is made of; material that may be used for some purpose. **2** a substance or things or belongings of an indeterminate kind or a quality not needing to be specified (*there's a lot of stuff about it in the newspapers; leave your stuff in the hall*). **3** a particular knowledge or activity (*knows her stuff*). **4 a** what a person is perceived to be made of; a person's capabilities or inward character. **b** the makings of future attainment or excellence (*it was the stuff of legend*). **5** esp. *Brit. dated* woollen fabric (esp. as distinct from silk, cotton, and linen). **6** valueless matter, trash, refuse, nonsense (*take that stuff away*). **7** (prec. by *the*) **a** *informal* an available supply of something, esp. drink or drugs. **b** *slang* money. **8** *N Amer. informal* **a** (in baseball) a pitcher's repertoire of pitches and his or her skill in using it. **b** (in baseball, tennis, etc.) the spin given to a ball in order to make it vary its course. ● *verb* **1** *transitive* **a** pack (a receptacle) tightly (*stuff a cushion with feathers; a head stuffed with weird notions*). **b** fill (a quantity of envelopes) with the same printed matter, as for a mass mailing. **2** *transitive* (foll. by *in, into*) force or cram (a thing) (*stuffed the socks in the drawer*). **3** *transitive* fill out the skin of (an animal or bird etc.) with material to restore the original shape (*a stuffed owl*). **4** *transitive* fill (poultry, vegetables, etc.) with a savoury or sweet mixture, esp. before cooking. **5 a** *transitive & reflexive* fill (a person or oneself) with food. **b** *transitive & intransitive* eat greedily. **6** *transitive* push, esp. hastily or clumsily (*stuffed the note behind the cushion*). **7** *transitive* (usu. in *passive*; foll. by *up*) block up (a person's nose etc.). **8** *transitive slang* (esp. as an expression of contemptuous dismissal) dispose of as unwanted (*you can stuff the job*). **9** *transitive N Amer.* place bogus votes in (a ballot box). **10** *transitive Brit. coarse slang offensive* have sexual intercourse with (a woman). □ **bit of stuff** *Brit. offensive* a woman regarded as an object of sexual desire. **do one's stuff** *informal* do what one has to. **get stuffed** *slang* an exclamation of dismissal, contempt, etc. **stuff and nonsense** *Brit.* an exclamation of incredulity or ridicule. **stuff it** *slang* an expression of rejection or disdain. **stuff one's face** eat a great deal or to excess. □ **stuff·er** *noun* (also in *combination*). [Old French *estoffe* (n.), *estoffer* (v.) equip, furnish, from Greek *stuphō* draw together]

stuffed animal *noun* **1** *N Amer.* a soft plush toy animal, such as a teddy bear. **2** an animal that has been stuffed as part of a taxidermic process.

stuffed shirt *noun informal* a pompous or prim person.

stuff gown *noun Brit. & Cdn* a gown worn by a barrister who is not a Queen's Counsel.

stuff·ing *noun* **1** padding used to stuff cushions etc. **2** a savoury mixture put inside a chicken, turkey, etc. before it is cooked (*sage and onion stuffing*). **3** a mixture of seasoned crumbled bread served with meat. □ **knock** (or **take**) **the stuffing out of** *informal* make feeble or weak; defeat.

stuffing box *noun* a box packed with material, to allow the working of an axle while remaining airtight.

stuff sack *noun* a bag, used esp. in camping, into which a sleeping bag, clothing, etc. can be stuffed or packed for ease of carrying or when not in use.

stuf·fy *adjective* (**stuf·fi·er**, **stuf·fi·est**) **1** (of a room or the atmosphere in it) lacking fresh air or ventilation; close. **2** dull or uninteresting. **3** (of a person's nose etc.) stuffed up. **4** (of a person) dull and conventional. □ **stuf·fi·ly** *adverb* **stuf·fi·ness** *noun*

stul·ti·fy /ˈstʌltəˌfaɪ/ *transitive verb* (**-fies**, **-fied**) make ineffective, useless, or futile, esp. as a result of tedious routine. □ **stul·ti·fi·ca·tion** /-fɪˈkeɪʃən/ *noun* **stul·ti·fier** *noun* [Late Latin *stultificare* from Latin *stultus* foolish]

stul·ti·fy·ing *adjective* extremely tedious or boring.
□ **stul·ti·fy·ing·ly** *adverb*

stum·ble ● *intransitive verb* **1** lurch forward or have a partial fall from catching or striking or misplacing one's foot. **2** (often foll. by *along*) walk unsteadily with repeated stumbles. **3** act in a blundering or hesitating manner, esp. make a mistake or repeated mistakes in speaking etc. **4** (foll. by *on, upon, across*) find or encounter by chance (*stumbled on a disused well*). ● *noun* an act of stumbling. □ **stum·bler** *noun* **stum·bling·ly** *adverb* [Middle English *stumble* (with euphonic *b*) corresponding to Norwegian *stumla*: related to STAMMER]

stumble·bum *noun* N Amer. informal a clumsy or inept person.

stum·bling block *noun* an obstacle or circumstance causing difficulty or hesitation.

stump ● *noun* **1** the projecting portion of the trunk of a cut or fallen tree that remains fixed in the ground. **2** the part remaining when a limb or other part of the body is amputated or severed. **3** the part of a broken tooth left in the gum. **4** a thing, e.g. a pencil or a candle, that has been worn down or reduced to a small part of its original length. **5** (in *pl.*) jocular the legs. **6** the stump of a tree, or other place, used by an orator to address a meeting. **7** *Cricket* each of the three uprights of a wicket. **8** a cylinder of rolled paper or other material with conical ends for softening pencil marks and other uses in drawing. ● *verb* **1** *transitive* (of a question etc.) be too hard for; puzzle. **2** *intransitive* walk stiffly or noisily as if on a wooden leg. **3** *transitive & intransitive* N Amer. traverse (a district) making speeches esp. for an election campaign. **4** *transitive* remove the stumps from (land). **5** *transitive Cricket* (esp. of a wicket-keeper) put (a batsman) out by touching the stumps with the ball while the batsman is out of the crease. □ **on the stump** informal engaged in political speech making and campaigning. **stump up** Brit. informal pay or produce (the money required). **up a** (or **the**) **stump** N Amer. slang **1** in difficulties. **2** pregnant. [Middle Dutch *stomp*, Old High German *stumpf*]

stump·age *noun* **1** standing timber considered with reference to its quantity or marketable value. **2** (in full **stumpage fee**) a tax charged for the privilege of cutting timber on government-owned land.

stumped *adjective* at a loss; baffled.

stump·er *noun* informal **1** a puzzling question. **2** a wicket-keeper.

stump farm *noun* (also **stump ranch**) N Amer. a tract of timberland that has been logged over, with large tree stumps remaining, sold as farm land.

stumpy *adjective* (**stump·i·er**, **stump·i·est**) short and thick.
□ **stump·i·ly** *adverb* **stump·i·ness** *noun*

stun *transitive verb* (**stunned**, **stun·ning**) **1** knock senseless; stupefy. **2** bewilder or astound due to something shocking, unbelievable or unexpected. **3** (of a sound) deafen temporarily. [Old French *estoner* ASTONISH]

stung past and past participle of STING.

stun grenade *noun* a grenade that stuns people with its sound and flash, without causing serious injury.

stun gun *noun* a gun which stuns a person or animal by means of an electric shock etc., without causing serious injury.

stunk past and past participle of STINK.

stunned *adjective* Cdn informal stupid; foolish.

stun·ner *noun* informal **1** a thing that stuns or dazes someone or something; an amazing or astounding thing. **2** a very attractive woman or girl.

stun·ning *adjective* informal **1** extremely impressive or attractive. **2** surprising or shocking (*a stunning revelation*). □ **stun·ning·ly** *adverb*

stun·sail /ˈstʌnsəl/ *noun* (also **stuns'l**) = STUDDING SAIL.

stunt[1] *transitive verb* retard the growth or development of.
□ **stunt·ed·ness** *noun* [stunt foolish (now dial.), Middle High German *stunz*, Old Norse *stuttr* short, from Germanic, perhaps related to STUMP]

stunt[2] ● *noun* **1** something unusual done to attract attention (*publicity stunt*). **2** an act notable or impressive on account of the skill, strength, or daring etc. required to perform it; an exciting or dangerous trick or manoeuvre. ● *intransitive verb* perform stunts, esp. aerobatics. [origin unknown: first used in 19th-c. US college athletics]

stunt double *noun* a person employed to take an actor's place in performing dangerous stunts.

stunt·man *noun* (*pl.* **-men**) a man employed to take an actor's place in performing dangerous stunts.

stunt·woman *noun* (*pl.* **-women**) a woman employed to take an actor's place in performing dangerous stunts.

stupa /ˈstuːpə/ *noun* a round usu. domed building erected as a Buddhist shrine. [Sanskrit *stūpa*]

stupe *noun* slang a foolish or stupid person.

stu·pe·fy /ˈstuːpəfaɪ, ˈstjuː-/ *transitive verb* (**-fies**, **-fied**) **1** make stupid or insensible (*stupefied with drink*). **2** stun with astonishment (*the news was stupefying*). □ **stu·pe·fa·cient** /-ˈfeɪʃənt/ *adjective & noun* **stu·pe·fac·tion** /-ˈfakʃən/ *noun* **stu·pe·fier** *noun* **stu·pe·fy·ing** *adjective* **stu·pe·fy·ing·ly** *adverb* [French *stupéfier* from Latin *stupefacere*, from *stupēre* 'be amazed']

stu·pen·dous /stuːˈpendəs, ˈstjuː-/ *adjective* amazing or prodigious, esp. in terms of size or degree (*a stupendous achievement*).
□ **stu·pen·dous·ly** *adverb* [Latin *stupendus* gerundive of *stupēre* be amazed at]

stu·pid ● *adjective* (**stu·pid·er**, **stu·pid·est**) **1** unintelligent, slow-witted, not clever (*a stupid man*). **2** showing lack of good judgment; foolish (*a stupid idea*). **3** uninteresting or boring. **4** in a state of stupor or lethargy. **5** obtuse; lacking in sensibility. **6** informal a general term of disparagement (*all you do is read your stupid books*). ● *noun* informal a stupid person. □ **stu·pid·ity** *noun* (*pl.* **-ities**). **stu·pid·ly** *adverb* [French *stupide* or Latin *stupidus* (as STUPENDOUS)]

stu·por *noun* **1** Med. a condition of near-unconsciousness characterized by great reduction in mental activity and responsiveness, caused by disease, narcotics, alcohol, etc. **2** a dazed, stunned, or torpid state.
□ **stu·por·ous** *adjective* [Middle English from Latin (as STUPENDOUS)]

sturdy *adjective* (**stur·di·er**, **stur·di·est**) **1** robust; strongly built. **2** vigorous and determined (*sturdy resistance*). □ **stur·di·ly** *adverb* **stur·di·ness** *noun* [Middle English 'reckless, violent', from Old French *esturdi, estourdi* past participle of *estourdir* stun, daze, ultimately from Latin *ex* EX-[1] + *turdus* thrush (taken as a type of drunkenness)]

stur·geon /ˈstɜːdʒən/ *noun* any large mailed shark-like fish of the family Acipenseridae etc. swimming upriver to spawn, used as food and a source of caviar and isinglass. [Old French *esturgeon*, ultimately from Germanic]

Stur·geon Falls a former town in NE central Ontario, situated on the Sturgeon River, about 35 km west of North Bay, now part of the town of West Nipissing; pop. (2001) 5,972.

Sturm und Drang /ˌʃtʊrm ʊnt ˈdraŋ/ *noun* **1** a literary and artistic movement in Germany in the late 18th c., characterized by the expression of emotional unrest and strong feeling and by a rejection of neoclassical literary norms. **2** a period of emotion, stress, or turbulence. [German, = storm and stress]

stut·ter ● *verb* **1** *intransitive* stammer, esp. by involuntarily repeating the first consonants of words. **2** *transitive* (often foll. by *out*) utter (words) in this way. **3** *intransitive* (esp. of a vehicle or engine) move or start with difficulty, making short sharp noises or movements. ● *noun* **1** the act or habit of stuttering. **2** an instance of stuttering. □ **stut·ter·er** *noun* [frequentative of Middle English (now dial.) *stut* from Germanic]

stutter-step N Amer. ● *intransitive verb* break one's stride while running by bringing one foot level with the other. ● *noun* this manoeuvre.

Stutt·gart /ˈstʊtɡɑːt, ˈʃtʊt-/ an industrial city in SW Germany, the capital of Baden-Württemberg, on the Neckar River; pop. (est. 2002) 575,400.

Stuy·ve·sant /ˈstaɪvəsənt/ **Peter** (Dutch name Petrus Stuyvesant) (c.1592–1672), Dutch colonial governor of the New Netherlands (1646–64), which later became the colony of New York.

sty[1] ● *noun* (*pl.* **sties**) **1** a pen or enclosure for pigs. **2** a filthy room or dwelling. ● *transitive & intransitive verb* (**sties**, **stied**) lodge in a sty. [Old English *stī*, prob. = *stig* hall (compare STEWARD), from Germanic]

sty[2] *noun* (also **stye**) (*pl.* **sties** or **styes**) an inflamed swelling on the edge of an eyelid. [*styany* (now dial.) = *styan eye* from Old English *stigend* sty, lit. 'riser' from *stīgan* rise + EYE, shortened as if = *sty on eye*]

Sty·gian /ˈstɪdʒiən/ *adjective* **1** (in Greek mythology) of or relating to the Styx. **2** often (**stygian**) literary dark, gloomy, indistinct. [Latin *stugius* from Greek *stugios* from *Stux -ugos* Styx, from *stugnos* hateful, gloomy]

style ● *noun* **1** a kind or sort, esp. in regard to appearance and form (*an elegant style of house*). **2** a manner of writing or speaking or performing (*written in a florid style*). **3** the distinctive manner of a person or school or period, esp. in relation to painting, architecture, furniture, dress, etc. **4 a** correct or conventional use of a language, esp. spelling, usage, and punctuation practices agreed upon by a particular newspaper, publishing house, etc. (often *attributive*: *style guide*; *style sheet*). **b** the correct way of designating a person or thing (*the correct style when addressing an archbishop is 'Your Grace'*). **5 a** a superior quality or manner (*do it in style*). **b** = FORM *noun* 9. **c** fashionableness or attractiveness of appearance or bearing (*she dresses with such style*). **6** a particular make, shape, or pattern (*in all sizes and styles*). **7** a method of reckoning dates (*Old Style; New Style*). **8** = STYLUS 1, 4. **9** *Bot.* the narrow extension of the ovary supporting the stigma. **10** *Zool.* a small slender pointed appendage. ● *transitive verb* **1** design or make etc. in a particular style. **2** designate with a particular name, description, or title. **3** arrange (hair) in a particular way. □ **style·less** *adjective* **style·less·ness** *noun* **styl·er** *noun* [Old French *stile, style* from Latin *stilus*: spelling *style* due to association with Greek *stulos* 'column']

-style *suffix* forming adjectives and adverbs with the sense 'in a manner characteristic of' (*peasant-style clothing; Japanese-style food; a revolution British-style*). ¶ The usage illustrated by the third example given above, with the noun coming first, is somewhat informal.

style book *noun* a manual of house style.

styl·et /'staɪlət/ *noun* **1** a slender pointed instrument; a stiletto. **2** *Med.* the stiffening wire of a catheter; a probe. **3** *Zool.* a small style, esp. a piercing mouthpart of an insect. [French *stilet* from Italian STILETTO]

styli *pl.* of STYLUS.

styl·in' *adjective* N Amer. *slang* hip, fashionable; cool.

styl·ish *adjective* **1** fashionable; elegant, chic. **2** having a superior quality, manner, etc. □ **styl·ish·ly** *adverb* **styl·ish·ness** *noun*

styl·ist *noun* **1 a** a person employed by a firm to create, coordinate, or promote new styles or designs, esp. of clothes or cars. **b** a hairdresser. **2 a** a writer noted for or aspiring to good literary style. **b** (in sports or music) a person who performs with style. **3** a person whose job is to arrange and coordinate food, clothes, etc. in a stylish and attractive way in photographs or films.

styl·is·tic *adjective* of or concerning esp. literary or artistic style. □ **styl·is·tic·ally** *adverb*

styl·is·tics *noun* the study of literary or linguistic style.

styl·ite /'staɪlaɪt/ *noun* Christianity *hist.* an ancient or medieval ascetic living on top of a pillar. [ecclesiastical Greek *stulitēs* from *stulos* pillar]

styl·ize *transitive verb* (also esp. *Brit.* **-ise**) (esp. as **styl·ized** *adjective*) paint, draw, etc. (a subject) in a fixed, conventional, or artificial style. □ **styl·iz·a·tion** *noun*

styl·oid /'staɪlɔɪd/ ● *adjective* resembling a stylus or pen. ● *noun* (in full **styloid process**) designating or pertaining to any of several slender pointed processes of bone, esp. that which projects from the base of the temporal bone. [modern Latin *styloides* from Greek *stuloeidēs* from *stulos* pillar]

sty·lus /'staɪləs/ *noun* (*pl.* **-li** /-laɪ/ or **-luses**) **1 a** an ancient implement for writing on wax etc., having a pointed end for inscribing characters and a flat broad end for erasing and smoothing the writing surface. **b** any sharp instrument or point for engraving, tracing, punching holes in paper, etc. **2** *Computing* an electrical device shaped like a pen, used esp. to design graphical images on a computer screen. **3 a** a hard, esp. diamond or sapphire, point on the arm of a turntable that follows a groove in a record and transmits recorded sound for reproduction; a needle. **b** a similar point used to produce such a groove when recording sound. **4** a pointer for indicating a time, position, etc., esp. the gnomon of a sundial. **5** a tracing point used to produce a written record in a seismograph, telegraph receiver, etc. [erroneous spelling of Latin *stilus*: compare STYLE]

sty·mie /'staɪmi/ ● *transitive verb* (**sty·mies, sty·mied, stymy·ing** or **sty·mie·ing**) **1** obstruct, thwart (a person, project, etc.) (*the threat of violence has stymied the peace talks*). **2 a** puzzle or perplex (a person). **b** place (a person) in a difficult situation. **3** *Golf* block (an opponent, an opponent's ball, or oneself) with a stymie. ● *noun* (*pl.* **-mies**) **1** *Golf* a situation on a green in which the path of a putt to the hole is obstructed by an opponent's ball. **2** a difficult or perplexing situation; a dilemma. [19th c.; origin unknown]

styp·tic /'stɪptɪk/ ● *adjective* (of a drug etc.) that checks bleeding. ● *noun* a styptic drug or substance. [Latin *stypticus* from Greek *stuptikos* from *stuphō* contract]

styptic pencil *noun* a stick of a styptic substance used to treat small cuts.

sty·rax /'staɪraks/ *noun* **1** storax resin. **2** any tree or shrub of the genus *Styrax*, e.g. the storax tree. [Latin from Greek *sturax*: compare STORAX]

sty·rene /'staɪriːn/ *noun* Chem. a liquid hydrocarbon, C_8H_8, easily polymerized and used in making plastics etc. [STYRAX + -ENE]

Styria /'stɪriːə/ a mountainous state of SE Austria; capital, Graz.

Styro·foam *noun* esp. N Amer. *proprietary* a variety of expanded polystyrene often used in the manufacture of insulation, disposable food containers, etc. [POLYSTYRENE + -O- + FOAM]

Styx /stɪks/ *Gk. & Rom. Myth* one of nine rivers in the underworld, over which Charon ferried the souls of the dead.

suable /'suːəbəl/ *adjective* liable to be sued; legally subject to legal process.

suasion /'sweɪʒən/ *noun* formal persuasion as opposed to force (*moral suasion*). □ **suasive** /'sweɪsɪv/ *adjective* [Old French *suasion* or Latin *suasio* from *suadēre suas-* urge]

suave /swɒv/ *adjective* (of a person, manners, etc.) charming, smooth; polite; sophisticated. □ **suave·ly** *adverb* **suave·ness** *noun* **suav·ity** /-vɪti/ *noun* (*pl.* **-ities**). [French *suave* or Latin *suavis* agreeable: compare SWEET]

sub *informal* ● *noun* **1** a submarine. **2** a sandwich made with a long roll or small loaf and filled with a variety of meats, cheeses, etc. **3 a** a substitute. **b** *N Amer.* a substitute teacher. **4** a subscription. **5** esp. *Brit.* a sub-editor. **6** *Econ.* a subsidiary. **7** *Brit.* a subsistence; an advance or loan against expected income. **8** *Military* a subaltern. ● *verb* (**subbed, sub·bing**) **1** *intransitive* (usu. foll. by *for*) act or work as a substitute for a person. **2** *transitive Brit.* copy-edit (a newspaper etc.). [abbreviation]

sub- *prefix* (also **suc-** before *c*, **suf-** before *f*, **sug-** before *g*, **sup-** before *p*, **sur-** before *r*, **sus-** before *c, p, t*) **1** at, to, or from a lower position (*subordinate; submerge; subtract; subsoil*). **2** secondary or inferior in rank or position (*subclass; subcommittee; sub-lieutenant; subtotal*). **3** somewhat, nearly; more or less (*subarctic; subaquatic*). **4** (forming verbs) denoting secondary action (*subdivide; sublet*). **5** denoting support (*subvention*). **6** *Chem.* (in names of compounds) denoting a relatively small or smaller than normal proportion of a component, esp. due to low oxidation state or the presence of another component. [from or after Latin *sub-* from *sub* under, close to, towards]

sub·acute *adjective* Med. (of a condition) between acute and chronic.

sub·adult *Zool.* ● *adjective* (of an animal) not fully adult. ● *noun* a subadult animal.

sub·alpine *adjective* **1** pertaining to or situated in the higher mountain slopes just below the timberline. **2** of or pertaining to the area at the foot of the Alps.

sub·altern /sʌbˈɒltərn, ˈsʌbəltərn/ ● *noun* **1** a person of inferior rank or status. **2** esp. *Brit. Military* an officer below the rank of captain, esp. a second lieutenant. ● *adjective* **1** of inferior rank; subordinate. **2** *Logic* (of a proposition) particular, not universal. [Late Latin *subalternus* from *alternus* ALTERNATE *adjective*]

sub·antarc·tic *adjective* of, pertaining to, or situated in regions immediately north of the Antarctic Circle.

sub·aqua·tic *adjective* **1** partly aquatic. **2** underwater.

sub·aque·ous *adjective* existing, formed, or taking place under water. □ **sub·aque·ous·ly** *adverb*

sub·arctic ● *noun* (usu. **Sub·arctic**) the region immediately south of the Arctic Circle. ● *adjective* characteristic of, pertaining to, or inhabiting this region.

sub·assembly *noun* (*pl.* **-assemblies**) **1** a unit assembled separately but designed to be incorporated with other such units into a larger manufactured product. **2 a** the stage of a product's manufacture in which such units are made (*the aircraft is currently in sub-assembly*). **b** the department in charge of this.

sub·atom·ic *adjective* **1 a** (of a particle) existing in an atom (*protons, neutrons, and electrons are subatomic particles*). **b** (of a process etc.) occurring within an atom. **2 a** smaller than an atom. **b** *informal* extremely small.

sub·basement *noun* a second basement below the main basement.

sub·branch *noun* a secondary or subordinate branch.

sub·cat·egory *noun* (*pl.* **-ies**) a secondary or subordinate category. □ **sub·cat·egor·iz·a·tion** *noun* **sub·cat·egor·ize** *transitive verb* (also esp. *Brit.* **-ise**).

sub·cellu·lar *adjective* **1** situated or occurring within a cell or cells. **2** smaller than a cell.

sub·class *noun* **1 a** a secondary or inferior class. **b** each of the groups or categories that constitute a class. **2** *Biol.* a taxonomic category below a class. □ **sub·classi·fi·ca·tion** *noun*

sub·clause *noun* esp. *Law* a subsidiary section of a clause.

sub·clav·ian /sʌbˈkleɪviən/ ● *adjective* **1** lying or extending under the collarbone. **2** designating or pertaining to either of the two main arteries serving the neck and arms. ● *noun* a subclavian vessel, nerve, or muscle. [modern Latin *subclavius* (as SUB-, *clavis* key): compare CLAVICLE]

sub·clinic·al *adjective* Med. (of a disease) not yet presenting definite or noticeable symptoms.

sub·com·mit·tee *noun* a body of people appointed by a committee, usu. composed of a selection of its own members, esp. to study or deal with a specific issue or an aspect of a larger matter.

sub·com·pact *N Amer.* ● *adjective* designating a car that is smaller than a compact, usu. having a wheelbase of less than 85 inches, and a 1 litre engine. ● *noun* a subcompact car.

sub·con·scious ● *noun* the part of the mind which influences actions etc. without one's full awareness. ● *adjective* **1** of, pertaining to, or existing in the subconscious. **2** operating or existing without one's full awareness (*subconscious impulses*). □ **sub·con·scious·ly** *adverb* **sub·con·scious·ness** *noun*

sub·con·tin·ent *noun* **1** a large section of a continent having a certain geographical or political identity or independence. **2** a large land mass, smaller than a continent, e.g. Greenland. □ **sub·con·tin·ent·al** *adjective*

sub·con·tract ● *verb* **1** *transitive* hire a person, company, or firm etc. to do (work) as part of a larger contract or project. **2** *intransitive* make or carry out a subcontract. ● *noun* an agreement in which an individual or firm agrees to perform all or a portion of a previous contract, esp. to supply materials, labour, etc.

sub·con·tract·or *noun* an individual or company that carries out work for a company as part of a larger contract.

sub·cor·ti·cal *adjective Anat.* pertaining to or situated in the region underlying a cortex, esp. that of the brain.

sub·crit·i·cal *adjective* **1** below a critical level, value, threshold, etc. **2** *Physics* containing or involving less than the critical mass.

sub·cul·ture ● *noun* **1 a** a cultural group within a larger or predominant culture but distinguished from it by factors such as class, ethnic background, religion, or residence, unified by shared beliefs or interests which may be at variance with those of the larger culture. **b** the system of beliefs, customs, and behaviour etc. typical of such a group. **2** a culture of micro-organisms started from another culture. ● *transitive verb* produce a subculture of (bacteria etc.). □ **sub·cul·tur·al** *adjective*

sub·cu·ta·neous /ˌsʌbkjuːˈteɪnɪəs/ *adjective* situated or introduced just under the skin. □ **sub·cu·ta·neous·ly** *adverb*

sub·dea·con *noun Christianity* **1** (in some Christian churches) a minister of the order next below a deacon. **2** a cleric or lay clerk acting as assistant to a deacon at the Eucharist.

sub·di·rec·to·ry *noun* (*pl.* **-ies**) *Computing* a directory that is itself contained in another directory.

sub·dis·ci·pline *noun* a subordinate branch of a discipline.

sub·di·vide *verb* **1** *transitive* **a** divide (a thing) into smaller parts or portions. **b** divide (a thing that has been divided) into smaller parts or portions. **2** *intransitive* divide into smaller parts, esp. after a previous division. **3** *transitive N Amer. & Austral.* divide (a tract of land) into plots for sale or development.

sub·di·vi·sion *noun* **1** *N Amer. & Austral.* an area of land divided into plots for sale or development. **2** *N Amer.* a housing development that has been built on such an area. **3** each of the parts into which a thing, esp. a previous division, is or may be divided; a secondary or subordinate division. **4** the act or an instance of subdividing.

sub·dom·in·ant *noun Music* the fourth note of the diatonic scale of any key.

sub·duc·tion *noun Geol.* the sideways and downward movement of the edge of a plate of the earth's crust into the mantle beneath a neighbouring lithospheric plate. □ **sub·duct** *transitive & intransitive verb*

subduction zone *noun Geol.* a long narrow region containing a trench through which a descending plate of the earth's crust is assimilated into the mantle during subduction.

sub·due *transitive verb* (**sub·dues**, **sub·dued**, **sub·du·ing**) **1** overcome or overpower (a person or animal etc.) by physical force or violence. **2** bring (a person etc.) under one's control by intimidation, persuasion, manipulation, etc. **3** check or restrain (an impulse, emotion, thought, etc.). **4** conquer and bring into subjection (an army, people, or country). [Middle English *sodewe* from Old French *so(u)duire* from Latin *subducere* (as SUB-, *ducere* lead, bring) used with the sense of *subdere* conquer (as SUB-, *-dere* put)]

sub·dued *adjective* **1** (of a colour, light, or sound, etc.) reduced in or lacking intensity or force. **2** (of a person) not showing much excitement, interest, or activity.

sub·dural /sʌbˈdjʊərəl/ *adjective Anat. & Med.* situated or occurring between the dura mater and the arachnoid membrane of the brain and spinal cord.

sub·edit *transitive verb* (**sub-edited**, **sub-editing**) *Brit.* = COPY-EDIT.

sub·editor *noun* **1** an assistant editor. **2** *Brit.* = COPY EDITOR.

sub·family *noun* (*pl.* **-ilies**) **1** *Biol.* a taxonomic category below a family. **2** any analogous subdivision of a family in a classification, such as in linguistics.

sub·floor *noun* a rough floor serving as a foundation for a finished floor in a building. □ **sub·floor·ing** *noun*

sub·freez·ing *adjective* (of a temperature etc.) below the freezing point.

sub·fusc /ˈsʌbfʌsk/ *adjective formal* dull; gloomy; drab. [Latin *subfuscus* from *fuscus* dark brown]

sub·genre *noun* a secondary or subordinate style of esp. literature or art.

sub·genus /sʌbˈdʒiːnəs/ *noun* (*pl.* **sub·genera** /-ˈdʒenərə/) *Biol.* a taxonomic category below a genus.

sub·glacial *adjective* existing or occurring under or at the bottom of a glacier.

sub·group *noun* **1** a subordinate group; a subdivision of a group. **2** *Math.* **a** a series of operations forming part of a larger group. **b** any group all of whose elements are elements of a larger group.

sub·head·ing *noun* (also **sub·head**) **1** a subordinate heading, headline, caption, or title in a chapter, article, etc. **2** a subordinate division in a classification.

sub·human ● *adjective* **1** (of an animal) closely related to, but of a lower order of being than, a human. **2** (of a person or behaviour) uncivilized, bestial; less than human. ● *noun* a subhuman person or creature.

sub·jacent /sʌbˈdʒeɪsənt/ *adjective* situated below; underlying. □ **sub·jacen·cy** *noun* [Latin *subjacēre* (as SUB-, *jacēre* lie)]

sub·ject ● *noun* **1 a** a topic or the theme of a discussion, investigation, or consideration. **b** a figure, incident, scene, etc. represented by an artist in a work of fiction, painting, photograph, etc. **c** (foll. by *of*) a person or thing towards whom or which a particular action, thought, or feeling is directed; a target or focus of attention, thought, dispute, etc. (*her comments have been the subject of recent debate*). **2** a particular department of art, history, science, etc. that is studied or taught in an academic institution (*math is her best subject*). **3** *Grammar* a word or phrase in a sentence indicating who or what performs the action of a verb or upon whom or which a verb is predicated, e.g. 'we' in the sentence *we ate ice cream* or 'my dog' in *my dog is clever*. **4 a** a person owing allegiance to and under the protection of a monarch or government (*the queen and her subjects*). **b** any person under the control of or owing obedience to another. **5** a person or corpse upon whom a medical treatment, study, or experiment is being performed. **6** *Philos.* **a** a thinking or feeling entity; the conscious mind; the ego, esp. as opposed to anything external to the mind. **b** the central substance or core of a thing as opposed to its attributes. **7** *Music* the theme of a fugue or sonata; the leading phrase or motif. **8** *Logic* the part of a proposition about which a statement is made. ● *adjective* (usu. foll. by *to*) **1** (foll. by *to*) susceptible to some esp. harmful or medical condition, occurrence, etc.; prone or vulnerable (*the patient is subject to infection*). **2** liable (*prices are subject to change without notice*). **3** dependent or conditional upon; resting on the assumption of (*the arrangement is subject to your approval*). **4** bound by law or regulation (*this offence is subject to a minimum $50 fine; subject to provincial sales tax*). **5** under the rule or domination of an individual or group, sovereign, country, etc. (*a subject nation*). ● *adverb* (foll. by *to*) conditionally upon (*subject to your consent, I propose to begin*). ● *transitive verb* (usu. foll. by *to*) **1** cause (a person or thing) to experience, undergo, or endure a specified treatment. **2** expose or make vulnerable to (*subjects herself to ridicule*). **3** subdue (a nation, person, etc.) to one's sway etc. □ **on the subject of** concerning, about. □ **sub·jec·tion** *noun* **sub·ject·less** *adjective* [Old French *suget* etc. from Latin *subjectus* past participle of *subjicere* (as SUB-, *jacere* throw)]

subject heading *noun* a heading in an index or catalogue under which references to a subject are listed.

sub·ject·ive ● *adjective* **1 a** (of art, written history, a person's views, etc.) proceeding from, or influenced by, an individual's personal thoughts and opinions; biased, not impartial or literal. **b** (of a person) tending to emphasize or be influenced by one's own feelings or opinions. **2** esp. *Philos.* proceeding from or belonging to the individual consciousness or perception; partial, misconceived, or distorted. **3** *Grammar* (of a case or word) constructed as appropriate to the subject of a sentence or verb. **4** (of a symptom etc.) that is felt or is experienced only by a patient, and may not be diagnosed by someone else, such as a doctor. ● *noun Grammar* **1** the subjective case. **2** a word or form in this case. □ **sub·jec·tive·ly** *adverb* **sub·jec·tiv·ity** *noun*

sub·jec·tiv·ism *noun Philos.* **1** the doctrine that knowledge, perception, morality, etc., are merely subjective and relative and that there is no external or objective truth. **2** a theory or method based exclusively on subjective facts. **3** the quality or condition of being subjective. □ **sub·jec·tiv·ist** *noun*

subject matter *noun* the substance or issues treated in a book, play, speech, etc.

sub judice /sʌb ˈdʒuːdəsi, sʊb ˈjuːdɪˌkei/ *adjective Law* under judicial consideration and therefore prohibited from public discussion elsewhere. [Latin, = under a judge]

sub·ju·gate /ˈsʌbdʒʊˌgeit/ *transitive verb* **1** bring (a country, people, etc.) into subjection; conquer, vanquish. **2** bring under domination or control; make subservient or dependent. □ **sub·ju·ga·tion** *noun* **sub·ju·ga·tor** *noun* [Late Latin *subjugare* bring under the yoke (as SUB-, *jugum* yoke)]

sub·junc·tive /səbˈdʒʌŋktɪv/ *Grammar* ● *noun* **1** (in full **subjunctive mood**) a mood of verbs used to express a condition, wish, fear, possibility, command, suggestion, uncertainty, or hypothetical situation, e.g. *if I were rich* or *I wish I were beautiful.* **2** a verb in this mood. ● *adjective* (of a verb or phrase) expressed in the subjunctive. [French *subjonctif -ive* or Late Latin *subjunctivus* from Latin *subjungere,* from *sub-* in addition + *jungere* to join, translation of Greek *hupotaktikos*]

sub·king·dom *noun Biol.* a taxonomic category below a kingdom.

sub·lease ● *noun* a transaction in which the lessee or tenant of a property leases it to another. ● *transitive verb* = SUBLET.

sub·lessee *noun* a person who holds a sublease.

sub·lessor *noun* a person who grants a sublease.

sub·let ● *transitive verb* (**sub·letting;** *past* and *past participle* **sublet**) **1** acquire a lease on (an apartment etc.) from a person who is leasing it from its owner. **2** rent out (an apartment etc.) that one is leasing from its owner. ● *noun* an apartment etc. that is being sublet.

sub·lethal *adjective* having an effect that is nearly lethal or fatal.

sub·lieuten·ant *noun Cdn & Brit.* a naval officer ranking next below lieutenant. Abbr.: **SLt**. ¶ See Usage Note at LIEUTENANT.

sub·lim·ate ● *verb* /ˈsʌblə.meit/ **1** *transitive* divert or channel the energy of (a primitive esp. sexual impulse) into a more highly valued or acceptable activity. **2** *Chem.* **a** *transitive* subject (a substance) to the action of heat to convert it into a vapour which, on cooling, is deposited in solid form. **b** *intransitive* (of a substance) pass from a solid state to a vapour, or from a gaseous state to a solid, without liquefaction. **3** *transitive* elevate or refine to a high degree of purity or excellence; idealize. ● *noun* /ˈsʌbləmət/ *Chem.* a refined or concentrated product; a product of sublimation. □ **sub·lim·a·tion** *noun* [Latin *sublimare sublimat-* SUBLIME *verb*]

sub·lime /səˈblaim/ ● *adjective* (**sub·lim·er, sub·lim·est**) **1** of the most exalted, grand, or noble kind; of a high intellectual, moral, or spiritual level (*sublime genius*). **2** (of nature, art, etc.) producing an overwhelming sense of awe, reverence, or high emotion, by reason of great beauty, vastness, or grandeur. **3** usu. *ironic* of the most extreme kind; supreme (*shows sublime indifference to the sufferings of others*). **4** *archaic* or *literary* dignified or lofty in bearing; proud, arrogant. ● *noun* a quality in art or nature etc. arousing or inspiring awe, reverence, terror, or high emotion in the person experiencing it. ● *transitive & intransitive verb Chem.* = SUBLIMATE *verb* 2. □ **from the sublime to the ridiculous** moving or ranging from what is serious or important to what is trivial or laughable. □ **sub·lime·ly** *adverb* **sub·lim·ity** /-ˈlɪməti/ *noun* [Latin *sublimis* (as SUB-, second element perhaps related to *limen* threshold, *limus* oblique)]

Sublime Porte *noun see* PORTE.

sub·lim·inal /səbˈlɪmənəl/ *Psych.* ● *adjective* **1** (of a stimulus, message, advertisement, etc.) operating below the threshold of sensation or consciousness; having an influence upon the mind without one being aware of it (*subliminal advertising*). **2** (of recognition, perception, etc.) occurring as a result of a process or stimulus of which one is unaware. ● *noun* something that is subliminal, esp. a subliminal message. □ **sub·lim·inal·ly** *adverb* [SUB- + Latin *limen -inis* threshold]

sub·lit·tor·al *adjective* **1** of or concerning the region from the line of the sea at low tide to the edge of the continental shelf. **2** (of plants, animals, deposits, etc.) living or found in this region.

Sub-Lt. *abbreviation* Sub-Lieutenant. ¶ In the Canadian Forces, the abbreviation *SLt* is used.

sub·lun·ary /sʌbˈluːnəri/ *adjective* **1** situated or existing beneath the moon. **2** of the world or worldly affairs; terrestrial, material, mundane. [Late Latin *sublunaris* (as SUB-, LUNAR)]

sub·lux·a·tion /sʌblʌkˈseiʃən/ *noun Med.* partial dislocation. [SUB- + Latin *luxat-,* past participle stem of *luxare,* from *luxus* 'dislocated']

sub·machine gun *noun* a hand-held lightweight automatic or semi-automatic weapon designed to shoot small-calibre ammunition.

sub·margin·al *adjective* (of land) not worth cultivating.

sub·ma·rine ● *noun* **1** a vessel capable of operating under water. **2** (in full **submarine sandwich**) = SUB *noun* 2. ● *adjective* living, occurring, or used under the surface of the sea (*submarine life*). ● *verb* **1** *transitive & intransitive Baseball* deliver (a pitch or the ball) sidearm or underhand. **2** *intransitive* voyage in or operate a submarine. **3** *intransitive* drop, sink; slide or fall under (*prices have submarined recently*).

sub·marin·er *noun* **1** /ˌsʌbˈmærənər/ a person who travels in or operates a submarine. **2** /ˌsʌbməˈriːnər/ *Baseball* a pitcher who throws with the arm at or below shoulder level; a sidearm or underhand pitcher.

sub·maxil·lary /ˌsʌbˈmæksɪləri/ *adjective* (esp. of a pair of salivary glands) beneath the upper jaw.

sub·medi·ant /sʌbˈmiːdiənt/ *noun Music* the sixth note of the diatonic scale of any key.

sub·menu *noun Computing* a secondary list of available commands, options, etc. displayed under a general heading listed in a menu.

sub·merge *verb* **1** *transitive* immerse, dip, or place in a liquid. **2** *transitive* overwhelm or inundate (a person) with work, problems, etc. **3** *transitive* conceal or suppress (an emotion etc.). **4** *intransitive* (of a submarine, its crew, a diver, etc.) dive below the surface of water. □ **sub·mer·gence** *noun* [Latin *submergere* (as SUB-, *mergere mers-* dip)]

sub·merged *adjective* **1** immersed, inundated, or buried in or beneath a liquid or substance. **2** suppressed, concealed, hidden. **3** *Bot.* growing entirely under water.

sub·merse *transitive verb* (esp. as **sub·mersed** *adjective*) submerge. [Latin *submers-* past participle stem of *submergere* SUBMERGE]

sub·mer·sible ● *noun* a submarine operating under water for short periods, used esp. for exploration. ● *adjective* **1** capable of being submerged. **2** intended or designed to operate or be used under water (*submersible pump*).

sub·mer·sion *noun* **1** the act or an instance of submerging. **2** the state of being submerged.

sub·micro·scop·ic *adjective* too small to be seen by an ordinary microscope.

sub·mini·ature *adjective* (esp. of electronic components, photographic equipment, etc.) of greatly reduced size.

sub·mis·sion *noun* **1** a thing that has been submitted for consideration, evaluation, or judgment. **2** humility, meekness, obedience, submissiveness (*showed great submission of spirit*). **3** *Law* **a** a contract in which parties in a dispute agree to submit to arbitration. **b** a matter referred to a third party, esp. a judge or jury, for arbitration. **4 a** the action or an instance of yielding to the authority or will of another; surrender. **b** (in wrestling) the surrender of a participant yielding to the pain of a hold.

sub·mis·sive *adjective* **1** obedient, subservient, meek. **2** willing to yield or back down. **3** (of an action, etc.) indicating subservience or a willingness to submit. □ **sub·mis·sive·ly** *adverb* **sub·mis·sive·ness** *noun* [SUBMISSION after *remissive* etc.]

sub·mit *verb* (**sub·mit·ted, sub·mit·ting**) **1** (usu. foll. by *to*) **a** *intransitive* cease resistance; give way; yield. **b** *reflexive* consent to undergo a certain treatment or abide by a certain condition or limitation etc.; surrender (oneself) to. **2** *transitive* present (an application, essay, contest entry, etc.) for consideration or decision. **3** *transitive* (usu. foll. by *to*) subject (a person or thing) to an operation, process, treatment, etc. (*submitted it to the flames*). **4** *transitive* esp. *Law* propose, suggest, or contend, esp. deferentially. □ **sub·mit·ter** *noun* [Latin *submittere* (as SUB-, *mittere miss-* send)]

sub·mul·tiple ● *noun* a number that can be divided exactly into a specified number. ● *adjective* being such a number.

sub·net·work *noun* (also **sub·net**) *Computing* **1** a system of dedicated computers responsible for communication functions in a system or network. **2** a smaller or subordinate network of computers within a larger one.

sub·normal *adjective* **1** less than or below the normal level (*subnormal temperatures*). **2** of a level of intelligence and general ability which is below a given standard of normality. □ **sub·normal·ity** *noun*

sub·note·book *noun* a computer that is smaller than a notebook but larger than a palmtop or personal digital assistant.

sub·nuclear *adjective Physics* occurring in or smaller than an atomic nucleus.

sub·ocean·ic *adjective* occurring or existing below the ocean or beneath the ocean floor.

sub·optimal *adjective* less than optimal; not of the highest level, standard, or quality, etc.

sub·orbit·al *adjective* **1** designating or having a trajectory that does not make a complete orbit of a planet. **2** situated below the orbit of the eye.

sub·order *noun* a taxonomic category between an order and a family. □ **sub·ordin·al** *adjective*

sub·ordin·ate ● *adjective* /səˈbɔːrdənət/ (often. foll. by *to*) **1** (of a person, position, etc.) of inferior rank; dependent upon the authority or power of another. **2** of inferior importance; secondary, minor. **3** (of a thing) dependent upon or subservient to a chief or principal thing of the same kind. ● *noun* /səˈbɔːrdənət/ a subordinate person or thing, esp. a person working under another's control or orders. ● *transitive verb* /səˈbɔːrdəˌneɪt/ (usu. foll. by *to*) **1** make inferior or secondary; treat or consider as less important or valuable. **2** bring into a subordinate position; make dependent or subservient. □ **sub·ordin·ate·ly** *adverb* **sub·ordin·a·tion** /-ˈneɪʃən/ *noun* [medieval Latin *subordinare*, *subordinat-* (as SUB-, Latin *ordinare* ordain)]

subordinate clause *noun* a clause, usu. introduced by a conjunction, that does not constitute a sentence itself but which depends on the principal clause that it modifies or in which it serves as a noun, e.g. 'that she has come' in *I hope that she has come*.

subordinated debt *noun Commerce* debt that, in the event of liquidation, can be claimed by an unsecured creditor only after the claims of secured creditors have been met.

sub·ordin·at·ing conjunction *noun* a conjunction that joins a subordinate clause to a main clause, e.g. 'because' in *I am happy because it is sunny*.

sub·orn /səˈbɔːrn/ *transitive verb* **1** induce or procure (a person) to commit an unlawful act by bribery or other means. **2** bribe or induce (a person) to give false testimony or commit perjury. **3** procure (false testimony) by bribery or other unlawful means. [Latin *subornare* incite secretly (as SUB-, *ornare* equip)]

sub·par *adjective* **1** poorer than usual; not as good as the average or what may be expected. **2** *Golf* below par.

sub·phylum /sʌbˈfaɪləm/ *noun* (*pl.* **sub·phyla** /-lə/) *Biol.* a taxonomic category below a phylum.

sub·plot *noun* a secondary or subordinate plot in a novel, play, etc.

sub·poena /səˈpiːnə/ ● *noun* a writ issued by a court or other authorized body requiring the attendance of a person at a stated time and place, usu. to testify or present evidence, subject to penalty for non-compliance. ● *transitive verb* (*past* and *past participle* **sub·poenaed**) **1** summon (a person) to appear in court as a witness. **2** require (evidence etc.) to be brought by a witness so that it may be presented in court. [Latin *sub poena* under penalty (the first words of the writ)]

sub·popu·la·tion *noun* **1** esp. *Biol.* an identifiable population forming part of or derived from a larger population. **2** *Statistics* a subgroup of a population.

sub·post office *noun* **1** *Cdn & Brit.* a small local post office offering fewer services than a main post office. **2** *Cdn* a postal outlet located within a drugstore, convenience store, etc., usu. offering limited postal services.

sub·pro·gram *noun Computing* = SUBROUTINE.

sub-region *noun* esp. *Ecology* a subdivision of a geographical region, usu. considered in terms of the plant and animal life it sustains. □ **sub-region·al** *adjective*

sub·roga·tion /ˌsʌbrəˈgeɪʃən/ *noun Law* the principle that a person paying a debt on behalf of another may succeed to the rights of that person in order to obtain restitution for that payment of debt. □ **sub·rogate** /ˈsʌbrəˌgeɪt/ *transitive verb* [Late Latin *subrogatio* from *subrogare* choose as substitute (as SUB-, *rogare* ask)]

sub rosa /sʌb ˈroːzə/ ● *adverb* in secrecy or confidence. ● *adjective* (usu. **sub-rosa**) (of communication, operations, etc.) secret, clandestine. [Latin, lit. 'under the rose', as emblem of secrecy]

sub·rou·tine *noun Computing* a routine designed to perform a frequently used operation within a program.

sub-Saharan *attributive adjective* from or forming part of the African regions south of the Sahara desert.

sub·scribe *verb* **1** *intransitive* (often foll. by *to*) arrange to receive a periodical, service, or series of tickets in exchange for payment. **2** *intransitive* (usu. foll. by *to*) express or feel agreement with an idea or resolution etc.; hold as a belief or opinion. **3** *transitive* write or sign (one's name) at the bottom of esp. a document as a witness or consenting party. **4** *transitive & intransitive* **a** (often foll. by *for*) pay or guarantee (a specified sum of money) for an issue of shares. **b** pledge or contribute (a specified sum of money) to a fund or charity etc. **5** *intransitive* (often foll. by *for*) *Brit.* apply or sign up to take part in (a class, activity, etc) (*compare* OVERSUBSCRIBE). [Latin *subscribere* (as SUB-, *scribere* script- write)]

sub·scrib·er *noun* **1** a person who pays a fee to receive regular issues of a periodical etc. **2** a person who pays a regular fee in order to receive a particular service, such as telephone or cable television service. **3** a person who purchases advance tickets to a series of theatrical productions, concerts, etc. **4** a person contributing money to a charity or towards the purchase of stock etc.

subscriber trunk dialling *noun Brit.* = DIRECT DIALING.

sub·script ● *noun* **1** a character, number, or symbol written or printed below the line or below and usu. to the right of another symbol (*compare* SUPERSCRIPT *noun*). **2** *Computing* a symbol, notionally written as a subscript but in practice usually not, used in a program, alone or with others, to specify one of the elements of an array. ● *adjective* written or printed below the line or below and to the right of another symbol. [Latin *subscriptus* (as SUBSCRIBE)]

sub·scrip·tion *noun* **1 a** an agreement to pay in advance for a specified number of consecutive issues of a periodical. **b** an agreement to purchase, in advance, tickets for a series of events (also *attributive*: *subscription series*). **c** an agreement to pay for and receive service from a cable television or telephone company etc. **2** an offer or agreement to purchase shares in a company. **3 a** a fee paid usu. in advance to purchase tickets for a series of events, a number of issues of a periodical, etc. **b** *Brit.* a fee paid regularly for membership in a society etc. **4** a sum of money donated to or raised by a charity, fund, etc. **5 a** a signature on a document etc. **b** agreement, assent.

sub·sea *adjective & adverb* beneath the surface of the sea.

sub·sec·tion *noun* a division of a section, esp. within a document or book.

sub·se·quence *noun* **1** /ˌsʌbˈsiːkwəns/ *Math.* a sequence derived from another by the omission of a number of terms. **2** /ˈsʌbsəkwəns/ the condition of being subsequent.

sub·se·quent /ˈsʌbsəkwənt/ *adjective* (usu. foll. by *to*) following a specified event etc. in time, esp. as a consequence. □ **sub·se·quent·ly** *adverb* [Old French *subsequent* or Latin *subsequi* (as SUB-, *sequi* follow)]

sub·serve *transitive verb* be instrumental in assisting, promoting, or furthering (a purpose, action, etc.).

sub·servi·ent /səbˈsɜːrvɪənt/ *adjective* **1** slavishly submissive, servile, obsequious. **2** (usu. foll. by *to*) serving as a means; instrumental. **3** (usu. foll. by *to*) subordinate. □ **sub·servi·ence** *noun* **sub·servi·ency** *noun* [Latin *subserviens subservient-* (as SUB-, SERVE)]

sub·set *noun* **1** a secondary part of a set. **2** *Math.* a set consisting of elements all of which are contained in another set.

sub-shrub *noun* a low-growing or small shrub. □ **sub-shrubby** *adjective*

sub·side *intransitive verb* **1** become calm or tranquil; die down; abate (*the excitement subsided*). **2** (of water) be reduced to a lower level. **3** (of the ground) cave in. **4** (of a building, ship, etc.) sink into the ground or water. **5** (of swelling etc.) be reduced, become less prominent. **6** (of a person) settle into a comfortable position (*subsided into a chair*). □ **sub·sid·ence** /-ˈsaidəns, ˈsʌbsədəns/ *noun* [Latin *subsidere* (as SUB-, *sidere* settle, related to *sedere* sit)]

sub·sidi·ary /səbˈsɪdieri, səbˈsɪdʒɜri/ ● *adjective* **1** serving to assist or supplement; auxiliary. **2** subordinate, secondary. ● *noun* (*pl.* **-aries**) **1** a company whose controlling interest is owned by a parent company. **2** a subsidiary thing or person; an accessory. [Latin *subsidiarius* (as SUBSIDY)]

sub·sid·ize /ˈsʌbsɪˌdaiz/ *transitive verb* (also esp. *Brit.* **-ise**) **1** reduce the cost of (a commodity or service) by subsidy (*government-subsidized housing*). **2** support (an organization, activity, person, etc.) by grants of money. **3** support financially in an indirect way (*our customers pay more to subsidize the high cost of rent here*). **4** pay money to secure the assistance or co-operation of (a person, organization, country, etc.). □ **sub·sid·iz·a·tion** *noun* **sub·sid·ized** *adjective*

sub·sidy /ˈsʌbsɪdi/ *noun* (*pl.* **-ies**) **1** money granted by a government to producers of certain goods to enable them to sell the goods to the public at a low price, to compete with foreign competition, or to avoid laying off employees. **2** money granted by a government to keep down the price of a service or commodity considered to be essential. **3** money granted to a charity, arts group, or other undertaking held to be in the public interest. **4** any grant or contribution of money. **5** money paid by one country to another in return for military, naval, or other aid. **6** *hist.* **a** a parliamentary grant to the sovereign for the needs of the state. **b** a tax levied on a particular occasion. [Anglo-French *subsidie* from Latin *subsidium* assistance]

sub·sist *intransitive verb* **1** (often foll. by *on*) maintain or support oneself; be sustained or kept alive (*manages to subsist on a meagre salary*). **2** remain in being; continue to exist. **3** (foll. by *in*) reside or exist in; be attributable to. □ **sub·sist·ent** *adjective* [Latin *subsistere* stand firm (as SUB-, *sistere* set, stand)]

sub·sist·ence *noun* **1** the means of supporting life; a livelihood. **2** the production of a sufficient quantity of goods required to sustain one's own existence or to support one's household, without producing a sufficient surplus for trade (also *attributive*: *subsistence farming*). **3 a** a minimal standard of living; a basic level of existence. **b** the income required to provide a minimal level of existence (also *attributive*: *subsistence wage*). **4** the state or an instance of subsisting.

subsistence level *noun* **1** the level of income required to provide no more than the bare necessities of life and to maintain a basic standard of living. **2** a basic standard of living.

sub·soil ● *noun* the layer of soil lying immediately under the surface soil (opp. TOPSOIL). ● *transitive verb* plow (land) deep enough to cut into the subsoil. □ **sub·soil·er** *noun*

sub·sonic *adjective* pertaining to, capable of, or designating speeds less than that of sound. □ **sub·sonic·ally** *adverb*

subsp. *abbreviation* (pl. **subspp.**) subspecies.

sub·space *noun* **1** *Math.* a space that is wholly contained in another space, or whose points or elements are all in another space. **2** (in science fiction) = HYPERSPACE.

sub·special·ty *noun* (pl. **-ties**) a secondary specialty within a branch of esp. science or medicine. □ **sub·special·ize** *intransitive verb* (also esp. *Brit.* **-ise**). **sub·special·ist** *noun*

sub·species *noun* (pl. same) *Biol.* a morphologically distinct subdivision of a species, esp. one geographically or ecologically isolated from other such subdivisions. □ **sub·specif·ic** *adjective*

sub·stance *noun* **1** the essential esp. solid matter of which a physical thing consists or is made. **2** a particular kind of material having a definite chemical composition and usu. uniform properties. **3** esp. *N Amer.* an intoxicating or narcotic chemical or drug, esp. an illegal one (*controlled substance*). **4 a** the content or inward nature of a thing as opposed to its superficial appearance or form (*this magazine is strong on style but weak on substance*). **b** steadiness or strength of character (*a man of substance*). **5 a** the essential point or theme conveyed in a work of fiction, account, argument, etc.; the actual meaning or gist. **b** concrete evidence (*his argument lacks substance; there is no substance to these rumours*). **6** wealth and possessions. **7** *Philos.* the essential nature underlying phenomena, which is subject to changes and accidents. □ **in substance 1** in reality. **2** generally; apart from details. [Old French from Latin *substantia* (as SUB-, *stare* stand)]

substance abuse *noun* esp. *N Amer.* the excessive use or misuse of any esp. addictive substance for its narcotic or stimulant effects; drug or alcohol abuse.

substance P *noun Biochem.* a polypeptide thought to be involved in the synaptic transmission of nerve impulses, esp. pain impulses.

sub·stan·dard *adjective* **1** of less than the required or normal quality or size; inadequate, inferior (*substandard housing*). **2** (of language) non-standard.

sub·stan·tial *adjective* **1** of real importance or value (*made a substantial contribution*). **2 a** of ample or considerable size or amount (*a substantial price increase*). **b** (of a meal or portion of food) ample and filling; nourishing. **3** of solid structure or build; stout (*a substantial house; a man of substantial stature*). **4** commercially successful; wealthy. **5** having substance or truth; essential, real (*substantial evidence*). □ **sub·stan·ti·al·ity** *noun* **sub·stan·tial·ly** *adverb*

sub·stan·ti·ate /səbˈstanʃɪˌeɪt/ *transitive verb* prove the truth of (a charge, statement, claim, etc.); demonstrate or verify by evidence. □ **sub·stan·ti·a·tion** *noun* [medieval Latin *substantiare* give substance to (as SUBSTANCE)]

sub·stan·tive /ˈsʌbstəntɪv/ ● *adjective* (also /səbˈstantɪv/) **1 a** having a firm or solid basis; important, significant. **b** of substantial extent or amount; considerable. **2** *Law* relating to rights and duties as opposed to forms of procedure. **3** having separate and independent existence. **4** *Grammar* (esp. of a verb, specifically the verb 'to be') expressing existence. **5** (of a dye) not needing a mordant. ● *noun Grammar* = NOUN. □ **sub·stan·tive·ly** *adverb* esp. *Grammar* [Old French *substantif -ive*, or Late Latin *substantivus* (as SUBSTANCE)]

sub·station *noun* **1** an outlet or establishment subordinate to a principal station (*postal substation*). **2** a station at which the high voltage of an electrical current from a generating station is reduced so that it is suitable for supply to consumers.

sub·stitu·ent /sʌbˈstɪtjʊənt/ *Chem.* ● *adjective* (of a group of atoms) replacing another atom or group in a compound, esp. replacing hydrogen in an organic compound. ● *noun* such a group. [Latin *substituere substituent-* (as SUBSTITUTE)]

sub·sti·tute ● *noun* **1 a** (also *attributive*) a thing that is or may be used in place of another, often to serve the same function but with a slightly different effect. **b** an artificial substance used as an alternative to a natural substance (*salt substitute*). **2 a** a person who is available or is used to perform the duties of another, esp. temporarily, such as during a holiday or illness. **b** a substitute teacher. **3** *Grammar* a word, such as a pronoun, that can be used in place of another. ● *verb* **1 a** *transitive* (often foll. by *for*) use or insert (a person or thing) in place of another (*substitute the new piece for the broken one; I'm going to substitute the rookie for our injured player*). **b** *intransitive* act as a substitute. **2** *transitive* disputed (usu. foll. by *with, by*) replace (a person or thing) with another. ¶ The use of *substitute* with the prepositions *by* or *with* should be avoided in standard English. The example *substitute dairy milk with soya milk* can be reworded as *substitute soya milk for dairy milk* (see sense 1 of the verb above). **3** *transitive Chem.* replace (an atom or group in a molecule) with another. □ **sub·sti·tut·able** *adjective* **sub·sti·tut·abil·ity** *noun* **sub·sti·tu·tion** *noun* **sub·sti·tu·tion·al** *adjective* **sub·sti·tu·tion·ary** *adjective* **sub·sti·tu·tive** *adjective* [Latin *substitutus* past participle of *substituere* (as SUB-, *statuere* set up)]

substitute teacher *noun N Amer.* a teacher who replaces another who is unable to teach because of illness etc.

sub·strate /ˈsʌbstreɪt/ *noun* **1** *Geol.* a layer of soil, earth, clay, or rock beneath the surface. **2** *Biol.* **a** the surface or material on which any particular organism grows. **b** the substance upon which an enzyme acts. **3** an underlying surface or foundation of a structure or development. [anglicized from SUBSTRATUM]

sub·strat·um /ˈsʌbˌstratəm, -ˌstreɪtəm/ *noun* (pl. **sub·strata**) **1** a foundation or basis (*the substratum of truth*). **2** = SUBSTRATE 1, 2. **3** *Linguistics* elements or features of a language identified as being relics of, or due to the influence of, an earlier extinct language. [modern Latin, past participle of Latin *substernere* (as SUB-, *sternere* strew): compare STRATUM]

sub·struc·ture *noun* an underlying or supporting structure.

sub·sume /səbˈsuːm, -ˈsjuːm/ *transitive verb* (often foll. by *in* or *under*) **1** include (a thing) in a larger group, class, or category; incorporate, absorb. **2** bring (a term, idea, category, etc.) into or under the heading of a broader one. □ **sub·sump·tion** *noun* [medieval Latin *subsumere* (as SUB-, *sumere sumpt-* take)]

sub·surface ● *noun* that which lies immediately below the surface of something, esp. the stratum or strata below the earth's surface. ● *adjective* existing, lying, or operating beneath the surface of earth, water, etc.

sub·system *noun* a self-contained system within a larger system.

sub·ten·ant *noun* a person who leases a property from a tenant. □ **sub·ten·ancy** *noun*

sub·tend *transitive verb* **1 a** (of a line, arc, figure, etc.) form (an angle) at a particular point when its extremities are joined at that point. **b** (of an angle or chord) have bounding lines or points that meet or coincide with those of (a line or arc). **2** *Bot.* (of a bract etc.) extend under so as to embrace, support, or enfold. [Latin *subtendere* (as SUB-, *tendere* stretch)]

sub·ter·fuge /ˈsʌbtəˌfjuːdʒ/ *noun* **1** a deceitful statement or action resorted to in an attempt to avoid blame, justify an argument, conceal something, etc. **2** the practice or policy of employing subterfuges. [French *subterfuge* or Late Latin *subterfugium* from Latin *subterfugere* escape secretly, from *subter* beneath + *fugere* flee]

sub·termin·al *adjective* nearly at the end.

sub·terran·ean /ˌsʌbtəˈreɪnɪən/ *adjective* **1** existing, occurring, or done under the earth's surface. **2** existing or kept out of sight; secret, concealed. □ **sub·terran·eous·ly** *adverb* [Latin *subterraneus* (as SUB-, *terra* earth)]

sub·text *noun* **1** an underlying, often distinct, theme in a piece of

Vowels: a *cat* ɑ *arm* e *bed* ɜr *her* ɜː *deux* ə *ago* ɪ *sit* i *cosy* iː *feed* ɒ *hot* ɔ *pore* ɔː *no* ʌ *run* ʊ *put*

writing, music, movie, or conversation. **2** the underlying theme of an event or period in history (*the sociological subtext of the Cold War*).
□ **sub·text·ual** *adjective*

sub·title ● *noun* **1** a secondary or additional title of a literary work, article, etc. **2 a** a translation or transcription of the dialogue of a movie printed at the bottom of the screen. **b** a caption explaining the plot of a silent movie. ● *transitive verb* provide (a book, movie, etc.) with a subtitle or subtitles. □ **sub·titled** *adjective*

subtle /ˈsʌtəl/ *adjective* (**subtler**, **subtlest**) **1 a** difficult to perceive or detect; not easily grasped or understood (*a subtle distinction*). **b** operating or performed imperceptibly or secretly (*we must try a subtle approach*). **2** (of scent, colour, etc.) faint, delicate, elusive (*subtle perfume*). **3 a** capable of making fine distinctions; perceptive; acute (*a subtle mind*). **b** cleverly or skilfully designed; elaborate, ingenious. **4** cunning or clever; crafty, wily. **5** devious, insidious. □ **subtly** *adverb* [Old French *sotil* from Latin *subtilis*]

subtle·ty /ˈsʌtəlti/ *noun* (*pl.* **-ties**) **1** something subtle. **2** a fine distinction or argument. **3** the quality or state of being subtle.

sub·tonic *noun Music* the note below the tonic, the seventh note of the diatonic scale of any key.

sub·total *noun* the total of one part of a group of figures to be added.

sub·tract *verb* **1** *transitive* (often foll. by *from*) deduct (a quantity or number) from another. **2** *intransitive* perform the arithmetical operation of subtraction (*do you know how to subtract?*). **3** *transitive* remove (a portion or thing) from another. □ **sub·trac·tion** *noun* **sub·tract·ive** *adjective* [Latin *subtrahere subtract-* (as SUB-, *trahere* draw)]

sub·trade *noun N Amer.* a specialist, such as an electrician or plumber, hired by a general contractor to perform part of a building job.

sub·tra·hend /ˈsʌbtrəˌhend/ *noun Math.* a quantity or number to be subtracted (*compare* MINUEND). [Latin *subtrahendus* gerundive of *subtrahere*: see SUBTRACT]

sub·tropic·al *adjective* **1** of or relating to the subtropics. **2** resembling or characteristic of the subtropics.

sub·tropics *plural noun* the regions adjacent to or bordering on the tropics.

sub·type *noun* a subordinate type, esp. a type included within a broader or more general type.

subu·late /ˈsʌbjələt, -leit/ *adjective Bot. & Zool.* slender and tapering to a point. [Latin *subula* awl]

sub·unit *noun* a distinct component, esp. each of two or more polypeptide chains in a large protein.

sub·urb *noun* **1** a residential district lying just beyond or just within the boundaries of a city. **2** (in *pl.*) the outlying part of a city or town composed of such districts. [Old French *suburbe* or Latin *suburbium* (as SUB-, *urbs urbis* city)]

sub·urban *adjective* **1** of, belonging to, situated in, or carried on in the suburbs. **2** *derogatory* having characteristics regarded as typical of the residents, architecture, or life of the suburbs; perceived as lacking the excitement, diversity, culture, or sophistication of residents or life in the city. □ **sub·urban·ite** *noun* **sub·urban·ize** *transitive verb* (also esp. *Brit.* **-ise**). **sub·urban·iz·a·tion** *noun* [Latin *suburbanus* (as SUBURB)]

suburban sprawl *noun N Amer.* the rapid and uncontrolled expansion of suburban areas.

sub·urb·ia *noun* **1** the suburbs collectively. **2** *derogatory* the social and cultural aspects of suburban life or residents.

sub·ven·tion *noun* a grant of money from a government etc.; a subsidy. [Old French from Late Latin *subventio -onis* from Latin *subvent-* assist (as SUB-, *venire* come)]

sub·ver·sive ● *adjective* (of a person, organization, activity, etc.) seeking to subvert (esp. a government). ● *noun* a subversive person; a revolutionary. □ **sub·ver·sive·ly** *adverb* **sub·ver·sive·ness** *noun*

sub·vert *transitive verb* esp. *Politics* overturn, overthrow, or upset (religion, government, morality, etc.). □ **sub·ver·sion** *noun* **sub·vert·er** *noun* [Old French *subvertir* or Latin *subvertere* (as SUB-, *vertere vers-* turn)]

sub·way *noun* **1** esp. *N Amer.* **a** an esp. urban railway most parts of which are underground. **b** a subway train or car. **c** a station on a subway line. **2 a** a tunnel beneath a road etc. **b** an underground passage for pipes, cables, etc.

sub·woof·er *noun* a loudspeaker component designed to reproduce very low bass frequencies.

sub·zero *adjective* (esp. of temperature) lower than zero.

sub·zone *noun* a subdivision of a zone.

suc- *prefix* assimilated form of SUB- before *c*.

suc·ceed *verb* **1** *intransitive* **a** (often foll. by *in*, *at*) accomplish one's purpose; have success; prosper (*succeeded in her ambition*). **b** (of a plan etc.) be successful. **2 a** *transitive* follow in order; come next after (*night succeeded day*). **b** *intransitive* (foll. by *to*) come next, be subsequent. **3** *intransitive* (often foll. by *to*) become the rightful or subsequent holder of an inheritance, office, title, property, etc. (*succeeded to the throne*). **4** *transitive* take over an office, property, inheritance, etc. from (*succeeded his father; succeeded the manager*). □ **nothing succeeds like success** one success leads to others. □ **suc·ceed·er** *noun* [Old French *succeder* or Latin *succedere* (as SUB-, *cedere cess-* go)]

succès de scandale /sʊkˌsei də skɑˈdal/ *noun* a book, play, etc. having great success because of its scandalous nature or associations. [French, lit. 'success of scandal']

succès d'estime /sʊkˌsei desˈtiːm/ *noun* a critical as opposed to a popular or commercial success. [French, lit. 'success of opinion or regard']

succès fou /sʊkˌsei ˈfuː/ *noun* a success marked by enthusiasm; a great success. [French, lit. 'crazy success']

suc·cess *noun* **1** the accomplishment of an aim; a favourable outcome (*their efforts met with success*). **2** the attainment of wealth, fame, or position (*spoiled by success*). **3** a thing or person that turns out well. [Latin *successus* (as SUCCEED)]

suc·cess·ful *adjective* **1** having or resulting in success. **2** prosperous; having wealth or status. □ **suc·cess·ful·ly** *adverb* **suc·cess·ful·ness** *noun*

suc·ces·sion *noun* **1 a** the process of following in order; succeeding. **b** a series of things or people in succession. **2 a** the right of succeeding to an office, inheritance, the throne, etc. **b** the act or process of so succeeding. **c** those having such a right. **3** *Ecology* the process by which a plant or animal community successively gives way to another until a stable climax community is reached (*compare* SERE³). **4 a** the rotation of crops. **b** the continuous cultivation of a crop throughout a season by successive sowings or plantings. **5** *Geol.* **a** a sequence of fossil forms representing an evolutionary series. **b** a group of strata representing a single chronological sequence. □ **in quick succession** following one another at short intervals. **in succession** one after another, without intervention. **in succession to** as the successor of. □ **suc·ces·sion·al** *adjective*

suc·ces·sive *adjective* following one after another. □ **suc·ces·sive·ly** *adverb*

suc·ces·sor *noun* (often foll. by *to*) a person who or thing which succeeds another in an office, function, or position.

successor state *noun* a state resulting from the partition of a previously existing country.

success story *noun* **1** a rise from poverty, insignificance, etc. to success. **2** such a successful person, thing, or venture.

suc·cinct /səˈsɪŋkt, səkˈsɪŋkt/ *adjective* briefly expressed; terse, concise. ¶ Though objected to by some, the pronunciation /səˈsɪŋkt/ is much more frequent than /səkˈsɪŋkt/ in Canada. □ **suc·cinct·ly** *adverb* **suc·cinct·ness** *noun* [Latin *succinctus* past participle of *succingere* tuck up (as SUB-, *cingere* gird)]

suc·cin·ic acid /sʌkˈsɪnɪk/ *noun Chem.* a crystalline dibasic acid derived from amber etc. □ **suc·cin·ate** /ˈsʌksɪˌneit/ *noun* [French *succinique* from Latin *succinum* amber]

succor *US var. of* SUCCOUR.

suc·co·tash /ˈsʌkəˌtaʃ/ *noun US* a dish of corn and lima beans boiled together. [Narragansett *msiquatash*]

Succoth *var. of* SUKKOT.

suc·cour (*US* **suc·cor**) ● *noun* aid; assistance, esp. in time of need. ● *transitive verb* assist or aid (esp. a person in danger or distress). [Old French *socours* from medieval Latin *succursus* from Latin *succurrere* (as SUB-, *currere curs-* run)]

suc·cu·bus /ˈsʌkjʊbəs/ *noun* (*pl.* **suc·cu·bi** /-ˌbai/) a female demon believed to have sexual intercourse with sleeping men. [Late Latin *succuba* prostitute, medieval Latin *succubus* from *succubare* (as SUB-, *cubare* lie)]

suc·cu·lent /ˈsʌkjʊlənt/ ● *adjective* **1** juicy; palatable. **2** *informal* desirable. **3** *Bot.* (of a plant, its leaves, or stems) thick and fleshy. ● *noun Bot.* a succulent plant, esp. a cactus. □ **suc·cu·lence** *noun* **suc·cu·lent·ly** *adverb* [Latin *succulentus* from *succus* juice]

suc·cumb /səˈkʌm/ *intransitive verb* (usu. foll. by *to*) **1** be forced to give way; be overcome (*succumbed to temptation*). **2** die as the result of a disease, wound, etc. (*succumbed to his injuries*). [Old French *succomber* or Latin *succumbere* (as SUB-, *cumbere* lie)]

uː mood ai my əi pipe au brown ʌu house ei day ɔi boy ã franglais ã Canadien ɔ̃ Brayon   (*see over for consonants*)

suc·cus·sion /səˈkʌʃən/ *noun* vigorous shaking, esp. in the preparation of a homeopathic remedy. □ **suc·cuss** *transitive verb* [Latin *succutere succuss-* (as SUB-, *cutere* = *quatere* 'shake')]

such ● *adjective* **1** (often foll. by *as*) of the kind or degree in question or under consideration (*such a person; such people; people such as these*). **2** (usu. foll. by *as to* + infin. *or that* + clause) so great; in such high degree (*not such a fool as to believe them; had such a fright that he fainted*). **3** of a more than normal kind or degree (*we had such an enjoyable evening; such foul language*). **4** of the kind or degree already indicated, or implied by the context (*there are no such things; such is life*). **5** *Law or formal* the aforesaid; of the aforesaid kind. ● *pronoun* **1** the thing or action in question or referred to (*such were his words; such was not my intention*). **2 a** *Commerce or informal* the aforesaid thing or things; it, they, or them (*those without tickets should purchase such*). **b** similar things; suchlike (*brought sandwiches and such*). □ **as such** as being what has been indicated or named (*a stranger is welcomed as such; there is no theatre as such*). **such-and-such** ● *adjective* (often foll by *a*) of a particular kind but not needing to be specified (*on such-and-such date; such-and-such a company*). ● *noun* a person or thing of this kind. **such as 1** of a kind that; like (*a person such as we all admire*). **2** for example (*insects, such as moths and bees*). **3** those who (*such as don't need help*). **such as it is** despite its shortcomings (*you are welcome to it, such as it is*). **such a one 1** (usu. foll. by *as*) such a person or such a thing. **2** *archaic* some person or thing unspecified. **such that** in such a manner that. [Old English *swilc, swylc* from Germanic: compare LIKE[1]]

such·like *informal* ● *adjective* of such a kind. ● *noun* things, people, etc. of such a kind.

Suchou see SUZHOU.

Suchow see XUZHOU.

suck ● *verb* **1** *transitive* draw (a fluid) into the mouth by contracting the lip muscles etc. to make a partial vacuum. **2** *transitive & intransitive* **a** draw milk or other fluid from or through (the breast etc. or a container). **b** extract juice from (a fruit) by sucking. **3** *transitive* **a** draw sustenance, knowledge, or advantage from (a book etc.). **b** imbibe or gain (knowledge, advantage, etc.) as if by sucking. **4 a** *transitive* apply the lips and mouth to and perform a sucking action on (the thumb etc.). **b** *transitive & intransitive* hold (a candy etc.) in the mouth. **5** *intransitive* esp. *N Amer. slang* be very bad, disagreeable, or disgusting. **6** *intransitive* make a sucking action or sound (*sucking at his pipe*). **7** *intransitive* (of a pump etc.) make a gurgling or drawing sound. **8** *transitive* (usu. foll. by *down, in*) engulf, smother, or drown in a sucking movement. **9** *transitive & intransitive* draw in some direction, esp. by producing a vacuum. **10** *transitive* (often foll. by *off*) *coarse slang* perform cunnilingus or esp. fellatio on. ● *noun* **1** the act or an instance of sucking, esp. the breast. **2** the drawing action or sound of a whirlpool etc. **3** (often foll. by *of*) a small draught of liquor. **4** *Cdn* a crybaby or sore loser; a person who refuses to participate or go along, esp. out of spite; a feeble, self-pitying person (see also SOOK). **5** *Cdn* a person who behaves obsequiously to those in authority, esp. a child. □ **give suck** *archaic* (of a mother, dam, etc.) suckle. **go suck an egg** see EGG[1]. **suck back** *N Amer. slang* drink thirstily. **suck dry 1** exhaust the contents of (a bottle etc.) by sucking. **2** exhaust (a person's sympathy, resources, etc.) as if by sucking. **suck in 1** absorb. **2** = sense 8 of *verb*. **3** draw in (the cheeks, the abdomen, etc.). **4** (usu. in *passive*) take in; cheat or deceive. **5** involve (a person) in an activity etc., esp. against his or her will. **suck it up** *N Amer. slang* accept a hardship. **suck up 1** (often foll. by *to*) *informal* behave obsequiously esp. for one's own advantage. **2** absorb. **suck wind** (or **air**) *N Amer.* gasp for air loudly after strenuous physical exertion. [Old English *sūcan*, = Latin *sugere*]

suck·er ● *noun* **1 a** a person or thing that sucks. **b** a sucking pig, newborn whale, etc. **2** *informal* **a** a gullible or easily deceived person. **b** (foll. by *for*) a person especially susceptible to. **3** esp. *N Amer. informal* a thing not specified by name (*I can't fix the sucker!*). **4** *N Amer. informal* a usu. round, flat hard candy on a small stick, held in the hand and sucked. **5 a** a rubber cup etc. that adheres to a surface by suction. **b** an organ enabling an organism to cling to a surface by suction. **6** *Bot.* a shoot springing from the rooted part of a stem, from the root at a distance from the main stem, from an axil, or occasionally from a branch. **7 a** any of various chiefly N American freshwater fishes of the family Catastomidae, related to carp, having a conformation of the lips which suggest that they feed by suction. **b** any of various fish that has a suctorial disc for adhering to surfaces. **8 a** the piston of a suction pump. **b** a pipe through which liquid is drawn by suction. ● *verb* **1** *transitive* esp. *N Amer. informal* fool, trick. **2** *Bot.* **a** *transitive* remove suckers from. **b** *intransitive* produce suckers. □ **there's a sucker born every minute** gullible people are not difficult to find.

sucker punch *noun* *N Amer.* an unexpected punch or blow. □ **sucker-punch** *transitive verb*

suck·hole esp. *Cdn & Austral. coarse slang* ● *noun* a sycophant. ● *intransitive verb* (**-holed, -holing**) behave obsequiously.

suckle *verb* **1** *transitive* feed (young) from the breast or udder. **2** *intransitive* feed by sucking the breast etc. □ **suck·ler** *noun* [Middle English, prob. back-formation from SUCKLING]

suck·ling *noun* an unweaned child or animal.

suck-up *noun* *N Amer. informal* a person who sucks up to a person in authority etc.; a sycophant.

sucky *adjective* (**suck·i·er, suck·i·est**) *slang* **1** *N Amer.* bad. **2** *Cdn* whiny, like a crybaby. □ **suck·i·ness** *noun*

suc·ra·lose /ˈsuːkrəloːs/ *noun* an artificial sweetener, synthetic chlorinated sucrose. [alteration of SUCROSE]

Sucre[1] /ˈsuːkreɪ/ the judicial capital and seat of the judiciary of Bolivia; pop. (est. 2001) 193,873. It is situated in the Andes, at an altitude of 2 700 m (8,860 ft.).

Sucre[2] /ˈsuːkreɪ/ **An·tonio José de** (1795–1830), Venezuelan revolutionary leader, president of Bolivia 1826–8. He served as Bolívar's chief of staff, liberating Ecuador (1822), Peru (1824), and Bolivia (1825) from the Spanish; the first president of Bolivia, he resigned following a Peruvian invasion (1828), and was later assassinated.

suc·rose /ˈsuːkroːs/ *noun* *Chem.* common sugar, a disaccharide obtained from sugar cane, sugar beet, etc. [French *sucre* SUGAR]

suc·tion ● *noun* **1** the act or an instance of sucking. **2 a** the production of a partial vacuum by the removal of air etc. in order to force in liquid etc. or procure adhesion. **b** the force produced by this process (*suction keeps the lid on*). ● *transitive verb* draw etc. using suction; suck. [Late Latin *suctio* from Latin *sugere suct-* SUCK]

suction cup *noun* a usu. rubber concave disc which can be made to adhere to a smooth surface by suction.

suction pump *noun* a pump for drawing liquid through a pipe into a chamber emptied by a piston.

suc·tor·ial /sʌkˈtɔːriəl/ *adjective* *Zool.* **1** adapted for or capable of sucking. **2** having a sucker for feeding or adhering. [modern Latin *suctorius* (as SUCTION)]

Sudan /suːˈdan/ (also **the Sudan**) **1** a country in NE Africa south of Egypt, with a coastline on the Red Sea; pop. (est. 2002) 37,090,298; capital, Khartoum. **2** a vast region of North Africa, extending across the width of the continent from the southern edge of the Sahara to the tropical equatorial zone in the south. The northern part of the region is known as the Sahel. □ **Sudan·ese** /ˌsuːdəˈniːz/ [Arabic *sūdān* (pl. of *sūdā* black), = country of the blacks]

su·dar·ium /suːˈderiəm/ *noun* (pl. **su·dar·ia**) **1** a cloth for wiping the face. **2** *Catholicism* = VERONICA 2. [Latin, = napkin, from *sudor* sweat]

suda·tor·ium /ˌsuːdəˈtɔːriəm/ *noun* (pl. **suda·tor·ia**) esp. *Rom. Hist.* **1** a hot-air or steam bath. **2** a room where such a bath is taken. [Latin, neuter of *sudatorius*, from *sudare* sweat]

Sud·bury a city in north central Ontario, about 125 km west of North Bay, now officially named Greater Sudbury; pop. (2001) 155,219. Situated near extensive sources of nickel, it lies at the centre of Canada's largest mining region. □ **Sud·bur·ian** /sʌdˈberiən, -ˈbəriən/ *noun* [*Sudbury* in Suffolk, England, birthplace of the wife of CPR superintendent J. Worthington *c.*1883]

sud·den *adjective* occurring or done unexpectedly or without warning; abrupt, hurried, hasty (*a sudden storm; a sudden departure*). □ **all of a sudden** unexpectedly; hurriedly; suddenly. **on a sudden** *archaic* suddenly. □ **sud·den·ly** *adverb* **sud·den·ness** *noun* [Old French *soudain* from Late Latin *subitanus* from Latin *subitaneus* from *subitus* sudden]

sudden death *noun* an extra period or session of play to decide a tied game etc., in which the winner is the first to take the lead (often *attributive: sudden-death overtime*).

sudden infant death syndrome *noun* *Med.* the unexplained death of a baby while sleeping. Abbr.: **SIDS**. *Also called* CRIB DEATH.

Su·deten·land /suːˈdeɪtənˌland/ an area in the northwest part of the Czech Republic, on the border with Germany. Allocated to the new state of Czechoslovakia after the First World War, it became an object of Nazi expansionist policies because of its large German population, and was ceded to Germany as a result of the Munich Agreement of September 1938. The area was returned to Czechoslovakia in 1945.

sudor·if·ic /ˌsuːdəˈrɪfɪk/ ● *adjective* (of a drug) causing sweating. ● *noun* a sudorific drug. [modern Latin *sudorificus* from Latin *sudor* sweat]

Consonants: b *but*   d *dog*   f *few*   g *get*   h *her*   j *yes*   k *cat*   l *leg*   m *man*   n *no*   p *pen*   r *red*   s *sit*

Sudra /ˈsuːdrə/ *noun* a member of the worker caste, lowest of the four Hindu castes. [Sanskrit *śūdra*]

suds ● *plural noun* **1** froth of soap and water. **2** *N Amer. informal* beer.
● *verb* **1** *intransitive* form suds. **2** *transitive* lather, cover, or wash in soapy water. □ **sudsy** *adjective* [originally = fen waters etc., of uncertain origin: compare Middle Dutch, Middle Low German *sudde*, Middle Dutch *sudse* marsh, bog, prob. related to SEETHE]

suds·er *noun N Amer. slang* a soap opera.

sue *verb* (**sues**, **sued**, **suing**) **1** *transitive & intransitive Law* institute legal proceedings against (a person). **2** *intransitive* (often foll. by *to*, *for*) *Law* make application to a law court for redress. **3** *transitive & intransitive* entreat (a person). **4** *intransitive* (often foll. by *for*) make entreaty for (*sued for peace*). **5** *transitive* (often foll. by *out*) make a petition in a law court for and obtain (a writ, pardon, etc.). □ **suer** *noun* [Anglo-French *suer* from Old French *siu-* etc. stem of *sivre* from Latin *sequi* follow]

suede /sweid/ *noun* (often *attributive*) **1** leather, orig. kidskin, with the flesh side rubbed to make a velvety nap. **2** a woven fabric resembling suede. [French (*gants de*) *Suède* (gloves of) Sweden]

suet /ˈsuːɪt/ *noun* the hard white fat on the kidneys or loins of oxen, sheep, etc., used to make dough etc. □ **suety** *adjective* [Anglo-French from Old French *seu* from Latin *sebum* tallow]

suete /swet/ *noun Cdn* (*Cape Breton*) a very strong southeasterly wind in the west coastal areas of the Cape Breton Highlands. [Acadian French, corruption of French *sud-est* 'southeast']

Sueto·nius /suːəˈtoːnɪəs/ (full name Gaius Suetonius Tranquillus) (AD *c*.69–*c*.150), Roman biographer and historian. His surviving works include *Lives of the Caesars*, covering the first 12 Roman emperors from Julius Caesar to Domitian.

suet pudding *noun* a pudding of flour, sugar, etc., and suet, usu. boiled or steamed.

Suez, Isthmus of /ˈsuːez/ an isthmus between the Mediterranean and the Red Sea, connecting Egypt and Africa to the Sinai peninsula and Asia. The port of Suez lies in the south, at the head of the Gulf of Suez, an arm of the Red Sea. The isthmus is traversed by the Suez Canal.

Suez Canal a shipping canal connecting the Mediterranean at Port Said with the Red Sea. Constructed between 1859 and 1869, it is 171 km (106 miles) long, providing the shortest route for sea traffic between Europe and Asia. It was closed between 1967 and 1975 as a consequence of the Six Day War.

Suez crisis a conflict following the nationalization of the Suez Canal, which had been neutral under British control, by President Nasser of Egypt in 1956. Britain, France, and Israel allied themselves to regain control, landing troops after Nasser's rejection of an ultimatum. Pressure from the US and USSR and criticism from many other countries, however, forced the withdrawal of forces. For his role in resolving the crisis, Lester Pearson, Canada's Secretary of State for External affairs, was awarded the 1957 Nobel Peace Prize.

suf- *prefix* assimilated form of SUB- before f.

suf·fer *verb* **1** *intransitive* undergo pain, grief, damage, etc. (*suffers acutely*; *your reputation will suffer*; *suffers from neglect*). **2** *transitive* undergo, experience, or be subjected to (pain, loss, grief, defeat, change, etc.) (*suffered intense pain*). **3** *transitive* put up with; tolerate. **4** *intransitive* (usu. foll. by *to* + infin.) *archaic* allow. ▪ **not suffer fools gladly** refuse to be patient with people one considers foolish, stupid, etc. □ **suf·fer·able** *adjective* **suf·fer·er** *noun* **suf·fer·ing** *noun* [Anglo-French *suffrir* from Latin *sufferre* (as SUB-, *ferre* bear)]

suf·fer·ance *noun* absence of objection rather than genuine approval; tolerance (*Charles was only here on sufferance*).

suf·fice /səˈfaɪs/ *intransitive verb* (often foll. by *for*, or *to* + infin.) be enough or adequate (*that will suffice for our purpose*; *suffices to prove it*). □ **suffice** (**it**) **to say** I shall content myself with saying. [Old French *suffire* (*suffis-*) from Latin *sufficere* (as SUB-, *facere* make)]

suf·fi·cien·cy /səˈfɪʃənsi/ *noun* (pl. **-cies**) **1** (often foll. by *of*) an adequate amount or adequate resources. **2** the condition or quality of being sufficient; adequacy.

suf·fi·cient /səˈfɪʃənt/ *adjective* sufficing, adequate, enough (*is sufficient for a family*; *didn't have sufficient funds*). □ **suf·fi·cient·ly** *adverb*

sufficient condition *noun Logic* a condition without which another condition cannot exist, and which in itself is sufficient for the other condition to exist.

suf·fix ● *noun* a verbal element added at the end of a word to form a derivative, e.g. *-ation*, *-fy*, *-ing*, *-itis*. ● *transitive verb* append, esp. as a suffix. □ **suf·fix·a·tion** *noun* [*suffixum*, *suffixus* past participle of Latin *suffigere* (as SUB-, *figere* fix- fasten)]

suf·fo·cate /ˈsʌfəkeit/ *verb* **1** *transitive* choke or kill by stopping breathing, esp. by pressure, fumes, etc. **2** *transitive* (often foll. by *by*, *with*) produce a choking or breathless sensation in, esp. by excitement, terror, etc. **3** *intransitive* be or feel suffocated or breathless. **4** *transitive* *informal* restrict, stifle. □ **suf·fo·cat·ing** *adjective* **suf·fo·cat·ing·ly** *adverb* **suf·fo·ca·tion** *noun* [Latin *suffocare* (as SUB-, *fauces* throat)]

Suf·folk[1] /ˈsʌfək/ a county of E England, on the coast of East Anglia; county town, Ipswich.

Suf·folk[2] /ˈsʌfək/ *noun* a breed of black-faced sheep. [SUFFOLK[1]]

Suffolk Punch see PUNCH 2.

suf·fra·gan /ˈsʌfrəgən/ ● *adjective* **1 a** designating a bishop in relation to his or her archbishop or metropolitan (*bishop suffragan*). **b** designating the see of such a bishop in relation to that of his or her archbishop or metropolitan. **2** *Anglicanism* designating a bishop appointed to help a diocesan bishop in the administration of a diocese; an auxiliary bishop. ● *noun* a suffragan bishop. [Anglo-French & Old French, representing medieval Latin *suffraganeus* assistant (bishop), from Latin *suffragium* (see SUFFRAGE): originally of a bishop summoned to vote in synod]

suf·frage /ˈsʌfrɪdʒ/ *noun* **1 a** the right of voting in political elections (*full adult suffrage*). **b** a view expressed by voting; a vote (*gave their suffrages for and against*). **c** opinion in support of a proposal etc. **2** (esp. in *pl.*) *Christianity* **a** a prayer made by a priest in the liturgy. **b** a short prayer made by a congregation esp. in response to a priest. [Latin *suffragium*, partly through French *suffrage*]

suf·fra·gette /sʌfrəˈdʒet/ *noun hist.* a woman engaged in esp. militant activity in favour of women's suffrage, esp. in the early 20th c.

suf·fra·gist /ˈsʌfrədʒɪst/ *noun* esp. *hist.* a person who advocates the extension of the suffrage, esp. to women. □ **suf·fra·gism** *noun*

suf·fuse /səˈfjuːz/ *transitive verb* **1** (of colour, moisture, etc.) spread from within to colour or moisten (*a blush suffused her cheeks*). **2** cover with colour etc. **3** spread throughout; fill (*a fragrance suffused the air*). □ **suf·fu·sion** *noun* [Latin *suffundere suffus-* (as SUB-, *fundere* pour)]

Sufi /ˈsuːfi/ *noun* (pl. **Sufis**) a member of any of various spiritual orders within Islam characterized by asceticism and mysticism. □ **Sufic** *adjective* **Suf·ism** *noun* [Arabic *ṣūfī*, perhaps from *ṣūf* wool (from the wool garment worn)]

sug- *prefix* assimilated form of SUB- before g.

sug·ar ● *noun* **1 a** a sweet crystalline substance obtained from various plants, esp. the sugar cane and sugar beet, used in cooking, confectionery, brewing, etc.; sucrose. **b** foods containing esp. refined sugar (*eat less sugar and more fresh fruit*). **2** *Chem.* any of a group of soluble usu. sweet-tasting crystalline carbohydrates found esp. in plants, e.g. glucose, and also in milk and blood. **3** *N Amer. informal* darling, dear (used as a term of address). **4** sweet words; flattery. **5** anything comparable to sugar encasing a pill in reconciling a person to what is unpalatable. **6** *slang* a narcotic drug, esp. heroin or LSD (taken on a lump of sugar). **7** *N Amer.* = MAPLE SUGAR. ● *interjection* expressing exasperation etc. ● *verb* **1** *transitive* sweeten with sugar. **2** *transitive* make (one's words, meaning, etc.) more pleasant or welcome. **3** *transitive* coat with sugar (*sugared almond*). **4** *intransitive* (in full **sugar off**) *N Amer.* make maple syrup or maple sugar by collecting and boiling maple sap. □ **sugar the pill** see PILL[1]. □ **sugar·less** *adjective* [Old French *sukere* from Italian *zucchero* prob. from medieval Latin *succarum* from Arabic *sukkar*]

sugar apple *noun* = SWEETSOP.

sugar beet *noun* a beet, *Beta vulgaris*, from which sugar is extracted.

sugar bush *noun N Amer.* a grove of sugar maples.

sugar camp *noun N Amer.* the buildings in a sugar bush where sugaring takes place.

sugar cane *noun* any perennial tropical grass of the genus *Saccharum*, esp. *S. officinarum*, with tall stout jointed stems from which sugar is extracted.

sugar-coat *transitive verb* (often as **sugar-coated** *adjective*) **1** cover or enclose (food) in sugar. **2** make superficially attractive. □ **sugar-coating** *noun*

sugar cookie *noun N Amer.* a sweet and rich plain cookie made from flour, sugar, butter, etc.

sugar cube *noun* a small compact cube of sugar crystals for dissolving in tea etc.

sugar daddy *noun slang* an elderly man who lavishes gifts on a young person esp. in return for sexual favours.

sugar house *noun* = SUGAR SHACK.

sugar·ing *noun* **1** (also **sugaring off**) *N Amer.* the making of maple

---

t *top* v *voice* w *we* z *zoo* ʃ *she* ʒ *vision* θ *thin* ð *this* ŋ *ring* x *loch* tʃ *chip* dʒ *jar*   (*see over for vowels*)

syrup or maple sugar by collecting and boiling the sap from esp. the sugar maple. **2** a method of removing unwanted hair by applying to the skin a sticky sugar mixture, which is then peeled off together with the hair.

sugaring-off party *noun N Amer.* a party in a sugar bush or sugar shack to celebrate sugaring.

sugar·loaf *noun* **1** a conical moulded mass of sugar. **2** (often *attributive*) anything with this shape, as a hill or mountain.

Sugar Loaf Mountain a rocky peak situated to the northeast of Copacabana Beach, in Rio de Janeiro, Brazil. It rises to a height of 390 m (1,296 ft.).

sugar lump *noun* = SUGAR CUBE.

sugar maple *noun* a N American maple, *Acer saccharum*, from the sap of which maple sugar and maple syrup are made.

sugar pie *noun Cdn* esp. (*Que.*) an open-faced or lattice-topped pie with a filling of brown or maple sugar mixed with cream and baked.

sugar plum *noun archaic* a small round candy of flavoured boiled sugar.

sugar rush *noun* a sudden but short-lived increase in energy, sometimes also accompanied by feelings of euphoria, caused by ingestion of simple sugars which raise the blood sugar level quickly.

sugar shack *noun N Amer.* **1** a building in which maple sap is boiled in making maple syrup or sugar. **2** esp. *Que.* a usu. small establishment in a sugar bush serving maple-flavoured dishes and other traditional fare.

sugar snap *noun* (in full **sugar snap pea**) a variety of pea eaten whole including the pod.

sugar water *noun* a thin syrup of sugar dissolved in water.

sugary *adjective* **1 a** containing esp. a high proportion of sugar. **b** resembling sugar. **2** excessively sweet or esp. sentimental. **3** falsely sweet or pleasant (*sugary compliments*). □ **sugar·i·ness** *noun*

sugg. *abbreviation* suggested.

sug·gest /sə'dʒest, sɒg-/ *transitive verb* **1** (often foll. by *that* + clause) propose (a theory, plan, or hypothesis) (*suggested to them that they should wait; suggested a different plan*). **2 a** cause (an idea, memory, association, etc.) to present itself; evoke (*poem suggests peace*). **b** hint at (*his behaviour suggests guilt*). □ **suggest itself** (of an idea etc.) come into the mind. [Latin *suggerere suggest-* (as SUB-, *gerere* bring)]

sug·gest·ible *adjective* open to suggestion; easily swayed. □ **sug·gest·ibil·ity** *noun*

sug·ges·tion *noun* **1** the act or an instance of suggesting; the state of being suggested. **2** a theory, plan, etc., suggested (*made a helpful suggestion*). **3** a slight trace; a hint (*a suggestion of garlic*). **4** *Psych.* **a** the insinuation of a belief etc. into the mind. **b** such a belief etc.

sug·gest·ive *adjective* **1** (usu. foll. by *of*) conveying a suggestion; evocative. **2** (esp. of a remark, joke, etc.) indecent, lewd; suggesting sex. □ **sug·gest·ive·ly** *adverb* **sug·gest·ive·ness** *noun*

Su·harto /sʊ'hɑːrtɔ/ (**Raden** (b.1921), Indonesian leader and general, president 1968–98.

Sui /sweɪ/ a dynasty which ruled in China AD 581–618, unifying the country and preparing the ground for the cultural flowering of the succeeding Tang dynasty.

sui·cid·al *adjective* **1** inclined to commit suicide. **2** of or concerning suicide. **3** self-destructive; fatally or disastrously rash. □ **sui·cid·al·ly** *adverb*

sui·cide ● *noun* **1 a** the intentional killing of oneself. **b** a person who commits suicide. **2** a self-destructive action or course (*political suicide*). **3** (*attributive*) *Military* designating a highly dangerous or deliberately suicidal operation etc. (*a suicide mission*). ● *intransitive verb* commit suicide. [modern Latin *suicida, suicidium* from Latin *sui* of oneself]

suicide bomber *noun* a person who deliberately commits suicide in attempting to destroy an enemy target, usu. by detonating bombs strapped to his or her body. □ **suicide bomb** *noun* **suicide bombing** *noun*

suicide pact *noun* an agreement between two or more people to commit suicide together.

suicide squeeze *noun see* SQUEEZE *noun* 7b.

suicide squeeze bunt *noun Baseball* a sacrifice bunt attempted while executing a suicide squeeze.

sui gen·er·is /suːi 'dʒenərɪs/ *adjective* of its own kind; unique. [Latin]

sui juris /suːi 'dʒʊərɪs/ *adjective Law* of age; independent. [Latin]

suint /swɪnt/ *noun* the natural grease in sheep's wool. [French from *suer* sweat]

suit ● *noun* **1 a** a set of outer clothes of matching material for men, consisting usu. of a jacket, pants, and sometimes a waistcoat. **b** a similar set of clothes for women usu. having a skirt instead of pants. **c** (esp. in *combination*) a set of clothes for a special occasion, occupation, etc. (*playsuit; bathing suit*). **2 a** any of the four sets (esp. spades, hearts, diamonds, clubs) into which a pack of cards is divided. **b** a player's holding in a suit (*his strong suit was clubs*). *See also* LONG SUIT 1, STRONG SUIT 1. **c** *Bridge* one of the suits as proposed trumps in bidding, frequently as opposed to no trumps. **3** a lawsuit. **4 a** a petition esp. to a person in authority. **b** the process of courting a woman (*paid suit to her*). **5** (usu. foll. by *of*) a set of armour, sails, etc. **6** *slang* a business executive. ● *verb* **1** *transitive* go well with (a person's figure, features, character, etc.); become. **2** *transitive & intransitive* meet the demands or requirements of; satisfy; agree with (*does not suit all tastes; can change the date if it doesn't suit*). **3** *transitive* make fitting or appropriate; accommodate; adapt (*suited her style to her audience*). □ **follow suit** *see* FOLLOW. **suit the action to the word** carry out a promise or threat at once. **suit oneself 1** do as one chooses. **2** find something that satisfies one. **suit up** *N Amer.* dress in clothing designed for a particular activity. [Old French *si(e)ute* from fem. past participle of a Romanic alteration of Latin *sequi* 'follow']

suit·able *adjective* (usu. foll. by *to, for*) well fitted for the purpose; appropriate. □ **suit·abil·ity** *noun* **suit·able·ness** *noun* **suit·ably** *adverb*

suit·case *noun* a usu. oblong case for carrying clothes etc., having a handle and a flat zippered or hinged lid. □ **live out of a suitcase** live temporarily with one's belongings still packed, esp. when travelling. □ **suit·case·ful** *noun* (*pl.* **-fuls**).

suit coat *noun N Amer.* a jacket worn as part of a suit.

suite /swiːt/ *noun* **1** a set of things belonging together, esp.: **a** a set of rooms in a hotel etc. for use by one person or group of people. **b** *N Amer.* a set of offices in an office building. **c** a set of furniture, usu. a sofa and armchairs etc., or table and chairs of the same design. **2** = APARTMENT 1a. **3** *Music* **a** a set of instrumental compositions, originally in dance style, to be played in succession. **b** a set of selected pieces from an opera, musical, ballet, etc., arranged to be played as one instrumental work. **4** a set of people in attendance; a retinue. **5** *Computing* a set of programs with a uniform design and the ability to share data. [French (as SUIT)]

suit·ed *adjective* appropriate; well fitted (*not suited to be an engineer*).

suit·ing *noun* cloth used for making suits.

suit·or *noun* **1** a man seeking to marry a specified woman; a wooer. **2** a plaintiff or petitioner in a lawsuit. **3** a prospective buyer of a business or corporation; the maker of a takeover bid. [Anglo-French *suitour* from Latin *secutor -oris*, from *sequi secut-* 'follow']

suk (also **sukh**) *var. of* SOUK.

Su·kar·no /suː'kɑːrnɔ/ (**Ach·mad** (1901–70), Indonesian leader, president 1945–67. A co-founder of the Indonesian National Party (1927), he was Indonesian leader during the Japanese occupation (1942–5) and led the struggle for independence, which was formally granted by the Netherlands in 1949; from the mid-1950s his dictatorial tendencies aroused opposition, and he was ousted by Suharto in 1967.

Sukho·tai /ˌsʊkə'taɪ/ (also **Sukho·thai**) a town in NW central Thailand; pop. (2002) 36,800. It was formerly the capital of an independent state of the same name, which flourished from the mid-13th to the mid-14th c. The ruins of the old city lie to the west of the modern town.

suki·yaki /ˌsʊki'jɒki/ *noun* a Japanese dish of sliced meat simmered with vegetables and sauce. [Japanese]

Suk·kot /sʊ'kɒt, 'sʌkəθ/ *noun* (also **Suc·coth**) the Jewish autumn harvest and thanksgiving festival commemorating the sheltering of the Israelites in the wilderness. [Hebrew *sukkōt* pl. of *sukkāh* thicket, hut]

Suk·kur /'sʌkər/ a city in SE Pakistan, on the Indus River; pop. (est. 1998) 329,000. Nearby is the Sukkur Barrage (completed in 1932), a dam constructed across the Indus which directs water from the river through irrigation channels to a large area of the Indus valley.

Sula·wesi /ˌsʊlə'weɪsi/ a mountainous island in the Greater Sunda group in Indonesia, situated to the east of Borneo; chief town, Ujung Pandang. It is noted as the habitat of numerous endemic species. The island was formerly called Celebes.

Sulay·ma·ni·yah /ˌsʊlɪmə'niːə/ (in full **As Sulaymaniyah** /as/, also **Sulai·ma·ni·ya**) a town in NE Iraq, in the mountainous region of S Kurdistan; pop. (2002) 643,200. Founded in 1781, it was an important trade centre on the route between Baghdad and Tabriz.

Vowels: a *cat* ɑ *arm* e *bed* ɜr *her* ɜː *deux* ə *ago* ɪ *sit* i *cosy* iː *feed* ɒ *hot* ɔ *pore* oː *no* ʌ *run* ʊ *put*

sul·cate /ˈsʌlkeit/ *adjective* grooved, fluted, channelled. [Latin *sulcatus*, past participle of *sulcare* furrow (as SULCUS)]

sul·cus /ˈsʌlkəs/ *noun* (*pl.* **sulci** /-saɪ/) *Anat.* a groove or furrow, esp. on the surface of the brain. [Latin]

Sulei·man I /ˈsuːlɪmən, ˌsuːleɪˈmɒn/ (also **Soli·man** or **Soly·man** /ˈsɒlɪmən/) (*c.*1494–1566), sultan of the Ottoman Empire 1520–66. Known as 'Suleiman the Magnificent', he was noted for his cultural achievements, and the Ottoman Empire reached its fullest extent under his rule.

sul·fa *var. of* SULPHA.

sulfa·nil·a·mide *var. of* SULPHANILAMIDE.

sul·fate *var. of* SULPHATE etc.

sul·fur *var. of* SULPHUR etc.

sulk ● *intransitive verb* indulge in a period of sullen esp. resentful silence or aloofness from others; be sulky. ● *noun* (also in *pl.*, prec. by *the*) a period of sulking (*has been in a sulk*; *got the sulks*). □ **sulk·er** *noun* [perhaps back-formation from SULKY]

sulky ● *adjective* (**sulk·i·er**, **sulk·i·est**) sullen, morose, or silent, esp. from resentment or ill temper. ● *noun* (*pl.* **-ies**) a light two-wheeled horse-drawn vehicle for one, esp. used in harness racing. □ **sulk·i·ly** *adverb* **sulk·i·ness** *noun* [perhaps from obsolete *sulke* hard to dispose of, of unknown origin]

Sulla /ˈsʌlə/ (full name Lucius Cornelius Sulla Felix) (138–78 BC), Roman general and politician. After concluding the war with Mithridates VI in the east in 85, Sulla invaded Italy in 83, ruthlessly suppressing his opponents; he was elected dictator in 82, and implemented constitutional reforms in favour of the Senate.

sul·len *adjective* **1** morose, resentful, sulky, unforgiving, unsociable. **2** dismal, melancholy (*a sullen sky*). □ **sul·len·ly** *adverb* **sul·len·ness** *noun* [16th-c. alteration of Middle English *solein* from Anglo-French from *sol* SOLE³]

Sul·li·van ▸ **1** Sir Ar·thur (Sey·mour) (1842–1900), English composer. His fame rests on the 14 light operas which he wrote in collaboration with the librettist W. S. Gilbert, including *The Mikado* (1885) and *The Gondoliers* (1889). **2** Ed·ward Vin·cent ('Ed') (1901–74), US television personality, who hosted the television variety program 'Toast of the Town' (1948–55), which later became the highly popular 'Ed Sullivan Show' (1955–71). **3** Louis (Henri) (1856–1924), US architect. He was an early pioneer of modern architecture, and is remembered for his dictum 'form follows function'.

sully *transitive verb* (**-lies**, **-lied**) **1** disgrace or tarnish (a person's reputation or character, a victory, etc.). **2** *literary* dirty; soil. [perhaps from French *souiller* (as SOIL²)]

Sully-Prudhomme /suˈli pruːˈdɒm/ **René Fran·çois Ar·mand** (pseudonym of René François Armand Prudhomme) (1839–1907), French poet. His early poems were sentimental, melancholy lyrics, as in the collection *Stances et poemes* (1865), while in his later works he attempted to turn abstract scientific and philosophical systems into epic verse, e.g. *La Justice* (1878) and *Le Bonheur* (1888); he was awarded the Nobel Prize for literature in 1901.

sul·pha *noun* (also **sul·fa**) any drug derived from sulphanilamide (often *attributive*: *sulpha drug*). [abbreviation]

sulpha·meth·ox·azole /ˌsʌlfəmeˈθɒksəzoːl/ *noun* (also **sulfa·meth·ox·azole**) a sulphonamide used to treat respiratory and urinary tract infections. [SULPHA + METHYL + OXY-² + AZO- + -OLE]

sulpha·nil·a·mide /ˌsʌlfəˈnɪləmaɪd/ *noun* (also **sulfa·nil·a·mide**) a colourless sulphonamide drug with antibacterial properties. [*sulphanilic* (SULPHUR, ANILINE) + AMIDE]

sul·phate (also **sul·fate**) ● *noun* a salt or ester of sulphuric acid. ● *transitive verb* (esp. as **sul·phat·ed** *adjective*) **1** combine with sulphur or sulphuric acid. **2** convert into a sulphate. □ **sul·pha·tion** *noun* [French *sulfate* from Latin *sulphur*]

sul·phide *noun* (also **sul·fide**) *Chem.* a binary compound of sulphur.

sul·phite *noun* (also **sul·fite**) *Chem.* a salt or ester of sulphurous acid. [French *sulfite* alteration of *sulfate* SULPHATE]

sul·phon·a·mide /sʌlˈfɒnəˌmaɪd/ *noun* (also **sul·fon·a·mide**) a substance derived from an amide of a sulphonic acid, able to prevent the multiplication of some pathogenic bacteria. [SULPHONE + AMIDE]

sul·phon·ate /ˈsʌlfəˌneɪt/ (also **sul·fon·ate**) *Chem.* ● *noun* a salt or ester of sulphonic acid. ● *transitive verb* convert into a sulphonate by reaction with sulphuric acid.

sul·phone /ˈsʌlfoːn/ *noun* (also **sul·fone**) an organic compound containing the SO₂ group united directly to two carbon atoms. □ **sul·phon·ic** /-ˈfɒnɪk/ *adjective* [German *Sulfon* (as SULPHUR)]

sul·phonyl·urea /ˌsʌlfənɪljuˈriːə/ *noun* (also **sul·fonyl·urea**) any of a group of compounds containing the group SO₂NHCONH, some of which are hypoglycemic drugs used to treat diabetes. [SULPHONE + -YL + UREA]

sulph·ox·ide /sʌlˈfɒksaɪd/ *noun* (also **sulf·ox·ide**) any organic compound containing the group SO joined to two carbon atoms. [SULPHUR + OXIDE]

sul·phur *noun* (also **sul·fur**) **1 a** a pale yellow non-metallic element having crystalline and amorphous forms, burning with a blue flame and a suffocating smell, and used in making gunpowder, matches, and sulphuric acid, in the vulcanizing of rubber, and as an antiseptic and fungicide. Symbol: **S**; at. no.: 16. **b** (*attributive*) like or containing sulphur. **2** the material of which hellfire and lightning were believed to consist. **3** any yellow butterfly of the family Pieridae. **4** a pale greenish-yellow colour. □ **sul·phury** *adjective* [Anglo-French *sulf(e)re*, Old French *soufre* from Latin *sulfur*, *sulp(h)ur*]

sulphur dioxide *noun* a colourless pungent gas formed by the burning of sulphur in air, used in manufacturing sulphuric acid and as a food preservative.

sul·phur·eous /sʌlˈfjʊrɪəs/ *adjective* (also **sul·fur·eous**) **1** of, like, or suggesting sulphur. **2** sulphur-coloured; yellow.

sul·phur·ic /sʌlˈfjʊrɪk/ *adjective* (also **sul·fur·ic**) *Chem.* containing hexavalent sulphur.

sulphuric acid *noun* a dense oily colourless highly acid and corrosive fluid much used in the chemical industry. *Chem.* formula: H₂SO₄.

sul·phur·ize /ˈsʌlfər̩aɪz/ *transitive verb* (also esp. *Brit.* **-ise**, also **sul·fur·ize**) impregnate, fumigate, or treat with sulphur, esp. in bleaching. □ **sul·phur·iz·a·tion** *noun*

sul·phur·ous /ˈsʌlfərəs/ *adjective* (also **sul·fur·ous**) **1 a** relating to or suggestive of sulphur, esp. in colour. **b** suggestive of burning sulphur, hellfire, etc.; fiery. **2** *Chem.* containing quadrivalent sulphur.

sulphurous acid *noun* an unstable weak acid used as a reducing and bleaching acid.

sulphur spring *noun* a spring impregnated with sulphur or its compounds.

Sul·pi·cian /sʌlˈpɪʃən/ *noun* a member of a Roman Catholic society of diocesan priests founded in Paris in 1641 and established in New France in 1657, concerned esp. with the training of priests. [from the church of Saint-*Sulpice* in Paris, the congregation's first seminary]

sul·tan *noun* **1 a** a Muslim sovereign. **b** (**the Sultan**) *hist.* the sultan of Turkey. **2** an absolute ruler. □ **sul·tan·ate** *noun* [French *sultan* or medieval Latin *sultanus* from Arabic *sulṭān* power, ruler, from *saluṭa* rule]

sul·tana /sʌlˈtɑːnə/ *noun* **1 a** a seedless raisin used in puddings, cakes, etc. **b** the small pale yellow grape producing this. **2** the mother, wife, concubine, or daughter of a sultan. [Italian, fem. of *sultano* = SULTAN]

sul·try *adjective* (**sul·tri·er**, **sul·tri·est**) **1** (of the atmosphere or the weather) hot or oppressive; close. **2** (of a person, character, etc.) passionate; sensual. □ **sul·tri·ly** *adverb* **sul·tri·ness** *noun* [obsolete *sulter* SWELTER]

Sulu Sea /ˈsuːluː/ a sea in the Malay Archipelago, encircled by the northeastern coast of Borneo and the western islands of the Philippines.

sum¹ ● *noun* **1** the total amount resulting from the addition of two or more items, facts, ideas, feelings, etc. (*the sum of two and three is five*; *the sum of their objections is this*). **2** a particular amount of money (*paid a large sum for it*). **3** an arithmetical problem (*could not work out the sum*). ● *transitive verb* (**summed**, **sum·ming**) find the sum of. □ **in sum** in brief. **sum up 1** (esp. of a judge) recapitulate or review the evidence in a case etc. **2** form or express an idea of the character of (a person, situation, etc.). **3** collect into or express as a total or whole. [Old French *summe* from Latin *summa* main part, fem. of *summus* highest]

sum² /sʊm/ *noun* (*pl.* **sumy**) the basic monetary unit of Uzbekistan. [Uzbek]

su·mac /ˈsuːmak/ *noun* (also **su·mach**) **1** any of various shrubs or trees of the genus *Rhus*, having cone-shaped clusters of reddish fruits. **2** the dried and ground leaves of this used in tanning and dyeing. **3** the fruits of the Mediterranean sumac, used as a spice, esp. in Middle Eastern cuisine. [Old French *sumac* or medieval Latin *sumac(h)* from Arabic *summāk*]

Su·ma·tra /sʊˈmɒtrə/ a large island of Indonesia, situated to the southwest of the Malay Peninsula, from which it is separated by the Strait of Malacca; chief city, Medan. □ **Su·ma·tran** *noun & adjective*

su·ma·trip·tan /suːməˈtrɪptan/ *noun* a generic drug used to relieve migraine headaches by constricting dilated blood vessels in the brain. [invented name]

Sumba /ˈsʊmbə/ (also called **Sandalwood Island**) an island of the Lesser Sunda group in Indonesia, lying to the south of the islands of Flores and Sumbawa; chief town, Waingapu.

Sum·bawa /sʊmˈbɒwə/ an island in the Lesser Sunda group in Indonesia, situated between Lombok and Flores.

sum·bitch noun US slang = SON OF A BITCH noun.

Sumer /ˈsuːmər/ an ancient region of SW Asia in present-day Iraq, comprising the southern part of Mesopotamia. It was the site in the 4th and 3rd millenniums BC of a thriving civilization of city states. Sumer joined with Akkad in the first half of the 2nd millennium BC to form the kingdom of Babylonia.

Sumer·ian /suːˈmeriən/ ● adjective of or relating to the early and non-Semitic element in the civilization of ancient Babylonia. ● noun **1** a member of the early non-Semitic people of ancient Babylonia. **2** the Sumerian language.

sumi-e /ˈsuːmieɪ/ noun a Japanese style of painting with brushes and ink. [Japanese sumi ink, blacking + e painting]

summa /ˈsuːmə/ noun (pl. **sum·mae** /-miː/) a summary of what is known of a subject. [Middle English from Latin: see SUM[1]]

summa cum laude /ˌsʊmə kʊm ˈlaʊdeɪ/ adverb & adjective esp. N Amer. (of a degree, diploma, etc.) of the highest standard; with the highest distinction. [Latin, = with highest praise]

sum·mar·ize transitive verb (also esp. Brit. **-ise**) make or be a summary of; sum up. □ **sum·mar·ist** noun **sum·mar·iz·er** noun

sum·mary ● noun (pl. **-ies**) a brief account; an abridgement. ● adjective **1** dispensing with needless details or formalities; brief (a summary account). **2** Law (of a trial etc.) without the customary legal formalities (summary justice). □ **sum·mar·i·ly** /səˈmerɪli/ adverb [Latin summarium from Latin summa SUM]

summary conviction noun a conviction made by a judge or magistrates without a jury.

summary conviction offence noun (also **summary offence**) Cdn a relatively minor criminal offence tried by a magistrate and without a jury or preliminary hearing (compare INDICTABLE OFFENCE).

summary jurisdiction noun the authority of a court to use summary proceedings and arrive at a judgment.

sum·ma·tion noun **1** the finding of a total or sum; an addition. **2** a summing-up. □ **sum·ma·tion·al** adjective **sum·ma·tive** adjective

sum·mer[1] ● noun **1** the warmest season of the year, in the northern hemisphere from June to August and in the southern hemisphere from December to February (see also INDIAN SUMMER). **2** the period from the summer solstice to the autumnal equinox. **3** the hot weather typical of summer. **4** (often foll. by of) the mature stage of life; the height of achievement, powers, etc. **5** (esp. in pl.) archaic a year (esp. of a person's age) (a child of ten summers). **6** (attributive) characteristic of or suitable for summer (summer clothes). ● verb **1** intransitive (usu. foll. by at, in) pass the summer. **2** transitive (often foll. by at, in) pasture (cattle). □ **sum·mer·less** adjective **sum·mery** adjective [Old English sumor]

sum·mer[2] noun a horizontal bearing beam, esp. one supporting joists or rafters. [Anglo-French sumer, somer pack horse, beam, Old French somier from Late Latin sagmarius from sagma from Greek sagma packsaddle]

summer camp noun esp. N Amer. a camp providing esp. outdoor recreational and sporting facilities during the summer, esp. for children.

summer·fallow /ˈsʌmərˌfaloː, -ˌfʊloː/ esp. Cdn ● noun agricultural land left fallow in the summer to allow moisture and nutrient levels to recover. ● transitive & intransitive verb lay (agricultural land) fallow during the summer.

summer house noun **1** a light building in a garden, park, etc. used for sitting in in fine weather. **2** a secondary residence occupied during the summer.

summer kitchen noun N Amer. an extra kitchen adjoining or separate from a house, used for cooking in hot weather.

Summer·land a district municipality in southern BC, situated on Okanagan Lake, north of Penticton; pop. (2001) 10,713. [so called because of the Okanagan Valley's warm, sunny climate]

summer pudding noun Cdn & Brit. a pudding of soft summer fruit encased in bread or sponge cake.

summer sausage noun N Amer. a dry or semi-dry sausage containing beef or pork, fermented and/or cooked and smoked to ensure good

keeping qualities. [originally produced in the winter for use in the summer]

summer savory noun see SAVORY[1].

summer school noun **1** esp. N Amer. a course of remedial or accelerating classes held in the summer. **2** a course of lectures, classes, etc. held during the summer.

Summer·side a city located on the southern shore of PEI, about 60 km west of Charlottetown; pop. (2001) 14,654. [Summerside House, the name of an inn, so called with reference to its position on the 'sunny side' of the island]

summer solstice noun the solstice at midsummer, at the time of the longest day, about 21 June in the northern hemisphere and 22 Dec. in the southern hemisphere; in Astronomy, the solstice in June.

summer squash noun see SQUASH[2] 1.

summer student noun **1** Cdn an esp. university student working at a job for the summer. **2** a university student attending lectures or working on a research fellowship during the summer.

summer theatre noun N Amer. **1** (also called **summer stock**) theatrical productions by a repertory company organized for the summer season, esp. at holiday resorts. **2** a theatre where such productions are put on.

summer·time noun the season or period of summer.

Summer Triangle noun the three bright stars, Vega, Altair, and Deneb, which are particularly conspicuous in the summer evening sky.

summer village noun Cdn (Alta.) a municipality having at least 60 parcels of land containing dwellings and fewer than 300 residents.

summing-up noun **1** a review of evidence and a direction given by a judge to a jury. **2** a recapitulation of the main points of an argument, case, etc.

sum·mit ● noun **1** the highest point, esp. of a mountain; the apex. **2** the highest degree of power, ambition, success, etc. **3** (in full **summit meeting, talks**, etc.) a discussion esp. between heads of government. ● transitive & intransitive verb Mountaineering reach the summit of (a mountain). [Old French somet, som(m)ete from som top, from Latin summum neuter of summus]

sum·mit·eer noun a participant in a summit meeting.

sum·mit·ry noun the practice of convening or holding summit meetings, or using them as a diplomatic device.

sum·mon transitive verb **1** call upon to appear, esp. as a defendant or witness in a law court. **2** (usu. foll. by to + infin.) call upon (summoned her to assist). **3** call together for a meeting or some other purpose (summoned the members to attend). **4** (often foll. by up) gather (courage, strength, energy, etc.) (summoned up her strength for the task). □ **sum·mon·able** adjective **sum·mon·er** noun [Old French somondre from Latin summonēre (as SUB-, monēre warn)]

sum·mons ● noun (pl. **sum·mons·es**) **1** an authoritative or urgent call to attend on some occasion or do something. **2 a** a call to appear before a judge or magistrate. **b** the writ containing such a summons. ● transitive verb esp. Law serve with a summons. [Old French somonce, sumunse from Latin summonita fem. past participle of summonēre: see SUMMON]

sum·mum bonum /ˌsʊməm ˈbɒnəm, ˈboː-/ noun the highest good, esp. as the end or determining principle in an ethical system. [Latin]

sumo /ˈsuːmoː/ noun a Japanese form of heavyweight wrestling in which a wrestler wins a bout by forcing his opponent outside a circle or making him touch the ground with any part of the body except the soles of the feet (also attributive: sumo wrestler). [Japanese]

sump noun **1** a pit, well, hole, etc. in which superfluous liquid collects in a basement, mine, cave, machine, etc. **2** a cesspool. [Middle English, = marsh, from Middle Dutch, Middle Low German sump, or (mining) German Sumpf, related to SWAMP]

sump pump noun a pump for removing waste water etc. from a sump.

sump·ter noun archaic a pack horse or other beast of burden. [Old French som(m)etier from Late Latin from Greek sagma -atos packsaddle: compare SUMMER[2]]

sump·tu·ary /ˈsʌmptʃuˌeri/ adjective relating to or denoting laws that limit private expenditure on food, clothing, and personal items (sumptuary laws). [Latin sumptuarius from sumptus cost, from sumere sumpt- take]

sump·tu·ous /ˈsʌmptʃuəs/ adjective rich, lavish, magnificent (a sumptuous setting). □ **sump·tu·os·ity** /-ˈɒsɪti/ noun **sump·tu·ous·ly** adverb **sump·tu·ous·ness** noun [Old French somptueux from Latin sumptuosus (as SUMPTUARY)]

Consonants:　b but　d dog　f few　g get　h her　j yes　k cat　l leg　m man　n no　p pen　r red　s sit

Sum·qayit /ˌsumkɒˈiːt/ an industrial city in E Azerbaijan, on the Caspian Sea; pop. (est. 2002) 279,200.

sum total *noun* = SUM *noun* 1.

Sumy /ˈsuːmi/ an industrial city in NE Ukraine, near the border with Russia; pop. (est. 2002) 288,200.

Sun. *abbreviation* Sunday.

sun ● *noun* 1 a the star around which the earth orbits and from which it receives light and warmth. **b** any similar star in the universe with or without planets. **2** the light or warmth received from the sun (*pull down the blinds and keep out the sun*). **3** *archaic* a day or a year. **4** *literary* a person or thing regarded as a source of glory, radiance, etc. **● *verb* (sunned, sun·ning) 1** *reflexive* bask in the sun. **2** *transitive* expose to the sun. **3** *intransitive* sun oneself. □ **beneath** (or **under**) **the sun** anywhere in the world. **in the sun** exposed to the sun's rays. □ **sun·less** *adjective* **sun·less·ness** *noun* **sun·like** *adjective* **sun·ward** *adjective & adverb* **sun·wards** *adverb* [Old English *sunne*, *sunna*]

sun-baked *adjective* dried or hardened or baked from the heat of the sun.

sun bath *noun* a period of exposing the body to the sun or a sun lamp.

sun·bathe *intransitive verb* bask in the sun, esp. to tan the body. □ **sun·bath·er** *noun*

sun·beam *noun* a ray of sunlight.

sun bear *noun* a small black bear, *Helarctos malayanus*, of SE Asia, with a light-coloured mark on its chest.

sun·bed *noun* *Brit.* = TANNING BED.

sun·belt *noun* a strip of territory receiving a high amount of sunshine, esp. (**the Sunbelt**), the region in the southern US stretching from California in the west to Florida in the east.

sun·bird *noun* any small bright-plumaged Old World bird of the family Nectariniidae, resembling a hummingbird.

sun·block *noun* a cream or lotion for protecting the skin from the sun.

sun·bonnet *noun* a bonnet of cotton etc. covering the neck and shading the face, esp. for children.

sun·burn ● *noun* inflammation of the skin caused by overexposure to the sun. ● *intransitive verb* suffer from sunburn. □ **sun·burned *adjective* (also **sun·burnt**).

sun·burst ● *noun* 1 something resembling the sun and its rays, e.g. an ornament, brooch, etc. **2** a sudden burst of sunshine, as from the sun appearing suddenly from behind clouds. **3** *Cdn* a trimming of fur around the hood of a parka. **● *adjective* 1** *Cdn* (of a parka or parka hood) trimmed with a sunburst. **2** resembling a sunburst in design, colour, etc.

sun·care *noun* the protection of the skin from damage by the sun.

sun·catch·er *noun* *N Amer.* an object made esp. of stained glass or coloured plastic hung in a window to sparkle in or refract incoming sunlight.

sun·dae *noun* a dish of ice cream topped with chocolate or butterscotch sauce, fruit, whipped cream, nuts, etc. [perhaps from SUNDAY]

Sunda Islands /ˈsʌndə/ a chain of islands in the southwestern part of the Malay Archipelago, consisting of two groups: the **Greater Sunda Islands**, which include Sumatra, Java, Borneo, and Sulawesi; and the **Lesser Sunda Islands**, which lie to the east of Java and include Bali, Sumbawa, Flores, Sumba, and Timor.

sun dance *noun* an annual ceremony held at midsummer by some Plains Aboriginal peoples, marked by several days of fasting, dancing, and induced visions.

Sun·dar·bans /ˈsundɑr͵bʌnz/ a region of swampland in the Ganges delta, extending from the mouth of the Hooghly River in West Bengal to that of the Tetulia in Bangladesh.

Sun·day ● *noun* the first day of the week, a Christian holiday and day of worship. ● *adverb* 1 on Sunday. **2** (**Sun·days**) on Sundays; each Sunday. [Old English *sunnandæg*, translation of Latin *dies solis*, Greek *hēmera hēliou* day of the sun]

Sunday best *noun* a person's best clothes, kept for use on Sundays and special occasions.

Sunday driver *noun* a person who drives chiefly on weekends, esp. slowly or unskilfully.

Sunday school *noun* **1** a school for the religious instruction of children on Sundays. **2** the members of such a school.

sun·deck *noun* **1** *N Amer.* a terrace or balcony positioned to catch the sun. **2** the upper deck of a steamer.

sun·der *transitive & intransitive verb* *archaic* or *literary* separate, sever. [Old English *sundrian*, from *āsundran* etc.]

Sun·der·land an industrial city in NE England, a port at the mouth of the Wear River; pop. (est. 2002) 180,700.

sun·dew *noun* any small insect-consuming bog plant of the family Droseraceae, esp. of the genus *Drosera* with hairs secreting drops of moisture.

sun·dial *noun* an instrument showing the time by the shadow of a pointer cast by the sun on to a graduated disc.

sun disc *noun* a winged disc, emblematic of the sun god.

sun dog *noun* a bright spot on a solar halo, frequently occurring in pairs on either side of the sun and prismatically coloured, caused by reflection of light by atmospheric ice crystals; a parhelion.

sun·down *noun* sunset.

sun·down·er *noun* **1** esp. *Brit. informal* an alcoholic drink taken at sunset. **2** *Austral.* a tramp who arrives at a sheep station etc. in the evening for food and shelter.

sun-drenched *adjective* **1** illuminated by sunshine. **2** (of a place) having very sunny weather.

sun·dress *noun* a sleeveless dress with a low neck and back, worn in hot weather.

sun-dried *adjective* dried by the sun, not by artificial heat.

sun·drops *noun* any of various plants of the genus *Oenothera* of the evening primrose family, with yellow flowers that open during the day, often grown in gardens.

sundry ● *adjective* various; several (*sundry items*). ● *noun* (*pl.* **-ries) (in *pl.*) items or oddments not mentioned individually. □ **all and sundry** everyone. [Old English *syndrig* separate, related to SUNDER]

sun·fish *noun* **1** any of various almost spherical fish, esp. a large ocean fish, *Mola mola*. **2** any of various small deep-bodied freshwater fishes of the family Centrarchidae, abundant in N America, and including the largemouth and smallmouth bass and the crappies.

sun·flower *noun* any very tall plant of the genus *Helianthus*, esp. *H. annus* with very large showy golden-rayed flowers, grown also for its seeds which yield an edible oil.

Sung¹ /suŋ/ (also **Song** /sɒŋ/) a dynasty that ruled in China AD 960–1279, a period of general prosperity, cultural flowering, and technological advance, marked by the first use of paper money and by advances in printing, firearms, shipbuilding, clockmaking, and medicine.

Sung² /sʌŋ/ **Al·fred** (born Sung Wang Moon) (b.1948), Chinese-born Canadian fashion designer.

sung *past participle of* SING.

sun·glass·es *plural noun* glasses tinted to protect the eyes from sunlight or glare. □ **sun·glassed** *adjective*

sun god *noun* the sun worshipped as a deity.

sun hat *noun* a hat designed to protect the head from the sun.

sun helmet *noun* *hist.* a helmet of cork etc. worn by explorers etc. in the tropics.

sunk *past and past participle of* SINK.

sunk·en *adjective* **1** that has been sunk. **2** beneath the surface; submerged. **3** (of the eyes, cheeks, etc.) hollow, depressed. **4** placed on a lower level than the surrounding area (*a sunken living room*).

sunk·er *noun* *Cdn* (*Nfld*) a reef or rocky shoal.

Sun King the nickname of Louis XIV of France.

sun-kissed *adjective* warmed or affected by the sun.

sun lamp *noun* **1** a lamp giving ultraviolet rays for an artificial suntan, therapy, etc. **2** a large lamp with a parabolic reflector used in filmmaking.

sun·light *noun* light from the sun. □ **sun·lit** *adjective*

Sunna /ˈsʌnə/ *noun* a traditional portion of Muslim law based on Muhammad's words or acts, accepted (together with the Quran) as authoritative by Muslims. [Arabic, = form, way, course, rule]

Sunni /ˈsuːni/ **● *noun* 1** one of the two main branches of Islam, commonly described as orthodox, and differing from the Shia in its understanding of the Sunna and in its rejection of Ali as Muhammad's first successor (*compare* SHIA). **2** (*pl.* same or **Sun·nis**) an adherent of this branch of Islam. **● *adjective* of or relating to Sunni.

sunny *adjective* (**sun·ni·er, sun·ni·est**) **1 a** bright with sunlight.

b exposed to or warmed by the sun. **2** cheery and bright in temperament. □ **sun·ni·ly** *adverb* **sun·ni·ness** *noun*

sunny side up *adjective* (of an egg) fried on one side only, with the unbroken yolk on the top.

sun parlour *noun N Amer.* = SUNROOM.

sun porch *noun N Amer.* an enclosed porch with more windows than exterior walls, designed to receive sunlight.

sun protection factor *noun see* SPF.

sun·ray *noun* **1** a sunbeam. **2** (in *pl.*) ultraviolet rays used therapeutically.

sun·rise *noun* **1** the sun's rising at dawn. **2** the coloured sky associated with this. **3** the time at which sunrise occurs.

sunrise industry *noun* a new and growing industry, esp. in electronics or telecommunications.

sun·roof *noun* a sliding part of the roof of a car that can be opened to let in air and sunlight.

sun·room *noun* a room with large windows, designed to receive sunlight.

sun·screen *noun* a cream or lotion rubbed on to the skin to protect it from the sun.

sun·set *noun* **1** the sun's setting in the evening. **2** the coloured sky associated with this. **3** the time at which sunset occurs. **4** the declining period of something. **5** (*attributive*) designating a provision under which an agency or program is to be disbanded or terminated at the end of a fixed period unless formally renewed (*sunset clause*).

sun·shade *noun* something that provides shade, as an awning or parasol.

sun·shine *noun* **1 a** the light of the sun. **b** an area lit by the sun. **c** the warmth of the sun. **2** fine weather. **3** cheerfulness; joy (*brought sunshine into her life*). **4** *informal* used as a friendly or sometimes threatening form of address. □ **sun·shiny** *adjective*

Sunshine Coast an informal name for the area along the southwestern coast of BC, north of Howe Sound on the Strait of Georgia. [with reference to the bright and pleasant weather along this section of the coast]

sun·spot *noun* one of the dark patches, changing in shape and size and lasting for varying periods, observed on the sun's surface.

sun·star *noun* any starfish of the genus *Solaster*, with many rays.

sun·stone *noun* a cat's-eye gem, esp. feldspar with embedded flecks of hematite etc.

sun·stroke *noun* acute prostration or collapse from the excessive heat of the sun.

sun·struck *adjective* **1** affected with sunstroke. **2** touched by the sun (*sunstruck glass*).

sun·suit *noun* any of various one- or two-piece suits worn (esp. by children) for play or leisure in warm weather.

sun·tan *noun* a brown colour of the skin caused by exposure to the sun (also *attributive: suntan lotion*). □ **sun·tanned** *adjective* **sun·tan·ning** *noun*

sun·trap *noun* a place sheltered from the wind and suitable for catching the sunshine.

sun-up *noun* esp. *N Amer.* sunrise.

sun visor *noun* **1** a fixed or movable shield at the top of a vehicle windshield to shield the eyes from the sun. **2** a half-moon shaped shade on an adjustable or elasticized headband, worn to protect the eyes from sunlight.

sun worshipper *noun* **1** a person who reveres the sun as a deity. **2** a person who sunbathes a great deal. □ **sun worship** *noun* **sun worshipping** *noun & adjective*

Sun Yat-sen /ˌsʊn jatˈsɛn/ (also **Sun Yixian** /ˌsʊn jiːˈʃiːˈan/) (1866–1925), Chinese Kuomintang leader, provisional president of the Republic of China 1911–12 and president of the Southern Chinese Republic 1923–5. Generally regarded in the West as the father of the modern Chinese state, he played a vital role in the successful revolution of 1911 in which the Manchu dynasty was overthrown; after 1923 he reorganized the Kuomintang along the lines of the Soviet Communist Party.

sup[1] ● *transitive verb* (**supped, sup·ping**) **1** take (soup, tea, etc.) by sips or spoonfuls. **2** esp. *Northern England informal* drink (alcohol). ● *noun* a sip of liquid. [Old English *sūpan*]

sup[2] *intransitive verb* (**supped, sup·ping**) (usu. foll. by *off, on*) *archaic* eat supper. [Old French *super, soper*]

sup- *prefix* assimilated form of SUB- before p.

super ● *adjective* **1** *informal* exceptional; splendid. **2** of or to an extreme or the highest degree, power, etc. ● *noun informal* **1** a superintendent. **2** *Theatre* a supernumerary actor. ● *interjection informal* expressing enthusiastic approval or assent. ● *adverb informal* extremely; excessively. [as SUPER-]

super- *combining form* forming nouns, adjectives, and verbs, meaning: **1** above, beyond, or over in place or time or conceptually (*superstructure; supernormal; superimpose*). **2** to a great or extreme degree (*superabundant; superhuman*). **3** extra good or large of its kind (*supertanker*). **4** of a higher kind, esp. in names of classificatory divisions (*superclass*). [from or after Latin *super-* from *super* above, beyond]

super·abound *intransitive verb* be very or too abundant.

super-absorb·ent *adjective* extremely absorbent.

super·abun·dant *adjective* abounding beyond what is normal or right. □ **super·abun·dance** *noun* **super·abun·dant·ly** *adverb*

super·annu·ate /ˌsuːpərˈanjuˌeit/ *transitive verb* **1** retire (a person) with a pension. **2** dismiss or discard as too old for use, work, etc. □ **super·annu·able** *adjective* [back-formation from SUPERANNUATED]

super·annu·at·ed /ˌsuːpərˈanjuˌeitəd/ *adjective* **1** retired because of age or disability. **2** too old for work or use; obsolete. [from medieval Latin *superannuatus* from Latin SUPER- + *annus* year]

super·annu·a·tion /ˌsuːpərˌanjuˈeiʃən/ *noun* **1** a pension paid to a retired person. **2** a regular payment made towards this by an employed person. **3** the process or an instance of superannuating.

Super Audio compact disc *noun proprietary* an audio recording format providing high-quality sound reproduction.

su·perb *adjective* **1** excellent; fine. **2** of the most impressive, splendid, grand, or majestic kind. □ **superb·ly** *adverb* **superb·ness** *noun* [French *superbe* or Latin *superbus* proud]

super·bike *noun* **1** a motorcycle with a nominal engine capacity of 750 cc or more. **2** a deluxe and often expensive model of bicycle.

Super Bowl *noun proprietary* (in American football) the deciding game played annually between the champions of the National Football Conference and the American Football Conference.

super·bug *noun* **1** a strain of bacteria that has become resistant to antibiotic drugs. **2** a microbe that is useful in biotechnology, esp. one which has been genetically engineered to enhance its usefulness for a particular purpose.

super·calen·der *transitive verb* give a highly glazed finish to (paper) by extra calendering.

super·car *noun* a high-performance sports car.

super·cargo *noun* (pl. **-goes**) an officer in a merchant ship managing sales etc. of cargo. [earlier *supracargo* from Spanish *sobrecargo* from *sobre* over + *cargo* CARGO]

super·charge *transitive verb* **1** (usu. foll. by *with*) charge (the atmosphere etc.) with energy, emotion, etc. **2** use a supercharger on (an internal combustion engine). □ **super·charged** *adjective*

super·char·ger *noun* a device supplying air or fuel to an internal combustion engine at above normal pressure to increase efficiency.

super·cili·ary /ˌsuːpərˈsɪliəri/ *adjective Anat.* of or concerning the eyebrow; over the eye. [Latin *supercilium* eyebrow (as SUPER-, *cilium* eyelid)]

super·cili·ous /ˌsuːpərˈsɪliəs/ *adjective* assuming an air of contemptuous indifference or superiority. □ **super·cili·ous·ly** *adverb* **super·cili·ous·ness** *noun* [Latin *superciliosus* (as SUPERCILIARY)]

super·class *noun* a taxonomic category between class and phylum.

super·clus·ter *noun Astronomy* a cluster of galaxies which themselves occur as clusters.

super·collid·er *noun* a collider in which superconducting magnets are used to accelerate particles to energies of millions of megavolts.

super·comput·er *noun* a powerful computer capable of dealing with complex problems. □ **super·comput·ing** *noun*

super·conduc·tiv·ity *noun Physics* the property of zero electrical resistance in some substances at very low absolute temperatures. □ **super·conduct·ing** *adjective* **super·conduct·ive** *adjective* **super·conduct·or** *noun*

super·contin·ent *noun Geol.* each of several large land masses thought to have divided to form the present continents in the geological past.

super·cool ● *verb Chem.* **1** *transitive* cool (a liquid) below its freezing point without solidification or crystallization. **2** *intransitive* (of a liquid) be cooled in this way. ● *adjective slang* very cool, relaxed, fine, etc.

Vowels: a *cat* ɑ *arm* e *bed* ɜr *her* ɜː *deux* ə *ago* ɪ *sit* i *cosy* iː *feed* ɒ *hot* ɔ *pore* oː *no* ʌ *run* ʊ *put*

super·crit·ic·al *adjective* **1** highly critical. **2** *Physics* of or relating to a mass of radioactive material in which the rate of a chain reaction increases over time.

super-duper *adjective informal* exceptional, super. [reduplication]

super·ego *noun* (*pl.* **-egos**) *Psych.* the part of the mind that acts as a conscience and responds to social rules.

super·eleva·tion *noun* the amount by which the outer edge of a curve on a road or railway is above the inner edge.

super·eroga·tion /ˌsuːpər̩erəˈɡeɪʃən/ *noun* the performance of more than duty requires. □ **super·eroga·tory** /-ɪˈrɒɡətɜri/ *adjective* [Late Latin *supererogatio* from *supererogare* pay in addition (as SUPER-, *erogare* pay out)]

super·family *noun* (*pl.* **-ilies**) a taxonomic category between family and order.

super·fat·ted *adjective* (of soap) containing extra fat.

super·feta·tion /ˌsuːpərfiːˈteɪʃən/ *noun* **1** *Med. & Zool.* a second conception during pregnancy giving rise to embryos of different ages in the uterus. **2** *Bot.* the fertilization of the same ovule by different kinds of pollen. **3** the accretion of one thing on another. [ultimately from Latin *superfetare* (as SUPER-, *fetus* FETUS)]

super·ficial /ˌsuːpərˈfɪʃəl/ *adjective* **1** of or on the surface; lacking depth (*a superficial knowledge; superficial wounds*). **2** swift or cursory (*a superficial examination*). **3** apparent but not real (*a superficial resemblance*). **4** (esp. of a person) having no depth of character or knowledge; shallow. **5** lacking substance or profundity; shallow (*the show had a very superficial plot*). **6** not involving a profound or serious issue; insignificant (*only superficial differences remain*). **7** *Commerce* (of a measure) involving the surface dimensions. □ **super·ficial·ity** /-ʃiˈalɪti/ *noun* (*pl.* **-ities**). **super·ficial·ly** *adverb* [Late Latin *superficialis* from Latin (as SUPERFICIES)]

super·ficies /ˌsuːpərˈfɪʃɪˌiːz/ *noun* (*pl.* same) *Math.* a surface. [Latin (as SUPER-, *facies* face)]

super·fine *adjective* **1** very fine; in very small granules (*superfine sugar*). **2** *Commerce* of extra quality.

super·fluid·ity *noun* the property of flowing without friction or viscosity, as in liquid helium below about 2.18 kelvins. □ **super·fluid** *noun & adjective*

super·fluity /ˌsuːpərˈfluːɪti/ *noun* (*pl.* **-ities**) **1** the state of being superfluous. **2** a superfluous amount or thing.

super·fluous /suːˈpɜrfluəs/ *adjective* more than enough, redundant, needless. □ **super·fluous·ly** *adverb* [Latin *superfluus* (as SUPER-, *fluere* to flow)]

super·fly *adjective informal* (of clothing or a person's appearance) bright and ostentatious.

super·giant *noun* a star of very great luminosity and size.

super giant slalom *noun Skiing* (also *informal* **super G**) a downhill event with a longer course and wider turns than a giant slalom.

super·glue ● *noun* any of various adhesives with an exceptional bonding capability. ● *transitive verb* (**-glues**, **-glued**, **-gluing** or **-glue·ing**) stick with superglue.

super·grass *noun Brit. informal* a police informer who implicates a large number of people.

super·group *noun* **1** a group made up of several related groups. **2 a** an exceptionally talented or successful rock group. **b** a rock group formed by star musicians from different groups.

super·heat *transitive verb Physics* **1** heat (a liquid) above its boiling point without vaporization. **2** heat (a vapour) above its boiling point (*superheated steam*). **3** heat to a very high temperature. □ **super·heat·er** *noun*

super·hero *noun* (*pl.* **-heroes**) a person or fictional character with extraordinary heroic attributes.

super·hetero·dyne /ˌsuːpərˈhetəroʊˌdaɪn/ ● *adjective* denoting or characteristic of a system of radio reception in which a local variable oscillator is tuned to beat at a constant ultrasonic frequency with carrier wave frequencies, making it unnecessary to vary the amplifier tuning and securing greater selectivity. ● *noun* a superheterodyne receiver. [SUPERSONIC + HETERODYNE]

super·high·way *noun N Amer.* a divided highway with two or more lanes in each direction.

super·human *adjective* **1** beyond normal human capability (*required a superhuman effort*). **2** higher than human (*a superhuman being*). □ **super·human·ly** *adverb*

super·impose *transitive verb* lay (a thing) on something else. □ **super·impos·able** *adjective* **super·impos·ition** *noun*

super·induce *transitive verb* introduce or induce in addition. □ **super·induc·tion** *noun*

super·intend *transitive & intransitive verb* **1** be responsible for the management or arrangement of (an activity etc.). **2** supervise (an institution, district, etc.). □ **super·intend·ence** *noun* **super·intend·ency** *noun* [ecclesiastical Latin *superintendere* (as SUPER-, INTEND), translation of Greek *episkopō*]

super·intend·ent ● *noun* **1 a** a person who superintends. **b** a director of an institution etc. **2** (in some Canadian municipal police forces) an officer ranking above staff inspector. **3** (in the Ontario Provincial Police) an officer ranking above inspector and below chief superintendent. **4** (in the Royal Newfoundland Constabulary) an officer ranking above inspector and below deputy chief. **5** (in the RCMP) an officer ranking above inspector and below chief superintendent. **6 a** (in the UK) a police officer above the rank of inspector. **b** (in the US) the head of a police department. **7** *N Amer.* a caretaker, esp. of an apartment building. **8** the chief administrator of a school division. ● *adjective* superintending.

Superior, Lake the largest and most northerly of the five Great Lakes, situated on the border between Canada and the US. With an area of 84 243 sq. km, it is the largest freshwater lake in the world. [so called with reference to the fact that its elevation is the highest among the Great Lakes]

su·peri·or ● *adjective* **1** in a higher position; of higher rank (*a superior officer; a superior court*). **2 a** above the average in quality etc. (*made of superior leather*). **b** having or showing a high opinion of oneself; supercilious (*had a superior air*). **3** (often foll. by *to*) **a** better or greater in some respect (*superior to its rivals in speed*). **b** above yielding, making concessions, paying attention, etc. (*is superior to bribery; superior to temptation*). **4** further above or out; higher, esp.: **a** *Astronomy* (of a planet) having an orbit further from the sun than the earth's. **b** *Zool.* (of an insect's wings) folding over others. **c** *Printing* (of figures or letters) placed above the line. **d** *Bot.* (of the calyx) above the ovary. **e** *Bot.* (of the ovary) above the calyx. ● *noun* **1** a person superior to another in rank, character, etc. **2** *Christianity* the head of a monastery or other religious institution (*Mother Superior; Father Superior*). **3** *Printing* a superior letter or figure. □ **su·peri·or·ly** *adverb* [Old French *superiour* from Latin *superior -oris*, comparative of *superus* that is above, from *super* above]

superior court *noun* (in Canada) the supreme court or courts of a province.

su·peri·or·ity *noun* the state of being superior.

superiority complex *noun Psych.* an undue conviction of one's own superiority to others.

super·jumbo *noun* an extremely large passenger aircraft, usu. containing between five hundred and one thousand seats.

su·perla·tive /suːˈpɜrlətɪv/ ● *adjective* **1** of the highest quality or degree (*superlative wisdom*). **2** *Grammar* (of an adjective or adverb) expressing the highest or a very high degree of a quality (e.g. *bravest, most fiercely*) (compare POSITIVE *adjective* 4b, COMPARATIVE *adjective* 3). ● *noun* **1** *Grammar* **a** the superlative expression or form of an adjective or adverb. **b** a word in the superlative. **2** something embodying excellence; the highest form of a thing. **3** (usu. in *pl.*) an expression of abundant praise. □ **su·perla·tive·ly** *adverb* **su·perla·tive·ness** *noun* [Old French *superlatif -ive* from Latin *superlatus* (as SUPER-, *latus* past participle of *ferre* take)]

super·lumin·al /ˌsuːpərˈluːmɪnəl/ *adjective Physics* of or having a speed greater than that of light. [SUPER- + Latin *lumen luminis* 'a light']

super·lun·ary /ˌsuːpərˈluːnɜri/ *adjective* **1** situated beyond the moon. **2** belonging to a higher world, celestial. [medieval Latin *superlunaris* (as SUPER-, LUNAR)]

super·man *noun* (*pl.* **-men**) **1** (esp. in Nietzschean philosophy) an ideal superior man of the future who achieves domination through integrity and creativity. **2** *informal* a man of exceptional strength or ability. [SUPER- + MAN, formed by G. B. Shaw after Nietzsche's German *Übermensch*]

super·mar·ket *noun* a large store selling foods, household goods, etc.

supermarket tabloid *noun* a tabloid newspaper sold in supermarkets, typically sensationalist and focusing on the lives of celebrities.

super·minis·ter *noun Cdn* a cabinet minister with responsibility for an important portfolio or a number of related portfolios.

super·model *noun* a highly-paid model employed in high-profile glamour modelling.

super·mom *noun N Amer. informal* a mother who fulfills all the duties of motherhood superlatively, esp. one who is also employed outside of the home.

su·per·nal /suːˈpɜːnəl/ *adjective* esp. *literary* **1** heavenly; divine. **2** of or concerning the sky. **3** lofty. □ **su·per·nal·ly** *adverb* [Old French *supernal* from Latin *supernus* from *super* above]

super·natant /ˌsuːpərˈneitənt/ esp. *Chem.* ● *adjective* floating on the surface of a liquid. ● *noun* a supernatant substance. [SUPER- + *natant* swimming, from Latin *natare* swim]

super·natur·al ● *adjective* attributed to or thought to reveal some force above the laws of nature; magical; mystical. ● *noun* (prec. *by the*) supernatural, occult, or magical forces, effects, etc.
□ **super·natur·al·ism** *noun* **super·natur·al·ist** *noun*
super·natur·al·ize *transitive verb* (also esp. *Brit.* **-ise**).
super·natur·al·ly *adverb* **super·natur·al·ness** *noun*

super·normal *adjective* beyond what is normal or natural.
□ **super·normal·ity** *noun*

super·nova *noun* (*pl.* **-novas** or **-novae**) *Astronomy* a star that suddenly increases very greatly in brightness because of an explosion ejecting most of its mass.

super·numer·ary /ˌsuːpərˈnuːmərˌeri, -njuː-/ ● *adjective* **1** in excess of the normal number; extra. **2** (of a person) engaged for extra work. **3** (of an actor) appearing on stage but not speaking. ● *noun* (*pl.* **-ies**) **1** an extra or unwanted person or thing. **2** a supernumerary actor. **3** a person engaged for extra work. [Late Latin *supernumerarius* (soldier) added to a legion already complete, from Latin *super numerum* beyond the number]

super·order *noun* *Biol.* a taxonomic category between order and class.

super·ordin·ate /ˌsuːpərˈɔːdɪnət/ ● *adjective* (usu. foll. by *to*) of superior importance or rank. ● *noun* **1** a superordinate person or thing; a superior. **2** *Linguistics* a word whose meaning implies or includes that of another. [SUPER-, after *subordinate*]

super·oxide *noun* a compound containing the anion O_2^-.

super·pose *transitive verb* (usu. foll. by *on*) esp. *Math.* place (a thing or a geometric figure) on or above something else, esp. so as to coincide.
□ **super·pos·ition** *noun*

super·power *noun* a state with supreme power and influence, esp. the US and, formerly, the USSR.

super·satur·ate *transitive verb* add to (esp. a solution) beyond saturation point. □ **super·satur·a·tion** *noun*

super·scribe *transitive verb* **1** write (an inscription) at the top of or on the outside of a document etc. **2** write an inscription over or on (a thing). □ **super·scrip·tion** *noun* [Latin *superscribere* (as SUPER-, *scribere* *script-* write)]

super·script ● *noun* a character, number, or symbol written or printed above the line and usu. to the right of another character (*compare* SUBSCRIPT *noun* 1). ● *adjective* written or printed above the line, esp. *Math.* (of a symbol) written above and to the right of another. [Latin *superscriptus* past participle of *superscribere*: see SUPERSCRIBE]

super·sede *transitive verb* **1 a** adopt or appoint another person or thing in place of. **b** set aside; cease to employ. **2** (of a person or thing) take the place of. □ **super·ses·sion** *noun* [Old French *superseder* from Latin *supersedēre* be superior to (as SUPER-, *sedēre* *sess-* sit)]

super·size ● *adjective* larger than average or standard sizes; extremely large. ● *noun* a thing which is extremely large, esp. a consumer product which is larger than standard sizes. ● *transitive verb* select or provide a larger portion than normal of (food).

Super Soaker *noun* *proprietary* a toy water gun into which air is pumped so as to eject a highly powered stream of water.

super·sonic *adjective* designating or having a speed greater than that of sound. □ **super·sonic·ally** *adverb*

super·sonics *plural noun* (treated as *sing.*) = ULTRASONICS.

super·star *noun* an extremely famous or renowned actor, film star, musician, etc. □ **super·star·dom** *noun*

super·state *noun* a powerful political state, esp. one formed from a federation of nations.

super·station *noun* a television station using satellite technology to broadcast over a very large area, esp. an entire continent.

super·sti·tion *noun* **1** irrational belief, esp. as based on fear of or reverence for the supernatural. **2** an irrational fear of the unknown or mysterious. **3** a practice, opinion, or religion based on these tendencies. **4** a widely held but unjustified idea of the effects or nature of a thing. □ **super·sti·tious** *adjective* **super·sti·tious·ly** *adverb* **super·sti·tious·ness** *noun* [Old French *superstition* or Latin *superstitio* (as SUPER-, *stare* *stat-* stand)]

super·store *noun* **1** a large supermarket selling a wide range of goods. **2** a very large store selling a particular type of merchandise (*appliance superstore*).

super·strat·um *noun* (*pl.* **-strata**) an overlying stratum.

super·struc·ture *noun* **1** the part of a building above its foundations. **2** a structure built on top of something else. **3** a concept or idea based on others. **4** the constructions above the upper deck of a ship. □ **super·struc·tur·al** *adjective*

super·tank·er *noun* a very large tanker ship.

super·terres·trial *adjective* **1** in or belonging to a region above the earth. **2** celestial.

super·title *noun* = SURTITLE.

super·tonic *noun* *Music* the note above the tonic, the second note of the diatonic scale of any key.

Super Tuesday *noun* *US* a day on which several states hold primary elections.

super·twist *adjective* designating varieties of liquid crystal display used in portable computers, in which to change state the plane of polarized light passing through the display is rotated by at least 180 degrees.

super·user *noun* a user of a computer system with special privileges needed to maintain and administer the system.

super·vene *intransitive verb* **1** occur as an interruption in or a change from some state. **2** ensue; follow closely on. □ **super·ven·ient** *adjective* **super·ven·tion** *noun* [Latin *supervenire* *supervent-* (as SUPER-, *venire* come)]

super VGA *abbreviation* see SVGA.

super·vise *transitive verb* **1** superintend, oversee the execution of (a task etc.). **2** oversee the actions or work of (a person). □ **super·vision** *noun* **super·visor** *noun* **super·visory** *adjective* [medieval Latin *supervidēre* *supervis-* (as SUPER-, *vidēre* see)]

super·weed *noun* an extremely robust or resistant (to herbicides or natural checks on growth) weed, esp. one feared to result from genetic modification of plants.

super·woman *noun* (*pl.* **-women**) *informal* a woman of exceptional strength or ability.

su·pin·ate /ˈsuːpɪˌneit/ *transitive & intransitive verb* **1** put (a hand or foreleg etc.) into a supine position (with the palm etc. upwards). **2** (of a person) turn (the foot) inward so that the weight falls on the outer side of the foot. □ **su·pin·a·tion** *noun*

su·pin·ator /ˈsuːpɪˌneitər/ *noun* *Anat.* a muscle in the forearm effecting supination.

su·pine /ˈsuːpain/ ● *adjective* **1** lying face upwards (*compare* PRONE 1a). **2** having the front or ventral part upwards; (of the hand) with the palm upwards. **3** inert, indolent; morally or mentally inactive. ● *noun* a Latin verbal noun used only in the accusative and ablative cases, esp. to denote purpose (e.g. *mirabile dictu* 'wonderful to relate'). □ **su·pine·ly** *adverb* **su·pine·ness** *noun* [Latin *supinus*, related to *super*: (n.) from Late Latin *supinum* neuter (reason unknown)]

sup·per *noun* **1** the evening meal, often the main meal of the day. **2** a light evening meal. **3** an evening social event, esp. one intended to raise money, at which a meal is served. □ **sing for one's supper** do something in return for a benefit. □ **sup·per·less** *adjective* [Old French *soper*, *super*]

supper·time *noun* **1** the time of day at which supper is customarily eaten (*I'll be there around suppertime*). **2** the time at which a supper is served (*it's suppertime, kids!*).

sup·plant *transitive verb* dispossess and take the place of, esp. by underhand means. □ **sup·plant·er** *noun* [Old French *supplanter* or Latin *supplantare* trip up (as SUB-, *planta* sole)]

sup·ple *adjective* (**sup·pler**, **sup·plest**) **1** bending and moving easily and gracefully; flexible. **2** not stiff or hard; easily manipulated.
□ **supple·ness** *noun* [Old French *souple* ultimately from Latin *supplex supplicis* submissive]

supple·jack *noun* any of various strong twining tropical shrubs, esp. *Berchemia scandens*.

supple·ly *var. of* SUPPLY².

sup·ple·ment ● *noun* **1** a thing or part added to remedy deficiencies (*dietary supplement*). **2** a part added to a book etc. to provide further information. **3** a separate section, esp. a colour magazine, added to a newspaper or periodical. **4** an additional charge payable for an extra service or facility. **5** *Math.* the amount by which an angle is less than 180° (*compare* COMPLEMENT *noun* 6). ● *transitive verb* provide a supplement for. □ **sup·ple·ment·al** *adjective* **sup·ple·ment·al·ly** *adverb* **sup·ple·men·ta·tion** *noun* [Latin *supplementum* (as SUB-, *plēre* fill)]

sup·ple·ment·ary *adjective* forming or serving as a supplement; additional. □ **sup·ple·men·tari·ly** *adverb*

sup·ple·tion /sə'pliːʃən/ *noun* the act or an instance of supplementing, esp. *Linguistics* the occurrence of unrelated forms to supply gaps in conjugation (e.g. *went* as the past of *go*). [Old French from medieval Latin *suppletio -onis* (as SUPPLY[1])]

sup·pli·ant /'sʌpliənt/ ● *adjective* **1** supplicating. **2** expressing supplication. ● *noun* a supplicating person. □ **sup·pli·ant·ly** *adverb* [French *supplier* beseech, from Latin (as SUPPLICATE)]

sup·pli·cate /'sʌplɪˌkeɪt/ *verb* **1** *transitive* petition humbly to (a person) or for (a thing). **2** *intransitive* (foll. by *to, for*) make a petition. □ **sup·pli·cant** *adjective & noun* **sup·pli·ca·tion** *noun* **sup·pli·ca·tory** *adjective* [Latin *supplicare* (as SUB-, *plicare* bend)]

sup·ply[1] ● *verb* (**-plies**, **-plied**) **1** *transitive* provide or furnish (a thing needed). **2** *transitive* (often foll. by *with*) provide (a person etc. with a thing needed). **3** *transitive* meet or make up for (a deficiency or need etc.). ● *noun* (*pl.* **-plies**) **1** the act or an instance of providing what is needed. **2** a stock, store, amount, etc., of something provided or obtainable (*a large supply of water*). **3** (in *pl.*) **a** food or other materials necessary for maintenance or for a specific activity. **b** the collected provisions and equipment for an army, expedition, etc. **c** a grant of money by Parliament for the costs of government (also *attributive*: *supply bill*). **4** (often *attributive*) a person, esp. a teacher or member of the clergy, acting as a temporary substitute for another. **5** (*attributive*) providing supplies or a supply (*supply officer*). □ **in short supply** available in limited quantity. **on supply** (of a schoolteacher etc.) acting as a supply. □ **sup·pli·er** *noun* [Old French *so(u)pleer* etc. from Latin *supplēre* (as SUB-, *plēre* fill)]

sup·ply[2] *adverb* (also **supple·ly**) in a supple manner.

supply and demand *noun Econ.* the amount or quantity of a product available and required, as factors regulating its price.

supply chain *noun* the sequence of processes involved in the production and distribution of a commodity (*supply chain management*).

supply line *noun* **1** (usu. in *pl.*) transportation or communication lines along which necessary supplies are delivered. **2** a conduit etc. through which something is supplied.

supply-side *adjective Econ.* denoting a policy of low taxation and other incentives to produce goods and invest (*supply-side economics*). □ **supply-sider** *noun*

supply teacher *noun Cdn & Brit.* = SUBSTITUTE TEACHER.

sup·port ● *transitive verb* **1** carry all or part of the weight of. **2** keep from falling or sinking or failing. **3 a** provide with a home and the necessities of life (*have a family to support*). **b** provide enough food and water to keep someone or something alive (*amazing that such a barren area can support any form of life*). **4** enable to last out; give strength to; encourage. **5** bear out; tend to substantiate or corroborate (a statement, charge, theory, etc.). **6 a** give help to, back up. **b** speak in favour of (a resolution etc.). **7** help (a person) by giving one's approval, sympathy, encouragement, etc. **8** be actively interested in (a particular political candidate, sports team, etc.). **9** (usu. as **supporting** *adjective*) take a part that is secondary to (a principal actor etc.). **10** occupy a position by the side of (a person) in order to give assistance or encouragement; assist by one's presence or attendance. **11** endure, tolerate (*can no longer support the noise*). **12** maintain or represent (a part or character) adequately. **13** contribute to the funds of (an institution). **14** (of a computer, operating system, etc.) allow the use or operation of (a program, device, etc.). **15** provide ongoing technical assistance for (a computer system etc.) once it is installed. ● *noun* **1** the act or an instance of supporting; the process of being supported. **2** a person or thing that supports. **3** encouragement or sympathy etc. given esp. to a person undergoing difficulties. **4** money paid by a divorced or separated person to his or her former spouse and/or their children. ● *adjective* (of hosiery) reinforced with elastic fibres in order to support the muscles and veins of the legs. □ **in support of** in order to support. □ **sup·port·able** *adjective* **sup·port·ably** *adverb* **sup·port·ing** *adjective* **sup·port·less** *adjective* [Old French *supporter* from Latin *supportare* (as SUB-, *portare* carry)]

sup·port·er *noun* **1** a person or thing that supports, esp. a person supporting a team or sport. **2** *Cdn* a person who pays education taxes to a usu. specified school system (*a separate school supporter*). **3** (in full **athletic supporter**) = JOCKSTRAP. **4** *Heraldry* the representation of an animal etc., usu. one of a pair, holding up or standing beside an escutcheon.

support group *noun* a group of people who meet on a regular basis

to provide mutual support by discussing a shared problem or experience.

sup·port·ive *adjective* providing support or encouragement. □ **sup·port·ive·ly** *adverb* **sup·port·ive·ness** *noun*

support price *noun* a minimum price guaranteed to a farmer for agricultural produce and maintained by subsidy etc.

support staff *noun* employees providing esp. clerical and administrative assistance.

sup·pose *transitive verb* (often foll. by *that* + clause) **1** assume, esp. in default of knowledge; be inclined to think (*I suppose they will return*; *what do you suppose she meant?*). **2** take as a possibility or hypothesis (*let's suppose you are right*). **3** (in *imperative*) as a formula of proposal (*suppose we go to the party*). **4** (of a theory or result etc.) require as a condition (*design in creation supposes a creator*). **5** (in *imperative* or *pres. part.* forming a question) in the circumstances that; if (*suppose they won't let you*; *supposing we stay*). **6** (in *passive*; foll. by *to* + infin.) be generally accepted or believed to be so (*is generally supposed to be wealthy*). **7** (in *passive*; foll. by *to* + infin.) be expected or required (*was supposed to write to you*). **b** (with *neg.*) not be allowed to (*you are not supposed to go in there*). **c** (with *neg.*) not be intended to (*we're not supposed to understand*). **8** (in *passive*; foll. by *to* + infin.) be intended (*just what is that supposed to mean?*). □ **I suppose so** an expression of hesitant agreement. □ **sup·pos·able** *adjective* [Old French *supposer* (as SUB-, POSE[1])]

sup·pos·ed *attributive adjective* generally accepted as being so; believed (*his supposed brother*). □ **sup·pos·edly** *adverb*

sup·pos·ition *noun* **1** a fact or idea etc. supposed. **2** the act or an instance of supposing. □ **sup·pos·ition·al** *adjective*

sup·posi·tory /sə'pɒzɪtɔri, -tri/ *noun* (*pl.* **-ies**) a medical preparation in the form of a cone, cylinder, etc., to be inserted into the rectum or vagina to melt. [medieval Latin *suppositorium*, neuter of Late Latin *suppositorius* placed underneath]

sup·press *transitive verb* **1** end the activity or existence of, esp. forcibly. **2** prevent (information, etc.) from being seen, heard, or known (*tried to suppress the report*). **3** arrest or stop (a cough, sneeze, etc.). **4** prevent (a feeling, reaction, etc.) from being expressed. **5 a** partly or wholly eliminate (electrical interference etc.). **b** equip (a device) to reduce such interference due to it. **6** *Psych.* keep out of one's consciousness. □ **sup·press·ible** *adjective* **sup·pres·sion** *noun* **sup·pres·sive** *adjective* **sup·pres·sor** *noun* [Latin *supprimere suppress-* (as SUB-, *premere* press)]

sup·pres·sant *noun* a suppressing or restraining agent (*cough suppressant*; *appetite suppressant*).

sup·pur·ate /'sʌpjəˌreɪt/ *intransitive verb* form pus; fester. □ **sup·pur·a·tion** *noun* **sup·pur·a·tive** /-rətɪv/ *adjective* [Latin *suppurare* (as SUB-, *purare* as PUS)]

supra /'suːprə/ *adverb* above or earlier on (in a text). [Latin, = above]

supra- /'suːprə/ *prefix* **1** above. **2** beyond, transcending (*supranational*). [from or after Latin *supra-* from *supra* above, beyond, before in time]

supra·nation·al *adjective* transcending national limits. □ **supra·nation·al·ism** *noun* **supra·nation·al·ity** *noun*

supra·orbit·al *adjective* situated above the orbit of the eye.

supra·renal *adjective* situated above the kidneys.

su·prem·a·cist /sə'preməsɪst, suː-/ *noun* a person who believes in or advocates the supremacy of a particular group, esp. determined by race or sex (also *attributive*: *supremacist group*). □ **su·prem·a·cism** *noun*

su·prem·acy /sə'preməsi, suː-/ *noun* (*pl.* **-cies**) **1** the state of being supreme in authority, rank, or power. **2** ultimate power or authority.

Supremacy, Act of either of two Acts of Parliament of 1534 and 1559 (esp. the former), laying down the position of the sovereigns Henry VIII and Elizabeth I as supreme heads of the Church of England and excluding the authority of the pope.

su·preme ● *adjective* **1** highest in authority, rank, or power. **2** of the highest quality or importance (*supreme achievement*). **3** greatest in amount or degree (*supreme stupidity*). **4** (of a penalty or sacrifice etc.) ultimate; resulting in death. ● *noun* **1** a rich velouté sauce made with reduced chicken stock and cream. **2** a dish of esp. chicken breasts served in this sauce. □ **reign** (or **rule**) **supreme 1** be dominant; hold supreme power, authority, or popularity. **2** be widespread or pervasive; be a prevalent feature. □ **su·preme·ly** *adverb* [Latin *supremus*, superlative of *superus* that is above, from *super* above]

Supreme Being *noun* a name given to an omnipotent deity; God.

Supreme Court *noun* the highest judicial court of appeal in a country, province, state, etc. hearing cases on civil, criminal, and constitutional matters.

---

t top   v voice   w we   z zoo   ʃ she   ʒ vision   θ thin   ð this   ŋ ring   x loch   tʃ chip   dʒ jar   *(see over for vowels)*

Supreme Soviet *noun* the governing council of the former Soviet Union consisting of two equal chambers, the Soviet of Union, composed of one delegate for every 300,000 citizens, and the Soviet of Nationalities, elected on a regional basis in the constituent republics and areas.

su·premo /sə'priːmoː, suː-/ *noun* (pl. **-premos**) esp. *Brit. informal* **1** a person who has supreme authority; a ruler or leader. **2** a person who is prominent in or in charge of an activity, movement, trend, etc. [Spanish, = SUPREME]

Supt. *abbreviation* Superintendent.

suq *var. of* SOUK.

sur-[1] *prefix* = SUPER- (*surcharge*; *surrealism*). [Old French]

sur-[2] *prefix* assimilated form of SUB- before *r*.

sura /'suːrə/ *noun* a chapter or section of the Quran. [Arabic *sūra*, prob. from Syriac *ṣūrṭā* scripture]

Sura·baya /ˌsuːrə'baiə/ a seaport in Indonesia, on the north coast of Java; pop. (2002) 2,729,300. Formerly the leading port of the Dutch East Indies, it is today Indonesia's principal naval base and its second largest city.

Sura·karta /ˌsuːrə'kɑrtə/ a city in central Java, Indonesia; pop. (est. 1995) 516,594.

sural /'sjuːrəl/ *adjective* of or relating to the calf of the leg (*sural artery*). [modern Latin *suralis* from Latin *sura* calf]

Surat /'suːrət, suː'rat/ a city in the state of Gujarat in W India, a port on the Tapti River near its mouth on the Gulf of Cambay; pop. (2001) 2,433,800. Noted for its textiles, gold and silver ware, it was the site of the first trading post of the East India Company, established in 1612.

sur·cease /sɜr'siːs/ esp. *N Amer. literary* ● *noun* **1** (usu. foll. by *from*) relief. **2** a cessation. ● *transitive & intransitive verb archaic* cease. [Old French *sursis*, past participle of Old French *surseoir* refrain, delay, from Latin (as SUPERSEDE), assimilated to CEASE]

sur·charge ● *noun* **1 a** a fee charged in addition to the normal cost of something (*a 10 per cent surcharge on imported goods*). **b** the payment of this fee or amount of money paid. **2** an excessive amount charged. **3** a mark printed on a postage stamp changing its value. **4** an overwhelming or excessive load or burden. ● *transitive verb* **1** exact a surcharge from (a person, company, etc.). **2** exact (a sum) as a surcharge. **3** mark (a postage stamp) with a surcharge.

sur·cin·gle /'sɜr,sɪŋgəl/ *noun* a strap or belt passed around the body of a horse to keep a blanket, pack, saddle, etc. in place. [Old French *surcengle* (as SUR-[1], *cengle* girth, from Latin *cingula* from *cingere* gird)]

sur·coat *noun hist.* **1** a loose robe, usu. embroidered with heraldic devices, worn over armour as part of the insignia of an order of knighthood. **2** an outer coat of rich material.

surd ● *adjective* **1** *Math.* (of a number) irrational. **2** *Phonetics* (of a sound) voiceless. ● *noun* **1** *Math.* an irrational number, esp. the root of an integer. **2** *Phonetics* a voiceless sound. [Latin *surdus* deaf, mute: sense 1 by mistranslating into Latin of Greek *alogos* irrational, speechless, through Arabic *jadr aṣamm* deaf root]

sure ● *adjective* **1** having or seeming to have adequate reason for a belief or assertion. **2** (often foll. by *of*, or *that* + clause) convinced (*he's guilty, I'm sure of it*; *I'm sure that she meant well*). **3** (foll. by *of*) having a confident anticipation or satisfactory knowledge of (*she's sure of the answer*). **4 a** reliable or unfailing (*a sure cure for the winter blahs*). **b** physically dependable; steady, secure (*a sure footing*). **5 a** (foll. by *to* + infin.) certain (*it's sure to rain*). **b** certain to come or happen etc.; inevitable (*a sure win*). **6** undoubtedly true or truthful (*one thing is sure: I'll never do that again*). ● *adverb informal* certainly, truly (*I'm sure glad you came*). ● *interjection* yes; of course. □ **as sure as eggs is** (or **are**) **eggs** without any doubt. **as sure as fate** quite certain. **sure as shootin'** *N Amer. informal* without a doubt. **be sure** (in *imperative* or *infinitive*; foll. by *that* + clause or *to* + infin.) take care to; not fail, neglect, or forget to (*be sure to turn the lights out*). **for sure** *informal* without doubt. **make sure 1** (often foll. by *that*) make or become certain; ensure. **2** (foll. by *of*) establish the truth or ensure the existence or happening of. **sure enough** *informal* **1** in fact; certainly (*I asked him to clean his room and, sure enough, he did*). **2** almost certainly (*they will come sure enough*). **sure of oneself** self-confident; self-assured. **to be sure 1** it is undeniable or admitted. **2** it must be admitted. □ **sure·ness** *noun* [Old French *sur* from Latin *securus* SECURE]

sure·fire *adjective informal* reliable, guaranteed, assured.

sure-footed *adjective* **1** treading safely without slipping or stumbling. **2** competent, unerring; not likely to fail or make a mistake. □ **sure-footed·ly** *adverb* **sure-footed·ness** *noun*

sure·ly *adverb* **1** certainly, assuredly, undoubtedly; indeed. **2** used to express a strong belief in the statement qualified, esp. in the face of possible dissent (*surely you don't believe that he's guilty*). **3** inevitably, without fail (*she seems to improve, slowly but surely*).

Sû·re·té /ˌsuːrə'tei/ *noun* (in full **Sû·re·té du Qué·bec**) *Cdn* the provincial police force of Quebec. [French, = 'police force', lit. 'safety']

sure thing esp. *N Amer. informal* ● *noun* a person or thing whose success is considered certain or guaranteed. ● *interjection* used to express consent to a proposal, request, or order.

sur·ety /'ʃʊrɪti/ *noun* (pl. **-eties**) **1** a person who assumes responsibility for the obligation of another, such as the payment of a debt or an appearance in court. **2 a** (in full **surety bond**) money given as a guarantee. **b** a guarantee or assurance. **3** certainty. **4** self-assurance. □ **of** (or **for**) **a surety** *archaic* certainly. **stand surety** become a surety (for).

surf ● *noun* **1** the swell of the sea breaking on the esp. shallow shore of a beach or a reef. **2** the foam produced by this. ● *verb* **1** *intransitive* ride the crest of a wave towards the shore, esp. on a surfboard or windsurfer. **2** *transitive* ride (a wave, swell, etc.) on a surfboard or windsurfer. **3** *transitive & intransitive* **a** *N Amer.* flip from one television channel to another in rapid succession using a remote control. **b** search or scan (the Internet) in order to sample a selection of sites. **4** *intransitive* glide or coast over snow etc. □ **surf·like** *adjective* **surfy** *adjective* [apparently from obsolete *suff*, of unknown origin, perhaps assimilated to *surge*]

sur·face ● *noun* **1 a** the outside part of something (*the earth's surface*). **b** the area of this. **2** any of the sides or faces of an object (*the polished surfaces of a diamond*). **3** the top or outside layer of something (*the surface of the road*). **4** the upper layer or top of the ground, a body of water, or any liquid. **5 a** the superficial level or appearance of a person or thing as opposed to feelings, qualities, etc. which may not be apparent on a casual view or consideration (*she seems quite happy on the surface*). **b** (*attributive*) superficial (*surface politeness*). **6** a relatively flat horizontal space or area used for some particular purpose or activity (*playing surface*). **7** *Geom.* a continuous extent having only two dimensions, length and width without thickness, whether plane or curved, finite or infinite. **8** (*attributive*) of or on the surface (*surface area*; *surface route*). ● *verb* **1** *transitive* cover (a road etc.) with a particular type of surface. **2** *intransitive* **a** rise to the surface of esp. water. **b** become visible, known, or apparent (*old animosities have started to surface*). **3** *intransitive* esp. *Brit. informal* wake up. □ **come to the surface** become perceptible after being hidden. □ **sur·facer** *noun* [French (as SUR-[1], FACE)]

surface-active *adjective* (of a substance, e.g. a detergent) able to affect the wetting or surface tension properties of a liquid.

sur·faced *adjective* (often in *combination*) having or having been furnished with a surface of a specified kind (*a shiny-surfaced gem*; *a hard-surfaced road*).

surface mail *noun* mail carried over land or sea (*compare* AIRMAIL).

surface noise *noun* background noise or hissing heard while playing a record, caused by imperfections in the grooves.

surface plate *noun* = COVER PLATE.

surface route *noun* a route that may be taken by a public transportation vehicle travelling on city streets, such as a bus or streetcar, as opposed to a subway.

surface structure *noun Linguistics* (in transformational grammar) the representation of grammatical or syntactic elements determining the form of a phrase or sentence (*compare* DEEP STRUCTURE).

surface temperature *noun* the temperature of a body of water or planet etc. taken at its surface.

surface tension *noun* the property that causes the surface of a liquid to behave as if it were covered with a weak elastic skin, caused by the tendency of the exposed surface to contract to the smallest possible area, and responsible for the concave profile of a meniscus.

surface-to-air *attributive adjective* (of a missile) designed to be fired from the ground or sea towards a target in the air, such as an aircraft.

surface-to-surface *attributive adjective* (of a missile) designed to be fired from one point on the ground or at sea and directed at a target elsewhere on the earth's surface.

surface water *noun* **1** water that collects on the surface of the ground. **2** the top layer of a body of water.

surf·act·ant /sɜr'faktənt/ *noun* a substance which reduces surface tension of a liquid. [*surface-active*]

surf and turf *noun N Amer.* a restaurant meal combining seafood (esp. lobster) and steak.

surf·board *noun* a long narrow fibreglass board with a small fin on the underside, on which a surfer stands or lies while being carried on the crest of a breaking wave towards the shore.

surf-casting *noun* (also **surf-fishing**) the act or sport of fishing from the shore by casting a line with usu. heavy tackle into the sea. □ **surf-cast** *intransitive verb* **surf-caster** *noun*

sur·feit /ˈsɜːrfət/ ● *noun* **1** (often foll. by *of*) a large or excessive amount. **2 a** excessive indulgence, formerly esp. in eating or drinking. **b** a feeling of satiety or illness resulting from overindulgence. ● *verb* (**sur·feit·ed, sur·feit·ing**) **1** *transitive* fill, supply, or feed to excess. **2** *transitive & intransitive* (foll. by *with*) be or cause to be wearied through excess. **3** *intransitive archaic* overeat. □ **sur·feit·ed** *adjective* [Old French *sorfe(i)t, surfe(i)t* (as SUPER-, Latin *facere fact-* do)]

surf·er *noun* **1 a** a person who participates in the sport of surfing, either recreationally or professionally. **b** (*attributive*) designating aspects or elements typical of the lifestyle, culture, language, etc. of a surfer (*surfer lingo; surfer shorts*). **2** *Computing* **a** a person who surfs the Internet. **b** a researcher who uses a variety of electronic databases to gather information.

surf guitar *noun* the style of guitar playing used in surf music.

sur·ficial /sɜːrˈfɪʃəl/ *adjective* of or relating to the earth's surface. [SURFACE after *superficial*]

surf·ing *noun* **1** the sport or activity of riding waves on a surfboard or windsurfer etc. **2** *Computing* an instance or the hobby of surfing the Internet. **3** *N Amer.* = CHANNEL SURFING.

surf music *noun* a style of pop music originating on the west coast of California in the early 1960s, characterized by high harmony vocals and lyrics related to the beach and surfing.

surf scoter *noun* a N American marine duck, *Melanitta perspicillata*.

surge ● *noun* **1** a sudden or violent rush, onset, or burst (*a surge of anger*). **2** a high rolling swell of water, esp. on the sea; a large or violent wave, a storm surge. **3** a rapid increase in price, activity, etc. over a short period. **4** a heavy forward or upward motion of a large or growing mass, volume, etc. (*the surge of the crowd*). **5** = POWER SURGE. **6** a growing strain of music or sound. ● *intransitive verb* **1** (of the sea etc.) rise and move forward in great waves; swell or heave with great force. **2 a** (of a crowd etc.) move forward suddenly or powerfully. **b** (of a person, vehicle, etc.) burst forward or ahead with sudden speed; accelerate. **3** show a large, sudden, usu. brief increase in magnitude, power, growth, etc. **4** (of a feeling, activity, etc.) increase suddenly and dramatically. [Old French *sourdre sourge-*, or *sorgir* from Catalan, from Latin *surgere* rise]

sur·geon *noun* **1** a medical practitioner qualified to practise surgery. **2** *Brit.* a medical officer in the armed forces. [Old French *serurgien* (as SURGERY)]

surgeon·fish *noun* any tropical marine fish of the genus *Acanthurus* with movable lancet-shaped spines on each side of the tail.

Surgeon General *noun* (*pl.* **Surgeons General**) **1** (in the US) the senior medical officer of the Bureau of Public Health or (in some states) a similar state authority. **2** the senior officer in medical service of the armed forces.

surgeon's knot *noun* a knot resembling a reef knot, originally used by doctors to tie ligatures.

sur·gery *noun* (*pl.* **-ies**) **1** the branch of medicine concerned with treatment of injuries or disorders of the body by incision, manipulation, or alteration of organs etc. **2** surgical treatment; an operation. **3** *esp. N Amer.* the part of or a room in a hospital where surgery is performed. **4** a detailed or extensive series of repairs, changes, or modifications made to something (*they hoped to perform major surgery on the new proposal before presenting it*). **5** *Brit.* **a** an office where a doctor, esp. a GP or dentist, sees and treats patients. **b** a place where an MP, lawyer, or other professional person gives advice. **c** a session of treatment or consultation. [Old French *surgerie* from Latin *chirurgia* from Greek *kheirourgia* handiwork, surgery, from *kheir* hand + *erg-* work]

surge suppressor *noun* (also **surge protector**) a device used to protect an electrical appliance etc. from damage in the event of a power surge. □ **surge suppression** *noun* (also **surge protection**).

surge tank *noun* a chamber connected by a T-joint to a water pipe in order to absorb surges of pressure by filling and drops in pressure by emptying.

sur·gical *adjective* **1** of, relating to, or performed by surgeons or surgery. **2** used or worn by surgeons or during surgery (*surgical gloves; surgical instruments*). **3** designating a swift and precise military attack,

esp. from the air (*surgical strike*). □ **sur·gical·ly** *adverb* [earlier *chirurgical* from *chirurgy* from Old French *sirurgie*: see SURGERY]

suri·cate /ˈsʊrɪˌkeɪt/ *noun* = MEERKAT. [French, of African origin]

su·rimi /suːˈriːmi/ *noun* a white relatively tasteless and odourless paste made from minced fish, used esp. to produce imitation crabmeat and lobster meat. [Japanese, lit. 'minced flesh']

Suri·name /ˌsʊrəˈnam, -ˈnɒmə/ (also **Suri·nam** /-ˈnam/) a country on the northeast coast of S America; pop. (est. 2002) 436,494; capital, Paramaribo. □ **Suri·nam·er** *noun* **Suri·nam·ese** /-nəˈmiːz/

sur·ly *adjective* (**sur·li·er, sur·li·est**) **1** rude, ill-natured, unfriendly; gruff. **2** hostile, belligerent. □ **sur·li·ly** *adverb* **sur·li·ness** *noun* [alteration of spelling of obsolete *sirly* haughty, from SIR + -LY[1]]

sur·mise /sɜːrˈmaɪz/ ● *transitive verb* (often foll. by *that* + clause) form an opinion that something may be true without sufficient evidence to be certain; infer, conjecture, suspect. ● *noun* an opinion formed without sufficient evidence for certainty; conjecture, speculation. [Old French fem. past participle of *surmettre* accuse, from Late Latin *supermittere supermiss-* (as SUPER-, *mittere* send)]

sur·mount *transitive verb* **1** overcome (an obstacle, difficulty, impediment, etc.). **2** (usu. in *passive*) (foll. by *by* or *with*) rest on top of; or be situated on or above (*a ring surmounted by a beautiful diamond*). **3** climb on top of or over (an obstacle). □ **sur·mount·able** *adjective*

sur·mul·let /sɜːrˈmʌlət/ *noun* a fish of tropical and subtropical oceans, related to the perch, and having two long barbels under the chin. [French *surmulet* from Old French *sor* red + *mulet* MULLET]

sur·name ● *noun* **1** a hereditary name common to all members of a family, as distinct from a given name; a family name. **2** *archaic* a name, title, or epithet added to a person's name or names, often indicating his or her birthplace, trade, familial relationship, or a prominent character trait, and sometimes becoming hereditary. ● *transitive verb* give a surname to; call (a person) by a surname.

sur·pass *transitive verb* **1** be greater, better than, or superior to; excel. **2** outdo (another person or thing) in degree or prominence (*crime has surpassed unemployment as the greatest concern among voters*). **3** go beyond, exceed (a certain limit etc.). **4** be beyond the range or capacity of; transcend (*so beautiful it surpasses description*). □ **sur·pass·able** *adjective* [French *surpasser* (as SUR-[1], PASS[1])]

sur·pass·ing *adjective* that surpasses what is ordinary; exceptional, matchless. □ **sur·pass·ing·ly** *adverb*

sur·plice /ˈsɜːrplɪs, -pləs/ *noun Christianity* a loose white vestment with wide sleeves, reaching the knees or feet and worn usu. over a cassock by clergy, choir members, altar servers, etc. □ **sur·pliced** *adjective* [Old French *sourpelis*, from medieval Latin *superpellicium* (as SUPER-, *pellicia* PELISSE)]

sur·plus ● *noun* **1** an amount left over when requirements have been met; what remains of what is needed or already used. **2 a** an excess of revenue over expenditure in a given period, esp. a fiscal year (*opp.* DEFICIT 2). **b** the excess value of a company's assets over the face value of its stock. **3 a** military supplies, such as clothing and camping gear, exceeding the requirements of the army or navy and sold to the public (also *attributive: surplus boots*). **b** (*attributive*) designating a store or outlet etc. selling such goods. ● *adjective* exceeding what is needed or used; excess. □ **sur·plus·age** *noun* [Old French *s(o)urplus* from medieval Latin *superplus* (as SUPER-, + *plus* more)]

surplus value *noun Econ.* the difference between the value of work done and the cost of the labour that has produced it.

sur·prise ● *noun* **1** an unexpected or astonishing event, circumstance, or thing. **2** the emotion caused by this; astonishment, shock, or amazement. **3** a gift or present. **4** a person or thing that achieves unexpected success (also *attributive: the surprise hit of the summer*). **5** an attack or approach made upon an unsuspecting victim (*they were caught by surprise*). **6** (*attributive*) unexpected; made or done etc. without warning (*a surprise visit; a surprise party*). **7** often *jocular* or *informal* a dish, esp. a casserole or stew, prepared with ingredients not made known to those to whom it is served (*tuna surprise*). ● *transitive verb* **1** cause (a person) to feel astonishment, shock, or amazement (*you surprised me with your answer; the news surprised her*). **2 a** startle (a person or animal) with a sudden or unexpected approach. **b** capture or attack by surprise. ● *interjection* used as an exclamation of triumph as a surprise is successfully revealed. □ **should come as no surprise** (a piece of information) should have been anticipated, guessed, or previously known. **surprise, surprise** *ironic* just as one might expect; this is no surprise at all. **take** (or **catch**) **by surprise** startle or astonish esp. with an unexpected encounter or statement. □ **sur·pris·ing** *adjective*

sur·pris·ing·ly *adverb* [Old French, fem. past participle of *surprendre* (as SUR-¹, *prendre* from Latin *praehendere* seize)]

sur·prised *adjective* (often foll. by *at, by, that* + clause, or *to* + infin.) **1** filled with mild astonishment or amazement. **2** shocked, scandalized.

sur·real *adjective* **1** having some of the qualities of surrealism; bizarre, unreal, dreamlike, fantastic. **2** = SURREALISTIC. □ **sur·real·ity** *noun* **sur·real·ly** *adverb* [back-formation from SURREALISM etc.]

sur·real·ism *noun* **1** (**Surrealism**) a 20th-c. movement in art and literature aiming to explore and express the subconscious mind and to move beyond the accepted conventions of reality by representing the irrational imagery of dreams using such techniques as automatism, the irrational juxtaposition of images, and the creation of mysterious symbols. **2** art or literature produced by or reminiscent of this movement. □ **sur·real·ist** (also **Surrealist**) *noun & adjective*

sur·real·is·tic *adjective* **1** based on, influenced by, or pertaining to Surrealism or the Surrealists. **2** characteristic or suggestive of Surrealism. □ **sur·real·is·tic·ally** *adverb*

sur·rebut·ter /ˌsərəˈbʌtər/ *noun Law* the plaintiff's reply to the defendant's rebutter. □ **sur·rebut·tal** *noun* [SUR-¹ + REBUTTER, after SURREJOINDER]

sur·rejoin·der /ˌsərəˈdʒɔɪndər/ *noun Law* the plaintiff's reply to the defendant's rejoinder. [SUR-¹ + REJOINDER]

sur·ren·der ● *verb* **1** *transitive* **a** give up possession or control of (something) to another, esp. on compulsion or demand; relinquish, yield. **b** abandon (hope etc.). **2** *intransitive* offer or give oneself up as a prisoner to esp. an enemy or the police; submit. **3** *intransitive & reflexive* (foll. by *to*) submit or abandon oneself entirely to some influence, emotion, course of action, etc. **4** *transitive Sport* give up or allow one or a number of (goals, runs, hits, yards, points, etc.). **5** *transitive* cancel (a life insurance policy) and receive back a portion of the premiums paid. **6** *transitive* give up (a lease) before its expiry. ● *noun* the act or an instance of surrendering. [Old French *surrendre* (as SUR-¹, RENDER)]

surrender value *noun* the amount payable to one who surrenders an insurance policy.

sur·rep·ti·tious /ˌsərəpˈtɪʃəs/ *adjective* **1** obtained, done, etc. in secret or by stealth or illicit means; clandestine. **2** acting stealthily or secretly; crafty, sly. □ **sur·rep·ti·tious·ly** *adverb* **sur·rep·ti·tious·ness** *noun* [Latin *surrepticius -itius* from *surripere surrept-* (as SUR-¹, *rapere* seize)]

Sur·rey 1 a city in southwestern BC, southeast of Vancouver; pop. (2001) 347,825. **2** a county of SE England; county town, Kingston-upon-Thames. □ **Surrey·ite** *noun* (in sense 1) [sense 1 after sense 2]

sur·rey *noun* (*pl.* **sur·reys**) esp. *US hist.* a light four-wheeled carriage with two seats facing forwards. [originally of an adaptation of the *Surrey cart*, originally made in Surrey, England]

sur·ro·gacy /ˈsərəgəsi/ *noun* the practice of surrogate motherhood.

sur·ro·gate /ˈsʌrəgət/ *noun* **1** a person or thing taking the place of another; a substitute. **2** a person appointed by authority to act in place of another, esp. in a specific role or office; a deputy. **3 a** a surrogate mother. **b** (*attributive*) relating to or involving surrogate motherhood (*surrogate adoption; surrogate parent*). **4** *Psych.* a person who fills the role of an absent or estranged relative, esp. a parent, in a child's upbringing (*his teacher became a sort of father surrogate*). [Latin *surrogatus* past participle of *surrogare* elect as a substitute (as SUR-¹, *rogare* ask)]

surrogate court *noun N Amer.* a court with jurisdiction over wills and estates of deceased persons.

surrogate mother *noun* **1** a woman who bears a child on behalf of another woman, either from her own egg fertilized by the other woman's partner or from the implantation in her uterus of a fertilized egg from the other woman. **2** a person or animal acting the role of mother. □ **surrogate motherhood** *noun* **surrogate mothering** *noun*

sur·round ● *transitive verb* **1** stand or be situated around; extend around, encircle. **2** (usu. foll. by *with*) **a** place a thing or things on all sides of or all around. **b** (*reflexive*) place people or things around (oneself); situate (oneself) amongst. **3** form the entourage of (a person) (*wealthy and influential people surround her*). **4** exist as a predominant aspect of; dominate (*the mystery that surrounds her disappearance*). ● *noun* **1** a structure or border placed around something (*tub surround; a fireplace with a tiled surround*). **2** the area around a place or thing; surroundings. **3** = SURROUND SOUND (also *attributive: surround speakers*). [Middle English = overflow, from Old French *s(o)uronder* from Late Latin *superundare* (as SUPER-, *undare* flow, from *unda* wave)]

sur·round·ing ● *adjective* located or situated around (*the city and surrounding regions*). ● *noun* (in *pl.*) all the objects, conditions, etc. that are around and may affect a person or thing.

surround sound *noun* a system of sound reproduction involving three or more speakers designed to create a more realistic effect for the listener by creating a sense of space and depth (*compare* AMBISONICS).

sur·tax ● *noun* **1** a higher rate of tax levied on personal incomes above a certain level. **2** any additional tax charged on something already taxed. ● *transitive verb* impose a surtax on.

Sur·title *noun proprietary* (esp. in opera) each of a sequence of captions projected above the stage, translating the text being sung.

sur·tout /sərˈtuː/ *noun hist.* a man's overcoat or frock coat. [French from *sur* over + *tout* everything]

Surt·sey /ˈsərtsi/ a small island to the south of Iceland, formed by a volcanic eruption in 1963.

sur·veil·lance /sərˈveɪləns/ *noun* **1** close observation or supervision, esp. of an enemy or suspected person. **2** a security device or system of security devices used to monitor premises and detect trespassers, burglars, shoplifters, etc. (also *attributive: surveillance camera*). [French from *surveiller* (as SUR-¹, *veiller* from Latin *vigilare* keep watch)]

sur·vey ● *noun* **1 a** a general and comprehensive discussion, description, view, consideration, or treatment of something. **b** (in full **survey course**) *N Amer.* an introductory academic course which gives a broad esp. historical overview of one subject. **2** a systematic collection and analysis of data relating to the opinions, habits, etc. of a population, usu. taken from a representative sample; an opinion poll. **3 a** the process or an act of surveying land or property. **b** a summary or report of the results or findings of this. **c** a map or plan based on the results obtained by surveying land. **d** a department carrying out the surveying of land. **4** a close inspection, investigation, or examination. ● *transitive verb* **1** make or present a general and comprehensive examination or assessment of (*survey the damage*). **2 a** record the views and opinions of (a person or group) in an opinion poll. **b** ascertain (the opinions etc.) of a person or group. **3** explore, measure, or determine the boundaries, extent, and ownership of (land, a property, etc.) in order to construct a map, plan, or detailed description. **4** examine and ascertain the condition, situation, or value of (a building etc.). [Old French *so(u)rveeir* (pres. stem *survey-*) from medieval Latin *supervidēre* (as SUPER-, *vidēre* see)]

sur·vey·ing *noun* **1** the scientific measurement of land for making maps, preparing for development, etc.; the business or occupation of a surveyor. **2** the act or an instance of exploring or measuring land, inspecting a building, etc.

sur·vey·or *noun* **1** a person whose occupation is the surveying of land and property. **2** = QUANTITY SURVEYOR. **3** *Brit.* an official inspector, esp. for measurement and valuation. **4** a person who conducts opinion polls or surveys.

surveyor general *noun* (*pl.* **sur·vey·ors gen·er·al**) *N Amer. hist.* a government official responsible for coordinating the survey of public lands in a particular region, province, state, etc.

sur·viv·able *adjective* **1** not fatal; able to be survived. **2** capable of surviving. □ **sur·viv·a·bil·ity** *noun*

sur·viv·al *noun* **1** the process or an instance of continuing to live, esp. after some tragic or disastrous event; continued existence. **2** the practice of coping with harsh or warlike conditions, as a leisure activity or training exercise. **3** a person, thing, or practice that has remained from a former time. □ **survival of the fittest** the continued existence of organisms which are best adapted to their environment, with the extinction of others, as a concept in the Darwinian theory of evolution.

sur·viv·al·ism *noun* **1** a policy of trying to ensure the survival of oneself, one's business, or one's social or national group, esp. in the face of competition or event of a natural disaster, catastrophic event, or foreign invasion. **2** the practising of outdoor survival skills as a sport or hobby. □ **sur·viv·al·ist** *noun & adjective*

survival kit *noun* a small pack filled with first aid supplies, emergency rations, and other materials that may be beneficial in the event of being stranded or lost.

survival suit *noun* a buoyant close-fitting thermal wetsuit designed to keep a person afloat in the event of a boating accident.

sur·vive *verb* **1** *intransitive* continue to live or exist, esp. after some event; remain alive or existent. **2** *transitive* live or exist longer than (*she survived her husband by three years; he is survived by his wife and three children*). **3** *transitive* remain alive after going through, or continue to

Consonants: b *but* d *dog* f *few* g *get* h *her* j *yes* k *cat* l *leg* m *man* n *no* p *pen* r *red* s *sit*

exist in spite of (a danger, accident, etc.) (*he has survived two strokes*). **4** *intransitive* remain in use or existence. **5** *transitive & intransitive informal* or *jocular* persevere; endure a difficult situation (*I don't know if I can survive another Winnipeg winter; how will I ever survive with no TV for a whole week?*). [Old French *sourvivre* from Latin *supervivere* (as SUPER-, *vivere* live)]

sur·viv·or *noun* **1** a person who survives or has survived, esp. one remaining alive after an event in which others die (*the blaze left only four survivors*). **2** *informal* a person who has a knack for overcoming difficulties or surviving afflictions unscathed (*she'll be okay, she's a survivor*). **3** *Law* a person who outlives others sharing a joint interest, esp. a joint tenant who inherits an estate upon the death of the other joint tenant.

survivor's guilt *noun* (also **survivor guilt**) guilt felt by someone who has survived a tragedy in which others died.

sur·viv·or·ship *noun* **1** the state or condition of being a survivor; survival. **2** *Law* a right depending on survival, esp. the right of the survivor of people with a joint interest to take the whole upon the death of the others. **3 a** the probability of surviving to a given age. **b** the proportion of a population that does this.

Surya /'suriə/ *Hinduism* the sun god of later Hindu mythology, originally one of several solar deities in the Vedic religion. [Sanskrit, = sun]

Sus. *abbreviation* Susanna (Apocrypha).

sus *var.* of SUSS.

sus- *prefix* assimilated form of SUB- before *c, p, t*.

Susa /'suːsə/ an ancient city of SW Asia, the capital in the 4th millennium BC of the kingdom of Elam and from the late 6th to the late 4th c. BC of the Persian Achaemenid dynasty.

Su·sanna ▶ **1** (in the Apocrypha) a woman of Babylon falsely accused of adultery by two elders but saved by the sagacity of Daniel. **2** the book of the Apocrypha telling the story of Susanna; in Catholic and Orthodox Bibles the story is included in the Book of Daniel.

sus·cep·ti·bil·ity /sə,septə'bɪlɪti/ *noun* (pl. **-ities**) **1** (often foll. by *to*) capacity to undergo or be affected by; sensitivity or vulnerability to. **2** (in *pl.*) a person's emotional capacity; sensibilities or feelings. **3** *Physics* the capacity of a substance for being magnetized, as measured by the ratio of magnetization to a magnetic field strength.

sus·cep·ti·ble /sə'septəbəl/ *adjective* **1 a** (*predicative*; usu. foll. by *to*) likely to be affected by; prone or vulnerable to (*susceptible to pain*). **b** vulnerable, esp. deficient in defences against a disease (*the virus attacks susceptible children*). **2** (foll. by *of*) *formal* capable of undergoing (an action or process); allowing, admitting of (*I consider this student susceptible of improvement*). **3** impressionable, sensitive; easily moved by emotion. □ **sus·cept·ibly** *adverb* [Late Latin *susceptibilis* from Latin *suscipere suscept-* (as SUB-, *capere* take)]

sushi /'suːʃi/ *noun* a Japanese snack of balls or squares of cold boiled rice flavoured with vinegar, salt, and sugar, and garnished with a variety of toppings, e.g. raw fish, egg, seaweed, or vegetables. [Japanese]

sushi bar *noun* **1** a bar or counter in a restaurant where patrons gather to eat sushi and drink. **2** a restaurant or establishment having a sushi bar.

sus·pect ● *transitive verb* **1 a** imagine (something) to be possible or likely (*the police suspect foul play*). **b** (usu. foll. by *that* + clause) be inclined to think (*I suspect that it might rain*). **2** (often foll. by *of*) believe to be guilty with insufficient proof or knowledge; doubt the innocence of. **3** (foll. by *to be*) believe tentatively, without clear ground. **4** doubt the genuineness or truth of; mistrust (*a broker whose honesty he had no reason to suspect*). ● *noun* a person suspected of an offence, evil intention, etc. ● *adjective* subject to or deserving of suspicion or distrust; questionable. □ **the usual suspects** *jocular* a group of people who are frequently and predictably present at events, called upon for comment, etc. [Latin *suspicere suspect-* (as SUB-, *specere* look)]

sus·pect·ed *noun* **1** imagined to be (*the suspected father of her baby*). **2** that one suspects of something which is not certain (*a suspected terrorist*). **3** (of an injury, ailment, disease, etc.) believed to have been suffered although not yet diagnosed or confirmed.

sus·pend *transitive verb* **1** attach (an object) to something above so that it hangs, usu. with free movement. **2** cause to remain in a floating or elevated position without attachment. **3** refrain from making, forming, or announcing (a judgment, opinion, etc.) until a later time; put off, defer, delay. **4** cancel or halt, esp. temporarily; render temporarily inactive or invalid (*they have suspended operations; the police suspended her driver's licence*). **5** forbid (a person) from performing a usual duty or participating in a usual activity for a temporary or indefinite period, esp. as a penalty (*was suspended from his job for two*

weeks without pay; the principal suspended them both for three days). **6** *Chem.* cause (particles) to be held in suspension. **7** *archaic* keep (an audience, listener, etc.) in suspense or expectation. □ **suspend disbelief** refrain from being skeptical about the believability of a work of fiction or its characters. **suspend payment** (of a company) fail to meet its financial engagements; admit insolvency. [Old French *suspendre* or Latin *suspendere suspens-* (as SUB-, *pendere* hang)]

suspended animation *noun* a temporary cessation of the vital functions without death.

suspended sentence *noun* a judicial sentence which is imposed but remains unenforced as long as the offender commits no further offence within a specified period.

sus·pend·er *noun* **1** (in *pl.*) *N Amer.* a pair of straps of usu. elastic material that may be worn over the shoulder and fastened to the waistband of a pair of pants to prevent them from falling down. **2** *Brit.*= GARTER 2.

suspender belt *noun Brit.* = GARTER BELT.

sus·pense *noun* **1** a state of uncertainty or expectation, accompanied by anxiety or excitement, about an awaited outcome, decision, etc. **2 a** a quality in a work of fiction that arouses excited expectation about the outcome, culprit, etc. in the mind of the viewer or reader. **b** a work of fiction containing this quality (also *attributive*: *suspense novel*). **c** works of this kind as a genre. **3** the condition of something that is in doubt or undecided (*the competition lacked suspense since everyone knew she would win*). **4** *Law* a suspension; the temporary cessation of a right etc. □ **keep in suspense** delay informing (a person) of important or useful information, thus heightening their excitement or anxiety. □ **sus·pense·ful** *adjective* **sus·pense·ful·ly** *adverb* [Old French *suspens* from past participle of Latin *suspendere* SUSPEND]

sus·pen·sion *noun* **1** the action of suspending or the condition of being suspended, esp. a temporary cessation or postponement. **2 a** a period during which one is prohibited from attending school or work, playing for a team, participating in an activity, etc. **b** a temporary revocation of a licence, contract, etc. **3** (in full **suspension system**) the system of springs and shocks that supports a vehicle on its axles. **4** a mixture in which small particles are distributed throughout a less dense liquid or gas. **5** *Music* the prolongation of a note of a chord to form a discord with the following chord. □ **(willing) suspension of disbelief** the voluntary withholding of skepticism on the part of the reader with regard to unbelievable characters or events in fiction.

suspension bridge *noun* a bridge consisting of a deck suspended from cables supported by towers at each end.

sus·pen·sive *adjective* having the power or effect of deferring or temporarily stopping the operation of something (*suspensive veto*).

sus·pen·sory *adjective* (of a ligament, muscle, bandage, etc.) holding an organ or limb etc. suspended.

sus·pi·cion *noun* **1** the feeling or state of mind of a person who suspects (*she viewed him with suspicion*). **2 a** the act or an instance of suspecting (*his actions raised suspicions*). **b** the state of being suspected (*is no longer under suspicion*). **3** a faint belief; a notion, inkling (*have a suspicion she's lying*). **4** a presumption of guilt based on evidence sufficient for arrest but not conviction (*was arrested on suspicion of murder*). □ **above suspicion** too obviously good etc. to be suspected. **under suspicion** suspected. [Anglo-French *suspeciun* from medieval Latin *suspectio -onis* from Latin *suspicere* (as SUSPECT): assimilated to French *suspicion* & Latin *suspicio*]

sus·pi·cious *adjective* **1 a** prone to suspicion; mistrustful, esp. of something or someone in particular (*tends to be suspicious of politicians*). **b** feeling suspicion; having one's suspicion aroused (*became suspicious when I didn't see her car*). **2** indicating suspicion (*a suspicious glance*). **3** inviting or justifying suspicion (*suspicious behaviour; a suspicious character*). □ **sus·pi·cious·ly** *adverb* **sus·pi·cious·ness** *noun*

Sus·que·hanna River /ˌsʌskwə'hanə/ a river of the northeastern US. It has two headstreams, one rising in New York State and one in Pennsylvania, which meet in central Pennsylvania. The river then flows 240 km (150 miles) south to Chesapeake Bay.

suss *slang* ● *transitive verb* **1** (usu. foll. by *out*) **a** investigate, check out (*I'll suss out the restaurants so we can decide where to eat*). **b** figure out. **2** esp. *Brit.* suspect of a crime. ● *noun Brit.* **1** shrewdness. **2** a suspect. **3** a suspicion; suspicious behaviour. □ **on suss** *Brit.* on suspicion (of having committed a crime). [abbreviation of SUSPECT, SUSPICION]

sussed *adjective Brit. slang* well informed; aware.

Sus·sex[1] a former county of S England. It was divided in 1974 into the counties of East Sussex and West Sussex.

Sus·sex² *noun* **1** a breed of long-coated, stocky, golden brown spaniel. **2** an English breed of speckled or red domestic fowl. [SUSSEX¹]

sus·tain ● *transitive verb* **1** provide with the basic necessities required to support or preserve life, livelihood, or existence; provide for the needs of (*water is required to sustain these trees*; *this industry sustains over 14,000 workers*). **2** endure, stand; bear up against. **3** undergo or suffer (defeat or injury etc.) (*she sustained a separated left shoulder*). **4** maintain or keep (an action or process) going continuously (*can she possibly sustain such an effort?*). **5** (of a court etc.) uphold or decide in favour of (an objection etc.). **6** give strength to; encourage, support. **7** substantiate or corroborate (a statement or charge). **8** hold up or support the weight of, esp. for a long period (*that ice is not thick enough to sustain your weight*). **9** *Music* hold (a note or chord) for an extended period. **10** *Theatre* continue to represent (a part, character, etc.) adequately. ● *noun Music* the effect or result of sustaining a note, esp. electronically. □ **sus·tained** *adjective* **sus·tain·er** *noun* **sus·tain·ing** *adjective* **sus·tain·ment** *noun* [Old French *so(u)stein-*, stressed stem of *so(u)stenir*, from Latin *sustinēre sustent-* (as SUB-, *tenēre* 'hold')]

sus·tain·able *adjective* **1** *Ecology* (esp. of development) that conserves an ecological balance by avoiding depletion of natural resources (*sustainable agriculture*; *sustainable forestry*). **2** that may be maintained, esp. at a particular level (*sustainable income*). □ **sus·tain·ably** *adverb* **sus·tain·a·bil·ity** *noun*

sustained-release *adjective* = SLOW-RELEASE.

sustained yield *noun* the quantity of a crop that can be periodically harvested without long-term depletion (also *attributive: sustained-yield forestry*).

sus·ten·ance /ˈsʌstənəns/ *noun* **1** a means of sustaining life; nourishment. **2** a means of subsistence; a livelihood. **3** the action or process of sustaining esp. life. [Anglo-French *sustenaunce* (as SUSTAIN)]

su·sur·ra·tion /ˌsuːsəˈreɪʃən/ *noun literary* a sound of whispering or rustling. □ **su·sur·rant** *adjective* **su·sur·rat·ing** *adjective*

su·sur·rus /suːˈsʌrəs/ *noun literary* a low soft whispering or rustling sound; a susurration. [Latin, of imitative origin]

Suth·er·land ▶ **1 Don·ald** (b.1935), Canadian actor. He has appeared in such diverse films as *Casanova* (1976), *Eye of the Needle* (1981), and *Bethune: The Making of a Hero* (1987). **2 Dame Joan** (b.1926), Australian operatic soprano. Noted for her dramatic coloratura roles, she is best known for her performance of the title role in Donizetti's *Lucia di Lammermoor* in 1959. **3 Kie·fer** (b.1966), Canadian film actor. His films include *Stand By Me* (1986), *Young Guns* (1988), *Flatliners* (1990), *A Few Good Men* (1992), and *Picking Up the Pieces* (1999). He is the son of Donald Sutherland and grandson of Tommy Douglas.

Sut·lej River /ˈsʌtledʒ/ a river of N India and Pakistan. Rising in the Himalayas in SW Tibet, it flows for 1 450 km (900 miles) westward through the Indian states of Himachal Pradesh and Punjab into Punjab province in Pakistan, where it joins the Chenab River to form the Panjnad, eventually to join the Indus. It is one of the five rivers that gave Punjab its name.

sut·ler /ˈsʌtlər/ *noun hist.* a person following an army and selling provisions etc. to the soldiers. [obsolete Dutch *soeteler* from *soetelen* befoul, perform mean duties, from Germanic]

Sutra /ˈsuːtrə/ *noun* **1** an aphorism or set of aphorisms in Hindu literature. **2** a narrative part of Buddhist literature. **3** Jainist scripture. [Sanskrit *sūtra* thread, rule, from *siv* SEW]

sut·tee /sʌˈtiː, ˈsʌti/ *noun* (also **sati**) (*pl.* **sut·tees** or **satis**) esp. *hist.* **1** the Hindu practice of a widow immolating herself on her husband's funeral pyre. **2** a widow who undergoes or has undergone this. [Hindi & Urdu from Sanskrit *satī* faithful wife, from *sat* good]

su·ture /ˈsuːtʃər/ ● *noun* **1** *Surgery* **a** the joining of the edges of a wound or incision by stitching. **b** a seam or stitch made during this procedure. **c** the material used to make surgical stitches. **2** the junction of two bones forming an immovable articulation, esp. each of the serrated borders between the bones of the skull. **3** *Bot. & Zool.* the junction, or line of junction, of contiguous parts, such as the line between adjacent whorls, chambers, or valves of a shell, the seam where the carpels of a pericarp join, etc. **4** *Geol.* the line of junction formed by the collision of two lithospheric plates. ● *transitive verb Surgery* stitch up (a wound or incision) with a suture. □ **su·tur·al** *adjective* **su·tured** *adjective* **su·ture·less** *adjective* [French *suture* or Latin *sutura* from *suere sut-* sew]

SUV /esjuːˈviː/ *noun* a sport-utility vehicle.

Suva /ˈsuːvə/ the capital of Fiji, situated on the southeast coast of the island of Viti Levu; pop. (est. 2002) 176,000.

Su·wan·nee River /səˈwɒni/ (also **Swa·nee River** /ˈswɒni/) a river

of the southeastern US. Rising in SE Georgia, it flows for some 400 km (250 miles) southwest through N Florida to the Gulf of Mexico.

Suwon /ˈsuːwɒn/ a city in S Korea, just south of Seoul; pop. (est. 1996) 755,550.

Suyin /suːˈjɪn/ **Han** (pseudonym of Elizabeth Comber) (b.1917), Chinese-born British writer and doctor. Born to a Chinese father and Belgian mother, she went to England in 1939 and trained as a doctor. Her works include the autobiographical novel *A Many Splendoured Thing* (1952) and a five-volume series of autobiography and Chinese history, starting with *The Crippled Tree* (1965).

su·zer·ain /ˈsuːzərən/ ● *noun* **1** a feudal overlord. **2** a sovereign or nation having some control over another nation that is internally autonomous. ● *adjective* supreme; holding the position of suzerain. □ **su·zer·ainty** *noun* [French, apparently from *sus* above, from Latin *sursum* upward, after *souverain* SOVEREIGN]

Su·zhou /suːˈdʒɔː/ (also **Su·chou**, **Soo·chow** /-ˈtʃaʊ/) a city in E China, in the province of Jiangsu, situated west of Shanghai on the Grand Canal; pop. (2002) 975,100. Founded in the 6th c. BC, it was the capital of the ancient Wu kingdom and a noted silk-manufacturing city.

Su·zuki¹ /səˈzuːki/ **David Taka·yoshi** (b.1936), Canadian geneticist and broadcaster. He is known esp. for his ardent environmentalism and for his popularization of science. He hosted CBC TV's *The Nature of Things* for ten years; his writing includes *Time to Change* (1994).

Su·zuki² /səˈzuːki/ *adjective* designating, pertaining to, or using a method of teaching the violin (esp. to young children), characterized by exercises involving large groups and parental participation. [Shin'ichi *Suzuki*, Japanese violin teacher d.1998]

Sv *symbol* sievert.

s.v. *abbreviation* (in a reference) under the word or heading given. [Latin *sub voce* (or *verbo*)]

Sval·bard /ˈsvɒlbɑːr/ a group of islands, including the island of Spitsbergen, in the Arctic Ocean about 640 km (400 miles) north of Norway; pop. (2002) 2,868.

svelte /svelt/ *adjective* slender, graceful, elegant. [French from Italian *svelto*]

Sven·gali /svenˈɡɑːli/ *noun* (*pl.* **Sven·galis**) a person who exercises a controlling or mesmeric influence on another, esp. for a sinister purpose. [a character in G. Du Maurier's *Trilby*]

Sverd·lovsk /svɜːrdˈlɒfsk/ a former name (1924–91) for YEKATERINBURG.

Sver·drup Islands /ˈsfɜːrdrəp, ˈsvɜːr-/ a group of islands in the NE Arctic Archipelago, including (from east to west) Axel Heiberg, Cornwall, Amund Ringnes and Ellef Ringnes islands. Together with the Parry Islands, they form the group known as the Queen Elizabeth Islands. [O. N. *Sverdrup*, Norwegian Arctic explorer d.1930]

Sve·tam·bara /ʃveˈtʌmbərə/ *noun* a member of one of the two principal sects of Jainism (the other is that of the Digambaras), which was formed AD *c.*80 and survives today in parts of India. The sect is characterized by asceticism and the wearing of white clothing. [Sanskrit, = white-clad]

SVGA *abbreviation* (also **Super VGA**) *Computing* a colour graphics adapter that is an upgrade of the VGA standard. [abbreviation of Super + VGA]

S-video *noun* a method of transmitting a video signal which separates the colour information from the brightness, to improve picture clarity.

SW *abbreviation* **1** southwest. **2** southwestern. **3** shortwave.

swab ● *noun* **1 a** an absorbent pad used in surgery for cleaning or applying medication to wounds. **b** a wad of cotton or other absorbent material fixed to the end of a rod and used for cleaning or applying medication. **c** a specimen of a secretion collected with a swab for examination. **2** a mop or other absorbent device for cleaning or mopping up. ● *transitive verb* (**swabbed**, **swab·bing**) **1** wipe or clean (a wound, ship's deck, etc.) with a swab. **2** absorb or apply (a substance) with a swab. [back-formation from *swabber*, via early modern Dutch *zwabber* from a Germanic base = 'splash, sway']

Swabia /ˈsweɪbiə/ a former duchy of medieval Germany. The region is now divided between SW Germany, Switzerland, and France. □ **Swa·bian** *adjective & noun*

swad·dle *transitive verb* **1** wrap (oneself or another or part of the body) in bandages, clothes, a blanket, etc. **2** wrap (a newborn child) in a blanket or swaddling clothes. **3** surround (a person or thing) with; smother (*we were swaddled in clouds of dust*). □ **swad·dled** *adjective* [Middle English from SWATHE + -LE⁴]

Vowels: a *cat* ɑ *arm* e *bed* ɜr *her* ɜː *deux* ə *ago* ɪ *sit* i *cosy* iː *feed* ɒ *hot* ɔ *pore* ɔː *no* ʌ *run* ʊ *put*

swad·dling clothes *plural noun hist.* narrow lengths of bandage wrapped around a newborn child to restrict its movements and quieten it.

swag ● *noun* **1** *slang* **a** the stolen goods carried off by a thief or burglar. **b** illicit gains. **2** a length of fabric or drapery fastened in such a way that it hangs loosely over a window, sagging in the middle. **3** an ornamental arrangement of flowers, leaves, or fruit. **4** *Austral. & NZ* a traveller's or miner's bundle of personal belongings. ● *verb* (**swagged, swag·ging**) **1** *transitive* hang (a curtain, cord, etc.) so that it sags in the middle; arrange in swags. **2** *intransitive* droop or hang heavily; sag. **3** *transitive* decorate or adorn with swags of flowers or leaves etc. [16th c.: prob. from Scandinavian]

swage /sweidʒ/ ● *noun* **1** a tool, die, or stamp for bending and shaping wrought iron etc. by hammering or pressure. **2** a circular or semicircular depression on an anvil. ● *transitive verb* shape (metal) with a swage. [French *s(o)uage* decorative groove, of unknown origin]

swag·ger ● *intransitive verb* **1** walk or behave with an air of confidence, self-importance, or toughness. **2** talk boastfully; brag. ● *noun* **1 a** an air or attitude of cockiness or toughness. **b** an air or attitude of smartness or flamboyance. **2** a swaggering gait or manner. **3** confident, boastful, or brash behaviour. □ **swag·ger·er** *noun* **swag·ger·ing** *adjective* **swag·ger·ing·ly** *adverb* [apparently from SWAG *verb* + -ER⁴]

swagger stick *noun* a short cane carried by a military officer.

swag·man *noun* (*pl.* **-men**) *Austral. & NZ* a vagabond or tramp. [from SWAG *noun* 4 + MAN]

Swa·hili /swɑˈhiːli, swɒ-/ ● *noun* (*pl.* same) **1** a member of a Bantu-speaking people of Zanzibar and adjacent coasts. **2** their language, used widely as a lingua franca in E Africa. ● *adjective* of or relating to the Swahili or their language. [Arabic *sawāhil*, pl. of *sāhil* 'coast']

swain *noun* **1** *archaic* a young man living or working in the country; a shepherd. **2** *literary or jocular* a young lover or suitor. [Old Norse *sveinn* lad = Old English *swān* swineherd, from Germanic]

Swain·son's hawk *noun* a dark-coloured hawk, *Buteo swainsoni*, found in western N America, esp. on the Prairies. [W. *Swainson*, English naturalist d.1855]

swale *noun esp. N Amer.* a low or hollow place, esp. a marshy depression or hollow between ridges. [16th c.: origin unknown]

swal·low¹ ● *verb* **1** *transitive & intransitive* cause or allow (food etc.) to pass down the throat. **2** *intransitive* perform the muscular movement of the esophagus required to do this (*my throat only hurts if I swallow*). **3** *transitive* **a** accept without opposition or protest; meekly put up with (an insult etc.). **b** accept (an unlikely assertion etc.) gullibly or unquestioningly. **4** *transitive* repress; resist the expression of (a feeling etc.) (*had to swallow my anger to continue*). **5** *transitive* (often foll. by *up*) engulf, absorb, or consume; cause to disappear. **5** *transitive* (of a business) cover an expense rather than passing it on to customers (*we're swallowing the GST*). ● *noun* **1** the act of swallowing. **2** an amount swallowed in one action. □ **swallow one's pride** humble oneself in order to admit guilt or error or to ask for a favour. □ **swal·low·able** *adjective* **swal·low·er** *noun* [Old English *swelg* (n.), *swelgan* (v.) from Germanic]

swal·low² *noun* any of various migratory swift-flying insect-eating birds of the family Hirundinidae, with a forked tail and long pointed wings. □ **one swallow does not make a summer** a single fortunate or satisfactory incident does not mean that what follows will be as good. [Old English *swealwe* from Germanic]

swal·low·tail *noun* **1** anything resembling the shape of a swallow's deeply forked tail. **2** any butterfly of the family Papilionidae with wings extended at the back to this shape. **3** (in full **swallowtail coat**) = TAILCOAT. □ **swallow-tailed** *adjective*

swam *past of* SWIM.

swami /ˈswɒmi/ *noun* (*pl.* **swamis**) **1** a Hindu male religious teacher. **2** *informal* an adviser or mentor. [Hindi *swāmī* master, prince, from Sanskrit *svāmin*]

Swam·mer·dam /ˈswɒmər,dam/ **Jan** (1637–80), Dutch naturalist and microscopist. He worked extensively on insects, describing their anatomy and life history, and classifying them into four groups; a pioneer in the use of lenses, he was the first to observe red blood cells.

swamp ● *noun* **1** a tract of low-lying ground in which water collects; an area of waterlogged ground; a bog or marsh. **2** a difficult or messy situation; a complication (*a bureaucratic swamp*). ● *verb* **1 a** *transitive* overwhelm, flood, or soak with water. **b** *intransitive* (of a boat) become filled with water and sink. **2** *transitive* overwhelm with a large amount of something (*swamped him with fan mail*). **3** *transitive & intransitive N Amer.* clear (a road) in a forest by felling trees, removing undergrowth, etc.,

esp. for hauling logs. □ **swampy** *adjective* (**swamp·i·er, swamp·i·est**). [17th c., = dial. *swamp* sunk (14th c.), prob. of Germanic origin]

swamp ash *noun* = BLACK ASH.

swamped *adjective* overwhelmed with work; extremely busy.

swamp·er *noun N Amer.* **1** *Cdn* a person who swamps logging roads. **2 a** *Cdn* (*BC*) an assistant to a truck driver. **b** *hist.* an apprentice to a teamster, in charge of maintaining the horses and helping with the transportation of freight. **3** *US* a native or inhabitant of a swampy region.

swamp fever *noun* **1** a contagious viral disease of horses, causing anemia, emaciation, and in many cases death. **2** = MALARIA.

swamp grass *noun* any of various grasses growing in low, wet places.

swamp·land *noun* land consisting of swamps.

swamp maple *noun* = RED MAPLE.

swamp oak *noun* **1** = PIN OAK. **2** = CASUARINA.

swamp sparrow *noun* a song sparrow, *Melospiza georgiana*, common in N America.

Swampy Cree *noun* **1** a member of a Cree people living in northern Manitoba and in the area of western James Bay and Hudson Bay. **2** the Cree dialect spoken by this people. [because the area they inhabit is mainly muskeg]

Swan, Sir Jo·seph Wil·son (1828–1914), English physicist and chemist. He devised an electric light bulb consisting of a carbon filament inside a glass bulb in 1860, and in 1883 formed a partnership with Thomas Edison to manufacture the bulbs.

swan ● *noun* any of several large web-footed swimming birds constituting the genera *Cygnus* and *Coscoroba* of the family Anatidae, characterized by a long and gracefully curved neck with all white (or, in the case of *Cygnus atratus*, black) plumage and black feet. ● *intransitive verb* (**swanned, swan·ning**) (usu. foll. by *about, around*, or *off*) esp. *Brit. informal* move or go aimlessly, casually, or with a superior air. □ **swan·like** *adjective & adverb* [Old English from Germanic]

swan dive *noun N Amer.* **1** a forward dive with the arms extended sideways until the diver is close to the surface of the water, at which point the arms are brought together over the head. **2** *jocular* a dramatic or spectacular fall, plunge, or dive.

Swa·nee River see SUWANNEE RIVER.

swank *informal* ● *noun* **1** style, elegance. **2** ostentation, flashiness, swagger. ● *intransitive verb* boast, show off. ● *adjective* esp. *N Amer.* (also **swanky** (**swan·ki·er, swan·ki·est**)) **1** posh, stylish. **2** pretentious, boastful. [19th c.: origin uncertain]

swan neck *noun esp. Brit.* = GOOSENECK. □ **swan-necked** *adjective*

swan·nery *noun* (*pl.* **-ies**) a place where swans are bred.

Swan River a river of Western Australia. Rising as the Avon to the southeast of Perth, it flows north and west through Perth to the Indian Ocean at Fremantle. It was the site of the first free European settlement in Western Australia.

swans·down *noun* **1** the fine down of a swan, used in trimmings. **2** a soft thick compact fabric of wool with a little silk or cotton. **3** a strong cotton fabric with a soft nap on one side (also *attributive*: *swansdown blanket*).

Swan·sea a city in S Wales, on the Bristol Channel; pop. (est. 2002) 170,500.

swan song *noun* the final work or performance of a writer, artist, etc. before retirement or death. [with reference to a song said to be sung by a swan as it dies]

swap (also **swop**) ● *transitive & intransitive verb* (**swapped, swap·ping**) exchange or trade (one thing for another). ● *noun* **1** an act of swapping one thing for another; a trade or exchange. **2** *Finance* a transaction in which two rates of interest on a certain principal are exchanged. **3** = SWAP MEET 1. □ **swap·pable** *adjective* **swap·per** *noun* [Middle English, originally = 'hit': prob. imitative]

swap meet *noun esp. N Amer.* **1** a gathering at which enthusiasts or collectors trade or exchange items of a particular kind. **2** a flea market.

SWAPO /ˈswɒpoʊ/ *abbreviation* South West Africa People's Organization.

swa·raj /swəˈrɑːdʒ/ *noun hist.* self-government or independence for India. □ **swarajist** *noun* [Sanskrit, = self-ruling: compare RAJ]

sward /swɔrd/ *noun literary* **1** the upper layer of soil usu. covered with grass or weeds; turf. **2** a covering or expanse of grass; lawn. [Old English *sweard* skin]

swarf /swɔrf/ *noun* waste debris produced by a machining operation esp. in the form of wet or greasy grit abraded from a grindstone or axle during use, metal filings or ribbons, stone chips, etc. [Old Norse *svarf* dust, from filing]

swarm[1] ● *noun* **1** a cluster of bees leaving the hive with the queen to establish a new colony. **2** a large number of insects or birds moving in a cluster. **3** (often foll. by *of*) a large or dense group of people, animals, or things, esp. when active or moving; a turbulent crowd. **4** a group of zoospores. ● *verb* **1** *intransitive* gather or proceed in a swarm or crowd. **2** *intransitive* (foll. by *with*) (of a place) be overrun, crowded, or infested (*in the summer the city swarms with tourists*). **3** *transitive* (of a large group of people or things) fill (an area or space); crowd (*students swarmed the halls*). **4** *transitive* gather around (a person), esp. in an aggressive or hostile manner (*photographers swarmed the popular star*). [Old English *swearm* from Germanic]

swarm[2] *transitive & intransitive verb* climb up (a rope or tree etc.), esp. in a rush, by clasping or clinging with the hands and knees. [16th c.: origin unknown]

swarm·ing *noun* a type of attack in which an individual is surrounded, taunted, and shoved by a group of attackers until the victim is too intimidated or confused to resist theft or assault.

swart /swɔrt/ *adjective* *archaic* dark in colour, swarthy. [Old English *sweart* from Germanic]

swarthy /ˈswɔrði/ *adjective* (**swar·thi·er**, **swar·thi·est**) of a dark colour or complexion. □ **swar·thi·ness** *noun* [var. of obsolete *swarty* (as SWART)]

swash[1] /swɒʃ/ ● *intransitive verb* **1** (of water etc.) splash about; make the sound of washing or of waves crashing against the shore. **2** *archaic* make a noise as of swords clashing or striking a shield. **3** *archaic* swagger. ● *noun* the action or sound of water dashing against the side of a cliff, ship, etc. [imitative]

swash[2] /swɒʃ/ *adjective* (of a letter) having a flourished stroke or strokes. [from earlier sense 'inclined obliquely': origin unknown]

swash·buck·ler /ˈswɒʃbʌklər/ *noun* **1** a swaggering adventurer or blustering ruffian. **2** a film, book, etc. portraying swashbuckling characters. [SWASH[1] + BUCKLER]

swash·buck·ling /ˈswɒʃbʌklɪŋ/ ● *adjective* acting like, or characteristic of the conduct of, a swashbuckler; noisily swaggering, blustering; ostentatiously daring. ● *noun* conduct characteristic of a swashbuckler.

swas·tika /ˈswɒstɪkə, ˈswɒstɪkə/ *noun* **1** an ancient symbol in the form of a cross with each of its four arms of equal length bent at right angles at the end, all in the same direction and usu. clockwise. **2** this symbol with clockwise continuations used as the emblem of Nazi Germany and adopted subsequently as the emblem of anti-Semitic and other racially motivated hate groups. [Sanskrit *svastika* from *svastí* well-being, from *sú* good + *astí* being]

SWAT /swɒt/ *noun* (in full **SWAT team**) a special detachment of some US law enforcement agencies trained to deal with terrorism and other dangerous situations such as hostage-takings. [acronym from Special Weapons and Tactics]

swat ● *verb* (**swat·ted**, **swat·ting**) **1** *transitive* crush (a fly etc.) with a sharp blow. **2** *transitive* hit hard and abruptly; slap, smack. **3** *intransitive* direct a blow at a target, esp. without hitting it (*swatted at the bee buzzing around her head*). ● *noun* a sharp slap or hit. [17th c. in the sense 'sit down': Northern English dial. & US var. of SQUAT]

swatch /swɒtʃ/ *noun* **1 a** a sample, esp. of cloth, fabric, or paint colours. **b** a collection of samples. **2 a** representative segment; a portion or section (*he appeals to a swatch of our listeners*). **3** *Cdn* (*Nfld*) an expanse of open water or ice, esp. one inhabited by seals. [17th c.: origin unknown]

swath /swɒθ/ ● *noun* (also **swathe** /sweɪð/) (*pl.* **swaths** /swɒθs, swɒðs/ or **swathes** /sweɪðs/) **1** a strip in a field or lawn that has been left clear after the passage of a mower, scythe, etc. **2** a row or line of grass, wheat, etc. as it falls or lies when mown or reaped. **3** a broad strip or long stretch of something (*had driven this swath of highway before*). ● *transitive verb* *N Amer.* cut (grain etc.) with a swather. □ **cut a wide swath 1** be effective in destruction. **2** make a grand or pompous display. [Old English *swæth, swathu*]

swathe /swɒð, sweɪð/ *transitive verb* **1** wrap (a person etc.) in bandages or clothes. **2** cover in or under; envelop (*the city was swathed in snow*). [Old English *swathian*]

swath·er /ˈswɒðər, ˈswɒθ-/ *noun* *N Amer.* a machine used to cut grain and deposit it in a row to dry and be collected.

Swatow /swɒˈtaʊ/ the former name for SHANTOU.

swat·ter *noun* = FLY SWATTER.

sway ● *verb* **1** *intransitive* **a** move slowly and rhythmically backwards and forwards or from side to side as if on a pivot (*tall grasses swaying in the breeze*). **b** rock awkwardly or unsteadily as if about to fall. **2** *intransitive* vacillate between two options or opinions; waver. **3** *transitive* **a** influence, affect, or direct the decision or opinion of (a person) (*hopes to sway the voters*). **b** control or direct the outcome of (an event) (*hopes to sway the election*). **4** *transitive* cause to move or swing from side to side (*sways her hips as she walks*). **5** *intransitive* bend, lean, or incline to one side. ● *noun* **1** a position of power, authority, or influence; clout. **2** a movement backwards and forwards or from side to side; a swaying motion. □ **hold sway** be supreme in power, control, influence, or popularity. [Middle English: compare Low German *swājen* be blown to and fro, Dutch *zwaaien* swing, wave]

sway-back *noun* an abnormally hollowed back (esp. of a horse); lordosis.

sway-backed *adjective* **1** (esp. of a horse) having a sway-back. **2** having an abnormal curve or sag; concave (*a sway-backed table*).

Swazi /ˈswɒzi/ ● *noun* (*pl.* same or **Swazis**) **a** a member of a people inhabiting Swaziland and parts of Mpumalanga in South Africa. **b** a native or national of Swaziland. **2** the Nguni language of this people. ● *adjective* of or relating to Swaziland, the Swazi, or their language. [*Mswati*, name of a former king of the Swazi]

Swazi·land /ˈswɒziˌlænd/ a small landlocked kingdom in southern Africa, bounded by South Africa and Mozambique; pop. (est. 2002) 1,123,605; capital, Mbabane.

swear ● *verb* (*past* **swore**; *past participle* **sworn**) **1** *transitive* **a** (often foll. by *to* + infin. or *that* + clause) state or promise solemnly or on oath. **b** promise to undertake, perform, or maintain (vengeance, allegiance, etc.); declare. **c** take (an oath). **2** *transitive* *informal* **a** state emphatically; insist (*he swore he hadn't seen it before*). **b** state or insist with near certainty; be almost certain (*you would swear this was real; I'd swear I've met you somewhere before*). **3** *transitive* cause to take an oath (*swore them to secrecy*). **4** *intransitive* **a** (often foll. by *at*) use profane or indecent language, esp. as an expletive or from anger. **b** use such language habitually (*he doesn't go out with girls who swear*). **5** *intransitive* (foll. by *by*) *informal* have or express great confidence or faith in (*I'll never use a computer, I swear by my old typewriter*). **6** *intransitive* (often foll. by *to, by, on*) appeal to a god or other sacred person or thing in confirmation of the truth of a solemn declaration or statement (*I swear to God; he swore on his mother's grave that it was true*). **7** *intransitive* (foll. by *to*; usu. in *neg.*) admit the certainty of (*could not swear to it*). **8** *transitive* (often foll. by *against*) make a sworn affirmation of (an offence) (*swear treason against*). ● *noun* a period of swearing. □ **swear blind** *informal* affirm emphatically. **swear in** induct into office etc. by administering an oath. **swear off** *informal* promise or vow to abstain from (drink etc.). **swear out** *N Amer.* obtain the issue of (a warrant for arrest) by making a charge on oath. **swear up and down** *N Amer.* swear or assert vehemently. □ **swear·er** *noun* **swear·ing** *noun* [Old English *swerian* from Germanic, related to ANSWER]

swearing-in *noun* a ceremony at which a person formally accepts the conditions of an office, tenure, assignment, etc., by swearing an oath.

swear word *noun* a profane or indecent word, esp. uttered as an expletive.

sweat ● *noun* **1** moisture exuded through the pores of the skin, esp. from heat, exertion, or nervousness. **2 a** a state or period of sweating (*broke out in a sweat*). **b** a period of time spent in a sweat lodge. **3** *informal* a state of anxiety (*was in a sweat about it*). **4** *informal* **a** drudgery, effort. **b** a laborious task or undertaking. **5** condensed moisture on a surface. **6** (in *pl.*) esp. *N Amer.* *informal* **a** = SWEATSUIT. **b** = SWEATPANTS. **c** = SWEATSHIRT. **7** = SWEAT BATH. ● *verb* (*past* and *past participle* **sweat·ed** or **sweat**) **1** *intransitive* exude sweat; perspire. **2** *intransitive* be terrified, suffering, etc. **3** *intransitive* (of a wall etc.) exhibit surface moisture. **4** *intransitive* drudge, toil. **5 a** *intransitive & transitive* exude or cause to exude or condense moisture in the form of drops on a surface, esp. as part of a manufacturing process. **b** *transitive* heat (meat or vegetables) slowly in fat or water to extract the juices. **c** *transitive* subject (hides or tobacco) to fermentation in manufacturing. **6** *transitive* emit (blood, gum, etc.) like sweat. **7** *transitive* make (a horse, athlete, etc.) sweat by exercise. **8** *transitive* cause to drudge or toil. **9** *transitive* *Metallurgy* subject (metal) to partial melting, esp. to fasten or join by solder without a soldering iron. **10** *transitive* *N Amer.* *informal* worry about (something) (*don't sweat the details*). □ **by the sweat of one's brow** by one's own hard work. **no sweat** *informal* **1** there is no need to worry. **2** without any difficulty. **sweat blood** *informal* **1** work strenuously. **2** be extremely anxious. **sweat bullets** *N Amer.* *slang* sweat profusely. **sweat one's guts out** *informal* work extremely hard, esp. excessively in comparison to the reward or to other people's expectations. **sweat it out** *informal* endure a difficult experience to the end. □ **sweat·proof** *adjective* [Old English *swāt* (n.), *swātan* (v., corresponding to Old High German *sweizzen* 'roast'), from Germanic: the noun altered from earlier *swote* in imitation of the verb]

sweat·band *noun* **1** a band of absorbent material, usu. elasticized terrycloth, worn around the head or wrist to soak up sweat. **2** a band of absorbent material lining a hat.

sweat bath *noun* **1** a structure filled with hot humid air to induce sweating. **2** the action of spending time in such a structure with the intention of sweating profusely.

sweat·box *noun* a very hot room or building.

sweat·ed *adjective* (of goods, workers, or labour) produced by or subjected to long hours under poor conditions.

sweat equity *noun* N Amer. unpaid labour that contributes to the value of something.

sweat·er *noun* **1** a knitted or crocheted garment covering the upper half of the body. **2** a sports jersey. □ **sweat·ered** *adjective* (also in combination).

sweater coat *noun* a knitted coat-like garment, usu. three-quarter length or full-length.

sweater set *noun* a woman's matching cardigan and sleeveless or short-sleeved sweater.

sweat gland *noun* a spiral tubular gland below the skin secreting sweat.

sweat lodge *noun* any of various structures heated by pouring water over hot stones, used by some Aboriginal groups to induce sweating, as for religious or medical purposes.

sweat·pants *plural noun* loose pants made of fleecy knit material with a drawstring or elasticized waist and often with elasticized cuffs, worn as casual attire or for sports.

sweat·shirt *noun* a loosely fitting long-sleeved top made of a fleecy knit material, worn as casual attire or for sports.

sweat·shop *noun* a factory, workshop, etc., esp. in the garment industry, where workers work long hours in unpleasant conditions for low pay.

sweat sock *noun* N Amer. a sock reaching to mid-calf, made of thick, absorbent, usu. white cotton or wool.

sweat·suit *noun* a suit of a sweatshirt and sweatpants, worn as casual attire or for sports.

sweaty *adjective* (**sweat·i·er, sweat·i·est**) **1** covered, damp with, or smelling of sweat (*a sweaty T-shirt*). **2** causing sweat. □ **sweat·i·ly** *adverb* **sweat·i·ness** *noun*

Swede *noun* **1 a** a native or national of Sweden. **b** a person of Swedish descent. **2** (**swede**) (in full **swede turnip**) esp. Brit. = RUTABAGA. [Middle Low German & Middle Dutch *Swēde*, prob. from Old Norse *Svíthjóth* from *Svíar* Swedes + *thjóth* people]

Sweden a country occupying the eastern part of the Scandinavian peninsula; pop. (est. 2002) 8,876,744, official language, Swedish; capital, Stockholm.

Sweden·borg /ˈswiːdənˌbɔːg/ **Eman·uel** (born Emanuel Swedberg) (1688–1772), Swedish scientist, theologian, and mystic. His speculative and inventive work anticipated later developments such as the nebular theory, crystallography, and flying machines; his mystical doctrines, which blended Christianity with elements of both pantheism and theosophy, were taken up by a group of followers, who founded the New Jerusalem Church in 1787. □ **Sweden·borg·ian** /ˌswiːdənˈbɔːgiən/ *adjective & noun* **Sweden·borg·ian·ism** *noun*

swede saw *noun* Cdn a type of hand saw with a bow-like tubular frame and many cutting teeth.

Swed·ish ● *adjective* of or relating to Sweden or its people or language. ● *noun* the language of Sweden.

Swedish massage *noun* a system of full-body massage first devised in Sweden, utilizing long strokes, kneading and friction techniques to relieve tension and stimulate circulation.

sweep ● *verb* (*past* and *past participle* **swept**) **1** *transitive* clean or clear (a room or area etc.) with or as with a broom. **2** *intransitive* (often foll. by *up*) clean a room etc. in this way. **3** *transitive* (often foll. by *up*) collect or remove (dirt or litter etc.) by sweeping. **4** *transitive* (foll. by *aside, away,* etc.) **a** push with or as with a broom. **b** dismiss or reject abruptly (*their objections were swept aside*). **5** *transitive* (foll. by *along, down,* etc.) carry or drive along with force. **6** *transitive* (foll. by *off, away,* etc.) remove or clear forcefully. **7** *transitive* traverse swiftly or lightly (*the wind swept the hillside*). **8** *transitive* impart a sweeping motion to (*swept his hand across*). **9** *transitive* swiftly cover or affect (*a new fashion swept the country*).

10 *intransitive* **a** glide swiftly; speed along with unchecked motion. **b** go majestically. **c** move suddenly and with force over an area (*fire swept through the building*). **11** *intransitive* (of geographical features etc.) have continuous extent. **12** *transitive* **a** pass over (something) in order to examine it or search for something (*searchlights swept the sky*). **b** drag (a river bottom etc.) to search for something. **c** examine (a building, telephone line, etc.) for electronic listening or recording devices. **13** *transitive* (of artillery etc.) include in the line of fire; cover the whole of. **14** *transitive* N Amer. win every event, award, or place in (a contest). ● *noun* **1** the act or motion or an instance of sweeping. **2** a curve in the road, a sweeping line of a hill, etc. **3** range or scope (*the long sweep of history*). **4** a sortie by aircraft. **5** (in *pl.*) *informal* = SWEEPSTAKES 1, 2. **6** a long oar worked from a barge etc. **7** the sail of a windmill. **8** a long pole mounted as a lever for raising buckets from a well. **9** N Amer. victory in all the games in a contest etc. by one team or competitor, or the winning of all the places in a single event. **10** *Electronics* the movement of a beam across the screen of a cathode ray tube. **11 a** a surprise raid by police through a neighbourhood, building, etc., to arrest suspected persons or seize illicit goods. **b** a comprehensive search for electronic listening or recording devices. **12** a survey of an area, esp. the night sky, made in an arc or circle. **13** (in *pl.*) N Amer. a survey of the popularity ratings of television programs, taken at regular intervals to determine advertising rates. **14** *Football* = END RUN 1. **15** = CHIMNEY SWEEP. **16** a piece of rubber affixed to the bottom of an exterior door to keep out drafts. □ **make a clean sweep of 1** completely abolish or expel. **2** win all the prizes etc. in (a competition etc.). **sweep away 1** abolish swiftly. **2** (usu. in *passive*) powerfully affect, esp. emotionally. **sweep the board 1** win all the money in a gambling game. **2** win all possible prizes etc. **sweep a person off his** (or **her**) **feet** affect a person with powerful emotion, esp. love. **sweep under the carpet** *see* CARPET. [Middle English *swepe* (earlier *swōpe*) from Old English *swāpan*]

sweep·back *noun* the angle at which an aircraft's wing is set back from a position at right angles to the body.

sweep·er *noun* **1** a person who cleans by sweeping. **2** a device for sweeping (*carpet sweeper*). **3** a person who or a vessel which sweeps for something under water. **4** Cdn **a** a tree growing close to and overhanging a stream or river. **b** a drifting tree or log in a stream or river. **5** *Curling* a player who sweeps in front of a moving rock with a broom or brush. **6** *Soccer* a defensive player positioned close to the goalkeeper and playing across the width of the field.

sweep·ing ● *adjective* **1** wide in range or effect (*sweeping changes*). **2** taking no account of particular cases or exceptions (*a sweeping statement*). **3** complete, overwhelming (*a sweeping victory*). **4** passing over a wide area (*a sweeping view*). ● *noun* (in *pl.*) dirt etc. collected by sweeping. □ **sweep·ing·ly** *adverb*

sweep second hand *noun* a second hand on a clock or watch, moving on the same dial as the other hands.

sweep·stakes *noun* (also **sweep·stake**) **1** a form of gambling in which all the money bet on the result of a contest is paid to the winner or winners. **2** a race with betting of this kind. **3** a prize or prizes won in a sweepstakes.

Sweet, Henry (1845–1912), English philologist and phonetician, whose works include *An Anglo-Saxon Reader* (1876), *A Handbook of Phonetics* (1877), and *A History of English Sounds* (1888).

sweet ● *adjective* **1 a** having the pleasant taste characteristic of sugar. **b** (in the names of baked goods) sweet-tasting, esp. Cdn (Nfld) containing molasses and raisins, and prepared chiefly at Christmas (*sweet bread; sweet loaf*). **2 a** smelling pleasant like roses or perfume etc.; fragrant. **b** (in the names of flowers, fruit, and vegetables) sweet-smelling or sweet-tasting (*sweet william; sweet potato*). **3** (of sound etc.) melodious or harmonious. **4 a** not salty, sour, or bitter. **b** fresh and pure (*the sweet air of the countryside*). **c** (of food) fresh, with flavour unimpaired by rottenness. **d** (of water) fresh and readily drinkable. **5** (of wine) having a sweet taste (*opp.* DRY *adjective* 2). **6** highly gratifying or attractive (*the sweet feeling of success*). **7** amiable, pleasant (*has a sweet nature*). **8** *informal* (of a person or thing) pretty, charming, endearing. **9** (foll. by *on*) *informal* fond of; in love with. **10** esp. *ironic* one's own; particular, individual (*takes his own sweet time*). **11** *slang* as an intensifier in phrases meaning 'nothing at all' (*sweet Fanny Adams*). **12** *informal* (of a deal etc.) not harsh or severe; with terms that are more lenient than deserved. **13** (often as *interjection*) used in expressions of assent or approval. ● *noun* **1** (in *pl.*) **a** N Amer. sweet foods, such as pie, cake, chocolate, etc. (*doesn't like sweets*). **b** Cdn (NB) = DAINTY *noun* 2. **2** Brit. a small shaped piece of confectionery usu. made with sugar or sweet chocolate. **3** Brit. a sweet dish forming a course of a meal; dessert. **4** a sweet part of something; sweetness. **5** (in *pl.*) delights, gratification. **6** (esp. as a form of address) sweetheart etc. □ **sweet·ish** *adjective* **sweet·ly** *adverb* [Old English *swēte*, from Germanic]

sweet alyssum *noun* see ALYSSUM 1.

sweet-and-sour *attributive adjective* cooked in a sauce containing sugar and vinegar or lemon juice etc. (*sweet-and-sour pork*).

sweet basil *noun* see BASIL.

sweet bay *noun* = BAY² 1.

sweet·bread *noun* the pancreas or thymus of an animal, used for food.

sweet-brier *noun* a wild rose, *Rosa eglanteria*, with small fragrant leaves and flowers.

sweet calamus *noun* = SWEET FLAG.

sweet cassava *noun* see CASSAVA.

sweet chestnut *noun* see CHESTNUT 1b.

sweet cicely *noun* a white-flowered aromatic umbelliferous plant, the North American *Osmorhiza claytoni* or the European *Myrrhis odorata*.

sweet clover *noun* any of various melilots.

sweet coltsfoot *noun* = BUTTERBUR.

sweet corn *noun* **1** a kind of corn with kernels having a high sugar content. **2** these kernels eaten as a vegetable.

sweet·en *verb* **1** *transitive & intransitive* make or become sweet or sweeter in smell, taste, or sound. **2** *transitive* make fresh or wholesome; purify (*use mouthwash to sweeten your breath*). **3** *transitive* make agreeable or less painful. **4** *transitive* increase the attractiveness or value of (a deal, proposal, etc.). **5** *transitive* esp. *US* increase (the collateral of a loan) by adding further securities. **6** *transitive* *Cards* *informal* increase the stakes (in a pot). □ **sweeten the pill** see PILL¹. □ **sweet·en·ing** *noun*

sweet·en·er *noun* **1** a substance used to sweeten food or drink, esp. any of various low-calorie sugar substitutes. **2** a thing that makes something more pleasant, agreeable, or tolerable. **3** *informal* a bribe or inducement.

sweet flag *noun* a plant of the arum family, *Acorus calamus*, with leaves resembling those of an iris and an aromatic root used medicinally.

sweet gale *noun* = BOG MYRTLE.

sweet·grass *noun* *N Amer.* **1** any of several fragrant grasses, esp. *Hierochloe odorata*, used in basket making and in smudging ceremonies. **2** any of various grasses or other plants relished by cattle for their sweet succulent foliage, esp. any of various marsh grasses of the genus *Glyceria*.

sweet·heart *noun* **1** a person with whom one is in love (*childhood sweethearts*). **2** a term of endearment (esp. as a form of address). **3** a lovable, amiable, or obliging person.

sweetheart deal *noun* (also **sweetheart contract**) *informal* an industrial agreement reached privately by employers and union leaders in their own interests.

sweetheart neckline *noun* a neckline on a dress, blouse etc. shaped like the top of a heart.

sweetheart rose *noun* *N Amer.* any of several roses having small pink, white, or yellow flowers particularly attractive as buds.

sweet·ie *noun* *informal* **1** (also **sweetie pie**) a term of endearment (esp. as a form of address). **2** = SWEETHEART 3. **3** *Brit.* a candy.

sweet·ing *noun* **1** a sweet-flavoured variety of apple. **2** *archaic* darling.

sweet marjoram *noun* see MARJORAM.

sweet·meat *noun* **1** an item of confectionery, such as a preserved or candied fruit, a sugared nut, etc. **2** a small fancy cake.

sweet·ness *noun* the quality of being sweet; fragrance, melodiousness, etc. □ **sweetness and light** a display of (esp. uncharacteristic) mildness and reason.

sweet pea *noun* any climbing plant of the genus *Lathyrus*, esp. *L. odoratus* with fragrant flowers in many colours.

sweet pepper *noun* a pepper with a relatively mild taste.

sweet potato *noun* **1** a tropical climbing plant, *Ipomoea batatas*, with sweet tuberous roots used for food. **2** the root of this.

sweet rocket *noun* see ROCKET² 1.

sweet shop *noun* esp. *Brit.* a candy store.

sweet·sop *noun* **1** a tropical American evergreen shrub, *Annona squamosa*. **2** the fruit of this, having a green rind and a sweet pulp.

sweet spot *noun* **1** the point on a bat, club, racquet, etc. at which it makes most effective contact with the ball. **2** a point that provides optimum performance.

sweet sultan *noun* a sweet-scented plant, *Centaurea moschata* or *C. suaveoleus*.

sweet talk *informal* ● *noun* flattery, blandishment. ● *transitive verb* (**sweet-talk**) flatter in order to persuade. □ **sweet-talking** *adjective*

sweet-tempered *adjective* amiable.

sweet tooth *noun* a liking for sweet-tasting things.

sweet violet *noun* a sweet-scented violet, *Viola odorata*.

sweet william *noun* a plant, *Dianthus barbatus*, with clusters of vivid fragrant flowers.

swell ● *verb* (*past participle* **swol·len** or **swelled**) **1** *intransitive & transitive* grow or cause to grow bigger or louder or more intense; expand; increase in force or intensity. **2** *intransitive & transitive* rise or raise up from the surrounding surface. **3** *intransitive* (foll. by *out*) bulge. **4** *intransitive* (of the heart as the seat of emotion) feel full of joy, pride, etc. **5** *intransitive* (foll. by *with*) be hardly able to restrain (pride etc.). ● *noun* **1** an act or the state of swelling. **2** the heaving of the sea with waves that do not break, e.g. after a storm. **3 a** a crescendo. **b** a mechanism in an organ etc. for obtaining a crescendo or diminuendo. **4** *informal* a person of distinction or of dashing or fashionable appearance. **5** a protuberant part. ● *adjective* **1** esp. *N Amer.* *informal* fine, splendid, excellent. **2** *informal* smart, fashionable. [Old English *swellan* from Germanic]

swelled head *noun* (also **swollen head**) *informal* inordinate conceit; excessive pride or vanity.

swell·ing *noun* **1** a swollen, distended, or protuberant part of something, esp. a part of the body enlarged as a result of disease or injury. **2** the process or an instance of swelling, becoming distended, or rising in intensity etc.

swel·ter ● *intransitive verb* (usu. as **swel·ter·ing** *adjective*) be uncomfortably hot. ● *noun* a sweltering atmosphere or condition. □ **swel·ter·ing·ly** *adverb* [base of (now dial.) *swelt* from Old English *sweltan* perish, from Germanic]

swept *past and past participle of* SWEEP.

swept-back *adjective* (of an aircraft wing) fixed at an acute angle to the fuselage, inclining outwards towards the rear.

swept-wing *adjective* (of an aircraft) having swept-back wings.

swerve ● *transitive & intransitive verb* change or cause to change direction, esp. abruptly. ● *noun* **1** a swerving movement. **2** divergence from a course. □ **swerv·er** *noun* [Middle English, representing Old English *sweorfan* SCOUR¹]

Swift, Jona·than (1667–1745), Irish satirist and poet. His greatest work, *Gulliver's Travels* (1726), is a satire on human society and institutions in the form of a fantastic tale of travels in imaginary lands; his other works include the ironic *A Modest Proposal* (1729), a pamphlet proposing that the children of the poor should be fattened to feed the rich. □ **Swift·ian** *adjective*

swift ● *adjective* **1** quick, rapid; soon coming or passing. **2** speedy, prompt (*a swift response; was swift to act*). **3** *informal* smart, clever (*not too swift*). ● *adverb* (*archaic* except in *combination*) swiftly (*swift-moving*). ● *noun* **1** any swift-flying insect-eating bird of the family Apodidae, with long wings and a superficial resemblance to a swallow. **2** a revolving frame for winding yarn etc. from. **3** *Cdn* an area of rapidly flowing current in a river. □ **swift·ly** *adverb* **swift·ness** *noun* [Old English, related to *swifan* move in a course]

Swift Current a city in SW central Saskatchewan, located on Swift Current Creek, 245 km west of Regina; pop. (2001) 14,821. [the name of the creek, from a translation of its Cree name *Kisiskatchewan*: compare SASKATCHEWAN RIVER]

swift fox *noun* a small fox, *Vulpes velox*, of N American prairies.

swift·ie *noun* *slang* **1** a deceptive trick. **2** a person who acts or thinks quickly.

swig ● *transitive & intransitive verb* (**swigged**, **swig·ging**) *informal* drink in large drafts. ● *noun* a large swallow of a beverage, esp. of liquor. □ **swig·ger** *noun* [16th c., originally as noun in obsolete sense 'liquor': origin unknown]

swile *noun* *Cdn* (*Nfld*) *archaic* a seal. □ **swil·er** *noun* **swil·ing** *noun* [irregular var. of SEAL²]

swill ● *verb* **1** *transitive & intransitive* drink greedily. **2** *transitive* (often foll. by *out*) *Brit.* rinse or flush; pour water over or through. ● *noun* **1** scraps of waste food, usu. mixed with water, for feeding pigs. **2** inferior liquor. **3** worthless matter; rubbish. □ **swil·er** *noun* [Old English *swillan*, *swilian*, of unknown origin]

swim ● *verb* (**swim·ming**; *past* **swam**; *past participle* **swum**) **1** *intransitive* propel the body through water by moving the arms and legs, or (of a fish) the fins and tail. **2** *transitive* **a** traverse (a stretch of water or its distance) by swimming. **b** compete in (a race) by swimming. **c** use (a particular stroke) in swimming. **3** *transitive* convey or propel by swimming. **4** *intransitive* float on or at the surface of a liquid (*bubbles swimming on the surface*). **5** *intransitive* appear to undulate or reel or whirl. **6** *intransitive* have a dizzy effect or sensation (*my head swam*). **7** *intransitive* (foll. by *in*, *with*) be flooded with liquid (*her eyes were swimming with tears*). **8** *intransitive* appear to move easily or quickly as if through water; glide along, through, etc. (*swam through the air*). ● *noun* **1** a period of or the act of swimming. **2** *Brit.* a deep pool frequented by fish in a river. □ **in the swim** involved in or acquainted with what is going on. **swim against the tide** act against prevailing opinion or tendency. □ **swim·mable** *adjective* **swim·mer** *noun* [Old English *swimman* from Germanic]

swim bladder *noun* a gas-filled sac in fish used to maintain buoyancy.

swim fin *noun* a flipper worn on the foot for underwater swimming.

swim·mer·et /ˈswɪməˌret/ *noun* (in crustaceans) an abdominal limb adapted for swimming.

swimmer's ear *noun* a painful infection of the ear canal usu. caused by bacteria.

swim·ming *noun* the action of swimming, esp. as a sport or recreation.

swimming bath *noun* (often in *pl.*) *Brit.* a public indoor swimming pool.

swimming costume *noun Brit.* = BATHING SUIT.

swimming hole *noun N Amer.* a place in a stream or river where it is deep enough for swimming.

swim·ming·ly *adverb* with easy and unobstructed progress.

swimming pool *noun* an artificial indoor or outdoor pool for swimming.

swim·suit *noun* an esp. one-piece bathing suit worn by women. □ **swim·suit·ed** *adjective*

swim trunks *plural noun* (also **swimming trunks**) *see* TRUNK 6.

swim·wear *noun* clothing worn for swimming.

Swin·burne, Alger·non Charles (1837–1909), English poet and critic. Associated with Rossetti and the Pre-Raphaelites, he came to fame with *Atalanta in Calydon* (1865), a drama in classical Greek form, and in *Songs before Sunrise* (1871), he expressed his hatred of authority and his support for Mazzini's struggle for Italian independence.

swin·dle ● *transitive verb* (often foll. by *out of*) **1** cheat (a person) of money, possessions, etc. (*was swindled out of all his savings*). **2** cheat a person of (money etc.) (*swindled all his savings out of him*). ● *noun* **1** an act of swindling. **2** a person or thing represented as what it is not. **3** a fraudulent scheme. □ **swind·ler** *noun* [back-formation from *swindler* from German *Schwindler* extravagant maker of schemes, swindler, from *schwindeln* be dizzy]

Swin·don an industrial town and railway centre in S England, formerly part of Wiltshire; pop. (est. 2001) 157,000.

swine *noun* (*pl.* same) **1** a pig. **2** (*pl.* **swine** or **swines**) *informal* **a** a term of contempt or disgust for a person. **b** a very unpleasant or difficult thing. □ **swin·ish** *adjective* (esp. in sense 2). **swin·ish·ness** *noun* [Old English *swīn* from Germanic]

swine fever *noun* an intestinal virus disease of pigs.

swine·herd *noun* a person who tends pigs.

swing ● *verb* (*past* and *past participle* **swung**) **1** *intransitive & transitive* move or cause to move with a to-and-fro or curving motion, as of an object attached at one end and hanging free at the other. **2** *intransitive & transitive* **a** sway. **b** hang so as to be free to sway. **c** oscillate or cause to oscillate. **3** *intransitive & transitive* revolve or cause to revolve. **4** *intransitive* move by gripping something and leaping etc. (*swung from tree to tree*). **5** *intransitive* go with a swinging gait (*swung out of the room*). **6** *intransitive* (foll. by *around*) move around to the opposite direction. **7** *intransitive* change from one opinion or mood to another. **8 a** *intransitive* (foll. by *at*) attempt to hit or punch. **b** *transitive* throw (a punch). **9 a** *intransitive* (also **swing it**) play music with swing (*see* sense 7c of *noun*). **b** *transitive* play (a tune or passage) with swing. **c** *intransitive* (of music) be played with swing. **10** *intransitive informal* **a** be lively, modern, or trendy. **b** be promiscuous. **11** *intransitive informal* (of a party etc.) be lively, successful, etc. **12** *transitive* have a decisive influence on (esp. voting etc.). **13** *transitive informal* deal with or achieve; manage. **14** *intransitive informal* be executed by hanging. ● *noun* **1** the act or an instance of swinging. **2** the motion of swinging. **3** the extent of swinging. **4** a swinging or smooth gait or rhythm or action. **5 a** a seat slung by ropes or chains etc. for swinging on or in. **b** a period of swinging on this. **6** an easy but vigorous continued

action. **7 a** jazz or dance music with an easy flowing but vigorous rhythm. **b** dance performed to this, esp. originally that popular in the late 1930s and early 1940s. **c** the rhythmic feeling or drive of this music. **8** a discernible change in opinion, esp. the amount by which votes or points scored etc. change from one side to another (often *attributive*: *swing riding*; *swing voter*). **9** an attempted punch. **10** (in musical theatre) a dancer who learns all the chorus dance parts in the show and thus can fill in for any dancer. **11** *N Amer.* a swift tour involving a number of stops. □ **get** (**back**) **into the swing of things** get used to (or return to) being easy and relaxed about an activity or routine one is engaged in. **in full swing** *see* FULL[1]. **swing the lead** *Brit. & Cdn informal* malinger; shirk one's duty. **swings and roundabouts** *Brit.* a situation affording no eventual gain or loss (from the phr. *lose on the swings what you make on the roundabouts*). □ **swing·er** *noun* (esp. in sense 10 of *verb*). [Old English *swingan* 'to beat', from Germanic]

swing·beat *noun Brit.* a form of dance music combining elements of rhythm and blues, soul, hip hop, and rap music.

swing bridge *noun* a bridge that can be swung to one side to allow the passage of ships.

swing coat *noun* a women's three-quarter-length loosely-cut coat made of lightweight fabric.

swinge /swɪndʒ/ *transitive verb* (**swinge·ing**) *archaic* strike hard; beat. [alteration of Middle English *swenge* from Old English *swengan* shake, shatter, from Germanic]

swinge·ing /ˈswɪndʒɪŋ/ *adjective* esp. *Brit.* **1** (of a blow) forcible. **2** huge or far-reaching, esp. in severity (*swingeing economies*).

swing·ing *adjective* **1** (of gait, melody, etc.) vigorously rhythmical. **2** *informal* **a** lively; modern; excellent (*the swinging sixties*). **b** promiscuous. □ **swing·ing·ly** *adverb*

swinging bridge *noun* a footbridge suspended from cables, which swings from side to side when walked on.

swinging door *noun* (also esp. *Brit.* **swing door**) a door able to open in either direction and close itself when released.

swingle·tree *noun* a crossbar pivoted in the middle, to which the traces are attached in a cart, plow, etc. [Middle English from Middle Dutch *swinghel* (as SWING, -LE[1]) + TREE *noun* 2]

swing·man *noun* (*pl.* **-men**) *N Amer.* a versatile player who can play effectively in different positions, esp. a basketball player who can play both guard and forward.

swing set *noun* a fixture in a park, yard, etc. having one or more swings and sometimes a slide.

swing shift *noun N Amer.* a work shift from afternoon to late evening.

swing-wing *noun* an aircraft wing that can move from a right-angled to a swept-back position.

swingy *adjective* (**swing·i·er**, **swing·i·est**) **1** (of music) characterized by swing (*see* SWING *noun* 7). **2** (of a skirt or dress) designed to swing with body movement. **3** *Curling* (of ice) on which the lateral movement of a rock is greater than normal.

swipe ● *verb* **1** *transitive & intransitive* hit hard and recklessly with a sweeping motion. **2** *transitive informal* steal. **3** *transitive* pass (a credit card, identity card, etc.) through an electronic device in order to read and process data magnetically encoded on it. ● *noun* **1** a quick swinging blow, or an attempt at this. **2** a sharp, antagonistic criticism, esp. made casually or in passing. □ **swip·er** *noun* [perhaps a variant of SWEEP]

swipe card *noun* a plastic card such as a credit card or ID card bearing magnetically encoded information which is read when the edge of the card is slid through an electronic device.

swirl ● *verb* **1** *intransitive & transitive* move or flow or carry along with or as with a whirling motion. **2** *transitive* give a twisted form to; twist or wind around in a curl. ● *noun* **1** a swirling motion of or in water, air, etc. **2** the act of swirling. **3** a twist or curl, esp. as part of a pattern or design. **4** commotion, disorder. □ **swirly** *adjective* [Middle English (originally as noun): originally Scots, perhaps of Low German or Dutch origin]

swish ● *verb* **1** *intransitive* move with or make a rustling or hissing sound. **2** *transitive* cause to make such a sound. **3** *transitive* swing (a stick etc.) audibly through the air, grass, etc. **4** *transitive* *Basketball* sink (a shot) without the ball touching the backboard or rim. ● *noun* **1** a swishing action or sound. **2** *N Amer. slang* an effeminate male homosexual. **3** *Basketball informal* a shot that goes through the basket without touching the backboard or rim. **4** *Cdn* (*Nfld & Maritimes*) liquor made by filling a recently emptied rum barrel with boiling water and rotating it every few days for a couple of weeks. ● *adjective* **1** esp. *Brit. informal* smart, fashionable. **2** *N Amer. slang* = SWISHY 2. [imitative]

swishy *adjective* **1** making a swishing sound. **2** *N Amer. slang* effeminate.

Swiss ● *adjective* of or relating to Switzerland or its people. ● *noun* (*pl.* same) **1** a native or national of Switzerland. **2** a person of Swiss descent. [French *Suisse* from Middle High German *Swiz*]

Swiss Army knife *noun* a pocket knife incorporating multiple blades and other tools, such as a screwdriver, can opener, pair of scissors, etc.

Swiss chard *noun* = CHARD.

Swiss cheese ● *noun* a mild hard yellow cheese with many large holes in it, originally made in Switzerland. ● *adjective* (**Swiss-cheese**) characterized by large holes or spaces.

Swiss cheese plant *noun* a climbing houseplant, *Monstera deliciosa*, with aerial roots and holes in the leaves.

Swiss guards *plural noun* Swiss mercenary troops employed formerly by sovereigns of France etc., and still at the Vatican.

Swiss roll *noun Brit. & Cdn* = JELLY ROLL.

Swiss steak *noun N Amer.* a dish of usu. less tender steak that has been pounded, floured, and cooked by braising with vegetables.

switch ● *noun* **1** a device for making and breaking the connection in an electric circuit. **2 a** a transfer, changeover, or deviation. **b** an exchange. **3** a slender flexible shoot cut from a tree. **4** a light tapering rod. **5** *N Amer.* a device at the junction of railway tracks for transferring a train from one track to another. **6** a tress of false or detached hair tied at one end, used in hairdressing. ● *verb* **1** *transitive* (foll. by *on*, *off*) **a** turn (an electrical device) on or off (*switch on the TV*). **b** start or stop the flow or operation of (water, electricity, etc.) by means of a tap, switch, etc. **c** display or cease to display (a quality or emotion) (*switched on the charm*). **2** *intransitive* change or transfer position, subject, etc. **3** *transitive* (often foll. by *over*) change or transfer. **4** *transitive* reverse the positions of; exchange (*switched chairs*). **5 a** *transitive* divert (a train etc.) on to another track by means of a switch. **b** *intransitive* (of a train) be diverted in this way. **6** *transitive* beat or flick with a switch. **7** *transitive & intransitive* move rapidly back and forth (*the cat switched her tail*). **8** *transitive Brit.* swing or snatch (a thing) suddenly (*switched it out of my hand*). □ **asleep at the switch** *see* ASLEEP. **switch off** *informal* cease to pay attention. **switch over** = senses 2, 3, 4 of the *verb*. □ **switch·able** *adjective* **switch·er** *noun* [earlier *swits*, *switz*, probably from Low German]

switch·back ● *noun* **1** *N Amer.* a hairpin bend in a zigzag road, trail, railway, etc. climbing a steep hill. **2** (often *attributive*) a railway or road with alternate sharp ascents and descents. **3** *Brit.* a roller coaster. ● *intransitive verb* **1** (of a road, trail, etc.) progress in a zigzag fashion up a slope. **2** (of a person or animal) climb a steeply ascending and descending road, trail, etc.

switch·blade *noun* a pocket knife with the blade released by a spring.

switch·board *noun* a central panel in an office etc. for the manual control of telephone connections.

switched-on *adjective Brit. informal* **1** up to date; aware of what is going on. **2** excited; under the influence of drugs.

switch·el *noun Cdn (Nfld) hist.* weak tea without milk and sweetened with molasses, drunk esp. by fishermen and sealers at sea. [origin unknown]

switch·eroo *noun N Amer. slang* a change, reversal, or exchange, esp. a surprising or deceptive one.

switch·gear *noun* **1** the switching equipment used in the transmission of electricity. **2** the switches or electrical controls in a motor vehicle.

switch·grass *noun* a tall rhizomatous N American grass, *Panicum virgatum*, which forms large clumps.

switch hitter *noun N Amer.* **1** *Baseball* a hitter who can bat either right- or left-handed. **2** *slang* a bisexual. □ **switch-hit** *intransitive verb* **switch-hitting** *adjective*

switch·man *noun* (*pl.* **-men**) *N Amer.* a person in charge of railway switches.

switch·over *noun* a change or exchange.

swith·er /'swɪðər/ *Scot.* ● *intransitive verb* hesitate; be uncertain. ● *noun* doubt or uncertainty. [16th c.: origin unknown]

Switz·er·land *noun* a landlocked country in central Europe; pop. (est. 2002) 7,301,994; capital, Berne. A neutral, mountainous country lying mainly in the Alps and the Jura, Switzerland is an international financial centre and the headquarters of several international organizations such as the Red Cross.

swiv·el /'swɪvəl/ ● *noun* (often *attributive*) a fastening or coupling device between two parts enabling one to revolve without turning the other.

● *transitive & intransitive verb* (**swiv·elled**, **swiv·el·ling**; esp. *US* **swiv·eled**, **swiv·el·ing**) turn on or as on a swivel. [Middle English from Old English *swīfan* sweep + -LE¹: compare SWIFT]

swivel chair *noun* a chair with a seat able to be turned horizontally.

swiz·zle¹ *informal* ● *noun* a mixed alcoholic drink esp. of rum or gin and bitters made frothy. ● *transitive verb* stir with or as with a swizzle stick. [19th c.: origin unknown]

swiz·zle² *noun Brit. informal* a thing that is disappointing or represents a mild swindle. [20th c.: prob. alteration of SWINDLE]

swizzle stick *noun* a stick used for stirring and frothing or flattening drinks.

swol·len ● *verb* past participle of SWELL. ● *adjective* enlarged, expanded, or increased by or as if by swelling (*a swollen ankle*; *the swollen river*).

swollen head *var. of* SWELLED HEAD.

swoon ● *intransitive verb* **1** *literary* faint. **2** enter a state of rapture or ecstasy (*the girls are swooning over the new English teacher*). ● *noun* an occurrence of fainting. □ **swoony** *adjective* [Middle English *swoune* perhaps back-formation from *swogning* (n.) from *iswogen* from Old English *geswogen* overcome]

swoop ● *verb* **1** *intransitive* (often foll. by *down*) descend rapidly like a bird of prey. **2** *intransitive* (often foll. by *on*) make a sudden attack from a distance. **3** *transitive* (often foll. by *up*) *informal* snatch the whole of at one swoop. ● *noun* **1** a swooping or snatching movement or action. **2** a sudden and unexpected attack. □ **at** (or **in**) **one fell swoop** *see* FELL⁴. [perhaps dial. var. of obsolete *swōpe* from Old English *swāpan*: see SWEEP]

swoosh ● *noun* **1** the noise of a sudden rush of liquid, air, etc. **2** a curved, wavy, or elliptical design as part of a corporate logo. ● *transitive & intransitive verb* move or cause to move with this noise. [imitative]

swop *var. of* SWAP.

sword /sɔrd/ *noun* **1** a weapon usu. of metal with a long blade and hilt with a hand guard, used esp. for thrusting or striking, and often worn as part of ceremonial dress. **2** (prec. by *the*) **a** slaughter, warfare. **b** the sword regarded as a symbol of military power, penal justice, etc. □ **put to the sword** kill, esp. in war. □ **sword-like** *adjective* [Old English *sw(e)ord* from Germanic]

sword-and-sorcery *noun* a genre of fiction characterized by heroic adventures and elements of fantasy.

sword·bear·er *noun* an official carrying the sovereign's etc. sword on a formal occasion.

sword dance *noun* a dance in which the performers brandish swords or step nimbly between and over swords laid on the ground. □ **sword dancer** *noun* **sword dancing** *noun*

sword·fern *noun* any of several ferns with long narrow fronds, esp. the N American *Polystichum munitum* and the tropical *Nephrolepis exaltata*.

sword fight *noun* a fight with swords. □ **sword fighting** *noun*

sword·fish *noun* a large marine fish, *Xiphias gladius*, with an extended sword-like upper jaw.

sword grass *noun* any of various grasses or sedges with sword-like leaves.

sword knot *noun* a ribbon or tassel attached to a sword hilt originally for securing it to the wrist.

sword of Damocles *noun* an imminent danger at a time of apparent happiness. [DAMOCLES]

sword·play *noun* **1** fencing. **2** repartee; cut-and-thrust argument.

swords·man *noun* (*pl.* **-men**) a person of (usu. specified) skill with a sword. □ **swords·man·ship** *noun*

sword stick *noun* a hollow walking stick containing a blade that can be used as a sword.

sword swallower *noun* a person ostensibly or actually swallowing sword blades as entertainment.

sword·tail *noun* a tropical fish, *Xiphophorus helleri*, with a long tail.

swore *past of* SWEAR.

sworn ● *verb* past participle of SWEAR. ● *adjective* bound by or as by an oath (*sworn enemies*).

swot *Brit. informal* ● *verb* (**swot·ted**, **swot·ting**) **1** *intransitive* study assiduously. **2** *transitive* (often foll. by *up*) study (a subject) hard or hurriedly. ● *noun* a person who studies hard. [dial. var. of SWEAT]

swum *past participle of* SWIM.

swung *past and past participle of* SWING.

swung dash *noun* a dash (~) with alternate curves.

-sy *suffix* forming diminutive nouns (*popsy*) and adjectives (*folksy*, *tipsy*).

sybar·ite /ˈsɪbəˌraɪt/ *noun* a person who is self-indulgent or devoted to sensuous luxury. □ **sybar·it·ic** /-ˈrɪtɪk/ *adjective* **sybar·it·ic·al** *adjective* **sybar·it·ic·al·ly** *adverb* **sybar·it·ism** *noun* [originally an inhabitant of Sybaris in S Italy, noted for luxury, from Latin *sybarita* from Greek *subaritēs*]

syca·mine /ˈsɪkəˌmɪn, -main/ *noun* Bible the black mulberry tree, *Morus nigra* (see Luke 17:6; in modern versions translated as 'mulberry tree'). [Latin *sycaminus* from Greek *sukaminos* mulberry tree, from Hebrew *šikmāh* sycamore, assimilated to Greek *sukon* fig]

syca·more /ˈsɪkəˌmɔr/ *noun* **1** an eastern N American plane tree, *Platanus occidentalis*, having greyish-brown peeling bark. *Also called* BUTTONBALL or BUTTONWOOD. **2** (in full **sycamore maple**) a large maple of Eurasia, *Acer pseudoplatanus*, with winged seeds, grown for its shade and timber. **3** Bible a fig tree, *Ficus sycomorus*, growing in the Middle East. [var. of SYCOMORE]

syce /saɪs/ *noun* (also **sice**) (esp. in India) a groom; a servant who looks after horses. [Hindustani from Arabic *sāʾis*, *sāyis*]

syco·more /ˈsɪkəˌmɔr/ *noun* = SYCAMORE 3. [Old French *sic(h)amor* from Latin *sycomorus* from Greek *sukomoros* from *sukon* fig + *moron* mulberry]

sy·co·nium /saɪˈkoːniəm/ *noun* (pl. **sy·co·nia**) Bot. a fleshy hollow receptacle developing into a multiple fruit as in the fig. [modern Latin from Greek *sukon* fig]

syco·phant /ˈsɪkəˌfant, ˈsaɪk-, -fənt/ *noun* a person who acts obsequiously towards someone in order to gain advantage; a servile flatterer. □ **syco·phancy** *noun* **syco·phant·ic** /-ˈfantɪk/ *adjective* **syco·phant·ic·al·ly** *adverb* [ultimately from Greek *sukophantēs* informer, from *sukon* fig + *phainō* show: the reason for the name is uncertain, and association with informing against the illegal exportation of figs from ancient Athens (recorded by Plutarch) cannot be substantiated]

Syden·ham /ˈsɪdənəm/ **Thom·as** (c.1624–89), English physician. He emphasized the healing power of nature, made a study of epidemics, wrote a treatise on gout, and explained the nature of the type of chorea that is named after him.

Sydenham's chorea *noun* chorea esp. in children as one of the manifestations of rheumatic fever; *also called* ST. VITUS'S DANCE.

Syd·ney 1 the capital of New South Wales in SE Australia; pop. (est. 2001) 4,085,578. Noted for its fine natural harbour, it is the country's largest city and chief port. **2** a metropolitan area of Cape Breton Island, situated near the eastern end of the island, on the Sydney River about 20 km southwest of Glace Bay. □ **Sydney·ite** *noun* (in sense 2) [sense 2 after T. Townshend, 1st Viscount *Sydney*, British Home Secretary d.1800]

Sydney Mines an urban community on Cape Breton Island, situated on the northwest side of Sydney Harbour, north of Sydney; pop. (1996) 17,294. [so named because of its position on *Sydney* Harbour and because it was formerly a noted coal-mining town]

Sydney·sider *noun* an inhabitant of Sydney, Australia.

syen·ite /ˈsaɪəˌnaɪt/ *noun* a grey crystalline rock of feldspar and hornblende with or without quartz. □ **syen·itic** /-ˈnɪtɪk/ *adjective* [French *syénite* from Latin *Syenites* (*lapis*) (stone) of *Syene* in Egypt]

Syk·tyv·kar /ˌsɪktɪfˈkʊr/ a city in NW Russia, capital of the autonomous republic of Komi; pop. (est. 2002) 227,800.

syl- *prefix* assimilated form of SYN- before l.

syl·lab·ary /ˈsɪləˌberi/ *noun* (pl. **-aries**) a list of characters representing syllables and (in some languages or stages of writing) serving the purpose of an alphabet.

syl·labi *pl.* of SYLLABUS.

syl·lab·ic /sɪˈlabɪk/ ● *adjective* **1** of, relating to, or based on syllables. **2** Prosody based on the number of syllables. **3** (of a symbol) representing a whole syllable. **4** articulated with distinct separation of syllables. **5** (of a style of singing, esp. plainsong) in which each syllable is sung to one note, i.e. with no slurs or runs. ● *noun* **1** a syllabic symbol. **2** (in pl.) = SYLLABARY. **3** a unit of sound capable by itself of forming a syllable. □ **syl·lab·ic·ally** *adverb* **syl·lab·icity** /-ˈbɪsɪti/ *noun*

syl·labi·ca·tion /ˌsɪləbɪˈkeɪʃən/ *noun* (also **syl·labi·fi·cat·ion** /-fɪˈkeɪʃən/) division into or articulation by syllables. □ **syl·lab·ify** *transitive verb* (**-fies**, **-fied**)

syl·lab·ize /ˈsɪləˌbaɪz/ *transitive verb* (also esp. Brit. **-ise**) divide into or articulate by syllables.

syl·la·ble /ˈsɪləbəl/ ● *noun* **1** a unit of pronunciation uttered without interruption, forming the whole or a part of a word and usu. having

one vowel sound often with a consonant or consonants before or after: there are two syllables in *water* and three in *inferno*. **2** a character or characters representing a syllable. **3** (usu. with *neg.*) the least amount of speech or writing (*did not utter a syllable*). ● *transitive verb* pronounce by syllables; articulate distinctly. □ **in words of one syllable** expressed plainly or bluntly. □ **syl·la·bled** *adjective* (also in combination). [Anglo-French *sillable* from Old French *sillabe* from Latin *syllaba* from Greek *sullabē* (as SYN-, *lambanō* take)]

syl·la·bub /ˈsɪləˌbʌb/ *noun* **1** a drink made of milk mixed with wine, cider, rum, etc. and often sweetened, spiced, and served warm. **2** a dessert made of cream or milk usu. mixed with white wine, flavoured, sweetened, and whipped to a thick but light consistency. [16th c.: origin unknown]

syl·la·bus /ˈsɪləbəs/ *noun* (pl. **syl·la·bus·es** or **syl·la·bi** /-ˌbaɪ/) **1 a** the program or outline of a course of study, teaching, etc. **b** Brit. a statement of the requirements for a particular academic examination. **2** Catholicism a summary of points decided by papal decree regarding heretical doctrines or practices. [modern Latin, originally a misreading of Latin *sittybas* accusative pl. of *sittyba* from Greek *sittuba* title slip or label]

syl·lep·sis /sɪˈlepsɪs/ *noun* (pl. **syl·lep·ses** /-siːz/) a figure of speech in which a word is applied to two others in different senses, e.g. *caught the train and a bad cold*, or to two others of which it grammatically suits one only, e.g. *neither they nor it is working* (compare ZEUGMA). □ **syl·lep·tic** *adjective* [Late Latin from Greek *sullēpsis* taking together, from *sullambanō*: see SYLLABLE]

syl·lo·gism /ˈsɪləˌdʒɪzəm/ *noun* **1** a form of reasoning in which a conclusion is drawn from two given or assumed propositions (premises): a common or middle term is present in the two premises but not in the conclusion, which may be invalid, e.g. *all trains are long*; *some buses are long*; *therefore some buses are trains*: the common term is *long*. **2** deductive reasoning as distinct from induction. □ **syl·lo·gis·tic** /-ˈdʒɪstɪk/ *adjective* **syl·lo·gis·tic·ally** *adverb* [Greek *sullogismos* from *sullogizomai* (as SYN-, *logizomai* to reason, from *logos* reason)]

syl·lo·gize /ˈsɪləˌdʒaɪz/ *verb* (also esp. Brit. **-gise**) **1** *intransitive* use syllogisms. **2** *transitive* put (facts or an argument) in the form of syllogism.

sylph /sɪlf/ *noun* **1** an elemental spirit of the air. **2** a slender graceful woman or girl. □ **sylph·like** *adjective* [modern Latin *sylphes*, German *Sylphen* (pl.), perhaps based on Latin *sylvestris* of the woods + *nympha* nymph]

sylva /ˈsɪlvə/ *noun* (also **silva**) (pl. **syl·vae** /-viː/ or **syl·vas**) **1** the trees of a region, epoch, or environment. **2** a treatise on or a list of such trees. [Latin *silva* a wood]

syl·van /ˈsɪlvən/ *adjective* (also **sil·van**) esp. *literary* **1 a** of the woods. **b** having woods; wooded. **2** rural.

Sylvan Lake a town in S central Alberta, west of Red Deer; pop. (2001) 7,493.

Syl·van·us var. of SILVANUS.

sym- *prefix* assimilated form of SYN- before *b*, *m*, *p*.

sym·bi·ont /ˈsɪmbiɒnt/ *noun* an organism living in symbiosis. [Greek *sumbiōn -ountos* part. of *sumbioō* live together (as SYMBIOSIS)]

sym·bi·o·sis /ˌsɪmbaɪˈoːsɪs, ˌsɪmbi-/ *noun* (pl. **sym·bi·o·ses** /-siːz/) **1 a** an interaction between two different organisms living in close physical association, usu. to the advantage of both (compare ANTIBIOSIS). **b** an instance of this. **2 a** a mutually advantageous association or relationship between persons. **b** an instance of this. □ **sym·bi·ot·ic** /-ˈɒtɪk/ *adjective* **sym·bi·ot·ic·ally** *adverb* [modern Latin from Greek *sumbiōsis* a living together, from *sumbioō* live together, *sumbios* companion (as SYN-, *bios* life)]

sym·bol ● *noun* **1** a thing conventionally regarded as typifying, representing, or recalling something, esp. an idea or quality (*white is a symbol of purity*). **2** a mark or character taken as the conventional sign of some object, idea, function, or process, e.g. the letters standing for the chemical elements or the characters in musical notation. ● *transitive verb* (**sym·bolled**, **sym·bol·ling**; *US* **sym·boled**, **sym·bol·ing**) symbolize. [Latin *symbolum* from Greek *sumbolon* mark, token (as SYN-, *ballō* throw)]

sym·bol·ic *adjective* (also **sym·bol·ic·al**) **1** of or serving as a symbol. **2** involving the use of symbols or symbolism. □ **sym·bol·ic·al·ly** *adverb*

symbolic logic *noun* the use of symbols to denote propositions etc. in order to assist reasoning.

sym·bol·ism *noun* **1 a** the use of symbols to represent ideas.

b symbols collectively. **2** an artistic and poetic movement or style using symbols and indirect suggestion rather than direct description to express ideas, emotions, etc. □ **sym·bol·ist** *noun* **sym·bol·is·tic** *adjective*

sym·bol·ize *transitive verb* (also esp. *Brit.* **-ise**) **1** be a symbol of. **2** represent by means of symbols. □ **sym·bol·iz·a·tion** *noun*

sym·bol·ogy /sɪmˈbɒlədʒi/ *noun* (*pl.* **-ogies**) **1** the branch of knowledge that deals with the use of symbols. **2** the use of symbols. **3** symbols collectively. □ **sym·bol·ogic·al** *adjective*

sym·metry /ˈsɪmətri/ *noun* (*pl.* **-ries**) **1 a** correct proportion of the parts of a thing; balance, harmony. **b** beauty resulting from this. **2 a** a structure that allows an object to be divided into parts of an equal shape and size and similar position to the point or line or plane of division. **b** the possession of such a structure. **c** approximation to such a structure. **3** the repetition of exactly similar parts facing each other or a centre. **4** *Bot.* the possession by a flower of sepals and petals and stamens and pistils in the same number or multiples of the same number. □ **sym·met·ric** /sɪˈmetrɪk/ *adjective* **sym·met·ric·al** *adjective* **sym·met·ric·al·ly** *adverb* **sym·met·rize** *transitive verb* (also esp. *Brit.* **-rise**) [obsolete French *symmétrie* or Latin *summetria* from Greek (as SYN-, *metron* measure)]

sym·path·ec·tomy /ˌsɪmpəˈθektəmi/ *noun* (*pl.* **-mies**) the surgical removal of a sympathetic ganglion etc.

sym·pa·thet·ic /ˌsɪmpəˈθetɪk/ *adjective* **1** of, showing, or expressing sympathy. **2** due to sympathy. **3** likeable or capable of evoking sympathy. **4** (of a person) friendly and co-operative. **5** (foll. by *to*) inclined to favour (a proposal etc.) (*was most sympathetic to the idea*). **6** (of a pain etc.) caused by a pain or injury to someone else or in another part of the body. **7** (of a sound, resonance, or string) sounding by a vibration communicated from another vibrating object. **8 a** designating the part of the autonomic nervous system consisting of nerves arising from ganglia near the middle part of the spinal cord that supply the internal organs, blood vessels, and glands, and balance the action of the parasympathetic nerves. **b** (of a nerve or ganglion) belonging to this system. □ **sym·pa·thet·ic·al·ly** *adverb*

sympathetic magic *noun* a type of magic, based on the belief of affinity between things or actions, that seeks to achieve an effect by performing an associated action or using an associated thing.

sym·pa·thize /ˈsɪmpəˌθaɪz/ *intransitive verb* (also esp. *Brit.* **-thise**) (often foll. by *with*) **1** feel or express sympathy; share a feeling or opinion. **2** agree with a sentiment or opinion. □ **sym·pa·thiz·er** *noun*

sym·patho·mi·met·ic /ˌsɪmpəθoːmɪˈmetɪk/ *adjective* (of a drug) producing physiological effects characteristic of the sympathetic nervous system by promoting the stimulation of sympathetic nerves.

sym·pa·thy /ˈsɪmpəθi/ *noun* (*pl.* **-thies**) **1** (often foll. by *with*) **a** the act of sharing or tendency to share in an emotion or sensation or condition of another person or thing. **b** (in *sing.* or *pl.*) compassion or commiseration; condolences. **2** (often foll. by *for*) a favourable attitude; approval. **3** (in *sing.* or *pl.*; often foll. by *with*) agreement (with a person etc.) in opinion or desire. **4** (*attributive*) in support of another cause (*sympathy strike*). □ **in sympathy** (often foll. by *with*) **1** having or showing or resulting from sympathy (with another). **2** by way of sympathetic action (*working to rule in sympathy*). [Latin *sympathia* from Greek *sumpatheia* (as SYN-, *pathēs* from *pathos* feeling)]

sym·pat·ico *var of.* SIMPATICO.

sym·pat·ric /sɪmˈpatrɪk/ *adjective* *Biol.* occurring within the same geographical area (compare ALLOPATRIC). [SYM- + Greek *patra* 'fatherland' + -IC]

sym·petal·ous /sɪmˈpetələs/ *adjective* *Bot.* having the petals united.

sym·phon·ic /sɪmˈfɒnɪk/ *adjective* relating to or having the form or character of a symphony. □ **sym·phon·ic·al·ly** *adverb*

symphonic poem *noun* = TONE POEM.

sym·phon·ist /ˈsɪmfənɪst/ *noun* a composer of symphonies.

sym·phony /ˈsɪmfəni/ *noun* (*pl.* **-ies**) **1** an elaborate composition usu. for full orchestra, and in several movements with one or more in sonata form. **2** an interlude for orchestra alone in a large-scale vocal work. **3** = SYMPHONY ORCHESTRA. **4** a harmoniously pleasing arrangement or juxtaposition of colours, shapes, sounds, etc. [Middle English, = harmony of sound, from Old French *symphonie* from Latin *symphonia* from Greek *sumphōnia* (as SYN-, *-phōnos* from *phōnē* sound)]

symphony orchestra *noun* a large orchestra suitable for playing symphonies etc.

sym·phy·sis /ˈsɪmfəsɪs/ *noun* (*pl.* **sym·phy·ses** /-ˌsiːz/) **1** the process of growing together. **2 a** a union between two bones esp. in the median plane of the body. **b** the place or line of this.

□ **sym·phys·eal** /-ˈfɪziəl/ *adjective* [modern Latin from Greek *sumphusis* (as SYN-, *phusis* growth)]

sym·po·dium /sɪmˈpoːdiəm/ *noun* (*pl.* **sym·po·dia**) *Bot.* the apparent main axis or stem of a vine etc., made up of successive secondary axes. □ **sym·po·dial** *adjective* [modern Latin (as SYN-, Greek *pous podos* foot)]

sym·po·sium /sɪmˈpoːziəm/ *noun* (*pl.* **sym·po·sia** /-ziə/) **1 a** a conference or meeting to discuss a particular subject. **b** a collection of essays or papers for this purpose. **2** a philosophical or other friendly discussion. **3** a drinking party, esp. of the ancient Greeks with conversation etc. after a banquet. [Latin from Greek *sumposion* in sense 3 (as SYN-, *-potēs* drinker)]

symp·tom /ˈsɪmptəm/ *noun* **1** *Med.* a change in the physical or mental condition of a person, regarded as evidence of a disorder (compare SIGN *noun* 11). **2** a sign of the existence of something. □ **symp·tom·less** *adjective* [Greek *sumptōma -atos* 'chance, symptom', from *sumpiptō* 'happen' (as SYN-, *piptō* 'fall')]

symp·tom·atic /ˌsɪmptəˈmatɪk/ *adjective* serving as a symptom. □ **symp·tom·atic·al·ly** *adverb*

symp·tom·atol·ogy /ˌsɪmptəməˈtɒlədʒi/ *noun* the branch of medicine concerned with the study and interpretation of symptoms.

syn. *abbreviation* **1** synonym. **2** synonymous.

syn- /sɪn/ *prefix* with, together, alike. [from or after Greek *sun-* from *sun* with]

syn·aer·esis *var. of* SYNERESIS.

syn·aes·the·sia *var. of* SYNESTHESIA.

syna·gogue /ˈsɪnəgɒg/ *noun* **1** the building where a Jewish assembly or congregation meets for religious observance and instruction. **2** the assembly itself. □ **syna·gog·al** /-ˈgɒgəl/ *adjective* [Old French *sinagoge* from Late Latin *synagoga* from Greek *sunagōgē* meeting (as SYN-, *agō* bring)]

syn·apo·morphy /sɪˈnapoːmɔrfi/ *noun* **1** *Biology* the possession by two organisms of a characteristic (not necessarily the same in each) that is derived from one characteristic in an organism from which they both evolved. **2** a characteristic derived in this way. □ **syn·apo·morph·ic** *adjective* [SYN- + APO- + Greek *morphē* 'form']

syn·apse /ˈsɪnaps, -ˈnaps, ˈsaɪn-/ *noun* *Anat.* **1** a junction of two nerve cells, consisting of a minute gap across which impulses pass by diffusion of a neurotransmitter. **2** (in *pl.*) the synapses in the brain, considered as an indicator of mental activity. □ **syn·ap·tic** *adjective* **syn·ap·tic·al·ly** *adverb* [Greek *synapsis* (as SYN-, *hapsis* from *haptō* join)]

syn·ap·sis /sɪˈnapsɪs/ *noun* (*pl.* **syn·ap·ses** /-siːz/) **1** *Anat.* = SYNAPSE. **2** *Biol.* the fusion of chromosome pairs at the start of meiosis.

sync (also **synch**) *informal* ● *noun* synchronization. ● *transitive & intransitive verb* (often foll. by *up*) synchronize. □ **in** (or **out of**) **sync** (often foll. by *with*) according or agreeing well (or badly). [abbreviation]

syn·carp·ous /sɪnˈkɑrpəs/ *adjective* (of a flower or fruit) having the carpels united (opp. APOCARPOUS). [SYN- + Greek *karpos* fruit]

synch *var. of* SYNC.

syn·chro *noun* **1** a synchronizing device. **2** synchronized swimming. **3** synchronized skating. [abbreviation]

synchro- *combining form* synchronized, synchronous.

syn·chro·cyclo·tron /ˌsɪŋkroːˈsaɪklətrɒn/ *noun* a cyclotron able to achieve higher energies by decreasing the frequency of the accelerating electric field as the particles increase in energy and mass.

syn·chro·mesh ● *noun* a system of gear changing, esp. in motor vehicles, in which the driving and driven gearwheels are made to revolve at the same speed during engagement by means of a set of friction clutches, thereby easing the change. ● *adjective* relating to or using this system. [abbreviation of *synchronized mesh*]

syn·chron·ic /sɪŋˈkrɒnɪk/ *adjective* describing a subject (esp. a language) as it exists at one point in time (opp. DIACHRONIC). □ **syn·chron·ic·al·ly** *adverb* [Late Latin *synchronus*: see SYNCHRONOUS]

syn·chron·icity /ˌsɪŋkrəˈnɪsɪti/ *noun* **1** the simultaneous occurrence of events which appear significantly related but have no discernible connection. **2** = SYNCHRONY 1.

syn·chron·ism /ˈsɪŋkrəˌnɪzəm/ *noun* **1** = SYNCHRONY. **2** the process of synchronizing sound and picture in cinematography, television, etc. □ **syn·chron·is·tic** *adjective* **syn·chron·is·tic·al·ly** *adverb* [Greek *sugkhronismos* (as SYNCHRONOUS)]

syn·chron·ize /ˈsɪŋkrənaɪz/ *verb* (also esp. *Brit.* **-ise**) **1 a** *transitive* cause to occur at the same time. **b** *intransitive* (often foll. by *with*) occur at the same time; be simultaneous. **2** *transitive* coordinate, combine (*we must synchronize our efforts*). **3** *transitive* carry out the synchronism of (a film). **4** *transitive* ascertain or set forth the correspondence in the date of

Vowels: a *cat* ɑ *arm* e *bed* ɜr *her* ɜː *deux* ə *ago* ɪ *sit* i *cosy* iː *feed* ɒ *hot* ɔ *pore* oː *no* ʌ *run* ʊ *put*

(events). **5** *transitive* cause (clocks etc.) to show a standard or uniform time. **b** *intransitive* (of clocks etc.) be synchronized. **6** *intransitive* operate in unison. □ **syn·chron·iz·a·tion** *noun* **syn·chron·iz·er** *noun*

syn·chron·ized skating *noun* figure skating performed in unison by a team of 12 or more skaters. □ **synchronized skater** *noun*

syn·chron·ized swimming *noun* a form of swimming in which participants perform coordinated dance-like leg and arm movements in time to music. □ **synchronized swimmer** *noun*

syn·chron·ous /ˈsɪŋkrənəs/ *adjective* (often foll. by *with*) **1** existing or occurring at the same time. **2** going at the same rate and exactly together; having coincident periods. **3** (of a motor or machine) having a speed exactly proportional to the current frequency. **4 a** (of a satellite) revolving around the parent planet at the same rate as the planet rotates. **b** (of an orbit) such that a satellite in it is synchronous. □ **syn·chron·ous·ly** *adverb* [Late Latin *synchronus* from Greek *sugkhronos* (as SYN-, *khronos* time)]

syn·chrony /ˈsɪŋkrəni/ *noun* **1** the state of being synchronic or synchronous. **2** the treatment of events etc. as being synchronous.

syn·chro·tron /ˈsɪŋkrəˌtrɒn/ *noun* *Physics* a cyclotron in which the magnetic field strength increases with the energy of the particles to keep their orbital radius constant.

synchrotron radiation *noun* *Physics* polarized radiation emitted by a charged particle spinning in a magnetic field.

syn·cline /ˈsɪŋklaɪn/ *noun* a fold in rock from whose axis the strata incline upwards on either side. □ **syn·clinal** *adjective* **syn·clinal·ly** *adverb* [*synclinal* (as SYN-, Greek *klinō* lean)]

synco·pate /ˈsɪŋkəpeɪt/ *transitive verb* **1** *Music* (often as **synco·pat·ed** *adjective*) **a** displace the beats or accents in (a passage) so that strong beats become weak and vice versa. **b** accent (a note) on a weak beat. **2** shorten (a word) by dropping interior sounds or letters, as *symbology* for *symbolology*, *Gloster* for *Gloucester*. □ **synco·pa·tion** *noun* **synco·pa·tor** *noun* [Late Latin *syncopare* swoon (as SYNCOPE)]

syn·cope /ˈsɪŋkəpi/ *noun* **1** *Grammar* the omission of interior sounds or letters in a word (*see* SYNCOPATE 2). **2** *Med.* a temporary loss of consciousness caused by a fall in blood pressure. □ **synco·pal** *adjective* [Late Latin *syncopē* from Greek *sugkopē* (as SYN-, *koptō* strike, cut off)]

syn·cre·tism /ˈsɪŋkrəˌtɪzəm/ *noun* **1** *Philos.* & *Theol.* the process or an instance of syncretizing. **2** *Linguistics* the merging of different inflectional varieties in the development of a language. □ **syn·cretic** /-ˈkretɪk/ *adjective* **syn·cre·tist** *noun* **syn·cre·tis·tic** /-ˈtɪstɪk/ *adjective* [modern Latin *syncretismus* from Greek *sugkrētismos*, from *sugkrētizō* (of two parties) 'combine against a third' (as SYN-, *krēs* 'Cretan', originally of ancient Cretan communities)]

syn·cre·tize /ˈsɪŋkrəˌtaɪz/ *transitive verb* (also esp. *Brit.* **-tise**) *Philos.* & *Theol.* attempt to unify or reconcile differing schools of thought, religions, etc.

syn·cyt·ium /sɪnˈsɪtɪəm/ *noun* (*pl.* **syn·cyt·ia** /-tɪə/) *Biol.* a mass of cytoplasm with several nuclei, not divided into separate cells. □ **syn·cytial** *adjective* [formed as SYN- + -CYTE + -IUM]

syn·dac·tyly /sɪnˈdaktɪli/ *noun* the condition of having some or all of the fingers or toes wholly or partly united as in webbed feet etc. [SYN- + Greek *daktulos* 'finger' + -Y³]

syn·dic *noun* **1** a government official in various countries. **2** *Brit.* a business agent of certain universities and corporations, esp. (at Cambridge University) a member of a committee of the senate. □ **syn·dic·al** *adjective* [French from Late Latin *syndicus* from Greek *sundikos* (as SYN-, *-dikos* from *dikē* justice)]

syn·dical·ism /ˈsɪndɪkəˌlɪzəm/ *noun* *hist.* a movement for transferring the ownership and control of the means of production and distribution to workers' unions. □ **syn·dical·ist** *noun* [French *syndicalisme* from *syndical* (as SYNDIC)]

syn·di·cate ● *noun* /ˈsɪndɪkət/ **1** a combination of individuals or commercial firms to promote some common interest. **2** an association or agency supplying material simultaneously to a number of newspapers, periodicals, etc. **3** a group of people who combine to buy or rent property, gamble, organize crime, etc. **4** a committee of syndics. ● *transitive verb* /ˈsɪndɪkeɪt/ **1** form into a syndicate. **2 a** publish (material) through a syndicate. **b** (esp. as **syn·di·ca·ted** *adjective*) publish the work of (a columnist, cartoonist, etc.) through a syndicate. **3** (esp. as **syndicated** *adjective*) make (a television or radio program) available to independent broadcasters. □ **syn·di·ca·tion** *noun* **syn·di·ca·tor** *noun* [French *syndicat* from medieval Latin *syndicatus* from Late Latin *syndicus*: see SYNDIC]

syn·drome /ˈsɪndrəʊm, -drəm/ *noun* **1 a** a group of symptoms or pathological signs which consistently occur together. **b** a condition

characterized by such a set of associated symptoms. **2** a characteristic combination of opinions, emotions, behaviour, etc. □ **syn·drom·ic** /-ˈdrɒmɪk/ *adjective* [modern Latin from Greek *sundromē* (as SYN-, *dromē* from *dramein* to run)]

syne /saɪn/ *Scot.* since. [contraction from Middle English *sithen* SINCE]

syn·ec·doche /sɪˈnekdəki/ *noun* a figure of speech in which a part is made to represent the whole or vice versa, e.g. *new faces at the meeting*; *Italy won by two goals.* □ **syn·ec·doch·ic** /-ˈdɒkɪk/ *adjective* **syn·ec·doch·ic·al** /-ˈdɒkəl/ *adjective* **syn·ec·doch·ic·al·ly** /-ˈdɒkɪkli/ *adverb* [Latin from Greek *sunekdokhē* (as SYN-, *ekdokhē* from *ekdekhomai* take up)]

syn·er·esis /sɪˈniːrɪsɪs/ *noun* (also **syn·aer·esis**) (*pl.* **syn·er·eses** /-ˌsiːz/) **1** the contraction of two vowels into a diphthong or single vowel. **2** the contraction of a gel accompanied by the separating out of liquid. [Late Latin from Greek *sunairesis* (as SYN-, *hairesis* from *haireō* take)]

syn·er·gist /ˈsɪnərdʒɪst/ *noun* a substance, organ, or other agent that participates in an effect of synergy.

syn·ergy /ˈsɪnərdʒi/ *noun* (also **syn·er·gism** /ˈsɪnərˌdʒɪzəm/) **1** the interaction or co-operation of two or more drugs, agents, organizations, etc., to produce an effect that exceeds or enhances the sum of their individual effects. **2** increased effectiveness, achievement, etc. produced by combined action, co-operation, etc. **3** an instance of this. □ **syn·er·get·ic** /-ˈdʒetɪk/ *adjective* **syn·er·gis·tic** *adjective* **syn·er·gis·tic·ally** *adverb* **syn·er·gize** *transitive verb* (also esp. *Brit.* **-gise**). [Greek *sunergos* working together (as SYN-, *ergon* work)]

syn·es·the·sia /ˌsɪnəsˈθiːʒə, -ziə/ *noun* (also **synaesthesia**) **1** *Psych.* the production of a mental sense impression relating to one sense by the stimulation of another sense, as in the association of certain sounds with colours. **2** a sensation produced in a part of the body by stimulation of another part. □ **syn·es·thet·ic** /-ˈθetɪk/ *adjective* [modern Latin from SYN- after *anaesthesia*]

syn·gamy /ˈsɪŋgəmi/ *noun* *Biol.* the fusion of gametes or nuclei in reproduction. [SYN- + Greek *gamos* marriage]

Synge /sɪŋ/ **(Ed·mund) John Mil·ling·ton** (1871–1909), Irish dramatist. At Yeats's suggestion, he went to live with the peasant community on the Aran Islands (1898–1902), an experience that inspired his plays *Riders to the Sea* (1905) and *The Playboy of the Western World* (1907).

syn·od /ˈsɪnəd/ *noun* **1** a church council attended by delegated clergy and sometimes laity (*see also* GENERAL SYNOD). **2** a group of churches whose representatives meet regularly; an ecclesiastical jurisdiction. **3** a Presbyterian ecclesiastical court above the presbyteries and subject to the General Assembly. **4** any meeting for debate. □ **syn·od·al** /ˈsɪnədəl/ *adjective* **syn·od·ic·al** /sɪˈnɒdɪkəl/ *adjective* [Late Latin *synodus* from Greek *sunodos* meeting (as SYN-, *hodos* way)]

syn·od·ic /sɪˈnɒdɪk/ *adjective* *Astronomy* **1** relating to or involving the conjunction of stars, planets, etc. **2** designating a month as measured from full moon to full moon, about 29½ days. [(as SYNOD)]

synodic period *noun* the time between the successive conjunctions of a planet with the sun.

syno·nym /ˈsɪnənɪm/ *noun* **1** a word or phrase that means exactly or nearly the same as another in the same language, e.g. *shut* and *close*. **2** a word denoting the same thing as another but suitable to a different context or containing a different emphasis, e.g. *serpent* for *snake*, *kill* for *slay*. **3** a word equivalent to another in some but not all senses, e.g. *ship* and *vessel*. **4** a taxonomic name having the same or nearly the same application as another, esp. one which has been superseded. □ **syno·nym·ic** /-ˈnɪmɪk/ *adjective* **syno·nym·ity** /-ˈnɪmɪti/ *noun* [Latin *synonymum* from Greek *sunōnumon* neuter of *sunōnumos* (as SYN-, *onoma* name): compare ANONYMOUS]

syn·onym·ous /sɪˈnɒnəməs/ *adjective* (often foll. by *with*) **1** having the same meaning; being a synonym (of). **2** (of a name, idea, etc.) suggestive of or associated with another (*blackflies are synonymous with summer*). □ **syn·onym·ous·ly** *adverb*

syn·onymy /sɪˈnɒnɪmi/ *noun* (*pl.* **-ies**) **1** the state of being synonymous. **2** a system or collection of synonyms. **3** the collocation of synonyms for emphasis, e.g. *in any shape or form*.

syn·op·sis /sɪˈnɒpsɪs/ *noun* (*pl.* **syn·op·ses** /-siːz/) **1** a summary or outline. **2** a brief general survey. □ **syn·op·size** *transitive verb* (also esp. *Brit.* **-sise**). [Late Latin from Greek (as SYN-, *opsis* seeing)]

syn·op·tic /sɪˈnɒptɪk/ ● *adjective* **1** of, forming, or giving a synopsis. **2** taking or affording a comprehensive mental view. **3** (**Synoptic**) designating any of the Gospels of Matthew, Mark, and Luke, which describe events from a similar point of view. **4** of the Synoptic Gospels.

---

uː m**oo**d aɪ m**y** əi p**i**pe au br**ow**n ʌu h**ou**se ei d**ay** ɔi b**oy** ã fr**an**glais ã Ca**na**dien ɔ Bra**yon** (*see over for consonants*)

5 giving a general view of weather conditions. ● *noun* a Synoptic Gospel. □ **syn·optic·al** *adjective* **syn·optic·ally** *adverb*

syn·ovial /saɪˈnoʊviəl, sɪ-/ *adjective* *Physiol.* denoting or relating to a viscous fluid lubricating joints and tendon sheaths. [modern Latin *synovia*, formed probably arbitrarily by Paracelsus]

synovial membrane *noun* a dense membrane of connective tissue secreting synovial fluid.

syn·ovitis /ˌsaɪnoʊˈvaɪtɪs, sɪn-/ *noun* inflammation of the synovial membrane.

syn·tac·tic /sɪnˈtaktɪk/ *adjective* of or according to syntax. □ **syn·tac·tic·al** *adjective* **syn·tac·tic·ally** *adverb* [Greek *suntaktikos* (as SYNTAX)]

syn·tag·ma /sɪnˈtagmə/ *noun* (also **syn·tagm** /ˈsɪntam/) (*pl.* **syn·tag·mas** or **syn·tag·mata** /-mətə/; **syn·tagms**) **1** a word or phrase forming a syntactic unit. **2** a systematic collection of statements. □ **syn·tag·matic** /-ˈmatɪk/ *adjective* **syn·tag·matic·ally** *adverb* [Late Latin from Greek *suntagma* (as SYNTAX)]

syn·tax /ˈsɪntaks/ *noun* **1 a** the order of words in which they convey meaning collectively by their connection and relation. **b** a set of rules for or an analysis of this. **2** *Computing* **a** the order and arrangement of words or symbols forming a logical sentence. **b** the rules by which elements in a formal system, programming language, etc., are combined. [French *syntaxe* or Late Latin *syntaxis* from Greek *suntaxis* (as SYN-, *taxis* from *tassō* arrange)]

synth /sɪnθ/ *noun informal* = SYNTHESIZER (also *attributive*: synth drums).

synth·ase /ˈsɪnθeɪz, -eɪs/ *noun* an enzyme which catalyzes the linking together of two molecules, esp. without the direct involvement of ATP. [SYNTHESIS + -ASE]

syn·the·sis /ˈsɪnθəsɪs/ *noun* (*pl.* **syn·the·ses** /-siːz/) **1** the process or result of building up separate elements, esp. ideas, into a connected whole, esp. into a theory or system. **2** a combination or composition. **3** *Chem.* the formation of a compound by combination of its elements or constituents, esp. the artificial production of compounds from their constituents as distinct from extraction from plants etc. **4** *Grammar* **a** the process of making compound and derivative words. **b** the tendency in a language to use inflected forms rather than groups of words, prepositions, etc. □ **syn·the·sist** *noun* [Latin from Greek *sunthesis* (as SYN-, THESIS)]

synthesis gas *noun* a gas used as a feedstock in the industrial synthesis of a chemical, esp. a mixture of hydrogen and carbon monoxide.

syn·the·size /ˈsɪnθəˌsaɪz/ *transitive verb* (also esp. *Brit.* **-sise**) **1** make (something) by synthesis, esp. chemically. **2** combine (a number of things) into a coherent whole. **3** (esp. as **syn·the·sized** *adjective*) **a** produce or imitate (a sound) electronically using a synthesizer. **b** characterize (music) by the use of a synthesizer or synthesizers (*a heavily synthesized dance track*).

syn·the·siz·er /ˈsɪnθɪˌsaɪzər/ *noun* an electronic musical instrument, esp. operated by a music keyboard, producing a wide variety of sounds by generating and combining signals of different frequencies. □ **syn·the·sist** /ˈsɪnθəsɪst/ *noun*

syn·thes·pian /sɪnˈθɛspiən/ *noun* a computer-generated character who may appear to interact with human actors in a film, or as part of an animated film using only such characters. [blend of SYNTHETIC + THESPIAN]

syn·thet·ase /ˈsɪnθəteɪz, -teɪs/ *noun* an enzyme which catalyzes a particular synthesis, esp. a ligase or a synthase. [SYNTHETIC + -ASE]

syn·thet·ic /sɪnˈθɛtɪk/ ● *adjective* **1 a** made by chemical synthesis, esp. to imitate a natural product (*synthetic rubber*). **b** artificial, imitation, invented. **2** (of emotions etc.) affected, insincere. **3** *Logic* (of a proposition) having truth or falsity determinable by recourse to experience (*compare* ANALYTIC 3). **4** of, pertaining to, involving, or using synthesis, or combination of parts into a whole; constructive. **5** *Linguistics* using combinations of simple words or elements in compounded or complex words (*compare* ANALYTIC 2). ● *noun* a synthetic substance. □ **syn·thet·ic·al** *adjective* **syn·thet·ic·ally** *adverb* [Greek *sunthetikos* from *sunthetos* from *suntithēmi* (as SYN-, *tithēmi* put)]

synthetic resin *noun* *Chem.* see RESIN *noun* 2.

syph /sɪf/ *noun informal* syphilis. [abbreviation]

syph·ilis /ˈsɪfɪlɪs/ *noun* a sexually transmitted disease progressing from infection of the genitals via the skin and mucous membrane to the bones, muscles, and brain. □ **syph·il·itic** /-ˈlɪtɪk/ *adjective & noun* [modern Latin from title (*Syphilis, sive Morbus Gallicus*) of a Latin poem (1530), from *Syphilus*, a character in it, the supposed first sufferer from the disease]

sy·phon esp. *Brit.* var. of SIPHON.

Syra·cuse 1 /ˈsaɪrəˌkjuːz/ a port on the east coast of Sicily; pop. (est. 2001) 121,000. Settled in 734 BC by colonists from Corinth, it became a flourishing centre of Greek culture, esp. in the 5th and 4th c. BC under the rule of Dionysius I and II. **2** /ˈsɪrəˌkjuːz/ a city in New York State, to the southeast of Lake Ontario; pop. (est. 2000) 147,306. The site of salt springs discovered by the French in 1654, it was an important centre of salt production during the 19th c. □ **Syra·cus·an** *noun & adjective*

Syrah /ˈsiːrə/ *noun* **1 a** a variety of black grape used in winemaking, grown originally in the Rhone valley of France, now also esp. in Australia and South Africa. **b** the vine that bears this grape. **2** a red wine produced from these grapes. [French, earlier *sirrah*: see SHIRAZ, where the early form *scyras* may have influenced the spelling]

Syr Darya River (also **Syr·dar·ya River**) see SIRDARYO RIVER.

Syria /ˈsɪriə/ a country in the Middle East with a coastline on the E Mediterranean Sea; pop. (est. 2002) 17,155,814; capital, Damascus. Ancient Syria also encompassed present-day Lebanon, Israel, Jordan, and parts of Iraq and Saudi Arabia. □ **Syr·ian** *adjective & noun*

Syr·iac /ˈsɪriak/ ● *noun* the language of ancient Syria, western Aramaic, now only in liturgical use in the Maronite and Syrian Catholic Churches, the Syrian Jacobite Church, and the Nestorian Church. ● *adjective* in or relating to this language.

syr·inga /sɪˈrɪŋgə/ *noun* **1** = MOCK ORANGE. **2** any plant of the genus *Syringa*, esp. the lilac. [modern Latin, formed as SYRINX (with reference to the use of its stems as pipestems)]

syr·inge /sɪˈrɪndʒ, ˈsɪr-/ ● *noun* **1** *Med.* **a** a tube with a nozzle and piston or bulb for sucking in and ejecting liquid in a fine stream. **b** (in full **hypodermic syringe**) a similar device with a hollow needle for insertion under the skin. **2** any similar device used in gardening, cooking, etc. ● *transitive verb* (**syr·ing·ing**) sluice or spray (the ear, a plant, etc.) with a syringe. [medieval Latin *syringa* (as SYRINX)]

syr·inx /ˈsɪrɪŋks/ *noun* (*pl.* **syr·inx·es** or **syr·ing·es** /sɪˈrɪndʒiːz/) **1** a set of pan pipes. **2** *Archaeology* a narrow gallery cut in rock in an ancient Egyptian tomb. **3** the lower larynx or song organ of birds. □ **syr·in·geal** /sɪˈrɪndʒiəl/ *adjective* [Latin *syrinx -ngis* from Greek *surigx suriggos* pipe, channel]

syr·phid /ˈsɔrfɪd/ ● *adjective* of or relating to the dipteran family Syrphidae, which includes the hoverflies. ● *noun* a fly of this family. [modern Latin *Syrphidae* from the genus name *Syrphis*, from Greek *surphos* 'gnat']

syr·up *noun* (*US* also **sir·up**) **1** any of various very sweet liquids used e.g. as a topping, to flavour a drink, to preserve canned fruit, as a form of medicine, etc. (*maple syrup*; *corn syrup*; *cough syrup*). **2** excessive sweetness of style or manner. **3** *Cdn* (*Nfld*) a fruit-flavoured drink of water and syrup; a cordial. □ **syr·upy** *adjective* [Old French *sirop* or medieval Latin *siropus* from Arabic *šarāb* beverage: compare SHERBET, SHRUB²]

sys·admin /ˈsɪsədˌmɪn/ *noun* *Computing* system administrator.

sys·op /ˈsɪsɒp/ *noun* *Computing* system operator.

sys·tem *noun* **1** a complex whole; a set of connected things, parts, institutions, etc.; an organized body of material or immaterial things (*railway system*; *school system*). **2** a set of devices functioning together. **3** *Physiol.* **a** a set of organs in the body with a common structure or function (*the digestive system*). **b** the human or animal body as a whole. **4 a** a method; considered principles of procedure or classification. **b** a classification. **5 a** a body of theory or practice relating to or prescribing a particular form of government, religion, etc. **b** (prec. by *the*) the prevailing political or social order, esp. regarded as oppressive and intransigent. **6** a method of choosing one's procedure in gambling etc. **7** *Computing* a group of related hardware units or programs or both, esp. when dedicated to a single application. **8** one of seven general types of crystal structure. **9** a major group of geological strata (*the Devonian system*). **10** *Physics* a group of associated bodies moving under mutual gravitation etc. **11** *Music* the braced staffs of a score. □ **get a thing out of one's system** *informal* be rid of a preoccupation or anxiety. □ **sys·tem·less** *adjective* [Greek *sustēma -atos* (as SYN-, *histēmi* set up)]

system administrator *noun* a person who administers a computer system or network.

sys·tem·atic *adjective* **1 a** methodical; done or conceived according to a plan or system. **b** (of a person etc.) acting according to a system; methodical (*a systematic administrator*). **2** of or pertaining to biological classification (*a systematic botanist*). **3** regular, deliberate (*a systematic liar*). □ **sys·tem·atic·ally** *adverb*

sys·tem·atics *plural noun* (usu. treated as *sing.*) the study or a system of classification; taxonomy.

sys·tem·atist /'sɪstəmətɪst, -'stemətɪst/ *noun* a person who constructs or follows an esp. biological classification. □ **sys·tem·atism** *noun*

sys·tem·atize *transitive verb* (also esp. *Brit.* **-atise**) **1** make systematic. **2** devise a system for. □ **sys·tem·atiz·ation** *noun* **sys·tem·atiz·er** *noun*

sys·tem·ic /sɪ'stemɪk/ *adjective* **1** *Physiol.* **a** of or concerning the whole body, not confined to a particular part (*systemic infection*). **b** (of blood circulation) other than pulmonary. **2** *Hort.* (of an insecticide, fungicide, etc.) entering the plant via the roots or shoots and passing through the tissues. **3** of or pertaining to a system, esp. in its entirety. □ **sys·tem·ic·ally** *adverb*

sys·tem·ize *transitive verb* = SYSTEMATIZE. □ **sys·tem·iz·a·tion** *noun* **sys·tem·iz·er** *noun*

system operator *noun Computing* a person who manages the operation of an electronic bulletin board. *Also called* SYSOP.

systems analysis *noun* the analysis of a complex process or operation in order to improve its efficiency, esp. by applying a computer system. □ **systems analyst** *noun*

systems operator *noun Computing* a person who controls or monitors the operation of complex esp. electronic systems.

systems theory *noun* the study of systems, esp. to find characteristics common to all systems or to classes of systems.

sys·tole /'sɪstəli/ *noun Physiol.* the contraction of the heart, when blood is pumped into the arteries (*compare* DIASTOLE). □ **sys·tol·ic** /-'stɒlɪk/ *adjective* [Late Latin from Greek *sustolē* from *sustellō* contract]

syzygy /'sɪzɪdʒi/ *noun* (*pl.* **-gies**) **1** *Astronomy* conjunction or opposition, esp. of the moon with the sun. **2** a pair of connected or correlated things. [Late Latin *syzygia* from Greek *suzugia* from *suzugos* yoked, paired (as SYN-, *zugon* yoke)]

Szcze·cin /'ʃtʃetʃin/ a city in NW Poland, a port on the Oder River near the border with Germany; pop. (est. 2000) 416,485.

Sze·chuan[1] /'setʃwɒn, 'seʃ-, -'wɒn/ (also **Sze·chwan**) *see* SICHUAN.

Sze·chuan[2] /'setʃwɒn, 'seʃ-, -'wɒn/ *noun* (also **Sze·chwan**) (*attributive*) designating food cooked in the distinctively spicy style of cuisine originating in Szechuan (*see* SICHUAN).

Szeged /'seged/ a city in S Hungary, a port on the Tisza River near the border with Serbia; pop. (est. 2002) 171,600.

Szell /sel/ **George** (1897–1970), Hungarian-born US conductor, pianist, and composer, who was noted for his interpretations of Wagner, Strauss, and Mahler.

Szent-Györgyi /sent'dʒɜrdʒi/ **Al·bert (von Nagyra·polt)** (1893–1986), Hungarian-born US biochemist, who was awarded the 1937 Nobel Prize for physiology or medicine for his research on vitamin C and muscular activity.

Szi·lard /'sɪlɑrd/ **Leo** (1898–1964), Hungarian-born US physicist and molecular biologist. He suggested the idea of nuclear chain reactions, and later became a central figure in the Manhattan Project to develop the atomic bomb; after the war he turned to experimental and theoretical studies in molecular biology and biochemistry.

Szym·bor·ska /shiːm'bɔrskə/ **Wis·ła·wa** (b.1923), Polish poet, winner of the Nobel Prize for literature in 1996.

Tt

T¹ *noun* (also **t**) (*pl.* **Ts** or **T's**) **1** the twentieth letter of the alphabet. **2** a T-shaped thing (esp. *attributive*: *T-joint*). **3** = T-SHIRT. □ **to a T** exactly; to a nicety.

T² *symbol* **1** *Chem.* the isotope tritium. **2** tera-. **3** tesla. **4** temperature. **5** tenor. **6** thiamine. **7** the time at which an event, esp. the launch of a spacecraft, is scheduled to occur (*T minus three minutes*).

t. *abbreviation* **1** ton(s). **2** tonne(s).

't *pronoun contraction of* IT (*'tis*).

-t¹ *suffix* = -ED² (*crept; sent*).

-t² *suffix* = -EST² (*shalt*).

T4 *noun* (in full **T4 slip**) *Cdn* an official statement issued by an employer, indicating one's employment income for the year, as well as the amount paid in employment insurance premiums and contributions to the Canada Pension Plan etc., used to calculate the amount of taxes owed and submitted with one's tax return.

TA ● *noun N Amer. informal* **1** TEACHING ASSISTANT. **2** teaching assistantship. ● *intransitive verb* (**TA'd, TA'ing**) *N Amer. informal* work as a teaching assistant.

Ta *symbol Chem.* the element tantalum.

ta *interjection Brit. informal* thank you. [infantile form]

tab¹ ● *noun* **1 a** a small flap or strip of material attached for grasping, fastening, or hanging up, or for identification. **b** a similar object as a decorative part of a garment etc. **2** *N Amer. informal* a bill or price (*picked up the tab*). **3** *Brit. Military* a marking on the collar distinguishing a staff officer. **4** esp. *N Amer.* a strip or ring of metal attached to the top of a canned drink and pulled to open the can. ● *transitive verb* (**tabbed, tab·bing**) **1** provide with a tab or tabs. **2** *N Amer.* designate, name, label (*was tabbed as her successor*). □ **keep tabs on** *informal* **1** keep account of. **2** have under observation or in check. [Middle English, origin uncertain: perhaps related to TAG¹]

tab² *noun* **1 a** a function on a computer keyboard or typewriter allowing the movement of the carriage, cursor, etc. to be pre-set. **b** the key used to advance the carriage or cursor this predetermined distance. **2** = TABULATOR 2. □ **tab·bing** *noun* [abbreviation of TABULATOR]

tab³ *noun slang* a tablet, esp. one containing an illicit drug (*LSD tabs*). [abbreviation]

tab⁴ *noun* tabloid. [abbreviation]

tab⁵ *noun* tablature. [abbreviation]

tab·ard /ˈtabərd/ *noun* **1** a herald's official coat emblazoned with the arms of the sovereign. **2** a woman's or girl's sleeveless jerkin. **3** *hist.* a knight's short emblazoned garment worn over armour. [Old French *tabart*, of unknown origin]

Ta·bas·co¹ /təˈbaskoː/ a state of SE Mexico, on the Gulf of Mexico; capital, Villahermosa.

Ta·bas·co² /təˈbaskoː/ *noun proprietary* a pungent sauce made from the fruit of *Capsicum frutescens*, used to flavour food. [TABASCO¹]

tab·bou·leh /təˈbuːliː/ *noun* a Syrian and Lebanese salad made with bulgur, parsley, onion, mint, lemon juice, oil, and spices. [Arabic *tabbūla*]

tabby *noun* (*pl.* **-bies**) **1** (also **tabby cat**) **a** a grey, orange, or brownish cat mottled or streaked with dark stripes. **b** any domestic cat, esp. female. **2** a kind of watered silk. **3** a plain weave. [French *tabis* (in sense 2) from Arabic *al-ʿattabiya* the quarter of Baghdad where tabby was manufactured: connection of other senses uncertain]

Taber /ˈteibər/ a town in S Alberta, east of Lethbridge; pop. (2001) 7,671. □ **Taber·ite** *noun* [originally *Tabor* after Mount Tabor in the Holy Land]

tab·er·nacle /ˈtabərˌnakəl/ *noun* **1** *hist.* a tent used as a sanctuary for the Ark of the Covenant by the Israelites during the Exodus. **2** *Christianity* a niche or receptacle esp. for the consecrated Eucharistic elements. **3** a place of worship. **4** *Bible* a fixed or movable habitation usu. of light construction. **5** *Naut.* a socket or double post for a hinged mast that can be lowered to pass under low bridges. [Old French from Latin *tabernaculum* tent, diminutive of *taberna* hut]

tab·la /ˈtablə, ˈtɒ-/ *noun Music* (in Indian music) a pair of small drums played with the hands. [Persian and Urdu *tablah*, Hindustani *tablā*, from Arabic *tabl* drum]

tab·la·ture /ˈtablətʃər/ *noun Music* a form of notation, esp. for the guitar or *hist.* the lute, in which lines, figures, and letters are used, e.g. with parallel lines representing the strings and numbers indicating the frets to be fingered. [French from Italian *tavolatura*, from *tavolare* 'set to music']

table ● *noun* **1 a** a piece of furniture with a flat top and one or more legs, providing a level surface for eating, writing, or working at, playing games on, etc. **b** (*attributive*) designating an object designed to sit or be used on a table (*table clock*). **2** a flat surface serving a specified purpose (*altar table*). **3 a** food provided in a household (*keeps a good table*). **b** a group seated at table for dinner etc. **4 a** a set of facts or figures systematically displayed, esp. in columns (*a table of contents*). **b** matter contained in this. **5** a flat surface for working on or for machinery to operate on. **6 a** a slab of wood or stone etc. for bearing an inscription. **b** matter inscribed on this. **7** = TABLELAND. **8** *Archit.* **a** a flat usu. rectangular vertical surface. **b** a horizontal moulding, esp. a cornice. **9 a** a flat surface of a gem. **b** a cut gem with two flat faces. **10** each half or quarter of a folding board for backgammon. **11** (*prec. by the*) = BARGAINING TABLE (*sought to draw them back to the table*). **12** any plane or level area (*water table*). ● *transitive verb Cdn & Brit.* bring forward for discussion or consideration at a meeting. **2** esp. *US* postpone consideration of (a matter). ¶ Because both of these contradictory meanings are in use in Canada, confusion may arise if the verb *table* is used outside of the strictly parliamentary context, where the first sense should be understood. As a result, it is better to use a different verb altogether, such as *present* or *postpone*, as the context requires. □ **at table** taking a meal at a table. **lay on the table 1** submit for discussion. **2** esp. *US* postpone indefinitely. **on the table** offered for discussion. **turn the tables** (often foll. by *on*) reverse one's relations (with), esp. by turning an inferior into a superior position (originally in backgammon). **under the table** *informal* **1** (of a transaction etc., esp. payment) done surreptitiously esp. to avoid taxes or duties. **2** very drunk after a meal or drinking bout. □ **table·ful** *noun* (*pl.* **-fuls**) **tabling** *noun* [Old French from Latin *tabula* plank, tablet, list]

tab·leau /ˈtabloː/ *noun* (*pl.* **tab·leaux** /-loːz/) **1** a picturesque presentation. **2** = TABLEAU VIVANT. **3** a dramatic or effective situation suddenly brought about. [French, = picture, diminutive of *table*: see TABLE]

tableau vivant /ˌtabloː ˈviːvã/ *noun* (*pl.* **tableaux vivants** pronunc. same) *Theatre* a silent and motionless group of people arranged to represent a scene. [French, lit. 'living picture']

table·cloth *noun* a cloth spread over the top of a table, esp. for meals.

table cream *noun* cream used in coffee, for pouring over desserts, etc.

Vowels: a *cat* ɑ *arm* e *bed* ɜr *her* ɜː *deux* ə *ago* ɪ *sit* i *cosy* iː *feed* ɒ *hot* ɔ *pore* oː *no* ʌ *run* ʊ *put*

table dance *noun N Amer.* a dance performed by a stripper at the table of a paying customer. □ **table dancer** *noun* **table dancing** *noun*

table d'hôte /ˌtablə ˈdoːt/ *noun* a meal consisting of a set menu at a fixed price, esp. in a hotel (*compare* À LA CARTE). [French, = host's table]

table hockey = TABLETOP HOCKEY.

table-hop *intransitive verb N Amer. informal* go from table to table in a restaurant etc. to socialize.

table knife *noun* a knife for use at meals, esp. in eating a main course.

table lamp *noun* a small usu. decorative lamp designed to stand on a table etc.

table·land *noun* an extensive elevated region with a level surface; a plateau.

table linen *noun* tablecloths, napkins, etc.

table manners *plural noun* decorum or correct behaviour while eating at table.

table mat *noun* a mat for protecting a tabletop from hot dishes, etc.

table·mate *noun* a person who shares a table with another.

Table Mountain a flat-topped mountain near the southwest tip of South Africa, overlooking Cape Town and Table Bay, rising to a height of 1 087 m (3,563 ft.).

table napkin *noun see* NAPKIN 1.

table runner *noun* a long narrow strip of cloth placed along the centre of a table.

table salt *noun* salt that is powdered or easy to powder for use at meals.

table saw *noun* esp. *N Amer.* a power tool consisting of a fixed circular saw mounted beneath a metal table with the blade projecting up through a slot.

table·side ● *adjective* (of food preparation etc.) performed adjacent to the table of a dining patron (*tableside service*). ● *adverb* next to the table of a dining patron (*flambéed tableside*).

table·spoon *noun* **1** a large spoon used for eating soup, cereal, etc. or for serving food. **2** a measuring spoon used in cooking, equal to ¹⁄₂ fluid ounce (approx. 15 ml). Abbr.: **tbsp**. **3** the amount held by either of these. □ **table·spoon·ful** *noun* (*pl.* **-fuls**)

tab·let *noun* **1** a small measured and compressed amount of a substance, esp. of a medicine or drug. **2** a flat slab of stone or wood, esp. for display or an inscription. **3** *Archit.* = TABLE 8. **4** *N Amer.* a writing pad. [Old French *tablete* from Romanic, diminutive of Latin *tabula* TABLE]

table talk *noun* miscellaneous informal talk at table.

table tennis *noun* an indoor game based on lawn tennis, played with small bats and a ball bounced on a table divided by a net.

table·top *noun* **1** the top or surface of a table. **2** (*attributive*) that can be placed or used on a tabletop.

tabletop hockey *noun N Amer.* a game played using a board or table resembling a miniature hockey rink, with players which can be made to move and shoot using connected rods running beneath the 'ice' surface and projecting at either end.

table·ware *noun* dishes, plates, implements, etc., for use at meals.

table wine *noun* ordinary wine for drinking with a meal.

tab·loid *noun* **1 a** a newspaper, usu. popular in style with bold headlines and large photographs, having pages half the size of those of the average broadsheet. **b** (*attributive*) designating highly sensational or lurid journalism etc. (*tabloid TV*). **2** anything in a compressed or concentrated form. □ **tab·loid·iz·a·tion** *noun* [originally the proprietary name of a medicine sold in tablets]

ta·boo ● *noun* (*pl.* **ta·boos**) **1** (also **tabu**) a system or the act of setting a person or thing apart as sacred or accursed. **2** a prohibition or restriction imposed by social custom. **3** a thing, activity, word, etc. so prohibited (*is still considered a taboo*). ● *adjective* **1** avoided or prohibited, esp. by social custom (*taboo words*). **2** (also **tabu**) designated as sacred and prohibited. ● *transitive verb* (**ta·boos, ta·booed**) **1** put (a thing, practice, etc.) under taboo. **2** exclude or prohibit by authority or social influence. [Tongan *tabu*]

ta·bor /ˈteibər/ *noun hist.* a small drum, esp. one used to accompany a pipe. [Old French *tabour, tabur*: compare TABLA, Persian *tabīra* drum]

Tab·riz /təˈbriːz/ a city in NW Iran; pop. (1996) 1,191,043.

tabu·lar /ˈtabjʊlər/ *adjective* **1** of or arranged in tables or lists. **2** broad and flat like a table. **3** (of a crystal) having two broad flat faces. **4** formed in thin plates. □ **tabu·lar·ly** *adverb* [Latin *tabularis* (as TABLE)]

tab·ula rasa /ˌtabjʊlə ˈrazə/ *noun* (*pl.* **tab·ulae rasae** /ˌtabjʊliː ˈraziː/)

1 a tablet with the writing erased; a clean slate. **2** the human mind (esp. at birth) viewed as having no innate ideas. [Latin, = scraped tablet]

tabu·late /ˈtabjʊˌleit/ *transitive verb* arrange (figures or facts) in tabular form. □ **tabu·la·tion** *noun* [Late Latin *tabulare tabulat-* from *tabula* table]

tabu·la·tor /ˈtabjʊˌleitər/ *noun* **1** a person or thing that tabulates. **2** a device on a typewriter for advancing to a sequence of set positions in tabular work.

tabun /ˈtɒbʊn/ *noun* an organic phosphorus compound used as a nerve gas. [German]

taca·ma·hac /ˈtakəməˌhak/ *noun* **1** a resinous gum obtained from certain tropical trees esp. of the genus *Calophyllum*. **2 a** the balsam poplar. **b** the resin of this. [obsolete Spanish *tacamahaca* from Aztec *tecomahiyac*]

tacet /ˈtasət, ˈtei-/ *intransitive verb Music* an instruction for a particular voice or instrument to be silent. [Latin, = is silent]

tach /tak/ *noun N Amer. informal* = TACHOMETER. [abbreviation]

Taché /taˈʃei/ **1 Alexandre-Antonin** (1823–94), Canadian Catholic missionary, priest, and archbishop. Arriving in the Red River Colony in 1845, he was ordained and learned Saulteaux, becoming a bishop in 1850. He helped restore order during the Red River Rebellion, founded many missions, and later fought vigorously for French and Catholic schools in Manitoba. **2 Sir Étienne-Paschal** (1795–1865), Canadian doctor and politician. He was elected to the new assembly for the Province of Canada in 1841 and held numerous posts in successive administrations. In 1864 he formed the Great Coalition which was ultimately responsible for Confederation, and he presided over the Quebec Conference.

Ta·ching *see* DAQING.

tach·ism /ˈtaʃɪzəm/ *noun* (also **tach·isme** /-ˈʃiːzm/) a form of action painting with dabs of colour arranged randomly to evoke a subconscious feeling. □ **tach·ist** /ˈtaʃɪst/ *noun* (also **tach·iste** /-ˈʃiːst/). [French *tachisme* from *tache* stain]

tacho- /ˈtakoː/ *combining form* speed. [Greek *takhos* speed]

tacho·graph /ˈtakəˌgraf/ *noun* a device used esp. in transport trucks and buses etc. for automatically recording speed and travel time.

tach·om·eter /təˈkɒmətər/ *noun* an instrument for measuring the rate of rotation of a shaft and hence the speed or velocity of a vehicle.

tachy- /ˈtaki/ *combining form* swift. [Greek *takhus* swift]

tachy·car·dia /ˌtakiˈkɑːdiə/ *noun Med.* an abnormally rapid heart rate. [TACHY- + Greek *kardia* heart]

tachyg·raphy /təˈkɪgrəfi/ *noun* **1** stenography, esp. that of the ancient Greeks and Romans. **2** the abbreviated medieval writing of Greek and Latin.

tachy·on /ˈtakiɒn/ *noun Physics* a hypothetical particle that travels faster than light. [TACHY- + -ON]

tacit /ˈtasɪt/ *adjective* understood or implied without being stated (*tacit consent*). □ **tacit·ly** *adverb* [Latin *tacitus* silent, from *tacēre* be silent]

taci·turn /ˈtasɪˌtɜːn/ *adjective* reserved in speech; saying little; uncommunicative. □ **taci·turn·ity** /-ˈtɜːnɪti/ *noun* **taci·turn·ly** *adverb* [French *taciturne* or Latin *taciturnus* (as TACIT)]

Taci·tus /ˈtasɪtəs/ (full name Publius, or Gaius, Cornelius Tacitus) (*c.*56–*c.*120), Roman historian. His major works on the history of the Roman Empire, only partially preserved, are the *Annals* (covering the years 14–68) and the *Histories* (69–96); they are written in an elevated and concise style, pervaded by a deep pessimism about the course of Roman history since the end of the Republic.

tack¹ ● *noun* **1 a** a small broad-headed sharp nail. **b** = THUMBTACK. **2** a long stitch used in fastening fabrics etc. lightly or temporarily together. **3 a** the direction in which a ship moves as determined by the position of its sails and regarded in terms of the direction of the wind (*starboard tack*). **b** a temporary change of direction in sailing made by turning the ship's head to the wind. **c** one of a consecutive series of such movements to port and starboard alternately, tracing a zigzag course, and made by a ship in order to reach a point to windward. **4** a course of action or policy (*try another tack*). **5** *Naut.* **a** a rope for securing the corner of some sails. **b** the corner to which this is fastened. **6** a sticky condition of varnish etc. ● *verb* **1** *transitive* fasten with or as if with tacks. **2** *transitive* stitch (pieces of cloth etc.) lightly together. **3** *transitive* (foll. by *to, on*) annex, append (a thing). **4** *intransitive* **a** change a ship's course by turning its head to the wind (*compare* WEAR² 2). **b** make a series of tacks in order to progress to windward. **5** *intransitive* change one's conduct or policy etc. □ **sharp as a tack** *see* SHARP.

---

uː m**oo**d ai m**y** əi p**i**pe au br**ow**n ʌu h**ou**se ei d**ay** ɔi b**oy** ã fr**an**glais ã C**an**adien ɔ̃ Br**ay**on   (*see over for consonants*)

☐ **tack·er** *noun* [Middle English *tak* etc., of uncertain origin: compare Bible *tache* clasp, link, from Old French *tache*]

tack² ● *noun* the saddle, bridle, etc., of a horse. ● *transitive verb* (often foll. by *up*) put tack on (a horse). [shortened from TACKLE]

tack cloth *noun N Amer.* a tacky cloth used in woodworking to remove sanding dust before applying finish etc.

tack·ham·mer *noun* a light hammer for driving tacks.

tackle ● *noun* **1** equipment for a task or sport (*fishing tackle*). **2** a mechanism, esp. of ropes, pulleys, blocks, hooks, etc., for lifting weights, managing sails, etc. (*block and tackle*). **3** a windlass with its ropes and hooks. **4** an act of tackling in football etc. **5** *Football* **a** the position next to the end of either the offensive or defensive line. **b** the player in this position. ● *transitive verb* **1** try to deal with (a problem or difficulty). **2 a** (esp. in football) apprehend forcefully or throw one's body at in order to stop or take down. **b** (in soccer etc.) obstruct, intercept, or stop (a player running with the ball). **3** (often foll. by *on*, *about*) initiate discussion with (a person), esp. with regard to a disputed issue. **4** secure or lift by means of tackle. ☐ **tack·ler** *noun* **tack·ling** *noun* [Middle English, probably via Middle Low German *takel* from *taken* 'lay hold of']

tackle block *noun* a pulley over which a rope runs.

tackle box *noun* esp. *N Amer.* a box with many compartments for storing and transporting fishing tackle.

tack room *noun* (also **tack shed** etc.) a room in a riding stable (or a shed etc.) where the saddles, bridles, etc. are kept.

tacky¹ *adjective* (**tack·i·er**, **tack·i·est**) (of glue or paint etc.) still slightly sticky after application. ☐ **tack·i·ness** *noun*

tacky² *adjective* (**tack·i·er**, **tack·i·est**) esp. *N Amer. informal* **1** showing poor taste or style. **2** tawdry or seedy. ☐ **tack·i·ly** *adverb* **tack·i·ness** *noun* [19th c.: origin unknown]

taco /ˈtɒkoː, ˈtɑːkoː/ *noun* (*pl.* **tacos**) a fried corn tortilla folded over and filled with ground meat, tomatoes, lettuce, shredded cheese, guacamole, etc. [Latin American Spanish]

taco chip *noun* a fried fragment of a corn tortilla, usu. flavoured, eaten cold like a potato chip.

tacon·ite /ˈtakənaɪt/ *noun* a type of chert used as an iron ore in parts of N America. [*Taconic* Range of mountains in eastern New York State + -ITE¹]

taco shell *noun* a usu. crisp folded tortilla used in making tacos.

tac·rine /ˈtakriːn/ *noun* a synthetic drug used in Alzheimer's disease to inhibit the breakdown of acetylcholine by cholinesterase and thereby enhance neurological function. [from TETRA- + ACRIDINE]

tact *noun* **1** adroitness in dealing with others or with difficulties arising from personal feeling. **2** intuitive perception of the right thing to do or say. [French from Latin *tactus* touch, sense of touch, from *tangere tact-* touch]

tac team *noun* = TACTICAL TEAM. [abbreviation]

tact·ful *adjective* having or showing tact. ☐ **tact·ful·ly** *adverb* **tact·ful·ness** *noun*

tac·tic *noun* a plan or method used to achieve something, esp. against an opponent. [modern Latin *tactica* from Greek *taktikē* (*tekhnē* art), from *taktos* ordered]

tac·tic·al *adjective* **1** of, relating to, or constituting tactics (*a tactical retreat*). **2** (of bombing or weapons) done or for use in immediate support of military or naval operations (*opp.* STRATEGIC 3). **3** adroitly planning or planned. **4** (of voting) aimed at preventing the strongest candidate from winning by supporting the next strongest. ☐ **tac·tic·ally** *adverb*

tactical team *noun* (also **tactical squad**) *N Amer.* a unit in a police force trained to handle especially volatile situations.

tac·tics *plural noun* **1** (also treated as *sing.*) the art of disposing armed forces esp. in contact with an enemy (*compare* STRATEGY 4a). **2** a the esp. immediate or short-range plans and means adopted in carrying out a scheme or achieving some end. **b** a skilful device or devices. ☐ **tac·ti·cian** /takˈtɪʃən/ *noun*

tac·tile /ˈtaktaɪl/ *adjective* **1** of or connected with the sense of touch. **2** perceived by touch. **3** designed to be perceived by touch. **4** (of a person) given to touching others, esp. as an unselfconscious expression of sympathy or affection. ☐ **tac·til·ity** /-ˈtɪlɪti/ *noun* [Latin *tactilis* from *tangere tact-* touch]

tact·less *adjective* having or showing no tact. ☐ **tact·less·ly** *adverb* **tact·less·ness** *noun*

tad *noun N Amer. informal* a small amount (often used as an adverb: *a tad too salty*). [19th c.: origin unknown]

ta-dah *interjection* (also **ta-da**) expressing triumph, a dramatic revelation, etc. [imitative of a trumpet fanfare]

Ta·dous·sac /ˈtaduːsak/ a village in NE central Quebec, situated on the north shore of the St. Lawrence, at the mouth of the Saguenay River, about 200 km northeast of Quebec City; pop. (2001) 870. [Montagnais *totouskak* breasts, with reference to two rounded hills to the west]

tad·pole *noun* the tailed aquatic larva of a frog, toad, or other amphibian from the time it leaves the egg until it loses its gills or tail and acquires legs. [Middle English *taddepolle* (as TOAD, POLL from the size of its head)]

Ta·dzhik *var.* of TAJIK.

Ta·dzhik·istan see TAJIKISTAN.

Tae Bo *noun* a fitness routine which combines elements of tae kwon do, boxing, and aerobics, performed to music. [TAE (KWON DO) + (BO)XING]

Taegu /taˈɡuː/ a city in SE South Korea; pop. (2002) 2,543,800. Nearby is the Haeinsa temple, established in AD 802, which contains 80,000 wooden printing blocks dating from the 13th c., engraved with compilations of Buddhist scriptures.

Tae·jon /taˈdʒɒn/ a city in central South Korea; pop. (2002) 1,386,800.

tae kwon do /taɪ kwɒn ˈdoː/ *noun* a modern Korean martial art similar to karate. [Korean, = art of hand and foot fighting]

taf·feta /ˈtafətə/ *noun* a fine lustrous silk or silk-like fabric. [Old French *taffetas* or medieval Latin *taffata*, ultimately from Persian *tāfta* past participle of *tāftan* twist]

taff·rail *noun Naut.* **1** the upper part of the flat portion of a ship's stern above the transom. **2** a rail around a ship's stern. [earlier *tafferel* from Dutch *taffereel* panel, diminutive of *tafel* (as TABLE): assimilated to RAIL¹]

taffy *noun* (*pl.* **-fies**) *N Amer.* **1** a chewy confection similar to toffee made from brown sugar or molasses boiled with butter and pulled until glossy. **2** *Cdn* a similar confection made by pouring hot maple syrup onto packed snow. [19th c.: origin unknown]

taffy apple *noun N Amer.* a confection consisting of an apple coated with taffy (sense 1).

taffy pull *noun N Amer.* a social occasion on which people gather to make taffy.

tafia /ˈtafiə/ *noun Caribbean* rum distilled from molasses etc. [18th c.: origin uncertain]

Taft, Wil·liam How·ard (1857–1930), US Republican politician, 27th president of the US 1909–13. His presidency is remembered for its dollar diplomacy in foreign affairs and for its tariff laws which were criticized as being too favourable to big business.

tag¹ ● *noun* **1 a** a label attached to or worn by a person or thing, esp. to indicate price, ownership, identity, etc. **b** a metal clip used to identify an animal or bird, esp. in order to trace its migratory patterns etc. **c** an electronic device that can be attached to a person or thing for monitoring purposes, e.g. to track offenders or to deter shoplifters. **d** a tag that authorizes a hunter to kill a certain type of animal (*a grizzly tag*). **2** *informal* an epithet or popular designation. **3** *Theatre* (in full **tag line**) **a** a closing speech addressed to the audience. **b** a trite quotation or stock phrase esp. used as a motto or slogan. **4** a metal or plastic point at the end of a shoelace to facilitate threading it through an eyelet; an aglet. **5 a** a short loop sewn on the back of a jacket, shirt, etc. so that it may be hung on a hook. **b** a loop of leather on the back of a boot used in pulling it on. **6 a** a loose or ragged end of something, such as a strand of rope. **b** a ragged lock of hair or of wool on a sheep. **c** the tip of an animal's tail, usu. of a different colour from the rest of the tail. **7** *Computing* a set of characters or symbols placed before or after a unit of data to make it readable in another form. **8 a** the refrain of a song. **b** a musical phrase added to the end of a piece. **9** a gang's or individual's identifying graffiti. ● *transitive verb* (**tagged**, **tag·ging**) **1** provide with a tag or tags. **2** (often foll. by *on*, *on to*) add, esp. as an afterthought; tack on. **3** *informal* follow closely or trail behind. **4** *Computing* label (an item of data) in order to identify it for subsequent processing or retrieval. **5** attach an identifying label to (an animal). **6** label radioactively (*see* LABEL *verb* 3). **7** shear away tags from (sheep). **8** *transitive & intransitive* paint graffiti (on). ☐ **tag along** (often foll. by *with*) go along with or accompany. ☐ **tagged** *adjective* [Middle English: origin unknown]

tag² ● *noun* **1** a children's game in which one player chases the others, and anyone who is caught then becomes 'it' and inherits the role of the pursuer. **2** = TELEPHONE TAG. **3** *Baseball* the act of tagging a runner. ● *verb* (**tagged**, **tag·ging**) **1** *transitive* touch (a player) in a game of tag. **2** *Baseball* **a** *transitive* touch (a runner) with the ball or a gloved hand

---

Consonants: b *but* d *dog* f *few* g *get* h *her* j *yes* k *cat* l *leg* m *man* n *no* p *pen* r *red* s *sit*

holding the ball. **b** *transitive* (foll. by *out*) put (a runner) out by doing this.
c *intransitive* (usu. foll. by *up*) (of a runner) return to and touch a base
before attempting to advance after a fly ball is caught. **d** *transitive* score
a hit or run off (a pitcher). **3** *transitive informal* strike (a person) with a
powerful punch or blow. [18th c.: origin unknown]

tag alder *noun* = SPECKLED ALDER.

Ta·gal·og /təˈgɑlɒg/ ● *noun* (*pl.* same or **Ta·gal·ogs**) **1** a member of
the principal people of the Philippine Islands. **2** the language of this
people, which belongs to the Malayo-Polynesian language group
although its vocabulary has been heavily influenced by Spanish with
some adaptations from Chinese and Arabic. ● *adjective* of or relating to
this people or language. [Tagalog from *taga* native + *ilog* river]

tag·along *N Amer.* ● *noun* a follower or companion, esp. one who is
uninvited or unwelcome. ● *adjective* **1** that is towed or trailed behind
something else. **2** (of a follower or companion) uninvited or
unwelcome.

Tag·an·rog /ˌtagənˈrɒg/ an industrial port in SW Russia, on the Gulf
of Taganrog, an inlet of the Sea of Azov; pop. (2002) 282,700.

tag day *noun N Amer.* a day on which contributions to a charity are
solicited in the street or at malls etc., with donors being given a small
identifying tag.

tag end *noun* **1** a loose end of something, esp. a strand of tinsel etc.
serving as the tail of an angler's fly. **2** esp. *N Amer.* = TAIL END.

ta·getes /təˈdʒiːtiːz/ *noun* any plant of the genus *Tagetes*, esp. any of
various marigolds with bright orange or yellow flowers. [modern Latin
from Latin *Tages* an Etruscan god]

tag·ger *noun* **1** a person who paints graffiti tags. **2** a computer
program that inserts tags in text.

ta·gine *var. of* TAJINE.

Tag·ish /ˈtagɪʃ/ ● *noun* (*pl.* same) **1** a member of an Aboriginal people
living esp. in the southern Yukon Territory. **2** the Athapaskan language
of this people. ● *adjective* of or relating to this people or their culture or
language. [Tagish, = 'fish trap']

taglia·telle /ˌtaljəˈteli/ *noun* **1** a type of pasta made in narrow ribbons.
2 a dish consisting of this pasta served with sauce etc. [Italian]

tag line *noun* = TAG¹ *noun* 3.

Tagli·oni /taliˈoːni/ **Marie** (1804–84), Swedish-born Italian dancer. The
most important ballerina of the romantic era, she conveyed an
impression of ethereal perfection, particularly when dancing the roles
of disembodied spirits such as the title role in *La Sylphide* (1832). She
gave artistic meaning to pointe work, which had previously been
merely a technical feat.

Ta·gore /təˈgɔr/ **Rab·in·dra·nath** (1861–1941), Indian writer and
philosopher. His poetry pioneered the use of colloquial Bengali, and he
won the Nobel Prize for literature in 1913 for *Gitanjali* (1912), a set of
poems modelled on medieval Indian devotional lyrics; he also wrote
philosophical plays, novels such as *Gora* (1929), and short fiction which
often commented on Indian national and social concerns.

tag sale *noun US* = GARAGE SALE.

tag team *noun* **1** a pair of wrestlers who fight as a team by alternately
competing in the ring against one of another paired team of
opponents (also *attributive*: *tag-team wrestling*). **2** two people completing a
single task as a team (also *attributive*: *tag-team approach*).

Tagus River /ˈteigəs/ a river in SW Europe, the longest river of the
Iberian peninsula, which rises in the mountains in E Spain and flows
over 1 000 km (625 miles) generally westward into Portugal, where it
turns southwestward, emptying into the Atlantic near Lisbon.

ta·hi·ni /təˈhiːni/ *noun* a paste or sauce made from ground sesame seeds.
[modern Greek *takhini*, from Arab *ṭaḥīnā*, from *ṭaḥana* grind, crush]

Ta·hi·ti /təˈhiːti/ an island in the central S Pacific, one of the Society
Islands, forming part of French Polynesia; pop. (2002) 180,000; capital,
Papeete.

Ta·hi·tian /təˈhiːʃən, -tiən/ ● *noun* **1** a native or inhabitant of Tahiti.
2 the Polynesian language of Tahiti. ● *adjective* of or relating to Tahiti,
its people, or language.

Tahl·tan /ˈtɒltən/ ● *noun* (*pl.* same or **Tahl·tans**) **1** a member of an
Aboriginal people living in the area of the Stikine River, BC. **2** the
Athapaskan language of this people. ● *adjective* of or relating to this
people or their culture or language. [origin uncertain]

tahr /tɑr/ *noun* any goatlike mammal of the genus *Hemitragus*, esp. *H.
jemlahicus* of the Himalayas. [Local (Himalayan) name]

tah·sil /taˈsiːl/ *noun* (in the Indian subcontinent) an administrative
division comprising several villages, formerly esp. for revenue
administration. [Urdu *taḥsīl* from Arabic, = collection]

Tai'an /taiˈɒn/ a city in NE China, in Shandong province; pop. (2002)
346,000.

tai chi /tai ˈtʃiː/ *noun* (in full **tai chi chuan** /tʃwɒn/) a Chinese martial
art and system of calisthenics consisting of sequences of very slow
controlled movements. [Chinese, = great ultimate boxing, from *tái*
'extreme' + *ji* 'limit' + *quán* 'fist, boxing']

Tai·chung /taiˈtʃʊŋ/ a city in west central Taiwan; pop. (2002)
1,033,600.

Ta'if /ˈtɒif/ a city in W Saudi Arabia, situated to the southeast of Mecca
in the Asir Mountains; pop. (est. 2002) 633,900. It is the unofficial seat
of government of Saudi Arabia during the summer.

Taig /teig/ *noun slang offensive* (in Northern Ireland) a Protestant name
for a Catholic. [var. of *Teague*, anglicized spelling of the Irish name
Tadhg, a nickname for an Irishman]

tai·ga /ˈtaigə/ *noun* any of the swampy coniferous forests of subarctic
N America, Europe, and Asia, usu. lying between Arctic tundra to the
north and aspen parkland or steppe to the south; the boreal forest.
[Russian]

tai·ko /ˈtɔikoː/ *noun* any of a variety of Japanese two-headed drums
made of a hollow wooden shell the opening of which is covered with
cowhide. [Japanese *tai* big + *ko* drum]

tail¹ ● *noun* **1** the rear part of an animal, esp. an elongation of the
vertebral column forming a flexible appendage that extends beyond
the rest of the body. **2 a** a thing resembling an animal's tail in shape
or position. **b** the rear end of anything, e.g. of a procession of people or
vehicles. **c** the inferior or weaker part of anything, esp. in a sequence.
3 a the rear part of an airplane, rocket, missile, etc., usu. including its
airfoil, rudder, or fins. **b** the rear part of a car or truck etc. **4 a** a
luminous trail of dust extending from the head of a comet and curving
away from the sun. **b** a nearly straight trail of ionized atoms lying in
the plane of a comet's orbit and blown away from the coma by the
solar wind and the effects of its magnetic field. **5 a** the hanging part
of the back of a coat. **b** = SHIRTTAIL. **6** (in *pl.*) *informal* **a** a tailcoat. **b** a
man's formal attire including tailcoat. **7** a twisted or braided tress of
hair, such as a pigtail or ponytail. **8 a** the image on the reverse of a
coin. **b** (in *pl.*) this side as a choice when tossing a coin (opp. HEAD 12).
9 an extra strip attached to the end of a kite. **10** *Cdn* the southeast
portion of the Grand Banks of Newfoundland, lying outside Canada's
320-km (200-mile) fishing zone (compare NOSE 6). **11** *informal* a person
who secretly watches or follows another, esp. as a detective or spy.
12 a *slang* the buttocks (*had to work my tail off to get the job done*). **b** *coarse
slang* the female genitals. **c** *coarse slang* women collectively regarded as
a means of male sexual gratification; sexual intercourse. **13 a** the part
of a letter, e.g. *y*, that extends below the line. **b** *Music* the stem of a note.
14 the slender backward prolongation of a butterfly's wing. **15** *Fishing*
a feathery spray of strands of tinsel, hair, etc. used to represent the
setae on a fly. **16** a calm stretch following rough water in a stream.
17 a comparative calm at the end of a gale. **18 a** the exposed end of a
slate or tile in a roof. **b** the unexposed end of a brick or stone in a wall.
● *verb* **1** *transitive & intransitive informal* follow closely and secretly; spy on.
2 *intransitive* (often foll. by *away*) (of an object in flight) deviate; drift,
carry, or curve away from a target. **3** *transitive* provide with a tail.
4 *transitive* dock the tail of (a lamb etc.). □ **on a person's tail** closely
following a person. **tail in** fasten (timber) by one end into a wall etc.
tail off (or **away**) diminish gradually; decrease in intensity, output,
production, etc. **with one's tail between one's legs** in a state of
dejection or humiliation. □ **tail·less** *adjective* [Old English *tægl*, *tægel*,
from Germanic]

tail² *Law* ● *noun* the limitation of the succession of land or other
property so that it cannot be bequeathed or sold but must pass to the
holder's descendants, failing which it reverts to the donor or the
donor's heirs or assigns. ● *adjective* so limited (*estate tail*; *fee tail*). □ **in
tail** under the limitation of tail. [Old French *taille* notch, cut, tax, from
taillier cut, ultimately from Latin *talea* twig]

tail·back *noun* **1** *Football* the running back who lines up furthest from
the line of scrimmage. **2** *Brit.* a long line of traffic backed up on a road
or highway etc.

tail·board *noun Brit.* = TAILGATE *noun*.

tail·bone *noun* **1** each of the caudal vertebrae in an animal. **2** =
COCCYX.

tail·coat *noun* a man's morning or evening coat with a long skirt
divided at the back into tails and cut away in front, worn as part of
formal dress.

tail covert *noun* each of the smaller feathers covering the bases of the
quill feathers of a bird's tail.

---

tail·dragger *noun* an airplane with a two-wheeled undercarriage and a third wheel under the tail rather than under the nose.

tailed *adjective* **1** (in *combination*) having a tail of a specified type, shape, colour, size, etc. (*white-tailed deer*). **2** having or provided with a tail.

tail end *noun* **1** the conclusion or final part (*the tail end of the movie*). **2** the back end of a thing; the part at the rear (*the tail end of the procession*).

tail-ender *noun* a person that lags behind or finishes near the end, such as in a race or competition (*opp.* FRONT-RUNNER).

tail feather *noun* a strong flight feather of a bird's tail.

tail fin *noun* **1** the caudal fin of a fish. **2** an upswept projection on the rear of a car. **3** a small projecting surface on the tail of an aircraft intended to provide stability.

tail·gate ● *noun* the hinged door at the back of a pickup truck, station wagon, or hatchback, esp. one which drops down forming a shelf to facilitate loading and unloading. ● *verb* N Amer. informal **1** *transitive & intransitive* follow (another vehicle) too closely. **2** *intransitive* attend or participate in a tailgate party. □ **tail·gater** *noun*

tailgate party *noun* N Amer. a party or barbecue held in the parking lot of a stadium etc., esp. before a football game or concert, in which participants gather around the open tailgates of their cars.

tail·hook *noun* a hook lowered from the tail of an aircraft to engage a steel cable stretched across the deck of an aircraft carrier, used in the event of a brake failure so that the plane does not roll beyond the edge of the runway.

tail·ing *noun* **1** (usu. in *pl.*) crushed stone and other waste produced in drilling, mining, or smelting ore. **2** the part of a beam or projecting brick etc. embedded in a wall.

tailings pond *noun* (also **tailing pond**) a large pool into which the tailings produced by mining and drilling etc. are drained.

tail light *noun* (also **tail lamp**) N Amer. a usu. red light on the back or at the rear of esp. a motor vehicle.

tailor ● *noun* a person who alters men's clothing and makes suits and jackets etc. to measure. ● *verb* **1** *transitive* design and make (clothing) esp. to meet the size requirements of a particular customer. **2** *transitive* design or adapt (something) to suit a specific need or purpose (*homes tailored to meet the needs of the elderly*). **3** *intransitive* work as a tailor. [Old French *tailleur* cutter, formed as TAIL²]

tailored *adjective* **1** (also in *combination*) made by a tailor, esp. in a specified way or style (*a well tailored blouse; a hand-tailored suit*). **2** (of clothing) well cut and closely fitted, not loose or sloppy; having the appearance of custom-made or tailor-made clothes. **3** having a neat design or appearance; trim, sleek (*this car has a tailored look*). **4** made to suit a specific purpose or need (*a tailored curriculum*).

tailor·ing *noun* **1** the business or occupation of a tailor. **2** the skill or workmanship of a tailor.

tailor-made ● *adjective* **1** (of clothing) made by a tailor to suit the needs of a particular customer; made-to-measure. **2** altered or designed to meet a specific need, purpose, or requirement. **3** (of a person, situation, etc.) ideally suited; perfect. **4** (of a cigarette) made in a factory, as opposed to being rolled by the smoker. ● *noun* **1** a tailor-made article of clothing. **2** a tailor-made cigarette.

tail·piece *noun* **1** an appendage attached to a thing to extend or conclude it. **2** a small decoration or illustration at the end of a book or chapter etc. (*compare* FRONTISPIECE 1). **3** a triangular piece of wood to which the lower ends of strings are fastened on some musical instruments. **4** a tube that extends from the drain of a sink to a trap.

tail·pipe *noun* the rear section of the exhaust pipe of a motor vehicle.

tail·plane *noun* a horizontal airfoil at the tail of an aircraft.

tail·race *noun* **1** a watercourse leading away from the turbine of a power station, a water wheel, a dam, etc. **2** a water channel used for the removal of tailings from a mine.

tail·spin ● *noun* **1** a state of chaos, panic, or loss of control. **2 a** a sharp or rapid decline. **b** *Sport* a slump. **3** a nose-first spiralling descent of an aircraft. ● *intransitive verb* (**-spin·ning**; past and past participle **-spun**) perform or fall into a tailspin.

tail·stock *noun* the adjustable part of a lathe holding the fixed spindle.

tail·water *noun* the water of a tailrace.

tail·wheel *noun* a wheel supporting the tail of an aircraft.

tail·wind *noun* a wind blowing in the direction of travel of an aircraft or vehicle.

Tai·myr Peninsula /taiˈmiːr/ (also **Tay·myr Peninsula**) a vast, almost uninhabited peninsula on the north coast of central Russia, extending into the Arctic Ocean and separating the Kara Sea from the Laptev Sea. Its northern tip is the northernmost point of Asia.

Tai·nan /taiˈnɒn/ a city on the southwest coast of Taiwan; pop. (2002) 746,300.

Taino /ˈtainoː/ ● *adjective* designating or pertaining to an extinct Arawak people formerly inhabiting the Greater Antilles and the Bahamas. ● *noun* (*pl.* **Tainos** or same) **1** a member of the Taino people. **2** the Arawak language of the Taino people. [Taino *taino* 'noble, lord']

taint ● *noun* **1** a trace, suggestion, or connotation of some bad or undesirable quality. **2** a corrupting influence; a cause of corruption or decay (*the taint of racism*). **3** a trace of rot, decay, or putrefaction, esp. an unpleasant scent or smell. ● *verb* **1** *transitive* contaminate, putrefy; cause to turn foul or rotten (*toxins have tainted the lake*). **2** *transitive* ruin, spoil (*tainted love*). **3** *transitive* (foll. by *with*) affect, esp. to a slight degree; imbue slightly with some bad or undesirable quality. **4** *intransitive* (of food) become putrid or rotten; spoil. □ **taint·ed** *adjective* **taint·less** *adjective* [Middle English, partly via Old French *teint(e)* from Latin *tinctus*, from *tingere* 'to dye', partly from ATTAINT]

tai·pan¹ /ˈtaipan/ *noun* the head of a foreign business in China. [Chinese]

tai·pan² /ˈtaipan/ *noun* a large dark brown venomous snake, *Oxyuranus scutellatus*, of northern Australia. [*dhayban*, its name in an extinct Aboriginal language of N Queensland]

Tai·pei /taiˈpei/ the capital of Taiwan; pop. (2002) 2,706,400.

Tai·ping Rebellion /taiˈpɪŋ/ a sustained uprising against the Qing dynasty in China 1850–64, led by the egalitarian Hong Xinquan (1814–64), who claimed to be a son of God. By the time the rebellion was defeated, some 20 million people had been killed.

Tai·wan /taiˈwɒn/ (official name **Republic of China**) an island country off the southeast coast of China; pop. (2002) 22,548,009; capital, Taipei. In 1949 Taiwan became the headquarters of the Kuomintang, which has held power continuously since then. In 1971 it lost its seat in the UN to the People's Republic of China, which regards Taiwan as one of its provinces. □ **Tai·wan·ese** /ˌtaiwɒˈniːz/ *adjective & noun*

Tai·yuan /ˌtaijuˈɒn/ a city in N China, capital of Shanxi province; pop. (2002) 1,883,200.

Ta·iz /taˈɪz/ (also **Ta'izz**) a city in SW Yemen; pop. (2002) 406,900. It was the administrative capital of Yemen from 1948 to 1962.

Taizé /ˈteizei/ *noun* a style of Christian worship characterized by the repetitive singing of simple harmonized tunes interspersed with reading, prayers, and periods of silence (also *attributive*: *Taizé prayer*). [the name of a village in Burgundy, France, the site of an ecumenical Christian community founded in 1948]

Tajik /tɒˈdʒiːk/ (also **Ta·dzhik**) ● *noun* **1** a native or inhabitant of the republic of Tajikistan. **2** the Iranian language of the Tajiks. ● *adjective* of or relating to Tajikistan, its people, or its language. [Persian, = 'someone who is neither an Arab nor a Turk']

Ta·jik·istan /tɒˌdʒiːkɪˈstan/ (also **Ta·dzhik·istan**) a mountainous republic in central Asia, north of Afghanistan; pop. (est. 2002) 6,719,567; capital, Dushanbe.

ta·jine /taˈʒiːn/ *noun* (also **ta·gine**) **1** a traditional shallow earthenware Moroccan cooking pot with a conical lid. **2** any of a variety of stews that may be cooked in this pot. [French from Arabic *ṭagīn*, perhaps ultimately from Greek]

Taj Mahal /ˌtɒʒ məˈhɒl, ˌtaʒ/ *noun* a mausoleum at Agra in N India, built by the Mogul emperor Shah Jahan (1592–1666) in memory of his favourite wife and completed *c.*1649. [perhaps a corruption of Persian *Mumtaz Mahal*, title of the wife of Shah Jahan, from *mumtāz* chosen one + *mahal* abode]

taka /ˈtaka/ *noun* the basic monetary unit of Bangladesh, equal to 100 poisha. [Bengali]

Tak·ak·kaw Falls /ˈtakəˌkɒ/ a waterfall in southeastern BC, which carries melted snow and ice from the Daly Glacier in the Rocky Mountains and drops 380 m into the Yoho River, in Yoho National Park. It is the second highest waterfall in Canada. [Cree, lit. 'it is magnificent']

take ● *verb* (*past* **took**; *past participle* **taken**) **1** *transitive* gather into one's hands or possession. **2** *transitive* pick out (an individual person or thing) from a group. **3** *transitive* deprive or rid a person of (a thing); steal, seize, carry away. **4** *transitive* capture by force (*have taken a hostage*). **5** *transitive* carry or bring with one (*you should take a jacket*). **6** *transitive* deliver or convey (a thing) to a person. **7** *transitive* receive or accept (something offered). **8** *transitive* gain use of or acquire by purchase or agreement (*the customer will take these three items*). **9** *transitive* receive (food, drink, a drug, etc.) voluntarily into one's body; swallow or inhale. **10** *transitive* (usu. foll. by *in* or *with*) add (milk, cream, sugar, etc.) to tea or coffee, esp. regularly (*I only take milk in my tea*). **11** *transitive* (often foll. by *with*) drink (tea or coffee) black or with specified ingredients. **12** *transitive* make use of (an opportunity, chance, advice, etc.). **13** *transitive* exercise, exert (*take caution*). **14** *transitive* own, assume, or accept (responsibility, blame, control, etc.). **15** *transitive* require or use up (*will only take a minute*). **16** *transitive* **a** experience or be affected by (a feeling or emotion) (*she took offence*). **b** (usu. foll. by *from* or *in*) feel or experience (comfort, consolation, etc.) as a result of; receive or derive from (*I take comfort from knowing that Rebecca is safe*). **17** *transitive* react to (something) in a specified way (*how did he take the news?*). **18** *transitive* accept without objection, opposition, or resentment; put up with, tolerate, bear, endure (*he can't take a joke; I've had just about all I can take*). **19** *transitive* occupy or engage oneself in; indulge in, esp. for exercise or leisure (*take a walk; take a nap*). **20** *transitive* undergo, experience (*she's taking treatments*). **21** *transitive* use as a means of transport (*takes the bus to work*). **22** *transitive* (of a vehicle) carry or convey (a person). **23** *transitive* (of a road etc.) lead (a person) to a specified place or in a specified direction. **24** *transitive* cause (a person or animal) to accompany one; conduct, escort (*he took the dog for a walk*). **25** *transitive* proceed to follow (a road etc.) or make (a turn) (*take the next left*). **26** *transitive* approach and attempt to pass or succeed in passing, clearing, or getting around (an obstruction) (*he took the corner too fast; she took every jump on the slope*). **27** *transitive* execute, make, or undertake; perform or effect (*Maggie just took her first steps; take a guess*). **28** *transitive* adopt or employ (measures etc.) (*they are taking steps to eliminate the problem*). **29** *transitive* venture upon (a gamble, risk, etc.). **30** *transitive* measure and record (a person's pulse, temperature, etc.). **31** *transitive* require (a particular size of shoes or clothing) for a correct fit (*she takes a size six*). **32** *transitive* ask for and write down (a name, address, etc.). **33** *transitive* write down (notes or minutes) based on a lecture, speech, meeting, etc. **34** *transitive* copy or borrow (an illustration, passage of text, etc.) from the work of another. **35** *transitive* derive (esp. a name or attribute) from a particular source (*takes its name from the inventor*). **36** *transitive* grasp mentally; understand (*I take your point*). **37** *transitive* (often foll. by *as* or *to mean*) understand, interpret (a person or thing) in a specified way (*I took it as a compliment; I took him to mean he wasn't staying*). **38** *transitive* (foll. by *for* or *to be*) suppose to be; consider or regard as (*do you take me for an idiot?*). **39** *transitive* receive instruction in (a subject) in a school, college, university, etc. **40** *transitive* **a** make (a photograph) with a camera. **b** have (a photograph of oneself) taken with a specified degree of success (*she takes a good picture*). **41** *transitive* bind oneself to an obligation etc. by the terms of (an oath, vow, etc.); accept the conditions of (an offer etc.). **42** *transitive* bring or receive (a person) into a specified condition or relation to oneself, as of marriage, employment, or custody. **43** *transitive* assume possession of (something symbolizing a particular role or occupation) (*I took her hand in marriage; taking the veil*). **44** *transitive* obtain after fulfilling the required conditions (*take a degree*). **45** *transitive* achieve through excellence of skill in competition; win (*she took first prize; they took the lead*). **46** *transitive* answer (a phone call). **47** *transitive informal* confront, attack, overcome, defeat (*I can take you, you're not so tough*). **48** *transitive informal* trick, cheat, or take advantage of (a person). **49** *transitive* inflict (revenge). **50** *transitive* terminate (a person's life). **51** *transitive Baseball* (of a batter) refrain from swinging at (a pitch). **52** *transitive Sport* attempt (a shot or swing etc.). **53** *transitive* proceed to occupy (*take a seat*). **54** *transitive* seek shelter or protection afforded by (refuge, cover, sanctuary, etc.). **55** *transitive* (foll. by *from*) subtract (*take 3 from 9*). **56** *transitive* hold, accommodate (*this jug takes two litres*). **57** *transitive* use or refer to as an example (*let's take Laurier for example*). **58** *transitive Grammar* have or require as part of the appropriate construction (*this verb takes an object*). **59** *transitive* have sexual intercourse with. **60** *transitive* (in *passive*; foll. by *by, with*) be attracted, charmed, or intrigued by. **61** *transitive* (in *passive*) *informal* or *jocular* be involved in a relationship; not be single or unattached. **62** *intransitive* be successful or effective (*the vaccine did not take*). **63** *intransitive* (of a plant, seed, etc.) begin to grow. **64** *transitive* catch, suffer, or contract (an illness etc.) (*she took a heart attack*). ● *noun* **1** **a** money taken or received in payment for or as the proceeds of a business transaction. **b** *N Amer.* the profits or earnings of business conducted esp. during a specific period (*the day's take*). **c** *informal* money acquired by theft or fraud. **2** the quantity of fish etc. caught at one time; a catch. **3** **a** a scene or sequence of film photographed continuously at one time. **b** an act of shooting a scene (*take one*). **4** *informal* an interpretation or assessment (*what's your take on the situation?*). **5** *informal* a visual, aural, or mental response (*a double take*). **6** **a** a sound recording of a concert or musical performance. **b** the act of making such a recording. □ **be taken ill** become ill, esp. suddenly. **have what it takes** *informal* have the necessary qualities etc. for success. **on the take** *slang* receiving bribes. **take account of** *see* ACCOUNT. **take action** *see* ACTION. **take advantage of** *see* ADVANTAGE. **take advice** *see* ADVICE. **take after** resemble (a parent or relative etc.), esp. in behaviour or attitudes. **take aim** *see* AIM. **take apart** **1** dismantle. **2** *informal* beat or defeat conclusively. **take aside** *see* ASIDE. **take away** **1** (foll. by *from*) diminish; weaken; detract from. **2** subtract. **3** remove or carry elsewhere. **4** *Brit.* = TAKE OUT 2. **take back** **1** retract (a statement). **2** convey (a person or thing) to his or her or its original position. **3** help (a person) recall or imagine an earlier time or incident. **4** **a** return (merchandise) to a store. **b** (of a store) accept such merchandise for return. **5** accept (a person) back into one's affections, into employment, etc. **6** *Printing* transfer to the previous line. **take a bow** *see* BOW[2]. **take breath** *see* BREATH. **take one's breath away** *see* BREATH. **take the cake** (or **biscuit**) *informal* be the most remarkable, outrageous, amusing, annoying, etc. **take care** *see* CARE. **take care of** *see* CARE. **take a chance** *see* CHANCE. **take charge** *see* CHARGE. **take a decision** esp. *Brit.* decide; make a decision. **take down** **1** write down or record (spoken words, information, etc.). **2** **a** disassemble (a structure) by dismantling. **b** remove (a fixture, decoration, etc.) from a hanging position. **3** (also **take down a peg**) humiliate. **4** *informal* **a** seize and wrestle to the ground; tackle. **b** defeat, subdue. **5** lower (one's pants or a similar article of clothing worn below the waist). **take effect** *see* EFFECT. **take for granted** *see* GRANT. **take fright** *see* FRIGHT. **take heart** be encouraged. **take hold** *see* HOLD[1]. **take ill** (or **sick**) *informal* become ill or sick. **take in** **1** draw or receive in (esp. air or moisture); absorb, swallow, inhale. **2** understand (*did you take that in?*). **3** *informal* go out to see (a movie etc.) (*shall we take in a show?*). **4** offer hospitality or shelter to (a person or animal). **5** make (an article of clothing) smaller. **6** cheat (*managed to take them all in*). **7** include or comprise. **8** furl (a sail). **9** perform (washing, sewing, etc.) at home for pay. **take in hand** **1** undertake; start doing or dealing with. **2** undertake the control or reform of (a person). **take into account** *see* ACCOUNT. **take it** **1** (often foll. by *that* + clause) assume (*I take it that you have finished*). **2** *informal* put up with or endure a difficult situation. **take it easy** *see* EASY. **take it from me** (or **take my word for it**) I can assure you. **take it upon oneself** (foll. by *to* + infin.) venture or presume. **take it or leave it** (esp. in *imperative*) an expression of indifference or impatience about another's decision after making an offer. **take it out on** relieve one's frustration or anger by attacking or treating harshly. **take a thing kindly** *see* KINDLY[1]. **take kindly to** *see* KINDLY[1]. **take one's leave of** *see* LEAVE[2]. **take a lot** (or **it**) **out of** exhaust the strength of. **take lying down** *see* LIE[1]. **take a person's name in vain** *see* VAIN. **take off** **1** **a** remove (clothing) from one's or another's body. **b** lose (weight). **2** **a** remove or lead away. **b** ask or order (a person) to leave one's job (*he's been taken off the case*). **3** deduct (part of an amount). **4** *informal* depart, esp. hastily (*took off in a fast car*). **5** *informal* mimic humorously. **6** jump from the ground. **7** become airborne. **8** (of a scheme, enterprise, etc.) become successful or popular. **9** have (a period) away from work. **10** remove or detach (something fastened or applied to a surface). **take oneself off** go away. **take on** **1** undertake (work etc.). **2** hire (an employee). **3** challenge or confront (an opponent or adversary). **4** acquire (a new meaning etc.). **take it on the chin** *see* CHIN. **take orders** *see* ORDER. **take out** **1** escort on a date or outing. **2** *N Amer.* buy (food etc.) at a restaurant for eating elsewhere. **3** **a** remove from within a place; extract. **b** carry (something) outside. **4** get (a licence or summons etc.) issued. **5** apply for and receive (a loan) from a bank. **6** borrow (a book etc.) from a library. **7** *slang* **a** *Sport* remove (a player) from play with a check, block, or tackle. **b** assassinate, murder. **8** *Bridge* remove (a partner or a partner's call) from a suit by bidding a different one or no trumps. **take a person out of himself** or **herself** make a person forget his or her worries. **take over** **1** succeed to the management or ownership of. **2** take control (of). **3** *Printing* transfer to the next line. **take part** *see* PART. **take place** *see* PLACE. **take a person's point** *see* POINT. **take root** *see* ROOT[1]. **take shape** *see* SHAPE. **take sides** *see* SIDE. **take some** (or **a lot of**) **doing** be hard to do. **take stock** *see* STOCK. **take that!** an exclamation accompanying a blow etc. **take one's time** not hurry. **take to** **1** adopt as a habit, practice, pastime, hobby, etc. (*she's taken to reading on the bus*). **2** form a liking for. **3** have recourse to (*when he gets lonely he takes to drinking*). **4** escape to; seek refuge in. **take to the cleaners** *see* CLEANER. **take to heart** *see* HEART. **take to one's heels** *see* HEEL[1]. **take to pieces** = TAKE APART 1. **take to task** *see* TASK. **take the trouble** = GO TO THE TROUBLE (*see* TROUBLE). **take up** **1** become interested or engaged in (an interest, pursuit, hobby, etc.). **2** adopt as a protege. **3** occupy (time or space). **4** begin (residence etc.). **5** resume after an interruption.

6 join in (a song, chorus, etc.). **7** accept (an offer etc.). **8** shorten (a garment). **9** go over the correct answers to (homework, an assignment, a test, etc.). **10** lift up. **11** absorb (*sponges take up water*). **12** take (a person) into a vehicle. **13** pursue (a matter etc.) further. **14** interrupt or question (a speaker). **take a person up on** accept (a person's offer etc.). **take up the gauntlet** accept a challenge. **take up with** begin to associate with. □ **take·able** *adjective* **tak·er** *noun* [Old English *tacan* from Old Norse *taka*]

take-away *noun* **1** *Football* an interception made or fumble forced by the defence (*compare* GIVEAWAY 4). **2** *Golf* the initial movement of the club at the beginning of a backswing. **3** *Brit.* = TAKEOUT 1.

take-charge *attributive adjective* esp. *N Amer.* characterized by leadership or authority (*a take-charge attitude*).

take·down *noun* **1** a wrestling manoeuvre in which an opponent is swiftly brought to the mat from a standing position. **2** *informal* a police raid or arrest. **3** a firearm with the capacity to have the barrel and magazine detached from the stock.

take-home *adjective* **1** that may be taken home. **2** (of pay or wages) remaining after taxes etc. have been deducted. **3** (of a test or exam) distributed to students to be written outside of class within a specified period of time.

take-home message *noun* a crucial piece of information that an audience etc. must retain.

take-it-or-leave-it *attributive adjective* characterized by or involving indifference; allowing acceptance or rejection (*a take-it-or-leave-it attitude*).

taken *past participle of* TAKE.

take-no-prisoners *attributive adjective* very aggressive or persistent; forceful (*a take-no-prisoners approach*).

take·off *noun* **1 a** the action or an instance of an aircraft becoming airborne. **b** the period during which this takes place (*please fasten your seat belts during takeoff*). **2 a** an act of mimicking, esp. a caricature or parody. **b** an imitation. **3 a** the moment of springing from the ground during a leap or jump. **b** a place from which one jumps. **4** the beginning of a new phase of accelerated or increased growth or development.

take·out *noun* **1** esp. *N Amer.* **a** food or a meal bought at a restaurant to be eaten off the premises (also *attributive*: *takeout food*). **b** a restaurant preparing food that may be bought and eaten elsewhere. **2** *Curling* a shot which removes an opponent's rock from play. **3** a pullout article in a newspaper or magazine.

take·over *noun* **1** the assumption of control or ownership of a business concern, esp. the buying out of one company by another. **2** a usu. hostile assumption of power or government; a military coup. **3** the act or an instance of taking over.

takeover bid *noun* an offer made to the shareholders of a company by an individual or organization to buy their shares at a specified price in order to gain control of that company.

take-up *noun* **1** an apparatus for gathering up film after exposure in a projector or camera. **2** esp. *Brit.* acceptance of something offered.

tak·in /ˈtakɪn/ *noun* a large shaggy horned ruminant, *Budorcas taxicolor*, of Tibet, Bhutan, and northern Burma (Myanmar), related to the muskox. [local Tibeto-Burman name]

tak·ing ● *adjective* **1** attractive or captivating. **2** catching or infectious. ● *noun* **1** the action or process of TAKE *verb* (*mine for the taking*). **2** (in *pl.*) = TAKE *noun* 1. □ **tak·ing·ly** *adverb*

Tak·li·ma·kan Desert /ˌtakləməˈkɒn/ (also **Takla Makan**) a desert in the Xinjiang autonomous region of NW China, lying between the Kunlun Shan and Tien Shan mountains and forming the greater part of the Tarim Basin.

Tako·radi /ˌtɑːkəˈrɒdi/ a seaport in W Ghana, on the Gulf of Guinea; pop. (2002) 86,400. It is part of the joint urban area of Sekondi-Takoradi and is one of the major seaports of West Africa.

tala[1] /ˈtɑːlə/ *noun* any of the traditional rhythmic patterns of Indian music. [Sanskrit *tāla* hand clapping]

tala[2] /ˈtɑːlə/ *noun* the basic monetary unit of Western Samoa, equal to 100 sene. [Samoan]

tal·aria /təˈlɛəriə/ *plural noun Gk & Rom. Myth* winged sandals or small wings attached to the ankles of some gods and goddesses, such as Mercury and Iris. [Latin, neuter pl. of *talaris* from *talus* ankle]

Tal·bot /ˈtɒlbət, ˈtal-/ **1 Thom·as** (1771–1853), Irish-born British soldier and Canadian colonial official. He was personal secretary to Governor Simcoe (1791–4). In 1801 he left the army and immigrated to Upper Canada, where he promoted settlement in the London area; by 1836 he had settled over 30,000 people in 29 townships. **2 Wil·liam Henry Fox** (1800–77), English scientist and pioneer of photography. He produced the first photograph on paper (1835) and discovered a process for producing a negative from which multiple positive prints could be made (1840), though the independently developed daguerreotype proved to be superior.

talc /talk/ ● *noun* **1** a monoclinic hydrated silicate of magnesium occurring as white, grey, or pale green masses or translucent laminae that are very soft and have a greasy feel, used esp. as a lubricant. **2** talcum powder. ● *transitive verb* (**talced, talc·ing**) treat (a surface) with talc to lubricate or dry it. □ **talcy** *adjective* [French *talc* or medieval Latin *talcum*, from Arabic *ṭalk* from Persian *talk*]

tal·cum /ˈtalkəm/ ● *noun* (in full **talcum powder**) a preparation of powdered talc, usu. scented or medicated for general cosmetic use. ● *transitive verb* (**tal·cumed, tal·cuming**) dust or treat with or as if with talcum powder. [medieval Latin: see TALC]

tale *noun* **1 a** a story or narrative, true or fictitious, told for interest or entertainment. **b** a literary composition cast in narrative form. **2 a** a report of an alleged fact, often malicious or in breach of confidence; a rumour. **b** (often in *pl.*) a false or fanciful statement; a lie. **3** a true account of improbable or extraordinary events. **4** *archaic* or *literary* a number or total. □ **live to tell the tale** survive an unpleasant or catastrophic event. [Old English *talu* from Germanic: compare TELL[1]]

tale-bearer *noun* a person who maliciously gossips or reveals secrets. □ **tale-bearing** *noun & adjective*

Ta·leg·gio /təˈledʒioː/ *noun* a type of soft Italian cheese made from cow's milk. [Italian, from the name of the *Taleggio* valley in Lombardy]

tal·ent *noun* **1** a special aptitude or faculty (*a talent for music*). **2 a** a person possessing exceptional skill or ability. **b** people of talent or ability collectively (*this team is loaded with talent*). **3** *Brit. informal* members of the opposite sex regarded in terms of sexual promise or desirability. **4 a** an ancient unit of weight, varying at different times and in different places, esp. one used by the Athenians and Romans, equivalent to nearly 26 kg (57 lb.). **b** such a weight of silver or gold used to represent a sum of money. □ **tal·ent·ed** *adjective* **tal·ent·less** *adjective* [Old English *talente* from Latin *talentum* 'sum of money', from Greek *talanton*; sense 1 is a figurative use with Biblical allusion to the parable of the talents (Matt. 25:14-30)]

talent pool *noun* a group of people seen as a source of talent.

talent scout *noun* a person looking for talented performers, esp. in sport and entertainment.

talent show *noun* a show consisting of performances by promising amateur entertainers, esp. ones hoping to enter show business professionally.

tales /ˈteɪliːz/ *noun Law* **1** a writ for summoning jurors to supply a deficiency. **2** a list of people who may be summoned. [Latin *tales* (*de circumstantibus*) such (of the bystanders), the first words of the writ]

tales·man /ˈteɪlzmən, ˈteɪlz-/ *noun* (*pl.* **-men**) *Law* a person summoned by a *tales*.

tale-teller *noun* **1** a person who tells stories. **2** a person who spreads malicious reports. □ **tale-telling** *noun*

tali *pl. of* TALUS[1].

Tal·i·ban /ˈtalɪban/ *noun* a fundamentalist Islamic movement founded in 1994, which steadily gained control of much of Afghanistan from early 1995, taking the capital (Kabul) in 1996 and setting up a repressive Islamic state until ousted by US military action in 2002. [Persian *ṭālibān*, plural of *ṭālib* 'seeker, enquirer, student,' so named because the movement reportedly began among Afghani students exiled in Pakistan]

tali·pes /ˈtalɪpiːz/ *noun Med.* = CLUB FOOT. [modern Latin from Latin *talus* ankle + *pes* foot]

tali·pot /ˈtalɪpɒt/ *noun* a tall S Indian palm, *Corypha umbraculifera*, with very large fan-shaped leaves that are used as sunshades etc. [Malayalam *tālipat*, Hindi *tālpāt* from Sanskrit *tālapattra* from *tāla* palm + *pattra* leaf]

tal·is·man /ˈtalɪzmən, ˈtalɪs-/ *noun* (*pl.* **tal·is·mans**) **1** an object, esp. an inscribed ring or stone, supposed to be endowed with magic powers esp. of averting evil from or bringing good luck to its holder. **2** a thing supposed capable of working wonders. □ **tal·is·man·ic** /-ˈmanɪk/ *adjective* **tal·is·man·ic·ally** *adverb* [French & Spanish, = Italian *talismano*, from medieval Greek *telesmon*, Greek *telesma* completion, religious rite, from *teleō* complete, from *telos* end]

talk ● *verb* **1** *intransitive* (often foll. by *to, with*) **a** converse or communicate ideas, information, or feelings by spoken words. **b** refer to a person for advice or information; consult (*I won't sign a thing until I've talked to my* *lawyer*). **c** *informal* negotiate, do business (*show me an offer, then we'll talk*). **2** *intransitive* have the power of speech. **3** *intransitive* (foll. by *about*) **a** have as the subject of discussion. **b** (in *imperative*) *informal* used to reinforce or emphasize as a clear or extreme example of (a thing) (*talk about dense! I explained it twice and he still didn't get it*). **4** *transitive* discuss (*we talked hockey all afternoon*). **5** *transitive* (often foll. by *to*) bring (a person) into a specified condition by talking (*talked himself hoarse; talked her to sleep*). **6** *transitive* **a** (foll. by *into*) persuade (a person) to agree to do something (*he talked me into buying his car*). **b** (foll. by *out of*) persuade (a person) not to do something (*she talked me out of quitting*). **7** *transitive* express or utter in words (*you're talking nonsense*). **8** *transitive informal* have in mind, think in terms of, envisage (*I'm talking six figures*). **9** *intransitive* reveal esp. secret information; betray secrets. **10** *intransitive* gossip (*people are starting to talk*). **11** *intransitive* **a** communicate without speaking, such as by writing, sign language, eye contact, etc. **b** have influence (*money talks*). **12** *transitive* use (a language) in speech (*is talking Spanish*). ● *noun* **1** conversation or talking. **2** a particular mode of speech (*baby talk*). **3** an informal address or lecture. **4 a** a rumour or gossip (*there is talk of a merger*). **b** the subject of rumour or gossip (*their success was the talk of the town*). **5** (often in *pl.*) formal discussions or negotiations between representatives of different countries, conflicting parties, etc. **6** empty promises or boasting. □ **know what one is talking about** have a thorough knowledge or understanding of a subject being discussed. **look who's talking** *informal* an expression of indignation or amusement at a person open to a criticism he or she has made of another. **now you're talking** *informal* now or at last you are saying, suggesting, etc. something that I agree with or approve of. **talk at** talk incessantly without consideration or concern for the thoughts and opinions of the person being addressed. **talk away 1** spend or consume (time etc.) in talking. **2** begin or carry on talking (*talk away! I'm listening*). **talk back** reply defiantly or with impudence. **talk big** *informal* talk boastfully. **talk is cheap** *informal* it is easier to announce one's intentions than to carry through with them. **talk down to** speak patronizingly or condescendingly to. **talk a person down 1** silence a person by greater loudness or persistence. **2** bring (a pilot or aircraft) to landing by radio instructions from the ground. **talk a person's ear off** *N Amer. informal* talk incessantly. **talk a good game** *informal* talk convincingly yet fail to act effectively. **talk the hind leg off a donkey** *informal* talk incessantly. **talk nineteen to the dozen** *see* DOZEN. **talk of 1** discuss or mention. **2** (often foll. by verbal noun) express some intention of (*talked of moving to Calgary*). **talk of the town** a prominent topic of local interest and popular discussion. **talk out 1** *Cdn & Brit.* prevent the passage of (a bill in Parliament) by prolonging discussion until the time of adjournment. **2** attempt to resolve by discussing. **talk over** discuss at length. **talk a person round** (or **over**) esp. *Brit.* gain agreement or compliance from a person by talking. **talk shop** talk, esp. tediously, about one's occupation, business, etc. **talk the talk** say things and make promises that will please or impress others and not offend (compare WALK THE WALK, *see* WALK). **talk tall** *informal* boast. **talk through** discuss thoroughly until a decision or resolution is reached. **talk a person through** guide a person in (a task) with continuous instructions. **talk through one's hat** (or *Brit.* **neck**) *informal* **1** exaggerate, bluff. **2** talk wildly or nonsensically. **talk to oneself** articulate one's thoughts to no one in particular and regardless of anyone present or listening. **talk tough** (often foll. by *on* or *about*) speak in a brash, boastful, or menacing manner. **talk trash** = TRASH TALK *verb*. **talk turkey** *see* TURKEY. **talk up** discuss (a subject) in order to arouse interest in it. **you should talk** *ironic* = LOOK WHO'S TALKING. [Middle English *talken*, frequentative verb from TALE or TELL[1]]

talk·athon *noun informal* a prolonged conversation or discussion.

talk·ative *adjective* fond of or given to talking; chatty. □ **talk·ative·ly** *adverb* **talk·ative·ness** *noun*

talk·back *noun* **1** (often *attributive*) a system of two-way communication by loudspeaker. **2** *Austral. & NZ* = PHONE-IN.

talked-about *adjective* widely discussed (*it's the most talked-about movie of the summer*).

talk·er *noun* **1** a person who talks. **2** a chatty or talkative person. **3** a person who gives talks or lectures; a speaker.

talk·fest *noun* = GABFEST.

talk·ie *noun informal* a movie with a soundtrack, as distinct from a silent film.

talk·ing ● *adjective* **1** that talks or is capable of talking (*a talking doll*). **2** (in *combination*) using a specified style or manner of speaking (*a smooth-talking politician*). **3** expressive (*talking eyes*). ● *noun in senses of* TALK *verb*. □ **talking of** *Brit.* = SPEAKING OF (*see* SPEAK).

talking book *noun* a recorded reading of a book, esp. for the blind.

talking drum *noun* each of a set of drums of different pitch which are beaten to transmit words in a tonal language, originating in W Africa.

talking head *noun informal* **1** a close-up shot on a television news broadcast or documentary etc. in which a reporter or newscaster is shown only from the shoulders up. **2** a person featured in such a shot.

talking picture *noun* (also **talking film**) a film with a soundtrack.

talking point *noun* **1** a topic suitable for or inviting discussion. **2** a fact supporting a decision, stance, or side in esp. a political debate.

talking shop *noun derogatory* **1** a centre for idle and unproductive talk; a place of argument rather than action. **2** an institution, committee, or organization, etc. that accomplishes little.

talking stick *noun* (among some N American Aboriginal groups) a carved staff used in gatherings, entitling the holder to speak to the group.

talking-to *noun informal* a reproof or reprimand; a lecture (*gave her a good talking-to*).

talk radio *noun* a radio format that features interviews, listener phone-ins, and discussions on sports or current events etc.

talk show *noun* esp. *N Amer.* a television or radio show in which people, esp. celebrities, are invited to talk informally about various topics (also *attributive*: talk-show host).

talk time *noun* the maximum length of time a cellular phone may be used before the battery will need to be recharged (compare STANDBY TIME, *see* STANDBY *noun* 3).

talky *adjective* **1** (of a book or theatrical production etc.) wordy or long-winded. **2** talkative.

tall ● *adjective* **1** (of a person or animal) of greater than average height. **2** of a specified height (*two metres tall*). **3** high relative to width or surrounding objects (*tall mountains*). **4** *informal* (of a statement or story) exaggerated, extravagant, unlikely. **5** *informal* (of language) pompous, arrogant. ● *adverb* **1** straight and erect (*stand tall*). **2** proudly. □ **tall·ish** *adjective* **tall·ness** *noun* [Middle English, representing Old English *getæl* swift, prompt]

Tal·la·has·see /ˌtaləˈhasi/ the state capital of Florida; pop. (2000) 150,624. □ **Tal·la·has·see·an** *noun & adjective*

tall·boy *noun* **1 a** a tall chest of drawers, often mounted on legs, usu. in two sections, one standing on the other. **b** = HIGHBOY. **2** *slang* a large can of beer.

tall drink *noun* a drink served in a tall glass.

Tal·ley·rand /ˈtaləˌrand/ (full surname Talleyrand-Périgord), **Charles Maurice de** (1754–1838), French statesman. Foreign minister under the Directory (1797–9) and Napoleon (1799–1807), he resigned (1807) and engaged in secret negotiations to have Napoleon deposed, becoming head of the new government after the fall of Napoleon (1814) and recalling Louis XVIII to the throne.

tall grass prairie *noun N Amer.* a prairie region characterized by certain tall moisture-favouring grasses.

Tal·linn /ˈtalɪn/ the capital of Estonia, a port on the Gulf of Finland; pop. (est. 2001) 403,891.

Tal·lis /ˈtaləs/ **Thomas** (*c.*1505–85), English composer. Organist of the Chapel Royal jointly with Byrd, he served under Henry VIII, Edward VI, Mary, and Elizabeth I; he is known mainly for his church music, esp. the 40-part motet *Spem in Alium*.

tal·lis /ˈtalɪs/ *noun* (also **tal·lit, tal·lith** /taˈlɪθ/, *pl.* **tal·li·tim, tal·li·thim** /talɪˈtiːm/) a shawl worn by Jewish men, esp. at prayer. [Rabbinical Hebrew *ṭallit* from *ṭillel* to cover]

tall order *noun* an exorbitant or unreasonable demand.

tal·low /ˈtaloʊ/ *noun* the harder kinds of esp. animal fat melted down for use in making candles, soap, etc. □ **tal·lowy** *adjective* [Middle English *talg, talug*, from Middle Low German *talg, talch*, of unknown origin]

tallow tree *noun* any of various trees, esp. *Sapium sebiferum* of China, yielding vegetable tallow.

tall ship *noun* a sailing ship with a high mast.

tally ● *noun* (*pl.* **-lies**) **1 a** a total score or amount. **b** the record of an amount, debt, score, etc. **2** *Sport* a goal or run scored. **3 a** a mark or number of marks used to represent a fixed number of things, e.g. a series of four vertical lines crossed by a diagonal line used to represent the number five. **b** a particular number, such as five, taken as a group or unit to facilitate counting. **4** *hist.* **a** a piece of wood scored across with notches for the items of an account and then split into halves, each party keeping one. **b** an account kept in this way. **5 a** a corresponding thing, counterpart, or duplicate. ● *verb* (**-lies, -lied**) **1** *transitive* **a** set down or record (a number etc.); register. **b** (often foll. by *up*) calculate the total of. **2** *transitive* amass, accumulate; achieve a total of. **3** *intransitive* agree or correspond; match. **4** *transitive & intransitive Sport* score (a run or goal etc.). [Anglo-French *tallie* from Latin *talea*: compare TAIL²]

tally·ho ● *interjection* a hunter's cry to the hounds upon sighting a fox. ● *noun* (*pl.* **-hos**) **1** the shout of 'tallyho!'. **2** *hist.* **a** any of various fast horse-drawn coaches or coach services. **b** *N Amer.* a large four-in-hand. ● *intransitive verb* (**-hoes, -hoed**) utter a cry of 'tallyho'. [compare French *taïaut*]

tally·man *noun* (*pl.* **-men**) **1** a person who keeps a tally. **2** *Brit.* a person who sells goods on credit, esp. from door to door.

tally sheet *noun* a piece of paper on which a tally is kept.

Tal·mud /ˈtalmʊd, -məd/ *noun* **1** the body of Jewish civil and ceremonial law and legend comprising the Mishnah and the Gemara. **2** either of two recensions of the Gemara, the Palestinian Talmud and the Babylonian Talmud, containing the commentary of scholars and jurists on the administration of Jewish law, compiled AD *c.*200–500. □ **Tal·mud·ic** /-ˈmʊdɪk/ *adjective* **Tal·mud·ic·al** /-ˈmʊdɪkəl/ *adjective* **Tal·mud·ist** *noun* [late Hebrew *talmûd* instruction, from Hebrew *lāmad* learn]

Talon /taˈlɔ̃/ **Jean** (*c.*1625–1694), French colonial administrator. The first intendant of New France (1665–8, 1669–72), he attempted to diversify the colony's economy by encouraging agriculture, fishing, lumbering, and industry as well as the traditional fur trade. While he succeeded in settling some 2,000 people in the colony, many of the industries he initiated failed when he returned to France.

talon /ˈtalən/ *noun* **1** a claw of an animal, esp. of a bird or beast of prey. **2 a** anything resembling this in form or appearance. **b** (often in *pl.*) a grasping human finger or hand. **3** the cards left after the deal in a card game. **4** a printed form attached to a bearer security that enables the holder to apply for a new sheet of coupons when the existing coupons have been used up. □ **tal·oned** *adjective* [Old French, = heel, ultimately from Latin *talus*: see TALUS¹]

talus¹ /ˈteɪləs/ *noun* (*pl.* **tali** /-laɪ/) *Anat.* a small bone in the foot, articulating with the tibia to form the ankle joint. *Also called* ANKLE BONE, ASTRAGALUS. [Latin, = ankle, heel]

talus² /ˈteɪləs/ *noun* (*pl.* **tal·us·es**) **1** *Geol.* a scree slope at the base of a mountain etc. consisting of material which has fallen from the face of the cliff above. **2** the sloping side of a wall or earthwork. [French: origin unknown]

tam *noun* (in full **tam-o'-shanter**) a round knitted or cloth cap of Scottish origin fitting closely around the brows but large and full above. [abbreviation of the name of the hero of Burns's *Tam o' Shanter*]

ta·male /təˈmɒli, -ˈmɑli/ *noun* a Mexican food of seasoned ground meat wrapped in cornmeal dough and steamed or baked in corn husks. [Latin American Spanish *tamal*, pl. *tamales*]

ta·man·dua /təˈmandjuːə/ *noun* any small Central and South American arboreal anteater of the genus *Tamandua*, with a prehensile tail used in climbing. [Portuguese from Tupi *tamanduà*]

tam·ar·ack /ˈtaməˌrak/ *noun* **1** any of several N American larches, esp. *Larix laricina*, found in wet places across most of Canada. **2** the wood from this. [Canadian French *tamarac*, prob. from Algonquian]

ta·mari /təˈmɑri/ *noun* a Japanese variety of rich wheat-free soy sauce. [Japanese]

tam·ar·in /ˈtamərɪn/ *noun* any of numerous small neotropical monkeys with fine silky coats and long bushy tails which belong to the genera *Saguinus* and *Leontopithecus*, and together with marmosets constitute the family Callithricidae. [French from Carib]

tam·ar·ind /ˈtamərɪnd/ *noun* **1** the fruit of the tree *Tamarindus indica*, a brown pod containing one to twelve seeds embedded in a soft brown sticky acid pulp, valued for its laxative qualities and also used to make esp. chutney and cold drinks. **2** the leguminous tree bearing this fruit, *Tamarindus indica*, with pinnate leaves and fragrant yellow red-streaked flowers, widely grown as a shade tree in tropical countries. [medieval Latin *tamarindus* from Arabic *tamr-hindī* Indian date]

tam·ar·isk /ˈtamərɪsk/ *noun* any shrub of the genus *Tamarix*, usu. with long slender branches and small pink or white flowers, that thrives by the sea. [Late Latin *tamariscus*, Latin *tamarix*]

Tamau·lipas /ˌtamauˈliːpas/ a state of NE Mexico with a coastline on the Gulf of Mexico; capital, Ciudad Victoria.

tam·bala /tamˈbɑlə/ *noun* (*pl.* same or **tam·balas**) a monetary unit of Malawi, equal to one-hundredth of a kwacha.

Tambo, Oli·ver (1917–93), South African politician. In 1944 he joined the African National Congress, organizing activities from abroad while the ANC was banned by the South African government (1960–90); during Nelson Mandela's long imprisonment he became acting

president of the ANC in 1967 and president in 1977, a position he held until 1991, when he gave it up in favour of the recently released Mandela.

tam·bour /ˈtambʊr/ *noun* **1** a flexible sliding shutter or door on a desk, cabinet, etc., made of strips of wood attached to a canvas backing (also *attributive*: *tambour cabinet*). **2 a** a circular frame consisting of one hoop fitting inside another, used to hold fabric taut while it is being embroidered. **b** material embroidered in this way. **3** a drum, esp. a small one with a deep tone. □ **tam·boured** *adjective* [French from *tabour* TABOR]

tam·boura /tamˈbʊrə/ *noun* (also **tam·bura**) *Music* a long-necked fretless type of lute with a round body and usu. four wire strings, used to provide a drone accompaniment in Indian music. [Arabic *ṭanbūra*]

tam·bour·ine /ˌtambəˈriːn/ *noun* a musical instrument consisting of a hoop with a skin stretched over one side and pairs of small jingling discs in slots around the circumference, played by shaking, striking, or drawing the fingers across the skin. [French, diminutive of TAMBOUR]

Tam·bov /tamˈbɒf/ an industrial city in SW Russia; pop. (2002) 309,200.

Tam·bur·laine see TAMERLANE.

tame ● *adjective* **1** reclaimed by human management from a naturally wild condition to a tractable or domesticated state. **2** (of an animal) gentle, accustomed to people; not showing the natural shyness, fear, or fierceness of a wild animal. **3 a** unlikely to harm, frighten, or offend (*a tame ski run; tame humour*). **b** lacking zest or vigour; insipid (*this hot sauce is pretty tame*). **4** *N Amer.* **a** (of land) cultivated. **b** (of a plant) produced by cultivation. **5** (of a person) co-operative, compliant, or servile. ● *transitive verb* **1** bring (a wild animal) under the control or into the service of humans. **2** reduce the intensity of (a person, emotion, etc.); calm, temper. **3** overcome the wildness of (a person etc.); control, subdue. **4** *N Amer.* cultivate (land). □ **tame·ly** *adverb* **tame·ness** *noun* **tamer** *noun* (also in *combination*). [Old English *tam* from Germanic]

Tam·er·lane /ˈtaməˌleɪn/ (also **Tam·bur·laine** /ˈtambɜː-/) (born Timur Lenk = 'lame Timur') (1336–1405), Mongol ruler of Samarkand 1369–1405. Leading a force of Mongols and Turks, between about 1364 and 1405 he conquered a large area including Persia, N India, and Syria, and established his capital at Samarkand; he defeated the Ottomans near Ankara in 1402, but died during an invasion of China.

Tam·il /ˈtamɪl/ ● *noun* **1** a member of a Dravidian people inhabiting the southern Indian subcontinent and parts of Sri Lanka. **2** the language of this people. ● *adjective* of this people or their language. □ **Tamil·ian** /-ˈmɪliən/ *noun & adjective* [(Portuguese, Dutch *Tamul* from) Tamil *Tamil* = Prakrit *Damila, Davila*, Sanskrit *Dramida, Dravida*. Compare DRAVIDIAN]

Tamil Nadu /ˌtamɪl naˈduː/ a state in the extreme southeast of the Indian peninsula, on the Coromandel Coast, with a largely Tamil-speaking, Hindu population; capital, Chennai.

Tam·many /ˈtaməni/ (in the US) **1** a fraternal and benevolent society of New York City, founded in 1789. **2** a political organization of the Democratic Party identified with this society; notorious for corruption, it dominated the political life of New York City during the 19th and early 20th c. by the use of bribes etc. [the name of an Aboriginal chief of the late 17th c. said to have welcomed William Penn]

Tammany Hall *noun* **1** any of the successive buildings used as the headquarters of Tammany. **2** the members of Tammany. **3** a corrupt political organization.

Tam·muz /ˈtamʊz/ *Myth* a Babylonian and Assyrian god, lover of Ishtar, corresponding to the Greek Adonis. He became the personification of the seasonal death and rebirth of crops.

tam-o'-shanter *noun* see TAM.

tam·oxi·fen /təˈmɒksɪfen/ *noun Pharm.* a drug which acts as an estrogen antagonist, used to treat breast cancer and infertility in women. [arbitrary formation based on *trans, amine, oxy-, phenol*, parts of the drug's chemical name]

tamp *transitive verb* (often foll. by *down*) **1** pound down or pack (earth, gravel, asphalt, etc.) in order to produce a firm base or level surface. **2 a** stuff or consolidate (tobacco) in a pipe. **b** pack (a pipe) with tobacco. **3** pack (a blasthole) full of clay, sand, etc., to concentrate the force of the explosion. **4** quash or suppress (a movement, speculation, etc.), esp. by forceful means. □ **tam·per** *noun* **tamp·ing** *noun* (in sense 1). [perhaps back-formation from French *tampin* (var. of TAMPION, taken as = *tamping*]

Tampa a port and resort on the west coast of Florida; pop. (2000) 303,619.

tamp·er *intransitive verb* (foll. by *with*) **1** meddle or interfere with, esp. so

---

Vowels: a *cat* ɑ *arm* e *bed* ɜr *her* ɜː *deux* ə *ago* ɪ *sit* i *cosy* iː *feed* ɒ *hot* ɔ *pore* ɔː *no* ʌ *run* ʊ *put*

as to cause alteration or harm. **2** make unauthorized alterations in (a document or file etc.). **3** contaminate (a drug or food product etc.) with a foreign substance. **4** exert a secret or corrupt influence upon; bribe. **5** *Sport* negotiate with a player who is under contract to another team. □ **tam·per·er** *noun* **tam·per·ing** *noun* [variant of TEMPER]

Tam·pere /ˈtampəˌrei/ a city in SW Finland; pop. (est. 2001) 197,774.

tamper-proof *adjective* (also **tamper-resistant**) not readily susceptible to tampering.

Tam·pi·co /tamˈpiːkoː/ one of Mexico's principal seaports, on the Gulf of Mexico; pop. (2000) 295,400.

tam·pion /ˈtampiən/ *noun* (also **tom·pion** /ˈtɒm-/) **1** a wooden stopper for the muzzle of a gun. **2** a plug e.g. for the top of an organ pipe. [Old French *tampon*, nasalized var. of *tapon*, related to TAP¹]

tam·pon /ˈtampɒn/ *noun* a soft plug of cotton or other material used to absorb secretions and stop the flow of blood etc. from an orifice or wound, esp. one inserted into the vagina during menstruation. [French: see TAMPION]

tam·pon·ade /tampəˈneid/ *noun* **1** (in full **cardiac tamponade**) compression of the heart by an accumulation of fluid in the pericardial sac. **2** the surgical use of a tampon.

tam-tam *noun* a large metal gong. [Hindi: see TOM-TOM]

tan¹ ● *noun* **1** a brown skin colour resulting from exposure to the sun or another source of ultraviolet light. **2** a yellowish-brown colour. **3** tanbark. ● *adjective* **1** of a yellowish-brown colour. **2** (of a person, their body, or a part of the body) brown in colour due to exposure to ultraviolet light. ● *verb* (**tanned**, **tan·ning**) **1** *transitive & intransitive* make or become brown by exposure to ultraviolet light. **2** *transitive* convert (rawhide) into leather by soaking in a liquid containing tannic acid or by the use of mineral salts etc. **3** *transitive slang* beat, thrash. □ **tanned** *adjective* **tan·ning** *noun* **tan·nish** *adjective* [Old English *tannian*, prob. from medieval Latin *tanare*, *tannare*, perhaps from Celtic]

tan² *abbreviation* tangent.

Tana, Lake /ˈtɒnə/ a lake in N Ethiopia, the source of the Blue Nile.

tan·ager /ˈtanədʒər/ *noun* any small New World bird of the subfamily Thraupinae, the male usu. having brightly coloured plumage. [modern Latin *tanagra* from Tupi *tangara*]

Tana·na·rive /ˌtananəˈriːv/ the former name (until 1975) for ANTANANARIVO.

tan·bark *noun* **1** the crushed bark of oak or other trees, used as a source of tannin for converting hides into leather. **2** leftover bark from tanning, used as a covering for paths etc. **3** a surface covered with this bark, esp. in a riding path or the floor of a circus ring.

Tan·cred /ˈtaŋkred/ (d.1112), Norman soldier, who was one of the leaders of the First Crusade (1096–9) and became regent of Antioch in 1101.

T. & A. *noun slang* TITS AND ASS.

tan·dem ● *noun* **1** a team of two people or arrangement of two machines working together in conjunction. **2** a bicycle or tricycle equipped with seats and pedals for two riders, one in front of the other. **3 a** two horses or dogs etc. harnessed one in front of the other. **b** a carriage or sled etc. drawn by animals harnessed in this way. ● *adjective* **1** co-operative, joint, dual; involving two people, organizations, etc. **2** involving two similar things, one behind the other. **3** (of an articulated truck or trailer) supported at the rear by two axles. ● *adverb* together, esp. one behind or after the other (*we were riding tandem*). □ **in tandem 1** one behind another. **2** alongside each other, together, in conjunction. [Latin, = at length (of time), used punningly]

tan·door /ˈtandʊr/ *noun* **1** a clay oven of a kind used originally in N India and Pakistan. **2** (*attributive*) designating food cooked in such an oven. [Urdu]

tan·doori /tanˈdʊri/ *noun* **1** a style of Indian cooking based on the use of a tandoor. **2** food or a dish cooked over charcoal in a tandoor (often *attributive*: *tandoori chicken*). [Hindustani]

Tang *noun* **1** a dynasty that ruled China AD 618–907, a period noted for territorial conquest and great wealth and regarded as the golden age of Chinese poetry and art. **2** (*attributive*) designating art and artifacts of this period. [Chinese *táng*]

tang *noun* **1** a sharp or penetrating taste, flavour, or smell. **2** a pointed projection on the blade of a knife, chisel, file, etc., by which the blade is held in the handle. **3** a characteristic quality. □ **tanged** *adjective* (in sense 2). [Old Norse *tange* point, tang of a knife]

Tanga /ˈtaŋgə/ one of the principal ports of Tanzania, situated in the northeast of the country on the Indian Ocean; pop. (2001) 198,300.

tanga /ˈtaŋgə/ *noun* **1** a skimpy pair of men's or women's underwear with a very narrow front and usu. an even narrower back. **2** a similar garment worn as a man's bathing suit or the lower half of a woman's bikini. [Portuguese, ultimately of Bantu origin]

Tan·gan·yika /ˌtaŋgəˈniːkə, -ˈnjiːkə/ see TANZANIA.

Tanganyika, Lake a lake in East Africa, in the Great Rift Valley. The deepest lake in Africa and the longest freshwater lake in the world, it forms most of the border of Congo (formerly Zaire) with Tanzania and Burundi.

tan·gelo /ˈtandʒəˌloː/ *noun* (*pl.* **-gelos**) **1** a hybrid citrus fruit, a cross between a tangerine and a grapefruit or pomelo. **2** the tree bearing this fruit. [TANGERINE + POMELO]

tan·gent /ˈtandʒənt/ ● *noun* *Math.* **1** a straight line touching a curve or curved surface so that it meets it at a point but does not intersect it at that point. **2** the ratio of the sides opposite and adjacent to an angle in a right-angled triangle. ● *adjective* **1** *Math.* (of a line or surface) touching, but not normally intersecting, another line or surface; that is a tangent. **2** touching. □ **on** (or **at**) **a tangent** diverging from a previous course of action or thought etc. (*the speaker went off on a tangent*). □ **tan·gency** *noun* (*pl.* **-cies**). [Latin *tangere tangent-* touch]

tan·gen·tial /tanˈdʒenʃəl/ *adjective* **1** *Math.* **a** of, pertaining to, or of the nature of a tangent. **b** acting or lying etc. in the direction of or along a tangent. **2** going off on a tangent; digressive, divergent (*tangential comments*). **3** that merely touches on a subject or matter; peripheral (*tangential evidence*). □ **tan·gen·tial·ly** *adverb*

Tan·ge·rang /ˈtaŋgərˌaŋ/ a city in NW Java, Indonesia, immediately southwest of Jakarta; pop. (est. 1990) 1,144,500.

tan·ger·ine /tandʒəˈriːn/ ● *noun* **1 a** a mandarin orange, esp. one with a sweeter or tangier flavour and darker colour of peel. **b** the tree bearing this fruit. **2** the colour of the peel of this fruit, a deep reddish orange. ● *adjective* of this colour. [originally *tangerine orange* from *Tanger* (former name of TANGIER)]

tan·gible /ˈtandʒɪbəl/ ● *adjective* **1** perceptible by touch; having material form (*tangible evidence*). **2** clearly intelligible; that can be grasped by the mind, not elusive or visionary (*tangible goals for the future*). **3** substantial, definite; that may be clearly viewed, evaluated, or calculated (*tangible assets; tangible results*). ● *noun* (usu. in *pl.*) a tangible thing, esp. an asset. □ **tan·gi·bil·ity** /-ˈbɪlɪti/ *noun* **tan·gibly** /-bli/ *adverb* [French *tangible* or Late Latin *tangibilis*, from *tangere* 'touch']

Tan·gier /tanˈdʒiːr/ (also **Tan·giers** /tanˈdʒiːrz/) a seaport on the northern coast of Morocco, on the Strait of Gibraltar commanding the western entrance to the Mediterranean; pop. (2002) 591,300.

tangle¹ ● *verb* **1 a** *transitive* (often foll. by *up*) twist, intertwine, or jumble (several strands of thread or string etc.) so that all the pieces are joined in a confused mass from which they may not be easily freed. **b** *intransitive* become twisted, intertwined, or jumbled. **2** *transitive* (in passive; often foll. by *up*) **a** become caught in a mess or tangle of rope, wires, etc. (*my foot is tangled in the extension cord*). **b** become embroiled in a difficult situation, controversy, affair, etc. **3** *intransitive* (foll. by *with*) *informal* become involved with (a person, organization, etc.), esp. in conflict or disagreement (*don't tangle with me*). **4** *transitive* complicate (a *tangled affair*). ● *noun* **1** a confused mass of twisted or intertwined hairs, threads, etc. that may not be easily separated. **2** a single long thread, cord, etc. coiled or knotted in a confusing manner; a snarl or ravel. **3** a confused or complicated state or situation; a dilemma, predicament, mess, etc. □ **tan·gled** *adjective* **tan·gly** *adjective* (**tan·gli·er**, **tan·gli·est**). [Middle English var. of obsolete *tagle*, of uncertain origin]

tangle² *noun* any of various seaweeds, esp. of the genus *Laminaria* or *Fucus*. [prob. from Norwegian *taangel* from Old Norse *thöngull*]

tango ● *noun* (*pl.* **tangos**) **1** a syncopated ballroom dance of Argentinian origin, performed with long dramatic gliding movements and abrupt pauses and changes in direction in 2/4 or 4/4 time. **2** a piece of music in the rhythm of this dance and usu. used as an accompaniment. ● *intransitive verb* (**-goes**, **-goed**) dance the tango. □ **it takes two to tango** both participants in a situation, esp. a dispute or conflict, must be held responsible. [Latin American Spanish]

tan·gram *noun* a Chinese geometrical puzzle consisting of a square cut into seven pieces, usu. five triangles, a rhomboid, and a square, which can be combined to make various shapes and figures. [19th c.: origin unknown]

Tang·shan /ˈtaŋˈʃan/ an industrial city in Hebei province, NE China; pop. (2002) 1,473,900. The city had to be rebuilt after a devastating earthquake in 1976, in which approximately 1 million people were killed or injured.

---

uː m**oo**d   ai m**y**   əi p**i**pe   au br**ow**n   ʌu h**ou**se   ei d**ay**   ɔi b**oy**   ɑ̄ fr**an**glais   ā Cana**di**en   ɔ̄ Bray**on**   (*see over for consonants*)

Tan·guy /tɑ̃'giː/ **Yves** (1900–55), French-born US painter. His surrealist works portray bleak unearthly landscapes with stark inanimate objects or ghostly life forms, as in *He Did What He Wanted* (1927) and *The Invisibles* (1951).

tangy *adjective* (**tang·i·er**, **tang·i·est**) having a strong, sharp flavour or scent; pungent. □ **tang·i·ness** *noun*

tan·ist /'tanɪst/ *noun hist.* the heir apparent to a Celtic chief, usu. his most vigorous adult relation, chosen by election. □ **tan·istry** *noun* [Irish & Gaelic *tánaiste* heir]

Tan·jung·ka·rang /ˌtandʒʊŋkəˈraŋ/ *see* BANDAR LAMPUNG.

tank ● *noun* **1** a large receptacle or storage chamber usu. for liquid or gas. **2** a heavy armoured fighting vehicle carrying guns and moving on a tracked carriage. **3** a container for the fuel supply in a motor vehicle, aircraft, etc. **4** = TANK TOP. **5** a pond or reservoir. **6** *esp. N Amer.* **a** a prison cell, esp. one for the temporary detention of more than one person (*drunk tank*). **b** *slang* a prison (*was in the tank for 3 years*). ● *verb* **1** *transitive* (usu. foll. by *up*) fill the tank of (a vehicle etc.) with fuel. **2** *informal* **a** *intransitive* (foll. by *up*) drink heavily; become drunk. **b** *transitive & reflexive* (often as **tanked up** *adjective*) inebriate oneself with alcoholic drink or drugs. **3** *informal* **a** *transitive* defeat utterly or completely. **b** *intransitive* fail utterly or completely. **4** *transitive & intransitive Sport informal* lose or fail to finish (a game or match) deliberately. **5** *intransitive informal* (of prices, market values, etc.) decline or decrease dramatically. □ **tank·ful** *noun* (*pl.* **-fuls**). **tank·less** *adjective* [Gujarati *tānkh* etc., perhaps from Sanskrit *tadāga* pond]

tan·ka /'taŋkə/ *noun* a Japanese poem in five lines and thirty-one syllables. [Japanese]

tank·age *noun* **1 a** storage in tanks. **b** a charge made for this. **2** the cubic content of a tank. **3** a kind of fertilizer obtained from refuse bones etc.

tank·ard /'taŋkərd/ *noun* **1** a tall mug with a handle and sometimes a hinged lid, esp. of silver or pewter for beer. **2** the contents of or an amount held by a tankard (*drank a tankard of ale*). [Middle English: origin unknown: compare Middle Dutch *tanckaert*]

tank·buster *noun* an aircraft or other device designed to combat tanks. □ **tank·bust·ing** *adjective*

tank car *noun esp. N Amer.* a railway car carrying a tank for transporting bulk liquids.

tank dress *noun* a sleeveless, close-fitting dress with a scoop neck.

tank engine *noun* a steam locomotive carrying fuel and water receptacles in its own frame, not in a tender.

tank·er *noun* a ship, aircraft, or road vehicle for carrying liquids or gases in bulk. □ **tanker·load** *noun*

tank farm *noun* an area of oil or gas storage tanks.

tank·ini *noun* a two-piece women's bathing suit combining a top half like a tank top and a bikini bottom. [blend of TANK TOP + BIKINI]

tank top *noun* a sleeveless upper garment with a scoop neck.

tank town *noun N Amer.* a small, unimportant town. [orig. a town at which steam locomotives had to stop to take on water]

tanned *adjective* **1** suntanned. **2** (of leather) that has been tanned.

tan·ner¹ *noun* **1** a person who tans hides. **2** a person who acquires a suntan.

tan·ner² *noun Brit. hist. slang* a sixpence. [19th c.: origin unknown]

tan·nery *noun* (*pl.* **-ies**) a place where hides are tanned.

Tann·häuser /'tan,hauzər, -,hɔizər/ (*c.*1200–*c.*1270), German poet. A minnesinger, he became a legendary figure as the knight who visited the grotto of Venus, repented, and sought absolution from the pope. His surviving works include lyrics and love poetry; he is commemorated in Wagner's opera *Tannhäuser* (1845).

tan·nic *adjective* **1** of or produced from tan. **2** (of wine) having an astringent flavour due to the presence of tannin. □ **tan·nate** *noun*

tan·nin *noun* (also **tannic acid**) any of a group of complex organic compounds found in tea, certain tree barks, and oak galls, used in leather production and as a mordant and astringent. [French *tanin* (as TAN¹, -IN)]

tanning bed *noun* a hinged device, lined with bulbs emitting ultraviolet light, in which a person lies to acquire an artificial tan.

tan·nish *adjective see* TAN¹.

Tan·noy /'tanɔi/ *noun Brit. proprietary* a type of public address system. [from *tantalum* alloy (rectifier)]

Tannu-Tuva /ˌtanuːˈtuːvə/ the former name for TUVA.

tansy *noun* (*pl.* **-sies**) any plant of the genus *Tanacetum*, esp. *T. vulgare* with yellow button-like flowers and aromatic leaves, formerly used in medicines and cookery. [Old French *tanesie* from medieval Latin *athanasia* immortality, from Greek]

tan·tal·ite /'tantə,lait/ *noun* a rare dense black mineral, the principal source of the element tantalum.

tan·tal·ize /'tantə,laiz/ *transitive verb* (also *esp. Brit.* **-ise**) **1** torment or tease by the sight or promise of what is unobtainable. **2** raise and then dash the hopes of; torment with disappointment. □ **tan·tal·iz·a·tion** *noun* **tan·tal·iz·er** *noun* [TANTALUS]

tan·tal·iz·ing /'tantə,laizɪŋ/ *adjective* (also *esp. Brit.* **-ising**) exciting interest, desire, hope, etc., often for the unobtainable. □ **tan·tal·iz·ing·ly** *adverb*

tan·ta·lum /'tantələm/ *noun* a rare hard white metallic element occurring naturally in tantalite, resistant to heat and the action of acids, and used in surgery and for electronic components. Symbol: **Ta**; at. no.: 73. [formed as TANTALUS with reference to its non-absorbent quality]

Tan·ta·lus /'tantələs/ *Gk Myth* a Lydian king, son of Zeus and father of Pelops. For his crimes (which included killing Pelops and offering his flesh to the gods) he was punished in Tartarus by being provided with fruit and water which receded when he reached for them.

tan·ta·lus /'tantələs/ *noun* a stand in which decanters may be locked up but visible. [TANTALUS]

tan·ta·mount *predicative adjective* (foll. by *to*) equivalent to (*was tantamount to a denial*). [from obsolete verb *tantamount* from Italian *tanto montare* 'amount to so much']

tan·tivy /tan'tɪvi/ *noun archaic* (*pl.* **-ies**) **1** a hunting cry. **2** a swift movement; a gallop or rush. [17th c.: perhaps imitative of hoof beats]

tant pis /tɑ̃ 'piː/ *interjection* so much the worse. [French]

Tan·tra /'tantrə/ *noun* any of a class of Hindu or Buddhist mystical and magical writings. □ **Tan·tric** *adjective* **Tan·trism** *noun* **Tan·trist** *noun* [Sanskrit, = loom, groundwork, doctrine, from *tan* stretch]

tantric sex *noun* a type of sexual practice based on Tantric beliefs, in which mental and physical self-control are exercised so as to heighten sexual arousal, prolong intercourse, and encourage multiple or extended orgasms.

tan·trum *noun* an outburst of bad temper or petulance (*threw a tantrum*). [18th c.: origin unknown]

Tan·za·nia /ˌtanzəˈniːə/ a country in East Africa with a coastline on the Indian Ocean; pop. (est. 2002) 37,187,939; capital, Dodoma. Tanzania consists of a mainland area (the former Tanganyika) and the island of Zanzibar. □ **Tan·za·nian** *adjective & noun*

Tao /'tau, 'dau/ *noun* **1** (in Taoism) the absolute being or principle underlying the universe; ultimate reality. **2** (in Confucianism) the way, method, or norm to be followed, esp. in conduct. [Chinese *dào* 'way, path, right way (of life), reason']

Taoi·seach /'tiːʃəx/ *noun* the prime minister of the Irish Republic. [Irish, = chief, leader]

Tao·ism /'tauɪzəm, 'dau-/ *noun* a Chinese philosophy based on the writings of Lao-tzu, advocating humility and religious piety. □ **Tao·ist** *noun* **Tao·istic** *adjective* [Chinese *dao* (right) way]

tap¹ ● *noun* **1** a device by which a flow of liquid or gas from a pipe or vessel can be controlled. **2** an act of tapping a telephone etc. **3** a tool for cutting the thread of a female screw. **4** the surgical withdrawal of fluid from a cavity etc. (*spinal tap*). ● *transitive verb* (**tapped**, **tap·ping**) **1 a** provide (a cask) with a tap. **b** let out (a liquid) by means of, or as if by means of, a tap. **2** draw sap from (a tree) by cutting or drilling into it. **3 a** obtain information or supplies or resources from. **b** extract or obtain; discover and exploit (*mineral resources to be tapped*; *tapping the skills of young people*). **4** connect a listening device to (a telephone or telegraph line etc.) to listen to a call or transmission. **5** cut a female screw thread in. **6** *Med.* drain (a cavity) of accumulated fluid. □ **on tap 1** (of beer etc.) ready to be drawn from a keg; not bottled or canned. **2** *informal* ready for immediate use; freely available. **tap into 1** obtain something from. **2** exploit. □ **tap·less** *adjective* **tap·pable** *adjective* [Old English *tæppian* (v.), *tæppa* (n.) from Germanic]

tap² ● *verb* (**tapped**, **tap·ping**) **1** *intransitive* (foll. by *at*, *on*) strike a gentle but audible blow. **2** *transitive* strike lightly (*tapped me on the shoulder*). **3** *transitive* (foll. by *against* etc.) cause (a thing) to strike lightly (*tapped a stick against the window*). **4** *intransitive* = TAP DANCE *verb*. **5** *transitive* (often foll. by *out*) **a** make a tap or taps (*tapped out the rhythm*). **b** write using a computer keyboard or typewriter. **6** *intransitive* walk with a tapping sound (*she tapped across the tiled floor*). **7** *transitive N Amer. informal* designate or select (someone) for a task or honour. ● *noun* **1 a** a light blow; a rap. **b** the sound of this (*heard a tap at the door*). **2 a** = TAP DANCE *noun* (also *attributive*: *goes to tap classes*). **b** a piece of metal attached to the toe and heel of a tap dancer's shoe to make the tapping sound. **3** (in *pl.*, usu. treated as *sing.*) *US* **a** a bugle call for lights to be put out in army quarters. **b** a similar signal at a military funeral. □ **tap·per** *noun* [Middle English *tappe* (imitative), perhaps through French *taper*]

tapa *noun* **1** the bark of a paper mulberry tree. **2** cloth made from this, used in the Pacific islands. [Polynesian]

tapas *plural noun* (often *attributive*) small savoury Spanish appetizers, esp. served with wine or beer. [Spanish]

tap dance ● *noun* a form of display dance performed wearing shoes fitted with metal taps, with rhythmical tapping of the toes and heels. ● *intransitive verb* perform a tap dance. □ **tap dancer** *noun* **tap dancing** *noun*

tape ● *noun* **1** a narrow strip of woven material for tying up, fastening, etc. **2 a** a strip of material stretched across the finishing line of a race. **b** a similar strip for marking off an area or forming a notional barrier. **3** (in full **adhesive tape**) a strip of opaque or transparent paper or plastic etc., esp. coated with adhesive for fastening, sticking, masking, insulating, etc. **4 a** = MAGNETIC TAPE. **b** a tape recording or tape cassette. **5** = TAPE MEASURE. ● *transitive verb* **1 a** tie up or join etc. with tape. **b** apply tape to. **2** (foll. by *off*) seal or mark off an area or thing with tape. **3** record on magnetic tape. **4** measure with tape. **5** wrap (a joint etc.) firmly with a bandage or tape to provide support. □ **have** (or **get**) **a person** or **thing taped** *Brit. informal* understand a person or thing fully. **on tape** recorded on magnetic tape. [Old English *tæppa, tæppe*, of unknown origin]

tape deck *noun* a piece of equipment for playing audiotapes, esp. as part of a stereo system.

tape-delay *noun* the use of a tape recording device to introduce an interval between recording and retransmitting. □ **tape-delayed** *adjective*

tape machine *noun* **1** = TAPE RECORDER. **2** = TICKER 2.

tape measure *noun* a strip of tape or thin flexible metal marked for measuring lengths.

tap·enade /tapəˈnad/ *noun* a Provençal dish, usu. served as an hors d'oeuvre, made mainly from puréed black olives, capers, and anchovies. [French, from Provençal *tapeno* caper + -ADE[1]]

tape player *noun* a tape recorder or tape deck.

taper ● *noun* **1** a wick coated with wax etc. for conveying a flame. **2** a slender candle. **3** gradual diminution in width or thickness. ● *verb* (often foll. by *off*) **1** *intransitive & transitive* diminish or reduce in thickness towards one end. **2** *transitive & intransitive* make or become gradually less. □ **taper·ing** *adjective* [Old English *tapur, -or, -er* wax candle, from Latin PAPYRUS, whose pith was used for candle wicks]

tape recorder *noun* a machine for recording sounds on magnetic tape and playing back the recording. □ **tape-record** *transitive verb* **tape recording** *noun*

tap·estry /ˈtapəstri/ *noun* (*pl.* **-ries**) **1 a** a thick textile fabric in which coloured weft threads are woven to form pictures or designs. **b** embroidery imitating this, usu. in wools on canvas. **c** a piece of such embroidery. **2** events or circumstances etc. compared with a tapestry in being intricate, interwoven, etc. (*life's rich tapestry*). □ **tap·est·ried** *adjective* [Old French *tapisserie* from *tapis* from Late Latin *tapetium* from Greek *tapētion* diminutive of *tapēs tapētos* tapestry]

ta·petum /təˈpiːtəm/ *noun* a light-reflecting part of the choroid membrane in the eyes of certain mammals, e.g. cats. [Late Latin from Latin *tapete* carpet]

tape·worm *noun* any flatworm of the class Cestoda, with a body like segmented tape, living as a parasite in the intestines.

ta·phon·omy /taˈfɒnəmi/ *noun* the science concerned with the process of fossilization. □ **tapho·nomic** /-fəˈnɒmɪk/ *adjective* **ta·phon·omist** *noun* [Greek *taphos* 'grave' + -NOMY]

tap-in *noun* a close-range shot requiring little force, esp. into the goal in hockey.

taping *noun* **1** the act or an instance of recording something on magnetic tape, esp. a session where an item is taped for later broadcast. **2** the act of applying tape or bandages etc.

tapi·oca /ˌtapiˈoːkə/ *noun* a starchy substance in hard white grains obtained from cassava and used for puddings etc. [Tupi-Guarani *tipioca* from *tipi* dregs + *og, ok* squeeze out]

tapir /ˈteipər, -pɪːr/ *noun* any nocturnal hoofed mammal of the genus *Tapirus*, native to Central and South America and Malaysia, having a short flexible protruding snout used for feeding on vegetation. □ **tapir·oid** *adjective & noun* [Tupi *tapira*]

tap pants *noun* *N Amer.* a type of loose-fitting women's underpants. [TAP[2], because orig. worn by tap dancers]

tapped-out *adjective* *N Amer. informal* **1** exhausted. **2** broke.

tap·pet *noun* a lever or projecting part used in machinery to give intermittent motion, often in conjunction with a cam. [apparently from TAP[2] + -ET[1]]

tap·room *noun* a room in which alcoholic drinks are available, esp. in a hotel.

tap·root *noun* a tapering root growing vertically downwards.

tap·ster *noun* a bartender. [Old English *tæppestre* originally fem. (as TAP[1], -STER)]

tap water *noun* water from a piped supply, esp. as opposed to bottled water.

ta·que·ria /takəˈriːə/ *noun* a Mexican restaurant specializing in tacos. [Mexican Spanish]

tar[1] ● *noun* **1** a dark thick inflammable liquid distilled from wood or coal etc. and used as a preservative of wood and iron, in making roads, as an antiseptic, etc. **2** a similar substance formed in the combustion of tobacco etc. ● *transitive verb* (**tarred, tar·ring**) **1** cover with tar. **2** mark or stain as with tar (*tarred the image of legitimate refugees*). □ **beat** (or **kick** or **whale** etc.) **the tar out of** *N Amer. slang* beat or thrash severely. **tar and feather** smear with tar and then cover with feathers as a punishment. **tarred with the same brush** be considered to have the same faults. [Old English *te(o)ru* from Germanic, related to TREE]

tar[2] *noun* *informal* a sailor. [abbreviation of TARPAULIN]

Tara a hill in County Meath in the Republic of Ireland, site in early times of the residence of the high kings of Ireland, still marked by ancient earthworks.

tara·bish /ˈtɑrbɪʃ/ *noun* *Cdn* (*Cape Breton*) a card game based on bridge. [origin unknown]

tara·did·dle *noun* (also **tarra·did·dle**) *informal* **1** a petty lie. **2** pretentious nonsense. [18th c.: compare DIDDLE]

tara·ma·sa·lata /ˌtarəmæsəˈlɑtə/ *noun* (also **tar·ama** /ˈtarəmə/) a pinkish pâté made from the roe of mullet or other fish with olive oil, seasoning, etc. [modern Greek *taramas* roe (from Turkish *tarama*) + *salata* SALAD]

Tara·naki /ˌtarəˈnaki/ the Maori name for Mount Egmont (see EGMONT, MOUNT).

tar·an·tel·la /ˌtarənˈtelə/ *noun* **1** a rapid whirling southern Italian dance in 6/8 time. **2** the music for this. [Italian, from TARANTO (because the dance was once thought to be a cure for a tarantula bite): compare TARANTULA]

Tar·an·tino /ˌterənˈtiːnoː/ **Quen·tin (Jer·ome)** (b.1963), US film director, screenwriter, and actor. Tarantino came to sudden prominence with *Reservoir Dogs* (1992), followed in 1994 by *Pulp Fiction*. Both aroused controversy for their amorality and violence, but also won much admiration for their wit, style, and structure.

tar·an·tism /ˈtarənˌtizəm/ *noun* *hist.* dancing mania, esp. that originating in S Italy among those who had (actually or supposedly) been bitten by a tarantula. [Italian *tarantismo* from TARANTO; compare TARANTULA]

Ta·ran·to /təˈrantoː/ a seaport and naval base in Apulia, SE Italy; pop. (2001) 201,349.

ta·ran·tula /təˈrantʃulə/ *noun* **1** any large hairy tropical spider of the family Theraphosidae, some of which are venomous. **2** a large black S European spider, *Lycosa tarentula*, whose bite was formerly held to cause tarantism. [Old Italian *tarantola*, from TARANTO]

Tar·awa /ˈtarəwə, təˈrɒwə/ an atoll in the S Pacific, one of the Gilbert Islands.

tar baby *noun* *N Amer. informal* a difficult problem, esp. one which is only aggravated by attempts to solve it. [from a doll smeared with tar to catch Brer Rabbit in a story by J. C. HARRIS[2]]

tar·boosh /tɑrˈbuːʃ/ *noun* a cap like a fez, sometimes worn as part of a turban. [Egyptian Arabic *ṭarbūš*, ultimately from Persian *sar-būš* head covering]

tardi·grade /ˈtɑrdɪˌgreid/ ● *noun* any minute freshwater invertebrate of the phylum Tardigrada, having a short plump body and four pairs of short legs. *Also called* WATER BEAR. ● *adjective* of or relating to this phylum. [French *tardigrade* from Latin *tardigradus* from *tardus* slow + *gradi* walk]

tar·dive dyskinesia *noun* a neurological disorder characterized by involuntary movements of the face and jaw. [*tardive* from French *tardif* (see TARDY)]

tardy *adjective* (**tard·i·er**, **tard·i·est**) **1** late; unpunctual, esp. consistently. **2** slow to act or come or happen. **3** delaying or delayed beyond the right or expected time. □ **tard·i·ly** *adverb* **tard·i·ness** *noun* [French *tardif*, *tardive*, ultimately from Latin *tardus* slow]

tare¹ *noun* **1** any of various vetches. **2** (in *pl.*) *New Testament* an injurious weed, probably darnel, resembling wheat when young (Matt. 13:24-30). [Middle English: origin unknown]

tare² *noun* **1** the weight of a wrapping, container, or receptacle in which goods are packed. **2** an allowance made for this. **3** the weight of a motor vehicle without its fuel or load. [French, = deficiency, tare, from medieval Latin *tara* from Arabic *ṭarḥa* what is rejected, from *ṭaraḥa* reject]

tar·ga *noun* (often *attributive*) a type of convertible sports car with a roof hood or panel that can be removed, esp. leaving a central roll bar for passenger safety (*targa roof*; *targa model*). [Italian, = shield, originally the name of a model of Porsche, probably named after the *Targa Florio*, a race held annually in Sicily]

tar·get ● *noun* **1** a mark or point fired or aimed at, esp. a round or rectangular object marked with concentric circles. **2 a** a person or thing aimed at, or exposed to gunfire etc. (*they were an easy target*). **b** a person, group, etc. which is the object of attention, a campaign, etc. (also *attributive*: *target audience*). **3** an objective or result aimed at (also *attributive*: *target date*). **4** a person or thing against whom criticism, abuse, etc., is or may be directed. **5** *archaic* a shield or buckler, esp. a small round one. ● *transitive verb* (**tar·get·ed**, **tar·get·ing**) **1** identify or single out (a person or thing) as an object of attention or attack. **2** aim or direct (*missiles targeted on major cities*; *should target our efforts where needed*). □ **on target 1** on the correct course to meet an objective. **2** accurate; exactly right. □ **tar·get·able** *adjective* [diminutive of Old French *targe* shield]

target language *noun* the language into which a text or speech is translated.

target practice *noun* the exercise of shooting (esp. with a gun) at a target in order to improve one's aim.

tar·iff ● *noun* **1 a** a duty on a particular class of imports or exports. **b** a list of duties or customs to be paid. **2** a table of fixed charges (*a hotel tariff*). ● *transitive verb* subject (goods) to a tariff. [French *tarif* from Italian *tariffa* from Turkish *tarife* from Arabic *taʿrīf(a)* from *ʿarrafa* notify]

Tarim River /tɑrˈiːm/ a river of NW China. It rises as the Yarkand in the Kunlun Shan mountains and flows for over 2 000 km (1,250 miles) generally eastward through the Tarim Basin, the driest region of Eurasia, petering out in the Lop Nor depression. For much of its course the river follows no clearly defined bed and is subject to much evaporation.

Tar·kov·sky /tɑrˈkɒfski/ **An·drei (Arsen·evich)** (1932–86), Russian film director. He rejected the constraints of socialist realism in the post-Stalin era in favour of a poetic and Impressionistic style. Films include *Ivan's Childhood* (1962), *Solaris* (1972), and *The Sacrifice* (1986), which won the special grand prize at Cannes.

tar·la·tan /ˈtɑrlətən/ *noun* a thin stiff open-weave muslin. [French *tarlatane*, prob. of Indian origin]

tar·mac ● *noun* **1** *proprietary* = TARMACADAM. **2** a surface made of this, e.g. a runway. ● *transitive verb* (**tarmac**) (**tar·macked**, **tar·mack·ing**) apply tarmacadam to. [abbreviation]

tar·mac·adam /ˌtɑrməˈkadəm/ *noun* a material of stone or slag bound with tar, used in paving roads etc. [TAR¹ + MACADAM]

tarn *noun* a small mountain lake. [Middle English *terne*, *tarne* from Old Norse]

tar·na·tion *interjection* N Amer. expressing exasperation. □ **in tarnation** used as an intensifier (*what in tarnation do you think you're doing?*). [from *tarnal*, dial. form of ETERNAL, + DAMNATION]

tar·nish ● *verb* **1** *transitive* lessen or destroy the lustre of (metal etc.). **2** *transitive* impair (one's reputation etc.). **3** *intransitive* (of metal etc.) lose lustre. ● *noun* **1 a** a loss of lustre. **b** a film of colour formed on an exposed surface of a mineral or metal. **2** a blemish; a stain. □ **tar·nish·able** *adjective* [French *ternir* from *terne* dark]

Tarn River a river of S France which rises in the Cévennes and flows 380 km (235 miles) generally southwestward through deep gorges before meeting the Garonne northwest of Toulouse.

taro *noun* (*pl.* **taros**) a tropical aroid plant, *Colocasia esculenta*, with tuberous roots used as food. *Also called* EDDO. [Polynesian]

tarot /ˈtaroʊ/ *noun* **1** (in *sing.* or *pl.*) **a** any of several games played with a pack of cards having five suits, the last of which is a set of permanent trumps. **b** a similar pack used in fortune-telling. **2 a** any of the trump cards. **b** any of the cards from a fortune-telling pack. [French *tarot*, Italian *tarocchi*, of unknown origin]

tarp *noun* N Amer. & Austral. *informal* a tarpaulin. [abbreviation]

tar·pan /ˈtɑrpan/ *noun* an extinct N European primitive wild horse. [Kirghiz Tartar]

tar·paper *noun* esp. N Amer. paper impregnated with tar, often used as a building material (also *attributive*: *tarpaper shack*). □ **tar·papered** *adjective*

tar·pau·lin /tɑrˈpɔlɪn/ *noun* **1** heavy-duty waterproof cloth esp. of tarred canvas. **2** a sheet or covering of this. **3 a** a sailor's tarred or oilskin hat. **b** *archaic* a sailor. [prob. from TAR¹ + PALL¹ + -ING¹]

Tar·peia /tɑrˈpeɪə, tɑrˈpiːə/ *Rom. Hist.* one of the Vestal Virgins, the daughter of a commander of the Capitol in Rome. According to legend she betrayed the citadel to the Sabines in return for what they wore on their arms, hoping to receive their golden bracelets; however, the Sabines killed her by throwing their shields onto her.

Tar·peian Rock /tɑrˈpiːən/ a cliff in ancient Rome, at the southwestern corner of the Capitoline Hill, over which murderers and traitors were hurled. [TARPEIA]

tar pit *noun* **1** a seepage of natural tar, esp. one in which animals have become trapped and their remains preserved. **2** a complicated or difficult problem; something in which one becomes bogged down.

tar·pon /ˈtɑrpɒn/ *noun* **1** a large silvery fish, *Megalops atlanticus*, common in the tropical Atlantic. **2** a similar fish, *Megalops cyprinoides*, of the Pacific ocean. [Dutch *tarpoen*, of unknown origin]

tar pond *noun* Cdn either of two lagoons containing waste sludge produced by the former steel mills in Sydney, NS.

Tar·quin /ˈtɑrkwɪn/ **1** (Latin name Lucius Tarquinius Priscus), semi-legendary Etruscan king of Rome *c.*616–*c.*578 BC. According to tradition, he was murdered by the sons of the previous king. **2** (Latin name Lucius Tarquinius Superbus; known as Tarquin the Proud), semi-legendary Etruscan king of Rome *c.*534–*c.*510 BC. Traditionally the seventh and last king of Rome, he was a cruel ruler and was ultimately expelled from the city after his son raped a woman called Lucretia; following his expulsion the Republic was founded.

tarra·did·dle *var. of* TARADIDDLE.

tar·ra·gon /ˈterəgɒn, ˈta-/ *noun* a bushy herb, *Artemisia dracunculus*, with leaves used to flavour salads, stuffings, vinegar, etc. [= medieval Latin *tarchon* from medieval Greek *tarkhōn*, perhaps through Arabic from Greek *drakōn* dragon]

Tar·rasa /təˈrasə/ (also **Ter·rassa**) an industrial city in Catalonia, NE Spain; pop. (est. 2001) 174,756.

tar·ry¹ *adjective* (**tar·ri·er**, **tar·ri·est**) of or like or smeared with tar.

tarry² *intransitive verb* (**tarries**, **tarried**) *archaic* or *literary* **1** defer coming or going. **2** linger, stay, wait. **3** be tardy. [Middle English: origin uncertain]

tar·sal ● *adjective* of or relating to the bones in the ankle. ● *noun* a tarsal bone. [TARSUS + -AL]

tar sand *noun* Geol. a deposit of sand impregnated with bitumen.

tarsi *pl. of* TARSUS.

tarsi- *combining form* (also **tarso-**) tarsus.

tar·sier /ˈtɑrsɪər/ *noun* any small large-eyed arboreal nocturnal primate of the genus *Tarsius*, native to Borneo, the Philippines, etc., with a long tail and long hind legs used for leaping from tree to tree. [French (as TARSUS), from the structure of its foot]

tarso- *var. of* TARSI-.

Tar·sus an ancient city in S Turkey, a present-day market town. It was the capital of Cilicia and the birthplace of St. Paul.

tar·sus *noun* (*pl.* **tarsi** /ˈtɑrsaɪ/) **1 a** the group of bones forming the ankle and upper foot. **b** the shank of a bird's leg. **c** the terminal segment of a limb in insects. **2** the fibrous connective tissue of the eyelid. [modern Latin from Greek *tarsos* flat of the foot, rim of the eyelid]

tart¹ *noun* a small, usu. open pie containing a fruit or sweet filling. [Old French *tarte* = medieval Latin *tarta*, of unknown origin]

tart² ● *noun* *slang* a prostitute; a promiscuous woman. ● *verb* (foll. by *up*) *informal* **1** *transitive* (usu. *reflexive*) improve the appearance of (oneself or a thing), esp. flashily or gaudily. **2** *intransitive* dress or make oneself up to look attractive. [prob. abbreviation of SWEETHEART]

tart³ *adjective* **1** sharp or acid in taste. **2** (of a remark etc.) cutting, bitter. □ **tart·ly** *adverb* **tart·ness** *noun* [Old English *teart*, of unknown origin]

tar·tan¹ *noun* **1** a pattern of coloured stripes crossing at right angles,

Vowels: a cat ɑ arm e bed ɜr her ɜː deux ə ago ɪ sit i cosy iː feed ɒ hot ɔ pore ɔː no ʌ run ʊ put

esp. a distinctive plaid of a sort orig. worn by the Scottish Highlanders to denote their clan. **2** woollen cloth woven in this pattern (often *attributive*: *a tartan scarf*). [perhaps from Old French *tertaine*, denoting a kind of cloth; compare with *tartarin*, a rich fabric formerly imported from the east through Tartary]

tar·tan² /ˈtɑrtən/ *noun hist.* a lateen-sailed single-masted ship used in the Mediterranean. [French *tartane* from Italian *tartana*, perhaps from Arabic *ṭarīda*]

Tar·tar (also **Tatar** except in sense 3 of *noun*) ● *noun* **1 a** a member of a group of Turkic peoples inhabiting parts of European and Asiatic Russia, especially parts of Siberia, the Crimea, the Caucasus, and districts along the Volga. **b** *hist.* a member of the combined forces of central Asian peoples, including Mongols and Turks, who under the leadership of Genghis Khan overran and devastated much of Asia and eastern Europe in the early 13th c., and under Tamerlane (14th c.) established a large empire in central Asia with its capital at Samarkand. **2** the Turkic language of these peoples. **3** (**tartar**) a violent-tempered or intractable person. ● *adjective* **1** of or relating to the Tartars. **2** of or relating to Central Asia east of the Caspian Sea. □ **Tar·tar·ian** *adjective* [Old French *Tartare* or medieval Latin *Tartarus*]

tar·tar *noun* **1** a hard deposit of saliva, calcium phosphate, etc., that forms on the teeth. **2** a deposit of acid potassium tartrate that forms a hard crust on the inside of a cask during the fermentation of wine. [medieval Latin from medieval Greek *tartaron*]

tar·tar·ic /tɑrˈtɑrɪk/ *adjective Chem.* of or produced from tartar.

tartaric acid *noun* a natural carboxylic acid found esp. in unripe grapes, used in baking powders and as a food additive.

tartar sauce *noun* a sauce of mayonnaise and chopped pickles, capers, etc. [French *sauce tartare* 'sauce of the Tartars']

Tar·tarus /ˈtɑrtərəs/ *Gk Myth* **1** a primeval god, offspring of Chaos. **2** a part of the underworld where the wicked suffered punishment for their misdeeds, esp. those such as Ixion and Tantalus who had committed some outrage against the gods. □ **Tar·tar·ean** /tɑrˈtɛriən/ *adjective*

Tar·tary /ˈtɑrtəri/ a historical region of Asia and E Europe, esp. the high plateau of central Asia and its northwestern slopes, which formed part of the Tartar Empire in the Middle Ages.

tarte Tatin /tɑrt taˈtã/ *noun* a type of upside-down apple tart consisting of pastry baked over slices of fruit arranged in caramelized sugar, served fruit side up after cooking. [French, from *tarte* 'pie' + *Tatin*, the surname of the sisters said to have created the dish]

tart·let *noun* a small tart.

tar·trate *noun Chem.* any salt or ester of tartaric acid.

tar·tra·zine /ˈtɑrtrə,ziːn/ *noun Chem.* a brilliant yellow dye derived from tartaric acid and used to colour food, drugs, and cosmetics.

tar·tufo /tɑrˈtuːfoʊ/ *noun* (*pl.* **-tufos**) a ball of ice cream with one flavour in the centre surrounded by another flavour, the whole often coated in cocoa or chopped nuts. [Italian, lit. = 'truffle']

tarty *adjective* (**tart·i·er**, **tart·i·est**) *informal* **1** (esp. of a woman) promiscuous; sleazy. **2** (of clothing, makeup, etc.) typical of that worn by prostitutes; immodest.

Tasche·reau /taʃˈroʊ/ **Louis-Alexandre** (1867–1952), Canadian lawyer and politician. As premier of Quebec 1920–36, he encouraged American investment and opposed social and economic reform.

taser /ˈteɪzər/ *noun* a weapon firing barbs attached by wires to batteries to cause temporary paralysis. [from the initial letters of Tom Swift's *electric rifle* (a fictitious weapon), after LASER]

Tashi lama /ˈtaʃi ˌlɑmə/ *noun* = PANCHEN LAMA.

Tash·kent /taʃˈkent/ the capital of Uzbekistan, in the western foothills of the Tien Shan mountains, in the far northeast of the country; pop. (2002) 2,150,000. One of the oldest cities in central Asia, Tashkent was an important centre on the trade route between Europe and the Orient.

task ● *noun* **1** a piece of work to be done or undertaken. **2** a difficult or unpleasant piece of work. ● *transitive verb* **1** make great demands on (a person's powers etc.). **2** assign a task to. □ **take to task** rebuke, scold. [Old Northern French *tasque* = Old French *tasche* from medieval Latin *tasca*, perhaps from *taxa* from Latin *taxare* TAX]

task force *noun* (also **task group**) **1** *Military* an armed force organized for a special operation. **2** a unit specially organized for a task.

task light *noun* a light fixture providing illumination for a spot on which a particular task is performed, e.g. a kitchen counter, rather than ambient lighting. □ **task lighting** *noun*

task·master *noun* a person who imposes a task or burden, esp. regularly or severely.

task·mis·tress *noun* a woman who imposes a task or burden, esp. regularly or severely.

Tas·man /ˈtazmən/ **Abel Jans·zoon** (1603–*c.*1659), Dutch navigator. Setting out in 1642 to explore Australian waters, he reached Tasmania and New Zealand, and in 1643 arrived at Tonga and Fiji.

Tas·man·ia /taz'meɪniə/ a state of Australia consisting of the mountainous island of Tasmania itself and several smaller islands; pop. (2001) 472,931; capital, Hobart. It is separated from the southeastern coast of mainland Australia by the Bass Strait. □ **Tas·man·ian** *noun & adjective*

Tasmanian devil *noun* a bearlike nocturnal flesh-eating marsupial, *Sarcophilus harrisii*, now found only in Tasmania.

Tasman Sea an arm of the S Pacific lying between Australia and New Zealand.

Tass *noun* the official news agency of the former Soviet Union, renamed ITAR-Tass in 1992. [the initials of Russian *Telegrafnoe agentstvo Sovetskogo Soyuza* Telegraphic Agency of the Soviet Union]

tas·sel ● *noun* **1** a tuft of loosely hanging threads or cords etc. attached for decoration to a cushion, scarf, cap, etc. **2** a tassel-like head of some plants, esp. a flower head with prominent stamens at the top of a corn stalk. ● *verb* (**tas·selled**, **tas·sel·ling**; esp. *US* **tas·seled**, **tas·sel·ing**) **1** *transitive* provide with a tassel or tassels. **2** *intransitive N Amer.* (of corn) form tassels. □ **tas·selled** *adjective* [Old French *tas(s)el* clasp, of unknown origin]

taste ● *noun* **1 a** the flavour of something, causing a particular sensation when it comes into contact with the tongue (*dislikes the taste of garlic*). **b** the sense by which a flavour is recognized (*was bitter to the taste*). **2** a small portion of food or drink taken as a sample. **3** a slight experience (*a taste of success*). **4** (often foll. by *for*) a liking or predilection (*has expensive tastes*; *is not to my taste*). **5** aesthetic discernment in art, literature, fashion, etc., esp. of a specified kind (*dresses in poor taste*). **6** a sense of what is tactful or polite etc. in a given situation; discretion. ● *verb* **1** *transitive* sample or test the flavour of (food etc.) by taking it into the mouth. **2** *transitive & intransitive* perceive the flavour of (*could taste the lemon*; *cannot taste with a cold*). **3** *transitive* (esp. with *neg.*) eat or drink a small portion of (*had not tasted food for days*). **4** *transitive* have experience of (*had never tasted failure*). **5** *intransitive* (often foll. by *of*) have a specified flavour (*tastes bitter*; *tastes of onions*). □ **a bad** (or **bitter** etc.) **taste** *informal* a strong feeling of distress or disgust following an experience. **taste blood** see BLOOD. **to taste** in the amount needed for a pleasing result (*add salt and pepper to taste*). [Old French *tast*, *taster* touch, try, taste, ultimately perhaps from Latin *tangere* touch + *gustare* taste]

taste bud *noun* any of the cells or nerve endings on the surface of the tongue by which things are tasted.

taste·ful *adjective* having, or done in, good taste. □ **taste·ful·ly** *adverb* **taste·ful·ness** *noun*

taste·less *adjective* **1** lacking flavour. **2** having, or done in, bad taste. □ **taste·less·ly** *adverb* **taste·less·ness** *noun*

taste·maker *noun N Amer.* a person or institution that determines or influences what is or will become stylish or fashionable.

tast·er *noun* **1** a person employed to test food or drink by tasting it, esp. for quality or *hist.* to detect poisoning. **2** an instrument etc. used in sampling or tasting. **3** a sample or foretaste.

taste test *noun* a usu. blind comparison of the flavours of two or more similar products. □ **taste-test** *transitive verb*

tast·ing *noun* a gathering at which food or drink (esp. wine) is tasted and evaluated.

tasting menu *noun* a prix-fixe menu of several small courses offered by a restaurant.

tasty *adjective* (**tast·i·er**, **tast·i·est**) **1** (of food) pleasing in flavour; appetizing. **2** *Brit.* attractive; very appealing. **3** *Brit.* very good; impressive. □ **tast·i·ly** *adverb* **tast·i·ness** *noun*

Tat a nickname for the Tatsenshini River.

tat¹ *noun Brit. informal* **1 a** a tatty or tasteless clothes; worthless goods. **b** rubbish, junk. **2** a shabby person. [back-formation from TATTY]

tat² *verb* (**tat·ted**, **tat·ting**) **1** *intransitive* do tatting. **2** *transitive* make by tatting. [19th c.: origin unknown]

tat³ *noun* see TIT-FOR-TAT.

ta-ta *interjection Brit. informal* goodbye. [19th c.: origin unknown]

ta·tami /təˈtɒmi/ *noun* (also **tatami mat**) a rush-covered straw mat forming a traditional Japanese floor covering. [Japanese]

Tatar var. of TARTAR.

Tatar·stan /ˌtatər'stan/ an autonomous republic in European Russia, in the valley of the Volga River; pop. (2002) 3,714,900; capital, Kazan.

tater noun slang = POTATO. [abbreviation]

Tatra Mountains /'tɒtrə/ (also **Tatras**) a range of mountains in E Europe on the Polish–Slovak border, the highest range in the Carpathians, rising to 2 655 m (8,710 ft.) at Mount Gerlachovsky.

Tats·hen·shini River /tatsen'ʃiːni/ a river in northwestern BC and SW Yukon, flowing first northward to Yukon, then generally southwestward through the St. Elias Mountains to join the Alsek River, which empties into the Pacific Ocean. [origin unknown]

tat·ter noun (usu. in pl.) a rag; an irregularly torn piece of cloth or paper etc. □ **in tatters** informal **1** torn to shreds. **2** (of a negotiation, argument, etc.) ruined, demolished. [Old Norse tötrar rags]

tat·ter·de·mal·ion /ˌtatərdɪ'maljən, -meil-/ informal ● noun a person in ragged or tattered clothing. ● adjective ragged or tattered; dilapidated. [TATTER or TATTERED: ending unexplained]

tat·tered adjective in tatters.

tat·ter·sall noun (also **tattersall check**) a fabric with a pattern of coloured lines forming squares like a tartan (also attributive: a tattersall shirt). [R. Tattersall, English horseman d.1795: from the traditional design of horse blankets]

tat·tie noun esp. Scot. informal = POTATO. [abbreviation]

tat·ting noun **1** a kind of knotted lace made by hand with a small shuttle and used for trimming etc. **2** the process of making this. [19th c.: origin unknown]

tat·tle ● verb **1** intransitive esp. N Amer. (often foll. by on) inform against a person; tell tales (she's always tattling; he tattled on me). **2 a** intransitive prattle, chatter; gossip idly. **b** transitive utter (words) idly. ● noun gossip; idle or trivial talk. [Middle Flemish tatelen, tateren (imitative)]

tat·tler noun **1** a person who tattles. **2** either of two sandpipers constituting the genus Heteroscelus, esp. (also **wandering tattler**) H. incanus, which is mainly grey with yellowish legs, and breeds in NW Canada.

tattle·tale noun N Amer. a person, esp. a child, who reveals (esp. discreditable) information about another's private affairs or behaviour.

tattletale grey ● noun **1** a dirty, off-white colour, as of inadequately washed clothes. **2** grey appearing in the hair on the head, esp. as revealing one's age. ● adjective of a tattletale grey colour.

tat·too¹ noun (pl. **tat·toos**) **1** an evening drum or bugle signal recalling soldiers to their quarters. **2** an elaboration of this with music and marching, presented as an entertainment. **3** a rhythmic tapping or drumming. [17th-c. tap-too from Dutch taptoe, lit. 'close the tap' (of the cask)]

tat·too² ● transitive verb (**tat·toos, tat·tooed**) **1** mark (the skin) with an indelible design by puncturing it and inserting pigment. **2** make (a design) in this way. ● noun (pl. **tat·toos**) a design made by tattooing. □ **tat·too·er** noun **tat·too·ist** noun [Polynesian]

tatty adjective (**tat·ti·er, tat·ti·est**) informal **1** tattered; worn and shabby. **2** inferior. **3** tawdry. □ **tat·ti·ly** adverb **tat·ti·ness** noun [originally Scots, = shaggy, apparently related to Old English tættec rag, TATTER]

Tatum /'teitəm/ **1 Ar·thur** (1910–56), US jazz pianist. A musician of great technical accomplishment, he performed chiefly in a trio with bass and guitar or as a soloist. **2 Ed·ward Law·rie** (1909–75), US biochemist. In collaboration with George Wells Beadle, he produced convincing evidence that a single gene codes for a single specific enzyme; they were awarded the Nobel Prize for physiology or medicine in 1958.

tau /tau, tɒ/ noun the nineteenth letter of the Greek alphabet (T, τ). [Greek]

tau cross noun a T-shaped cross.

taught past and past participle of TEACH.

taunt ● noun a thing said in order to anger or wound a person. ● transitive verb **1** assail with taunts. **2** reproach (a person) contemptuously. □ **taunt·er** noun **taunt·ing·ly** adverb [16th c., in phr. taunt for taunt from French tant pour tant tit for tat, hence a smart rejoinder]

tau particle noun Physics an unstable, heavy, and charged elementary particle of the lepton class.

taupe /tɒːp/ ● noun a grey with a tinge of another colour, usu. brown. ● adjective of this colour. [French, = MOLE¹]

Taupo, Lake /'taupɒ/ (called in Maori **Taupo·moana**) the largest lake of New Zealand, in the centre of North Island. The town of Taupo is situated on its northern shore.

taur·ine¹ /'tɔriːn/ noun Biochem. a sulphur-containing amino acid important in the metabolism of fats. [Greek tauros 'bull' + -INE⁴]

taur·ine² /'tɔriːn, -rain/ adjective of or like a bull; bullish. [Latin taurinus from taurus bull]

Taur·us noun **1** a constellation between Gemini and Aries, traditionally regarded as contained in the figure of a bull. **2 a** the second sign of the zodiac. **b** a person born when the sun is in this sign, usu. between April 20 and May 20. □ **Taur·ean** adjective & noun [Latin, = bull]

Taurus Mountains a range of mountains in S Turkey, parallel to the Mediterranean coast. Rising to a height of 3 734 m (12,250 ft.) at Mount Aladaë, the range forms the southern edge of the Anatolian plateau.

taut adjective **1** (of a rope, muscles, etc.) tight; not slack. **2** (of nerves) tense. **3** (of a ship etc.) in good order or condition. □ **taut·en** transitive & intransitive verb **taut·ly** adverb **taut·ness** noun [Middle English touht, togt, perhaps = TOUGH, influenced by tog- past participle stem of obsolete tee (Old English tēon) pull]

tauto- combining form the same. [Greek, from tauto, to auto the same]

tau·tog /tɒ'tɒg/ noun a fish, Tautoga onitis, found off the Atlantic coast of N America, used as food. [Narragansett tautauog (pl.)]

tau·tol·o·gy /tɒ'tɒlədʒi/ noun (pl. **-gies**) **1** the saying of the same thing twice over in different words, esp. as a fault of style, e.g. arrived one after the other in succession. **2** a statement that is necessarily true. □ **tau·to·log·ic·al** adjective **tau·to·log·ic·ally** adverb **tau·tol·o·gist** noun **tau·tol·o·gize** intransitive verb (also esp. Brit. **-gise**) **tau·tol·o·gous** /-ləgəs/ adjective [Late Latin tautologia from Greek (as TAUTO-, -LOGY)]

tauto·mer /'tɒtə,mɜr/ noun Chem. a substance that exists as two mutually convertible isomers in equilibrium. □ **tauto·mer·ic** /-'merik/ adjective **tauto·mer·ism** /-'tɒmə,rizəm/ noun [TAUTO- + -MER]

Tav·ener /'tavənər/ **Sir John** (b.1944), English composer. His work, much of it religious choral music, is greatly influenced by his Russian Orthodox faith.

tav·ern noun **1** a drinking establishment, esp. one serving beer and wine but not hard liquor. **2** hist. an inn or public house. [Old French taverne from Latin taberna hut, tavern]

tav·erna /tə'vɜrnə/ noun a Greek café or restaurant. [modern Greek (as TAVERN)]

taw¹ transitive verb make (hide) into leather without the use of tannin, esp. by soaking in a solution of alum and salt. □ **tawer** noun [Old English tawian from Germanic]

taw² noun **1** a large marble. **2** a game of marbles. **3** a line from which players throw marbles. [18th c.: origin unknown]

tawd·ry ● adjective (**tawd·ri·er, tawd·ri·est**) **1** showy but worthless. **2** over-ornamented, gaudy, vulgar. **3** base; despicable. ● noun cheap or gaudy finery. □ **tawd·ri·ly** adverb **tawd·ri·ness** noun [earlier as noun: short for tawdry lace, originally St. Audrey's lace from Audrey = Etheldrida, patron saint of Ely]

tawny ● adjective (**tawn·i·er, tawn·i·est**) of an orange- or yellow-brown colour. ● noun this colour. □ **tawn·i·ness** noun [Anglo-French tauné, Old French tané from tan TAN¹]

tawny eagle noun a brownish African or Asian eagle, Aquila rapax.

tawny owl noun **1** a reddish-brown European owl, Strix aluco. **2** (**Tawny Owl**) Cdn an assistant adult leader of a Brownie pack.

tax ● noun **1** a contribution to government revenue compulsorily levied on individuals, property, or businesses. **2** (usu. foll. by on, upon) a strain or heavy demand; an oppressive or burdensome obligation. ● transitive verb **1** impose a tax on (persons or goods etc.). **2** deduct tax from (income etc.). **3** make heavy demands on (a person's powers or resources etc.) (you really tax my patience). **4** (foll. by with) confront (a person) with a wrongdoing etc. **5** Law examine and assess (costs etc.). □ **tax·able** adjective **tax·er** noun [Old French taxer from Latin taxare censure, charge, compute, perhaps from Greek tassō fix]

taxa pl. of TAXON.

tax-and-spend noun (attributive) (of a government policy or its proponents) advocating high taxes and government expenditure on programs beyond the basic responsibilities of government, esp. as an impetus to the economy.

tax·a·tion noun **1** the fact or condition of being taxed. **2** the act of taxing. **3** revenue raised by taxes.

Consonants: b but d dog f few g get h her j yes k cat l leg m man n no p pen r red s sit

tax avoidance *noun* the arrangement of financial affairs to minimize payment of tax.

tax base *noun* the taxpayers on which a (esp. municipal) government depends, considered collectively.

tax bite *noun N Amer. informal* an amount that one is compelled to pay as tax, esp. as a proportion of income.

tax bracket *noun* a range of incomes taxed at a given rate.

tax break *noun informal* a tax concession or advantage allowed by government.

Tax Court of Canada *noun Cdn* a federal court with jurisdiction to hear appeals on matters involving esp. income taxes, employment insurance, the Canada Pension Plan, etc.

tax credit *noun* a sum that may be deducted from the amount of tax owing. □ **tax-creditable** *adjective Cdn.*

tax-deductible *adjective* (of expenses) that may be deducted from income before the amount of tax to be paid is calculated.

tax disc *noun Brit.* a paper disc displayed on the windshield of a motor vehicle, certifying payment of excise duty.

tax dollar *noun N Amer.* a dollar paid as tax.

tax evasion *noun* the illegal nonpayment or underpayment of income tax. □ **tax evader** *noun*

tax-exempt *adjective* esp. *N Amer.* **1** (of income) not subject to taxation. **2** (of a security etc.) earning income that is not subject to taxation.

tax-free *adjective* exempt from taxes.

tax grab *noun* an excessive or unjustified tax demand by a government, esp. when disguised as other forms of payment, e.g. licence fees etc.

tax haven *noun* a country etc. where income tax is low.

tax holiday *noun* a period of tax exemption or tax reduction, esp. one of a fixed duration, granted as an incentive by a government.

taxi ● *noun* (*pl.* **taxis**) **1** (also **taxi·cab**) a car with a driver that may be hired for journeys, esp. one with a meter that records the fare to be paid. **2** a boat, airplane, etc. similarly used. ● *verb* (**taxis**, **taxied**, **taxi·ing**) **1 a** *intransitive* (of an aircraft or pilot) move along the ground under the machine's own power before takeoff or after landing. **b** *transitive* cause (an aircraft) to taxi. **2** *intransitive* go in a taxi. [abbreviation of *taximeter cab*]

taxi dancer *noun* a dancing partner available for hire.

taxi·dermy /'taksɪ,dɜrmi/ *noun* the art of preparing, stuffing, and mounting the skins of animals or birds etc. in lifelike poses. □ **taxi·der·mal** *adjective* **taxi·der·mic** *adjective* **taxi·der·mist** *noun* [Greek *taxis* arrangement + *derma* skin]

taxi driver *noun* a driver of a taxi.

taxi·meter /'taksɪ,miːtɜr/ *noun* an automatic device fitted to a taxi, recording the fare payable. [French *taximètre* from *taxe* tariff, TAX + -METER]

tax·ing *adjective* tiring or demanding; requiring great physical or mental effort.

taxis /'taksɪs/ *noun* **1** *Surgery* the restoration of displaced bones or organs by manual pressure. **2** *Biol.* the movement of a cell or organism in response to an external stimulus. [Greek from *tassō* arrange]

taxi stand *noun* (also esp. *Brit.* **taxi rank**) a place where taxis wait to be hired.

taxi·way *noun* a route along which an aircraft can taxi when moving to or from a runway.

tax·man *noun* (*pl.* **-men**) *informal* **1** an inspector or collector of taxes. **2** the personification of the government department dealing with taxes.

Tax·ol *noun proprietary* a compound obtained from the bark of certain yews, which inhibits the growth of some tumours. [Latin *taxus* yew + -OL[1]]

taxon /'taksən/ *noun* (*pl.* **taxa**) any taxonomic group. [back-formation from TAXONOMY]

tax·on·omy /tak'sɒnəmi/ *noun* **1** the science of the classification of living and extinct organisms. **2** the practice of this. □ **taxo·nomic** *adjective* **taxo·nomic·al** *adjective* **taxo·nomic·ally** *adverb* **tax·ono·mist** *noun* [French *taxonomie* (as TAXIS, Greek *-nomia* distribution)]

tax·pay·er *noun* a person who pays taxes. □ **tax·pay·ing** *adjective*

tax relief *noun* remission of a proportion of income tax.

tax return *noun* a declaration of income for taxation purposes.

tax revolt *noun* a widespread refusal to pay a tax.

tax shelter *noun* a financial arrangement, such as an investment, intended to minimize payment of tax. □ **tax-sheltered** *adjective*

tax year *noun* = FISCAL YEAR.

Tay the longest river in Scotland, flowing 192 km (120 miles) eastward through Loch Tay, entering the North Sea through the Firth of Tay.

tay·berry *noun* (*pl.* **-berries**) a dark red soft fruit produced by crossing the blackberry and raspberry. [*Tay* in Scotland (where introduced in 1977)]

Tay·lor ▸ 1 Dame Eliza·beth Rose·mond (b.1932), English-born US actress. She began her career as a child star in films such as *National Velvet* (1944), and went on to star in many films, including *Cat on a Hot Tin Roof* (1958) and *Who's Afraid of Virginia Woolf?* (1966), for which she won an Oscar. **2 Zach·ary** (1784–1850), US Whig politician, 12th president of the US 1849–50. He became a national hero after his victories in the war with Mexico (1846–8), and as president, he came into conflict with Congress over his desire to admit California to the Union as a free state (without slavery).

Taylor·ism *noun* the principles or practice of scientific management and work efficiency as practised in a system known as the Taylor System, characterized by the division of factory work into the smallest and simplest jobs. □ **Taylor·ist** *adjective* [from F. W. *Taylor*, US engineer d.1915]

Tay–Sachs disease /teiˈsaks/ *noun Med.* an inherited metabolic disorder in which certain lipids accumulate in the brain, causing spasticity and death in childhood. [W. *Tay*, English ophthalmologist d.1927 and B. *Sachs*, US neurologist d.1944]

Tay·side a former local government region in E Scotland, dissolved in 1996.

taz·za /'tɒtsə/ *noun* a saucer-shaped cup, esp. one mounted on a foot. [Italian]

TB *abbreviation* **1 a** tubercle bacillus. **b** tuberculosis. **2** torpedo boat.

Tb *symbol Chem.* the element terbium.

TBA *abbreviation* to be announced.

T-ball *noun N Amer.* a form of baseball for young children, in which the ball is placed on a stand in front of the batter instead of being thrown by the pitcher.

T-bar *noun* **1** (in full **T-bar lift**) a type of ski lift in the form of a series of inverted T-shaped metal bars for towing skiers uphill. **2** a metal bar with a T-shaped cross-section. **3** (often *attributive*) a T-shaped fastening on a shoe or sandal.

Tbil·isi /təbə'liːsi/ the capital of Georgia; pop. (2002) 1,382,900. From 1845 until 1936 its name was Tiflis.

T-bill *noun* TREASURY BILL.

T-bone ● *noun* **a** a T-shaped bone, esp. in steak from the thin end of a loin. **b** such a steak. ● *transitive verb* (usu. in *passive*) *N Amer. informal* (of a car or truck) run into or collide with (another vehicle) on the side.

tbsp *abbreviation* = TABLESPOON 2.

TBT *abbreviation* = TRIBUTYLTIN.

Tc *symbol* the element technetium.

TCDD *abbreviation* tetrachlorodibenzoparadioxin (see DIOXIN).

T cell *noun* = T LYMPHOCYTE.

Tchai·kov·sky /tʃaiˈkɒfski/ **Pyotr Ilich** (1840–93), Russian composer. His music is melodious, expressive, and, esp. in his later symphonies (including his sixth symphony, the 'Pathétique', 1893), melancholy; his works include the ballets *Swan Lake* (1877), *The Sleeping Beauty* (1890), and *The Nutcracker* (1892), the overture *1812* (1880), and the operas *Eugene Onegin* (1879) and *The Queen of Spades* (1890). □ **Tchai·kov·skian** *adjective*

tchotch·ke /'tʃɒtʃki/ *noun N Amer. informal* a knick-knack (*Laurie is happy to sell tchotchkes to ballet audiences*). [Yiddish *tshatshke* from Polish *czaczko*]

TCM *abbreviation* traditional Chinese medicine.

TCP *abbreviation proprietary* a disinfectant and germicide. [trichlorophenylmethyliodasalicyl]

TCP/IP *abbreviation* Transmission Control Protocol/Internet Protocol, the obligatory standard to be used by any system connecting to the Internet.

TD *abbreviation* **1** touchdown. **2** *Irish* Teachta Dála, Member of the Dáil.

TDD *abbreviation N Amer.* Telecommunication Device for the Deaf.

Te *symbol Chem.* the element tellurium.

te *var. of* TI[2].

tea *noun* **1 a** (in full **tea plant**) an evergreen shrub or small tree, *Camellia sinensis*, of India, China, etc. **b** its dried leaves. **2 a** a drink

---

t *top*　v *voice*　w *we*　z *zoo*　ʃ *she*　ʒ *vision*　θ *thin*　ð *this*　ŋ *ring*　x *loch*　tʃ *chip*　dʒ *jar*　　　(*see over for vowels*)

made by infusing tea leaves in boiling water. **b** a cup of this. **3** a similar drink made from the leaves of other plants or from another substance (*camomile tea*; *beef tea*). **4 a** esp. *Brit.* a light afternoon meal consisting of tea, bread, cakes, etc. **b** esp. *Brit.* a cooked (esp. early) evening meal. **c** esp. *N Amer.* an afternoon reception at which tea is served. **d** *Cdn* (*Nfld*) an afternoon or early evening social gathering in a church hall etc. at which a light meal is offered for sale. □ **tea and sympathy** *Brit. informal* hospitable behaviour towards a troubled person. [17th-c. *tay*, *tey*, probably via Dutch *tee* from Chinese (Amoy dialect) *te*, = Mandarin dialect *cha*]

tea bag *noun* a small perforated paper or cloth bag containing tea leaves for infusion.

tea ball *noun* esp. *N Amer.* a ball of perforated metal which is filled with tea leaves and placed in a teapot for infusion.

tea·berry *noun* (*pl.* **-berries**) = CHECKERBERRY.

tea biscuit *noun* *Cdn* a small baked foodstuff, leavened with baking powder or soda, often containing raisins or currants.

tea bread *noun* a kind of light, sweet bread eaten as a snack with tea etc.

tea break *noun* esp. *Brit.* a short break from work during which food or drink may be consumed.

tea bun *noun* *Cdn* (*Nfld*) = TEA BISCUIT.

tea caddy *noun* a container for tea.

tea·cake *noun* *Brit.* a flat, round, sweet bread, often with raisins or currants, usu. eaten toasted and buttered.

tea ceremony *noun* an elaborate Japanese ritual of serving and drinking tea, as an expression of Zen Buddhist philosophy.

Teach, Ed·ward (known as 'Blackbeard') (d.1718), English pirate, whose exploits in the W Indies and along the coast of Virginia and the Carolinas are the subject of numerous legends.

teach *verb* (*past and past participle* **taught**) **1 a** *transitive* give systematic information to (a person) or about (a subject or skill). **b** *intransitive* practise this professionally. **c** *transitive* enable (a person) to do something by instruction and training (*taught me to swim*; *taught me how to dance*). **2** *transitive* **a** advocate as a moral etc. principle (*my parents taught me forgiveness*). **b** communicate, instruct in (*suffering taught me patience*). **3** *transitive* (foll. by *to* + infin.) **a** induce (a person) by example or punishment to do or not to do a thing (*that will teach you to sit still*; *that will teach you not to laugh*). **b** *informal* make (a person) disinclined to do a thing (*I will teach you to interfere*). □ (**one can't**) **teach an old dog new tricks** (one cannot) successfully make old people change their ideas, methods of work, etc. **teach a person a lesson** *see* LESSON. **teach school** *N Amer.* be a teacher in a school. **teach to the test** teach exclusively or predominantly material that one knows will appear on a test. [Old English *tæcan*, from a Germanic root meaning 'show']

teach·able *adjective* **1** (of a subject) that can be taught or imparted by instruction, training, etc. **2** apt at learning. □ **teach·abil·ity** *noun*

teachable moment *noun* a situation or event that serendipitously offers an opportunity to educate people about a topic.

teach·er *noun* a person who teaches, esp. in a school. □ **teach·er·ish** *adjective* **teach·er·ly** *adjective*

teach·er·age *noun* *N Amer.* a house or lodgings provided for a teacher by a school.

teacher's aide *noun* an assistant employed esp. in an elementary school to help the teaching staff in a variety of ancillary and supervisory duties.

teachers' college *noun* *N Amer.* (also **teachers college**) **1** a faculty of education within a university. **2** a college for training teachers.

teacher's pet *noun* the favourite or favoured student of a teacher.

tea chest *noun* *Brit. & Cdn* a light metal-lined wooden box in which tea is packed for transport.

teach-in *noun* **1** an informal debate on a matter of public, usu. political interest, originally between the staff and students of a university. **2** a conference attended by members of a profession on topics of common concern. **3** an informal lecture or discussion for disseminating information. **4** a series of these.

teach·ing *noun* **1** the profession of a teacher. **2** (often in *pl.*) what is taught; a doctrine.

teaching assistant *noun* a graduate student hired to assist a professor, esp. by marking assignments and teaching seminars. Abbr.: **TA.** □ **teaching assistantship** *noun*

teaching hospital *noun* a hospital associated with a university, where medical students receive practical training.

tea cozy *noun* an insulated cover placed over a teapot to keep the contents hot.

tea·cup *noun* a cup from which tea is drunk, usu. with a matching saucer.

tea dance *noun* an afternoon tea with dancing.

tea doll *noun* *Cdn* (*Nfld*) (among the Innu of Labrador) a rag doll designed to be packed with two or three pounds of tea, thus serving as a means of transporting tea in the bush as well as a child's toy.

tea garden *noun* a garden or open-air enclosure where tea and other refreshments are served to the public.

tea house *noun* a restaurant, esp. in China or Japan, where tea and other refreshments are served.

teak *noun* **1** a large deciduous tree, *Tectona grandis*, native to India and SE Asia. **2** (in full **teakwood**) its hard durable timber, used esp. in shipbuilding and furniture. [Portuguese *teca* from Malayalam *tēkka*]

tea·kettle *noun* = KETTLE 1. □ **ass** (or **tail**) **over teakettle** *N Amer. slang* head over heels.

teal ● *noun* (*pl.* same or **teals**) **1** any of various small freshwater ducks of the genus *Anas*, esp. the green-winged teal, *A. crecca*, the male of which has a chestnut head and a green stripe, and the blue-winged teal, *A. discors*, which has a chalky blue forewing and a green speculum. **2** a dark greenish-blue colour. ● *adjective* (in full **teal blue**; hyphenated when *attributive*) of this colour. [Middle English, related to Middle Dutch *tēling*, of unknown origin]

tea lady *noun* esp. *Brit.* a woman employed to make tea in offices etc.

tea leaf *noun* **1** a dried leaf of tea. **2** (esp. in *pl.*) these after infusion or as dregs, the patterns formed by which are interpreted by fortune tellers. **3** *Brit. rhyming slang* a thief.

tea light *noun* a small candle in a shallow round metal case, used in an ornamental holder for decoration or in a stand for a teapot to keep tea warm.

team ● *noun* **1** a set of players forming one side in a game or contest (*a hockey team*); (also *attributive*: *team jacket*). **2** two or more persons working together. **3 a** a set of draft animals. **b** one animal or more in harness with a vehicle. ● *verb* **1** *intransitive & transitive* (usu. foll. by *up*) join in a team or in common action (*decided to team up with them*). **2** *transitive* harness (horses etc.) in a team. **3** *transitive* *N Amer.* convey or transport (goods etc.) by means of a team. **4** *transitive* (foll. by *with*) match or coordinate (clothes). [Old English *tēam* 'team of draught animals', of Germanic origin: related to German *Zaum* 'bridle', also to TEEM[1] and TOW[1]]

team·mate *noun* a fellow member of a team or group.

team player *noun* a person who plays or works well as a member of a team and is not solely concerned with his or her own glory. □ **team play** *noun*

team spirit *noun* willingness to act as a member of a group rather than as an individual.

team·ster *noun* **1** *N Amer.* a truck driver, esp. a member of the Teamsters Union. **2** a driver of a team of animals.

team-teaching *noun* teaching by a team of teachers working together. □ **team-teach** *transitive & intransitive verb*

team·work *noun* the combined action of a team, group, etc., esp. when effective and efficient.

tea party *noun* a social occasion at which tea is served, esp. in the late afternoon.

tea plant *noun* see TEA *noun* 1a.

tea·pot *noun* a pot with a handle, spout, and lid, in which tea is brewed and from which it is poured.

tea·poy *noun* a small three- or four-legged table esp. for use in serving tea. [Hindi *tīn*, *tir-* three + Persian *pāī* foot: sense and spelling influenced by TEA]

tear[1] /ter/ ● *verb* (*past* **tore**; *past participle* **torn**) **1** *transitive* (often foll. by *up*) pull apart or to pieces with some force (*tear it in half*; *tore up the letter*). **2** *transitive* **a** make a hole or rent in by tearing (*have torn my coat*). **b** make (a hole or rent). **3** *transitive* (foll. by *away*, *off*, etc.) pull violently or with some force (*tore the book away from me*; *tore off the cover*; *tore a page out*; *tore down the notice*). **4** *transitive* violently disrupt or divide (*the country was torn by civil war*; *torn by conflicting emotions*). **5** *intransitive* *informal* go or travel hurriedly or impetuously (*tore across the road*). **6** *intransitive* undergo tearing (*the curtain tore down the middle*). **7** *intransitive* (foll. by *at* etc.) pull violently or with some force. ● *noun* **1** a hole or other damage caused by tearing. **2** a torn part of cloth etc. **3** *N Amer.* **a** a spree. **b** *Sport* a winning streak; a successful run (*on a tear*). □ **be torn between** have difficulty in choosing between. **tear apart 1** destroy, divide utterly. **2** search (a place) exhaustively. **3** criticize forcefully. **4** distress greatly. **tear down** demolish. **tear one's hair out** behave with extreme desperation or anger. **tear into 1** attack verbally; reprimand. **2** make a vigorous start on (an activity). **tear oneself away** leave despite a strong desire to stay. **tear to shreds** *informal* refute or criticize thoroughly. **that's torn it** *Brit. informal* that has spoiled things, caused a problem, etc. □ **tear·able** *adjective* **tear·er** *noun* [Old English *teran*, from Germanic]

tear² /tiːr/ ● *noun* **1** a drop of clear salty liquid appearing in or flowing from the eyes, as a result of emotion, physical irritation, pain, etc. **2** a tear-like thing; a drop. ● *intransitive verb N Amer.* (of the eyes) fill with tears. □ **in tears** crying; shedding tears. **without tears** presented so as to be learned or done easily. □ **teary** *adjective* [Old English *tēar*]

tear·away *noun Brit.* **1** an impetuous or reckless young person. **2** a hooligan.

tear·down *noun N Amer.* a house bought to be promptly demolished and replace with a new, larger one.

tear·drop *noun* **1** a single tear. **2** a thing resembling a teardrop in shape, esp. a jewel.

tear duct *noun* a passage through which tears pass to the eye or from the eye to the nose.

tear·ful *adjective* **1** crying or inclined to cry. **2** causing or accompanied with tears; sad (*a tearful goodbye*). □ **tear·ful·ly** *adverb* **tear·ful·ness** *noun*

tear gas ● *noun* a gas that causes severe irritation to the eyes, used in warfare or riot control to disable opponents or make crowds disperse (often *attributive*: *tear-gas canister*). ● *transitive verb* (**tear-gas**) (**-gases**, **-gassed**, **-gassing**) attack with tear gas.

tear·ing /ˈteriŋ/ *adjective* extreme, overwhelming, violent (*in a tearing hurry*).

tear-jerker *noun informal* a sentimental story, film, etc., calculated to evoke sadness or sympathy. □ **tear-jerking** *noun & attributive adjective*

tear·less *adjective* not shedding tears. □ **tear·less·ly** *adverb*

tear-off *attributive adjective* (of a sheet of paper etc.) that can be removed by tearing off usu. along a perforated line.

tea room *noun* **1** a small restaurant or café where tea and other refreshments are served. **2** *N Amer. slang* a public washroom used as a meeting place by gay men.

tea rose *noun* a hybrid rose bush bearing flowers with a scent resembling that of tea.

tear sheet *noun* **1** a magazine or newspaper page containing an advertisement, photograph, story, etc., which is clipped and sent to the advertiser, photographer, etc. as proof of insertion. **2** a page that can be removed from a newspaper or magazine etc. for use separately.

tear-stained *adjective* wet or marked with tears (*her tear-stained face*).

tease ● *verb* **1** *transitive* **a** make fun of (a person or animal) playfully or unkindly or annoyingly. **b** tempt or allure, esp. sexually, while refusing to satisfy the desire aroused. **2** *intransitive* tease a person or animal. **3** *transitive* esp. *N Amer.* comb (the hair) from the ends towards the scalp to make it look thicker. **4** *transitive* gently pull or comb (something tangled) into separate strands. ● *noun* **1** *informal* a person fond of teasing. **2** an instance of teasing (*it was only a tease*). □ **tease out 1** separate by disentangling. **2** extract, obtain or ascertain, esp. by painstaking effort (*to tease out the truth*). □ **teas·ing·ly** *adverb* [Old English *tǣsan* from West Germanic]

tea·sel (also **tea·zel**, **tea·zle**) ● *noun* **1** any plant of the genus *Dipsacus*, with large prickly heads that were formerly dried and used to raise the nap on woven cloth. **2** a device used as a substitute for teasels. ● *transitive verb* dress (cloth) with teasels. [Old English *tǣs(e)l*, = Old High German *zeisala* (as TEASE)]

teas·er *noun* **1** *informal* a hard question or task. **2** a teasing person. **3** esp. *N Amer.* a short introductory advertisement, esp. an excerpt or sample designed to stimulate interest or curiosity. **4** an inferior animal used to excite another animal before it serves or is served by the stud animal.

tea service *noun* (also **tea set**) a matching teapot, milk jug, and sugar bowl (often also including a matching coffee pot and tray), for serving tea.

tea shop *noun* = TEA ROOM 1.

tea·spoon *noun* **1** a small spoon for stirring coffee, tea, etc. **2** an amount held by this, esp. as a unit of measure in cooking, equal to ¹/₃ tablespoon (approx. 5 ml). Abbr.: **tsp.** □ **tea·spoon·ful** *noun* (*pl.* **-fuls**).

tea strainer *noun* a small device for straining tea.

teat /tiːt, tɪt/ *noun* **1** a mammary nipple, esp. of an animal. **2** esp. *Brit.* a thing resembling this, esp. a rubber nipple on a baby's or animal's feeding bottle. [Old French *tete*, prob. of Germanic origin, replacing TIT²]

tea table *noun* a usu. small table at which tea is served.

tea time *noun* the time in the afternoon when tea is served.

tea towel *noun Cdn, Brit.*, etc. a thin linen or cotton towel for drying washed dishes etc.

tea tray *noun* a tray from which tea is served.

tea tree *noun* **1** any of various aromatic Australasian flowering shrubs and small trees esp. of the genus *Leptospermum*. **2** an ornamental red-berried shrub, *Lycium barbarum*, of the nightshade family.

tea trolley *noun Cdn & Brit.* (also *N Amer.* **tea wagon**) a small wheeled trolley from which tea is served.

tea·zel (also **tea·zle**) *var. of* TEASEL.

tech *informal* ● *noun* **1** (esp. in phr. **high-tech**) technology. **2** a technician. **3** a technical college or school. **4** technology stocks. ● *adjective* technical. □ **techy** *adjective* [abbreviation]

tech·ie *noun* (also **tek·kie**) (*pl.* **-ies**) *informal* an expert in or enthusiast for technology, esp. computing.

tech·ne·tium /tekˈniːʃiəm, -ʃəm/ *noun Chem.* an artificially produced radioactive metallic element occurring in the fission products of uranium. Symbol: **Tc**; at. no.: 43. [modern Latin from Greek *tekhnētos* artificial, from *tekhnē* art]

tech·nic·al ● *adjective* **1** of or involving or concerned with the mechanical arts and applied sciences (*technical school; a technical education*). **2** of or relating to a particular subject or craft etc. (*technical terms*). **3** (of a book or discourse etc.) using technical language; requiring special knowledge to be understood. **4** due to mechanical failure (*technical difficulties*). **5** legally such; such in strict interpretation (*technical assault; lost on a technical point*). **6** of or relating to the technique of an art form, esp. as contrasted to the emotional, lyrical etc. aspects. **7** of or relating to technological equipment (*technical support*). ● *noun* esp. *N Amer.* **1** a vehicle, esp. a truck, with mounted machine guns etc. **2** a gunman who rides in such a truck. [Latin *technicus* from Greek *tekhnikos* from *tekhnē* art]

technical foul *noun Basketball* a penalty for a conduct violation such as abusive language or unsportsmanlike conduct, rather than for contact with another player, consisting of a free throw awarded to the other team.

tech·nic·al·ity *noun* (*pl.* **-ities**) **1** the state of being technical. **2** a technical expression. **3** a technical point or detail (*was acquitted on a technicality*).

technical knockout *noun Boxing* a termination of a fight by the referee on the grounds of a contestant's inability to continue, the opponent being declared the winner. Abbr.: **TKO**.

tech·nic·al·ly *adverb* **1** with reference to the technique displayed (*a technically accomplished violinist*). **2** according to the facts of a case, the exact meaning of words, etc.; strictly.

tech·ni·cian *noun* **1** a person employed to look after technical equipment and do practical work in a laboratory etc. **2** an expert in the practical application of a science. **3** a person skilled in the technique of an art or craft.

Techni·color *noun* (often *attributive*) **1** proprietary a process of colour cinematography using synchronized monochrome films, each of a different colour, to produce a colour print. **2** (usu. **technicolor** or **technicolour**) *informal* **a** vivid colour. **b** artificial brilliance. □ **dream in Technicolor** see DREAM. □ **techni·col·ored** *adjective* [TECHNICAL + COLOR]

tech·nics *noun* **1** technology. **2** technical terms, details, methods, etc. [Latin *technicus* from Greek *tekhnikos* from *tekhnē* art]

tech·nique *noun* **1 a** a manner of esp. artistic execution or performance in relation to mechanical or formal details. **b** skill or ability in this area. **2** a means or method of doing or achieving something; a knack or trick. [French (as TECHNICAL)]

techno ● *noun* a style of popular dance music making extensive use of electronic instruments and synthesized sound (also in *combination*: *techno-funk; techno-rock*). ● *adjective* of, pertaining to, or characterized by technology; technologically advanced (*techno trends*). [abbreviation of TECHNOLOGICAL]

techno- *combining form* relating to or using technology (*techno-economy*). [abbreviation of TECHNOLOGICAL]

techno·babble *noun informal* incomprehensible technical jargon.

tech·noc·racy /tekˈnɒkrəsi/ *noun* (*pl.* **-cies**) **1** the government or control of society or industry by technical experts. **2** an instance or application of this.

techno·crat *noun* an exponent or advocate of technocracy. □ **techno·crat·ic** *adjective*

tech·noid /ˈteknɔid/ ● *noun informal* = TECHIE. ● *adjective* in the style of techno music.

techno·logic·al /ˌteknəˈlɒdʒikəl/ *adjective* of or using technology. □ **techno·logic·ally** *adverb*

tech·nol·ogy *noun* (*pl.* **-gies**) **1** the study or use of the mechanical arts and applied sciences. **2** the application of this to practical tasks in industry. **3** a tool etc. used for this. □ **tech·nol·o·gist** *noun*
tech·nol·o·gize *transitive verb* (also esp. *Brit.* **-gise**) [Greek *tekhnologia* systematic treatment, from *tekhnē* art]

technology transfer *noun* the transfer of new technology or advanced technological information from developed to underdeveloped countries.

techno·phile ● *noun* an enthusiast about new technology. ● *adjective* **1** of or relating to a technophile. **2** compatible with new technology. □ **techno·philia** *noun* **techno·phil·ic** *adjective*

techno·phobe *noun* a person who fears, dislikes, or avoids new technology. □ **techno·phobia** *noun* **techno·phob·ic** *adjective*

techno·thriller *noun* a novel or movie in the thriller genre whose plot centres on (usu. military) science and technology.

tec·ton·ic /tekˈtɒnik/ *adjective* **1** of or relating to building or construction. **2** *Geol.* relating to the deformation of the earth's crust or to the structural changes caused by this (*see* PLATE TECTONICS). □ **tec·ton·ic·ally** *adverb* [Late Latin *tectonicus* from Greek *tektonikos* from *tektōn -onos* carpenter]

tec·ton·ics /tekˈtɒniks/ *noun* **1** *Archit.* the art and process of producing practical and aesthetically pleasing buildings. **2** *Geol.* the study of large-scale structural features (*compare* PLATE TECTONICS).

tec·tor·ial membrane /tekˈtɔriəl/ *noun Anat.* the membrane covering the organ of Corti in the inner ear. [Latin *tectorium* a cover (as TECTRIX)]

tec·trix /ˈtektriks/ *noun* (*pl.* **tec·tri·ces** /-ˌsiːz, -ˈtraisiːz/) = COVERT *noun* 2. [modern Latin from Latin *tegere tect-* cover]

Tecum·seh¹ /təˈkʌmsi/ a town in SW Ontario, east of Windsor; pop. (2001) 25,105. [TECUMSEH²]

Tecum·seh² /tiˈkʌmsə/ (*c.*1768–1813), Shawnee chief. He established a Confederacy, was led into a war with the US over the issue of Aboriginal lands, and was defeated at Tippecanoe (1811); during the War of 1812 he was made a brigadier general by the British, and was killed in battle.

Ted *noun* (also **ted**) *Brit. informal* a Teddy boy. [abbreviation]

ted *transitive verb* (**ted·ded**, **ted·ding**) turn over and spread out (grass, hay, or straw) to dry or for a bedding etc. □ **ted·der** *noun* [Old Norse *tethja* spread manure, from *tad* hay, *toddi* small piece]

teddy *noun* (*pl.* **-dies**) **1** (in full **teddy bear**) a soft toy bear. **2** a woman's undergarment combining camisole and panties. [pet form of the names *Edward*, *Theodore*, in sense 1 with reference to *Theodore* Roosevelt, US president d.1919, famous as a bear hunter]

Teddy boy *noun Brit. informal* a youth, esp. of the 1950s, affecting an Edwardian style of dress and appearance, usu. a long jacket and narrow trousers. [*Teddy*, pet form of *Edward*]

Te Deum /tiː ˈdiːəm, tei ˈdeiəm/ *noun* **1 a** a Christian hymn beginning *Te Deum laudamus*, 'We praise Thee, O God'. **b** the music for this. **2** an expression of thanksgiving or exultation. [Latin]

tedi·ous /ˈtiːdiəs/ *adjective* tiresomely long or boring. □ **tedi·ous·ly** *adverb* **tedi·ous·ness** *noun*

tedi·um /ˈtiːdiəm/ *noun* the state of being tedious; boredom. [Latin *taedium* from *taedēre* to weary]

tee¹ *noun* = T¹. [phonetic spelling]

tee² ● *noun* **1** *Golf* **a** a cleared space from which a golf ball is struck at the beginning of play for each hole. **b** a small support of wood or plastic from which a ball is struck at a tee. **2** a mark aimed at in curling etc. **3** *Football* a stand on which the ball is placed for a kickoff. ● *transitive verb* (**tees**, **teed**) (often foll. by *up*) *Golf* place (a ball) on a tee ready to strike it. □ **tee off 1** *Golf* play a ball from a tee. **2** *informal* start, begin. **3** *informal* make angry; annoy. [earlier (17th-c.) *teaz*, of unknown origin: in sense 2 perhaps = TEE¹]

tee-hee (also **te-hee**) ● *noun* **1** a titter. **2** a restrained or contemptuous laugh. ● *intransitive verb* (**tee-hees**, **tee-heed**) titter or laugh in this way. [imitative]

tee line *noun Curling* a straight line painted across the middle of the circle, perpendicular to the centre line.

teem¹ *intransitive verb* **1** be abundant (*fish teem in these waters*). **2** (foll. by *with*) be full of or swarming with (*teeming with fish*; *teeming with ideas*). □ **teem·ing** *adjective* [Old English *tēman* etc. give birth to, from Germanic, related to TEAM]

teem² *intransitive verb* (of water etc.) flow copiously; pour (*it was teeming with rain*). [Old Norse *tœma* from *tómr* (adj.) empty]

teen ● *adjective* = TEENAGE. ● *noun* = TEENAGER. □ **teen·dom** *noun* [abbreviation of TEENAGE, TEENAGER]

-teen *suffix* forming the names of numerals from 13 to 19. [Old English inflected form of TEN]

teen·age *adjective* relating to or characteristic of teenagers. □ **teen·aged** *adjective*

teen·ager *noun* a person from 13 to 19 years of age.

teens *plural noun* **1** the years of one's life from 13 to 19 (*in one's teens*). **2** the years of a century from 13 to 19. **3** the units of a scale of temperature from 13 to 19.

teen·sy *adjective* (**teen·si·er**, **teen·si·est**) *informal* = TEENY.

teensy-weensy *adjective* = TEENY-WEENY.

teeny *adjective* (**teen·i·er**, **teen·i·est**) *informal* tiny. [var. of TINY]

teeny·bop·per *noun informal* a young teenager, usu. a girl, who keenly follows the latest fashions in clothes, pop music, etc.

teeny-weeny *adjective* very tiny.

tee-off *noun* the beginning of a round of golf, when players tee off (often *attributive*: *tee-off time*).

tee·pee *noun* (also **te·pee**, **tipi**) a conical tent used by Plains Aboriginal peoples, made of skins, cloth, or canvas on a frame of poles. [Sioux or Dakota *tīpī*]

teepee ring *noun* a circle of stones used to anchor the covering of a teepee.

tee-shirt *var. of* T-SHIRT.

tee shot *noun Golf* an initial shot from a tee.

tee·ter *intransitive verb* **1** totter; stand or move unsteadily. **2** hesitate; be indecisive. □ **teeter on the brink** (or **edge**) be in imminent danger (of disaster etc.). [var. of dial. *titter*]

teeter-totter *noun N Amer.* = SEE-SAW.

teeth *pl. of* TOOTH.

teethe *intransitive verb* grow or cut baby teeth. □ **teeth·ing** *noun*

teething problems *plural noun* (also **teething troubles**) initial difficulties in an enterprise etc., regarded as temporary.

teething ring *noun* (also **teeth·er**) a small ring of plastic, hard rubber, etc. for an infant to bite on while teething.

tee·total ● *adjective* advocating or characterized by total abstinence from alcoholic drink. ● *intransitive verb* (**tee·total·led**, **tee·total·ling**; also esp. *US* **tee·totaled**, **tee·total·ing**) practise or advocate teetotalism. □ **tee·total·ism** *noun* [reduplication of TOTAL]

tee·total·ler *noun* (also esp. *US* **tee·total·er**) a person advocating or practising abstinence from alcoholic drink.

tee·totum /tiːˈtoːtəm/ *noun* **1** a spinning top with four sides lettered to determine whether the spinner has won or lost. **2** any top spun with the fingers. [T (the letter on one side) + Latin *totum* the whole (stakes), for which T stood]

teff *noun* an African cereal, *Eragrostis tef.* [Amharic *ṭēf*]

te·fil·lin /təˈfilin/ *plural noun* Jewish phylacteries. [Aramaic *tĕpillīn*]

TEFL /ˈtefəl/ *abbreviation* teaching of English as a foreign language.

Tef·lon *noun* **1** *proprietary* polytetrafluoroethylene, esp. used as a non-stick coating for kitchen utensils. **2** (*attributive*) (of a politician etc.) having an undamaged reputation, in spite of scandal or misjudgment; able to deflect criticism on to others. [*tetra-* + *fluor-* + *-on*]

Tegu·ci·galpa /təˌɡuːsiˈɡalpə/ capital of Honduras; pop. (2002) 1,186,400.

tegu·ment /ˈteɡjʊmənt/ *noun* an integument, esp. of a flatworm. [Latin *tegumentum* from *tegere* cover]

te-hee *var. of* TEE-HEE.

Teh·ran /teiˈran, te-, -ˈrɒn/ the capital of Iran, situated in the foothills of the Elburz Mountains; pop. (2002) 7,722,900.

Teil·hard de Char·din /ˈtaijar də ʃarˈdã/ **Pierre** (1881–1955), French Jesuit philosopher and paleontologist. He is best known for his theory, blending science and Christianity, that humanity is evolving mentally and socially towards a perfect spiritual state; his major works include *The Phenomenon of Man* (1955).

Consonants: b *but* d *dog* f *few* g *get* h *her* j *yes* k *cat* l *leg* m *man* n *no* p *pen* r *red* s *sit*

Te·jano /təˈhɑːnəʊ/ *noun* (*pl.* **-janos**) a native or inhabitant of Texas who is of Mexican origin or ancestry (often *attributive*: *Tejano music*). [American Spanish, alteration of *Texano* Texan]

Tekak·witha /ˌtekaˈkwiːθə/ **Ka·te·ri** (1656–1680), Mohawk mystic, the first Native North American to be beatified (1980).

Te Kan·awa /te ˈkɑːnəwə/ **Dame Kiri (Jan·ette)** (b.1944), New Zealand operatic soprano. She made her debut in London in 1970 and since then has sung in the world's leading opera houses, esp. in works by Mozart, Strauss, and Verdi.

tek·kie *var. of* TECHIE.

tek·tite *noun* Geol. a small roundish glassy body of unknown origin occurring in various parts of the earth. [German *Tektit* from Greek *tēktos* molten, from *tēkō* melt]

tel. *abbreviation* (also **Tel.**) telephone.

tela·mon /ˈteləˌmən, -ˌmɒn/ *noun* (*pl.* **tela·mon·es** /-ˈmoːniːz/) *Archit.* a male figure used as a pillar to support an entablature. [Latin *telamones* from Greek *telamōnes* pl. of *Telamōn*, the father of Ajax in Greek mythology]

Tel Aviv /ˌtel əˈviːv/ (also **Tel Aviv-Jaffa**) a city on the Mediterranean coast of Israel; pop. (2000) 354,400 (with Jaffa).

tel·co *noun* (*pl.* **-cos**) a telecommunications company. [abbreviation]

tele- *combining form* **1** at or to a distance (*telekinesis*). **2** forming names of instruments for operating over long distances (*telescope*). **3** television (*telecast*). **4** done by means of the telephone (*telemarketing*). [Greek *tēle-* from *tēle* far off: sense 3 from TELEVISION: sense 4 from TELEPHONE]

tele·bank·ing *noun* a method of banking in which the customer conducts transactions by telephone, esp. by means of a computerized system using Touch-Tone dialling or speech-recognition technology.

tele·cast ● *noun* a television broadcast. ● *transitive verb* transmit by television. □ **tele·cast·er** *noun*

tele·cine /ˈteləˌsɪni/ *noun* **1** the broadcasting of movies on television. **2** equipment for doing this.

tele·com *noun* (also *Brit.* **tele·coms, tele·comms**) (*attributive*) telecommunications (*see* TELECOMMUNICATION 2). [abbreviation]

tele·com·muni·ca·tion *noun* **1** communication over a distance by telephone, radio, television, etc. **2** (usu. in *pl.*) the branch of technology concerned with this.

tele·com·mute *intransitive verb* work from home, communicating by modem, telephone, fax, etc. □ **tele·com·mut·er** *noun* **tele·com·mut·ing** *noun*

tele·con·fer·ence *noun* a conference with participants in different locations linked by telecommunication devices. □ **tele·con·fer·en·cing** *noun*

tele·fax *noun* **1** facsimile transmission (*see* FACSIMILE *noun* 2). **2** a document etc. sent by facsimile transmission. [abbreviation]

tele·film *noun* a film made for or broadcast on television.

tele·gen·ic /ˌteləˈdʒenɪk/ *adjective* having an appearance or manner that looks pleasing on television. □ **tele·gen·ic·ally** *adverb* [TELEVISION + *-genic* in PHOTOGENIC]

tele·gram *noun* a message sent by telegraph and then usu. delivered in written or printed form. [TELE- + -GRAM, after TELEGRAPH]

tele·graph ● *noun* **1** a system of or device for transmitting messages or signals to a distant place esp. by making and breaking an electrical connection. **2** (*attributive*) used in this system (*telegraph wire*). ● *verb* **1** *transitive* send a message by telegraph to. **2** *transitive* send by telegraph. **3** *transitive* give an advance indication of. **4** *intransitive* make signals (*telegraphed to me to come up*). □ **tele·graph·er** /ˈteləˌɡrɑːfər, tɪˈleɡrəfər/ *noun* [French *télégraphe* (as TELE-, -GRAPH)]

tele·graph·ese /ˌteləɡrəˈfiːz/ *noun* informal or jocular abbreviated language; concise elliptical style.

tele·graph·ic *adjective* **1** of or by telegraphs or telegrams. **2** economically worded. □ **tele·graph·ic·ally** *adverb*

teleg·raph·ist /tɪˈleɡrəfɪst/ *noun* a person skilled in or employed in telegraphy.

telegraph key *noun* a device for making and breaking the electric circuit of a telegraph system.

telegraph plant *noun* an E Indian plant, *Desmodium gyrans* (*Codariocalyx motorius*), whose leaves have a jerking motion in response to warmth.

teleg·raphy /tɪˈleɡrəfi/ *noun* the science or practice of using or constructing telegraphs.

Tel·egu *var. of* TELUGU.

tele·health *noun* the delivery of health services, expertise, and information at a distance through the use of information technology and telecommunications.

tele·kin·esis /ˌtelɪkɪˈniːsɪs/ *noun* Psych. movement of objects at a distance supposedly by paranormal means. □ **tele·kin·etic** /-ˈnetɪk/ *adjective* **tele·kin·etic·ally** *adverb* [modern Latin (as TELE-, Greek *kinēsis* motion, from *kineō* move)]

Te·lema·chus /təˈleməkəs/ *Gk Myth* the son of Odysseus and Penelope.

Tele·mann /ˈteləˌman/ **Georg Phil·ipp** (1681–1767), German composer and organist. His work reflects a variety of influences, particularly French composers such as Lully, and his prolific output includes 600 overtures, 44 Passions, 12 complete services, and 40 operas.

tele·mark /ˈteləˌmɑːk/ *Skiing* ● *noun* a swing turn with one ski advanced and the knee bent, used to change direction or stop short. ● *intransitive verb* perform this turn. [*Telemark* in Norway]

tele·mar·ket·ing *noun* the marketing of goods etc. by means of usu. unsolicited telephone calls. □ **tele·mar·ket·er** *noun*

tele·matics *noun* the branch of information technology which deals with the long-distance transmission of computerized information. □ **tele·matic** *adjective*

tele·medi·cine *noun* = TELEHEALTH.

tele·mes·sage *noun* a message sent by telephone or telex and delivered in written form.

tele·meter /ˈteləˌmiːtər, təˈlemɪtər/ ● *noun* an apparatus for recording the readings of an instrument and transmitting them by radio. ● *verb* **1** *intransitive* record readings in this way. **2** *transitive* transmit (readings etc.) to a distant receiving set or station. □ **tele·met·ric** *adjective* **telem·etry** /tɪˈlemətri/ *noun*

tele·novela /ˌtelənɒˈvelə/ *noun* (esp. in Latin America) a Spanish-language or Portuguese-language soap opera. [Spanish or Portuguese, from *tele* (in *televisión* 'television'+ *novela* 'novel']

tele·ol·ogy /ˌteliˈɒlədʒi, ˌtiː-/ *noun* (*pl.* **-gies**) *Philos.* **1** the explanation of phenomena by the purpose they serve rather than by postulated causes. **2** (in Christian theology) the doctrine of design and purpose in the material world. □ **teleo·logic** *adjective* **teleo·logic·al** *adjective* **teleo·logic·al·ly** *adverb* **tele·ol·o·gism** *noun* **tele·ol·o·gist** *noun* [modern Latin *teleologia* from Greek *telos teleos* end + -LOGY]

tele·oper·ator /ˌteliˈɒpəreɪtər/ *noun* any remote-controlled machine which mimics or responds to the actions of a human controller at a distance. □ **tele·oper·at·ed** *adjective* **tele·oper·ation** *noun*

tele·ost /ˈteliɒst, ˈtiːl-/ ● *noun* any fish of the subclass Teleostei, comprising the bony fishes and including most familiar kinds of fish except sharks, rays, sturgeons, and lungfishes. ● *adjective* of or relating to this subclass. [Greek *teleo-* 'complete' + *osteon* 'bone']

tele·path /ˈteləˌpaθ/ *noun* a telepathic person. [back-formation from TELEPATHY]

telep·athy /təˈlepəθi/ *noun* the supposed communication or perception of thoughts or ideas by extrasensory means. □ **tele·path·ic** /ˌteləˈpaθɪk/ *adjective* **tele·path·ic·ally** *adverb* **telep·a·thist** *noun* [TELE- 'distant' + -PATHY 'feeling']

tele·phone ● *noun* **1** an apparatus for transmitting sound (esp. speech) over a distance, esp. by converting acoustic vibrations to electrical signals. **2** a system of communication using a network of telephones. ● *transitive & intransitive verb* = PHONE¹. □ **on** (or **over**) **the telephone** by use of or using the telephone. □ **tele·phon·er** *noun* **tele·phon·ic** /teləˈfɒnɪk/ *adjective* **tele·phon·ic·ally** *adverb* [TELE- + -PHONE.]

telephone banking *noun* = TELEBANKING.

telephone book *noun* a book listing telephone subscribers and numbers in a particular area.

telephone booth *noun* a public booth or enclosure from which telephone calls can be made.

telephone box *noun* Brit. = TELEPHONE BOOTH.

telephone directory *noun* = TELEPHONE BOOK.

telephone number *noun* **1** a number assigned to a particular telephone and used in making connections to it. **2** (often in *pl.*) Brit. informal a number with many digits, esp. representing a large sum of money.

telephone pole *noun* a pole supporting telephone wires.

telephone tag *noun* a situation in which two people try repeatedly to return each other's telephone calls but fail to make contact because when either calls the other cannot answer.

teleph·onist /tɪˈlefənɪst/ *noun* Brit. an operator in a telephone exchange or at a switchboard.

teleph·ony /tɪˈlefəni/ *noun* the use or a system of telephones.

tele·photo ● *noun* (*pl.* **-photos**) (in full **telephoto lens**) a lens with a longer focal length than standard, giving a narrow field of view and a magnified image. ● *adjective* of or using such a lens (*a telephoto shot*).

tele·play *noun* a play written for production on television.

tele·port *transitive verb* (esp. in science fiction) transport or be transported across space and distance instantly. □ **tele·port·a·tion** *noun* **tele·porter** *noun* [TELE- + PORT⁵]

tele·pres·ence *noun* **1** the use of virtual reality technology esp. for remote control of machinery or for apparent participation in distant events. **2** a sensation of being elsewhere created in this way.

tele·print·er *noun* a device for transmitting telegraph messages as they are keyed, and for printing messages received.

tele·prompt·er *noun* N Amer. a device, unseen by the audience, displaying a magnified television script to a speaker or performer.

tele·robotic *adjective* of, pertaining to, or designating a machine or mechanized system whose operation is controlled remotely through the use of telecommunications. □ **tele·robot** *noun* **tele·robotic·ally** *adverb* **tele·robotics** *noun*

tele·sales *plural noun* selling by means of the telephone.

tele·scope ● *noun* **1** an optical instrument using lenses or mirrors or both to make distant objects appear nearer and larger. **2** = RADIO TELESCOPE. ● *verb* **1** *transitive* press or drive (sections of a tube, colliding vehicles, etc.) together so that one slides into another like the sections of a folding telescope. **2** *intransitive* close or be driven or be capable of closing in this way. **3** *transitive* compress so as to occupy less space or time. [Italian *telescopio* or modern Latin *telescopium* (as TELE-, -SCOPE)]

tele·scop·ic *adjective* **1 a** of, relating to, or made with a telescope (*telescopic observations*). **b** visible only through a telescope (*telescopic stars*). **2** (esp. of a lens) able to focus on and magnify distant objects. **3** consisting of sections that telescope. □ **tele·scop·ic·ally** *adverb*

telescopic sight *noun* a small telescope mounted as a sight on a firearm or surveying instrument.

tele·shop·ping *noun* the ordering of goods by customers using a telephone or direct computer link.

tele·text *noun* a news and information service, in the form of text and graphics, from a computer source transmitted to televisions with appropriate receivers.

tele·theatre *noun* N Amer. an off-track betting facility where horse races are shown on television.

tele·thon *noun* an exceptionally long television program, esp. one featuring live performers, broadcast to raise money for a charity.

tele·type ● *noun* a kind of teleprinter. ● *verb* **1** *intransitive* operate a teleprinter. **2** *transitive* send by means of a teleprinter.

tel·evan·gel·ist *noun* esp. N Amer. an evangelical preacher who appears regularly on television to promote beliefs and appeal for funds. □ **tel·evan·gel·ism** *noun*

tele·vise *transitive verb* transmit by television. [back-formation from TELEVISION]

tele·vision *noun* **1** a system for reproducing on a screen visual images converted (usu. with sound) into electrical signals and transmitted esp. by radio waves. **2** (in full **television set**) a device with a screen for receiving these signals. **3** the medium, art form, or occupation of broadcasting on television. **4** the programs broadcast on television (*watched television last night*). [TELE- 'distant'+ VISION]

tele·visual *adjective* relating to or suitable for television. □ **tele·visual·ly** *adverb*

tele·work *intransitive verb* = TELECOMMUTE. □ **tele·work·er** *noun* **tele·work·ing** *noun*

telex (also **Telex**) ● *noun* **1** an international system of telegraphy with printed messages transmitted and received by teleprinters using the public telecommunications network. **2** a message sent this way. ● *transitive verb* send or communicate with by telex. [TELEPRINTER + EXCHANGE]

Tell, Wil·liam (German name Wilhelm Tell), legendary hero of the liberation of Switzerland from Austrian oppression, who was required to hit with an arrow an apple placed on the head of his son; the events are placed in the 14th c., but there is no evidence for a historical person of this name.

tell¹ *verb* (*past* and *past participle* **told**) **1** *transitive* relate or narrate in speech or writing; give an account of (*tell me a story*). **2** *transitive* make known; express in words; divulge (*tell me your name; tell me what you want*). **3** *transitive* reveal or signify to (a person) (*your face tells me everything*). **4** *transitive* **a** utter (*don't tell lies*). **b** warn (*I told you so*).

5 *intransitive* **a** (often foll. by *of, about*) divulge information or a description; reveal a secret (*I told of the plan; promise you won't tell*). **b** (foll. by *on*) *informal* inform against (a person). **6** *transitive* (foll. by *to* + infin.) give (a person) a direction or order (*tell them to wait; do as you are told*). **7** *transitive* assure (*it's true, I tell you*). **8** *transitive* explain in writing; instruct (*this book tells you how to cook*). **9** *transitive* decide, determine, distinguish (*cannot tell which button to press; how do you tell one from the other?*). **10** *intransitive* **a** (often foll. by *on*) produce a noticeable effect (*every disappointment tells; the strain was beginning to tell on me*). **b** reveal the truth (*time will tell*). **c** have an influence (*the evidence tells against you*). **11** *transitive* count (votes) at a meeting, election, etc. □ **as far as one can tell** judging from the available information. **tell apart** distinguish between (usu. with *neg.* or *interrogative: could not tell them apart*). **tell it like it is** *informal* relate the facts of a matter realistically or honestly, holding nothing back. **tell me about it** *informal* used as an ironic acknowledgement of one's familiarity with a difficult or unpleasant situation or experience described by someone else. **tell me another** *informal* an expression of incredulity. **tell off 1** *informal* reprimand, scold. **2** count off or detach for duty. **tell on** tattle on; reveal a person's activities, esp. to a person in authority. **tell a tale** be significant or revealing. **tell tales** report a discreditable fact about another. **tell (the) time** determine the time from the face of a clock or watch. **there is no telling** it is impossible to know (*there's no telling what may happen*). **tell you what** *informal* used to introduce a suggestion. **you're telling me** *informal* I agree wholeheartedly. □ **tell·able** *adjective* [Old English *tellan*, from Germanic]

tell² *noun* Archaeology an artificial mound in the Middle East etc. formed by the accumulated remains of ancient settlements. [Arabic *tall* hillock]

tell-all *adjective* designating books etc. in which a person reveals all about their life, esp. the most sordid details.

Tell el-Amarna see AMARNA, TELL EL-.

Tel·ler, Ed·ward (1908–2003), Hungarian-born US physicist. He worked on the first atomic reactor, later working on the first atomic bombs at Los Alamos; he studied the feasibility of producing a fusion bomb, and work under his guidance after the Second World War led to the detonation of the first hydrogen bomb in 1952.

tell·er *noun* **1** a person employed to receive and pay out money in a bank etc. **2** a person who tells esp. stories (*a teller of tales*). **3** a person who counts (votes).

tell·ing *adjective* **1** having a marked effect; striking. **2** significant. □ **tell·ing·ly** *adverb*

telling-off *noun* (*pl.* **tellings-off**) Brit. informal a reproof or reprimand.

tell·tale *noun* **1** (*attributive*) that reveals or betrays (*a telltale smile*). **2** Brit. a tattletale. **3** a device for automatic monitoring or registering of a process etc.

tel·lur·ic /teˈlʊrɪk/ *adjective* **1** of the earth as a planet. **2** of the soil. **3** Chem. of tellurium, esp. in its higher valence. [Latin *tellus -uris* earth: sense 3 from TELLURIUM]

tel·lur·ium /teˈlʊriəm/ *noun* Chem. a rare brittle lustrous silver-white element occurring naturally in ores of gold and silver, used in semiconductors. Symbol: **Te**; at. no.: 52. □ **tel·lur·ide** /ˈteljʊˌraid/ *noun* **tel·lur·ite** /ˈteljʊˌrəit/ *noun* [Latin *tellus -uris* earth, prob. named in contrast to *uranium*]

telly *noun* (*pl.* **-lies**) esp. Brit. informal **1** television. **2** a television set. [abbreviation]

tel·net Computing ● *noun* **1** a network protocol that allows a user on one computer to log in to another computer that is part of the same network. **2** a program that establishes a connection from one computer to another by means of such a protocol. **3** a link thus established. ● *intransitive verb* log in or connect to a remote computer using a telnet program. [from TEL(ECOMMUNICATION + NET(WORK)]

telo·mer·ase /ˈteləmɪreɪz/ *noun* the enzyme in a eukaryote that repairs the telomeres of the chromosomes so that they do not become progressively shorter during successsive rounds of chromosome replication.

telo·mere /ˈteləmɪr/ *noun* the end of a chromosome, which consists of repeated sequences of DNA that perform the function of ensuring that each cycle of DNA replication has been completed. [Greek *telos* end + *meros* part]

telo·phase /ˈteləfeiz, ˈtiːl-/ *noun* Biol. the final stage of cell division, in which the nuclei of the daughter cells are formed. [Greek *telos* 'end' + PHASE]

telos /ˈtelɒs, ˈtiː-/ *noun* an ultimate object or aim. [Greek = end]

Vowels: a cat ɑ arm e bed ɜr her ɜː *deux* ə ago ɪ sit i cosy iː feed ɒ hot ɔ pore ɔː no ʌ run ʊ put

tel·son /ˈtelsən/ *noun* the last segment in the abdomen of crustaceans and arachnids. [Greek, = limit]

Te·lugu /ˈteləˌɡuː/ *noun* (also **Tel·egu**) (*pl.* same or **Tel·ugus**) **1** a member of a Dravidian people in SE India. **2** the language of this people, spoken mainly in Andhra Pradesh. [Telugu]

Te·mag·ami, Lake /təˈmɒɡəmi/ a lake in NE Ontario, situated north of Lake Nipissing and west of Lake Timiskaming. [Ojibwa, = deep lake]

tem·blor /temˈblɔr, -ˈblɔr/ *noun* US an earthquake. [Latin American Spanish]

tem·er·ari·ous /ˌteməˈreriəs/ *adjective literary* reckless, rash.
□ **tem·er·ari·ous·ly** *adverb* [Latin *temerarius* from *temere* rashly]

tem·er·ity /təˈmerɪti/ *noun* excessive confidence or boldness; audacity. [Latin *temeritas* from *temere* rashly]

Témis·ca·mingue, Lac /teiˈmiːskamɑ̃ɡ/ see TIMISKAMING, LAKE.

Témis·coua·ta, Lac /teiˈmiːskwɒtə/ a lake in E Quebec, situated southeast of Rivière-du-Loup. [Mi'kmaq, = deep lake]

Temne /ˈtemni/ ● *noun* **1** a member of a people of Sierra Leone. **2** the Niger-Congo language of this people, the main language of Sierra Leone. ● *adjective* of or relating to this people or their language. [the name in Temne]

temp.[1] *abbreviation* temperature.

temp.[2] *abbreviation* in the time of (*temp. Henry I*). [Latin *tempore* ablative of *tempus* time]

temp *informal* ● *noun* **1** a temporary employee, esp. a secretary. **2** a temperature (*temps in the teens*). ● *intransitive verb* work as a temp. [abbreviation]

tem·peh /ˈtempə/ *noun* a fermented soybean product, usu. eaten fried. [Indonesian *tempe*]

tem·per ● *noun* **1** habitual or temporary disposition of mind esp. as regards composure. **2** irritation or anger (*in a fit of temper*). **3** a tendency to have fits of anger (*have a temper*). **4** composure or calmness (*lose one's temper*). **5** the condition of metal as regards hardness and elasticity. ● *transitive verb* **1** bring (metal or clay) to a proper hardness or consistency. **2** (foll. by *with*) moderate or mitigate (*temper justice with mercy*). **3** tune or modulate (a piano etc.) so as to distance intervals correctly. □ **out of temper** angry, peevish. □ **tem·pered** *adjective* [Old English *temprian* (v.) from Latin *temperare* 'mingle': influenced by Old French *temprer*, *tremper*]

tem·pera /ˈtempərə/ *noun* **1** a method of painting using an emulsion of powdered pigment typically held together with egg yolk and water. **2** this emulsion. [Italian, in *pingere a tempera* 'paint in distemper']

tem·per·ament /ˈtempərəmənt, -pərmənt/ *noun* **1** a person's distinct nature and character, esp. as permanently affecting behaviour; natural disposition, personality (*a nervous temperament; the artistic temperament*). **2** a creative or spirited personality (*was full of temperament*). **3** an adjustment of intervals in tuning a piano etc. so as to fit the scale for use in all keys, esp. (**equal temperament**) an adjustment in which the 12 semitones are at equal intervals. [Latin *temperamentum* (as TEMPER)]

tem·per·ament·al /ˌtempərəˈmentəl, -pər-/ *adjective* **1** of or having temperament (*a temperamental aversion to hard work*). **2 a** (of a person) liable to erratic or moody behaviour. **b** (of a thing, e.g. a machine) working unpredictably; unreliable. □ **tem·per·ament·al·ly** *adverb*

tem·per·ance *noun* **1** moderation or self-restraint esp. in eating and drinking. **2 a** total or partial abstinence from alcoholic drink. **b** (*attributive*) advocating or enjoined with abstinence. [Anglo-French *temperaunce* from Latin *temperantia* (as TEMPER)]

tem·per·ate *adjective* **1** avoiding excess; self-restrained. **2** moderate. **3 a** (of a region or climate) characterized by mild temperatures. **b** (of a plant, tree, etc.) growing in a region characterized by mild temperatures. □ **tem·per·ate·ly** *adverb* **tem·per·ate·ness** *noun* [Latin *temperatus* past participle of *temperare*: see TEMPER]

temperate zone *noun* the belt of the earth between the frigid and the torrid zones.

tem·per·ature *noun* **1** the degree or intensity of heat of a substance, the air, etc. in relation to others, esp. as shown by a thermometer or perceived by touch etc. **2** *Med.* the degree of internal heat of the body. **3** *informal* a body temperature above the normal (*have a temperature*). □ **take a person's temperature** ascertain a person's body temperature, esp. as a diagnostic aid. [French *température* or Latin *temperatura* (as TEMPER)]

temperature inversion *noun Meteorol.* = INVERSION 4.

-tempered *combining form* having a specified temper or disposition

(*bad-tempered; hot-tempered*). □ **-temperedly** *adverb* **-temperedness** *noun*

tem·pest *noun* **1** a violent windy storm. **2** violent agitation or tumult. □ **tempest in a teapot** N Amer. great agitation over a trivial matter. [Old French *tempest(e)*, ultimately from Latin *tempestas* season, storm, from *tempus* time]

tem·pes·tu·ous /temˈpestʃuəs/ *adjective* **1** stormy. **2** (of a person, emotion, relationship, etc.) turbulent, violent, passionate. □ **tem·pes·tu·ous·ly** *adverb* **tem·pes·tu·ous·ness** *noun*

tempi *pl.* of TEMPO.

Tem·plar /ˈtemplər/ *noun hist.* = KNIGHT TEMPLAR.

tem·plate /ˈtempleit, -plət/ *noun* **1 a** a pattern or gauge, usu. a piece of thin board or metal plate, used as a guide in cutting or drilling metal, stone, wood, etc. **b** a flat card or plastic pattern esp. for cutting cloth for patchwork etc. **2** a timber or plate used to distribute the weight in a wall or under a beam etc. **3** *Computing* a stored pattern for a document or part of a document from which new documents or parts of documents may be made. **4** *Biochem.* a nucleic acid molecule that acts as a pattern for the sequence of assembly of a protein, nucleic acid, or other large molecule. [originally *templet*, prob. from TEMPLE[3] + -ET[1]: influenced by *plate*]

Tem·ple ▸ **1** Shir·ley (married name Shirley Temple Black) (b.1928), US actress and diplomat. In the 1930s she became the foremost child star of her day with a succession of films, including *Bright Eyes* (1934) in which she sang 'On the Good Ship Lollipop'. As an adult she became active in Republican politics, serving as the US representative to the United Nations (1969–70) and in other diplomatic postings. **2 Sir Thom·as** (1615–74), English colonial administrator. As one of three partners who obtained the rights to commerce and government in Nova Scotia in 1654, he became sole governor in 1662 but had to return the colony to France in 1670.

temple[1] *noun* **1** a building devoted to the worship, or regarded as the dwelling place, of a god or gods or other objects of religious reverence. **2** *hist.* any of three successive religious buildings of the Jews in Jerusalem. **3** *N Amer.* a synagogue. **4** a place of Christian public worship, esp. a Mormon church. **5** a place in which God is regarded as residing, esp. a Christian's person or body. **6** any large imposing building devoted to a particular interest etc. (*a temple of the arts*). [Old English *temp(e)l*, reinforced in Middle English by Old French *temple*, from Latin *templum* open or consecrated space]

temple[2] *noun* **1** the flat part of either side of the head between the forehead and the ear. **2** either of the two side pieces on a pair of glasses extending from the frame toward the ear (*compare* ARM[1] 4g). [Old French, ultimately from Latin *tempora* pl. of *tempus*]

temple[3] *noun* a device in a loom for keeping the cloth stretched. [Old French, originally the same word as TEMPLE[2]]

tempo *noun* (*pl.* **-pos** or **tempi**) **1** *Music* the speed at which a passage of music is or should be played. **2** the rate of motion or activity (*the tempo of the war is quickening*). [Italian from Latin *tempus* time]

tem·por·al[1] /ˈtempərəl/ *adjective* **1** of worldly as opposed to spiritual affairs; of this life; secular as opposed to ecclesiastical. **2** of or relating to time. **3** *Grammar* relating to or denoting time or tense (*temporal conjunction*). □ **tem·por·al·ly** *adverb* [Old French *temporel*, or from Latin *temporalis* from *tempus -oris* 'time']

tem·por·al[2] /ˈtempərəl/ *adjective Anat.* of or situated in the temples of the head (*temporal artery; temporal bone*). [Late Latin *temporalis* from *tempora* 'the temples' (as TEMPLE[2])]

temporal bone *noun* either of two bones forming part of the side of the skull on each side and enclosing the middle and inner ear.

tem·por·al·ity /ˌtempəˈralɪti/ *noun* (*pl.* **-ities**) **1** the state of existing within or having some relationship with time. **2** temporariness. **3** (usu. in *pl.*) a secular possession, esp. the properties and revenues of a religious corporation or an ecclesiastic.

temporal lobe *noun* each of the paired lobes of the brain lying beneath the temples, including areas concerned with the understanding of speech.

tem·por·ary /ˈtempəreri/ ● *adjective* lasting or meant to last only for a limited time (*temporary buildings; temporary relief*). ● *noun* (*pl.* **-ies**) a person employed temporarily. □ **tem·por·ar·i·ly** *adverb* **tem·por·ar·i·ness** *noun* [Latin *temporarius* from *tempus -oris* time]

tem·por·ize /ˈtempəˌraiz/ *intransitive verb* (also esp. *Brit.* **-ise**) **1** avoid committing oneself so as to gain time; employ delaying tactics. **2** comply temporarily with the requirements of the occasion. □ **tem·por·iz·a·tion** *noun* **tem·por·iz·er** *noun* [French *temporiser* bide one's time, from medieval Latin *temporizare* delay, from *tempus -oris* time]

tem·po·ro·man·dib·u·lar /ˌtempɜroˈmanˈdɪbjʊlər/ *adjective* of or pertaining to the hinge joint between the temporal bone and the lower jaw. [TEMPORAL[2] + MANDIBULAR (see MANDIBLE)]

temporomandibular joint syndrome *noun* a condition caused by poor alignment of the temporomandibular joint, accompanied by limitation of jaw movement, clicking of the joint, and often headaches in the temples.

Tem·pra·nillo /ˌtemprɔˈnɪloː/ *noun* **1** a type of black grape grown in Spain. **2** a red Rioja wine made from such grapes. [Spanish *temprano*, 'early', because the grape ripens early]

tempt *transitive verb* **1** entice or incite (a person) to do a wrong or forbidden thing (*tempted him to steal it*). **2** allure, attract. **3** risk provoking (esp. an abstract force or power) (*would be tempting fate to try it*). **4** *archaic* make trial of; try the resolution of (*God did tempt Abraham*). □ **be tempted to** be strongly disposed to (*I am tempted to question this*). □ **tempt·able** *adjective* [Old French *tempter* test, from Latin *temptare* handle, test, try]

temp·ta·tion *noun* **1 a** the act or an instance of tempting; the state of being tempted; incitement esp. to wrongdoing. **b** (**the Temptation**) the tempting of Christ by the Devil (see Matt. 4). **2** an attractive thing or course of action. **3** *archaic* putting to the test.

tempt·er *noun* **1** a person who tempts. **2** (**the Tempter**) the Devil.

tempt·ing *adjective* **1** attractive, inviting. **2** enticing to evil, wrongdoing, etc. □ **tempt·ing·ly** *adverb*

tempt·ress *noun* a woman who tempts.

tem·pura /temˈpʊrɔ/ *noun* (in Japanese cuisine) fish, shellfish, or vegetables, fried in batter. [Japanese]

ten ● *noun* **1** one more than nine. **2** a symbol for this (10, x, X). **3** a size etc. denoted by ten. **4** ten o'clock. **5** a card with ten pips. **6** a set of ten. **7** a ten-dollar bill, ten-pound note, etc. **8** (*in pl.*) the digit second from the right of a whole number in decimal notation, representing a multiple of ten less than a hundred (*numbered in the tens of thousands*). ● *adjective* **1** that amount to ten. **2** (as a round number) several (*ten times as easy*). □ **hang ten** see HANG. [Old English *tien*, *tēn* from Germanic]

ten. *abbreviation* tenuto.

ten·able /ˈtenəbəl/ *adjective* **1** that can be maintained or defended against attack or objection (*a tenable position; a tenable theory*). **2** (foll. by *for*, *by*) (of an office etc.) that can be held for (a specified period) or by (a specified class of person). □ **ten·abil·ity** *noun* [French from *tenir* hold, from Latin *tenēre*]

ten·ace /ˈtenɔs/ *noun Bridge* **1** two cards, one ranking next above, and the other next below, a card held by an opponent. **2** the holding of such cards. [French from Spanish *tenaza*, lit. 'pincers']

ten·a·cious /tɔˈneɪʃɔs/ *adjective* **1** holding fast. **2** persistent, stubborn. **3** strongly cohesive. **4** adhesive, sticky. **5** (of memory) retentive. **6** (often foll. by *of*) keeping a firm hold of property, principles, life, etc.; not readily relinquishing. □ **ten·a·cious·ly** *adverb* **ten·acity** /tɔˈnasɪti/ *noun* [Latin *tenax -acis* from *tenēre* hold]

ten·ancy /ˈtenɔnsi/ *noun* (*pl.* **-cies**) **1** the status of a tenant; possession as a tenant. **2** the duration or period of this. **3** occupation of any position, condition, etc.

ten·ant /ˈtenɔnt/ ● *noun* **1** a person, business, etc. who rents a residence, premises, etc. from the owner. **2** (often foll. by *of*) the occupant of a place. **3** *Law* a person holding real property by private ownership. ● *transitive verb* occupy as a tenant. □ **ten·ant·less** *adjective* [Old French, pres. part. of *tenir* hold, from Latin *tenēre*]

tenant farmer *noun* a person who farms rented land.

ten·antry *noun* the tenants of an estate etc.

Ten·cel /ˈtensel/ *noun proprietary* a fibre obtained from wood pulp using recyclable solvents; a fabric made of this. [an invented word]

tench *noun* (*pl.* same) a European freshwater fish, *Tinca tinca*, of the carp family. [Old French *tenche* from Late Latin *tinca*]

Ten Commandments *plural noun* (usu. prec. by *the*) (in Christian and Jewish belief) the divine rules of conduct given by God to Moses on Mount Sinai.

tend[1] *intransitive verb* **1 a** (usu. foll. by *to*) be apt or inclined (*tends to lose his temper*). **b** (usu. foll. by *towards*) suggest or exhibit a tendency towards (a quality etc.). **2** lead, conduce. **3** be moving; be directed; hold a course (*tends in our direction; tends downwards; tends to the same conclusion*). [Old French *tendre* stretch, from Latin *tendere tens-* or *tent-*]

tend[2] *verb* **1** *transitive* take care of, look after, be responsible for (*tends the

sick; tending their flock; tending the fire; tending bar; tending goal*). **2** *intransitive* (foll. by *to*) esp. *N Amer.* give attention to. [Middle English from ATTEND]

ten·dency *noun* (*pl.* **-cies**) **1** (often foll. by *to*, *towards*) a leaning or inclination; a way in which a person or thing is likely to behave. **2** a group within a larger political party or movement. **3** a direction in which something moves or changes.

ten·den·tious /tenˈdenʃɔs/ *adjective derogatory* (of writing etc.) calculated to promote a particular cause or viewpoint; having an underlying purpose. □ **ten·den·tious·ly** *adverb* **ten·den·tious·ness** *noun*

ten·der[1] *adjective* (**ten·der·er**, **ten·der·est**) **1** easily cut or chewed, not tough (*tender steak*). **2** easily touched or wounded, susceptible to pain or grief (*a tender heart; a tender conscience*). **3** easily hurt, sensitive (*tender skin; a tender place*). **4** delicate, fragile (*a tender reputation*). **5** loving, affectionate, fond (*tender parents; wrote tender verses*). **6** requiring tact or careful handling, ticklish (*a tender subject*). **7** (of age) early, immature (*of tender years*). □ **ten·der·ly** *adverb* **ten·der·ness** *noun* [Old French *tendre* from Latin *tener*]

ten·der[2] ● *verb* **1** *transitive* **a** offer, present (one's services, apologies, resignation, etc.). **b** offer (money etc.) as payment. **2** *intransitive* (often foll. by *for*) make a tender for the supply of a thing or the execution of work. **3** *transitive* invite bids for (a contract). ● *noun* **1** an offer, esp. an offer in writing to execute work or supply goods at a fixed price. **2** the auctioning of an item of value, e.g. a contract, to bidders. **3** money or other commodities that may be legally tendered or offered in payment (see LEGAL TENDER). □ **put out to tender** seek tenders with respect to (work etc.). □ **ten·der·er** *noun* [Old French *tendre*: see TEND[1]]

ten·der[3] *noun* **1** a person who looks after people or things. **2** a ship attending a larger one to supply stores, convey passengers or orders, etc. **3** a special railway car closely coupled to a steam locomotive to carry fuel, water, etc. [Middle English from TEND[2] or from ATTENDER (as ATTEND)]

tender-crisp *adjective* (of a vegetable) cooked briefly so as to become softened on the outside but remain crunchy on the inside.

ten·der·foot *noun* (*pl.* **-foots** or **-feet**) a newcomer or novice, esp. in the bush or in the Scouts or Guides.

tender-hearted *adjective* having a tender heart, easily moved by pity etc. □ **tender-hearted·ness** *noun*

ten·der·ize *transitive verb* (also esp. *Brit.* **-ise**) make tender, esp. make (meat) tender by pounding, marinating, etc. □ **ten·der·iz·er** *noun*

ten·der·loin *noun* **1** a tender cut of meat from the inside of a loin of beef or pork. **2** *N Amer. slang* a district of a city where vice and corruption are prominent. [sense 2 apparently with reference to the bribes made to the police to persuade them to turn a blind eye]

tender mercies *plural noun ironic* attention or treatment which is not in the best interests of its recipient.

ten·din·itis *noun* (also **ten·don·itis**) inflammation of a tendon, most commonly from overuse but also from infection or rheumatic disease.

ten·don *noun* **1** a cord or strand of strong fibrous tissue attaching a muscle to a bone etc. **2** (in a quadruped) = HAMSTRING *noun* 2. □ **ten·din·ous** *adjective* [French *tendon* or medieval Latin *tendo -dinis* from Greek *tenōn* 'sinew', from *teinō* 'stretch']

ten·dril *noun* **1** each of the slender leafless shoots, often growing in a spiral form, by which some climbing plants cling for support. **2 a** a slender curl, e.g. of hair. **b** part of a usu. immaterial thing which entwines itself pervasively or clings like a plant tendril (*tendrils of smoke*). [prob. from obsolete French *tendrillon* diminutive of obsolete *tendron* young shoot, ultimately from Latin *tener* TENDER[1]]

Tene·brae /ˈtenɔˌbreɪ/ *noun* **1** (in the Western Church) any of various offices for the last three evenings of Holy Week, at which candles are successively extinguished. **2** this office set to music. [Latin, = darkness]

tene·brous /ˈtenɔbrɔs/ *adjective literary* dark, gloomy. [Old French *tenebrus* from Latin *tenebrosus* (as TENEBRAE)]

tene·ment /ˈtenɔmɔnt/ *noun* **1** a building with apartments or rooms rented cheaply, esp. in a poor area of a city. **2** a dwelling place. **3 a** a piece of land held by an owner. **b** *Law* any kind of permanent property, e.g. lands or buildings, held from a superior. [Old French from medieval Latin *tenementum* from *tenēre* hold]

Tene·rife /ˌtenɔˈriːf/ a volcanic island in the Atlantic, the largest of the Canary Islands; pop. (2001) 701,034; capital, Santa Cruz.

ten·esi /ˈtenesiː/ *noun* (*pl.* same) a monetary unit of Turkmenistan, equal to one-hundredth of a manat.

ten·et /ˈtɛnət/ *noun* a doctrine, dogma, or principle held by a group or person. [Latin, third person singular of *tenēre* hold]

ten·fold *adjective & adverb* **1** ten times as much or as many. **2** consisting of ten parts.

ten-four *interjection* your message has been received and understood (used in radio communication etc.). [originally one of several signals beginning with 'ten-' used in the US for police radio communication]

10-gallon hat *noun* = COWBOY HAT.

tenge /ˈtɛŋgeɪ/ *noun* a monetary unit of Kazakhstan, equal to 100 tiyn. [Kazakh and Turkmen, lit. = 'coin, ruble']

Teng Hsiao-p'ing see DENG XIAOPING.

Ten Lost Tribes of Israel *see* LOST TRIBES.

Tenn. *abbreviation* Tennessee.

Ten·nant, Ver·on·ica (b.1947), English-born Canadian ballet dancer noted for her dramatic interpretations. She made her National Ballet debut in 1965; she performed in a wide range of ballets with many of the world's leading male dancers, including Rudolf Nureyev. Since her retirement from dancing, she has worked as a dance video producer.

ten·ner *noun esp. Brit informal* a ten-dollar bill or ten-pound note.

Ten·nes·see a state in the central southeastern US; pop. (2000) 5,689,283; capital, Nashville. □ **Ten·nes·sean** *noun*

Tennessee River a river in the southeastern US, flowing some 1 400 km (875 miles) in a great loop, generally westward through Tennessee and Alabama, then northward to re-enter Tennessee, joining the Ohio River in W Kentucky.

Tennessee walking horse *noun* a lightly built breed of horse developed in Tennessee and distinguished by its specialized natural gait.

Ten·niel /ˈtɛnjəl/ **Sir John** (1820–1914), English illustrator and cartoonist. He worked as a cartoonist for the magazine *Punch* between 1851 and 1901, but is best known for his illustrations for Lewis Carroll's *Alice's Adventures in Wonderland* (1865) and *Through the Looking Glass* (1871).

ten·nis *noun* either of two games (court tennis and esp. lawn tennis) in which two or four players strike a ball with racquets over a net stretched across a court. [Middle English *tenetz, tenes*, etc., apparently from Old French *tenez* 'take, receive', called by the server to an opponent, imperative of *tenir* take]

tennis ball *noun* a ball used in playing tennis, esp. a hollow rubber ball with a felt or felt-like covering used in lawn tennis.

tennis court *noun* a court used in playing tennis.

tennis elbow *noun* a painful inflammation of the tendons in the elbow caused by playing tennis or engaging in other activities involving repetitious movement of the elbow joint.

tennis racquet *noun* a racquet used in playing tennis.

tennis shoe *noun* **1** a light canvas or leather soft-soled shoe used in tennis. **2** esp. *US* a similar shoe suitable for general casual wear; a running shoe.

ten·no *noun* (*pl.* **-nos**) the Emperor of Japan viewed as a divinity. [Japanese]

Tenny·son /ˈtɛnɪsən/ **Al·fred, 1st Baron Tenny·son of Ald·worth and Fresh·water** (1809–92), English poet, best known for his verse narratives on themes from ancient and medieval mythology, as in 'The Lady of Shalott' (1832), 'The Lotus-Eaters' (1832), 'Morte d'Arthur' (1842), and *Idylls of the King* (1859), and for 'The Charge of the Light Brigade' (1854). All his poetry is characterized by richness and musicality of language. His greatest work, *In Memoriam* (1850) was written after the death of his close friend Arthur Hallam. He was made Poet Laureate in 1850. □ **Tenny·son·ian** /ˌtɛnɪˈsoːnɪən/ *adjective*

Te·noch·ti·tlán /teˌnɒtʃtiˈtlɒn/ the ancient capital of the Aztec Empire, which was founded *c.*1320 on the site of present-day Mexico City. In 1521 the Spanish conquistador Cortés, having deposed the Aztec emperor Montezuma and overthrown his empire, razed Tenochtitlán and established Mexico City.

ten·on /ˈtɛnən/ ● *noun* a projecting piece of wood made for insertion into a corresponding cavity (esp. a mortise) in another piece. ● *transitive verb* **1** cut as a tenon. **2** join by means of a tenon. [French from *tenir* hold, from Latin *tenēre*]

tenor *noun* **1 a** a singing voice between baritone and alto or counter-tenor, the highest of the ordinary adult male range. **b** a singer with this voice. **c** a part written for it. **2 a** an instrument, esp. a saxophone or viola, of which the range is roughly that of a tenor voice. **b** the largest bell of a peal or set. **3** (usu. foll. by *of*) the general purport or drift of a document or speech. **4** (usu. foll. by *of*) a settled or

prevailing course or direction, esp. the course of a person's life or habits. **5** *Law* **a** the actual wording of a document. **b** an exact copy. [Old French *tenour* from Latin *tenor -oris* from *tenēre* hold]

tenor clef *noun Music* a sign that indicates that the second highest line of the staff represents middle C.

tenor·ist *noun* a person who sings a tenor part or esp. who plays a tenor saxophone or other tenor instrument.

tenor·man *noun* (*pl.* **-men**) a person who plays tenor saxophone.

teno·syno·vitis /ˌtɛnoːˌsainoˈvaitɪs/ *noun* inflammation and swelling of a tendon sheath, usu. in the wrist, often caused by repetitive movements such as typing. [Greek *tenōn* tendon + SYNOVITIS]

ten·pin *noun* **1** a pin used in 10-pin bowling. **2** (often in *pl.*) *N Amer.* = 10-PIN BOWLING. □ **ten·pin·ner** *noun*

10-pin bowling *noun* a variety of bowling in which players have two chances to knock down sets of ten pins using a large hard rubber ball.

ten·rec /ˈtɛnrɛk/ *noun* any hedgehog-like tailless insect-eating mammal of the family Tenrecidae, esp. *Tenrec ecaudatus* native to Madagascar. [French *tanrec*, from Malagasy *tàndraka*]

TENS /tɛnz/ *abbreviation* TRANSCUTANEOUS ELECTRICAL NERVE STIMULATION.

tense¹ ● *adjective* **1** stretched tight, strained (*tense cord; tense muscle*). **2** in a state of, causing, or characterized by nervous strain or tension (*tense nerves; a tense moment*). **3** *Phonetics* pronounced with the vocal muscles tense. ● *transitive & intransitive verb* make or become tense. □ **tense up** become tense. □ **tense·ly** *adverb* **tense·ness** *noun* [Latin *tensus* past participle of *tendere* stretch]

tense² *noun Grammar* **1** a form taken by a verb to indicate the time (also the continuance or completeness) of the action etc. (*present tense; imperfect tense*). **2** a set of such forms for the various persons and numbers. □ **tense·less** *adjective* [Old French *tens* from Latin *tempus* time]

ten·sile /ˈtɛnsaɪl, -səl/ *adjective* **1** of or relating to tension. **2** capable of being drawn out or stretched. [medieval Latin *tensilis* (as TENSE¹)]

tensile strength *noun* resistance to breaking under tension.

ten·sion ● *noun* **1** the act or an instance of stretching; the state of being stretched; tenseness. **2** mental strain or excitement. **3** a strained (political, social, etc.) state or relationship. **4** *Mech.* the strained condition resulting from forces acting in opposite directions away from each other. **5** electromagnetic force (*high tension; low tension*). **6** the degree of tightness of stitches in knitting and machine sewing. ● *transitive verb* subject to tension. □ **ten·sion·al** *adjective* [French *tension* or Latin *tensio* (as TEND¹)]

ten·sion·er *noun* a device for applying tension to a seat belt, cable, pipeline, etc.

ten·sor /ˈtɛnsər/ *noun* **1** *Anat.* a muscle that tightens or stretches a part of the body. **2** *Math.* a generalized form of vector involving an arbitrary number of indices. □ **ten·sor·ial** /-ˈsɔːrɪəl/ *adjective* [modern Latin (as TEND¹)]

Tensor bandage *noun Cdn proprietary* a wide elasticized bandage used to tape injured joints to provide support.

ten-speed *noun* (in full **ten-speed bicycle**) esp. *N Amer.* a bicycle with geared wheels allowing ten different gear ratios, esp. one with a light frame and with handlebars curling forwards and downwards.

ten-spot *noun informal* **1** a ten-dollar bill or ten-pound note. **2** a playing card with ten pips.

tent¹ ● *noun* **1** a portable shelter or dwelling of canvas, cloth, etc., supported by a pole or poles and stretched by cords or loops attached to pegs driven into the ground. **2** (*attributive*) composed of or occurring in or under a tent or tents (*tent city; tent show*). **3** *Med.* = OXYGEN TENT. ● *verb* **1** *transitive* **a** cover with or as with a tent. **b** cover (a dish) with a tent-like lid of foil etc. **2** *intransitive* **a** encamp in a tent. **b** dwell temporarily. **3** *transitive & intransitive* form into a tent-like shape, esp. with sides etc. meeting at a top point or ridge. □ **fold one's tent** give up. □ **tent·ed** *adjective* **tent·ing** *noun* **tent-like** *adjective* [Old French *tente*, ultimately from Latin *tendere* stretch]

tent² *noun* a piece (esp. a roll) of cloth inserted into a wound or natural opening to keep it open. [Old French *tente* from *tenter* probe (as TEMPT)]

ten·tacle /ˈtɛntəkəl/ *noun* **1** a long slender flexible appendage of an (esp. invertebrate) animal, used for feeling, grasping, or moving. **2** a thing used like a tentacle as a feeler etc. **3** *Bot.* a sensitive hair or filament. **4** (usu. in *pl.*) a strong esp. insidious binding force. □ **ten·tacled** *adjective* (also in *combination*). **ten·tac·u·lar** /-ˈtakjʊlər/ *adjective* **ten·tac·u·late** /-ˈtakjʊlət/ *adjective* [modern Latin *tentaculum* from Latin *tentare = temptare* (see TEMPT) + *-culum* -CULE]

ten·ta·tive /ˈtɛntətɪv/ ● *adjective* **1** done by way of trial, experimental, provisional. **2** hesitant, not definite (*tentative suggestion; tentative acceptance*). ● *noun* an experimental proposal or theory.
□ **ten·ta·tive·ly** *adverb* **ten·ta·tive·ness** *noun* [medieval Latin *tentativus*, from *tentare*, variant of *temptare* 'handle, try']

tent caterpillar *noun* the gregarious larva of any of several moths of the family Lasiocampidae, esp. of the genus *Malacosoma*, which spins a tent-like web of silk.

tent city *noun* a very large collection of tents, esp. erected in an emergency or in protest.

ten·ter *noun* **1** a machine for stretching cloth to dry in shape. **2** = TENTERHOOK. [medieval Latin *tentorium* (as TEND[1])]

ten·ter·hook *noun* any of the hooks to which cloth is fastened on a tenter. □ **on tenterhooks** in a state of suspense or mental agitation due to uncertainty.

tent flap *noun* a flap at the entrance to a tent.

tent fly *noun* a piece of canvas or other material stretched over a tent leaving an open space but keeping off sun and rain.

tenth ● *noun* **1** the position in a sequence corresponding to the number 10 in the sequence 1-10. **2** something occupying this position. **3** one of ten equal parts of a thing. **4** *Music* **a** an interval or chord spanning an octave and a third in the diatonic scale. **b** a note separated from another by this interval. ● *adjective* that is the tenth. ● *adverb* in the tenth place; tenthly. □ **tenth·ly** *adverb*

tent peg *noun* (also **tent stake**) any of the pegs to which the cords of a tent are attached.

tent pole *noun* a pole supporting a tent.

tent revival *noun* N Amer. an evangelistic or charismatic prayer gathering held in a tent.

tent ring *noun* Cdn a ring of stones for holding down a tent, teepee, etc., esp. as encountered indicating a past campsite.

tent stitch *noun* **1** a series of parallel diagonal stitches. **2** such a stitch.

tent trailer *noun* N Amer. a trailer consisting of a wheeled frame and a collapsible tent.

tenu·ous /ˈtɛnjuːəs/ *adjective* **1** slight, of little substance; insignificant, meagre (*tenuous connection*). **2** (of a distinction etc.) oversubtle. **3** thin, slender, small. **4** rarefied. □ **tenu·ity** *noun* **tenu·ous·ly** *adverb* **tenu·ous·ness** *noun* [Latin *tenuis*]

ten·ure /ˈtɛnjər/ *noun* **1** a condition, or form of right or title, under which (esp. real) property is held. **2 a** the holding or possession of an office or property. **b** the period of this (*during his tenure of office*). **3** guaranteed permanent employment, esp. as a teacher or lecturer after a probationary period. [Old French from *tenir* hold, from Latin *tenēre*]

ten·ured /ˈtɛnjərd/ *adjective* **1** (of an official position) carrying a guarantee of permanent employment. **2** (of a teacher, lecturer, etc.) having guaranteed tenure of office.

tenure-track *adjective* (also **tenure-stream**) designating an employment structure whereby the holder of a (usu. academic) post is guaranteed consideration of eventual tenure (*tenure-track appointment*).

ten·uto /təˈnuːtoː/ *Music* ● *adverb & adjective* (of a note etc.) sustained, given its full time value (*compare* LEGATO, STACCATO). ● *noun* (*pl.* **-utos**) a note or chord played tenuto. [Italian, = held]

teo·calli /ˌtiːəˈkali/ *noun* (*pl.* **teo·callis**) a temple of the Aztecs or other Mexican peoples, usu. on a truncated pyramid. [Nahuatl from *teotl* god + *calli* house]

teo·sinte /ˌtiːəˈsɪnti/ *noun* a subspecies of corn (*Zea mays*) grown as fodder. [French from Nahuatl *teocintli*]

Teo·tihua·cán /teɪˌoːtiːwəˈkɒn/ the largest city of pre-Columbian America, situated about 40 km (25 miles) northeast of Mexico City. Built c.300 BC, it reached its zenith AD c.300–600, when it was the centre of an influential culture which spread throughout Meso-America. By 650 it was declining as a major power, and it was sacked by the invading Toltecs c.900. Among its monuments are palatial buildings, plazas, and temples, including the Pyramids of the Sun and the Moon and the temple of Quetzalcóatl.

tepal /ˈtiːpəl, ˈtɛpəl/ *noun* a segment of the outer whorl in a flower having no differentiation between petals and sepals. [French *tépale*, as blend of PETAL and SEPAL]

te·pee var. of TEEPEE.

teph·ra /ˈtɛfrə/ *noun* fragmented rock etc. ejected by a volcanic eruption. [Greek, = ash]

Tepic /teˈpiːk/ a city in W Mexico, capital of the state of Nayarit; pop. (2000) 265,800.

tepid /ˈtɛpɪd/ *adjective* **1** slightly warm. **2** unenthusiastic. □ **tepid·ity** *noun* **tepid·ly** *adverb* **tepid·ness** *noun* [Latin *tepidus* from *tepēre* be lukewarm]

tep·pan·yaki /ˈtɛpənjaki/ *noun* a Japanese dish of meat or fish, fried with vegetables on a hot steel plate forming the centre of the dining table. [Japanese, from *teppan* steel plate + *yaki* fry]

te·quila /təˈkiːlə/ *noun* a Mexican spirit made by distilling the fermented sap of an agave. [*Tequila*, a town in Mexico where the drink was first produced]

tequila sunrise *noun* a cocktail containing tequila and grenadine.

ter- *combining form* three; threefold (*tercentenary; tervalent*). [Latin *ter* thrice]

tera- *combining form* **1** denoting a factor of 10^{12} (*terawatt*). **2** *Computing* (in the binary system) denoting a multiple of 2^{40} (i.e. 1 099 511 627 776) (*terabyte; terabit*). [Greek *teras* monster]

tera·byte *noun* *Computing* 1 099 511 627 776 (i.e. 2^{40}) bytes as a measure of data capacity, or loosely 1 000 000 000 000 bytes.

tera·flop *noun* *Computing* a unit of computing speed equal to 10^{12} floating-point operations per second.

ter·aph /ˈtɛrəf/ *noun* (*pl.* **ter·aph·im**, also used as *sing.*) a small image as a domestic deity or oracle of the ancient Hebrews. [Late Latin *theraphim*, Greek *theraphin* from Hebrew *ṯʳāpîm*]

tera·to- /ˈtɛrətoː/ *combining form* monster; malformation. [Greek *teras -atos* monster]

tera·to·gen /təˈratədʒən/ *noun* Med. an agent or factor causing malformation of an embryo. □ **tera·to·gen·ic** /ˌtɛrətəˈdʒɛnɪk/ *adjective* **tera·to·gen·icity** /təˌratədʒəˈnɪsɪti/ *noun*

tera·tol·ogy /ˌtɛrəˈtɒlədʒi/ *noun* **1** *Biol.* the scientific study of animal or vegetable monstrosities. **2** mythology relating to fantastic creatures, monsters, etc. □ **tera·to·logic·al** /-təˈlɒdʒɪkəl/ *adjective*

tera·toma /ˌtɛrəˈtoːmə/ *noun* Med. a tumour of heterogeneous tissues, esp. of the gonads.

tera·watt *noun* a unit of power equal to 10^{12} watts or a million megawatts.

ter·bium *noun* Chem. a silvery metallic element of the lanthanide series. Symbol: **Tb**; at. no.: 65. [modern Latin, named after *Ytterby*, a village in Sweden where it was discovered]

ter·buta·line /tɜrˈbjuːtəliːn/ *noun* Med. a synthetic compound with bronchodilator properties, used especially in the treatment of asthma. [TER- + BUTYL + -INE 4]

terce *noun* Christianity the office of the third canonical hour of prayer, originally said at the third hour of the day (i.e. 9 a.m.). [var. of TIERCE]

ter·cel /ˈtɜrsəl/ *noun* Falconry the male of the hawk, esp. a peregrine or goshawk. [Old French *tercel*, ultimately a diminutive of Latin *tertius* third, perhaps from a belief that the third egg of a clutch produced a male bird, or that the male was one-third smaller than the female]

ter·cen·ten·ary /ˌtɜrsɛnˈtɛnri, -ˈtiːnri/ ● *noun* (*pl.* **-aries**) **1** a tercentennial. **2** a celebration of this. ● *adjective* of or relating to a tercentenary.

ter·cen·ten·nial /ˌtɜrsɛnˈtɛniəl/ ● *noun* a three-hundredth anniversary. ● *adjective* **1** lasting three hundred years or occurring every three hundred years. **2** of or concerning a tercentennial.

ter·cet /ˈtɜrsət/ *noun* Prosody a set or group of three lines rhyming together or connected by rhyme with an adjacent triplet. [French from Italian *terzetto* diminutive of *terzo* third, from Latin *tertius*]

tere·binth /ˈtɛrəbɪnθ/ *noun* a small S European tree, *Pistacia terebinthus*, yielding resin formerly used as a source of turpentine. [Old French *terebinte* or Latin *terebinthus* from Greek *terebinthos*]

ter·edo /təˈriːdoː/ *noun* (*pl.* **-edos**) = SHIPWORM. [Latin from Greek *terēdōn* from *teirō* rub hard, wear away, bore]

Ter·ence (Latin name Publius Terentius Afer) (c.190–159 BC), Roman comic dramatist. His six surviving comedies, set in Athens and using the same stock characters as are found in Plautus, include *The Eunuch*.

Ter·eng·ganu see TRENGGANU.

ter·eph·thal·ic acid /tɛrəfˈθalɪk/ *noun* Chem. the *para*-isomer of phthalic acid, used in making plastics and other polymers. [*terebic* from TEREBINTH, + PHTHALIC ACID]

Ter·esa, Mother (also **Ther·esa**) (born Agnes Gonxha Bojaxhiu) (1910–97), Roman Catholic nun and missionary, born in what is now Macedonia of Albanian parentage. From 1928 onward, she devoted herself to helping the destitute in India, particularly in Calcutta, and founded the Order of Missionaries of Charity; she was awarded the Nobel Peace Prize in 1979, and beatified by Pope John Paul II in 2003.

Ter·esa of Ávila /ˈavɪlə/ **St.** (1515–82), Spanish Carmelite nun and mystic, a Doctor of the Church. Seeking to return the Carmelite Order to its original discipline and observances, she instituted the 'discalced' reform movement, establishing the first of a number of convents in 1562 and encouraging St. John of the Cross to found a similar monastic order; her spiritual writings include *The Way of Perfection* (1583) and *The Interior Castle* (1588). Feast day, 15 Oct.

Ter·esa of Li·sieux /liːˈzjɜː/ **St.** (also **Thé·rèse**) (born Marie-Françoise Thérèse Martin) (1873–97), French Carmelite nun. After her death from tuberculosis her cult grew through the publication of her autobiography *L'Histoire d'une âme* (1898), teaching that sanctity can be attained through continual renunciation in small matters and not only through extreme self-mortification. Feast day, 3 Oct.

Ter·esh·kova /ˌterəʃˈkoːvə/ **Val·en·tina (Vlad·i·mir·ovna)** (b.1937), Russian cosmonaut. In June 1963 she became the first woman in space; her spacecraft returned to earth after three days in orbit.

Tere·sina /ˌtereˈziːnə/ a river port in NE Brazil, on the Paranaíba River; pop. (2002) 705,900.

ter·ete /təˈriːt/ *adjective Biol.* smooth and rounded; cylindrical. [Latin *teres -etis*]

ter·gi·ver·sate /ˈtɜːdʒɪvɜːseɪt/ *intransitive verb* **1** equivocate; make conflicting or evasive statements. **2** be apostate; change one's party or principles. □ **ter·gi·ver·sa·tion** *noun* **ter·gi·ver·sa·tor** *noun* [Latin *tergiversari* turn one's back, from *tergum* back + *vertere vers-* turn]

teri·yaki *noun* **1** (in Japanese cuisine) fish or meat marinated in soy sauce etc. and grilled. **2** this sauce. [Japanese from *teri* gloss, lustre + *yaki* grill]

term ● *noun* **1** a word or phrase used to express a definite concept, esp. in a particular branch of study etc. (*a technical term*). **2** (in *pl.*) language used; mode of expression (*answered in no uncertain terms*). **3** (in *pl.*) a relation or footing (*we are on familiar terms*). **4** (in *pl.*) **a** conditions or stipulations (*cannot accept your terms; do it on your own terms*). **b** financial charges (*my terms are very reasonable*). **5 a** a limited period of some state or activity (*for a term of five years*). **b** a period over which operations are conducted or results contemplated (*in the short term*). **c** a period of some weeks, alternating with holiday or vacation, during which instruction is given in a school etc. or during which a law court holds sessions. **d** a period of imprisonment. **e** a period of tenure. **6** *Logic* a word or words that may be the subject or predicate of a proposition. **7** *Math.* **a** each of the two quantities in a ratio. **b** each quantity in a series. **c** a part of an expression joined to the rest by + or –, e.g. *a*, *b*, *c* in *a* + *b* – *c*. **8** the completion of a normal length of pregnancy. **9** an appointed day, esp. for payment of money due. **10** (*attributive*) designating a life insurance policy which provides a payment on death within a specified period, and which has no value once this term has expired. **11** *Law* an interest in land for a fixed period. **12** = TERMINUS 5. ● *transitive verb* denominate, call; assign a term to (*the music termed classical*). □ **bring to terms** cause to accept conditions. **come to terms** agree on conditions; come to an agreement. **come to terms with 1** reconcile oneself to (a difficulty etc.). **2** conclude an agreement with. **in terms of 1** in the language peculiar to, using as a basis of expression or thought. **2** as regards, with reference to. **make terms** conclude an agreement. **be on good** (or **friendly**, etc.) **terms with** have a good relationship with. □ **term·er** *noun* (esp. in *combination*). **term·ly** *adjective & adverb* [Old French *terme* from Latin TERMINUS]

ter·ma·gant /ˈtɜːməɡənt/ ● *noun* **1** an overbearing or ill-tempered woman. **2** (**Termagant**) *hist.* an imaginary deity of violent and turbulent character, often appearing in morality plays. ● *adjective* violent, turbulent, shrewish. [Middle English *Tervagant* from Old French *Tervagan* from Italian *Trivigante*]

term deposit *noun Cdn* an amount of money, usu. between $1,000 and $5,000, deposited with a financial institution for a fixed term, usu. between 30 days and a year, at a fixed interest rate, and which can be withdrawn before term on payment of a penalty.

ter·min·able /ˈtɜːmɪnəbəl/ *adjective* **1** that may be terminated. **2** coming to an end after a certain time (*terminable annuity*).

ter·min·al ● *adjective* **1 a** (of a disease) ending in death, fatal. **b** (of a patient) in the last stage of a fatal disease. **c** (of a morbid condition) forming the last stage of a fatal disease. **d** *informal* very great; irreparable (*terminal laziness*). **2** of or forming a limit or terminus (*terminal station*). **3 a** *Zool.* etc. ending a series (*terminal joints*). **b** *Bot.* borne at the end of a stem etc. **4** of or done etc. each term (*terminal accounts*; *terminal examinations*). ● *noun* **1** a terminating thing; an

extremity. **2** a terminus for trains or long-distance buses. **3** a departure and arrival building for air passengers at an airport. **4** a point of connection for closing an electric circuit. **5** a device for entering data into a computer or receiving its output, esp. one that can be used by a person as a means of two-way communication with a computer, e.g. a keyboard and monitor. **6** = TERMINUS 5. **7** an installation where grain, oil, etc. is stored at the end of a rail line or pipeline, or at a port. **8** a patient suffering from a terminal illness. □ **ter·minal·ly** *adverb*

terminal elevator *noun* a large grain elevator to which grain is shipped from country elevators for bulk accumulation before onward shipment, usu. by water.

terminal velocity *noun* a velocity of a falling body such that the resistance of the air etc. prevents further increase of speed under gravity.

ter·min·ate *verb* **1** *transitive & intransitive* bring or come to an end. **2** *transitive* end (a pregnancy) by artificial means before the fetus is viable. **3** *transitive* bound, limit. **4** *transitive* fire (an employee).

ter·min·a·tion *noun* **1** the act or an instance of terminating; the state of being terminated. **2** *Med.* an induced abortion. **3** an ending or result of a specified kind (*a happy termination*). **4** dismissal from employment. **5** the point or part in which something ends. **6** a word's final syllable or letters or letter esp. as an element in inflection or derivation. □ **bring to a termination** make an end of.

ter·min·ator *noun* **1** a person or thing that terminates. **2** the dividing line between the light and dark part of a planetary body. **3** (*attributive*) designating a gene, seed, etc. that has been artificially created or altered so as to produce an infertile plant.

ter·mi·ner *see* OYER AND TERMINER.

ter·mini *pl.* of TERMINUS.

ter·min·ol·ogy *noun* (*pl.* **-gies**) **1** the system of terms used in a particular subject. **2** the science of the proper use of terms. □ **ter·min·o·logic·al** *adjective* **ter·min·o·logic·ally** *adverb* **ter·min·ol·o·gist** *noun* [German *Terminologie* from medieval Latin TERMINUS term]

ter·minus *noun* (*pl.* **ter·mini** or **ter·minus·es**) **1 a** the end of a railway, bus route, etc. **b** a station at this point. **2** a point at the end of a pipeline etc. **3** a final point, a goal. **4** *Math.* the end point of a vector etc. **5** *Archit.* a figure of a human bust or an animal ending in a square pillar from which it appears to spring, originally as a boundary marker. [Latin, = end, limit, boundary]

terminus ad quem /ad ˈkwem/ *noun* the finishing point of an argument, policy, period, etc. [Latin, = end to which]

terminus ante quem /anti ˈkwem/ *noun* the finishing point of a period; the latest possible date for something. [Latin, = end before which]

terminus a quo /ɒ ˈkwoː/ *noun* the starting point of an argument, policy, period, etc. [Latin, = end from which]

terminus post quem /poːst ˈkwem/ *noun* the starting point of a period; the earliest possible date for something. [Latin, = end after which]

ter·mit·ary /ˈtɜːmɪtəri/ *noun* (*pl.* **-aries**) (also **ter·mit·ari·um** /tɜːmɪˈteriəm/; *pl.* **ter·mit·aria** /-ˈteriə/) a nest of termites, usu. a large mound of earth.

ter·mite *noun* a small ant-like social insect of the order Isoptera, destructive to timber. [Late Latin *termes -mitis*, alteration of Latin *tarmes* after *terere* rub]

term of endearment *noun* a pet name or other term used to convey love or fondness.

term paper *noun N Amer.* an essay or dissertation representative of the work done during a term.

terms of reference *noun* points referred to an individual or body of persons for decision or report; the scope of an inquiry etc.; a definition of this.

terms of trade *noun* the ratio between prices paid for imports and those received for exports.

tern *noun* a bird of the subfamily Sterninae, like a gull but usu. smaller and with a long forked tail, esp. the common tern *Sterna hirundo* or the arctic tern *S. paradisaea*. [of Scandinavian origin: compare Danish *terne*, Swedish *tärna* from Old Norse *therna*]

tern·ary /ˈtɜːnəri/ *adjective* **1** composed of three parts or constituents. **2** *Math.* using three as a base (*ternary scale*). **3** *Music* designating a form in which the first subject is repeated after an interposed second subject in a related key. [Latin *ternarius* from *terni* three each]

terne /tɜːn/ *noun* **1** (in full **terne metal**) a lead alloy with about 20 per cent tin and often antimony. **2** (in full **terne plate**) thin sheet iron or steel coated with an alloy of lead and tin. [prob. from French *terne* 'dull': compare TARNISH]

ter·pene *noun Chem.* any of a large group of unsaturated cyclic hydrocarbons found in the essential oils of plants, esp. conifers and oranges. [*terpentin* obsolete var. of TURPENTINE]

Terp·sich·ore /tɜrpˈsɪkəri/ *Gk & Rom. Myth* the Muse of lyric poetry and dance. [Greek, = delighting in dance]

terp·sich·or·ean /ˌtɜrpsɪˈkɔriən, -kəˈriːən/ *adjective* of or relating to dancing. [TERPSICHORE]

Ter·race a city in west central BC, situated on the Skeena River, 147 km east of Prince Rupert; pop. (2001) 12,109. □ **Ter·racite** *noun* [with reference to a series of four benchlands along the north side of the river]

ter·race ● *noun* **1 a** each of a series of flat areas formed on a slope and used for cultivation. **b** a similar levelled top of a natural slope or raised level area adjoining a house. **2** a level paved area next to a house. **3** the flat roof of a house, esp. in warm climates, where the roof is used as a cool resting area. **4 a** a row of houses on a raised level or along the top or face of a slope. **b** *Brit.* a row of houses built in one block of uniform style. **5** *Geol.* a horizontal shelf or bench on a slope leading to a river, sea, etc. **6** *Brit.* **a** a flight of wide shallow steps as for spectators at a sports ground. **b** (in *pl.*) the spectators occupying such steps. ● *transitive verb* (esp. as **ter·raced** *adjective*) form into or provide with a terrace or terraces. □ **ter·ra·cing** *noun* [Old French, ultimately from Latin *terra* 'earth']

terrace house *noun Brit.* (also **ter·raced house**) any of a row of houses joined by party walls; a row house.

terra·cotta ● *noun* **1 a** unglazed usu. brownish-red earthenware used chiefly as an ornamental building material, in flowerpots etc., and in modelling. **b** a statuette of this. **2** the brownish-red colour of terracotta. ● *adjective* of a brownish-red colour. [Italian, 'baked earth']

terra firma *noun* dry land, firm ground. [Latin, = firm land]

terra·form *transitive verb* (esp. in science fiction) transform (a planet) so as to resemble the earth. □ **terra·formed** *adjective* **terra·form·er** *noun* [Latin *terra* 'earth' + TRANSFORM]

ter·rain *noun* **1** ground, a tract of land, esp. with regard to its physical characteristics or their capacity for use by a military tactician, traveller, etc. **2** a particular area of knowledge; a sphere of influence or action. [French, ultimately from Latin *terrenum*, neuter of *terrenus*, from *terra* 'earth']

terra in·cog·nita /ˌtɛrə ɪŋkɒɡˈniːtə, ɪnˈkɒɡnɪtə/ *noun* an unknown or unexplored region. [Latin, = unknown land]

Ter·ran ● *adjective* (in science fiction) of or relating to the planet earth. ● *noun* an inhabitant of the planet earth.

ter·rane /təˈreɪn/ *noun* a fault-bounded area or region with a distinctive stratigraphy, structure, and geological history, which is different from those of adjacent areas, esp. a fragment of a tectonic plate, bounded by strike-slip faults. [as TERRAIN]

Terra Nova National Park a park in E Newfoundland, situated at the head of Bonavista Bay, southeast of Gander. [Latin, lit. 'new land']

ter·ra·pin /ˈtɛrəpɪn/ *noun* any of various N American edible freshwater turtles of the family Emydidae. [Algonquian]

ter·rar·ium /təˈrɛriəm/ *noun* (*pl.* **ter·rar·iums** or **ter·rar·ia**) **1** a vivarium for small land animals. **2** a sealed transparent globe etc. containing growing plants. [modern Latin from Latin *terra* earth, after AQUARIUM]

ter·raz·zo /tɛˈratsoː, -ˈrazoː/ *noun* (*pl.* **-zos**) a flooring material of stone chips set in concrete and given a smooth surface. [Italian, = terrace]

Terre·bonne /tɛrˈbɒn/ a town in south central Quebec, situated on the north shore of the Rivière des Mille-Îles, northeast of Laval; pop. (2001) 80,531. [French, lit. 'good earth', with reference to the fertile soil in the area]

terre·plein /ˈtɛrpleɪn/ *noun* a level space where a battery of guns is mounted. [originally a sloping bank behind a rampart: French *terre-plein* from Italian *terrapieno* from *terrapienare* fill with earth, from *terra* earth + *pieno* from Latin *plenus* full]

ter·res·trial /təˈrɛstriəl/ ● *adjective* **1** of or on or relating to the earth; earthly. **2 a** of or on dry land. **b** *Zool.* living on or in the ground (opp. AQUATIC, ARBOREAL, AERIAL). **c** *Bot.* growing in the soil (opp. EPIPHYTIC (see EPIPHYTE), AQUATIC). **3** *Astronomy* (of a planet) similar in size or composition to the earth, as Mercury, Venus, and Mars. **4** of this world, worldly. **5** *Brit.* (of broadcasting) not using satellites. ● *noun* an inhabitant of the earth. □ **ter·res·trial·ity** *noun* **ter·res·trial·ly** *adverb* [Latin *terrestris* from *terra* earth]

terrestrial globe *noun* a globe representing the earth.

terrestrial magnetism *noun* the magnetic properties of the earth as a whole.

ter·ret *noun* each of the loops or rings on a horse harness for the driving reins to pass through. [Old French *to(u)ret* diminutive of TOUR]

ter·rible *adjective* **1** *informal* **a** dreadful, awful (*the accident was terrible*). **b** very bad (*terrible cigars*) (also as an intensifier: *a terrible bore*). **2** *informal* very incompetent (*terrible at tennis*). **3** (*predicative*) *informal* ill (*he ate too much and feels terrible*). **4** (*predicative*; often foll. by *about*) *informal* full of remorse (*I feel terrible about it*). **5** causing terror; fit to cause terror; formidable. □ **ter·rible·ness** *noun* [French from Latin *terribilis*, from *terrēre* 'frighten']

terrible two *noun* esp. *N Amer. informal* **1** a two-year-old child regarded as typically troublesome. **2** (in *pl.*) this age (*is in his terrible twos*).

ter·ribly *adverb* **1** *informal* very, extremely (*he was terribly nice about it*). **2** in a terrible manner.

ter·rico·lous /tɛˈrɪkələs/ *adjective* living on or in the earth. [Latin *terricola* earth dweller, from *terra* earth + *colere* inhabit]

ter·rier *noun* **1** any of various breeds of dog originally used for turning out foxes etc. from their earths. **2** an eager or tenacious person or animal. [Old French (*chien*) *terrier* from medieval Latin *terrarius* from Latin *terra* earth]

ter·rif·ic *adjective* **1** *informal* **a** excellent (*did a terrific job*). **b** of great size or intensity. **c** excessive (*making a terrific noise*). **2** *archaic* causing terror. □ **ter·rif·ic·ally** *adverb* [Latin *terrificus* from *terrēre* frighten]

ter·ri·fy *transitive verb* (**-fies**, **-fied**) fill with terror; frighten severely (*terrified them into submission*; *is terrified of dogs*). □ **ter·ri·fy·ing** *adjective* **ter·ri·fy·ing·ly** *adverb* [Latin *terrificare* (as TERRIFIC)]

ter·ri·gen·ous /tɛˈrɪdʒənəs/ *adjective Geol.* derived from the land, esp. (of a marine deposit) made of material eroded from the land. [Latin *terrigenus* 'earth-born']

ter·rine /təˈriːn/ *noun* **1 a** a kind of pâté, usu. coarse textured, cooked in and often served from a terrine. **b** esp. *hist.* a dish of meat, poultry, or game, stewed in a large covered earthenware vessel. **2** a usu. oval earthenware vessel, esp. one in which pâté is cooked, served, or sold. [original form of TUREEN]

ter·ri·tor·ial /ˌtɛrəˈtɔriəl/ ● *adjective* **1** of land (*territorial conquests*). **2** limited to a district (*the right was strictly territorial*). **3** (of a person or animal etc.) inclined to claim and become especially defensive of an area. **4** (usu. **Territorial**) of or relating to any of the Territories of Canada or other countries. ● *noun* (**Territorial**) *Brit.* a member of the Territorial Army. □ **ter·ri·tor·ial·ity** /-ˈalɪti/ *noun*

Territorial Army *noun* (in full **Territorial and Army Volunteer Reserve**) *Brit.* a volunteer force locally organized to provide a reserve of trained and disciplined soldiers for use in an emergency.

Territorial Court *noun Cdn* a court established in a Territory by Territorial legislation, usu. having both criminal and civil divisions, which conducts hearings by judge alone on offences of a relatively minor nature.

territorial waters *plural noun* the waters under the jurisdiction of a country, esp. the part of the sea within a stated distance of the shore, traditionally three miles from low-water mark.

ter·ri·tory *noun* (*pl.* **-ies**) **1** the extent of the land under the jurisdiction of a ruler, country, city, etc. **2** (**Territory**) **a** (in Canada) a region which has not been admitted as a province but which is governed by an elected legislative assembly, but with a commissioner in a role analogous to a lieutenant governor in a province. There are three territories: Yukon, the Northwest Territories, and Nunavut. **b** a region administered by the US federal government having an appointed governor and an elected legislature but without the full rights of a state. **c** any similar division of other countries such as Australia and France. **3 a** a conceptual subdivision of a subject or area; a sphere or domain (*she's brought classical music into the territory of pop music*). **b** an area of responsibility, knowledge, or concern (*computer problems are Owen's territory*). **4** the district over which a sales representative or agent operates. **5** *Zool.* **a** an area defended by an animal or group of animals against others of the same species. **b** the part of a city a person or group of people is associated with. **6** *Sport* an area of a playing surface, esp. one defended by a team or player (*hit the ball into foul territory*). **7** a large tract of land. [Latin *territorium* from *terra* land]

ter·roir /tɛrˈwɑr/ *noun* **1** the total natural environment in which a particular wine is produced, including factors such as the soil, topography, and climate, thought to give the wine a distinctive taste. **2** (in full **goût de terroir** /ˌɡuːdətɛrˈwɑr/) the characteristic taste and

---

Consonants: b *but* d *dog* f *few* g *get* h *her* j *yes* k *cat* l *leg* m *man* n *no* p *pen* r *red* s *sit*

flavour imparted to a wine by the environment in which it is produced. [French, lit. 'soil']

ter·ror *noun* **1** extreme fear or dread. **2 a** a person or thing that causes terror. **b** *informal* or *jocular* an exasperating or troublesome person, esp. a child (*the twins are holy terrors*). **c** *Sport* a dreaded or formidable opponent. **3** the use of organized intimidation; terrorism. **4** (**the Terror**; also **the Reign of Terror**) the period of the French Revolution between mid-1793 and July 1794 when the ruling Jacobin faction, dominated by Robespierre, attempted to eliminate domestic and foreign opposition to the radical Revolution through a series of extreme political, economic, and military reforms. During the course of the Terror, 40,000 French citizens were executed, 1,300 in its last six weeks (also **the Great Terror**) in Paris alone. It ended with the fall and execution of Robespierre. [Old French *terrour* from Latin *terror -oris* from *terrēre* frighten]

ter·ror·ism *noun* **1** the systematic employment of violence and intimidation to coerce a government or community, esp. into acceding to specific political demands. **2** an act of terrorizing, esp. continued over an extended period; persecution. □ **ter·ror·ist** *noun* **ter·ror·is·tic** *adjective*

ter·ror·ize *transitive verb* (also esp. *Brit.* **-ise**) **1** fill with terror. **2** coerce by terror; use terrorism against. **3** bully, harass, persecute, torment.

terror-stricken *adjective* (also **terror-struck**) overwhelmed with terror; terrified.

Terry, Dame (Alice) Ellen (1847–1928), English actress. As Henry Irving's leading lady at the Lyceum Theatre in London (1878–1902), she played in many of his Shakespearean productions, notably in the roles of Desdemona, Portia, and Beatrice; she also acted in plays by George Bernard Shaw, with whom she conducted a long correspondence.

terry cloth *noun N Amer.* (also **terry**) an absorbent cotton pile fabric with the loops uncut, used for making esp. towels and bathrobes (also *attributive*: *terry cloth robe*). [18th c.: origin unknown]

terse *adjective* (**ters·er**, **ters·est**) **1** (of language) brief, concise, to the point. **2** (of a person's manner or speech) brusque, curt, abrupt. □ **terse·ly** *adverb* **terse·ness** *noun* [Latin *tersus* past participle of *tergēre* wipe, polish]

ter·tian /ˈtɜrʃən/ *adjective* (of a fever) recurring every forty-eight hours. [Latin (*febris*) *tertiana*, from *tertius* 'third' (the fever recurring every third day by inclusive reckoning)]

ter·tiary /ˈtɜrʃəri/ ● *adjective* **1** third in order or rank etc. **2** (**Tertiary**) *Geol.* of or relating to the first period in the Cenozoic era, lasting from about 65 to 2 million years ago, during which mammals evolved rapidly, becoming the dominant land vertebrates. **3** designating the sector of the economy or workforce concerned with services, such as transportation and leisure etc. **4** *Chem.* **a** (of an organic compound) having the characteristic functional group located on a saturated carbon atom which is itself bonded to three other carbon atoms. **b** (of an amine) derived from ammonia by replacement of three hydrogen atoms by organic radicals. **5** *Med.* of or pertaining to the third or late stage of a disease, esp. syphilis. **6** *Brit.* = POST-SECONDARY. ● *noun* **1** *Geol.* the Tertiary period. **2** a member of the third order of a monastic body. [Latin *tertiarius* from *tertius* third]

tertium quid /ˌtɜrʃiəm ˈkwɪd, ˌtɜrtjəm/ *noun* a third thing, indefinite and undefined, related in some way to two definite or known things, but distinct from both. [Latin, apparently translation of Greek *triton ti*]

Ter·tul·lian /tɜrˈtʌliən/ (Latin name Quintus Septimius Florens Tertullianus) (*c*.160–*c*.240), early Christian theologian, born in Carthage. His writings include Christian apologetics and attacks on pagan idolatry and Gnosticism.

terza rima /ˌtɛrtsə ˈriːmə, ˌtɛrtsə/ *noun Prosody* a form of iambic verse of Italian origin, consisting of triplets in which the middle line of each triplet rhymes with the first and third line of the next (*aba bcb cdc* etc.), as in Dante's *Divine Comedy*. [Italian, = third rhyme]

ter·zet·to /tɛrtˈsetɔː/ *noun* (*pl.* **-tos** or **ter·zet·ti** /-tiː/) *Music* a vocal or instrumental trio. [Italian: see TERCET]

TESL /ˈtɛsəl/ *abbreviation* teaching of English as a second language.

Tesla /ˈtɛslə/ **Nikola** (1856–1943), Croatian-born US electrical engineer and inventor. Working for Westinghouse, he developed the first alternating current induction motor and made contributions to long-distance electrical power transmission; he also studied high-frequency current, developing several forms of oscillators and the Tesla coil, and developed a wireless guidance system for ships.

tesla /ˈtɛslə/ *noun* the SI unit of magnetic flux density, equal to one weber per square metre or 10,000 gauss. Abbr.: **T**. [TESLA]

Tesla coil *noun* a form of induction coil for producing high-frequency alternating currents. [TESLA]

Tes·lin Lake /ˈtɛzlɪn/ a long, narrow lake straddling the border between Yukon Territory and northwestern BC, situated southeast of Whitehorse. [possibly from Tagish *teslintoo* long, narrow water]

TESOL /ˈtɛsɒl/ *abbreviation* **1** teaching of English to speakers of other languages. **2** teachers of English to speakers of other languages.

TESSA /ˈtɛsə/ *noun* (also **Tessa**) *Brit.* tax exempt special savings account.

tes·sel·lat·ed /ˈtɛsəˌleɪtəd/ *adjective* (also **tes·sel·ated**) **1** (of a floor, wall, etc.) composed of or decorated with small blocks of variously coloured material arranged in a pattern or mosaic. **2** composed of or arranged in or as if in a mosaic. **3** *Bot.* & *Zool.* having colours or surface divisions in regularly arranged squares or patches. □ **tes·sel·late** *transitive verb* [Latin *tessellatus* or Italian *tessellato* from Latin *tessellare* from *tessella* diminutive of TESSERA]

tes·sel·la·tion /ˌtɛsəˈleɪʃən/ *noun* (also **tes·sel·a·tion**) **1 a** an arrangement of shapes, colours, minute parts, etc., closely fitted together. **b** *Geom.* an arrangement of esp. identical polygons in a pattern without gaps or overlapping. **2** a piece of tessellated work; a mosaic. **3** an act or instance of tessellating; the state of being tessellated.

tes·sera /ˈtɛsərə/ *noun* (*pl.* **tes·serae** /-ˌriː/) **1** a small square block of marble, glass, tile, etc., used in a mosaic. **2** *Gk & Rom. Hist.* a small square tablet of wood or bone etc. used as a token or ticket. □ **tes·ser·al** *adjective* [Latin from Greek, neuter of *tesseres, tessares* four]

Tes·sin see TICINO.

tes·si·tura /ˌtɛsəˈtʊrə/ *noun Music* the range within which most tones of a voice part fall. [Italian, = TEXTURE]

test¹ ● *noun* **1 a** a critical examination or trial of the qualities, genuineness, or suitability of a person or thing (*we are carrying out tests on the new product*). **b** the method by which such qualities are tested (*we're using a beta test on the new software*). **c** (*attributive*) designating equipment or materials etc. used in a test (*test facilities*). **2 a** a procedure for assessing a person's aptitude, competence, skill, or intelligence. **b** a set of questions on an academic subject to be answered without assistance (*spelling test*). **3** a procedure performed in order to determine a person's physical or psychological condition (*pregnancy test*; *Rorschach test*). **4** (often foll. by *of*) a situation requiring a person to demonstrate a particular ability or strength (*talking to her is a real test of your patience*). **5** a standard for comparison or trial; a criterion (*it does not stand up to our test*). **6** *Chem.* **a** a procedure for examining a substance under known conditions or with a specific reagent to determine its identity or the presence or absence of some constituent, activity, etc. **b** a substance by means of which this may be done. **7** (*attributive*) designating esp. fishing line having a strength or capacity of a specified weight (*20-pound test line*). ● *verb* **1** *transitive* subject (a person or thing) to a close or critical examination; evaluate by experiment. **2** *transitive* (often foll. by *for*) subject (a substance) to a chemical test (*tested his blood for alcohol*). **3** (usu. foll. by *for*) **a** *transitive* & *intransitive* apply or carry out a test on a person or thing (*they're testing for HIV*). **b** *transitive* achieve or receive a specific result (*tested positive for banned substances*). **4** *transitive* try the patience or endurance of (a person); tax. □ **put to the test** cause to undergo a test. **stand** (or **withstand) the test of time** be or remain popular after the passage of a long period of time. **test out** subject (a theory etc.) to a practical test; try out. **test the water(s)** judge people's feelings or opinions before taking further action. **test whether** perform a test to see; check. □ **test·able** *adjective* **test·abil·ity** *noun* **test·ed** *adjective* **test·ing** *noun* [Old French from Latin *testu(m)* earthen pot, collateral form of *testa* TEST²]

test² *noun* the shell of some invertebrates, esp. foraminifers and tunicates. □ **tes·ta·ceous** *adjective* [Latin *testa* tile, jug, shell, etc.: compare TEST¹]

testa *noun* (*pl.* **tes·tae** /ˈtɛstiː/) *Bot.* a seed coat. [Latin (as TEST²)]

Test Acts *plural noun* various acts that made the holding of public office in Britain conditional on profession of the established religion, effectively excluding Catholics, Nonconformists, and non-Christians. In England such an act was repealed in 1828, although laws imposing similar conditions on university entrance remained until 1871. *See also* CATHOLIC EMANCIPATION, PENAL LAWS.

tes·ta·ment *noun* **1** *Bible* **a** (**Testament**) either of the main divisions of the Christian Bible (*see* OLD TESTAMENT, NEW TESTAMENT). **b** (**Testament**) a copy of the New Testament. **c** = COVENANT 3. **2** (usu. foll. by *to*) evidence, proof; a tribute (*it is a testament to your loyalty*). **3 a** a will (*last will and testament*). **b** a legacy; something bequeathed. [Latin *testamentum* will (as TESTATE): in early Christian Latin rendering Greek *diathēkē* covenant]

tes·ta·ment·ary *adjective* **1** made, bequeathed, or appointed by will. **2** of or relating to a will.

tes·tate ● *adjective* having left a valid will at death. ● *noun* a testate person. [Latin *testatus* past participle of *testari* testify, make a will, from *testis* witness]

tes·ta·tor /tə'steitɔr/ *noun* a person who has made a will, esp. one who dies testate.

tes·ta·trix /tə'steitriks/ *noun* a woman who has made a will, esp. one who dies testate.

test ban *noun* an agreement among several countries to discontinue the testing of nuclear weapons.

Test-Ban Treaty an international agreement not to test nuclear weapons in the atmosphere, in space, or under water, signed in 1963 by the US, the UK, and the USSR, and later signed by more than 100 governments, with the notable exceptions of France and China.

test bed *noun* **1** a testing site. **2** equipment for testing machines, esp. aircraft engines, before acceptance for general use.

test card *noun Brit.* = TEST PATTERN.

test case *noun* **1** *Law* an action brought to ascertain the law, thereby setting a precedent for other cases involving the same principle. **2** a person, thing, or set of circumstances used to test something.

test drive ● *transitive verb* **1** drive (a car or truck etc.) in order to assess its quality and performance before buying it. **2** run (software) to sample its features and assess its suitability. **3** *informal* sample (a product) prior to purchase. ● *noun* **1** a drive taken to assess the performance of a car or truck etc. one is thinking of buying. **2** an act or instance of trying out any product, such as computer software, prior to purchase. □ **test driver** *noun*

test·ee *noun* a person subjected to a test.

test·er¹ *noun* **1** a device or instrument used to test something (*circuit tester*). **2** a person who conducts a test of esp. a product. **3 a** a small amount of a perfume or cosmetic for a customer to sample before purchase. **b** the bottle from which this is dispensed.

test·er² *noun* a canopy, esp. over a four-poster bed. [medieval Latin *testerium, testrum, testura*, ultimately from Latin *testa* tile]

tes·tes *pl.* of TESTIS.

test fire *transitive & intransitive verb* fire (a gun or missile) experimentally.

test flight *noun* a flight during which the performance of an aircraft is tested. □ **test-fly** *transitive verb*

tes·ticle *noun* either of the two glandular organs in male humans and other mammals, which contain the sperm-producing cells and are usu. enclosed in the scrotum. □ **tes·ticu·lar** /te'stikjələr/ *adjective* [Latin *testiculus* diminutive of *testis* witness (of virility)]

test·ify *verb* (-**fies**, -**fied**) **1** *Law* **a** *intransitive* appear as a witness to give evidence in a court of law. **b** *transitive* (often foll. by *that*) state under oath in a court of law; swear (*testified that she had been with him that night*). **2** *transitive* (usu. foll. by *that*) affirm or declare, esp. based on first-hand knowledge or prior experience. **3** *intransitive* (often foll. by *to*) bear witness; attest (*I can testify to the quality of her work*). **4** *transitive & intransitive* (of a thing) serve as proof or evidence of (*his poetry testifies to his torment*). □ **testify against** give testimony that may help to convict (a defendant). □ **testi·fier** *noun* [Latin *testificari* from *testis* witness]

testi·mon·ial *noun* **1 a** a written or oral statement attesting to the quality of esp. a product or service and recommending it to others. **b** a certificate of a person's character, conduct, or qualifications. **2** a gift presented to a person, esp. in public, as a mark of esteem, in acknowledgement of services, etc.; a tribute (also *attributive*: *testimonial dinner*).

testi·mony *noun* (*pl.* -**ies**) **1** *Law* **a** evidence or the body of evidence presented under oath in a court of law by one or more witnesses (*her whereabouts were confirmed by the testimony of three witnesses*). **b** an act of presenting evidence; a statement given under oath. **2** a declaration or statement of fact. **3** (usu. foll. by *to*) evidence, proof; a demonstration (*the pyramids are testimony to the engineering skills of the ancient Egyptians*). **4** *archaic* an open acknowledgement or profession, esp. of religious faith or experience. **5** *Bible* the Ten Commandments. [Latin *testimonium* from *testis* witness]

testing ground *noun* a place or situation where something may be tried out to assess its suitability or acceptability before being used, implemented, or adopted on a larger scale.

tes·tis /'testis/ *noun* (*pl.* **tes·tes** /-tiːz/) a testicle. [Latin, = witness: compare TESTICLE]

test-market ● *transitive verb* introduce (a new product or service) in a limited region in order to assess consumer response. ● *noun* (usu. **test market**) a limited area that serves as the market for a new product.

test match *noun* an international cricket or rugby match, esp. one of a series of matches, played between representative teams from certain countries.

tes·tos·ter·one /te'stɒstərəʊn/ *noun* **1** a steroid hormone that stimulates the development of male secondary sexual characteristics, produced in the testicles and, in very much smaller quantities, in the ovaries and adrenal cortex. **2** *informal* (also in *combination*) stereotypical machismo (*testosterone-charged lyrics*). [TESTIS + STEROL + -ONE]

test paper *noun* **1** the sheet on which a student writes the answers to a test. **2** *Chem.* a paper impregnated with a substance changing colour under known conditions.

test pattern *noun* esp. *N Amer.* a still television picture transmitted outside normal program hours and designed for use in judging the quality and position of the image.

test pilot *noun* a pilot who test-flies aircraft. □ **test-pilot** *transitive verb*

test spin *noun informal* = TEST DRIVE *noun*.

test tube *noun* **1** a cylindrical vessel of thin transparent glass, having a closed rounded bottom at one end, used in laboratories etc. to hold small amounts of liquid for analysis and experimentation. **2** (*attributive*, usu. **test-tube**) designating procedures and operations carried out artificially or under laboratory conditions (*test-tube fertilization*).

test-tube baby *noun informal* a baby conceived by in vitro fertilization.

tes·tu·do /te'stuːdɔː, te'stjuː-/ *noun* (*pl.* -**dos** or **tes·tu·di·nes** /-di,niːz/) *Rom. Hist.* **1** a movable screen with an arched roof used to protect besieging troops. **2** a protective screen formed by a body of troops in close array by holding their shields in overlapping fashion above their heads. [Latin *testudo -dinis*, lit. 'tortoise' (as TEST²)]

testy *adjective* (**test·i·er**, **test·i·est**) irritable, touchy. □ **test·i·ly** *adverb* **test·i·ness** *noun* [Anglo-French *testif* from Old French *teste* head (as TEST²)]

tet·an·ic /tə'tanik/ *adjective* **1** of, pertaining to, characterized by, or characteristic of tetanus. **2** designating tonic muscular contraction. [Latin *tetanicus* from Greek *tetanikos* (as TETANUS)]

teta·nus /'tetnəs, 'tetənəs/ *noun* **1** a disease caused by the bacterium *Clostridium tetani*, marked by rigidity and spasms of the voluntary muscles. **2** *Physiol.* the prolonged contraction of a muscle caused by rapidly repeated stimuli. [Latin from Greek *tetanos* muscular spasm, from *teinō* stretch]

tet·any /'tetəni/ *noun* a disease with intermittent muscular spasms caused by malfunction of the parathyroid glands and a consequent deficiency of calcium. [French *tétanie* (as TETANUS)]

tetchy *adjective* (**tetch·i·er**, **tetch·i·est**) easily angered or annoyed; peevish, irritable. □ **tetch·i·ly** *adverb* **tetch·i·ness** *noun* [prob. from *tecche, tache* blemish, fault, from Old French *teche, tache*]

tête-à-tête /ˌteta'tet/ ● *noun* **1** a conversation between two people. **2** an S-shaped sofa, enabling two people to sit face to face. ● *adverb* **1** together in private (*they spoke tête-à-tête*). **2** facing each other; face to face (*we were seated tête-à-tête*). ● *adjective* involving or attended by only two people; private. [French, lit. 'head-to-head']

tête-bêche /tet'beʃ/ ● *adjective* (of a postage stamp) printed upside down or sideways relative to the next stamp in the same row. ● *noun* a stamp printed upside down or sideways. [French from *tête* head + *béchevet* double bed-head]

teth·er ● *noun* **1** a rope etc. by which an animal is tied to confine it to the spot. **2** anything that attaches, binds, or confines. ● *transitive verb* **1** tie or confine (an animal etc.) with a tether. **2** bind by circumstances or conditions. □ **at the end of one's tether** = AT THE END OF ONE'S ROPE (see END). [Old Norse *tjothr* from Germanic]

tether·ball *noun N Amer.* a game in which people use their hands or paddles to hit a ball suspended on a cord from an upright post, the winner being the first person to wind the cord completely around the post.

Tethys /'teθis/ **1** *Gk Myth* a goddess of the sea, daughter of Uranus (Heaven) and Gaia (Earth). **2** *Astronomy* satellite III of Saturn, the ninth closest to the planet, discovered by Cassini in 1684 (diameter 1 050 km). **3** *Geol.* an ocean formerly separating the supercontinents of Gondwanaland and Laurasia, the forerunner of the present-day Mediterranean. □ **Tethy·an** /'teθiən/ *adjective*

Tet·lit Gwich'in /'tiːtlit 'gwitʃin/ ● *noun* a member of a Gwich'in people, esp. living in or originating from the community of Fort McPherson, NWT. ● *adjective* of or relating to this people or their culture. [Gwich'in, ='people of the headwaters']

Tet Offensive (in the Vietnam War) a surprise offensive launched by the Viet Cong and the North Vietnamese army in Jan.–Feb. 1968, timed to coincide with the first day of the Tet (Vietnamese New Year). Although eventually repulsed, the attack shook American confidence and hastened the withdrawal of US forces.

Té·touan /teiˈtwɒn/ a city in N Morocco; pop. (2002) 330,100.

tetra *noun* (*pl.* same or **tet·ras**) any of various small, often brightly coloured tropical fish of the characin family, frequently kept in aquariums. [abbreviation of modern Latin *Tetragonopterus* (literally 'tetragonal finned'), former genus name]

tetra- *combining form* (also **tetr-** before a vowel) **1** four (*tetrapod*). **2** *Chem.* (forming names of compounds) containing four atoms or groups of a specified kind (*tetroxide*). [Greek from *tettares* four]

tetra·chlor·ide *noun* *Chem.* a compound of four atoms of chlorine with some other element or radical (*carbon tetrachloride*).

tetra·cyc·lic /ˌtetrəˈsɪklɪk/ *adjective* **1** *Chem.* (of a compound) having a molecular structure of four fused hydrocarbon rings. **2** *Bot.* (of a flower) having four circles or whorls.

tetra·cy·cline /ˌtetrəˈsəikliːn, -lɪn/ *noun* **1** a tetracyclic compound, $C_{22}H_{24}N_2O_8$, which is a broad spectrum antibiotic. **2** any of several antibiotics structurally related to this compound, used to treat various kinds of infection. [TETRACYCLIC + -INE⁴]

tet·rad *noun* **1** a group of four. **2** *Biol.* **a** a group of four cells or spores etc. **b** a group of four homologous chromatids formed during meiotic division. **3** a square block of four 1-km squares within a 10-km square, used as a unit in biological recording.

tetra·ethyl lead /ˌtetrəˈhiːθəl/ *noun* a colourless oily toxic liquid, $Pb(C_2H_5)_4$, formerly added to gasoline as an anti-knock agent.

tetra·gon *noun* a quadrangle.

tet·rag·on·al /tɪˈtraɡənəl/ *adjective* **1** *Mineralogy* belonging to or being a crystal system in which there are three mutually perpendicular crystallographic axes, two being equal and the third of a different length. **2** of or like a quadrangle; quadrangular.

Tetra·gram·ma·ton /ˌtetrəˈɡraməˌtɒn/ *noun* the Hebrew name of God transliterated in four letters as YHVH or JHVH, often regarded as ineffable and treated as a mysterious symbol of God (*compare* YAHWEH, JEHOVAH). [Greek (as TETRA-, *gramma*, *-atos* letter)]

tetra·hed·rite /ˌtetrəˈhiːdrəit/ *noun* a metallic grey mineral consisting of native sulphide of antimony, iron, and copper, typically occurring as tetrahedral crystals.

tetra·hed·ron /ˌtetrəˈhiːdrən, -ˈhedrən/ *noun* (*pl.* **-hed·rons** or **-hedra**) a solid figure or object with four plane faces, esp. (in full **regular tetrahedron**) one with four equal equilateral triangular faces.
□ **tetra·hed·ral** *adjective*

tetra·hydro·can·nabi·nol /ˌtetrəˌhaidrəkəˈnabɪnəl/ *noun see* THC.

tet·ral·ogy /teˈtralədʒi, -ˈtrɒlədʒi/ *noun* (*pl.* **-ogies**) **1** a group of four related literary or operatic works. **2** *Gk Hist.* a series of four plays, three tragic and one satyric, performed in Athens at the festival of Dionysus.

tet·ram·eter /teˈtramətər/ *noun* *Prosody* a line of four metrical feet.

Tetra Pak *noun* *proprietary* a kind of plasticized cardboard carton for packaging milk and other drinks, folded from a single sheet into a box shape, originally tetrahedral, now usu. rectangular.

tetra·plegia /ˌtetrəˈpliːdʒiə/ *noun* *Med.* = QUADRIPLEGIA.
□ **tetra·plegic** *adjective & noun* [modern Latin (as TETRA-, Greek *plēgē* blow, strike)]

tetra·ploid /ˈtetrəˌplɔid/ *Biol.* ● *adjective* (of an organism or cell) having four times the haploid set of chromosomes. ● *noun* a tetraploid organism or cell. □ **tetra·ploidy** *noun*

tetra·pod *noun* *Zool.* **1** an animal with four feet or limbs. **2** a member of the group Tetrapoda, which includes all vertebrates higher than fishes, i.e. amphibians, reptiles, birds, and mammals. [modern Latin *tetrapodus* from Greek *tetrapous* (as TETRA-, *pous podos* foot)]

tet·rarch /ˈtetrɑrk/ *noun* **1** *Rom. Hist.* the governor of a fourth part of a country or province. **2** one of four joint rulers. [Late Latin *tetrarcha* from Latin *tetrarches* from Greek *tetrarkhēs* (as TETRA-, *arkhō* rule)]

tetra·valent /ˌtetrəˈveilənt/ *adjective* *Chem.* having a valence of four; quadrivalent.

tetri *noun* (*pl.* same) a monetary unit of Georgia, equal to one-hundredth of a lari. [Georgian]

tetro·do·toxin /teˌtroːdəˈtɒksən/ *noun* a poisonous substance found in the ovaries of certain pufferfishes which affects the action of nerve cells. [modern Latin *Tetrodon* former genus name for a variety of pufferfish, + TOXIN]

tet·rox·ide /teˈtrɒksaid/ *noun* *Chem.* any oxide containing four atoms of oxygen in its molecule or empirical formula.

tet·ter *noun* *archaic* or *dialect* any of various skin diseases of humans, horses, etc., such as ringworm, eczema, impetigo, etc. [Old English *teter*]

Teut. *abbreviation* Teutonic.

Teuto- /ˈtuːtoː, ˈtjuː-/ *combining form* forming nouns and adjectives with the sense 'Teutonic'.

Teu·ton /ˈtuːtən, ˈtjuː-/ *noun* **1** a member of a Teutonic nation, esp. a German. **2** *hist.* a member of a northern European tribe recorded from the 4th c. BC which combined with others to carry out raids on northeastern and southern France until heavily defeated in 102 BC. [Latin *Teutones*, *Teutoni*, from an Indo-European base meaning 'people' or 'country']

Teu·ton·ic /tuːˈtɒnɪk, tjuː-/ ● *adjective* **1 a** German. **b** displaying the characteristics stereotypically attributed to Germans. **2** *hist.* of or pertaining to the Teutons. **3** *dated* designating or pertaining to the Germanic branch of the Indo-European language family or the Germanic-speaking peoples. ● *noun dated* = GERMANIC 1.

Teutonic Knights a military order of German knights, originally enrolled *c.*1191 as the Teutonic Knights of St. Mary of Jerusalem. After participating in the Crusades they turned their attentions against Prussia and E Europe, eventually becoming a great sovereign power through conquest. The order was re-established as an honorary ecclesiastical institution in 1834 and maintains a titular existence.

TeV *abbreviation* tera-electron volt(s).

Tews·ley /ˈtjuːzli/ **Rob·ert** (b.1972), English ballet dancer, noted for his musicality, dramatic ability, elegance, and purity of line.

Tex. *abbreviation* Texas.

Tex·ada Island /teksˈeidə/ a long, narrow island in the Strait of Georgia, situated off the southwestern coast of mainland BC, from which it is separated by the Malaspina Strait. [F. de *Tejada*, Spanish naval commander *c.*1791]

Texas a state in the southern US, on the border with Mexico, with a coastline on the Gulf of Mexico; pop. (2000) 20,851,820; capital, Austin. The area formed part of Mexico until 1836, when it declared independence and became a republic. It became the 28th state of the US in 1845. □ **Tex·an** *adjective & noun*

Texas gate *noun* *Cdn* (*West*) = CATTLE GUARD.

Texas leaguer *noun* *Baseball* a shallow fly ball or pop-up that falls between the infield and outfield; a bloop single or double.

Texas Longhorn *noun* a breed of cattle once common in the southwestern US, distinguished by long horns and able to thrive in dry regions.

Texas mickey *noun* *Cdn informal* a 130-ounce bottle of alcohol, esp. rye whisky.

Tex-Mex ● *noun* **1** a Texan style of cooking characterized by the adaptation of Mexican ingredients and influences, such as tacos, enchiladas, ground beef, etc., with more moderate use of hot flavourings such as chilies. **2** a style of dance music originated by the Tejanos and characterized esp. by the use of accordion. **3** the variety of Mexican Spanish spoken in Texas. ● *adjective* of or relating to the blend of Texan and Mexican cooking, music, language, or culture, existing or originating in the southwestern US. [*Texan* + *Mexican*]

text *noun* **1 a** the wording of something written or printed; the actual words, phrases, and sentences as written. **b** the wording adopted by an editor as the most faithful representation of the author's original work (*the authoritative text*). **2** the main written or printed part of a book as distinct from notes, illustrations, appendices, etc. **3** the original words of an author or document, esp. in the original language, form, and order as opposed to a translation, revision, paraphrase, or commentary. **4** data in textual form, esp. as stored, processed, or displayed in a word processor or text editor. **5 a** a textbook. **b** (in *pl.*) books prescribed for study. **6** a short passage from the Scriptures, esp. one quoted as illustrative of a belief, doctrine, or moral, or chosen as the subject or starting point for a sermon. **7** a subject or theme.
□ **text·less** *adjective* [Old Northern French *texte* from Latin *textus* tissue, literary style (in medieval Latin = Gospel) from Latin *texere* text-weave]

text·book ● *noun* a book giving instruction in a particular, esp. academic, subject (*a math textbook*). ● *attributive adjective* conforming to or corresponding to a standard or type that is prescribed or widely held by theorists (*a textbook case*). □ **text·book·ish** *adjective*

---

uː mo**od** ai m**y** əi p**ipe** au br**own** ʌu h**ouse** ei d**ay** ɔi b**oy** ã fr**anglais** ã C**anadien** ɔ̃ Br**ayon** (*see over for consonants*)

text editor *noun Computing* = EDITOR 5. □ **text editing** *noun*

text file *noun Computing* a file used to store data in textual form.

tex·tile ● *noun* **1** any woven fabric. **2** any of various fabrics which do not require weaving. **3** natural or synthetic fibres or yarns suitable for being spun and woven or manufactured into cloth etc. **4** (in *pl.*) the manufacture or production of woven or unwoven fabrics. ● *adjective* **1** used in or relating to the production of textiles (*textile mill*). **2** suitable for weaving (*textile materials*). **3** woven. [Latin *textilis* (as TEXT)]

text messaging *noun* the sending of a message in text over the Internet, to appear on the display screen of a wireless phone or pager, often characterized by the use of abbreviations for phrases, since the number of characters that can be sent is limited. □ **text message** *noun*

text processing *noun Computing* word processing.

text·ual *adjective* **1** of, concerning, or contained in a text (*textual errors*). **2** based on, following, or conforming to the text of a work (*textual analysis*). □ **text·ual·ly** *adverb*

textual criticism *noun* the study of the content and message of esp. Biblical writings. *Also called* LOWER CRITICISM (*compare* HIGHER CRITICISM).

text·ual·ist *noun* a person who adheres strictly to text, esp. that of the Bible. □ **text·ual·ism** *noun*

text·u·al·ity *noun* (*pl.* **-ities**) **1** the medium of textual language. **2** strict adherence to a text; textualism.

tex·ture ● *noun* **1 a** the surface of a thing assessed in terms of its roughness, smoothness, softness, etc. by the senses of esp. sight and touch. **b** the feel of food or wine in the mouth (*the sauce had a light creamy texture*). **2** a discernible roughness or bumpiness on a surface (*the stone is polished until it has no texture*). **3** the physical or perceived structure and composition of the constituent parts or formative elements of something, such as soil or rock. **4** *Art* the representation of the tactile quality and nature of a surface in a photograph, painting, etc. **5** *Music* the quality of sound created by the combination of the different elements of a work or passage. **6** the quality of a piece of writing, esp. with reference to imagery, alliteration, etc. **7** the character, appearance, or tactile quality of textile fabric as determined by its weave or arrangement of threads. **8** one's life, society, etc. seen in terms of a particular arrangement and assortment of events and individuals etc. ● *transitive verb* provide with a texture. □ **tex·tur·al** *adjective* **tex·tur·al·ly** *adverb* **tex·ture·less** *adjective* **tex·tur·ous** *adjective* [Latin *textura* weaving (as TEXT)]

tex·tured *adjective* **1** having a discernible texture; not smooth or flat (*the walls were covered with textured plaster*). **2** (in *combination*) having a specified kind of texture (*coarse-textured brick*). **3** having a distinctive or characteristic texture (*textured harmonies*).

textured vegetable protein *noun* spun or extruded vegetable protein, usu. made to simulate the texture, taste, and appearance of meat. Abbr.: **TVP**.

texture mapping *noun Computing* a method of assigning an object the appearance of a particular texture without explicitly modelling it as part of the surface geometry, used esp. in grey-scale images and maps.

tex·tur·ize *transitive verb* (also esp. *Brit.* **-ise**) impart a particular texture to (hair, fabric, food, etc.). □ **tex·tur·ized** *adjective*

TFT *abbreviation* thin film transistor, denoting a technology used to make flat colour display screens, usu. for high-end portable computers.

TG *abbreviation* transformational grammar.

TGIF *abbreviation informal* thank God (or goodness) it's Friday.

TGV *noun* a type of high-speed French passenger train. [acronym from French *Train à Grande Vitesse* high-speed train]

Th *symbol* the element thorium.

Th. *abbreviation* Thursday.

-th¹ *suffix* (also **-eth**) forming ordinal and fractional numbers from *four* onward (*fourth*; *thirtieth*). [Old English *-tha, -the, -otha, -othe*]

-th² *suffix* forming nouns denoting an action or process: **1** from verbs (*birth*; *growth*). **2** from adjectives (*breadth*; *filth*; *length*). [Old English *-thu, -tho, -th*]

-th³ *var. of* -ETH².

Thack·eray /ˈθakɜri/ **Wil·liam Make·peace** (1811–63), Indian-born English novelist. *Vanity Fair* (1847–8), a vivid portrayal of early 19th-c. society, satirized upper-middle class pretensions through its central character Becky Sharp; later novels include *Pendennis* (1848–50), and *The Virginians* (1857–9).

Thai /taɪ/ ● *noun* (*pl.* same or **Thais**) **1 a** a native or inhabitant of Thailand. **b** a member of the people forming the largest ethnic group in Thailand and also inhabiting neighbouring regions. **2** the language of Thailand. ● *adjective* of or relating to Thailand or its people or language. [Thai, = free]

Thai·land /ˈtaɪland/ a kingdom in SE Asia; pop. (2002) 62,354,402; capital, Bangkok. The country was known as Siam until 1939.

Thailand, Gulf of an inlet of the South China Sea between the Malay Peninsula to the west and Thailand and Cambodia to the east. It was formerly known as the Gulf of Siam.

Thai stick *noun* strong cannabis in leaf form, twisted into a small, tightly packed cylinder ready for smoking.

thal·amus /ˈθaləməs/ *noun* (*pl.* **thal·ami** /-ˌmaɪ/) **1** *Anat.* either of two masses of grey matter lying between the cerebral hemispheres on either side of the third ventricle, which relay sensory information and act as a centre for pain perception. **2** *Bot.* the receptacle of a flower. □ **thal·amic** /θəˈlamɪk, ˈθaləmɪk/ *adjective* [Latin from Greek *thalamos* an inner room or woman's apartment]

thal·as·semia /θaləˈsiːmiə/ *noun* (also **thal·as·saemia**) *Med.* any of a group of hereditary hemolytic diseases caused by faulty hemoglobin synthesis and widespread in Mediterranean, African, and Asian countries. [Greek *thalassa* 'sea' (because first known around the Mediterranean) + -EMIA]

thal·as·sic /θəˈlasɪk/ *adjective literary* of the sea or seas, esp. small or inland seas. [French *thalassique* from Greek *thalassa* sea]

thal·as·so·ther·apy /θəˌlasoʊˈθerəpi/ *noun* a therapeutic treatment using sea water. □ **thal·as·so·ther·apist** *noun* [Greek *thalassa* 'sea' + THERAPY]

thal·er /ˈtalər/ *noun hist.* a German silver coin. [German *T(h)aler*: see DOLLAR]

Thales /ˈθeɪliːz/ (c.624–c.545 BC), Greek philosopher, mathematician, and astronomer, of Miletus. He was held by Aristotle to be the founder of physical science, and is also credited with founding geometry; he proposed that water was the primary substance from which all things were derived, and represented the earth as floating on an underlying ocean.

thali /ˈtali/ *noun* **1** a metal platter or flat dish on which Indian food is served. **2** an Indian meal consisting of a selection of assorted dishes, esp. served on such a platter. [Hindi *thālī* from Sanskrit *sthālī*]

Thalia /θəˈlaɪə/ *Gk & Rom. Myth* the Muse of comedy.

thal·ido·mide /θəˈlɪdəˌmaɪd/ *noun* **1** a drug formerly used as a sedative but found in 1961 to cause fetal malformation when taken by a mother early in pregnancy. **2** (*attributive*) designating a baby or child etc. born with a congenital abnormality due to the effects of thalidomide. [from *(ph)thal(ic acid)* + (im)*ido* + (i)*mide*]

thal·li *pl. of* THALLUS.

thal·lium /ˈθaliəm/ *noun Chem.* a rare soft white metallic element, occurring naturally in zinc blende and some iron ores. Symbol: **Tl**; at. no.: 81. □ **thal·lic** *adjective* [formed as THALLUS, from the green line in its spectrum]

thal·lus /ˈθaləs/ *noun* (*pl.* **thal·li** /-laɪ/) a plant body, such as in algae, fungi, lichens, etc., without vascular tissue and not differentiated into root, stem, and leaves. □ **thal·loid** *adjective* [Latin from Greek *thallos* green shoot, from *thallō* bloom]

thal·weg /ˈtalveg/ *noun Geog.* the line of fastest descent from any point on land, esp. one connecting the deepest points along a river channel or the lowest points along a valley floor. [German from *Thal* valley + *Weg* way]

Thames River /temz/ **1** a river of S England, flowing 338 km (210 miles) eastward from the Cotswolds in Gloucestershire through London to the North Sea. **2** a river in SW Ontario, which rises near Stratford and flows southwestward through Woodstock, London, and Chatham to empty into Lake St. Clair. [sense 2 after sense 1]

than *conjunction* **1** introducing the second element in a comparison (*you are older than he is*; *you are older than he*). ¶ It is also possible to say *you are older than him*, with *than* treated as a preposition, esp. in less formal contexts. **2** introducing the second element in a statement of difference (*anyone other than me*). **3** (foll. by *to* + infin.) in a statement expressing hypothesis or consequence (*we would be better to proceed than to stop*). **4** when (*we had no sooner arrived than it started to rain*). [Old English *thanne* etc., originally the same word as THEN]

thana·tol·ogy /ˌθanəˈtɒlədʒi/ *noun* the branch of science that deals with death, its causes and phenomena, and with the effects of approaching death and the needs of the terminally ill and their families. □ **thana·to·logic·al** /ˈθanətəˈlɒdʒəkəl/ *adjective* **thana·tol·o·gist** *noun* [Greek *thanatos* 'death' + -LOGY]

Thana·tos /ˌθæˈnatoːs/ *noun Psych.* (in Freudian psychology) the urge for destruction or self-destruction (*opp.* EROS 2b). [Greek lit. 'death']

thane *noun hist.* **1** (in Anglo-Saxon England) a man who held land from an English king or other superior by military service, ranking between ordinary freemen and hereditary nobles. **2** (in medieval Scotland) a man who held land from a king and ranked with the son of an earl. □ **thane·dom** *noun* [Old English *theg(e)n* servant, soldier, from Germanic]

thank ● *transitive verb* **1** express gratitude to (*thanked her for the present*). **2** hold responsible (*you can thank yourself for that*). ● *noun* (in *pl.*) **1** gratitude (*expressed his heartfelt thanks*). **2** an expression of gratitude (*give thanks to Heaven*). ● *interjection* (in *pl.*) (also **thanks a lot**) **1** used as an expression of gratitude; thank you (*thanks for your help*). **2** *ironic* used to express disappointment, anger, etc. at the action of another. □ **give thanks** say grace at a meal. **I will thank you to** *ironic* (implying reproach) I'd rather you would; I would ask you to (*I'll thank you to mind your own business!*). **no thanks to** despite. **thank goodness** (or **God** or **heavens** etc.) **1** *informal* an expression of relief or pleasure. **2** an expression of pious gratitude. **thanks to** as a (good or bad) result of (*thanks to my quick thinking; thanks to your stupid idea*). [Old English *thancian, thanc* from Germanic, related to THINK]

thank·ful *adjective* **1** grateful, appreciative, pleased, relieved. **2** (of words or acts) expressive of thanks. □ **thank·ful·ness** *noun*

thank·ful·ly *adverb* **1** in a thankful manner. **2** let us be thankful; fortunately (*thankfully, nobody was hurt*).

thank·less *adjective* **1** not expressing or feeling gratitude; ungrateful. **2** (of a task etc.) giving no pleasure or profit; not likely to win or receive thanks. □ **thank·less·ly** *adverb* **thank·less·ness** *noun*

Thanks·giv·ing *noun* **1** *Cdn* **a** (in full **Thanksgiving Day**) an annual holiday, originally for giving thanks to God for the success of the harvest, celebrated on the second Monday in October. **b** (in full **Thanksgiving weekend**) the long weekend ending with Thanksgiving Day. **2** *US* **a** (in full **Thanksgiving Day**) a similar holiday observed annually on the fourth Thursday in November. **b** (in full **Thanksgiving weekend**) the long weekend beginning with Thanksgiving Day and usu. lasting until Sunday. **3** (**thanksgiving**) **a** the expression of thanks or gratitude, esp. to God. **b** a form of words used for this. **4** (**thanksgiving**) a public celebration, marked with religious services, held as an expression of gratitude for divine favour.

thank you ● *interjection* **1** a polite formula acknowledging and expressing gratitude for a gift, favour, service, inquiry into one's health, etc. **2** used to emphasize a preceding statement, esp. one implying refusal or denial (*I said no, thank you*). ● *noun informal* **1** an instance of expressing gratitude or appreciation (*we would like to extend a warm thank you to all our customers*). **2** (*attributive*) (usu. **thank-you**) designating a gesture etc. intended as a way of expressing appreciation or gratitude (*thank-you gift*).

Thant /ˈθant/ **U** (1909–74), Burmese diplomat, Secretary-General of the United Nations 1961–71. He helped to resolve several international crises, including the Cuban missile crisis (1962), the India-Pakistan conflict in Kashmir (1965), and the Arab-Israeli Six Day War (1967).

Thar Desert /tɑr/ (also known as **Great Indian Desert**) a desert region to the east of the Indus River, lying in the Rajasthan and Gujarat states of NW India and the Punjab and Sind regions of SE Pakistan.

Tharp, Twyla (b.1942), US dancer and choreographer. Her numerous works blend ballet and modern dance styles, incorporating elements of American popular culture, and include *Deuce Coupe* (1973) *Push Comes to Shove* (1976) and several Broadway shows.

that ● *demonstrative pronoun* (*pl.* **those**) **1** the person or thing indicated, named, or understood, esp. when observed by the speaker or when familiar to the person addressed (*I heard that; who is that in the garden?; I knew that before; that's not fair*). **2** (contrasted with *this*) the further or less immediate or obvious etc. of two (*this bag is much heavier than that*). **3** the action, behaviour, or circumstances just observed or mentioned (*don't do that again*). **4** (esp. in relative constructions) the one, the person, etc., described or specified in some way (*those who have cars can take the luggage; those unfit for use; a table like that described above*). **5** (*pl.* **that**) used instead of *which* or *whom* to introduce a defining clause, esp. one essential to identification (*the book that you sent me; there is nothing here that matters*). **6** (on the telephone etc.) the person spoken to (*who is that?*). **7** *Brit. informal* referring to a strong feeling just mentioned (*'Are you glad?' 'I am that'*). ● *demonstrative adjective* (*pl.* **those**) **1** designating the person or thing indicated, named, understood, etc. (*compare* sense 1 of *pronoun*) (*look at that dog; what was that noise?; things were easier in those days*). **2** contrasted with *this* (*compare* sense 2 of *pronoun*) (*this bag is*

heavier than that one). **3** expressing strong feeling (*I will not soon forget that day*). ● *adverb* **1** to such a degree; so (*have done that much; I won't go that far*). **2** *informal* very (*not that good*). **3** at which, on which, etc. (*at the speed that he was going he could not stop; the day that I first met her*). ¶ Often omitted in this sense, e.g. *the day I first met her.* ● *conjunction* introducing a subordinate clause indicating: **1** a statement or hypothesis (*they say that he is better; there is no doubt that he meant it*). **2** a purpose (*we live that we may eat*). **3** a result (*I am so sleepy that I cannot keep my eyes open*). **4** a reason or cause (*is it that she's busy?*). **5** a wish (*Oh, that summer were here!*). ¶ Often omitted in senses 1 and 3, e.g. *they say he is better.* □ **all that** very (*I'm not all that tired*). **and all that** (or **and that**) *informal* and all or various things associated with or similar to what has been mentioned. **like that 1** of that kind (*is fond of books like that*). **2** in that manner, as you are doing, as he has been doing, etc. (*wish they would not talk like that*). **3** *informal* without effort (*did the job like that*). **4** of that character (*you'll have to forgive him, he's like that about money*). **that is** (or **that is to say**) a formula introducing or following an explanation of a preceding word or words. **that's** *informal* you are (by virtue of present or future obedience etc.) (*that's a good boy*). **that's more like it** an acknowledgement of improvement. **that's right** an expression of approval or assent. **that's that** a formula concluding a narrative or discussion or indicating completion of a task. **that there** *slang* = sense 1 of *adjective*. **that will do** no more is needed or desirable. [Old English *thæt*, nominative & accusative sing. neuter of demonstrative pron. & adj. *se, sēo, thæt* from Germanic; *those* from Old English *thās* pl. of *thes* THIS]

that·away *adverb esp. N Amer. informal* or *jocular* **1** (esp. with reference to the route taken by an object of pursuit) in that direction (*he went thataway*). **2** in that manner; like that.

thatch ● *noun* **1 a** a covering for a roof made of straw, reeds, palm leaves, or similar material. **b** the material used to make such a covering. **c** (*attributive*) designating a hut, cottage, roof, etc. having such a covering. **2 a** a matted layer of plant debris etc. on a lawn. **b** material forming such a layer. **3** *informal* a covering of some material, such as the hair of the head. **4 a** any of several palms used for thatching, e.g. the palmetto thatch, *Thrinax parviflora.* **b** the leaves of this tree used for thatching. ● *transitive verb* **1** cover (a roof or a building) with thatch. **2** remove (thatch) from a lawn; dethatch. □ **thatch·er** *noun* **thatch·ing** *noun* [Old English *theccan* 'cover']

thatched *adjective* **1** made of, covered, or roofed with thatch (*thatched hut*). **2 a** covered with something resembling thatch. **b** arranged in a manner similar to thatch (*thatched hair*).

Thatch·er ▶ **1 Mar·garet Hilda, Baron·ess Thatch·er of Kes·teven** (b.1925), English Conservative politician, prime minister 1979–90. Britain's first woman prime minister, she emphasized monetarist policies, privatization of nationalized industries, and anti-union legislation; she was renowned for her determination and resolve (she had been dubbed the 'Iron Lady' as early as 1976), esp. in her handling of the Falklands War of 1982, and resigned after a leadership challenge. **2 (Wil·bert) Ross** (1917–71), Canadian politician, Liberal premier of Saskatchewan 1964–71.

Thatch·er·ism *noun* the political and economic policies advocated by Margaret Thatcher. □ **Thatch·er·ite** *noun & adjective*

thauma·turge /ˈθɔməˌtɜrdʒ/ *noun* (also **thauma·tur·gist** /ˈθɔməˌtɜrdʒəst/) a person who works wonders or performs miracles. □ **thauma·tur·gic** *adjective* **thauma·tur·gic·al** *adjective* **thauma·turgy** *noun* [medieval Latin *thaumaturgus* from Greek *thaumatourgos* (adj.) from *thauma -matos* marvel + *-ergos* -working]

thaw ● *verb* **1** *intransitive* (often foll. by *out*) **a** (of ice, snow, or something that is frozen) pass into a liquid or unfrozen state. **b** (of a person or part of the body) warm up after being very cold. **2** *intransitive* (usu. prec. by *it* as subject) (of the weather) become warm enough to melt snow and ice etc. (*it began to thaw*). **3** *transitive* (often foll. by *out*) cause (something frozen or very cold) to melt or warm up; defrost. **4** *transitive & intransitive* make or become animated or amicable after a period of hostility or animosity. ● *noun* **1** the act or an instance of thawing. **2** a period of warmer weather marked by the rise of temperature above the freezing point and the melting of snow and ice. **3** *Politics* a reduction in the hostility or formality of relations; an increase in friendliness or cordiality. [Old English *thawian* from West Germanic; origin unknown]

THC *abbreviation* tetrahydrocannabinol, the active principle of cannabis.

the ● *definite article* **1** denoting one or more people or things already mentioned, under discussion, implied, or familiar (*gave the man a wave; will let the matter drop; shot myself in the foot*). **2** serving to describe as unique (*the Queen; the St. Lawrence*). **3 a** (foll. by defining adj.) which is, who are, etc. (*ignored the embarrassed Mr. Smith; Edward the Seventh*). **b** (foll. by adj. used *absol.*) denoting a class described (*from the sublime to* *the ridiculous).* **4** best known or best entitled to the name (with *the* stressed: *no relation to the Kipling; this is the book on this subject).* **5** used to indicate a following defining clause or phrase (*the book that you borrowed; the best I can do for you; the bottom of a well).* **6 a** used to indicate that a singular noun represents a species, class, etc. (*the cat loves comfort; is there a future for the novel?; plays the harp well).* **b** used with a noun which figuratively represents an occupation, pursuit, etc. (*went on the stage; too fond of the bottle).* **c** (foll. by the name of a unit) a, per (*20 kilometres to the litre).* **d** designating a disease, affliction, etc. (*the measles; the blues).* **7** (foll. by a unit of time) the present, the past (*man of the moment; questions of the day; book of the month).* **8** *Brit. informal* my, our. **9** *Brit.* used before the surname of the chief of a Scottish or Irish clan (*the Grant).* **10** *Brit. dialect* (esp. in Wales) used with a noun characterizing the occupation of the person whose name precedes. ● *adverb* (preceding comparatives in expressions of proportional variation) in or by that (or such a) degree; on that account (*the more the merrier; the more he gets the more he wants).* □ **all the** in the full degree to be expected (*that makes it all the worse).* **so much the** (tautologically) so much, in that degree (*so much the worse for him).* [(adj.) Old English, replacing *se, sēo, that* (= THAT), from Germanic: (adv.) from Old English *thȳ, thē,* instrumental case]

the·atre *noun* (also **the·ater**) **1 a** a building or an outdoor facility in which plays etc. are performed in front of an audience. **b** a movie theatre. **2 a** forms of entertainment performed in theatres, such as plays, opera, dance, or music. **b** theatrical or dramatic entertainment of a specified quality (*makes good theatre).* **c** in names of theatrical, esp. dance, companies (*Toronto Dance Theatre).* **3 a** the writing, production, and performance of plays. **b** the drama of a particular author, period, or place (*Restoration theatre).* **4 a** a place where action takes place in public view; a scene or field of action (*the theatre of war).* **b** (*attributive*) designating weapons intermediate between tactical and strategic (*theatre nuclear missiles).* **5** (in full **operating theatre**) = OPERATING ROOM. **6** a room or hall for lectures etc. with seats in tiers. [Old French *t(h)eatre* from Latin *theatrum* from Greek *theatron* from *theaomai* behold]

theatre·goer *noun* a person who often attends theatres. □ **theatre·going** *noun & adjective*

theatre-in-the-round *noun* a dramatic performance on a stage surrounded by spectators on at least three sides.

theatre of the absurd *noun* drama portraying the futility and anguish of human struggle in a senseless and inexplicable world.

theat·ric·al ● *adjective* **1** of or for the theatre; of acting or actors. **2 a** (of a manner, speech, or gesture) calculated for effect; showy, histrionic. **b** (of a person) artificial, affected. ● *noun* **1** (usu. in *pl.*) a dramatic performance (*amateur theatricals).* **2** (usu. in *pl.*) a professional actor or actress. **3** (in *pl.*) theatrics. □ **theat·ric·al·ism** *noun* **theat·ric·al·ity** *noun* **theat·ric·al·ize** *transitive verb* (also esp. *Brit.* **-ise).** **theat·ric·al·iza·tion** *noun* **theat·ric·al·ly** *adverb*

theatrical release *noun* the release of a film in movie theatres.

theat·rics *plural noun* **1** showy dramatic gestures, exaggerated behaviour and display of emotion; histrionics (*the lawyer tried to impress the jury with courtroom theatrics).* **2** the art of staging or performing plays.

thebe /ˈθeɪbeɪ/ *noun* (*pl.* same) a monetary unit of Botswana, equal to one-hundredth of a pula. [Setswana, = shield]

Thebes /θiːbz/ **1** the Greek name for an ancient city of Upper Egypt, whose ruins are situated on the Nile about 675 km (420 miles) south of Cairo. It was the capital of ancient Egypt under the 18th dynasty (*c.*1550–1290 BC). **2** a city in Greece, in Boeotia, northwest of Athens. Traditionally founded by Cadmus and the seat of the legendary king Oedipus, Thebes became a major military power in ancient Greece following the defeat of the Spartans at the battle of Leuctra in 371 BC, and was destroyed by Alexander the Great in 336 BC. □ **Theb·an** *adjective & noun*

theca /ˈθiːkə/ *noun* (*pl.* **thecae** /-siː/) **1** *Bot.* a receptacle, sheath, or cell, esp. one enclosing some organ, part, or structure. **2** *Anat.* an envelope of hormonally active cells enclosing a tertiary or a mature ovarian follicle. [Latin from Greek *thēkē* case]

thé dan·sant /ˌteɪ dɑˈsɑ̃/ *noun* = TEA DANCE. [French]

thee *pronoun* objective case of THOU[1]. [Old English]

theft *noun* **1** the act or an instance of stealing. **2** *Law* dishonest appropriation of another's property with intent to deprive him or her of it permanently. [Old English *thīefth, thēofth,* later *thēoft,* from Germanic (as THIEF)]

the·ine /ˈθiːiːn/ *noun* caffeine, esp. that obtained from tea and originally thought to be a different substance. [modern Latin *thea* tea + -INE[4]]

their *possessive adjective* (*attributive*) **1** of or belonging to them or themselves (*their house; their own business).* **2** (**Their**) (in titles) that they are (*Their Majesties).* **3** disputed as a third person sing. indefinite meaning 'his or her' (*has anyone lost their keys?).* ¶ See Usage Note at THEY. [Old Norse *theirra* of them, genitive pl. of *sá* THE, THAT]

theirs *possessive pronoun* **1** the one or ones belonging to or associated with them (*it is theirs; theirs are over here).* **2** disputed the one or ones belonging to an indefinite singular antecedent (*each of them brought theirs).* □ **of theirs** of or belonging to them (*a friend of theirs).*

their·selves *pronoun disputed* = THEMSELVES. ¶ *Theirselves* is not generally considered acceptable in written or even spoken language.

the·ism /ˈθiːɪzəm/ *noun* belief in the existence of gods or a god, esp. one God supernaturally revealed to man (*compare* DEISM), who created and intervenes in the universe. □ **the·ist** *noun* **the·is·tic** *adjective* **the·is·tic·al** *adjective* **the·is·tic·al·ly** *adverb* [Greek *theos* god + -ISM]

The·lon River /ˈθiːlɒn/ a river in northern Canada, 904 km long, which rises east of Great Slave Lake in the NWT, flows through Nunavut to Baker Lake, and empties into Chesterfield Inlet on Hudson Bay. [Chipewyan, = whitefish]

them ● *pronoun* objective case of THEY (*I saw them).* **2** *informal* they (*it's them again; is older than them).* **3** disputed him or her; used in relation to a singular noun or pronoun of undetermined gender (*if anyone comes, ask them to wait).* ¶ See Usage Note at THEY. ● *adjective slang* or *dialect* those (*them bones).* [Middle English *theim* from Old Norse: see THEY]

the·mat·ic /θiˈmatɪk/ ● *adjective* **1** of or relating to subjects or topics (*thematic philately; the arrangement of the anthology is thematic).* **2** *Music* of melodic subjects (*thematic treatment).* **3** *Grammar* **a** of or belonging to a theme (*thematic vowel; thematic form).* **b** (of a form of a verb) having a thematic vowel. ● *noun* (in *pl.*; treated as *sing.* or *pl.*) the themes or subjects in a text esp. for study or discussion. □ **the·mat·ic·al·ly** *adverb*

thema·tize /ˈθiːmətaɪz/ *transitive verb* (also esp. *Brit.* **-tise**) make thematic; present or select as a theme or topic of discourse. □ **thema·tiz·a·tion** *noun*

theme ● *noun* **1 a** a subject or topic on which a person speaks, writes, or thinks; a topic of discussion etc. **b** a dominant subject or motif in a work of art; a topic of composition. **2** *Music* a prominent or frequently recurring melody or group of notes in a composition. **3** = THEME SONG 1. **4** *US* a school exercise, esp. an essay, on a given subject. **5** *Grammar* the stem of a noun or verb; the part to which inflections are added, esp. composed of the root and an added vowel. **6** (*attributive*) denoting a restaurant or pub in which the decor and food and drink served suggest a particular country, historical period, or other ambience (*theme bars sprang up in town centres).* ● *transitive verb* (esp. as **themed** *adjective*) design (an event, leisure park, restaurant, etc.) around a theme to unify ambience, decor, etc. [ultimately from Greek *thema -matos* from *tithēmi* set, place]

theme park *noun* an amusement park organized around a unifying idea.

theme song *noun* (also *Brit.* **theme tune**) **1** esp. *N Amer.* a distinctive tune used to introduce a particular program or performer on television or radio. **2** a recurrent melody in a musical play or film.

Them·is /ˈθemɪs/ *Gk Myth* a goddess, daughter of Uranus (Heaven) and Gaia (Earth), although sometimes also identified with Gaia. In Homer she was the personification of order and justice, who convened the assembly of the gods.

The·mis·to·cles /θiˈmɪstəˌkliːz/ (*c.*528–462 BC) Athenian statesman. Under his command the Athenian fleet which he had built up defeated the Persian fleet at Salamis in 480; in the following years he lost influence, was ostracized in 470, and eventually fled to the Persians in Asia Minor, where he died.

them·self *pronoun disputed* = THEMSELVES 3 (*anyone can hurt themself).*

them·selves *pronoun* **1 a** emphatic form of THEY or THEM. **b** reflexive form of THEM; (*compare* HERSELF). **2** in their normal state of body or mind (*are quite themselves again).* **3** (also **them·self**) disputed (referring back to an indefinite pronoun) himself, herself; himself or herself (*everyone kept it to themselves).* ¶ The use of *themselves* or *themself* in sense 3 is considered erroneous by some people. See Usage Note at THEY. □ **be themselves** act in their normal, unconstrained manner.

then ● *adverb* **1** at that time; at the time in question (*was then too busy; then comes the trouble; the then existing laws).* **2 a** next, afterwards; after that (*then he told me to come in).* **b** and also (*then, there are the children to consider).* **c** after all (*it is a problem, but then that is what we are here for).* **3 a** in that case; therefore; it follows that (*then you should have said so).* **b** if what you say is true (*but then why did you take it?).* **c** (implying grudging or impatient concession) if you must have it so (*all right then, have it your own way*). **d** used parenthetically to resume a narrative etc. (*the policeman, then, knocked on the door*). ● *attributive adjective* (often in combination) that or who was such at the time (*the then artistic director*). ● *noun* that time (*until then*). □ **but then** but, that being so; but on the other hand. **then again** on the other hand (*see* HAND). **then and there** immediately and on the spot. [Old English *thanne, thonne*, etc., from Germanic, related to THAT, THE]

thence *adverb* (also **from thence**) *archaic* or *literary* **1** from that place or source. **2** for that reason. **3** = THENCEFORTH. [Middle English *thennes* from Old English *thanon(e)* etc. from West Germanic]

thence·forth *adverb* (also **from thenceforth**) *archaic* or *literary* from that time onward.

thence·for·ward *adverb archaic* or *literary* thenceforth.

theo- *combining form* God or gods. [Greek from *theos* god]

theo·bro·mine /θiə'broʊmiːn/ *noun* a bitter white alkaloid obtained from cacao seeds, related to caffeine. [*Theobroma* cacao genus: modern Latin from Greek *theos* god + *brōma* food, + -INE⁴]

theo·cen·tric *adjective* having God as its centre. □ **theo·cen·trism** *noun*

theoc·racy /θiː'ɒkrəsi/ *noun* (*pl.* **-cies**) **1** a form of government by God or a god directly or by a priestly order etc. claiming divine commission. **2** a state so governed. □ **theo·crat** *noun* **theo·crat·ic** *adjective*

Theoc·ri·tus /θiː'ɒkrɪtəs/ (*c.*310–*c.*250 BC), Greek poet, born in Sicily. His bucolic idylls, hexameter poems presenting the song contests and love songs of imaginary shepherds, were the model for Virgil's *Eclogues* and for subsequent pastoral poetry. □ **Theoc·ri·tean** /θiː,ɒkrɪ'tiːən/ *adjective*

theod·icy /θiː'ɒdɪsi/ *noun* (*pl.* **-cies**) **1** the vindication or defence of divine providence in view of the existence of evil. **2** an instance of this. [THEO- + Greek *dikē* justice]

theod·o·lite /θiː'ɒdə,laɪt/ *noun* a surveying instrument for measuring horizontal and vertical angles with a rotating telescope. [16th c. *theodelitus*, of unknown origin]

Theo·dora /θiə'dɔːrə/ (*c.*500–48), Byzantine empress, wife of Justinian. She is reputed (according to Procopius) to have led a dissolute life in her early years, and later became noted for her intellect and learning; as Justinian's closest adviser, she exercised a considerable influence on political affairs and the theological questions of the time.

Theo·dor·akis /,θiədə'rɒkɪs/ **Mikis** (b.1925), Greek composer and politician. A member of the Greek Parliament 1964–7, he was imprisoned by the new military government for his left-wing political activities (1967–70), but released after worldwide protests. His compositions include the ballet *Antigone* (1958), the score for the film *Zorba the Greek* (1965), and the opera *Kostas Kariotakis* (1985).

Theo·doric /θiː'ɒdərɪk/ (known as Theodoric the Great) (*c.*454–526), king of the Ostrogoths 471–526. He invaded Italy in 488 and completed its conquest in 493, establishing a kingdom with the capital at Ravenna; at its greatest extent his empire included the Italian mainland, Sicily, Dalmatia, and parts of Germany.

Theo·do·sius I /θiːə'doʊsiəs/ (known as Theodosius the Great; full name Flavius Theodosius) (*c.*346–95), Roman emperor 379–95. He was proclaimed co-emperor (379) by the Emperor Gratian (359–83), took control of the Eastern Empire, and later installed his son on the western throne (393); a pious Christian, he banned all forms of pagan worship in 391.

theog·ony /θiː'ɒgəni/ *noun* (*pl.* **-nies**) **1** the genealogy of the gods. **2** an account of this. [THEO- + Greek *-gonia* begetting]

theo·lo·gian /θiə'loʊdʒən/ *noun* a person trained in theology.

theo·logic·al /θiə'lɒdʒɪkəl/ *adjective* of theology. □ **theo·logic·ally** *adverb*

theological virtue *noun* one of the principal virtues of Christian theology: faith, hope, and charity (*compare* CARDINAL VIRTUE).

theol·ogy /θiː'ɒlədʒi/ *noun* (*pl.* **-gies**) **1 a** the branch of knowledge dealing with esp. theistic religion; the study of the nature, attributes, and governance of God. **b** a particular system or theory of (esp. Christian) religion. **c** the rational analysis of a religious faith. **2** a system of theoretical principles, esp. an impractical or rigid ideology. □ **theol·o·gist** *noun* **theol·o·gize** *transitive & intransitive verb* (also esp. *Brit.* **-gise**). [Old French *theologie* from Latin *theologia* from Greek (as THEO-, -LOGY)]

theoph·any /θiː'ɒfəni/ *noun* (*pl.* **-ies**) a visible manifestation of God or a god. [ultimately from Greek *theophaneia*, as THEO- + *phainein* show]

Theo·phras·tus /θiə'fræstəs/ (*c.*370–*c.*287 BC), Greek philosopher and scientist. He continued the method and research of his teacher Aristotle, with a particular emphasis on empirical observation; his few surviving works include treatises on botany and other scientific subjects, and the *Characters*, a collection of sketches of psychological types.

theo·phyl·line /θiə'fɪliːn, -lɪn/ *noun* an alkaloid similar to theobromine, found in tea leaves. [irreg. from modern Latin *thea* tea + Greek *phullon* leaf + -INE⁴]

the·orbo /θiː'ɔːboʊ/ *noun* (*pl.* **-orbos**) a two-necked musical instrument of the lute class much used in the 17th c. □ **the·orb·ist** *noun* [Italian *tiorba*, of unknown origin]

theor·em /'θiːrəm, 'θiːərəm/ *noun* esp. *Math.* **1** a general proposition not self-evident but proved by a chain of reasoning; a truth established by means of accepted truths (*compare* PROBLEM 4b). **2** a rule in algebra etc., esp. one expressed by symbols or formulae (*binomial theorem*). [French *théorème* or Late Latin *theorema* from Greek *theōrēma* speculation, proposition, from *theōreō* look at]

theor·etic /θiə'retɪk/ ● *adjective* = THEORETICAL. ● *noun* (in *sing.* or *pl.*) the theoretical part of a science etc.

theor·etic·al /θiə'retɪkəl/ *adjective* **1** concerned with knowledge but not with its practical application. **2** based on theory rather than experience or practice. **3** existing only in theory; ideal, hypothetical. □ **theor·etic·al·ly** *adverb*

theor·eti·cian /,θiːrə'tɪʃən/ *noun* a person concerned with the theoretical aspects of a subject.

theor·ist *noun* a holder or inventor of a theory or theories.

theor·ize *verb* (also esp. *Brit.* **-ise**) **1** *intransitive* form or construct theories; indulge in theories. **2** *transitive* consider or devise in theory. □ **theor·iz·a·tion** *noun* **theor·iz·er** *noun*

theory *noun* (*pl.* **-ies**) **1** a supposition or system of ideas explaining something, esp. one based on general principles independent of the particular things to be explained (*opp.* HYPOTHESIS 2) (*atomic theory; theory of evolution*). **2** a speculative (esp. fanciful) view (*one of my pet theories*). **3** (the sphere of) abstract knowledge or speculative thought (*this is all very well in theory, but how will it work in practice?; has been studying theory*). **4** the principles on which a subject of study is based (*the theory of music; economic theory*). **5** *Math.* a collection of propositions to illustrate the principles of a subject (*probability theory; theory of equations*). [Greek *theōria* from *theōros* spectator, from *theōreō* look at]

theos·o·phy /θiː'ɒsəfi/ *noun* any of various philosophies professing to achieve a knowledge of God by spiritual ecstasy, direct intuition, or special individual relations, esp. a modern movement following Hindu and Buddhist teachings and seeking universal fellowship. □ **theo·soph·ic** /θiə'sɒfɪk/ *adjective* **theo·soph·ic·al** /θiə'sɒfɪkəl/ *adjective* **theos·o·phist** *noun* [medieval Latin *theosophia* from late Greek *theosophia* from *theosophos* wise concerning God (as THEO-, *sophos* wise)]

The Pas /ðə 'pɒ/ a town in west central Manitoba, situated on the Saskatchewan River, about 125 km southeast of Flin Flon; pop. (2001) 5,795. [ultimately from Cree *opasquaow* narrows between wooded banks]

Thera /'θiːrə/ a Greek island in the S Cyclades. Transformed by a violent volcanic eruption in about 1500 BC (which may have provided the basis for the myth of Atlantis), it now consists of the remaining eastern rim of the volcano, with steep cliffs rising above a lagoon. There are important archaeological sites, remains of an ancient Minoan civilization. The island is also called Santorini.

thera·peut·ic /,θerə'pjuːtɪk/ *adjective* **1** of, for, or contributing to the cure of disease. **2** contributing to general, esp. mental, well-being (*finds walking therapeutic*). □ **thera·peut·ic·ally** *adverb*

therapeutic abortion *noun* an abortion performed for the physical or mental health of the pregnant woman.

therapeutic cloning *noun* a technique for producing new human cells or organs using genetic material from the person requiring a transplant or other treatment.

thera·peut·ics /,θerə'pjuːtɪks/ *plural noun* (usu. treated as *sing.*) the branch of medicine concerned with the treatment of disease and the action of remedial agents. [ultimately from Greek *therapeutika* from *therapeuō* wait on, cure]

ther·apist *noun* a person who practises or administers therapy, esp. a psychotherapist.

ther·ap·sid /θe'ræpsɪd/ ● *noun* a fossil reptile of the order Therapsida, related to the ancestors of mammals. ● *adjective* of or relating to this order. [modern Latin *Therapsida*, from Greek *thēr* 'beast' + (*h*)*apsis* -*idos* 'arch' (referring to the structure of the skull)]

ther·apy *noun* (*pl.* **-apies**) **1** the treatment of physical or mental disorders, other than by surgery. **2** a particular type of such treatment. □ **ther·ap·ize** *transitive verb* (also esp. *Brit.* **-ise**) [modern Latin *therapia* from Greek *therapeia* healing]

Thera·vada /ˌθerəˈvʊdə/ *noun* a more conservative form of Buddhism, practised in Sri Lanka, Burma (now Myanmar), Thailand, etc. [Pali *theravāda* from *thera* elder, old + *vāda* speech, doctrine]

there ● *adverb* **1** in, at, or to that place or position (*lived there for some years; goes there every day*). **2** at that point (in speech, performance, writing, etc.) (*there he stopped*). **3** in that respect (*I agree with you there*). **4** used for emphasis in calling attention (*hello there!; there goes the bell; that bike there is mine*). **5** used to indicate the fact or existence of something (*there is a house on the corner*). ● *noun* that place (*lives somewhere near there*). ● *interjection* **1** expressing confirmation, triumph, satisfaction, etc. (*there! what did I tell you?*). **2** used to soothe a child etc. (*there, there, never mind*). □ **be there for someone** be ready to give support etc. **have been there before** *slang* know all about it. **so there** *informal* expressing defiance or defiant triumph. **there and then** immediately and on the spot. **there it is** that is the situation; nothing can be done about it. **there you are** (or **go**) *informal* **1** this is what you wanted etc. **2** expressing confirmation, triumph, resignation, etc. [Old English *thær, ther* from Germanic, related to THAT, THE]

there·abouts *adverb* (also **there·about**) **1** near that place (*ought to be somewhere thereabouts*). **2** near that number, quantity, etc. (*two litres or thereabouts*).

there·after *adverb* *formal* after that.

there·at *adverb* *archaic* **1** at that place. **2** on that account. **3** after that.

there·by *adverb* by that means, as a result of that. □ **thereby hangs a tale** much could be said about that.

there·for *adverb* *formal* for that object or purpose.

there·fore *adverb* for that reason; accordingly, consequently.

there·from *adverb* *archaic* from that or it.

there·in *adverb* *formal* **1** in or into that place etc. **2** in that respect; in that matter.

there·in·after *adverb* *formal* later in the same document etc.

there·in·to *adverb* *archaic* into that place.

ther·emin /ˈθerəmin/ *noun* an electronic musical instrument in which the tone is generated by two high-frequency oscillators and the pitch controlled by the movement of the performer's hand towards and away from the circuit. [L. *Theremin*, Russian inventor d.1993]

there·of *adverb* *formal* of that or it.

there·on *adverb* *archaic* on that or it (of motion or position).

there's *contraction* **1** there is. **2** esp. *Brit. informal* you are (by virtue of present or future obedience etc.) (*there's a dear*).

Ther·esa, Moth·er see TERESA, MOTHER.

Thé·rèse of Li·sieux, St. see TERESA OF LISIEUX, ST.

there·to *adverb* *formal* that or it.

there·to·fore *adverb* *formal* before that time.

there·under *adverb* *formal* **1** in accordance with that. **2** stated below that (in the document etc.).

there·unto *adverb* *archaic* to that or it.

there·upon *adverb* **1** in consequence of that. **2** soon or immediately after that. **3** *archaic* upon that (of motion or position).

there·with *adverb* *archaic* **1** with that. **2** soon or immediately after that.

ther·mal ● *adjective* **1** of, for, or producing heat. **2** promoting the retention of heat (*thermal underwear*). **3** of or pertaining to a process of computer printing in which fine heated pins form characters on heat-sensitive paper (*thermal printer; thermal paper*). ● *noun* **1** a rising current of heated air (used by gliders, balloons, and birds to gain height). **2** (in *pl.*) thermal underwear. □ **ther·mal·ly** *adverb*

thermal conductivity *noun* the rate at which heat passes through a substance, expressed as the amount of heat that flows per unit time through unit area with a temperature gradient of one degree per unit distance.

thermal imaging *noun* the technique of using the heat given off by an object etc. to produce an image of it or locate it.

thermal spring *noun* a spring of naturally hot water.

ther·mic *adjective* of or relating to heat.

thermi·dor *see* LOBSTER THERMIDOR.

ther·mion /ˈθɜrmiˌɒn/ *noun* an ion or electron emitted by a substance at high temperature. □ **ther·mion·ic** *adjective* **ther·mion·ics** *plural noun* (treated as *sing.*). [THERMO- + ION]

thermionic valve *noun* (also **thermionic tube**) a device giving a flow of thermionic electrons in one direction, used esp. in the rectification of a current and in radio reception.

ther·mis·tor /θɜrˈmɪstər/ *noun* *Electricity* a resistor whose resistance is greatly reduced by heating, used for measurement and control. [*thermal resistor*]

ther·mite *noun* a mixture of finely powdered aluminum and iron oxide that produces a very high temperature on combustion (used in welding and for incendiary bombs). [German *Thermit* (as THERMO-, -ITE¹)]

thermo- *combining form* denoting heat. [Greek from *thermos* hot, *thermē* heat]

thermo·baric *adjective* denoting or relating to a very large fuel-air bomb which ignites into a fireball when detonated, creating a powerful wave of pressure that sucks out oxygen from any confined spaces nearby. [THERMO- + Greek *barus* 'heavy']

thermo·chem·istry *noun* the branch of chemistry dealing with the quantities of heat evolved or absorbed during chemical reactions. □ **thermo·chem·ical** *adjective*

thermo·cline *noun* **1** a temperature gradient, esp. an abrupt one in a body of water. **2** a layer of water marked by an abrupt temperature change. [THERMO- + Greek *klinō* 'to slope']

thermo·couple *noun* a thermoelectric device for measuring temperature, consisting of two wires of different metals connected at two points, a voltage being developed between the two junctions in proportion to the temperature difference.

thermo·dynam·ics *plural noun* (usu. treated as *sing.*) the science of the relations between heat and other (mechanical, electrical, etc.) forms of energy. □ **thermo·dynam·ic** *adjective* **thermo·dynam·ic·ally** *adverb* **thermo·dynami·cist** *noun*

thermo·elec·tric *adjective* relating to electricity produced by a temperature difference. □ **thermo·elec·tri·city** *noun*

thermo·gen·esis *noun* the production of heat, esp. in a human or animal body. □ **thermo·genic** *adjective*

thermo·gram *noun* a record made by a thermograph.

thermo·graph *noun* **1** an instrument that gives a continuous record of temperature. **2** an apparatus used to obtain an image produced by infrared radiation from an esp. human or animal body.

therm·og·raphy *noun* **1** the taking or use of infrared thermograms, esp. to detect tumours. **2** a process of printing, photocopying, etc. which imitates embossing by applying heat to ink and powder to create a raised image. □ **thermo·graph·ic** *adjective*

thermo·karst *noun* topography in which the eventual melting of permafrost has produced hollows, hummocks, etc., reminiscent of karst.

thermo·labile /ˌθɜrmoˈleɪbaɪl, -bɪl/ *adjective* (of a substance) unstable when heated.

thermo·lumin·es·cence /ˌθɜrmoˌluːmɪˈnesəns/ *noun* the property of becoming luminescent when pre-treated and subjected to high temperatures, used esp. as a means of dating ancient artifacts. □ **thermo·lumin·es·cent** *adjective*

therm·oly·sis /θɜrˈmɒlɪsɪs/ *noun* decomposition by the action of heat.

therm·om·eter /θɜrˈmɒmɪtər/ *noun* an instrument for measuring temperature, esp. a graduated thin glass tube containing mercury or alcohol which expands when heated. □ **thermo·met·ric** /ˌθɜrməˈmetrɪk/ *adjective* **therm·om·etry** *noun*

thermo·nuclear *adjective* **1** relating to or using nuclear reactions that occur only at very high temperatures. **2** relating to or characterized by weapons using thermonuclear reactions.

Thermo·pane *noun* *proprietary* an insulating double-glazed windowpane.

thermo·phile /ˈθɜrmoˌfaɪl/ ● *noun* a bacterium etc. growing optimally at high temperatures. ● *adjective* of or being a thermophile. □ **thermo·phil·ic** /-ˈfɪlɪk/ *adjective*

thermo·plas·tic ● *adjective* (of a substance) that becomes soft and plastic on heating and hard and rigid on cooling, and is able to repeat these processes. ● *noun* a thermoplastic substance.

Therm·opy·lae /θɜrˈmɒpəˌliː/ *noun* a pass between the mountains and the sea in Greece, about 200 km (120 miles) northwest of Athens, originally narrow but now much widened by the recession of the sea. In 480 BC it was the scene of the heroic defence by 6,000 Greeks, under the command of Leonidas, against the Persian army of Xerxes I.

Consonants: b *but*   d *dog*   f *few*   g *get*   h *her*   j *yes*   k *cat*   l *leg*   m *man*   n *no*   p *pen*   r *red*   s *sit*

thermo·regu·la·tion *noun* the regulation of temperature, esp. of body temperature. □ **thermo·regu·late** *intransitive verb* **thermo·regu·la·tory** *noun*

Ther·mos *noun* (in full **Thermos bottle**) *proprietary* an insulated flask for keeping a liquid hot or cold, esp. with a double lining enclosing a vacuum. [Greek *thermos* 'hot']

thermo·set·ting *adjective* (of plastics) setting permanently when heated. □ **thermo·set** *adjective*

thermo·sphere *noun* the region of the atmosphere beyond the mesosphere, characterized by an increase of temperature with height.

thermo·stable *adjective* (of a substance) stable when heated. □ **thermo·stabil·ity** *noun*

thermo·stat *noun* a device that automatically regulates temperature, or that activates a device when the temperature reaches a certain point. □ **thermo·stat·ic** *adjective* **thermo·stat·ic·ally** *adverb*

thero·pod /ˈθiːrəpɒd/ ● *noun* a saurischian dinosaur of the group *Theropoda*, comprising mainly bipedal carnivores, including tyrannosaurs and the possible ancestors of birds. ● *adjective* of or relating to this group. [Greek *thēr* 'beast' + *pous podos* 'foot']

the·saur·us /θəˈsɔːrəs/ *noun* (pl. **the·saur·us·es** or **the·sauri** /-raɪ/) **1** a book that lists words in groups of synonyms and related concepts. **2** a dictionary or encyclopedia. **3** a treasury. [Latin from Greek *thēsauros* 'treasure']

these *pl.* of THIS.

The·seus /ˈθiːsiəs/ *Gk Myth* the son of Poseidon (or of Aegeus, king of Athens) and husband of Phaedra. The legendary hero of Athens, he slew the Cretan Minotaur with the help of Ariadne.

thesis /ˈθiːsɪs/ *noun* (pl. **theses** /-siːz/) **1** a proposition to be maintained or proved. **2** a dissertation, esp. by a candidate for a degree. **3** /ˈθiːsɪs, ˈθesɪs/ an unstressed syllable or part of a metrical foot in Greek or Latin verse (*opp.* ARSIS). [Late Latin from Greek, = putting, placing, a proposition etc., from *the*- root of *tithēmi* place]

thesp *noun informal* = THESPIAN.

thes·pian /ˈθespiən/ ● *adjective* of or relating to tragedy or drama. ● *noun* an actor or actress. [THESPIS]

Thes·pis /ˈθespɪs/ (6th c. BC), Greek dramatic poet. He is regarded as the founder of Greek tragedy, having been named by Aristotle as the originator of the role of the actor in addition to the traditional chorus.

Thess. *abbreviation* Thessalonians (New Testament).

Thes·sa·lon·ians /ˌθesəˈloʊniənz/ either of two books of the New Testament, the earliest letters of St. Paul, written from Corinth to the new Church at Thessalonica.

Thes·sa·lon·iki /ˌθesələˈniːki/ (also **Sal·on·ika**, **Sal·on·ica** /səˈlɒnɪkə/, Latin **Thes·sal·on·ica** /ˌθesəˈlɒnɪkə, -ləˈnaɪkə/) a seaport in NE Greece; pop. (2002) 407,800. A major port and the second largest city in Greece, it is the capital of the present-day Greek region of Macedonia.

Thes·saly /ˈθesəli/ (Greek **Thes·salía** /ˌθesaˈliːa/) a region of NE Greece. □ **Thes·sa·lian** /θeˈseɪliən/ *adjective & noun*

theta /ˈθiːtə/ *noun* **1** the eighth letter of the Greek alphabet (Θ, ϑ). **2** (*attributive*) of or pertaining to electrical activity observed in the brain under certain conditions, consisting of oscillations having a frequency of 4 to 7 hertz (*theta rhythm; theta waves*). [Greek]

Thet·ford Mines an asbestos-mining city in south central Quebec, about 90 km northeast of Sherbrooke; pop. (2001) 26,323. [*Thetford* in Norfolk, England]

Thetis /ˈθetɪs/ *Gk Myth* a sea nymph, mother of Achilles.

theur·gy /ˈθiːɜːdʒi/ *noun* **1** supernatural or divine agency esp. in human affairs. **2** the art of securing this. □ **theur·gic** *adjective* **theur·gical** *adjective* [Late Latin *theurgia* from Greek *theourgia* from *theos* god + *-ergos* working]

thew /θjuː/ *noun* (esp. in *pl.*) *literary* **1** muscular strength. **2** mental or moral vigour. □ **thewy** *adjective* [Old English *thēaw* usage, conduct, of unknown origin]

they *pronoun* (obj. **them**; possessive **their**, **theirs**) **1** the people, animals, or things previously named or in question (*pl.* of HE, SHE, IT). **2** people in general (*they say we are wrong*). **3** those in authority (*they have raised the fees*). **4** *disputed* as a third person sing. indefinite pronoun meaning 'he or she' (*anyone can come if they want to*). ¶ The use of *they* instead of 'he or she' is common in spoken English and increasingly so in written English, although still deplored by some people. It is particularly useful when the sex of the person is unspecified or unknown and the writer wishes to avoid the accusation of sexism that can arise from the use of *he*. Similarly, *their* can replace 'his' or 'his or

her' and *themselves* 'himself' or 'himself or herself', e.g. *Everyone must provide their own lunch; Did anyone hurt themselves in the accident?* [Middle English *thei*, obj. *theim*, from Old Norse *their* nominative pl. masc., *theim* dative pl. of *sá* THE that]

they'd *contraction* **1** they had. **2** they would.

they'll *contraction* **1** they will. **2** they shall.

they're *contraction* they are.

they've *contraction* they have.

thia·mine /ˈθaɪəmɪn/ *noun* (also **thia·min**) a vitamin of the B complex, found in unrefined cereals, beans, and liver, a deficiency of which causes beriberi. Symbol: **T**. *Also called* VITAMIN B$_1$. [THIO- + *amin* from VITAMIN]

thick ● *adjective* **1 a** of great or specified extent between opposite surfaces (*a thick wall; a wall two metres thick*). **b** of large diameter (*a thick rope*). **2 a** (of a line etc.) broad; not fine. **b** (of script or type, etc.) consisting of thick lines. **3 a** arranged closely; crowded together; dense. **b** numerous. **4** (usu. foll. by *with*) densely covered or filled (*air thick with snow*). **5 a** firm in consistency; containing much solid matter; viscous (*a thick paste; thick soup*). **b** made of thick material (*a thick coat*). **6** muddy, cloudy; impenetrable by sight (*thick darkness*). **7** *informal* (of a person) stupid, dull. **8 a** (of a voice) indistinct. **b** (of an accent) very marked. **9** *informal* intimate or very friendly (esp. *thick as thieves*). **10** (of one's head) suffering from a headache, hangover, etc. ● *noun* a thick or dense part of anything. ● *adverb* thickly (*snow lay thick on the ground*). □ **a bit thick** *Brit. informal* unreasonable or intolerable. **in the thick of 1** at the busiest or most intense part of. **2** heavily occupied with. **lay it** (or **something**) **on thick** exaggerate. **thick and fast** in great quantity or large numbers, and rapidly or in quick succession (*plaudits arrived thick and fast*). **thick on the ground** abundant; in great quantity. **through thick and thin** under all conditions; in spite of all difficulties. □ **thick·ish** *adjective* **thick·ly** *adverb* [Old English *thicce* (adj. & adv.), from Germanic]

thick ear *noun Brit. slang* the external ear swollen as a result of a blow (esp. *give a person a thick ear*).

thick·en *verb* **1** *transitive & intransitive* make or become thick or thicker. **2** *intransitive* become more complicated (*the plot thickens*). □ **thick·en·er** *noun*

thick·en·ing *noun* **1** the process of becoming thick or thicker. **2** a substance used to thicken liquid. **3** a thickened part.

thick·et *noun* **1** a tangle of shrubs or trees. **2** a dense, oppressive quantity (*a thicket of PR men*). [Old English *thiccet* (as THICK, -ET¹)]

thick·head *noun informal* a stupid person; a blockhead. □ **thick-headed** *adjective* **thick-headed·ness** *noun*

thick·ness *noun* **1** the state of being thick. **2** the extent to which a thing is thick. **3** a layer of material of a certain thickness (*three thicknesses of cardboard*). **4** a part that is thick or lies between opposite surfaces (*steps cut in the thickness of the wall*).

thick·set *adjective* **1** heavily or solidly built. **2** set or growing close together.

thick skin *noun* **1** a thick or hard skin or outer layer. **2** *informal* insensitivity to reproach or criticism; callousness. □ **thick-skinned** *adjective*

thick-skulled *adjective* (also **thick-witted**) stupid, dull; slow to learn.

thief *noun* (pl. **thieves**) a person who steals esp. secretly and without violence. [Old English *thēof* from Germanic]

Thiers /tjeɪ/ (**Louis**) **Adolphe** (1797–1877), French statesman and historian, who led the peace negotiations following the Franco-Prussian War (1871), helped to plan the economic and military reconstruction of France, and was first president of the Third Republic (1871–3); his works include *Histoire de la Révolution française* (1823–7) and *Histoire du consulat et de l'empire* (1845–62).

thieve *verb* **1** *intransitive* (esp. as **thiev·ing** *adjective*) be a thief. **2** *transitive* steal (a thing). [Old English *thēofian* (as THIEF)]

thiev·ery *noun* the act or practice of stealing; theft.

thieves *pl.* of THIEF.

thiev·ish *adjective* **1** given to stealing. **2** of, pertaining to, or characteristic of a thief or thieves; stealthy (*thievish aims*). □ **thiev·ish·ly** *adverb* **thiev·ish·ness** *noun*

thigh *noun* **1** the part of the human leg between the hip and the knee. **2** a corresponding part in other animals. □ **-thighed** *adjective* (in combination). [Old English *thēh, thēoh, thīoh*, Old High German *dioh*, Old Norse *thjó* from Germanic]

thigh bone *noun* = FEMUR.

thigh-high ● *adjective* reaching to the thighs (*thigh-high boots; a thigh-high skirt*). ● *noun* (in *pl.*) thigh-high stockings etc.

thigh-slapper *noun informal* an exceptionally funny joke, description, etc. □ **thigh-slapping** *adjective*

thim·ble *noun* **1 a** a metal or plastic cap, usu. with a closed end, worn to protect the finger and push the needle in sewing. **b** = THIMBLEFUL. **2** *Mech.* a short metal tube or ferrule etc. **3** *Naut.* a metal ring concave on the outside and fitting in a loop of spliced rope to prevent chafing. [Old English *thȳmel* (as THUMB, -LE¹)]

thimble·berry *noun* (*pl.* **-berries**) any of several N American raspberries with thimble-shaped fruit.

thimble cookie *noun N Amer.* a round cookie with a jam-filled depression in the centre formed by pressing a thimble into the dough.

thimble·ful *noun* (*pl.* **-fuls**) a small quantity, esp. of liquid to drink.

thimble·rig *noun* a game often involving sleight of hand, in which three inverted thimbles or cups are moved about, contestants having to spot which is the one with a pea or other object beneath; a shell game. □ **thimble·rigger** *noun* [THIMBLE + RIG in obsolete sense 'trick, dodge']

thi·mero·sal /ˈθaɪˈmɛrəˌsal/ *noun* a crystalline antiseptic, C₉H₉HgNaO₂S. [THIO- + *mer* from MERCURY + *sal* from SALICYLATE]

Thim·phu /ˈtɪmpuː, ˈθɪm-/ (also **Thim·bu** /ˈtɪmbuː, ˈθɪm-/) the capital of Bhutan; pop. (2000) 53,600.

thin ● *adjective* (**thin·ner, thin·nest**) **1** having the opposite surfaces close together; of small thickness or diameter. **2 a** (of a line) narrow or fine. **b** (of a script or type etc.) consisting of thin lines. **3** made of thin material (*a thin dress*). **4** lean; not plump. **5 a** not dense or copious (*thin hair; a thin haze*). **b** not full or closely packed (*a thin audience*). **6** of slight consistency (*a thin paste*). **7** weak; lacking an important ingredient (*thin blood; a thin voice*). **8** (of an excuse, argument, disguise, etc.) flimsy or transparent. **9** (of a business, market, etc.) not very active or busy. **10** (of the plot of a story etc.) not very complicated or intriguing. ● *adverb* thinly (*cut the bread very thin*). ● *verb* (**thinned, thin·ning**) **1** *transitive & intransitive* make or become thin or thinner. **2** *transitive & intransitive* (often foll. by *out*) reduce; make or become less dense or crowded or numerous. **3** *transitive* (often foll. by *out*) remove some of a crop of (seedlings, saplings, etc.) or some young fruit from (a vine or tree) to improve the growth of the rest. □ **on thin ice** see ICE. **thin edge (**or **end) of the wedge** see WEDGE¹. **thin on the ground** see GROUND¹. **thin on top** balding. **wear thin** see WEAR¹. □ **thin·ly** *adverb* **thin·ness** *noun* **thin·ning** *adjective* [Old English *thynne* from Germanic]

thin air *noun* a state of invisibility or non-existence (*vanished into thin air*).

thin blue line *noun* (also **thin red line** etc.) the police or military seen as the only defence against crime, lawlessness, invasion, etc. [from the colour of police or military uniforms]

thin client *noun Computing* a client terminal with minimal processing power and storage capacity, esp. one with no hard disk.

thine *possessive pronoun archaic* or *dialect* **1** the one or ones belonging to thee. **2** (*attributive* before a vowel) = THY. [Old English *thīn* from Germanic]

thin-film *adjective* **1** (of a process or device) using or involving a very thin solid or liquid film. **2** *Electronics* denoting a miniature circuit or device consisting of a thin layer of metal or semiconductor on a ceramic or glass substrate.

thing *noun* **1** a material or non-material entity, idea, action, etc., that is or may be thought about or perceived. **2** an inanimate material object (*take that thing away*). **3** an unspecified object or item (*have a few things to buy*). **4** an act, idea, or utterance (*a silly thing to do*). **5** an event (*an unfortunate thing to happen*). **6** a quality (*patience is a useful thing*). **7** (with reference to a person) expressing pity, contempt, or affection (*poor thing!; a dear old thing*). **8** a specimen or type of something (*the latest thing in hats*). **9** *informal* one's special interest or concern (*not my thing at all*). **10** a thought, point for consideration, etc. (*and another thing...*). **11** *informal* a matter of or concerning (a preceding word) (*it's a pride thing*). **12** *Brit. informal* something remarkable (*now there's a thing!*). **13** (prec. by *the*) *informal* **a** what is conventionally proper or fashionable (*the latest thing*). **b** what is needed or required (*your suggestion was just the thing*). **c** (often foll. by *about, with*) what is important or to be considered (*the thing with them is they're always late; the thing is, shall we go or not?*). **14** (in *pl.*) personal belongings or clothing (*where have I left my things?*). **15** (in *pl.*) equipment (*painting things*). **16** (in *pl.*) affairs in general (*not in the nature of things*). **17** (in *pl.*) circumstances or conditions (*things look good*). **18** (in *pl.* with a following adjective) all that is so describable (*all things Greek*). **19** (in *pl.*) *Law* property. □ **be all things to all men** (or **people**) **1** please everyone, typically by regularly altering one's behaviour or opinions in order to conform to those of others. **2** be able to be interpreted or used differently by different people to their own satisfaction. **do one's own thing** *informal* pursue one's own interests or inclinations. **do things to** *informal* affect remarkably. **have a thing about** (or **for, with**) *informal* be obsessed about; be peculiarly interested in, repulsed by, etc. **make a thing of** *informal* **1** regard as essential. **2** cause a fuss about. **one** (or **just one**) **of those things** *informal* something unavoidable or to be accepted. □ **thing·ness** *noun* [Old English from Germanic]

thingy *noun* (also **thing·a·ma·jig, thing·a·ma·bob, thing·uma-**; also **thing·ummy**) a person or thing whose name one has forgotten or does not know or does not wish or care to mention. [THING + meaningless suffix]

thin·horn sheep *noun* a mountain sheep, *Ovis dalli* (of which there are two subspecies, DALL SHEEP and STONE SHEEP), with long, slender, pointed horns flaring away from the head.

think ● *verb* (*past* and *past participle* **thought**) **1** *transitive* (often foll. by *that* + clause) be of the opinion (*we think that they will come*). **2** *transitive* (foll. by *that* + clause or to + infin.) judge or consider (*is thought to be a fraud*). **3** *intransitive* **a** exercise the mind positively with one's ideas etc.; form connected ideas; meditate, cogitate (*let me think for a moment*). **b** have the capacity to do this. **4** *intransitive* (foll. by *of* or *about*) **a** consider; be or become mentally aware of (*think of you constantly*). **b** form or entertain the idea of; imagine to oneself (*couldn't think of such a thing*). **c** choose mentally; hit upon (*think of a number*). **5** *transitive* have a half-formed intention (*I think I'll stay*). **6** *transitive* form a conception of (*cannot think how you do it*). **7** *transitive* bring into or out of a specified condition by thinking (*cannot think away a toothache*). **8** *transitive* recognize the presence or existence of (*the child thought no harm*). **9** *transitive* (foll. by *to* + infin.) intend or expect (*thinks to deceive us*). **10** *transitive* (foll. by *to* + infin.) remember (*did not think to lock the door*). **11** *intransitive informal* (of a computer) process data. ● *noun informal* an act of thinking (*must have a think about that*). □ **have another think coming** be greatly mistaken. **think again** revise one's plans or opinions. **think ahead** direct one's thoughts to a future event or situation and plan for it. **think aloud** utter one's thoughts as soon as they occur. **think back to** recall (a past event or time). **think better of** change one's mind about (an intention) after reconsideration. **think big** see BIG *adverb* 3. **think fit** see FIT¹. **think for oneself** have an independent mind or attitude. **think little** (or **nothing**) **of** consider to be insignificant or unremarkable. **think much** (or **highly**) **of** have a high opinion of. **think on** (or **upon**) *archaic* think of or about. **think out 1** consider carefully. **2** produce (an idea etc.) by thinking. **think over** reflect upon in order to reach a decision. **think through** reflect fully upon (a problem etc.). **think twice** use careful consideration, avoid hasty action, etc. **think up** *informal* devise; produce by thought. [Old English *thencan thōhte gethōht* from Germanic]

think·able *adjective* that can be imagined as something that could possibly happen or be true; conceivable.

think·er *noun* **1** a person who thinks, esp. in a specified way (*an original thinker*). **2** a person with a skilled or powerful mind.

think·ing ● *adjective* **1** using thought or rational judgment; cogitative. **2** thoughtful, reflective, intellectual. ● *noun* opinion or judgment. □ **a thinking person's** (or **man's, woman's**) designed for intelligent people; designating an intellectual version of a designated thing etc. (*a thinking person's sitcom*). **put on one's thinking cap** *informal* meditate on a problem.

think piece *noun* an article containing discussion, analysis, opinion, etc., rather than facts or news.

think tank *noun* a body of experts, as a research organization, providing advice and ideas on specific national or commercial problems.

thin·ner *noun* a volatile liquid used to dilute paint etc.

thin·nings *plural noun* plants, trees, etc. which have been removed to improve the growth of those remaining.

thin red line *noun* see THIN BLUE LINE.

thin-skinned *adjective* **1** (esp. of fruit) having a thin skin or outer layer. **2** sensitive to reproach or criticism; easily upset.

Thin·su·late *noun proprietary* a thin batting made from very fine propylene fibres trapping tiny pockets of air to provide high thermal insulation with little bulk or weight. [blend of THIN + INSULATE]

thio- /ˈθaɪəʊ/ *combining form* sulphur, esp. replacing oxygen in compounds (*thio-acid*). [Greek *theion* sulphur]

thiol /ˈθaɪɒl/ *noun* *Chem.* any organic compound containing an alcohol-like group but with sulphur in place of oxygen. *Also called* MERCAPTAN. [THIO- + -OL¹]

thio·pen·tal sodium /ˌθaɪoʊˈpɛntəl/ *noun* a barbiturate drug used as a general anaesthetic and a hypnotic, and (reputedly) as a truth drug. *Also called* PENTOTHAL. [THIO- + PENTOBARBITAL]

thio·sul·phate /ˌθaɪoʊˈsʌlfeɪt/ *noun* (also **thio·sul·fate**) a sulphate in which one oxygen atom is replaced by sulphur.

third ● *noun* **1** the position in a sequence corresponding to that of the number 3 in the sequence 1–3. **2** something occupying this position. **3** each of three equal parts of a thing. **4** = THIRD GEAR. **5** *Music* **a** an interval or chord spanning three consecutive notes in the diatonic scale, e.g. C to E. **b** a note separated from another by this interval. **6** *Baseball* **a** the third inning. **b** = THIRD BASE. **7** *Football* = THIRD DOWN. **8** *Curling* = VICE-SKIP. **9** *Brit.* **a** a place in the third class in an examination. **b** a person having this. ● *adjective* that is the third. ● *adverb* in the third place; thirdly. □ **third·ly** *adverb* [Old English *third(d)a*, *thridda* from Germanic]

third age *noun* esp. *Brit.* the period in life of active retirement; old age.

third base *noun* *Baseball* **1** the third of the bases that must be touched to score a run. **2** the position of the player covering this base and the area of the infield surrounding it. □ **third baseman** *noun*

third-best ● *adjective* of third quality. ● *noun* a thing in this category.

third class ● *noun* **1** a set of persons or things grouped together as third-best. **2** the third-best accommodation in a train, ship, etc. **3** *Brit.* **a** the third highest division in an examination or test. **b** a place in this. ● *adjective* (often hyphenated when *attributive*) **1** belonging to, travelling by, etc. the third class. **2** of lower quality; inferior. ● *adverb* by the third class (*travels third-class*).

third degree ● *noun* long and severe questioning esp. by police to obtain information or a confession. ● *adjective* (**third-degree**) denoting burns of the most severe kind, affecting lower layers of tissue.

third down *noun* *Football* the third of three attempts (four in American football) to advance the ball ten yards in order to achieve a new first down.

third eye *noun* **1** *Hinduism & Buddhism* the 'eye of insight' in the forehead of an image of a deity, esp. the god Shiva. **2** the faculty of intuitive insight or prescience. **3** the pineal gland in certain vertebrates.

third force *noun* a group, as a political party, acting as a check on conflict between two opposing groups.

third gear *noun* the third (and in cars often next to highest) in a sequence of gears.

third-hand ● *adjective* **1** (of goods) previously owned or used by two or more consecutive owners. **2** (of information etc.) obtained after having passed from the original source through two or more intermediaries. ● *adverb* (**third hand**) through two or more intermediaries (*heard the news third hand*).

Third International *noun* = COMINTERN.

third party ● *noun* **1** a party or person besides the two primarily concerned. **2** a person involved incidentally. **3** a political party other than the two (or more) most important. **4** *Law* a person against whom a defendant commences a claim for all or part of the plaintiff's claim (also *attributive*: *third party claim*). ● *adjective* *Cdn & Brit.* (of insurance) covering damage or injury suffered by a person other than the insured (*third party liability insurance*).

third person *noun* *Grammar see* PERSON 4.

third rail *noun* **1** (in some electric railways) an extra rail which conveys the current. **2** esp. *US Politics* a highly controversial and therefore politically dangerous area of public policy.

third-rate *adjective* inferior; very poor in quality.

third reading *noun* a third presentation of a bill to a legislative assembly, in Canada to debate it for the last time in the House of Commons before it passes to the Senate, in the US to consider it for the last time, and in the UK to debate committee reports.

Third Reich *noun* the Nazi regime, 1933–45.

Third Republic *noun* *hist.* **1** the republican regime in France between the fall of Napoleon III (1870) and the German occupation of 1940. **2** this period in France.

third-string *attributive adjective* *N Amer.* (esp. of an athlete) inferior. □ **third-stringer** *noun*

Third Wave *noun* the current phase of economic, social, and cultural change (following the agrarian and industrial waves), in which knowledge is the primary productive force.

third way *noun* any option regarded as an alternative to two extremes.

third wheel *noun* *informal* a third person joining a couple in a social situation more suitable for just the couple.

Third World *noun* (usu. prec. by *the*) the developing countries of Asia, Africa, and Latin America.

thirst ● *noun* **1** an intense physical need or craving to drink something, associated with dehydration and a dryness of the throat and mouth. **2** a strong desire or craving (*a thirst for power*). ● *intransitive verb* (usu. foll. by *for*) **1** feel thirst. **2** have a strong desire. [Old English *thurst*, *thyrstan* from West Germanic]

thirst-quench·ing *adjective* that satisfies or is capable of satisfying thirst. □ **thirst-quench·er** *noun*

thirsty *adjective* (**thirst·i·er**, **thirst·i·est**) **1** having a need or desire to drink. **2** (of land, a crop, etc.) dry; needing moisture. **3** (often foll. by *for*) eager. **4** *informal* causing thirst (*thirsty work*). □ **thirst·i·ly** *adverb*

thir·teen ● *noun* **1** one more than twelve, or three more than ten. **2** a symbol for this (13, xiii, XIII). **3** a size etc. denoted by thirteen. **4 a** a group of thirteen people or things. **b** the thirteenth person or thing of a set or series (*chapter thirteen*). ● *adjective* that amount to thirteen. □ **thir·teenth** *adjective, noun & adverb* [Old English *thrēotīene* (as THREE, -TEEN)]

Thirteen Colonies *hist.* the 17th- and 18th-c. British colonies in N America (Virginia, Massachusetts, Maryland, Connecticut, Rhode Island, N Carolina, S Carolina, New York, New Jersey, Delaware, New Hampshire, Pennsylvania, and Georgia) that ratified the Declaration of Independence in 1776, thereby becoming the founding states of the US.

thirty ● *noun* (*pl.* **-ties**) **1** the product of three and ten. **2** a symbol for this (30, xxx, XXX). **3** (in *pl.*) the numbers from 30 to 39, esp. the years of a century or of a person's life. **4 a** a group of thirty people or things. **b** the thirtieth person or thing of a set or series. **5** (in *combination*) thirty minutes past (a specified hour) (*four-thirty*). ● *adjective* that amount to thirty. □ **thirty-first, -second**, etc. the ordinal numbers between thirtieth and fortieth. **thirty-one, -two**, etc. the cardinal numbers between thirty and forty. □ **thir·ti·eth** *adjective, adverb, & noun* **thirty·fold** *adjective & adverb* [Old English *thritig* (as THREE, -TY²)]

thirty·ish *adjective* *informal* approximately thirty, esp. in age.

Thirty-nine Articles *plural noun* statements of doctrine in the *Book of Common Prayer* historically accepted as representing the teaching of the Church of England.

thirty-second note *noun* *N Amer.* *Music* a note having the time value of half a sixteenth note and represented by a large dot with a three-hooked stem.

thirty-second rest *noun* *N Amer.* *Music* a rest having the time value of a thirty-second note.

thirty·some·thing *informal* ● *noun* **1** an undetermined age between thirty and forty. **2** a person of this age. ● *adjective* **1** characteristic of the tastes and lifestyle of this group. **2** between thirty and forty years of age. [popularized as a catchphrase by the US television show *Thirtysomething* first broadcast in 1987]

30-30 *noun* **1** a rifle that fires a cartridge .30 inch in diameter. **2** a .30 inch cartridge.

Thirty Thousand Islands a group of islands and islets along the eastern shore of Georgian Bay in south central Ontario.

Thirty Years War a prolonged European war 1618–48. Though it began as a struggle between the Catholic Holy Roman Emperor and some of his German Protestant states, the war gradually drew in most of the major European military powers and became a fight for continental hegemony with France, Sweden, Spain, and the Holy Roman Empire as the major protagonists. When the Treaty of Westphalia ended the fighting, Bourbon France had emerged as the pre-eminent European power.

this ● *demonstrative pronoun* (*pl.* **these**) **1** the person or thing indicated, close by, already named, or understood (*can you see this?*; *this is my cousin*). **2** (contrasted with *that*) the person or thing that is closer or more immediately in mind. **3 a** the action, behaviour, or circumstances, under consideration (*this just won't do*; *what do you think of this?*). **b** what is about to be demonstrated or announced (*listen to this*). **4** (on the telephone) **a** the person speaking. **b** the person spoken to. ● *demonstrative adjective* (*pl.* **these**) **1** designating the person or thing close by etc. (*compare senses 1, 2 of pronoun*). **2** (of time) **a** the present or current (*I'm busy all this week*). **b** relating to today (*this morning*). **c** just past or to come (*we haven't seen her these three weeks*; *we will meet again this*

Tuesday). **3** *informal* (in narrative) designating a person or thing previously unspecified (*so this guy comes up and grabs my hand*). ● *adverb* to this degree or extent; to a height or extent indicated by a gesture of the hand or hands (*knew Kyle when he was this high*; *I love you this much*). □ **these days** = NOWADAYS. **this here** *slang* this particular (person or thing). **this much** the amount or extent about to be stated (*I know this much, she's not here*). [Old English, neuter of *thes*]

this and that *noun informal* various unspecified things.

Thisbe /ˈθɪzbi/ *Rom. Myth* a Babylonian girl, lover of Pyramus.

this·tle /ˈθɪsəl/ *noun* **1** any of various prickly plants of the genera *Carduus*, *Cirsium*, and *Carlina*, which have tubular, chiefly purple flowers in globular heads, esp. any of those occurring as weeds. **2** any of several prickly plants of other families. **3** one of these plants as the national emblem of Scotland. [Old English *thistel* from Germanic]

thistle·down *noun* **1** the light feathery down of a thistle seed. **2** thistle seeds collectively, esp. as carried along by the wind.

this world *noun* the present world or state of existence as opposed to an imagined or future existence, esp. mortal life as opposed to life after death. □ **this-worldli·ness** *noun* **this-worldly** *attributive adjective*

thith·er *adverb archaic* or *formal* to or towards that place. [Old English *thider*, alteration (influenced by HITHER) of *thæder*]

thix·otropy /θɪkˈsɒtrəpi/ *noun* the property displayed by certain gels of becoming temporarily fluid when shaken or stirred etc., and of reverting back to a gel when left to stand. □ **thixo·trop·ic** /ˌθɪksəˈtrɒpɪk/ *adjective* [Greek *thixis* touching + *tropē* turning]

tho' *archaic* or *informal var.* of THOUGH.

thole¹ /θoːl/ *noun* (in full **thole-pin**) a vertical pin or peg in the side or gunwale of a boat which serves as the fulcrum for an oar, esp. either of a pair forming an oarlock. [Old English *thol* fir tree, peg]

thole² /θoːl/ *transitive verb Scot.* or *archaic* **1** undergo or suffer (pain, grief, etc.). **2** permit or admit of. [Old English *tholian* from Germanic]

thol·os /ˈθɒlɒs/ *noun* (*pl.* **thol·oi** /-lɔɪ/) *Gk Hist.* a dome-shaped tomb, esp. of the Mycenaean period. [Greek]

Thom /tɒm/ **Ron·ald James** (1923–86), Canadian architect. His first large project was the design of Massey College, University of Toronto (1963); he also designed colleges and residences for Trent University (1963–79), the Shaw Festival Theatre in Niagara-on-the-Lake (1973), and the Metropolitan Toronto Zoo (1974).

Thom·as ▸ **1 Aud·rey Grace** (b.1935), US-born Canadian novelist and short-story writer. Her novels include *Mrs Blood* (1970) and *Goodbye Harold Good Luck* (1986). Her work is at its best when studying the daily minutiae of women's lives. **2 Dylan Mar·lais** (1914–53), Welsh poet. His poems, such as 'Do not go gentle into that good night', are usu. romantic in feeling and rhetorical in style. He also wrote the radio play *Under Milk Wood* (1954). **3 St.**, an Apostle, who said that he would not believe that Christ had risen again until he had seen and touched his wounds (John 20:24–9); the story is the origin of the nickname 'doubting Thomas'. Feast day, 21 December.

Thom·as à Kem·pis /ə ˈkɛmpɪs/ (born Thomas Hemerken) (c.1380–1471), German Augustinian canon and theologian. He wrote a number of ascetic treatises and is the probable author of *On the Imitation of Christ* (c.1415–24), a manual of spiritual devotion.

Thom·as Aqui·nas, St. see AQUINAS.

Thom·as More, St. see MORE.

Thom·ism /ˈtoːmɪzəm/ *noun* the philosophical or theological doctrine developed by St. Thomas Aquinas. □ **Thom·ist** *noun* **Thom·is·tic** /-ˈmɪstɪk/ *adjective* [Thomas (AQUINAS)]

Thomp·son¹ /ˈtɒmsən/ a nickel-mining city in north central Manitoba, situated on the Burntwood River, about 725 km north of Winnipeg; pop. (2001) 13,256. [J. F. *Thompson*, president of the International Nickel Co. c.1957]

Thomp·son² /ˈtɒmsən/ **1 Sir Ben·ja·min, Count Rum·ford** (1753–1814), US-born English physicist, who is noted for his research on the relationship between mechanical work and heat. **2 Daley** (b.1958), English athlete. He won a number of major decathlon titles in the 1980s, including gold medals in the Olympic Games of 1980 and 1984. **3 David** (1770–1857), English-born Canadian fur trader, explorer, and surveyor. Apprenticed to the Hudson's Bay Company at age 14, he was the first to make comprehensive maps of the western territory that became part of Canada in 1870; he also charted the official boundary between Canada and the US from the St. Lawrence to the Lake of the Woods. **4 Ed·ward Pal·mer** ('E.P.') (1924–93), English historian and activist. A leading Marxist social historian, he was also known for his outspoken advocacy of nuclear disarmament; his works include *The Making of the English Working Class* (1963) and *Witness Against the Beast*

(1993), a study of William Blake. **5 Emma** (b.1959), English actress and screenwriter. Her films include *Henry V* (1989), *Howards End* (1992), for which she won an Oscar for best actress, and *Sense and Sensibility* (1995), for which she also wrote the Oscar-winning screenplay. **6 Sir John Spar·row David** (1845–94), Canadian judge and politician, Conservative prime minister of Canada 1892–94. Elected as a member of the Nova Scotia assembly in 1877, he was Attorney General 1878–82, and premier in 1882. In 1885 he entered the Macdonald Cabinet as minister of justice. He followed J.J.C. Abbott as prime minister in 1892, and died at Windsor Castle two years later. □ **Thomp·son·ian** /ˌtɒmˈsoːniːən/ *adjective*

Thomp·son³ /ˈtɒmsən/ *noun* = NLAKA'PAMUX. [THOMPSON RIVER]

Thompson raisin *noun* a dark brown seedless raisin made by drying Thompson grapes in the sun.

Thompson River a river in SE central BC, 489 km long (to the head of the North Thompson), which rises in the Cariboo Mountains and flows generally southwestward through Kamloops to join the Fraser River west of Merritt. [David THOMPSON]

Thompson seedless grape *noun* a thin-skinned, light-green sweet grape much grown in California for raisins or as table grapes. [W. *Thompson*, 19th-c. British-born California grape-grower who developed the hybrid]

Thom·son ▸ **1 Sir George Paget** (1892–1975), English physicist, who demonstrated the wave-particle nature of elementary particles; he was awarded the Nobel Prize for physics in 1937. **2** his father, **Sir Jo·seph John** (1856–1940), English physicist, discoverer of the electron, the existence of which he deduced from his experiments on the deflection of cathode rays in magnetic and electric fields; he received the 1906 Nobel Prize for physics for his research into the electrical conductivity of gases. **3 Roy Her·bert, 1st Baron Thom·son of Fleet** (1894–1976), Canadian-born British newspaper proprietor and media entrepreneur. In 1931 he opened his own radio station in North Bay, Ontario. He then built up his N American press and radio holdings before acquiring his first British newspaper, the *Scotsman*, in 1952, the year he settled in Britain. By the mid 1960s the Thomson Organization had become an international corporation, with interests in publishing, printing, television, and travel. **4 Thom·as John** ('Tom') (1877–1917), Canadian painter. After modest beginnings, he became friends with painters such as J.E.H. MacDonald, Fred Varley, Arthur Lismer, and A.Y. Jackson. He began sketching and painting in Algonquin Park in 1912, and spent a great deal of his time there; he drowned in the park in 1917. **5 Vir·gil** (1896–1989), US composer. His lyrical style shows the influence of US hymns and folk music and his contact with the French composers of Les Six; his works include the operas *Four Saints in Three Acts* (1928) and *The Mother of Us All* (1947). **6 Sir Wil·liam**, see KELVIN.

-thon *combining form* = -ATHON.

thong *noun* **1** a narrow strip of hide or leather used esp. as a lace, cord, strap, rein, or as the lash of a whip. **2** *N Amer.*, *Austral.*, & *NZ* = FLIP-FLOP 2. **3 a** a skimpy garment for the lower body, consisting of narrow strips of cloth or leather attached to a piece of material that covers the genitals but not the buttocks. **b** (*attributive*) designating articles of clothing that resemble this (*thong bikini*; *thong panties*). □ **thonged** *adjective* [Old English *thwang*, *thwong*, from Germanic]

Thor *Scand. Myth* the god of thunder, the weather, agriculture, and the home, the son of Odin and Frigga; he is represented as armed with a hammer, and Thursday is named after him.

thor·ax /ˈθɔːraks/ *noun* (*pl.* **thor·ax·es** or **thor·aces** /ˈθɔːrəˌsiːz/) **1** *Anat.* & *Zool.* **a** the part of the body of a mammal between the neck and the abdomen, including the cavity enclosed by the ribs, breastbone, and dorsal vertebrae, and containing the chief organs of circulation and respiration. **b** the corresponding part of a bird, reptile, amphibian, or fish. **2** *Zool.* the middle section of the body of an arthropod, between the head and abdomen. □ *adjective* **thor·acic** /θɔˈrasɪk/ *adjective* [Latin from Greek *thōrax -akos* 'breastplate']

Thora·zine /ˈθɔːrəziːn/ *noun proprietary* = CHLORPROMAZINE.

Thor·eau /θɔˈroː/ **Henry David** (1817–62), US essayist and poet. A central figure of Transcendentalism with his friend and mentor Ralph Waldo Emerson, Thoreau is best known for *Walden, or Life in the Woods* (1854), an account of his two-year experiment in self-sufficiency living in a hut by Walden Pond, near Concord, Mass.; his essay *Civil Disobedience* (1849) influenced Mahatma Gandhi's policy of passive resistance. □ **Thor·eau·vian** *adjective & noun*

thor·ium *noun* a radioactive metallic element occurring naturally in monazite, used in electronic equipment and as a source of nuclear energy. Symbol: **Th**; at. no.: 90. [THOR]

Consonants: b *but* d *dog* f *few* g *get* h *her* j *yes* k *cat* l *leg* m *man* n *no* p *pen* r *red* s *sit*

Thorn see TORUŃ.

thorn *noun* **1** a stiff sharp-pointed projection on a plant. **2** a thorn-bearing bush, shrub, or tree, such as the hawthorn. **3** a cause of pain, grief, irritation, or trouble. **4 a** the name of the letter used in Old and Middle English, Gothic, and Old Saxon to represent the voiced and voiceless dental fricatives /ð/ and /θ/, eventually superseded by the digraph th. **b** the name of a letter used in Old Norse and Icelandic to represent the voiceless dental fricative /θ/. □ **a thorn in one's side** (or **flesh**) a constant annoyance. □ **thorn·less** *adjective* **thorn·proof** *adjective* [Old English from Germanic]

thorn·apple *noun* **1** a plant of the nightshade family, *Datura stramonium*, native to N America, bearing large funnel-shaped white or mauve flowers. *Also called* JIMSON WEED (*see* JIMSON). **2** the fruit of this plant, a capsule covered with long spines and containing poisonous seeds.

thorn·back *noun* a ray, *Raja clavata*, with spines on the back and tail.

Thorn·dike, Dame Agnes Sybil (1882–1976), English actress. She was noted for her versatility and performances in a wide range of stage roles, including the title part of the first London production of Shaw's *St. Joan* (1924).

thorn·tail *noun* any S American hummingbird of the genus *Popelairia*.

thorny *adjective* (**thorn·i·er, thorn·i·est**) **1** having many thorns. **2** (of a subject, issue, problem, etc.) difficult to handle or resolve; delicate. □ **thorn·i·ly** *adverb* **thorn·i·ness** *noun*

Thor·old a city in S Ontario, immediately south of St. Catharines; pop. (2001) 18,048. □ **Thorold·ite** *noun* [Sir J. *Thorold*, British Member of Parliament d.1815]

thor·ough /'θəːrəʊ, 'θʌrəʊ, 'θʌrə/ *adjective* **1** applied to or affecting every part or detail; not superficial (*she has a thorough understanding of the problem*). **2** done with great care and completeness (*she did a thorough job*). **3** (of a person) taking pains to do something carefully and completely (*Carl may be slow, but he's very thorough*). **4** absolute, utter (*a thorough nuisance*). □ **thorough·ly** *adverb* **thorough·ness** *noun* [originally as adv. and prep. in the senses of *through*, from Old English *thuruh* var. of *thurh* THROUGH]

thorough bass *noun* a bass part for a keyboard instrument extending through a piece of esp. baroque music, notated with figures to indicate the harmony.

thorough·bred ● *noun* **1** a purebred animal, esp. a horse (also *attributive:* thoroughbred racing). **2** (**Thoroughbred**) a racehorse of a breed originating from English mares and Arab stallions, whose ancestry for several generations is fully documented. **3** a distinguished or first-rate person or thing. ● *adjective* **1** of pure breed. **2** of outstanding quality; distinguished, remarkable.

thorough·fare *noun* **1 a** a road or path open at both ends through which esp. traffic may pass. **b** a main road or highway. **2** *N Amer.* a navigable waterway, esp. a channel for shipping.

thorough·going *adjective* **1** extremely thorough; not superficial (*a thoroughgoing attack*). **2** (*attributive*) absolute, utter; out-and-out (*a thoroughgoing idiot*).

Thorpe, James Fran·cis ('Jim') (1888–1953), US athlete. He played football and baseball professionally and won gold medals for the decathlon and pentathlon at the 1912 Olympics, although these were later withdrawn because of his professional status.

Thors·havn see TÓRSHAVN.

Thos. *abbreviation* Thomas.

those *pl.* of THAT.

Thoth /θəʊθ, ˈtoːt/ *Egyptian Myth* a moon god, the god of wisdom, justice, and writing and patron of the sciences. He was closely associated with Ra and was his messenger, which led the Greeks to identify him with Hermes; he is most often represented in human form with the head of an ibis surmounted by the moon's disc and crescent.

thou¹ /ðaʊ/ *pronoun* (*obj.* **thee**; *possessive* **thy** or **thine**; *pl.* **ye** or **you**) second person singular pronoun, now replaced by *you* except in some formal, liturgical, dialect, and poetic uses. [Old English *thu* from Germanic]

thou² /ðaʊ/ *noun* (*pl.* same or **thous**) *informal* a thousand, esp. a thousand dollars (*she makes 50 thou a year*). [abbreviation]

though ● *conjunction* **1** (often prec. by *even*) despite the fact that (*even though it was early we went to bed; though I may be hungry, I will not eat*). **2** (introducing a possibility) even if (*ask him though he may well refuse*). **3** and yet; but still; however; nevertheless (*she read on, though not to the very end*). **4** in spite of being (*the portions were small though expensive*). ● *adverb informal* **1** however; all the same (*I wish you had told me, though*). **2** (used as an intensifier after a question or emphatic statement)

indeed, truly ('*She's awfully smart.' 'Isn't she, though?'*). □ **as though** = AS IF (*see* AS¹). [Old Norse *thó* etc., corresponding to Old English *thēah*, from Germanic]

thought¹ *noun* **1** the process or power of thinking; the faculty of reason. **2** the intellectual activity or way of thinking characteristic of or associated with a particular time, people, group, etc. (*medieval European thought; a school of thought*). **3 a** sober reflection or consideration (*a lot of thought went into this*). **b** deep meditation or contemplation (*was lost in thought*). **4 a** a piece of reasoning produced by thinking; an idea (*I just had a thought*). **b** (usu. in *pl.*) what one is thinking; an opinion or assessment of a person or thing (*what are your thoughts on the subject?; keep your thoughts to yourself*). **5** (often in *pl.*) attention (*we turn our thoughts to summer*). **6 a** regard, concern, consideration (*did it without any thought of the consequences*). **b** (in *pl.*) sympathy (*our thoughts are with you*). **7** (foll. by *of* + verbal noun or *to* + infin.) a hope, intention, or expectation; a notion (*gave up all thoughts of winning; had no thought to go*). **8** the mere contemplation (*the thought of it makes me nervous*). **9** the subject of one's thinking (*my one thought was to get away*). □ **give thought to** consider; think about. **on second thought** contrary to what one originally decided or announced. **without a second thought** without giving a matter full or proper consideration. [Old English *thōht* (as THINK)]

thought² *past and past participle of* THINK.

thought crime *noun* **1** unorthodox or controversial thinking, considered as a criminal offence or socially unacceptable. **2** an instance of this. [coined by George Orwell in *Nineteen Eighty-four* (1949)]

thought experiment *noun* a mental assessment of the implications of a hypothesis.

thought·ful *adjective* **1** (often foll. by *of*) showing thought or consideration for others; considerate, kind (*it was thoughtful of you to call*). **2** showing signs of careful thought or consideration (*a thoughtful gift; a thoughtful approach to the game*). **3 a** absorbed in meditation; deep in thought. **b** given to contemplation; prudent, reflective. □ **thought·ful·ly** *adverb* **thought·ful·ness** *noun*

thought·less *adjective* **1** lacking in consideration for others; inconsiderate, tactless. **2** showing a lack of concern for the possible consequences of one's actions; careless. **3** resulting from a lack of thought (*a thoughtless mistake*). □ **thought·less·ly** *adverb* **thought·less·ness** *noun*

thought out *adjective* (usu. with qualifying adverb) produced by mental effort (usu. hyphenated when *attributive:* a carefully thought-out plan).

thought police *noun informal* an authoritarian special interest group that monitors others for signs of behaviour or views it considers deviant, inappropriate, or politically incorrect. [with reference to the *Thought Police* in George Orwell's *Nineteen Eighty-four* (1949)]

thought-provoking *adjective* (of an article, question, etc.) that prompts others to further contemplation of matters or issues raised.

thought transference *noun* telepathy.

thought wave *noun* a supposed pattern of energy by which it is claimed that thoughts are transferred from one person to another.

thou·sand ● *noun* (*pl.* **thou·sands** or (in sense 1) **thou·sand**) (in *sing.* prec. by *a* or *one*) **1** the product of a hundred and ten. **2** a symbol for this (1,000, m, M). **3** a set of a thousand things. **4 a** (in *pl.*) the numbers usu. between 1000 and 10,000, esp. referring to dollars (*I don't know the exact cost but it will be somewhere in the thousands*). **b** (in *sing.* or *pl.*) *informal* a large number. ● *adjective* that amount to a thousand. □ **thousand·fold** *adjective & adverb* **thou·sandth** *adjective, adverb, & noun* [Old English *thūsend* from Germanic]

Thousand Island *noun* designating a piquant mayonnaise salad dressing made with tomatoes, chili sauce, finely chopped boiled egg, onion, green pepper, and occasionally celery or pickle. [from the THOUSAND ISLANDS in the St. Lawrence, where this dressing was first made]

Thousand Islands 1 a group of islands (estimated counts vary in number from 1,150 to 1,800) situated in a widening of the St. Lawrence River, between Kingston and Brockville in SE Ontario. Some of the islands (including Wolfe Island, the largest) belong to Canada and some to the US. **2** a group of about 100 small islands in the SW Java Sea, forming part of Indonesia.

Thrace an ancient country lying west of the Black Sea and north of the Aegean, originally inhabited by a warlike Indo-European people. Conquered by Philip II of Macedon in 342 BC, it became a Roman province in AD 46. It is now divided between Turkey, Bulgaria, and Greece. □ **Thra·cian** *adjective & noun*

Thrale, Hes·ter Lynch see PIOZZI.

thrall *noun literary* **1** (often foll. by *to*) a condition or state of or like slavery or servitude; subjection to a person, power, or influence (*she lived in thrall to the needs of her aging mother*). **2** (often foll. by *of*) power, influence, or control (*he never escaped the thrall of alcohol*). **3** one who is controlled by or dependent upon a person, power, or influence; a slave. □ **thrall·dom** *noun* (also **thral·dom**). [Old English *thrǣl* from Old Norse *thrǣll*, perhaps from a Germanic root = run]

thrash ● *verb* **1** *transitive* beat severely with a stick or whip, esp. as a punishment. **2** *transitive* a *Sport informal* defeat (an opponent) convincingly. **b** criticize or scold severely (*his new book was thrashed by the critics*). **3** *intransitive* (foll. by *around, about*) move or fling the body, limbs, etc., about violently, esp. in panic or helplessness; flail (*thrashed around in the water, shouting for help*). **4** *intransitive* lash about like a flail or whip (*the branches thrashed in the wind*). **5** *intransitive* (of a ship) make way against the wind or tide. **6** *transitive* = THRESH 1. ● *noun* **1** (in full **thrash metal**) a style of fast loud heavy metal rock music similar to speed metal but with a greater presence of punk elements (also *attributive: thrash band*). **2** an act of thrashing. **3** *informal* a party, esp. a lavish one. □ **thrash out 1** discuss (a matter etc.) at length in order to reach a solution or consensus. **2** establish (a plan, solution, etc.) after discussing a matter thoroughly. □ **thrash·ing** *noun* **thrashy** *adjective* (in sense 1 of *noun*). [Old English *therscan*, later *threscan*, from Germanic]

thrash·er[1] *noun* **1** a person that plays or listens to thrash music. **2** a person or thing that thrashes. **3** = THRESHER 2.

thrash·er[2] *noun* any of several N American songbirds of the family Mimidae, with greyish or brownish plumage and a slightly down-curved bill, esp. the **brown thrasher**, *Toxostoma rufum*, which has a reddish-brown back and pale speckled underside. [perhaps from English dial. *thrusher* = THRUSH[1]]

thrash metal *noun* = THRASH *noun* 1.

thread ● *noun* **1 a** a fine strand made by drawing out and twisting the fibres of flax, cotton, wool, silk, etc. **b** a length of this. **2** a length of thin cord composed of two or more strands twisted together used esp. in sewing and weaving. **3** anything resembling thread in fineness and length, such as a thin stream of liquid or a filament of a spider's web. **4 a** anything regarded as threadlike with reference to its continuity or connectedness, such as the sequence of events or ideas continuing through the whole course of a narrative, argument, one's life, etc. **b** a continuous or persistent feature of something, esp. one combining with other features to form a pattern or texture (*a common thread running throughout her works*). **5** the spiral ridge running along the outside of a screw or inside of a nut. **6 a** a single fibre of material in an article of clothing (*a loose thread*). **b** (in *pl.*) *informal* clothes. **7** *Computing* **a** a group of linked messages posted on the Internet that share a common subject or theme. **b** a programming structure or process formed by linking a number of separate elements or subroutines, esp. each of the tasks executed concurrently in multi-threading. ● *verb* **1** *transitive* **a** pass a thread through the eye of (a needle). **b** (often foll. by *through*) pass (string etc.) through a hole or series of holes. **2** *transitive* put (beads) on a string. **3 a** *transitive & intransitive* (often foll. by *through*) make (one's way) through a crowd etc. (*threaded her way through the heavy traffic*). **b** *transitive* make one's way through (a narrow or obstructed passage, a crowd, etc.). **4** *transitive* form a screw thread on. **5** *transitive Sport* (esp. in hockey and football) complete (a pass) to a teammate through a crowd of players. **6** *transitive* feed (a strip of material) through a piece of machinery, such as film through a projector. □ **hang by a thread** be in a precarious state, position, etc. □ **thread·er** *noun* **thread·like** *adjective* [Old English *thrǣd* from Germanic]

thread·bare *adjective* **1** (of fabric, clothing, carpeting, etc.) so worn that the nap is lost and the thread visible. **2 a** having lost effect, freshness, or force through overuse (*a threadbare plot*). **b** weak or insubstantial (*a threadbare excuse*). **3** (of a person) wearing threadbare clothing.

thread·ed *adjective* **1** (of a pipe, bolt, etc.) fitted with a thread. **2** *Computing* **a** (of a list or tree) containing extra linkages as well as a pointer from each item to the following node. **b** (of a program etc.) formed from or involving a set of separate units, sections, modules, etc., which may be linked into a continuous sequence.

thread·fin *noun* any small tropical fish of the family Polynemidae, with long streamers from its pectoral fins.

thread·worm *noun* any of various esp. parasitic threadlike nematode worms, e.g. the pinworm.

thready *adjective* (**thread·i·er, thread·i·est**) **1** (of a person's pulse)

barely perceptible. **2** (of a voice or sound) lacking fullness; feeble, faint. **3** of or like a thread.

threat *noun* **1** a declaration of an intention to take some hostile action, esp. an expression of an intention to inflict pain, injury, damage, etc. unless a particular demand or set of demands is met (*a death threat; a threat to shut off our water unless we pay the bill*). **2** an indication of the approach or imminent occurrence of something unwelcome or undesirable (*the threat of war; a threat of rain in the forecast*). **3** a person or thing regarded as a likely cause of harm or damage etc. (*she is a security threat*). [Old English *thrēat* affliction etc., from Germanic]

threat·en *verb* **1** *transitive & intransitive* (often foll. by *with*) make a threat or threats against (a person) (*threatened him with a knife*). **2** *transitive* **a** declare one's intention of inflicting (punishment, injury, etc.), esp. in retaliation for something done or not done (*she is threatening legal action unless he agrees to her demands*). **b** (foll. by *to* + infin.) express an intention or promise (*they threatened to quit*). **3** *transitive* appear likely or certain to cause or do (something undesirable) (*the epidemic threatens to kill thousands*). **4** *transitive* jeopardize or endanger (*pollution is threatening the water supply*). **5** *transitive & intransitive* be a sign or indication of the approach or imminent occurrence of (something undesirable); portend (*those clouds threaten rain*). **6** *transitive* intimidate or frighten. [Old English *thrēatnian* (as THREAT)]

threat·ened *adjective* **1** (of a species etc.) in danger of becoming rare or extinct; at risk of becoming endangered. **2** intimidated. **3** having been vowed or portended. **4** in jeopardy or danger.

threat·en·ing *adjective* **1** designed or tending to menace or intimidate (*a threatening letter*). **2** foreboding (*threatening storm clouds*). □ **threat·en·ing·ly** *adverb*

three ● *noun* **1 a** one more than two, or seven less than ten. **b** a symbol for this (3, iii, III). **2** a size etc. denoted by three. **3** three o'clock. **4 a** a group of three people or things. **b** the third person or thing of a set or series (*I'm on book three*). **5** a card with three pips. **6** *Basketball* a three-point field goal. ● *adjective* that amount to three. □ **three cheers** see CHEER. **three sheets to the wind** see SHEET[2]. [Old English *thrī* from Germanic]

three-and-a-half *noun Cdn* (*Que.*) an apartment having a kitchen, living room, bedroom, and bathroom.

three-bagger *noun Baseball informal* (also **three-base hit**) = TRIPLE *noun* 3.

three-card monte *noun* see MONTE 2.

three-card trick *noun* a card game in which players bet on which of three cards lying face down is the queen.

three-chord *adjective* **1** (of a song) based on three guitar chords. **2** *usu. derogatory* **a** (of a song) repetitive and simple. **b** (of a musician) seeming to know only three chords; not particularly creative or talented.

three-colour *adjective* **1** having, using, or consisting of three colours. **2** designating or relating to a process of reproducing natural colours by combining or superimposing photographic images in the three primary colours. □ **three-coloured** *adjective*

three-cornered *adjective* **1** having three corners; triangular. **2** relating to or involving three individuals or groups etc.

3-D ● *adjective* **1** having or presenting a three-dimensional image or appearance (*a 3-D movie*). **2** used to produce a three-dimensional image or appearance (*3-D glasses*). ● *noun* a format that presents three-dimensional images (*the movie is in 3-D*).

three-day eventer *noun* = EVENTER.

three-day eventing *noun* = EVENTING.

three-decker *noun* **1** something with three decks, layers, or divisions. **2** a sandwich made with three slices of bread.

three-dimension·al *adjective* **1 a** having or appearing to have length, width, and depth. **b** producing the appearance of having length, width, and depth (*three-dimensional effects*). **2** (of literature etc.) vivid, realistic. □ **three-dimension·al·ity** *noun* **three-dimensional·ize** *transitive verb* (also esp. *Brit.* **-ise**). **three-dimension·al·ly** *adverb*

three·fold ● *adjective* **1** three times as much or as many. **2** consisting of three parts. ● *adverb* to or by three times the number.

3G *adjective* (of telephone technology) third-generation.

three-handed *adjective* (esp. of a game of cards) involving three players.

three-in-one *attributive adjective* designating a single device or unit that performs three separate functions or consists of three parts that can be used separately.

Vowels: a cat   ɑ arm   e bed   ɜr her   ɜː deux   ə ago   ɪ sit   i cosy   iː feed   ɒ hot   ɔ pore   oː no   ʌ run   ʊ put

three-legged *adjective* having or supported by three legs.

three-legged race *noun* a race run by teams of two, one member of each team having the left leg tied to the right leg of the other.

three-line whip *noun* a written notice calling on members of a political party to attend a parliamentary vote, underlined three times to denote urgency.

three-martini lunch *noun N Amer. informal* a lavish lunch, esp. one charged to a business expense account.

Three Mile Island an island in the Susquehanna river near Harrisburg, Pennsylvania, site of a nuclear power station. In 1979 an accident caused damage to the reactor core, an incident that provoked strong reactions against the nuclear industry in the US and precipitated a reassessment of safety standards.

three-on-one *noun* (*pl.* **-ones**) **1** *Hockey* a rush led by three players against one defender and a goalie (also *attributive*: *a three-on-one break*). **2** *Basketball* a rush led by three players against one defender.

three-on-three *noun* a scaled-down game of basketball involving two teams of three players playing on a schoolyard court or half court and usu. shooting at only one basket.

three-peat *N Amer. Sport informal* ● *noun* a third consecutive win of a particular championship by one player or team. ● *intransitive verb* win a particular championship for a third consecutive time. [from THREE + (RE)PEAT]

three·pence /ˈθrepəns, ˈθrʊpəns/ *noun Brit.* the sum of three pence, esp. before decimalization.

three·penny /ˈθrəpəni/ *adjective Brit.* costing three pence, esp. before decimalization.

three-phase *adjective* (of an electric generator, motor, etc.) designed to supply or use simultaneously three separate alternating currents of the same voltage, but with phases differing by a third of a period.

three-piece ● *adjective* **1** consisting of three matching or related parts (*a three-piece band; a three-piece furniture suite*). **2** (of a suit) consisting of matching pants, jacket, and vest. ● *noun* (also **three-piecer**) an ensemble or group consisting of three matching or related components, members, etc.

three-pitch *noun Cdn* a variety of softball in which the batter cannot draw a walk, having only three chances to hit a ball delivered underhand by a teammate.

three-ply *adjective* consisting of three layers, strands, or thicknesses.

three-point *adjective Basketball* **1** (of a field goal, basket, shot, etc.) that is worth three points if successfully completed. **2** relating to the shooting of three-point field goals (*three-point range*). **3** (*attributive*) designating a play in which a player who is fouled while successfully completing a two-point field goal is awarded a free throw which, if made, would result in a third point.

three-point·er *noun Basketball* a three-point basket.

three-point landing *noun* the landing of an aircraft on the two main wheels and the tailwheel or nose wheel simultaneously.

three-point turn *noun* a method of turning a vehicle around in a narrow space by moving in three arcs, forwards, backwards, and forwards again.

three-prong *adjective Electricity* **1** (of an outlet) that has been grounded and is thus capable of receiving a plug with three pins or prongs. **2** (of a plug) that has three pins or prongs and is designed to fit in a grounded outlet.

three-pronged *adjective* having three aspects, stages, aims, or lines of attack (*three-pronged attack*).

three-quarter ● *noun* **1** (in *pl.*) three of the four equal parts into which something is or may be divided (*three-quarters of an hour*). **2** (in full **three-quarter back**) *Rugby* each of three or four players playing behind the halfbacks. ● *adjective* **1** consisting of or measuring three-quarters of the normal amount (*a three-quarter length coat*). **2** (of a portrait or view etc.) **a** showing the figure as far as the hips. **b** showing three-quarters of the face; between full face and profile. ● *adverb* (**three-quarters**) to the extent of three-quarters (*the tank is three-quarters full*).

three-ring binder *noun* a ring binder with three rings.

three-ring circus *noun N Amer.* **1** a circus with three rings for simultaneous performances. **2 a** a showy or extravagant display. **b** a scene of confusion or disorder.

three score *noun archaic* sixty.

three-season *adjective* designating a building, piece of equipment, article of clothing, etc. that is suitable for use in spring, summer, and fall.

three-sixty *noun* (*pl.* **-sixties**) *informal* a spin of 360°; a complete turn or revolution.

three·some *noun* **1** a group of three people. **2** an (esp. sexual) activity in which three people participate.

three-star *adjective* **1** (of a hotel, restaurant, etc.) given three stars in a grading in which this denotes a high quality, usu. one or two grades below the highest. **2** having or designating a military rank distinguished by three stars on the epaulette of the uniform.

three strikes and you're out *noun* (also **three strikes**) *informal* (in the US) legislation by which a person convicted of a serious felony for the third time would face a mandatory life sentence.

three-way *adjective* **1** involving three participants (*a three-way tie*). **2** designating or relating to a trilight bulb (*three-way bulb; three-way socket*). **3** (of a loudspeaker) having three separate drive units for different frequency ranges; having a woofer, tweeter, and mid-range speaker.

three-wheel·er *noun* a vehicle with three wheels, esp. a kind of small all-terrain vehicle.

thren·ody /ˈθrenədi/ *noun* (*pl.* **-odies**) a song of lamentation, esp. for the dead; a dirge. □ **thren·odic** /-ˈnɒdɪk/ *adjective* **thren·od·ist** /ˈθrenədɪst/ *noun* [Greek *thrēnōidia* from *thrēnos* wailing + *ōidē* ODE]

threo·nine /ˈθriːəˌniːn/ *noun Biochem.* a hydrophilic amino acid widely present in proteins and essential in the human diet. [*threose* (name of a sugar), ultimately from Greek *eruthros* red + -INE⁴]

thresh /θreʃ, θraʃ/ *transitive & intransitive verb* **1** shake, beat, or mechanically treat (wheat etc.) to separate the grain from the husk and straw, esp. with a flail or by the action of a revolving mechanism. **2** = THRASH *verb* 1, 3. □ **thresh·ing** *noun* [var. of THRASH]

thresh·er /ˈθreʃər, ˈθraʃər/ *noun* **1 a** a person that threshes grain. **b** a threshing machine. **2** (in full **thresher shark**) a shark, *Alopias vulpinus*, with a long upper lobe to its tail with which it lashes the water to direct its prey.

thresher·man *noun* (*pl.* **-men**) *N Amer. hist.* a person who participates in the annual threshing of grain.

threshing floor *noun* a prepared hard level surface on which grain is threshed, esp. with a flail.

threshing machine *noun hist.* a machine for separating grain from the straw or husk.

thresh·old /ˈθreʃəʊld, -həʊld/ *noun* **1 a** a strip of wood or stone forming the bottom of a doorway and crossed upon entering a house or room. **b** the entrance to a house or building etc. **c** the boundary of a region. **2** the point just before a new situation, period of life, etc. begins (*on the threshold of victory*). **3** *Physiol. & Psych.* a limit below which a stimulus causes no reaction (*pain threshold*). **4** the magnitude that must be exceeded for a certain reaction, phenomenon, result, or condition to occur or be manifested. **5** a step in a scale of wages or taxation at which increases become due or mandatory, usu. operative in specified conditions, such as a rise in the cost of living. [Old English *therscold, threscold*, etc., related to THRASH in the sense 'tread']

threw *past of* THROW.

thrice *adverb archaic or literary* **1** three times. **2** (esp. in *combination*) highly (*thrice-blessed*). [Middle English *thries* from *thrie* (adv.) from Old English *thrīwa, thriga* (as THREE, -S³)]

thrift *noun* **1** prudent financial management; the habit of saving money and spending it carefully; frugality. **2** (in full **thrift institution**) *US* a savings and loan association. **3** a European plant, *Armeria maritima*, having dense heads of small pink flowers, leafless stems, and dense rosettes of linear leaves. *Also called* SEA PINK. [Old Norse (as THRIVE)]

thrift shop *noun* (also **thrift store**) a store that sells second-hand merchandise, esp. clothing, with proceeds often going to charity (also *attributive: thrift-shop dresses*).

thrifty *adjective* (**thrift·i·er, thrift·i·est**) **1** economical, frugal. **2** healthy, thriving. □ **thrift·i·ly** *adverb* **thrift·i·ness** *noun*

thrill ● *noun* **1** a powerful and often sudden feeling of excitement, exhilaration, or emotion (*the thrill of scoring the winning goal*). **2 a** a thing that causes such a feeling of excitement or exhilaration (*his new book was a real thrill*). **b** an exciting or exhilarating event or experience (*it was a thrill to meet her*). **3** intense excitement (*the thrill has not gone out of our marriage*). **4** *Med.* **a** a vibration, pulsation, or throb. **b** a vibratory movement or resonance heard in auscultation. ● *verb* **1** *transitive* cause (a person) to feel intense excitement. **2** *transitive* thoroughly please or delight. **3** *intransitive* (usu. foll. by *at* or *to*) feel or become excited (*thrilled at the sound of her voice*). **4** *intransitive* quiver or throb with or as if with emotion. □ **thrill·ing** *adjective* **thrill·ing·ly** *adverb* [thirl (now dial.) from Old English *thyrlian* pierce, from *thŷrel* hole, from *thurh* THROUGH]

thrilled *adjective* **1** thoroughly pleased or delighted. **2** overwhelmed with excitement.

thrill·er *noun* **1** an exciting or sensational movie or novel etc., esp. a suspenseful one involving mystery, crime, or espionage. **2** a person or thing that thrills or excites.

thrill-kill *noun* a murder or series of murders committed for no purpose other than the excitement of doing it.

thrill ride *noun* a particularly dramatic or fast ride, esp. at an amusement park.

thrill-seeker *noun* **1** a person who enjoys the excitement of participating in dangerous activities. **2** usu. *derogatory* a person seeking thrills. □ **thrill-seeking** *adjective & noun*

thrips *noun* (*pl.* same) a member of the order Thysanoptera, of minute dark-coloured insects, typically having slender bodies and four fringed wings, many of which are pests of various plants. [Latin from Greek, = woodworm]

thrive *intransitive verb* (*past* **thrived** or **throve**; *past participle* **thrived** or **thriv·en**) **1** (of a child, plant, or animal) grow vigorously, flourish. **2** be or become successful or prosperous (*the tourist industry thrives during the summer*). □ **thrive on 1** (of an animal etc.) depend upon for growth or sustenance. **2** (of a person) depend upon for the strength or motivation required to succeed; be driven or encouraged by (*she thrives on pressure*). □ **thriv·ing** *adjective* [Old Norse *thrífask* reflexive of *thrífa* grasp]

thro' *var. of* THROUGH.

throat *noun* **1** the front part of the neck beneath the chin and above the collarbone. **2** the windpipe or gullet. **3** anything resembling or compared to a throat, such as a narrow passage or entranceway. **4** the part of a chimney or furnace etc. immediately above the fireplace, which narrows down to the neck. **5** = BARREL *noun* 7. **6** *literary* a voice. □ **be at each other's** (or **one another's**) **throats** quarrel violently. **cut one's own throat** bring about one's own downfall. **ram** (or **thrust** etc.) **down a person's throat** force a person to accept (a thing). □ **-throated** *adjective* (in *combination*). [Old English *throte, throtu* from Germanic]

throat singing *noun* **1** *Cdn.* (in Inuit culture) a type of singing, usu. performed by two women face to face, uttering deep, rhythmic sounds evocative of animal and bird noises, sometimes with a competitive aspect. **2** a vocal technique of simultaneously producing distinct harmonic overtones and lower throaty tones, esp. as practised in Tibetan and other east Asian cultures.

throaty *adjective* (**throat·i·er**, **throat·i·est**) **1** (of a voice) rough, husky; hoarse. **2** produced or modified in the throat; deep, guttural (*a throaty laugh; a throaty cough*). □ **throat·i·ly** *adverb* **throat·i·ness** *noun*

throb ● *intransitive verb* (**throbbed**, **throb·bing**) **1** (of the heart or pulse) beat or palpitate, esp. with more than usual force or rapidity. **2** pulsate or vibrate, esp. with a deep audible rhythm. **3** ache with a recurrent or pulsating pain (*my head is throbbing*). ● *noun* **1** a palpitation or (esp. violent) pulsation. **2** a throbbing; a rhythmic esp. audible beat or vibration. [Middle English, apparently imitative]

throe *noun* (usu. *in pl.*) **1** a violent pang, esp. of childbirth or death. **2** anguish, torment. □ **in the throes of 1** struggling with the task of. **2** in the midst of (esp. a volatile or emotional situation). [Middle English *throwe* perhaps from Old English *thrēa, thrawu* calamity, alteration of perhaps by assoc. with *woe*]

throm·bi *pl. of* THROMBUS.

throm·bin *noun* a plasma protein which acts as an enzyme to convert fibrinogen to fibrin and so promote the clotting of blood. [as THROMBUS + -IN]

thrombo- *combining form Med. & Biochem.* of, pertaining to, or involving the clotting of blood. [Greek *thrombus* THROMBUS]

throm·bo·cyte /ˈθrɒmbəˌsəɪt/ *noun* a cell or platelet which circulates in the blood of vertebrates and is responsible for coagulation.

throm·bo·cyto·penia /ˌθrɒmbəˌsəɪtəˈpiːniə/ *noun Med.* deficiency of platelets in the blood. □ **throm·bo·cyto·penic** *adjective* [THROMBOCYTE + Greek *penia* 'poverty']

throm·bo·embol·ism /ˌθrɒmbəʊˈɛmbəˌlɪzm/ *noun* an embolism of a blood vessel caused by a thrombus dislodged from another site.

throm·bose /θrɒmˈbəʊz/ *transitive & intransitive verb* affect with or undergo thrombosis. [back-formation from THROMBOSIS]

throm·bo·sis /θrɒmˈbəʊsɪs/ *noun* (*pl.* **throm·bo·ses** /-siːz/) a local coagulation or clotting of the blood in a part of the circulatory system.

throm·bot·ic /-ˈbɒtɪk/ *adjective* [modern Latin from Greek *thrombōsis* curdling (as THROMBUS)]

throm·bus /ˈθrɒmbəs/ *noun* (*pl.* **throm·bi** /-bəɪ/) a blood clot that forms on the wall of a blood vessel or a chamber of the heart, esp. in such a way that it impedes or obstructs the flow of blood. [modern Latin from Greek *thrombos* lump, blood clot]

throne ● *noun* **1** an ornate, elaborate, and usu. raised chair occupied by a deity, monarch, pope, bishop, etc., esp. on ceremonial occasions. **2 a** the position, office, power, or dignity of a sovereign (*a claim to the throne*). **b** the occupant of a throne; a monarch or ruler. **3** *Christianity* a member of the third order of the nine ranks of heavenly beings (see ORDER *noun* 19). **4** *informal* or *jocular* a toilet. ● *transitive verb* place on or as if on a throne. □ **throne·less** *adjective* [Old French *trone* from Latin *thronus* from Greek *thronos* high seat]

throne room *noun* **1** a room containing a throne, esp. one used for audiences with a monarch. **2** *informal* or *jocular* a bathroom.

Throne Speech *noun Cdn* = SPEECH FROM THE THRONE.

throng ● *noun* (often foll. by *of*) a crowd or multitude of esp. people. ● *verb* **1** *transitive & intransitive* gather or assemble in or around (*crowds thronged the streets*). **2** *intransitive* travel in large numbers (*on weekends people throng to the malls*). [Middle English *thrang, throng*, Old English *gethrang*, from verbal stem *thring- thrang-*]

thros·tle *noun* a song thrush. [Old English from Germanic: related to THRUSH[1]]

throt·tle ● *noun* **a** (in full **throttle valve**) a valve controlling the flow of fuel or steam etc. in an engine. **b** (in full **throttle control** or **throttle lever**) a lever or pedal operating this valve. ● *verb* **1** *transitive* choke or strangle. **2** *transitive* stifle or suppress (words, a rumour, etc.). **3** *transitive & intransitive* control the flow of gas or steam to (an engine etc.). □ **throttle back** (or **down**) close the throttle of (an engine or vehicle) in order to slow down or stop. □ **throt·tler** *noun* [Middle English *throtel* (v.), perhaps from THROAT + -LE[4]: (n.) perhaps a diminutive of THROAT]

through ● *preposition* **1 a** from one end to the other of (*we drove through Saskatchewan*). **b** going in one side or end and out the other of (*through the tunnel*). **c** beyond; past (*she drove through a stop sign*). **2** between or among (*ran through the trees*). **3 a** from beginning to end of; over each one or part of (*she read through the letter*). **b** during the whole temporal extent of (*we worked through lunch*). **4 a** by means of (*I heard about it through an ad in the paper*). **b** due to; because of (*he lost it through carelessness*). **5** *N Amer.* up to and including (*Monday through Friday*). ● *adverb* **1 a** from side to side, end to end, or beginning to end of a body or space (*I read the letter through; may I pass through?*). **b** all the way; to the end of a journey (*we walked through to the garden*). **2** past or across a barrier or space (*there was a gate but the guard let us through*). **3** successfully past a particular stage or test (*our team made it through to the finals*). **4** so as to be connected by telephone (*the operator will put you through*). ● *attributive adjective* **1** (of a flight etc.) that travels the whole distance or journey without interruption or change. **2** (of traffic) going through a place to a destination. **3** (of a road, route, etc.) open at both ends, allowing a continuous journey. □ **be through** *informal* **1** (often foll. by *with*) have finished (*I'm through with the newspaper, you can have it now*). **2** (often foll. by *with*) cease to have dealings; terminate a relationship with (*he and his girlfriend are through*). **3** have no further prospects; be washed up (*is through as a politician*). **through and through 1** thoroughly; in every respect. **2** repeatedly through; through again and again. [Old English *thurh* from West Germanic]

through-ball *noun Soccer* a forward pass that goes through the opposing team's defence.

through-composed *adjective* = DURCHKOMPONIERT.

through·out ● *preposition* **1** through all of; in or to every part of; everywhere in (*was known throughout southwestern Ontario*). **2** during the whole time, extent, or length of; from beginning to end (*we cried throughout the funeral*). ● *adverb* **1** in every part or respect (*the timber was rotten throughout*). **2** during the whole time (*it was a dull speech but I stayed awake throughout*).

through·put *noun* **1** the amount of material put through a process, esp. in manufacturing or computing. **2** processing or handling capacity.

through·way *noun N Amer.* (also esp. *US* **thru·way**) an expressway.

throve *past of* THRIVE.

throw ● *verb* (*past* **threw**; *past participle* **thrown**) **1** *transitive* project (something) with force from the hand or arm through the air, esp. in a particular direction; cast, hurl, fling. **2** *transitive* force violently, esp. in a particular direction or into a particular position; cause to be thrust or

Consonants: b *but*   d *dog*   f *few*   g *get*   h *her*   j *yes*   k *cat*   l *leg*   m *man*   n *no*   p *pen*   r *red*   s *sit*

shot through the air (*the wind threw the ship onto the rocks*; *the snow blower threw the snow onto the lawn*). **3** *transitive* cause to pass into or out of a particular state or condition, esp. suddenly or unexpectedly (*it threw her life into turmoil; the news threw us into a panic*). **4** *transitive* turn or move (part of the body) quickly or suddenly (*threw his arms around her*). **5** *transitive* **a** emit or project (a beam, ray, or light). **b** cast (a shadow). **6** *transitive* (of a ventriloquist) project (the voice) so that it seems to be coming from a source other than the speaker. **7** *transitive* direct (a kiss, wink, look, insult, etc.) at a person. **8** *transitive* **a** give, deliver, or aim (a punch). **b** (often foll. by *on*) *Hockey* deliver (a hit or bodycheck) on an opponent. **9** *transitive* **a** *Sport* (often foll. by *down*) (esp. in wrestling or football) bring (an opponent) to the ground; tackle. **b** (of a horse) cause (its rider) to fall off. **10** *transitive informal* (often foll. by *off*) baffle, confuse, disconcert (*the question really threw me*). **11** *transitive* have (a tantrum or fit etc.). **12** *transitive* host (a party, barbecue, etc.). **13** *transitive* (foll. by *on* or *off*) put on or remove (clothes or an article of clothing) hastily (*throw a jacket on and let's go*). **14** *Baseball & Football* **a** *intransitive* start or participate in a game as a pitcher or quarterback (*who's throwing for the Expos tonight?*). **b** *transitive & intransitive* pitch, pass, or deliver (the ball), esp. in a specified manner or direction (*she threw to the first baseman; he threw deep into the end zone*). **c** *transitive* (of a pitcher in baseball) earn or achieve (a strikeout, complete game, etc.). **15** *transitive informal* lose (a game or race etc.) deliberately. **16** *transitive* move (a switch or lever) in order to turn something on. **17** *transitive* put (a vehicle) into a particular gear (*threw the car into third*). **18** *transitive* **a** cause (a die or dice) to fall on a surface, esp. by releasing or propelling them from the hand. **b** obtain (a specified number) by throwing a die or dice. **19 a** *transitive & intransitive* form (ceramic ware) on a potter's wheel. **b** *transitive* turn (wood etc.) on a lathe. **c** *transitive* twist (silk etc.) into thread or yarn. **20** *transitive* (often foll. by *into*) alter or change deftly into another form or shape. ● *noun* **1** an act of throwing. **2** the distance a thing is or may be thrown (*a stone's throw*). **3** *N Amer.* **a** (in full **throw rug**) a light rug or piece of decorative fabric used as a casual covering for furniture. **b** a light shawl or afghan. **4** the act of throwing an opponent or being thrown in wrestling. **5** (prec. by *a*) *informal* each; per item or turn (*$20 a throw*). **6 a** the movement of a crank, cam, or eccentric wheel. **b** the extent of this motion measured on a straight line passing through the centre of motion. **c** the distance between the centre of the crankpins and the centre of the crankshaft. **7** *Geol. & Mining* **a** a fault in strata. **b** the amount of vertical displacement caused by this. **8** the distance moved by the pointer of an instrument etc. □ **throw around** (or **about**) **1** throw in various directions. **2** spend (one's money) in a reckless or ostentatious manner. **throw away 1** dispose of or discard (something no longer wanted), esp. by putting it in the garbage. **2 a** waste or fail to make use of (an opportunity etc.). **b** (often foll. by *on*) waste (money, one's life, etc.) in foolish ventures, on undeserving people, etc. **3** discard (a card). **4** *Theatre* speak (lines) with deliberate underemphasis. **throw back 1** (usu. in *passive*; foll. by *on*) force (a person) to rely on something (*was thrown back on his savings*). **2** pull aside (curtains, bedclothes, etc.), esp. with a sharp movement. **3** swallow (a drink) quickly and in one gulp. **throw caution to the wind** see CAUTION. **throw cold water on** see COLD. **throw a person a curve** confuse someone by doing or saying something unexpected. **throw down** fling, hurl, or bring to the ground or floor. **throw down the gauntlet** (or **glove**) issue a challenge. **throw dust in a person's eyes** see DUST. **throw for** *N Amer. Football* (of a quarterback) amass (a specified number of yards, interceptions, etc.) by passing the ball. **throw good money after bad** incur further loss in a hopeless attempt to recoup a previous loss. **throw one's hand in 1** *Cards* fold. **2** give up; withdraw from a contest. **throw in 1** include at no extra cost. **2** add or make (a remark) casually. **3 a** (in basketball or soccer) throw (the ball) in bounds. **b** (in baseball) return (the ball) from the outfield. **throw in one's lot with** see LOT. **throw in the towel** (or **sponge**) **1** admit defeat. **2** (of a boxer or a boxer's attendant) throw the towel or sponge used between rounds into the air as a token of defeat. **throw light on** see LIGHT¹. **throw off 1** confuse or distract (a person speaking, thinking, or acting) from the matter in hand. **2** discard; contrive to get rid of. **3** write or utter in an offhand manner. **throw oneself at** make eager or overt advances upon (someone) regarded as a potential romantic partner or spouse. **throw oneself into** engage vigorously in. **throw oneself on** (or **upon**) **1** rely completely on (*he threw himself on the mercy of the court*). **2** attack. **throw open 1** open (a window or door etc.) wide and usu. suddenly. **2** (often foll. by *to*) make vulnerable or accessible. **3** invite general discussion on (a question). **throw out 1** discard or dispose of (something no longer wanted), esp. by putting it in the garbage. **2 a** force (a troublemaker, trespasser, unruly patron, etc.) to leave the premises. **b** evict (a tenant etc.) from a house or apartment. **c** *Sport* (of

an official) eject (a player, manager, or coach) from a game as a disciplinary measure. **3** wrench or dislocate (one's back, shoulder, hip, etc.). **4** put forward tentatively. **5 a** reject (a proposal or bill) in Parliament. **b** dismiss (a case or charges) in a court of law. **6** *Baseball* put (a runner) out by throwing the ball to the base before he or she reaches it. **7** cause to project or extend; build (a bridge or pier etc.). **8** *Brit.* = THROW OFF 1. **throw over** desert or abandon. **throw stones** see STONE. **throw together 1** prepare or assemble hastily. **2** introduce; cause to meet. **throw up 1** vomit. **2** abandon. **3** resign from. **4** erect hastily. **5** bring to notice. **6** lift (a sash window) quickly. **throw one's weight around** (or **about**) *informal* act with unpleasant self-assertiveness. □ **throw·able** *adjective* **throw·er** *noun* (also in *combination*). [Old English *thrāwan* twist, turn, from West Germanic]

throw·away ● *adjective* **1** meant to be discarded after esp. one use; disposable (*throwaway diapers*). **2** (of a line, word, etc.) deliberately underemphasized for effect. **3** disposed to throwing things away; wasteful (*throwaway society*). ● *noun* **1** something that is meant to be discarded after esp. one use. **2** *N Amer.* printed material meant to be discarded once read, such as a flyer or advertising supplement. **3** *N Amer.* a child or youth who has been cast out or rejected by family or society (also *attributive*: *throwaway children*).

throw·back *noun* (often foll. by *to*) **1** a person who embodies the principles, views, and characteristics of an earlier era. **2** a thing, such as a song, that recalls a similar thing of a previous era. **3** reversion to ancestral character.

throw cushion *noun N Amer.* (also **throw pillow**) one of usu. several small cushions placed on a chair or chesterfield.

throw-in *noun* (in basketball and soccer) the act of throwing the ball in bounds from the sidelines during play.

throw rug *noun see* THROW *noun* 3a.

thru *preposition & adverb N Amer. informal* through.

thrum¹ ● *verb* (**thrummed**, **thrum·ming**) **1** *transitive & intransitive* play (a stringed instrument) monotonously or unskilfully. **2** *intransitive* (often foll. by *on*) drum idly (*rain thrummed on the roof*). **3** *intransitive* produce or emit a low hum or thrumming sound, esp. monotonously or continuously. ● *noun* **1** a low monotonous hum or drone, such as that of a car or machinery operating. **2 a** music consisting of the unskilled or monotonous playing of a guitar or other stringed instrument. **b** the sound of a guitar being thrummed. [imitative]

thrum² ● *noun* loose strands or wisps of unspun wool or raw fleece etc. twisted and knitted into a toque or mitten etc. ● *transitive verb* (**thrummed**, **thrum·ming**) knit thrums into a mitten or toque etc. at regular intervals. □ **thrummed** *adjective* **thrum·ming** *noun* [Old English from Germanic]

thrush¹ *noun* any small or medium-sized songbird of the family Turdidae. [Old English *thrysce* from Germanic: compare THROSTLE]

thrush² *noun* **1 a** a fungal disease, candidiasis, characterized by white patches on the inside of the mouth and throat and on the tongue. **b** this disease affecting any other part of the body, esp. the vagina, and characterized by pain and severe itching. **2** inflammation affecting the frog of a horse's foot. [17th c.: origin unknown]

thrust ● *verb* (*past* and *past participle* **thrust**) **1** *transitive* push or shove with a sudden force or impulse (*thrust the letter into my pocket; a reporter thrust a microphone into her face*). **2** *transitive* **a** (foll. by *on*) impose (a thing) forcibly on a person; enforce acceptance of (a thing) (*had this task thrust on me at the last minute*). **b** (usu. foll. by *into*) force (a person) into some condition or course of action (*the scandal has thrust him into the limelight*). **3 a** *transitive & intransitive* (often foll. by *through* or *past*) make (one's way) forcibly; advance through a crowd or past an obstacle etc. (*she thrust past me abruptly*). **b** *intransitive* make a sudden lunge forward. **c** *intransitive* (foll. by *at* or *through*) lunge forward with a pointed weapon; stab. ● *noun* **1** a sudden or forcible push or lunge. **2** the propulsive force exerted by the propeller of a ship or aircraft, or developed by a jet or rocket engine. **3** (often foll. by *of*) **a** the principal theme or gist of remarks, an argument, etc. **b** the aim or underlying principle of an undertaking, movement, etc. **4** a caustic, critical, or witty remark aimed at a person. **5 a** a lunge or attack with a pointed weapon. **b** a strong attempt to penetrate an enemy's line or territory. **6** (in full **thrust fault**) *Geol.* a low-angle reverse fault in which older strata is displaced horizontally over newer. **7** the lateral pressure exerted by an arch or other structure against an abutment or support. □ **thrust oneself in** interfere. [Middle English *thruste* etc. from Old Norse *thrýsta*]

thrust·er *noun* **1** a small rocket engine on a spacecraft, used to make alterations in its flight path or altitude. **2 a** (in full **bow thruster**) a propeller located on the bow of a boat or ship used esp. when docking.

---

t *top*   v *voice*   w *we*   z *zoo*   ʃ *she*   ʒ *vision*   θ *thin*   ð *this*   ŋ *ring*   x *loch*   tʃ *chip*   dʒ *jar*   (*see over for vowels*)

b each of several jets or propellers on an offshore rig etc., used for accurate manoeuvring and maintenance of position.

thrust stage *noun* an open stage that extends into the auditorium giving the audience seating around the sides.

thru·way *esp. US var. of* THROUGHWAY.

Thu·cydi·des /θuːˈsɪdɪˌdiːz/ (*c*.455–*c*.400 BC), Greek historian. His *History of the Peloponnesian War* covers events up to about 411 and presents an analysis of the origins and course of the war.

thud ● *noun* a dull low sound like that of a blow on something soft. ● *intransitive verb* (**thud·ded**, **thud·ding**) produce or fall with a thud. □ **thud·ding·ly** *adverb* [prob. from Old English *thyddan* thrust]

thug *noun* **1 a** a vicious ruffian; a violent criminal or gangster. **b** *derogatory* a person regarded as a threat or menace; a punk or bully. **2** (**Thug**) *hist.* a member of a religious organization of professional robbers and assassins in India, who strangled their victims. □ **thug·gery** *noun* **thug·gish** *adjective* **thug·gish·ly** *adverb* **thug·gish·ness** *noun* [Hindi & Marathi *ṭhag* swindler]

thug·gee *noun hist.* the system of robbery and assassination practised by the Thugs. [Hindi *ṭhagī* (as THUG)]

thuja /ˈθuːjə/ *noun* any evergreen coniferous tree of the genus *Thuja*, with small leaves closely pressed to the branches; arborvitae. [modern Latin from Greek *thuia*, an African tree]

Thule **1** /ˈθuːli/ a country described by the ancient Greek explorer Pytheas (*c*.310 BC) as being six days' sail north of Britain, variously identified with Iceland, the Shetland Islands, and, most plausibly, Norway. It was regarded by the ancients as the northernmost part of the world (compare ULTIMA THULE). **2** /ˈtuːli/ an Inuit culture widely distributed from Alaska to Greenland AD *c*.100–1400. Members of the culture hunted whales, seals, walrus, and caribou, lived in semi-permanent houses with whalebone frames located by the sea in winter and probably in tents made of animal skin located inland in summer, and travelled by kayak or dog-drawn sled. **3** /ˈtuːli/ a settlement on the northwest coast of Greenland, founded in 1910 by the Danish explorer Knud Rasmussen (1879–1933). A US air base is located nearby.

thul·ium /ˈθuːliəm, ˈθjuː-/ *noun* a soft metallic element of the lanthanide series, occurring naturally in apatite. Symbol: **Tm**; at. no.: 69. [modern Latin from Latin THULE]

thumb ● *noun* **1 a** the short thick first digit of the human hand, opposable to the fingers. **b** a corresponding digit of the hand or foot of other animals. **2** the part of a glove meant for a thumb. ● *verb* **1** *intransitive* turn the pages of a book with or as if with a thumb (*thumbed through the directory*). **2** *transitive* make (a book or its pages etc.) dirty or worn by or as if by repeated handling with the thumb (*a well-thumbed book*). **3** *transitive* solicit or obtain (a ride etc.) by signalling with a closed fist and raised thumb to passing vehicles while standing at the side of a road or highway. **4** *transitive* touch, feel, handle, or depress etc. with the thumb. □ **be all thumbs** be clumsy; lack manual dexterity. **thumb one's nose** (usu. foll. by *at*) **1** hold one's thumb to the bottom of the nose with the hand open and fingers spread out as a gesture of derision or contempt. **2** mock, deride, or scorn. **thumbs-down** an indication of rejection or failure. **thumbs-up** an indication of success or approval. **under a person's thumb** completely under a person's influence or sway. □ **thumbed** *adjective* (also in *combination*). **thumb·less** *adjective* [Old English *thūma* from a West Germanic root = swell]

thumb index ● *noun* a set of labelled notches cut into the side of a dictionary, diary, etc. for easy reference. ● *transitive verb* provide (a book etc.) with these. □ **thumb-indexed** *adjective*

thumb·nail *noun* **1** the nail of a thumb. **2 a** a brief or concise descriptive account. **b** (*attributive*) designating a description etc. that is short and concise (*a thumbnail sketch*). **3** *Computing* a small picture of a larger image or page layout, often used as a link on a web page.

thumb piano *noun* a musical instrument of southern Africa consisting of a set of keys or tongues attached to a resonator, which are plucked by the thumb and forefingers.

thumb·print *noun* **1** an impression of a thumb used esp. for identification. **2** a distinguishing trait or characteristic.

thumb·screw *noun* **1** an instrument of torture for crushing the thumbs. **2** a screw with a flattened head for turning with the thumb and forefinger.

thumb-sucker *noun* **1** a child that habitually sucks his or her thumb. **2** *informal* a serious article in a newspaper or periodical. □ **thumb-sucking** *noun & adjective*

thumb·tack *N Amer.* ● *noun* a pin with a flat head that may be pushed into a bulletin board for fastening a notice or message etc. ● *transitive verb* fasten (a note, message, artwork, etc.) to a wall or bulletin board etc. using a thumbtack or thumbtacks.

thumb·wheel *noun* a control device for electrical or mechanical equipment in the form of a wheel operated with the thumb.

thump ● *verb* **1** *transitive* beat or strike heavily esp. with the fist (*threatened to thump me*). **2** *intransitive* throb or pulsate strongly (*my heart was thumping*). **3** *intransitive* step or tread heavily; stomp. **4** *intransitive* (usu. foll. by *on*) pound with the hand, esp. to attract attention (*thumped on the door until they let him in*). **5** *transitive informal* achieve a resounding victory over. **6** *transitive & intransitive* play (a tune etc.) with a heavy touch. ● *noun* **1** a dull heavy blow, as with the fist or a blunt instrument. **2** the sound of this. □ **thump·er** *noun* [imitative]

thump·ing ● *adjective* **1** *informal* exceptionally large; huge, walloping (*a thumping majority; a thumping lie*). **2** that thumps. ● *noun* **1** a series of repeated thumps or the sound of this. **2** *informal* a thorough beating. □ **thump·ing·ly** *adverb*

thun·der ● *noun* **1** a loud rumbling or crashing noise accompanying a flash of lightning, caused by the sudden heating and expansion of gases along the channel of the discharge. **2** a resounding loud deep noise (*the thunder of applause*). **3** powerful, vehement, or terrifying speech. ● *verb* **1** *intransitive* (prec. by *it* as subject) (of thunder) sound (*it thundered all night*). **2** *intransitive* make or proceed with a noise suggestive of thunder (*bison thundered across the prairie*). **3** *transitive* utter or communicate in a loud voice or forceful manner; shout, roar ('*Out of my sight!*' *he thundered*). **4** *intransitive* **a** speak loudly, angrily, or with bombast; rant. **b** (usu. foll. by *against*) criticize or denounce loudly or vehemently. □ **steal a person's thunder** spoil the effect of another's idea, action, etc. by expressing or doing it first. □ **thun·der·er** *noun* **thun·dery** *adjective* [Old English *thunor* from Germanic]

Thunder Bay a city and port in NW Ontario, situated at the head of Lake Superior on Thunder Bay; pop. (2001) 109,016. [the name of the bay, with reference to the thunderbird]

thunder·bird *noun* a mythical bird which, according to the legends of many N American Aboriginal peoples, created the thunder with its beating wings and the lightning with its flashing eyes.

thunder·bolt *noun* **1** a flash of lightning with a simultaneous crash of thunder. **2 a** a bolt of lightning believed to be used as an agent of divine punishment or destruction. **b** the representation of a bolt or shaft of lightning wielded by various gods, such as Jupiter and Thor. **3** a sudden and unexpected occurrence or item of news.

thunder·clap *noun* **1** a crash of thunder. **2** a very loud, sudden noise (also *attributive*: *thunderclap voice*). **3** something startling or unexpected.

thunder·cloud *noun* **1** a cumulonimbus cloud with a towering or spreading top, which is charged with electricity and produces thunder and lightning. **2** something threatening or dreadful.

thunder·head *noun esp. N Amer.* a tall cumulonimbus cloud with an anvil-shaped top extending horizontally, usu. portending a thunderstorm.

thun·der·ing *adjective informal* **1** very great or excessive; immense (*a thundering nuisance*). **2** (of a sound or thing producing sound) as loud as thunder. □ **thun·der·ing·ly** *adverb*

thunder mug *noun N Amer. informal* a chamber pot.

thun·der·ous *adjective* **1** powerful, violent, very hard or heavy (*a thunderous headache; a thunderous collision*). **2** very loud; rumbling or resounding like thunder. □ **thun·der·ous·ly** *adverb*

thunder·shower *noun esp. N Amer.* a rain shower accompanied by thunder and lightning.

thunder·storm *noun* a storm with thunder and lightning, and usu. heavy rain or hail.

thunder·struck *adjective* amazed, astonished; overwhelmingly surprised or startled. □ **thunder·strik·ing** *adjective*

thunder thighs *plural noun jocular or derogatory* grotesquely fat or muscular thighs.

thunk[1] *informal* = THUD. [imitative]

thunk[2] *informal esp. jocular past and past participle of* THINK.

Thur. *abbreviation* Thursday.

Thur·ber, James Gro·ver (1894–1961), US humorist and cartoonist. He published many of his essays, stories, and sketches in the *New Yorker* magazine, and among his many collections are *My Life and Hard Times* (1933) and *My World — And Welcome to It* (1942), which contains the story 'The Secret Life of Walter Mitty'. □ **Thurber·esque** *adjective*

Vowels: a *cat*   ɑ *arm*   e *bed*   ɜr *her*   ɜ: *deux*   ə *ago*   ɪ *sit*   i *cosy*   iː *feed*   ɒ *hot*   ɔ *pore*   oː *no*   ʌ *run*   ʊ *put*

thur·ible /ˈθʊərəbəl/ *noun* a censer. [Old French *thurible* or Latin *t(h)uribulum* from *thus thur-* incense (as THURIFER)]

thur·ifer /ˈθʊərɪfər/ *noun* an acolyte carrying a censer. [Late Latin from *thus thuris* incense, from Greek *thuos* sacrifice + *-fer* -bearing]

Thur·in·gia /θjʊˈrɪndʒiə/ a state of central Germany; capital, Erfurt.

Thurs. *abbreviation* Thursday.

Thurs·day ● *noun* the fifth day of the week, following Wednesday. ● *adverb* **1** on Thursday. **2** (**Thursdays**) on Thursdays; each Thursday. [Old English *thunresdæg*, *thur(e)sdæg*, day of thunder, representing Late Latin *Jovis dies* day of Jupiter]

thus *adverb formal* **1 a** in this way; in the manner that has been shown or indicated. **b** as follows; in the manner about to be shown or indicated. **2** therefore, consequently; as a result. **3** so; to the degree or extent indicated (*thus far*). [Old English (= Old Saxon *thus*), of unknown origin]

thus·ly *adverb* thus. ¶ The word *thusly* is generally regarded as a superfluous synonym for *thus* except in those instances where it is used with deliberate irony or humour.

Thut·mose III /θʊtˈmoːsə, -ˈmoːs/ (d.1426 BC), Egyptian king, 1479–26 BC. He extended Egyptian rule to Syria and Nubia, and the prosperity of his reign was reflected in the building program he undertook at Karnak.

thwack ● *noun* **1** a sharp resonant sound as produced esp. by one flat surface striking another. **2** a heavy blow producing such a sound. ● *transitive verb* lash, slap, or whack (a person or thing), esp. with something flat, such as the palm of one's hand. [imitative]

thwart /θwɔːt/ ● *transitive verb* successfully oppose (a person or thing); foil, frustrate, block. ● *noun* a structural member extending across a boat, esp. a seat in a rowboat or canoe. [Old Norse *thvert* neuter of *thverr* transverse = Old English *thwe(o)rh* from Germanic]

thy *possessive pronoun* (*attributive*) (also **thine** before a vowel) of or belonging to thee: now replaced by *your* except in some formal, liturgical, dialect, and poetic uses. [Middle English *thī*, reduced from *thīn* THINE]

thy·la·cine /ˈθaɪləsiːn/ *noun* a Tasmanian doglike carnivorous marsupial with stripes across the rump, now possibly extinct. [modern Latin *Thylacinus* from Greek *thulakos* 'pouch']

thyme /taɪm/ *noun* any herb or shrub of the genus *Thymus* with aromatic leaves, esp. *T. vulgare* grown for culinary use. [Old French *thym* from *thymum* from Greek *thumon* from *thuô* burn a sacrifice]

thymi *pl.* of THYMUS.

thy·mi·dine /ˈθaɪmədaɪn/ *noun Biochem.* a nucleoside of thymine that is found in DNA. [THYMINE + -IDINE]

thy·mine /ˈθaɪmiːn/ *noun Biochem.* a pyrimidine found in all living tissue as a component base of DNA. [*thymic* (as THYMUS) + -INE⁴]

thy·mol /ˈθaɪmɒl/ *noun Chem.* a white crystalline phenol obtained from oil of thyme and used esp. as an antiseptic, preservative, or flavouring.

thy·mus /ˈθaɪməs/ *noun* (*pl.* **thy·mu·ses** or **thymi** /-maɪ/) (in full **thymus gland**) *Anat.* a lymphoid organ situated near the base of the neck of vertebrates which is the site of maturation of T-lymphocytes, in humans becoming much smaller at the approach of puberty. □ **thym·ic** *adjective* [modern Latin from Greek *thumos*]

thy·ris·tor /θaɪˈrɪstər/ *noun* esp. *Brit. Electronics* a semiconductor rectifier in which the current between two electrodes is controlled by a signal applied to a third electrode. [Greek *thura* gate + TRANSISTOR]

thyro- /ˈθaɪrəʊ/ *combining form* of, pertaining to, or connected with the thyroid gland or cartilage.

thy·roid /ˈθaɪrɔɪd/ ● *noun* **1 a** (in full **thyroid gland**) a large ductless gland in the neck of vertebrates which secretes hormones regulating growth and development through control of the rate of metabolism. **b** an extract prepared from the thyroid gland of animals and used to treat hypothyroid conditions, such as goitre and cretinism. **2** (in full **thyroid cartilage**) the largest of the cartilages of the larynx, consisting of two broad four-sided plates joined in front at an angle, enclosing the vocal cords and, in men, forming the Adam's apple. ● *adjective* of, pertaining to, or connected with the thyroid (*thyroid artery*). [obsolete French *thyroide* or modern Latin *thyroides*, irreg. from Greek *thureoeidēs* from *thureos* oblong shield]

thyro·toxi·co·sis /ˌθaɪrəʊˌtɒksɪˈkoːsəs/ *noun Med.* a disorder involving overactivity of the thyroid gland.

thy·rox·ine /θaɪˈrɒksən/ *noun* (also **thy·rox·in**) the main hormone produced and secreted by the thyroid gland which increases the metabolic rate and regulates growth and development in animals. [THYROID + OX- + -INE⁴]

thyr·sus /ˈθɜːrsəs/ *noun* (*pl.* **thyr·si** /-saɪ/) *Gk & Rom. Hist.* a staff or spear tipped with an ornament like a pine cone, carried by Bacchus and his followers. [Latin from Greek *thursos*]

thy·self *pronoun archaic emphatic & reflexive form of* THOU¹, THEE.

Ti *symbol* the element titanium.

ti¹ /tiː/ (also **ti tree**) *noun* any woody plant of the genus *Cordyline* and related genera, esp. *C. terminalis* with edible roots, cultivars of which are frequently grown as houseplants. [Tahitian, Maori, etc.]

ti² /tiː/ *noun* (also **te**) **1** (in tonic sol-fa) the seventh note of a major scale. **2** the note B in the fixed-do system. [earlier *si*: French from Italian, perhaps from *Sancte Iohannes*: see GAMUT]

Tia·mat /ˈtiəmɒt/ (in Babylonian myth) a monstrous primeval being, a dragon who was the mother of the first Babylonian gods; she was slain by Marduk.

Tian·an·men /tiˈɛnənmɛn/ *noun* **1** (in full **Tiananmen Square**) a large public square in the centre of Beijing long used as a site for festivals and rallies. It attracted worldwide attention in spring 1989 when a demonstration involving hundreds of thousands of student-led pro-democracy protesters was suppressed by government troops, who opened fire on the unarmed protesters, killing over 2,000. **2** this demonstration. [Chinese, lit. 'heavenly peace']

Tian·jin /tjenˈdʒɪn/ (also **Tien·tsin**) a port in NE China, in Hubei province; pop. (2002) 6,746,500.

Tian Shan see TIEN SHAN.

ti·ara /tiˈɛrə, -ˈɑːrə/ *noun* **1** a woman's jewelled ornamental coronet or headband worn on the front of the hair. **2** a three-crowned diadem formerly worn by a pope. **3** *hist.* a turban worn by ancient Persian kings. □ **ti·araed** *adjective* [Latin from Greek, of unknown origin]

Ti·ber·ias, Lake /taɪˈbiːriəs/ an alternative name for the Sea of Galilee (see GALILEE, SEA OF).

Ti·ber·ius /taɪˈbiːriəs/ (full name Tiberius Julius Caesar Augustus) (42 BC–AD 37), Roman emperor AD 14–37. Following a distinguished military career, he became the adopted successor of his stepfather and father-in-law Augustus. As emperor he sought to continue Augustus's policies but became increasingly tyrannical toward the end of his reign, which was marked by a growing number of treason trials and executions.

Tiber River /ˈtaɪbər/ a river of central Italy, upon which Rome stands. It rises in the Tuscan Apennines and flows 405 km (252 miles) generally southwestward, entering the Tyrrhenian Sea at Ostia.

Ti·bes·ti Mountains /tɪˈbesti/ a mountain range in north central Africa, in the Sahara in N Chad and S Libya, rising to 3 415 m (11,201 ft.) at Emi Koussi, the highest point in the Sahara.

Tibet /tɪˈbet/ a mountainous country in Asia on the northern side of the Himalayas, since 1965 forming an autonomous region of China; pop. (1999) 2,560,000; capital, Lhasa. Most of the territory forms a high plateau with an average elevation of over 4 000 m (12,500 ft.).

Tibet·an /tɪˈbetən/ ● *noun* **1 a** a native or inhabitant of Tibet. **b** a person of Tibetan descent. **2** the language of Tibet. ● *adjective* of or relating to Tibet or its language.

Tibetan Buddhism *noun* the religion of Tibet, a form of Mahayana Buddhism. The head of the religion is the Dalai Lama, who was also head of the Tibetan state until the Chinese annexation of the country.

Tibeto-Burman ● *adjective* **1** pertaining to Tibet and Burma (Myanmar). **2** designating or pertaining to a group of Sino-Tibetan languages spoken in Asia or the peoples speaking any of these languages. ● *noun* the Tibeto-Burman group of languages.

tibia /ˈtɪbiə/ *noun* (*pl.* **tib·iae** /-bi͵iː/ or **tib·ias**) **1** *Anat.* the inner and larger of the two bones of the lower leg extending from the knee to the ankle, articulating at its upper end with the fibula. *Also called* SHIN BONE. **2** the corresponding part in other tetrapod animals, esp. the tibiotarsus of a bird. **3** the fourth segment of the leg in insects. □ **tib·ial** *adjective* [Latin, = shin bone]

tibio·tar·sus /ˌtɪbioːˈtɑːrsəs/ *noun* (*pl.* **tibio·tar·si** /-saɪ/) the bone in a bird corresponding to the tibia, fused at the lower end with the proximal bones of the tarsus.

tic *noun* **1 a** a disorder characterized by a repeated habitual spasmodic twitching of one or more muscles, esp. of the face, largely involuntary and accentuated under stress. **b** = TIC DOULOUREUX. **2** a habitual mannerism or idiosyncrasy; a habit or quirk. [French from Italian *ticchio*]

tic dou·lou·reux /tɪk duːləˈruː/ *noun* trigeminal neuralgia. [TIC + French *douloureux* 'painful']

Ti·cino /tɪˈtʃiːnoː/ (French **Tes·sin** /tesɑ̃/; German **Tes·sin** /ˈtesiːn/) a predominantly Italian-speaking canton in S Switzerland, on the Italian border; capital, Bellinzona.

tick¹ ● *noun* **1 a** the regular slight click made by a watch or clock. **b** the short soft metallic sound of two things clicking together. **2** a check mark. **3** esp. *Brit. informal* a moment; an instant. **4** *Stock Exch.* the smallest recognized amount by which the price of a commodity or stock etc. may fluctuate. ● *verb* **1** *intransitive* **a** (of a clock etc.) operate with or make a tick. **b** (foll. by *away, down*) (of time) pass. **2** *intransitive* (of a mechanism) operate, function, work (*take it apart to see how it ticks*). **3** *transitive* (often foll. by *off*) mark (an item on a list, a box or option on an application form, a written answer, etc.) with a tick. □ **in two ticks** *Brit. informal* in a very short time. **tick off** *informal* **1** *N Amer.* annoy, irritate. **2** *Brit.* reprimand. **tick over 1** (of a person, project, etc.) be working or functioning at a basic or minimum level. **2** *Brit.* (of an engine etc.) idle. **what makes a person tick** *informal* what makes a person behave in a certain way; a person's motivation. [Middle English: compare Dutch *tik*, Low German *tikk* touch, tick]

tick² *noun* **1** any of various bloodsucking acarids of the families Argasidae and Ixodidae, which attach themselves to the skin of dogs, cattle, and other mammals, and may transmit disease to humans. **2** any of various parasitic flies of the families Hippoboscidae, infesting birds and sheep etc., and Nycteribiidae, infesting bats. [Old English *ticca* (recorded as *ticia*); Middle English *teke, tyke*: compare Middle Dutch, Middle Low German *tēke*, Old High German *zēcho*]

tick³ *noun* *Cdn & Brit. informal* credit (*buy it on tick*). [apparently an abbreviation of TICKET in phr. *on the ticket*]

tick⁴ *noun* **1** a case or cover filled with feathers etc. to form a mattress or pillow. **2** = TICKING. [Middle English *tikke, tēke* from West Germanic from Latin *theca* from Greek *thēkē* case]

tick-borne *adjective* (of a disease) transmitted by ticks.

ticked *adjective* (in full **ticked off**) *informal* angry, displeased.

tick·er *noun* **1** *informal* **a** the heart. **b** a watch. **2** *N Amer.* a telegraphic or electronic machine that prints out data on a strip of paper, esp. stock market information or news reports. **3** a band of headlines running across the bottom of the screen on a television newscast.

ticker·tape *noun* **1** a long narrow strip of paper on which a ticker prints esp. stock prices. **2** this or similar material, such as streamers, ribbon, or confetti, thrown from windows to greet a celebrity in a motorcade (also *attributive*: *tickertape parade*).

tick·et ● *noun* **1 a** a written or printed piece of paper or card entitling the holder to enter a place, watch or participate in an event, travel by public transport, etc. **b** a similar printed card making the bearer eligible for a raffle, draw, or sweepstakes. **c** a receipt for an item left temporarily for safe keeping, such as at a coat check. **2** an official notification of a traffic violation (*parking ticket; speeding ticket*). **3** esp. *N Amer.* **a** a list of candidates for election nominated by a political party or group; a slate. **b** the declared principles or policies of a political party or group. **4** a tag or label attached to an item and giving its name, price, or other details. **5** *Cdn* a negotiable cash receipt issued to a farmer by the manager of a grain elevator for grain received. **6 a** (foll. by *to*) a means of reaching or achieving (*this promotion is my ticket to upper management*). **b** (foll. by *out*) something enabling a person to leave an unfavourable location or situation (*hoped this course would be his ticket out of unemployment*). **7** (prec. by *the*) *informal* the ideal, correct, or required thing (*that's just the ticket*). **8** a person or thing, esp. a performer or performance, the popularity of which is judged according to its availability or accessibility (*the Dirty Realists are the hottest ticket in town right now!*). **9** a certificate of qualification as a ship's master, pilot, etc. **10** *Cdn hist.* = LOCATION TICKET. **11** *Brit.* a certificate of discharge from the army. ● *verb* (**ticket·ed, ticket·ing**) **1 a** *transitive* issue a ticket to (the driver of a vehicle). **b** *transitive & intransitive* place a parking ticket on the windshield of (a car). **2** *transitive* attach a ticket to; label. **3** *transitive* **a** issue (a person) with a ticket for a trip. **b** *informal* (usu. in *passive*) designate (a person) for a particular role or destiny (*is ticketed to be the starting goalie*). □ **write one's own ticket** dictate one's own terms. □ **ticket·ed** *adjective* **ticket·less** *adjective* [obsolete French *étiquet* from Old French *estiquet(te)* from *estiquier, estechier* fix, from Middle Dutch *steken*]

ticket agent *noun* a person who sells tickets to esp. theatrical or sporting events. □ **ticket agency** *noun*

ticket collector *noun* a person who is employed to collect tickets, esp. from passengers on a train.

ticket holder *noun* a person who has purchased a ticket for a sporting or theatrical event, concert, etc.

tickety-boo *adjective* *Cdn & Brit. informal* just fine; all right; in order. [20th c.: origin uncertain]

tick fever *noun* (in humans or cattle) a bacterial or rickettsial fever transmitted by the bite of a tick.

tick·ing *noun* a strong durable usu. striped linen or cotton fabric used esp. to cover mattresses and pillows. [TICK⁴ + -ING¹]

tick·lace /ˈtɪkəlˌas/ *noun* (also **tickle-ass**) *Cdn (Nfld)* = KITTIWAKE. [imitative of its cry]

tickle¹ ● *verb* **1 a** *transitive* lightly touch, stroke, or poke (a person or part of a person's body) in such a way that the nerves are excited, producing a reflex spasmodic movement and usu. laughter. **b** *intransitive* (of a part of the body) be affected by this sensation (*my throat tickles*). **c** *intransitive* cause this sensation (*this sweater tickles*). **2** *transitive* amuse, delight, or excite (a person, curiosity, a sense of humour, etc.) (*this dessert will tickle your palate; I was tickled by the thought of it*). **3** *transitive* prime (a carburetor, esp. on a motorcycle) by allowing extra fuel to pass through it prior to starting. ● *noun* **1** an act of tickling. **2** a tickling sensation (*a tickle in my throat*). □ **tickled pink** (or **to death**) *informal* extremely amused or pleased. **tickle the ivories** *see* IVORY. □ **tick·ler** *noun* **tick·ly** *adjective* [Middle English, prob. frequentative of TICK¹]

tickle² *noun* *Cdn (Nfld & Maritimes)* **1** a narrow strait or channel between islands or between an island and the mainland, esp. one that is difficult to navigate. **2** an entrance to a harbour that is narrow and difficult to navigate. [perhaps from TICKLE¹ *verb*]

tick·lish *adjective* **1** sensitive to tickling. **2** (of a matter to be dealt with etc.) requiring careful treatment or handling; tricky, delicate. **3** (of a person) touchy; easily offended, irritated, or upset. □ **tick·lish·ness** *noun*

tick-tock *noun* the ticking sound of esp. a large clock.

tick-trefoil *noun* any of various leguminous plants of the genus *Desmodium* with seed pods which stick to clothing, fur, etc.

ticky-tacky ● *noun* inferior or cheap material, esp. used in suburban building. ● *adjective* made of ticky-tacky; cheap, in poor taste. [prob. reduplication of TACKY²]

tic-tac-toe *noun* (also **tick-tack-toe**) **1** *N Amer.* a children's game in which players attempt to complete a row of three Xs or three Os marked alternately on a square grid of nine squares drawn on paper or a blackboard etc. **2** *Hockey* **a** a swift three-way passing play that results in a scoring opportunity. **b** (*attributive*) designating a skilful style of play involving quick accurate passes.

tidal *adjective* of, related to, or affected by the tides; ebbing and flowing periodically (*tidal basin; tidal river*). □ **tidal·ly** *adverb*

tidal bore *noun* = BORE³.

tidal flat *noun* = FLAT¹ *noun* 2b.

tidal pool *noun* *N Amer.* a usu. large pool of water that remains on a shore or beach etc. after the tide has receded.

tidal wave *noun* **1** the undulation of the surface of the sea which passes around the earth and causes high tide as its highest point reaches each successive place. **2** (not in technical use) an exceptionally large ocean wave, esp. one caused by an underwater earthquake or volcanic eruption. *Also called* TSUNAMI. **3 a** a widespread manifestation of feeling, opinion, etc. **b** a large or overwhelming quantity or amount of something.

tid·bit *noun* *N Amer.* **1** a small piece of food; a dainty morsel or delicacy. **2** an interesting or piquant item of news or information. [Middle English *tyd bit*, perhaps from dial. *tid* soft, tender + BIT¹]

tid·dler *noun* esp. *Brit. informal* **1** a small fish, esp. a stickleback or minnow. **2** an unusually small thing or person. [perhaps related to TIDDLY² and archaic *tittlebat*, a childish form of STICKLEBACK]

tid·dly¹ *adjective* (**tid·dli·er, tid·dli·est**) esp. *Brit. informal* slightly drunk. [19th c., earlier = a drink: origin unknown]

tid·dly² *adjective* (**tid·dli·er, tid·dli·est**) *Brit. informal* little.

tiddly·wink *noun* **1** a small plastic counter flicked into a cup by being pressed on its edge by a larger one. **2** (in *pl.*) this game. [19th c.: perhaps related to TIDDLY¹]

tide ● *noun* **1 a** the alternate rising and falling of the sea, usu. twice each lunar day in a given place, occurring due to the attraction of the moon and sun. **b** the alternate inflow and outflow of water on a shore or coast produced by this (see EBB *noun* 1, FLOOD *noun* 3). **c** the water as affected by this. **2** the course or trend of opinion, luck, or events (*we must stem the tide of opposition; the third goal turned the tide in our favour*). **3** the flow or movement of a large amount of something (*stop the tide of illegal drugs coming into the country*). **4** (*archaic except when in combination*) a particular time or season (*Eastertide*). ● *intransitive verb* drift with or as if with the tide. □ **tide over** enable or help (a person) to get through esp. a difficult period (*the money will tide me over until Friday; a snack will tide you over until dinner*). □ **tide·less** *adjective* [Old English *tīd* from Germanic, related to TIME]

tide·land *noun* *N Amer.* land that is submerged at high tide.

tide line *noun* **1** the level reached by the sea water at high tide. **2** a mark left on the shore by the water at this level.

tide·mark *noun* **1** a tide line. **2** esp. *Brit.* a mark left on a surface indicating the level reached by water.

tide pool *noun* = TIDAL POOL.

tide rip *noun* = RIP².

tide table *noun* a table indicating the times and levels of high and low tides at a particular place.

tide·water *noun* **1** water carried or affected by tides. **2** *N Amer.* a region situated on tidewater (also *attributive: tidewater port*).

tide·way *noun* **1** a channel in which a tide runs, esp. the tidal part of a river. **2** the ebb or flow in a tidal channel.

tid·ings *plural noun* *literary* news, information. [Old English *tīdung*, prob. from Old Norse *títhindi* events, from *títhr* occurring]

tidy ● *adjective* (**tidi·er, tidi·est**) **1** neat, orderly; methodically arranged. **2** (of a person) **a** having a clean and neat appearance. **b** inclined to keep things neat. **3** free of complications; convenient (*the movie had a very tidy ending*). **4** *informal* considerable (*it cost a tidy sum*). ● *transitive verb* (**tidies, tidied**) (often foll. by *up*) **1** make (a room, oneself, etc.) neat; put or arrange in good order. **2** (also foll. by *away*) put (things) away for the sake of tidiness (*tidy up the mess on the floor; tidy away the dishes*). ● *noun* (*pl.* **tidies**) **1** an act or period of tidying (*I have to give the place a quick tidy before they come*). **2** *Brit.* a receptacle for holding scraps or small objects, esp. on a desk or in a kitchen sink. **3** esp. *US* an antimacassar. □ **tidi·ly** *adverb* **tidi·ness** *noun* [Middle English, = timely etc., from TIDE + -Y¹]

tie ● *verb* (**tied, tying**) **1** *transitive* **a** (often foll. by *together*) bind or fasten (two things) with rope or string etc. **b** (often foll. by *to, on*) fasten or secure (a person or thing) to another with rope or string etc. **c** (often foll. by *up*) confine or restrict the movement of (a person or thing) with rope or string etc. **2** *transitive* **a** form (a string, ribbon, shoelace, necktie, etc.) into a knot or bow. **b** make (a knot or bow) in a piece of rope or string etc. **c** secure (an article of clothing, esp. a shoe or boot) by tying a lace, belt, etc. **3** *transitive* (usu. in *passive*) **a** be closely or inextricably linked to (a person or thing) (*the success of the company is tied to the fortunes of the industry as a whole*). **b** bind or restrict (a person) with an obligation or responsibility etc. **4 a** *transitive & intransitive* (often foll. by *for, at*) finish a game, event, or competition with the same score or standing as (an opponent or opponents) (*the teams tied at three; we tied them for first place*). **b** *transitive* make (a game or score) even (*the goal tied the game*). **c** *transitive* match or equal (a record). **5** *transitive* *Fishing* make (an artificial fly) by dressing a hook with strands of silk and feathers etc. **6** *transitive* *Music* **a** connect (written notes) with a tie or ligature. **b** perform (two notes) as one unbroken tone. **7** *transitive* join (rafters etc.) with a crosspiece etc. ● *noun* **1** a rope, cord, or chain, etc. used for fastening or tying something (*a twist-tie*). **2** a strip of material worn around the neck under the collar and tied with a knot in front. **3** (often in *pl.*) something uniting or restricting people or things; a link or connection, esp. a bond or obligation (*ties to the mob; all economic ties have been severed*). **4 a** a game or competition etc. in which two or more opponents have or finish with the same score (*our team has one win and two ties so far*). **b** the condition of having the same score as an opponent (*the game ended in a tie*). **5** *N Amer.* a wooden or concrete beam laid horizontally to support the rails of a subway or train track. **6** (also **tie beam**) a rod or beam holding parts of a structure together. **7** *Music* a curved line above or below two notes of the same pitch indicating that they are to be played for the combined duration of their time values. **8** *N Amer.* = TIE STALL (also *attributive: tie barn*). □ **fit to be tied** *informal* very angry. **have one's hands tied** see HAND. **tie down 1** fasten or secure with rope to a fixed point. **2** limit or restrict (a person), esp. with responsibility or commitment. **tie in** (foll. by *with*) make or be relevant to or consistent with; fit. **tie the knot** see KNOT¹. **tie one on** *N Amer.* get drunk. **tie up 1** bind or fasten securely with cord etc. **2** (usu. in *passive*) fully occupy or engage (a person), esp. in business or a meeting etc. **3** hinder or obstruct; prevent from acting freely. **4 a** complete (an undertaking etc.). **b** take care of (loose ends). **5** invest or reserve (capital etc.) so that it is not immediately available for use. **6** moor (a boat). **7** secure or tether (an animal). □ **tied** *adjective* **tie·less** *adjective* [Old English *tīgan, tēgan* (v.), *tēah, tēg* (n.) from Germanic]

tie-back *noun* a decorative strip of fabric or cord for holding a curtain back from the window.

tie·break·er *noun* (also **tie·break**) esp. *Sport* **1** a means of determining the winner when two competitors are tied. **2** a goal or point etc. that gives a person or team the lead in a tie game. □ **tie·break·ing** *adjective*

tie clip *noun* an ornamental clip for holding a necktie in place.

tied *adjective* *Brit.* **1** (of a house) occupied subject to the tenant's working for its owner. **2** (of a pub etc.) bound to supply the products of a particular brewery only.

Tiede·mann, Mount /ˈtiːdəmən/ a peak (3 848 m) in the Coast Mountains of SW central BC, situated east of Mount Waddington. [H. O. *Tiedeman*, CPR surveyor d.1891]

tie-down *noun* **1** a device, esp. a cord or strap, used to secure or fasten something (also *attributive: tie-down chain*). **2** a place on an airfield where an airplane may be anchored with ropes running from underneath the wings to eyebolts set in the ground.

tie-dye ● *noun* **1** a method of producing coloured patterns on fabric or a garment by tying parts of it so that they receive less dye than other parts when the fabric is dyed. **2** a garment etc. dyed in this way (also *attributive: tie-dye T-shirt*). ● *transitive verb* dye (fabric or a garment) using this method. □ **tie-dyed** *adjective*

tie-in *noun* **1** a connection or association; a link. **2 a** a joint promotion of related items esp. featuring promotional merchandise produced to take advantage of the success of a movie or television series etc. **b** an item marketed in such a promotion (also *attributive*).

Tien Shan /tjen ˈʃan/ (also **Tian Shan**) a range of mountains lying to the north of the Tarim Basin in the Xinjiang autonomous region and E Kyrgyzstan. Extending for about 2 500 km (1,500 miles), it rises to 7 439 m (24,406 ft.) at Pik Pobedy.

Tien·tsin see TIANJIN.

tie pin *noun* an ornamental pin for holding a necktie in place.

Tiep·olo /ˈtiːɛpəˌloː, ˈtjep-/ **Gio·van·ni Bat·tis·ta** (1696–1770), Italian painter. A leading rococo artist, he used dramatic foreshortening, translucent colour, and settings of theatrical splendour in his numerous frescoes and altarpieces, which include the *Antony and Cleopatra* frescoes in the Palazzo Labia, Venice (*c.*1750).

tier¹ /tiːr/ *noun* **1** each of a series of rows or horizontal units placed one above another in a structure, such as in theatre seating. **2** a rank, grade, or stratum. □ **tiered** *adjective* (also in *combination*). [earlier *tire* from French from *tirer* draw, elongate, from Romanic]

tier² /tair/ *noun* a person who ties something, esp. a person who ties artificial flies for fishing.

tierce /tiːrs/ *noun* **1** *Music* an interval of two octaves and a major third. **2** *Christianity* = TERCE. [Old French *t(i)erce* from Latin *tertia* fem. of *tertius* third]

Tier·ra del Fuego /tiˌɛrə del ˈfweiɡoː/ an island at the southern extremity of S America, separated from the mainland by the Strait of Magellan. It is now divided between Argentina and Chile. [Spanish, lit. 'land of fire']

tie stall *noun* *N Amer.* a stall in a barn in which a cow may be tied (also *attributive: a tie-stall barn*).

tie-up *noun* **1 a** a connection, a link. **b** a business partnership, merger, or takeover, etc. **2** *N Amer.* **a** a stoppage, esp. of labour or business. **b** a traffic jam. **3** *N Amer.* = TIE STALL.

TIFF /tɪf/ *noun* *Computing* a file format used widely in desktop publishing for representing colour or grey-scale images. [acronym from tagged image file format]

tiff *noun* a petty quarrel; a minor argument, disagreement, or rift. [18th c.: origin unknown]

Tif·fany, Louis Com·fort (1848–1933), US glass-maker and interior decorator. He was the son of Charles Louis Tiffany (1812–1902), who founded the New York jewellers Tiffany and Company; a leading exponent of American art nouveau, he produced stained glass and mosaic in a distinctive style, as well as iridescent glass vases and lamps.

tif·fany *noun* (in full **tiffany lamp**) any of various lamps with stained-glass shades, esp. a suspended ceiling lamp with a polygonal shade scalloped around the bottom edge. [L.C. TIFFANY]

tif·fin *noun* (esp. in British India) a light meal eaten esp. at midday; lunch. [apparently from *tiffing* sipping]

Tif·lis /tɪfˈliːs/ the official Russian name (1845–1936) for TBILISI.

tiger *noun* **1** a large powerful carnivorous feline, *Panthera tigris*, tawny yellow in colour with blackish transverse stripes and a white belly, found in several races in parts of Asia. **2** a person of great energy, strength, or courage. **3** (also **tiger economy**) a dynamic economy of one of the smaller East Asian countries, especially that of Singapore,

Taiwan, or South Korea. □ **have a tiger by the tail** be engaged in an undertaking etc. which proves unexpectedly difficult but cannot easily or safely be abandoned. □ **tiger·ish** *adjective* [Old French *tigre* from Latin *tigris* from Greek *tigris*]

tiger beetle *noun* any flesh-eating beetle of the family Cicindelidae, with spotted or striped wing covers.

tiger cat *noun* any moderate-sized feline resembling the tiger, e.g. the ocelot, serval, or margay.

tiger lily *noun* a tall E Asian lily, *Lilium tigrinum*, with flowers of dull orange spotted with black or purple, naturalized in N America.

tiger moth *noun* any moth of the family Arctiidae, having richly spotted and streaked wings suggesting a tiger's skin.

tiger salamander *noun* a large N American salamander, *Ambystoma tigrinum*, which is black with yellow patches or stripes.

tiger's eye *noun* (also **tiger eye**) a yellowish-brown semi-precious variety of quartz with a silky iridescent lustre.

tiger shark *noun* an aggressive shark of warm seas, *Galeocerdo cuvieri*, with dark vertical stripes on the body.

tiger shrimp *noun* a large shrimp marked with dark bands, of the genus *Penaeus*.

tight ● *adjective* **1** set or fastened securely in place so as not to move or to move only with difficulty (*the lid is quite tight*). **2** (of a rope, surface, muscle, etc.) drawn or stretched so as to be tense; not loose, slack, or relaxed. **3** (of clothing etc.) fitting very closely or too closely. **4 a** (of money etc.) scarce; not easily obtainable. **b** (of a money market) in which money is scarce. **5** dense, compact (*roll it into a tight ball*). **6 a** (of control etc.) strictly imposed. **b** (of a deadline, budget, etc.) allowing no leeway. **c** (of a schedule) having no free time; packed with appointments, meetings, events, etc. **7** difficult to deal with or manage; resolved or achieved by a narrow margin (*a tight squeeze*; *a tight situation*). **8** (usu. in *combination*) of such close texture as to be impervious to a specified thing (*airtight*; *watertight*). **9** (of a corner or curve) having a short radius. **10** (of a game, competition, etc.) close. **11** *informal* on terms of close friendship; intimate. **12** *informal* drunk. **13** *informal* (of a person) cheap, stingy. **14** (of a musical group or concert etc.) well organized or coordinated (*we wanted to produce a tight show*). ● *adverb* tightly (*hold on tight!*). □ **run a tight ship** *N Amer.* maintain the efficiency of an organization, company, etc., with strict management. **sit tight 1** remain in one's seat. **2** do nothing, either as a safeguard against making a mistake or so as to wait for an opportunity to get what one wants. **sleep tight!** *see* SLEEP. □ **tight·ly** *adverb* **tight·ness** *noun* [prob. alteration of *thight* from Old Norse *théttr* watertight, of close texture]

tight-assed *adjective* esp. *N Amer.* (also esp. *Brit.* **tight-arsed**) *slang* **1** rigidly conventional and uptight; straightlaced. **2** stingy, cheap. □ **tight-ass** *noun* (also *attributive*).

tight·en *transitive & intransitive verb* (often foll. by *up*) make or become tight or tighter. □ **tighten one's belt** *see* BELT.

tight end *noun* Football **1** an offensive end who lines up next to the tackle and may be used either as a blocker or to receive passes. **2** this position.

tight-fisted *adjective* stingy, cheap. □ **tight-fisted·ness** *noun*

tight-fitting *adjective* **1** (of clothing) fitting very close to the body. **2** that fits snugly or securely (*a tight-fitting lid*).

tight-lipped *adjective* **1** refusing to discuss esp. a particular matter; secretive, reticent (*remains tight-lipped about her plans*). **2** with the lips pursed, esp. in anger.

tightly knit *adjective* (also **tight-knit**) = CLOSE-KNIT.

tight·rope *noun* **1** a rope or wire stretched tightly high above the ground, on which acrobats perform. **2** a delicate or risky situation.

tightrope walker *noun* an acrobat who performs on a tightrope. □ **tightrope walk** *noun* **tightrope walking** *noun*

tights *plural noun* a one-piece article of clothing made usu. of knitted nylon, designed to cover the hips and each of the legs and feet, worn esp. by women and also forming part of the costume worn by male or female dancers, acrobats, etc.

tight·wad *noun* esp. *N Amer. slang* a cheap or miserly person. □ **tight·wad·dery** *noun*

Tiglath-pileser I /ˌtɪɡlæθpaɪˈliːzɜːr/ (*fl.* 12th–11th c. BC) king of Assyria *c.*1115–*c.*1077 BC. He extended Assyrian territory further into Asia Minor, taking Cappadocia and reaching Syria, as well as expanding his kingdom to the upper Euphrates and defeating the king of Babylonia.

Tiglath-pileser III /ˌtɪɡlæθpaɪˈliːzɜːr/ (known as 'Pulu') (died *c.*727 BC), king of Assyria *c.*745–727 BC. He brought the Assyrian Empire to the

height of its power, subduing large parts of Syria and Palestine, and, towards the end of his reign, conquering Babylonia and ascending the Babylonian throne under the name of Pulu.

tigon /ˈtaɪɡən/ *noun* (also **tig·lon** /ˈtaɪɡlən/) the offspring of a tiger and a lioness (*compare* LIGER). [blend of TIGER + LION]

Ti·gray /ˈtiːɡreɪ/ (also **Tigre**) a province of Ethiopia, in the north of the country, bordering Eritrea; capital, Mekele. □ **Ti·gray·an** /tɪˈɡreɪən/ *adjective & noun* (also **Tigre·an**).

tig·ress *noun* **1** a female tiger. **2** a fierce or passionate woman.

Tig·ris River /ˈtaɪɡrɪs/ a river in SW Asia, the more easterly of the two rivers of ancient Mesopotamia. It rises in the mountains of E Turkey and flows 1 850 km (1,150 miles) southeastward through Iraq, passing Baghdad, to join the Euphrates, forming the Shatt al-Arab, which flows into the Persian Gulf.

Tihwa /ˈtiːˈhwɒ/ the former name (until 1954) for URUMQI.

Tiju·ana /tiəˈwɒnə/ a town in NW Mexico, situated just south of the US frontier; pop. (2000) 1,148,700.

Tikal /tiˈkɒl/ an ancient Mayan city in the tropical Petén region of N Guatemala, with great plazas, pyramids, and palaces. It flourished AD 300–800, reaching its peak towards the end of that period.

tiki /ˈtɪki/ (*pl.* **tikis**) ● *noun* (in Maori and Polynesian culture) a large wooden or small greenstone image of a human figure, often worn as a neck pendant. ● *adjective* designating a style of music or ambience suggestive of the tropical islands of the South Pacific (*tiki bar*).

tiki·nagan /tɪkəˈnɒɡən/ *noun Cdn* = CRADLEBOARD. [Cree *tikina:kan*]

tikka /ˈtɪkə, ˈtiːkə/ *noun* (usu. in *combination*) an Indian dish of marinated meat, esp. chicken or lamb, threaded on skewers and grilled. [Punjabi *ṭikkā*]

'til (also **til**) *informal* = UNTIL.

ti·lapia /tɪˈlapiə, -ˈleɪp-/ *noun* a freshwater cichlid fish of the African genus *Tilapia* or a related genus, widely introduced for food. [modern Latin]

Til·burg an industrial city in the S Netherlands, in the province of North Brabant; pop. (2002) 193,400.

Til·bury /ˈtɪlbəri/ the principal container port of London and SE England, on the north bank of the Thames River.

til·bury /ˈtɪlbəri/ *noun* (*pl.* **-ies**) *hist.* a light open two-wheeled carriage. [after the inventor's name]

tilde /ˈtɪldə/ *noun* a mark (˜), placed over a letter, e.g. over a Spanish *n* when pronounced *ny* (as in *señor*) or a Portuguese *a* or *o* when nasalized (as in *São Paulo*). [Spanish, ultimately from Latin *titulus* TITLE]

tile ● *noun* **1** a thin slab of baked clay, usu. of a regular shape, used in series for paving a floor, lining a wall or fireplace, covering a roof, etc. **2** a similar piece of glazed ceramic, cork, linoleum, slate, etc., used for similar purposes. **3** tiles collectively. **4** a hollow, usu. cylindrical pipe made of clay, concrete, or plastic, used for draining land, roads, etc. **5** a thin flat piece used in a game, such as in Scrabble or mah-jong. ● *transitive verb* **1** cover with tiles. **2** lay drainage tile in. □ **on the tiles** *informal* enjoying a night out in a wild or reckless manner, esp. drinking (*went out for a night on the tiles*). □ **tiled** *adjective* **tiler** *noun* [Old English *tigule*, *-ele*, from Latin *tegula*]

tile bed *noun* = SEPTIC FIELD.

tile·fish *noun* (*pl.* same or **tile·fish·es**) any of various fishes of the family Malacanthidae, having elongated or compressed bodies, esp. the brightly coloured *Lopholatilus chamaeleonticeps*, caught for food in deep waters off the Atlantic coast of N America.

tiling *noun* **1** the profession or an instance of covering a surface with tiles. **2 a** work consisting of tiles. **b** tiles collectively. **3** the occupation or an instance of laying drainage tiles.

till¹ = UNTIL. ¶ *Till* is an accepted variant of *until* and may be used interchangeably with it except at the beginning of a sentence, where *until* is preferred in formal writing and speech, as in the example, *Until she finishes her homework, she won't be allowed to play.* [Old English & Old Norse *til* to, related to TILL³]

till² *noun* a cash register or drawer for money in a store etc. □ **have one's hand in the till** used in reference to theft from one's place of work. [Middle English: origin unknown]

till³ *transitive verb* **1** prepare and use (land, soil, etc.) for growing crops. **2** plow (land, a field, etc.). □ **till·able** *adjective* [Old English *tilian* strive for, cultivate, from Germanic]

till⁴ *noun* stiff clay containing boulders, sand, etc. deposited by melting glaciers and ice sheets. [17th c. (Scots): origin unknown]

till·age *noun* **1** the action or process of tilling land. **2** tilled land.

till·er¹ *noun* a horizontal bar fitted to the head of a boat's rudder to turn it in steering. [Anglo-French *telier* weaver's beam, from medieval Latin *telarium* from Latin *tela* web]

till·er² ● *noun* **1** (in full **tiller shoot**) a lateral shoot from the base of the stem, esp. of a cereal grass. **2** = SUCKER 6. ● *intransitive verb* put forth lateral shoots or tillers. □ **till·er·ing** *noun* [apparently representing Old English *telgor*, extended from *telga* bough]

till·er³ *noun* **1** a machine or implement used for breaking up or cultivating soil. **2** a person who tills soil or cultivates a crop.

Til·ley, Sir Sam·uel Leon·ard (1818–96), Canadian politician, Father of Confederation. First elected to the New Brunswick Assembly as a Liberal in 1850, he attended both the Charlottetown and Quebec Conferences as a supporter of Confederation. He served in the Macdonald Cabinet as minister of customs (1867–73) and finance (1878–85), and was Lieutenant-Governor of New Brunswick 1878–93.

Till·son·burg a town in SW central Ontario, southeast of London; pop. (2001) 14,052. □ **Till·son·burg·er** *noun* [G. *Tillson*, early settler *c.*1825]

tilt¹ ● *verb* **1 a** *intransitive* lean from the vertical or incline from the horizontal; assume a slanted position. **b** *transitive* cause to lean, slant, or slope. **2** *intransitive* (often foll. by *towards*) incline towards a particular opinion. **3** *transitive* **a** bias or influence (a decision, verdict, etc.) in favour of a particular person or thing (*the defendant's passionate testimony may have tilted the case in her favour*). **b** aim or direct (something) towards a particular audience or objective (*their advertising is tilted at middle-aged men*). **4** *intransitive* **a** challenge; take on. **b** *hist.* rush or charge at in a joust. **5** *transitive Film* move (a camera) in a vertical plane. ● *noun* **1** a slanting or sloping position; a lean. **2** an inclination or bias. **3 a** an encounter between opponents (*the two teams engaged in an entertaining tilt*). **b** *hist.* a joust between two knights on horseback with lances, each attempting to throw the other from the saddle. **4** a function of some cars and trucks etc. that enables the height and angle of the steering wheel to be adjusted. **5** *Film* the upward or downward pivoting movement of a camera across the screen. **6** (in full **pelvic tilt**) an exercise designed to relieve back ailments by thrusting the pelvis forward. □ **full** (or **at full**) **tilt 1** at full speed. **2** with the utmost force or energy. □ **tilt·er** *noun* [Middle English *tilte* perhaps from an Old English form related to *tealt* unsteady, from Germanic: weapon senses of unknown origin]

tilt² *noun Cdn* (*Nfld.*) **1** a small shack, cabin, or hut characterized by a sloping roof, used seasonally by fishermen and trappers. **2** a rudimentary tent or shelter consisting of a sealskin or canvas covering; a lean-to. [Old English *teld* = Old High German *zelt* tent]

Tilt-a-Whirl *noun* (*N Amer.*) *proprietary* a fairground ride consisting of several cars that spin upon a revolving, tilting platform.

tilth *noun* **1** the condition of cultivated soil (*a fine tilth*). **2** tillage. [Old English *tilth(e)* (as TILL³)]

tilt-rotor *adjective* designating a type of aircraft with rotors that can be tilted to allow the machine either to manoeuvre like a helicopter or fly like a conventional airplane.

Tim. *abbreviation* Timothy (New Testament).

tim·bale *noun* **1** /tɑ̃'bal/ **a** a dish consisting of meat, fish, or vegetables in a creamy sauce, or fruit etc. served in a drum-shaped china or copper mould, a pastry shell, or a similar crust made of rice or pasta. **b** the mould, shell, or crust in which this is served. **2** /tam'bali/ (usu. in *pl.*) each of a pair of single-headed drums played with drumsticks, used esp. in Latin American dance music. [sense 1 from French, sense 2 from Spanish, both ultimately from Arabic *aṭ-ṭabl* 'the drum']

tim·ber ● *noun* **1** wood that has been prepared for use as building material, in carpentry, etc. **2 a** a beam or piece of wood forming or capable of forming part of a building or structure. **b** (usu. in *pl.*) the pieces of wood forming the ribs, bends, or frames of a ship's hull. **3 a** large standing trees suitable for timber. **b** trees in their natural state not considered as building material. **c** an area of woodland or forest. ● *interjection* a warning cry that a tree is about to fall. □ **tim·ber·ing** *noun* [Old English, = building, from Germanic]

timber berth *noun Cdn* = BERTH *noun* 8.

timber cruiser *noun N Amer.* = CRUISER 4. □ **timber cruising** *noun*

tim·bered *adjective* **1** (esp. of a building) made wholly or partly of timber. **2** (of land, a region, etc.) covered with trees; wooded (*timbered mountains*).

timber frame ● *noun* **1** a usu. factory-prepared section of timber framework used in the construction of houses and barns etc. **2** a house or barn etc. built using a timber framework. ● *adjective* **1** (usu. **timber-framed**) (usu. *attributive*) having a frame of esp. large timbers.

2 (*attributive*) (of a house) built using usu. factory-prepared sections of timber framework. □ **timber framer** *noun*

timber·jack *noun N Amer.* = LOGGER.

timber·land *noun N Amer.* land covered with forest yielding timber.

timber licence *noun Cdn Forestry* a licence to cut timber from a berth conditional upon payment of dues to the government.

timber limit *noun Cdn* = LIMIT *noun* 3.

timber·line *noun N Amer.* **1** the altitudinal level on a mountain above which no trees grow. **2** = TREELINE 1.

timber rights *plural noun Cdn Forestry* the rights to cut timber of a certain diameter in a specified region, which are controlled by the provincial government and may be obtained in exchange for payment.

timber slide *noun Cdn* = SLIDE *noun* 10.

timber wolf *noun* = WOLF *noun* 1.

tim·bre /'tambər, 'tãbrə/ *noun* the distinctive character or quality of a sound, esp. that of a musical voice or instrument, apart from its pitch and intensity. □ **tim·bral** *adjective* [French from Romanic from medieval Greek *timbanon* from Greek *tumpanon* drum]

tim·brel /'tɪmbrəl/ *noun archaic* a tambourine or similar instrument. [diminutive of Middle English *timbre* from Old French (as TIMBRE, -LE²)]

Tim·buk·tu /,tɪmbʌk'tuː/ (also **Tim·buc·too**) a town in N Mali; pop. (est. 2002) 34,600. Founded by the Tuareg in the 11th c., it became a Muslim centre of learning and a major trading centre for gold and salt on the trans-Saharan trade routes. **2** any remote or outlandish place in a faraway country (*from here to Timbuktu*).

time ● *noun* **1** the indefinite and continuous duration of existence seen as a series of events progressing from the past through the present into the future. **2 a** the passage of time regarded as affecting people or things (*time heals all wounds; time will tell*). **b** (**Time**; in full **Father Time**) the personification of time, esp. as an old man with a scythe and hourglass. **3** (in *sing.* or *pl.*) **a** a more or less definite portion of time in history, esp. belonging to particular events or circumstances (*the time of Confederation; prehistoric times*). **b** the period contemporary with a specified person (*in Laurier's time*). **c** (prec. by *the*) the era being considered (*scientists of the time*). **d** the prevailing conditions of a period or era (*hard times; times have changed*). **4** (prec. by *a*) an indefinite period (*waited for a time*). **5 a** a portion of time available to do something; free time (*I have some time this afternoon; I'm wasting my time*). **b** the amount of time required to do something (*we don't have time for a walk*). **6 a** (usu. in *combination*) a recognizable part of a day or year (*lunchtime; springtime*). **b** a point in the course of a day expressed by hours and minutes past midnight or noon (*what time is it?; the time is 12:15*). **7** time or an amount of time as measured or determined by a conventional standard (*eight o'clock Eastern Daylight Time; she ran the race in record time*). **8 a** an occasion (*last time I saw you*). **b** an event or occasion qualified in some way (*we had a good time*). **9** a suitable moment or occasion (*let's set a time to meet; now is the time to strike*). **10** *Cdn* (*Maritimes & Nfld*) a festive gathering of friends and relatives, esp. in celebration of an event, such as a wedding. **11** a lifetime (*will last my time*). **12 a** *informal* a prison sentence (*is doing time*). **b** an apprenticeship (*served my time*). **13 a** the date or expected date of death or of childbirth (*my time is drawing near*). **b** a period of gestation. **14** measured time spent at work. **15 a** the rhythm of a piece of music, as shown by division into bars and expressed by a time signature. **b** the tempo characteristic of a type of music, esp. used as the tempo for a particular piece (*this should be played in waltz time*). **c** the duration of a note. **16 a** *Sport* a time out. **b** *Brit.* closing time at a bar or pub. **17** *Cdn* (*Nfld.*) a party or celebration, usu. marking a particular holiday or community event. ● *interjection* **1** (also **time out**) *Sport* used by a player or coach to ask an official for a time out during a game. **2** *Brit.* used to announce closing time at a bar. ● *transitive verb* **1** measure and record the amount of time taken by (a process or activity, or a person doing it). **2** choose or establish a suitable occasion for (*time your remarks carefully; I timed my vacation to coincide with hers*). **3** esp. *Sport* execute (a jump, shot, etc.) at a calculated instant. **4** regulate the duration or interval of; establish times of operation for. **5** arrange the time of arrival of (a train etc.) (*trains are timed to arrive on the hour*). □ **against time** with utmost speed, in order to finish by a certain time (*working against time*). **ahead of one's time** having ideas too enlightened or advanced to be accepted by one's contemporaries. **ahead of time** in advance of an event or occurrence; earlier, beforehand. **all the time 1** constantly (*nags all the time*). **2** at all times (*leaves a light on all the time*). **3** during the whole of the time referred to (often despite some contrary expectation etc.) (*we never noticed, but he was there all the time*). **at one time 1** in or during a known but unspecified past period. **2** simultaneously (*ran three businesses at one time*). **at the same time 1** simultaneously; at a time that is the same for all. **2** nevertheless (*I must tell you the news, but at the same time, I don't want to upset you*). **at a time** separately or in successive groups of a specified number each (*ask your questions one at a time; came three at a time*). **at times** occasionally, periodically. **before one's time 1** prematurely (*old before her time*). **2** before one was born or present etc. (*that was before my time*). **call time 1** *Sport* ask an official for a time out. **2** *Brit.* announce closing time at a bar or pub. **find the time** make arrangements to one's schedule so that there is enough time for a particular activity. **for the time being** for the present; until some other arrangement is made. **give a person the time of day 1** tell a person what time it is. **2** (with *neg.*) *slang* refuse to help or talk or pay attention to a person; snub, ignore. **half the time** *informal* **1** very often, esp. too often (*I couldn't tell if he was being serious half the time*). **2** in a relatively short period (*she did the job in half the time*). **have no time for 1** be unable or unwilling to spend time on. **2** dislike. **have the time 1** be able to spend the time needed. **2** know what time it is. **have a time of it** undergo trouble or difficulty. **in no** (or **less than no**) **time 1** very soon. **2** very quickly. **in one's own good** (or **sweet**) **time** at a pace decided by oneself. **in one's own time** outside working hours. **in time 1** not late, punctual (*was in time to catch the bus*). **2** eventually (*in time you may agree*). **3** in accordance with a given rhythm or tempo, esp. of music. **in one's time** during the prosperous period of a person's life or career; in one's heyday (*in his time he was a great hurdler*). **keep good** (or **bad**) **time 1** (of a clock etc.) record time accurately (or inaccurately). **2** be habitually punctual (or not punctual). **keep time** move or sing etc. in time. **know the time of day** be well informed. **long time no see** see LONG¹. **lose no time** (often foll. by *in* + verbal noun) act immediately (*lost no time in cashing the cheque*). **make time 1** (usu. foll. by *for* or *to* + infin.) find an opportunity to spend time with a person or participate in some activity, esp. while one is already very busy. **2** (usu. foll. by *with*) esp. *US slang* make sexual advances (to a person). **not before time** not too soon; timely. **no time** *informal* a very short interval (*it was no time before they came*). **out of time** at an inappropriate time. **pass the time of day** *informal* exchange a greeting or casual remarks. **time after time 1** repeatedly, on many occasions. **2** in many instances. **time and** (or **time and time**) **again** on many occasions. **time and motion** (usu. *attributive*) concerned with measuring the efficiency of industrial and other operations. **the time of day** the hour by the clock. **the time of one's life** a thrilling, exciting, or extremely enjoyable occasion or moment. **time of the month** *informal* or *euphemism* a woman's menstrual period. **time was** there was a time (*time was when I could do that*). [Old English *tīma* from Germanic]

time and a half *noun* an increased amount of money paid to an employee for overtime work, equal to one and a half times the pay the employee would normally earn for working the same number of hours.

time bomb *noun* **1** a bomb designed to explode at a pre-set time. **2 a** a situation on the verge of becoming a crisis or disaster if not defused in time. **b** an unpredictable or moody person, esp. one whose psychological stability is questioned.

time capsule *noun* **1** a sealed box etc. containing objects chosen as representative of life at a particular time, buried for discovery in the future. **2** an old town, building, etc. which has remained largely unchanged for a long time.

time clock *noun* **1** a clock with a mechanism that records an employee's hours of arrival and departure by stamping these times on a card inserted in it by the employee as he or she enters and leaves. **2** *Sport* the clock on a scoreboard indicating the amount of time remaining to be played in a game or portion of a game.

time code *noun* a coded signal on videotape or film giving information about the frame number, time of recording or exposure, scene, camera, etc.

time-consum·ing *adjective* (of a process, activity, etc.) that requires a large or inconvenient amount of time to complete.

time exposure *noun* **1** a method of taking a photograph in which the film is exposed for longer than the maximum normal shutter setting. **2** a picture taken using this method.

time factor *noun* the passage of time as a limitation on what can be achieved.

time frame *noun* a specific period of time in which something occurs, has occurred, or is planned to occur.

time-honoured *adjective* (also **time-honored**) (of a custom, tradition, etc.) that is revered or respected as a result of having been observed, practised, etc. for many years.

time immemorial *noun* (also **time out of mind**) a longer time than anyone can remember or trace (*these lands have been inhabited from time immemorial*).

time·keep·er *noun* **1** an official responsible for recording time, esp. at a competition or game. **2 a** a device that records time, such as a watch or clock, esp. regarded in terms of its accuracy (*a good timekeeper*). **b** a person regarded in terms of punctuality. □ **time·keep·ing** *noun*

time lag *noun* an interval of time between related events, esp. a cause and its effect.

time-lapse *adjective* designating or pertaining to a method of taking a sequence of photographs using frames taken at long intervals to photograph a slow process, and shown continuously as if at normal speed.

time·less *adjective* not affected by the passage of time; remaining popular, effective, significant, etc., over time (*a timeless truth; timeless beauty*). □ **time·less·ly** *adverb* **time·less·ness** *noun*

time limit *noun* the period of time within which a task must be accomplished or completed.

time·line *noun* **1** a line graduated in years on which esp. historical events are marked, used to teach or learn the dates and order of important events in history. **2** a schedule for a project etc. showing the dates by which certain stages must be completed in order for the project to be ready on time.

time lock *noun* a lock with a timer which prevents its being unlocked until a set time. □ **time-locked** *adjective*

time·ly *adjective* (**time·li·er**, **time·li·est**) opportune; occurring, done, or made at a suitable or appropriate time. □ **time·li·ness** *noun*

time machine *noun* an imaginary machine capable of transporting a person backwards or forwards in time.

time off *noun* a period of time spent away from work, esp. taken for rest or recreation; a vacation.

time out *noun* esp. *N Amer.* **1** *Sport* a short stoppage in play requested usu. by a coach or a player so that a team can consider or discuss strategy, attend to an injured player, etc. **2** a short break or period away from an activity. **3** a brief period during which children are sent to their bedrooms to calm down and reconsider their behaviour. **4** (usu. **time·out**) *Computing* a cancellation or cessation that automatically occurs when a predefined interval of time has passed without a certain event occurring.

time·piece *noun* an instrument, such as a clock or watch, for measuring the passage of time.

timer *noun* **1** a device that measures elapsed time, esp. one that sounds to indicate that a certain amount of time has passed, often used for cooking. **2** a device that can be set to turn an appliance etc. on or off at a pre-set time. **3** a person responsible for keeping track of time.

time-release *adjective* denoting something, esp. a drug preparation, that releases an active substance gradually.

times ● *noun* used following a number to express multiplication of what follows (*two times six is twelve; I'm ten times better than I used to be*). ● *adverb* multiplied by (*the party will cost $10 times the number of people coming*).

time saver *noun* an activity, method, tool, etc., that reduces the amount of time required to do something. □ **time-saving** *adjective*

time scale *noun* the time allowed for or taken by a sequence of events in relation to a broader period of time.

time-sensitive *adjective* that must be completed, performed, arranged, etc. at or by a certain time (*a time-sensitive delivery*).

time series *noun* *Statistics* a series of values of a quantity obtained at successive times, usu. with equal intervals between them.

time-server *noun* a person who changes his or her views to suit the prevailing circumstances, fashion, etc. □ **time-serving** *adjective*

time-share *noun* **1** a property that is owned jointly by several people under a time-sharing arrangement (also *attributive*: *time-share condominium*). **2** a share in a property owned jointly under a time-sharing arrangement.

time-sharing *noun* **1** an arrangement in which a vacation home is jointly owned or rented by several people, each of whom is entitled to use it for a fixed limited period of time each year. **2** the simultaneous use of a single computer system by several users stationed at different terminals and performing different operations.

time sheet *noun* a sheet on which the hours worked by an employee are recorded.

time-shift ● *transitive verb* tape (a television show) on a VCR in order to watch it at a later date. ● *noun* a movement from one time or setting to another, esp. in a movie, novel, etc. (*continual time-shifts make the plot hard to follow*).

time signal *noun* an audible signal or announcement of the exact time of day, esp. broadcast on the radio.

time signature *noun Music* an indication of tempo following a clef, expressed as a fraction with the numerator giving the number of beats in each bar and the denominator giving the basic note value of each beat.

time slot *noun* = SLOT¹ *noun* 3b.

time span *noun* a period of time, usu. of a specified length (*the study was performed over a twelve-week time span*).

times table *noun Math.* **1** a chart showing the products of a number when multiplied by each of the numbers from one to twelve, learned and often memorized by children in school. **2** (in *pl.*) the times tables for each of a range of numbers, esp. those from one to twelve (*do you know your times tables?*).

time-stamp *noun* **1** a record printed on or affixed to a document, item of mail, etc. indicating the time it was received, sent, or generated. **2** *Computing* a piece of data attached to a digital file indicating when the file was received, sent or generated.

time switch *noun Brit.* a switch acting automatically at a pre-set time.

time-table ● *noun* **1** a list or plan of the times or dates when successive things are to occur or be done; a schedule or timeline. **2 a** a student's schedule indicating the days and times of classes. **b** a schedule of departure and arrival times of buses, trains, airplanes, etc. **●** *transitive verb* outline or arrange (events etc.) in a timetable; schedule.

time-tested *adjective* that has, over time, been proven or shown to be effective, useful, or accurate; reliable (*a time-tested remedy*).

time travel *noun* travel through time into the past or the future, esp. as a feature of science fiction. □ **time traveller** *noun*

time trial *noun* a race in which participants are individually timed, often used to determine qualifiers and their starting positions for a later race.

time warp *noun* **1** (in science fiction) an imaginary or hypothetical distortion of space in relation to time that causes or enables a person to remain stationary in time or to travel backwards or forwards in time. **2** a state in which the styles, attitudes, etc. of a past period are retained (*stuck in a 1950s time warp*).

time-waster *noun* **1** a person who wastes time. **2** a thing that causes time to be wasted.

time-wasting ● *adjective* that wastes time. **●** *noun* the act of wasting time.

time-worn *adjective* **1** antiquated. **2** adversely affected by age or time (*a time-worn building*). **3** trite; hackneyed (*a time-worn phrase*).

time zone *noun* each of the longitudinal divisions of the globe throughout which a standard time is used, being one hour or one half-hour behind that of the division to its east.

timid *adjective* **1** easily frightened; apprehensive, meek, shy. **2** characterized by or indicating a fear or shyness (*a timid handshake*). □ **timid·ity** *noun* **timid·ly** *adverb* **timid·ness** *noun* [French *timide* or Latin *timidus* from *timēre* fear]

tim·ing *noun* **1** the ability to act or speak at the right time in order to achieve the greatest effect. **2** the time or period of time chosen for an event etc. **3** the act of recording time. **4** the regulation of the opening and closing of valves in an internal combustion engine.

Ti·misk·a·ming, Lake /təˈmɪskəˌmɪŋ/ (also **Lac Té·mis·ca·mingue**) a long, narrow lake in NE Ontario and NW Quebec, forming part of the border between the two provinces. The southern portion is narrow and quite deep, while the northern portion is wider and more shallow. [Algonquin *timi-s-timing* there is deep and shallow water]

Timi·şoara /ˌtiːmiˈʃwɑrə/ an industrial city in W Romania; pop. (est. 2002) 340,000.

Tim·mins a city in NE central Ontario, situated 298 km north of Sudbury; pop. (2001) 43,686. [N. and H. *Timmins*, founders of the city *c*.1911]

Timor /ˈtiːmɔr/ the largest of the Lesser Sunda Islands, in the S Malay Archipelago; pop. (est. 2002), East Timor 948,300, West Timor 3,888,300. The island was formerly divided into Dutch West Timor and Portuguese East Timor. In 1950 West Timor (chief town, Kupang) was absorbed into the newly formed Republic of Indonesia. In 1975 East Timor (chief town, Dili) declared itself independent but was invaded and occupied by Indonesia in 1976. It gained official independence in 2002. □ **Timor·ese** /ˌtiːmɔrˈiːz/ *noun & adjective*

timor·ous /ˈtɪmərəs/ *adjective* **1** timid; easily alarmed. **2** frightened. □ **timor·ous·ly** *adverb* **timor·ous·ness** *noun* [Old French *temoreus* from medieval Latin *timorosus* from Latin *timor* from *timēre* fear]

Timor Sea an arm of the Indian Ocean between Timor and NW Australia.

Tim·othy /ˈtɪməθi/ **1 St.** (1st c. AD), convert and disciple of St. Paul. Traditionally he was the first bishop of Ephesus and was martyred in the reign of the Roman emperor Nerva. Feast day, Jan. 22 or 26. **2** either of two books of the New Testament, epistles of St. Paul addressed to St. Timothy.

tim·othy /ˈtɪməθi/ *noun* (in full **timothy grass**) a fodder grass, *Phleum pratense*. [Timothy Hanson, who introduced it in Carolina *c*.1720]

tim·pani /ˈtɪmpəni/ *plural noun* (also **tym·pani**) kettledrums. □ **tim·pan·ist** *noun* [Italian, pl. of *timpano* = TYMPANUM]

tin ● *noun* **1** a silvery-white malleable metallic element resisting corrosion, occurring naturally in cassiterite and other ores, and used esp. in alloys and for plating thin iron or steel sheets to form tin plate. Symbol: **Sn**; at. no.: 50. **2 a** a container made of tin (*a cookie tin*). **b** esp. *Brit.* a hermetically sealed container made of tin, tin plate, or aluminum, in which food is preserved and sold; a can. **c** esp. *Brit.* a baking pan. **3** = TIN PLATE. **4** *Brit. slang* money. **●** *transitive verb* (**tinned**, **tin·ning**) **1** seal (food) in an airtight tin for preservation. **2** cover or coat with tin. □ **tinned** *adjective* [Old English from Germanic]

tina·mou /ˈtɪnəˌmuː/ *noun* any S American bird of the family Tinamidae, resembling a grouse but related to the rhea. [French from Galibi *tinamu*]

Tin·ber·gen /ˈtɪnˌbɜrɡən/ **1 Jan** (1903–94), Dutch economist. In 1969 he shared with Ragnar Frisch the first Nobel Prize for economics, awarded for his pioneering work on econometrics. **2** his brother, **Niko·laas** (1907–88), Dutch zoologist and ethologist. From his classical studies on herring gulls, sticklebacks, and wasps, he found that much animal behaviour was innate and stereotyped, and he introduced the concept of displacement activity; he shared a Nobel Prize in 1973 with von Frisch and Lorenz.

tin can *noun* a metal can used to preserve food, esp. a used empty one.

tinc·ture /ˈtɪŋktʃər/ **●** *noun* **1** (often foll. by *of*) a slight infusion of an element or quality; a tinge, trace, or hint. **2** a medicinal solution, usu. in alcohol, of the active constituents of a naturally occurring substance, esp. one of plant origin. **●** *transitive verb* (often foll. by *with*) imbue or affect slightly with (a quality, colour, etc.). [Latin *tinctura* dyeing (as TINGE)]

Tin·dal /ˈtɪndəl/ (also **Tin·dale**) var. of TYNDALE.

tin·der *noun* a dry substance, such as bits of wood, that readily catches fire, used to start a fire from a spark struck with a flint. □ **tin·dery** *adjective* [Old English *tynder*, *tyndre* from Germanic]

tinder·box *noun* **1** *hist.* a box containing tinder, flint, and steel, formerly used for kindling fires. **2** a volatile or explosive person, thing, or situation.

tine *noun* any of a series of projecting points or prongs, such as on a fork, comb, cultivating tool, the antler of a deer, etc. □ **tined** *adjective* (also in *combination*). [Old English *tind*]

tinea /ˈtɪniə/ *noun Med.* ringworm. [Latin, = moth, worm]

tin ear *noun informal* **1** an inability to perceive the subtle meaning of a speech, joke, etc. **2** tone-deafness.

tin·foil *noun* = FOIL² 1c.

ting ● *noun* a thin clear high-pitched sound made by a small bell or glass etc. when struck. **●** *transitive & intransitive verb* emit or cause to emit this sound. [imitative]

tinge ● *transitive verb* (**tinged**, **tinge·ing** or **tin·ging**) (usu. in *passive*; often foll. by *with*) **1** give a slight shade of a usu. specified colour to; tint or modify the colour of (*Maggie has blond hair tinged with red*). **2** modify or affect slightly with the addition of a small amount of a characteristic or quality (*regret tinged with satisfaction*). **●** *noun* **1** a trace of some colour. **2** a trace or trace of something, esp. a quality or emotion. [Latin *tingere tinct-* dye, stain]

tin glaze *noun* a glaze for pottery made white and opaque by the addition of tin oxide. □ **tin glazed** *adjective*

tin·gle ● *noun* **1** a slight prickling or stinging sensation, usu. felt in a limb that has been exposed to cold or which has fallen asleep. **2** a slight tickling sensation or goosebumps as a result of stimulation or excitement. **●** *transitive & intransitive verb* experience or cause this sensation. [Middle English, perhaps var. of TINKLE]

tin·gly *adjective* (**tin·gli·er**, **tin·gli·est**) causing or characterized by tingling.

tin god *noun* **1** a self-important person. **2** an object of unjustified veneration.

tin hat *noun informal* a steel helmet worn esp. by soldiers.

tin·horn *N Amer. slang* ● *noun* a pretentious but unimpressive or insignificant person. ● *adjective* pretentious but unimpressive.

tin·ker ● *intransitive verb* **1** (foll. by *with*, *at*) **a** work in an amateurish or desultory way, esp. to adjust or mend machinery etc. **b** meddle, tamper. **2** (usu. foll. by *with*) make minor adjustments to; refine. ● *noun* **1** an itinerant mender of kettles and pans etc. **2** *Scot. & Irish* a gypsy. **3** a period of tinkering. **4** a clumsy or unskilful worker. □ **not give a tinker's damn** (or **cuss**) not care at all. □ **tin·ker·er** *noun* **tin·ker·ing** *noun* [Middle English: origin unknown]

Tin·ker·toy *noun proprietary* **1** a type of building toy consisting of short coloured dowels that may be inserted into round connecting blocks. **2** (*attributive*) *jocular* designating anything resembling a Tinkertoy model, esp. in appearance or simplicity.

tin·kle ● *verb* **1** *intransitive & transitive* make or cause to make a succession of short light ringing sounds. **2** *intransitive informal* or *euphemism* urinate. ● *noun* **1** a tinkling sound. **2** *informal* or *euphemism* an act of urinating. **3** *Brit. informal* a telephone call (*will give you a tinkle on Monday*). □ **tinkle the ivories** see IVORY. □ **tin·kly** *adjective* [Middle English from obsolete *tink* to chink (imitative)]

tin Liz·zie *noun informal* an old or decrepit car.

tin·ner *noun* **1** a tinsmith. **2** a person who mines tin.

tin·nitus /tɪˈnaɪtəs/ *noun Med.* a ringing in the ears. [Latin from *tinnire* tinnit- ring, tinkle, of imitative origin]

tin·ny *adjective* (**tin·ni·er**, **tin·ni·est**) **1 a** having a sound like that of tin being struck. **b** (of music, esp. on a recording) thin and metallic, missing the lower frequencies. **2** (of a metal object) flimsy, insubstantial. □ **tin·ni·ly** *adverb* **tin·ni·ness** *noun*

tin opener *noun* = CAN OPENER.

Tin Pan Alley *noun informal* or *derogatory* **1** the pop music industry, esp. as associated with the production and exploitation of popular song for commercial gain. **2** (*attributive*) designating musicians, composers, music, etc., associated with or characteristic of the pop music industry. [nickname for 28th Street in New York, the original centre of the US pop music industry, due to the supposed resemblance of pop music to the clanging of pots and pans]

tin plate *noun* sheet iron or sheet steel coated with tin.

tin-plated *adjective* coated with tin. □ **tin-plate** *transitive verb*

tin·pot *adjective* crude, second-rate, inferior (*a tinpot navy*).

tin·sel ● *noun* **1** glittering metallic strands or threads used for decoration, esp. on a Christmas tree. **2** cheap or superficial brilliance or splendour; showiness, gaudiness, glitz. ● *transitive verb* (**tin·selled**, **tin·sel·ling** or **tin·seled**, **tin·sel·ing**) **1** adorn with tinsel. **2** give a speciously attractive or showy appearance to. □ **tin·selled** *adjective* (also **tin·seled**). **tin·sel·ly** *adjective* (also **tin·sely**). [Old French *estincele* spark, from Latin *scintilla*]

Tinsel·town *informal* = HOLLYWOOD. [from the superficial glamour of the film industry]

tin·smith *noun* a person who manufactures or repairs items of tin and tin plate. □ **tin·smith·ing** *noun*

tin·snips *noun* a pair of hand-held shears used to cut sheet metal.

tin soldier *noun* a toy soldier made of metal.

tin·stone *noun* = CASSITERITE.

tint ● *noun* **1 a** a shade, colour, or hue. **b** (in painting) a particular colour obtained by adding a pigment to a base. **2** a faint colour spread over the surface of something to give a specified tone to a different colour. **3** a semi-permanent hair dye. **4** *Printing* **a** a uniform halftone shaded effect produced with a series of parallel lines or dots. **b** a solid coloured background on which lettering or an illustration etc. is printed. ● *transitive verb* **1** apply a tint to (hair, paint, a picture, etc.); colour. **2** give (eyeglasses, window glass, etc.) a darker tone or colour in order to decrease the strength of light passing through. □ **tint·ed** *adjective* **tint·er** *noun* [alteration of earlier *tinct* from Latin *tinctus* dyeing (as TINGE), perhaps influenced by Italian *tinto*]

Tin·tagel /tɪnˈtadʒəl/ a village on the coast of N Cornwall, SW England. Nearby are the ruins of Tintagel Castle, the legendary birthplace of King Arthur and a stronghold of the Earls of Cornwall from the 12th to the 15th c.

tinta·marre /tantəˈmɑr/ *noun Cdn* a noisy parade, esp. the annual celebration on National Acadian Day, August 15, involving a procession, the banging of pots and pans, playing of musical instruments, etc. [French, =ˈdin']

T-inter·sec·tion *noun* an intersection shaped like the letter *T*, at which one road joins another at right angles without crossing it.

tin·tin·nabu·la·tion /ˌtɪntɪˌnabjuˈleɪʃən/ *noun* a ringing or tinkling of bells. [as Latin *tintinnabulum* tinkling bell, from *tintinnare* reduplication of *tinnire* ring]

Tin·tor·etto /ˌtɪntəˈretoː/ (born Jacopo Robusti) (*c.*1518–94), Italian painter. Unusual viewpoints, striking juxtapositions in scale, and bold chiaroscuro effects are typical features of his works, among the most famous of which are the huge canvas *Paradiso* (after 1577) hanging in the main hall of the Doges' Palace in Venice, and his paintings of the life of the Virgin, the life of Christ, and the Passion (1576–88) in the halls of the Scuola di San Rocco, also in Venice.

tin·type *noun* a photograph taken as a positive on a thin tin or iron plate coated with enamel.

tin·ware *noun* articles made of tin or tin plate.

tin whistle *noun* = PENNYWHISTLE.

tiny *adjective* (**tini·er**, **tini·est**) very small; minuscule, minute. □ **tini·ly** *adverb* **tini·ness** *noun* [obsolete *tine*, *tyne* (adj. & n.) small, a little: Middle English, of unknown origin]

-tion *suffix* forming nouns denoting action, such as *contemplation*, or a resulting state or condition, such as *completion* or *protection* (see -ION, -ATION, -ITION, -UTION). [from or after French *-tion* or Latin *-tio -tionis*]

tip¹ ● *noun* **1** an extremity or end, esp. of a small or tapering thing (*tips of the fingers; the northern tip of the island*). **2** a small piece or part attached to or over the end of something. **3** the topmost joint of a fishing rod. **4** (usu. in *pl.*) a leaf bud of tea. ● *transitive verb* (**tipped**, **tip·ping**) **1** provide or adorn with a tip. **2** colour or mark the tip of. □ **on the tip of one's tongue** about to be remembered (*his name is on the tip of my tongue*). **the tip of the iceberg** a small evident part of something known to be much larger or more significant. □ **tipped** *adjective* (also in *combination*). [Old Norse *typpi* (n.), from Germanic (related to TOP¹): prob. reinforced by Middle Dutch & Middle Low German *tip*]

tip² ● *verb* (**tipped**, **tip·ping**) **1** (often foll. by *up*) **a** *intransitive* assume a slanting or leaning position. **b** *transitive* cause to assume a slanting position. **2** (usu. foll. by *over*) **a** *intransitive* become overturned; fall or turn over. **b** *transitive* cause (something) to be overturned. **3** *transitive* **a** tilt (a container) in order to empty its contents (*tipped the bottle to his lips*). **b** (usu. foll. by *into*) pour out or spill (the contents of a container) (*tipped the water into the sink*). **4** *transitive* strike or touch lightly. **5** *transitive* **a** *Hockey* deflect (a shot or the puck) toward the net in an attempt to score. **b** *Baseball* (of a batter) barely hit (a pitch or the ball) foul or into the catcher's glove. **c** *Basketball* tap (a rebound) lightly toward the basket in an attempt to score. ● *noun* **1** a gentle push or slight tilt. **2** *Hockey* an act of deflecting the puck. **3** *Baseball* an act of tipping a pitch or ball (*compare* FOUL TIP). **4** *Basketball* the act or an instance of tapping a ball towards the basket. **5** *Basketball* = TIPOFF 3. **6** *Brit.* **a** a place where garbage is dumped. **b** *informal* a messy or untidy place. □ **tip the balance** settle a matter that was previously undetermined. **tip one's hand** unintentionally reveal one's intentions. **tip one's hat** (or **cap**) **1** raise or touch one's hat or cap in greeting or acknowledgement. **2** (usu. foll. by *to*) acknowledge or thank. **tip off** *Basketball* (of two teams) begin a game with a jump ball. **tip the scales** see SCALE². [Middle English: origin uncertain]

tip³ ● *noun* **1** a small sum of money given in appreciation for a service rendered. **2** a useful suggestion or piece of advice. **3** a piece of private or special information, esp. regarding an investment or bet. ● *transitive verb* (**tipped**, **tip·ping**) **1** give a small sum of money to (a person) in appreciation for a service given. **2** *Brit.* name as the likely winner of a race or contest etc. □ **tip off** *informal* give (a person) advance warning or confidential information, esp. discreetly or covertly. **tip a person the wink** esp. *Brit. informal* give a person private information. [17th c.: origin uncertain]

tipi *var. of* TEEPEE.

tip-in *noun Hockey & Basketball* a goal or basket scored on a tip.

tip·off *noun* **1** a warning or piece of information etc. given discreetly or confidentially. **2** something that serves as a warning; a sign or indication. **3** *Basketball* a jump ball at the start of a game.

tip·per *noun* **1** a person who gives or leaves a tip in appreciation for a service given. **2** *Brit.* a dump truck (also *attributive*: *tipper truck*).

Tip·per·ary /ˌtɪpəˈreri/ a county in the centre of the Republic of Ireland, in the province of Munster; county town, Clonmel.

tip·pet *noun* **1** *Fishing* a length of twisted nylon or hair to which a hook is attached. **2** a short cape or stole worn by women around the neck and shoulders. **3** a similar garment worn as part of some official costumes, esp. by some members of the clergy. [Middle English, prob. from TIP¹]

tipping fee *noun N Amer.* a fee levied for waste dumped in a landfill site.

tipping point *noun* the point at which something permanently changes, after the force for such a change has been steadily growing.

tip·ple ● *verb* **1** *intransitive* drink intoxicating liquor habitually. **2** *transitive* drink (liquor) repeatedly in small amounts. ● *noun informal* an alcoholic drink. □ **tip·pler** *noun* [Middle English, back-formation from *tippler*, of unknown origin]

tippy *adjective* (**tip·pi·er**, **tip·pi·est**) *N Amer. informal* unstable; liable to tip over.

tippy·toe *N Amer. informal* = TIPTOE.

tip·sheet *noun* a publication offering readers information, advice, and predictions, esp. on wagering or the stock market.

tip·staff *noun* **1** a sheriff's officer. **2** a metal-tipped staff carried as a symbol of office. [contraction of *tipped staff*, i.e. tipped with metal]

tip·ster *noun* a person who provides tips or confidential information, esp. about betting at horse races.

tipsy *adjective* (**tipsi·er**, **tipsi·est**) **1** slightly drunk. **2** caused by or showing intoxication (*a tipsy grin*). **3** = TIPPY. □ **tipsi·ly** *adverb* **tipsi·ness** *noun* [prob. from TIP² = inclined to lean, unsteady: for *-sy* compare FLIMSY, TRICKSY]

tip·toe ● *noun* the tips of the toes. ● *intransitive verb* (**tip·toes**, **tip·toed**, **tip·toe·ing**) **1** walk gently with the heels raised and one's weight supported by the toes and balls of the feet. **2** (usu. foll. by *around*) cautiously avoid (*tiptoed around the issue*). ● *adjective* **1** characterized by standing or walking on tiptoe. **2** extremely cautious or careful. ● *adverb* (also **on tiptoe**) (stand etc.) on the toes and balls of the feet with the heels raised.

tip-top *informal* ● *adjective* excellent. ● *noun* the highest point of excellence.

tip-up ● *noun N Amer.* (in ice fishing) a rod or arm that supports the line and tilts up to indicate that a fish has been hooked. ● *adjective* that may be tipped, tilted, or folded up, e.g. a tip-up seat in a theatre.

ti·rade /'taireid/ *noun* a long vehement rant or outburst, esp. in denunciation of a particular thing. [French, = long speech, from Italian *tirata* volley, from *tirare* pull, from Romanic]

tira·mi·su /ˌtiːrəmiˈsuː, -ˈmiːsuː/ *noun* an Italian dessert consisting of layers of sponge cake or biscuit soaked in coffee and brandy or liqueur, filled with mascarpone cheese and topped with cocoa powder. [Italian *tira mi sù*, lit. 'pick me up']

Tir·ana /tɪˈrɒnə/ (also **Tir·anë**) the capital of Albania, on the Ishm River in central Albania; pop. (est. 2002) 404,000.

tire¹ *verb* **1 a** *transitive* (often foll. by *out*) make weak or exhausted through exercise etc. **b** *intransitive* become weak or exhausted from exertion. **2** (usu. foll. by *of*) **a** *transitive* (in *passive*) exhaust the patience or interest of; bore (*I am tired of their excuses*). **b** *intransitive* have one's interest or patience exhausted by; become fed up with. □ **tiring** *adjective* [Old English *tēorian*, of unknown origin]

tire² *noun* (*Brit.* **tyre**) a rubber covering, either solid or hollow and inflated, placed around each of the wheels of a vehicle to give a soft contact with the road. [Middle English, perhaps = archaic *tire* headdress]

tired *adjective* **1** (often foll. by *out*) weak, exhausted, or fatigued from exercise or exertion. **2** (of an idea etc.) overused; trite. **3** (of vegetables, flowers, etc.) limp, no longer fresh. □ **tired·ly** *adverb* **tired·ness** *noun*

tire iron *noun N Amer.* a steel bar with a flat tip, used to remove a tire from the rim of a wheel.

tire-kicker *noun informal* a person who asks to test or be shown an item for sale (esp. an expensive one) without any intention of purchasing it.

tire·less *adjective* showing or characterized by inexhaustible energy; indefatigable (*Janet is a tireless worker*). □ **tire·less·ly** *adverb* **tire·less·ness** *noun*

Ti·resi·as /taiˈriːsiəs/ *Gk Myth* a blind Theban prophet, so wise that even his ghost had its wits and was not a mere phantom; legends account variously for his wisdom and blindness, and some stories also state that he spent seven years as a woman.

tire·some *adjective* **1** wearisome, tedious. **2** *informal* annoying (*you are becoming awfully tiresome*). □ **tire·some·ly** *adverb* **tire·some·ness** *noun*

Tîrgu Mureş /ˌtiːrgu 'mʊreʃ/ a city in central Romania, on the Mureş River; pop. (2002) 162,800.

Tir·ich Mir /ˌtiːrɪtʃ 'miːr/ the highest peak in the Hindu Kush, in NW Pakistan, rising to 7 690 m (25,230 ft.).

Tir-nan-Og /ˌtiːrnaˈnoːg/ *Irish Myth* a land of perpetual youth, the Irish equivalent of Elysium. [Irish, = land of the young]

Tir·pitz /'tɜrpɪts, 'tiːr-/ **Al·fred von** (1849–1930), German admiral. As secretary of state of the German ministry of marine (1897–1916), he was responsible for the enormous growth of the German navy in the years leading up to the First World War.

Tirso de Mol·ina /'tiːrsoː dei məˈliːnə/ (pseudonym of Gabriel Téllez) (1584–1648), Spanish dramatist, who was the creator of the prototype of Don Juan in his play *El Burlador de Sevilla* (1630).

'tis *archaic* it is. [contraction]

tis·ane /tɪˈzan/ *noun* a medicinal infusion formerly made with barley, now usu. made with dried herbs; herbal tea. [French from Latin *ptisana* from Greek *ptisanē* peeled barley]

Ti·siph·one /tɪˈsɪfəni/ *Gk Myth* one of the Furies.

tis·sue *noun* **1** the material of which an animal or plant body, or any of its parts or organs, is composed, consisting of an aggregation of specialized cells (*muscle tissue; nervous tissue*). **2 a** (in full **facial tissue**) a disposable piece of thin soft absorbent paper for blowing one's nose, drying one's eyes, etc. **b** (in full **toilet tissue**) = TOILET PAPER. **3** = TISSUE PAPER. **4** (foll. by *of*) an intricate mass, series, or network of things (*a tissue of lies*). **5** any of various rich or fine materials of a delicate or gauzy texture. □ **tis·suey** *adjective* [Old French *tissu* rich material, past participle of *tistre* from Latin *texere* weave]

tissue culture *noun Biol. & Med.* **1** the growth in an artificial medium of cells derived from living tissue. **2** a culture of this kind.

tissue paper *noun* thin translucent paper, often coloured, used esp. for wrapping fragile articles or gifts.

tissue plasminogen activator *noun* a naturally occurring substance in the walls of blood vessels that is capable of dissolving blood clots in the coronary arteries. Abbr.: **TPA**.

Tisza River /'tiːsa/ a river in SE Europe, the longest tributary of the Danube, which rises in the Carpathian Mountains of W Ukraine and flows 960 km (600 miles) westward into Hungary, then southward, joining the Danube in Serbia northwest of Belgrade.

Tit. *abbreviation* Titus (New Testament).

tit¹ *noun* any of various small birds esp. of the family Paridae. [prob. from Scandinavian]

tit² *noun* **1** *informal* a nipple; a teat. **2** *slang* a woman's breast. □ **go tits up** *slang* = GO BELLY UP (see BELLY). [Old English: compare Middle Low German *titte*]

tit³ *noun Brit. coarse slang* a term of contempt for a person. [20th c.: perhaps from TIT²]

Ti·tan /'taitən/ *noun* **1** (often **titan**) a person or organization of very great power, importance, or strength (*a corporate titan*). **2** *Gk Myth* a member of a family of early gigantic gods, the offspring of Heaven and Earth, who contended for the sovereignty of heaven and were overthrown by Zeus. [Middle English from Latin from Greek]

Ti·tan·ia /taiˈtaniə, tɪ-, -ˈteiniə/ **1** (in medieval folklore) the queen of the fairies, and wife of Oberon. **2** *Astronomy* the largest satellite of Uranus, the 14th closest to the planet (diameter 1 600 km).

Titanic /taiˈtanɪk/ a British passenger liner, supposedly unsinkable and the largest ship in the world when she was built, that struck an iceberg off the coast of Newfoundland on her maiden voyage in April 1912 and sank with the loss of 1,490 lives.

ti·tan·ic¹ /taiˈtanɪk/ *adjective* **1** huge, gigantic, colossal. **2** of or like the Titans. □ **ti·tan·ic·ally** *adverb*

ti·tan·ic² /taiˈtanɪk, tɪ-/ *adjective Chem.* of titanium, esp. in quadrivalent form. □ **titan·ate** /'taitə,neit, 'tɪ-/ *noun*

ti·tan·ium /taiˈteiniəm, tɪ-/ *noun Chem.* a grey metallic element occurring naturally in many clays etc., and used to make strong light alloys that are resistant to corrosion. Symbol: **Ti**; at. no.: 22. [Greek (as TITAN) + -IUM, after *uranium*]

titanium dioxide *noun* (also **titanium oxide**) the oxide TiO_2, an inert compound occurring naturally as the mineral rutile, used esp. as a white pigment in the production of paints and plastics.

tit·bit *noun Brit.* = TIDBIT.

titch *noun informal* **1** *Brit.* a small person. **2** *N Amer.* a small amount. [*Tich*, stage name of Harry Relph (d.1928), English music hall comedian]

titchy *adjective* (also **titch·ie**) (**titch·i·er**, **titch·i·est**) *Brit. informal* very small; tiny.

titer *var. of* TITRE.

tit·fer *noun Brit. slang* a hat. [abbreviation of *tit-for-tat*, rhyming slang]

tit-for-tat *noun* a situation in which a blow, injury, insult, etc. is given in retaliation for one received (also *attributive*: *tit-for-tat insults*). [= earlier *tip* (TIP[2]) *for tap*]

tithe /taɪð/ ● *noun* **1** *hist.* one-tenth of the annual produce of agriculture, formerly taken as a tax for the support of the Church and clergy. **2 a** a tenth of an individual's income, pledged or donated to a church. **b** any tax or donation, usu. of one-tenth of a person's income. **3** a tenth part or very small amount of anything. ● *verb* **1** *transitive & intransitive* (often foll. by *to*) pay one-tenth of (one's earnings etc.), esp. towards the support of a church and clergy. **2** *transitive* impose the payment of a tithe on (a person). □ **tith·able** *adjective* [Old English *teogotha* tenth]

tithe barn *noun hist.* a barn built to store agricultural tithes.

tith·ing /ˈtaɪðɪŋ/ *noun* **1** the practice of taking or paying a tithe. **2** *Brit. hist.* **a** ten householders living close together and collectively responsible for each other's behaviour. **b** the district occupied by them.

Tith·onus /tɪˈθoʊnəs/ *Gk Myth* a Trojan prince with whom the goddess Aurora fell in love. She asked Zeus to make him immortal but omitted to ask for eternal youth, and he became very old and decrepit although he talked perpetually. Tithonus prayed her to remove him from this world and she changed him into a grasshopper, which chirps ceaselessly.

titi /ˈtiːtiː/ *noun* (*pl.* **titis**) any long-coated S American monkey of the genus *Callicebus.* [Tupi]

Ti·tian /ˈtɪʃən/ (Italian name Tiziano Vecellio) (*c.*1488–1576), Italian painter, generally considered to be the most important painter of the 16th-c. Venetian school. His large output of paintings, which are noted for their rich colour, includes religious and mythological scenes, e.g. *Madonna with Saints and Members of the Pesaro Family* (1519–*c.*1528) and *Bacchus and Ariadne* (*c.*1518–23). □ **Titian·esque** *adjective*

ti·tian /ˈtɪʃən/ *adjective* (also **Titian**) (of hair) bright golden auburn. [from TITIAN, by association with the auburn hair portrayed in many of his works]

Ti·ti·caca, Lake /ˌtɪtɪˈkɒkə/ a lake in the Andes, on the border between Peru and Bolivia. At an altitude of 3 809 m (12,497 ft.), it is the highest large lake in the world.

tit·il·late /ˈtɪtəˌleɪt/ *transitive verb* **1** excite, arouse, or stimulate, esp. sexually. **2** delight, amuse. □ **tit·il·lat·ing** *adjective* **tit·il·lat·ing·ly** *adverb* **tit·il·la·tion** *noun* [Latin *titillare titillat-*]

titi·vate /ˈtɪtɪˌveɪt/ *transitive verb* **1** adorn. **2** (often *reflexive*) put the finishing touches to. □ **titi·va·tion** *noun* [earlier *tidivate*, perhaps from TIDY after *cultivate*]

title ● *noun* **1** the name given to a book, work of art, piece of music, etc. **2** the formal heading of each section of a legal document, statute, book, etc. **3 a** the title page of a book or its contents. **b** a book regarded in terms of its title (*published 20 new titles*). **4** a caption or credit in a movie, television show, etc. **5 a** a form of nomenclature indicating a person's status or rank, either appended to a person's name, e.g. *Dr., Mrs., Dame, Lieutenant*, or used as a form of address or reference, e.g. *Your Majesty.* **b** a description indicating a person's role, job, or function, e.g. *Queen, Editor-in-Chief, Assistant Coach.* **6** *Sport* a championship. **7** *Law* **a** the right to the possession of land or property. **b** the evidence of such a right; title deeds. **c** (foll. by *to*) a just or recognized claim. **8** (*attributive*) **a** designating a song featured on an album of the same name (*title track*). **b** designating the role or part in a play etc. from which the title of the piece is taken (*played the title role in the musical 'Oliver'*). **9** *Christianity* **a** a guarantee of support required by a candidate for ordination. **b** each of the parish churches in Rome under a cardinal. ● *transitive verb* give a title to. [Old French from Latin *titulus* placard, title]

titled *adjective* having a title of nobility or rank.

title deed *noun* a legal document containing or constituting evidence of ownership.

title·hold·er *noun* a person who holds a title, esp. the reigning champion in a sport.

title page *noun* a page at the beginning of a book giving the title, author, and usu. the name and location of the publisher.

titlist *noun esp. N Amer.* a titleholder.

tit·mouse *noun* (*pl.* **tit·mice**) any of various small songbirds of the family Paridae, esp. of the genus *Parus.* [Middle English *titmōse* from TIT[1] + Old English *māse* titmouse, assimilated to MOUSE]

Tito /ˈtiːtoʊ/ (born Josip Broz) (1892–1980), Yugoslav military and political leader, prime minister 1945–53 and president 1953–80. He organized a Communist resistance to the German occupation of Yugoslavia in 1941, and emerged as head of the new government at the end of the war; he defied Stalin over policy in the Balkans in 1948, established Yugoslavia as a non-aligned Communist state with a federal constitution, and was made president for life in 1974. □ **Tito·ism** *noun* **Tito·ist** *noun & adjective*

Tito·grad /ˈtiːtoʊˌɡrad/ a former name (1946–93) for PODGORICA.

ti·trate /ˈtaɪtreɪt/ *transitive verb Chem.* ascertain the amount of a constituent in (a solution) by slowly adding measured volumes of a suitable reagent of known concentration until the point when the reaction just begins or ceases to occur. □ **ti·trat·able** *adjective* **ti·tra·tion** *noun*

titre /ˈtaɪtər/ *noun* (also **titer**) **1** *Chem.* the concentration of a solution as determined by titration. **2** *Med.* the concentration of an antibody, as determined by finding the highest dilution at which it is still active. [French, = TITRE]

tits and ass *noun coarse slang* crude or gratuitous sexuality, esp. as featured in a movie or magazine etc.

tit·ter ● *intransitive verb* laugh or giggle, esp. in a nervous or embarrassed manner. ● *noun* a restrained or nervous giggle. [imitative]

tit·tle *noun* **1** the smallest part of something; a minute and insignificant amount; a whit. **2** a small written or printed stroke or dot. [Middle English from Latin (as TITLE)]

tittle-tattle ● *noun* petty gossip. ● *intransitive verb* gossip, chatter. [reduplication of TATTLE]

tit·tup ● *intransitive verb* (**tit·tupped, tit·tup·ping** or **tit·tuped, tit·tup·ing**) (esp. of a horse or rider) gallop, canter, or proceed with a bouncing or bobbing motion. ● *noun* a bouncing canter or movement. [perhaps imitative of hoof beats]

titty *noun* (*pl.* **-ties**) *slang* = TIT[2].

titu·ba·tion /ˌtɪtjuːˈbeɪʃən/ *noun Med.* unsteadiness in posture or gait, esp. a rhythmic nodding of the head and trunk due to a cerebellar disease. [Latin *titubatio* from *titubare* totter]

titu·lar /ˈtɪtjʊlər/ *adjective* **1** being what is specified in name or title only without having the attributes or exercising the functions implied by it (*titular ruler; titular sovereignty*). **2** from whom or which a title or name is taken (*the book's titular hero*). **3** of or relating to a title. □ **titu·lar·ly** *adverb* [French *titulaire* or modern Latin *titularis* from *titulus* TITLE]

titular bishop *noun* a bishop deriving his title from a see no longer in existence, esp. in a non-Christian country.

Titus /ˈtaɪtəs/ **1** (full name Titus Vespasianus Augustus; born Titus Flavius Vespasianus) (AD 39–81), Roman emperor 79–81, son of Vespasian. He ended a revolt in Judea with the conquest of Jerusalem (70), helped to complete the Colosseum, and provided relief for the survivors of the eruption of Vesuvius (79). **2 a St.** (1st c. AD), Greek churchman. A convert and helper of St. Paul, he was traditionally the first bishop of Crete. Feast day (in the Eastern Church) 23 August; (in the Western Church) 6 February. **b** a book of the New Testament, an epistle of St. Paul addressed to St. Titus.

Tiu /ˈtiːuː/ (in Germanic mythology) the god of war and the sky, after whom Tuesday is named.

tix *plural noun informal* tickets.

tiyin /tiːˈjɪn/ *noun* (*pl.* same) a monetary unit of Kyrgyzstan and Uzbekistan equal to one-hundredth of a som. [Kirghiz]

tiyn /tiːˈjən/ *noun* a monetary unit in Kazakhstan, equal to one-hundredth of a tenge. [Kazakh]

tizzy *noun* (*pl.* **-zies**) (also **tiz, tizz**; *pl.* **-es**) *informal* a flustered, agitated, or hysterical state; a panic of excitement or nervousness (*seeing him sends Katherine into a tizzy*). [20th c.: origin unknown]

T-joint *noun* a joint shaped like the letter *T*, at which one pipe joins another at right angles without crossing it.

TKO ● *noun Boxing* a technical knockout. ● *transitive verb* (**TKO's, TKO'd, TKO'ing**) **1** *Boxing* defeat (an opponent) by technical knockout. **2** *informal* thwart (a person), esp. at the last minute to prevent completion of a task (*I would have been on time but I got TKO'd by a subway delay*). ● *abbreviation Boxing* technical knockout.

Tl *symbol* the element thallium.

Tlax·cala /tlɒsˈkɒlə/ **1** a state of east central Mexico. **2** its capital city; pop. (est. 2000) 73,200. □ **Tlax·calan** *adjective & noun*

TLC *abbreviation informal* tender loving care.

Tlem·cen /tlemˈsen/ a city in NW Algeria; pop. (est. 2002) 134,100. From the 13th to the 15th c. it was the capital of the Berber dynasty. It has notable mosques and medieval buildings.

Tlin·git /ˈtlɪŋɡɪt/ ● *noun* (*pl.* same or **Tlin·gits**) **1** a member of an Aboriginal people living on the islands and coast of SE Alaska and northern BC. **2** the language of this people. ● *adjective* of or relating to this people or their culture or language. [Tlingit *ɬi:ngít* person]

T lymphocyte *noun Physiol.* a lymphocyte of a type produced by the thymus gland and active in the immune response. *Also called* T CELL. [T for *thymus*]

TM *abbreviation* **1** trademark. **2** transcendental meditation.

Tm *symbol* the element thulium.

TMJ *abbreviation* **1** the temporomandibular joint. **2** = TEMPOROMANDIBULAR JOINT SYNDROME.

TMR *abbreviation* MOUNT ROYAL 2.

TN *abbreviation* Tennessee (in official postal use).

tn *abbreviation* **1** *US* ton(s). **2** town.

TNT *abbreviation* trinitrotoluene, a high explosive that is relatively insensitive to shock and can be conveniently melted, formed from toluene by substitution of three hydrogen atoms with nitro groups.

T.O. an informal name for Toronto. [abbreviation of Toronto, Ontario]

to ● *preposition* **1** introducing a noun: **a** expressing what is reached, approached, or touched (*fell to the ground*; *drove to Alberta*; *put her face to the window*; *five minutes to six*). **b** expressing what is aimed at: often introducing the indirect object of a verb (*throw it to me*; *explained the problem to them*). **c** as far as; until (*went on to the end*; *will be staying from Tuesday to Friday*). **d** to the extent of (*were all drunk to a man*; *was starved to death*). **e** expressing what is followed (*according to instructions*; *made to order*; *dance to the music*). **f** expressing what is considered or affected (*am used to that*; *that is nothing to me*). **g** expressing what is caused or produced (*turn to stone*; *tear to shreds*). **h** expressing what is compared (*nothing to what it once was*; *comparable to any other*; *equal to the occasion*; *won the game by a score of three to two*). **i** expressing what is increased (*add it to mine*). **j** expressing what is involved or composed as specified (*there is nothing to it*; *more to him than meets the eye*). **k** (**to the**) *Math.* indicating the power (exponent) to which a number is raised (*ten to the minus thirty-three*). **2** introducing the infinitive: **a** as a verbal noun (*to get there is the priority*). **b** expressing purpose, consequence, or cause (*we eat to live*; *left him to starve*; *am sorry to hear that*). **c** as a substitute for *to* + infinitive (*wanted to come but was unable to*). ● *adverb* **1** in the normal or required position or condition (*come to*; *heave to*). **2** in a nearly closed position (*close the door to*). [Old English *tō* (adv. & prep.) from West Germanic]

toad *noun* **1** any frog-like amphibian of the family Bufonidae, esp. of the genus *Bufo*, breeding in water but living chiefly on land, esp. any of those that have a dry warty skin and walk rather than leap. **2** any of various similar amphibians including the Suriname toad. **3** a repulsive or loathsome person. □ **toad·let** *noun* [Old English *tādige*, *tādde*, *tāda*, of unknown origin]

toad·flax *noun* **1** any plant of the genus *Linaria* or *Chaenorrhinum*, with flax-like leaves and spurred yellow or purple flowers. **2** a related plant, *Cymbalaria muralis*, with lilac flowers and ivy-shaped leaves.

toad-in-the-hole *noun Brit.* sausages or other meat baked in Yorkshire pudding batter.

toad·stool *noun* a non-technical name for the spore-bearing structure of various fungi, usu. poisonous or inedible, consisting of a round flat cap that surmounts a slender stalk or stipe.

toady ● *noun* (*pl.* **-ies**) a person who behaves servilely towards another; a sycophant. ● *intransitive verb* (**-ies**, **-ied**) (often foll. by *to*, *up to*) behave servilely or obsequiously towards a person; fawn upon, flatter. □ **toady·ing** *adjective* **toady·ish** *adjective* **toady·ism** *noun* [contraction of *toad-eater*, originally a charlatan's shill who ate or pretended to eat toads, then regarded as poisonous, to demonstrate the charlatan's skill in expelling poison]

to and fro ● *adverb* **1** backwards and forwards. **2** repeatedly between the same points. ● *noun* (usu. **to-and-fro**; *pl.* **tos-and-fros**) **1** movement to and fro. **2** vacillation, indecision, or debate on an issue. □ **toing and froing** constant bustling movement or travelling back and forth, here and there, or from any one spot to another.

toast ● *noun* **1** sliced bread dried and browned on both sides by exposure to dry heat. **2 a** a very brief speech or tribute offered in honour of a person, occasion, institution, etc., prior to drinking, esp. at a formal dinner or celebration. **b** a call by the speaker to other guests to endorse this tribute by raising their glasses before drinking. **3 a** a person (formerly esp. a woman), institution, etc. in whose honour a company is asked to drink. **b** (foll. by *of*) a person or thing that is extremely popular or celebrated among a specified group of people or in a specified place etc. (*she's the toast of the town*). **4** *N Amer. informal* a

person or thing that is or is about to be in trouble or severe difficulty (*if I don't get this done on time I'm toast*). ● *verb* **1** *transitive* cook or brown (bread, almonds, marshmallows, etc.) by exposure to a source of radiant heat. **2** *intransitive* (of bread etc.) become brown in this way. **3** *transitive* warm (one's feet, oneself, etc.) at a fire etc. **4** *transitive* drink to the health or in honour of (a person or thing). [Old French *toster* roast, ultimately from Latin *torrēre tost-* parch: sense 3a of the noun reflects the notion that a woman's name flavours the drink as spiced toast would]

toast·er *noun* a device used to toast bread etc., esp. an electrical appliance that automatically shuts off when the toast is ready.

toaster oven *noun* a tabletop electrical appliance used as a toaster and as a small oven.

toast·master *noun* an official responsible for announcing or proposing toasts at a public ceremony.

toast·mis·tress *noun* a female official responsible for announcing or proposing toasts at a public ceremony.

toasty *adjective* (**toast·i·er**, **toast·i·est**) **1** comfortably warm. **2** (of wine) characterized by the aroma of maturation in small French oak casks. **3** like or resembling toast. □ **toast·i·ness** *noun*

to·bac·co *noun* (*pl.* **-cos**) **1** a narcotic and addictive preparation of the dried leaves esp. of the plant *Nicotiana tabacum* and hybrids, which is esp. smoked or chewed for its relaxing effects, and used for ceremonial and religious purposes among some N American Aboriginal groups. **2** = TOBACCO PLANT. [Spanish *tabaco*, of uncertain origin]

tobacco mosaic virus *noun* a virus that causes mosaic disease in tobacco and similar effects in other plants, much used in biochemical research.

Tobacco Nation *noun* = PETUN.

to·bac·co·nist *noun* a person who deals in tobacco, esp. the owner of a store selling tobacco, pipes, cigars, cigarettes, and other assorted items.

tobacco pipe *noun* see PIPE *noun* 2a.

tobacco plant *noun* any of several plants of the genus *Nicotiana* of the nightshade family, esp. *N. tabacum* and its cultivars grown for their narcotic leaves which are used for smoking, and other cultivated varieties grown for their fragrant flowers, or for the production of insecticides (see TOBACCO).

To·bago see TRINIDAD AND TOBAGO.

Toba·go·nian /ˌtəˈbeɪˈɡoʊnɪən/ ● *noun* a native or inhabitant of Tobago. ● *adjective* of or relating to the island of Tobago.

to-be *adjective* (usu. in *combination*) that will soon become what is specified; future (*I saw my bride-to-be escorted by my mother-in-law-to-be*).

To·bique River /toʊˈbiːk/ a river in NW New Brunswick, which flows southwestward from the west central part of the province to join the Saint John River south of Grand Falls. [N. *Toubic*, Maliseet chief d.1767]

Tobit /ˈtoʊbɪt/ **1** a pious Jew during the Babylonian Captivity, described in the Apocrypha. **2** a book of the Apocrypha telling the story of Tobit.

to·bog·gan *esp. N Amer.* ● *noun* **1** a long narrow sled without runners, bent or curled upwards at the front, which may be drawn by a rope over compacted snow or ice or used to coast down hills. **2** a similar wooden sled, sometimes equipped with steel runners, usu. drawn by dogs or having a motor, used to transport supplies etc. over snow. ● *intransitive verb* **1** ride on a toboggan. **2** coast down hills on a toboggan. □ **toboggan down** slide or coast down (a slope, slide, or hill) on a toboggan. □ **to·bog·gan·er** *noun* **to·bog·gan·ing** *noun* [Canadian French *tabaganne* from Mi'kmaq *topaǥan* sled]

toboggan slide *noun* **1** *informal* a rapid and usu. irreversible decline. **2** = SLIDE *noun* 8.

To·bruk /təˈbrʊk/ a port on the Mediterranean coast of NE Libya; pop. (2002) 146,800. It was the scene of fierce fighting during the North African campaign in the Second World War.

Toby jug *noun* (also **Toby**) a beer mug in the form of a stout old man wearing a long full-skirted coat and a three-cornered hat. [familiar form of the name *Tobias*]

To·can·tins /ˌtoʊkənˈtiːns/ a river of S America, which rises in central Brazil and flows 2 640 km (1,640 miles) northward, joining the Pará to enter the Atlantic through a large estuary at Belém.

toc·cata /təˈkɑːtə/ *noun* a brisk musical composition for a keyboard instrument, having the air of an improvisation and designed to demonstrate the performer's touch and technique. [Italian, fem. past participle of *toccare* touch]

Toch·ar·ian /təˈkɛriən/ ● *noun* **1** an extinct Indo-European language spoken by a central Asian people that lived in the first millennium AD.

2 a member of the central Asian people speaking this language. ● *adjective* of or in this language. [French *tocharien* from Latin *Tochari* from Greek *Tokharoi* a Scythian tribe]

tock ● *noun* a short, hollow sound, deeper and more resonant than a tick. ● *intransitive verb* make this sound. [imitative]

to·coph·er·ol /ˌtɒˈkɒfɜrɒl/ *noun* any of several closely related fat-soluble alcohols that occur in plant oils, wheat germ, egg yolk, and leafy vegetables, and which are antioxidants essential in the diets of animals and humans. *Also called* VITAMIN E. [Greek *tokos* offspring + *pherō* bear + -OL[1]]

Tocque·ville /ˈtɒkvɪl/ **Alex·is Charles Henri Mau·rice Clé·rel de** (1805–59), French sociologist and historian, whose principal works are *La démocratie en Amérique* (1835–40) and *L'Ancien Régime* (1856), a social and political study of pre-revolutionary France.

toc·sin *noun* **1** an alarm signal sounded by ringing a bell or bells. **2** a warning or signal. [French from Old French *touquesain*, from Provençal *tocasenh* from *tocar* TOUCH + *senh* signal bell]

to·day ● *adverb* **1** on or in the course of this present day (*shall we go today?*). **2** nowadays, in modern times. ● *noun* **1** this present day (*today is my birthday*). **2** modern times. □ **a week today** next week on this same day; one week from today. [Old English *tō dæg* on (this) day (as TO, DAY)]

Todd, Alex·an·der Ro·ber·tus, Baron (1907–97), Scottish biochemist, who was awarded the 1957 Nobel Prize for chemistry for his work in determining the chemical structure of nucleotides.

tod·dle ● *intransitive verb* **1** walk with short unsteady steps like those of a small child. **2** *informal* **a** take a casual or leisurely walk. **b** (usu. foll. by *off, along*) depart. ● *noun* a casual or awkward walk or stroll. [16th-c. *todle* (Scots & Northern English), of unknown origin]

tod·dler *noun* a child who has just recently learned to walk, usu. between the ages of a year and a half and three years.
□ **toddler·hood** *noun*

toddy *noun* (*pl.* **-dies**) **1** an alcoholic drink made with esp. rum or whisky and hot water, usu. flavoured with lemon juice and sweetened with sugar or honey. **2** the sugary sap of certain kinds of palm, fermented to produce arrack. [Hindustani *tāṛī* from *tāṛ* palm, from Sanskrit *tāla* palmyra]

to-do *noun* a commotion or fuss. [*to do* as in *what's to do* (= to be done)]

to-do list *noun* a list of chores, projects, assignments, etc. that one must or hopes to complete.

tody /ˈtoːdi/ *noun* (*pl.* **todies**) any of several small insect-eating Caribbean birds of the genus *Todus*, which have green backs and red throats and are related to the kingfishers. [French *todier* from Latin *todus*, a small bird]

toe ● *noun* **1** any of the five terminal projections of the foot. **2** the corresponding part of an animal. **3** the part of an item of footwear that covers the toes. **4** *Figure Skating* **a** = TOE PICK. **b** = TOE LOOP. **5** a part resembling a toe or the toes in shape or position, esp. the lower end, tip, or point of something (*the toe of a glacier*). **6** the tip of the head of a golf club. ● *verb* (**toes, toed, toeing**) **1** *transitive* touch (esp. a line or mark) with the toe of one's shoe (*the runners toed the starting line*). **2** *transitive* strike or direct (an object) with the toe (*toed the ball at the net*). **3** (foll. by *in, out*) **a** *intransitive* walk with the toes pointed in or out. **b** *transitive* cause (a pair of objects, such as wheels, speakers, etc.) to converge or diverge slightly at the front. **4** *transitive Golf* strike (the ball) with the toe of the club. □ **make a person's toes curl** excite or thrill a person. **on one's toes** alert, ready. **step** (or **tread**) **on a person's toes** offend or threaten a person by encroaching upon their privileges or responsibilities, esp. unintentionally. **toe the line** conform to a general policy or principle, esp. unwillingly or under pressure. **toe to toe 1** directly in front of and facing (another or each other). **2** (of adversaries, rivals, opponents, etc.) in competition or conflict. **turn up one's toes** *informal* die. □ **toe·less** *adjective* [Old English *tā* from Germanic]

toea /ˈtoːeiə/ *noun* (*pl.* same) a monetary unit of Papua New Guinea, equal to one-hundredth of a kina. [Motu, = 'cone-shaped shell']

toe·cap *noun* the reinforced outer covering of the toe of a boot or shoe.

toe·clip *noun* a moulded plastic or metal clip that holds the front of a cyclist's shoe to the pedal of a bike to prevent the foot from slipping.

toed *adjective* (in *combination*) **1** (of an animal) having toes of a specified number or kind (*three-toed sloth*). **2** (of a shoe, boot, etc.) having a toe of a specified kind (*steel-toed boots*).

toe·hold *noun* **1** a small foothold. **2** a favourable position from which a minor advantage may be gained or influence or support increased

minimally. **3** *Wrestling* a hold in which the opponent's toe is seized and the leg forced backwards.

toe jam *noun* *informal* an accumulation of dirt, dead skin cells, etc. between the toes or under the toenails.

toe loop *noun* *Figure Skating* a loop jump in which the toe of the free skate is dug into the ice to assist the takeoff from the opposite foot.

toe·nail ● *noun* **1** the nail at the tip of each toe. **2** a nail driven obliquely through the end of a board or beam etc. ● *transitive verb* fasten (a board etc.) with a toenail or toenails.

toe pick *noun* *Figure Skating* a jagged toothed edge on the front tip of a skate blade, used to dig into the ice when completing various technical manoeuvres, esp. jumps.

toe·rag *noun* *Brit. slang* a term of contempt for a person. [earlier = tramp, vagrant, from the rag wrapped round the foot in place of a sock]

toe rubber *noun* (usu. in *pl.*) *Cdn* one of a pair of galoshes that extends from the heel of a man's shoe under the sole and over the tip of the toe.

toe shoe *noun* *N Amer.* = POINTE SHOE.

toe-tapping *adjective* denoting music, esp. folk tunes, with a lively beat that inspires listeners to tap their feet.

toff *noun* esp. *Brit. informal* a distinguished, wealthy, or well-dressed person. [perhaps a perversion of *tuft* = titled undergraduate (from the gold tassel formerly worn on the cap)]

tof·fee *noun* **1** a hard and often brittle candy that softens when sucked or chewed, made by boiling sugar and butter, often with other ingredients or flavourings such as nuts. **2** esp. *Brit.* a small individual piece of this. □ **for toffee** *Brit. informal* (prec. by *can't* etc.) (denoting incompetence) at all (*they couldn't sing for toffee*). [earlier TAFFY]

toffee-apple *noun Brit.* an apple covered with a thin coating of toffee.

toffee-nosed *adjective Brit. slang* snobbish, pretentious.

tofu /ˈtoːfuː/ *noun* a pale curd of varying consistency made from soybean milk and used as a source of protein esp. in vegetarian recipes and Asian cuisine. [Japanese *tōfu* from Chinese *dòufu*, from *dòu* beans + *fŭ* rot, turn sour]

tofu burger *noun* = SOYA BURGER.

tog *informal* ● *noun* (in *pl.*) clothes, esp. several articles of clothing constituting a single outfit (*ski togs*). ● *transitive & intransitive verb* (**togged, tog·ging**) (foll. by *out, up*) dress up, esp. elaborately or stylishly. [apparently abbreviation of 16th-c. cant *togeman(s)*, *togman*, from French *toge* or Latin *toga*: see TOGA]

toga /ˈtoːgə/ *noun* **1** *Rom. Hist.* a loose flowing outer garment made of a single piece of cloth and covering the whole body apart from the right arm. **2** a robe or gown of office. □ **toga'd** *adjective* (also **togaed**). [Latin, related to *tegere* cover]

to·geth·er ● *adverb* **1** in company or conjunction (*we built it together*). **2** simultaneously; at the same time (*let's all sing together*). **3** in notional combination; collectively (*makes more than all of us put together*). **4** with coherence or combination of parts or elements belonging to a single body or thing; so as to form a connected, united, or coherent whole (*I hope this mixture holds together*). **5** (of two or more people, parts, etc.) into association, proximity, contact, or union; so as to unite (*tied them together; put two and two together*). **6** into one gathering, company, or body (*called all the employees together*). **7** (of two people) one with another, esp. in a relationship (*we're getting back together*). **8** *informal* **a** into an organized state (*get your things together*). **b** into a rational state of mind (*pull yourself together*). **9** without interruption; consecutively (*they could talk for hours together*). ● *adjective informal* composed, self-assured, well organized; free of emotional difficulties or inhibitions. □ **keep it together** stay in control. **together with** as well as; in addition to. [Old English *tōgædere* from TO + *gædre* together: compare GATHER]

to·geth·er·ness *noun* **1** a feeling of comfort proceeding from a close and harmonious bond or association with others, esp. friends or family; fellowship, camaraderie. **2** the condition of being together.

tog·gle ● *noun* **1** a short decorative crosspiece sewn on one side of esp. a coat or other garment, which may be pushed through a loop or hole on the other side in order to button it up. **2** *Computing* a key or command that is always operated in the same way but has opposite effects on successive occasions, e.g. activating and deactivating a particular function. **3** a pin or other crosspiece put through the eye of a rope, a link of a chain, etc., to keep it in place. **4** a pivoted barb on a harpoon. ● *verb* **1** *Computing* **a** *intransitive* (often foll. by *between*) switch from one function or state of operation to another by using a toggle. **b** *transitive & intransitive* (usu. foll. by *on* or *off*) activate or deactivate (a

Vowels: a *cat* ɑ *arm* e *bed* ɜr *her* ɜː *deux* ə *ago* ɪ *sit* i *cosy* iː *feed* ɒ *hot* ɔ *pore* oː *no* ʌ *run* ʊ *put*

feature or function etc.) using a toggle. **2** *transitive* provide or fasten with a toggle. [18th-c. Naut.: origin unknown]

toggle bolt *noun N Amer.* any of various bolts used for mounting pictures, shelving, etc., to drywall, having wings that close for passage through a drilled hole but spring open after passing through so that the bolt cannot be withdrawn.

toggle switch *noun* **1** an electric switch operated by means of a short projecting lever that is moved usu. up and down. **2** *Computing* = TOGGLE *noun* 2.

Togli·at·ti /tɒˈljati/ (Russian **Toly·at·ti** /tɑˈljatti/) an industrial city and river port in SW Russia, on the Volga River; pop. (2002) 727,600. It was formerly called Stavropol.

Togo /ˈtoːɡoː/ a country in West Africa on the Gulf of Guinea; pop. (est. 2002) 5,285,501; capital, Lomé. □ **Togo·lese** /ˌtoːɡəˈliːz/ *adjective & noun*

To·ho·ku /toːˈhoːkuː/ a region of Japan, on the island of Honshu; capital, Sendai.

toil ● *intransitive verb* **1** work laboriously or incessantly. **2** make slow painful progress (*toiled along the path*). ● *noun* prolonged or intensive labour; drudgery. □ **toil·er** *noun* [Anglo-French *toiler* (v.), *toil* (n.), dispute, from Latin *tudiculare* stir about, from *tudicula* machine for bruising olives, related to *tundere* beat]

toile /twɒl/ *noun* **1** any of various linen or cotton fabrics. **2** a garment reproduced in muslin or other cheap material for fitting or for making copies. [French *toile* cloth, from Latin *tela* web]

toi·let *noun* **1 a** a bathroom fixture for defecation and urination, consisting of a large porcelain basin usu. with a hinged lid and seat and a tank from which running water is flushed to rinse the basin. **b** a room containing such a fixture. **2** the process of washing, dressing, arranging one's hair, etc. (*make one's toilet*). **3** the cleansing of part of the body after an operation or at the time of childbirth. □ **go into** (or **down**) **the toilet** *N Amer.* **1** go into sharp decline, esp. in quality. **2** become irrecoverably lost. [French *toilette* cloth, wrapper, diminutive from *toile*: see TOILE]

toilet paper *noun* (also **toilet tissue**) a long continuous perforated sheet of soft absorbent paper wound around a cardboard roll, used for cleaning oneself after defecating or urinating.

toilet roll *noun* a roll of toilet paper.

toi·letry *noun* (pl. **-ries**) (usu. in pl.) any of various articles or cosmetics used in washing and dressing, such as soap, shampoo, deodorant, etc.

toilet table *noun* esp. *Brit.* = DRESSING TABLE.

toi·lette /twɒˈlet/ *noun* = TOILET 2. [French: see TOILET]

toilet training *noun* the process of teaching a young child to use the toilet. □ **toilet train** *transitive verb*

toilet water *noun* = EAU DE TOILETTE.

toils *plural noun literary* **1** a net or snare. **2** (usu. foll. by *of*) a difficult situation or undesirable position from which one cannot easily extricate oneself. [pl. of *toil* from Old French *toile* cloth, from Latin *tela* web]

toil·some *adjective* involving or requiring great effort or a struggle; laborious.

toil-worn *adjective* worn or worn out by toil.

Tojo, **Hi·deki** (1884–1948), Japanese military and political leader, prime minister 1941–4. He initiated the Japanese attack on Pearl Harbor, and by 1944 he had assumed virtual control of all political and military decision-making; after Japan's surrender in 1945 he was tried and hanged as a war criminal.

toka·mak /ˈtoːkəmak/ *noun Physics* a toroidal apparatus for producing controlled fusion reactions in hot plasma. [Russian acronym, from *toroidal'naya kamera s magnitnym polem* 'toroidal chamber with magnetic field']

To·kay /təˈkeɪ/ *noun* **1** a sweet aromatic wine made near Tokaj in Hungary. **2** a similar wine produced elsewhere, esp. in California and Australia.

toke *N Amer. slang* ● *noun* **1** a drag on a cigarette containing a narcotic substance, esp. marijuana. **2** a marijuana cigarette. ● *intransitive verb* (often foll. by *up*) smoke or take a drag on a marijuana cigarette. [20th c.: origin unknown]

Tok·elau /ˌtoːkəˈlaʊ/ a group of three islands in the W Pacific, between Kiribati and Western Samoa, forming an overseas territory of New Zealand; pop. (2001) 1,445.

tok·en ● *noun* **1 a** a visible or tangible representation of something abstract or immaterial; a thing serving as a sign or symbol (*their handshake was a token of reconciliation*). **b** a thing given as an expression of affection, or to be kept as a memento or souvenir. **2 a** a stamped piece of metal or plastic, often similar to a coin, used as a limited medium of exchange, such as on a bus or subway, in a casino, or in certain coin-operated machines. **b** esp. *Brit.* a gift certificate. **3** a person chosen as a nominal representative of a minority or under-represented group, usu. in order to pre-empt charges of discrimination. **4** *Computing* **a** the smallest meaningful unit of information in a sequence of data. **b** a unique sequence of bits granting permission to transmit information in a token ring. **5** a thing serving as evidence of authenticity or as a guarantee. ● *attributive adjective* **1** chosen out of tokenism as a nominal representative of a minority group (*the token woman on the committee*). **2** done or made as a matter of form; nominal or perfunctory (*token effort*). **3** conducted briefly to demonstrate strength of feeling (*token resistance; token strike*). **4** serving to acknowledge a principle only (*a token payment*). □ **by the same token 1** in the same way; similarly. **2** moreover. **in token of** as a sign, symbol, or evidence of. [Old English *tāc(e)n* from Germanic, related to TEACH]

token·ism *noun* esp. *Politics* the principle or practice of granting minimum concessions, esp. to minority or under-represented groups, as a token gesture to appease public pressure, comply with legal requirements, etc. □ **token·is·tic** *adjective*

token ring *noun Computing* a network architecture configured in such a way that each node must receive a token from an adjacent node before it can transmit information to another.

Tok Pisin /tɒk ˈpɪsɪn/ *noun* an English-based creole used as a commercial and administrative language by over 2 million people in Papua New Guinea. [Tok Pisin = 'pidgin talk']

Toku·ga·wa /ˌtɒkuˈɡɒwə/ the last shogunate in Japan, founded by Tokugawa Ieyasu (1543–1616) and in power 1603–1867. The period was marked by almost complete international isolation: Japanese people were forbidden to travel abroad, and a few traders in Nagasaki were the only foreigners allowed in the country.

Tokyo the capital of Japan and capital of Kanto region; pop. (2002) 8,180,500. Formerly called Edo, it was the centre of the military government under the shoguns (1603–1867). It was renamed Tokyo in 1868, when it replaced Kyoto as the imperial capital. □ **Tokyo·ite** *noun & adjective*

tolar /ˈtɒlɑr/ *noun* the basic monetary unit of Slovenia, equal to 100 stotins. [Slovene]

told *past and past participle of* TELL[1].

tole *noun* **1** enamelled or lacquered tin-plated sheet iron used for making decorative metalwork. **2** (*attributive*) **a** designating articles made of lacquered sheet iron (*tole vase*). **b** denoting the method of painting or lacquering tin plate. [French *tôle* sheet iron, from dial. *taule* table, from Latin *tabula* a flat board]

To·ledo 1 /təˈleidoː/ a city in central Spain on the Tagus River, capital of Castilla-La Mancha region; pop. (2001) 69,450. Toledan steel and sword blades have been famous since the 1st c. BC. **2** /təˈliːdoː/ an industrial city and port on Lake Erie, in NW Ohio; pop. (2000) 313,619. □ **To·led·an** *adjective*

tol·er·able /ˈtɒlərəbəl/ *adjective* **1** able to be endured; bearable. **2** reasonably good; passable, mediocre. □ **tol·er·abil·ity** *noun* **tol·er·ably** *adverb*

tol·er·ance /ˈtɒlərəns/ *noun* **1** a willingness or ability to accept or allow without protest or irritation (*has no tolerance for mediocrity*). **2** the disposition to adopt a liberal attitude towards the opinions or acts of others, esp. those of other religions or ethnic backgrounds. **3** the capacity to withstand or endure. **4 a** the ability of an organism to withstand some particular environmental condition. **b** the ability to endure large doses of active drugs, or to resist the action of a toxin etc. **5** an allowable variation in any measurable property.

tol·er·ant /ˈtɒlərənt/ *adjective* **1** disposed to adopt a liberal attitude towards the beliefs and opinions of others. **2** (usu. foll. by *of*) patient, forgiving; willing to allow or put up with. **3** able to withstand the action of a drug, toxin, etc. **4** able to withstand a (usu. specified) environmental condition (*drought tolerant*). □ **tol·er·ant·ly** *adverb*

tol·er·ate /ˈtɒləˌreɪt/ *transitive verb* **1** allow the existence, practice, or occurrence of without authoritative interference or proscription. **2** endure or allow with patience, leniency, or understanding; put up with. **3** sustain or endure (pain, suffering, etc.). **4** be capable of continued subjection to (a drug, radiation, etc.) without harm. □ **tol·er·ator** *noun* [Latin *tolerare tolerat-* endure]

tol·er·a·tion *noun* **1** the acceptance of forms of religion at variance from those officially recognized by a country or state. **2** = TOLERANCE.

Toleration Act an act of the British Parliament of 1689 granting freedom of worship to dissenters (excluding Roman Catholics and Unitarians) on certain conditions. Its real purpose was to unite all Protestants under William III against the deposed Roman Catholic James II.

Tol·kien /'tɒːlkiːn, 'tɒl-/ **John Ron·ald Reuel** (1892–1973), South African-born English novelist and scholar. He is famous for the fantasy adventures *The Hobbit* (1937) and *The Lord of the Rings* (1954–5), which are set in Middle Earth, an imaginary land peopled by hobbits and other mythical creatures. □ **Tolkien·esque** *adjective*

toll[1] *noun* **1** a sum of money charged for permission to travel along a road or highway etc., the proceeds of which are used for its maintenance (also *attributive*: *toll bridge*). **2** the loss or damage caused by a disaster etc., esp. the number of deaths or casualties (*death toll*). **3** *N Amer.* a charge for a long-distance telephone call. □ **take its toll** cause or be accompanied by loss, damage, injury, etc. [Old English from medieval Latin *toloneum* from Late Latin *teloneum* from Greek *telōnion* toll house, from *telos* tax]

toll[2] ● *verb* **1** *transitive* ring (a bell) with a slow succession of uniform strokes. **2** (of a bell) **a** *intransitive* sound with a slow succession of uniform strokes. **b** *transitive* announce or mark (a death etc.) in this way. **c** *transitive* strike (the hour). ● *noun* the action or sound of a bell as it tolls or is struck. [Middle English, special use of (now dial.) *toll* entice, pull, from an Old English root *-tyllan*]

toll booth *noun* a booth at a bridge or highway etc. where tolls are collected.

toll-free ● *adjective* (esp. of a telephone call, number, or service) that can be made, used, or accessed without charge. ● *adverb* without charge.

toll·gate ● *noun* **1** a gate preventing passage until a toll is paid. **2** *Cdn* a barrier imposed illegally on business or trade etc. pending payment of a bribe or tribute. ● *transitive & intransitive verb* *Cdn* block or hinder (a business contract etc.) pending payment of a bribe or tribute.

toll·gat·ing *noun Cdn* the illegal practice of paying or extorting a bribe or tribute for the right to do business with or within a province, country, etc.

toll house *noun* a house at a tollgate or toll bridge, used by a toll collector.

toll·house cookie *noun* *US* a chocolate chip cookie.

Tol·mie /'tɒlmi/ **Simon Fraser** (1867–1937), Canadian politician, Conservative premier of BC 1928–33.

Tol·pud·dle martyrs /'tɒl,pʌdəl/ six farm labourers from the village of Tolpuddle in Dorset, whose sentence in 1834 to seven years' transportation for attempting to form a trade union caused widespread protests.

Tol·stoy /'tɒːlstɔi, 'tɒl-/ **Leo** (Russian name Count Lev Nikolaevich Tolstoi) (1828–1910), Russian writer. He is best known for the novels *War and Peace* (1863–9), an epic tale of the Napoleonic invasion and the lives of three aristocratic families, and *Anna Karenina* (1873–7), describing a married woman's passion for a young officer and her tragic fate. □ **Tolstoy·an** *noun & adjective*

tolt /tɒːlt/ *noun Cdn* (*Nfld*) an isolated knoll or mound rising above the surrounding plain. [Brit. dial. *tolt* a ridge of trees]

Tol·tec /'tɒltek/ ● *noun* **1** a member of a Nahuatl people that flourished in Mexico before the Aztecs. **2** the language of this people. ● *adjective* of or relating to this people or their language. □ **Tol·tec·an** *adjective* [Spanish *tolteca* from Nahuatl *toltecatl*, lit. 'person from Tula' (ancient Toltec city)]

tolu /tə'luː, 'tɒːluː/ *noun* a fragrant brown balsam obtained from either of two S American trees, *Myroxylon balsamum* or *M. toluifera*, and used in perfumery and medicine. [Santiago de *Tolu* in Colombia]

To·lu·ca /tə'luːkə/ (in full **Toluca de Lerdo** /dei 'lerdoː/) a city in central Mexico, capital of the state of Mexico; pop. (2000) 666,596. It lies at the foot of the extinct volcano Nevado de Toluca, at an altitude of 2 680 m (8,793 ft.).

tolu·ene /'tɒljuːˌiːn/ *noun* (also **tolu·ol** /'tɒljuːɒl/) a colourless aromatic liquid hydrocarbon derivative of benzene, originally obtained from tolu, now obtained from coal tar and petroleum, and used esp. as a solvent as well as in the manufacture of explosives. *Also called* METHYL BENZENE. □ **tolu·ic** *adjective* [TOLU + -ENE]

Tol·yat·ti see TOGLIATTI.

tom[1] *noun* **1** = TOMCAT *noun*. **2** a male of various other animals, such as a turkey. [abbreviation of the name *Thomas*]

tom[2] *noun* = TOM-TOM 2.

toma·hawk ● *noun* a tool or weapon with a handle and a sharp stone or iron cutting head, formerly used by some N American Indians. ● *transitive verb* strike, cut, or kill with a tomahawk. [Virginia Algonquian]

toma·til·lo /tɒmə'tɪloː/ *noun* (*pl.* **-los**) esp. *US* **1** a purplish edible fruit. **2** a Mexican ground cherry, *Physalis philadelphica*, bearing this. [Spanish, diminutive of *tomate* TOMATO]

to·mato /tə'meitoː, -'maːtoː/ *noun* (*pl.* **-toes**) **1** a glossy, usu. bright red and spherical pulpy edible fruit, eaten both raw and cooked as a vegetable. **2** a solanaceous plant, *Lycopersicon esculentum*, bearing this. □ **to·mato·ey** *adjective* [17th-c. *tomate*, = French or Spanish & Portuguese, from Mexican *tomatl*]

tomato clam cocktail *noun* a drink consisting of tomato juice mixed with clam juice.

tomb /tuːm/ *noun* **1** a large esp. underground vault for the burial of the dead. **2** an excavation in the earth or in rock to receive a corpse. **3** a monument erected over a person's burial place. **4** (prec. by *the*) *literary* the state of death. [Old French *tombe* from Late Latin *tumba* from Greek *tumbos*]

Tom·baugh /'tɒmbɒ/ **Clyde Wil·liam** (1906–97), US astronomer. His chief interest was the search for undiscovered planets, and his extensive examination of photographic plates led to his discovery of the planet Pluto on 13 March 1930.

tom·bo·la /tɒm'boːlə/ *noun Brit.* a kind of raffle or draw in which tickets are drawn from a turning drum-shaped container, esp. at a fair or fete. [French *tombola* or Italian from *tombolare* tumble]

tom·bo·lo /'tɒmboːloː/ *noun* (*pl.* **-los**) a spit joining an island to the mainland. [Italian, = sand dune]

Tom·bouc·tou see TIMBUKTU 1.

tom·boy *noun* a girl whose behaviour, pastimes, and style of dress are considered typical of those of a young boy. □ **tom·boy·ish** *adjective* **tom·boy·ish·ly** *adverb* **tom·boy·ish·ness** *noun*

tomb·stone *noun* a slab of stone, usu. engraved with an epitaph, placed upright or laid flat over a person's grave as a memorial.

tom·cat ● *noun* a male cat. ● *intransitive verb* (**-catted**, **-cat·ting**) *slang* (of a man) pursue women promiscuously for sexual gratification.

tom·cod *noun* (*pl.* same) *N Amer.* (also **tommy·cod**) any of various small marine fishes, now esp. either of two fishes of the genus *Microgadus*, *M. tomcod* of the W Atlantic and *M. proximus* of the E Pacific, and the related *Urophycis floridana*.

Tom Collins *noun* an iced cocktail of gin with soda, lemon or lime juice, and sugar. [20th c.: origin unknown]

Tom, Dick, and Harry *noun* (usu. prec. by *any*, *every*) usu. *derogatory* ordinary people taken at random (*the last thing we want is to have every Tom, Dick, and Harry show up at our party*).

tome /toːm/ *noun* **1** a large, heavy, learned book or volume of a work. **2** *informal* or *jocular* a book, esp. one that is excessively long or dull. [French from Latin *tomus* from Greek *tomos* section, volume, from *temnō* cut]

-tome *combining form* forming nouns meaning: **1** an instrument for cutting (*microtome*). **2** a section or segment. [Greek *tomē* a cutting, *-tomos* -cutting, from *temnō* cut]

to·men·tum /tə'mentəm/ *noun* (*pl.* **to·men·ta**) **1** *Bot.* matted woolly down on stems and leaves. **2** *Anat.* the tufted inner surface of the pia mater in the brain. □ **to·men·tose** /tə'mentoːs, 'toː-/ *adjective* **to·men·tous** *adjective* [Latin, = cushion-stuffing]

tom·fool *noun* **1** a foolish or silly person; a buffoon. **2** (*attributive*) foolish, stupid (*a tomfool idea*).

tom·fool·ery *noun* (*pl.* **-eries**) **1** foolish behaviour; nonsense. **2** an instance of this.

tommy *noun* (*pl.* **-mies**) (also **Tommy**) *informal* a British private soldier. [*Tommy* (*Thomas*) *Atkins*, a name used in specimens of completed official forms]

tommy bar *noun Brit.* a short bar used with a wrench to tighten or loosen a bolt.

tommy·cod *noun* (*pl.* same) *N Amer.* = TOMCOD.

Tommy gun *noun* a type of submachine gun. [J. T. *Thompson*, US Army officer d.1940, its co-inventor]

tommy-rot *noun dated slang* nonsense.

tomo·gram /'tɒməˌgram/ *noun* a visual record obtained by tomography.

tom·og·raphy /tə'mɒgrəfi/ *noun* any of various techniques which provide images of successive plane sections of the human body or other solid objects using X-rays or ultrasound, now usu. processed by

Consonants: b *but*   d *dog*   f *few*   g *get*   h *her*   j *yes*   k *cat*   l *leg*   m *man*   n *no*   p *pen*   r *red*   s *sit*

computer to give a three-dimensional image. □ **tomo·graph·ic** /toːməˈgrafɪk/ adjective [Greek tomē a cutting + -GRAPHY]

to·mor·row ● noun **1** the day after today. **2** the future, esp. the near future. ● adverb **1** on the day after today. **2** at some future time. □ **like** (or **as if) there is no tomorrow** with no regard for the future; recklessly. [TO + MORROW: compare TODAY]

Tomsk an industrial city in S Siberian Russia, a port on the Tom River; pop. (2002) 483,800.

Tom Thumb noun **1** a very short male person. **2** (also **tom thumb**) **a** a dwarf variety of cultivated flower or vegetable. **b** a small wildflower, esp. bird's-foot trefoil. [the name of the tiny hero of a fairy tale]

tom-tom noun **1** a simple hand-beaten drum associated with North American Aboriginal, African, or Eastern cultures. **2** a small to medium-sized drum used esp. as part of a drum kit. [Hindi tamtam, imitative]

-tomy combining form forming nouns denoting cutting, esp. in surgery (laparotomy). [Greek -tomia cutting, from temnō cut]

ton ● noun **1** (in full **short ton**) esp. N Amer. a unit of weight equal to 2,000 lb. avoirdupois (907.19 kg). **2** (in full **long ton**) Brit. a unit of weight equal to 2,240 lb. avoirdupois (1016.05 kg). **3** = METRIC TON. **4 a** (in full **displacement ton**) a unit of measurement of a ship's weight or volume in terms of its displacement of water with the load line just immersed, equal to 2,240 lb. (1016.05 kg) or 35 cu. ft. (0.99 cubic metres). **b** (in full **freight ton**) a unit of weight or volume of cargo, equal to a metric ton (1 000 kg) or 40 cu. ft. **5 a** (in full **gross ton**) a unit of gross internal capacity, equal to 100 cu. ft. (2.83 cubic metres). **b** (in full **net** or **register ton**) an equivalent unit of net internal capacity. **6** a unit of refrigerating power able to freeze 2,000 lb. of ice at 0°C in 24 hours. **7** a measure of capacity for various materials, esp. 40 cu. ft. of timber. **8** (usu. in pl.) informal a large number or amount (tons of things to do; has a ton of stuff to learn). **9** esp. Brit. slang **a** a speed of 100 mph. **b** a sum of £100. **c** a score of 100. ● adverb (usu. in pl.) informal much, a lot (am feeling tons better). □ **weigh a ton** informal be very heavy. [originally the same word as TUN: differentiated in the 17th c.]

tonal adjective **1 a** of or relating to tone or tonality. **b** designating or pertaining to music using conventional keys and harmony. **2** (of a language) expressing semantic differences by varying the intonation given to words or syllables of a similar sound. □ **ton·al·ly** adverb

ton·al·i·ty noun (pl. **-ities**) **1** Music **a** the relationship between the tones of a musical scale. **b** the observance of a single tonic key as the basis of a composition. **2** the tone or colour scheme of a picture.

tondo noun (pl. **tondi**) a circular painting or relief. [Italian, = round (plate), from rotondo from Latin rotundus round]

tone ● noun **1** a musical or vocal sound, esp. with reference to its pitch, quality, and strength. **2** (often in pl.) modulation of the voice expressing a particular feeling or mood (a cheerful tone; suspicious tones). **3** a manner of expression in writing. **4** Music **a** a musical sound, esp. of a definite pitch and character. **b** an interval of a major second, e.g. C–D. **5 a** the general effect of colour or of light and shade in a photograph, painting, etc. **b** the tint or shade of a colour. **6 a** the general spirit or character of something (her opening statement set the tone for the meeting; the new houses lower the tone of the neighbourhood). **b** an attitude or sentiment expressed in a letter, speech, etc. **7** (of the body) the state of being firm and strong (good muscular tone). **8** a state of good or specified health or quality. **9** Phonetics **a** an accent on one syllable of a word. **b** a way of pronouncing a word or syllable with a specific intonation to distinguish it from others of a similar sound (Mandarin Chinese has four tones). ● verb **1** transitive give the desired tone to. **2** transitive modify the tone of. **3** transitive strengthen, firm (tone the skin). **4** intransitive (often foll. by to) attune. **5** transitive Photog. give (a monochrome picture) an altered colour in finishing by means of a chemical solution. **6** intransitive undergo a change in colour by toning. □ **tone down 1** make or become softer in tone of sound or colour. **2** make less strong or extreme. **tone up 1** make or become stronger in tone of sound or colour. **2** strengthen (muscles etc.). **3** make (a statement etc.) more emphatic. □ **tone·less** adjective **tone·less·ly** adverb [Old French ton or Latin tonus from Greek tonos tension, tone, from teinō stretch]

tone arm noun the movable arm supporting the pickup of a record player.

tone control noun a switch for varying the proportion of high and low frequencies in reproduced sound.

tone-deaf adjective unable to perceive differences of musical pitch accurately. □ **tone-deafness** noun

tone-on-tone adjective (of a fabric or design) dyed with or using different shades of the same colour.

tone poem noun an extended orchestral composition, usu. in one movement and freer in form than a symphony, on a descriptive or rhapsodic theme.

toner noun **1** a chemical bath for toning a photographic print. **2** a powdered ink used in laser printers and photocopiers. **3** an astringent lotion applied to the face to control oiliness and tighten pores.

tone-row noun = SERIES 8.

tong[1] noun a Chinese guild, association, or secret society. [Chinese tang meeting place]

tong[2] transitive verb (**tonged, tong·ing**) **1** esp. Brit. style (the hair) using a curling iron. **2** collect (oysters etc.) using tongs.

Tonga a country in the S Pacific consisting of an island group southeast of Fiji; pop. (est. 2002) 106,137; capital, Nuku'alofa. The kingdom of Tonga consists of about 170 volcanic and coral islands, of which thirty-six are inhabited.

tonga noun a light horse-drawn two-wheeled vehicle used in India. [Hindi tāṅgā]

Ton·gan ● adjective of or relating to the island of Tonga or its people or language. ● noun **1** a native or national of Tonga. **2** the Polynesian language spoken in Tonga.

Ton·ga·ri·ro, Mount /ˌtɒŋɡəˈriːrəʊ/ a mountain in North Island, New Zealand. It rises to a height of 1 968 m (6,457 ft.) and is held sacred by the Maoris.

tongs plural noun (also **pair of tongs** singular) an instrument with two hinged or sprung arms for grasping and holding things. [pl. of tong from Old English tang(e) from Germanic]

Tong·shan /tɒŋˈʃan/ a former name (1912–45) for XUZHOU.

tongue ● noun **1** the fleshy muscular organ in the mouth used in tasting, licking, and swallowing, and (in humans) for speech. **2** the tongue of an ox etc. as food. **3** the faculty of or a tendency in speech (a sharp tongue). **4** a particular language (his native tongue is German). **5 a** thing like a tongue in shape or position, esp.: **a** a long low promontory. **b** a strip of leather etc., attached at one end only, under the laces in a shoe. **c** the clapper of a bell. **d** the pin of a buckle. **e** the projecting strip on a wooden etc. board fitting into the groove of another. **f** a vibrating slip in the reed of some musical instruments. **g** a jet of flame. **h** the pole by which a wagon or other vehicle may be drawn along. ● verb (**tongues, tongued, tonguing**) **1** transitive produce staccato etc. effects with (a flute etc.) by means of tonguing. **2** intransitive use the tongue in this way. **3** transitive kiss with the tongue. **4** transitive touch or move with the tongue; lick up. □ **find** (or **lose**) **one's tongue** be able (or unable) to express oneself after a shock etc. **the gift of tongues** the power of speaking in unknown languages, regarded as one of the gifts of the Holy Spirit (Acts 2). **give tongue 1** speak one's thoughts. **2** (of hounds) bark, esp. on finding a scent. **with one's tongue hanging out** eagerly or expectantly. **with one's tongue in one's cheek** insincerely or ironically. □ **tongued** adjective (also in combination). **tongue·less** adjective [Old English tunge from Germanic, related to Latin lingua]

tongue-and-groove noun (usu. attributive) panelling etc. with a projecting strip down one side and a groove down the other.

tongue depressor noun Med. a flat wooden stick for pressing down the tongue, esp. to allow inspection of the mouth or throat.

tongue-in-cheek ● adjective ironic; slyly humorous. ● adverb insincerely or ironically.

tongue-kissing noun kissing with the tongue inserted in the other's mouth. □ **tongue-kiss** transitive & intransitive verb

tongue-lashing noun a severe scolding or reprimand.

tongue-tie noun a speech impediment due to a malformation of the tongue.

tongue-tied adjective **1** too shy or embarrassed to speak. **2** having a tongue-tie.

tongue trooper noun Cdn slang (in Quebec) a provincial government official responsible for enforcing the province's language laws, esp. by monitoring commercial signs in stores, restaurants, etc.

tongue twister noun a sequence of words difficult to pronounce quickly and correctly, e.g. She sells seashells by the seashore.

tongue-twisting adjective difficult to articulate.

tongue-wagging noun excessive talking or gossiping.

tonguing noun Music the technique of playing a wind instrument using the tongue to articulate certain notes.

---

t top   v voice   w we   z zoo   ʃ she   ʒ vision   θ thin   ð this   ŋ ring   x loch   tʃ chip   dʒ jar   (see over for vowels)

tonic ● *noun* **1** an invigorating medicine or medicinal agent. **2** anything serving to invigorate. **3** = TONIC WATER. **4** *Music* the first degree of a scale, forming the keynote of a piece (*see* KEYNOTE 3). ● *adjective* **1** serving as a tonic; invigorating. **2** *Music* denoting the first degree of a scale. **3 a** designating or involving continuous muscular contraction without relaxation. **b** restoring normal tone to organs. [French *tonique* from Greek *tonikos* (as TONE)]

tonic accent *noun Phonetics* an accent marked by a change of pitch within a syllable.

ton·icity /tɒːˈnɪsɪti/ *noun* **1** the state of being tonic. **2** a healthy elasticity of muscles etc.

tonic sol-fa *noun Music* a system of notation used esp. in teaching singing, with do as the keynote of all major keys and la as the keynote of all minor keys.

tonic water *noun* a carbonated drink containing quinine, often used as a mix with gin.

to·night ● *noun* the evening or night of the present day. ● *adverb* on the present or approaching evening or night. [TO + NIGHT: compare TODAY]

tonka bean *noun* the black fragrant seed of a S American tree, *Dipteryx odorata*, used in perfume etc. [*tonka*, its name in Guyana, + BEAN]

Ton·kin /tɒnˈkɪn/ a mountainous region of northern Vietnam, centred on the delta of the Red River. Formerly part of China, it became a French protectorate in 1883. It was part of French Indochina from 1887 until 1946.

Tonkin, Gulf of an arm of the South China Sea, bounded by the coasts of S China and northern Vietnam. Its chief port is Haiphong.

Tonlé Sap /ˌtɒnlei ˈsap/ a lake in central Cambodia, linked to the Mekong river by the Tonlé Sap river. On the northwest shore stand the ruins of the ancient city of Angkor, capital of the former Khmer Empire.

ton-mile *noun* one ton of goods carried one mile, as a unit of traffic.

ton·nage /ˈtʌnɪdʒ/ *noun* **1** weight in tons. **2** a ship's internal cubic capacity or freight-carrying capacity measured in tons. **3** the total carrying capacity esp. of a country's mercantile marine. **4** a charge per ton on freight or cargo. [originally in sense 'duty on a tun of wine': Old French *tonnage* from *tonne* TUN: later from TON]

tonne /tʌn/ *noun* = METRIC TON. [French: see TUN]

ton·neau /tʌˈnoʊ/ *noun* **1** the part of a motor vehicle occupied by the back seats, esp. in an open car. **2** = TONNEAU COVER. [French, lit. cask, tun]

tonneau cover *noun* a removable flexible cover for the passenger seats in an open car, boat, etc., when they are not in use.

ton·sil *noun* either of two small masses of lymphoid tissue on each side of the root of the tongue. □ **ton·sil·lar** *adjective* [French *tonsilles* or Latin *tonsillae* (pl.)]

tonsil hockey *noun jocular slang* French kissing.

tonsil·lec·tomy *noun* (*pl.* **-mies**) the surgical removal of the tonsils.

ton·sil·litis *noun* inflammation of the tonsils.

ton·sor·ial /tɒnˈsɔːriəl/ *adjective* usu. *jocular* of or relating to a hairdresser or hairdressing. □ **ton·sor·ial·ly** *adverb* [Latin *tonsorius* from *tonsor* barber, from *tondēre tons-* shave]

ton·sure /ˈtɒnʃər/ ● *noun* **1** the shaving of the crown of the head or the entire head, esp. of a person entering a priesthood or monastic order. **2** a bare patch made in this way. ● *transitive verb* give a tonsure to. □ **ton·sured** *adjective* [Old French *tonsure* or Latin *tonsura* (as TONSORIAL)]

ton·tine /ˈtɒntiːn, -ˈtiːn/ *noun* an annuity shared by subscribers to a loan, the shares increasing as subscribers die until the last survivor gets all, or until a specified date when the remaining survivors share the proceeds. [French, from the name of Lorenzo *Tonti* of Naples, originator of tontines in France *c.* 1653]

Ton·ton Ma·coute /tɔ̃tɔ̃ maˈkuːt/ *noun* (*pl.* **Ton·tons Ma·coutes** *pronunc.* same) a member of a militia formed in 1961 by President F. Duvalier of Haiti, notorious for its brutal and arbitrary behaviour, disbanded in 1986. [Haitian French, said to allude to an ogre of folk tales]

Tony *noun* (*pl.* **Tonys**) (also **Tony award**) any of the awards given annually by the American Theatre Wing for excellence in some aspect of theatre. [the nickname of Antoinette Perry, US actress and producer d.1946]

tony *adjective* (**toni·er, toni·est**) *N Amer. informal* stylish, fashionable, high-class (*a tony neighbourhood*).

too *adverb* **1** to a greater extent than is desirable, permissible, or possible for a specified or understood purpose (*too colourful for my taste*; *too large to fit*). **2** in addition, also (*are they coming too?*). **3** *informal* very; extremely (*you're too kind*). **4** moreover (*we must consider, too, the time of year*). □ **none too 1** rather less than (*feeling none too good*). **2** barely. **too bad** *see* BAD. **too much, too much for** *see* MUCH. **too right** *see* RIGHT. [stressed form of TO, from 16th-c. spelled *too*]

too·dle *N Amer. var. of.* TOOTLE.

toodle-oo *interjection informal* (also **too·dles**) goodbye. [perhaps from French *à tout à l'heure* 'see you soon']

took *past of* TAKE.

tool ● *noun* **1 a** any device or implement used to carry out mechanical functions whether manually or by a machine. **b** an item of software for interactive applications. **2** a thing used in an occupation or pursuit (*the tools of one's trade*; *reference tools*). **3** a person used as a mere instrument by another. **4** *coarse slang* the penis. **5 a** a distinct design in the tooling of a book. **b** a small stamp or roller used to make this. ● *verb* **1** *transitive* work or shape (stone, wood, etc.) with a tool. **2** *transitive* impress a design on (a leather book cover, belt, etc.). **3** *intransitive* (foll. by *along, around,* etc.) *slang* drive or ride, esp. in a casual or leisurely manner. **4** *transitive & intransitive* (often foll. by *up*) equip with tools. □ **tool up 1** *slang* arm oneself. **2** equip oneself. □ **tool·er** *noun* [Old English *tōl* from Germanic]

tool·bar *noun* a row or column of icons on a computer screen which can be clicked on to execute frequently used commands.

tool belt *noun* a usu. leather belt with pouches and loops for holding tools, worn by carpenters etc.

tool box *noun* **1** (also **tool chest**) a box or container for keeping tools in. **2** *Computing* **a** a set of software tools. **b** the set of programs or functions accessible from a single menu.

tool·ing *noun* **1** the process of dressing stone or wood with a chisel etc. **2** the impressing of ornamental designs on leather, esp. on the covers of books, with heated tools. **3** the designs so formed.

tool kit *noun* (also **tool·set**) **1** a set of tools. **2** *Computing* a set of software tools, usu. designed for a specific application. **3** a repertoire of techniques used to solve problems, make decisions, etc. (*the manager's tool kit*).

tool·maker *noun* a person who makes and maintains precision tools. □ **tool·making** *noun*

tool·push *noun* (also **tool·pusher**) a worker directing the drilling on an oil rig.

tool shed *noun* a shed in which tools etc. are stored.

toon *noun informal* **1** = CARTOON *noun* 1, 2, 3. **2** a cartoon character. [shortened form; also with punning allusion to TUNE *noun*]

toon·ie *noun Cdn informal* the Canadian two-dollar coin. [after LOONIE]

toot ● *noun* **1** a short sharp sound as made by a horn, trumpet, or whistle. **2** *slang* cocaine or a snort of cocaine. **3** *N Amer. slang* a drinking binge; a spree. ● *verb* **1** *transitive* sound (a horn etc.) with a short sharp sound. **2** *intransitive* give out such a sound. **3** *intransitive slang* break wind. □ **toot one's own horn** praise oneself; boast. □ **toot·er** *noun* [probably from Middle Low German *tūten*, or imitative]

tooth ● *noun* (*pl.* **teeth**) **1** each of a set of hard bony enamel-coated structures in the jaws of most vertebrates, used for biting and chewing. **2** a toothlike part or projection, e.g. the cog of a gearwheel, the point of a saw or comb, etc. **3** (often foll. by *for*) one's sense of taste; an appetite or liking (*in pl.*) force or effectiveness (*the penalties give the contract teeth*). ● *verb* **1** *transitive* provide with teeth. **2** *intransitive* (of cogwheels) engage, interlock. □ **armed to the teeth** completely and elaborately armed or equipped. **fight tooth and nail** fight very fiercely. **get one's teeth into** devote oneself seriously to. **in the teeth of 1** in spite of (opposition or difficulty etc.). **2** contrary to (instructions etc.). **3** directly against (the wind etc.). **set a person's teeth on edge** see EDGE. □ **toothed** *adjective* (also in *combination*). **tooth·like** *adjective* [Old English *tōth* (pl. *tēth*) from Germanic]

tooth·ache *noun* a (usu. prolonged) pain in a tooth or teeth.

tooth·brush *noun* a small brush with a long narrow handle, for cleaning the teeth.

toothbrush moustache *noun* a short bristly moustache trimmed to a rectangular shape.

toothed whale *noun* a whale of the suborder Odonticeti, having teeth rather than baleen plates, including sperm whales, killer whales, and dolphins and porpoises.

tooth fairy *noun* (in folk legend) a fairy who leaves a small amount of money for a child in exchange for a baby tooth placed under the child's pillow at night.

tooth·less *adjective* **1** having no teeth. **2** lacking the means of compulsion or enforcement; ineffectual.

tooth·paste *noun* a usu. minty-tasting paste for cleaning the teeth, applied with a toothbrush.

tooth·pick *noun* a small sharp instrument, usu. of wood or plastic, for removing small pieces of food lodged between the teeth.

tooth powder *noun* powder for cleaning the teeth, applied with a toothbrush.

tooth·some *adjective* **1** (of food) delicious, appetizing. **2** alluring; sexy. □ **tooth·some·ly** *adverb*

tooth·wort /ˈtuːθwɜrt, -wɔrt/ *noun* **1** any of various cruciferous plants of the genus *Dentaria* of eastern N America, esp. *Dentaria diphylla*, with white flowers and an edible root. *Also called* PEPPER ROOT, CRINKLEROOT. **2** a Eurasian parasitic plant, *Lathraea squamaria*, with toothlike root scales.

tooth·y *adjective* (**tooth·i·er**, **tooth·i·est**) having or showing large, numerous, or prominent teeth (*a toothy grin*). □ **tooth·i·ly** *adverb*

too·tle ● *verb* **1** *intransitive* (also *N Amer.* **too·dle**) (usu. foll. by *along*, *around*, etc.) *informal* move casually or aimlessly. **2** *intransitive* toot gently or repeatedly. **3** *transitive* play (a wind instrument). ● *noun* an act of tootling.

too-too *adjective & adverb informal* extreme, excessive(ly).

toots /tʊts/ *noun N Amer. slang* used as a familiar form of address, esp. to a woman or girl. ¶ Often *offensive* if used to a stranger. [prob. abbreviation of TOOTSIE]

toot·sie /ˈtʊtsi/ *noun* (*pl.* **-sies**) **1** (usu. in *pl.*) *informal* usu. *jocular* a foot; a toe. **2** *esp. N Amer. slang* **a** a woman; a female lover. **b** a prostitute. [jocular diminutive: alteration of FOOT]

toot sweet *adverb informal* right away, immediately (*she wanted the document toot sweet*). [Anglicized form of French *tout de suite*]

top¹ ● *noun* **1** the highest point or part (*the top of the mountain*). **2 a** the highest rank or place (*a lawyer at the top of her profession*). **b** *esp. Brit.* the upper end or head (*the top of the table*). **3** the upper surface of a thing, esp. of the ground, a table, etc. **4** the upper part of a thing, esp.: **a** a garment covering the upper part of the body. **b** the upper part of a shoe or boot. **c** the stopper of a bottle. **d** the lid of a jar, pot, or other container. **e** *esp. Brit.* the creamy part of milk. **f** the folding roof of a car, baby carriage, etc. **g** the upper edge or edges of a page or pages in a book (*gilt top*). **5** the utmost degree; height (*shouted at the top of his voice*). **6** *Baseball* the first half of an inning, in which the visiting team bats. **7** the beginning (of a piece of music, scene in a play, etc.) (*let's start again from the top*). **8** the high-frequency component of reproduced sound. **9 a** (in *pl.*) *informal* a person or thing of the best quality (*he's tops at golf*). **b** the best or choicest part (*top of the morning*). **10** (esp. in *pl.*) the leaves etc. of a plant grown esp. for its root (*turnip tops*). **11** (usu. in *pl.*) a bundle of long wool fibres prepared for spinning. **12** *Naut.* a platform round the head of each of the lower masts of a sailing ship, serving to extend the topmost rigging or carry guns. **13** (in *pl.*) *esp. Bridge* the two or three highest cards of a suit. **14** *Brit.* = TOP GEAR (*climbed the hill in top*). **15** = TOPSPIN. ● *adjective* **1** highest in position (*the top shelf*). **2** highest in degree, importance, or skill (*at top speed*; *the top job*; *the world's top athletes*). ● *transitive verb* (**topped**, **top·ping**) **1** provide with a top, cap, etc. (*cake topped with icing*). **2** remove the top of (a tree, plant, fruit, etc.). **3 a** be higher or better than; surpass. **b** be at the top of (*topped the list*). **4** reach the top of (a hill etc.). **5** *Golf etc.* **a** hit (a ball) above the centre. **b** make (a stroke) in this way. **6** *Brit. slang* **a** execute esp. by hanging, kill. **b** (*reflexive*) commit suicide. □ **at the top** in the highest rank of a profession etc. (**at**) **tops** *esp. N Amer.* at the most. **come to the top** win distinction. **from top to toe** from head to foot; completely. **off the top of one's head** *see* HEAD. **on top 1** in a superior position; above. **2** on the upper part of the head (*bald on top*). **on top of 1** fully in command of. **2** in close proximity to. **3** in addition to. **at the** (or **on**) **top of one's game** in top form. **the top of the hour** the beginning of the hour. **on top of the world** *informal* exuberant. **over the top 1** *esp. hist.* over the parapet of a trench (and into battle); into action. **2** (hyphenated when *attributive*) to excess, beyond reasonable limits; outrageous (*that joke was over the top*). **top off** (or **up**) **1** put an end or the finishing touch to (a thing). **2** = TOP UP 1b. **top out 1** reach a peak; stop rising (*prices topped out at around $200*). **2** put the highest stone on (a building). **top up 1 a** add to; bring up to a certain level (*topped up EI benefits*). **b** fill up (a glass or other partly full container). **2** top up something for (a person) (*your glass is empty; may I top you up?*). □ **top·most** *adjective* [Old English *topp*]

top² *noun* a toy, usu. conical, spherical, or pear-shaped, spinning on a

point when set in motion by hand, string, etc. [Old English, of uncertain origin]

Top 40 *noun* (also **Top Forty**) the forty most popular songs or recordings in the music charts at a given time.

topaz /ˈtoʊpaz/ *noun* a transparent or translucent aluminum silicate mineral, usu. yellow, used as a gem. [Old French *topaze* from Latin *topazus* from Greek *topazos*]

top banana *noun slang* **1** *N Amer.* a leader of an organization etc. **2** a comedian topping the bill.

top boot *noun esp. hist.* a boot with a high top esp. of a different material or colour.

top brass *noun see* BRASS *noun* 6.

top-class *adjective* of the best quality or highest order; first-class.

top·coat *noun* **1** an overcoat. **2** an outer coat of paint etc. **3** a clear coat of nail polish applied on top of a coat of coloured nail polish to prevent it from chipping.

top dog *noun informal* a victor or master.

top dollar *noun esp. N Amer.* a high or the highest price.

top-down *attributive adjective* **1** proceeding from the top downwards. **2** proceeding from the general to the particular. **3** denoting a system of government or management in which actions and policies are initiated at the highest level; hierarchical.

top drawer ● *noun* **1** the uppermost drawer in a chest etc. **2** *informal* high social position or origin. ● *attributive adjective* (**top-drawer**) *informal* of the highest quality or esp. social level.

top dressing *noun* **1** the application of manure or fertilizer to the top of the earth instead of plowing it in. **2** manure so applied. **3** a superficial show. □ **top-dress** *transitive verb*

tope¹ *intransitive verb archaic* or *literary* drink alcohol to excess, esp. habitually. □ **toper** *noun* [perhaps from obsolete *top* quaff]

tope² *noun Ind.* a grove, esp. of mangoes. [Telugu *tōpu*, Tamil *tōppu*]

tope³ *noun* = STUPA. [Punjab *tōp* from Prakrit & Pali *thūpo* from Sanskrit STUPA]

tope⁴ *noun* a small shark, *Galeorhinus galeus*. [perhaps from Cornish]

topee *var. of* TOPI¹.

To·pe·ka /təˈpiːkə/ the state capital of Kansas; pop. (2000) 122,377.

top-end *adjective* = HIGH-END.

top-flight *adjective* in the highest rank of achievement.

top·gal·lant /tɒpˈɡalənt, təˈɡalənt/ *noun* the mast, sail, yard, or rigging immediately above the topmast and topsail of a sailing ship.

top gear *noun Brit.* the highest gear in a motor vehicle or bicycle.

top-grade *adjective* of the best quality or highest order.

top gun *noun esp. N Amer. informal* **1** an ace fighter pilot. **2** an important person, company, etc.

top-hamper *noun* an encumbrance on top, esp. the upper sails and rigging of a ship.

top hat *noun* a man's formal hat with a high cylindrical crown. □ **top-hatted** *adjective*

top-heavy *adjective* **1** disproportionately heavy at the top so as to be in danger of toppling. **2 a** (of an organization, business, etc.) having a disproportionately large number of people in senior administrative positions. **b** overcapitalized. **3** *informal* (of a woman) having a disproportionately large bust. □ **top-heavily** *adverb* **top-heaviness** *noun*

To·phet /ˈtoʊfɪt/ *noun Bible* hell. [name of a place in the Valley of Hinnom near Jerusalem used for idolatrous worship, including the sacrifice of children, and later for burning refuse: from Hebrew *tōpet*]

top-hole *adjective Brit. informal* first-rate.

topi¹ /ˈtoʊpi/ *noun* (also **topee**) (*pl.* **topis** or **topees**) *Anglo-Indian* a pith helmet. [Hindi *ṭopī*]

topi² /ˈtoʊpi/ *noun* (*pl.* **topis** or same) a large usu. reddish-brown antelope of African grassland, *Damaliscus lunatus*, with a sloping back, esp. one of E African coastal race. [West African name]

topi·ary /ˈtoʊpiˌeri/ ● *adjective* concerned with or formed by clipping shrubs, trees, etc. into ornamental or animal forms (*topiary garden*). ● *noun* (*pl.* **-aries**) **1** topiary art. **2** a piece or example of topiary work. □ **topi·ar·ist** *noun* [French *topiaire* from Latin *topiarius* landscape gardener, from *topia opera* fancy gardening, from Greek *topia* pl. diminutive of *topos* place]

topic *noun* **1** a theme for a book, discourse, essay, sermon, etc. **2** the subject of a conversation or argument. [Latin *topica* from Greek (*ta*

---

uː m**oo**d   aɪ m**y**   əɪ p**i**pe   aʊ br**ow**n   ʌʊ h**ou**se   eɪ d**ay**   ɔɪ b**oy**   ã fr**an**glais   ã Ca**na**dien   ɔ̃ Br**ay**on   (*see over for consonants*)

topika topics, as title of a treatise by Aristotle from *topos* a place, a commonplace]

top·ic·al *adjective* **1** of or pertaining to current affairs or a subject in the news etc. (*a topical song*). **2** dealing with a place; local. **3** *Med.* (of an ailment, medicine, etc.) affecting or applied externally to a part of the body. **4** of or concerning topics. □ **top·ic·al·ity** *noun* **top·ic·al·ly** *adverb*

top·knot *noun* **1** a bun or tuft of hair worn on the crown of the head. **2** esp. *hist.* a decorative knot or bow of ribbon worn on the head (esp. in the 18th. c.). **3** a tuft or crest growing on the head.

top·less *adjective* **1** without or seeming to be without a top. **2 a** (of clothes) having no upper part. **b** (of a person) wearing such clothes; bare-breasted. **c** (of a place, esp. a beach) where women go topless. □ **top·less·ness** *noun*

top-level *adjective* of the highest level of importance, prestige, etc.

top·line ● *noun* the profile line of an animal's back from the centre of the shoulders to the end of the hip bones. ● *attributive adjective* (**top-line**) **1** of the highest quality; top-of-the-line. **2** (esp. of an entertainment act) considered worthy of top billing.

top·lofty *adjective* US *informal* haughty. □ **top·loft·i·ness** *noun*

top·mast *noun* the mast next above the lower mast on a sailing ship.

top·most *adjective* uppermost.

top-notch *adjective informal* first-rate. □ **top-notcher** *noun*

top note *noun* the dominant initial scent in a perfume.

topo /ˈtɒpɒ/ ● *noun* **1** topography. **2** a topographical map. ● *adjective* topographical.

top of mind *adjective* (of an issue, product, marketing campaign, etc.) of which the public is very much aware (also *attributive: top-of-mind issues*).

top-of-the-line *adjective* (also esp. *Brit.* **top-of-the-range**) the most expensive (and usu. highest quality) of a group of similar products (*a top-of-the-line stereo system*).

top·og·raphy /təˈpɒɡrəfi/ *noun* **1 a** a detailed description, representation on a map, etc., of the natural and artificial features of a town, district, etc. **b** such features. **2** *Anat.* the mapping of the surface of the body with reference to the parts beneath. □ **top·og·raph·er** *noun* **top·o·graph·ic** /-ˈɡrafɪk/ **top·o·graph·ic·al** *adjective* **top·o·graph·ic·ally** *adverb* [Late Latin *topographia* from Greek from *topos* place]

topoi *pl. of* TOPOS.

top·ol·ogy /təˈpɒlədʒi/ *noun Math.* **1** the study of geometrical properties and spatial relations unaffected by the continuous change of shape or size of figures. **2** the way in which constituent parts are interrelated or arranged. □ **top·o·logic·al** /ˌtɒpəˈlɒdʒɪkəl/ *adjective* **top·o·logic·ally** *adverb* **top·ol·o·gist** *noun* [German *Topologie* from Greek *topos* place]

topo·nym /ˈtɒpənɪm/ *noun* **1** a place name. **2** a descriptive place name, usu. derived from a topographical feature of the place.

top·onymy /təˈpɒnɪmi/ *noun* the study of the place names of a region. □ **topo·nym·ic** /-ˈnɪmɪk/ *adjective* [Greek *topos* place + *onoma* name]

topos /ˈtɒpɒs, ˈtɒpɔːs, -pɒs/ *noun* (*pl.* **topoi** /ˈtɒpɔɪ/) a stock theme in literature etc. [Greek, = commonplace]

top·per *noun* **1** a thing that tops. **2** *informal* = TOP HAT. **3** esp. *N Amer.* a woman's short loose jacket or coat. **4** *N Amer.* a short curtain, often ruffled or shirred, hung at the top of a window.

top·ping ● *noun* a garnish, top layer, sauce, etc. put on top of food (*sundaes with a choice of five toppings; bread crumb topping*). ● *adjective* **1** pre-eminent in position, rank, etc. **2** *Brit. dated slang* excellent.

top·ple *transitive & intransitive verb* **1** (usu. foll. by *over*) totter and fall (over), or cause to do so. **2** overthrow or be overthrown (*the government was toppled by a coup*). [TOP[1] + -LE[4]]

top·sail /ˈtɒpseɪl, -səl/ *noun* **1** the square sail, or each of two such sails, next above the lowest on a sailing ship. **2** a fore-and-aft sail above the gaff.

top secret *adjective* of the highest secrecy.

top seed *noun Sport* the top-ranked competitor or team in a tournament etc. □ **top-seeded** *adjective*

top shelf *informal* ● *noun Hockey* the highest part of the net, just beneath the crossbar. ● *adverb Hockey* (shoot or score) at or into this part of the net (*he went top shelf on the goalie's glove side*). ● *attributive adjective* first-rate (*a top-shelf drummer*).

top·side ● *noun* the side of a ship above the waterline. ● *adverb* on or to the upper deck of a ship.

Top-Sider *noun* (usu. in *pl.*) *proprietary* a casual shoe designed to be worn on boats, typically made of leather or canvas with a rubber sole; a deck shoe.

top·soil *noun* the surface layer of soil (*opp.* SUBSOIL).

top·spin *noun* a fast forward spinning motion imparted to a ball in tennis etc. by hitting it forward and upward.

top·stitch *transitive verb* make a row of neat, esp. decorative, stitches on the right side of (a garment etc.). □ **top·stitch·ing** *noun*

Topsy *noun* □ (**just growed**) **like Topsy** a person, institution, custom etc. has come into existence nobody knows when or how. [from the name of a character in Harriet Beecher Stowe's *Uncle Tom's Cabin*]

topsy-turvy ● *adverb & adjective* **1** upside down. **2** in utter confusion. ● *noun* utter confusion. □ **topsy-turvily** *adverb* **topsy-turviness** *noun* [apparently from TOP[1] + obsolete *terve* overturn]

top-tier *adjective* = TOP-LEVEL.

top-up *noun Brit.* an addition; something that serves to top up (esp. a partly full glass).

top·water *adjective N Amer.* (of a bait) that floats on top of the water.

toque *noun* **1** /tuːk/ (also **tuque**) *Cdn* a close-fitting knitted hat, often with a tassel or pompom on the crown. **b** a long knitted stocking cap. **2** /toːk/ a woman's small brimless hat. **3** /toːk/ *hist.* a small cap or bonnet for a man or woman. **4** /toːk/ a tall white hat with a full pouched crown, worn by chefs. [French, apparently = Italian *tocca*, Spanish *toca*, of unknown origin; sense 1 by assimilation from Canadian French *tuque*]

tor *noun* a hill or rocky peak, esp. in Devon or Cornwall. [Old English *torr*: compare Gaelic *tòrr* bulging hill]

Torah *noun* **1** (usu. prec. by *the*) **a** the Pentateuch. **b** a scroll containing this. **2** the will of God as revealed in Mosaic law. [Hebrew *tōrāh* instruction]

Tor·bay 1 a popular seaside resort in Devon, SW England; pop. (est. 1998) 123,000. **2** a town in SE Newfoundland, situated on the Avalon Peninsula on Tor Bay, just north of St. John's; pop. (2001) 5,474. [sense 2 prob. from sense 1]

torc *noun* (also **torque**) *hist.* a necklace of twisted metal, esp. of the ancient Gauls and Britons.

torch ● *noun* **1 a** a piece of wood, cloth, etc., soaked in a flammable substance and lighted for illumination. **b** any similar lamp, e.g. an oil lamp on a pole. **2** (also **electric torch**) *Brit.* = FLASHLIGHT 1. **3** a source of heat, illumination, or enlightenment (*bore aloft the torch of freedom*). **4** esp. *N Amer.* a blowtorch. ● *transitive verb N Amer. slang* set fire to, esp. as an act of arson. □ **carry a torch for** suffer from unrequited love for. **pick up the torch** carry on with the work of someone unable to continue. **put to the torch** destroy by burning. [Old French *torche* from Latin *torqua* from *torquēre* twist]

torch·bear·er *noun* **1** a person who leads the way in an attempt to reform, inspire, etc. **2** a person who carries a usu. ceremonial torch.

tor·chère /tɔːrˈʃer/ *noun* **1** = TORCHIERE. **2** a tall stand with a small table for a candlestick etc. [French (as TORCH)]

tor·chi·ere /tɔːrʃiˈer/ *noun* a floor lamp having the light bulb in an upturned saucer-shaped shade at the top of the pole. [var. of TORCHÈRE]

torch·light ● *noun* the light of a torch or torches. ● *adjective* done or accompanied by torchlight (*a torchlight parade*). □ **torch·lit** *adjective*

tor·chon /ˈtɔːrʃən, -ʃɔ̃/ *noun* (in full **torchon lace**) coarse bobbin lace with geometrical designs. [French, = duster, dishcloth, from *torcher* wipe]

torch song *noun* a melancholy or sentimental romantic song with a slow tempo. □ **torch singer** *noun*

torchy *adjective* characteristic of torch songs or a torch singer.

tore[1] *past of* TEAR[1].

tore[2] *noun* = TORUS 1, 4. [French from Latin *torus*: see TORUS]

torea·dor /ˈtɔːriəˌdɔr/ *noun* a bullfighter, esp. one on horseback. [Spanish from *torear* fight bulls, from *toro* bull, from Latin *taurus*]

toreador pants *noun* women's close-fitting calf-length pants.

tor·ero /təˈrerəʊ/ *noun* (*pl.* **-eros**) a bullfighter, esp. one on foot. [Spanish from *toro*: see TOREADOR]

tori *pl. of* TORUS.

toric /ˈtɔːrɪk/ *adjective* **1** *Geom.* having the form of a torus or part of a torus. **2** (esp. of a lens) having a surface curved like part of a torus, the radius of curvature having a minimum value in one direction and a maximum value in the direction at right angles to this.

torii /ˈtɔːriː/ *noun* (*pl.* same) the gateway of a Shinto shrine, with two uprights and two crosspieces. [Japanese]

Consonants: b *but* d *dog* f *few* g *get* h *her* j *yes* k *cat* l *leg* m *man* n *no* p *pen* r *red* s *sit*

tor·ment ● *noun* **1** severe physical or mental suffering; anguish (*was in torment*). **2** a cause of this (*his shyness made public speaking a torment*). ● *transitive verb* **1** subject to torment (*tormented with worry*). **2** tease or worry excessively (*enjoyed tormenting the teacher*). □ **tor·ment·ing·ly** *adverb* **tor·ment·or** *noun* [Old French *torment, tormenter* from Latin *tormentum* 'instrument of torture', from *torquēre* to twist]

tor·men·til /ˈtɔːməntɪl/ *noun* a Eurasian plant, *Potentilla erecta*, with bright yellow flowers and a highly astringent rootstock. [Old French *tormentille* from medieval Latin *tormentilla*, of unknown origin]

Tor·men·tine, Cape /ˈtɔːməntaɪn/ the easternmost point of New Brunswick, extending into the Northumberland Strait, opposite the town of Borden, PEI.

torn ● *verb* past participle of TEAR¹. ● *adjective* **1** that has been torn or violently pulled apart (*torn jeans; torn ligaments*). **2** anxious because having to make a painful choice between two options (*I feel really torn*).

tor·na·do *noun* (*pl.* **-does**) **1** a violent storm with very strong circular winds over a small area, often accompanied by a funnel-shaped cloud. **2** (in W Africa) a thundery squall at the beginning or end of the rainy season. **3** a violent or destructive person or thing. □ **tor·nadic** /-ˈnadɪk/ *adjective* [apparently assimilation of Spanish *tronada* thunderstorm (from *tronar* to thunder) to Spanish *tornar* to turn]

Torn·gat Mountains a mountain range on the Quebec–Labrador border, situated along the northeastern end of the Ungava Peninsula. [from Inuktitut *Torngarsuak* Great Spirit, i.e. controller of all spirits]

Tor·nio River /ˈtɔːnioː/ a river which rises in NE Sweden and flows generally southward, forming the border between Sweden and Finland before emptying into the Gulf of Bothnia.

tor·oid /ˈtɔːrɔɪd/ *noun* a figure resembling a torus. □ **tor·oid·al** /tɔːˈrɔɪdəl/ *adjective*

To·ron·to the capital city of Ontario and largest municipality in Canada, situated in the southern part of the province, on Lake Ontario near its western end; pop. (2001) 2,481,494. □ **To·ron·to·nian** /təˌrɒnˈtoːniən/ *noun* [Mohawk *tkaronto* trees standing in the water, with reference to ancient fish weirs set up between Lakes Simcoe and Couchiching]

Toronto couch *noun* Cdn (esp. West) = WINNIPEG COUCH.

Toronto Islands a group of eleven islands off the northwestern shore of Lake Ontario, just south of Toronto.

tor·pedo /tɔːˈpiːdoː/ ● *noun* (*pl.* **-oes**) **1 a** a self-propelled underwater missile, usu. cylindrical with a pointed or tapered nose, fired at a ship and exploding on impact. **b** (in full **aerial torpedo**) a similar device dropped from an aircraft. **2** = ELECTRIC RAY. **3** *US* an explosive device on a railway line detonated by pressure to give a warning signal. ● *transitive verb* (**-oes, -oed**) **1** destroy or attack with a torpedo. **2** make (a policy, institution, plan, etc.) ineffective or inoperative; destroy. □ **damn the torpedoes** *N Amer. slang* let us proceed aggressively without fear of the dangers or concern for the consequences. □ **torpedo-like** *adjective* [Latin, = numbness, electric ray, from *torpēre* be numb]

torpedo boat *noun* a small fast lightly armed warship for carrying or discharging torpedoes.

torpedo tube *noun* a tube from which torpedoes are fired by using compressed air or an explosive charge.

tor·pid *adjective* **1 a** sluggish, inactive. **b** dull, apathetic. **2** (of a part of the body etc.) numb. **3** (of a hibernating animal) dormant. □ **tor·pid·ity** *noun* **tor·pid·ly** *adverb* [Latin *torpidus* (as TORPOR)]

tor·por /ˈtɔːpər/ *noun* a torpid state. [Latin from *torpēre* be sluggish]

torque /tɔːk/ ● *noun* **1** *Mech.* a twisting or rotating force, causing rotation in a mechanism. **2** *var.* of TORC. ● *transitive verb* **1** apply torque or a twisting force to. **2** (often foll. by *up*) *N Amer. informal* heighten; increase (sound, intensity, etc.). □ **tor·quey** *adjective* [Latin *torquēre* 'to twist': in sense 1 via French, and Latin *torques*]

torque converter *noun* a device to transmit the correct torque from the engine to the axle in a motor vehicle.

Tor·que·mada /ˌtɔːkəˈmɒdə, -ˈmɑːdə/ **Tomás de** (*c.*1420–98), Spanish cleric and grand inquisitor. A Dominican monk, he persuaded Ferdinand and Isabella to institute the Inquisition in 1478; he was appointed Inquisitor-General of Spain in 1483, and became known for his ruthless suppression of heresy.

torr *noun* (*pl.* same) a unit of pressure used in measuring partial vacuums, equal to 133.32 pascals. [TORRICELLI]

tor·rent *noun* **1** a rushing stream of water, lava, etc. **2** (in *pl.*) a great downpour of rain (*came down in torrents*). **3** (usu. foll. by *of*) a violent or copious flow (*a torrent of abuse*). □ **tor·ren·tial** /tɒˈrenʃəl/ *adjective*

tor·ren·tial·ly *adverb* [French from Italian *torrente* from Latin *torrens -entis* scorching, boiling, roaring, from *torrēre* scorch]

Tor·reón /ˌtɒreiˈɒn/ a city in north central Mexico, west of Monterrey; pop. (est. 2000) 505,000.

Tor·res Strait /ˈtɒrəs/ a channel separating the northern tip of Queensland, Australia, from the island of New Guinea, linking the Arafura Sea and the Coral Sea.

Tor·ri·cel·li /ˌtɒrɪˈtʃeli/ **Evan·gel·ista** (1608–47), Italian mathematician and physicist. His most important invention was the mercury barometer, with which he demonstrated that the atmosphere exerts a pressure sufficient to support a column of mercury in an inverted closed tube. □ **Tor·ri·cel·lian** *adjective*

tor·rid *adjective* **1 a** (of the weather) very hot and dry. **b** (of land etc.) parched by such weather. **2** (of language or actions) emotionally charged; passionate, intense. **3** successful; hard to contain or stop (*a torrid offence; a torrid economy*). □ **tor·rid·ity** *noun* **tor·rid·ly** *adverb* [French *torride* or Latin *torridus*, from *torrēre* 'parch']

torrid zone *noun* the central belt of the earth between the Tropics of Cancer and Capricorn.

Tórs·havn /ˈtɔːshaun/ (also **Thors·havn**) the capital of the Faeroe Islands, a port on the island of Strømø; pop. (est. 2002) 17,100.

tor·sion *noun* **1** twisting, esp. of one end of a body while the other is held fixed. **2** *Math.* the extent to which a curve departs from being planar. **3** *Bot.* the state of being twisted into a spiral. **4** *Med.* the twisting of the cut end of an artery after surgery etc. to impede bleeding. □ **tor·sion·al** *adjective* **tor·sion·al·ly** *adverb* [Old French from Late Latin *torsio -onis* from Latin *tortio* (as TORT)]

torsion bar *noun* a bar forming part of a vehicle suspension, twisting in response to the motion of the wheels, and absorbing their vertical movement.

torso *noun* (*pl.* **-sos**) **1 a** the trunk of the human body. **b** the part of the human body between the pelvis or waist and the shoulders. **2** a statue of a human consisting of the trunk alone, without head or limbs. **3** an unfinished or mutilated work (esp. of art, literature, etc.). [Italian, = stalk, stump, torso, from Latin *thyrsus*]

tort *noun* Law a breach of duty (other than under contract) for which damages can be obtained in a civil court by the person wronged. [Old French from medieval Latin *tortum* wrong, neuter past participle of Latin *torquēre* tort- twist]

torte *noun* an elaborate rich cake, esp. one with ground nuts as an ingredient and having multiple layers. [German]

tor·tel·lini /ˌtɔːtəˈliːni/ *noun* small squares of pasta stuffed with meat, cheese, etc., rolled and formed into tight ring-shaped pouches. [Italian, pl. of *tortello*, diminutive of *tortello* 'small cake, fritter']

tort·fea·sor /ˈtɔːtˌfiːzər/ *noun* Law a person guilty of tort. [Old French *tort-fesor, tort-faiseur*, etc. from *tort* wrong, *-fesor, faiseur* doer]

torti·col·lis /ˌtɔːtɪˈkɒlɪs/ *noun* Med. a rheumatic etc. disease of the muscles of the neck, causing twisting and stiffness. [modern Latin from Latin *tortus* crooked + *collum* neck]

tor·tilla /tɔːˈtiːə/ *noun* (esp. in Mexican cooking) a thin round bread made with either cornmeal or wheat flour and usu. filled with meat, cheese, beans, etc. [Spanish diminutive of *torta* cake, from Late Latin]

tortilla chip *noun* (usu. in *pl.*) a fried segment of a corn tortilla, often covered with a cheesy or spicy powdered coating, eaten cold like a potato chip.

tor·tious /ˈtɔːʃəs/ *adjective* Law constituting a tort; wrongful. [Anglo-French *torcious* from *torcion* extortion, from Late Latin *tortio* torture: see TORSION]

tor·toise /ˈtɔːtəs/ *noun* **1** any slow-moving land or freshwater reptile of the family Testudinidae, encased in a scaly or leathery domed shell, and having a retractile head and elephantine legs. **2** a slow-moving person or thing. **3** tortoiseshell; tortoiseshell colour. □ **tortoise-like** *adjective & adverb* [Middle English *tortuce*, Old French *tortue*, from medieval Latin *tortuca*, of uncertain origin]

tor·toise·shell ● *noun* **1** the yellowish-brown mottled or clouded outer shell of some turtles, used for decorative combs, jewellery, etc. **2 a** = TORTOISESHELL CAT. **b** = TORTOISESHELL BUTTERFLY. ● *adjective* **1** having the colouring or appearance of tortoiseshell. **2** made of tortoiseshell or a synthetic substitute.

tortoiseshell butterfly *noun* any of various butterflies, esp. of the genus *Aglais* or *Nymphalis*, with wings mottled like tortoiseshell.

tortoiseshell cat *noun* a domestic cat, usu. female, with a mottled black, orange, and cream or white coat.

Tor·tola /tɔːˈtoːlə/ the principal island of the British Virgin Islands in

T
UV

the W Indies. Its chief town, Road Town, is the capital of the Virgin Islands.

tor·trix /ˈtɔːtrɪks/ *noun* any moth of the family Tortricidae, the larvae of which live inside rolled leaves. [modern Latin, fem. of Latin *tortor* twister: see TORT]

tor·tuous /ˈtɔːtʃuːəs/ *adjective* **1** full of twists and turns (*followed a tortuous route*). **2** not direct or straightforward; unnecessarily complex (*a tortuous legal battle; a tortuous line of argument*). □ **tor·tuos·ity** /-ˈɒsɪtɪ/ *noun* (*pl.* **-ities**). **tor·tuous·ly** *adverb* [Old French from Latin *tortuosus* from *tortus* a twist (as TORT)]

tor·ture ● *noun* **1** the infliction of severe bodily pain esp. as a punishment or a means of interrogation or intimidation. **2** severe physical or mental suffering (*the torture of defeat*). ● *transitive verb* **1** subject to physical or mental torture. **2** force out of a natural position or state. □ **tor·tur·er** *noun* **tor·tur·ous** *adjective* **tor·tur·ous·ly** *adverb* [French from Late Latin *tortura* twisting (as TORT)]

Toruń /ˈtɔrʊn/ (German **Thorn** /tɔrn/) an industrial city in N Poland, on the Vistula River; pop. (est. 2000) 204,322.

torus *noun* (*pl.* **tori** or **torus·es**) **1** *Geom.* a surface or solid formed by rotating a closed curve, esp. a circle, about a line in its plane but not intersecting it, e.g. like a ring doughnut. **2** a thing of this shape, esp. a large ring-shaped chamber used in physical research. **3** *Archit.* a large convex moulding, usu. semicircular in cross-section, esp. as the lowest part of the base of a column. **4** *Anat.* a smooth ridge of bone or muscle. **5** *Bot.* the receptacle of a flower. [Latin, = swelling, bulge, cushion, etc.]

Tor·vill and Dean English figure skating duo consisting of Jayne Torvill (b.1957) and Christopher (Colin) Dean (b.1958). They won the ice dancing gold medal in the 1984 Winter Olympic Games and a bronze medal in the 1994 Olympics.

Tory ● *noun* (*pl.* **-ies**) **1** *informal* (in Canada and the UK) a member or supporter of a Conservative party. **2** *hist.* (in England) a member of the party that opposed the exclusion of James II and later supported the established religious and political order and gave rise to the Conservative Party (*opp.* WHIG 1). **3** *US hist.* a loyal colonist during the American Revolution. ● *adjective informal* (in Canada and the UK) of or relating to a Conservative party. □ **Tory·ism** *noun* [originally = Irish outlaw, prob. from Irish from *tóir* pursue]

Tos·ca·nini /ˌtɒskəˈniːnɪ/ **Ar·turo** (1867–1957), Italian conductor. He made his conducting debut in 1886, and was contracted as musical director by La Scala, Milan, before becoming a conductor at the Metropolitan Opera, New York; among the works he premiered were Puccini's *La Bohème* (1896) and *Turandot* (1926).

tosh *noun Brit. informal* rubbish, nonsense. [19th c.: origin unknown]

toss ● *verb* **1** *transitive* (often foll. by *to, away, aside, out,* etc.) throw lightly or carelessly or easily. **2** *transitive & intransitive* roll about, throw, or be thrown, restlessly or from side to side (*the ship tossed on the ocean; was tossing and turning all night; tossed her head angrily*). **3 a** *transitive* throw (a coin) into the air to decide a choice etc. by the side on which it lands. **b** *intransitive* (often foll. by *for*) settle a question or dispute in this way (*tossed for it*). **c** *transitive* (often foll. by *for*) settle a dispute with (a person) in this way (*will toss you for it*). **4** *transitive* **a** (of a horse etc.) throw (a rider) off its back. **b** (of a bull etc.) throw (a person etc.) up with the horns. **c** throw (a pancake) up so that it flips on to the other side in the frying pan. **5** *transitive* coat (food) with dressing etc. by stirring with a light up-and-down motion. **6** *transitive* bandy about in debate; discuss (*tossed the question back and forth*). **7** *transitive informal* discard, get rid of (*the government should toss the proposal*). ● *noun* **1** the act or an instance of tossing (a coin, the head, etc.). **2** *N Amer.* a game or competition in which something is tossed (*egg toss; ring toss*). □ **argue the toss** see ARGUE. **not give a toss** esp. *Brit. informal* not care at all. **toss one's cookies** see COOKIE[1]. **toss in** *N Amer.* add (an ingredient or element) to a mixture, concoction, etc., esp. casually (*tossed in a few glissandos*). **toss off 1** dispatch (work) rapidly or without effort (*tossed off an omelette*). **2** drink in one gulp. **3** utter in an offhand manner (*tossed off a few witty lines*). **toss out** = THROW OUT 1, 2, 4, 5, 6 (see THROW). [16th c.: origin unknown]

toss cushion *noun N Amer.* (also **toss pillow**) = THROW CUSHION.

toss·er *noun* **1** a person or thing that tosses. **2** *Brit. coarse slang* an unpleasant or contemptible person.

toss·pot *noun* a habitual drinker.

toss-up *noun* **1** a situation in which either of two alternatives is equally possible or equally attractive (*it's a toss-up whether he wins*). **2** the tossing of a coin.

tos·ta·da /təˈstɑːdə/ *noun* (also **tos·ta·do** /təˈstɑːdəʊ/ *pl.* **-dos**) a corn tortilla topped with a seasoned mixture of beans, ground meat, and vegetables. [Spanish, past participle of *tostar* to toast]

tot¹ *noun* **1** a small child (*a tiny tot*). **2** a shot of liquor. [18th c., of dial. origin]

tot² *verb* (**tot·ted, tot·ting**) **1** *transitive* (usu. foll. by *up*) add (figures etc.). **2** *intransitive* (foll. by *up*) (of items) mount up. [abbreviation of TOTAL or of Latin *totum* the whole]

total ● *adjective* **1** complete, comprising the whole or all (*the total number of people*). **2** absolute, unqualified (*in total ignorance; total abstinence*). **3** *Astronomy* (of an eclipse) in which the whole disc (of the sun, moon, etc.) is obscured. ● *noun* a total number or amount. ● *verb* (**to·talled, total·ling**; esp. *US* **to·taled, total·ing**) **1** *transitive* **a** amount in number to (*they totalled 131*). **b** find the total of (things, a set of figures, etc.). **2** *intransitive* (foll. by *to, up to*) amount to, mount up to. **3** *transitive N Amer. slang* wreck (a car etc.) completely. ● *adverb* in total (*there were fifty people total*). [Old French from medieval Latin *totalis* from *totus* entire]

to·tali·tar·ian /təʊˌtælɪˈteərɪən/ ● *adjective* **1** of or relating to a centralized dictatorial form of government requiring complete subservience to the state. **2** demanding strict obedience in all matters; authoritarian. ● *noun* a person advocating such a system. □ **to·tali·tar·ian·ism** *noun*

to·tal·ity /təʊˈtælɪtɪ/ *noun* **1 a** the complete amount or sum. **b** the quality of being total; entirety. **2** *Astronomy* the time during which an eclipse is total.

total·ize *verb* (also esp. *Brit.* **-ise**) **1** *transitive* collect into a total; find the total of. **2** *transitive & intransitive* (of a corporation or societal institution) subsume (other institutions) in establishing an all-pervading influence. □ **total·iz·a·tion** *noun*

total·iz·er *noun* (also esp. *Brit.* **-iser**) **1** a device showing the number and amount of bets staked on a race, to facilitate the division of the total among those backing the winner. **2** a person or thing which totalizes.

total·ly *adverb* **1** completely; absolutely (*totally destroyed; totally different backgrounds*). **2** *informal* as an intensifier (*yes, I can totally help you out*).

Total Quality Management *noun* (in industry) a systematic approach to improving the quality of products and customer service etc., while reducing costs.

total recall *noun* the ability to remember every detail of one's experience clearly.

total war *noun* a war in which all available weapons and resources are employed.

tote¹ esp. *N Amer. informal* ● *transitive verb* carry (*toting a gun*). ● *noun* **1** = TOTE BAG. **2** any large container for storage or transportation, esp. in agricultural use. □ **toter** *noun* (also in *combination*). **-toting** *adjective* (in *combination*). [17th-c. US, prob. of dial. origin]

tote² *noun slang* (in full **tote board**) a totalizer. [abbreviation]

tote³ *transitive verb* (esp. foll. by *up*) *N Amer.* find the total of (things, a set of figures, etc.) (*toted up the cost*).

tote bag *noun* esp. *N Amer.* a large open bag with handles, usu. made of fabric, esp. canvas.

to·tem /ˈtəʊtəm/ *noun* **1 a** (among some N American Aboriginal peoples) the emblem or symbol of a clan or family, usually the animal or plant that the family claims as its mythical ancestor. **b** an image of this. **2** an emblem or symbol. □ **to·tem·ic** /-ˈtemɪk/ *adjective* **totem·ism** *noun* **totem·ist** *noun* **totem·is·tic** *adjective* [Algonquian]

totem pole *noun* **1** a pole on which family crests or totems are carved or hung. **2** a hierarchy (*high on the office totem pole*).

tote road *noun N Amer.* a rough temporary road used esp. to convey provisions to a work camp.

t'other *adjective & pronoun* (also **tother**) *dialect or jocular* the other. [Middle English *the tother*, for earlier *thet other* = *the other* (*thet* obsolete neuter of *the*]

to·tipo·tent /təʊˈtɪpətənt/ *adjective* (of a cell) capable of differentiating into any other related kind of cell or (in some organisms) a complete individual. □ **to·tipo·tency** *noun* [from *toti-* combining form of Latin *totus* whole + POTENT]

tot lot *noun informal* a playground for young children.

toto see IN TOTO.

tot·ter ● *intransitive verb* **1** stand or walk unsteadily or feebly (*tottered out of the pub*). **2 a** shake or rock as if about to collapse. **b** (of an institution, government, etc.) be about to fall. ● *noun* an unsteady or shaky movement or gait. □ **tot·ter·ing** *adjective* **tot·tery** *adjective* [Middle Dutch *touteren* to swing]

totty *noun Brit. informal* girls or women collectively regarded as sexually desirable.

tou·can /ˈtuːkan/ *noun* any tropical American fruit-eating bird of the family Ramphastidae, with an immense beak and brightly coloured plumage. [Tupi *tucana*, Guarani *tucã*]

touch ● *verb* **1** *transitive* come into or be in physical contact with (another thing) at one or more points. **2 a** *transitive* (often foll. by *with*) bring the hand etc. into contact with (*touched her arm*). **b** *intransitive* bring esp. the hand into contact with something; handle, manipulate (*don't touch!*). **3 a** *intransitive* (of two things etc.) be in or come into contact with one another (*the balls were touching*). **b** *transitive* bring (two things) into mutual contact (*they touched hands*). **4** *transitive* rouse tender or painful feelings in (*was touched by his appeal*). **5** *transitive* strike lightly (*just touched the wall with the back bumper*). **6** *transitive* (usu. with *neg.*) **a** disturb or interfere with (*don't touch my things*). **b** have any dealings with (*won't touch bricklaying*). **c** consume; use up; make use of (*dare not touch alcohol; has not touched her breakfast; need not touch your savings*). **7** *transitive* **a** deal with (a subject) lightly or in passing (*touched the matter of their expenses*). **b** concern (*it touches you closely*). **8** *transitive* **a** reach or rise as far as, esp. momentarily (*the thermometer touched 35°*). **b** (usu. with *neg.*) approach in excellence etc. (*can't touch him for style*). **9** *transitive* affect slightly; modify (*pity touched with fear*). **10** *transitive* affect in a way specified or implied by the context; transform (*has touched many lives*). **11** *transitive* (often foll. by *in*) esp. *Art* mark lightly, put in (features etc.) with a brush, pencil, etc. **12** *transitive* **a** strike (the keys, strings, etc. of a musical instrument). **b** strike the keys or strings of (a piano etc.). **13** *transitive* (usu. foll. by *for*) *slang* ask for and get money etc. from (a person) as a loan or gift (*touched him for $5*). **14** *transitive* injure slightly (*blossom touched by frost*). **15** *transitive Math.* be tangent to (a curve). ● *noun* **1** the act or an instance of touching, esp. with the body or hand (*felt a touch on my arm*). **2 a** the faculty of perception through physical contact, esp. with the fingers (*has no sense of touch in her right arm*). **b** the qualities of an object etc. as perceived in this way (*the soft touch of silk*). **3** a small amount; a slight trace (*a touch of salt; a touch of class*). **4 a** a musician's manner of playing keys or strings. **b** the manner in which the keys or strings respond to touch. **c** an artist's or writer's style of workmanship, writing, etc. (*has a delicate touch*). **5 a** a distinguishing quality or trait (*a rather amateur touch*). **b** a special skill or proficiency (*have lost my touch*). **6** (esp. in *pl.*) **a** a light stroke with a pen, pencil, etc. **b** a slight alteration or improvement (*this speech needs a few touches*). **7** (prec. by *a*) slightly (*is a touch too arrogant*). **8** *slang* **a** the act of asking for and getting money etc. from a person. **b** a person from whom money etc. is so obtained. **9** *Soccer & Rugby* the part of the field outside the sidelines. **10** *archaic* a test with or as if with a touchstone (*put it to the touch*). □ **at a touch** when touched, however lightly (*opened at a touch*). **be a soft touch** see SOFT TOUCH. **get** (or **put**) **in touch with** come or cause to come into communication with; contact. **in touch** (often foll. by *with*) **1** in communication (*we're still in touch after all these years*). **2** up to date, esp. regarding news etc. (*keeps in touch with events*). **3** aware, conscious, empathetic (*not in touch with her own feelings*). **lose touch** (often foll. by *with*) **1** cease to be informed. **2** cease to correspond with or be in contact with another person. **lose one's touch** not show one's customary skill. **out of touch** (often foll. by *with*) **1** not in correspondence. **2** not up to date or modern. **3** lacking in awareness or sympathy (*out of touch with her son's beliefs*). **to the touch** when touched (*was cold to the touch*). **touch all the bases** see BASE[1]. **touch at** (of a ship) call at (a port etc.). **touch base** see BASE[1]. **touch bottom 1** reach the bottom of water with one's feet. **2** be at the lowest or worst point. **touch a chord** see CHORD[2]. **touch down 1** (of an aircraft or spacecraft) make contact with the ground in landing. **2** *Rugby* touch the ground with the ball behind one's own or esp. the opponent's goal line. **touch off 1** explode by touching with a match etc. **2** initiate (a process, incident, etc.) suddenly (*touched off a long controversy*). **touch on** (or **upon**) **1** treat (a subject) briefly, refer to or mention casually. **2** verge on (*that touches on impudence*). **touch up 1** give finishing touches to or retouch (a picture, writing, etc.). **2** *slang* **a** caress so as to excite sexually. **b** sexually molest. **3** strike (a horse) lightly with a whip. **touch wood** touch something wooden with the hand to avert ill luck. **would not touch with a 10-foot** (or **barge**) **pole** refuse to be associated or concerned with (a person or thing). □ **touch·able** *adjective* **touch·ably** *adverb* **touch·er** *noun* **touch·less** *adjective* [Old French *touche*: prob. imitative, imitating a knock]

touch and go ● *adjective* uncertain regarding the outcome; precarious (*it was touch and go whether we'd catch our flight; a touch-and-go situation*). ● *noun* (*pl.* **touch and goes**, **go's**) a manoeuvre in which an aircraft touches the ground as in landing and immediately takes off again.

touch·down *noun* **1 a** *Football* the act or an instance of scoring six points by being in possession of the ball in the opposing side's end zone. **b** *Rugby* an act of touching the ground behind the opposing side's goal with the ball held in the hands, to score points. **2** the act or an instance of an aircraft making contact with the ground during landing.

tou·ché /tuːˈʃeɪ/ *interjection* **1** the acknowledgement of a hit by a fencing opponent. **2** the acknowledgement of a justified accusation, a witticism, or a point made in reply to one's own. [French, past participle of *toucher* TOUCH]

touched *adjective* **1** in senses of TOUCH *verb*. **2** (also in phr. **touched in the head**) *informal* slightly mad.

touch football *noun N Amer.* a form of football in which the ball carrier need only be touched to be stopped.

touch hole *noun hist.* a small hole in a gun for igniting the charge.

touch·ing ● *adjective* exciting tender feeling or sympathy; moving (*a touching incident; touching confidence*). ● *preposition literary* concerning; about. □ **touch·ing·ly** *adverb*

touch judge *noun Rugby* a linesman.

touch·line *noun Soccer & Rugby* either of the lines marking the side boundaries of the field.

touch-me-not *noun* any of various plants of the genus *Impatiens*, with ripe seed capsules that spring open when touched.

touch·pad *noun* **1** a usu. square area on a flat panel that needs only to be touched to activate an electrical device. **2** a panel including these.

touch screen *noun Computing* an input device that responds to the touch of a finger or stylus by transmitting the coordinates of the touched area to the computer.

touch-sensitive *adjective* **1** (of a computer input device, esp. a screen) operated by the touch of a finger, stylus, etc. **2** designating an electronic musical keyboard which responds dynamically to the varying force of a player's touch.

touch·stone *noun* **1** a fine-grained dark schist or jasper used for testing alloys of gold etc. by observing the colour of the mark which they make on it. **2** a thing which serves to test the genuineness or value of anything; a standard or criterion.

Touch-Tone *noun* (*attributive*) proprietary designating a telephone system in which a different single tone is generated by each of the numbered buttons pushed to make a call (*compare* ROTARY PHONE).

touch type *transitive & intransitive verb* type without looking at the keys. □ **touch typing** *noun* **touch typist** *noun*

touch-up *noun* a quick restoration or improvement (of paintwork, a piece of writing, etc.) (also *attributive*: *touch-up paint*).

touchy *adjective* (**touch·i·er**, **touch·i·est**) **1** apt to take offence; over-sensitive. **2** delicate; requiring careful handling (*a touchy subject*). □ **touch·i·ly** *adverb* **touch·i·ness** *noun* [perhaps alteration of TETCHY, influenced by TOUCH]

touchy-feely *adjective* displaying, encouraging, or relating to an uninhibited sharing of thoughts and emotions, often associated with physical touching, hugging, etc., as the basis of relationships.

tough ● *adjective* **1** hard to break, cut, tear, or chew; durable; strong. **2** (of a person) able to endure hardship; hardy. **3** unyielding, stubborn; difficult (*it was a tough job; a tough customer; that's a tough question*). **4** *informal* **a** acting sternly; hard (*get tough with; be tough on*). **b** (of circumstances, luck, etc.) severe, unpleasant, hard, unjust. **5** (of a law, policy, etc.) demanding; strictly enforced. **6** *informal* **a** rough, aggressive, or violent (*tough kids; tough talk*). **b** characterized by hardship or violence (*a tough neighbourhood*). ● *noun* a tough person, esp. a ruffian or criminal. ● *interjection ironic* that is unfortunate (used unsympathetically or defiantly to underscore an unfortunate condition or circumstance which another must face) (*Can't find your coat? Tough!*). □ **be a tough sell** *N Amer.* be difficult to convince others about (*knew their proposal would be a tough sell*). **hang tough** see HANG. **have it tough** be hard-pressed or in difficulty. **talk tough** see TALK. **tough as nails** *N Amer.* extremely tough (also *attributive*: *a tough-as-nails competitor*). **tough** (**it**) **out** *informal* endure or withstand (difficult conditions). □ **tough·ish** *adjective* **tough·ly** *adverb* **tough·ness** *noun* [Old English *tōh*]

tough·en *transitive & intransitive verb* make or become tough. □ **tough·en·er** *noun*

tough guy *noun informal* a hard, aggressive, or unyielding person (also, with hyphen, *attributive*: *his tough-guy swagger*).

tough·ie *noun* (also **toughy** *pl.* **-ies**) *informal* a tough person or problem.

tough love noun esp. N Amer. promotion of a person's welfare, esp. that of an addict, child, or criminal, by enforcing certain constraints on them, or requiring them to take responsibility for their actions.

tough luck informal ● noun bad luck, misfortune. ● interjection (also coarse slang **tough shit, tough titty**) often ironic that is unfortunate.

tough-minded adjective **1** realistic, not sentimental. **2** determined, resolute, stubborn. □ **tough-minded·ness** noun

tough nut noun = HARD NUT.

tough sledding noun see SLEDDING.

Tou·lon /tuːˈlɔ̃/ a port and naval base on the Mediterranean coast of S France; pop. (1999) 159,389.

Tou·louse /tuːˈluːz/ a city in SW France on the Garonne River, principal city of the Midi-Pyrénées region; pop. (1999) 390,350.

Toulouse-Lautrec /tuːˌluːz loːˈtrek/ **Henri (Marie Ray·mond) de** (1864–1901), French painter and lithographer. His reputation is based on his colour lithographs from the 1890s, depicting actors, music-hall singers, prostitutes, and waitresses in Montmartre; these include the *Moulin Rouge* series (1894).

tou·pée /tuːˈpeɪ/ noun a wig or artificial hairpiece to cover a bald spot. [French *toupet* hair tuft, diminutive of Old French *toup* tuft (as TOP¹)]

toup·ie /ˈtuːpi/ noun Cdn a round boneless smoked ham. [perhaps from French, = spinning top]

tour ● noun **1 a** a journey from place to place as a holiday. **b** an excursion, ramble, or walk (*made a tour of the garden*). **c** an organized and guided trip, excursion, or visit (also *attributive*: *tour bus*). **2** (in full **tour of duty**) **a** a period of duty on military or diplomatic service. **b** the time to be spent at a particular post. **3** a series of performances, matches, etc., at different places on a route through a country, around the world, etc. (*the band's European tour*; *the pro golf tour*). ● verb **1** intransitive make a tour (*toured through India*; *the company has been touring for four months*). **2** transitive make a tour of (a country etc.). □ **on tour** (esp. of a musical or dramatic performer, sports team, etc.) touring. [Old French *to(u)r* from Latin *tornus* from Greek *tornos* lathe]

tour·aco var. of TURACO.

tour de force noun (pl. **tours de force** pronunc. same) a feat of skill or strength; an impressive performance, achievement, or creation. [French]

tour d'hori·zon /tuːrdɔriˈzɔ̃/ noun (pl. **tours d'horizon** pronunc. same) a broad general survey. [French, lit. = 'tour of the horizon']

tour en l'air /tuːrɑ̃ˈleɪr/ noun (pl. **tours en l'air** pronunc. same) a jump in ballet in which the dancer jumps straight upward and turns around at least once before landing. [French, lit. 'turn in the air']

tour·er noun **1** in senses of TOUR verb. **2** a vehicle, esp. a car, for touring.

Tour·ette's syndrome /tʊˈrets/ noun (also **Tour·ette Syndrome**) a neurological disorder characterized by involuntary tics and vocalizations and the compulsive utterance of obscenities. [G. de la Tourette, French neurologist d.1904]

touring car noun hist. a car with room for passengers and much luggage.

tour·ism noun the business or industry of attracting and providing accommodation and services for visitors and travellers on holiday.

tour·ist noun a person making a visit or tour as a holiday; a person travelling for pleasure (often *attributive*: *tourist accommodation*). □ **tour·is·tic** adjective **tour·is·tic·ally** adverb

tourist class noun the lowest class of passenger accommodation in a ship, aircraft, etc.

tourist home noun N Amer. a home offering overnight accommodation for travellers.

tourist trap noun a place where tourists are exploited, e.g. where all goods and services are excessively expensive.

tour·isty adjective usu. derogatory appealing to or visited by many tourists.

tour·ma·line /ˈtɜːrməliːn, ˈtʊr-/ noun a boron aluminum silicate mineral of various colours, possessing unusual electrical properties, and used in electrical and optical instruments and as a gemstone. [French from Sinhalese *toramalli* porcelain]

tour·na·ment /ˈtɜːrnəmənt, ˈtʊr-/ noun **1** any contest of skill or series of contests involving a number of competitors (*chess tournament*; *tennis tournament*). **2** hist. **a** a pageant in which jousting with blunted weapons took place. **b** a meeting for jousting between single knights for a prize etc. [Old French *torneiement* from *tornier* TOURNEY]

tour·ne·dos /ˈtʊrnəˌdoʊ/ noun (pl. same /-ˌdoʊz/) a small round thick cut from a fillet of beef. [French, from *tourner* to turn + *dos* back]

tour·ney /ˈtɜːrni, ˈtʊr-/ ● noun (pl. **-neys**) a tournament. ● intransitive verb (**-neys, -neyed**) take part in a tournament. [Old French *tornei* (n.), ultimately from Latin *tornus* a turn]

tour·ni·quet /ˈtɜːrnəkət, ˈtʊr-, -ˌkeɪ, -ˌkiː/ noun a device for stopping the flow of blood through an artery by twisting a bar etc. in a ligature or bandage so as to tighten it. [French prob. from Old French *tournicle* coat of mail, TUNICLE, influenced by *tourner* TURN]

tour of duty noun see TOUR noun 2.

tour operator noun a travel agent specializing in package holidays.

Tours /tʊr/ an industrial city in west central France, on the Loire; pop. (1999) 132,820.

tour·tière /tɔrˈtjɛr/ noun a French-Canadian meat pie consisting esp. of ground pork and spices with a flaky double crust, traditionally served at Christmas. [Canadian French from French dialect, = pie dish]

tou·sle /ˈtaʊsəl, ˈtaʊzəl/ ● transitive verb **1** make (esp. the hair) untidy; rumple. **2** handle roughly or rudely. ● noun a tousled mass of hair etc. [frequentative of (now dialect) *touse*, Old English, related to Old High German *zirzuson*, *erzüsen* 'tear to pieces']

tousle-haired adjective having untidy hair.

Tous·saint L'Ouver·ture /tuːsɑ̃ luːverˈtʊːr/ **Pierre Domi·nique** (c.1743–1803), Haitian revolutionary leader. The leader of a slaves' rebellion in 1791, he was appointed Governor General by the revolutionary government of France in 1797. In 1802 Napoleon Bonaparte (wishing to restore slavery) ordered his forces to regain control of the island, and Toussaint was imprisoned in France.

tout ● verb **1** transitive extol, recommend, advocate. **2** intransitive solicit patronage persistently; pester customers (*touting outside the store*). **3** transitive (of a vendor etc.) **a** try to sell (goods or services), esp. persistently. **b** solicit the patronage of (a customer, passersby, etc.) persistently. **4** intransitive **a** N Amer. offer racing tips for a share of the resulting profit. **b** Brit. spy out the movements and condition of racehorses in training. ● noun **1** a person employed in touting. **2** Brit. **a** person who sells tickets etc. at inflated prices; a scalper. □ **tout·ed** adjective **tout·er** noun [Middle English *tūte* look out = Middle English (now dial.) *toot* (Old English *tōtian*) from Germanic]

tout court /tuː ˈkʊr/ adverb without addition; simply (*think of themselves as Scottish-Canadian rather than Canadian tout court*). [French, lit. 'very short']

tout de suite /tuːt ˈswiːt/ adverb immediately; at once. [French]

tou·ton /ˈtaʊtən/ noun Cdn (Nfld) a deep-fried flat round of bread dough, eaten with molasses. [origin unknown]

to·var·ich /təˈvɑːrɪʃ/ noun (also **to·var·ish**) (in the former USSR) comrade (esp. as a form of address). [Russian *tovarishch*]

TOW abbreviation tube-launched, optically-guided, wire-guided (missile).

tow¹ /toʊ/ ● transitive verb **1** (of a motor vehicle, horse, or person controlling it) pull (a boat, another motor vehicle, a trailer, etc.) along by a rope, tow bar, etc. **2** pull (a person or thing) along behind one. **3** (often foll. by *away*; often in *passive*) remove (a motor vehicle) to a pound, garage, etc. (*my car got towed again for illegal parking*). ● noun **1** the act or an instance of towing; the state of being towed. **2** N Amer. Forestry a set of boomed logs gathered to be towed. **3** N Amer. a mechanism for pulling skiers etc. up a hill. □ **in tow 1** (also **under tow**) being towed. **2** accompanying, often as a charge or as an admirer etc. □ **tow·able** adjective **tow·age** /-ɪdʒ/ noun [Old English *togian* from Germanic, related to TUG]

tow² /toʊ/ noun **1** the coarse and broken part of flax or hemp prepared for spinning. **2** a loose bunch of rayon etc. strands. [Middle Low German *touw* from Old Saxon *tou*, related to Old Norse *tó* wool]

to·ward /təˈwɔrd, twɔrd/ ● preposition (also **to·wards**) **1** in the direction of (*set out toward town*). **2** as regards; in relation to (*his attitude towards death*). **3** as a contribution to; for (*put this toward your expenses*). **4** near (*towards the end of our journey*). ¶ As forms of the preposition, *toward* and *towards* are equally common in Canada; the fact that this dictionary lists *toward* first should not discourage the use of *towards*. ● adjective /twɔrd, tɔrd/ **1** about to take place; in process. **2** docile, apt. **3** promising, auspicious. [Old English *tōweard* (adj.) future (as TO, -WARD)]

tow bar noun a bar for towing a trailer etc.

tow·boat noun a boat used to tow other boats, barges, etc.

towel ● noun **1** a piece of rough-surfaced absorbent, usu. terry cloth, used for drying oneself or a thing after washing. **2** absorbent paper used for this. **3** a cloth used for drying plates, dishes, etc.; a tea towel. ● verb (**tow·elled, towel·ling**; US **tow·eled, towel·ing**) (N Amer. also foll. by *off*) **1** transitive (often *reflexive*) wipe or dry with a towel.

2 *intransitive* wipe or dry oneself with a towel. [Old French *toail(l)e* from Germanic]

towel·ette *noun* a small moistened tissue for wiping esp. the hands or face, often individually wrapped.

towel·ling *noun* (also *US* **towel·ing**) **1** in senses of TOWEL *verb*. **2** absorbent cloth, esp. cotton or linen with uncut loops, used as material for towels.

towel rack *noun* a frame for hanging towels on.

tow·er ● *noun* **1 a** a tall narrow building or structure, either standing alone or forming part of a castle, church, etc. **b** a fortress etc. comprising or including a tower. **c** a tall structure housing machinery, apparatus, operators, etc. (*cooling tower*; *control tower*). **d** (also *Brit.* **tower block**) a tall building containing offices or apartments. **2** a lofty pile or mass (*a tower of books*). **3** a casing for computer components which stands upright, either alone or on a desk etc. **4** *hist.* a tall movable structure used in storming a fortified place. **5** a place of defence; a protection. ● *intransitive verb* (usu. foll. by *above*, *high*, *over*) reach or be high or above; be superior. □ **tow·ered** *adjective* [Old English *torr*, & Middle English *tūr*, Anglo-French & Old French *tur* etc., from Latin *turris* from Greek]

tower·ing *adjective* **1** high, lofty (*towering peaks*). **2** extremely eminent, exalted (*a towering intellect*). **3** violent (*towering rage*). □ **tower·ing·ly** *adverb*

Tower of Babel *Bible* a tower built in an attempt to reach heaven, which God frustrated by confusing the language of its builders (Gen. 11).

Tower of London (also **the Tower**) a fortress by the Thames just east of the City of London, begun in 1078, and used over the centuries as a state prison and as a repository for the crown jewels.

tower of strength *noun* a person or thing that gives strong and reliable support.

tow·head·ed *adjective* having very light-coloured or unkempt hair. □ **tow·head** *noun* [TOW²]

tow·hee /ˈtauhiː, toː-/ *noun* any of several buntings of the genus *Pipilo*, of brush and woodland in N America, esp. *P. erythrophthalmus*, having a black back, rust sides, and a white breast. [imitative of its call]

tow line *noun* a rope or line used in towing.

Town, Har·old Bar·ling (1924–90), Canadian artist. A major figure in the group Painters Eleven (1954–60), he was the most widely-known visual artist in English Canada from the late 1950s to the late 1960s.

town *noun* **1 a** an urban area with a name, defined boundaries, and local government, usu. larger than a village and smaller than a city. **b** any densely populated area, esp. as opposed to the country or suburbs. **c** the people of a town (*the whole town knows of it*). **d** the government, administration, or employees of a town. **2 a** the central business or shopping area in a neighbourhood (*just going into town*). **b** *Brit.* London or the chief city or town in one's neighbourhood (*went up to town*). **3** the permanent residents of a university town as distinct from the members of the university (*compare* GOWN 4). □ **go to town** *informal* act or work with energy or enthusiasm. **on the town** *informal* enjoying the entertainments, esp. the nightlife, of a town; celebrating. □ **town·let** *noun* **town·ward** *adjective & adverb* **town·wards** *adverb* [Old English *tūn* enclosure, from Germanic]

town council *noun* the elective governing body in a town. □ **town councillor** *noun*

town crier *noun* *hist.* an officer employed by a town council etc. to make public announcements in the streets or marketplace.

town·ee *var. of* TOWNIE.

Townes, Charles Hard (b.1915), US physicist. He invented the maser in 1954, and later showed that an optical maser (a laser) was possible, though the first working laser was constructed by others; he shared the Nobel Prize for physics in 1964.

town father *noun see* FATHER 9.

town hall *noun* **1** a building for the administration of local government, having public meeting rooms etc. **2** (also **town hall meeting**) *N Amer.* a meeting or television broadcast allowing people to express their opinions on political issues to political leaders.

town·house *noun* **1** (*N Amer.* also **town·home**) any of a row of usu. similar joined houses, two or three storeys high, along a street; a row house. **2** an urban residence, esp. of a person with a house in the country. **3** *Brit.* a town hall.

town·ie *noun* (also **town·ee**) *derogatory* a person living in a town, esp. as opposed to those living in the country or (in a university town) a student etc.

town line *noun* *Cdn* (*Ont.*) a road separating two municipalities, esp. townships.

town meeting *noun* **1** *N Amer.* a general assembly of the inhabitants of a town. **2** *US* a meeting of the voters of a town for the transaction of public business.

town planner *noun* = URBAN PLANNER. □ **town planning** *noun*

town·scape *noun* **1** the visual appearance of a town or towns. **2** a picture of a town.

towns·folk *noun* the inhabitants of a particular town or towns.

Towns·hend /ˈtaunzend/ **Pete** (b.1945), English rock guitarist, singer, and songwriter, who was a founding member of The Who (1964–83).

town·ship *noun* **1** *N Amer.* a division of a county with some corporate powers. **2** *N Amer.* (in areas of W Canada and the US surveyed into ranges and townships) a district six miles square, containing thirty-six sections. **3** *hist.* an urban area in South Africa set aside for black occupation. **4** *Brit. hist.* **a** a community inhabiting a manor, parish, etc. **b** a manor or parish as a territorial division. **c** a small town or village forming part of a large parish.

Town·ships *noun Cdn* (*prec. by the*) = EASTERN TOWNSHIPS. □ **Town·ship·per** *noun*

town·site *noun N Amer.* (esp. *Cdn*) **1** the site of a town, esp. a tract of land set apart by legal authority to be occupied by a town, and usu. surveyed and laid out with streets etc. **2** an unincorporated town in a national park etc.

towns·man *noun* (*pl.* **-men**) an inhabitant of a town; a fellow citizen. □ **towns·woman** *noun*

towns·people *plural noun* the people of a town.

tow·path *noun* a path beside a river or canal, originally used for towing barges by horse.

tow rope *noun* = TOW LINE.

tow truck *noun N Amer.* a truck used to tow away motor vehicles, e.g. by hoisting and dragging them or by conveying them on a flat bed.

tox·emia /tɒkˈsiːmiə/ *noun* (also esp. *Brit.* **tox·aemia**) **1** blood poisoning. **2** a condition in pregnancy characterized by increased blood pressure. □ **tox·em·ic** *adjective* [as TOXI- + -EMIA]

toxi- *combining form* (also **toxico-, toxo-**) poison; poisonous, toxic.

toxic ● *adjective* **1** of or relating to poison (*toxic symptoms*). **2** poisonous (*toxic gas*). **3** caused by poison (*toxic anemia*). **4** *informal* (of a relationship, state of mind, etc.) harmful, unhealthy (*toxic shame*). ● *noun* (in *pl.*) toxic substances. □ **toxic·ally** *adverb* **tox·icity** *noun* [medieval Latin *toxicus* 'poisoned' via Latin *toxicum* from Greek *toxikon* (*pharmakon*) '(poison for) arrows', from *toxon* 'bow', *toxa* 'arrows']

toxi·cant /ˈtɒksɪkənt/ *noun* a toxic substance, esp. one used as a pesticide etc.

toxi·col·ogy *noun* the scientific study of poisons. □ **toxi·co·logic·al** *adjective* **toxi·col·o·gist** *noun*

toxic shock syndrome *noun Med.* acute septicemia in women, typically caused by bacterial infection from a retained tampon, IUD, etc. Abbr.: **TSS**.

tox·in *noun* a poison produced by a living organism, esp. one formed in the body and stimulating the production of antibodies. [TOXIC + -IN]

tox·oid *noun* a chemically modified toxin from a pathogenic micro-organism, which is no longer toxic but is still antigenic and can be used as a vaccine.

toxo·plas·mo·sis *noun Med.* a disease caused by infection with the protozoan *Toxoplasma gondii*, transmitted esp. through poorly prepared food or in cat feces and dangerous in unborn children. [TOXO- (see TOXI-) + PLASMA + -OSIS]

toy ● *noun* **1 a** a plaything, esp. for a child. **b** (often *attributive*) a model or miniature replica of a thing, esp. as a plaything (*toy boat*). **2 a** a thing, esp. a gadget or instrument, regarded as providing amusement or pleasure. **b** a task or undertaking regarded in an unserious way. **3** (usu. *attributive*) a diminutive breed or variety of dog etc. ● *intransitive verb* (usu. foll. by *with*) **1 a** consider something casually or without serious intent (*toyed with the idea of going to the Yukon*). **b** deal with something or someone thoughtlessly; trifle or amuse oneself with (*toying with her affections*). **2 a** move a material object idly (*toyed with her necklace*). **b** nibble at food etc. unenthusiastically (*toyed with a peach*). □ **toy·like** *adjective* [Middle English: origin unknown]

toy boy *noun informal* a much younger male lover.

toyi-toyi /ˈtɔitɔi/ *noun* (in S Africa) a dance step characterized by high-stepping movements, typically performed at protest gatherings or marches.

---

t top v voice w we z zoo ʃ she ʒ vision θ thin ð this ŋ ring x loch tʃ chip dʒ jar (*see over for vowels*)

toy·land *noun informal* the toy industry.

Toyn·bee, Ar·nold (Jo·seph) (1889–1975), English historian. In his 12-volume *Study of History* (1934–61) he surveyed the history of different civilizations, tracing in them a pattern of growth, maturity, and decay and concluding that contemporary Western civilization is in the last of these stages.

toy·town *noun* (usu. *attributive*) resembling a model of a town; seemingly diminutive.

TPA *abbreviation* TISSUE PLASMINOGEN ACTIVATOR.

Tpr *abbreviation* (also **Tpr.**) TROOPER 1.

TQM *abbreviation* TOTAL QUALITY MANAGEMENT.

tr. *abbreviation* transitive.

tra·bec·u·la /trəˈbekjʊlə/ *noun* (*pl.* **tra·bec·u·lae** /-ˌliː/) **1** *Anat.* a supporting band or bar of connective or bony tissue, esp. dividing an organ into chambers. **2** *Bot.* a beam-like projection or process within a hollow structure. □ **tra·bec·u·lar** *adjective* **tra·bec·u·late** /-lət/ *adjective* [Latin, diminutive of *trabs* beam]

Trab·zon /ˈtrabzən/ (also **Trebi·zond** /ˈtrebəˌzɒnd/) a port on the Black Sea in N Turkey; pop. (2002) 203,700.

trace¹ ● *transitive verb* **1 a** observe, discover, or find vestiges or signs of by investigation. **b** (often foll. by *along, through, to,* etc.) follow or mark the track or position of (*traced their footprints in the mud*; *traced the outlines of a wall*). **c** (often foll. by *back*) follow to its origins (*can trace my family to the 12th century*; *the report has been traced back to you*). **2** (often foll. by *over*) copy (a drawing etc.) by drawing over its lines on a superimposed piece of translucent paper, or by using carbon paper. **3** (often foll. by *out*) mark out, delineate, sketch, or write esp. laboriously (*traced out a plan of the district*; *traced out his vision of the future*). **4** pursue one's way along (a path etc.). ● *noun* **1 a** a sign or mark or other indication of something having existed; a vestige (*no trace remains of the settlement*; *has the traces of a vanished beauty*). **b** a very small quantity. **c** an amount of rainfall etc. too small to be measured. **2** a track or footprint left by a person or animal. **3** a track left by the moving pen of an instrument etc. **4** a line on the screen of a cathode ray tube showing the path of a moving spot. **5** a curve's projection on or intersection with a plane etc. **6** *N Amer.* the track made by the passage of any person or thing; a beaten path, a trail. □ **trace·able** *adjective* **trace·abil·ity** *noun* **trace·less** *adjective* [Old French *trace* (n.), *tracier* (v.) from Latin *tractus* drawing: see TRACT¹]

trace² *noun* **1** each of the two side straps, chains, or ropes by which a horse draws a vehicle. **2** a long strap attached to a sled dog's harness, by which it pulls the sled. □ **kick over the traces** become insubordinate or reckless. [Old French *trais*, pl. of TRAIT]

trace element *noun* **1** a chemical element occurring in minute amounts. **2** (also **trace mineral**) a chemical element required only in minute amounts by living organisms for normal growth.

trace fossil *noun* a fossil that represents a burrow, footprint, etc., of an organism.

tracer *noun* **1** a person or thing that traces. **2** *Military* a bullet etc. that is visible in flight because of flames etc. emitted (also *attributive*: *tracer bullet*). **3** an artificially produced radioactive isotope capable of being followed through the body by the radiation it produces. **4** a person whose business is the tracing of missing persons, property, etc.

tracery *noun* (*pl.* **-ies**) **1** ornamental stone openwork esp. in the upper part of a Gothic window. **2** a fine or delicate decorative pattern. **3** a natural object finely patterned. □ **tracer·ied** *adjective*

trachea /ˈtreɪkɪə, trəˈkiːə/ *noun* (*pl.* **trach·eae** /-kiːiː/) **1** the passage reinforced by rings of cartilage, through which air reaches the bronchial tubes from the larynx; the windpipe. **2** each of the air passages in the body of an insect etc. **3** any duct or vessel in a plant. □ **trach·eal** /ˈtreɪkɪəl/ *adjective* **trach·eate** /ˈtreɪkɪˌeɪt/ *adjective* [medieval Latin *trachia* from Greek *trakheia* (*artēria*) rough (artery), from *trakhus* rough]

tracheo- /ˈtreɪkɪəʊ/ *combining form* trachea.

trach·eot·omy /ˌtreɪkɪˈɒtəmi, ˌtraki-/ *noun* (also **trach·eos·tomy** /-ˈɒstəmi/) (*pl.* **-tomies**) **1** a surgical operation to make an opening in the trachea, esp. so that the patient can breathe through it via a curved tube. **2** the opening so made.

tra·choma /trəˈkoːmə/ *noun* a contagious disease of the eye with inflamed granulation on the inner surface of the lids. [modern Latin from Greek *trakhōma* from *trakhus* rough]

trach·yte /ˈtreɪkəɪt, ˈtrak-/ *noun* a light-coloured volcanic rock rough to the touch. □ **trach·yt·ic** /trəˈkɪtɪk/ *adjective* [French from Greek *trakhutēs* roughness (as TRACHOMA)]

tracing *noun* **1** a copy of a drawing etc. made by tracing. **2** = TRACE¹ *noun* 3. **3** the act or an instance of tracing.

tracing paper *noun* translucent paper used for making tracings.

track¹ ● *noun* **1 a** a mark or marks left by a person, animal, or thing in passing. **b** (in *pl.*) such marks, esp. footprints. **2** a rough path, esp. one beaten by use. **3** a continuous railway line (*laid three miles of track*). **4 a** a racecourse for horses etc. **b** *Sport* a prepared course for runners etc. **c** esp. *N Amer. Sport* the athletic events, esp. running, which take place on a track (*track coach*; *competes in track*). **d** = WARNING TRACK. **5 a** a section of a compact disc, phonograph record, cassette tape, etc., containing one song etc. **b** one of several lengthwise divisions of a strip of magnetic tape, containing one sequence of signals; a channel. **c** that which is recorded on such a strip (*annoyed by the laugh track*; *laid down the drum track*). **6 a** a line of travel, passage, or motion (*followed the track of the hurricane*). **b** the path travelled by a ship, aircraft, etc. (compare COURSE *noun* 2c). **7** *US Education* = STREAM *noun* 4. **8 a** a continuous band around the wheels of a tank, tractor, etc. **9** the transverse distance between a vehicle's wheels. **10 a** a course of action or conduct; a way of proceeding. **b** a line of reasoning or thought (*this track proved fruitless*). **11** = CAREER PATH (*tenure-track*). **12** (in full **track mark**) (usu. in *pl.*) *slang* a line on the skin made by repeated injections of an addictive drug. ● *verb* **1** *transitive* **a** follow the track of (an animal, person, spacecraft, etc.). **b** trace the movements of. **2** *transitive* **a** follow (a course, development, etc.). **b** follow the course or development of (*tracked the students through high school*). **3** *intransitive* (often foll. by *back, in,* etc.) (of a film or television camera) move in relation to the subject being filmed. **4** *intransitive* (of a stylus) follow a groove in a record. **5** *intransitive* (of wheels) run so that the back ones are exactly in the track of the front ones. **6** *transitive N Amer.* **a** make a track with (dirt etc.) from the feet. **b** leave such a track on (a floor etc.). **7** *transitive US Education* assign (a pupil) to a course of study according to ability. □ **in one's tracks** *informal* where one stands, there and then (*stopped him in his tracks*). **keep** (or **lose**) **track of** follow (or fail to follow) the course or development of. **make tracks** *informal* go or run away. **make tracks for** *informal* go in pursuit of or toward. **off the track** away from the subject. **on a person's track 1** in pursuit of him or her. **2** in possession of a clue to a person's conduct, plans, etc. **on the right** (or **wrong**) **track** following the right (or wrong) line of inquiry. **on** (or **off**) **track** following (or deviating from) the desired direction or goal. **on the wrong side of the tracks** *informal* in a poor or less prestigious part of town. **track down** reach or capture by tracking. [Old French *trac*, perhaps from Low German or Dutch *tre(c)k* 'draught' etc.]

track² *verb* **1** *transitive* tow (a boat) by rope etc. from a bank. **2** *intransitive* travel by being towed. [apparently from Dutch *trekken* to draw etc., assimilated to TRACK¹]

track·age *noun* the tracks or lines of a railway system collectively.

track and field *noun* esp. *N Amer.* athletic events comprising track events (such as sprints, hurdles, etc.) and field events (such as throwing and jumping competitions).

track·ball *noun Computing* a small ball that is rotated in a holder to move a cursor on a screen.

tracked *adjective* (of a wheeled vehicle) equipped with tracks (see TRACK¹ *noun* 8).

track·er *noun* **1** a person or thing that tracks. **2** a police dog tracking by scent. **3** a wooden connecting rod in the mechanism of an organ.

track·ing *noun* **1** in senses of TRACK *verb*. **2** in a VCR, the alignment of the tape with the tape head, which may need to be adjusted for tapes recorded on another machine. **3** *Electricity* the formation of a conducting path over the surface of an insulating material. **4** *US Education* the streaming of school pupils.

tracking shot *noun Film* a shot during which the camera is moved, e.g. along a track, esp. to follow the subject.

tracking station *noun* an establishment set up to track objects in the sky.

tracking stock *noun N Amer.* shares issued by a parent company to track the performance of a subsidiary or division.

track-laying *noun* the laying of railway track. □ **track·lay·er** *noun*

track·less *adjective* **1** without a track or tracks; untrodden. **2** leaving no track or trace. **3** (esp. of a vehicle) not running on a track. □ **track·less·ness** *noun*

track light *noun* (usu. in *pl.*) one of a line of lights fitted on a metal or plastic strip, each of which can be positioned individually. □ **track lighting** *noun*

track meet *noun* an event at which various races and other athletic contests are held.

track·pad *noun* *Computing* a small pad with which the actions of a cursor etc. can be controlled by the movement of a finger along its surface.

track pants *plural noun* loose pants, usu. with elasticized cuffs, worn casually or by an athlete etc. for exercising or jogging.

track·point *noun* *Computing* a nib, esp. built into a keyboard, which can be manipulated by a finger to move a cursor etc.

track record *noun* the past achievements of a person or an organization.

track shoe *noun* a shoe with a flat rubber sole, worn by runners or as casual footwear.

track·side *noun* (often *attributive*) the area beside a railway line or racetrack.

track suit *noun* a loose warm two-piece suit worn by an athlete etc. for exercising or jogging.

track·way *noun* **1** a beaten path, esp. made by prehistoric animals. **2** *Brit.* an ancient roadway.

tract[1] *noun* **1** a region or area of indefinite, esp. large, extent (*pathless desert tracts*). **2** *Anat.* an area of an organ or system (*respiratory tract*). [Latin *tractus* drawing, from *trahere tract-* draw, pull]

tract[2] *noun* a short treatise in pamphlet form esp. on a religious or political subject. [apparently abbreviation of Latin *tractatus* TRACTATE]

tract[3] *noun* *Catholicism & Music* an anthem replacing the alleluia in some Masses. [medieval Latin *tractus* (*cantus*) drawn-out (song), past participle of Latin *trahere* draw]

tract·able *adjective* **1** (of a person) easily handled; manageable; docile. **2** (of material etc.) pliant, malleable. □ **tract·abil·ity** *noun* **tract·ably** *adverb* [Latin *tractabilis* from *tractare* handle, frequentative of *trahere tract-* draw]

Tract·arian·ism *noun hist.* = OXFORD MOVEMENT. □ **Tract·arian** *adjective & noun* [after *Tracts for the Times*, published in Oxford 1833–41 and outlining the movement's principles]

trac·tate /'trakteɪt/ *noun* a treatise. [Latin *tractatus* from *tractare*: see TRACTABLE]

tract house *noun* (also **tract home**) *N Amer.* one of a number of similar houses built as part of a real estate development. □ **tract housing** *noun*

trac·tion *noun* **1** the grip of a tire, footwear, etc. on the ground. **2** the act of drawing or pulling a thing over a surface, esp. a road or track (*steam traction*). **3 a** a sustained pulling on a limb, muscle, etc., by means of pulleys, weights, etc. to maintain the positions of fractured bones, correct deformity, etc. **b** the state of being subjected to such a pull (*was in traction for a month after the accident*). **c** contraction, e.g. of a muscle. □ **trac·tive** *adjective* [French *traction* or medieval Latin *tractio* from Latin *trahere tract-* draw]

traction control *noun* a feature on some motor vehicles which automatically reduces engine power when the wheels spin on slippery patches of road.

traction engine *noun* a steam or diesel engine for drawing heavy loads on roads, fields, etc.

trac·tor *noun* a powerful motor vehicle used for hauling etc., esp. one with large treaded rear wheels used to haul farm machinery. [Late Latin *tractor* (as TRACTION)]

tractor beam *noun* (in science fiction) a beam of energy that can irresistibly draw objects such as space ships or keep them stationary.

tractor cap *noun* = BASEBALL CAP.

tractor pull *noun* *N Amer.* a competition in which tractors pull increasingly heavy loads.

tractor-trailer *noun* *N Amer.* an articulated truck consisting of a powerful cab pulling a large detachable trailer; a transport truck.

tractor train *noun* *Cdn* (*North*) a train of sleds pulled by a tractor etc.

Tracy[1] /tra'siː/ a former town in south central Quebec, situated at the confluence of the Richelieu and St. Lawrence rivers, just south of Lac Saint-Pierre, now merged with Sorel into the city of Sorel-Tracy; pop. (2001) 12,390. [A. de Prouville de *Tracy*, military governor of New France d.1670]

Tracy[2], **Spen·cer** (1900–67), US actor. He won Oscars for his performances in *Captains Courageous* (1937) and *Boys' Town* (1938), and later co-starred with Katharine Hepburn in films such as *Adam's Rib* (1949) and *Guess Who's Coming to Dinner?* (1967).

trad *informal* ● *noun* esp. *Brit.* traditional jazz. ● *adjective* traditional. [abbreviation]

trade ● *noun* **1 a** buying and selling. **b** buying and selling conducted between nations etc.; the exchange of goods between peoples (also *attributive*: *trade goods*). **c** business conducted for profit (esp. as distinct from a profession) (*a butcher by trade*). **d** business of a specified nature or time (*Christmas trade*; *tourist trade*). **2** a skilled handicraft esp. requiring an apprenticeship (*learned a trade*; *his trade is plumbing*). **3** (usu. prec. by *the*) the people engaged in a specific trade (*the trade will never agree to it*). **4** *N Amer.* **a** a transaction, esp. a swap. **b** *Sport* an exchange of players between two or more franchises or teams. **5** (usu. in *pl.*) a trade wind. ● *verb* **1** *intransitive* (often foll. by *in*, *with*) engage in trade; buy and sell (*trades in plastic novelties*; *we trade with Japan*). **2** *transitive* **a** exchange in commerce; barter (goods). **b** exchange (insults, blows, etc.). **c** esp. *N Amer.* (foll. by *for*) swap, exchange. **d** *N Amer.* exchange products or commodities with (a person) (*I'll trade you for it*). **e** *N Amer. Sport* (of a franchise or team) relinquish the rights to (a player) to another team in exchange for the rights to one or more of theirs or for other considerations (*was traded to Vancouver*). **3** *intransitive* (usu. foll. by *with*, *for*) have a transaction with a person for a thing. **4** *intransitive* (of shares, currency, etc.) be bought and sold (*the dollar is trading lower this month*; *trades on the Toronto Stock Exchange*). □ **trade in** (often foll. by *for*) exchange (esp. a used car etc.) in part payment for another. **trade off** exchange, esp. as a compromise. **trade on** take advantage of (a person's credulity, one's reputation, etc.). **trade up** sell something in order to buy a better or more expensive replacement. □ **trad·able** *adjective* **trade·able** *adjective* [Middle Low German *trade* 'track' from Old Saxon *trada*, Old High German *trata*: related to TREAD]

trade balance *noun* = BALANCE OF TRADE.

trade barrier *noun* a policy or regulation that restricts trade between countries, provinces, etc.

trade book *noun* a book published by a commercial publisher and intended for general readership.

trade commissioner *noun* a government official stationed in another jurisdiction to promote trade etc.

trade·craft *noun* **1** skill or art in connection with a trade or calling. **2** skill in espionage and intelligence work.

trade deficit *noun* (also **trade gap**) the extent by which a country's imports exceed its exports.

trade fair *noun* = TRADE SHOW.

trade goods *plural noun* goods exchanged between countries, peoples, etc.

trade-in *noun* a thing, esp. a car, exchanged in part payment for another.

trade jargon *noun* **1** the jargon used within a trade or industry. **2** (also **trade language**) a pidgin spoken by merchants or traders.

trade journal *noun* a periodical containing news etc. concerning a particular trade.

trade·mark ● *noun* **1** a logo, word, or words, secured by legal registration or established by use as representing a company, product, etc. **2** a distinctive characteristic etc. ● *adjective* characteristic or distinctive (*dressed in his trademark baggy pants*). ● *transitive verb* (usu. as **trade·marked** *adjective*) **1** provide with a trademark. **2** register as a trademark.

trade name *noun* **1** a name by which a thing is called in a trade. **2** a name given to a product; a brand name. **3** a name under which a business operates.

trade-off *noun* a balance achieved between two desirable but incompatible features; a compromise, bargain.

trade paper *noun* = TRADE JOURNAL.

trader *noun* **1 a** a person engaged in trading. **b** a person who trades stocks. **2 a** a fur trader. **b** the manager of a trading post. **3** a merchant ship.

trade route *noun* a route followed by traders or trading vessels.

trad·es·can·tia /ˌtradəˈskantiə/ *noun* any plant of the genus *Tradescantia*, with blue, white, or pink three-petalled flowers, esp. spiderwort, *T. virginiana*, of eastern N America cultivated in gardens, and the trailing wandering Jew frequently grown as a houseplant. [modern Latin from J. *Tradescant*, English naturalist d.1638]

trade secret *noun* **1** a secret device, technique, formula, etc., used esp. by a business. **2** *jocular* any secret.

trade show *noun* a gathering of members of a trade or industry for the exhibition of the latest technology, products, developments, etc.

trades·man *noun* (*pl.* **-men**) **1** a person engaged in a trade, esp. a skilled craftsman. **2** *Brit.* a shopkeeper. □ **trades·woman** *noun* (*pl.* **-women**).

trades·people *plural noun* people engaged in trade; tradesmen or tradeswomen and their families.

trade union *noun* (also *Brit.* **trades union**) an organized association of workers formed to protect and further their rights and interests and to bargain collectively with employers; a labour union. □ **trade unionism** *noun* **trade unionist** *noun*

trade war *noun* a situation in which governments act aggressively in international markets to promote their own countries' trading interests.

trade-weight·ed *adjective* (esp. of exchange rates) weighted according to the importance of the trade with the various countries involved.

trade wind *noun* a wind blowing continually towards the equator and deflected westward. [from an obsolete adverbial use of *trade*: *blow trade* = blow regularly]

trad·ing *noun* the act of engaging in trade.

trading card *noun N Amer.* a small card depicting a figure or figures from popular culture, esp. sports, for collecting or trading.

trading floor *noun* the area in a stock exchange etc. where dealing is done.

trading post *noun* (also **trading station**) a store or other place for conducting trade, usu. in remote areas, esp. originally established by colonial powers to trade with Aboriginal peoples.

trading stamp *noun* a stamp formerly given to customers by some stores which was exchangeable in large numbers for various articles.

trad·i·tion *noun* **1 a** a custom, opinion, or belief handed down to posterity esp. orally or by practice. **b** this process of handing down. **2** an established practice or custom (*going camping on the Labour Day weekend is a tradition in our family*). **3** artistic, literary, etc. principles based on experience and practice; any one of these (*stage tradition*; *traditions of the Dutch School*). **4** *Theol.* doctrine or a particular doctrine etc. claimed to have divine authority without documentary evidence, esp.: **a** the oral teaching of Christ and the Apostles. **b** the laws held by the Pharisees to have been delivered by God to Moses. **c** the words and deeds of Muhammad not in the Quran. □ **trad·i·tion·less** *adjective* [Old French *tradicion* or Latin *traditio* from *tradere* hand on, betray (as TRANS-, *dare* give)]

trad·i·tion·al *adjective* of, based on, or obtained by tradition. □ **trad·i·tion·al·ly** *adverb*

trad·i·tion·al·ism *noun* **1** respect or support for tradition, esp. in contrast with modern practices or styles. **2** a philosophical system referring all religious knowledge to divine revelation and tradition. □ **trad·i·tion·al·ist** *noun* **trad·i·tion·al·is·tic** *adjective* **trad·i·tion·alize** *transitive & intransitive verb*

tradition-bound *adjective* not departing from tradition; not innovative (*a tradition-bound company*).

tra·duce /trəˈduːs, -ˈdjuːs/ *transitive verb* speak ill of; misrepresent. □ **tra·ducer** *noun* [Latin *traducere* disgrace (as TRANS-, *ducere* duct-lead)]

Tra·fal·gar, Battle of /trəˈfalɡər/ the decisive naval battle of the Napoleonic Wars, fought on 21 Oct. 1805 off the cape of Trafalgar on the south coast of Spain, in which the British fleet under Nelson (who was killed in the action) thoroughly defeated the combined fleets of France and Spain, thus thwarting Napoleon's projected invasion of Britain.

traf·fic ● *noun* **1** (often *attributive*) **a** vehicles moving on a public road or highway, esp. of a specified kind, density, etc. (*heavy traffic on the 401*; *traffic sign*). **b** such movement in the air, at sea, or by rail. **c** people moving, esp. on foot (*a carpet worn by heavy traffic*). **2** (usu. foll. by *in*) trade, esp. illegal (*the traffic in drugs*). **3 a** the transportation of goods, the coming and going of people or goods by road, rail, air, sea, etc. **b** the persons or goods so transported. **4** dealings or communication between people etc. (*had no traffic with them*). **5** the messages, signals, etc., transmitted through a communications system; the flow or volume of such signals. ● *verb* (**traf·ficked**, **traf·fick·ing**) **1** *intransitive* (usu. foll. by *in*) **a** deal in something, esp. illegally (*trafficked in narcotics*). **b** engage in (*traffics in half-truths*). **2** *transitive* deal in; barter. □ **traf·fick·er** *noun* **traf·fic·less** *adjective* [French *traf(f)ique*, Spanish *tráfico*, Italian *traffico*, of unknown origin]

traffic calming *noun* (often *attributive*) the deliberate slowing of traffic, esp. along residential streets, by building speed bumps, obstructions, etc.

traffic circle *noun N Amer.* a road junction at which traffic moves in one direction around a central island.

traffic cone *noun* PYLON 1.

traffic cop *noun* **1** a police officer who directs the flow of traffic, esp. by gesturing while standing in the road. **2** *informal* a person who directs the conflicting forces or interests in an organization etc. to ensure smooth operation.

traffic engineer *noun* a person engaged in the design and planning of roads and the control of traffic. □ **traffic engineering** *noun*

traffic island *noun* a paved or grassed area in a road to divert traffic, provide a refuge for pedestrians, etc.

traffic jam *noun* traffic at a standstill because of volume, construction, an accident, etc.

traf·ficked *adjective* (of a roadway, route, etc.) used by an esp. specified amount of traffic (*a heavily trafficked road*).

traffic light *noun* (usu. in *pl.*) each of a set of automatic lights, usu. red, amber, and green, for controlling road traffic, esp. at intersections.

traffic pattern *noun* **1** a pattern in the air above an airport of permitted lanes for aircraft to follow after takeoff or prior to landing. **2** the characteristic distribution of traffic on a route.

traffic sign *noun* a sign conveying information, a warning, etc., to road traffic.

traffic staff sergeant *noun* (in the Ontario Provincial Police) an officer ranking above sergeant and below sergeant major responsible for traffic duty.

traffic warden *noun Brit.* a uniformed official employed to help control road traffic and esp. parking.

traga·canth /ˈtraɡəˌkanθ/ *noun* a white or reddish gum from a plant, *Astragalus gummifer*, used as a vehicle for drugs, dye, etc. [French *tragacante* from Latin *tragacantha* from Greek *tragakantha*, name of a shrub, from *tragos* goat + *akantha* thorn]

tra·gedi·an /trəˈdʒiːdiən/ *noun* **1** a writer of tragedies. **2** an actor in tragedy.

tra·gedi·enne /trəˌdʒiːdɪˈen/ *noun* an actress in tragedy.

tra·gedy /ˈtradʒədi/ *noun* (*pl.* **-ies**) **1** a serious accident, crime, or natural catastrophe. **2 a** a sad event; a calamity (*the team's defeat is a tragedy*). **b** a tragic element; tragic circumstances. **3 a** a dramatic representation dealing with tragic events and with an unhappy ending, esp. concerning the downfall of the protagonist. **b** the tragic genre (*compare* COMEDY 1). [ultimately from Greek *tragōidia*, apparently 'goat song' from *tragos* goat + *ōidē* song]

tra·gic /ˈtradʒɪk/ *adjective* **1** sad; calamitous; greatly distressing (*a tragic tale*). **2** of, or in the style of, tragedy (*tragic drama*; *a tragic actor*). □ **tra·gic·al** *adjective* **tra·gic·ally** *adverb* [French *tragique* from Latin *tragicus* from Greek *tragikos* from *tragos* goat: see TRAGEDY]

tragi·com·edy /ˌtradʒɪˈkɒmədi/ *noun* (*pl.* **-edies**) **1 a** a play having a mixture of comedy and tragedy. **b** plays of this kind as a genre. **2** an event etc. having tragic and comic elements. □ **tragi·comic** *adjective* **tragi·comic·ally** *adverb*

trago·pan /ˈtraɡəˌpan/ *noun* any Asian pheasant of the genus *Tragopan*, with erect fleshy horns on its head. [Latin from Greek from *tragos* goat + *Pan* the god Pan]

trahison des clercs /ˌtraiˌzɔ̃ dei ˈkler/ *noun* the betrayal of standards, scholarship, etc., by intellectuals. [French, title of a book by J. Benda (1927)]

Trail a city in southern BC, situated at the mouth of Trail Creek, on the Columbia River, about 25 km south of Castlegar and 10 km north of the border with Washington state; pop. (2001) 7,575. □ **Trail·ite** *noun* [the name of the creek, so called because it marked the Columbia River end of the Dewdney Trail]

trail ● *noun* **1 a** a track left by a thing, person, etc., moving over a surface (*left a trail of wreckage*; *a slug's slimy trail*). **b** a track, scent, or other trace followed in hunting, seeking, etc. (*we're on the trail*; *paper trail*). **2 a** a beaten or maintained path or track, esp. through a park, wild region, etc., often for a specified traffic (*scenic trail*; *ski trail*). **b** a route into or through wild territory, followed by a wave of migrants, prospectors, etc. **c** *N Amer.* a highway route designated for its interest to tourists (*the Cabot Trail*). **d** *Cdn* (in Alberta) a major arterial road through a city (*dropped her off near Yellowhead Trail and 66th St.*). **e** a tour or series of performances, shows, etc. (*on the festival trail*). **3** a part dragging behind a thing or person; an appendage (*a trail of smoke*; *a condensation trail*). **4** the rear end of a gun carriage, resting or sliding on the ground when the gun is unlimbered. ● *verb* **1** *transitive & intransitive* draw, be drawn, or appear to draw along behind (*with the children trailing*; *trailing smoke*). **2** *intransitive* (often foll. by *behind*) walk wearily; lag; straggle.

3 *transitive* follow the trail of; pursue (*trailed him to his home*).
4 a *intransitive* be losing in a game or other contest (*trailing by three points*). **b** *transitive* have fewer points in a game, series, etc. than (one's opponent) (*trails St. John's by five points*). **5** *intransitive* (usu. foll. by *away*, *off*) peter out; tail off. **6** *intransitive* **a** (of a plant etc.) grow or hang over a wall, along the ground etc. **b** (of a garment etc.) hang loosely. **7** *transitive* (often *reflexive*) drag (oneself, one's limbs, etc.) along wearily etc.
□ **trail one's coat** deliberately provoke a quarrel, fight, etc. [Old French *traillier* to tow, or from Middle Low German *treilen* haul, from Latin *tragula* dragnet]

trail bike *noun* a light motorcycle for use in rough terrain; a dirt bike.

trail·blaz·er *noun* **1** a person who marks a new track through wild country. **2** a pioneer; an innovator. □ **trail-blazing** *noun & attributive adjective*

trail-breaker *noun* a person who clears a path through rough terrain, deep snow, etc. □ **trail-breaking** *noun*

trail·er ● *noun* **1** a vehicle towed by another, esp.: **a** the rear section of a tractor-trailer. **b** an open cart. **c** a platform for transporting a boat etc. **d** *N Amer.* a camper, mobile home, house trailer, or other towed vehicle with living accommodations. **2** a series of brief extracts from a film etc., used to advertise it in advance; a preview. **3** a person or thing that trails. **4** a trailing plant. ● *transitive & intransitive verb* transport or travel by trailer. □ **trailer·able** *adjective*

trailer home *noun N Amer.* = MOBILE HOME.

trailer park *noun N Amer.* (also **trailer camp**, **trailer court**) a place where mobile homes or other trailers may be parked for holiday or more permanent accommodation.

trailer trash *noun N Amer.* a poor, lower-class, esp. boorish white person typified as living in a mobile home.

trail·head *noun N Amer.* the starting point of a trail.

trail·ing arbutus *noun N Amer.* the mayflower, *Epigaea repens*.

trail·ing edge *noun* **1** the rear edge of an aircraft's wing etc. **2** *Electronics* the part of a pulse in which the amplitude diminishes (*opp.* LEADING EDGE).

Traill, Cath·ar·ine Parr (born Catharine Parr Strickland) (1802–99), English-born Canadian pioneer, writer, and botanist. She and her husband emigrated to Canada in 1832, and settled near Peterborough, Ont. There, she wrote her best-known book, *The Backwoods of Canada* (1836), an account of her first three years in the new country; she was the elder sister of writer Susanna Moodie.

trail mix *noun* esp. *N Amer.* a mixture of nuts, dried fruit, chocolate chips, etc., esp. as a snack eaten by hikers etc.

Trail of '98 *Cdn* the route taken by stampeders during the Klondike gold rush of 1898, including the Chilkoot Pass.

trail ride *noun N Amer.* a ride on horseback along a trail esp. through rugged country. □ **trail riding** *noun*

trail·side *adjective N Amer.* situated or occurring near a trail.

train ● *verb* **1 a** *transitive* (often foll. by *to* + infin.) teach (a person, animal, oneself, etc.) a specified skill esp. by practice (*trained the dog to beg*; *was trained in midwifery*). **b** *intransitive* undergo this process (*has trained as a teacher*). **2** *transitive & intransitive* bring or come into a state of physical efficiency by exercise, diet, etc.; undergo physical exercise, esp. for a specific purpose (*trained me for the high jump*; *the team trains every evening*). **3** *transitive* cause (a plant) to grow in a required shape (*trained the peach tree up the wall*). **4** *transitive* (usu. as **trained** *adjective*) improve the abilities of (the mind, eye, voice, etc.) as a result of instruction, practice, etc. **5** *transitive* (often foll. by *on*) point or aim (a gun, camera, etc.) at an object etc. **6** *intransitive informal* go by train. ● *noun* **1 a** a series of railway cars drawn by a locomotive. **b** *Cdn* (North) = TRACTOR TRAIN. **2** something dragged along behind or forming the back part of a dress, robe, etc. (*wore a dress with a long train*; *the train of the peacock*). **3** a succession or series of people, things, events, etc. (*a long train of camels*; *interrupted my train of thought*; *a train of ideas*). **4** a body of followers; a retinue (*a train of admirers*). **5** a succession of military vehicles etc., including artillery, supplies, etc. (*baggage train*). **6** a line of gunpowder etc. to fire an explosive charge. **7** a series of connected wheels or parts in machinery. □ **in train** properly arranged or directed. **in a person's train** following behind a person.
□ **train·able** *adjective* **train·abil·ity** *noun* **train·less** *adjective* [Old French *trainer*, *trahiner*, ultimately from Latin *trahere* draw]

train·band *noun hist.* any of several divisions of London citizen soldiers, esp. in the Stuart period.

trained seal *noun* **1** a seal trained to perform tricks for the amusement of the public. **2** a person who does another's bidding unthinkingly.

train·ee *noun* (often *attributive*) a person undergoing training.
□ **trainee·ship** *noun*

train·er *noun* **1** a person who trains. **2 a** a person who trains athletes, horses, etc., as a profession. **b** a person who attends to the medical and physical well-being of athletes, esp. on a team. **3** an aircraft or device simulating it used to train pilots. **4** *Brit.* a soft running shoe of leather, canvas, etc.; an athletic shoe. **5** a piece of equipment used for training; an exercise machine.

train·ing *noun* **1** the act or process of teaching or learning a skill, discipline, etc. (*physical training*). **2** the process of developing physical fitness and efficiency by diet and exercise. **3** (*attributive*) designating a thing designed or modified to facilitate the learning of a skill etc. (*training pants*). □ **go into training** begin physical training. **in training 1** undergoing physical training. **2** physically fit as a result of this. **out of training 1** no longer training. **2** physically unfit.

training camp *noun* the gathering of members of a sports team for organized physical training prior to the start of a new season. **2** any camp where training takes place.

training ground *noun* any setting where one learns or develops specific skills, attributes, etc.

training school *noun* **1** (also **training college**) a college or school where students are trained in a particular profession or occupation. **2** *N Amer.* a vocational institution for juvenile delinquents.

training ship *noun* a ship on which young people are taught seamanship etc.

training shoe *noun* = TRAINER 4.

training wheel *noun N Amer.* a small wheel fitted to each side of the rear wheel of a bicycle to stabilize it for a child learning to ride.

train·load *noun* a number of people, or quantity of goods etc., transported by train.

train·man *noun* (*pl.* **-men**) a railway employee working on trains.

train-mile *noun* one mile travelled by one train, as a unit of traffic.

train oil *noun* oil obtained from the blubber of a whale (esp. of a right whale). [obsolete *train*, *trane* train oil, from Middle Low German *trān*, Middle Dutch *traen*, apparently = TEAR²]

train·spot·ter *noun Brit.* **1** a person whose hobby is observing trains and recording locomotive numbers. **2** a derogatory term for an obsessive follower of any specialized hobby. □ **train·spot·ting** *noun*

train tracks *plural noun* **1** railway tracks. **2** *slang* orthodontic braces.

train wreck *noun* **1** an act or instance of a train crashing. **2** the wreckage resulting from this. **3** *informal* any situation characterized by chaos or disorder.

traipse /treips/ *informal* ● *intransitive verb* **1** tramp or trudge wearily. **2** walk aimlessly or carelessly. **3** (often foll. by *around*) go on errands. ● *noun* a tedious journey on foot. [16th-c. *trapes* (v.), of unknown origin]

trait /treit/ *noun* **1** a distinguishing feature or characteristic esp. of a person. **2** *Genetics* an inherited or inheritable characteristic (*a recessive trait*). [French from Latin *tractus* (as TRACT¹)]

trai·tor *noun* (often foll. by *to*) a person who is treacherous or disloyal, esp. to his or her country. □ **trai·tor·ous** *adjective* **trai·tor·ous·ly** *adverb* [Old French *traît(o)ur* from Latin *traditor -oris* from *tradere*: see TRADITION]

Tra·jan /ˈtreidʒən/ (Latin name Marcus Ulpius Traianus) (*c.*53–117), Roman emperor 98–117. During his reign Dacia (now NW Romania) was annexed as a province and many public works were undertaken.

tra·jec·tory /trəˈdʒektəri/ *noun* (*pl.* **-ies**) **1 a** the path described by a projectile flying or an object moving under the action of given forces. **b** a notional path or direction taken by someone or something. **2** *Math* a curve or surface cutting a system of curves or surfaces at a constant angle. [(originally adj.) from medieval Latin *trajectorius* from Latin *traicere traject-* (as TRANS-, *jacere* throw)]

Tra·lee /trəˈliː/ a port on the southwest coast of the Republic of Ireland; the county town of Kerry; pop. (2002) 20,800.

tram¹ *noun* **1** esp. *Brit.* = STREETCAR. **2** *N Amer.* = GONDOLA 3. **3** a four-wheeled vehicle used in coal mines. [Middle Low German & Middle Dutch *trame* balk, beam, barrow-shaft]

tram² *noun* double silk thread used for the weft of some velvets and silks. [French *trame* from Latin *trama* weft]

tram·car *noun hist.* a streetcar.

tram·line *noun Brit.* **1** (usu. in *pl.*) a rail for a streetcar. **2** an inflexible principle or course of action etc.

tram·mel ● *transitive verb* (**tram·melled**, **tram·mel·ling**; also **tram·meled**, **tram·mel·ing**) impede the free action of; hinder, constrain. ● *noun* **1** (usu. in *pl.*) an impediment to free movement; a hindrance (*the trammels of domesticity*). **2** a triple dragnet for fish, which are trapped in a pocket formed when they attempt to swim through. **3** an instrument for drawing ellipses etc. with a bar sliding in upright grooves. [in sense 'net' from Old French *tramail* from medieval Latin *tramaculum, tremaculum*, perhaps formed as TRI- + *macula* (MAIL²): later history uncertain]

tra·mon·tana /trəmɒn'tanə/ *noun* a cold north wind in the Adriatic. [Italian: see TRAMONTANE]

tra·mon·tane /trə'mɒntein/ ● *adjective* **1** situated or living on the other side of mountains, esp. the Alps as seen from Italy. **2** (from the Italian point of view) foreign; barbarous. ● *noun* **1** a tramontane person. **2** = TRAMONTANA. [Italian *tramontano* from Latin *transmontanus* beyond the mountains (as TRANS-, *mons montis* mountain)]

tramp ● *verb* **1** *intransitive* **a** walk heavily and firmly (*tramping around upstairs*). **b** go on foot, esp. a distance. **2** *transitive* **a** cross on foot, esp. wearily or reluctantly. **b** cover (a distance) in this way (*tramped forty miles*). **3** *transitive* (often foll. by *down*) tread on; trample; stamp on. **4** *intransitive* live as a tramp. ● *noun* **1** an itinerant vagrant or beggar; a hobo. **2** esp. *N Amer. slang* derogatory a promiscuous woman. **3** the sound of a person, or esp. people, walking, marching, etc., or of horses' hooves. **4** a journey on foot, esp. protracted. **5** an iron plate protecting the sole of a boot used for digging. **6** a merchant ship running on no regular line or route (also *attributive: tramp steamer*). □ **tramp·er** *noun* **tramp·ish** *adjective* **trampy** *adjective* [Middle English *trampe* from Germanic]

tram·ple ● *transitive verb* **1** tread under foot. **2** press down or crush in this way. **3** disregard with contempt; put down. ● *noun* the sound or act of trampling. □ **trample on** (or **over**) **1** tread heavily on. **2** treat roughly or with contempt; disregard (a person's feelings etc.). □ **tramp·ler** *noun*

tram·po·line /,trampə'liːn, 'trampə,liːn/ ● *noun* a strong fabric sheet connected by springs to a horizontal frame, used by gymnasts etc. for somersaults, as a springboard, etc. ● *intransitive verb* use a trampoline. □ **tram·po·lin·er** *noun* **tram·po·lin·ist** *noun* [Italian *trampolino* from *trampoli* stilts]

tram·way *noun* **1** (also *hist.* **tram road**) a crude road with wooden, stone, or metal tracks for wheels, used in mining etc. **2 a** rails for a streetcar. **b** a streetcar system.

trance ● *noun* **1 a** a sleep-like or half-conscious state without response to stimuli. **b** a hypnotic or cataleptic state. **2** such a state as entered into by a medium. **3** a state of extreme exaltation or rapture; ecstasy. **4** a stunned or dazed state. **5** a state of mental absorption or abstraction from external things. **6** a form of hypnotically rhythmic and atmospheric techno music (also *attributive: trance dance*). ● *transitive verb literary* = ENTRANCE². □ **trance·like** *adjective* [Old French *transe* from *transir* depart, fall into a trance, from Latin *transire*: see TRANSIT]

tranche /trɑːnʃ/ *noun* a portion, esp. of income, or of a block of shares. [French, = slice (as TRENCH)]

trank *slang* ● *noun* (usu. in *pl.*) a tranquilizer. ● *transitive verb* (esp. as **tranked** *adjective*) tranquilize. [abbreviation]

tran·ny *noun* (pl. **-nies**) *slang* **1** *N Amer. Mech.* transmission. **2** esp. *Brit. informal* a transistor radio. **3** a transsexual or transvestite. [abbreviation]

tran·quil /'trankwɪl/ *adjective* calm, serene, unruffled. □ **tran·quil·ity** /-'kwɪlɪti/ *noun* **tran·quil·ly** *adverb* [French *tranquille* or Latin *tranquillus*]

tran·quil·ize *transitive verb* (also **tran·quil·lize, -lise**) make tranquil, esp. by a drug etc. □ **tran·quil·iz·ing** *adjective*

tran·quil·izer *noun* (also **tran·quil·lizer, -liser**) a person or thing which tranquilizes, esp. a drug used to diminish tension or anxiety.

trans- *prefix* **1** across, beyond (*transcontinental; transgress*). **2** on or to the other side of (*transatlantic*) (opp. CIS-). **3** through (*transcutaneous*). **4** into another state or place (*transform; transcribe*). **5** surpassing, transcending (*transfinite*). **6** *Chem.* **a** (of an isomer) having the same atom or group on opposite sides of a given plane in the molecule (compare CIS- 4). **b** having a higher atomic number than (*transuranic*). [from or after Latin *trans* across]

trans *adjective* transsexual.

trans·act *transitive verb* perform or carry through (business). □ **trans·act·or** *noun* [Latin *transigere transact-* (as TRANS-, *agere* do)]

trans·action *noun* **1 a** a piece of esp. commercial business done; a deal (*a profitable transaction*). **b** *N Amer.* = TRADE 4b. **c** the management of business etc. **2** (in *pl.*) published reports of discussions, papers read, etc., at the meetings of a learned society.

trans·action·al *adjective* **1** in senses of TRANSACTION. **2** *Psych.* of,

pertaining to, or involving interpersonal communication viewed as transactions of attitude between participants.

trans·alpine *adjective* beyond the Alps, esp. from the Italian point of view. [Latin *transalpinus* (as TRANS-, *alpinus* ALPINE)]

Transalpine Gaul see GAUL¹.

trans·amin·ase /tranz'amɪneɪs/ *noun* an enzyme which catalyzes the transfer of an amino group from one molecule to another. [TRANS- + AMINO + -ASE]

trans·atlan·tic *adjective* **1** crossing or spanning the Atlantic (*a transatlantic flight*). **2** beyond the Atlantic, esp.: **a** *Brit.* North American. **b** *N Amer.* European. □ **trans·atlan·tic·ally** *adverb*

trans·axle *noun* an integral driving axle and differential gear in a motor vehicle. [TRANSMISSION + AXLE]

trans·bor·der *adjective* that crosses, or is situated on or pertains to both sides of a border (*transborder shopping; a transborder meeting*).

trans·bound·ary *adjective* that crosses, or is situated on or pertains to both sides of a boundary.

trans-Canada ● *adjective* spanning, including, or involving all of Canada. ● *noun* (**Trans-Canada**) (prec. by *the*) (in full **Trans-Canada Highway**) a highway spanning Canada from St. John's to Victoria, formally opened in 1962 and completed in 1970.

Trans·cau·casia /,tranzkɔ'keɪʒə/ a region lying to the south of the Caucasus mountains, between the Black Sea and the Caspian, and comprising the republics of Georgia, Armenia, and Azerbaijan. □ **Trans·cau·casian** *adjective*

trans·ceiv·er /tran'siːvər/ *noun* any device which is both a transmitter and receiver of signals, e.g. a radio transceiver, modem, etc.

tran·scend /tran'send/ *transitive verb* **1** be beyond the range or grasp of (human experience, reason, belief, etc.). **2** excel; surpass. **3** be above or independent of; go beyond or exceed the limits of. [Old French *transcendre* or Latin *transcendere* (as TRANS-, *scandere* climb)]

tran·scend·ent /tran'sendənt/ ● *adjective* **1** excelling, surpassing (*transcendent merit*). **2** transcending human experience. **3** *Philos.* **a** higher than or not included in any of Aristotle's ten categories in scholastic philosophy. **b** not realizable in experience in Kantian philosophy. **4** (esp. of the supreme being) existing apart from, not subject to the limitations of, the material universe (opp. IMMANENT 2). ● *noun Philos.* a transcendent thing. □ **tran·scend·ence** *noun* **tran·scend·en·cy** *noun* **tran·scend·ent·ly** *adverb*

tran·scen·dent·al /,transen'dentəl/ ● *adjective* **1** = TRANSCENDENT. **2 a** (in Kantian philosophy) presupposed in and necessary to experience; a priori. **b** (in Schelling's philosophy) explaining matter and objective things as products of the subjective mind. **c** (esp. in Emerson's philosophy) regarding the divine as the guiding principle in man. **3 a** visionary, abstract. **b** vague, obscure. **4** *Math.* (of a function) not capable of being produced by the algebraical operations of addition, multiplication, and raising to a power, or the inverse operations. ● *noun* a transcendental term, conception, etc. □ **tran·scen·dent·al·ly** *adverb*

tran·scen·dent·al·ism *noun* **1** transcendental philosophy, belief, thought, etc. **2** exalted or visionary language. □ **tran·scen·dent·al·ist** *noun*

Transcendental Meditation *noun proprietary* a method of detaching oneself from problems, anxiety, etc., by silent meditation and repetition of a mantra.

trans·code *transitive & intransitive verb* convert from one form of coded representation to another. □ **trans·coder** *noun*

trans·contin·ent·al ● *adjective* (of a railway etc.) extending across a continent. ● *noun* a transcontinental railway or train. □ **trans·contin·ent·al·ly** *adverb*

tran·scribe *transitive verb* **1** make a copy of, esp. in writing. **2** transliterate. **3** write out (shorthand, notes, etc.) in ordinary characters or continuous prose. **4 a** record for subsequent reproduction. **b** broadcast in this form. **5** arrange (music) for a different instrument etc. **6** synthesize (a nucleic acid, usu. RNA) using an existing nucleic acid (usu. DNA) as a template, so that the genetic information in the latter is copied. **7** represent (a speech sound or spoken word) in a written form using phonetic characters. □ **tran·scrib·er** *noun* [Latin *transcribere transcript-* (as TRANS-, *scribere* write)]

tran·script *noun* **1 a** a written or recorded copy. **b** something transcribed. **2** any copy. **3** a written record of public proceedings etc. **4** *N Amer.* an official record of a student's grades etc. **5** a length of RNA or DNA that has been transcribed respectively from a DNA or RNA template. [Old French *transcrit* from Latin *transcriptum* neuter past participle: see TRANSCRIBE]

tran·script·ase /tran'skrɪpteɪz/ *noun* an enzyme which catalyzes the formation of RNA from a DNA template during transcription, or (**reverse transcriptase**) the formation of DNA from an RNA template in reverse transcription.

tran·scrip·tion *noun* **1 a** the action or process of transcribing something. **b** an instance of this. **2** a transcript or copy. **3** *Biol.* the process by which genetic information represented by a sequence of DNA nucleotides is copied into newly synthesized molecules of RNA, with the DNA serving as a template. □ **tran·scrip·tion·al** *adjective* **tran·scrip·tion·al·ly** *adverb* **tran·scrip·tion·ist** *noun*

trans·cul·tur·al *adjective* pertaining to or involving more than one culture; cross-cultural.

trans·cu·ta·neous /ˌtranzkjuː'teɪniəs/ *adjective* through or by the skin.

transcutaneous electrical nerve stimulation *noun Med.* a treatment for pain involving the application of an electric current through electrodes attached to the skin. Abbr.: **TENS**.

trans·der·mal *adjective Med.* (of a drug) applied through the skin, esp. from an adhesive patch, and absorbed slowly into the body.

trans·duce *transitive verb* **1** convert (energy, esp. in the form of a signal) into a different medium or form of energy. **2 a** transfer (genetic material) from one cell to another with a virus or virus-like particle. **b** subject (a cell) to such transfer. □ **trans·duc·tion** *noun* [back-formation from TRANSDUCER]

trans·du·cer *noun* any device for converting a signal from one medium of transmission to another, esp. a non-electrical signal into an electrical one, e.g. pressure into voltage. [Latin *transducere* 'lead across' (as TRANS-, *ducere* 'lead')]

tran·sect ● *transitive verb* /tran'sekt/ cut across or transversely. ● *noun* /'transekt/ a line or strip across the earth's surface or through any object, along which a survey or observations are made.
□ **tran·sec·tion** *noun* [TRANS- + Latin *secare sect-* cut]

tran·sept /'transept/ *noun* **1** either arm of the part of a cross-shaped church at right angles to the nave (*north transept; south transept*). **2** this part as a whole. □ **tran·sept·al** /-'septəl/ *adjective* [modern Latin *transeptum* (as TRANS-, SEPTUM)]

tran·sex·ual *var. of* TRANSSEXUAL.

trans fat *noun* (in full **trans fatty acid**) any unsaturated fatty acid with the same atoms on opposite sides of its double bonds, found frequently in margarines and cooking oils as a result of hydrogenation during processing. [TRANS- 6a]

trans·fec·tion *noun* the introduction of free nucleic acid into a eukaryotic cell. □ **trans·fect** *transitive verb* [TRANS- + INFECTION]

trans·fer ● *verb* (**trans·ferred**, **trans·fer·ring**) **1** *transitive* (often foll. by *to*) **a** move (a thing etc.) from one place to another (*transferred the bag from the car to the station; transferred the money into another account*). **b** hand over the possession of (property, rights, etc.) to a person (*transferred her membership to her son*). **2** *transitive & intransitive* move or change to another department, school, group, etc. **3** *intransitive* change from one route, airport, station, etc., to another on a journey. **4** *transitive* **a** reroute (a telephone connection) to another line, department, etc. **b** reroute the telephone connection of (a caller) to another line, department, etc. (*I'll transfer you*). **5** *transitive* convey or apply (a drawing or design) from one surface to another, esp. from a prepared sheet. **6** *transitive* change (the sense of a word etc.) by extension or metaphor. **7** *transitive* copy (data etc.) using a different medium. ● *noun* **1** the act or an instance of transferring or being transferred. **2** *N Amer.* a ticket allowing a journey to be continued on another route etc. **3 a** design etc. conveyed or to be conveyed from one surface to another. **b** a small usu. coloured picture or design on paper, which is transferable to another surface. **4** a person who is or is to be transferred. **5 a** the conveyance of property, a right, etc. **b** a document effecting this. **6** = TRANSFER PAYMENT. □ **trans·fer·ee** *noun* **trans·fer·or** *noun* esp. *Law.* [French *transférer* or Latin *transferre* (as TRANS-, *ferre lat-* bear)]

trans·fer·able *adjective* capable of being transferred.
□ **trans·fer·abil·ity** *noun*

transferable vote *noun* a vote that can be transferred to a voter's second choice if the first choice is eliminated.

trans·fer·ase /'transfəreɪs/ *noun* an enzyme which catalyzes the transfer of a particular group from one molecule to another.
[TRANSFER + -ASE]

trans·fer·ence /'transfərəns/ *noun* **1** the act or an instance of transferring; the state of being transferred. **2** *Psych.* the redirection of childhood emotions to a new object, esp. to a psychoanalyst.

transfer fee *noun* esp. *Brit.* a fee paid from one soccer club to another for the transfer of a player.

transfer payment *noun* a direct payment from a government not made in exchange for goods or services, e.g. to an individual or family in the form of an employment insurance payment or family allowance, or (in Canada) esp. to another level of government.

trans·fer·ral *noun* = TRANSFER *noun* 1.

trans·fer·rin /trans'ferɪn/ *noun* a protein transporting iron in blood serum. [TRANS- + Latin *ferrum* 'iron']

transfer RNA *noun* RNA conveying an amino acid molecule from the cytoplasm to a ribosome for use in protein synthesis etc. Abbr.: **tRNA**.

transfer station *noun* a facility where garbage is collected for compression etc. before being trucked to a landfill site.

trans·fig·ur·a·tion *noun* **1** a change of form or appearance. **2 a** Christ's appearance in radiant glory to three of his disciples (Matt. 17:2, Mark 9:2–3). **b** (**Transfiguration**) the festival of Christ's transfiguration.

trans·figure *transitive verb* change in form or appearance, esp. so as to elevate or idealize.

trans·finite /trans'faɪnaɪt/ *adjective* **1** beyond or surpassing the finite. **2** *Math.* (of a number) exceeding all finite numbers.

trans·fix *transitive verb* **1** pierce with a sharp implement or weapon. **2** (usu. in *passive*) root (a person) to the spot with fascination, astonishment, fear, etc.; paralyze the faculties of. □ **trans·fixion** *noun*

trans·form ● *verb* **1 a** *transitive* make a thorough or dramatic change in the form, outward appearance, character, etc., of. **b** *intransitive* (often foll. by *into*, *to*) undergo such a change. **2** *transitive Electricity* change the voltage etc. of (a current). **3** *transitive Math.* change (a mathematical entity) by transformation. ● *noun Math. & Linguistics* the product of a transformation. □ **trans·form·able** *adjective* **trans·form·a·tive** *adjective*

trans·form·a·tion *noun* **1** the act or an instance of transforming; the state of being transformed. **2** *Zool.* a complete change of form at metamorphosis, esp. of insects, amphibians, etc. **3** the induced or spontaneous change of one element into another. **4** *Math.* a change from one geometrical figure, expression, or function to another of the same value, magnitude, etc. **5** *Biol.* **a** the modification of a eukaryotic cell from its normal state to a malignant state. **b** the genetic alteration of a cell by introduction of extraneous DNA, esp. by a plasmid. **6** *Linguistics* a process, with reference to particular rules, by which one grammatical pattern of sentence structure can be converted into another, or the underlying meaning of a sentence can be converted into a statement of syntax.

trans·form·a·tion·al *adjective* relating to or involving transformation. □ **trans·form·a·tion·ally** *adverb*

transformational grammar *noun Linguistics* a grammar that describes a language by means of transformation (see TRANSFORMATION 6).

trans·form·er *noun* **1** an apparatus for reducing or increasing the voltage of an alternating current. **2** a person or thing that transforms.

trans·fuse /tranz'fjuːz/ *transitive verb* **1** permeate (*purple dye transfused the water; was transfused with gratitude*). **2 a** transfer (blood) from one person or animal to another. **b** inject (liquid) into a blood vessel to replace lost fluid. **c** treat (a person) with a blood transfusion.
□ **trans·fusion** *noun* [Latin *transfundere transfus-* (as TRANS-, *fundere* pour)]

trans·gen·dered *adjective* (also **trans·gender**) having an identity which does not conform unambiguously to conventional notions of male or female gender, esp. undergoing, or having undergone, sex change procedures.

trans·genic /tranz'dʒenɪk/ *adjective Biol.* (of an animal or plant) having genetic material introduced from another species.

trans·genics *noun* the branch of biology concerned with transgenic organisms.

trans·gress *verb* **1** *transitive & intransitive* contravene or go beyond the bounds or limits set by (a commandment, law, etc.). **2** *transitive Geol.* (of the sea) spread over (the land). □ **trans·gres·sive** *adjective*
trans·gres·sor *noun* [French *transgresser* or Latin *transgredi transgress-* (as TRANS-, *gradi* go)]

trans·gres·sion *noun* **1** an act or instance of transgressing. **2** a violation of law, duty or command.

tran·ship *var. of* TRANSSHIP.

trans·histor·ical *adjective* (also **trans·histor·ic**) having significance that transcends the historical; universal, eternal.

trans·hu·mance /trans'hju:məns/ *noun* the seasonal moving of livestock to a different region. [French from *transhumer* from Latin TRANS- + *humus* ground]

tran·si·ent /'tranziənt/ ● *adjective* of short duration; momentary; passing; impermanent (*life is transient; of transient interest*). ● *noun* **1 a** a temporary visitor, worker, etc. **b** a vagrant; a tramp. **2** *Electricity* a brief current etc. □ **tran·si·ence** *noun* **tran·si·en·cy** *noun* **tran·si·ent·ly** *adverb* [Latin *transire* (as TRANS-, *ire* go)]

trans·illu·min·ate *transitive verb* pass a strong light through for inspection, esp. for medical diagnosis. □ **trans·illu·min·a·tion** *noun*

tran·sis·tor /tran'zɪstər/ *noun* **1** a semiconductor device with three connections, capable of amplification in addition to rectification. **2** (in full **transistor radio**) a portable radio with transistors. [blend of TRANSFER + RESISTOR]

tran·sis·tor·ize *transitive verb* (also esp. Brit. **-ise**) design or equip with, or convert to, transistors.

tran·sit ● *noun* **1** the act or process of going, conveying, or being conveyed, esp. over a distance (*transit by rail; made a transit of the lake*). **2** a passage or route (*the overland transit*). **3** *N Amer.* the local conveyance of passengers on public routes. **4 a** the apparent passage of a celestial body across the meridian of a place. **b** the passage of an inferior planet across the face of the sun, or of a moon etc. across the face of a planet. **5** a surveying instrument for measuring horizontal angles. ● *verb* (**tran·sit·ed, tran·sit·ing**) **1** *transitive* make a transit across. **2** *intransitive* make a transit. □ **in transit** while going or being conveyed. [Latin *transitus*, from *transire* (as TRANSIENT)]

transit camp *noun* a camp for the temporary accommodation of soldiers, refugees, etc.

transit instrument *noun* (also **transit circle**) a telescope mounted so as to move only on a north-south line, for observing the transit of a celestial body across the meridian.

tran·si·tion ● *noun* **1 a** a passing or change from one place, state, condition, etc., to another (*an age of transition; a transition from plain to hills*). **b** passage in thought, speech, or writing, from one subject to another. **2** *Music* a momentary modulation. **3** *Physics* a change in an atomic nucleus or orbital electron with emission or absorption of radiation. ● *transitive & intransitive verb* undergo or cause to undergo a transition. □ **tran·si·tion·al** *adjective* **tran·si·tion·ally** *adverb* [French *transition* or Latin *transitio* (as TRANSIT)]

transition element *noun* *Chem.* (also **transition metal**) any of a set of metallic elements in the periodic table whose uncombined atoms have partly filled *d* or *f* orbitals and the ability to form coloured complexes.

transition game *noun* *N Amer. Sport* (in hockey, basketball, etc.) a team's ability to switch quickly from offensive to defensive play, or vice versa.

transition house *noun* (also **transition home**) *Cdn* a home operated by a social service agency, esp. for abused women.

tran·si·tive /'tranzɪtɪv/ ● *adjective* **1** *Grammar* (of a verb or sense of a verb) that takes a direct object (whether expressed or implied), e.g. *saw* in *saw the donkey, saw that she was ill* (opp. INTRANSITIVE). **2** *Logic* (of a relation) such as to be valid for any two members of a sequence if it is valid for every pair of successive members. ● *noun* a transitive verb. □ **tran·si·tive·ly** *adverb* **tran·si·tive·ness** *noun* **tran·si·tiv·ity** *noun* [Late Latin *transitivus* (as TRANSIT)]

tran·si·tory /'tranzɪ,tɔri/ *adjective* not permanent, brief, transient. □ **tran·si·tor·i·ness** *noun*

transit shelter *noun* a shelter from the rain etc. for those waiting for a transit vehicle, e.g. a bus or streetcar.

transit visa *noun* a visa allowing only passage through a country.

transit·way *noun* any roadway, railway, etc. used for transit, esp. one reserved for public transit.

Trans·jordan *the* former name of an area of Palestine east of the Jordan River, now part of the Hashemite Kingdom of Jordan (see JORDAN[1]). □ **Trans·jor·dan·ian** *noun & adjective*

Trans·kei /tran'skaɪ/ *a* former homeland established in South Africa for the Xhosa people, now part of the province of Eastern Cape.

trans·late *verb* **1** *transitive & intransitive* **a** (often foll. by *into*) express the sense of (a word, sentence, speech, book, etc.) in another language. **b** do this as a profession etc. (*translates for the UN*). **2** *intransitive* (of a literary work etc.) be translatable, bear translation (*does not translate well*). **3** *transitive* express (an idea, book, etc.) in another, esp. simpler,

form. **4** *transitive* interpret the significance of; infer as (*translated his silence as dissent*). **5** *transitive* move or change, esp. from one person, place, or condition, to another (*was translated by joy*). **6** *intransitive* (foll. by *into*) result in; be converted into; manifest itself as. **7** *transitive* Christianity **a** remove (a bishop) to another see. **b** remove (a saint's relics etc.) to another place. **8** *transitive* Bible convey to heaven without death; transform. **9** *transitive* Mech. **a** cause (a body) to move so that all its parts travel in the same direction. **b** impart motion without rotation to. **10** *transitive* Biol. make use of (a sequence of nucleotides) as a template for a sequence of amino acids. □ **trans·lat·able** *adjective* **trans·lat·abil·ity** *noun* [Latin *translatus*, past participle of *transferre*: see TRANSFER]

trans·la·tion *noun* **1** the act or an instance of translating. **2** a written or spoken rendering of the meaning of a word, speech, book, etc., in another language. **3** *Biol.* the process by which a sequence of nucleotide triplets in a messenger RNA molecule gives rise to a specific sequence of amino acids during synthesis of a polypeptide or protein. □ **trans·la·tion·al** *adjective* **trans·la·tion·al·ly** *adverb*

trans·la·tor *noun* **1** a person or hand-held device that translates from one language into another. **2** a program that translates from one (esp. programming) language into another.

trans·liter·ate /tranz'lɪtə,reɪt/ *transitive verb* represent (a word etc.) in the closest corresponding letters of a different alphabet or language. □ **trans·liter·a·tion** *noun* **trans·liter·ator** *noun* [TRANS- + Latin *littera* letter]

trans·lo·cate *transitive verb* **1** move from one place to another. **2** *Physiol. & Biochem.* (usu. in *passive*) transport (a dissolved substance) within an organism, esp. in the phloem of a plant, or actively across a cell membrane. **3** *Biol.* move (a portion of a chromosome) to a new position on the same or another chromosome. □ **trans·loca·tion** *noun*

trans·lu·cent /tranz'lu:sənt/ *adjective* **1** allowing light to pass through diffusely; semi-transparent. **2** transparent. □ **trans·lu·cence** *noun* **trans·lu·cen·cy** *noun* **trans·lu·cent·ly** *adverb* [Latin *translucēre* (as TRANS-, *lucēre* shine)]

trans·lunar *adjective* **1** lying beyond the moon. **2** of or relating to space travel or a trajectory towards the moon.

trans·mar·ine *adjective* situated or going beyond the sea. [Latin *transmarinus* from *marinus* MARINE]

trans·mem·brane *adjective* existing or occurring across a cell membrane.

trans·mi·grant /tranz'maɪgrənt/ ● *adjective* passing through, esp. a country on the way to another. ● *noun* a migrant or alien passing through a country etc.

trans·mi·grate /,tranzmaɪ'greɪt/ *intransitive verb* **1** (of the soul) pass into a different body; undergo metempsychosis. **2** migrate. □ **trans·mi·gra·tion** *noun* **trans·mi·gra·tor** *noun* **trans·migra·tory** /-'maɪgrətɔri/ *adjective*

trans·mis·sion *noun* **1** the act or an instance of transmitting; the state of being transmitted. **2** a broadcast radio or television program. **3** the mechanism by which power is transmitted from an engine to the axle in a motor vehicle. [Latin *transmissio* (as TRANS-, MISSION)]

transmission line *noun* a conductor or conductors, esp. a cable, carrying electricity over large distances with minimum losses.

trans·mit *transitive verb* (**trans·mit·ted, trans·mit·ting**) **1 a** pass or hand on; transfer (*transmitted the message; how diseases are transmitted*). **b** communicate (ideas, emotions, etc.). **2 a** allow (heat, light, sound, electricity, etc.) to pass through; be a medium for. **b** be a medium for (ideas, emotions, etc.) (*his message transmits hope*). **3** broadcast (a radio or television signal, message, etc.). □ **trans·mis·si·bil·ity** *noun* **trans·mis·sible** *adjective* **trans·mis·sive** *adjective* **trans·mit·table** *adjective* **trans·mit·tal** *noun* [Latin *transmittere* (as TRANS-, *mittere* miss- send)]

trans·mit·tance *noun* *Physics* the ratio of the light energy falling on a body to that transmitted through it.

trans·mit·ter *noun* **1** a person or thing that transmits. **2** a set of equipment used to generate and transmit electromagnetic waves carrying messages, signals, etc., esp. those of radio or television. **3** = NEUROTRANSMITTER.

trans·mog·rify /tranz'mɒgrɪ,faɪ/ *transitive & intransitive verb* (**-fies, -fied**) *jocular* transform or be transformed, esp. in a magical or surprising manner. □ **trans·mog·rifi·ca·tion** *noun* [17th c.: origin unknown]

trans·mon·tane /tranz'mɒnteɪn, -s'mɒnteɪn, -'teɪn/ *adjective* = TRAMONTANE. [Latin *transmontanus*: see TRAMONTANE]

trans·mu·ta·tion /,tranzmju:'teɪʃən/ *noun* **1** the act or an instance of transmuting or changing into another form etc. **2** *Alchemy* the supposed process of changing base metals into gold. **3** *Physics* the changing of one element into another by nuclear bombardment etc. **4** *Biol.* Lamarck's theory of the change of one species into another. □ **trans·mu·ta·tion·al** *adjective* **trans·mu·ta·tion·ist** *noun*

trans·mute /tranz'mjuːt/ *transitive & intransitive verb* **1** change the form, nature, or substance of. **2** *Alchemy* subject (base metals) to transmutation. □ **trans·mut·able** *adjective* **trans·mut·abil·ity** *noun* **trans·mu·ta·tive** /-təɪv/ *adjective* **trans·mut·er** *noun* [Latin *transmutare* (as TRANS-, *mutare* change)]

trans·nation·al ● *adjective* extending beyond national boundaries. ● *noun* a transnational company. □ **trans·nation·al·ly** *adverb*

trans·ocean·ic *adjective* **1** situated beyond the ocean. **2** concerned with crossing the ocean (*transoceanic flight*).

tran·som /'transəm/ *noun* **1** a horizontal bar of wood or stone across a window or the top of a door (*compare* MULLION). **2** each of several beams fixed across the sternpost of a ship. **3** a strengthening crossbar. **4** *N Amer.* = TRANSOM WINDOW. □ **over the transom** *N Amer.* offered or sent without the prior agreement of the recipient; (esp. of a manuscript etc.) uncommissioned, unsolicited. □ **tran·somed** *adjective* [Middle English *traversayn*, *transyn*, *-ing*, from Old French *traversin* from *traverse* TRAVERSE]

transom window *noun* **1** a window divided by a transom. **2** a window placed above the transom of a door or larger window.

tran·sonic *adjective* relating to speeds close to that of sound. [TRANS- + SONIC, after *supersonic* etc.]

trans-Pacific *adjective* **1** on the other side of the Pacific Ocean. **2** crossing the Pacific Ocean.

trans·par·en·cy /trans'perənsi/ *noun* (*pl.* **-cies**) **1** the condition of being transparent. **2** *Photog.* a positive transparent photograph mounted between glass plates or in a frame to be viewed using a slide projector. **3** a clear plastic page containing usu. written information, projected on a wall or screen using an overhead projector. **4** a picture, inscription, etc., made visible by a light behind it. **5** the quality of transactions and activities in business, government, etc., being open to examination by the public.

trans·par·ent /trans'perənt/ *adjective* **1** allowing light to pass through so that bodies can be distinctly seen (*compare* TRANSLUCENT). **2 a** (of a disguise, pretext, etc.) easily seen through. **b** (of a motive, quality, meaning, etc.) easily discerned; evident; obvious. **3** (of a person etc.) easily understood; frank; open. **4** *Physics* transmitting heat or other electromagnetic rays without distortion. **5** *Computing* (of a program, process, etc.) not giving any indication of its presence; operating in a manner which the general user does not perceive, or such that other software does not need to take account of it. **6** (of transactions and activities in business, government, etc.) open to examination by the public. □ **trans·par·ent·ly** *adverb* [Old French from medieval Latin *transparens* from Latin *transparēre* shine through (as TRANS-, *parēre* appear)]

trans·person·al *adjective* **1** transcending the personal. **2** *Psych.* (esp. in psychotherapy) of or relating to the exploration of transcendental states of consciousness beyond personal identity.

tran·spire *verb* **1** *intransitive* **a** (prec. by *it* as subject) turn out; prove to be the case (*it transpired he knew nothing about it*). **b** (of a secret or something unknown) leak out; come to be known. **2** *intransitive* occur; happen (*nobody knows what transpired between them*). **3** *transitive & intransitive* emit (vapour, sweat, etc.), or be emitted, through the skin or lungs; perspire. **4** *intransitive* (of a plant or leaf) release water vapour. □ **tran·spir·a·tion** /transpə'reɪʃən/ *noun* [French *transpirer* or medieval Latin *transpirare* (as TRANS-, Latin *spirare* 'breathe')]

trans·plant ● *transitive verb* /tranz'plant/ **1 a** plant in another place (*transplanted the petunias*). **b** move to another place (*a Winnipegger transplanted to Toronto*). **2** *Surgery* transfer (living tissue or an organ) and implant in another part of the body or in another body. ● *noun* /'tranzplant/ **1** *Surgery* **a** the transplanting of an organ or tissue. **b** such an organ etc. **2** a thing, esp. a plant, transplanted. **3** *N Amer. informal* a person not native to his or her place of residence. □ **trans·plant·able** *adjective* **trans·plant·a·tion** *noun* **trans·plant·er** *noun*

tran·spond·er *noun* a device for receiving a radio signal and automatically transmitting a different signal. [TRANSMIT + RESPOND]

trans·port ● *transitive verb* **1** take or carry (a person, goods, troops, baggage, etc.) from one place to another. **2** *hist.* take (a criminal) to a penal colony; deport. ● *noun* **1** an act or instance of transporting or carrying; conveyance. **2 a** a system of conveying people, goods, etc., from place to place. **b** esp. *Brit.* the means of this (*our transport has*

arrived). **3 a** a ship, aircraft, etc. used to carry soldiers, supplies, etc. **b** = TRANSPORT TRUCK. **4** (esp. in *pl.*) vehement emotion (*transports of joy*). **5** *hist.* a transported convict. [Old French *transporter* or Latin *transportare* (as TRANS-, *portare* carry)]

trans·port·able *adjective* **1** capable of being transported. **2** *hist.* (of an offender or an offence) punishable by transportation. □ **trans·port·abil·ity** *noun*

trans·por·ta·tion *noun* **1** the act or process of transporting something; conveyance of people, goods, etc. **2 a** a system of conveying. **b** esp. *N Amer.* the means of this. **3** *hist.* removal to a penal colony.

transport café *noun Brit.* = TRUCK STOP.

trans·port·ed *adjective* (usu. foll. by *with*) affected with strong emotion.

trans·port·er *noun* **1** a person or device that transports. **2** a vehicle used to transport other vehicles or large pieces of machinery etc. by road.

transport truck *noun N Amer.* a large, long truck, used esp. for conveying goods long distances.

trans·pose *transitive verb* **1 a** cause (two or more things) to change places. **b** change the position of (a thing) in a series. **2** change the order or position of (words or a word) in a sentence. **3** (often foll. by *up*, *down*) *Music* write or play in a different key from the original. **4** *Algebra* transfer (a term) with a changed sign to the other side of an equation. □ **trans·pos·able** *adjective* **trans·pos·er** *noun* [Middle English, = transform, from Old French *transposer* (as TRANS-, Latin *ponere* put)]

trans·pos·ition *noun* the act or an instance of transposing; the state of being transposed. □ **trans·pos·ition·al** *adjective*

trans·poson /trans'poːzɒn/ *noun* a chromosomal segment that can undergo transposition, esp. a segment of bacterial DNA that can be translocated as a whole between chromosomal, phage, and plasmid DNA in the absence of a complementary sequence in the host DNA. [blend of TRANSPOSITION + -ON]

trans·put·er *noun* a high-performance microprocessor with integral memory designed for parallel processing. [TRANSISTOR + COMPUTER]

trans·racial *adjective* across or crossing racial boundaries.

trans·sex·ual (also **tran·sexual**) ● *adjective* having the physical characteristics of one sex and the supposed psychological characteristics of the other. ● *noun* **1** a transsexual person. **2** a person whose sex has been changed by surgery. □ **trans·sex·u·al·ism** *noun* **trans·sex·u·al·ity** *noun*

trans·ship *transitive verb* (also **tran·ship**) *intransitive* (**-shipped**, **-ship·ping**) transfer from one ship or form of transport to another. □ **trans·ship·ment** *noun*

tran·sub·stan·ti·a·tion /ˌtransəbˌstanʃiˈeɪʃən/ *noun* (in Roman Catholic and Orthodox belief) the conversion in the Eucharist, after consecration, of the whole substance of the bread and wine into the body and blood of Christ, only the appearances of bread and wine remaining. [medieval Latin (as TRANS-, SUBSTANCE)]

tran·sude /tran'suːd, -'sjuːd/ *intransitive verb* (of a fluid) pass through the pores or interstices of a membrane etc. □ **tran·sud·a·tion** *noun* [French *transsuder* from Old French *tressuer* (as TRANS-, Latin *sudare* sweat)]

trans·uran·ic /ˌtranzjʊˈranɪk/ *adjective Chem.* (of an element) having a higher atomic number than uranium.

Trans·vaal /tranz'vɒl/ (also **the Transvaal**) a former province in NE South Africa, lying north of the Vaal River. Once the core of the Boer republic, it was annexed by Britain in 1877; resistance to British rule led to the Boer Wars. In 1994 it was divided into the provinces of Northern Transvaal (now Limpopo), Eastern Transvaal (now Mpumalanga), Pretoria-Witwatersrand-Vereeniging (now Gauteng), and the eastern part of North-West Province.

trans·valu·a·tion *noun* an alteration of values; a re-evaluation. □ **trans·value** *transitive verb*

trans·ver·sal ● *adjective* (of a line) cutting a system of lines. ● *noun* a transversal line. □ **trans·ver·sal·ity** *noun* **trans·ver·sal·ly** *adverb*

trans·verse /'tranzvɜrs/ *adjective* situated, arranged, or acting in a crosswise direction. □ **trans·verse·ly** *adverb* [Latin *transvertere* *transvers-* turn across (as TRANS-, *vertere* turn)]

transverse flute *noun* a flute having the mouthpiece in the side near one end.

transverse wave *noun Physics* a wave in which the medium vibrates at right angles to the direction of its propagation.

trans·ves·tite /tranz'vestəɪt/ *noun* a person, esp. a man, who dresses in the clothes of the opposite sex, esp. as a sexual stimulus.

---

t top   v voice   w we   z zoo   ʃ she   ʒ vision   θ thin   ð this   ŋ ring   x loch   tʃ chip   dʒ jar   (*see over for vowels*)

□ **trans·ves·tism** *noun* [German *Transvestismus* from TRANS- + Latin *vestire* clothe]

Tran·syl·vania /ˌtransɪlˈveɪnɪə/ a large tableland region of NW Romania, separated from the rest of the country by the Carpathian Mountains and the Transylvanian Alps. □ **Tran·syl·van·ian** *adjective*

trap¹ ● *noun* **1 a** an enclosure or device, often baited, for catching animals, usu. by affording a way in but not a way out. **b** *Cdn (Nfld)* a large box-shaped fishing net used in inshore waters to catch migrating cod and salmon. **c** a device with bait for killing vermin, esp. = MOUSETRAP 1. **2 a** a trick betraying a person into speech or an act (*is this question a trap?*). **b** an unpleasant situation from which escape is difficult (*fell into the trap of taking on new debts to pay off the old ones*). **3** an arrangement to catch an unsuspecting person, e.g. a speeding motorist. **4** a device for hurling an object such as a clay pigeon into the air to be shot at. **5 a** a curve in a drainpipe etc. that fills with liquid and forms a seal against the upward passage of gases. **b** a device for preventing the passage of steam etc. **6** *slang* the mouth (*shut one's trap*). **7** *Golf* a bunker. **8** *Football* a tactical play in which an attacking team permits a defensive player to cross the line of scrimmage in order to block him from the side, so enabling the ball carrier to move unopposed through the gap created. **9** a two-wheeled carriage (*a pony and trap*). **10** = TRAP DOOR 1. **11** *Brit.* a compartment from which a greyhound is released at the start of a race. **12** (esp. in *pl.*) *informal* a percussion instrument esp. in a jazz band. **13** = NEUTRAL-ZONE TRAP.
● *verb* (**trapped, trap·ping**) **1** *transitive* catch (an animal or fish) in a trap. **2** *intransitive* **a** catch wild animals in traps for their fur. **b** set traps for game. **3** *transitive* catch or catch out (a person) by means of a trick, plan, etc. **4** *transitive* **a** stop and retain in a trap. **b** cause a person to be unable to leave a location (*they were trapped on the ice*). **5** *transitive* provide (a place) with traps. **6** *transitive Baseball* catch (a ball) just after it has hit the ground. **7** keep (something) in a particular place and prevent it from escaping (*trapped the puck*). □ **trap out** deplete the supply of fur-bearing animals in a region through trapping. [Old English *treppe, træppe*, related to Middle Dutch *trappe*, medieval Latin *trappa*, of uncertain origin]

trap² *transitive verb* (**trapped, trap·ping**) (often foll. by *out*) **1** provide with trappings. **2** adorn. [obsolete *trap* (n.): Middle English from Old French *drap*: see DRAPE]

trap³ *noun* (in full **trap·rock**) any dark-coloured igneous rock, fine-grained and columnar in structure, esp. basalt. [Swedish *trapp* from *trappa* stair, from the often stair-like appearance of its outcroppings]

trap⁴ *noun* (usu. in *pl.*) *slang* a trapezius muscle. [abbreviation]

trap boat *noun N Amer.* = TRAP SKIFF.

trap door *noun* **1** a door or hatch in a floor, ceiling, or roof, usu. flush with the surface. **2** a buttoned flap covering the buttocks on long underwear.

trap door spider *noun* any of various spiders, esp. of the family Ctenizidae, that make a hinged trap door at the top of their nest.

trap·eze *noun* **1** a crossbar or set of crossbars suspended by ropes used as a swing for acrobatics etc. **2** a harness attached by a cable to a sailboat's mast, enabling a sailor to balance the boat by leaning backwards far out over the windward side. □ **trap·ez·ist** *noun* [French *trapèze* from Late Latin *trapezium*: see TRAPEZIUM]

tra·pez·ium /trəˈpiːzɪəm/ *noun* (*pl.* **tra·pez·ia** or **tra·pez·iums**) **1** *N Amer.* a quadrilateral with no two sides parallel. **2** *Brit.* a quadrilateral with only one pair of sides parallel. [Late Latin from Greek *trapezion* from *trapeza* table]

tra·pez·ius /trəˈpiːzɪəs/ *noun* (*pl.* **tra·pezii** /-zɪaɪ/) *Anat.* either of a pair of large triangular muscles extending over the back of the neck and shoulders.

trap·ez·oid /ˈtrapəˌzɔɪd/ *noun* **1** *N Amer.* a quadrilateral with only one pair of sides parallel. **2** *Brit.* a quadrilateral with no two sides parallel. □ **trap·ez·oid·al** *adjective* [modern Latin *trapezoides* from Greek *trapezoeidēs* (as TRAPEZIUM)]

trap·line *noun N Amer.* **1** a series of traps set outdoors for catching animals. **2** the trail along which a trapper walks to check his or her traplines. **3** the general area in which a trapper has his or her traplines set up.

trap·per *noun* **1** a person who traps wild animals esp. to obtain furs. **2** *Hockey* a goalie's catching glove.

trap·pings *plural noun* **1** outward signs, objects, ceremonies, etc. esp. as an indication of status (*the trappings of office*). **2** the harness of a horse esp. when ornamental. [Middle English (as TRAP²)]

Trap·pist ● *noun* a member of a branch of the Cistercian order founded in 1664 at La Trappe in Normandy and noted for an austere rule including a vow of silence. ● *adjective* of or relating to this order. [French *trappiste* from *La Trappe*]

trap·rock *noun see* TRAP³.

traps *plural noun Brit. informal* personal belongings; baggage. [perhaps contraction from TRAPPINGS]

trap shooting *noun* the sport of shooting at clay pigeons launched into the air from a trap. □ **trap shooter** *noun*

trap skiff *noun Cdn (Nfld & Maritimes)* a fishing boat used esp. in the cod fishery.

trash ● *noun* **1** esp. *N Amer.* garbage, refuse. **2 a** things of poor workmanship, quality, or material; worthless stuff. **b** literary or artistic work of an inferior quality. **3** nonsense; foolish talk. **4** a worthless person or persons. **5** the refuse of crushed sugar canes and dried stripped leaves and tops of sugar cane used as fuel. ● *transitive verb* **1** esp. *N Amer. informal* wreck, destroy. **2** esp. *N Amer. informal* expose the worthless nature of; disparage. **3** strip (sugar canes) of their outer leaves to speed up the ripening process. [Middle English: origin unknown]

trash can *noun* esp. *N Amer.* a garbage can.

trash cover *noun Cdn* crop residue left on top of the soil to prevent erosion and moisture loss.

trashed *adjective* **1** *informal* very drunk. **2** destroyed, wrecked.

trash fish *noun* a fish sold for animal feed etc. rather than human consumption.

trash talk esp. *US informal* ● *noun* **1** *Sport* ostentatiously insulting or boastful rhetoric delivered with the intention of demoralizing, intimidating, or humiliating an opponent. **2** any derisory or boastful statement. ● *verb* (**trash-talk**) **1** *intransitive* deliver trash talk; badmouth an opponent. **2** *transitive* demoralize or attempt to demoralize (an opponent) with trash talk. □ **trash-talker** *noun* **trash-talking** *noun & adjective*

trashy *adjective* (**trash·i·er, trash·i·est**) **1** of poor quality; cheap, inferior. **2** (of a person) worthless, disreputable. □ **trash·i·ly** *adverb* **trash·i·ness** *noun*

Trás-os-Montes /ˌtraʒuːʃˈmɒnteʃ/ a mountainous region of NE Portugal, north of the Douro River. [Portuguese, = beyond the mountains]

trat·tor·ia /ˌtratəˈriːə/ *noun* an Italian restaurant. [Italian]

trau·ma /ˈtrɒmə/ *noun* (*pl.* **trau·mas**) **1 a** *Psych.* emotional shock following a stressful event, sometimes leading to long-term neurosis. **b** (in general use) a distressing or emotionally disturbing experience etc. **2** any physical wound or injury. **3** physical shock following this, characterized by a drop in body temperature, mental confusion, etc. □ **trau·ma·tize** *transitive verb* (also esp. *Brit.* **-tise**). **trau·ma·tiz·a·tion** *noun* [Greek *trauma traumatos* 'wound']

trau·mat·ic /trəˈmatɪk/ *adjective* **1** of or causing trauma. **2** (in general use) distressing; emotionally disturbing (*a traumatic experience*). **3** of or for wounds. □ **trau·mat·ic·ally** *adverb*

trauma·tism /ˈtrɒməˌtɪzəm/ *noun* **1** the action of a trauma. **2** a condition produced by this.

tra·vail /trəˈveɪl, ˈtraveɪl/ *literary* ● *noun* **1** painful or laborious effort. **2** the pangs of childbirth. ● *intransitive verb* undergo a painful effort, esp. in childbirth. [Old French *travail, travaillier*, ultimately from medieval Latin *trepalium* instrument of torture, from Latin *tres* three + *palus* stake]

trav·el ● *transitive & intransitive verb* (**trav·elled, trav·el·ling**; esp. *US* **trav·eled, trav·el·ing**) **1** *intransitive* go from one place to another; make a journey esp. of some length or abroad. **2** *transitive* **a** journey along or through (a country). **b** cover (a distance) in travelling. **3** *intransitive* withstand a long journey (*wines that do not travel*). **4** *intransitive* go from place to place as a salesperson. **5** *intransitive* move or proceed in a specified manner or at a specified rate (*light travels faster than sound*). **6** *intransitive informal* move quickly. **7** *intransitive* pass esp. in a deliberate or systematic manner from point to point (*the photographer's eye travelled over the scene*). **8** *intransitive Basketball* make two or more steps' progress in any direction while carrying (esp. instead of dribbling) the ball, in violation of the rules. **9** *intransitive* (of a machine or part) move or operate in a specified way. **10** *intransitive* (of deer etc.) move onward in feeding. **11** *intransitive* (of a dancer or dance step) cover a relatively large expanse of floor. ● *noun* **1 a** the act of travelling, esp. in foreign countries. **b** (often in *pl.*) a period of this (*have returned from their travels*). **2** (*attributive*) suitable for use when travelling because of size, portability, dual voltage, etc. (*travel alarm*). **3** the range, rate, or mode of motion of a part in machinery. □ **trav·el·ling** *noun* [Middle English, originally = TRAVAIL]

travel agency *noun* a company which makes transportation, accommodation, etc. arrangements for travellers. □ **travel agent** *noun*

trav·elled *adjective* experienced in travelling (also in *combination*: *much-travelled*).

trav·el·ler *noun* (also esp. US **trav·el·er**) **1** a person who travels or is travelling. **2** *Brit.* = COMMERCIAL TRAVELLER. **3** *Brit.* a gypsy. **4** (also **New Age traveller**) a person who embraces New Age values and leads an itinerant and unconventional lifestyle. **5** a moving mechanism, esp. a travelling crane.

traveller's cheque *noun* a cheque for a fixed amount that may be cashed on signature, usu. internationally.

traveller's joy *noun* a wild clematis, *Clematis vitalba*.

traveller's tale *noun* an incredible and probably untrue story.

travelling crane *noun* a crane able to move on rails, esp. along an overhead support.

travelling salesman *noun* a male sales representative who travels about to sell his wares.

travelling wave *noun Physics* a wave in which the medium moves in the direction of propagation.

trav·el·ogue *noun* a film, book, or illustrated lecture about travel. [TRAVEL after MONOLOGUE etc.]

travel-sick *adjective* suffering from nausea caused by motion in travelling. □ **travel sickness** *noun*

tra·verse /trəˈvɜrs, ˈtravərs/ ● *verb* **1** *transitive* travel or lie across (*traversed the country; a pit traversed by a beam*). **2** *transitive* consider or discuss the whole extent of (a subject). **3** *transitive* turn (a large gun) horizontally. **4** *transitive Law* deny (an allegation) in pleading. **5** *transitive* thwart, frustrate, or oppose (a plan or opinion). **6** *intransitive* (of the needle of a compass etc.) turn on or as on a pivot. **7** *intransitive* (of a horse) walk obliquely. **8** *intransitive* make a traverse in climbing. ● *noun* **1** a sideways movement. **2** an act of traversing. **3** a thing, esp. part of a structure, that crosses another. **4** a gallery extending from side to side of a church or other building. **5 a** a single line of survey, usu. plotted from compass bearings and chained or paced distances between angular points. **b** a tract surveyed in this way. **6** *Naut.* a zigzag line taken by a ship because of contrary winds or currents. **7** a skier's similar movement on a slope. **8** the sideways movement of a part in a machine. **9 a** a sideways motion across a rock face from one practicable line of ascent or descent to another. **b** a place where this is necessary. **10** *Military* a pair of right-angle bends in a trench to avoid enfilading fire. **11** *Law* a denial, esp. of an allegation of a matter of fact. **12** the act of turning a large gun horizontally to the required direction. □ **tra·vers·able** *adjective* **tra·ver·sal** *noun* **tra·vers·er** *noun* [Old French *traverser* from Late Latin *traversare, transversare* (as TRANSVERSE)]

trav·er·tine /ˈtravərˌtiːn/ *noun* a white or light-coloured calcareous rock deposited from springs. [Italian *travertino, tivertino* from Latin *tiburtinus* of Tibur (Tivoli) near Rome]

trav·es·ty /ˈtravəsti/ ● *noun* (pl. **-ties**) a grotesque misrepresentation or imitation (*a travesty of justice*). ● *transitive verb* (**-ties**, **-tied**) make or be a travesty of. [(originally adj.) from French *travesti* past participle of *travestir* disguise, change the clothes of, from Italian *travestire* (as TRANS-, *vestire* clothe)]

tra·vois /ˈtravwɒ/ *noun* (pl. same /-vwɒz/) *hist.* a V-shaped frame of teepee poles pulled by dogs or horses, used by Plains Aboriginal peoples to carry teepee covers and other possessions. [earlier *travail* from French, perhaps the same word as TRAVAIL]

trawl ● *verb* **1** *intransitive* (often foll. by *through, for*) **a** fish with a trawl or seine. **b** search thoroughly. **2** *transitive* **a** catch by trawling. **b** search thoroughly through (*trawled the schools for new trainees*). ● *noun* **1** an act of trawling. **2** (in full **trawl net**) a large wide-mouthed fishing net dragged by a boat along the sea bottom. **3** (in full **trawl line**) *N Amer.* a long buoyed sea-fishing line supporting short lines with baited hooks. [prob. from Middle Dutch *traghelen* to drag (compare *traghel* dragnet), perhaps from Latin *tragula*)]

trawl·er *noun* **1** a boat used for trawling. **2** a person who trawls.

trawl·er·man *noun* (pl. **-men**) a man who works on a trawler.

tray *noun* **1 a** a flat shallow vessel usu. with a raised rim for carrying, storing, or collecting items. **b** something carried on a tray (*a tray of drinks; cheese tray*). **2** a shallow lidless box forming a compartment of a box, cabinet, trunk, etc. □ **tray·ful** *noun* (pl. **-fuls**). [Old English *trīg* from Germanic, related to TREE]

tray table *noun* **1** a tray with legs which can be folded out, forming a stand or table. **2** a small rectangular table that folds down from the back of a seat on an airliner, train, etc.

treach·er·ous /ˈtretʃərəs/ *adjective* **1** guilty of or involving treachery; disloyal, traitorous. **2** deceptive, unreliable. **3** (of ground, ice, conditions, etc.) dangerous, hazardous. □ **treach·er·ous·ly** *adverb* [Old French *trecherous* from *trecheor* a cheat, from *trechier, trichier*: see TRICK]

treach·ery /ˈtretʃəri/ *noun* (pl. **-eries**) **1** violation of faith or trust; betrayal. **2** an instance of this.

treacle /ˈtriːkəl/ *noun* **1** esp. *Brit.* **a** a syrup produced in refining sugar; golden syrup. **b** molasses. **2** cloying sentimentality or flattery. □ **treacly** *adjective* [Middle English *triacle* from Old French from Latin *theriaca* from Greek *thēriakē* antidote against venom, fem. of *thēriakos* (adj.) from *thērion* wild beast]

tread ● *verb* (**trod**; **trod·den** or **trod**) **1** *intransitive* (often foll. by *on*) **a** set down one's foot; walk or step. **b** (of the foot) be set down. **2** *transitive* **a** walk on. **b** (often foll. by *down*) press or crush with the feet. **3** *transitive* perform (steps etc.) by walking (*trod a few paces*). **4** *transitive* make (a hole etc.) by treading. **5** *intransitive* (foll. by *on*) suppress; subdue mercilessly. **6** *transitive* make a track with (dirt etc.) from the feet. **7** *transitive* (often foll. by *in, into*) press down into the ground with the feet (*trod dirt into the carpet*). **8** *transitive & intransitive* (of a male bird) copulate with (a hen). ● *noun* **1** a manner or sound of walking (*recognized the heavy tread*). **2** the top surface of a step or stair. **3** the thick moulded part of a vehicle tire for gripping the road. **4 a** the part of a wheel that touches the ground or rail. **b** the part of a rail that the wheels touch. **5** the part of the sole of a shoe that rests on the ground. **6** (of a male bird) copulation. □ **tread the boards** be an actor; appear on the stage. **tread water** (**tread·ed** or **trod**) **1** maintain an upright position in the water by moving the feet with a walking movement and the hands with a sideways circular motion. **2** fail to advance. □ **tread·ed** *adjective* **tread·er** *noun* [Old English *tredan* from West Germanic]

treadle /ˈtredəl/ ● *noun* a lever worked by the foot and imparting motion to a machine. ● *intransitive verb* work a treadle. [Old English *tredel* stair (as TREAD)]

tread·mill *noun* **1** a device for producing motion by the weight of persons or animals stepping on steps on the inner surface of a revolving upright wheel. **2** an exercise machine consisting of a continuous moving belt on which a person walks or jogs. **3** monotonous routine work.

trea·son *noun* **1** (in full **high treason**) violation by a subject of allegiance to the sovereign or to the state, esp. by attempting to kill or overthrow the sovereign or to overthrow the government. **2** any betrayal of trust; treachery. □ **trea·son·ous** *adjective* [Old French *traïson*, from Latin *traditio* handing over (as TRADITION)]

trea·son·able *adjective* involving or guilty of treason. □ **trea·son·ably** *adverb*

treas·ure ● *noun* **1 a** wealth or riches stored or accumulated, esp. in the form of gems, precious metals, etc. **b** a hoard of such wealth. **2** a thing valued for its rarity, workmanship, associations, etc. (*art treasures*). **3** *informal* a much loved or highly valued person. ● *transitive verb* **1** value highly; cherish, prize (*I treasure his friendship*). **2** store (something valuable) for preservation or future use. □ **treas·ur·able** *adjective* [Old French *tresor*, ultimately from Greek *thēsauros*: see THESAURUS]

treasure chest *noun* **1** a chest for holding or storing treasure. **2** a collection of valuable or delightful things.

treasure house *noun* **1** a building or room in which treasure is kept; a treasury. **2** an abundant source of something valuable (*a treasure house of information*).

treasure hunt *noun* **1** a search for treasure. **2** a game in which players seek a hidden object from a series of clues.

treas·ur·er *noun* **1** a person appointed to administer the funds of a society, corporation, municipality, etc. **2** an officer authorized to receive and disburse public revenues.

treasure trove *noun* **1** *Law* treasure of unknown ownership which is found hidden in the ground etc. and is declared the property of the Crown. **2** a collection of valuable or delightful things.

treas·ury *noun* (pl. **-ies**) **1** a place or building where treasure is stored. **2** the funds or revenue of a state, institution, or society. **3** (**Treasury**) **a** the department managing the public revenue of a country. **b** the offices and officers of this. **c** the place where the public revenues are kept. **4** = TREASURY BILL.

treasury bill *noun* a bill of exchange issued by the government to raise money for temporary needs.

Treasury Board *noun Cdn* a committee of the Privy Council responsible for reviewing and prioritizing planned government expenditures and programs etc.

treasury bond *noun* a government bond issued by the Treasury.

Treasury Branch *noun Cdn* (in Alberta) one of a network of savings banks operated by the government of Alberta.

treat ● *verb* **1** *transitive* act or behave towards or deal with (a person or thing) in a certain way (*treated me kindly*; *treat it as a joke*). **2** *transitive* deal with or apply a process to; act upon to obtain a particular result (*treat it with acid*). **3** *transitive* apply medical care or attention to. **4** *transitive* present or deal with (a subject) in literature or art. **5** *transitive* (often foll. by *to*) **a** provide with food or drink or entertainment at one's own expense (*treated us to dinner*). **b** provide with a special gift or indulgence (*treated myself to a pedicure*). **6** *intransitive* (often foll. by *with*) negotiate terms (with a person). **7** *intransitive* (often foll. by *of*) give a spoken or written exposition. ● *noun* **1** an event or circumstance (esp. when unexpected or unusual) that gives great pleasure. **2** a meal, entertainment, etc., provided by one person for the enjoyment of another or others. **3** *N Amer.* a candy, cookie, or other small sweet food item. **4** (*prec. by a*) *Brit.* extremely good or well (*they looked a treat*; *has come on a treat*). □ **treat·able** *adjective* **treat·er** *noun* **treat·ing** *noun* [Old French *traitier* from Latin *tractare* handle, frequentative of *trahere* tract- draw, pull]

trea·tise /ˈtriːtɪs/ *noun* a written work dealing formally and systematically with a subject. [Anglo-French *tretis* from Old French *traitier* TREAT]

treat·ment *noun* **1** a process or manner of behaving towards or dealing with a person or thing (*received rough treatment*). **2** the application of medical care or attention to a patient. **3 a** a manner of treating a subject in literature or art. **b** a preparatory version of a screenplay, including descriptions of sets and of the camerawork required. **4** subjection to the action of a chemical, physical, or biological agent. **5** (*prec. by the*) *informal* the customary way of dealing with a person, situation, etc. (*got the full treatment*).

treaty *noun* (*pl.* **-ies**) **1 a** a formally concluded and ratified agreement between states. **b** the document embodying such an agreement. **2** an agreement between individuals or parties, esp. for the purchase of property. **3** (in Canada and the US) an agreement between a government and a Native people in which the Native group ceded the rights to land in exchange for reserves, small cash payments, annual payments to band members, continued fishing and hunting rights, and other considerations. □ **take treaty** *Cdn hist.* (of a Native group) agree to a treaty with the federal government. [Anglo-French *treté* from Latin *tractatus* TRACTATE]

treaty band *noun Cdn* an Aboriginal band that has signed a treaty with the federal government.

treaty Indian *noun Cdn* a status Indian who is a member of a treaty band.

treaty port *noun hist.* a port that a country was bound by treaty to keep open to foreign trade.

treaty rights *plural noun Cdn* the rights, e.g. that of holding land on a reserve, granted to a group of Aboriginal people under the terms of a treaty.

Treb·bi·ano /ˈtrebianoː/ *noun* **1** a variety of vine and grape widely cultivated in Italy and elsewhere. **2** the dry aromatic white wine produced from this grape. [Italian, from the River *Trebbia* in northern central Italy]

Trebi·zond see TRABZON.

treble ● *adjective* **1** (of a voice) high-pitched. **2** *Music* = SOPRANO (esp. of an instrument or with reference to a boy's voice). **3** esp. *Brit.* **a** threefold. **b** triple. **c** three times as much or many (*treble the amount*). ● *noun* **1 a** *Music* = SOPRANO (esp. a boy's voice or part, or an instrument). **b** a high-pitched voice. **2** the high-frequency output of a radio, record player, etc., corresponding to the treble in music. **3** a treble quantity or thing. **4** *Darts* a hit on the narrow ring enclosed by the two middle circles of a dartboard, scoring treble. **5** *Brit. Sport* three victories or championships in the same game, sport, etc. ● *verb* esp. *Brit.* **1** *transitive & intransitive* make or become three times as much or many; increase threefold; multiply by three. **2** *transitive* amount to three times as much as. [Old French from Latin *triplus* TRIPLE; in the musical sense because it was the highest part in a three-part contrapuntal composition]

treble clef *noun Music* a sign that indicates that the second lowest line of the staff represents the G above middle C.

treble hook *noun* a fish hook with three points.

Treb·linka /treˈblɪŋkə/ a Nazi concentration camp in Poland in the Second World War, where a great many of the Jews of the Warsaw ghetto were murdered.

trebu·chet /ˈtrebjuˌʃet, -bəʃət/ *noun* (also **treb·uck·et** /ˈtrebʌkɪt, ˈtriː-/) *hist.* **1** a military machine used in siege warfare for throwing stones etc. **2** a tilting balance for accurately weighing light articles. [Old French from *trebucher* overthrow, ultimately from Frankish]

tre·cento /treiˈtʃentoː/ *noun* the style of Italian art and literature of the 14th c. [Italian, = 300 used with reference to the years 1300-99]

Tree, Sir Her·bert (Draper) Beer·bohm (1853–1917), English actor and theatre manager, who was known for his lavishly spectacular productions of Shakespeare.

tree ● *noun* **1 a** a perennial plant with a woody self-supporting main stem or trunk when mature and usu. unbranched for some distance above the ground (*compare* SHRUB[1]). **b** any similar plant having a tall erect usu. single stem, e.g. palm tree. **2** a piece or frame of wood etc. for various purposes (*shoetree*). **3** *archaic* or *poet.* **a** a gibbet. **b** a cross, esp. the one used for Christ's crucifixion. **4** (in full **tree diagram**) *Math.*, *Computing, etc.* a branching figure or graph in which processes, relationships, etc., are represented by points or nodes joined by lines. **5** = FAMILY TREE. **6** = CHRISTMAS TREE. **7** = SADDLE TREE. ● *transitive verb* **1** force to take refuge in a tree. **2** esp. *US* put into a difficult position. □ **grow on trees** (usu. with *neg.*) be plentiful. **out of one's tree** *informal* crazy. □ **treed** *adjective* **tree·less** *adjective* **tree·less·ness** *noun* **tree·like** *adjective* [Old English *trēow* from Germanic]

tree·creep·er *noun* any small creeping bird, esp. of the family Certhiidae, feeding on insects in the bark of trees.

tree diagram *noun see* TREE *noun* 4.

tree farm *noun* an area of land where trees are grown for commercial purposes.

tree fern *noun* a large fern, esp. of the family Cyatheaceae, with an upright trunk-like stem.

tree frog *noun* any arboreal tailless amphibian, esp. of the family Hylidae, climbing by means of adhesive discs on its digits.

tree hopper *noun* any insect of the family Membracidae, living in trees.

tree house *noun* a structure built in the branches of a tree for children to play in.

tree hugger *noun* esp. *N Amer. informal* a person who cares for trees or the environment; an environmentalist.

tree·line *noun* **1** (in the northern hemisphere) the latitudinal limit north of which no trees grow. **2** = TIMBERLINE 1.

tree·nail *noun* (also **tre·nail**) a hard wooden pin for securing timbers etc.

tree of heaven *noun* an Asian tree, *Ailanthus altissima*, with pinnate leaves, frequently planted as an ornamental for its clusters of winged seeds which turn reddish yellow in the fall.

tree of Jesse *noun* an illustration of a tree showing the descent of Jesus from Jesse, with the intermediate descendants placed on scrolls of foliage branching out of each other.

tree of knowledge *noun Bible* the tree in the Garden of Eden bearing the forbidden fruit.

tree of life *noun* = THUJA.

tree peony *noun* a large shrub, *Paeonia suffruticosa*, bearing white or pink magenta-blotched flowers, which is native to China, Tibet, and Bhutan, and from which are derived many cultivated varieties, producing single or double flowers in many colours.

tree ring *noun* a ring in a cross-section of a tree, produced by one year's growth.

tree shrew *noun* any small insect-eating arboreal mammal of the family Tupaiidae having a pointed nose and bushy tail.

tree sparrow *noun* **1** *N Amer.* a N American finch, *Spizella arborea*, inhabiting grassland areas. **2** *Brit.* a sparrow, *Passer montanus*, inhabiting woodland areas.

tree spiking *noun* an act of environmental protest in which long nails are driven into trees to make cutting down the trees with a chainsaw dangerous.

tree surgeon *noun* a person who prunes trees and treats decayed or damaged trees in order to preserve them. □ **tree surgery** *noun*

tree swallow *noun* a N American swallow *Tachycineta bicolor*, with a steel-blue back and white underparts, frequenting marshes and bodies of water, and nesting in cavities in trees or in bird boxes.

tree toad noun = TREE FROG.

tree tomato noun a S American shrub, *Cyphomandra betacea*, with edible egg-shaped red fruit.

tree·top noun the topmost part of a tree.

tree trunk noun the trunk of a tree.

trefa /ˈtreifə/ adjective (also **tref** /treif/) not kosher. [Hebrew *ṭˀrēpāh* 'the flesh of an animal torn', from *ṭārap* rend]

tre·foil /ˈtrefɔil, ˈtriː-/ ● noun 1 any leguminous plant of the genus *Trifolium*, with leaves of three leaflets and flowers of various colours, esp. clover. 2 any plant with similar leaves. 3 a three-lobed ornamentation, esp. in tracery windows. 4 a thing arranged in or with three lobes. ● adjective of or concerning a three-lobed plant, window tracery, etc. □ **tre·foiled** adjective (also in *combination*). [Anglo-French *trifoil* from Latin *trifolium* (as TRI-, *folium* leaf)]

trek ● verb (**trekked**, **trek·king**) 1 a *intransitive* travel or make one's way on foot, esp. arduously (*trekking through the forest*). b *intransitive* & *transitive* hike, esp. in difficult country (*trek the Torngat Mountains*). 2 *intransitive* esp. *South Africa hist.* migrate or journey with one's belongings by ox cart. 3 *intransitive South Africa* (of an ox) draw a vehicle or pull a load. ● noun 1 a a journey or walk made by trekking (*it was a trek to the nearest laundromat*). b each stage of such a journey. 2 an organized migration of a body of persons. □ **trek·ker** noun [South African Dutch *trek* (n.), *trekken* (v.) draw, travel]

Trek·kie noun (also **Trek·ker**) *slang* a fan of *Star Trek*, a TV science fiction drama series.

trel·lis ● noun a lattice or grating of light wooden or metal bars used esp. as a support for fruit trees or creepers and often fastened against a wall. ● *transitive verb* (**trel·lised**, **trel·lis·ing**) 1 provide with a trellis. 2 support (a vine etc.) with a trellis. [Old French *trelis* ultimately from Latin *trilix* three-ply (as TRI-, *licium* warp thread)]

trema·tode /ˈtremə,toːd/ noun any parasitic flatworm of the class Trematoda, esp. a fluke, equipped with hooks or suckers, e.g. a liver fluke. [modern Latin *Trematoda* from Greek *trēmatōdēs* perforated, from *trēma* hole]

Trem·blant, Mont /trãˈblũ/ a peak in south central Quebec, situated in the Laurentian Mountains, north of Montreal (968 m). [French, lit. 'trembling mountain', with reference to its Aboriginal mythology, i.e. mountain of the spirits]

Trem·blay, Michel (b.1942), French-Canadian playwright and novelist. His plays, including *Les Belles-Soeurs* (1968), are noteworthy for their portrayal of working-class Quebeckers and their use of joual. He has also published a series of novels based on the Montreal neighbourhood of Plateau Mont-Royal.

trem·ble ● *intransitive verb* 1 shake involuntarily from fear, excitement, weakness, etc. 2 be in a state of extreme apprehension (*trembled at the very thought of it*). 3 move in a quivering manner (*leaves trembled in the breeze*). ● noun 1 a trembling state or movement; a quiver (*couldn't speak without a tremble*). 2 (in *pl.*) a disease (esp. of cattle) marked by trembling. □ **trem·bling·ly** adverb [Old French *trembler* from medieval Latin *tremulare* from Latin *tremulus* TREMULOUS]

trem·bling aspen noun (also **trembling poplar**) a poplar found across Canada, *Populus tremuloides*, with leaves that tremble in a slight breeze. *Also called* QUAKING ASPEN.

trem·bly adjective (**trem·bli·er**, **trem·bli·est**) *informal* trembling; agitated.

tre·men·dous /trɪˈmendəs/ adjective 1 awe-inspiring, fearful, overpowering. 2 remarkable, considerable, excellent (*a tremendous explosion; gave a tremendous performance*). □ **tre·men·dous·ly** adverb [Latin *tremendus*, gerundive of *tremere* tremble]

trem·olo /ˈtreməloː/ noun (*pl.* **trem·o·los**) *Music* 1 a tremulous effect produced on musical instruments or in singing: a by rapid reiteration of a note, esp. on bowed stringed instruments or on an organ. b by rapid alternation between two notes. c by rapid repeated slight variation in the pitch of a note, e.g. on an electric guitar. *Compare* VIBRATO. 2 a device in an organ producing a tremolo. [Italian (as TREMULOUS)]

trem·or /ˈtremər/ ● noun 1 a shaking or quivering. 2 a thrill (of fear or exultation etc.). 3 (in full **earth tremor**) a slight earthquake. ● *intransitive verb* undergo a tremor or tremors. [Old French *tremour* & Latin *tremor* from *tremere* tremble]

tremu·lous /ˈtremjʊləs/ adjective 1 trembling or quivering (*in a tremulous voice*). 2 (of a line etc.) drawn by a tremulous hand. 3 timid or

vacillating. □ **tremu·lous·ly** adverb **tremu·lous·ness** noun [Latin *tremulus* from *tremere* tremble]

tre·nail var. of TREENAIL.

trench ● noun 1 a long narrow usu. deep depression or ditch. 2 *Military* a this dug by troops to stand in and be sheltered from enemy fire. b (in *pl.*) a defensive system of these, as used in the First World War. 3 a long narrow deep depression in the ocean bed. 4 *informal* = TRENCH COAT 2. ● verb 1 *transitive* dig a trench or trenches in (the ground). 2 *transitive* turn over the earth of (a field, garden, etc.) by digging a succession of adjoining ditches. 3 *intransitive* (foll. by *on, upon*) *archaic* a encroach. b verge or border closely. □ **in the trenches** actively involved in the practical details or hard work connected with a project. [Old French *trenche* (n.) *trenchier* (v.), ultimately from Latin *truncare* TRUNCATE]

tren·chant /ˈtrentʃənt/ adjective 1 (of a style or language etc.) incisive, terse, vigorous. 2 *archaic* or *literary* sharp, keen. □ **tren·chan·cy** noun **tren·chant·ly** adverb [Old French, part. of *trenchier*: see TRENCH]

trench coat noun a loose belted double-breasted raincoat. [originally a waterproof coat that was part of the uniform of British officers in the trenches in the First World War]

trench·er noun 1 esp. *hist.* a wooden or earthenware platter for serving food. 2 a machine, usu. self-propelled, used in digging trenches. [Old French *trencheoir* from *trenchier*: see TRENCH]

trench·er·man noun (*pl.* **-men**) a person who eats well, or in a specified manner (*a good trencherman*).

trench fever noun a highly infectious disease transmitted by lice, that infested soldiers in the trenches in the First World War.

trench foot noun a painful condition of the feet caused by long immersion in cold water or mud and marked by blackening and death of surface tissue.

trench mortar noun a light simple mortar for throwing bombs from a front trench into enemy trenches.

trench warfare noun 1 *Military* hostilities carried on from more or less permanent trenches. 2 a protracted dispute in which the parties maintain entrenched positions while persistently attacking their opponents.

trend ● noun a general direction and tendency (esp. of events, fashion, or opinion etc.). ● *intransitive verb* 1 bend or turn away in a specified direction. 2 be chiefly directed; have a general and continued tendency. [Old English *trendan* from Germanic: compare TRUNDLE]

trend line noun a line indicating the general course or tendency of something, e.g. a geographical feature or set of points on a graph.

trend·oid *informal* often *derogatory* ● adjective trendy; self-consciously or extravagantly fashionable. ● noun a person who sets or follows fashions; a trendy.

trend·setter noun a person who leads the way in fashion etc. □ **trend·setting** adjective

trend·spot·ter noun a person who observes (or seeks to predict) the changing tide of fashion, in dress, ideas, consumer culture, etc.

trendy *informal* ● adjective (**trend·i·er**, **trend·i·est**) often *derogatory* fashionable; following fashionable trends. ● noun (*pl.* **-ies**) a fashionable person. □ **trend·i·ly** adverb **trend·i·ness** noun

Treng·ganu /treŋˈɡʊnuː/ (also **Ter·eng·ganu** /ˌtereŋ-/) a state of Malaysia, on the east coast of the Malay Peninsula; capital, Kuala Trengganu.

Trent, Council of an ecumenical council of the Roman Catholic Church, held in three sessions between 1545 and 1563 in Trento, northern Italy. Prompted by the opposition of the Reformation, the council clarified and redefined the Church's position on certain issues, abolished many of the abuses that had been prevalent, and strengthened the authority of the papacy. The overall effect was to provide the Church with a solid foundation for the Counter-Reformation.

Trent Hills a town in SE Ontario, about 45 km northeast of Cobourg; pop. (2001) 12,569.

Trentino-Alto Adige /tren,tiːnoː,altoː ˈaltoː ˈaːdiˌdʒeɪ/ a region of NE Italy; pop. (1990) 891,420; capital, Bolzano. Situated on the border with Austria, it includes the Dolomites.

Tren·to /ˈtrentoː/ a city on the Adige River in N Italy; pop. (2001) 104,844. A medieval ecclesiastic principality, it was the scene of the Council of Trent in 1545–63.

Tren·ton 1 the state capital of New Jersey; pop. (2000) 85,403. 2 a former city in SE Ontario, situated on the Bay of Quinte at the mouth of the Trent River, about 20 km west of Belleville, now part of the city of Quinte West; pop. (2001) 16,770. □ **Tren·ton·ian** *noun* (in sense 2) [sense 2 a shortening of *Trentown*, after Canada's TRENT RIVER]

Trent River 1 the chief river of central England, which rises in Staffordshire and flows 275 km (170 miles) generally northeastward, uniting with the Ouse River 25 km (15 miles) west of Hull to form the Humber estuary. **2** a river in SE Ontario, which rises in Rice Lake, just north of Cobourg, and flows generally southeastward to Lake Ontario at Trenton.

Trent-Severn Waterway a waterway, completed in 1920, allowing navigation from Lake Ontario to Georgian Bay, formed by the Trent Canal and the Severn River. The canal, completed two years earlier, links Lake Ontario through a series of lakes, rivers (including the Trent River) and artificial channels to Lake Simcoe; the Severn River provides the necessary link from Lake Simcoe to a point on Georgian Bay, west of Gravenhurst.

tre·pan /trɪˈpan/ ● *noun* **1** a cylindrical saw formerly used by surgeons for removing part of the bone of the skull. **2** a borer for sinking shafts. ● *transitive verb* (**tre·panned, tre·pan·ning**) perforate (the skull) with a trepan. □ **trep·an·a·tion** /ˌtrepəˈneɪʃən/ *noun* **tre·pan·ning** *noun* [medieval Latin *trepanum* from Greek *trupanon* from *trupaō* bore, from *trupē* hole]

tre·pang /trɪˈpaŋ/ *noun* = BÊCHE-DE-MER 1. [Malay *trīpang*]

tre·phine /trɪˈfaɪn, -ˈfiːn/ ● *noun* an improved form of trepan with a guiding centre pin. ● *transitive verb* operate on with this. □ **treph·in·a·tion** /ˌtrefɪˈneɪʃən/ *noun* [originally *trafine*, from Latin *tres fines* three ends, apparently formed after TREPAN]

trep·i·da·tion /ˌtrepɪˈdeɪʃən/ *noun* **1** a feeling of fear or alarm; perturbation of the mind. **2** tremulous agitation. **3** the trembling of limbs, e.g. in paralysis. □ **trepi·da·tious** *adjective* **trepi·da·tious·ly** *adverb* [Latin *trepidatio* from *trepidare* be agitated, tremble, from *trepidus* alarmed]

très /treɪ/ *adverb* very. [French]

tres·pass /ˈtrespas/ ● *intransitive verb* **1** (usu. foll. by *on, upon*) make an unlawful or unwarrantable intrusion (esp. on land or property). **2** (foll. by *on*) make unwarrantable claims (*shall not trespass on your hospitality*). **3** (foll. by *against*) *literary* or *archaic* offend. ● *noun* **1** *Law* a voluntary wrongful act against the person or property of another, esp. unlawful entry to a person's land or property. **2** *archaic* a sin or offence. □ **tres·pass·er** *noun* [Old French *trespasser* pass over, trespass, *trespas* (n.), from medieval Latin *transpassare* (as TRANS-, PASS¹)]

tress ● *noun* **1** a long lock of human (esp. female) hair. **2** (in *pl.*) a woman's or girl's head of hair. ● *transitive verb* arrange (hair) in tresses. □ **tressed** *adjective* (also in *combination*). **tressy** *adjective* [Old French *tresse*, perhaps ultimately from Greek *trikha* threefold]

tres·tle *noun* **1** a supporting structure for a table etc., consisting of two frames fixed at an angle or hinged or of a bar supported by two divergent pairs of legs. **2** (in full **trestle table**) a table consisting of a board or boards laid on trestles or other supports. **3** (in full **tres·tle·work**) an open braced framework to support a bridge etc. **4** (in full **trestle tree**) *Naut.* each of a pair of horizontal pieces on a lower mast supporting the topmast etc. [Old French *trestel*, ultimately from Latin *transtrum* 'beam']

trestle bridge *noun* a bridge supported on trestles.

tre·ti·noin /trəˈtɪnɔɪn/ *noun* retinoic acid, applied topically in the treatment of acne and other skin disorders. [*t-* of unknown origin + *retino-* (in RETINOL *noun*) + -IN]

tre·vally /trɪˈvali/ *noun* (pl. **-lies**) any Australian fish of the genus *Caranx*, used as food. [prob. alteration of *cavally*, a kind of fish, from Spanish *caballo* horse, from Latin (as CAVALRY)]

Tre·vel·yan /trɪˈvɛljən/ **George Mac·aulay** (1876–1962), English historian, who is best known for his *English Social History* (1944).

Trev·ino /trəˈviːnɔː/ **Lee (Buck)** (b.1939), US golfer, who was the first player to win the US Open, the British Open, and the Canadian Open championships in a single year (1971).

Tre·vith·ick /trəˈvɪθɪk/ **Rich·ard** (1771–1833), English engineer, who built the world's first steam railway locomotive (1804).

trews /truːz/ *plural noun Brit.* a pair of pants, esp. close-fitting tartan trousers formerly worn by certain Scottish regiments. [Irish *trius*, Gaelic *triubhas* (sing.); compare TROUSERS]

T. Rex *noun* a Tyrannosaurus rex (*see* TYRANNOSAUR).

trey /treɪ/ *noun* (pl. **treys**) **1** *Basketball informal* a three-point field goal. **2** a three in dice or cards. [Old French *trei*, *treis* three, from Latin *tres*]

tri- /traɪ/ *combining form* **1** forming nouns and adjectives meaning three or three times. **2** *Chem.* (forming the names of compounds) containing three atoms or groups of a specified kind (*triacetate*). [Latin & Greek from Latin *tres*, Greek *treis* three]

tri·able /ˈtraɪəbəl/ *adjective* (of a case or person etc.) that may be tried in court; liable to a judicial trial.

tri·acet·ate /traɪˈasəˌteɪt/ *noun* **1** a cellulose derivative containing three acetate groups. **2** a synthetic fibre made from this.

tri·ac·tor /ˈtraɪˌaktɜr/ *noun Cdn* a bet on the first three finishers in a horse race, specifying their order of finish (*compare* EXACTOR). [blend of TRI- + EXACTOR]

triad /ˈtraɪad/ *noun* **1** a group of three people or things. **2** *Music* a chord of three notes, consisting of a given note with the third and fifth notes of its scale. **3** (usu. **Triad**) any of several Chinese secret societies in various countries, usu. involved in criminal activities. **4** *Chem.* a trimeric unit within a polymer. □ **triad·ic** *adjective* **triad·ic·al·ly** *adverb* [ultimately from Greek *trias -ados* from *treis* three]

tri·age /ˈtriːaʒ, -ɒʒ, -ˈaʒ, -ˈɒʒ/ ● *noun* **1** the process of determining the order in which a large number of injured or ill patients will receive medical treatment, with priority usu. given to those patients with the most severe ailments or the greatest chance of survival. **2** the process of prioritizing a large number of people or things requiring attention (*promising students are favoured in a system of educational triage*). ● *transitive & intransitive verb* prioritize; sort out by triage. [French from *trier*: compare TRY]

trial ● *noun* **1** a judicial examination and determination of issues between parties by a judge with or without a jury (*stood trial for murder*). **2 a** the process or an instance of testing the ability, quality, performance, etc. of a thing, esp. before reaching a final decision about it (*the new vaccine has undergone extensive trials*). **b** the state or condition of a person or thing being tested or tried out (*on trial*). **3 a** a frustrating or exasperating experience, thing, or person. **b** (in *pl.*; usu. foll. by *of*) the frustrating aspects of something (*the trials and tribulations of being an artist*). **4** any of various races or competitions to evaluate the speed and overall abilities of athletes, vehicles, or animals (*time trials*; *sheepdog trials*). ● *transitive & intransitive verb* (**trialled, trial·ling**; esp. *US* **trialed, trial·ing**) subject to or undergo a test to assess performance. □ **on trial 1** being tried in a court of law. **2** being tested; to be chosen or retained only if found suitable or satisfactory. [Anglo-French *trial*, *triel* from *trier* TRY]

trial and error *noun* a method of finding the most effective way of completing a task, resolving a situation, etc., by experimenting with various unsuccessful approaches until a suitable one is found.

trial balloon *noun* an announcement or experiment made in order to see how a new policy will be received. [translation of French *ballon d'essai*]

trial court *noun* a court of first instance (opp. COURT OF APPEAL).

Trial Division *noun Cdn* (in PEI and Newfoundland and Labrador) a division of the Supreme Court, with judges appointed federally, which has jurisdiction over a wide range of civil and criminal cases, and hears appeals from lower provincial courts.

trial·ist *noun* a person who takes part in a sports trial or time trial etc.

trial lawyer *noun N Amer.* a lawyer practising in a trial court.

trial run *noun* **1** a preliminary test of the performance of a new procedure, technology, etc. **2** = TEST DRIVE *noun* 1.

tri·angle *noun* **1** a plane closed figure with three sides and angles. **2** a three-sided object, area, etc. having this shape (*she folded the napkins into triangles*). **3** any three things not in a straight line, with imaginary lines joining them (*the airline is increasing service in the Toronto-Ottawa-Montreal triangle*). **4** *Music* a percussion instrument consisting of a steel rod bent into the shape of a triangle and sounded by striking it with a small thin rod. **5** a situation or relationship involving three people (*love triangle*). **6** a flat wooden or plastic instrument in the form of a right-angled triangle used for drawing straight lines and square angles. [ultimately from Latin *triangulus* 'three-cornered']

tri·angu·lar /traɪˈaŋɡjʊlər/ *adjective* **1** arranged in the form or shape of a triangle; having three corners or sides. **2** (of a pyramid) having a three-sided base. **3** involving three people or parties (*a triangular relationship*). □ **tri·angu·lar·ity** /-ˈlerɪti/ *noun* **tri·angu·lar·ly** *adverb*

tri·angu·late /traɪˈaŋɡjuːˌleɪt/ *verb* **1 a** *transitive* arrange in the shape of a triangle. **b** *intransitive* adopt a triangular shape. **2** *transitive* divide (an area) into triangles for surveying purposes. **3** *transitive* **a** measure and map (an area) by the use of triangles with a known base length and base angles. **b** determine (a height, distance, etc.) in this way. □ **tri·angu·la·tion** *noun*

Tri·as·sic /traɪˈasɪk/ *Geol.* ● *adjective* of or relating to the earliest period of the Mesozoic era, lasting from about 248 to 213 million years ago, during which dinosaurs became numerous and mammals first emerged. ● *noun* this geological period or system. [Late Latin *trias* (as TRIAD), because the strata are divisible into three groups]

tri·ath·lon /traɪˈaθlɒn/ *noun* an athletic contest in which competitors engage in three different events, usu. swimming, cycling, and long-distance running. □ **tri·ath·lete** *noun* [TRI- after DECATHLON]

tri·atom·ic /ˌtraɪəˈtɒmɪk/ *adjective Chem.* **1** containing three or more atoms in one molecule. **2** having three replacement atoms or radicals.

tri·axial /traɪˈaksɪəl/ *adjective* having three axes.

tri·az·ine /ˈtraɪəˌziːn/ *noun* any of a group of chemical compounds whose molecules contain an unsaturated ring of three carbon and three nitrogen atoms. [TRI- + AZO- + -INE]

tribal ● *adjective* of, relating to, or characteristic of a tribe or tribes. ● *noun* (usu. in *pl.*) a member of a tribal community, esp. in the Indian subcontinent. □ **tribal·ly** *adverb*

tribal council *noun N Amer.* an organization encompassing a number of Aboriginal communities that have grouped together for social, political, and sometimes economic strength.

tribal·ism *noun* **1** the condition of existing as a separate tribe or tribes; tribal organization. **2** loyalty to one's own tribe or social group. □ **tribal·ist** *noun* **tribal·is·tic** *adjective*

tri-band esp. *Brit.* ● *adjective* designating a type of cellphone or other communication device capable of operating on three GSM frequencies, allowing use worldwide. ● *noun* one of these devices.

tribe *noun* **1 a** a group of families claiming descent from a common ancestor, sharing a common culture, religion, dialect, etc., and usu. occupying a specific geographical area and having a recognized leader. **b** a group of Aboriginal peoples sharing a common ancestry, language, culture and name. **2 a** *Jewish Hist.* each of the twelve divisions of the Israelites claiming descent from the twelve sons of Jacob. **b** *Rom. Hist.* each of the political divisions of the Roman people. **c** *Gk Hist.* each of the divisions of the ancient Greek people, originally on the basis of common ancestry, later forming a political unit. **3 a** a group or community of people united by a shared profession or hobby etc. (*the whole tribe of actors*). **b** a large family. **4** *Biol.* a group of related animals or plants, esp. one ranking between genus and the subfamily. [Middle English, originally in pl. form *tribuz*, *tribus* from Old French or Latin *tribus* (sing. & pl.)]

tribes·man *noun* (*pl.* **-men**) a member of a tribe or of one's own tribe, esp. one who is male.

Tribes of Israel (also called the **Twelve Tribes of Israel**) the twelve divisions of ancient Israel, each traditionally descended from one of the twelve sons of Jacob. Ten of the tribes (Asher, Dan, Gad, Issachar, Levi, Manasseh, Naphtali, Reuben, Simeon, and Zebulun, known as the *Lost Tribes*) were deported to captivity in Assyria *c.*720 BC, leaving only the tribes of Judah and Benjamin. *See also* LOST TRIBES.

tribes·person *noun* (*pl.* **tribes·people**) a member of a tribe.

tribes·woman *noun* (*pl.* **-women**) a female member of a tribe.

tribo- /ˈtraɪbəʊ-, ˈtrɪbəʊ-/ *combining form* rubbing or friction. [Greek *tribos* rubbing]

tribo·elec·tric /ˌtraɪbəʊɪˈlektrɪk, ˌtrɪb-/ *adjective* concerning electricity generated by friction.

trib·ol·ogy /traɪˈbɒlədʒi/ *noun* the branch of science and technology concerned with interacting surfaces in relative motion, and thus with friction, wear, lubrication, and the design of bearings. □ **tribo·logic·al** *adjective*

tribo·lumin·es·cence /ˌtraɪbəʊˌluːmɪˈnesəns, ˌtrɪbəʊ-/ *noun* the emission of light from a substance when rubbed, scratched, etc.

tribu·la·tion /ˌtrɪbjʊˈleɪʃən/ *noun* great trouble or suffering. [Old French from ecclesiastical Latin *tribulatio -onis* from Latin *tribulare* press, oppress, from *tribulum* sledge for threshing, from *terere trit-* rub]

tri·bu·nal /traɪˈbjuːnəl, trɪ-/ *noun* **1** a board appointed to adjudicate in some matter, esp. one appointed by a government to investigate a matter of public concern. **2** a court of justice. **3 a** a seat or bench for a judge or judges. **b** *Rom. Hist.* a raised platform in a Roman basilica on which the magistrates' seats were placed. **4 a** a place of judgment. **b** judicial authority (*the tribunal of public opinion*). [French *tribunal* or Latin *tribunus* (as TRIBUNE²)]

trib·une¹ /ˈtrɪbjuːn, -ˈbjuːn/ *noun* **1** a popular leader who attempts to protect the rights and interests of the people, often by demagogic means. **2** *Rom. Hist.* **a** (in full **tribune of the people**) an official appointed to protect the rights and interests of the plebeians. **b** (in full

military tribune) a legionary officer. □ **trib·un·ate** /-nət/ *noun* **trib·une·ship** *noun* [Latin *tribunus*, prob. from *tribus* tribe]

trib·une² /ˈtrɪbjuːn/ *noun* **1 a** an apse in a basilica containing a bishop's throne. **b** a bishop's throne. **2** a raised area or gallery with seats. **3** a dais or rostrum. [French from Italian from medieval Latin *tribuna* TRIBUNAL]

tribu·tary /ˈtrɪbjʊˌteri/ ● *noun* (*pl.* **-ies**) **1** a stream or river flowing into a larger river or lake. **2** *hist.* a person or nation required to pay a tax or tribute to another. ● *adjective* **1** (of a river etc.) that flows into a larger river or lake. **2** *hist.* required to pay or paying a tribute or tax.

trib·ute /ˈtrɪbjuːt/ *noun* **1 a** an act, statement, or gift made or given as a gesture of respect, admiration, or affection for a person (*paid tribute to her achievements*; *they left a floral tribute on his grave*). **b** a show, concert, album, etc., produced to honour the life, career, or work of esp. an artist or entertainer (also *attributive*: *tribute album*). **2** (foll. by *to*) a thing attributable to or indicative of a praiseworthy quality or act (*their success is a tribute to their perseverance*; *his recovery is a tribute to the skill of his doctors*). **3** *hist.* **a** a payment made periodically by one nation or ruler to another as a sign of dependence or submission or to ensure peace and protection. **b** an obligation to pay this (*was laid under tribute*). **4** any donation of esp. money exacted or extorted. [Middle English from Latin *tributum* neuter past participle of *tribuere tribut-* assign, originally divide between tribes (*tribus*)]

tri·butyl·tin /ˌtraɪbjuːˈtɪltɪn/ *noun* **1** an organic radical in which tetravalent tin is covalently linked to three butyl radicals. **2** any of various compounds containing this radical, some of which are used as pesticides, esp. in paints and wood preservatives.

trice *noun* □ **in a trice** in a moment; instantly. [Middle English *trice* (v.) pull, haul, from Middle Dutch *trīsen*, Middle Low German *trissen*, related to Middle Dutch *trīse* windlass, pulley]

tri·cen·ten·nial /ˌtraɪsenˈteniəl/ *noun* = TERCENTENNIAL *noun*.

tri·cep *noun informal* a triceps muscle. ¶ Although *tricep* is becoming more common in informal use, *triceps* remains standard as the singular noun. [back-formation from TRICEPS]

tri·ceps /ˈtraɪseps/ *noun* (*pl.* same) any muscle having three heads or points of attachment at one end, esp. the large extensor muscle at the back of the upper arm. [Latin, = three-headed (as TRI-, *-ceps* from *caput* head)]

tri·cera·tops /traɪˈserəˌtɒps/ *noun* a plant-eating dinosaur of the Cretaceous genus *Triceratops*, having a bony horn on the snout, two longer ones above the eyes, and a bony frill around the neck. [modern Latin from Greek *trikeratos* three-horned + *ōps* face]

tri·china /trɪˈkiːnə/ *noun* (*pl.* **tri·chinae** /-niː/) a minute parasitic nematode worm of the genus *Trichinella*, esp. *T. spiralis* which causes trichinosis. [modern Latin from Greek *trikhinos* of hair: see TRICHO-]

trich·in·osis /ˌtrɪkɪˈnəʊsɪs/ *noun* a disease caused by infection with trichinae, often from poorly cooked infected meat, whose larvae penetrate the intestinal wall, migrate around the body, and encyst in muscular tissue, causing fever, pain, and stiffness.

tri·chloro·ethyl·ene /ˌtraɪklɔːrəʊˈeθəliːn/ *noun Chem.* a colourless non-flammable volatile liquid, used as a solvent and a cleaner.

tricho- /ˈtrɪkəʊ/ *combining form* of, pertaining to, or resembling hair or hairs. [Greek *thrix trikhos* hair]

trich·ol·ogy /trɪˈkɒlədʒi, traɪ-/ *noun* the study of the structure, functions, and diseases of the hair. □ **trich·ol·o·gist** *noun*

trich·ome /ˈtraɪkəʊm/ *noun Bot.* a hair, scale, prickle, or other outgrowth from the epidermis of a plant. [Greek *trikhōma* from *trikhoō* cover with hair (as TRICHO-)]

tricho·mon·ad /ˌtrɪkəˈmɒnad/ *noun* any flagellate protozoan of the genus *Trichomonas*, parasitic in humans, cattle, and fowls.

tricho·mon·iasis /ˌtrɪkəməˈnaɪəsɪs/ *noun* any of various infections caused by trichomonads parasitic on the urinary tract, vagina, or digestive system.

tri·chot·omy /traɪˈkɒtəmi/ *noun* (*pl.* **-ies**) a division (esp. sharply defined) into three parts, classes, or categories, esp. of human nature into body, soul, and spirit. □ **tri·chot·om·ous** *adjective* [Greek *trikha* threefold, from *treis* three, after DICHOTOMY]

tri·chro·mat·ic /ˌtraɪkrəˈmatɪk/ *adjective* **1** having or using three colours. **2** of or pertaining to the perception of colours or their reproduction in printing and photography etc., by the combination of images formed in three widely different single colours, often red, green, and purple.

tri·city /ˈtraɪˌsɪti/ *noun* (*pl.* **-cities**) a metropolitan area consisting of three adjoining but independent cities (also *attributive*: *tricity area*).

trick ● *noun* **1** an action or scheme undertaken to fool, outwit, or deceive. **2** an optical illusion or figment of the imagination (*a trick of the light*). **3** a special technique; a knack or special way of doing something. **4 a** a feat of skill or dexterity (*the magician performed several tricks*). **b** an unusual action learned by an animal, e.g. shaking a paw or rolling over and playing dead. **5** a mischievous or underhanded act; a prank, a practical joke (*he played a dirty trick on us*). **6** a peculiar or characteristic habit or mannerism (*has a trick of repeating himself*). **7** (*attributive*) done to deceive, mystify, or to create an illusion (*trick photography; trick question*). **8** *slang* **a** a prostitute's client. **b** a prostitute's session with a client. **9 a** the cards played in a single round of a card game, usu. one from each player. **b** such a round of play. **c** a point gained as a result of this. **10** (*attributive*) designating a limb or joint that is unsound and liable to weaken suddenly and without warning (*a trick knee*). ● *transitive verb* **1** deceive by a trick; outwit. **2 a** (usu. foll. by *into* + verbal noun) lure or induce by trickery; fool (*his parents tricked me into marrying him*). **b** (foll. by *out of*) cheat, defraud; cause (a person) to relinquish or lose something by deceitful means (*they tricked him out of his inheritance*). **3** (usu. foll. by *out* or *up* + *in* or *with*) adorn, decorate, dress up, esp. showily; deck out (*she was tricked out in a fur jacket and leather boots; the walls were tricked up with posters*). □ **up to one's old tricks** *informal* involved in a former bad habit or reprehensible pattern of behaviour. **do** (or **turn**) **the trick** *informal* accomplish one's purpose; achieve the required result. **how's tricks?** *informal* how are you? **not miss a trick** see MISS¹. **try every trick in the book** attempt every method or technique that can be used to achieve what one wants. **turn a trick** *slang* (of a prostitute) have a session with a client. **up to a person's tricks** aware of the mischief a person is likely to attempt. [Old French dial. *trique*, Old French *triche* from *trichier* deceive, of unknown origin]

trick·ery *noun* (*pl.* **-eries**) the use of tricks or deception.

trickle ● *intransitive verb* **1** (esp. of a liquid) flow in a thin stream or drops; percolate, seep (*water trickled through the crack*). **2** come, go, or pass gradually (*people are trickling into the auditorium; the news has trickled out*). **3** (foll. by *down*) (esp. of wealth or information) be dispersed or distributed among recipients at various levels in diminishing amounts. ● *noun* **1** a thin or dripping stream of liquid. **2** a slow passage, procession, or flow (*traffic slows to a trickle*). [Middle English *trekel, trikle*, prob. imitative]

trickle charger *noun* a device for charging a storage battery at a low rate over a long period. □ **trickle charge** *transitive verb*

trickle-down *noun* **1** the spread or dissemination of wealth, information, an emotion, etc., from concentrated levels at a limited number of sources through or among many recipients in diminishing amounts. **2** (*attributive*) designating or relating to the economic theory that government benefits favouring large companies will result in increased profits for smaller companies and their suppliers etc., and improvements in the economy at all levels.

trick of the trade *noun* a clever way of doing a job, known and used by experienced members of a particular industry or profession.

trick-or-treat esp. *N Amer.* ● *noun* a Halloween custom in which children, dressed in costumes, knock on the doors of neighbours soliciting a treat of esp. candy, threatening, in accordance with tradition, to commit a prank if denied. ● *intransitive verb* (of children) call on neighbours on Halloween, asking for candy or other treats. ● *interjection* (usu. **trick or treat!**) shouted by children while trick-or-treating. □ **trick-or-treater** *noun*

trick·ster *noun* **1** a person who enjoys playing pranks and practical jokes on others; a joker. **2** a person who deceives others for esp. financial or political gain; a fraud or cheat.

trick·sy *adjective* (**trick·si·er, trick·si·est**) **1** full of tricks; mischievous, playful. **2** = TRICKY 1. □ **trick·si·ness** *noun* [TRICK: for -*sy* compare FLIMSY, TIPSY]

tricky *adjective* (**trick·i·er, trick·i·est**) **1** difficult, challenging; requiring care and adroitness (*driving was tricky because of the rain*). **2** awkward; difficult to manage or operate (*this lock is quite tricky*). **3** crafty, adroit, or deceitful. □ **trick·i·ly** *adverb* **trick·i·ness** *noun*

tri·clin·ic /traɪˈklɪnɪk/ *adjective* **1** (of a mineral) forming crystals having three unequal axes, all obliquely inclined. **2** denoting or pertaining to the system classifying triclinic crystalline substances. [TRI- + *klinō* incline]

tri·col·our /ˈtraɪˌkʌlər/ (also esp. *US* **tri·col·or**) ● *noun* (also /ˈtrɪkələr/) a flag of three colours, esp. the French national flag of blue, white, and red. ● *adjective* (also **tri·col·oured**) having three colours.

tri·corne /ˈtraɪkɔrn/ (also **tri·corn**) ● *adjective* **1** having three corners or horns. **2** (of a hat) having a brim turned up on three sides. ● *noun* a tricorne hat. [French *tricorne* or Latin *tricornis* (as TRI-, *cornu* horn)]

tri·cot /ˈtriːkoː/ *noun* a fine sheer knitted fabric made of either natural or synthetic fibres, usu. having a ribbed pattern. [French, = knitting, from *tricoter* knit, of unknown origin]

tri·cus·pid /traɪˈkʌspəd/ ● *noun* **1** a tooth with three cusps or points. **2** a heart valve formed of three triangular segments. ● *adjective* (of a tooth) having three cusps or points.

tri·cycle /ˈtraɪsɪkəl/ ● *noun* a vehicle, esp. ridden by children, having three wheels, two on an axle at the back and one at the front, driven by pedals in the same way as a bicycle. ● *intransitive verb* ride a tricycle. □ **tri·cyc·list** *noun*

tri·cyclic /traɪˈsaɪklɪk, -ˈsɪk-/ ● *adjective* having three rings or circles. ● *noun* Pharm. any of a number of antidepressant drugs having molecules with three fused rings.

tri·dent /ˈtraɪdənt/ *noun* **1** a three-pronged spear, esp. as an attribute of Poseidon (Neptune) or Britannia. **2** (**Trident**) **a** any of a class of US nuclear-powered submarines designed to carry ballistic missiles. **b** a submarine-launched ballistic missile designed to be carried by such a submarine. [Latin *tridens trident-* (as TRI-, *dens* tooth)]

tri·den·tate /traɪˈdenteɪt/ *adjective* having three teeth or prongs. [TRI- + Latin *dentatus* toothed]

Tri·den·tine /traɪˈdentaɪn/ *adjective* of, relating to, or in accordance with the Council of Trent (see TRENT, COUNCIL OF). [medieval Latin *Tridentinus* from *Tridentum* Trent]

Tridentine Mass *noun* the eucharistic liturgy used by the Roman Catholic Church from 1570 to 1964.

tri·duum /ˈtrɪdjuəm/ *noun Christianity* a period of three days of religious observance, esp. Holy Thursday, Good Friday, and Holy Saturday. [Latin (as TRI-, *dies* day)]

tried ● *transitive & intransitive verb* past and past participle of TRY. ● *adjective* proven or tested by experience or examination.

tried-and-true *adjective* proven reliable by experience.

tri·enni·al /traɪˈenɪəl/ ● *adjective* **1** recurring every three years. **2** lasting three years. ● *noun* an event recurring every three years. □ **tri·enni·al·ly** *adverb* [Late Latin *triennis* (as TRI-, Latin *annus* year)]

tri·enni·um /traɪˈenɪəm/ *noun* (*pl.* **tri·enni·ums** or **tri·ennia** /-nɪə/) a period of three years.

Trier /triːr/ a city on the Mosel River in Rhineland-Palatinate, western Germany; pop. (2002) 99,200. Established *c.*400 BC, Trier is one of the oldest cities in Europe.

trier /ˈtraɪər/ *noun* **1** a person who tests something. **2** *Law* a person appointed to decide whether a challenge to a juror is well-founded.

Tri·este /triˈest/ a city in NE Italy, the largest port on the Adriatic and capital of Friuli-Venezia Giulia region; pop. (2001) 209,520.

tri·facial /traɪˈfeɪʃəl/ *adjective* = TRIGEMINAL.

tri·fecta /traɪˈfektə/ *noun* **1** *N Amer., Austral., & NZ Racing* = TRIACTOR. **2** a group of three related events or people (*the movie won a trifecta of awards at the ceremony*). [TRI- + PERFECTA]

trif·fid *noun* esp. *Brit.* (in science fiction) one of a race of predatory plants which are capable of growing to a gigantic size and are possessed of locomotor ability and a poisonous sting. [coined by John Wyndham in *Day of the Triffids* (1951)]

tri·fid /ˈtraɪfɪd/ *adjective* esp. *Biol.* partly or wholly split into three divisions or lobes. [Latin *trifidus* (as TRI-, *findere fid-* split)]

tri·fle ● *noun* **1** a dessert consisting of sponge cake soaked in liquor, esp. sherry, covered with custard, jam, whipped cream, and fruit. **2 a** a small amount of money (*it was sold for a trifle*). **b** (prec. by *a*) somewhat (*she was a trifle annoyed*). **3** a thing of little value or importance. ● *intransitive verb* **1** (foll. by *with*) treat someone or something with a lack of seriousness or respect; dally, fool around. **2** talk or act frivolously. □ **tri·fler** *noun* [Old French *truf(f)le* by-form of *trufe* deceit, of unknown origin]

trif·ling *adjective* **1** of little importance or significance; petty, trivial. **2** frivolous, not serious. □ **trif·ling·ly** *adverb*

tri·focal /traɪˈfoːkəl/ ● *noun* (in *pl.*) a pair of eyeglasses having lenses with three parts, each with a different focal length. ● *adjective* having three focuses.

tri·foli·ate /traɪˈfoːlɪət/ *adjective* **1** (of a compound leaf) having three leaflets. **2** (of a plant) having such leaves.

tri·for·ium /traɪˈfɔrɪəm/ *noun* (*pl.* **tri·for·ia**) a gallery or arcade above the arches of the nave, choir, and transepts of a church. [Anglo-Latin, of unknown origin]

tri·fur·cate /ˈtraɪfɜrkət/ *adjective* (also **tri·fur·cated** /ˈtraɪfɜrˌkeɪtəd/) divided into three branches, esp. like the prongs of a fork.

trig *informal* ● *noun* trigonometry. ● *adjective* trigonometrical.

tri·gem·in·al /traɪˈdʒɛmɪnəl/ *adjective* **1** designating or pertaining to the fifth and largest pair of cranial nerves, which divide into three branches, the ophthalmic, maxillary, and mandibular nerves, supplying the front half of the head. **2** designating or pertaining to a form of neuralgia of the trigeminal nerve, which may involve any of its three branches, often causing severe pain. [Latin *trigeminus* born as a triplet (as TRI-, *geminus* born at the same birth) + -AL]

trig·ger ● *noun* **1 a** a movable lever for releasing a spring or catch and so setting off a mechanism. **b** a catch that may be depressed by the finger in order to release the hammer of a gunlock. **2** an event or occurrence etc. that sets off a reaction or chain reaction. ● *transitive verb* **1** set (an action or process) in motion; initiate, precipitate. **2** fire (a gun) by the use of a trigger. □ **quick on the trigger** quick to react or respond. □ **trig·gered** *adjective* [17th-c. *tricker* from Dutch *trekker* from *trekken* pull: compare TREK]

trigger finger *noun* the finger with which one pulls the trigger of a gun, usu. the forefinger of the right hand.

trig·ger·fish *noun* (*pl.* same or **-fishes**) any usu. tropical marine fish of the family Balistidae, in which the first spine on the dorsal fin can be depressed by pressing on the second.

trigger-happy *adjective* **1** apt to shoot with little or no provocation. **2** liable to act or react rashly and heedless of possible consequences.

trig·ger·man *noun informal* **1** a gunman. **2** *Hockey* an offensive player responsible for taking a shot on goal.

trigger point *noun* **1** a particular circumstance or situation which causes an event to occur (*the dictator's refusal to withdraw was the trigger point for military action*). **2** *Physiology & Medicine* a sensitive area of the body, stimulation or irritation of which causes a specific effect in another point, esp. a tender area in a muscle which causes generalized musculoskeletal pain when overstimulated.

Trig·lav /ˈtriːɡlaf/ a mountain in the Julian Alps, NW Slovenia, near the Italian border. Rising to 2 863 m (9,392 ft.), it is the highest peak in the mountains east of the Adriatic.

tri·gly·cer·ide /traɪˈɡlɪsəraɪd/ *noun Chem.* any ester formed from glycerol and three acid radicals, including the main constituents of fats and oils.

tri·glyph /ˈtraɪɡlɪf/ *noun Archit.* a block or tablet with three vertical grooves alternating with metopes in a Doric frieze. [Latin *triglyphus* from Greek *trigluphos* (as TRI-, *gluphē* carving)]

tri·gon /ˈtraɪɡɒn/ *noun* **1** *archaic* a triangle. **2** *hist.* a lyre or harp with a triangular shape. [Latin *trigonum* from Greek *trigōnon* neuter of *trigōnos* three-cornered (as TRI-, -GON)]

tri·gon·al /ˈtrɪɡənəl/ *adjective* **1** triangular; of or relating to a triangle. **2** designating or belonging to a crystal system characterized by crystals having three equal axes separated by equal angles that are not right angles. **3** *Biol.* triangular in cross-section. [medieval Latin *trigonalis* (as TRIGON)]

trig·on·om·e·try /ˌtrɪɡəˈnɒmətri/ *noun* the branch of mathematics dealing with the relations between the sides and angles of triangles, esp. as expressed by trigonometric functions, and including the theory of triangles, of angles, and of elementary periodic functions. □ **trig·on·o·met·ric** /-nəˈmɛtrɪk/ *adjective* **trig·on·o·met·ric·al** *adjective* [modern Latin *trigonometria* (as TRIGON, -METRY)]

tri·gram /ˈtraɪɡram/ *noun* (also **tri·graph**) **1** a group of three letters representing one sound. **2 a** a figure drawn with three lines. **b** each of the eight figures composed of three whole or unbroken parallel lines, occurring in the ancient Chinese text *I Ching*.

tri·halo·meth·ane /ˌtraɪhaloˈmɛθeɪn/ *noun Chem.* any of the compounds formed by substitution of halogen atoms for three of the hydrogen atoms of methane, certain of which, created as a by-product of the chlorination of drinking water, are considered carcinogenic.

tri·hed·ral /traɪˈhiːdrəl/ *adjective* having three surfaces.

trike *noun informal* **1** a tricycle. **2** a kind of ultralight aircraft. [abbreviation]

tri·lat·er·al /traɪˈlatərəl/ *adjective* **1** of, on, or with three sides; three-sided. **2** involving or shared by three countries, esp. as parties to an agreement concerning trade and finance (*trilateral trade negotiations*). □ **tri·lat·er·al·ism** *noun* **tri·lat·er·al·ist** *noun & adjective*

tril·by *noun* (*pl.* **-bies**) a soft felt hat with a narrow brim and indented crown. □ **tril·bied** *adjective* [name of the heroine in G. du Maurier's novel *Trilby* (1894), in the stage version of which such a hat was worn]

tri-level *adjective* having three levels, storeys, or floors (*a tri-level building; a tri-level government proposal*).

tri·light /ˈtraɪləɪt/ *noun Cdn* **1** a light bulb that can be adjusted to shine at any of three degrees of brightness. **2** (*attributive*) designating a lamp, socket, switch, etc., used with or using such a bulb.

tri·linear /traɪˈlɪnɪər/ *adjective* of or having three lines.

tri·lingual /traɪˈlɪŋɡwəl, -juːəl/ *adjective* **1** able to speak three languages, esp. fluently. **2** spoken or written in three languages. □ **tri·lingual·ism** *noun*

tri·liter·al /traɪˈlɪtərəl/ *adjective* **1** consisting of three letters. **2** (of a Semitic language) having roots consisting of three consonants.

tri·lith·on /ˈtraɪlɪθɒn/ *noun* (also **tri·lith** /ˈtraɪlɪθ/) a prehistoric monument consisting of three stones, esp. two uprights surmounted by a lintel. □ **tri·lith·ic** /-ˈlɪθɪk/ *adjective* [Greek *trilithon* (as TRI-, *lithos* stone)]

trill ● *noun* **1** a musical effect produced with the voice or an instrument, in which a quavering or tremulous sound is produced by a rapid alternation of two notes a tone or semitone apart. **2** a usu. high-pitched sound resembling this, such as the warbling song of a bird. **3** the pronunciation of *r* with a vibration of the tongue. ● *verb* **1** *intransitive* produce a trill. **2** *transitive* **a** sing or play (a song etc.) with a trill. **b** pronounce (the letter *r*) with a trill. [Italian *trillo* (n.), *trillare* (v.)]

Tril·ling, **Lionel** (1905–75), US literary critic, whose works include *The Liberal Imagination* (1950), *The Opposing Self* (1955), and *Sincerity and Authenticity* (1972).

tril·lion *noun* (*pl.* same or (in sense 3) **tril·lions**) **1** a million million (1,000,000,000,000 or 10^{12}). **2** *Brit.* (formerly) a million million million (1,000,000,000,000,000,000 or 10^{18}). **3** (in *pl.*) *informal* a very large number (*they've spent trillions of dollars renovating their cottage*). □ **tril·lion·aire** *noun* **tril·lionth** *adjective & noun* [French *trillion* or Italian *trilione* (as TRI-, MILLION), after BILLION]

tril·lium *noun* any of various usu. N American plants of the genus *Trillium*, of the lily family, bearing a whorl of three leaves at the summit of the stem and in the middle a solitary flower with three white or brightly coloured petals. The floral emblem of Ontario. [modern Latin, apparently from Swedish *trilling* 'triplet']

trilo·bite /ˈtraɪləbaɪt/ *noun* any of numerous extinct marine arthropods of the subphylum Trilobita, which had a body divided into an anterior solid head, a segmented thorax or trunk, and a posterior tail, and which are found abundantly as fossils in Paleozoic rocks. [modern Latin *Trilobites* (as TRI-, Greek *lobos* lobe)]

tril·ogy /ˈtrɪlədʒi/ *noun* (*pl.* **-ogies**) **1** a group or series of three related novels, theatrical works, etc., often produced by a single author and unified by a common theme or set of characters. **2** *Gk Hist.* a set of three connected tragedies performed at the festival of Dionysus in Athens. [Greek *trilogia* (as TRI-, -LOGY)]

trim ● *verb* (**trimmed**, **trim·ming**) **1** *transitive* make (something) neat or of regular size or shape, esp. by cutting away irregular or unwanted parts (*she trimmed the hedge*). **2** *transitive* (foll. by *off*, *away*) remove or cut away (irregular, uneven, or unwanted parts), esp. to reduce something to a regular shape (*he always trims the fat off his meat*). **3** *transitive* **a** reduce the size, amount, or number of (a budget, payroll, costs, etc.). **b** eliminate (superfluous costs, jobs, etc.) (*they trimmed six players off the roster*). **4** *transitive* **a** decorate, finish, or adorn with ornaments etc. (*she trimmed the dress with lace; tonight we'll trim the Christmas tree*). **b** (often foll. by *up*) make (a person) neat in dress and appearance. **5** *transitive* adjust the balance of (a ship or aircraft) by distributing its cargo evenly. **6 a** *transitive* arrange (a ship's sails) to suit the wind. **b** *intransitive* modify one's attitude in order to stand well with opposing parties. ● *noun* **1** a haircut to shorten a person's hair without changing the hairstyle. **2** decorative material or other ornamentation, usu. of a contrasting design or colour, added to clothing or upholstery (*a plain blue dress with a frilly trim*). **3** decorative wood mouldings used esp. as a border around the windows, doorways, and walls of a house (*paint the walls first, then the trim*). **4** ornamental finishing pieces mounted on the outside of a car or truck etc. **5** esp. *Brit.* condition, state, or order, esp. of readiness or fitness (*she has a month to get in trim for the race*). **6** the balance or inclination of an aircraft. ● *adjective* **1** neat, tidy, spruce. **2** in proper order; well arranged or equipped. **3** slender, slim, esp. as a sign of physical fitness. □ **in trim 1** having a neat or healthy appearance. **2** *Naut.* in the state of being prepared for sailing. □ **trim·ly** *adverb* **trim·ness** *noun* [perhaps from Old English *trymman*, *trymian* make firm, arrange: but there is no connecting evidence between Old English and 1500]

tri·maran /ˈtraɪməran/ *noun* a sailing vessel similar to a catamaran, with three hulls side by side. [TRI- + CATAMARAN]

Trim·ble, **David** (b.1944), Northern Irish Protestant Unionist leader. He shared the 1998 Nobel Peace Prize with Catholic Nationalist John

t top   v voice   w we   z zoo   ʃ she   ʒ vision   θ thin   ð this   ŋ ring   x loch   tʃ chip   dʒ jar   (see over for vowels)

Hume for their efforts in securing the accord known as the 'Good Friday Agreement'.

trimer /ˈtraɪmər/ *noun Chem.* a compound whose molecule is composed of three molecules of a monomer. □ **tri·mer·ic** /-ˈmerɪk/ *adjective*

tri·mes·ter /ˈtraɪˌmestər, -ˈmes-/ *noun* **1** a period of three months. **2** one-third of the length of human pregnancy. **3** *N Amer.* each of three terms of an academic year at some universities and high schools. [French *trimestre* from Latin *trimestris* (as TRI-, *-mestris* from *mensis* month)]

tri·meter /ˈtrɪmɪtər/ *noun Prosody* a verse line of three feet. [Latin *trimetrus* from Greek *trimetros* (as TRI-, *metron* measure)]

tri·meth·o·prim /traɪˈmeθəprɪm/ *noun* an antibiotic often used in conjunction with sulphamethoxazole to treat respiratory and urinary tract infections. [TRI- + METHYL + OXY-² + PYRIMIDINE]

trim·mer *noun* **1** a device or instrument, esp. an electric one, for trimming (esp. hair, grass, hedges, etc.). **2** *Archit.* a short beam or timber across an opening, such as a hearth, to carry the ends of truncated joists. **3** a person who trims something. **4** a small capacitor used to tune a radio set.

trim·ming *noun* **1** ornamentation or decoration, esp. for a hat or other articles of clothing. **2** (in *pl.*) *informal* accessories, the usual accompaniments, esp. the garnishes and side dishes traditionally served with the main course of a particular meal. **3** (in *pl.*) pieces cut off in trimming.

trim-tab *noun* an adjustable tab or airfoil attached to the wing or tail etc. of an airplane, used to stabilize it during flight.

Tri·murti /trɪˈmɜrti/ *Hinduism* the triad formed by the gods Brahma, Vishnu, and Shiva. [Sanskrit from *tri* three + *mūrti* form]

Trin·coma·lee /ˌtrɪŋkəməˈliː/ the principal port of Sri Lanka, on the east coast; pop. (2002) 82,600.

trine /traɪn/ ● *adjective* **1** *Astrology* designating or pertaining to the aspect of two heavenly bodies 120° (one-third of the zodiac) apart. **2** threefold, triple; made up of three parts. ● *noun Astrology* a trine aspect. [Old French *trin trine* from Latin *trinus* threefold, from *tres* three]

Trini·dad and To·bago /ˈtrɪnɪˌdad, təˈbeɪɡoʊ/ a country in the W Indies consisting of two islands off the northeast coast of Venezuela; pop. (est. 2002) 1,163,724; capital, Port of Spain (on Trinidad). Much the larger of the two islands is Trinidad, with Tobago to the northeast.

Trini·dad·ian /ˌtrɪnɪˈdadiən/ ● *noun* a native or inhabitant of Trinidad. ● *adjective* of or relating to the island of Trinidad or its people.

Trini·tar·ian /ˌtrɪnɪˈteriən/ ● *noun* a person who believes in the doctrine of the Trinity. ● *adjective* **1** of, pertaining to, or believing in the doctrine of the Trinity. **2** (**trinitarian**) composed or consisting of three parts. □ **Trini·tar·ian·ism** *noun*

tri·nitro·tolu·ene /traɪˌnaɪtroʊˈtɒljuːˌiːn/ *noun* (also **tri·nitro·tolu·ol**) = TNT.

Trin·ity /ˈtrɪnɪti/ *noun (pl.* **-ities**) **1** (also **Holy Trinity**) *Theol.* **a** the three modes of being of the Christian Godhead as conceived in orthodox Christian belief; the Father, Son, and Holy Spirit as constituting one God. **b** the existence of God in three persons. **2** (often foll. by *of*) a group of three people or things. [Old French *trinité* from Latin *trinitas -tatis* triad (as TRINE)]

Trinity Bay a large inlet of the N Atlantic, extending deeply into the coast of SE Newfoundland, separating the Avalon and Bonavista peninsulas. [perhaps so called on Trinity Sunday *c.*1500]

Trinity Sunday *noun* the first Sunday after Pentecost, observed in honour of the Trinity.

trin·ket *noun* a small ornament or piece of jewellery etc., esp. one having little worth or value. □ **trin·ket·ry** *noun* [16th c.: origin unknown]

tri·nom·ial /traɪˈnoʊmiəl/ ● *noun* an algebraic expression consisting of three terms connected by a plus or minus sign. ● *adjective* consisting of three terms. [TRI- after BINOMIAL]

trio *noun (pl.* **trios**) **1** a set or group of three. **2** *Music* **a** a composition for three performers. **b** a group of three performers. **c** the alternative section in a minuet, scherzo, march, or similar movement, usu. in a different key or style from the preceding and following passages. [French & Italian from Latin *tres* three, after *duo*; sense 2c from the fact that such sections were originally written for two oboes and a bassoon]

tri·ode /ˈtraɪoʊd/ *noun* **1** a thermionic valve having three electrodes, usu. an anode, a cathode, and a grid. **2** a semiconductor rectifier having three connections. [TRI- + ELECTRODE]

trio·let /ˈtraɪələt, ˈtriːələt/ *noun* a poem of eight (usu. eight-syllabled)

lines rhyming *abaaabab*, the first line recurring as the fourth and seventh and the second as the eighth. [French (as TRIO)]

tri·ox·ide /traɪˈɒksaɪd/ *noun Chem.* an oxide containing three oxygen atoms.

trip ● *verb* (**tripped**, **trip·ping**) **1 a** *transitive* (often foll. by *up*) cause (a person) to stumble or fall by entangling the feet. **b** *intransitive* (often foll. by *over*) stumble or fall, esp. by suddenly catching the foot against an obstacle. **2** *transitive* (usu. foll. by *up*) **a** cause (a person) to make a mistake or blunder. **b** expose the error of (a person), esp. by detecting an inconsistency in their facts or calculations. **3** *intransitive* make an error, esp. in calculation or articulation. **4** *intransitive* **a** run or dance with quick light steps. **b** (of a rhythm, words, etc.) flow lightly and gracefully. **5** *intransitive* esp. *Cdn* make a journey or expedition through rough country, esp. in a canoe (*we went canoe tripping in Algonquin Park*). **b** make an excursion to a place. **6** *transitive* **a** release or depress (a catch or lever etc.) in order to activate a mechanism (*he tripped the switch and the lights came on*). **b** activate (a mechanism) in this way (*she tripped the lights*). **7** *intransitive* (often foll. by *out*) *informal* undergo a hallucinatory experience induced by drugs. ● *noun* **1** a journey or excursion, either one made repeatedly on a particular usu. short route or one taken for pleasure (*a quick trip to the drugstore; a three-week trip to Europe*). **2 a** an act of causing a person to stumble or blunder. **b** a stumble or blunder. **3** an illusory or self-indulgent activity or attitude; an intense and usu. temporary enthusiasm or preoccupation (*he was caught up in this fitness trip; power trip; guilt trip*). **4** *informal* a hallucinatory experience caused by a drug. **5 a** an intense or exhilarating experience. **b** an exciting or stimulating person. **6** a contrivance for a tripping mechanism etc. **7** a nimble step. □ **trip the light fantastic** *jocular* dance. [Old French *triper, tripper,* from Middle Dutch *trippen* skip, hop]

tri·part·ite /traɪˈpɑrtaɪt/ *adjective* **1** divided into or consisting of three parts. **2** shared by or involving three parties. **3** *Bot.* (of a leaf) divided into three segments almost to the base. [Latin *tripartitus* (as TRI-, *partitus* past participle of *partiri* divide)]

trip computer *noun* an electronic odometer, typically with extra capabilities such as the ability to calculate fuel consumption.

tripe *noun* **1** the first or second stomach of a ruminant, esp. an ox or cow, prepared as food. **2** *informal* something considered worthless or foolish; nonsense, garbage. [Old French, of unknown origin]

trip-hammer ● *noun* a heavy mechanical hammer that is raised by mechanical means and then dropped by a tripping device, such as a cam. ● *intransitive verb* (esp. of the heart) pound or throb with a heavy beat like that of a trip-hammer.

trip-hop *noun* esp. *Brit.* a style of popular music combining the rhythm and instrumentation of hip hop with elements borrowed from earlier genres, such as jazz and progressive rock. □ **trip-hopper** *noun*

triph·thong /ˈtrɪfθɒŋ, ˈtrɪp-/ *noun* **1** a sequence of three vowel sounds pronounced as a single syllable (as in *fire*). **2** three vowel characters representing the sound of a single vowel (as in *b*eau) (compare DIPHTHONG). [French *triphtongue* (as TRI-, DIPHTHONG)]

tri·plane /ˈtraɪpleɪn/ *noun* an early type of airplane having three sets of wings, one above the other.

triple ● *adjective* **1** consisting of three usu. equal parts or things; threefold. **2** involving three parties. **3** three times as much or many (*triple the amount; triple thickness*). **4** *Figure Skating, Dance, etc.* (of a jump, pirouette, etc.) involving three revolutions (*triple lutz; triple toe loop*). ● *adverb* to three times the amount or extent (*the cars were triple parked*). ● *noun* **1** a threefold number or amount. **2** a set of three. **3** *Baseball* a hit that enables the batter to reach third base. **4** *Figure Skating, Dance, etc.* a jump, spin, etc. involving three revolutions. ● *verb* **1** *transitive & intransitive* multiply or increase by three. **2** *Baseball* **a** *intransitive* hit a triple. **b** *transitive* (foll. by *in* or *home*) drive (a baserunner) in by hitting a triple. □ **trip·ly** *adverb* [Old French *triple* or Latin *triplus* from Greek *triplous*]

Triple A *noun* = AAA 1, 4, 5 (also *attributive*: *Triple-A credit rating; Triple-A outfielder*).

Triple Alliance *noun* any of a number of notable alliances of three countries or states, including those made in 1668 between England, the Netherlands, and Sweden against France, in 1717 between Britain, France, and the Netherlands against Spain, in 1865 between Argentina, Brazil, and Uruguay against Paraguay, and in 1882 between Germany, Austria-Hungary, and Italy against France and Russia.

triple crown *noun* **1** the title awarded to the winner of three important events. **2 a** *Cdn* the title awarded to the horse that wins the Queen's Plate, the Prince of Wales Stakes, and the Breeders' Stakes. **b** *US* the title awarded to the horse that wins the Preakness, Belmont Stakes, and Kentucky Derby. **3** the title awarded to the baseball player who finishes the year leading the league in batting average, home runs, and runs batted in.

triple-decker *noun* something with three decks, layers, or levels, e.g. a sandwich made with three pieces of bread and two layers of filling, or a three-storey building.

triple-double *noun* *Basketball* the achievement of a player who reaches double figures in any three categories of personal statistics, such as points, rebounds, and assists, in a single game.

Triple Entente *noun* an early 20th-c. alliance between Britain, France, and Russia which formed the basis of the Allied powers in the First World War.

Triple-E Senate *noun* *Cdn* a proposed senate that would have more effective powers than the existing Senate and which would consist of elected members equally representing the provinces, as introduced and advocated by Alberta premier Don Getty in the late 1980s. [from the three E's of Equal, Elected, and Effective]

triple jump *noun* a field event in which athletes attempt to achieve the greatest distance on a jump that involves a hop followed by a long step and a leap. □ **triple jumper** *noun*

triple play *noun* *Baseball* a play in which three players, usu. the batter and two baserunners, are put out.

triple rhyme *noun* a rhyme including three syllables.

triple sec *noun* a colourless orange-flavoured liqueur. [French lit. 'thrice dry']

trip·let *noun* **1** (usu. in *pl.*) each of three children or animals born at one birth. **2 a** a group of three equal notes played in the time of two. **b** a group of three successive lines of verse, esp. when rhyming together and of the same length. **3** *Chem.* an atomic or molecular state characterized by two unpaired electrons with parallel spins. **4** a set of three people or things. [TRIPLE + -ET¹, after *doublet*]

triple-team *transitive & intransitive verb* *Sport* (of a team) use or assign three players to cover (an opponent).

triple threat *noun* a person skilled in three aspects of a profession or field, or having expertise in three separate professions or fields.

triple time *noun* musical time with three beats to the bar; waltz time.

triple whammy *noun* *informal* a threefold blow or setback.

tri·plex /'traipleks, 'trɪ-/ ● *noun* (*pl.* **-ex·es**) *N Amer.* a residential building divided into three apartments, esp. a three-storey dwelling with a separate apartment on each floor. ● *adjective* triple or threefold. [Latin *triplex -plicis* (as TRI-, *plic-* fold)]

trip·li·cate ● *adjective* /'trɪplɪkət/ **1** existing in three examples or copies. **2** having three corresponding parts. ● *noun* /'trɪplɪkət/ each of a set of three copies or corresponding parts. ● *transitive verb* /'trɪplɪˌkeɪt/ **1** make in three copies. **2** multiply by three. □ **in triplicate** (written, printed, produced, etc.) in three identical or exactly corresponding copies. □ **trip·li·ca·tion** *noun* [Latin *triplicatus* past participle of *triplicare* (as TRIPLEX)]

trip·li·city /trɪ'plɪsɪti/ *noun* (*pl.* **-ties**) **1** the state of being triple. **2** a group of three things. [Late Latin *triplicitas* from Latin TRIPLEX]

trip·loid /'trɪplɔɪd/ *Biol.* ● *noun* an organism or cell having three times the haploid set of chromosomes. ● *adjective* of or being a triploid. □ **trip·loidy** *noun* [modern Latin *triploides* from Greek (as TRIPLE)]

trip·man *noun* (*pl.* **-men**) *Cdn hist.* a man hired for temporary duty on a fur brigade, paid by the trip.

trip·meter *noun* an instrument used to record the distance travelled by a vehicle during a particular trip.

tri·pod /'traɪpɒd/ *noun* **1** a stand with three usu. adjustable and collapsible legs for supporting a camera or telescope etc. **2** a three-legged stool, seat, or table, etc. **3** *Gk Hist.* a three-legged bronze altar at Delphi on which the priestess sat to deliver oracles. □ **tri·pod·al** /traɪ'pɒdəl, 'trɪpədəl/ *adjective* [Latin *tripus tripodis* from Greek *tripous* (as TRI-, *pous podos* foot)]

Trip·oli /'trɪpəli/ **1** the capital and chief port of Libya, on the Mediterranean coast in the northwest of the country; pop. (2002) 1,223,300. **2** a port in NW Lebanon; pop. (2002) 208,700. □ **Tri·pol·itan** /trə'pɒlɪtən/ *noun & adjective*

trip·oli /'trɪpəli/ *noun* = ROTTENSTONE. [French from TRIPOLI]

Trip·oli·tania /ˌtrɪpəlɪ'teɪniə/ a coastal region surrounding Tripoli in North Africa, in what is now NE Libya. Its name is Latin, referring to three Phoenician cities which were established there in the 7th c. BC: Oea (now Tripoli), Leptis Magna, and Sabratha. □ **Trip·oli·tan·ian** *adjective & noun* [Latin *Tripolis* three cities]

tri·pos /'traɪpɒs/ *noun* *Brit.* the final honours exam that must be written to complete a bachelor's degree at Cambridge University. [as TRIPOD,

with reference to the stool on which graduates sat to deliver a satirical speech at the degree ceremony]

trip·per *noun* **1** esp. *Cdn* (*North*) a person who makes an expedition through rough country, esp. by canoe. **2 a** a person who goes on a journey or short trip, esp. for pleasure (*day tripper*). **b** *Brit.* a sightseer, a tourist.

trip·ping *noun* **1** esp. *Cdn* (*North*) the activity of travelling through rough country, esp. by canoe. **2** *Hockey* **a** an illegal act of causing an opponent to fall by obstructing him or her with one's stick, leg, or foot, etc. **b** a minor penalty assessed for this.

trip·ping·ly *adverb* with great ease and rapidity (*this word probably doesn't come trippingly off your tongue*).

trip·py *adjective* (**trip·pi·er**, **trip·pi·est**) *informal* (of music, poetry, etc.) producing an effect resembling that of a psychedelic drug.

trip·tych /'trɪptɪk/ *noun* **1** a picture or relief carving on three panels, usu. hinged vertically together and often used as an altarpiece. **2** a set of three artistic works, usu. meant to be viewed, displayed, or performed together. **3** a set of three writing tablets hinged or tied together. [TRI-, after DIPTYCH]

Trip·ura /'trɪpʊrə/ a small state in the far northeast of India, on the eastern border of Bangladesh; capital, Agartala. An ancient Hindu kingdom, Tripura once covered a large area including Bengal, Assam, and parts of Burma.

trip·wire *noun* **1** a wire stretched close to the ground in order to trip up trespassers, enemies, etc., or to activate an alarm when disturbed. **2** a comparatively weak military force employed as a first line of defence, engagement with which will trigger the intervention of strong forces.

tri·reme /'traɪriːm/ *noun hist.* a galley with three banks of oars. [French *trirème* or Latin *triremis* (as TRI-, *remus* 'oar')]

tri·sac·char·ide /traɪ'sakəˌraɪd/ *noun* *Chem.* a sugar consisting of three linked monosaccharides.

tri·sect /traɪ'sekt/ *transitive verb* cut or divide into three (usu. equal) parts. □ **tri·sec·tion** *noun* **tri·sect·or** *noun* [TRI- + Latin *secare sect-* cut]

tri·service *noun* the three armed forces, army, navy, and air force (also attributive: *tri-service commander*).

tri·shaw /'traɪʃɔː/ *noun* a light three-wheeled vehicle operated by pedals, used in the Far East as a taxi to chauffeur passengers. [TRI- + RICKSHAW]

tris·kai·deka·phobia /ˌtrɪskaɪˌdekə'fɔːbiə/ *noun* fear or superstition regarding the number thirteen. [Greek *treiskaideka* 'thirteen' + -PHOBIA]

tris·kel·ion /traɪ'skeliən, trɪ-/ *noun* a symbolic figure of three legs or lines radiating from a common centre. [Greek TRI- + *skelos* leg]

tris·mus /'trɪzməs/ *noun* *Med.* = LOCKJAW. [modern Latin from Greek *trismos* = *trigmos* a scream, grinding]

tri·sodium phosphate /traɪ'səʊdiəm/ *noun* a water-soluble compound, $Na_3PO_412H_2O$, occurring as crystals, used esp. as a detergent for removing grease stains from asphalt, washing walls prior to painting, etc. Abbr.: **TSP**.

tri·somy /'traɪsəmi/ *noun* *Med.* (*pl.* **-ies**) a condition in which an extra copy of a chromosome is present in the cell nuclei, causing developmental abnormalities. □ **tri·som·ic** /ˌtraɪ'səʊmɪk/ *adjective* [TRI- + -SOME³]

trisomy-21 *noun* *Med.* the most common form of Down's syndrome, caused by an extra copy of chromosome number 21 in the cell nuclei.

Tris·tan /'trɪstən/ (also **Tris·tram** /'trɪstrəm/) (in medieval legend) a knight who was the lover of Iseult. In one version of the tale, a love potion caused Tristan and Iseult to fall in love as they were travelling to her wedding with King Mark of Cornwall. Tristan fled to Brittany but sent for Iseult to heal him when wounded by a poisoned weapon. The ship in which she approached bore a white sail, the agreed signal that she was aboard, but Tristan's wife informed him that the sail was black and Tristan died of despair, following which Iseult killed herself.

Tris·tan da Cunha /ˌtrɪstən də 'kuːnə/ the largest of a small group of volcanic islands in the S Atlantic, 2 112 km (1,320 miles) southwest of the British colony of St. Helena, of which it is a dependency; pop. (2002) 320. Its original inhabitants were shipwrecked sailors. □ **Tris·tan·ian** /trɪ'steɪniən/ *noun & adjective* [*Tristão da Cunha*, Portuguese admiral who discovered it in 1506]

tri·state /'traɪsteɪt/ *noun* *US* a region consisting of three bordering states or the adjoining parts of three bordering states (also attributive: *tristate community*).

trist·esse /trɪsˈtes/ *noun* sadness, sorrow, melancholy. [French]

tri·sulph·ide *noun* a compound of an element or radical with three atoms of sulphur.

tri·syllab·ic /ˌtraɪsəˈlæbɪk/ *adjective* (of a word or metrical foot) having three syllables.

trite *adjective* **1** (of a phrase, opinion, etc.) stale through constant use or repetition; hackneyed, commonplace, worn out. **2** (of a work, novel, etc.) containing or characterized by stale or commonplace ideas, subjects, etc. □ **trite·ly** *adverb* **trite·ness** *noun* [Latin *tritus* past participle of *terere* rub, wear down]

triti·at·ed /ˈtrɪtiːˌeɪtəd/ *adjective* containing tritium; having had an atom of ordinary hydrogen replaced by tritium.

triti·cale /trɪtəˈkeɪli/ *noun* a high-protein hybrid between wheat, *Triticum aestivum*, and rye, *Secale cereale*, used by the brewing industry, in some baked goods, and as feed for livestock. [modern Latin from the genus names *Triti(cum)* wheat + *(Se)cale* rye]

trit·ium /ˈtrɪtiəm/ *noun Chem.* a radioactive isotope of hydrogen with a mass about three times that of ordinary hydrogen, which occurs naturally in minute amounts and is produced artificially, esp. for use in fusion reactors. Symbol: **T** or **³H**. [modern Latin from Greek *tritos* third]

trito- /ˈtraɪtoː, ˈtrɪtoː/ *combining form* third. [Greek *tritos* third]

Tri·ton /ˈtraɪtən/ *noun* **1** *Gk Myth* the son of Poseidon and Amphitrite, usu. represented as a man with a fish's (sometimes a horse's) tail carrying a trident and trumpet made from a conch shell; Tritons are sometimes regarded as constituting a class of minor sea gods or mermen. **2** *Astronomy* the largest satellite of Neptune (diameter 2 700 km), the seventh closest to the planet, discovered in 1846. **3** (**triton**) any marine gastropod mollusc of the family Cymatiidae, with a long conical shell. [Latin from Greek *Tritōn*]

tri·ton /ˈtraɪtən/ *noun* a subatomic particle composed of one proton and two neutrons, the nucleus of the tritium atom.

tri·tone /ˈtraɪtoːn/ *noun Music* an interval of an augmented fourth, comprising three whole tones.

trit·ur·ate /ˈtrɪtʃərˌreɪt/ *transitive verb* reduce to fine particles or a powder by rubbing, crushing, or grinding; pulverize. □ **trit·ur·a·tion** *noun* [Latin *triturare* 'thresh grain' from *tritura* rubbing (as TRITE)]

tri·umph ● *noun* **1** a great success, achievement, or victory; a major accomplishment (*a triumph of engineering; a triumph over a rival*). **2** the state of being successful or victorious (*she raised her fist in triumph*). **3** the thrill, joy, or satisfaction of success or victory; exultation. **4** *Rom. Hist.* the processional entry of a victorious general and his army into Rome. ● *intransitive verb* (often foll. by *over*) be successful or victorious; prevail. [Old French *triumphe* (n.), from Latin *triump(h)us* prob. from Greek *thriambos* hymn to Bacchus]

tri·umph·al /traɪˈʌmfəl/ *adjective* done, used, or made to celebrate or commemorate a success or victory (*triumphal procession; triumphal arch*).

tri·umph·al·ism /traɪˈʌmfəlɪzəm/ *noun* extreme or ostentatious pride or excessive exultation over one's achievements or those of one's country, party, etc. □ **tri·umph·al·ist** *adjective & noun*

tri·umph·ant /traɪˈʌmfənt/ *adjective* **1** victorious or successful. **2** exultant. □ **tri·umph·ant·ly** *adverb*

tri·um·vir /traɪˈʌmvɜr/ *noun* (*pl.* **tri·um·virs** or **tri·um·vi·ri** /-raɪ/) a member of a triumvirate. [Latin, originally in pl. *triumviri*, back-formation from *trium virorum* genitive of *tres viri* three men]

tri·um·vir·ate /traɪˈʌmvɜrət/ *noun* **1 a** a group of three people in a joint position of power or authority. **b** *Rom. Hist.* a committee of three public officers overseeing administrative departments. The term is used specifically of the unofficial coalition of Julius Caesar, Pompey, and Crassus in 60 BC (the *First Triumvirate*) and of the office to which Antony, Lepidus, and Octavian were appointed in 43 BC (the *Second Triumvirate*). **2** a group of three people. **3** a set of three things.

tri·une /ˈtraɪjuːn/ *adjective* (esp. with reference to the Trinity) that is three in one; that constitutes or consists of three persons or things in unity. [TRI- + Latin *unus* one]

tri·valent /traɪˈveɪlənt/ *adjective Chem.* **1** having a valence of three. **2** (of a vaccine) providing immunity against three strains of an infective agent. □ **tri·valence** *noun*

Tri·van·drum /trɪˈvændrəm/ the capital of the state of Kerala, a port on the southwest coast of India; pop. (2001) 744,700.

triv·et /ˈtrɪvət/ *noun* **1** a low, flat, usu. three-legged cast iron or ceramic stand placed under a hot kettle, pot, or serving dish to protect the surface of a table. **2** a similar stand with three or more legs used to keep something raised while being heated or cooked in a pot, roasting pan, or over a fire. [Middle English *trevet*, apparently from Latin *tripes* (as TRI-, *pes pedis* foot)]

trivia /ˈtrɪviə/ *plural noun* (treated as *sing.*) **1** *N Amer.* unimportant but interesting or amusing tidbits of factual information, esp. on a particular subject, often used as the basis for quizzes or games (*movie trivia; hockey trivia*). **2** unimportant or inconsequential matters or details; trifles. [modern Latin, pl. of TRIVIUM, influenced by TRIVIAL]

triv·ial *adjective* **1** of little importance or consequence; trifling. **2** commonplace, ordinary, trite. **3** *Math.* (of a solution etc.) in which all variables or unknowns are equal to zero. □ **triv·ial·ity** *noun* (*pl.* **-ities**). **triv·ial·ly** *adverb* [Latin *trivialis* commonplace, from *trivium*: see TRIVIUM]

triv·ial·ize *transitive verb* (also esp. *Brit.* **-ise**) diminish or downplay the importance, significance, or value of; minimize, belittle. □ **triv·ial·iz·a·tion** *noun*

triv·ium /ˈtrɪviəm/ *noun hist.* (in the Middle Ages) the lower division of a university course of study, comprising grammar, rhetoric, and logic (*compare* QUADRIVIUM). [Latin, = place where three roads meet (as TRI-, *via* road)]

tri·week·ly *adjective* **1** produced or occurring three times each week. **2** produced or occurring once every three weeks.

-trix *suffix* (*pl.* **-trices** /trɪsiːz, ˈtraɪ-/ or **-trixes**) forming feminine agent nouns corresponding to masculine nouns in *-tor*, esp. in *Law* (*executrix*). [Latin *-trix -tricis*]

tRNA *abbreviation* TRANSFER RNA.

Troad /ˈtroːad/ an ancient region of NW Asia Minor, of which Troy was the chief city.

Tro·bri·and Islands /ˈtroːbriənd/ a small group of islands in the SW Pacific, in Papua New Guinea, situated off the southeast tip of the island of New Guinea. □ **Tro·bri·and·er** *noun*

tro·car /ˈtroːkɑr/ *noun* a surgical instrument used for withdrawing fluid from a body cavity, consisting of a shaft with a three-sided cutting point enclosed in a cannula. [French *trois-quarts*, *trocart* from *trois* three + *carre* (Latin *quadra*) side, face, from the triangular appearance of this device]

tro·chaic /troːˈkeɪɪk/ *Prosody* ● *adjective* (esp. of a rhythm or meter etc.) using or characterized by the use of a trochee or trochees. ● *noun* (usu. in *pl.*) trochaic verse. [Latin *trochaicus* from Greek *trokhaikos* (as TROCHEE)]

tro·chan·ter /troːˈkæntər/ *noun* **1** *Anat.* any of several bony protuberances by which muscles are attached to the upper part of the femur or thigh bone. **2** *Zool.* the second segment of the leg in insects. □ **tro·chan·ter·ic** /ˌtroːkænˈterɪk/ *adjective* [French from Greek *trokhantēr* from *trekhō* run]

tro·chee /ˈtroːkiː/ *noun Prosody* a metrical foot consisting of one long or stressed syllable followed by one short or unstressed syllable (*compare* IAMB). [Latin *trochaeus* from Greek *trokhaios* (*pous*) running (foot), from *trekhō* run]

troch·lea /ˈtrɒkliə/ *noun* (*pl.* **troch·leae** /-liˌiː/) *Anat.* a structure or arrangement of parts resembling a pulley, with a smooth surface over which some other part slides, e.g. the groove at the lower end of the humerus, with which the ulna articulates at the elbow. □ **troch·lear** *adjective* [Latin, = pulley, from Greek *trokhilia*]

tro·choid /ˈtroːkɔɪd/ ● *adjective* **1** *Anat.* (of a joint) in which one bone rotates freely around a central axis. **2** *Math.* (of a curve) traced by a point on a radius of a circle rotating along a straight line or another circle. ● *noun* a trochoid joint or curve. [Greek *trokhoeidēs* wheel-like, from *trokhos* wheel]

trod *past and past participle of* TREAD.

trod·den *past participle of* TREAD.

trog·lo·dyte /ˈtrɒgləˌdaɪt/ ● *noun* **1** a cave dweller, esp. of prehistoric times. **2** *derogatory* **a** a person regarded as living in wilful ignorance, esp. of current trends and subjects; a conservative or old-fashioned person. **b** a base, degenerate, or primitive person. **3** a person living in seclusion; a hermit. ● *adjective* **1** dwelling in caves. **2** ignorant; old-fashioned, unmannerly, or uncouth. □ **trog·lo·dyt·ic** /-ˈdɪtɪk/ *adjective* [Latin *troglodyta* from Greek *trōglodutēs* from the name of an Ethiopian people, after *trōglē* hole]

tro·gon /ˈtroːgɒn/ *noun* any tropical bird of the genus *Trogon* or the family Trogonidae, widely distributed in tropical and subtropical forests, having a short thick bill and soft plumage of varied and often brilliant colour. [modern Latin from Greek *trōgōn* from *trōgō* gnaw]

troi·ka /ˈtrɔɪkə/ *noun* **1 a** a Russian carriage or sleigh drawn by a team of three horses. **b** this team of horses. **2** a group of three people working together, esp. in an administrative or managerial capacity; a triumvirate. **3** a group of three people or things. [Russian from *troe* three]

Troi·lus /ˈtrɔɪləs/ *Gk Myth* a Trojan prince, the son of Priam and Hecuba, killed by Achilles; in medieval legends of the Trojan War he was the forsaken lover of Cressida.

Trois-Pistoles /trwɒpiˈstɔl/ a town in E Quebec, situated on the south shore of the St. Lawrence, about 50 km southwest of Rimouski; pop. (2001) 3,635. [perhaps with reference to a sailor's silver goblet, lost while dipping for water and worth three *pistoles* (French, = gold coins)]

Trois-Rivières /trwɑriˈvjɛr/ a city in south central Quebec, situated on the St. Lawrence, at the mouth of the Rivière Saint-Maurice, roughly midway between Montreal and Quebec City; pop. (2001) 126,438. [French, lit. 'three rivers', so called with reference to the river's three outlets at its mouth, formed by the presence of two islands]

Tro·jan /ˈtroːdʒən/ ● *adjective* of or relating to ancient Troy or its inhabitants. ● *noun* **1** a native or inhabitant of Troy. **2** a person of great energy, courage, or endurance (*works like a Trojan*). [Latin *Troianus* from *Troia* Troy]

Trojan Horse *noun* **1** a hollow wooden statue of a horse in which the Greeks are said to have concealed themselves to enter Troy. **2** a seemingly innocuous person or device that eludes a person's defences to bring about his or her downfall. **3** *Computing* a program that breaches the security of a computer system, esp. by ostensibly functioning as part of a legitimate program, in order to erase, corrupt, or remove data.

Trojan War *Gk Myth* the ten-year siege of Troy by a coalition of Greeks, described in Homer's *Iliad*. The Greeks were attempting to recover Helen, wife of Menelaus, who had been abducted by the Trojan prince Paris. The war ended with the capture of the city by a trick: the Greeks ostensibly ended the siege but left behind a group of men concealed in a hollow wooden horse so large that the city walls had to be breached for it to be drawn inside. (See also TROY.)

troll[1] /ˈtroːl/ *noun Scand. Myth* a member of a race of grotesque dwarfs (or, formerly, giants) usu. dwelling in caves or under bridges. □ **troll·ish** *adjective* [Old Norse & Swedish *troll*, Danish *trold*]

troll[2] /ˈtroːl/ ● *verb* **1** esp. *N Amer. Fishing* **a** *intransitive* fish by drawing bait along in the water behind a moving boat. **b** *transitive* draw (a lure or baited line) behind a boat. **c** *transitive* practise this method of fishing in (a particular stretch of water). **2** *intransitive* (foll. by *for*) **a** esp. *N Amer.* attempt to catch a particular type of fish using this method. **b** pursue, seek; go looking or searching. **3** *intransitive* sing out in a carefree jovial manner. **4** *intransitive* esp. *Brit.* walk, stroll. ● *noun* **1** an act or method of trolling for fish. **2** a baited line or lure used in this. [Middle English 'stroll, roll': compare Old French *troller* quest, Middle High German *trollen* stroll]

troll·er /ˈtroːlər/ *noun* esp. *N Amer. Fishing* **1** a person who trolls for fish. **2** a fishing boat used for trolling.

trol·ley /ˈtrɒli/ *noun* (also **trol·ly**; *pl.* **-leys, -lies**) **1 a** a small cart on wheels or casters used for serving food. **b** *Brit.*= SHOPPING CART 1. **c** a small wheeled cart for other purposes, e.g. carrying luggage. **2** a grooved metallic pulley receiving current from an overhead electric wire and conveying this by a pole etc. to the motor of a trolley bus or streetcar. **3 a** (in full **trolley bus**) a bus powered by electricity from an overhead cable. **b** (in full **trolley car**) *US* = STREETCAR. **4** esp. *Brit.* any small wheeled cart running on rails, such as in a mine or factory. □ **off one's trolley** esp. *Brit.* = OFF ONE'S ROCKER (see ROCKER). [of dial. origin, perhaps from TROLL[2]]

troll·ing motor *noun N Amer. Fishing* a quiet low-powered motor suitable for a boat used in trolling.

trol·lop /ˈtrɒləp/ *noun* **1** a promiscuous woman. **2** a prostitute. [17th c.: perhaps related to TRULL]

Trol·lope /ˈtrɒləp/ **An·thony** (1815–82), English novelist. A prolific writer, he is best known for two series of novels: one set in the imaginary county of Barsetshire and telling of the lives of the local clergy, gentry, etc. including *The Warden* (1855), *Barchester Towers* (1857), and *The Last Chronicle of Barset* (1867); and the other dealing with the social and political world of London, known as the 'Palliser' novels (1864–80). □ **Trol·lop·ian** /trəˈloːpiːən/ *adjective & noun*

trom·bone *noun* **1** a large brass wind instrument with a sliding tube, analogous to the valves of other wind instruments, used to increase and decrease its length, thereby varying its tone. **2** a person who plays or is playing a trombone. □ **trom·bon·ist** *noun* [French or Italian, from Italian *tromba* TRUMPET]

trom·mel /ˈtrɒməl/ *noun Mining* a rotating cylindrical screen or sieve used for washing and sizing ores, coal, gravel, etc. [German, = drum]

tromp *verb* esp. *N Amer. informal* **1** *intransitive* march with a heavy step; trudge, stomp. **2** *transitive* trample. [alteration of TRAMP]

trompe l'oeil /trɔ̃pˈlɔɪ/ *noun* an optical illusion, esp. a still-life painting designed to deceive the spectator by giving an illusion of reality (also *attributive*). [French, lit. 'deceives the eye']

-tron *suffix Physics* forming nouns denoting: **1** a subatomic particle (*positron*). **2** a device or machine, esp. a particle accelerator (*betatron*). **3** a kind of electron tube, esp. a thermionic valve (*ignitron*). [after ELECTRON]

Trond·heim /ˈtrɒndhaɪm/ a fishing port in west central Norway; pop. (2002) 141,600. Founded by Olaf I Tryggvason, it was the capital of Norway during the Viking period.

troop ● *noun* **1** an assembled company of people or animals. **2 a** a detachment of police officers or soldiers etc., esp. a unit of artillery and armoured formation. **b** (in *pl.*) soldiers or armed forces. **3** a cavalry unit commanded by a captain. **4** a group of Scouts or Girl Guides usu. consisting of three or more patrols. ● *intransitive verb* (foll. by *in, out, off,* etc.) walk, march, or proceed in large numbers, in or as if in a troop. □ **troop the colour** esp. *Brit.* transfer a flag ceremonially at a public mounting of garrison guards. [French *troupe*, back-formation from *troupeau* diminutive of medieval Latin *troppus* flock, prob. of Germanic origin]

troop carrier *noun* a large aircraft, armoured vehicle, etc., for transporting military troops.

troop·er *noun* **1** (also **Trooper**) a private in an armoured or cavalry unit. Abbr.: **Tpr. 2** *US*= STATE TROOPER. **3** *informal* a resilient, hard-working, reliable, or uncomplaining person. ¶ Although historically this sense derives from *trouper*, 'a member of a troupe', it has become assimilated with *trooper* in the sense of 'a soldier', which has resulted in *trooper* becoming the more common spelling for this sense. **4** a cavalry horse. **5** esp. *Brit.* a troopship. □ **swear like a trooper** swear constantly.

troop·ship *noun* a ship used for transporting military troops.

trope /troːp/ *noun* a literary or rhetorical device consisting of the figurative use of a word or phrase. [Latin *tropus* from Greek *tropos* turn, way, trope, from *trepō* turn]

troph·ic /ˈtrɒfɪk/ *adjective* **1** of or concerned with nutrition (*trophic nerves*). **2** (of a hormone) stimulating the production or another specific hormone from an endocrine gland. [Greek *trophikos* from *trophē* nourishment, from *trephō* nourish]

-trophic /ˈtroːfɪk, ˈtrɒfɪk/ *combining form* **1** relating to nutrition (*autotrophic, oligotrophic*). **2** relating to maintenance or regulation, esp. by a hormone (*corticotrophic, gonadotrophic*). □ **-trophism, -trophy** *combining forms.*

tropho- /ˈtrɒfoː/ *combining form* nourishment.

tropho·blast /ˈtrɒfoːˌblast/ *noun* a layer of cells or a membrane surrounding an embryo, which supplies it with nourishment and later forms most of the placenta. □ **tropho·blas·tic** *adjective*

tro·phy /ˈtroːfi/ *noun* (*pl.* **-phies**) **1** an ornamental commemorative object, such as a gold or silver cup, awarded as a prize for excellence or an outstanding achievement, such as in sports or academics. **2** an animal or part of an animal captured in hunting and displayed as a memorial, e.g. a deer's antlers. **3** an animal that is hunted and usu. kept to prove the skill of the hunter (also *attributive: trophy fish*). **4** *derogatory* a person or thing regarded as having been obtained to enhance a person's status by association (also *attributive: trophy home; trophy wife*). **5** *Gk & Rom. Hist.* a structure consisting of the weapons etc. of a defeated army set up as a memorial of victory. [French *trophée* from Latin *trophaeum* from Greek *tropaion* from *tropē* rout, from *trepō* turn]

trop·ic ● *noun* **1** (**Tropic**) either of two terrestrial parallels of latitude 23°26′ north (**Tropic of Cancer**) or south (**Tropic of Capricorn**) of the equator, defining the torrid zone and representing, respectively, the northernmost and southernmost limits at which the sun can be directly overhead. **2** (**Tropic**) each of two corresponding circles on the celestial sphere where the sun appears to turn after reaching its greatest declination. **3** (in *pl.*) the region between the Tropics of Cancer and Capricorn; the torrid zone and parts immediately adjacent. ● *adjective* = TROPICAL 1. [Latin *tropicus* from Greek *tropikos* from *tropē* turning, from *trepō* turn]

-tropic *combining form* **1** turning towards (*heliotropic*). **2** affecting (*psychotropic*). **3** = -TROPHIC 2.

trop·ic·al ● *adjective* **1** pertaining to, occurring in, or characteristic of

t top   v voice   w we   z zoo   ʃ she   ʒ vision   θ thin   ð this   ŋ ring   x loch   tʃ chip   dʒ jar   (see over for vowels)

the tropics (*tropical rainforest*; *tropical diseases*). **2** resembling the tropics in climate; very hot and humid. **3** (esp. of clothing) suitable for wearing or using in the tropics (*a tropical shirt*). ● *noun* a tropical plant. □ **trop·ic·al·ly** *adverb*

tropical cyclone *noun* = CYCLONE 2.

tropical storm *noun* a tropical cyclone with winds ranging from 30 to 64 knots (63–118 km/h), often associated with heavy rain.

tropical year *noun* see YEAR 1.

tropic bird *noun* any seabird of the family Phaethontidae, with very long central tail feathers.

Tropic of Cancer *noun* see TROPIC noun 1.

Tropic of Capricorn *noun* see TROPIC noun 1.

trop·ism /ˈtroʊpɪzəm/ *noun* **1** *Biol.* the turning of all or part of an organism in a particular direction by growth, bending, or locomotion, in response to an external stimulus. **2** any sort of tendency or inclination. [Greek *tropos* turning, from *trepō* turn]

tropo·logic·al /ˌtrɒpəˈlɒdʒɪkəl/ *noun* **1** of, pertaining to, or involving the figurative use of words. **2** of, pertaining to, or involving a figurative interpretation, esp. of the Scriptures. □ **trop·ol·ogy** /trəˈpɒlədʒi/ *adjective* [Late Latin *tropologia* from Greek *tropologia* (as TROPE)]

tropo·pause /ˈtrɒpəˌpɔz, ˈtroʊ-/ *noun* the upper limit of the troposphere, separating it from the stratosphere, at which temperature ceases decreasing with height. [TROPOSPHERE + PAUSE]

tropo·sphere /ˈtrɒpəˌsfɪr, ˈtroʊ-/ *noun* the lowest region of the atmosphere, extending to a height of between 8 and 18 km and marked by convection and a general decrease of temperature with height (*compare* STRATOSPHERE, IONOSPHERE). □ **tropo·spher·ic** /-ˈsfiːrɪk, -ˈsfɛrɪk/ *adjective* [Greek *tropos* turning + SPHERE]

trop·po *adverb Music* too much (qualifying a tempo indication). □ **ma non troppo** but not too much. [Italian]

Trot *noun informal usu. derogatory* a Trotskyist. [abbreviation]

trot ● *verb* (**trot·ted, trot·ting**) **1** *intransitive* (of a person) run with short strides at a moderate pace. **2** *intransitive* (of a horse) proceed at a pace faster than a walk in which the legs move in diagonal pairs almost together. **3** *intransitive informal* walk, go. **4** *transitive* cause (esp. a horse) to proceed at a trot. ● *noun* **1** a trotting pace or gait (*proceed at a trot*). **2** a run at this pace (*he rounded the bases on his home run trot*). **3** (**the trots**) *slang* an attack of diarrhea. □ **on the trot** *informal* **1** continually busy (*kept them on the trot*). **2** *Brit.* in succession (*she won four on the trot*). **trot out 1** lead out and show off the paces of (a horse). **2** produce or introduce (as if) for inspection and approval, esp. tediously or predictably. [Old French *troter* from Romanic & medieval Latin *trottare*, of Germanic origin]

troth /troʊθ/ *noun archaic* **1** faith, loyalty. **2** truth. □ **plight** (or **pledge**) **one's troth** pledge one's word esp. in marriage or betrothal. [Middle English *trowthe*, for Old English *trēowth* TRUTH]

trot·line *noun* a length of line supporting shorter lines with baited hooks at intervals, strung across the width of a stream or river.

Trot·sky, Leon (born Lev Davidovich Bronstein) (1879–1940), Russian revolutionary. He helped to organize the October Revolution with Lenin, and built up the Red Army that eventually defeated the White Russian forces in the Russian Civil War; after Lenin's death he was defeated in the struggle for power by Stalin, exiled (1929), and murdered by a Stalinist assassin in Mexico.

Trot·sky·ism *noun* the political or economic principles of Trotsky, which called for a worldwide socialist revolution. □ **Trot·sky·ist** *noun* **Trot·sky·ite** *noun derogatory*.

trot·ter *noun* **1** a horse bred or trained for harness racing. **2** (usu. in *pl.*) **a** the foot of certain animals, esp. the pig, eaten as food. **b** *jocular* a human foot.

trot·ting *noun* = HARNESS RACING.

trou /traʊ/ *plural noun* □ **drop trou** esp. *US informal* (usu. of men) pull down one's pants; strip naked. [shortening of TROUSERS]

trou·ba·dour /ˈtruːbəˌdɔr/ *noun* **1** any of a number of French medieval lyric poets composing and singing in Provençal esp. on the themes of chivalry and courtly love, living in S France, E Spain, and N Italy between the 11th and 13th c. **2** a singer or poet. [French from Provençal *trobador* from *trobar* find, invent, compose in verse]

trouble ● *noun* **1 a** difficulty, problems, complications; a hard time (*we're having trouble with the car*). **b** disturbance of the mind or feelings; worry, distress. **2 a** inconvenience, bother; unpleasant or unnecessary exertion (*he went to a lot of trouble*). **b** a cause of this (*the child was no trouble*). **3** (usu. foll. by *with*) an annoying, disconcerting, or problematic

feature or aspect (*the trouble with you is your attitude; the trouble with Tuesday is that it's supposed to rain*). **4** a faulty condition or operation (*kidney trouble; engine trouble*). **5 a** fighting, disturbance (*this is a family establishment, we don't want any trouble*). **b** (in *pl.*) political or social unrest, public disturbances. **c** (**the Troubles**) any of various rebellions, civil wars, and periods of unrest in Ireland, esp. in 1919–23 and in Northern Ireland from 1968. **6** disagreement, strife (*she is having trouble at home; he and his wife are having trouble*). ● *verb* **1** *transitive* cause distress or anxiety to; disturb, worry (*we were troubled by the news*). **2** *transitive, intransitive, & reflexive* subject or be subjected to inconvenience, bother, or unpleasant exertion (*sorry to trouble you; don't trouble yourself; don't trouble to explain*). **3** *transitive* afflict; cause pain etc. to (*she is troubled with arthritis*). **4** *intransitive* be disturbed or worried (*don't trouble about it*). □ **ask for trouble** *informal* invite danger or difficulty by rash or indiscreet behaviour. **be no trouble** cause no inconvenience or nuisance. **go to the** (or **some**) **trouble** devote one's time or energy to do something. **in trouble 1** involved in a matter likely to bring censure or punishment. **2** *euphemism* pregnant while unmarried. **look for trouble** *informal* **1** aggressively seek to cause trouble. **2** invite trouble. **take the trouble** = GO TO THE TROUBLE. [Old French *truble* (n.), *turbler* (v.), ultimately from Latin *turbidus* TURBID]

trouble and strife *noun* esp. *Brit. rhyming slang* a wife.

troubled *adjective* **1 a** feeling worry, distress, anxiety, or apprehension (*a troubled mind*). **b** indicating worry or distress (*a troubled look*). **2** fraught with trouble, problems, unrest, turmoil, etc. (*a troubled childhood; the financially troubled company*). **3** physically unsettled or disturbed; not calm (*troubled waters*).

trouble-free *adjective* **1** free of problems, complications, or difficulties (*a trouble-free journey*). **2** that is unlikely to malfunction or require maintenance (*a trouble-free automobile*).

trouble light *noun N Amer.* a heavy-duty portable light fixture consisting of a socket enclosed in a steel cage powered by a long extension cord, that may be suspended by a hook to provide light for work conducted in poorly lit areas.

trouble·maker *noun* a person who habitually causes trouble. □ **trouble·making** *noun & attributive adjective*

trouble·shoot·er *noun* **1** a person who detects and corrects faults in machinery, computer equipment, etc. **2** a mediator who specializes in resolving esp. industrial or diplomatic disputes. □ **trouble·shoot** *transitive & intransitive verb* (*past* and *past participle* **-shot**). **trouble·shoot·ing** *noun*

trouble·some *adjective* **1** that causes problems or difficulty (*a troublesome child*). **2** distressing, worrisome, disconcerting (*troublesome news*). **3** fraught with problems, complications, or turmoil (*a troublesome period*). □ **trouble·some·ness** *noun*

trouble spot *noun* a place where difficulties regularly occur.

trough /trɒf/ *noun* **1 a** a long narrow open receptacle for water, animal feed, etc. **b** *jocular* the source of wealth or prosperity, characterized as a trough from which people feed greedily like pigs (*the trough of political patronage*). **2 a** a narrow channel or conduit for conveying a liquid. **b** = EAVESTROUGH. **3** *Meteorol.* an elongated region of low barometric pressure (*compare* RIDGE 4). **4** a hollow between two wave crests. **5** the lowest point of something, esp. the lowest level of economic activity or prosperity. **6 a** a broad elongated depression or valley; a narrow syncline (*Labrador Trough*). **b** an elongated depression of the sea floor. [Old English *trog* from Germanic]

trounce *transitive verb* **1** defeat decisively or convincingly. **2** beat, thrash. □ **troun·cing** *noun* [16th c., = afflict: origin unknown]

troupe /truːp/ *noun* a company of actors or dancers etc. [French, = TROOP]

trouper /ˈtruːpər/ *noun* **1** a member of esp. a theatrical troupe; a performer, esp. an experienced one. **2** = TROOPER 3.

trouser role *noun* a young male role played by a woman in an opera, play, etc.

trou·sers *plural noun* **1** an outer garment reaching from the waist usu. to the ankles, divided into two parts to cover the legs. *Also called* PANTS. **2** (**trou·ser**) (*attributive*) designating a part or parts of such a garment (*trouser leg; trouser pockets*). □ **wear the trousers** see WEAR[1]. □ **trou·sered** *adjective* **trouser·less** *adjective* [archaic *trouse* (sing.) from Irish & Gaelic *triubhas* TREWS: pl. form after *drawers*]

trouser suit *noun Brit.* = PANTSUIT.

trous·seau /ˈtruːsoʊ, truːˈsoʊ/ *noun* (*pl.* **trous·seaux** or **trous·seaus** /-soʊz/) the clothes collected by a bride for her marriage. [French, lit. bundle, diminutive of *trousse* TRUSS]

trousseau tea *noun Cdn dated* a party hosted by a bride's mother for neighbours and acquaintances, at which shower and wedding gifts, the bride's trousseau, contents of her hope chest, etc. are displayed.

trout *noun* (*pl.* same or **trouts**) **1** any of various freshwater fish of the genus *Salmo* of the northern hemisphere, valued as food. **2** a similar fish of the family Salmonidae (*see also* SALMON TROUT). **3** *slang derogatory* a woman, esp. an old or ill-tempered one. **4** *Cdn* (*Nfld*) *informal* a term of affectionate address (*that's right, me old trout*). [Old English *truht* from Late Latin *tructa*]

trout·ing *noun N Amer.* the action of fishing for trout, esp. as a recreational activity.

trout lily *noun* any of several plants of the genus *Erythronium*, with bell-shaped flowers and often mottled leaves.

trou·vaille /truːˈvaɪ/ *noun* **1** a lucky find or discovery. **2** a sudden inspiration, thought, or idea. [French from *trouver* find]

trou·vère /truːˈvɛr/ *noun* any of a group of French medieval poets composing *chansons de geste* and fabliaux, living in N France between the 11th and 14th c. [Old French *trovere* from *trover* find: compare TROUBADOUR]

trove *noun* = TREASURE TROVE. [Anglo-French *trové* from *trover* find]

trov·er *noun Law* **1** the action of finding and assuming possession of personal property. **2** a common-law action to recover the value of personal property illegally converted by another to his or her own use. [Old French *trover* find]

trow /traʊ, troʊ/ *transitive verb archaic* think, believe. [Old English *trūwian*, *trēowian*, related to TRUCE]

Trow·bridge /ˈtroʊbrɪdʒ/ a town in SW England, the county town of Wiltshire; pop. (2002) 31,200.

trow·el /ˈtraʊəl/ ● *noun* **1** a small hand-held tool with a flat metal blade, used to apply and spread mortar, cement, plaster, etc. **2** a hand-held gardening tool resembling a small shovel, consisting of a pointed scoop-like blade attached to a handle, used for lifting plants or earth. ● *transitive verb* (**trow·elled, trow·el·ling**; esp. *US* **trow·eled, trow·eling**) **1** dig, move, or apply with a trowel. **2** apply plaster etc. to (a wall etc.) with a trowel. [Old French *truele* from Latin *trulla* scoop, diminutive of *trua* ladle etc.]

Troy in Homeric legend, the city of King Priam that was besieged for ten years by the Greeks. Once thought to exist only in legend, it is now believed to have been situated on the NE Aegean coast of Turkey until it was sacked and destroyed by fire in the mid-13th c. BC.

troy *noun* (in full **troy weight**) a system of weights used for precious metals and gems, based on a pound of 12 ounces or 5,760 grains (also *attributive*: *troy ounce*). [Middle English, prob. from TROYES[1], the French town where the system was first used.]

Troyes[1] /trwɑ/ a town in N France, on the Seine River; pop. (1999) 60,958. It was capital of the former province of Champagne.

Troyes[2] see CHRÉTIEN DE TROYES.

trs. *abbreviation* transpose (letters or words etc.).

tru·ant /ˈtruːənt/ ● *noun* **1** a student who stays away from school without leave or explanation. **2** a person absent from work. ● *adjective* (of a person or behaviour etc.) idle, wandering, negligent, shirking, absent. ● *intransitive verb* (also **play truant**) be absent or stay away from school or work. □ **truan·cy** *noun* (*pl.* **-cies**). [Old French, prob. ultimately from Celtic: compare Welsh *truan*, Gaelic *truaghan* wretched]

truant officer *noun N Amer.* a person charged with investigating truancy.

truce *noun* **1** a temporary suspension of hostilities, usu. for a limited period, between warring armies or factions or between bickering individuals in a private feud or quarrel. **2** an agreement or treaty effecting this. [Middle English *trew(e)s* (pl.) from Old English *trēow*, related to TRUE]

Tru·cial States a group of Arab sheikdoms on the Persian Gulf, since 1971 forming the United Arab Emirates. The Trucial States had a special treaty relationship with Britain following the signing of a maritime truce in 1836.

truck[1] ● *noun* **1** esp. *N Amer.* any of various kinds of large sturdy road vehicle used for a variety of purposes. **2 a** any of a variety of wheeled carts and platforms used to transport goods. **b** (in full **hand truck**) a sturdy upright metal frame with two wheels and a short perpendicular shelf used to move large appliances, boxes, etc. **3** a pivoted undercarriage with two or more pairs of wheels, mounted to the underside of a railway car. **4** each of two axle units on a skateboard or roller skate, to which the wheels are attached. **5** *Brit.* an open railway vehicle for carrying freight. **6 a** *Naut.* a wooden disc at the top of a mast

with holes for halyards. **b** a small solid wheel or roller. ● *verb* **1** *transitive* deliver or convey by truck. **2** *intransitive N Amer.* drive a truck, esp. for a living. **3** *intransitive N Amer. informal* go or proceed at a casual pace. □ **truck·ful** *noun* [perhaps short for TRUCKLE in sense 'wheel, pulley']

truck[2] ● *noun* **1** the action or practice of bartering or trading by exchange of commodities. **2** esp. *US* fruit and vegetables grown for sale (*truck crops*). **3** *informal* small miscellaneous items or wares; odds and ends. **4** esp. *hist.* **a** the payment of wages in kind or as vouchers rather than money. **b** (in full **truck system**) the system or practice of such payment. ● *transitive & intransitive verb* deal, barter, exchange. □ **have no truck with** avoid dealing, interacting, or associating with. [Old French *troquer* (unrecorded) = *trocare*, of unknown origin]

truck bomb *noun* a terrorist bomb concealed in or under a truck.

truck·er *noun* esp. *N Amer.* **1** a person who drives a truck, esp. a person who drives a transport truck or tractor-trailer etc. for a living. **2** a company dealing in long-distance transportation of goods.

truck farm *noun* esp. *US* a usu. small farm growing fruit and vegetables for sale; a market garden. □ **truck farmer** *noun* **truck farming** *noun*

truck·ing *noun N Amer.* the action or business of transporting goods by truck.

truckle *intransitive verb* (foll. by *to*) assume a subordinate or inferior position; submit, yield, back down. [originally = 'sleep in a truckle bed', from obsolete *truckle* wheel, pulley, from Anglo-French *trocle* from Latin *trochlea* pulley]

truckle bed *noun Brit.* = TRUNDLE BED.

truck·load *noun* esp. *N Amer.* **1** the quantity of goods that is or can be transported in a truck. **2** (usu. foll. by *of*) *informal* a large quantity or amount. □ **by the truckload** in large quantities or amounts.

truck stop *noun N Amer.* a roadside restaurant or diner, often having a gas station on the premises, catering to highway travellers, esp. truckers.

trucu·lent /ˈtrʌkjʊlənt/ *adjective* **1** vehemently defiant. **2** aggressive, belligerent, pugnacious. **3** fierce, vicious, scathing. □ **trucu·lence** *noun* **trucu·lent·ly** *adverb* [Latin *truculentus* from *trux trucis* fierce]

Tru·deau /truːˈdoʊ, ˈtruːdoʊ/ Pierre (El·liott) (1919–2000), Canadian politician, Liberal prime minister of Canada 1968–79 and 1980–4. As prime minister, he was noted for his commitment to federalism and official bilingualism. Trudeau also achieved the transfer of remaining constitutional powers from Britain to Canada in 1982 and the entrenchment of individual and minority rights in the Canadian Charter of Rights and Freedoms.

Trudeau·mania /ˌtruːdoʊˈmeɪniə/ *noun Cdn* widespread popularity of, and fascination with, Pierre Elliott Trudeau among the Canadian public, esp. during the election campaign of 1968.

trudge ● *verb* **1** *intransitive* walk laboriously, or without energy or spirit, but steadily and persistently. **2** *transitive* travel (a road or specified distance etc.) in this way. ● *noun* a steady laborious walk. □ **trudg·er** *noun* [16th c.: origin unknown]

true ● *adjective* **1** in accordance or consistent with fact or reality (*a true story*). **2** genuine, authentic; really or strictly so called; not spurious or counterfeit (*a true friend; the true heir to the throne*). **3** (often foll. by *to*) loyal or faithful (*true to one's word*). **4** (foll. by *to*) closely conforming (to a standard or expectation etc.) (*true to form; true to life*). **5** correctly positioned, fitted, balanced, or aligned; level, square. **6** exact, accurate, precise (*a true aim; a true copy*). **7** (also **it is true**) certainly, admittedly (*true, it would cost more, but it would be worth it*). **8** (of a compass bearing) measured relative to true north. **9** reliable, trusty, sure (*a true sign*). **10** *archaic* honest, upright (*twelve good men and true*). ● *adverb* **1** in a sincere or genuine manner; truly (*tell me true*). **2** accurately (*aim true*). **3** conforming with the ancestral type; without variation (*breed true*). ● *transitive verb* (**trues, trued, tru·ing** or **true·ing**) (often foll. by *up*) bring into the correct, exact, or required form, position, alignment, shape, etc. □ **come true** actually happen or transpire; be realized. **out of true** not in the correct or exact position. **too good to be true** better than one could have hoped or imagined. **true to form** (or **type**) being or behaving as expected. **true to life** accurately representing or consistent with real life (also *attributive*: *true-to-life example*). □ **true·ness** *noun* [Old English *trēowe*, *trȳwe*, from the Germanic noun represented by TRUCE]

true believer *noun* **1** a person who trusts or sincerely believes (*she is a true believer in homeopathic remedies*). **2** an ardent or fanatical supporter of esp. a political or religious movement or cause; a zealot (also *attributive*: *a true-believer environmentalist*). □ **true-believing** *adjective*

uː mo**o**d   aɪ my   ɔɪ p**i**pe   aʊ br**o**wn   ʌʊ h**o**use   eɪ day   ɔɪ boy   ā fr**a**nglais   ã Canadien   ɔ̄ Brayon   (*see over for consonants*)

true bill *noun US* a bill of indictment found by a grand jury to be supported by sufficient evidence to justify the hearing of a case.

true-blue *adjective* **1** steadfastly loyal or devoted. **2** real; genuine.

true-born *adjective* of genuine or legitimate birth.

true-false *adjective* (also **true and false**) **1** designating a type of test question consisting of a statement designed to elicit either the response 'true' or 'false'. **2** designating a test consisting of such questions.

true grit *noun* strength of character.

true-heart·ed *adjective* faithful, loyal.

true horizon *noun see* HORIZON 1c.

true life *noun* **1** reality; actual life or existence. **2** (*attributive*; usu. **true-life**) designating things resembling or occurring in reality (*a true-life story*).

true love *noun* **1** genuine love. **2** a sweetheart.

true north *noun* **1** north according to the earth's axis, not magnetic north. **2** (**True North**, prec. by *the*) *Cdn informal* or *jocular* Canada.

Truf·faut /truːˈfoʊ/ **Fran·çois** (1932–84), French film director, producer, writer, and actor. In 1959 he directed his first feature film, *Les Quatre cents coups*, a work which established him as a leading director of the *nouvelle vague*; his other films include *Jules et Jim* (1961), *La Nuit américaine* (1973); *Day for Night*, which won an Oscar for best foreign film, and *The Last Metro* (1980).

truf·fle *noun* **1** any strong-smelling underground fungus of the order Tuberales, regarded as a great culinary delicacy and collected in France and N Italy with the help of trained dogs or pigs. **2** a round soft chocolate, often flavoured with alcohol. [prob. from Dutch *truffel* from obsolete French *truffle*, ultimately from Latin *tubera* pl. of TUBER]

truf·fled *adjective* stuffed or garnished with truffles.

trug *noun Brit.* a shallow oblong basket usu. made of wooden strips and used esp. for carrying garden produce, flowers, etc. [perhaps a dial. var. of TROUGH]

tru·ism *noun* **1** a self-evident or indisputable truth, esp. a trivial or hackneyed one, e.g. *nothing lasts forever*. **2** a proposition that states nothing beyond what is implied in any of its terms. □ **tru·is·tic** *adjective*

Tru·jil·lo¹ /truːˈhiːjɔː/ a city on the coast of NW Peru; pop. (2002) 600,900.

Tru·jil·lo² /truːˈhiːjɔː/ **Rafael** (born Rafael Léonidas Trujillo Molina; known as 'Generalissimo') (1891–1961), Dominican leader, president of the Dominican Republic 1930–8 and 1942–52. Although he was formally president for only two periods, he wielded dictatorial powers from 1930 until his assassination in 1961.

Truk Islands /trʌk/ a group of about fourteen volcanic islands and atolls in the W Pacific, in the Caroline Islands group, forming part of the Federated States of Micronesia; pop. (est. 2002) 77,900. It was the site of a Japanese naval base during the Second World War.

trull *noun archaic* a prostitute. [16th c.: compare German *Trulle*, TROLLOP]

truly *adverb* **1 a** sincerely, genuinely (*truly grieved*). **b** (used as an emphatic affirmative) very, really (*I am truly frustrated*). **2** really, indeed (*truly, I do not know*). **3** faithfully, loyally (*served them truly*). **4** accurately, truthfully (*is not truly depicted; has been truly stated*). **5** rightly, properly (*well and truly*). **6** used in formulaic closings of letters (*yours truly*).

Tru·man, Harry S. (1884–1972), US Democratic politician, 33rd president of the US 1945–53. He authorized the use of the atomic bomb against Hiroshima and Nagasaki (1945), and his administration introduced the Marshall Plan of emergency aid to war-shattered European countries (1948) and helped to establish NATO (1949); he later involved the US in the Korean War. □ **Truman·esque** *adjective*

Truman Doctrine *noun hist.* the principle that the US should give support to countries or peoples threatened by Soviet forces or Communist insurrection. First expressed in 1947 by Harry Truman, the doctrine was seen by the Communists as an open declaration of the Cold War.

trump¹ ● *noun* **1** (in *pl.*) *Cards* the suit determined, usu. by cutting or bidding, to rank above the other three during a deal or game (*hearts are trumps*). **2** (in full **trump card**) **a** a playing card of this suit. **b** a card cut or turned up to determine this suit. **3** (in full **trump card**) an important resource available to a person but held, usu. secretly, in reserve until an opportune moment when it may be used or revealed to gain a decisive advantage; a secret weapon. **4** *informal* an admirable, helpful, or reliable person. ● *verb* **1 a** *transitive* defeat (a card or its player) with a trump. **b** *intransitive* play a trump card when another suit has been led. **2** *transitive informal* **a** foil or thwart (a person, proposal,

etc.), esp. with an unexpected move at the last minute or by means of a previously secret resource. **b** surpass; gain an unexpected advantage over. □ **trump up** fabricate or invent (an accusation, excuse, etc.). **turn up trumps** *Brit. informal* **1** turn out better than expected. **2** be greatly successful or helpful. [corruption of TRIUMPH in the same (now obsolete) sense]

trump² *noun archaic* the sound or a blast of a trumpet (*the final trump*). [Old French *trompe* from Frankish: prob. imitative]

trumped-up *adjective* (of a charge, allegation, etc.) fabricated, invented.

trump·ery ● *noun* (pl. **-eries**) **1** a worthless, useless, or trifling article. **2** nonsense, garbage. **3** worthless finery. ● *adjective* **1** showy but of little use or value (*trumpery jewels*). **2** delusive, shallow, empty (*trumpery arguments*). [Old French *tromperie* from *tromper* deceive]

trum·pet ● *noun* **1 a** any of a family of brass wind instruments with a bright, powerful, and penetrating tone, consisting of a straight or curved tube with a flared bell and most commonly three valves. **b** a person who plays or is playing a trumpet. **2** anything resembling a trumpet in shape, such as the tubular corona of a daffodil. **3** anything resembling the sound of a trumpet. ● *verb* (**trum·pet·ed**, **trum·pet·ing**) **1** *transitive* herald, announce, celebrate, or proclaim loudly. **2** *intransitive* **a** blow or play a trumpet. **b** make a loud sound like that of a trumpet (*the angry elephant trumpeted in the jungle*). [Old French *trompette* diminutive (as TRUMP²)]

trumpet creeper *noun* = TRUMPET VINE.

trum·pet·er *noun* **1** a person who plays a trumpet. **2 a** any of various birds having a loud cry resembling the sound of a trumpet, including each of three crane-like birds of the family Psophiidae, which are stout ground-dwelling birds of S American forests. **b** a particular variety of domestic pigeon.

trumpeter swan *noun* a large N American wild swan, *Cygnus buccinator*, with a black bill and a loud, trumpet-like, guttural call.

trumpet honeysuckle *noun* an evergreen scarlet-flowered honeysuckle, *Lonicera sempervirens*, of the eastern US.

trumpet vine *noun* (also **trumpet creeper**) either of two climbing shrubs constituting the genus *Campsis* of the Bignoniaceae family, with orange or red trumpet-shaped flowers, *C. radicans* of the eastern US, and the Chinese *C. grandiflora*.

trun·cate ● *transitive verb* /ˈtrʌŋkeɪt, trʌŋˈkeɪt/ **1** shorten or diminish by cutting off the top or end part of; cut short, mutilate. **2** *Geom.* & *Mineralogy* replace (an edge or a vortex) with a plane face, esp. so as to make equal angles with the adjacent faces; ● *adjective* /ˈtrʌŋkeɪt/ *Bot.* & *Zool.* ending abruptly as if cut off transversely at the base or tip. □ **trun·ca·tion** *noun* [Latin *truncare truncat-* maim]

trun·cat·ed *adjective* **1 a** having been shortened or reduced by or as if by cutting or mutilation. **b** limited in depth or scope; narrow (*a truncated view*). **2** *Geom.* & *Mineralogy* (of a figure, crystal, etc.) having an edge or vortex replaced by a plane face, esp. one equally inclined to the adjacent faces. **3** *Bot.* & *Zool.* = TRUNCATE.

trun·cheon /ˈtrʌntʃən/ *noun* **1** *Brit.* a short club or cudgel, esp. carried by a police officer. **2** a staff or baton carried as a symbol of office or authority. [Old French *tronchon* stump, ultimately from Latin *truncus* trunk]

trun·dle *verb* **1** *intransitive* move or roll on a wheel or wheels, esp. heavily or noisily. **2** *intransitive* go or move, esp. heavily, noisily, or at a steady pace. **3** *transitive* push (a wheeled vehicle) along. [Old English *trendel* circle (as TREND)]

trundle bed *noun* esp. *N Amer.* a low bed on wheels that can be stored under a larger bed.

trunk *noun* **1** the main stem of a tree as distinct from its branches and roots. **2** the human body, or that of an animal, considered apart from the limbs and head. **3** the mobile elongated prehensile snout of an elephant, containing the passages to the nostrils and also used to draw in and spray water for cooling. **4** a large box with a hinged lid for transporting luggage, clothes, etc. **5** *N Amer.* a compartment at the rear of most cars, used to transport luggage etc. **6** (in *pl.*) a man's garment worn for swimming, boxing, etc., either loose-fitting shorts or close-fitting briefs. **7** the main part of any structure, esp. one that branches off into smaller parts (*water flows from tributary valleys into the trunk valley*). **8** the main body of a blood vessel, artery, or nerve etc. **9** an enclosed duct or conduit for cables, ventilation, etc. □ **trunk·ful** *noun* (pl. **-fuls**). **trunk·less** *adjective* [Old French *tronc* from Latin *truncus*]

trunk·ing *noun* a system or an arrangement of electrical or telephone lines or cables, or of conduits for these.

trunk line *noun* **1** a main railway line or route. **2** a large or main pipeline for oil or gas, esp. one from a production field to a refinery or terminal. **3** a telephone line running between exchanges.

trunk road noun **1** Cdn an access road, esp. one used for logging. **2** (also **trunk route**) esp. Brit. an important main road.

trun·nel noun = TREENAIL.

trun·nion noun **1** either of a pair of cylindrical projections on opposite sides of a cannon or mortar, by which it is pivoted on its carriage. **2** either of any similar pair of opposing pins or pivots on which a piece of machinery is supported. [French trognon core, tree trunk, of unknown origin]

Truro /ˈtrʊrɔː, ˈtrʊrɒ/ **1** the county town of Cornwall, in SW England; pop. (1998) 16,900. **2** a town in north central Nova Scotia, situated about 100 km northeast of Halifax; pop. (2001) 11,457. □ **Truro·nian** noun [sense 2 after sense 1]

truss ● noun **1** a metal or wooden structural framework, esp. consisting of rafters, posts, and struts, supporting a roof or bridge etc. **2** a medical device used to provide even pressure on a hernia, usu. consisting of a padded belt fitted with straps. **3** a compact terminal cluster of flowers or fruit. **4** a large corbel supporting a monument. **5** Naut. a heavy iron ring securing the lower yards to a mast. ● transitive verb **1** tie or skewer the wings and legs of (a fowl etc.) to the body for cooking. **2** (often foll. by up) tie up (a person) by binding the arms close to the body. **3** support (a roof or bridge etc.) with a truss or trusses. □ **truss·er** noun [Old French trusser (v.), trusse (n.), of unknown origin]

trust ● noun **1 a** faith or confidence in the loyalty, veracity, reliability, strength, etc., of a person or thing. **b** the state or condition of being trusted or relied on. **2** the obligation or responsibility placed on a person who is trusted or relied on (she is in a position of trust). **3** reliance on the truth of a statement etc. without examination. **4** a confident expectation. **5** a person or thing upon whom one relies or depends (God is our sole trust). **6** a thing or person committed to one's care; a charge. **7** Law **a** the fiduciary obligation placed on a person by making that person the nominal owner of property to be used for the enjoyment and benefit of another. **b** the property or estate held in this way. **c** the legal relationship between the nominal owner and the property. **8 a** a body of trustees. **b** an organization managed by trustees. **9** a group of associated companies in a particular area of business, organized to reduce or defeat competition, lessen mutual expenses, etc., esp. one in which a central committee of trustees holds a majority or all of the stock and has a controlling vote in each company, prohibited by law in some jurisdictions, including the US. **10** commercial credit (obtained goods on trust). ● verb **1** transitive **a** have or place faith or confidence in the loyalty, veracity, reliability, honour, etc. of (a person or thing). **b** (foll. by to + clause) rely upon; have confidence in the ability of (a person or thing) (I trust our dog to come when called). **2** transitive (foll. by with) allow (a person) to have, use, or be responsible for something with confidence that it will be properly used or cared for (I would trust him with my life). **3** transitive believe the veracity of (a person or statement etc.) (I seldom trust what I read in that newspaper). **4** transitive (often foll. by that + clause) have faith, confidence, or hope that a thing is occurring or will occur (I trust you will not be late; I trust that she is recovering). **5** intransitive (foll. by in) place reliance on (we trust in you). **6** intransitive (foll. by to) place (esp. undue) reliance on (shall have to trust to luck). **7** transitive (foll. by for) allow credit to (a customer) for goods. □ **in trust** Law held on the basis of trust (see sense 7 of noun). **on trust 1** on credit. **2** on the basis of trust or confidence. **take on trust** accept (an assertion, claim, etc.) without evidence or investigation. **not trust a person as far as one can throw him or her** not trust a person at all. **trust a person to do something!** it is characteristic or predictable for a person to act in such a way (trust her to be late, she always is!). □ **trust·able** adjective

trust·ed adjective **trust·er** noun [Old Norse traust from traustr strong: (v.) from Old Norse treysta, assimilated to the noun]

trust·a·far·ian noun esp. Brit. a wealthy young (white) person with a bohemian lifestyle. [blend of TRUST (in TRUST FUND) and RASTAFARIAN]

trust·bust·er noun esp. US a person or agency employed to dissolve trusts, esp. a government official responsible for the enforcement of antitrust legislation. □ **trust·bust·ing** noun & adjective

trust company noun a company formed to act as a trustee or to deal with trusts, esp. one that offers banking services.

trust·ee noun **1** Law a person given control or powers of administration of property held in trust with a legal obligation to administer it solely for the purposes specified. **2** any of a group of people appointed to manage the affairs of an institution etc. **3** Cdn an elected member of a school board. **4** a state made responsible for the government of an area. □ **trustee·ship** noun

trust·ful adjective inclined to trust; not feeling or showing suspicion. □ **trust·ful·ly** adverb **trust·ful·ness** noun

trust fund ● noun a fund of money, securities, etc. held in trust. ● (**trust-fund**) adjective derogatory (of a young person) financially supported, usu. by wealthy parents or other relatives, and thus spared the need to work hard for a living (trust-fund baby).

trust·ing adjective inclined to trust others, esp. characteristically; trustful. □ **trust·ing·ly** adverb **trust·ing·ness** noun

trust territory noun a territory under the trusteeship of the United Nations or of a country designated by them.

trust·worthy adjective deserving of trust; reliable, dependable, etc. □ **trust·worthi·ness** noun

trusty ● adjective (**trust·i·er, trust·i·est**) archaic or jocular trustworthy (a trusty steed). ● noun (pl. **-ies**) informal a prisoner who is given special privileges for good behaviour. □ **trust·i·ly** adverb **trust·i·ness** noun

Truth, So·jour·ner (adopted name of Isabella Van Wagener) (c.1797–1883), US abolitionist and feminist. She was born into slavery, freed in 1827, and spent the remainder of her life campaigning for the women's rights movement and for the abolition of slavery; she published The Narrative of Sojourner Truth in 1850.

truth noun (pl. **truths** /truːθs, truːðz/) **1** the quality or a state of being true; conformity to fact or reality; genuineness, authenticity (she doubted the truth of the statement; there may be some truth in it). **2 a** what is true; the matter or circumstance as it really is (I want to discover the truth about what happened that night; the truth of the matter is that I forgot). **b** a true statement; a report or account consistent with fact and reality. **3** something held or accepted as true; a fixed or established principle (one of the fundamental truths). **4** accuracy of delineation or representation, esp. in art or literature; lifelike quality. **5** ideal or spiritual reality as a subject of revelation or an object of esp. philosophical or religious interpretation or quest. □ **in truth** literary truly, really. **to tell the truth** (also **if truth be told** or **truth to tell**) to be honest; frankly. [Old English triewth, trēowth (as TRUE)]

truth commission noun an official body charged with the investigation of claims of human rights abuses, esp. during a previous government or regime.

truth·ful adjective **1** habitually speaking the truth; sincere, honest. **2** (of an artistic or literary representation etc.) accurate, realistic, true to life. **3** (of a story etc.) true. □ **truth·ful·ly** adverb **truth·ful·ness** noun

Truth or Dare noun a game in which each participant, in turn, must choose between answering honestly a personal question or carrying out a dare put to him or her by one of the other players.

truth serum noun (also **truth drug**) any of various drugs supposedly able to induce a person to tell the truth.

truth squad noun Politics a group of people with the task of questioning the truth of statements made by members of an opposing party.

truth table noun **1** Logic a tabular representation of the truth or falsity of a complex proposition as determined by the possible combinations of truth values of its components. **2** Computing a table representing the outputs from all possible combinations of input.

truth value noun Logic the value of truth or falsehood assigned to a proposition considered within a certain set of conditions.

try ● verb (**tries, tried**) **1** intransitive make an effort with a view to success (often foll. by to + infin.; informal foll. by and + infin.: tried to be on time; try and be early; I shall try hard). ¶ Use with and is uncommon in the past tense and in negative contexts (except in imperative). **2** transitive make an effort to achieve (tried my best; had better try something easier). **3** transitive **a** test (the quality of a thing) by use or experiment. **b** test the qualities of (a person or thing) (try it before you buy; have you tried the salad?). **4** transitive make severe demands on (a person, quality, etc.) (my patience has been sorely tried). **5** transitive examine the effectiveness or usefulness of for a purpose (try cold water; have you tried kicking it?). **6** transitive ascertain the state of fastening of (a door, window, etc.). **7** transitive **a** investigate and decide (a case or issue) judicially. **b** subject (a person) to trial (will be tried for murder). **8** transitive make an experiment in order to find out (let us try which takes longest). **9** intransitive (foll. by for) **a** apply or compete for. **b** seek to reach or attain (am going to try for a gold medal). **10** transitive (often foll. by out) **a** extract (oil) from fat by heating. **b** treat (fat) in this way. ● noun (pl. **tries**) **1** an effort to accomplish something; an attempt (give it a try). **2** Rugby the act of touching the ball down behind the opposing goal line, scoring points and entitling the scoring side to a kick at goal. □ **try (on) for size** try out or test for suitability. **try one's hand** see how skilful one is, esp. at the first attempt. **try it on** *Brit. informal* **1** test another's patience. **2** attempt to outwit or deceive another person. **try on** put on (clothes etc.) to see if they fit or suit the wearer. **try out 1 a** put to the test. **b** test thoroughly. **2** esp. *N Amer.* (often foll. by *for*) undergo a test in the hope of being selected for a role, a position on a sports team, etc; audition. [Middle English, = separate, distinguish, etc., from Old French *trier* sift, of unknown origin]

try·ing *adjective* annoying, vexatious; hard to endure.

try·out *noun* esp. *N Amer.* (often in *pl.*) **1** a test of the qualities or performance of a person or thing. **2** a gathering of prospective members of a team, troupe, etc. for such testing.

tryp·ano·some /'trɪpənə,soːm, trɪ'panə-/ *noun Med.* any protozoan parasite of the genus *Trypanosoma* having a long trailing flagellum and infesting the blood etc. [Greek *trupanon* borer + -SOME³]

tryp·ano·som·ia·sis /,trɪpənəsə'maɪəsɪs, trɪ'panə-/ *noun* any of several diseases caused by a trypanosome and usu. transmitted by biting insects, including sleeping sickness and Chagas' disease.

tryp·sin /'trɪpsɪn/ *noun* a digestive enzyme which hydrolyzes proteins, and is secreted by the pancreas. □ **tryp·tic** *adjective* [Greek *tripsis* friction, from *tribō* rub (because it was first obtained by rubbing down the pancreas with glycerine)]

tryp·to·phan /'trɪptə,fan/ *noun Biochem.* an amino acid essential in the diet of vertebrates. [as TRYPSIN + -*phan* from Greek *phainō* appear]

try·sail /'traɪsəl/ *noun* a small strong fore-and-aft sail set on the mainmast or other mast of a sailing vessel in heavy weather.

try square *noun* an L-shaped carpenter's square for verifying right angles.

tryst /trɪst/ ● *noun* an esp. secret meeting between lovers. ● *intransitive verb* keep a tryst. [Middle English, variant of obsolete *trist* an appointed station in hunting, from French *triste* or medieval Latin *trista, tristra*]

Tsao-chuang see ZAOZHUANG.

tsar *var. of* CZAR.

tsar·evich *var. of* CZAREVICH.

tsar·ina *var. of* CZARINA.

Tsar·it·syn /tsɒ'riːtsɪn/ a former name (until 1925) for VOLGOGRAD.

Tsaw·was·sen /tsə'wɒsən/ part of the district municipality of Delta, BC, where the principal ferry terminal for service to Vancouver Island is located. [Halkomelem, = 'looking towards the sea']

TSE *abbreviation hist.* Toronto Stock Exchange.

tse·tse /'tsiːtsi, 'tiːtsi/ *noun* any fly of the genus *Glossina* native to Africa, that feeds on human and animal blood with a needle-like proboscis and transmits trypanosomiasis (sleeping sickness). [Setswana]

TSH *abbreviation* thyroid-stimulating hormone.

T-shirt *noun* (also **tee-shirt**) a short-sleeved casual top, usu. of a cotton knit fabric and having the form of a T when spread out. □ **T-shirt·ed** *adjective*

Tsilh·qot'in /tsɪl'koːtɪn/ ● *noun* **1** a member of an Athapaskan people inhabiting the basin of the Chilcotin River valley, between the Coast Mountains and the Fraser River in BC. **2** the Athapaskan language of this people. ● *adjective* of or relating to this people or their culture or language. [Tsilhqot'in, = 'ochre river people', in reference to red and yellow mineral substances used for dyes]

Tsim·shian /'tsɪmʃiːən, -ʃən/ ● *noun* (*pl.* same or **Tsim·shians**) **1** a member of a group of Aboriginal peoples living in coastal and interior northern BC. **2** the group of languages spoken by the Tsimshian and related Aboriginal peoples. ● *adjective* of or relating to this people or their culture or language. [Tsimshian *čamsián*, lit. 'inside the Skeena River']

Tsi·nan see JINAN.

Tsing·hai see QINGHAI.

Tsi·tsi·kamma Forest /,tsiːtsiː'kɒmə/ an area of dense natural forest, now a national park, on the south coast of South Africa.

tsk *interjection, noun, & verb* (also **tsk tsk**; *verb* **tsk-tsk**) = TUT (*see* TUT-TUT).

Tskhin·vali /'tskɪnvəli/ the capital of South Ossetia.

Tson·ga /'tsɒŋɡə/ *noun* **1** (*pl.* same or **-gas**) a member of a people living in Transvaal, southern Mozambique, and southern Zimbabwe. **2** the Bantu language of this people. [a local name, from either Tsonga or Zulu]

tso·tsi /'tsɒtsi/ *noun* (*pl.* **tso·tsis**) (in S Africa) a young black urban criminal. [perhaps a Sotho corruption of ZOOT SUIT]

TSP *abbreviation* TRISODIUM PHOSPHATE.

tsp. *abbreviation* teaspoonful.

T-square *noun* a T-shaped instrument for drawing parallel lines or right angles.

TSR *noun Computing* a program which stays in the computer's memory once it has been executed and remains ready to be reactivated instantly, without subsequently-activated programs needing to be terminated. [terminate and stay resident]

TSS *abbreviation* TOXIC SHOCK SYNDROME.

tsu·nami /tsuː'nɒmi/ *noun* (*pl.* **tsu·namis**) a long high sea wave caused by underwater earthquakes or other disturbances. *Also called* TIDAL WAVE. [Japanese from *tsu* harbour + *nami* wave]

tsu·ris /'tsuːris/ *noun* esp. *US informal* trouble, woe. [Yiddish *tsores*, pl. of *tsore* 'trouble']

Tsu·shima /tsuː'ʃiːmə/ a Japanese island in the Korea Strait, between S Korea and Japan. In 1905 it was the scene of the destruction of a Russian naval fleet by the Japanese.

Tsuu T'ina /tsuː'tɪnə/ *noun* = SARCEE. [Sarcee, = 'many people']

Tswana /'tswɒnə/ *noun* (also **Se·tswa·na** /se'tswɒnə/) **1** a southern African people living in Botswana and neighbouring areas. **2** a member of this people. **3** = SETSWANA. ¶ *Setswana* is now the preferred form for the language. [Bantu (compare SETSWANA)]

TSX *abbreviation* Toronto Stock Exchange.

TTL *abbreviation* (*attributive*) *Photog.* designating the viewing or metering of a subject through the lens of a camera rather than through a separate viewfinder or meter. [through the lens]

TTY *abbreviation* teletypewriter.

TTYL *abbreviation* talk to you later.

TU *abbreviation* Trade Union.

Tu. *abbreviation* Tuesday.

Tua·motu Archipelago /,tuːə'moːtuː/ a group of about 80 coral islands forming part of French Polynesia, in the S Pacific; pop. (2002) 18,300. It is the largest group of coral atolls in the world. The islands of Mururoa and Fangataufa have been used by the French since 1966 for nuclear testing.

Tua·reg /'twɑreg/ ● *noun* (*pl.* same or **Tua·regs**) **1** a member of a Berber group of nomads of the western and central Sahara, now concentrated mainly in Algeria, Mali, Niger, and western Libya. **2** the Berber dialect of the Tuareg. ● *adjective* of or relating to this people or their language. [Berber]

tua·tara /,tuːə'tɑrə/ *noun* a large lizard-like reptile, *Sphenodon punctatus*, unique to certain small islands of New Zealand, having a crest of soft spines extending along its back. [Maori from *tua* on the back + *tara* spine]

Tuatha Dé Dan·aan /,tuhə dei 'danən/ *plural noun Irish Myth* the members of an ancient race who inhabited Ireland before the historical Irish. Formerly believed to have been a real people, they are credited with the possession of magical powers and great wisdom. [Irish, = people of the goddess Danaan]

tub ● *noun* **1** an open flat-bottomed usu. round container for various purposes. **2** a bathtub. **3** a tub-shaped (usu. plastic) carton. **4** the amount a tub will hold. **5 a** *informal* a clumsy slow boat. **b** a stout roomy boat for rowing practice. **6** (in mining) a container for conveying ore, coal, etc. **7** *informal* (usu. *derogatory*) a fat person. ● *transitive & intransitive verb* (**tubbed**, **tub·bing**) plant, place, bathe, or wash in a tub. □ **tub·ful** *noun* (*pl.* **-fuls**). [Middle English, prob. of Low German or Dutch origin: compare Middle Low German, Middle Dutch *tubbe*]

tuba /'tuːbə, 'tjuːbə/ *noun* (*pl.* **tubas**) **1** a large, very low-pitched valved brass wind instrument. **2** a tuba player. [Italian from Latin, = trumpet]

tubal /'tuːbəl, 'tjuːbəl/ *adjective Anat.* of or relating to a tube, esp. the Fallopian or bronchial tubes.

tubal ligation *noun* the ligation of the Fallopian tubes as a means of sterilization.

tubby *adjective* (**tub·bi·er**, **tub·bi·est**) (of a person) fat. □ **tub·bi·ness** *noun*

tube ● *noun* **1** a long hollow rigid or flexible cylinder, esp. for holding or carrying air, liquids, etc. **2** a soft metal or plastic cylinder sealed at one end and having a screw cap at the other, for holding a semi-liquid substance ready for use (*a tube of toothpaste*). **3 a** *Anat. & Zool.* a hollow cylindrical organ in the body (*bronchial tubes*; *Fallopian tubes*). **b** *Bot.* a hollow cylindrical structure in a plant. **4 a** a cathode ray tube esp. in a television set. **b** (*prec. by the*) esp. *N Amer. informal* television. **5** *Brit.* (often prec. by *the*) *informal* the London underground railway system (*went by tube*). **6** *N Amer.* a thermionic valve. **7** = INNER TUBE. **8** (*attributive*) designating a close-fitting skirt or sleeveless cylindrical dress or top, esp. of elasticized fabric (*tube top*). **9** the cylindrical body of a wind instrument. ● *transitive verb* **1** equip with tubes. **2** enclose in a tube. □ **down the tube** (or **tubes**) esp. *N Amer.* = DOWN THE DRAIN (see DRAIN). **have one's tubes tied** *informal* receive a tubal ligation. □ **tube·less** *adjective* (esp. in sense 7 of *noun*). **tube·like** *adjective* [French *tube* or Latin *tubus*]

tube pan *noun N Amer.* a round baking pan with a hollow vertical tube in the centre, used to bake ring-shaped cakes.

tuber *noun* **1 a** the short thick rounded part of a stem or rhizome, usu. found underground and covered with modified buds, e.g. in a potato. **b** the similar root of a dahlia etc. **2** *Anat.* a lump or swelling. [Latin, = hump, swelling]

tu·ber·cle /ˈtuːbərkəl, ˈtjuː-/ *noun* **1** a small rounded protuberance esp. on a bone. **2** a small rounded swelling on the body or in an organ, esp. a nodular lesion characteristic of tuberculosis in the lungs etc. **3** a small tuber; a wart-like growth. [Latin *tuberculum*, diminutive of *tuber*: see TUBER]

tubercle bacillus *noun* a bacterium causing tuberculosis.

tu·ber·cu·lar /tuːˈbɜrkjʊlər/ ● *adjective* (also **tu·ber·cu·lous**) of or having tubercles or tuberculosis. ● *noun* a person with tuberculosis. [from Latin *tuberculum* (as TUBERCLE)]

tu·ber·cu·la·tion /tʊˌbɜrkjʊˈleɪʃən/ *noun* **1** the formation of tubercles. **2** a growth of tubercles.

tu·ber·cu·lin /tʊˈbɜrkjʊlɪn/ *noun* a sterile protein extract from cultures of tubercle bacillus, used in the diagnosis and (formerly) the treatment of tuberculosis.

tuberculin test *noun* a hypodermic injection of tuberculin to detect a tubercular infection.

tu·ber·cu·lo·sis /tʊˌbɜrkjʊˈloːsɪs/ *noun* an infectious disease caused by the bacillus *Mycobacterium tuberculosis*, characterized by tubercles, esp. in the lungs. *Abbr.:* **TB**. *See also* PULMONARY TUBERCULOSIS.

tuber·ose¹ /ˈtuːbəˌroːs, ˈtjuːbə-/ *adjective* **1** covered with tubers; knobby. **2** of or resembling a tuber. **3** bearing tubers. □ **tuber·os·ity** /-ˈrɒsɪti/ *noun*

tuber·ose² /ˈtuːbəˌroːz, ˈtuːbroːz, ˈtjuː-/ *noun* a plant, *Polianthes tuberosa*, native to Mexico, having heavily scented white funnel-like flowers and strap-shaped leaves.

tu·ber·ous /ˈtuːbərəs, ˈtjuːbərəs/ *adjective* = TUBEROSE¹.

tube skate *noun Cdn* an ice skate with the blade running along a hollow metal tube.

tube sock *noun N Amer.* an elasticized sock with no shaping for the heel.

tube steak *noun N Amer. slang* a wiener.

tube·well *noun* a well consisting of an iron pipe with a solid steel point and lateral perforations near the end, which is driven into the earth until a water-bearing stratum is reached, when a suction pump is applied to the upper end.

tube·worm *noun* a worm which constructs or secretes a tube in which it lives.

tubi·fex /ˈtuːbɪˌfeks, ˈtjuːbɪ-/ *noun* any red annelid worm of the genus *Tubifex*, found in mud at the bottom of rivers and lakes and used as food for aquarium fish. [modern Latin from Latin *tubus* tube + *-fex* from *facere* make]

tub·ing *noun* **1 a** a length of tube. **b** a quantity of tubes; tubes collectively. **2** *N Amer.* a recreational activity in which one sits in an inflated oversized inner tube and floats down a river, is pulled by a boat, or slides down a snow-covered hill.

Tub·man ▸ 1 Har·riet (Ross) (*c.*1820–1913), US abolitionist. She escaped from slavery (1849) and subsequently helped hundreds of Southern slaves to escape to the northern US and Canada through the Underground Railroad. **2 Wil·liam Vacan·arat Shad·rach** (1895–1971), Liberian leader, president 1944–71. He introduced universal adult suffrage and representation of all Liberians in the national legislature.

tub of lard *noun informal derogatory* a fat person.

tub-thumper *noun informal* a ranting preacher or orator. □ **tub-thumping** *adjective & noun*

Tu·bu·ai Islands /ˌtuːbuːˈaɪ/ (also called **Austral Islands**) a group of volcanic islands in the S Pacific, forming part of French Polynesia; chief town, Mataura (on the island of Tubuai); pop. (2002) 7,800.

tubu·lar /ˈtuːbjʊlər, ˈtjuː-/ *adjective* **1** tube-shaped. **2** having or consisting of tubes. **3** (of furniture etc.) made of tubular pieces.

tubular bells *noun* an orchestral instrument consisting of a row of vertically suspended brass tubes that are struck with a hammer.

tu·bule /ˈtuːbjuːl, ˈtjuː-/ *noun* a small tube in a plant or an animal body. [Latin *tubulus*, diminutive of *tubus* tube]

tu·bu·lin /ˈtuːbjʊlɪn, ˈtjuː-/ *noun Biochem.* a protein that is the main constituent of the microtubules of living cells.

tuch·us /ˈtʊxʊs/ *noun* (also **tuch·is**) *N Amer. informal* the buttocks. [as TUSH²]

tuck ● *verb* **1** *transitive* (often foll. by *in, up*) **a** draw, fold, or turn the outer or end parts of (cloth or clothes etc.) close together so as to be held; thrust in the edge of (a thing) so as to confine it (*tucked his shirt into his pants; tucked the sheet under the mattress*). **b** thrust in the edges of bedclothes around (a person) (*came to tuck me in*). **2** *transitive* draw together into a small space (*tucked her legs under her; the bird tucked its head under its wing*). **3** *transitive* **a** stow (a thing) away in a specified place or way (*tucked it in a corner; tucked it out of sight*). **b** (usu. in *passive*) hide away, seclude (*a town tucked away in the foothills*). **4** *intransitive* (often foll. by *down*) bring one's knees to one's chest; curl oneself into a ball. **5** *transitive* **a** make a stitched fold in (material, a garment, etc.). **b** shorten, tighten, or ornament with stitched folds. **6** *transitive Brit.* hit (a ball) to the desired place. ● *noun* **1** a flattened usu. stitched fold in material, a garment, etc., often one of several parallel folds for shortening, tightening, or ornament. **2** (in full **tuck position**) **a** (in diving, gymnastics, etc.) a position with the knees bent upwards into the chest and the hands clasped round the shins. **b** (in skiing) a tight crouched position, with the chest bent down to the knees and the arms close by the sides; a squatting position. **3** *informal* a cosmetic surgical operation (*nip and tuck; tummy tuck*). **4** *Brit. informal* food, esp. cakes and sweets eaten by children. □ **tuck in** *informal* eat food heartily. **tuck into** (or **away**) *informal* eat (food) heartily (*tucked into their dinner; could really tuck it away*). [Middle English *tukke, tokke,* from Middle Dutch, Middle Low German *tucken,* = Old High German *zucchen* pull, related to TUG]

tucka·more /ˈtʌkəmɔr/ *noun Cdn* (*Nfld*) **1** a stunted tree or bush, esp. a spruce or juniper, with creeping roots and interlacing branches. **2** dense scrub formed by such trees or bushes. [obsolete sense of TUCK = 'tug' + Middle English *more* 'tree root']

tucker ● *noun* **1** a person or thing that tucks. **2** *hist.* a piece of lace or linen etc. in or on a woman's bodice. **3** *Austral. informal* food. ● *transitive verb* (esp. in *passive*; often foll. by *out*) *N Amer. informal* tire, exhaust. □ **best bib and tucker** see BIB¹.

tucker box *noun* (also **tucker bag**) *Cdn & Austral. informal* a container for food.

tuck-in *noun Brit. informal* a large meal.

tuck·ing *noun* a series of usu. stitched tucks in material or a garment.

tuck-pointing *noun* brickwork pointing with coloured mortar with a narrow groove which is filled with fine white lime putty allowed to project slightly (see POINTING 2). □ **tuck-point** *transitive & intransitive verb*

tuck position *noun* see TUCK *noun* 2.

tuck shop *noun* **1** *Cdn* a small store within a hospital, hotel, apartment block, etc., selling snacks and daily necessities to residents or guests. **2** *Brit.* a small store, esp. near or in a school, selling food to children.

Tuc·son /ˈtuːsɒn/ a city in SE Arizona; pop. (2000) 486,699.

'tude *noun N Amer.* = ATTITUDE 3. [abbreviation]

-tude *suffix* forming abstract nouns (*altitude; attitude; solitude*). [from or after French *-tude* from Latin *-tudo -tudinis*]

Tudor *hist.* ● *adjective* **1** of, characteristic of, or associated with the royal family of England ruling 1485–1603 or this period. **2** of or relating to the architectural style of this period, or one in imitation of it, esp. with half-timbering and elaborately decorated houses. ● *noun* **1** a member of the Tudor royal family. **2** a house with Tudor architecture. [Owen *Tudor* of Wales, grandfather of Henry VI]

Tudor·beth·an /tuːdərˈbiːθən, ˈtjuː-/ *adjective Brit.* (of a house etc.) imitating Tudor and Elizabethan styles in design. [blend of TUDOR and ELIZABETHAN 1]

Tudor rose *noun* a conventional five-lobed figure of a rose, esp. a red rose encircling a white one.

Tues. *abbreviation* (also **Tue.**) Tuesday.

Tues·day ● *noun* the third day of the week, following Monday. ● *adverb* **1** on Tuesday. **2** (**Tuesdays**) on Tuesdays; each Tuesday. [Old English *Tīwesdæg* from *Tīw* TIU]

tufa /ˈtuːfə, ˈtjuː-/ *noun* **1** a porous rock composed of calcium carbonate and formed around mineral springs. **2** = TUFF. □ **tufa·ceous** /-'feiʃəs/ adjective [Italian, var. of *tufo*: see TUFF]

tuff noun rock formed by the consolidation of volcanic ash. □ **tuff·aceous** /-tʌ'feiʃəs/ adjective [French *tuf*, *tuffe* from Italian *tufo* from Late Latin *tofus*]

tuf·fet noun **1** a low seat. **2** = TUFT. [var. of TUFT]

tuft ● noun a bunch or collection of threads, grass, feathers, hair, etc., held or growing together at the base. ● verb **1** transitive provide with a tuft or tufts. **2** transitive make depressions at regular intervals in (upholstery etc.) by passing a thread through. **3** intransitive grow in tufts. □ **tufty** adjective [Middle English, prob. from Old French *tofe*, *toffe*, of unknown origin: for -t compare GRAFT¹]

tuft·ed adjective **1** having or growing in a tuft or tufts. **2** (of a bird) having a tuft of feathers on the head.

tuft·ing noun **1** in senses of TUFT verb. **2** (in northern Canada) **a** a handicraft in which plucked moosehair or caribou hair is dyed, gathered in tufts, stitched in patterns on a background of fabric or leather, and finally contoured or sculpted with clippers. **b** a product of such handiwork.

tug ● verb (**tugged**, **tug·ging**) **1** transitive & intransitive pull hard or violently; jerk (*tugged it from my grasp*; *tugged at my sleeve*). **2** transitive tow (a ship etc.) by means of a tugboat. **3** intransitive toil, struggle; go laboriously. ● noun **1** a hard, violent, or jerky pull (*gave a tug on the rope*). **2** a sudden strong emotional feeling (*felt a tug as I watched them go*). **3** a small powerful boat for towing larger boats and ships. **4** an aircraft towing a glider. **5** (of a horse's harness) a loop from a saddle supporting a shaft or trace. □ **tug·ger** noun [Middle English *togge*, *tugge*, intensive from Germanic: see TOW¹]

tug·boat noun = TUG noun 3.

tug-of-war noun **1** a contest in which two teams pull at opposite ends of a rope until one drags the other over a central line. **2** an intense struggle between two opponents.

tu·grik /'tuːɡriːk/ noun the basic monetary unit of Mongolia, equal to 100 mongos. [Mongolian]

tuile /twiːl/ noun a thin curved cookie, usu. made with almonds. [French, = 'tile']

tu·ition /tjuː'iʃən, tjuː-/ noun **1** N Amer. a fee paid for education or instruction. **2** teaching or instruction, esp. if paid for. □ **tu·ition·al** adjective [Old French from Latin *tuitio -onis* from *tueri tuit-* watch, guard]

Tuk /tʌk/ a nickname for Tuktoyaktuk. [abbreviation]

Tuk·toyak·tuk /tʌktɔi'jɒktək/ a hamlet located in the northwesternmost part of the NWT, on the shore of the Beaufort Sea, about 140 km northeast of Inuvik; pop. (2001) 930. [Inuvialuktun *tuktuujaartuq* rock caribou place, so called with reference to a legend about a shaman hunter who turned two caribou into protruding rocks as they were attempting to escape into the sea]

tuk-tuk /'tuktuk/ noun (in Thailand) a three-wheeled motorized vehicle used as a taxi. [imitative]

Tuk·tut No·gait National Park /,tuːktʊt 'nɒɡait/ a park in the NWT, 425 km northeast of Inuvik, bordering on Nunavut and the Amundsen Gulf, established in 1996 to protect the calving grounds of the barren ground caribou. [Inuvialuktun, = 'young caribou']

Tula /'tuːlə/ **1** an industrial city in European Russia, to the south of Moscow; pop. (est. 2002) 497,500. **2** the ancient capital city of the Toltecs in Mexico, usu. identified with a site near the town of Tula in Hidalgo State, central Mexico.

tu·lar·emia /,tuːlə'riːmiə/ noun (also **tu·lar·aemia**) a severe infectious disease of animals transmissible to humans, caused by the bacterium *Pasteurella tularense* and characterized by ulcers at the site of infection, fever, and loss of weight. □ **tu·lar·emic** adjective [modern Latin from *Tulare* County in California, where it was first observed]

tulip noun **1** any bulbous spring-flowering plant of the genus *Tulipa*, esp. one of the many cultivated forms with showy cup-shaped flowers of various colours and markings. **2** a flower of this plant. [originally *tulipa(n)* from modern Latin *tulipa* from Turkish *tul(i)band* from Persian *dulband* TURBAN (from the shape of the expanded flower)]

tulip·o·mania noun (also **tulip mania**) **1** hist. a trading phenomenon in Holland in 1637, when a flurry of financial speculation rapidly inflated the price of tulip bulbs before prices suddenly crashed. **2** analogous behaviour by modern investors.

tulip poplar noun = TULIP TREE.

tulip tree noun any of various trees, esp. *Liriodendron tulipifera* of eastern N America, producing tulip-like flowers.

tulip·wood noun a fine-grained pale timber produced by the tulip tree.

Tull, Jeth·ro (1674–1741), English agriculturalist. He had a profound effect on agricultural practice with his invention of the seed drill (1701), which could sow seeds in accurately spaced rows at a controlled rate.

Tul·la·more /,tʊlə'mɔːr/ the county town of Offaly, in the Republic of Ireland; pop. (est. 2002) 10,500.

tulle /tuːl/ noun a soft fine net used in veils, tutus, etc. [*Tulle* in SW France, where it was first made]

tul·li·bee /'tʌlɪbiː/ noun any of various N American whitefishes of the genus *Coregonus*. [Canadian French *toulibi*, ultimately from Ojibwa]

Tulsa /'tʌlsə/ a city on the Arkansas River in NE Oklahoma; pop. (2000) 393,049.

tulsi /'tʊlsiː/ noun a kind of basil, *Ocimum sanctum*, which is cultivated by Hindus as a sacred plant. [Hindi]

tum noun informal the stomach. [abbreviation of TUMMY]

tum·ble ● verb **1** intransitive & transitive fall or cause to fall suddenly, clumsily, or headlong. **2** intransitive **a** fall rapidly in amount etc. (*prices tumbled*). **b** fall in ruins; collapse, topple. **3** intransitive (often foll. by *around*, *about*) roll or toss erratically or helplessly to and fro. **4** intransitive move or rush in a headlong or blundering manner (*the children tumbled out of the car*). **5** intransitive (often foll. by *to*) informal grasp the meaning or hidden implication of an idea, circumstance, etc. (*they quickly tumbled to our intentions*). **6** transitive overturn; fling or push roughly or carelessly. **7** intransitive perform gymnastic or acrobatic feats, esp. somersaults. **8** transitive rumple or disarrange; pull about; disorder. **9** transitive clean (castings, gemstones, etc.) in a tumbler (see TUMBLER 4). ● noun **1** a sudden or headlong fall (*Jason took a tumble down the stairs*). **2** a somersault or other acrobatic feat. **3** an untidy or confused state. [Middle English *tumbel* from Middle Low German *tummelen*, Old High German *tumalōn* frequentative of *tūmōn*: compare Old English *tumbian* to dance]

tumble·down adjective falling or fallen into ruin; dilapidated.

tumble dry transitive & intransitive verb dry (clothing etc.) in a clothes dryer with a heated rotating drum.

tumble·home noun the inward inclination of the upper part of a ship's or boat's side.

tum·bler noun **1** a drinking glass with no handle or foot, formerly with a rounded bottom so as not to stand upright, now with a thick heavy base. **2** an acrobat or gymnast, esp. one performing somersaults. **3 a** a pivoted piece in a lock that holds the bolt until lifted by a key. **b** a notched pivoted plate in a gunlock. **4** (also **tumbling box**, **tumbling barrel**) a revolving drum or barrel containing an abrasive substance, in which castings, gemstones, etc., are cleaned by friction. **5** a kind of pigeon that turns over backwards in flight. **6** an electrical switch worked by pushing a small sprung lever. □ **tumbler·ful** noun (pl. **-fuls**).

tumble·weed noun N Amer. & Austral. any of various plants, esp. of arid regions, that form a globular bush that breaks off in late summer and is tumbled about by the wind, e.g. *Amaranthus albus*.

tum·brel /'tʌmbrəl/ noun (also **tum·bril** /-rɪl/) hist. **1** an open cart in which condemned persons were conveyed to their execution, esp. to the guillotine during the French Revolution. **2** a two-wheeled covered cart for carrying tools, ammunition, etc. **3** a cart that tips to empty its load, esp. one carrying dung. [Old French *tumberel*, *tomberel* from *tomber* fall]

tu·me·fy /'tuːmɪ,fai, 'tjuː-/ verb (**-fies**, **-fied**) **1** intransitive swell, inflate; be inflated. **2** transitive cause to do this. [French *tuméfier* from Latin *tumefacere* from *tumēre* swell]

tu·mes·cent /tjuː'mesənt, tjuː-/ adjective **1** becoming tumid; swelling. **2** swelling as a response to sexual stimulation. □ **tu·mes·cence** noun [Latin *tumescere* (as TUMEFY)]

tumid /'tuːmɪd, 'tjuː-/ adjective **1** (of parts of the body etc.) swollen, inflated. **2** (of a style etc.) inflated, bombastic. [Latin *tumidus* from *tumēre* swell]

tummy noun (pl. **-mies**) informal the stomach. [childish pronunciation of STOMACH]

tummy tuck noun informal cosmetic surgery in which excess abdominal fat and skin is removed; an abdominoplasty.

tumor·i·gen·ic /,tuːmərə'dʒenɪk, ,tjuː-/ adjective capable of causing tumours. □ **tumor·i·gen·icity** /-dʒe'nɪsiti/ noun

tu·mour noun (also **tumor**) an abnormal swelling or enlargement in any part of the body, esp. a permanent swelling without

---

Consonants: b *but*   d *dog*   f *few*   g *get*   h *her*   j *yes*   k *cat*   l *leg*   m *man*   n *no*   p *pen*   r *red*   s *sit*

inflammation, caused by excessive continued growth and proliferation of cells in a tissue, which may be either benign or malignant. □ **tumor·ous** *adjective* [Latin *tumor* from *tumēre* swell]

tump·line *noun N Amer.* a sling for carrying a load on the back, with a strap which passes around the forehead. [ultimately from Algonquian *mattump* + LINE¹]

tu·mult /ˈtjuːmʌlt, ˈtuː-, -məlt, ˈtʌmʌlt/ *noun* **1** an uproar or din, esp. of a disorderly crowd. **2** an angry demonstration by a mob; a riot; a public disturbance. **3** a conflict of emotions in the mind. **4** commotion, agitation, disturbance. [Old French *tumulte* or Latin *tumultus*]

tu·mul·tu·ous /təˈmʌltʃʊəs, tuː-, tjuː-, -tjʊəs/ *adjective* **1** noisily vehement; uproarious; making a tumult (*a tumultuous welcome*). **2** disorderly; characterized by commotion or disturbance. **3** agitated. □ **tu·mul·tu·ous·ly** *adverb*

tu·mu·lus /ˈtuːmjʊləs, ˈtjuː-/ *noun* (*pl.* **tu·mu·li** /-ˌliː/) an ancient burial mound or barrow. [Latin from *tumēre* swell]

tun ● *noun* **1** a large beer or wine cask. **2** a brewer's fermenting vat. **3** a measure of capacity, equal to 210 imperial gallons or 252 US gallons (about 955 litres). ● *transitive verb* (**tunned, tun·ning**) store (wine etc.) in a tun. [Old English *tunne* from medieval Latin *tunna*, prob. of Gaulish origin]

tuna¹ *noun* (*pl.* same or **tunas**) **1** any of several large marine food and game fishes of the mackerel family, of the genera *Thunnus, Euthynnus, Katsuwonus*, and closely related genera, having a rounded body and pointed snout and found in warm seas worldwide, esp. the very large *Thunnus thynnus*. **2** (also **tuna fish**) the flesh of the tuna, often tinned in oil or water. [Latin American Spanish, from Spanish *atún*]

tuna² /ˈtuːnə, ˈtjuː-/ *noun* **1** a prickly pear, esp. *Opuntia tuna*. **2** the fruit of this. [Spanish from Haitian]

tun·able *adjective* that may be tuned. □ **tun·abil·ity** *noun*

Tunb Islands /ˈtuːnəb/ two small islands (Greater and Lesser Tunb) in the Persian Gulf, administered by the emirate of Ras al Khaimah until occupied by Iran in 1971.

tun·dish /ˈtʌndɪʃ/ *noun* an intermediate reservoir in metal founding.

tun·dra *noun* a vast level treeless Arctic region usu. with a marshy surface and underlying permafrost. [Lappish]

Tundra Buggy *noun Cdn proprietary* a large wheeled sightseeing bus used to take tourists into polar bear country.

tundra swan *noun* a swan, *Cygnus columbianus*, breeding in Alaska and the low Arctic.

tundra tire *noun Cdn* a wide airplane tire inflated to low pressure, used to operate from rough terrain.

tundra wolf *noun* the larger of two subspecies of wolf in the Canadian Far North, with white, grey or brown fur, inhabiting the mainland.

tune ● *noun* **1** a melody with or without harmony. **2** a song (*the Dirty Realists play some cool tunes*). **3** the proper musical pitch or intonation; harmony (*in tune; out of tune*). ● *verb* **1** *transitive* put (a musical instrument) in tune. **2 a** *transitive* adjust (a radio receiver, television, etc.) to a particular frequency, channel, etc. **b** *intransitive* (usu. foll. by *in*) adjust a radio receiver, television, etc. to the required signal or channel (*tuned in to their favourite station*). **c** *transitive* (in *passive*) cause to be interested in, watching, or listening to a broadcast etc. (*a sunbather tuned to the ball game*). **3** *transitive* adjust (an engine etc.) to run smoothly and efficiently. **4** *transitive* (foll. by *to*) adjust or adapt to a required or different purpose, situation, etc. **5** *intransitive* (foll. by *with*) be in harmony with. □ **in tune 1** having the correct pitch or intonation (*sings in tune*). **2** (usu. foll. by *with*) harmonizing with one's company, surroundings, etc. **out of tune 1** not having the correct pitch or intonation (*always plays out of tune*). **2** (usu. foll. by *with*) clashing with one's company etc. **stay tuned 1** continue to watch or listen to a broadcast etc. **2** *informal* more news or information is forthcoming. **to the tune of** *informal* to the considerable sum or amount of. **tune in** (often foll. by *to*) *informal* become acquainted with or aware of. **tune out 1** stop tuning in to a broadcast etc. **2** become oblivious to (something) or to one's surroundings. **tune up 1** (of a musician) bring one's instrument to the proper or uniform pitch. **2** bring to the most efficient condition. [Middle English: unexplained variant of TONE]

tune·ful *adjective* melodious, musical. □ **tune·ful·ly** *adverb* **tune·ful·ness** *noun*

tune·less *adjective* **1** unmelodious, unmusical. **2** out of tune. □ **tune·less·ly** *adverb* **tune·less·ness** *noun*

tun·er *noun* **1** a person who tunes musical instruments, esp. pianos. **2 a** a device for tuning a radio receiver. **b** a radio receiver. **3** an electronic device for tuning a guitar etc.

tune·smith *noun informal* a songwriter.

tune-up *noun* esp. *N Amer.* **1** an act or instance of making esp. minor adjustments to a motor vehicle etc. to ensure optimum performance. **2** *Sport* (often foll. by *for*) an event that serves as a practice for a subsequent event.

tung *noun* a tree, *Aleurites fordii*, native to China, bearing poisonous fruits containing seeds that yield oil. [Chinese *tong*]

tung oil *noun* the oil of the tung used in paints and varnishes.

tung·sten *noun Chem.* a steel-grey dense metallic element with a very high melting point, occurring naturally in scheelite and used for the filaments of electric lamps and for alloying steel etc. Symbol: **W**; at. no.: 74. □ **tung·state** *noun* [Swedish from *tung* heavy + *sten* stone]

tungsten carbide *noun* a very hard black substance used in making dies and cutting tools.

Tun·gus /ˈtʊŋʊs, tʊŋˈuːs/ *noun* (*pl.* same) **1** a member of a people of E Siberia. **2** the Altaic language of this people. [Yakut]

Tun·gus·ka /tʊŋˈɡuːskə/ two rivers in Siberian Russia, the **Lower Tunguska** and **Stony Tunguska**, flowing westward into the Yenisei River through the forested, sparsely-populated Tunguska Basin. The area was the scene, in 1908, of a devastating explosion believed to have been due to the disintegration in the atmosphere of a meteorite or small comet.

tunic *noun* **1 a** a close-fitting short coat of police or military etc. uniform. **b** a loose often sleeveless garment usu. reaching to about the knees, as worn in ancient Greece and Rome. **c** a loose, knitted, women's upper garment reaching to mid-thigh, usu. worn over leggings, a skirt, blouse, or pants. **d** a loose sleeveless usu. belted dress worn over a blouse, esp. as part of a girl's school uniform. **e** any of various loose, pleated dresses gathered at the waist with a belt or cord. **f** a tunicle. **2** *Zool.* the rubbery outer coat of an ascidian etc. **3** *Bot.* **a** any of the concentric layers of a bulb. **b** the tough covering of a part of this. **4** *Anat.* a membrane enclosing or lining an organ. [French *tunique* or Latin *tunica*]

tuni·cate /ˈtuːnɪkət, ˈtjuː-, -ˌkeɪt/ ● *noun* any marine animal of the subphylum Urochordata having a rubbery or hard outer coat, including sea squirts. ● *adjective* **1** *Zool.* of or relating to this subphylum. **2 a** *Zool.* enclosed in a tunic. **b** *Bot.* having concentric layers. [Latin *tunicatus* past participle of *tunicare* clothe with a tunic]

tu·nicle /ˈtuːnɪkəl, ˈtjuː-/ *noun* a short vestment worn over an alb, esp. by an Anglican subdeacon. [Old French *tunicle* or Latin *tunicula* diminutive of *tunica* tunic]

tun·ing *noun* **1** in senses of TUNE *verb*. **2** the action or process of tuning something (*an electronic instrument requires no tuning*). **3** the extent to which a musical instrument, performance, or ensemble is in tune (*the violinist's tuning is uncertain, and the tone harsh*). **4** a particular key or set of pitches to which an instrument, esp. one with strings, is tuned (*the guitar is in D-A-D-G-A-D tuning*). **5** the facility on a radio allowing for the reception of different stations, frequencies, or wavelengths. **6** *Electronics* the variation of the resonant frequency of an oscillatory circuit.

tuning fork *noun* a two-pronged steel fork that gives a particular note when struck, used in tuning musical instruments etc.

Tunis /ˈtuːnɪs, ˈtjuː-/ the capital of Tunisia, a port on the Mediterranean coast of North Africa; pop. (2000) 690,600.

Tu·ni·sia /tʊˈniːziə, -ˈniːs-, -ˈnɪs-, tjuː-, -ˈniːʒə/ a country in North Africa; pop. (est. 2002) 9,815,644; capital, Tunis. Tunisia has a Mediterranean coastline and extends south into the Sahara Desert. □ **Tu·ni·sian** *adjective & noun*

tun·ket *noun N Amer.* euphemism (esp. in exclamatory phr. **what** or **where** or **how** etc. **in tunket**) hell. [origin unknown]

tun·nel ● *noun* **1** an artificial underground passage through a hill or under a road or river etc., esp. for a railway or road to pass through, or in a mine. **2** an underground passage dug by a burrowing animal. **3** a long enclosed passageway or corridor through a building etc., e.g. from the dressing room to the playing area in a sports stadium. **4** any fictional or theoretical means of passage from one time, universe, etc. to another. **5** a prolonged period of difficulty or suffering (esp. in metaphors, e.g. *a light at the end of the tunnel*). **6** a tube containing a driveshaft etc. **7** a canal or hollow groove in the body (*carpal tunnel*). ● *verb* (**tun·nelled, tun·nel·ling**; also esp. US **tun·neled, tun·nel·ing**) **1** *intransitive* (foll. by *through, into,* etc.) make a tunnel through (a hill etc.). **2** *transitive* make (one's way) by tunnelling. **3** *intransitive Physics* (of a subatomic particle) pass through a potential barrier. □ **tun·nel·ler** *noun* [Old French *tonel* diminutive of *tonne* TUN]

tunnel diode *noun Electronics* a two-terminal semiconductor diode using tunnelling electrons to perform high-speed switching operations.

tunnel vision *noun* **1** vision that is defective in not adequately including objects away from the centre of the field of view. **2** *informal* **a** concentration focused on a limited or single objective, perception, etc. (also *attributive*: *a tunnel-vision approach*). **b** inability to be diverted or swayed from this.

tunny *noun* (*pl.* same or **-nies**) esp. *Brit.* = TUNA¹. [French *thon* from Provençal *ton*, from Latin *thunnus* from Greek *thunnos*]

tup ● *noun* **1** esp. *Brit.* a male sheep; a ram. **2** the striking head of a piledriver, etc. ● *transitive verb* (**tupped, tup·ping**) esp. *Brit.* (of a ram) copulate with (a ewe). [Middle English *toje, tupe*, of unknown origin]

tu·pelo /ˈtuːpəˌloː, ˈtjuː-/ *noun* (*pl.* **-pelos**) **1** any of various Asian and N American deciduous trees of the genus *Nyssa*, with colourful foliage and growing in swampy conditions. **2** the wood of this tree. [Creek from *ito* tree + *opilwa* swamp]

Tupi /ˈtuːpi/ ● *noun* (*pl.* same or **Tupis**) **1** a member of an Aboriginal people native to the Amazon valley. **2** the language of this people. ● *adjective* of or relating to this people or language. [S American Aboriginal name]

Tupi-Guarani ● *noun* (*pl.* same or **Tupi-Guaranis**) **1** a member of a S American people of Tupi, Guarani, or other related stock. **2** a S American Aboriginal language family including Tupi and Guarani. ● *adjective* of or relating to this people or language family.

tupik /ˈtuːpɪk/ *noun* a traditional skin tent used by Inuit groups during the summer. [Inuktitut *tupiq*]

-tuple /ˈtʌpəl/ *combining form* esp. *Math.* forming nouns and adjectives with preceding algebraic symbol with the sense 'consisting of as many parts or elements as indicated by the symbol' (*n-tuple*). [from the ending of QUINTUPLE, OCTUPLE, etc.]

Tu·po·lev /ˈtuːpələf/ **An·drei (Nik·olai·evich)** (1888–1972), Russian aeronautical engineer. He produced Russia's first jet bomber (1946) and jet passenger plane. With his son Alexei (1925–2001) he designed the world's first supersonic airliner, which first flew in December 1968 but was never commercially viable.

tup·pence *noun* *Brit.* = TWOPENCE. [phonetic spelling]

tup·penny /ˈtʌpəni/ *adjective* *Brit.* = TWOPENNY. [phonetic spelling]

Tup·per ▸ Sir Charles (1821–1915), Canadian Conservative politician, sixth prime minister of Canada (1896). Elected premier of Nova Scotia in 1864, he attended all three Confederation conferences. In 1867 he entered the House of Commons and was a member of the Macdonald Cabinet from 1870. He was prime minister for barely two months before being defeated by Laurier's Liberals.

Tup·per·ware *noun* *proprietary* a range of plastic containers for storing food. [*Tupper*, name of the manufacturer, + WARE¹]

tuque *noun* *var. of* TOQUE 1. [Canadian French, ultimately from a pre-Romance form *tukka* 'gourd, hill']

tura·co /ˈtʊrəˌkoː/ *noun* (also **tour·aco**) (*pl.* **-acos**) any African bird of the family Musophagidae, with crimson and green plumage and a prominent crest. [French from native West African name]

tur·ban *noun* **1** a man's headdress, consisting of a length of cotton or silk wound around a cap or the head, worn esp. by Muslims and Sikhs. **2** a woman's headdress or hat resembling this. □ **tur·baned** *adjective* [16th c. (also *tulbant* etc.), ultimately from Turkish *tülbent* from Persian *dulband*: compare TULIP]

tur·bel·lar·ian /ˌtɜːbəˈleəriən/ ● *noun* any usu. free-living flatworm of the class Turbellaria of fresh or salt water or damp earth, having a ciliated surface. ● *adjective* of or relating to this class. [modern Latin *Turbellaria* from Latin *turbella* diminutive of *turba* crowd: see TURBID]

tur·bid *adjective* **1** (of a liquid or colour) muddy, thick; not clear. **2** (of a style etc.) confused, disordered. □ **tur·bid·ity** *noun* **tur·bid·ly** *adverb* [Latin *turbidus* from *turba* a crowd, a disturbance]

tur·bin·ate /ˈtɜːbɪnət/ *adjective* **1** shaped like a spinning top or inverted cone. **2** (of a shell) with whorls decreasing rapidly in size. **3** *Anat.* (esp. of some nasal bones) shaped like a scroll.

tur·bine /ˈtɜːbaɪn/ *noun* a rotary motor or engine driven by a flow of water, steam, gas, wind, etc., esp. to produce electrical power. [French from Latin *turbo -binis* spinning top, whirlwind]

tur·bit /ˈtɜːbɪt/ *noun* a breed of domestic pigeon of stout build with a neck frill and short beak. [apparently from Latin *turbo* top, from its figure]

tur·bo *noun* (*pl.* **-bos**) **1 a** = TURBOCHARGER. **b** a motor vehicle equipped with this. **2** = TURBINE.

turbo- *combining form* turbine.

turbo·charge *transitive verb* (esp. as **turbo·charged** *adjective*) **1** supply (a motor, a vehicle, etc.) with a turbocharger; use a turbocharger on. **2** *informal* greatly increase the efficiency, power, or speed of.

turbo·char·ger *noun* a supercharger driven by a turbine powered by the engine's exhaust gases.

turbo·diesel *noun* **1** a turbocharged diesel engine. **2** a vehicle powered by this.

turbo·fan *noun* **1** a jet engine in which a turbine-driven fan provides additional thrust. **2** an aircraft powered by this.

turbo·jet *noun* **1** a jet engine in which the jet also operates a turbine-driven compressor for the air drawn into the engine. **2** an aircraft powered by this.

turbo·prop *noun* **1** a jet engine in which a turbine is used as in a turbojet and also to drive a propeller. **2** an aircraft powered by this.

turbo·shaft *noun* a gas turbine that powers a shaft for driving heavy vehicles, generators, pumps, etc.

turbo·super·charger *noun* = TURBOCHARGER.

tur·bot /ˈtɜːbət/ *noun* **1** the Greenland halibut. **2** a large speckled European flatfish, *Scophthalmus maximus*, having a broad scaleless diamond-shaped body covered with bony tubercles, valued for food. **3** any of various similar fishes. [Old French from Old Swedish *törnbut* from *törn* thorn + *but* BUTT³]

tur·bu·lence /ˈtɜːbjʊləns/ *noun* **1 a** an irregularly fluctuating flow of air or fluid. **b** a disturbed state caused by this. **2** *Meteorol.* stormy conditions as a result of atmospheric disturbance. **3** a disturbance, commotion, or tumult.

tur·bu·lent /ˈtɜːbjʊlənt/ *adjective* **1** disturbed; in commotion. **2** (of a flow of air etc.) varying irregularly; causing disturbance. **3** tumultuous. **4** insubordinate, riotous. □ **tur·bu·lent·ly** *adverb* [Latin *turbulentus* from *turba* crowd]

Turco- *combining form* (also **Turko-**) Turkish; Turkish and. [medieval Latin (as TURK)]

Tur·co·man *var. of* TURKOMAN.

turd *noun* *coarse slang* **1** a lump of excrement. **2** a term of contempt for a person. [Old English *tord* from Germanic]

tu·reen /təˈriːn, tjʊ-/ *noun* a deep covered dish for serving soup etc. [earlier *terrine, -ene* from French *terrine* large circular earthenware dish, fem. of Old French *terrin* earthen, ultimately from Latin *terra* earth]

turf ● *noun* (*pl.* **turfs** or **turves**) **1 a** a layer of grass etc. with earth and matted roots as the surface of grassland. **b** a piece of this cut from the ground. **c** esp. *N Amer. informal* artificial turf (*would rather play on grass than on turf*). **2** a slab of peat for fuel. **3** (prec. by *the*) **a** a horse racing generally. **b** a general term for racecourses. **4 a** an area regarded as being under the control of a particular person or group; one's personal territory. **b** one's sphere of influence or activity. ● *transitive verb* **1** (often as **turfed** *adjective*) cover (ground) with turf. **2** (esp. foll. by *out*) *informal* expel or eject (a person or thing). [Old English from Germanic]

Tur·fan Depression /ˈtɜːfan, tɑːˈfan/ a low-lying area in Xinjiang, W China, descending to 154 m (505 ft.) below sea level, with an area of 50 000 sq. km (20,000 sq. miles). It is China's lowest point below sea level.

turf war *noun* (also **turf battle**) a fight or struggle over spheres of influence or control.

turfy *adjective* (**turf·i·er, turf·i·est**) like turf; grassy.

Tur·genev /tɜːˈɡenjef/ **Ivan (Serge·evich)** (1818–83), Russian novelist, dramatist, and short-story writer. His novels (e.g. *Rudin*, 1856), plays (*A Month in the Country*, 1850), and short stories (e.g. the collection *A Sportsman's Sketches*, 1852) examine individual lives to illuminate the social, political, and philosophical issues of the day. His novel *Fathers and Sons* (1862) depicts the rise of Russian nihilism.

tur·ges·cent /tɜːˈdʒesənt/ *adjective* becoming turgid; swelling.

tur·gid /ˈtɜːdʒɪd/ *adjective* **1** swollen, inflated, enlarged. **2** (of language) pompous, bombastic. □ **tur·gid·ity** *noun* [Latin *turgidus* from *turgēre* swell]

tur·gor /ˈtɜːɡɔː/ *noun* *Bot.* the rigidity of cells due to the absorption of water. [Late Latin (as TURGID)]

Turin /ˈtjʊərɪn, ˈtjuː-, tjʊˈrɪn/ a city in NW Italy on the Po River, capital of Piedmont region; pop. (2001) 857,433. Turin was the capital of the kingdom of Sardinia from 1720 and a centre of the Risorgimento in the 19th c. It was the first capital of a unified Italy (1861–4).

Tur·ing /ˈtjʊərɪŋ/ **Alan Mathi·son** (1912–54), English mathematician. He developed the concept of a theoretical computing machine in 1937, a key step in the development of the first computer, carried out important work on code breaking during the Second World War, and investigated artificial intelligence.

Turing test *noun Computing* a test for intelligence in a computer, which requires that a human should be unable to distinguish it from another human by the replies to questions put to both. [TURING]

tu·ris·ta /tuˈriːstə/ *noun N Amer.* **1** a tourist in a Spanish-speaking country. **2** diarrhea experienced by a traveller, esp. in a Latin American country. [Spanish, = 'tourist']

Turk *noun* **1 a** a native or national of Turkey. **b** a person of Turkish descent. **2** a member of a Central Asian people from whom the Ottomans derived, speaking Turkic languages. **3** *see* YOUNG TURK. [ultimately from Persian & Arabic *Turk*, of unknown origin]

Tur·kana /tərˈkɒnə/ ● *noun* (*pl.* same) **1** a member of an East African people living between Lake Turkana and the Nile. **2** the Nilotic language of the Turkana. ● *adjective* of or relating to the Turkana or their language. [Nilotic]

Turkana, Lake a salt lake in NW Kenya, with no outlet.

Turk·estan /ˌtərkəˈstan/ (also **Turk·istan**) a region of central Asia between the Caspian Sea and the Gobi Desert, inhabited mainly by Turkic peoples. It is divided by the Pamir and Tien Shan mountains into W Turkestan, which comprises present-day Turkmenistan, Kazakhstan, Uzbekistan, Tajikistan, and Kyrgyzstan, and E Turkestan, which comprises the Xinjiang autonomous region of China.

Tur·key a country comprising the whole of the Anatolian peninsula in W Asia, with a small enclave in SE Europe to the west of Istanbul; pop. (2002) 67,308,928; capital, Ankara.

tur·key *noun* (*pl.* **-keys**) **1** a large mainly domesticated game bird, *Meleagris gallopavo*, originally of N America, having dark plumage with a green or bronze sheen, prized as food esp. on festive occasions including Christmas and Thanksgiving. **2** the flesh of the turkey as food. **3** *N Amer. slang* **a** a theatrical failure; a flop. **b** a stupid or inept person. **4** *see* COLD TURKEY. □ **talk turkey** *N Amer. informal* talk frankly and straightforwardly; get down to business. [16th c.: short for *turkeycock* or *turkeyhen*, originally applied to the guinea fowl which was imported through Turkey, and then erroneously to the N American bird]

turkey shoot *noun* **1** a competition for marksmen originally using live turkeys as targets. **2** *Military* the easy shooting of a large number of enemy units.

turkey vulture *noun* (also **turkey buzzard**) a N American vulture, *Cathartes aura*, having a white beak and legs and dark plumage.

Turki /ˈtərki/ ● *noun* (*pl.* same) **1** the Turkic languages, esp. those of central Asia, collectively. **2** a member of a Turkic-speaking people. ● *adjective* of or relating to these languages or their speakers. [Persian *turkī* (as TURK)]

Turk·ic /ˈtərkɪk/ ● *adjective* of or relating to a large group of Altaic languages including Turkish, Azerbaijani, and Kyrgyz, or the peoples speaking them. ● *noun* the Turkic languages collectively.

Turk·ish ● *adjective* of or relating to Turkey, or to the Turks or their language. ● *noun* this language.

Turkish bath *noun* **1** a hot-air or steam bath followed by washing, massage, etc. **2** (in *sing.* or *pl.*) a building for this.

Turkish carpet *noun* a wool carpet with a thick pile and traditional bold design.

Turkish coffee *noun* a strong black coffee served, usu. sweetened, with the grounds.

Turkish delight *noun* a firm jellylike candy usu. eaten in cubes coated in powdered sugar.

Turkish towel *noun* a towel made of cotton terry.

Turk·istan *see* TURKESTAN.

Turk·men /ˈtərkmən/ ● *noun* (*pl.* same or **Turk·mens**) **1** a member of any of various Turkic peoples inhabiting the region east of the Caspian Sea and south of the Aral Sea, comprising Turkmenistan and parts of Iran and Afghanistan. **2** the Turkic language of these peoples. ● *adjective* of or relating to these peoples or their language. [Persian *turkmān* from Turkish *türkmen*; also influenced by Russian *turkmen*]

Turk·men·istan /tərkˌmenɪˈstan/ (also **Turk·men·ia** /tərkˈmiːniə/) a republic in central Asia, lying between the Caspian Sea and Afghanistan; pop. (est. 2002) 4,688,963; capital, Ashgabat. Turkmenistan is dominated by the Karakum Desert, which occupies about 90 per cent of the country. It was previously part of Turkestan.

Turko- *var.* of TURCO-.

Turko·man /ˈtərkoːmən/ *noun & adjective* (also **Tur·co·man**) (*pl.* **-mans**)

= TURKMEN [medieval Latin *Turcomannus*, French *turcoman* from Persian *turkmān* (see TURKMEN)]

Turks and Cai·cos Islands /tərks, ˈkeikɒs/ a British dependency in the W Indies, comprising two island groups between Haiti and the Bahamas; pop. (2002) 18,738; capital, Cockburn Town (on the island of Grand Turk).

Turk's cap *noun* **1** a martagon lily or other plant with turban-like flowers. **2** a gourd shaped like a turban.

Turk's head *noun* a turban-like ornamental knot.

Turku /ˈtərkuː/ an industrial port in SW Finland; pop. (2001) 173,686.

tur·meric /ˈtərmərɪk/ *noun* **1** a tropical Asian plant, *Curcuma longa*, of the ginger family, yielding aromatic rhizomes used as a spice and for yellow dye. **2** this rhizome powdered and used as a spice esp. in curry powder. [16th-c. forms *tarmaret* etc. perhaps from French *terre mérite* and modern Latin *terra merita*, of unknown origin]

tur·moil *noun* **1** violent confusion; agitation. **2** disturbance, tumult, trouble. [16th c.: origin unknown]

turn ● *verb* **1** *transitive & intransitive* move around a fixed point or central axis; rotate, revolve (*turn the wheel; the wheel turns; the key turns in the lock*). **2** *transitive & intransitive* reverse the position of, so that the back faces forward, the bottom faces up, or the inside faces out (*turn around and face the audience; grill the meat on one side, then turn it over; turn the shirt inside out*). **3 a** *intransitive* take a new direction (*turn left at the lights*). **b** *intransitive* (of a road) bend, curve. **4** *transitive* go around (a corner). **5** *transitive* change the course or direction of; aim, direct (*she turned her eyes away*). **6** *transitive & intransitive* (usu. foll. by *to* or *from*) focus or conclude focusing (one's thoughts or attention) on a particular subject etc. **7** *intransitive* (foll. by *to*) **a** apply oneself to; set about (*turned to doing the ironing*). **b** have recourse to (*he turned to her for help*). **8** *transitive & intransitive* (foll. by *into*) change in nature, form, or condition; transform (*she has turned the book into a play; he turned into a frog*). **9** *transitive & intransitive* cause to become or become (*they have turned crazy*). **10** *transitive & intransitive* (foll. by *against*) make or become hostile to (*our actions have turned them against us*). **11** *intransitive* (foll. by *on*) **a** become hostile towards; attack (*the dog suddenly turned on its owner*). **b** *Baseball* hit (a pitch) with great force. **12 a** *intransitive* (of hair or leaves) change colour. **b** *transitive* cause (the hair) to change colour. **13 a** *intransitive* (of milk) become sour. **b** *transitive* cause (milk) to become sour. **14 a** *intransitive* (of the stomach) be nauseated. **b** *transitive* cause (the stomach) to become nauseated. **15** *transitive* reach the age of (*he has turned 40*). **16 a** *transitive* flip (a page of a book) in order to read or write on the other side. **b** *intransitive* (foll. by *to*) go to (a particular page or passage). **17** *intransitive* become an informer. **18** *intransitive* (of the head) become giddy. **19** *transitive* translate (*turn it into French*). **20** *transitive* twist or sprain (an ankle). **21** *intransitive* (foll. by *on*) depend on; be determined by (*it all turns on the weather tomorrow*). **22** *transitive* send or put into a specified place or condition; cause to go (*he turned the cattle out into the field*). **23** *transitive Baseball* execute (a double play). **24** *transitive* perform (a somersault etc.). **25** *transitive* make or earn (a profit etc.) (*she turned a quick buck*). **26** *transitive* (often foll. by *aside*) divert (a bullet). **27** *transitive* blunt (the edge of a knife, slot of the head of a screw, etc.). **28** *transitive* shape (an object) on a lathe. **29** *transitive* give an elegant form to (*turn a compliment*). **30** *transitive* (esp. as **turned** *adjective*) *Printing* invert (type) to make it appear upside down (*a turned comma*). **31** *transitive* pass around (the flank etc. of an army) in order to attack it from the side or rear. **32** *intransitive* (of the tide) change from flood to ebb or vice versa. ● *noun* **1** an act of turning around on an axis; a total or partial revolution (*a single turn of the handle*). **2 a** an act of turning or facing another way; a change of direction (*took a sudden turn to the left*). **b** a point at which a turning or change occurs. **3 a** a place where a road turns off or branches onto another (*I think we took a wrong turn*). **b** a place where a road, river, etc., changes direction; a bend. **4** a change of the tide from ebb to flow or from flow to ebb. **5** a change in circumstances or in the course of events, esp. for better or worse. **6** the transition from one period of time to the next (*the turn of the century*). **7** an opportunity or obligation etc. that comes successively to each of several people (*it's my turn to wash the dishes*). **8** a period of work done by a group of people in succession; a shift. **9** a short walk or ride (*a turn in the garden*). **10** the halfway point in a round of golf. **11** an act or deed, esp. one that does good or harm to another (*one good turn deserves another*). **12** *informal* a momentary shock or feeling of concern (*the news gave me quite a turn*). **13** a variation or particular manner of linguistic expression, esp. for effect (*turn of phrase*). **14** *N Amer. Forestry* a load of logs yarded or hauled in a single trip. **15** *Music* a melodic ornament consisting of a group of three, four, or five notes, comprising the principal note and the note one degree above or below it. **16** esp. *Brit.* a short performance on stage or in a circus etc. **17** a tendency or disposition (*is of a mechanical turn of* mind). **18** one round in a coil of rope etc. **19** purpose (*served my turn*). **20** *Printing* **a** inverted type as a temporary substitute for a missing letter. **b** a letter turned the wrong side up. **21 a** *Brit.* the difference between the buying and selling price of stocks etc. **b** a profit made from this. □ **at every turn** at every change of circumstance, at each new stage; continually. **by turns** one after the other in regular succession; alternately. **in turn** in succession; one by one. **in one's turn** when one's turn or opportunity comes. **not know which way** (or **where**) **to turn** be unsure how to act, whom to trust, etc.; be completely at a loss. **not turn a hair** *see* HAIR. **on the turn 1** changing. **2** (of milk) becoming sour. **3** at the turning point. **out of turn 1** at a time when it is not one's turn. **2** inappropriately; ill advisedly or tactlessly (*did I speak out of turn?*). **take turns** act or work alternately or in succession. **to a turn** (esp. cooked) to exactly the right degree etc. **turn around 1** (also **turn about**) turn and face the opposite direction. **2** adopt an opposite course or policy. **3** begin to show an opposite trend or movement. **4** receive, process, and send (passengers, goods, etc.) out again. **turn away 1** turn and face another direction; avert one's eyes. **2** refuse to accept or admit; reject, send away. **turn back 1** return, go back the way one has come. **2** fold back. **turn one's back on** *see* BACK. **turn a blind eye** *see* BLIND. **turn the corner 1** make a turn at an intersection onto a perpendicular street. **2** pass the critical point in an illness, difficulty, etc.; begin to make noticeable improvement. **turn a person's crank** *slang* (usu. with *neg.*) amuse, thrill, or excite a person. **turn a deaf ear** *see* DEAF. **turn down 1** reject (a proposal, application, etc.). **2** reduce the volume or strength of (sound, heat, etc.) by turning a knob etc. **3** fold down (bedsheets etc.). **turn one's hand to** *see* HAND. **turn a person's head** *see* HEAD. **turn an honest penny** earn money fairly. **turn in 1** hand in, submit. **2** achieve or register (a performance, score, etc.). **3** *informal* go to bed. **4** fold inwards. **5** incline inwards (*his toes turn in*). **6** hand over (a suspect etc.) to the authorities. **turn in one's grave** *see* GRAVE[1]. **turn loose 1** release and set free (an animal). **2** allow (a person) to go where, or do as, he or she pleases. **turn off 1 a** stop the flow or operation of (water, electricity, etc.) by means of a tap, switch, etc. **b** operate (a tap, switch, etc.) to achieve this. **2 a** enter a side road. **b** (of a side road) lead off from another road. **3** *informal* cause to lose interest (*turned me right off with their complaining*). **turn of speed** the ability to go fast when necessary. **turn on 1 a** start the flow or operation of (water, electricity, etc.) by means of a tap, switch, etc. **b** operate (a tap, switch, etc.) to achieve this. **c** activate, begin to use (charm, genius, etc.). **2** *informal* excite, arouse; stimulate the interest of, esp. sexually. **3** *informal* introduce to or make aware of (*she turned me on to classical music*). **turn on one's heel** *see* HEEL[1]. **turn out 1** (often foll. by *to* + infin. or *that* + clause) prove to be the case; result (*turned out to be true; we shall see how things turn out*). **2** extinguish (a light etc.). **3** *informal* assemble; attend a meeting etc. **4** expel. **5** produce (manufactured goods etc.). **6** dress or equip (*well turned out*). **7** empty (a pocket) to see the contents. **8** empty or clean out (a room etc.). **9** *informal* **a** get out of bed. **b** go out of doors. **10** *Military* call (a guard) from the guardroom. **11** (of a ballet dancer) rotate the legs outwards in the hip sockets. **turn over 1** turn from one side onto another; bring the reverse or underside into view (*turn over the page*). **2** upset; cause to fall over. **3 a** cause (an engine) to run. **b** (of an engine) start running. **4** consider thoroughly. **5** (foll. by *to*) **a** transfer the care or conduct of (a person or thing) to (a person) (*shall turn it all over to my deputy*). **b** = TURN IN 6. **6** *N Amer. Sport* lose possession of (the ball or puck) to the opposing team. **7** do business to the amount of (*turns over $5000 a week*). **turn round** esp. *Brit.* = TURN AROUND. **turn the tables** *see* TABLE. **turn tail** run away from something feared; flee. **turn the tide** reverse the trend of events. **turn to account** *see* ACCOUNT. **turn turtle** *see* TURTLE. **turn up 1** increase the volume or strength of (sound, heat, etc.) by turning a knob etc. **2** place upwards. **3** discover or reveal. **4** be found, esp. by chance (*it turned up in a bus depot*). **5** happen or present itself; (of a person) put in an appearance (*a few people turned up late*). **6** shorten (a garment) by increasing the size of the hem. [Old English *tyrnan*, *turnian* from Latin *tornare* from *tornus* lathe, from Greek *tornos* lathe, circular movement]

turn·about *noun* **1** a change or reversal of direction. **2** an abrupt change of opinion or policy etc. **3** an act of repaying an injury or offence in kind (*turnabout is fair play*).

turn·around *noun* **1 a** an abrupt or unexpected reversal of a trend, attitude, opinion, fortune, etc. **b** an improvement or recovery, esp. in business. **2 a** the process of receiving, processing, and sending out again. **b** the process of unloading and reloading an airplane, ship, etc. **c** the amount of time required for such processes (*a seven-day turnaround*). **3** esp. *US* a place where vehicles can turn around, such as at the end of a street.

turn·buckle *noun* a device for tightly joining two ropes, cables, wires, etc., consisting of two eyebolts that screw into a threaded coupling that, when turned, brings the eyebolts closer together or moves them further apart, thereby adjusting the tension.

turn·coat *noun* a person who changes sides in a conflict, dispute, etc.; a traitor.

turn·down ● *noun* **1** a rejection or refusal. **2** an act of turning down the sheets of a bed, esp. as a courtesy performed in a hotel (also *attributive*: turndown service). **3** a downturn. ● *attributive adjective* (esp. of a collar) that is or may be turned down.

Turn·er ▸ **1 John Napier** (b.1929), English-born Canadian Liberal politician, seventeenth prime minister of Canada (1984). He served in the Trudeau cabinet, most notably as minister of justice (1968–72) and minister of finance (1972–5). Chosen federal Liberal leader in 1984, he served as prime minister for only 80 days; he resigned as party leader in 1990. **2 Jo·seph Mal·lord Wil·liam** (1775–1851), English landscape painter. He specialized in landscapes and seascapes, such as *The Fighting Téméraire* (1838), whose most characteristic feature is their treatment of light; in later paintings such as *Rain, Steam and Speed* (1844) his hazy swirling representation of light and other atmospheric conditions foreshadowed the work of the Impressionists and abstract art. **3 Tina** (born Anna Mae Bullock) (b.1940), US rock and soul singer. In 1956 Turner and her husband formed the Ike and Tina Turner Revue. She left the Revue and their marriage in 1976 and built a solo career. She starred in the film *Mad Max Beyond Thunderdome* (1985). Albums include *Private Dancer* (1984). □ **Turn·er·esque** *adjective* (in sense 2).

turn·er *noun* **1** a thing that turns or is used for turning, such as a spatula. **2** a person who turns wood on a lathe.

Turner's syndrome *noun* (also **Turner syndrome**) a congenital syndrome affecting females in which the cells contain only one instead of two X chromosomes, characterized by developmental abnormalities including the absence of ovaries, webbing of the neck, and shortness of stature. [H. H. *Turner*, US physician d.1970]

turn·ing *noun* **1 a** the act or practice of using a lathe. **b** work or an article produced on a lathe. **2** esp. *Brit.* a place where one road turns off onto another; a turn.

turning circle *noun* (also **turning radius**) the smallest circle in which a car, ship, etc., can turn without reversing.

turning point *noun* **1** a moment at which a decisive change occurs in one's life, a process, a game, etc. **2** an incident that causes or results in decisive change.

tur·nip *noun* **1** *N Amer.* = RUTABAGA. **2 a** a cruciferous plant, *Brassica rapa*, with a large white globular root and sprouting leaves. **b** this root used as a vegetable. □ **fall off a turnip truck** (or **cart**) *N Amer.* (usu. with *neg.*) be foolish or simple-minded. □ **tur·nipy** *adjective* [earlier *turnep(e)* from *neep* from Latin *napus*: first element of uncertain origin]

turnip tops *plural noun* (also **turnip greens**) the leaves of the white turnip eaten as a vegetable.

turn·key ● *noun* (*pl.* **-keys**) *archaic* a jailer. ● *adjective* of or involving the provision of a complete product or service that is ready for immediate use (*turnkey Internet servers; the fantasy of the turnkey house*).

turn·off *noun* **1** a road that leads away from a larger or more important one. **2** *informal* something that causes disgust or a loss of interest.

turn of the century ● *noun* the period at the end of one century and beginning of the next, esp. around 1900. ● *adjective* (usu. **turn-of-the-century**) used, manufactured, or existing at the end of the 19th c. and beginning of the 20th c.

turn-on *noun* *informal* a thing or person that thrills, excites, or causes esp. sexual stimulation or arousal.

turn·out *noun* **1** the number of people attending or participating in an event, such as a meeting or a vote (*officials were disappointed by the low voter turnout for the municipal election*). **2** the quantity of goods produced in a given time. **3** *N Amer.* a place where animals may be turned out to graze. **4** *Dance* **a** the outward rotation of the leg in the hip socket. **b** the ability to achieve this (*she has good turnout*). **5** a set or display of equipment, clothes, etc. **6** *N Amer.* a widened place in a road for vehicles to pass each other or park temporarily.

turn·over *noun* **1** the amount of money made in a business in a given time. **2** the rate at which a particular asset or product is sold and replaced. **3** the rate at which employees join and leave a company, tenants move into and out of housing, etc. **4** a small usu. triangular or semicircular pie, made by folding a piece of pastry over onto itself to enclose a usu. sweet filling. **5** *N Amer. Sport* a loss of possession of the ball or puck to the opposing team.

turn·pike *noun* **1** *US* a highway maintained by tolls. **2** a tollgate. **3** *hist.* a spiked barrier fixed in or across a road or passage, as a defence against a sudden attack.

turn signal *noun N Amer.* each of a pair of flashing lights on either side of a motor vehicle used to indicate when it is about to turn or change lanes.

turn·stile *noun* a mechanical gate consisting of usu. four revolving arms fixed to a vertical post allowing people through singly, and usu. functioning in one direction only.

turn·stone *noun* any wading bird of the genus *Arenaria*, related to the plover, that looks under stones for small animals to eat.

turn·table *noun* **1** a circular revolving platform spinning a phonograph record that is being played. **2** the unit housing this; a record player. **3** *Railways* a circular revolving platform for turning a railway locomotive or other vehicle.

turn·tabl·ist *noun* a hip hop disc jockey who manipulates a phonograph record while it is playing on a turntable to produce a new, improvised piece of music.

turn-up *noun Brit.* **1** *informal* an unexpected, usu. pleasant, occurrence; a surprise. **2** = CUFF¹ 2.

tur·pen·tine /ˈtɜrpəntaɪn/ ● *noun* **1** (also **oil of turpentine**) a volatile essential oil with a pungent odour, obtained by distilling gum turpentine or pine wood, used esp. as a solvent and thinner for paints and stains, and in medical liniments. **2** (in full **crude turpentine** or **gum turpentine**) any of various viscous oleoresins which exude from coniferous trees, esp. pines, and can be distilled to yield gum rosin and oil of turpentine. **3** any of various conifers and other trees yielding turpentine or a similar resin, including the terebinth tree, *Pistacia terebinthus* and the related *P. palaestina*. ● *transitive verb* apply turpentine to. [Old French *ter(e)bentine* from Latin *ter(e)binthina* (*resina* 'resin') (as TEREBINTH)]

tur·pi·tude /ˈtɜrpɪˌtuːd, -ˌtjuːd/ *noun formal* baseness, depravity, wickedness. [French *turpitude* or Latin *turpitudo* from *turpis* disgraceful, base]

turps *noun informal* oil of turpentine. [abbreviation]

tur·quoise /ˈtɜrkɔɪz, -kwɔɪz/ ● *noun* **1** a semi-precious stone, usu. opaque and of a sky-blue to blue-green colour, consisting of hydrated copper aluminum phosphate. **2** the colour of this mineral, usu. a greenish-blue. ● *adjective* of this colour. [Old French *turqueise* (later *-oise*) Turkish (stone)]

turr *noun Cdn* (*Nfld*) = MURRE. [prob. imitative of MURRE and the sound made by this bird]

tur·ret *noun* **1** a small tower, usu. projecting from the wall of a building, such as a castle, as a decorative addition. **2** a low flat usu. revolving armoured tower or enclosure for a gun and gunners in a ship, aircraft, fort, or tank. **3** an attachment for a lathe, drill, etc. that holds various tools or bits and may be rotated to access the one required to do a particular job. □ **tur·ret·ed** *adjective* [Old French *to(u)rete* diminutive of *to(u)r* TOWER]

tur·tle *noun* **1** any of various marine or freshwater reptiles of the order Testudines, encased in a shell of bony plates, and having flippers or webbed toes used in swimming. **2** the flesh of the turtle, esp. used for soup. □ **turn turtle** turn over, capsize. [apparently alteration of *tortue*: see TORTOISE]

turtle bean *noun* a black bean.

turtle·dove *noun* any wild dove of the genus *Streptopelia*, esp. *S. turtur*, noted for its soft cooing and its affection for its mate and young. [archaic *turtle* (in the same sense) from Old English *turtla*, *turtle* from Latin *turtur*, of imitative origin]

turtle·head *noun* any of several plants of the genus *Chelone*, of eastern N America, with lipped flowers said to resemble a turtle's head.

Turtle Island (among some N American Aboriginal peoples) a name for the continent of N America, thought of as the shell of a giant turtle surrounded by oceans.

turtle·neck *noun N Amer.* **a** a high round turned-over collar, esp. on a knitted garment. **b** a garment having this type of neck. **2** *Brit.* = MOCK TURTLENECK.

turtle shell ● *noun* = TORTOISESHELL *noun* 1. ● *adjective* (**turtle·shell**) = TORTOISESHELL *adjective*.

turves *rare pl.* of TURF.

Tus·can ● *noun* **1** an inhabitant of Tuscany. **2** the classical Italian language of Tuscany. ● *adjective* **1** of or relating to Tuscany or the Tuscans. **2** *Archit.* designating or pertaining to the simplest of the five classical orders, resembling Doric but devoid of all ornament.

Tus·cany /ˈtʌskəni/ a region of west central Italy, on the Ligurian Sea; capital, Florence.

Tus·ca·rora /ˌtʌskəˌrɔrə/ ● *noun* **1** a member of an Iroquois people living in southern Ontario and western New York, the last member to join the Iroquoian confederacy. **2** the Iroquoian language of this people. ● *adjective* of or relating to this people or their language or culture. [Iroquois, from Tuscarora *skaroˈren* hemp gatherers, their self-designation]

tush¹ *noun* **1** a long pointed tooth, esp. a canine tooth of a horse. **2** the stunted tusk of some Indian elephants. [Old English *tusc* TUSK]

tush² /tʊʃ/ *noun* (also **tush·ie**, **tushy** (*pl.* **-ies**)) esp. *N Amer. slang* the buttocks. [Yiddish *tokhes* from Hebrew *taḥat* 'beneath']

tush³ *interjection archaic* expressing strong disapproval or scorn. [Middle English: imitative]

tusk *noun* **1** a long pointed tooth, esp. protruding from a closed mouth, as in the elephant, walrus, etc. **2** anything resembling a tusk in appearance, such as a tusk-like tooth of a human. □ **tusked** *adjective* (also in *combination*). **tusky** *adjective* [Middle English alteration of Old English *tux* var. of *tusc*: compare TUSH¹]

tusk·er *noun* an animal, such as an elephant or wild boar, having esp. well-developed tusks.

tus·sah /ˈtʌsə/ *noun* (also **tus·sore** /ˈtʌsɜr, ˈtʌsɔr/) **1** an Indian or Chinese silkworm, *Antherea mylitta*, yielding strong but coarse brown silk. **2** (in full **tussah silk**) silk from this and some other silkworms. [Urdu from Hindi *tasar* from Sanskrit *tasara* shuttle]

tus·sive /ˈtʌsɪv/ *adjective* of, relating to, or producing a cough. [Latin *tussis* cough]

tus·sle ● *noun* a struggle, scuffle, or conflict, esp. a minor or playful one. ● *intransitive verb* engage in a tussle. [originally Scots & Northern English, perhaps diminutive of *touse*: see TOUSLE]

tus·sock /ˈtʌsək/ *noun* a tuft or clump of grass etc. forming a small hill. □ **tus·socky** *adjective* [16th c.: perhaps alteration of dial. *tusk* tuft]

tussock grass *noun* any of various grasses growing in large tussocks, esp. the north temperate hair grass *Deschampsia cespitosa*.

tussock moth *noun* any of various moths of the family Lymantriidae, whose larvae have long dorsal tufts of hairs and are usu. pests of trees.

tus·sore *var.* of TUSSAH.

tut *var.* of TUT-TUT.

Tut·ankh·amen /ˌtuːtənˈkɒmən/ (also **Tut·ankh·amun** /-kɒˈmuːn/) (died *c.*1352 BC), Egyptian pharaoh of the 18th dynasty, reigned *c.*1361–*c.*1352 BC, who is primarily known because of the rich and varied contents of his tomb, discovered virtually intact by the English archaeologist Howard Carter in 1922.

Tut·cho·ne /tuːˈtʃoːni, tuːˈʃoːni/ ● *noun* (*pl.* same or **Tut·cho·nes**) **1** a member of an Aboriginal people living in the area of the Yukon River. **2** the Athapaskan language of this people. ● *adjective* of or relating to this people or their culture or language. [from Tutchone *dechän* 'wood']

tu·tel·age /ˈtuːtələdʒ, ˈtjuː-/ *noun* **1** instruction, teaching, education (*made vast improvements under her tutelage*). **2** protection, care, guardianship. **3** the condition or duration of being supervised by a tutor or guardian. [Latin *tutela* from *tuēri* tuit- or tut- watch]

tu·tel·ary /ˈtuːtələri, ˈtjuː-/ *adjective* **1** serving as a guardian, protector, or patron (*tutelary saint*). **2** of or relating to a guardian (*tutelary authority*). [Late Latin *tutelaris*, Latin *-arius* from *tutela*: see TUTELAGE]

tu·tor ● *noun* **1** a private teacher, either one in general charge of a person's education or employed to give a student additional instruction in a particular subject or subjects. **2** esp. *Brit.* a university teacher supervising the studies of assigned undergraduates. ● *verb* **1** *transitive* act as a tutor; teach or assist (a student) privately, esp. in a particular subject. **2** *intransitive* work as a tutor. □ **tutor·ship** *noun* [Latin, from *tuēri* tut- watch]

tu·tor·ial /tuːˈtɔriəl, tjuː-/ ● *adjective* of or relating to a tutor or tuition. ● *noun* **1** a period of instruction given by a teaching assistant at a university to a small group of students. **2** a period of instruction given privately by a tutor, to either a single pupil or small group. **3** any training session or seminar (*we had a tutorial on the new equipment at work today*). **4** *Computing* a program that enables a user to learn how to use a type of software by offering onscreen instruction interspersed with practice exercises.

Tutsi /ˈtʊtsi/ *noun* (*pl.* same or **Tutˈsis**) a member of a Bantu-speaking people forming a minority of the population of Rwanda. [Bantu]

tutti /ˈtuːti/ *Music* ● *adverb* with all voices or instruments together. ● *noun* (*pl.* **tuttis**) a passage to be performed in this way. [Italian, pl. of *tutto* all]

tutti-frutti /ˌtuːtiˈfruːti/ *noun* (*pl.* **-fruttis**) **1** a candy or dessert, esp. ice cream, consisting of or flavoured with a mixture of chopped preserved fruits and nuts. **2** an artificial flavour combining the tastes of several fruits. [Italian, = all fruits]

tut-tut (also **tut**) ● *interjection* expressing rebuke, impatience, or contempt. ● *noun* an exclamation of 'tut-tut' or the sound of consecutive clicks of the tongue against the alveolar ridge. ● *intransitive verb* (**-tutted**, **-tutting**) **1** exclaim 'tut-tut'. **2** express disapproval. [imitative]

Tutu /ˈtuːtuː/ **Desˈmond (Mpilo)** (b.1931), South African clergyman, archbishop of Cape Town from 1986 to 1996. As general secretary of the South African Council of Churches (1979–84) he became a leading voice in the struggle against apartheid, calling for economic sanctions against South Africa and emphasizing non-violent action; he was awarded the Nobel Peace Prize in 1984.

tutu /ˈtuːtuː/ *noun* a female ballet dancer's costume with a long, flowing bell-shaped skirt of layered tulle or a short, stiff skirt of layered net standing out from the hips. [French, childish alteration of *cucu*, diminutive of *cul* buttocks]

Tuva /ˈtuːvə/ (formerly **Tannu-Tuva** /ˌtanu-/) an autonomous republic in south central Russia, on the border with Mongolia; pop. (est. 2002) 308,200; capital, Kyzyl. □ **Tuvan** *noun & adjective*

Tuˈvaˈlu /tuːˈvɒluː/ a country in the SW Pacific consisting of a group of nine main islands, the former Ellice Islands; pop. (est. 2002) 11,146; capital, Funafuti. The Ellice Islands formed part of the British colony of the Gilbert and Ellice Islands but separated from the Gilberts (later Kiribati) after a referendum in 1975. □ **Tuˈvaˈluan** /ˌtuːvəˈluːən, tuːˈvɒluːən/ *adjective & noun*

tu-whit, tu-whoo *noun* a representation of the cry of an owl. [imitative]

tux *noun* N Amer. *informal* = TUXEDO.

tuxˈedo /tʌkˈsiːdoː/ *noun* (*pl.* **-edos** or **-edoes**) N Amer. **1** a dress suit worn esp. by men on formal occasions, consisting of a usu. black jacket and matching pants, often trimmed in silk, traditionally worn with a black tie, cummerbund, and white dress shirt. **2** the formal coat or jacket worn as part of this suit. □ **tuxˈedoed** *adjective* [after a country club at *Tuxedo* Park, New York where this garment was first worn]

TV *noun* television. [abbreviation]

TV dinner *noun* esp. N Amer. a prepared frozen single-serving meal packaged in a compartmentalized tray in which it is heated.

Tver /tver/ an industrial port in European Russia, on the Volga River northwest of Moscow; pop. (est. 2002) 453,800. It was known as Kalinin from 1931 until 1991.

TVP *abbreviation proprietary* = TEXTURED VEGETABLE PROTEIN.

TV table *noun* (also **TV tray**) N Amer. one of usu. a set of small portable folding tables with a detachable tray forming the tabletop, from which a person sitting in an easy chair or on a chesterfield may eat, as while watching television.

twadˈdle /ˈtwɒdəl/ ● *noun* useless, senseless, silly, or dull talk, ideas, or writing. ● *intransitive verb* indulge in this. [alteration of earlier *twattle*, alteration of TATTLE]

Twain ▸ **1 Mark** (pseudonym of Samuel Langhorne Clemens) (1835–1910), US novelist and humorist. His novels *The Adventures of Tom Sawyer* (1876) and *The Adventures of Huckleberry Finn* (1885) give a vivid portrayal of life along the Mississippi, combining picaresque adventure with moral commentary. **2 Shaˈnia** (born Eileen Regina Edwards) (b.1965), Canadian country singer. Her second album, *The Woman in Me* (1995), sold 19 million copies worldwide; her follow-up album, *Come on Over* (1997), became the best-selling country album of all time, with international sales of 34 million. Her 2002 release, *UP!*, was issued in country, pop, and world music mixes.

twain *adjective & noun archaic* two. [Old English *twegen*, masc. form of *twā* TWO]

twang ● *noun* **1 a** a strong ringing sound made by the plucked string of a musical instrument or bow. **b** any sound resembling this. **2 a** a nasal quality of pronunciation or intonation characteristic of the speech of an individual, area, country, etc. **b** an accent having such a quality. ● *verb* **1 a** *intransitive* ring, resound, or resonate with a sound like that of a plucked string. **b** *transitive* cause (a bow, arrow, etc.) to produce this sound (*she twanged the rubber band*). **2** *transitive* usu.

derogatory play (a tune or instrument) in this way. **3** *transitive* utter with a nasal twang. □ **twangy** *adjective* [imitative]

'twas *archaic* it was. [contraction]

twat /twɒt/ *noun coarse slang* **1** the female genitals. **2** esp. *Brit.* a contemptible person. [17th c.: origin unknown]

twayˈblade *noun* any orchid of the genus *Listera* etc., with green or purple flowers and a single pair of leaves. [*tway* var. of TWAIN + BLADE]

tweak ● *transitive verb* **1** pinch and twist sharply; pull with a sharp jerk; twitch. **2** make fine adjustments to (a mechanism). **3** taunt; jibe at; pique; tease (*opposition members tweaked the leader over the recent political fiasco*). ● *noun* an instance of tweaking. [prob. alteration of dial. *twick* & TWITCH]

twee *adjective* (**tweer**; **tweest**) usu. *derogatory* affectedly dainty, quaint, or sentimental. □ **tweeˈness** *noun* [childish pronunciation of SWEET]

tweed *noun* **1** a rough-surfaced woollen cloth of varying texture, usu. of mixed flecked colours, originally produced in Scotland. **2** (in *pl.*) clothes made of tweed. [originally a misreading of *tweel*, Scots form of TWILL, influenced by assoc. with the TWEED RIVER]

Tweedleˈdum and Tweedleˈdee *plural noun* a pair of persons or things that are virtually indistinguishable. [the names originally applied to the rival composers Handel and Bononcini in a 1725 satire by John Byrom, and later popularized as twin characters in Lewis Carroll's *Through the Looking-Glass*]

Tweed River a river which rises in the Southern Uplands of Scotland and flows 155 km (97 miles) generally eastward, crossing into NE England and entering the North Sea at Berwick-upon-Tweed. For part of its lower course it forms the border between Scotland and England.

Tweedsˈmuir see BUCHAN.

tweedy *adjective* (**tweedˈiˈer**, **tweedˈiˈest**) **1** of or relating to tweed cloth. **2** often dressed in tweed cloth (usu. with connotations of dowdiness, heartiness, bluffness, or professorial demeanour). □ **tweedˈiˈness** *noun*

tween ● *noun* = TWEEN-AGER. ● *adjective* = TWEEN-AGE (see TWEEN-AGER).

'tween *preposition archaic* or *literary* = BETWEEN. [contraction]

tween-ager (also **tweenˈie**) N Amer. a person who has not yet, or has only recently, become a teenager, usu. between the ages of 8 and 14. □ **tween-age** *adjective*

'tween decks *noun Naut.* the space between the decks of a ship.

tweenˈer *noun informal* a person or thing considered to be in between two other recognized categories or types.

tweet ● *noun* the chirp of a small bird. ● *intransitive verb* make a chirping noise. [imitative]

tweetˈer *noun* a loudspeaker designed to reproduce high frequencies (*compare* WOOFER).

tweeze *transitive verb* esp. N Amer. **1** pinch or grab with or as if with tweezers. **2** pluck (the eyebrows) with tweezers. [back-formation from TWEEZERS]

tweezˈers *plural noun* a small pair of pincers used for picking up tiny objects, plucking eyebrows, removing splinters, etc. [extended form of *tweezes* (compare *pincers* etc.) pl. of obsolete *tweeze* case for small instruments, from *etweese* = French *étuis*, pl. of *étui* ETUI]

twelfth ● *noun* **1** the position in a sequence corresponding to the number 12. **2** the person or thing corresponding to the number 12 in a category, series, etc., identified contextually, such as a day of the month or (following a proper name) a specified monarch or pope etc. (*her birthday is the twelfth of July; King Charles XII of Sweden*). **3** each of twelve equal parts of a thing. **4** *Music* **a** an interval or chord spanning an octave and a fifth in the diatonic scale. **b** a note separated from another by this interval. ● *adjective* that is the twelfth. ● *adverb* in the twelfth place; twelfthly. □ **twelfthˈly** *adverb*

Twelfth Day *noun* 6 Jan., the twelfth day after Christmas, the festival of the Epiphany.

Twelfth Night *noun* **1** the evening of 5 Jan., the eve of the Epiphany. **2** = TWELFTH DAY.

twelve ● *noun* **1** one more than eleven; the sum of ten and two, or the product of two and six. **2** a symbol for this (12, xii, XII). **3** twelve people or things identified contextually, such as years of age, points in a game, minutes, inches, etc. **4** a size etc. denoted by twelve. **5** twelve o'clock. **6** (**the Twelve**) the twelve apostles. ● *adjective* that amount to twelve. [Old English *twelf(e)* from Germanic, prob. related to TWO]

twelveˈfold *adjective & adverb* **1** twelve times as much or as many. **2** consisting of twelve parts.

twelve·month *noun archaic* a year; a period of twelve months.

twelve-pack *noun N Amer.* a case of twelve items sold together, esp. bottles or cans of beer.

12-step *adjective* designating or pertaining to a program designed to help addicts overcome esp. a drug or alcohol dependency, based on progressing through twelve stages towards recovery. □ **12-stepper** *noun* **12-stepping** *noun*

Twelve Tables a set of laws drawn up in ancient Rome in 451 and 450 BC, embodying the most important rules of Roman law.

twelve-tone *adjective* (also **twelve-note**) pertaining to or designating music using the twelve chromatic notes of the octave on an equal basis without dependence on a key system.

Twelve Tribes of Israel *see* TRIBES OF ISRAEL.

twenty ● *noun (pl.* **-ties**) **1** the product of two and ten. **2** a symbol for this (20, xx, XX). **3** twenty people or things identified contextually, such as years of age, points in a game, minutes, etc. **4** (in *pl.*) the numbers from 20 to 29, esp. the years of a century or of a person's life. **5** *informal* a large indefinite number (*have told you twenty times*). **6** a twenty-dollar bill, twenty-pound note, etc. ● *adjective* that amount to twenty. □ **twenty-first, -second**, etc. the ordinal numbers between twentieth and thirtieth. **twenty-one, -two**, etc. the cardinal numbers between twenty and thirty. □ **twen·ti·eth** *adjective, adverb & noun* **twenty·fold** *adjective & adverb* [Old English *twentig* (perhaps as TWO, -TY²)]

24-7 *adverb* twenty-four hours a day, seven days a week; constantly (*the store is open 24-7*).

24 Sussex Drive *noun Cdn* the official residence of the prime minister in Ottawa, since 1951.

twenty-one *noun N Amer.* = BLACKJACK¹ 1.

twenty questions *noun* a parlour game in which one party is allowed twenty questions (answered by either 'yes' or 'no') to discover the object of the other's thoughts.

twenty-six *noun Cdn* a 26-ounce bottle of liquor.

twenty·some·thing ● *noun* **1** an undetermined age between twenty and thirty. **2** a person of this age or generation. ● *adjective* **1** characteristic of the tastes and lifestyle of this group. **2** between twenty and thirty years of age. [after THIRTYSOMETHING]

20/20 *adjective* (also **twenty-twenty**) denoting vision of normal acuity. □ **hindsight is 20/20** it is much easier to understand and criticize events, decisions, etc. after the fact than while they are occurring or being made.

twenty-two *noun* a .22-calibre gun or cartridge.

'twere *archaic* it were. [contraction]

twerp *noun slang* a foolish, pathetic, or insignificant person; a pipsqueak, a nobody. □ **twerpy** *adjective* [20th c.: origin unknown]

Twi /twi/ ● *noun* **1** one of the two main varieties of Akan spoken in Ghana, the other being the mutually intelligible Fanti. **2** a member of a Twi-speaking people inhabiting Ghana. ● *adjective* of or pertaining to the Twi or their people. [Kwa]

twi·bill /'twaibɪl/ *noun hist.* a double-bladed battle-axe. [Old English from *twi-* double + BILL³]

twice *adverb* **1** on two successive occasions; two times (*we went out twice; take these pills twice a day*). **2** in double degree or quantity (*twice as good*). [Middle English *twiges* from Old English *twige* (as TWO, -S³)]

twid·dle *verb* **1 a** *transitive* cause to rotate lightly or delicately with the fingers; twirl, adjust (*she twiddled the pen, wondering what to write*). **b** *intransitive* (often foll. by *with*) play idly; fiddle, tinker. **2** *intransitive* move in a twirling manner (*the baton twiddled in the air*). □ **twiddle one's thumbs** move one's thumbs around each other with the fingers linked together, esp. as a sign of boredom or impatience. **2** have nothing to do. □ **twid·dler** *noun* **twid·dly** *adjective* [apparently imitative, after *twirl, twist*, and *fiddle, piddle*]

twig¹ *noun* **1** a small branch or shoot of a tree or shrub. **2** *Anat.* a small branch of an artery etc. □ **twigged** *adjective* (also in *combination*).

twiggy *adjective* [Old English *twigge* from a Germanic root *twi-* (unrecorded) as in TWICE, TWO]

twig² *verb* (**twigged, twig·ging**) *informal* **1 a** *transitive* understand; grasp the meaning or nature of. **b** *intransitive* (often foll. by *to*) become conscious or aware of; catch on. **2** *transitive* recognize, perceive, observe. [18th c.: origin unknown]

twig furniture *noun N Amer.* a style of rustic furniture made from the branches and twigs of esp. willow trees.

twi·light *noun* **1 a** the soft glowing light from the sky when the sun is below the horizon, esp. in the evening. **b** any faint light resembling this. **2** the period or time of day when this occurs, esp. in the evening. **3** an intermediate condition or period, esp. one of decline or destruction (also *attributive: twilight years of life*). **4** a state of imperfect knowledge or understanding. [Middle English from Old English *twi-* two (in uncertain sense) + LIGHT¹]

twilight sleep *noun* a state of partial narcosis or stupor without total loss of consciousness, in particular a state induced by an injection of morphine and scopolamine, formerly popular for use during childbirth.

twilight zone *noun* any physical or conceptual area lying undefined or intermediate between two distinct fields or regions, having characteristics of both but belonging to neither (*professional wrestling exists in a twilight zone between sport and entertainment*).

twi·lit *adjective* (also **twi·light·ed**) dimly illuminated by or as if by twilight.

twill *noun* **1** a woven fabric with a surface of diagonal parallel ridges, produced by passing the weft threads over one and under two or more threads of the warp, instead of over and under in regular succession. **2** the method of weaving this fabric. [Northern English var. of obsolete *twilly*, Old English *twili*, from *twi-* double, after Latin *bilix* (as BI-, *licium* thread)]

'twill *archaic* it will. [contraction]

Twil·lin·gate a town off the northeastern coast of Newfoundland, situated on South Twillingate Island, about 100 km north of Gander; pop. (2001) 2,651. □ **Twil·lin·gater** *noun* [Pointe de *Toulinguet* in Brest, France]

twin ● *noun* **1** each of two children or animals born at the same time to the same mother, having developed from the same ovum (*identical twins*) or two separately fertilized ova (*fraternal twins*) (also *attributive: twin sisters*). **2** either of two closely related or similar things; a counterpart (also *attributive: twin houses*). **3** either of two parts, usu. identical, working in unison (also *attributive: twin cylinder engine*). **4 a** (*attributive*) denoting a twin-size mattress, bed, sheets, etc. (*see* TWIN-SIZE). **b** such a bed or mattress. **5** *Mineralogy* a composite crystal consisting of two usu. equal and similar crystals having reversed, rotated, or shifted positions with respect to each other, united along a plane or interpenetrating. **6** (**the Twins**) the zodiacal sign or constellation Gemini. **7** a twin-engined aircraft. ● *verb* (**twinned, twin·ning**) **1 a** *transitive* couple, join, unite (two people or things) closely or intimately. **b** *intransitive* (often foll. by *with*) be or become coupled or joined; pair. **2** *intransitive* (in *passive*) *Mineralogy* (of two crystals) grow to form twin crystals. **3** *transitive* (usu. in *passive*) establish official links between (two cities or towns, esp. in different countries) for the purposes of friendship and cultural exchange. **4** *transitive* build a second two-lane highway (alongside an existing one) so as to create a divided highway. □ **twin·ning** *noun* **twin·ship** *noun* [Old English *twinn* double, from *twi-* two: compare Old Norse *tvinnr*]

twin·berry *noun (pl.* **-berries**) *N Amer.* any of various honeysuckles with berries borne in pairs.

twin bill *noun informal* **1** *Baseball* = DOUBLEHEADER 1a. **2** = DOUBLE FEATURE.

twin-cam *attributive adjective* (esp. of an engine) having two camshafts.

twin city *noun* **1** (**Twin Cities**) *N Amer.* two neighbouring cities situated close together, such as St. Paul and Minneapolis, Minnesota or (formerly) Fort William and Port Arthur, Ontario, before they merged and became Thunder Bay. **2** each of a pair of usu. international cities with official ties for the purposes of friendship and cultural exchange.

twine ● *noun* a strong cord or string made of the twisted strands of hemp, cotton, sisal, etc. ● *verb* **1** *transitive* **a** join together (two or more strands etc.) by twisting (*she twined her hair into a braid*). **b** (often foll. by *with*) twist or join (one thing, strand, etc.) with another (*I twined my arm with hers*). **2** *intransitive* (of two things) become joined, linked, or tangled (*their lives twined inextricably the moment they met*). **3** *transitive* (often foll. by *around*) wind or wrap (one or more strands etc.) (*I twined the rope around a tree*). **4** *transitive* form (a garland or wreath etc.) by twisting or weaving flowers, leaves, etc. **5** *intransitive* (of a plant) grow in a twisting or winding manner (*the morning glories twined up the trellis*). □ **twin·er** *noun* [Old English *twin, twigin* linen, ultimately from the stem of *twi-* two]

twin-engined *adjective* (also **twin-engine**) (of an aircraft etc.) having two engines.

twin·flower *noun* a low plant of the honeysuckle family, *Linnaea borealis*, with pairs of bell-shaped flowers.

twinge ● *noun* **1** a sudden sharp physical pain (*she felt a twinge in her shoulder*). **2** a sudden emotional pang (*a twinge of conscience; a twinge of* guilt). ● *transitive & intransitive verb* cause or experience a twinge. [*twinge* (v.) pinch, wring, from Old English *twengan* from Germanic]

twi-night *adjective Baseball* designating or pertaining to a doubleheader beginning with a game played in the late afternoon in daylight and concluding with a game played in the evening under artificial light. [TWI(LIGHT) + NIGHT]

twink·ie *noun* (also **twink, twinky** *pl.* **-ies**) esp. *US derogatory* **1** a weak or feeble person; a wimp. **2** a homosexual. [perhaps from *Twinkie* proprietary name for a brand of cream-filled cupcake (*compare* CREAM PUFF 1, 2)]

twin·kle ● *intransitive verb* **1** (of a star or light etc.) shine with rapid alternation between brightness and faintness. **2** (of the eyes) have a bright lively expression, esp. of amusement. **3** (of the feet in dancing) move lightly and rapidly. ● *noun* **1** a sparkle or gleam of the eyes, esp. as a reflection of liveliness, youthfulness, or mischievousness. **2** a brief or intermittent flash, flicker, or gleam of light; a glimmer. **3 a** a blink or wink of the eye. **b** a brief moment; an instant. □ **twink·ler** *noun* **twink·ly** *adjective* [Old English *twinclian*]

twinkle·toes *noun informal* a person who is nimble and quick on their feet.

twink·ling ● *noun* the action of twinkling. ● *adjective* that twinkles. □ **in a twinkling** (or **the twinkling of an eye**) in an instant.

twin-screw *adjective* (of a ship) having two propellers on separate shafts with opposite twists.

twin-set *noun* esp. *Brit.* = SWEATER SET.

twin-size *adjective* (also **twin-sized**) designating the smallest standard size of a mattress, usu. 98 by 191 cm (38.5 by 75 in.), or of the bed frame, sheets, etc. designed for such a mattress.

twirl ● *verb* **1** *transitive & intransitive* spin, turn, or rotate rapidly or quickly (*she twirled the baton in the air; he twirled around and faced them*). **2** *transitive* roll or twist between the thumb and forefinger (*he twirled his moustache*). ● *noun* **1** a twirling motion. **2** a twirling object or shape, such as a flourish made with a pen. □ **twirl·er** *noun* **twirly** *adjective* [16th c.: prob. alteration (by association with *whirl*) of obsolete *tirl* TRILL]

twist ● *verb* **1 a** *transitive* distort the shape of (something usu. long and thin) by turning two ends in opposite directions or by turning one end while the other remains fixed. **b** *transitive* cause (something long and thin, such as a string, wire, or strand of hair) to coil around an axis, thus imparting a spiral shape to it. **c** *intransitive* assume a spiral or twisted form by being distorted in this way. **2** *transitive* **a** wind (strands of hemp, cotton, etc.) together to form a rope. **b** form (a rope etc.) by winding strands of hemp or cotton etc. **c** (foll. by *with, in with*) interweave (*she twisted her hair with ribbon*). **3** *transitive* (often foll. by *around*) wind or coil (a thread etc.) around something. **4** *transitive, intransitive, & reflexive* turn (oneself or a part of one's body) around partly or completely in order to face another direction. **5 a** *transitive* accidentally turn (one's ankle, knee, etc.) sharply, so as to strain and injure the ligaments or tendons. **b** *transitive* deliberately turn (someone else's arm etc.) around violently in order to cause pain or injury. **c** *transitive* screw up or contort (one's face or features), esp. in pain, anger, or contempt. **d** *intransitive* (of the face or features) be contorted. **6** *transitive* distort or misrepresent (facts or someone's meaning, intentions, etc.). **7** *transitive* **a** apply a rotating movement to (*she nervously twisted the ring around her finger*). **b** (foll. by *off*) remove by twisting (*twist the top off the jar*). **8** *intransitive* rotate or turn, or be capable of this (*falling leaves twisted in the air*). **9** *intransitive* (of a road, river, person, etc.) follow a very winding path. **10** *intransitive* dance the twist. **11** *transitive Brit. informal* cheat (a person). ● *noun* **1** an act or an instance of twisting. **2** a thing formed by or as by twisting; a twisted form or shape, such as a spiral ornamentation in the stem of a wineglass. **3** a bend or curve in a road or path, esp. one followed immediately by a curve in the opposite direction. **4 a** a complication, esp. an unexpected or ironic development in a story or in a person's life (*this mystery novel has a great twist at the end*). **b** a slight change made to an existing model, usu. to add interest or flair (*the classic old story with a modern twist*). **5** usu. *derogatory* an eccentric inclination or attitude, esp. a peculiar mental bent. **6 a** a curled piece of lemon peel to flavour a drink. **b** an item of food having a spiral or twisted shape (*pasta twists; cinnamon twists*). **7** (prec. by *the*) a dance in which the upper and lower body are swivelled back and forth in opposite directions, popular in the early 1960s. **8** a sprain or strain of a limb. **9 a** a rope or cord made by winding together strands of hemp or cotton etc. **b** a fine strong silk thread used by tailors etc. **10** *N Amer. hist.* tobacco rolled and twisted into a thick cord. **11** the rifling bore of a gun. **12** *Physics* **a** a twisting strain or force; torque. **b** forward motion combined with rotation about an axis, e.g. the movement of a screw.

13 *N Amer.* = FRENCH TWIST. **14** *Brit.* a drink made of two ingredients mixed together. **15** *Brit. informal* a swindle. **16** a carpet with a tightly curled pile. □ **round the twist** *Brit. informal* = ROUND THE BEND (see BEND[1]). **twist a person's arm** *informal* apply coercion to a person to overcome their reluctance to do something. **twist around one's finger** see FINGER. **twist of fate** an ironic reversal of fortune. **twist the knife** cause further damage or mental pain, in addition to some previously inflicted. **twist in the wind** be left in a state of painful suspense or uncertainty. □ **twist·able** *adjective* **twisty** *adjective* (**twist·i·er, twist·i·est**). [Middle English, related to TWIN, TWINE]

twist·ed *adjective* **1** (of a person, their mind, or values) morally warped; perverted. **2** (of a story) having many complications and unexpected changes of plot; intricate in a way that strains credulity. **3** misshapen, mangled (*the wrecked car was left a heap of twisted metal*). **4** (of an ankle etc.) sprained. **5** entwined. **6** (of the face or the features) contorted.

twisted pair *noun* a pair of conductors twisted about each other in a cable.

twisted stalk *noun* any of several N American and Asian plants of the genus *Streptopus*, of the lily family, bearing bell-shaped flowers on bent or twisted stalks.

twist·er *noun* **1** *N Amer.* a tornado. **2** esp. *Brit. informal* a swindler; a dishonest person. **3** a person or thing that twists.

twist-tie ● *noun* a small strip of plastic-covered wire which can be looped around something, typically the neck of a plastic bag, and fastened by twisting the two ends together. ● *transitive verb* (**-ties, -tied, -tying**) fasten with a twist-tie.

twit[1] *noun slang* a silly or foolish person. [originally dial.: perhaps from TWIT[2]]

twit[2] *transitive verb* (**twit·ted, twit·ting**) reproach or scold, esp. in a good-humoured or teasing manner. [16th-c. *twite* from *atwite* from Old English *ætwitan* reproach with, from *æt* at + *witan* blame]

twitch ● *verb* **1 a** *intransitive* (of the features, muscles, limbs, etc.) move or contract spasmodically. **b** *transitive* move (part of the body) spasmodically. **2** *transitive* give a short sharp pull at; jerk, tug. ● *noun* **1 a** a sudden involuntary contraction or movement of a muscle etc. **b** a pang; a twinge (*a twitch of irritation*). **2** a sudden sharp pull or jerk. **3** a loop of cord attached to a stick, used to restrain a horse during veterinary operations by twisting the stick to tighten the loop around the animal's upper lip. [Middle English from Germanic: compare Old English *twiccian*, dial. *twick*]

twitch·er *noun Brit. informal* a birdwatcher who tries to get sightings of rare birds.

twitch grass *noun* = COUCH[2]. [var. of QUITCH]

twitchy *adjective* (**twitch·i·er, twitch·i·est**) **1** having a tendency to twitch. **2** nervous, fidgety.

twit·ter ● *verb* **1** *intransitive* **a** (of a bird) chirp with a succession of light tremulous sounds. **b** (of a person) laugh, titter. **2 a** *intransitive* talk rapidly in a tremulous voice; chatter. **b** *transitive* utter or express in this way. ● *noun* **1** a light tremulous chirp. **2** *informal* a state of excitement. **3** a giggle or titter. □ **twit·ter·er** *noun* **twit·tery** *adjective* [imitative]

'twixt *preposition archaic* = BETWIXT. [contraction]

twiz·zle *noun Figure Skating* a turn executed with one skate blade on the ice. [imitative, after TWIST]

two ● *noun* **1** one more than one; the sum of one unit and another unit. **2** a symbol for this (2, ii, II). **3** two people or things identified contextually, such as parts or divisions, years of age, points in a game, etc. **4** a size etc. denoted by two. **5** two o'clock. **6** a card with two pips. ● *adjective* that amount to two. □ **in two** in or into two pieces. **in two shakes** see SHAKE. **or two** denoting several (*a thing or two*). **put two and two together** make (esp. an obvious) inference from what is known or evident. **that makes two of us** *informal* I am in the same position or am of the same opinion. **two by two** in pairs. **two can play at that game** *informal* I am equally capable of using a person's strategy, to their disadvantage (*she thinks she can beat me by cheating, but two can play at that game*). **two a penny** *Brit.* see PENNY. [Old English *twā* (fem. & neuter), *tū* (neuter), with Germanic cognates and related to Sanskrit *dwau, dwe,* Greek & Latin *duo*]

two-and-a-half *noun Cdn (Que.)* an apartment having two rooms, typically a combined kitchen/living room and a bedroom, plus a bathroom.

two-bagger *noun* (also **two-base hit**) *Baseball* = DOUBLE 4.

two-bit *adjective N Amer. informal* **1** cheap, worthless, minor, small-time. **2** worth twenty-five cents.

two bits *noun N Amer. informal* twenty-five cents.

Consonants: b *but* d *dog* f *few* g *get* h *her* j *yes* k *cat* l *leg* m *man* n *no* p *pen* r *red* s *sit*

two-by-four *noun* a length of timber that has a rectangular cross-section of $1^1/_2$ inches by $3^1/_2$ inches (3.8 cm by 8.9 cm) when trimmed, or 2 inches by 4 inches (5.1 cm by 10.2 cm) when untrimmed.

two cents *plural noun* (in full **two cents' worth**) *N Amer. informal* an unsolicited opinion.

two-cycle *adjective N Amer.* = TWO-STROKE.

2-D ● *adjective* having or portraying a two-dimensional appearance. ● *noun* a format that presents two-dimensional images.

two-dimen·sion·al *adjective* **1** having or appearing to have length and width but no depth. **2** lacking depth or substance; superficial. □ **two-dimen·sion·al·ity** *noun* **two-dimen·sion·al·ly** *adverb*

two-edged *adjective* double-edged.

two-faced *adjective* insincere, deceitful, hypocritical.

two·fer /ˈtuːfər/ *noun esp. US slang or jocular* **1** a coupon entitling a person to buy two tickets for a theatrical performance for the price of one. **2** any two items regarded as being obtained for the price of one. [representing a pronunciation of 'two for one']

two-fisted *adjective N Amer.* tough, aggressive, vigorous.

two·fold *adjective & adverb* **1** twice as much or as many. **2** consisting of two parts.

two-four *noun Cdn informal* a case of twenty-four bottles of beer.

2,4-D *noun* a slightly soluble white to yellow crystalline powder, $C_8H_6O_3Cl_2$, that forms the active ingredient in many herbicides.

two-handed *adjective* **1** using or requiring the use of two hands. **2** (of a card game) for two players.

two-hander *noun* **1** a play for two actors. **2** *Hockey slang* a two-handed slash.

two-on-one *noun* (pl. **-ones**) **1** *Hockey* a rush led by two players against one defender and a goalie (also *attributive: two-on-one break*). **2** *Basketball* a rush led by two players against one defender.

two·pence /ˈtʌpəns/ *noun Brit.* **1** the sum of two pence, esp. before decimalization. **2** *informal* (esp. with *neg.*) a thing of little value (*don't care twopence*).

two·penny /ˈtʌpəni/ *adjective Brit.* **1** costing two pence, esp. before decimalization. **2** (also **twopenny-halfpenny** /ˌtʌpnɪˈheɪpni/) *informal* cheap, worthless.

two per cent *noun* (also **2 per cent**, **2%**) *N Amer.* partly skimmed milk containing two per cent milk fat.

two-piece ● *adjective* (esp. of a suit, snowsuit, bathing suit, etc.) consisting of two matching items. ● *noun* (also **two-piecer**) a two-piece suit or bathing suit etc.

two-ply ● *adjective* consisting of two strands or thicknesses. ● *noun* two-ply wool or wood etc.

two-pronged *adjective* having two aspects, stages, aims, or lines of attack.

two-seater *noun* a vehicle or aircraft with two seats.

two-sided *adjective* **1** having two sides. **2** having two aspects; controversial.

two solitudes *plural noun Cdn* the anglophone and francophone populations of Canada, portrayed as two cultures coexisting independent of and isolated from each other. [from *Two Solitudes* (1945) a novel by Hugh MacLennan]

two·some *noun* **1** two people together. **2** a game, dance, etc., for two people.

two-spirit·ed *noun* (of an Aboriginal person) gay or lesbian.

two-step *noun, verb, & adjective* ● *noun* a ballroom dance for couples involving a sliding step in march or polka time. ● *intransitive verb* dance the two-step. ● *adjective* involving two successive actions or stages.

two-stroke *adjective* **1** (of an internal combustion engine) having its power cycle completed in one up-and-down movement of the piston. **2** (of a vehicle) having a two-stroke engine.

two-time *informal* ● *transitive verb* **1** be unfaithful to (esp. a lover or spouse). **2** swindle, double-cross. ● *adjective* having achieved a specified distinction twice (*two-time champion*). □ **two-timer** *noun*

two-tone *adjective* having two colours or two shades of the same colour. □ **two-toned** *adjective*

'twould *archaic* it would. [contraction]

two-way *adjective* **1** involving two participants. **2** (of a radio) capable of transmitting and receiving signals. **3** (of a loudspeaker) having two separate drive units for different frequency ranges, a woofer and a tweeter. **4** (of traffic etc.) moving in two esp. opposite directions. **5** (of a

tap etc.) permitting fluid etc. to flow in either of two channels or directions.

two-way mirror *noun* a panel of glass that is transparent from one side but reflects light and images from the other.

two-wheel drive *noun* a system in a motor vehicle which supplies power to either the front or back wheels (*see* FRONT-WHEEL DRIVE, REAR-WHEEL DRIVE).

two-wheel·er *noun* a vehicle with two wheels. □ **two-wheeled** *adjective*

Twp. *abbreviation* Township.

TX *abbreviation* (in official postal use) Texas.

-ty¹ *suffix* forming nouns denoting quality or condition (*cruelty*; *plenty*). [Old French *-té*, *-tet* from Latin *-tas -tatis*: compare -ITY]

-ty² *suffix* forming cardinal numerals from 20 to 90 denoting tens (*twenty*; *thirty*; *ninety*). [Old English *-tig*]

Ty·burn /ˈtaɪbɜrn/ a place in London, England where public hangings were held *c.*1300–1783.

ty·coon /taɪˈkuːn/ *noun* **1** a business magnate. **2** *hist.* a title applied by foreigners to the shogun of Japan 1854–68. □ **ty·coon·ery** *noun* [Japanese *taikun* great lord, from Chinese *dà* great + *jūn* prince]

tyee /ˈtaɪiː/ *noun Cdn* (*BC*) a chinook salmon, esp. one weighing more than 13.6 kg (30 lb.) (*see* CHINOOK 2). [Chinook Jargon, from Nuu-chah-nulth *ta·yi*: elder brother, chief]

tying *pres. part. of* TIE.

tyke *noun* **1** *informal* a small child. **2** *Cdn* **a** an initiation level of sports competition for young children. **b** a player at this level. **3** a dog, esp. a mongrel or mutt. **4** *esp. Brit.* an unpleasant or ill-mannered man. [Old Norse *tík* bitch]

Ty·len·ol /ˈtaɪlənɒl/ *noun N Amer. proprietary* acetaminophen.

Tyler ▸ **1 John** (1790–1862), US Whig politician, 10th president of the US 1841–5. He succeeded William Henry Harrison as president and was noted for securing the annexation of Texas (1845). **2 Wat** (full name Walter Tyler) (d.1381), English revolutionary, who led the Peasants' Revolt (1381) against the newly imposed poll tax of Richard II; he was killed by the Lord Mayor of London and several other royal supporters.

tym·pana *pl. of* TYMPANUM.

tym·pani *var. of* TIMPANI.

tym·pan·ic /tɪmˈpanɪk/ *adjective* **1** *Anat.* of, relating to, or having a tympanum. **2** resembling or acting like a drumhead.

tympanic bone *noun Anat.* (in mammals) a bone of annular or tubular form supporting the eardrum and surrounding part of the external auditory meatus, forming part of the temporal bone in adults.

tympanic membrane *noun Anat.* = EARDRUM.

tym·pa·num /ˈtɪmpənəm/ *noun* (pl. **tym·pa·na** /-nə/ or **tym·pa·nums**) **1** *Anat.* **a** = MIDDLE EAR. **b** = EARDRUM. **2** *Zool.* the membrane covering the hearing organ on the leg of an insect. **3** *Archit.* a vertical triangular space forming the centre of a pediment. **4** *Archit.* **a** a similar space over a door between the lintel and an arch. **b** a carving on this space. **5** a drum, esp. a hand drum of ancient Greece and Rome. [Latin from Greek *tumpanon* drum, from *tuptō* strike]

Tyn·dale /ˈtɪndəl/ **William** (also **Tin·dal**; **Tin·dale**) (*c.*1494–1536), English translator and Protestant martyr. Faced with ecclesiastical opposition to his project for translating the Bible into English, he went abroad in 1524, and translated the New Testament (*c.*1525–6), the Pentateuch (1530), and Jonah (1531); in 1535 he was arrested, charged with heresy, and subsequently strangled and burned at the stake.

Tyn·dall /ˈtɪndəl/ **John** (1820–93), Irish physicist. He studied the absorbency and transmission of heat by gases and liquids; he also worked on the transmission of sound, and the scattering of light by suspended particles, becoming the first person to explain the blue colour of the sky.

Tyndall stone *noun* (also **Tyndall limestone**) *Cdn* a variety of mottled dolomitic limestone quarried near Winnipeg, noted for the presence of a large number of fossils. [after *Tyndall* Manitoba where it is quarried, named after John TYNDALL]

Tyn·dar·eus /tɪnˈdɛrɪəs/ *Gk Myth* a king of Sparta, husband of Leda.

Tyne and Wear /ˈtaɪn ənd wɪːr/ a former metropolitan county of NE England.

Tyne River a river in NE England, formed by the confluence of two headstreams, the North Tyne, which rises in the Cheviot Hills, and the South Tyne, which rises in the N Pennines. It flows 50 km (31 miles) generally eastward, entering the North Sea at Tynemouth.

Tyne·side an industrial conurbation on the banks of the Tyne River, in NE England, stretching from Newcastle-upon-Tyne to the coast. □ **Tyne·sider** noun

Tyn·wald /ˈtɪnwɒld/ noun the parliament of the Isle of Man. [Old Norse thing-völlr place of assembly, from thing assembly + völlr field]

type ● noun **1 a** a class of people or things distinguished by common essential characteristics. **b** a kind or sort (I don't like that type of coffee). **2** a person, thing, or event serving as an illustration, symbol, or characteristic specimen of another, or of a class. **3** (in combination) made of, resembling, or functioning as. **4 a** a person of a particular specified or contextually implied character (he's the strong silent type; she's not the type to pick a fight). **b** (prec. by possessive) the kind of person to whom one is attracted (he's not my type). **5 a** the general form, structure, or character distinguishing a particular group or class of things. **b** an object, conception, or work of art serving as a model for subsequent artists. **6** Printing **a** a character for printing, originally a metal casting from a matrix, reproducing a punch on which a letter or other character was engraved. **b** such pieces collectively, esp. with reference to size or font. **c** printed characters produced by type collectively (printed in large type). **7** Biol. an organism having or chosen as having the essential characteristics of its taxonomic group and giving its name to the next highest taxonomic group, e.g. the genus Solanum (potato) is said to be the type genus of the family Solanaceae. **8** Theol. a foreshadowing in the Old Testament of a person or event of the Christian dispensation. **9** a device on either side of a medal or coin. ● verb **1** transitive & intransitive **a** write with a typewriter. **b** use a computer keyboard. **2** transitive be a type or example of. **3** transitive **a** assign to a type; classify. **b** Biol. & Med. determine the type to which (blood, tissue, etc.) belongs. **4** transitive = TYPECAST. □ **in type** Printing composed and ready for printing. □ **typal** adjective [French type or Latin typus from Greek tupos impression, figure, type, from tuptō strike]

Type A noun (pl. **Type A's**) **1** a personality type characterized by ambition, impatience, and aggressive competitiveness, thought to be particularly susceptible to stress. **2** a person of this personality type.

Type B noun (pl. **Type B's**) **1** a personality type characterized as easygoing and thought to have low susceptibility to stress. **2** a person of this personality type.

type·cast transitive verb (past and past participle **-cast**) (usu. in passive) **1** assign (an actor) repeatedly to the same type of role which he or she has often played successfully in previous productions or which seems to fit his or her personality. **2** consider (a person) as fitting a stereotype; pigeonhole. □ **type·cast·ing** noun

typed adjective **1** classified as or having a certain character or type. **2** (of a document) produced with a computer keyboard and printer, typewriter, etc.; not handwritten.

type·face noun **1 a** the particular style, appearance, size, etc. of a type or set of types. **b** Computing the design of a particular font. **2 a** the inked part of type. **b** the impression made by this.

type locality noun (also **type site**) Archaeology & Geol. a site where specimens regarded as defining the characteristics of a culture, stratigraphic level, etc., are found.

type·script noun a typewritten document.

type·set·ter noun Printing **1** a person who composes type. **2** a machine used for setting textual matter in type. □ **type·set** transitive & intransitive verb (**-set·ting**; past and past participle **-set**). **type·set·ting** noun

type specimen noun Biol. & Geol. the original specimen which, though not necessarily the most characteristic representative of a species, is used to name and describe a new species.

type·writ·er noun a machine for producing characters like those used in printing by means of keys which, when pressed one at a time, cause a type mounted on a bar or ball to strike a sheet of paper inserted around a roller, through an inked ribbon. □ **type·writ·ing** noun

type·writ·ten adjective produced with a typewriter.

ty·phoid /ˈtaɪfɔɪd/ ● noun **1** (in full **typhoid fever**) a severe infectious fever caused by the bacterium Salmonella typhi, involving a rash, myalgia, and in some cases delirium and intestinal inflammation. **2** a similar disease of animals. ● adjective resembling or characteristic of typhus. □ **ty·phoid·al** /ˌtaɪˈfɔɪdəl/ adjective [TYPHUS + -OID]

Typhoid Mary noun **1** a person who transmits a disease widely without showing its symptoms. **2** a transmitter of undesirable opinions, sentiments, etc. [nickname of Mary Mallon, Irish-born cook who transmitted typhoid fever in the US, d.1938]

Ty·phon /ˈtaɪfən/ Gk Myth a monster with 100 serpent heads, who was cast by Zeus into Tartarus, and who was held to be the source of winds which cause shipwreck and devastation.

ty·phoon /taɪˈfuːn/ noun a violent storm occurring in or around the Indian subcontinent, esp. a tropical cyclone occurring in the region of the Indian or W Pacific Oceans. □ **ty·phon·ic** /-ˈfɒnɪk/ adjective [partly from Portuguese tufão from Arabic ṭūfān (perhaps from Greek tuphōn whirlwind); reinforced by Chinese dial. tai fung big wind]

ty·phus /ˈtaɪfəs/ noun any of a group of acute infectious fevers caused by rickettsiae, often transmitted by lice or fleas, and characterized by a purple rash, headaches, fever, and usu. delirium. [modern Latin from Greek tuphos smoke, stupor, from tuphō to smoke]

typ·i·cal /ˈtɪpɪkəl/ adjective **1** serving as a characteristic example; representative (a typical high school student). **2** characteristic of or serving to distinguish a type (a typical feature of Maritime architecture). **3** (often foll. by of) conforming to expected esp. undesirable behaviour, attitudes, etc. (is typical of them to forget; They're late again? Typical.). **4** symbolic. □ **typ·i·cal·ity** /-ˈkalɪti/ noun **typ·i·cal·ly** adverb [medieval Latin typicalis from Latin typicus from Greek tupikos (as TYPE)]

typ·i·fy /ˈtɪpɪˌfaɪ/ transitive verb (**-fies, -fied**) **1** be a representative example of; embody the characteristics of. **2** serve as an emblem or symbol of; symbolize. [Latin typus TYPE + -FY]

typ·ist noun a person who types or uses a typewriter, esp. professionally.

typo noun (pl. **typos**) informal an error in typed or printed material, resulting from a mistake in typing or in arranging and setting types etc. [abbreviation of 'typographical (error)']

typ·og·raph·er /taɪˈpɒɡrəfər/ noun a person skilled in typography.

typ·og·raphy /taɪˈpɒɡrəfi/ noun **1** the art or practice of printing. **2** the process of printing; the process of setting and arranging types and printing from them. **3** the style and appearance of printed matter. □ **typo·graph·ic** /-pəˈɡrafɪk/ adjective **typo·graph·ic·al** adjective **typo·graph·ic·al·ly** adverb [French typographie or modern Latin typographia (as TYPE, -GRAPHY)]

typ·ol·ogy /taɪˈpɒlədʒi/ noun (pl. **-gies**) **1 a** the branch of knowledge that deals with classes with common characteristics. **b** a classification of esp. human behaviour or characteristics according to type. **2** the branch of religion that deals with esp. Biblical symbolic representation. □ **typo·logic·al** adjective **typo·logic·al·ly** adverb **typ·olo·gist** noun

Tyr /tɪːr/ Scand. Myth the god of battle, identified with Mars.

tyr·a·mine /ˈtaɪrəmiːn/ noun Biochem. a derivative of tyrosine occurring naturally in cheese and other foods and affecting the sympathetic nervous system. [TYROSINE + AMINE]

tyr·an·nical /tɪˈranɪkəl, tə-, taɪ-/ adjective **1** of or pertaining to a tyrant or tyranny (a tyrannical regime). **2** resembling or characteristic of a tyrant or tyranny (his upbringing was tyrannical and harsh). □ **tyr·an·nical·ly** adverb [Old French tyrannique from Latin tyrannicus from Greek turannikos (as TYRANT)]

tyr·an·ni·cide /tɪˈranəˌsaɪd, tə-, taɪ-/ noun **1** the act or an instance of killing a tyrant. **2** the killer of a tyrant. □ **tyr·an·ni·cid·al** adjective [French from Latin tyrannicida, -cidium (as TYRANT, -CIDE)]

tyr·an·nize /ˈtɪrəˌnaɪz/ verb (also esp. Brit. **-nise**) **1** transitive rule, control, or behave oppressively or cruelly towards. **2** intransitive (usu. foll. by over) exercise power or control oppressively or cruelly. [French tyranniser (as TYRANT)]

tyr·an·no·saur /təˈranəsɔr, taɪ-, ti-/ noun (also **tyr·an·no·saur·us** /-ˌranəˈsɔrəs/) a huge bipedal carnivorous saurischian dinosaur of the Upper Cretaceous, Tyrannosaurus rex, having powerful hind legs and jaws, a large well-developed tail, and small claw-like front legs. [Greek turannos TYRANT, after dinosaur]

tyr·anny /ˈtɪrəni/ noun (pl. **-nies**) **1 a** the arbitrary, cruel, and excessive exercise of power, control, or authority. **b** (often foll. by of) an unduly oppressive influence (the tyranny of public opinion). **2** cruel and oppressive government by more than one person. **3** a tyrannical act; tyrannical behaviour. **4** Gk Hist. **a** rule by a tyrant. **b** a period of this. **c** a state ruled by a tyrant. □ **tyr·an·nous** adjective **tyr·an·nous·ly** adverb

tyr·ant /ˈtaɪrənt/ noun **1** an oppressive or cruel ruler. **2** any person exercising power oppressively or cruelly. **3** Gk Hist. an absolute ruler who seizes power without legal right. [Old French from Latin tyrannus from Greek turannos]

tyrant flycatcher noun any of various small birds of the New World family Tyrannidae, including flycatchers, phoebes, pewees, and kingbirds, which catch insects by a short flight from a perch. [so called because of the aggressive behaviour of the kingbird towards other birds approaching its nest]

Tyre /taɪr/ a port on the Mediterranean in S Lebanon; pop. (2002)

Vowels: a cat ɑ arm e bed ɜr her ɜː deux ə ago ɪ sit i cosy iː feed ɒ hot ɔ pore ɔː no ʌ run ʊ put

16,000. Founded in the 2nd millennium BC as a colony of Sidon, it was for centuries a Phoenician port and trading centre.

tyre Brit. var. of TIRE[2].

Tyr·ian /ˈtɪrɪən/ ● *adjective* of or relating to ancient Tyre. ● *noun* a native or citizen of Tyre.

Tyrian purple *noun* see PURPLE *noun* 2.

tyro /ˈtaɪˌrəʊ/ *noun* (*pl.* **tyros**) a beginner or novice. [medieval Latin *tyro*, Latin *tiro*, young soldier, recruit]

Tyrol /tɪˈrəʊl/ **1** an Alpine state of W Austria; capital, Innsbruck. **2** the region comprising this and parts of northern Italy. □ **Tyrol·ean** /tɪˈrəʊlɪən, -rəˈliːən/ *adjective* **Tyrol·ese** /-ˈliːz/ *adjective & noun*

Ty·rone /tɪˈrəʊn/ one of the Six Counties of Northern Ireland, formerly an administrative area; pop. (1981) 143,900; chief town, Omagh.

tyro·pita /tɪˈrɒpiːtə/ *noun* (in Greek cuisine) a savoury pie with a filling of feta and sometimes other cheeses and eggs in phyllo pastry. [Greek, from *tyrí* 'cheese' + *pita* 'pie']

tyro·sine /ˈtaɪrəsiːn/ *noun* Chem. a hydrophilic amino acid present in many proteins and important in the synthesis of some hormones etc. [formed irregularly from Greek *turos* 'cheese' + -INE[4]]

Tyr·rhene /ˈtɪriːn/ *adjective & noun* (also **Tyr·rhen·ian** /tɪˈriːnɪən/) *archaic* = ETRUSCAN. [Latin *Tyrrhenus*]

Tyrrhenian Sea a part of the Mediterranean Sea between mainland Italy and the islands of Sicily and Sardinia.

Tyson ► **Ian and Syl·via** (born Sylvia Fricker), Canadian folk duo. They were key performers in the folk revival of the early '60s with hits like 'Four Strong Winds' (1962).

Tyu·men /tjuːˈmen/ a city in W Siberian Russia, in the eastern foothills of the Ural Mountains; pop. (est. 2002) 507,000. Founded in 1586 on the site of a 14th-c. Tartar town, it is regarded as the oldest city in Siberia.

Tyvek *noun* proprietary a type of lightweight, waterproof material made from polyethylene fibres, used variously but esp. for protective clothing and in house construction.

Tzad·dik /ˈtsɒdɪk/ *noun* (*pl.* **Tzad·dik·im** /tsɒˈdɪkɪm/) Judaism **1** a person of exemplary righteousness. **2** a Hasidic spiritual leader or sage. [Hebrew *ṣaddīq* just, righteous]

tza·tziki /tsatˈsiːki/ *noun* a Greek side dish of yogourt with cucumber, garlic, and sometimes mint. [modern Greek from Turkish]

tze·dakah /tseˈdɒkə/ *noun* Judaism the obligation to help fellow Jews; charity. [Hebrew *ṣĕdāqāh* righteousness]

tzim·mes /ˈtsɪməs/ *noun* (*pl.* same) (in Jewish cuisine) a stew of sweetened vegetables or vegetables and fruit, sometimes with meat. [Yiddish *tsimes*, of unknown origin]

T-zone *noun* the central part of a person's face, including the forehead, nose, and chin, esp. as having oilier skin than the rest of the face.

Tzu-po see ZIBO.

---

uː mood   ai my   əi pipe   au brown   ʌu house   ei day   ɔi boy   ɑ̃ franglais   ã Canadien   ɔ̃ Brayon   (see over for consonants)

Uu

U¹ *noun* (also **u**) (*pl.* **Us** or **U's**) **1** the twenty-first letter of the alphabet. **2** a U-shaped object or curve (esp. *in combination: U bolt*).

U² *adjective* esp. *Brit. informal* **1** upper class. **2** supposedly characteristic of the upper class. [abbreviation]

U³ /uː/ *adjective* a Burmese title of respect before a man's name. [Burmese]

U⁴ *abbreviation* (also **U.**) university (*U of T*).

U⁵ *symbol* **1** *Chem.* the element uranium. **2** uracil.

U⁶ *pronoun informal* you (*While-U-Wait; U-pick*).

U⁷ *noun informal* a university (*I'm taking classes at the U*). [abbreviation]

u *symbol* = MICRO- 2. [substituted for the original symbol μ]

UAE *abbreviation* United Arab Emirates.

UAR *abbreviation* United Arab Republic.

UAV *abbreviation* unmanned aerial vehicle.

UAW *abbreviation* United Auto Workers.

Uban·ghi Shari /juːˌbaŋgi ˈʃɑri/ a former name (until 1958) for the CENTRAL AFRICAN REPUBLIC.

über- /ˈuːbər/ *combining form* representing the supreme example of its kind; ultimate (often with connotations of power, arrogance, etc.). [after ÜBERMENSCH]

Über·mensch /ˈuːbərˌmenʃ/ *noun* = SUPERMAN 1. [German]

-ubility /jʊˈbɪlɪti/ *suffix* forming nouns from, or corresponding to, adjectives in *-uble* (*solubility; volubility*). [Latin *-ubilitas:* compare -ITY]

ubi·qui·tous /juːˈbɪkwɪtəs/ *adjective* **1** present everywhere or in several places simultaneously. **2** often encountered. □ **ubi·qui·tous·ly** *adverb* **ubi·qui·tous·ness** *noun* **ubi·quity** *noun* [modern Latin *ubiquitas* from Latin *ubique* everywhere, from *ubi* where]

-uble /jʊbəl/ *suffix* forming adjectives meaning 'that may or must (be)' (*see* -ABLE) (*soluble; voluble*). [French from Latin *-ubilis*]

-ubly /jʊbli/ *suffix* forming adverbs corresponding to adjectives in *-uble*.

U-boat *noun hist.* a German submarine. [German *U-boot* = *Unterseeboot* undersea boat]

UC *abbreviation* (in Canada) United Church.

u.c. *abbreviation* upper case.

Uc·cel·lo /uːˈtʃelo/ **Paolo** (born Paolo di Dono) (c.1397–1475), Italian painter. He is associated with the early use of perspective in painting, and his surviving works include the series of three panels including *The Rout of San Romano* (c.1454–c.1457) and *The Hunt*, one of the earliest-known paintings on canvas.

UCW *abbreviation* (in Canada) United Church Women.

UDA *abbreviation* Ulster Defence Association (a Loyalist paramilitary organization).

ud·der *noun* the mammary gland of cattle, sheep, etc., hanging as a bag-like organ with several teats. □ **ud·dered** *adjective* (also in *combination*). [Old English *ūder* from West Germanic]

UDI *abbreviation* unilateral declaration of independence.

Ud·mur·tia /ʊdˈmərtiə/ (also called **Ud·murt Republic**) an autonomous republic in central Russia; pop. (est. 2002) 1,608,100; capital, Izhevsk.

udon /ˈuːdɒn/ *noun* (in Japanese cooking) a thick strip of pasta made from wheat flour. [Japanese]

UDR *abbreviation* Ulster Defence Regiment.

UEFA /juːˈeifə, -ˈiːfə/ *abbreviation* Union of European Football Associations.

UEL *abbreviation Cdn* UNITED EMPIRE LOYALIST.

U-ey *noun slang* a U-turn.

UFA *abbreviation Cdn* United Farmers of Alberta.

Ufa /uːˈfɒ/ the capital of Bashkiria, in the Ural Mountains; pop. (est. 2002) 1,094,900.

UFFI /ˈʌfi/ *noun Cdn* urea formaldehyde foam insulation. [acronym]

UFO /juːˈefˈoː/ *noun* (*pl.* **UFOs**) an unidentified flying object, esp. one supposed to have come from outer space. [abbreviation]

ufol·ogy /juːˈfɒlədʒi/ *noun* the study of UFOs. □ **ufolo·gist** *noun* **ufo·logic·al** /-ˈlɒdʒɪkəl/ *adjective*

Ugan·da /juːˈgandə/ a landlocked country in East Africa; pop. (est. 2002) 24,699,073; capital, Kampala. □ **Ugan·dan** *adjective & noun*

Uga·rit /ˈuːgəˌrit/ an ancient port in N Syria, an important commercial city during the Late Bronze Age, to which period belong a palace, temples, and private residences containing legal, religious and administrative cuneiform texts in Sumerian, Akkadian, Hurrian, Hittite and Ugaritic languages. The last of these was written in an early form of the Phoenician alphabet. □ **Uga·rit·ic** /ˌuːgəˈrɪtɪk/ *adjective & noun*

ugh /ə, ʌg, ʌx/ *interjection* **1** expressing disgust or horror. **2** the sound of a cough or grunt. [imitative]

Ugli /ˈʌgli/ *noun* (*pl.* **Ug·lies**) *proprietary* a mottled green and yellow citrus fruit, a hybrid of a grapefruit and tangerine. [UGLY]

ugli·fy *transitive verb* (**-fies, -fied**) make ugly. □ **ugli·fi·ca·tion** *noun*

ugly ● *adjective* (**ugli·er, ugli·est**) **1** unpleasing or repulsive to see or hear (*an ugly scar; spoke with an ugly snarl*). **2** unpleasantly suggestive; discreditable (*ugly rumours*). **3** threatening, dangerous (*the sky has an ugly look*). **4** morally repulsive; vile (*ugly vices*). **5** characterized by violence or hostility (*an ugly confrontation*). ● *noun* (*pl.* **ug·lies**) (in *pl.*) ugly or unpleasant things. □ **ugli·ness** *noun* [Old Norse *uggligr* to be dreaded, from *ugga* to dread]

ugly American *noun* an American who behaves offensively abroad.

ugly customer *noun* an unpleasantly formidable person.

ugly duckling *noun* a person who turns out to be beautiful or talented etc. against all expectations. [with reference to a cygnet in a brood of ducks in a tale by Hans Christian Andersen]

Ug·rian /ˈuːgriən, ˈjuː-/ ● *adjective* = UGRIC *adjective*. ● *noun* **1** a person of Ugric stock. **2** = UGRIC *noun*.

Ug·ric /ˈuːgrɪk, ˈjuː-/ ● *adjective* **1** of or relating to the eastern branch of Finnic peoples, esp. the Magyars. **2** of or relating to the group of Finno-Ugric languages including Magyar. ● *noun* the Ugric group of languages. [Russian *Ugry*, the name of a people dwelling east of the Urals]

uh *interjection* esp. *N Amer.* expressing the inarticulate sound made by a speaker who hesitates or is uncertain what to say.

UHF *abbreviation* ultra-high frequency.

uh-huh *interjection informal* expressing assent or a noncommittal response to a question or remark.

uh·lan /ˈuːlɒn, ˈjuːlən/ *noun hist.* a cavalryman armed with a lance in some European armies, esp. the former German army. [French & German from Polish (h)ulan from Turkish oğlan youth, servant]

uh-oh *interjection* expressing sudden concern, worry, etc.

Consonants: b *but*   d *dog*   f *few*   g *get*   h *her*   j *yes*   k *cat*   l *leg*   m *man*   n *no*   p *pen*   r *red*   s *sit*

UHT *abbreviation* ultra-high-temperature sterilization (used to designate esp. dairy products sterilized at very high temperatures so that they can keep without refrigeration).

uh-uh *interjection* expressing a negative response to a question or remark; no. [imitative]

UI *abbreviation* (in Canada) unemployment insurance.

UIC *abbreviation Cdn* **1** *hist.* Unemployment Insurance Commission. **2** *informal* unemployment insurance (*has been living on UIC*).

Uigh·ur /ˈwiːɡɜr/ ● *noun* (*pl.* same or **-urs**) **1** a member of a Turkic people prominent in Central Asia from the 8th to the 12th c. and now living mostly in northwestern China. **2** their language. ● *adjective* of or pertaining to the Uighurs.

uil·lean pipes /ˈɪljən/ *noun* a form of Irish bagpipe in which the bag is inflated by bellows worked by the elbow. [Irish *píob* 'pipe' + *uillean*, genitive singular of *uille* 'elbow']

Uist /ˈjuːɪst/ two small islands in the Outer Hebrides, off the west coast of Scotland, North Uist and South Uist, lying to the south of Lewis and Harris, separated from each other by the island of Benbecula.

Uj·jain /ˈuːdʒaɪn/ a city of west central India in Madhya Pradesh; pop. (2001) 429,900. It is one of the seven holy cities of Hinduism. [Hindi, = one who conquers with pride]

U-joint *noun* = UNIVERSAL JOINT.

Ujung Pan·dang /uːˌdʒʊŋ panˈdaŋ/ the chief seaport of the island of Sulawesi in Indonesia; pop. (2002) 1,170,200.

UK *abbreviation* United Kingdom.

ukase /juːˈkeɪz/ *noun* **1** an arbitrary command. **2** *hist.* an edict of the Czarist Russian government. [Russian *ukaz* ordinance, edict, from *ukazat´* show, decree]

Uke /juːk/ *noun* (also **Ukie** /ˈjuːki/) *Cdn dated* a Ukrainian. [abbreviation]

Ukraine /juːˈkreɪn/ (also **the Ukraine**) a country in E Europe, to the north of the Black Sea; pop. (est. 2002) 48,396,470; capital, Kiev.

Ukrain·ian /juːˈkreɪniən/ ● *noun* **1** a native of Ukraine. **2** the Slavic language of Ukraine. ● *adjective* of or relating to Ukraine or its people or language.

Ukrainian Catholic ● *adjective* of or pertaining to an Eastern Church of the Catholic communion under the jurisdiction of the Metropolitan of Lviv, including large communities in Canada and the US. ● *noun* a member of this Church.

Ukrainian Christmas *noun* Christmas as celebrated by Ukrainian Christians on 7 Jan.

Ukrainian Easter egg *noun* = PYSANKA.

Ukrainian Greek Orthodox *adjective* = UKRAINIAN ORTHODOX.

Ukrainian Orthodox *adjective* of or pertaining to any of various Eastern Orthodox Churches of Ukrainian ethnicity, including large communities in Ukraine, Canada and the US.

uku·lele /ˌjuːkəˈleɪli/ *noun* a small four-stringed Hawaiian (originally Portuguese) guitar. [Hawaiian, = jumping flea]

Ulala /ˌuːlɒˈlɒ/ a former name (until 1932) for GORNO-ALTAISK.

Ulan Bator /ˌuːlɒnˈbɒtɜr/ (also **Ulan·baatar**) the capital of Mongolia; pop. (est. 2000) 760,077. It was founded in the 17th c. and developed as a religious centre around a Buddhist monastery. It was known as Urga until 1924.

Ulan·ova /uːˈlɒnəvə/ **Gal·ina (Ser·geev·na)** (1910–98), Russian ballet dancer. Over a long career in Leningrad and Moscow she gave notable interpretations of 19th-c. ballets, such as *Swan Lake* and *Giselle*, and created the role of Juliet (her interpretation of which became legendary) in Prokofiev's *Romeo and Juliet.*

Ulan-Ude /uːˌlɒnuːˈdeɪ/ an industrial city in S Siberian Russia, capital of the republic of Buryatia; pop. (est. 2002) 370,800.

-ular /jʊlər/ *suffix* forming adjectives, sometimes corresponding to nouns in *-ule* (*pustular*) but often without diminutive force (*angular*; *granular*). □ **-ularity** /-ˈlerɪti/ *suffix* [from or after Latin *-ularis* (as *-ULE*, *-AR¹*)]

ul·cer /ˈʌlsər/ *noun* **1 a** an open sore on an external or internal surface of the body, often forming pus. **b** = PEPTIC ULCER. **2 a** a moral blemish. **b** a corroding or corrupting influence etc. □ **ul·cered** *adjective* **ul·cer·ous** *adjective* [Latin *ulcus -eris*, related to Greek *helkos*]

ul·cer·ate /ˈʌlsəreɪt/ *transitive & intransitive verb* (often as **ul·cer·at·ed** *adjective*) form into or affect with an ulcer. □ **ul·cer·a·tion** *noun* **ul·cera·tive** /-rətɪv/ *adjective*

-ule *suffix* forming diminutive nouns (*capsule*; *globule*). [from or after Latin *-ulus, -ula, -ulum*]

ulema /ˈuːlɪmə/ *noun* **1** a body of Muslim doctors of sacred law and theology. **2** a member of this. [Arabic *ʽulamā* pl. of *ʽālim* learned, from *ʽalama* know]

-ulent /jʊlənt/ *suffix* forming adjectives meaning 'abounding in, full of' (*fraudulent*; *turbulent*). □ **-ulence** *suffix.* [Latin *-ulentus*]

Ul·has·nagar /uːlhəsˈnʌɡɜr/ a city in W India, in the state of Maharashtra; pop. (2001) 472,900.

ul·lage /ˈʌlɪdʒ/ *noun* **1** the amount by which a cask, bottle, etc. falls short of being full. **2** loss by evaporation or leakage. [Anglo-French *ulliage*, Old French *ouillage* from *ouiller* fill up, ultimately from Latin *oculus* eye, with reference to the bunghole]

Ulm /ʊlm/ an industrial city on the Danube in Baden-Württemberg, S Germany; pop. (est. 2002) 116,300.

ulna /ˈʌlnə/ *noun* (*pl.* **ulnae** /-niː/) **1** the thinner and longer bone in the forearm, on the side opposite to the thumb (*compare* RADIUS 3). **2** *Zool.* a corresponding bone in an animal's foreleg or a bird's wing. □ **ulnar** *adjective* [Latin, related to Greek *ōlenē* and ELL¹]

-ulous /jʊləs/ *suffix* forming adjectives (*fabulous*; *populous*). [Latin *-ulosus*, *-ulus*]

Ul·pian /ˈʌlpiən/ (Latin name Domitius Ulpianus) (died *c.*228), Roman jurist, born in Phoenicia. His numerous legal writings provided one of the chief sources for Justinian's *Digest* of 533.

Ulsan /ˈuːlsɒn/ an industrial port on the south coast of S Korea; pop. (2002) 870,300.

Ul·ster 1 a former province of Ireland, in the north of the island. The nine counties of Ulster are now divided between Northern Ireland (Antrim, Down, Armagh, Londonderry, Tyrone, and Fermanagh) and the Republic of Ireland (Cavan, Donegal, and Monaghan). **2** (loosely) Northern Ireland.

ul·ster *noun* a man's long loose overcoat of rough cloth. [ULSTER, where it was originally sold]

Ulster·man *noun* (*pl.* **-men**) a native of Ulster.

Ulster·woman *noun* (*pl.* **-men**) a female native of Ulster.

ult. *abbreviation* ultimo.

ul·ter·ior /ʌlˈtiːriər/ *adjective* **1** existing in the background, or beyond what is evident or admitted; hidden, secret (*ulterior motive*). **2** situated beyond. **3** more remote; not immediate; in the future. [Latin, = further, more distant]

ul·tim·ate /ˈʌltɪmət/ ● *adjective* **1** last, final. **2** beyond which no other exists or is possible (*the ultimate analysis*). **3** fundamental, primary, unanalyzable (*ultimate truths*). **4** maximum (*ultimate tensile strength*). **5** *informal* unsurpassed, best (*the ultimate car wash*). ● *noun* **1** (prec. by *the*) the best achievable or imaginable. **2** a final or fundamental fact or principle. **3** a non-contact field sport resembling football but using a Frisbee, in which passes may be made in any direction, but running with the Frisbee is prohibited. □ **ul·tim·acy** /-məsi/ *noun* **ul·tim·ate·ly** *adverb* [Late Latin *ultimatus*, past participle of *ultimare* 'come to an end']

ul·tima Thule /ˌʌltɪmə ˈθuːli/ *noun* **1** a faraway unknown region. **2** the highest or uttermost point or degree attained or attainable. [Latin, = furthest Thule, a remote northern region]

ul·ti·matum /ˌʌltɪˈmeɪtəm/ *noun* (*pl.* **ul·ti·matums** or **ul·ti·mata**) a final demand or statement of terms by one party, the rejection of which by another could cause a breakdown in relations, war, or an end of co-operation etc. [Latin neuter past participle of *ultimare*: see ULTIMATE]

ul·timo /ˈʌltɪˌmoː/ *adjective archaic* of last month (*the 28th ultimo*). [Latin *ultimo mense* in the last month]

ul·timo·geni·ture /ˌʌltɪmoːˈdʒɛnɪtʃɜr/ *noun* a system in which the youngest son has the right of inheritance (*compare* PRIMOGENITURE 2). [Latin *ultimus* last, after PRIMOGENITURE]

ul·tra ● *adjective* **1** favouring extreme views or measures, esp. in religion or politics. **2** going beyond what is usual or ordinary; extreme. ● *adverb* very, extremely; excessively. ● *noun* an extremist. [originally as abbreviation of French *ultra-royaliste*: see ULTRA-]

ultra- *combining form* **1** extreme(ly), excessive(ly) (*ultra-conservative*; *ultra-modern*). **2** beyond; on the other side of (*opp.* CIS-). [Latin *ultra* beyond]

ultra·centri·fuge /ˌʌltrəˈsɛntrɪˌfjuːdʒ/ *noun* a high-speed centrifuge used to separate small particles and large molecules in a liquid and to determine their sedimentation rate (and hence their size). □ **ultra·centri·fu·ga·tion** /-fjuːˈɡeɪʃən/ *adjective*

ultra·fil·tra·tion *noun* filtration using a filter fine enough to retain large molecules, viruses, and colloidal particles.

ultra-high *adjective* **1** extremely high. **2** (of a frequency) in the range 300 to 3000 megahertz.

ultra·ism *noun* the holding of extreme positions in politics, religion, etc. □ **ultra·ist** *noun*

ultra·light ● *noun* N Amer. a very small, light, low-speed, one- or two-seater aircraft with an open frame. ● *adjective* extremely light.

ultra-marathon *noun* a running or cycling race over a distance longer than that of a marathon, esp. 50 km, 50 miles, 70 km, or more. □ **ultra-marathon·er** *noun*

ultra·marine ● *noun* **1 a** a brilliant blue pigment originally obtained from lapis lazuli. **b** an imitation of this from powdered fired clay, sodium carbonate, sulphur, and resin. **2** the colour of this. ● *adjective* of this colour. [medieval Latin *ultramarinus* beyond the sea (as ULTRA-, MARINE), because lapis lazuli was brought from beyond the sea]

ultra·micro·scope *noun* an optical microscope used to reveal very small particles by means of light scattered by them.

ultra·micro·scop·ic *adjective* **1** too small to be seen by an ordinary optical microscope. **2** of or relating to an ultramicroscope.

ultra·mon·tane /ˌʌltrəˈmɒntein/ ● *adjective* **1** situated on the other side of the Alps from the point of view of the speaker. **2 a** advocating supreme papal authority in matters of faith and discipline. **b** Cdn hist. (in Quebec) advocating the subordination of the state to the Catholic Church. ● *noun* **1** a person living on the other side of the Alps. **2** a person advocating ultramontane views (compare GALLICAN).
□ **ultra·mon·tan·ism** /-ˈmɒntənɪzəm/ *noun* **ultra·mon·tan·ist** *noun* [medieval Latin *ultramontanus* (as ULTRA-, Latin *mons montis* mountain)]

ultra·mun·dane /ˌʌltrəˈmʌndein/ *adjective* lying beyond the world or the solar system. [Latin *ultramundanus* (as ULTRA-, *mundanus* from *mundus* world)]

ultra·sonic *adjective* of or involving sound waves with a frequency above the upper limit of human hearing. □ **ultra·sonic·ally** *adverb*

ultra·sonics *plural noun* (usu. treated as sing.) the science and application of ultrasonic waves.

ultra·sound *noun* **1** sound having an ultrasonic frequency. **2** ultrasonic waves. **3** Med. a (also **ultra·sono·graphy** /ˌʌltrəsəˈnɒɡrəfi/) an esp. diagnostic procedure using echoes of ultrasonic pulses to delineate objects or areas of different density in the body. **b** an image of a subject produced by such a procedure.

ultra·struc·ture *noun* Biol. fine structure not visible with an optical microscope. □ **ultra·struc·tur·al** *adjective*

Ultra·suede *noun* proprietary a synthetic non-woven fabric resembling suede.

ultra·violet *adjective* Physics of or using electromagnetic radiation having a wavelength shorter than that of the violet end of the visible spectrum but longer than that of X-rays.

ultra vires /ˌʌltrə ˈvaɪˌriːz, ˌʊltrə ˈviːreiz/ *adverb & predicative adjective* beyond one's legal power or authority. [Latin]

ulu /ˈuːluː/ *noun* an Inuit knife consisting of a semicircular or crescent-shaped blade and a handle centred behind the non-cutting edge, traditionally used by women. [Inuktitut]

ulu·late /ˈʌljuˌleit, ˈjuː-/ *intransitive verb* howl, wail; make a hooting cry. □ **ulu·lant** *adjective* **ulu·la·tion** *noun* [Latin *ululare ululat-* (imitative)]

Ul·un·di /ʊˈlʊndi/ a town in KwaZulu-Natal, South Africa. Founded in 1873 as the capital of Zululand, it was restored as the capital of the former homeland of KwaZulu in the early 1980s.

Ul·ya·nov /uːˈljɒnɒf/ **Vlad·i·mir Ilich**, see LENIN.

Ul·ya·novsk /uːˈljɒnɒfsk/ the former name (1924–92) of SIMBIRSK.

Ulys·ses /juːˈlɪsiːz, ˈjuːlɪsiːz/ **1** the Roman name for Odysseus. **2** a space probe of the European Space Agency, launched in 1990 to investigate the polar regions of the sun.

um ● *interjection* expressing hesitation or a pause in speech. ● *intransitive verb* (also **um and ah**, (**ummed and ahhed**, **umming and ahhing**)) express hesitation or indecision.

-um var. of -IUM 1.

Umay·yad /ʊˈmaijad/ (also **Omay·yad** /ɒˈmai-/) ● *adjective* of or relating to a Muslim dynasty, which included the family of the prophet Muhammad, that ruled the Islamic world from AD 660 (or 661) to 750 and later ruled Moorish Spain 756–1031. ● *noun* a member of this dynasty.

um·bel /ˈʌmbəl/ *noun* Bot. a flower cluster in which stalks nearly equal in length spring from a common centre and form a flat or curved surface, as in parsley. □ **um·bel·late** /-bəˌleit/ *adjective* **um·bel·lule** /-ˈbeljuːl/ *adjective* [obsolete French *umbelle* or Latin *umbella* sunshade, diminutive of UMBRA]

um·bel·lif·er /ʌmˈbelɪfər/ *noun* any plant of the family Umbelliferae bearing umbels, including parsley and carrot. □ **um·bel·lif·er·ous** /-bəˈlɪfərəs/ *adjective* [obsolete French *umbellifère* from Latin (as UMBEL, *-fer* bearing)]

um·ber ● *noun* **1** a natural pigment like ochre but darker and browner. **2** the colour of this. ● *adjective* **1** of this colour. **2** dark, dusky. [French (*terre d'*)*ombre* or Italian (*terra di*) *ombra* = shadow (earth), from Latin UMBRA or *Umbra* fem. of *Umber* Umbrian]

um·bil·ic·al /ʌmˈbɪlɪkəl/ ● *attributive adjective* **1** of, situated near, or affecting the navel. **2** linking, connecting. **3** inseparably linked. ● *noun* a flexible supply or control line, hose, etc., esp. from a main source to a site otherwise difficult to access. □ **um·bil·ic·al·ly** *adverb*

umbilical cord *noun* **1** a flexible cordlike structure containing blood vessels and attaching a fetus to the placenta. **2** Astronaut. a supply cable linking a missile to its launcher, or an astronaut in space to a spacecraft.

um·bil·icate /ʌmˈbɪlɪkət/ *adjective* **1** shaped like a navel. **2** having an umbilicus.

um·bil·icus /ʌmˈbɪlɪkəs/ *noun* (pl. **um·bil·ici** /-ˌsaɪ/) **1** Anat. the navel. **2** Bot. & Zool. a navel-like formation. **3** Math a point in a surface through which all cross-sections have the same curvature. [Latin, related to Greek *omphalos* and to NAVEL]

um·bles *plural noun* the edible offal of deer etc. [Middle English var. of NUMBLES]

umbo /ˈʌmbəʊ/ *noun* (pl. **umbos** or **umbo·nes** /-ˈbəʊniːz/) **1** the boss of a shield, esp. in the centre. **2** Bot. & Zool. a rounded knob or protuberance. □ **umbo·nal** *adjective* **umbo·nate** /-nət/ *adjective* [Latin *umbo -onis*]

umbra *noun* (pl. **um·bras** or **um·brae**) **1** the fully shaded inner region of a shadow cast by an opaque object, esp. Astronomy the area on the earth or moon experiencing the total phase of an eclipse (compare PENUMBRA 1a). **2** the dark central part of a sunspot. □ **um·bral** *adjective* [Latin, = shade]

um·brage /ˈʌmbrɪdʒ/ *noun* **1** offence; a sense of slight or injury (esp. give or take umbrage at). **2** archaic **a** shade. **b** what gives shade.
□ **um·bra·geous** /ʌmˈbreidʒəs/ *adjective* [Old French, ultimately from Latin *umbraticus* from *umbra*: see UMBRA]

um·brel·la *noun* **1** a light portable device for protection against rain, strong sun, etc., consisting of a usu. circular canopy of cloth mounted by means of a collapsible metal frame on a central stick. **2** protection or patronage. **3** (often *attributive*) a coordinating or unifying agency (*umbrella organization*). **4** a screen of fighter aircraft or a curtain of fire put up as a protection against enemy aircraft. **5** Zool. the gelatinous disc of a jellyfish etc., which it contracts and expands to move through the water. □ **um·brel·laed** *adjective* **um·brella-like** *adjective* [Italian *ombrella*, diminutive of *ombra* shade, from Latin *umbra*: see UMBRA]

umbrella bird *noun* any S American bird of the genus *Cephalopterus*, with a black radiating crest and long wattles.

umbrella pine *noun* **1** = STONE PINE. **2** a Japanese evergreen conifer, *Sciadopitys verticillata*, with leaves in umbrella-like whorls, planted as an ornamental.

umbrella stand *noun* a stand for holding closed upright umbrellas.

umbrella stroller *noun* N Amer. a stroller which can be folded up to resemble a closed umbrella.

umbrella tree *noun* any of various trees with whorls of radiating leaves, esp. a small N American magnolia, *Magnolia tripetala*, and an Australian tree, *Schefflera actinophylla*, often grown as a houseplant.

Um·bria /ˈʌmbriə/ a region of central Italy, in the valley of the Tiber; capital, Perugia.

Um·brian /ˈʌmbriən/ ● *adjective* of or relating to Umbria. ● *noun* **1** the language of ancient Umbria, related to Latin. **2** an inhabitant of ancient Umbria.

umi·ak /ˈuːmiˌak/ *noun* a large, open, flat-bottomed boat made by stretching an animal hide over a wooden frame, traditionally used by Inuit women. [Inuktitut *umiaq*]

um·laut /ˈʊmlaʊt/ ● *noun* **1** a mark (¨) used over a vowel, esp. in Germanic languages, to indicate a vowel change. **2** such a vowel change, e.g. German *Mann*, *Männer*, English *man*, *men*, due to *i*, *j*, etc. (now usu. lost or altered) in the following syllable. ● *transitive verb* modify (a form or a sound) by an umlaut. [German from *um* about + *Laut* sound]

umma /ˈʊmə/ *noun* (also **ummah**) the whole community of Muslims bound together by ties of religion. [Arabic, lit. = 'people, community']

Umm al Qai·wain /ˌʊm al kaiˈwain/ **1** one of the seven member states of the United Arab Emirates; pop. (2002) 45,800. **2** its capital city.

Vowels: a cat   ɑ arm   e bed   ɜr her   ɜː deux   ə ago   ɪ sit   i cosy   iː feed   ɒ hot   ɔ pore   ɔː no   ʌ run   ʊ put

ump esp. *N Amer. informal* ● *noun* an umpire, esp. in baseball. ● *verb* **1** *intransitive* act as umpire. **2** *transitive* act as umpire in (a game). [abbreviation]

umph *var. of* OOMPH 1.

um·pire ● *noun* **1** a person chosen to enforce the rules and settle disputes in various sports, e.g. baseball. **2** a person chosen to arbitrate between disputants, or to ensure fair play. ● *verb* **1** *intransitive* (usu. foll. by *for*, *in*, etc.) act as umpire. **2** *transitive* act as umpire in (a game etc.). [Middle English, later form of *noumpere* from Old French *nonper* not equal (as NON-, PEER²): for loss of *n*- compare ADDER]

ump·teen *slang* ● *adjective* indefinitely many; a lot of. ● *pronoun* indefinitely many. □ **ump·teenth** *adjective* **umpty** *adjective* [jocular formation on -TEEN]

Um·tata /ʊmˈtɒtə/ the former capital of Transkei; pop. (est. 1983) 80,000.

un-¹ *prefix* **1** added to adjectives and participles and their derivative nouns and adverbs, meaning: **a** not: denoting the absence of a quality or state (*unusable*; *uncalled for*; *uneducated*; *unfailing*; *unofficially*; *unhappiness*). **b** the reverse of, usu. with an implication of approval or disapproval, or with some other special connotation (*unselfish*; *unsociable*; *unscientific*). **2** (less often) added to nouns, meaning 'a lack of' (*unrest*; *untruth*). ¶ The number of words that can be formed with this prefix (and similarly with *un-²*) is potentially as large as the number of adjectives in use; consequently only a selection, being considered the most current or semantically noteworthy, can be given here. ¶ Words meaning 'the reverse of' (see sense 1b above) often have neutral counterparts in *non-* (see NON- 6) and counterparts in *in-* (see IN-¹), e.g. *unadvisable*. ¶ In the case of some words with the prefix *un-*, there is ambiguity as to which prefix is meant, e.g. *undressed* can mean either 'not dressed' or 'no longer dressed'. [Old English from Germanic, related to Latin *in-*]

un-² *prefix* added to verbs and (less often) nouns, forming verbs denoting: **1** the reversal or cancellation of an action or state (*undress*; *unlock*; *unsettle*). **2** deprivation or separation (*unmask*). **3** release from (*unburden*; *uncage*). **4** causing to be no longer (*unman*). ¶ See the third note at un-¹. [Old English *un-*, *on-* from Germanic]

un-³ *prefix Chem.* denoting 'one', combined with other numerical roots (*nil* = 0, *bi* = 2, etc.) to form names of recently discovered elements based on the atomic number, e.g. *unnilhexium* = element 106. [Latin *unus* 'one']

'un *pronoun informal* one (*raised four young 'uns*; *that's a good 'un*). [dialect variant]

un·abashed *adjective* not ashamed, embarrassed, or discouraged in circumstances in which others might be. □ **un·abash·ed·ly** *adverb*

un·abated *adjective* not abated; undiminished.

un·able *adjective* (usu. foll. by *to* + infin.) not able; lacking ability.

un·abridged *adjective* (of a text etc.) complete; not abridged.

un·ab·sorbed *adjective* not absorbed.

un·academ·ic *adjective* **1** not academic (esp. not scholarly or theoretical). **2** (of a person) not suited to academic study.

un·accent·ed *adjective* **1** not accented; not emphasized. **2** (of speech) not having a foreign accent.

un·accept·able *adjective* not acceptable. □ **un·accept·abil·ity** *noun* **un·accept·ably** *adverb*

un·accom·mo·dat·ing *adjective* not accommodating; disobliging.

un·accom·pan·ied *adjective* **1** not accompanied, alone. **2** *Music* without accompaniment.

un·account·able *adjective* **1** unable to be explained. **2** unpredictable or strange in behaviour. **3** not responsible. □ **un·account·abil·ity** *noun* **un·account·ably** *adverb*

un·account·ed *adjective* of which no account is given. □ **unaccounted for** unexplained; not included in an account.

un·accus·tomed *adjective* **1** (usu. foll. by *to*) not accustomed. **2** not customary; unusual (*his unaccustomed silence*). □ **un·accus·tomed·ly** *adverb*

un·achiev·able *adjective* not achievable.

un·acknow·ledged *adjective* not acknowledged.

un·ac·quaint·ed *adjective* (usu. foll. by *with*) not acquainted.

un·adapt·able *adjective* not adaptable.

un·adapt·ed *adjective* not adapted.

un·ad·dressed *adjective* (esp. of a letter etc.) without an address.

un·ad·jacent *adjective* not adjacent.

un·admit·ted *adjective* not admitted.

un·adorned *adjective* not adorned; plain.

un·adul·ter·ated *adjective* **1** not adulterated; pure; concentrated. **2** sheer, complete, utter (*unadulterated nonsense*).

un·adven·tur·ous *adjective* not adventurous.

un·adver·tised *adjective* not advertised.

un·advised *adjective* **1** indiscreet; rash. **2** not having had advice. □ **un·advis·ed·ly** *adverb*

un·aesthet·ic /ˌʌnɛsˈθɛtɪk/ *adjective* **1** not aesthetically pleasing. **2** lacking the principles of good taste. □ **un·aesthet·ic·ally** *adverb*

un·affect·ed *adjective* **1** (usu. foll. by *by*) not affected. **2** free from affectation; genuine; sincere. □ **un·affect·ed·ly** *adverb* *noun*

un·affec·tion·ate *adjective* lacking or not showing affection.

un·affili·ated *adjective* not affiliated.

un·afford·able *adjective* not affordable.

un·afraid *adjective* not afraid.

un·aggres·sive *adjective* not aggressive.

un·aid·ed *adjective* not aided; without help.

un·air-condi·tioned *adjective* not air-conditioned.

un·aired *adjective* **1** that has not been aired or ventilated. **2** that has not been broadcast.

un·alien·able *adjective Law* = INALIENABLE.

un·aligned *adjective* **1** = NON-ALIGNED. **2** not physically aligned.

un·alike *adjective* not alike; different.

un·allevi·ated *adjective* not alleviated; relentless.

un·allied *adjective* not allied; having no allies.

un·allow·able *adjective* not allowable.

un·alloyed /ˌʌnəˈlɔɪd, ʌnˈal-/ *adjective* **1** not alloyed; pure. **2** complete; utter (*unalloyed joy*).

un·alter·able *adjective* not alterable. □ **un·alter·ably** *adverb*

un·altered *adjective* not altered; remaining the same.

un·ambigu·ous *adjective* not ambiguous; clear or definite in meaning. □ **un·ambigu·ous·ly** *adverb*

un·ambi·tious *adjective* not ambitious; without ambition. □ **un·ambi·tious·ly** *adverb*

un·ambiva·lent /ˌʌnamˈbɪvələnt/ *adjective* (of feelings etc.) not ambivalent; straightforward.

un-American *adjective* **1** not in accordance with American characteristics etc. **2** contrary to the interests of the US; (in the US) treasonable. □ **un-American·ism** *noun*

un·ampli·fied *adjective* not amplified.

un·amused *adjective* not amused.

un·ana·lyz·able *adjective* (also **un·ana·lys·able**) not able to be analyzed.

un·ana·lyzed *adjective* (also **un·ana·lysed**) not analyzed.

un·aneled /ˌʌnəˈniːld/ *adjective archaic* not having received extreme unction.

unani·mous /juːˈnanɪməs/ *adjective* **1** all in agreement (*the committee was unanimous*). **2** (of an opinion, vote, etc.) held or given by general consent (*the unanimous choice*). □ **unan·im·ity** /-nəˈnɪmɪti/ *noun* **unani·mous·ly** *adverb* [Late Latin *unanimis*, Latin *unanimus* from *unus* one + *animus* mind]

un·an·nounced *adjective* not announced; without warning (of arrival etc.).

un·answer·able *adjective* **1** unable to be answered (*an unanswerable question*). **2** unable to be refuted (*has an unanswerable case*). □ **un·answer·ably** *adverb*

un·an·swered *adjective* **1** not answered. **2** (of a goal scored by one team) not matched by a goal scored by the other team (*scored three unanswered goals in the third period*).

un·antici·pated *adjective* not anticipated.

un·apolo·get·ic *adjective* not apologetic or sorry. □ **un·apolo·get·ic·ally** *adverb*

un·appar·ent *adjective* not apparent.

un·appeal·able *adjective* esp. *Law* not able to be appealed against.

un·appeal·ing *adjective* not appealing; unattractive.

un·appeas·able *adjective* that cannot be appeased.

un·appeased *adjective* not appeased.

un·appetiz·ing *adjective* (also esp. *Brit.* **un·appetis·ing**) not appetizing. □ **un·appetiz·ing·ly** *adverb*

un·appre·ci·ated *adjective* not appreciated.

un·appre·cia·tive *adjective* not appreciative.

un·appre·hend·ed *adjective* **1** not perceived by the intellect. **2** not arrested.

un·approach·able *adjective* **1** not approachable; remote, inaccessible. **2** (of a person) unfriendly. □ **un·approach·abil·ity** *noun* **un·approach·ably** *adverb*

un·appro·pri·ated *adjective* **1** not allocated or assigned. **2** not taken into possession by anyone.

un·approved *adjective* not approved or sanctioned.

un·apt *adjective* **1** (usu. foll. by *for*) not suitable. **2** (usu. foll. by *to* + infin.) not apt.

un·argu·able *adjective* not arguable; certain. □ **un·argu·ably** *adverb*

un·armed *adjective* not armed; without weapons.

un·articu·lated *adjective* not articulated or distinct.

un·ascer·tain·able /ˌʌnasɜrˈteinəbəl/ *adjective* not ascertainable.

un·ascer·tained /ˌʌnasɜrˈteind/ *adjective* not ascertained; unknown.

un·ashamed *adjective* **1** feeling no guilt, shameless. **2** blatant; bold. □ **un·asham·ed·ly** *adverb*

un·asked *adjective* (often foll. by *for*) not asked, requested, or invited.

un·asked-for *adjective* (usu. *attributive*) (esp. of advice) not sought or requested.

un·assail·able *adjective* unable to be attacked or questioned. □ **un·assail·abil·ity** *noun* **un·assail·ably** *adverb*

un·assert·ive *adjective* (of a person) not assertive or forthcoming; reticent. □ **un·assert·ive·ly** *adverb* **un·assert·ive·ness** *noun*

un·assigned *adjective* not assigned.

un·assim·il·ated *adjective* not assimilated. □ **un·assim·il·able** *adjective*

un·assist·ed *adjective* **1** not assisted. **2** *Hockey* (of a goal) scored by a player who takes possession of the puck from the opposing team rather than receiving it from a teammate.

un·associ·ated *adjective* (often foll. by *with*) having no connection or association.

un·assuaged /ˌʌnəˈsweidʒd/ *adjective* not assuaged. □ **un·assuage·able** *adjective*

un·assumed *adjective* *Cdn* (of a road) not taken over for maintenance by a local authority; privately owned.

un·assum·ing *adjective* not pretentious or arrogant; modest. □ **un·assum·ing·ly** *adverb*

un·ath·let·ic *adjective* not athletic.

un·attached *adjective* **1** (often foll. by *to*) not attached, esp. to a particular body, organization, etc. **2** not engaged or married; not having a boyfriend or girlfriend.

un·attain·able *adjective* not attainable. □ **un·attain·ably** *adverb*

un·attempt·ed *adjective* not attempted.

un·attend·ed *adjective* **1 a** unsupervised; alone (*don't leave your child unattended*). **b** with the owner not present (*unattended cars will be towed*). **2** (usu. foll. by *to*) not made the object of one's attention, concern, etc.; not dealt with (*letters unattended to*).

un·attract·ive *adjective* not attractive. □ **un·attract·ive·ly** *adverb* **un·attract·ive·ness** *noun*

un·attribut·able *adjective* (esp. of information) that cannot or may not be attributed to a source etc.

un·attribut·ed *adjective* (of a painting, quotation, etc.) not attributed to a source etc.

un·audit·ed *adjective* (of accounts etc.) not audited.

un·authen·ti·cated *adjective* not authenticated.

un·author·ized *adjective* (also esp. *Brit.* **un·author·ised**) **1** not authorized. **2** (of a biography) written without the consent and co-operation of the subject.

un·avail·able *adjective* not available. □ **un·avail·abil·ity** *noun*

un·avail·ing *adjective* not availing; achieving nothing; ineffectual. □ **un·avail·ing·ly** *adverb*

un·avoid·able *adjective* not avoidable; inevitable. □ **un·avoid·abil·ity** *noun* **un·avoid·ably** *adverb*

un·avowed *adjective* not avowed.

un·aware ● *adjective* (usu. foll. by *of*, or *that* + clause) not aware (*unaware of her presence*). ● *adverb* = UNAWARES. □ **un·aware·ness** *noun*

un·awares *adverb* without being aware of a situation (*caught them unawares*). [earlier *unware(s)* from Old English *unwær(es)*: see WARE²]

un·backed *adjective* **1** not supported. **2** (of a horse etc.) having no backers. **3** (of a chair, picture, etc.) having no back or backing.

un·baked *adjective* not baked or not yet baked; raw.

un·bal·ance ● *transitive verb* upset the physical or mental balance of (*unbalanced by the blow; the shock unbalanced him*). ● *noun* lack of balance; instability, esp. mental.

un·bal·anced *adjective* **1** not balanced. **2** (of a mind or a person) unstable or deranged.

un·ban *transitive verb* (**un·banned**, **un·ban·ning**) remove a ban or prohibition from (a publication, person, group, etc.); lift official restrictions on. □ **un·ban·ning** *noun*

un·bap·tized *adjective* not baptized.

un·bar *transitive verb* (**un·barred**, **un·bar·ring**) **1** remove a bar or bars from (a gate etc.). **2** unlock.

un·bear·able *adjective* not bearable. □ **un·bear·ably** *adverb*

un·beat·able *adjective* **1** not beatable; unable to be defeated. **2** superlative, excellent; that cannot be improved (*unbeatable prices*).

un·beat·en *adjective* **1** not beaten. **2** (of a record etc.) not surpassed.

un·beauti·ful *adjective* not beautiful; ugly. □ **un·beauti·ful·ly** *adverb*

un·becom·ing *adjective* **1** (esp. of clothing) not flattering or suiting a person. **2** (often foll. by *to*, *for*) not fitting; indecorous or unsuitable. □ **un·becom·ing·ly** *adverb*

un·befit·ting *adjective* not befitting; unsuitable.

un·be·knownst /ˌʌnbɪˈnoːnst/ *adjective* (also **un·be·known**) (foll. by *to*) without the knowledge of (*was there all the time unbeknownst to us*). [UN-¹ + *beknown* (archaic) = KNOWN + -*st*]

un·belief *noun* lack of belief, esp. in religious matters. □ **un·believ·er** *noun* **un·believ·ing** *adjective* **un·believ·ing·ly** *adverb*

un·believ·able *adjective* not believable; incredible. □ **un·believ·abil·ity** *noun* **un·believ·ably** *adverb*

un·belt·ed *adjective* not wearing or fastened by a belt.

un·bend *verb* (*past* and *past participle* **un·bent**) **1** *transitive & intransitive* change from a bent position; straighten. **2** *intransitive* relax from strain or severity; become affable. **3** *transitive* *Naut.* **a** unfasten (sails) from yards and stays. **b** cast (a cable) loose. **c** untie (a rope). □ **un·bend·able** *adjective*

un·bend·ing *adjective* **1** not bending; inflexible. **2** firm; austere (*unbending rectitude*).

un·biased *adjective* not biased; impartial.

un·bibli·cal *adjective* **1** not in or authorized by the Bible. **2** contrary to the Bible.

un·bid·den *adjective* **1** not commanded or invited (*arrived unbidden*). **2** without conscious effort; spontaneous.

un·bind *transitive verb* (*past* and *past participle* **un·bound**) release from bonds or binding.

un·bleached *adjective* not bleached.

un·blem·ished *adjective* not damaged or marked in any way.

un·blessed *adjective* (also *archaic* **un·blest**) not blessed.

un·blink·ing *adjective* **1** not blinking. **2** steadfast; not hesitating. **3** stolid; cool. □ **un·blink·ing·ly** *adverb*

un·block *transitive verb* remove an obstruction from (esp. a pipe, drain, etc.); open up, clear.

un·blush·ing *adjective* **1** not blushing. **2** unashamed; frank. □ **un·blush·ing·ly** *adverb*

un·bolt *transitive verb* release (a door etc.) by drawing back the bolt.

un·bolt·ed *adjective* **1** not bolted. **2** (of flour etc.) not sifted.

un·born *adjective* **1** not yet born (*an unborn child*). **2** never to be brought into being (*unborn hopes*).

un·bosom /ʌnˈbuzəm/ *transitive verb* **1** (*reflexive*) unburden (oneself) of one's thoughts, secrets, etc. **2** disclose (thoughts, secrets, etc.).

un·both·ered *adjective* not bothered; unconcerned.

un·bound¹ *adjective* **1** not bound or tied up. **2** unconstrained. **3 a** (of a book) not having a binding. **b** having paper covers. **4** (of a substance or particle) in a loose or free state.

un·bound² *past* and *past participle of* UNBIND.

un·bound·ed *adjective* not bounded; infinite (*unbounded optimism*).

un·bowed *adjective* (usu. *predicative*) undaunted; not having submitted to pressure or demands.

un·branched *adjective* not having or divided into branches.

un·brand·ed *adjective* **1** (of a product) not bearing a brand name. **2** (of livestock) not branded with the owner's mark.

un·breach·able *adjective* not able to be breached.

un·break·able *adjective* not breakable.

un·breath·able *adjective* foul, noxious (*unbreathable air*).

un·bridge·able *adjective* unable to be bridged.

Consonants: b *but*   d *dog*   f *few*   g *get*   h *her*   j *yes*   k *cat*   l *leg*   m *man*   n *no*   p *pen*   r *red*   s *sit*

un·bridled *adjective* unconstrained (*unbridled insolence*).

un·brok·en *adjective* **1** not broken. **2** not tamed (*an unbroken horse*). **3** not crushed in health or spirit; not subdued or weakened. **4** (of ground) not broken up by digging etc. **5** not interrupted or disturbed (*unbroken sleep*). **6** not surpassed (*an unbroken record*).

un·bruised *adjective* not bruised.

un·buckle *transitive verb* release the buckle of (a strap, shoe, etc.).

un·budge·able *adjective* *informal* that cannot be moved.

un·built *adjective* not yet built or (of land etc.) not yet built on.

un·bun·dle *transitive verb* **1** unpack; remove from a bundle. **2** market or price (goods or services) as individual items rather than as part of a package. **3** split (a company) into separate businesses.

un·bur·den *transitive verb* **1** relieve of a burden. **2** (esp. *reflexive*; often foll. by *to*) relieve (oneself, one's conscience, etc.) by confession etc. □ **un·bur·dened** *adjective*

un·buried *adjective* not buried.

un·burned *adjective* (also **un·burnt**) **1** not consumed by fire. **2** not scorched; not affected or damaged by fire etc.

un·bury *transitive verb* (**-buries, -buried**) **1** remove from the ground etc. after burial. **2** unearth (a secret etc.).

un·busi·ness·like *adjective* not businesslike.

un·but·ton *verb* **1** *transitive* **a** unfasten (a coat etc.) by taking the buttons out of the buttonholes. **b** unbutton the clothes of (a person). **2** *intransitive informal* relax from tension or formality; become communicative.

un·but·toned *adjective* **1** not buttoned. **2** *informal* communicative, unrestrained, informal.

un·caged *adjective* **1** released from or not confined to a cage. **2** not provided with cages.

un·called *adjective* not summoned or invited. □ **un·called for** (hyphenated when *attributive*) (of an opinion, action, etc.) impertinent or unnecessary (*an uncalled-for remark*).

un-Canadian *adjective* not in accordance with Canadian characteristics, practices, etc.

un·canny *adjective* (**un·can·ni·er, un·can·ni·est**) **1** seemingly supernatural; mysterious. **2** of an unsettling accuracy, intensity, etc. (*an uncanny resemblance*). □ **un·can·ni·ly** *adverb* **un·can·ni·ness** *noun*

un·canon·ical *adjective* not canonical. □ **un·canon·ical·ly** *adverb*

un·cap *transitive verb* (**un·capped, un·cap·ping**) remove the cap from (a jar, bottle, etc.).

un·cared-for *adjective* disregarded; neglected.

un·caring *adjective* **1** neglectful. **2** lacking compassion.

un·carpet·ed *adjective* not covered or provided with a carpet or carpeting.

un·case *transitive verb* remove from a cover or case.

un·cashed *adjective* not cashed.

un·cas·tra·ted *adjective* not castrated.

un·cata·logued *adjective* (*US* **un·cata·loged**) not catalogued.

un·catch·able *adjective* not able or likely to be caught.

un·cat·egor·iz·able *adjective* that cannot be assigned to a category.

un·caught *adjective* not caught.

un·ceas·ing *adjective* not ceasing; continuous (*unceasing effort*). □ **un·ceas·ing·ly** *adverb*

UNCED *abbreviation* United Nations Conference on Environment and Development.

un·ceded *adjective* (of land) that has not been officially ceded to a government by an Aboriginal group by means of a treaty.

un·celeb·rated *adjective* not publicly acclaimed.

un·cen·sored *adjective* not censored.

un·cere·moni·ous *adjective* **1** lacking ceremony or formality. **2** abrupt; discourteous. □ **un·cere·moni·ous·ly** *adverb*

un·cer·tain *adjective* **1** not certainly knowing or known (*uncertain what it means; the result is uncertain*). **2** unreliable (*his aim is uncertain*). **3** changeable, erratic (*uncertain weather*). **4** not confident; hesitant. □ **in no uncertain terms** clearly and forcefully. □ **un·cer·tain·ly** *adverb*

un·cer·tain·ty *noun* (*pl.* **-ties**) **1** the fact or condition of being uncertain. **2** an uncertain matter or circumstance.

uncertainty principle *noun* (in full **Heisenberg uncertainty principle** after W. HEISENBERG) *Physics* the principle that the momentum and position of a particle cannot both be precisely determined at the same time.

un·certi·fied *adjective* **1** not attested as certain. **2** not guaranteed by a certificate of competence etc. **3** not certified as insane.

un·chain *transitive verb* **1** remove the chains from. **2** release; liberate.

un·chal·lenge·able *adjective* not challengeable; unassailable. □ **un·chal·lenge·ably** *adverb*

un·chal·lenged *adjective* not challenged.

un·chal·len·ging *adjective* not presenting a challenge or other stimulation.

un·change·able *adjective* not changeable; immutable, invariable. □ **un·change·abil·ity** *noun* **un·change·ably** *adverb*

un·changed *adjective* not changed; unaltered.

un·chan·ging *adjective* not changing; remaining the same. □ **un·chan·ging·ly** *adverb*

un·chap·er·oned *adjective* without a chaperone.

un·char·ac·ter·is·tic *adjective* not characteristic. □ **un·char·ac·ter·is·tic·ally** *adverb*

un·charged *adjective* not charged (esp. in senses 3, 7, 8 of CHARGE *verb*)

un·charis·mat·ic *adjective* lacking charisma.

un·charit·able *adjective* unkind, harsh, and unsympathetic. □ **un·charit·able·ness** *noun* **un·charit·ably** *adverb*

un·chart·ed *adjective* not charted, mapped, or surveyed.

uncharted waters *plural noun* (also **uncharted territory**) a situation that one has not experienced before.

un·char·tered *adjective* **1** not furnished with a charter; not formally privileged or constituted. **2** unauthorized; illegal.

un·chaste *adjective* not chaste. □ **un·chas·tity** *noun*

un·chas·tened *adjective* not sorry; unbowed.

un·checked *adjective* **1** not checked. **2** freely allowed; unrestrained (*unchecked violence*).

un·chic *adjective* not chic.

un·chival·rous *adjective* not chivalrous; rude. □ **un·chival·rous·ly** *adverb*

un·chosen *adjective* not chosen.

un·chris·tian *adjective* **1** contrary to Christian principles, esp. uncaring or selfish. **2** not Christian.

un·churched *adjective* not associated with a church; not churchgoing.

un·cial /ˈʌnsɪəl, -ʃəl/ ● *adjective* **1** of or written in majuscule writing with rounded unjoined letters found in manuscripts of the 4th–8th c., from which modern capitals are derived. **2** of or relating to an inch or an ounce. ● *noun* **1** an uncial letter. **2** an uncial style or manuscript. [Latin *uncialis* from *uncia* inch: sense 1 in Late Latin sense of *unciales litterae*, the original application of which is unclear]

un·circum·cised *adjective* **1** not circumcised. **2** *archaic* spiritually impure; heathen.

un·civil *adjective* ill-mannered; impolite.

un·civil·ized *adjective* (also esp. *Brit.* **un·civil·ised**) **1** not civilized. **2** rough; uncultured.

un·clad *adjective* not clad; naked.

un·claimed *adjective* not claimed.

un·clasp *transitive verb* **1** loosen the clasp or clasps of. **2** release the grip of (a hand etc.).

un·classi·fi·able *adjective* not classifiable.

un·classi·fied *adjective* **1** not classified. **2** (of state information) not secret.

uncle *noun* **1 a** the brother of one's father or mother. **b** an aunt's husband. **2** *informal* a name given by children to a male family friend. **3** *Cdn* (*Nfld*) a term of respectful address to an older man in the community. **4** *slang* esp. *hist.* a pawnbroker. □ **cry** (or **say** or **yell**) **uncle** *N Amer. informal* surrender; admit defeat; yell for mercy. [Anglo-French *uncle*, Old French *oncle* from Late Latin *auunculus* from Latin *avunculus* maternal uncle: see AVUNCULAR]

-uncle *suffix* forming nouns, usu. diminutives (*carbuncle*). [Old French *-uncle, -oncle* or Latin *-unculus, -la*, a special form of *-ulus* -ULE]

un·clean *adjective* **1** not clean. **2** unchaste. **3** unfit to be eaten; ceremonially impure. **4** *Bible* (of a spirit) wicked. □ **un·clean·ness** *noun*

un·cleaned *adjective* not cleaned.

un·clean·li·ness *noun* lack of cleanliness.

un·clear *adjective* **1** not clear or easy to understand; obscure, uncertain. **2** (of a person) doubtful, uncertain (*I'm unclear as to what you mean*). □ **un·clear·ly** *adverb*

---

un·cleared *adjective* **1** (of land) not cleared of trees etc. **2** not cleared away or up. **3** (of a cheque etc.) not cleared.

un·clench *verb* **1** *transitive* release (clenched hands, features, teeth, etc.). **2** *intransitive* (of clenched hands etc.) become relaxed or open.

Uncle Sam *noun informal* a personification of the federal government or citizens of the US (*will fight for Uncle Sam*). [prob. expanded from *US* United States]

Uncle Tom *noun derogatory* a black man considered to be servile, cringing, etc. [with reference to the hero of H. B. Stowe's *Uncle Tom's Cabin* (1852)]

un·climbed *adjective* (of a peak, rock face, etc.) not previously climbed. □ **un·climb·able** *adjective*

un·clip *transitive verb* release from being fastened or held with a clip.

un·clog *transitive verb* (**un·clogged, un·clog·ging**) unblock (a drain, pipe, etc.).

un·clothe *transitive verb* **1** remove the clothes from. **2** strip of leaves or vegetation (*trees unclothed by the wind*). **3** expose, reveal. □ **un·clothed** *adjective*

un·cloud·ed *adjective* **1** not clouded; clear; bright. **2** untroubled (*unclouded serenity*).

un·clut·tered *adjective* not cluttered; not containing too many objects, details, or elements.

unco /ˈʌŋkoː/ *Scot.* ● *adjective* strange, unusual; notable. ● *adverb* remarkably; very. ● *noun* (*pl.* **uncos**) **1** a stranger. **2** (in *pl.*) news. □ **the unco guid** /ɡɪd/ *esp. derogatory* the rigidly religious. [Middle English, var. of UNCOUTH]

un·coat·ed *adjective* not covered with a coating of some substance.

un·coil *transitive & intransitive verb* unwind.

un·collect·ed *adjective* **1** left awaiting collection. **2** (of money) not collected or claimed. **3** (of literary work) not gathered into a collection for publication.

un·col·onized *adjective* not colonized.

un·col·oured *adjective* (also **un·col·ored**) **1** having no colour. **2** not having been coloured. **3** not influenced; impartial. **4** not exaggerated.

un·combed *adjective* (of hair) not combed.

un·com·bined *adjective* (esp. of a chemical element) not combined with something else.

un·com·fort·able *adjective* **1** not comfortable. **2** uneasy; causing or feeling disquiet (*an uncomfortable silence*). □ **un·com·fort·ably** *adverb*

un·com·mer·cial *adjective* **1** not commercial. **2** contrary to commercial principles.

un·com·mit·ted *adjective* **1** not committed. **2** unattached to any specific political cause or group.

un·com·mon *adjective* **1** not common; unusual; remarkable. **2** remarkably great etc. (*an uncommon fear of spiders*). □ **un·com·mon·ly** *adverb*

un·com·muni·ca·tive *adjective* not wanting to communicate; taciturn.

un·com·pen·sated *adjective* not compensated.

un·com·peti·tive *adjective* not competitive.

un·com·plain·ing *adjective* not complaining; resigned. □ **un·com·plain·ing·ly** *adverb*

un·com·plet·ed *adjective* not completed; incomplete.

un·compli·cated *adjective* not complicated; simple; straightforward.

un·compli·ment·ary *adjective* not complimentary; insulting.

un·com·pre·hend·ing *adjective* not comprehending. □ **un·com·pre·hend·ing·ly** *adverb*

un·com·pressed *adjective* not compressed.

un·compro·mis·ing *adjective* unwilling to compromise; stubborn; unyielding. □ **un·compro·mis·ing·ly** *adverb*

un·con·cealed *adjective* not concealed; obvious.

un·con·cern *noun* lack of concern; indifference; apathy. □ **un·con·cerned** *adjective* **un·con·cern·ed·ly** *adverb*

un·con·dition·al *adjective* not subject to conditions; complete (*unconditional surrender*). □ **un·con·dition·al·ly** *adverb*

un·con·di·tioned *adjective* **1** not subject to conditions or to an antecedent condition. **2** (of behaviour etc.) not determined by conditioning; natural.

unconditioned reflex *noun* an instinctive response to a stimulus.

un·con·fi·dent *adjective* not confident.

un·con·fined *adjective* not confined; boundless.

un·con·firmed *adjective* not confirmed.

un·con·form·able *adjective* **1** not conformable or conforming. **2** (of rock strata) not having the same direction of stratification. □ **un·con·form·ably** *adverb*

un·con·form·ity *noun* (*pl.* **-ities**) *Geol.* **1** a large break in the chronological sequence of layers of rock. **2** the surface of contact between two groups of unconformable strata.

un·con·gen·ial *adjective* not congenial.

un·con·nect·ed *adjective* **1** not physically joined. **2** not connected or associated. **3** (of speech etc.) disconnected; not joined in order or sequence (*unconnected ideas*). □ **un·con·nect·ed·ly** *adverb* **un·con·nect·ed·ness** *noun*

un·con·quer·able *adjective* not conquerable.

un·con·quered *adjective* not conquered or defeated.

un·con·scion·able *adjective* **1 a** having no conscience. **b** contrary to conscience. **2 a** unreasonably excessive (*an unconscionable length of time*). **b** not right or reasonable. □ **un·con·scion·ably** *adverb* [UN-¹ + obsolete *conscionable* from *conscions*, obsolete variant of CONSCIENCE]

un·con·scious ● *adjective* not conscious (*unconscious of any change; fell unconscious on the floor; an unconscious prejudice*). ● *noun* that part of the mind which is inaccessible to the conscious mind but which affects behaviour, emotions, etc. (*compare* COLLECTIVE UNCONSCIOUS). □ **un·con·scious·ly** *adverb* **un·con·scious·ness** *noun*

un·con·secrat·ed *adjective* not consecrated.

un·con·sid·ered *adjective* **1** not considered; disregarded. **2** (of a response etc.) immediate; not premeditated.

un·con·sol·able /ˌʌnkənˈsoːləbəl/ *adjective* unable to be consoled; inconsolable.

un·con·soli·dat·ed *adj.* not consolidated.

un·con·sti·tu·tion·al *adjective* not in accordance with the political constitution or with procedural rules. □ **un·con·sti·tu·tion·al·ity** *noun* **un·con·sti·tu·tion·al·ly** *adverb*

un·con·strained *adjective* not constrained or compelled.

un·con·strict·ed *adjective* not constricted.

un·con·struct·ed *adjective* *N Amer.* (of a garment) made with little or no interfacing, stiffening, or other material which would give definition to its shape; designed to fit loosely or easily rather than to emphasize structure.

un·con·sumed *adjective* not consumed.

un·con·sum·mated *adjective* not consummated.

un·con·tain·able *adjective* not containable.

un·con·tamin·ated *adjective* not contaminated; pure, unpolluted.

un·con·ten·tious *adjective* not controversial.

un·con·test·ed *adjective* not contested.

un·contra·dict·ed *adjective* not contradicted.

un·con·trived *adjective* not planned; not artificially created.

un·con·trol·lable *adjective* not controllable. □ **un·con·trol·labi·li·ty** *noun* **un·con·trol·lably** *adverb*

un·con·trolled *adjective* not controlled; unrestrained, unchecked.

un·contro·ver·sial *adjective* not controversial. □ **un·contro·ver·sial·ly** *adverb*

un·con·ven·tion·al *adjective* not bound by convention or custom; unusual; unorthodox. □ **un·con·ven·tion·al·ity** *noun* **un·con·ven·tion·al·ly** *adverb*

un·con·vert·ed *adjective* not converted.

un·con·vinced *adjective* not convinced.

un·con·vin·cing *adjective* not convincing. □ **un·con·vin·cing·ly** *adverb*

un·cooked *adjective* not cooked; raw.

un·cool *adjective slang* not stylish or fashionable; not having street credibility. □ **un·cool·ness** *noun*

un·co·opera·tive *adjective* not co-operative. □ **un·co·opera·tive·ly** *adverb*

un·co·ordin·ated *adjective* **1** not coordinated. **2** (of a person, a person's movements etc.) clumsy.

un·cork *transitive verb* **1** draw the cork from (a bottle etc). **2** *informal* unleash.

un·cor·rect·ed *adjective* not corrected.

un·cor·robor·ated *adjective* (esp. of evidence etc.) not corroborated.

un·cor·rupt·ed *adjective* not corrupted.

un·count·able *adjective* inestimable, immense (*uncountable wealth*). □ **un·count·ably** *adverb*

uncountable noun *noun* a noun that cannot form a plural or be used with the indefinite article, e.g. *happiness*.

un·count·ed *adjective* **1** not counted. **2** very many; innumerable.

un·couple *verb* **1** *transitive* unfasten, disconnect, detach. **2** *transitive* release (railway cars) from couplings. **3** *intransitive* (of a couple) separate at the end of a relationship; split up. □ **un·coupled** *adjective*

un·couth /ʌnˈkuːθ/ *adjective* **1** (of a person, manners, appearance, etc.) lacking in ease and polish; uncultured, rough (*uncouth voices*; *behaviour was uncouth*). **2** *archaic* not known; desolate; wild; uncivilized (*an uncouth place*). □ **un·couth·ly** *adverb* **un·couth·ness** *noun* [Old English *uncūth* unknown (as UN-¹ + *cūth* past participle of *cunnan* know, CAN¹)]

un·coven·ant·ed /ʌnˈkʌvənəntəd/ *adjective* **1** not bound by a covenant. **2** not promised by or based on a covenant, esp. God's covenant.

un·cov·er *transitive verb* **1** remove a cover or covering from. **2** make known; disclose (*uncovered the truth at last*).

un·cov·ered *adjective* **1** not covered by a roof, clothing, etc. **2** not wearing a hat.

un·crack·able *adjective* (of a code etc.) that cannot be cracked.

un·creat·ed *adjective* existing without having been created; not created.

un·creat·ive *adjective* not creative.

un·cred·it·ed *adjective* not acknowledged as the author, actor, etc.

un·crit·ic·al *adjective* **1** not critical; complacently accepting. **2** not in accordance with the principles of criticism. □ **un·crit·ic·al·ly** *adverb*

un·cross *transitive verb* remove (the limbs, knives, etc.) from a crossed position.

un·crowd·ed *adjective* not filled or likely to fill with crowds.

un·crowned *adjective* **1** not crowned. **2** having the status but not the name of (*the uncrowned king of boxing*).

UNCTAD *abbreviation* United Nations Conference on Trade and Development.

unc·tion /ˈʌŋkʃən/ *noun* **1 a** the act of anointing with oil etc. as a religious rite. **b** the oil etc. so used. **2 a** soothing words or thought. **b** excessive or insincere flattery. **3 a** the act of anointing for medical purposes. **b** an ointment so used. **4 a** a fervent or sympathetic quality in words or tone caused by or causing deep emotion. **b** a pretense of this. [Latin *unctio* from *ung(u)ere unct-* anoint]

unc·tuous /ˈʌŋktʃʊəs/ *adjective* **1** (of behaviour, speech, etc.) unpleasantly flattering. **2** (esp. of minerals) having a greasy or soapy feel; oily. □ **unc·tuous·ly** *adverb* **unc·tuous·ness** *noun* [medieval Latin *unctuosus* from Latin *unctus* anointing (as UNCTION)]

un·culti·vated *adjective* (esp. of land) not cultivated.

un·cul·tured *adjective* not cultured, unrefined.

un·cured *adjective* **1** not cured. **2** (of pork etc.) not salted or smoked.

un·curl *transitive & intransitive verb* relax from a curled position, untwist.

un·cur·tained *adjective* not curtained.

un·cut *adjective* **1** not cut. **2** (of a book) with the pages not cut open or with untrimmed margins. **3** (of a book, film, etc.) complete; uncensored. **4** (of a stone, esp. a diamond) not shaped by cutting. **5** (of alcohol, a drug, etc.) undiluted, unadulterated.

un·dam·aged *adjective* not damaged; intact.

un·dated *adjective* not provided or marked with a date.

un·daunt·ed *adjective* not daunted. □ **un·daunt·able** *adjective*

un·dead ● *adjective* (esp. of a vampire etc. in fiction) technically dead but still animate. ● *noun* (prec. by *the*; treated as *pl.*) those who are undead.

un·decid·able *adjective* that cannot be established or refuted; uncertain. □ **un·decid·abil·ity** *noun*

un·decid·ed ● *adjective* **1** not settled or certain (*the question is undecided*). **2** hesitating; irresolute (*undecided about their relative merits*). ● *noun* a person who is undecided, esp. as regards a vote.

un·deciph·er·able *adjective* not decipherable.

un·declared *adjective* not declared.

un·decor·ated *adjective* **1** not adorned; plain. **2** not honoured with an award.

un·defeat·ed *adjective* not defeated.

un·defend·ed *adjective* not defended.

un·defiled *adjective* not defiled; pure.

un·defined *adjective* **1** not defined. **2** not clearly marked; vague, indefinite. □ **un·defin·able** *adjective*

un·delete *transitive verb* *Computing* cancel the deletion of (text or a file).

un·deliv·ered *adjective* **1** not delivered or handed over. **2** not set free or released. □ **un·deliv·er·able** *adjective*

un·demand·ing *adjective* not demanding.

un·demo·crat·ic *adjective* not democratic. □ **un·demo·crat·ic·ally** *adverb*

un·demon·strated *adjective* not demonstrated.

un·demon·stra·tive *adjective* not expressing feelings etc. outwardly; reserved. □ **un·demon·stra·tive·ly** *adverb*

un·deni·able *adjective* **1** unable to be denied or disputed; certain. **2** excellent (*was of undeniable character*). □ **un·deni·ably** *adverb*

un·dent·ed *adjective* **1** (of a surface) not dented. **2** (foll. by *by*) not affected.

un·depend·able *adjective* not to be depended upon; unreliable.

under ● *preposition* **1 a** in or to a position lower than; below; beneath (*fell under the table*; *under the left eye*). **b** within, on the inside of (a surface etc.) (*wore a vest under his shirt*). **2 a** inferior to; less than (*a captain is under a major*; *is under 18*). **b** at or for a lower cost than (*was under $20*). **3 a** subject or liable to; controlled or bound by (*lives under oppression*; *under pain of death*; *born under Saturn*; *the country prospered under him*). **b** undergoing (*is under repair*). **c** classified or subsumed in (*that book goes under biology*; *goes under many names*). **4** at the foot of or sheltered by (*hid under the wall*; *under the cliff*). **5** planted with (a crop). **6** powered by (sail, steam, etc.). **7** following (another player in a card game). ● *adverb* **1** in or to a lower position or condition (*kept him under*). **2** *informal* in or into a state of unconsciousness (*put him under for the operation*). ● *adjective* lower (*the under jaw*). □ **under one's arm** see ARM¹. **under arms** see ARM². **under one's belt** see BELT. **under one's breath** see BREATH. **under canvas** see CANVAS. **under a cloud** see CLOUD. **under control** see CONTROL. **under the counter** see COUNTER¹. **under cover** see COVER *noun* 4. **under fire** see FIRE. **under foot** see FOOT. **under a person's nose** see NOSE. **under separate cover** in another envelope. **under the sun** anywhere in the world. **under water** in and covered by water. **under the weather** see WEATHER. □ **under·most** *adjective* [Old English from Germanic]

under- *prefix in senses of* UNDER: **1** below, beneath (*undercarriage*; *underground*). **2** lower in status; subordinate (*undersecretary*). **3** insufficiently, incompletely (*undercook*; *underdeveloped*).

under·achieve *intransitive verb* do less well than might be expected (esp. scholastically). □ **under·achieve·ment** *noun* **under·achiev·er** *noun*

under·active *adjective* (esp. of a gland) insufficiently active.

under·age *adjective* **1** not old enough, esp. not yet of adult status. **2** (of an activity) carried on by a person below the legal age for the activity (*underage drinking*).

under·appre·ci·ated *adjective* not appreciated according to one's merits.

under·arm ● *adjective* **1** *Sport* = UNDERHAND *adjective* 1. **2** in, of, or for the armpit (*underarm deodorant*). ● *adverb* = UNDERHAND *adverb*. ● *noun* the armpit.

under·belly *noun* (*pl.* **-bel·lies**) **1** the undersurface of an animal, vehicle, etc. **2** an area, region, etc. vulnerable to attack. **3** a hidden, unpleasant, or criminal part of society.

under·bid ● *transitive & intransitive verb* (**under·bid·ding**; *past and past participle* **under·bid**) **1** make a lower bid than (a person). **2** *Bridge etc.* bid less on (one's hand) than its strength warrants. ● *noun* **1** such a bid. **2** the act or an instance of underbidding.

under·bid·der *noun* **1** the person who makes the bid next below the highest. **2** *Bridge etc.* a player who underbids.

under·body *noun* (*pl.* **-bodies**) the undersurface of the body of an animal, vehicle, etc.

under·boss *noun* N Amer. the second-highest person in rank in a crime syndicate.

under·brush *noun* N Amer. undergrowth in a forest.

under·capit·al·ize *transitive verb* (also esp. *Brit.* **-ise**) (esp. as **under·capit·al·ized** *adjective*) provide (a business etc.) with insufficient capital to achieve a desired result.

under·card *noun* Boxing a contest placed second on the billing.

under·car·riage *noun* **1** the supporting frame of a vehicle. **2** a structure of wheels or floats beneath an aircraft to receive the impact on landing and support the aircraft on the ground, water, etc.

under·charge *transitive verb* **1** charge too little for (a thing) or to (a person). **2** give less than the proper charge to (a gun, an electric battery, etc.).

under·class *noun* a subordinate social class.

under·clothes *plural noun* clothes worn under others, esp. next to the skin; underwear.

under·cloth·ing *noun* underclothes collectively.

under·coat *noun* **1 a** a preliminary layer of paint under the finishing coat. **b** the paint used for this. **2** an animal's under layer of hair or down. **3** a coat worn under another. □ **under·coat·ing** *noun*

under·cook *transitive verb* cook insufficiently. □ **under·cooked** *adjective*

under·cover *adjective* (usu. *attributive*) **1** surreptitious. **2** engaged in spying, esp. by working with or among those to be observed (*undercover agent*).

under·croft *noun* a crypt. [Middle English from UNDER- + *croft* crypt, from Middle Dutch *crofte* cave, from medieval Latin *crupta* for Latin *crypta*: see CRYPT]

under·cur·rent *noun* **1** a current below the surface. **2** an underlying often contrary feeling, activity, or influence (*an undercurrent of protest*).

under·cut ● *transitive verb* (-cut·ting; *past* and *past participle* -cut) **1** sell or work at a lower price or lower wages than. **2** *Golf etc.* strike (a ball) so as to make it rise high. **3 a** cut away the part below or under (a thing). **b** cut away material to show (a carved design etc.) in relief. **4** render unstable or less firm, undermine. ● *noun* **1** *N Amer.* a notch cut in a tree trunk to guide its fall when felled. **2** any space formed by the removal or absence of material from the lower part of something. **3** *Brit.* the underside of a sirloin.

under·devel·oped *adjective* **1** not fully developed; immature. **2** (of a country etc.) below its potential economic level. **3** *Photog.* not developed sufficiently to give a normal image. □ **under·devel·op·ment** *noun*

under·dog *noun* **1** a person, team, etc. thought to be in a weaker position, and therefore not likely to win a competition, fight, etc. **2** a person who is in a state of inferiority or subjection.

under·done *adjective* **1** not thoroughly done. **2** (of food) lightly or insufficiently cooked.

under·draw·ing *noun* a preliminary sketch, subsequently covered with layers of paint.

under·dressed *adjective* dressed too plainly or too lightly.

under·edu·cated *adjective* poorly educated; with insufficient literacy skills.

under·empha·size *transitive verb* (also esp. *Brit.* -sise) place an insufficient degree of emphasis on. □ **under·empha·sis** *noun* (pl. -empha·ses)

under·employed *adjective* **1** employed at a task that uses less than one's full talents or abilities. **2** employed less than full-time. **3** (of a facility etc.) used less than it could be. □ **under·employ·ment** *noun*

under·esti·mate ● *transitive verb* **1** fail to recognize the strength, skill, talent, etc. of a person, esp. an opponent. **2** form too low an opinion or estimate of. ● *noun* an estimate that is too low. □ **under·esti·ma·tion** *noun*

under·expose *transitive verb* **1** *Photog.* use too short an exposure or too narrow an aperture with (a film) or when photographing (a subject), resulting in a darkened picture. **2** expose (a person etc.) too little to the public eye. □ **under·expo·sure** *noun*

under·fed *adjective* insufficiently fed.

under·floor *attributive adjective* situated or operating beneath the floor (*underfloor heating*).

under·flow *noun* an undercurrent.

under·foot *adverb* **1** beneath one's feet; on the ground. **2** sitting, lying, etc. right at or around one's feet so as to obstruct or inconvenience; in the way. **3** in a state of subjection.

under·fund·ed *adjective* not having sufficient funding. □ **under·fund** *transitive verb* **under·fund·ing** *noun*

under·fur *noun* an inner layer of short fur or down underlying an animal's outer fur.

under·garment *noun* an article of underclothing.

under·gird *transitive verb* **1** make secure underneath. **2** strengthen, support (*trust undergirds love*).

under·glaze ● *adjective* **1** (of painting on porcelain etc.) done before the glaze is applied. **2** (of colours) used in such painting. ● *noun* underglaze painting.

under·go *transitive verb* (3rd sing. present -goes; past -went; past participle -gone) experience.

under·grad *noun & adjective* *informal* = UNDERGRADUATE. [abbreviation]

under·gradu·ate ● *noun* a student at a university who has not yet completed a bachelor's degree. ● *adjective* **1** of or related to an undergraduate or undergraduates. **2** of or related to the course of study of a student completing a bachelor's degree (*undergraduate education*).

under·ground ● *adverb* **1** beneath the surface of the ground. **2** into hiding or some secret activity. ● *adjective* **1** situated beneath the surface of the ground. **2 a** secret, hidden, not open to the public. **b** designating a secret group, movement, or activity, esp. one aiming to subvert an established order or a ruling power (*underground army*). **3 a** of or pertaining to a subculture seeking to provide radical alternatives to the socially accepted or established mode. **b** unconventional, experimental (*underground press*). ● *noun* **1** a secret group or activity, esp. aiming to challenge or subvert a ruling power. **2** a subculture seeking to provide radical alternatives to the socially accepted or established mode. **3** *Brit.* a subway system. **4** a place below the surface of the earth.

underground economy *noun* financial transactions not officially declared or recorded.

Underground Railroad *noun* (also *Cdn* **Underground Railway**) *hist.* a secret network of safe houses and transportation established to help fugitive slaves escape from the southern US to Canada and the Free States of the American North in the years before the Civil War.

under·growth *noun* a dense growth of shrubs etc., esp. under large trees.

under·hand ● *adjective* **1** *Sport* (of a throw, pitch, serve, etc.) performed with the hand lower than the level of the shoulders. **2** = UNDERHANDED 1, 2. ● *adverb* (throw or pitch etc.) with the hand lower than the level of the shoulder. ● *transitive verb* throw (a ball etc.) with the hand below the level of the shoulder.

under·hand·ed ● *adjective* **1** deceptive, crafty, not above board. **2** secret, clandestine, surreptitious. **3** = UNDERHAND 1. ● *adverb* = UNDERHAND.

Under·hill ▶ 1 Bar·bara Ann (b.1963), Canadian figure skater. She began pairs skating with Paul Martini in 1978, and they won the world Junior championships that year; they were Canadian champions 1979–83, and won the world gold medal in Ottawa in 1984. **2 Frank Haw·kins** (1889–1971), Canadian historian and political theorist. A history professor at the Universities of Saskatchewan (until 1927) and Toronto (until 1955), Underhill was the first president of the League for Social Reconstruction, and the main author of the CCF's Regina Manifesto (1933). He also wrote extensively for *Canadian Forum*.

under·lay¹ ● *transitive verb* (past and past participle -laid) lay something under (a thing) to support or raise it. ● *noun* **1** a thing laid under another, esp. material laid under a carpet or mattress as protection or support. **2** the manner in which the words are fitted to the notes of a piece of vocal music. □ **under·lay·ment** *noun*

under·lay² past of UNDERLIE.

under·lie *transitive verb* (-lying; past -lay; past participle -lain) **1** lie or be situated under (a stratum etc.). **2** (of a principle, reason, etc.) be the basis of (a doctrine, law, conduct, etc.) **3** exist beneath the superficial aspect of.

under·line ● *transitive verb* **1** draw a line under (a word etc.) to give emphasis or draw attention or indicate italic or other special type. **2** emphasize, stress. ● *noun* **1** a line drawn under a word etc. **2** a caption below an illustration. □ **under·lin·ing** *noun*

under·ling *noun* usu. *derogatory* a subordinate.

under·lip *noun* the lower lip of a person, animal, or insect.

under·lying ● *verb pres. part. of* UNDERLIE. ● *adjective* **1** lying under or beneath the surface. **2 a** having a visible effect though not immediately obvious or openly present (*an underlying cause*). **b** fundamental, basic (*underlying principle*).

under·manned *adjective* having too few people such as crew or staff.

under·mine *transitive verb* **1** weaken, injure, destroy, ruin (a person, reputation, health, etc.) by secret or insidious means. **2** wear away the base or foundation of (*rivers undermine their banks*). **3** dig a tunnel or excavate beneath (a wall etc.). □ **under·miner** *noun* [Middle English from UNDER- + MINE²]

under·neath ● *preposition* **1** at or to a lower place than: directly below. **2** below or behind a covering of (*she wore a shirt underneath her sweater*). ● *adverb* **1** at or to a lower place. **2** directly beneath or covered by something (*the cat was underneath the covers*). ● *noun* the lower surface or part. ● *adjective* lower. [Old English *underneothan* (as UNDER + *neothan*: compare BENEATH)]

under·nour·ished *adjective* insufficiently nourished.
□ **under·nourish·ment** *noun*

under·pad *noun* a layer of soft foam laid under carpeting to provide cushioning and protect the floor.

under·paid ● *verb past and past participle of* UNDERPAY. ● *adjective* (of an employee) receiving a salary that is considered incommensurate with one's qualifications or the amount or type of work one is required to do.

under·paint·ing *noun* paint subsequently overlaid with another layer or with a finishing coat.

under·pants *plural noun* an article of underclothing worn to cover the hips, crotch, and sometimes the thighs.

under·part *noun* the lower part or underside of anything, esp. an animal.

under·pass *noun* a section of road or a walkway providing a passage beneath another road, railway, etc.

under·pay *transitive verb* (*past* and *past participle* **-paid**) pay (an employee etc.) too little. □ **under·pay·ment** *noun*

under·per·form *verb* **1** *intransitive* perform less well or be less profitable than expected. **2** *transitive* perform less well or be less profitable than. □ **under·per·form·ance** *noun* **under·per·form·er** *noun*

under·pin *transitive verb* (**-pinned**, **-pin·ning**) **1** form the basis for; support, strengthen. **2** support or strengthen (a building etc.) from below, esp. by laying a solid foundation.

under·pin·ning *noun* **1** a thing or structure that supports or strengthens. **2** (in *pl.*) a basis, foundation, or underlying principle.

under·plant *transitive verb* (usu. foll. by *with*) plant or cultivate the ground surrounding (a tall plant) with smaller ones.

under·play *verb* **1** *transitive* play down the importance of. **2** *transitive & intransitive Theatre* **a** perform with deliberate restraint. **b** underact.

under·popu·lated *adjective* having an insufficient or very small population. □ **under·popu·la·tion** *noun*

under·powered *adjective* **1 a** lacking full electrical, mechanical, etc. power. **b** lacking sufficient amplification. **2** with insufficient authority.

under·price *transitive verb* **1** price lower than what is usual or appropriate. **2** undercut (a competitor) in price.

under·priv·il·eged ● *adjective* **1** less privileged than others; deprived. **2** not enjoying the normal standard of living or rights in a society. ● *noun* (prec. by *the*; treated as *pl.*) underprivileged people.

under·rate *transitive verb* have too low an opinion of; underestimate. □ **under·rated** *adjective*

under-report *transitive verb* fail to report (news, data, etc.) fully.

under-represent *transitive verb* provide with inadequate or insufficient representation.

under-resourced *adjective* having insufficient financial or other resources.

under·ripe *adjective* not sufficiently ripe.

under·score ● *verb* = UNDERLINE. ● *noun* **1** = UNDERLINE. **2** the character _ used in email addresses etc. to represent a word break or blank space.

under·sea *adjective* below the sea or the surface of the sea, submarine.

under·secre·tary *noun* (*pl.* **-taries**) a subordinate official, esp. a junior minister or senior civil servant.

under·sell *transitive verb* (*past* and *past participle* **-sold**) **1** sell at a lower price than (another seller). **2** sell at less than the true value.

under·served *adjective* inadequately served.

under·sexed *adjective* having unusually weak sexual desires.

under-sheriff *noun* a deputy sheriff.

under·shirt *noun* N Amer. a light usu. cotton knitted short-sleeved or sleeveless shirt with no collar worn as an article of underclothing.

under·shoot *verb* (*past* and *past participle* **-shot**) **1** *transitive & intransitive* (of an aircraft) land short of (a runway etc.). **2** *transitive* fall short of or below (a target, goal, etc.).

under·shorts *plural noun* N Amer. men's underpants.

under·shot *adjective* having the chin, jaw, or lower teeth projecting beyond the upper teeth.

under·side *noun* (also in *pl.*) the lower side or bottom; the surface underneath.

under·signed *adjective* whose signature is appended below (*we, the undersigned, wish to state...*).

under·sized *adjective* (also **under·size**) of less than the usual size.

under·skirt *noun* a skirt worn under another; a petticoat.

under·slung *adjective* **1** supported from above. **2** (of a vehicle chassis) hanging lower than the axles.

under·sold *past and past participle of* UNDERSELL.

under·sow *transitive verb* (*past participle* **under·sown**) **1** sow (a later-growing crop) on land already seeded with another crop. **2** (foll. by *with*) sow land already seeded with (a crop) with a later-growing crop.

under·staffed *adjective* having too few staff. □ **under·staff·ing** *noun*

under·stand *verb* (*past* and *past participle* **-stood**) **1** *transitive* perceive the meaning of (words, a person, etc.) (*I can't understand you when you use technical words; he understood the joke*). **2** *transitive* perceive the significance, explanation, or cause of (*I don't understand why he came; she could not understand why it was such a big deal*). **3 a** *transitive* have a sympathetic awareness of the character or nature of; know how to deal with, be sympathetic to (*I understand your concern; nobody really understands me*). **b** *transitive & intransitive* accept without anger or resentment (*if you can't come, I'll understand*). **4 a** *transitive & intransitive* (often foll. by *about*) be conversant or familiar with, have a mastery of (a subject, skill, etc.) (*she understands about politics; he understands hockey*). **b** *transitive* be sufficiently acquainted with (a language) to be able to interpret the meaning of the words employed. **5** *transitive* (often foll. by *that* + clause) accept as true without positive knowledge or certainty; learn, gather, infer (*I understand that you are engaged; am I to understand that you refuse?*). **6** *transitive* supply (a word) mentally (*the verb may be either expressed or understood*). **7** *intransitive* have understanding (in general or in particular) (*you don't have to explain, I understand perfectly*). □ **understand each other 1** know each other's views or feelings. **2** be in agreement or collusion. [Old English *understandan* (as UNDER-, STAND)]

under·stand·able *adjective* **1** that one might expect; natural or reasonable (*it is understandable that a beginner would make such a mistake*). **2** that may be easily understood; comprehensible (*the instructions were very understandable*). □ **under·stand·abil·ity** *noun* **under·stand·ably** *adverb*

under·stand·ing ● *noun* **1** the ability to reason and comprehend; intellect. **2 a** an individual's perception or interpretation of a situation etc. **b** a person's knowledge of a subject. **3** an agreement; a thing agreed upon, esp. informally (*had an understanding with the rival company; consented only on this understanding*). **4** harmony in opinion or feeling (*disturbed the good understanding between them*). **5** sympathetic awareness or tolerance; empathy. ● *adjective* **1 a** sympathetic to others' feelings. **b** of a forgiving nature. **2** having understanding, insight, or good judgment. □ **under·stand·ing·ly** *adverb*

under·state *transitive verb* **1** express in greatly or unduly restrained terms. **2** represent (a thing) as being less than it actually is. □ **under·stater** *noun*

under·stated *adjective* **1** (of fashion, architecture, appearance, etc.) restrained in style or colour; not showy, simple (*the decor is refreshingly understated*). **2** stated or expressed in unduly restrained terms (*understated irony*). □ **under·stated·ly** *adverb* **under·stated·ness** *noun*

under·state·ment *noun* **1** a statement that expresses an idea etc. in mild or restrained terms (*to say that she was displeased would be an understatement: she was furious!*). **2** the quality of being understated or restrained in style or appearance. **3** the action or practice of understating.

under·steer ● *noun* a tendency of a car or truck etc. to turn less sharply than was intended. ● *intransitive verb* (of a vehicle) have such a tendency.

under·stood ● *verb past and past participle of* UNDERSTAND. ● *adjective* **1** inferred or implied without being explicitly stated. **2** accepted or agreed upon. **3 a** properly interpreted or perceived. **b** capable of being properly interpreted or perceived (*he could not make himself understood*).

under·storey *noun* (*pl.* **-storeys**) (also **under·story** *pl.* **-stories**) **1** a layer of vegetation beneath the main canopy of a forest. **2** the plants forming this.

under·study esp. *Theatre* ● *noun* (*pl.* **-studies**) a person who studies another's role or duties in order to perform at short notice in the absence of the other. ● *transitive verb* (**-studies**, **-studied**) **1** study (a role etc.) as an understudy. **2** act as an understudy to (a person).

under·surface *noun* the lower surface or surface underneath; the underside.

under·take *transitive verb* (*past* **under·took**; *past participle* **under·taken**) **1** take on (an obligation, responsibility, task, etc.); commit oneself to perform. **2** (usu. foll. by *to* + infin.) accept an obligation, promise.

---

t top   v voice   w we   z zoo   ʃ she   ʒ vision   θ thin   ð this   ŋ ring   x loch   tʃ chip   dʒ jar   (*see over for vowels*)

under·taker *noun* a person whose business is to make arrangements for funerals; a funeral director.

under·tak·ing *noun* **1** work etc. undertaken; an enterprise (*a serious undertaking*). **2** a pledge or promise. **3** the management of funerals as a profession.

under-the-counter *adjective* (of merchandise) not available in stores without a licence, prescription, or special permission, and thus often purchased and sold illegally.

under-the-table *adjective informal* (of a transaction etc., esp. payment) done surreptitiously esp. to avoid taxes or duties.

under·things *plural noun informal* (esp. women's) underclothing.

under·tone *noun* **1** a subdued tone of sound or colour. **2** an underlying quality. **3** an undercurrent of feeling.

under·took *past of* UNDERTAKE.

under·tow *noun* **1** a current below the surface of the sea moving in the opposite direction to the surface current. **2** an underlying feeling or influence, esp. one that is not expressed openly.

under·trained *adjective* inadequately trained.

under·trick *noun Bridge* a trick by which the declarer falls short of his or her contract.

under·use ● *transitive verb* use below the optimum level. ● *noun* insufficient use.

under·util·ized *adjective* (also esp. *Brit.* **-ised**) underused. □ **under·util·iz·a·tion** *noun* **under·util·ize** *transitive verb*

under·value *transitive verb* (**-values**, **-valued**, **-valu·ing**) **1** value insufficiently. **2** underestimate. □ **under·valu·a·tion** *noun*

under·vest *noun* = UNDERSHIRT.

under·water ● *adjective* **1** living or situated below the surface of the water. **2** designed to be used or done under the surface of the water. ● *adverb* under water.

under·way *predicative adjective* **1** (of a process, project, activity, etc.) having been instigated; in progress. **2** (of a person) having begun an activity etc. **3** *Naut.* (of a ship) in motion, having begun to move through the water.

under·wear *noun* **1** underclothing. **2** underpants.

under·weight *adjective* **1** weighing less than is normal or desirable. **2** (also **under·weight·ed**) *Finance* having less investment in a particular area than is considered desirable or appropriate.

under·went *past of* UNDERGO.

under·whelm *transitive verb jocular* fail to impress. □ **under·whelm·ing** *adjective* **under·whelm·ing·ly** *adverb* [after OVERWHELM]

under·wing *noun* **1 a** a wing partly covered by another, such as the hindwing of an insect. **b** the underside of a bird's wing. **2** (*attributive*) designating something located or occurring beneath the wing or wings of an aircraft (*underwing rockets*).

under·wire *noun* **1** *N Amer.* a thin semicircular support of wire stitched into the underside of each cup of a bra (also *attributive*: *underwire bra*). **2** *N Amer.* a bra with such a support. □ **under·wired** *Brit. adjective*

under·wood *noun* undergrowth.

under·work *verb* **1** *transitive* impose too little work on. **2** *intransitive* do too little work.

under·world *noun* **1** the part of society comprising those who live by organized crime and immorality. **2** the mythical abode of the dead under the earth.

under·write *transitive verb* (*past* **under·wrote**; *past participle* **under·writ·ten**) **1 a** sign, issue, and accept liability under (an insurance policy). **b** insure (a person, property, etc.). **c** assume liability up to (a certain amount). **2 a** guarantee (an undertaking or venture etc.) by assuming responsibility for any losses or debts incurred. **b** pay for or contribute financially towards. **3** guarantee the sale of (shares in a new company) by agreeing to purchase a certain percentage of shares not bought by the public. **4** write below (*the underwritten names*).

under·writer *noun* **1** a person who examines a risk, decides whether or not it can be insured, and if it can, works out a premium to be charged, usu. on the basis of the frequency of past claims for similar risks. **2** a financial institution that guarantees to buy a certain proportion of any unsold shares when a new investment security is offered to the public.

un·descend·ed *adjective Med.* (of a testicle) remaining in the abdomen instead of descending normally into the scrotum.

un·deserved *adjective* (of a reward or punishment) not deserved. □ **un·deserv·ed·ly** *adverb*

un·deserv·ing *adjective* not deserving.

un·desir·able ● *adjective* not desirable; objectionable, unpleasant. ● *noun* (usu. in *pl.*) an objectionable or unpleasant person, animal, insect, etc. □ **un·desir·abil·ity** *noun* **un·desir·ably** *adverb*

un·desired *adjective* not desired.

un·detect·able *adjective* not detectable. □ **un·detect·ably** *adverb*

un·detect·ed *adjective* not detected; unobserved, unnoticed.

un·deter·mined *adjective* = UNDECIDED.

un·deterred *adjective* not deterred.

un·devel·oped *adjective* not developed.

un·deviat·ing *adjective* not deviating; steady, constant. □ **un·deviat·ing·ly** *adverb*

un·diag·nosed *adjective* not diagnosed.

undid *past of* UNDO.

und·ies *plural noun informal* (esp. women's) underclothes. [abbreviation]

un·differ·en·ti·ated *adjective* not differentiated.

un·digest·ed *adjective* **1** not digested. **2** (esp. of information, facts, etc.) not properly arranged or considered.

un·digni·fied *adjective* lacking dignity.

un·dilut·ed *adjective* **1** not diluted. **2** complete, utter.

un·dimin·ished *adjective* not diminished or lessened.

un·dimmed *adjective* not weakened, lessened, or made dim. □ **un·dim·mable** *adjective*

un·dine /ˈʌndiːn/ *noun* a female water spirit; a nymph. [modern Latin *undina* (word invented by Paracelsus) from Latin *unda* wave]

un·diplo·mat·ic *adjective* tactless. □ **un·diplo·mat·ic·ally** *adverb*

un·direct·ed *adjective* aimless; lacking direction; unfocused.

un·disci·plined *adjective* lacking discipline; not disciplined. □ **un·disci·pline** *noun*

un·dis·closed *adjective* not revealed or made known.

un·dis·cov·ered *adjective* not discovered.

un·dis·crim·in·at·ing *adjective* **1** lacking taste or good judgment. **2** not selective, indiscriminate.

un·dis·cussed *adjective* not discussed. □ **un·dis·cuss·able** *adjective*

un·dis·guised *adjective* not disguised or concealed; open, candid. □ **un·dis·guis·ed·ly** *adverb*

un·dis·mayed *adjective* not dismayed.

un·dis·puted *adjective* **1** not disputed or called into question. **2** universally acknowledged or accepted; generally recognized as being (*the undisputed champion*).

un·dis·tin·guished *adjective* **1** lacking any distinguishing characteristic or feature (*an undistinguished square building*). **2** unremarkable, mediocre (*an undistinguished author*).

un·dis·trib·ut·ed *adjective* not distributed.

un·dis·turbed *adjective* not disturbed or interfered with.

un·divid·ed *adjective* not divided or shared; whole, entire (*gave him my undivided attention*).

undo ● *verb* (*3rd sing. present* **-does**; *past* **-did**; *past participle* **-done**) **1 a** *transitive* unfasten or untie (a coat, button, knot, etc.). **b** *intransitive* become unfastened (*how does this necklace undo?*). **c** unfasten the clothing of (a person). **2** *transitive* restore to the original form or condition; annul, cancel (*cannot undo the past*). **3** *transitive* ruin the prospects, reputation, or morals of. ● *noun* (*pl.* **undos**) *Computing* **1** a feature of some programs that allows the user to reverse the effect of the last action or actions, including restoring deletions. **2** the key on some keyboards that controls this feature.

un·doable *adjective* that cannot be done.

un·dock *transitive & intransitive verb* **1** separate (a spacecraft) from another in space. **2** take (a ship) out of a dock.

un·docu·ment·ed *adjective* **1** *N Amer.* not having the appropriate legal document or licence. **2** not proved by or recorded in documents.

un·doing *noun* **1 a** ruin, downfall, destruction. **b** the cause of this. **2** the process of reversing what has been done. **3** the action of opening or unfastening.

un·domes·ti·cated *adjective* not domesticated.

un·done *adjective* **1** not done; incomplete (*left the job undone*). **2** not fastened or tied (*left the buttons undone*; *undone shoelaces*). **3** *archaic* ruined.

un·doubt·ed *adjective* certain, not questioned, not regarded as doubtful.

un·doubt·ed·ly *adverb* beyond doubt; without question; certainly, definitely.

un·drained *adjective* not drained.

un·dramat·ic *adjective* **1** lacking a dramatic quality or effect. **2** understated; unremarkable. □ **un·dramat·ic·ally** *adverb*

un·draped *adjective* **1** not covered with drapery. **2 a** not hidden or concealed. **b** naked.

un·dreamed of *adjective* (also **un·dreamt of**) (usu. hyphenated when *attributive*) not considered or imagined; completely unexpected and usu. very pleasing.

un·dress ● *verb* **1** *intransitive* take off one's clothes. **2** *transitive* take the clothes off (a person). ● *noun* **1 a** *Military* a uniform or clothing worn on ordinary rather than ceremonial occasions (also *attributive*: *undress cap*) (opp. FULL DRESS). **b** casual or informal clothing. **2** the state of being naked or only partially clothed.

un·dressed *adjective* **1** not or no longer dressed; partly or wholly naked. **2** (of leather etc.) not treated. **3** (of food) not having a dressing.

un·drink·able *adjective* unable to be consumed by drinking; unsuitable for drinking.

Und·set /ˈunset/ **Sig·rid** (1882–1949), Norwegian novelist, whose works include the trilogy *Kristin Lavransdatter* (1920–22); she was awarded the Nobel Prize for literature in 1928.

undue *adjective* **1** excessive, disproportionate; unwarranted. **2** inappropriate, improper, unjust. □ **un·duly** *adverb*

undue influence *noun Law* influence that causes a person to act contrary to his or her own free will or without adequate attention to the consequences.

un·dulant /ˈʌndjʊlənt/ *adjective* moving like waves; fluctuating.

undulant fever *noun* brucellosis in humans, which can lead to chronic intermittent fever and chiefly affects the reticuloendothelial system.

un·dulate ● *intransitive verb* /ˈʌndjʊˌleɪt, -dʒʊˌleɪt/ **1** have a wavy or rippling outline or appearance (*the undulating landscape*). **2** have a wavelike motion; move with a smooth regular rising and falling or rippling back and forth (*the snake undulates through the grass*). ● *adjective* /ˈʌndjʊlət, -dʒʊlət/ wavy, going alternately up and down or from side to side (*leaves with undulate margins*). [Late Latin *undulatus* from Latin *unda* wave]

un·dula·tion /ˌʌndjʊˈleɪʃən, -dʒʊ-/ *noun* **1** a wavy motion or form, a gentle rise and fall. **2** each wave of this. **3** a set of wavy lines.

un·dyed *adjective* not dyed.

un·dying *adjective* eternal, never-ending (*undying love*).

un·earned *adjective* **1** not earned. **2** *Baseball* (of a run) resulting from an error or passed ball.

unearned income *noun* income from interest payments or investments etc. as opposed to salary, wages, or fees.

un·earth *transitive verb* **1** discover by investigation, searching, or while rummaging; bring to light. **2** uncover by the removal of earth; dig up.

un·earth·ly *adjective* **1 a** not of this world (*unearthly creature*). **b** eerie, supernatural, mysterious. **2** not typical of this world; rare, uncommon (*unearthly beauty*). **3** *informal* absurdly early or inconvenient (*an unearthly hour*). □ **un·earth·li·ness** *noun*

un·ease *noun* lack of ease, anxiety, discomfort, distress.

un·easy *adjective* (**un·easi·er**, **un·easi·est**) **1** (of a person) apprehensive, nervous, troubled; uncomfortable in mind or body. **2** characterized by or causing nervousness or restlessness; disturbing (*an uneasy silence*). **3** tenuous, shaky (*an uneasy alliance*). □ **un·easi·ly** *adverb* **un·easi·ness** *noun*

un·eat·able *adjective* that is not in a condition to be eaten (*compare* INEDIBLE).

un·eaten *adjective* not eaten.

un·econom·ic *adjective* not economic; incapable of being profitably operated etc.

un·econom·ic·al *adjective* not economical; wasteful.

un·edify·ing *adjective* not edifying, esp. uninstructive or degrading. □ **un·edify·ing·ly** *adverb*

un·edited *adjective* not edited.

un·educat·ed *adjective* not educated. □ **un·educ·able** *adjective*

un·elect·able *adjective* (of a candidate, party, etc.) unworthy of, or unsuitable for, election.

un·elect·ed *adjective* not elected.

un·embar·rassed *adjective* not embarrassed.

un·embel·lished *adjective* not embellished or decorated.

un·emotion·al *adjective* not emotional; lacking emotion. □ **un·emotion·al·ly** *adverb*

un·emphat·ic *adjective* not emphatic. □ **un·emphat·ic·ally** *adverb*

un·employ·able ● *adjective* not qualified or suitable for paid employment. ● *noun* **1** (often in *pl.*) an unemployable person. **2** (prec. by *the*; treated as *pl.*) unemployable people collectively. □ **un·employ·abil·ity** *noun*

un·em·ployed ● *adjective* **1** not having paid employment; out of work. **2** not in use. ● *noun* (prec. by *the*; treated as *pl.*) unemployed people.

un·employ·ment *noun* **1** the state of being unemployed. **2** the condition or extent of this in a country or region etc., esp. the number or percentage of unemployed people (*unemployment was lower in the West last month*). **3** *Cdn informal* = UNEMPLOYMENT INSURANCE (*some people work while on unemployment*).

unemployment benefit *noun* (also *US* **unemployment compensation**) a regular payment made by a government or, in the US, a trade union, to an unemployed person.

unemployment insurance *noun Cdn* = EMPLOYMENT INSURANCE. Abbr.: **UI**. ¶ No longer in official use though common in unofficial use.

un·en·closed *adjective* not enclosed.

un·encum·bered *adjective* not encumbered; free of any encumbrance.

un·end·ing *adjective* having or apparently having no end. □ **un·end·ing·ly** *adverb* **un·end·ing·ness** *noun*

un·en·dowed *adjective* not endowed.

un·endur·able *adjective* that cannot be endured. □ **un·endur·ably** *adverb*

un·enforce·able *adjective* (of a contract, law, etc.) impossible to enforce.

un·enforced *adjective* not enforced.

un·en·gaged *adjective* not engaged; uncommitted.

un-English *adjective* **1** not characteristic of the English language. **2** not characteristic of or derived from the culture or inhabitants of England.

un·enjoy·able *adjective* not enjoyable.

un·enlight·ened *adjective* not enlightened. □ **un·enlight·en·ing** *adjective*

un·enter·pris·ing *adjective* not enterprising.

un·enthusi·as·tic *adjective* not enthusiastic. □ **un·enthusi·as·tic·ally** *adverb*

un·envi·able *adjective* unpleasant, undesirable (*I had the unenviable task of telling him that he was being dismissed*). □ **un·envi·ably** *adverb*

un·equal *adjective* **1** not equal in amount, size, value, etc. **2** (usu. foll. by *to*) inadequate in ability or resources etc. (*unequal to the task*). **3 a** (of a contest, conflict, treaty, etc.) not evenly balanced; favouring one side (*an unequal bargain*). **b** inconsistent; varying or variable (*unequal distribution*). □ **un·equal·ly** *adverb*

un·equalled *adjective* (also esp. *US* **un·equaled**) **1** superior to all others. **2** (foll. by *by*) not matched or surpassed.

un·equipped *adjective* not equipped.

un·equivo·cal *adjective* not ambiguous; plain, unmistakable. □ **un·equivo·cal·ly** *adverb* **un·equivo·cal·ness** *noun*

un·err·ing *adjective* **1** not missing the intended target; certain, sure. **2** not failing or making a mistake; true. □ **un·err·ing·ly** *adverb*

UNESCO /juːˈnɛskoʊ/ *abbreviation* (also **Unesco**) United Nations Educational, Scientific, and Cultural Organization.

un·escort·ed *adjective* not escorted.

un·essen·tial ● *adjective* **1** not essential (*compare* INESSENTIAL). **2** not of the first importance. ● *noun* an unessential part or thing.

un·estab·lished *adjective* not established.

un·ethical *adjective* not ethical, esp. unscrupulous in business or professional conduct. □ **un·ethical·ly** *adverb*

un·even *adjective* **1** not level or smooth. **2** not consistent, regular, or uniform. **3** (of a competition) unequal. □ **un·even·ly** *adverb* **un·even·ness** *noun*

uneven bars *plural noun* esp. *N Amer.* two horizontal bars placed close together and raised on supports, one higher than the other, used in women's gymnastic competitions.

un·event·ful *adjective* not eventful. □ **un·event·ful·ly** *adverb* **un·event·ful·ness** *noun*

un·exam·ined *adjective* not examined.

un·exampled *adjective* having no precedent or parallel.

un·excep·tion·able *adjective* to whom or to which no exception can be taken; perfectly satisfactory or adequate. ¶ *Unexceptionable* should not be confused with *unexceptional*. Note the difference in meaning between *Her new book is unexceptionable* (i.e. it contains nothing that would cause objections) and *Her new book is unexceptional* (i.e. it is mediocre). □ **un·excep·tion·ably** *adverb*

---

uː mood   aɪ my   əi pipe   au brown   ʌu house   ei day   ɔi boy   ɑ̃ franglais   ã Canadien   ɔ̃ Brayon   (*see over for consonants*)

un·excep·tion·al *adjective* not out of the ordinary; usual, normal. ¶ See Usage Note at UNEXCEPTIONABLE. □ **un·excep·tion·al·ly** *adverb*

un·excit·able *adjective* not easily excited.

un·excit·ed *adjective* not excited.

un·excit·ing *adjective* not exciting; dull.

un·exhaust·ed /ˌʌnɪɡˈzɔːstəd/ *adjective* not used up, spent, or brought to an end.

un·expect·ed ● *adjective* not expected; surprising. ● *noun* (prec. by *the*; usu. treated as *sing.*) an unexpected thing or unexpected things collectively. □ **un·expect·ed·ly** *adverb* **un·expect·ed·ness** *noun*

un·expired *adjective* that has not yet expired.

un·explain·able *adjective* inexplicable. □ **un·explain·ably** *adverb*

un·explained *adjective* not explained.

un·explod·ed *adjective* (usu. *attributive*) (of a bomb etc.) that has not exploded.

un·exploit·ed *adjective* (of resources etc.) not exploited.

un·explored *adjective* not explored.

un·exposed *adjective* not exposed.

un·expressed *adjective* not expressed or made known (*unexpressed fears*).

un·expur·gated *adjective* (esp. of a text etc.) complete and containing all the original material; uncensored.

un·fading *adjective* *literary* that never fades.

un·fail·ing *adjective* **1** unlimited, inexhaustible (*an unfailing source of comfort*). **2** unceasing, constant (*unfailing devotion*). **3** certain, reliable (*unfailing accuracy*). □ **un·fail·ing·ly** *adverb*

un·fair *adjective* **1** not just, reasonable, or objective (*unfair criticism*). **2** not according to the rules (*unfair play*). **3** dishonest (*obtained by unfair means*). □ **un·fair·ly** *adverb* **un·fair·ness** *noun*

un·faith·ful *adjective* **1** (of a person) not faithful, esp. to a sexual partner. **2** (of behaviour) disloyal. □ **un·faith·ful·ly** *adverb* **un·faith·ful·ness** *noun*

un·falter·ing *adjective* not faltering; steady, resolute. □ **un·falter·ing·ly** *adverb*

un·famil·iar *adjective* not familiar. □ **un·famili·ar·ity** *noun*

un·fashion·able *adjective* not fashionable. □ **un·fashion·ably** *adverb*

un·fasten *transitive verb* **1** loosen. **2** open the fastening or fastenings of. **3** detach.

un·fastened *adjective* **1** that has not been fastened. **2** that has been loosened, opened, or detached.

un·fathom·able *adjective* incapable of being fathomed. □ **un·fathom·ably** *adverb*

un·fathomed *adjective* **1** of unascertained depth. **2** not fully explored or known.

un·favour·able *adjective* (also **un·favor·able**) not favourable or beneficial; adverse, unpropitious. □ **un·favour·ably** *adverb*

un·fazed *adjective* *informal* untroubled; not disconcerted. □ **un·faz·able** *adjective*

un·feas·ible *adjective* not feasible; impractical. □ **un·feas·ibil·ity** *noun* **un·feas·ibly** *adverb*

unfed *adjective* not fed; hungry.

un·feel·ing *adjective* **1** unsympathetic, harsh, not caring about others' feelings. **2** lacking sensation or sensitivity (*my unfeeling hands*). □ **un·feel·ing·ly** *adverb*

un·feigned *adjective* genuine, sincere.

un·felt *adjective* not felt.

un·femin·ine *adjective* **1** not characteristically or stereotypically feminine. **2** not regarded as suitable or appropriate for a woman.

un·fenced *adjective* not provided with fences.

un·ferment·ed *adjective* not fermented.

un·fertil·ized *adjective* (also esp. *Brit.* **un·fertil·ised**) not fertilized.

un·fettered *adjective* unrestrained, unrestricted. □ **un·fetter** *transitive verb*

un·filial *adjective* not befitting a son or daughter.

un·filled *adjective* not filled.

un·film·able *adjective* (of a book etc.) impossible to adapt for film.

un·filtered *adjective* **1** not filtered. **2** (of a cigarette) not provided with a filter.

un·finished *adjective* **1** not finished; incomplete. **2** (of wood furniture etc.) having no finishing coat; unpainted, unstained, unvarnished, etc. □ **un·finish·able** *adjective*

unfinished business *noun* **1** a task or tasks that must be completed. **2** *Psych. informal* unresolved issues.

unfit *adjective* **1** not fitted or suited. **2** not provided with fittings.

un·fit·ting *adjective* not fitting, proper, or right; unbecoming.

un·fixed *adjective* **1** not fixed, determined, or secure. **2** (of a person) unsettled, uncertain.

un·flag·ging *adjective* tireless, persistent. □ **un·flag·ging·ly** *adverb*

un·flap·pable *adjective* *informal* imperturbable; remaining calm in a crisis. □ **un·flap·pabil·ity** *noun* **un·flap·pably** *adverb*

un·flatter·ing *adjective* not flattering. □ **un·flatter·ing·ly** *adverb*

un·flavoured *adjective* (also **un·flavored**) not flavoured.

un·fledged *adjective* **1** (of a person) inexperienced. **2** (of a bird) not yet fledged.

un·flinch·ing *adjective* not showing reluctance, hesitation, indecision, or fear; unwavering, direct. □ **un·flinch·ing·ly** *adverb*

un·focused *adjective* (also **un·focussed**) not focused.

un·fold *verb* **1** *transitive* open the fold or folds of, spread out. **2** *intransitive* develop, become clear (*the plot begins to unfold*). **3** *intransitive* become opened out. **4** *transitive* reveal, explain, or make clear (a thought, idea, mystery, etc.). □ **un·fold·ing** *noun* **un·fold·ment** *noun US.*

un·forced *adjective* **1** not produced by effort; easy, natural. **2** not compelled or constrained. □ **un·forced·ly** *adverb*

un·ford·able *adjective* that cannot be forded.

un·fore·see·able *adjective* not foreseeable.

un·fore·seen *adjective* not foreseen.

un·forget·table *adjective* that cannot be forgotten; memorable, wonderful (*an unforgettable experience*). □ **un·forget·tably** *adverb*

un·forgiv·able *adjective* without any justifiable motive; inexcusable, indefensible, disgraceful. □ **un·forgiv·ably** *adverb*

un·forgiv·en *adjective* not forgiven.

un·forgiv·ing *adjective* not forgiving. □ **un·forgiv·ing·ly** *adverb*

un·formed *adjective* **1** not formed. **2** shapeless. **3** not developed.

un·forth·coming *adjective* **1** not willing to divulge information. **2** not ready or made available when needed or wanted.

un·forti·fied *adjective* not fortified.

un·fortu·nate ● *adjective* **1 a** having bad fortune; unlucky. **b** unhappy. **2** regrettable (*it is unfortunate that you could not have been here*). **3** unsuitable, inappropriate, or inauspicious (*a most unfortunate choice of words; a very pretty sweater but a rather unfortunate colour*). ● *noun* (usu. in *pl.*) an unfortunate person.

un·fortu·nate·ly *adverb* **1** (qualifying a whole sentence) it is unfortunate that. **2** in an unfortunate manner.

un·found·ed *adjective* having no basis in fact; unsubstantiated, not valid (*the rumour was unfounded; your fears are completely unfounded*).

un·framed *adjective* (esp. of a picture) not framed.

un·free *adjective* deprived or devoid of liberty. □ **un·free·dom** *noun*

un·freeze *verb* (*past* **un·froze**; *past participle* **un·frozen**) **1** *transitive* cause to thaw. **2** *intransitive* thaw. **3** *transitive* remove restrictions from, make (assets, credits, etc.) realizable.

un·frequent·ed *adjective* not frequented.

un·friend·ly *adjective* (**un·friend·li·er**, **un·friend·li·est**) **1** not friendly. **2** (in *combination*) *informal* not helpful or beneficial to (*ozone-unfriendly*). □ **un·friend·li·ness** *noun*

un·frock *transitive verb* = DEFROCK.

un·froze *past of* UNFREEZE.

un·frozen ● *verb past participle of* UNFREEZE. ● *adjective* not frozen.

un·fruit·ful *adjective* **1** not producing good results, unprofitable. **2** not producing fruit or crops. □ **un·fruit·ful·ly** *adverb*

un·fulfilled *adjective* not fulfilled. □ **un·fulfill·able** *adjective* **un·fulfill·ing** *adjective* **un·fulfill·ment** *noun*

un·fund·ed *adjective* not funded.

un·funny *adjective* (**un·funni·er**, **un·funni·est**) not amusing, although meant to be. □ **un·funni·ness** *noun*

un·furl *verb* **1** *transitive* spread or open out (a sail, flag, etc.) to its greatest length or width. **2** *intransitive* become spread out or fully extended.

un·furnished *adjective* **1** (of an apartment etc.) without furniture. **2** (often foll. by *with*) not provided or supplied.

un·fussy *adjective* not fussy. □ **un·fussi·ly** *adverb*

un·gain·ly *adjective* awkward, clumsy, ungraceful (*he walks in long ungainly strides*). □ **un·gain·li·ness** *noun* [UN-[1] + obsolete *gainly* graceful, ultimately from Old Norse *gegn* straight]

un·gal·lant *adjective* not gallant. □ **un·gal·lant·ly** *adverb*

Un·ga·va, District of /ʊŋˈɡɒvə/ *hist.* a district (1895–1912) of the North-West Territories, occupying what is now roughly the Ungava Peninsula. [from Inuktitut, meaning uncertain: perhaps = toward the open water, unknown land, or place to the south]

Un·ga·va Bay a large, wide inlet of Hudson Strait, indenting the northeastern coast of Quebec.

Un·ga·va Peninsula a large peninsula comprising most of N Quebec, bounded by Hudson Bay to the west, Hudson Strait and Ungava Bay to the north, Labrador to the east and the Eastmain River to the south. Located in the northwest is a large, almost perfectly circular meteoritic crater measuring over 3 km in diameter and almost 500 m in depth.

un·gener·ous *adjective* not generous; mean. □ **un·gener·ous·ly** *adverb*

un·gentle *adjective* not gentle. □ **un·gently** *adverb*

un·gentle·man·ly *adjective* not gentlemanly.

un·gifted *adjective* not gifted or talented.

un·glamor·ous *adjective* **1** lacking glamour or appeal. **2** mundane.

un·glazed *adjective* not glazed.

un·gloved *adjective* not wearing a glove or gloves.

un·glued *adjective* **1** having no glue, unstuck. **2** *N Amer.* discomposed, confused, crazy. □ **come** (or **become**) **unglued** *N Amer.* **1 a** fall apart, lose one's composure. **b** become crazy. **2** fall into a state of chaos or disarray.

un·godly *adjective* **1** impious, wicked. **2** *informal* outrageous (*an ungodly hour to arrive*). □ **un·godli·ness** *noun*

un·govern·able *adjective* uncontrollable, violent. □ **un·govern·ably** *adverb*

un·grace·ful *adjective* not graceful. □ **un·grace·ful·ly** *adverb*

un·gracious *adjective* not cordial, courteous, or polite; rude or unkind to others. □ **un·gracious·ly** *adverb*

un·gram·mat·ic·al *adjective* contrary to the rules of grammar. □ **un·gram·mat·ic·al·ity** *noun* (*pl.* **-ies**). **un·gram·mat·ic·al·ly** *adverb*

un·grasp·able *adjective* **1** that cannot be grasped or seized. **2** that cannot be comprehended.

un·grate·ful *adjective* **1** not feeling or showing gratitude. **2** not pleasant or acceptable. □ **un·grate·ful·ly** *adverb* **un·grate·ful·ness** *noun*

un·greased *adjective* **1** not lubricated with grease. **2** (of a cookie sheet etc.) not coated with butter or shortening etc. prior to cooking.

un·ground·ed *adjective* **1** having no basis or justification; unfounded. **2** *N Amer. Electricity* (of an electrical outlet etc.) not grounded. **3** (foll. by *in*) not properly instructed (in a subject etc.).

un·grudging *adjective* not grudging. □ **un·grudging·ly** *adverb*

un·guard *transitive verb Cards* place (a high card) at risk of capture by discarding a lower protecting card.

un·guard·ed *adjective* **1 a** (of a person) not on one's guard; candid, open. **b** resulting from such candidness (*she told me so in an unguarded moment*). **2** careless, thoughtless, incautious (*an unguarded remark*). **3** not guarded; vulnerable. □ **un·guard·ed·ly** *adverb*

un·guent /ˈʌŋɡwənt/ *noun* a soft substance, such as a perfumed oil, used esp. as an ointment. [Latin *unguentum* from *unguere* anoint]

un·guess·able *adjective* that cannot be guessed or imagined.

un·guid·ed *adjective* not guided in a particular path or direction; left to take its own course.

un·guis /ˈʌŋɡwɪs/ *noun* (*pl.* **un·gues** /-wiːz/) **1** *Bot.* the narrow base of a petal. **2** *Zool.* a nail or claw. [Latin]

un·gu·late /ˈʌŋɡjʊlət, -ˌleɪt/ ● *adjective* hoofed. ● *noun* a hoofed mammal. [Late Latin *ungulatus* from Latin *ungula*, diminutive of *unguis* a nail or claw]

un·hallowed *adjective* **1** not consecrated. **2** not sacred; unholy, wicked.

un·ham·pered *adjective* not hampered.

un·hand *transitive verb archaic* or *jocular* **1** take one's hands off (a person). **2** release from one's grasp.

un·hand·some *adjective* not handsome.

un·handy *adjective* **1** not easy to handle or manage; awkward. **2** not skilful in using the hands.

un·happy *adjective* (**un·happi·er**, **un·happi·est**) **1 a** not happy, miserable. **b** (often foll. by *with*, *about*) displeased, dissatisfied, upset. **2** unsuccessful, unfortunate, regrettable. **3** causing or associated with misfortune; inauspicious (*an unhappy omen*). □ **un·happi·ly** *adverb* **un·happi·ness** *noun*

un·harmed *adjective* not harmed.

un·har·moni·ous *adjective* not harmonious.

un·harness *transitive verb* remove a harness from. □ **un·har·nessed** *adjective*

un·hatched *adjective* (of an egg etc.) not hatched.

UNHCR *abbreviation* United Nations High Commissioner for Refugees.

un·health·ful *adjective* harmful to health, unwholesome. □ **un·health** *noun*

un·healthy *adjective* (**un·healthi·er**, **un·healthi·est**) **1** not in good health. **2** not conducive to good physical, mental, or emotional health or well-being (*an unhealthy diet; an unhealthy relationship*). **3** not indicative of good health; unwholesome (*an unhealthy complexion*). **4** inappropriate, perverse (*he maintains an unhealthy attachment to her*). □ **un·healthi·ly** *adverb* **un·healthi·ness** *noun*

un·heard *adjective* not heard.

unheard of *adjective* (usu. hyphenated when *attributive*) **1** unknown, unfamiliar. **2** unprecedented, not previously attempted or considered. **3** outrageous, preposterous.

un·heat·ed *adjective* not heated.

un·heed·ed *adjective* not heeded; disregarded.

un·heed·ing *adjective* not giving heed; heedless. □ **un·heed·ing·ly** *adverb*

un·help·ful *adjective* not helpful. □ **un·help·ful·ly** *adverb*

un·herald·ed *adjective* not heralded; unannounced.

un·hero·ic *adjective* not heroic. □ **un·hero·ic·ally** *adverb*

un·hesitat·ing *adjective* **1** without pause, uncertainty, or hesitation (*an unhesitating reply*). **2** without interruption; relentless, constant (*her unhesitating generosity and kindness*). □ **un·hesitat·ing·ly** *adverb*

un·hewn *adjective* (of stone) not hewn.

un·hin·dered *adjective* not hindered.

un·hinge *transitive verb* **1** take (a door etc.) off its hinges. **2 a** unsettle or unbalance (a person); make crazy. **b** throw (a situation etc.) into chaos or confusion. **3** detach, separate, or dislodge.

un·hinged *adjective* unsettled, unbalanced, disordered, confused.

unhip *adjective informal* not hip; not aware of or consistent with the latest trends or styles.

un·histor·ical *adjective* not historical. □ **un·histor·ical·ly** *adverb*

un·hitch *transitive verb* **1** release from a hitched state. **2** unhook, unfasten.

un·hit·table *adjective* (esp. of a pitched baseball) that cannot be hit.

un·hol·ster *transitive verb* remove from a holster.

un·holy *adjective* (**un·holi·er**, **un·holi·est**) **1** evil, wicked. **2** *informal* dreadful, terrible (*this room is an unholy mess!*). **3** not holy. **4** denoting an alliance or collaboration with potentially harmful implications between two or more parties that are not natural allies. □ **un·holi·ness** *noun*

un·hook *transitive verb* **1** remove from a hook or hooks. **2** unfasten by releasing a hook or hooks.

un·hoped for *adjective* (usu. hyphenated when *attributive*) not hoped for or expected.

un·horse *transitive verb* **1** throw or drag from a horse. **2** (of a horse) throw (a rider). **3** dislodge, overthrow.

un·human *adjective* **1** not human. **2** superhuman. **3** inhuman, brutal.

un·hurried *adjective* not hurried. □ **un·hurried·ly** *adverb*

un·hurt *adjective* not hurt.

un·husked *adjective* not having the husk removed.

un·hygien·ic *adjective* not hygienic. □ **un·hygien·ic·ally** *adverb*

un·hyphen·ated *adjective* not hyphenated.

uni- *combining form* one; having or consisting of one. [Latin from *unus* one]

uni *noun Brit. informal* a university.

Uni·ate /ˈjuːniˌət, -ˌeɪt/ ● *adjective* of or relating to any community of Christians in E Europe or the Near East that acknowledges papal supremacy but retains its own liturgy etc. ● *noun* a member of such a community. [Russian *uniyat* from *uniya* from Latin *unio* UNION]

uni·axial /ˌjuːniˈaksɪəl/ *adjective* having a single axis. □ **uni·axial·ly** *adverb*

uni·body *noun* (*pl.* **-bodies**) a single moulded unit forming both the bodywork and chassis of a vehicle.

uni·brow *noun* eyebrows that meet above the nose, giving the appearance of a single eyebrow.

uni·cameral /ˌjuːnɪˈkamərəl/ *adjective* with a single legislative chamber.

un·iced *adjective* not covered with icing.

UNICEF /ˈjuːnəˌsef/ *abbreviation* United Nations Children's Fund. [acronym of the original name 'United Nations International Children's Emergency Fund']

uni·cellu·lar /ˌjuːnɪˈseljələr/ *adjective* (of an organism, organ, tissue, etc.) consisting of a single cell.

uni·corn /ˈjuːnɪkɔrn/ *noun* **1 a** a fabulous animal usually represented as a horse with a single straight horn projecting from its forehead. **b** a heraldic representation of this, with a twisted horn, a deer's feet, a goat's beard, and a lion's tail. **2** a team of three horses, two abreast and one in front, used to draw a carriage or coach. [Old French *unicorne* from Latin *unicornis*, from UNI- + *cornu* 'horn', translation of Greek *monocerōs*]

uni·cycle /ˈjuːnɪˌsaɪkəl/ *noun* a single-wheeled cycle, esp. as used by acrobats. □ **uni·cyc·list** *noun*

un·ideal·ized *adjective* (also esp. *Brit.* **-ised**) not represented as perfect or ideal; unembellished.

un·iden·ti·fi·able *adjective* unable to be identified.

un·iden·ti·fied *adjective* not identified.

uni·dimen·sion·al /ˌjuːnɪdaɪˈmenʃənəl/ *adjective* having (only) one dimension; one-dimensional.

uni·direc·tion·al /ˌjuːnɪdɪˈrekʃənəl, ˌjuːnɪdaɪ-/ *adjective* having only one direction of motion, operation, etc. □ **uni·direc·tion·al·ly** *adverb*

uni·fi·ca·tion /ˌjuːnɪfɪˈkeɪʃən/ *noun* **1** the act or an instance of unifying; the state of being unified. **2** *Cdn* the action or policy of merging the traditional army, navy, and air force into a single combined force. □ **uni·fi·ca·tory** *adjective*

Unification Church *noun* a religious organization founded in 1954 in Korea by Sun Myung Moon (*compare* MOONIE).

Unified Family Court *noun Cdn* (in Newfoundland and Labrador) a division of the Supreme Court which has jurisdiction over all aspects of family law, including divorce, custody, adoption, etc.

unified field theory *noun Physics* a theory that seeks to explain all the field phenomena (e.g. gravitation and electromagnetism: *see* FIELD *noun* 8) formerly treated by separate theories.

uni·form ● *adjective* **1** not changing in form or character; the same, unvarying (*present a uniform appearance; all of uniform size and shape*). **2** conforming to the same standard, rules, or pattern. **3** constant in the course of time (*uniform acceleration*). **4** (of a tax, law, etc.) not varying with time or place. ● *noun* **1** uniform distinctive clothing worn by members of the same body, e.g. by soldiers, police, members of a sports team, etc. **2** clothing, usu. white or in pastel colours, worn by nurses and other members of medical professions. **3** a style of dress typical of a certain group (*jeans and a T-shirt–the uniform of teenagers*). **4** a police officer wearing a uniform. ● *transitive verb* **1** clothe in uniform (*a uniformed officer*). **2** make uniform. □ **uni·formed** *adjective* **uni·form·ly** *adverb* [French *uniforme* or Latin *uniformis* (as UNI-, FORM)]

uni·formi·tar·ian /ˌjuːnɪˌfɔrmɪˈteriən/ ● *adjective* of the theory that geological processes are always due to continuously and uniformly operating forces. ● *noun* a holder of this theory. □ **uni·formi·tar·ian·ism** *noun*

uni·form·ity /ˌjuːnɪˈfɔrmɪti/ *noun* (*pl.* **-ities**) the state of being uniform; sameness, consistency.

unify /ˈjuːnɪˌfaɪ/ *transitive & intransitive verb* (**-fies, -fied**) make united or uniform. □ **uni·fied** *adjective* **uni·fi·er** *noun* **uni·fy·ing** *adjective* [French *unifier* or Late Latin *unificare* (as UNI-, -FY)]

un·ignor·able *adjective* that cannot be ignored. □ **un·ignor·ably** *adverb*

uni·lat·eral /ˌjuːnɪˈlatərəl/ *adjective* **1** performed by or affecting only one person or party (*unilateral disarmament; unilateral declaration of independence*). **2** one-sided. **3** (of leaves) all on the same side of the stem. **4** (of a line of descent) through ancestors of one sex only. □ **uni·lat·eral·ism** *noun* **uni·lat·eral·ly** *adverb*

uni·lin·gual /ˌjuːnɪˈlɪŋɡwəl, -ˈlɪŋɡjuəl/ *esp. Cdn* ● *adjective* **1** able to speak only one language. **2** spoken or written in or involving only one language. ● *noun* a unilingual person. □ **uni·lin·gual·ism** *noun* **uni·lin·gual·ist** *adjective* **uni·lin·gual·ly** *adverb*

uni·locu·lar /ˌjuːnɪˈlɒkjʊlər/ *adjective Bot. & Zool.* single-chambered.

un·imagin·able *adjective* impossible to imagine. □ **un·imagin·ably** *adverb*

un·imagina·tive *adjective* lacking imagination; stolid, dull. □ **un·imagina·tive·ly** *adverb* **un·imagina·tive·ness** *noun*

un·imagined *adjective* not imagined.

un·impaired *adjective* not impaired.

un·impeach·able *adjective* giving no opportunity for censure; beyond reproach or question. □ **un·impeach·ably** *adverb*

un·impeded *adjective* not impeded.

un·import·ance *noun* lack of importance.

un·import·ant *adjective* not important.

un·impos·ing *adjective* unimpressive.

un·im·pressed *adjective* not impressed.

un·impres·sion·able *adjective* not impressionable.

un·impres·sive *adjective* not impressive. □ **un·impres·sive·ly** *adverb*

un·improved *adjective* **1** not made better or improved. **2** not made use of. **3** (of land) not used for agriculture or building; not developed.

un·incor·por·ated *adjective* **1** not formed into a corporation. **2** not incorporated or united.

un·infect·ed *adjective* not infected.

un·inflect·ed *adjective* **1** *Grammar* (of a language) not having inflections. **2** not changing or varying. **3** not bent or deflected.

un·influ·enced *adjective* not influenced.

un·influ·en·tial *adjective* having little or no influence.

un·inform·a·tive *adjective* not informative; giving little information.

un·informed *adjective* **1** not informed or instructed. **2** ignorant, uneducated.

un·inhabit·able *adjective* that cannot be inhabited.

un·inhabit·ed *adjective* not inhabited.

un·inhibit·ed *adjective* not inhibited. □ **un·inhibit·ed·ly** *adverb*

un·initi·ated *adjective* not initiated; not admitted or instructed.

un·injured *adjective* not injured.

un·inspired *adjective* not imaginative or inspiring; dull.

un·inspir·ing *adjective* not inspiring.

un·install *transitive verb* (**un·installed, un·install·ing**) remove an installed program from a computer system.

un·instruct·ed *adjective* not instructed or informed.

un·insu·lated *adjective* not insulated.

un·insur·able *adjective* that cannot be insured.

un·insured *adjective* not insured.

un·intelli·gent *adjective* not intelligent. □ **un·intelli·gent·ly** *adverb*

un·intelli·gible *adjective* not intelligible. □ **un·intelli·gi·bil·ity** *noun* **un·intelli·gibly** *adverb*

un·intend·ed *adjective* not intended.

un·inten·tion·al *adjective* not intentional. □ **un·inten·tion·al·ly** *adverb*

un·inter·est·ed *adjective* **1** not interested. **2** unconcerned, indifferent. □ **un·inter·est·ed·ly** *adverb* **un·inter·est·ed·ness** *noun*

un·inter·est·ing *adjective* not interesting. □ **un·inter·est·ing·ly** *adverb* **un·inter·est·ing·ness** *noun*

un·inter·rupt·ed *adjective* not interrupted. □ **un·inter·rupt·ed·ly** *adverb*

un·inter·rupt·ible *adjective* that cannot be interrupted.

uni·nucle·ate /ˌjuːnɪˈnuːkliət, -ˈnjuː-/ *adjective Biol.* having a single nucleus.

un·invent·ive *adjective* not inventive. □ **un·invent·ive·ness** *noun*

un·investi·gated *adjective* not investigated.

un·invited *adjective* not invited.

un·inviting *adjective* not inviting; unattractive, repellent.

un·involved *adjective* not involved.

union *noun* **1 a** the act or an instance of uniting; the state of being united. **b** (**the Union**) *hist.* the uniting of the English and Scottish crowns in 1603, of the English and Scottish parliaments in 1707, or of Great Britain and Ireland in 1801. **2 a** a whole resulting from the combination of parts or members. **b** a political unit formed in this way, esp. the US, the UK, the USSR, or South Africa. **3** (**the Union**) *US hist.* the body of northern states in the American Civil War. **4 a** = LABOUR UNION. **b** a group of people united for a common cause. **5** marriage, matrimony. **6** concord, agreement (*lived together in perfect union*). **7** *Math.* the totality of the members of two or more sets. **8** a part of a flag with a device emblematic of union, normally occupying the upper corner next to the staff. **9** a joint or coupling for pipes etc. **10** (**Union**) (in the UK) **a** a general social club and debating society at some universities and colleges. **b** the buildings or accommodation of such a society. **11** a fabric of mixed materials, e.g. cotton with linen or silk. [Old French *union* or ecclesiastical Latin *unio* unity, from Latin *unus* one]

union-busting *noun N Amer.* tactics undertaken by corporations to weaken or eliminate unions in the workplace. □ **union-buster** *noun*

union card *noun* a card that identifies a person as a member of a particular labour union.

Union Government *noun Cdn hist.* the coalition government that governed Canada from 1917–1920.

union·ist *noun* **1 a** a member of a labour union. **b** an advocate of labour unions. **2** (usu. **Unionist**) an advocate of union, esp.: **a** a person opposed to the rupture of the parliamentary union between Great Britain and Northern Ireland (formerly between Great Britain and Ireland). **b** a member of a political party having these aims. **c** *hist.* a person who opposed secession during the American Civil War. □ **union·ism** *noun*

union·ize *transitive & intransitive verb* (also esp. *Brit.* **-ise**) bring or come under the organization or rules of a labour union. □ **union·iz·a·tion** *noun* **union·ized** *adjective*

un-ionized *adjective* (also esp. *Brit.* **-ionised**) not ionized.

Union Jack *noun* **1** the national ensign of the United Kingdom, formed by the union of the crosses of St. George, St. Andrew, and St. Patrick. **2** (**union jack**) (in the US) a jack consisting of the union from the national flag.

Union Nationale /ˌuːnjɔ̃ nasjəˈnal/ *noun Cdn hist.* (in Quebec) a provincial political party identified with conservative French-Canadian nationalism. Founded to contest the 1935 provincial election, it held power in Quebec uninterrupted from 1944 to 1960, under Maurice Duplessis.

Union of Serbia and Montenegro a federation consisting of the republics of Serbia and Montenegro, established in 2003 from the former federal republic of Yugoslavia; pop. (est. 2002) 10,656,929; federal capital, Belgrade.

Union of Soviet Socialist Republics the full name of the SOVIET UNION. Abbr.: **USSR**.

union scale *noun* = SCALE³ 6.

union shop *noun* a store, factory, trade, etc., in which employees must belong to a labour union or join one within an agreed time.

Union Territory any of several territories of India which are administered by the central government.

unip·ar·ous /juːˈnɪpərəs/ *adjective* **1** producing one offspring at a birth. **2** *Bot.* having one axis or branch.

uni·polar /ˌjuːnɪˈpoːlər/ *adjective* **1** (esp. of an electric or magnetic apparatus) showing only one kind of polarity. **2** *Biol.* (of a nerve cell etc.) having only one pole. **3** (of psychiatric illness) characterized by either depressive or (more rarely) manic episodes but not both. □ **uni·polar·ity** *noun*

unique *adjective* **1** of which there is only one; unequalled; having no like, equal, or parallel (*your position was unique*; *this vase is considered unique*). **2** *disputed* unusual, remarkable (*the most unique person I ever met*). **3** (foll. by *to*) limited in occurrence to a particular area, situation, etc. (*that species is unique to this part of Canada*). ¶ In sense 1, *unique* should not be qualified by adverbs such as *absolutely*, *most*, and *quite* because it is an absolute concept. The use of *unique* in sense 2 is regarded as incorrect by some people. □ **unique·ly** *adverb* **unique·ness** *noun* [French from Latin *unicus* from *unus* one]

un·ironed *adjective* (esp. of clothing, linen, etc.) not ironed.

un·iron·ic *adjective* not ironic; to be taken at face value. □ **un·ironic·al·ly** *adverb*

uni·serial /ˌjuːnɪˈsiːriəl/ *adjective Bot. & Zool.* arranged in one row.

uni·sex /ˈjuːnɪˌseks/ *adjective* (of clothing, hairstyles, etc.) designed to be suitable for both sexes.

uni·sex·ual *adjective* **1 a** of one sex. **b** *Bot.* having stamens or pistils but not both. **2** unisex. □ **uni·sex·u·al·ity** *noun*

un-Islamic *adjective* contrary to Islamic principles.

uni·son /ˈjuːnɪsən/ ● *noun* **1** *Music* **a** identity in pitch of two or more sounds or notes. **b** the sounding of notes or melodies at the same pitch, or at pitches one or more octaves apart, by different voices or instruments together (*sang unison on the first and last verses*). **2** agreement, concord (*acted in perfect unison*). ● *adjective Music* coinciding in pitch. □ **in unison** together; as one (*read the poem in unison*). [Old French *unison* or Late Latin *unisonus* (as UNI-, *sonus* SOUND¹)]

un·issued *adjective* not issued.

unit *noun* **1 a** an individual thing, person, or group regarded as single and complete, esp. for purposes of calculation. **b** each of the (smallest) separate individuals or groups into which a complex whole may be analyzed (*the family as the unit of society*). **2** (also *attributive*) a quantity chosen as a standard in terms of which other quantities may be expressed (*unit of heat*; SI *unit*; *unit area*). **3** *N Amer., Austral. & NZ* a private residence forming one of several in a large building or group of buildings; an apartment etc. **4** a device with a specified function forming part of a complex mechanism. **5** a piece of furniture for fitting with others like it or made of complementary parts. **6 a** a group with a special function in an organization. **b** a subdivision of a larger military grouping. **7** a group of buildings, wards, etc., in a hospital. **8** a portion of a school course centring on a particular theme (*just finished a unit on insects*). **9** *Cdn (PEI)* = SCHOOL UNIT. **10** the number 'one'. **11** *Brit.* the smallest share in a unit trust. [Latin *unus*, prob. after DIGIT]

uni·tard /ˈjuːnɪtɑrd/ *noun* a tight-fitting one-piece garment of stretchable fabric which covers the body from the shoulders to the toes or ankles. [UNI- + LEOTARD]

Uni·tar·ian /ˌjuːnɪˈteriən/ ● *noun* **1** a person who believes that God is not a Trinity but one person. **2** a member of a religious body maintaining this and advocating freedom from formal dogma or doctrine. ● *adjective* of or relating to the Unitarians. □ **Uni·tar·ian·ism** *noun* [modern Latin *unitarius* from Latin *unitas* UNITY]

uni·tary /ˈjuːnɪteri/ *adjective* **1** of a unit or units. **2** marked by unity or uniformity. **3** of or relating to a system of government in which the powers of the separate constituent parts are vested in a central body. □ **uni·tar·ily** *adverb* **uni·tar·ity** /-ˈterɪti/ *noun*

unit cell *noun Geol.* the smallest repeating group of atoms, ions, or molecules in a crystal.

unit cost *noun* the cost of producing or purchasing one item of manufacture, calculated by dividing the total cost of a batch by the number of units.

unite *verb* **1** *transitive & intransitive* join together; make or become one; combine. **2** *transitive & intransitive* join together for a common purpose or action (*united in their struggle against injustice*). **3** *transitive & intransitive* join in marriage. **4** *transitive* possess (qualities, features, etc.) in combination (*united anger with mercy*). **5** *intransitive & transitive* form or cause to form a physical or chemical whole (*oil will not unite with water*). □ **uni·tive** /ˈjuːnɪtɪv/ *adjective* [Latin *unire unit-* from *unus* one]

united ● *adjective* **1** joined together for a common purpose. **2** joined politically. **3** joined together by love or sympathy. **4** in agreement. **5** (**United**) *Cdn* of, relating to, or belonging to the United Church. ● *noun* (**United**) *Cdn* a member of the United Church. □ **united·ly** *adverb*

United Arab Emirates an independent state on the south coast of the Persian Gulf, west of the Gulf of Oman; population (1996) 2,500,000; capital, Abu Dhabi. It was formed in 1971 by the federation of the independent sheikdoms formerly called the Trucial States: Abu Dhabi, Ajman, Dubai, Fujairah, Ras al Khaimah, Sharjah, and Umm al Qaiwain. Abbr.: **UAE**.

United Arab Republic a former political union established by Egypt and Syria in 1958. It was seen as the first step towards the creation of a pan-Arab union in the Middle East, but only Yemen (1958–66) entered into loose association with it and Syria withdrew following a coup in 1961. Egypt retained the name United Arab Republic until 1971. Abbr.: **UAR**.

United Canada *hist.* the political union of Canada West (formerly Upper Canada) and Canada East (formerly Lower Canada), lasting from 1841 to 1867.

United Church *noun* (in full **United Church of Canada**) (in Canada) a Protestant denomination formed in 1925 by the merger of the Methodist and Congregationalist Churches together with the majority of Presbyterians.

United Empire Loyalist *noun Cdn* = LOYALIST 2. Abbr.: **UEL**.

United Farmers *noun Cdn* any of various political groups growing out of provincial farmers' organizations.

United Kingdom (in full **United Kingdom of Great Britain and Northern Ireland**) a country of W Europe consisting of England, Wales, Scotland, and Northern Ireland; pop. (2001) 58,789,194; capital, London. Abbr.: **UK**. (See also BRITAIN, GREAT BRITAIN.)

United Nations *noun* **1** an international organization of countries set up in 1945, in succession to the League of Nations, to promote international peace, security, and co-operation. Its members now number more than 150 and include most sovereign states of the world. Its headquarters are in New York. Abbr.: **UN**. **2** *hist.* (during World War II) the nations that in 1942 agreed to stand united against the Axis powers.

United Provinces *hist.* **1** = UNITED CANADA. **2** the seven Dutch provinces of Friesland, Gelderland, Groningen, Holland, Overijssel, Utrecht, and Zeeland, which formed a union under the Treaty of Utrecht in 1579 following their successful rebellion against Spanish rule, leading to the formation of the Dutch Republic.

United States (in full **United States of America**) a country occupying most of the southern half of N America and including also Alaska and the Hawaiian Islands; pop. (2002) 280,562,489; capital, Washington, DC. Abbr.: **US**, **USA**.

unit·hold·er *noun Cdn & Brit.* a person with a holding in a mutual fund or unit trust.

unit price *noun* the price charged for each unit of goods supplied.

unit train *noun N Amer.* a train carrying only one substance, esp. a natural resource.

unit trust *noun Brit.* = MUTUAL FUND.

unity *noun* (*pl.* **-ties**) **1** oneness; being one, single, or individual; being formed of parts that constitute a whole; due interconnection and coherence of parts (*disturbs the unity of the idea; the pictures lack unity; national unity*). **2** harmony or concord between persons etc. (*lived together in unity*). **3** a thing forming a complex whole (*a person regarded as a unity*). **4** *Math.* the number 'one', the factor that leaves unchanged the quantity on which it operates. **5** *Theatre* each of the three dramatic principles requiring limitation of the supposed time of a drama to that occupied in acting it or to a single day (**unity of time**), use of one scene throughout (**unity of place**), and concentration on the development of a single plot (**unity of action**). [Old French *unité* from Latin *unitas -tatis* from *unus* one]

Univ. *abbreviation* University.

uni·valent ● *adjective* **1** /ˌjuːnɪˈveɪlənt/ *Chem.* having a valence of one. **2** /juːˈnɪvələnt/ *Biol.* (of a chromosome) remaining unpaired during meiosis. ● *noun* /juːˈnɪvələnt/ *Biol.* a univalent chromosome.

uni·valve /ˈjuːnɪˌvalv/ *Zool.* ● *adjective* having one valve. ● *noun* a univalve mollusc.

uni·ver·sal ● *adjective* **1** of, belonging to, or done etc. by all persons or things in the world or in the class concerned; applicable to all cases (*the feeling was universal; met with universal approval*). **2** *Logic* (of a proposition) in which something is asserted of all of a class (*opp.* PARTICULAR 5). ● *noun* **1** *Logic* a universal proposition. **2** *Philos.* **a** a term or concept of general application. **b** a nature or essence signified by a general term. □ **uni·ver·sal·ity** *noun* **uni·ver·sal·ly** *adverb*

universal donor *noun* a person of blood group O, who can in theory donate blood to recipients of any ABO blood group.

uni·ver·sal·ist *noun* **1** a person who is learned in many subjects or who has a wide range of interests etc. **2** a person advocating loyalty to and concern for others without regard to national allegiance. **3** *Theol.* a person who believes that all mankind will eventually be saved. **4** a member of an organized body of Christians who believe this. □ **uni·ver·sal·ism** *noun* **uni·ver·sal·is·tic** *adjective*

uni·ver·sal·ize *transitive verb* (also esp. *Brit.* **-ise**) **1** apply universally; give a universal character to. **2** bring into universal use; make available for all. □ **uni·ver·sal·iz·a·tion** *noun*

universal joint *noun* a coupling or joint which can transmit rotary power by a shaft at any selected angle.

universal language *noun* an artificial language intended for use by all nations.

Universal Product Code *noun* a bar code printed on the packaging of many consumer goods and used esp. in retail sales and inventory control. Abbr.: **UPC**.

universal remote *noun* a single remote control that can be used to operate a range of devices, e.g. a stereo, TV, DVD player, etc.

universal suffrage *noun* a suffrage extending to all adults with minor exceptions.

universal time *noun* Greenwich time calculated from midnight at the Greenwich meridian.

uni·verse *noun* **1** all existing things; the cosmos. **2** all of humanity. **3** a sphere of activity, existence, interest, etc. (*he is the centre of her universe*). **4** *Statistics & Logic* all the objects under consideration. [French *univers* from Latin *universum* neuter of *universus* combined into one, whole, from UNI- + *versus* past participle of *vertere* turn]

uni·ver·sity *noun* (*pl.* **-ties**) **1** an educational institution designed for instruction of students in many branches of advanced learning,

conferring degrees in various faculties, and often embodying colleges and similar institutions. **2** the members of this collectively. [Old French *université* from Latin *universitas -tatis* the whole (world), in Late Latin college, guild (as UNIVERSE)]

uni·vocal /ˌjuːnɪˈvoːkəl, juːˈnɪvəkəl/ ● *adjective* (of a word etc.) having only one proper meaning. ● *noun* a univocal word. □ **uni·vocal·ity** /ˌjuːnɪvɒˈkaliti/ *noun* **uni·vocal·ly** *adverb*

Unix /ˈjuːnɪks/ *noun Computing proprietary* a multi-user operating system. [UNI- + respelling of -ICS, on the pattern of an earlier, less compact system called *Multics*]

un·just *adjective* not just, contrary to justice or fairness. □ **un·just·ly** *adverb* **un·just·ness** *noun*

un·justi·fi·able *adjective* not justifiable. □ **un·justi·fi·ably** *adverb*

un·justi·fied *adjective* not justified.

un·kempt *adjective* **1** untidy, of neglected appearance. **2** uncombed, dishevelled. [UN-¹ + archaic *kempt* past participle of *kemb* comb, from Old English *cemban*]

un·kept *adjective* **1** (of a promise, law, etc.) not observed; disregarded. **2** not tended; neglected.

un·kill·able *adjective* that cannot be killed.

un·kind *adjective* **1** not kind. **2** harsh, cruel. □ **un·kind·ly** *adverb* **un·kind·ness** *noun*

un·kink *verb* **1** *transitive* remove the kinks from; straighten. **2** *intransitive* lose kinks; become straight.

un·knot *transitive verb* (**un·knot·ted**, **un·knot·ting**) release the knot or knots of, untie.

un·know·able ● *adjective* that cannot be known. ● *noun* **1** an unknowable thing. **2** (**the Unknowable**) the postulated absolute or ultimate reality. □ **un·know·abil·ity** *noun*

un·know·ing ● *adjective* (often foll. by *of*) not knowing; ignorant, unconscious. ● *noun* ignorance (*cloud of unknowing*). □ **un·know·ing·ly** *adverb*

un·known ● *adjective* (often foll. by *to*) not known, unfamiliar (*her purpose was unknown to me*). ● *noun* **1** an unknown thing or person. **2** an unknown quantity (*equation in two unknowns*). □ **unknown to** without the knowledge of (*did it unknown to me*). □ **un·known·ness** *noun*

Unknown Soldier *noun* an unidentified representative member of a country's armed forces killed in war, given burial with special honours in a national memorial.

un·labelled *adjective* (also esp. *US* **un·labeled**) not labelled; without a label.

un·lace *transitive verb* **1** undo the lace or laces of. **2** unfasten or loosen in this way.

un·lade *transitive verb* **1** take the cargo out of (a ship). **2** discharge (a cargo etc.) from a ship.

un·laden *adjective* not laden.

un·lady·like *adjective* not ladylike.

un·laid¹ *adjective* not laid.

un·laid² *past and past participle of* UNLAY.

un·lament·ed *adjective* not lamented.

un·lash *transitive verb* unfasten (a thing lashed down etc.).

un·latch *verb* **1** *transitive* release the latch of. **2** *transitive & intransitive* open or be opened in this way.

un·law·ful *adjective* not lawful; illegal, not permissible. □ **un·law·ful·ly** *adverb* **un·law·ful·ness** *noun*

un·lay *transitive verb* (*past and past participle* **un·laid**) *Naut.* untwist (a rope). [UN-² + LAY¹]

un·lead·ed /ʌnˈledəd/ ● *adjective* **1** (of gasoline etc.) without added lead. **2** not covered, weighted, or framed with lead. ● *noun* unleaded gasoline etc.

un·learn *transitive verb* (*past and past participle* **un·learned** or **un·learnt**) **1** discard from one's memory. **2** rid oneself of (a habit, false information, etc.).

un·learned¹ *adjective* not well educated; untaught, ignorant.

un·learned² *adjective* (also **un·learnt**) **1** that has not been learned (*an unlearned lesson*). **2** that does not need to be learned; innate (*an unlearned behaviour*).

un·leash *transitive verb* **1** release (something powerful or destructive). **2** set free to engage in pursuit or attack.

un·leav·ened *adjective* not leavened; made without yeast or other raising agent.

un·less *conjunction* if not; except when (*shall go unless I hear from you; will* *make it home by 8 unless the train is late).* [ON or IN + LESS, assimilated to UN-¹]

un·let·tered *adjective* **1** illiterate. **2** not well educated.

un·liber·ated *adjective* not liberated.

un·licensed *adjective* (also **un·licenced**) not licensed, esp. without a licence to sell alcoholic drink.

un·light·ed *adjective* **1** not provided with light. **2** not set burning.

un·like ● *adjective* **1** not like; different from (*is unlike both his parents*). **2** uncharacteristic of (*such behaviour is unlike her*). **3** dissimilar, different. ● *preposition* differently from (*acts quite unlike anyone else*). □ **un·like·ness** *noun*

un·like·able *adjective* (also **un·likable**) not easy to like; unpleasant.

un·like·ly *adjective* (**un·like·li·er**, **un·like·li·est**) **1** improbable (*an unlikely story*). **2** (foll. by *to* + infin.) not to be expected to do something (*she's unlikely to be available*). **3** unpromising (*an unlikely candidate*). □ **un·like·li·hood** *noun* **un·like·li·ness** *noun*

un·lim·ber *transitive verb* **1** free (a gun) from its limber ready for use. **2** esp. *US* unpack or unfasten (something) ready for use.

un·lim·it·ed *adjective* without limit; unrestricted; very great in number or quantity (*has unlimited possibilities; an unlimited expanse of sea*). □ **un·lim·it·ed·ness** *noun*

un·lined¹ *adjective* **1** (of paper etc.) without lines. **2** (of a face etc.) without wrinkles.

un·lined² *adjective* (of a garment etc.) without lining.

un·link *transitive verb* **1** undo the links of (a chain etc.). **2** detach or set free by undoing or unfastening a link or chain.

un·list·ed *adjective* **1** esp. *N Amer.* (of a telephone number) not listed in a telephone directory. **2** not included in a published list, esp. (of a security) not eligible for trading on an exchange.

un·listen·able *adjective* (esp. of music) impossible or unbearable to listen to. □ **un·listen·ably** *adverb*

unlit *adjective* not lit.

un·liv·able *adjective* that cannot be lived or lived in.

un·lived-in *adjective* **1** appearing to be uninhabited. **2** unused by the inhabitants.

un·load *verb* **1** *transitive & intransitive* remove a load from (a vehicle etc.). **2** *transitive* remove (a load) from a vehicle etc. **3** *transitive* remove the charge from (a firearm etc.). **4** *transitive informal* get rid of. **5** (often foll. by *on*) *informal* **a** *transitive* divulge (information). **b** *transitive & intransitive* give vent to (feelings). □ **un·load·er** *noun*

un·lock *verb* **1** *transitive* **a** release the lock of (a door, box, etc.). **b** release or disclose by unlocking. **2** *transitive* release thoughts, feelings, etc., from (one's mind etc.). **3** *intransitive* become unlocked.

un·locked *adjective* not locked.

un·looked-for *adjective* unexpected, unforeseen.

un·loose *transitive verb* (also **un·loosen**) loose; set free.

un·lov·able *adjective* not lovable. □ **un·lov·abil·ity** *noun*

un·loved *adjective* not loved.

un·love·ly *adjective* not attractive; unpleasant, ugly. □ **un·love·li·ness** *noun*

un·lov·ing *adjective* not loving. □ **un·lov·ing·ly** *adverb* **un·lov·ing·ness** *noun*

un·lucky *adjective* (**un·luck·i·er**, **un·luck·i·est**) **1** not fortunate or successful. **2** wretched. **3** bringing bad luck. **4** ill-judged. □ **un·luck·i·ly** *adverb*

un·made *adjective* **1** not made. **2** destroyed, annulled.

un·make *transitive verb* (*past* and *past participle* **un·made**) undo the making of; destroy, depose, annul.

un·man *transitive verb* (**un·manned**, **un·man·ning**) deprive of supposed manly qualities (e.g. self-control, courage); cause to weep etc.; discourage.

un·man·age·able *adjective* not (easily) managed, manipulated, or controlled. □ **un·man·age·ably** *adverb*

un·man·aged *adjective* **1** not handled or directed in a controlled way. **2** (of land etc.) left wild; in a natural state.

un·man·ly *adjective* not manly. □ **un·man·li·ness** *noun*

un·manned *adjective* **1** not manned. **2** overcome by emotion etc.

un·man·nered *adjective* lacking affectation; straightforward.

un·man·ner·ly *adjective* **1** without good manners. **2** (of actions, speech, etc.) showing a lack of good manners.

un·mapped *adjective* **1** not represented on a usu. geographical or chromosome map. **2** unexplored.

un·marked *adjective* **1** not marked (*an unmarked police car*). **2** not noticed.

un·market·able *adjective* not marketable.

un·married *adjective* not married; single.

un·mask *verb* **1** *transitive* **a** remove the mask from. **b** expose the true character of. **2** *intransitive* remove one's mask. □ **un·mask·er** *noun*

un·match·able *adjective* that cannot be matched.

un·matched *adjective* not matched or equalled.

un·meant *adjective* not meant or intended.

un·measur·able *adjective* that cannot be measured. □ **un·measur·ably** *adverb*

un·meas·ured *adjective* **1** not measured. **2** limitless.

un·medi·ated *adjective* with no intervention; directly perceived.

un·melt·ed *adjective* not melted.

un·memor·able *adjective* not memorable. □ **un·memor·ably** *adverb*

un·men·tion·able ● *adjective* that cannot (properly) be mentioned. ● *noun* **1** (in *pl.*) *jocular* **a** undergarments. **b** *archaic* trousers. **2** a person or thing not to be mentioned.

un·men·tioned *adjective* not mentioned.

un·merci·ful *adjective* merciless. □ **un·merci·ful·ly** *adverb*

un·merit·ed *adjective* not merited.

unmet *adjective* (of a quota, demand, goal, etc.) not achieved or fulfilled.

un·metered *adjective* not metered.

un·meth·od·ic·al *adjective* not methodical. □ **un·meth·od·ic·al·ly** *adverb*

un·mind·ful *adjective* (often foll. by *of*) not mindful; unaware.

un·miss·able *adjective* that cannot or should not be missed.

un·mistak·able *adjective* that cannot be mistaken or doubted, clear. □ **un·mistak·abil·ity** *noun* **un·mistak·ably** *adverb*

un·miti·gated *adjective* **1** not mitigated or modified. **2** absolute, unqualified (*an unmitigated disaster*). □ **un·miti·gated·ly** *adverb*

un·mixed *adjective* not mixed.

unmixed blessing *noun* a thing having advantages and no disadvantages.

un·mod·er·at·ed *adjective Computing* (of a newsgroup etc.) whose content is not screened before being made available.

un·modern·ized *adjective* (also esp. *Brit.* **-ised**) (of a house etc.) not modernized; retaining the original features.

un·modi·fied *adjective* not modified.

un·modu·lated *adjective* not modulated.

un·molest·ed *adjective* not molested.

un·mon·itored *adjective* not monitored.

un·moor *verb* **1** *transitive & intransitive* release the moorings of (a vessel). **2** *transitive* weigh all but one anchor of (a vessel).

un·mother·ly *adjective* not motherly.

un·moti·vated *adjective* without motivation; without a motive.

un·mould *transitive verb* (also **un·mold**) remove (a dessert etc.) from a mould or pan.

un·mount·ed *adjective* not mounted.

un·mourned *adjective* not mourned.

un·moved *adjective* **1** not moved. **2** not changed in one's purpose. **3** not affected by emotion. □ **un·movable** *adjective* (also **un·move·able**).

un·moving *adjective* **1** not moving; still. **2** not emotive.

un·mown *adjective* not mown.

un·muf·fle *transitive verb* **1** remove a muffler from (a face, bell, etc.). **2** free of something that muffles or conceals. □ **un·muf·fled** *adjective*

un·music·al *adjective* **1** not pleasing to the ear. **2** unskilled in or indifferent to music. □ **un·music·al·ity** *noun* **un·music·al·ly** *adverb*

un·muz·zle *transitive verb* **1** remove a muzzle from. **2** relieve of an obligation to remain silent.

un·name·able *adjective* that cannot be named, esp. too bad to be named.

un·named *adjective* not named.

un·natur·al *adjective* **1** contrary to nature or the usual course of nature; not normal. **2 a** lacking natural feelings. **b** extremely cruel or wicked. **3** artificial. **4** affected. □ **un·natur·al·ly** *adverb* **un·natur·al·ness** *noun*

un·navig·able *adjective* not navigable.

un·neces·sary *adjective* **1** not necessary. **2** more than is necessary

---

t *top*   v *voice*   w *we*   z *zoo*   ʃ *she*   ʒ *vision*   θ *thin*   ð *this*   ŋ *ring*   x *loch*   tʃ *chip*   dʒ *jar*   (*see over for vowels*)

(with *unnecessary care*). □ **un·neces·sar·ily** *adverb*
un·neces·sar·i·ness *noun*

un·need·ed *adjective* not needed.

un·nerve *transitive verb* deprive of courage or confidence. □ **un·nerv·ing** *adjective* **un·nerv·ing·ly** *adverb*

un·notice·able *adjective* not easily seen or noticed. □ **un·notice·ably** *adverb*

un·noticed *adjective* not noticed.

un·num·bered *adjective* **1** not marked with a number. **2** not counted. **3** countless.

UNO /ˈjuːnəʊ/ *abbreviation* United Nations Organization.

un·oaked *adjective* (of wine) not matured in an oak container.

un·objec·tion·able *adjective* not objectionable; acceptable. □ **un·objec·tion·ably** *adverb*

un·obliging *adjective* not obliging; unhelpful, uncooperative.

un·ob·scured *adjective* not obscured.

un·observ·able *adjective* not observable; imperceptible.

un·observ·ant *adjective* not observant.

un·ob·served *adjective* not observed.

un·ob·struct·ed *adjective* not obstructed.

un·obtain·able *adjective* that cannot be obtained.

un·obtru·sive *adjective* not making oneself or itself noticed. □ **un·obtru·sive·ly** *adverb* **un·obtru·sive·ness** *noun*

un·occu·pied *adjective* not occupied.

un·offend·ing *adjective* not offending; harmless, innocent.

un·official *adjective* **1** not officially authorized or confirmed. **2** not characteristic of officials. □ **un·official·ly** *adverb*

un·oiled *adjective* not oiled.

un·opened *adjective* not opened.

un·opposed *adjective* not opposed.

un·or·dained *adjective* not ordained.

un·ordin·ary *adjective* not ordinary.

un·organ·ized *adjective* (also esp. *Brit.* **-ised**) not organized (*compare* DISORGANIZE).

un·origin·al *adjective* lacking originality; derivative. □ **un·origin·al·ity** *noun* **un·origin·al·ly** *adverb*

un·orna·ment·ed *adjective* not ornamented.

un·ortho·dox *adjective* not orthodox. □ **un·ortho·doxy** *noun*

un·osten·ta·tious *adjective* not ostentatious. □ **un·osten·ta·tious·ly** *adverb*

un·owned *adjective* **1** unacknowledged. **2** having no owner.

un·pack *verb* **1** *transitive & intransitive* open and remove the contents of (a package, luggage, etc.). **2** *transitive* take (a thing) out from a package etc. **3** *transitive* unload (a vehicle etc.).

un·paid *adjective* (of debt, a person, work, etc.) not paid.

un·paint·ed *adjective* not painted.

un·paired *adjective* **1** not arranged in pairs. **2** not forming one of a pair.

un·palat·able /ʌnˈpalətəbəl/ *adjective* **1** not pleasant to taste. **2** (of an idea, suggestion, etc.) disagreeable, distasteful. □ **un·palat·abil·ity** *noun*

un·paral·leled *adjective* having no parallel or equal.

un·pardon·able *adjective* that cannot be pardoned. □ **un·pardon·ably** *adverb*

un·parlia·ment·ary *adjective* contrary to proper parliamentary usage.

unparliamentary language *noun* swear words or abuse.

un·pasteur·ized *adjective* not pasteurized.

un·patent·ed *adjective* not patented.

un·patri·ot·ic *adjective* not patriotic. □ **un·patri·ot·ic·ally** *adverb*

un·paved *adjective* not paved.

un-PC *adjective* not politically correct.

un·peeled *adjective* not peeled.

un·peg *transitive verb* (**un·pegged**, **un·peg·ging**) **1** unfasten by the removal of pegs. **2** cease to maintain or stabilize (prices etc.).

un·peopled *adjective* not populated.

un·per·ceived *adjective* not perceived; unobserved.

un·percep·tive *adjective* not perceptive.

un·perfect·ed *adjective* not perfected.

un·perfor·ated *adjective* not perforated.

un·per·formed *adjective* not performed.

un·per·fumed *adjective* not perfumed.

un·person *noun* a person whose name or existence is denied or ignored.

un·persuad·able *adjective* not able to be persuaded; obstinate.

un·persuad·ed *adjective* not persuaded.

un·persua·sive *adjective* not persuasive. □ **un·persua·sive·ly** *adverb*

un·per·turbed *adjective* not perturbed.

un·philo·soph·ic·al *adjective* (also **un·philo·soph·ic**) **1** not according to philosophical principles. **2** lacking philosophy.

un·pick *transitive verb* undo (stitching, a knot, an agreement, etc.).

un·picked *adjective* **1** not selected. **2** (of a flower) not plucked.

un·pictur·esque *adjective* not picturesque.

un·pin *transitive verb* (**un·pinned**, **un·pin·ning**) unfasten or detach by or as if by removing a pin or pins.

un·pitied *adjective* not pitied.

un·pity·ing *adjective* not pitying.

un·place·able *adjective* that cannot be placed or classified (*her accent was unplaceable*).

un·placed *adjective* not placed, esp. not placed as one of the first three finishing in a race etc.

un·planned *adjective* not planned.

un·plant·ed *adjective* not planted.

un·play·able *adjective* **1** *Sport* (of a ball) that cannot be struck or returned. **2** that cannot be played. □ **un·play·ably** *adverb*

un·pleas·ant *adjective* not pleasant; displeasing; disagreeable. □ **un·pleas·ant·ly** *adverb* **un·pleas·ant·ness** *noun*

un·pleas·antry *noun* (*pl.* **-ries**) **1** unkindness. **2** (in *pl.*) **a** unpleasant comments. **b** unpleasant problems.

un·pleas·ing *adjective* not pleasing.

un·plowed *adjective* (also **un·ploughed**) not plowed.

un·plucked *adjective* not plucked.

un·plug *transitive verb* (**un·plugged**, **un·plug·ging**) **1 a** disconnect (an electrical device) by removing its plug from the socket. **b** disconnect (an electrical cord or plug) from a socket. **2** unclog. **3** remove a stopper or plug from.

un·plugged *adjective* **1** that has been unplugged. **2** (of rock music, etc.) performed or played on instruments without electric amplification.

un·plumbed *adjective* **1** not plumbed. **2** not fully explored or understood. □ **un·plumb·able** *adjective*

un·poetic *adjective* (also **un·poet·ic·al**) not poetic.

un·point·ed *adjective* **1** having no point or points. **2 a** not punctuated. **b** (of written Hebrew etc.) without vowel points. **3** (of masonry or brickwork) not pointed.

un·pol·ished *adjective* **1** not polished; rough. **2** without refinement; crude.

un·polit·ic·al *adjective* not concerned with politics. □ **un·polit·ic·al·ly** *adverb*

un·pollut·ed *adjective* not polluted.

un·popu·lar *adjective* not popular; not liked by the public or by people in general. □ **un·popu·lar·ity** *noun*

un·popu·lated *adjective* not populated.

un·posed *adjective* not in a posed position, esp. for a photograph.

un·pos·sessed *adjective* **1** (foll. by *of*) not in possession of. **2** not possessed.

un·pow·ered *adjective* (of a boat, vehicle, etc.) propelled other than by fuel.

un·prac·tised *adjective* (also **un·prac·ticed**) **1** not experienced or skilled. **2** not put into practice.

un·preced·ent·ed *adjective* **1** having no precedent; unparalleled. **2** novel. □ **un·preced·ent·ed·ly** *adverb*

un·predict·able *adjective* that cannot be predicted. □ **un·predict·abil·ity** *noun* **un·predict·ably** *adverb*

un·predict·ed *adjective* not predicted or foretold.

un·preju·diced *adjective* not prejudiced.

un·premedi·tat·ed *adjective* not previously thought over, not deliberately planned; unintentional.

un·pre·pared *adjective* not prepared (in advance); not ready. □ **un·prepared·ness** *noun*

un·prepos·sess·ing *adjective* not prepossessing; unattractive.

un·pre·scribed *adjective* (esp. of drugs) not prescribed.

un·present·able *adjective* not presentable.

un·pressed *adjective* not pressed, esp. (of clothing) unironed.

un·pressur·ized *adjective* (also esp. *Brit.* **-ised**) not pressurized.

un·pretend·ing *adjective* unpretentious.

un·preten·tious *adjective* not making a great display; simple, modest. □ **un·preten·tious·ly** *adverb* **un·preten·tious·ness** *noun*

un·priced *adjective* not having a price or prices fixed, marked, or stated.

un·primed *adjective* not primed.

un·prin·cipled *adjective* lacking or not based on good moral principles.

un·print·able *adjective* that cannot be printed, esp. because too indecent or libellous or blasphemous.

un·print·ed *adjective* not printed.

un·prob·lem·at·ic *adjective* causing no difficulty. □ **un·prob·lem·at·ic·ally** *adverb*

un·pro·cessed *adjective* (esp. of food, raw materials) not processed.

un·product·ive *adjective* not productive. □ **un·product·ive·ly** *adverb*

un·profes·sion·al *adjective* **1** contrary to professional standards of behaviour etc. **2** not belonging to a profession; amateur. □ **un·profes·sion·al·ly** *adverb*

un·profit·able *adjective* not profitable. □ **un·profit·ably** *adverb*

UNPROFOR /ˈʌnprəfɔːr/ *abbreviation* United Nations Protection Force.

un·progres·sive *adjective* not progressive.

un·promis·ing *adjective* not likely to turn out well. □ **un·promis·ing·ly** *adverb*

un·prompt·ed *adjective* spontaneous.

un·pro·nounce·able *adjective* that cannot be pronounced.

un·propi·tious *adjective* not propitious.

un·protect·ed *adjective* **1** not protected. **2** (of sexual intercourse) performed without a condom or other contraceptive.

un·protest·ing *adjective* not protesting.

un·prov·able *adjective* that cannot be proven. □ **un·prov·abil·ity** *noun*

un·proven *adjective* (also **un·proved**) not proven.

un·provid·ed *adjective* (usu. foll. by *with*) not furnished, supplied, or equipped.

un·pro·voked *adjective* (of a person or act) without provocation.

un·publi·cized *adjective* (also esp. *Brit.* **-cised**) not publicized.

un·pub·lished *adjective* not published. □ **un·publish·able** *adjective*

un·punc·tual *adjective* not punctual.

un·punc·tu·ated *adjective* not punctuated.

un·punish·able *adjective* that cannot be punished.

un·pun·ished *adjective* not punished.

un·puri·fied *adjective* not purified.

un·put·down·able *adjective* *informal* (of a book) so engrossing that one has to go on reading it.

un·quali·fied *adjective* **1 a** not having the necessary qualifications. **b** not competent (*unqualified to give an answer*). **2** not legally or officially qualified (*an unqualified practitioner*). **3** not modified or restricted; complete (*unqualified assent; unqualified success*).

un·quanti·fi·able *adjective* impossible to quantify. □ **un·quanti·fied** *adjective*

un·quench·able *adjective* that cannot be quenched.

un·quenched *adjective* not quenched.

un·question·able *adjective* that cannot be disputed or doubted. □ **un·question·ably** *adverb*

un·questioned *adjective* **1** not disputed or doubted; definite, certain. **2** not interrogated or investigated.

un·question·ing *adjective* **1** asking no questions. **2** done etc. without asking questions. □ **un·question·ing·ly** *adverb*

un·quiet *adjective* **1** restless, agitated, stirring. **2** perturbed, anxious.

un·quote /ˈʌnkwoːt/ *adverb* (in speech, reading aloud, etc.) indicating the presence of closing quotation marks (compare QUOTE *adverb*).

un·quoted *adjective* not quoted, esp. on a stock exchange.

un·ranked *adjective* (in sports etc.) that has not been ranked or considered a contender.

un·rated *adjective* **1** not having received a rating. **2** *N Amer.* (of a movie) not allocated an official classification, typically because regarded as unsuitable for general release.

un·ravel *verb* (**un·ravelled, un·ravel·ling;** also esp. *US* **un·raveled,**

un·ravel·ing) **1** *transitive* cause to be no longer ravelled, tangled, or intertwined. **2** *transitive* probe and solve (a mystery etc.). **3** *transitive* undo (a fabric, esp. a knitted one). **4** *intransitive* become disentangled or unknitted. **5** *intransitive* come apart, collapse (*our plans have unravelled*).

un·reach·able *adjective* that cannot be reached.

un·react·ive *adjective* having little tendency to react chemically.

un·read *adjective* **1** (of a book etc.) not read. **2** (of a person) not well-read.

un·read·able *adjective* **1** too dull or too difficult to be worth reading. **2** illegible. □ **un·read·abil·ity** *noun* **un·read·ably** *adverb*

un·ready[1] *adjective* **1** not ready. **2** not prompt in action.

un·ready[2] *adjective* *archaic* lacking good advice; rash (*Ethelred the Unready*). [UN-[1] + REDE, assimilated to UNREADY[1]]

un·real *adjective* **1** not real. **2** imaginary, illusory. **3** *N Amer. & Austral.* slang incredible, amazing. □ **un·real·ity** *noun* **un·real·ly** *adverb*

un·real·is·tic *adjective* not realistic. □ **un·real·is·tic·ally** *adverb*

un·real·iz·able *adjective* that cannot be realized.

un·real·ized *adjective* not realized.

un·reason *noun* lack of reasonable thought or action.

un·reason·able *adjective* **1** going beyond the limits of what is reasonable or equitable (*unreasonable demands*). **2** not guided by or listening to reason. □ **un·reason·able·ness** *noun* **un·reason·ably** *adverb*

un·reasoned *adjective* not reasoned.

un·reason·ing *adjective* not reasoning.

un·recep·tive *adjective* not receptive.

un·recip·ro·cat·ed *adjective* not reciprocated.

un·reckoned *adjective* not calculated or taken into account.

un·recog·niz·able *adjective* (also esp. *Brit.* **-nisable**) that cannot be recognized. □ **un·recog·niz·ably** *adverb*

un·recog·nized *adjective* (also esp. *Brit.* **-nised**) not recognized.

un·recon·ciled *adjective* not reconciled.

un·recon·struct·ed *adjective* **1** not reconciled or converted to the current political orthodoxy. **2** not rebuilt.

un·record·ed *adjective* not recorded.

un·recover·able *adjective* not recoverable.

un·recyc·lable *adjective* not recyclable.

un·redeem·able *adjective* that cannot be redeemed.

un·re·deemed *adjective* not redeemed.

un·reel *transitive & intransitive verb* unwind from or as if from a reel.

un·ref·ereed *adjective* not refereed.

un·refined *adjective* not refined.

un·reflect·ing *adjective* not thoughtful; not engaging in reflection or thought. □ **un·reflect·ing·ly** *adverb*

un·reflect·ive *adjective* not reflective. □ **un·reflect·ive·ly** *adverb*

un·reformed *adjective* not reformed.

un·regard·ed *adjective* not regarded.

un·regen·er·ate ● *adjective* not regenerate; obstinately wrong or bad. ● *noun* an unregenerate person. □ **un·regen·er·ate·ly** *adverb*

un·regis·tered *adjective* not registered.

un·regulat·ed *adjective* not regulated.

un·re·hearsed *adjective & adverb* not rehearsed.

un·re·inforced *adjective* not reinforced.

un·relat·ed *adjective* not related.

un·released *adjective* not released, esp. (of a recording, film, etc.) to the public.

un·relent·ing *adjective* **1** not relenting or yielding. **2** unmerciful. **3** not abating or relaxing. □ **un·relent·ing·ly** *adverb*

un·reli·able *adjective* not reliable; erratic. □ **un·reli·abil·ity** *noun* **un·reli·ably** *adverb*

un·relieved *adjective* **1** lacking the relief given by contrast or variation. **2** not aided or assisted. □ **un·reliev·ed·ly** *adverb*

un·remark·able *adjective* not remarkable; uninteresting. □ **un·remark·ably** *adverb*

un·remarked *adjective* **1** not mentioned or remarked upon. **2** unnoticed.

un·remem·bered *adjective* not remembered; forgotten.

un·remit·ting *adjective* never relaxing or slackening, incessant. □ **un·remit·ting·ly** *adverb*

un·remorse·ful *adjective* lacking remorse.

---

uː m**oo**d ai m**y** əi p**i**pe au br**ow**n ʌu h**ou**se ei d**ay** ɔi b**oy** ã fr**an**glais ā Canadi**en** ɔ̃ Br**ayon**   (*see over for consonants*)

un·remuner·a·tive *adjective* bringing no, or not enough, profit or income.

un·repeat·able *adjective* **1** that cannot be done, made, or said again. **2** too indecent to be said again.

un·repent·ant *adjective* not repentant, impenitent. □ **un·repent·ant·ly** *adverb*

un·report·ed *adjective* not reported.

un·rep·re·sent·a·tive *adjective* not representative.

un·rep·re·sent·ed *adjective* not represented.

un·repressed *adjective* not repressed.

un·request·ed *adjective* not requested or asked for.

un·requit·ed /ˌʌnrɪˈkwɔɪtəd/ *adjective* **1** (of love etc.) not reciprocated. **2** (of a yearning etc.) unsatisfied.

un·resent·ful *adjective* lacking resentment.

un·reserved *adjective* **1** not reserved (*unreserved seats*). **2** without reservations; absolute (*unreserved confidence*). **3** free from reserve (*an unreserved nature*). □ **un·reserv·ed·ly** *adverb*

un·resist·ed *adjective* not resisted.

un·resist·ing *adjective* not resisting. □ **un·resist·ing·ly** *adverb*

un·resolv·able *adjective* (of a problem, conflict, etc.) that cannot be resolved.

un·resolved *adjective* **1 a** uncertain how to act, irresolute. **b** uncertain in opinion, undecided. **2** (of questions etc.) undetermined, undecided, unsolved. **3** not broken up or dissolved.

un·respon·sive *adjective* not responsive. □ **un·respon·sive·ness** *noun*

un·rest *noun* a state of disturbance and dissatisfaction accompanied by angry protest, violence, etc.

un·rest·ful *adjective* not restful.

un·rest·ing *adjective* not resting.

un·restored *adjective* not restored.

un·restrained *adjective* not restrained.

un·restrict·ed *adjective* not restricted.

un·returned *adjective* **1** not reciprocated or responded to. **2** not having returned or been returned.

un·revealed *adjective* not revealed; secret. □ **un·reveal·ing** *adjective*

un·revised *adjective* not revised; in an original form.

un·reward·ed *adjective* not rewarded.

un·reward·ing *adjective* not rewarding or satisfying.

un·rhymed *adjective* not rhymed.

un·riddle *transitive verb* solve or explain (a mystery etc.).

un·rig *transitive verb* (**un·rigged**, **un·rig·ging**) remove the rigging from (a ship).

un·right·eous *adjective* not righteous; unjust, wicked, dishonest. □ **un·right·eous·ness** *noun*

un·ripe *adjective* not ripe.

un·rivalled *adjective* (also esp. *US* **un·rivaled**) having no equal; peerless.

un·road·worthy *adjective* not roadworthy.

un·roll *verb* **1** *transitive & intransitive* open out from a rolled-up state. **2** *intransitive* (of a landscape) appear stretched out before the viewer. **3** *intransitive* (of events) happen one after the other.

un·roman·tic *adjective* not romantic. □ **un·roman·tic·ally** *adverb*

un·rope *verb* **1** *transitive* detach by undoing a rope. **2** *intransitive Mountaineering* detach oneself from a rope.

un·round·ed *adjective* not rounded.

un·ruf·fled *adjective* **1** not agitated or disturbed; calm. **2** not physically ruffled or made rough.

un·ruly *adjective* (**un·ruli·er**, **un·ruli·est**) not easily controlled or disciplined, disorderly. □ **un·ruli·ness** *noun* [Middle English from UN-¹ + *ruly* from RULE]

un·sad·dle *transitive verb* **1** remove the saddle from (a horse etc.). **2** dislodge from a saddle.

un·safe *adjective* not safe. □ **un·safe·ly** *adverb*

unsafe sex *noun* sexual activity in which precautions are not taken to reduce the risk of spreading sexually transmitted diseases.

un·said¹ *adjective* not said or uttered.

un·said² *past and past participle of* UNSAY.

un·salar·ied *adjective* not salaried.

un·sale·able *adjective* (also **un·salable**) not saleable.

un·salt·ed *adjective* not salted.

un·salvage·able *adjective* not salvageable.

un·sancti·fied *adjective* not sanctified.

un·sanc·tioned *adjective* not sanctioned.

un·sani·tary *adjective* not sanitary.

un·satis·fac·tory *adjective* not satisfactory; poor, unacceptable.

un·satis·fied *adjective* not satisfied.

un·satis·fy·ing *adjective* not satisfying.

un·satur·ated *adjective* **1** *Chem.* (of a compound, esp. a fat or oil) having double or triple bonds in its molecule and therefore capable of further reaction. **2** not saturated. □ **un·satur·a·tion** *noun*

un·saved *adjective* not saved.

un·savoury *adjective* (also **un·savory**) **1** disagreeable to the taste, smell, or feelings; disgusting. **2** disagreeable, unpleasant (*an unsavoury character*). **3** morally offensive. □ **un·savour·i·ness** *noun*

un·say *transitive verb* (*past* and *past participle* **un·said**) retract (a statement).

un·say·able *adjective* **1** that cannot be said. **2** that would be improper to mention.

un·scal·able *adjective* that cannot be scaled.

un·scarred *adjective* not scarred or damaged.

un·scathed /ʌnˈskeɪðd/ *adjective* without suffering any injury.

un·scent·ed *adjective* not scented.

un·sched·uled *adjective* not scheduled.

un·scholar·ly *adjective* not scholarly.

un·schooled *adjective* **1** uneducated, untaught. **2** not sent to school. **3** untrained, undisciplined.

un·scien·tif·ic *adjective* **1** not in accordance with scientific principles. **2** not familiar with science. □ **un·scien·tif·ic·ally** *adverb*

un·scram·ble *transitive verb* restore from a scrambled state, esp. interpret (a scrambled transmission etc.). □ **un·scram·bler** *noun*

un·scratched *adjective* not scratched; not harmed or injured at all.

un·screened *adjective* **1** not investigated or checked, esp. for security or medical problems. **2** not provided with a screen. **3** (of a film or TV program etc.) not shown on a screen or aired.

un·screw *verb* **1** *transitive & intransitive* unfasten or be unfastened by turning or removing a screw or screws or by twisting like a screw. **2** *transitive* loosen (a screw, lid, etc.).

un·script·ed *adjective* (of a speech etc.) delivered without a prepared script; unplanned, unrehearsed.

un·scrip·tur·al *adjective* against or not in accordance with Scripture.

un·scrupu·lous *adjective* having no scruples, unprincipled. □ **un·scrupu·lous·ly** *adverb* **un·scrupu·lous·ness** *noun*

un·seal *transitive verb* break the seal of; open (a letter, receptacle, etc.).

un·sealed *adjective* not sealed.

un·search·able *adjective* inscrutable.

un·season·able *adjective* **1** (esp. of weather) not appropriate to the season. **2** untimely, inopportune. □ **un·season·ably** *adverb*

un·season·al *adjective* not typical of, or appropriate to, the time or season.

un·seasoned *adjective* **1** not flavoured with salt, herbs, etc. **2** (esp. of timber) not matured. **3** inexperienced.

un·seat *transitive verb* **1** remove from power or office, esp. in an election. **2** dislodge from a seat, esp. on horseback.

un·sea·worthy *adjective* not seaworthy. □ **un·sea·worthi·ness** *noun*

un·secured *adjective* not secured.

un·see·able *adjective* that cannot be seen.

un·seed·ed *adjective* *Sport* (of a player) not seeded.

un·see·ing *adjective* **1** not seeing; unobservant. **2** blind. □ **un·see·ing·ly** *adverb*

un·seem·ly *adjective* (**un·seem·li·er**, **un·seem·li·est**) **1** indecent. **2** unbecoming. □ **un·seem·li·ness** *noun*

un·seen *adjective* **1** not seen. **2** invisible. **3** (of a passage for translation) not previously read or prepared.

un·segment·ed *adjective* not divided into segments.

un·segre·gated *adjective* not segregated.

un·seiz·able *adjective* that cannot be seized or grasped.

un·select·ed *adjective* not selected.

un·select·ive *adjective* not selective.

un·self·con·scious *adjective* not self-conscious. □ **un·self·con·scious·ly** *adverb* **un·self·con·scious·ness** *noun*

un·self·ish *adjective* willing to put the needs of others before one's

---

Consonants: b but   d dog   f few   g get   h her   j yes   k cat   l leg   m man   n no   p pen   r red   s sit

own needs, wishes, etc. □ **un·self·ish·ly** adverb **un·self·ish·ness** noun

un·sell·able adjective not sellable.

un·sensa·tion·al adjective not sensational.

un·senti·ment·al adjective not sentimental. □ **un·senti·men·tal·ity** noun **un·senti·men·tal·ly** adverb

un·separ·ated adjective not separated.

un·serious adjective not serious; lighthearted. □ **un·serious·ness** noun

un·service·able adjective not serviceable; unfit for use.

un·serviced adjective Cdn (esp. of a campsite) not serviced with electricity etc.

un·set adjective not set.

un·set·tle verb **1** transitive disturb the settled state or arrangement of; discompose. **2** transitive derange. **3** intransitive become unsettled. □ **un·set·tling** adjective **un·set·tling·ly** adverb

un·set·tled adjective **1** not (yet) settled. **2** worried and uneasy. **3** liable or open to change or further discussion. **4** (of a bill etc.) unpaid. **5** restless, unstable; continually changing. □ **un·settled·ness** noun

un·sewn adjective not sewn.

un·sex transitive verb **1** deprive (a person) of the qualities of her or his sex. **2** castrate or spay (an animal). □ **un·sexed** adjective

un·sexy adjective (**un·sexi·er, un·sexi·est**) **1** not sexually attractive or stimulating; not appealing. **2** unfashionable or unexciting.

un·shackle transitive verb **1** release from shackles. **2** set free.

un·shaded adjective not shaded.

un·shak·able adjective (also **un·shake·able**) that cannot be shaken; firm. □ **un·shak·ably** adverb

un·shaken adjective not shaken.

un·shape·ly adjective not shapely.

un·shared adjective not shared.

un·shaven adjective not shaved; not having shaved. □ **un·shaven·ness** noun

un·sheathe transitive verb remove (a knife etc.) from a sheath.

un·shed adjective not shed.

un·shelled adjective (of nuts, peas, etc.) not (yet) extracted from the shell.

un·shel·tered adjective not sheltered.

un·shield·ed adjective not shielded or protected.

un·ship transitive verb (**un·shipped, un·ship·ping**) **1** remove or discharge (a cargo or passenger) from a ship. **2** esp. Naut. remove (an object, esp. a mast or oar) from a fixed position.

un·shock·able adjective that cannot be shocked. □ **un·shock·ably** adverb

un·shod adjective not wearing shoes.

un·shorn adjective not shorn.

un·shov·elled adjective (also esp. US **un·shov·eled**) not shovelled, e.g. of snow or a snowy sidewalk etc.

un·showy adjective not showy.

un·shrink·able adjective (of fabric etc.) not liable to shrink.

un·sight·ed adjective **1** blind. **2** prevented from seeing by an obstruction.

un·sightly adjective unpleasant to look at, ugly. □ **un·sightli·ness** noun [from UN-¹ + obsolete sightly pleasant to look at]

un·signed adjective **1** not signed. **2** not having signed a contract.

un·sink·able adjective that cannot be sunk. □ **un·sink·abil·ity** noun

un·sized¹ adjective **1** not made to a size. **2** not sorted by size.

un·sized² adjective (of fabric, paper, or a wall) not treated with size.

un·skil·ful adjective (also **un·skill·ful**) not skilful. □ **un·skil·ful·ly** adverb

un·skilled adjective lacking or not needing special skill or training.

un·sleep·ing adjective not or never sleeping.

un·sliced adjective (esp. of a loaf of bread when it is bought) not having been cut into slices.

un·sling transitive verb (past and past participle **un·slung**) remove (something) from the place where it has been slung or suspended.

un·smiling adjective not smiling. □ **un·smiling·ly** adverb

un·smoked adjective **1** not cured by smoking (unsmoked bacon). **2** not consumed by smoking (an unsmoked cigar).

un·snap transitive verb (**un·snapped, un·snap·ping**) undo, unfasten, or open with a snap.

un·snarl transitive verb disentangle.

un·sociable adjective not sociable, disliking the company of others. □ **un·sociabil·ity** noun

un·social adjective **1** not social; not suitable for, seeking, or conforming to society. **2** outside the normal working day (unsocial hours). **3** anti-social.

un·soiled adjective not soiled or dirtied.

un·sold adjective not sold.

un·solicit·ed adjective not asked for.

un·solv·able adjective that cannot be solved, insoluble. □ **un·solv·abil·ity** noun

un·solved adjective not solved.

un·sophis·ti·cated adjective **1** not having or showing much experience of the world and social situations. **2** not complicated or refined; basic (unsophisticated equipment). **3** not adulterated or artificial.

un·sort·ed adjective not sorted.

un·sought adjective **1** not searched out or sought for. **2** unasked; without being requested.

un·sound adjective **1** unhealthy, diseased. **2** rotten, weak. **3 a** ill-founded, fallacious. **b** unorthodox, heretical. **4** unreliable. **5** wicked. □ **of unsound mind** insane. □ **un·sound·ness** noun

un·sound·ed¹ adjective **1** not uttered or pronounced. **2** not made to sound.

un·sound·ed² adjective unfathomed.

un·sparing adjective **1** giving freely and generously. **2** severe; merciless. □ **un·sparing·ly** adverb

un·speak·able adjective **1** that cannot be expressed in words. **2** indescribably bad or objectionable. □ **un·speak·ably** adverb

un·speak·ing adjective not speaking; silent.

un·special·ized adjective not specialized.

un·specif·ic adjective not specific; general, inexact.

un·speci·fied adjective not specified.

un·spec·tacu·lar adjective not spectacular; dull.

un·spent adjective **1** not expended or used. **2** not exhausted or used up.

un·spirit·ual adjective not spiritual; earthly, worldly.

un·spoiled adjective **1** (also esp. Brit. **un·spoilt**) not spoiled. **2** not plundered.

un·spoken adjective **1** understood without being expressed verbally. **2** not uttered as or expressed in speech.

un·spon·sored adjective not supported or promoted by a sponsor.

un·spool verb **1** transitive & intransitive unwind from or as if from a spool. **2 a** transitive screen (a film). **b** intransitive (of a film) be screened.

un·sport·ing adjective not sportsmanlike; not fair or generous. □ **un·sport·ing·ly** adverb

un·sports·man·like adjective (of behaviour, an act, etc.) dishonourable, unseemly; unfair.

unsportsmanlike conduct noun a penalty imposed in various sports for unprofessional or unseemly conduct, e.g. pulling the hair of one's opponent.

un·spot·ted adjective **1 a** not marked with a spot or spots. **b** morally pure. **2** unnoticed.

un·sprayed adjective not sprayed, esp. (of crops etc.) with a pesticide.

un·sprung adjective not provided with a spring or springs.

un·spun adjective not spun; not formed or prepared by spinning.

un·stable adjective **1** not stable. **2** changeable. **3** showing a tendency to sudden mental or emotional changes. **4** (of weather, an air mass, etc.) likely to produce precipitation. □ **un·stabil·ized** adjective **un·stably** adverb

un·stained adjective not stained.

un·stamped adjective **1** not marked by stamping. **2** not having a stamp affixed.

un·stated adjective not stated or declared.

un·steady adjective (**un·steadi·er, un·steadi·est**) **1** not steady or firm. **2** changeable, fluctuating. **3** not uniform or regular. □ **un·steadi·ly** adverb **un·steadi·ness** noun

un·sterile adjective (of a syringe etc.) not sterile.

un·stick transitive verb (past and past participle **un·stuck**) separate (a thing stuck to another). □ **come unstuck** informal come to grief, fail.

un·stiff·en transitive & intransitive verb lose or cause to lose stiffness; loosen, relax.

un·stimu·lat·ing adjective not stimulating.

un·stint·ed *adjective* given without restraint; liberal (*they received unstinted praise*).

un·stint·ing *adjective* given or giving without restraint; unsparing (*he was unstinting in his praise*). □ **un·stint·ing·ly** *adverb*

un·stitch *transitive verb* undo the stitches of.

un·stop *transitive verb* (**un·stopped**, **un·stop·ping**) **1** free from obstruction. **2** remove the stopper from.

un·stop·pable *adjective* that cannot be stopped or prevented. □ **un·stop·pabil·ity** *noun* **un·stop·pably** *adverb*

un·stop·per *transitive verb* remove the stopper from.

un·strained *adjective* **1** not subjected to straining or stretching. **2** not injured by overuse or excessive demands. **3** not forced or produced by effort. **4** not passed through a strainer.

un·strap *transitive verb* (**un·strapped**, **un·strap·ping**) undo the strap or straps of.

un·stressed *adjective* **1** (of a word, syllable, etc.) not pronounced with stress. **2** not subjected to stress.

un·string *transitive verb* (*past* and *past participle* **un·strung**) **1** remove or relax the string or strings of (a bow, guitar, etc.). **2** remove from a string. **3** (esp. as **un·strung** *adjective*) unnerve.

un·struc·tured *adjective* **1** not structured. **2** informal. **3** (of a garment, esp. a jacket) unlined.

un·stuck *past* and *past participle of* UNSTICK.

un·studied *adjective* **1** easy, natural, spontaneous. **2** not having or having been studied.

un·stuffy *adjective* **1** informal, casual. **2** not stuffy.

un·stylish *adjective* **1** lacking style. **2** unfashionable.

un·sub·scribe *intransitive verb* remove oneself from an esp. computer mailing list etc.

un·sub·stan·tial *adjective* having little or no solidity, reality, or factual basis.

un·sub·stan·ti·ated *adjective* not substantiated.

un·subtle *adjective* not subtle; obvious, clumsy. □ **un·subtly** *adverb*

un·success·ful *adjective* not successful. □ **un·success·ful·ly** *adverb*

un·suit·able *adjective* not suitable. □ **un·suit·abil·ity** *noun* **un·suit·ably** *adverb*

un·suit·ed *adjective* (usu. foll. by *for, to*) not suited (to); inappropriate; not fit (for).

un·sullied *adjective* not sullied.

un·sung *adjective* **1** unrecognized, unknown. **2** not sung.

un·super·vised *adjective* not supervised.

un·support·able *adjective* **1** that cannot be endured. **2** indefensible.

un·support·ed *adjective* not supported.

un·support·ive *adjective* not giving support.

un·sure *adjective* not sure. □ **un·sure·ly** *adverb* **un·sure·ness** *noun*

un·surfaced *adjective* (of a road etc.) not provided with a surface.

un·surpass·able *adjective* that cannot be surpassed.

un·surpassed *adjective* not surpassed.

un·surprised *adjective* not surprised.

un·surpris·ing *adjective* not surprising. □ **un·surpris·ing·ly** *adverb*

un·surveyed *adjective* not surveyed.

un·suspect·ed *adjective* not suspected.

un·suspect·ing *adjective* not suspecting. □ **un·suspect·ing·ly** *adverb*

un·suspi·cious *adjective* not suspicious.

un·sustain·able *adjective* not sustainable. □ **un·sustain·ably** *adverb*

un·sustained *adjective* not sustained.

un·swayed *adjective* uninfluenced, unaffected.

un·sweet·ened *adjective* not sweetened.

un·swept *adjective* not swept.

un·swerv·ing *adjective* **1** steady, constant. **2** not turning aside. □ **un·swerv·ing·ly** *adverb*

un·sworn *adjective* **1** (of a person) not subjected to or bound by an oath. **2** not confirmed by an oath.

un·symmet·ric·al *adjective* not symmetrical.

un·sympa·thet·ic *adjective* not sympathetic. □ **un·sympa·thet·ic·ally** *adverb*

un·system·atic *adjective* not systematic. □ **un·system·atic·ally** *adverb*

un·taint·ed *adjective* not tainted.

un·talent·ed *adjective* not talented.

un·tame·able *adjective* (also **un·tamable**) that cannot be tamed.

un·tamed *adjective* not tamed, wild.

un·tan·gle *transitive verb* **1** free from a tangled state. **2** free from entanglement.

un·tanned *adjective* not tanned.

un·tapped *adjective* not (yet) tapped (*untapped resources*).

un·tar·nished *adjective* not tarnished.

un·tasted *adjective* not tasted.

un·taught *adjective* **1** not instructed by teaching; ignorant. **2** not acquired by teaching; natural, spontaneous.

un·taxed *adjective* not required to pay or not attracting taxes.

un·teach·able *adjective* **1** incapable of being instructed. **2** that cannot be imparted by teaching.

un·tempered *adjective* not tempered.

un·tenable /ʌnˈtɛnəbəl/ *adjective* (of an argument, position, etc.) not tenable; that cannot be defended. □ **un·tenabil·ity** *noun*

un·tenant·ed *adjective* not occupied by a tenant.

un·tend·ed *adjective* not tended; neglected.

un·ten·dered *adjective* (of a contract) not put out to tender.

un·tenured *adjective* not tenured.

Unter·mensch /ˈʊntɜːmɛnʃ/ *noun* (*pl.* **-menschen** /-menʃən/) a person considered racially or socially inferior. [German]

un·test·ed *adjective* not tested or proved. □ **un·test·able** *adjective*

un·tethered *adjective* not tethered.

un·thanked *adjective* not thanked.

un·thank·ful *adjective* not thankful.

un·thawed *adjective* frozen; not thawed.

un·think·able *adjective* **1** that cannot be imagined or grasped by the mind. **2** *informal* highly unlikely or undesirable. □ **un·think·ably** *adverb*

un·think·ing *adjective* **1** not thinking. **2** characterized by thoughtlessness or absence of thought. □ **un·think·ing·ly** *adverb*

un·thought *adjective* (often foll. by *of*) not thought of.

un·thread *transitive verb* **1** take the thread out of (a needle etc.). **2** disentangle.

un·threat·en·ing *adjective* not threatening or aggressive; safe.

un·thrifty *adjective* **1** wasteful, extravagant, prodigal. **2** not thriving or flourishing. □ **un·thrift·i·ness** *noun*

un·tidy *adjective* (**un·tidi·er**, **un·tidi·est**) not neat or orderly. □ **un·tidily** *adverb* **un·tidiness** *noun*

un·tie *transitive verb* (*pres. part.* **un·tying**) **1** undo (a knot etc.). **2** unfasten the cords etc. of (a package etc.). **3** release from bonds or attachment.

un·tied *adjective* not tied.

until ● *preposition* **1** up to or as late as (*wait until six o'clock; did not return until night*). **2** up to the time of (*faithful until death; waited until the end*). ● *conjunction* **1** up to the time when (*wait until I return*). **2** so long that (*laughed until I cried*). [originally northern Middle English *untill* from Old Norse *und* as far as + TILL¹]

un·tilled *adjective* not tilled.

un·time·ly ● *adjective* **1** inopportune. **2** (esp. of death) premature. □ **un·time·li·ness** *noun*

un·tinged *adjective* not tinged.

un·tiring *adjective* tireless. □ **un·tiring·ly** *adverb*

un·titled *adjective* having no title.

unto *preposition* archaic = TO preposition (in all uses except as the sign of the infinitive); (*do unto others; faithful unto death; take unto oneself*). [Middle English from UNTIL, with TO replacing northern TILL¹]

un·told *adjective* **1** not told. **2** not (able to be) counted or measured (*untold misery*).

un·touch·able ● *adjective* **1** that may not or cannot be touched. **2** that may not be harmed, criticized, disrupted, etc. ● *noun* **1** a member of a hereditary Hindu group held to defile members of higher castes on contact. ¶ Use of the term, and social restrictions accompanying it, were declared illegal under the Indian constitution in 1949. **2** an untouchable person or thing. □ **un·touch·abil·ity** *noun*

un·touched *adjective* **1** not touched. **2** not affected physically, not harmed, modified, used, or tasted. **3** not affected by emotion. **4** not discussed.

un·touristy *adjective* (also **un·tourist·ed**) **1** not visited by many tourists. **2** not altered to appeal to tourists.

Vowels: a *cat* ɑ *arm* e *bed* ɜː *her* ɜ: *deux* ə *ago* ɪ *sit* i *cosy* iː *feed* ɒ *hot* ɔ *pore* ɔː *no* ʌ *run* ʊ *put*

un·toward *adjective* **1** inconvenient, unlucky. **2** unseemly, improper.

un·trace·able *adjective* that cannot be traced.

un·traced *adjective* not traced.

un·tracked *adjective* **1** not marked with tracks from skis etc. **2** having no previously trodden track; unexplored.

un·trad·ition·al *adjective* not traditional; unusual.

un·trained *adjective* not trained; unskilled.

un·tram·melled *adjective* (also esp. *US* **un·tram·meled**) not deprived of freedom of action or expression; not restricted or hampered (*a mind untrammelled by convention*).

un·trans·formed *adjective* that has not or has not been transformed.

un·trans·lat·able *adjective* that cannot be translated (satisfactorily). □ **un·trans·lat·abil·ity** *noun* **un·trans·lat·ed** *adjective*

un·trav·elled *adjective* (also esp. *US* **un·trav·eled**) **1** that has not travelled. **2** that has not been travelled over or through.

un·treat·able *adjective* (esp. of a disease) that cannot be treated.

un·treat·ed *adjective* **1** (of a patient, disease, or other condition) not given medical care. **2** not improved, preserved, or altered by the use of a chemical, physical or biological agent (*untreated sewage poured into the sea*).

un·trendy *adjective informal* not trendy.

un·tried *adjective* **1** not tried or tested. **2** inexperienced. **3** not yet tried by a judge.

un·trimmed *adjective* **1** left uncut or in an irregular shape. **2** not adorned.

un·trod·den *adjective* not trodden; stepped on, or traversed.

un·troubled *adjective* not troubled; calm, tranquil.

un·true *adjective* **1** not true, contrary to what is the fact. **2** (often foll. by *to*) not faithful or loyal. **3** deviating from an accepted standard. □ **un·truly** *adverb*

un·trust·worthy *adjective* not trustworthy. □ **un·trust·worthi·ness** *noun*

un·truth *noun* (*pl.*) **1** the state of being untrue, falsehood. **2** a false statement (*told me an untruth*).

un·truth·ful *adjective* not truthful. □ **un·truth·ful·ly** *adverb* **un·truth·ful·ness** *noun*

un·tuck *transitive verb* free (a shirt, bedclothes, etc.) from being tucked in or up.

un·tuned *adjective* **1** not in tune, not made tuneful. **2** (of a radio receiver etc.) not tuned to any one frequency. **3** not in harmony or concord, disordered.

un·turned *adjective* not turned over, around, away, etc. □ **leave no stone unturned** *see* STONE.

un·tutored *adjective* **1** uneducated, untaught. **2** simple, unsophisticated.

un·twist *transitive & intransitive verb* open from a twisted or spiralled state.

un·tying *pres. part. of* UNTIE.

un·typ·ical *adjective* not typical; unusual. □ **un·typ·ical·ly** *adverb*

un·usable *adjective* not usable.

un·used *adjective* **1 a** not in use. **b** never having been used. **2** (foll. by *to*) not accustomed.

un·usual *adjective* **1** not usual. **2** exceptional, remarkable, strange. □ **un·usual·ly** *adverb* **un·usual·ness** *noun*

un·utter·able *adjective* inexpressible; beyond description (*unutterable torment*; *an unutterable fool*). □ **un·utter·ably** *adverb*

un·uttered *adjective* not uttered or expressed.

un·vaccin·at·ed *adjective* not vaccinated.

un·valued *adjective* **1** not regarded as valuable. **2** not having been valued.

un·van·quished *adjective* not vanquished.

un·var·nished *adjective* **1** not varnished. **2** (of a statement or person) plain and straightforward (*the unvarnished truth*).

un·vary·ing *adjective* not varying. □ **un·vary·ing·ly** *adverb*

un·veil *transitive verb* **1** remove a veil from. **2** remove a covering from (a statue, plaque, etc.) as part of the ceremony of the first public display. **3** disclose, reveal, make publicly known. □ **un·veil·ing** *noun*

un·venti·lat·ed *adjective* not provided with a means of ventilation.

un·veri·fi·able *adjective* that cannot be verified.

un·veri·fied *adjective* not verified.

un·versed *adjective* (usu. foll. by *in*) not experienced or skilled.

un·viable *adjective* not viable.

un·visit·ed *adjective* not visited.

un·voiced *adjective* **1** not spoken or expressed. **2** *Phonetics* not voiced.

un·waged *adjective* **1** (of a person) not receiving a wage; out of work; doing unpaid work. **2** (of work) not recompensed with wages; unpaid.

un·walled *adjective* without enclosing walls.

un·want·ed *adjective* not wanted.

un·warlike *adjective* not warlike.

un·warned *adjective* not warned or forewarned.

un·warrant·able *adjective* indefensible, unjustifiable. □ **un·warrant·ably** *adverb*

un·warrant·ed *adjective* **1** unauthorized. **2** unjustified.

un·wary *adjective* **1** not cautious. **2** (often foll. by *of*) not aware of possible danger etc. □ **un·wari·ly** *adverb*

un·washed *adjective* **1** not washed. **2** not usually washed or clean. *See also* GREAT UNWASHED.

un·watch·able *adjective* disturbing or not interesting to watch.

un·watched *adjective* not watched.

un·watered *adjective* not watered.

un·waver·ing *adjective* not wavering. □ **un·waver·ing·ly** *adverb*

un·weaned *adjective* not weaned.

un·wear·able *adjective* that cannot be worn.

un·wearied *adjective* **1** not wearied or tired. **2** never becoming weary, indefatigable. **3** unremitting.

un·weary·ing *adjective* persistent.

un·weathered *adjective* not weathered.

un·wed *adjective* unmarried.

un·wed·ded *adjective* unmarried.

un·weight *transitive verb* (esp. as **un·weight·ed** *adjective*) remove the weight from.

un·welcome *adjective* not welcome or acceptable; displeasing.

un·welcom·ing *adjective* **1** having an inhospitable atmosphere. **2** hostile; unfriendly.

un·well *predicative adjective* not in good health; (somewhat) ill.

un·whole·some *adjective* **1** not promoting, or detrimental to, physical or moral health; unhealthy, insalubrious. **2** unhealthy-looking. □ **un·whole·some·ly** *adverb*

un·wieldy *adjective* (**un·wield·i·er**, **un·wield·i·est**) cumbersome, clumsy, or hard to manage, owing to size, shape, weight, etc. □ **un·wield·i·ness** *noun* [Middle English from UN-¹ + *wieldy* active (now dial.) from WIELD]

un·will·ing *adjective* not willing or inclined; reluctant. □ **un·will·ing·ly** *adverb* **un·will·ing·ness** *noun*

un·wind *verb* (*past* and *past participle* **un·wound**) **1 a** *transitive* draw out (a thing that has been wound). **b** *intransitive* become drawn out after having been wound. **2** *intransitive & transitive informal* relax.

un·wink·ing *adjective* **1** not winking. **2** watchful, vigilant.

un·win·nable *adjective* that cannot be won.

un·wired *adjective* **1** *informal* not having access to the Internet. **2** not fitted with or reliant on electric or fibre optic cables.

un·wisdom *noun* lack of wisdom, folly, imprudence.

un·wise *adjective* **1** (of a person etc.) foolish, imprudent. **2** injudicious. □ **un·wise·ly** *adverb*

un·wit·nessed *adjective* not witnessed.

un·wit·ting *adjective* **1** not knowing; unaware of the state of the case (*an unwitting offender*). **2** unintentional, inadvertent. □ **un·wit·ting·ly** *adverb* [Old English *unwitende* (as UN-¹, WIT²)]

un·woman·ly *adjective* not womanly; not befitting a woman.

un·wont·ed /ʌnˈwɒntəd/ *adjective* not customary or usual. □ **un·wont·ed·ly** *adverb*

un·work·able *adjective* not workable; impracticable. □ **un·work·abil·ity** *noun*

un·worked *adjective* not cultivated, mined, or carved.

un·world·ly *adjective* **1** spiritually-minded. **2** spiritual. **3** inexperienced; unsophisticated. □ **un·world·li·ness** *noun*

un·worn *adjective* not worn or impaired by wear.

un·worried *adjective* not worried; calm.

un·worthy *adjective* (**un·worthi·er**, **un·worthi·est**) **1** (often foll. by *of*) not worthy or befitting the character of a person etc. **2** discreditable, unseemly. **3** contemptible, base. **4** having or possessing insufficient merit, excellence, or worth; not deserving. □ **un·worthi·ly** *adverb* **un·worthi·ness** *noun*

un·wound[1] *adjective* not wound or wound up.

un·wound[2] *past and past participle of* UNWIND.

un·wound·ed *adjective* not wounded, unhurt.

un·wrap *verb* (**un·wrapped**, **un·wrap·ping**) **1** *transitive* remove the wrapping from. **2** *transitive* open or unfold. **3** *transitive* unfold, reveal, disclose. **4** *intransitive* become unwrapped.

un·wrin·kled *adjective* free from wrinkles, smooth.

un·writ·able *adjective* that cannot be written.

un·writ·ten *adjective* **1** not written. **2** (of a law etc.) resting originally on custom or judicial decision, not on statute. **3** (of a convention etc.) not expressed in words, implicit.

un·yield·ing *adjective* **1** not yielding to pressure etc. **2** firm, obstinate. □ **un·yield·ing·ly** *adverb* **un·yield·ing·ness** *noun*

un·yoke *transitive verb* release from a yoke.

unzip *verb* (**un·zipped**, **un·zip·ping**) **1** *transitive* unfasten the zipper of. **2** *intransitive* unfasten a zipper (esp. in disrobing). **3** *transitive* Computing decompress (a previously compressed file).

up ● *adverb* **1** at, in, or towards a higher place or position (*jumped up in the air*; *what are they doing up there?*). **2** to or in a place regarded as higher, esp.: **a** northwards (*up in Yellowknife*). **b** *Brit.* towards a major city or a university (*went up to London*). **3** *informal* ahead etc. as indicated (*went up front*). **4 a** to or in an erect position or condition (*stood it up*). **b** to or in a prepared or required position (*wound up the watch*). **c** in or into a condition of efficiency, activity, or progress (*stirred up trouble*; *the house is up for sale*; *the hunt is up*; *the surf is up*). **5** in a stronger or winning position or condition (*our team was up three goals*; *am $10 up on the transaction*). **6** (of a computer) running and available for use. **7** to the place or time in question or where the speaker etc. is (*a child came up to me*; *went straight up to the door*; *has been fine up till now*). **8** at or to a higher price or value (*our costs are up*; *shares are up*). **9 a** completely or effectually (*burn up*; *eat up*; *tear up*; *use up*). **b** more loudly or clearly (*speak up*). **10** in a state of completion; denoting the end of availability, supply, etc. (*time is up*). **11** into a compact, accumulated, or secure state (*pack up*; *save up*; *tie up*). **12** out of bed (*are you up yet?*). **13** (of the sun etc.) having risen. **14** happening, esp. unusually or unexpectedly (*something is up*). **15 a** *Baseball* at bat. **b** next in line or in order of business. **16** taught or informed (*is well up in French*). **17** (usu. foll. by *before*) appearing for trial etc. (*was up before the parole board*). **18** *Brit.* (of a road etc.) being repaired. **19** (of a jockey) in the saddle. **20** towards the source of a river. **21** inland. **22** (of the points etc. in a game): **a** registered on the scoreboard. **b** forming the total score for the time being. **23** upstairs, esp. to bed (*are you going up yet?*). **24** (of a theatre curtain) raised etc. to reveal the stage. **25** (as *interjection*) get up. **26** (of a ship's helm) with rudder to leeward. **27** in rebellion. ● *preposition* **1** upwards along, through, or into (*climbed up the ladder*). **2** from the bottom to the top of. **3** along (*walked up the road*). **4 a** at or in a higher part of (*is situated up the street*). **b** towards the source of (a river). ● *adjective* **1** directed upwards. **2** full of energy, enthusiastic (*that Word Lady always sounds so up in the morning*). **3** *Brit.* of travel towards a capital or centre (*the up train*; *the up platform*). **4** ready and willing; game (*are you up for a game of pool?*). **5** (of a computer system) functioning properly (*when will we be back up?*). ● *noun* a period of good fortune (*we've had our ups and downs*). ● *verb* (**upped**, **up·ping**) **1** *intransitive informal* start up; begin abruptly to say or do something (*upped and hit him*). **2** *transitive* increase or raise, esp. abruptly (*upped all their prices*). □ **be all up with** (with *it* as subject) be disastrous or hopeless for (a person). **up and...** denoting the action of doing something suddenly (*she up and told him*; *he up and died*). **on the up and up** *informal* **1** esp. *N Amer.* honest(ly); on the level. **2** *Brit.* steadily improving. **something is up** *informal* something unusual or undesirable is afoot or happening. **up against 1** in or into contact with. **2** *informal* confronted with (*up against a problem*). **up against it** *informal* in great difficulties. **up and around** (or **about**, **doing**) having risen from bed; active. **up close** very close(ly). **up and down 1** back and forth (along) (*have been up and down the road four times already*). **2** in every direction. **3** *informal* in varying health or spirits. **swear up and down** see SWEAR. **up for** available for or being considered for (office etc.). **up hill and down dale** up and down hills, or confronting many obstacles, on an arduous journey or in the fulfillment of an arduous task. **up in the air** see AIR. **up in arms** see ARM[2]. **up on** informed about (a matter or subject). **up the spout** see SPOUT. **up sticks** see STICK[1]. **up to 1** until (*up to the present*). **2** not more than (*you can have up to five*). **3** less than or equal to (*sums up to $100*). **4 a** incumbent on (*it is up to you to tell them*). **b** to be decided by (*I'll leave it up to you*). **5** capable of or fit for (*am not up to a long walk*). **6** occupied or busy with (*what have you been up to?*). **up to date** see DATE[1]. **up to the mark** see MARK[1]. **up to snuff** see SNUFF[2]. **up to speed** see SPEED. **up to one's old tricks** see TRICK.

up to a person's tricks see TRICK. **up with** *interjection* expressing support for a stated person or thing. **up yours** *coarse slang* expressing contemptuous defiance or rejection. **what's up?** *informal* **1** what is going on? **2** what is the matter? [Old English *up(p)*, *uppe*, related to Old High German *ūf*]

up- *prefix in senses of* UP, added: **1** as an adverb to verbs and verbal derivations, = 'upwards' (*upcurved*; *update*). **2** as a preposition to nouns forming adverbs and adjectives (*upcountry*; *uphill*). **3** as an adjective to nouns (*upland*; *upstroke*).

up·along *Cdn* (*Nfld*) ● *adverb* to or on a location away from a person or place, esp. to or on mainland Canada (*went upalong*). ● *noun* such a location (*from upalong*).

up-and-coming *adjective informal* (of a person) making good progress and likely to succeed. □ **up-and-comer** *noun*

up and running *adjective & adverb* functioning; in operation.

Upani·shad /uːˈpanɪˌʃad/ *noun* each of a series of philosophical compositions concluding the exposition of the Vedas. □ **Upani·shad·ic** /-ˈʃadɪk/ *adjective* [Sanskrit from *upa* near + *ni-ṣad* sit down]

upas /ˈjuːpəs/ *noun* **1** (in full **upas tree**) a Javanese tree, *Antiaris toxicaria*, yielding a milky sap used as arrow poison. **2** the poisonous sap of upas and other trees. [Malay *ūpas* poison]

up·beat ● *noun* an unaccented beat in music. ● *adjective informal* optimistic or cheerful.

up·braid *transitive verb* (often foll. by *with*, *for*) chide or reproach (a person). □ **up·braid·ing** *noun* [Old English *upbrēdan* (as UP-, *brēdan* = *bregdan* BRAID in obsolete sense 'brandish')]

up·bring·ing *noun* **1** the bringing up of a child; education. **2** the manner of this. [obsolete *upbring* to rear (as UP-, BRING)]

UPC *abbreviation* UNIVERSAL PRODUCT CODE.

up·cast ● *noun* **1** the act of casting up; an upward throw. **2** *Mining* a shaft through which air leaves a mine. ● *transitive verb* (*past* and *past participle* **up·cast**) cast up.

up·chuck *verb & noun N Amer. slang* vomit.

up-close-and-personal *adjective informal* intimate, cozy.

up·com·ing *adjective* esp. *N Amer.* forthcoming; about to happen.

up·coun·try *adverb & adjective* inland; towards the interior of a country.

up·court *adverb Basketball* towards the opponent's end of the court.

up·date ● *transitive verb* **1** make more modern or up-to-date, esp. by replacing old material, methods, etc. or including new material. **2** provide (a person) with the latest information about something. ● *noun* **1** the act or an instance of updating. **2** an updated version; a set of updated information. □ **up·dat·able** *adjective* (also **update·able**). **up·dated** *adjective* **up·dater** *noun*

Up·dike, **John (Hoyer)** (b.1932), US novelist, poet, and short-story writer. His quartet of novels *Rabbit, Run* (1960), *Rabbit Redux* (1971), *Rabbit is Rich* (1981), and *Rabbit at Rest* (1990) is a small-town tragicomedy tracing the career of a former basketball player. □ **Updik·ean** *adjective*

updo *noun* a hairstyle in which the hair is piled high on the head.

up·draft *noun* (also **up·draught**) an upward draft.

up·end *verb* **1** *transitive & intransitive* set or become upside down or so that one end is at the top. **2** *transitive* knock over; cause to fall down. **3** *intransitive* (of a duck etc.) dip the head below water and raise the tail into the air, when feeding in shallow water. **4** *transitive Sport* defeat.

up·field *adverb* = DOWNFIELD.

up·front *informal* ● *adverb* (usu. **up front**) **1** at the front; in front. **2** (of payments) in advance. ● *adjective* **1** honest, open, frank. **2** (of payments) made in advance. **3** at the front or most prominent.

up·grade ● *verb* **1** *transitive* raise (something) to a higher standard. **2** *transitive* improve (equipment, machinery, etc.) esp. by replacing components. **3** *intransitive* replace (components of) one's equipment, software, etc. with improved versions. **4** *transitive & intransitive* move to a higher category in a hierarchy (*upgraded to business class*). ● *noun* **1** the act or an instance of upgrading. **2** an upgraded piece of equipment etc. □ **up·grade·abil·ity** *adjective* (also **up·grad·abil·ity**) esp. *Computing*. **up·grade·able** *adjective* (also **up·grad·able**) esp. *Computing*.

up·grader *noun* **1** a type of oil refinery which is designed to make heavy crude oil light enough to be processed in normal refineries. **2** a person who upgrades or improves, esp. a person who changes to upgraded software etc.

up·growth *noun* the process or result of growing upwards.

up·heav·al *noun* **1** a violent or sudden change or disruption. **2** *Geol.* an upward displacement of part of the earth's crust. **3** the act or an instance of heaving up.

up·heave *verb* **1** *transitive* heave or lift up, esp. forcibly. **2** *intransitive* rise up.

up·hill ● *adverb* in an ascending direction up a hill, slope, etc. ● *adjective* **1** sloping up; ascending. **2** arduous, difficult (*an uphill struggle*). ● *noun* an upward slope.

up·hold *transitive verb* (*past* and *past participle* **up·held**) **1** confirm or maintain (a decision etc., esp. of another). **2** give support or countenance to (a person, practice, etc.). **3** maintain unimpaired and intact. □ **up·hold·er** *noun*

up·hol·ster /ʌpˈoːlstər, ʌpˈhoːl-/ *transitive verb* provide (furniture) with upholstery. [back-formation from UPHOLSTERER]

up·hol·ster·er *noun* a person who upholsters furniture, esp. professionally. [obsolete *upholster* (n.) from UPHOLD (in obsolete sense 'keep in repair') + -STER]

up·hol·stery *noun* **1** textile covering, padding, springs, etc., for furniture. **2** an upholsterer's work.

UPI *abbreviation* United Press International.

up ice *adverb* *Hockey* towards the opponent's end of the rink.

U-pick *N Amer.* ● *adjective* designating an orchard or farm where customers pick produce directly from the fields etc. ● *noun* such a farm or orchard.

up-island *adverb & adjective* *Cdn* towards or of the northern or more remote parts of Vancouver Island.

up·keep *noun* **1** maintenance in good condition. **2** the cost or means of this.

up·land ● *noun* high or hilly country. ● *adjective* of or relating to this.

up·lift ● *transitive verb* **1** raise; lift up. **2** elevate or stimulate morally or spiritually. ● *noun* **1** the act or an instance of being raised. **2** *Geol.* the raising of part of the earth's surface. **3** *informal* a morally or spiritually elevating influence. **4** support for the bust etc. from a garment. □ **up·lift·er** *noun* **up·lift·ing** *adjective* (esp. in sense 2 of *verb*).

up·light *noun* a light placed or designed to throw illumination upwards. □ **up·light·ing** *noun*

up·link ● *noun* a communications link to a satellite. ● *transitive verb* (esp. as **up·linked** *adjective*) provide with or send by an uplink.

up·load *Computing* ● *transitive & intransitive verb* **1** transfer (data) to a larger storage device or to a central system. **2** *Cdn* shift (costs) from a lower level of government to higher one. ● *noun* (usu. *attributive*) a transfer of data to a larger storage device or to a central system (*upload feature*).

up·market *adjective & adverb* = UPSCALE.

upon *preposition* = ON. ¶ *Upon* is sometimes more formal than *on*, but is the only idiomatic choice in *once upon a time* and in uses such as *row upon row of seats* and *Christmas is almost upon us*. [Middle English from UP + ON *preposition*, after Old Norse *upp á*]

up·per[1] ● *adjective* **1** situated above another part (*the upper atmosphere*; *the upper lip*). **2** higher in position or status (*the upper class*). **3** (**Upper**) **a** situated on higher ground (*Upper Egypt*). **b** situated to the north (*Upper California*). **4** (often **Upper**) *Geol. & Archaeology* designating a younger, and hence usu. shallower, part of a stratigraphic division, archaeological deposit, etc., or the period in which it was formed or deposited. ● *noun* the part of a boot or shoe above the sole. □ **on one's uppers** esp. *Brit. informal* extremely short of money.

up·per[2] *noun* *slang* a stimulant drug, esp. an amphetamine.

Upper Arrow Lake a long, narrow lake in south central BC, lying in the Columbia River valley and part of the Columbia River system. It extends southward from Revelstoke some 100 km.

Upper Austria a state of NW Austria; capital, Linz.

Upper Canada 1 *hist.* the mainly English-speaking region of Canada north of the Great Lakes and west of the Ottawa River, in what is now the southern portion of Ontario. It was a British colony from 1791 to 1841, when it was united with Lower Canada to form the Province of Canada. **2** esp. *Maritimes* Ontario. □ **Upper Canadian** *noun & adjective*

Upper Canada Rebellion *see* REBELLIONS OF 1837.

Upper Canada Village a living museum of a 19th-c. community, situated in Morrisburg, a village in SE Ontario on the St. Lawrence about 40 km southwest of Cornwall. [so called to reflect the area's early Upper Canadian heritage]

upper case ● *adjective* designating the larger characters used in printing and writing, often differing in shape as well as size from the lower case forms. ● *noun* an upper case letter. [originally designating the upper of a typesetter's cases, which traditionally held the type for such characters]

upper chamber *noun* = UPPER HOUSE.

upper class ● *noun* the highest class of society. ● *adjective* (**upper-class**) of the upper class.

upper·class·man *noun* (pl. **-men**) esp. *US* a junior or senior student in a high school or college.

upper crust *noun* (hyphenated when *attributive*) *informal* the upper class.

upper·cut ● *noun* an upwards blow delivered with the arm bent. ● *transitive verb* hit with an uppercut.

Upper Great Lakes Lakes Superior, Michigan, and Huron.

upper hand *noun* dominance or control; an advantage.

upper house *noun* the usu. smaller body in a bicameral legislature, often representing regional or sectional interests, esp. (in Canada) the Senate.

upper middle class ● *noun* the class of society between the middle and upper classes. ● *adjective* (**upper-middle-class**) of the upper middle class.

upper·most ● *adjective* **1** highest in place or rank. **2** predominant. ● *adverb* at or to the highest or most prominent position.

Upper Volta former name (until 1984) of BURKINA FASO.

upper·works *noun* the part of a ship that is above the water when fully laden.

uppish *adjective* *informal* self-assertive or arrogant.

uppity *adjective* *informal* **1** impertinent; arrogant. **2** snobbish. □ **uppiti·ness** *noun* (also **uppity·ness**) [fanciful from UP]

Upp·sala /ˈʊpˈsɒlə/ a city in E Sweden; pop. (est. 2000) 189,569. Its university, founded in 1477, is the oldest in N Europe.

up·raise *transitive verb* (esp. as **up·raised** *adjective*) raise to a higher level.

up·right ● *adjective* **1** erect, vertical (*an upright posture*; *stood upright*). **2** (of a piano) with vertical strings. **3** (of a person or behaviour) righteous; strictly honourable or honest. **4** (of a picture, book, etc.) greater in height than width. ● *noun* **1** a post or rod fixed upright esp. as a structural support. **2** (usu. in *pl.*) a goalpost, esp. in football. **3** an upright piano. ● *transitive verb* raise or restore to an upright or vertical position. □ **up·right·ness** *noun*

up·ris·ing *noun* **1** a rebellion or revolt. **2** the action or an act of rising or uprising.

up·river ● *adverb* at or towards a point nearer the source of a river. ● *adjective* situated or occurring upriver.

up·roar *noun* **1** a tumult; a violent disturbance. **2** a sustained protest; an expression of outrage. [Dutch *oproer* from *op* up + *roer* confusion, assoc. with ROAR]

up·roar·ious *adjective* **1** very noisy. **2** provoking loud laughter. □ **up·roar·ious·ly** *adverb* **up·roar·ious·ness** *noun*

up·root *verb* **1** *transitive* pull (a plant etc.) up from the ground. **2** *transitive* displace (a person) from an accustomed location. **3** *transitive* eradicate, destroy. **4** *intransitive* move away from one's accustomed location or home. □ **up·root·ed·ness** *noun*

up·rush *noun* an upward rush, esp. of emotion.

UPS *abbreviation* uninterruptible power supply.

upsa·daisy *var.* of UPSY-DAISY.

ups and downs *plural noun* **1** rises and falls. **2** alternate good and bad fortune.

up·scale *adjective & adverb* *N Amer.* towards or relating to the more expensive or more affluent sector of the market.

up·sell *intransitive verb* attempt to persuade a customer to buy something additional or more expensive.

upset ● *verb* (**upset·ting**; *past* and *past participle* **upset**) **1** *transitive & intransitive* overturn or be overturned. **2** *transitive* disturb the composure of (*was very upset by the news*). **3** *transitive* disturb (the digestion) (*anti-inflammatories may upset the stomach*). **4** *transitive* disrupt (*upset all their plans*). **5** *transitive* defeat (a favoured opponent). ● *noun* **1** a condition of upsetting or being upset (*a stomach upset*). **2** a surprising victory over a favoured opponent. ● *adjective* **1** disturbed (*an upset stomach*). **2** distressed, esp. emotionally (*the child was upset*). □ **upset·ter** *noun* **upset·ting·ly** *adverb*

upset price *noun* the lowest acceptable selling price of a property in an auction etc.; a reserve price.

upset stomach *noun* a temporary slight disorder of the digestive system.

up·shift ● *verb* **1** *intransitive* move to a higher gear in a motor vehicle. **2** *transitive* esp. *US* increase (*upshifted the penalties*). ● *noun* a movement upwards, esp. a change to a higher gear.

up·shot *noun* (usu. prec. by *the*) the final or eventual outcome or conclusion.

up·side ● *noun* **1** (often *attributive*) the upper side or surface of something. **2** the positive aspect of something; an advantage. **3** an upward movement of share prices etc. ● *preposition N Amer. slang* on or against (esp. in phr. **slap** (or **whack** etc.) **someone upside the head**).

upside down ● *adverb* **1** with the upper part where the lower part should be; in an inverted position. **2** in or into total disorder (*everything was turned upside down*). ● *adjective* (also **upside-down** *attributive*) that is positioned upside down; inverted. [Middle English, originally *up so down*, perhaps = 'up as if down']

upside-down cake *noun* a cake baked with fruit in a syrup at the bottom, and inverted for serving.

up·sides *Brit. informal* ● *adverb* **1** alongside. **2** (foll. by *with*) equal with (a person) by revenge, retaliation, etc. ● *preposition* alongside. [*upside* = top part]

up·si·lon /ˈjuːpsɪˌlɒn, ʌpˈsailən/ *noun* the twentieth letter of the Greek alphabet (Υ, υ). [Greek, = slender U, from *psilos* 'slender', with reference to the need to distinguish upsilon from the diphthong *oi*: in late Greek the two had the same pronunciation]

up·size *transitive & intransitive verb* increase in size.

up·slope *adverb* towards the higher end of a slope.

up·stage ● *adjective & adverb* **1** nearer the back of a theatre stage. **2** snobbish(ly). ● *transitive verb* **1** (of an actor) move upstage to make (another actor) face away from the audience. **2** divert attention from (a person) to oneself; outshine.

up·stairs ● *adverb* **1** to or on an upper floor. **2** to or in a more influential position or higher authority. **3** *informal* mentally, in the head (*doesn't have much upstairs*). ● *adjective* situated upstairs. ● *noun* an upper floor. □ **the Man Upstairs** *informal jocular* God.

up·stand·ing *adjective* **1** standing up. **2** honest or straightforward.

up·start ● *noun* a person who has risen suddenly to prominence, esp. one who behaves arrogantly. ● *adjective* **1** that is an upstart. **2** of or characteristic of an upstart.

up·state *US* ● *noun* part of a state remote from its large cities, esp. the northern part of New York State. ● *adjective* of or relating to this part. ● *adverb* in or to this part. □ **up·stater** *noun*

up·stream ● *adverb* against the flow of a stream etc. ● *adjective* moving upstream.

up·stroke *noun* a stroke made or written upwards.

up·surge *noun* **1** an upward surge; a rise (as in feelings etc.). **2** a rapid growth in number or size.

up·swept *adjective* **1** (of the hair) combed to the top of the head. **2** curved or sloped upwards.

up·swing *noun* an upward movement or trend.

upsy-daisy *interjection* (also **upsa·daisy**, **oopsy daisy**) expressing encouragement to a child who is being lifted or has fallen. [earlier *up-a-daisy*]

up·take *noun* **1** *informal* understanding; comprehension (*slow on the uptake*). **2** the act or an instance of taking up. **3** absorption or incorporation of something by a living system (*oxygen uptake*).

up·tempo *adjective & adverb* at a fast or an increased tempo.

up·thrust *noun* **1** upward thrust, e.g. of a fluid on an immersed body. **2** *Geol.* = UPHEAVAL 2.

up·tick *noun N Amer.* an increase, esp. a small one.

up·tight *adjective informal* **1** nervously tense or angry. **2** *N Amer.* rigidly conventional.

up·time *noun* time during which a machine, esp. a computer, is in operation.

up-to-date see DATE¹.

up-to-the-minute *adjective* (usu. *attributive*) latest; most modern.

up·town *N Amer.* ● *adjective* **1** of or in the upper or northward part of a city outside of downtown. **2** of or characteristic of an affluent area or people. ● *noun* **1** *Cdn* the central business district, esp. of a small town. **2** the upper or northward part of a city outside of downtown. ● *adverb* in or into the area designated as uptown. □ **up·town·er** *noun*

up·trend *noun* an upward tendency.

up·turn ● *noun* **1** an upward trend; an improvement. **2** an upheaval. ● *transitive verb* turn up or upside down.

UPU *abbreviation* Universal Postal Union.

up·ward ● *adverb* (also **up·wards**) towards what is higher, superior, larger in amount, more important, or earlier. ● *adjective* moving,

extending, pointing, or leading upward. □ **upwards of** more than (*found upwards of forty specimens*).

up·ward·ly *adverb* in an upward direction.

upwardly mobile *adjective* able or aspiring to advance socially or professionally.

upward mobility *noun* social or professional advancement.

up·well·ing *noun* **1** a welling upwards, esp. the rising of cold water from the bottom of the sea, often bringing with it a renewed source of nutrients. **2** the water that has risen in this way.

up·wind *adjective & adverb* against the direction of the wind.

Ur /ɜr/ an ancient Sumerian city formerly on the Euphrates, in S Iraq. It was one of the oldest cities of Mesopotamia, dating from the 4th millennium BC, and according to the Bible was Abraham's place of origin. Spectacular royal tombs and vast ziggurats dating from the period *c.*2600–2000 BC have been excavated there.

ur- /ʊr/ *combining form* (also **Ur-**) used in words denoting the earliest, original, or primitive stage of a historical or cultural episode, movement, development, or entity (*an ur-language predating all others*). [German]

ura·cil /ˈjʊrəsɪl/ *noun Biochem.* a pyrimidine derivative found in living tissue as a component base of RNA. Symbol: **U**. [UREA + ACETIC]

ur·aemia *Brit. var. of* UREMIA.

ur·aeus /jʊˈriːəs/ *noun* a representation of the sacred asp or snake, symbolizing supreme power, esp. worn on the headdresses of ancient Egyptian divinities and sovereigns. [modern Latin from Greek *ouraios*, representing the Egyptian word for 'cobra']

Ural-Altaic /ˌjʊrəlˈteɪɪk/ *adjective* of, relating to, or denoting a hypothetical language group formerly proposed to include both the Uralic and the Altaic languages.

Ural·ic /jʊˈralɪk/ ● *adjective* **1** of, relating to, or denoting a family of languages spoken from northern Scandinavia to western Siberia, comprising the Finno-Ugric and Samoyedic groups. **2** of or relating to the Ural Mountains or the surrounding areas. ● *noun* the Uralic languages collectively.

Ural Mountains /ˈjʊrəl/ (also **Urals**) a mountain range in N Russia, extending 1 600 km (1,000 miles) southward from the Arctic Ocean to the Aral Sea, in Kazakhstan, rising to 1 894 m (6,214 ft.) at Mount Narodnaya. It forms the boundary between Europe and Asia.

Ur·ania /jʊˈreɪniə/ *Gk & Rom. Myth* the Muse of astronomy. [Greek, = heavenly]

ur·an·ium /jʊˈreɪniəm/ *noun* a heavy radioactive metallic chemical element of the actinide series occurring naturally in pitchblende and other ores, which is capable of nuclear fission and therefore used as a source of nuclear energy. Symbol: **U**; at. no.: 92. □ **ur·an·ic** /-ˈranɪk/ *adjective* [modern Latin, from URANUS: compare *tellurium*]

urano-¹ /ˈjʊrəno/ *combining form* forming words with the sense 'pertaining to the sky or heavens'. [Greek *ouranos* heaven(s)]

urano-² /ˈjʊrəno/ *combining form* forming words with the sense 'containing, composed of, or having the structure of uranium'.

Ura·nus /jʊˈreɪnəs, ˈjʊrən-/ **1** *Gk Myth* a personification of heaven or the sky, the most ancient of the Greek gods and first ruler of the universe. He was overthrown and castrated by his son Cronus. **2** *Astronomy* the seventh planet from the sun in the solar system, orbiting between Jupiter and Neptune at an average distance of 2 870 million km from the sun; equatorial diameter 50 800 km. □ **Ur·an·ian** /jʊˈreɪniən/ *adjective*

urban *adjective* **1** of, living in, or situated in a town or city (*an urban population*) (opp. RURAL). **2** *N Amer.* designating music, or radio stations playing it, performed by black artists, esp. R & B, hip hop, reggae, soca, jazz, and gospel. [Latin *urbanus* from *urbs urbis* city]

Urban II /ˈɜrbən/ (born Odo) (*c.*1035–99), French ecclesiastic, pope 1088–99. He initiated the First Crusade at the Council of Clermont (1095), and continued the church reforms begun by Pope Gregory VII.

Urban VI /ˈɜrbən/ (born Bartolomeo Prignano) (*c.*1318–89), Italian ecclesiastic, pope 1378–89. His election as pope inaugurated the Great Schism in the Western Church (1378–1417).

ur·bane /ɜrˈbeɪn/ *adjective* elegant and refined in manner and style; courteous, sophisticated, suave. □ **ur·bane·ly** *adverb* [French *urbain* or Latin *urbanus*: see URBAN]

urban forest *noun* the trees and shrubbery found in a city.

urban guerrilla *noun* a terrorist operating in an urban area.

urban heat island *noun* = HEAT ISLAND.

ur·ban·ism *noun* **1** the development of an urban community;

urbanization. **2** the character or way of life of a city. **3** a study of the development or way of life of a city. □ **ur·ban·ist** *noun* (in sense 3).

ur·ban·ite *noun* a resident of a city.

ur·ban·ity /ɜrˈbanɪti/ *noun* (*pl.* **-ities**) **1** an urbane quality; refinement of manner. **2** the state, condition, or character of a city; urban life.

ur·ban·ize *transitive verb* (also esp. *Brit.* **-ise**) **1** make (a mainly rural area) urban. **2** destroy the rural quality of (a community). □ **ur·ban·iz·a·tion** *noun*

urban legend *noun* (also **urban myth**) an unverifiable, usu. apocryphal story, widely recounted as if true, which typically depicts outlandish or sensational happenings in a plausible contemporary setting.

urban municipality *noun* any incorporated city, town, village, resort village, summer village, or township.

urban planner *noun* a person who plans the construction, growth, and development of urban communities as a profession. □ **urban planning** *noun*

urban renewal *noun* the process of rejuvenating derelict or dilapidated districts of a city through slum clearance and redevelopment.

urban sprawl *noun* the uncontrolled expansion of urban areas.

urban village *noun* a small self-contained district or community within a city or town, with residential housing, shops, and services within walking distance.

ur·ceo·late /ˈɜrsiələt/ *adjective Bot.* having the shape of a pitcher, with a large body and small mouth. [Latin *urceolus* diminutive of *urceus* pitcher]

ur·chin *noun* **1** a poor, dirty, and ill-clothed child, esp. in an urban area. **2** = SEA URCHIN. **3** *archaic* **a** a hedgehog. **b** a goblin or elf. [Middle English *hirchon*, *urcheon* from Old Northern French *herichon*, Old French *heriçon*, ultimately from Latin (*h*)*ericius* hedgehog]

Urdu /ˈʊrduː/ *noun* an Indo-Aryan language closely related to Hindi with an admixture of Persian and Arabic words, now the official language of Pakistan and also used in India. [Persian (*zabān i*) *urdū* 'language of (the) camp' (because it developed as a lingua franca after the Muslim invasions between the occupying armies and the local people of the region around Delhi), *urdū* being from Turkic *ordū*: see HORDE]

-ure /ɜr/ *suffix* **1** forming nouns denoting action or process (*censure*; *closure*; *seizure*). **2** forming nouns denoting result (*creature*; *scripture*). **3** forming collective nouns (*legislature*; *nature*). **4** forming nouns denoting function (*judicature*; *ligature*). [from or after Old French *-ure* from Latin *-ura*]

urea /jʊˈriːə/ *noun* a soluble crystalline compound which is the main nitrogenous breakdown product of protein metabolism in mammals, is excreted in their urine, and is used esp. as a fertilizer, de-icing agent, and in the manufacture of synthetic resins. [modern Latin from French *urée* from Greek *ouron* urine]

urea formaldehyde *noun* a plastic, resin, or foam made by condensation of urea with formaldehyde, used esp. for insulation.

ur·emia /jʊˈriːmiə/ *noun* (*Brit.* **ur·aemia**) *Med.* a raised level in the blood of urea and other waste compounds that are normally eliminated by the kidneys. □ **ur·emic** (*Brit.* **ur·aemic**) *adjective* [Greek *ouron* urine + *haima* blood]

ur·eter /jʊˈriːtər/ *noun* either of two tubes which convey urine from the kidney to the bladder or cloaca. □ **ur·eter·al** *adjective* **ur·eter·ic** /ˌjʊrɪˈtɛrɪk/ *adjective* [French *uretère* or modern Latin *ureter* from Greek *ourētēr* from *oureō* urinate]

ur·eth·ane /ˈjʊrəˌθeɪn/ ● *noun* **1** = POLYURETHANE. **2** a crystalline amide, ethyl carbamate, formerly used as an anaesthetic. ● *transitive verb* coat with a polyurethane finish. [French *uréthane* (as UREA, ETHANE)]

ur·ethra /jʊˈriːθrə/ *noun* (*pl.* **ur·ethrae** /-riː/ or **ur·ethras**) the tube or canal through which urine is carried out of the body from the bladder, and which in the male also conveys semen. □ **ur·eth·ral** *adjective* **ur·eth·ritis** /-rɪˈθraɪtɪs/ *noun* [Late Latin from Greek *ourēthra* (as URETER)]

Urey /ˈjʊri/ **Har·old Clay·ton** (1893–1981), US chemist. He discovered deuterium in 1932 and developed a technique for obtaining heavy water; he also developed theories on the formation of the planets and of the possible synthesis of organic compounds in the earth's primitive atmosphere, and was awarded the Nobel Prize for chemistry in 1934.

Urga /ˈɜrgə/ the former name (until 1924) for ULAN BATOR.

urge ● *transitive verb* **1** (often foll. by *on*) drive, hasten, or impel with force or encouragement (*he urged the horses forward*; *she urged her teammates on*). **2** (often foll. by *to* + infin.) encourage or entreat earnestly or persistently; exhort (*we urged them to go*). **3** (often foll. by *on*, *upon*)

advocate (an action or argument etc.) pressingly or emphatically (to a person). **4** (often foll. by *that* + clause) advocate or recommend eagerly or insistently (*we urge caution*; *we urge that they should be cautious*). **5** present or state earnestly or insistently in argument, justification, or defence (*I must urge the seriousness of this problem*). ● *noun* a strong impulse, desire, or tendency. □ **ur·ging** *noun* [Latin *urgēre* press, drive]

ur·gency *noun* (*pl.* **-cies**) **1** the state, condition, or fact of being urgent. **2** a pressing or urgent need.

ur·gent *adjective* **1** demanding or requiring immediate action or attention; pressing (*an urgent need for help*). **2** expressing a need for prompt action or attention; insistent (*an urgent call for help*). □ **ur·gent·ly** *adverb*

-uria /ˈjʊriə/ *combining form* forming nouns denoting abnormal conditions of urine production, composition, etc., or disorders characterized by these (*dysuria*; *glycosuria*). [modern Latin from Greek *-ouria* (as URINE)]

Uriah /jʊˈraɪə/ (in the Bible) a Hittite officer in David's army, husband of Bathsheba, whom David caused to be killed in battle (2 Sam. 11).

uric /ˈjʊrɪk/ *adjective* of or relating to urine.

uric acid *noun* a crystalline acid, which is the end product of purine metabolism in primates and carnivores, is excreted in their urine, and is the main nitrogenous excretory product in birds, reptiles, and insects.

Uriel /ˈjʊriəl/ one of the four chief archangels in Jewish apocryphal writings.

urin·al /ˈjʊrənəl/ *noun* **1 a** a ceramic plumbing fixture for men to urinate into, usu. equipped with a flushing mechanism. **b** a washroom containing these. **2** any receptacle for urination, such as a chamber pot.

urin·aly·sis /ˌjʊrɪˈnalɪsɪs/ *noun* (*pl.* **urin·aly·ses** /-ˌsiːz/) the analysis of urine by physical, chemical, and microscopical means to test for the presence of disease or drugs etc.

urin·ary /ˈjʊrɪnˌɛri/ *adjective* **1** of or relating to urine. **2** affecting or occurring in the urinary system (*urinary diseases*).

urin·ate /ˈjʊrəˌneɪt/ *intransitive verb* discharge urine. □ **urin·a·tion** *noun*

urine /ˈjʊrɪn/ *noun* the pale yellow fluid containing waste products filtered from the blood by the kidneys, stored in the bladder, and discharged at intervals through the urethra. □ **urin·ous** *adjective* [Old French from Latin *urina*]

URL /ɜrl, uˌɑrˈel/ *noun Computing* the address used to specify the location of a website on the Internet. [acronym from *universal* (or *uniform*) *resource locator*]

urn *noun* **1** a large decorative vase or container with a rounded usu. egg-shaped body and a pedestal. **2** any usu. ornamental vessel, vase, or container used to store or bury the ashes of the cremated dead. **3** a large metal container with a tap, in which coffee or tea is made and kept hot. [Latin *urna*, related to *urceus* pitcher]

uro-¹ /ˈjʊroː/ *combining form* forming words with the sense 'pertaining to, present in, or derived from urine'. [Greek *ouron* urine]

uro-² /ˈjʊroː/ *combining form* forming words with the sense 'pertaining to or designating a posterior or caudal part, region, or process'. [Greek *oura* tail]

uro·genital /ˌjʊroːˈdʒɛnɪtəl/ *adjective* of, pertaining to, or affecting both the urinary and genital organs.

uro·ol·ogy /jʊˈrɒlədʒi/ *noun* the branch of medicine that deals with disorders of the kidney and urinary tract. □ **uro·logic·al** *adjective* **uro·logic·al** *adjective* **ur·ol·o·gist** *noun*

uro·pygium /ˌjʊroːˈpɪdʒiəm/ *noun* the rump of a bird, supporting the tail feathers. [medieval Latin from Greek *ouropugion*]

Ur·quhart /ˈɜrkɑrt/ **Jane** (b.1949), Canadian writer. Of her novels, *Away* (1993) won the Governor General's Award, and *The Stone Carvers* (2001) was a finalist for both the Governor General's Award and the Giller Prize.

Ursa Major /ˌɜrsə ˈmeɪdʒər/ *noun* = BIG DIPPER. [Latin, = greater bear]

Ursa Minor /ˌɜrsə ˈmaɪnər/ *noun* = LITTLE DIPPER. [Latin, = lesser bear]

ur·sine /ˈɜrsaɪn/ *adjective* of or like a bear. [Latin *ursinus* from *ursus* bear]

Ur·sula, St. /ˈɜrsjʊlə/ a legendary British saint and martyr, said to have been put to death with 11,000 virgins after being captured by Huns near Cologne while on a pilgrimage. The legend probably developed from an incident of the 4th c. or earlier.

Ur·su·line /ˈɜrsjʊˌlɪn, -laɪn/ ● *noun* a nun of an Augustinian order founded by St. Angela in 1535 for nursing the sick and teaching girls. ● *adjective* of or relating to this order. [St. URSULA, the founder's patron saint]

urti·caria /ˌɜːrtɪˈkeɪriə/ *noun Med.* = HIVES. [modern Latin from Latin *urtica* nettle, from *urere* burn]

Uru·guay /ˈjɜːrə,gweɪ, ˈjʊr-, ˈɜr-/ a country on the Atlantic coast of S America south of Brazil; pop. (est. 2002) 3,386,575; capital, Montevideo. □ **Uru·guay·an** /-ˈgweɪən/ *adjective & noun*

Uruk /ˈuːrʊk/ an ancient city in S Mesopotamia, to the northwest of Ur (known also by its Biblical name **Erech**). One of the greatest cities of Sumer, it was built in the 5th millennium BC and was the seat of the legendary hero Gilgamesh. Excavations have revealed ziggurats and temples dedicated to the sky god Anu.

Urum·qi /ʊˈrʊmtʃi/ (also **Urum·chi**) the capital of the Xinjiang autonomous region in NW China; pop. (est. 2002) 1,363,100. It was a major trading centre on the ancient caravan routes of central Asia, and developed during the 20th c. into the main industrial centre of the region. [Mongolian, lit. 'fine pasture']

urus /ˈjʊrəs/ *noun* = AUROCHS. [Latin from Germanic]

US *abbreviation* **1** United States. **2** Undersecretary. **3** unserviceable.

us *pronoun* **1** *objective case of* WE (*they saw us*). **2** *informal* = WE (*it's us again*). **3** *N Amer. informal* ourselves, to or for ourselves (*we've got to get us one of those!*). **4** *informal* = ME[1] (*give us a kiss*). [Old English *ūs* from Germanic]

USA *abbreviation* **1** United States of America. **2** United States Army.

usable *adjective* (also **use·able**) that can be used. □ **usabil·ity** *noun*

USAF *abbreviation* United States Air Force.

usage *noun* **1** the action or an instance of using something or of being used; employment, use. **2 a** habitual or customary practice, esp. as creating a right, obligation, or standard. **b** established or customary use of words, expressions, constructions, etc. in a language, esp. as opposed to what is prescribed. **3** a manner of using or treating; treatment (*damaged by rough usage*).

usance /ˈjuːzəns/ *noun* the time allowed by commercial usage or law for the payment of foreign bills of exchange.

USB *abbreviation* universal serial bus.

USD *abbreviation* US dollars.

USDA *abbreviation* United States Department of Agriculture.

use ● *transitive verb* **1 a** employ (something) for a particular purpose; (*can I use the phone?*; *use your discretion*). **b** employ or avail oneself of (something) regularly (*she uses the subway to get to work*). **2 a** (in *past*; foll. by *to* + infin.) did, was, or had in the past as a customary practice or continuous state (*I used to be a dancer*; *it didn't use to rain so often*). **b** (usu. in *passive*; foll. by *to*) familiar by habit; accustomed (*not used to hard work*). **3** exploit (a person or thing) for one's own ends (*he's just using you to make his girlfriend jealous*; *he used the bad weather as an excuse for not coming*). **4** treat (a person) in a specified manner (*they used him shamefully*). **5** *esp. N Amer.* take (drugs, alcohol, etc.) regularly. ● *noun* **1** the act of using or the state of being used; application to a purpose (*the use of force*). **2** the manner or mode of using, employing, or utilizing something (*she put it to good use*). **3** the right or power of using (*lost the use of my right arm*). **4** advantage, value, usefulness (*a flashlight would be of some use right now*). **5** need or occasion for employing something; necessity, demand, call (*would you have any use for this radio?*). **6** habitual, usual, or common practice (*long use has accustomed me to it*). **7** the characteristic ritual and liturgy of a church or diocese etc. **8** *Law hist.* the holding of land or property by one person for the sole benefit or profit of another. □ **could use** *informal* **1** would like to have; want. **2** would be in a position to benefit from; need. **have no use for 1** do not need. **2** dislike or be impatient with. **it's** (or **there's**) **no use** it would be pointless to; it will not help to (*there's no use trying to talk to her when she's like this*). **make use of 1** employ, apply. **2** benefit from. **use it or lose it 1** an opportunity etc., if not taken advantage of, may not be made available again. **2** something, e.g. a skill, may become lost or unusable through neglect. **use a person's name** quote a person as an authority or reference etc. **use up 1** consume completely, use all of. **2** find a use for (something remaining). **3** exhaust or wear out e.g. with overwork. [Old French *us*, *user*, ultimately from Latin *uti us-* use]

used *adjective* having been previously owned; second-hand.

use·ful *adjective* **1** that can be used for a practical purpose; beneficial. **2** of use or value to someone; helpful (*he's quite useful around the house*). **3** *informal* reasonably effective or successful (*Sara is their most useful player*). □ **make oneself useful** be helpful. □ **use·ful·ly** *adverb* **use·ful·ness** *noun*

use·less *adjective* **1** failing to fulfill the intended purpose or produce the desired results (*this knife is useless*). **2** serving no purpose (*useless information*). **3** *informal* incompetent, ineffectual (*I'm useless at swimming*). □ **use·less·ly** *adverb* **use·less·ness** *noun*

Use·net *noun* any of a number of services designed to help users access information on a network, usu. consisting of an index of newsgroups arranged according to subject matter.

user *noun* **1** a person using something. **2** a person or organization making use of a computer system. **3** *informal* a drug addict. **4** one who manipulates others for personal advantage. **5** *Law* the continued use, exercise, or enjoyment of a right; presumptive right arising from use (*right of user*).

user-defined *adjective Computing* that has been specified or varied by a user. □ **user-definable** *adjective*

user fee *noun* a small fee charged for a service, esp. an additional amount of money or tax charged for a service that is paid for or subsidized by the government.

user-friendly *adjective* **1** *Computing* (of a system, program, software, etc.) designed to make the user's task as easy as possible, esp. by offering onscreen instructions, prompts, and feedback. **2** *informal* or *jocular* easy to read, use, or understand. □ **user-friendli·ness** *noun*

user group *noun Computing* a newsgroup exchanging technical information, advice, and services.

user interface *noun Computing* the means of communication between a user and a system, referring esp. to the use of input/output devices with supporting software (compare GRAPHICAL USER INTERFACE).

user·name *noun* (also **user ID**) *Computing* an identification used in conjunction with a password by a person with access to a computer network.

user-pay *noun* esp. *Cdn* designating a program the costs of which are paid for by user fees.

USGS *abbreviation* United States Geological Survey.

ush·er ● *noun* **1** a person who shows people to their seats in a theatre, stadium, church, etc. **2** an attendant of the groom at a wedding, responsible for greeting guests at the church and showing them to their seats. **3** a doorkeeper at a court etc. **4** *Brit.* an officer walking before a person of rank. ● *transitive verb* **1** (usu. foll. by *into*) show or guide (a person) into a room, to a seat, etc. (*ushered us into the room*). **2** (foll. by *in*) be the forerunner of (an era, age, movement, etc.). **3** act as usher to. [Anglo-French *usser*, Old French *uissier*, var. of *huissier* from medieval Latin *ustiarius* for Latin *ostiarius* from *ostium* door]

usher·ette *noun* a woman who shows people to their seats, esp. in a theatre or stadium etc.

Usher of the Black Rod *noun Cdn* = BLACK ROD 1.

Üskü·dar /ˌuːskuˈdɑr/ a suburb of Istanbul, on the eastern side of the Bosporus where it joins the Sea of Marmara; pop. (2000) 495,118. During the Crimean War, when it was known as Scutari, Florence Nightingale set up a hospital in the British army barracks there.

USN *abbreviation* United States Navy.

Us·pa·llata Pass /ˌuːspəˈjɒtə/ a pass over the Andes near Santiago, Chile. The principal route across the Andes, it links Argentina with Chile. At its highest point stands a statue, 'Christ of the Andes', erected in 1904.

us·que·baugh /ˈʌskwɪˌbɒb/ *noun* esp. *Irish & Scot.* whisky. [Irish & Scots Gaelic *uisge beatha* water of life: compare WHISKY]

USS *abbreviation* United States Ship.

USSR *abbreviation hist.* Union of Soviet Socialist Republics.

Us·ta·ba·kan·skoe /ˌuːstabəˈkɒnskɔːjə/ the former name (until 1931) for ABAKAN.

Us·tashe /uːˈstɒʃi/ *plural noun* (also treated as *sing.*) (also **Us·tasha**, **Us·tashas**, **Us·tashi**) the members of a Croatian extreme nationalist movement that ruled Croatia with Nazi support after the German invasion and partition of Yugoslavia in 1941, massacring hundreds of thousands of Serbs, Jews, and members of the resistance movement before being forced to flee at the end of the war. [Serbo-Croat *Ustaše* rebels]

Us·ti·nov /ˈjuːstɪˌnɒf/ **Sir Peter (Alex·an·der)** (1921–2004), English actor, director, and dramatist, of Russian descent. He wrote and acted in a number of plays including *Romanoff and Juliet* (1956), and his films include *Spartacus* (1960) and *Death on the Nile* (1978); he was also well known as a mimic, raconteur, broadcaster, and novelist.

usu. *abbreviation* usually.

usual ● *adjective* such as commonly occurs, or is observed or done; customary, habitual, regular (*I woke up at my usual hour*; *they offer the usual services*; *more than the usual number of rainy days in March*). ● *noun informal* **1** (prec. by *the*) what is customary or habitual ('*What did you talk about?*' '*Oh, the usual.*'). **2** (prec. by *the*, *my*, etc.) the drink or meal a person habitually orders in a bar or restaurant. □ **as usual** as is or was commonly the case (*they were late,*

Consonants: b *but*   d *dog*   f *few*   g *get*   h *her*   j *yes*   k *cat*   l *leg*   m *man*   n *no*   p *pen*   r *red*   s *sit*

as usual). **than usual** than is or was customary or habitual (*I ate less than usual today*). □ **usu·al·ness** *noun* [Old French *usual*, *usuel* or Late Latin *usualis* (as USE)]

usu·al·ly *adverb* **1** as a rule; generally speaking; normally. **2** in a usual or customary manner.

usu·fruct /ˈjuːzuːˌfrʌkt, -zjuː-/ *noun* **1** (in Roman and Scots law) the right of enjoying the use and income from another's property without destroying, damaging, or diminishing the property. **2** (often foll. by *of*) enjoyment or profitable possession (*unrestricted usufruct of common lands*). □ **usu·fruc·tu·ary** /-ˈfrʌktʃuːeri/ *adjective & noun* [medieval Latin *usufructus* from Latin *usus* (*et*) *fructus* from *usus* USE + *fructus* FRUIT]

Usum·bura /ˌuːzəmˈbʊərə/ the former name (until 1962) for BUJUMBURA.

usur·er /ˈjuːzərər, ˈjuːʒ-/ *noun* a person who practises usury.

usur·ious /juːˈzɜːriəs, ˈjuːʒ-/ *adjective* **1** of, involving, or practising usury. **2** (of interest) taken or charged by usury; exorbitant, excessive. □ **usur·ious·ly** *adverb*

usurp /jʊˈsɜrp, -ˈzɜrp/ *transitive verb* **1** seize or assume (another's position or authority) by force. **2** take possession of (land etc.) unlawfully. □ **usurp·a·tion** *noun* **usurp·er** *noun* [Old French *usurper* from Latin *usurpare* seize for use]

usury /ˈjuːzəri, ˈjuːʒ-/ *noun* **1** the act or practice of lending money at interest, esp. at an exorbitant, excessive, or illegal rate. **2** interest on money lent at such a rate. [medieval Latin *usuria* from Latin *usura* (as USE)]

UT *abbreviation* Utah (in official postal use).

Utah /ˈjuːtɑː/ a state in the western US; pop. (2000) 2,233,169; capital, Salt Lake City. Mormons fleeing persecution arrived there in 1847; statehood was refused until these renounced polygamy—a dispute which led to the Utah War (1857–58). Utah became the 45th state of the US in 1896. □ **Utah·an** (also **Utahn**) /ˈjuːtɒən/ *adjective & noun*

UTC *abbreviation* CO-ORDINATED UNIVERSAL TIME.

Ute /juːt/ ● *noun* **1** a member of a Shoshone Aboriginal people inhabiting parts of Colorado, Utah, and New Mexico. **2** the language of this people. ● *adjective* of, pertaining to, or designating the Ute or their language. [Spanish *Yuta* an unidentified Aboriginal language]

ute /juːt/ *noun* Austral. & NZ *informal* a pickup truck. [abbreviation of 'utility truck']

uten·sil /juːˈtensəl/ *noun* a tool or implement for domestic use, esp. any of those objects found in a kitchen and used for eating or preparing food (*cooking utensils*). [Old French *utensile* from medieval Latin, neuter of Latin *utensilis* usable (as USE)]

uter·ine /ˈjuːtərˌɪn, -raɪn/ *adjective* **1** of or relating to the uterus. **2** born of the same mother but not the same father (*sister uterine*).

uter·us /ˈjuːtərəs/ *noun* (pl. **uter·us·es** or **uteri** /-ˌraɪ/) the womb. [Latin]

U Thant /ˈuː ˈθænt/ see THANT.

Uther Pendragon /ˌjuːθər penˈdræɡən, ˌuːθ-/ (in Arthurian legend) king of the Britons and father of Arthur.

UTI *abbreviation* urinary tract infection.

utili·dor /juːˈtɪlədɔr/ *noun* Cdn (*North*) an enclosed insulated conduit running above ground and carrying water, sewerage, and electricity between houses in settlements built on permafrost. [blend of UTILITY + CORRIDOR]

utili·tar·ian /ˌjuːtɪlɪˈteriən/ ● *adjective* **1** designed to be practically useful rather than attractive; functional. **2** of or pertaining to the doctrine of utilitarianism. ● *noun* an adherent of utilitarianism.

utili·tar·ian·ism /ˌjʊtɪlɪˈteriəˌnɪzəm/ *noun* the doctrine that an action is right in so far as it promotes happiness, and that the guiding principle of conduct should be to achieve the greatest benefit or happiness for the greatest number of people.

util·ity /juːˈtɪlɪti/ ● *noun* (pl. **-ies**) **1** the condition or quality of being useful or beneficial. **2** (usu. in *pl.*) a useful thing; a thing able to satisfy human needs. **3 a** (often in *pl.*) = PUBLIC UTILITY. **b** (in *pl.*) shares in a public utility. **c** (in *pl.*) electricity, natural gas, etc. as provided by a public utility. **4** *Computing* = UTILITY PROGRAM. ● *attributive adjective* **1** designating things made for utility; useful, functional rather than attractive (*utility furniture*). **2** *Baseball* designating a substitute player, esp. an infielder, who is capable of playing several different positions. **3** N Amer. designating the lowest grade of domestic meat, e.g. of an animal that is missing a part. [Old French *utilité* from Latin *utilitas -tatis* from *uti* use]

utility knife *noun* N Amer. any of a range of small all-purpose heavy-duty work knives with sharp replaceable, usu. retractable, blades.

utility pole *noun* N Amer. a pole used to carry wires above the ground; a telephone or hydro pole.

utility program *noun* *Computing* a program for carrying out a routine function.

utility room *noun* a room equipped with domestic appliances such as a freezer, washing machine and dryer, or water heater.

utility vehicle *noun* (also **utility truck**) **1** N Amer. = SPORT-UTILITY. **2** Austral. & NZ = PICKUP 1.

util·ize /ˈjuːtəˌlaɪz/ *transitive verb* (also esp. Brit. **-ise**) make use of; use effectively for a practical purpose. □ **util·iz·able** *adjective* **util·iz·a·tion** *noun* [French *utiliser* from Italian *utilizzare* from Latin *utilis* from *uti* 'use']

-ution /ˈuːʃən, ˈjuːʃən/ *suffix* forming nouns, = -ATION (*solution*). [French from Latin *-utio*]

ut·most ● *adjective* **1** greatest in amount or degree; most extreme, ultimate (*an issue of the utmost importance*). **2** furthest, most remote; outermost (*the utmost limits*). ● *noun* (prec. by *the*) **1** that which is greatest in degree, amount, or extent (*these shoes offer the utmost in durability*). **2** the extreme limit, the ultimate degree (*my patience was tested to the utmost*). **3** the greatest or best of one's ability or power (*we performed to our utmost*). □ **do one's utmost** do all that one can. [Old English *ūt(e)mest* (as OUT, -MOST)]

Uto-Aztec·an /ˌjuːtoːˈæztekən/ ● *noun* a language family of Central America and western N America. ● *adjective* of or pertaining to this language. [UTE + AZTEC + -AN]

uto·pia /juːˈtoːpiə/ *noun* (also **Utopia**) **1** an imaginary or hypothetical place or state of things considered to be perfect; a condition of social or political perfection. **2** an impossibly ideal scheme, esp. for social or political improvement. [modern Latin, lit. 'no place', from Greek *ou* not + *topos* place, title of a book (1516) by Thomas More]

uto·pian /juːˈtoːpiən/ (also **Utopian**) ● *adjective* **1** of, pertaining to, or characteristic of a utopia. **2** impossibly ideal or perfect; idealistic. ● *noun* an idealistic reformer. □ **uto·pian·ism** *noun*

Utrecht /ˈjuːtrekt/ a city in the central Netherlands, capital of a province of the same name; pop. (est. 2002) 232,800.

Utrecht, Peace of a series of treaties (1713–14) ending the War of the Spanish Succession. The terms granted the throne of Spain to Philip V of France, but forbade the union of the French and Spanish thrones; the succession of the House of Hanover to the British throne was secured and the former Spanish territories in Italy were ceded to the Hapsburgs. See also UTRECHT, TREATY OF.

Utrecht, Treaty of a treaty (1713) signed by Britain and France as part of the Peace of Utrecht ending the War of the Spanish Succession (see UTRECHT, PEACE OF). The treaty ended the North American phase of the war (see QUEEN ANNE'S WAR) by obliging France to cede the Hudson Bay drainage area, all claims to Newfoundland, as well as Port-Royal and much of Acadia to Britain, though France retained Cape Breton and Île Saint-Jean (Prince Edward Island).

utri·cle /ˈjuːtrɪkəl/ *noun* **1** any of various small cells or sacs found in animals and plants. **2** (also **utric·u·lus** /juːˈtrɪkjʊləs/; pl. **-li** /-laɪ/) the larger of the two divisions of the membranous labyrinth of the inner ear. □ **utric·u·lar** /juːˈtrɪkjʊlər/ *adjective* [French *utricule* or Latin *utriculus* diminutive of *uter* leather bag]

Utri·llo /uˈtriːoʊ/ **Mau·rice** (1883–1955), French painter. He painted street scenes of Paris, esp. of the Montmartre district.

Uttar·anch·al /ˈʊtərəntʃəl/ a state in northern India, formed in 2000 from the northern part of Uttar Pradesh; capital, Dehra Dun.

Uttar Pra·desh /ˌʊtər prəˈdeʃ/ a large state in N India, bordering on Tibet and Nepal; capital, Lucknow. The most populous state, it was formed in 1950 from the United Provinces of Agra and Oudh.

ut·ter¹ *attributive adjective* complete, total, absolute, unqualified (*utter misery; an utter fool*). □ **utter·ly** *adverb* [Old English *ūtera*, *ūttra*, comparative adj. from *ūt* OUT]

ut·ter² *transitive verb* **1** emit audibly (*uttered a startled cry*). **2** speak or say (words, a phrase, a prayer, etc.). **3** *Law* issue or circulate (a forged document, counterfeit money or cheques, etc.). □ **utter·er** *noun* [Middle Dutch *ūteren* make known, assimilated to UTTER¹]

utter·ance *noun* **1** the act or an instance of uttering. **2** a thing spoken. **3 a** the power of speaking. **b** a manner of speaking. **4** *Linguistics* an uninterrupted chain of spoken or written words not necessarily corresponding to a single or complete grammatical unit.

utter·most *adjective & noun* = UTMOST.

Utu·lei /ˈuːtuːleɪ/ the executive capital of American Samoa, pop. (1990) 930.

U-turn ● *noun* **1** an act of driving a vehicle in a U-shaped course in order to turn around and travel in the opposite direction. **2** a reversal of policy. ● *intransitive verb* perform a U-turn.

UV *abbreviation* **1** ultraviolet. **2** ultraviolet radiation (*UV levels*; *UV protection*).

UVA *abbreviation* ultraviolet radiation of relatively long wavelengths.

UVB *abbreviation* ultraviolet radiation of relatively short wavelengths.

UVC *abbreviation* ultraviolet radiation of very short wavelengths, which does not penetrate the earth's ozone layer.

uvea /ˈjuːvɪə/ *noun* a pigmented layer which is the middle vascular coat of the eye, composed of the choroid, iris, and ciliary body of the eye, lying beneath the outer layer. [medieval Latin from Latin *uva* grape]

UV Index *noun* an index used to represent the intensity of the sun's ultraviolet rays, ranging from 'low' (less than 4) to 'extreme' (more than 9), determined by weighting quantities of incoming UV radiation at different wavelengths according to how effective these are in reddening human skin.

uvula /ˈjuːvjʊlə/ *noun* (*pl.* **uvu·lae** /-ˌliː/) **1** a fleshy extension of the soft palate hanging above the throat. **2** a similar process in the bladder or cerebellum. [Late Latin, diminutive of Latin *uva* grape]

uvu·lar /ˈjuːvjʊlər/ ● *adjective* **1** of or relating to the uvula. **2** articulated with the back of the tongue and the uvula, as in *r* in French. ● *noun* a uvular consonant.

Ux·bridge a township in south central Ontario, about 70 km northeast of Toronto; pop. (2001) 17,377. [*Uxbridge* in Greater London, England]

ux·or·ial /ʌkˈzɔːrɪəl/ *adjective* of or relating to a wife.

ux·ori·cide /ʌkˈzɔːrəˌsaɪd/ *noun* **1** the act of killing one's wife. **2** a person who commits such an act. [Latin *uxor* wife + -CIDE]

ux·ori·ous /ʌkˈzɔːrɪəs/ *adjective* **1** greatly or excessively fond of one's wife; doting. **2** (of behaviour etc.) showing such fondness.
□ **ux·ori·ous·ness** *noun* [Latin *uxoriosus* from *uxor* wife]

Uz·bek /ˈʌzbek, ˈʊz-/ *noun* **1** a member of a Turkic people living mainly in Uzbekistan. **2** the language of this people. [Uzbek]

Uz·bek·istan /ʌzˌbekɪˈstan, ʊz-/ an independent republic in central Asia, lying south and southeast of the Aral Sea; pop. (est. 2002) 25,563,441; capital, Tashkent.

Uzi /ˈuːzi/ *noun* (in full **Uzi machine gun** or **Uzi machine pistol**) a type of submachine gun of Israeli design. [from *Uziel* Gal, the name of the Israeli army officer who designed it]

Vv

V¹ *noun* (also **v**) (*pl.* **Vs** or **V's**) **1** the twenty-second letter of the alphabet. **2** a V-shaped thing. **3** (as a Roman numeral) five.

V² *symbol* **1** *Chem.* the element vanadium. **2 a** volt(s). **b** voltage, potential difference. **3** volume.

v. *abbreviation* **1** verse. **2** verso. **3** versus. **4** very. **5** *vide.* **6** velocity.

V-1 *noun hist.* a type of German flying bomb used in the Second World War. [abbreviation of German *Vergeltungswaffe* reprisal weapon]

V-2 *noun hist.* a type of German rocket-powered missile used in the Second World War. [abbreviation of German *Vergeltungswaffe* reprisal weapon]

V6 *noun* (*pl.* **V6's**) **1** an engine with six cylinders forming a V shape. **2** a vehicle with such an engine.

V8 *noun* (*pl.* **V8's**) **1** an engine with eight cylinders forming a V shape. **2** a vehicle with such an engine.

VA *abbreviation* **1** US Veterans' Administration (*VA hospital*). **2** Vice Admiral. **3** Virginia (in official postal use). **4** Vicar Apostolic. **5** *Brit.* Order of Victoria and Albert.

Va. *abbreviation* Virginia.

Vaal River /vɒl/ a river of South Africa, the chief tributary of the Orange River, rising in the Drakensberg Mountains and flowing 1 200 km (750 miles) southwestward to the Orange River near Douglas, in Northern Cape. For much of its length it forms the border between North-West Province and Free State.

vac *noun informal* **1** a vacuum cleaner. **2** *Brit.* a vacation. [abbreviation]

va·cancy /'veikənsi/ *noun* (*pl.* **-cies**) **1** the state of being vacant or empty. **2** an available room in a hotel, apartment building, etc. **3** an unoccupied position; a job opening. **4** emptiness of mind; lack of intelligence. **5** *Mineralogy* a defect in a crystal lattice consisting of the absence of an atom or ion from a position where there should be one.

vacancy rate *noun* the percentage of rental properties that are vacant at a given time.

va·cant /'veikənt/ *adjective* **1** containing no objects; empty. **2** (of land, a building, etc.) uninhabited (*a vacant lot*). **3** (of a place, room, etc.) unoccupied; not in use (*a vacant seat*). **4** (of a post or position) available. **5** characterized by or exhibiting a lack of attention, intelligence, or thought (*a vacant stare*). □ **va·cant·ly** *adverb* [Old French *vacant* or Latin *vacare* (as VACATE)]

vacant possession *noun Brit.* the right of a purchaser to exclusive use of a property or premises upon completion of the sale.

va·cate /'veikeit, və'keit/ *transitive verb* **1** leave or cease to occupy (a house, room, etc.). **2** give up tenure of (a post etc.). **3** *Law* annul (a judgment or contract etc.). [Latin *vacare vacat-* be empty]

va·ca·tion /vei'keiʃən/ ● *noun* **1** *N Amer.* a period of several days or weeks spent away from work or school etc., used esp. for recreation and travel; a holiday. **2** *Brit.* the annual fixed period during which esp. universities and courts are closed. **3** the act of vacating a house or position etc. ● *intransitive verb N Amer.* take or spend a vacation. □ **va·ca·tion·er** *noun* **va·ca·tion·ist** *noun*

vacation farm *noun* (also **holiday farm**) a working farm on which people may spend a vacation.

vacation·land *noun N Amer.* an area that attracts or caters to tourists and vacationers.

vacation pay *noun Cdn* the wages which an employee is entitled, under federal law, to receive either as paid vacation, or in lieu of paid vacation, amounting to four per cent of the year's salary or six per cent for an employee who has worked for a single employer for six or more consecutive years.

vac·cin·ate /'vaksɪˌneit/ *transitive & intransitive verb* inoculate with a vaccine to procure immunity from a disease; immunize. □ **vac·cin·a·tion** *noun* **vac·cin·a·tor** *noun*

vac·cine /vak'siːn, 'vaksiːn/ *noun* **1** an antigenic preparation used to stimulate the production of antibodies and procure immunity from one or several diseases. **2** *hist.* the cowpox virus used in vaccination against smallpox. **3** *Computing* a program designed to protect a computer system from the effect of destructive software such as a virus. [Latin *vaccinus* from *vacca* cow]

vac·cinia /vak'sɪniə/ *noun Med.* = COWPOX. [modern Latin (as VACCINE)]

vacil·late /'vasɪˌleit/ *intransitive verb* **1** fluctuate in opinion or resolution; waver between different opinions, options, actions, etc. **2** sway unsteadily; waver. □ **vacil·lat·ing** *adjective* **vacil·la·tion** *noun* [Latin *vacillare vacillat-* sway]

vacua *pl. of* VACUUM.

vacu·ity /və'kjuːɪti/ *noun* (*pl.* **-ities**) **1 a** absolute emptiness. **b** an empty or vacant space; a void. **2 a** complete absence of ideas; vacancy of mind or thought. **b** an empty or inane thing.

vacu·ole /'vakjuˌɒl/ *noun Biol.* a small cavity or vesicle in organic tissue, esp. a tiny space within the cytoplasm of a cell containing air, fluid, food particles, etc. □ **vacu·ol·ar** *adjective* **vacu·ol·at·ed** *adjective* **vacu·ol·a·tion** *noun* [French, diminutive of Latin *vacuus* empty]

vacu·ous /'vakjuːəs/ *adjective* **1** unintelligent, expressionless (*a vacuous stare*). **2** lacking substance or content; meaningless (*a vacuous criticism*). **3** empty. **4** idle, indolent. □ **vacu·ous·ly** *adverb* **vacu·ous·ness** *noun* [Latin *vacuus* empty (as VACATE)]

vac·uum /'vakjuːm/ ● *noun* (*pl.* **vac·uums** or **vacua** /-jʊə/) **1** a space entirely devoid of matter. **2** a space or vessel from which the air has been completely or partly removed by a pump etc. **3 a** a place or situation etc., marked by an absence of the usual, former, or expected contents (*the vacuum created by the death of his wife*). **b** a place or situation etc. in which one is insulated from external influences; a state of isolation. **4** (*pl.* **vac·uums**) **a** a vacuum cleaner. **b** a device which cleans dirt off the floor and walls of a swimming pool by suction. **5** a decrease of pressure below the normal atmospheric value. ● *verb informal* **1** *transitive & intransitive* clean (a room, carpet, swimming pool, etc.) with a vacuum. **2** *transitive* remove (dust etc.) with or as if with a vacuum cleaner. [modern Latin, neuter of Latin *vacuus* empty]

vacuum brake *noun* an emergency brake system used esp. on trains, in which the brake is operated by negative pressure caused by the condensation of steam or the exhaustion of air.

vacuum cleaner *noun* an electrical appliance for removing dust from carpets, other flooring, soft furnishings, etc., by suction.

vacuum flask *noun Brit.* = THERMOS.

vacuum packed *adjective* **1** (esp. of food) sealed in an airtight package or container from which some or all of the air has been removed, usu. in order to preserve freshness. **2** (of a package or container etc.) hermetically sealed after the partial removal of air.

vacuum pump *noun* a pump for producing a vacuum.

vacuum tube *noun* a sealed glass tube containing a near-vacuum for the free passage of electric current, esp. one used as a thermionic valve.

VAD *abbreviation* **1** VOLUNTARY AID DETACHMENT. **2** a member of this.

vade mecum /ˌvadi'miːkəm, ˌveidi'meikəm/ *noun* **1** a handbook or

Vowels: a *cat* ɑ *arm* e *bed* ɜr *her* ɜː *deux* ə *ago* ɪ *sit* i *cosy* iː *feed* ɒ *hot* ɔ *pore* ɔː *no* ʌ *run* ʊ *put*

manual kept or carried with one for ready reference. **2** anything useful kept readily available for use. [French from modern Latin, = go with me]

VAdm *abbreviation Cdn* VICE ADMIRAL.

Vado·dara /vəˈdoːdərə/ (also known as **Bar·oda**) a city in the state of Gujarat, W India; pop. (2001) 1,306,000. It was the capital of the former state of Baroda.

Vaduz /vaˈduts/ the capital of Liechtenstein; pop. (est. 2002) 5,300.

vaga·bond /ˈvagəˌbɒnd/ ● *noun* **1** a person who roams or wanders from place to place with no settled habitation and no visible means of support; a tramp or hobo, esp. an idle or dishonest one. **2** *informal* a disreputable, idle, or worthless person; a rascal or scamp. ● *adjective* **1** roving, straying, or wandering. **2** resembling or pertaining to a homeless wanderer. □ **vaga·bond·age** *noun* [Old French *vagabond* or Latin *vagabundus* from *vagari* wander]

vagal /ˈveigəl/ *adjective* of, related to, or affecting the vagus nerve.

Vagan·ova /vəˈɡɒnəvə/ **Agrip·pina Jacov·levna** (1879–1951), Russian dancer and teacher. Russian ballet owes its great virtuosity to the teaching system she developed, synthesizing the most important schools and styles throughout the world, now also much used outside of Russia.

va·gary /ˈveigəri/ *noun* (pl. **-ies**) a capricious, outlandish, or eccentric act or notion; a caprice or whim (*the vagaries of Fortune*). □ **va·gari·ous** /vəˈɡeriəs/ *adjective* [Latin *vagari* wander]

vagi pl. of VAGUS.

va·gina /vəˈdʒainə/ *noun* (pl. **va·ginas** or **va·ginae** /-niː/) **1** the canal leading from the vulva to the cervix of the uterus in women and most female mammals. **2** a sheath formed around a stem by the base of a leaf. □ **vagin·al** /ˈvadʒənəl/ *adjective* **vagin·itis** /ˌvadʒiˈnaitis/ *noun* [Latin, = sheath, scabbard]

vagina den·tata /denˈteitə/ *noun Psych.* the motif or theme of a vagina equipped with teeth, which occurs in myth, folklore, and fantasy, and is said to symbolize fear of castration, the dangers of sexual intercourse, etc.

vagin·is·mus /ˌvadʒiˈnizməs/ *noun* a painful spasmodic contraction of the vagina in response to physical contact or pressure, esp. in sexual intercourse.

va·grant /ˈveigrənt/ ● *noun* **1** a person with no settled home or regular work. **2** a person who roams or wanders. ● *adjective* **1** characteristic of or relating to a vagrant or vagrancy. **2** wandering or roving (*a vagrant musician*). **3** *literary* random; occurring unpredictably (*vagrant inspiration; vagrant discoveries*). □ **va·gran·cy** *noun* [Anglo-French *vag(a)raunt*, perhaps alteration of Anglo-French *wakerant* etc. by assoc. with Latin *vagari* wander]

vague /veig/ *adjective* **1** (of a statement etc.) couched in general, indefinite, or imprecise terms; lacking in details or particulars (*gave a vague answer*). **2** (of an idea, notion, feeling, etc.) not definite, clear, or fully established; difficult to formulate. **3** lacking physical definiteness of form or outline; indistinctly seen or perceived. **4** (of a person or mind) imprecise; inexact in thought, expression, or understanding. □ **vague·ly** *adverb* **vague·ness** *noun* [French *vague* or Latin *vagus* wandering, uncertain]

vagus /ˈveigəs/ *noun* (pl. **vagi** /-gai/) *Anat.* either of the tenth pair of cranial nerves, which supply the upper digestive tract and the organs of the chest cavity and abdomen. [Latin: see VAGUE]

vail *verb archaic* **1** *transitive* lower (a weapon etc.) or remove (one's hat or crown etc.) as a sign of submission or respect. **2** *intransitive* yield, submit. [Middle English from obsolete *avale* from Old French *avaler* to lower, from *a val* down, from *val* VALE]

vain *adjective* **1** having an excessively high opinion of one's own appearance, abilities, worth, etc.; conceited. **2** useless, ineffectual, futile (*in the vain hope of dissuading them*). **3** empty, trivial, unsubstantial (*vain boasts*). □ **in vain** without success; ineffectually, uselessly (*it was in vain that we protested*). **take a person's name in vain** mention a person's name (formerly esp. that of God) casually or irreverently, such as when swearing. □ **vain·ly** *adverb* **vain·ness** *noun* [Old French from Latin *vanus* empty, without substance]

vain·glory *noun literary* boastfulness; extreme vanity. □ **vain·glor·i·ous** *adjective* **vain·glor·i·ous·ly** *adverb* **vain·glor·i·ous·ness** *noun* [Middle English, after Old French *vaine gloire*, Latin *vana gloria*]

vair *noun archaic* or *hist.* fur obtained from a variety of Russian red squirrel with grey back and white belly, used widely in the 13th and 14th c. for linings and trimmings. [Old French from Latin (as VARIOUS)]

Vaish·nava /ˈvaiʃnava/ *noun Hinduism* a devotee of Vishnu. [Sanskrit *vaiṣṇavá*]

Vais·ya /ˈvəisjə/ *noun* **1** the third of the four great Hindu castes, comprising the merchants and agriculturalists. **2** a member of this caste. [Sanskrit *vaiśya* peasant, labourer]

va·lance /ˈvalans, veil-/ *noun* a short ornamental curtain hung around a bedstead or above a window etc. in order to conceal the frame or supporting hardware. □ **va·lanced** *adjective* [Middle English, ultimately from Old French *avaler* descend: see VAIL]

Val-Bélair /valbeiˈler/ a former town in SE central Quebec, now part of the city of Québec; pop. (2001) 21,332. [blend of the names of two former communities: *Val-Saint-Michel* + *Bélair* (an informal name for the seigneury of Guillaume-Bonhomme)]

Val-d'Or /valˈdɔr/ a gold-mining city in NW central Quebec, about 450 km northwest of Montreal; pop. (2001) 31,430. [French, lit. 'valley of gold']

vale *noun archaic* or *literary* a valley. □ **vale of tears** *literary* the world or one's earthly existence regarded as a place of trouble or suffering. [Old French *val* from Latin *vallis, valles*]

val·edic·tion /ˌvaləˈdikʃən/ *noun* **1** the act or an instance of bidding farewell. **2** a statement or address etc. made upon bidding farewell. [Latin *valedicere valedict-* (from *vale* imperative of *valēre* be well or strong + *dicere* say), after *benediction*]

val·edic·tor·ian /ˌvalədikˈtɔriən/ *noun N Amer.* a person who gives a valedictory.

val·edic·tory /ˌvaləˈdiktəri/ ● *noun* (pl. **-ies**) **1** *N Amer.* a speech or address given by a student of a graduating class at a school or university as a part of the graduation exercises. **2** any statement or address made upon leaving or bidding farewell. ● *adjective* of, pertaining to, or performed as a valedictory (*valedictory address*).

va·lence /ˈveiləns/ *noun* (also *Brit.* **va·len·cy**) esp. *N Amer.* **1 a** the power or capacity of an atom or group to combine with or displace other atoms or groups in the formation of compounds, equivalent to the number of hydrogen atoms that it could combine with or displace. **b** the combining power of an antibody. **2** *Linguistics* the power of a verb to govern other elements in the same sentence, equivalent to the number of noun phrases with which it combines. [Late Latin *valentia* power, competence, from *valēre* be well or strong]

valence electron *noun* any of the electrons in the outermost shell of an atom involved in its forming a chemical bond with another.

Va·len·cia /vəˈlensiə/ **1** an autonomous region of E Spain, on the Mediterranean coast. It was formerly a Moorish kingdom (1021–1238). **2** its capital, a port on the Mediterranean coast; pop. (2001) 746,612. **3** a city in N Venezuela; pop. (1991) 1,457,200.

Valencia orange *noun* a variety of orange much grown in the southern US, with a sweet juicy flesh, few seeds, and thin, smooth peel. [VALENCIA]

Va·len·ciennes /vaˌlãsiˈen/ *noun* a variety of fine bobbin lace. [*Valenciennes* in NE France, where it was made in the 17th and 18th c.]

va·len·cy /ˈveilənsi/ *noun* (pl. **-cies**) *Brit.* = VALENCE.

Valentine, St. either of two early Italian saints (who may have been the same person) traditionally commemorated on 14 Feb.: a Roman priest martyred *c.*269, and a bishop of Terni martyred at Rome. St. Valentine was regarded as the patron of lovers, a tradition which may be connected with the old belief that birds pair on 14 Feb. or with the pagan fertility festival of Lupercalia (15 Feb.).

val·en·tine *noun* **1** a note, card, or gift, traditionally sent anonymously, given as a token of love or affection on Valentine's Day. **2** a person courted as a sweetheart on Valentine's Day. [St. VALENTINE]

Valentine's Day *noun* (in full **St. Valentine's Day**) 14 February, observed in honour of St. Valentine and celebrated with the courting of sweethearts and the exchange of valentines and other tokens of affection.

Val·en·tino /ˌvalənˈtiːnoː/ **Ru·dolph** (born Rodolfo Guglielmi di Valentina d'Antonguolla) (1895–1926), Italian-born US actor. He became a leading star of silent films in the 1920s, and became known as the 'Great Lover' playing the romantic hero in films such as *The Sheikh* (1921) and *Blood and Sand* (1922).

Val·era see DE VALERA.

Val·er·ian /vəˈliːriən/ (Latin name Publius Licinius Valerianus) (d.260), Roman emperor 253–60. He became emperor following the murder of Gallus (reigned 251–3), and appointed his son Gallienus as joint ruler; during his reign Valerian renewed the persecution of the Christians initiated by Decius.

val·er·ian /vəˈliːriən/ *noun* **1** any of various flowering plants of the family Valerianaceae, esp. the common valerian, *Valerian officinalis*, with pink or white flowers and a strong smell liked by cats. **2** a bitter-tasting drug derived from the rootstock of this plant, used as a sedative. [Old French *valeriane* from medieval Latin *valeriana (herba)*, apparently fem. of *Valerianus* of Valerius]

Val·éry /valer'iː/ **(Am·broise) Paul (Tous·saint Jules)** (1871– 1945), French poet, essayist, and critic. His poetry, influenced by symbolist poets such as Mallarmé and blending lyricism, rich imagery, and intellectual eloquence, includes *La Jeune parque* (1917) and *Le Cimetière marin* (1922).

valet /va'lei, 'va-/ ● *noun* **1** a male servant who attends to a gentleman's clothes, etc. **2** a hotel employee with similar duties for guests. **3** an attendant responsible for parking the cars of patrons of esp. a restaurant or hotel. **4** *N Amer.* a rack on which clothing may be hung. ● *intransitive verb* (**valeted, valet·ing**) work as a valet. [French, = Old French *valet, vaslet*, VARLET: related to VASSAL]

valet parking *noun* a service provided at a restaurant, club, or airport whereby an attendant parks and retrieves patrons' vehicles. □ **valet parker** *noun*

val·etu·din·ar·ian /ˌvalɪˌtjuːdɪˈneriən/ ● *noun* **1** a person who is chronically in poor health; an invalid. **2** a person who is obsessively or unduly concerned about his or her health. ● *adjective* **1** in poor health; infirm. **2** constantly or unduly concerned with one's health. [Latin *valetudinarius* in ill health, from *valetudo -dinis* health, from *valēre* be well]

val·gus /'valgəs/ *noun* a deformity involving the outward displacement of the foot or hand. [Latin, = knock-kneed]

Val·halla /val'halə/ *noun* **1** *Scand. Myth* the hall in which the souls of those who have died in battle feast with Odin for eternity. **2** *informal* or *jocular* a place or state of perfect bliss; paradise. [modern Latin from Old Norse *Valhöll* from *valr* the slain + *höll* HALL]

vali·ant /'valjənt/ *adjective* (of a person or conduct) brave, courageous, heroic. □ **vali·ant·ly** *adverb* [Anglo-French *valiaunt*, Old French *vaïlant*, ultimately from Latin *valēre* be strong]

valid *adjective* **1** (of an argument, assertion, objection, etc.) well-founded and defensible; sound. **2 a** executed with the proper formalities; legally binding and acceptable (*a valid contract*). **b** not having reached its expiry date (*this credit card is no longer valid*). **3** having legitimacy, authenticity, or authority (*valid information*). □ **valid·ity** *noun* **valid·ly** *adverb* [French *valide* or Latin *validus* strong (as VALIANT)]

valid·ate *transitive verb* **1** make or declare legally valid. **2** lend force or validity to. **3** demonstrate or support the truth or value of (*workshops are designed to validate children's own creativity*). **4** check or prove the validity or accuracy of (something) (*validate incoming data against authority files*). **5** (of a store, restaurant, etc.) stamp (a customer's parking ticket) so that they are entitled to free or discounted parking. □ **valid·a·tion** *noun*

val·ine /'valiːn, vei-/ *noun Biochem.* an amino acid that is an essential nutrient for vertebrates and a general constituent of proteins. [VAL(ERIAN) + -INE⁴]

val·ise /və'liːs/ *noun* a small piece of luggage similar to a suitcase or portmanteau. [French from Italian *valigia* corresponding to medieval Latin *valisia*, of unknown origin]

Val·ium /'valiəm/ *noun proprietary* the drug diazepam used as a tranquilizer and relaxant. [20th c.: origin uncertain]

Val·kyrie /'valkɪri, val'kiːri/ *noun Scand. Myth* each of Odin's twelve handmaidens who hovered over battlefields and conducted the fallen warriors of their choice to Valhalla. [Old Norse *Valkyrja*, lit. 'chooser of the slain' from *valr* the slain + (unrecorded) *kur-, kuz-* related to CHOOSE]

Valla·do·lid /ˌvalədə'liːd/ **1** a city in N Spain, capital of Castilla-León region; pop. (2001) 318,293. It was the principal residence of the kings of Castile in the 15th c. and capital of Spain until 1561. **2** the former name (until 1828) of MORELIA.

val·lecu·la /və'lekjolə/ *noun* (pl. **val·lecu·lae** /-ˌliː/) *Anat. & Bot.* a groove or furrow. [Late Latin, diminutive of Latin *vallis* valley]

Valle d'Aosta /ˌvalei dei'ɒstə/ a mountainous region in the northwest corner of Italy; capital, Aosta.

Val·let·ta /və'letə/ the capital and chief port of Malta; pop. (est. 2002) 7,000; urban harbour area pop. (est. 2002) 195,900.

val·ley *noun* (pl. **-leys**) **1 a** a low usu. elongated area more or less enclosed by hills and typically having a stream flowing through it. **b** the extensive tract of land drained by a single large river system. **2** any depression or hollow resembling or compared to this. **3** *Archit.* an internal angle formed by the junction of two sloping sides of a roof, or

by the slope of a roof and a wall. [Old French *valee*, ultimately from Latin *vallis, valles*: compare VALE]

Valley East a former town in north central Ontario, now part of Greater Sudbury; pop. (2001) 22,374. [with reference to the area's agricultural valley]

Valley·field = SALABERRY-DE-VALLEYFIELD.

Valley Forge the site on the Schuylkill River in Pennsylvania, about 32 km (20 miles) northwest of Philadelphia, where George Washington's Continental Army spent the bitterly cold winter of 1777– 78, during the American Revolution, in conditions of extreme hardship.

Valley girl *noun* esp. *US informal* or *derogatory* a fashionable and affluent teenage girl from the San Fernando Valley in S California, speaking a variety of slang characterized by the use of filler words such as *like* and *totally* and a limited group of adjectives expressing approval or disapproval.

val·lum *noun Rom. Hist.* a defensive wall or rampart of earth, sods, and stone. [Latin, collective noun from *vallus* stake]

Va·lois /'valwɒ/ **1** the French royal house from the accession of Philip VI, successor to the last Capetian king, in 1328 to the death of Henry III (1589), when the throne passed to the Bourbons. **2 Dame Nin·ette de**, see DE VALOIS.

valor *var. of* VALOUR.

valor·ize *transitive verb* (also esp. *Brit.* **-ise**) **1** raise or fix the price or value of (a commodity etc.) by artificial means, esp. by government intervention. **2** give validity to; make valid. □ **valor·iz·a·tion** *noun* [back-formation from *valorization* from French *valorisation* (as VALOUR)]

valour *noun* (also **valor**) personal courage, esp. in battle. □ **valor·ous** *adjective* [Old French from Late Latin *valor -oris* from *valēre* be strong]

Val·pa·raí·so /ˌvalpə'raizoː/ the principal port of Chile, in the centre of the country, near the capital, Santiago; pop. (est. 2002) 301,700.

Val·poli·cella /ˌvalpolɪ'tʃelə/ *noun* a red Italian wine made in the Valpolicella region NW of Verona.

valu·able ● *adjective* **1** of material or monetary value; precious. **2** of great use or benefit; having considerable importance or worth. ● *noun* (usu. in *pl.*) a valuable thing, esp. a small article of personal property such as jewellery. □ **valu·ably** *adverb*

valu·a·tion *noun* **1 a** an estimation of a thing's monetary value, esp. by a professional appraiser. **b** the estimated monetary value. **2** an appraisal of something with respect to excellence or merit. □ **valu·ate** *transitive verb* **valu·ator** *noun*

value ● *noun* **1** the worth, usefulness, or importance of a thing; relative merit or status according to the estimated utility of a thing. **2 a** the material or monetary worth of a thing; the amount of money, goods, etc., for which a thing can be exchanged or traded. **b** the monetary worth as estimated or appraised professionally; valuation. **3** the amount of a commodity, medium of exchange, etc., considered to be the equivalent of something (*the insurance company paid us full value for our lost property*). **4** the worth or quality of something compared to the price paid for it. **5** the ability of a thing to serve a specified purpose or cause a specified effect (*shock value; R-value*). **6** (in *pl.*) the principles or moral standards of a person or social group; the generally accepted or personally held judgment of what is valuable or important in life. **7** *Music* the length or duration of a sound signified by a note. **8 a** *Math.* the amount represented by an algebraic term or expression. **b** *Physics & Chem.* the numerical measure of a quantity or a number denoting magnitude on some conventional scale (*the value of gravity at the equator*). **9** (foll. by *of*) **a** the meaning (of a word etc.). **b** the quality of a spoken sound; the sound represented by a letter. **10** the relative rank or importance of a playing card, chess piece, etc., according to the rules of the game. **11** the relation of one part of a picture to others with respect to light and shade; the part being characterized by a particular tone. ● *transitive verb* (**val·ues, val·ued, valu·ing**) **1** (often in *passive*, foll. by *at*) estimate the value of; appraise (esp. professionally) (*their house is valued at $400,000*). **2** consider of worth or importance; have a high opinion of (*I value his friendship*). [Old French, fem. past participle of *valoir* be worth, from Latin *valēre*]

value added ● *noun* the amount by which the value of an article is increased at each stage of its production, exclusive of initial costs. ● *adjective* (**value-added**) **1** (of food, goods, etc.) having features or ingredients added to the basic line or model to justify an increase in price and thereby enhance the profit margin for the producer and retailer. **2** (of a company) offering specialized or extended services in a commercial area.

value-added tax *noun* a tax on the amount by which the value of an article has been increased at each stage of its production or distribution.

value chain *noun Business* the process by which a company acquires raw materials, converts them into goods or services, markets them, and then provides after-sale service.

value-free *adjective* free from criteria imposed by subjective values or standards.

value judgment *noun* an estimate of esp. moral or artistic merit based on personal opinion rather than facts.

value·less *adjective* having no value. □ **value·less·ness** *noun*

valu·er *noun Brit.* an appraiser.

value system *noun* the set of connected or interdependent values of a person or social group.

valve *noun* **1** a device for controlling the passage of air, steam, water, etc. through a pipe, esp. an automatic device allowing movement in one direction only. **2** *Anat. & Zool.* a membranous fold in a hollow organ or tubular structure of the circulatory system, digestive tract, etc. which automatically closes to prevent the reflux of blood or other contents. **3** *Music* a device for extending the range of pitch of a brass instrument by increasing or decreasing the effective length of the tube. **4** each of the two shells of an oyster, mussel, etc. **5** *Bot.* each of the segments into which a capsule or dry fruit dehisces. **6** *Brit.* = VACUUM TUBE. □ **valved** *adjective* (also in *combination*). **valve·less** *adjective* [Latin *valva* leaf of a folding door]

val·vul·ar *adjective* **1** esp. *Med.* of, relating to, or affecting a valve or valves, esp. the valves of the heart. **2** having the form or function of a valve. [modern Latin *valvula*, diminutive of Latin *valva*]

val·vul·itis /ˌvalvjʊˈlaɪtɪs/ *noun* inflammation of the valves of the heart.

vam·brace /ˈvambreɪs/ *noun hist.* a piece of armour for the forearm. [Old French *avant-bras* from *avant* before (see AVAUNT) + *bras* arm]

va·moose /vaˈmuːs/ *intransitive verb N Amer.* (often in *imperative*) *slang* leave, disappear, take off. [Spanish *vamos* let us go]

vamp¹ *noun* **1** the part of a boot or shoe covering the front of the foot. **2** *Music* a short simple introductory passage or accompaniment, sometimes improvised and usu. repeated several times until otherwise instructed. ● *transitive verb* **1** (often foll. by *up*) **a** compile or piece together out of old materials. **b** restore or repair. **2** *Music* play (a passage or accompaniment etc.) as a vamp (*the guitarist vamped the intro*). **3** put a new vamp on (a boot or shoe). [Middle English from Old French *avantpié* from *avant* before (see AVAUNT) + *pied* foot]

vamp² *informal* ● *noun* a woman who uses sexual attraction to exploit men. ● *verb* **1** *intransitive* behave as a vamp. **2** *transitive* act as a vamp towards (usu. a man). □ **vamp·ish** *adjective* **vampy** *adjective* [abbreviation of VAMPIRE]

vam·pire *noun* **1** a ghost or reanimated corpse supposed to leave its grave at night to suck the blood of sleeping people, often represented as a human figure with long pointed canine teeth. **2** a person who preys ruthlessly on others. □ **vam·piric** /vamˈpiːrɪk/ *adjective* [French *vampire* or German *Vampir* from Magyar *vampir* perhaps from Turkish *uber* witch]

vampire bat *noun* any of various tropical esp. S American bats of the family Desmodontidae, which have sharp incisors for piercing flesh and lap the blood of large mammals.

vam·pir·ism *noun* **1** belief in the existence of vampires. **2** the practices of a vampire.

Van, Lake /van/ a large salt lake in the mountains of E Turkey.

van¹ *noun* **1 a** any of a range of covered vehicles, usu. smaller than a truck, with space in the back for cargo and usu. enclosed with no side windows. **b** *N Amer.* a similar vehicle, larger than a car, for carrying passengers. **c** esp. *Brit.* = CARAVAN 2b. **2** *Brit.* a railway carriage for mail or luggage or for the use of the guard. [abbreviation of CARAVAN]

van² *noun* = VANGUARD.

van·ad·ium /vəˈneɪdiəm/ *noun Chem.* a hard grey metallic transition element occurring naturally in several ores, used in small quantities to strengthen some steels. Symbol: **V**; at. no.: 23. □ **van·ad·ate** /ˈvanəˌdeɪt/ *noun* [modern Latin from Old Norse *Vanadís* name of the Scandinavian goddess Freya + -IUM]

Van Allen /van ˈalən/ **James Al·fred** (b.1914), US physicist, who discovered the Van Allen belts surrounding the earth.

Van Allen belt *noun* each of two regions partly surrounding the earth at heights of several thousand kilometres, containing intense radiation and high-energy charged particles trapped by the earth's magnetic field. [J.A. VAN ALLEN]

Van·brugh /ˈvanbrə, vanˈbruː/ **Sir John** (1664–1726), English

dramatist and architect. As a dramatist he is known for the comedies *The Relapse* (1696) and *The Provok'd Wife* (1697); one of the chief exponents of English baroque architecture, his major works include Castle Howard in Yorkshire (1702) and Blenheim Palace in Oxfordshire (1705), both produced in collaboration with Hawksmoor.

Van Buren /van ˈbjʊrən/ **Mar·tin** (1782–1862), US Democratic politician, 8th president of the US 1837–41. His measure to place government funds, previously held in private banks, in an independent treasury caused many Democrats to join the Whig party.

vanco·mycin /ˌvankoˈmaɪsən/ *noun* a bacterial antibiotic used against resistant strains of streptococcus and staphylococcus. [*vanco-* (of unknown origin) + -MYCIN]

Van·cou·ver¹ a city and port in the southwest corner of mainland BC, about 50 km north of the border with Washington state; pop. (2001) 545,671 (urban agglomeration pop. 1,986,965). □ **Van·cou·ver·ite** *noun* [G. VANCOUVER²]

Van·cou·ver², **George** (1757–98), English navigator. After accompanying Captain James Cook on his second and third voyages, he took command of a naval expedition exploring the coasts of Australia, New Zealand, and Hawaii (1791–2); he later charted much of the west coast of N America between S Alaska and California.

Vancouver, Mount a peak (over 4 780 m) in the St. Elias Mountains, situated on the Yukon/Alaska border, southeast of Mount Logan. [G. VANCOUVER²]

Vancouver Island a large island off the Pacific coast of Canada, in southwestern BC. The provincial capital, Victoria, is situated at its southeasternmost tip. [G. VANCOUVER²]

Vancouver special *noun Cdn* (*BC*) a style of house common in Vancouver having a low-pitched roof, a brick lower storey including the bedrooms and a stucco upper storey with sliding glass doors from the living area opening onto a narrow, metal-railed balcony on the front of the house.

van·dal ● *noun* **1** a person who wilfully or maliciously destroys or damages property. **2** (**Vandal**) a member of a Germanic people that ravaged Gaul, Spain, N Africa, and Rome in the 4th–5th c., destroying many books and works of art. ● *adjective* of or relating to the Vandals. □ **Van·dal·ic** /vanˈdalɪk/ *adjective* (in sense 2 of *noun*). [Latin *Vandalus* from Germanic]

van·dal·ism *noun* wilful or malicious destruction of or damage to private or public property.

van·dal·ize *transitive verb* (also esp. *Brit.* **-ise**) destroy or damage wilfully or maliciously.

Van de Graaff generator /ˌvan də ˈɡraf/ *noun Electricity* a machine devised to generate electrostatic charge by means of an endless vertical belt collecting charge from a voltage source and transferring it to a large insulated metal dome, where a high voltage is produced. [R. J. *van de Graaff*, US physicist d.1967]

Van·der·bijl·park /ˈvandərbail,park/ a steel-manufacturing city in South Africa, in the province of Gauteng, south of Johannesburg; pop. (2002) 281,700 (with Vereeniging).

Van·der·bilt /ˈvandər,bilt/ **Cor·nel·ius** (1794–1877), US businessman and philanthropist. He amassed a fortune from shipping and railways.

van der Waals /van dər ˈwɒls/ **Jo·han·nes Did·er·ik** (1837–1923), Dutch physicist, who proposed the equation, which now bears his name, linking the pressure, volume, and temperature of a gas; he was awarded the Nobel Prize for physics in 1910.

van der Waals forces *plural noun Chem.* short-range attractive forces between uncharged molecules. [J.D. VAN DER WAALS]

Van Die·men's Land /van ˈdiːmənz/ the former name (until 1855) for TASMANIA.

Van Doos /van ˈduːz/ *plural noun Cdn informal* the Royal 22e Régiment (the Royal 22nd Regiment), a French-speaking Canadian infantry regiment. [corruption of French *vingt-deux* twenty-two]

Van Dyck /van ˈdɔik/ **Sir An·thony** (also **Van·dyke**) (1599–1641), Flemish painter. His portraits of members of the English court of Charles I, noted for their refinement of style and elegant composition, determined the course of portraiture in England for more than 200 years.

Van·dyke /vanˈdɔik/ ● *noun* **1** each of a series of large points forming a border on lace or cloth etc. **2** a cape or collar etc. with these. **3** = VANDYKE BEARD. ● *adjective* in the style of dress, esp. with pointed borders, common in portraits by Van Dyck. [Sir A. VAN DYCK, anglicized *Vandyke*]

Vandyke beard *noun* a neat pointed beard.

Vandyke brown ● *noun* a deep rich brown. ● *adjective* (hyphenated when *attributive*) of this colour.

vane *noun* **1** = WEATHER VANE. **2** a blade of a screw propeller or a windmill etc. **3** the sight of surveying instruments, a quadrant, etc. **4** the flat part of a bird's feather formed by the barbs. **5** a broad flat projecting surface designed to guide the motion of a projectile, e.g. an arrow. □ **vaned** *adjective* [Middle English, southern & western var. of obsolete *fane* from Old English *fana* banner, from Germanic]

Vän·ern, Lake /ˈveɪnɜrn/ a lake in SW Sweden, the largest lake in Sweden and the third largest in Europe.

Van Eyck /van ˈaik/ **Jan** (c.1370–1441), Flemish painter. His best-known works include the altarpiece *The Adoration of the Lamb* (known as the Ghent Altarpiece, 1432) in the church of St. Bavon in Ghent and the portrait *The Arnolfini Marriage* (1434).

vang *noun* Naut. each of two guy ropes running from the end of a gaff to the deck. [earlier *fang* = 'gripping device': Old English from Old Norse *fang* grasp, from Germanic]

Van Gogh /van ˈɡoː, -ɡɒx/ **Vin·cent Wil·lem** (1853–90), Dutch painter. A Post-Impressionist painter, he used bright colours for expressive or symbolic purposes, and broad, vigorous, swirling brush strokes; among his best-known works are several studies of sunflowers and *A Starry Night* (1889).

van·guard *noun* **1** the foremost part of an army or fleet advancing or ready to advance. **2** the leaders of a movement or of opinion etc. **3** the forefront of a movement, field of activity, etc. [earlier *vandgard*, *(a)vantgard*, from Old French *avan(t)garde* from *avant* before (see AVAUNT) + *garde* GUARD]

Van Horne, Sir Wil·liam Cor·nel·ius (1843–1915), American-born Canadian railway official. Appointed general manager of the CPR in 1882, he was responsible for the rapid completion of the line from Montreal to Port Moody. After becoming president of the CPR in 1888, he developed a telegraph service and the Empress line of steamships, and founded the CP Hotel chain, personally helping to design the Banff Springs and Château Frontenac.

Van·ier[1] /ˈvanjei/ a former city in E Ontario, completely surrounded by and now part of the city of Ottawa; pop. (1996) 17,632. **2** /vanˈjei/ a former town in SE central Quebec, completely surrounded by and now part of Quebec City; pop. (2001) 11,054. [Georges VANIER[2]]

Van·ier[2] /ˈvanjei/ **1 Georges(-Philéas)** (1888–1967), Canadian diplomat, Governor General 1959–67. During World War II he served (from 1943) as minister to all allied governments in exile in London; from 1944–53 he was ambassador to France. **2** his son **Jean** (b.1928), Canadian spiritual leader. In 1964 he established in France a home called L'Arche where handicapped people could live with him; similar homes are now found in Canada, the US, India, and other countries. Through his life, work, and writing, he expresses the concept that each person has a distinct value as a human being.

Vanier Cup *noun* Cdn a trophy awarded annually to the winner of the Canadian interuniversity football championship. [Georges VANIER[2]]

van·illa /vəˈnɪlə, -ˈnelə/ ● *noun* **1 a** any tropical climbing orchid of the genus *Vanilla*, esp. *V. planifolia*, with fragrant flowers. **b** (in full **vanilla bean**) the fruit of these. **2** a substance obtained from the vanilla bean or synthesized and used to flavour ice cream and other foods. ● *adjective* = PLAIN-VANILLA. [Spanish *vainilla* pod, diminutive of *vaina* sheath, pod, from Latin VAGINA]

vanilla sugar *noun* granulated white sugar flavoured with vanilla.

vanilla wafer *noun* N Amer. a plain, round, vanilla-flavoured cookie, usu. used to make cookie-crumb pie crusts.

van·il·lin /vəˈnɪlɪn/ *noun* a sweet-smelling crystalline aldehyde which is the chief essential constituent of vanilla.

Vanir /vɒˈniːr/ Scand. Myth a group of gods, often associated with fertility, assimilated into the AESIR after a war between the two.

van·ish *verb* **1** *intransitive* **a** disappear suddenly. **b** disappear gradually; fade away. **2** *intransitive* cease to exist. **3** *intransitive* go away. **4** *intransitive* Math. become zero. **5** *transitive* cause to disappear. [Old French *e(s)vaniss-* stem of *e(s)vanir* ultimately from Latin *evanescere* (as EX-[1], *vanus* empty)]

van·ish·ing point *noun* **1** the point at which receding parallel lines viewed in perspective appear to meet. **2** the state of complete disappearance of something.

van·itas /ˈvanɪtas/ *noun* a still-life painting of a 17th-century Dutch genre containing symbols of death or change as a reminder of their inevitability. [Latin, = 'vanity']

van·ity *noun* (pl. **-ities**) **1 a** conceit and desire for admiration of one's personal attainments or attractions. **b** excessive concern with one's physical appearance. **c** something about which one is vain. **2 a** futility or unsubstantiality (*the vanity of human achievement*). **b** an unreal thing. **3** ostentatious display. **4** a unit consisting of a sink set into a flat top with cupboards beneath, esp. in a bathroom. **5** N Amer. a dressing table. [Old French *vanité* from Latin *vanitas -tatis* (as VAIN)]

vanity plate *noun* (also **vanity licence plate**) N Amer. a vehicle licence plate bearing a distinctive or personalized combination of letters, numbers, or both.

vanity publisher *noun* (also **vanity press**) a publisher who publishes only at the author's expense. □ **vanity publishing** *noun*

van Ley·den see LUCAS VAN LEYDEN.

van·quish *transitive verb* literary conquer or overcome. □ **van·quish·er** *noun* [Old French *vencus* past participle and *venquis* past tense of *veintre*, from Latin *vincere*: assimilated to -ISH[1]]

Van·taa /ˈvantɑ/ a city in S Finland; pop. (est. 2001) 179,856.

van·tage *noun* **1** (also **vantage point**) a place affording a good view or prospect. **2** Brit. Tennis = ADVANTAGE 4. [Anglo-French from Old French *avantage* ADVANTAGE]

van't Hoff /vant ˈhɒf/ **Jaco·bus Hen·dri·cus** (1852–1911), Dutch chemist, who applied the laws of thermodynamics to chemical reactions, and in organic chemistry studied the spatial arrangements of groups attached to a carbon atom; he was awarded the first Nobel Prize for chemistry in 1901.

Vanu·atu /ˌvanuːˈatuː/ a country consisting of a group of islands in the SW Pacific; pop. (est. 2002) 196,178; capital, Vila. Formerly called the New Hebrides. □ **Vanu·atu·an** *adjective* & *noun*

vapid /ˈvapɪd/ *adjective* insipid; lacking interest; flat, dull (*vapid moralizing*). □ **vap·id·ity** *noun* (pl. **-ities**). **vap·id·ly** *adverb* [Latin *vapidus*]

vapor var. of VAPOUR.

vap·or·etto /vapəˈretɔ/ *noun* (pl. **vap·or·etti** or **-ettos**) (in Venice) a canal boat (originally a steamboat, now a motorboat) used for public transport. [Italian, = small steamboat, diminutive of *vapore* from Latin *vapor* 'steam']

vapor·ize *transitive* & *intransitive verb* (also esp. Brit. **-ise**) convert or be converted into vapour. □ **vapor·iz·a·tion** *noun*

vapor·iz·er *noun* a device that vaporizes substances, esp. for medicinal inhalation.

va·pour (also **vapor**) ● *noun* **1** moisture or another substance diffused or suspended in air, e.g. mist or smoke. **2** Physics a gaseous form of a normally liquid or solid substance (compare GAS 1). **3** a medicinal agent for inhaling. **4** (in pl.) archaic a state of depression or melancholy thought to be caused by exhalations of vapour from the stomach. ● *intransitive verb* **1** rise as vapour. **2** make idle boasts or empty talk. □ **vapor·ous** *adjective* **vapour·ing** *noun* [Old French *vapour* or Latin *vapor* steam, heat]

vapour barrier *noun* a thin layer of waterproof material, e.g. polyethylene film, used to protect insulation by blocking the passage of moisture from the interior space.

vapour lock *noun* **1** an interruption in the flow of a liquid through a fuel line or other pipe as a result of vaporization of the liquid. **2** US informal a sudden inability to perform to one's usual standards (*the president suffered from vapour lock in press conferences*).

vapour pressure *noun* the pressure of a vapour in contact with its liquid or solid form.

vapour trail *noun* = CONTRAIL.

vapour·ware *noun* (also **vapor·ware**) Computing slang software that as yet exists only in the plans or publicity material of its developers.

va·quero /vəˈkeroː/ *noun* (pl. **-queros**) N Amer. (esp. in Spanish-speaking areas) a cowherd or cattle driver. [Spanish, from *vaca* cow: compare Portuguese *vaqueiro*]

var. *abbreviation* **1** variety. **2** variant.

var·ac·tor /vəˈraktər/ *noun* a semiconductor diode with a capacitance dependent on the applied voltage. [*varying reactor*]

Var·an·asi /vəˈrɒnəsi/ (formerly **Ben·ares** /bəˈnɑriːz/) a city on the Ganges, in Uttar Pradesh, N India; pop. (2001) 1,100,700. It is a holy city and a place of pilgrimage for Hindus, who undergo ritual purification in the Ganges.

Var·an·gian /vəˈrandʒiən/ ● *noun* any of the Scandinavian rovers who penetrated into Russia in the 9th–10th c. AD, establishing the Rurik dynasty and reaching Constantinople. ● *adjective* of or relating to the Varangians. [medieval Latin *Varangus*, ultimately from Old Norse, = confederate]

Vara·thane *noun* proprietary a type of oil- or water-based polyurethane finish used esp. on wood.

var·ec /ˈverek/ *noun* **1** seaweed. **2** = KELP. [French *varec(h)* from Old Norse: related to WRECK]

Va·rennes /vaˈren/ a town in south central Quebec, situated on the south shore of the St. Lawrence, northeast of Montreal; pop. (2001) 19,653. [R. Gaultier de *Varennes*, former governor of Trois-Rivières d.1689]

var·eny·ky /vaˈrenəki, ˌverəˈniːki/ *plural noun N Amer.* dough dumplings stuffed with mashed potato, cheese, etc., boiled and then optionally fried, and usu. served with onions, sour cream, etc.; perogies. [Ukrainian]

Va·rèse /vaˈrez/ **Edgar(d)** (1883–1965), French-born US composer. His works, known for their use of dissonance and their experimentation with unusual sounds and instrument combinations, include *Ionisation* (1931), for percussion, piano, and two sirens, and *Poème électronique* (1958).

Var·gas /ˈvɑrɡəs/ **Getúlio Dor·nel·les** (1883–1954), Brazilian leader, president 1930–45 and 1951–4. He introduced fiscal, educational, electoral, and land reforms, but his regime was totalitarian and repressive, and he was overthrown in a coup in 1945. He returned to power in 1951, but his government was unpopular and he committed suicide after widespread calls for his resignation.

Var·gas Llosa /ˌvɑrɡəs ˈjoːsə/ **Jorge Mario Pedro** (b.1936), Peruvian novelist, dramatist, and essayist. His fiction often contains elements of myth and fantasy, and is frequently critical of the political situation in Peru; his novels include *The Time of the Hero* (1963), *Aunt Julia and the Scriptwriter* (1977), and *The War of the End of the World* (1982).

vari·able ● *adjective* **1 a** that can be varied or adapted (*a rod of variable length; the pressure is variable*). **b** (of a gear) designed to give varying speeds. **2** apt to vary; not constant; unsteady (*a variable mood; variable fortunes*). **3** *Math.* (of a quantity) indeterminate; able to assume different numerical values. **4** (of wind or currents) tending to change direction. **5** *Astronomy* (of a star) periodically varying in brightness. **6** *Bot. & Zool.* (of a species) including individuals or groups that depart from the type. **7** *Biol.* (of an organism or part of it) tending to change in structure or function. ● *noun* **1** a variable thing or quantity. **2** *Math.* **a** a variable quantity. **b** a symbol, such as *x*, *y*, or *z*, that represents this. **3** *Naut.* **a** a shifting wind. **b** (in *pl.*) the region between the NE and SE trade winds. □ **vari·abil·ity** *noun* **vari·ably** *adverb*

variable-geometry *adjective* denoting a swing-wing aircraft.

vari·ance *noun* **1** difference of opinion; dispute, disagreement; lack of harmony (*at variance among ourselves; a theory at variance with all known facts*). **2** *Law* a discrepancy between statements or documents. **3** *Statistics* a quantity equal to the square of the standard deviation. **4** *N Amer. Law* an official dispensation, esp. from a building regulation or zoning bylaw.

vari·ant ● *adjective* **1** differing in form or details from the main one (*a variant spelling*). **2** having different forms (*forty variant types of pigeon*). **3** variable or changing. ● *noun* a variant form, spelling, type, reading, etc.

vari·ate *noun Statistics* **1** a quantity having a numerical value for each member of a group. **2** a variable quantity, esp. one whose values occur according to a frequency distribution.

vari·a·tion *noun* **1** the act or an instance of varying. **2** departure from a former or normal condition, action, or amount, or from a standard or type (*prices are subject to variation*). **3** the extent of this. **4** a thing that varies from a type. **5** *Music* a repetition (usu. one of several) of a theme in a changed or elaborated form. **6** *Astronomy* a deviation of a heavenly body from its mean orbit or motion. **7** *Math.* a change in a function etc. due to small changes in the values of constants etc. **8** *Dance* a solo that is part of a full-length ballet, pas de deux, etc. □ **variations on a** (or **the**) **theme** different versions of one idea or thing (*his culinary skills amounted to variations on the theme of meat loaf*). □ **vari·a·tion·al** *adjective*

vari·cella /ˌverɪˈselə/ *noun Med.* **1** = CHICKEN POX. **2** (in full **vari·cella zos·ter**) a herpesvirus causing chicken pox and shingles. [modern Latin, irreg. diminutive of VARIOLA]

vari·ces *pl.* of VARIX.

vari·co·cele /ˈverɪkəˌsiːl/ *noun* a mass of varicose veins in the spermatic cord. [formed as VARIX + -CELE]

vari·col·oured *adjective* (also **vari·col·ored**) **1** variegated in colour. **2** of various or different colours. [Latin *varius* VARIOUS + COLOURED]

vari·cose *adjective* (esp. of the veins of the legs) affected by a condition causing them to become dilated and swollen. □ **vari·cosed** *adjective* **vari·cos·ity** /ˌverɪˈkɒsɪti/ *noun* [Latin *varicosus* from VARIX]

var·ied *adjective* showing variety; diverse.

varied thrush *noun* a thrush of western N America, *Ixoreus naevius*, with a dark grey back and bars on the reddish-orange breast and head, with reddish-orange bars on the wings.

varie·gate /ˈverəˌɡeit, -riəˌɡeit/ *transitive verb* **1** mark with irregular patches of different colours. **2** diversify in appearance, esp. in colour. □ **varie·ga·tion** *noun* [Latin *variegare variegat-* from *varius* various]

varie·gat·ed *adjective* **1** *Bot.* (of plants) having leaves containing two or more colours. **2** marked or characterized by variety or diversity.

var·iet·al /vəˈraiətəl/ ● *adjective* **1** esp. *Bot. & Zool.* of, forming, or designating a variety. **2** (of wine) made from a single designated variety of grape. ● *noun* a wine made from a single, designated variety of grape. □ **var·iet·al·ly** *adverb*

var·iety /vəˈraiəti/ *noun* (*pl.* **-ieties**) **1** diversity; absence of uniformity; many-sidedness; the condition of being various (*not enough variety in our lives*). **2** a quantity or collection of different things (*for a variety of reasons*). **3 a** a class of things different in some common qualities from the rest of a larger class to which they belong. **b** a specimen or member of such a class. **4** (foll. by *of*) a different form of a thing, quality, etc. **5** *Biol.* **a** a subspecies. **b** a cultivar. **c** an individual or group usually fertile within the species to which it belongs but differing from the species type in some qualities capable of perpetuation. **6** a mixed sequence of dances, songs, comedy acts, etc. (usu. *attributive*: *a variety show*). [French *variété* or Latin *varietas* (as VARIOUS)]

variety store *noun N Amer.* = CONVENIENCE STORE.

Vari·focal /ˌverɪˈfoʊkəl/ *proprietary* ● *adjective* having a focal length that can be varied, esp. of a lens that allows an infinite number of focusing distances for near, intermediate, and far vision. ● *noun* (in *pl.*) Varifocal eyeglasses.

vari·form *adjective* having various forms. [Latin *varius* + -FORM]

va·rio·la /vəˈraiələ/ *noun Med.* smallpox. [medieval Latin, = pustule, pock (as VARIOUS)]

vari·om·eter /ˌverɪˈɒmɪtər/ *noun* **1** a device for varying the inductance in an electric circuit. **2** a device for indicating an aircraft's rate of change of altitude.

vari·orum /ˌveriˈɔrəm/ ● *adjective* **1** (of an edition of a text) having notes by various editors or commentators. **2** (of an edition of an author's works) including variant readings. ● *noun* a variorum edition. [Latin from *editio cum notis variorum* edition with notes by various (commentators): genitive pl. of *varius* VARIOUS]

vari·ous *adjective* **1** different, diverse (*too various to form a group*). **2** more than one, several (*for various reasons*). **3** individual or separate (*the various members of the staff*). □ **vari·ous·ly** *adverb* **vari·ous·ness** *noun* [Latin *varius* changing, diverse]

var·is·tor /vəˈrɪstər/ *noun* a semiconductor diode with resistance dependent on the applied voltage. [*varying resistor*]

varix /ˈverɪks/ *noun* (*pl.* **vari·ces** /ˈverɪˌsiːz/) **1** *Med.* **a** a permanent abnormal dilation of a vein or artery. **b** a vein etc. dilated in this way. **2** each of the ridges across the whorls of a univalve shell. [Latin *varix* -*icis*]

var·let /ˈvɑrlət/ *noun archaic* **1** a rascal. **2** a servant or groom, esp. a knight's attendant. [Old French, var. of *vaslet*: see VALET]

Var·ley /ˈvɑrliː/ **Fred·erick Hors·man** (1881–1969), English-born Canadian painter. After emigrating to Canada in 1912, he worked as a commercial illustrator in Toronto and became friends with Tom Thomson and Frank Carmichael. In 1920 he became one of the founding members of the Group of Seven, though throughout his career he travelled more widely than the other members, and also painted more portraits.

var·mint *noun N Amer. informal jocular* **1** a destructive or undesirable wild animal. **2** a troublesome or objectionable person. [var. of *varmin*, VERMIN]

Varna a port and resort in E Bulgaria, on the west shores of the Black Sea; pop. (est. 2001) 314,539.

var·na *noun* each of the four Hindu castes. [Sanskrit, = colour, class]

var·nish ● *noun* **1** a resinous solution used to give a hard shiny transparent coating to wood, metal, paintings, etc. **2 a** any other preparation for a similar purpose. **b** *Brit.* = NAIL POLISH. **3** external appearance or display without an underlying reality. **4** artificial or natural glossiness. **5** a superficial polish of manner. ● *transitive verb* **1** apply varnish to. **2** gloss over (a fact). □ **var·nish·er** *noun* [Old French *vernis* from medieval Latin *veronix* fragrant resin, sandarac, or medieval Greek *berenikē* prob. from *Berenice* in NE Libya]

var·roa *noun* (also **varroa mite**) a microscopic mite, *Varroa jacobsoni*, which is a debilitating parasite of the honeybee, causing loss of honey production. [Marcus *Varro*, Roman scholar d.27 BC]

Consonants: b *but* d *dog* f *few* ɡ *get* h *her* j *yes* k *cat* l *leg* m *man* n *no* p *pen* r *red* s *sit*

var·si·ty *adjective* **1** designating sports played at the university or college level. **2** *N Amer.* designating the most advanced level of athletic competition in a high school etc. (*played on her school's varsity basketball team*). [shortening of UNIVERSITY, reflecting an archaic pronunciation]

Var·sol *noun Cdn proprietary* mineral spirits. [blend of *varnish*-maker's *solvent*]

Var·u·na /ˈvʌrʊnə/ *Hinduism* one of the oldest of the gods in the Rig-Veda. Originally the sovereign lord of the universe and guardian of cosmic law, he is known in later Hinduism as god of the waters.

varve *noun* annually deposited layers of clay and silt in a lake used to determine the chronology of glacial sediments. [Swedish *varv* layer]

vary *verb* (**-ies, -ied**) **1** *transitive* make different; modify, diversify (*seldom varies the routine; the style is not sufficiently varied*). **2** *intransitive* **a** undergo change; become or be different (*the temperature varies from 20° to 30°*). **b** be of different kinds (*her mood varies*). **3** *intransitive* (foll. by *as*) be in proportion to. □ **vary·ing** *adjective* **vary·ing·ly** *adverb* [Old French *varier* or Latin *variare* (as VARIOUS)]

varying hare *noun* = ARCTIC HARE.

vas /vas/ *noun* (*pl.* **vasa** /ˈveɪsə/) *Anat.* a vessel or duct. [Latin, = vessel]

Vas·ari /vəˈsɑːri/ **Gior·gio** (1511–74), Italian painter, architect, and biographer. He designed the Uffizi palace in Florence and painted the mannerist frescoes depicting the history of Florence and the Medici family in the Palazzo Vecchio. His book *Lives of the Most Excellent Painters, Sculptors and Architects* (1550, enlarged 1568) laid the basis for later art historical study in the West.

Vasco da Gama /ˈvaskoː/ see GAMA.

vas·cu·lar /ˈvaskjʊlər/ *adjective* of, made up of, or containing vessels for conveying blood or sap etc. (*vascular functions; vascular tissue*). □ **vas·cu·lar·ity** *noun* [modern Latin *vascularis* from Latin VASCULUM]

vascular bundle *noun Bot.* a strand of conducting vessels in the stem or leaves of a plant, usu. with phloem on the outside and xylem on the inside.

vas·cu·lar·ize /ˈvaskjʊlɜraɪz/ *transitive verb* (also esp. *Brit.* **-ise**) *Med.* & *Anat.* (usu. in *passive*) make vascular, develop (esp. blood) vessels in. □ **vas·cu·lar·iz·a·tion** *noun*

vascular plant *noun* a plant with conducting tissue.

vas·cu·litis /ˌvaskjuˈlaɪtɪs/ *noun Med.* inflammation of a blood vessel or blood vessels.

vas·cu·lum /ˈvaskjʊləm/ *noun* (*pl.* **vas·cu·la**) a botanist's (usu. metal) collecting case with a lengthwise opening. [Latin, diminutive of VAS]

vas def·er·ens /ˈdefəˌrenz/ *noun* (*pl.* **vasa def·er·en·tia** /ˌdefəˈrenʃiə/) *Anat.* the spermatic duct from the testicle to the urethra.

vase /vɒz, veiz, veis/ *noun* a vessel, usu. tall and cylindrical, used as an ornament or container, esp. for flowers. [French from Latin VAS]

vas·ec·tomy /vəˈsektəmi/ *noun* (*pl.* **-mies**) the surgical removal of part of each vas deferens esp. as a means of sterilization. □ **vas·ec·to·mize** *transitive verb* (also esp. *Brit.* **-mise**).

Vas·el·ine /ˈvasəˌliːn/ ● *noun proprietary* a type of petroleum jelly used as an ointment, lubricant, etc. ● *transitive verb* (**vaseline**) treat with Vaseline. [irreg. from German *Wasser* 'water' + Greek *elaion* oil]

vaso- /ˈveizo/ *combining form* a vessel, esp. a blood vessel (*vasoconstrictive*). [Latin *vas*: see VAS]

vaso·active /ˌveizoˈaktɪv/ *adjective* = VASOMOTOR.

vaso·con·stric·tion /ˌveizoːkənˈstrɪkʃən/ *noun* the constriction of blood vessels. □ **vaso·con·stric·ting** *adjective* **vaso·con·strict·ive** *adjective* **vaso·con·strict·or** *noun*

vaso·dila·tion /ˌveizoːdaiˈleiʃən/ *noun* (also **vaso·dila·ta·tion** /-dailei'teiʃən/) the dilatation of blood vessels. □ **vaso·dila·tor** *noun* **vaso·dila·tory** *adjective*

vaso·motor /ˈveizoːˌmoːtər/ *adjective* causing constriction or dilatation of blood vessels.

vaso·pres·sin /ˌveizoːˈpresɪn/ *noun* a pituitary hormone acting to reduce diuresis and increase blood pressure. *Also called* ANTIDIURETIC HORMONE.

vas·sal *noun* **1** *hist.* a holder of land by feudal tenure on conditions of homage and allegiance. **2** a humble dependant. □ **vas·sal·age** *noun* [Old French from medieval Latin *vassallus* retainer, of Celtic origin: the root *vassus* corresponding to Old Breton *uuas*, Welsh *gwas*, Irish *foss*: compare VAVASOUR]

vast ● *adjective* **1** immense, huge; very great (*a vast expanse of water; a vast crowd*). **2** *informal* great, considerable (*makes a vast difference*). ● *noun literary* a vast space (*the vast of heaven*). □ **vast·ly** *adverb* **vast·ness** *noun* [Latin *vastus* void, immense]

VAT /ˌviːˈeiˈtiː, vat/ *abbreviation* (in the UK) value-added tax.

vat ● *noun* **1** a large tank or other vessel, esp. for holding liquids or something in liquid in the process of brewing, tanning, dyeing, etc. **2** a dyeing liquor in which a textile is soaked to take up a colourless soluble dye afterwards coloured by oxidation in air. ● *transitive verb* (**vat·ted, vat·ting**) place or treat in a vat. [Middle English, southern & western var. of *fat*, Old English *fæt* from Germanic]

vatic /ˈvatɪk/ *adjective formal* prophetic or inspired. [Latin *vates* prophet]

Vati·can /ˈvatɪkən/ *noun* (prec. by *the*) **1** the palace and official residence of the Pope in Rome. **2** papal government. □ **Vati·can·ism** *noun* [French *Vatican* or Latin *Vaticanus* name of a hill in Rome]

Vatican City an independent papal state in the city of Rome, the seat of government of the Roman Catholic Church; pop. (est. 2002) 1,000. It covers an area of 44 hectares (109 acres) around St. Peter's Basilica and the palace of the Vatican, and is extended to some outlying buildings such as the pope's summer residence, Castel Gandolfo.

Vatican Council *noun* an ecumenical council of the Roman Catholic Church, esp. that held in 1869–70 or that held in 1962–5.

Vatican II *noun* the Second Vatican Council, held in 1962–65, which effected liturgical and organizational reforms in the Roman Catholic Church, promoted ecumenism, and emphasized the role of the laity.

vati·cin·ate /vaˈtɪsɪˌneɪt/ *transitive & intransitive verb formal* prophesy. □ **vati·cin·a·tion** *noun* [Latin *vaticinari* from *vates* prophet]

vatu /ˈvatuː/ *noun* (*pl.* same) the basic monetary unit of Vanuatu. [Bislama]

Vau·ban /voːˈbã/ **Sébas·tian Le Pres·tre de** (1633–1707), French marshal and military engineer, noted for his writings on siege warfare. His fortresses on France's frontiers were in large part responsible for maintaining Louis XIV's military might.

Vaud /voː/ a canton on the shores of Lake Geneva in W Switzerland; capital, Lausanne. It is noted for its wines.

vaude·ville /ˈvɒdvɪl, ˈvɒdəˌvɪl/ *noun* **1** a form of variety entertainment popular esp. in the US from about 1880 until the early 1930s, featuring a mixture of specialty acts such as burlesque comedy and song and dance. **2** a stage play on a trivial theme with interspersed songs (also *attributive*: *vaudeville act*). □ **vaude·vil·lian** *adjective & noun* [French, originally derived from convivial song esp. any of those composed by O. Basselin, 15th-c. poet born at *Vau de Vire* in Normandy]

Vau·dreuil /voːˈdrɜj/ **1 Phil·ippe de Ri·gaud de Vau·dreuil, Mar·quis de** (*c.*1643–1725), French soldier and colonial administrator. Appointed commander of the French troops in Canada in 1687, he was governor of Montreal 1698–1703 and governor of New France 1703–25. As governor he established a number of fur trading posts in Iroquois territory, and used an alliance with the Abenaki to hold back the spread of Massachusetts. **2** his son, **Pierre de Ri·gaud de Vau·dreuil de Ca·va·gnial, Mar·quis de** (1698–1778), French-Canadian soldier and colonial administrator. After serving as governor of Louisiana (1742–53), he was appointed the only Canadian-born Governor General of New France (1755–60). Responsible for overall military affairs during the Seven Years War, he disagreed with Montcalm over how to conduct the war; in the end he surrendered the colony to the English in 1760 in an attempt to protect the citizens from further suffering.

Vau·dreuil-Dorion /voːˌdrɜjˈdoriɔ̃/ a city in south central Quebec, southwest of Montreal; pop. (2001) 19,920. [VAUDREUIL + DORION]

Vaughan¹ /vɒn/ a city in south central Ontario, on the northwestern edge of Toronto; pop. (2001) 182,022. [B. *Vaughan*, British politician d.1835]

Vaughan² /vɒn/ **Sarah Lois ('Sassy')** (1924–90), US jazz singer and pianist. Originally associated with bebop, she performed as a soloist from 1945, and became internationally famous for her vocal range, her use of vibrato, and her improvising skills.

Vaughan Williams, **Ralph** (1872–1958), English composer. His works frequently reflect his interest in Tudor composers and English folk songs; among his most notable compositions are the *Fantasia on a Theme by Thomas Tallis* (1910), *A London Symphony* (1914), the Mass in G minor (1922), and numerous popular hymn tunes.

vault ● *noun* **1 a** an arched roof. **b** a continuous arch. **c** a set or series of arches whose joints radiate from a central point or line. **2** a vaultlike covering (*the vault of heaven*). **3** an underground chamber, esp. as a place of interment beneath a church or in a cemetery etc. (*family vault*). **4** a place of storage, esp. for valuables (*bank vault*). **5** an act of vaulting. **6** *Anat.* the arched roof of a cavity. ● *verb* **1** *intransitive* leap or spring, esp. while supporting oneself using one or both hands or with the help of a pole. **2** *transitive* spring over (a gate etc.) in this way. **3** *transitive* (esp. as **vault·ed**) **a** make in the form of a vault.

b provide with a vault or vaults. □ **vault·er** noun [Old French voute, vaute, ultimately from Latin volvere roll]

vault·ing ● noun **1** arched work in a vaulted roof or ceiling. **2** a gymnastic or athletic exercise in which participants vault over obstacles. ● adjective **1** excessively confident or presumptuous (vaulting ambition). **2** used to vault or in vaulting (a vaulting pole). □ **vault·ing·ly** adverb

vaulting horse noun a wooden block to be vaulted over by gymnasts.

vaunt literary ● verb **1** intransitive boast, brag. **2** transitive boast of; extol boastfully. ● noun a boast. [Anglo-French vaunter, Old French vanter from Late Latin vantare from Latin vanus VAIN]

vaunt·ed adjective highly praised, esp. to excess.

vava·sour /ˈvavəˌsʊr/ noun hist. a vassal owing allegiance to a great lord and having other vassals under him. [Old French vavas(s)our from medieval Latin vavassor, perhaps from vassus vassorum VASSAL of vassals]

va-va-voom adjective (also **va-va-va-voom**) (of a woman) having a particularly sexy body. [origin unknown]

Vavi·lov /ˈvavɪˌlɒf/ **Niko·lai Ivan·ovich** (1887–c.1943), Soviet plant geneticist. He did much to improve the yields of Soviet agriculture, and located the centres of origin of many cultivated plants; however, his views conflicted with official Soviet ideology (dominated by the theories of T. D. Lysenko) and he was arrested in 1940, dying later in a labour camp.

VC abbreviation **1** VICTORIA CROSS. **2** Vice-Chairman. **3** Vice-Chancellor. **4** Vice-Consul. **5** Viet Cong. **6** venture capital.

V-chip noun a device that, when installed in a TV set or receiver, can be programmed by the user to block or scramble any TV program that contains an undesirable level of violence, sex, or bad language (as indicated by a code inserted into the signal by the broadcaster). [VIEWER + (MICRO)CHIP; the v is now more usually interpreted as the initial letter of VIOLENCE]

VCR noun an electrical apparatus used in conjunction with a television for recording broadcast material onto videotape and for playing back videocassettes. [abbreviation of videocassette recorder]

VD abbreviation VENEREAL DISEASE.

VDT abbreviation VIDEO DISPLAY TERMINAL.

VDU abbreviation video (or visual) display unit (see VIDEO DISPLAY TERMINAL).

VE abbreviation Victory in Europe (in 1945).

've abbreviation (chiefly after pronouns) = HAVE (I've; they've).

veal noun **1** calf's flesh. **2** a calf raised for veal. [Old French veiaus veel from Latin vitellus diminutive of vitulus calf]

Veb·len /ˈvɛblən/ **Thor·stein Bunde** (1857–1929), US economist and social scientist. His book The Theory of the Leisure Class (1899) was a critique of capitalism in which he coined the phrase 'conspicuous consumption'; his other works include The Theory of Business Enterprise (1904).

vec·tor ● noun **1** Math. & Physics a quantity having direction as well as magnitude, esp. as determining the position of one point in space relative to another (radius vector). **2** (attributive) Computing denoting a type of graphical representation using lines to construct the outside of objects. **3** a course to be taken by an aircraft. **4** an organism, typically a biting insect or tick, that transmits a disease or parasite from one animal or plant to another. ● transitive verb **1** direct (an aircraft in flight) to a desired point. **2** change or alter the direction of (the thrust of a jet engine) in order to steer an aircraft etc. □ **vec·tor·ial** adjective **vec·tor·ize** transitive verb (also esp. Brit. **-ise**) (in sense 1 of noun). [Latin, = carrier, from vehere vect- convey]

Veda /ˈveɪdə, ˈviː-/ noun (in sing. or pl.) the most ancient Hindu scriptures, esp. four collections called Rig-Veda, Sāma-Veda, Yajur-Veda, and Atharva-Veda. [Sanskrit vēda, lit. (sacred) knowledge]

Ve·dan·ta /vɪˈdɑntə, veˈdɒn-/ noun **1** the Upanishads. **2** the Hindu philosophy based on these, esp. in its monistic form. □ **Ve·dan·tic** adjective **Ve·dan·tist** noun [Sanskrit vedānta (as VEDA, anta end)]

VE day noun 8 May, the day marking the Allied victory in Europe in 1945.

Vedda /ˈvedə/ noun a Sri Lankan aboriginal. [Sinhalese veddā hunter]

ved·ette /vəˈdet/ noun **1** a leading star of stage or screen. **2** a mounted sentry positioned beyond an army's outposts to observe the movements of the enemy. [French, = scout, from Italian vedetta, veletta from Spanish velar watch, from Latin vigilare]

Vedic /ˈveɪdɪk, ˈviː-/ ● adjective of or relating to the Veda or Vedas. ● noun the language of the Vedas, an older form of Sanskrit.

vee noun **1** the letter V. **2** a thing shaped like a V.

vee·jay noun informal = VJ.

vee·na /ˈviːnə/ noun an Indian stringed musical instrument with a fretted fingerboard and a gourd at either end. [Sanskrit & Hindi viṇā]

veep noun esp. N Amer. informal a vice-president. [from the initials VP]

veer¹ ● intransitive verb **1 a** change direction or course, esp. suddenly. **b** (of a conversation, or a person's behaviour or opinions) change suddenly. **2** (of the wind) change direction clockwise (compare BACK verb 5). **3** Naut. = WEAR² 2. ● noun a change of course or direction. [French virer from Romanic, perhaps alteration of Latin gyrare GYRATE]

veer² transitive verb Naut. slacken or let out (a rope, cable, etc.). [Middle Dutch vieren]

veery /ˈviːri/ noun a N American woodland thrush, Catharus fuscescens. [perhaps imitative]

veg¹ /vedʒ/ noun informal a vegetable or vegetables. [abbreviation]

veg² /vedʒ/ intransitive verb (**veg·ges**, **vegged**, **veg·ging**) esp. N Amer. (often foll. by out) relax in a mindless or passive manner. [abbreviation of VEGETATE]

Vega /ˈviːgə/ noun Astronomy a brilliant blue star, the brightest in the constellation Lyra and the fifth-brightest in the sky. [Spanish or medieval Latin Vega from Arabic, = the falling vulture]

Vega Car·pio /ˌveɪgə ˈkɑrpioʊ/ **Lope Felix de** (1562–1635), Spanish dramatist and poet. Regarded as the founder of Spanish drama, he is said to have written 1,500 plays, of which several hundred survive, covering a wide range of genres from the historical and sacred to contemporary plays of intrigue and chivalry.

veg·an /ˈviːgən, ˈveɪ-, ˈvedʒən/ ● noun a person who does not eat or use animal products. ● adjective using or containing no animal products. □ **vegan·ism** noun [contraction of VEGETARIAN]

Vegas = LAS VEGAS.

vege·table ● noun **1** any plant or edible fungus whose leaves, roots, tubers, fruit, seeds, or flowers are used for food, e.g. lettuce, potatoes, carrots, tomatoes, and mushrooms. **2** informal **a** a person who is incapable of normal intellectual activity, esp. through brain injury etc. **b** a person lacking in animation or living a monotonous life. ● adjective **1** of, derived from, relating to, or comprising plants or plant life, esp. as distinct from animal life or mineral substances. **2** of or relating to vegetables as food. **3 a** unresponsive to stimulus (vegetable behaviour). **b** uneventful, monotonous (a vegetable existence). [Old French vegetable or Late Latin vegetabilis animating (as VEGETATE)]

vegetable butter noun a vegetable fat with the consistency of butter.

vegetable ivory noun a hard white material obtained from the endosperm of the ivory nut.

vegetable oil noun an oil derived from plants, e.g. canola oil, olive oil, corn oil.

vegetable tallow noun a vegetable fat used as tallow.

vegetable wax noun an exudation of certain plants such as sumac.

vege·tal adjective **1** of or having the nature of plants (vegetal growth). **2** vegetative.

vege·tar·ian ● noun a person who abstains from animal food, esp. that from slaughtered animals, though often not eggs and dairy products. ● adjective **1** of or relating to vegetarians or vegetarianism. **2 a** containing no meat. **b** containing no animal products. □ **vege·tar·ian·ism** noun [irreg. from VEGETABLE + -ARIAN]

vege·tate verb **1** intransitive live an uneventful or monotonous life. **2** intransitive esp. N Amer. relax in a mindless or passive manner (went home and spent the evening vegetating). **3** transitive (usu. in passive) be covered or provided with vegetation or plant life (esp. of a specified kind). **4** intransitive grow as plants do; fulfill vegetal functions. [Latin vegetare animate, from vegetus from vegēre be active]

vege·ta·tion noun **1** plants collectively; plant life (luxuriant vegetation; no sign of vegetation). **2** the process of vegetating. □ **vege·ta·tion·al** adjective

vege·ta·tive adjective **1** of, relating to, or concerned with growth and development as distinct from reproduction. **2** of or relating to vegetation or plant life. **3** (of reproduction) asexual. **4** (of a person or way of life) dull, unthinking, or inactive. □ **vege·ta·tive·ly** adverb

veg·gie (also **vegie**) informal ● noun **1** esp. N Amer. a vegetable. **2** a vegetarian. ● adjective made of vegetables; vegetarian (veggie burger). [abbreviation]

Vegre·ville /ˈvegrəvɪl/ a town in east central Alberta, about 100 km east of Edmonton; pop. (2001) 5,376. It is the site of the Ukrainian Pysanka Festival and home to a giant pysanka monument. [Fr. V. Végréville, Oblate missionary d.1903]

Vowels: a cat ɑ arm e bed ɜr her ɜː deux ə ago ɪ sit i cosy iː feed ɒ hot ɔ pore ɔː no ʌ run ʊ put

vehe·ment /ˈviːəmənt/ *adjective* showing or caused by strong feeling; forceful, ardent (*a vehement protest; vehement desire*). □ **vehe·mence** *noun* **vehe·ment·ly** *adverb* [French *véhément* or Latin *vehemens -entis*, perhaps from *vemens* (unrecorded) deprived of mind, assoc. with *vehere* carry]

vehicle /ˈviːəkəl/ *noun* **1** any conveyance for transporting people, goods, etc., esp. on land. **2** a medium for thought, feeling, etc. **3** a liquid etc. as a medium for suspending pigments, drugs, etc. **4** a song, play, film, etc. that is intended or serves to display the leading actor or performer to the best advantage. **5** the literal meaning of a word or words used metaphorically. □ **ve·hicu·lar** /vɪˈhɪkjʊlər/ *adjective* [French *véhicule* or Latin *vehiculum* from *vehere* carry]

veil ● *noun* **1** a piece of fabric worn, esp. by women, over the head or face for concealment, to protect the face from the sun, dust, etc., or traditionally as part of a bride's attire. **2** a piece of fabric as part of a nun's headdress, resting on the head and shoulders. **3** a curtain, esp. that separating the sanctuary in the Jewish Temple. **4** something that conceals, covers, or disguises (*under the veil of friendship; a veil of mist*). **5** *Photog.* slight fogging. **6** = VELUM. ● *transitive verb* cover or conceal with or as if with a veil. □ **beyond the veil** in the unknown state of life after death. **draw a veil over** avoid discussing or calling attention to. **take the veil** become a nun. [Anglo-French *veil(e)* from Latin *vela* pl. of VELUM]

veiled *adjective* **1** (of a person) wearing a veil. **2** partially concealed or disguised (*veiled threats*).

veil·ing *noun* **1** light fabric used for veils etc. **2** a veil.

vein ● *noun* **1 a** any of the anatomical tubes by which blood is conveyed to the heart (*compare* ARTERY 1). **b** (in general use) any blood vessel (*has German blood in her veins*). **2** a nervure of an insect's wing. **3** a slender bundle of tissue forming a rib in the framework of a leaf. **4** a streak or stripe of a different colour in wood, marble, cheese, etc. **5** a fissure in rock filled with ore or other deposited material. **6** a source of a particular characteristic (*a rich vein of humour*). **7** a distinctive feature or quality (*a vein of humour in her work*). **8** a manner or style; a mood (*in a more serious vein*). ● *transitive verb* fill or cover with or as with veins. □ **veined** *adjective* **vein·like** *adjective* **veiny** *adjective* (**vein·i·er**, **vein·i·est**). [Old French *veine* from Latin *vena*]

vein·ing *noun* a pattern of streaks or veins.

ve·la·men /vɪˈleɪmən/ *noun* (*pl.* **ve·la·mi·na** /-mɪnə/) an enveloping membrane esp. of an aerial root of an orchid. [Latin from *velare* cover]

velar /ˈviːlər/ *adjective* **1** of a veil or velum. **2** *Phonetics* (of a sound) pronounced with the back of the tongue near the soft palate. [Latin *velaris* from *velum*: see VELUM]

Ve·láz·quez /vəˈlaskwez/ **Diego Rod·rí·guez de Silva y** (1599–1660), Spanish painter. After his appointment as court painter to Philip IV in 1623, he painted many notable portraits, in a natural and simple style; among the best-known are *Pope Innocent X* (1650) and *Las Meninas* (*c.*1656).

Vel·cro *proprietary* ● *noun* a fastener for clothes etc. consisting of two strips of nylon fabric, one looped and one burred, which adhere when pressed together. ● *transitive verb* fasten with Velcro. □ **Vel·croed** *adjective* [French *velours croché* hooked velvet]

veld /velt/ *noun* (also **veldt**) *South Africa* open country; grassland. [Afrikaans from Dutch, = FIELD]

veli·ger /ˈviːlɪdʒər/ *noun* *Zool.* the free-swimming larva of a mollusc, with a ciliated velum. [VELUM + Latin *-ger* 'bearing']

vel·leity /veˈliːɪti/ *noun* *formal* a wish or inclination not strong enough to lead to action (*you went on about how lovely it would be to escape the city, but it was just a velleity*). [medieval Latin *velleitas*, from *velle* 'to wish']

vel·lum *noun* **1 a** fine parchment originally from the skin of a calf. **b** a manuscript written on this. **2** smooth writing paper imitating vellum. [Old French *velin* (as VEAL)]

velo·cim·eter /ˌveləˈsɪmɪtər/ *noun* an instrument for measuring velocity.

vel·oci·pede /vəˈlɒsɪˌpiːd/ *noun* *hist.* **1** an early form of bicycle propelled by pressure from the rider's feet on the ground. **2** any early form of bicycle or tricycle. [French *vélocipède* from Latin *velox -ocis* swift + *pes pedis* foot]

vel·oci·rap·tor /vəˈlɒsɪˌraptər/ *noun* a small bipedal carnivorous dinosaur of the genus *Velociraptor*, of the Cretaceous period, with an enlarged curved claw on each hind foot. [modern Latin, from Latin *velox -ocis* 'swift' + RAPTOR]

vel·ocity /vəˈlɒsɪti/ *noun* (*pl.* **-ties**) **1** the measure of the rate of movement of a usu. inanimate object in a given direction. **2** speed in a given direction. **3** (in general use) speed. [French *vélocité* or Latin *velocitas* from *velox -ocis* swift]

velo·drome /ˈveləˌdrəʊm/ *noun* an arena with a usu. banked track for cycle racing. [French *vélodrome* from *vélo* bicycle (as VELOCITY, -DROME)]

velour /vəˈlʊr/ *noun* any of various fabrics with a velvet-like finish, used for clothing, upholstery, etc. [French *velours* velvet, from Old French *velour, velous* from Latin *villosus* hairy, from *villus*: see VELVET]

ve·lou·té /vəluˈteɪ/ *noun* a sauce made from chicken stock and cream thickened with a mixture of butter and flour. [French, = velvety]

velum /ˈviːləm/ *noun* (*pl.* **vela**) a membrane, membranous covering, or flap. [Latin, = sail, curtain, covering, veil]

vel·vet ● *noun* **1** a closely woven fabric of silk, cotton, etc., with a thick short pile on one side. **2** the furry skin on a deer's growing antler. **3** anything smooth and soft like velvet. ● *adjective* of, like, or soft as velvet. □ **vel·vet·ed** *adjective* **vel·vety** *adjective* [Old French *veluotte* from *velu* velvety, from medieval Latin *villutus* from Latin *villus* tuft, down]

vel·vet·een *noun* a cotton fabric with a pile like velvet but not as thick.

velvet glove *noun* outward gentleness, esp. cloaking firmness or strength (*compare* IRON FIST).

velvet·leaf *noun* a plant of the mallow family *Abutilon theophrasti*, with velvety heart-shaped leaves, naturalized in N America.

velvet revolution *noun* a non-violent political revolution, esp. the sequence of events in Czechoslovakia which led to the ending of Communist rule in late 1989.

Ven. *abbreviation* Venerable.

vena cava /ˌviːnə ˈkeɪvə/ *noun* (*pl.* **venae cavae** /-niː -viː/) each of usu. two veins carrying blood into the heart. [Latin, = hollow vein]

venal /ˈviːnəl/ *adjective* **1** (of a person) willing to act dishonestly or immorally, or to sacrifice principles, for money. **2** characterized by or associated with corruption or bribery. □ **ve·nal·ity** /-ˈnalɪti/ *noun* [Latin *venalis* from *venum* thing for sale]

ven·a·tion /vɪˈneɪʃən/ *noun* the arrangement of veins in a leaf or an insect's wing etc., or the system of venous blood vessels in an organism. [Latin *vena* vein]

vend *transitive verb* **1** offer (merchandise) for sale. **2** *Law* sell. □ **vend·ible** *adjective* [French *vendre* or Latin *vendere* sell]

vend·ee /venˈdiː/ *noun* *Law* the buying party in a sale, esp. of property.

ven·det·ta /venˈdetə/ *noun* **1** a blood feud in which the family of a murdered person seeks vengeance on the murderer or the murderer's family, orig. as prevalent in Corsica and Sicily. **2** a prolonged bitter quarrel. [Italian from Latin *vindicta*: see VINDICTIVE]

vending machine *noun* a coin-operated machine for the sale of small items, e.g. pop, snacks, etc.

Ven·dôme /vãˈdoːm/ **Louis Jo·seph de** (1654–1712), French soldier and marshal, who served as a commander during the War of the Spanish Succession.

vend·or *noun* **1** *Law* the seller in a sale, esp. of property. **2** a person who sells, esp. at an outdoor stand, in a stadium, etc. (*curbside hot dog vendors*). **3** = VENDING MACHINE.

ven·du /vãˈduː/ *noun* (*pl.* **ven·dus**) *Cdn derogatory* a Québécois who is viewed as having sold out or become assimilated to English-Canadian society. [French, lit. = 'sold']

ven·eer ● *noun* **1 a** a thin covering of fine wood or other surface material applied to a coarser wood. **b** a layer in plywood. **2** (often foll. by *of*) a deceptive outward appearance of a good quality etc. ● *transitive verb* **1** apply a veneer to (wood, furniture, etc.). **2** disguise (an unattractive character etc.) with a more attractive manner etc. [earlier *fineer* from German *furni(e)ren* from Old French *fournir* FURNISH]

vene·punc·ture *var. of* VENIPUNCTURE.

ven·er·able /ˈvenərəbəl/ *adjective* **1** entitled to veneration on account of character, age, associations, etc. (*a venerable priest; venerable relics*). **2** *Catholicism* as the title of a deceased person who has attained a certain degree of sanctity but has not been fully beatified or canonized. **3** as the title of an archdeacon in the Anglican Church. □ **ven·er·abil·ity** *noun* **ven·er·ably** *adverb*

ven·er·ate *transitive verb* **1** regard with deep respect. **2** revere on account of sanctity etc. □ **ven·er·a·tion** *noun* [Latin *venerari* adore, revere]

ve·nereal /vəˈniːriəl/ *adjective* **1** of or relating to sexual desire or intercourse. **2** relating to venereal disease. [Latin *venereus* from *venus veneris* sexual love]

venereal disease *noun* any of various diseases contracted chiefly by sexual intercourse with a person already infected. Abbr.: **VD**. *Also called* SEXUALLY TRANSMITTED DISEASE.

ven·ery[1] /'vɛnərɪ/ *noun archaic* sexual indulgence. [medieval Latin *veneria* (as VENEREAL)]

ven·ery[2] /'vɛnərɪ/ *noun archaic* hunting. [Old French *venerie* from *vener* to hunt, ultimately from Latin *venari*]

Ven·etia /vɛ'niːʃə/ (Italian **Ven·eto** /'vɛnetəʊ/) a region of NE Italy; capital, Venice.

Ven·etian /vɪ'niːʃən/ ● *noun* **1** a native or citizen of Venice. **2** the Italian dialect of Venice. **3** (**venetian**) = VENETIAN BLIND. ● *adjective* of Venice. [Old French *Venicien*, assimilated to medieval Latin *Venetianus* from *Venetia* Venice]

venetian blind *noun* a window blind consisting of a number of adjustable horizontal slats to control the light.

Venetian glass *noun* delicate glassware made at Murano near Venice.

Venetian red *noun* **1** a reddish pigment of ferric oxides. **2** a strong reddish brown.

Venetian window *noun* a window with three separate openings, the central one being arched and highest.

Vene·zuela /ˌvɛnə'zweɪlə/ a republic on the north coast of S America, with a coastline on the Caribbean Sea; pop. (est. 2002) 24,287,670; capital, Caracas. □ **Vene·zuelan** *adjective & noun*

ven·geance /'vɛndʒəns/ *noun* **1** punishment inflicted or retribution exacted for wrong to oneself or to a person etc. whose cause one supports. **2** the desire for revenge. □ **with a vengeance** in a higher degree than was expected or desired; in the fullest sense (*punctuality with a vengeance*). [Old French from *venger* avenge, from Latin (as VINDICATE)]

venge·ful *adjective* **1** vindictive; seeking vengeance. **2** characterized by or demonstrating a desire for revenge. □ **venge·ful·ly** *adverb* **venge·ful·ness** *noun* [obsolete *venge* avenge (as VENGEANCE)]

veni·al /'viːnɪəl/ *adjective* (of a sin or fault) pardonable, excusable; not mortal. □ **veni·al·ity** *noun* **veni·al·ly** *adverb* [Old French from Late Latin *venialis* from *venia* forgiveness]

Ven·ice a city in NE Italy, capital of Venetia region; pop. (est. 2001) 266,181. Situated on a lagoon of the Adriatic, it is built on numerous islands that are separated by canals and linked by bridges. It was a powerful republic in the Middle Ages and from the 13th to the 16th c. a leading sea power and important centre of art and music.

veni·punc·ture /'viːnəˌpʌŋktʃər/ *noun* (also **vene·punc·ture**) *Med.* the puncture of a vein esp. with a hypodermic needle to withdraw blood or for an intravenous injection. [Latin *vena* vein + PUNCTURE]

veni·son /'vɛnɪsən, -zən/ *noun* a deer's flesh as food. [Old French *veneso(u)n* from Latin *venatio -onis* hunting, from *venari* to hunt]

Ven·ite /vɪ'naɪtɪ/ *noun* **1** Psalm 95 used as a canticle. **2** a musical setting of this. [Latin, = 'come ye', its first word]

Venn diagram /vɛn/ *noun* a diagram of usu. circular areas representing mathematical sets, the areas intersecting where they have elements in common. [J. Venn, English logician d.1923]

ven·om /'vɛnəm/ *noun* **1** a poisonous fluid secreted by snakes, scorpions, etc., usu. transmitted by a bite or sting. **2** strong, bitter feeling or language; malice, spite. □ **ven·omed** *adjective* [Old French *venim*, var. of *venin* ultimately from Latin *venenum* poison]

ven·om·ous *adjective* **1 a** containing, secreting, or injecting venom. **b** (of a snake etc.) inflicting poisonous wounds by this means. **2** (of a person etc.) virulent, spiteful, malignant. □ **ven·om·ous·ly** *adverb*

ven·ous /'viːnəs/ *adjective* **1** of or full of veins. **2** (of blood) deoxygenated and of a dusky red colour (opp. ARTERIAL 1b). [Latin *vena* vein + -OUS]

vent[1] ● *noun* **1** (also **vent hole**) a hole or opening allowing motion of air etc. out of or into a confined space. **2** an outlet; free passage or play (*gave vent to their indignation*). **3** the anus esp. of a lower animal, serving for both excretion and reproduction. **4** an aperture or outlet through which volcanic products are discharged at the earth's surface. **5** a touch hole of a gun. **6** a flue of a chimney. ● *verb* **1** *transitive* **a** make a vent in (a cask etc.). **b** (often as **vented** *adjective*) provide (a machine, space, etc.) with a vent. **2 a** *transitive* give vent or free expression to (*vented my anger*). **b** *intransitive* release one's frustrations, esp. orally (*I'm a good listener when she needs to vent*). □ **vent one's spleen on** scold or ill-treat without cause. [partly French *vent* from Latin *ventus* wind, partly French *évent* from *éventer* expose to air, from Old French *esventer*, ultimately from Latin *ventus* wind]

vent[2] *noun* a slit in a garment, esp. in the lower edge of the back of a coat. [Old French *fente* slit, ultimately from Latin *findere* cleave]

venti·fact /'vɛntɪˌfakt/ *noun* a stone shaped by windblown sand. [Latin *ventus* wind + *factum* neuter past participle of *facere* make]

venti·late *transitive verb* **1 a** cause air to circulate freely in (a room etc.). **b** provide with a vent or vents. **c** (of wind etc.) blow upon or through so as to purify or freshen. **2** submit (a question, grievance, etc.) to public consideration and discussion. **3** *Med.* **a** oxygenate (the blood). **b** admit or force air into (the lungs). □ **venti·la·tion** *noun* [Latin *ventilare ventilat-* blow, winnow, from *ventus* wind]

venti·la·tor *noun* **1** an appliance or aperture for ventilating a room etc. **2** *Med.* = RESPIRATOR 2.

Ven·to·lin /'vɛntəlɪn/ *noun proprietary* a preparation of salbutamol. [perhaps from VENTILATE + -OL[1] + -IN]

ven·tral *adjective* **1** *Anat. & Zool.* of or on the abdomen (compare DORSAL 1). **2** *Bot.* of the front or lower surface. □ **ven·tral·ly** *adverb* [obsolete *venter* abdomen, from Latin *venter ventr-*]

ventral fin *noun* either of the ventrally placed fins on a fish.

ven·tricle *noun* **1** either of the two muscular lower chambers of the heart (in some animals, a single chamber), which pump the blood to the arteries and through the body. **2** each of four fluid-filled cavities in the brain, formed by enlargements of the central canal of the spinal cord. **3** the recess or space on each side of the larynx between the vestibular folds and the vocal cords. □ **ven·tri·cu·lar** /vɛn'trɪkjʊlər/ *adjective* [Latin *ventriculus* diminutive of *venter* belly]

ven·trilo·quism /vɛn'trɪləˌkwɪzəm/ *noun* (also **ven·trilo·quy** /vɛn'trɪləkwɪ/) the skill of speaking or uttering sounds so that they seem to come from the speaker's dummy or a source other than the speaker. □ **ven·trilo·quial** /ˌvɛntrɪ'ləʊkwɪəl/ *adjective* **ven·trilo·quist** *noun* **ven·trilo·quize** *intransitive verb* (also esp. *Brit.* **-quise**). [ultimately from Latin *ventriloquus* ventriloquist, from *venter* belly + *loqui* speak]

ventro- *combining form* the underside or abdomen. [from Latin *venter ventr-* belly]

ven·ture ● *noun* **1 a** an undertaking of a risk. **b** a risky enterprise. **2** a business enterprise involving risk. ● *verb* **1** *intransitive* dare; not be afraid (*did not venture to stop them*). **2** *intransitive* (usu. foll. by *out* etc.) dare to go somewhere dangerous or unpleasant. **3** *transitive* dare to put forward (an opinion, suggestion, etc.). **4 a** *transitive* expose to risk; stake (a bet etc.). **b** *intransitive* take risks. **5** *intransitive* (foll. by *on, upon*) dare to engage in etc. (*ventured on a longer journey*). □ **nothing ventured, nothing gained** one cannot expect to achieve anything without taking risks. [from ADVENTURE]

venture capital *noun* **1** money invested in a project in which there is a substantial element of risk, esp. money invested in a new venture or an expanding business in exchange for shares in the business. **2** (*attributive*) designating a company investing in such ventures.

venture capitalist *noun* a supplier of venture capital for investment.

ven·tur·er *noun* **1** *hist.* a person who undertakes or shares in a trading venture. **2** (**Venturer**) *Cdn* a member of a level (ages 14–17) in Scouting.

venture·some *adjective* **1** disposed to take risks. **2** risky.

Ven·turi /vɛn'tʃʊrɪ/ **Rob·ert (Charles)** (b.1925), US architect and writer. He reacted against the prevailing International Style of the 1960s and pioneered the development of postmodernist architecture; his writings include *Complexity and Contradiction in Architecture* (1966).

ven·turi /vɛn'tʃʊrɪ/ *noun* (*pl.* **ven·turis**) (in full **venturi tube**) a tube with a narrower middle section for measuring flow rate or exerting suction. [G. B. Venturi, Italian physicist d.1822]

venue /'vɛnjuː/ *noun* **1 a** an appointed site or meeting place, as for a sports event, meeting, concert, etc. **b** a building for such a meeting or event (*downtown's newest venue*). **2** *Law* **a** *hist.* the county or other place within which a jury must be gathered and a cause tried (originally the neighbourhood of the crime etc.). **b** the location of a trial. [French, = a coming, fem. past participle of *venir* come, from Latin *venire*]

ven·ule /'vɛnjuːl/ *noun Anat.* a small vein adjoining the capillaries. [Latin *venula* diminutive of *vena* vein]

Venus ▸ **1** *Rom. Myth* a goddess, identified with Aphrodite (the Greek goddess of love) in classical Rome though apparently a spirit of kitchen gardens in earlier times. **2** *literary* **a** a beautiful woman. **b** sexual love; amorous influences or desires. **3** *Astronomy* the second planet from the sun in the solar system, orbiting between Mercury and the earth at an average distance of 108 million km from the sun; the planet is almost equal in size to the earth, with a diameter of 12 104 km. □ **Venus·ian** /vɪ'njuːzɪən, -'nuː-/ *adjective & noun*

Venus flytrap *noun* a flesh-consuming plant, *Dionaea muscipula*, with leaves that close on insects etc.

Consonants: b *but*   d *dog*   f *few*   g *get*   h *her*   j *yes*   k *cat*   l *leg*   m *man*   n *no*   p *pen*   r *red*   s *sit*

ver·acious /vəˈreiʃəs/ *adjective formal* **1** speaking or disposed to speak the truth. **2** (of a statement etc.) true or meant to be true. [Latin *verax veracis* from *verus* true]

ver·acity /vəˈrasiti/ *noun* **1** truthfulness, honesty. **2** accuracy (of a statement etc.). [French *veracité* or medieval Latin *veracitas* (as VERACIOUS)]

Vera·cruz /ˌverəˈkruːz/ **1** a state of east central Mexico, with a long coastline on the Gulf of Mexico; capital, Jalapa Enriquez. **2** a city and port of Mexico, in Veracruz state, on the Gulf of Mexico; pop. (2000) 535,500.

ver·an·da /vəˈrandə/ *noun* (also **ver·an·dah**) **1** a usu. roofed porch or external gallery along one or more sides of a house, esp. the front. **2** *Austral. & NZ* a roof over a sidewalk in front of a shop. [Hindi *varandā* from Portuguese *varanda* railing, balustrade]

ve·rapa·mil /vəˈrapəmil/ *noun* a synthetic compound which acts as a calcium antagonist and is used to treat angina pectoris and cardiac arrhythmias. [from *v(al)er(onitr)il(e)* (from VALERIAN + NITRILE), with the insertion of *-apam-* (of unknown origin)]

verb *noun Grammar* a word used to indicate an action, state, or occurrence, and forming the main part of the predicate of a sentence, e.g. *hear, become, happen*. [Old French *verbe* or Latin *verbum* word, verb]

ver·bal ● *adjective* **1** of or concerned with words (*made a verbal distinction*). **2** oral, not written (*gave a verbal statement*). ¶ Some people reject this use of *verbal* as illogical, and prefer *oral*. However, *verbal* is the usual term in expressions such as *verbal communication*, *verbal contract*, and *verbal evidence*. **3** *Grammar* of or in the nature of a verb (*verbal inflections*). **4** literal (*a verbal translation*). **5** talkative, articulate. ● *noun Grammar* **1** a verbal noun. **2** a word or words functioning as a verb. □ **ver·bal·ly** *adverb* [French *verbal* or Late Latin *verbalis* (as VERB)]

verbal diarrhea *noun jocular* tendency to talk too much; extreme verbosity.

ver·bal·ism *noun* **1** a verbal expression, a word. **2** predominance of or concentration on the merely verbal over reality or meaning; minute attention to words. □ **ver·bal·ist** *noun*

ver·bal·ize *verb* (also esp. *Brit.* **-ise**) **1** *transitive* express in words. **2** *intransitive* be verbose. **3** *transitive* make (a noun etc.) into a verb. □ **ver·bal·iz·a·tion** *noun* **ver·bal·iz·er** *noun*

verbal noun *noun Grammar* a noun formed as an inflection of a verb and partly sharing its constructions, e.g. *smoking* in *smoking is forbidden*: see -ING[1].

ver·batim /vərˈbeitim/ *adverb & adjective* in exactly the same words; word for word (*copied it verbatim*; *a verbatim report*). [medieval Latin (adv.), from Latin *verbum* word]

ver·bena /vərˈbiːnə/ *noun* any plant of the genus *Verbena*, bearing clusters of fragrant flowers. [Latin, = sacred bough of olive etc., in medieval Latin, = vervain]

ver·bi·age /ˈvɜrbiədʒ/ *noun* needless accumulation of words; verbosity. [French from obsolete *verbeier* chatter, from *verbe* word: see VERB]

ver·bose /vərˈboːs/ *adjective* using or expressed in more words than are needed. □ **ver·bose·ly** *adverb* **ver·bos·ity** /-ˈbɒsiti/ *noun* [Latin *verbosus* from *verbum* word]

ver·boten /vərˈboːtən, ver-/ *adjective* forbidden, esp. by an authority. [German]

Ver·chères[1] /verˈʃer/ a municipality in south central Quebec, situated on the south shore of the St. Lawrence, northeast of Montreal; pop. (2001) 4,782. [F. Jarret de *Verchères*, regimental officer and first seigneur d.1700]

Ver·chères[2] /verˈʃer/ **Marie-Madeleine Jar·ret de** (1678–1747), French-Canadian heroine, noted for her defence in 1692 of the family fort from an Iroquois attack.

ver·dant /ˈvɜrdənt/ *adjective* **1** (of grass etc.) green, fresh-coloured. **2** (of a field etc.) covered with green grass etc. □ **ver·dan·cy** *noun* **ver·dant·ly** *adverb* [perhaps from Old French *verdeant* part. of *verdoier* be green, ultimately from Latin *viridis* green]

verd-antique /ˌvɜrdanˈtiːk/ *noun* **1** ornamental usu. green serpentine. **2** a green encrustation on ancient bronze. **3** green porphyry. [obsolete French, = antique green]

ver·derer /ˈvɜrdɜrər/ *noun Brit.* a judicial officer of royal forests. [Anglo-French (earlier *verder*), Old French *verdier*, ultimately from Latin *viridis* green]

Verdi /ˈverdi/ **Giu·seppe (For·tu·nino Fran·cesco)** (1813–1901), Italian composer. His many operas, including such standards as *Rigoletto* (1851), *La Traviata* (1853), and *Aida* (1871), are notable for strong characterization, original orchestration, and memorable tunes; he also wrote a Requiem (1874). □ **Verdi·an** *noun & adjective*

ver·dict *noun* **1** a decision on an issue of fact in a civil or criminal cause or an inquest. **2** a decision or an opinion given after testing, examining, or experiencing something. [Anglo-French *verdit*, Old French *voirdit* from *voir, veir* true, from Latin *verus* + *dit* from Latin DICTUM saying]

ver·di·gris /ˈvɜrdigris, -ˌgriːs/ *noun* a bright bluish-green incrustation formed on copper or brass by atmospheric oxidation, consisting of basic copper carbonate. [Old French *verte-gres, vert de Grece* green of Greece]

Ver·dun /vɜrˈdʌn/ a former city in south central Quebec, on the southeastern part of the Island of Montreal near Île des Soeurs, now part of the city of Montreal; pop. (2001) 60,564. [shortening of *Saverdun*, a village in S France, birthplace of Z. Dupuy, an early landowner in the area *c.*1662]

Verdun, Battle of /vɜrˈdʌn/ a long and severe battle of the First World War, fought in 1916 at the fortified town of Verdun in NE France. The French, initially unprepared, eventually repelled a prolonged German offensive but suffered heavy losses.

ver·dure /ˈvɜrdjər, -dʒər/ *noun* **1** green vegetation. **2** the greenness of this. [Old French from *verd* green, from Latin *viridis*]

Ver·eeni·ging /fəˈriːnəkiŋ, -ˈreinəxiŋ/ a city in South Africa, in the province of Gauteng; pop. (2002) 392,400 (with Vanderbijlpark).

Vereeniging, Treaty of the treaty which terminated the Second Boer War in 1902.

verge[1] ● *noun* **1** an edge or border. **2** an extreme limit beyond which something happens (*on the verge of tears*). **3** *Brit.* a grass edging of a road, flower bed, etc. **4** *Archit.* an edge of tiles projecting over a gable. **5** a wand or rod carried before a bishop, dean, etc., as an emblem of office. ● *intransitive verb* (foll. by *on*) border on; approach closely (*verging on the ridiculous*). [Old French from Latin *virga* 'rod']

verge[2] *intransitive verb* incline downwards or in a specified direction. [Latin *vergere* bend, incline]

ver·ger /ˈvɜrdʒər/ (also **vir·ger**) esp. *Anglicanism* **1** an official in a church who acts as caretaker and attendant. **2** an officer who bears the staff before a bishop etc. [Anglo-French (as VERGE[1])]

Ver·gil see VIRGIL.

ver·idi·cal /vəˈridikəl/ *adjective* **1** *formal* truthful. **2** *Psych.* (of visions etc.) coinciding with reality. □ **ver·idi·cal·ly** *adverb* [Latin *veridicus* from *verus* true + *dicere* say]

veri·est *adjective* (superlative of VERY) real, extreme (*the veriest fool knows that*).

veri·fi·ca·tion *noun* **1** the process or an instance of establishing the truth or validity of something. **2** *Philos.* the establishment of the validity of a proposition empirically. **3** the process of verifying procedures laid down in weapons agreements.

ver·ify *transitive verb* (**-fies, -fied**) **1** establish the truth or correctness of by examination or demonstration (*must verify the statement; verified my figures*). **2** (of an event etc.) bear out or fulfill (a prediction or promise). **3** *Law* append an affidavit to (pleadings); support (a statement) by testimony or proofs. □ **veri·fi·able** *adjective* **veri·fi·ably** *adverb* **veri·fi·er** *noun* [Old French *verifier* from medieval Latin *verificare* from *verus* true]

Veri·gin /ˈveriːgin/ **Peter Vasil·evich** (1859–1924), Russian-born religious leader. Exiled to Siberia after becoming the leader of the Doukhobors in 1886, he eventually followed more than 7,000 of his people to Canada in 1903. He developed an economically viable community in BC, but after his death the community fell into disarray.

ver·ily /ˈverili/ *adverb archaic* really, truly.

veri·sim·ili·tude /ˌverisiˈmilituːd, -ˌtjuːd/ *noun* **1** the appearance or semblance of being true or real. **2** a statement etc. that merely seems true. □ **veri·sim·ilar** /-ˈsimilər/ *adjective* [Latin *verisimilitudo* from *verisimilis* probable, from *veri* genitive of *verus* true + *similis* like]

ver·ism /ˈviːrizəm/ *noun* realism in literature or art. □ **ver·ist** *noun* **ver·is·tic** *adjective* [Latin *verus* or Italian *vero* true + -ISM]

ver·ismo /veˈrizmoː/ *noun* (esp. of opera) realism. [Italian (as VERISM)]

verit·able /ˈveritəbəl/ *adjective* real; rightly so called (*a veritable feast*). □ **verit·ably** *adverb* [Old French (as VERITY)]

véri·té /veriˈtei/ *noun* (esp. in combination) realism or naturalism in the arts, esp. in film (*cinéma-vérité; television vérité*). [French, = truth]

ver·ity /ˈveriti/ *noun* (pl. **-ities**) **1** a true statement, esp. one of fundamental import. **2** truth. [Old French *verité, verté* from Latin *veritatis* from *verus* true]

---

t *top*   v *voice*   w *we*   z *zoo*   ʃ *she*   ʒ *vision*   θ *thin*   ð *this*   ŋ *ring*   x *loch*   tʃ *chip*   dʒ *jar*   (*see over for vowels*)

ver·jus /ˈvɜːdʒuːs/ *noun* (also **ver·juice**) **1** an acidic juice obtained from crabapples, sour grapes, etc., and formerly used in cooking and medicine. **2** bitter feelings, thoughts, etc. [Old French *vertjus* from *vert* green + *jus* JUICE]

Ver·khne·udinsk /ˌverxnjeˈuːdɪnsk/ the former name (until 1934) for ULAN-UDE.

Ver·laine /verˈlen/ **Paul (Marie)** (1844–96), French lyric poet, a leading symbolist. His work, including *Poèmes saturniens* (1867), *Fêtes galantes* (1869), and *Romances sans paroles* (1874), is noted for its simplicity and musicality and uses the themes of eroticism and religious mysticism. He was influenced by Rimbaud and was for a time his lover, but the relationship ended when Verlaine shot and wounded Rimbaud.

Ver·meer /vɜːˈmiːr/ **Jan** (1632–75), Dutch painter. His domestic genre scenes, distinguished by their clear design and treatment of light, often depict a single figure engaged in an ordinary task, e.g. *The Kitchen Maid* (c.1658); his other works include a self-portrait, the *Allegory of Art* (c.1665).

ver·meil /ˈvɜːmeil, -mɪl/ ● *noun* **1** silver gilt. **2** an orange-red garnet. **3** *literary* vermilion. ● *adjective literary* vermilion. [Old French: see VERMILION]

vermi- /ˈvɜːmi/ *combining form* worm. [Latin *vermis* worm]

vermi·celli /ˌvɜːmɪˈtʃeli/ *noun* pasta made in long slender threads. [Italian, pl. of *vermicello* diminutive of *verme* from Latin *vermis* worm]

vermi·cide /ˈvɜːmɪˌsaɪd/ *noun* a substance that kills worms.

vermi·compost·ing /ˈvɜːmɪˌkɒmpəʊstɪŋ/ *noun* composting using earthworms to convert organic waste into fertilizer. □ **vermi·compost·er** *noun*

ver·micu·lar /vɜːˈmɪkjʊlər/ *adjective* **1** like a worm in form or movement; vermiform. **2** *Med.* of or caused by intestinal worms. **3** marked with close wavy lines. [medieval Latin *vermicularis* from Latin *vermiculus* diminutive of *vermis* worm]

ver·micu·late /vɜːˈmɪkjʊlət/ *adjective* (also **ver·micu·lat·ed** /-ˌleɪtəd/) **1** = VERMICULAR. **2** worm-eaten. □ **ver·micu·la·tion** *noun* [Latin *vermiculatus* past participle of *vermiculari* be full of worms (as VERMICULAR)]

ver·micu·lite /vɜːˈmɪkjʊlaɪt/ *noun* **1** a hydrated silicate resulting from the alteration of mica etc., esp. an aluminosilicate of magnesium. **2** this material in flakes used as a medium for growing plants, for insulation, etc. [as VERMICULATE + -ITE[1]]

vermi·culture /ˈvɜːmɪˌkʌltʃər/ *noun* the cultivation of earthworms, esp. in vermicomposting.

vermi·form /ˈvɜːmɪˌfɔːrm/ *adjective* worm-shaped.

vermiform appendix *noun see* APPENDIX 1.

vermi·fuge /ˈvɜːmɪˌfjuːdʒ/ ● *adjective* that expels intestinal worms. ● *noun* a drug that does this.

ver·mil·ion /vɜːˈmɪljən/ ● *noun* **1** cinnabar. **2 a** a brilliant red pigment made by grinding this or artificially. **b** the colour of this. ● *adjective* of this colour. [Old French *vermeillon* from *vermeil* from Latin *vermiculus* diminutive of *vermis* worm]

Vermilion Pass a pass through the Rocky Mountains, over 1 600 m high, situated on the BC–Alberta border, west of Banff. [see VERMILION RIVER]

Vermilion River a river on the BC–Alberta border, which rises in the Rocky Mountains near Banff and flows 70 km southward to drain into the Kootenay River. [so called with reference to the presence of the red, yellow and orange ochre beds of nearby mineral springs]

ver·min /ˈvɜːmɪn/ *noun* (usu. treated as *pl.*) **1** mammals and birds injurious to game, crops, etc., e.g. rodents and noxious insects. **2** parasitic worms or insects. **3 a** vile or contemptible persons. **b** a person of this type. □ **ver·min·ous** *adjective* [Old French *vermin*, *-ine*, ultimately from Latin *vermis* 'worm']

Ver·mont /vɜːˈmɒnt/ a state in the northeastern US, on the border with Canada; pop. (est. 1990) 562,760; capital, Montpelier. It became the 14th state of the US in 1791. □ **Ver·mont·er** *noun*

ver·mouth /vɜːˈmuːθ/ *noun* a fortified wine flavoured with aromatic herbs. [French *vermout* from German *Wermut* WORMWOOD]

ver·nacu·lar /vɜːˈnækjʊlər/ ● *noun* **1** the language or dialect of a particular country (*Latin gave place to the vernacular*). **2** the language of a particular clan or group. **3** informal speech. ● *adjective* **1** (of language) of one's native country; not of foreign origin or of learned formation. **2** (of architecture) concerned with ordinary rather than monumental buildings. □ **ver·nacu·lar·ly** *adverb* [Latin *vernaculus* domestic, native, from *verna* slave born in the master's home]

ver·nal *adjective* of, in, or appropriate to spring (*vernal equinox; vernal breezes*). [Latin *vernalis* from *vernus* from *ver* spring]

vernal equinox *noun* = SPRING EQUINOX.

vernal grass *noun* a sweet-scented European grass, *Anthoxanthum odoratum*, grown for hay.

ver·na·tion /vɜːˈneɪʃən/ *noun Bot.* the arrangement of leaves in a leaf bud (*compare* AESTIVATION 1). [modern Latin *vernatio* from Latin *vernare* bloom (as VERNAL)]

Verne /ˈvɜːrn, ˈvern/ **Jules** (1828–1905), French novelist. Regarded as one of the first writers of science fiction, he is best known for the adventure stories *Journey to the Centre of the Earth* (1864), *Twenty Thousand Leagues under the Sea* (1870), and *Around the World in Eighty Days* (1873).

ver·nier /ˈvɜːrniər/ *noun* a small movable graduated scale for obtaining fractional parts of subdivisions on a fixed main scale of a barometer, sextant, calipers, etc. [P. *Vernier*, French mathematician d.1637]

vernier engine *noun* an auxiliary engine for slight changes in the motion of a space rocket etc.

ver·nis·sage /ˌvernɪˈsɒʒ/ *noun* a private view of an exhibit of paintings etc. before public exhibition. [French, = varnishing]

Ver·non /ˈvɜːrnən/ a city in south central BC, 117 km southeast of Kamloops; pop. (2001) 33,494. [F. G. *Vernon*, early settler and later chief commissioner of lands and works c.1887]

Verny /ˈverni/ the former name (until 1921) for ALMATY.

Ver·ona /vəˈrɔːnə/ a city on the Adige River, in NE Italy; pop. (est. 2001) 243,474.

ver·onal /ˈverənəl/ *noun* a sedative drug, a derivative of barbituric acid. [German, from VERONA]

Vero·nese /ˌverəˈneɪzi/ **Paulo** (born Paolo Caliari) (c.1528–88), Italian painter. Of his numerous paintings, dealing mainly with religious, allegorical, and historical subjects, his richly-coloured feast scenes, e.g. *The Marriage at Cana* (1562), and his series of frescoes in the Villa Maser near Treviso (1561) are the best known.

ver·on·ica /vəˈrɒnɪkə/ *noun* **1** any plant of the genus *Veronica* or *Hebe*, esp. speedwell. **2 a** a cloth supposedly impressed with an image of Christ's face. **b** any similar picture of Christ's face. **3** *Bullfighting* the movement of a matador's cape away from a charging bull. [medieval Latin from the name *Veronica*: in sense 2 from the association with St. Veronica]

Ver·on·ica, St. /vəˈrɒnɪkə/ a woman of Jerusalem who offered her headcloth to Christ on the way to Calvary, to wipe the blood and sweat from his face. The cloth is said to have retained the image of his features.

Ver·ra·zano /verəˈtsɒnəʊ/ **Gio·van·ni da** (also **Ver·raz·zano**) (c.1485–c.1528), Italian navigator, who, in the service of France, explored the eastern coast of N America (1524), being the first European to see the sites of present-day New York harbour and Narragansett Bay.

Ver·roc·chio /vəˈrɒːˌkjəʊ/ **An·drea del** (born Andrea di Cioni) (1435–88), Italian sculptor, painter, and goldsmith, who is known for his bronze sculpture of *David* (c.1475) in Florence, and the bronze equestrian statue of the *condottiere* Bartolomeo Colleoni in Venice (begun 1481).

ver·ruca /vəˈruːkə/ *noun* (pl. **ver·rucae** /-siː/ or **ver·rucas**) a wart or similar growth. □ **ver·ru·cose** /ˈveruˌkəʊz/ *adjective* **ver·ru·cous** /ˈverʊkəs/ *adjective* [Latin]

Ver·sace /verˈsɒtʃeɪ/ **Gianni** (1947–97), Italian fashion designer, known for his daring designs.

Ver·sailles /verˈsaɪ/ *noun* an immense and magnificent palace built for Louis XIV near the town of Versailles, southwest of Paris.

Versailles, Treaty of 1 a treaty which terminated the American Revolution in 1783. **2** a treaty signed in 1919 as part of the formal end of the First World War, redividing the territory of the defeated Central Powers, restricting Germany's armed forces, and establishing the League of Nations.

ver·sant /ˈvɜːrsənt/ *noun* **1** the extent of land sloping in one direction. **2** the general slope of land. [French from *verser* from Latin *versare* frequentative of *vertere vers-* turn]

ver·sa·tile /ˈvɜːrsəˌtaɪl/ *adjective* **1** turning easily or readily from one subject or occupation to another; capable of dealing with many subjects (*a versatile mind*). **2** (of a device etc.) having many uses. **3** *Bot. & Zool.* moving freely about or up and down on a support (*versatile antenna*). □ **ver·sa·til·ity** /-ˈtɪlɪti/ *noun* [French *versatile* or Latin *versatilis* (as VERSANT)]

verse ● *noun* **1 a** metrical composition in general (*wrote pages of verse; also attributive: verse drama*). **b** a particular type of this (*English verse*).

2 a a metrical line in accordance with the rules of prosody. **b** a group of a definite number of such lines. **c** a stanza of a poem or song with or without refrain. **d** a poem. **3** each of the short numbered divisions of a chapter in the Bible or other scripture. **4 a** a versicle. **b** a passage (of an anthem etc.) for solo voice. ● *transitive verb* **1** express in verse. **2** (usu. *reflexive*; foll. by *in*) instruct; make knowledgeable. [Old English *fers* from Latin *versus* a turn of the plow, a furrow, a line of writing, from *vertere vers-* turn: in Middle English reinforced by Old French *vers* from Latin *versus*]

versed *adjective* (foll. by *in*) experienced or skilled in; knowledgeable about. [French *versé* or Latin *versatus* past participle of *versari* be engaged in (as VERSANT)]

versed sine *noun* unity minus cosine.

vers·icle /ˈvɜrsɪkəl/ *noun* each of the short sentences in a liturgy said or sung by a priest etc. and alternating with responses.

versi·colour /ˈvɜrsɪˌkʌlər/ *adjective* (also **versi·color**) **1** changing or varying in colour; iridescent. **2** of various colours; variegated. [Latin from *versus* past participle of *vertere* turn + COLOUR]

versi·fy *verb* (**-fies, -fied**) **1** *transitive* turn into or express in verse. **2** *intransitive* compose verses. □ **versi·fi·ca·tion** *noun* **versi·fi·er** *noun*

ver·sion *noun* **1** an account of a matter from a particular person's point of view (*told them my version of the incident*). **2** a book or work etc. in a particular edition or translation (*Revised Standard Version*). **3** a form or variant of a thing as adapted, performed, etc. **4** a piece of translation, esp. as a school exercise. **5** *Med.* the manual turning of a fetus in the womb to improve presentation. [French *version* or medieval Latin *versio* from Latin *vertere vers-* turn]

vers libre /ver ˈliːbrə/ = FREE VERSE. [French]

verso /ˈvɜrsoː/ *noun* (*pl.* **versos**) **1 a** the left-hand page of an open book. **b** the back of a printed leaf of paper or manuscript (*opp.* RECTO 2). **2** the reverse of a coin. [Latin *verso* (*folio*) on the turned (leaf)]

verst /vɜrst/ *noun* a Russian measure of length, about 1.07 km (0.66 mile). [Russian *versta*]

ver·sus *preposition* **1** against (esp. in legal and sports use). *Abbr.:* **v., vs. 2** as opposed to; in contrast with. [Latin, = towards, in medieval Latin against]

vert[1] /vɜrt/ *noun & adjective* Heraldry green. [Old French from Latin *viridis* green]

vert[2] *slang* ● *noun* a vertical surface, esp. the lift of a skateboarding ramp etc. ● *adjective* vertical.

ver·te·bra /ˈvɜrtəbrə/ *noun* (*pl.* **ver·te·brae** /-briː, -breɪ/) **1** each segment of the backbone. **2** (in *pl.*) the backbone. □ **ver·te·bral** *adjective* [Latin from *vertere* turn]

ver·te·brate /ˈvɜrtəˌbreɪt, -brət/ ● *noun* any animal of the subphylum Vertebrata, having a spinal column, including mammals, birds, reptiles, amphibians, and fishes. ● *adjective* of or relating to the vertebrates.

ver·tex /ˈvɜrteks/ *noun* (*pl.* **ver·ti·ces** /-tɪˌsiːz/ or **vertex·es**) **1** the highest point; the top or apex. **2** *Math* **a** each angular point of a polygon, polyhedron, etc. **b** a meeting point of two lines that form an angle. **c** the point at which an axis meets a curve or surface. **3** *Anat.* the crown of the head. [Latin *vertex -ticis* whirlpool, crown of a head, vertex, from *vertere* turn]

ver·ti·cal /ˈvɜrtɪkəl/ ● *adjective* **1** at right angles to a horizontal plane, perpendicular. **2** in a direction from top to bottom of a picture etc. **3** of or at the vertex or highest point. **4** at, or passing through, the zenith. **5** *Anat.* of or relating to the crown of the head. **6** involving all the levels in an organizational hierarchy or stages in the production of a class of goods (*vertical integration*). ● *noun* **1** a vertical line or plane. **2** (in *pl.*) (in full **vertical blinds**) a window blind consisting of a number of adjustable vertical slats to control the light. **3** (in full **vertical drop**) the difference in elevation between the top and bottom of a mountain, ski run, etc. **4** (in full **vertical tasting**) a sampling of several vintages of the same wine. □ **ver·ti·cal·ity** /-ˈkalɪti/ *noun* **ver·ti·cal·ly** *adverb* [French *vertical* or Late Latin *verticalis* (as VERTEX)]

vertical angles *plural noun* *Math.* each of the pairs of opposite angles made by two intersecting lines.

vertically challenged *adjective* *jocular* (of a person) short.

vertical takeoff *noun* the takeoff of an aircraft directly upwards.

vertical thinking *noun* deductive reasoning (*opp.* LATERAL THINKING).

ver·ti·cil /ˈvɜrtɪsɪl/ *noun* *Bot.* & *Zool.* a whorl; a set of parts arranged in a circle around an axis. [Latin *verticillus* whorl of a spindle, diminutive of VERTEX]

ver·ti·gin·ous /vɜrˈtɪdʒɪnəs/ *adjective* of, causing, or affected by vertigo. □ **ver·ti·gin·ous·ly** *adverb* [Latin *vertiginosus* (as VERTIGO)]

ver·ti·go /ˈvɜrtɪgoː/ *noun* a condition with a sensation of whirling and a tendency to lose balance; dizziness, giddiness. [Latin *vertigo -ginis* whirling, from *vertere* turn]

vertu *var. of* VIRTU.

ver·vain /ˈvɜrveɪn/ *noun* any of various herbaceous plants of the genus *Verbena*, esp. *V. officinalis* with small blue, white, or purple flowers. [Old French *verveine* from Latin VERBENA]

verve *noun* enthusiasm, vigour, spirit, esp. in artistic or literary work. [French, earlier = a form of expression, from Latin *verba* words]

ver·vet /ˈvɜrvət/ *noun* a small grey African monkey, *Cercopithecus aethiops*. [French]

Ver·woerd /fərˈvʊrt/ **Hen·drik (Frensch)** (1901–66), Dutch-born South African politician, prime minister 1958–66. He developed the segregation policy of apartheid, banned the ANC and the Pan-Africanist Congress (1960), and withdrew South Africa from the Commonwealth, declaring it a republic (1961); he was assassinated by a parliamentary secretary.

very ● *adverb* **1** in a high degree (*did it very easily; had a very bad cough; am very much better*). **2** in the fullest sense (foll. by *own* or superlative adj.: *at the very latest; do your very best; my very own room*). ● *adjective* **1** real, true, actual; truly such (usu. prec. by *the, this, his, etc.* emphasizing identity, significance, or extreme degree: *the very thing we need; those were her very words*). **2** *archaic* real, genuine (*very God*). □ **not very 1** in a low degree. **2** far from being. **very good** (or **well**) a formula of consent or approval. **the very same** *see* SAME. [Old French *verai*, ultimately from Latin *verus* true]

very high frequency *noun see* VHF.

Very light /ˈveri/ *noun* a flare projected from a pistol for signalling or temporarily illuminating the surroundings. [E. W. *Very*, US inventor d.1910]

Very pistol /ˈveri/ *noun* a gun for firing a Very light.

Very Reverend *noun* **1** (in Canada) the title of the moderator or a former moderator of the United Church. **2** the title of a dean etc.

Vesa·lius /vɪˈseɪliəs/ **An·dreas** (1514–64), Flemish anatomist. He held that traditional theories of anatomy were seriously flawed because based on the bodies of apes; his major work, *De humani corporis fabrica* (1543), contained accurate descriptions of human anatomy.

ves·ica /ˈvesɪkə/ *noun* **1** *Anat.* & *Zool.* a bladder, esp. the urinary bladder. **2** *Art* = MANDORLA. □ **vesi·cal** *adjective* [Latin]

ves·icle /ˈvesɪkəl/ *noun* **1 a** *Anat.* & *Biol.* a small fluid-filled bladder, sac, or vacuole. **b** *Bot.* an air-filled swelling in a seaweed etc. **2** *Geol.* a small cavity in volcanic rock produced by gas bubbles. **3** *Med.* a blister. □ **ves·icu·lar** /vəˈsɪkjʊlər/ *adjective* **ves·icu·la·tion** /vəˌsɪkjʊˈleɪʃən/ *noun* [French *vésicule* or Latin *vesicula*, diminutive of VESICA]

Ves·pa·sian /vesˈpeɪʒən/ (Latin name Titus Flavius Vespasianus) (AD 9–79), Roman emperor 69–79 and founder of the Flavian dynasty. His reign saw the restoration of financial and military order and the initiation of a public building program which included the rebuilding of the Capitol and the beginning of the construction of the Colosseum (75).

ves·per *noun* **1** *literary* Venus as the evening star. **2** *literary* evening. **3** (in *pl.*) **a** the office of the sixth canonical hour of prayer, originally said towards evening. **b** evening prayer. [Latin *vesper* 'evening (star)': sense 3 partly from Old French *vespres* via ecclesiastical Latin *vesperas* from Latin *vespera* 'evening']

ves·per·tine /ˈvespərˌtaɪn, -tɪn/ *adjective* **1** *Bot.* (of a flower) opening in the evening. **2** *Zool.* active in the evening. **3** *Astronomy* setting near the time of sunset. **4** of or occurring in the evening. [Latin *vespertinus* from *vesper* evening]

ves·pi·ary /ˈvespiːˌeri/ *noun* (*pl.* **-aries**) a nest of wasps. [irreg. from Latin *vespa* wasp, after *apiary*]

ves·pine /ˈvespaɪn/ *adjective* of or relating to wasps. [Latin *vespa* wasp]

Ves·pucci /veˈspuːtʃi/ **Amer·igo** (1451–1512), Italian merchant and explorer. He made two voyages to the New World (1499–1500; 1501–2) during which he explored the Brazilian coastline; the Latin form of his first name is believed to have given rise to the name of America.

ves·sel *noun* **1** a hollow receptacle esp. for liquid, e.g. a cask, cup, pot, bottle, or dish. **2** a ship or boat, esp. a large one. **3 a** *Anat.* a duct or canal etc. holding or conveying blood or other fluid, esp. = BLOOD VESSEL. **b** *Bot.* a woody duct carrying or containing sap etc. **4** *Bible* or *jocular* a person regarded as the recipient or exponent of a quality (*a weak vessel*). [Anglo-French *vessel(e)*, Old French *vaissel(le)* from Late Latin *vascellum* diminutive of *vas* vessel]

---

uː m**oo**d   aɪ m**y**   əi p**i**pe   au br**ow**n   ʌu h**ou**se   ei d**ay**   ɔi b**oy**   ã fr**an**glais   ã Cana**dien**   ɔ̃ Bra**yon**   (*see over for consonants*)

vest ● *noun* **1 a** *N Amer. & Austral.* a sleeveless and collarless, usu. V-necked garment covering the shoulders and reaching the waist or hip, often with a buttoned front, worn over a shirt. **b** any sleeveless garment worn for a specified purpose (*bulletproof vest*). **2** *Brit.* = UNDERSHIRT. ● *verb* **1** *transitive* (esp. in *passive*; foll. by *with, in*) bestow or confer (powers, authority, etc.) on (a person). **2** *transitive* (foll. by *in*) confer (property or power) on (a person) with an immediate fixed right of immediate or future possession. **3** *intransitive* (foll. by *in*) (of property, a right, etc.) come into the possession of (a person). **4 a** *transitive archaic* clothe. **b** *intransitive Christianity* put on vestments. □ **close to the vest** *N Amer.* cautious(ly), careful(ly), guarded(ly). [(n.) French *veste* from Italian *veste* from Latin *vestis* garment: (v.) Middle English, originally past participle from Old French *vestu* from *vestir* from Latin *vestire vestit-* clothe]

Vesta ▶ **1** *Rom. Myth* the goddess of the hearth and household. Her temples contained no image but a fire which was kept constantly burning and was tended by the Vestal Virgins. **2** *Astronomy* asteroid 4, discovered in 1807; it is the brightest asteroid and the third largest (diameter 501 km).

vesta *noun hist.* a short wooden or wax match. [VESTA]

ves·tal ● *adjective* **1** chaste, pure. **2** of or relating to the Roman goddess Vesta. ● *noun* **1** a chaste woman. **2** *Rom. Hist.* a vestal virgin.

vestal virgin *noun Rom. Hist.* a virgin consecrated to Vesta and vowed to chastity, who shared the charge of maintaining the sacred fire burning on the goddess's altar.

vest·ed *adjective* **1** *in senses of* VEST *verb.* **2** absolute, fixed; not contingent. **3** established by law or tradition.

vested interest *noun* **1** *Law* an interest (usu. in land or money held in trust) recognized as belonging to a person. **2 a** a personal interest in a state of affairs, usu. with an expectation of gain. **b** (usu. in *pl.*) a person or group with such an interest.

Ves·ter·ålen /ˈvestəˌrɒlən/ a group of islands of Norway, north of the Arctic Circle.

ves·ti·bule /ˈvestɪˌbjuːl/ *noun* **1 a** an antechamber, hall, or lobby just inside the outer door of a building, e.g. where coats may be left. **b** the area between two sets of doorways at the main entrance of a church etc. **2** *N Amer.* an enclosed space between railway passenger cars. **3** *Anat.* **a** a chamber or channel connected with others. **b** the central cavity of the labyrinth of the inner ear. □ **ves·tib·u·lar** /-ˈstɪbjʊlər/ *adjective* [French *vestibule* or Latin *vestibulum* entrance court]

ves·tige /ˈvestɪdʒ/ *noun* **1** a trace or piece of evidence; a sign (*vestiges of an earlier civilization; found no vestige of their presence*). **2** a slight amount; a particle (*without a vestige of clothing; showed not a vestige of decency*). **3** *Biol.* a part or organ of an organism that is reduced or functionless but was well developed in its ancestors. [French from Latin *vestigium* footprint]

ves·ti·gial /veˈstɪdʒiəl, -dʒəl/ *adjective* **1** being a vestige or trace. **2** *Biol.* (of an organ) atrophied or functionless from the process of evolution (*a vestigial wing*). □ **ves·ti·gial·ly** *adverb*

vest·ment *noun* **1** (usu. in *pl.*) any of the official robes of clergy, choristers, etc., worn during divine service, e.g. a chasuble. **2** a garment, esp. an official or state robe. [Old French *vestiment, vestement* from Latin *vestimentum* (as VEST)]

vest-pocket *attributive adjective N Amer.* **1** small enough to fit into a small pocket as on a vest. **2** very small (*vest-pocket parks in urban areas*).

vest-pocket park *noun N Amer.* = POCKET PARK.

ves·try *noun* (pl. **-tries**) **1** a room or building attached to a church for keeping vestments in. **2 a** esp. *Anglicanism* a meeting of the members of a parish. **b** a body of parishioners meeting in this way. [Old French *vestiaire, vestiarie,* from Latin *vestiarium* (as VEST)]

vestry·man *noun* (pl. **-men**) a member of a vestry.

ves·ture /ˈvestʃər/ ● *noun literary* **1** garments, dress. **2** a covering. ● *transitive verb* clothe. [Old French from medieval Latin *vestitura* (as VEST)]

Vesu·vius /vəˈsuːviəs/ an active volcano near Naples, in S Italy, 1 277 m (4,190 ft.) high. It violently erupted in AD 79, burying the towns of Pompeii and Herculaneum.

vet[1] ● *noun informal* a veterinarian. ● *transitive verb* (**vet·ted, vet·ting**) **1** make a careful and critical examination of (a scheme, work, candidate, etc.). **2** examine or treat (an animal). [abbreviation]

vet[2] *noun N Amer. informal* an esp. military veteran. [abbreviation]

vetch *noun* any plant of the genus *Vicia,* esp. *V. sativa,* largely used for silage or fodder. [Anglo-French & Old Northern French *veche* from Latin *vicia*]

vetch·ling *noun* any of various plants of the genus *Lathyrus,* related to vetch.

vet·er·an *noun* **1** a person who has grown old in or had long experience of esp. military service or an occupation (*a war veteran; a veteran of the theatre; a veteran goalie*). **2** *N Amer.* an ex-serviceman or servicewoman. **3** (*attributive*) of or for veterans. [French *vétéran* or Latin *veteranus* (adj. & n.) from *vetus -eris* old]

Veterans Day *noun* (in the US) a public holiday held on November 11 to honour US veterans and victims of all wars.

vet·er·in·ar·ian /ˌvetrɪˈneriən, ˌvetərɪ-/ *noun N Amer.* a person qualified to treat diseased or injured animals.

vet·er·in·ary /ˈvetrɪˌneri, ˈvetərɪ-/ ● *adjective* of or for diseases and injuries of esp. farm and domestic animals, or their treatment. ● *noun* (pl. **-ies**) a veterinary surgeon. [Latin *veterinarius* from *veterinae* cattle]

veterinary surgeon *noun* esp. *Brit.* a veterinarian.

vet·iver /ˈvetɪvər/ *noun* = CUSCUS[1]. [French *vétiver* from Tamil *veṭṭivēru* from *vēr* root]

veto /ˈviːtoʊ/ ● *noun* (pl. **-oes**) **1 a** a constitutional right to reject a legislative enactment. **b** the right of a permanent member of the UN Security Council to reject a resolution. **c** such a rejection. **d** an official message conveying this. **2** a prohibition (*put one's veto on a proposal*). ● *transitive verb* (**-oes, -oed**) **1** exercise a veto against (a measure etc.). **2** forbid authoritatively. [Latin, = I forbid, with reference to its use by Roman tribunes of the people in opposing measures of the Senate]

vex *transitive verb* **1** anger esp. by a slight or a petty annoyance; irritate, annoy. **2** puzzle, confound. **3** distress mentally; grieve, afflict. □ **vex·ing** *adjective* [Old French *vexer* from Latin *vexare* shake, disturb]

vex·a·tion *noun* **1** the act or an instance of vexing; the state of being vexed. **2** an annoying or distressing thing.

vex·a·tious *adjective* **1** such as to cause vexation. **2** *Law* not having sufficient grounds for action and seeking only to annoy the defendant. □ **vex·a·tious·ly** *adverb*

vexed *adjective* **1** irritated, angered. **2** (of a problem, issue, etc.) difficult and much discussed; problematic. □ **vex·ed·ly** *adverb*

vexil·lol·ogy /ˌveksɪˈlɒlədʒi/ *noun* the study of flags. □ **vexil·lol·o·gist** *noun* [Latin *vexillum* flag + -LOGY]

vex·il·lum /vekˈsɪləm/ *noun* (pl. **vex·il·la**) **1** *Rom. Hist.* military standard, esp. of a maniple. **2** *Bot.* the large upper petal of a papilionaceous flower. **3** *Zool.* the vane of a feather. [Latin from *vehere vect-* carry]

Vez·ina Trophy *noun* a trophy awarded annually in the NHL to the goalie voted most valuable to his team. [G. Vézina, Canadian goaltender d.1926]

V-formation *noun* a formation, esp. of flying geese, airplanes, etc., resembling the letter V.

VFR *abbreviation Aviation* = VISUAL FLIGHT RULES.

VG *abbreviation* **1** very good. **2** Vicar-General.

VGA *abbreviation Computing* video graphics array, a standard for graphics adapters originally capable of generating a 640 by 480 pixel 16-colour screen.

VHF *abbreviation* very high frequency (designating radio waves of frequency *c.*30– *c.*300 MHz and wavelength *c.*1–10 metres).

VHS *abbreviation proprietary* Video Home System (one of the standard formats for videocassettes).

VI *abbreviation* Virgin Islands.

via /ˈviːə, ˈvaɪə/ *preposition* **1** by way of; through (*Montreal to Rome via Paris; via satellite*). **2** by means of; with the aid of (*tried to improve the economy via fiscal restraint*). [Latin, ablative of *via* way, road]

Via Appia see APPIAN WAY.

vi·able /ˈvaɪəbəl/ *adjective* **1** (of a plan etc.) feasible; practicable, esp. from an economic standpoint. **2 a** (of a seed or spore) able to germinate. **b** (of a plant, animal, etc.) capable of living or developing normally under particular environmental conditions. **3** *Med.* (of a fetus or unborn child) able to live after birth. □ **vi·abil·ity** *noun* [French from *vie* 'life', from Latin *vita*]

via dol·or·osa /ˌviːə ˌdɒləˈroʊzə/ *noun* **1** the route believed to have been taken by Christ through Jerusalem to Calvary. **2** an extremely painful experience requiring strength or courage to bear. [Latin, = sorrowful way]

via·duct /ˈvaɪəˌdʌkt/ *noun* **1** a long bridge-like structure, esp. a series of arches, carrying a road or railway across a valley, low-lying ground, etc. **2** such a road or railway. [Latin *via* way, after AQUEDUCT]

Vi·ag·ra /vaɪˈagrə/ *noun proprietary* the drug sildenafil citrate, taken

Consonants: b *but* d *dog* f *few* g *get* h *her* j *yes* k *cat* l *leg* m *man* n *no* p *pen* r *red* s *sit*

orally as a tablet in the treatment of male impotence. [origin unknown]

vi·al /ˈvaɪəl/ *noun* a small (usu. cylindrical glass) vessel esp. for holding liquid medicines. [Middle English, var. of *fiole* etc.: see PHIAL]

via media /ˌvaɪə ˈmiːdiə, -ˈmiːdiə, ˌvaɪə-/ *noun literary* a middle way or compromise between extremes. [Latin]

viand /ˈvaɪənd/ *noun formal* **1** an article of food. **2** (in *pl.*) provisions, victuals. [Old French *viande* food, ultimately from Latin *vivenda*, neuter pl. gerundive of *vivere* to live]

vi·ati·cal /vaɪˈatɪkəl/ *adjective* designating or relating to an arrangement whereby a person having a terminal illness (esp. AIDS) sells his or her life insurance policy to a third party for less than its mature value so that he or she can benefit from the proceeds while alive (*viatical settlement*).

vi·ati·cum /vaɪˈatɪkəm/ *noun* (*pl.* **vi·ati·ca**) **1** the Eucharist as given to a person near or in danger of death. **2** provisions or an official allowance of money for a journey. [Latin, neuter of *viaticus* from *via* road]

vibe *noun informal* **1** (often in *pl.*) vibration, esp. in the sense of feelings or atmosphere communicated (*the house had bad vibes*). **2** (in *pl.*) = VIBRAPHONE. [abbreviation]

vi·bracu·lum /vaɪˈbrakjʊləm/ *noun* (*pl.* **vi·bracu·la**) *Zool.* a whip-like structure of bryozoans used to bring food within reach by lashing movements. [modern Latin (as VIBRATE)]

Vi·bram *noun proprietary* a kind of moulded rubber sole used esp. on climbing boots.

vi·brant /ˈvaɪbrənt/ *adjective* **1** full of life and energy; exciting. **2** (of colours etc.) bright and striking. **3** vibrating. **4** (often foll. by *with*) (of a person or thing) thrilling, quivering (*vibrant with emotion*). **5** (of sound) resonant. □ **vi·bran·cy** *noun* **vi·brant·ly** *adverb*

vi·bra·phone /ˈvaɪbrəfoʊn/ *noun* a percussion instrument of tuned metal bars with motor-driven resonators and metal tubes giving a vibrato effect. □ **vi·bra·phon·ist** *noun* [VIBRATO + -PHONE]

vi·brate /ˈvaɪbreɪt/ *verb* **1** *intransitive & transitive* move or cause to move continuously and rapidly to and fro; oscillate. **2** *intransitive Physics* move unceasingly to and fro, esp. rapidly. **3** *intransitive* (of a sound) throb; continue to be heard. **4** *intransitive* (foll. by *with*) quiver, thrill (*vibrating with passion*). **5** *intransitive* (of a pendulum) swing to and fro. [Latin *vibrare vibrat-* shake, swing]

vi·bra·tile /ˈvaɪbrəˌtaɪl/ *adjective* **1** capable of vibrating. **2** *Biol.* (of cilia etc.) used in vibratory motion. [VIBRATE, after *pulsatile* etc.]

vi·bra·tion /vaɪˈbreɪʃən/ *noun* **1** the act or an instance of vibrating; a continuous rapid shaking movement or sensation. **2** *Physics* (esp. rapid) motion to and fro esp. of the parts of a fluid or an elastic solid whose equilibrium has been disturbed or of an electromagnetic wave. **3** (in *pl.*) **a** a mental (esp. occult) influence. **b** a characteristic atmosphere or feeling in a place, regarded as communicable to people present in it. □ **vi·bra·tion·al** *adjective*

vi·bra·to /vɪˈbrɑːtoʊ/ *noun Music* a rapid slight variation in pitch in singing or playing a stringed or wind instrument, producing a tremulous effect (*compare* TREMOLO). [Italian, past participle of *vibrare* VIBRATE]

vi·bra·tor /ˈvaɪbreɪtər/ *noun* a device that vibrates or causes vibration, esp. an electric or other instrument used in massage or for sexual stimulation. □ **vi·bra·tory** /-brəˌtɔːri/ *adjective*

vib·rio /ˈvɪbrioʊ/ *noun* (*pl.* **vib·rios**) *Biol. & Med.* a water-borne bacterium of the genus *Vibrio* etc., typically shaped like a curved rod with a flagellum, and including the cholera bacterium. [modern Latin, from Latin *vibrare* VIBRATE]

vi·bris·sae /vaɪˈbrɪsiː/ *plural noun* **1** the stiff coarse sensitive hairs growing on the face, esp. around the mouth, of most mammals, such as a cat's whiskers. **2** the bristle-like feathers growing near the mouth of certain birds that catch insects in flight. [Latin (as VIBRATE)]

vibro- *combining form* vibrating.

vi·bur·num /vaɪˈbɜːrnəm/ *noun* any shrub of the genus *Viburnum*, usu. with white flowers, e.g. the guelder rose and wayfaring tree. [Latin, = wayfaring tree]

Vic. *abbreviation* Victoria.

vic·ar /ˈvɪkər/ *noun* **1 a** (in the Church of England) an incumbent of a parish where tithes formerly passed to a chapter or religious house or layman (*compare* RECTOR). **b** (in other Anglican churches) a member of the clergy deputizing for another. **2** *Catholicism* a representative or deputy of a bishop. **3** a cleric or choir member appointed to sing certain parts of a cathedral service. □ **vic·ari·ate** /vəˈkeriət/ *noun* [Old French *vicaire* from Latin *vicarius* substitute, from *vicis*: see VICE³]

vic·ar·age /ˈvɪkərɪdʒ/ *noun* the residence or benefice of a vicar.

vicar apostolic *noun Catholicism* a Roman Catholic missionary or titular bishop.

vicar-general *noun* (*pl.* **vicars-general**) **1** an Anglican official serving as a deputy or assistant to a bishop or Archbishop. **2** *Catholicism* an ecclesiastical officer assisting or representing a bishop in matters of jurisdiction or administration.

vic·ari·ous /vɪˈkeriəs, vaɪ-/ *adjective* **1** experienced, enjoyed, or undergone second-hand by imagining one's own participation in the experiences of another (*vicarious pleasure*). **2** performed, accomplished, or undergone on behalf of another (*vicarious suffering*). **3** deputed, delegated (*vicarious authority*). □ **vic·ari·ous·ly** *adverb* **vic·ari·ous·ness** *noun* [Latin *vicarius*: see VICAR]

Vicar of Christ *noun* the Pope.

vice¹ *noun* **1 a** illegal or grossly immoral conduct; extreme corruption or depravity. **b** a particular form of this, esp. involving prostitution or drugs etc. **c** an immoral, dissolute, or illegal habit or practice. **2** a defect in character or behaviour; a personal flaw or bad habit (*drunkenness was not among his vices*). **3** a fault or bad habit in a horse etc. [Old French from Latin *vitium*]

vice² esp. *Brit.* var. of VISE.

vice³ *preposition* in the place of; in succession to. [Latin, ablative of *vix* (recorded in oblique forms in *vic-*) change]

vice⁴ *noun informal* a vice-president, vice-principal, etc.

vice- *combining form* forming nouns meaning 'next in rank or authority to' or 'acting as a substitute or deputy for' (*vice-chairperson; vice-governor*). [Latin *vice* 'in place of' (as VICE³)]

vice admiral *noun* (also **Vice Admiral**) a naval officer ranking below admiral and above rear admiral. Abbr.: **VAdm**.

vice-chancel·lor *noun* **1** the deputy of a chancellor. **2** *Cdn & Brit.* the acting representative of the chancellor of a university, discharging most of the administrative duties.

vice·ger·ent /vaɪsˈdʒɛrənt/ ● *adjective* exercising delegated power. ● *noun* a person appointed to discharge the office of another; a deputy. □ **vice·ger·ency** *noun* (*pl.* **-cies**). [medieval Latin *vicegerens* (as VICE³, Latin *gerere* carry on)]

vice-president *noun* **1** a government official who ranks immediately below the president and assumes the role and responsibilities of the president in the event of his or her inability to govern due to absence, illness, or death. **2** an executive officer deputizing for a president and often overseeing a division of a corporation etc. □ **vice-presiden·cy** *noun* (*pl.* **-cies**). **vice-presiden·tial** *adjective*

vice-princi·pal *noun* the assistant to a principal, esp. in a school, college, or university.

vice·regal *adjective* of or relating to a Governor General or viceroy.

vice·reine /ˈvaɪsreɪn/ *noun* **1** the wife of a viceroy. **2** a woman who exercises authority over a colony or province etc. on behalf of a sovereign. [French (as VICE-, *reine* queen)]

vice·roy /ˈvaɪsrɔɪ/ *noun* a person who exercises authority over a colony or province etc. on behalf of a sovereign. □ **vice·roy·al·ty** *noun* [French (as VICE-, *roy* king)]

vice-skip *noun Curling* the third player on a curling rink. Also called THIRD.

vice squad *noun* a special unit of a police force for the enforcement of laws related to prostitution, drug trafficking, illegal gambling, etc.

vice versa /ˌvaɪs ˈvɜːrsə, ˌvaɪsə-/ *adverb* with the order of the terms or conditions changed; the other way around (*I'll help you and vice versa*). [Latin, = the position being reversed (as VICE³, *versa* ablative fem. past participle of *vertere* turn)]

Vichy /ˈviːʃi/ a town in south central France; pop. (1999) 26,528. A noted spa town, it is the source of an effervescent mineral water. The town was the headquarters during the Second World War of the regime that was set up after the German occupation of N France, to administer unoccupied France and the colonies. Never recognized by the Allies, the regime functioned as a puppet government for the Nazis.

vichys·soise /ˌviːʃiˈswɑːz, ˌvɪ-/ *noun* a thick soup made of puréed leeks and potatoes with cream, usu. served chilled. [French *crème vichyssoise glacée*, lit. 'iced cream soup of Vichy']

vicin·age /ˈvɪsɪnədʒ/ *noun* a neighbourhood; a surrounding district or vicinity. [Old French *vis(e)nage*, ultimately from Latin *vicinus* neighbour]

vicin·al /ˈvɪsɪnəl, -ˈsaɪnəl/ *adjective* **1** neighbouring, adjacent. **2** *Chem.* (of substituted groups or atoms) in neighbouring or adjacent positions on a carbon ring or chain. [French *vicinal* or Latin *vicinalis* from *vicinus* neighbour]

vicin·ity /vəˈsɪnɪti/ *noun* (*pl.* **-ities**) **1** the area within a limited distance of a place. **2** (foll. by *to*) the state of being near or close; proximity. □ **in the vicinity of 1** near (*in the vicinity of the park*). **2** approximately (*in the vicinity of $300,000*). [Latin *vicinitas* (as VICINAL)]

vi·cious /ˈvɪʃəs/ *adjective* **1** malevolent, spiteful, wicked (*vicious sarcasm*). **2** savage, brutal (*a vicious dog; a vicious slaying*). **3** fierce, intense, severe (*a vicious storm*). **4** of, pertaining to, or characterized by vice or immorality. □ **vi·cious·ly** *adverb* **vi·cious·ness** *noun* [Old French *vicious* or Latin *vitiosus* from *vitium* VICE¹]

vicious circle *noun* (also **vicious cycle**) an unbroken sequence of reciprocal cause and effect; an action and reaction that intensify each other.

vicis·si·tude /vɪˈsɪsɪˌtuːd, -ˌtjuːd/ *noun* (in *pl.*) changes in circumstance; uncertainties or variations of fortune or outcome.
□ **vicis·si·tud·in·ous** *adjective* [French *vicissitude* or Latin *vicissitudo* *-dinis* from *vicissim* by turns (as VICE²)]

Vick·ers, Jona·than Stew·art ('Jon') (b.1926), Canadian tenor. He performed all over the operatic world from the early 1950s until his retirement in 1988, and is known for his interpretations of Handel, Wagner, and Britten.

Vick·rey, Wil·liam S. (1914–1996), Canadian-born economist, co-winner (with James A. Mirrlees) of the 1996 Nobel Prize for economics.

Vicks·burg a city on the Mississippi River, in W Mississippi; pop. (2000) 26,400. In 1863, during the American Civil War, it was successfully besieged by Union forces. Its loss effectively split the secessionist states in half, bringing the end of the war much nearer.

Vi-Co /ˈvaɪkoː/ *noun* *Cdn* (*Sask.*) *proprietary* chocolate milk.

vic·tim *noun* **1** a person who suffers or dies as a result of an event or circumstance. **2** a person harmed, injured, or destroyed as a result of their own or another's ambition, passion, pursuit of wealth, etc. (*he is a victim of his own success*). **3** a person fooled or taken advantage of; a dupe (*fell victim to a hoax*). **4** *hist.* a living creature sacrificed to a deity or in a religious rite. **5** a person who has come to feel helpless and passive in the face of misfortune or ill-treatment (also *attributive: a victim mentality*). □ **fall victim to** succumb to or suffer as a result of. □ **vic·tim·hood** *noun* [Latin *victima*]

victim impact statement *noun* a statement issued by the victim of a crime, describing how he or she has been harmed by the offence, esp. as used in determining a sentence.

vic·tim·ize *transitive verb* (also esp. *Brit.* **-ise**) **1** make a victim of; cause (a person etc.) to suffer harm, inconvenience, discomfort, etc. **2** single out (a person) for punishment or unfair treatment.
□ **vic·tim·iz·a·tion** *noun* **vic·tim·iz·er** *noun*

victim·less crime *noun* a crime perceived as having no victims, esp. because of the willing participation of all involved, e.g. prostitution.

vic·tim·ol·ogy *noun* **1** the study of the victims of crime or discrimination, the psychological effects on them of their experience, and methods of recovery. **2** the possession of an outlook, arising from real or imagined victimization, which seems to glorify and indulge the state of being a victim.

vic·tor *noun* a person or country etc. that succeeds in overcoming or defeating an adversary or opponent. [Anglo-French *victo(u)r* or Latin *victor* from *vincere vict-* conquer]

Vic·tor Em·man·uel II (1820–78), king of Sardinia 1849–61 and Italy 1861–78. In 1859 he led his army to victory against the Austrians, and in 1860 entered the papal territories around French-held Rome to join his forces with those of Garibaldi; after being crowned first king of a united Italy in Turin in 1861, he continued to add to his kingdom, acquiring Venetia in 1866 and Rome in 1870.

Vic·tor Em·man·uel III (1869–1947), king of Italy 1900–46. He invited Mussolini to form a government in 1922, and during the Second World War acted to dismiss Mussolini and conclude an armistice; he abdicated in favour of his son in 1946, but a republic was established the same year by popular vote and both he and his son went into exile.

Vic·toria¹ 1 a state of SE Australia; pop. (est. 2001) 4,822,663; capital, Melbourne. **2** the capital of Hong Kong; pop. (2001) 1,035,000. **3** the capital city of BC, a port situated on the southeastern tip of Vancouver Island; pop. (2001) 74,125 (urban agglomeration pop. 311,902). **4** the capital of the Seychelles, a port on the island of Mahé; pop. (est. 2002) 22,800. [Queen VICTORIA²]

Vic·toria² ▸ 1 (1819–1901), queen of Great Britain and Ireland 1837–

1901 and empress of India 1876–1901. She married her cousin Prince Albert in 1840, and had the longest reign in British history, a time during which Britain became a powerful and prosperous imperial nation. **2 Tomás Luis de** (1548–1611), Spanish composer of religious music, one of the greatest of the 16th c. His masses, motets, requiem, and other music are dramatic and colourful.

Victoria, Lake (also **Victoria Ny·an·za** /niˈanzə/) the largest lake in Africa, with shores in Uganda, Tanzania, and Kenya, and drained by the Nile.

vic·toria *noun* **1** a low light four-wheeled carriage with a collapsible top, seats for two passengers, and a raised driver's seat. **2** a gigantic S American water lily, *Victoria amazonica*. **3** (also **victoria plum**) *Brit.* a large red luscious variety of plum. [Queen VICTORIA²]

Victoria Cross *noun* a medal awarded to members of the Commonwealth armed forces for conspicuous acts of bravery, instituted by Queen Victoria in 1856.

Victoria Day *noun* *Cdn* (also *BC, Nfld* **Queen's Birthday**) a holiday falling on the Monday immediately preceding 25 May.

Victoria Falls a spectacular waterfall 109 m (355 ft.) high, on the Zambezi River, on the Zimbabwe–Zambia border.

Victoria Island a large island in the Arctic Archipelago, situated off the northern coast of Nunavut. The northwest part belongs to the NWT while the eastern and southern part belong to Nunavut. With an area of 217 291 sq. km, it is the second largest island in Canada. [Queen VICTORIA²]

Victoria Lake a lake in SW central Newfoundland, situated south of Red Indian Lake and west of Meelpaeg Lake. [prob. after Queen VICTORIA²]

Vic·tor·ian ● *adjective* **1** of or characteristic of the reign of Queen Victoria. **2** associated with attitudes attributed to this time, esp. of prudery and moral strictness. **3** resembling or typical of the architectural style of this time, characterized by lavish ornamentation set in forms of neoclassicism and Gothic revival. ● *noun* **1** a person of this time. **2** a resident of a place called Victoria. □ **Vic·tor·ian·ism** *noun*

Vic·tor·iana *plural noun* **1** articles, esp. collectors' items and furniture, of the Victorian period. **2** attitudes characteristic of this period.

Victoria Nile the upper part of the White Nile, between Lake Victoria and Lake Albert. (See NILE RIVER.)

Victorian Order of Nurses *noun* *Cdn* a non-profit community-based health organization that provides home care for the elderly and chronically ill.

Victoria Peak 1 a mountain, 2 163 m (7,099 ft.) high, on Vancouver Island, about 60 km west of Campbell River. **2** a mountain on Hong Kong Island, rising to 554 m (1,818 ft.). [Queen VICTORIA²]

Vic·toria·ville a city in south central Quebec, north of Sherbrooke; pop. (2001) 38,841. [Queen VICTORIA²]

vic·tor·ious *adjective* **1** having won a victory; conquering, triumphant. **2** of or characterized by victory (*a victorious cheer*). □ **vic·tor·ious·ly** *adverb*

vic·tory *noun* (*pl.* **-ies**) **1 a** the state of having overcome or conquered an adversary in battle. **b** the state of having defeated an opponent in a game, competition, election, court trial, etc. **2** an instance of this; a triumph. **3** an instance of achieving success in some endeavour or of overcoming an obstacle or difficulty. [Anglo-French *victorie*, from Latin *victoria* (as VICTOR)]

Victory Bond *noun* *hist.* any of various bonds issued during the First and Second World Wars in Canada, Britain, and Australia to help finance the war effort.

Victory Garden *noun* *hist.* a garden planted to grow food during the Second World War.

victory lap *noun* *N Amer.* **1** a triumphant circuit of the grounds of a sports stadium completed by the victorious athlete. **2** any behaviour considered unduly triumphant.

Vic·tro·la /vɪkˈtroːlə/ *noun* esp. *hist.* *proprietary* a kind of gramophone driven by clockwork. [the *Victor* Talking Machine Co. + -OLA]

vict·ual /ˈvɪktʃuəl, ˈvɪtl/ ● *noun* (usu. in *pl.*) food, provisions. ● *verb* (**vict·ualled, vict·ual·ling**; *US* **vict·ualed, vict·ual·ing**) **1** *transitive* supply or feed (a person) with victuals. **2** *transitive & intransitive* eat, consume. [Old French *vitaille* from Late Latin *victualia*, neuter pl. of Latin *victualis* from *victus* food]

vict·ual·ler /ˈvɪktʃuələr, ˈvɪtlər/ *noun* (*US* **vict·ual·er**) **1** a person who serves food and drink for a living. **2** a ship carrying provisions for other ships.

vi·cu·ña /vɪˈkjuːnə/ *noun* **1** a S American mammal, *Vicugna vicugna*, related to the llama, with fine silky wool. **2 a** a fine fabric made from the wool of the vicuña. **b** a synthetic material made to resemble this. [Spanish from Quechua]

vid *noun informal* = VIDEO. [abbreviation]

Vidal[1] /vɪˈdɒl/ **Gore** (born Eugene Luther Vidal) (b.1925), US novelist, dramatist, and essayist. His novels, usu. satirical comedies, include *Myra Breckenridge* (1968), about the lurid adventures of a transsexual, and *Creation* (1981); his essays form a satirical commentary on US political and cultural life.

Vidal[2] *noun* (in full **Vidal Blanc**) **1** a hybrid variety of white wine grape widely grown in Ontario, used. esp. in icewines. **2** a wine made from this grape. [Jean-Louis *Vidal*, 20th-c. French winemaker]

vi·dal·ia /vaɪˈdeɪlɪə/ *noun* a sweet onion of the southern US. [the city of *Vidalia*, Georgia]

vide /ˈviːdeɪ/ *transitive verb* (as an instruction in a reference to a passage in a book etc.) see, consult. [Latin, imperative of *vidēre* see]

vide·licet /vəˈdeɪlɪˌsɛt/ *adverb* = VIZ. [Latin from *vidēre* see + *licet* it is permissible]

video ● *noun* (*pl.* **videos**) **1** the process of recording, reproducing, or broadcasting visual images on magnetic tape or disk (also *attributive*: *video equipment*). **2** the visual element of television broadcasts. **3 a** a recording made on videotape or disk, esp. one commercially produced and available for sale or rent on videocassette, DVD, etc. **b** = MUSIC VIDEO. **4 a** a videocassette or DVD (*the movie will be available on video this fall*). **b** = VIDEOTAPE 1. ● *transitive verb* (**-eos**, **-eoed**) = VIDEOTAPE. [Latin *vidēre* see, after AUDIO]

video arcade *noun* = ARCADE 3.

video camera *noun* (also **video·cam**) a camera used to record images on videotape etc. or to transmit images to a monitor screen.

video card *noun* Computing the circuit board that enables a monitor to display graphics.

video·cas·sette *noun* a length of videotape enclosed in a sealed plastic casing, suitable for use in a video camera or VCR.

videocassette recorder *noun* = VCR.

video conference *noun* an arrangement in which television sets linked by telephone lines are used to enable a group of people in different places to communicate with each other in sound and vision. □ **video conferencing** *noun*

video diary *noun* a series of video recordings made by an individual over a period of time, focusing on a period of his or her life, a certain event, the progress of a particular venture or project etc.

video·disc *noun* an optical disk on which visual material is recorded for reproduction on a television screen.

video display terminal *noun* (also **video display unit**) Computing a device for displaying on a screen data stored in a computer, usu. incorporating a keyboard for manipulating the data. Abbr.: **VDT** (or **VDU**).

video film *noun* esp. *Brit.* a film on videocassette.

video game *noun* any of a variety of games that can be played by using a joystick, buttons, etc. to manipulate computer-generated images displayed on a television screen, computer monitor, or the screen of an arcade game.

vid·eog·raphy /ˌvɪdɪˈɒɡrəfi/ *noun* the process or art of making videos. □ **vid·eog·raph·er** *noun*

video jockey *noun* = VJ.

video lottery terminal *noun* a government-regulated gambling machine that offers a selection of esp. card games on a video screen and rewards a winner in credit rather than coin, usu. located in a bar, restaurant, casino, or racetrack. Abbr.: **VLT**.

video-on-demand *noun* a pay-per-view television service that allows a customer to select from a list of programs, which may be accessed from a server through a telephone line at any time.

video·phile *noun* an enthusiast for videos or video technology.

video·phone *noun* a telephone incorporating a television screen allowing communication in both sound and vision.

video recorder *noun* = VCR.

video recording *noun* **1** the action or process of recording something on videotape. **2** = VIDEO 3a.

video signal *noun* a signal that contains all the information required for producing a television image.

video store *noun* a retail establishment that rents and sells esp. movie videos and video games, and also rents the equipment required to play these.

video·tape ● *noun* **1** magnetic tape for recording television pictures and sound. **2 a** a length of this. **b** a videocassette, esp. one on which nothing has been recorded. **3** a video recording, esp. one commercially produced and available for sale or rent on videocassette. ● *transitive verb* make a recording of (a person, an event, etc.) on videotape.

videotape recorder *noun* **1** a device used to record images and sound onto an open spool of videotape, used esp. in television broadcasting. Abbr.: **VTR**. **2** = VCR.

vid·screen *noun informal* a video screen.

vie *intransitive verb* (**vying**) (often foll. by *with*) compete, contend (*they vied with each other for her attention; the two teams are vying for the title*). [prob. from Middle English (as ENVY)]

vi·elle /viˈɛl/ *noun* a hurdy-gurdy. [French from Old French *viel(l)e*; see VIOL]

Vien·na /viˈɛnə/ the capital of Austria, situated in the northeast of the country on the Danube River; pop. (2001) 1,562,700. From 1278 to 1918 it was the seat of the Hapsburgs. It has long been a centre of the arts and esp. music. □ **Vien·nese** /viəˈniːz/ *adjective & noun*

Vienna sausage *noun* a small frankfurter, esp. canned.

Vien·tiane /ˌvjɛnˈtjɒn/ the capital and chief port of Laos, on the Mekong River; pop. (est. 2002) 189,600.

Viet Cong /ˌviːɛtˈkɒŋ/ *noun* (*pl.* same) a member of the Communist guerrilla movement in Vietnam which fought the South Vietnamese government forces 1954–75 with the support of the North Vietnamese army and opposed the South Vietnam and US forces in the Vietnam War. [Vietnamese, lit. 'Vietnamese Communist']

Viet·minh /ˌviːɛtˈmɪn/ *noun* (*pl.* same) a member of a Communist-dominated nationalist movement, formed in 1941, that fought for Vietnamese independence from French rule. Members of the Vietminh later joined with the Viet Cong in the Vietnam War. [Vietnamese *Viet-Nam Dôc-Lâp Dong-Minh* Vietnamese Independence League]

Viet·nam /ˌviːɛtˈnam, -ˈnɒm, ˈviːɛt-/ a country in SE Asia, with a coastline on the South China Sea; pop. (est. 2002) 81,098,416; capital, Hanoi. Vietnam was partitioned along the 17th parallel between Communist North Vietnam (capital, Hanoi) and non-Communist South Vietnam (capital, Saigon) in 1954, but reunified under a Communist government in 1976 after the end of the Vietnam War. [Vietnamese *Viet* name of the inhabitants + *nam* south]

Viet·nam·ese /ˌviːˌɛtnəˈmiːz, ˈviːɛtnə-/ ● *adjective* of or relating to Vietnam, its inhabitants, or language. ● *noun* (*pl.* same) **1** a native or national of Vietnam. **2** the language of Vietnam.

Vietnam War a war between Communist North Vietnam and US-backed South Vietnam. After the partition of Vietnam in 1954, guerrilla campaigns by the North to unite the country as a Communist state fuelled US concern over the possible spread of Communism in SE Asia. A US army was sent to Vietnam after 1964, eventually numbering 400,000, but the war aroused immense controversy and resentment at home, and all US forces were withdrawn by 1973; the North Vietnamese captured the southern capital Saigon to end the war in 1975. The war caused millions of Vietnamese casualties, while American dead numbered 55,000.

view ● *noun* **1** range of vision; extent of visibility (*came into view; in full view of the crowd*). **2 a** what is seen from a particular point; a scene or prospect (*a fine view of the mountains; a room with a view*). **b** a picture etc. representing this. **3 a** an opinion or belief concerning a particular subject or thing (*she holds strong views on morality*). **b** a mental attitude; an outlook (*took a favourable view of the matter*). **c** a manner of considering a thing (*took a long-term view of the situation*). **4** a visual examination, inspection, or survey. **5** an opportunity for a formal visual inspection; a viewing (*a private view of the exhibition*). **6** an instance of viewing, e.g. a television program (*pay-per-view*). ● *verb* **1** *transitive* inspect or examine in a formal or official manner (*we are going to view the house*). **2** *transitive* catch sight of; spy, see. **3** *transitive* regard or approach in a particular manner; consider (*they viewed her with suspicion*). **4** *transitive Computing* read or examine (a document or the contents of a file) in a window in which changes and corrections cannot be made. **5** *transitive & intransitive* watch (television or a program on television). □ **have in view 1** have as one's object. **2** bear (a circumstance) in mind in forming a judgment etc. **in view of 1** considering; on account of. **2** so as to be seen by; within the visible range of. **on view** being shown (for observation or inspection); being displayed or exhibited. **with a view to 1** with the hope or intention of. **2** with the aim of attaining or achieving (*with a view to marriage*). □ **view·able** *adjective* [Anglo-French *v(i)ewe*, Old French *vëue* fem. past participle from *vëoir* see, from Latin *vidēre*]

view·er noun **1** a person who views, watches, or looks at something; an observer, a spectator. **2** a person watching television. **3** a device for looking at photographic slides or transparencies etc.

view·er·ship noun **1** the audience for a television program or channel etc. **2** the number of viewers comprising this audience.

view·find·er noun a device on a camera showing the field of view of the lens, used in framing and focusing a picture.

view·ing noun **1** an opportunity or occasion to view. **2** the activity or a period of watching television. **3** N Amer. an opportunity for mourners to see the body of a deceased person for a final time prior to a funeral.

view·less adjective **1** not having or affording a view. **2** lacking opinions.

view·point noun **1** a point of view; a mental standpoint from which a matter is considered. **2** a place or position from which a view or prospect may be seen.

view·port noun **1** a window in a ship or spacecraft etc. **2** Computing = WINDOW 6.

View Royal a town situated at the southeastern end of Vancouver Island, just west of Esquimalt; pop. (2001) 7,271. [so called with reference to the beautiful view of *Royal* Roads Bay, which lies to the south]

view·screen noun a screen on which images can be viewed, esp. on consumer electronics and in science fiction.

view·shed noun the area visible from a given point of view, esp. considered as land worth conserving for its scenic value.

vig noun = VIGORISH.

Vigée-Lebrun /vi,ʒeilə'brã/ **(Marie Louise) Élisa·beth** (1755–1842), French painter known for her portraits, esp. those of Marie Antoinette and Lady Hamilton.

vi·gesi·mal /vɪ'dʒesɪməl, vai–/ adjective **1** of twentieths or twenty. **2** calculated, counted, or proceeding by twenties. [Latin *vigesimus* from *viginti* twenty]

vigil /'vɪdʒəl/ noun **1** a stationary and peaceful demonstration in support of a particular cause, usu. without speeches or other explicit advocacy of the cause, and often with some suggestion of mourning. **2** an occasion or period of keeping awake for any reason during a time usually devoted to sleep, esp. to keep watch or pray. **3** Christianity the eve of a festival or holy day as an occasion for religious observance. **4** (in pl.) prayers said or sung at a nocturnal service. [Old French *vigile* from Latin *vigilia* from *vigil* awake]

vigi·lance /'vɪdʒələns/ noun the quality of being alert to harm or danger; watchfulness, circumspection, caution. [French *vigilance* or Latin *vigilantia* from *vigilare* keep awake (as VIGIL)]

vigilance committee noun N Amer. a self-appointed body of citizens established to maintain justice and order in a community lacking well-established procedures for such matters.

vigi·lant /'vɪdʒələnt/ adjective extremely wary and heedful of harm or danger; attentive, alert, on one's guard. □ **vigi·lant·ly** adverb

vigi·lante /vɪdʒə'lanti/ noun a person, often a member of a group, who undertakes law enforcement and executes summary justice in the absence or perceived inadequacy of legally constituted law enforcement bodies. □ **vigi·lan·tism** noun [Spanish, = vigilant]

Vi·gneault /vi:'njoː/ **Gilles** (b.1928), Canadian singer, songwriter, and poet. He began singing his own material in 1959, and his song 'Mon Pays' (1964) became a Québécois anthem.

vi·gne·ron /'viːnjə,rɔ̃/ noun a person who cultivates grapevines for winemaking. [French from *vigne* VINE]

vi·gnette /vɪn'jet/ noun **1 a** a brief descriptive account, anecdote, essay, or character sketch. **b** a short evocative usu. self-contained episode in a play, novel, movie, etc. **2** an illustration or decorative design on a blank space in a book, usu. at the beginning or end of a chapter or on the title page, not enclosed in a definite border. **3** a photograph or portrait showing only the head and shoulders with the edges gradually shaded off into the background. [French, diminutive of *vigne* VINE]

vignet·ting /vɪn'jetɪŋ/ noun **1** the technique of producing vignettes, esp. in photography. **2** a darkening of the periphery of an image resulting from the loss of light as it passes through an optical system.

Vigny /vi:'nji:/ **Al·fred Vic·tor, Comte de** (1797–1863), French poet, novelist, and dramatist, whose several volumes of verse reveal his philosophy of stoic resignation; other works include his historical novel *Cinq-Mars* (1826) and the play *Chatterton* (1835), whose hero epitomizes the romantic notion of the poet as an isolated genius.

Vigo¹ /'viːɡoː/ a port on the Atlantic in Galicia, NW Spain; pop. (est. 2001) 287,282.

Vigo² /viːˈɡoː/ **Jean** (1905–34), French film director. His experimental films, such as *Zéro de conduite* (1933) and *L'Atalante* (1934), combine lyrical, surrealist, and realist elements.

vigor var. of VIGOUR.

vig·or·ish /'vɪɡərɪʃ/ noun US slang **1** the percentage deducted by a bookie from a gambler's winnings. **2** the rate of interest charged by a usurer on a loan. [prob. from Yiddish, from Russian *vyigrysh* profit, winnings]

vig·or·ous adjective **1 a** (of a person, animal, etc.) physically strong, healthy and robust. **b** (of a plant) growing actively; flourishing. **2** characterized by, requiring, or involving physical force or energy. **3** (of language etc.) powerful, vehement, rousing. **4** full of or exhibiting operative force or vitality. □ **vig·or·ous·ly** adverb **vig·or·ous·ness** noun

vig·our noun (also **vig·or**) **1** active physical strength or energy. **2** a flourishing physical condition. **3** powerful operative force; intensity of effect or operation (*the storm's vigour*). **4** mental or emotional strength, intensity, or vitality as shown in thought or speech or in literary style. [Old French *vigour* from Latin *vigor -oris* from *vigēre* be lively]

Vi·jaya·wada /,vidʒaiə'wɒdə/ a city on the Krishna River in Andhra Pradesh, SE India; pop. (2001) 825,400.

Vi·king /'vɔikɪŋ/ ● noun **1** any of the Scandinavian seafaring pirates and traders who raided and settled in parts of NW Europe and other coastal territories on the North Atlantic in the 8th–11th c. **2** either of two US space probes sent to Mars in 1975, each of which consisted of an orbiter and a soft lander that conducted experiments on the surface. ● adjective of or relating to the Vikings or their time. [Old Norse *vikingr*, perhaps from Old English *wicing* from *wic* camp]

Vila /'viːlə/ (also **Port Vila**) the capital of Vanuatu, on the southwest coast of the island of Efate; pop. (est. 2002) 33,900.

vile adjective **1** disgusting. **2** morally base; depraved, shameful. **3** informal abominably bad or unpleasant (*vile weather*). **4** archaic worthless. □ **vile·ly** adverb **vile·ness** noun [Old French *vil* vile from Latin *vilis* cheap, base]

vili·fy /'vɪlə,fai/ transitive verb (**-fies, -fied**) speak or write about in an abusively disparaging manner. □ **vili·fi·ca·tion** noun **vili·fi·er** noun [Middle English in sense 'lower in value', from Late Latin *vilificare* (as VILE)]

Villa /'viːjə/ **Pan·cho** (born Doroteo Arango) (1878–1923), Mexican revolutionary. Having played a prominent role in the revolution of 1910–11, he overthrew the dictatorial regime of General Victoriano Huerta in 1914, in collaboration with Venustiano Carranza; later that year, he and Zapata rebelled against Carranza and fled to the north of the country. He was eventually assassinated.

vil·la /'vɪlə/ noun **1** a luxurious country residence, esp. in continental Europe. **2** Rom. Hist. a large country house with an estate. **3** Brit. a detached or semi-detached house in a residential district. [Italian & Latin]

vil·lage noun **1 a** a group of houses and associated buildings, larger than a hamlet and smaller than a town, esp. in a rural area. **b** the inhabitants of a village regarded as a community. **2** a self-contained district or community within a city or town, regarded as having features characteristic of a village. **3** N Amer. a small municipality with limited corporate powers. □ **vil·la·ger** noun **vil·la·gey** adjective [Old French from Latin *villa*]

village idiot noun **1** a person of very low intelligence living and well known in a village. **2** a foolish or simple-minded person.

Villa·her·mosa /,viːjəɛr'mosə/ (in full **Villa·her·mosa de San Juan Bau·tis·ta** /dei ,san hwɒn bau'tiːstə/) a city in SE Mexico, capital of the state of Tabasco; pop. (2000) 625,500.

vil·lain /'vɪlən/ noun **1** a person guilty or capable of great wickedness. **2** the character in a play, novel, etc., whose evil actions or motives are important in the plot; the antagonist of the hero. **3** informal usu. jocular a rascal or rogue. **4** Brit. informal a professional criminal. **5** archaic a simple or unsophisticated person; a rustic or boor. □ **villain of the piece** the person responsible for mishandling or interfering with a situation, esp. in business or politics. □ **vil·lain·ess** noun **vil·lain·ize** transitive verb [Old French *vilain*, ultimately from Latin *villa*: see VILLA]

vil·lain·ous adjective **1** characteristic of a villain; depraved, wicked. **2** atrocious, abominable. □ **vil·lain·ous·ly** adverb

vil·lainy noun (pl. **-ies**) **1** conduct or behaviour characteristic of a villain. **2** a wicked act or deed; a crime.

Villa-Lobos /,vɪlə'loːbɔːs/ **Hei·tor** (1887–1959), Brazilian composer. His works often incorporate Brazilian folk music, as in the series of 14 *Chôros* (1920–9), scored in the style of Puccini, and the nine *Bachianas*

Consonants: b *but*   d *dog*   f *few*   g *get*   h *her*   j *yes*   k *cat*   l *leg*   m *man*   n *no*   p *pen*   r *red*   s *sit*

brasileiras (1930–45), arranged in counterpoint after the manner of Bach.

vil·lan·elle /ˌvɪləˈnel/ *noun* a usu. pastoral or lyric poem consisting normally of five three-line stanzas and a final quatrain, with only two rhymes throughout, and some lines repeated. [French from Italian *villanella* fem. of *villanello* rural, diminutive of *villano* (as VILLAIN)]

-ville *combining form* esp. *N Amer. informal* forming words designating a place, situation, etc. having a specified quality (*hicksville; dullsville*). [French *ville* town, as in the names of many N American cities and towns]

vil·lein /ˈvɪlən/ *noun hist.* a feudal tenant entirely subject to a lord or attached to a manor. □ **vil·lein·age** /ˈvɪlənɪdʒ/ *noun* [Middle English, var. of VILLAIN]

Ville-Marie /viːlmaˈriː/ a former Catholic missionary colony (est. 1642) on Île de Montréal, on the site of the present-day city of Montreal. [the Virgin MARY]

Ville·neuve /ˈvɪlnəv/ **1 Gilles** (1950–1982), Canadian racing driver. Although his career ended with his early death in a racing accident, in his time he was Canada's foremost racing driver, winning Grand Prix and Formula races across N America and Europe from 1974. **2** his son, **Jacques** (b.1971), Canadian racing driver. Following his father into the Grand Prix and Formula circuits, he won the Indianapolis 500 in 1995 and the world Formula One championship in 1997.

Vil·liers /ˈvɪlərz, ˈvɪljərz/ **George**, see BUCKINGHAM².

Vil·lon /viːˈjɔ̃/ **François** (born François de Montcorbier or François des Loges) (b.1431), French lyric poet. His riotous and dissipated life resulted in several periods of imprisonment. His famous poem 'Ballade des dames du temps jadis' is known for its refrain 'Mais où sont les neiges d'antan?' ('Where are the snows of yesteryear?').

vil·lus /ˈvɪləs/ *noun* (*pl.* **vil·li** /-laɪ/) **1** *Anat.* any of numerous short slender hairlike projections on some membranes, esp. in the mucous membrane of the chorion or small intestines. **2** *Bot.* (in *pl.*) long soft hairs covering fruit and flowers etc. □ **vil·lous** *adjective* [Latin, = shaggy hair]

Vil·ni·us /ˈvɪlniəs/ the capital of Lithuania; pop. (est. 1999) 578,334.

vim *noun informal* vigour, energy. [perhaps from Latin, accusative of *vis* energy]

Vimy Ridge, Battle of /ˈviːmi/ *noun* an Allied attack on the German position of Vimy Ridge, near Arras in France, during the First World War. One of the key positions on the Western Front, it had resisted earlier French and British assaults before it was taken by Canadian troops on 9 April 1917 at the cost of heavy casualties.

vin·ai·grette /ˌvɪnəˈɡret/ *noun* a dressing served with salads and cold meats, made with oil, vinegar, and various seasonings. [French, diminutive of *vinaigre* VINEGAR]

vinar·ter·ta /ˈvɪnəˌtertə/ *noun Cdn* an Icelandic dessert consisting of several layers of white cake with a prune filling. [Icelandic]

vin·blas·tine /vɪnˈblastiːn/ *noun* a cytotoxic alkaloid obtained from the Madagascar periwinkle, *Catharanthus roseus*, used to treat lymphomas and other cancers. [modern Latin *Vinca* former genus name of the periwinkle + -BLAST + -INE⁴]

Vin·cent de Paul, St. /ˌvɪnsənt də ˈpɒl/ (1581–1660), French priest who devoted his life to caring for the poor and sick. He established the Congregation of the Mission (the Lazarists) in 1624, and in 1633 was co-founder of the Daughters of Charity (Sisters of Charity of St. Vincent de Paul). Feast day, 27 Sept. (formerly 19 July).

Vin·cen·tian /vɪnˈsenʃən/ *noun see* LAZARIST.

Vinci *see* LEONARDO DA VINCI.

vin·cris·tine /vɪnˈkrɪstiːn/ *noun* a cytotoxic alkaloid obtained from the Madagascar periwinkle, *Catharanthus roseus*, used to treat acute leukemia and other cancers. [as VINBLASTINE, second element prob. from CRISTA]

vin·cu·lum /ˈvɪŋkjʊləm/ *noun* (*pl.* **vin·cu·la**) **1** a bond or tie. **2** *Algebra* a horizontal line drawn over a group of terms to show they are to be treated as a unit in the operation that follows, e.g. $a + b \times c = ac + bc$, but $a + b \times c = a + bc$. [Latin, = bond, from *vincire* bind]

vin·da·loo /vɪndəˈluː/ *noun* a heavily spiced hot Indian curry dish made with meat, fish, or poultry. [prob. from Portuguese *vin d'alho* 'wine and garlic (sauce)', from *vinho* 'wine' + *alho* 'garlic']

vin·di·cate *transitive verb* **1** clear (a person, oneself, etc.) of blame, suspicion, or criticism by evidence or demonstration. **2** uphold or establish the truth or validity of (something disputed). **3** justify (one's actions, conduct, etc.). □ **vin·di·ca·tion** *noun* **vin·di·ca·tor** *noun* [Latin *vindicare* claim, avenge, from *vindex -dicis* claimant, avenger]

vin·dic·tive *adjective* **1** tending to seek revenge. **2** characterized by this

tendency; vengeful, spiteful (*a vindictive criticism*). □ **vin·dic·tive·ly** *adverb* **vin·dic·tive·ness** *noun* [Latin *vindicta* vengeance (as VINDICATE)]

vine *noun* **1** any climbing or trailing woody-stemmed plant, esp. of the genus *Vitis*, bearing grapes. **2** a slender trailing or climbing stem. □ **viny** *adjective* [Old French *vi(g)ne* from Latin *vinea* vineyard, from *vinum* wine]

vin·egar *noun* **1** a sour liquid consisting mainly of dilute acetic acid, produced by the oxidation of the alcohol in wine or cider etc., and used as a condiment or food preservative. **2** sour behaviour or character. **3** energy, vitality (*see* PISS AND VINEGAR). □ **vin·egared** *adjective* **vin·egary** *adjective* [Old French *vyn egre*, ultimately from Latin *vinum* wine + *acer*, *acre* sour]

vine maple *noun* a shrubby maple tree of the east coast of N America, *Acer circinatum*, with seven- to nine-lobed leaves.

vin·ery /ˈvaɪnəri/ *noun* (*pl.* **-eries**) **1** a greenhouse for grapevines. **2** a vineyard.

vine·yard /ˈvɪnjərd/ *noun* a plantation of grapevines, esp. one cultivated for winemaking. □ **vine·yard·ist** *noun*

vinho verde /ˌviːnjɔ ˈverdei/ *noun* a young Portuguese wine, not allowed to mature. [Portuguese, lit. 'green wine']

vini- /ˈvɪni/ *combining form* wine. [Latin *vinum*]

vini·cul·ture /ˈvɪnɪˌkʌltʃər/ *noun* the cultivation of grapes for the production of wine. □ **vini·cul·tur·ist** *noun*

vi·nif·era /vaɪˈnɪfərə/ ● *adjective* of, derived from, or designating the vine *Vitis vinifera* or its grape, native to Europe and also widely cultivated in N America. ● *noun* (*pl.* same or **vi·nif·eras**) the vinifera wine or grape. [modern Latin]

vini·fi·ca·tion /ˌvɪnɪfɪˈkeɪʃən/ *noun* the conversion of grape juice etc. into wine by fermentation. □ **vini·fy** /ˈvɪnɪfaɪ/ *transitive verb* (**-fies, -fied**).

vining /ˈvaɪnɪŋ/ *adjective* (of a plant) that grows as a vine (*vining vegetables*).

Vin·land /ˈvɪnlənd/ the region of the northeast coast of N America which was visited in the 11th c. by Norsemen led by Leif Ericsson. The exact location is uncertain: sites from the northernmost tip of Newfoundland, where Viking remains have been found, to Cape Cod and even Virginia have been proposed. [so named because vines were found growing there]

Vin·ny·tsya /ˈviːnɪtsjə/ (Russian **Vin·ni·tsa** /ˈviːnɪtsə/) a city in central Ukraine; pop. (est. 2001) 357,000.

vino /ˈviːnoː/ *noun informal* or *jocular* wine. [Spanish & Italian, = wine]

vin or·di·naire /ˌvæ̃ ɔrdiˈner/ *noun* cheap table wine. [French, = ordinary wine]

vin·ous /ˈvaɪnəs/ *adjective* **1** of, like, or associated with wine. **2** given to or resulting from indulgence in wine. [Latin *vinum* wine]

Vin·son Mas·sif /ˈvɪnsən maˈsiːf/ the highest mountain range in Antarctica, in Ellsworth Land, rising to 5 140 m (16,863 ft.).

vin·tage /ˈvɪntədʒ/ ● *noun* **1 a** the year in which the grapes are picked for the production of a particular wine. **b** the wine made from these grapes. **2** a wine of high quality from a single identified year and district. **3** the process of gathering grapes for winemaking. **4 a** the year or period when a thing was made or produced (*a car of pre-war vintage*). **b** a thing made in a particular year or period. ● *adjective* **1** being of high quality and earlier time (*a vintage house*). **2** characteristic of the best period of a person's work or career. **3** (of wine) produced in an exceptional or outstanding year. [alteration (influenced by VINTNER) of Middle English *vendage*, *vindage* from Old French *vendange* from Latin *vindemia* from *vinum* wine + *demere* remove]

vint·ner /ˈvɪntnər/ *noun* a person who makes or sells wine. [Old French *vinetier* from medieval Latin *vinetarius* from Latin *vinetum* vineyard, from *vinum* wine]

viny *adjective see* VINE.

vinyl *noun* **1** *Chem.* the radical –CH:CH₂ derived from ethylene by removal of a hydrogen atom (usu. *attributive*: *vinyl group*). **2** any plastic made by polymerizing a compound containing the vinyl group, esp. polyvinyl chloride. **3 a** a gramophone record. **b** gramophone records collectively, esp. as opposed to audiotapes and compact discs. [Latin *vinum* 'wine' + -YL]

Vi·ogn·ier /viːˈɒnjeɪ/ *noun* **1** a variety of white wine grape, grown traditionally in the northern Rhone region of France, but also elsewhere since the 1980s, noted for producing wine with a floral, fruity aroma and for its relative scarcity. **2** a white wine made from this grape. [French]

viol /ˈvaɪəl/ *noun* a musical instrument of the Renaissance and Baroque periods, having five, six, or seven strings, often with frets, played with a bow and held vertically on the knees or between the legs. [Old French *viole* from Provençal *viola*, *viula*, prob. ultimately from Latin *vitulari* be joyful]

vi·o·la¹ /vɪˈoːlə/ *noun* **1 a** a four-stringed musical instrument of the violin family, larger than the violin and of lower pitch. **b** a person who plays or is playing a viola. **2** a viol. [Italian & Spanish, prob. from Provençal: see VIOL]

vi·o·la² /vaɪˈoːlə, viː-/ *noun* **1** any plant of the genus *Viola*, including the pansy and violet. **2** a cultivated hybrid of this genus. [Latin, = violet]

viol·aceous /ˌvaɪəˈleɪʃəs/ *adjective* **1** of a violet colour; purplish blue. **2** *Bot.* of the violet family Violaceae.

viola da brac·cio /vɪˌoːlə də ˈbrɒtʃoː/ *noun* any member of the violin family, as opposed to a viola da gamba.

viola da gamba /vɪˌoːlə də ˈɡambə/ *noun* a viol held between the player's legs, esp. one corresponding to the modern cello.

viola d'amore /vɪˌoːlə daˈmɔreɪ/ *noun* a tenor viol, similar in size to the viola, with a wavy outline and sound holes and no frets.

vio·late /ˈvaɪəˌleɪt/ *transitive verb* **1** fail to observe or comply with (*violate an agreement*; *violate a law*). **2 a** treat irreverently; desecrate, defile (a sanctuary etc.). **b** fail to respect; disregard (*violate tradition*). **3** break in or intrude upon, disturb (a person's privacy etc.). **4** assault sexually; rape. □ **vio·la·tion** *noun* **vio·la·tor** *noun* [Latin *violare* treat violently]

vio·lence *noun* **1** the esp. illegal exercise of physical force to cause injury or damage to a person or property; violent behaviour. **2** great force or strength; vehemence, severity, intensity (*the bomb exploded with violence*). **3** strength or intensity of emotion; fervour, passion. □ **do violence to 1** misinterpret, misapply, or distort. **2** cause harm or injury to.

vio·lent *adjective* **1 a** involving or characterized by the use of great physical force, esp. in order to cause injury (*a violent game*). **b** involving an unlawful use of force (*violent crime*). **2** (of a person) tending to use aggressive physical force, esp. to injure or intimidate others. **3** operating with great and usu. destructive physical force (*a violent storm*). **4** passionate, intense, extreme (*a violent contrast*; *violent dislike*; *a violent pain*). **5** (of death) resulting from external force or from poison (compare NATURAL *adjective* 2). □ **vio·lent·ly** *adverb* [Old French from Latin *violentus*]

vio·let ● *noun* **1 a** any plant of the genus *Viola* with usu. purple, blue, yellow, or white flowers. **b** any of various plants resembling the sweet violet. **2** the bluish-purple colour seen at the end of the spectrum opposite red. ● *adjective* of a bluish-purple colour. [Old French *violet(te)* diminutive of *viole* from Latin VIOLA²]

vio·lin *noun* **1** a musical instrument with four strings of treble pitch, rested on the shoulder beneath the chin and played with a bow. **2** a violin player. □ **vio·lin·ist** *noun* **vio·lin·ist·ic** *adjective* [Italian *violino* diminutive of VIOLA¹]

viol·ist *noun* a person who plays a viola.

Viollet-le-Duc /viːjəˈleɪ lə ˈduːk/ **Eu·gène Em·man·uel** (1814–79), French architect. His *Dictionnaire raisonné de l'architecture française du XIe au XVIe siècle* (1858–75) was instrumental in sustaining the Gothic Revival in France. Among the restorations he supervised were Amiens Cathedral and the fortifications at Carcassonne.

vio·lon·cello /ˌviːələnˈtʃeloː, ˌvaɪə-/ *noun* (*pl.* **-cellos**) *formal* = CELLO. □ **vio·lon·cellist** *noun* [Italian]

VIP /ˌviːaɪˈpiː/ *noun* (*pl.* **VIPs**) a very important person, esp. a high-ranking official, guest, or business associate (also *attributive*: *VIP lounge*). [acronym from *very important person*]

vi·pas·sana /vɪˈpasənə/ *noun* (in Buddhism) meditation involving concentration on the body or its sensations, or the insight which this provides. [Pali, lit. 'inward vision']

vi·per /ˈvaɪpər/ *noun* **1** any venomous snake of the family Viperidae, including the pit vipers, adders, and puff adders. **2** a malignant or treacherous person. □ **viper·ish** *adjective* **viper-like** *adjective*

viper·ous *adjective* [French *vipère* or Latin *vipera* from *vivus* alive + *parere* bring forth]

viper·ine /ˈvaɪpəraɪn/ *adjective* **1** of, pertaining to, or designating the subfamily Viperinae, which comprises the true vipers, or the family Viperidae which contains it. **2** resembling a viper.

viper's bugloss *noun* a stiff bristly blue-flowered plant, *Echium vulgare*.

viper's grass *noun* = SCORZONERA.

viper's nest *noun* a group of people prone to malicious and spiteful attacks upon one another.

vir·ago /vɪˈrɑːɡoː, -ˈreɪɡoː/ *noun* (*pl.* **-agos**) **1** a domineering, abusive, or ill-tempered woman. **2** *archaic* a strong and courageous woman, esp. a warrior. [Old English from Latin, = female warrior, from *vir* man]

viral /ˈvaɪrəl/ *adjective* of or caused by a virus. □ **viral·ly** *adverb*

viral load *noun* the amount of a virus (esp. HIV) present in the blood.

viral marketing *noun* a marketing technique whereby information about a company's goods or services is passed electronically from one Internet user to another. [from the idea of the information being passed on like a computer virus.]

Vir·chow /ˈvɜrkoː/ **Ru·dolf (Karl)** (1821–1902), German physician and pathologist, founder of cellular pathology.

vir·elay /ˈvɪrəˌleɪ/ *noun* a song or short lyric poem, originating in 14th-c. France, usu. consisting of stanzas composed of short lines and rhymes variously arranged. [Old French *virelai*]

vir·eo /ˈvɪrioː/ *noun* (*pl.* **-eos**) any small plain songbird of the family Vireonidae, inhabiting woodlands throughout the western hemisphere. [Latin, perhaps = greenfinch]

vir·es·cence /vɪˈresəns/ *noun* **1** greenness. **2** *Bot.* the abnormal development of chlorophyll in petals normally of some bright colour, resulting in greenness. □ **vir·es·cent** *adjective* [Latin *virescere*, inceptive of *virēre* be green]

vir·ger *var. of* VERGER.

Vir·gil /ˈvɜrdʒəl/ (also **Ver·gil**) (Latin name Publius Vergilius Maro) (70–19 BC), Roman poet. His three works are the pastoral *Eclogues*, the *Georgics*, a didactic poem on farming, and the *Aeneid*, an epic poem relating the wanderings of the Trojan hero Aeneas (legendary founder of Rome) after the fall of Troy. □ **Vir·gil·ian** /vɜrˈdʒɪliən/ *adjective*

vir·gin ● *noun* **1** a person who has never had sexual intercourse. **2 a** (**the Virgin**) the Blessed Virgin Mary (see MARY 1). **b** a picture or statue etc. representing the Blessed Virgin Mary. **3** *informal* a naive, innocent, or inexperienced person (*a political virgin*). **4** a member of any order of women under a vow of chastity. **5** a female insect producing eggs without impregnation. **6** (**the Virgin**) the zodiacal sign or constellation Virgo. ● *adjective* (usu. *attributive*) **1 a** being a virgin. **b** of or befitting a virgin (*virgin modesty*). **2** not yet used, explored, or exploited (*virgin prairie*). **3** undefiled, spotless. **4** (of olive oil) obtained from the first pressing of olives etc.; unrefined. **5** (of clay) not yet fired. **6** (of metal) freshly produced from smelted ore rather than from scrap metal. **7** (of wool) that has never, or only once, been spun or woven. **8** (of an insect) producing eggs without impregnation. [Old French *virgine* from Latin *virgo -ginis*]

vir·gin·al *adjective* **1** that is a virgin. **2** that belongs or relates to a virgin. **3** that befits, resembles, or is characteristic of a virgin. □ **vir·gin·al·ly** *adverb*

vir·gin·als *noun* (also **vir·gin·al**) an early keyboard instrument resembling a spinet and set in a box, played esp. in the 16th and 17th c. □ **vir·gin·al·ist** *noun* [from VIRGINAL, perhaps from its use by young women]

virgin birth *noun* **1** the doctrine of Christ's birth from a mother who was a virgin. **2** parthenogenesis.

virgin forest *noun* a forest in its untouched natural state.

Vir·gin·ia¹ a state of the eastern US, on the Atlantic coast; pop. (2000) 7,078,515; capital, Richmond. It was the site of the first permanent European settlement in N America in 1607 and was one of the original thirteen states of the Union (1788). □ **Vir·gin·ian** *noun & adjective*

Vir·gin·ia² *noun* **1** a variety of tobacco grown and produced in Virginia. **2** a cigarette made of this.

Virginia Algonquian *noun* the Algonquian language (now extinct) of the Powhatans.

Virginia Beach a city and resort on the Atlantic coast of SE Virginia; pop. (est. 2000) 425,257.

Virginia bluebell *noun* (also **Virginian cowslip**) a spring-flowering plant of eastern N America, *Mertensia virginica*, with blue, bell-shaped flowers.

Virginia creeper *noun* a N American vine, *Parthenocissus quinquefolia*, cultivated for ornament.

Virginia Falls a waterfall (90 m) in the southwestern NWT, situated on the South Nahanni River. [*Virginia*, daughter of F. Hunter, US explorer *c.*1928]

Virginia opossum *noun see* OPOSSUM 1.

Virginia reel *noun N Amer.* a country dance of US origin, in which couples, arranged in a double line facing their partners, complete steps shouted by a caller or fiddler.

Virginia stock *noun see* STOCK *noun* 11.

Virgin Islands a group of Caribbean islands at the eastern extremity of the Greater Antilles, divided between British and US administration. The British Virgin Islands consists of about forty islands in the northeast of the group; pop. (est. 2002) 21,272; capital, Road Town (on Tortola). The remaining islands (about fifty) constitute the US unincorporated territory of the Virgin Islands; pop. (est. 2002) 123,498; capital, Charlotte Amalie (on St. Thomas).

vir·gin·ity /noun/ **1** the state of being a virgin. **2** the state of being fresh, pure, or untouched. **3** innocence, inexperience.

Virgin Mary[1] the mother of Jesus (see MARY 1).

Virgin Mary[2] /noun (pl. **Marys**)/ a drink of tomato juice without vodka (compare BLOODY MARY[2]).

Virgin Queen Queen Elizabeth I of England.

virgin's bower /noun/ any of various kinds of clematis, esp. the N American *Clematis virginiana*.

Vir·go /ˈvɜrgoː/ /noun (pl. **-gos**)/ **1** a constellation on the celestial equator between Leo and Libra, containing several bright stars including Spica and a dense cluster of galaxies, which is traditionally regarded as representing a maiden or goddess associated with the harvest. **2 a** the sixth sign of the zodiac. **b** a person born when the sun is in this sign, usu. between 23 August and 22 September. □ **Vir·go·an** /noun & adjective/ [Old English from Latin, = virgin]

vir·gule /ˈvɜrgjuːl/ /noun/ a slanting line used to mark a pause in a line of medieval manuscripts or a division of lines in poetry; a solidus. [French, = comma, from Latin *virgula* diminutive of *virga* rod]

viri·des·cent /ˌvɪrəˈdesənt/ /adjective/ approaching green in colour; greenish. □ **viri·des·cence** /noun/ [Late Latin *viridescere* from Latin *viridis* green]

vir·id·ian /vəˈrɪdiən/ ● /noun/ **1** a bright bluish-green chromium oxide pigment. **2** the colour of this pigment. ● /adjective/ of this colour; bluish-green. [Latin *viridis* green]

vir·ile /ˈviːraɪl, -əl/ /adjective/ **1** of, belonging to, or characteristic of a man; manly; masculine. **2** (of a person) full of the strength, vigour, or energy typically attributed to men. **3** (of a man) having a strong sexual drive or procreative ability. □ **vir·il·ity** /vəˈrɪlɪti/ /noun/ [French *viril* or Latin *virilis* from *vir* man]

vir·il·iz·a·tion /ˌvɪrəlaɪˈzeɪʃən/ /noun/ (also **vir·il·ism** /ˈvɪrəˌlɪzəm/, esp. Brit. **vir·il·is·a·tion**) Med. the abnormal development of secondary male characteristics in a female, usu. as a result of excess androgen production. □ **vir·il·ize** (also esp. Brit. **-ise**) /transitive & intransitive verb/

vir·ion /ˈvairiən/ /noun/ the complete infective form of a virus outside a host cell, with a core and a capsid. [VIRUS + -I- + -ON]

vir·oid /ˈvaɪˌrɔɪd/ /noun/ an infectious entity affecting plants, similar to a virus but smaller and consisting only of nucleic acid without a protein coat.

vir·ol·ogy /vaɪˈrɒlədʒi/ /noun/ the branch of science that deals with the study of viruses. □ **viro·logic·al** /adjective/ **viro·logic·al·ly** /adverb/ **vir·ol·o·gist** /noun/

virtu /vɜrˈtuː/ /noun/ (also **vertu**) **1 a** an interest or expertise in the fine arts. **b** curios or *objets d'art* collectively. **2** the merit or excellence inherent in a thing or in a person. [Italian *virtù* VIRTUE, virtu]

vir·tu·al /adjective/ **1** that is such in essence or effect, though not recognized as such in name or according to strict definition (*she married a virtual stranger*). **2** *Computing* **a** not physically existing but made by software to appear to do so from the point of view of the program or user (*virtual memory; virtual circuit*). **b** designating or existing or experienced in an environment created by virtual reality. **3** *Physics* designating particles and processes that cannot be directly detected and occur over very short intervals of time and space with correspondingly indefinite energy and momenta. **4** *Optics* designating the apparent focus or image resulting from the effect of reflection or refraction upon rays of light. □ **vir·tu·al·ity** /noun/ **vir·tu·al·ize** /transitive verb/ [medieval Latin *virtualis* from Latin *virtus* after Late Latin *virtuosus*]

virtual community /noun/ *Computing* a group of users who communicate regularly in cyberspace.

vir·tu·al·ly /adverb/ **1** in effect; practically; as far as essential qualities or facts are concerned. **2** nearly, almost.

virtual memory /noun/ *Computing* an apparent increase in the amount of available RAM, which is actually supported by data held in secondary storage, e.g. a hard disk, transfer between the two being made automatically as required.

virtual private network /noun/ *Computing* a set of computers connected via the Internet or other public network, using encryption etc. to ensure security, allowing them to communicate as if on a private network.

virtual reality /noun/ **1** the computer-generated simulation of a three-dimensional image or environment that can be interacted with in a seemingly real or physical way by a person using special electronic equipment, such as a helmet with a screen inside or gloves fitted with sensors. **2** the software or technology used to generate this environment.

vir·tue /noun/ **1** conformity of life and conduct with moral principles; voluntary adherence to recognized laws or standards of conduct; moral excellence. **2** a particular form of moral excellence; a manifestation of the influence of moral principles in life or conduct (*patience is a virtue*). **3** chastity or sexual purity, traditionally esp. of women. **4** a particular beneficial quality or feature inherent in or pertaining to something; an advantage (*she extolled the virtues of the proposed legislation*). **5** *archaic* inherent worth or merit (*there is no virtue in such drugs*). **6** *Christianity* a member of the seventh order of the nine ranks of heavenly beings (*see ORDER noun 19*). □ **by** (or **in**) **virtue of** on the strength or basis of; due to (*got the job by virtue of his experience*). **make a virtue of necessity** derive some credit or benefit from an unwelcome obligation. [Old French *vertu* from Latin *virtus -tutis* from *vir* man]

vir·tu·oso /ˌvɜrtʃuˈoːsoʊ, -tjuː-, -zoː/ ● /noun (pl. **vir·tu·osi** or **-osos**)/ **1** a person who has mastered the technique of a fine art, esp. music. **2** a person with outstanding technical skill in any sphere. ● /adjective/ requiring or displaying the skills of a virtuoso (*she is playing a virtuoso piece*). □ **vir·tu·os·ic** /-ˈɒsɪk/ /adjective/ **vir·tu·os·ity** /-ˈɒsɪti/ /noun/ [Italian, = learned, skilful, from Late Latin (as VIRTUE)]

vir·tu·ous /adjective/ **1** possessing or displaying moral rectitude. **2** chaste. □ **vir·tu·ous·ly** /adverb/ **vir·tu·ous·ness** /noun/

virtuous circle /noun/ (also **virtuous cycle**) a beneficial recurring cycle of cause and effect (*compare* VICIOUS CIRCLE).

vir·u·lent /ˈvirʊlənt, ˈvirjʊ-/ /adjective/ **1** violently bitter or rancorous; full of acrimony or hostility (*virulent abuse*). **2 a** (of a disease) malignant or severe. **b** (of micro-organisms) capable of producing disease. **3** possessing venomous or poisonous qualities. □ **viru·lence** /noun/ **viru·lent·ly** /adverb/ [Latin *virulentus* (as VIRUS)]

virus /noun/ **1 a** a submicroscopic organism that can multiply only inside living host cells, has a non-cellular structure lacking any intrinsic metabolism and usu. comprising a single DNA or RNA molecule inside a protein coat, and is usu. pathogenic. **b** an infection with such an organism. **2** = COMPUTER VIRUS. **3** a harmful, corrupting, or malignant influence. [Latin, = slimy liquid, poison]

Vis. /abbreviation/ Viscount.

visa /ˈviːzə/ /noun/ **1** an endorsement on a passport etc. showing that it has been found correct, esp. as allowing the holder to enter or leave a country. **2** the term for which such an endorsement remains valid (*overstayed their visa*). [French from Latin *visa* neuter pl. past participle of *vidēre* see]

vis·age /ˈvɪzɪdʒ/ /noun/ literary a face, a countenance. □ **vis·aged** /adjective/ (also in *combination*). [Old French from Latin *visus* sight (as VISA)]

Vi·sakha·pat·nam /vɪˌsɒkəˈpʌtnəm/ a port on the coast of Andhra Pradesh, in SE India; pop. (2001) 969,600.

vis-à-vis /ˌviːzəˈviː/ ● /preposition/ **1** in relation to; compared with. **2** opposite to; facing. ● /adverb/ facing one another. ● /noun (pl. same)/ **1** a person or thing facing another, esp. in some dances. **2** a person occupying a corresponding position in another group. [French, = face to face, from *vis* face, from Latin (as VISAGE)]

Visc. /abbreviation/ Viscount.

vis·cacha /vɪsˈkatʃə/ /noun/ any S American burrowing rodent of the genus *Lagidium* of the chinchilla family, having valuable fur. [Spanish from Quechua (h)*uiscacha*]

vis·cera /ˈvɪsərə/ /plural noun/ the interior organs in the great cavities of the body, e.g. heart, liver, esp. in the abdomen, e.g. the intestines. [Latin, pl. of *viscus*: see VISCUS]

vis·cer·al /ˈvɪsərəl/ /adjective/ **1** of the viscera. **2** relating to inward feelings or instinct rather than conscious reasoning. □ **vis·cer·al·ly** /adverb/

vis·cid /ˈvɪsɪd/ /adjective/ glutinous, sticky. [Late Latin *viscidus* from Latin *viscum* birdlime]

visco·elas·tic /ˌvɪskoʊəˈlastɪk/ /adjective/ (of a substance) exhibiting both elastic and viscous behaviour. □ **visco·elas·ti·city** /noun/

vis·com·eter /vɪsˈkɒmɪtər/ /noun/ an instrument for measuring the viscosity of liquids. □ **visco·met·ric** /adjective/ **vis·com·etry** /noun/

Vis·conti /vɪsˈkɒnti/ **Lu·chino** (full name Don Luchino Visconti, Conte di Modrone) (1906–76), Italian film and theatre director. Born into an aristocratic family, he became a Marxist and his neo-realist films reflect his commitment to social issues; they include *Obsession* (1942), *The Leopard* (1963), and *Death in Venice* (1971).

vis·cose /ˈvɪskəʊs, -kəʊz/ *noun* **1** a form of cellulose in a highly viscous state suitable for drawing into yarn. **2** rayon made from this. [Late Latin *viscosus* (as VISCOUS)]

vis·cos·ity /vɪˈskɒsɪti/ *noun* (*pl.* **-ities**) **1** the quality or degree of being viscous. **2** *Physics* **a** (of a fluid) internal friction, the resistance to flow. **b** a quantity expressing this.

vis·count /ˈvaɪkaunt/ *noun* a nobleman ranking between an earl or count and a baron. □ **vis·count·cy** *noun* (*pl.* **-cies**) [Anglo-French *viscounte*, Old French *vi(s)conte* from medieval Latin *vicecomes -mitis* (as VICE-, COUNT²)]

vis·count·ess /ˈvaɪkauntɪs/ *noun* **1** a viscount's wife or widow. **2** a woman holding the rank of viscount in her own right.

Viscount Melville Sound a large arm of the Arctic Ocean, situated between Victoria and Melville islands. [R. S. Dundas, 2nd *Viscount Melville*, English statesman d.1851]

vis·cous /ˈvɪskəs/ *adjective* **1** glutinous, sticky. **2** semi-liquid. **3** *Physics* having a high viscosity; not flowing freely. [Anglo-French *viscous* or Late Latin *viscosus* (as VISCID)]

vis·cus /ˈvɪskəs/ *noun* (*pl.* **vis·cera** /ˈvɪsərə/) (usu. in *pl.*) any of the soft internal organs of the body. [Latin]

vise /vaɪs/ (also esp. *Brit.* **vice**) ● *noun* an instrument, esp. attached to a workbench, with two movable jaws between which an object may be clamped so as to leave the hands free to work on it. ● *transitive verb* secure in a vise. □ **vise·like** *adjective* [Middle English, = winding stair, screw, from Old French *vis* from Latin *vitis* vine]

Vise-Grip *noun N Amer.* proprietary (often in *pl.*) pliers whose jaws can be locked into position.

Vish·in·sky see VYSHINSKY.

Vish·nu /ˈvɪʃnuː/ *Hinduism* one of the major gods, originally a minor Vedic god but now the preserver of the cosmos in the Hindu triad with Shiva and Brahma. He is considered to have descended to earth nine times to save the world in various incarnations or avatars such as Rama, Krishna, and the historical Buddha; the tenth incarnation will herald the end of the world. □ **Vishnu·ism** *noun* [Sanskrit *Vishnu*]

visi·bil·ity /ˌvɪzɪˈbɪlɪti/ *noun* **1** the state of being visible; ability to be seen. **2** the range or possibility of vision as determined by the conditions of light and atmosphere (*visibility was down to 50 metres*). **3** the degree to which something impinges on public awareness or attracts attention (*product visibility*).

vis·ible /ˈvɪzɪbəl/ *adjective* **1 a** that can be seen by the eye. **b** (of light) within the range of wavelengths to which the eye is sensitive. **2** that can be perceived or ascertained; apparent, open (*has no visible means of support*; *spoke with visible impatience*). **3** in a position of public prominence; attracting attention. □ **vis·ibly** *adverb* [Old French *visible* or Latin *visibilis* from *vidēre vis-* see]

visible horizon *noun* see HORIZON 1b.

visible minority *noun esp. Cdn* **1** an ethnic group whose members are clearly racially distinct from those of the predominant race in a society. **2** a member of such an ethnic group.

Visi·goth /ˈvɪzɪˌɡɒθ/ *noun* **1** a West Goth, a member of the branch of the Goths who settled in France and Spain in the 5th c. and ruled much of Spain until 711. **2** *informal* an uncivilized or barbarous person. □ **Visi·goth·ic** *adjective* [Late Latin *Visigothus*]

vi·sion ● *noun* **1** the act or faculty of seeing, sight (*has impaired his vision*). **2 a** a thing or person seen in a dream or trance. **b** a supernatural or prophetic apparition. **3** a thing or idea perceived vividly in the imagination (*the romantic visions of youth*; *had visions of warm sandy beaches*). **4** imaginative insight. **5** ability to plan or form policy in a far-sighted way, e.g. in politics. **6** a person etc. of unusual beauty. ● *verb* **1** *transitive* see or present in or as in a vision. **2** *intransitive* experience a vision, have a vision quest. **3** *intransitive* (esp. as **vi·sion·ing** *noun*) explore or express a vision of how one would like the future to be. □ **vi·sion·less** *adjective* [Old French from Latin *visio -onis* (as VISIBLE)]

vi·sion·ary ● *adjective* **1** having vision or foresight. **2** given to seeing visions. ● *noun* (*pl.* **-ies**) a visionary person.

vision quest *noun* (among some N American Aboriginal peoples) a sacred ceremony in which an individual, often a teenage boy, goes to a secluded place to fast and communicate with the spiritual world, often through visions.

visit ● *verb* (**visit·ed**, **visit·ing**) **1** *transitive & intransitive* go or come to see (a person, place, etc.) as an act of friendship or ceremony, on business or for a purpose, or from interest. **b** *transitive* go or come to see

for the purpose of official inspection, supervision, consultation, or correction. **2** *transitive* reside temporarily with (a person) or at (a place). **3** *intransitive* be a visitor. **4** *transitive* (of a disease, calamity, etc.) come upon, attack. **5** *transitive* **a** *Bible* (foll. by *with*) punish (a person). **b** (often foll. by *on*) inflict something harmful or unpleasant on. **6** *intransitive N Amer.* **a** (foll. by *with*) go to see (a person) esp. socially. **b** (usu. foll. by *with*) converse, chat. **7** *transitive* access and view (a website). ● *noun* **1 a** an act of visiting, a call on a person or at a place (*was on a visit to some friends*; *paid him a long visit*). **b** temporary residence with a person or at a place. **2** (foll. by *to*) an occasion of visiting a doctor, dentist, etc. **3** a formal or official call for the purpose of inspection etc. **4** *N Amer.* a chat. □ **vis·it·able** *adjective* [Old French *visiter* or Latin *visitare* go to see, frequentative of *visare* view, from *vidēre vis-* see: the noun perhaps from French *visite*]

vis·it·ant *noun* **1** a visitor, esp. a supposedly supernatural one. **2** a migratory bird present in a locality for part of the year (*winter visitant*).

vis·it·a·tion *noun* **1** a visit, esp. a formal one. **2** a divorced person's visit with his or her child or children in the custody of a former spouse, granted as a right by a court. **3** a visit with a sick person in a hospital, a prison inmate, etc. **4** (**Visitation**) **a** the visit of the Virgin Mary to Elizabeth related in Luke 1:39-56. **b** the feast commemorating this on 31 May or 2 July. **5** an official visit of inspection, esp. a bishop's examination of a church in his diocese. **6** *informal* an unduly protracted visit or social call. **7** trouble or difficulty regarded as a divine punishment. **8** the boarding of a vessel belonging to another state to learn its character and purpose. **9** *N Amer.* a gathering with the family of a deceased person before the funeral, usu. with the opportunity to pay one's last respects to the deceased.

vis·it·ing ● *noun* paying a visit or visits. ● *attributive adjective* **1** that visits (*visiting nurse*). **2** (of an academic etc.) having been invited from one institution to spend some time at another (*a visiting professor*). **3** pertaining to visits (*visiting hours*).

visiting card *noun* = CALLING CARD 1.

visiting fireman *noun N Amer. slang* a visitor given especially cordial treatment.

visiting hours *plural noun* a designated time when visitors may call, esp. to see a patient in hospital etc.

visiting nurse *noun N Amer.* a trained nurse who visits those in need of medical attention in their homes.

vis·itor *noun* **1** a person who visits a person or place. **2** *Sport* a team competing in the opposing side's home stadium, rink, etc. **3** = VISITANT 2. □ **visi·tor·ial** *adjective*

visitor centre *noun* a building in a tourist area in which exhibitions etc. are displayed as an introduction to the locality.

visitors' book *noun* = GUEST BOOK.

visor /ˈvaɪzər/ *noun* **1 a** a movable part of a helmet covering the face. **b** *N Amer.* the projecting front part of a cap. **c** a half-moon shaped shade on an adjustable or elasticized headband, worn to protect the eyes from strong light. **d** *hist.* a mask or disguise. **2** a movable flap at the top of a windshield inside a car to protect the eyes from glare. □ **vis·ored** *adjective* [Anglo-French *viser*, Old French *visiere* from *vis* face, from Latin *visus*: see VISAGE]

vista *noun* **1** a long narrow view as between rows of trees. **2** a scenic wide view; a prospect or panorama. **3** a mental view of a long succession of remembered or anticipated events (*opened up new vistas to her ambition*). [Italian, = view, from *visto* seen, past participle of *vedere* see, from Latin *vidēre*]

Vis·tula River /ˈvɪstjʊlə/ a river in Poland which rises in the Carpathian Mountains and flows 940 km (592 miles) generally northward, through Cracow and Warsaw, to the Baltic near Gdańsk.

vis·ual ● *adjective* of, concerned with, or used in seeing. ● *noun* (usu. in *pl.*) **1** a visual image or display, a picture. **2** the visual element of a film or television broadcast. □ **visu·al·ity** *noun* **visu·al·ly** *adverb* [Late Latin *visualis* from Latin *visus* sight, from *vidēre* see]

visual aid *noun* a film, model, etc., as an aid to learning.

visual angle *noun* the angle formed at the eye by rays from the extremities of an object viewed.

visual art *noun* (often in *pl.*) any art meant to be appreciated mainly or exclusively through sight, e.g. graphic art, sculpture, etc. □ **visual artist** *noun*

visual display unit *noun esp. Brit. Computing* = VIDEO DISPLAY TERMINAL. Abbr.: **VDU**.

visual field *noun* field of vision.

visual flight rules *plural noun* rules for navigating aircraft by sight rather than by using instruments only or ground control. Abbr.: **VFR**.

Consonants: b *but*   d *dog*   f *few*   g *get*   h *her*   j *yes*   k *cat*   l *leg*   m *man*   n *no*   p *pen*   r *red*   s *sit*

vis·ual·ize *transitive verb* (also esp. *Brit.* **-ise**) **1** make visible esp. to one's mind (a thing not visible to the eye). **2** make visible to the eye. □ **vis·ual·iz·able** *adjective* **vis·ual·iz·a·tion** *noun*

visual purple *noun* = RHODOPSIN.

vital ● *adjective* **1 a** essential to the existence or functioning of a thing or to the matter in hand; indispensable; extremely important (*a vital question; secrecy is vital*). **b** paramount, very great (*of vital importance*). **2** of, concerned with, or essential to organic life (*vital energy; vital functions*). **3** full of life or activity; lively. **4** *archaic* fatal to life or to success etc. (*a vital error*). ● *noun* (in *pl.*) the body's vital organs, e.g. the heart and brain. □ **vital·ly** *adverb* [Old French from Latin *vitalis* from *vita* life]

vital capacity *noun* the volume of air that can be expelled from the lungs after taking the deepest possible breath.

vital force *noun* **1** (in Bergson's philosophy) life force. **2** any mysterious vital principle.

vital·ism *noun* *Biol.* the doctrine that life originates in a vital principle distinct from chemical and other physical forces. □ **vital·ist** *noun* **vital·is·tic** *adjective*

vital·ity *noun* **1** liveliness, animation. **2** the ability to sustain life, life power. **3** (of an institution, language, etc.) the ability to endure and to perform its functions.

vital·ize *transitive verb* (also esp. *Brit.* **-ise**) **1** endow with life. **2** infuse with vigour. □ **vital·iz·a·tion** *noun*

vital signs *plural noun* clinical measurements that indicate the state of a person's essential body functions, esp. pulse rate, temperature, respiration rate, and blood pressure.

vital statistics *plural noun* **1** the number of births, marriages, deaths, etc. **2** *jocular* the measurements of a woman's bust, waist, and hips.

vita·min /ˈvʌɪtəmɪn/ *noun* **1** any of a group of organic compounds essential in small amounts for many living organisms to maintain normal health and development. **2** (usu. in *pl.*) a pill providing any of these as a dietary supplement. [originally *vitamine* from Latin *vita* life + AMINE, because originally thought to contain an amino acid]

vitamin A *noun* = RETINOL.

vitamin B₁ *noun* = THIAMINE.

vitamin B₂ *noun* = RIBOFLAVIN.

vitamin B₃ *noun* = NIACIN.

vitamin B₆ *noun* = PYRIDOXINE.

vitamin B₁₂ *noun* = CYANOCOBALAMIN.

vitamin B complex *noun* a group of vitamins which, although not chemically related, are often found together in the same foods.

vitamin C *noun* = ASCORBIC ACID.

vitamin D *noun* any of a group of vitamins found in liver and fish oils, essential for the absorption of calcium and the prevention of rickets in children and osteomalacia in adults.

vitamin D₂ *noun* = CALCIFEROL.

vitamin D₃ *noun* = CHOLECALCIFEROL.

vitamin E *noun* = TOCOPHEROL.

vitamin H *noun* = BIOTIN.

vita·min·ize *transitive verb* (also esp. *Brit.* **-ise**) (esp. as **vita·min·ized** *adjective*) add vitamins to.

vitamin K *noun* any of a group of vitamins found mainly in green leaves and essential for the blood clotting process.

vitamin K₁ *noun* = PHYLLOQUINONE.

vitamin K₂ *noun* = MENAQUINONE.

vitamin M *noun* esp. *N Amer.* = FOLIC ACID.

Vi·tebsk see VITSEBSK.

vi·tel·lin /vɪˈtɛlɪn, vaɪ-/ *noun* *Chem.* the chief protein constituent of the yolk of an egg. [VITELLUS + -IN]

vi·tel·line /vɪˈtɛlʌɪn, vaɪ-, -lɪn/ *adjective* of or relating to the yolk of an egg or the contents of the ovum. [medieval Latin *vitellinus* (as VITELLUS)]

vitelline membrane *noun* the yolk sac.

vi·tel·lus /vɪˈtɛləs, vaɪ-/ *noun* **1** the yolk of an egg. **2** the contents of the ovum. [Latin, = yolk]

viti·ate /ˈvɪʃɪˌeɪt/ *transitive verb* **1** impair the quality or efficiency of; corrupt, debase, contaminate. **2** make invalid or ineffectual. □ **viti·a·tion** *noun* [Latin *vitiare* from *vitium* VICE¹]

viti·cul·ture /ˈvɪtɪˌkʌltʃər/ *noun* the cultivation of grapevines; the science or study of this. □ **viti·cul·tur·al** *adjective* **viti·cul·tur·ist** *noun* [Latin *vitis* vine + CULTURE]

Viti Levu /ˌviːti ˈleːvuː/ the largest of the Fiji islands. Its chief settlement is Suva.

viti·ligo /vɪtɪˈlaɪɡəʊ/ *noun* *Med.* a condition in which the pigment is lost from areas of the skin, causing whitish patches. [Latin]

Vi·toria /vɪˈtɔːrɪə/ a city in N Spain, capital of the Basque Provinces; pop. (est. 2001) 218,902.

Vi·tória /vɪˈtɔːrɪə/ a port in E Brazil; pop. (2000) 291,889.

vit·reous /ˈvɪtrɪəs/ *adjective* **1** of, or of the nature of, glass. **2** like glass in hardness, brittleness, transparency, structure, etc. (*vitreous enamel*). [Latin *vitreus* from *vitrum* glass]

vitreous humour *noun* (also **vitreous body**) *Anat.* a transparent jellylike tissue filling the eyeball.

vitri·fy /ˈvɪtrɪˌfaɪ/ *transitive & intransitive verb* (**-fies**, **-fied**) convert or be converted into glass or a glasslike substance esp. by heat. □ **vitri·fi·ca·tion** *noun* [French *vitrifier* or medieval Latin *vitrificare* (as VITREOUS)]

vi·trine /vɪˈtriːn/ *noun* a glass display case. [French from *vitre* glass]

vit·ri·ol /ˈvɪtrɪˌɒl, ˈvɪtrɪəl/ *noun* **1** sulphuric acid or a sulphate, originally one of glassy appearance. **2** caustic or hostile speech, criticism, or feeling. [Old French *vitriol* or medieval Latin *vitriolum* from Latin *vitrum* glass]

vit·ri·ol·ic /ˌvɪtrɪˈɒlɪk/ *adjective* (of speech or criticism) caustic or hostile.

Vit·ruv·ius /vɪˈtruːvɪəs/ (full name Marcus Vitruvius Pollio) (*fl.* 1st c. BC), Roman architect and military engineer, who wrote an influential ten-volume treatise on architecture, largely based on Greek sources, which deals with all aspects of building. □ **Vit·ruv·ian** *adjective*

Vit·sebsk /ˈviːtsjebsk/ (Russian **Vi·tebsk** /vɪtjebsk/) a city in NE Belarus; pop. (est. 2002) 335,200.

vitta /ˈvɪtə/ *noun* (*pl.* **vit·tae** /ˈvɪtiː/) **1** *Bot.* a resin canal in the fruit of some plants. **2** *Zool.* a stripe of colour. [Latin, = band, chaplet]

vittle *informal var. of* VICTUAL *noun.*

vi·tu·per·ate /vɪˈtuːpəˌreɪt, -ˈtjuː-, vaɪ-/ *verb* **1** *transitive* revile, abuse; find fault with in strong or violent language. **2** *intransitive* employ abusive language. □ **vi·tu·per·a·tion** *noun* **vi·tu·per·a·tive** /-rətɪv/ *adjective* **vi·tu·per·ator** *noun* [Latin *vituperare* from *vitium* VICE¹]

Vitus, St. /ˈvʌɪtəs/ (died *c.*300), Christian martyr. Said to have been martyred during the reign of Diocletian, he was invoked against rabies and as the patron of epileptics and people suffering certain nervous disorders, including St. Vitus's dance (Sydenham's chorea). Feast day, 15 June.

viv·ace /vɪˈvɒtʃeɪ/ *Music* ● *adverb* in a lively and brisk manner. ● *adjective* (of a musical passage) played or to be played vivace. ● *noun* a vivace passage in music. [Italian from Latin (as VIVACIOUS)]

viv·acious /vɪˈveɪʃəs, vaɪ-/ *adjective* lively, sprightly, animated. □ **viv·acious·ly** *adverb* **viv·acious·ness** *noun* **viv·acity** /vɪˈvasɪti/ *noun* [Latin *vivax* -*acis* from *vivere* live]

Viv·aldi /vɪˈvɒldi/ **An·tonio (Lucio)** (1678–1741), Italian composer and violinist. He wrote some 500 concertos, many of them, like his well-known *The Four Seasons* (1725), for the violin, which he helped to establish as a solo instrument. He also wrote many operas and sacred vocal compositions of which his *Gloria* is the best known.

viv·ar·ium /vaɪˈvɛərɪəm, vɪ-/ *noun* (*pl.* **viv·ar·iums** or **viv·ar·ia** /-rɪə/) a place artificially prepared for keeping animals in (nearly) their natural state; an aquarium or terrarium. [Latin, = warren, fish pond, from *vivus* living, from *vivere* live]

viva voce /ˌviːvə ˈvɒtʃeɪ, ˈvɔːtʃeɪ/ *adjective* spoken, oral. ● *adverb* out loud, orally. ● *noun* an oral examination for an academic qualification. [medieval Latin, = with the living voice]

viver·rid /vɪˈvɛrɪd, vaɪ-/ ● *noun* any mammal of the family Viverridae, including civets, mongooses, and genets. ● *adjective* of or relating to this family. [Latin *viverra* ferret + -ID³]

vivid *adjective* **1 a** (of light or colour) strong, intense, glaring (*a vivid flash of lightning; of a vivid green*). **b** brilliantly coloured or lit. **2 a** (of an impression, description, etc.) clear, striking, graphic. **b** (of a mental faculty) capable of strong and distinct impressions, producing clear images; active (*has a vivid imagination; have a vivid recollection of the scene*). **3** (of a person) lively, vigorous. □ **vivid·ly** *adverb* **vivid·ness** *noun* [Latin *vividus* from *vivere* live]

viv·ify *transitive verb* (**-fies**, **-fied**) enliven, animate, make lively or living. □ **vivi·fi·ca·tion** *noun* [French *vivifier* from Late Latin *vivificare* from Latin *vivus* living, from *vivere* live]

viv·ip·ar·ous /vɪˈvɪpərəs, vaɪ-/ *adjective* **1** *Zool.* bringing forth young alive, not hatching them by means of eggs (*compare* OVIPAROUS). **2** *Bot.* producing bulbs or seeds that germinate while still attached to the

---

t *top*   v *voice*   w *we*   z *zoo*   ʃ *she*   ʒ *vision*   θ *thin*   ð *this*   ŋ *ring*   x *loch*   tʃ *chip*   dʒ *jar*   (see over for vowels)

parent plant. □ **vivi·par·ity** /ˌvɪvɪˈperɪti/ *noun* **viv·ip·ar·ous·ly** *adverb* [Latin *viviparus* from *vivus*: see VIVIFY]

vivi·sect /ˈvɪvɪˌsekt, -ˈsekt/ *transitive verb* perform vivisection on. [back-formation from VIVISECTION]

vivi·sec·tion /ˌvɪvɪˈsekʃən/ *noun* **1** dissection or other painful treatment of living animals for purposes of scientific research. **2** unduly detailed or ruthless criticism. □ **vivi·sec·tion·al** *adjective* **vivi·sec·tion·ist** *noun* **vivi·sec·tor** /ˈvɪvɪˌsektər/ *noun* [Latin *vivus* living (see VIVIFY), after DISSECTION (as DISSECT)]

vixen *noun* **1** a female fox. **2** a spiteful or quarrelsome woman. □ **vixen·ish** *adjective* [Middle English *fixen* from Old English, fem. of FOX]

Vi·yella /vaɪˈelə/ *noun proprietary* a fabric made from a twilled mixture of cotton and wool. [from *Via Gellia*, a valley in Derbyshire where it was first made]

viz. *adverb* (usu. introducing a gloss or explanation) namely; that is to say; in other words (*came to a firm conclusion, viz. that we were right*). [abbreviation of VIDELICET, *z* being medieval Latin symbol for abbreviation of *-et*]

viz·ier /ˈvɪziːr, vɪˈzɪːr/ *noun hist.* a high official in some Muslim countries, esp. in Turkey under Ottoman rule. □ **viz·ier·ship** *noun* [ultimately from Arabic *wazīr* caliph's chief counsellor]

VJ *abbreviation* video jockey, a person who introduces music videos on television etc. [after DJ]

VJ day *noun* 15 August, 1945, the day Japan ceased fighting in the Second World War, or 2 September of the same year, when Japan formally surrendered.

Vlach /vlak/ ● *noun* a member of a Romanic people inhabiting Romania and parts of the former Soviet Union. ● *adjective* of or relating to this people. [Bulgarian from Old Slavic *Vlachŭ* Romanian etc. from Germanic, = foreigner]

Vladi·kav·kaz /ˌvladɪkafˈkɒs/ a city in SW Russia, capital of the autonomous republic of North Ossetia; pop. (est. 2002) 313,100. It was formerly known as Ordzhonikidze (1931–44 and 1954–93) and Dzaudzhikau (1944–54).

Vlad·i·mir /ˈvladəˌmiːr, vləˈdiːmiːr/ a city in European Russia, east of Moscow; pop. (est. 2002) 336,100.

Vladimir I /ˈvladəˌmiːr/ (known as Vladimir the Great; canonized as St. Vladimir) (956–1015), grand prince of Kiev 980–1015. After marrying a sister of the Byzantine emperor Basil II (*c.*987) he converted to Christianity, a move which resulted in Christianity in Russia and Ukraine developing in close association with the Orthodox rather than the Western Church. Feast day, 15 July.

Vladi·vos·tok /ˌvladəˈvɒstɒk/ a city in the extreme southeast of Russia, on the coast of the Sea of Japan, capital of Primorsky; pop. (est. 2002) 596,800. It is the chief port of Russia's Pacific coast and terminus of the Trans-Siberian Railway.

vlei /fleɪ/ *noun South Africa* a hollow in which water collects during the rainy season. [Dutch dial. from Dutch *vallei* valley]

VLF *abbreviation* very low frequency (designating radio waves of frequency *c.*3–30 kHz and wavelength *c.*10–100 km).

VLSI *abbreviation Computing* very large-scale integration, the technology integrating over 100,000 transistors on a single chip.

VLT *abbreviation* VIDEO LOTTERY TERMINAL.

Vltava River /ˈvəltəvə/ (also traditionally called **Mol·dau**) a river of the Czech Republic, which rises in the Bohemian Forest on the German–Czech border and flows 435 km (270 miles) generally northward, passing through Prague before joining the Elbe north of the city.

V-neck *noun* (often *attributive*) **1** (also **V-neckline**) a neck of a pullover etc. with straight sides meeting at an angle in the front to form a V. **2** a garment with this. □ **V-necked** *adjective*

V.O. *abbreviation* voice-over.

VOC *abbreviation* volatile organic compound.

vocab /ˈvoːkab/ *noun informal* vocabulary. [abbreviation]

voc·able /ˈvoːkəbəl/ *noun* a word, esp. with reference to form rather than meaning. [French *vocable* or Latin *vocabulum* from *vocare* call]

vo·cabu·lary /vəˈkabjuˌleri/ *noun* (pl. **-ies**) **1** (the (principal) words used in a language or a particular book or branch of science etc. or by a particular author (*scientific vocabulary; the vocabulary of Shakespeare*). **2** a list of these, arranged alphabetically with definitions or translations. **3** the range of words known to an individual (*his vocabulary is limited*). **4** a set of artistic or stylistic forms or techniques, esp. a range of movements in dance etc. [medieval Latin *vocabularius, -um* (as VOCABLE)]

vocal ● *adjective* **1** of or concerned with or uttered by the voice (*a vocal communication*). **2** expressing one's feelings freely in speech (*was very vocal about his rights*). **3** (of music) written for or produced by the voice with or without accompaniment (*compare* INSTRUMENTAL *adjective* 2). **4** *Phonetics* voiced. **5** *literary* (of trees, water, etc.) endowed with a voice or a similar faculty. ● *noun* **1** (in *sing.* or *pl.*) the sung part of a musical composition. **2** a musical performance with singing. □ **vocal·ity** /voːˈkalɪti/ *noun* **vocal·ly** *adverb* [Latin *vocalis* (as VOICE)]

vocal cords *plural noun* (also **vocal folds**) folds of the lining membrane of the larynx near the opening of the glottis, which vibrate in the airstream when close together to produce voiced sounds.

vo·cal·ic /voːˈkalɪk/ *adjective* of or consisting of a vowel or vowels.

vocal·ise /ˈvoːkəˈliːz/ *noun Music* **1** a singing exercise using individual syllables or vowel sounds. **2** a vocal passage consisting of a melody without words. **3** *derogatory* a technical vocal display. [French, from *vocaliser* 'to vocalize']

vocal·ism *noun* **1** the use of the voice in speaking or singing. **2** a vowel sound or system.

vocal·ist *noun* a singer, esp. of jazz or popular songs.

vocal·ize *verb* (also esp. *Brit.* **-ise**) **1** *transitive* **a** form (a sound) or utter (a word) with the voice. **b** make sonant (*f* is vocalized into *v*). **2** *intransitive* utter a vocal sound. **3** *transitive* articulate, express. **4** *transitive* write (Hebrew etc.) with vowel points. **5** *intransitive Music* sing with several notes to one vowel. **6** *transitive* (usu. in *passive*) change (a consonant) to a semi-vowel or vowel. □ **vocal·iz·a·tion** *noun*

vo·ca·tion *noun* **1 a** a strong feeling of fitness for a particular career or occupation. **b** a divine call to the religious life. **2 a** a person's employment, esp. regarded as requiring dedication. **b** a trade or profession. [Old French *vocation* or Latin *vocatio* from *vocare* call]

vo·ca·tion·al *adjective* **1** of or relating to an occupation or employment. **2** (of education or training) directed at a particular esp. manual or technical occupation and its skills (*vocational school*). □ **vo·ca·tion·al·ism** *noun* **vo·ca·tion·al·ize** *transitive verb* (also esp. *Brit.* **-ise**). **vo·ca·tion·al·ly** *adverb*

voca·tive /ˈvɒkətɪv/ *Grammar* ● *noun* the case of nouns, pronouns, and adjectives used in addressing or invoking a person or thing. ● *adjective* of or in this case. [Old French *vocatif -ive* or Latin *vocativus* from *vocare* call]

vo·cif·er·ate /vəˈsɪfəˌreɪt/ *verb* **1** *transitive* utter (words etc.) noisily. **2** *intransitive* shout, bawl. □ **vo·cif·er·a·tion** *noun* [Latin *vociferari* from *vox* voice + *ferre* bear]

vo·cif·er·ous /voːˈsɪfərəs/ *adjective* **1** (of a person, speech, etc.) noisy, clamorous. **2** insistently and forcibly expressing one's views. □ **vo·cif·er·ous·ly** *adverb* **vo·cif·er·ous·ness** *noun*

vo·coder /ˈvoːˌkoːdər/ *noun* a synthesizer that produces sounds from an analysis of speech input. □ **vo·co·dered** *adjective* (VOICE + CODE)

vod·ka *noun* **1** a colourless alcoholic spirit made by distillation of rye etc. **2** a drink of this. [Russian, diminutive of *voda* water]

vogue /voːg/ *noun* **1** (prec. by *the*) the prevailing fashion. **2** popular use or currency (*has had a great vogue*). □ **in vogue** in fashion, generally current. □ **vo·guish** *adjective* [French from Italian *voga* rowing, fashion, from *vogare* row, go well]

vogue word *noun* a word currently fashionable.

vo·guing /ˈvoːgɪŋ/ *noun* solo dancing with movements reminiscent of a fashion model's posing and posturing. [from the fashion magazine *Vogue*]

voice ● *noun* **1 a** a sound formed in the larynx etc. and uttered by the mouth, esp. human utterance in speaking, shouting, singing, etc. (*heard a voice; spoke in a low voice*). **b** the ability to produce this (*has lost her voice*). **c** this regarded as characteristic of an individual. **2 a** the use of the voice; utterance, esp. in spoken or written words (esp. *give voice*). **b** an opinion so expressed; the expressed will of the people, a group, etc. **c** the right to express an opinion (*I have no voice in the matter*). **d** an agency by which an opinion is expressed. **3** *Grammar* a form or set of forms of a verb showing the relation of the subject to the action (*active voice; passive voice*). **4** *Music* **a** a vocal part in a composition. **b** a constituent part in a fugue. **5** *Phonetics* sound uttered with resonance of the vocal cords, not with mere breath. **6** (usu. in *pl.*) the supposed utterance of an invisible guiding or directing spirit. **7** the distinctive tone or style of a literary work or author. ● *transitive verb* **1** give utterance to; express (*the letter voices our opinion*). **2** (esp. as **voiced** *adjective*) *Phonetics* utter with vibration of the vocal cords, e.g. *b, d, g, v, z.* **3** *Music* regulate the tone quality of (organ pipes). **4** (of an actor) provide the voice for a character in an animated film. □ **in voice** (or **good voice**) in proper vocal condition for singing or speaking. **with**

Vowels: a *cat* ɑ *arm* e *bed* ɜr *her* ɜː *deux* ə *ago* ɪ *sit* i *cosy* iː *feed* ɒ *hot* ɔ *pore* oː *no* ʌ *run* ʊ *put*

one voice unanimously. □ **-voiced** *adjective* **voicer** *noun* (in sense 3 of *verb*). **voi·cing** *noun* [Old French *vois* from Latin *vox vocis*]

voice box *noun* the larynx.

voice·less *adjective* **1** dumb, mute, speechless. **2** *Phonetics* uttered without vibration of the vocal cords, e.g. *f, k, p, s, t.* □ **voice·less·ly** *adverb* **voice·less·ness** *noun*

voice mail *noun* a system for electronically storing, processing, and reproducing verbal messages left through the conventional telephone network.

voice mailbox *noun* an electronic file storing an individual's voice mail messages.

voice message *noun* a message left on a voice mail system.

voice-over *noun* narration in a film etc. not accompanied by a picture of the speaker.

voice print *noun* a visual record of speech, analyzed with respect to frequency, duration, and amplitude.

voice vote *noun* a vote taken by noting the relative strength of calls of *yea* and *nay*.

voi·cing *noun Jazz* the tonal quality of a group of musical instruments in an ensemble; a blend of instrumental sound.

void ● *adjective* **1 a** empty, vacant. **b** (foll. by *of*) lacking; free from (*a style void of affectation*). **2** esp. *Law* (of a contract, deed, promise, etc.) invalid, not binding (*null and void*). **3** useless, ineffectual. **4** (often foll. by *in*) *Cards* (of a hand) having no cards in a given suit. ● *noun* **1** an empty space, a vacuum (*vanished into the void; cannot fill the void made by death*). **2** an unfilled space in a wall or building. **3** (often foll. by *in*) *Cards* the absence of cards in a particular suit. ● *verb* **1** *transitive* render invalid. **2** *transitive & intransitive* empty the contents of esp. the bowels or bladder; excrete. □ **void·able** *adjective* **void·ness** *noun* [Old French dial. *voide*, Old French *vuide, vuit*, related to Latin *vacare* VACATE: v. partly from AVOID, partly from Old French *voider*]

void·ed *adjective* **1** in senses of VOID verb. **2** *Heraldry* (of a bearing) having the central area cut away so as to show the field.

voila /vwɒˈlɒ/ *interjection* expressing satisfaction or ease of accomplishment. [French from imperative of *voir* see + *là* there]

voile /vɔil, vwɒl/ *noun* a thin semi-transparent material. [French, = VEIL]

voir dire /vwɑr ˈdiːr/ *noun* **1** a preliminary examination by a judge or counsel of the competence of a witness or juror. **2** an investigation into the admissibility of evidence, held during a trial. [Old French *voir* true, truth + *dire* say]

Voi·sine /vwɒˈziːn/ **Roch** (b.1963), Canadian pop singer and songwriter. Of Acadian origin, he sings in both English and French and is hugely popular in Quebec and France. Two of his albums have received Victoire trophies for the best album in the French-speaking world.

Voj·vod·ina /vɔiˈvɒdɪnə/ a mainly Hungarian-speaking province of N Serbia, on the Hungarian border; pop. (est. 1991) 2,013,900; capital, Novi Sad.

vol. *abbreviation* volume.

volant /ˈvoːlənt/ *adjective Zool.* flying, able to fly. [French from *voler* from Latin *volare* fly]

volar /ˈvoːlər/ *adjective Anat.* of the palm or sole. [Latin *vola* hollow of hand or foot]

vola·tile /ˈvɒlə,tail, -təl/ ● *adjective* **1** evaporating rapidly (*volatile salts*). **2** changeable; unstable. **3** lively, lighthearted. **4** apt to break out into violence. **5** transient. **6** *Computing* designating memory whose contents are destroyed on the removal of power to the memory. ● *noun* a volatile substance. □ **vola·tile·ness** *noun* **vola·til·ity** /-ˈtɪlɪti/ *noun* [Old French *volatil* or Latin *volatilis* from *volare volat-* fly]

volatile oil *noun* = ESSENTIAL OIL.

vola·til·ize /vəˈlatɪ,laiz/ *verb* (also esp. *Brit.* **-ise**) **1** *transitive* cause to evaporate. **2** *intransitive* evaporate. □ **vola·til·iz·a·tion** *noun*

vol-au-vent /ˈvɒloː,vɑ̃/ *noun* a (usu. small) round case of puff pastry filled with meat, fish, etc., and sauce. [French, lit. 'flight in the wind']

vol·can·ic /vɒlˈkanɪk/ ● *adjective* of, like, or produced by a volcano. ● *noun* (usu. in *pl.*) a rock or mineral formed by volcanic action. □ **vol·can·ic·al·ly** *adverb* **vol·can·ic·ity** /,vɒlkəˈnɪsɪti/ *noun*

volcanic bomb *noun* a mass of ejected lava usu. rounded and sometimes hollow.

volcanic glass *noun* obsidian.

vol·can·ism /ˈvɒlkənɪzəm/ *noun* (also **vul·can·ism** /ˈvʌl-/) volcanic activity or phenomena.

vol·ca·no /vɒlˈkeinoː/ *noun* (pl. **-noes**) **1** a mountain or hill having an opening or openings in the earth's crust through which lava, cinders,

steam, gases, etc., are or have been expelled continuously or at intervals. **2 a** a state of things likely to cause a violent outburst. **b** a violent esp. suppressed feeling. [Italian from Latin *Volcanus* VULCAN]

vol·can·ol·ogy /,vɒlkəˈnɒlədʒi/ *noun* (also **vul·can·ol·ogy** /,vʌl-/) the scientific study of volcanoes. □ **vol·cano·logic·al** *adjective* **vol·can·ol·o·gist** *noun*

vole *noun* any small rat-like or mouselike plant-eating rodent of the family Cricetidae. [originally *vole-mouse* from Norwegian from *voll* field + *mus* mouse]

Volga /ˈvɒlgə/ the longest river in Europe, which rises in NW Russia and flows 3 688 km (2,292 miles) generally eastward to Kazan, where it turns southeastward to the Caspian Sea.

Vol·go·grad /ˈvɒlgə,grad/ an industrial city in SW Russia, situated at the junction of the Don and Volga rivers; pop. (2002) 987,400. The city was called Tsaritsyn until 1925, and Stalingrad from then until 1961. (See also STALINGRAD, BATTLE OF.)

vol·ition /vəˈlɪʃən/ *noun* **1** the exercise of the will. **2** the power of willing. □ **of** (or **by**) **one's own volition** voluntarily. □ **vol·ition·al** *adjective* [French *volition* or medieval Latin *volitio* from *volo* I wish]

volk /fɒlk/ *noun* **1** the Afrikaner people. **2** the German people (esp. with reference to Nazi ideology). [Afrikaans (from Dutch), German = nation, people]

völk·isch /ˈfɜlkɪʃ/ *adjective* populist, nationalist, racist. [German]

vol·ley ● *noun* (pl. **-leys**) **1 a** the simultaneous discharge of a number of weapons. **b** the bullets etc. discharged in a volley. **2** (usu. foll. by *of*) a rapid emission of many things at once in quick succession (*a volley of insults*). **3 a** the return of a ball, shuttlecock, etc. in play in tennis etc. before it touches the ground. **b** a series of these. **4** *Soccer* the kicking of a ball in play before it touches the ground. **5** *Volleyball* a pass etc. made with the fingertips. **6** *Cricket* **a** a ball pitched right up to the batsman or the stumps without bouncing. **b** the pitching of the ball in this way. ● *verb* (**-leys, -leyed**) **1** *transitive & intransitive Sport* return or send (a ball) by a volley. **2** *transitive & intransitive* discharge (bullets, abuse, etc.) in a volley. **3** *intransitive* (of bullets etc.) fly in a volley. **4** *intransitive* (of guns etc.) sound together. □ **vol·ley·er** *noun* [French *volée*, ultimately from Latin *volare* fly]

vol·ley·ball *noun* **1** a game for two usu. six-player teams in which a large inflated ball is hit back and forth over a net with the fingers, fist, or forearm. **2** the ball used in this game.

Vol·ogda /ˈvɒləgdə/ a city in NW Russia; pop. (est. 2002) 303,500.

vols. *abbreviation* volumes.

Vol·scian /ˈvɒlʃən/ ● *noun* **1** a member of an ancient people formerly inhabiting eastern Latium, in conflict with Rome from the 5th c. BC until finally defeated in 304 BC. **2** the Italic language of the Volscians. ● *adjective* of or pertaining to the Volscians or their language. [Latin *Volsci*]

volt[1] *noun* the SI unit of electromotive force, the difference of potential that would carry one ampere of current against one ohm resistance. Abbr.: **V**. [VOLTA]

volt[2] *var.* of VOLTE.

Volta /ˈvoːltə, ˈvɒl-/ **Ales·san·dro Giu·seppe An·tonio Ana·sta·sio, Count** (1745–1824), Italian physicist. He invented a number of important electrical instruments, including the electrophorus and the condensing electroscope, but is best known for the voltaic pile or electrochemical battery (1800), which was the first device to produce a continuous electric current.

volt·age *noun* electromotive force or potential difference expressed in volts.

vol·taic *adjective archaic* of electricity from a primary battery; galvanic (*voltaic battery*).

Vol·taire /vɒlˈter/ (pseudonym of François-Marie Arouet) (1694–1778), French writer, dramatist, and poet, a leading figure of the Enlightenment. His radical political and religious views and satirical writings brought him frequently into conflict with the Establishment; major works include *Lettres philosophiques* (1734) and *Candide* (1758), a satirical tale attacking Leibniz's optimism.

volt·am·eter /vɒlˈtamɪtər/ *noun* an instrument for measuring an electric charge.

volt·am·metry /vɒlˈtamətri/ *noun* a technique for identifying and finding the concentrations of various ions in solution by plotting the relation of current and voltage in a micro-electrode. □ **volt·am·met·ric** /-ˈmetrɪk/ *adjective* [VOLT[1] + AMPERE + -METRY]

Volta River /ˈvɒltə/ a river of West Africa, which is formed in central Ghana by the junction of its headwaters, the Black Volta, the White

Volta, and the Red Volta, which rise in Burkina Faso. At Akosombo in SE Ghana the river has been dammed, creating Lake Volta, which is one of the world's largest artificial lakes.

volte /vɒlt, voːlt/ *noun* (also **volt**) **1** *Fencing* a quick movement to escape a thrust. **2** a sideways circular movement of a horse. [French from Italian *volta* turn, fem. past participle of *volgere* turn, from Latin *volvere* roll]

volte-face /vɒltə ˈfas/ *noun* **1** a complete reversal of position in argument or opinion. **2** the act or an instance of turning around. [French from Italian *voltafaccia*, ultimately from Latin *volvere* roll + *facies* appearance, face]

volt·meter *noun* an instrument for measuring electric potential in volts.

vol·uble /ˈvɒljubəl/ *adjective* speaking or spoken vehemently, incessantly, or fluently (*voluble spokesman*; *voluble excuses*). □ **volu·bil·ity** /-ˈbɪlɪti/ *noun* **vol·uble·ness** *noun* **vol·ubly** *adverb* [French *voluble* or Latin *volubilis* from *volvere* roll]

vol·ume *noun* **1 a** a set of sheets of paper, usu. printed, and bound together; a book, esp. one of a matching set or series (*issued in three volumes*; *a library of 12,000 volumes*). **b** several consecutive issues of a magazine etc. esp. designed to be bound together as a book. **c** *hist.* a scroll of papyrus etc., an ancient form of book. **2 a** solid content, bulk. **b** the space occupied by a substance. **c** (usu. foll. by *of*) an amount or quantity (*large volume of business*). **d** the amount of space in a container. **3 a** quantity or power of sound. **b** a knob etc. controlling this, as on stereo equipment. **c** fullness of tone. **4** (foll. by *of*) **a** a moving mass of water etc. **b** (usu. in *pl.*) a wreath or coil or rounded mass of smoke etc. □ **speak volumes** *see* SPEAK. □ **vol·umed** *adjective* (also in *combination*). [Old French *volum(e)* from Latin *volumen -minis* roll, from *volvere* to roll]

volu·met·ric *adjective* of or relating to measurement by volume. □ **volu·met·ric·ally** *adverb* [VOLUME + METRIC]

vo·lu·min·ous /vəˈluːmɪnəs, vəˈljuː-/ *adjective* **1** large in volume; bulky. **2** (of drapery, a skirt, etc.) loose and ample. **3** consisting of many volumes. **4** (of a writer) producing many books. □ **vo·lu·min·ous·ly** *adverb* **vo·lu·min·ous·ness** *noun*

vol·um·ize *transitive verb* (also esp. *Brit.* **-ise**) increase the bulk or volume of (esp. hair).

vol·un·tar·ism /ˈvɒləntəˌrɪzəm/ *noun* **1** the principle of relying on voluntary action rather than compulsion, esp. as regards social welfare. **2** *Philos.* the doctrine that the will is a fundamental or dominant factor in the individual or the universe. □ **vol·un·tar·ist** *noun* [irreg. from VOLUNTARY]

vol·un·tary /ˈvɒlənˌteri/ ● *adjective* **1** done, acting, or able to act of one's own free will; not constrained or compulsory, intentional (*a voluntary donation*). **2** unpaid (*voluntary work*). **3** (of an institution) **a** supported by voluntary contributions. **b** staffed by volunteers. **4** brought about, produced, etc., by voluntary action. **5** (of a movement, muscle, or limb) controlled by the will. **6** (of a confession by a criminal) not prompted by a promise or threat. **7** not accidental; intentional (*voluntary manslaughter*). **8** *Law* (of a conveyance or disposition) made without return in money or other consideration. ● *noun* (*pl.* **-ies**) **1** an organ solo played before, during, or after a church service. **2** the music for this. □ **vol·un·tar·i·ly** *adverb* **vol·un·tar·i·ness** *noun* [Old French *volontaire* or Latin *voluntarius* from *voluntas* will]

Voluntary Aid Detachment *noun* (in the UK) a group of organized voluntary first aid and nursing workers, founded in 1909.

voluntary simplicity *noun* a philosophy or way of life that rejects materialism and is characterized by minimal consumption, environmental responsibility, and community co-operation.

vol·un·teer /ˌvɒlənˈtiːr/ ● *noun* **1** a person who voluntarily takes part in an enterprise or offers to undertake a task. **2** a person who enrols voluntarily for military service. **3** a person who works for an organization voluntarily and without pay. **4** (*attributive*) designating an organization etc. composed of volunteers (*volunteer fire department*). **5** (usu. *attributive*) a self-sown plant. ● *verb* **1** *transitive* (often foll. by *to* + infin.) undertake or offer (one's services, a remark or explanation, etc.) voluntarily. **2** *intransitive* (often foll. by *for*) make a voluntary offer of one's services; be a volunteer. **3** *transitive* (usu. in *passive*; often foll. by *for*, or *to* + infin.) often *ironic* assign or commit (a person) to a particular esp. 'voluntary' undertaking, esp. without consultation.

vol·un·teer·ism /vɒlənˈtiːrɪzəm/ *noun* esp. *N Amer.* the involvement of volunteers, esp. in community service.

vo·lup·tu·ary /vəˈlʌptʃʊˌeri/ ● *noun* (*pl.* **-aries**) a person given up to luxury and sensual pleasure. ● *adjective* concerned with luxury and sensual pleasure. [Latin *volupt(u)arius* (as VOLUPTUOUS)]

vo·lup·tu·ous /vəˈlʌptʃʊəs, -tju-/ *adjective* **1** of, tending to, occupied with, or derived from, sensuous or sensual pleasure. **2** suggestive of sensuous or sensual pleasure; sensuously or sensually pleasing. **3** (of a woman) curvaceous and sexually desirable. □ **vo·lup·tu·ous·ly** *adverb* **vo·lup·tu·ous·ness** *noun* [Old French *voluptueux* or Latin *voluptuosus* from *voluptas* pleasure]

vol·ute /ˈvɒljuːt, vəˈljuːt, -ˈluːt/ ● *noun* **1** *Archit.* a spiral scroll characteristic of Ionic capitals and also used in Corinthian and composite capitals. **2 a** any marine gastropod mollusc of the genus *Voluta*. **b** the spiral shell of this. ● *adjective* esp. *Bot.* rolled up. □ **vol·uted** *adjective* [French *volute* or Latin *voluta* fem. past participle of *volvere* roll]

Volzh·sky /ˈvɒlʒski/ an industrial city in SW Russia, on the Volga; pop. (est. 2002) 286,300.

vomer /ˈvoːmər/ *noun Anat.* the small thin bone separating the nostrils in humans and most vertebrates. [Latin, = ploughshare]

vomit ● *verb* (**vomit·ed**, **vomit·ing**) **1** *transitive & intransitive* eject (matter) from the stomach through the mouth. **2** *transitive* (of a volcano, chimney, etc.) eject violently, belch forth. ● *noun* matter vomited from the stomach. [Middle English, ultimately from Latin *vomere* vomit- or frequentative Latin *vomitare*]

vomi·tor·ium /ˌvɒmɪˈtɔːriəm/ *noun* (*pl.* **vomi·tor·ia**) *Rom. Hist.* **1** a vomitory. **2** a place in which, according to popular misconception, the ancient Romans are supposed to have vomited during feasts to make room for more food. [Latin; see VOMITORY]

vomi·tory /ˈvɒmɪtəri/ ● *adjective* emetic. ● *noun* (*pl.* **-ies**) *Rom. Hist.* each of a series of passages for entrance and exit in an amphitheatre or theatre. [Latin *vomitorius* (adj.), *-um* (n.) (as VOMIT)]

vomit·ous *adjective* esp. *N Amer.* nauseating.

vomity *adjective* like or smelling of vomit.

VON *abbreviation Cdn* **1** VICTORIAN ORDER OF NURSES. **2** a VON nurse.

von Braun see BRAUN 3.

Von Gencsy /vɒnˈgentsi/ **Eva** (1924–96), Hungarian-born Canadian dancer and choreographer. Emigrating to Canada in 1948, she joined the Royal Winnipeg Ballet, and moved to Ballets Chiriaeff in Montreal in 1953. In 1957 she turned to jazz, both performing and teaching, and in 1972 founded Les Ballets Jazz de Montréal, serving as artistic director and choreographer until 1979.

Von·ne·gut /ˈvɒnəgət/ **Kurt** (b.1922), US novelist and short-story writer. His works blend elements of realism, science fiction, fantasy, and satire; they include *Cat's Cradle* (1963) and *Slaughterhouse Five, or The Children's Crusade* (1969).

von Neu·mann /von ˈnjuːmən/ **John** (1903–57), Hungarian-born US mathematician, whose most influential contributions were in the harnessing of nuclear energy for both military and peaceful uses, and the design and use of high-speed electronic computing machines.

von Wil·le·brand's disease *noun* an inherited disorder characterized by a tendency to bleed, caused by deficiency or abnormality of a plasma coagulation factor. [E.A. *von Willebrand* Finnish physician d.1949]

voo·doo ● *noun* **1 a** a religion practised in the W Indies (esp. Haiti) and the southern US, characterized by sorcery and spirit possession, and combining elements of traditional African religious rites with Roman Catholic ritual. **b** a person skilled in this. **c** a voodoo spell. **2** *informal* seemingly magical ability (*working her voodoo again*). **3** (*attributive*) designating an impracticable or seemingly mystical approach to solving scientific or practical problems (*voodoo economics*). ● *transitive verb* (**voo·doos**, **voo·dooed**) affect by voodoo; bewitch. □ **voo·doo·ism** *noun* **voo·doo·ist** *noun* [Louisiana French *voudou* from Fon *vodu* tutelary deity, fetish]

voodoo doll *noun* a small figure in the likeness of a real person, the tormenting or hexing of which supposedly affects the person.

vor·acious /vəˈreɪʃəs/ *adjective* **1** greedy in eating, ravenous. **2** very eager in some activity; insatiable (*a voracious reader*). □ **vor·acious·ly** *adverb* **vor·acious·ness** *noun* **vor·acity** /vəˈrasɪti/ *noun* [Latin *vorax* from *vorare* devour]

Vor·arl·berg /ˈfɔːrɑːrlˌbɜːrg/ an Alpine state of W Austria; capital, Bregenz.

Vor·on·ezh /vəˈrɒnɛʒ/ a city in Russia, south of Moscow; pop. (est. 2002) 905,600.

Voro·shi·lov·grad /ˌvɒrəˈʃiːləfˌgrad/ a former name (1935–91) for LUHANSK.

-vorous /vərəs/ *combining form* forming adjectives meaning 'feeding on' (*carnivorous*). □ **-vora** /vərə/ *combining form* forming names of groups. **-vore** /vɔr/ *combining form* forming names of individuals. [Latin *-vorus* from *vorare* devour]

Vor·ster /ˈfɔrstər, ˈvɔr-/ **Bal·thazar Jo·han·nes** (known as 'John') (1915–83), South African politician, prime minister 1966–78 and president 1978.

vor·tex *noun* (*pl.* **vor·ti·ces** /vɔrtɪˌsiːz/ or **vor·tex·es**) **1 a** a mass of whirling fluid, esp. a whirlpool or whirlwind. **2** any whirling motion or mass. **3** a system, occupation, pursuit, etc., viewed as swallowing up or engrossing those who approach it (*the vortex of society*). **4** *Physics* a portion of fluid whose particles have rotatory motion. □ **vor·ti·cal** *adjective* **vor·ti·city** /vɔrˈtɪsɪti/ *noun* [Latin *vortex -icis* eddy, var. of VERTEX]

vor·ti·cella /ˌvɔrtɪˈsɛlə/ *noun* any sedentary protozoan of the family Vorticellidae, consisting of a tubular stalk with a bell-shaped ciliated opening. [modern Latin, diminutive of VORTEX]

vor·ti·cist /ˈvɔrtɪsɪst/ *noun* **1** *Art* an artist of a British movement c. 1914–15 influenced by futurism and cubism and characterized by harsh machine-like forms. **2** *Metaphysics* a person regarding the universe, with Descartes, as a plenum in which motion propagates itself in circles. □ **vor·ti·cism** *noun*

Vosges /voːʒ/ a mountain system of E France, in Alsace near the border with Germany.

vo·tary /ˈvoʊtəri/ *noun* (*pl.* **-ies**) **1** a devoted follower of a religion, deity, or cult, esp. one who is bound, by vow, to the worship of God. **2** (often foll. by *of*) a devoted follower, adherent or advocate of a person, cause, occupation, or pursuit. [Latin *vot-*: see VOTE]

vote ● *noun* **1 a** a formal expression of choice or opinion by means of a ballot, show of hands, etc., concerning esp. a choice of candidate or approval or rejection of a motion or resolution. **b** a ballot or ticket used for recording one's choice (*we will know the winner once the votes have been counted*). **2** the collective votes that are or may be given by or for a particular group (*we hope to win the francophone vote; the Conservative vote has increased*). **3** (usu. prec. by *the*) the right to vote, esp. in general elections; suffrage. **4 a** an opinion expressed or decision reached by a majority of votes (*a vote of confidence*). **b** a resolution passed or grant of appropriation authorized by Parliament. ● *verb* **1** *intransitive* **a** (often foll. by *for, against, in favour of,* or *to* + infin.) express a choice or preference by casting a vote. **b** (foll. by *on*) register or express one's opinion regarding (*they vote on the proposal today*). **2** *transitive* (usu. foll. by *to, in favour of,* or *that*) decide by a majority of votes (*striking workers have voted to accept the latest proposal*). **3** *transitive* support (a candidate, party, side, etc.) habitually or in a particular election (*I vote Liberal*). **4** *transitive* pronounce or declare by formal ballot or general consent (*her classmates voted her most likely to succeed; he was voted the league's MVP*). **5** *transitive* (often foll. by *that* + clause, *to*) *informal* announce one's proposal (*I vote that we all go home*). □ **put to a** (or **the**) **vote** submit to a decision by voting. **vote down** defeat (a proposal etc.) in a vote. **vote in** elect (a candidate) by votes. **vote out** dismiss (an incumbent) from office etc. by voting. **vote with one's feet** *informal* indicate an opinion by one's presence or absence. □ **vot·able** *adjective* **vote·less** *adjective* [Middle English from past participle stem *vot-* of Latin *vovēre* vow]

vote-getter *noun informal* **1** a candidate in an election (*four of the top five vote-getters were women*). **2** a policy introduced prior to or during an election campaign in an attempt to sway voters. □ **vote-getting** *noun*

vote of censure *noun* = VOTE OF NON-CONFIDENCE.

vote of confidence *noun* (also **vote of support**) **1** a vote showing that the majority support the policy of the governing body etc. **2** an indication from a person of his or her support for or approval of another, their work, etc.

vote of non-confidence *noun Cdn* (also esp. *US & Brit.* **vote of no confidence**) a vote indicating that the majority does not support a policy of the governing party, as a result of which the governing party is usu. forced to resign.

vot·er *noun* **1** a person eligible to vote in an election. **2** a person voting.

voters list *noun* a list of the names and addresses of those who are eligible to vote in an upcoming general election or referendum.

vot·ing booth *noun N Amer.* = POLLING BOOTH.

vot·ing machine *noun* (esp. in the US) an apparatus at a polling station on which votes may be registered automatically.

vot·ing shares *plural noun* (also **voting stock**) shares in a company that entitle the holder to vote at the annual general meeting and any other meetings of the company.

vo·tive /ˈvoʊtɪv/ *adjective* **1** offered or undertaken in fulfillment of a vow or as a thanksgiving (*votive offering*). **2** expressive of a vow, desire, or wish (*votive prayer*). [Latin *votivus* (as VOTE)]

votive candle *noun* **1** (also **votive light**) (in some Christian denominations) a candle, often contained in a glass vase, that may be lit as a symbol of prayer, usu. in front of a religious image. **2** a type of squat household candle, usu. tapering at the top and often scented, used for decoration.

votive Mass *noun Catholicism* a Mass that does not correspond to the order of the day but is said for a special intention, at the choice of the celebrant.

vouch *verb* **1** *intransitive* (foll. by *for*) take responsibility for or express confidence in (a person or thing); guarantee the reliability of. **2** *intransitive* (foll. by *for*) confirm or verify the truth or existence of something by providing proof or assurance (*experts vouched for the painting's authenticity*). [Old French *vo(u)cher* summon etc., ultimately from Latin *vocare* call]

vouch·er *noun* **1** a document which can be exchanged for goods or services, or which entitles the holder to a reduction in the price of something (*a $5.00 gift voucher*). **2** esp. *Brit.* a document establishing the payment of money for goods received; a receipt (*she signed the credit card voucher and handed it to the clerk*). **3** a person who vouches for a person, statement, etc.

vouch·safe *transitive verb formal* **1** give as a gift or privilege (*she would not vouchsafe me a reply*). **2** permit, allow, or agree.

vous·soir /ˈvuːswɑr/ *noun* each of the wedge-shaped or tapered stones or bricks forming an arch or vaulting. [Old French *vossoir* etc., from popular Latin *volsorium*, ultimately from Latin *volvere* roll]

vow ● *noun* **1** a solemn promise made to God, another deity, or a saint, to perform an action or adopt a particular way of life. **2 a** a solemn undertaking or resolve (*I made a vow never to speak to her again*). **b** (foll. by *of*) a solemn promise to observe a specified state or condition (*a vow of silence*). **3** (in *pl.*) **a** the promises by which a monk or nun is bound to poverty, chastity, and obedience. **b** the promises of fidelity made during a marriage ceremony. **4** (usu. as **baptismal vows**) the promises given at baptism by the baptized person or by sponsors. ● *transitive verb* **1** promise or undertake solemnly (*she vowed that she would never return*). **2** make a solemn resolve or threat to inflict (injury) or exact (revenge). **3** dedicate or consecrate to a deity. □ **under a vow** bound by a vow one has made. [Old French *vo(u)*, from Latin (as VOTE)]

vow·el *noun* **1** a speech sound made with vibration of the vocal cords but without audible friction, more open than a consonant and capable of forming a syllable. **2** a letter of the alphabet representing such a sound, such as *a, e, i, o, u*. □ **vow·elled** (also esp. *US* **vow·eled**) *adjective* (also in *combination*). **vowel·less** *adjective* [Old French *vouel, voiel* from Latin *vocalis (littera)* VOCAL (letter)]

vowel point *noun* each of a set of marks used to indicate a vowel in Hebrew, Syriac, and Arabic.

voxel /ˈvɒksɛl/ *noun Computing* each of an array of discrete elements into which a representation of a three-dimensional object is divided; a three-dimensional pixel. [blend of VOLUME + ELEMENT, with *-x* inserted for ease of pronunciation]

vox pop *noun informal* **1** popular opinion as represented by informal comments from members of the public. **2** statements or interviews of this kind. [abbreviation of VOX POPULI]

vox pop·uli /ˌvɒks ˈpɒpjʊˌli/ *noun* general public opinion, popular belief or rumour. [Latin, lit. 'the voice of the people']

voy·age ● *noun* a journey, esp. a long one by water, air, or in space. ● *verb* **1** *intransitive* make a voyage. **2** *transitive* traverse, esp. by water or air. [Old French *voiage* from Latin *viaticum*]

voy·ager *noun* **1** a person who makes a voyage; a traveller. **2** (**Voyager**) either of two US space probes that surveyed and photographed the outer planets, including Jupiter, Saturn, Uranus, and Neptune, and their respective moons, from 1977–1989. **3** *Cdn* = VOYAGEUR.

voy·ageur /ˌvɔɪəˈʒɜr, ˌvwɑdjaˈʒɜr/ *noun esp. Cdn hist.* a usu. French-speaking or Metis canoeman employed by merchants in Montreal to transport goods to and from trading posts in the interior. □ **voy·aging** *noun* [French, lit. 'voyager' (as VOYAGE)]

voyageur canoe *noun Cdn* = CANOT DU NORD.

voyageur sash *noun Cdn* = CEINTURE FLÉCHÉE.

voy·eur /vɔɪˈjɜr/ *noun* **1** a person who derives sexual gratification from the covert observation of others as they undress or engage in sexual activities. **2** a powerless or passive observer, esp. one who derives an inordinate amount of enjoyment from observing a situation without participating in it. [French, from *voir* 'see']

voy·eur·ism /ˈvɔɪjər,ɪzm, ,vɔɪˈjɜr-/ *noun* the practice or state or an instance of being a voyeur; voyeuristic behaviour. ◻ **voy·eur·is·tic** *adjective* **voy·eur·is·tic·ally** *adverb*

VP *abbreviation* Vice-President.

VPN *abbreviation* VIRTUAL PRIVATE NETWORK.

VQA *noun Cdn* (often *attributive*) designating a Canadian wine certified by the Vintners Quality Alliance, a body of winemakers, wine merchants, and federal government officials, as meeting certain standards of taste and conforming to statutory regulations.

VR *abbreviation* **1** virtual reality. **2** Queen Victoria. **3** variant reading. [sense 2 from Latin *Victoria Regina*]

VRAM *noun Electronics* a type of RAM used in computer display cards. [abbreviation of *video* RAM]

VRML *abbreviation* virtual reality modelling language.

vroom ● *intransitive verb* **1** (esp. of a car or engine) make a roaring or revving noise, suggestive of great speed. **2** (of a car or truck etc.) travel at high speed. ● *noun* the roaring sound of an engine. ● *interjection* an imitation of such a sound. [imitative]

vs. *abbreviation* versus.

VSE *abbreviation hist.* Vancouver Stock Exchange.

V-shaped *adjective* having a shape or a cross-section resembling the letter V.

V sign *noun* **1** a sign of the letter V made with the first two fingers pointing up and the palm of the hand facing outwards, as a symbol of victory. **2** *Brit.* a similar sign made with the back of the hand facing outwards, as a gesture of abuse, contempt, etc.

VSOP *abbreviation* Very Special (or Superior) Old Pale (brandy).

VT *abbreviation* Vermont (in official postal use).

Vt. *abbreviation* Vermont.

VTO *abbreviation* vertical takeoff.

VTOL /ˈviːtɒl/ *noun* an aircraft capable of landing and taking off vertically (*compare* STOL). [acronym from Vertical TakeOff and Landing]

VTR *abbreviation* = VIDEOTAPE RECORDER 1.

vug *noun Mineralogy* a small pocket or cavity in a rock, lined with tiny crystals. [Cornish *vooga*]

Vuil·lard /vwiːˈjɑr/ **(Jean) Édouard** (1868–1940), French painter and graphic artist. A member of the Nabi group, he produced decorative panels, murals, paintings, and lithographs, and his most typical subjects were domestic interiors and portraits.

Vul·can *Rom. Myth* the god of fire, identified with the Greek Hephaestus.

vul·can·ism *noun* = VOLCANISM.

vul·can·ite *noun* a hard black vulcanized rubber, ebonite.

vul·can·ize *transitive verb* (also esp. *Brit.* **-ise**) treat (rubber or rubber-like material) with sulphur at a high temperature to increase its durability and elasticity. ◻ **vul·can·iz·a·tion** *noun* **vul·can·iz·er** *noun*

vul·can·ol·ogy *var. of* VOLCANOLOGY.

vul·gar *adjective* **1** likely to offend; indecent, rude, obscene (*a vulgar joke*). **2** displaying or proceeding from ignorance or a lack of refinement, manners, or taste (*a vulgar habit; vulgar tastes*). **3 a** popular, common. **b** of or characteristic of the common people, plebeian. ◻ **vul·gar·ly** *adverb* [Latin *vulgaris* from *vulgus* common people]

vulgar fraction *noun* a fraction expressed by numerator and denominator, not decimally.

vul·gar·ian /vʌlˈɡeriən/ *noun* a vulgar person.

vul·gar·ism *noun* **1** a coarse or obscene word or expression. **2** an instance of coarse or uneducated behaviour.

vul·gar·ity *noun* (*pl.* **-ities**) **1** the quality of being vulgar. **2** an instance of this.

vul·gar·ize *transitive verb* (also esp. *Brit.* **-ise**) **1** make (a person, manners, etc.) vulgar; infect with vulgarity. **2** make widely known or accessible to the public; popularize. ◻ **vul·gar·iz·a·tion** *noun*

vulgar Latin *noun* any of the popular and informal dialects of Latin spoken in classical times, esp. those from which the Romance languages developed.

vulgar tongue *noun* the national or vernacular language, esp. formerly as opposed to Latin.

Vul·gate /ˈvʌlɡeit, -ɡət/ *noun* **1 a** the Latin version of the Bible prepared mainly by St. Jerome in the late 4th c. **b** the official Roman Catholic Latin text of the Bible as revised in 1592. **2** (**vulgate**) the traditionally accepted text of any author. **3** (**vulgate**) common or colloquial speech. [Latin *vulgata* (*editio* edition), fem. past participle of *vulgare* make public, from *vulgus*: see VULGAR]

vul·ner·able *adjective* **1** able to be physically or emotionally hurt. **2** liable to damage or harm, esp. from aggression or attack (*a vulnerable position*). **3** (foll. by *to*) exposed or susceptible to a destructive agent or influence etc. (*vulnerable to attack; vulnerable to criticism*). **4** *Bridge* (of a side) liable to increased penalties or bonuses as a result of having won a game. ◻ **vul·ner·abil·ity** *noun* (*pl.* **-ities**). **vul·ner·ably** *adverb* [Late Latin *vulnerabilis* from Latin *vulnerare* to wound, from *vulnus -eris* wound]

vul·pine /ˈvʌlpain/ *adjective* **1** resembling or characteristic of a fox. **2** crafty, cunning. [Latin *vulpinus* from *vulpes* fox]

vul·ture *noun* **1** any of various large birds of prey of the family Cathartidae or Accipitridae, most of which have a mainly bald head and neck, feeding chiefly on carrion and reputed to gather with others in anticipation of a death. **2** a ruthless or rapacious person, esp. one who preys upon those who are vulnerable or weak. ◻ **vul·tur·ine** /ˈvʌltʃəˌriːn/ *adjective* **vul·tur·ous** *adjective* [Anglo-French *vultur* from Latin *vulturius*]

vul·va /ˈvʌlvə/ *noun* (*pl.* **vul·vas**) the external female genitals, consisting (in humans) of the labia, clitoris, and vaginal opening. ◻ **vul·val** *adjective* **vul·var** *adjective* [Latin, = womb]

Vun·tut Gwitchin /ˈvʊntʌt ˈɡwɪtʃɪn/ ● *noun* a member of a Gwich'in people living in Yukon, esp. in and around the community of Old Crow. [Gwich'in, =ʻpeople of the lakes']

Vun·tut National Park /ˈvʊntʌt/ a park in N Yukon, surrounding the Porcupine River area, north of the community of Old Crow. It was established to preserve the surrounding wetlands and the habitat of the Porcupine caribou herd. [Gwich'in, = 'among the lakes']

vv. *abbreviation* **1** verses. **2** volumes.

VX *noun* (also **VX gas** or **VX nerve agent**) a colourless and odourless organophosphorous nerve agent that blocks the transmission of impulses in a person's central nervous system, rapidly causing convulsions, respiratory failure, and death. [British and US military code name]

Vyat·ka /ˈvjɒtkə/ an industrial town in north central European Russia, on the Vyatka River; pop. (est. 2002) 464,100. It was formerly known as Kirov (1934–92).

vying *pres. part. of* VIE.

Vysh·in·sky /vɪˈʃɪnski/ **An·drei Yanu·ary·evich** (also **Vish·in·sky**) (1883–1954), Soviet lawyer and diplomat. The chief prosecutor in Stalin's 'purge trials' of the 1930s, he became foreign minister (1949–53) and principal Soviet delegate at the United Nations (1945–9; 1953–4).

Vowels: a cat ɑ arm e bed ɜr her ɜː *deux* ə ago ɪ sit i cosy iː feed ɒ hot ɔ pore ɔː no ʌ run ʊ put

Ww

W¹ *noun* (also **w**) (*pl.* **Ws** or **W's**) the twenty-third letter of the alphabet.

W² *abbreviation* (also **W.**) **1** watt(s). **2** West; Western. **3** women's (size). **4** Welsh.

W³ *symbol Chem.* the element tungsten.

w *abbreviation* (also **w.**) **1** with. **2** wife. **3** weight. **4** width.

WA *abbreviation* **1** Washington (State) (in official postal use). **2** Western Australia.

Waac /wak/ *noun hist.* **1** the Women's Army Auxiliary Corps. **2** a member of this, esp. in Britain from 1917–19 or in the US from 1942–8. [acronym]

Waaf /waf/ *noun Brit. hist.* **1** the Women's Auxiliary Air Force. **2** a member of this (1939–48). [acronym]

waah *interjection* expressing wailing. [imitative]

Waal River /wɒl/ a river of the south central Netherlands. The most southerly of two major distributaries of the Rhine, it flows for 84 km (52 miles) from the point where the Rhine forks, just west of the border with Germany, to the estuary of the Meuse (Maas) on the North Sea.

WAC *noun* **1 a** the US Women's Army Corps. **b** /wak/ a member of this. **2** the Women's Action Coalition. [acronym]

Wace /ˈweɪs/ **Rob·ert** (c.1100–c.1171), Anglo-Norman poet, who wrote the *Roman de Brut* and *Roman de Rou*, a history of the dukes of Normandy.

wack esp. *US slang* ● *adjective* **1** bad, harmful. **2** unfashionable, boring. ● *noun* = WACKO. [prob. back-formation from WACKY]

wacke /ˈwakə/ *noun hist.* a greyish-green or brownish rock resulting from the decomposition of basaltic rock. [German from Middle High German *wacke* large stone, Old High German *wacko* pebble]

wacked *var. of* WHACKED.

wacko (also **whacko**) *N Amer. slang* ● *adjective* crazy, insane. ● *noun* (*pl.* **-os** or **-oes**) a person who is crazy or insane; a lunatic. [WACKY + -O]

wacky *adjective* (also **whacky**) (**-ier, -iest**) *informal* crazy, madcap, goofy. □ **wack·i·ly** *adverb* **wack·i·ness** *noun* [originally dial., = left-handed, from WHACK]

wad ● *noun* **1 a** a small mass, clump, or ball of soft material (*a wad of bubble gum*). **b** a compact bundle of soft, loose, or pliable material used for stuffing or packing. **2 a** a number of banknotes or papers etc. stacked or rolled together. **b** (in *sing.* or *pl.*) a large quantity of esp. money. **3** a disc or plug of paper, cloth, or felt retaining the powder and shot in position in a gun or cartridge. ● *transitive verb* (**wad·ded, wad·ding**) **1** press, crumple, or arrange (soft material) into a wad or wadding. **2** plug (the barrel of a gun) with a wad. □ **shoot one's wad** *N Amer.* do all that one can do. [perhaps related to Dutch *watten*, French *ouate* padding, cotton wool]

wad·ding *noun* **1** any soft, loose, or pliable material of cotton or wool etc. used to line, stuff, or pad garments, quilts, etc., or to pack fragile articles. **2** any material from which the wads for guns are made.

Wad·ding·ton, Mir·iam (born Miriam Dworkin) (1917–2004), Canadian poet. Her first book of poetry, *Green World*, was published in 1945; many volumes of poems, a collection of short stories, and numerous essays and articles followed.

Wad·ding·ton, Mount a peak in the Coast Mountains of SW central BC, situated northwest of Bute Inlet. It rises to a height of over 4 000 m. [A. P. Waddington, English-born Canadian businessman d.1872]

wad·dle ● *intransitive verb* walk with short steps and a clumsy rocking

or swaying motion, like a stout short-legged person or a bird with short legs set far apart, such as a duck, penguin, or goose. ● *noun* a waddling gait. [perhaps frequentative of WADE]

wade ● *verb* **1** *intransitive* walk through a deep liquid or soft substance that acts as an impediment to motion, such as water, mud, or snow. **2** *intransitive* (often foll. by *through*) go laboriously or doggedly through a tedious task, a long or uninteresting book, etc. **3** *transitive* walk through (water etc.). ● *noun* a period of wading. □ **wade in** (or **into**) *informal* involve oneself energetically. [Old English *wadan* from Germanic, = go (through)]

wader *noun* **1** (in *pl.*) high waterproof boots, or a waterproof garment for the legs and body, worn esp. for fishing. **2 a** *N Amer.* any large, long-necked, long-legged wading bird, as a heron, stork, or crane. **b** a wading bird, esp. any of various birds of the order Charadriiformes. **3** a person who wades.

wadi /ˈwɒdi/ *noun* (also **wady**) (*pl.* **wadis** or **wadies**) a rocky watercourse in North Africa etc., dry except in the rainy season. [Arabic *wādī*]

Wadi Halfa /ˌwɒdi ˈhalfə/ a town in N Sudan, on the border with Egypt. It is situated on the Nile at the southern end of Lake Nasser and is the terminus of the railway from Khartoum.

wad·ing bird *noun* any usu. long-legged wader that finds its food in shallow waters or along the shore.

wad·ing pool *noun N Amer.* a shallow pool for children to play in.

WAF *abbreviation* (in the US) **1** Women in the Air Force. **2** /waf/ a member of the WAF.

wafer *noun* **1** a very thin light crisp cookie. **2** a thin disc of unleavened bread used in the Eucharist. **3** *Electronics* a very thin slice of a semiconductor crystal used as the substrate for solid state circuitry. **4** a disc of red paper stuck on a legal document instead of a seal. **5** *hist.* a small disc of dried paste formerly used for fastening letters, holding papers together, etc. [Anglo-French *wafre*, Old Northern French *waufre*, Old French *gaufre* (compare GOFFER) from Middle Low German *wāfel* waffle: compare WAFFLE²]

wafer·board *noun* esp. *Cdn* a rigid sheet or panel ranging in thickness from 6.5 mm (¹/₄ inch) to 19 mm (³/₄ inch), composed of randomly arranged wood chips, larger than those of particleboard, bonded with resin (compare PARTICLEBOARD).

wafer-thin ● *adjective* very thin. ● *adverb* very thinly (*cut it wafer-thin*).

waf·fle¹ ● *intransitive verb* **1** (esp. *N Amer.*) waver in opinion or resolve; vacillate, equivocate. **2** (esp. *Brit.*) (often foll. by *on*) indulge in rambling aimless speech or writing. ● *noun* **1** verbose but aimless talk or writing. **2** (**Waffle**) *Cdn hist.* a caucus of NDP members organized in 1969 to promote a socialist and nationalist agenda, which included the replacement of US private ownership of Canadian industry with Canadian public ownership, the establishment of an independent Canadian labour movement, the right of Quebec to self-determination, and the advancement of the feminist movement. □ **waf·fler** *noun* (also **Waffler** in sense 2 of *noun*) **waf·fly** *adjective* [originally dial., frequentative of *waff* = yelp, yap (imitative)]

waf·fle² *noun* **1** a crisp pancake with a grid pattern of indentations on each side. **2** (*attributive* or in *combination*) designating esp. fabrics with a texture resembling that of a waffle (*waffle-knit sweater*). [Dutch *wafel*, *waefel* from Middle Low German *wāfel*: compare WAFER]

waffle iron *noun* an appliance used to bake waffles, consisting of two hinged metal pans with a grid pattern, which forms indentations on the waffle as it cooks.

waft ● verb **1** intransitive float or glide gently through or as if through the air or over water. **2** transitive carry or send gently through or as if through the air. ● noun **1** (usu. foll. by of) a scent passing through the air or carried by a breeze; a whiff. **2** Naut. a flag etc. knotted in the middle, formerly used as a distress signal. [originally 'convoy (ship etc.)', back-formation from obsolete waughter, wafter armed convoy ship, from Dutch or Low German wachter from wachten to guard]

wag[1] ● verb (**wagged, wag·ging**) transitive & intransitive shake, wave, or sway to and fro or from side to side, esp. in a rapid energetic manner (she wagged her finger at me in reproach). ● noun a single wagging motion (with a wag of his tail). □ **the tail that wags the dog** a subordinate or unimportant person exercising control over the organization etc. of which he or she is a member. **tongues** (or **chins** or **jaws**) **wag** there is talk or gossip. [Middle English waggen from root of Old English wagian sway]

wag[2] noun a humorist; a joker or wit. [prob. from obsolete waghalter one likely to be hanged (as WAG[1], HALTER)]

wage ● noun **1** (in sing. or pl.) **a** a payment made by an employer to an employee in exchange for work or service rendered. **b** a fixed regular payment, usu. daily or weekly, made by an employer to a manual or unskilled worker (compare SALARY). **2** (in pl.) Econ. the part of total production that is the return to labour as earned income as distinct from the remuneration received by capital as unearned income. **3** (in sing. or pl.) literary reward, recompense, requital (the wage of sin is death). ● transitive verb conduct, carry on (a war, conflict, campaign, etc.). [Anglo-French wage, Old French g(u)age, from Germanic, related to GAGE[1], WED]

wage claim noun a demand for an increase in pay made by an employee or union etc. to an employer.

wage earner noun a person who works for wages. □ **wage-earning** attributive adjective

wage labour noun **1** the portion of the labour force working for wages. **2** the body of workers receiving wages from one employer. **3** work for which wages are paid. □ **wage labourer** noun

wager ● verb **1** transitive & intransitive stake (esp. a sum of money) on the outcome of an uncertain event or on an undecided or unresolved matter. **2** transitive (usu. foll. by that + clause) **a** make a bet that (a certain outcome, result, etc.) will occur (I'll wager that my team beats yours). **b** informal confidently assert; be certain (I'll wager they've left by now). ● noun **1** an instance of wagering; a betting transaction. **2** a thing, esp. a sum of money, laid down as a stake. □ **wager·ing** noun [Anglo-French wageure from wager (as WAGE)]

wager of battle noun hist. a form of trial in which a defendant's guilt or innocence was decided by single combat between the parties or their champions.

wager of law noun hist. a form of trial in which the defendant was required to produce witnesses who would swear to his or her innocence.

wage scale noun a graduated scale of wage rates for different levels of work.

wage slave noun a person dependent on income from employment of an extremely arduous or menial nature. □ **wage slavery** noun

wage worker noun = WAGE EARNER.

wag·gery noun (pl. **-ies**) **1** waggish behaviour, joking. **2** a waggish action or remark, a joke.

wag·gish adjective amusing, witty, facetious, tongue-in-cheek (a waggish columnist; a waggish remark). □ **wag·gish·ly** adverb **wag·gish·ness** noun

wag·gle informal ● verb **1** transitive & intransitive move with short movements from side to side or up and down. **2** intransitive Golf swing the head of one's club back and forth over the ball before playing a shot. ● noun a waggling motion. □ **wag·gly** adjective [WAG[1] + -LE[4]]

Wag·ner /ˈvɒɡnər/ (**Wil·helm**) **Rich·ard** (1813–83), German composer. He made a major contribution to the history of opera with his development of music drama, synthesizing music, drama, verse, legend, and spectacle; his works include Der Ring des Nibelungen (The Ring of the Nibelung), four operas based on Germanic sagas, Tristan and Isolde (1859), and the Siegfried Idyll (1870) for orchestra.

Wag·ner·ian /vɒɡˈneriən/ ● adjective **1** of, relating to, or characteristic of Wagner or his music and theories of musical and dramatic composition. **2** grandiose, highly dramatic. ● noun an admirer of Wagner or his music.

wag·on noun (also esp. Brit. **wag·gon**) **1** a large sturdy four-wheeled

vehicle, usu. drawn by horse or tractor, for transporting heavy or bulky loads, esp. an open cart for carrying hay etc. with an elongated body and extended framework attached to the sides. **2** hist. a covered horse-drawn vehicle used for the conveyance of goods and passengers by road. **3** N Amer. a child's small four-wheeled cart made of wood, metal, or plastic, drawn by hand and used for carrying light loads or passengers. **4** esp. N Amer. **a** = STATION WAGON. **b** = PADDY WAGON. **5** a cart or trolley for serving tea or meals. **6** (in full **water wagon**) a vehicle for carrying water, esp. one used to clean the streets. **7** Brit. a railway freight car, esp. an open one. □ **fix a person's wagon** N Amer. slang get even with a person. **off the wagon** (or **water wagon**) informal again indulging in alcoholic drinks after a period of temperance. **on the wagon** (or **water wagon**) informal abstaining from alcoholic drinks. [earlier wagon, wag(h)en, from Dutch wag(h)en, related to Old English wægn WAIN]

wagon burner noun Cdn offensive slang a N American Indian.

wag·on·er noun (also esp. Brit. **wag·gon·er**) a person who drives a wagon.

wag·on·ette noun (also esp. Brit. **wag·gon·ette**) a four-wheeled horse-drawn pleasure vehicle, open or with a removable cover, with facing seats along the sides and one or two seats arranged crosswise in the front.

wag·on·load noun (also esp. Brit. **wag·gon·load**) as much as a wagon can carry.

wagon train noun N Amer. esp. hist. a succession of wagons, esp. a train of covered wagons and horses used by migrating pioneers or settlers.

wag·tail noun any small bird of the genus Motacilla with a long tail in frequent motion.

Wah·habi /wəˈhɒbi/ noun (also **Wa·habi**) (pl. **-habis**) a member of a strictly orthodox Sunni Muslim sect founded in the 18th c. by Muhammad ibn Abd al-Wahhab, who called for a return to the earliest doctrines and practices of Islam as embodied in the Quran and Sunna. □ **Wah·ha·bism** noun (also **Wa·ha·bism**). [Abd al-Wahhab]

wahoo[1] /waˈhuː/ noun a large marine fish of the Scombridae family, Acanthocybium solanderi, which is a streamlined and fast-swimming predator and is found in all tropical seas. [20th c.: origin unknown]

wahoo[2] interjection N Amer. = YAHOO[2].

wah-wah noun (also **wa-wa**) Music **1** an effect achieved on brass instruments by alternately applying and removing a mute, or on an electric guitar by using a pedal to control the output from the amplifier. **2** a device for producing this effect on an electric guitar, consisting of a pedal and circuit box. [imitative]

waif noun **1** a homeless and helpless person, esp. a neglected, abandoned, or starved child. **2** an extremely thin person. **3** a lost or ownerless article. □ **waifs and strays 1** homeless or neglected children. **2** odds and ends. □ **waif·ish** adjective **waif·like** adjective [Anglo-French waif, Old Northern French gaif, prob. of Scandinavian origin]

Wai·kato /waiˈkɒtoː/ the longest river of New Zealand, which flows 434 km (270 miles) generally northwestward from Lake Taupo, at the centre of North Island, to the Tasman Sea.

Wai·ki·ki /ˌwaikiˈkiː/ a beach resort, a suburb of Honolulu, on the island of Oahu, in Hawaii.

wail ● noun **1** a long loud plaintive inarticulate high-pitched cry of pain, grief, or despair. **2** a sound resembling or suggestive of this. ● intransitive verb **1** utter a wail or wails. **2** (of the wind etc.) produce a sound like that of a person wailing (the ambulance siren wailed). **3** (often foll. by about) complain or lament persistently and bitterly. **4** (often foll. by away) (of esp. a rock or jazz musician) play with great intensity or emotion. □ **wail·er** noun **wail·ing·ly** adverb [Old Norse, related to WOE]

Wail·ing Wall noun = WESTERN WALL.

wain noun archaic a wagon. [Old English wæg(e)n, wæn, from Germanic, related to WAY, WEIGH]

wain·scot ● noun panelling of oak or other wood lining, esp. covering the lower part of a wall of a room. ● transitive verb (**wain·scot·ted**, also **wain·scot·ed**, **wain·scot·ting**, also **wain·scot·ing**) line (a wall or room etc.) with wainscot. [Middle Low German wagenschot, apparently from wagen WAGON + schot of uncertain meaning]

wain·scot·ting noun (also **wain·scot·ing**) **1 a** a wainscot. **b** wainscots collectively. **2** the material used for this.

Wain·wright a town in east central Alberta, southwest of Lloydminster; pop. (2001) 5,117. [W. Wainwright, vice-president of both the Grand Trunk and the Grand Trunk Pacific railways d.1914]

wain·wright noun a person who makes wagons.

WAIS *abbreviation* wide area information server.

waist *noun* **1 a** the part of the human body below the ribs and above the hips, usu. of smaller circumference than these; the narrower middle part of the normal human figure. **b** the circumference of this part of the body. **2 a** the part of a garment encircling or covering the waist (*his pants have an elasticized waist*). **b** the horizontal seam joining the upper and lower parts of a dress, often encircling the waist but sometimes raised to below the bust or lowered to the hips. **3** the narrow middle part of a violin, hourglass, etc. **4** the constriction between the thorax and abdomen of a wasp or ant etc. **5** the middle part of a ship, between the forecastle and the quarterdeck. □ **waist·ed** *adjective* (also in *combination*). [Middle English *wast*, perhaps from Old English from the root of WAX²]

waist·band *noun* a band of material fitting around the waist and forming the upper part of a skirt, pair of pants, etc.

waist·coat *noun* a man's formal vest, usu. buttoned and worn over a shirt and under a jacket.

waist-deep ● *adjective* **1** (of water, snow, etc.) so deep as to reach the waist. **2** (often foll. by *in*) submerged to the waist. ● *adverb* immersed up to the waist.

waist-high ● *adjective* as tall or high as one's waist (*a waist-high fence*). ● *adverb* at or up to the level of one's waist (*the ball crosses the plate waist-high; the weeds grow waist-high*).

waist·line *noun* **1** a person's waist, usu. with reference to its circumference (*chocolate is bad for the waistline*). **2** = WAIST 2.

wait ● *verb* **1** *intransitive* (often foll. by *for, until, while*, etc.) remain inactive for a specified period of time or until some expected event occurs (*wait for the signal; wait till your mother gets home; wait while I put on my shoes*). **2** *intransitive* (usu. foll. by *for*) remain for a time without something promised or expected (*we had to wait for the bus; this is the chance I've been waiting for*). **3** *intransitive* (foll. by *for*) stop or slow down so that a person catches up or is not left behind (*wait for me!*). **4** *transitive* = AWAIT (esp. in phr. **wait one's turn**). **5** *intransitive* be ready or available (*exotic islands waiting to be discovered*). **6** *intransitive* **a** (of a matter, work, etc.) be neglected or unresolved for some time. **b** be delayed or postponed (*our trip will have to wait until I've finished my work*). **7** *transitive* defer (a meal etc.) until a person's arrival (*don't wait supper for me*). ● *noun* **1** a period of waiting (*had a long wait for the train*). **2** the action or process of watching out for an enemy or lurking in ambush (esp. in phr. **lie in wait**). **3** (in *pl.*) esp. *Brit. hist.* a small band of street musicians and singers performing carols. □ **can't wait** is very impatient (*I can't wait to see what she bought me*). **wait a minute** (or **second**) used when one has just noticed something or had a sudden idea or inspiration. **wait and see** await the progress of events before acting (also *attributive: wait-and-see approach*). **wait for it!** *informal* **1** do not begin before the proper moment. **2** used to create an interval of suspense before saying something unexpected or amusing. **waiting to happen** likely to happen imminently (*a disaster waiting to happen*). **wait on 1 a** attend to the needs of. **b** take orders from and serve meals to (a patron or patrons in a restaurant). **c** serve (a customer in a store). **2** remain in expectation of; wait for. **3** pay a respectful visit to. **wait out** esp. *N Amer. informal* remain inactive during; wait for the end of (*wait out the rain*). **wait tables** (or **on tables**) work in a restaurant taking orders from patrons and serving their meals. **wait up 1** (often foll. by *for*) not go to bed until a person arrives or an event happens. **2** (in *imperative*) used to urge a person to stop or slow down so that one can catch up. **(just) you wait!** used to imply a threat, warning, or promise. □ **wait·ing** *noun* [Old Northern French *waitier* from Germanic, related to WAKE¹]

wait-a-bit *noun* a plant with hooked thorns etc. that catch the clothing.

wait·er *noun* **1** a person, esp. a man, who works in a restaurant waiting tables. **2** a tray or salver. **3** a person who waits for a time, event, or opportunity.

waiting game *noun* a tactic used in a competition, business negotiation, etc., in which one refrains from acting in the earlier part in order to gain advantage or be more effective at a later stage.

waiting list *noun* a list of people waiting for something not immediately available, such as accommodation at a restaurant or hotel, an appointment for a type of medical treatment, etc.

waiting period *noun* a specified period of time that must pass before one is able or allowed to do something.

waiting room *noun* a room, such as in a doctor's or dentist's office or railway station, where one may wait for an appointment, train, etc.

wait-list esp. *N Amer.* ● *noun* a waiting list. ● *transitive verb* (usu. in *passive*) place the name of (a person) on a waiting list.

wait·person *noun* (*pl.* **-persons** or **-people**) a waiter or waitress (used to avoid sexual distinction).

wait·ress ● *noun* a woman who works in a restaurant waiting tables. ● *intransitive verb* work as a waitress. □ **wait·ress·ing** *noun*

wait staff *noun N Amer.* the waitpersons of a restaurant collectively.

wait state *noun Computing* (of an operating system, central processing unit, etc.) the condition of being unable to process further instructions due to being occupied with some other task.

waive *transitive verb* **1** decline to take advantage of (a right, claim, opportunity, etc.); relinquish. **2** refrain from insisting upon (a rule, requirement, etc.); forgo. **3** refrain from charging or imposing (a penalty, cost, fee, etc.). **4** *N Amer. Sport* **a** (of a team) give up the rights to (a player) for the purposes of a trade, demotion, or unconditional release. **b** (of a team) refrain from exercising the right to sign (a player) from another team in the same league. [Anglo-French *weyver*, Old French *gaiver* allow to become a WAIF, abandon]

waiv·er *noun* **1** the act or an instance of waiving a right, claim, etc. **2** a formal document recording this, e.g. one guaranteeing that a party will not be held responsible for damage or injury sustained in the course of an activity. **3** *N Amer. Sport* **a** a team's waiving of the right to sign a player from another team in the same league before he or she is demoted, traded, or unconditionally released. **b** (in *pl.*) the process in which teams waive the right to sign or claim such a player (*he has cleared waivers; he was picked up on waivers*).

waka·me /'wakamei/ *noun* an edible brown seaweed, typically in dried form, used in Chinese and Japanese cookery. [Japanese]

Waka·shan /'wɒkə,ʃan/ *noun* an Aboriginal language family of the west coast of N America, including such languages as Haisla, Heiltsuk, Kwakwala, and Nuu-chah-nulth. [*Wakash*, a former name for the Nuu-chah-nulth, from Nuu-chah-nulth *wakaš* 'bravo!', + -AN]

wake¹ ● *verb* (*past* **woke** or **waked**; *past participle* **woken** or **waked**) **1** (often foll. by *up*) **a** *intransitive* come out of the state of sleep or unconsciousness. **b** *transitive* rouse from sleep or unconsciousness. **2** *transitive & intransitive* (often foll. by *up*) become or cause to become alert, attentive, or aware. **3** *transitive* (usu. foll. by *up*) disturb (a place) with noise (*he woke up the whole house with his music*). **4** *transitive* stir or evoke (an emotion, memory, etc.). **5** *transitive* (*past* usu. **waked**) keep watch or vigil beside the body of (a dead person) before burial; hold a wake for. **6** *intransitive & transitive* rise or raise from the dead. ● *noun* **1 a** a watch or vigil held by relatives and friends beside the body of a dead person before burial. **b** a gathering of friends and relatives to celebrate and remember the life of a person who has died, usu. over food and drink. **2** *hist.* **a** a vigil commemorating the dedication of a church. **b** a festival held on this occasion. □ **waker** *noun* [Old English *wacan* (recorded only in past *woc*), *wacian* (weak form), related to WATCH: sense 'vigil' perhaps from Old Norse]

wake² *noun* **1** the track left on the water's surface by a moving vessel. **2** turbulent air left behind a moving aircraft. **3** the trail left by anything that has passed (*the storm left a path of destruction in its wake*). □ **in the wake of 1** behind, following. **2** in the aftermath of; as a result or consequence of. [prob. from Middle Low German from Old Norse *vǫk* hole or opening in ice]

wake·board *noun* a surfboard-like board used in wakeboarding.

wake·board·ing *noun* a water sport in which participants ride on a short, wide board resembling a surfboard, towed by a motorboat.

Wake·field a town and metropolitan district in northern England, formerly part of West Yorkshire; pop. (est. 2002) 74,300.

wake·ful *adjective* **1** unable to sleep. **2** (of a night etc.) passed with little or no sleep. **3** vigilant, alert. □ **wake·ful·ly** *adverb* **wake·ful·ness** *noun*

waken *transitive & intransitive verb* make or become awake. [Old Norse *vakna* from Germanic, related to WAKE¹]

wake-robin *noun N Amer.* any of various trilliums, esp. the red-flowered *Trillium erectum*.

wake-up call *noun* esp. *N Amer.* **1** a telephone call made to wake a person up, esp. one requested from a hotel employee by a guest. **2 a** an act of drawing attention to a problem or concern. **b** a surprising and esp. distressing incident etc. symptomatic of and drawing attention to a larger problem or concern requiring immediate action.

wakey-wakey *interjection* used to wake a person up.

waking *adjective* being or occurring while one is awake (*in her waking hours; waking dreams*).

Waks·man, **Sel·man Abra·ham** (1888–1973), Russian-born US microbiologist. He discovered the bacterium *Streptomyces griseus* (1915) and isolated streptomycin (1943), which was developed into the first effective drug against tuberculosis; he was awarded a Nobel Prize in 1952.

Wal·achia see WALLACHIA.

Wal·cott, **Derek Alton** (b.1930), West Indian poet and playwright, whose works examine the conflict between West Indian and West Indian culture, and include the play *Dream on Monkey Mountain* (1967), the collection *In a Green Night: Poems 1948–60* (1962), and the epic poem *Omeros* (1990); he was awarded the Nobel Prize for literature in 1992.

Wal·den a former town in north central Ontario, now part of Greater Sudbury; pop. (2001) 10,101. [blend of the former town and township names *Waters* + *Lively* + *Denison*, a tribute to *Walden Pond*, where H. D. Thoreau lived in the mid-19th c.]

Wal·den·ses /wɒlˈdɛnsiːz/ *plural noun* a puritan religious sect originally in S France, now chiefly in Italy and the US, founded *c.*1170 and much persecuted. □ **Wal·den·sian** *adjective & noun* [medieval Latin from Peter *Waldo* of Lyons, founder]

Wald·heim /ˈvɒlthaɪm/ **Kurt** (b.1918), Austrian diplomat and politician, Secretary-General of the United Nations 1972–81, president of Austria 1986–92. During his presidential campaign he denied allegations that as an army intelligence officer he had direct knowledge of Nazi atrocities during the Second World War; he was subsequently cleared in court of charges relating to his war record.

Waldo, **Caro·lyn** (b.1964), Canadian synchronized swimmer. One of the first Canadians to excel in this sport, she swept the 1986 world championships in Madrid, and won two gold medals (one solo and one duet) in the 1988 Olympics.

Wal·dorf salad *noun* a salad made with diced apples, walnuts, and usu. celery, dressed with mayonnaise. [*Waldorf*-Astoria Hotel in New York, where this salad was first served]

Wal·dorf school *noun* a private academic institution based on the anthroposophical ideas of Rudolf Steiner, such as the belief that the human consciousness can and must be trained to rise above attention to material things. [German *die Freie Waldorfschule* 'the Free Waldorf School', the first school Steiner established, for children of employees at the Waldorf-Astoria cigarette factory in Stuttgart]

wale *noun* **1 a** a ridge or raised line of threads on a woven fabric, such as corduroy. **b** the texture of a fabric with such lines. **2** *Naut.* any of the broad thick timbers forming the side of a ship. **3** any of the horizontal bands woven around the body of a basket. **4** = WELT 1. [Old English *walu* stripe, ridge]

Wales a principality of Great Britain and the United Kingdom, to the west of central England; pop. (est. 2001) 2,903,085; capital, Cardiff. Wales is mainly mountainous and forms a large peninsula extending into the Irish Sea. It has retained a distinct cultural identity, and the Welsh language, spoken by about half a million people, is widely used.

Wa·łę·sa /vaˈwɛnsə/ **Lech** (b.1943), Polish union leader, president of Poland 1990–95. He founded the trade union movement Solidarity (1980), and was awarded the Nobel Peace Prize in 1983 for his efforts to establish workers' rights.

walk ● *verb* **1** *intransitive* **a** (of a person or other biped) progress at a natural pace, except when speed is desired, by lifting and setting down each foot in turn, never having both feet off the ground at once. **b** progress with similar movements (*walked on his hands*; *walked on stilts*). **c** (of a quadruped) proceed at the slowest pace, always having at least two feet on the ground at once. **2** *intransitive* **a** travel or go on foot (*Rebecca walks to work*). **b** exercise in this way (*he walks for two hours each day*). **3** *transitive* travel on foot over or through (*walking the halls*). **4** *transitive* **a** escort or accompany on foot (*he walked me home*). **b** lead (a dog or horse etc.) at a walking pace. **5** *transitive* move (a large heavy object) by rocking it on alternate edges in a manner suggestive of walking. **6** *intransitive* (of a ghost) roam or appear. **7** *Baseball* **a** *intransitive* (of a batter) reach first base by taking four balls from the pitcher. **b** *transitive* (of a pitcher) allow (a batter) to go to first base by throwing four balls. **c** *transitive* (foll. by *in* or *home*) force in (a run) by issuing a walk to a batter with the bases loaded. **8** *intransitive* *Basketball* take two or more steps with the ball without dribbling; travel. **9** *intransitive* *N Amer.* *slang* **a** be released from suspicion or from a charge. **b** = WALK OUT 2. ● *noun* **1** a short journey on foot for exercise or pleasure; a stroll (*we went for a walk*). **2 a** the slowest gait or pace of a person or animal (*go at a walk*). **b** the particular manner of walking of a person or animal (*I recognized her by her walk*). **3 a** a usual or favourite place for walking. **b** a place intended or suitable for walking. **4** *N Amer.* a sidewalk or the paved path leading from this to a house or building (*shovelled the front walk*). **5** a distance to be walked usu. defined by a specified amount of time required to traverse it on foot (*it's about a ten-minute walk from here*; *it's quite a walk to the store*). **6** (also **walk·athon**) a sponsored event in which participants walk a certain distance for charity. **7** *Baseball* a free pass to first base awarded to a batter who has taken four balls from a pitcher. □ **in a walk** esp. *N Amer. Sport* easily; without effort (*they won the game in a walk*). **walk around** (or **about**) stroll. **walk all over** *informal* **1** defeat easily. **2** take advantage of. **walk away** (**from**) **1** refuse to confront or become involved with. **2** survive (an accident etc.) without serious injury. **3** easily outdistance (an opponent) in a race. **walk away with** *informal* = WALK OFF WITH. **walk the boards** be an actor. **walk in** (often foll. by *on*) enter or arrive, esp. unexpectedly or with surprising ease. **walk in the park** (often with neg.) *N Amer.* a feat or accomplishment achieved with ease. **walk into** *informal* encounter through unwariness (*walked into the trap*). **walk off 1** depart (esp. abruptly). **2** ease the effects of (a meal, injury, etc.) by walking (*walked off his anger*). **walk a person off his** (or **her**) **feet** (or **legs**) exhaust a person with walking. **walk off the job** go on strike. **walk off with** *informal* **1** steal. **2** win easily. **walk on air** see AIR. **walk out 1** depart suddenly in anger or protest. **2** go on strike. **walk out on** desert, abandon. **walk over 1** *informal* = WALK ALL OVER. **2** traverse (a racecourse) at a walking pace to win a race with little or no opposition. **walk the plank** see PLANK. **walk the streets 1** be a prostitute. **2** traverse the streets esp. in search of work etc. **walk tall** *informal* feel justifiable pride. **walk through 1** rehearse (a scene in a play or movie etc.). **2** guide (a person) carefully through each stage of a procedure. **walk up to** approach (a person) for a conversation etc. **walk the walk** carry through on promises made (*compare* TALK THE TALK, *see* TALK). [Old English *wealcan* roll, toss, wander, from Germanic]

walk·able *adjective* (of a distance or area) capable of being walked; not too large to be walked.

walk·about *noun* **1** esp. *Brit.* a protracted walk or tour, esp. one taking in a number of places. **2** esp. *Brit.* an informal stroll among a crowd by a visiting dignitary. **3** *Austral.* a period of wandering in the bush by an Australian Aborigine. □ **go walkabout** *Austral.* go on a walkabout.

walk·athon *noun* = WALK 6.

Walk·em /ˈwɒkəm/ **George An·thony** (1834–1908), Irish-born Canadian lawyer and politician. A member of the BC colonial Legislative Council (1864–70), he was elected to the provincial legislature in 1871. As premier 1874–6 and 1878–82, he struggled with Ottawa over the failure to begin the promised Pacific railway.

Walk·er ▶ **1 Alice Mal·sen·ior** (b.1944), US writer and critic. She won international acclaim for her epistolary novel *The Color Purple* (1982); her other works include *In Search of Our Mothers' Gardens: Womanist Prose* (1983), a collection of critical essays, and the novel *Possessing the Secret of Joy* (1992), an indictment of female genital mutilation. **2 Hiram** (1816–99), US-born Canadian distiller and businessman. Although he lived in Canada for only five years (1859–64), he founded a distillery, a railway, and a new town, Walkerville (now part of Windsor, Ont.). **3 Hor·atio** (1858–1938), Canadian painter. He is known esp. for his vivid portrayals of habitant life on the Île d'Orléans in the late 19th and early 20th c.

walk·er *noun* **1** a person who walks, esp. one who walks for exercise or recreation. **2** a wheeled framework with a sling or seat that supports a baby within reaching distance of the ground so that he or she can learn to walk. **3** a usu. tubular metal frame with two wheels and/or rubberized ferrules, used by disabled or old people to help them walk. **4** esp. *US* a male escort paid to accompany usu. wealthy women in public or at social engagements.

Walk·er·ton a former town in SW central Ontario, about 100 km northwest of Guelph, now part of Brockton township; pop. (2001) 4,851. □ **Walk·er·ton·ian** *noun* [J. *Walker*, local miller d.1873, and his son William, who laid out the area in village lots]

walk·ies esp. *Brit.* ● *interjection* a command to a dog to prepare for a walk. ● *plural noun* *informal* or *jocular* a walk or period of walking, esp. with a dog. □ **go walkies** *informal* or *jocular* **1** go for a walk. **2** go missing (*some equipment went walkies*).

walkie-talkie *noun* a small portable radio transmitter and receiver that provides two-way communication.

walk-in ● *attributive adjective* **1** (of a storage area) large enough to walk into (*walk-in closet*). **2** designating a commercial establishment or medical facility etc. that serves customers and patients without appointments (*a walk-in clinic*). **3** designating the clientele of such an establishment or facility (*walk-in customers*). ● *noun* **1** a business or medical facility that serves customers without appointments. **2** a client of such an establishment or facility.

walk·ing ● *noun* the activity or an instance of taking a walk, esp. for recreation or exercise. ● *adjective* **1** that can, does, or appears to walk. **2** used or worn for walking (*walking stick*; *walking boots*). **3** done on foot

Vowels: a cat ɑ arm e bed ɜr her ɜː deux ə ago ɪ sit i cosy iː feed ɒ hot ɔ pore ɔː no ʌ run ʊ put

(*a walking tour of the city*). **4** a person regarded as embodying the qualities of a specified thing (*stay out of his way, he's a walking disaster*; *she's a walking encyclopedia of baseball trivia*).

walking bass *noun* a bass part in 4/4 time in which a note is played on each beat of the bar and which typically moves up and down the scale in small steps.

walking fern *noun* a N American evergreen fern, *Camptosorus rhizophyllus*, with fronds that root at the ends.

walking frame *noun* = WALKER 3.

walking papers *plural noun* N Amer. *informal* notice of dismissal.

walking plow *noun* N Amer. a type of agricultural plow drawn esp. by a horse or team of horses and guided by a person from behind.

walking shoe *noun* a sturdy, comfortable shoe for walking.

walking shorts *plural noun* a pair of loose-fitting shorts extending as far as the knee.

walking stick *noun* **1** a stick carried when walking, used esp. to provide extra support. **2** esp. *US* = STICK INSECT.

walking tour *noun* a tour of a city or region conducted on foot rather than by bus or train.

walking wounded *plural noun* **1** war casualties capable of walking despite their injuries. **2** *informal* a body of people suffering from illnesses, injuries, or mental or emotional difficulties.

Walk·man *noun* (*pl.* **-mans**) *proprietary* a type of personal stereo consisting of a radio or cassette or compact disc player and lightweight headphones.

walk of life *noun* a person's profession or social rank.

walk-on *noun* **1** a small role or part with no or little speaking in a dramatic production. **2** an actor who plays such a role. **3** N Amer. *Sport* a player who tries out for a team despite not having been drafted or officially invited.

walk·out ● *noun* **1** a sudden angry departure, esp. in protest. **2** a strike called by workers (*compare* LOCKOUT). **3** N Amer. a doorway or passageway providing access to the outside or another room. ● *attributive adjective* designating a room or building etc. with access to the outside (*a walkout basement*).

walk·over *noun* **1** a horse race in which the eventual winner is unchallenged, having merely to walk over the finish line in order to record the victory. **2** an easy victory or achievement.

walk-through ● *noun* **1** a rough rehearsal of a theatrical production or film. **2** an unchallenging role in a theatrical production or film. **3** a perfunctory or lacklustre performance. ● *attributive adjective* designating a building etc. permitting access from either end (*a walk-through garden*).

walk-up N Amer. ● *adjective* **1** (of a building) allowing access to the upper floors only by stairs. **2** (of an apartment, office, etc.) located in such a building. ● *noun* **1** a building with no elevator, in which access to the upper floors is possible only by stairs. **2** an apartment or office etc. located in such a building.

walk·way *noun* **1** any passage or path designed for or used by pedestrians. **2** a pedestrian passageway connecting different buildings or different parts of a building. **3** a paved path, such as one running through a garden or from the entrance of a house etc. to the sidewalk.

Wal·kyrie /val'ki:ri, 'valkɜri/ *var. of* VALKYRIE.

wall ● *noun* **1 a** a continuous and usu. vertical structure of little thickness in proportion to its length and height, enclosing, protecting, or dividing a space or supporting a roof. **b** the surface of a wall, esp. inside a room (*hung the picture on the wall*). **2 a** a vertical rock face, such as one that lies exposed on the steep side of a mountain, or one excavated in a quarry or mine. **b** *Mining* the surface of rock adjacent to or enclosing a seam or vein etc. (*crystals lining the wall of the cavity*). **3** *Anat.* the outermost layer or enclosing membrane etc. of an organ or hollow structure etc. (*stomach wall*). **4** *Baseball* the barrier enclosing the playing field at its outermost limit, extending along the curved perimeter of the outfield from one foul line to the other. **5** a thing or group of things serving as an obstacle or barrier (*a wall of security guards*). **6** an immaterial thing resembling a wall in terms of its imposing nature or in its ability to isolate or protect (*a wall of sound*; *a wall of secrecy*). ● *transitive verb* **1** (usu. foll. by *off*, *in*) surround, fortify, or enclose with or as if with a wall or walls. **2** (usu. foll. by *off*, *up*) block, seal, or close (a space etc.) with a wall. **3** (foll. by *up*) confine or enclose within a sealed space. □ **between you and me and the wall** *informal* in strict confidence. **go to the wall 1** (usu. foll. by *for*) esp. N Amer. do everything in one's power to help another, often putting oneself at risk in the process. **2** esp. *Brit.* **a** be defeated. **b** go out of business. **hit the wall 1** (of a long-distance or marathon runner)

reach the point of onset of extreme fatigue at which the body's stores of energy are virtually exhausted. **2** reach a point at which one can proceed no further. **off the wall** N Amer. *informal* unorthodox, unconventional (also *attributive*: *off-the-wall notions*). **up the wall** *informal* crazy or furious (*this song drives me up the wall*). **walls have ears** one should be cautious about what one says lest it be overheard. □ **walled** *adjective* (also in *combination*). **wall-less** *adjective* [Old English from Latin *vallum* rampart, from *vallus* stake]

wal·la·by /'wɒləbi/ *noun* (*pl.* **-bies**) any of various marsupials of the family Macropodidae, smaller than kangaroos, and having large hind feet and long tails. [Dharuk *walabi* or *waliba*]

Wal·lace ▸ **1 Al·fred Rus·sel** (1823–1913), English naturalist. He independently formulated a theory of evolution based on natural selection identical to that of Charles Darwin, but credit for the theory has been attached somewhat arbitrarily to Darwin. **2 Sir Wil·liam** (*c.*1270–1305), Scottish national hero. A leader of Scottish resistance to Edward I, he defeated the English army at Stirling (1297); he was defeated at the battle of Falkirk (1298), and subsequently captured and executed by the English.

Wal·lace·burg a former town in SW Ontario, situated about 50 km south of Sarnia on the Sydenham River, now part of the city of Chatham-Kent; pop. (2001) 11,114. □ **Wal·lace·burg·er** *noun* [Sir W. WALLACE]

Wal·lachia /wɒ'leikiə/ (also **Wa·lachia**) a former principality of SE Europe, between the Danube and the Transylvanian Alps. In 1861 it was united with Moldavia to form Romania. □ **Wal·lach·ian** *noun & adjective*

wal·lah /'wɒlə/ *noun* **1** (often in *combination*) a person concerned with or in charge of a usu. specified thing, business, etc. (*we bought our tickets from the ticket wallah*). **2** *slang* a person doing a routine administrative job. [Hindi *-wālā* suffix = -ER[1]]

wal·la·roo /,wɒlə'ru:/ *noun* a large brownish-black kangaroo, *Macropus robustus*. [Dharuk *wolaru*]

wall ball *noun* N Amer. a variety of baseball played in a schoolyard by two or more players, in which the batter's strike zone is represented by a box drawn on a wall, and singles, doubles, triples, and home runs are achieved by hitting a tennis ball past certain designated landmarks.

wall·board *noun* = DRYWALL.

wall chart *noun* a chart or poster designed for display on the wall of a classroom or conference room as a source of information, a training or teaching aid, etc.

wall·cov·er·ing *noun* any of various materials used to cover and decorate interior walls, such as a tapestry or wallpaper.

Wal·len·berg /'vɒlən,bɜrg/ **Raoul** (1912-?), Swedish diplomat, who helped thousands of Hungarian Jews to escape from the Nazis by issuing them Swedish passports (1944); in 1945 he was arrested by the Soviets, taken to Moscow, and imprisoned, and although the Soviet authorities stated that he had died in prison in 1947, his fate remains uncertain.

Wal·ler, Fats (born Thomas Wright Waller) (1904–43), US jazz pianist, songwriter, bandleader, and singer, who is known for the songs 'Ain't Misbehavin'' (1928) and 'Honeysuckle Rose' (1929).

wal·let *noun* **1 a** a flat pocket-sized folding case, usu. made of leather, for keeping money, credit cards, identification, etc. on one's person. **b** a person's financial resources. **2** *archaic* a bag for carrying food etc. on a journey, esp. as used by a pilgrim or beggar. [prob. from Anglo-French *walet* (unrecorded), perhaps from Germanic]

wal·ley /'wɒli/ *noun Figure Skating* a jump taking off from the back inside edge of the skating foot, completing one complete reverse rotation in the air, and landing on the back outside edge of the same foot. [origin unknown]

wall·eye *noun* **1** a large N American freshwater fish, *Stizostedion vitreum*, which has large prominent eyes and is valued as a food and sport fish. *Also called* PICKEREL or PIKE-PERCH. **2 a** an eye with a streaked, white, or parti-coloured iris. **b** an eye with an opaque cornea. **3** an eye squinting outwards. [back-formation from WALLEYED]

wall·eyed *adjective* **1** having one or both eyes with a streaked or whitish iris or opaque cornea. **2** having a divergent squint. **3** having wide and glaring eyes, as if from anger or excitement. [Old Norse *vagleygr* from *vagl* (unrecorded: compare Icelandic *vagl* film over the eye) + *auga* EYE]

wall fern *noun* an evergreen polypody, *Polypodium vulgare*, with very large leaves.

wall·flower *noun* **1 a** a fragrant spring garden plant, *Cheiranthus cheiri*, with esp. brown, yellow, or dark red clustered flowers. **b** any of various flowering plants of the genus *Cheiranthus* or *Erysimum*, growing wild on old walls or stony ground. **2** *informal* a shy or socially awkward person. **3** a person sitting out at a dance for lack of partners.

wall hanging *noun* a usu. large decorative tapestry etc. hung for display on an interior wall.

wall-hung *adjective* = WALL-MOUNTED.

Wal·lis, Sir Barnes (Nev·ille) (1887–1979), English inventor. He pioneered geodetic construction in his designs for the R100 airship (1930) and the Wellington bomber used in the Second World War, and designed the bouncing bomb used against the Ruhr dams in Germany in 1943.

Wal·lis and Fu·tuna Islands /ˈwɒlɪs, fuːˈtuːnə/ an overseas territory of France comprising two groups of islands to the west of Samoa in the central Pacific; pop. (est. 2002) 15,585; capital, Mata-Utu.

wall-mounted *adjective* (often *attributive*) that is or may be attached by a bracket or other support to a wall (*a wall-mounted telephone*).

Wal·loon /wɒˈluːn/ ● *noun* **1** a member of a French-speaking people inhabiting S and E Belgium and neighbouring parts of France (*compare* FLEMING[2]). **2** the French dialect spoken by this people. ● *adjective* of or concerning the Walloons or their language. [French *Wallon* from medieval Latin *Wallo -onis* from Germanic: compare WELSH]

wal·lop *informal* ● *transitive verb* (**wal·loped, wal·lop·ing**) **1 a** pound or strike with great force. **b** spank; beat. **2** esp. *Sport* defeat decisively. ● *noun* **1** a heavy or resounding blow. **2 a** the ability to deliver such a blow. **b** the capacity to create a powerful impact or impression (*this tearjerker of a film packs quite an emotional wallop*). □ **wal·lop·er** *noun* [earlier senses 'gallop', 'boil', from Old Northern French (*walop* n. from) *waloper*, Old French *galoper*: compare GALLOP]

wal·lop·ing ● *noun* **1** a sound thrashing. **2** a decisive victory. ● *adjective* **1** huge, whopping (*a walloping profit*). **2** powerful.

wal·low ● *intransitive verb* **1** (esp. of an animal) lie or roll around in mud, sand, water, etc. **2** (of a boat or aircraft) roll from side to side (*oil tankers wallowing heavily in the storm*). **3** (usu. foll. by *in*) indulge in unrestrained self-pity, misery, sensuality, pleasure, etc. (*wallows in nostalgia*). ● *noun* **1** the act or an instance of wallowing. **2** a place used by buffalo, rhinoceros, etc., for wallowing. **3** a depression in the ground caused by this. □ **wal·low·er** *noun* [Old English *walwian* roll, from Germanic]

wall painting *noun* a mural or fresco.

wall·paper ● *noun* **1** decorative paper printed or embossed with designs, usu. sold in a roll and cut into strips to be pasted on interior walls as decoration. **2** *Computing* an optional background pattern or picture displayed onscreen, esp. one used in a windows-based system. **3** usu. *derogatory* a plain or common thing or collection of these regarded as constituting an unobtrusive atmosphere or backdrop etc. ● *transitive verb* decorate with wallpaper.

wall pennywort *noun* see PENNYWORT 1.

wall pepper *noun* a succulent stonecrop, *Sedum acre*, with a pungent taste.

wall plate *noun* **1** any of various often decorative plates used to cover electrical fixtures or hardware, such as a plastic cover for a switch or receptacle. **2** timber placed horizontally in or on a wall as a support for joists or rafters.

wall rue *noun* a small fern, *Asplenium ruta-muraria*, with leaves like rue, growing on walls and rocks.

wall space *noun* space on the surface of a wall available for use, e.g. for displaying pictures.

Wall Street *noun* a street at the south end of Manhattan, where the New York Stock Exchange and other leading US financial institutions are located. The name is used allusively to refer to the American money market or financial interests.

Wall Street Crash the collapse of prices on the New York Stock Exchange in Oct. 1929, a major factor giving impetus to the early stages of the Depression.

Wall Street·er *noun* esp. *US* a Wall Street banker or financier, esp. involved in the New York stock market.

wall tent *noun* N *Amer.* a large tent with nearly perpendicular sides.

wall-to-wall *attributive adjective* **1** (of carpeting) covering the entire floor area; extending from one wall to another. **2** filling a space or area entirely (*wall-to-wall restaurants*). **3** endless; exclusive of all else (*wall-to-wall sports coverage; wall-to-wall insults*).

wall unit *noun* a piece of furniture with shelves and cupboards for storing and displaying books, curios, stereo equipment, etc., intended to stand against a wall in esp. a living room etc.

wally *noun* (pl. **-lies**) *derogatory* a foolish or inept person; a nerd or geek. [origin uncertain, perhaps shortened form of *Walter*]

wally·ball *noun* US a game resembling volleyball played in an indoor court like that used for squash or racquetball. [blend of WALL *noun* + VOLLEYBALL]

wal·nut *noun* **1** any tree of the genus *Juglans*, having aromatic leaves and drooping catkins, e.g. the N American black walnut, *J. nigra*. **2** the nut of these trees, esp. the English walnut, consisting of an edible kernel in a ridged shell covered with a thick green husk. **3** the timber of the walnut tree, used in cabinetmaking. [Old English *walh-hnutu* from Germanic NUT]

Wal·pole /ˈwɒlpəʊl/ **1 Hor·ace, 4th Earl of Or·ford** (1717–97), English writer and Whig politician. He wrote *The Castle of Otranto* (1764), one of the first Gothic novels, and is also noted for his contribution to the Gothic revival in architecture, converting his home near London into a Gothic castle (*c.*1753–76). **2** his father **Sir Rob·ert, 1st Earl of Or·ford** (1676–1745), English Whig politician, first lord of the Treasury and Chancellor of the Exchequer 1715–17 and 1721–42. He is generally recognized as the first British prime minister in the modern sense, having presided over the Cabinet for George I and George II during his second term as first lord of the Treasury and Chancellor.

Wal·pole Island /ˈwɒlpəʊl/ an island in SW Ontario, situated in Lake St. Clair, 48 km (30 miles) south of Sarnia. It is the site of an Indian reserve.

Wal·pur·gis night /valˈpʊrɡɪs/ *noun* the eve of May 1, when witches are alleged to meet on the Brocken mountain in Germany and hold revels with the Devil. [German *Walpurgisnacht* from *Walpurgis* genitive of St. *Walpurga* English nun (8th c.) + *Nacht* NIGHT]

wal·rus *noun* (pl. **wal·rus·es**) a large amphibious long-tusked Arctic mammal, *Odobenus rosmarus*, related to the seal and sea lion. [prob. from Dutch *walrus, -ros*, perhaps by metathesis after *walvisch* 'whale-fish' from word represented by Old English *horschwæl* 'horse-whale']

walrus moustache *noun* a long thick drooping moustache.

Wal·sall /ˈwɒlsɒl/ an industrial town in West Midlands, England; pop. (est. 2002) 173,900.

Walsh, Mount /wɒlʃ/ a peak (4 505 m) in SW Yukon Territory, situated on the border with Alaska, in the St. Elias mountain range. [J. M. *Walsh*, territorial commissioner and North West Mounted Police officer d.1905]

Wal·sing·ham /ˈwɒlsɪŋəm/ **Sir Fran·cis** (*c.*1530–90), English politician. As secretary of state (1573–90) to Elizabeth I he developed a domestic and foreign spy network that led to the detection of numerous plots against Elizabeth I and the gathering of intelligence about the Spanish Armada.

Wal·ter /ˈvɒltɜr/ **Bruno** (born Bruno Walter Schlesinger) (1876–1962), German-born US conductor, who was particularly renowned for his interpretations of Mozart, Mahler, Brahms, and Bruckner.

Wal·ter Mit·ty *noun* (pl. **Wal·ter Mit·tys**) a person who indulges in daydreams, esp. of a life much more exciting and glamorous than his or her real life (often *attributive*: *lives in a Walter Mitty world*). [a hero of James Thurber's short story *The Secret Life of Walter Mitty*]

Wal·ther von der Vogel·weide /ˈvɒltɜr fɒn dɛr ˈfoːɡəlvaɪdə/ (*c.*1170–*c.*1230), German singer and composer, who is considered one of the greatest of German minnesingers.

Wal·ton /ˈwɒltən/ **1 Er·nest Thom·as Sin·ton** (1903–95), Irish physicist. See COCKCROFT. **2 Izaak** (1593–1683), English writer. His book *The Compleat Angler* (1653; largely rewritten, 1655), combines practical information on fishing with folklore, interspersed with pastoral songs and ballads. **3 Sir Wil·liam (Tur·ner)** (1902–83), English composer, whose works include *Façade* (1921–3), a setting of poems by Edith Sitwell for recitation, the Viola Concerto (1928–9), and the oratorio *Belshazzar's Feast* (1930–1).

waltz ● *noun* **1** a dance in triple time performed by couples who rotate and progress around the floor. **2** the usu. flowing and melodious music for this. ● *verb* **1** *intransitive* dance a waltz. **2** *intransitive* (often foll. by *in, out, around*, etc.) *informal* move lightly, casually, with deceptive ease, etc. (*waltzed in and took first prize*). **3** *transitive* **a** move (a person) in a waltz. **b** cause a person to move rapidly or easily (*was waltzed off to Paris*). □ **waltz Matilda** see MATILDA[2]. □ **waltz·er** *noun* [German *Walzer* from *walzen* revolve]

Wam·pa·noag /ˈwɒmpəˈnoːɒɡ/ ● *noun* a member of a N American Aboriginal people of southeastern Massachusetts and the eastern shore of Narragansett Bay. ● *adjective* of or relating to this people or their culture. [Narragansett, lit. 'easterners']

Consonants: b *but* d *dog* f *few* g *get* h *her* j *yes* k *cat* l *leg* m *man* n *no* p *pen* r *red* s *sit*

wam·pum /'wɒmpəm/ *noun hist.* small, cylindrical blue and white beads cut from the shell of the quahog and woven into strings or belts by Aboriginal peoples of the eastern woodlands and Atlantic coast of N America to be used as a medium of exchange or to record treaties. [Algonquian *wampumpeag* from *wap* white + *umpe* string + *-ag* pl. suffix]

WAN /wan/ *noun* WIDE-AREA NETWORK. [acronym]

wan /wɒn/ *adjective* **1** (of a person's complexion or appearance) pale, pallid, sickly; exhausted; worn. **2** (of a star etc. or its light) partly obscured; faint. **3** *archaic* (of night, water, etc.) dark, black. □ **wanly** *adverb* [Old English *wann* dark, black, of unknown origin]

wand *noun* **1 a** a supposedly magic stick used in casting spells by a fairy, magician, etc. **b** a stick used by a conjuror for effect. **2** a slender rod carried or used as a marker in the ground. **3** a small applicator for mascara etc., usu. with a brush at one end. **4** a hand-held electronic device which can be passed over a bar code to read the data this represents. **5** a hand-held metal detector, esp. as used in security screening at airports etc. **6** a staff symbolizing some officials' authority. **7** *informal* a conductor's baton. [Old Norse *vendr*, prob. from Germanic: compare WEND, WIND²]

wan·der ● *verb* **1** *intransitive* (often foll. by *in, off,* etc.) go about from place to place aimlessly. **2** *intransitive* **a** (of a person, river, road, etc.) wind about; diverge; meander. **b** (of esp. a person) get lost; leave home; stray from a path etc. **3** *intransitive* **a** talk or think incoherently; be inattentive or delirious. **b** (of a talk, words, thoughts, etc.) be incoherent; lack focus. **4** *transitive* cover while wandering (*wanders the world*). ● *noun* the act or an instance of wandering (*went for a wander around the garden*). □ **wan·der·er** *noun* **wan·der·ing** *noun* (esp. in *pl.*). [Old English *wandrian* (as WEND)]

wandering Jew *noun* **1** (in medieval legend) a man who insulted Jesus on the day of the Crucifixion and was condemned to roam the earth until the Second Coming. **2** any of various creeping or trailing plants, esp. any of several variegated varieties of tradescantia grown as houseplants.

wandering sailor *noun* the moneywort or ivy-leaved toadflax.

Wander·jahr /'vɒndər,jɑr/ *noun* (pl. **Wanderjahre** /-,jɑrə/) a year spent travelling abroad, typically immediately before or after a university or college course. [German, lit. 'wander year']

wander·lust *noun* a strong desire to travel. [German]

wan·deroo /,wɒndə'ruː/ *noun* a langur, *Semnopithecus vetulus*, of Sri Lanka. [Sinhalese *wanderu* monkey]

wane ● *intransitive verb* **1** (of the moon) decrease in apparent size after the full moon (*compare* WAX² 1). **2** decrease in power, vigour, importance, brilliance, size, etc.; decline. ● *noun* **1** the process of waning. **2** a defect of a plank etc. that lacks square corners. □ **on the wane** waning; declining. □ **waney** *adjective* (in sense 2 of *noun*). [Old English *wanian* lessen, from Germanic]

Wang Jing Wei /,waŋ dʒɪŋ 'weɪ/ (also **Wang Ching-wei**) (1883–1944), Chinese revolutionary, who struggled with Chiang Kai-shek for control of the Kuomintang during the early 1930s, and was installed by the Japanese as head of a puppet regime in Nanking (1940–44).

wan·gle /'waŋɡəl/ *informal* ● *transitive verb* (often *reflexive*) obtain (a favour etc.) by scheming etc. (*wangled himself a free trip*). ● *noun* the act or an instance of wangling. □ **wan·gler** *noun* [19th-c. printers' slang: origin unknown]

wan·igan /'wanɪɡən/ *noun* N *Amer.* a watertight box or receptacle for cooking supplies and food, as used by canoeists or at a lumber camp. [Algonquian]

wank *coarse slang* ● *transitive & intransitive verb* (often foll. by *off*) masturbate. ● *noun* **1** an act of masturbating. **2** = WANKER. ¶ Usually considered a taboo word. [20th c.: origin unknown]

Wan·kel engine /'waŋkəl, 'vaŋ-/ *noun* a rotary internal combustion engine with a continuously rotated and eccentrically pivoted nearly triangular piston. [F. *Wankel*, German engineer d.1988]

wank·er *noun coarse slang* **1** a contemptible or ineffectual person. **2** a person who masturbates. ¶ Usually considered a taboo word.

wanna *contraction informal* want to (*I wanna win*).

wanna·be /'wɒnəbi/ *noun slang* often *derogatory* a person who tries to emulate a particular celebrity, follow the lifestyle of a particular group, etc.; an aspirant (also *attributive*: *all those wannabe guitar heroes*). [representing informal pronunciation of *want to be*]

want ● *verb* **1** *transitive* **a** (often foll. by *to* + infin.) desire; wish for possession of; need (*wants a toy train; wants it done immediately; wanted to leave; wanted him to leave*). **b** need or desire (a person, esp. sexually). **c** require to be attended to in esp. a specified way (*the garden wants weeding*). **d** (foll. by *to* + infin.) *informal* ought; should; need (*you want to*

pull *yourself together; you don't want to overdo it*). **2** *intransitive* (usu. foll. by *for*) lack; be deficient (*wants for nothing*). **3** *intransitive* (foll. by *in, out*) esp. N *Amer. informal* desire to be in, out, etc. (*wants in on the deal*). ● *noun* **1** (often foll. by *of*) **a** a lack, absence, or deficiency (*could not go for want of time; shows great want of judgment*). **b** poverty; need (*living in great want; in want of necessities*). **2 a** a desire for a thing etc. (*meets a long-felt want*). **b** a thing so desired (*can supply your wants*). □ **do not want to** am unwilling to. [Old Norse *vant* neuter of *vanr* lacking = Old English *wana*, formed as WANE]

want ad *noun* N *Amer.* a classified newspaper advertisement, esp. seeking employees.

want·ed *adjective* (of a suspected criminal etc.) sought by the police.

want·ing *adjective* **1** lacking (in quality or quantity); deficient, not equal to requirements (*wanting in judgment; the standard is sadly wanting*). **2** absent, not supplied or provided. □ **be found wanting** fail to meet requirements.

want list *noun* (also **wants list**) a list of desired stamps, books, etc., circulated among dealers by a collector etc.

wan·ton /'wɒntən/ ● *adjective* **1** capricious; random; arbitrary; motiveless (*wanton destruction; wanton wind*). **2** licentious; lewd; sexually promiscuous. **3** luxuriant; unrestrained. **4** *archaic* playful; lively (*a wanton child*). ● *noun literary* an immoral or licentious person, esp. a woman. ● *intransitive verb literary* behave wantonly. □ **wan·ton·ly** *adverb* **wan·ton·ness** *noun* [Middle English *wantowen* (wan- UN-¹ + *towen* from Old English *togen* past participle of *tēon* discipline, related to TEAM)]

WAP *abbreviation* Wireless Application Protocol, a set of protocols enabling cellphones and other radio devices to be connected to the Internet.

wapen·take /'wɒpən,teik, 'wap-/ *noun Brit. hist.* (in areas of England with a large Viking population) a division of a shire; a hundred. [Old English *wǣpen(ge)tæc* from Old Norse *vápnatak* from *vápn* weapon + *tak* taking, from *taka* TAKE: perhaps with reference to voting in assembly by show of weapons]

wap·iti /'wɒpiti/ *noun* (pl. **wap·itis**) a N American deer, *Cervus canadensis*. Also called ELK. [Cree *wapitik* white deer]

Wa·pusk National Park /wɒ'pʌsk/ a park in northeast Manitoba on the coast of Hudson Bay, extending south of Churchill. It is noted for its polar bears. [Cree, = 'white bear']

war ● *noun* **1 a** armed hostilities between esp. nations; conflict (*war broke out; war zone*). **b** a specific conflict or the period of time during which such conflict exists (*was before the war*). **2** the operations by which armed hostilities are carried out; warfare as a profession or art. **3 a** hostility or contention between people, groups, etc. (*war of words*). **b** (often foll. by *on*) a sustained campaign against crime, disease, poverty, etc. **c** sustained rivalry or competition, e.g. between companies (*the cola war*). *See also* PRICE WAR, FARE WAR. **4** N *Amer.* a children's card game for two in which each player shows a card and the higher card takes both, with a tie resulting in a number of cards being staked and the winner of the next draw taking them all; the game ends when one player wins all the cards. ● *intransitive verb* (**warred**, **war·ring**) engage in a war. □ **at war** (often foll. by *with*) engaged in a war. **go to war 1** declare or begin a war. **2** (of a soldier etc.) see active service. [Middle English *werre* from Anglo-French, Old Northern French var. of Old French *guerre*]

War·beck /'wɔrbek/ **Per·kin** (1474–99), Flemish claimant to the English throne. Encouraged by Yorkists in England and on the Continent, he claimed to be Richard, Duke of York, in an attempt to overthrow Henry VII; he was captured, imprisoned, and later executed.

war·bird *noun informal* a fighter aircraft.

war·ble¹ ● *verb* **1** *intransitive & transitive* sing in a gentle trilling birdlike manner. **2** *transitive* **a** speak or utter in a warbling manner. **b** express in a song or verse (*warbled his love*). ● *noun* a warbled song or utterance. □ **war·bly** *adjective* [Old Northern French *werble(r)* from Frankish *hwirbilōn* whirl, trill]

war·ble² *noun* **1** a hard lump on a horse's back caused by the galling of a saddle. **2 a** a swelling or abscess caused by the larva of a warble fly beneath the skin of cattle etc. **b** the larva causing this. [16th c.: origin uncertain]

warble fly *noun* any of various flies of the genus *Hypoderma*, infesting the skin of cattle and horses.

war·bler *noun* **1** a person, bird, etc. that warbles. **2** any small insect-eating bird of the family Sylviidae or, in N America, Parulidae, including the blackpoll, not always remarkable for their song.

war bond *noun* a bond issued by a government to help finance war expenditures.

war bonnet *noun* a headdress worn as part of traditional dress by some N American Indian (esp. Plains) peoples, esp. one with feathers attached to a headband and extending down the back.

war bride *noun* a woman who marries an esp. foreign serviceman met during a war.

War·burg /ˈwɔːbɜːg/ **Otto Hein·rich** (1883–1970), German biochemist, who researched intracellular respiration and the action of respiratory enzymes; he was awarded the Nobel Prize for physiology or medicine in 1931.

war canoe *noun* **1** any of several very large canoes suitable for warfare, formerly used by various cultures. **2** a very large canoe for 14 paddlers used in racing.

war chest *noun* a store of funds for a war or any other esp. political campaign.

war cloud *noun* an esp. international situation threatening war.

war correspondent *noun* a correspondent reporting from a scene of war.

war council *noun* **1** a group of military officers, elected officials, etc., convened to decide strategy for a war. **2** a meeting held to plan a response to an emergency etc.

war crime *noun* a crime violating the international laws of war. □ **war criminal** *noun*

war cry *noun* **1** a phrase or name shouted to rally one's troops. **2** a party slogan etc.

Ward ▸ 1 Dame Bar·bara (Mary), Baron·ess Jack·son (1914–81), English economist, conservationist, and journalist, whose works include *Spaceship Earth* (1966) and *Only One Planet* (1972). **2 Mrs. Hum·phry** (née Mary Augusta Arnold) (1851–1920), English writer and anti-suffrage campaigner, who is best known for several novels dealing with social and religious themes, esp. *Robert Elsmere* (1888). **3 Max·well Wil·liam** (b.1921), Canadian aviator and businessman. In 1953 he founded Wardair, which was very successful as a charter airline until bought out by Canadian Airlines in 1989.

ward ● *noun* **1** a separate room or division of a hospital, prison, etc. (*maternity ward*). **2** an esp. municipal administrative or electoral division. **3 a** a minor under the care of a guardian appointed by the parents or a court. **b** (in full **ward of the government**) a minor or mentally deficient person placed under the protection of a government or children's aid society. **4** a territorial division of the Mormon Church presided over by a bishop. **5** (in *pl.*) the corresponding notches and projections in a key and a lock. ● *transitive verb archaic* guard; protect. □ **ward off 1** parry (a blow). **2** avert, turn away (danger, poverty, etc.). [Old English *weard, weardian* from Germanic: reinforced in Middle English by Old Northern French *warde*, variant of Old French *garde* GUARD]

-ward /wəd/ *suffix* (also **-wards**) added to nouns of place or destination and to adverbs of direction and forming: **1** adverbs (usu. **-wards**) meaning 'toward the place etc.' (*moving backwards; set off homewards*). **2** adjectives (usu. **-ward**) meaning 'turned or tending toward' (*a downward look; an onward rush*). **3** (less commonly) nouns meaning 'the region toward or about' (*look to the eastward*). [from or after Old English *-weard*, from a Germanic root meaning 'turn']

war dance *noun* a dance performed before a battle, ceremonially, or to celebrate victory.

war dead *plural noun* people killed in war.

war·den *noun* **1** (usu. in *combination*) a supervising official (*game warden; park warden*). **2** *Cdn* the head of a county council. **3 a** esp. *N Amer.* a prison governor. **b** the governor of an institution at a university or college (*warden of residences*). **c** *Brit.* the president or governor of a school, hospital, youth hostel, etc. **4** = CHURCHWARDEN 1. □ **war·den·ship** *noun* [Old Northern French *wardein* var. of Old French *g(u)arden* GUARDIAN]

ward·er *noun* **1** *Brit.* a prison officer. **2** a guard. □ **ward·ress** /ˈwɔːdrəs/ *noun* [Anglo-French *wardere, -our* from Old Northern French *warder*, Old French *garder* to GUARD]

ward-heeler *noun* *N Amer.* usu. *derogatory* a minor party worker in elections etc. □ **ward-heeling** *noun & adjective*

ward·robe *noun* **1** a large movable or built-in cupboard or closet with shelves, hooks, rails, etc., for storing clothes. **2** a person's entire stock of clothes. **3** the costume department or costumes of a performing arts company etc. **4** a department of a royal household in charge of clothing. [Old Northern French *warderobe*, Old French *garderobe* (as GUARD, ROBE)]

wardrobe mistress *noun* a woman in charge of a theatrical or film wardrobe.

wardrobe trunk *noun* a trunk fitted with rails, shelves, etc. for use as a travelling wardrobe.

ward·room *noun* **1** a room in a warship for the use of commissioned officers. **2** these officers collectively.

-wards *var. of* -WARD.

ward·ship *noun* **1** a guardian's care or tutelage (*under his wardship*). **2** the condition of being a ward.

ware¹ *noun* **1** (esp. in *combination*) things of the same kind, esp. ceramics or cutlery (*chinaware; silverware; hardware*). **2** (usu. in *pl.*) **a** articles for sale (*displayed his wares*). **b** a person's skills, talents, etc. **3** ceramics etc. of a specified material, factory, or kind (*Wedgwood ware; Delftware*). **4** (in *combination*) a kind of software (*groupware*). [Old English *waru* from Germanic, perhaps originally = 'object of care', related to WARE³]

ware² *transitive verb* (also **'ware**) (esp. in hunting) look out for; avoid (usu. in *imperative*: *ware hounds!*). [Old English *warian* from Germanic (as WARE³), & from Old Northern French *warer*]

ware³ *predicative adjective archaic* aware. [Old English *wær* from Germanic]

ware·house ● *noun* **1** a building in which esp. retail goods are stored and from which they are distributed to retailers etc.; a repository. **2** a wholesale or large retail store. ● *transitive verb* **1** deposit or store (goods) temporarily in a warehouse. **2** *N Amer. informal* shut up (esp. a person) in a prison or hospital etc. and forget about or ignore. □ **ware·hous·er** *noun* **ware·house·man** *noun* (*pl.* **-men**).

warehouse club *noun* an organization which operates from a large, warehouse-like store, and sells goods in bulk quantities at very low prices to customers who must first become club members.

warehouse party *noun* a large (usu. illegal) organized public party with dancing, held in a warehouse or similar building; a rave.

warez /werz/ *noun* **1** illegal copies of software, distributed through computer bulletin boards or Internet sites. **2** a counterculture centred on the distribution of pirated software, pornographic images, etc., and the online discussion of such activities. [probably a respelling of *wares*]

war·fare *noun* **1** the activity of fighting a war, esp. of a particular type (*chemical warfare*). **2** an aggressive or violent conflict or struggle.

war·farin /ˈwɔːfərɪn/ *noun* a water-soluble anticoagulant derived from coumarin used esp. as a rat poison and in the treatment of thrombosis. [Wisconsin Alumni Research Foundation + *-arin*, after COUMARIN]

war fever *noun* an enthusiasm for war.

war game ● *noun* **1** a military exercise testing or improving tactical knowledge etc. **2** a battle etc. conducted with counters representing military units. ● *transitive verb* (**war-game**) examine or test (a strategy) by playing it through. □ **war-gaming** *noun*

war·head *noun* the explosive head of a missile, torpedo, or similar weapon.

War·hol /ˈwɔːhɒl, -hɔːl/ **Andy** (born Andrew Warhola) (*c.*1928–87), US painter, graphic artist, and filmmaker. A leading exponent of pop art, he first achieved fame in the early 1960s with a series of silkscreen prints and acrylic paintings of familiar objects (such as Campbell's soup cans), Marilyn Monroe, etc., treated with objectivity and precision. □ **War·hol·ian** /-ˈhɔːlɪən/ *adjective*

war·horse *noun* **1** *hist.* a knight's or trooper's powerful horse. **2** *informal* a veteran of any activity, esp. a soldier, politician, etc.; a dependable or stalwart person or thing. **3** a thing which is frequently used or very familiar, esp. a work of art which is frequently performed.

war·like *adjective* **1** threatening war; hostile. **2** martial; soldierly. **3** of or for war; military (*warlike preparations*).

war·lock *noun* a sorcerer or wizard; a man who practises witchcraft. [Old English *wær-loga* traitor, from *wær* covenant: *loga* related to LIE²]

war·lord *noun* a military commander or commander-in-chief, esp. a regional military commander with more or less independent control of an area or military group. □ **war·lord·ism** *noun*

warm ● *adjective* **1** of or at a fairly or comfortably high temperature. **2** (of clothes etc.) providing warmth (*needs warm gloves*). **3 a** (of a person, action, feelings, etc.) sympathetic; cordial; friendly; loving (*a warm welcome; has a warm heart*). **b** enthusiastic; hearty (*was warm in her praise*). **4** animated, heated, excited (*a warm exchange of views*). **5** *informal* **a** (of a participant in esp. a children's game of seeking) close to the object etc. sought. **b** near to guessing or finding out a secret. **6** (of a colour, light, etc.) containing red, yellow, or orange tones. **7** *Hunting* (of a scent) fresh and strong. ● *verb* **1** *transitive* **a** make warm (*fire warms the room*). **b** excite; make cheerful (*warms the heart*). **2** *intransitive* **a** (often foll. by *up*) become warm (*while the dinner was warming up*). **b** (often foll. by *to*) become animated, enthusiastic, or sympathetic (*warmed to his subject*). ● *noun* **1** the act of warming; the state of being warmed (*gave it a warm; had a nice warm by the fire*). **2** the warmth of the atmosphere etc.

□ **warm the bench** (or **pine**) *Sport* be made to sit inactively and not participate in a game etc. **warm up 1** (of an athlete, performer, etc.) prepare oneself by light exercise or practice immediately before the start of a contest or other form of physical exertion. **2** become or cause to become warmer. **3** (often foll. by *to*) (of a person) become enthusiastic etc. (about). **4** (of an engine, electrical equipment, etc.) reach a temperature for efficient working. **5** reheat (food). **6** amuse or entertain (an audience or crowd) so as to make them more receptive to the main act. □ **warm·er** *noun* (also in *combination*). **warm·ing** *noun* **warm·ish** *adjective* **warm·ly** *adverb* **warm·ness** *noun* [Old English *wearm* from Germanic]

warm and fuzzy *adjective N Amer. informal* = WARM FUZZY *adjective*.

warm-blooded *adjective* **1** (of an organism) having warm blood; mammalian (see HOMEOTHERM). **2** ardent, passionate.
□ **warm-blooded·ness** *noun*

warm down *noun* a session of gentle exercise after strenuous physical exercise.

War Measures Act *noun* (in Canada) a statute of 1914 conferring on the federal cabinet the power to govern by decree in times of war or national emergency, and suspending freedoms to allow for the arrest and detention of citizens on suspicion only rather than on reasonable or probable grounds. *See* OCTOBER CRISIS.

warmed-over *adjective* esp. N Amer. **1** (of food etc.) reheated or stale. **2** (of an idea or product) stale; second-hand (*warmed-over communism*).

war memorial *noun* a monument etc. commemorating those killed in a war.

warm front *noun* the leading edge of an advancing mass of warm air.

warm fuzzy *N Amer. informal* ● *noun* (*pl.* **-ies**) a feeling of emotional warmth or pleasant satisfaction as a visceral reaction to something (*donating to environmental causes always gave them the warm fuzzies*). ● *adjective* (also **warm and fuzzy**) pertaining to, evoking, or evoked by such a reaction (*warm fuzzy images; a warm fuzzy feeling*).

warm-hearted *adjective* having a warm heart; kind, friendly.
□ **warm-hearted·ly** *adverb* **warm-hearted·ness** *noun*

warming hut *noun* a hut or shelter along a cross-country ski trail in which skiers may rest, often with a wood stove or other form of heating.

war·monger /ˈwɔr،mɒŋɡər, -ˌmʌŋɡər/ *noun* a person who seeks to bring about or promote war. □ **war·monger·ing** *noun & adjective*

warmth *noun* **1 a** the state of being warm. **b** moderate heat. **2** a friendly or loving attitude, personality, etc.

warm-up *noun* **1** a session of preparatory exercise or practice for a contest, performance, etc. **2** (*attributive*) **a** designating clothing worn during an esp. athletic warm-up (*warm-up suit*). **b** designating an act that performs prior to the main attraction at a concert etc. (*warm-up band*). **3** (often in *pl.*) an esp. knitted or fleece garment worn over other clothing to provide warmth during warm-up exercises.

warn *verb* **1** *transitive & intransitive* **a** (often foll. by *of*, or *that* + clause, or *to* + infin.) inform of danger, unknown circumstances, etc. (*warned them of the danger; warned her that she was being watched; warned him to expect a visit; the sign warned of the danger*). **b** (often foll. by *against*) inform (a person etc.) about a specific danger, hostile person, etc. (*warned her against trusting him; the notice warned against unsupervised swimming*). **2** *transitive* (usu. with *neg.*) admonish; tell forcefully (*has been warned not to go*). **3** *transitive* give (a person) cautionary notice regarding conduct etc. (*I've warned you many times*). □ **warn off 1** warn (a person) to keep away (from). **2** *Brit.* prohibit from attending races, esp. at a specified course. □ **warn·er** *noun* [Old English *war(e)nian, wearnian*, ultimately from Germanic: related to WARE³]

warn·ing ● *noun* **1** in senses of WARN *verb*. **2** anything that serves to warn; a hint or indication of difficulty, danger, etc. **3** an indication of any impending event (*without warning*). ● *attributive adjective* serving to warn or indicate. □ **take warning** take heed; beware; recognize the danger. □ **warn·ing·ly** *adverb*

warning track *noun Baseball* a track or strip of gravel etc. running along the perimeter of a baseball field to give fielders warning of the proximity of the wall, stands, etc., esp. that portion along the farthest perimeter of the outfield.

War of 1812 a conflict between the US and the UK 1812–14. British interference in US trade during the Napoleonic Wars led to American calls for the annexation of British North America and finally to a declaration of war on 18 June 1812. Most of the fighting occurred along the Canadian border. After the changing of hands of a number of forts, and the burning of public buildings in York (Toronto) and

Washington, the Treaty of Ghent restored all conquered territories to their pre-war owners.

War of American Independence *see* AMERICAN REVOLUTION.

war of attrition *noun* a prolonged war (e.g. World War I) in which military strategy is based on the calculation that the enemy's manpower and material resources will be exhausted before one's own as a result of numerous battles, usu. involving massive losses on both sides.

war of nerves *noun* an attempt to wear down an opponent by psychological means, as by the use of hostile or subversive propaganda to undermine morale and cause confusion.

war of words *noun* a sustained conflict conducted by means of the spoken or written word; a propaganda war.

warp ● *verb* **1** *transitive & intransitive* **a** make or become bent or twisted out of shape, esp. by the action of heat, damp, etc. **b** make or become perverted, bitter, or strange (*too much TV warps the mind*). **2 a** *transitive* haul (a ship) by a rope attached to a fixed point. **b** *intransitive* progress in this way. **3** *transitive* silt over (land) with warp, by flooding. **4** *transitive* arrange (threads) as a warp. ● *noun* **1 a** a state of being warped, esp. of shrunken or expanded timber. **b** perversion, bitterness, etc. of the mind or character. **2** the threads stretched lengthwise in a loom to be crossed by the weft. **3** a rope used in towing or warping, or attached to a trawl net. **4** sediment etc. left esp. on poor land by standing water. **5** (in science fiction) an imaginary or hypothetical distortion in space in relation to time (*time warp; space warp*). **6** (*attributive*) of or pertaining to warp speed (*warp drive; warp factor*). □ **warp·age** *noun* (esp. in sense 1a of *verb*). [Old English *weorpan* throw, *wearp* from Germanic]

war paint *noun* **1** paint used to adorn the body before battle, esp. by some N American Aboriginal peoples. **2** *informal* elaborate makeup.

warp and woof *plural noun* two fundamental constituent elements of a thing (*the warp and woof of Canadian culture*).

war party *noun* a band of warriors esp. seeking battle.

war·path *noun* **1** *hist.* the path or route taken by a warlike expedition of N American Aboriginal peoples. **2** *informal* any hostile course or attitude (*is on the warpath again*).

warped *adjective* **1** in senses of WARP *verb*. **2** (of a person, mind, attitude, etc.) perverted, twisted, sick; bizarre.

war·plane *noun* a military aircraft, esp. one equipped for fighting, bombing, etc.

war poet *noun* a poet writing at the time of and on the subject of war, esp. one on military service during World War I.

warp speed *noun* **1** (in science fiction) travelling speed faster than that of light. **2** *informal* an extraordinarily high speed.

war·rant ● *noun* **1 a** anything that authorizes a person or an action (*have no warrant for this*). **b** a person so authorizing (*I will be your warrant*). **2 a** a written authorization, money voucher, travel document, etc. (*travel warrant*). **b** a written authorization allowing police to search premises, arrest a suspect, etc. **c** a certificate entitling the holder to subscribe for shares of a company. **3** a certificate of service rank held by a warrant officer. ● *transitive verb* **1** justify; make necessary or appropriate in the circumstances (*nothing can warrant his behaviour*). **2** guarantee or attest to esp. the genuineness of an article, the worth of a person, etc. [Old Northern French *warant*, var. of Old French *guarant, -and* from Frankish *werēnd* from *giwerēn* be surety for]

war·rant·able *adjective* (of an action or statement) able to be authorized or sanctioned; justifiable. □ **war·rant·abil·ity** *noun*

war·ran·tee *noun* a person to whom a warranty is given.

warrant officer *noun* **1** (also **Warrant Officer**) (in the Canadian Army and Air Force) a non-commissioned officer of a rank below master warrant officer and above sergeant. Abbr.: **WO**. **2** an officer of a similar rank in other armies.

war·ranty *noun* (*pl.* **-ties**) **1** a manufacturer's written promise as to the extent to which defective goods will be repaired, replaced, etc. **2** (usu. foll. by *for* + verbal noun) an authority or justification. **3** an undertaking by an insured person of the truth of a statement or fulfillment of a condition.

War·ren ▸ 1 Earl (1891–1974), US judge, chief justice of the US Supreme Court 1953–69. He headed the commission of inquiry (known as the Warren Commission) held in 1964 into the assassination of John F. Kennedy; the commission found that Lee Harvey Oswald was the sole gunman, a decision that has since been much disputed. **2 Rob·ert Penn** (1905–89), US poet, novelist, and critic. An advocate of New Criticism, he collaborated with the US critic Cleanth Brooks (1906–94) in writing such critical works as *Understanding Poetry* (1938) and

Understanding Fiction (1943); he also wrote several novels, including *All the King's Men* (1946), and many volumes of poetry.

war·ren noun **1 a** a network of interconnecting rabbit burrows. **b** a piece of ground occupied by this. **2** a densely populated or labyrinthine building or district. [Anglo-French & Old Northern French *warenne*, Old French *garenne* game park, from Germanic]

war·ring adjective **1** rival, antagonistic, fighting (*warring factions*). **2** conflicting (*warring principles*).

War·ring·ton an industrial town on the Mersey River in NW England, formerly part of Cheshire; pop. (est. 2002) 84,100.

war·rior noun **1** a person experienced or distinguished in fighting in an armed force etc. **2** (*attributive*) **a** of or relating to a warrior. **b** martial (*a warrior nation*). [Old Northern French *werreior* etc., Old French *guerreior* etc. from *werreier*, *guerreier* 'make WAR']

war room noun **1** a room from which a war is directed. **2** a room in which business or political strategy is planned.

War·saw the capital of Poland, on the Vistula River; pop. (est. 2000) 1,610,471.

Warsaw Convention noun an international agreement (1929) on compensation and liability in international air travel.

Warsaw Pact *hist.* a treaty of mutual defence and military aid signed at Warsaw on 14 May 1955 by Communist states of Europe under Soviet leadership, in response to the admission of West Germany to NATO; collectively, the group of states which signed the treaty. Following the collapse of the Communist system the Pact was dissolved in 1991.

war·ship noun an armoured ship used in war.

Wars of Religion *See* FRENCH WARS OF RELIGION.

Wars of the Roses the civil wars arising from the dynastic struggle between the followers of the House of York (with the white rose as its emblem) and the House of Lancaster (with the red rose) in 15th-century England. The struggle was largely ended in 1485 by the defeat and death of the Yorkist king Richard III at the battle of Bosworth Field and the accession of the Lancastrian Henry Tudor (Henry VII), who united the two houses by marrying Elizabeth, daughter of Edward IV.

war-surplus attributive adjective designating items or *matériel* discarded by the military and made available to the public (*war-surplus binoculars*).

wart noun **1** a small benign growth on the skin, usu. hard and rounded, caused by a virus-induced abnormal growth of skin cells and thickening of the epidermis. **2** any protuberance, as on the skin of an animal, surface of a plant, etc. □ **warts and all** informal with no attempt to conceal blemishes or inadequacies. □ **wart·ed** adjective **warty** adjective [Old English *wearte*]

wart·hog noun an African wild pig of the genus *Phacochoerus*, with a large head and warty lumps on its face, and large curved tusks.

war·time noun the period during which a war is waged (often *attributive*: *wartime rationing*).

war-torn adjective racked or devastated by war.

war-weary adjective (esp. of a population) exhausted and dispirited by war. □ **war-weariness** noun

war whoop noun a war cry or howl made on rushing into battle.

War·wick[1] /ˈwɒrɪk/ the county town of Warwickshire, in central England, on the Avon River; pop. (est. 2002) 23,300.

War·wick[2] /ˈwɒrɪk/ **Earl of** (title of Richard Neville; known as 'the Kingmaker') (1428–71), English statesman. During the Wars of the Roses he fought first on the Yorkist side, helping Edward IV to gain the throne in 1461; having lost influence at court he then fought on the Lancastrian side, briefly restoring Henry VI to the throne in 1470.

War·wick·shire /ˈwɒrɪkʃɪr/ a county of central England; county town, Warwick.

war widow noun a woman whose husband has been killed in war.

wary /ˈweri/ adjective (**wari·er**, **wari·est**) **1** on one's guard; given to caution; circumspect. **2** (foll. by *of*) cautious, suspicious (*am wary of buying used cars*). **3** showing or done with caution or suspicion (*a wary expression*). □ **wari·ly** adverb **wari·ness** noun [WARE[2] + -Y[1]]

war zone noun an area in which a war takes place.

was 1st & 3rd sing. past of BE.

was·abi /wəˈsɒbi/ noun a cruciferous plant, *Eutrema wasabi*, with a thick green root which tastes like strong horseradish and is used in Japanese cooking, usu. ground as an accompaniment to raw fish. [Japanese]

Was·aga Beach /wəˈseɪgə/ a town in south central Ontario, situated at the mouth of the Nottawasaga River where it empties into Nottawasaga Bay, northwest of Barrie; pop. (2001) 12,419. It is a popular summer resort. □ **Was·aga Beach·er** noun [as NOTTAWASAGA BAY]

Wash. abbreviation Washington.

wash ● verb **1** transitive cleanse (oneself or a part of oneself, clothes, etc.) with liquid, esp. water and usu. soap or detergent. **2** transitive (foll. by *out*, *off*, *away*, etc.) remove (a stain or dirt) in this way. **3** intransitive wash oneself or esp. one's hands and face. **4** intransitive wash clothes etc. **5** intransitive (of fabric or dye) bear washing without damage. **6** intransitive (foll. by *off*, *out*) (of a stain etc.) be removed by washing. **7** transitive moisten, water (*tear-washed eyes; a rose washed with dew*). **8** transitive (of a river, sea, etc.) touch (a country, coast, etc.) with its waters. **9 a** transitive (of moving liquid) carry along in a specified direction (*a wave washed him overboard; was washed up on the shore*). **b** intransitive be carried in this way (*shells wash up on the beaches*). **10** transitive **a** scoop out (*the water had washed a channel*). **b** erode, denude (*sea-washed cliffs*). **11** intransitive (foll. by *over*, *along*, etc.) sweep, move, or splash. **12** transitive sift (ore) by the action of water. **13** transitive **a** brush a thin coat of watery paint or ink over (paper in watercolour painting etc., or a wall). **b** (foll. by *with*) coat (inferior metal) with gold etc. ● noun **1** the act or an instance of washing; the process of being washed (*give them a good wash; only needed one wash*). **2** a quantity of clothes for washing or just washed (*your pants are in the wash*). **3** the visible or audible motion of agitated water or air, esp. due to the passage of a ship etc. or aircraft. **4 a** soil swept off by water; alluvium. **b** a sandbank exposed only at low tide. **c** the dry bed of an intermittent stream. **d** an expanse or pool of shallow water. **5** kitchen slops and scraps given to pigs. **6** a liquid to spread over a surface to cleanse, heal, or colour. **7 a** a thin coating of watercolour, wall-colouring, or metal. **b** an expanse of colour appearing to have been washed on (*a wash of warm orange twilight*). **8** malt etc. fermenting before distillation. **9** a lotion or cosmetic. **10** a balanced outcome; a situation or result which is of no net benefit to either of two opposing sides, values, etc. □ **come out in the wash** informal be clarified, or (of contingent difficulties) be resolved or removed, in the course of time. **wash one's dirty laundry in public** see DIRTY LAUNDRY. **wash down 1** wash completely (esp. a large surface or object). **2** (usu. foll. by *with*) accompany or follow (food) with a drink. **wash one's hands** euphemism use the toilet. **wash one's hands of** renounce responsibility for. **wash out 1** clean the inside of (a thing) by washing. **2** clean (a garment etc.) by brief washing. **3 a** rain out (an event etc.). **b** informal cancel. **4** (of a flood, downpour, etc.) make a breach in (a road etc.). **5** fail, drop out (*washed out of med school*). **6** = sense 2 of verb **wash up 1** wash (dishes, cutlery, etc.) after use. **2** N Amer. wash one's face and hands. **won't wash** informal (of an argument etc.) will not be believed or accepted. [Old English *wæscan* etc. from Germanic, related to WATER]

Wash, the an inlet of the North Sea on the east coast of England between Norfolk and Lincolnshire.

wash·able adjective that can be washed, esp. without damage. □ **wash·abil·ity** noun

wash-and-wear adjective **1** (of a fabric or garment) easily washed, drying readily, and not requiring to be ironed. **2** (of a haircut) requiring little or no styling after washing.

wash basin noun a basin for washing one's hands, face, etc.

wash·board noun **1 a** a board of ribbed wood or a sheet of corrugated zinc on which clothes are scrubbed in washing. **b** this used as a percussion instrument, played with the fingers. **2** N Amer. a dirt or gravel road whose surface has become corrugated as a result of weather and usage (also *attributive*: *washboard road*). **3** (*attributive*) designating any corrugated surface (*has a washboard stomach*).

wash·cloth noun N Amer. a small terry cloth for washing oneself; a face cloth.

wash·day noun a day on which clothes etc. are washed.

washed out adjective (hyphenated when *attributive*) **1** faded by washing. **2** pale. **3** informal limp, enfeebled.

washed up adjective esp. N Amer. slang defeated, having failed.

wash·er noun **1 a** a person or thing that washes. **b** a washing machine. **2** a flat ring of rubber, metal, leather, etc., inserted at a joint to tighten it and prevent leakage. **3** a similar ring placed under the head of a screw, bolt, etc., or under a nut, to disperse its pressure. □ **washer·less** adjective

washer·man noun (pl. **-men**) a man whose occupation is washing clothes, linen, etc.

washer·woman noun (pl. **-women**) a woman whose occupation is washing clothes, linen, etc.

wash house noun a building where clothes are washed.

wash·ing noun **1** a quantity of clothes for washing or just washed. **2** the act of washing clothes.

Consonants:　b *but*　d *dog*　f *few*　g *get*　h *her*　j *yes*　k *cat*　l *leg*　m *man*　n *no*　p *pen*　r *red*　s *sit*

washing machine *noun* a machine for washing clothes and linen etc.

washing powder *noun Brit.* powdered laundry detergent.

washing soda *noun* sodium carbonate, used dissolved in water for washing and cleaning.

Wash·ing·ton[1] **1** a state of the northwestern US, on the Pacific coast; pop. (est. 2000) 5,894,121; capital, Olympia. **2** the capital of the US; pop. (est. 2000) 572,059. It is co-extensive with the District of Columbia, a Federal district on the Potomac River with boundaries on the states of Virginia and Maryland. □ **Wash·ing·ton·ian** /ˌwɒʃɪŋˈtəːnɪən/ *noun & adjective* [G. WASHINGTON[2]]

Wash·ing·ton[2] ▸ **1 Booker Talia·ferro** (1856–1915), US educator. An emancipated slave, he pursued a career in teaching, and emerged as a leading commentator for black Americans at the turn of the century; he published his influential autobiography, *Up from Slavery*, in 1901. **2 George** (1732–99), US politician, 1st president of the US 1789–97. He was the commander of the Continental Army during the American Revolution, eventually winning a decisive victory at Yorktown, Virginia (1781); he chaired the convention at Philadelphia (1787) that drew up the American constitution and, two years later, he was unanimously elected president.

Wash·ing·ton, Mount a peak (1 590 m) on Vancouver Island, west of Courtenay.

washing-up *noun Brit.* **1** the process of washing dishes etc. after use. **2** used dishes etc. for washing.

wash·out *noun* **1** *Geol.* a narrow river channel that cuts into pre-existing sediments. **2** a breach in a road, railway track, etc., caused by flooding. **3** *informal* **a** a fiasco; a complete failure. **b** a person who has failed or dropped out.

wash·rag *noun N Amer.* = WASHCLOTH.

wash·room *noun* **1** *esp. Cdn* a room with toilet facilities; a bathroom. **2** *esp. N Amer.* a room with facilities for washing oneself. □ **go to the washroom** *esp. Cdn euphemism* defecate or urinate.

wash·stand *noun* a piece of furniture to hold a basin, jug of water, soap, etc. for washing oneself with.

wash·tub *noun* a tub or vessel for washing clothes etc.

washy *adjective* (**wash·i·er**, **wash·i·est**) (of colour) faded-looking, thin, faint.

wasn't *contraction* was not.

WASP /wɒsp/ (also **Wasp**) *N Amer. usu. derogatory* ● *noun* **1** a white Protestant of Anglo-Saxon descent. **2** a middle-class North American white Protestant. ● *adjective* of, pertaining to, being, or typical of a WASP or WASPs. □ **WASP·ish** *adjective* (also **Wasp·ish**). **WASPy** *adjective* (also **Waspy**). [white Anglo-Saxon Protestant]

wasp *noun* a stinging often flesh-eating insect of the order Hymenoptera, esp. of the genus *Vespula*, with black and yellow stripes and a very thin waist. □ **wasp·like** *adjective* [Old English *wæfs, wæps, wæsp*, from West Germanic: perhaps related to WEAVE[1] (from the web-like form of its nest)]

wasp·ish *adjective* irritable, petulant. □ **wasp·ish·ly** *adverb* **wasp·ish·ness** *noun*

wasp waist *noun* a very slender waist. □ **wasp-waisted** *adjective*

was·sail /ˈwɒseɪl, ˈwɒsəl/ *archaic* ● *noun* **1** a festive occasion, esp. during the Christmas season. **2** a usu. alcoholic drink consumed on such an occasion, e.g. mulled wine. ● *intransitive verb* **1** make merry; celebrate with drinking etc. **2** go from house to house at Christmastime singing carols and songs. □ **was·sail·er** *noun* [Middle English *wæs hæil* etc. from Old Norse *ves heill*, corresponding to Old English *wes hāl* 'be in health', a form of salutation: compare HALE[1]]

Was·ser·mann test /ˈwɒsərmən/ *noun* a test for syphilis using the reaction of the patient's blood serum. [A. von *Wassermann*, German pathologist d.1925]

wast /wɒst, wəst/ *archaic or dialect 2nd sing. past of* BE.

wast·age /ˈweɪstɪdʒ/ *noun* **1** an amount wasted. **2** loss or destruction of something, esp. something valuable that has not been used or kept carefully. **3** (in full **natural wastage**) *esp. Brit.* loss of employees because they retire or move to other jobs; attrition.

waste ● *verb* **1** *transitive* use to no purpose or for inadequate result or extravagantly (*waste time*). **2** *transitive* fail to use (esp. an opportunity). **3** *transitive* (often foll. by *on*) **a** give (advice etc.), utter (words etc.), without effect. **b** (often in *passive*) fail to be appreciated or used properly (*she was wasted on him*; *I feel wasted in this job*). **4** *transitive & intransitive* (often foll. by *away*) wear gradually away; make or become weak; wither. **5** *transitive literary* ravage, devastate. **6** *transitive* treat as wasted or valueless. **7** *intransitive* be expended without useful effect.

8 *transitive esp. N Amer.* **a** beat up. **b** kill, murder. ● *adjective* **1** superfluous; no longer serving a purpose. **2** (of a district etc.) not inhabited or cultivated; desolate (*waste ground*). ● *noun* **1** the act or an instance of wasting; extravagant or ineffectual use of an asset, of time, etc. **2 a** waste material or food; refuse; useless remains or by-products. **b** excrement. **3** a waste region; a desert etc. **4** the state of being used up; diminution by wear and tear. **5** *Law* damage to an estate caused by an act or by neglect, esp. by a tenant. □ **go to waste** be wasted. **lay waste** ravage, devastate. **waste one's breath** *see* BREATH. **waste not, want not** extravagance leads to poverty. **waste words** *see* WORD. □ **wast·er** *noun* [Old Northern French *wast(e)*, var. of Old French *g(u)ast(e)*, from Latin *vastus* 'unoccupied, uncultivated']

waste·basket *noun esp. N Amer.* a receptacle for waste paper.

waste bin *noun esp. Brit.* a bin for waste paper, refuse, etc., used indoors or outdoors.

wast·ed *adjective* **1** *in senses of* WASTE *verb*. **2** *predicative adjective esp. N Amer. slang* **a** worn out; exhausted. **b** intoxicated by alcohol or drugs.

waste disposal *noun* (often *attributive*) the disposing of waste products, garbage, etc., esp. as a public or corporate process.

waste·ful *adjective* **1** extravagant. **2** causing or showing waste. □ **waste·ful·ly** *adjective* **waste·ful·ness** *noun*

waste ground *noun* an area of unused land, esp. one left undeveloped in an urban area.

waste·land *noun* **1** an unproductive or useless or devastated area of land. **2** a place or time considered spiritually or intellectually barren.

waste management *noun* the collection, disposal, treatment, or recycling of waste.

waste paper *noun* spoiled or valueless paper.

waste·paper basket *noun* = WASTEBASKET.

waste product *noun* (esp. in *pl.*) a useless by-product of manufacture or of an organism or organisms.

waste stream *noun* the mass of waste generated e.g. by a city for disposal etc.

waste water *noun* **1** water that has served an esp. industrial purpose, allowed to run away. **2** sewage.

wast·rel /ˈweɪstrəl/ *noun* a wasteful or good-for-nothing person.

wat /wɒt/ *noun* a Buddhist monastery or temple in Thailand or Cambodia. [Thai from Sanskrit *vāṭa* enclosure]

watch ● *verb* **1** *transitive* keep the eyes fixed on; look at attentively. **2** *transitive* **a** keep under observation; follow observation. **b** monitor or consider carefully; pay attention to (*have to watch my weight*; *watched their progress with interest*). **c** be careful to prevent damage or harm to (*watch your head*). **3** *intransitive* (often foll. by *for*) be in an alert state; be vigilant; take heed (*watch for the holes in the road*; *watch for an opportunity*). **4** *intransitive* (foll. by *over*) look after; take care of. **5** *intransitive archaic* remain awake for devotions etc. ● *noun* **1** a small portable timepiece for carrying on one's person. **2** a state of alert or constant observation or attention. **3** *Naut.* **a** a usu. four-hour spell of duty. **b** each of the halves into which a ship's crew is divided to take alternate watches. **4** *hist.* a watchman or group of watchmen, esp. patrolling the streets at night. **5** a former division of the night (*the watches of the night*). **6** *hist.* irregular Highland troops in the 18th c. □ **on the watch** waiting for an expected or feared occurrence. **on watch** on lookout duty. **watch one's back** be alert to danger. **watch the clock** *see* CLOCK[1]. **watch it** (or **oneself**) *informal* be careful. **watch one's mouth** *see* MOUTH. **watch out 1** (often foll. by *for*) be on one's guard. **2** as a warning of immediate danger. **watch one's step** proceed cautiously. □ **watch·able** *adjective* [Old English *wæcce* (n.), related to WAKE[1]]

watch·band *noun N Amer.* a strap for fastening a watch on the wrist.

watch cap *noun esp. N Amer.* a close-fitting usu. dark knitted cap, as used in bad weather by sailors.

watch case *noun* the outer metal case enclosing the works of a watch.

watch chain *noun* a metal chain for securing a pocket watch.

watch·dog ● *noun* **1** a dog kept to guard property etc. **2** a person or body monitoring others' rights, behaviour, etc. ● *transitive verb* (**-dogged**, **-dog·ging**) maintain surveillance over.

watch·er *noun* a person who watches or observes or follows something closely (often in *combination*: *birdwatcher*; *Commons-watcher*).

watch·ful *adjective* **1** watching or observing closely; alert; on the watch. **2** *archaic* wakeful. □ **watch·ful·ly** *adverb* **watch·ful·ness** *noun*

watch glass *noun* **1** a glass disc covering the face of a watch. **2** a similar disc used in a laboratory etc. to hold material for use in experiments.

watch·ing brief *noun* a state of interest maintained in a proceeding not directly or immediately concerning one.

watch·keep·ing *noun* keeping a lookout, esp. as a member of a watch on board ship. □ **watch·keep·er** *noun*

watch·maker *noun* a person who makes and repairs watches and clocks. □ **watch·making** *noun*

watch·man *noun* (pl. **-men**) **1** a man employed to look after an empty building etc. at night. **2** *archaic or hist.* a member of a night street patrol.

watch·spring *noun* the mainspring of a watch.

watch strap *noun* = WATCHBAND.

watch·tower *noun* a tower from which observation can be kept.

watch·word *noun* **1** a phrase summarizing a guiding principle; a slogan. **2** *hist.* a military password.

wat·er ● *noun* **1** a colourless transparent odourless tasteless liquid compound of oxygen and hydrogen. Chem. formula: H_2O (*see also* HEAVY WATER). **2** a liquid consisting chiefly of this and found in seas, lakes, and rivers, in rain, and in secretions of organisms. **3** an expanse of water; a sea, lake, river, etc. **4** (in *pl.*) part of a sea or river (*in Icelandic waters*). **5** (often as **the waters**) mineral water at a spa etc. **6** the state of a tide (*high water*). **7** a solution of a specified substance in water (*lavender water*). **8** *archaic* the quality of the transparency and brilliance of a gem, esp. a diamond. **9** *Business* an amount of nominal capital added by watering (*see* sense 10 of *verb*). **10** (*attributive*) **a** found in or near water. **b** of, for, or worked by water. **c** involving, using, or yielding water. **11 a** urine. **b** (also in *pl.*) the amniotic fluid discharged from the womb before childbirth. ● *verb* **1** *transitive* sprinkle or soak with water. **2** *transitive* supply (a plant) with water. **3** *transitive* give water to (an animal) to drink. **4** *intransitive* (of the mouth or eyes) secrete water as saliva or tears. **5** *transitive* (usu. as **watered** *adjective*) (of silk etc.) having irregular wavy glossy markings. **6** *transitive* (usu. foll. by *down*) adulterate (beer, milk, etc.) with water. **7** *transitive* (of a river etc.) supply (a place) with water. **8** *intransitive* (of an animal) go to a pool etc. to drink. **9** *intransitive* (of a ship, engine, etc., or the person in charge of it) take in a supply of water. **10** *transitive Business* increase (a company's debt, or nominal capital) by the issue of new shares without a corresponding addition to assets. □ **blow out of the water** *see* BLOW¹. **by water** using a ship etc. for travel or transport. **dead in the water** *see* DEAD. **hold water** *see* HOLD¹. **in deep water** (or **waters**) in serious trouble or difficulty. **in** (or **into**) **hot water** *see* HOT WATER. **keep one's head above water** *see* HEAD. **like water** lavishly, profusely. **like water off a duck's back** *see* DUCK¹. **make one's mouth water** cause one's saliva to flow, stimulate one's appetite or anticipation. **make water 1** urinate. **2** (of a ship) take in water. **muddy the water(s)** *see* MUDDY. **of the first water 1** (of a diamond) of the greatest brilliance and transparency. **2** of the finest quality or extreme degree. **off the water wagon** *see* WAGON. **on the water wagon** *see* WAGON. **throw** (or **pour**) **cold water on** *see* COLD. **water down 1** dilute with water. **2** (often as **watered down** *adjective*) make less vivid, forceful, or horrifying. **water under the bridge** past events accepted as past and irrevocable. □ **water·less** *adjective* [Old English *wæter* from Germanic, related to WET]

water arum *noun* a plant of the arum family, *Calla palustris*, found across Canada, with a white spathe and yellow spadix and fruit in a cluster of red berries. Also called ARUM LILY, WILD CALLA.

water bag *noun* a bag of leather, canvas, etc., for holding water.

water balloon *noun* N Amer. a water-filled toy balloon used in games, bursting on being dropped or mishandled.

water-based *adjective* (usu. *attributive*) (of a solution, substance, etc.) having water as the main ingredient.

water bear *noun* = TARDIGRADE *noun*.

Water Bearer *noun* = WATER CARRIER.

water·bed *noun* a bed with a mattress of rubber or plastic etc. filled with water.

water beetle *noun* any of numerous beetles that live in water, esp. carnivorous beetles of the family Dytiscidae, and scavenging beetles of the family Hydrophilidae.

water birch *noun* a birch of western N America, *Betula occidentalis*, often growing in thickets in wet places. Also called BLACK BIRCH, RIVER BIRCH.

water bird *noun* a bird frequenting esp. fresh water.

water birth *noun* a birth in which the mother spends the final stages of labour in a birthing pool, with delivery taking place either in or out of the water.

water blister *noun* a blister containing a colourless fluid, not blood or pus.

water boatman *noun* any aquatic bug of the family Corixidae, swimming with oar-like hind legs.

water bomber *noun* Cdn an aircraft used to drop water on forest fires, esp. one which scoops up its load by skimming the surface of a lake etc. □ **water bombing** *noun*

water-borne *adjective* **1** (of goods etc.) conveyed by or travelling on water. **2** (of a disease) communicated or propagated by contaminated water.

water boy *noun* N Amer. **1** a boy whose job it is to fetch water for or hand water to labourers, athletes, etc. **2** *informal* a person in a subservient position or role.

water·buck *noun* any of various African antelopes of the genus *Kobus*, frequenting riverbanks.

water buffalo *noun* a large Asiatic buffalo, *Bubalus arnee*, with large curved horns, which occurs widely as a domesticated beast of burden.

water cannon *noun* a device giving a powerful jet of water to disperse a crowd etc.

Water Carrier *noun* (also **Water Bearer**) the zodiacal sign or constellation Aquarius.

water chestnut *noun* **1** an aquatic plant, *Trapa natans*, bearing an edible seed. **2 a** (in full **Chinese water chestnut**) a tropical sedge, *Eleocharis tuberosa*, with rushlike leaves arising from a corm. **b** this corm used as food.

water clock *noun* a clock measuring time by the flow of water.

water closet *noun* dated **1** a flush toilet. **2** a room containing this.

water·col·our *noun* (also **water·color**) **1** artists' paint made of pigment to be diluted with water and not oil. **2** a picture painted with this. **3** the art of painting with watercolours. □ **water·col·our·ist** *noun*

water-cooled *adjective* cooled by the circulation of water.

water cooler *noun* a vessel in which water is cooled and kept cool, esp. a tank of cooled drinking water in a workplace as a setting for informal conversation or gossip (also, with hyphen, *attributive*: *water-cooler rumours*).

water·course *noun* **1** a brook, stream, or artificial water channel. **2** the bed along which this flows.

water·craft *noun* (pl. same) N Amer. any boat.

water·cress *noun* a hardy perennial cress, *Nasturtium officinale*, growing in running water, with pungent leaves used in salad etc.

water cure *noun* = HYDROPATHY.

water cycle *noun* the circulation of water from the atmosphere, where water vapour condenses and falls as precipitation, to the earth where it collects as liquid or ice, and back to the atmosphere through evaporation or transpiration.

water diviner *noun* a person who dowses (*see* DOWSE¹) for water.

water·er *noun* **1** a receptacle for drinking water for animals. **2** a person or thing that waters.

water·fall *noun* a stream, river, or artificial watercourse flowing over a precipice or down a steep hillside.

water feature *noun* a pond or fountain in a garden.

Water·ford /ˈwɔtərfərd/ **1** a county of the Republic of Ireland, in the southeast, in the province of Munster; county town, Waterford; main administrative centre, Dungarvan. **2** its county town, a port on an inlet of St. George's Channel; pop. (est. 2002) 46,000, a centre for crystal manufacture.

water·fowl *noun* (usu. collect. as *pl.*) birds frequenting water, esp. swimming game birds.

water·fowl·ing *noun* N Amer. the hunting of waterfowl for sport or food. □ **water·fowl·er** *noun*

water·front *noun* esp. urban land adjoining a river, lake, harbour, etc. (also *attributive*: *waterfront condos*). □ **cover the waterfront** N Amer. cover every aspect of something.

water garden *noun* a garden with pools or a stream, for growing aquatic plants.

Water·gate a US political scandal in which people hired by the Republican Party's committee to re-elect President Nixon were caught breaking into the national headquarters of the Democratic Party in an attempt to plant bugs during the 1972 election campaign, leading

Vowels: a cat   ɑ arm   e bed   ɜr her   ɜː *deux*   ə ago   ɪ sit   i cosy   iː *feed*   ɒ hot   ɔ pore   ɔː no   ʌ run   ʊ put

ultimately to the president's resignation in 1974. [the *Watergate* building in Washington, DC, where the break-in occurred]

water·gate *noun* **1** a floodgate. **2** a gate giving access to a river etc.

water gauge *noun* a glass tube etc. indicating the height of water in a reservoir, boiler, etc.

water·glass *noun* **1** a solution of sodium or potassium silicate used for preserving eggs, as a vehicle for fresco painting, and for hardening artificial stone. **2** a tube with a glass bottom enabling objects under water to be observed. **3** (usu. **water glass**) a glass for holding usu. drinking water.

water hammer *noun* a knocking noise in a water pipe when a tap is suddenly turned off.

water hazard *noun see* HAZARD 5.

water heater *noun* a device for heating (esp. domestic) water.

water hemlock *noun* a poisonous umbelliferous plant, *Cicuta maculata*, found in marshes. *Also called* COWBANE.

water·hen *noun* **1** = COOT 1. **2** = MOORHEN.

water hole *noun* a shallow depression in which water collects; a pond, a pool.

water hyacinth *noun* a tropical river weed, *Eichhornia crassipes*.

water ice *noun* **1** a confection of flavoured and frozen water and sugar etc.; a sorbet, slush, etc. **2** *Astronomy* frozen water or water vapour.

water·ing *noun* the act or an instance of supplying water or (of an animal) obtaining water.

watering can *noun* a portable container with a long spout usu. ending in a perforated sprinkler, for watering plants.

watering hole *noun* **1** a pool of water from which animals regularly drink; a water hole. **2** *slang* a bar.

watering place *noun* **1** = WATERING HOLE 1. **2** a spa or seaside resort. **3** a place where water is obtained.

water jump *noun* a place where a horse in a steeplechase etc. must jump over water.

water·leaf *noun* any of several N American woodland plants of the genus *Hydrophyllum*, with bell-shaped flowers and leaves looking as if stained with water.

water level *noun* **1 a** the surface of the water in a lake etc. **b** the height of this. **2** = WATER TABLE.

water lily *noun* any aquatic plant of the family Nymphaeaceae, with broad flat floating leaves and large solitary cup-shaped flowers.

water·line *noun* **1 a** the line along which the surface of water touches the side of a floating body; water level. **b** such a line marked on a ship for use in loading. **2** a pipe or hose used as a conduit for water.

water·logged *adjective* **1** saturated with water. **2** (of a boat etc.) hardly able to float from being saturated or filled with water. **3** (of ground) made useless by being saturated with water. [*waterlog* (v.), from WATER + LOG[1], prob. originally = 'reduce (a ship) to the condition of a log']

water·log·ging *noun* the saturating of esp. horticultural soil with water.

Wat·er·loo[1] /wɒtɜrˈluː/ a city in SW central Ontario, forming a conurbation with Kitchener, which lies immediately to the southeast; pop. (2001) 86,543. [see WATERLOO, BATTLE OF]

Wat·er·loo[2] *noun* a decisive defeat; an irrevocable end (esp. in phr. **meet one's Waterloo**). [see WATERLOO, BATTLE OF]

Waterloo, Battle of a battle fought on 18 June 1815 near the village of Waterloo (in what is now Belgium), in which Napoleon's army was defeated by the British and Prussians. Attempting to exploit a temporary separation of the British and Prussian armies, Napoleon attacked the outnumbered British force; the British (under the Duke of Wellington) were able to hold off the French until the arrival of the Prussians forced the French to retreat. Under the pressure of the allied pursuit Napoleon's army disintegrated completely, effectively ending his bid to return to power.

water lot *noun* a lot along a shoreline.

water main *noun* the main pipe in a water supply system.

water·man *noun* (*pl.* **-men**) **1** a person working on a boat or among boats. **2** an oarsman as regards skill in keeping the boat balanced.

water·mark ● *noun* a faint design made in some paper during manufacture, visible when held against the light, identifying the maker etc. ● *transitive verb* mark with this.

water meadow *noun* esp. *Brit.* a meadow periodically flooded by a stream.

water·melon *noun* a large smooth green melon, *Citrullus lanatus*, with red pulp and watery juice.

water meter *noun* a device for measuring and recording the amount of water supplied to a house etc.

water milfoil *noun see* MILFOIL 2.

water mill *noun* a mill worked by a water wheel.

water moccasin *noun see* MOCCASIN 3.

water nymph *noun* a nymph regarded as inhabiting or presiding over water.

water of crystallization *noun* water forming an essential part of the structure of some crystals.

water ouzel *noun* = DIPPER 1.

water park *noun* a public recreation area with water slides, wave pools, swimming pools, etc.

water pennywort *noun see* PENNYWORT 2.

water pepper *noun* an aquatic herb, *Polygonum hydropiper*. *Also called* SMARTWEED.

Water Pik *noun proprietary* a device for cleaning the teeth by directing a jet of water at them.

water pill *noun* a diuretic pill.

water pipe *noun* **1** a pipe for conveying water. **2** a hookah.

water pistol *noun* a toy pistol shooting a jet of water.

water plantain *noun* any plant of the genus *Alisma*, e.g. *A. triviale*, of wet places of eastern N America, with small white flowers and plantain-like leaves.

water polo *noun* a game played in a swimming pool, in which teams of seven swimmers attempt to throw an inflated ball into the other team's goal.

water power *noun* **1** mechanical force derived from the weight or motion of water. **2** a fall in the level of a river, as a source of this force.

water·proof ● *adjective* impervious to water. ● *noun* esp. *Brit.* a waterproof garment or material. ● *transitive verb* make waterproof. □ **water·proof·ness** *noun*

water rat *noun* **1** N *Amer.* = MUSKRAT. **2** *Brit.* = WATER VOLE 2.

water repellent ● *adjective* not easily penetrated by water (also, with hyphen, *attributive*: *a water-repellent fabric*). ● *noun* a coating, stain, etc. applied to a surface to make it water repellent.

water-resist·ant *adjective* (of a fabric, wristwatch, etc.) able to resist, but not entirely prevent, the penetration of water. □ **water resistance** *noun*

Wat·ers, Muddy (born McKinley Morganfield) (1915–83), US blues singer and guitarist, who became famous with his song 'Rollin' Stone' (1950) and later recorded such hits as 'Got My Mojo Working' (1957).

water·scape *noun* **1** a picturesque view or prospect including water. **2** a representation of such a view, esp. a painting.

water scorpion *noun* any aquatic bug of the family Nepidae, living submerged and breathing through a bristle-like tubular tail.

water·shed *noun* **1** a line of separation between waters flowing to different rivers, basins, or seas. **2** a turning point in affairs. **3** the area drained by a single lake or river and its tributaries; a drainage basin. [WATER + *shed* ridge of high ground (related to SHED[2]), after German *Wasserscheide*]

water·side *noun* the margin of a sea, lake, or river (also *attributive*: *a waterside theatre*).

water ski ● *noun* (*pl.* **skis**) each of a pair of long thin boards, or a single board, strapped to the feet to enable a person pulled by a motorboat to skim over the surface of the water. ● *intransitive verb* (**water-ski**) (**-skis**, **-skied**; **-skiing**) be pulled along the water's surface while on a water ski or skis. □ **water skier** *noun* **water skiing** *noun*

water·slide *noun* a usu. high or long recreational slide, down which water cascades, esp. into a swimming pool.

water snake *noun* any of various snakes that frequent fresh water, esp. harmless colubrid snakes of the genus *Nerodia*.

water softener *noun* an apparatus or substance for softening hard water.

water-soluble *adjective* soluble in water.

water sport *noun* (usu. in *pl.*) a sport practised on water, such as water skiing, windsurfing, etc.

water·spout *noun* a gyrating column of water and spray formed by a whirlwind between sea and cloud.

water starwort *noun* any plant of the genus *Callitriche*, growing in water.

water supply *noun* the provision and storage of water, or the amount of water stored, for the use of a town, house, etc.

water table *noun* a level below which the ground is saturated with water.

water taxi *noun* a small usu. motor-driven boat for hire for transporting passengers, usu. over short distances.

water·tight *adjective* **1** (of a joint, container, vessel, etc.) closely fastened or fitted or made so as to prevent the passage of water. **2** (of an argument etc.) unassailable.

Water·ton Lakes National Park a park in the southwestern corner of Alberta, on the border with Montana. It was linked with Montana's Glacier National Park in 1932 to form the first international peace park, and has since been designated a World Heritage Site. [ultimately after C. Waterton, English naturalist d.1865]

water torture *noun* a form of torture in which the victim is exposed to the incessant dripping of water on the head, or the sound of dripping.

water tower *noun* a tower with an elevated tank to give pressure for distributing water.

water vole *noun* **1** *N Amer.* a semi-aquatic vole of N America, *Microtus richardsoni*, which burrows into the banks of rivers and streams. **2** either of two larger similar Eurasian voles of the genus *Arvicola*.

water·way *noun* **1** a navigable channel. **2** a route for travel by water.

water·weed *noun* any of various aquatic plants, esp. Canadian or American waterweed, *Elodea canadensis*.

water wheel *noun* a wheel driven by water to work machinery, or to raise water.

water wings *plural noun* inflated floats fixed on the arms of a person learning to swim.

water·works *noun* **1** an establishment for managing a water supply. **2** *informal* the shedding of tears (esp. in phr. **turn on the waterworks**). **3** *informal* the urinary system.

wat·ery *adjective* **1** containing too much water. **2** too thin in consistency. **3** of, characteristic of, or of the consistency of water. **4** (of the eyes) suffused or running with water. **5** (of colour) pale. **6** (of the sun, moon, or sky) rainy-looking. □ **water·i·ness** *noun*

watery grave *noun* the bottom of the sea, a lake, etc. as a place where a person lies drowned.

Wat·son ▶ 1 James Dewey (b.1928), US biologist. Together with F. H. C. Crick he proposed a model for the structure of the DNA molecule (see CRICK), later recounting the discovery in *The Double Helix* (1968); he shared a Nobel Prize with Crick and M. H. F. Wilkins in 1962. **2 John Broad·us** (1878–1958), US psychologist, founder of the school of behaviourism. He viewed behaviour as determined by an interplay between genetic endowment and environmental influences, and held that the role of the psychologist was to discern, through observation and experimentation, which behaviour was innate and which was acquired. **3 Sheila** (1909–98), Canadian novelist and critic. Her novel *The Double Hook* (1959) is seen as marking the beginning of contemporary writing in Canada; she has also published several collections of stories, including *Five Stories* (1984).

Wat·son Lake 1 a small lake in S Yukon Territory, situated just east of the Liard River, where it crosses the border with BC. **2** a town situated 16 km to the east, on the Alaska Highway; pop. (2001) 912. □ **Wat·son Laker** *noun* [F. Watson, early settler c.1898]

Watson-Watt, Sir Rob·ert Alex·ander (1892–1973), Scottish physicist. He produced a system for locating thunderstorms by means of their radio emissions, and went on to lead a team that developed radar into a practical system for locating aircraft.

Watsu /ˈwɒtsuː/ *noun* *proprietary* a form of shiatsu massage that takes place in water. [blend of WATER + SHIATSU]

Watt, James (1736–1819), Scottish engineer. He greatly improved the efficiency of the Newcomen steam engine by condensing the spent steam in a separate chamber, allowing the cylinder to remain hot.

watt *noun* the SI unit of power, equivalent to one joule per second, corresponding to the rate of energy in an electric circuit where the potential difference is one volt and the current one ampere. Symbol: **W**. [WATT]

watt·age *noun* an amount of electrical power expressed in watts, esp. the operating power of an appliance etc.

Wat·teau /wɒˈtoː/ **(Jean) An·toine** (1684–1721), French painter. An initiator of the rococo style in painting, he is also known for his invention of the pastoral genre known as the *fête galante*, an imaginary and rather theatrical world; his best-known painting is *L'Embarquement pour l'île de Cythère* (1717).

watt-hour *noun* the energy used when one watt is applied for one hour.

wat·tle[1] /ˈwɒtəl/ ● *noun* **1 a** interlaced rods and split rods as a material for making fences, walls, etc. **b** (in *sing.* or *pl.*) rods and twigs for this use. **2** an Australian acacia with long pliant branches, with bark used in tanning and golden flowers used as the national emblem. ● *transitive verb* **1** make of wattle. **2** enclose or fill up with wattles. [Old English *watul*, of unknown origin]

wat·tle[2] *noun* a loose fleshy appendage on the head or throat of a turkey or other birds. □ **wat·tled** *adjective* [16th c.: origin unknown]

wattle and daub *noun* (also, with hyphens, *attributive*) a network of rods and twigs plastered with mud or clay as a building material.

Watts /wɒts/ **Isaac** (1674–1748), English hymn writer and poet, who is remembered for hymns such as 'O God, Our Help in Ages Past' (1719).

Waugh /wɔː/ **Eve·lyn (Ar·thur St. John)** (1903–66), English novelist. His early novels were social satires, while *Brideshead Revisited* (1945), a complex story of an old Roman Catholic family, was more sombre and serious in tone; later works include his trilogy (based on his wartime experiences) *Men at Arms* (1952).

wave ● *verb* **1 a** *intransitive* (often foll. by *to*) move a hand etc. to and fro in greeting or as a signal (*waved to me across the street*). **b** *transitive* move (a hand etc.) in this way. **2 a** *intransitive* show a sinuous or sweeping motion as of a flag, tree, or a field of wheat etc., in the wind; flutter, undulate. **b** *transitive* impart a waving motion to. **3** *transitive* brandish (a sword etc.) as an encouragement to followers etc. **4** *transitive* tell or direct (a person) by waving (*waved them away*; *waved them to follow*). **5** *transitive* express (a greeting etc.) by waving (*waved goodbye to them*). **6** *transitive* give an undulating form to (hair, drawn lines, etc.); make wavy. **7** *intransitive* (of hair etc.) have such a form; be wavy. ● *noun* **1** a moving ridge or swell of water between two depressions; any of a succession of undulations which travel over the surface of a body of water. **2** a long body of water curling into an arched form and breaking on the shore. **3 a** a thing compared to this, e.g. a body of persons in one of successive advancing groups. **b** (usu. prec. by *the*) a wavelike effect produced by a crowd at a sporting event etc., whereby adjoining sections successively stand or raise hands momentarily. **4** a gesture of waving. **5 a** the process of waving the hair. **b** an undulating form produced in the hair by waving. **6 a** a temporary occurrence or increase of a condition, emotion, or influence (*a wave of enthusiasm*). **b** a specified period of widespread weather (*heat wave*). **7** *Physics* **a** a periodic disturbance of the particles of a substance which may be propagated without net movement of the particles, as in the passage of undulating motion, heat, sound, etc. (see also STANDING WAVE, TRAVELLING WAVE). **b** a single curve in the course of this motion. **8** *Electricity* a similar variation of an electromagnetic field in the propagation of light or other radiation through a medium or vacuum. **9** (in *pl.*; prec. by *the*) *literary* the sea; water. □ **make waves** *informal* **1** cause trouble. **2** create a significant impression. **wave aside** dismiss as intrusive or irrelevant. **wave down** wave to (a vehicle or its driver) as a signal to stop. **wave off 1** signal an approaching person or thing to stop approaching. **2** (in hockey etc.) disallow (a goal). □ **wave·less** *adjective* **wave·like** *adjective & adverb* [Old English *wafian* (v.) from Germanic: (n.) also alteration of Middle English *wawe*, *wage*]

wave·band *noun* a range of (esp. radio) wavelengths between certain limits.

wave equation *noun* a differential equation expressing the properties of motion in waves.

wave·form *noun* *Physics* a curve showing the shape of a wave at a given time.

wave·front *noun* *Physics* a surface containing points affected in the same way by a wave at a given time.

wave function *noun* a function satisfying a wave equation and describing the properties of a wave.

wave·guide *noun* *Electricity* a metal tube etc. confining and conveying microwaves.

wave·length *noun* **1** the distance between successive crests of a wave, esp. points in a sound wave or electromagnetic wave. Symbol: λ. **2** this as a distinctive feature of radio waves from a transmitter. **3** *informal* a particular mode or range of thinking and communicating (*we don't seem to be on the same wavelength*).

wave·let *noun* a small wave on water.

wave mechanics *noun* a method of analysis of the behaviour esp. of atomic phenomena with particles represented by wave equations (see QUANTUM MECHANICS).

wave·num·ber *noun* *Physics* the number of waves in a unit distance.

Consonants: b *but* d *dog* f *few* g *get* h *her* j *yes* k *cat* l *leg* m *man* n *no* p *pen* r *red* s *sit*

wave-particle *adjective* designating the twofold description of matter and energy in terms of two seemingly incompatible concepts: waves and particles.

wave pool *noun* a large swimming pool with an apparatus for producing waves for recreation.

wav·er *intransitive verb* **1** be or become unsteady; falter; begin to give way. **2** be irresolute or undecided between different courses or opinions; be shaken in resolution or belief. **3** (of a light) flicker. □ **waver·er** *noun* **waver·ing·ly** *adverb* **wav·ery** *adjective* [Old Norse *vafra* flicker, from Germanic, related to WAVE]

wave theory *noun hist.* the theory that light is propagated through the ether by a wave motion imparted to the ether by the molecular vibrations of the radiant body.

wave train *noun* a group of waves of equal or similar wavelengths travelling in the same direction.

wavy *adjective* (**wav·i·er**, **wav·i·est**) (of a line or surface) having waves or alternate contrary curves (*wavy hair*). □ **wav·i·ly** *adverb* **wav·i·ness** *noun*

Wawa /ˈwɒˌwɒ/ part of the township of Michipicoten in north central Ontario, situated about 200 km north of Sault Ste. Marie. [Ojibwa, = wild goose, with reference to Wawa Lake, a site where the geese flock during the spring and fall]

wa-wa *var. of* WAH-WAH.

wax¹ ● *noun* **1** a sticky mouldable yellowish substance secreted by bees as the material of honeycomb cells; beeswax. **2** a white translucent material obtained from this by bleaching and purifying and used for candles, as a basis of polishes, and for other purposes. **3** any similar substance, typically a lipid or hydrocarbon (*earwax, paraffin wax*). **4** a session of waxing (in sense 2 of *verb*). **5** *informal* **a** a phonograph record. **b** material for the manufacture of this. **6** (*attributive*) made of wax. ● *transitive verb* **1** cover, polish, or treat with wax. **2** remove unwanted hair from (the legs etc.) by applying wax and peeling off the wax and hairs together. **3** *informal* defeat resoundingly. **4** *informal* record for the phonograph. □ **the whole ball of wax** the full complement of related or necessary things. □ **wax·er** *noun* **wax·ing** *noun* (esp. in sense 2 of *verb*) **wax·like** *adjective* [Old English *wæx, weax*]

wax² *intransitive verb* **1** (of the moon between new and full) have a progressively larger part of its visible surface illuminated, increasing in apparent size. **2** become larger or stronger. **3** pass into a specified state or mood (*wax lyrical*). □ **wax and wane** undergo alternate increases and decreases. [Old English *weaxan*]

wax³ *noun Brit. slang* a fit of anger. [19th c.: origin uncertain: perhaps from WAX² *wroth* etc.]

wax bean *noun* a yellow-podded bean.

wax·berry *noun* (*pl.* -berries) **1** any of various plants with berries with a waxy coating, esp. a wax myrtle. **2** the fruit of this.

wax·bill *noun* any of various birds esp. of the family Estrildidae, with usu. red bills resembling the colour of sealing wax.

waxed paper *noun* (also **wax paper**) paper impregnated with wax to make it waterproof or greaseproof.

waxen *adjective* **1** having a smooth pale translucent surface as of wax. **2** able to receive impressions like wax. **3** *archaic* made of wax.

Wax·man, Al·bert Sam·uel ('Al') (1935–2001), Canadian actor and director. The star of CBC TV's 'King of Kensington' (1975–80), for which he earned an ACTRA award in 1976, he also appeared in and directed many movies.

wax museum *noun* esp. *N Amer.* a gallery etc. exhibiting wax figures of esp. famous people.

wax myrtle *noun* the bayberry, *Myrica cerifera*.

wax palm *noun* **1** a S American palm, *Ceroxylon alpinum*, with its stem coated in a mixture of resin and wax. **2** a carnauba.

wax paper *var. of* WAXED PAPER.

wax tree *noun* an Asian tree, *Rhus succedanea*, having white berries which yield wax.

wax·wing *noun* any bird of the genus *Bombycilla*, with a crest and often with small tips like red sealing wax to some wing feathers.

wax·work *noun* **1 a** an object, esp. a lifelike dummy, modelled in wax. **b** the making of waxworks. **2** (in *pl.*) an exhibition of wax dummies.

waxy *adjective* (**wax·i·er**, **wax·i·est**) resembling wax in consistency or in its surface. □ **wax·i·ly** *adverb* **wax·i·ness** *noun*

way ● *noun* **1** a road, track, path, etc., for passing along. **2** a course or route for reaching a place, esp. the best one (*asked the way to Sherbrooke*). **3** a place of passage into a building, through a door, etc. (*could not find the way out*). **4 a** a method or plan for attaining an object (*that is not the way to do it*). **b** the ability to obtain one's object (*has a way with him*). **5 a** a person's desired or chosen course of action. **b** a custom or manner of behaving; a personal peculiarity (*has a way of forgetting things; that's just her way; things had a way of going badly*). **6** a specific manner of life or procedure (*soon got into the way of it*). **7** the normal course of events (*that is always the way*). **8** (also *N Amer. informal* **ways**) a travelling distance; a length traversed or to be traversed (*is a long way away; a good ways down the road*). **9 a** an unimpeded opportunity of advance. **b** a space free of obstacles. **10** a region or ground over which advance is desired or natural. **11** advance in some direction; impetus, progress (*pushed my way through*). **12** movement of a ship etc. (*gather way; lose way*). **13** the state of being engaged in movement from place to place; time spent in this (*met them on the way home; with songs to cheer the way*). **14** a specified direction (*step this way; which way are you going?; one-way traffic*). **15** (in *pl.*) parts into which a thing is divided (*split it three ways*). **16** *informal* the scope or range of something (*want a few things in the stationery way*). **17** a person's line of occupation or business. **18** a specified condition or state (*things are in a bad way*). **19** a respect (*is useful in some ways*). **20 a** (in *pl.*) a structure of timber etc. down which a new ship is launched. **b** parallel rails etc. as a track for the movement of a machine. ● *adverb informal* **1** at or to a considerable distance or extent (*you're way off the mark; my daughter is way ahead of others her age in reading*). **2** much (*I was cycling way too fast*). **3** extremely; really (*the guys behind the bar were way cool*). □ **across the way** (in a street etc.) facing or opposite. **be on one's way 1** set off; depart. **2** be in the course of a journey etc. **by the way 1** incidentally; as a more or less irrelevant comment. **2** during a journey. **by way of 1** through; by means of. **2** as a substitute for or as a form of (*did it by way of apology*). **3** with the intention of (*asked by way of discovering the truth*). **come one's way** become available to one; become one's lot. **find a way** discover a means of obtaining one's object. **get** (or **have**) **one's way** (or **have it one's own way** etc.) get what one wants; ensure one's wishes are met. **give way 1 a** make concessions; yield. **b** fail to resist; yield. **2** (often foll. by *to*) concede precedence (to). **3** (of a structure etc.) be dislodged or broken under a load; collapse. **4** (foll. by *to*) be superseded by. **5** (foll. by *to*) be overcome by (an emotion etc.). **6** (of rowers) row hard. **go all the way 1** go the whole distance. **2** do something wholeheartedly or completely. **3** *informal* engage in sexual intercourse. **go out of one's way** (often foll. by *to* + infin.) make a special effort (*went out of their way to help*). **go one's own way** act independently, esp. against contrary advice. **go one's way 1** leave, depart. **2** (of events, circumstances, etc.) be favourable to one. **go a person's way** accompany a person (*are you going my way?*). **go way back** = GO BACK 2b (see GO¹). **have it both ways** see BOTH. **in the family way** see FAMILY. **in its way** if regarded from a particular standpoint appropriate to it. **in no way** not at all; by no means. **in a way** in a certain respect but not altogether or completely. **in the** (or **one's**) **way** forming an obstacle or hindrance. **lead the way 1** act as guide or leader. **2** show how to do something. **look the other way 1** ignore what one should notice. **2** disregard an acquaintance etc. whom one sees. **make way 1** (often foll. by *for*) allow room for others to proceed. **2** achieve progress. **make one's way** proceed. **my way or the highway** *N Amer. informal* said to assert the view that there is no alternative (apart from leaving) to accept the speaker's opinions or policies. **one way or another** by some means. **on the** (or **one's**) **way 1** in the course of a journey etc. **2** having progressed (*is well on the way to completion*). **3** *informal* (of a child) conceived but not yet born. **on the way out** *informal* going down in status, estimation, or favour; going out of fashion. **the other way around** (or **about**) in an inverted or reversed position or direction. **out of the way 1** no longer an obstacle or hindrance. **2** disposed of; settled. **3** (of a person) imprisoned or killed. **4** (with *neg.*) common or unremarkable (*nothing out of the way*). **5** (of a place) remote, inaccessible. **out of one's way** not on one's intended route. **put a person in the way of** give a person the opportunity of. **way back** *informal* long ago. [Old English *weg* from Germanic: (adv.) from AWAY]

-way *suffix* = -WAYS.

way·bill *noun* **1** a document on which a shipper, courier, etc. records details of the sender, recipient, weight, etc. of an item to be transported. **2** a list of passengers or parcels on a vehicle.

way·farer *noun* a traveller, esp. on foot. □ **way·far·ing** *noun*

wayfaring tree *noun* a white-flowered European and Asian shrub, *Viburnum lantana*, common along roadsides, with berries turning from green through red to black.

way·lay *transitive verb* (*past* and *past participle* **way·laid**) **1** lie in wait for. **2** stop to rob or interview. □ **way·lay·er** *noun*

---

way·mark *noun* a natural or artificial object as a guide to travellers, esp. walkers.

Wayne ▶ **1 John** (born Marion Michael Morrison; known as 'the Duke') (1907–79), US actor. Remembered as the archetypal cowboy hero, he appeared in many classic westerns, notably *Stagecoach* (1939), *Red River* (1948) and *True Grit* (1969), for which he won an Oscar. **2 John Louis** 'Johnny' *see* WAYNE AND SHUSTER.

Wayne and Shuster Canadian comedy duo comprising Johnny Wayne (1918–90) and Frank Shuster (1916–2002). In a career spanning four decades from the 40s to the 80s, on both radio and television, they became immensely popular for their comedy skits combining slapstick, visual humour, and puns.

way of life *noun* the principles or habits governing all one's actions etc.

way of the Cross *noun* a series of images representing the stations of the cross, esp. in a church or on the road to a shrine.

way of the world *noun* the customary manner of proceeding, behaving, etc.

way of thinking *noun* one's customary opinion of matters.

way-out *adjective informal* **1** unusual, eccentric. **2** avant-garde, progressive. **3** excellent, exciting.

way·point *noun* **1** a stopping place, esp. on a journey. **2** the computer-checked coordinates of each stage of a flight, sea journey, etc. (also *attributive: waypoint identification*).

-ways *suffix* forming adjectives and adverbs of direction or manner (*sideways*) (*compare* -WISE[1]).

ways and means *plural noun* **1** methods of achieving something. **2** methods of raising government revenue.

way·side *noun* **1** the side or margin of a road. **2** the land at the side of a road. □ **fall by the wayside 1** fail to continue in an endeavour or undertaking (after Luke 8:5). **2** be discarded.

wayside cross *noun* a cross or crucifix erected by the side of a road or at an intersection.

way station *noun N Amer.* **1** a minor station on a railway. **2** a point marking progress in a certain course of action etc.

way·ward *adjective* **1** childishly self-willed or perverse; capricious. **2** erratic; unaccountable or freakish. □ **way·ward·ly** *adverb*

way·ward·ness *noun* [obsolete *awayward* turned away, from AWAY + -WARD: compare FROWARD]

wazoo /wəˈzuː/ *noun N Amer. informal* a person's buttocks or anus. □ **up** (or **out**) **the wazoo** in great quantities. [20th c.: origin unknown]

Wb *abbreviation* weber(s).

WC *abbreviation* water closet.

WCC *abbreviation* WORLD COUNCIL OF CHURCHES.

W/Cdr. *abbreviation* Wing Commander.

WCTU *abbreviation* Woman's Christian Temperance Union.

we *pronoun* (*obj.* **us**; *poss.* **our**, **ours**) **1** (*pl. of* I[2]) used by and with reference to more than one person speaking or writing, or one such person and one or more associated persons. **2** used for or by a royal person in a proclamation etc. and by a writer or editor in a formal context. **3** people in general (*compare* ONE *pronoun* 2). **4** *informal* = I[2]. **5** *informal* (often implying condescension) you (*how are we feeling today?*). [Old English from Germanic]

weak *adjective* **1** deficient in strength, power, or number; fragile; easily broken or bent or defeated. **2** deficient in vigour; sickly, feeble (*weak health; a weak imagination*). **3 a** deficient in resolution; easily led (*a weak character*). **b** (of an action or features) indicating a lack of resolution (*a weak surrender; a weak chin*). **4** unconvincing or logically deficient (*weak evidence; a weak argument*). **5** (of a mixed liquid or solution) watery, thin, dilute (*weak tea*). **6** of a low standard, slipshod. **7** (of a syllable etc.) unstressed. **8** (of prices or a market) having a downward tendency. **9** *Grammar* in Germanic languages: **a** (of a verb) forming inflections by the addition of a suffix to the stem. **b** (of a noun or adjective) belonging to a declension in which the stem originally ended in -*n* (*opp.* STRONG *adjective* 22b). □ **weak·ish** *adjective* [Old Norse *veikr* from Germanic]

weak·en *transitive & intransitive verb* make or become weak or weaker.

weaker sex *noun offensive* women collectively.

weak·fish *noun* (*pl.* same or **-fishes**) *N Amer.* a marine fish of the genus *Cynoscion*, used as food. [obsolete Dutch *weekvisch* from *week* soft (formed as WEAK) + *visch* FISH[1]]

weak grade *noun Grammar* an unstressed ablaut form.

weak interaction *noun Physics* the weakest form of interaction between elementary particles.

weak-kneed *noun informal* lacking resolution.

weak·ling *noun* a feeble person or animal.

weak link *noun* a weak or defective element which renders the whole vulnerable.

weak·ly ● *adverb* in a weak manner. ● *adjective* (**weak·li·er**, **weak·li·est**) sickly, not robust.

weakly interacting massive particle *noun see* WIMP.

weak-minded *adjective* **1** mentally deficient. **2** lacking in resolution.

weak moment *noun* a time when one is unusually compliant or temptable.

weak·ness *noun* **1** the state or condition of being weak. **2** a weak point; a defect. **3** the inability to resist a particular temptation. **4** (foll. by *for*) a self-indulgent liking (*have a weakness for chocolate*).

weak·side *noun Football* the side of an offensive line with the fewer number of players (also *attributive: weakside linebacker*).

weak sister *noun esp. N Amer.* a weak, ineffectual, or unreliable member of a group.

weak spot *noun* (or **weak point**) **1** a place where defences are assailable. **2** a flaw in an argument or character or in resistance to temptation.

weal[1] /wiːl/ *noun* = WELT 1. [var. of WALE, influenced by obsolete *wheal* suppurate]

weal[2] *noun literary* welfare, prosperity; good fortune. [Old English *wela* from West Germanic (as WELL[1])]

Weald /wiːld/ *noun* (also **weald**) (prec. by *the*) *Brit.* a formerly wooded district including parts of Kent, Surrey, and East Sussex. [Old English, = *wald* WOLD]

Weald·en /ˈwiːldən/ *Brit.* ● *adjective* **1** of the Weald. **2** resembling the Weald geologically. ● *noun* a series of Lower Cretaceous freshwater deposits above Jurassic strata and below chalk, best exemplified in the Weald.

wealth *noun* **1** riches; abundant possessions. **2** the state of being rich. **3** (foll. by *of*) an abundance or profusion (*a wealth of new material*). **4** *archaic* welfare or prosperity. [Middle English *welthe*, from WELL[1] or WEAL[2] + -TH[2], after *health*]

wealth tax *noun* a tax on personal capital.

wealthy *adjective* (**wealth·i·er**, **wealth·i·est**) having an abundance esp. of money. □ **wealth·i·ly** *adverb*

wean *transitive verb* **1** accustom (an infant or other young mammal) to food other than (esp. its mother's) milk. **2** (often foll. by *from, away from, off*) disengage (from a habit etc.) esp. gradually. **3** (foll. by *on*; esp. in *passive*) nourish with or expose to from an early age (*was weaned on talk shows and sitcoms*). [Old English *wenian* accustom, from Germanic: compare WONT]

wean·er *noun* a young animal recently weaned.

wean·ling *noun* a newly-weaned animal etc.

weapon *noun* **1** a thing designed or used or usable for inflicting bodily harm, e.g. a gun or knife. **2** a means employed for trying to gain an advantage (*irony is a double-edged weapon; new weapons against disease*). □ **weap·oned** *adjective* (also in *combination*). **weapon·less** *adjective* [Old English *wæp(e)n*]

weapon·ize *verb* **1** *transitive* adapt for use as a weapon. **2** *intransitive* establish a nuclear arsenal in a form capable of being immediately used. **3** *transitive* install weapons in.

weapon of mass destruction *noun* a nuclear, biological, or chemical weapon able to cause widespread devastation and loss of life.

weap·on·ry *noun* weapons collectively.

weapons-grade *adjective* designating fissile material of a suitable quality for making nuclear weapons.

wear[1] ● *verb* (*past* **wore**; *past participle* **worn**) **1** *transitive* have on one's person as clothing or an ornament etc. (*is wearing shorts; wears earrings*). **2** *transitive* be dressed habitually in (*wears green*). **3** *transitive* exhibit or present (a facial expression or appearance) (*wore a frown; the day wore a different aspect*). **4** (often foll. by *away, down*) **a** *transitive* injure the surface of, or partly obliterate or alter, by rubbing, stress, or use. **b** *intransitive* undergo such injury or change. **5** *transitive & intransitive* (foll. by *off, away*) rub or be rubbed off. **6** *transitive* **a** make (a hole etc.) by constant rubbing or dripping etc. **b** make (a path etc.) by repeated travel along the same route. **7** *transitive & intransitive* (often foll. by *out*) exhaust, tire or be tired. **8** *transitive* (foll. by *down*) overcome by persistence. **9** *intransitive* **a** remain for a specified time in working order or a presentable state; last long. **b** (foll. by *well, badly, etc.*) endure continued use or life. **10 a** *intransitive* (of time) pass, esp. tediously. **b** *transitive* (usu. foll. by *on*) pass (time) gradually away. **11** *transitive Brit. informal* (usu. with *neg.*)

Vowels: a *cat* ɑ *arm* e *bed* ɜr *her* ɜː *deux* ə *ago* ɪ *sit* i *cosy* iː *feed* ɒ *hot* ɔ *pore* ɔː *no* ʌ *run* ʊ *put*

tolerate, accept (*they won't wear that excuse*). ● *noun* **1** the act of wearing or the state of being worn (*suitable for informal wear*). **2** things worn; clothing suitable for a specified purpose or part of the body (esp. in *combination*: *sportswear*; *footwear*). **3** (also **wear and tear**) damage sustained from continuous use. **4** the capacity for resisting wear and tear (*still a great deal of wear left in it*). □ **in wear** being regularly worn. **wear one's heart on one's sleeve** *see* HEART. **wear off** lose effectiveness or intensity. **wear out 1** use or be used until no longer usable. **2** tire or be tired out. **wear thin 1** (of patience, excuses, etc.) begin to fail. **2** tax one's patience or interest. **wear the pants** (or **trousers**) be the dominant partner in a marriage or relationship. **wear** (or **wear one's years**) **well** *informal* remain young-looking. □ **wear·able** *adjective & noun* **wear·abil·ity** *noun* **wear·er** *noun* [Old English *werian* from Germanic]

wear² *verb* (*past* and *past participle* **wore**) **1** *transitive* bring (a ship) about by turning its head away from the wind. **2** *intransitive* (of a ship) come about in this way (compare TACK¹ *verb* 4a). [17th c.: origin unknown]

wear·ing *adjective* **1** tiring; stressful; frustrating. **2** tedious. □ **wear·ing·ly** *adverb*

weari·some /ˈwɪːrɪsəm/ *adjective* tedious; tiring by monotony or length. □ **weari·some·ly** *adverb* **weari·some·ness** *noun*

weary ● *adjective* (**weari·er**, **weari·est**) **1** unequal to or disinclined for further exertion or endurance; tired. **2** (foll. by *of*) no longer interested in or enthusiastic about. **3** tiring or tedious. ● *transitive & intransitive verb* (**-ies**, **-ied**) make or grow weary. □ **weari·ly** *adverb* **weari·ness** *noun* **weary·ing·ly** *adverb* [Old English *wērig*, *wærig* from West Germanic]

wea·sel ● *noun* **1** any of various small carnivorous mammals of the family Mustelidae, with a slender body, including ermines, minks, and ferrets, and noted for their ferocity, esp. the long-tailed weasel of N America, *Mustela frenata*, having a brown and yellow coat, or the least weasel of N America and Eurasia, *M. nivalis*, with a very short tail and brown and white coat. **2** *informal* a deceitful, sneaky, or treacherous person. ● *verb* (**wea·seled**, **wea·sel·ing**; also esp. *Brit.* **wea·selled**, **wea·sel·ling**) **1** *intransitive* esp. *N Amer.* equivocate or quibble. **2** *intransitive* (foll. by *out*) default on an obligation. □ **weasel one's way into** obtain by cunning, sneakiness, etc. (*weaseled his way into their affection*). □ **weasel·ly** *adjective* [Old English *wesle*, *wesule* from West Germanic]

weasel word *noun* (usu. in *pl.*) a word that is intentionally ambiguous or misleading, esp. as part of a statement that deliberately avoids commitment.

weath·er ● *noun* **1** the state of the atmosphere at a place and time as regards temperature, cloudiness, dryness, sunshine, wind, and precipitation etc. **2** a news report concerning the weather (*listened to the weather*). **3** bad weather; destructive rain, frost, wind, etc. (*had not been expecting weather*). **4** (*attributive*) *Naut.* windward (*on the weather side*). ● *verb* **1** *transitive* expose to or affect by atmospheric changes, esp. deliberately to dry, season, etc. (*weathered timber*). **2** *transitive* (usu. in *passive*) discolour or partly disintegrate (rock or stones) by exposure to air. **b** *intransitive* be discoloured or worn in this way. **3** *transitive* make (boards or tiles) overlap downwards to keep out rain etc. **4** *transitive* **a** come safely through (a storm). **b** survive (a difficult period etc.). **5** *transitive* (of a ship or its crew) get to the windward of (a cape etc.). □ **keep a** (or **one's**) **weather eye on** (or **open**) be watchful. **make heavy weather of** *informal* exaggerate the difficulty or burden presented by (a problem, course of action, etc.). **under the weather** *informal* **1** slightly unwell. **2** in low spirits. **weathered in** unable to depart, proceed, etc. because of bad weather. [Old English *weder*]

weather-beaten *adjective* worn, damaged, or discoloured by exposure to wind, rain, etc.

weather·board ● *noun* **1** = CLAPBOARD. **2** a sloping board attached to the bottom of an outside door to keep out the rain etc. ● *transitive verb* fit or supply with weatherboards. □ **weather·board·ing** *noun* (in sense 1 of *noun*).

weather·cock *noun* **1** a weather vane in the form of a rooster. **2** an inconstant, changeable, or trendy person.

weather forecast *noun* an analysis of the state of the weather with an assessment of likely developments over a certain time. □ **weather forecaster** *noun* **weather forecasting** *noun*

weather glass *noun* dated a barometer.

weath·er·ing *noun* **1** the action of the weather on materials etc. exposed to it. **2** exposure to adverse weather conditions (*see* WEATHER *verb* 1).

weather·ize *transitive verb* *N Amer.* make (a building) impervious to the weather by insulation, double glazing, etc. □ **weather·iz·a·tion** *noun*

weath·er·ly *adjective* *Naut.* **1** (of a ship) making little leeway. **2** capable of keeping close to the wind.

weather·man *noun* (*pl.* **-men**) **1** a man who broadcasts a weather forecast. **2** a meteorologist.

weather map *noun* a diagram showing the future or current state of the weather over a large area.

weather·proof ● *adjective* resistant to the effects of bad weather, esp. rain. ● *transitive verb* make weatherproof. □ **weather·proofed** *adjective* **weather·proof·ing** *noun*

weather side *noun* the side from which the wind is blowing (*opp.* LEE SIDE; *see* LEE 2).

weather station *noun* an observation post for recording meteorological data.

weather·strip ● *noun* a piece of material used to make a door or window proof against rain or wind. ● *transitive verb* (**-stripped**, **-strip·ping**) apply a weatherstrip to. □ **weather·strip·ping** *noun*

weather·tight *adjective* (of a dwelling) sealed against rain, wind, etc.

weather vane *noun* a revolving pointer mounted on a spire or other high place to show the direction of the wind.

weather-worn *adjective* weather-beaten; damaged by storms etc.

weave¹ ● *verb* (*past* **wove**; *past participle* **woven** or **wove**) **1** *transitive* **a** form (fabric) by interlacing long threads in two directions. **b** form (thread) into fabric in this way. **2** *intransitive* **a** make fabric in this way. **b** work at a loom. **3** *transitive* make (a basket or wreath etc.) by interlacing rods or flowers etc. **4** *transitive* **a** contrive, devise, or construct (a poem, spell, narrative, etc.), esp. skilfully. **b** intermingle or blend in closely as if by weaving; work up (separate elements) into an intricate and connected whole. ● *noun* a style of weaving. [Old English *wefan*]

weave² *intransitive verb* (*past* **weaved** or **wove**; *past participle* **weaved** or **woven**) move repeatedly from side to side; take an intricate course to avoid obstructions. [prob. from Middle English *weve*, var. of *waive* from Old Norse *veifa* WAVE]

weav·er *noun* **1** a person whose occupation is weaving. **2** (in full **weaver bird**) any tropical bird of the family Ploceidae, building elaborately woven nests.

weav·ing *noun* **1** the action of creating woven materials. **2** something woven, esp. a decorative hanging.

web ● *noun* **1** a network of fine threads constructed by a spider to catch its prey, from fluid secreted from its spinnerets. **2 a** a complete network or connected series (*a web of social problems*). **b** (also **Web**; usu. prec. by *the*) = WORLD WIDE WEB. **c** a snare or trap (*a web of deceit*). **3 a** a membrane between the toes of a swimming animal or bird. **b** the vane of a bird's feather. **4 a** a woven fabric. **b** an amount woven in one piece. **5 a** a large roll of paper used in a continuous printing process. **b** an endless wire mesh on rollers, on which this is made. **6** a thin flat part connecting thicker or more solid parts in machinery etc. ● *verb* (**webbed**, **web·bing**) **1** *transitive* weave a web on. **2** *intransitive* weave a web. □ **webby** *adjective* [Old English *web*, *webb*]

Webb, (Mar·tha) Bea·trice (née **Pot·ter**) (1858–1943) and her husband, **Sid·ney (James), Baron Pass·field** (1859–1947), English socialists, economists, and historians. Prominent members of the Fabian Society, they helped to establish the London School of Economics (1895), and together wrote several important books on socio-political theory and history.

webbed *adjective* **1 a** (of a bird's foot etc.) having the digits connected by a membrane or fold of skin. **b** (of fingers or toes) united by a fold of skin. **2** covered with or as if with a web.

web·bing *noun* a web or woven fabric, esp. strong narrow closely-woven fabric used for supporting upholstery, for belts, etc.

web browser *noun* a program used to locate and access hypertext documents on the Internet.

web·cam *noun* a video camera connected to a computer connected to the Internet, so that its images can be seen by Internet users.

web·cast *noun* a live video broadcast of an event transmitted over the Internet. □ **web·cast·ing** *noun*

web-enabled *adjective* designating or relating to hardware, software, or electronic data adapted for use on the Internet, or the users or producers of such technologies (*a web-enabled television*; *each of these three companies is web-enabled*).

Weber /ˈveɪbər/ **1 Carl Maria (Frie·drich Ernst) von** (1786–1826), German composer. He is regarded as the founder of the German romantic school of opera, and his works include *Der Freischütz* (1817–

21), *Euryanthe* (1822–3), and *Oberon* (1826). **2 Ernst Hein·rich** (1795–1878), German physiologist and anatomist, who is noted for his studies of sensory response. **3 Max** (1864–1920), German economist and sociologist. He was one of the founders of modern sociology, and in his celebrated book *The Protestant Ethic and the Spirit of Capitalism* (1904), he argued that there was a direct relationship between the Protestant work ethic and the rise of Western capitalism; other works include *Economy and Society* (1922). **4 Wil·helm Eduard** (1804–91), German physicist. He proposed a unified system for electrical units, determined the ratio between the units of electrostatic and electromagnetic charge, and devised a law of electrical force (later replaced by Maxwell's field theory). □ **Weber·ian** /veiˈbɪrɪən/ *adjective*

weber /ˈveibɜr/ *noun* the SI unit of magnetic flux, causing the electromotive force of one volt in a circuit of one turn when generated or removed in one second. ¶ Abbr.: **Wb**. [W. E. WEBER]

Web·ern /ˈveibɜrn/ **Anton (Frie·drich Ernst) von** (1883–1945), Austrian composer. A leading exponent of serialism, his music is marked by its brevity.

web-footed *adjective* having the toes connected by webs.

web·log *noun* a frequently updated website typically run by one person and consisting of interesting excerpts and personal observations, usu. with hyperlinks to other sites; an online journal or diary. □ **web·log·ger** *noun*

web·master *noun* a person who designs and develops websites.

web offset *noun* offset printing on a web of paper.

web page *noun* a hypertext document that is accessible via the World Wide Web.

web ring *noun* a number of websites with related content, offering links to one another in such a way that a person may view each of them in turn rather than repeatedly going back to a single referring site.

web server *noun* **1** a program providing access to World Wide Web documents, which accepts requests from web browsers, and delivers the required hypertext documents. **2** the computer or computer system on which such a program runs, and on which the documents are stored.

web·site *noun* **1** a hypertext document or a set of linked documents, usually associated with a particular person, organization, or topic, that is held on a computer system and can be accessed via the World Wide Web. **2** the computer system that holds such a hypertext document or documents.

Web·ster ▸ 1 Dan·iel (1782–1852), US politician, who was a noted orator, and served as a senator (1827–41; 1845–50) and as secretary of state (1841–3; 1850–52). **2 John** (*c.*1580–*c.*1625), English dramatist. He wrote several plays in collaboration with other dramatists but his reputation rests on two revenge tragedies, *The White Devil* (1612) and *The Duchess of Malfi* (1623). **3 Noah** (1758–1843), US lexicographer and philologist. His *American Dictionary of the English Language* (1828) in two volumes was the first dictionary to give comprehensive coverage of American usage.

web·work *noun* a web-like mesh or system of links; a network.

web·worm *noun N Amer.* a gregarious caterpillar spinning a large web in which to sleep or to feed on enclosed foliage.

Wed. *abbreviation* Wednesday.

wed *verb* (**wed·ding**; *past* and *past participle* **wed·ded** or **wed**) **1** usu. *formal* or *literary* **a** *transitive & intransitive* marry. **b** *transitive* join in marriage. **2** *transitive* unite (*wed efficiency to economy*). [Old English *weddian* to pledge]

we'd *contraction* **1** we had. **2** we should; we would.

wed·ded *adjective* **1** of or in marriage (*wedded bliss*). **2** (foll. by *to*) obstinately attached or devoted (*to a pursuit etc.*).

Wed·dell Sea /ˈwedəl/ an arm of the Atlantic Ocean, off the coast of Antarctica. [J. *Weddell*, British explorer d.1834]

wed·ding *noun* **1** a marriage ceremony (considered by itself or with the associated celebrations). **2** an act or instance of uniting or joining.

wedding band *noun* = WEDDING RING.

wedding cake *noun* a cake served at a wedding reception, esp. a multi-tiered fruitcake with white icing.

wedding day *noun* the day or anniversary of a wedding.

wedding dress *noun* a dress designed to be worn by a bride at a wedding, esp. a long white one, often with a train.

wedding march *noun* a march played at the entrance of the bride or the exit of the couple at a wedding.

wedding night *noun* the night after a wedding (esp. with reference to its consummation).

wedding party *noun* **1** the principal figures at a wedding, including the bride, groom, maid or matron of honour, best man, and often including bridesmaids, groomsmen, a flower girl, ring bearer, etc. **2** *Brit.* the whole group of people gathered for a wedding.

wedding ring *noun* (also **wedding band**) a ring that is given during a wedding ceremony and worn afterwards to show that the person wearing it is married.

wedge¹ ● *noun* **1** a piece of wood or metal etc. tapering to a sharp edge, that is driven between two objects or parts of an object to secure or separate them. **2** anything resembling or acting as a wedge (*a wedge of cheese*; *troops formed a wedge*; *drove an emotional wedge between them*). **3** a golf club with a wedge-shaped head. **4 a** a women's shoe with a solid wedge-shaped sole which is higher at the heel and lower toward the front of the foot. **b** such a sole. ● *verb* **1** *transitive* tighten, secure, or fasten by means of a wedge (*wedged the door open*). **2** *transitive* force open or apart with a wedge. **3** *transitive & intransitive* (foll. by *in*, *into*) pack or thrust (a thing or oneself) tightly in or into. □ **thin edge** (or **end**) **of the wedge** *informal* an action or procedure of little importance in itself, but likely to more serious developments. □ **wedge·like** *adjective* [Old English *wecg*]

wedge² *transitive verb* prepare (pottery clay) for use by kneading and throwing down. [17th c.: origin uncertain]

wedge-shaped *adjective* **1** shaped like a solid wedge. **2** V-shaped.

wedg·ie *noun informal* **1** a woman's shoe with a wedge sole (*see* WEDGE¹ 4). **2** *N Amer.* a practical joke in which the victim's underpants are pulled up tightly between the buttocks.

Wedg·wood¹, Jo·siah (1730–95), English potter, who earned an international reputation with the pottery factories that he established in Staffordshire in the 1760s; his designs were often based on antique relief sculptures.

Wedg·wood² *noun proprietary* **1** ceramic ware made by Josiah Wedgwood and his successors, esp. a kind of fine stoneware usu. with a white cameo design. **2** the characteristic blue colour of this stoneware.

wed·lock *noun* the married state. □ **born in** (or **out of**) **wedlock** born of married (or unmarried) parents. [Old English *wedlāc* marriage vow, from *wed* pledge (related to WED) + *-lāc* suffix denoting action]

Wed·nes·day /ˈwenzdei, -di/ ● *noun* the fourth day of the week, following Tuesday. ● *adverb* **1** on Wednesday. **2** (**Wednesdays**) on Wednesdays; each Wednesday. [Middle English *wednesdei*, Old English *wōdnesdæg* day of (the god) Odin]

Weds. *abbreviation* Wednesday.

wee¹ *adjective* (**weer** /ˈwiːɜr/; **weest** /ˈwiːɪst/) **1** *informal* very small in amount or extent (*a wee bit late*). **2** esp. *Scot.* small in size or stature. □ **the wee hours** *see* HOUR. [originally Scots noun, from northern Middle English *wei* (small) quantity, from Anglian *wēg*]

wee² esp. *Brit. slang* ● *noun* urine. ● *intransitive verb* urinate. [imitative]

weed ● *noun* **1** a wild plant growing where it is not wanted. **2 a** *informal* a thin weak-looking or contemptibly feeble person. **b** *slang* an inferior horse. **3** *slang* **a** marijuana. **b** tobacco. ● *verb* **1** *transitive* **a** clear (an area) of weeds. **b** remove unwanted parts from. **2** *transitive* (foll. by *out*) **a** sort out (inferior or unwanted parts, elements, etc.) for removal. **b** rid (a quantity or company) of inferior or unwanted members etc. **3** *intransitive* cut off or uproot weeds. □ **weed·er** *noun* **weed·less** *adjective* [Old English *wēod*, of unknown origin]

weed·bed *noun N Amer.* an area of a lake etc. with many weeds, esp. as frequented by fish.

Weed Eater *noun proprietary* = WEED WHACKER.

weed-grown *adjective* overgrown with weeds.

weed inspector *noun* an official in charge of controlling the growth of harmful weeds.

weed killer *noun* a substance used to destroy weeds.

weed·line *noun N Amer.* the edge of a weedbed.

weeds *plural noun* (in full **widow's weeds**) *archaic* deep mourning worn by a widow. [Old English *wǣd(e)* garment, from Germanic]

weed whacker *noun N Amer.* a hand-held motorized garden tool used to trim grass, weeds, etc.

weedy *adjective* (**weed·i·er**, **weed·i·est**) **1** having many weeds. **2** (esp. of a person) weak, feeble; of poor stature. □ **weed·i·ness** *noun*

week *noun* **1** a period of seven consecutive days thought of as either from Sunday to Saturday or from Monday to Sunday. **2** a period of seven days counted from or beginning with a usu. specified point (*three weeks since we were there*). **3** one week of the year devoted to a specific event, holiday, cause, or activity (*Grey Cup week*; *Earth Week*; *reading week*). **4** the period of five days from Monday to Friday. **5** the period during which one works in a week (*a 35-hour week*). **6** (in *pl.*) *informal* a long time (*I haven't seen you in weeks*). **7** *Brit.* a week after (a specified day) (*Tuesday week*; *tomorrow week*). [Old English *wice* from Germanic, prob. originally = sequence]

week·day *noun* any of the days from Monday to Friday (also *attributive*: *weekday mornings*).

week·end ● *noun* **1** the period from Friday evening to Sunday evening. **2** this period extended slightly (*a three-day weekend*). ● *adjective* **1** held on or over a weekend. **2** carrying out a specific activity or hobby, or fulfilling a particular role, only on weekends. **3** for use on weekends. ● *intransitive verb* spend a weekend.

weekend bag *noun* a piece of luggage of a size suitable for holding the clothes and personal items necessary for a weekend.

week·ender *noun* a person who spends weekends away from home.

weekend warrior *noun N Amer. informal* or *jocular* a person who participates in an activity only in his or her spare time, esp. on weekends.

week-long *adjective* lasting for a week (*a week-long festival*).

week·ly ● *adjective* **1** done, produced, or occurring once a week. **2** calculated or determined by the week (*a weekly salary*; *a weekly rate*). ● *adverb* once a week; from week to week. ● *noun* (*pl.* **-lies**) a weekly newspaper or periodical.

week·night *noun* each of the nights of a week not falling on a weekend, i.e. from Monday to Thursday.

ween /wiːn/ *transitive verb archaic* be of the opinion; think, suppose. [Old English *wēnan* from Germanic]

wee·nie¹ *noun N Amer.* = WIENER 1. [alteration of WIENER]

wee·nie² *noun N Amer.* **1** *derogatory* (as a term of contempt) an objectionable, feeble, or insignificant person; a wimp, geek, or nerd. **2** *slang* the penis. [from WEENY]

weeny *adjective* (also **ween·sy**) (**wee·ni·er**, **wee·ni·est** or **ween·si·er**, **ween·si·est**) *informal* tiny. [WEE¹ after *tiny, teeny*]

weep ● *verb* (*past* and *past participle* **wept**) **1** *intransitive* express grief or misery etc. by tears usu. accompanied by sobs and moans; cry. **2** *intransitive* (foll. by *for*) shed tears for; bewail, lament. **3** *transitive* & *intransitive* shed or exude (liquid, drops of water or moisture, condensation, etc.). ● *noun* a fit or period of weeping. [Old English *wēpan* from Germanic (prob. imitative)]

weep·er *noun* **1 a** a person who weeps or is prone to weeping. **b** *hist.* a hired mourner at a funeral. **2** (usu. in *pl.*) *hist.* anything worn as a conventional badge of mourning, such as a man's crape hatband or a woman's black crape veil. **3 a** an emotional or sentimental ballad or song. **b** = WEEPIE.

weep·ie *noun* (also **weepy**) (*pl.* **-ies**) *informal* a sentimental or emotional movie, novel, or play, etc.; a tearjerker.

weep·ing ● *adjective* **1** (of a tree) having drooping branches (*weeping willow*). **2** that cries or weeps. ● *noun* the act of shedding tears.

weeping bed *noun* = SEPTIC FIELD.

weeping fig *noun* = FICUS BENJAMINA.

weeping tile *noun* a perforated plastic pipe used for drainage, esp. around building foundations and in septic fields.

weeping willow *noun* any of several ornamental willows with drooping branches and slender yellowish-green leaves.

weepy *adjective* (**weep·i·er**, **weep·i·est**) *informal* **1** inclined to cry or weep; sad, tearful. **2** (of a movie or novel etc.) intended to evoke a tearful reaction. □ **weep·i·ly** *adverb* **weep·i·ness** *noun*

wee·vil /ˈwiːvəl/ *noun* **1** any destructive beetle of the family Curculionidae, with its head extended into a beak or rostrum and feeding esp. on grain. **2** any insect damaging stored grain. □ **wee·vily** *adjective* [Middle Low German *wevel* from Germanic]

wee-wee *noun informal* = PEE-PEE 1. [20th c.: origin unknown]

weft *noun* **1 a** the threads woven across a warp to make fabric. **b** yarn used for this. **2** strips of cane, straw, etc. used as filling in weaving baskets or mats etc. **3** a thing that is spun or woven. [Old English *weft(a)*: related to WEAVE¹]

Weg·ener /ˈveigənər/ **Al·fred Lo·thar** (1880–1930), German meteorologist and geologist, who was the first serious proponent of the theory of continental drift.

Wehr·macht /ˈvermɒxt/ *noun hist.* the German armed forces, esp. the army, from 1921–1945. [German, = defensive force]

Wei /wei/ the name of several dynasties which ruled in China, especially that of AD 386–535.

Wei·fang /weiˈfaŋ/ a city in Shandong province, E China; pop. (est. 1999) 621,125.

wei·gela /waiˈgiːlə, -ˈdʒiː-, ˈwaigələ/ *noun* any of various Asian shrubs of the genus *Weigela*, of the honeysuckle family, with pink, white or red flowers, grown as an ornamental. [modern Latin, from C. E. *Weigel*, German physician d.1831, + -A¹]

weigh *verb* **1** *transitive* determine the heaviness of (a body or substance), esp. using scales. **2** *transitive* (often foll. by *out*) **a** use scales to measure and remove a definite quantity of (a substance) from a larger supply. **b** distribute in exact amounts by weight. **3** *transitive* **a** consider the relative value, importance, or desirability of; estimate with a view to choice, rejection, or preference (*weighed the options*; *weighed the merits of the candidates*). **b** (foll. by *against, with*) compare (one consideration) with another. **4** *intransitive* have or be equal to a specified degree of heaviness (*this weighs three kilograms*; *he weighs more than I do*). **5** *intransitive* have a usu. specified degree of importance (*this issue will weigh heavily on the outcome*). **6** *intransitive* (usu. foll. by *on*) be a source of worry or concern (to); lie heavy (upon) (*it's been weighing on her mind for some time*). □ **weigh anchor** take the anchor up. **weigh down 1** bring or keep down by exerting weight. **2** be oppressive or burdensome to (*weighed down with worries*). **weigh in 1** (of a boxer, jockey, etc.) have one's weight checked officially. **2** (foll. by *at*) have a specified weight officially recorded at a weigh-in (*the prizewinning salmon weighed in at 18.2 kg*). **3 a** bring one's weight or influence to bear; contribute to a discussion, undertaking, etc. **b** (foll. by *with*) introduce or contribute (something) to an undertaking etc. (*the whole family weighed in with offers of help*). **weigh into** *informal* attack (physically or verbally). **weigh up** *Brit. informal* consider carefully; evaluate (a person, situation, etc.). **weigh with** be of importance to. **weigh one's words** carefully choose a sensitive or tactful way of expressing something. □ **weigh·er** *noun* [Old English *wegan* from Germanic, related to WAY]

weigh-in *noun* an official weighing of a person or thing, such as a boxer prior to a bout or an angler's catch at the end of a competition.

weigh scale *noun* (also **weigh station**) *N Amer.* a large metal platform at the side of a highway where trucks are required to be weighed to ensure that they do not exceed the legal limit for the road.

weight ● *noun* **1** *Physics* **a** the force experienced by a body as a result of the earth's gravitational pull (*compare* MASS¹ *noun* 8). **b** any similar force with which a body tends to a centre of attraction. **2** the heaviness of a body regarded as a property of it; its relative mass giving rise to a downward force (*she is twice your weight*; *it is held in position by its weight*). **3 a** the quantitative expression of a body's weight (*it has a weight of three pounds*). **b** a unit or system of units used for measuring or expressing how much a body weighs (*troy weight*). **4** a body of a known weight for use in weighing. **5** a heavy body used to hold something down, to drive the mechanism of a clock, as a sinker in fishing, etc. **6 a** a heavy mass or load. **b** an emotional burden; a worry or responsibility etc. (*a weight off my mind*). **7 a** a power to persuade, convince, or impress; influence, sway (*carried weight with the public*). **b** the heaviest part; preponderance (*the weight of evidence was against them*). **8** *Statistics* a relative value assigned to a factor or observation, esp. a multiplier associated with any of a set of numerical quantities that are added together. **9 a** (in *pl.*) heavy blocks or discs of metal, barbells, etc. designed to be used in lifting and other exercises to improve or demonstrate physical strength and fitness. **b** = SHOT¹ 7. **10** (in full **weight class**) each of a series of divisions to which an athlete in some sports, e.g. boxing, may be assigned, according to how much he or she weighs (*flyweight*; *heavyweight*). **11** (usu. in *combination*) the relative weight of a fabric or garment as a measure of its quality or suitability for a particular use or season (*a lightweight spring jacket*; *dress-weight cotton*). ● *transitive verb* **1 a** supply with an additional weight. **b** (usu. foll. by *down*) hold down with a weight or weights. **2** devise or manipulate (a rule or law etc.) so that it favours a particular individual, group, or goal over others (*legislation weighted in favour of the working class*). **3** *Statistics* multiply (the components of an average) by factors reflecting their relative importance. **4** (foll. by *with*) impede or burden. **5** assign a handicap weight to (a horse). □ **pull one's weight** see PULL. **throw one's weight around** (or **about**) see THROW. **worth one's** (or **its**) **weight in gold** extremely valuable, useful, or helpful. □ **weight·ed** *adjective* [Old English (*ge*)*wiht*: compare WEIGH]

weight·ing *noun* **1** emphasis or priority (*they will give due weighting to quality as well as price*). **2** an allocated proportion of something, esp. an investment (*the company continues to recommend a 35 per cent weighting in bonds*).

weight·less *adjective* **1** lacking or apparently lacking weight. **2** (of an orbiting satellite etc.) not apparently acted on by gravity, either due to a locally weak gravitational field, or because both the body and its surroundings are freely and equally accelerating under the influence of the field. **3** lacking substance, importance, or significance. □ **weight·less·ly** *adverb* **weight·less·ness** *noun*

weight·lift·ing *noun* the sport or exercise of lifting heavy weights. □ **weight·lift·er** *noun*

weight loss *noun* **1** a decrease in body weight. **2** (*attributive*; usu. **weight-loss**) designed to promote or achieve a reduction in body weight (*weight-loss clinic*).

weight room *noun* a room where weights and related equipment are kept and used for physical training.

weight training *noun* physical conditioning or training involving the use of weights. □ **weight train** *intransitive verb*

weighty *adjective* (**weight·i·er**, **weight·i·est**) **1** of considerable weight; heavy. **2** of great importance or significance. **3** (of an argument, speech, etc.) producing a powerful effect; convincing, persuasive. **4** (of a person) having great authority or stature; influential. □ **weight·i·ly** *adverb* **weight·i·ness** *noun*

Weil /'vaɪl/ **Si·mone** (1909–43), French essayist, philosopher, and mystic, whose reputation is based on the posthumous publication of such autobiographical works as *Waiting for God* (1949) and *Notebooks* (1951–6).

Weill /'vaɪl/ **Kurt** (1900–50), German composer, resident in the US from 1935. He is best known for the operas he wrote in collaboration with Bertolt Brecht, political satires which evoke the harsh decadence of the pre-war period in Germany; these include *The Rise and Fall of the City of Mahagonny* (1927) and *The Threepenny Opera* (1928).

Wei·mar /'vaɪmɑr/ a city in Thuringia, central Germany; pop. (2002) 62,200. It was famous in the late 18th and early 19th c. for its intellectual and cultural life; both Goethe and Schiller lived and worked here.

Wei·mar·aner /ˌwaɪməˈrɑnər, ˌvaɪ-/ *noun* (also **weimaraner**) a breed of pointer, with a short usu. grey coat and drooping ears, originally bred as a hunting dog in the Weimar region. [German, from WEIMAR]

Weimar Republic the German republic of 1919–33. Faced with huge reparation costs deriving from the Treaty of Versailles, as well as soaring inflation and high unemployment, the country saw a growth in right-wing support which led ultimately to the rise of Hitler and the Nazis. [WEIMAR, where its constitution was drawn up]

Wein·zweig /'vaɪntsvaɪg/ **John Jacob** (b.1913), Canadian composer and teacher. He was the first Canadian composer to explore the use of the twelve-tone scale; his compositions include the ballet *Red Ear of Corn* (1949).

Weir /wiːr/ **Mi·chael Rich·ard** ('Mike') (b.1970), Canadian golfer. He joined the PGA tour in 1997, and won the World Golf Championship in 2000 and the Masters in 2003.

weir /wiːr/ *noun* **1** a dam built across a river to raise the level of water upstream or regulate its flow. **2** an enclosure of stakes and netting set in a stream or river etc., used for trapping fish. [Old English *wer* from *werian* dam up]

weird /wiːrd/ ● *adjective* **1** strange, unusual, out of the ordinary, bizarre. **2** suggestive of fate or the supernatural; unearthly, unnatural, uncanny. **3** *archaic* connected with fate, esp. having or claiming preternatural power to control a person's destiny (*weird sisters*). ● *noun* esp. *Scot. archaic* a person's appointed lot or destiny; fate (esp. in phr. **dree one's weird**, see DREE). □ **weird out** *slang* **1** make or become uncharacteristically depressed or upset. **2** induce a sense of disbelief or alienation in (a person). □ **weird·ly** *adverb* **weird·ness** *noun* [(earlier as noun) from Old English *wyrd* destiny, from Germanic]

weirdo /'wiːrdoʊ/ *noun* (also **weirdy** /'wiːrdi/) (*pl.* **weird·os** or **weird·ies**) *informal* a strange or abnormal person.

Weis·mann /'vaɪsmən/ **Au·gust (Frie·drich Leo·pold)** (1834–1914), German biologist, one of the founders of modern genetics. He expounded the theory of germplasm and suggested that variability in individuals came from the recombination of chromosomes during reproduction. □ **Weis·mann·ism** *noun*

Weiss·mul·ler /'vaɪs.mʊlər/ **Peter John ('John·ny')** (1904–84), US swimmer and actor. He won three Olympic gold medals in 1924 and two in 1928, and later achieved wider recognition as the star of the Tarzan films of the 1930s and 1940s.

Weiz·mann /'vaɪzmən, 'vaɪtsmən/ **Chaim (Az·riel)** (1874–1952), Russian-born Israeli politician, president 1949–52. A supporter of Zionism from the early 1900s, he participated in the negotiations that led to the Balfour Declaration (1917), which outlined British support for a Jewish homeland in Palestine; he became Israel's first president in 1949.

welch *var. of* WELSH.

wel·come ● *noun* **1** a kind or hospitable reception given to a visitor or stranger upon arriving (*we gave them a warm welcome*). **2** a greeting or reception of a specified (usu. friendly or unfriendly) kind (*he received a cool welcome from his in-laws*). ● *interjection* used to greet a visitor or guest, esp. expressing pleasure at the arrival (*welcome home!*). ● *transitive verb* **1 a** greet or receive with pleasure; give a friendly reception to (*welcomed them home*). **b** (foll. by *with*) greet or receive with something of a specified kind (*the audience welcomed him with boos*). **2** be pleased at or receptive to the prospect of (something) (*we welcome your comments*). ● *adjective* **1** that one receives with pleasure (*a welcome guest*; *welcome news*). **2** (foll. by *to*, *to* + *infin.*) freely allowed or cordially invited (*you are welcome to anything in the fridge*; *she's welcome to use the car*). □ **make welcome** receive hospitably. **wear out** (or **overstay** or **outstay**) **one's welcome** *N Amer.* inconvenience one's host by staying longer than is reasonable or expected. **welcome aboard!** *jocular* (with allusion to nautical usage) a greeting to a person joining a particular group, starting a job, etc. **you're** (or **you are**) **welcome** a polite response to an expression of thanks, signifying that the recipient of a favour is without obligation to the giver. □ **wel·com·er** *noun* **wel·com·ing** *adjective* **wel·com·ing·ly** *adverb* [originally Old English *wilcuma* one whose coming is pleasing, from *wil-* desire, pleasure + *cuma* comer, with later change to *wel-* WELL[1] after Old French *bien venu* or Old Norse *velkominn*]

welcome mat *noun N Amer.* **1** a doormat typically bearing some message of greeting, such as *Welcome*. **2** anything used to invite, entice, or solicit investors, customers, etc. (*the company has thrown down the welcome mat to potential investors*).

welcome tax *noun Cdn (Que.)* a municipal tax levied on all house purchases in the Province of Quebec. [translation of French *taxe de bienvenue*]

Welcome Wagon *noun N Amer.* **1** *proprietary* an organization of people who make newcomers in a community welcome by providing gifts, samples of local merchants' wares, etc. **2** (**welcome wagon**) *informal* a group of people delegated to greet a visitor, guest, or newcomer in a community.

weld[1] ● *transitive verb* **1 a** hammer or press (pieces of heated iron or steel) into one piece. **b** join (pieces of metal or plastic etc.) by melting, using local heat provided by an electric arc, oxyacetylene torch, or laser, usu. with the addition of extra metal. **c** form or repair by welding (*she welded this candlestick*). **2** bring together (arguments, members of a group, etc.) into an effectual or homogeneous whole. ● *noun* a welded joint. □ **weld·able** *adjective* **weld·abil·ity** *noun* [alteration (prob. influenced by past participle) of WELL[2] *verb* in obsolete sense 'melt or weld (heated metal)']

weld[2] *noun* **1** a plant, *Reseda luteola*, yielding a yellow dye. **2** *hist.* this dye. [Old English *w(e)alde* (unrecorded): compare Middle Dutch *woude*, Middle Low German *walde*]

weld·er *noun* **1** a person who welds, esp. as a profession. **2** a torch etc. used in welding.

wel·fare *noun* **1** well-being, happiness; health and prosperity of a person or a community etc. **2 a** the organized provision for the basic esp. physical and economic well-being of needy members of a community by statutory procedure or social effort. **b** financial support given for this purpose. □ **on welfare** *N Amer.* receiving financial assistance from the government for basic living needs.

welfare roll *noun N Amer.* (usu. in *pl.*) a list of people entitled to welfare benefits.

welfare state *noun* **1** a system whereby the government of a country etc. undertakes to protect the health and well-being of its citizens, esp. those in financial or social need, by means of grants, pensions, allowances, etc. **2** a country practising this system.

welfare work *noun* various programs and efforts organized for the welfare of the poor, disabled, or disadvantaged. □ **welfare worker** *noun*

wel·far·ism *noun* the principles or policies associated with a welfare state. □ **wel·far·ist** *noun*

wel·kin /'welkɪn/ *noun poet.* sky; the upper air. [Old English *wolcen* cloud, sky]

Wel·kom /'welkəm, 'vel-/ a town in central South Africa, in Free State; pop. (2002) 226,100.

well[1] ● *adverb* (**bet·ter**, **best**) **1** in an acceptable or satisfactory manner (*you have worked well*). **2** with some talent or distinction (*plays the piano well*). **3** in a way appropriate to the facts or circumstances (*you did well to tell me*). **4** in a kind way (*treated me well*). **5** thoroughly, carefully (*polish it well*). **6** with heartiness or approval; favourably (*speak* *well of*; *the book was well reviewed*). **7** with equanimity or good nature (*he took it well*). **8** probably, reasonably, indeed (*you may well be right*; *you may well ask*; *we might well take the risk*). **9** to a considerable extent (*she is well over forty*; *we found out well in advance*). **10** intimately; closely, in detail (*she knows you well*). **11** successfully, fortunately (*it turned out well*). **12** luckily, opportunely (*well met!*). **13** with a fortunate outcome; without disaster (*were well rid of them*). **14** profitably (*did well for themselves*). **15** comfortably, abundantly, liberally (*we live well here*; *the job pays well*). **16** *informal* used with preceding adverb to form intensive phrases (*I should bloody well hope so!*). ● *adjective* (**bet·ter**, **best**) **1** (usu. *predicative*) in good health; free or recovered from illness (*are you feeling well?*; *was not a well person*). **2** (*predicative*) **a** in a satisfactory state or position (*all is well*). **b** proper, advisable (*it would be well to inquire*). ● *interjection* **1** expressing surprise, insistence, resignation, etc. (*well I never!*; *oh well, at least we tried*). **2** used to resume or continue speaking, esp. after a pause (*well...who was it?*; *well anyway, as I was saying*). □ **all's well that ends well** the inconvenience of a problem or matter is negligible as long as it is resolved satisfactorily. **as well 1** also, in addition; to an equal extent. **2** (also **just as well**) with equal reason or result; with no loss of advantage or need for regret (*we might as well go home*; *it would be just as well to stop*). **3** *Cdn* furthermore, moreover (*As well, Winnipeggers are very friendly*). ¶ Only Canadians use *as well* in a sentence-initial position like this. **as well as** in addition to. **leave** (or **let**) **well enough alone** refrain from trying to improve something that is already satisfactory. **well and good** expressing dispassionate acceptance of a statement or decision etc. **well and truly** decisively, completely. **well worth** certainly worth (*well worth a visit*; *well worth visiting*). ¶ A hyphen is normally used in combinations of *well-* when used attributively, but not when used predicatively, e.g. *a well-made coat* but *the coat is well made*. [Old English *wel*, *well* prob. from the same stem as WILL[1]]

well[2] ● *noun* **1** a shaft sunk into the ground to obtain water, oil, natural gas, etc. **2** a natural source or spring of water. **3 a** the open space or shaft in a building enclosing a staircase or housing an elevator. **b** a deep narrow space in the middle of a building or group of buildings, to provide light and ventilation. **4** a receptacle, reservoir, or depression designed to hold liquid, such as one in a dish for gravy or in a desk for ink. **5** a deep receptacle, compartment, or recess, such as that in the trunk of a car in which a spare tire is kept. **6** (foll. by *of*) a source, esp. a copious one (*a well of information*). **7** *Brit.* a railed area in a courtroom where solicitors sit. ● *intransitive verb* **1** (foll. by *up*, *out*) gather, gush, or spring as in or from a fountain (*she felt anger welling up inside her*). **2** (foll. by *up*) (of eyes) be filled with tears. [Old English *wella* (= Old High German *wella* wave, Old Norse *vella* boiling heat), *wellan* boil, melt, from Germanic]

we'll *contraction* we shall; we will.

well acquainted *adjective* (usu. foll. by *with*) familiar.

well-adjust·ed *adjective* **1** *Psych.* mentally and emotionally stable. **2** in a state of proper adjustment.

well-advised *adjective* **1** (usu. foll. by *to* + infin.) (of a person) prudent, wise (*would be well-advised to wait*). **2** (of an action etc.) carefully thought out.

well-aimed *adjective* **1** (of a jibe or criticism) incisive, biting. **2** precisely directed; accurate.

Wel·land /'weland/ a city in S Ontario, situated about 20 km south of St. Catharines; pop. (2001) 48,402. □ **Wel·land·er** *noun* [see WELLAND RIVER]

Welland Canal a canal, almost 44 km long, which links Lake Ontario (at St. Catharines) to Lake Erie (at Port Colborne), overcoming a 99.4 m difference in height between the two bodies of water and bypassing Niagara Falls. It forms part of the St. Lawrence Seaway.

Welland River a river in S Ontario, rising southwest of Hamilton and flowing gradually southeast to the city of Welland, where it turns northeast. Its flow is diverted into the Queenston-Chippawa Power Canal shortly before its mouth on the Niagara River just above Niagara Falls. [after the *Welland River* in Lincolnshire, England]

well-appoint·ed *adjective* furnished with all of the necessary equipment, accessories, or desirable features (*a well-appointed kitchen*).

well-attend·ed *adjective* (of a meeting etc.) attended by a large number of people.

well-balanced *adjective* **1** having no constituent lacking or in excess; regulated to ensure a proper balance (*a well-balanced diet*). **2** sane, sensible.

well-behaved *adjective* having or demonstrating good manners or conduct.

well-being *noun* a happy, healthy, and prosperous state or condition; moral or physical welfare.

well-born *adjective* of noble family.

well-bred *adjective* **1** demonstrating qualities indicative of a good upbringing, such as refined speech, courteous behaviour, and excellent manners. **2** (of an animal) of good or pure stock.

well-built *adjective* **1** of solid and reliable construction. **2** (of a person) well-proportioned with a strong, sturdy, or muscular build.

well-chosen *adjective* (of words etc.) carefully selected for effect.

well-conditioned *adjective* in good physical condition; healthy.

well-connect·ed *adjective* having powerful or influential relatives, friends, associates, contacts, etc.

well-construct·ed *adjective* **1** (of a building, furniture, etc.) constructed in a sound or practical way. **2** (of a text) with a clear or carefully-planned structure.

well-defined *adjective* clearly marked, outlined, or indicated; having definite shape, structure, or guidelines.

well-deserved *adjective* rightfully merited or earned.

well-designed *adjective* **1** (of furniture, living space, etc.) designed for practical use. **2** of a good design (*well-designed poster*).

well-developed *adjective* **1** fully developed or grown; mature. **2** of generous size.

well-disposed *adjective* (often foll. by *toward*) having a good disposition or friendly feeling (for).

well-document·ed *adjective* supported or attested by much documentary evidence.

well done ● *adjective* **1** (of meat) thoroughly cooked. **2** (of a task etc.) performed or executed skilfully or effectively. ● *interjection* expressing approval of a person's actions.

well-dressed *adjective* wearing clothes of good quality.

well-earned *adjective* fully deserved.

well-educat·ed *adjective* having received a high level of education.

well-endowed *adjective* **1** well provided with talent or resources. **2** *euphemism* **a** (of a woman) having large breasts. **b** (of a man) = WELL-HUNG.

well equipped *adjective* **1** having a plentiful supply of equipment. **2** (foll. by *to* + infin., *for*) having the necessary requirements or resources (*she is well equipped to deal with the situation*).

Welles /'welz/ **(George) Orson** (1915–85), US film director and actor. He produced, directed, wrote, and acted in the critically acclaimed *Citizen Kane* (1941), based on the life of the newspaper tycoon William Hearst; his other films include *The Lady of Shanghai* (1948) and *The Third Man* (1949). □ **Welles·ian** *adjective*

well-estab·lished *adjective* **1** (of a custom, rule, etc.) long-standing. **2** firmly entrenched in a profession, role, or position; proven (*a well-established artist*).

well-fed *adjective* **1** having had plenty to eat. **2** *euphemism* plump, overweight.

well-formed *adjective* **1** correctly or attractively proportioned or shaped. **2** *Logic* designating any sequence of symbols conforming to the formation rules of a logical system. **3** *Linguistics* formed according to stated grammatical rules. □ **well-formed·ness** /-'fɔrmədnəs/ *noun*

well-founded *adjective* (of a belief, suspicion, statement, etc.) having a foundation in fact or reason; based on strong evidence.

well-groomed *adjective* **1** (of a person) having a clean and neat appearance with carefully tended hair, clothes, etc. **2** (of an animal) having a clean and brushed coat. **3** (of ski trails etc.) properly maintained or looked after.

well-ground·ed *adjective* **1** = WELL-FOUNDED. **2** (often foll. by *in*) having a good training in or knowledge of the basic principles of a subject.

well·head *noun* **1** a structure built over an oil or gas well. **2** = WELLSPRING.

well-heeled *adjective* *informal* wealthy.

well·house *noun* a small building or room enclosing a well and its apparatus.

well-hung *adjective* *slang* (of a man) having large genitals.

wel·lie *var. of* WELLY.

well-informed *adjective* possessing or communicating much knowledge in general or of a specified subject.

Wel·ling·ton[1] the capital of New Zealand, situated at the southern tip of North Island; pop. (2001) 167,190. □ **Wel·ling·ton·ian** /ˌwelɪŋ'tɔːniːən/ *noun & adjective* [WELLINGTON[2]]

---

uː mood   aɪ my   əi pipe   au brown   ʌu house   ei day   ɔi boy   ã franglais   ã Canadien   ɔ̃ Brayon   (*see over for consonants*)

Wel·ling·ton², **1st Duke of** (title of Arthur Wellesley; known as the 'Iron Duke') (1769–1852), Irish-born British soldier and Tory politician, prime minister 1828–30 and 1834. He served as commander of British forces in the Peninsular War (1808–14), and defeated Napoleon at the Battle of Waterloo (1815), thus ending the Napoleonic Wars (1800–15).

wel·ling·ton noun (also **Wellington**, in full **wellington boot**) (usu. in *pl.*) esp. *Brit.* a waterproof rubber or plastic boot usu. reaching the knee, worn in wet or muddy conditions. [WELLINGTON²]

well-intentioned *adjective* having or showing good intentions.

well-kept *adjective* **1** kept in good order or condition. **2** carefully preserved; not revealed (*a well-kept secret*).

well-knit *adjective* (of a person) compact; not loose-jointed or sprawling.

well-known *adjective* **1** known to many; widely known, famous. **2** intimately or thoroughly known.

well-liked *adjective* regarded with favour or approval; popular.

well-lit *adjective* (also **well-lighted**) suitably provided with light or lighting; sufficiently illuminated.

well-loved *adjective* regarded with great affection; dearly loved.

well-made *adjective* strongly or skilfully constructed, prepared, or devised.

well-maintained *adjective* **1** kept in good repair. **2** kept up to date (*well-maintained inventory*).

well-mannered *adjective* having or demonstrating good manners; courteous, polite.

well-marked *adjective* clearly defined, distinct; easy to distinguish or recognize.

well-matched *adjective* **1** compatible, suited; fit to be a pair. **2** (of opponents or adversaries) evenly matched; having similar or offsetting strengths and weakness.

well-meaning *adjective* **1** (of a person) having or demonstrating good intentions, esp. despite being misguided or unhelpful. **2** (also **well-meant**) (of advice etc.) based on good intentions but usu. ineffective or ill-advised.

well·ness noun the state of being well or in good health.

well-nigh *adverb* very nearly; almost (*it was well-nigh impossible*).

well off *adjective* **1** having plenty of money. **2** in a fortunate situation or position.

well-oiled *adjective* *informal* **1 a** sufficiently or generously lubricated. **b** (of an organization, operation, etc.) running smoothly. **2** drunk.

well-ordered *adjective* neatly, carefully, or properly composed or arranged.

well-organized *adjective* **1** skilfully or carefully organized; planned in detail. **2** (of a person) orderly; able to organize personal activities.

well-paid *adjective* **1** (of a person) amply rewarded for a job. **2** (also **well-paying**) (of a job) that pays well.

well placed *adjective* **1** set in a good place or position; properly, conveniently, or judiciously placed. **2** holding a position of influence, authority, or high social standing. **3** (foll. by *to* + infin.) in a suitable position; easily able (*you are well placed to know*).

well-planned *adjective* **1** of careful or practical design. **2** (of an event, program, etc.) planned or structured carefully with attention to detail.

well pleased *adjective* highly gratified or satisfied.

well-prepared *adjective* **1** prepared with care. **2** having prepared thoroughly (for an interview, exam, etc.).

well-preserved *adjective* **1** having remained in good condition over time (*a well-preserved artifact*). **2** (of an elderly person) showing little sign of aging.

well-propor·tioned *noun* having good, graceful, or correct proportions.

well-read *adjective* knowledgeable through much reading.

well-received *adjective* favourably received or reviewed.

well-rounded *adjective* **1** (of a person) having or showing a fully developed personality combined with a wide range of knowledge and interests. **2** well-balanced, full, and varied (*a well-rounded life; a well-rounded team*). **3** (of a phrase etc.) complete and well expressed.

Wells ▸ **1 Clyde** (b.1937), Canadian politician, Liberal premier of Newfoundland 1989–96. First elected to the Newfoundland House of Assembly 1966–71, he served briefly in the Smallwood cabinet. He gained national attention as premier for his opposition to the Meech Lake Accord. **2 Her·bert George** (1866–1946), English novelist. He wrote some of the earliest science fiction novels, such as *The Time Machine* (1895) and *The War of the Worlds* (1898), and his socialism was

reflected in several comic novels about lower-middle-class life, including *Kipps* (1905) and *The History of Mr. Polly* (1910). □ **Wells·ian** *adjective* (in sense 2).

well-spent *adjective* (esp. of money or time) used profitably or judiciously.

well-spoken *adjective* (of a person) speaking articulately and grammatically or with an accent considered to be refined.

well·spring *noun* **1** the place where a spring breaks out of the ground; the source of a stream or river. **2** (usu. foll. by *of*) an esp. abundant source (*melancholy is the wellspring of creativity*).

well-stocked *adjective* having an abundant supply.

well-suited *adjective* (usu. foll. by *to*, *for*) suitable.

well-support·ed *adjective* **1** attended by many. **2** supported by much evidence.

well-taken *adjective* (of a point or argument) accepted as valid.

well-thought-of *adjective* having a good reputation; esteemed, respected.

well-thought-out *adjective* carefully planned or devised in advance.

well-thumbed *adjective* (of a book or page etc.) bearing marks of frequent handling.

well-timed *adjective* done or occurring at an appropriate or convenient time; opportune, timely.

well-to-do *adjective* comfortably wealthy or prosperous.

well-travelled *adjective* **1** having travelled extensively. **2** (of a path etc.) much frequented.

well-trodden *adjective* frequently walked on.

well-turned *adjective* **1** (of a compliment, phrase, or verse) elegantly expressed. **2** elegantly shaped, fashioned, or displayed.

well-uphol·stered *adjective* **1** (of a chair etc.) padded, comfortable. **2** *jocular* (of a person) fat.

well-used *adjective* **1 a** used properly or frequently. **b** worn from frequent handling or use. **2** (of a road or path etc.) frequently travelled.

well versed *adjective* (usu. foll. by *in*) very learned, experienced, or skilled in (a subject, field, art, etc.); knowledgeable about.

well-wisher *noun* a person who wishes one well; a person conveying his or her congratulations, sympathies, wishes of luck or success, etc. to another.

well-worn *adjective* **1** decrepit, shabby, or worn out from extensive use or handling. **2** (of a phrase or idea etc.) trite, hackneyed.

welly *noun* (also **wel·lie**) (*pl.* **-lies**) esp. *Brit. informal* a wellington boot. [abbreviation]

Wels·bach /ˈwelzbak/ **Carl Auer von**, see AUER.

Welsh ● *adjective* of or relating to Wales or its people or language.
● *noun* **1** the Celtic language of Wales. **2** (prec. by *the*; treated as *pl.*) the people of Wales. □ **Welsh·ness** *noun* [Old English *Welisc*, *Wælisc*, etc., from Germanic from Latin *Volcae*, the name of a Celtic people]

welsh *intransitive verb* (also **welch**) (usu. foll. by *on*) **1** fail or refuse to pay or repay money owed, esp. from a loan or wager (*he welshes on gambling debts*). **2** fail or refuse to honour or fulfill a promise or obligation (*she welshed on our agreement*). □ **welsh·er** *noun* [19th c.: origin unknown]

Welsh corgi *noun* see CORGI.

Welsh dresser *noun* a type of sideboard with open shelves above a cupboard and drawers.

Welsh harp *noun* a harp with three rows of strings.

Welsh·man *noun* (*pl.* **-men**) a man who is Welsh by birth or descent.

Welsh onion *noun* a species of onion, *Allium fistulosum*, forming clusters of bulbs.

Welsh rabbit *noun* (also **Welsh rarebit**) a dish of melted and seasoned cheese on toast.

Welsh·woman *noun* (*pl.* **-women**) a woman who is Welsh by birth or descent.

welt ● *noun* **1** a ridge raised on the flesh by the impact of a rod, whip, etc., or by an allergic reaction. **2** a strip of leather etc. sewn around the edge of a shoe upper and attached to the sole. **3** a strip of reinforced material on the edge or seam of an article of clothing as a border or binding. ● *transitive verb* **1** (usu. in *passive*) cause a welt to develop on (a person or part of the body) **2** provide (an article of clothing) with a welt. [Middle English *welte*, *walt*, of unknown origin]

Welt·an·schau·ung /ˌveltanˈʃauʊŋ/ *noun* (*pl.* **-en**) = WORLD VIEW. [German from *Welt* world + *Anschauung* perception]

wel·ter¹ ● *noun* a confused mixture of things or people. ● *intransitive* *verb* **1** toss, roll. **2** (foll. by *in*) lie prostrate or wallow in blood etc. [Middle Dutch, Middle Low German *welteren*]

wel·ter² *noun* **1** a heavy rider or boxer. **2** a thing exceptionally big or heavy for its kind. [19th c.: origin unknown]

welter·weight *noun* **1** a weight class in certain sports intermediate between lightweight and middleweight, in the amateur boxing scale 63.5-67 kg but differing for professionals and wrestlers. **2** a boxer etc. of this weight.

Welt·schmerz /ˈvɛltʃmɛrts/ *noun* a feeling of pessimism; an apathetic or vaguely yearning outlook on life. [German from *Welt* world + *Schmerz* pain]

Welty /ˈwɛlti/ **Eu·dora** (1909–2001), US novelist, short-story writer, and critic. Her novels chiefly focus on life in the American South and contain Gothic elements, as in *Delta Wedding* (1946) and *The Optimist's Daughter* (1972).

Wemba-wemba /ˈwɛmbəˌwɛmbə/ *noun* an Aboriginal language of SE Australia, now extinct.

wen¹ *noun* a sebaceous cyst on or under the skin, esp. on the head. [Old English *wen, wenn,* of unknown origin: compare Dutch *wen,* Middle Low German *wene,* Low German *wehne* tumour, wart]

wen² *noun* (also **wyn** /wɪn/) a runic letter in Old and Middle English, later replaced by *w.* [Old English, var. of *wyn* joy (see WINSOME), used because it begins with this letter: compare THORN 4]

Wen·ces·las, St. /ˈwɛnsəsləs/ (also **Wen·ces·laus**; known as 'Good King Wenceslas') (*c.*907–29), Duke of Bohemia. He worked to Christianize the people of Bohemia but was murdered by his brother Boleslaus; he later became venerated as a martyr and hero of Bohemia. Feast day, 28 Sept.

Wen·ces·laus /ˈwɛnsəsləs/ (also **Wen·ces·las**) (1361–1419), king of Bohemia (as Wenceslaus IV) 1378–1419. He became king of Germany and Holy Roman emperor in the same year as he succeeded to the throne of Bohemia, but was deposed by the German Electors in 1400.

wench ● *noun* **1** *jocular* a girl or young woman. **2** *archaic* a prostitute or mistress. **3** *archaic* a female servant. ● *intransitive verb* *archaic* (of a man) consort with prostitutes. □ **wench·er** *noun* [Middle English *wenche, wenchel* from Old English *wencel* child: compare Old English *wancol* weak, tottering]

Wen-Chou see WENZHOU.

Wend /wɛnd/ *noun* a member of a Slavic people of N Germany, now inhabiting E Saxony. □ **Wend·ish** *adjective* [German *Wende* from Old High German *Winida,* of unknown origin]

wend *intransitive verb* go. □ **wend one's way** make one's way. [Old English *wendan* turn, from Germanic, related to WIND²]

wen·di·go *noun* var. of WINDIGO.

Wen-Do /ˈwɛndoʊ/ *noun* *Cdn proprietary* a program of self-defence designed for women, which emphasizes awareness and avoidance of potentially dangerous situations as well as appropriate reactions, including, as a last resort, physical attacks directed against the particularly vulnerable areas of an assailant's body. [lit. 'women's way', from Anglo-Saxon *cwēne* woman + Japanese *dō* way]

Wendy house *noun* *Brit.* a structure resembling a house for children to play in. [after the house built around *Wendy* in J. M. Barrie's *Peter Pan*]

Wens·ley·dale *noun* **1** a variety of hard flaky white or blue veined cheese made from cow's milk. **2** a sheep of a breed with long wool. [*Wensleydale* in Yorkshire]

went *past of* GO¹.

wentle·trap *noun* any marine snail of the genus *Clathrus,* with a spiral shell of many whorls. [Dutch *wenteltrap* winding stair, spiral shell]

Wen·zhou /wɛnˈdʒoʊ/ (also **Wen-Chou** /-ˈtʃoʊ/) an industrial city in Zhejiang province, E China; pop. (est. 2001) 730,800.

wept *past of* WEEP.

were *2nd sing. past, pl. past, and past subjunctive of* BE.

we're *contraction* we are.

were- /wer, wiːr/ *combining form* used to denote a person imagined to be able to change at times into a specified animal (*were-rat; were-snake*). [back-formation from WEREWOLF]

weren't *contraction* were not.

were·wolf /ˈwerwʊlf, ˈwiːr-/ *noun* (*pl.* **-wolves**) a mythical being who at times changes from a person to a wolf. [Old English *werewulf:* first element perhaps from Old English *wer* man = Latin *vir*]

wer·gild /ˈwergɪld/ *noun* (also **wer·geld** /-geld/) *hist.* (in Germanic and Anglo-Saxon law) the price put on a person according to his or her rank, payable as a fine or compensation by a person guilty of homicide

or certain other crimes. [Old English *wergeld,* Anglo-Latin *weregildum,* from *wer* man + *gield* yield]

Wer·ner /ˈvɜrnɜr/ **Al·fred** (1866–1919), French-born Swiss chemist. In 1893 he announced the theory of chemical coordination, proposing a secondary or residual form of valence to explain the structures of coordination compounds; he was awarded the Nobel Prize for chemistry in 1913.

wert *archaic 2nd sing. past of* BE.

Weser River /ˈveɪzɜr/ a river of NW Germany, which is formed at the junction of the Werra and Fulda rivers in Lower Saxony and flows 292 km (182 miles) northward to the North Sea near Bremerhaven.

Wes·ley /ˈwesli, ˈwez-/ **1 Charles** (1707–88) English clergyman, poet, and hymn writer, co-founder of Methodism. He published over 4,500 hymns, including 'Hark, the herald angels sing', 'Christ the Lord is ris'n today', and 'Rejoice, the Lord is King'. **2** his brother **John** (1703–91), English preacher and co-founder of Methodism. He devoted his life to evangelistic work, travelling throughout Britain winning many converts; despite his wish for Methodism to remain within the Church of England, it formally separated in 1791. □ **Wes·ley·an** *noun & adjective* **Wes·ley·an·ism** *noun*

Wes·sex /ˈwesəks/ the kingdom of the West Saxons, established in Hampshire in the early 6th c. and gradually expanded by conquest to include much of S England. Under Alfred the Great and his successors it formed the nucleus of the Anglo-Saxon kingdom of England. The name was revived in the 19th c. by Thomas Hardy to designate the southwestern counties of England (esp. Dorset) in which his novels are set.

West ▸ **1 Ben·ja·min** (1738–1820), US-born English painter. His portrait *The Death of General Wolfe* (1771) depicted its subject in contemporary rather than classical dress, signifying a new departure in English historical painting. **2 Mae** (1892–1980), US actress and dramatist. She made her name on Broadway in her comedies *Sex* (1926) and *Diamond Lil* (1928), which were memorable for their frank approach to sexuality; her films include *She Done Him Wrong* (1933) and *Klondike Annie* (1936). **3 Na·than·ael** (pseudonym of Nathan Weinstein) (1903–40), US novelist, who is known principally for two macabre and tragic novels, *Miss Lonelyhearts* (1933) and *The Day of the Locust* (1939).

west ● *noun* **1** the point of the horizon where the sun sets at the equinoxes (cardinal point 90° to the left of north). **2** the compass point corresponding to this. **3** the direction in which this lies. **4** (usu. **the West**) **a** Europe and the countries of the western hemisphere as distinguished from those of the regions or countries lying to the east of the Mediterranean, esp. China, Japan, and other countries of E Asia; the Occident in contrast to the Orient. **b** *hist.* the non-Communist countries of Europe and N America. **5** (usu. **the West**) **a** the western part of a country or city etc. **b** *Cdn* the part of the country west of the Ontario-Manitoba border. **c** *US* the States lying to the west of the Mississippi. **d** *hist.* the territory west of the Allegheny Mountains, outside of the Thirteen Colonies. **6** (**West**) *Bridge* a player occupying the position designated 'west'. ● *adjective* **1** toward, at, near, or facing west. **2** coming from the west (*west wind*). ● *adverb* **1** toward, at, or near the west. **2** (foll. by *of*) further west than. [Old English]

West Bank a region west of the Jordan River and northwest of the Dead Sea. It contains Jericho, Hebron, Nablus, Bethlehem, and other settlements; 97 per cent of its inhabitants are Palestinian Arabs. It became part of Jordan in 1948 and was occupied by Israel following the Six Day War of 1967. In 1993 an agreement was signed which granted limited autonomy to the Palestinians, including the withdrawal of Israeli troops and the establishment of a Palestinian police force; however, political unrest and violence have continued to plague the region. □ **West Banker** *noun*

West Bengal a state in E India; capital, Calcutta. It was formed in 1947 from the predominantly Hindu area of former Bengal. □ **West Bengali** /ˈbenˌɡoli, -ˈɡali/ *noun & adjective*

west·bound *adjective* travelling or leading westwards.

West Brom·wich /ˈbrɒmɪtʃ/ an industrial town in the West Midlands of England; pop. (est. 2002) 143,900.

West Country the southwestern counties of England.

West End *noun* **1** the district of London (England) lying between Charing Cross Road and Park Lane, noted for its many theatres and fashionable shops. **2** the western part of any city or town. □ **West Ender** *noun*

west·er *intransitive verb* (of the sun) travel westward; draw near the west. □ **west·er·ing** *adjective*

west·er·ly ● *adjective & adverb* **1** in a western position or direction. **2** (of a wind) blowing from the west. ● *noun* (*pl.* **-lies**) a wind blowing from the west.

west·ern ● *adjective* **1** of or in the west; inhabiting the west. **2** lying or directed toward the west. **3** (esp. of a wind) blowing from the west. **4** (**Western**) **a** of or relating to the Occident or (formerly) the non-Communist countries of Europe and N America (*see* WEST *noun* 4). **b** of or related to the Canadian or American West (*see* WEST *noun* 5). ● *noun* **1** a film or novel of a genre depicting life in the N American West in the 19th and early 20th c., usu. featuring cowboys in heroic roles, gunfights, etc. **2** *N Amer.* **a** = WESTERN SANDWICH. **b** = WESTERN OMELETTE. ● *adverb* (ride etc.) in the manner of a cowboy, in a relaxed style with a deep-seated saddle and almost straight legs.
□ **west·ern·most** *adjective*

Western Australia a state comprising the western part of Australia; pop. (est. 2001) 1,906,114; capital, Perth. □ **Western Australian** *noun & adjective*

Western blot *noun* *Biochem.* an adaptation of the Southern blot procedure, used to identify specific peptide and amino acid sequences (*compare* SOUTHERN BLOT). □ **Western blotting** *noun* [punningly after SOUTHERN BLOT]

Western Cape a province of SW South Africa, formerly part of Cape Province; capital, Cape Town.

Western Church *noun* the part of the Christian Church including the Catholic Church and the Protestant Churches, as distinct from the Orthodox or Eastern Churches.

Western Civ. *abbreviation* Western Civilization.

Western Cordillera the system of mountain ranges and intervening valleys etc. on the western side of N America.

Western Empire *see* ROMAN EMPIRE.

west·ern·er *noun* (also **Westerner**) a native or inhabitant of the western part of any country or of any country of the western hemisphere.

Western Front the zone of fighting in western Europe in the First World War, in which the German army engaged the armies to its west. Trench warfare was the front's distinctive feature; battles were inconclusive with heavy casualties on both sides.

Western Ghats *see* GHATS, THE.

western hemisphere *noun* the half of the earth containing North and South America and the surrounding waters.

Western Isles 1 an alternative name for the Hebrides (see HEBRIDES, THE). **2** an administrative region of Scotland, consisting of the Outer Hebrides; administrative centre, Stornoway.

west·ern·ize *transitive verb* (also **Westernize, -ise**) influence with or convert to Western ideas and customs etc., esp. the ideas and customs of Occidental countries. □ **west·ern·iz·a·tion** *noun* **west·ern·iz·er** *noun*

western omelette *noun* *N Amer.* an omelette made with diced onion, ham, and often green peppers.

Western provinces *plural noun* Manitoba, Alberta, Saskatchewan, and British Columbia (*compare* ATLANTIC PROVINCES, CENTRAL PROVINCES).

western red cedar *noun see* RED CEDAR.

Western Roman Empire *see* ROMAN EMPIRE.

Western Sahara a region of NW Africa, on the Atlantic coast between Morocco and Mauritania; pop. (est. 2002) 256,177; capital, La'youn. The region was formerly an overseas Spanish province, called Spanish Sahara. □ **Western Saharan** *adjective*

Western Samoa *see* SAMOA. □ **Western Samoan** *noun & adjective*

western sandwich *noun* *N Amer.* a toasted sandwich in which the filling is a western omelette.

Western Wall *noun* the remaining part of the wall of Herod's temple in Jerusalem destroyed in AD 70, where Jews traditionally pray and lament on Fridays. *Also called* WAILING WALL.

western yew *noun see* PACIFIC YEW.

Western Zhou *see* ZHOU.

West Flanders a province of NW Belgium; capital, Bruges. (See also FLANDERS.)

West Germanic *noun* a group of the Germanic branch of Indo-European languages that includes High and Low German, English, Frisian, and Dutch.

West Germany *hist.* the Federal Republic of Germany (see GERMANY).

West Glamorgan a former county of S Wales, formed in 1974 and dissolved in 1996.

West Highland white terrier *noun* (also **West·ie**) a small terrier with short legs, a white coat, and an erect tail and ears.

West Indian satinwood *noun see* SATINWOOD 1b.

West Indies *noun* a chain of islands extending from the Florida peninsula to the coast of Venezuela, lying between the Caribbean and the Atlantic. They consist of three main island groups: the Greater and Lesser Antilles and the Bahamas, with Bermuda lying further to the north. The islands presently comprise a number of independent states and British, French, Dutch, and US dependencies. □ **West Indian** *adjective & noun* [named by Columbus in 1492 because he thought he had discovered the coast of India]

west·ing *noun* *Naut.* the distance travelled westward as measured from either a defined north–south grid line or a meridian.

West·ing·house, George (1846–1914), US engineer. He held over 400 patents, but is best known for vacuum-operated safety brakes on railway vehicles and electrically controlled signals for railways; he championed the use of alternating current (through Nikola Tesla), and built up a huge company to manufacture his products.

West·lock a town in central Alberta, situated about 80 km north of Edmonton; pop. (2001) 4,817. [blend of *Westgate* + *Lock*hart, two early settlers *c.*1912]

West·meath /westˈmiːð/ a county of the Republic of Ireland, in the province of Leinster; county town, Mullingar.

West Midlands a former metropolitan county of central England.

West·min·ster /ˈwestˌmɪnstər/ (also **City of Westminster**) an inner borough of London (England), which contains the Houses of Parliament and many government offices. The name is used allusively to refer to the British Parliament.

Westminster, Statute of *noun* a statute of 1931 recognizing the equality of status of the Commonwealth dominions as autonomous communities within the British Empire, and giving their legislatures independence from British control.

Westminster chimes *plural noun* the pattern of chimes struck at successive quarters by Big Ben in the British Houses of Parliament, used for other clocks and doorbells.

Westminster Confession *noun* a statement of Presbyterian doctrine adopted by the General Assembly at Edinburgh in 1647.

West·mor·land /ˈwestmərlənd/ a former county of NW England. In 1974 it was united with Cumberland and northern parts of Lancashire to form the county of Cumbria.

West·mount a former city in south central Quebec, now part of the city of Montreal; pop. (2001) 19,727. Traditionally, the community of Westmount is an enclave of wealthy anglophones. □ **West·mount·er** *noun* [so called with reference to its location on the western slope of Mount Royal]

West Nile virus *noun* (also **West Nile fever**) a mosquito-borne virus and the disease it causes, usu. a mild fever but sometimes a fatal encephalitis. [from the West part of the Nile river, where the virus originated]

West Nipissing a town in NE central Ontario, about 35 km west of North Bay, including the former town of Sturgeon Falls and surrounding area; pop. (2001) 13,114.

west-northwest *noun* the direction or compass point midway between west and northwest.

Wes·ton, Wil·lard Gar·field (1893–1978), Canadian manufacturer. The son of biscuit manufacturer George Weston, he took over the family business in 1924, and developed it into one of the largest food conglomerates in Canada, expanding into the international market.

Weston-super-Mare /ˌwestənˌsuːpərˈmer/ a resort in SW England, on the Bristol Channel; pop. (2002) 73,400.

West·phal·ia /westˈfeɪlɪə/ a former province of NW Germany. In 1946 the major part of the province was incorporated in the state of North Rhine–Westphalia, the northern portion becoming part of Lower Saxony. □ **West·phal·ian** *noun & adjective*

Westphalia, Treaty of the peace (1648) which ended the Thirty Years War.

West Pointer *noun* an officer trained at the US military academy at West Point, in SE New York State.

West Side *noun* the western part of any of several N American cities or boroughs, esp. the island borough of Manhattan, New York.

west-southwest *noun* the direction or compass point midway between west and southwest.

West Sussex a county of SE England; county town, Chichester. It was formed in 1974 from part of the former county of Sussex.

Vowels: a *cat* ɑ *arm* e *bed* ɜr *her* ɜː *deux* ə *ago* ɪ *sit* i *cosy* iː *feed* ɒ *hot* ɔ *pore* oː *no* ʌ *run* ʊ *put*

West Vancouver a district municipality in southwestern BC, lying to the west of North Vancouver; pop. (2001) 41,421.

West Virginia a state of the eastern US; pop. (est. 2000) 1,808,344; capital, Charleston. It separated from Virginia during the American Civil War (1861) and became the 35th state of the US in 1863. □ **West Virginian** *noun & adjective*

west·ward ● *adjective & adverb* (also **west·wards**) toward the west. ● *noun* a westward direction or region.

West Yorkshire a former metropolitan county of N England.

wet ● *adjective* (**wet·ter**, **wet·test**) **1** covered, dampened, or soaked with water or another liquid (*my hands are wet; a wet towel*). **2** (of the weather etc.) rainy (*a wet day; the wet season*). **3** (of paint, ink, etc.) not yet dried. **4** used or done with water (*wet shampoo; a wet shave*). **5** (of ingredients in a recipe) liquid, such as water, oil, eggs, etc. **6** (of a baby) having urinated; having a diaper that needs to be changed. **7** *informal* **a** of or pertaining to alcohol, esp. as drunk in substantial quantities (*a wet lunch*). **b** (of a country, of legislation, etc.) favouring or permitting the sale of alcohol. **8** esp. *Brit. informal* feeble, inept. **9** *slang* (of the activities of an intelligence organization, esp. the KGB) involving bloodshed, esp. assassination. **10** *Brit. Politics informal* (of a politician) Conservative with liberal tendencies. ● *transitive verb* (**wet·ting**; *past* and *past participle* **wet** or **wet·ted**) **1** dampen, soak, make wet. **2 a** urinate in or on (*wet the bed*). **b** *reflexive* urinate involuntarily (*I laughed so hard I nearly wet myself*). ● *noun* **1** moisture; liquid that makes something wet. **2** precipitation or a period of this (*come in out of the wet*). **3** esp. *Brit. informal* a feeble or inept person. **4** *informal* a person who is in favour of the sale and consumption of alcohol. **5** *Fishing* = WET FLY. **6** *Brit. Politics informal* a Conservative politician with liberal tendencies. □ **all wet** *N Amer.* completely wrong or mistaken. **wet the baby's head** *informal* celebrate the birth of a baby with a drink. **wet behind the ears** immature, inexperienced. **wet through** (or **to the skin**) with one's clothes soaked. **wet one's whistle** *informal* drink. □ **wetly** *adverb* **wet·ness** *noun* **wettable** *adjective* **wet·ting** *noun* **wet·tish** *adjective* [Old English *wǣt* (adj. & n.), *wǣtan* (v.), related to WATER: in Middle English replaced by past participle of the verb]

Wet·as·ki·win /wəˈtaskəwɪn/ a city in central Alberta, about 75 km south of Edmonton; pop. (2001) 11,154. [ultimately from Cree *Witaskiwinik* place of peace, with reference to a nearby site where the Cree and Blackfoot made peace *c.*1867]

wet·back *noun US informal* or *derogatory* a Mexican labourer who enters the US illegally. [originally with reference to the practice of swimming across the Rio Grande from Mexico to the US]

wet bar *noun N Amer.* a bar or counter in the home equipped with a sink and running water, from which drinks are served.

wet blanket *noun informal* a person who spoils the fun of others by a lack of enthusiasm.

wet dream *noun* an erotic dream with involuntary ejaculation of semen.

wet fly *noun* an artificial fly allowed to sink below the surface of the water.

weth·er /ˈweðər/ *noun* a castrated ram. [Old English]

wet·land *noun* (often in *pl.*) a marsh, swamp, bog, or other stretch of land that is frequently saturated with water (also *attributive*: *wetland vegetation*).

wet look ● *noun* **1** a shiny surface given esp. to clothing materials. **2** a shiny or wet appearance achieved by applying a type of gel to the hair. ● *attributive adjective* (**wet-look**) having or giving a shiny or wet appearance.

wet nurse ● *noun* a woman employed to breastfeed another's baby. ● *transitive verb* (usu. **wet-nurse**) **1** breastfeed (another's baby). **2** *informal* treat as if helpless; pamper, spoil.

wet snow *noun* large cohesive flakes of snow that fall when the temperature is above or slightly below the freezing point, accumulating in dense heavy masses.

wet·suit *noun* a close-fitting one-piece rubber garment worn by scuba divers, surfers, etc., to protect them from the cold.

Wet'suwet'en /wətˈsuːwətˌen/ ● *noun* **1** a member of an Aboriginal people living in north-central BC, along the Skeena River. **2** the Athapaskan language of this people. ● *adjective* of or relating to this people or their language or culture. [Wet'suwet'en, = 'of the lower drainage']

wetting agent *noun* a chemical that can be added to a liquid to reduce its surface tension and allow it to penetrate or spread over a material more easily.

wet·ware *noun* brain cells regarded as chemical materials organized so as to perform arithmetic or logical operations. [after HARDWARE, SOFTWARE]

we've *contraction* we have.

Wex·ford /ˈweksfərd/ **1** a county of the Republic of Ireland, in the southeast in the province of Leinster. **2** its county town, a port on the Irish Sea; pop. (2002) 16,500.

Wey·burn /ˈweibɜrn/ a city in SE central Saskatchewan, situated on the Souris River, 115 km southeast of Regina; pop. (2001) 9,534. [the name of a CPR construction contractor, or perhaps the name of his brother-in-law *c.*1893]

Wey·den /ˈvaidən/ **Ro·gier van der** (French name Rogier de la Pasture) (*c.*1400–64), Flemish painter, who was particularly influential in the development of Dutch portrait painting; his major works include *The Last Judgement* and *The Deposition in the Tomb* (both *c.*1450).

Wey·mouth /ˈweiməθ/ a resort and port on the coast of Dorset, S England; pop. (est. 2002) 53,000.

w.f. *abbreviation* wrong font.

WFTU *abbreviation* World Federation of Trade Unions.

WHA *abbreviation N Amer. hist.* World Hockey Association.

whack *informal* ● *transitive verb* **1** strike or beat forcefully with a sharp slap or blow. **2** *N Amer. slang* kill. ● *noun* **1** a sharp or resounding blow. **2** *slang* a turn; an attempt. **3** *slang* **a** esp. *Brit.* a share or portion. **b** (usu. foll. by *of*) a large number or amount (*a whole whack of people*). □ **have** (or **take**) **a whack at** *slang* attempt. **out of whack** esp. *N Amer. slang* **1** out of order; malfunctioning. **2** (of calculations, figures, etc.) maladjusted, skewed, awry. **whack off** *N Amer. coarse slang* masturbate. □ **whack·er** *noun* **whack·ing** *noun* [imitative, or alteration of THWACK]

whacked *adjective* (also **wacked**) **1** (usu. foll. by *out*) esp. *N Amer.* **a** mad, crazy, wild. **b** high or intoxicated on drugs or alcohol. **2** (sometimes foll. by *out*) tired out; exhausted.

whack·ing esp. *Brit. informal* ● *adjective* very large. ● *adverb* very (*whacking great news*).

whacko[1] *interjection Brit. slang* expressing delight or enjoyment.

whacko[2] *var. of* WACKO.

whacky *var. of* WACKY.

whale[1] *noun* (*pl.* **whales** or **whale**) any of various large marine mammals of the order Cetacea, having a streamlined fishlike body, forelimbs modified as fins, and a tail with horizontal flukes, and which breathes through a nasal opening on top of the head. □ **a whale of a** *informal* an exceptionally good or large etc. [Old English *hwæl*]

whale[2] *transitive verb* esp. *N Amer. informal* beat, thrash. [var. of WALE]

whale·back *noun* **1** anything shaped like a whale's back (also *attributive*: *whaleback waves*). **2** a large elongated mound, hill, or sand dune.

whale·boat *noun* a long narrow double-bowed boat formerly used for whaling, now used esp. as a lifeboat.

whale·bone *noun* **1** an elastic horny substance which grows in a series of thin parallel plates in the upper jaw of baleen whales, serving to strain plankton from the sea water. *Also called* BALEEN. **2** a strip of this esp. used as a stiffening in stays and dresses etc.

whale oil *noun* oil from the blubber of whales.

whal·er *noun* (also **whale·man**) a person engaged in the business of whaling. **2 a** a ship used in whaling. **b** a whaleboat.

whale shark *noun* a large tropical whale-like shark, *Rhincodon typus*, feeding on plankton close to the surface, the largest living fish.

whale-watch *N Amer.* ● *noun* an excursion made by boat in the hope of observing whales in their natural habitat. ● *intransitive verb* go on an excursion to observe whales.

whal·ing *noun* the hunting and killing of whales, esp. for their oil, meat, or whalebone.

wham *informal* ● *noun* the sound of forcible impact. ● *interjection* expressing such a sound. ● *verb* (**whammed**, **wham·ming**) **1** *intransitive* make such a sound or impact. **2** *transitive* strike with force. □ **wham-bam** *informal* (esp. with reference to sexual intercourse) (with) quick forceful or violent action (also *attributive*: *wham-bam techniques*). [imitative]

whammy *noun* (*pl.* **-mies**) esp. *US informal* **1** an evil or unlucky influence; a hex or curse. **2** (esp. in phr. **double whammy**) a powerful or unpleasant effect or a problematic situation. [20th c.: from WHAM + -Y[1]]

whammy bar *noun Music* a bar or lever attached to the bridge of an electric guitar which, when depressed, lowers the tension of the strings to reduce their pitch, with repeated depression and release producing a tremolo effect.

whang *informal* ● *verb* **1** *intransitive* produce a loud resonating or ringing sound under or as if under a forceful blow. **2** *transitive & intransitive* strike heavily and loudly. ● *noun* a loud resonating or ringing sound or blow. [imitative]

whan·gee /waŋˈgiː/ *noun* **1** a Chinese or Japanese bamboo of the genus *Phyllostachys*. **2** a cane made from this. [Chinese *huang* old bamboo sprouts]

whap /wɒp, wap/ *esp. N Amer.* ● *noun* **1** a hard slap as if with a flat object or the palm of the hand. **2** the sound of this. ● *transitive verb* strike or slap forcefully, esp. with or as if with a flat object or the palm of the hand. [Middle English: dial. *wap*, of unknown origin]

wharf ● *noun* (*pl.* **wharves** or **wharfs**) a level quayside structure to which a ship may be moored to load and unload. ● *transitive verb* **1** moor (a ship) at a wharf. **2** unload and store (goods) on a wharf. [Old English *hwearf*]

wharf·age *noun* **1** the provision of accommodation or storage at a wharf. **2** a fee for this.

wharf·in·ger /ˈwɔrfɪndʒɜr/ *noun* an owner or keeper of a wharf. [prob. ultimately from WHARFAGE]

Whar·ton, Edith (New·bold) (1862–1937), US novelist and short-story writer. Her novels, many of them set in New York high society, are chiefly preoccupied with the often tragic conflict between social and individual fulfillment; they include *The House of Mirth* (1905), *Ethan Frome* (1911) and *The Age of Innocence* (1920).

wharves *pl.* of WHARF.

what ● *interrogative adjective* **1** used in asking the identity of a choice made from an indefinite or definite set of alternatives (*what books have you read?*). **2** *informal* = WHICH *interrogative adjective* (*what book have you chosen?*). ● *adjective* (usu. in exclamation) how great or remarkable (*what luck!*). ● *relative adjective* the or any...that (*will give you what help I can*). ● *pronoun* (corresponding to the functions of the *adj.*) **1 a** used in asking the identity or name of a thing or things specified, indicated, or understood (*what is wrong?; I don't know what you mean*). **b** used in asking the character, function, occupation, etc. of a person or persons specified, indicated, or understood (*what are you going to be when you grow up?*). **2** (asking for a remark to be repeated) = what did you say? **3** asking for repetition, clarification, or confirmation of something disputed or not completely understood (*you did what?; what, you want me to do it?*). **4 a** how much (*what pain you must have suffered!; what is it going to cost?*). **b** how great (*what a save!*). **5** (prec. by *or*) *informal* representing the unknown final alternative in a set of proposed options (*I didn't know if she was scared, nervous, or what; is this terrific or what!*). **6** (as relative *pron.*) that or those which; a, the, or any thing which (*what followed was worse; tell me what you think*). ● *adverb* to what extent (*what does it matter?*). ● *interjection* **1** expressing surprise or astonishment (*what, that's it?*). **2** expressing disbelief and inviting repetition or confirmation of a previous remark. □ **what about** what is your position on or opinion of (*what about me?; what about a game of tennis?*). **what for** *informal* **1** why? for what reason? **2** a severe reprimand (esp. in phr. **give a person what for**). **what have you** *informal* (prec. by *or*) anything else similar. **what if? 1** what would result etc. if. **2** what would it matter if. **what is more** and as an additional point; moreover. **what next?** *informal* what more absurd, shocking, or surprising thing is possible? **what of?** what is the news concerning? **what of it?** why should that be considered significant? **what's his** (or **her**) **name** (also **what's his** (or **her**) **face**) a person whose name one cannot recall, does not know, or does not wish to specify. **what's what** *informal* what things are useful or important. **what's with** *informal* what is the matter with? what has happened to? what is the reason for? **what with** *informal* on account of; because of (usu. several things). [Old English *hwæt*]

what·chama·callit /ˈwʌtʃəməˌkɒlɪt, wɒt-/ (also **what·cha·callit** /ˈwʌtʃəˌkɒlɪt, wɒt-/, **what-d'you-call-it**) *noun* a thing the proper name of which one cannot recall, does not know, or does not wish to mention. [representing a pronunciation of *what you may call it*]

what·ever ● *pronoun* **1** anything or everything (*lend me whatever you can; do whatever it takes*). **2** no matter what (*whatever happens, I'll be ready; whatever it is, it's coming this way*). **3** representing an unknown final alternative, usu. in a set of proposed options (*he'll drink wine, beer, whatever*). **4** what in any way (*whatever can you mean?*) ● *adjective* **1** any...that (*whatever money you can lend me will help*). **2** any; no matter what (*whatever garbage he writes sells*). **3** (used as a perfunctory designation of anything a speaker is reluctant or unable to describe

specifically) denoting an unnamed person or thing (*for whatever reason, she left early*). **4** = WHATSOEVER *adjective* 1.

what-if ● *adjective* based on speculation or conjecture; hypothetical. ● *noun* speculation as to what might have been had antecedent conditions been different.

what·not *noun* **1** (usu. prec. by *and*) other similar items (*a drawer full of paper, pens, and whatnot*). **2** an unspecified or trivial thing. **3** a stand with shelves used for keeping or displaying small objects.

what say ● *interjection* pardon? what did you say? ● *adverb* indicating a suggestion or proposition to which a reply is expected (*what say we go to a movie?*).

whats·it *noun* **1** = WHATCHAMACALLIT. **2** = WHAT'S HIS NAME (see WHAT). [representing a pronunciation of *what is it (called)*]

what·so·ever ● *adjective* **1** (predicative; with *neg.*) at all; of any kind (*there is no doubt whatsoever*). **2** *archaic* = WHATEVER *adjective* 1, 2. ● *pronoun archaic* = WHATEVER *pronoun* 1, 2.

wheat *noun* **1** any cereal plant of the genus *Triticum*, bearing dense four-sided seed spikes. **2** its grain, used in making flour etc. □ **separate the wheat from the chaff** see CHAFF. [Old English *hwǣte* from Germanic, related to WHITE]

wheat berry *noun* a whole wheat kernel.

Wheat Board *noun* *Cdn* a Crown corporation responsible for the sale of all wheat and barley produced in Western Canada and destined for export or domestic human consumption.

wheat·ear /ˈwiːtɪr/ *noun* any small migratory bird of the mainly Old World genus *Oenanthe*, esp. with a white belly and rump. [apparently from *wheatears* (see WHITE, ARSE)]

wheat·en *adjective* **1** made of the grain or flour of wheat. **2** of the colour of ripe wheat, usu. a pale gold.

wheaten terrier *noun* a soft-coated breed of terrier originally developed in Ireland and distinguished by its pale golden wavy coat.

wheat germ *noun* the embryo of the wheat grain.

wheat grass *noun* any of several N American grasses of the genus *Agropyron*, grown as fodder.

wheat·meal *noun* *Brit.* flour made from wheat with some of the bran and germ removed.

wheat pool *noun* *Cdn* a grain farmers' co-operative in Western Canada for the sale of wheat and other cereal crops.

Wheat·stone, Sir Charles (1802–75), English physicist and inventor. In the 1830s he collaborated with Sir W. F. Cooke (1806–79) to develop the electric telegraph, and he later devised the Wheatstone bridge (based on an idea of the mathematician Samuel Christie) and the rheostat.

Wheatstone bridge *noun* an apparatus for measuring electrical resistances by equalizing the potential at two points of a circuit. [WHEATSTONE]

whee *interjection* expressing delight or excitement. [imitative]

whee·dle *verb* **1** *transitive & intransitive* attempt to coax or persuade (a person) by flattery or endearments. **2** *transitive* (often foll. by *out*) talk or coax a person into giving up possession of (something); obtain or acquire by wheedling. □ **wheed·ler** *noun* **wheed·ling** *adjective* **wheed·ling·ly** *adverb* [perhaps from German *wedeln* fawn, cringe, from *Wedel* tail]

wheel ● *noun* **1** a solid disc or circular frame with spokes radiating from the centre, attached or able to be attached at its centre to an axle around which it revolves, used to facilitate the motion of a vehicle or for various mechanical purposes. **2** anything resembling a wheel in function or appearance (*roulette wheel; a wheel of brie*). **3** a machine etc. of which a wheel is an essential part (*spinning wheel; potter's wheel*). **4** (in *pl.*) *slang* a car. **5** = STEERING WHEEL. **6** a recurring course of actions or events; an endless cycle (*wheel of life*). **7** (in *pl.*, usu. foll. by *of*) the driving or animating force (*wheels of industry*). **8** a motion like that of a wheel, esp. the movement of a line of people with one end as a pivot. **9** *hist.* a large wheel used in various ways as an instrument of torture. **10** *slang* a person of considerable importance; a big wheel. **11** a set of short lines concluding a stanza. ● *verb* **1** *transitive & intransitive* turn or rotate on an axis or pivot. **2** (often foll. by *around, about*) **a** *intransitive* change direction or face another way, esp. quickly or suddenly. **b** *transitive* cause to do this. **3** *transitive* (often foll. by *in, out*) push or pull (a wheeled thing, esp. a cart, bicycle, or stroller, or its load or occupant). **4** *intransitive* move in circles or curves (*seagulls wheeled overhead*). **5** *intransitive* (of a line of people) swing around in line with one end as a pivot. □ **at the wheel 1** (also **behind the wheel**) driving a car or truck etc. **2** directing a ship. **3** in control of affairs. **wheel and deal** engage in political or commercial scheming. **wheels within

wheels 1 intricate machinery. **2** *informal* indirect or secret agencies. □ **wheeled** *adjective* (also in *combination*). **wheel·less** *adjective* **wheel-like** *adjective* [Old English *hwēol, hwēogol*]

wheel·barrow *noun* a shallow open container for moving small loads, with a wheel at one end and two legs and two handles at the other.

wheel·base *noun* the distance between the front and rear axles of a vehicle.

wheel·chair *noun* **1** a chair on wheels for an invalid or a disabled person. **2** (*attributive*) **a** designating a sport or activity participated in by athletes in wheelchairs (*wheelchair basketball*). **b** designating an athlete participating in such an activity.

wheel clamp *noun Brit.* a clamp for locking to the wheel of an illegally parked car or truck etc. in order to temporarily immobilize it.

Wheel·er, Anne (b.1946), Canadian filmmaker. She is known for her films *A War Story* (1981), based on her father's experiences as a Japanese POW, and *Cowboys Don't Cry* (1988); her films are distinguished by strong characters living through extraordinary times or situations.

wheel·er *noun* **1** (in *combination*) a vehicle having a specified number of wheels (*an 18-wheeler*). **2** a wheelwright. **3** = WHEELHORSE 1.

wheeler-dealer *noun* a person who wheels and deals (*see* WHEEL). □ **wheeler-dealing** *noun*

wheel·horse *noun N Amer.* **1** a horse harnessed next to the wheels of a vehicle or nearest the driver and behind another. **2** *informal* an experienced and conscientious member of a political party.

wheel·house *noun* **1** a structure enclosing a large wheel, esp. the structure on a ship containing the steering wheel. **2** *Baseball slang* the area over the plate where a pitch is most likely to be hit by a particular batter.

wheel·ie *noun slang* the stunt of riding a bicycle or motorcycle for a short distance with the front wheel off the ground. □ **pop a wheelie** perform this stunt.

wheel-lock *noun* **1** an old kind of gunlock having a steel wheel to rub against flint etc. **2** a gun with this type of gunlock.

wheel·man *noun* (*pl.* **-men**) esp. *US* **1** a driver of a wheeled vehicle, esp. the driver of a getaway car in a burglary or holdup. **2** a cyclist. **3** *Naut.* a helmsman.

wheel of Fortune *noun* the wheel which Fortune is fabled to turn in order to determine the fates of humans; a metaphor for luck and the mutability of personal circumstances.

wheels·man *noun* (*pl.* **-men**) *N Amer. Naut.* a steersman.

wheel·spin *noun* rotation of a vehicle's wheels without traction.

wheel·wright /ˈwiːlraɪt/ *noun* a person who makes or repairs esp. wooden wheels.

wheeze /wiːz/ ● *intransitive verb* **1** breathe with an audible congested whistling sound, due to dryness or obstruction of the air passages. **2** make a similar whistling or rasping sound (*the bus wheezed to a stop*). ● *noun* **1** a sound of or resembling wheezing. **2** *informal* **a** a hackneyed running joke or comic phrase. **b** *Brit.* a clever scheme. □ **wheez·er** *noun* **wheez·i·ly** *adverb* **wheez·i·ness** *noun* **wheezy** *adjective* [prob. from Old Norse *hvæsa* to hiss]

Whel·an /ˈweɪlən/ **Ed·ward** (1824–67), Irish-born Canadian journalist and politician. He was elected to the PEI legislative assembly in 1847. The leading journalistic voice supporting the Reformers on the question of Responsible Government, he was also a strong supporter of Confederation.

whelk¹ /welk/ *noun* any predatory marine gastropod mollusc of the family Buccinidae, esp. the edible kind of the genus *Baccinum*, having a spiral shell. [Old English *wioloc, weoloc*, of unknown origin: perhaps influenced by WHELK²]

whelk² *noun* a pimple. [Old English *hwylca* from *hwelian* suppurate]

whelm /welm/ *transitive verb archaic* **1** cover with a great mass of water or earth etc.; engulf. **2** overpower emotionally; overwhelm. [Old English *hwelman* (unrecorded) = *hwylfan* overturn]

whelp /welp/ ● *noun* **1 a** a young dog; a puppy. **b** the young of various other animals, such as seals or mink. **2 a** usu. *jocular* a young child. **b** an ill-mannered child or youth. ● *transitive & intransitive verb* (of a female animal, esp. a bitch or seal) give birth to (a whelp or whelps). □ **in whelp** (of a female animal) pregnant. [Old English *hwelp*]

when ● *interrogative adverb* **1** at what time? **2** how soon? **3** how long ago? **4** on what occasion? under what circumstances? (*when is it best to ask?*). ● *adverb N Amer. informal* in the past (*I can say I knew her when*). ● *relative adverb* (prec. by *time* etc.) at or on which (*there are times when I could cry*). ● *conjunction* **1 a** at the time that, on the occasion that (*come when it is convenient; when I was your age*). **b** at any time that, on any

occasion that (*I smile when I hear her voice*). **2** although; considering that (*why stand when you could sit?*). **3** at which time; after which; but just then (*he was nearly asleep when the phone rang*). **4** while on the contrary, whereas (*she gave me $5.00 when she really meant to give me $10.00*). ● *pronoun* what time? (*till when can you stay?; since when have you been married?*). ● *noun* time, occasion, date (*fixed the where and when*). [Old English *hwanne, hwenne*]

whence /wens/ *formal* ● *adverb* from what place? (*whence did they come?*). ● *conjunction* **1** to the place from which (*return whence you came*). **2** (often prec. by *place* etc.) from which (*the source whence these errors arise*). **3** and thence (*whence it follows that*). ¶ Although it is historically well-established, some speakers and writers of English avoid the expression *from whence* which they consider redundant on the grounds that *from* is implied in the meaning of *whence* and does not need to be repeated. [Middle English *whannes, whennes* from *whanne, whenne* from Old English *hwanon(e)* whence, formed as WHEN + -s³: compare THENCE]

whence·so·ever /ˌwenssoːˈevɜr/ *adverb & conjunction formal* from whatever place or source.

when·ever ● *conjunction & adverb* **1** at whatever time; on whatever occasion. **2** every time that. □ **or whenever** *informal* or at any similar time.

when-issued *adjective Finance* of or relating to trading in securities that have not yet been issued.

when·so·ever ● *conjunction & adverb formal* = WHENEVER.

where ● *interrogative adverb* **1** in or at what place or position? (*where is the milk?*). **2** to what place? (*where are you going?*). **3 a** in what book or passage of a book? (*where did you read that?*). **b** from whom? from what source? (*where did you hear that?*). **4** in what direction or respect? (*where are you going with this argument?; where does it concern us?*). **5** in what situation or condition? (*where does that leave us?*). **6** at what point or stage? (*where did we go wrong?*). ● *relative adverb* (prec. by *place* etc.) in or to which (*places where they meet*). ● *conjunction* **1** in, at, or to the place in which (*put it where we can all see it*). **2** in the situation or circumstances in which (*give credit where credit is due*). **3** *N Amer. informal* that (*I see where the jewellery store was robbed again*). ● *pronoun* what place? (*where do you come from?; where are you going to?*). ● *noun* a place, esp. the or a place at which something happens, has happened, or will happen (*see WHEN noun*). [Old English *hwǣr, hwār*]

where·abouts ● *adverb* /ˌweərəˈbʌuts/ where or approximately where? (*whereabouts are they?*). ● *noun* /ˈweərəˌbʌuts/ (treated as *sing.* or *pl.*) the place in or near which a person or thing is; the approximate location. ¶ Although it is more common for *whereabouts* to take a plural verb, it may be used correctly with a singular verb (*her whereabouts are not known; the whereabouts of the purse and its contents remains a mystery*).

where·after /werˈaftɜr/ *conjunction formal* after which.

where·as /werˈaz/ *conjunction* **1** in contrast or comparison with the fact that (*I like coffee whereas she will only drink tea*). **2** (esp. in legal preambles) taking into consideration the fact that; seeing that; since.

where·at /werˈat/ *conjunction archaic* **1** at which place or point. **2** for which reason.

where·by *conjunction* **1** by means of which; in which (*a process whereby public concerns may be expressed*). **2** according to which; under the terms of which (*a deal whereby she will receive a 10 per cent royalty*).

where·fore ● *adverb archaic* **1** for what cause, purpose, or reason? why? **2** on account of which; as a result of which. ● *conjunction formal* which being the case; for which reason. ● *noun* a reason (*never mind the whys and wherefores*).

where·from /werˈfrʌm, -ˈfrɒm/ *conjunction archaic* from which place, from where; whence.

where·in *formal* ● *conjunction* in which thing, matter, fact, place, etc. ● *adverb* in what place or respect?

where·of *formal* ● *conjunction* of which or whom (*the person whereof she writes*). ● *adverb* of what? □ **know whereof one speaks** recognize or understand what one is talking about.

where·on *archaic* ● *conjunction* on what or which. ● *adverb* on what?

where·so·ever *conjunction & adverb archaic or formal* = WHEREVER.

where·to *formal* ● *conjunction* to which. ● *adverb* to what?

where·upon /ˈweərəˌpɒn, ˌweərəˈpɒn/ *conjunction* upon the occurrence of which; immediately after and as a consequence of which.

wher·ever ● *adverb* in or to whatever place. ● *conjunction* in every place that. □ **or wherever** *informal* or in any similar place.

where·with /werˈwɪθ, -ˈwɪð/ *conjunction archaic* with which; by means of which.

where·with·al /ˈwerwɪˌθɒl, -ˌðɒl/ *noun informal* the means by which to do something.

---

t top   v voice   w we   z zoo   ʃ she   ʒ vision   θ thin   ð this   ŋ ring   x loch   tʃ chip   dʒ jar   (*see over for vowels*)

wher·ry /ˈweri/ *noun* (*pl.* **-ries**) **1** a light rowboat usu. for carrying passengers. **2** a large light barge. [Middle English: origin unknown]

whet /wet/ *transitive verb* (**whet·ted, whet·ting**) **1** sharpen (a tool or weapon). **2** stimulate (the appetite, a desire, interest, etc.). □ **whet·ter** *noun* (also in *combination*). [Old English *hwettan* from Germanic]

wheth·er *conjunction* **1** introducing an indirect question or an expression of doubt or choice between alternatives, in which the final alternative is introduced by *or* or *or whether* (*I'm not sure whether it's Monday or Tuesday*). **2** introducing an indirect question, simple inquiry, or opinion, in which the second alternative is implied only (*I wonder whether we should go; I doubt whether it matters*). **3** introducing a statement that is applicable whichever of the possibilities given is true (*whether he likes it or not, he has to do it*). [Old English *hwæther, hwether*]

whet·stone *noun* **1** a shaped fine-grained stone used to sharpen tools and cutlery etc. by grinding. **2** a thing that sharpens the senses etc.

whew /hwjuː/ *interjection* expressing relief, surprise, or exhaustion as from heat or exertion. [imitative: compare PHEW]

whey /wei/ *noun* the watery liquid that remains when milk forms curds. [Old English *hwæg, hweg* from Low German]

whey-faced *adjective* pale, esp. with fear or anxiety.

which ● *interrogative adjective* used in asking the identity of a choice from a definite set of alternatives (*which John are you talking about?; tell me which book you prefer; which way should we go?*). ● *relative adjective* being the thing or things just referred to, usu. introducing a clause not essential for identification (*the newspaper comes regularly at 6:00, by which time I am usually up; he might not come tonight, in which case I won't see him until tomorrow*). ● *interrogative pronoun* **1** which person or persons (*which of you is responsible?*). **2** which thing or things (*tell me which you prefer*). ● *relative pronoun* **1** introducing a clause that describes or states something additional about the antecedent but which is not essential for identification (compare THAT *pronoun* 5) (*this house, which happens to be for sale, was built in the 1880s*). **2** used in place of *that* after *in* or *that* (*there is the house in which I was born; that which you have just seen*). □ **which is which** a phrase used when two or more people or things are difficult to distinguish from each other. [Old English *hwilc*]

which·ev·er *adjective & pronoun* **1** either or any of a definite set of people or things that (*take whichever you like; take whichever one you like*). **2** no matter which (*whichever one wins, they both get a prize*).

which·so·ev·er *adjective & pronoun archaic* = WHICHEVER.

whick·er /ˈwɪkər/ ● *intransitive verb* (of a horse) give a soft breathy whinny. ● *noun* such a whinny or similar sound. [imitative]

whid·ah *var. of* WHYDAH.

whiff ● *noun* **1** a puff or breath of air, smoke, etc. (*we came outside for a whiff of fresh air*). **2** a smell or odour (*he caught the whiff of her perfume as she passed*). **3** (foll. by *of*) a trace or suggestion (*a whiff of danger*). **4** *Baseball informal* a strikeout. ● *verb* **1** *transitive* sniff, get a slight smell of. **2** *transitive & intransitive* blow or puff lightly. **3** *Baseball informal* **a** *intransitive* (of a batter) strike out. **b** *transitive* (of a pitcher) strike (a batter) out. [imitative]

whif·fle /ˈwɪfəl/ ● *verb* **1** *transitive & intransitive* (of the wind) blow gently. **2** *transitive* make the sound of or like wind blowing gently. **3** *transitive & intransitive* flutter (*the bird whiffled its feathers; leaves whiffled in the wind*). ● *noun* a slight movement of air.

whiffle·tree /ˈwɪfəlˌtriː/ *noun N Amer.* = SWINGLETREE. [var. of WHIPPLETREE]

whiffy /ˈwɪfi/ *adjective* (**whiff·i·er, whiff·i·est**) *informal* having an unpleasant smell.

Whig /wɪg/ *noun hist.* **1** a member of the English (later British) reforming and constitutional party that after 1688 sought the supremacy of Parliament and was eventually succeeded in the 19th c. by the Liberal Party (*opp.* TORY 3). **2 a** a member of a 19th-c. US political party established in 1834 in opposition to the Democratic Party, favouring a protective tariff and strong central government, succeeded by the Republican Party. **b** a colonist who supported the American Revolution. □ **Whig·gery** *noun* **Whig·gish** *adjective* [prob. a shortening of Scots *whiggamer, -more*, nickname of 17th-c. Scottish rebels, from *whig* to drive + MARE¹]

while ● *noun* a period of time considered with respect to its duration, usu. a relatively short one (*we waited for a while, then left; a short while ago I received this letter*). ● *conjunction* **1** during the time that (*while we were away our house was broken into*). **2** in spite of the fact that (*while I admit there are problems, I believe they can be resolved*). **3** when on the contrary; whereas (*I take my coffee black while they prefer theirs with cream*). ● *transitive verb* (foll. by *away*) pass (a period of time) in a leisurely or pleasant

manner. ● *relative adverb* (prec. by *time* etc.) during which; when (*the summer while I was abroad*). □ **all the while** during the whole time (that). **worth while** (or **worth one's while**) worth the time or effort spent; worth doing, beneficial, profitable, advantageous. [Old English *hwil*: (conj.) abbreviation of Old English *thā hwīle the*, Middle English *the while that*]

whiles *conjunction archaic* = WHILE. [originally in the adverbs *somewhiles, otherwhiles*]

whil·om /ˈwailəm/ *archaic* ● *adverb* formerly, once. ● *adjective* former, erstwhile (*my whilom friend*). [Old English *hwīlum* dative pl. of *hwīl* WHILE]

whilst /wailst/ *adverb & conjunction* esp. *Brit.* while. [WHILES: compare AGAINST]

whim *noun* **1** a spontaneous and unaccountable idea or decision; a fanciful or capricious notion. **2** capriciousness. [17th c.: origin unknown]

whim·brel /ˈwɪmbrəl/ *noun* a small curlew, esp. *Numenius phaeopus*, with a striped head and a trilling call. [WHIMPER (imitative): compare DOTTEREL]

whim·per ● *verb* **1** *intransitive* make feeble, querulous, or plaintive sounds expressive of fear, pain, or distress; cry and whine softly. **2** *transitive* say in a whimpering voice. ● *noun* **1** a feeble intermittent cry; a whimpering sound. **2** a dull, disappointing, or anticlimactic note or tone (*the conference ended on a whimper*). □ **whim·per·ing·ly** *adverb* [imitative, from dial. *whimp* 'to whimper', of imitative origin]

whim·si·cal /ˈwɪmzəkəl/ *adjective* **1** spontaneous; inspired by whim. **2 a** proceeding from whimsy; imaginative or playful (*a whimsical sense of humour*). **b** unconventional, fanciful, or quaint (*a whimsical set of furnishings*). □ **whim·si·cal·i·ty** /-ˈkaləti/ *noun* **whim·si·cal·ly** *adverb*

whim·sy /ˈwɪmzi/ *noun* (*pl.* **-sies**) **1** an unpredictable, fanciful, or playful quality or condition. **2** a spontaneous or capricious notion or fancy; a whim. [related to WHIM-WHAM: compare *flimsy*]

whim-wham /ˈwɪmwam/ *noun archaic* **1** a toy or trinket. **2** = WHIM 1. [reduplication: origin uncertain]

whin /wɪn/ *noun* (in *sing.* or *pl.*) gorse. [prob. Scandinavian: compare Norwegian *hvine*, Swedish *hven*]

whin·chat /ˈwɪntʃat/ *noun* a small brownish songbird, *Saxicola rubetra*, of Eurasia and N Africa. [WHIN + CHAT²]

whine ● *noun* **1** a subdued, prolonged, plaintive cry or wail suggesting pain, distress, or complaint. **2** a shrill prolonged sound resembling this. **3 a** a complaining tone of voice. **b** an instance of feeble or undignified complaining. ● *verb* **1** *intransitive* emit or utter a whine. **2** *intransitive* complain in a querulous tone, esp. about unimportant things. **3** *transitive* say or express in a whining tone. □ **whin·er** *noun* **whin·ing·ly** *adverb* **whiny** *adjective* (**whin·i·er, whin·i·est**) (also **whiney**). [Old English *hwīnan*]

whing·ding *var. of* WINGDING.

whinge /wɪndʒ/ (*pres. part.* **whin·ging, whinge·ing**) esp. *Brit. informal* ● *intransitive verb* whine or grumble in a peevish complaining manner; gripe. ● *noun* a peevish complaint or gripe. □ **whin·ger** *noun* [Old English *hwinsian* from Germanic]

whinny /ˈwɪni/ ● *noun* (*pl.* **-nies**) **1** a gentle high-pitched neigh, usu. expressing pleasure. **2** a sound resembling this. ● *intransitive verb* (**-nies, -nied**) give a whinny. [imitative: compare WHINE]

whip ● *noun* **1** a flexible switch or a rod with a leather lash attached, used for urging animals on or for flogging. **2 a** a member of a political party appointed to monitor and control its conduct and tactics and to ensure the attendance and voting of its members in debates. **b** the whips' written notice requesting or requiring attendance for voting at a division etc., variously underlined according to the degree of urgency (*three-line whip*). **c** (prec. by *the*) the discipline and instructions associated with being a member of a party. **3** a light fluffy dessert made with whipped cream or beaten eggs. **4** a slender unbranched shoot. **5** a simple rope-and-pulley apparatus for hoisting light objects. ● *verb* (**whipped, whip·ping**) **1** *transitive* beat or urge with a whip. **2** *transitive* (usu. foll. by *into*) bring (a person) into a usu. specified condition or state (*he whipped them into a fury; she whipped us into shape*). **3** *transitive* beat (cream or eggs etc.) into a froth. **4** *intransitive* move suddenly or quickly (*she whipped around in time to see him; the car whipped past us; I have to whip out to the store*). **5** *transitive informal* throw or propel with great force or speed (*she whipped the ball*). **6** *transitive slang* defeat convincingly (*he whipped me in the race*). **7** *transitive Fishing* cast a line over (a stretch of water) repeatedly. **8** *transitive* wind rope or twine around (something) to bind it. **9** *transitive Brit. slang* steal (*who whipped my pen?*). **10** *transitive* sew with overcast stitches. □ **whip off 1** remove (an article of clothing) hurriedly. **2** produce or complete in a short amount

Vowels:　a cat　ɑ arm　e bed　ɜr her　ɜː deux　ə ago　ɪ sit　i cosy　iː feed　ɒ hot　ɔ pore　oː no　ʌ run　ʊ put

of time. **whip on** urge into action. **whip out** draw out or remove suddenly (*whipped out a knife*). **whip up 1** prepare in a short amount of time or with ease (*whipped up a meal*). **2** excite or stir up (feeling etc.). □ **whip·less** *adjective* **whip-like** *adjective* **whip·per** *noun* [Middle English (h)*wippen* (v.), prob. from Middle Low German & Middle Dutch *wippen* swing, leap, dance]

whip·cord *noun* **1** a strong ribbed worsted fabric. **2** a tightly twisted cord such as is used for making the lash of a whip.

whip hand *noun* **1** the hand in which one holds the whip used to urge a horse. **2** (usu. prec. by *the*) the advantage or control in a situation.

whip kick *noun* a type of kick used with some swimming strokes, e.g. breaststroke, elementary backstroke, etc., in which the lower legs are bent, rotated outwards, and brought quickly back together in a horizontal position.

whip·lash ● *noun* **1** damage to the neck or spine caused by a severe jerk of the head, esp. as in a car accident. **2** the flexible end of a whip. **3** a blow with a whip. **4** a sharp reaction; a backlash. ● *verb* **1** *transitive* shake or jerk violently causing a whiplash effect. **2** *intransitive* move suddenly and forcefully like the lash of a whip.

whipped *adjective* **1** that has been whipped. **2** *N Amer. informal* tired, exhausted.

whipped cream *noun* heavy cream beaten until stiff and used as a topping or filling for desserts.

whipped topping *noun* an artificial substitute for whipped cream.

whip·per·snap·per *noun* **1** a presumptuous or intrusive young person. **2** a child. [perhaps for *whipsnapper*, implying noise and unimportance]

Whip·per·snip·per *noun* *Cdn & Austral. proprietary* a hand-held motorized garden tool used to trim grass, weeds, etc.

whip·pet /ˈwɪpɪt/ *noun* a dog of a breed that is a cross between a greyhound and a terrier or spaniel, used for racing. [prob. from obsolete *whippet* move briskly, from *whip it*]

whip·ping *noun* **1** a beating or flogging with a whip. **2** *Sport* a sound defeat. **3** cord used to wind around or bind something.

whipping boy *noun* **1** a person blamed for the mistakes or incompetence of another, esp. a superior; a scapegoat. **2** *hist.* a boy educated with a young prince and punished instead of him.

whipping cream *noun* heavy cream, usu. with 35% milk fat, often with stabilizers and thickeners added so as to be suitable for whipping.

whipping post *noun* *hist.* a post to which offenders were tied for public whippings.

whipple·tree /ˈwɪpəlˌtriː/ *noun* = SWINGLETREE. [apparently from WHIP + TREE]

whip·poor·will /ˈwɪpərˌwɪl/ *noun* a N American bird of the goatsucker family, *Caprimulgus vociferus*, with a loud cry uttered repeatedly at dusk and during the night. [imitative of its cry]

whippy *adjective* (**whip·pi·er**, **whip·pi·est**) flexible, springy. □ **whip·pi·ness** *noun*

whip-round *noun* *Brit. informal* an informal collection of money from a group of people.

whip·saw esp. *N Amer.* ● *noun* **1** a saw with a narrow blade usu. operated by two people pulling at either end of its frame. **2** something that is disadvantageous in two ways (*the whipsaw of inflation and recession*). ● *transitive verb* (past participle **-sawed** or **-sawn**) **1** *transitive* cut with a whipsaw. **2** *transitive* (usu. in *passive*) *slang* subject to two opposing and usu. harmful influences or forces. **3** *intransitive* fluctuate between two extremes.

whip scorpion *noun* any arachnid of the order Uropygi, with a long slender tail-like appendage, which secretes an irritating vapour.

whip snake *noun* any of various long slender snakes of the family Colubridae.

whip·stitch ● *noun* an overcast stitch. ● *transitive verb* sew with overcast stitches.

whip·stock *noun* the handle of a whip.

whip·worm *noun* any of various parasitic worms of the family Trichuridae, esp. worms of the genus *Trichuris* which infest the intestines of domestic animals.

whir /wɜːr/ (also **whirr**) ● *noun* a continuous droning, humming, or buzzing sound like that of machinery or the fluttering of a bird's wings (*the whir of electric fans*). ● *intransitive verb* (**whirred**, **whir·ring**) **1** make this sound. **2** move swiftly with such a sound (*the cyclists whirred away*). [Middle English, prob. Scandinavian: compare Danish *hvirre*, Norwegian *kvirra*, perhaps related to WHIRL]

whirl ● *verb* **1** *transitive & intransitive* turn around rapidly, esp. repeatedly.

2 *transitive & intransitive* (often foll. by *away*) convey or travel swiftly, esp. in a vehicle. **3** *intransitive* **a** (of the brain, senses, etc.) seem to spin; be dizzy or confused. **b** (of thoughts etc.) follow each other in bewildering succession. ● *noun* **1** a swift circling or whirling movement (*she vanished in a whirl of dust*). **2** *informal* an attempt (*give it a whirl*). **3** a state of intense activity; a frantic series of events (*the political whirl*). **4** a state of confusion (*my mind is in a whirl*). □ **whirl·er** *noun* **whirl·ing** *adjective* [Middle English: (v.) from Old Norse *hvirfla*: (n.) from Middle Low German & Middle Dutch *wervel* spindle & Old Norse *hvirfill* circle, from Germanic]

whirli·gig /ˈwɜːrlɪɡɪɡ/ *noun* **1** anything having a rapid circling movement (also *attributive*: *whirligig contraption*). **2** any of various toys that are whirled or spun around, such as a toy with four arms like miniature windmill sails which whirl around when it is moved through the air. **3** a merry-go-round. **4** anything characterized by constant frantic activity or change (*the whirligig of time*). **5** (in full **whirligig beetle**) any of various freshwater beetles of the family Gyrinidae, which have paddle-like legs and are found in large numbers circling rapidly over the surface of still water. [WHIRL + obsolete *gig* a spinning top]

whirling dervish *noun* a member of any of various Muslim religious fraternities who has taken vows of poverty and austerity and whose order includes the practice of dancing or howling as a spiritual exercise.

whirl·pool *noun* **1 a** a powerful circular eddy in a body of water that draws or sucks objects to its centre, usu. caused by the meeting of adverse currents. **b** anything resembling this, such as a destructive or absorbing agency or a turbulent swirling mass. **2** (in full **whirlpool bath**) a large bathtub with underwater jets of hot, usu. aerated, water, used for physiotherapy or relaxation.

whirl·wind *noun* **1** a small rotating storm of wind in which a vertical usu. funnel-shaped column of air whirls rapidly around a core of low pressure and moves progressively over land or water. **2** (*attributive*) very rapid or hasty (*a whirlwind romance; a whirlwind tour*). **3** a confused tumultuous process. **4** an active, impetuous, or reckless person. □ **reap the whirlwind** suffer the consequences of one's own offence.

whirly·bird *noun* *informal* a helicopter.

whirr *var. of* WHIR.

whisht /hwɪʃt/ *verb* (also **whist** /hwɪst/) esp. *Scot. & Irish dialect* **1** *intransitive* (esp. as *imperative*) be quiet; hush. **2** *transitive* quieten. [imitative]

whisk ● *verb* **1** *transitive* brush lightly with a sweeping movement (*she whisked the hair from her face*). **2** *transitive* (usu. foll. by *away*, *off*) **a** take, seize, or remove with a sudden sweeping motion (*the waiter whisked the plate away*). **b** convey quickly (*he whisked her off to the hospital*). **3** *transitive* **a** whip (cream, eggs, etc.) with a whisk. **b** (foll. by *in*, *together*) add or combine (ingredients) with a whisk. **4** *intransitive* go quickly; rush, dart (*a car whisked past*). ● *noun* **1** a whisking action or motion. **2** a utensil consisting of wire hoops attached to a handle, used for beating eggs or cream etc. lightly. **3** (in full **whisk broom**) a bundle of straw, grass, or synthetic bristles bound at one end around a usu. short handle, used to sweep dust or debris from a surface. [Middle English *wisk*, prob. Scandinavian: compare Old Norse *visk* wisp]

whis·ker *noun* **1 a** any of the hairs growing on a person's face. **b** (in *pl.*) these hairs collectively growing on esp. a man's chin, upper lip, or cheek; a moustache or beard. **2** each of a number of long projecting hairs growing on the face of many mammals, such as dogs, cats, and seals. **3** *informal* a small distance or amount; a narrow margin (*came within a whisker of succeeding; won by a whisker*). **4** a single hairlike crystal of a metal measuring only a few microns in thickness, characterized by a tensile strength much greater than that of the bulk material. □ **whis·kered** *adjective* **whis·kery** *adjective* [WHISK + -ER[1]]

whisky *noun* (also **whis·key**) (*pl.* **-kies** or **-keys**) **1** an alcoholic liquor distilled esp. from rye, malted barley, or corn. **2** a drink of this. ¶ Irish whiskey and bourbon whiskey are usually spelled *whiskey*. [abbreviation of obsolete *whiskybae*, var. of USQUEBAUGH]

whisky blanc /ˌwɪskiˈblɒnk/ *noun* *Cdn* (*Que.*) a type of colourless whisky made from distilled grain alcohol. [French, lit. 'white whisky']

whisky fort *noun* (also **whisky post**) *Cdn hist.* an establishment selling whisky illegally to the Aboriginal peoples of the Canadian west in the late 19th c.

whisky jack *noun* *Cdn* = GREY JAY. [alteration of *whisky-john*, corruption of Cree *wiskatjan*, Montagnais *wi:skača:n* 'blacksmith', possibly with reference to the grey and black plumage]

whisky trader *noun* *Cdn* (*West*) & *US Northwest hist.* a person selling whisky illegally, esp. a nomadic American outlaw trading with the Aboriginal peoples north of the Montana border in the late 19th c.

whis·per ● *verb* **1** *transitive & intransitive* **a** say or speak in a soft breathy voice without vibration of the vocal cords, esp. for the sake of secrecy or intimacy. **b** say or speak in a low barely audible tone. **2 a** *intransitive* speak or converse in private, esp. to conspire or to exchange rumours about a person or thing. **b** *transitive* (in *passive*) be rumoured. **3** *intransitive* (of leaves, wind, water, etc.) make a soft rustling or murmuring sound that resembles whispering. **●** *noun* **1** whispering speech (*talking in whispers*). **2** something whispered. **3 a** a rumour or piece of gossip. **b** (usu. with *neg.*) a suggestion or hint. **4** a soft rustling or whispering sound. □ **whis·per·er** *noun* **whis·per·ing** *noun* [Old English *hwisprian*]

whispering campaign *noun* a systematic circulation of a rumour, esp. in order to denigrate a person or thing.

whispering gallery *noun* a usu. circular gallery situated under a dome, whose acoustic properties are such that a whisper may be heard around its entire circumference.

whist¹ /wɪst/ *noun* a card game for four players grouped into pairs, in which points are scored according to the number of tricks won and, in some forms, by the highest trumps or honours held by each pair. [earlier *whisk*, perhaps from WHISK (with reference to whisking away the tricks): perhaps assoc. with WHIST²]

whist² *var. of* WHISHT.

whist drive *noun* a social occasion or tournament at which whist is played, with players changing tables and partners from deal to deal until an individual overall winner is declared.

whis·tle ● *noun* **1** a clear shrill sound made by forcing breath through the narrow opening made by contracting the lips or through a space between the teeth constricted by the tip of the tongue. **2** a similar sound made by a bird, the wind, a projectile, etc. **3 a** a small device that produces such a sound when blown, used esp. as a signal. **b** a simple musical instrument resembling a pipe or recorder. **●** *verb* **1** *intransitive* sound or emit a whistle. **2** *intransitive* give a signal or call for attention or express surprise, approval, or derision by whistling. **3** *transitive & intransitive* produce (a tune etc.) consisting of a series of whistled sounds of various pitch. **4** *transitive* summon, announce, or signal by whistling or blowing a whistle (*the referee whistled the play dead*). **5** *intransitive* (of a kettle, train, etc.) emit a clear shrill sound produced by the passage of steam etc. through a small opening. **6** *intransitive* (of the wind, a projectile, etc.) move or fly past with a whistle. □ **as clean** (or **clear** or **dry**) **as a whistle** very clean or clear or dry. **blow the whistle on** *informal* **1** call attention to (a questionable or illicit activity) in order to have it brought to an end. **2** inform on (those responsible) for such an activity. **whistle Dixie** *N Amer.* be overly optimistic. **whistle in the dark** pretend to be unafraid. [Old English (*h*)*wistlian* (v.), (*h*)*wistle* (n.) of imitative origin: compare Old Norse *hvísla* whisper, Middle Swedish *hvisla* whistle]

whistle-blower *noun* a person who calls attention to a questionable or illicit activity in an attempt to have it brought to an end. □ **whistle-blowing** *adjective & noun*

whistle·punk *noun* esp. *Cdn* (*BC*) *Forestry dated* a member of a logging crew who relays to the donkeyman the hooktender's signal that the logs have been secured with chokers and may be hauled away.

Whist·ler¹ /ˈwɪslər/ a district municipality and ski resort in SW central BC, at Mount Whistler; pop. (2001) 8,896. □ **Whist·ler·ite** *noun*

Whist·ler² ▸ **James (Ab·bott) Mc·Neill** (1834–1903), US painter and etcher. He mainly painted in one or two colours, and sought to achieve harmony of colour and tone, as in the portrait *Arrangement in Grey and Black: The Artist's Mother* (1872) and the landscape *Old Battersea Bridge: Nocturne – Blue and Gold* (c.1872–5). □ **Whist·ler·ian** /ˌwɪsˈlɪəriən/ *adjective*

Whistler, Mount a peak in SW central BC, about 60 km northeast of Squamish. [so called with reference to the whistling marmots that dwell on its slopes]

whist·ler *noun* **1 a** a person who whistles. **b** a thing which makes a whistling sound. **2** any bird of the genus *Pachycephala*, with a whistling cry. **3** (also **whistling marmot**) = HOARY MARMOT.

whis·tle stop *noun* **1** *N Amer.* **a** the train station of a small town at which trains stop only when given a particular signal indicating that a passenger is waiting to board. **b** a small or unimportant town. **2 a** politician's brief stop in a town to give an electioneering speech during a campaign tour. **3** (*attributive*) designating a journey or tour with brief stops made at many of the small towns along the way.

Whit /wɪt/ *adjective* connected with, belonging to, or following Pentecost (*Whit Monday*; *Whit weekend*). [Old English *Hwīta Sunnandæg*, lit. 'white

Sunday', prob. from the white robes of the newly-baptized at Pentecost]

whit /wɪt/ *noun* (usu. with *neg.*) the least possible amount (*not a whit better*). □ **every whit** the whole; wholly. **not a** (or **no**) **whit** not at all. [earlier *w(h)yt* apparently alteration of WIGHT in phr. *no wight* etc.]

Whit·by /ˈwɪtbi/ a town in S Ontario, situated on Lake Ontario, just west of Oshawa; pop. (2001) 87,413. [*Whitby*, a seaside town in North Yorkshire, England]

Whit·church-Stouff·ville /ˌwɒttʃˈɜrtʃˈstoːvɪl/ a town in south central Ontario, southeast of Aurora; pop. (2001) 22,008. [*Whitchurch*, prob. after one of several places in either England or Wales, + *Stouffville*, after A. *Stouffer*, local miller and settler d.1851]

White ▸ **1 Pat·rick (Vic·tor Mar·tin·dale)** (1912–90), English-born Australian novelist. He is best known for the novels *The Tree of Man* (1955) and *Voss* (1957); he was awarded the Nobel Prize for literature in 1973. **2 Rob·ert** ('Bob') (b.1935), Irish-born Canadian labour leader. He founded the Canadian Autoworkers Union in 1985, and in 1992 he was elected head of the Canadian Labour Congress. He is also active in the NDP. **3 Ter·ence Han·bury** (1906–64), English novelist, who is best known for his four novels on the Arthurian legend, published under the title *The Once and Future King* (1958).

white ● *adjective* **1** having a colour like that of fresh snow or milk, produced by reflection, transmission, or emission of all wavelengths of visible light without absorption, being fully luminous and devoid of any hue. **2** (esp. of the skin) approaching such a colour; pale, esp. in the face (*turned as white as a sheet*). **3** (also **White**) **a** designating or belonging to any of various peoples having light-coloured skin, usu. of European origin; Caucasian. **b** of, relating to, or characteristic of white people or their culture. **c** predominantly inhabited by or consisting of white people (*a white neighbourhood*). **4 a** (of hair) having lost its colour esp. in old age. **b** (of a person) white-haired. **5 a** (of a plant) having white flowers or pale-coloured fruit (*white hyacinth*). **b** (of a tree) having light-coloured bark etc. (*white ash*; *white poplar*). **6** (of wine) made from white grapes or dark grapes with the skins removed, and of an amber, golden, or pale yellow colour. **7** (of coffee) having milk or cream added. **8** (of metal or an object made of metal) silvery grey and lustrous. **9** transparent, colourless (*white glass*). **10** esp. *literary* morally or spiritually pure; innocent, untainted. **11** *hist.* pertaining to or supporting a royalist cause; counter-revolutionary or reactionary (*white guard*; *white army*). **●** *noun* **1** a white colour. **2** a white substance, such as paint or dye (*he covered the wall with white*). **3** the white or light-coloured part of anything. **4** the translucent viscous fluid surrounding the yolk of an egg, which turns white when cooked; albumen. **5** the visible part of the eyeball around the iris. **6** a thing distinguished by white colour, such as a breed of cattle, hog, or rabbit. **7 a** white clothing or material (*dressed in white*). **b** (in *pl.*) white clothes as worn in tennis, as a naval uniform, etc. **c** (in *pl.*) white linen or clothing etc. separated from coloured laundry for washing. **8** (also **White**) a member of a light-skinned race. **9 a** (in a game or sport) a white piece, ball, etc. **b** the player using such pieces. **10** any part of a sheet of paper not printed on. **●** *transitive verb archaic* make white. □ **white out 1** make or become white. **2** (often in *passive*) obliterate or conceal with whiteness, as with snow. **3** cover (a typewritten or printed error) with correction fluid. □ **white·ly** *adverb* **white·ness** *noun* **whit·ish** *adjective* [Old English *hwīt*]

white admiral *noun* a butterfly with a white band across its wings.

white ant *noun* a termite.

white ash *noun* an ash of eastern N America, *Fraxinus americana*.

white·bait *noun* (*pl.* same) (usu. *pl.*) a small silvery-white fish caught in large numbers and eaten whole, comprising the young of herrings and sprats.

white·beam *noun* a rosaceous tree, *Sorbus aria*, having red berries and leaves with a white downy underside, planted as an ornamental.

white birch *noun* a birch tree found across Canada, *Betula papyrifera*, with white bark that peels in strips, traditionally used by some N American Aboriginal peoples for making canoes. *Also called* PAPER BIRCH.

white blood cell *noun* any of various colourless nucleated cells found in the blood, lymph, and connective tissue, which produce antibodies and which migrate through the walls of vessels to the sites of injuries, where they surround and isolate dead tissue, foreign bodies, and bacteria. *Also called* LEUKOCYTE.

white·board *noun* a board with a white surface, which can be written on with a felt-tipped marker and wiped clean.

white bread ● *noun* bread of a light colour, made from usu. bleached wheat flour from which the bran and germ have been removed, as

Consonants: b *but*   d *dog*   f *few*   g *get*   h *her*   j *yes*   k *cat*   l *leg*   m *man*   n *no*   p *pen*   r *red*   s *sit*

distinguished from brown bread. ● *adjective* (**white-bread**) *N Amer.*
1 of, belonging to, or representative of the white middle class;
bourgeois. **2** straightlaced, conventional, inoffensive; bland or
innocuous.

white·cap *noun* (usu. in *pl.*) a wave or breaker with a foamy white
crest. □ **white·capped** *adjective*

white cedar *noun* any of several N American conifers, esp. the eastern
white cedar, *Thuja occidentalis*.

white cell *noun* = WHITE BLOOD CELL.

white chocolate *noun* a mixture of cocoa butter, milk, and sugar, of
a consistency like chocolate.

white Christmas *noun* Christmas with snow on the ground.

white·coat *noun* **1** a young seal, having a coat of white fur. **2** the fur
or skin of this seal.

white coat *noun* a white lab coat, worn by doctors, scientists,
laboratory workers, etc. □ **men in white coats** *jocular* attendants in
a mental asylum. □ **white-coated** *adjective*

white-collar *adjective* **1** designating, pertaining to, or performing
non-manual, esp. clerical, administrative, or professional, work. **2 a** (of
a crime) non-violent, esp. involving fraud, embezzlement, income tax
evasion, etc. **b** (of a person) guilty of such a crime.

White·court a town in central Alberta, situated on the Athabasca
River, about 175 km northwest of Edmonton; pop. (2001) 8,334. [W.
White, the area's first postmaster, who brought the mail from
Green*court*, a town about 30 km to the southeast, *c*.1909]

white currant *noun* a cultivar of red currant with pale edible berries.

whited sepulchre *noun* a hypocrite. [with reference to Matt. 23:27]

white dwarf *noun* a small faint very dense star lying below the main
sequence, representing the stable phase assumed by stars of a
relatively low mass when their nuclear reactions cease.

white elephant *noun* an item or property that is no longer useful or
wanted, esp. one that is difficult to maintain or dispose of. [from the
story that kings of Siam would present a rare albino elephant, highly
venerated in some Asian countries, to unpopular courtiers in order to
ruin them by the cost of its maintenance]

white elm *noun* = AMERICAN ELM.

White Ensign *noun Brit.* a white flag, with the Union Jack or a
national flag in the upper corner, flown at the stern of naval ships in
Commonwealth countries other than Canada.

white·face *noun* the white makeup of a clown or actor.

white-faced *adjective* **1** (of an animal etc.) having white facial
markings or a naturally white face. **2** having a face that is or has
become pale, as with fear. **3** having a face that has been made white
with makeup.

White Fathers *plural noun* an international order of Roman Catholic
brothers and priests involved in missionary work in Africa since 1868.

white feather *noun* a symbol of cowardice. [with reference to the
fact that a white feather in the tail of a game bird is considered a mark
of bad breeding]

White·field, George (1714–70), English Methodist preacher,
instrumental in promoting Methodism in the US.

white finger disease *noun* = RAYNAUD'S DISEASE.

white·fish *noun* **1** (*pl.* same or **-fishes**) any freshwater fish of the
genus *Coregonus* etc., of the trout family, and used esp. for food, esp.
Coregonus clupeaformis of lakes and large rivers throughout northern
N America. **2** (**white fish**) any fish with pale flesh, such as cod,
haddock, plaice, etc.

Whitefish Bay a bay at the southeastern end of Lake Superior,
situated just west of Sault Ste. Marie.

white flag *noun* the flag traditionally hoisted to signal the wish to
surrender or for a period of truce. □ **raise** (or **wave** or **run up**) **the
white flag** admit defeat in an argument, contest, etc.

white flour *noun* fine wheat flour, usu. bleached, from which most of
the bran and germ have been removed.

white·fly *noun* (*pl.* **-flies**) any small insect of the family Aleyrodidae,
having wings covered with white powder and feeding on the sap of
shrubs, crops, etc.

White Friar *noun* a Carmelite.

white gas *noun* = NAPHTHA.

white gold *noun* any of various silver-coloured alloys of gold used in
jewellery.

white goods *plural noun* **1** household linen. **2** large domestic

electrical equipment that is conventionally white, such as
refrigerators, washing machines, and other appliances.

White·hall a street in Westminster, London (England), on which many
government offices are located. The name is used allusively to refer to
the British Civil Service. [after the former royal palace of *White Hall*,
originally a residence of Cardinal Wolsey]

White·head, Al·fred North (1861–1947), English philosopher and
mathematician. He is remembered chiefly for *Principia Mathematica*
(1910–13), a treatise on mathematical logic which he wrote with his
pupil Bertrand Russell; he later turned his attention to the
construction of a metaphysical system, the details of which he
published in *Process and Reality* (1929).

white·head *noun informal* a white or white-topped pimple.

white heat *noun* **1** the temperature at which metal radiates a white
light. **2** a state of intense passion or activity.

white hope *noun* a person expected to bring success to an
organization or group etc.

White·horse the capital (and only) city of Yukon Territory, situated
on the Yukon River in the territory's southern region, about 90 km
north of the border with BC; pop. (2001) 19,058. Whitehorse is the
centre of a copper-mining and fur-trapping region. [named after the
Whitehorse Rapids of the Yukon River, prob. with reference to the
resemblance of the white waters to the manes of horses]

white-hot *adjective* **1** at a heat sufficient to cause metal to radiate a
white light. **2** in an intense emotional state, esp. one of passion or
anger. **3** extremely successful, popular, or in demand.

White House *noun* **1 a** the official residence of the US President in
Washington, DC. **b** the US President or the executive branch of the US
government. **2** the Russian parliament building.

white knight *noun* **1** a person who comes to the aid of someone; an
unexpected saviour. **2** *Stock Exch.* a welcome company bidding for a
company facing an unwelcome takeover bid.

white-knuckle *attributive adjective* (also **white-knuckled**) **1** (esp. of
an airplane or amusement park ride) causing fear or terror. **2** (of a
participant) feeling fear or terror.

white lead *noun* a mixture of lead carbonate and hydrated lead oxide
used as pigment in paint or mixed with linseed oil to make putty.

white lie *noun* a harmless or trivial untruth, esp. one told in order to
avoid hurting someone's feelings.

white light *noun* colourless light, e.g. sunlight.

white lightning *noun N Amer. slang* inferior or illicitly distilled whisky;
moonshine.

white magic *noun* magic involving the invocation of good spirits and
used for beneficent or harmless purposes.

white man's burden *noun* the supposed responsibility of white
Europeans and N Americans to advance civilization, education,
religion, public health, etc., in underdeveloped parts of the world,
used as a justification for colonization. [from *The White Man's Burden*
poem by R. KIPLING]

white matter *noun* the whitish tissue in the vertebrate central
nervous system consisting mainly of nerve fibres, situated below the
grey matter of the cortex and next to the core of the spinal cord.

white meat *noun* **1** any meat that is pale in colour when cooked, such
as veal or poultry. **2** the breast meat of poultry.

white mulberry *noun see* MULBERRY.

whit·en *transitive & intransitive verb* make or become white.
□ **whit·en·ing** *noun*

whit·en·er *noun* **1** a thing that whitens, such as a bleaching agent for
clothes or a polish for teeth. **2** a soluble powder added to coffee as a
substitute for cream.

white night *noun* **1** a sleepless night. **2** a night when it never
properly gets dark, as in high latitudes in summer. [translation of
French *nuit blanche*]

White Nile the name for the main, western branch of the Nile
between the Ugandan–Sudanese border and its confluence with the
Blue Nile at Khartoum. (See NILE RIVER.)

white noise *noun* noise having nearly equal intensities at all the
frequencies of its range.

white oak *noun* any of various oaks with leaves with rounded lobes,
esp. *Quercus alba*, of the eastern US and southern Ontario and Quebec.

white·out *noun* **1 a** a weather condition in which the horizon and
physical features of snow-covered country are indistinguishable due to
uniform light diffusion. **b** a dense blizzard that reduces visibility. **2** =
CORRECTION FLUID.

white pages *plural noun* (usu. treated as *sing.*) a telephone directory or section of this containing the phone numbers and addresses of residential and business subscribers listed alphabetically (*compare* BLUE PAGES, YELLOW PAGES).

white·paint·ing *noun Cdn* the renovation or reclamation of a house, building, or neighbourhood in a derelict part of a city's urban core. □ **white·paint·er** *noun*

white paper *noun* **1** (also **White Paper**) an official report prepared by an appointed committee, summarizing the results of an investigation into an issue, policy, or proposed legislation, and outlining the government's intention regarding it. **2** an authoritative report on an item of particular interest issued by any organization.

White Pass a pass (889 m) through the Coast Mountains of northwestern BC, situated on the border with Alaska, about 120 km south of Whitehorse. It was used heavily by those en route to Dawson during the Klondike gold rush. [T. *White*, Canadian politician d.1888]

white pelican *noun* a pelican with white plumage, *Pelecanus erythrorhynchos*, breeding from the Prairie provinces south to Central America.

white pepper *noun* the ripe or husked ground or whole berries of *Piper nigrum* as a condiment.

white perch *noun* a fish related to the basses, *Morone americana*, of eastern N America.

white picket fence *noun see* PICKET FENCE.

white pine *noun* any of several N American pines with needles in bundles of five and soft wood, esp. the eastern white pine, *Pinus strobus*, and the western white pine, *Pinus monticola*.

white pizza *noun* a pizza made without tomato sauce.

white poplar *noun* a Eurasian poplar, *Populus alba*, with lobed leaves covered with dense white down beneath.

white rabbit *interjection* uttered upon waking on the first day of the month to supposedly bring good fortune to the speaker for the rest of the month.

White River a river in W Yukon Territory, 265 km long, which rises in the St. Elias Mountains and flows generally northeastward to join the Yukon River south of Dawson. [so called because of its colour, a result of the suspended volcanic ash in its waters]

White Rock[1] a city on the coast of southwestern BC, situated about 40 km southeast of Vancouver and immediately north of the border with Washington state; pop. (2001) 18,250. □ **White Rocker** *noun* [so called with reference to a large white rock on its beach, a landmark for mariners]

White Rock[2] *noun* a variety of white Plymouth Rock chickens.

white rose *noun* the emblem of Yorkshire or the House of York.

White Russia an alternative name for BELARUS.

White Russian ● *noun* **1** a Belarussian. **2** a drink made with vodka, cream, and crème de cacao or coffee-flavoured liqueur. ● *adjective* Belarussian.

white sale *noun* a sale of household linen.

White Sands an area of white gypsum salt flats in central New Mexico, designated a national monument in 1933. It is surrounded by a large missile testing range, which, in 1945, as part of the Manhattan Project, was the site of the detonation of the first nuclear weapon.

white sauce *noun* a sauce made with flour, melted butter, and milk or cream.

White Sea an inlet of the Barents Sea on the coast of NW Russia.

white shark *noun* = GREAT WHITE SHARK.

white-shoe *adjective US slang* **1** designating or relating to esp. a law firm or corporation predominantly owned by or employing members of the white upper class. **2** designating or relating to a person employed by or associated with such a law firm or corporation.

white slave *noun* a woman who is trapped, forced, or sold into prostitution, usu. abroad. □ **white slavery** *noun*

white sock *noun* = STOCKING 5.

white spirit *noun Brit.* = MINERAL SPIRITS.

white spruce *noun* any of several spruce trees of N America, esp. *Picea glauca*, found across Canada, and used for lumber and wood pulp.

white stuff *noun N Amer. informal* snow.

white sugar *noun* refined sugar from which the molasses has been removed.

white supremacy *noun* a belief that whites are innately superior to non-whites. □ **white supremacist** *noun*

white-tailed deer *noun* (also **white·tail**, **whitetail deer**) a deer,

Odocoileus virginianus, which has a white underside to the tail and is found from Canada to northern S America.

white·throat *noun* a warbler, *Sylvia communis*, with a white patch on the throat.

white tie *noun* **1** a man's white bow tie worn as part of full evening dress. **2** full formal evening dress (also *attributive*: *white-tie affair*).

white trash *noun* (*pl.* same) *N Amer. derogatory* **1** a member of the class of poor lower-class whites. **2** the members of this class collectively. **3** (*attributive*; **white-trash**) belonging or pertaining to or characteristic of the white lower class.

white vinegar *noun* colourless vinegar made from grain alcohol.

white·wall *noun* (in full **whitewall tire**) an automotive tire with a white side wall.

white·wash ● *noun* **1** a solution of lime and water, or of whiting, size, and water, for whitening walls etc. **2** something that conceals faults or mistakes in order to clear or uphold the reputation of a person or institution; a cover-up. **3** *Sport* a victory in which the opponent fails to score or is defeated by a lopsided margin. ● *transitive verb* **1** cover with whitewash. **2** attempt to clear or uphold the reputation of (a person, institution, etc.) by concealment of faults or mistakes. **3** *Sport* defeat (an opponent) convincingly, esp. in a shutout. □ **white·wash·er** *noun*

white·water ● *noun* **1** a stretch of turbulent foamy water in a river caused by a steep drop or by large rocks in the riverbed. **2** the surf or a stretch of clear or frothy sea water, esp. on a beach or shoal. ● *attributive adjective* **1** designating a river or stretch of a river where there is whitewater. **2** designating an activity or event that takes place on such a river (*whitewater rafting*; *whitewater rodeo*). **3** designating a person who participates in such an activity or event.

white wedding *noun* a wedding at which the bride wears a formal white wedding dress.

white whale *noun* = BELUGA 1.

white-winged scoter *noun* a mainly black scoter, *Melanitta fusca*, with a white patch on the wing and a white circle around each eye.

white·wood *noun* any light-coloured wood that has not been finished with a paint, stain, or varnish.

whit·ey *noun* (also **Whit·ey**) (*pl.* **-eys**) *slang offensive* **1** a white person. **2** white people collectively.

white Zinfandel *noun* a pale pink, sweet, often slightly carbonated California wine made from Zinfandel grapes and other varieties.

whith·er /ˈwɪðər/ *archaic* ● *adverb* **1 a** to what place? **b** to what result or end? **2** (*prec. by place* etc.) to which (*the house whither we were walking*). ● *conjunction* **1** to the or any place to which (*go whither you will*). **2** to which place (*we saw a house, whither we walked*). [Old English *hwider* from Germanic: compare HITHER, THITHER]

whith·er·so·ever /ˌwɪðərsoʊˈevər/ *adjective & conjunction archaic* to any place to which.

whit·ing[1] /ˈwəɪtɪŋ/ *noun* any of various fishes of the cod family with pearly-white flesh and white coloration. [Middle Dutch *wijting*, apparently formed as WHITE + -ING[3]]

whit·ing[2] *noun* ground chalk used to make whitewash, metal polish, putty, etc.

whit·low /ˈwɪtloʊ/ *noun* an inflammation near a fingernail or toenail. [Middle English *whitflaw*, *-flow*, apparently = WHITE + FLAW[1] in the sense 'crack', but perhaps of Low German origin: compare Dutch *fijt*, Low German *fit* whitlow]

Whit·man /ˈwɪtmən/ **Wal·ter** (1819–92), US poet. He published the first edition of *Leaves of Grass*, incorporating 'I Sing the Body Electric' and 'Song of Myself', in 1855; written in free verse, the collection celebrates democracy, sexuality, the self, and the liberated American spirit in union with nature. □ **Whit·man·esque** *adjective*

Whit·ney /ˈwɪtni/ **1 Eli** (1765–1825), US inventor. He devised the mechanical cotton gin (patented 1794), as well as conceiving the idea of mass-producing interchangeable parts; he first applied this method in his fulfillment of a US government contract (1797) to supply muskets. **2 Sir James Pliny** (1843–1914), Canadian lawyer and politician, Conservative premier of Ontario 1905–14. First elected to the Ontario legislature in 1888, he became leader of the Conservative opposition in 1896, rebuilt the party, and broke the Liberals' 33-year reign in 1905. As premier, he created Ontario's provincial hydroelectric power system.

Whit·ney, Mount a mountain in the Sierra Nevada in California. Rising to 4 418 m (14,495 ft.), it is the highest peak in the continental US outside Alaska.

Vowels:　a cat　ɑ arm　e bed　ɜr her　ɜ: deux　ə ago　ɪ sit　i cosy　iː feed　ɒ hot　ɔ pore　ɔː no　ʌ run　ʊ put

Whit·sun /ˈwɪtsən/ ● *noun* (also **Whit Sunday**) = PENTECOST.
● *adjective* = WHIT. [Middle English, from *Whitsun Day* = Whit Sunday]

Whit·sun·tide /ˈwɪtsənˌtaɪd/ *noun Brit.* the weekend or week including Pentecost.

Whit·ti·er /ˈwɪtiːər/ **John Green·leaf** (1807–92), US poet and abolitionist. He wrote poetry for the abolitionist cause and is best known for his poems on rural themes.

Whit·ting·ton /ˈwɪtɪŋtən/ **Sir Rich·ard ('Dick')** (d.1423), English merchant and Lord Mayor of London. Legend tells of his arrival in London with his cat, and how he was about to leave the city when the church bells told him to stay.

Whit·tle /ˈwɪtəl/ **Sir Frank** (1907–96), English aeronautical engineer, test pilot, and one of the inventors of the jet aircraft engine; his engine made its maiden flight in 1941.

whit·tle /ˈwɪtəl/ *verb* **1** *transitive & intransitive* cut, shape, or pare (wood, a stick, etc.) by carving thin shavings from the surface with a knife. **2** *intransitive* **a** (often foll. by *away*) make repeated reductions to (*whittled away at the deficit*). **b** (often foll. by *down*) reduce or diminish by repeated subtractions (*whittled down the waiting list*). [var. of Middle English *thwitel* long knife, from Old English *thwītan* to cut off]

whiz /wɪz/ (also **whizz**) *informal* ● *noun* **1** the sibilant humming or buzzing sound made by the friction of a body moving through the air at great speed. **2** (also **wiz**) *informal* a person who is remarkable or skilful in some usu. specified respect (*is a whiz at chess*). **3** *slang* an act of urinating. ● *verb* (**whiz·zes**, **whizzed**, **whiz·zing**) **1** *intransitive* make or emit a sibilant humming or buzzing sound. **2** *intransitive* move with or as if with such a sound. **3** *transitive* cause to make such a sound, esp. by rotating rapidly in a blender or food processor etc. **4** *intransitive slang* urinate. □ **whiz·zer** *noun* [imitative: in sense 2 of *noun* influenced by WIZARD]

whiz-bang /ˈwɪzbaŋ/ *informal* ● *adjective* **1** fast-paced, lively, spectacular. **2** technologically innovative or advanced; up to date, modern (*whiz-bang computer graphics*). ● *noun* a high-velocity shell from a small-calibre gun, whose passage is heard before the gun's report.

whiz kid *noun informal* an exceptionally bright or successful young person.

WHL *abbreviation* Western Hockey League.

WHO *abbreviation* World Health Organization.

who *pronoun* (*obj.* **whom** or *informal* **who**; *possessive* **whose**) **1 a** what or which person or persons? (*who called?; you know who it was; whom or who did you see?*). ¶ In the last example *whom* is correct but *who* is common in less formal contexts. **b** what sort of person or persons? (*who am I to object?*). **2** (a person) that (*anyone who wishes can come; the woman whom you met; the man who you saw*). ¶ In the last two examples *whom* is correct but *who* is common in less formal contexts. **3** and or but he, she, they, etc. (*gave it to Cheryl, who passed it on to Sherry*). **4** *archaic* the or any person or persons that (*whom the gods love die young*). □ **who cares?** I don't care. **who goes there?** *see* GO¹. **who knows?** I don't know. [Old English *hwā* from Germanic: *whom* from Old English dative *hwām, hwæm*: *whose* from genitive *hwæs*]

whoa /woː/ *interjection* **1** commanding a horse or other animal to come to a stop. **2** *jocular* demanding a person to stop or slow down. [var. of HO¹]

who'd *contraction* **1** who had. **2** who would.

who-does-what *attributive adjective* (of a dispute etc.) concerning which group of workers should do a particular job.

who·dun·it /huːˈdʌnɪt/ *noun* (also **who·dun·nit**) *informal* a story about the detection of a crime, esp. murder; a mystery. [= *who done* (illiterate for *did*) *it?*]

who·ev·er *pronoun* (*obj.* **whom·ev·er** or *informal* **who·ev·er**; *possessive* **whos·ev·er**) **1** the or any person or persons who (*whoever comes is welcome*). **2** though anyone (*whoever else objects, I do not; whosever it is, I want it*). **3** *informal* (as an intensive) who ever; who at all (*whoever heard of such a thing?*). **4** (usu. foll. by *or*) *informal* any or some similar person (*give it to me or whoever*).

whole ● *adjective* **1** not less than; all there is of; entire, complete (*waited a whole year; tell the whole truth; the whole school knows*). **2** unbroken, intact (*the whale swallowed him whole*). **3** containing all the proper or essential constituents. **4** *archaic* healthy, uninjured. ● *noun* **1** a thing made up of combined or connected parts; a thing complete in itself. **2** all there is of a thing (*spent the whole of the summer by the sea*). **3** (foll. by *of*) all members, inhabitants, etc., of (*the whole of Hamilton knows it*). ● *adverb* in every way; entirely (*that's a whole different matter*). □ **as a whole** in its entirety. **go the whole hog** *see* HOG. **on the whole** taking everything relevant into account; in general (*it was, on the whole, a good report*). **a whole lot** *see* LOT. **a whole new** (or **different**) **ball game** *informal* **1** a separate issue or matter very different from the one currently under discussion or consideration. **2** a new situation very different from the present one. **the whole nine yards** *slang* everything; every item, aspect, member, etc. **the whole shooting match** *see* SHOOTING. □ **whole·ness** *noun* [Old English *hāl*]

whole blood *noun* blood to which an anticoagulant has been added but which is otherwise unchanged after it is obtained from a donor, used for transfusions.

whole cloth ● *noun* cloth of the full size as manufactured, as opposed to a cut piece used to make a garment. ● *adjective* (usu. **whole-cloth**) *N Amer.* not based on fact; false, fabricated. □ **out of whole cloth** *N Amer.* with no basis in fact or reality (*he invents rumours out of whole cloth*).

whole food *noun* food that has not been unnecessarily processed or refined, such as brown rice.

whole-grain *adjective* (of cereal products) made with or containing the whole grain, including the bran and the germ (*whole-grain bread*).

whole·heart·ed *adjective* **1** (of a person) completely devoted or committed. **2** (of an action etc.) done with all possible effort, attention, or sincerity. □ **whole·heart·ed·ly** *adverb* **whole·heart·ed·ness** *noun*

whole-life insurance *noun* a life insurance policy for which the premiums are payable throughout the remaining life of the person insured.

whole·meal *noun Brit.* = WHOLE WHEAT.

whole milk *noun* milk from which no fat has been removed.

whole note *noun N Amer. Music* a note having the time value of four quarter notes or two half notes and represented by a hollow ring.

whole number *noun Math* a number without fractions; an integer.

whole rest *noun N Amer. Music* a rest having the time value of a whole note.

whole·sale ● *noun* the selling of goods in large quantities to be retailed by others (*compare* RETAIL). ● *adjective* **1** of, pertaining to, or involved in wholesale (*a wholesale distributor*). **2** done on a large scale; extensive (*wholesale changes*). ● *adverb* **1** at a wholesale price (*I can get it for you wholesale*). **2** on a large scale. ● *verb* **1** *transitive* sell (goods) wholesale. **2** *intransitive* (usu. foll. by *for, at*) (of goods) be sold wholesale, esp. for a specified price. □ **whole·saler** *noun* [Middle English: originally *by whole sale*]

whole·some *adjective* **1** promoting physical health or well-being (*wholesome food*). **2** promoting mental or moral health (*wholesome curiosity; wholesome pursuits*). **3** having a sound physical or moral constitution. **4** indicative of good health (*wholesome appearance*). □ **whole·some·ly** *adverb* **whole·some·ness** *noun* [Middle English, prob. from Old English (unrecorded) *hālsum* (as WHOLE, -SOME¹)]

whole-tone scale *noun Music* a scale consisting entirely of tones, with no semitones.

whole wheat *noun* wheat with none of the bran or germ removed (also *attributive*: *whole wheat flour*).

whol·ism *var. of* HOLISM.

who'll *contraction* who will; who shall.

wholly *adverb* **1** entirely, completely; without limitation. **2** solely, exclusively.

wholly owned *adjective* designating a company all of whose shares are owned by another company (*a wholly owned subsidiary*).

whom *objective case of* WHO.

whom·ever *objective case of* WHOEVER.

whomp *esp. N Amer. informal* ● *noun* a loud dull heavy sound. ● *verb* **1** *transitive* bang or strike heavily with a dull heavy sound; thump. **2** *intransitive* make a dull heavy banging sound. [imitative]

whom·so *archaic objective case of* WHOSO.

whom·so·ever *objective case of* WHOSOEVER.

whoop /wuːp, wʊp, huːp/ ● *noun* **1** a loud cry of or as of excitement etc. **2** a long rasping indrawn breath in whooping cough. ● *intransitive verb* utter a whoop. □ **no big whoop** *N Amer. slang* no big deal. **whoop it up** *esp. N Amer. informal* **1** engage in revelry. **2** arouse enthusiasm. [Middle English: imitative]

whoop-de-do /ˈwuːpdəˌduː/ (also **whoop-de-doo**) *N Amer. slang* ● *noun* **1** a fuss, a commotion. **2** a party or other festive event. ● *interjection* expressing exultation or (*ironic*) indifference.

whoop·ee *informal* ● *interjection* /wʊˈpiː/ expressing exuberant joy.

---

uː m**oo**d   aɪ m**y**   əɪ p**i**pe   au br**ow**n   ʌu h**ou**se   eɪ d**a**y   ɔɪ b**oy**   ā fr**an**glais   ã C**an**adien   ɔ̃ Br**ay**on   (*see over for consonants*)

● *noun* /'wʊpi/ exuberant enjoyment or revelry. □ **make whoopee** *informal* **1** rejoice noisily or hilariously. **2** make love.

whoopee cushion *noun* a rubber cushion used in a practical joke, that when sat on makes a sound like the breaking of wind.

whoop·er /'wuːpər, 'huːpər/ *noun* **1** a whooping crane. **2** a whooping swan.

whoop·ing cough /'wuːpɪŋ, 'huːpɪŋ/ *noun* an infectious bacterial disease, esp. of children, with a series of short violent coughs followed by a whoop. *Also called* PERTUSSIS.

whoop·ing crane *noun* a large endangered N American crane, *Grus americana*, with mainly white plumage, which passes through the Prairie provinces in migration between N Alberta and Texas.

whoop·ing swan *noun* a swan, *Cygnus cygnus*, with a characteristic whooping sound in flight.

whoops *interjection* *informal* expressing surprise or apology, esp. on making an obvious mistake. [var. of OOPS]

whoop-up *noun* *Cdn informal* a noisy celebration or party.

whoosh /wuːʃ, wʊʃ/ (also **woosh**) ● *transitive & intransitive verb* move or cause to move with a rushing sound. ● *noun* a sudden movement accompanied by a rushing sound. ● *interjection* an exclamation imitating this. [imitative]

whop = WHAP.

whop·per *noun* *slang* **1** something big of its kind. **2** a blatant or gross lie.

whop·ping *adjective* *slang* very big (*a whopping lie; a whopping fish*).

whore /hɔr, hʊr/ ● *noun* **1** a prostitute. **2** *derogatory* a promiscuous woman. ● *intransitive verb* **1** (of a man) seek or chase after whores. **2** act as a whore. □ **whore·dom** *noun* [Old English *hōre* from Germanic]

who're *contraction* who are.

whore·house *noun* a brothel.

whore·monger /'hɔr,mɒŋgər, -mʌŋgər, 'hʊr-/ *noun* (also **whore·master**) a sexually promiscuous man; a lecher.

whore·son /'hɔrsən, 'hʊr-/ *noun* *archaic* a disliked person.

whor·ish /'hɔrɪʃ, 'hʊr-/ *adjective* of or like a whore. □ **whor·ish·ly** *adverb* **whor·ish·ness** *noun*

whorl /wɔrl, wɜrl/ *noun* **1** a ring of leaves or other organs round a stem of a plant. **2** one turn of a spiral, esp. on a shell. **3** a convolution, a coil. **4** a complete circle in a fingerprint. **5** *archaic* a small wheel on a spindle steadying its motion. □ **whorled** *adjective* [Middle English *wharwyl, whorwil*, apparently var. of WHIRL: influenced by *wharve* (n.) = whorl of a spindle]

whortle·berry /'wɜrtəl,beri/ *noun* (*pl.* **-berries**) a bilberry. [16th c.: dial. form of *hurtleberry*, Middle English, of unknown origin]

who's *contraction* who is.

whose ● *pronoun* of or belonging to which person (*whose is this book?*). ● *adjective* of whom or which (*whose book is this?; the boy, whose name was Gabriel; the house whose roof was damaged*).

whose·so *archaic* *possessive of* WHOSO.

whose·soever *possessive of* WHOSOEVER.

whos·ever /huːˈzɛvər/ *possessive of* WHOEVER.

whoso /'huːsoʊ/ *pronoun* *archaic* = WHOEVER. [Middle English, = WHO + SO¹, from Old English *swā hwā swā*]

who·soever /,huːsoʊˈɛvər/ *pronoun* *archaic* = WHOEVER.

who's who *noun* **1** the significant people in a given field. **2** a list or directory with facts about notable persons.

who've *contraction* who have.

whump /wʌmp/ ● *verb* **1** *intransitive* make or move or knock with a dull thudding sound. **2** *transitive* strike heavily or with a dull thudding sound. ● *noun* a dull thudding sound, as of a body landing heavily. [imitative]

whup /wʌp/ *transitive verb* esp. *US* **1** whip, beat. **2** defeat soundly. [Scots var. of WHIP]

why ● *adverb* **1 a** for what reason or purpose (*why did you do it?; I do not know why you came*). **b** on what grounds (*why do you say that?*). **2** (prec. by *reason* etc.) for which (*the reasons why I did it*). ● *interjection* expressing: **1** surprised discovery or recognition (*why, it's you!*). **2** impatience (*why, of course I do!*). **3** reflection (*why, yes, I think so*). **4** objection (*why, what is wrong with it?*). ● *noun* (*pl.* **whys**) a reason or explanation (*whys and wherefores*). □ **why so?** on what grounds?; for what reason or purpose? [Old English *hwī, hwȳ* instrumental of *hwæt* WHAT from Germanic]

why·dah /'wɪdə/ *noun* (also **whi·dah**) any small African weaver bird of the genus *Vidua*, the male having mainly black plumage and tail

feathers of great length. [originally *widow bird*, altered from assoc. with *Whidah* (now Ouidah) in Benin]

WI *abbreviation* **1** West Indies. **2** WOMEN'S INSTITUTE. **3** Wisconsin (in official postal use).

Wiar·ton /'wairtən/ a former town in SW Ontario, on the eastern side of the Bruce Peninsula northwest of Owen Sound, noted for its Groundhog Day festival, during which an albino groundhog, 'Wiarton Willie' is awoken from hibernation; pop. (2001) 2,349.
□ **Wiar·ton·ian** *noun* [*Wiarton Place* near Maidstone, Kent, the birthplace of Sir Edmund Walker Head, governor of Canada 1854–61]

Wicca /'wɪkə/ *noun* the religious cult of modern witchcraft, a goddess-worshipping, shamanistic nature religion. □ **Wic·can** *adjective & noun* [Old English *wicca* WITCH]

wich- *var. of* WYCH-.

Wich·ita /'wɪtʃɪˌtɔ/ a city in S Kansas, on the Arkansas River; pop. (est. 2000) 344,284.

wick¹ ● *noun* a strip or thread of fibrous or spongy material feeding a flame with fuel in a candle, lamp, etc. ● *transitive verb* (often foll. by *away*) esp. *N Amer.* (esp. of fabric) absorb or draw off (moisture) by capillary action. □ **dip one's wick** *coarse slang* (of a man) have sexual intercourse. **get on a person's wick** *Brit.* *informal* annoy a person. [Old English *wēoce, -wēoc* (compare Middle Dutch *wiecke*, Middle Low German *wēke*), of unknown origin]

wick² *noun* *dialect* (except in compounds e.g. *bailiwick*, and in place names e.g. *Warwick*) **1** a town, hamlet, or district. **2** a dairy farm. [Old English *wīc*, prob. from Germanic from Latin *vicus* street, village]

wick·ed *adjective* (**wick·ed·er, wick·ed·est**) **1** sinful, iniquitous, given to or involving immorality. **2** spiteful, ill-tempered; intending or intended to give pain. **3** playfully malicious. **4** *informal* foul; very bad; formidable (*wicked weather; a wicked cough*). **5** *slang* excellent, remarkable. □ **wicked·ly** *adverb* **wicked·ness** *noun* [Middle English from obsolete *wick* (perhaps adj. use of Old English *wicca* wizard) + -ED¹ as in *wretched*]

wick·er *noun* braided twigs or osiers etc. as material for chairs, baskets, mats, etc. [Middle English, from Eastern Scandinavian: compare Swedish *viker* willow, related to *vika* bend]

wicker·work *noun* **1** wicker. **2** things made of wicker.

wick·et *noun* **1** *N Amer.* a station for an employee in a ticket office, bank, etc., often closed by a window. **2** (in full **wicket door** or **wicket gate**) a small door or gate esp. beside or in a larger one or closing the lower part only of a doorway. **3** *Cricket* **a** a set of three stumps with the bails in position defended by a batsman. **b** the ground between two wickets. **c** the state of this (*a slow wicket*). **d** a pair of batsmen batting at the same time. **4** *N Amer.* a croquet hoop. □ **on a good** (or **sticky**) **wicket** *Brit. informal* in a favourable (or unfavourable) position. [Anglo-French *wiket*, Old French *guichet*, of uncertain origin]

wicket-keeper *noun* *Cricket* the fielder stationed close behind a batsman's wicket.

wicki·up /'wɪkiˌʌp/ *noun* a hut used by some N American Aboriginal peoples, consisting of a frame covered with grass etc. [Fox *wikiyap*]

Wick·liffe /'wɪklɪf/ (also **Wi·clif**) var. of WYCLIFFE.

Wick·low /'wɪkloʊ/ **1** a county of the Republic of Ireland, in the east, in the province of Leinster. **2** its county town, on the Irish Sea; pop. (est. 2000) 7,600.

Wicks, Al·fred ('Ben') (1926–2000), English-born Canadian cartoonist and writer. One of Canada's best known and most prolific cartoonists, his work combined humour with often harsh political comment.

wid·der·shins var. of WITHERSHINS.

wide ● *adjective* **1 a** measuring much or more than other things of the same kind across or from side to side. **b** considerable; more than is needed (*a wide margin*). **2** (following a measurement) in width (*a metre wide*). **3** extending far; embracing much; of great extent (*has a wide range; has wide experience; reached a wide public*). **4** not tight or close or restricted; loose. **5 a** *Brit.* free, liberal; unprejudiced (*takes wide views*). **b** not specialized; general. **6** open to the full extent (*staring with wide eyes*). **7 a** (foll. by *of*) not within a reasonable distance of. **b** at a considerable distance from a point or mark. **8** *Brit. slang* shrewd; skilled in sharp practice. **9** (in *combination*) extending over the whole of (*nationwide*). ● *adverb* **1** to the full extent (*her eyes opened wide*). **2** far from a particular point or mark (*he shoots! and the shot goes wide*). **3** at or near the side of the field; toward the boards or sideline (*skated wide and made the shot*). ● *noun* *Cricket* a ball judged to pass the wicket beyond the batsman's reach and so scoring a run. □ **give a wide berth to** see

BERTH. **wide of the mark** see MARK[1]. □ **wide·ness** noun [Old English wīd (adj.), wīde (adv.) from Germanic]

wide-angle attributive adjective (of a lens) having a short focal length and hence a field covering a wide angle.

wide-area network noun Computing a communications network similar to a local area network but having longer communications links, typically between buildings or different sites. Abbr.: **WAN**.

wide awake adjective **1** fully awake. **2** informal wary, knowing.

wide-band adjective having a wide band of frequencies or wavelengths.

wide-body noun (often attributive) a large jet airplane with a cabin divided by two aisles rather than one. □ **wide-bodied** adjective

wide boy noun Brit. slang a man skilled in dishonest practices.

wide-eyed adjective surprised, amazed, or naive.

wide·ly adverb **1** to a wide extent; far apart (widely spaced). **2** extensively (widely read; widely distributed). **3** by many people (it is widely thought that; widely accepted). **4** considerably; to a large degree (holds a widely different view).

wid·en transitive & intransitive verb make or become wider. □ **widen·er** noun

wide open adjective **1** fully open. **2** stretching over an outdoor expanse (wide open spaces). **3** (esp. of a contest) of which the outcome is not predictable. **4** (predicative: often foll. by to) exposed or vulnerable (esp. to attack).

wide-ranging adjective covering an extensive range.

wide receiver noun Football (also **wide·out**) a player positioned on the wide side of the offensive line used mainly to receive passes.

wide·screen attributive adjective designed with or for a screen presenting a wide field of vision in relation to its height.

wide·spread adjective widely distributed or disseminated.

widg·eon /ˈwɪdʒən/ noun (also **wi·geon**) a species of dabbling duck, esp. the baldpate of N America or Anas penelope of Europe. [16th c.: origin uncertain]

widg·et noun informal **1** any gadget or device. **2** Computing a component of a user interface that operates in a particular way. [perhaps alteration of GADGET]

wid·ow ● noun **1** a woman who has lost her husband by death and has not married again. **2** informal a woman whose husband is often away on a specified activity (golf widow). **3** the short last line of a paragraph at the top of a page or column (compare ORPHAN noun 3). ● transitive verb make into a widow or widower. [Old English widewe, related to Old High German wituwa, Sanskrit vidhávā, Latin viduus bereft, widowed, Greek ēïtheos unmarried man]

widow bird noun a whydah.

wid·owed adjective bereft by the death of a spouse (my widowed mother).

wid·ower noun a man who has lost his wife by death and has not married again.

widow·hood noun the state or period of being a widow.

widow-maker noun N Amer. & Austral. slang **1** a dead branch caught high in a tree which may fall on a person below. **2** any dangerous thing usu. operated by people, e.g. an aircraft, piece of equipment, etc.

widow's mite noun a small money contribution made by a person who can ill afford it.

widow's peak noun a V-shaped growth of hair towards the centre of the forehead.

widow's walk noun N Amer. a railed or balustraded platform built on the roof, originally in early New England houses, esp. for providing an unimpeded view of the sea.

widow's weeds plural noun see WEEDS.

width noun **1** measurement or distance from side to side. **2** a large extent. **3** breadth or liberality of thought, views, etc. **4** a strip of material of a particular width (you'll need two widths of fabric for each curtain). **5** the distance between the sides of a swimming pool (can swim two widths). □ **width·ways** adverb **width·wise** adverb [17th c. (as WIDE, -TH²) replacing wideness]

Wiebe /ˈwiːb/ **Rudy (Henry)** (b.1934), Canadian writer. He is best known for his novels, often set among his own people, the Mennonites, and other ethnic minority groups, such as Canada's Aboriginal peoples; these include The Temptations of Big Bear (1973) and The Mad Trapper (1980).

Wie·land /ˈwiːlənd/ **Joyce** (1931–98), Canadian artist and filmmaker. She held her first exhibition of paintings in 1960, and began work in experimental film in the late 1960s. She is known for her film The Far Shore (1976).

wield /wiːld/ transitive verb **1** hold and use (a weapon or tool). **2** exert or command (power or authority etc.). □ **wield·er** noun [Old English wealdan, wieldan from Germanic]

wieldy adjective (**wield·i·er**, **wield·i·est**) easily wielded, controlled, or handled.

Wie·ner /ˈwiːnər/ **Nor·bert** (1894–1964), US mathematician, who established the science of cybernetics in the late 1940s.

wie·ner /ˈwiːnər/ noun esp. N Amer. **1** a frankfurter. **2** = WEENIE² 2. [German, abbreviation of Wienerwurst, lit. 'Vienna sausage']

wiener roast noun N Amer. an outdoor social gathering at which wieners are roasted or boiled over an open fire.

Wiener schnitzel /ˈviːnər/ noun a breaded and fried pork or veal cutlet.

wie·nie var. of WEENIE.

Wies·baden /ˈviːsˌbɒdən/ a city in western Germany, the capital of Hesse, situated on the Rhine opposite Mainz; pop. (est. 2002) 266,000. It has been a popular spa town since Roman times.

Wie·sel /ˈviːzəl/ **Elie** (full name Eliezer Wiesel) (b.1928), Romanian-born US human rights campaigner, novelist, and academic. A survivor of the Auschwitz and Buchenwald concentration camps, he emigrated to the US in 1956 and subsequently emerged as a leading authority on the Holocaust, documenting and publicizing Nazi war crimes perpetrated against Jews and others during the Second World War; he was awarded the Nobel Peace Prize in 1986.

Wie·sen·thal /ˈviːzənˌtɒl/ **Simon** (b.1908), Austrian Jewish investigator of Nazi war crimes. After spending 1942 to 1945 in Nazi labour and concentration camps, he began his long campaign to bring Nazi war criminals to justice; enlisting the help of West German, Israeli, and other government agents, he traced some 1,000 unprosecuted criminals, including Adolf Eichmann.

wife noun (pl. **wives**) **1** a married woman esp. in relation to her husband. **2** archaic a woman, esp. an old or uneducated one. **3** (in combination) a woman engaged in a specified activity (fishwife; housewife; midwife). □ **have** (or **take**) **to wife** archaic marry (a woman). □ **wife·hood** noun **wife·less** adjective **wife·like** adjective **wife·ly** adjective **wife·li·ness** noun [Old English wīf woman: ultimate origin unknown]

wife swapping noun informal the exchange of marital partners for sexual purposes within a group of friends or acquaintances.

Wif·fle ball noun proprietary **1** a light perforated ball used in a type of baseball. **2** a game played with such a ball. [variant of WHIFFLE]

wig¹ noun **1** an artificial head of hair esp. to conceal baldness or as a disguise or part of a costume, or worn by a judge or lawyer. **2** a hairpiece. □ **wigged** adjective (also in combination), **wig·less** adjective [abbreviation of PERIWIG: compare WINKLE]

wig² verb (**wigged**, **wig·ging**) intransitive (usu. foll. by out) lose control of one's emotions. [apparently from WIG¹ in slang or informal sense 'rebuke' (19th c.)]

wigeon var. of WIDGEON.

wig·gle informal ● transitive & intransitive verb move or cause to move irregularly and quickly from side to side etc. ● noun an act of wiggling. □ **wig·gler** noun [Middle Low German & Middle Dutch wiggelen: compare WAG¹, WAGGLE]

wiggle room noun a limited capacity to manoeuvre or negotiate, esp. in order to modify a previous statement or decision; an allowance made for the possibility of error or change.

wig·gly adjective (**wig·gli·er**, **wig·gli·est**) informal **1** moving with a wiggle. **2** having small irregular undulations or bends (a wiggly line).

wight /waɪt/ noun archaic a person (wretched wight). [Old English wiht = thing, creature, of unknown origin]

Wight, Isle of see ISLE OF WIGHT.

Wig·ner /ˈwɪgnər/ **Eu·gene Paul** (1902–95), Hungarian-born US physicist, who was awarded the 1963 Nobel Prize for physics for his introduction of the concept of parity into nuclear physics.

Wig·town·shire /ˈwɪgtənˌʃɪr/ a former county of SW Scotland. It became a part of the region of Dumfries and Galloway in 1975.

wig·wag /ˈwɪgwæg/ intransitive verb (**wig·wagged**, **wig·wag·ging**) informal **1** move lightly to and fro. **2** wave flags in this way in signalling. [reduplication from WAG¹]

wig·wam /ˈwɪgwɒm/ noun (among some N American Aboriginal peoples) a house consisting of bent saplings stuck in the ground in a dome shape and covered with birch bark. [Ojibwa wigwaum, Algonquin wikiwam their house]

Wil·ber·force /ˈwɪlbərˌfɔrs/ **Wil·liam** (1759–1833), English politician and social reformer. He successfully campaigned for the abolition of the slave trade in the British West Indies (1807), and later throughout the British Empire (1833).

Wilberforce Falls a waterfall in western Nunavut, 49 m high, situated on the Hood River, west of Bathurst Inlet. [WILBERFORCE]

wilco /ˈwɪlkoː/ *interjection informal* expressing compliance or agreement, esp. acceptance of instructions received by radio. [abbreviation of *will comply*]

wild ● *adjective* **1** (of an animal or plant) in its original natural state; not domesticated or cultivated (esp. of species or varieties allied to others that are not wild). **2** not civilized; barbarous. **3** (of an area of land etc.) not cultivated or settled by people. **4** unrestrained, disorderly, uncontrolled (*a wild youth; wild hair*). **5** tempestuous, violent (*a wild night*). **6 a** intensely eager; excited, frantic (*wild with excitement; wild delight*). **b** (of looks, appearance, etc.) indicating distraction. **c** (foll. by *about*) *informal* enthusiastically devoted to (a person or subject). **7** *informal* infuriated, angry (*makes me wild*). **8** haphazard, ill-aimed, rash (*a wild guess; a wild shot; a wild venture*). **9** (of a horse, game bird, etc.) shy; easily startled. **10** *informal* exciting, delightful. **11** *informal* amazing, incredible (*a wild story*). **12** (of a card) having any rank chosen by the player holding it (*the joker is wild*). ● *adverb* in a wild manner (*shooting wild*). ● *noun* (usu. in *pl.*) a wilderness. □ **in the wild** in an uncultivated etc. state. **in** (or **out in**) **the wilds** *informal* far from normal habitation. **run wild** grow or stray unchecked or undisciplined. **wild and woolly** uncouth; lacking refinement. □ **wild·ish** *adjective* **wild·ly** *adverb* **wild·ness** *noun* [Old English *wilde* from Germanic]

wild bergamot *noun see* BERGAMOT[1] 3a.

wild boar *noun see* BOAR 1.

wild calla *noun* = WATER ARUM.

wild card *noun* **1** a card having any rank chosen by the player holding it. **2** *Computing* a character that will match any character or sequence of characters in a filename etc. **3** *Sport* an extra player or team chosen to enter a competition at the organizers' discretion after the regular places have been taken. **4** an unpredictable person or thing.

wild carrot *noun* = QUEEN ANNE'S LACE.

wild·cat ● *noun* **1** a smallish cat of a non-domesticated kind; esp. *Felis sylvestris* of Eurasia and Africa, with a grey and black coat and bushy tail, or *N Amer.* a bobcat. **2** a hot-tempered or violent person. **3** an exploratory oil well. **4** a sudden and unofficial strike. ● *adjective* (*attributive*) **1** esp. *N Amer.* reckless; financially unsound. **2** (of a strike) called at short notice, usu. without union backing.

wild·cat·ter *noun N Amer.* **1** a prospector who sinks wildcat oil wells. **2** a person who promotes or participates in risky business enterprises. **3** a wildcat striker.

wild-caught *attributive adjective* (of an animal) caught in and taken from the wild.

wild cucumber *noun* a climbing plant of the cucumber family, *Echinocystis lobata*, found east of the Rockies and bearing a prickly fleshy fruit.

Wilde /waɪld/ **Oscar (Fin·gal O'Flaher·tie Wills)** (1854–1900), Irish dramatist, novelist, poet, and wit. His plays, e.g. *Lady Windermere's Fan* (1892) and *The Importance of Being Earnest* (1895) are characterized by brilliantly witty lines and sharp social observation; he also wrote the novel *The Picture of Dorian Gray* (1890) and *The Ballad of Reading Gaol* (1898), which described his imprisonment for homosexual activity. □ **Wild·ean** /ˈwaɪldɪən/ *adjective*

wilde·beest /ˈwɪldəˌbiːst, ˈvɪl-/ *noun* = GNU. [Afrikaans (as WILD, BEAST)]

Wild·er /ˈwaɪldər/ **1 Billy** (born Samuel Wilder) (1906–2002), Austrian-born US film director and screenwriter, whose films include *Double Indemnity* (1944), *Sunset Boulevard* (1950), *Some Like It Hot* (1959), and *The Apartment* (1960); the latter won Oscars for best script, director, and picture. **2 Thorn·ton (Niven)** (1897–1975), US novelist and dramatist. His work is particularly concerned with the universality of human experience, irrespective of time or place; his works include the novel *The Bridge of San Luis Rey* (1927) and the plays *Our Town* (1938) and *The Skin of Our Teeth* (1942).

wild·er /ˈwɪldər/ *transitive verb archaic* **1** lead astray. **2** bewilder. [perhaps based on WILDERNESS]

wil·der·ness *noun* **1** a wild, uncultivated, and uninhabited region (often *attributive*: *wilderness area*). **2** part of a garden left with an uncultivated appearance. **3** (foll. by *of*) a confused assemblage of things. □ **in the wilderness** out of political office. **voice in the**

wilderness an unheeded advocate of reform. [Old English *wildēornes* from *wild dēor* wild deer]

wild·fire *noun* **1** a destructive or uncontrollable fire, esp. in a forest. **2** *hist.* a combustible liquid, esp. Greek fire, formerly used in warfare. **3** = WILL-O'-THE-WISP 1. □ **spread like wildfire** spread with great speed.

wild·flower *noun* a flowering plant growing in a natural state without human intervention.

wild·fowl *noun* (*pl.* same) (usu. in *pl.*) a game bird, esp. an aquatic one.

wild ginger *noun* a N American plant, *Asarum canadense*, with large heart-shaped leaves and a rootstock tasting of ginger.

wild goose chase *noun* a foolish or hopeless and unproductive quest.

wild grape *noun* any of several species of grape, *Vitis*, found esp. in eastern N America.

wild horse *noun* **1** a horse not domesticated or broken in. **2** (in *pl.*) *informal* even the most powerful influence etc. (*wild horses would not drag the secret from me*).

wild hyacinth *noun* = BLUEBELL 2.

wild·ing[1] / ˈwaɪldɪŋ/ *noun US* the activity or an instance of a gang of youths going on a violent rampage through the streets, parks, etc., attacking or mugging people at random along the way.

wild·ing[2] / ˈwaɪldɪŋ/ *noun* (also **wild·ling**) **1** a plant sown by natural agency, esp. a wild crabapple. **2** the fruit of such a plant.

wild leek *noun* a wild onion of eastern N America, *Allium tricoccum*.

wild licorice *noun* = LICORICE ROOT 1.

wild·life *noun* wild animals collectively (often *attributive*: *wildlife biologist*; *wildlife sanctuary*).

wild lily of the valley *noun* = CANADA MAYFLOWER.

wild marjoram *noun see* MARJORAM.

wild oat *noun* a European grass, *Avena fatua*, naturalized in N America, similar to the cultivated oat. □ **sow one's wild oats** *see* OAT.

wild pitch *noun Baseball* a pitch which is not hit by the batter and cannot be stopped by the catcher, enabling a baserunner to advance.

wild rice *noun* any tall grass of the genus *Zizania*, yielding edible grains.

wild rose *noun* any of several species of uncultivated rose, *Rosa*, e.g. *R. acicularis*, the floral emblem of Alberta.

wild sarsaparilla *noun see* SARSAPARILLA 4.

wild silk *noun* **1** silk from wild silkworms. **2** an imitation of this from short silk fibres.

wild type *noun* a strain or characteristic which prevails in natural conditions, as distinct from an atypical mutant.

Wild West *noun* the western regions of the US in the 19th c., when they were lawless frontier districts.

wild·wood *noun literary* uncultivated or unfrequented woodland.

wile /waɪl/ *noun* (usu. in *pl.*) a stratagem; a trick or cunning procedure. [Middle English *wīl*, perhaps from Scandinavian (Old Norse *vél* craft)]

wil·ful *adjective* (also **will·ful**) **1** (of an action or state) intentional, deliberate (*wilful murder*; *wilful neglect*; *wilful disobedience*). **2** (of a person) obstinate, headstrong. □ **wil·ful·ly** *adverb* **wil·ful·ness** *noun*

Wil·helm I /ˈvɪlhelm/ *see* WILLIAM I 4.

Wil·helm II /ˈvɪlhelm/ *see* WILLIAM II 2.

Wil·helm·ina I /ˌwɪləˈmiːnə/ (full name Wilhelmina Helena Pauline Maria) (1880–1962), queen of the Netherlands 1890–1948. She maintained a government-in-exile in London (1940–5) during the Second World War, and abdicated in 1948 in favour of her daughter Juliana.

Wil·helms·haven /ˈvɪlhelmzˌhɒfən/ a port and resort in NW Germany, on the North Sea; pop. (1998) 88,950. It was a major naval base until 1945.

wili·ness *noun see* WILY.

Wilkes /wɪlks/ **1 Charles** (1798–1877), US naval officer and explorer, who explored Antarctica (*c*.1840). During the American Civil War he caused an international incident by removing two Confederate commissioners from a British ship. **2 John** (1725–97), English journalist and politician, who became known as a champion of liberty for his support of the parliamentary reform movement.

Wilkes Land a region of Antarctica with a coast on the Indian Ocean. It is claimed by Australia.

Wil·kins ▸ 1 Sir (George) Hu·bert (1888–1958), Australian polar explorer, who explored the Arctic by air (1928) and by submarine (1931). **2 Mau·rice (Hugh Fred·erick)** (b.1916), New Zealand-born

English biochemist and molecular biologist. Studying the structure of the DNA molecule by means of X-ray diffraction analysis, he and his colleague Rosalind Franklin provided the evidence for and confirmed the double helix structure proposed by F. H. C. Crick and J. D. Watson in 1953; Wilkins, Crick, and Watson shared a Nobel Prize for their work on DNA in 1962.

will[1] *auxiliary verb & transitive* (3rd sing. present **will**; past **would**) (foll. by infin. without *to*, or *intr.*; present and past only in use) **1** expressing the future tense in statements, commands, or questions (*you will regret this*; *they will leave at once*; *will you go to the party?*). **2** expressing a wish or intention (*I will return soon*). **3** expressing desire, consent, or inclination (*will you have a sandwich?*; *come when you will*; *the door will not open*). **4** expressing ability or capacity (*the jar will hold a kilo*). **5** expressing habitual or inevitable tendency (*accidents will happen*; *will sit there for hours*). **6** expressing probability or expectation (*that will be my wife*). □ **will do** *informal* expressing willingness to carry out a request. ¶ See Usage Note at SHALL. [Old English *wyllan*, (unrecorded) *willan* from Germanic: related to Latin *volo*]

will[2] ● *noun* **1** the faculty by which a person decides or is regarded as deciding on and initiating action (*the mind consists of the understanding and the will*). **2** (also **will-power**) control exercised by deliberate purpose over impulse; self-control (*has a strong will*; *overcame his shyness by willpower*). **3** a deliberate or fixed desire or intention (*a will to live*). **4** energy of intention; the power of effecting one's intentions or dominating others. **5** directions (usu. written) in legal form for the disposition of one's property after death (*make one's will*). **6** disposition towards others (*good will*). **7** what one desires or ordains (*thy will be done*). ● *verb* **1** *transitive* have as the object of one's will; intend unconditionally (*what God wills*; *willed that we should succeed*). **2** *intransitive* exercise willpower. **3** *transitive* instigate or impel or compel by the exercise of willpower (*you can will yourself into contentment*). **4** *transitive* bequeath by the terms of a will (*shall will my money to charity*). □ **at will** whenever one pleases. **have one's will** obtain what one wants. **what is your will?** what do you wish done? **where there's a will there's a way** determination will overcome any obstacle. **a will of one's own** obstinacy; wilfulness of character. **with the best will in the world** however good one's intentions. **with a will** energetically or resolutely. □ **willed** *adjective* (also in *combination*). **will·er** *noun* **will-less** *adjective* [Old English *willa* from Germanic]

Wil·lan /ˈwɪlən/ **(James) Healey** (1880–1968), English-born Canadian composer, organist, and choir director. In all he composed over 800 works, including operas and symphonies, as well as many liturgical pieces; these include *An Apostrophe to the Heavenly Hosts* (1921) for unaccompanied choir. Through his more than 50 years of teaching he influenced several generations of composers, organists, and singers.

Willem·stad /ˈwɪləm,stat, ˈvɪl-/ the capital of the Netherlands Antilles, situated on the southwest coast of the island of Curaçao; pop. (est. 2002) 58,400.

wil·let /ˈwɪlət/ *noun* (pl. same) a large grey and white N American shorebird, *Catoptrophorus semipalmatus*, with a loud call. [*pill-will-willet*, imitative of its call]

will·ful *var. of* WILFUL.

Wil·liam, Prince (b.1982), older son of the Prince of Wales.

William I ▶ **1** (known as William the Conqueror) (*c.*1027–87), the first Norman king of England 1066–87. The illegitimate son of Robert, Duke of Normandy, he claimed the English throne on the death of Edward the Confessor, stating that Edward had promised it to him; he invaded England, defeated Harold II at the Battle of Hastings (1066), was crowned king, and introduced Norman institutions and customs (including feudalism and administrative and legal practices). **2** (known as William the Lion) (1143–1214), grandson of David I, king of Scotland 1165–1214. He attempted to reassert Scottish independence but was forced to pay homage to Henry II of England after being captured by him in 1174. **3** (known as 'William the Silent') (1533–84), prince of Orange and count of Nassau. He was made stadtholder of Holland, Zeeland, and Utrecht (1559) by Philip II of Spain, and later led the revolt against Spanish rule in the Netherlands (1568–76); he was assassinated. **4** (German name Wilhelm I) (1797–1888), king of Prussia 1861–88 and emperor of Germany 1871–88. He became the first emperor of Germany after Prussia's victory against France in 1871, and the latter part of his reign was marked by the rise of German socialism, to which he responded with harsh repressive measures.

William II ▶ **1** (known as William Rufus) (*c.*1060–1100), son of William the Conqueror, king of England 1087–1100. He was killed by an arrow while out hunting; whether this was an assassination or an accident remains unclear. **2** (German name Kaiser Wilhelm) (1859–1941), emperor of Germany 1888–1918. After forcing his chief minister,

Bismarck, to resign in 1890 he proved unable to exercise a strong or consistent influence over German policies, which became increasingly militaristic in foreign affairs; he was unable to prevent the outbreak of the First World War (1914), and abdicated in 1918.

William III (known as William of Orange) (1650–1702), king of Great Britain and Ireland 1689–1702. He was stadtholder of the Netherlands from 1672 and married Mary, daughter of the future James II, in 1677; in 1688 he landed in England at the invitation of disaffected politicians, deposed James II, and, having accepted the Declaration of Rights, was crowned along with his wife the following year.

William IV (known as 'the Sailor King') (1765–1837), son of George III, king of Great Britain and Ireland 1830–7. He served in the Royal Navy from 1779, rising to Lord High Admiral in 1827, and came to the throne after the death of his brother George IV; in 1834 he intervened in political affairs by imposing his own choice of prime minister (the Conservative Robert Peel), despite a Whig majority in Parliament.

William of Malmes·bury /ˈmɒmzberi, -briˌ/ (*c.*1095–*c.*1143), English chronicler, whose major works were the *Gesta Regum Anglorum*, a history of England from 449 to 1120, and its sequel, the *Historia novella*, covering the period from 1128 to 1142.

William of Occam /ˈɒkəm/ (also **Ock·ham**) (*c.*1285–1349), English philosopher and Franciscan friar. His form of nominalist philosophy saw God as beyond human powers of reasoning, and things as provable only by experience or by scriptural authority — hence his maxim, known as *Occam's razor*, that the fewest possible assumptions should be made in explaining anything; he distinguished between faith and reason, advocated a radical separation of the Church from the world, denied the pope all temporal authority, and conceded large powers to the laity and their representatives.

William of Orange see WILLIAM III.

William Rufus see WILLIAM II 1.

Wil·liams ▶ **1 Hank** (born Hiram Williams) (1923–53), US country singer and songwriter, whose songs include 'Why Don't you Love me?', 'Your Cheatin' Heart', and 'Move it on Over'. **2 Jody** (b.1950), American activist who was awarded the 1997 Nobel Peace Prize for her campaign to bring about an international ban on anti-personnel land mines. **3 John (Chris·to·pher)** (b.1941), Australian guitarist and composer, who is noted for an eclectic repertoire that includes both classical and popular music. **4 Robin (Mc·Laur·im)** (b.1952), American actor and comedian. He began his career in television with *Mork and Mindy* in 1978, and went on to star in many films, including *Good Will Hunting* (1997), for which he won an Oscar, *Dead Poets Society* (1989), and *Mrs. Doubtfire* (1993). **5 Rowan** (b.1950), Welsh Anglican churchman and theologian, Archbishop of Canterbury since 2002. **6 Theo·dore Sam·uel ('Ted')** (1918–2002), US baseball player. An outfielder with the Boston Red Sox (1939–60), he had a lifetime batting average of .344, hit 521 career home runs, and was the last player to have a batting average over .400 in a single season (.406 in 1941). **7 Ten·nes·see** (born Thomas Lanier Williams) (1911–83), US dramatist. He achieved success with the semi-autobiographical *The Glass Menagerie* (1944) and *A Streetcar Named Desire* (1947), plays which deal with the tragedy of vulnerable heroines living in fragile fantasy worlds shattered by brutal reality; his later plays increasingly feature Gothic and macabre elements, and include *Cat on a Hot Tin Roof* (1955), *Suddenly Last Summer* (1958), and *The Night of the Iguana* (1962). **8 Venus** (b.1980) and **Se·rena** (b.1981), American tennis players. The sisters hold numerous grand slam titles, and in the 2000 Olympic Games, Venus won a gold medal for the ladies' singles and, with Serena, a further gold for the doubles. **9 Wil·liam Car·los** (1883–1963), US poet, essayist, novelist, and short-story writer. His poetry illuminates the ordinary by vivid, direct observation, and is characterized by avoidance of emotional content and the use of the vernacular; his works include the long poem *Paterson* (1946–58) and the essay collection *In the American Grain* (1925).

Wil·liams·burg /ˈwɪljəmz,bɜrg/ a city in SE Virginia, between the James and York rivers; pop. (2000) 11,988. A large part of the town has been restored and reconstructed so that it appears as it was during the colonial era.

Williams Lake 1 a lake in central BC, situated 120 km south of Quesnel. **2** a city situated just off its northwestern shore; pop. (2001) 11,153. □ **Williams Laker** *noun* [Chief *William*, leader of a Shuswap band *c.*1861]

William the Conqueror see WILLIAM I 1.

wil·lie *var. of* WILLY.

wil·lies *plural noun informal* nervous discomfort (*she gives me the willies*). [19th c.: origin unknown]

will·ing *adjective* **1** ready to consent or undertake (*a willing ally*; *am willing to do it*). **2** given or done etc. by a willing person (*willing hands*; *willing help*). □ **will·ing·ly** *adverb* **will·ing·ness** *noun*

Wil·ling·don /ˈwɪlɪŋdən/ **Free·man Freeman-Thomas, 1st Mar·quess of** (1866–1941), British politician, Governor General of Canada 1926–31. He was the first Governor General to act solely as the agent of the monarch.

Wil·lis·ton Lake /ˈwɪlɪstən/ a large reservoir in north central BC. Created in 1968 by the damming of the Peace River's headwaters, the lake is used today to transport local timber to pulp mills and sawmills at Mackenzie. [R. *Williston*, minister of lands and forests 1956–72]

will-o'-the-wisp *noun* **1** a phosphorescent light seen on marshy ground, perhaps resulting from the combustion of gases. **2** an elusive person. **3** a delusive hope or plan. [originally *Will with the wisp*: *wisp* = handful of (lighted) hay etc.]

wil·low *noun* **1** a tree or shrub of the genus *Salix*, growing usu. near water in temperate climates, with small flowers borne on catkins, and pliant branches yielding osiers for baskets, etc. **2** a cricket bat. [Old English *welig*]

willow grouse *noun* = WILLOW PTARMIGAN.

willow herb *noun* any plant of the genus *Epilobium*, with narrow leaves and pink or purple flowers.

willow pattern *noun* a conventional pottery design of blue on white china etc. representing a Chinese scene in which a willow tree is a prominent feature.

willow ptarmigan *noun* a ptarmigan, *Lagopus lagopus*, with large amounts of white plumage even in summer.

willow warbler *noun* (also **willow wren**) a small Eurasian woodland bird, *Phylloscopus trochilus*, with a tuneful song.

wil·lowy *adjective* **1** lithe, slender, and graceful. **2** having or bordered by willows.

will·power *var. of* WILL[2] *noun* 2.

Wills, Helen (New·ing·ton) (1905–98), US tennis player, who won the US singles title seven times (1923–25, 1927–29, and 1931), and the Wimbledon title eight times (1927–30, 1932–33, 1935, and 1938).

willy *noun* (also **wil·lie**) (*pl.* **-lies**) *slang* the penis.

willy-nilly ● *adverb* **1** whether one likes it or not. **2** haphazardly, at random. ● *adjective* existing or occurring willy-nilly. [later spelling of *will I, nill I* I am willing, I am unwilling]

Wil·mot /ˈwɪlmət/ **Mon·tagu** (d.1766), British army officer. After serving in Nova Scotia from 1746, he was appointed Lieutenant-Governor of Nova Scotia in 1763 and Governor in 1764; during his term extensive amounts of land were granted to speculators, who often did little to encourage settlement.

Wil·son ▸ 1 Ber·tha (b.1923), Scottish-born Canadian lawyer and judge. The first female judge appointed to the Supreme Court of Canada, she is known for her judgments in cases involving human rights, discrimination, and child custody. **2 Charles Thom·son Rees** (1869–1959), Scottish physicist, who invented the cloud chamber (1895) in an attempt to reproduce the conditions in which clouds are formed in nature; by 1911 he had a chamber in which the track of an ion could be made visible, and this became a major tool of particle physicists in subsequent years. He shared a Nobel Prize for physics in 1927. **3 Ethel Davis** (1888–1980), South African-born Canadian novelist and essayist. Her many collections of stories include *Love and Salt Water* (1956) and *Mrs. Golightly and Other Stories* (1961). **4 (James) Har·old, Baron Wil·son of Rie·vaulx** (1916–95), English Labour politician, prime minister 1964–70 and 1974–6. His government introduced a number of social reforms, including reducing the voting age to 18, liberalizing the laws on divorce, homosexuality, and abortion, and introducing comprehensive schooling. **5 (Thom·as) Wood·row** (1856–1924), US Democratic politician, 28th president of the US 1913–21. He initially kept the US out of the First World War, but, following the German reintroduction of unrestricted submarine warfare, entered the war on the Allied side in April 1917; his conditions for a peace treaty, as set out in his 'Fourteen Points' speech (1918), and his plan for the formation of the League of Nations were crucial in the international negotiations surrounding the end of the war, and he was awarded the Nobel Peace Prize in 1919.
□ **Wil·son·ian** /wɪlˈsoːnɪən/ *adjective & noun*

wilt¹ ● *verb* **1** *intransitive* (of a plant, leaf, or flower) wither, droop. **2** *intransitive* (of a person) lose one's energy, flag, tire, droop. **3** *transitive* cause to wilt. ● *noun* **1** the action or an act of wilting. **2** a plant disease causing wilting. [originally dial.: perhaps alteration of *wilk*, *welk*, of Low German or Dutch origin]

wilt² *archaic* 2nd person sing. of WILL[1].

Wil·ton *noun* a kind of woven carpet with a thick pile. [*Wilton* in S England]

Wilts. *abbreviation* Wiltshire.

Wilt·shire /ˈwɪltʃɪr/ a county of S England; county town, Trowbridge.

wily /ˈwaɪli/ *adjective* (**wili·er**, **wili·est**) full of wiles; crafty, cunning. □ **wili·ness** *noun*

Wimble·don /ˈwɪmbəldən/ an annual international tennis championship on grass, held in the London suburb of Wimbledon. Now one of the world's major tennis championships, it has been played since 1877.

wim·min *var. of* WOMYN.

WIMP /wɪmp/ *noun* any of several hypothetical subatomic particles which have relatively large mass but which interact only weakly with ordinary matter, postulated as the main constituents of the dark matter of the universe. [acronym from the initial letters of weakly interacting massive particle]

wimp *noun* *informal* a feeble or ineffectual person. □ **wimp out** demonstrate one's feebleness by failing to act or by avoiding an undertaking; chicken out. □ **wimp·ish** *adjective* **wimp·ish·ly** *adverb* **wimp·ish·ness** *noun* **wimpy** *adjective* [20th c.: origin uncertain]

wim·ple *noun* a linen or silk headdress covering the neck and the sides of the face, formerly worn by women and still worn by some nuns. [Old English *wimpel*]

win ● *verb* (**win·ning**; *past* and *past participle* **won**) **1** *transitive* acquire or secure as a result of a fight, contest, bet, litigation, or some other effort (*won some money*; *won my admiration*). **2** *transitive* be victorious in (a fight, game, race, etc.). **3** *intransitive* **a** be the victor; win a race or contest etc. (*who won?*; *persevere, and you will win*). **b** make one's way or become by successful effort. **4** *transitive* reach by effort (*win the summit*; *win the shore*). **5** *transitive* obtain (ore) from a mine. ● *noun* a victory in a game or bet etc. □ **win the day** be victorious in battle, argument, etc. **win out** overcome obstacles. **win over** persuade, gain the support of. **you can't win** *informal* there is no way to succeed. **you can't win them all** *informal* a resigned expression of consolation on failure.
□ **win·nable** *adjective* [Old English *winnan* toil, endure: compare Old High German *winnan*, Old Norse *vinna*]

wince ● *intransitive verb* grimace, tense, or shrink away involuntarily in pain, embarrassment, or distress. ● *noun* a wincing movement.
□ **win·cer** *noun* **win·cing·ly** *adverb* [Old French *guenchir* turn aside: compare WINCH, WINK]

winch ● *noun* **1** a hoisting or hauling apparatus consisting of a horizontal drum or axle around which a rope, cable, or chain passes, turned by a crank or motor. **2** a windlass. **3** *Brit.* the reel of a fishing rod. ● *transitive verb* lift with a winch. □ **winch·er** *noun* [Old English *wince* from Germanic: compare WINCE]

Win·ches·ter¹ /ˈwɪntʃestər/ the county town of Hampshire, in S England; pop. (est. 2002) 38,000. It became capital of the West Saxon kingdom of Wessex in 519.

Win·ches·ter² *noun* **1** *proprietary* a breech-loading repeating rifle. **2** (in full **Winchester disk** or **drive**) *Computing* a (usu. fixed) disk drive in a sealed unit containing a high-capacity hard disk and the read/write heads (so called because its original numerical designation corresponded to that of the rifle's calibre). [named after O. F. *Winchester* d.1880, US manufacturer of the rifle]

Winck·el·mann /ˈvɪŋkəlmən/ **Jo·hann (Joa·chim)** (1717–68), German archaeologist and art historian. His best-known work, *History of the Art of Antiquity* (1764), was a seminal text in the neoclassical movement, and was particularly influential in popularizing the art and culture of ancient Greece.

wind¹ /wɪnd/ ● *noun* **1 a** air in more or less rapid natural motion, esp. from an area of high pressure to one of low pressure. **b** a current of wind blowing from a specified direction or otherwise defined (*north wind*; *bitter wind*). **2 a** breath as needed in physical exertion or in speech. **b** the power of breathing without difficulty while running or making a similar continuous effort (*let me recover my wind*). **c** a spot below the centre of the chest where a blow temporarily paralyzes breathing. **3** mere empty words; meaningless rhetoric. **4** gas generated in the bowels etc. by indigestion; flatulence. **5 a** an artificially produced current of air, esp. for sounding an organ or other wind instrument. **b** air stored for use or used as a current. **c** (usu. in *pl.*) a wind instrument. **d** a player of a wind instrument. **e** (in *pl.*) wind instruments collectively. **6** a scent carried by the wind, indicating the presence or proximity of an animal etc. ● *transitive verb* **1** cause (a person) to have difficulty breathing as a result of exertion or a blow. **2** renew the wind of by rest (*stopped to wind the horses*). **3** make breathe quickly and deeply by exercise. **4** *Brit.* burp (a baby). **5** detect the presence of by a scent. **6** /waind/ (*past* and *past participle* **wind·ed** or **wound** /waund/) *literary* sound (a bugle or call) by blowing. □ **before the wind** helped by the wind's force. **close to** (or **near**) **the wind 1** sailing as nearly against the wind as is consistent with using its force. **2** *informal* verging on indecency or dishonesty. **get wind of 1** detect by smell. **2** begin to suspect; hear a rumour of. **get** (or **have**) **the wind up** *informal* be alarmed or frightened. **how** (or **which way**) **the wind blows** (or **lies**) **1** what is the state of opinion. **2** what developments are likely. **in the wind** happening or about to happen. **in the wind's eye** directly against the wind. **like the wind** swiftly. **off the wind** *Naut.* with the wind on the quarter. **on a wind** *Naut.* against a wind on either bow. **on the wind** (of a sound or scent) carried by the wind. **put the wind up** *informal* alarm or frighten. **take the wind out of a person's sails** frustrate a person by anticipating an action or remark etc. **to the winds** (or **four winds**) **1** in all directions. **2** into a state of abandonment or neglect. **wind and weather** exposure to the effects of the elements. **wind** (or **winds**) **of change** a force or influence for reform. □ **wind·ed** *adjective* (also in *combination*). **wind·less** *adjective* [Old English]

wind² /waind/ ● *verb* (*past* and *past participle* **wound** /waund/) **1** *intransitive* go in a circular, spiral, curved, or crooked course (*the path winds up the hill*). **2** *transitive* make (one's way) by such a course (*wind your way up to bed*; *wound their way into our affections*). **3** *transitive* wrap closely; surround with or as with a coil (*wound the blanket around me*; *wound my arms around the child*; *wound the child in my arms*). **4 a** *transitive* coil; provide with a coiled thread etc. (*wind the ribbon on to the card*; *wound thread on a spool*; *winding wool into a ball*). **b** *intransitive* coil; (of wool etc.) coil into a ball (*the creeper winds around the pole*; *the wool wound into a ball*). **5** *transitive* wind up (a clock etc.). **6** *transitive* hoist or draw with a windlass etc. (*wound the cable car up the mountain*). ● *noun* **1** a bend or turn in a course. **2** a single turn when winding. □ **wind down 1** lower by winding. **2** (of a mechanism) unwind. **3** (of a person) relax. **4** draw gradually to a close. **wind off** unwind (string, wool, etc.). **wind up 1** coil the whole of (a piece of string etc.). **2** esp. *Brit.* tighten the coiling or coiled spring of (esp. a clock etc.). **3 a** *informal* increase the tension or intensity of (*wound myself up to fever pitch*). **b** irritate or provoke (a person) to the point of anger. **4** bring to a conclusion; end (*wound up his speech*). **5** *Brit. Commerce* **a** arrange the affairs of and dissolve (a company). **b** (of a company) cease business and go into liquidation. **6** *informal* arrive finally; end in a specified state or circumstance (*you'll wind up in prison*; *wound up owing $100*). **7** draw back the arm in preparation for a throw, shot, etc. **wound up** *adjective* (of a person) excited or tense or angry. [Old English *windan*, related to WANDER, WEND]

wind·age /'wIndIdʒ/ *noun* **1** the friction of air against the moving part of a machine. **2 a** the effect of the wind in deflecting a missile. **b** an allowance for this. **3** the difference between the diameter of a gun's bore and its projectile, allowing the escape of gas.

Win·daus /'vIndaus/ **Adolf** (1876–1959), German organic chemist. He did pioneering work on the chemistry and structure of steroids and their derivatives, notably cholesterol, and investigated the D vitamins and vitamin B₁; he was awarded the Nobel Prize for chemistry in 1928.

wind·bag *noun informal derogatory* a person who talks a lot but says little of any value.

wind·blown *adjective* **1** carried by the wind (*windblown snow*). **2** made untidy by the wind (*windblown hair*). **3** (of trees) made to grow in a certain shape by strong prevailing winds.

wind·bound *adjective* unable to sail because of contrary winds.

wind·break *noun* an obstacle, such as a row of trees, a fence, wall, etc. serving to break the force of the wind and shelter houses, crops, or animals.

wind·break·er *noun N Amer.* a kind of wind-resistant outer jacket with close-fitting neck, cuffs, and hip band.

wind·burn *noun* inflammation of the skin caused by exposure to the wind. □ **wind·burned** *adjective* (also **wind·burnt**).

wind·cheat·er *noun Brit.* = WINDBREAKER.

wind chill *noun* the cooling effect of wind blowing on a person or surface.

wind chill factor *noun* a measure or scale of the combined effect of low temperature and wind speed on body temperature.

wind chimes *plural noun* small pieces of glass, metal, etc. suspended from a frame so as to sound against one another in the wind.

wind-down *noun informal* a gradual lessening of excitement or reduction of activity.

wind energy *noun* energy obtained from harnessing the wind with windmills, wind turbines, etc.

wind·er *noun* a winding mechanism esp. of a clock or watch.

Win·der·mere /'wIndər,mɪːr/ (also **Lake Windermere**) a lake in Cumbria, in the southeastern part of the Lake District. At about 17 km (10 miles) in length, it is the largest lake in England.

wind·fall *noun* **1** an unexpected gift of money, piece of good luck, etc. **2** an apple or other fruit blown to the ground by the wind. **3** *N Amer.* **a** a branch or tree blown down by the wind. **b** timber thus blown down.

wind farm *noun* a group of energy-producing windmills or wind turbines.

wind·flower *noun* an anemone.

wind gap *noun* a dried-up former river valley through ridges or hills.

wind gauge *noun* **1** an anemometer. **2** an apparatus attached to the sights of a gun enabling allowance to be made for the wind in shooting.

Wind·hoek /'wInthʊk, 'vInt-/ the capital of Namibia, situated in the centre of the country; pop. (est. 2002) 194,00.

wind·hover /'wInd,hʌvər/ *noun Brit.* a kestrel.

Win·di·go /'wIndIgoː/ *noun* (in the folklore of Northern Algonquian peoples) a cannibalistic giant; a person who has been transformed into a monster by the consumption of human flesh. [Ojibwa *wintiko*]

wind·ing ● *noun* **1** in senses of WIND² *verb*. **2** curved or sinuous motion or movement. **3 a** a thing that is wound around or coiled. **b** Electricity coils of wire as a conductor around an armature etc. ● *adjective* following a curving, sinuous, or meandering course or path (*a winding river*).

winding sheet *noun* a sheet in which a corpse is wrapped for burial.

wind instrument *noun* a musical instrument in which sound is produced by the player blowing a current of air through or across a mouthpiece.

wind·jam·mer *noun* a merchant sailing ship.

wind·lass /'wIndləs/ ● *noun* a machine with a horizontal axle for hauling or hoisting. ● *transitive verb* hoist or haul with a windlass. [alteration of (perhaps by assoc. with dial. *windle* to wind) of obsolete *windas* from Old French *guindas* from Old Norse *vindáss* from *vinda* WIND² + *áss* pole]

wind machine *noun* a device for producing a blast of air or the sound of wind, used esp. in the theatre etc.

wind·mill ● *noun* **1** a mill, pump, or generator driven by the action of the wind on its rotating sails or blades. **2** esp. *Brit.* = PINWHEEL *noun* 1. ● *transitive & intransitive verb* whirl or fling (one's limbs) around in a manner suggestive of a windmill. □ **tilt at windmills** attack an imaginary enemy or grievance (with reference to Don Quixote, who attacked windmills, thinking that they were giants).

win·dow *noun* **1 a** an opening in a wall, roof, or vehicle etc., usu. with glass in fixed, sliding, or hinged frames, to admit light or air etc. and allow the occupants to see out. **b** the glass filling this opening (*have broken the window*). **2** a space for display behind the front window of a store. **3** an aperture in a wall etc. through which customers are served in a bank, ticket office, etc. **4** an opportunity to observe or learn. **5** an opening or transparent part in an envelope to show an address. **6** *Computing* a defined area on a display screen in which a part of a file or image can be displayed. **7 a** an interval during which atmospheric and astronomical circumstances are suitable for the launch of a spacecraft. **b** any interval or opportunity for action. **8** strips of metal foil dispersed in the air to obstruct radar detection. **9** a range of electromagnetic wavelengths for which a medium is transparent. □ **out** (**of**) **the window** *informal* no longer taken into account. □ **win·dowed** *adjective* (also in *combination*). **win·dow·less** *adjective* [Old Norse *vindauga* from WIND¹, EYE)]

window box *noun* a long narrow box placed on an outside windowsill, used for growing flowers.

window cleaner *noun* **1** a person who is employed to clean windows. **2** a substance or object used for cleaning windows.

window dressing *noun* **1** the art of arranging a display in a store window etc. **2** an adroit presentation of facts etc. to give a deceptively favourable impression. □ **window dresser** *noun*

window frame *noun* a supporting frame for the glass of a window.

win·dow·ing *noun Computing* the use of windows for the simultaneous display of parts of different files, images, etc.

window ledge *noun* = WINDOWSILL.

t top v voice w we z zoo ʃ she ʒ vision θ thin ð this ŋ ring x loch tʃ chip dʒ jar (*see over for vowels*)

window of opportunity *noun* a favourable opportunity for doing something that must be seized immediately if it is not to be missed.

win·dow·pane *noun* a pane of glass in a window.

window seat *noun* **1** a seat below a window, esp. in a bay or alcove. **2** a seat next to a window in an aircraft, train, restaurant, etc.

window shade *noun* a blind.

window-shop *transitive verb* look at goods displayed in store windows, usu. without buying anything. □ **window-shopper** *noun*

window·sill *noun* a sill below a window.

window treatment *noun* a blind, curtain, or other drapery for a window.

wind·pipe *noun* the air passage from the throat to the lungs; the trachea.

wind power *noun* power derived from harnessing the wind with windmills, wind turbines, etc.

wind·proof *adjective* (esp. of an outer garment) impervious to wind.

wind·row /'windrō/ *noun* **1** a line of raked hay, sheaves, etc., laid out for drying by the wind. **2** *N Amer.* a long pile or row of leaves, dust, etc. heaped up by or as if by the wind. **3** *Cdn* a ridge of snow, gravel, etc. heaped along the side of a road by a snowplow, grader, etc.

wind sail *noun* a canvas funnel conveying air to the lower parts of a ship.

Wind·scale /'windskeil/ a former name of SELLAFIELD.

wind·screen *noun Brit.* = WINDSHIELD.

wind shear *noun* a variation in wind velocity at right angles to the wind's direction.

wind·shield *noun N Amer.* a glass window across the front of a motor vehicle or aircraft.

windshield wiper *noun N Amer.* a device consisting of a rubber blade on an arm, moving in an arc, for keeping a windshield clear of rain etc.

wind·sock *noun* a cylinder or cone of fabric on a mast to show the direction of the wind at an airfield etc.

Wind·sor[1] 1 an industrial city and port in SW Ontario, situated at the mouth of the Detroit River and Lake St. Clair, opposite Detroit; pop. (2001) 208,402. **2** a town in south central Quebec, situated on the Rivière Saint-François, northwest of Sherbrooke; pop. (2001) 5,321. □ **Wind·sor·ite** *noun* (in sense 1). [*Windsor* in Berkshire, S England, the site of the royal residence at Windsor Castle]

Wind·sor[2] ▸ 1 the name in current use by the British royal family. The name, previously Saxe-Coburg-Gotha, was changed in 1917 in response to wartime anti-German feeling. **2 Duke of**, the title conferred on Edward VIII on his abdication in 1936.

Windsor chair *noun* a wooden dining chair with a semicircular back supported by upright rods.

wind sprint *noun* a form of exercise involving moving from a walk or slow run to a faster run and repeatedly reversing the process.

wind·storm *noun* a storm with very strong wind but little or no rain, snow, etc.

wind·surf·ing *noun* the sport of riding on water on a sailboard. □ **wind·surf** *intransitive verb* **wind·surf·er** *noun*

wind·swept *adjective* exposed to or swept back by the wind.

wind·throw *noun* **1** the uprooting and blowing down of trees by the wind. **2** trees so uprooted.

wind tunnel *noun* a tunnel-like device for producing an airstream of known velocity past models of aircraft, buildings, etc., in the study of wind flow or wind effects on the full-size object.

wind·up /'waindʌp/ ● *noun* **1** a conclusion; a finish. **2 a** *Baseball* the drawing back of the arm as part of the pitcher's throwing motion. **b** *Hockey* the drawing back of the stick as part of a player's shooting motion. **3** a device operated by being wound up, as a toy. **4** *Brit. informal* a deliberate attempt to annoy or provoke someone. ● *adjective* operated by being wound up.

wind·ward ● *adjective & adverb* on the side from which the wind is blowing (*opp.* LEEWARD). ● *noun* the windward region, side, or direction (*to windward; on the windward of*). □ **get to windward of 1** place oneself there to avoid the smell of. **2** gain an advantage over.

Windward Islands a group of islands in the E Caribbean. Constituting the southern part of the Lesser Antilles, they include Martinique, St. Lucia, Barbados, St. Vincent and the Grenadines, and Grenada. [with reference to their position further upwind, in terms of the prevailing southeasterly winds, than the Leeward Islands]

windy[1] /'windi/ *adjective* (**wind·i·er**, **wind·i·est**) **1** stormy with wind (*a windy night*). **2** exposed to the wind; windswept (*a windy plain*). **3** *informal* wordy, verbose, empty (*a windy speech*). **4** *Brit.* generating or characterized by flatulence. **5** *Brit. informal* nervous, frightened. □ **wind·i·ly** *adverb* **wind·i·ness** *noun* [Old English *windig*]

windy[2] /'waindi/ *adjective* that winds, winding (*a narrow windy path*).

wine *noun* **1** fermented grape juice as an alcoholic drink. **2** a fermented drink resembling this made from other fruits etc. as specified (*elderberry wine; ginger wine*). **3** the dark red colour of red wine. □ **wine and dine** entertain or be entertained with food and drink. □ **wine·less** *adjective* [Old English *wīn* from Germanic from Latin *vinum*]

wine bar *noun* a bar or small restaurant where wine is the main drink available.

wine·berry *noun* (*pl.* **-berries**) **1 a** a deciduous bristly shrub, *Rubus phoenicolasius*, from China and Japan, producing scarlet berries used in cooking. **b** this berry. **2** = MAKO².

wine·bib·ber *noun archaic* or *literary* a tippler or drunkard. [WINE + *bib* to tipple]

wine cellar *noun* **1** a cellar for storing wine. **2** the contents of this.

wine cooler *noun* **1** a beverage of wine, soda water, and fruit flavours. **2** a usu. insulated bucket-like container for holding ice cubes to chill a bottle of wine.

wine·glass *noun* **1** a glass for wine, usu. with a stem and foot. **2** the contents of this.

wine grower *noun* a cultivator of grapes for wine. □ **wine-growing** *noun & adjective*

wine gum *noun Cdn & Brit.* a small, chewy, fruit-flavoured candy made with gelatin.

wine list *noun* a list of wines available in a restaurant etc.

wine·maker *noun* a producer of wine; a wine grower.

wine·making *noun* (often *attributive*) the production of wine, either commercially or as a hobby.

wine·press *noun* a press in which grapes are squeezed in making wine.

wine rack *noun* a frame with compartments for holding bottles of wine in a horizontal position.

win·ery /'wainəri/ *noun* (*pl.* **-ies**) esp. *N Amer.* an establishment where wine is made.

Wine·sap *noun N Amer.* a medium-sized, deep red eating and cooking apple, with yellow patches and tiny white dots.

wine·skin *noun* a whole skin of a goat etc. sown up and used to hold wine.

wine steward *noun* (also **wine waiter**) a waiter responsible for serving wine.

wine tasting *noun* **1** the act of judging the quality of wine by tasting it. **2** an occasion for this. □ **wine taster** *noun*

wine vinegar *noun* vinegar made from wine.

winey *adjective* (also **winy**) (**winier**, **winiest**) resembling wine in taste or appearance.

Win·frey, Oprah (b.1954), American talk-show host and actress, famous for *The Oprah Winfrey Show*.

wing ● *noun* **1** each of the limbs or organs by which a bird, bat, or insect is able to fly. **2** anything resembling or analogous to a wing in form or function. **3** either of a pair of rigid horizontal structures extending on either side of an aircraft that support it in the air. **4** (in *pl.*) a badge depicting a pair of wings awarded to a person or worn on a uniform to symbolize that he or she is a certified pilot. **5** part of a building which projects or is extended in a certain direction from the main or central part (*lived in the north wing*). **6** a section of a political party or group holding more progressive or reactionary views than those of the more moderate centre (*see* RIGHT WING, LEFT WING). **7** esp. *Hockey & Soccer* **a** the area along the side of a playing surface (*he skated down the wing and fired a shot on goal*). **b** the position of the forward player who covers this area. **c** a player at this position; a winger. **8 a** either of the flanks on the right or left side of the main body of an army or fleet in battle array. **b** an operational unit of some air forces consisting of two or more squadrons. **9** (in *pl.*) the sides of a theatre stage out of view of the audience. **10** *Anat. & Bot.* a lateral part or projection of an organ or structure. **11** a cut of beef from the short loin, including the thirteenth rib (also *attributive: wing steak*). **12** *Brit.* = FENDER 1a, c. ● *verb* **1 a** *intransitive* fly through the air, on wings or in an aircraft or as if so (*bats winging overhead; the ball came winging through the air*). **b** *transitive* make (one's way) through the air. **2** *transitive* (usu. in *passive*) equip with wings. **3** *transitive* **a** enable to fly; give swiftness to (*fear winged my steps*). **b** esp. *N Amer.* cause to sail or soar through the air;

throw. **4** *transitive* shoot (a bird) in the wing. □ **give** (or **lend**) **wings to** speed up (a person or a thing). **on the wing** flying or in flight. **on a wing and a prayer** with only the slightest chance of success. **spread** (or **stretch**) **one's wings** test or develop one's abilities. **take under one's wing** treat as a protege. **take wing** fly away; soar. **waiting in the wings** awaiting one's opportunity to fill a position expected to become available. **wing it** *informal* improvise; speak or act without preparation. □ **winged** *adjective* (also in *combination*). **wing·less** *adjective* **wing·let** *noun* **wing-like** *adjective* [Middle English pl. *wenge, -en, -es* from Old Norse *vængir*, pl. of *vængr*]

wing·back *noun* **1** *N Amer. Football* **a** an offensive back who lines up next to an end. **b** the position of this player. **2** = WINGBACK CHAIR.

wingback chair *noun* (also **wing chair**) an armchair with side pieces projecting forward at the top of a high back.

wing·beat *noun* one complete cycle of movements made by the wing of a bird etc. in flying.

wing-case *noun* either of a pair of modified toughened forewings which cover the functional wings of certain insects, such as a beetle.

wing collar *noun* a high stiff shirt collar with the corners turned down, usu. worn with formal dress.

wing commander *noun* (currently in the RAF or *hist.* in the RCAF) an officer ranking below group captain and above a squadron leader.

wing·ding *noun* (also **whing·ding**) *N Amer. informal* a wild party; a festive social gathering or celebration. [20th c.: origin unknown]

wing·er *noun* **1** *esp. Hockey & Soccer* a forward who plays on the wing. **2** (in *combination*) a person affiliated with a specified political wing (*left winger*).

wing forward *noun Rugby* a forward who plays on the part of the field close to the sidelines.

wing·man *noun* (*pl.* **-men**) the pilot of an aircraft which is positioned behind and to one side of the leading aircraft, as in attack formation.

wing nut *noun* **1** a threaded nut with flat projections so that it may be tightened or loosened by hand with the thumb and forefinger, without the aid of a wrench. **2** *N Amer. slang* a crazy person; an idiot.

wing shooting *noun* the sport or practice of shooting birds while they are in flight. □ **wing shooter** *noun*

wing shot *noun* **1** a shot aimed at a flying bird. **2** a person skilled at wing shooting.

wing·span *noun* (also **wing·spread**) the maximum lateral extent of the wings of a bird or aircraft, measured from tip to tip.

wing tip *noun* **1** the tip of the wing of an aircraft, bird, bat, or insect. **2** *N Amer.* **a** a usu. perforated toecap with a backward extending point and curved sides. **b** (usu. **wing·tip**, in full **wingtip shoe**) a shoe having such a toecap.

wingy *adjective* (**wing·i·er**, **wing·i·est**) *Cdn informal* crazy, flighty, loopy.

Win·isk River /wɪˈnɪsk/ a river in N Ontario, 475 km long, which rises some 50 km north of Thunder Bay and flows generally northeastward to Hudson Bay. [Cree, = woodchuck]

wink ● *intransitive verb* **1** close and open one eye, esp. in a deliberate, intimate, or collusive manner, to convey a message to a person, or as a signal of friendliness. **2** (of a light etc.) twinkle; shine or flash intermittently. **3** (usu. foll. by *out*) disappear or go out suddenly. ● *noun* **1** an act of closing and opening the eye, esp. as a signal. **2** a brief moment; an instant (*our trade surplus will vanish in a wink*). **3** (usu. with *neg.*) *informal* a very brief or the shortest possible period of sleep (*I didn't sleep a wink*). □ **as easy as winking** *informal* very easy. **wink at** purposely avoid seeing (an offence, impropriety, etc.); pretend not to notice. **wink-wink, nudge-nudge** = NUDGE, NUDGE, WINK, WINK (*see* NUDGE). [Old English *wincian* from Germanic: compare WINCE, WINCH]

win·kle ● *noun* any edible marine gastropod mollusc of the genus *Littorina*, abundant in the intertidal zone of rocky coasts; a periwinkle. ● *transitive verb* (foll. by *out*) extract (*winkled the information out of them*). □ **wink·ler** *noun* [abbreviation of PERIWINKLE²: compare WIG¹]

winkle-picker *noun Brit. informal* a shoe with a long pointed toe, popular in the 1950s.

Wink·ler a town in S Manitoba, situated about 125 km southwest of Winnipeg, near the border with N Dakota; pop. (2001) 7,943. □ **Wink·ler·ite** *noun* [V. *Winkler*, lumber merchant and local legislator c.1892]

win·less *adjective* esp. *N Amer.* characterized by an absence of victories (*their pitcher is winless in four starts; a six-game winless streak*).

Win·ne·bago /ˌwɪnəˈbeigo/ *noun N Amer.* proprietary a recreational vehicle.

win·ner *noun* **1** a person, team, racehorse, etc. that is victorious in a competition. **2** a goal, run, card, etc. that decides the outcome of a game or competition. **3** *informal* a successful or highly promising idea, enterprise, etc.

winner's circle *noun* **1** an area at a racetrack where horses are unsaddled after a race and where awards are presented to the jockeys, trainers, and owners of winning horses. **2** the category of those who have achieved success or victory in any event or endeavour.

winner-take-all *attributive adjective* **1** denoting a conflict in which victory is outright or the successful competitor alone is rewarded. **2** denoting the attitude or approach of a person whose sole objective is outright victory.

win·ning ● *adjective* **1** victorious, successful (*the winning entry*). **2** that determines the outcome of a game or competition (*the winning run*). **3** denoting a streak of consecutive victories uninterrupted by losses or ties (*a four-game winning streak*). **4** attractive, persuasive (*a winning smile; winning ways*). ● *noun* **1** the action of being victorious (*winning is everything*). **2** (in *pl.*) money won esp. in gambling. □ **win·ning·ly** *adverb*

win·ning·est *adjective N Amer. Sport informal* that has won the most often; that has recorded or achieved the most victories.

winning post *noun* a post marking the end of a race.

Win·ni·peg the capital of Manitoba, situated in the southeastern part of the province at the confluence of the Assiniboine and Red rivers, south of Lake Winnipeg; pop. (2001) 619,544. □ **Win·ni·peg·ger** *noun* [as WINNIPEG, LAKE]

Winnipeg, Lake a large lake in central Manitoba, representing (together with Lake Winnipegosis and Lake Manitoba) the bottom of former glacial Lake Agassiz. Occupying an area of 24 387 sq. km, it has a maximum depth of only 18 m. [Cree and Ojibwa *ouenpig* murky water, with reference to the cloudiness of the water where the river drains into the lake]

Winnipeg couch *noun Cdn* a couch with no arms or back, that converts into a double bed.

Winnipeg General Strike *noun Cdn hist.* a large general strike, 15 May–25 June 1919, in Winnipeg, involving over 30,000 labourers dissatisfied with low wages, poor working conditions, and the lack of a collective bargaining process. The strike, which was supported by many public sector workers, crippled the city for over a month before the federal government intervened, arresting several of the strike's leaders and placing the city under military rule, effectively forcing the strikers back to work.

Winnipeg goldeye *noun Cdn* = GOLDEYE.

Win·ni·peg·osis, Lake /ˌwɪnəpegˈoːsɪs/ a lake in W Manitoba, situated west of Lake Winnipeg and north of Lake Manitoba. [diminutive of Cree and Ojibwa *ouenpig*: see WINNIPEG, LAKE]

Winnipeg River a river in SE Manitoba, 813 km long, which rises in Lake of the Woods in NW Ontario and flows northwestward to Lake Winnipeg. [as WINNIPEG, LAKE]

win·now /ˈwɪno/ *transitive verb* **1** expose (grain) to the wind or to a current of air so that unwanted lighter particles of chaff are separated or blown away. **2** (foll. by *out, from*) separate (chaff) from grain by exposing it to a current of air. **3** (often foll. by *down*) subject to a process which separates the various parts or components, esp. the good from the bad (*winnow down the number of candidates*). **4** (often foll. by *out, from*) **a** extract or obtain (something valuable or desirable) by separating it from something undesirable (*winnow out the best players from a group of prospects*). **b** eliminate or clear away (something undesirable) by separating it from something useful (*winnow the lies from the truth*). □ **win·now·er** *noun* (in senses 1, 2). [Old English *windwian* (as WIND¹)]

wino /ˈwaino/ *noun* (*pl.* **winos**) *slang* a habitual excessive drinker of cheap wine; an alcoholic, esp. one who is destitute.

win·some /ˈwɪnsəm/ *adjective* (of a person, looks, or manner) winning, attractive, engaging. □ **win·some·ly** *adverb* **win·some·ness** *noun* [Old English *wynsum* from *wyn* JOY + -SOME¹]

win·ter ● *noun* **1 a** the fourth and coldest season of the year, beginning at the end of fall and lasting until the start of spring. **b** *Astronomy* the period from the winter solstice to the spring equinox. **2** cold or wintry weather typical of this season. **3** a time or state of old age, decay, affliction, hostility, emotional coldness, etc. **4** (in *pl.*) *literary* a specified number of years, esp. of a person's age (*a man of fifty winters*). ● *attributive adjective* **1** characteristic of winter (*winter weather*). **2** done or occurring in winter (*winter sports*). **3** suitable for use in winter (*winter coat*). **4 a** (of plants or animals) active or flourishing in winter. **b** (of crops) sown in fall for harvesting the following year. ● *verb* **1** *intransitive* (usu. foll. by *in*) spend the winter (*her family winters in Florida*). **2** (often foll. by *over*) **a** *intransitive* (of animals) find or be provided with food and shelter in the winter. **b** *transitive* keep or maintain (animals or plants) during the winter. □ **win·ter·ly** *adjective* [Old English from Germanic, prob. related to WET]

winter aconite *noun* any plant of the genus *Eranthis*, with yellow buttercup-like flowers blooming in the early spring.

winter·berry *noun* (*pl.* **-berries**) any of several deciduous N American hollies with non-prickly leaves and with berries which persist through the winter, esp. *Ilex verticillata*.

winter carnival *noun* N Amer. an organized festival featuring various outdoor winter sports and activities, such as dogsled and snowmobile races, ice sculptures, etc.

winter city *noun* a city subject to long and harsh winters.

winter club *noun* Cdn an organization that offers access to various recreational facilities for activities such as skating and curling throughout the winter.

winter creeper *noun* any of various evergreen shrubs of the genus *Euonymus*, esp. varieties of *E. fortunei*.

win·ter·er *noun* Cdn hist. = WINTERING PARTNER.

winter feed ● *transitive verb* feed or maintain (livestock) during winter when pasturage is frozen or covered with snow. **● *noun*** food supplied to livestock during the winter.

winter·green *noun* **1** any of several plants esp. of the genus *Pyrola*, *Gaultheria*, or *Chimaphila*, remaining green through the winter. **2** (in full **wintergreen oil**) an oil containing methyl salicylate, originally distilled from the leaves of *G. procumbens* but now usu. made synthetically, which is used medicinally in lotions and creams etc. and as a flavouring.

winter ice road *noun* Cdn = WINTER ROAD.

win·ter·ing ground *noun* (usu. in *pl.*) the region to which animals, esp. birds, migrate in the winter.

win·ter·ing partner *noun* (also **win·ter·er**) Cdn hist. a stockholding member and representative of a fur-trading company, esp. the North West Company or Hudson's Bay Company, stationed year-round at a trading post in the northern interior to negotiate the acquisition of furs.

win·ter·ize *transitive verb* (also esp. Brit. **-ise**) esp. N Amer. adapt or prepare (a home, cottage, car, etc.) for use in cold weather. □ **win·ter·iz·a·tion** *noun* **win·ter·ized** *adjective*

winter jasmine *noun* a jasmine, *Jasminum nudiflorum*, with yellow flowers.

winter·kill N Amer. **● *noun*** **1** the death of plants or animals as a result of exposure to frost, snow, and extreme cold. **2** a plant, part of a plant, or animal that has died in this way. **● *verb*** **1** *transitive* kill (usu. in *passive*) (plants or animals) by exposure to frost, snow, and extreme cold. **2** *intransitive* (of a plant or animal) die from exposure to cold etc.

Win·ter·peg a jocular nickname for Winnipeg. [with reference to its cold winters]

winter range *noun* N Amer. land suitable for grazing to which animals migrate in the winter.

winter road *noun* Cdn (*North*) a secondary road made of compacted snow or ice, often plowed over a frozen lake or ground impassable in the summer.

winter savory *noun* see SAVORY[1].

winter solstice *noun* the time of year when the sun appears at its lowest altitude above the horizon at noon and daylight is at a minimum, occurring in the northern hemisphere when the sun reaches its southernmost point in the sky on about 22 Dec., or in the southern hemisphere when it reaches its northernmost point on about 21 June.

winter sports *plural noun* sports performed on snow or ice esp. in winter, such as skiing, figure skating, hockey, etc.

winter squash *noun* N Amer. see SQUASH[2] 1.

winter·time *noun* the season of winter.

winter wheat *noun* wheat that is planted in the fall and harvested the following summer. *Compare* SPRING WHEAT.

Win·throp /ˈwɪnˌθrɒp/ **1 John** (1588–1649), English colonist, the first governor of the Massachusetts Bay Colony and the dominant figure among the Puritan founders of New England. **2** his son, **John** (1606–76), English colonist, who was the governor of Connecticut (1657–76).

win·try *adjective* (also **win·tery**) ; **win·tri·er**, **win·tri·est**) **1** characteristic of or affected by winter (*wintry weather*; *a wintry landscape*). **2** (of a smile, greeting, etc.) lacking warmth or enthusiasm; dismal, cheerless. □ **win·tri·ness** *noun*

win-win *adjective* designating or pertaining to a situation which is beneficial to both parties involved.

winy *var. of* WINEY.

wipe ● *transitive verb* **1** clean or dry the surface of by rubbing with a cloth or towel etc. (*wipe the table*; *wipe your feet before coming inside*). **2** spread or apply (a soft or liquid substance) over a surface by rubbing with a soft cloth or the hand etc. **3** (often foll. by *away*, *off*) **a** clear or remove (moisture, dirt, a spill, etc.) from something (*wiped the mess off the table*; *wipe your tears away*). **b** remove or eliminate completely (*the village was wiped off the map*; *wipe that smile off your face!*). **4** (often foll. by *from*) remove or erase (a thought, memory, etc.) from one's mind. **5 a** erase (data, a recording, etc.) from a computer disk, videotape, etc. **b** erase data from (a medium). **● *noun*** **1** an act of wiping (*give the floor a wipe*). **2** a disposable piece of absorbent paper or cloth, usu. treated with a cleaning agent, for wiping something clean. **3** an effect in which an existing film or video image seems to be wiped away by a new one as the boundary between them moves across the screen. □ **wipe down** clean (esp. a vertical surface) by wiping. **wipe the floor with** *informal* inflict a humiliating defeat on. **wipe off** annul (a debt etc.). **wipe out 1 a** greatly or completely reduce the strength or significance of; destroy, annihilate (*wiped out the competition*; *the whole population was wiped out*). **b** efface, obliterate (*wipe it out of my memory*). **2** *slang* murder. **3** *informal* **a** (of a surfer) fall or be knocked from one's surfboard. **b** fall, skid, or crash. **4** clean the inside of. **5** avenge (an insult etc.). **wipe the slate clean** see SLATE. **wipe up** clear or remove (a liquid etc.) by wiping or absorbing it with a cloth. □ **wipe·able** *adjective* [Old English *wīpian*: compare Old High German *wīfan* wind round, Gothic *weipan* crown: related to WHIP]

wiped out *adjective* **1** annihilated, destroyed. **2** esp. N Amer. financially ruined, penniless. **3** esp. N Amer. *informal* tired out, exhausted.

wipe·out *noun* **1** a fall, crash, or accident, esp. while surfing, skiing, skating, etc. **2** *informal* a dismal failure. **3** an instance of destruction or annihilation. **4** the obliteration of one radio signal by another.

wiper *noun* **1** = WINDSHIELD WIPER. **2** *Electricity* a moving component that rotates or slides to make electrical contact with one or more terminals.

Wir·ad·huri /wɜrˈadʒɜri/ *noun* an Aboriginal language of SE Australia, now extinct.

wire ● *noun* **1 a** metal drawn out into the form of a fine thread or thin flexible rod. **b** a piece of this. **2** a single line of esp. copper wire, or several of these braided or twisted together, usu. insulated and used as a conductor of electrical current. **3** esp. N Amer. *informal* **a** dated a telegram. **b** = NEWS WIRE. **4** an electronic listening device, esp. one which can be concealed on a person; a bug. **5 a** a line or cable made of several strands of wire twisted or braided together for strength. **b** several strands of wire woven or arranged into a mesh or netting (*chicken wire*). **6** N Amer. a wire stretched across and above a racetrack at the starting and finish line. **7** (*attributive*) made of wire (*a wire coat hanger*). **● *transitive verb*** **1** fit, fasten, strengthen, or secure with a wire (*wired my jaw shut*). **2** (often foll. by *up*) *Electricity* furnish (a building etc.) with electrical circuits, fibre optic cabling, telephone lines, etc. **3** fit (a person) with a concealed listening device. **4** esp. N Amer. *informal* **a** dated convey (a message) by telegraph. **b** arrange to have (money) sent, formerly by telegraph, now usu. by some other means. □ **by wire** by telegraph. **down to the wire** see DOWN[1]. **get one's wires crossed** see CROSS. **under the wire** N Amer. just in time. **wire-to-wire** N Amer. from start to finish. [Old English *wīr*]

wire brush ● *noun* **1** a brush with stiff wire bristles used for removing rust, paint, or dirt from hard surfaces, esp. metal. **2** either of a pair of thin sticks with long wire bristles for producing a soft hissing sound on drums, cymbals, etc. **● *transitive verb*** (usu. **wire-brush**) clean with a wire brush.

wire cutters *plural noun* (also **wire cutter**) a tool or pair of pliers used to cut wire.

wired *adjective* **1** *slang* hyper, strung out, or antsy, esp. due to the effects of a drug or stimulant, such as caffeine. **2 a** fitted with electrical connections or electric or fibre optic cables. **b** *informal* having access to the Internet. **3** supported, strengthened, or stiffened with wire. □ **wired for sound** fitted with or wearing an electronic listening device.

wire gauge *noun* **1** a gauge for measuring the diameter of wire. **2** a standard series of sizes in which wire etc. is made.

wire gauze *noun* a stiff gauze woven from wire.

wire grass *noun* any of various grasses with tough wiry stems.

wire-hair *noun* any dog or breed of dog, esp. a terrier, having a rough coat of a stiff and wiry texture. □ **wire-haired** *adjective*

Consonants: b *but*   d *dog*   f *few*   g *get*   h *her*   j *yes*   k *cat*   l *leg*   m *man*   n *no*   p *pen*   r *red*   s *sit*

wire·less ● *adjective* designating or pertaining to any of various devices, communication systems, etc., esp. cell phones etc., not requiring wires, esp. employing radio transmission. ● *noun* **1** esp. *Brit.* *dated* a radio. **2** (in full **wireless telegraphy**) = RADIO-TELEGRAPHY.

wire-puller *noun* esp. *N Amer. informal* a person, esp. a politician, who exerts control or influence from behind the scenes. □ **wire-pulling** *noun*

wire-rimmed *adjective* (of a pair of eyeglasses) having a frame made of wire.

wire rims *plural noun* a pair of wire-rimmed eyeglasses.

wire rope *noun* rope made of strands of wire twisted together.

wire service *noun N Amer.* a news agency that supplies syndicated news stories to its subscribers, e.g. newspapers, radio and television stations.

wire stripper *noun* (often in *pl.*) a tool for removing the insulation from electrical wires.

wire·tap ● *noun* **1** an act of tapping a telephone line, esp. as a means of surveillance. **2** a device used to do this. ● *transitive verb* **1** tap the telephone lines of (a house or building etc.). **2** monitor (a conversation etc.) by means of a wiretap. □ **wire·tap·per** *noun* **wire·tap·ping** *noun*

wire wheel *noun* a wheel with narrow metal spokes joining the rim to the hub, esp. on a sports car.

wire·worm *noun* the larva of the click beetle, causing damage to crop plants.

wir·ing *noun* **1** a system of electrical wires in an apparatus or building. **2** the installation of electrical wires.

wiry /'waɪrɪ/ *adjective* (**wiri·er**, **wiri·est**) **1** resembling wire in texture or appearance, esp. stiff and flexible (*wiry hair*). **2** (of a person) thin and sinewy. **3** made of wire. □ **wiri·ness** *noun*

Wis. *abbreviation* Wisconsin.

Wis·con·sin /wɪs'kɒnsən/ a state in the northern US, bordering on Lakes Superior and Michigan; pop. (est. 2000) 5,363,675; capital, Madison. □ **Wis·con·sin·ite** *noun*

Wisd. *abbreviation* Wisdom of Solomon (Apocrypha).

wis·dom *noun* **1** the state of being wise. **2** experience and knowledge together with the power of applying them critically or practically. **3** sagacity, prudence; common sense. **4** wise sayings, thoughts, etc., regarded collectively. **5** (**Wisdom**) = WISDOM OF SOLOMON. □ **in his** (or **her** etc.) **wisdom** usu. *ironic* in the belief that it would be best (*the committee in its wisdom decided to abandon the project*). [Old English *wīsdōm* (as WISE[1], -DOM)]

Wisdom of Solomon *noun* a book of the Apocrypha ascribed to Solomon and containing a meditation on wisdom; the book is thought actually to date from about 1st c. BC–1st c. AD. In Catholic Bibles it is often referred to as the **Book of Wisdom**.

wisdom tooth *noun* each of four hindmost teeth on either side of the upper and lower jaws, which usu. erupt around the age of 20 and which may be removed if they cause pain.

wise[1] *adjective* **1 a** having experience and knowledge and the ability to apply them judiciously. **b** (of an action, behaviour, etc.) proceeding from, consistent with, or demonstrating knowledge, judgment, or discernment. **2** sagacious, prudent, sensible, discreet. **3** having knowledge; learned, erudite. **4** suggestive of wisdom (*with a wise nod of the head*). **5** *N Amer. informal* **a** alert, crafty. **b** impudent, cocky. □ **wise to** *informal* aware of, esp. so as to know what to do or how to act. **none the** (or **no**) **wiser** knowing no more than before. **put a person wise** (often foll. by *to*) *informal* inform a person (about). **wise after the event** able to understand and assess an event or circumstance after its implications have become obvious. **wise off** (often foll. by *at*) esp. *US* make wisecracks (at a person). **wise up** become informed, aware, or enlightened. **without anyone's being the wiser** undetected. □ **wise·ly** *adverb* [Old English *wīs* from Germanic]

wise[2] *noun archaic* way, manner, or degree (*in solemn wise*; *on this wise*). □ **in no wise** not at all. [Old English *wīse* from Germanic from WIT[2]]

-wise[1] *suffix* **1** forming adjectives and adverbs meaning 'in the manner, form, or direction of' (*crosswise*; *clockwise*; *lengthwise*) (compare -WAYS). **2** *informal* forming adverbs meaning 'in terms of, regarding' (*music-wise the band is a success but they need to improve image-wise*). ¶ Invented combinations of this sort are usually considered inelegant.

-wise[2] *suffix* forming adjectives meaning 'mindful and careful of, having or showing common sense regarding' (*a media-wise celebrity*; *a penny-wise investor*).

wise·acre *noun* **1** a foolish person with an air or affectation of wisdom. **2** = WISE GUY 1. [Middle Dutch *wijsseggher* soothsayer, prob. from Old High German *wissago*, *wizago*, assimilated to WISE[1], ACRE]

wise·ass *noun* (also *attributive*) esp. *N Amer. slang* = WISE GUY 1.

wise·crack *informal* ● *noun* a witty or sarcastic remark. ● *verb* **1** *intransitive* make a wisecrack. **2** *transitive* say (something) in a snide, facetious, or sarcastic manner. □ **wise·crack·er** *noun* **wise·crack·ing** *noun & adjective*

wise guy *noun informal* **1** a smug or cocky person who makes sarcastic quips or comments, esp. in order to display cleverness (also *attributive*: *wise-guy attitude*). **2** *US slang* a person involved in organized crime.

Wise·man, Adele (1928–92), Canadian author and educator. She has written novels, including *The Sacrifice* (1956, Governor General's Award) and *Crackpot* (1974), a play, *Testimonial Dinner and Old Women at Play* (1978), and a collection of essays, *Memoirs of a Book-Molesting Childhood* (1987).

wise man *noun* **1** a learned or prudent man, esp. one chosen as an adviser in political matters. **2** a man who practises magic, esp. each of the three Magi.

wis·ent /'wiːzənt/ *noun* the European bison, *Bison bonasus*. [German: compare BISON]

wise woman *noun* **1** a learned or prudent woman, esp. one chosen as an adviser in political matters. **2** *hist.* a female magician or witch, esp. a harmless or beneficent one who deals in charms against disease, bad luck, etc.

wish ● *verb* **1** *transitive* (often foll. by *that* + clause) have as a desire or aspiration (esp. something that cannot or is unlikely to occur) (*I wish I were you*; *I wish I played in the NHL*). **2** *transitive* have as an intention or hope (*I wish to travel once I have completed my education*). **3** *transitive* demand or request (*I wish you wouldn't do that*; *I wish you to go*). **4** *intransitive* (often foll. by *for*) have or express a desire or yearning for (esp. something not easily or likely to be obtained) (*I wish for a million dollars*). **5** *transitive* have or express one's hopes for (the success or well-being etc. of another) (*wish me luck!*; *I wish you no harm*; *she wished me a happy birthday*). **6** *transitive* (usu. with *neg.*, foll. by *on*, *upon*) foist on a person (*I wouldn't wish that on anyone*). ● *noun* **1 a** a desire, request, or aspiration. **b** an expression of this. **2** a thing desired (*got my wish*). □ **best** (or **good**) **wishes** hopes felt or expressed for another's happiness etc. **if wishes were horses** (**beggars would ride**) everybody would be rich, talented, successful, etc. if wishing were all that was required. **the wish is father to the thought** we believe a thing because we wish it true. □ **wish·er** *noun* (in sense 5 of *verb*; also in *combination*). [Old English *wȳscan*, Old High German *wunsken* from Germanic, ultimately related to WEEN, WONT]

wish·bone *noun* **1** a forked bone between the neck and breastbone of a bird, traditionally removed from the carcass of cooked fowl and broken between two people, the longer portion entitling the holder to make a wish. **2** an object of similar shape. **3** a wishbone-shaped element in the independent suspension of a vehicle, having two arms which are hinged to the chassis at their ends and to the wheel at their joint (compare DOUBLE-WISHBONE SUSPENSION).

wish·ful *adjective* full of desire, longing, or yearning; having or expressing a wish. □ **wish·ful·ly** *adverb* **wish·ful·ness** *noun*

wish-fulfill·ment *noun* a tendency for an unconscious or acknowledged desire to be satisfied in fantasy or dreams.

wishful thinking *noun* belief or expectation founded on wishes rather than on what one has reason to suppose to be true.

wishing well *noun* a well or a structure shaped like one into which one throws a coin with the belief that a wish made at the same time will come true.

wish list *noun* a list of wishes, desires, aspirations, or objectives.

wishy-washy *adjective* **1** (of a person) indecisive, irresolute, feeble. **2** lacking strength or substance; insipid (*a wishy-washy article*). **3** (of tea, soup, etc.) weak, watery. [reduplication of WASHY]

wisp *noun* **1** several strands of hair or pieces of grass or hay; a small bundle of hay, grass, hair, etc. **2** a thin faint diffuse trace or streak of smoke etc. (*wisps of cloud*). **3** a person or thing that is slender or delicate (*a wisp of a child*). **4** (usu. foll. by *of*) a hint or suggestion (*a wisp of hope*). □ **wispy** *adjective* (**wisp·i·er**, **wisp·i·est**). **wisp·i·ly** *adverb* **wisp·i·ness** *noun* [Middle English: origin uncertain: compare West Frisian *wisp*, and WHISK]

wist *past and past participle of* WIT[2].

wis·teria /wɪ'stiːriə/ *noun* (also **wis·taria** /-'steriə/) any climbing plant of the genus *Wisteria*, with hanging racemes of blue, purple, or white flowers. [C. Wistar (or Wister), US anatomist d.1818]

wist·ful *adjective* (of a person, looks, etc.) yearningly or mournfully expectant or wishful. □ **wist·ful·ly** *adverb* **wist·ful·ness** *noun* [apparently assimilation of obsolete *wistly* (adv.) intently (compare WHISHT) to *wishful*, with corresponding change of sense]

wit[1] *noun* **1 a** the apt, clever, unexpected, and humorous expression of thought or juxtaposition of contrasting ideas and expressions, calculated to delight an audience (*conversation sparkling with wit*). **b** the ability to give intellectual pleasure by means of this in speech or writing. **2** a person possessing such an ability; a cleverly humorous person. **3** (often in *pl.*) mental or intellectual power; intelligence, quick understanding (*a battle of wits*). □ **at one's wits'** (or **wit's**) **end** in a state of utter perplexity or despair. **have** (or **keep**) **one's wits about one** be vigilant or mentally alert. **live by one's wits** live by ingenious or crafty expedients, without a settled occupation. **match wits with** contend with someone intellectually. **out of one's wits** mad, insane. **scare** (or **frighten**) **the wits out of** frighten severely. □ **wit·ted** *adjective* (in sense 3; also in *combination*). [Old English *wit(t)*, *gewit(t)* from Germanic]

wit[2] *transitive & intransitive verb* (1st & 3rd sing. present **wot** /wɒt/; past and past participle **wist**) (often foll. by *of*) *archaic* know. □ **to wit** that is to say; namely. [Old English *witan* from Germanic]

witch ● *noun* **1** a person, usu. a woman, who practises magic or sorcery, esp. one supposed to have dealings with evil spirits and to be able to perform supernatural acts with their help. **2** a follower or practitioner of the religious cult of modern witchcraft; a Wiccan. **3** an ugly or malevolent old woman; a hag. ● *transitive verb archaic* bewitch. □ **witch·ing** *adjective & noun* **witch·like** *adjective* **witchy** *adjective* (**witch·i·er**, **witch·i·est**). [Old English *wicca* (masc.), *wicce* (fem.), related to *wiccian* (v.) practise magic arts]

witch- *var. of* WYCH-.

witch·craft *noun* **1 a** the practices of a witch, esp. the use of magic and sorcery. **b** the use of supernatural power supposed to be possessed by a person in league with the devil or evil spirits. **2** the practices and beliefs of the Wiccans. **3** bewitching power, charm, or influence, as exercised by eloquence or beauty.

witch doctor *noun* a person who professes to cure disease and counteract witchcraft by magic, esp. a tribal magician.

witch·ery *noun* **1** witchcraft. **2** bewitching power or influence.

witches' brew *noun* (also **witch's brew**) **1** a magic brew prepared by witches. **2** any harmful, suspicious, or disgusting concoction or blend of elements.

witches' Sabbath *noun see* SABBATH 4.

witch·etty /ˈwɪtʃəti/ *noun* (*pl.* **-ties**) (also **witchetty grub**) a large white larva of an Australian beetle or moth, eaten as food by Aborigines. [Adnyamathanha, an Aboriginal language]

witch·grass *noun* = QUACK GRASS.

witch hazel *noun* **1** any N American shrub of the genus *Hamamelis*, with bark yielding an astringent lotion. **2** this lotion, esp. from the leaves of *H. virginiana*.

witch hunt *noun* **1** *hist.* a search for and persecution of people suspected of witchcraft. **2** a malicious campaign directed against a particular group of people with unpopular or unorthodox views or behaviour, formerly esp. communists. □ **witch-hunting** *noun*

witching hour *noun* midnight, when witches are supposedly active. [with reference to Shakespeare's *Hamlet* III. ii. 377 'the witching time of night']

with *preposition* expressing: **1** an instrument or means used (*cut with a knife*; *can walk with assistance*). **2** association or company (*lives with his mother*; *works with IBM*; *lamb with mint sauce*). **3** separation or release (*break with tradition*; *could not bear to part with it*). **4** cause or origin (*shiver with fear*; *in bed with measles*). **5** possession, attribution (*the man with dark hair*; *a vase with handles*). **6** circumstances; accompanying conditions (*sleep with the window open*; *a holiday with all expenses paid*). **7** manner adopted or displayed (*behaved with dignity*; *spoke with vehemence*; *handle with care*; *won with ease*). **8** agreement or harmony (*sympathize with*; *I believe with you that it can be done*). **9** disagreement, antagonism, competition (*incompatible with*; *stop arguing with me*). **10** responsibility or care for (*the decision rests with you*; *leave the child with me*). **11** material (*made with gold*). **12** addition or supply; possession of as a material, attribute, circumstance, etc. (*fill it with water*; *threaten with dismissal*; *decorate with holly*). **13** reference or regard (*be patient with them*; *how are things with you?*; *what do you want with me?*; *there's nothing wrong with expressing one's opinion*). **14** relation or causative association (*changes with the weather*; *keeps pace with the cost of living*). **15** an accepted circumstance or consideration (*with all your faults, we like you*). □ **away** (or **in** or **out** etc.) **with** (as interjection) take, send, or put (a person or thing) away, in, out, etc. **be with a person 1** agree with and support a person. **2** *informal* follow a person's meaning (*are you with me?*). **one**

with part of the same whole as. **with child** (or **young**) *archaic* pregnant. **with it** esp. *N Amer. informal* **1 a** up to date; conversant with modern or fashionable trends or ideas. **b** (*attributive*; **with-it**) fashionable (*with-it clothes*). **2** alert, attentive. **with that** thereupon. [Old English, prob. shortened from a Germanic prep. corresponding to Old English *wither*, Old High German *widar* against]

with·al /wɪˈðɔl/ *archaic* ● *adverb* moreover; as well; at the same time. ● *preposition* (placed after its expressed or omitted object) with (*what shall he fill his belly withal?*). [Middle English from WITH + ALL]

with·draw *verb* (*past* **with·drew**; *past participle* **with·drawn**) **1** *transitive* pull or draw aside or back (*withdrew my hand*). **2** *transitive* discontinue, cancel, retract (*withdrew my support*; *the promise was later withdrawn*). **3 a** *transitive* remove (a person etc.) from a position, situation, competition, etc. (*withdrew the child from school*). **b** *intransitive* remove oneself from a position or situation etc. (*she was forced to withdraw from competition*; *the troops withdrew from battle*). **4** *transitive* take (money) out of an account. **5** *intransitive* retire from a society or community, from public life, etc. **b** become reserved or uncommunicative. **6** *transitive & intransitive* retract (an unparliamentary remark) made during a parliamentary debate, esp. at the insistence of other MP's. [Middle English from *with-* away (as WITH) + DRAW]

with·drawal *noun* **1 a** the act or an instance of withdrawing (*the withdrawal of troops*). **b** the removal of money from a place of deposit. **2** the process of ceasing to take an addictive drug, often associated with unpleasant and sometimes life-threatening physical reactions (*withdrawal symptoms*). **3** *Psych.* a psychological state or process characterized by apathy, depression, or a retreat from objective reality, usu. as a response to severe stress or physical danger. **4** = COITUS INTERRUPTUS.

with·drawing-room *noun archaic* = DRAWING-ROOM 1.

with·drawn *adjective* **1** abnormally shy and unsociable; mentally detached or isolated. **2** (of a place) private, secluded.

withe /wɪθ, wɪð, waɪð/ (also **withy** /ˈwɪði/) (*pl.* **withes** or **-ies**) *noun* a strong flexible shoot esp. of willow or osier, or several of these twisted together, used for tying a bundle of wood, binding planks of a raft, etc. [Old English *withthe*, *withig* from Germanic, related to WIRE]

with·er /ˈwɪðər/ *verb* **1** *transitive & intransitive* (of a plant) become or cause to become dry and shrivelled. **2** *transitive & intransitive* (often foll. by *away*) lose or deprive of vigour, vitality, youth, or freshness. **3** *intransitive* (often foll. by *away*) **a** cease to flourish; decline, fall into decay. **b** (in Marxist theory) (of the state) disappear as no longer being necessary after the dictatorship of the proletariat has effected the necessary changes in society. **4** *transitive* mortify (a person) with a look of extreme contempt. [Middle English, apparently var. of WEATHER differentiated for certain senses]

wither·ing *adjective* **1** scornful, scathing (*a withering glare*). **2** fading, decaying. □ **wither·ing·ly** *adverb*

with·ers *plural noun* the highest part of the back of a horse, sheep, ox, etc., lying between the shoulder blades. [shortening of (16th-c.) *widersome* (or *-sone*) from *wider-*, *wither-* against (compare WITH), as the part that resists the strain of the collar: second element obscure]

wither·shins /ˈwɪðərʃɪnz/ *adverb* (also **wid·der·shins** /ˈwɪd-/) esp. *Scot.* **1** in a direction contrary to the sun's course (considered as unlucky). **2** counter-clockwise. [Middle Low German *weddersins* from Middle High German *widdersinnes* from *wider* against + *sin* direction]

with·hold *transitive verb* (*past* and *past participle* **-held**) **1** (often foll. by *from*) restrain or hold back from action. **2** keep back (what belongs to, is due to, or is desired by another); refuse to give, grant, or allow (*withhold one's consent*; *withhold the truth*). □ **with·hold·er** *noun* [Middle English from *with-* away (as WITH) + HOLD[1]]

with·hold·ing tax *noun* **1** a tax levied by some countries on interest or dividends paid to a person resident outside that country. **2** *US* a portion of an employee's salary or wages deducted by the employer and paid directly to the government in order to reduce the amount of income tax owed by the employee at the end of the year.

with·in ● *preposition* **1** inside; enclosed or contained by. **2 a** not beyond or exceeding (*within one's means*). **b** not transgressing (*within the law*; *within reason*). **3** not further off than (*within three miles of a station*; *within shouting distance*; *within an inch of his life*). **4** before the end of (a period of time) (*arrived within minutes*). **5** *Brit.* lying within an area implied, e.g. *Bishopsgate Within*, i.e. within the walls of London. ● *adverb archaic* or *literary* **1** inside; to, at, or on the inside; internally. **2** indoors (*is anyone within?*). **3** in spirit (*make me pure within*). □ **within doors** in or into a house. **within one's grasp** *see* GRASP. **within reach** (or **sight**) **of** near enough to be reached or seen. [Old English *withinnan* on the inside (as WITH, *innan* (adv. & prep.) within, formed as IN)]

Vowels: a *cat* ɑ *arm* e *bed* ɜr *her* ɜ: *deux* ə *ago* ɪ *sit* i *cosy* i: *feed* ɒ *hot* ɔ *pore* oː *no* ʌ *run* ʊ *put*

with·out ● *preposition* **1** not having, feeling, or showing (*came without any money*; *acted without hesitation*; *sang without any emotion*). **2** with freedom from (*without fear*; *without embarrassment*). **3** in the absence of (*cannot live without you*; *the train left without us*). **4** with neglect or avoidance of (*do not leave without telling me*). **5** *archaic* outside (*without the city wall*). **6** *Brit.* lying outside of an area implied, e.g. *Bishopsgate Without*, i.e. outside of the walls of London. ● *adverb archaic* or *literary* **1** outside (*seen from without*). **2** out of doors (*remained shivering without*). **3** in outward appearance (*rough without but kind within*). □ **without end** infinite, eternal. [Old English *withūtan* (as WITH, *ūtan* from outside, formed as OUT)]

with·stand *verb* (*past* and *past participle* **-stood**) **1** *transitive* maintain one's position against; resist, oppose (*withstood the attack*). **2** *transitive* tolerate, endure, bear (*this plant will withstand the harsh climate*). **3** *intransitive* make opposition; offer resistance. [Old English *withstandan* from *with-* against (as WITH) + STAND]

withy /ˈwɪði/ *noun* (*pl.* **-ies**) **1** a willow of any species. **2** *var. of* WITHE.

wit·less *adjective* **1** lacking wisdom or sense; foolish, stupid. **2** crazy, out of one's mind. □ **wit·less·ly** *adverb* **wit·less·ness** *noun*

wit·ness ● *noun* **1** a person present at some event or occurrence and able to give information about it from observation. **2** *Law* **a** a person giving testimony under oath in a court of law. **b** testimony, evidence, confirmation (*he was bribed to give false witness*). **3** *Law* **a** a person selected or appointed to be present at a transaction etc. in order to testify to its having taken place. **b** a person who signs a document attesting to its proper execution. **4** (foll. by *to*, *of*) a person or thing whose existence, condition, etc., attests or proves something (*this village is a witness to the ravages of war*). **5** (**Witness**) = JEHOVAH'S WITNESS. ● *verb* **1** *transitive* be a witness of (an event etc.); experience by personal observation (*did you witness the accident?*). **2** *transitive* **a** sign (a document) as a witness of its authenticity. **b** formally be present as a witness of (a transaction etc.). **3** *transitive* (of a place, time, etc.) be associated with (a fact or event); be the scene or setting of (*Europe witnessed massive political change in the late 1980s*). **4** *transitive* (as *imperative*) introducing an illustration of the preceding statement (*he is an accomplished musician: witness his performance last week*). **5** *intransitive* (foll. by *to*, *against*) give or serve as evidence. **6** *intransitive* publicly assert one's religious convictions, esp. in an attempt to convert others. □ **bear witness to 1** attest the truth of. **2** state one's belief in. **call to witness** appeal to for confirmation etc. [Old English *witnes* (as WIT¹, -NESS)]

witness box *Cdn & Brit.* (also esp. *N Amer.* **witness stand**) an enclosure in a court of law from which witnesses give evidence.
¶ *Witness box* is the term in official use in Canadian courts.

Wit·ten·berg /ˈvɪtənˌbɜrg/ a town in eastern Germany, on the Elbe River northeast of Leipzig; pop. (2002) 49,100. In 1517 Martin Luther initiated the Protestant Reformation by nailing his ninety-five theses to the door of a church here.

wit·ter /ˈwɪtər/ *intransitive verb* (often foll. by *on*) esp. *Brit. informal* speak tediously and at length on trivial matters. [20th c.: prob. imitative]

Witt·gen·stein /ˈvɪtgənˌʃtaɪn/ **Lud·wig (Josef Jo·hann)** (1889–1951), Austrian-born philosopher. In the *Tractatus Logico-philosophicus* (1921), he contended that language achieves meaning by 'picturing' things by established conventions; principal among his later works (all published posthumously) is *Philosophical Investigations* (1953), in which he showed that some philosophical problems are simply a result of a misunderstanding of the nature of language. □ **Witt·gen·stein·ian** /-ˈʃtaɪniən/ *adverb*

wit·ti·cism /ˈwɪtɪˌsɪzəm/ *noun* a witty remark. [coined by Dryden (1677) from WITTY, after *criticism*]

wit·ting *adjective* **1** (often foll. by *of*) aware. **2** intentional. □ **wit·ting·ly** *adverb*

witty *adjective* (**wit·ti·er**, **wit·ti·est**) **1** (of a person) capable of or given to saying or writing clever and amusing things. **2** (of speech or writing etc.) characterized by wit or humour (*a witty remark*). □ **wit·ti·ly** *adverb* **wit·ti·ness** *noun*

Wit·wa·ters·rand, the /wɪtˈwɔtɜrz,rand/ (also called **the Rand**) a region of South Africa, around the city of Johannesburg, consisting of a series of parallel rocky ridges. The region contains rich gold deposits, first discovered in 1886.

wi·vern *var. of* WYVERN.

wives *pl. of* WIFE.

wiz *var. of* WHIZ *noun* 2.

wiz·ard ● *noun* **1** a man who practises magic; a sorcerer. **2** a person noted for his or her remarkable ability within a certain sphere; a genius or expert (*she is a financial wizard*; *he's a wizard in the kitchen*). **3** *Computing* a software tool that operates automatically to guide a user

through a particular process. ● *adjective Brit. slang* wonderful, excellent. □ **wiz·ard·ly** *adjective* [Middle English from WISE¹ + -ARD]

wiz·ardry *noun* **1** the art or practice of a wizard. **2 a** remarkable skill or expertise in a particular field or activity. **b** a result of this.

wiz·ened /ˈwɪzənd/ *adjective* (also **wizen**) shrivelled or wrinkled, esp. with age. [past participle of *wizen* shrivel, from Old English *wisnian* from Germanic]

wk. *abbreviation* **1** week. **2** work.

wks. *abbreviation* weeks.

Wm. *abbreviation* William.

WMD *abbreviation* weapon of mass destruction.

WNW *abbreviation* west-northwest.

WO *abbreviation* WARRANT OFFICER.

wo *interjection* = WHOA. [var. of *who* (interj.), HO¹]

w/o *abbreviation* without.

woad *noun hist.* **1** a cruciferous plant, *Isatis tinctoria*, yielding a blue dye now superseded by indigo. **2** the dye formerly obtained from this. [Old English *wād* from Germanic]

wob·ble ● *verb* **1 a** *intransitive* sway or rock erratically from side to side. **b** *transitive* cause to do this. **2** *intransitive* stand or proceed unsteadily; stagger. **3** *intransitive* (of the voice or a sound) quaver, pulsate. **4** *intransitive* hesitate or waver between different opinions or courses of action. ● *noun* **1** the action or an act of wobbling. **2** an instance of vacillation or pulsation. [earlier *wabble*, corresponding to Low German *wabbeln*, Old Norse *vafla* waver, from Germanic: compare WAVE, WAVER, -LE⁴]

wob·bler *noun* **1** a person or thing that wobbles. **2** a fishing lure that wobbles and does not spin. □ **throw a wobbler** *Brit.* = THROW A WOBBLY (see WOBBLY).

Wob·bly /ˈwɒbli/ *noun* (*pl.* **-blies**) a member of the Industrial Workers of the World. [20th c.: origin unknown]

wob·bly *adjective* (**wob·bli·er**, **wob·bli·est**) **1** wobbling or tending to wobble; unsteady. **2** (of a line, handwriting, etc.) not straight or regular; shaky, wavy, undulating (*a wobbly line*). **3** wavering, vacillating, uncertain (*the economy was wobbly*). □ **throw a wobbly** *Brit. slang* lose one's composure or temper in a fit of panic, nerves, anger, etc. □ **wob·bli·ness** *noun*

Wode·house /ˈwʊdhaʊs/ **Sir Pel·ham Gren·ville** (1881–1975), English-born US writer. Among his prolific output of humorous novels and short stories, his best-known are those depicting the leisured English upper-class world of the vapid Bertie Wooster and his ever-reliable valet, Jeeves, the first of which appeared in 1917. □ **Wode·hous·ian** /-ˈhaʊziən/ *adjective*

Woden /ˈwoʊdən/ *see* ODIN.

wodge *noun* (usu. foll. by *of*) esp. *Brit. informal* a chunk or lump. [alteration of WEDGE¹]

woe *noun* **1** misfortune, distress, bitter grief. **2** (in *pl.*) troubles, misfortunes. □ **woe betide** (or **to**) there will be unfortunate consequences for (*woe betide you if you are late*). **woe is me** an exclamation of distress. [Old English *wā*, *wǣ* from Germanic]

woe·begone /ˈwoʊbɪˌgɒn/ *adjective* **1** sad, miserable, or dismal in appearance. **2** *archaic* overwhelmed or afflicted with misfortune, distress, sorrow, or grief. [WOE + *begone* = surrounded, from Old English *begān* (as BE-, GO¹)]

woe·ful *adjective* **1** afflicted with sorrow, distress, or misfortune (*a woeful expression*). **2** causing sorrow or affliction. **3** very bad or poor; wretched, pitiful, dreadful (*woeful ignorance*). □ **woe·ful·ly** *adverb* **woe·ful·ness** *noun*

wog *noun slang offensive* a foreigner, esp. a non-white one. [20th c.: origin unknown]

wog·gle *noun* a leather etc. ring through which the ends of a Scout's neckerchief are threaded. [20th c.: origin unknown]

Wöh·ler /ˈvɜːlər/ **Frie·drich** (1800–82), German chemist. He demonstrated that organic compounds could be made from inorganic compounds, and was the first to isolate the elements aluminum and beryllium.

wok *noun* a large bowl-shaped frying pan used in esp. Chinese cooking. [Cantonese]

woke *past of* WAKE¹.

woken *past participle of* WAKE¹.

wold /woʊld/ *noun* a tract of high open uncultivated land or moor. [Old English *wald* from Germanic, perhaps related to WILD: compare WEALD]

Wolf /vɒlf/ **1 Frie·drich Au·gust** (1759–1824), German classical scholar. Considered the founder of philology, he is particularly noted for his study of the genesis and authorship of the Homeric poems. **2 Hugo (Phil·ipp Jakob)** (1860–1903), Austrian composer. He produced some 300 songs notable for their emotionally charged melodic line and striking harmonies in the accompaniment.

wolf ● *noun* (*pl.* **wolves**) **1** a wild flesh-eating tawny-grey mammal related to the dog, esp. *Canis lupus*, hunting in packs. *Also called* GREY WOLF, TIMBER WOLF. **2** the skin, hide, or fur of this animal. **3** *slang* **a** a person compared to a wolf, esp. with regard to the animal's ferocity or rapacity. **b** a man who habitually pursues or seduces women. ● *transitive verb* (often foll. by *down*) devour (food) ravenously. □ **cry wolf** raise repeated false alarms (so that a genuine one is disregarded). **have** (or **hold**) **a wolf by the ears** be in a precarious position; be in a predicament where any course of action presents problems. **keep the wolf from the door** have enough money to provide for oneself or one's family. **throw to the wolves** sacrifice (a friend or colleague) in order to avert danger or difficulties for oneself. **wolf in sheep's clothing** a person whose hostile intentions are concealed by a pretense of friendliness. □ **wolf·ish** *adjective* **wolf·ish·ly** *adverb* **wolf·like** *adjective & adverb* [Old English *wulf*]

wolf cub *noun* **1** a young wolf. **2** (**Wolf Cub**) the former name for CUB 2.

wolf-dog *noun* a hybrid between a domestic dog and a wolf.

Wolfe, James (1727–59), English general. As one of the leaders of the expedition sent to seize French Canada, he played a vital part in the capture of Louisbourg on Cape Breton Island in 1758. The following year he commanded the attack on the French capital, the city of Quebec. He was fatally wounded while leading his troops to victory on the Plains of Abraham, the scene of the battle which led to British control of Canada.

Wolfe Island a small island in Lake Ontario, situated at the entrance to the St. Lawrence River, just south of Kingston. Over 125 sq. km in area, it is the largest of the Thousand Islands. [WOLFE]

wolf·er *noun* esp. *N Amer.* (*West*) *hist.* a person who hunts wolves.

wolf·fish *noun* any of various aggressive large deepwater marine fishes of the family Anarhichadidae which have long bodies and large doglike teeth.

wolf·hound *noun* a dog of any of several large breeds, e.g. a borzoi, originally kept for hunting wolves.

wolf pack *noun* **1** any group of people or things which operate as a hunting and attacking pack, such as a group of submarines or aircraft. **2** a number of wolves naturally associating as a group, esp. for hunting.

wolf·ram /ˈwʊlfrəm/ *noun* **1** tungsten. **2** wolframite. [German: perhaps from *Wolf* WOLF + *Rahm* cream, or Middle High German *rām* dirt, soot]

wolf·ram·ite /ˈwʊlfrəˌmaɪt/ *noun* a monoclinic tungstate of iron and manganese, which occurs as black to brown crystals, blades, granules, and masses, and is the chief ore of tungsten.

Wolf River *noun* *N Amer.* a large variety of cooking apple. [*Wolf River*, Wisconsin, near which it was first grown]

wolfs·bane *noun* an aconite, esp. *Aconitum lycoctonum*.

Wolfs·burg /ˈvɒlfsbɜrg/ an industrial city on the Mittelland Canal in Lower Saxony, NW Germany; pop. (est. 2002) 117,500.

wolf·skin *noun* **1** the skin or pelt of a wolf. **2** an article of clothing made of this.

wolf's milk *noun* any of several spurges, esp. the European leafy spurge, *Euphorbia esula*, naturalized in N America.

wolf spider *noun* any ground-dwelling spider of the family Lycosidae, hunting instead of trapping its prey.

Wolf·ville a town in central Nova Scotia, situated on Minas Basin and the Cornwallis River, about 80 km northwest of Halifax; pop. (2001) 3,658. It is the site of Acadia University. [E. De *Wolf*, early postmaster and judge *c.*1786]

wolf whistle ● *noun* a rising and falling whistle imitating the howl of a wolf, made esp. by a man to express his admiration of a woman's appearance. ● *intransitive verb* (**wolf-whistle**) make such a whistling sound.

wolf willow *noun* *Cdn* = SILVERBERRY.

Wol·las·ton /ˈwʊləstən/ **Wil·liam Hyde** (1766–1828), English chemist and physicist. He pioneered powder metallurgy, developed while he was attempting to produce malleable platinum, demonstrated that static and current electricity were the same, and was the first to observe the dark lines in the solar spectrum.

Wollaston Lake a lake in NE Saskatchewan, situated northwest of Reindeer Lake. [WOLLASTON]

Wollaston Peninsula a broad peninsula of the southwestern coast

of Victoria Island. It is formed by Prince Albert Sound, an inlet of Amundsen Gulf.

Wol·lon·gong /ˈwɒlənˌgɒŋ/ a city on the coast of New South Wales, SE Australia; pop. (est. 2002) 261,800.

Woll·stone·craft /ˈwʊlstənˌkrɑft/ **Mary** (1759–97), English writer and feminist. Her best-known work, *A Vindication of the Rights of Woman* (1792), defied Rousseau's assumptions about male supremacy and championed educational equality for women; in 1797 she married William Godwin and died shortly after giving birth to their daughter Mary, who was later to marry Percy Bysshe Shelley.

Wolof /ˈwɒlɒf/ ● *noun* (*pl.* same or **Wol·ofs**) **1** a member of an African people of Senegal and Gambia. **2** the Niger-Congo language of this people. ● *adjective* of or designating the Wolof or their language. [Wolof]

Wolse·ley /ˈwʊlzli/ **Gar·net Jo·seph Wolse·ley, 1st Vis·count** (1833–1913), British soldier. Sent to Canada as assistant quartermaster general in 1861, he commanded the 1870 expedition to Red River. He served as commander-in-chief of the British army 1895–1900.

Wol·sey /ˈwʊlzi/ **Thom·as** (known as Cardinal Wolsey) (*c.*1474–1530), English clergyman and statesman. He dominated foreign and domestic policy in the early part of Henry VIII's reign and held the positions of Archbishop of York (1514–30), cardinal (1515–30), and Lord Chancellor (1515–29); he incurred royal displeasure through his failure to secure the papal dispensation necessary for Henry's divorce from Catherine of Aragon, was charged with treason, and died on his way to trial in London.

Wol·ver·hamp·ton /ˌwʊlvərˈhamptən/ an industrial city in the Midlands, northwest of Birmingham; pop. (est. 2001) 236,573.

wol·ver·ine /ˌwʊlvərˈiːn, ˈwʊl-/ *noun* **1** a carnivorous animal, *Gulo luscus* of N America or *Gulo gulo* of Europe, of the weasel family, resembling a small bear, with dark brown fur and a long bushy tail. **2** the fur of the wolverine. [16th-c. *wolvering*, formed obscurely from *wolv-*, stem of WOLF]

wolves *pl. of* WOLF.

woman ● *noun* (*pl.* **women**) **1** an adult female person. **2** (as second element in *combination*) an adult female person having a specified nationality, status, character, profession, occupation, or interest; a female person associated with something specified (*businesswoman*; *Frenchwoman*). **3** (*attributive*) female (*women friends*). **4** *informal* a wife or female sexual partner. **5** the female human person, esp. viewed as a type (*how does woman differ from man?*). **6** (prec. by *the*) the character or qualities traditionally associated with women; the feminine aspect of a person (*brought out the woman in me*). **7** a man with characteristics traditionally associated with women. **8 a** *hist.* a female servant. **b** a queen's female attendant ranking below lady (*woman of the bedchamber*). ● *transitive verb* (**womanned**, **woman·ning** or **womaned**, **woman·ing**) provide with esp. a crew or staff of women. □ **woman·less** *adjective* **woman·like** *adjective* [Old English *wīfmon*, *-man* (as WIFE, MAN), a formation peculiar to English, the ancient word being WIFE]

woman·hood *noun* **1 a** the state or condition of being a woman. **b** the state of being a grown woman; female maturity. **2** the disposition, character, or qualities traditionally attributed to women. **3** women collectively; womankind.

woman·ish *adjective* **1** usu. *derogatory* (of a man) effeminate, unmanly. **2** suitable to or characteristic of a woman. □ **woman·ish·ly** *adverb*

woman·ism *noun* *N Amer.* advocacy of or enthusiasm for the rights and achievements of women, esp. that form promoted by some black women writers, characterized by an emphasis on celebrating the contribution of women to society as a whole. □ **woman·ist** *adjective & noun* [WOMAN + -ISM, adopted by A. WALKER as more relevant to Black people than FEMINISM]

woman·ize *verb* (also esp. *Brit.* **-ise**) **1** *intransitive* (of a man) pursue or engage in casual sexual encounters with women; philander. **2** *transitive* make womanish. □ **woman·iz·er** *noun*

woman·kind *noun* women collectively.

woman·ly *adjective* (of a woman) having or showing qualities traditionally associated with women; not masculine or girlish. □ **woman·li·ness** *noun*

woman·power *noun* women available for work or service etc.

womb /wuːm/ *noun* **1** the organ in the body of a woman or female mammal in which offspring are carried, protected, and nourished before birth; the uterus. **2** a place of origin, development, or growth. **3** a hollow space, cavity, or shelter. □ **womb·like** *adjective* [Old English *wamb*, *womb*]

Consonants: **b** *but*   **d** *dog*   **f** *few*   **g** *get*   **h** *her*   **j** *yes*   **k** *cat*   **l** *leg*   **m** *man*   **n** *no*   **p** *pen*   **r** *red*   **s** *sit*

wom·bat /ˈwɒmbat/ *noun* any burrowing plant-eating Australian marsupial of the family Vombatidae, resembling a small bear, with short legs. [Aboriginal]

women *pl. of* WOMAN.

women·folk *plural noun* **1** women collectively; womankind. **2** the women of a particular family, household, or other group.

Women's Institute *noun* an organization founded to enable women in rural areas to meet regularly and engage in various cultural activities, social work, etc. Now worldwide, it was first established by Adelaide Hoodless in Stoney Creek, Ontario, in 1897. Abbr.: **WI.**

women's lib *noun* (also **Women's Lib**) *informal* = WOMEN'S LIBERATION.

women's libber *noun informal* a supporter of women's liberation.

women's liberation *noun* **1** the liberation of women from inequalities and subservient status in relation to men, and from sexist attitudes from which these result. **2** (also **Women's Liberation**, in full **Women's Liberation Movement**) = WOMEN'S MOVEMENT.

women's movement *noun* (also **Women's Movement**) a broad movement campaigning for women's liberation and for the recognition and extension of women's rights.

women's rights *plural noun* the human rights of women, esp. those that promote or secure legal and social equality with men.

women's room *noun N Amer.* = LADIES' ROOM.

women's shelter *noun N Amer.* an establishment offering refuge, protection, and counselling to women who are victims of esp. domestic assault or abuse, and their children.

women's studies *plural noun* (usu. treated as *sing.*) a course of academic studies focusing on women and their role in society, as well as their history and literature.

women's suffrage *noun* **1** the right of women to vote. **2** (also **Women's Suffrage**, in full **Women's Suffrage Movement**) a movement campaigning for this.

womens·wear *noun* clothes for women.

womyn /ˈwɪmɪn/ *plural noun* (also **wim·min**) women. [alteration of *women*, adopted by some feminists to avoid the ending *-men*]

won[1] /wɒn/ *noun* (*pl.* same) the basic monetary unit of North and South Korea, equal to 100 chon. [Korean]

won[2] past and past participle of WIN.

Won·der, Stev·ie (born Steveland Judkins Morris) (b.1950), US singer, songwriter, and musician. He became a recording artist with Motown in 1961, and although at first a soul singer, from the 1970s his repertoire has broadened to include rock, funk, and romantic ballads; among his albums are *Innervisions* (1973) and *Songs in the Key of Life* (1976).

won·der ● *noun* **1** the emotion excited by the perception of something unexpected, unfamiliar, or inexplicable, esp. surprise or astonishment mingled with admiration, perplexity, or curiosity. **2** an amazing, remarkable, or astonishing person or thing. **3** (*attributive*) having marvellous or amazing properties or qualities (*a wonder drug; Sleuth the Wonder Dog*). **4** a miraculous or surprising thing (*it is a wonder you were not hurt*). ● *verb* **1** *transitive* desire or be curious to know (*I wonder what time it is*). **2** *intransitive* (usu. foll. by *about*) speculate with curiosity or doubt (*I wonder about him sometimes*). **3** *transitive* used to express a tentative inquiry or polite request (*I was wondering if you might be free tomorrow night?*). **4** *intransitive* (often foll. by *at*, or *to* + infin.) be filled with wonder or great surprise. **5** *transitive* (foll. by *that* + clause) be surprised to find. □ **I shouldn't wonder** *informal* it would not surprise me; I think it likely. **no** (or **small**) **wonder** (often foll. by *that* + clause) it is natural or hardly surprising; one might have guessed (*no wonder she looks tired, she hasn't slept in three days!*). **wonders will never cease** an exclamation of extreme (usu. delightful) surprise. **work** (or **do**) **wonders** **1** perform miracles. **2** achieve remarkable success. □ **won·der·er** *noun* [Old English *wundor, wundrian*, of unknown origin]

won·der·ful *adjective* **1** very remarkable or admirable (*a wonderful meal*). **2** *informal* marvellous, terrific (*I feel wonderful*). **3** that arouses wonder or astonishment. □ **won·der·ful·ly** *adverb* **won·der·ful·ness** *noun*

won·der·ing *adjective* filled with wonder; marvelling (*their wondering gaze*). □ **won·der·ing·ly** *adverb*

won·der·land *noun* **1** an imaginary world of marvels or surprises. **2** an actual place of remarkable or incredible beauty (*a winter wonderland*).

won·der·ment *noun* **1** a state of surprise or awe. **2** a cause of surprise or awe; a wonderful thing.

wonder·struck *adjective* reduced to silence by wonder.

wonder-worker *noun* a person who performs wonders or miracles. □ **wonder-working** *attributive adjective*

won·drous /ˈwʌndrəs/ *literary* ● *adjective* wonderful. ● *adverb* wonderfully (*wondrous kind*). □ **won·drous·ly** *adverb* [alteration of obsolete *wonders* (adj. & adv.), = genitive of WONDER (compare -s[3]) after *marvellous*]

wonk /wɒŋk/ *noun N Amer. slang* usu. *derogatory* **1** a studious or hard-working person, esp. one who is obsessively devoted to academic studies at the expense of social activities; a nerd. **2** (in full **policy wonk**) esp. *US* a person who takes an unnecessary interest in minor details of policy. □ **wonk·ery** *noun* **wonk·ish** *adjective* **wonk·ish·ness** *noun* [20th c.: origin unknown]

wonky *adjective* (**wonk·i·er, wonk·i·est**) *informal* **1** crooked, loose, unsteady. **2** faulty, unreliable, askew. **3** esp. *US* unattractive, boring. □ **wonk·i·ly** *adverb* **wonk·i·ness** *noun* [fanciful formation]

wont /wɒnt/ ● *predicative adjective* (foll. by *to* + infin.) accustomed (*as we were wont to say*). ● *noun* what is customary, one's habit (*as is my wont*), [Old English *gewunod* past participle of *gewunian* from *wunian* dwell]

won't *contraction* will not.

wont·ed /ˈwɒntəd/ *attributive adjective* habitual, accustomed, usual.

won ton /ˈwɒntɒn/ *noun* (in Chinese cooking) a small round dumpling of dough containing a savoury filling, sometimes deep-fried and served as an accompaniment to a meal, but more commonly boiled and served in a broth. [Cantonese *wăn t'ān*]

woo *transitive verb* (**woos, wooed**) **1** court; seek the hand or love of (esp. a woman). **2** seek the favour or support of (*trying to woo voters*). **3** try to win, gain, or achieve (fame, fortune, etc.). **4** coax, entreat, or importune. □ **woo·er** *noun* [Old English *wōgian* (intr.), *āwōgian* (tr.), of unknown origin]

Wood, Henry Wise (1860–1941), US-born Canadian farmer and political leader. As president (1916–31) of the United Farmers of Alberta he was one of the most powerful political figures in Alberta, believing that rural people needed to band together to offset the growing power of industrialists, bankers, and professionals.

Wood, Mount a peak (over 4 800 m) in SW Yukon Territory, in the St. Elias mountain range. [Z. T. Wood, NWMP officer d.1915]

wood *noun* **1 a** a hard fibrous material that forms the main substance of the trunk or branches of a tree or shrub. **b** this cut for timber or for fuel, or for use in crafts, manufacture, etc. **2** = WOODS. **3** (prec. by *the*) wooden storage, esp. a cask, for wine etc. (*poured straight from the wood*). **4** a wooden-headed golf club, or any club with a head relatively broad from face to back. □ **wood·less** *adjective* [Old English *wudu, wi(o)du*]

wood alcohol *noun* methanol.

wood·bine *noun* any of various climbing plants esp. the N American Virginia creeper, *Parthenocissus quinquefolia*, and the European wild honeysuckle, *Lonicera periclymenum*.

wood bison *noun* (also **wood buffalo**) a subspecies of the N American bison found in wooded parts of western Canada, somewhat larger than the plains bison.

wood·block *noun* **1** a block from which woodcuts are made. **2** each of the small pieces of wood used in making a parquet floor, often arranged in a pattern.

wood·box *noun* a large usu. wooden box built near a fireplace, stove, etc., for storing firewood.

Wood Buffalo (formerly called **Fort McMurray**) a regional municipality in NE Alberta, situated at the confluence of the Clearwater and Athabasca rivers, over 400 km northeast of Edmonton; pop. (2001) 41,466.

Wood Buffalo National Park the largest park in Canada, occupying a large portion of NE Alberta and an area of the NWT south of Great Slave Lake. Designated a World Heritage Site, the park is a preserve for the world's largest free-roaming herd of wood and plains bison.

wood-burner *noun* a wood-burning stove.

wood-burning *adjective* using wood as fuel; heated or driven by the burning of wood.

wood·carv·er *noun* **1** a person who carves designs in relief on wood. **2** a tool for carving wood.

wood·carv·ing *noun* **1** (also *attributive*) the act or process of carving wood. **2** (also *attributive*) the art or skill of woodcarving. **3** a design in wood produced by this art.

wood chip *noun* a small piece of wood, used in quantity for burning, filling in a garden, etc.

wood·chuck *noun* a reddish-brown and grey N American marmot, *Marmota monax*. Also called GROUNDHOG. [alteration by association with WOOD of Algonquian name: compare Narragansett *ockutchaun*]

Wood·cock, George (1912–95), Canadian author and essayist. He founded the journal *Canadian Literature* in 1959, and edited it until 1977; he also wrote numerous books, including *The Canadians* (1976) and *Northern Spring* (1986).

wood·cock *noun* (*pl.* same) any game bird of the genus *Scolopax*, inhabiting woodland.

wood·craft *noun* esp. *N Amer.* **1** skill in woodwork. **2** knowledge of woodland esp. in camping, scouting, etc.

wood·cut *noun* **1** a relief cut on a block of wood sawn along the grain. **2** a print made from this, esp. as an illustration in a book. **3** the technique of making such reliefs and prints.

wood·cut·ter *noun* **1** a person who cuts wood, esp. one who fells trees. **2** a maker of woodcuts. □ **wood·cut·ting** *adjective & noun*

wood duck *noun* a N American wild duck, *Aix sponsa*, the male of which has a striking iridescent green and blue head with white stripes.

wood·ed *adjective* having woods or many trees.

wood·en *adjective* **1** made of wood. **2** like wood. **3 a** stiff, clumsy, or stilted; without animation or flexibility (*wooden movements; a wooden performance*). **b** expressionless (*a wooden stare*). □ **wood·en·ly** *adverb* **wooden·ness** *noun*

wood engraving *noun* **1** a relief cut on a block of wood sawn across the grain. **2** a print made from this. **3** the technique of making such reliefs and prints. □ **wood engraver** *noun*

wooden horse *noun* = TROJAN HORSE 1.

wood fern *noun* any of various woodland ferns of the genus *Dryopteris*, found across N America.

wood fibre *noun* fibre obtained from wood esp. as material for paper.

wood-fired *adjective* using wood as fuel (*pizza from a wood-fired oven*).

wood grain *noun* **1** the grain of wood. **2** a surface or finish imitating this.

wood·land *noun* wooded country, woods (often *attributive: woodland scenery*). □ **wood·land·er** *noun*

woodland caribou *noun* a caribou of a population found in forested areas of Canada, larger than the barren ground caribou.

Woodland Cree *noun* **1** a member of any of the Cree peoples who live in forested areas (as opposed to the Plains). **2** the dialect of Cree spoken by this people.

wood lily *noun* any of various shade-loving plants, esp. the trillium.

wood·lot *noun N Amer.* a treed plot of land, esp. on a farm, from which firewood may be obtained.

wood·louse *noun* (*pl.* **-lice**) esp. *Brit.* = SOWBUG.

wood·man *noun* (*pl.* **-men**) **1** a forester. **2** a woodcutter.

wood·mouse *noun* (*pl.* **-mice**) a field mouse.

wood nymph *noun* a dryad or hamadryad.

wood·peck·er *noun* any bird of the family Picidae that climbs and taps tree trunks in search of insects.

wood·pile *noun* a pile of wood, esp. for fuel.

wood poppy *noun* a plant of eastern N America, *Stylophorum diphyllum* of the poppy family, with leaves and flowers resembling the greater celandine.

wood pulp *noun* wood fibre reduced chemically or mechanically to pulp as raw material for paper.

wood·rat *noun* any rat of the N American genus *Neotoma*, most species of which build houses of twigs and other found materials, esp. the pack rat.

wood·ruff *noun* a white-flowered plant of the genus *Galium*, esp. *G. odoratum* grown for the fragrance of its whorled leaves when dried or crushed.

wood·rush *noun* any grassy herbaceous plant of the genus *Luzula*.

Woods, Tiger (born Eldrick Woods) (b.1975), American golfer. In 2000 he became the youngest player to win all four of golf's grand slam events.

Woods, Lake of the see LAKE OF THE WOODS.

woods *plural noun* growing trees densely occupying a tract of land. □ **out of the woods** out of danger or difficulty.

wood screw *noun* see SCREW *noun* 2.

wood·shed *noun* a shed where wood for fuel is stored. □ **something nasty in the woodshed** *Brit. informal* a shocking or distasteful thing kept secret. **take someone to the woodshed** *N Amer. informal*

discreetly reprimand or punish (originally by giving a child a spanking out of sight in the woodshed).

wood·sia /ˈwʊdziə/ *noun* any of various woodland ferns of the genus *Woodsia*, with lacy fronds. [J. *Woods*, English architect and botanist d.1864 + -IA¹]

woods·man *noun* (*pl.* **-men**) **1** a person who lives in or frequents the woods for hunting, camping, etc. **2** a person skilled in woodcraft. □ **woods·man·ship** *noun*

wood·smoke *noun* the smoke from a wood fire.

wood sorrel *noun* any of various plants of the genus *Oxalis* with trifoliate leaves, e.g. *O. montana*, found east of the Rockies, with white flowers streaked with purple.

wood stain *noun* a commercially-produced substance for colouring wood.

Wood·stock 1 a city in SW central Ontario, about 40 km northeast of London; pop. (2001) 33,061. **2** a town in W New Brunswick, situated on the Saint John River, 104 km (65 miles) northwest of Fredericton; pop. (2001) 5,198. **3** a small town in New York State, situated in the southeast near Albany. Noted as an artists' colony, it gave its name in the summer of 1969 to a huge rock festival held some 96 km (60 miles) to the southwest, which came to symbolize the youth culture of the period. □ **Wood·sto·nian** (in sense 1) *noun* [sense 1 after *Woodstock* in Oxfordshire, England; sense 2 possibly after W. H. C. Bentinck, 3rd Duke of Portland, Viscount *Woodstock* and prime minister of Great Britain d.1809]

wood stove *noun* a wood-burning stove.

Woods·worth, James Shaver (1874–1942), Canadian Methodist minister, social worker, and politician. The most prominent promoter of the social gospel, he entered the House of Commons as a Winnipeg MP representing the Independent Labour Party in 1921. In 1933 he was chosen as the first leader of the CCF, a position he held until his death.

woodsy *adjective N Amer.* like or characteristic of woods.

wood thrush *noun* a large brown and white N American thrush, *Hylocichla mustelina*.

wood tick *noun* a tick which infests wild and domestic animals and is often found clinging to plants, esp. of the genus *Dermacentor*.

wood warbler *noun* **1** a European woodland bird, *Phylloscopus sibilatrix*, with a trilling song. **2** any American warbler of the family Parulidae.

Wood·ward ▸ 1 Charles (1842–1937), Canadian merchant and politician. In 1892 he opened a store in Vancouver selling groceries and shoes, and ten years later he incorporated as Woodward Department Stores Ltd. In 1924 he was elected as a Liberal MLA. **2 Rob·ert Burns** (1917–79), US organic chemist. He was the first to synthesize a wide range of complex organic compounds, including quinine, cholesterol, cortisone, strychnine, chlorophyll, and vitamin B_{12}, and was awarded the Nobel Prize for chemistry in 1965.

wood·wind *noun* (often *attributive*) **1** (*collective*) the wind instruments of the orchestra that were (mostly) originally made of wood, e.g. the flute and clarinet. **2** (usu. in *pl.*) an individual instrument of this kind or its player (*the woodwinds are out of tune*).

wood·work *noun* **1** the making of things in wood. **2** things made of wood, esp. the wooden parts of a building. □ **crawl** (or **come**) **out of the woodwork** *informal* (of something unwelcome) emerge from obscurity into (unwelcome) prominence. □ **wood·work·er** *noun* **wood·work·ing** *noun*

wood·worm *noun* **1** the wood-boring larva of the furniture beetle. **2** the damaged condition of wood affected by this.

woody ● *adjective* (**wood·i·er, wood·i·est**) **1** (of a region) wooded; abounding in woods. **2** like or of wood (*a woody stem*). **●** *noun* (*pl.* **-ies**) *informal* **1** a wood duck. **2** *US* a station wagon with wood or imitation wood panelling on the sides. **3** *coarse slang* an erection. □ **wood·i·ness** *noun*

wood·yard *noun* a yard where wood is used or stored.

woody nightshade *noun* see NIGHTSHADE 1.

woof¹ ● *noun* the gruff bark of a dog. **●** *verb* **1** *intransitive* give a woof. **2** *transitive* (often foll. by *down*) *informal* consume ravenously. **3** *intransitive & transitive US informal* talk (to) or say (something) ostentatiously or aggressively. [imitative]

woof² *noun* = WEFT. [Old English *ōwef*, alteration of *ōwebb* (after *wefan* WEAVE¹), formed as A-², WEB: influenced by *warp*]

woof·er *noun* a loudspeaker designed to reproduce low frequencies (compare TWEETER). [WOOF¹ + -ER¹]

wool *noun* **1** fine soft wavy hair from the fleece of sheep, goats, etc. **2 a** yarn produced from this hair. **b** cloth or clothing made from it.

3 any of various wool-like substances (*steel wool*). **4** soft short under-fur or down. **5** *informal* a person's hair, esp. when short and curly. □ **pull the wool over a person's eyes** deceive a person. □ **wool-like** *adjective* [Old English *wull*]

Woolf /wʊlf/ **(Ade·line) Vir·ginia** (née Stephen) (1882–1941), English novelist, essayist, and critic. A central figure in the Bloomsbury group, she was a principal exponent of modernism, and her novels, which include *Mrs. Dalloway* (1925), *To the Lighthouse* (1927), and *The Waves* (1931), are characterized by a stream-of-consciousness technique and poetic Impressionism; her non-fiction includes *A Room of One's Own* (1929), a major work of the women's movement.

wool·gath·er·ing *noun* absent-mindedness; dreamy inattention. □ **wool·gather** *intransitive verb*

wool·grow·er *noun* a breeder of sheep for wool.

wool·len (also **wool·en**) ● *adjective* made wholly or partly of wool, esp. from short fibres. ● *noun* **1** a fabric produced from wool. **2** (in *pl.*) woollen garments.

Wool·ley /ˈwʊli/ **Sir (Charles) Leon·ard** (1880–1960), English archaeologist. He directed a joint British–American excavation of the Sumerian city of Ur (in what is now southern Iraq) (1922–34) which discovered rich royal tombs and thousands of clay tablets providing valuable information on everyday life of the period.

wool·ly ● *adjective* (**wool·li·er**, **wool·li·est**) **1** bearing or naturally covered with wool or wool-like hair; downy. **2** resembling or suggesting wool (*woolly clouds*). **3** made of (esp. knitted) wool; woollen. **4** (of a sound) indistinct. **5** (of thought) vague or confused. **6** lacking in definition, luminosity, or incisiveness. ● *noun* (*pl.* **-lies**) *informal* a woollen garment, esp. a knitted pullover. □ **wild and woolly** see WILD. □ **wool·li·ness** *noun*

woolly bear *noun* **1** a large hairy caterpillar, esp. of the tiger moth. **2** the small hairy larva of a carpet beetle, destructive to textiles, insect collections, etc.

Wool·sack *noun* **1** (in the UK) the Lord Chancellor's wool-stuffed seat in the House of Lords. **2** the position of Lord Chancellor.

wool·shed *noun* *Austral. & NZ* a large shed for shearing and baling wool.

Wool·worth, Frank Win·field (1852–1919), US businessman. He opened his first store selling inexpensive items in 1879, and gradually built up a large chain of US department stores; these later became an international retail organization.

woom·era /ˈwuːmərə/ *noun Austral.* **1** an Aboriginal stick for throwing a dart or spear more forcibly. **2** a club used as a missile. [Dharuk *wamara*]

woosh *var. of* WHOOSH.

woozy /ˈwuːzi/ *adjective* (**woozi·er**, **woozi·est**) *informal* **1** dizzy or unsteady. **2** dazed or slightly drunk. **3** vague. □ **woozi·ly** *adverb* **woozi·ness** *noun* [19th c.: origin unknown]

wop *noun slang offensive* an Italian. [20th c.: origin uncertain: perhaps from Italian *guappo* bold, showy, from Spanish *guapo* dandy]

Worces·ter /ˈwʊstər/ a cathedral city in W England, on the Severn River, the administrative centre of Worcestershire; pop. (est. 2002) 86,200. It was the scene in 1651, during the English Civil War, of a battle in which Cromwell defeated a Scottish army under Charles II. It has been a centre of porcelain manufacture since 1751.

Worces·ter·shire /ˈwʊstərʃɪr/ a county of west central England, part of Hereford and Worcester between 1974 and 1996.

Worcestershire sauce *noun* (Brit. **Worcester sauce**) *N Amer.* a pungent sauce containing soy, vinegar, and seasoning, first made in Worcester.

word ● *noun* **1** a sound or combination of sounds forming a meaningful element of speech, usu. shown with a space on either side of it when written or printed, used as part (or occas. as the whole) of a sentence. **2** speech, esp. as distinct from action (*bold in word only*). **3** one's promise or assurance (*gave us their word*). **4** (in *sing.* or *pl.*) a thing said, a remark or conversation. **5** (in *pl.*) the text of a song or an actor's part. **6** (in *pl.*) angry talk (*they had words*). **7 a** news; a message (*send word*). **b** a rumour (*word is she's left town*). **8** a command, password, or motto (*gave the word to begin*). **9** a basic unit of the expression of data in a computer. **10** (**the Word**) **a** any divine message. **b** the Gospel. **c** Jesus. **d** the Bible. ● *transitive verb* put into words; select words to express (*how shall we word that?*). □ **be as good as one's word** fulfill (or exceed) what one has promised. **break one's word** fail to do what one has promised. **have no words for** be unable to express. **have a word** (often foll. by *with*) speak briefly (to). **in other words** expressing the same thing differently. **in so many words** explicitly or bluntly. **in a** (or **one**) **word** briefly. **keep one's word** do what

one has promised. **my** (or **upon my**) **word** an exclamation of surprise or consternation. **not the word for it** not an adequate or appropriate description. **of few words** taciturn. **of one's word** reliable in keeping promises (*a woman of her word*). **on** (or **upon**) **my word** a form of asseveration. **put into words** express in speech or writing. **take a person at his** or **her word** interpret a person's words literally or exactly. **take a person's word for it** believe a person's statement without investigation etc. **too ... for words** too ... to be adequately described (*was too funny for words*). **waste words** talk in vain. **word for word** in exactly the same or (of translation) corresponding words. **words fail me** an expression of disbelief, dismay, etc. **a word to the wise** a piece of advice etc. given in the hope that it will be sufficient to change a person's behaviour etc. □ **word·age** *noun* **word·less** *adjective* **word·less·ly** *adverb* **word·less·ness** *noun* [Old English from Germanic]

-word *suffix* appended to a (frequently capitalized) letter of the alphabet to denote a word beginning with that letter, esp. denoting a word which is taboo slang or otherwise likely to give offence, or one having negative connotations in a particular (esp. a political) context. See F-WORD.

word association *noun* the bringing to mind of one word in response to another, esp. as a revelation of the contents and character of a person's subconscious.

word·book *noun* a book with lists of words; a vocabulary or dictionary.

word division *noun* the practice of splitting words between two lines of a printed text by means of a hyphen.

word game *noun* a game involving the making or selection etc. of words.

word·ing *noun* **1** a form of words used. **2** the way in which something is expressed.

word of honour *noun* an assurance given upon one's honour.

word of mouth *noun* spoken communication between people as a means of transmitting information (*word of mouth is the only way to find out about this*).

word order *noun* the sequence of words in a sentence, esp. affecting meaning etc.

word painting *noun* a vivid description in writing.

word-perfect *adjective* knowing one's part etc. by heart.

word-picture *noun* a piece of word-painting.

word·play *noun* use of words to witty effect, esp. by punning.

word processor *noun* a computer system for electronically storing, manipulating, editing, and usu. displaying and printing text entered from a keyboard. □ **word-process** *transitive verb* **word processing** *noun*

word·smith *noun* a skilled user or maker of words.

Words·worth ▶ **1 Dor·othy** (1771–1855), English diarist, William Wordsworth's sister and devoted companion. She kept detailed diaries such as her *Grasmere Journal* (1800–3), which, as well as providing a biographical perspective on her brother, document her intense response to nature. **2 Wil·liam** (1770–1850), English poet. With Coleridge he created the English Romantic movement; together they published the *Lyrical Ballads* (1798), a collection of poems (including Wordsworth's 'Tintern Abbey') which attacked the poetical conventions of the 18th c. Much of his work was inspired by the Lake District, where he lived with his sister Dorothy for much of his life. Among his many poems are the ode 'Intimations of Immortality' (1807), sonnets, such as 'Surprised by Joy' and 'I Wandered Lonely as a Cloud' (both 1815), and the posthumously published autobiographical *The Prelude* (1850). □ **Words·worth·ian** *noun & adjective*

word wrap *noun* in word processing, the automatic shifting of a word too long to fit on a line to the beginning of the next line.

wordy *adjective* (**word·i·er**, **word·i·est**) **1** using or expressed in many or too many words; verbose. **2** consisting of words. □ **word·i·ly** *adverb* **word·i·ness** *noun*

wore[1] *past of* WEAR[1].

wore[2] *past and past participle of* WEAR[2].

work ● *noun* **1** the application of mental or physical effort to a purpose; the use of energy. **2 a** a task to be undertaken. **b** the materials used or made by work; the result of an action; an achievement; a thing made. **4** a person's employment or occupation etc., esp. as a means of earning income (*looked for work; is out of work*). **5 a** a literary or musical composition. **b** (in *pl.*) all such by an author or composer etc. **6** actions or experiences of a specified kind (*good work!; this is thirsty work*). **7 a** (in *combination*) things or parts made of a specified material or with specified tools etc. (*ironwork*; *needlework*). **b** *archaic* needlework. **8** (in *pl.*) the operative part of a clock or machine. **9** *Physics* the exertion of force overcoming resistance or producing molecular change (*convert heat into work*). **10** (in *pl.*) *informal* all that is available; everything needed. **11** (in *pl.*) *Brit.* operations of building or repair (*major building works*). **12** (in *pl.*; often treated as *sing.*) esp. *Brit.* a place where manufacturing is carried on. **13** (usu. in *pl.*) *Theol.* a meritorious act. **14** (usu. in *pl.* or in *combination*) a defensive structure (*earthworks*). **15** (in *combination*) **a** ornamentation of a specified kind (*latticework*). **b** articles having this. ● *verb* **1** *intransitive* (often foll. by *at*, *on*) do work; be engaged in bodily or mental activity. **2** *intransitive* **a** be employed in certain work (*works in industry*; *works as a secretary*). **b** (foll. by *with*) be the workmate of (a person). **3** *intransitive* (often foll. by *for*) make efforts; conduct a campaign (*works for peace*). **4** *intransitive* (foll. by *in*) be a craftsman (in a material). **5** *intransitive* operate or function, esp. effectively (*how does this machine work?*; *your idea will not work*). **6** *intransitive* (of a part of a machine) run, revolve; go through regular motions. **7** *transitive* carry on, manage, or control (*cannot work the machine*). **8** *transitive* **a** put or keep in operation or at work; cause to toil (*this mine is no longer worked*; *works the staff very hard*). **b** cultivate (land). **9** *transitive* **a** bring about; produce as a result (*worked miracles*). **b** *informal* arrange (matters) (*worked it so that we could go*; *can you work things for us?*). **10** *transitive* knead, hammer; bring to a desired shape or consistency. **11** *transitive* do, or make by, needlework etc. **12** *transitive & intransitive* (cause to) progress or penetrate, or make (one's) way, gradually or with difficulty in a specified way (*worked our way through the crowd*; *worked the peg into the hole*). **13** *intransitive* (foll. by *loose* etc.) gradually become (loose etc.) by constant movement. **14** *transitive* artificially excite (*worked themselves into a rage*). **15** *transitive* solve (a mathematical problem). **16** *transitive* **a** purchase with one's labour instead of money (*work one's passage*). **b** obtain by labour the money for (one's way through university etc.). **17** *intransitive* (foll. by *on*, *upon*) have influence. **18** *intransitive* be in motion or agitated; cause agitation, ferment (*his features worked violently*; *the yeast began to work*). **19** *intransitive Naut.* sail against the wind. □ **at work** in action or engaged in work. **get worked up** become angry, excited, or tense. **give a person the works 1** *informal* give or tell a person everything. **2** *informal* treat a person harshly. **3** *slang* kill a person. **have one's work cut out** be faced with a hard task. **in the works** esp. *N Amer.* being planned, worked on, or produced. **set to work** begin or cause to begin operations. **work away** (or **on**) continue to work. **work one's fingers to the bone** *see* BONE. **work in** find a place for. **work it** *informal* bring it about; achieve a desired result. **work off** get rid of by work or activity. **work out 1** solve (a mathematical problem) or find out (an amount) by calculation. **2** be calculated (*the total works out to 230*). **3** give a definite result (*this multiplication problem will not work out*). **4** have a specified result (*the plan worked out well*). **5** provide for the details of (*has worked out a scheme*). **6** accomplish or attain with difficulty (*work out one's salvation*). **7** exhaust with work (*the mine is worked out*). **8** engage in physical exercise or training. **work over 1** examine thoroughly. **2** *informal* treat with violence. **work a** (or **the**) **room** (or **crowd**) *informal* make the rounds of people gathered in a room, in order to make a favourable impression. **work to rule** (esp. as a form of job action) follow official working rules exactly in order to reduce output and efficiency. **work up 1** bring gradually to an efficient state. **2** (foll. by *to*) advance gradually to a climax. **3** elaborate or excite by degrees. **4** learn (a subject) by study. **work one's will** (foll. by *on*, *upon*) *archaic* accomplish one's purpose on (a person or thing). **work wonders** *see* WONDER. □ **work·less** *adjective* [Old English *weorc* etc.]

work·able *adjective* **1** that can be worked or will work. **2** that is worth working; practicable, feasible (*a workable quarry*; *a workable scheme*). □ **work·abil·ity** *noun* **work·ably** *adverb*

work·aday *adjective* **1** ordinary, everyday, practical. **2** fit for, used, or seen on workdays.

work·ahol·ic *noun informal* a person addicted to work; a person who voluntarily works excessively hard, esp. for too long. □ **work·ahol·ism** *noun* [blend of WORK + ALCOHOLIC]

work·around *noun Computing* a method for overcoming a problem or limitation in a program or system.

work basket *noun* (also **work bag**) a basket or bag etc. containing sewing materials.

work bee *noun N Amer.* a social gathering at which communal work is performed.

work·bench *noun* a bench for doing mechanical or practical work, esp. carpentry.

work·book *noun* **1** a student's book that provides information on a subject together with exercises. **2** a student's notebook; a scribbler.

work·boot *noun* a sturdy leather boot worn esp. by people engaged in manual labour.

work·box *noun* a box for holding tools, materials for sewing, etc.

work camp *noun* **1** a prison camp enforcing a regime of hard labour. **2** a camp at which community work is done esp. by young volunteers.

work·day *noun* esp. *N Amer.* **1** a day on which work is usually done. **2** the part of the day devoted to work (*the union is campaigning for a shorter workday*).

work·er *noun* **1** a person who works, esp. one who does a particular type of work (*factory workers*; *rescue workers*). **2 a** a person who works in a specified way (*a slow worker*). **b** a person who works hard (*she's quite the worker!*). **3** a neuter or undeveloped female of various social insects, esp. a bee or ant, that does the basic work of its colony.

worker priest *noun* a Roman Catholic priest who engages part-time in secular work.

workers' compensation *noun* money paid to a person to compensate for injury suffered on the job.

work ethic *noun* the principle that hard work is intrinsically virtuous or worthy of reward.

work·fare *noun* a welfare system which requires some work or training from those receiving benefits. [blend of WORK + WELFARE]

work·flow *noun* the organization of the sequence of industrial, administrative, etc. processes through which a piece of work passes from initiation to completion.

work·force *noun* **1** the workers engaged or available in an industry etc. **2** the number of such workers.

work·group *noun Computing* a group of people who have simultaneous access via a computer network to shared software and data, which enables them to work together on projects.

work·horse *noun* **1** a horse used for heavy work, e.g. plowing, hauling, etc., rather than riding or racing. **2** a person, machine, etc. that does a great amount of work.

work·house *noun* **1** *Brit. hist.* a public institution in which the destitute of a parish received board and lodging in return for work done. **2** *US* a house of correction for petty offenders.

work·ing ● *adjective* **1 a** having a job; employed (*the working poor*). **b** having a job that involves physical labour (*a working man*). **c** spent in work or employment (*all his working life*). **2** functioning or able to function (*a working model of a steam engine*). **3** preliminary; that is good enough as a basis for work, argument, etc. and may be improved later (*the book's working title*). ● *noun* **1** the activity of work. **2** (often in *pl.*) the act or manner of functioning of a thing (*the workings of the human mind*). **3** (usu. in *pl.*) **a** a mine or quarry. **b** the part of this in which work is being or has been done (*disused mine workings*).

working capital *noun* capital that is needed and used in running a business, and not invested in its buildings, equipment, etc.

working class ● *noun* the class of people who are employed for wages, esp. in manual or industrial work. ● *adjective* (**working-class**) of or relating to the working class.

working day *noun* esp. *Brit.* = WORKDAY.

working drawing *noun* a drawing to scale, serving as a guide for construction or manufacture.

working girl *noun* **1** *informal* a girl or woman who goes out to earn her living. **2** *N Amer. slang* a prostitute.

working group *noun* (also *Brit.* **working party**) a group of people appointed to study a particular problem or advise on some question.

working hours *plural noun* hours normally devoted to work.

working hypothesis *noun* a hypothesis used as a basis for action.

working knowledge *noun* an adequate level of knowledge or expertise in a specified area, esp. the use of a language.

working lunch *noun* a lunch at which business is conducted.

work·ing·man *noun* (*pl.* **-men**) *N Amer.* a man who works for wages, esp. in manual or industrial work.

working order *noun* the condition in which a machine works (satisfactorily or as specified).

working week *noun* esp. *Brit.* = WORKWEEK.

work-in-progress *noun* work undertaken but not yet completed.

work·load *noun* the amount of work to be done by an individual etc.

work·man *noun* (*pl.* **-men**) **1** a man employed to do manual labour. **2** a person considered with regard to skill in a job (*a good workman*).

work·man·like *adjective* characteristic of a good workman; showing practised skill.

work·man·ship *noun* **1** the degree of skill in doing a task, or of quality in the product made. **2** a thing made or created by a specified person etc.

work·mate *noun* a person with whom one works.

work of art *noun* a fine picture, poem, or building etc.

work·out *noun* a session of physical exercise or training.

work·people *plural noun* people in paid employment.

work·piece *noun* a thing worked on with a tool or machine.

work·place *noun* a place at which a person works; an office, factory, etc.

work·room *noun* a room for working in, esp. one equipped for a certain kind of work.

work·sheet *noun* **1** a paper for recording work done or in progress. **2** a paper listing questions or activities for students etc. to work through.

work·shop ● *noun* **1** a room or building in which goods are manufactured. **2 a** a meeting for concerted discussion and practical work on a particular subject, in which a group of people share their knowledge and experience (*a writing workshop*). **b** the members of such a group. ● *transitive verb* (**work·shopped**, **work·shop·ping**) present a workshop performance of (a dramatic work), esp. in order to explore aspects of the production before it is staged formally.

work-shy *adjective* disinclined to work.

work site *noun* a site where an industry is located or where labour takes place.

work·song *noun* a song sung while engaged in physical labour.

work·space *noun* **1** space in which to work. **2** an area rented or sold for commercial purposes. **3** *Computing* a memory storage facility for temporary use.

work·station *noun* **1** a computer terminal or the desk etc. where this is located. **2** a location on an assembly line at which an operation in a manufacturing process is carried out.

work study *noun* a system of assessing methods of working so as to achieve the maximum output and efficiency.

work surface *noun* a flat surface for working on, e.g. a counter or table.

work table *noun* a table for working at.

work·top *noun* esp. *Brit.* a work surface, esp. in a kitchen.

work-to-rule *noun* the act or an instance of working to rule.

work·up *noun* **1** a diagnostic examination of a patient. **2 a** the process of bringing a ship into seaworthy condition. **b** an instance of this.

work·wear *noun* hard-wearing clothes worn by people performing manual labour etc.

work·week *noun* N *Amer.* the number of days or hours per week devoted or allotted to work.

world *noun* **1 a** the earth, or a planetary body like it. **b** its countries and their inhabitants. **c** all people; the earth as known or in some particular respect. **2 a** the universe or all that exists; everything. **b** everything that exists outside oneself (*dead to the world*). **3 a** the time, state, or scene of human existence. **b** (prec. by *the*, *this*) mortal life. **4** secular interests and affairs. **5** human affairs; their course and conditions; active life (*how goes the world with you?*). **6** average, respectable, or fashionable people or their customs or opinions. **7** all that concerns or all who belong to a specified class, time, domain, or sphere of activity (*the medieval world*; *the sports world*). **8** (foll. by *of*) a vast amount (*that makes a world of difference*). **9** (*attributive*) affecting many nations, of all nations (*world politics*; *a world champion*; *world record*). □ **be worlds apart** be completely different in attitudes, opinions, etc. (*politically, they're worlds apart*). **bring into the world** give birth to or attend at the birth of. **come into the world** be born. **for all the world** (foll. by *like*, *as if*) precisely (*looked for all the world as if they were real*). **in the world** of all; at all (used as an intensifier in questions) (*what in the world is it?*). **man** (or **woman**) **of the world** a person experienced and practical in human affairs. **out of this world** informal extremely good etc. (*the food was out of this world*). **see the world** travel widely; gain wide experience. **think the world of** have a very high regard for. **the** (or **all the**) **world over** throughout the world. **the world to come** supposed life after death. **world without end** forever. □ **world·er** *noun* (also in *combination*). [Old English w(e)orold, world from a Germanic root meaning 'age': related to OLD]

World Bank *noun* the International Bank for Reconstruction and Development, an organization administering economic aid between member nations.

world beat *noun* = WORLD MUSIC.

world-beater *noun* a person or thing surpassing all others.

world-class *adjective* of a quality or standard regarded as high throughout the world.

World Council of Churches *noun* an association established in 1948 to promote unity among the many different Christian Churches. Its member Churches number over 300 and include virtually all Christian traditions except Roman Catholicism and Unitarianism. Its headquarters are in Geneva.

World Court *noun* = INTERNATIONAL COURT OF JUSTICE.

World Cup *noun* any of various international sports competitions (or the trophies awarded for them), esp. a competition in soccer instituted in 1930 and held every fourth year between national teams who qualify from regional preliminary rounds.

world-famous *adjective* known throughout the world.

World Health Organization *noun* an agency of the United Nations, headquartered in Geneva, established in 1948 to promote health and control communicable diseases. Abbr.: **WHO**.

World Heritage Site *noun* a natural or man-made site, area, or structure recognized as being of outstanding international importance and therefore as deserving special protection. Sites are nominated by countries to the World Heritage Convention (an organization of UNESCO), which decides whether or not to declare them World Heritage Sites.

world language *noun* **1** a language in use throughout the world. **2** a language used in many countries.

world line *noun* *Physics* a curve in space-time joining the positions of a particle throughout its existence.

world·ly *adjective* (**world·li·er**, **world·li·est**) **1** temporal or earthly (*worldly goods*). **2** engrossed in temporal affairs, esp. the pursuit of wealth and pleasure. **3** experienced in life, sophisticated. □ **world·li·ness** *noun*

worldly-minded *adjective* intent on worldly things.

worldly wisdom *noun* prudence as regards one's own interests.

worldly-wise *adjective* having worldly wisdom.

world music *noun* **1** traditional local or ethnic music, esp. from the developing world. **2** a style of commercial pop music incorporating elements of such folk traditions.

world power *noun* a nation having power and influence in world affairs.

World Series *noun* a North American professional baseball championship played after the end of the season between the champions of the American League and the National League. It was first played in 1903.

world's fair *noun* an international exhibition of the industrial, scientific, technological, and artistic achievements of the participating nations.

world-shaking *adjective* of supreme importance.

world view *noun* a comprehensive view or philosophy of life, the world, and the universe.

world war *noun* a war involving many important nations.

World War I *noun* = FIRST WORLD WAR.

World War II *noun* = SECOND WORLD WAR.

World War III *noun* a hypothetical future world war, esp. one involving the destruction of the planet through the use of nuclear weapons.

world-weary *adjective* weary of the world and life on it. □ **world-weari·ness** *noun*

world·wide ● *adjective* affecting, occurring in, or known in all parts of the world. ● *adverb* throughout the world.

World Wide Web *noun* an international computer network incorporating multimedia techniques and using hypertext links to access and retrieve information. Abbr.: **WWW**.

worm ● *noun* **1** any of various types of creeping or burrowing invertebrate animals with long slender bodies and no limbs, esp. segmented in rings or parasitic in the intestines or tissues. **2** the long slender larva of an insect, esp. in fruit or wood. **3** (in *pl.*) intestinal or other internal parasites. **4** a blindworm or slow-worm. **5** a maggot supposed to eat dead bodies in the grave. **6** an insignificant or contemptible person. **7 a** the spiral part of a screw. **b** a short screw working in a worm gear. **8** the spiral pipe of a still in which the vapour is cooled and condensed. **9** the ligament under a dog's tongue.

10 *Computing* a program designed to sabotage a computer or computer network, esp. a self-duplicating program which can operate without becoming incorporated into another program. ● *verb* **1** *intransitive & transitive* (often *reflexive*) move with a crawling motion (*wormed through the bushes*; *wormed our way through the bushes*). **2** *intransitive & reflexive* (foll. by *into*) insinuate oneself into a person's favour, confidence, etc. **3** *transitive* (foll. by *out*) obtain (a secret etc.) by cunning persistence (*managed to worm the truth out of them*). **4** *transitive* cut the worm of (a dog's tongue). **5** *transitive* rid (a plant or dog etc.) of worms. □ **the worm turns** a meek person retaliates after being pushed too far. □ **worm·er** *noun* **worm·like** *adjective* [Old English *wyrm*]

worm casting *noun* (also **worm·cast**) a convoluted mass of earth left on the surface by a burrowing earthworm.

worm-eaten *adjective* **1 a** eaten into by worms. **b** rotten, decayed. **2** old and dilapidated.

worm fishing *noun* fishing with worms as bait.

worm gear *noun* an arrangement of a toothed wheel worked by a short revolving cylinder bearing a screw thread.

worm·hole *noun* **1** a hole made by a burrowing worm or insect in wood, fruit, books, etc. **2** *Physics* a hypothetical connection between widely separated regions of space-time.

Worms /ˈvɜrmz, vɔrmz/ an industrial town in western Germany, on the Rhine northwest of Mannheim; pop. (1998) 80,622. It was the scene in 1521 of the condemnation of Martin Luther's teaching (*see* Diet of Worms).

worm's-eye view *noun* a view as seen from below or from a humble position.

worm·wheel *noun* the wheel of a worm gear.

worm·wood *noun* **1** any herbaceous plant or woody shrub of the genus *Artemisia*, with a bitter aromatic taste, esp. *A. absinthium*, used in the preparation of vermouth and absinthe and in medicine. **2** bitter mortification or a source of this. [Middle English, alteration of obsolete *wormod* from Old English *wormōd*, *wermōd*, after *worm*, *wood*: compare VERMOUTH]

wormy *adjective* (**worm·i·er**, **worm·i·est**) **1** full of worms. **2** worm-eaten. □ **worm·i·ness** *noun*

worn ● *verb* past participle of WEAR¹. ● *adjective* **1** damaged by use or wear. **2** looking tired and exhausted. **3** (in full **well-worn**) (of a joke etc.) stale; often heard.

worn out *adjective* **1** exhausted. **2** worn, esp. to the point of being no longer usable (often *attributive*: *a worn-out engine*).

wor·ried *adjective* **1** uneasy, troubled in the mind. **2** suggesting worry (*a worried look*).

wor·ri·ment *noun* esp. *US* **1** the act of worrying or state of being worried. **2** a cause of worry.

wor·ri·some *adjective* causing or apt to cause worry or distress. □ **wor·ri·some·ly** *adverb*

worry ● *verb* (**-ries**, **-ried**) **1** *intransitive* give way to anxiety or unease; allow one's mind to dwell on difficulty or troubles. **2** *transitive* harass, importune; be a trouble or anxiety to. **3** *transitive* **a** (of a dog etc.) shake or pull repeatedly with the teeth. **b** attack repeatedly. ● *noun* (*pl.* **-ries**) **1** a thing that causes anxiety or disturbs a person's tranquility. **2** a disturbed state of mind; anxiety; a worried state. **3** a dog's worrying of its quarry. □ **not to worry** *informal* there is no need to worry. **worry along** (or **through**) manage to advance by persistence in spite of obstacles. **worry oneself** (usu. in *neg.*) take needless trouble. □ **wor·ried·ly** *adverb* **wor·rier** *noun* **worry·ing** *adjective* **worry·ing·ly** *adverb* [Old English *wyrgan* strangle, from West Germanic]

worry beads *plural noun* a string of beads manipulated with the fingers to occupy or calm oneself.

worry·wart *noun informal* a person who habitually worries unduly.

worse ● *adjective* **1** bad to a greater degree or on a greater scale; less good or desirable. **2** (*predicative*) in or into worse health or a worse condition (*is getting worse*). ● *adverb* more badly or more ill. ● *noun* **1** a worse thing or things (*you might do worse than accept*). **2** (prec. by *the*) a worse condition (*a turn for the worse*). □ **none the worse** (often foll. by *for*) not adversely affected (by). **or worse** or as an even worse alternative. **the worse for wear 1** damaged by use. **2** injured. **3** drunk. **worse luck** *see* LUCK. **worse off** in a worse (esp. financial) position. [Old English *wyrsa*, *wiersa*]

worsen *transitive & intransitive verb* make or become worse.

wor·ship ● *noun* **1 a** homage or reverence paid to a deity, esp. in a formal service. **b** the acts, rites, or forms of worship. **2** adoration or devotion comparable to religious homage shown towards a person

or principle (*the worship of wealth*; *regarded them with worship in their eyes*). **3** *archaic* worthiness, merit; recognition given or due to these; honour and respect. ● *verb* (**wor·shipped**, **wor·ship·ping**; also esp. *US* **wor·shiped**, **wor·ship·ing**) **1** *transitive* adore as divine; honour with religious rites. **2** *transitive* idolize or regard with adoration (*worships the ground she walks on*). **3** *intransitive* attend public worship. **4** *intransitive* be full of adoration. □ **Your** (or **His** or **Her**) **Worship** esp. *Cdn & Brit.* a title of respect used to or of a mayor, certain magistrates, etc. □ **wor·ship·per** *noun* (also esp. *US* **wor·ship·er**). [Old English *weorthscipe* (as WORTH, -SHIP)]

wor·ship·ful *adjective* **1** (usu. **Worshipful**) a title given to officers of certain organizations. **2** full of worship; adoring (*worshipful fans*). **3** *archaic* entitled to honour or respect. **4** *archaic* imbued with a spirit of veneration. □ **wor·ship·ful·ly** *adverb*

worst ● *adjective* worse than any other person or thing of a similar kind; most bad. ● *adverb* worse than anyone or anything else of a similar kind; most badly. ● *noun* the worst part, event, circumstance, or possibility (*the worst of the storm is over*; *prepare for the worst*). ● *transitive verb* get the better of; defeat, outdo. □ **at its** etc. **worst** in the worst state. **at worst** (or **the worst**) in the worst possible case. **get** (or **have**) **the worst of it** be defeated. **if** (**the**) **worst comes to** (**the**) **worst** if the worst happens. **in the worst way** to an extreme degree (*wants to win in the worst way*). [Old English *wierresta*, *wyrresta* (adj.), *wyrst*, *wyrrest* (adv.)]

worst-case *adjective* designating or pertaining to the worst of the possible foreseeable outcomes, scenarios, etc.

worst·ed /ˈwɜrstəd/ ● *noun* **1** a fine smooth yarn spun from combed long staple wool. **2** fabric made from this. ● *adjective* made of worsted. [*Worste(a)d* in Norfolk, England]

wort /wɜrt, wɔrt/ *noun* **1** *archaic* (except in names) a plant or herb (*liverwort*; *St. John's wort*). **2** the infusion of malt which after fermentation becomes beer. [Old English *wyrt*: related to ROOT¹]

worth ● *predicative adjective* (governing a noun like a preposition) **1** of a value equivalent to (*is worth $50*; *is worth very little*). **2** such as to justify or repay; deserving; bringing compensation for (*worth doing*; *not worth the trouble*). **3** possessing or having property amounting to (*is worth a million dollars*). ● *noun* **1** what a person or thing is worth; the (usu. specified) merit of (*of great worth*; *persons of worth*). **2** the equivalent of money in a commodity (*ten dollars' worth of gas*). □ **for all one is worth** *informal* with one's utmost efforts; without reserve. **for what it is worth** without a guarantee of its truth or value. **worth it** *informal* worth the time or effort spent. **worth one's salt** *see* SALT. **worth while** (or **one's while**) *see* WHILE. [Old English *w(e)orth*]

worth·less *adjective* without value or merit. □ **worth·less·ly** *adverb* **worth·less·ness** *noun*

worth·while *adjective* that is worth the time or effort spent; of value or importance. □ **worth·while·ness** *noun*

worthy ● *adjective* (**worth·i·er**, **worth·i·est**) **1** estimable; having some moral worth; deserving respect (*lived a worthy life*). **2** esp. *jocular* (of a person) entitled to recognition (*the worthy citizens of the town*). **3 a** (foll. by *of* or *to* + infin.) deserving (*worthy of a mention*; *worthy to be remembered*). **b** (foll. by *of*) adequate or suitable to the dignity etc. of (*in words worthy of the occasion*). ● *noun* (*pl.* **-ies**) **1** a worthy person. **2** a person of some distinction. **3** *jocular* a person. □ **worth·i·ly** *adverb* **worth·i·ness** *noun* [Middle English *wurthi* etc. from WORTH]

-worthy *combining form* forming adjectives meaning: **1** deserving of (*blameworthy*; *noteworthy*). **2** suitable or fit for (*newsworthy*; *roadworthy*).

wot *see* WIT².

Wotan /ˈwoːtɒn/ *see* ODIN.

wotch·er /ˈwɒtʃər/ *interjection Brit. slang* a form of casual greeting. [corruption of *what cheer*]

would *auxiliary verb* (*3rd sing.* **would**) *past of* WILL¹, used esp.: **1** (in the 2nd and 3rd persons, and often in the 1st: *see* SHOULD). **a** in reported speech (*he said he would be home by evening*). **b** to express the conditional mood (*they would have been killed if they had gone*). **2** to express habitual action (*would wait for her every evening*). **3** to express a question or polite request (*would they like it?*; *would you come in, please?*). **4** to express probability (*I guess she would be over fifty by now*). **5** (foll. by *that* + clause) *literary* to express a wish (*would that you were here*). **6** to express consent (*they would not help*). [Old English *wolde*, past of *wyllan*: see WILL¹]

would-be *attributive adjective* often *derogatory* desiring or aspiring to be (a *would-be politician*).

wouldn't *contraction* would not. □ **I wouldn't know** *informal* (as is to be expected) I do not know.

wouldst /wʊdst/ *archaic* 2nd sing. past of WOULD.

wound[1] ● *noun* **1** an injury done to living tissue by a cut or blow etc., esp. beyond the cutting or piercing of the skin. **2** an injury to a person's reputation or a pain inflicted on a person's feelings. **3** *literary* the pangs of love. ● *transitive verb* inflict a wound on (*wounded soldiers; wounded feelings*). □ **wound·ing·ly** *adverb* [Old English *wund* (n.), *wundian* (v.)]

wound[2] *past and past participle of* WIND[2] (*compare* WIND[1] *verb* 6).

wound·ed *noun* suffering from or damaged by a wound or wounds. □ **wound·ed·ness** *noun*

Wounded Knee, Battle of the last major confrontation (1890) between the US army and Aboriginal peoples, in which more than 150 largely unarmed Sioux men, women, and children were massacred at the village of Wounded Knee on a reservation in South Dakota.

wound·wort /ˈwuːndwɜrt, -wɔrt/ *noun* any of various plants esp. of the genus *Stachys*, formerly supposed to have healing properties.

wove[1] *past of* WEAVE[1].

wove[2] *adjective* (of paper) made on a wire-gauze mesh and so having a uniform unlined surface. [var. of *woven*, past participle of WEAVE[1]]

woven *past participle of* WEAVE[1].

wow[1] ● *interjection* expressing astonishment or admiration. ● *noun slang* a sensational success. ● *transitive verb slang* impress or excite greatly. [originally Scots: imitative]

wow[2] *noun* a slow pitch-fluctuation in sound reproduction, perceptible in long notes. [imitative]

wow·ser /ˈwauzər/ *noun Austral. slang* **1** a puritanical fanatic. **2** a spoilsport. **3** a teetotaller. [20th c.: origin uncertain]

WP *abbreviation* word processor or processing.

w.p. *abbreviation* weather permitting.

WPC *abbreviation* (in the UK) woman police constable.

Wpg. *abbreviation* Winnipeg.

w.p.m. *abbreviation* words per minute.

WRAC *abbreviation* (in the UK) Women's Royal Army Corps.

wrack[1] *noun* **1** seaweed cast up or growing on the shore. **2** a wreck or wreckage. **3** = RACK[2]. **4** = RACK[5] *noun*. [Middle Dutch *wrak* or Middle Low German *wra(c)k*, a parallel formation to Old English *wræc*, related to *wrecan* WREAK: compare WRECK, RACK[5]]

wrack[2] *var. of.* RACK[1] *verb* 1.

WRAF *abbreviation* (in the UK) Women's Royal Air Force.

wraith *noun* **1** a ghost or apparition. **2** the spectral appearance of a living person supposed to portend that person's death. □ **wraith·like** *adjective* [16th-c. Scots: origin unknown]

Wran·gel Island /ˈraŋɡəl/ an island in the Arctic Ocean, off the coast of NE Russia. [Baron F. *Wrangel*, Russian admiral and explorer d.1870]

wran·gle ● *noun* a heated or prolonged argument, altercation, or dispute. ● *verb* **1** *intransitive* engage in a wrangle. **2** *transitive* get (a thing) from a person by argument or persuasion. **3** *transitive N Amer.* herd (horses, cattle, etc.). □ **wran·gling** *noun* [Middle English, prob. from Low German or Dutch: compare Low German *wrangelen*, frequentative of *wrangen* to struggle, related to WRING]

wran·gler *noun* **1** *N Amer.* a cowboy. **2** a person who wrangles. **3** a person who supervises and handles animals used on a film set.

wrap ● *verb* (**wrapped, wrap·ping**) **1** *transitive* (often foll. by *up*) envelop in folded or soft encircling material (*wrap it up in paper; wrap a gift*). **2** *transitive* **a** (foll. by *around, about*) arrange or draw (a pliant covering) around (a person) (*wrapped the scarf closer around me*). **b** use (oneself or a part of one's body) to embrace a person (*wrapped her arms around his neck; wrapped herself around him*). **3** *transitive* (foll. by *around*) *slang* crash (a vehicle) into a stationary object. **4** *transitive & intransitive* finish filming (a movie, video, etc.). **5** *Computing* **a** *transitive* cause (a word or other unit of text) to be carried over to a new line automatically as the right margin is reached. **b** *intransitive* (of a word etc.) be so carried over. ● *noun* **1** a shawl or scarf or other such addition to clothing. **2** esp. *N Amer.* material used for wrapping. **3** the completion of the filming of a movie, video, etc. **4** a sandwich of any of a variety of fillings wrapped in a tortilla. □ **take the wraps off** disclose. **under wraps** in secrecy. **wrap oneself in the flag** *see* FLAG[1]. **wrapped up in** engrossed or absorbed in. **wrap up 1** finish off, bring to completion (*wrapped up the deal in two days*). **2** put on warm clothes (*wrap up well*). [Middle English: origin unknown]

wrap·around ● *adjective* **1** (of a garment, esp. a woman's skirt or top) designed to wrap around the body. **2** curving or extending around at the edges. ● *noun* anything that wraps around.

wrap-over *Brit.* ● *attributive adjective* (of a garment) having no seam at one side but wrapped around the body and fastened. ● *noun* such a garment.

wrap party *noun* a party held to celebrate the completion of filming.

wrap·per *noun* **1** a thing in which something is wrapped, esp. a flexible piece of paper, cellophane, foil, etc. forming a protective covering for a product (*candy wrappers*). **2** a cover enclosing a newspaper or similar packet for mailing. **3** a paper cover of a book or magazine, usu. detachable. **4** a loose enveloping robe or gown. **5** a tobacco leaf of superior quality enclosing a cigar.

wrap·ping *noun* (often in *pl.*) material used to wrap; wrappers, wrapping paper, etc.

wrapping paper *noun* strong or decorative paper for wrapping gifts etc.

wrap-up ● *noun* a summary, esp. of news; a conclusion (*a wrap-up of the day's events*). ● *adjective* that concludes or sums up a program, book, etc.

wrasse /ras/ *noun* any bright-coloured marine fish of the family Labridae with thick lips and strong teeth. [Cornish *wrach*, var. of *gwrach*, = Welsh *gwrach*, lit. 'old woman']

wras·sle *transitive & intransitive verb N Amer. dialect* = WRESTLE *verb*.

wrath /raθ/ *noun* extreme anger. [Old English *wræththu* from *wrāth* WROTH]

Wrath, Cape /raθ/ a headland at the northwestern tip of the mainland of Scotland.

wrath·ful *adjective literary* extremely angry. □ **wrath·ful·ly** *adverb* **wrath·ful·ness** *noun*

WRCNS *abbreviation Cdn hist.* Women's Royal Canadian Naval Service.

wreak /riːk/ *transitive verb* **1** (usu. foll. by *upon*) give vent or expression to (vengeance, anger etc.). **2** cause (damage etc.) (*the hurricane wreaked havoc on the crops*). □ **wreak·er** *noun* [Old English *wrecan* drive, avenge, etc., from Germanic: compare WRACK[1], WRECK, WRETCH]

wreath /riːθ/ *noun* (pl. **wreaths** /riːðz, riːθs/) **1** flowers or leaves fastened in a ring esp. as an ornament for a person's head or a building or for laying on a grave etc. as a mark of honour or respect. **2** (foll. by *of*) something shaped like a wreath (*wreaths of cloud*). [Old English *writha* from *writhan* WRITHE]

wreathe /riːð/ *verb* **1** *transitive* encircle as, with, or like a wreath. **2** *transitive* (foll. by *round*) put (one's arms etc.) round (a person etc.). **3** *intransitive* (of smoke etc.) move in the shape of wreaths. **4** *transitive* form (flowers, silk, etc.) into a wreath. **5** *transitive* make (a garland). [partly back-formation from archaic *wrethen* past participle of WRITHE; partly from WREATH]

wreck ● *noun* **1 a** the destruction or disablement esp. of a ship. **b** a ship that has suffered a wreck (*the shores are strewn with wrecks*). **2** a greatly damaged or disabled building, vehicle, aircraft, etc. **3** a person whose health, esp. mental health, has been damaged or destroyed (*had become a physical and mental wreck*). **4** *N Amer.* a crash or collision on a road, railway, etc. **5** (foll. by *of*) a wretched remnant or disorganized set of remains. **6** *Law* goods etc. cast up by the sea. ● *verb* **1** *transitive* cause the wreck of; damage or destroy. **2** *transitive* completely ruin (hopes, chances, etc.). **3** *intransitive* suffer a wreck. **4** *intransitive N Amer.* deal with wrecked vehicles etc. [Anglo-French *wrec* etc. (compare VAREC) from a Germanic root meaning 'to drive': compare WREAK]

wreck·age *noun* **1** wrecked material. **2** the remnants of a wreck. **3** the action or process of wrecking.

wrecked *adjective* **1** involved in a shipwreck (*wrecked sailors*). **2** ruined, destroyed. **3** *informal* **a** intoxicated by alcohol or drugs. **b** tired.

wreck·er *noun* **1** a person or thing that wrecks or destroys. **2** esp. *N Amer.* a person employed in demolition, or in recovering a wrecked ship or its contents. **3** *N Amer.* a person who breaks up damaged vehicles for spare parts and scrap. **4** *N Amer.* a vehicle or train used in recovering a damaged one.

wreck·house winds *plural noun Cdn* extremely strong winds which blow across Cape Ray from the Long Range Mountains in Newfoundland.

wreck·ing *noun* esp. *N Amer.* the demolition of old cars, buildings, etc., often to obtain usable scrap.

wrecking ball *noun* (also **wrecker's ball**) a heavy metal ball which may be swung from a crane into a building to demolish it.

wrecking bar *noun* a steel bar with one end chisel-shaped for prying and the other end bent and split to form a claw.

Wren[1], **Sir Chris·to·pher** (1632–1723), English architect. Following the Great Fire of London (1666), he was responsible for the design of the new St. Paul's Cathedral (1675–1711) and many of the city's churches; among his other works are Greenwich Observatory (1675) and a partial rebuilding of Hampton Court (1689–94).

Wren² *noun* **1** (in the UK) a member of the Women's Royal Naval Service. **2** (in Canada) a member of the Women's Royal Canadian Naval Service. [originally in pl., from abbreviation WRNS]

wren *noun* any small usu. brown short-winged songbird of the family Troglodytidae, esp. *Troglodytes troglodytes* of N America and Eurasia, having an erect tail. [Old English *wrenna*]

wrench ● *noun* **1** a violent twist or oblique pull or act of tearing off. **2** a tool for gripping and turning a nut on a bolt etc. **3** an instance of painful uprooting or parting (*leaving home was a great wrench*). ● *transitive verb* **1** twist or pull violently around or sideways. **2** (often foll. by *off, away*, etc.) pull off with a wrench. **3** injure (a limb, etc.) by undue twisting or stretching; sprain (*wrenched my ankle*). **4** distort (facts) to suit a theory etc. [(earlier as verb:) Old English *wrencan* twist]

wrench·ing *adjective N Amer.* painfully traumatic.

wrest *transitive verb* **1** force or wrench away from a person's grasp. **2** (foll. by *from*) obtain by effort or with difficulty. **3** distort into accordance with one's interests or views (*wrest the law to suit themselves*). [Old English *wrǣstan* from Germanic, related to WRIST]

wres·tle ● *verb* **1** *intransitive* (often foll. by *with*) take part in a fight, either as sport or in earnest, that involves grappling with one's opponent and trying to throw or force him to the ground. **2** *transitive* force (someone) into a particular position or place by fighting in such a way (*wrestled his opponent to the ground*). **3** *intransitive* **a** (foll. by *with, against*) struggle, contend. **b** (foll. by *with*) do one's utmost to deal with (a task, difficulty, etc.). **4** *transitive N Amer.* throw (a calf etc.) for branding. **5** *transitive* move with efforts as if wrestling. ● *noun* **1** a contest in which two opponents grapple and try to throw each other to the ground esp. as an athletic sport under a code of rules. **2** a hard struggle. □ **wrest·ler** *noun* [Old English (unrecorded) *wrǣstlian*: compare Middle Low German *wrostelen*, Old English *wraxlian*]

wrest·ling *noun* the sport or activity in which opponents grapple with each other, trying to throw or hold one another down on the ground.

wretch *noun* **1** an unfortunate or unhappy person. **2** often *jocular* an evil or wicked person. [Old English *wrecca* from Germanic]

wretch·ed *adjective* **1** unhappy or miserable. **2** of very poor quality. **3** ill or unwell (*I feel wretched today*). **4** despicable; contemptible. **5** used to express annoyance (*this wretched car refuses to start*). □ **wretch·ed·ly** *adverb* **wretch·ed·ness** *noun*

wrig·gle ● *verb* **1** *intransitive* (of a worm etc.) twist or turn its body with short writhing movements. **2** *intransitive* (of a person or animal) make wriggling motions. **3** *transitive & intransitive* (foll. by *along* etc.) move or go in this way (*wriggled into the corner; wriggled her hand into the hole*). **4** *transitive* make (one's) way by wriggling. **5** *intransitive* practise evasion. ● *noun* an act of wriggling. □ **wriggle out of** *informal* avoid on a contrived pretext. □ **wrig·gler** *noun* **wrig·gly** *adjective* [Middle Low German *wriggelen* frequentative of *wriggen*]

Wright ▸ **1 Frank Lloyd** (1869–1959), US architect. He advocated an 'organic' architecture, characterized by a close relationship between building and landscape, and the nature of the materials used, as can be seen in the Kaufmann House (known as 'Falling Water') in Pennsylvania (1935–9), which incorporates a natural waterfall into its design; other notable buildings include the Guggenheim Museum of Art in New York (1956–9). **2 Or·ville** (1871–1948) and **Wil·bur** (1867–1912), US aviation pioneers. In 1903 at Kitty Hawk, N Carolina, the Wright brothers were the first to make brief, powered, sustained, and controlled flights in an airplane which they had designed and built themselves. ▸ **Wright·ian** *noun & adjective*

wright *noun* a maker or builder (usu. in *combination*: *playwright; shipwright*). [Old English *wryhta, wyrhta* from West Germanic]

wring ● *transitive verb* (*past* and *past participle* **wrung**) **1 a** squeeze tightly. **b** (often foll. by *out*) squeeze and twist esp. to remove liquid. **2** twist forcibly; break by twisting. **3** distress or torture. **4** extract by squeezing. **5** (foll. by *out, from*) obtain by pressure or importunity; extort. ● *noun* an act of wringing; a squeeze. □ **wring a person's hand** clasp it forcibly or press it with emotion. **wring one's hands** clasp them as a gesture of great distress. **wring the neck of** kill (a chicken etc.) by twisting its neck. [Old English *wringan*, related to WRONG]

wring·er *noun* a device for wringing water from washed clothes etc. □ **put through the wringer** *informal* subject to a very stressful experience.

wring·ing *adjective* (in full **wringing wet**) so wet that water can be wrung out.

wrin·kle ● *noun* **1** a slight crease or depression in the skin such as is produced by age. **2** a similar mark in another flexible surface. **3** *informal* a minor difficulty; a snag. **4** a clever innovation in technique etc.; a new development. ● *verb* **1** *transitive* make wrinkles in. **2** *intransitive* form wrinkles; become marked with wrinkles. □ **wrin·kled** *adjective* [originally representing Old English *gewrinclod* sinuous]

wrink·ly ● *adjective* (**wrink·li·er, wrink·li·est**) having many wrinkles. ● *noun* (also **wrink·lie**) (*pl.* **-lies**) *Brit. slang offensive* an old or middle-aged person.

wrist ● *noun* **1** the joint connecting the hand with the forearm. **2** the corresponding part in an animal. **3** the part of a garment covering the wrist. **4** = WRIST PIN. ● *transitive verb Hockey* shoot (the puck) with a wrist shot. □ **slap on the wrist** a mild rebuke or reprimand. [Old English from Germanic, prob. from a root related to WRITHE]

wrist·band *noun* **1** a band forming or concealing the end of a shirt sleeve; a cuff. **2** a strip of material worn around the wrist to absorb sweat. **3** a strap or band attached to a watch worn around the wrist. **4** a bracelet used for identification, e.g. while in hospital or as admission to an event etc.

wrist·let *noun* a band or ring worn on the wrist.

wrist pin *noun Mech.* a stud projecting from a crank etc. as an attachment for a connecting rod.

wrist rest *noun* a padded support for resting the wrists while typing etc.

wrist shot *noun Hockey* (also **wrist·er**) a shot taken by sweeping the puck along the ice with a fluid motion before releasing it.

wrist-slap *noun* a mild rebuke or reprimand.

wrist·watch *noun* a watch worn on a strap or band around the wrist.

wristy *adjective* (esp. of a shot in cricket, tennis, etc.) involving or characterized by movement of the wrist.

writ¹ *noun* **1** a form of written command in the name of a sovereign, court, government, etc., to act or abstain from acting in some way. **2** a government document ordering an election. □ **drop the writ** *Cdn* call an election. **serve a writ on** deliver a writ to (a person). **one's writ runs** one has authority (as specified). [Old English (as WRITE)]

writ² *archaic past participle of* WRITE. □ **writ large** in magnified or emphasized form.

write *verb* (*past* **wrote**; *past participle* **writ·ten**) **1** *intransitive* mark paper or some other surface by means of a pen, pencil, etc., with symbols, letters, or words. **2** *transitive* form (such symbols etc.). **3** *transitive* form the symbols that represent or constitute (a word or sentence, or a document etc.). **4** *transitive* fill or complete (a sheet, cheque, etc.) with writing. **5** *transitive & intransitive* record (data) in a computer memory. **6** *transitive* (esp. in passive) indicate (a quality or condition) by one's or its appearance (*guilt was written on his face*). **7** *transitive* compose (a text, article, novel, etc.) for written or printed reproduction or publication; put into literary etc. form and set down in writing. **8** *intransitive* be engaged in composing a text, article, etc. (*writes for the local newspaper*). **9** *intransitive* **a** (foll. by *to*) write and send a letter (to a recipient). **b** communicate by writing (*she hardly ever writes*). **10** *transitive* write and send a letter to (a person) (*wrote him last week*). **11** *transitive* convey (news, information, etc.) by letter (*wrote that they would arrive next Friday*). **12** *transitive Cdn & South Africa* take (an exam or test) (*I wrote Prof. Weldon's Middle English exam last week*). **13** *intransitive* write in a cursive hand, as opposed to printing individual letters. **14** *transitive* state in written or printed form (*it is written that*). **15** *transitive* cause to be recorded. **16** *transitive* underwrite (an insurance policy). **17** *transitive* (foll. by *into, out of*) include or exclude (a character or episode) in a story by suitable changes of the text. **18** *transitive archaic* describe in writing. □ **nothing to write home about** *informal* of little interest or value. **write down 1** record or take note of in writing. **2** reduce the nominal value of (stock, goods, etc.). **write in 1** send a suggestion, query, etc., in writing to an organization, esp. a broadcasting station. **2** esp. *US* add (an extra name) on a list of candidates when voting. **write off 1** write and send a letter. **2** to note the deduction of money in an account, financial statement or tax return, esp. to record the cancelling of a sum as a business expense, bad debt, depreciated stock, etc. (*the company wrote off the loss as a bad debt; he could write off his art supplies on his tax return*). **3** damage (a vehicle etc.) so badly that it cannot be repaired. **4** dismiss as insignificant. **write out 1** write in full or in finished form. **2** exhaust (oneself) by writing. **write up 1** write a full account of. **2** praise or bring to public attention in writing (*the concert was written up in the newspapers*). **3** make entries to bring (a diary etc.) up to date. □ **writ·able** *adjective* [Old English *writan* scratch, score, write, from Germanic: originally used of symbols inscribed with sharp tools on stone or wood]

write·down noun a reduction in the estimated or nominal value of stock, assets, etc.

write-in noun esp. US an instance of writing in (see WRITE IN 2).

write·off noun 1 a thing written off, esp. a vehicle too badly damaged to be repaired. 2 a person or thing that is given up as being hopeless, useless, or pointless (the entire weekend was a writeoff). 3 a an act of cancelling a debt because there is no chance that it will be paid. b an act of writing off an expense, etc.

write-once adjective Computing denoting a memory or storage device, typically an optical one, on which data, once written, cannot be modified.

write protect noun (often attributive) a means to protect the data in a storage device from being erased (turn off the write-protect tab). □ **write-protect·ed** adjective

writ·er noun 1 a person who writes or has written something. 2 a person who writes books; an author. 3 a person who writes screenplays.

writer-in-residence noun a writer holding a usu. temporary residential post in a university etc. in order to share his or her professional insights with students and faculty.

writer·ly adjective 1 characteristic of a professional author. 2 consciously literary.

writer's block noun a (usu. temporary) inability to express one's thoughts in writing due to a lack of inspiration.

writer's cramp noun a muscular spasm in the hands due to excessive writing.

write-up noun informal a written or published account, a review.

writhe /raið/ verb 1 intransitive twist or roll oneself about in or as if in acute pain. 2 intransitive suffer severe mental discomfort or embarrassment (writhed with shame; writhed at the thought of it). 3 transitive twist (one's body etc.) about. [Old English writhan, related to WREATHE]

writ·ing noun 1 a group or sequence of letters or symbols. 2 = HANDWRITING. 3 (usu. in pl.) a piece of literary work done; a book, article, etc. 4 the work or profession of a writer (turned to writing late in life). 5 (**Writings**) the Hagiographa. □ **in writing** in written form (give me your request for funding in writing). **the writing** (or **handwriting**) **is on the wall** there are clear signs of approaching failure or disaster.

writing desk noun a desk for writing at, esp. with compartments for papers etc.

writing pad noun a pad (see PAD¹ noun 2) of paper for writing on.

writing paper noun paper for writing (esp. letters) on.

writ·ten ● verb past participle of WRITE. ● adjective that has been or is to be done in writing (a written agreement; a written exam). □ **have something written all over one** informal used to convey that the presence of a particular quality or feeling is clearly evident. **written in stone** fixed, unchangeable.

WRNS abbreviation (in the UK) Women's Royal Naval Service.

Wroc·ław /ˈvrɒtswɒf/ an industrial city on the Oder river in W Poland; pop. (est. 2000) 633,857.

wrong ● adjective 1 mistaken; not true; in error (gave a wrong answer; we were wrong to think that). 2 unsuitable; less or least desirable (the wrong road; a wrong decision). 3 contrary to law or morality (it is wrong to steal). 4 amiss; out of order, in or into a bad or abnormal condition (something wrong with my heart; my watch has gone wrong). 5 designating the side of fabric that will not be on the outside of the garment etc. ● adverb (usually placed last) in a wrong manner or direction; with an incorrect result (guessed wrong; told them wrong). ● noun 1 what is morally wrong; a wrong action. 2 injustice; unjust action or treatment (suffer wrong). ● transitive verb 1 treat unjustly; do wrong to. 2 mistakenly attribute bad motives to; discredit. □ **do wrong** commit sin; transgress, offend. **do wrong to** malign or mistreat (a person). **get in wrong with** incur the dislike or disapproval of (a person). **get off on the wrong foot** begin badly; make a bad start. **get wrong 1** misunderstand (a person, statement, etc.). 2 obtain an incorrect answer to. **get** (or **get hold of**) **the wrong end of the stick** misunderstand completely. **go down the wrong way** (of food) enter the windpipe instead of the gullet. **go wrong 1** take the wrong path. 2 stop functioning properly. 3 depart from virtuous or suitable behaviour. **in the wrong** responsible for a quarrel, mistake, or offence. **on the wrong side of 1** out of favour with (a person). 2 somewhat more than (a stated age). **wrong side out** inside out. **wrong way round** in the opposite or reverse of the normal or desirable orientation or sequence etc. □ **wrong·ly** adverb **wrong·ness** noun [Old English wrang from Old Norse rangr awry, unjust, related to WRING]

wrong·doer noun a person who behaves immorally or illegally. □ **wrong·doing** noun

wrong-foot transitive verb informal 1 (in tennis, soccer, etc.) play so as to catch (an opponent) off balance. 2 disconcert; catch unprepared.

wrong·ful adjective 1 characterized by unfairness or injustice. 2 contrary to law. 3 (of a person) not entitled to the position etc. occupied. □ **wrong·ful·ly** adverb **wrong·ful·ness** noun

wrongful dismissal noun unjust dismissal from employment.

wrong-headed adjective perverse and obstinate. □ **wrong-headed·ly** adverb **wrong-headed·ness** noun

wrote past of WRITE. □ **that's all she wrote** N Amer. informal that's it; that's the end.

wroth /roːθ, rɒθ/ predicative adjective archaic angry. [Old English wrāth from Germanic]

wrought ● verb archaic past and past participle of WORK. ● adjective 1 (of metals) beaten out or shaped by hammering. 2 (often in combination) worked or made (cleverly wrought; well-wrought).

wrought iron noun a tough malleable form of iron suitable for forging or rolling, not cast.

wrung past and past participle of WRING. □ **wrung out** exhausted.

wry adjective (**wryer, wry·est** or **wrier, wri·est**) 1 (of humour) dry and mocking. 2 (of a face or smile etc.) contorted in disgust, disappointment, or mockery. 3 distorted or turned to one side. □ **wryly** adverb **wry·ness** noun [wry (v.) from Old English wrigian tend, incline, in Middle English deviate, swerve, contort]

wry·neck noun 1 (usu. **wry neck**) = TORTICOLLIS. 2 any bird of the genus Jynx of the woodpecker family, able to turn its head over its shoulder.

WSW abbreviation west-southwest.

wt. abbreviation weight.

WTO abbreviation World Trade Organization.

Wu noun a dialect of Chinese spoken in the Jiangsu and Zhejiang Provinces. [Chinese]

Wuhan /wuːˈhan/ a port in E China, the capital of Hubei province, situated at the confluence of the Han and the Yangtze rivers; pop. (est. 2002) 4,454,800.

Wu-hsi see WUXI.

Wunder·kam·mer /ˈvʊndəˌkaməʳ/ noun (pl. **Wunder·kam·mern**) a place where a collection of curiosities and rarities is exhibited. [German, literally 'wonder chamber']

wunder·kind /ˈvʊndəʳkɪnt/ noun informal (pl. **wunder·kinds** or **wunder·kinder**) a person who achieves great success while relatively young. [German from Wunder wonder + Kind child]

Wundt /vʊnt/ **Wil·helm** (1832–1920), German philosopher and physiologist. He was the founder of psychology as an independent and scientific discipline, and felt that the major task of the psychologist was to analyze human consciousness, which could be broken down into simpler fundamental units.

Wup·per·tal /ˈvʊpəʳˌtɒl/ an industrial city in western Germany, in North Rhine-Westphalia, northeast of Düsseldorf; pop. (est. 2002) 368,600.

Wur·lit·zer /ˈwɜːʳlɪtsəʳ/ noun proprietary a large pipe organ or electric organ, esp. one used in the movie theatres of the 1930s. [Rudolf Wurlitzer, German-born US instrument maker]

wurst /vʊrst, vɜːʳst/ noun sausage, esp. of a German or Austrian type. [German]

Würz·burg /ˈvɜːʳtsbɜːʳg/ an industrial city on the Main River in Bavaria, S Germany; pop. (est. 2002) 125,300.

wuss /wʊs/ noun (also **wussy** pl. **-sies**) esp. N Amer. slang an inept, feeble, or cowardly person. □ **wussy** noun & adjective [20th c.: origin unknown]

Wuxi /wuːˈʃiː/ (also **Wu-hsi**) a city on the Grand Canal in Jiangsu province, E China; pop. (est. 2002) 1,126,000.

WV abbreviation West Virginia (in official postal use).

W.Va. abbreviation West Virginia.

WWF abbreviation World Wildlife Fund.

WW I abbreviation N Amer. World War I.

WW II abbreviation N Amer. World War II.

WWW abbreviation World Wide Web.

WY abbreviation Wyoming (in official postal use).

Wyan·dot /ˈwaɪəndɒt/ (also **Wyan·dotte** esp. in sense 2 of noun) ● noun 1 a a member of a N American Aboriginal people originally of Ontario, now living esp. in Oklahoma. b the Iroquoian language of this people. **2 a** a domestic fowl of a medium-sized American breed. **b** this breed. ● *adjective* of or relating to the Wyandots or their language or culture. [French *Ouendat* from the Aboriginal name *Wendat*]

wych- /wɪtʃ/ *combining form* (also **wich-**, **witch-**) in names of trees with pliant branches. [Old English *wic(e)* apparently from a Germanic root meaning 'bend': related to WEAK]

wych elm *noun* a species of elm, *Ulmus glabra*.

Wych·er·ley /ˈwɪtʃərli/ **Wil·liam** (*c*.1640–1716), English dramatist. His Restoration comedies, notably *The Country Wife* (1675), are characterized by their acute social criticism, particularly of sexual morality and marriage conventions.

wych-hazel /ˈwɪtʃ,heizəl/ *noun* **1** *var. of* WITCH HAZEL. **2** = WYCH ELM.

Wyc·liffe /ˈwɪklɪf/ **John** (also **Wyc·lif**; **Wick·liffe**; **Wic·lif**) (*c*.1330–84), English religious reformer, theologian, and philosopher. He upheld the Bible as the sole guide for doctrine, questioned the scriptural basis of the papacy, and instituted the first English translation of the complete Bible. □ **Wyc·liff·ite** *noun & adjective*

wye *noun* N *Amer.* a triangular arrangement of three sections of railway track, used for turning locomotives around. [reproducing the pronunciation of the letter *y*]

Wye River a river which rises in the Cambrian Mountains of W Wales and flows 208 km (132 miles) generally southeastward, entering the Severn estuary at Chepstow. In its lower reaches it forms part of the border between Wales and England.

Wyeth /ˈwaiəθ/ **An·drew New·ell** (b.1917), US painter. His paintings of rural scenes are noted for their precision and detail, and often convey a sense of loneliness or nostalgia; they include *Christina's World* (1948).

wyn *var. of* WEN².

Wyn·ette /waiˈnet/ **Tammy** (born Tammy Wynette Pugh) (1942–98), US country singer. Her unique lamenting voice brought her success with songs such as 'Apartment No. 9' (1966) and 'Stand by Your Man' (1968).

Wyo. *abbreviation* Wyoming.

Wyo·ming /waiˈoːmɪŋ/ a state in the west central US; pop. (est. 2000) 493,782; capital, Cheyenne. □ **Wyo·ming·ite** *noun*

WYSIWYG /ˈwɪziwɪg/ *adjective* (also **wysiwyg**) *Computing* denoting the representation of text onscreen in a form exactly corresponding to its appearance on a printout. [acronym from *what you see is what you get*]

wy·vern /ˈwaivɜrn/ *noun* (also **wi·vern**) *Heraldry* a winged two-legged dragon with a barbed tail. [Old French *wivre*, *guivre* from Latin *vipera*: for *-n* compare BITTERN]

Xx

X¹ *noun* (also **x**) (*pl.* **Xs** or **X's**) **1** the twenty-fourth letter of the alphabet. **2** (as a Roman numeral) ten. **3** (*usu.* **x**) *Algebra* the first unknown quantity. **4** *Math.* the first coordinate. **5** an unknown or unspecified number or person etc. **6** a cross-shaped symbol esp. used: **a** to indicate position (*X marks the spot*). **b** to indicate incorrectness. **c** to symbolize a kiss. **d** to symbolize a vote. **e** as the signature of a person who cannot write.

X² *abbreviation* the drug Ecstasy.

-x *suffix* forming the plural of some nouns in *-u* taken from French (*beaux*; *tableaux*). [French]

X-acto knife *noun* *N Amer.* *proprietary* a small utility knife with a fine very sharp blade, used for crafts, hobbies, etc.

Xan·adu /ˈzanədu:/ *noun* used to convey an impression of a place as almost unattainably luxurious or beautiful (*three architects and a planner combine to create a Xanadu*). [alteration of *Shang-tu*, the name of an ancient city in SE Mongolia, as portrayed in Coleridge's poem *Kubla Khan* (1816)]

Xanax /ˈzanaks/ *noun* *proprietary* alprazolam, a drug of the benzodiazepine group used in the treatment of anxiety.

Xan·kän·di /ˌxɒnkənˈdiː/ (called in Russian **Step·ana·kert**) the capital of Nagorno-Karabakh in S Azerbaijan; pop. (est. 2002) 56,300.

xan·than gum /ˈzanθən/ *noun* a polysaccharide produced by fermentation and used in foods as a gelling agent, thickener, etc. [modern Latin, from *Xanthomonas campestris* bacteria that produces it + *-AN*]

xan·thate /ˈzanθeit/ *noun* any salt or ester of xanthic acid.

xan·thic /ˈzanθɪk/ *adjective* yellowish. [Greek *xanthos* yellow]

xanthic acid *noun* any colourless unstable acid containing the -OCS₂H group.

xan·thine /ˈzanθiːn/ *noun* *Biochem.* a purine derivative found in blood and urine which is a breakdown product of nucleic acids and is the parent compound of caffeine and other alkaloids. [Greek *xanthos* 'yellow' + *-INE⁴*]

Xan·thip·pe /zanˈθɪpi/ (also **Xan·tip·pe** /zanˈtɪpi/) (5th c. BC), wife of the philosopher Socrates. Her reputed bad temper has made her proverbial as a shrew.

xan·tho·ma /zanˈθɔːmə/ *noun* (*pl.* **xan·tho·mas** or **xan·tho·mata**) *Med.* **1** a skin disease characterized by irregular yellow patches. **2** such a patch. [as XANTHIC + -OMA]

xan·tho·phyll /ˈzanθəfɪl/ *noun* any of various oxygen-containing carotenoids associated with chlorophyll, some of which cause the yellow colour of leaves in autumn. [as XANTHIC + Greek *phullon* leaf]

Xavier, St. Fran·cis /ɪɡˈzeivjər, ˈzeivjɜr/ (known as the 'Apostle of the Indies') (1506–52), Spanish missionary. One of the original seven Jesuits, he was ordained in 1537, and from 1540 onward made a series of missionary journeys to S India, Malacca, the Moluccas, Sri Lanka, and Japan. Feast day, 3 December.

X-C *abbreviation* (also **XC**, **X-country**) *N Amer.* cross-country (*X-C skiing*).

X chromosome *noun* a sex chromosome of which the number in female cells is twice that in male cells. [X as an arbitrary label + CHROMOSOME]

Xe *symbol* the element xenon.

xebec /ˈziːbek/ *noun* (also **zebec**, **zebeck**) *hist.* a small three-masted Mediterranean vessel with lateen and usu. some square sails.

[alteration (influenced by Spanish *xabeque*) of French *chebec*, via Italian *sciabecco* from Arabic *šabāk*]

Xen·akis /zeˈnɒkɪs/ **Ian·nis** (1922–2001), Romanian-born French composer and architect. His music uses computer-aided calculations and electronic instruments, and a composition style in which a random sequence of notes is produced according to mathematical probabilities, as in *Pithoprakta* (1955–6).

xeno- /ˈzenoː, ˈziːnoː/ *combining form* **1 a** foreign. **b** a foreigner. **2** other. [Greek *xenos* strange, foreign, stranger]

xeno·biol·ogy /ˌzenoːbaiˈɒlədʒi, ˈziːnoː-/ *noun* (esp. in science fiction) the investigation of extraterrestrial life forms. □ **xeno·biol·o·gist** *noun*

xeno·biot·ic /ˌzenoːbaiˈɒtɪk/ *adjective* relating to or denoting a substance, typically a synthetic chemical, that is foreign to the body or to an ecological system.

xeno·graft /ˈzenoːgraft, ˈziːnoː-/ *noun* a tissue graft from a donor of a different species from the recipient.

xeno·lith /ˈzenəlɪθ, ˈziːn-/ *noun* *Geol.* an inclusion within an igneous rock mass, usu. derived from the immediately surrounding rock. □ **xeno·lith·ic** *adjective*

xenon /ˈzenɒn, ˈziːnɒn/ *noun* a heavy colourless odourless inert gaseous element occurring in traces in the atmosphere and used in fluorescent lamps. Symbol: **Xe**; at. no.: 54. [Greek, neuter of *xenos* strange]

Xen·opha·nes /zeˈnɒfəˌniːz/ (*c.*570–*c.*480 BC), Greek philosopher and poet. He was a proponent of a form of monotheism, arguing that there is a single eternal self-sufficient Consciousness which influences the universe (with which it is identical) through thought.

xeno·phobe /ˈzenəˌfoːb, ˈziːn-/ *noun* a person given to xenophobia.

xeno·phobia /ˌzenəˈfoːbiə, ˌziːn-/ *noun* a deep dislike of foreigners. □ **xeno·phob·ic** *adjective* **xeno·phobic·al·ly** *adverb*

Xeno·phon /ˈzenəfɒn/ (*c.*435–*c.*354 BC), Greek historian, writer, and military leader. In 401 he joined the campaign of the Persian prince Cyrus the Younger against Artaxerxes II, and after the death of Cyrus led an army of 10,000 Greek mercenaries on a 1 500 km (900 mile) retreat to the Black Sea. His works include the *Anabasis*, the *Hellenica*, and three works concerning the life and teachings of Socrates.

xeno·trans·plant·a·tion /ˌziːnoːtransplanˈteiʃən/ *noun* the transplantation of organs or tissues from a member of one species to a member of another, esp. the transplantation of animal organs into humans. □ **xeno·trans·plant** *noun*

Xer /ˈeksər/ *noun* *informal* a member of Generation X. [abbreviation]

xeran·the·mum /ziːˈranθɪməm/ *noun* a composite plant of the genus *Xeranthemum*, with dry everlasting composite flowers. [modern Latin from *xēros* dry + *anthemon* flower]

xeric /ˈziːrɪk/ *adjective* *Ecology* having or characterized by dry conditions. [as XERO- + -IC]

xeri·scap·ing /ˈzeriskeipɪŋ/ *noun* environmental design of park or residential land utilizing a variety of methods to minimize the need for water, fertilizer, and labour. □ **xeri·scape** *noun* [XERIC + LANDSCAPING (see LANDSCAPE)]

xero- /ˈziːroː, ˈzeroː/ *combining form* dry. [Greek *xēros* dry]

xero·derma /ˌziːrəˈdɜrmə/ *noun* any of various diseases characterized by extreme dryness of the skin, esp. ichthyosis. [modern Latin (as XERO-, Greek *derma* skin)]

xer·og·raphy /ziːˈrɒgrəfi, ze-/ *noun* a dry copying process in which black or coloured powder adheres to parts of a surface remaining electrically charged after exposure of the surface to light from an image of the document to be copied. □ **xero·graph·ic** *adjective* **xero·graph·ic·ally** *adverb* [XERO- + -GRAPHY]

xer·oph·il·ous /zɪˈrɒfɪləs, zeˈ-/ *adjective* (of a plant) adapted to extremely dry conditions.

xero·phyte /ˈzɪːrəˌfəɪt, ˈzeˈ-/ *noun* a plant able to grow in very dry conditions, e.g. in a desert. □ **xero·phyt·ic** *adjective*

Xerox /ˈzɪːrɒks/ ● *noun* **1** proprietary a machine for copying by xerography. **2** a copy made using this machine. ● *transitive verb* (**xerox**) reproduce by this process. [invented from XEROGRAPHY]

Xerxes I /ˈzɜːrksiːz/ (c.519–465 BC), son of Darius I, king of Persia 486–465. He led an expedition against Greece, and in 480 won victories by sea at Artemisium and by land at Thermopylae; defeats at Salamis (480) and Plataea (479) forced him to withdraw from Greece.

X factor *noun* a critical or unknown element.

Xhosa /ˈkɔːsə, ˈkɒ-/ ● *noun* **1** (pl. same or **Xho·sas**) a member of a Bantu-speaking people forming the second largest ethnic group in South Africa after the Zulus. **2** the language of this people, forming part of the Nguni language group. ● *adjective* of or relating to this people or language. [Nguni]

xi /sai, gzai, zai/ *noun* the fourteenth letter of the Greek alphabet (Ξ, ξ). [Greek]

Xia·men /ʃɒˈmen/ (also **Hsia-men**; also called **Amoy**) a port in Fujian province, SE China; pop. (est. 2002) 729,800.

Xian /ʃiːˈan/ (also **Hsian, Sian**) an industrial city of central China, capital of Shaanxi province; pop. (est. 2002) 2,951,900. In 1974 the discovery was made nearby of the burial place of the Qin emperor Shi Huangdi (c.259–210 BC), who is buried in an elaborate tomb complex guarded by a 'terracotta army': 10,000 life-size pottery soldiers and horses. [Chinese, lit. 'western peace']

Ximen·es de Cis·ner·os see JIMÉNEZ DE CISNEROS.

Xing·jian /ʃɪŋˈdʒen/ **Gao** (b.1940), Chinese dramatist and novelist , winner of the 2000 Nobel Prize for literature. He fled China in 1987 after years of harassment by Communist authorities, and his works were banned in China after he wrote about the Tiananmen Square demonstrations in 1989.

Xingú /ʃɪŋˈguː/ a S American river, which rises in the Mato Grosso of W Brazil and flows 1 979 km (1,230 miles) generally northward to join the Amazon delta.

Xi·ning /ʃiːˈnɪŋ/ (also **Hsi·ning, Si·ning**) a city in north central China, capital of Qinghai province; pop. (est. 2002) 890,900.

Xin·ji·ang /ˌʃɪndʒiˈaŋ/ (also **Sin·ki·ang**) an autonomous region of NW China, on the border with Mongolia and Kazakhstan; pop. (est. 2000) 19,250,000; capital, Urumqi.

-xion /kʃən/ *suffix* forming nouns (see -ION) from Latin participial stems in -x- (fluxion).

xiph·oid /ˈzɪfɔɪd/ *adjective* Biol. sword-shaped. [Greek xiphoeidēs from xiphos sword]

xiphoid process *noun* the cartilaginous process at the lower end of the sternum.

XL *abbreviation* (esp. of clothing) extra large.

X-linked *adjective* of or relating to a gene carried on the X chromosome.

Xmas /ˈkrɪsməs, ˈeksməs/ *noun informal* = CHRISTMAS. [abbreviation, with X for the initial chi of Greek Khristos Christ]

XML *abbreviation* Extensible Mark-up Language.

X-rated *adjective* (usu. attributive) indecent, pornographic (X-rated humour; an X-rated movie). [from X, a film classification formerly applied to films suitable for adults only]

X-ray /ˈeksreɪ/ (also **x-ray**) ● *noun* **1** (in pl.) electromagnetic radiation of short wavelength, able to pass through opaque bodies. **2** an image made by the effect of X-rays on a photographic plate, esp. showing the position of bones etc. by their greater absorption of the rays. **3** (attributive) denoting an apparent or supposed faculty for seeing through objects (X-ray vision). ● *transitive verb* photograph, examine, or treat with X-rays. [translation of German x-Strahlen (pl.) from Strahl ray, so called because when discovered in 1895 the nature of the rays was unknown]

X-ray astronomy *noun* the branch of astronomy concerned with the X-ray emissions of celestial bodies.

X-ray crystallography *noun* the study of crystals and their structure by means of the diffraction of X-rays by the regularly spaced atoms of a crystalline material.

X-ray tube *noun* a device for generating X-rays by accelerating electrons to high energies and causing them to strike a metal target from which the X-rays are emitted.

XS *abbreviation* (esp. of clothing) extra small.

X's and O's *noun* = TIC-TAC-TOE 1.

X-treme *adjective informal* designating sports etc. performed in extreme conditions.

xu /suː/ *noun* (pl. same) a monetary unit of Vietnam, equal to one-hundredth of a dong. [Vietnamese from French sou]

Xu·zhou /ʃuːˈdʒɔː/ (also **Hsu-chou, Su·chow**) a city in Jiangsu province, E China; pop. (est. 2002) 1,106,500. It was formerly known as Tongshan (1912–45).

Xwe Nal Mewx *var. of* SNE NAY MUXW.

XXL *abbreviation* (esp. of clothing) extra, extra large.

XXX *adjective* = X-RATED.

xylem /ˈzaɪləm/ *noun Bot.* woody tissue (compare PHLOEM). [Greek xulon wood]

xylene /ˈzaɪliːn/ *noun Chem.* one of three isomeric hydrocarbons formed from benzene by the substitution of two methyl groups, obtained from wood etc. [formed as XYLEM + -ENE]

xyli·tol /ˈzaɪlɪtɒl/ *noun* a sweet-tasting crystalline alcohol, present in some plant tissues and used as an artificial sweetener in foods. [XYLO- + -ITE[1] + -OL[1]]

xylo- /ˈzaɪlɔː/ *combining form* wood. [Greek xulon wood]

xylo·phone /ˈzaɪləˌfəʊn/ *noun* a musical instrument of wooden or metal bars graduated in length and struck with a small wooden hammer or hammers. □ **xylo·phon·ist** *noun* [Greek xulon wood + -PHONE]

Yy

Y¹ *noun* (also **y**) (*pl.* **Ys** or **Y's**) **1** the twenty-fifth letter of the alphabet. **2** (usu. **y**) *Algebra* the second unknown quantity. **3** *Math.* the second coordinate. **4 a** a Y-shaped thing, esp. an arrangement of lines, piping, roads, etc. **b** a forked clamp or support.

Y² *abbreviation* (also **Y.**) **1** yen. **2** *N Amer.* **a** = YMCA. **b** = YWCA. **c** = YMHA. **d** = YWHA.

Y³ *symbol* the element yttrium.

y. *abbreviation* year(s).

-y¹ *suffix* (also **-ey**) forming adjectives: **1** from nouns and adjectives, meaning: **a** full of; having the quality of (*messy; icy; horsey*). **b** addicted to (*boozy*). **2** from verbs, meaning 'inclined to', 'apt to' (*runny; sticky*). [from or after Old English *-ig* from Germanic]

-y² *suffix* (also **-ey, -ie**) forming diminutive nouns, pet names, etc. (*granny; Sally; nightie; Mickey*). [Middle English (originally Scots)]

-y³ *suffix* forming nouns denoting: **1** state, condition, or quality (*courtesy; orthodoxy; modesty*). **2** an action or its result (*colloquy; remedy; subsidy*). [from or after French *-ie* from Latin *-ia, -ium*, Greek *-eia, -ia*: compare -ACY, -ERY, -GRAPHY, and others]

ya¹ *informal* ● *interjection* yes. ● *pronoun* you. [reproducing pronunciations]

ya² *noun* (in full **ya pear**) a medium-sized Asian pear with a light, rusty skin and ovoid shape. [Chinese]

yab·ber *intransitive verb informal* chatter. [orig. from an Australian Aboriginal language, possibly influenced by *jabber, yammer*]

yacht /jɒt/ ● *noun* **1** a light sailing vessel, esp. equipped for racing. **2** a larger usu. power-driven vessel equipped for cruising. **3** a light vessel for travel on sand or ice. ● *intransitive verb* race or cruise in a yacht. □ **yacht·ing** *noun* [early modern Dutch *jaghte* = *jaghtschip* fast pirate ship, from *jag(h)t* chase, from *jagen* to hunt + *schip* SHIP]

yacht·ie /ˈjɒti/ *noun informal* a yachtsman.

yachts·man *noun* (*pl.* **-men**) a person who sails yachts.

yack (also **yackety-yack**) *informal var. of* YAK².

yada yada yada *interjection* used to indicate that further details are predictable or contextually evident from what has preceded. [imitative]

yaf·fle *noun* *Cdn* (*Nfld*) an armful or small load, esp. of cod, firewood, etc. [origin unknown]

Yafo /ˈjɒfɔː/ the Hebrew name for JAFFA¹.

Yag·ara /ˈjɒɡɑrə/ *noun* an Aboriginal language of the area around Brisbane, Australia, now extinct.

yage /ˈjɒheɪ/ *noun* = AYAHUASCA. [American Spanish]

ya·hoo¹ ● *noun* (*pl.* **-hoos**) a coarse, brutish, or uncivilized person. ● *adjective* characteristic of a yahoo. □ **yahoo·ism** *noun* [name of an imaginary race of brutish creatures in Swift's *Gulliver's Travels* (1726)]

ya·hoo² *interjection* an exclamation of excitement, triumph, etc.

yahr·zeit /ˈjɑrtsəɪt/ *noun* (among Jews) the anniversary of someone's death, esp. a parent's. [Yiddish, lit. 'anniversary time']

Yah·weh /ˈjɒweɪ/ *noun* (also **Yah·veh** /ˈjɒveɪ/) a form of the Hebrew name of God used in the Bible. Formed from the four consonants YHVH (the Tetragrammaton) with added vowels, the word became regarded as too sacred to pronounce and was often replaced by *adonai* (my lord); this led to YHVH being incorrectly vocalized as *Jehovah*. Compare JEHOVAH.

Yah·wist /ˈjɒwɪst/ *noun* (also **Yah·vist** /-vɪst/) the postulated author or authors of parts of the Hexateuch in which God is regularly named *Yahweh*. □ **Yah·wis·tic** *adjective*

Yajur-Veda /ˌjʌdʒʊrˈveɪdə, -ˈviːdə/ one of the four Hindu Vedas, a collection of sacrificial formulae in early Sanskrit used in the Vedic religion by the priest in charge of sacrificial ritual. [Sanskrit, from *yajus* ritual worship + *vĕda* VEDA]

yak¹ *noun* a long-haired humped Tibetan ox, *Bos grunniens*. [Tibetan *gyag*]

yak² (also **yack, yackety-yack**) *informal* often *derogatory* ● *noun* trivial, meaningless, or unduly persistent conversation. ● *intransitive verb* (**yakked, yak·king**) (often foll. by *away, about*) engage in such conversation; chatter. □ **yak·ker** *noun* [imitative]

yaki·tori /jɑkɪˈtɔːri/ *noun* a Japanese dish of skewered grilled chicken pieces. [Japanese, from *yaki* 'grilling, toasting' + *tori* 'bird']

Yakut /jɑˈkʊt/ *noun* (*pl.* same or **Yakuts**) **1** a member of an indigenous people living in scattered settlements in northern Siberia. **2** the Turkic language of this people.

Ya·ku·tia /jəˈkuːtiə/ (official name **Republic of Sakha**) an autonomous republic in E Russia; pop. (est. 2002) 916,000; capital, Yakutsk. It is the largest of the sovereign republics and the coldest inhabited region of the world, with 40 per cent of its territory lying north of the Arctic Circle.

Ya·kutsk /jəˈkʊtsk/ a city in E Russia, on the Lena river, capital of the republic of Yakutia; pop. (est. 2002) 192,500.

ya·kuza /jəˈkuːzə/ *noun* (*pl.* same) **1** a Japanese gangster or racketeer; a member of a Japanese organized crime gang. **2** (in *pl.*) Japanese organized crime gangs. [Japanese *ya* 'eight' + *ku* 'nine' + *za* 'three', with reference to the worst kind of hand in a gambling game]

Yale, Elihu (1649–1721), English merchant and philanthropist, born in Boston, Massachusetts, who endowed Yale College (later Yale University) in New Haven, Connecticut in 1718.

Yalie /ˈjeɪli/ *noun informal* a student or graduate of Yale University in Connecticut.

y'all *contraction US informal* you-all.

Yalta Conference /ˈjɒltə/ a meeting of Allied leaders which took place in Feb. 1945 at the Crimean port of Yalta, at which Churchill, Roosevelt, and Stalin planned the final stages of the Second World War and the subsequent territorial division of Europe.

Yalu River /ˈjɑluː/ a river of E Asia, which rises in the mountains of Jilin province in NE China and flows about 800 km (500 miles) generally southwestward to the Yellow Sea, forming most of the border between China and N Korea. In November 1950 the advance of UN troops towards the Yalu River precipitated the Chinese invasion of N Korea.

yam *noun* **1 a** any tropical or subtropical climbing plant of the genus *Dioscorea*. **b** the edible starchy tuber of this. **2** esp. *US* a sweet potato. [Portuguese *inhame* or Spanish *iñame*, prob. of W African origin]

Yama /ˈjɑmə/ *Hindu Myth* the first man to die. He became the guardian, judge, and ruler of the dead, and is represented as carrying a noose and riding a buffalo.

Yama·moto /ˌjɑməˈmoːtoː/ **Iso·roku** (1884–1943), Japanese admiral. He was commander-in-chief of the Combined Fleet (air and naval forces) during the Second World War, and planned the Japanese attack on Pearl Harbor (1941); his fleet was defeated at the Battle of Midway (1942).

---

t *top*   v *voice*   w *we*   z *zoo*   ʃ *she*   ʒ *vision*   θ *thin*   ð *this*   ŋ *ring*   x *loch*   tʃ *chip*   dʒ *jar*   (*see over for vowels*)

yam bean *noun* a Central American climbing plant of the pea family, cultivated for its edible tubers (jicama).

yam·mer *informal* ● *verb* **1** *intransitive* whine or complain; grumble. **2** *intransitive* **a** make a loud noise; talk loudly. **b** talk incessantly with little substance. **3** *transitive* utter complainingly. **4** *intransitive* (esp. of an animal) howl or wail. ● *noun* an act or a sound of yammering. □ **yam·mer·er** *noun* [Old English *geōmrian* from *geōmor* sorrowful]

Yam·ous·sou·kro /ˌjamuːˈsuːkroː/ the capital of the Ivory Coast; pop. (2002) 195,500. It replaced Abidjan as the capital in 1983.

Yan·cheng /janˈtʃeŋ/ (also **Yen-cheng**) a city in Jiangsu province, E China; pop. (est. 2002) 278,900.

Yang Chen Ning (b.1922), Chinese-born US physicist, who, with Tsun-Dao Lee, was awarded the 1957 Nobel Prize for physics for their discovery that parity is not conserved in the weak interaction.

yang *noun* (in Chinese philosophy) the active male principle of the universe (compare YIN). [Chinese]

Yan·gon /janˈɡɒn/ the official Burmese name for RANGOON.

Yang·shao /janˈʃau/ an ancient civilization of northern China during the 3rd millennium BC, characterized by painted pottery with naturalistic designs of fish and human faces and abstract patterns of triangles, spirals, arcs, and dots.

Yang·tze /ˈjantsi/ (also called **Chang Jiang**) the principal river of China, which rises as the Jinsha in the Tibetan highlands and flows 6 380 km (3,964 miles) southward then generally eastward through central China, entering the East China Sea at Shanghai.

Yank *noun informal* often *derogatory* an inhabitant of the US; an American. [abbreviation of YANKEE]

yank *informal* ● *verb* **1** *transitive & intransitive* pull sharply or with a jerk. **2** *transitive* N Amer. remove, withdraw, or cancel abruptly. ● *noun* a sudden hard pull. □ **yank someone's chain** *see* CHAIN. [19th c.: origin unknown]

Yan·kee *informal* ● *noun* **1** often *derogatory* = YANK. **2** US an inhabitant of New England or one of the northern States. **3** *hist.* a Federal soldier in the Civil War. ● *adjective* of, relating to, or characteristic of a Yankee or Yankees (*Yankee ingenuity*). [18th c.: origin uncertain: perhaps from Dutch *Janke* diminutive of *Jan* John, attested (17th c.) as a nickname]

Yano·mami /ˈjanəˌmɒmi/ *noun* (also **Yano·mamö** /-ˌmɒmɔː/) (*pl.* same) **1** a member of an indigenous people living in the forests of S Venezuela and N Brazil. **2** either of the two related languages of this people. [the name in Yanomami, literally 'people']

Yan·qui *noun* a variant of YANKEE, typically used in Latin American contexts. [Spanish]

Yan·tai /janˈtaɪ/ (also **Yen-tai**) a port on the Yellow Sea in Shandong province, E China; pop. (est. 2002) 474,200.

Yaoun·dé /jaˈʊndeɪ/ the capital of Cameroon; pop. (est. 2002) 1,122,500.

yap ● *intransitive verb* (**yapped, yap·ping**) **1** bark shrilly or fussily. **2** *informal* talk noisily, foolishly, or complainingly. ● *noun* **1** a shrill bark; a yelp. **2** idle, tiresome, or insistent chatter. **3** *slang* the mouth (*shut your yap!*). □ **yap·per** *noun* [imitative]

yap·ok /ˈjapɒk/ *noun* a semi-aquatic Central and South American opossum, *Chironectes minimus*, which has grey fur with dark bands. [*Oyapok, Oiapoque*, N Brazilian river]

yappy *adjective* (**-pi·er, -pi·est**) (of a dog) inclined to yap.

yard[1] *noun* **1** a unit of linear measure equal to 3 feet (0.9144 metre). **2** this length of material (*a yard and a half of cloth*). **3** a square or cubic yard, esp. of sand, topsoil, etc. **4** a cylindrical spar tapering to each end slung across a mast for a sail to hang from. □ **by the yard** at great length. **the whole nine yards** *informal see* WHOLE. [Old English *gerd* from West Germanic]

yard[2] ● *noun* **1** a piece of enclosed ground, esp. attached to a building. **2** N Amer. & Austral. the area at the front or back of a house, usu. including a lawn and sometimes also gardens etc. **3** an enclosed piece of ground used for a particular business or purpose (*lumberyard; stockyard*). **4** = RAILWAY YARD. **5** N Amer. a place where deer or moose etc. congregate, esp. during the winter months. **6** Forestry = LANDING 3. **7** (**the Yard**) Brit. informal = SCOTLAND YARD. ● *transitive verb* **1** put (cattle) into a stockyard. **2** Forestry move (logs or felled trees) from the felling site to the landing. [Old English *geard* enclosure, region, from Germanic: compare GARDEN]

yard·age *noun* **1** a number of yards of material etc. **2** a distance measured in yards (*tried hard to gain yardage, but failed*). **3 a** the use of a stockyard etc. **b** payment for this.

yard·arm *noun* the outer extremity of a ship's yard (*see* YARD[1] 4). □ **the sun is over the yardarm** *informal* it is past noon (and

therefore traditionally late enough in the day to start consuming alcohol).

yard·bird *noun* US slang **1** a new military recruit. **2** a convict.

yard·er[1] *noun* Forestry an engine or vehicle used to move logs from the bush to a yard, landing, etc.

yard·er[2] *noun* (in *combination*) Sport designating a kick, throw, etc. in which the ball travels the specified number of yards (*a 64-yarder*).

yard goods *plural noun* fabrics woven in standard lengths for sale by linear measure.

yard·light *noun* a strong light suspended on a pole, used to illuminate a farmyard.

yard·man *noun* (*pl.* -**men**) **1** a person working in a railway or lumber yard. **2** a person who does various outdoor jobs.

yard·master *noun* the manager of a railway yard.

yard of ale *noun* Brit. **1** a deep slender beer glass, about a yard long and holding two to three pints. **2** the contents of this.

yard sale *noun* N Amer. a sale of used household items and other possessions, held in the front yard of a private house.

yard·stick *noun* **1** a measuring rod a yard long, usu. divided into inches etc. **2** a standard used for comparison.

yard·work *noun* N Amer. gardening and other maintenance work required in the yard of a residence.

Yaren /ˈjarən/ the capital of Nauru; pop. (est. 1992) 672.

Yar·mouth /ˈjɑːrməθ/ a town and port on the southwestern coast of Nova Scotia, about 280 km southwest of Halifax; pop. (2001) 7,561. □ **Yar·mouth·ian** *noun* [*Yarmouth*, Massachusetts]

yar·mul·ke /ˈjɑːrmʊlkə/ *noun* (also **yar·mul·ka**) a skullcap worn by Jewish men. [Yiddish]

yarn ● *noun* **1** any spun thread, esp. for knitting, weaving, rope making, etc. **2** *informal* a long or rambling story or discourse. ● *intransitive verb informal* tell yarns. [Old English *gearn*]

Yaro·slavl /ˈjɑːrəsˌlɒvl/ a port in European Russia, on the Volga River northwest of Nizhni Novgorod; pop. (est. 2002) 611,300.

yar·row *noun* any perennial herb of the genus *Achillea*, esp. milfoil. [Old English *gearwe*, of unknown origin]

yash·mak /ˈjaʃmak/ *noun* a veil concealing the face except the eyes, worn by some Muslim women when in public. [Arabic *yašmak*, Turkish *yaşmak*]

yat·ter *verb & noun informal* chatter, gossip. [imitative, perhaps after YAMMER + CHATTER; compare YAP, NATTER]

yaw ● *intransitive verb* **1** (of a ship) deviate temporarily from its course, esp. through faulty steering or adverse weather conditions. **2** (of an aircraft, missile, etc.) rotate about a vertical axis. ● *noun* the yawing of a ship etc. from its course. [16th c.: origin unknown]

yawl *noun* **1** a two-masted fore-and-aft sailing boat with the mizzen-mast stepped far aft. **2** *hist.* a ship's jolly boat with four or six oars. [Middle Low German *jolle* or Dutch *jol*, of unknown origin: compare JOLLY[2]]

yawn ● *verb* **1** *intransitive* open the mouth wide and inhale esp. when sleepy or bored. **2** *intransitive* (esp. as **yawn·ing** *adjective*) (of a chasm etc.) gape, be wide open (*a yawning gap*). **3** *transitive* utter or say with a yawn. ● *noun* **1** an act of yawning. **2** *informal* a boring or tedious idea, activity, etc. □ **yawn·ing·ly** *adverb* [Old English *ginian, geonian*]

yawn·er *noun* **1** a boring or tedious idea, activity, etc. **2** a person who yawns.

yawp N Amer. ● *noun* **1** a harsh or hoarse cry. **2** foolish talk. **3** complaining or querulous talk. ● *intransitive verb* **1** make a loud, harsh cry. **2** talk complainingly or querulously. □ **yawp·er** *noun* [Middle English (imitative)]

yaws *plural noun* (usu. treated as *sing.*) a contagious tropical skin disease with large red swellings. [17th c.: origin unknown]

yay[1] *interjection* slang (also **yea, yeah**) expressing triumph, approval, or encouragement. [perhaps alteration of YEAH]

yay[2] *adverb* N Amer. informal (with adjectives of size, height, etc.) so, this (*about yay big*). [probably variant of YEA]

Yb *symbol* the element ytterbium.

Y chromosome *noun* a sex chromosome occurring only in male cells. [*Y* as an arbitrary label + CHROMOSOME]

yclept /ɪˈklept/ *adjective* archaic called (by the name of). [Old English *gecleopod* past participle of *cleopian* call, from Germanic]

yd. *abbreviation* yard (measure).

yds. *abbreviation* yards (measure).

ye[1] *pronoun* archaic pl. of THOU[1]. [Old English *ge* from Germanic]

ye² *adjective* *pseudo-archaic* = THE (*Ye Olde Book Shoppe*). [var. spelling from the *y*-shaped letter THORN (representing *th*) in the 14th c.]

yea /jeɪ/ ● *interjection* **1** yes. **2** = YAY¹. ● *adverb* indeed, even (*ready, yea eager*). ● *noun* **1** the word 'yea'. **2** an affirmative answer or assent, esp. in voting. □ **the yeas have it** = *the ayes have it* (see AYE¹). [Old English *gea, ge* from Germanic]

Yea·ger /ˈjeɪgɜr/ **Charles El·wood 'Chuck'** (b.1923), US pilot. He became the first person to break the sound barrier when he piloted the Bell X-1 rocket research aircraft to a level-flight speed of 670 mph in 1947.

yeah *adverb* *informal* **1** yes. **2** = YAY¹. □ **oh yeah?** expressing incredulity. **yeah, right** expressing scornful disbelief or contradiction. [casual pronunciation of YES]

year *noun* **1** (also **astronomical year, solar year, tropical year**) the time occupied by the earth in one revolution around the sun, 365 days, 5 hours, 48 minutes, and 46 seconds in length (*compare* SIDEREAL YEAR). **2** (also **calendar year, civil year**) the period of 365 days (**common year**) or 366 days (see LEAP YEAR) from 1 January to 31 December, used for reckoning time in ordinary affairs. **3 a** a period of the same length as this starting at any point (*four years ago*). **b** such a period in terms of a particular activity etc. occupying its duration (*school year; tax year*). **4** (in *pl.*) age or time of life (*young for his years*). **5** (usu. in *pl.*) *informal* a very long time (*it took years to get served*). **6 a** group of students entering university etc. in the same academic year. □ **in the year of Our Lord** (foll. by the year) in a specified year AD. **of the year** chosen as outstanding in a particular year (*employee of the year*). **a year and a day** the period specified in some legal matters to ensure the completion of a full year. **the year dot** see DOT¹. **year in, year out** continually over a period of years. [Old English *gē(a)r* from Germanic]

year·book *noun* **1** an annual publication dealing with events or aspects of the (usu. preceding) year. **2** *N Amer.* a book published by the graduating class of a school etc., commemorating the events of the past year and usu. including photographs of all the students.

year-end *noun* the end of esp. the financial year (often *attributive*: *year-end profits*).

year·ling ● *noun* **1** an animal between one and two years old. **2** a racehorse in the calendar year after the year of foaling. ● *adjective* a year old; having existed or been such for a year (*a yearling heifer*).

year-long *adjective* lasting a year or the whole year.

year·ly ● *adjective* **1** done, produced, or occurring once a year. **2** of or lasting a year. ● *adverb* once a year; from year to year.

yearn /jɜrn/ *intransitive verb* (usu. foll. by *for, after*, or *to* + infin.) have a strong emotional longing. □ **yearn·er** *noun* **yearn·ing** *noun & adjective* **yearn·ing·ly** *adverb* [Old English *giernan* from a Germanic root meaning 'eager']

year of grace *noun* a specified year AD.

year-round ● *adjective* existing etc. throughout the year. ● *adverb* throughout the year.

yeast *noun* **1** a greyish-yellow fungous substance obtained esp. from fermenting malt liquors and used as a fermenting agent, to raise bread, etc. **2** any of various unicellular fungi in which vegetative reproduction takes place by budding or fission. □ **yeast·less** *adjective* **yeast·like** *adjective* [Old English *gist, giest* (unrecorded)]

yeast infection *noun* = THRUSH² 1.

yeasty *adjective* (**yeast·i·er, yeast·i·est**) **1** frothy or tasting like yeast. **2** in a ferment. **3** working like yeast. **4** (of talk etc.) light and superficial. □ **yeast·i·ly** *adverb* **yeast·i·ness** *noun*

Yeats /jeɪts/ **Wil·liam But·ler** (1865–1939), Irish poet and dramatist. He was prominent in Ireland's cultural, literary, and theatrical revival, and his later poetry is noted for its lyrical style and the influence of symbolism, mysticism, and the occult; his works include the play *The Countess Cathleen* (1892) and verse collections such as *The Tower* (1928), which includes the poems 'Sailing to Byzantium' and 'Leda and the Swan'. He was awarded the Nobel Prize for literature in 1923. □ **Yeats·ian** *adjective*

yech /jex, jek/ *interjection* (also **yecch**) expressing disgust. [imitative]

yee-haw *interjection* (also **yee-hah**) *N Amer.* expressing enthusiasm or exuberance.

yeesh *interjection* *N Amer.* *informal* expressing frustration, exasperation, etc. [origin unknown]

yegg *noun* *N Amer.* *slang* a travelling burglar or safecracker. [20th c.: perhaps a surname]

ye gods! *interjection* an exclamation of astonishment.

Yekat·er·in·burg /jəˌkatəˈriːnbɜrg/ (also **Ekat·er·in·burg**) an industrial city in central Russia, in the eastern foothills of the Urals; pop. (est. 2002) 1,260,000. It was founded by Peter the Great in 1721. Between 1924 and 1991 it was known as Sverdlovsk.

Yekat·er·ino·dar /jəˌkatəˈriːnəˌdɑr/ (also **Ekat·er·ino·dar**) a former name (until 1922) for KRASNODAR.

Yekat·er·ino·slav /jəˌkatəˈriːnəˌslɒf/ (also **Ekat·er·ino·slav**) a former name (1787–1926) for DNIPROPETROVSK.

Yeliza·vet·pol /jəˌlizəˈvjetpɒl/ (also **Eliza·vet·pol**) the former Russian name (1804–1918) for GÄNCÄ.

yell ● *noun* **1** a loud sharp cry of pain, anger, fright, encouragement, delight, etc. **2** a shout. **3** *N Amer.* an organized cry, used esp. to support a sports team. ● *transitive & intransitive verb* make or utter with a yell. □ **yell·ing** *noun* [Old English *g(i)ellan* from Germanic]

yel·low ● *adjective* **1** of the colour between green and orange in the spectrum, of lemons, egg yolks, or gold. **2** of the duller colour of faded leaves, ripe wheat, etc. **3 a** having a yellow skin or complexion as a result of jaundice etc. **b** usu. *offensive* designating or pertaining to Oriental people. **4** *informal* cowardly. **5** (of newspapers etc.) unscrupulously sensational. ● *noun* **1** a yellow colour or pigment. **2** yellow clothes or material (*dressed in yellow*). **3 a** a yellow ball, piece, etc., in a game or sport. **b** the player using such pieces. **4** a yellow light as part of a set of traffic lights, indicating that the intersection should be cleared. **5** (usu. in *combination*) a yellow moth or butterfly. ● *transitive & intransitive verb* make or become yellow. □ **yellow·ish** *adjective* **yellow·ly** *adverb* **yellow·ness** *noun* **yel·lowy** *adjective* [Old English *geolu, geolo* from West Germanic, related to GOLD]

yellow-bellied sapsucker *noun* a sapsucker, *Sphyrapicus varius*, with black and white stripes on the head, a red crest and yellow belly, found throughout most of N America.

yellow-belly *noun* **1** *informal* a coward. **2** any of various fish with yellow underparts. □ **yellow-bellied** *adjective*

yellow bile *noun* *hist.* bile as one of the four bodily humours, characterized as hot and dry, and associated with a peevish or irascible temperament (*compare* HUMOUR *noun* 5). Also called CHOLER.

yellow-billed loon *noun* a loon, *Gavia adamsii*, very similar in appearance to the common loon but with a whitish-yellow bill, which breeds in the Arctic.

yellow birch *noun* a birch of eastern Canada, *Betula alleghaniensis*, providing hardwood lumber for furniture and construction.

yellow·cake *noun* impure uranium oxide obtained during processing of uranium ore.

yellow cedar *noun* a false cypress of the Pacific coast of N America, *Chamaecyparis nootkatensis*, planted as an ornamental.

yellow fever *noun* an often fatal tropical virus disease characterized by fever and jaundice.

yellow·fin *noun* (also **yellowfin tuna**) a widely distributed, commercially important tuna, *Thunnus albacares*, that has yellow anal and dorsal fins.

yellow flag *noun* **1** a flag displayed by a ship in quarantine. **2** an iris, *Iris pseudacorus*, with slender sword-shaped leaves and yellow flowers. **3** *Motorsport* a yellow flag used to signal to drivers that there is a hazard such as oil or a crashed car ahead.

yellow·hammer *noun* **1** *N Amer.* a flicker with yellow plumage. **2** a common Eurasian bunting, *Emberiza citrinella*, of which the male has a yellow head, neck, and breast. [16th c.: origin of *hammer* uncertain]

Yellow·head Pass a pass through the Rocky Mountains, situated on the BC–Alberta border, west of Jasper. At an elevation of 1 131 m, it is the Continental Divide's lowest crossing. [translation of French *Tête Jaune*, the nickname of P. Bostonais, a fair-haired Iroquois trapper d.1827]

yellow jack *noun* **1** = YELLOW FEVER. **2** = YELLOW FLAG 1.

yellow jacket *noun* *N Amer.* a wasp of the genus *Vespula*, with black and yellow markings.

yellow jersey *noun* a jersey worn by the overall leader in a cycling race at the end of a day, and presented to the final winner.

Yellow·knife¹ the capital (and only) city of the NWT, situated in the south central part of the region at the mouth of the Yellowknife River, where it empties into the North Arm of Great Slave Lake; pop. (2001) 16,541. It was founded in 1935 as a gold-mining town. □ **Yellow·knifer** *noun* [YELLOWKNIFE²]

Yellow·knife² *noun* (pl. same or **Yellow·knives**) a member of an Aboriginal people formerly living around the Coppermine River; they are now absorbed into the Chipewyan. [so called because they made knives from copper]

---

u: m**oo**d ai m**y** əi p**i**pe au br**ow**n ʌu h**ou**se ei d**ay** ɔi b**oy** ɑ̃ fr**an**glais ã Canad**ien** ɔ̃ Bray**on**   (*see over for consonants*)

yellow·legs *noun* (*pl.* same) either of two migratory sandpipers with yellow legs, *Tringa melanoleuca* or *T. flavipes*.

yellow line *noun* (in the UK) a line painted along the side of the road in yellow either singly or in pairs to denote parking restrictions.

Yellow Pages *noun proprietary* a telephone directory or section of one printed on yellow paper, listing business subscribers according to the goods or services they offer.

yellow pepper *noun* the yellow ripe fruit of the sweet pepper, *Capsicum annuum*, used as a vegetable.

yellow perch *noun* a perch, *Perca flavescens*, with yellowish flanks marked by wide black bands, widespread throughout N America east of the Rockies, and much fished for food.

yellow peril *noun offensive* the political or military threat regarded as emanating from Asian peoples, esp. the Chinese.

yellow pine *noun* any of various pines with needles in bundles of twos or threes and hard wood.

yellow rattle *noun* a yellow-flowered plant of the genus *Rhinanthus*.

yellow ribbon *noun* a yellow ribbon attached to a building, tree, etc., as a tribute to an absent person, esp. a soldier, or as a sign to welcome someone home after an absence.

Yellow River the second largest river in China, which rises in the mountains of west central China and flows over 4 830 km (3,000 miles) in a huge semicircle before entering the gulf of Bo Hai.

Yellow Sea an arm of the East China Sea, separating the Korean peninsula from the east coast of China.

yellow spot *noun* = MACULA 2.

Yellow·stone National Park a US national park on the Wyoming–Montana border, noted for its many geysers, hot springs, and mud volcanoes. [after the *Yellowstone* River, a tributary of the Missouri which runs through it]

yellow streak *noun informal* a trait of cowardice.

yellow·tail *noun* (*pl.* same or **yellow·tails**) a marine fish which has yellow coloration on the tail, esp. a fish of the jack family.

yellow·throat *noun* any of several New World warblers of the genus *Geothlypis*, esp. *G. trichas* of N America, the male of which has a black mask and yellow underparts.

Yellow Transparent *noun Cdn* an early yellow-skinned apple used for cooking and eating.

yellow·wood *noun* a small leguminous tree of eastern N America, *Cladrastis lutea*, with yellow wood which yields a yellow dye, planted as an ornamental.

yelp ● *noun* a sharp shrill cry of or as of a dog in pain or excitement. ● *intransitive verb* utter a yelp. □ **yelp·er** *noun* [Old English *gielp(an)* boast (imitative): compare YAWP]

Yelt·sin /ˈjeltsɪn/ **Boris Nikola·evich** (b.1931), Russian leader, president of the Russian Federation 1991–99. In 1990 he was elected president of the Russian Soviet Federative Socialist Republic, and shortly afterwards he and his supporters resigned from the Communist Party, creating a powerful opposition movement; on the breakup of the USSR (1991) he became president of the independent Russian Federation.

Yemen /ˈjemən/ a country in the south and southwest of the Arabian peninsula; pop. (est. 2002) 18,701,257; capital, San'a. □ **Yem·eni** *noun & adjective*

Yem·en·ite /ˈjemənaɪt/ ● *noun* **1** = YEMENI. **2** a Jew who was, or whose ancestors were, formerly resident in Yemen. ● *adjective* of, relating to, or designating a Yemeni Arab or a Yemeni Jew.

yen¹ *noun* (*pl.* same) the chief monetary unit of Japan. [Japanese from Chinese *yuan* round, dollar]

yen² *informal* ● *noun* a longing or yearning. ● *intransitive verb* (**yenned**, **yen·ning**) feel a longing. [orig. in the sense 'craving (of a drug addict) for a drug' from Chinese *yǎn*]

Yen-cheng see YANCHENG.

Yeni·sei River /ˌjenəˈseɪ/ a river in Siberia, which rises in the mountains on the Mongolian border and flows 4 106 km (2,566 miles) generally northward to the Arctic coast, emptying into the Kara Sea.

yenta *noun* (also **yente**) *N Amer. slang* a gossip or busybody. [Yiddish, originally a personal name]

Yen-tai see YANTAI.

yeo·man /ˈjoːmən/ *noun* (*pl.* **-men**) **1** *Brit. esp. hist.* a man holding and cultivating a small landed estate. **2** *Brit. hist.* a person qualified by possessing free land of an annual value of 40 shillings to serve on juries, vote for the knight of the shire, etc. **3** *Brit.* a member of the yeomanry force. **4** *Brit. hist.* a servant in a royal or noble household.

5 (**Yeoman**) (in full **Chief Yeoman of Signals**) a signaller in the Canadian Navy or the Royal Navy, responsible for transmitting both visual and radio signals. **6** a petty officer of the US Navy performing clerical duties on board ship. □ **yeo·man·ly** *adjective* [Middle English *yoman*, *yeman*, etc., prob. from YOUNG + MAN]

Yeoman of the Guard *noun* **1** a member of the British sovereign's bodyguard. **2** (in general use) a warder in the Tower of London.

yeo·man·ry /ˈjoːmənri/ *noun* (*pl.* **-ries**) **1** a body of yeomen. **2** *Brit. hist.* a volunteer cavalry force raised from the yeoman class (1794–1908).

yeoman service *noun* (also **yeoman's service**, **yeoman work**) efficient or useful help in need.

Yeoman Usher *noun Brit.* the deputy of Black Rod.

yeow *interjection* expressing a howl of pain.

yep *adverb & noun* (also **yup**) *N Amer. informal* = YES. [corruption]

-yer *var.* of -IER esp. after *w* (*lawyer*).

yerba maté /ˈjɜːbə ˌmateɪ/ *noun* = MATÉ. [Spanish, = herb maté]

Yere·van /ˌjerəˈvan/ the capital of Armenia; pop. (est. 2002) 1,258,000.

yes ● *adverb* **1** equivalent to an affirmative sentence: the answer to your question is affirmative, it is as you say or as I have said, the statement etc. made is correct, the request or command will be complied with, the negative statement etc. made is not correct. **2** (in answer to a summons or address) an acknowledgement of one's presence. ● *noun* **1** an utterance of the word *yes*. **2** an affirmation or assent. **3** a vote in favour of a proposition. □ **yes?** **1** indeed? is that so? **2** what do you want? **yes and no** that is partly true and partly untrue. [Old English *gēse*, *gīse*, prob. from *gīa sīe* may it be (*gīa* is unrecorded)]

ye·shiva /jəˈʃiːvə/ *noun* (also **ye·shivah**) **1** an Orthodox Jewish college or seminary. **2** an Orthodox Jewish elementary school, teaching both religious and secular subjects. [Hebrew *yĕšībāh*, from *yāšab* sit]

yes-man *noun* (*pl.* **-men**) *informal* a weak person who always agrees with people in authority in order to gain their approval.

yester- *combining form poet.* or *archaic* of or relating to yesterday (*yester-eve*). [Old English *geostran*]

yes·ter·day ● *adverb* **1** on the day before today. **2** in the recent past. **3** *informal* extremely urgently; immediately (*they want delivery yesterday!*). ● *noun* **1** the day before today. **2** the recent past. [Old English *giestran dæg* (as YESTER-, DAY)]

yesterday's man *noun* a man, esp. a politician, whose career is finished or past its peak.

yesterday's news *noun* a person or thing that is no longer of interest.

yes·ter·year *noun literary* **1** last year. **2** the past.

yet ● *adverb* **1** as late as, or until, now or then (*there is yet time; your best work yet*). **2** (with *neg.* or *interrogative*) so soon as, or by, now or then (*it is not time yet; hasn't he finished yet?*). **3** again; in addition (*more and yet more*). **4** in the remaining time available; before all is over (*I will do it yet*). **5** (foll. by *comparative*) even (*a yet more difficult task*). **6** nevertheless; and in spite of that; but for all that (*it is strange, and yet it is true*). **7** as an ironic intensive at the end of a sentence: too; what's more (*his own mother yet!*). ● *conjunction* but at the same time; but nevertheless (*I won, yet what good has it done?*). □ **as yet** see AS¹. **nor yet** and also not (*won't listen to me nor yet to you*). [Old English *gīet(a)*, = Old Frisian *iēta*, of unknown origin]

yeti /ˈjeti/ *noun* = ABOMINABLE SNOWMAN. [Tibetan]

Yev·tu·shenko /ˌjevtuːˈʃeŋkɒ/ **Yev·geni Alek·san·dro·vich** (b.1933), Russian poet of Ukrainian descent, who incurred official hostility because of the outspokenness of some of his poetry, notably *Babi Yar* (1961), which strongly criticized Russian anti-Semitism.

yew *noun* **1** any dark-leaved evergreen coniferous tree or shrub of the genus *Taxus*, having seeds enclosed in a fleshy red aril, and historically often planted in churchyards. **2** its wood, used formerly as a material for bows and still in cabinetmaking. [Old English *īw*, *ēow* from Germanic]

Y-fronts *plural noun Brit. proprietary* = JOCKEY SHORTS.

Ygg·dra·sil /ˈɪɡdrəsɪl/ *Scand. Myth* a huge ash tree located at the centre of the earth, with three roots, one extending to Niflheim (the underworld), one to Jotunheim (land of the giants), and one to Asgard (land of the gods). [Old Norse *yg(g)drasill* from *Yggr* Odin + *drasill* horse]

YHVH see TETRAGRAMMATON.

Yichun /jiːˈtʃʊn/ (also **I-chun** /iː-/) a city in Heilongjiang province, NE China; pop. (est. 2002) 954,600.

Yid *noun slang offensive* a Jew. [back-formation from YIDDISH]

Yid·dish ● *noun* a vernacular used by Jews in or from central and eastern Europe, originally a German dialect with words from Hebrew and several modern languages, and written using Hebrew characters. ● *adjective* of or relating to this language. [German *jüdisch* Jewish]

Yid·dish·er *dated* ● *noun* a person speaking Yiddish. ● *adjective* Yiddish-speaking.

Yid·dish·ism *noun* **1** a Yiddish word, idiom, etc., esp. one adopted into another language. **2** advocacy of Yiddish culture.

Yid·dish·keit *noun* the quality of being Jewish; the Jewish way of life or its customs or practices. [Yiddish *yidishkeyt*]

yield ● *verb* **1** *transitive & intransitive* produce or return as a fruit, profit, or result (*the land yields crops; the investment yielded 15 per cent*). **2** *transitive* give up; surrender, concede; comply with a demand for (*yielded the fortress*). **3** *intransitive* (often foll. by *to*) a surrender; make submission. **b** give consent or change one's course of action in deference to; respond as required to (*yielded to persuasion*). **4** *intransitive* (foll. by *to*) be inferior or confess inferiority to (*I yield to none in understanding the problem*). **5** *intransitive* (foll. by *to*) give right-of-way to other traffic. **6** *intransitive* US allow another the right to speak in a debate etc. ● *noun* **1** an amount yielded or produced; an output. **2** the income produced by an investment. □ **yield·er** *noun* [Old English *g(i)eldan* pay, from Germanic]

yield curve *noun Finance* a curve on a graph in which the yield of fixed-interest securities is plotted against the length of time they have to run to maturity.

yield·ing *adjective* **1** compliant, submissive. **2** (of a substance) able to bend; not stiff or rigid. □ **yield·ing·ness** *noun*

yikes *interjection slang* an expression of surprise or sudden apprehension. [origin unknown]

yin *noun* (in Chinese philosophy) the passive female principle of the universe (*compare* YANG). [Chinese]

Yin·chuan /jɪnˈtʃwan/ the capital of Ningxia autonomous region, on the Yellow River; pop. (est. 2002) 628,200.

ying·yang *noun* □ **up the yingyang** *N Amer. slang* in large quantities or to a large degree (*charged up the yingyang for it*). [origin unknown]

yin-yang *noun* the harmonious interaction of the female and male forces of the universe.

yin-yang symbol *noun* a circle divided by an S-shaped line into a dark and a light segment, representing respectively yin and yang.

yip *N Amer.* ● *intransitive verb* (**yipped**, **yip·ping**) **1** = YELP *verb*. **2** talk loudly, insistently, complainingly or naggingly (*he's always yipping at me about something*). ● *noun* = YELP *noun*. [imitative]

yip·pee *interjection* expressing delight or excitement.

yip·pie *noun* (also **Yippie**) a member of a group of politically active hippies. [Youth International Party, after HIPPIE]

yips *plural noun* extreme nervousness causing a golfer to miss easy putts. [origin unknown]

-yl *suffix Chem.* forming nouns denoting a radical (*ethyl; hydroxyl; phenyl*).

ylang-ylang /ˈiːlaŋˌiːlaŋ/ *noun* (also **ilang-ilang**) **1** a Malayan tree, *Cananga odorata*, from the fragrant yellow flowers of which a perfume is distilled. **2** the perfume itself. [Tagalog *ilang-ilang*]

YMCA *abbreviation* Young Men's Christian Association.

YMHA *abbreviation* Young Men's Hebrew Association.

Ymir /ˈiːmɪr/ *Scand. Myth* the primeval giant from whose body the gods created the world.

-yne *suffix Chem.* forming names of unsaturated compounds containing a triple bond (*ethyne*).

yo *interjection slang* calling attention, expressing encouragement or excitement, or as a greeting.

yob *noun Brit. slang* a rude, noisy or aggressive young person. □ **yob·bery** *noun* **yob·bish** *adjective* **yob·bish·ness** *noun* [back slang for BOY]

yobbo *noun* (pl. **-bos**) *Brit. slang* = YOB.

yocto- *combining form* denoting a factor of 10^{-24}. [adapted from OCTO-, on the pattern of *peta-, exa-*, etc.]

yod *noun* **1** the tenth and smallest letter of the Hebrew alphabet. **2** the semi-vowel /j/, which has the sound of the letter yod. [Hebrew *yōd* from *yad* hand]

yodel ● *transitive & intransitive verb* (**yo·delled**, **yodel·ling** or **yo·deled**, **yodel·ing**) sing with melodious inarticulate sounds and frequent changes between falsetto and the normal voice, in the manner of Swiss and Tyrolean mountaineers. ● *noun* a yodelling cry. □ **yodel·ler** *noun* (also **yodel·er**). [German *jodeln*]

yoga *noun* **1** a Hindu system of philosophic meditation and asceticism designed to effect reunion with the universal spirit. **2** a system of esp. posture and breathing exercises used to attain control of the body and

mind. **3** = HATHA YOGA. □ **yogic** *adjective* [Hindustani from Sanskrit, = union]

yogh /jɒɡ/ *noun* a Middle English letter used for certain values of *g* and *y*. [Middle English]

yogi *noun* a person proficient in yoga. □ **yog·ism** *noun* [Hindustani from YOGA]

yo·gourt *noun* (also **yo·gurt**, **yo·ghurt**) a semi-solid slightly tart food prepared from milk fermented by added bacteria, usu. sweetened or flavoured with fruit etc. [French from Turkish *yoğurt*]

Yog·ya·karta /ˌjɒɡjəˈkɑːtə/ (also **Jog·ja·karta** /ˌdʒɒɡdʒə-/) a city in south central Java, Indonesia; pop. (est. 2002) 417,900. It was formerly the capital of Indonesia (1945–9).

yo-heave-ho *interjection & noun* = HEAVE-HO.

yo-ho *interjection* (also **yo-ho-ho**) **1** used to attract attention. **2** = YO-HEAVE-HO.

Yoho National Park a park in southeastern BC, situated on the border with Alberta, just west of Lake Louise. It was established in 1886. [ultimately from Cree, = awe]

yoke ● *noun* **1** a wooden crosspiece fastened over the necks of two oxen etc. and attached to the plow or wagon to be drawn. **2** (*pl.* same or **yokes**) a pair (of oxen etc.). **3** an object like a yoke in form or function, e.g. a wooden bar held across the shoulders for carrying a pair of pails. **4** a fitted part of a garment, usu. placed across the shoulders or around the hips, from which the rest hangs. **5** sway, dominion, or servitude, esp. when oppressive. **6** a bond or union, esp. that of marriage. **7** *Rom. Hist.* an uplifted yoke, or an arch of three spears symbolizing it, under which a defeated army was made to march. **8 a** (in an airplane) a double handle somewhat resembling a steering wheel, by which the elevators are controlled. **b** *Naut.* the crossbar of a rudder to whose ends ropes are fastened. **9** a crossbar on which a bell swings. **10** a bar of soft iron between the poles of an electromagnet. ● *verb* **1** *transitive* put a yoke on. **2** *transitive* couple or unite (a pair). **3** *transitive* (foll. by *to*) link (one thing) to (another). **4** *intransitive* match or work together. [Old English *geoc* from Germanic]

yokel *noun* a country bumpkin. [perhaps from dial. *yokel* green woodpecker]

Yoko·hama /ˌjɔːkɔːˈhɒmə/ a seaport on the island of Honshu, Japan; pop. (2002) 3,483,600. Originally a small fishing village, Yokohama developed as a major port and is now the second largest city in Japan.

yolk¹ *noun* **1** the yellow inner part of an egg that nourishes the young before it hatches. **2** *Biol.* the corresponding part of any animal ovum. □ **yolked** *adjective* (also in *combination*). **yolk·less** *adjective* **yolky** *adjective* [Old English *geol(o)ca* from *geolu* YELLOW]

yolk² *noun* = SUINT. [Old English, back-formation from *eowucig* 'full of natural grease', ultimately from *ēuwu* EWE]

yolk sac *noun* a membrane enclosing the yolk of an egg.

Yom Kip·pur /jɒm kɪˈpʊr/ *noun* the most solemn religious fast of the Jewish year, eight days after the Jewish New Year, marked by fasting and prayers of repentance. *Also called* DAY OF ATONEMENT. [Hebrew]

Yom Kippur War the Israeli name for the Arab–Israeli conflict in 1973, called by the Arabs the **October War**. Israel was attacked on the festival of Yom Kippur (in that year, 6 Oct.): Egyptian forces crossed the Suez Canal and attacked from the south while Syrian forces attacked from the Golan Heights (occupied by Israel since the Six Day War) from the north. In less than three weeks the Syrians were repulsed and the Egyptians were surrounded; international pressure forced a ceasefire.

yomp *intransitive verb Brit. slang* march with heavy equipment over difficult terrain. [20th c.: origin unknown]

yon *literary & dialect* ● *adjective & adverb* yonder. ● *pronoun* yonder person or thing. [Old English *geon*]

yon·der ● *adverb* over there; at some distance in that direction; in the place indicated by pointing etc. ● *adjective* situated yonder. ● *noun* (in phr. **the wild** (or **wide**) **blue yonder**) the distance; a remote place. [Middle English: compare Old Saxon *gendra*, Gothic *jaindrē*]

yoni /ˈjoːni/ *noun* esp. *Hinduism* a figure or representation of the female genitals as a sacred symbol or object. [Sanskrit, = source, womb, female genitals]

yonks *plural noun Brit. slang* a long time (*haven't seen you for yonks*). [20th c.: origin unknown]

yoof /juːf/ *noun* esp. *Brit. slang* youth; young people collectively.

yoo-hoo ● *interjection* used to attract a person's attention. ● *transitive & intransitive verb* call 'yoo-hoo' to.

yore *noun literary* □ **of yore** formerly; in or of old days. [Old English *gēara, gēare*, etc., adv. forms of uncertain origin]

York 1 a former city in S Ontario, now part of the city of Toronto; pop. (2001) 150,255. **2** the former name (1793–1834) for the city of Toronto. **3** a city on the Ouse River in N England, formerly part of Yorkshire; pop. (est. 2002) 101,800. [senses 1 and 2 ultimately in honour of the Duke of *York*: see JAMES II 2]

York, Cape a cape extending into the Torres Strait at the northeast tip of Australia, in Queensland. It is the northernmost point of the continent of Australia.

York, House of the English royal house descended from Edmund of Langley (1341–1402), 1st Duke of York, which ruled England from 1461 (Edward IV) until the defeat and death of Richard III in 1485; the House of York fought the Wars of the Roses with the House of Lancaster, both houses being branches of the Plantagenet line.

York boat *noun Cdn hist.* a type of large, shallow-draft inland cargo boat used for transportation esp. of furs and trade goods in the Prairies. [YORK FACTORY]

York Factory a remote historic site in NE Manitoba, located on the shore of Hudson Bay, at the mouth of the Hayes River. Built by the Hudson's Bay Co. in 1684, it served as a principal trading depot until 1957. [Duke of *York*, HBC governor: see JAMES II 2]

York·ist ● *noun hist.* a follower of the House of York or of the White Rose party supporting it in the Wars of the Roses (compare LANCASTRIAN). ● *adjective* of or concerning the House of York.

Yorks. *abbreviation* Yorkshire.

York·shire /ˈjɔrkʃɪr/ a former county of N England, traditionally divided into East, West, and North Ridings. Since 1996 the northern part of the Yorkshire area has formed the county of North Yorkshire, while the rest consists of unitary authorities.

York·shire·man *noun* (pl. **-men**; fem. **York·shire·woman**, pl. **-women**) a native of Yorkshire.

Yorkshire pudding *noun* a puffy baked mixture of flour, eggs, and milk, usu. eaten with roast beef. [YORKSHIRE]

Yorkshire terrier *noun* a small long-haired blue-grey and tan kind of terrier.

York·ton a city in SE central Saskatchewan, situated 187 km northeast of Regina; pop. (2001) 15,107. [after the *York* Farmers Colonization Co., a group who established the city *c*.1882 and who hailed from *York* County, Ontario]

Yor·uba /ˈjɒrubə/ ● *noun* 1 (pl. **-ubas** or same) a member of an African people inhabiting the west coast, esp. Nigeria. **2** the language of this people. ● *adjective* of or relating to the Yorubas or their language. [Yoruba]

Yosem·ite National Park /joːˈsemɪti/ a US national park in the Sierra Nevada in central California. Yosemite Valley, in the centre of the park, is noted for its sheer granite cliffs such as the mile-high rock face of El Capitan and several spectacular waterfalls, including Yosemite Falls, the highest waterfall in the US, with a drop of 739 m (2,425 ft.).

Yoshkar-Ola /jaʃˌkɑrəˈlɒ/ the capital of the Russian republic of Mari El, east of Nizhni Novgorod; pop. (est. 2000) 249,200.

yotta- *combining form* denoting a factor of 10^{24}. [formed like YOCTO-, apparently adapted from Italian *otto* 'eight']

you ● *pronoun* (obj. **you**; possessive **your**, **yours**) **1** used with reference to the person or persons addressed or one such person and one or more associated persons. **2** (with a noun) in an exclamatory statement (*you fools!*). **3** (in general statements) one, a person, anyone, or everyone (*it's hard work, but you get used to it*). ● *noun* the personality or essential nature of the person or persons being addressed (*that dress just isn't you*). □ **you and yours** you together with your family, property, etc. [Old English *ēow* accusative & dative of *gē* YE¹ from West Germanic: supplanting *ye* because of the more frequent use of the obj. case, and *thou* and *thee* as the more courteous form]

you-all *pronoun US informal* you (usu. more than one person).

you'd *contraction* **1** you had. **2** you would.

you-know-what *noun* (also **you-know-who**) a thing or person unspecified but understood.

you'll *contraction* you will; you shall.

Young ▶ 1 Brig·ham (1801–77), US Mormon leader. He became a Mormon (1832), succeeded Joseph Smith as the movement's leader (1844), and established its headquarters at Salt Lake City, Utah (1847); he also served as governor of the territory of Utah (1850–7). **2 Den·ton True** ('Cy') (1867–1955), US baseball player. He pitched for various teams in his 22-year major-league career, and his record of 511 wins has yet to be matched; since 1956 the trophy honouring baseball's best pitchers has been named after him. **3 Sir John**, see LISGAR.

4 Les·ter Wil·lis (1909–59), US jazz tenor saxophonist, who was a leading jazz musician in the 1930s and 1940s. **5 Neil (Per·ci·val)** (b.1945), Canadian singer, songwriter, and guitarist. He played with the group Buffalo Springfield (1966–8), and won a reputation as an emotive songwriter with a pessimistic view of humankind. Albums include *Harvest* (1972) and *Sleeps with Angels* (1994). **6 Thom·as** (1773–1829), English physicist, physician, and Egyptologist. His major work in physics concerned the wave theory of light, which he supported with the help of advanced experiments in optical interference; he also played a major part in deciphering the Rosetta Stone.

young ● *adjective* (**young·er**, **young·est**) **1** not far advanced in life, development, or existence; not yet old. **2 a** immature or inexperienced. **b** youthful. **3** felt in or characteristic of youth (*young love*; *young ambition*). **4** representing young people (*Young Liberals*). **5** distinguishing a son from his father (*young Jones*). **6** (**young·er**) **a** distinguishing one person from another of the same name (*the younger Pitt*). **b** *Scot.* the heir of a landed commoner. ● *noun* (collective) offspring, esp. of animals before or soon after birth. □ **with young** (of an animal) pregnant. □ **young·ish** *adjective* **young·ling** *noun* [Old English *g(e)ong* from Germanic]

young blood *noun* see BLOOD.

Young Italy a movement founded by Giuseppe Mazzini in 1831 to work towards a united Italian republic, a significant stimulus to the Risorgimento.

young lady *noun* **1 a** a young (esp. unmarried) woman. **b** a girl. **2** *informal* a girlfriend or sweetheart.

young man *noun* **1 a** a man who is young. **b** a boy. **2** *informal* a boyfriend or sweetheart.

young offender *noun* a young criminal, esp. (in Canada) one older than 12 and younger than 18 years of age.

young person *noun Law* **1** a young man or young woman. **2** (in the UK) a person generally between 14 and 17 years of age.

Young Pretender see STUART 2.

young·ster *noun* a child or young person.

young thing *noun archaic* or *informal* an indulgent term for a young person.

Young Turk *noun* **1** a member of a group of reformers in the Ottoman Empire in the late 19th and early 20th centuries, who carried out the revolution of 1908 and deposed the sultan Abdul Hamid II. **2** a young person eager for radical change to the established order.

young 'un *noun informal* a youngster.

young woman *noun* **1** a woman who is young. **2** *informal* a girlfriend or sweetheart.

your *possessive adjective* (attributive) **1** of or belonging to you or yourself or yourselves (*your house*; *your own business*). **2** (**Your**) (in titles) that you are (*Your Majesty*). **3** *informal* usu. derogatory much talked of; well known (*why not ask your self-styled 'expert'*). **4** belonging to or associated with an unspecified person (*my classroom is the second door on your left*). [Old English *ēower* genitive of *gē* YE¹]

Your·cenar /ˈjusəˌnɑr/ **Mar·guer·ite** (born de Crayencour) (1903–87), Belgian writer. Her work reflects her interest in male homosexuality, notably in the novel *Alexis ou le Traité du vain combat* (1929). Many of her novels are meticulous historical reconstructions, including *Mémoires d'Hadrian* (1951). She was the first woman elected to the Académie française (1980).

you're *contraction* you are.

yours *possessive pronoun* **1** the one or ones belonging to or associated with you (*it is yours*; *yours are over there*). **2** your letter (*yours of the 10th*). **3** introducing a formula ending a letter (*yours ever*). □ **of yours** of or belonging to you (*a friend of yours*).

your·self *pronoun* (pl. **your·selves**) **1 a** emphatic form of YOU. **b** reflexive form of YOU. **2** in your normal state of body or mind (*are quite yourself again*). □ **be yourself** act in your normal, unconstrained manner. **how's yourself?** *slang* how are you? (esp. after answering a similar inquiry).

yours truly *noun informal* myself, me; I (*has a picture of yours truly on the cover*). □ **yours truly** used as a conventional formula preceding a signature.

youse *pronoun* (also **yous**) *dialect* or *informal* you (usu. more than one person). ¶ Generally considered unacceptable in writing or cultivated speech. [YOU + -S¹]

youth *noun* **1** the state of being young; the period between childhood and adult age. **2** the vigour or enthusiasm, inexperience, or other characteristic of this period. **3** an early stage of development etc. **4** a young person (esp. male). **5** (treated as *pl.*) young people collectively (*creating jobs for youth*). [Old English *geoguth* from Germanic, related to YOUNG]

youth court *noun* a court which has jurisdiction over all cases involving young offenders or youths.

youth·ful *adjective* **1** young, esp. in appearance or manner. **2** having the characteristics of youth (*youthful impatience*). **3** having the freshness or vigour of youth (*a youthful complexion*). □ **youth·ful·ly** *adverb* **youth·ful·ness** *noun*

youth hostel *noun* a place where (esp. young) travellers can stay cheaply for the night. □ **youth hosteller** *noun*

youth·quake *noun* the series of radical political and cultural upheavals occurring among students and young people in the 1960s.

you've *contraction* you have.

You·ville /juːˈviːl/ **St. Marie-Marguer·ite d'** (1701–1771), Canadian businesswoman and lay sister. Widowed in 1730, she carried on the family business. In 1740 she and four other women formed a group which in 1755 became the Sisters of Charity of the Hôpital Général, or Grey Nuns. She returned to France in 1763. She was the first Canadian-born person to be beatified (1959) and was canonized in 1994.

yowl ● *noun* a loud wailing cry of or as of a cat or dog in pain or distress. ● *intransitive verb* utter a yowl. [imitative]

yo-yo ● *noun* (*pl.* **yo-yos**) **1** a toy consisting of a pair of discs with a deep groove between them in which string is attached and wound, and which can be spun alternately downward and upward by its weight and momentum as the string unwinds and rewinds. **2** a thing that repeatedly falls and rises again. **3** *slang* a stupid or incompetent person. ● *adjective* characterized by repeated upward and downward movement, fluctuation, etc. ● *intransitive verb* (**yo-yoes**, **yo-yoed**) **1** play with a yo-yo. **2** move up and down; fluctuate. [20th c.: origin unknown]

yo-yo dieting *noun* the phenomenon of repeatedly dieting and then regaining the weight so lost. □ **yo-yo dieter** *noun*

Ypres /ˈiːprə/ a town in NW Belgium, near the border with France, in the province of West Flanders; pop. (1999) 35,071.

Ypres, Battle of any of three battles on the Western Front near Ypres during the First World War. In the first battle (Oct.–Nov. 1914) Allied forces prevented the Germans breaking through to the Channel ports; the second battle (Apr.–May 1915), in which the 1st Canadian Division first saw combat, was an inconclusive trench conflict in which poison gas was used for the first time, while the third battle (1917) was the slaughter of Passchendaele (*see* PASSCHENDAELE, BATTLE OF).

yr. *abbreviation* **1** year(s). **2** your.

yrs. *abbreviation* **1** years. **2** yours.

YST *abbreviation* YUKON STANDARD TIME.

YT *abbreviation* **1** Yukon Territory. **2** YUKON TIME.

YTD *abbreviation* year to date.

yt·ter·bium /ɪˈtɜːbiəm/ *noun Chem.* a silvery metallic element of the lanthanide series occurring naturally as various isotopes. Symbol: **Yb**; at. no.: 70. [modern Latin from *Ytterby* in Sweden]

yt·tri·um /ˈɪtriəm/ *noun Chem.* a greyish metallic element resembling the lanthanides, occurring naturally in uranium ores and used in making superconductors. Symbol: **Y**; at. no.: 39. [formed as YTTERBIUM]

Yuan /juːˈɒn/ a dynasty that ruled China AD 1259–1368, established by the Mongols under Kublai Kahn; it was succeeded by the Ming dynasty.

yuan /juˈɒn/ *noun* (*pl.* same) the chief monetary unit of China. [Chinese, = 'round, dollar']

Yuan Jiang /juˌɒn ˈdʒjaŋ/ the Chinese name for the Red River (*see* RED RIVER 2).

Yuca·tán /ˌjuːkəˈtɒn, ˌjukəˈtan/ a state of SE Mexico, at the northern tip of the Yucatán Peninsula; capital, Mérida.

Yucatán Peninsula a peninsula in S Mexico, lying between the Gulf of Mexico and the Caribbean Sea.

yuc·ca /ˈjʌkə/ *noun* any N American white-flowered liliaceous plant of the genus *Yucca*, with sword-like leaves. [Carib]

yuck¹ (also **yuk**) *slang* ● *interjection* an expression of strong distaste or disgust. ● *noun* something messy or repellent. [origin unknown]

yuck² *var. of* YUK¹.

yucky *adjective* (also **yukky**) (**-ier**, **-iest**) *slang* **1** messy, repellent. **2** sickly, sentimental. **3** distasteful, contemptible.

Yugo·slav /ˈjuːɡəˌslɒv, -slav/ ● *noun* a native or national of Yugoslavia. ● *adjective* of or relating to Yugoslavia or its people. [Austrian German *Jugoslav* from Serbian *jugo-* from *jug* south + SLAV]

Yugo·slav·ia /ˌjuːɡəˈslɒviə, -ˈslaviə/ a former federation of Slavic states in SE Europe, in the Balkans. The country was formed as the Kingdom of Serbs, Croats, and Slovenians, at the end of the First World War. It comprised Serbia, Montenegro, and the former Slavic provinces of the Austro-Hungarian Empire, and assumed the name of Yugoslavia in 1929; capital, Belgrade. After the Second World War, it emerged as a Communist federal republic. In 1990, four of the six constituent republics (Slovenia, Croatia, Bosnia-Herzegovina and Macedonia) seceded; the two remaining republics, Serbia and Montenegro, declared a new federal republic of Yugoslavia in 1992, but its name was changed to the Union of Serbia and Montenegro in 2003. □ **Yugo·slav·ian** *adjective & noun*

yuk¹ (also **yuck**) *informal* ● *transitive & intransitive verb* **1** laugh heartily. **2** fool around. ● *noun* **1** a hearty laugh. **2** something, such as a joke, that causes hearty laughter. □ **yuk it up** joke around. [origin uncertain]

yuk² *var. of* YUCK¹.

yu·kata /juˈkatə/ *noun* a light cotton kimono, frequently with stencil designs, worn after a bath or as a housecoat. [Japanese *yu* 'hot water' + *kata(bira)* 'light kimono']

Yu·kawa /juːˈkɒwə/ **Hideki** (1907–81), Japanese physicist, who was awarded the 1949 Nobel Prize for physics for his prediction in 1935 of the existence of the pi meson (pion).

yukky *var. of* YUCKY.

Yukon, District of *hist.* a district (1895–98) of the North-West Territories, corresponding to what is now Yukon Territory. [see YUKON RIVER]

Yukon Gold *noun* a large, yellow-fleshed, smooth-skinned, early-maturing variety of potato.

Yukon Party *noun* a conservative political party active in Yukon territorial politics.

Yukon River a river of northwestern N America, 3 185 km long, rising south of Whitehorse and flowing generally northwestward through Dawson into Alaska, where it flows southwestward to the Bering Sea. [Gwich'in *Yukunah* great river]

Yukon Standard Time *noun* = PACIFIC STANDARD TIME.

Yukon stove *noun Cdn* (*North*) a simple stove used for cooking and heating, often consisting of an oil drum on legs. [YUKON TERRITORY]

Yukon Territory a territory of NW Canada, on the border with Alaska; pop. (2001) 28,674; capital, Whitehorse. The capital was Dawson until 1953. □ **Yukon·er** *noun* [as YUKON, DISTRICT OF]

Yukon Time *noun* = PACIFIC TIME.

yule *noun* (in full **yule·tide**) *archaic* or *literary* the Christmas festival. [Old English *gēol(a)*: compare Old Norse *jól*]

yule log *noun* **1** a large log burned in the hearth on Christmas Eve. **2** a log-shaped rolled cake eaten at Christmas, usu. iced in chocolate made to look like bark.

yum *interjection* (also **yum-yum**) expressing pleasure from eating or the prospect of eating. [imitative]

yum·my *adjective* (**yum·mi·er**, **yum·mi·est**) *informal* tasty, delicious.

Yun·nan /juːˈnan/ a province of SW China, on the border with Vietnam, Laos, and Burma; capital, Kunming. □ **Yun·nan·ese** *noun & adjective*

yup¹ *var. of* YEP.

yup² *noun* = YUPPIE.

Yupik /ˈjuːpɪk/ ● *noun* **1** a member of a group of Aboriginal peoples living in coastal areas of Alaska and NE Siberia. **2** any of the languages spoken by the Yupik. ● *adjective* of or relating to this people or their culture or language. [Yupik *Yup'ik* 'real person']

yup·pie *noun* (also esp. *Brit.* **yuppy**) (*pl.* **-pies**) *informal*, usu. *derogatory* a young, affluent, middle-class professional person, esp. one working in a city and characterized by careerism and acquisitiveness for trendy status symbols. □ **yup·pie·dom** *noun* [young urban professional]

yup·pi·fy *transitive verb* (**-fies**, **-fied**) (esp. as **yup·pi·fied** *adjective*) *informal* make typical of or suitable for yuppies. □ **yup·pi·fi·ca·tion** *noun*

yurt /jʊrt, jɜrt/ *noun* **1** a circular tent of felt, skins, etc., on a collapsible framework, used by nomads in Mongolia and Siberia. **2** a semi-subterranean hut, usu. of timber covered with earth or turf. [Russian *yurta* via French *yourte* or German *Jurte* from Turkish *jurt*]

Yuz·ovka /ˈjuːzəfkə/ a former name (1872–1924) for DONETSK.

YWCA *abbreviation* Young Women's Christian Association.

YWHA *abbreviation* Young Women's Hebrew Association.

---

uː m**oo**d   ai m**y**   əi p**i**pe   au br**ow**n   ʌu h**ou**se   ei d**ay**   ɔi b**oy**   ɑ̃ fr**an**glais   ã Canadi**en**   ɔ̃ Bray**on**   (*see over for consonants*)

Zz

Z /zed, ziː/ *noun* (also **z**) (*pl.* **Zs** or **Z's**) **1** the twenty-sixth letter of the alphabet. **2** (usu. **z**) *Algebra* the third unknown quantity. **3** *Math.* the third coordinate. **4** *Chem.* atomic number.

zaba·glione /ˌzabaˈljoːnei/ *noun* a dessert consisting of egg yolks, sugar, and (esp. Marsala) wine, whipped to a frothy texture over gentle heat and served warm or cold. [Italian]

Zabrze /ˈzabʒə/ an industrial and mining city in Upper Silesia, S Poland; pop. (est. 2000) 197,910. From 1915 to 1945, it was a German city bearing the name Hindenburg.

Zaca·tecas /ˌzakəˈteikas/ **1** a state of north central Mexico. **2** its capital, a silver-mining city situated at an altitude of 2 500 m (8,200 ft.); pop. (2000) 113,900.

Zach·ar·ias /ˌzakəˈraiəs/ (also **Zech·ar·iah**) *New Testament* the father of John the Baptist.

zaf·tig /ˈzaftɪg/ *adjective* N Amer. informal (of a woman) plump; having a full, rounded figure. [Yiddish, from German *saftig* juicy]

zag ● *noun* a sharp change of direction in a zigzag course. ● *intransitive verb* (**zagged**, **zag·ging**) perform a zag. [ZIGZAG]

Zaga·zig /ˈzagəˌzig/ (also **Zaqa·ziq**) a city in the Nile delta, N Egypt; pop. (est. 2002) 305,800.

Zag·reb /ˈzɒgreb/ the capital of Croatia; pop. (2001) 691,724.

Zag·ros Mountains /ˈzagrɒs/ a range of mountains in W Iran, rising to 4 548 m (14,921 ft.) at Zard Kuh. Most of Iran's oil fields lie along the western foothills.

zai·batsu /zaiˈbatsuː/ *noun* (*pl.* same) a Japanese business cartel or conglomerate. [Japanese, from *zai* wealth + *batsu* clique]

zai·deh *noun* (also **zaida, zaidy**) = ZEDA.

Zaire /zɒˈiːr/ (also **Zaïre**) the former name (1960–97) for CONGO. □ **Zair·ean** *adjective & noun* (also **Zair·ian**).

zaire /zɒˈiːr/ *noun* the basic monetary unit of Congo (formerly Zaire), equal to 100 makuta. [from Zaire, local name of the Congo River]

Zaire River *see* CONGO RIVER.

zakat /zəˈkɒt/ *noun* obligatory payment made annually under Islamic law on certain kinds of property and used for charitable and religious purposes. [Arabic, = 'almsgiving']

Zam·bezi River /zamˈbiːzi/ a river of East Africa, which rises in NW Zambia and flows for 2 560 km (1,600 miles) southward through Angola and Congo (formerly Zaire) to the Victoria Falls near Maramba, turning eastward along the border between Zambia and Zimbabwe, before crossing central Mozambique and entering the Indian Ocean. It is dammed in two places to form the Kariba and Cabora Bassa lakes.

Zam·bia /ˈzambiə/ a landlocked country in central Africa, divided from Zimbabwe by the Zambezi River; pop. (est. 2002) 9,959,037; capital, Lusaka. Zambia was formerly the British protectorate of Northern Rhodesia (see RHODESIA). □ **Zam·bian** *adjective & noun*

Zam·bo·anga /ˌzamboːˈaŋgə/ a port on the west coast of Mindanao, in the S Philippines; pop. (est. 2000) 601,794.

Zam·boni /ˌzamˈboːni/ *noun* N Amer. proprietary a tractor-like machine incorporating mechanisms for shaving the ice surface of a rink and spraying water on it to provide a clean smooth surface. [F.J. *Zamboni*, US inventor d.1988]

zam·in·dar /zəˈmiːndɑr/ *noun* (also **zem·in·dar**) (in India) the owner of a large agricultural estate. [Urdu, from Persian *zamīndār*, from *zamīn* land + *dār* holder]

ZANU /ˈzanuː/ *abbreviation* Zimbabwe African National Union.

Zan·uck /ˈzanək/ **Dar·ryl Fran·cis** (1902–79), US film producer. He co-founded Twentieth Century pictures (1933), merged with the Fox Company (1935), remained controlling executive of Twentieth Century Fox, and was president from 1965 until his retirement in 1971.

zany ● *adjective* (**zan·i·er, zan·i·est**) comically idiotic; crazily ridiculous. ● *noun* (*pl.* **-ies**) **1** a foolish or eccentric person; a buffoon. **2** *hist.* an attendant clown awkwardly mimicking a chief clown in shows. □ **zan·i·ly** *adverb* **zan·i·ness** *noun* [French *zani* or Italian *zan(n)i*, Venetian form of *Gianni, Giovanni* John]

Zan·zi·bar /ˈzanzəˌbɒr/ an island off the coast of East Africa, part of Tanzania; pop. (est. 2002, with Pemba) 934,400. The island has its own administration and retains considerable autonomy. □ **Zan·zi·bari** *adjective & noun*

Zao·zhuang /zauˈdʒwaŋ/ (also **Tsao-chuang** /tʃauˈtʃwaŋ/) a city in Shandong province, E China; pop. (est. 2002) 472,100.

zap *slang* ● *verb* (**zapped, zap·ping**) **1** *transitive* **a** kill or destroy; deal a sudden blow to. **b** hit forcibly (*zapped the ball over the net*). **2** *intransitive & transitive* **a** move quickly and vigorously. **b** *intransitive* use a remote control to move rapidly between television channels. **3** *transitive* overwhelm emotionally. **4** *transitive* Computing erase or change (a file, an item in a program, etc.). **5 a** *intransitive* (foll. by *through*) fast-forward or rewind a videotape to skip a section. **b** *transitive* delete or skip over (a television commercial or commercials), e.g. by fast-forwarding a videotape. **6** *transitive* N Amer. informal cook (food) in a microwave. ● *noun* **1** energy, vigour. **2** a strong emotional effect. ● *interjection* expressing the sound or impact of a bullet, ray gun, etc., or any sudden event. [imitative]

Zap·ata /zəˈpatə/ **Emil·iano** (1879–1919), Mexican revolutionary. In 1911 he participated in the revolution led by Francisco Madero (1873–1913), and when Madero failed to redistribute land to the peasants, Zapata attempted to implement his own program of agrarian reform by adopting guerrilla tactics; he later joined forces with Pancho Villa and others, overthrowing General Huerta (1854–1916) in 1914.

zapa·te·ado /ˌzɒpəˈtiːˈdɒ/ *noun* (*pl.* **-ados**) **1** a flamenco dance with rhythmic stamping of the feet. **2** this technique or action. [Spanish from *zapato* shoe]

Zapa·tista /ˌzapəˈtiːstə/ *noun* **1** *hist.* a supporter of Emiliano Zapata. **2** a member or supporter of a revolutionary force espousing ideals for social and agrarian reform similar to those of Zapata, and which launched a popular uprising in the southern Mexican state of Chiapas in January 1994.

Zapf *noun* the name of several typefaces designed by Hermann Zapf, German type designer b.1918.

Zapo·pan /ˌzapɒˈpan/ a city in the state of Jalisco, Mexico, noted for its basilica; pop. (est. 2000) 912,000.

Zapo·rizh·zhya /ˌzapɒˈrɪʒjə/ an industrial city of Ukraine, on the Dnieper River; pop. (est. 2001) 814,000. It was known until 1921 as Aleksandrovsk.

Zapo·tec /ˈzapəˌtek/ ● *noun* **1** (*pl.* same or **-tecs**) a member of an Aboriginal people inhabiting the region around Oaxaca in SW Mexico. **2** the language of this people. ● *adjective* of or relating to the Zapotec or their language. [Spanish from Nahuatl]

Zappa, Frank (born Francis Vincent Zappa) (1940–93), US rock singer, musician, and songwriter. He formed the Mothers of Invention in 1965, and later pursued a successful solo career, in which he frequently combined flowing guitar improvisations with scatological

---

Consonants: b *but* d *dog* f *few* g *get* h *her* j *yes* k *cat* l *leg* m *man* n *no* p *pen* r *red* s *sit*

humour; he was also a composer of avant-garde orchestral and electronic music.

zap·per *noun slang* **1** a remote control for a television, VCR, etc. **2** a device, person, or technique that kills or does away with something, esp. insects.

zappy *adjective* (**zap·pi·er**, **zap·pi·est**) *informal* lively, energetic.

ZAPU /'zapu:/ *abbreviation* Zimbabwe African People's Union.

Zaqa·ziq see ZAGAZIG.

Zara·thus·tra /ˌzarə'θu:strə/ the Avestan name for the Persian prophet ZOROASTER. □ **Zara·thus·tri·an** *adjective & noun*

zar·eba /zə'ri:bə/ *noun* (also **zar·iba**) **1** a hedged or palisaded enclosure for the protection of a camp or village in Sudan etc. **2** a defensive force or barrier. [Arabic *zarība* cattle pen]

Zaria /'zɑriə/ a city in N Nigeria; pop. (est. 2002) 898,900.

Zarqa /'zɑrkə/ (also **Az Zarqa**) a city in N Jordan, northeast of Amman; pop. (2002) 491,300.

zar·zuela /zɑr'zweilə/ *noun* **1** a Spanish traditional form of musical comedy. **2** a Spanish dish of various kinds of seafood cooked in a rich sauce. [Spanish: apparently from a place name]

zax *noun* a slater's chopper, with a point for making nail holes. [Old English *seax* knife, from Germanic]

za·zen /zɒ'zen/ *noun* Zen meditation, usu. conducted in the lotus position. [Japanese, from *za* 'sitting' + *zen* (see ZEN)]

zeal *noun* **1** earnestness or fervour in advancing a cause or rendering service. **2** hearty and persistent endeavour. [ecclesiastical Latin *zelus* from Greek *zēlos*]

Zea·land the principal island of Denmark, situated between the Jutland peninsula and the southern tip of Sweden. Its chief city is Copenhagen.

zeal·ot /'zelət/ *noun* **1** an uncompromising or extreme partisan; a fanatic. **2** (**Zealot**) *hist.* a member of a Jewish sect in Palestine during the 1st c. AD that advocated the overthrow of Roman rule. □ **zeal·ot·ry** *noun* [ecclesiastical Latin *zelotes* from Greek *zēlōtēs* (as ZEAL)]

zeal·ous /'zeləs/ *adjective* full of zeal; enthusiastic. □ **zeal·ous·ly** *adverb* **zeal·ous·ness** *noun*

zea·xan·thin /zi:ə'zanθɪn/ *noun* a carotenoid pigment found in corn and egg yolk, used as a colouring. [*Zea*, genus name for corn, + XANTHIC + -IN]

zebec (also **ze·beck**) *var. of* XEBEC.

zebra /'zi:brə, 'zeb-/ *noun* **1** any of various African quadrupeds, esp. *Equus burchelli*, related to the ass and horse, with black and white stripes. **2** (*attributive*) with alternate dark and pale stripes. [Italian or Portuguese from Congolese]

zebra crossing *noun Brit.* a pedestrian crossing marked by broad black and white stripes on the road.

zebra mussel *noun* a tiny mussel of the genus *Dreissena*, which proliferates rapidly and adheres in large numbers to any surface, thus becoming a pest by clogging water intake pipes etc.

zebu /'zi:bu:/ *noun* a humped ox, *Bos indicus*, of India, E Asia, and Africa. [French *zébu*, of unknown origin]

Zebu·lun /'zebjʊlən/ (also **Zebu·lon**) **1** a Hebrew patriarch, son of Jacob and Leah (Gen. 30:20). **2** the tribe of Israel traditionally descended from him.

Zech. *abbreviation Bible* Zechariah.

Zech·ar·iah /ˌzekə'raiə/ **1** a Hebrew minor prophet of the 6th c. BC. **2** a book of the Bible containing his prophecies, urging the restoration of the Temple, and some later material. **3** see ZACHARIAS.

zed *noun Cdn & Brit.* the letter Z. [French *zède* from Late Latin *zeta* from Greek ZETA]

zeda /'zeidə/ *noun* (among Jewish people) grandfather. [Yiddish *zeide*]

Zed·ekiah /ˌzedə'kaiə/ *Bible* the last king of Judea, who rebelled against Nebuchadnezzar and was carried off to Babylon into captivity (2 Kings 24–5, 2 Chron. 36).

zedo·ary /'zedoˌeri/ *noun* an aromatic ginger-like substance made from the rootstock of E Indian plants of the genus *Curcuma* and used in medicine, perfumery, and dyeing. [medieval Latin *zedoarium* from Persian *zidwār*]

zee *noun N Amer.* the letter Z. □ **catch** (or **bag**) **some zees** *slang* get some sleep. [17th c.: var. of ZED]

Zee·brugge /'zi:ˌbrʊgə/ a seaport on the coast of Belgium, linked by canal to Bruges.

Zee·land /'zi:lənd/ an agricultural province of the SW Netherlands, at the estuary of the Maas and Scheldt rivers; capital, Middelburg.

Zee·man /'zi:mən/ **Pieter** (1865–1943), Dutch physicist, who was awarded the 1902 Nobel Prize for physics for his discovery of the Zeeman effect.

Zeeman effect *noun Physics* the splitting of the spectrum line into several components by a magnetic field.

Zef·fi·rel·li /ˌzefə'reli/ **G. Fran·co Corsi** (b.1923), Italian film and theatre director. He began to direct his own operatic productions in the 1950s, becoming known for the opulence of his sets and costumes; his films include *Romeo and Juliet* (1968), *Brother Sun, Sister Moon* (1973), and a film version of the opera *La Traviata* (1983).

zein /'zi:ɪn/ *noun Biochem.* the principal protein of corn. [modern Latin *Zea*, genus name of corn + -IN]

Zeiss /zais/ **Carl** (1816–88), German optical instrument maker, who established the company named after him (1846) which produces precision optical instruments, including microscopes, lenses, binoculars, and cameras.

zeit·geist /'tsaitgaist, 'zaitgaist/ *noun* **1** the spirit of the times. **2** the trend of thought and feeling in a period. □ **zeit·geisty** *adjective* [German from *Zeit* time + *Geist* spirit]

zem·in·dar *var. of* ZAMINDAR.

Zen ● *noun* a form of Mahayana Buddhism emphasizing the value of meditation and intuition. ● *adjective* having characteristics thought to be typical of Zen Buddhism, esp. tranquility, minimalism, resignation, etc. □ **Zen·ist** *noun* (also **Zen·nist**). **Zen·like** *adjective* [Japanese, = meditation]

zen·ana /ze'nɒnɒ/ *noun* the part of a house for the seclusion of women of high-caste families in India and Iran. [Hindustani *zenāna* from Persian *zanāna* from *zan* woman]

Zend /zend/ *noun* an interpretation of the Avesta, each Zend being part of the Zend-Avesta. [Persian *zand* interpretation]

Zend-Avesta *noun* the Zoroastrian sacred writings of the Avesta or text and Zend or commentary.

zen·do *noun* a place for Zen Buddhist meditation and study. [Japanese, from ZEN + *dō* 'hall']

ze·nith /'zi:nɪθ, 'zen-/ *noun* **1** the part of the celestial sphere directly above an observer (*opp.* NADIR). **2** the highest or culminating point in prosperity, power, etc. □ **ze·nith·al** *adjective* [Old French *cenit* or medieval Latin *cenit*, ultimately from Arabic *samt (ar-ra's)* path (over the head)]

zenithal projection *noun* a projection of part of a globe onto a plane tangential to the centre of the part, showing the correct directions of all points from the centre.

Zeno /'zi:nɒ/ **1** (known as Zeno of Elea) (fl. 5th c. BC), Greek philosopher. He defended Parmenides' theories by formulating paradoxes which set out to demonstrate that motion and plurality are illusions. **2** (known as Zeno of Citium) (c.335–c.263 BC), Greek philosopher. He founded the school of Stoic philosophy in Athens in about 300, and his influence on the development of Stoicism was considerable, particularly in the field of ethics.

zeo·lite /'zi:əˌlait/ *noun* each of a number of minerals consisting mainly of hydrous silicates of calcium, sodium, and aluminum, able to act as cation exchangers. □ **zeo·lit·ic** /-'lɪtɪk/ *adjective* [Swedish & German *zeolit* from Greek *zeō* boil + -LITE (from their characteristic swelling and fusing under the blowpipe)]

Zeph. *abbreviation Bible* Zephaniah.

Zepha·niah /ˌzefə'naiə/ **1** a Hebrew minor prophet of the 7th c. BC. **2** a book of the Bible containing his prophecies.

zephyr /'zefɜr/ *noun literary* a mild gentle wind or breeze. [ZEPHYRUS]

Zephyr·us /'zefərəs/ *Gk Myth* the personification of the west wind.

Zep·pelin[1] /'zepəlin/ **Fer·di·nand Adolf Aug·ust Hein·rich, Count von** (1838–1917), German aviation pioneer, who developed the dirigible airship which is named after him.

Zep·pelin[2] /'zepəlin/ *noun hist.* a large dirigible airship of the early 20th c., originally for military use. [ZEPPELIN[1]]

zepto- *combining form* denoting a factor of 10^{-21}. [adapted from SEPTI-, on the pattern of *peta-, exa-*, etc.]

Zer·matt /'zɜrmat/ an Alpine ski resort and mountaineering centre near the Matterhorn, in S Switzerland; pop. (est. 1989) 4,200.

zero ● *noun* (*pl.* **zeros**) **1 a** the figure 0. **b** no quantity or number; nil. **2** a point on the scale of an instrument from which a positive or negative quantity is reckoned. **3** (in full **zero hour**) **a** the hour at which a planned, esp. military, operation is timed to begin. **b** a crucial

t *top* v *voice* w *we* z *zoo* ʃ *she* ʒ *vision* θ *thin* ð *this* ŋ *ring* x *loch* tʃ *chip* dʒ *jar* (*see over for vowels*)

moment. **4** the lowest point; a nullity or nonentity. ● *adjective* that amounts to zero; no, not any (*zero subscribers; zero tolerance*). ● *transitive verb* (**zeroes**, **zeroed**) **1** adjust (an instrument etc.) to zero point. **2** set the sights of (a gun) for firing. ▢ **zero in on 1** take aim at. **2** focus one's attention on. [French *zéro* or Italian *zero* from Old Spanish from Arabic *ṣifr* CIPHER]

zero-emission *adjective* designating a motor vehicle which does not emit pollutant gases (*zero-emission vehicles*).

zero gravity *noun* the state or condition in which there is no apparent force of gravity acting on a body, either because the force is locally weak, or because both the body and its surroundings are freely and equally accelerating under the force.

zero option *noun* a disarmament proposal for the total removal of certain types of weapons on both sides.

zero-sum *adjective* (of a game, political situation, etc.) in which whatever is gained by one side is lost by the other so that the net change is always zero.

zeroth /ˈziːrəʊθ/ *adjective* immediately preceding what is regarded as 'first' in a series.

zero tolerance *noun* a policy of rigorously punishing all infractions against a law, behavioural code, etc., no matter how minor.

zest *noun* **1** piquancy; a stimulating flavour or quality. **2 a** keen enjoyment or interest. **b** (often foll. by *for*) relish. **c** gusto (*entered into it with zest*). **3** the outer, coloured, covering of the peel of a citrus fruit, grated and used as a flavouring. ▢ **zest·ful** *adjective* **zest·ful·ly** *adverb* **zesty** *adjective* (**zest·i·er**, **zest·i·est**). [French *zeste* orange or lemon peel, of unknown origin]

zest·er *noun* a kitchen utensil for obtaining zest from citrus fruit by scraping or peeling.

zeta /ˈziːtə/ *noun* the sixth letter of the Greek alphabet (Z, ζ). [Greek *zēta*]

zetta- *combining form* denoting a factor of 10^{21}. [formed like ZEPTO-, apparently adapted from Italian *sette* 'seven']

zeug·ma /ˈzuːɡmə, ˈzjuː-/ *noun* a rhetorical figure by which a single word is made to refer to two or more words in a sentence, esp. when applying to them in different senses. ▢ **zeug·mat·ic** *adjective* [Latin from Greek *zeugma -atos* from *zeugnumi* to yoke, *zugon* yoke]

Zeus /zuːs, zjuːs/ *Gk Myth* the supreme god, the son of Cronus (whom he dethroned) and Rhea, and husband of Hera. He was the protector and ruler of humankind, the dispenser of good and evil, and the god of weather and atmospheric phenomena (rain, thunder, etc.); he was identified by the Romans with Jupiter.

Zeux·is /ˈzuːksɪs, ˈzjuː-/ (*fl.* late 5th c. BC), Greek painter. His works (none of which survive) are only known through the records of ancient writers, who make reference to monochrome techniques, his use of shading to create an illusion of depth, and his verisimilitude.

Zhang·jia·kou /ˌdʒaŋdʒɪəˈkəʊ/ (also **Chang-chiakow** /ˌtʃaŋ-tʃɪəˈkaʊ/) a city situated on the Great Wall in Hebei province, NE China; pop. (est. 2002) 878,600.

Zhan·jiang /dʒanˈdʒjaŋ/ (also **Chan-chiang** /tʃanˈtʃjaŋ/) a port in Guangdong province, S China; pop. (est. 2002) 615,800.

Zhda·nov /ˈʒdɒnɒf/ the former name (1948–89) for MARIUPOL.

Zhe·jiang /dʒeˈdʒjaŋ/ (also **Che·kiang** /tʃeˈkjaŋ/) a province of E China; capital, Hangzhou.

Zheng·zhou /dʒeŋˈdʒəʊ/ (also **Cheng·chow** /tʃeŋˈtʃaʊ/) the capital of Henan province, in NE central China; pop. (est. 2002) 2,153,400.

Zhen·jiang /dʒenˈdʒjaŋ/ (also **Chen-chiang** /tʃenˈtʃjaŋ/, **Chin·kiang** /tʃɪnˈkjaŋ/) a port in Jiangsu province, on the Yangtze River, E China; pop. (est. 2002) 569,700.

Zhong·shan /dʒɒŋˈʃan/ (also **Chung-shan** /tʃʊŋ-/) a city in Guangdong province, SE China; pop. (est. 2002) 316,600.

Zhou /dʒəʊ/ (also **Chou** /ʃəʊ/) a dynasty which ruled in China from the 11th century BC to 256 BC, commonly divided into *Western Zhou* (which ruled from a western capital until 771 BC) and *Eastern Zhou* (which ruled after 771 BC from a capital based in the east). The rule of the Eastern Zhou, although weak and characterized by strife, saw the Chinese classical age of Confucius and Lao-tzu.

Zhou Enlai /ˌdʒəʊ enˈlaɪ/ (also **Chou En-lai** /ˌtʃəʊ enˈlaɪ/) (1898–1976), Chinese Communist leader, prime minister of China 1949–76. One of the founders of the Chinese Communist Party, he joined Sun Yat-sen in 1924 and organized the revolt in Shanghai in 1927, before forming a partnership with Mao Zedong; on the formation of the People's Republic of China in 1949 he became premier and also served as foreign minister (1949–58).

Zhu De /ˈdʒuː ˈdeɪ/ (also **Chu Teh** /ˈtʃuː ˈteɪ/) (1886–1976), Chinese military leader and politician. After joining Mao Zedong in 1928, he became the founder and commander-in-chief of the Chinese Red Army (1930–54), later renamed the People's Liberation Army (1946), and led these forces on the Long March (1934–35).

Zhu·kov /ˈʒuːkɒf/ **Georgi Kon·stan·tin·ovich** (1896–1974), Soviet military leader. He was responsible for much of the planning of the Soviet Union's campaigns in the Second World War, defeating the Germans at Stalingrad (1943), lifting the siege of Leningrad (1944), and leading the final assault on Germany (1945) which resulted in the capture of Berlin.

Zhyto·myr /ʒɪˈtɒmiːr/ an industrial city in central Ukraine; pop. (est. 2001) 284,000.

Zia ul-Haq /ˌzɪə ʊlˈhak/ **Muham·mad** (1924–88), Pakistani political and military leader, president 1978–88. As chief of staff he led the bloodless coup which deposed President Zulfikar Bhutto in 1977, and as president, he banned all political parties and began to introduce strict Islamic laws; he died in an air crash, possibly as the result of sabotage.

Zibo /ziːˈbɔː, dzəˈbɔː/ (also **Tzu-po** /tsuːˈpɔː/) a city in Shandong province, E China; pop. (est. 2002) 2,887,600.

zi·dovu·dine /zaɪˈdɒvjuːˌdiːn/ *noun* = AZT. [arbitrary alteration of chemical name *azidothymidine*]

Zieg·feld /ˈziːɡfeld/ **Flor·enz** (1869–1932), US theatre manager, who produced a series of revues in New York, based on those of the Folies-Bergère, entitled the *Ziegfeld Follies*.

zig ● *noun* an abrupt angled movement, esp. in a zigzag course. ● *intransitive verb* (**zigged**, **zig·ging**) perform a zig. [ZIGZAG]

zig·gu·rat /ˈzɪɡəˌrat/ *noun* **1** a rectangular stepped tower in ancient Mesopotamia, surmounted by a temple. **2** something having this shape. [Assyrian *ziqquratu* pinnacle]

zig·zag ● *noun* **1** a line or course having abrupt alternate right and left turns. **2** (often in *pl.*) each of these turns. ● *adjective* **1** having the form of a zigzag; alternating right and left. **2** (of sewing machine stitches) produced in a zigzag, used for neatening unfinished edges etc. ● *adverb* with a zigzag course. ● *intransitive verb* (**zig·zagged**, **zig·zag·ging**) move in a zigzag course. [French from German *zickzack*]

zilch *noun* esp. N Amer. slang nothing. [20th c.: origin uncertain]

zil·lion *noun* informal an indefinite large number. ▢ **zil·lionth** *adjective & noun* [Z (perhaps = unknown quantity) + MILLION]

zil·lion·aire *noun* informal a very rich person.

Zim·babwe /zɪmˈbɒbwi, -weɪ/ a landlocked country in SE Africa, divided from Zambia by the Zambezi River; pop. (est. 2002) 11,376,676; capital, Harare. Zimbabwe was formerly known as Southern Rhodesia (see RHODESIA). ▢ **Zim·bab·wean** *adjective & noun*

Zin *noun* a Zinfandel wine.

zinc *noun Chem.* a white metallic element occurring naturally as zinc blende, and used as a component of brass, in galvanizing sheet iron, and in electric batteries. Symbol: **Zn**; at. no.: 30. [German *Zink*, of unknown origin]

zinc blende *noun* see BLENDE.

zinc chloride *noun* a white crystalline deliquescent solid used as a preservative, antiseptic, and flux.

zinc oxide *noun* a powder used as a white pigment and in medicinal ointments.

zinc sulphate *noun* a white water-soluble compound used as a mordant.

zine /ziːn/ *noun* (also **'zine**) informal a magazine, esp. a fanzine. [abbreviation]

Zin·fan·del /ˈzɪnfəndel/ *noun* **1** a red, white, or rosé wine made esp. in California. **2** the black grape from which this is made. [origin unknown]

zing informal ● *noun* **1** vigour, energy. **2** a short, high-pitched buzzing or ringing sound, as of a bullet moving through the air. **3** zest, liveliness (*lemon juice adds zing to this cheesecake*). ● *verb* **1** *intransitive* move swiftly or with a shrill sound. **2** *transitive* N Amer. criticize or rebuke (a person) severely. ▢ **zingy** *adjective* (**zing·i·er**, **zing·i·est**). [imitative]

zing·er *noun* esp. N Amer. slang **1** a witty or pointed remark. **2** an unexpected turn of events or piece of news. **3** an outstanding person or thing.

Zinne·mann /ˈzɪnəmən/ **Fred** (1907–97), Austrian-born US film director. He joined MGM in 1937 and won Oscars for the short *That Mothers Might Live* (1938) and the feature films *From Here to Eternity*

Vowels: a cat ɑ arm e bed ɜr her ɜ: deux ə ago ɪ sit i cosy iː feed ɒ hot ɔ pore ɔː no ʌ run ʊ put

(1953) and *A Man For All Seasons* (1966), noted for their meticulous realism.

zin·nia *noun* a composite plant of the chiefly Mexican genus *Zinnia*, often grown for their showy flowers. [J. G. Zinn, German physician and botanist d.1759]

Zin·ov·iev /zɪˈnoːvi̯əf/ **Grig·ori Yevse·evich** (born Ovsel Gershon Aronov Radomyslsky) (1883–1936), Russian revolutionary, chairman of Comintern 1919–26. He was arrested by Stalin (1935), convicted of treason in the assassination of the Soviet politician Sergei Kirov (1888–1934), and executed.

Zin·zen·dorf /ˈzɪnzəndorf/ **Count Niko·laus Lud·wig von** (1700–60), German Protestant theologian, who founded the Moravian Church (c.1722).

Zion /ˈzaiən/ *noun* (also **Sion** /ˈsaiən/) **1** one of the two hills and also the citadel of ancient Jerusalem. The name came to signify Jerusalem itself and, allegorically, the heavenly city or kingdom of heaven. **2** the Jewish religion or people. **3** the region of Palestine as the Jewish homeland and as the symbol of Judaism. **4** the Christian Church. [Old English from ecclesiastical Latin *Sion* from Hebrew *ṣiyôn*]

Zion·ism *noun* a movement originally for the re-establishment and now the development of a Jewish nation in what is now Israel. □ **Zion·ist** *noun*

zip ● *noun* **1** a light fast sound, as of a bullet passing through air. **2** energy, vigour. **3** zest (*these chili peppers have a lot of zip!*). **4** *N Amer. informal* nothing, zero; zilch. **5** esp. *Brit.* **a** (in full **zip fastener**) = ZIPPER *noun*. **b** (*attributive*) having a zipper (*zip bag*). **6** a zip code. ● *verb* (**zipped, zip·ping**) **1** *transitive & intransitive* (often foll. by *up*) fasten with a zipper. **2** *intransitive* move with zip or at high speed. **3** *transitive Computing* compress (a file or files) using a program called PKZIP, or (more generally) any similar program. □ **zip one's lip** *slang* keep quiet. [imitative]

zip code *noun US* a system of postal codes consisting of five- or nine-digit numbers. [zone improvement plan]

zip file *noun* a computer file that has been compressed.

zip gun *noun N Amer. informal* a cheap homemade or makeshift gun.

zip-lock *adjective* (also **zip-top**) *N Amer.* designating a plastic bag with a special strip along the two open edges so that it can be sealed shut by pressing them together and readily reopened or resealed.

zip·per esp. *N Amer.* ● *noun* a fastening device of two flexible strips with interlocking projections closed or opened by pulling a slide along them. ● *transitive verb* **1** (often foll. by *up*) fasten with a zipper. **2** provide with a zipper. □ **zip·pered** *adjective*

zippo *noun* (also **zip·ola**) *N Amer. informal* = ZIP *noun* 4.

zippy *adjective* (**zip·pi·er, zip·pi·est**) *informal* **1** bright, fresh, lively. **2** fast, speedy. □ **zip·pi·ly** *adverb* **zip·pi·ness** *noun*

zip-up *attributive adjective* able to be fastened with a zip fastener.

zir·con *noun* a zirconium silicate of which some translucent varieties are cut into gems (see HYACINTH 5, JARGON²). [German *Zirkon*: compare JARGON²]

zir·co·nia /zɜrˈkoːniə/ *noun* zirconium dioxide, used in ceramics, refractory coatings, etc., and in fused form as a synthetic substitute for diamonds in jewellery.

zir·co·nium /zɜrˈkoːniəm/ *noun Chem.* a grey metallic element occurring naturally in zircon and used in various industrial applications. Symbol: **Zr**; at. no.: 40. [modern Latin from ZIRCON + -IUM]

Ziska /ˈzɪskə/ **Jan** (also **Žižka** /ˈʒɪʃkə/) (c.1376–1424), Bohemian soldier, who led the Hussite rebellion against the Holy Roman emperor Sigismund (1420–4).

zit *noun slang* a pimple. [20th c.: origin unknown]

zith·er /ˈzɪðər/ *noun* a musical instrument consisting of a flat wooden sound box with numerous strings stretched across it, placed horizontally and played with the fingers and a plectrum. □ **zith·er·ist** *noun* [German (as CITTERN)]

ziti /ˈziːtiː/ *plural noun* pasta in the form of tubes resembling large macaroni. [Italian, prob. from dial. *zito* 'bridegroom' because traditionally served at weddings]

zizz *informal* ● *noun* **1** a whizzing or buzzing sound. **2** a short sleep. ● *intransitive verb* **1** make a whizzing sound. **2** doze or sleep. [imitative]

zloty /ˈzlɒti/ *noun* (*pl.* same or **zlotys**) the chief monetary unit of Poland, equal to 100 groszy. [Polish, lit. 'golden']

Zn *symbol* the element zinc.

zo·di·ac /ˈzoːdiˌak/ *noun* **1 a** a belt of the heavens within about 8° of the ecliptic, including all apparent positions of the sun, moon, and most familiar planets, and divided into twelve parts (signs) named after constellations (Aries, Taurus, Gemini, Cancer, Leo, Virgo, Libra, Scorpio, Sagittarius, Capricorn, Aquarius, Pisces) and used in astrology. **b** a diagram of these signs. **2** (**Zodiac**) *proprietary* a kind of inflatable rubber dinghy, esp. one powered by an outboard motor. **3** a complete cycle, circuit, or compass. [Old French *zodiaque* from Latin *zodiacus* from Greek *zōidiakos* from *zōidion* sculptured animal figure, diminutive of *zōion* animal]

zo·di·ac·al /zoˈdaiəkəl/ *adjective* of or in the zodiac.

zodiacal light *noun* a luminous area of sky shaped like a tall triangle occasionally seen in the east before sunrise or in the west after sunset, esp. in the tropics.

zoe·trope /ˈzoːətroːp/ *noun* a 19th-c. optical toy consisting of a cylinder with a series of pictures on the inner surface that, when viewed through slits with the cylinder rotating, give an impression of continuous motion. [formed irregularly from Greek *zōē* 'life' + -*tropos* 'turning']

Zog I /ˈzɒg/ (full name Ahmed Bey Zogu) (1895–1961), Albanian leader, prime minister 1922–4, president 1925–8, and king 1928–39. His autocratic rule resulted in a period of relative political stability, but when Albania was invaded by Italy in 1939, Zog went into exile; he abdicated in 1946.

Zohar /ˈzoːhɑr/ *noun* the chief text of the Jewish Kabbalah, presented as an allegorical or mystical interpretation of the Pentateuch. [Hebrew, lit. = 'light, splendour']

Zola /ˈzoːlə/ **Émile Édouard Charles An·toine** (1840–1902), French novelist and critic. His series of 20 naturalistic novels collectively entitled *Les Rougon-Macquart* (1871–93) chronicles the lives of two families over several generations, and sets out to show how human behaviour is determined by environment and heredity; novels in the series include *Nana* (1880), *Germinal* (1885), and *La Terre* (1887). He is also remembered for his outspoken support of Alfred Dreyfus in his pamphlet *J'accuse* (1898). □ **Zola·esque** *adjective*

zoll·ver·ein /ˈtsɒlfəˌrain/ *noun hist.* a customs union, esp. of German states in the 19th c. [German]

zom·bie *noun* **1** *informal* a dull, apathetic, or exceedingly tired person. **2** a corpse said to be revived by witchcraft. **3** *Cdn slang* (during World War II) a conscript, orig. for national defence as opposed to overseas service. **4** a drink consisting of several kinds of rum mixed with fruit juice and sugar. □ **zombie·like** *adjective* **zom·bi·fi·ca·tion** *noun* **zom·bi·fied** *adjective* **zom·bi·fy** *transitive verb* [Kikongo *zumbi* fetish]

zon·a·tion *noun* distribution in zones, esp. (*Ecology*) of plants into zones characterized by the dominant species.

zone ● *noun* **1** an area having particular features, properties, purpose, or use (*danger zone; erogenous zone*). **2** any well-defined region of more or less belt-like form. **3 a** an area between two exact or approximate concentric circles. **b** a part of the surface of a sphere enclosed between two parallel planes, or of a cone or cylinder etc., between such planes cutting it perpendicularly to the axis. **4** (in full **time zone**) a range of longitudes where a common standard time is used. **5** *Geol. etc.* a range between specified limits of depth, height, etc., esp. a section of strata distinguished by characteristic fossils. **6** *Geog.* any of five divisions of the earth bounded by circles parallel to the equator (see FRIGID ZONE, TEMPERATE ZONE, TORRID ZONE). **7** an encircling band or stripe distinguishable in colour, texture, or character from the rest of the object encircled. ● *transitive verb* **1** encircle as or with a zone. **2** arrange or distribute by zones. **3 a** divide (a city, land, etc.) into areas subject to particular planning restrictions. **b** designate (a specific area) for use or development in this manner. □ **in the zone** in a state of perfect concentration leading to optimum mental or physical performance. **zone out** *N Amer. slang* lose concentration; cease paying attention. □ **zonal** *adjective* **zon·ing** *noun* (in sense 3 of *verb*). [French *zone* or Latin *zona* girdle, from Greek *zōnē*]

zoned-out *adjective informal* inattentive, as if intoxicated by drugs or alcohol.

zonk *slang* ● *verb* **1** *transitive* hit or strike. **2** (foll. by *out*) **a** *transitive* overcome, overwhelm, knock out. **b** *intransitive* fall heavily asleep. ● *noun* (often as *interjection*) the sound of a blow or heavy impact. [imitative]

zonked *adjective* (also **zonked out**) *informal* **1** under the influence of drugs or alcohol. **2** tired, exhausted.

zoo *noun* **1** a place where wild animals are kept for exhibition to the public, breeding, study, etc. **2** any busy, noisy place (*it's a zoo in the lobby*). **3** a diverse or motley collection of people or things. [abbreviation of ZOOLOGICAL GARDEN]

zoo- /ˈzuːə, ˈzoːə/ *combining form* of animals or animal life. [Greek *zōio-* from *zōion* animal]

zoo·geog·ra·phy /ˌzuːədʒɪˈɒɡrəfi, ˌzoː-/ *noun* the branch of zoology dealing with the geographical distribution of animals.
□ **zoo·geo·graph·ic** *adjective* **zoo·geo·graph·ic·al** *adjective*

zooid /ˈzuːɔid, ˈzoː-/ *noun* **1** a more or less independent invertebrate organism arising by budding or fission. **2** a distinct member of an invertebrate colony. □ **zooid·al** *adjective*

zoo·keep·er *noun* a person employed in a zoo to care for the animals.

zoo·logic·al /ˌzuːəˈlɒdʒɪkəl, ˌzoːə-/ *adjective* of or relating to zoology.
□ **zoo·logic·al·ly** *adverb*

zoological garden *noun* (also **zoological gardens**) = zoo 1.

zo·ology /zuːˈɒlədʒi, zoː-/ *noun* the scientific study of animals, esp. with reference to their structure, physiology, classification, and distribution. □ **zo·olo·gist** *noun*

zoom ● *verb* **1** *intransitive* move quickly, esp. with a low-pitched humming or buzzing sound. **2 a** *intransitive* cause an airplane to mount at high speed and a steep angle. **b** *transitive* cause (an airplane) to do this. **3 a** *intransitive* alter the field of view of a camera by varying the focal length of a zoom lens, esp. (foll. by *in* (*on*)) so as to close up on a subject without losing focus. **b** *transitive* cause (a lens or camera) to do this. **c** *Computing* (usu. foll. by *in* or *out*) alter the representation of an image or document on a computer screen so as to make it appear larger or smaller. **4** *intransitive* (of prices, costs, etc.) rise sharply. ● *noun* **1** an airplane's steep climb. **2** a zooming camera shot. **3** a zoom lens. [imitative]

zoom·able *adjective* *Computing* (of a digital map or image) that can be viewed at various levels of detail and magnification.

zoom lens *noun* a lens with a variable focal length, esp. one able to change focal length without losing focus.

zoo·morph·ic /ˌzuːəˈmɔrfɪk, ˌzoːə-, zuːˈmɔrfɪk/ *adjective* **1** dealing with or represented in animal forms. **2** having gods of animal form.
□ **zoo·morph·ism** *noun*

zoono·sis /ˌzuːəˈnoːsɪs, zoːə-/ *noun* (pl. **-ses** /-siːz/) any of various diseases which can be transmitted to humans from animals.
□ **zoo·not·ic** *adjective* [ZOO- + Greek *nosos* disease]

zoo·phyte /ˈzuːəˌfəit, ˈzoːə-/ *noun* any of various sessile invertebrate animals that resemble plants or flowers, such as a coral, sea anemone, or sponge. □ **zoo·phyt·ic** /-ˈfɪtɪk/ *adjective*

zoo·plank·ton /ˌzuːəˈplaŋktən, zoːə-/ *noun* the animal component of plankton, consisting of small animals and the immature stages of larger animals.

zoo·spore /ˈzuːəˌspɔr, ˈzoːə-/ *noun* a spore of fungi, algae, etc. capable of motion.

zoot suit *noun* *informal* a man's suit of an exaggerated style popular in the 1940s, characterized by a long draped jacket with padded shoulders and high-waisted tapering trousers. □ **zoot-suited** *adjective* [rhyming on SUIT]

zoot-suiter *noun* *informal* a person wearing a zoot suit.

zoo·xan·thel·la /ˌzoːəzanˈθelə/ *noun* (pl. **zoo·xan·thel·lae**) a yellowish-brown symbiotic dinoflagellate present in large numbers in the cytoplasm of many marine invertebrates. [modern Latin *zoo-* 'of animals' + Greek *xanthos* 'yellow' + diminutive *ella*]

zori *noun* (pl. **zoris**) a Japanese sandal, having a simple thong between the toes and a flat sole originally of straw but now often of rubber or felt etc. [Japanese]

zor·il /ˈzɒrɪl/ *noun* (also **zor·ille**) a flesh-eating African mammal, *Ictonyx striatus*, of the skunk and the weasel family. [French *zorille* from Spanish *zorrilla* diminutive of *zorro* fox]

Zoro·as·ter /ˌzɒroˈastər/ (Avestan name Zarathustra) (*c.*628–*c.*551 BC), Persian prophet and founder of Zoroastrianism. According to tradition he was born in Persia, and began to preach the tenets of what was later called Zoroastrianism after receiving a vision from Ahura Mazda.

Zoro·as·trian /ˌzɒroˈastriən/ (also **Zara·thus·tri·an** /ˌzerəˈθustriən/) ● *adjective* of or relating to Zoroaster (or Zarathustra) or the dualistic religious system taught by him or his followers in the Zend-Avesta, based on the concept of a conflict between a spirit of light and good and a spirit of darkness and evil. ● *noun* a follower of Zoroaster.
□ **Zoro·as·trian·ism** *noun*

Zor·rilla y Moral /zəˈriːə iː mɔːˈral/ **José** (1817–93), Spanish poet and dramatist, whose works include the verse collection *Cantos del trovador* (1841) and the play *Don Juan Tenorio* (1844). He was the dominant figure of Spanish nationalist Romanticism and his work was viewed as quintessentially Spanish, with picturesque characters, involved plots, and flights of lyricism.

Zouave /zuːˈɒv, zwɒv/ *noun* **1** a member of a French light-infantry corps originally formed of Algerians and long retaining their original

oriental uniform. **2** *hist.* (in full **Papal Zouave**) a member of a troop of soldiers (of whom about 400 were from French Canada) formed in Rome for the defence of the pope, 1860–71. [French from *Zouaoua*, name of a tribe]

zouk /zuːk/ *noun* an exuberant style of popular music, originating in the Antilles, combining Caribbean and Western elements and characterized by a strong fast beat derived from Antillean drumming. [Antillean French Creole, lit. 'to party']

zounds /zaundz/ *interjection* *archaic* expressing surprise or indignation. [(*God*)'s *wounds* (i.e. those of Christ on the Cross)]

zowie *interjection* (also **zowee**) *N Amer.* expressing astonishment, admiration, or delight. [alteration of wow¹]

ZPG *abbreviation* zero population growth.

Zr *symbol* *Chem.* the element zirconium.

Zsig·mon·dy /ˈʃɪgmɒndi/ **Rich·ard (Adolph)** (1865–1929), Austrian-born German chemist. He investigated the properties of various colloidal solutions, esp. of gold in glass or water, and invented the ultramicroscope for counting colloidal particles; he was awarded the Nobel Prize for chemistry in 1925.

zuc·chet·to /zuːˈketo, tsuː-/ *noun* (pl. **-tos**) a Roman Catholic ecclesiastic's skullcap, black for a priest, purple for a bishop, red for a cardinal, and white for a pope. [Italian *zucchetta* diminutive of *zucca* gourd, head]

zuc·chi·ni /zuːˈkiːni/ *noun* (pl. same or **zuc·chi·nis**) esp. *N Amer.* & *Austral.* a green-skinned summer squash, similar in appearance to a cucumber. [Italian, pl. of *zucchino* diminutive of *zucca* gourd]

Zug /tsuːg/ (French **Zoug** /zuɡ/) **1** a mainly German-speaking canton in central Switzerland. The smallest canton, it joined the confederation in 1352. **2** its capital; pop. (2002) 23,200.

zug·zwang /ˈtsuktsvaŋ/ *noun* *Chess* an obligation to move in one's turn even when this must be disadvantageous. [German from *Zug* move + *Zwang* compulsion]

Zuider Zee /ˌzaidər ˈziː, ˈzei/ a former large shallow inlet of the North Sea, in the Netherlands. In 1932 a dam across its entrance was completed, and since then large parts of it have been drained and reclaimed as agricultural land. The remainder forms the freshwater lake of the IJsselmeer. [Dutch, = southern sea]

Zuker·man /ˈzukərmən/ **Pin·chas** (b.1948), Israeli violinist and conductor, internationally known as a soloist and performer of chamber music. Since 1998 he has been Music Director of the National Arts Centre in Ottawa.

Zulu ● *noun* **1** a member of a Bantu-speaking people forming the largest ethnic group in South Africa. **2** the language of this people.
● *adjective* of or relating to the Zulus or their language. [Zulu *umzulu*, pl. *amazulu*]

Zulu·land see KwaZulu.

Zuni /ˈzuːni, ˈzuːnji/ (also **Zuñi** /ˈzuːnji/) ● *noun* **1** a member of a Pueblo people of New Mexico. **2** the language of this people. ● *adjective* of or relating to the Zuni or their language. [a river in New Mexico]

zuppa /ˈtsuːpə, ˈzuːpə/ *noun* (in full **zuppa di pesce** /di ˈpeʃe/) fish soup. [Italian, lit. 'soup']

Zur·ich /ˈzurɪk, ˈzjuː-/ a city in north central Switzerland, situated on Lake Zurich; pop. (est. 2002) 339,300. The largest city in Switzerland, it is a major international financial centre.

Zweig /zwaig/ **Stef·an** (1881–1942), Austrian biographer, essayist, and playwright, who is primarily noted for his biographical essays and full-length biographies, which include *Marie Antoinette* (1932) and *Right to Heresy* (1935), on Erasmus.

zwie·back /ˈzwiːbak/ *noun* a sweet rich egg bread, sliced and baked again until crisp. [German, = twice baked]

Zwing·li /ˈzwɪŋli, ˈtsvɪŋli/ **Ul·rich** (1484–1531), Swiss Protestant reformer. A major figure in the Swiss Reformation, he attacked the idea of purgatory, the invocation of saints, monasticism, and other orthodox doctrines; he rejected Luther's doctrine of consubstantiation. □ **Zwing·li·an** *noun* & *adjective*

zwit·ter·ion /ˈzwɪtəˌraiən, ˈtsvɪ-/ *noun* a molecule or ion having separate positively and negatively charged groups. □ **zwit·ter·ion·ic** *adjective* [German from *Zwitter* a hybrid]

Zwory·kin /ˈzwɒrɪkɪn, zvəˈriːkɪn/ **Vlad·i·mir (Kuz·mich)** (1889–1982), Russian-born US physicist and television pioneer. He invented an electronic television input device, which incorporated a screen scanned by an electron beam and sent an electric signal to a cathode ray tube adapted to receive the image; this had been developed into the first practical television camera by about 1929.

Consonants: b *but* d *dog* f *few* g *get* h *her* j *yes* k *cat* l *leg* m *man* n *no* p *pen* r *red* s *sit*

Zyban /ˈzaiban/ *noun proprietary* an antidepressant drug, bupropion, used as an aid in quitting smoking.

zy·deco /ˈzaidəkoː/ *noun* a kind of dance music originally from southern Louisiana, combining blues and Cajun influences and often performed on guitar, violin, and accordion. [Louisiana Creole, possibly from French *les haricots* in a dance tune title]

zygo- /ˈzaigoː/ *combining form* joining, pairing. [Greek *zugo-* from *zugon* yoke]

zygo·dac·tyl /ˌzaigoːˈdaktɪl/ ● *adjective* (of a bird) having two toes pointing forward and two backward. ● *noun* such a bird. ☐ **zygo·dac·tyl·ous** *adjective*

zy·go·ma /zaiˈgoːmə, zɪ-/ *noun* (*pl.* **zy·go·mata** /-tə/) the bony arch of the cheek formed by connection of the zygomatic and temporal bones at the edge of the eye socket. ☐ **zygo·mat·ic** /ˌzaigəˈmatik, ˌzɪ-/ *adjective* [Greek *zugōma -atos* from *zugon* yoke]

zygomatic arch *noun* = ZYGOMA.

zy·gote /ˈzaigoːt/ *noun Biol.* a cell formed by the union of two gametes; a fertilized ovum. ☐ **zy·got·ic** /-ˈgɒtik/ *adjective* **zy·got·ic·ally** *adverb* [Greek *zugōtos* yoked, from *zugoō* to yoke]

zym·ase /ˈzaimeis/ *noun* a mixture of enzymes obtained from yeast which catalyze the breakdown of sugars in alcoholic fermentation. [French from Greek *zumē* leaven]

zym·ot·ic /zaiˈmɒtik, zɪ-/ *adjective* of, relating to, or denoting an infectious disease. [Greek *zumōtikos* (as ZYMASE)]

zym·urgy /ˈzaimɜrdʒi/ *noun* the branch of applied chemistry dealing with the use of fermentation in brewing etc. [Greek *zumē* leaven, after *metallurgy*]

zzz *interjection* used to imitate the sound of a person sleeping or snoring.

---

t *top*   v *voice*   w *we*   z *zoo*   ʃ *she*   ʒ *vision*   θ *thin*   ð *this*   ŋ *ring*   x *loch*   tʃ *chip*   dʒ *jar*   (*see over for vowels*)

Appendices

A. PUNCTUATION MARKS

1. General remarks

The purpose of punctuation is to mark out strings of words into manageable groups and help clarify their meaning (or in some cases to prevent a wrong meaning being deduced). The marks most commonly used to divide a piece of prose or other writing are the period, the semicolon, and the comma, with the strength of the dividing or separating role diminishing from the period to the comma. The period marks the main division into sentences; the semicolon joins sentences (as in this sentence); and the comma (which is the most flexible in use and causes the most problems) separates smaller elements with the least loss of continuity. Brackets and dashes also serve as separators—often more strikingly than commas, as in this sentence.

2. Capital letter   C

2.1.1 This is used for the first letter of the word beginning a sentence in most cases:

She decided not to come. Later she changed her mind.

2.1.2 A sentence or clause contained in a subordinate or parenthetic role within a larger one does not normally begin with a capital letter:

I have written several letters (there are many to be written) and hope to finish them tomorrow.

2.1.3 In the following, however, the sentence is a separate one and therefore does begin with a capital letter:

We have more than one option. (You have said this often before.) So we should think carefully before acting.

2.1.4 A capital letter also begins sentences that form quoted speech:

The assistant turned and replied, "I think it works."

2.2 The use of capital letters for proper names, titles, etc. is discussed in section C of this appendix.

3. Period   •

3.1 This is used to mark the end of a sentence when it is a statement (and not a question or exclamation). In prose, sentences marked by periods normally represent a discrete or distinct statement; more closely connected or complementary statements are joined by a semicolon (as here).

3.2.1 Periods are used to mark abbreviations (*Wed., Gen., p.m.*). They are often omitted in abbreviations that consist entirely of capital letters (*CBC, EDT, RRSP*), and in acronyms that are pronounced as a word rather than a sequence of letters (*Intelsat*), and should be omitted in abbreviations for SI units (*Hz, kg, cm*).

3.2.2 If an abbreviation with a period comes at the end of a sentence, another period is not added:

They have a collection of many animals, including dogs, cats, tortoises, snakes, etc.

but

They have a collection of many animals (dogs, cats, tortoises, snakes, etc.).

3.3 A sequence of three periods is used to mark an ellipsis or omission in a sequence of words, especially when forming an incomplete quotation. When the omission occurs at the end of a sentence, a fourth point is added as the period of the whole sentence:

He left the room, slammed the door, . . . and went out.

The report said: "There are many issues to be considered, of which the most important are money, time, and personnel. . . . Let us consider personnel first."

3.4 A period is used as a decimal point (*10.5%; $1.65*), and to separate the domains of an email address or URL (*www.oup.com*). It is commonly used in British practice to divide hours and minutes in giving time (*6.15 p.m.*), where a colon is standard in North American use.

4. Semicolon   ;

4.1.1 The main role of the semicolon is to unite sentences that are closely associated or that complement or parallel each other in some way, as in the following:

In the north of the city there is a large industrial area with few dwellings; further east is the university.

To err is human; to forgive, divine.

4.1.2 It is often used as a stronger division in a sentence that already includes divisions by means of commas:

He came out of the house, which lay back from the road, and saw her at the end of the path; but instead of continuing towards her, he hid until she had gone.

4.2 It is used in a similar way in lists of names or other items, to indicate a stronger division:

I would like to thank the managing director, Jennifer Dunbar; my secretary, Raymond Martin; and my assistant, David Singh.

5. Comma   ,

5.1 Use of the comma is more difficult to describe than other punctuation marks, and there is considerable variation in practice. Essentially, it is used to give detail to the structure of sentences, especially longer ones, and make their meaning clear. Too many commas can be distracting; too few can make a piece of writing difficult to read or, worse, difficult to understand.

5.2.1 The comma is used to separate the main clauses of a sentence when they are not sufficiently close in meaning or content to form a continuous unpunctuated sentence, and are not distinct enough to warrant a semicolon. A conjunction such as *and, but, yet*, etc., is normally used:

The road runs through a beautiful wooded valley, and the railway line follows it closely.

5.2.2 It is considered incorrect to join the clauses of a compound sentence without a conjunction. In the following sentence, the comma should either be replaced by a semicolon, or be retained and followed by *and*:

I like skating very much, I go to the local rink every day after school.

5.2.3 It is also considered incorrect to separate a subject from its verb with a comma:

Those with the smallest incomes and no other means, should get more support.

5.3.1 Commas are usually inserted between adjectives coming before a noun:

An enterprising, ambitious person.

A cold, damp, poorly heated room.

5.3.2 But the comma is omitted when the last adjective has a closer relation to the noun than the others:

A distinguished foreign politician.

5.4 An important role of the comma is to prevent ambiguity, especially after a verb used intransitively where it might otherwise be taken to be transitive:

With the police pursuing, the people shouted loudly.

She did not want to leave, from a feeling of loyalty.

In the valley below, the houses appeared very small.

5.5.1 Commas are used in pairs to separate elements in a sentence that are not part of the main statement:

I would like you all, ladies and gentlemen, to raise your glasses.

There is no truth, as far as I can see, to this rumour.

It appears, however, that we were wrong.

5.5.2 It is also used to separate a relative clause from its antecedent when the clause is not serving an identifying function:

The picture, which was hanging above the fireplace, was a present.

In the above sentence, the information in the *which* clause is incidental to the main statement; without the comma, it would form an essential part of it in identifying which picture is being referred to (and could be replaced by *that*):

The picture which/that was hanging above the fireplace was a present.

5.6.1 Commas are used to separate items in a list or sequence. Usage varies as to the inclusion of a comma before *and* in the last item; the practice in this dictionary is to include it:

The following will compete in the first heat: Cohen, Sallese, Paterson, and Roy.

5.6.2 A final comma before *and*, when used regularly and consistently, has the advantage of clarifying the grouping at a composite name occurring at the end of a list:

Officials gathered from Prince Edward Island, Nova Scotia, and Newfoundland and Labrador.

5.7 In numbers of four or more figures, a comma is often used to separate each group of three consecutive figures starting from the right (e.g. *10,135,793*). In metric practice, a space is used instead of a comma or period to separate each group of three consecutive figures (*10 135 793*).

5.8 A comma is used to introduce a quotation of a complete sentence:

Joan exclaimed, "Isn't he fabulous!".

and substitutes for a period at the end of a quotation if this is followed by a continuation of the sentence:

"I've never seen such a fabulous dancer," said Joan.

6. Colon :

6.1 The main role of the colon is to separate main clauses when there is a step forward from the first to the second, especially from introduction to main point, from general statement to example, from cause to effect, and from premise to conclusion:

There is something I forgot to tell you: your mother called earlier.

It was not easy: to begin with, we had to raise the necessary capital.

The weather was bad: so we decided to stay home.

(In this example, a comma could be used, but the emphasis on cause and effect would be greatly reduced.)

6.2 It also introduces a list of items. In this use a dash should not be added:

This recipe requires the following: semi-sweet chocolate, cream, egg whites, and sugar.

6.3 It is used to introduce, more formally and emphatically than a comma would, speech or quoted material:

I told them last week: "Do not under any circumstances open this box."

6.4 It is used to divide hours and minutes in giving time (*6:30 p.m.*).

7. Question mark ?

7.1.1 This is used in place of the period to show that the preceding sentence is a question:

Would you like another cup of coffee?

She actually volunteered to do it?

7.1.2 It is not used when the question is implied by indirect speech:

I asked you if you would like another cup of coffee.

7.2 It is used (often in brackets) to express doubt or uncertainty about a word or phrase immediately following or preceding it:

Jean Talon, born (?) 1625.

They were then seen boarding a bus (to Kingston?).

8. Exclamation mark !

This is used after an exclamatory word, phrase, or sentence expressing any of the following:

8.1 Absurdity:

That's preposterous!

8.2 Command or warning:

Watch out!

8.3 Contempt or disgust:

Your hands are filthy!

8.4 Emotion or pain:

I love this song!

Ouch! That hurts!

8.5 Enthusiasm:

I can't wait to see you!

8.6 Wish or regret:

If only I could fly!

8.7 Wonder, admiration, or surprise:

Isn't that beautiful!

9. Apostrophe ,

9.1.1 The main use is to indicate the possessive case, as in *Julie's book*, *the boys' mother*, etc. It comes before the *s* in singular and plural nouns not ending in *s*, as in *the girl's games* and *the women's games*. It comes after the *s* in plural nouns ending in *s*, as in *the girls' games*.

9.1.2 In singular nouns ending in *s* practice differs between (for example) *Charles'* and *Charles's*; in some cases the shorter form is preferable for reasons of sound, as in *Xerxes' fleet*, in *Jesus' name*.

9.1.3 It is also used to indicate a place or business, e.g. *the butcher's*. In this use it is often omitted in some names, e.g. *Tim Hortons, Shoppers Drug Mart, Smiths Falls*.

9.2 It is used to indicate a contraction, e.g. *we're, mustn't, o'clock*.

9.3 It is sometimes used to form a plural of individual letters or numbers, although this use is diminishing. It is helpful in *dot your i's and cross your t's*, but unnecessary in *MPs* and *1940s*.

9.4 For its use as a quotation mark, see section 10.

10. Quotation marks   " "

10.1 The main use is to indicate direct speech and quotations. Quotation marks are used at the beginning and end of quoted material:

> She said, "I have something to tell you."

10.2 The closing quotation marks should come after any punctuation mark which is part of the quoted matter, but before any mark which is not:

> They shouted, "Watch out!".
>
> They were described as "an unruly bunch".

10.3 Punctuation dividing a sentence of quoted speech is put inside the quotation marks:

> "Go away," he said, "and don't ever come back."

10.4 Quotation marks are also placed around cited words and phrases:

> What does "integrated circuit" mean?

10.5 A quotation within a quotation is put in single quotation marks:

> "Have you any idea," he said, "what 'integrated circuit' means?"

This is the practice followed by most North American publishers. British publishers use single quotation marks for a first quotation and double quotation marks for a quotation within:

> Have you any idea,' he said, 'what "integrated circuit" means?'

11. Brackets   ([ ])

11.1 The types of brackets used in normal punctuation are round brackets ( ), also known as parentheses, and square brackets [ ].

11.2 The main use of round brackets is to enclose explanations and extra information or comment:

> He was (and still is) a rebel.
>
> Congo (formerly Zaire).
>
> He spoke at length about his Weltanschauung (world view).

11.3 They are used to give references and citations:

> Wilfrid Laurier (1841–1919).
>
> A discussion of integrated circuits (see p. 38).

11.4 They are used to enclose reference letters or figures, e.g. *(1), (a)*.

11.5 They are used to enclose optional words:

> There are many (apparent) difficulties.

(In this example, the difficulties may or may not be only apparent.)

11.6.1 Square brackets are used less often. The main use is to enclose extra information attributable to someone (normally an editor) other than the writer of the surrounding text:

> Robert walked in, and his sister [Sara] greeted him.

11.6.2 They are used in some contexts to convey special kinds of information, especially when round brackets are also used for other purposes: for example, in this dictionary they are used to give the etymologies at the end of entries.

12. Dash   —

12.1 A single dash is used to indicate a pause, whether a hesitation in speech or to introduce an explanation or expansion of what comes before it:

> We must try to help—before it's too late.
>
> We then saw the reptiles—snakes, crocodiles, that sort of thing.

12.2 A pair of dashes is used to indicate asides and parentheses, like the use of commas as explained at 5.5.1 above, but forming a more distinct break:

> He refused to tell anyone—least of all his wife—about that embarrassing moment during the medical exam.

12.3 It is sometimes used to indicate an omitted word, for example a coarse word or part of a coarse word in reported speech:

> "Let's get the f— out of here," he said.

12.4 It is also used to sum up a list before carrying on with a sentence:

> Chocolates, flowers, champagne—all these would be appreciated.

12.5 When a proper dash cannot be produced, two hyphens (with no space before or after) can be used instead.

13. Hyphen   -

13.1 The hyphen has two main functions: to link words or elements of words into longer words and compounds, and to mark the division of a word at the end of a line in print or writing.

13.2.1 The use of the hyphen to connect words to form compound words is diminishing in English. It is often retained to avoid awkward collisions of letters, as in *twist-tie*.

13.2.2 The hyphen serves to connect words that have a syntactic link, as in *soft-centred candies* and *French-speaking people*, where the reference is to candies with soft centres and people who speak French, rather than soft candies with centres and French people who can speak (which would be the sense conveyed if the hyphens were omitted). It is also used to avoid more extreme kinds of ambiguity, as in *twenty-odd people*.

13.2.3 A particularly important use of the hyphen is to link compounds and phrases used attributively, as in *a well-known man* (but *the man is well known*), and *water-cooler gossip* (but *gossip around the water cooler*).

13.2.4 It is also used to connect elements to form words in cases such as *re-enact* (where the collision of two e's would be awkward), *re-form* (= to form again, to distinguish it from *reform*), and some other prefixed words such as those in *anti-, non-, over-,* and *post-*. Usage varies in this regard, and much depends on how well established and clearly recognizable the resulting formation is. When the second element is a name, a hyphen is usual (as in *anti-Darwinian*).

13.2.5 It is used to indicate a common second element in all but the last of a list, e.g. *two-*, *three-*, or *fourfold*.

13.3 The hyphen used to divide a word at the end of a line is a different matter, because it is not a permanent feature of the spelling. The general principle to follow is to insert the hyphen where it will least distract the reader, usually (but not always) at a syllable break.

B. SPELLING RULES

1. General Remarks

Canadian spelling practices vary widely, sometimes coinciding with American spellings, sometimes with British. In certain tendencies Canadians are quite consistent, hardly ever using the British spellings *tyre*, *gaol*, and *kerb*, and usually avoiding American spellings such as *check* (for a bank draft) and *maneuver*. In other cases our usage is divided: please refer to section 6 below for guidance on Canadian preferences regarding suffix variants such as *-ise/-ize* and *-our/-or*. In most cases Canadians have the luxury of being able to select either set of spelling conventions, as long as variants of the same word are not mixed indiscriminately within a single piece of writing. For specific points of uncertainty, the main part of the dictionary should be consulted. In this dictionary, the spelling favoured by Canadians always appears as the headword with the less common variant in brackets.

2. *i* before *e*

For words pronounced with an "ee" sound, the traditional rule "*i* before *e* except after *c*" is fairly reliable. The exceptions are (a) *seize*, (b) *either* and *neither* (if you pronounce them that way; also *heinous*, *inveigle*), (c) Latin words such as *prima facie*, *species*, and *superficies*, and (d) words in which a stem ending in *e* is followed by a suffix beginning with *i*, e.g. *caffeine*, *casein*, *codeine*, *plebeian*, *protein*. Note that the syllable *-feit* is so spelled, e.g. *counterfeit*, *forfeit*, *surfeit*, and that *mischief* is spelled like *chief*.

Words pronounced with an "ay" or long "i" sound generally have *-ei-*: *beige*, *heinous*, *reign*, *veil*, *eiderdown*, *height*, *kaleidoscope*. Words with other sounds follow no rules and must simply become familiar to the eye, e.g. *foreign* and *sovereign* (related to *reign*), *friend*, *heifer*, *leisure*, *Madeira*, *sieve*, *their*, *view*, *weir*, *weird*.

3. Doubling consonants

When a suffix beginning with a vowel (such as *-able*, *-ed*, *-er*, *-ing*, or *-ish*) or *-y* is added to a word ending in a consonant, the consonant is usually doubled if it is a single consonant preceded by a single vowel, and comes at the end of a stressed syllable. So *controllable*, *dropped*, *permitted*, *bigger*, *trekking*, *beginning*, *transferring*, *reddish*, *forgotten*, but *sweated*, *sweeter*, *appealing*, *greenish* (more than one vowel), *planting* (more than one consonant), *balloted*, *happened*, *preferable*, *profiting*, *rocketing* (not ending a stressed syllable). If the final unstressed syllable can stand alone as a single word, then the final consonant, if it is preceded by a single vowel, may still be doubled, e.g. *kidnapped*, *worshipped*, *formatted*, *outcropped*, *programmed*, although note that *invalided* and (in British and most Canadian writing) *benefited* are exceptions to this rule. Other variable or exceptional verbs include *canvas*, *coif*, and *target*. Verbs ending in a vowel followed by *-c* generally form inflections in *-cked*, *-cking*, e.g. *bivouac*, *mimic*, *picnic*.

While all varieties of English agree in doubling an *l* if it follows a single vowel in a stressed syllable (e.g. *dispelled*, *gelled*, *propelled*) and in not doubling it if it follows more than one vowel (e.g. *heeled*, *mailed*, *coolish*), practice differs regarding an *l* that follows a single vowel in an unstressed syllable (e.g. in *label*, *travel*, *jewel*): Canadians and the British double the *l*

(*labelled*, *travelling*, *jeweller*), whereas Americans do not (*labeled*, *traveling*, *jeweler*,). With infinitives, however, the most common Canadian practice agrees with the American in using a double *l* (e.g. *appall*, *enthrall*) rather than with the British (*appal*, *enthral*). There are exceptions to the above guidelines: Canadians and the British double the *l* in *woollen*, and agree with Americans in not doubling the *l* in *paralleled*, *devilish*. Note also the variability of *cruel(l)er*, *cruel(l)est*.

The letter *s* is not usually doubled before the suffix *-es*, either in plural nouns, e.g. *focuses*, *gases*, *pluses*, *yeses*, or in the present tense of verbs, e.g *focuses*, *gases*. However verbal forms in *-s(s)ed*, *-s(s)ing* are variable, and doubling only after stressed syllables is often preferable, e.g. *gassing*, *nonplussed*, but *biased* and (usually) *focused*, *focusing*.

The consonants *h*, *w*, *x*, and *y* are never doubled: *hurrahed*, *guffawed*, *mower*, *boxing*, *stayed*. Silent consonants are also never doubled: *crocheting*, *précising*.

4. Dropping silent *e*

A final silent *e* is usually dropped when adding a suffix beginning with a vowel, e.g. *bluish*, *bravest*, *continuous*, *queued*, *refusal*, *writing*. Exceptions are noted below:

4.1 before *-ing* The *e* is retained in *dyeing*, *singeing*, and *swingeing* to distinguish them from *dying*, *singing*, and *swinging*. It is sometimes retained in *ag(e)ing*, *blu(e)ing*, *cu(e)ing*, *glu(e)ing*, *ru(e)ing*, *spong(e)ing*, and *ting(e)ing*. It is also retained for words ending in *-ee* and *-oe*, e.g. *canoeing*, *fleeing*, *hoeing*, *shoeing*, *tiptoeing*. Otherwise it is dropped: *charging*, *icing*, *lunging*, *staging*, etc.

4.2 words ending in -ce or -ge The *e* is retained to preserve the sound of the consonant, e.g. *advantageous*, *courageous*, *noticeable*, *manageable*, *peaceable*.

4.3 before -able The dropping of *e* before *-able* is very unpredictable. The main part of the dictionary should be consulted for specific points of concern.

4.4 before -age The *e* is usually dropped: *cleavage*, *dosage*, *wastage*. Exceptions: *acreage*, *mileage*. Note also that *linage* and *lineage* are different words.

4.5 before -y The *e* is usually dropped: *bony*, *icy*, *grimy*. Exceptions: (a) after *u* (*gluey*); (b) after *g* (*cottagey*, *villagey*, but optional in *cag(e)y*, *stag(e)y*); (c) after *c* (*dicey*, optional in *pric(e)y*, *spac(e)y*, *pac(e)y*, but otherwise dropped, e.g. *bouncy*, *chancy*, *fleecy*, *lacy*, etc.). The *e* is retained in *holey* to distinguish it from *holy*, and an extra *e* is added to separate two *y*s, e.g. *clayey*. It may be retained or added for clarity in more unusual words. e.g. *chocolatey*, *echoey*.

A silent *e* is not usually dropped when adding a suffix beginning with a consonant, e.g. *useful*, *homeless*, *safely*, *movement*, *whiteness*, *lifelike*, *awesome*. Exceptions: *argument*, *awful*, *duly*, *ninth*, *truly*, *wholly*. When such a suffix is added to certain words ending in *-dge*, Canadian English prefers dropping the *e* in some cases (e.g. *judgment*), while in other instances it does not (*acknowledgement*, *abridgement*). The main part of the dictionary should be consulted for specific points of concern.

5. Forming plurals

5.1 Simple nouns Regular plurals are formed by adding *s*, or after *s*, *sh*, *ss*, *z*, *x*, *ch* (unless pronounced "hard") by adding *es*: *books*, *boxes*, *pizzas*, *queues*, *arches*, *stomachs*. An apostrophe should not be used. Nouns ending in *-y* preceded by a consonant (or *-quy*) form plurals ending in *-ies*, e.g. *rubies*, *soliloquies*, but *boys*, *monkeys*. Exceptions: *lay-bys*, *standbys*, most names (e.g. *the Kennedys*). Nouns ending in *-f* or *-fe* (not *-ff*, *-ffe*) may form plurals in *-ves*, either always (e.g. *halves, leaves*) or optionally (e.g. *hooves, scarves*), or may always have regular plurals (e.g. *beliefs, chiefs*); these should be checked in the main part of the dictionary. Nouns ending in *-o* or *-i* are variable and should be checked in the main part of the dictionary; a number of long-established English words have only plurals in *-oes* (e.g. *heroes, potatoes, tomatoes*), but plurals in *-os* are common and are usual among words which are less naturalized (e.g. *arpeggios*), or are formed by abbreviation (e.g. *kilos*), or have a vowel preceding the *-o* (e.g. *radios*). Nouns ending in *-ful* form regular plurals in *-fuls* (see Usage Note at CUPFUL). Only the letter *z* is regularly doubled in forming plurals: *fezzes, quizzes,* but *gases, yeses* (see "Doubling consonants" above). Nouns ending in *-man* or *-woman* form plurals in *-men* and *-women*, e.g. *chairmen, spokeswomen,* etc., but note *caimans, talismans, Turkomans*. Other irregular plurals are noted in the main text of the dictionary.

5.2 Compound nouns Most compound nouns pluralize the last element: *break-ins, forget-me-nots, major generals, ne'er-do-wells, man-hours*. Exceptions include: (*a*) nouns followed by prepositional phrases, e.g. *commanders-in-chief, daughters-in-law, ladies-in-waiting, men-of-war, rights-of-way*; (*b*) nouns denoting persons, followed by adverbs, e.g. *hangers-on, passersby, runners-up*; (*c*) nouns followed by adjectives, e.g. *heirs presumptive, notaries public, Governors General* (though terms in common use, especially if hyphenated, may not follow this rule, e.g. *Secretary-Generals*); (*d*) nouns denoting people and containing *man* or *woman*, which pluralize both elements, e.g. *women friends, menservants, gentlemen farmers*.

5.3 Foreign and classical plurals Words adopted into English generally form regular English plurals, but words not fully naturalized may form the plural as in the language of origin, e.g. *cherubim, lire, virtuosi*. Many words of Greek and Latin origin retain classical plurals, though they may be used only in technical contexts, e.g. *formulae, indices, topoi*. In general, in forming classical plurals, *-us* becomes *-i* (occasionally *-era* or *-ora*); *-a* becomes *-ae*; *-um* and *-on* become *-a*; *-ex* and *-ix* become *-ices*; *-nx* becomes *-nges*; *-is* becomes *-es* or *-ides*; and *-os* becomes *-oi*. Note that many nouns regularly form only English plurals, e.g. *agendas, irises, octopuses, phoenixes, Thermoses*. Care should be taken with words ending in *-a*, e.g. *addenda, bacteria, criteria, phenomena,* and *strata* are plural, but *nebula* and *vertebra* are singular.

6. Common suffixes

Several common suffixes occur in different forms which may cause spelling difficulties: users of the dictionary should be careful to check if unsure of accepted usage. The most frequent sources of uncertainty in Canadian English are as follows:

6.1 -er/re Canadian writers overwhelmingly prefer the *-re* spellings in words such as *centre, fibre, theatre, lustre, meagre, sombre, spectre,* etc. The *-er* spellings preferred in American English can be found in Canadian writing and are acceptable provided that consistency governs their use. The words *acre, cadre, euchre, lucre, massacre, mediocre, ogre,* and *wiseacre* are never spelled *-er*. Note also the usage indicated in the entries for *meter* and *metre* in the main part of the dictionary.

6.2 -ce/-se In standard British use and most Canadian use, *licence* and *practice* are nouns, *license* and *practise* are verbs; in American use the *-ise* form is used for both noun and verb. Note also the distinction between *prophesy* and *prophecy*.

6.3 -ise-/-ize/, -yse/-yze The verbal ending *-ize* has been in general use since the 16th century; it is favoured in North American English and in much British writing. However, the alternative spelling *-ise* is used, especially in Britain, and may be adopted provided that its use is consistent. A number of verbs always end in *-ise*, notably *advertise, chastise, despise, disguise, franchise, merchandise, surmise,* and all verbs ending in *-cise, -prise, -vise* (including *comprise, excise, supervise, surprise, televise,* etc.), but *-ize* is always used in *prize, capsize, size, realize, specialize, civilize*. Canadian English tends to prefer *-yze* for the words *catalyze, analyze,* and *paralyze,* although it is not uncommon to find these words—especially *analyze*—also ending in *-yse* in Canadian writing.

6.4 -our/-or Canadian English tends to favour the suffix *-our* for words like *colour, honour, odour, rigour,* etc., although *-or* is also common in Canadian writing. Note that certain words are always spelled with *-or* (e.g. *error, stupor, tremor*), and that words that can be spelled either *-or* or *-our* drop the *u,* even in British English, when the endings *-ation, -iferous, -ific, -ize,* and *-ous* are added (e.g. *coloration, odoriferous, honorific, glamorize, humorous,* but note that Canadian and British English usually prefer *colourist, honourable, savoury*). It is advisable to check such spellings in the dictionary.

7. ae and oe

The use of the printed ligatures æ and œ is becoming rare, and there is a trend in favour of replacing these with simple *e*. Although Canadian English tends to follow this convention, there are still some instances in which Canadians prefer to retain *ae* or *oe* (e.g. *amoeba, archaeology*). Other exceptions include proper names and words derived from them (e.g. *Aeschylus, Oedipus, Caesarean*). The main part of the dictionary should be consulted for specific points of concern.

C. CAPITALIZATION

The use of capital letters in punctuating sentences has been discussed above; their use to distinguish proper nouns or "names" from ordinary words is subject to wide variation in practice. The standard Oxford University Press style is outlined below, but the most important criterion is consistency within a single piece of writing.

1. Capital letters are used for the names of people and places (*Terry Fox, Prince Edward Island, Robson Street, the Mad Trapper*); the names of peoples and languages and derived words directly relating to them (*Canadian, Quebecer, Englishman, Inuktitut, Americanism*); the names of institutions and institutional groups (*the Crown, the Government, the Department of Health, the National Museum of Natural Sciences*); the names of religious institutions and denominations and their adherents (*Judaism, Muslim, the United Church*) and of societies and organizations (*the Law Society of Upper Canada*); the names of months and days (*June, Monday, New Year's Day*); abstract qualities personified (*the Face of Nature, O Death!*) or used as sobriquets (a *Green* = ecological activist); and names of other non-personal things (*the Flying Dutchman*).

Note that *the Anglican Church* is an institution, but *the Anglican church* is a building; a *Democrat* belongs to a political party, but a *democrat* simply supports democracy; *Northern Ireland* is a name with recognized status, but *northern England* is not.

2. A capital letter is used for words derived from a proper name, if the connection with the name is direct, or felt to be continuing (*Christian, Homeric, Marxism*), but not if it is more remote or conventional (*chauvinistic, quixotic, guillotine*).

3. A capital letter is used by convention in many names that are trademarks (*Xerox, Cineplex, Arborite*) or are otherwise associated with a particular manufacturer etc. Some proprietary terms are now conventionally spelled with a lower case initial (*aspirin, pablum, jeep*), and this is generally true of established verbs derived from proprietary terms (*to xerox, to skidoo*).

4. Capital letters are used in titles of courtesy or rank, including compound titles (*the Right Honourable Lester B. Pearson, Dame Emma Albani, Governor General, Lieutenant Commander, Her Excellency*).

5. A capital letter is used for the personal pronoun *I* and for the interjection *O*.

6. A capital letter is used for the name of a deity (*God, Father, Allah, Great Spirit*). However, the use of capitals in possessive determiners and possessive pronouns (*in His name*) is now generally considered old-fashioned.

7. Capital letters are used for the first and other important words in titles of books, newspapers, plays, movies, television programs, etc., and in headings and captions (*The Merchant of Venice, Pride and Prejudice, Book of Common Prayer, New Testament, Talmud, Guide to the Use of the Dictionary*).

8. Capital letters are used for historical events and periods (*the Dark Ages, the Renaissance, the First World War*); also for geological time divisions, but not for certain archaeological periods (*Devonian, Paleozoic,* but *neolithic*).

9. Capital letters are frequently used in abbreviations, with or without periods (*TSN, M.B.A.*).

10. A capital letter is used for a compass direction when abbreviated (*N, NE, NNE*) or when denoting a region (*cold weather in the North*).

D. ITALICIZATION

Italic type makes a word or phrase stand out from its context. It is used especially in the following ways:

1. For titles of books, plays, major musical works, works of art, long poems, periodical publications, and individual ships, trains, aircraft, etc.: *Henry V, The Magic Flute, The Diviners,* Michelangelo's *David, The Globe and Mail,* HMCS *Protecteur.*

The articles *The* or *A* may or may not be part of a full title: the *Vancouver Sun, The Gazette.* Unless the exact title is to be cited, the article may be omitted if the work is well known or has already been cited: Darwin's *Origin of Species.*

2. For foreign words and phrases, when still perceived as foreign. When a foreign word becomes sufficiently naturalized, it is printed in roman. Headwords in this dictionary use italic or roman based on the current frequency of use in English. Words which would normally be printed in roman are sometimes italicized for consistency when other related words are being used, or when an English word exists with the same spelling, as with *pension* for a Continental boarding house.

3. For the Latin names of genera and species.

4. For distinguishing a word or phrase from the surrounding text, especially to emphasize it, or when mentioning a technical word for the first time. Italics may be used, for example, to distinguish stage directions in plays; in dictionaries, they typically distinguish markers for parts of speech, labels concerning register or restriction of use, and example sentences.

5. Italic type is not used for the following:

5.1 Titles of chapters in books, articles in periodicals, shorter poems, individual television and radio programs; these may be referred to in quotation marks: her article "Joan of Arc and the Action Française" in the *The Journal of French History,* "Sonnet VI" in *Selected Poems.*

5.2 The names of sacred texts or their subdivisions; quotation marks are not used: the Quran, Genesis, Epistle to the Romans.

5.3 Musical works identified by a description (Beethoven's Fifth Symphony).

5.4 Names of buildings or of types of vehicle (the Colosseum, Maple Leaf Gardens, a Honda Accord).

5.5 Most short abbreviations, including units of measurement (ad hoc, cf., e.g., ibid., i.e., km, pro tem, q.v.).

6. If a piece of text is already printed in italics, then the function of italicization is taken by roman type: She was reading *On the Use of* Verfremdungseffekt *in Brecht's Plays.*

E. OFFENSIVE LANGUAGE AND SEXISM

In general, terms should be avoided which convey an impression of over-generalization, describing people as though they were merely instances of a particular feature, or especially imposing on them a depreciatory stereotype. Words referring to race or to a physical or mental handicap which have been used as terms of abuse, or have been associated with discrimination, are frequently therefore avoided even in their original neutral senses. Register labels are used in the dictionary to label terms that may be considered derogatory or offensive, and usage notes are used in several cases to suggest appropriate alternatives.

Words and phrases that describe women and men in ways that stereotype them on the basis of their sex are often avoided where possible. Terms for occupations or titles which are unnecessarily marked for gender may be replaced with gender-neutral terms (*police officer* instead of *policeman, flight attendant* instead of *stewardess, spokesperson* instead of *spokeswoman* or *spokesman*), and there are suitable alternatives for most words in which *man* is used as a prefix (*synthetic* for *man-made, workforce* for *manpower, humankind* or *people* for *mankind*). The extending of this tendency to cover words with only tenuous etymological ties to sex is not generally accepted. Many words containing the letters *man* derive not from the word *man* but from the Latin root *man(u),* "hand" (*manufacture, manipulate, manuscript*), and attempts to replace such words for their perceived association with gender may result in writing that is awkward or imprecise.

The English language lacks a third person singular pronoun or possessive adjective applying neutrally to both sexes. The older convention of using *he, him, his* for both sexes (e.g. *Each member must pay his membership fees*) is now eschewed by many writers. Acceptable alternatives include (i) rephrasing in the plural (e.g. *All members must pay their membership fees*); (ii) using both pronouns or possessives (e.g. *Each member must pay his or her membership fee*), although this is often cumbersome; *his/her* and *he/she* (or even *s/he*) are awkward to read aloud. The use of *they* and *their* in the singular is common in informal speech (e.g. *Each member must pay their membership fee*), and many commentators have softened their opposition to it, in spite of the fact that several continue to regard the plural pronoun as ungrammatical and advise against using it in formal writing and speech.

PRIME MINISTERS OF CANADA

John A. Macdonald	1867—73	Conservative
Alexander Mackenzie	1873—78	Liberal
John A. Macdonald	1878—91	Conservative
John J.C. Abbott	1891—92	Conservative
John S.D. Thompson	1892—94	Conservative
Mackenzie Bowell	1894—96	Conservative
Charles Tupper	1896	Conservative
Wilfrid Laurier	1896—1911	Liberal
Robert L. Borden	1911—20	Conservative
Arthur Meighen	1920—21	Conservative
W.L. Mackenzie King	1921—26	Liberal
Arthur Meighen	1926	Conservative
W.L. Mackenzie King	1926—30	Liberal
Richard B. Bennett	1930—35	Conservative
W.L. Mackenzie King	1935—48	Liberal
Louis S. St. Laurent	1948—57	Liberal
John G. Diefenbaker	1957—63	Progressive Conservative
Lester B. Pearson	1963—68	Liberal
Pierre Elliott Trudeau	1968—79	Liberal
Joseph Clark	1979—80	Progressive Conservative
Pierre Elliott Trudeau	1980—84	Liberal
John Turner	1984	Liberal
Brian Mulroney	1984—93	Progressive Conservative
Kim Campbell	1993	Progressive Conservative
Jean Chrétien	1993—2004	Liberal
Paul Martin	2004—	Liberal

GOVERNORS GENERAL OF CANADA

Viscount Monck of Ballytrammon	1867—69
Baron Lisgar of Lisgar and Bailieborough	1869—72
The Marquess of Dufferin and Ava	1872—78
The Marquess of Lorne	1878—83
The Marquess of Lansdowne	1883—88
Baron Stanley of Preston	1888—93
The Earl of Aberdeen	1893—98
The Earl of Minto	1898—1904
Earl Grey	1904—11
The Duke of Connaught and Strathearn	1911—16
The Duke of Devonshire	1916—21
Viscount Byng of Vimy	1921—26
Viscount Willingdon of Ratton	1926—31
The Earl of Bessborough	1931—35
Baron Tweedsmuir of Elsfield	1935—40
The Earl of Athlone	1940—46
Earl Alexander of Tunis	1946—52
Vincent Massey	1952—59
Georges Vanier	1959—67
Roland Michener	1967—74
Jules Léger	1974—79
Edward Schreyer	1979—84
Jeanne Sauvé	1984—90
Ramon Hnatyshyn	1990—95
Roméo LeBlanc	1995—99
Adrienne Clarkson	1999—

The conversion factors are not exact unless so marked. They are given only to the accuracy likely to be needed in everyday calculations.

1. IMPERIAL AND AMERICAN, WITH METRIC EQUIVALENTS

Linear measure

1 inch	= 25.4 millimetres exactly
1 foot = 12 inches	= 0.3048 metre exactly
1 yard = 3 feet	= 0.9144 metre exactly
1 (statute) mile = 1,760 yards	= 1.609 kilometres
1 int. nautical mile = 1.150779 miles	= 1.852 km exactly

Square measure

1 square inch	= 6.45 sq. centimetres
1 square foot = 144 sq. in.	= 9.29 sq. decimetres
1 square yard = 9 sq. ft.	= 0.836 sq. metre
1 acre = 4,840 sq. yd.	= 0.405 hectare
1 square mile = 640 acres	= 259 hectares

Cubic measure

1 cubic inch	= 16.4 cu. centimetres
1 cubic foot = 1,728 cu. in.	= 0.0283 cu. metre
1 cubic yard = 27 cu. ft.	= 0.765 cu. metre

Capacity measure

Name	System	Equal to	Metric
fluid oz.	imperial	1/20 imp. pint	28.41 ml
	US (liquid)	1/16 US pint	29.57 ml
gill	imperial	1/4 pint	142.07 ml
	US (liquid)	1/4 pint	118.29 ml
pint	imperial	20 fl.oz.(imp.)	568.26 ml
	US (liquid)	16 fl.oz.(US)	473.18 ml
	US (dry)	1/2 quart	550.61 ml
quart	imperial	2 pints	1.1365 litres
	US (liquid)	2 pints	0.9464 litre
	US (dry)	2 pints	1.1012 litres
gallon	imperial	4 quarts	4.546 litres
	US (liquid)	4 quarts	3.785 litres
peck	imperial	2 gallons	9.092 litres
	US (dry)	8 quarts	8.810 litres
bushel	imperial	4 pecks	36.369 litres
	US (dry)	4 pecks	35.239 litres

Avoirdupois weight

1 grain	= 0.065 gram
1 dram	= 1.772 grams
1 ounce = 16 drams	= 28.35 grams
1 pound = 16 ounces = 7,000 grains	= 0.45359237 kilogram exactly
1 stone = 14 pounds	= 6.35 kilograms
1 quarter = 2 stones	= 12.70 kilograms
1 hundredweight = 4 quarters = 112 lb.	= 50.80 kilograms
1 (long) ton = 20 cwt. = 2,240 lb.	= 1.016 tonnes
1 short ton = 2,000 pounds	= 0.907 tonne

2. METRIC, WITH IMPERIAL EQUIVALENTS

Linear measure

1 millimetre	= 0.039 inch
1 centimetre = 10 mm	= 0.394 inch
1 decimetre = 10 cm	= 3.94 inches
1 metre = 100 cm	= 1.094 yards
1 decametre = 10 m	= 10.94 yards
1 hectometre = 100 m	= 109.4 yards
1 kilometre = 1000 m	= 0.6214 mile

Square measure

1 square centimetre	= 0.155 sq. inch
1 square metre = 10 000 sq. cm	= 1.196 sq. yards
1 are = 100 sq. metres	= 119.6 sq. yards
1 hectare = 100 ares	= 2.471 acres
1 square kilometre = 100 ha	= 0.386 sq. mile

Cubic measure

1 cubic centimetre	= 0.061 cu. inch
1 cubic metre = one million cu. cm	= 1.308 cu. yards

Capacity measure

1 millilitre	= 0.002 pint (imperial)
1 centilitre = 10 ml	= 0.018 pint
1 decilitre = 100 ml	= 0.176 pint
1 litre = 1000 ml	= 1.76 pints
1 decalitre = 10 l	= 2.20 gallons (imperial)
1 hectolitre = 100 l	= 2.75 bushels (imperial)

Weight

1 milligram	= 0.015 grain
1 centigram = 10 mg	= 0.154 grain
1 decigram = 100 mg	= 1.543 grain
1 gram = 1000 mg	= 15.43 grain
1 decagram = 10 g	= 5.64 drams
1 hectogram = 100 g	= 3.527 ounces
1 kilogram = 1000 g	= 2.205 pounds
1 tonne (metric ton) = 1000 kg	= 0.984 (long) ton

3. SI UNITS

Base units

Physical quantity	Name	Abbr. or symbol
length	metre	m
mass	kilogram	kg
time	second	s
electric current	ampere	A
temperature	kelvin	K
amount of substance	mole	mol
luminous intensity	candela	cd

Supplementary units

Physical quantity	Name	Abbr. or symbol
plane angle	radian	rad
solid angle	steradian	sr

Derived units with special names

Physical quantity	Name	Abbr. or symbol
frequency	hertz	Hz
energy	joule	J
force	newton	N
power	watt	W
pressure	pascal	Pa
electric charge	coulomb	C
electromotive force	volt	V
electric resistance	ohm	Ω
electric conductance	siemens	S
electric capacitance	farad	F
magnetic flux	weber	Wb
inductance	henry	H
magnetic flux density	tesla	T
luminous flux	lumen	lm
illumination	lux	lx

4. TEMPERATURE

Celsius (or Centigrade): Water boils (under standard conditions) at 100° and freezes at 0°
Fahrenheit: Water boils at 212° and freezes at 32°
Kelvin: Water boils at 373.15 kelvins and freezes at 273.15 kelvins.

Celsius	Fahrenheit
–50°	–58°
–40°	–40°
–30°	–22°
–20°	–4°
–17.8°	0°
–10°	14°
0°	32°
10°	50°
20°	68°
30°	86°
40°	104°
50°	122°
60°	140°
70°	158°
80°	176°
90°	194°
100°	212°

To convert Celsius into Fahrenheit: multiply by 9, divide by 5, and add 32.
To convert Fahrenheit to Celsius: subtract 32, multiply by 5, and divide by 9.

5. METRIC PREFIXES

	Abbr. or symbol	Factor
deca-	da	10
hecto-	h	10^2
kilo-	k	10^3
mega-	M	10^6
giga-	G	10^9
tera-	T	10^{12}
peta-	P	10^{15}
exa-	E	10^{18}
deci-	d	10^{-1}
centi-	c	10^{-2}
milli-	m	10^{-3}
micro-	μ	10^{-6}
nano-	n	10^{-9}
pico-	p	10^{-12}
femto-	f	10^{-15}
atto-	a	10^{-18}

Pronunciations and derivations of these are given at their alphabetical places in the dictionary. They may be applied to any units of the metric system: hectogram (abbr. hg) = 100 grams; kilowatt (abbr. kW) = 1000 watts; megahertz (MHz) = 1 million hertz; centimetre (cm) = $^1/_{100}$ metre; microvolt (μV) = one millionth of a volt; picofarad (pF) = 10^{-12} farad, and are sometimes applied to other units (megabit).

6. POWER NOTATION

This expresses concisely any power of ten (any number that is composed of factors of 10), and is sometimes used in the dictionary. 10^2 or ten squared = $10 \times 10 = 100$; 10^3 or ten cubed = $10 \times 10 \times 10 = 1,000$. Similarly, $10^4 = 10,000$ and $10^{10} = 1$ followed by ten zeros = 10,000,000,000. Proceeding in the opposite direction, dividing by ten and subtracting one from the index, we have $10^2 = 100$, $10^1 = 10$, $10^0 = 1$, $10^{-1} = ^1/_{10}$, $10^{-2} = ^1/_{100}$, and so on; $10^{-10} = 1/10,000,000,000$.

7. BINARY SYSTEM

Only two units (0 and 1) are used, and the position of each unit indicates a power of two.

One to ten written in binary form:

	eights (2^3)	fours (2^2)	twos (2^1)	one
1				1
2			1	0
3			1	1
4		1	0	0
5		1	0	1
6		1	1	0
7		1	1	1
8	1	0	0	0
9	1	0	0	1
10	1	0	1	0

i.e. ten is written as 1010 ($2^3 + 0 + 2^1 + 0$); one hundred is written as 1100100 ($2^6 + 2^5 + 0 + 0 + 2^2 + 0 + 0$).

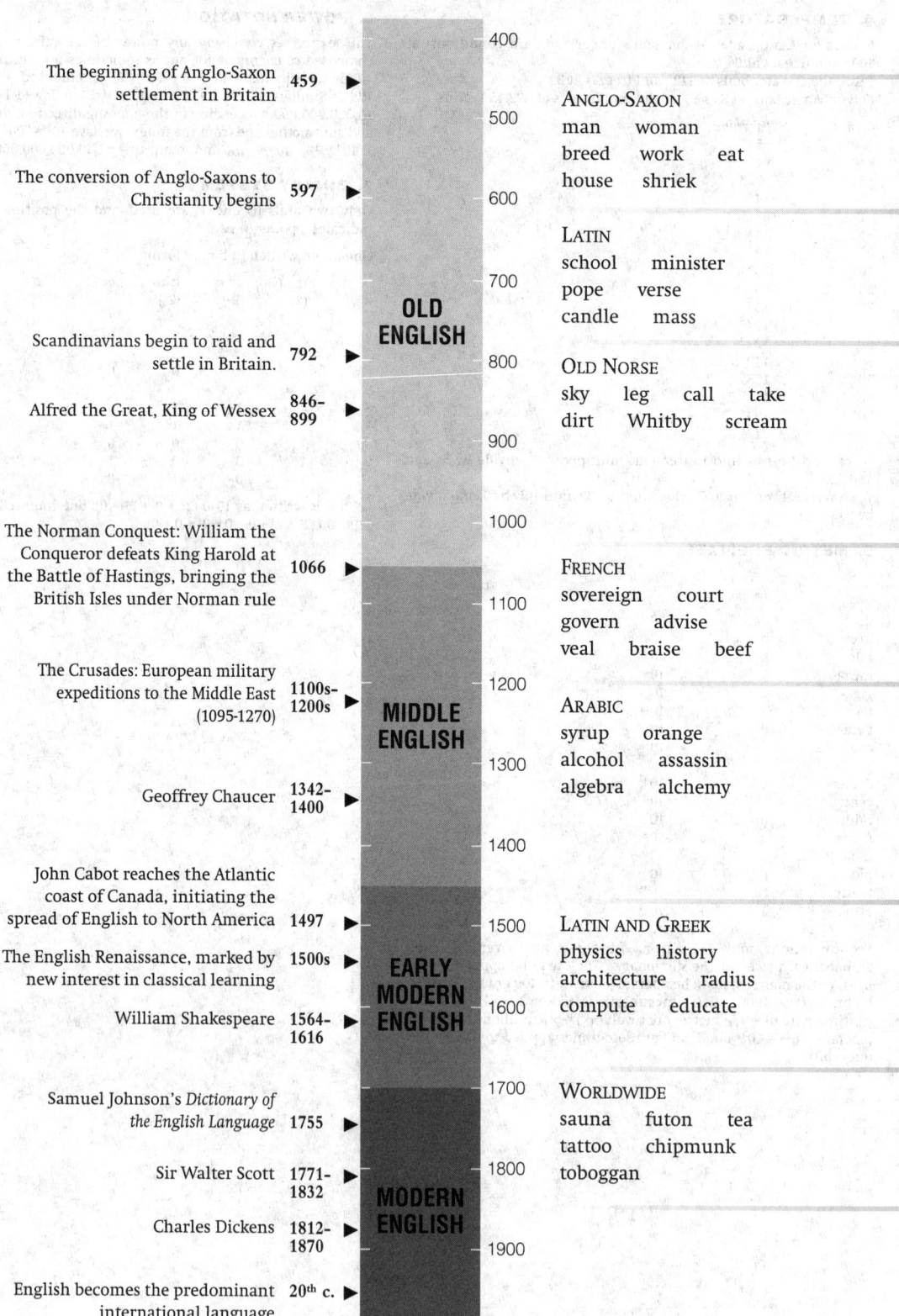

The beginning of Anglo-Saxon settlement in Britain — 459

The conversion of Anglo-Saxons to Christianity begins — 597

Scandinavians begin to raid and settle in Britain. — 792

Alfred the Great, King of Wessex — 846–899

The Norman Conquest: William the Conqueror defeats King Harold at the Battle of Hastings, bringing the British Isles under Norman rule — 1066

The Crusades: European military expeditions to the Middle East (1095-1270) — 1100s–1200s

Geoffrey Chaucer — 1342–1400

John Cabot reaches the Atlantic coast of Canada, initiating the spread of English to North America — 1497

The English Renaissance, marked by new interest in classical learning — 1500s

William Shakespeare — 1564–1616

Samuel Johnson's *Dictionary of the English Language* — 1755

Sir Walter Scott — 1771–1832

Charles Dickens — 1812–1870

English becomes the predominant international language — 20th c.

OLD ENGLISH

MIDDLE ENGLISH

EARLY MODERN ENGLISH

MODERN ENGLISH

400
500
600
700
800
900
1000
1100
1200
1300
1400
1500
1600
1700
1800
1900
2000

ANGLO-SAXON
man   woman
breed   work   eat
house   shriek

LATIN
school   minister
pope   verse
candle   mass

OLD NORSE
sky   leg   call   take
dirt   Whitby   scream

FRENCH
sovereign   court
govern   advise
veal   braise   beef

ARABIC
syrup   orange
alcohol   assassin
algebra   alchemy

LATIN AND GREEK
physics   history
architecture   radius
compute   educate

WORLDWIDE
sauna   futon   tea
tattoo   chipmunk
toboggan

History of The English Language

ANGLO-SAXON English developed from Anglo-Saxon (also known as Old English), the language brought to Britain by Germanic tribes (the Angles, Saxons, and Jutes), in the fifth century AD. These invaders gave England its name, "the land of the Angles", and provided the language with many common basic terms.

LATIN At the end of the sixth century, a group of monks came as missionaries from Rome to strengthen Christianity in Britain. The words that came into English from Latin at this time are mainly connected with religion and learning.

OLD NORSE In the ninth and tenth centuries, invaders came from Scandinavia and occupied a large part of eastern England and northern Britain. Many everyday words in modern English come from their language, Old Norse, which is related to Anglo-Saxon, and many place names end in -by from their word for village.

FRENCH When Britain was conquered by the Normans in 1066, French became the language of the ruling classes. Many words in modern English that describe government and the legal system, as well as terms connected with cooking, came from French at this time.

ARABIC During the Christian military expeditions to the Middle East in the twelfth and thirteenth centuries, English Crusaders came into contact with the Arab world and brought many of their words back to Britain. These words tended to relate to Islam, to Arab society and culture, and to learning, particularly in the fields of mathematics and astronomy.

LATIN AND GREEK Many words of Latin origin came into English through French, but the Renaissance of the fifteenth and sixteenth centuries brought new interest in classical learning and an influx of words from Latin and Greek. Latin and Greek continue to be used in the invention of new words, particularly in the fields of science and technology.

WORLDWIDE Beginning with English colonization of North America in the sixteenth century, English spread to many parts of the world where it was influenced by the native languages of these lands. English speakers today take words from a wide variety of other languages for phenomena that have no existing English name.

ENGLISH TODAY As a result of absorbing words from all of these sources, English often has many synonyms from different languages to express the same idea, such as *fear* (from Old English), *terror* (from French), *alarm* (from Italian), *trepidation* (from Latin), and *angst* (from German).

Arabic					Hebrew			Greek			Russian	
Alone	Final	Medial	Initial									
ا	ـا		ا	'alif	'	א	aleph	'	A α	alpha	a	А а	a
ب	ـب	ـبـ	بـ	bā'	b	ב	beth	b, bh	B β	beta	b	Б б	b
ت	ـت	ـتـ	تـ	tā'	t				Γ γ	gamma	g	В в	v
ث	ـث	ـثـ	ثـ	thā'	th	ג	gimel	g, gh				Г г	g
ج	ـج	ـجـ	جـ	jīm	j	ד	daleth	d, dh	Δ δ	delta	d	Д д	d
ح	ـح	ـحـ	حـ	ḥā'	ḥ	ה	he	h				Е е	e, ye
خ	ـخ	ـخـ	خـ	khā'	kh	ו	waw	w	E ε	epsilon	e	Ё ё	yo
د	ـد			dāl	d				Z ζ	zeta	z	Ж ж	zh
ذ	ـذ			dhāl	dh	ז	zayin	z	H η	eta	ē	З з	z
ر	ـر			rā'	r				Θ θ	theta	th	И и	i
ز	ـز			zay	z	ח	ḥeth	ḥ				Й й	i
س	ـس	ـسـ	سـ	sīn	s	ט	ṭeth	ṭ	I ι	iota	i	К к	k
ش	ـش	ـشـ	شـ	shīn	sh	י	yodh	y	K κ	kappa	k	Л л	l
ص	ـص	ـصـ	صـ	ṣād	ṣ	כ ך	kaph	k, kh	Λ λ	lambda	l	М м	m
ض	ـض	ـضـ	ضـ	ḍād	ḍ	ל	lamedh	l	M μ	mu	m	Н н	n
ط	ـط	ـطـ	طـ	ṭā'	ṭ	מ ם	mem	m	N ν	nu	n	О о	o
ظ	ـظ	ـظـ	ظـ	ẓā'	ẓ	נ ן	nun	n	Ξ ξ	xi	x	П п	p
ع	ـع	ـعـ	عـ	'ayn	'	ס	samekh	s	O o	omicron	o	Р р	r
غ	ـغ	ـغـ	غـ	ghayn	gh	ע	'ayin	'	Π π	pi	p	С с	s
ف	ـف	ـفـ	فـ	fā'	f	פ ף	pe	p, ph	P ρ	rho	r, th	Т т	t
ق	ـق	ـقـ	قـ	qāf	q	צ ץ	ṣadhe	ṣ	Σ σ ς	sigma	s	У у	u
ك	ـك	ـكـ	كـ	kāf	k	ק	qoph	q	T τ	tau	t	Ф ф	f
ل	ـل	ـلـ	لـ	lām	l	ר	resh	r	Y υ	upsilon	u	Х х	kh
م	ـم	ـمـ	مـ	mīm	m	ש	śin	ś	Φ φ	phi	ph	Ц ц	ts
ن	ـن	ـنـ	نـ	nūn	n	ש	shin	sh	X χ	chi	kh	Ч ч	ch
ه	ـه	ـهـ	هـ	hā'	h	ת	taw	t, th	Ψ ψ	psi	ps	Ш ш	sh
و	ـو			wāw	w				Ω ω	omega	ō	Щ щ	shch
ى	ـى	ـيـ	يـ	yā'	y							Ъ ъ	" ('hard sign')
												Ы ы	y
												Ь ь	' ('soft sign')
												Э э	e
												Ю ю	yu
												Я я	ya

List of Abbreviations

Abbreviations in general use (such as etc., i.e., and those for books of the Bible) are explained in the dictionary itself. Some abbreviations may appear in italics.

abbr.	abbreviation	Geom.	Geometry	orig.	origin, original(ly)
absol.	absolute(ly)	Gk	Greek		
adj.	adjective			Parl.	Parliament
adv.	adverb	hist.	with historical	part.	participle
Amer.	America, American		reference	Pharm.	Pharmacology
Anat.	Anatomy			Philos.	Philosophy
Archit.	Architecture	Ind.	Indian (of the	Photog.	Photography
assoc.	associated, association		subcontinent	phr.	phrase
Austral.	Australia, Australian		comprising India,	Physiol.	Physiology
aux.	auxiliary		Pakistan, and	pl.	plural
			Bangladesh)	poet.	poetical
Biochem.	Biochemistry	infin.	infinitive	Polit.	Politics
Biol.	Biology	interj.	interjection	pop.	population
Bot.	Botany	interrog.	interrogative	poss.	possessive
Brit.	British, in British use	intr.	intransitive	prec.	preceded
		irreg.	irregular(ly)	prep.	preposition
c.	century			pres.	present
c.	*circa*	lit.	literally	prob.	probably, probable
Cdn	Canada, Canadian			pron.	pronoun
Chem.	Chemistry, Chemical	masc.	masculine	pronunc.	pronunciation
collect.	collective(ly)	Math.	Mathematics	Psych.	Psychology, Psychiatry
comb.	combination,	Mech.	Mechanics		
	combining	Med.	Medicine	Rom.	Roman
conj.	conjunction	Meteorol.	Meteorology		
Crystallog.	Crystallography	Mil.	Military	Scand.	Scandinavian
		Mineral.	Mineralogy	Scot.	Scottish
dial.	dialect	Mus.	Music	sing.	singular
				Stock Exch.	Stock Exchange
Econ.	Economics	n.	noun		
ellipt.	elliptical(ly)	N Amer.	North America,	Theol.	Theology
Engin.	Engineering		North American	tr.	transitive
esp.	especial(ly)	Naut.	Nautical		
est.	estimated	neg.	negative	US	American
		neut.	neuter	usu.	usually
fem.	feminine	n.pl.	noun plural		
fl.	*floruit* (flourished)	NZ	New Zealand	v.	verb
foll.	followed, following			var.	variant(s)
		obj.	objective		
Geog.	Geography	opp.	opposite (of), (as)	Zool.	Zoology
Geol.	Geology		opposed (to)		